CHILTON'S MOTORCYCLE and ATV REPAIR MANUAL 1945-85

Publisher & Editor-In-Chief Kerry A. Freeman, S.A.E.
Executive Editors Dean F. Morgantini, S.A.E., W. Calvin Settle Jr., S.A.E.
Managing Editor Nick D'Andrea
Senior Editors Debra Gaffney, Jacques Gordon, Michael L. Grady, Kevin M. G. Maher, Richard J. Rivele, S.A.E., Richard T. Smith, Jim Taylor, Ron Webb
Project Managers Larry Braun, S.A.E., A.S.C., Thomas P. Browne III, Joseph DeFrancesco, Robert E. Doughten, Benjamin E. Greisler, A.S.E., Martin J. Gunther, Craig P. Nangle, A.S.E., Ernest H. Ralph, A.S.E., S.A.E., Richard Schwartz
Editorial Staff Jaffer A. Ahmad, Bradley Bower, James Carr, Robert A. Chabot, William C. Cottman, A.S.E., Leonard Davis, A.S.E., Michael DiFurio Jr., S.A.E., Sam Fiorani, Matthew E. Frederick, William C. Friedauer, Edward J. Giacomucci, A.S.E., S.A.E., Al Gibbs, Herbert Guie Jr, Dawn M. Hoch, David E. Jester, Lori Johnson, A.S.E., William Kessler, Kenneth F. Konzelman, Neil J. Leonard, A.S.E., James R. Marotta, Robert McAnally, Raymond K. Moore, Norman D. Norville, A.S.E., Christine L. Nuckowski, Eric S. Peterson, A.S.E., Charles Ramsey, A.S.E., Roy Ripple, A.S.E., Paul Shanahan, Larry E. Stiles, Gordon L. Tobias, Albert A. Wood, A.S.E.
Production Manager Andrea M. Steiger
Assistant Production Manager Marsha Park Herman
Production Specialists Christina Davis, Kimberly T. Hayes, Joseph C. McGinty, Elizabeth E. Thompson
Director of Manufacturing Mike D'Imperio
Manufacturing Manager Robin Norman
OFFICERS
Senior Vice President Ronald A. Hoxter

CHILTON BOOK COMPANY

ONE OF THE **DIVERSIFIED PUBLISHING COMPANIES,**
A PART OF **CAPITAL CITIES/ABC,INC.**

Manufactured in

Chilton Way, Radnor, PA 19089
ISBN 0-8019-7635-9
Library of Congress Catalog Card No. 85-47957

678901234 32109876

USING THIS BOOK

Chilton's **MOTORCYCLE REPAIR MANUAL** has been designed for maximum ease of use by the experienced owner or mechanic, while providing, at the same time, detailed information on basic concepts and procedures which are needed by the beginner.

To accomplish this goal, a "General Information" section is included at the end of the manual, and the novice should refer to this first before attempting the operations outlined in the individual model sections.

The "General Information" section contains all of the basic information necessary for motorcycle maintenance and tune-up, including such items as tips on lubrication, decarbonization, cable and chain care and adjustments, breaker points, ignition timing and the use of timing lights, spark plug readings, and carburetor theory and troubleshooting.

While most of the information contained in "General Information" is applicable to the great majority of motorcycles, exceptions and special cases will, of course, be noted in the individual sections.

Necessary specifications are included either in the test or collected in charts at the end of the related section.

SAFETY NOTICE

Proper service and repair procedures are vital to the safe, reliable operation of all motor vehicles, as well as the personal safety of those performing repairs. This manual outlines procedures for servicing and repairing vehicles using safe effective methods. The procedures contain many NOTES, CAUTIONS and WARNINGS which should be followed along with standard safety procedures to eliminate the possibility of personal injury or improper service which could damage the vehicle or compromise its safety.

It is important to note that repair procedures and techniques, tools and parts for servicing motor vehicles, as well as the skill and experience of the individual performing the work vary widely. It is not possible to anticipate all of the conceivable ways or conditions under which vehicles may be serviced, or to provide cautions as to all of the possible hazards that may result. Standard and accepted safety precautions and equipment should be used when handling toxic or flammable fluids, and safety goggles or other protection should be used during cutting, grinding, chiseling, prying, or any other process that can cause material removal or projectiles.

Some procedures require the use of tools specially designed for a specific purpose. Before substituting another tool or procedure, you must be completely satisfied that neither your personal safety, nor the performance of the vehicle will be endangered.

Contents

Harley-Davidson V-Twins

MODEL COVERAGE

XL (900)
XLH (900)
XLCH (900)
XL-1000
XLH-1000
XLCH-1000
FL/FLH Duo-Glide
FL/FLH Electra Glide
FX/FXE Super Glide

INDEX

MAINTENANCE

NOTE: *Common maintenance procedures are explained in detail in "General Information."*

LUBRICATION

Changing Engine Oil

1. Run the engine until normal operating temperature is reached.
2. Position the motorcycle so that it will stand straight up or lean slightly to the right.
3. Remove oil filter cap and drain plug in oil tank. Turn the engine over a few times to remove any oil remaining in the sump. It is not necessary to drain the crankcase as there is only a small amount of oil remaining.
4. Install drain plug. Pour one quart of kerosene into the oil tank. Rock the motorcycle gently from side-to-side. Remove drain plug and drain kerosene from oil tank.
5. Clean oil filters thoroughly and dry by blowing them with compressed air.
6. Reinstall drain plug and add proper quantity and grade of oil.

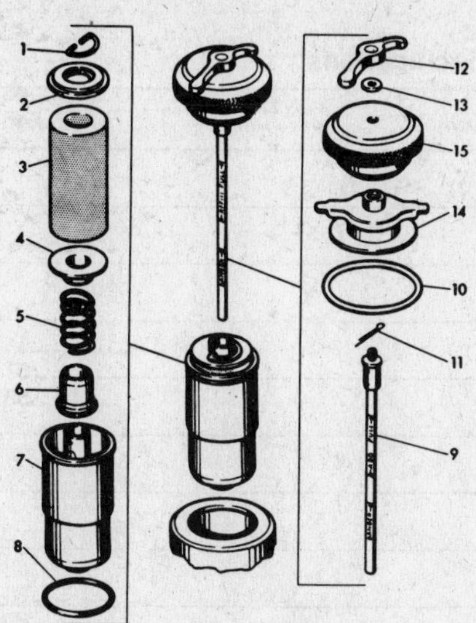

Oil tank filter

1. Filter clip
2. Cap seal washer
3. Filter element
4. Filter lower retainer
5. Cup spring
6. Cup seal
7. Cup
8. O-ring
9. Dipstick and valve assembly
10. Cap gasket
11. Cap cotter pin
12. Capscrew
13. Cap washer
14. Capnut
15. Cap top

Changing Transmission Oil

SPORTSTER

1. Stand the motorcycle upright and remove the oil level plug from the chaincase bottom.
2. Fill the transmission through the large screw hole in the chaincase cover with engine oil until overflow begins from the oil level plug hole.

General Specifications

Sportster	*XL, XLH*	*XLCH*	*XLH (1000 cc)*	*XLCH (1000 cc)*
DIMENSIONS				
Wheelbase (in.)	①	57	58½	58½
Overall Length (in.)	②	83¼	87¼	87¼
Overall Width (in.)	34	③	33	32
Overall Height (in.)	40½	42	40½	42
Ground Clearance (in.)	④	⑤	⑪	⑫
CAPACITIES				
Fuel Tank (U.S. gal.)	4.0	2.2	4.0/2.2	4.0/2.2
Oil Tank (quarts)	3	3	3	3
Transmission (pints)	1½	1½	1½	1½
ENGINE				
Number of Cylinders	2	2	2	2
Type	45 degree, V-type, four-cycle, OHV			
Bore (in.)	3.00	3.00	3.188	3.188
(mm)	76.2	76.2	81	81
Stroke (in.)	3.8125	3.8125		
(mm)	76.2	76.2		
Piston Displacement (cu in.)	53.9	53.9	60.9	60.9
(cc)	883	883	997.5	997.5
Torque	⑩	⑥	52 ft lbs @ 3800 rpm	
Compression Ratio	⑦	⑪	9.0 : 1	9.0 : 1
TRANSMISSION				
Type	Constant mesh-foot shift			
GEAR RATIOS				
First gear	10.63 : 1⑧	10.63 : 1⑧	11.16 : 1	11.16 : 1⑨
Second gear	7.69 : 1	7.69 : 1	8.08 : 1	8.08 : 1
Third gear	5.82 : 1	5.82 : 1	6.11 : 1	6.11 : 1
Fourth gear	4.21 : 1	4.21 : 1	4.42 : 1	4.42 : 1
First gear		11.74 : 1⑩		
Second gear		8.50 : 1		
Third gear		6.43 : 1		
Fourth gear		4.66 : 1		

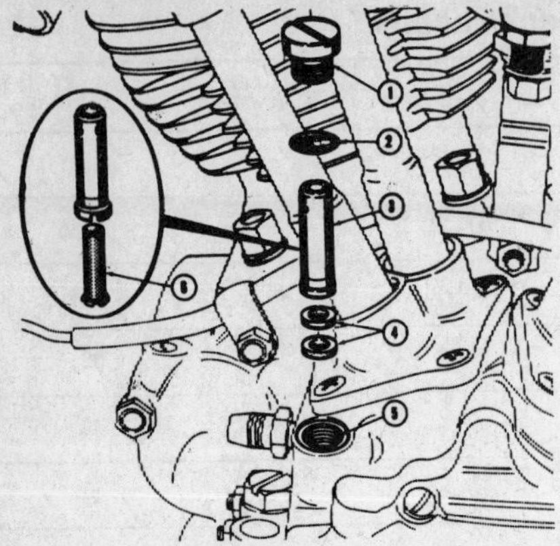

Hydraulic pushrod screen

1. Oil screen body cap
2. Oil screen body gasket
3. Oil screen body
4. Crankcase body seal (2)
5. Crankcase oil screen body hole
6. Crankcase oil screen

3. Secure both plugs when overflow ceases.
4. Change oil annually or every 5,000 miles.

GLIDE MODELS

1. Remove the transmission oil filler plug to check level. The motorcycle must be standing upright.
2. Remove the drain plug to change the oil.
3. Refill with oil to the level of the filler opening.
4. Change the oil annually or every 5,000 miles.

Changing Fork Oil

FL/FLH

It is not necessary to change the fork oil unless leakage has been noted.

1. On non-adjustable forks, remove the upper bracket bolt at the very top of each fork tube.
2. On adjustable forks, remove the fork cover side panels or headlight housing and fork filler screws.
3. Remove the drain bolts from the bottom of the sliders, pumping the forks up and down to remove all the oil.
4. Refit the drain plugs and fill each fork leg with 6½ oz of Harley-Davidson Type B fork oil. Add 7 oz if the forks have been disassembled.
5. Refit the bracket bolts or filler screws.

FX/FXE

It is not usually necessary to change fork oil unless leakage has been noted.

1. Remove the front wheel and fender.
2. Remove the cap from the top of each fork tube. Remove the drain plugs from the fork sliders.
3. Loosen the bolt at the very bottom of each slider a few turns. Move the sliders up and down to drain all the oil.
4. Secure slider bolts and drain plugs. Fill each fork tube with the correct quantity of Harley-Davidson Type B fork oil. For 1972 and earlier models: 5½ oz. For 1973 and later models: 5 oz.

Add 1 oz to the above quantities if the forks have been disassembled.

General Specifications (cont.)

Sportster	*XL, XLH*	*XLCH*	*XLH (1000 cc)*	*XLCH (1000 cc)*
Sportster		*Front*	*Rear*	
TIRE DATA				
XL, XLH (1965–66)		3.50 x 18	3.50 x 18	
XLH (1967–1969)		3.25/3.50 x 19	4.00 x 18	
XLCH (1969 & earlier)		3.25/3.50 x 19	4.25 x 18	
XLH (1970 & later)		3.75 x 19	4.25 x 18	
XLCH (1970 & later)		3.75 x 19	4.25 x 18	

① Wheelbase (in.)
1965–66: 56½
1967 and later: 58½

② Overall length (in.)
1965–66: 87
1967–72: 89

③ Overall width (in.)
1965–66: 29½
1967 and later 34

④ Ground Clearance (in.)
1965–66: 2½ (min.)
1967 and later: 6⅞

⑤ Ground Clearance (in.)
1965–66: 4⅛ (min.)
1967 and later: 6⅞

⑥ Torque
XL: 48 ft lbs @ 3600 rpm
XLH: 52 ft lbs @ 3800 rpm

⑦ Compression Ratio
XL: 7.5 : 1
XLH: 9.0 : 1

⑧ Gear Ratio
XL & XLH: 1965–66
XLH & XLCH: 1967 (optional)

⑨ Gear Ratio
XL && XLH: 1967 and later (standard)

⑩ Gear Ratio
XLCH: 1970–71

⑪ Ground Clearance (in.)
1972: 6¾
1973 and later: 7¼

⑫ Ground Clearance (in.)
1972: 6½
1973 and later: 7¼

General Specifications

Glide Models	*FL & FLH (1969 & earlier)*	*FL & FLH (1970 & later)*	*FX/FXE*
DIMENSIONS			
Wheelbase (in.)	60.0	61.5	62.7
Overall Length (in.)	92.0	89.0	92.0
Overall Width	35.0	38.5	33.0
CAPACITIES			
Fuel Tank (large) (U.S. gal.)	5.0	5.0	3.6
(small) (U.S. gal.)	3.5	3.5	—
Reserve Tank (large) (U.S. gal.)	1.2	1.2	①
(small) (U.S. gal.)	1.0	1.0	—
Oil Tank (quarts)	4	4	4
Transmission (pints)	1.5	1.5	1.5
ENGINE			
Number of Cylinders	2	2	2
Type		45 degree, V-type, four-cycle, OHV	
Bore (in.)	$3\frac{7}{16}$	$3\frac{7}{16}$	$3\frac{7}{16}$
(mm)	87.3	87.3	87.3
Stroke (in.)	$3\frac{31}{32}$	$3\frac{31}{32}$	$3\frac{31}{32}$
(mm)	100.8	100.8	100.8

SPORTSTER

On 1972 and earlier models, it is not necessary to change the fork oil unless leakage has been noted.

On 1973 and later models, change fork oil every 5,000 miles.

Refer to the FX/FXE section preceding for procedures. Oil type and quantity are the same for the Sportsters 1970 and later.

For 1968–69 models, add 4½ oz to each leg.

For 1967 and earlier models, add 3½ oz to each leg.

Add 1 oz extra if adding oil to forks which have been disassembled.

Primary Chain Lubrication

SPORTSTER

The Sportster's primary chain is automatically oiled through a port between the chain and transmission compartments.

GLIDE MODELS

Oil is supplied to the primary drive chain through an oil line which is connected to metering orifice in the oil pump.

Drive Chain Lubrication

1. Loosen the oiler screw locknut (if fitted) and turn the adjusting screw to the right to decrease flow, and to the left to increase flow.

   NOTE: *It is important that the screw is never moved more than a fraction. Small adjustments make a great difference in oil flow.*

2. Hold adjusting screw with screwdriver and tighten locknut.
3. Check for proper rate of flow. Oil should be deposited on chain at the rate of two or three drops a minute.

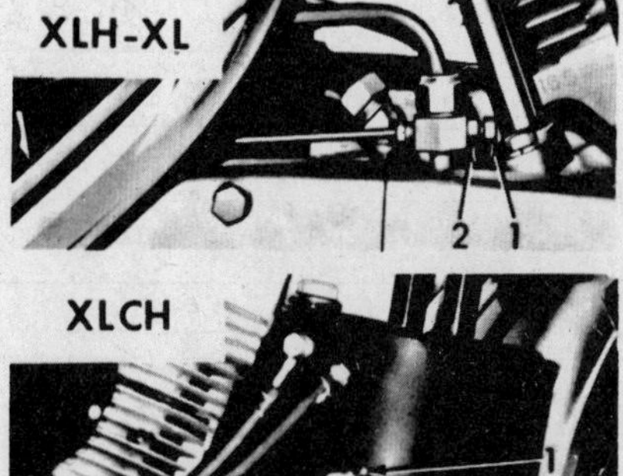

Sportster drive chain oiler (early)

1. Adjusting screw
2. Adjusting screw lock nut (early 1970)

Chain Oiler Maintenance

1. The primary chain oiler (Glide models) needs no attention under normal conditions. If the chain oiler will not pass oil, it is probably clogged. Remove the oriface screw and washer from the oil pump and blow out the passage with compressed air.
2. The drive chain oiler should be checked every 2,000 miles.

General Specifications (cont.)

Glide Models	*FL & FLH (1969 & earlier)*	*FL & FLH (1970 & later)*	*FX/FXE*
Piston Displacement (cu in.)	73.66	73.66	73.66
(cc)	1207	1207	1207
TORQUE (ft lbs)			
FL	62 @ 3200 rpm	62 @ 3200 rpm	
FLH	65 @ 3200 rpm	65 @ 3200 rpm	
FX			65 @ 3200 rpm
COMPRESSION RATIO			
FL	7.25 : 1	7.25 : 1	
FLH	8.00 : 1	8.00 : 1	
FX			8.00 : 1
TRANSMISSION			
Type	Constant mesh, hand or foot shift		
GEAR RATIOS (Internal) Three-Speed			
First Gear	2.71 : 1	2.71 : 1	
Second Gear	1.50 : 1	1.50 : 1	
Third Gear	1.00 : 1	1.00 : 1	
Reverse	2.66 : 1	2.66 : 1	
Four-Speed			
First Gear	3.00 : 1	3.00 : 1	②
Second Gear	1.82 : 1	1.82 : 1	1.82 : 1
Third Gear	1.23 : 1	1.23 : 1	1.23 : 1
Fourth Gear	1.00 : 1	1.00 : 1	1.00 : 1
NUMBER OF SPROCKET TEETH			
Clutch	37	37	37
Transmission	22	22	23
Rear Wheel	51	51	51
NUMBER OF SPROCKET TEETH			
Engine—Three-Speed Trans.			
(Solo) FLH	24	24	
FL	23	23	
(Sidecar) FLH	22	22	
FL	19	19	
Four-Speed			
(Solo)	23/24	23/24	23/24
(Sidecar)	22	22	22

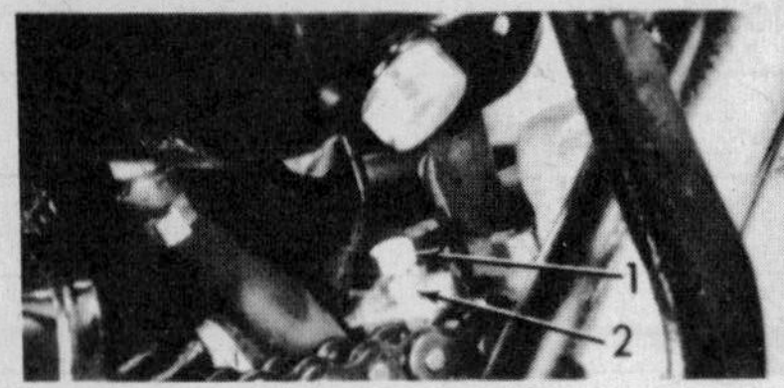

Sportster drive chain oiler (late)

Glide models chain oiler adjustment points

3. If an oiler screw locknut is fitted, back it off as far as possible. Turn the screw in, counting the number of turns before it reaches its seat.
4. Remove the screw. Blow out the line with compressed air.
5. Install the screw, turn it in until it contacts the seat, then back it off the number of turns which were counted (Step 3). Tighten the locknut, if fitted.
6. Normal setting is ¼ turn open (Glide) and ¾ turns open (Sportster).

SERVICE CHECKS AND ADJUSTMENTS

Fuel Strainer

The fuel strainer is located in the top of the supply valve inside of the fuel tank. The strainer can be cleaned in the following manner:

1. Drain the fuel tank.
2. Remove the supply valve.
3. Remove the dirt lying at the lip of the hole where the supply valve was removed.

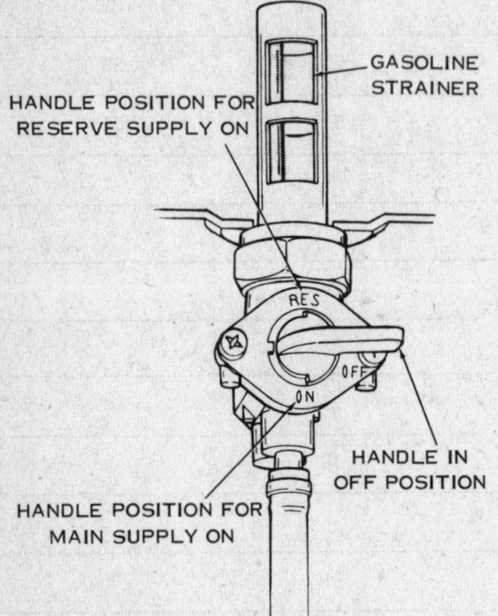

Fuel petcock (1975 and later)

General Specifications (cont.)

Glide Models	*FL & FLH (1969 & earlier)*	*FL & FLH (1970 & later)*	*FX/FXE*
OVERALL GEAR RATIOS (Three-Speed) (Solo)			
FLH			
First Gear	9.69	9.69	
Second Gear	5.36	5.36	
Third Gear	3.57	3.57	
FL			
First Gear	10.01	10.01	
Second Gear	5.60	5.60	
Third Gear	3.73	3.73	
FLH (Sidecar)			
First Gear	10.57	10.57	
Second Gear	5.84	5.84	
Third Gear	3.90	3.90	
FL			
First Gear	12.20	12.20	
FL			
Second Gear	6.75	6.75	
Third Gear	4.50	4.50	
(Four-Speed) (Solo) (23-tooth engine sprocket)			
First Gear	11.19	11.19	③
Second Gear	6.79	6.79	6.51
Third Gear	4.59	4.59	4.40
Fourth Gear	3.73	3.73	3.57
(24-tooth engine sprocket)			
First Gear	10.74	10.74	④
Second Gear	6.50	6.50	6.24
Third Gear	4.39	4.39	4.21
Fourth Gear	3.57	3.57	3.42
(Sidecar)			
First Gear	11.69	11.69	⑤
Second Gear	7.09	7.09	6.80
Third Gear	4.79	4.79	4.60
Fourth Gear	3.90	3.90	3.73

4. Clean strainer and blow dry with compressed air.
5. Replace the supply valve.

This operation should be performed every 2,000 miles or when needed.

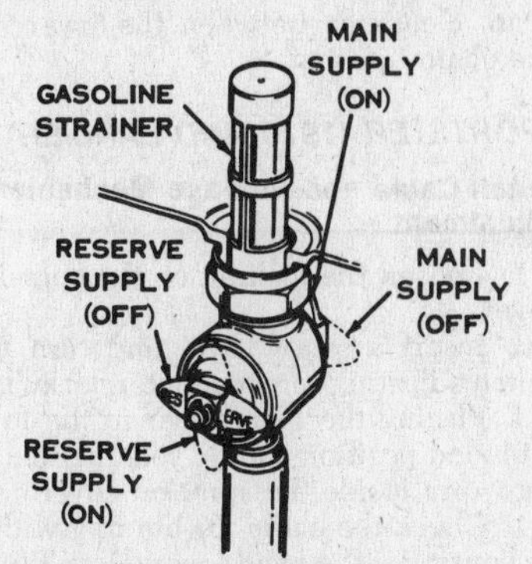

Fuel petcock (1974 and earlier)

NOTE: *On 1975 and later valves, be sure it is set to the "off" position when the engine is not running.*

Air Cleaner

The metal mesh-type filter need never be replaced, but should be cleaned every 1,000 miles in a safe solvent and lightly coated with engine oil. For *extremely* dusty conditions, this should be performed every 100 miles or at least once a day.

The corrugated paper-type element should be blown free of dirt every 1,000 miles, or more often in dusty conditions. If the surfaces are oily or sooty, the element can be cleaned with a safe solvent. When the element ceases to come clean, it must be replaced. Never coat it with oil.

The plastic foam-type element uses oil in the same manner as the metal mesh air cleaner and requires service at the same intervals. A sooty surface is normal but when the surface pores become clogged or the surface becomes mottled, cleaning is necessary. Remove the filter from the screen and wash it in a nonflammable solvent. When completely dry, soak it in engine oil, work the oil in until it is an even color, and allow the excess to drain off. The filter is now ready to be replaced. Replace the element so that the three grooves are towards the screen.

Clutch Adjustment

GLIDE MODELS

Foot Control Adjustment

1. Remove chain housing cover.
2. Place the foot pedal in the fully engaged position (toe down).
3. Loosen the pushrod adjusting screw locknut, and turn the adjusting screw until the end of the clutch release lever has about ⅛ in. free-play before the clutch disengages. Turning the screw to the right will decrease the movement and to the left will increase the movement.
4. Secure the locknut while holding the adjusting screw with a screwdriver and recheck the adjustment.
5. Check that there is ¼ in. clearance

General Specifications (cont.)

Glide Models	*FL & FLH (1969 & earlier)*	*FL & FLH (1970 & later)*	*FX/FXE*
TIRE DATA			
Front	5.10 x 16	5.10 x 16	3.75 x 19
Rear	5.10 x 16	5.10 x 16	5.10 x 16
TIRE PRESSURE			
Solo—front (psi)	20	20	24
rear (psi)	24	24	24
One Passenger			
front (psi)	20	20	24
rear (psi)	26	26	26
Sidecar			
front (psi)	22	22	
rear (psi)	26	26	
sidecar (psi)	20	20	

① Reserve tank (large) (U.S. gal.)
1972–74: 0.7
1975 and later: 0.6

② First gear
1974 and earlier: 3.00 : 1
1975 and later: 2.45 : 1

③ First gear
1972–74: 10.71
1975 and later: 9.91

④ First gear
1972–74: 10.25
1975 and later: 9.48

⑤ First gear
1972–74: 11.20
1975 and later: 10.33

between the lever and the starter drive housing.
6. The foot pedal should clear the bearing cover to prevent the rod from bending.

Hand Control Adjustment

1. Loosen the adjusting sleeve until there is about ¼ in. free movement at the hand lever before disengagement begins.
2. Turn the sleeve out for less lever play, or in for more, and secure the locknut.
3. If the above steps fail to correct the problem, or if the sleeve has already been adjusted all the way out, go on to the following steps.

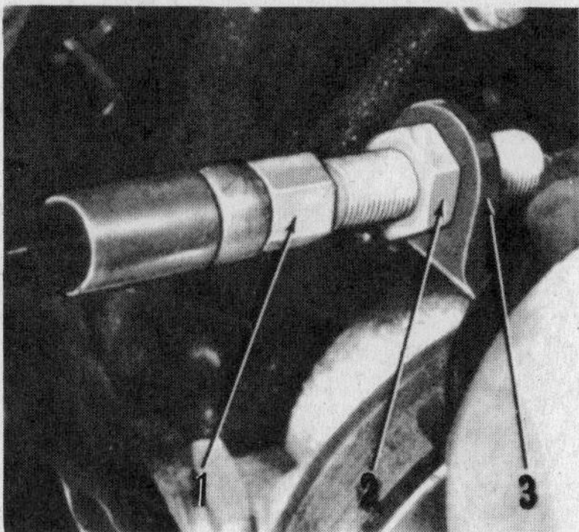

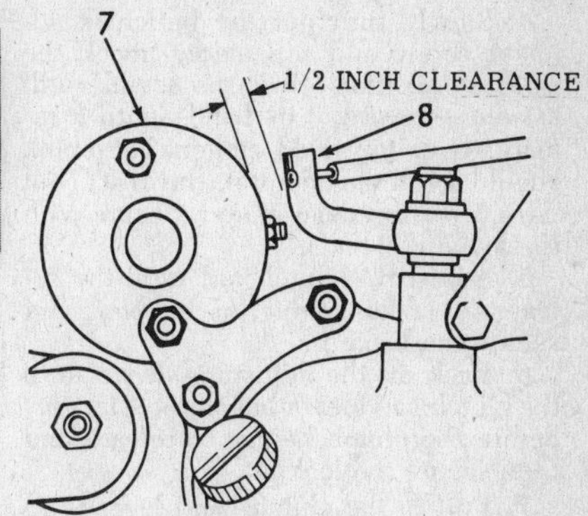

Hand clutch adjustment

1. Clutch cable adjusting sleeve
2. Sleeve lock nut
3. Bracket
4. Clutch push rod adjusting screw lock nut
5. Clutch adjusting screw
6. Clutch spring adjusting nuts
7. Starter motor
8. Clutch release lever

4. Move the clutch release lever until all the slack in the actuating mechanism has been taken up. You will notice a difference in lever motion.

5. If, at this point, there is not ⅜–⅝ in. between the lever and the starter motor, take the following steps.

a. Loosen the sleeve locknut and turn the sleeve to the right until it is resting against the locknut.

b. Remove the clutch cover and loosen the pushrod locknut. Turn the adjusting screw clockwise to move the release lever backward, or counterclockwise to move it forward.

c. Secure the locknut while holding the adjusting screw with a screwdriver when the lever is about ½ in. from the starter motor.

d. Secure the clutch cover using a new gasket and a gasket sealer.

6. Repeat Steps 1 and 2 to complete the adjustment.

Hand Lever Cable Removal and Installation

1. Turn the adjusting sleeve to the right until it seats against the locknut.

2. Remove the cable by lifting the ferrule clear of the anchor pin and sliding it through the slot.

3. Replace with the pin slot toward the inside.

4. Replace pin-type assemblies with the open end facing down.

Hand Clutch Booster Control Adjustment

The routine adjustment that is made to maintain the correct amount of hand lever play is done in the following manner:

1. Loosen the control-coil adjusting sleeve locknut and turn the adjusting sleeve to the right until there is one or more inches of play at the hand lever.

2. Loosen the bellcrank adjusting screw locknut and turn in the adjusting screw until the bellcrank will no longer cross top dead center when shifted by hand.

3. Loosen the upper adjuster nut which controls the tension of the clutch booster spring. Loosen it all the way.

4. Slowly turn out the bellcrank adjuster screw and repeatedly check the release position that the crank will assume—moving it by hand—until it remains over top dead center. The crank should reach the end of its travel at about ⅛ in. over top dead center. Secure with the locknut.

5. Adjust the clutch rod until the release lever has about 1/16 in. play, and secure the locknut.

6. Back off the adjusting sleeve until the clutch hand lever has about ½ in. play before the clutch begins to release and then secure the locknut.

7. Pull in the clutch hand lever to its stop and tighten the lower adjuster nut for the booster-spring tension until the hand lever remains in. Slowly loosen the nut until the lever returns to the fully extended position.

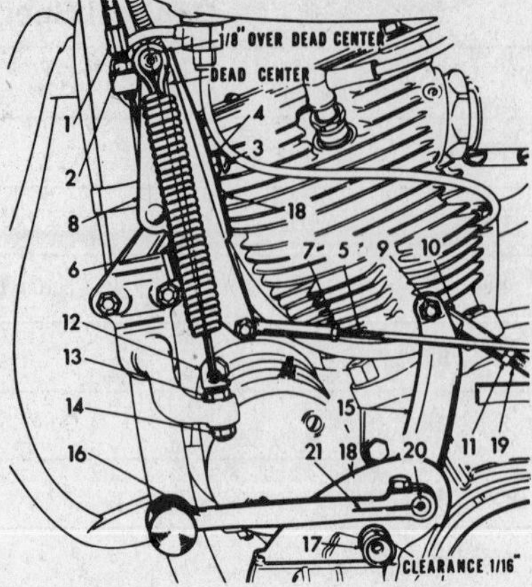

Hand clutch booster control adjustment

1. Control coil sleeve
2. Control coil adjusting sleeve locknut
3. Bellcrank adjusting screw
4. Bellcrank adjusting screw locknut
5. Clutch lever rod
6. Clutch control booster spring
7. Clutch lever rod locknut
8. Clutch control booster bellcrank
9. Shifter rod end bolt
10. Shifter rod end
11. Shifter rod end locknut
12. Clutch booster spring tension adjuster
13. Clutch booster spring tension upper adjuster nut
14. Clutch booster spring tension lower adjuster nut
15. Gearshifter lever
16. Gearshifter foot lever and rubber pedal
17. Foot lever cover mounting stud (1964 and earlier)
18. Grease gun fittings (2)
19. Shifter rod
20. Foot lever positioning mark
21. Foot lever clamping slot

8. Secure the upper adjuster nut which controls the tension of the booster spring.

The following procedure may help to eliminate hand lever stiffness, failure of the bellcrank to resume its position, or slipping or dragging of the clutch.

HAND LEVER
ANCHOR PIN
CONTROL CABLE FERRULE
SLOT OPEN END MUST FACE TOWARD INSIDE OF LEVER

1. Back off the clutch lever rod locknut and adjust the rod until the actuating lever has about ½ in. of play.

2. Move the actuating lever forward until all slack is taken up.

3. Check and make sure that there is a ¼ in. clearance between the lever rod and chain housing.

SPORTSTER (1970 AND EARLIER)

Clutch Cable and Release Mechanism Adjustment

1. Loosen the locknut on the sprocket cover.

2. Insert a screwdriver and turn the clutch adjusting screw counterclockwise.

3. Placing the hand lever in the fully extended position should seat the releasing worm inside the sprocket cover.

4. Check the cable for binding within its housing if the hand lever doesn't fully return to its seat.

5. Turn the cable adjusting sleeve at the hand lever until the worm almost reaches its stop.

6. Turn the adjusting screw clockwise until there is play in ⅛ of the hand lever's total movement. This is indicated by slightly increased tension on the lever as it approaches the released position.

7. While holding the adjusting screw steady, secure the locknut. Test-ride the motorcycle to check for slipping or dragging.

Clutch Spring Adjustment

1. Disconnect the battery ground wire from the negative terminal on XLH models.

2. Remove the left footrest and rear brake lever from their splined shafts.

3. On 1966 and earlier models, remove the stoplight switch from its mount, without disconnecting the wires, and place it out of the way.

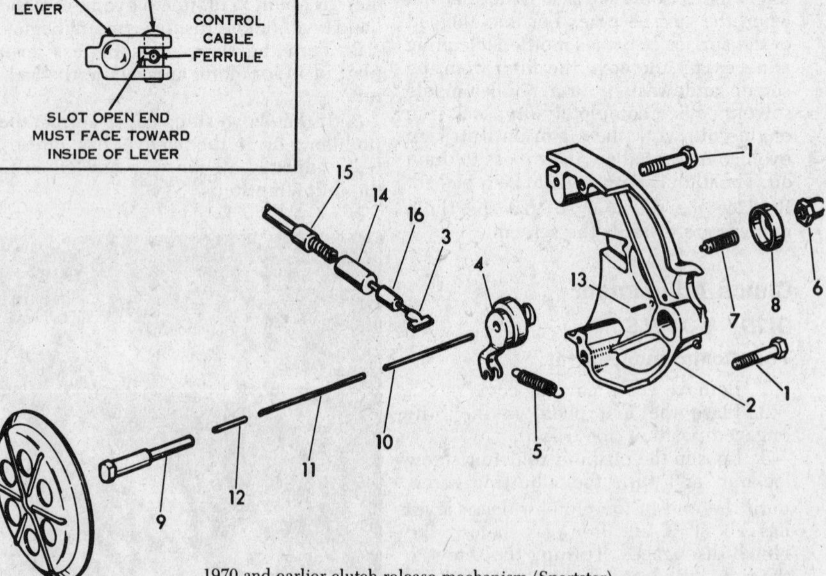

1970 and earlier clutch release mechanism (Sportster)

1. Sprocket cover bolts (2)
2. Sprocket cover
3. Control cable end
4. Clutch release worm and lever
5. Clutch release worm and lever spring
6. Clutch adjusting screw locknut
7. Clutch adjusting screw
8. Clutch release worm cover
9. Clutch release rod—left
10. Clutch release rod—right
11. Clutch release rod—right center
12. Clutch release rod—left center
13. Sprocket cover roll pin
14. Clutch cable felt seal retainer
15. Clutch cable ferrule
16. Clutch cable felt seal

4. Place a drip pan under the chain cover and remove the cover and gasket.
5. Remove the clutch cover screws, retainers, cover, and gasket. Tap the cover gently to remove it, but do not pry on it as this may warp it and cause leaks.
6. Tighten the adjusting nuts, one-half turn at a time, making sure that they seat in their locked position against the adjusting plate after each turn. The nuts have hex-heads of 7/16 and ½ in. sizes.
7. When properly adjusted the pressure plate should be uniformly 3/16 in. from the outside of the spring cup flanges.
8. If tightened beyond 7/64 in. clearance, the clutch will not release. The necessity of such an adjustment would indicate worn or oily clutch plates. Excessive tightness will damage the clutch release rods.

SPORTSTER (1971 AND LATER)

Clutch Cable and Release Mechanism Adjustment

1. Turn the cable adjuster in until there is a goodly amount of play in the cable.
2. Remove the plug from the primary chain compartment cover. Loosen the adjusting screw locknut and turn the adjusting screw in until resistance is felt. Turn it in about 2 more turns.
3. Turn the cable adjuster out until there is no free play (but no tension) in the cable. Tighten the cable adjuster locknut. The cable is now properly adjusted.
4. Back off the adjusting screw until it turns easily. Turn it in gently until resistance is felt, then back if off ¼ to ½ turn and tighten the locknut.
5. Check clutch operation and reset if necessary.

Clutch Spring Adjustment: 1971–Early 1974

1. The procedure is essentially the same as described for 1970 and Earlier Sportster.
2. When properly adjusted, the pressure plate should be 11/32 in. from the outer surface of the outer drive plate.
3. If tightened beyond 5/16 in. clearance, the clutch will not release. Such an adjustment will damage the clutch release rods.

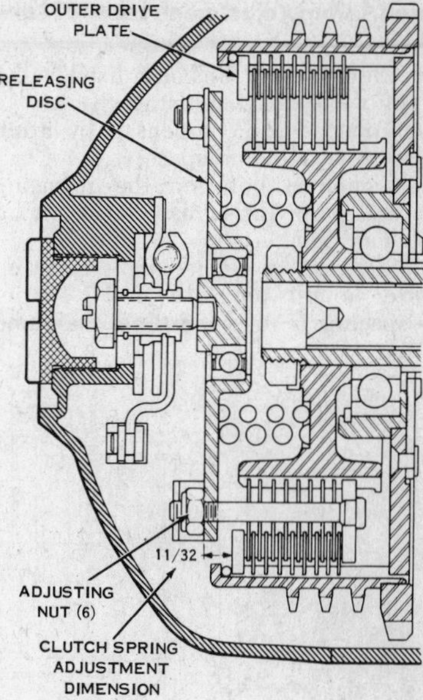

Clutch adjustment (1971–early 1974)

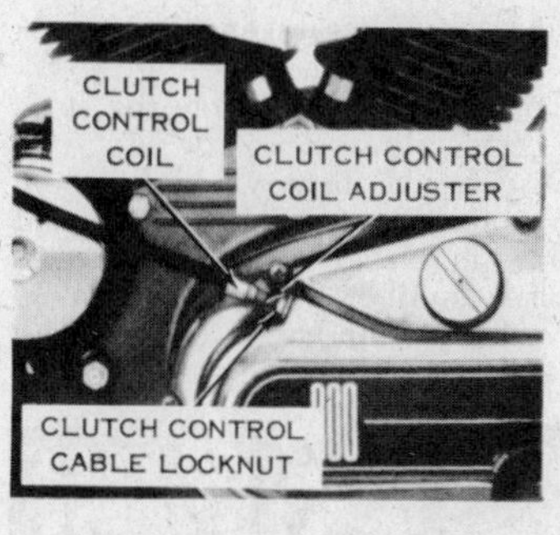

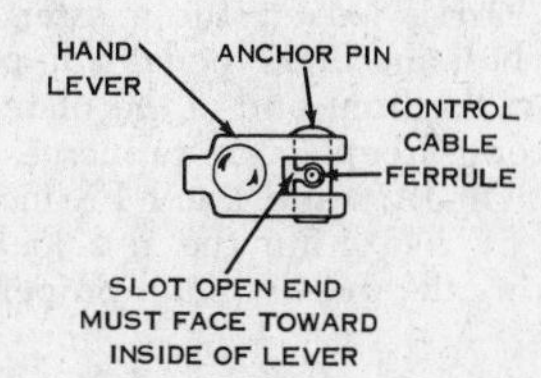

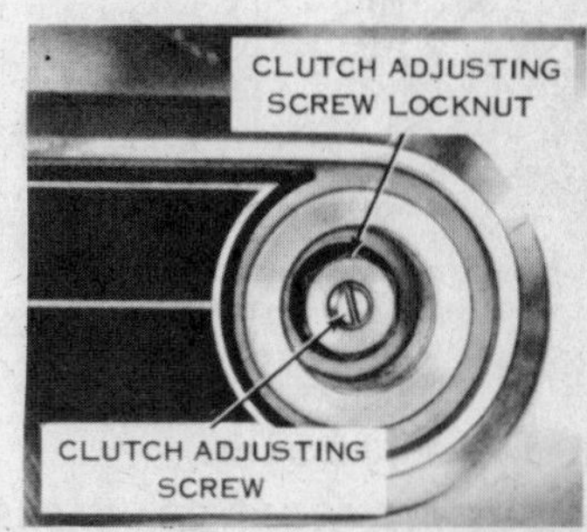

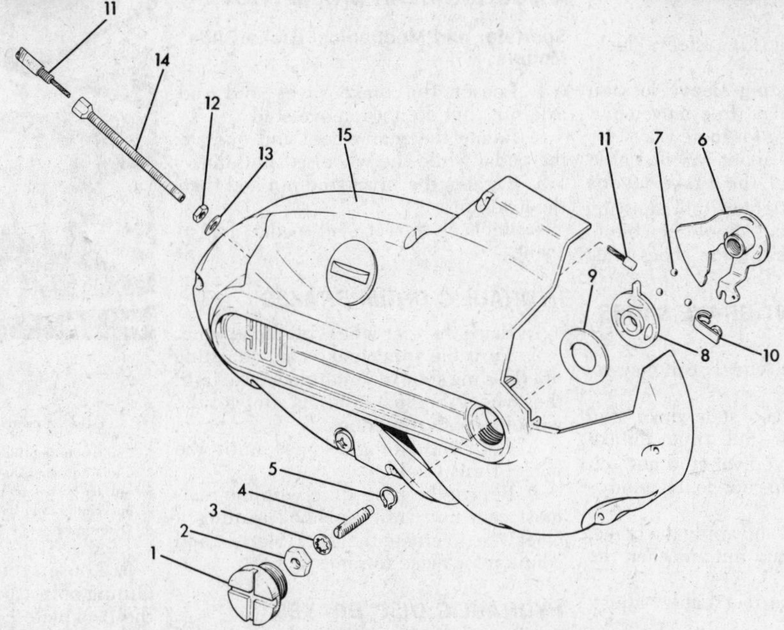

1971 and later Sportster clutch release mechanism

1. Access plug, clutch release adjusting screw
2. Lock nut, adjusting screw
3. Lockwasher, adjusting screw
4. Screw, clutch release adjusting
5. Retaining ring, Truarc
6. Release ramp and lever
7. Ball (3)
8. Release ramp
9. Washer
10. Cable coupling
11. Cable and coil assy.
12. Lock nut, coil adjusting sleeve
13. Washer, coil adjusting sleeve
14. Sleeve, coil adjusting
15. Primary chain case cover

Clutch Spring Adjustment: Late 1974 and Later

1. Clutch spring tension is fixed by the length of the six clutch stud spacers. As clutch plates wear, compensate by fitting shorter than standard spacers.
2. Clearance between the releasing disc and outer drive plate must not be less than ⅛ in.
3. Standard spacer length is 1.530 in. Shorter lengths are 1.440 and 1.450 in. All spacers in use must be the same length.

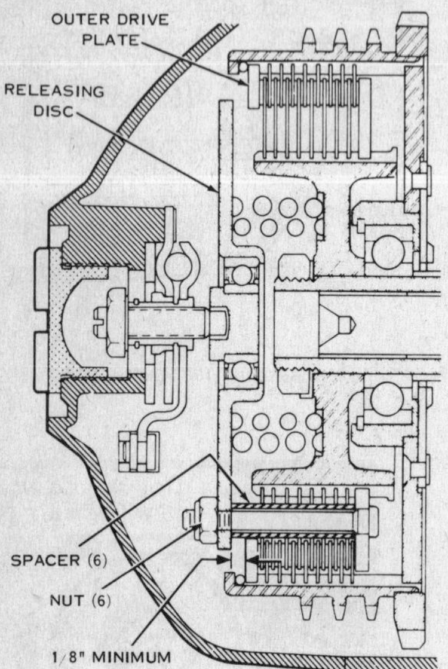

Clutch adjustment (late 1974 and later)

Brake Adjustments

ADJUSTING FRONT BRAKE CABLE (ALL MODELS)

1. Loosen the adjusting sleeve locknut.
2. Turn the adjusting sleeve locknut clockwise for less play (free movement) and counterclockwise for more play.
3. When there is about ³/₁₆ in. cable play, or when ¼ of the brake lever's movement is free, tighten the adjusting sleeve nut. The wheel should be able to spin freely; if it doesn't, the shoes must be centered (adjusted).

ADJUSTING FRONT BRAKE SHOES (ALL MODELS)

1. Raise the front wheel so it may rotate freely.
2. Loosen the brake shoe pivot stud nut and sleeve nut. (Substitute "brake shoe pivot stud" for "pivot stud nut" on Sportsters. Loosen this but do not remove it).
3. Spin the wheel and apply the brake. Tighten the pivot stud nut and then the axle sleeve nut.
4. Recheck for correct cable adjustment.

ADJUSTING REAR WHEEL BRAKE LINKAGE

Sportster and Mechanical Brake Glide Models

1. Turn the brake rod adjusting nut clockwise to tighten the brake and counterclockwise to loosen it. The nut has a lip which serves as a stop against the clevis pin in the operating lever. Using a screwdriver as a lever against the brake operating lever, pry it forward, and turn the adjusting nut. This saves wear on the nut's lip.
2. There should be 1¼ in. of play in the brake pedal before the brakes begin to operate. If the brakes still drag, center the shoes.

HYDRAULIC DRUM BRAKE

1969 and Earlier

1. Expose the piston pushrod link by sliding the rubber boot away from the master cylinder.
2. Adjust the piston rod so that the foot pedal moves freely about 1½ in. before the brake begins to operate.
3. Back off the locknut and turn the plunger clockwise to shorten the pushrod, and counterclockwise to lengthen it.
4. Test for free movement and secure the locknut.

1970 and Later

1. Freeplay of the brake pedal (before the pushrod contacts the piston in the master cylinder) should be about ¹/₁₆ in.
2. If adjustment is necessary (FL/FLH), loosen the master cylinder rear bolt and brake pedal stop plate bolt. Move the front end of the plate down to decrease freeplay, up to increase it.
3. On 1972 and Later FX models, adjust by loosening the rod locknut and turning the rod to obtain proper play.

ADJUSTING REAR BRAKE SHOES

Sportster and Mechanical Brake Glide Models

1. Loosen the brake pivot stud and axle nuts but do not remove stud.
2. Rotate the rear wheel and operate the pedal while the wheel is spinning.
3. Tighten the pivot stud nut and then the axle nut.
4. Recheck for correct pedal adjustment.

HYDRAULIC DRUM BRAKES

1. Raise the rear wheel off the ground.
2. Turn the front brake cam adjusting nut (leading shoe) counterclockwise until the wheel begins to drag. Rotate the wheel in both directions.
3. Turn the nut clockwise until the wheel turns freely.
4. Repeat the procedure with the rearmost cam nut (trailing shoe), turning it clockwise to create the drag (Step 2), and counterclockwise to remove it.

HYDRAULIC DISC BRAKES

The hydraulic disc brakes are self-adjusting. Fluid levels in front and rear master cylinders should be checked every 1,000 miles.

Primary Chain Adjustment

Check the primary chain every 2,000 miles for correct adjustment. Chain adjustment can be checked through the oil filter opening which is located near the top of the chain housing cover. A properly adjusted chain will have free up-and-down movement in the upper strand as follows:

Chain slack with cold engine—⅝ to ⅞ in.

Chain slack with warm engine—⅜ to ⅝ in.

Glide models rear brake shoe adjustment

1. Leading brake shoe adjusting cam nut
2. Trailing brake shoe adjusting cam nut

To adjust the chain, follow the steps below.

1. Disconnect battery cable from starter motor. Remove left foot rest and rear brake foot lever.
2. Place an oil drain pan under clutch. Remove front chain cover screws, chain cover and gasket.

Glide models primary chain adjustment

1. Chain adjusting shoe
2. Chain adjusting shoe bracket
3. Bracket backplate
4. Backplate center bolt
5. Outer plate
6. Support bracket
7. Primary chain oiler
A. Adjusting holes
B. Adjusting holes

3. Loosen the chain adjusting shoe retaining bolts (three bolts on the Sportster, the backplate center bolt on Glide models). Raise shoe to tighten chain and lower to loosen chain.
4. Tighten retaining bolts. Check adjustment of chain.
5. Replace gasket, chain cover and secure with front chain cover screws. Reconnect battery cable to starter motor. Replace foot rest and brake lever.

Sportster primary chain adjustment

1. Drive chain
2. Chain adjuster shoe
3. Support bracket
4. Support bracket bolts (2)
5. Support bracket brace
6. Brace bolt

Rear Chain Adjustment

Check the rear chain adjustment every 1,000 miles. A properly adjusted rear chain will have a ½ in. movement midway between the mainshaft and the rear wheel drive sprocket. Adjustment should be checked at several points along chain. Chain is adjusted as follows:

Sportster

1. Loosen the axle nut.
2. Loosen the right and left adjusting stud locknuts. Loosen the anchor bolt on 73 models.
3. Turn both adjusting stud locknuts clockwise the same number of turns to tighten the chain and counterclockwise to loosen it. While loosening the chain, tap the axle forward with a soft mallet.
4. Secure the locknut against the adjusting nut and measure the distance from the locknut to the outer end of the adjusting stud. Both should be the same to ensure correct alignment.
5. Spin the wheel and look for wobbling of the sprocket which would indicate poor alignment.

Sportster drive chain adjustment

1. Rear axle nut
2. Adjusting stud lock nut
3. Adjusting stud nut
4. Adjusting stud
5. Anchor bolt (1973)

6. The chain should have ½ in. of play midway between the mainshaft and the rear wheel sprocket.
7. Secure the axle nut and adjusting stud locknut. Adjust the brake rod if necessary.

GLIDE MODELS

1972 and Earlier

1. Remove the axle nut and washer from right-side and loosen the brake sleeve nut, brake anchor stud nut (left-side), and adjusting screw locknuts.
2. Proceed as described in the "Sportster" section.

Glide models rear chain adjustment (1972 and earlier)

1. Brake sleeve nut
2. Wheel adjusting screw locknut
3. Wheel adjusting screw
4. Brake anchor stud nut

1973 and Later

1. Remove cotter pin and loosen brake anchor cable nut. Loosen axle nut.
2. Adjust chain by turning adjusting nuts. Turn adjusting nuts an equal number of turns to keep wheel in alignment. To move axle forward it may be necessary to tap lightly on the ends of studs.
3. Tighten axle nuts and brake anchor cable nut, replace cotter pin. Check chain adjustment.

Periodic Maintenance Intervals

OIL

WEEKLY
- Rear chain

EVERY 2,000 MILES
- Clutch hand lever
- Brake hand lever
- Clutch control cable
- Front brake cable
- Throttle cable
- Spark cable
- Clutch booster lever rod clevis
- Shifter lever linkage
- Rear brake rod clevis
- Front brake cable clevis
- Saddle post bearing
- Generator bearing

Recommended Tire Pressure ①

	Front Tire Size	*Front Tire Pressure*	*Rear Tire Size*	*Rear Tire Pressure*
SPORTSTER				
1966 and earlier XL, XLH	3.25/3.50 x 19	14 lbs	4.00 x 18	18 lbs
1967 and later XL, XLH	3.50 x 18	16 lbs	3.50 x 18	20 lbs
1969 and earlier XLCH	3.25/3.50 x 19	16 lbs	4.00 x 18	18 lbs
1970 and later (all models)	3.75 x 19	24 lbs	4.25 x 18	30 lbs
GLIDE MODELS				
Solo	5.10 x 16	20 lbs	5.10 x 16	24 lbs
	5.00 x 16	12 lbs	5.10 x 16	18 lbs
	3.75 x 19	24 lbs	5.10 x 16	24 lbs
Rider and one passenger	5.10 x 16	20 lbs	5.10 x 16	26 lbs
	3.00 x 16	12 lbs	5.10 x 16	20 lbs
	3.75 x 19	24 lbs	5.10 x 16	26 lbs
Rider, one sidecar passenger or 150 lb load	5.10 x 16	22 lbs	5.10 x 16	26 lbs
	5.00 x 16	12 lbs	5.00 x 16	20 lbs
Sidecar wheel	5.10 x 16	20 lbs		
	5.00 x 16	14 lbs		

① Based on rider weight of 150 lbs. For every 50 lbs. over this, increase pressure 2 psi (rear) and 1 psi (front).

Periodic Maintenance Intervals

SERVICE

WEEKLY
- Check battery level
- Check tire pressure
- Adjust chain
- Adjust clutch
- Adjust brakes
- Check brake fluid
- Tighten nuts, bolts, and wheel spokes

EVERY 1,000 MILES OR 2 MONTHS (SUMMER) OR 1 MONTH (WINTER)
- Clean air cleaner
- Change engine oil (during winter or dusty conditions)
- Check transmission oil
- Check rear chain oiler

EVERY 2,000 MILES OR 4 MONTHS (SUMMER) OR 2 MONTHS (WINTER)
- Adjust tappets
- Clean and adjust contact points
- Adjust primary chain
- Clean tappet oil screen
- Change engine oil
- Change fuel filter
- Check primary chain oiler

EVERY 5,000 MILES OR 12 MONTHS
- Adjust ignition timing
- Replace spark plugs
- Replace oil filter element
- Replace contact points
- Replace air filter element
- Change transmission oil
- Change fork oil ('73 and later Sportster)
- Check generator
- Check alternator
- Check shock bushings
- Check front and swing arm bearings
- Rotate tires

EVERY 10,000 MILES
- Check oil pressure

GREASE

EVERY 2,000 MILES
- Front brake shaft
- Front wheel hub
- Rear brake shaft
- Rear bake crossover shaft
- Rear wheel hub
- Swing arm pivot bearing
- Body frame bearing
- Clutch release worm
- Clutch release cable housing
- Clutch pushrod bearing
- Clutch booster bearing
- Clutch pedal bearing
- Foot shift lever
- Rear brake pedal bearing
- Kick-starter shaft
- Master cylinder lever
- Rear axle bearing
- Saddle bearing and post
- Tachometer drive gear
- Speedometer drive

EVERY 5,000 MILES
- Throttle control spiral
- Spark control spiral
- Speedometer cable
- Tachometer cable
- Contact breaker camshaft and advance unit
- Compensating sprocket
- Sidecar wheel hub
- Generator bearing
- Front wheel hub
- Rear wheel hub

EVERY 10,000 MILES
- Repack rear fork pivot bearing

EVERY 50,000 MILES
- Repack steering head bearings

Recommended Lubricants

Engine and Transmission	
Below 40° F	Special Light (58)
Above 40° F	Medium Heavy (75)
High temperature or sustained high speed	Regular Heavy (105)
Front Forks	
Harley-Davidson Type-B	

TUNE-UP

NOTE: *Common tune-up procedures are explained in detail in "General Information."*

CONTACT BREAKER POINTS

There are four types of contact breakers in use on all Harley-Davidson V-Twins. The points should be checked for gap and surface condition at the first 500 and 1,000 miles, and every 2,000 miles thereafter.

Single Contact Breaker with Manual Advance

This system has one pair of points which regulate the spark in both cylinders simultaneously. The narrow lobe of the cam times the front cylinder and the wide lobe times the rear cylinder. Both cylinders operate from a single ignition coil which fires both spark plugs, but at different stages of the combustion cycle. If the front cylinder is firing, the rear is dormant, since no combustible mixture is present during the exhaust stroke. Manual rotation of the circuit breaker base provides advanced or retarded timing.

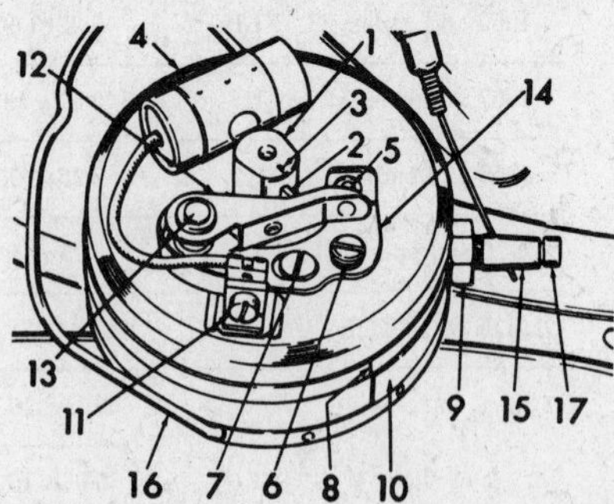

Single contact breaker, manual advance

1. Breaker cam
2. Fiber cam follower
3. Cam timing mark
4. Condenser
5. Contact points
6. Lockscrew
7. Eccentric adjusting screw
8. Timing mark
9. Adjusting stud locknut
10. Timing adjusting stud plate
11. Wire stud screw
12. Circuit breaker lever
13. Pivot stud
14. Contact point and support
15. Timing adjusting stud
16. Cover retainer
17. Control wire lockscrew

ADJUSTMENT

1. Turn the engine over until the points are fully open to their widest gap. Loosen the point lock screw.
2. Rotate the eccentric adjusting screw until the points open far enough to insert a feeler gauge of 0.020 in.
3. Secure the lockscrew and check gap against any movement which may have occurred when securing the screw.

Single Contact Breaker with Automatic Advance

(GLIDE MODELS TO 1969 SPORTSTER MODELS TO 1970

This type of contact breaker works the same way as the manual advance type, except that the spark is automatically advanced through the action of flyweights in the contact breaker base as the engine speed increases.

Adjustment

The points on the automatic advance type are set in the same manner as on the manual advance type.

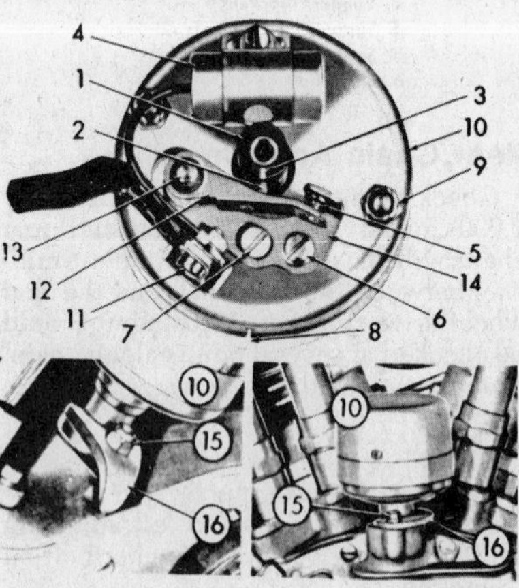

Single contact breaker, automatic advance (early)

1. Breaker cam
2. Fiber cam follower
3. Cam timing mark
4. Condenser
5. Contact points
6. Adjustable point lock screw
7. Eccentric adjusting screw
8. Timing marks (1965) model
9. Circuit breaker head nut (2)
10. Circuit breaker head
11. Wire stud screw
12. Circuit breaker lever
13. Pivot stud
14. Contact point and support
15. Stem clamp nut
16. Stem clamp

Double Contact Breaker

This system has individual contact point sets and coils for each cylinder. The single lobe cam on the timer shaft has a single mark which aligns with the fiber cam follower for each set of points when the points are open to their fullest travel. Therefore, the cam opens each set of points once every crankshaft rotation.

ADJUSTMENT

1. Loosen the front cylinder (indicated by an "F" on the breaker base) breaker point lock screw.
2. Set the front points to 0.022 in. by manipulating the eccentric adjusting screw until the proper gap is obtained. Check the gap with a wire feeler gauge. There should be a slight drag on the gauge when removing it.
3. Secure the lock screw and check gap against possible movement caused by securing the lock screw.

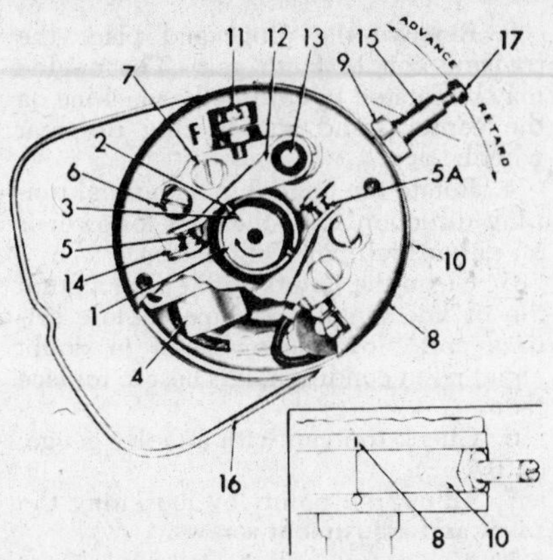

Double contact breaker

1. Cam
2. Fiber cam follower
3. Cam timing mark
4. Condenser
5. Front cylinder contact points
5A. Rear cylinder contact points
6. Lockscrew
7. Adjusting screw
8. Timing mark
9. Adjusting stud locknut
10. Timing adjusting plate
11. Wire stud screw
12. Circuit breaker lever
13. Pivot stud
14. Contact point and support
15. Timing adjusting stud
16. Cover retainer
17. Control wire lockscrew

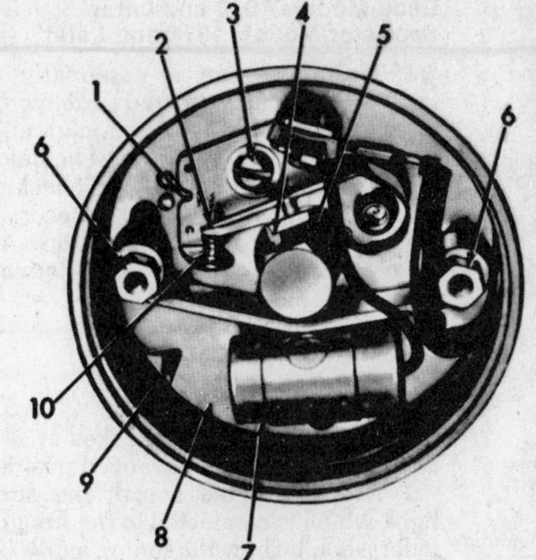

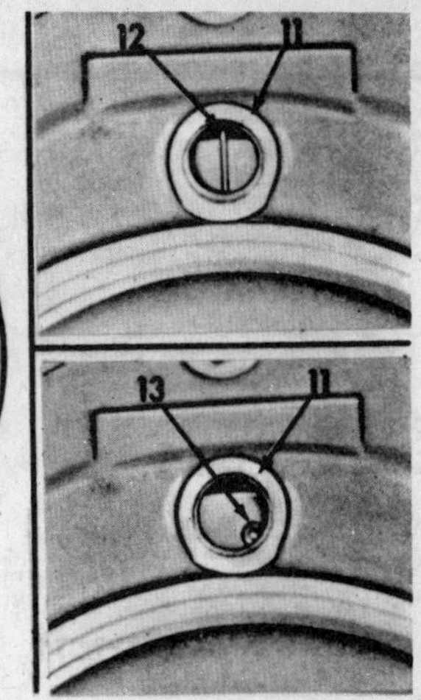

Contact breaker, Glide models (1970 and later), Sportster (1971 and later)

1. Contact point adjusting notch
2. Moving contact points
3. Stationary contact point lockscew
4. Cam follower
5. Breaker cam
6. Circuit breaker plate screws (2)
7. Condenser
8. Circuit breaker plate
9. Circuit breaker plate adjusting notch
10. Contacts
11. Timing inspection hole
12. Advance (35°) timing mark on flywheel
13. Retarded (5° BTDC) position of piston top dead center mark on flywheel

4. Follow the above procedure on the rear set of points.

5. Check ignition timing any time the rear set of points are adjusted as this will affect the timing. Consult "Ignition Timing" section for procedures.

Single Contact Breaker with Automatic Advance

GLIDE MODELS 1970 AND LATER SPORTSTER MODELS 1971 AND LATER

This type of circuit breaker is the same as the "Single Contact Breaker With Automatic Advance." If, during point gap setting procedures, a discrepancy of 0.004 in. or more is discovered, the breaker cam must be checked for eccentric travel.

Adjustment

1. Turn the engine over until the points are open to their widest gap. Loosen the point lock screw.

2. Use a small screwdriver at the pry point (adjusting notch) until a gap of 0.018 in. is obtained.

3. Secure the lockscrew and check for movement caused by securing the lock screw.

IGNITION TIMING

1. Timing should not be checked until breaker points are cleaned and properly gapped.

2. Static and dynamic (strobe light) timing are both possible. If the static method is used, support the rear wheel off the ground, remove the plugs, engage the transmission, and turn the wheel to rotate the engine. Always rotate the engine in the normal direction of rotation.

3. Telescoping the front pushrod cover will allow valve motion to be observed for static timing. The piston comes up for the compression (ignition) stroke just after the intake valve closes.

4. For dynamic timing, crankcase view plug No. 96295-65 is available to prevent oil spray.

Static Timing

MANUAL ADVANCE

1. Remove the inspection hole cap from the left side of the crankcase. Telescope the front pushrod cover. Remove point cover.

2. Turn the engine in the normal direction of rotation until the front intake valves closes. Turn the engine very slowly from this point on until the timing mark for the front cylinder is aligned in the inspection hole as illustrated.

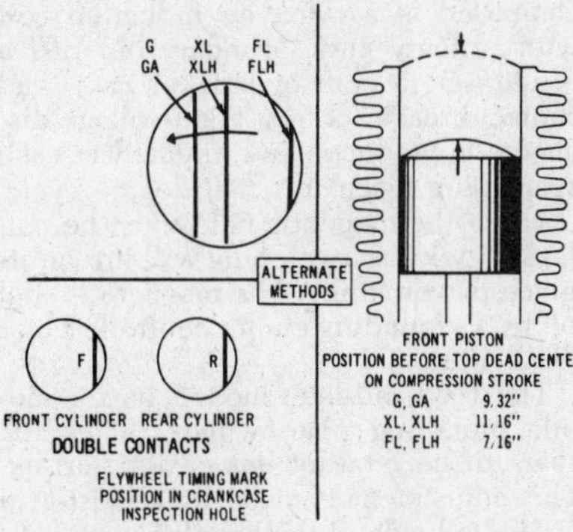

Timing marks for all models with manual timing advance

3. Check that the timing mark on the breaker point base aligns with the end of the timing adjusting plate.

4. Rotate the breaker point head counterclockwise until it reaches its stop (full advance position).

5. At this point the timing mark on the breaker cam should align with the fiber heel of the breaker points. If it does not, loosen the timing adjusting stud locknut and move the head until alignment is achieved.

Procede with the timing procedure accordingly:

6. On single contact breaker models, hook up the timing lamp. With the points in the fully advanced position, and flywheel marks correctly aligned as illustrated earlier, the points should just begin to open as indicated by the reaction of the test light. If they do not, loosen the adjusting stud locknut and move the base until the light reacts with the timing marks properly positioned. Tighten locknut and retard the timing; then advance it and check that the points open. Rotate the engine one full revolution and check that the points open at the proper time.

7. On double contact breaker models, connect the test lamp to the point wire for the front cylinder (yellow). Align the front cylinder timing mark ("F") as shown. Check test light reaction (fully advanced) as for the single contact breaker (Step 6). Repeat the procedure with the other set of points. If the rear cylinder points to not open at the correct time, adjust by changing the point gap rather than moving the base.

AUTOMATIC ADVANCE

NOTE: *Static timing is not recommended since it will result in timing being slightly retarded. On automatic advance models, a strobe light should be used.*

Glide Models to 1969 Sportster Models to 1970

1. Remove the plug from the inspection hole on the left of the crankcase. Telescope the front pushrod cover and remove the breaker point cover.

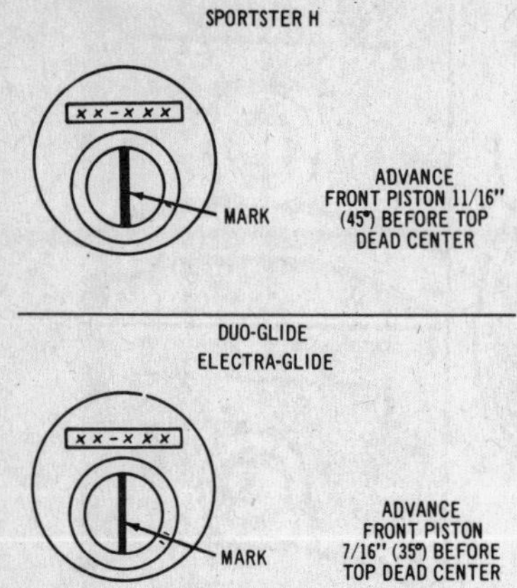

Timing marks for all models with automatic timing advance

2. Turn the engine in the normal direction of rotation until the front cylinder intake valve closes, then continue turning slowly until the flywheel advance timing mark is aligned in the very center of the inspection hole.

3. The cam must be turned clockwise as far as possible (full advance position) and held there while checking the timing.

4. At this point, the timing mark on the top of the cam should align with the breaker point fiber heel. If it does not, shift the breaker head so that alignment is obtained:

a. A limited adjustment is available on 1965 models due to slotted holes in the timer plate in which the base studs ride. Loosen the contact breaker head nuts and shift the base by prying between the plate lip and the base stud with a screwdriver.

b. If this is not enough, the entire shaft must be loosened, lifted free, and rotated a couple of teeth until the follower and the cam mark are in alignment. This will cause the base timing marks to go out of alignment.

c. When the cam and fiber align, while in the fully advanced position, secure the timer plate nuts. Overtightening will cause distortion of the timer base plate and affect timing.

d. On 1966 and later models there is a clamp on the contact breaker stem to allow a 360° adjustment range. Loosen the clamp bolts and turn the head clockwise to retard or counterclockwise to advance the timing to attain alignment.

5. The cam must be turned clockwise as far as possible when checking alignment as noted previously. This is the full advance position.

6. Hook up the test light. The points must begin to open just as the advanced flywheel mark is aligned in the center of the inspection hole. If adjustment is necessary, loosen the nut or bolts and rotate the breaker point head so that the light reacts just as the flywheel advanced mark is in the center of the inspection hole. Be sure the cam is held in the full advance position as this is checked.

Glide Models 1970 and Later Sportster Models 1971 and Later

1. The procedure is essentially the same as for earlier models except that there is no preliminary cam mark alignment necessary. The cam must be held in the full advance position when checking.

2. If timing adjustment is necessary, loosen the two breaker plate screws and rotate the plate until proper timing is achieved.

Dynamic Timing

ALL MODELS

1. Timing should be checked at about 2,000 rpm or the full advanced position.

2. At that engine speed, the strobe light, which is connected to the front cylinder, should show the timing marks centered in the inspection hole.

3. If adjustment is necessary, rotate either the breaker point head or the breaker plate, depending on model. Refer to "Static Timing" or the illustrations.

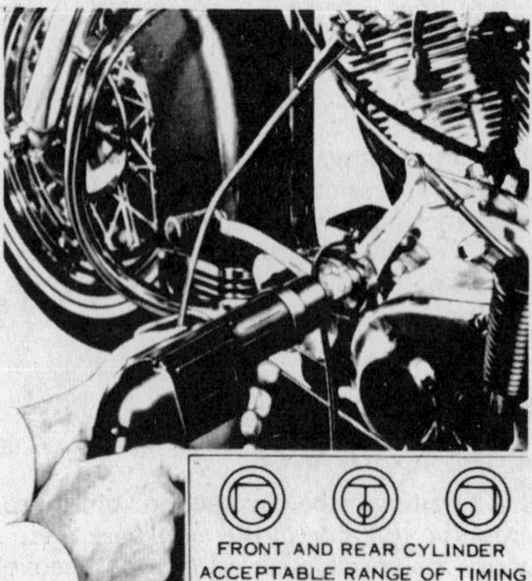

Timing with a strobe light

SPORTSTER XLCH MAGNETO

The magneto is a generating system composed of a rotor, an induction coil with primary and secondary circuits, a condenser, a contact breaker cam, and contact breaker points. High-voltage discharge is produced and directed to each spark plug twice in a 360 degree cycle, because the magnetic field must be collapsed twice so each plug will fire on its given power stroke. The magneto is shut off by a grounding circuit controlled by a "kill" button.

The 1965 and later models have a mobile mounting plate which allows the spark to be retarded for easier starting. This adjustment is made by a twist-grip on the left-side of the handlebar.

Adjusting Contact Breaker Points

1. The points should be examined for proper gap and surface 1,500 miles after installation and then at intervals of 2,000 miles.

2. Remove the carburetor, air cleaner, and magneto cover.

3. Remove the plugs and place the transmission in High gear. The engine may be rotated by setting the machine on the center stand and turning the rear wheel.

4. Rotate the engine in its normal running direction until the cam follower is on either high point of the cam.

5. Clean the points with either a point file or fine metal sandpaper before setting, and blow clean. When in doubt about point condition, it is best to replace them.

6. Check the gap with a feeler gauge. (0.015 in.).

7. Adjust the points by loosening the pivot and adjustment screws.

Setting Ignition Timing

Ignition is timed with the spark advanced and is correctly set when the forward piston is 45 degrees ($^{11}/_{16}$) in.) before top dead center. This corresponds to the flywheel timing mark position when it is in the center of the inspection hole. Whenever the points are replaced, or at least annually, the timing should be set.

The 1965–1967 models have an adjusting screw which, when turned clockwise, advances the timing. A counterclockwise adjustment retards the timing. Applying mild pressure to the magneto housing will cause it to follow the movement of the adjusting screw. The correct amount of spark retardation is obtained by backing off the setting stop screw until there is a distance of $^{3}/_{16}$ in. between its head and seat. Adjust the screw only one turn; more will affect retarded timing.

Late 1967 XLCH models have a slot and pin in the base plate which serves the same function as the adjustment screw.

1. Remove the magneto cover, timing inspection hole plug, and spark plugs. Telescope or remove the front intake pushrod cover so that valve motion can be observed.

2. Place the transmission in High gear and put the motorcycle on its center stand so that the engine can be turned by rotating the rear wheel.

3. Set the contacts points.

4. Turn the engine until the exposed valve closes (travels to its highest point). Slowly rotate the engine in its normal running direction until the timing mark is aligned in the center of the inspection hole.

5. Align the timing marks on the magneto base and mounting plate.

6. If the narrow cam lobe is not located counterclockwise from the cam follower and the breaker points aren't beginning to open, the magneto must be adjusted. Be sure the spark is fully advanced.

7. On 1965 to early 1967 models, an adjustment can be made with the magneto advance stop screw.

8. If alignment, which will not interfere with the air cleaner, cannot be made through adjustment of the screw, or if it is a fixed-position magneto, lift up the magneto until its drive gears become unmeshed. Turn the cam the amount it was

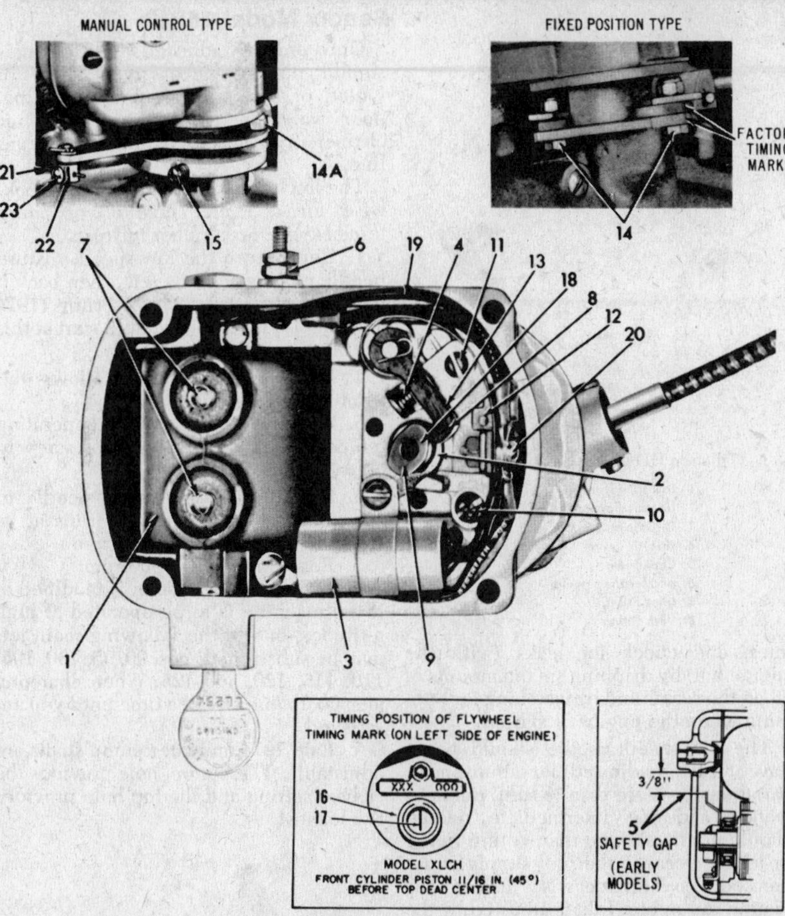

Sportster magneto

1. Induction coil
2. Rotor
3. Condenser
4. Circuit breaker points
5. Safety gap (1964 and earlier)
6. Ignition cut-out terminal
7. Coil secondary terminal spring
8. Cam follower
9. Cam
10. Pivot screw
11. Adjusting screw
12. Adjusting stud
13. Cam oiler felt
14. Magneto mounting bolts and nuts (1964 and earlier)
14A. Magneto mounting bolts (1965)
15. Magneto advance stop screw (1965 and later)
16. Timing inspection hole
17. Timing mark
18. Narrow cam lobe
19. Coil lead wire
20. Breaker point terminial
21. Control wire (1965)
22. Swivel block (1965)
23. Control wire set screw (1965)

out of position and replace the magneto. Repeat this until the proper point timing is obtained and then secure the magneto.

9. A timing or continuity light is one accurate means of determining when the points begin to open. Attach one test lead to the terminal post or point spring and the other to a ground. When the points break contact the light will go out. An emergency method is to place cellophane between the points and to tug gently on it. When the points begin to open, the cellophane will be released.

10. A strobe light provides the most accurate setting since it is done with the engine running. This takes up any endplay and automatically advances the timing. Leads are attached to the front plug, ground, and the positive battery terminal. Timing view plug, part HD (No. 96295-65), must be used to prevent oil spray. The engine should be operating at between 1,500 and 2,000 rpm.

11. Recheck ignition timing, always rotating the engine in the direction of normal operation. Never overtighten the coil lead wire as this may damage insulators and cause a short circuit.

VALVE TAPPET ADJUSTMENT

Sportster

Valve tappets must be adjusted with the engine cold. Adjust the tappets after the first 500 and 1,000 miles, and thereafter at every 2,000 miles.

1. Press down on the pushrod cover retaining spring and remove the cover spring keeper.
2. Block up the telescoped cover so it doesn't slip down.
3. Rotate the engine until the valve that is to be adjusted is at its lowest position.
4. Loosen the tappet adjusting screw locknut and turn the adjusting screw into the tappet body until the pushrod is free and will shake slightly. Hold the pushrod just below the cylinder head and shake it toward the front and rear of the engine.
5. Gently turn the adjusting screw toward the pushrod until nearly all play is removed. Secure the tappet screw locknut against the tappet body.

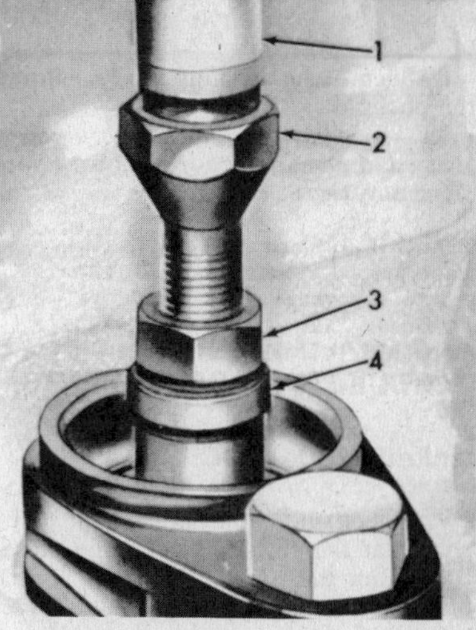

Sportster tappet adjustment

1. Push rod
2. Tappet adjusting screw
3. Tappet adjusting screw locknut
4. Tappet body

6. Check adjustment again for a slight amount of shake and the ability to rotate freely without any rough spots or binding.
7. Both ends of the valve covers must seat on the cork washers during reassembly.
8. Perform the above operations on the remaining three valve tappets.

Glide Models

Tappet adjustment is not necessary unless the engine has been disassembled. Adjustment must be made on a cold engine.

1. Remove the pushrod cover cap spring retainers.
2. Each tappet must be adjusted when at its lowest position. This can be found by rotating the engine until the corresponding valve of the other cylinder is fully open.
3. Loosen the tappet adjusting screw locknut and turn the adjusting screw into the tappet body so that the pushrod is shortened and will shake slightly.
4. Hold the pushrod with a wrench and turn the adjusting screw down to lengthen the rod until all of the play is taken up.

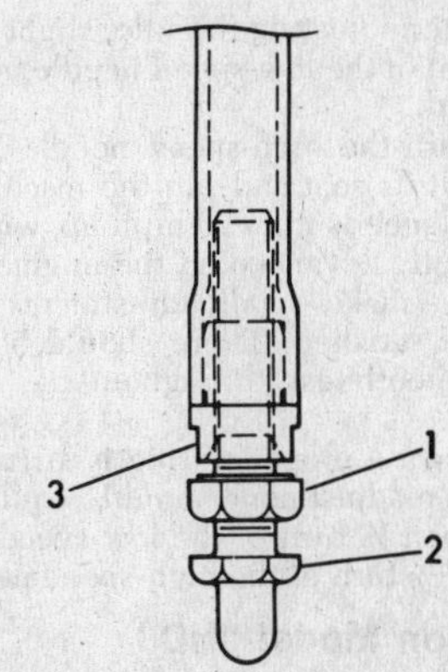

Glide models tappet adjustment

1. Locknut 2. Adjusting screw 3. Pushrod

5. Mark the adjusting screw position with chalk and turn it down four full turns.

6. Secure the locknut while holding the pushrod steady.

NOTE: *Allow the hydraulic units to bleed down after adjustment before turning the engine over to adjust the next one.*

7. Install the pushrod cover spring cap retainers.

CARBURETOR ADJUSTMENTS

Linkert Model "DC"

1. Check the cable adjustment to be sure that the throttle opens and closes fully. Run the engine until the normal operating temperature is reached.

2. Turn the low- and high-speed needles gently to their seat, and back the low-speed needle out 1½ turns so that the engine will start. You may wish to turn the idle stop screw clockwise to raise the idle speed slightly.

3. With the choke in the fully opened position and the spark fully advanced, turn low-speed needle in slowly until the engine misses and runs irregularly. Turn the needle out counterclockwise until the engine runs smoothly with the throttle closed. A slightly richer mixture, obtained by turning the needle in, will aid starting and overall performance.

4. Adjust the throttle stop screw until 700–900 rpm idle speed is obtained.

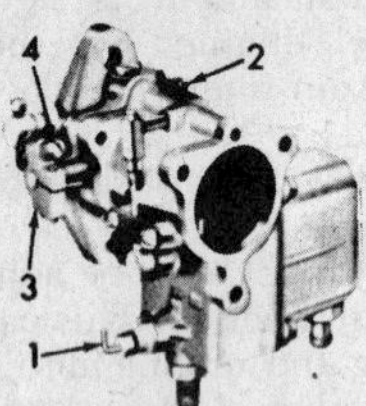

Linkert model DC carburetor adjustment

1. High-speed needle
2. Low-speed needle
3. Throttle lever
4. Throttle stop screw

5. After adjusting the idle, slight readjustment of the low-speed needle may be required.

6. Turn the high-speed needle ¾–1¼ turns off its seat and run the machine at various speeds from 20 mph up, with the spark fully advanced. If the engine runs roughly, make small adjustments until you are satisfied. There should be uniform smoothness throughout the speed range.

7. Once a proper setting is arrived at, further readjustment should require no more than ⅛ turn of the low-speed needle and ¼ turn of the high-speed needle.

Tillotson Model "HD"

Before attempting an adjustment, examine all mountings, filters, screens, and lines, and check for leaks (with the engine hot) by dripping small amounts of oil on the seams and by watching for bubbling when the engine is started.

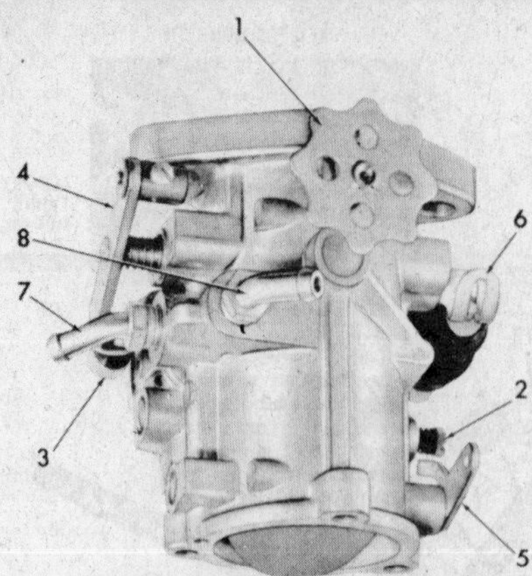

Tillotson HD carburetor adjustments

1. Low-speed needle
2. Intermediate speed needle
3. Throttle stop screw
4. Throttle lever
5. Choke lever
6. Accelerating pump
7. Inlet fitting
8. Vent fitting

The low-speed needle should never have to be readjusted for atmospheric variations by more than ⅛ turn, richer or leaner, and the intermediate needle should not need more than ¼ turn richer or leaner because the fuel supply is decreased; counterclockwise makes the engine run richer. Idle is adjusted by the idle stop screw.

If atmosphere, altitude, or modifications to the engine or exhaust system renders adjustment ineffectual, the following main jets may be substituted: 0.049, 0.051, 0.053 (Electra-Glide standard jet), 0.055, 0.057, (Sportster standard jet), 0.059, 0.061, or 0.063.

1. Loosen the cable adjustment so that the throttle lever will open and close fully in response to handlebar manipulation.

2. Turn both the low and intermediate-speed needles in to their seats and then back out about ⅞ turn. This adjustment will allow the engine to start but will cause it to run too richly.

3. When the engine reaches normal operating temperature, open the choke all the way and fully advance the spark.

4. Set the throttle stop screw so the engine idles at about 2,000 rpm.

5. Turn the intermediate needle in both directions until the engine runs at its smoothest, with no surge, and with a constant rpm pulse. When the optimal setting is achieved, back the needle out ⅛ turn so the mixture is slightly rich.

6. Adjust the idle stop screw so the engine runs at about 900–1,000 rpm.

7. Adjust the idle needle in the same manner as the intermediate needle.

8. Recheck both needle adjustments. The idle mixture is made richer by turning the adjusting screw to the right and is made leaner by turning it to the left. The main nozzle provides a richer mixture when the screw is turned to left and leaner when turned to the right.

Bendix Model 16P12

Once properly adjusted, major changes should not be necessary. Check for fouled or bad plugs, improper timing, poor valve adjustment, clogged air cleaner, or air leaks at the manifold or gas line.

The low-speed needle is turned clockwise for a leaner mixture or counterclockwise for a richer mixture.

1. Gently turn the low-speed mixture needle clockwise to its seat, then back it out 1½ turns (1972–73) or 2¼ turns (1974 and later). The engine should start at this setting but will run too richly.

2. Make sure the cable allows the throttle to close fully.

3. With the engine at normal operating temperature, set the throttle stop screw to 700–900 rpm.

4. Readjust the low-speed needle to the point where the engine runs at its smoothest and at its highest rpm.

5. Reset idle to 700–900 rpm.

6. If the exhaust system is modified or if the machine is to be operated at high altitudes, one of the following main jets may be substituted: nos. 90, 95, 100, 105, 110, 115, 120, and 125. When changing jets, go up one size at a time until you are satisfied.

7. Late 1971 and later pump shafts are adjustable. The bottom hole provides the richest setting and the top hole provides the leanest.

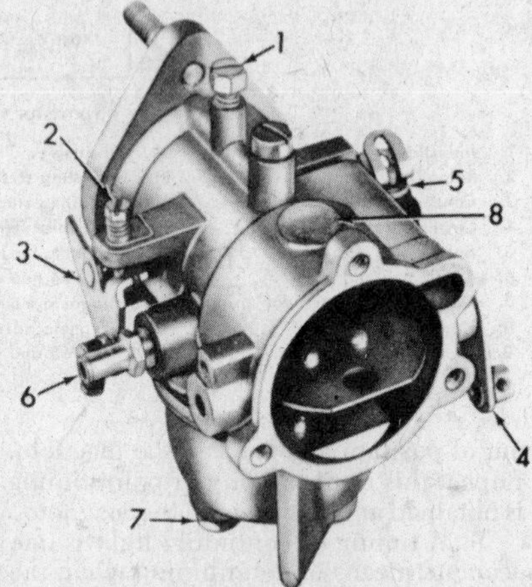

Bendix 16P12 carburetor adjustments

1. Low-speed mixture needle
2. Throttle stop screw
3. Throttle lever
4. Choke lever
5. Accelerating pump
6. Inlet fitting
7. Bowl drain plug

Keihin

1. Turn the low speed mixture screw in gently until it is seated, then back it out 1½ turns.

2. Adjust the throttle stop screw to allow engine idle at desired speed. This should be 700–900 rpm.

3. Adjust the low speed mixture screw (on warm engine) turning it in and out so that the highest or smoothest idle is obtained.

Turning the mixture screw in will lean out the mixture; turning it out will richen

Keihin carburetor adjustments

3. Screw
10. Screw, throttle stop
12. Screw, low speed mixture
17. Lever, throttle
38. Fitting
40. Plate, choke
41. Lever, choke
42. Flange, mtg.
43. Lever, accel. pump
44. Rocker arm
45. Spring, rocker arm

Tune-Up Specifications

	Sportster	*Glide Models*
IGNITION TIMING		
Point gap	①	②
Dwell	③	④
Ignition timing (retarded)	⑤	5° (1/64 in.) BTC
Ignition timing (advanced)	⑥	35° (7/16 in.) BTC
SPARK PLUGS		
Plug gap (magneto ignition)	0.020 in.	——
Plug gap (battery ignition)	0.025–0.030 in.	0.025–0.030 in.
Plug heat range (average use)	⑦	⑧
Installation torque	⑨	⑨
TAPPET ADJUSTMENT		
Clearance (cold)	no lash	1/8 (4 turns) from seat

① Point gap
magneto ignition: 0.015 in.
battery ignition 1970 and earlier: 0.020 in.
battery ignition 1971 and later: 0.018 in.

② Point gap
1969 and earlier single breaker: 0.020 in.
1969 and earlier double breaker: 0.022 in.
1970 and later: 0.018 in.

③ Dwell
1971 and earlier: 90° at 2000 rpm
1972 and later: 140° at 2000 rpm

④ Dwell
1971 and earlier: 90° at 2000 rpm
1972 and later: 140° at 2000 rpm

⑤ Ignition timing (retarded)
1971 and earlier: 15° (5/64 in.) BTC
1972 and later: 10° (1/32 in.) BTC

⑥ Ignition timing (advanced)
1971 and earlier: 45° (11/16 in.) BTC
1972 and later: 40° (17/32 in.) BTC

⑦ Plug heat range
1965–1969: #4
1970 and later: #5

⑧ Plug heat range
1974 and earlier: #3–4
1975 and later: #5–6

⑨ Installation torque
Iron heads: 20 ft lbs
Aluminum heads: 15 ft lbs

the mixture. The screw will probably have to be turned in slightly from the 1½ turn position.

4. Readjust the throttle stop screw, if necessary, so that idle speed is 700–900 rpm.

5. The carburetor is fitted with an accelerator pump. The pump has an adjustable screw which controls the amount of fuel injected. Standard setting for this screw gives a distance of about ¼ in. (6 mm) between the stop and the end of the screw. Increase fuel by turning the screw out. Decrease by turning the screw in.

6. The pump rocker arm spring controls duration and has three possible positions on the rocker arm. The center notch is the standard position.

7. The main jet may be changed for high altitude. Standard main jet size is 185 meaning the the jet will pass 185cc of fuel per minute. Alternate jets are available from 160 to 185 in steps of 5cc.

ENGINE AND TRANSMISSION

ENGINE REMOVAL AND INSTALLATION

Sportster

1. Remove the seat, drain the gas and oil, and remove the gas tank. The following steps pertain to the right-side of the machine:
2. Remove the air cleaner assembly.
3. Disconnect the throttle and choke cables at the carburetor.
4. Remove the top center engine support bolt, taking note of the number and placement of the spacer shims.
5. Remove the exhaust assemblies.
6. Disconnect the spark plug cable from the contact breaker or magneto.
7. Remove the starter crank and spring.
8. Place the transmission in Fourth gear and remove the right footrest and the shifter lever (1974 and earlier). On 1975 and later machines, remove the right footrest and brake lever.
9. Remove the transmission sprocket cover. Disconnect the clutch cable. On 1975 and later machines, detach the shifter link from the arm of the shifter pedal cross shaft.
10. Remove the drive chain from the countershaft sprocket.
11. Remove the oil return line.
12. Remove the oil vent and oil feed lines. Remove the breather pipe.
13. Remove the clutch cable and oil pressure switch.
14. Disconnect the speedometer cable. Remove the lower front safety guard bolt. The following steps pertain to the left-side of the machine:
15. Loosen, but do not remove, the top front engine mounting bolt.
16. Remove the remaining three, front engine mounting bolts.
17. Remove the tool box (1966 and earlier XLH).
18. Remove the battery tie rod support (1966 and earlier XLH).
19. Disconnect the battery ground wire and the spark plug cables.
20. Remove the horn and engine support bracket.
21. Disconnect the throttle cable and support bracket at the carburetor.
22. Remove the battery cover and disconnect both terminal leads on XLH models.
23. Remove the oil vent line at the crankcase (1966 and earlier models).
24. Disconnect the contact breaker-to-coil lead.
25. Remove the battery, battery carrier, and oil tank.
26. Remove the regulator ground strap and the two, top rear, engine mounting bolts.
27. Remove the rear brake lever and return spring on 1974 and earlier models or the gearshift foot lever on 1975 and later models, and the stop switch on 1966 and earlier models.
28. Remove the left footrest.
29. Remove the two, lower rear, engine mounting bolts.
30. Remove the top front engine mounting bolt.
31. With the engine tilted forward, lift it up and out of the left side of the frame.

Glide Models

For cylinder work with the engine still in the frame, complete the following steps:

1. Remove the instrument cover mounting base screw and pry off the cover side plate.
2. Remove the seat.
3. Remove the shift lever bottom bolts to remove the gas tank on hand-shift models.
4. Drain the gas tank and remove it.
5. Remove the cylinder head bracket, taking note of the number and position of the spacers for reassembly.
6. Remove the spark plugs and disconnect the battery ground wire.
7. Remove the carburetor manifold clamps and the air cleaner assembly.
8. Disconnect the throttle and choke cables from the carburetor, then remove the fuel and vent lines, carburetor, and its support bracket.
9. Disconnect the exhaust pipes at the cylinders. Disconnect and reposition the regulator without removing it. Follow the steps below to remove the engine crankcase from the frame:
10. Remove the left footrest, primary chaincase cover, compensating sprocket, or shaft nut. Remove the chain adjuster mounting bolt and clutch assembly.
11. Remove the engine sprocket shaft chain cover. Loosen the transmission base mounting bolts. Remove the inner chainguard-to-transmission mounting bolts.
12. Remove the clutch hub, shaft key, starter housing chainguard nuts, solenoid wire, inner chainguard from mainshaft, chain oiler hose at oil pump, and the remaining hoses.
13. Disconnect the coil leads, generator wires, and oil switch wire.
14. Drain the oil tank and remove the oil lines at the oil pump. Remove the crankcase breather tube.
15. Remove the right footrest and the brake master cylinder assembly.
16. Remove the exhaust system.
17. Remove the front and rear engine mounting bolts. The engine may now be lifted clear of the frame through the right side.

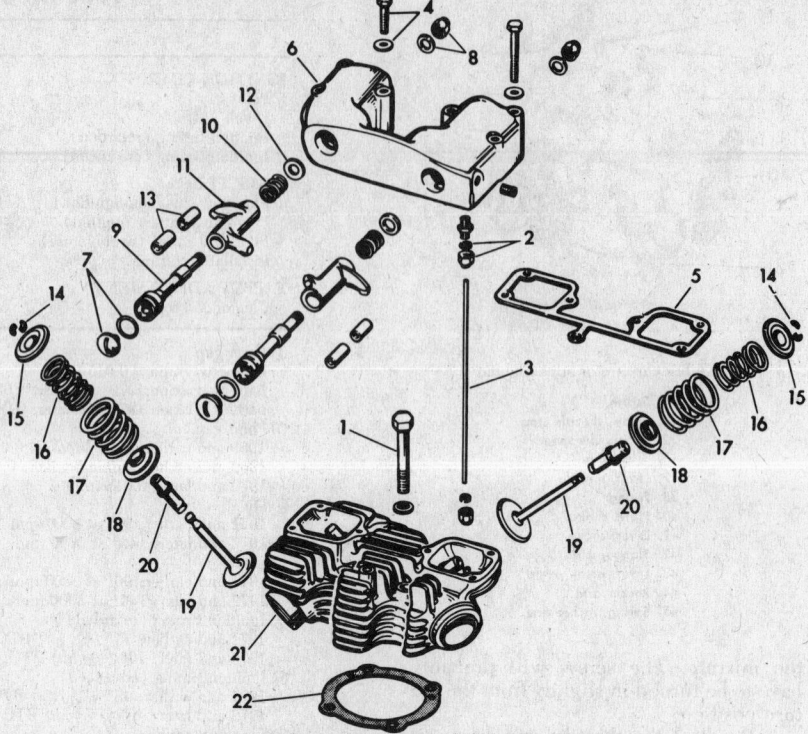

Sportster cylinder head assembly

1. Cylinder head bolt and washer (4)
2. Oil line and rubber sleeve (2)
3. Rocker arm cover-to-crankcase oil line
4. Rocker arm cover screw and washer (7)
5. Rocker arm cover gasket (2)
6. Rocker arm cover
7. Rocker arm shaft screw and O-ring
8. Rocker arm shaft acorn nut and washer (2 each)
9. Rocker arm shaft (2)
10. Rocker arm spring
11. Rocker arm (2)
12. Rocker arm spacer (2)
13. Rocker arm bushing (4)
14. Valve key (4)
15. Valve spring under collar (2)
16. Inner valve spring (2)
17. Outer valve spring (2)
18. Valve spring lower collar (2)
19. Intake and exhaust valve
20. Intake and exhaust valve guide
21. Cylinder head
22. Cylinder head gasket

CYLINDER HEAD AND VALVES

Sportster

REMOVAL

1. Strip the motorcycle as described in "Engine Removal" following Steps 1–6, 20, 21, and 24.
2. Remove the air cleaner assembly, carburetor support bracket, carburetor, manifold clamps, and manifold.
3. Remove the oil line nuts and rubber sleeves.
4. Remove the spark plugs.
5. Remove the pushrod cover spring keepers while holding the spring retainers down.
6. Telescope the valve covers.
7. Rotate the engine until there is clearance at both tappets. The valves are now closed.
8. Remove the cylinder head bolts and washers.
9. If necessary gently tap the base of the head with a soft mallet to loosen it and lift the entire assembly free through the left side of the frame. Lightly oil the piston crown and cylinder.
10. Separate the pushrods and mark them for replacement in their original positions.

DISASSEMBLY

1. Remove the rocker arm cover bolts and washers.
2. Remove the rocker arm cover, tapping it gently with a soft mallet to loosen it if necessary.
3. Inspect the rocker arm surfaces, for excessive wear, where they contact the valve stems and pushrods.
4. Check the rocker arm shaft and bushing for excessive play.
5. If replacement of the above items is necessary, remove the rocker arm shaft, O-ring, acorn nut, and washer.
6. Drift the shaft from the cover and remove the rocker arm spring, arm, and spacer, and separate them for replacement in their original positions. It is not a good idea to mix parts since this will affect clearances and since some parts are not interchangeable.

CAUTION: *Intake and exhaust rocker arms are not interchangeable.*

7. Compress the valve springs using Valve Spring Compressor (H-D Part No. 96600-36), or any suitable spring compressor and remove the valve keys spring collar, springs, and valves. Separate the parts for replacement in their original positions.

INSPECTION

1. Clean all parts in a suitable solution and blow them dry, taking care to blow all passages clear.
2. Replace the oil line nut rubber sleeve and the gaskets if worn. Replace the shaft O-ring.
3. Inspect the rocker arm and shaft for wear and replace them if necessary. Rocker arm pads may be ground free of pitting or uneven wear.
4. Replace shaft bushings if play exceeds 0.002 in. Bushings are a press-fit and must be drifted out from the acorn nut side. Inserting a ⅝–11 thread tap will aid in the drifting procedure. Line-ream the new bushing with Reamer (H-D Part No. 94804-57) or a suitable substitute.
5. Soak the head in a suitable solvent until all of the carbon deposits are soft, then gently scrape it clean and brush it with a wire brush, taking care not to scratch the head face.

6. Blow the cylinder head and passages clear and clean again in a suitable solvent.

7. Inspect the valve and valve seat for a pitted or corroded condition which may adversely affect seating. Consult "Valve and Valve Seat Refacing" for procedures or replace. Seats which are cracked or loose must be replaced as described in "Valve Seat Insert Replacement."

8. Remove the valve head and the stem carbon deposits with a wire wheel or blunt knife, taking care not to scratch or nick the surface. The stem may be polished with fine emery cloth or steel wool. Warped, bent, or otherwise damaged valves must be replaced.

9. Intake valve guides may be cleaned up with a 5/16 in. reamer and the exhaust valves with a 11/32 in. reamer.

10. Inspect the guides for excessive stem clearance. Consult "Engine Specifications" for proper measurements.

11. Replace the pushrods if warped, bent, or flattened at the ball ends.

12. Inspect the valve springs and check for proper tension and length. Springs which are more than ⅛ in. shorter or which have 5 lbs less tension than listed in "Engine Specifications" must be replaced. A Valve Spring Tester (H-D Part No. 96797-47), or a suitable substitute, may be used. If the springs are still their original length, they may be used even if their strength isn't checked.

PUSHROD REMOVAL AND INSTALLATION

1. Rotate the engine until the tappet is at its lowest position.

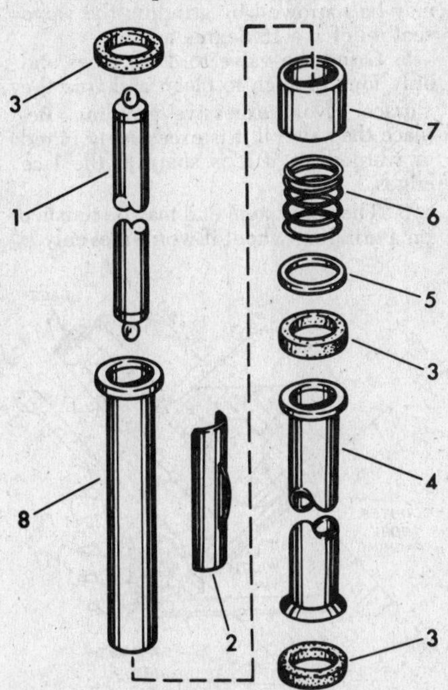

Sportster pushrod assembly

1. Pushrod
2. Cover spring keeper
3. Cover cork washer (3)
4. Lower cover
5. Cover screw washer
6. Cover spring
7. Spring retainer
8. Upper cover

2. Turn up the adjusting screw locknut until it is seated against the adjusting screw.

3. Turn down the adjusting screw, into the tappet body, until it reaches its seat.

4. Pry the pushrod up and to the side, taking care not to bind the upper end in the rocker housing, and remove the rod and cover assembly.

5. Install new cork cover washers in the rocker cover and tappet guide, taking care not to damage them. Install a new cork washer in the pushrod cover also, taking care to seat all washers.

6. Assemble the pushrod assembly in the reverse order of disassembly and adjust tappets as described in "Valve Tappet Adjustment."

ASSEMBLY

Assemble in reverse order of disassembly. Note the following:

1. Lightly oil the valve seats and stems.

2. Place the lower valve spring collar over the guides, taking care to seat it properly.

3. Install the springs and upper collars, and use a compressor to replace the valve keys. Keys are easily handled by placing a dab of grease on a screwdriver tip, and can be temporarily secured until the springs are released by greasing the key grooves.

4. Install the rocker arm spacer, spring, and arm.

5. Lightly oil the rocker arm shaft and install it so that the spring ends are flush with the spacer and arm.

6. Secure the shaft O-ring, shaft screw, acorn nut washer, and acorn nut. Check arm action for binding.

7. Check to see that the cylinder head and rocker arm surfaces are still clean and apply a thin coat of aluminum paint to the head face if a cover gasket is not to be used.

8. Carefully install the cover gasket, if applicable, and install the cover in either case.

9. Turn the screws to a snug fit and then turn each ⅛–¼ turn at a time until the cover is secure.

INSTALLATION

Install in the reverse order of disassembly. Note the following:

1. Cylinder and head faces must be absolutely clean.

2. Lightly oil or grease both sides of a new head gasket and align it on the cylinder.

3. With the valve tappets in their lowest position, install the head assembly. Pushrods must seat in the tappet screw and pushrod sockets.

4. Insert the oil line in the head and crankcase fittings.

5. Secure the cylinder bolts in the same manner as the rocker cover bolts and torque them to 65 ft lbs.

6. Position the rubber, oil line nut sleeves and secure the nuts.

7. Install the intake manifold and replace the rubber O-rings before installing the carburetor. Correct alignment of these units is critical as air leaks adversely affect performance. The cylinder may have to be shifted slightly to provide proper manifold alignment.

8. Adjust the tappets as described in "Valve Tappet Adjustment."

9. Assemble the remaining parts in the reverse order of disassembly.

Glide Models

REMOVAL

1. Refer to Steps 1–9 under "Engine Removal and Installation."

2. Remove the carburetor and manifold.

3. Disconnect the cylinder head oil lines.

4. Remove the spring cap retainers on the pushrod covers. Remove the head bolts. Lift the cylinder head and remove the pushrods and covers. Remove the head.

5. Mark the pushrod locations for reassembly.

DISASSEMBLY

1. Remove the rocker arm cover.

2. Check the rocker arm pads and ball sockets for wear. Check the shaft for play. If removal is necessary, remove the rocker arm shaft screw and o-ring. Remove the acorn nut and washer. Drift the shaft from the cover and remove the rocker arm and spacer.

3. Mark all parts so that they can be assembled in their original positions.

4. Compress the valves springs with tool No. 96600-36 or a suitable substitute. Remove valve and spring assembly.

INSPECTION

1. Consult Sportster "Cylinder Head Inspection."

2. Bearing faces, with dowel pins removed, may be sanded with emery cloth to reduce clearances. A suitable reamer (such as Reamer HD Part No. 94804-57) may be used to line-ream the bearing.

3. Gently strike the edges of the bearings, while assembled, to align parts before the checking fit.

4. Continually sand, clean, check clearances, and repeat until the desired fit is obtained.

ASSEMBLY AND INSTALLATION

Assemble in reverse order of disassembly. Note the following:

1. Assemble the valve assemblies as described in Sportster "Cylinder Head Assembly."

2. If the rocker arm is not free, the lifters will not fill with oil.

3. Replace rocker arm cover using aluminum paint on the cover faces, unless the model is equipped with a gasket as on 1971 and later models.

4. Raise the valve end with a screwdriver when the cover is installed to prevent rocker arm jamming on 1966 and later models.

5. See Sportster "Cylinder Head Installation" for torquing and carburetor assembly procedures.

6. Adjust the tappets as described in "Valve Tappet Adjustment."

7. Assemble remaining parts in reverse order of disassembly.

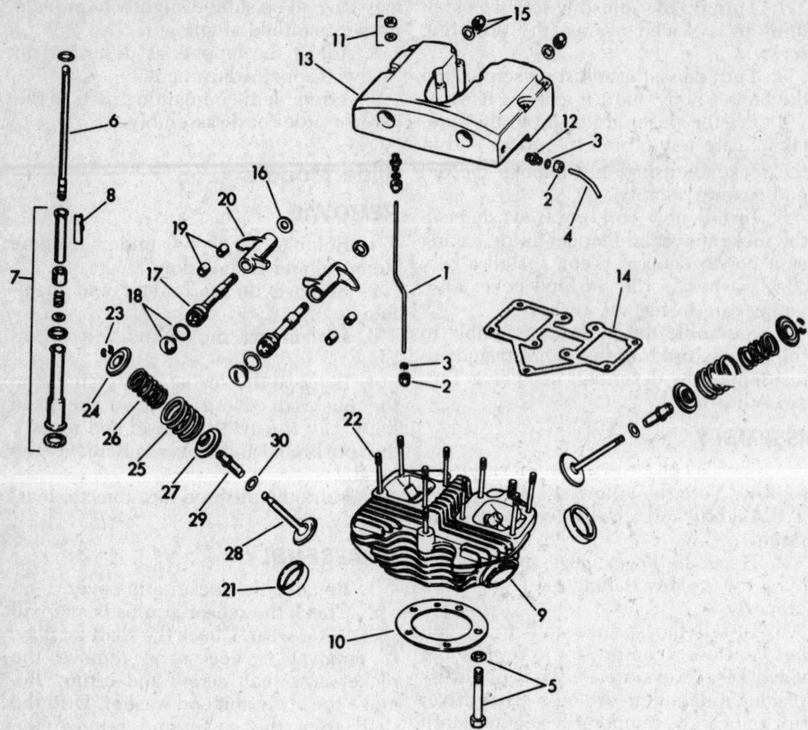

Glide models cylinder head assembly

1. Overhead oil feed line
2. Feed line nut (3)
3. Feed line rubber sleeve (3)
4. Cylinder interconnecting oil line
5. Head bolt and washer (5)
6. Pushrod (2)
7. Pushrod cover (2)
8. Spring cap retainer (2)
9. Cylinder head
10. Cylinder head gasket
11. Rocker housing nut and washer (5)
12. Oil feed line nipple
13. Rocker arm housing
14. Rocker housing gasket
15. Rocker arm shaft acorn nut and washer
16. Rocker arm spacer (2)
17. Rocker arm shaft (2)
18. Rocker arm shaft screw and O-ring (2 each)
19. Rocker arm bushing (4)
20. Rocker arm (2)
21. Valve seat insert (one exhaust, one intake)
22. Rocker housing stud (8)
23. Valve key (2)
24. Upper valve spring collar (2)
25. Outer valve spring (2)
26. Inner valve spring (2)
27. Lower spring collar (2)
28. Valve (one exhaust, one intake)
29. Valve guide (one exhaust, one intake)
30. Valve guide gasket (2)

Valve Guides and Seats

REPLACEMENT VALVE GUIDES

Sportster

1. Valve guide clearance must be within 0.003–.005 in. Guides must be replaced if play exceeds 0.002 in.
2. Using a shouldered drift or an arbor press, remove the valve guides from the valve head side.
3. Carefully tap the new guide squarely into place and ream it with a suitable reamer to remove any possible high spots.
4. Ream the guides, with a 5/16 in. reamer for the exhaust guides, and a 11/32 in. reamer for the intake guides, to assure a smooth and perfectly round fit. 1972 and later models require Valve Guide Reamer (H-D Part No. 94830-47) or another suitable reamer.

Glide Models

1. Same as Steps 1–3 for the Sportster.
2. Exhaust valve guide clearance must be within 0.004–0.006 in. Intake valve guide clearance must be within 0.002–0.004 in. Guides must be replaced when play exceeds 0.002 in.

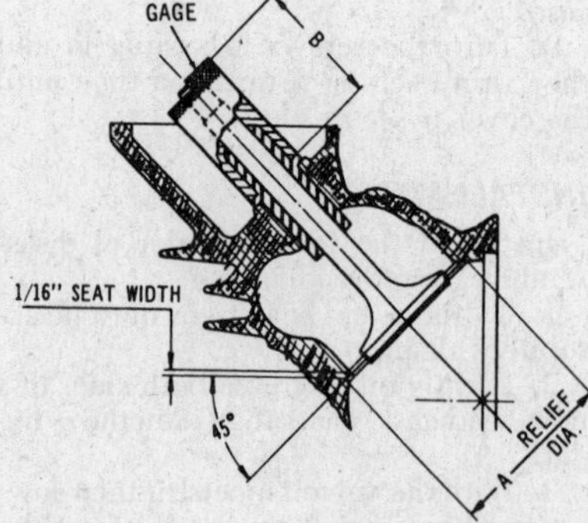

Model	Valve	Relief Dia. A	B Max.	B Min.
XL	Int.	1.75	1.420 (all)	1.375 (all)
	Exh.	1.62		
XLH	Int.	1.87		
	Exh.	1.62		

Sportster (1969 and earlier) valve seat tolerances

3. Oversize guides are available in 0.001–0.006 in. oversizes.
4. Ream out the guides with Valve Guide Reamer (H-D Part No. 94830-47) or a suitable substitute.

Valve Seats

Cylinder heads may be returned to the factory to have new seats installed.

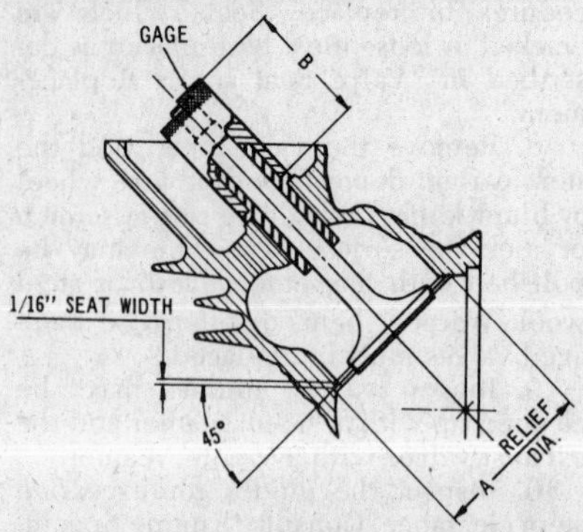

Valve	Relief Dia. A	B Max.	B Min.
Int.	2.120	1.420	1.375
Exh.	1.62		

Sportster (1970 and later) valve seat tolerances

REFACING VALVES AND SEATS

1. If the valve guides are to be replaced, do so before refacing the valves and seats.
2. Use Valve Grinding Tool (H-D Part No. 96550-36) or one of the many commercial grinding tools available.
3. Grind the seat to a 45 degree angle so that the seat is 1/16 in. wide.
4. If the seat is wider than 1/16 in., it may be narrowed by grinding the valve seat relief at a 15 degree angle.
5. Grind the valve to 45 degrees and only long enough to clean and true the surface. Avoid excessive grinding. Replace the valve if it is excessively pitted or warped, or if it is sharp at the face edges.
6. The valve stem end may be finished on a grinding wheel if worn unevenly.

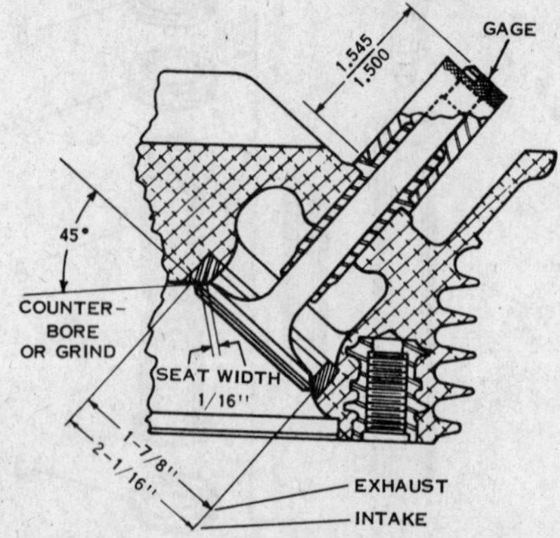

Glide models valve seat tolerances

LAPPING VALVES AND SEATS

1. After the valve faces and seats are ground, apply a light coat of fine lapping compound and insert the valve in the guide.

2. Rotate the valve several times with a grinding tool while applying light pressure at the face and seat by pulling on the valve stem. This may also be done by hand. A good way is to put a piece of gas line over the stem and hold the head so the stem is up. Rotate it several times and then check as described below.

3. To check for a well-seated valve, clean the seat and face thoroughly and insert the valve. Apply light pressure to the seat and face, then pour some gasoline on the valve from the combustion chamber side. If it takes several seconds (10–15 is a good indication) before leakage occurs, lapping has been successful.

CYLINDERS AND PISTONS

All Models

DISASSEMBLY

1. Remove the cylinder head as described in "Cylinder Head Removal."

2. Clean the crankcase thoroughly at the cylinder base. The front cylinder must be removed first on Glide models.

3. Remove the cylinder base nuts and raise the cylinder high enough to place a clean, oily rag over the crankcase to prevent foreign objects from falling in.

4. Rotate the engine until the piston is at its lowest point and lift the cylinder free.

5. Discard the cylinder base gasket.

6. Remove the cylinder compression rings with a ring expander. Rings can also be removed by prying one end free and blocking the other end or by pulling both ends free of the piston. If the rings will not clear the piston completely, work them off slowly, taking care not to scratch or nick the piston surface. Once removed, rings should be replaced.

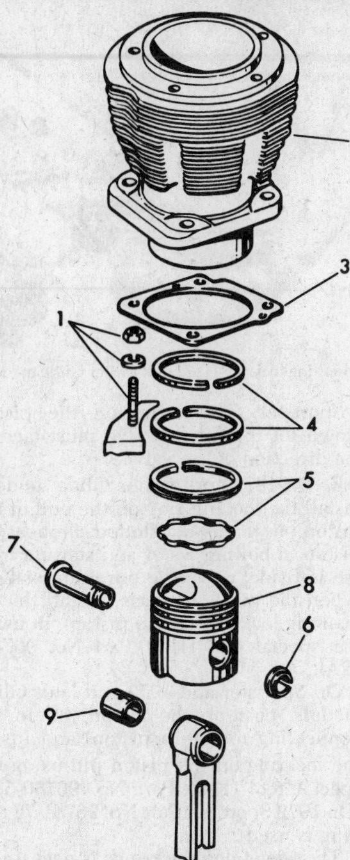

Glide models cylinder and piston assembly

1. Cylinder base stud nut and washer (4)
2. Cylinder
3. Cylinder base gasket
4. Piston rings (2 compression)
5. Oil control piston ring and expander spring
6. Piston pin lockring (2)
7. Piston pin
8. Piston
9. Piston pin bushing

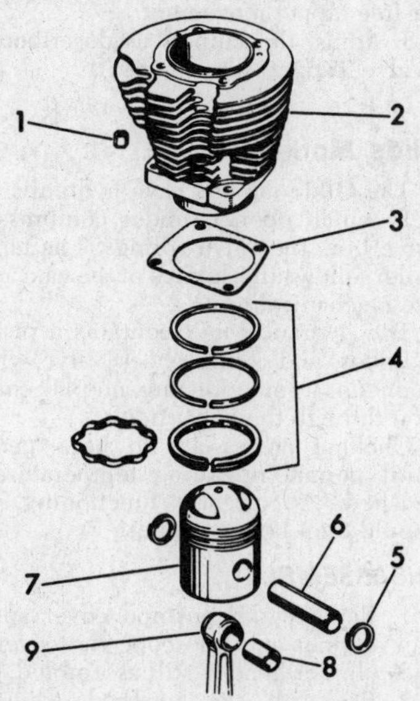

Sportster cylinder and piston assembly

1. Cylinder base nut (4)
2. Cylinder
3. Cylinder base gasket
4. Set piston rings
5. Piston pin lockring (2)
6. Piston pin
7. Piston
8. Piston pin bushing
9. Connecting rod

7. Pry the piston pin lock rings free and discard them. Glide models (1972 and earlier) have a lipped piston pin lock ring. Use Tool No. 96780-32A to push out the right-side ring and pry it off.

8. Push out the piston pin from the piston until it can be removed. Mark the pistons for reassembly in the original cylinders.

9. Remove the piston pin bushing, if necessary, using Piston Pin Bushing Tool (H-D Part No. 95970-32A), and Connecting Rod Clamping Tool (H-D Part No. 95952-33) or remove the connecting rod and support the rod around piston bore then drift it free. Consult "Connecting Rod Small End Bushing Replacement."

INSPECTION

1. Inspect the piston pin and pin bushing for a pitted, scored, or loose condition and replace if necessary. Pins are a hand-press fit with about 0.001 in. clearance. If the pin and pin bushing fit is more than 0.002 in. loose, replace worn parts as described.

2. On Sportsters, the front rod must have no more than $^{11}/_{64}$ in. axial or radial play and no more than $^{3}/_{64}$ in. for the rear before lower bearing replacement is indicated.

3. On Glide models, the rod bearing should be replaced when either rod has more than $^{3}/_{32}$ in. side shake at the upper end or appreciable up and down play.

CYLINDER BORE REFINISHING

1. Measure cylinder bore by taking measurements from front to rear and side to side with an inside micrometer at both ½ in. from the top of the cylinder. Repeat at the bottom of ring travel to determine cylinder roundness.

2. Measure piston diameter perpendicular to the wrist pin at the base of the piston skirt to check for roundness.

3. Subtract the piston diameter from the cylinder bore to arrive at a clearance measurement.

4. Refinishing is necessary if the cylinders are scuffed, scored, or worn greater than 0.002 in.

5. Oversize pistons should be fitted when cylinder wear is greater than 0.002 in.

6. If wear exceeds 0.002 in., the cylinders must be bored to the next standard oversize and fitted with suitable pistons and rings.

7. Oversized pistons and rings are available in 0.005, 0.010, 0.020, 0.030, 0.040, 0.050, 0.060, and 0.070 in. oversizes.

8. When it becomes necessary to exceed the 0.070 in. oversize, new cylinders are required.

9. New pistons of the same original size may be used if the cylinders are not worn in excess of 0.002 in. if damage does not make boring necessary, and total piston clearance is 0.002–0.006 in. Replace the rings and rough up the cylinder walls with no. 150 carborundum emery cloth.

10. Refinish the cylinders with a hone or boring bar, and then with a finishing hone. If the cylinders are not badly scored or worn, a hone alone should suffice.

11. Bore to slightly less than the nearest oversize if badly worn or scored, and then finish with a hone to the exact size.

PISTON RING ASSEMBLY

1. Replace the rings even if the same pistons are to be used.

2. Rough up the cylinder walls with carborundum emery cloth to facilitate ring seating.

3. The top two ring grooves are for the compression rings. The lowest groove is for the oil control ring.

4. Consult "Engine Specifications" for ring and piston fit and gap specifications.

5. Ring gap is determined with the piston crown ½ in. from the top of the cylinder. Lay the ring to be checked on top of the piston and check the gap with a feeler gauge.

6. Use standard size pistons and rings in standard bores or match oversize rings and pistons in oversized bores. Oversized rings are available in 0.010 in. gradations from 0.010–0.070 in. Regardless of the oversize, the proper gap is the stan-

dard gap. A smaller gap may cause ring failure. If necessary, increase gap with a fine-cut file.

7. Using a ring expander, slip the oil ring in place and then the two compression rings. Rings are fit with the chamfered or dotted side up. Later models may have one side of the ring marked "TOP" which must face upwards when the ring is installed.

8. Stagger ring gaps 120° before assembling the piston in the cylinder.

CONNECTING ROD SMALL END BUSHING REPLACEMENT

1. Bushings are a hand-press fit and must be tight in the rod.

2. If the pin clearance exceeds 0.002 in., there are two possible methods of correction:

a. Ream the bushing oversize and use an oversize pin. This involves reaming the piston holes as well.

b. Install a new bushing and ream it to fit a standard pin. This is the preferred method.

3. Remove bushings by either of the following methods:

a. Remove the rod and support it around the bushing bore then drift the bushing fee.

b. Assemble Piston Pin Bushing Tool (H-D Part No. 95970–32) and Connecting Rod Clamping Fixture (H-D Part No. 95952-33), and drive the bushing free.

4. Replace the bushings with the oil slot aligned with the rod oil slot.

5. Using Reamer (H-D Part No. 94800-26) or a suitable replacement, ream the bushing to size, or ream it nearly to size and finish with a hone. This is the preferred method.

6. The bushing should now afford 0.001 in. pin clearance: a slight shake when the pin is in the bushing.

ASSEMBLY

Assemble in reverse order of disassembly. Note the following:

1. Rings should be replaced if they have been removed. Gaps must be staggered 120° around the piston. Fit with the chamfered or dotted or "TOP" side up.

2. Glide models: Install the pistons so that the piston boss web is to the right-side of the engine or in the original position. The web is a small ridge underneath the piston.

Piston web is installed on the right of the engine

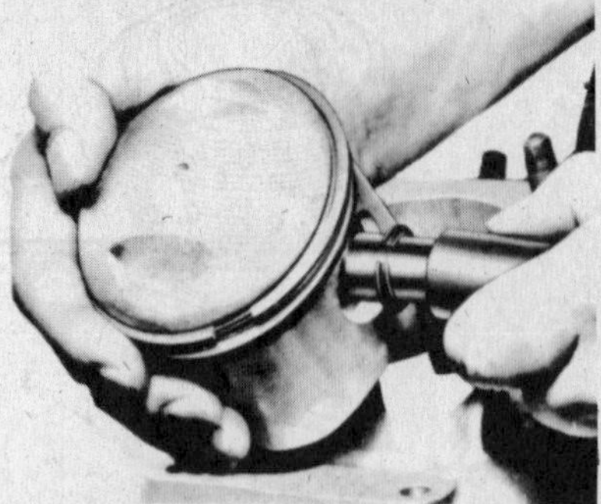

Installing lockring (1972 and earlier Glide models)

Sportster: The relief on the piston crown for the intake valve must face in the direction of the valve.

3. On 1972 and earlier Glide models, install the locking ring on the end of the piston pin that is not slotted. Preheat the piston in boiling water and starting from the left-side, drive the pin into position. When the pin is in place, install the remaining lockring on the piston pin using the special tool (H-D Part No. 96780-32A).

On Sportster and 1973 and later Glide models, position the piston pin in the connecting rod (thru piston) and install the lockring on the piston pin using the special tool (H-D Part No. 96780-58A) (On 1972 Sportster Part No. 96781-72 tool plug is used).

The use of new lockrings is necessary.

4. Lubricate the cylinder walls, pistons, pins, and bushings.

5. Assemble the cylinder using a ring compressing device if so desired.

Installing lockring (Sportster and 1973 and later Glide models)

VALVE TAPPETS AND TAPPET GUIDE

Sportster

REMOVAL

1. Remove the tappet guide screw and tappet adjusting screw.

2. Remove the tappet guide with Tappet Guide Puller (H-D 95724-57) or a suitable gear puller. Cam gears must be in place during this operation or damage to the camshaft bushings will result.

3. Remove the tappet guide O-ring, tappet body, and the tappet and roller assembly.

4. Mark the tappet assemblies for reassembly in their correct locations.

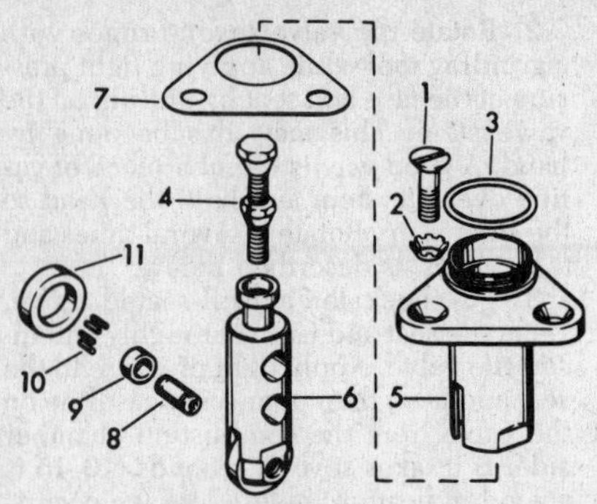

Tappet assembly (Sportster)

1. Tappet guide screw (2)
2. Tappet guide screw lockwasher (2)
3. Valve cover guide gasket
4. Tappet screw with nut
5. Tappet guide
6. Tappet
7. Tappet guide gasket
8. Roller pin
9. Roller race
10. Needle rollers (25 small or 20 large)
11. Roller

INSTALLATION

Assemble in reverse order of disassembly. Note the following:

1. Lightly lubricate the tappet assembly with engine oil before assembly.

2. The roller must seat correctly on the cam and in the guide.

3. Block up the tappet, at its limit of travel, to keep it from falling into the crankcase during installation.

4. Place the O-ring and guide gasket on the guide.

5. Turn the adjusting screw and nut into the tappet and insert the tappet in the guide.

6. With the guide screw holes aligned, insert the guide into the crankcase and tap gently with a soft mallet until the guide is seated.

7. Secure the assembly and recheck for free tappet movement.

8. Adjust the tappets as described in "Valve Tappet Adjustment."

Glide Models

The Glide models have hydraulic tappets which operate under compression force from the valve springs. The tappet roller follows the surface of the cam as do the mechanical units.

The hydraulic unit contains a piston, cylinder, and a ball check valve which maintains a self-adjusting, no-play condition through the valve train.

Clicking noises are to be expected until normal operating temperature is reached. A correctly functioning unit should then become quiet.

DISASSEMBLY

1. Remove the pushrod cover spring cap retainer and telescope the covers if the cylinder head is still assembled.

2. Back off the pushrod adjusting screw until the rod can be lifted free of the ball socket.

3. Remove the tappet guide screws and hydraulic units.

4. Gently tap the guides with a soft mallet to loosen them. The tappets and

guides can be removed together by pressing the tappet tops against the guide sides with thumb and forefinger, and then by lifting them clear. Do not allow the tappets to fall into the gearcase through the tappet guide mounting holes.

5. Remove the pushrod cork washers from the guides.

6. Remove the tappet from the bottom of the guide.

7. Remove the guide gasket.

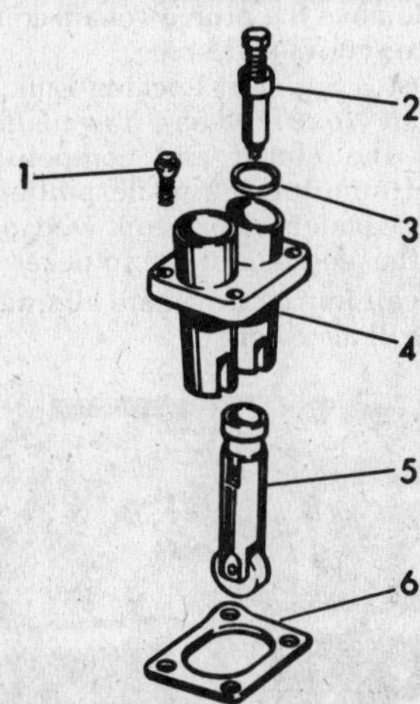

Tappet assembly (Glide models)

1. Tappet guide screw (4)
2. Pushrod hydraulic unit (2)
3. Pushrod cover cork washer (2)
4. Tappet guide
5. Tappet and roller assembly (2)
6. Tappet guide gasket

INSPECTION

1. Clean all parts except the gaskets and hydraulic units in a suitable solvent and blow dry. Do not mix parts.

2. Remove the hydraulic piston and spring from the cylinder, wash them in a suitable solution, and blow them dry.

3. Clear all of the oil passages with compressed air or a piece of wire.

4. Inspect all parts for a worn or damaged condition and replace where necessary.

5. Inspect the cam condition through the gearcase guide ports.

6. Replace the entire tappet as a rule, but roller assemblies only may be replaced, if necessary, by drilling or pressing out the roller pin and installing a roller replacement kit. Rollers should have 0.0005–0.001 in. play on the bearings and about 0.008 in. sideplay.

7. Replace worn parts if the tappet fit in the guide exceeds 0.001 in.

8. The guide is press-fit into the crankcase and must be replaced if play exceeds 0.0005–0.001 in.

9. If the tappet adjusting screw is worn hollow due to pushrod action, it must be replaced to ensure accurate adjustment.

10. Replace the rubber O-rings and gaskets if necessary.

CHECKING PUSHROD OPERATION

1. Check to make sure that the ball valve and seat are clean and dry.

2. Insert the piston in the cylinder.

3. Holding the piston in a vertical position, press down until the spring begins to seat on the cylinder. The cylinder base hole should not be covered.

4. Maintain this pressure for six seconds and then release. The piston should bounce back.

5. If the piston fails to return, repeat Steps 3 and 4 while covering the hole. If the piston does not bounce back, replace the unit. If the piston does bounce back, the ball is not seating and the unit must be replaced.

6. Check for a clogged oil screen beneath the large cap screw near the rear tappet guide before replacing the units. If the tappet operates correctly without the screen in place, the problem was not in the hydraulic units. Consult "Gearcase Disassembly" for screen removal procedures.

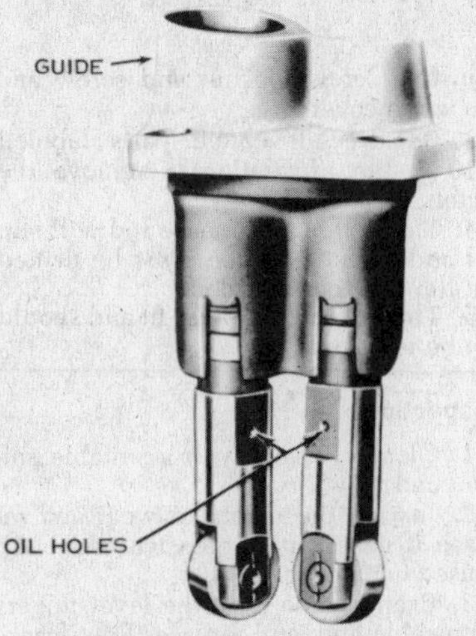

Assembling tappets in guide (Glide models)

ASSEMBLY

Assemble in reverse order of disassembly. Note the following:

1. Insert the tappets into the guides so that the flat surfaces with oil holes are toward the center of the guide.

2. Place a dry guide gasket in position and insert the guide into the gearcase while holding the tappets with the thumb and forefinger. Secure the guide screws. Tighten to 10 ft lbs.

3. Assemble the cork washers and hydraulic units.

4. Adjust the tappets as described in "Valve Tappet Adjustment."

CLUTCH

Glide Models

DISASSEMBLY

1. Remove the chainguard of chain housing cover.

2. Remove the pushrod adjusting screw locknut and place a ⅛ in. thick washer of 1¾ in. diameter, with a ⅜ in. hole, over the adjusting screw.

3. Secure it with a locknut and tighten until the spring guide stud nuts are free.

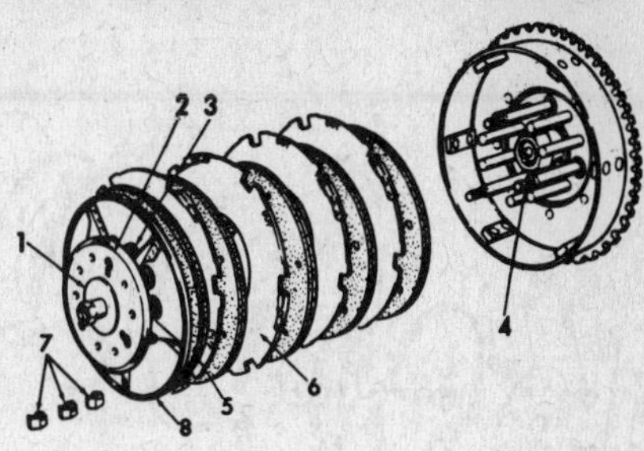

Removing clutch plates (Glide models)

1. Flat washer
2. Spring collar
3. Spring
4. Clutch hub nut
5. Friction discs (5)
6. Steel discs (4)
7. Spring tension adjusting nuts (3)
8. Outer disc

4. Remove the stud nuts and slip out the releasing disc, springs, pressure plate, adjusting screw, and adjusting screw locknut as an assembly.

5. Slide out the friction and steel discs.

6. Loosen the starter motor to provide clearance for removing the clutch sprocket and chain.

7. Remove the engine sprocket nut with Sprocket Nut Wrench (H-D Part No. 94545-26) or a suitable substitute and pull the sprocket off the shaft. A 1.0 in. socket can also be used.

8. Lift the primary chain so that it is free from the clutch sprocket and remove the clutch sprocket.

9. Remove the clutch gear nut and washer using H-D Clutch Hub Nut Wrench, Part No. 94645-41. This nut has a left-hand thread, and the tool is best used in conjunction with a soft mallet. Any socket which fits the nut properly can also be used.

10. Pull the clutch hub with Claw Puller (H-D Part No. 95960-41A). Most small gear pullers will also work.

11. Remove the bearing plate springs from the hub pins.

12. Remove the bearing retainer from the hub.

INSPECTION

1. Clean all parts in a suitable solvent and blow them dry.

2. Examine all parts for wear and replace any friction disc linings that are glazed, grooved, worn down to the rivets, oil-impregnated, cracked or chipped.

3. Glazed friction discs can sometimes be salvaged by soaking them in white gas for several hours and roughing them with a medium grade sandpaper. Make certain that all traces of gas are removed before reinstalling. This is not a recommended practice but will serve temporarily.

4. Steel discs can be reused unless they are burned or grooved, or if buffer balls do not snap back when depressed.

5. Replace the clutch hub roller bearing if, after cleaning and repacking, it sticks or fails to revolve smoothly.

6. Clutch springs may be tested for compression with the Valve Spring Tester, Part No. 96797-47 or an automotive tester. 1967 and earlier models have springs whose free length is 1 31/64 in.

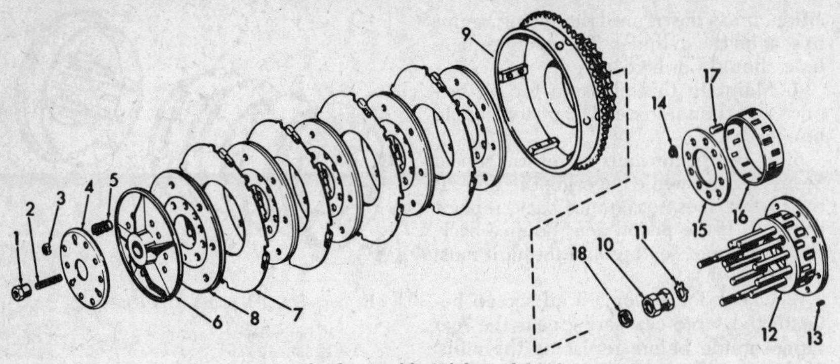

Clutch assembly (Glide models)

1. Pushrod adjusting screw locknut
2. Adjusting screw
3. Spring tension adjusting nut (3)
4. Spring collar
5. Spring (10)
6. Outer disc (pressure plate)
7. Steel disc (4)
8. Friction disc (5)
9. Clutch shell
10. Clutch hub nut
11. Hub nut lockwasher
12. Clutch hub
13. Clutch hub key
14. Bearing plate spring (3)
15. Bearing plate
16. Bearing retainer
17. Bearing roller
18. Bearing nut seal

and compress to 42–52 lbs at 1⅛ in. 1968 and later models have a free length of $1^{45}/_{64}$ in. and compress to 30–38 lbs. at 1¼ in. Springs not meeting these specifications should be replaced.

ASSEMBLY

1. Assemble the springs on the releasing disc and place the pressure plate on them, taking care to seat each spring properly.
2. Turn the pushrod adjusting screw into the releasing disc.
3. Lay the washer, as described in "Clutch Disassembly," loosely over the adjusting screw and secure it with the pushrod adjusting screw locknut.
4. Before securing the locknut, check spring alignment and correct if necessary, using a ⅜ in. rod as an aligning tool.
5. Place the hub on the gear shaft with the splines engaged, and secure it with the lockwasher and gear nut. Set the washer in one of the nut's slots with a punch.
6. Slide the clutch sprocket and key ring on the hub.
7. Light grease the ball bearings.
8. Slide the clutch discs on in the order shown in the illustration. The disc which is closest to the hub should be a friction disc, then a steel disc, and so on with buffers staggered in different spline ways. Steel discs are installed with the "out" stamp facing out.
9. Slip the releasing assembly on the hub studs, and secure it with the spring guide stud nuts as described in "Clutch Spring Adjustment."
10. When reassembling, the back of the pressure plate to the front of the clutch releasing disc is $^{31}/_{32}$ in. for 1967 and earlier models, and $1^{1}/_{32}$ in. for 1968 and later models.
11. Adjust the clutch control and release lever.

Sportster

RELEASE MECHANISM

Disassembly

1. Remove the sprocket cover and disengage the clutch cable.
2. Disengage the spring, remove the adjusting screw locknut and screw and the worm cover.
3. Remove all clutch parts labeled 1–10 in the illustration to remove the clutch release rods.
4. The left clutch release rod will slip out and the other three must be drifted out from the clutch side.
5. The roll pin is a press-fit and should not be removed.

Inspection

1. Clean all parts with a suitable solvent and blow dry.
2. Inspect the worm for wear and replace if necessary. Excessive wear will cause clutch drag.
3. Examine the fit of the lever fingers with cable end, and replace if not firm.
4. The correct length of the lever spring is $1^{25}/_{32}$ in. and must be replaced if worn or damaged.
5. Examine the tips of the clutch release rods for wear, roll the rods on a flat surface to check for warping, and replace if necessary.

Assembly

Assemble in reverse order of disassembly. Note the following:

1. Dip the rod ends in oil before installing.
2. Slip in the left release rod from the clutch gear end, and slip in the left center, right center, and right release rods from the sprocket side.
3. Assemble clutch parts 10-1 (see illustration) as described in the "Clutch Assembly" section.
4. Assemble the worm, spring, cover, adjusting screw, and locknut to the sprocket cover and check for smooth movement.
5. Place the cover on the starter shaft and engage the cable end with the lever; secure the cover.
6. Lubricate the worm with a suitable grease through the worm fitting.
7. Check the motion of the worm and be sure it seats against the roll pins.
8. Install the remaining parts.
9. Adjust the clutch release mechanism.
9. Adjust the clutch release mechanism.

1970 AND EARLIER CLUTCH

Disassembly

1. Remove the chain and clutch covers, and all associated hardware.
2. Remove the hub stud nuts, spring-tension adjusting plate, spring cups, and releasing disc.
3. Slide out the 14 clutch plates and backing plate by tipping the engine or lifting them out with a hooked piece of wire.
4. Remove the primary chain adjuster brace capscrews and brace.
5. Use a Sprocket Locking Link Tool (H-D Part No. 97200-55), if available, to prevent the clutch and compensating sprocket from turning while pulling the hub. A wooden door stop wedged in below the compensating sprocket or a suitable air impact driver are alternatives which will also work.

Clutch hub nut removal (Sportster)

1. Front chain adjuster brace and cap screws
2. Front chain adjuster
3. Sprocket locking link tool
4. Clutch lock plate
5. Clutch hub
6. Clutch shell
7. Clutch hub nut wrench
8. Front chain
9. Sprocket

Removing the clutch hub (Sportster)

1. Clutch hub puller
2. Compensating sprocket shaft wrench

6. Bend the ears of the hub nut lockwasher away from the hub and remove the left release rod.
7. Using a Clutch Lock Plate (H-D Part No. 97175-55) and a Hub Wrench (H-D Part No. 94647-52), remove the clutch hub nut. An old steel clutch plate can be drilled out to substitute for the lockplate and an appropriate size socket can be used instead of the hub wrench.
8. Pry the hub nut lockwasher free and discard it.
9. Pry the oil seal free from the clutch gear end.
10. Remove the clutch hub from the clutch gear splines with a Hub Puller

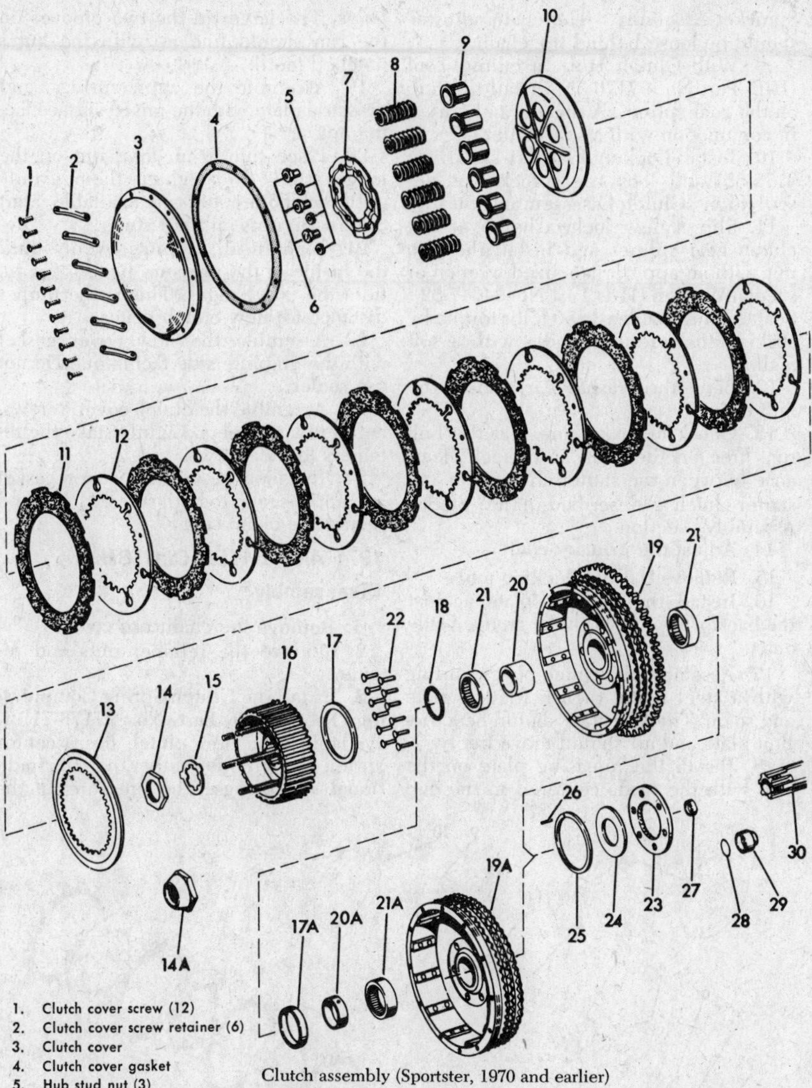

1. Clutch cover screw (12)
2. Clutch cover screw retainer (6)
3. Clutch cover
4. Clutch cover gasket
5. Hub stud nut (3)
6. Hub stud nut—long (3)
7. Pressure plate
8. Clutch spring (6)
9. Backing plate cup (6)
10. Releasing disc
11. Friction drive plate (7)
12. Driven plate (7)
13. Backing plate
14. Hub nut (1967 XLH)
14A. Hub nut (1966 and earlier)
15. Hub nut lockwasher
16. Clutch hub assembly
17. Clutch hub oil seal (1967 XLH)
17A. Clutch hub oil seal (1966 and earlier)
18. Clutch hub O-ring (1967 XLH)
19. Clutch shell (1967 XLH)
19A. Clutch shell (1966 and earlier)
20. Clutch hub spacer (1967 XLH)
20A. Clutch hub spacer (1966 and earlier)
21. Needle bearing (2—1967 XLH)
21A. Needle bearing (1—1966 and earlier)
22. Sprocket rivet (12)
23. Starter clutch
24. Sprocket bearing washer (variable-size)
25. Sprocket hub washer
26. Sprocket hub washer pin
27. Clutch gear (pushrod) oil seal
28. Clutch gear extension O-ring (1966 and earlier)
29. Clutch gear extension (1966 and earlier)
30. Clutch gear

Clutch assembly (Sportster, 1970 and earlier)

(H-D Part No. 95960-52) or suitable gear puller.

11. On 1967 XLH models, remove the O-ring from its groove in the clutch gear.

12. Remove the gear shaft nut by using the Compensating Sprocket Shaft Wrench H-D Part No. 94557-55), and remove the clutch shell, primary chain, and engine sprocket. As an alternative method, punches can be inserted in the sprocket holes, and levered with a screwdriver.

13. Remove the clutch hub spacer.

14. Remove the clutch gear extension and O-ring by tapping it with a soft mallet. This applies only to 1966 and earlier models.

Inspection

1. Inspect the clutch cover for damage which might cause leaks and use a new gasket for reassembly.

2. New springs have a free-length of 1⅝ in. and if any spring is too short, damaged from heat, or worn, the set should be replaced.

3. Inspect the clutch release disc for grooves, excessive wear, or a warped condition, and replace if necessary.

4. Inspect the clutch friction plates for wear, grooves, or oil saturation. If the plates are worn but not oily, they may be cleaned with medium grade sandpaper.

5. Driven clutch plates can be reused if they are only slightly discolored but they must still be smooth.

6. Replace the hub nut lockwasher.

7. Inspect the clutch hub spacer and needle bearing for excessive play and wear. Replace the spacer, if necessary.

8. Carefully pry the oil seal from the clutch sprocket and expand it to check for wear or damage. Replace if in doubt or if hairline cracks are present.

9. Examine and replace the clutch shell if excessive wear, grooving, worn or loose keys, worn or broken teeth, loose rivets, or a damaged sealing surface is present.

10. Loose rivets can be replaced if this is the only fault. Set the rivets until they are flush to 0.010 in. above the starter clutch face or 0.080 in. between the rivet head and bottom of the sprocket tooth for key securing rivets. Seal both sides with a solvent-proof sealer.

11. Inspect the starter clutch teeth for wear or damage, and consult the "Clutch Sprocket Needle Bearing and Starter Clutch" section for replacement procedures.

12. Inspect the clutch gear oil seal, by expanding the seal surface, and replace it if hair line cracks or other damage is present.

13. Replace the clutch hub rubber O-ring, if it is worn or damaged.

CLUTCH SPROCKET NEEDLE BEARING AND STARTER CLUTCH REPLACEMENT

1. Remove the oil seal and sprocket rivets to gain access to the clutch sprocket needle bearings, washers, and starter clutch. Bearings and the sprocket hub washer pin are a press-fit.

2. Replace the bearing by pressing from the inside on the bearing's printed side to a depth of 0.025–0.029 in. from the shell's inner face to the bearing's lip.

3. Press the roll pin until it extends 0.08 in. from the sprocket face.

4. On 1967 XLH models, the two bearings are pressed in the same way. The first seats to 1.010–0.015 in. from the shell to the bearing's inner face, the second is pressed from the starter clutch side until it is flush with the first.

5. Align the hub washer countersunk hole with the washer pin and mount the washer.

6. Insert the appropriate sized variable washer in the starter clutch.

7. With the starter clutch on the back plate, check clearance between the washer and the clutch with a feeler gauge. Exert pressure on the plate and try different washers until 0.001–0.0021 in. clearance is arrived at. Washers come in thicknesses which vary by .002 in.

8. Insert the rivets into the countersunk holes from within the shell and set to 0.010 in. maximum above the clutch face. Seal both sides of the rivets with a solvent proof sealer.

9. Press the hub oil seal in place with the lip facing into the shell.

COMPENSATION SPROCKET

Removal

1. Loosen the clutch shell and primary chain as described in "Clutch Disassembly."

2. Remove the sprocket shaft nut using Shaft Nut Wrench (H-D Part No. 94557-57) or a one-inch hex socket or wrench.

3. Slip the spring, sliding cam sleeve, sliding cam sprocket, and primary chain

and clutch shell off shaft as an assembly. Use Sprocket Shaft Extension Puller (H-D Part No. 96015-56) or a suitable substitute to remove the shaft extension if desired.

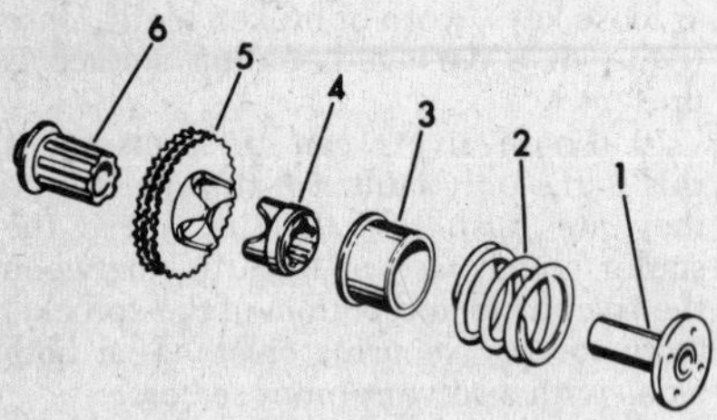

Compensating sprocket assembly

1. Sprocket shaft nut
2. Sprocket spring
3. Sprocket sliding cam sleeve
4. Sprocket sliding cam
5. Engine sprocket
6. Sprocket shaft extension

Inspection

1. Clean all parts with a suitable solvent and blow them dry.
2. Inspect the sprocket teeth, shaft splines, and sliding surfaces for excessive wear or damage, and replace if necessary.
3. The cam and extension must be a matched set, so replace both or neither.
4. If the spring is damaged there will be primary chain noise even when the chain is properly tensioned. Replace it if this is the case.

Installation

1. Set the shaft extension with Sprocket Shaft Bearing Tool (H-D Part No. 97081-54) as described in the "Crankcase Assembly" section. A socket can also be used as a drift.
2. Lightly grease the extension splines and assemble the sprocket, chain and clutch shell.
3. Slide on the sleeve, spring, shaft nut, and cam, taking care to align the splines.
4. Secure the clutch shell and sprocket shaft nut.
5. Assemble the chain cover and associated hardware.

1970 AND EARLIER CLUTCH

Assembly

1. All parts must be clean, dry, and oil-free.
2. Lightly coat the release rod tips in oil and slide them into the clutch gear with the right rod first, then the right center, left center, and left rod last.
3. On 1966 and earlier models, press the gear extension into the clutch gear and seal it with aluminum paint.
4. Insert the hub nut O-ring and oil seal.
5. Lightly grease the needle roller bearings and compensating sprocket shaft extension.
6. Press-fit the roller bearing in the clutch shell.
7. Install the hub spacer and O-ring on the clutch gear.
8. Assemble the compensating sprocket as described in "Compensating Sprocket Assembly." The chain adjuster should be loose behind the chain.
9. With Clutch Hub Installing Tool (H-D Part No. 97170-55) install the hub on the gear splines. A socket can be used in conjunction with a soft mallet.
10. Install Locking Plate (H-D Part No 9175-55) and lock the sprocket as described in "Clutch Disassembly" Step 5.
11. Slip a new lockwasher over the clutch gear splines and install the hub nut with an appropriate sized wrench or special Wrench (H-D Part No. 94647-52). Seat the nut to at least 150 ft lbs torque by striking the wrench handle with a soft mallet.
12. Bend the washer ear against the hub nut.
13. Check to make sure that the hub runs free on the shaft and check clearance between the starter clutch gear and starter clutch as described in the "Starter Assembly" section.
14. Adjust the primary chain.
15. Remove the hub locking tools.
16. Install the backing plate against the back of the hub with the grooved side out.
17. Assemble the clutch plates starting with a steel plate, then a friction plate and so on. The last plate should be a friction plate and all should move freely.
18. Install the releasing plate on the hub with the studs centered in the cup holes. The larger of the two grooves on the rim should line up with the hub's notched tooth.
19. Assemble the cups, springs, and pressure plate with the raised surface facing out.
20. Place the ½ in. long nut on the longer studs and tighten them evenly until the shorter studs are available. Start the 7/16 in. nuts on their studs.
21. Tighten all six nuts evenly until the inside of the pressure plate is 3/16 in. from the cup flanges. This is the proper distance for new clutch plates.
22. Assemble the new cover gasket with the graphite side facing out. Do not use sealer.
23. Assemble the clutch cover, screws, and screw retainers. Lightly stake the retainers to the screws.
24. Install a new chain cover gasket and apply sealer to both sides. Mount and secure the chain cover.

1971 AND LATER CLUTCH

Disassembly

1. Remove the chaincase cover.
2. Remove the retainer nuts and retainer.
3. Install the Clutch Spring Compressing Tool (H-D Part No. 97178-71) if available. The new clutch has a center spring configuration rather than the traditional six springs. The pressure on the

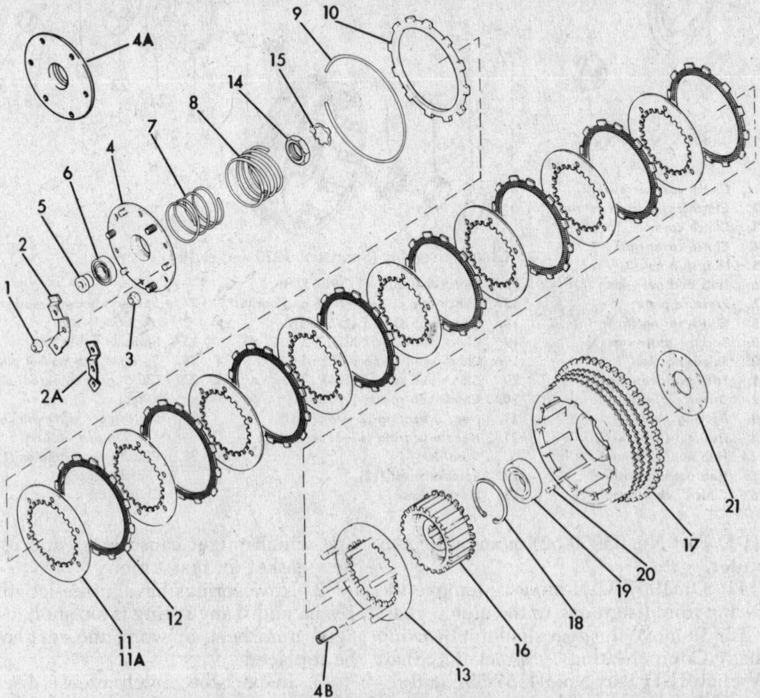

Clutch assembly (Sportster, 1971 and later)

1. Nut, retainer (3) (Early 1971) (6) (Late 1971 to early 1974)
2. Retainer (3) (Early 1971)
2A. Retainer (6) (Late 1971 to early 1974)
3. Nut, pressure plate (6)
4. Releasing disc (To early 1974)
4A. Releasing disc (Late 1974 and later)
4B. Stud spacer (6) (Late 1974 and later)
5. Releasing disc collar
6. Releasing disc bearing
7. Spring, inner
8. Spring, outer
9. Retaining ring, outer drive plate
10. Outer drive plate
11. Driven plate (8) (1971 to early 1974)
11A. Driven plate (8) (Late 1974 and later)
12. Driven plate (8)
13. Pressure plate
14. Hub nut
15. Hub nut lockwasher
16. Clutch hub assy.
17. Clutch shell
18. Retaining ring, clutch shell bearing
19. Bearing, clutch shell
20. Rivet, starter clutch (12)
21. Starter clutch

Clutch retaining parts (1971–early 1974)

1. Retainer nut (6)
2. Retainer (6)
3. Adjusting nut (beneath retainer) (6)
4. Clutch releasing disc

releasing disc won't bend the disc if the spring tension nuts are loosened diagonally, one turn at a a time and then removed.

4. Remove the releasing disc, inner and outer springs, and Compressing Tool (if used).

5. Remove the retaining ring from the clutch shell groove and pull all of the clutch plates free as a unit by pulling on the pressure plate studs.

6. Consult "1970 and Earlier Clutch Disassembly" to complete disassembly.

Inspection

1. Inspect the clutch springs for heat damage and replace any spring under the following free-length limits: inner springs are to be $2\frac{5}{16}$ in.; 1970–71 outer springs are to be $1\frac{3}{4}$ in., and 1972 and later outer springs are to be $2\frac{1}{2}$ in.

2. If the clutch shell bearing action is rough or has excessive play, it may be replaced by arbor-pressing it in and out after the retaining ring is removed with snapring pliers.

3. Check the releasing disc bearing action for roughness or excessive play and replace if necessary.

4. Consult "1970 and Earlier Inspection" for additional procedures.

Assembly

1. Consult "1970 and Earlier Clutch Assembly."

2. On late 1974 and later machines, be sure the stud spacers are installed.

3. The clutch nuts (1971–early 1974) should be tightened to yield a distance of $\frac{11}{32}$ in from the outer drive plate to the outer side of the releasing disc.

TIMING GEARCASE

Sportster

DISASSEMBLY

1. Remove the exhaust pipe assemblies, footrest, shift lever, or footrest and brake pedal on 1975 and later bikes, breather pipe, contact breaker or magneto, as described in "Contact Breaker Assembly" or "Magneto Removal," and pushrods as described in "Pushrod Removal and Installation."

2. Drain the oil, remove the gearcase cover screws, and remove the cover from its dowel pins by tapping it with a soft mallet or hammer and wood block where the cover projects beyond the gearcase. Remove the cover gasket.

3. Remove the tappets and guides.

4. Disconnect the clutch cable.

5. Remove the rear cylinder exhaust, rear cylinder intake, front cylinder exhaust, and front cylinder intake cam gears

Removing gearcase cover (1970 and earlier)

1. Exhaust pipe clamp (2)
2. Footrest
3. Gearshift foot lever
4. Breather pipe
5. Circuit breaker
6. Gearcase cover
7. Pushrod (4)
8. Gearcase cover screws (11)
9. Clutch cable

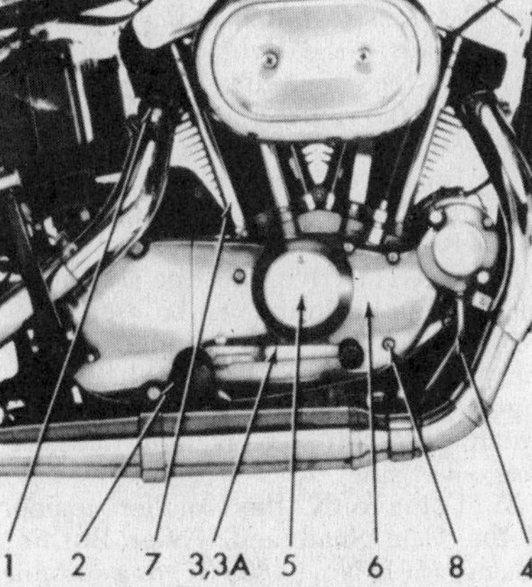

Removing gearcase cover (1971 and later)

1. Exhaust pipe port clamp (2)
2. Footrest
3. Gearshift foot lever (1974 and earlier)
3A. Brake lever (1975 and later)
4. Breather pipe
5. Circuit breaker
6. Gearcase cover
7. Pushrod (4)
8. Gearcase cover screw (11)

and cam gear plates. Gear lobes are numbered from 1–4 to designate their positions from the back to the front of the gearcase. Remove and separate the gear shaft shims for replacement in their original positions.

6. Remove the idler gear and its fiber washer by lifting the generator away from the crankcase.

7. Remove the pinion gear with Pinion Gear Puller (H-D Part No. 96830-51) or a suitable substitute.

8. Remove the oil pump drive gear.

INSPECTION

1. Clean all of the parts except the cover gasket in a suitable solvent and blow dry with compressed air.

2. Clean the inside of the gearcase, taking care to keep the solvent from soaking through the crankcase.

3. Inspect all parts for wear or damage and replace as necessary. Bushings need not be removed unless wear or damage makes replacement necessary.

4. Inspect the crankcase oil screen for a clogged condition and clean or replace as necessary. Probe the screen hole with a hooked piece of wire to check for foreign objects.

5. Replace the idler gear bushing or shaft if worn.

6. Replace the gear assemblies when excessive lash is present, the teeth are damaged or the cams are worn or pitted.

7. Blow the crankcase relief pipe clear with compressed air.

8. Inspect breather oil separator seal ring for free action.

9. If shaft clearance in the cover bushings exceeds 0.0005–0.001 in. by 0.001 in. or more, bushing replacement is necessary. Replace the bushings also if the flanges are worn.

10. If the shaft clearance in the bearings exceed 0.0005–0.0025 in., bearing replacement is necessary.

11. Inspect the cam gear plates for wear or damage and replace if necessary.

12. Replace the pinion gear if clearance is present, since any lash will cause noisy operation.

13. Oil separator bushings must have free-play and $\frac{1}{16}$ in. running clearance with the generator oil slinger washer.

14. Remove the cam gear needle bearing with needle bearing puller (H-D Part No. 95760-69 or disassemble the crankcase as described in "Crankcase Disassembly" and arbor press them out. Press on the printed side of the bearing only when replacing, (Tool No. 97273-60) taking care to press the bearing in absolutely straight. Laying a flat piece of metal over the bearing will protect it. Press until flush with the mating surface.

15. Remove the gearcase cover bushings with crankcase cam gear shaft bushing remover (H-D Part No. 95760-69), or a suitable substitute.

16. Drift the crankcase bushings out from the flywheel side with a suitable drift, or use the above special tool if the crankcase is still assembled.

17. Press the front cylinder exhaust bushing into the gearcase cover with the oil hole toward the rear of the cover. Place a flat plate over the flange to protect it, and press until the flange sits flush on

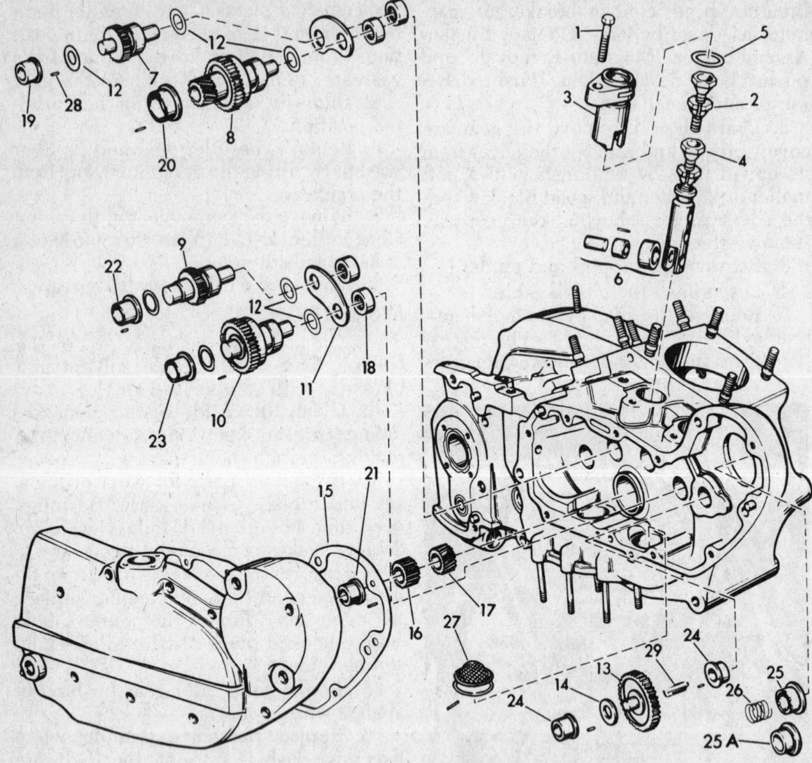

Gearcase and tappet assembly

1. Tappet guide screw
2. Tappet screw with nut
3. Tappet guide
4. Tappet and roller
5. Tappet guide O-ring
6. Tappet roller kit
7. Rear cylinder exhaust cam gear
8. Rear cylinder intake cam gear
9. Front cylinder intake cam gear
10. Front cylinder exhaust cam gear
11. Cam gear plate (2)
12. Camshaft washer—0.005–0.007 in.
13. Idler gear
14. Idler gear shaft fiber washer
15. Gearcase cover gasket
16. Flywheel shaft pinion gear
17. Oil pump drive gear
18. Cam gear needle roller bearing (4)
19. Rear exhaust cam gear shaft bushing
20. Cam gear and timer shaft bushing
21. Pinion gear shaft bushing
22. Front intake cam gear shaft bushing
23. Front exhaust cam gear shaft bushing
24. Idler gear shaft bushing (2)
25A. Oil separator bushing
27. Crankcase oil strainer, retainer pin and gasket
28. Gearcase cover bushing pin (7)
29. Idler gear shaft

the mating surface. Drill, with a No. 31 drill, 9/32 in. deep. Secure the pin slightly below the bushing and peen the bushing around the pin. Using the bushing boss hole as a guide, drill a 5/32 in. oil hole through the bushing.

18. Press the front and rear cylinder intake bushings into the gearcase cover with the narrow section of the flange pointing downward. Repeat the above drilling operation.

19. Press the rear cylinder exhaust bushing flush with the oil feed pump seat from the outside. Repeat the above dowel pin installation, but do not peen the bushing.

20. Press the pinion gear shaft bushing into the cover with the oil hole pointing 30 degrees forward of its vertical centerline.

21. Arbor-press the crankcase side bushings in place, with the crankcase disassembled, from the gearcase side with the flange notch pointing upward. Repeat the above pin securing procedures.

22. To line-ream the cam gear and timer bushings, insert the Camshaft and Timer Shaft Bushing Reamer (H-D) Part No. 94803-37) "T" portion through the right crankcase from the flywheel side without turning the reamer and assemble the larger portion of the tool. Start the larger portion in the timer shaft bushing and assemble the gearcase cover. Always secure the cover with at least four screws when reaming and always turn the reamer to the right until bottom is reached, then withdraw it while still turning to the right. A suitable substitute reamer may be used if care is taken.

23. Line-ream the pinion shaft bushing with Pinion Shaft Bushing Reamer (H-D Part No. 94812-37) or a suitable substitute. The cover must be assembled and a guide bushing must be used.

24. Ream the rear cylinder exhaust cam gear bushings with Oiler Shaft Bushing Reamer (H-D Part No. 94811-36) or a suitable substitute. Work from the gearcase cover side.

25. Using only the smaller reamer of the Cam Shaft and Timer Bushing Reamer (H-D No. 94803-37) or a suitable substitute, line-ream the front cylinder exhaust and intake bushings, taking care not to remove more metal than necessary.

CAM GEAR END PLAY

End play must be checked before final assembly.

1. Temporarily install the two cam gear plates without the shims. The bevelled side of the shaft holes should face outwards towards the cams.

2. Install the cam gears. Assemble the case cover with gasket dry and tighten it securely.

3. Turn the engine over until the No. 1 cam gear lobe is facing up (look through the tappet guide hole in the crankcase).

4. Pry the cam gear towards the case cover with a screwdriver. With a feeler gauge, measure the clearance between the camshaft shoulder and the gear plate. It should be 0.001–0.005 in.

If necessary, add the proper number of 0.005 or 0.007 in. shims until end play is correct.

5. Repeat the procedure with the remaining gears.

6. Check that the gears rotate freely.

BREATHER VALVE TIMING

1. Turn the engine until the flywheel timing mark is directly in the center of the inspection hole.

2. Install the spiral gear, the marked side facing towards the pinion gear. The gear must be fitted so that the timing hole in the breather sleeve gear is in the center of the slot in the breather bushing.

3. Install the pinion gear. The pinion gear outer face must be exactly 5/16 in. from the gearcase joint face.

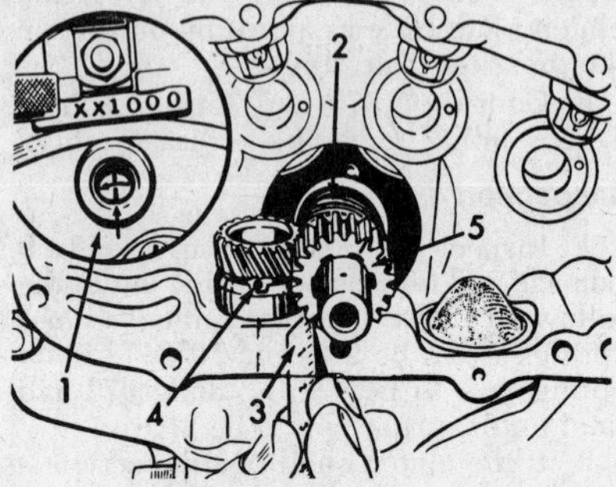

Breather valve timing

1. Flywheel timing mark
2. Oil pump drive gear (spiral gear)
3. Measurement
4. Timing hole in breather sleeve gear
5. Pinion gear

ASSEMBLY

1. Install the cam gear plates, bevelled side of the shaft holes facing the cams.

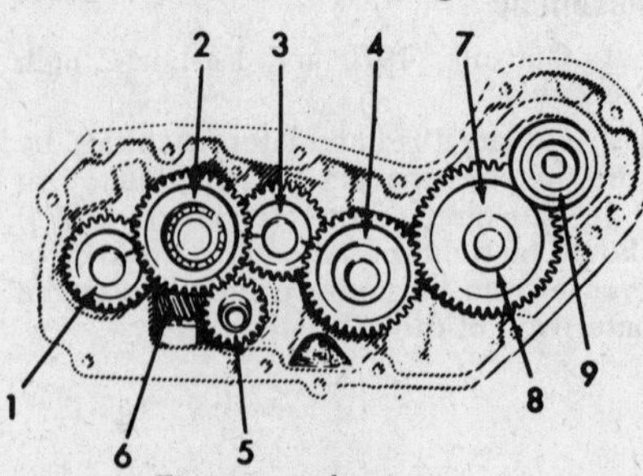

Timing gear alignment

1. Rear exhaust cam gear
2. Rear intake cam gear
3. Front intake cam gear
4. Front exhaust cam gear
5. Pinion gear
6. Crankcase breather sleeve gear
7. Intermediate gear (has no timing mark)
8. Intermediate gear fiber washer
9. Generator drive gear

2. Lubricate the shafts and install the gears 1 through 4 with the marks aligned.
3. Install the idler gear with the fiber washer on the cover side.
4. The remainder of the procedure is the reverse of disassembly.

Glide Models

DISASSEMBLY

1. Remove the pushrods, tappets, hydraulic units, and tappet guides.
2. Remove the oil screen cap, gasket, springs, and screen.
3. Remove the circuit breaker assembly including breaker cam and advance assembly.
4. Remove the gearcase cover screws and tap the cover with a plastic mallet or the like to remove it. 1973 and later cover and gasket are different from earlier models.
5. Remove the breather valve spacing washer and gear.
6. Remove the cam gear, spacer, and thrust washer.
7. Remove the pinion gear shaft nut (left-hand thread). Pull off the pinion gear with Part No. 96830-51. The tool has left-hand threads.
8. Remove the key, gear shaft pinion spacer, oil pump pinion shaft gear, and key.
9. Remove the oil pump drive gear shaft lockring, drive gear, and key.
10. Remove the oil pump.

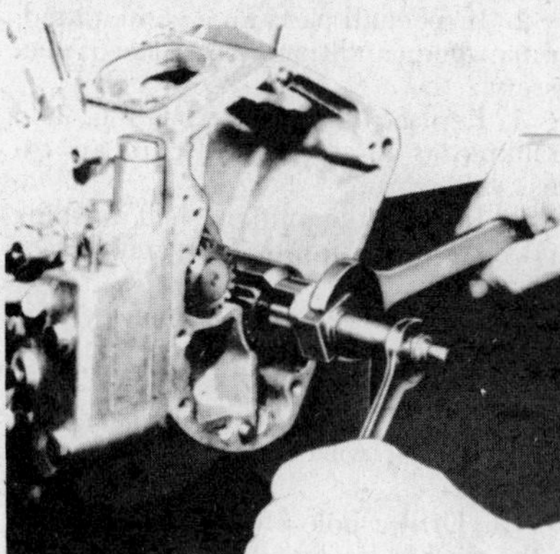

Removing the pinion gear

INSPECTION

1. Inspect the oil screen. Clean or replace if damaged or plugged.
2. Inspect the cam gear and gear bushings for wear. If bushing to shaft clearance exceeds the standard specification by 0.001 in. or more, install new bushings.
3. Check pinion shaft play in the right main roller bearing. Replace the bearings if play exceeds the standard specification by 0.001 in. or more.
4. Check the needle bearing for wear. If the camshaft is worn 0.003 in. or more, replace the camshaft and bearing.
5. To remove the needle bearing use Tool No. 95760-69 which does not necessitate splitting the crankcases. Install with No. 97272-60 pressing it in from the end with manufacturer's stamp. Install new bearing from the gearcase side.
6. Pinion shaft main roller bearings are replaced after splitting the crankcases.
7. Check the gears for wear. Assemble the pinion and cam gear without end spacer and check that there is no backlash and that the cam gear can be moved back and forth along the shaft axis without restriction.
8. To replace the gearcase cover bushings, remove the pinion shaft cover bushing with Tool No. 95760-69.
9. To install a new bushing, position it so that the bushing oil hole is directly in line with the lubrication channel outlet in the cover. Press in the bushing until the top is flush with the bushing boss in the cover. Center punch a new dowel pin location at least 1/8 in. from the original location. Drill No. 31 is used to make a hole 3/16 in. deep. Press in bushing until it bottoms on the shoulder in cover hole. Continue drilling dowel pin hole to 9/32 in. from top to bushing. Install a new dowel pin and peen edges of hole to lock the pin in place. On 1973 and later models, the flat on the bushing must line up with the oil hole in the cover.
10. To replace the camshaft cover bushing, use Tool No. 95760-69 to remove the old bushing.
11. Make a mark on the outside of the bushing boss to locate the original dowel pin hole. Press in a new bushing until the shoulder is against the cover boss. Locate a new dowel pin hole at least 1/8 in from the original hole. Drill a No. 31 hole exactly 9/32 in. deep. Install a new pin and peen the edges over to secure it.
12. Drill a 5/32 in. lubrication hole through the bushing, using the oil hole in the bushing boss as a guide.
13. The bushings must be line-reamed. To ream the pinion shaft bushing, insert the reamer pilot into the right crankcase roller bearing race.
14. Insert a 9/16 in. pinion shaft cover bushing reamer (No. 94805-57) through the pilot and push into cover bushing until it bottoms. Then turn it one turn. Rotate the reamer in the same direction during extraction.
15. To ream the cam gear cover bushing, use a 1 in. expansion reamer and ream to 1.002–1.003 in.

ASSEMBLY

1. Check breather gear end-play. Assemble the breather gear and gasket to the case. Install the spacer washer on the end of the breather gear. Place a straightedge across the gearcase at the spacer. Measure the distance between the straightedge and the spacer. Subtract 0.006 in. (gasket compression). The resultant figure is the end-play. It should be 0.001–0.005 in. If greater, insert a thicker spacer.
2. Check cam gear end play. Install the thrust washer, spacer, and cam gear. Position the gasket and secure the cover.
3. Measure the end-play between the cam gear and the cover bushing through

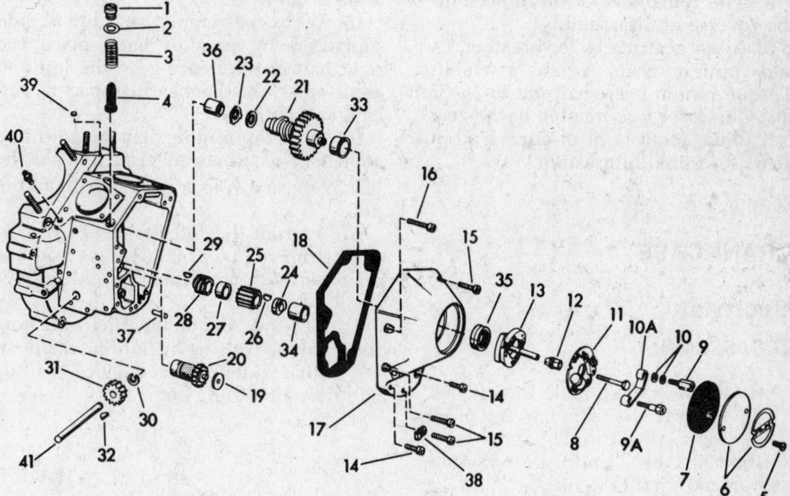

Gearcase assembly

1. Oil screen cap
2. Cap seal
3. Oil screen spring
4. Oil screen
5. Circuit breaker cover screws (2)
6. Circuit breaker cover
7. Circuit breaker cover gasket
8. Circuit breaker cam assembly bolt
9. Circuit breaker screw (2) (1970)
9A. Circuit breaker plate screw (1971 and later)
10. Circuit breaker plate screw lockwasher and washer (1970)
10A. Retainer (1971 and later)
11. Circuit breaker plate assembly
12. Circuit breaker cam
13. Circuit breaker advance assembly
14. Gear cover screw, 1 in. (2)
15. Gear cover screw, 1 1/4 in (3)
16. Gear cover screw, 1 3/4 in. (1)
17. Gear cover
18. Gear cover gasket
19. Breather gear washer
20. Breather gear
21. Cam gear
22. Cam gear spacing washer
23. Cam gear thrust washer
24. Gear shaft nut
25. Pinion gear
26. Pinion gear key
27. Pinion gear spacer
28. Oil pump pinion shaft gear
29. Oil pump pinion shaft gear key
30. Oil pump drive gear lockring
31. Oil pump drive gear
32. Oil pump drive gear key
33. Gear cover camshaft bushing
34. Gear cover pinion shaft bushing
35. Camshaft oil seal
36. Camshaft needle bearing
37. Cover dowel pin (2)
38. Wire clip
39. Welch plug
40. Oil line fitting
41. Oil pump shaft

Timing gear marks aligned

the tappet guide hole. It should be 0.001–0.005 in. Replace the spacer with one of a different thickness to bring the clearance into specification, if necessary.

4. The remainder of the procedure is the reverse of disassembly.

5. Align gear marks for breather, cam, and pinion gears when assembling. Torque pinion gear shaft nut to 25–35 ft lbs. Check for free rotation of the gears.

6. Pour about ¼ qt of engine oil over gears for initial lubrication.

CRANKCASE

Sportster

DISASSEMBLY

1. Remove the engine from frame.
2. Remove the cylinders and pistons.
3. Remove the oil pumps as described in the "Lubrication Systems" section and drain the oil.
4. Remove the contact breaker.
5. Remove the generator and starter.
6. Remove the tappets.
7. Remove the sprocket shaft extension with a sprocket shaft extension puller (H-D Part no. 96015-56) or a suitable substitute. Solid sprocket models can be removed with a claw puller.
8. Remove the speedometer drive unit, right crankcase bolts, stud lock nuts, rear mount bolts, battery carrier or oil tank bracket, rear engine mount, and top center crankcase stud.
9. Loosen the top of the crankcase by tapping it with a soft mallet and separate the cases.
10. Pry the pinion bearing shaft snap-ring from the shaft and remove the shaft bearing washer, roller bearings, and bearing retainers.

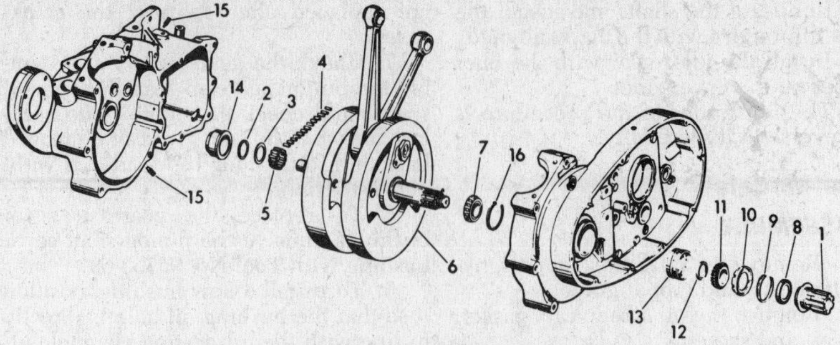

Crankshaft assembly (Sportster)

1. Sprocket shaft extension
2. Pinion shaft bearing snap ring
3. pinion shaft bearing washer
4. Pinion shaft roller bearing (13)
5. Pinion shaft roller bearing retainer
6. Connecting rod and flywheel assembly
7. Sprocket shaft Timken bearing right half
8. Sprocket shaft oil seal
9. Sprocket shaft bearing spring ring (outer)
10. Sprocket shaft bearing spacer
11. Sprocket shaft Timken bearing left half
12. Sprocket shaft Timken bearing spacer
13. Sprocket shaft Timken bearing outer race
14. Pinion shaft bushing
15. Pinion shaft bearing bushing screw (2)
16. Sprocket shaft bearing spring ring (inner)

11. Remove the transmission as described in "Transmission Disassembly."
12. Arbor-press the sprocket shaft to remove the flywheel assembly from the left case. If drifted free, flywheel alignment will be lost.
13. Remove the Timken bearing right half with a sprocket shaft bearing puller (H-D Part No. 96015-52) or a suitable substitute if flywheel is to be disassembled or if the bearing is to be replaced.
14. Pry free the sprocket shaft oil seal and spring with a pointed instrument and replace both.
15. With the crankcase clutch side supported by parallel bars, place the right half of the bearing on the left and arbor-press out the bearing spacers, left half, and outer race.
16. With the pinion shaft secured in a copper or wood-jawed vise, remove the lock plate screw, lock plate, and crankpin nut.
17. Loosen the left flywheel by striking its rim at a point 90 degrees from the crankpin with a soft mallet and remove the flywheel.
18. Separate the connecting rods from the crankpin bearing by holding the bearing with a suitably sized piece of pipe and lifting the rods free.
19. Remove and separate the bearing for reassembly.
20. Remove the lock plate screws, lock plates, and sprocket and crank pin lock nuts.
21. Tap the flywheels with a soft mallet to loosen the shafts and remove the shafts and keys.

INSPECTION

1. Clean all parts in a suitable solvent and blow dry. Blow all oil holes clear.
2. Inspect all parts for a worn, pitted, or damaged condition and replace if necessary.
3. Replace the rods, bearing, and crankpin as an assembly if parts are excessively worn.
4. Inspect the pinion shaft bushing and shaft for wear or damage and replace if necessary.
5. Inspect the sprocket shaft bearing assembly for wear or damage. Timken rollers must be replaced in sets.
6. Replace worn or damaged flywheel thrust washers in the following manner:

   a. Drill a hole slightly deeper than the washer on its outer edge using a ⅛ in. drill.

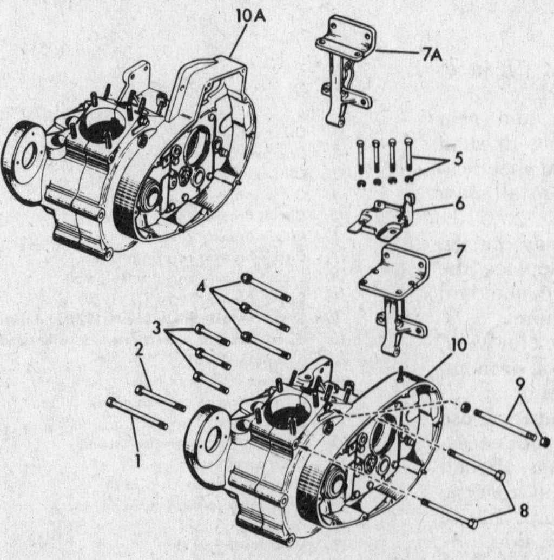

Crankcase assembly

1. Crankcase mounting bolt 5/16 x 4-7/16"
2. Crankcase mounting bolt 5/16 x 4-1/16"
3. Crankcase mounting bolt 5/16 x 2-3/8" (3)
4. Crankcase rear mounting stud and lock nut (3)
5. Engine rear mounting bolt and lockwasher (4) (1966 and earlier), (2) (1967 and later)
6. Battery carrier (1966 and earlier)
7. Engine rear mount (1966 and earlier)

7A. Engine rear mount (1967 and later)

8. Crankcase bolt (2)
9. Crankcase stud and lock nut (center)
10. Crankcase (1966 and earlier)

10A. Crankcase (1967 and later)

Figure following name of part indicates quantity necessary for one complete assembly.

b. Pry the washer free with a pointed tool.

c. File the staked flywheel material smooth with emery paper and thoroughly clean the washer seat.

d. Insert a new washer taking care to seat it fully.

e. Secure the washer by center punching the flywheel around the washer.

7. Lap worn connecting rod races until there is no wear on the shoulder and both rods will accept the same size rollers. The lapping tool must fit in the bearing race snugly before compound is applied. Connecting rod lapping arbor (H-D Part No. 96740-36) or a suitable substitute, used at 150–200 rpm in a lathe, will provide the best results. Use a smooth motion.

8. Secure the pinion shaft to the right flywheel making sure all parts are completely clean.

9. Secure the pinion shaft key.

10. Secure the pinion shaft in a copper or wood-jawed vise and tightly secure the pinion shaft nut with a crankpin and flywheel nut wrench (H-D Part No. 94546-41) until the lockplate notches line up with the nut edges. Do not use additional leverage as damage will result.

11. Secure the crankpin and nut in the above manner.

12. Fit the rod bearings in the following manner:

a. Assemble the thoroughly cleaned sprocket and pinion shafts to the flywheel. If the lockwasher screw holes won't line up, increase the tightness of the shaft nut.

b. Secure the crank pin in the left flywheel.

c. Secure the flywheel and sprocket shaft with the crank pin in a vertical position in a copper or wood-jawed vise.

d. Install a connecting rod bearing set on the crankpin and check for a plug fit of both rods. If necessary, lap the tighter of the two rods until both are even.

e. Check for correct fit by subtracting one half the specified running clearance from the roller size.

f. The upper end rod furthest from the flywheel should have side shake of 1/32–3/64 in. Bearings must not extend beyond the rod edges.

13. Replace the pinion shaft bushing and bearing. Place the arbor guide sleeve (H-D Part No. 96728-56), or a suitable substitute, through the Timken bearing from the inside of the case, and fit the bearings to a running clearance of 0.0008–0.001 in. A slightly looser fit is recommended for sustained high speed driving.

ASSEMBLY

1. Secure the thoroughly cleaned left fly wheel and sprocket shaft in a copper or wood-jawed vise and assemble the crank pin and right flywheel.

2. Check flywheel alignment with a straight edge. Alternately tighten the crank pin nut slightly and recheck alignment until secure. A soft mallet can be used to aid alignment. This method generally provides alignment to within 0.002 in.

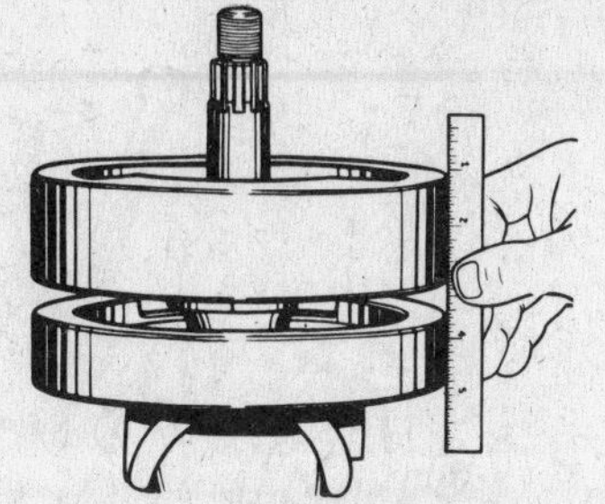

Checking flywheel alignment

3. Press one rod against the flywheel thrust washer and measure play between the opposite rod and washer with a feeler gauge. Check for the following if play is less than 0.006 in.:

a. Flywheels and crank pin tapers were oily during assembly allowing crankpin nuts to be overtightened.

b. Flywheel thrust washers are improperly seated.

c. Flywheel tapered holes are worn to excessive clearance.

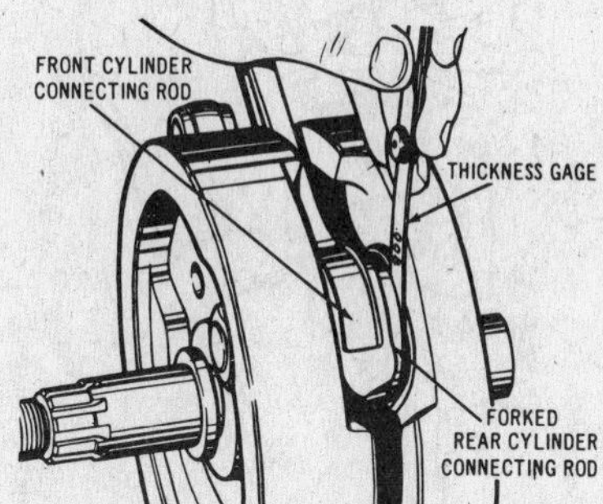

Measuring rod side clearance

d. Cracks at the flywheel tapered holes.

4. If play is greater than 0.010 in., wait until the flywheels are trued before correcting.

5. True the flywheels with a truing device (H-D Part No. 96650-30) in the following manner:

a. Place the flywheel assembly in the device and adjust until the centers are snug.

b. Rotate the flywheels and mark the high point with chalk. Loosen the device slightly and align using the three following methods.

NOTE: *(A) or (B) should be done before (C).*

(A). A C-clamp can be used on the rims directly opposite the crankpin along with moderate blows to the rim at the crank pin with a soft mallet.

(B). A hardwood wedge can be driven between the wheels directly opposite the crankpin. Moderate blows with a soft mallet are the safest way to perform this operation.

(C). Strike the wheel, at about 90 degrees from the crank pin, with a firm blow with a soft mallet.

c. Repeat Steps (A) and (B) above. If truing procedures were effective, shaft play should be 0.001 in. or less. The factory device has 0.002 in. gradations. Check for a cracked flywheel, enlarged tapered hole or worn sprocket or pinion shafts if repeated truing attempts fail.

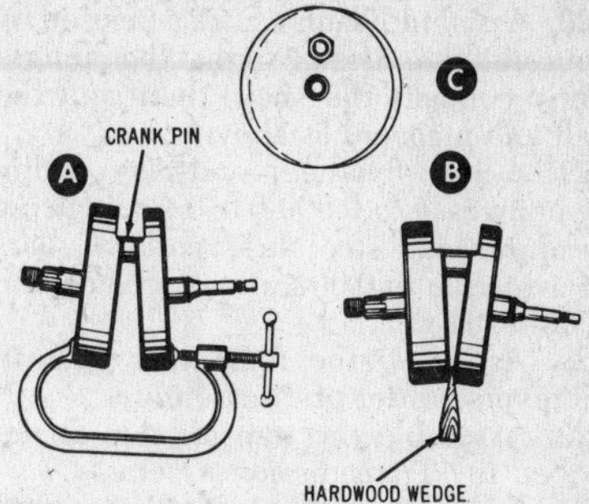

Aligning the flywheels

d. Secure the crank pin nuts tightly when the flywheels are true, then recheck on device. Minor adjustments may be made without loosening the crankpin nuts.

6. An alternate method is to use a dial indicator, and a lathe or some other means of rotating the flywheels on a steady plane.

7. Replace the sprocket shaft bearing inner spring ring.

8. Support the left crankcase, crankcase side up, on an arbor press and press the Timken bearing outer race in until it seats on the spring ring. Sprocket shaft bearing tool (H-D Part No. 97081-54) or an arbor press may be used for all of these operations.

9. Secure the flywheel assembly in a copper or wood-jawed vise with the sprocket shaft up.

10. Install a flywheel support plate (H-D Part No. 96137-52) or a suitable substitute between the flywheel halves.

11. Press the bearing right half on the shaft with a 1 in. I.D. (inside diameter) x 6 in. steel tube until the bearing seats on the shaft shoulder.

12. Slip the sprocket shaft bearing spacer in place and lubricate the bearing with engine oil.

13. Insert the sprocket shaft through the bearing outer race in the left and press the left half of the bearing in place until it is seated, taking care not to damage it. Both bearing halves must be tight against their spacers.

14. Place the notched side of the sprocket shaft bearing spacer on the shaft and gently press it into place or use a suitable screw type extractor until the spacer is tight against the outer bearing race.

15. Install the outer spring ring and oil seal with the lipped side in.

16. Press the sprocket shaft extension in place until seated with the shaft and extension splines aligned.

17. Assemble the pinion shaft bearing, bearing washer, and a new bearing snap-ring, taking care to seat the snap-ring in the shaft groove.

18. Measure the flywheel end-play with a flywheel end-play gauge (H-D Part No. 96700-38) on the sprocket shaft.

19. Adjust the gauge pin until it gently touches the case. Push the shaft to the left and measure the clearance with a feeler gauge.

20. A dial indicator can also be used by securing the indicator so that the plunger gently contacts the shaft, then shift the shaft and measure as above.

21. Adjust flywheel end-play within the crankcase to 0.009-0.013 in. by using the appropriate steel thrust collar. Collars are available in 0.004 in. gradations from 0.066-0.102 in.

22. Assemble the remaining parts in the reverse order of disassembly.

23. Assemble the transmission as described in "Transmission Assembly."

24. Coat the crankcase joint faces with a non-hardening sealer.

25. Apply engine oil to the pinion shaft bearing; assemble and secure the crankcase halves.

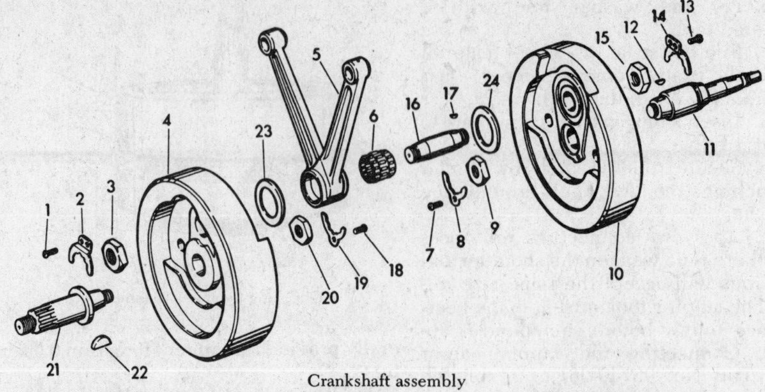

Crankshaft assembly

1. Lock plate screw (4)
2. Lock plate (2)
3. Crank pin nut (2)
4. Left flywheel
5. Connecting rods (one forked, one single end)
6. Bearing rollers and retainers
7. Lock plate screw (see item 1)
8. Lock plate (2)
9. Gear shaft nut (2)
10. Right flywheel
11. Pinion shaft
12. Pinion shaft key
13. Lock plate screw (see item 1)
14. Lock plate (see item 2)
15. Crank pin lcck nut (see item 3)
16. Crank pin
17. Crank pin key
18. Lock plate screw (see item 1)
19. Lock plate (see item 8)
20. Sprocket shaft nut (see item 9)
21. Sprocket shaft
22. Sprocket shaft key
23. Flywheel washer (2)
24. Flywheel washer (see item 23)

Glide Models

DISASSEMBLY

1–6. Same as for the Sportster.

7. Remove the gearcase assembly.

8. Remove the 3/8 x 3 1/4 in. crankcase bolts, 5/16 x 5 in. studs, breather stud and chain oiler, 5/16 x 6 in. stud, and 11/32 x 5 13/16 in. studs.

9. With the gear case side up, tap the crankcase with a soft mallet and remove the crankcase right half, spiral lock ring, and bearing washers and bearing retainer assembly.

10. Remove the sprocket shaft spacer (1968 and earlier models) and secure the pinion shaft in a copper or wood-jawed vise with the left case up.

11. Remove the left-hand threaded sprocket shaft bearing nut with the sprocket shaft bearing nut wrench (H-D Part No. 97235-55A) or a suitable substitute.

12. With the left case supported on parallel bars, arbor-press the sprocket shaft until the flywheel assembly comes free and remove the sprocket bearing half, washer, and spacer.

13. Pry the flywheel side outer snap-ring free (1968 and earlier models).

14. Arbor-press the bearing outer race press plug (H-D Part No. 97194-57) or a suitable drift to prevent damage to the races (1968 and earlier models).

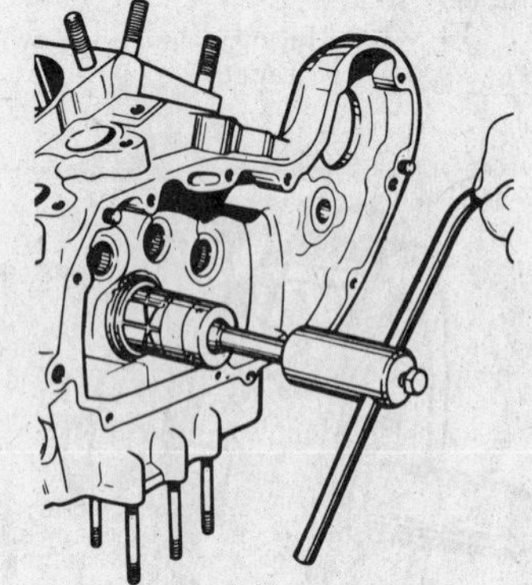

Lapping the pinion shaft bearing race

15. Using a suitably sized brass drift and hammer, tap the bearing race free from the opposite side. Remove the outer race snap-ring with a 1/8 in. punch or any suitable pointed instrument if the bearing set is to be replaced. This is easily done by tapping the ring through the oil hole (1969 and later models).

16. Consult Sportster "Crankcase Disassembly" for sprocket bearing inner half removal instructions. Use a bearing puller (H-D Part No. 96015-56). Leave the assembly in the vise.

17. Insert a 5 x 1/2 in. rod through the flywheel holes to secure them. Disassemble as directed in Sportster "Disassembly."

INSPECTION

Consult Sportster "Inspection."

ASSEMBLY

Assemble in the reverse order of disassembly. Note the following:

1. Install the outer race snap-ring in the left case.

2. With the case supported on parallel bars, press the bearing outer races and snap-ring into the crankcase bushing. Use an outer race press plug (H-D Part No. 97194-57) or a suitable drift to press them in, one at a time, until sealed with the wider end out.

3. Install the bearing and spacer on the sprocket shaft, with the shaft in case and the outer bearing halves as described in Sportster "Crankcase Assembly."

4. The bearing must not be preloaded (under excessive tension). If shaking the case half does not reveal a slight amount of play in the case bearing half, or if the flywheel assembly will not rotate freely, the bearing must be removed and a 0.003 in. shim (H-D Part No. 23741-55) added to spacers. Assemble and recheck for play.

5. Slip the inner bearing washer, bearings, and outer washer in place on the pinion shaft and secure a new spiral lock ring in the shaft groove.

6. Apply a non-hardening sealer to the joint surface and secure the cases with the 5/16 x 6 in. and the 11/32 x 5 13/16 in. studs.

7. Consult Sportster "Crankcase Assembly" for flywheel end-play checking and correcting procedures.

8. Secure the case halves.

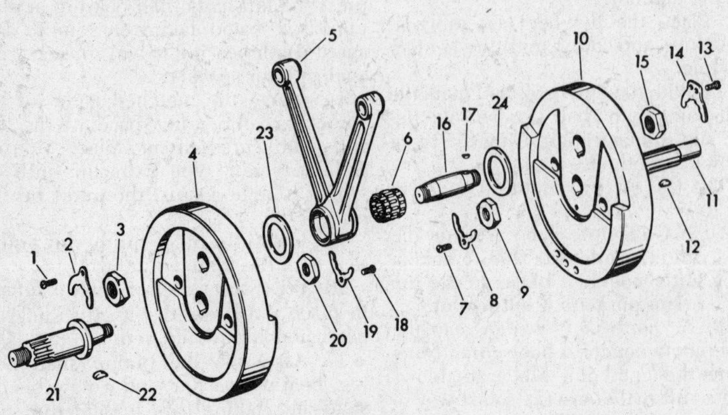

Crankshaft assembly

1. Crank pin lock plate screw
2. Crank pin nut lock plate
3. Crank pin nut
4. Flywheel (left)
5. Connecting rods
6. Crank pin roller and retainer set
7. Pinion shaft lock plate screw
8. Pinion shaft nut lock plate
9. Pinion shaft nut
10. Flywheel (right)
11. Pinion shaft
12. Pinion shaft key
13. Crank pin lock plate screw
14. Crank pin nut lock plate
15. Crank pin nut
16. Crank pin
17. Crank pin key
18. Sprocket shaft lock plate screw
19. Sprocket shaft nut lock plate
20. Sprocket shaft nut
21. Sprocket shaft
22. Sprocket shaft key
23. Crank pin boss washer (left)
24. Crank pin boss washer (right)

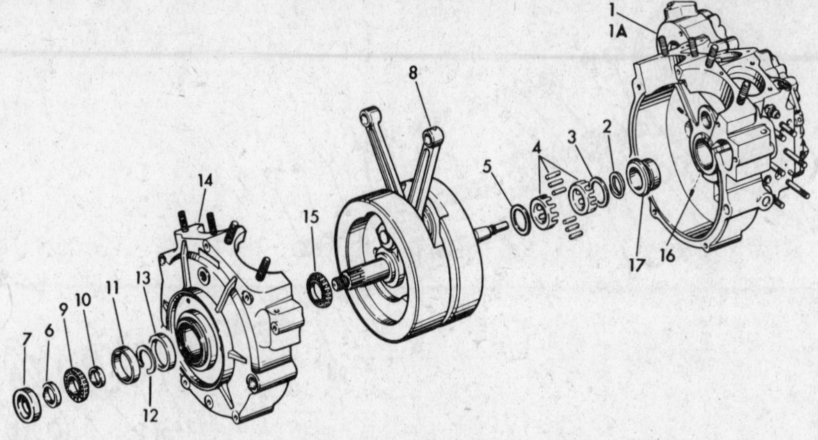

Crankcase assembly (Glide models)

1. Right crankcase half (1970–72)
1A. Right crankcase half (1973 & later)
2. Spiral lock ring
3. Bearing washer (2)
4. Bearings and retainer
5. Bearing washer (see item 3)
6. Sprocket shaft spacer
7. Sprocket shaft bearing seal
8. Flywheel and rod assembly
9. Sprocket bearing half
10. Bearing inner spacer
11. Bearing outer race
12. Outer race snap ring
13. Bearing outer race
14. Left crankcase half
15. Sprocket bearing half
16. Pinion shaft bearing race lock screw (2)
17. Pinion shaft bearing race

Note: Keep parts 9, 10, 11, 12, 13 and 15 as a set. Do not transpose or interchange parts.

TRANSMISSION

Sportster

CRANKCASE AND TRANSMISSION DISASSEMBLY

This section only applies if such work as overhauling the crankcase or flywheel is to be done. Otherwise the transmission can be serviced through the access cover.

1. Disassemble the crankcase as described in "Crankcase Disassembly."
2. Remove the first gear washer and first gear from the countershaft.
3. Free the assembled mainshaft.
4. Remove Second gear.
5. Remove the gear shifter cam cap screw and retainer ring, and then the shifter mechanism will come free of the access cover.
6. Remove the First gear washer, Third gear, and the shifter fork from the countershaft and remove the assembled countershaft.
7. For further information, consult "Shifter Mechanism Disassembly" and "Mainshaft and Countershaft Disassembly."

SHIFTER LINKAGE (1975 AND LATER)

Removal

1. Loosen the rear exhaust pipe at the cylinder and position it out of the way.
2. Remove the muffler for the front cylinder.
3. Remove the right footrest and brake pedal.
4. Remove the sprocket cover.
5. Mark the position of the shifter pedal relative to its shaft. Remove the pinch bolts and pull off the pedal.
6. On the right side of the machine, disconnect the rear end of the shifter link by removing the lockring and pulling the shifter link from the cross shaft arm.
7. The pivot end may be removed from the shifter link after loosening the locknut. When removing the pivot end, count the number of turns necessary to get it off the link for reassembly.

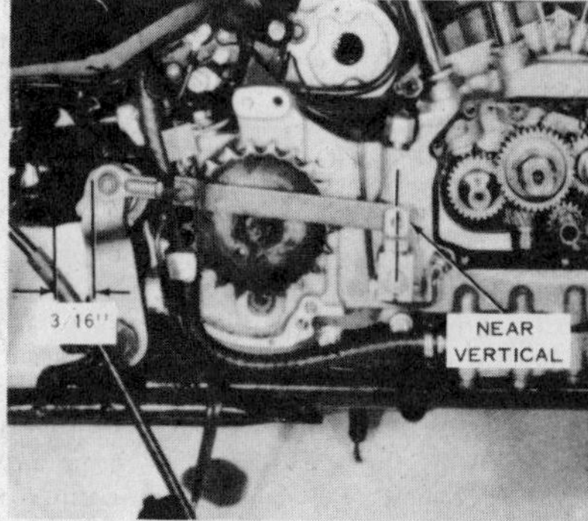

Shift linkage adjustment (1975 and later Sportster)

Installation

1. With the transmission in fourth gear, position the shifter pedal on its shaft so that it is ⅛ in. from the bottom of the footrest rubber when at the top limit of its travel.
2. With the pedal in this position, the cross shaft arm should be $^3/_{16}$ in. from the swing arm. Turn the pivot end in or out on its shaft to achieve adjustment.
3. If adjustment to these dimensions is not possible, proceed as follows: remove the gearcase cover. Remove the clevis lever from the shifter shaft after removing the pinch bolt. Mark the position of the lever on the shaft before removal. Move the lever one spline in either direction to achieve clearances outlined in Steps 1–2, above.

TRANSMISSION ACCESS COVER REMOVAL

1. With a drip pan under the clutch, remove the footrest, stoplight switch, brake pedal (74 and earlier) or shifter pedal (75 and later), chaincase cover, clutch, primary chain, and compensating sprocket assembly by consulting the "Clutch Disassembly" section.

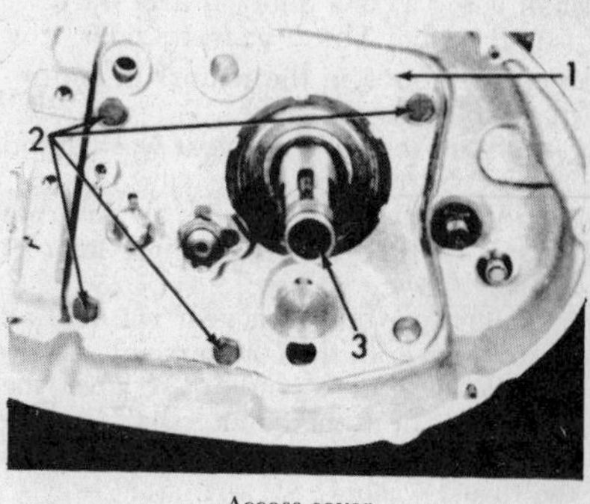

Access cover

1. Access cover
2. Access cover capscrews (4)
3. Clutch gear oil seal
4. Hub nut rubber O-ring (XLCH, 1966 and earlier XLH)

2. Loosen the front cylinder exhaust pipe and muffler; remove the starter crank assembly, right footrest, and shifter lever. Remove the sprocket cover, starter crank gear, starter clutch gear, and starter crankshaft as described in the "Starter" section.
3. Loosen the mainshaft nut.
4. Remove the drive-chain master link and remove the chain.
5. Remove the mainshaft nut, lockwasher, sprocket, oil seal retainer screws and lockwashers, oil seal, seal retainer, and gasket from the mainshaft. If the sprocket requires assistance from a claw puller, make certain that at least two teeth are grasped by the puller or else damage will result.
6. Remove the access cover cap bolts.
7. Pry the clutch gear oil seal free and replace it.
8. Remove the hub nut rubber O-ring from the groove in the clutch gear (if applicable).
9. Pull the access cover free with Transmission Access Cover Puller (H-D Part No. 95560-57) or an appropriate sized gear puller

SHIFTER MECHANISM DISASSEMBLY

1. Remove Second gear from the mainshaft, cap screw, retainer ring, and washer. Using snap-ring pliers, remove the cam retaining ring and slide it off the camshaft thrust washer.
2. Remove the gear shifter cam, pawl carrier, pawl carrier support, and pawl carrier support shims (if applicable). Remove the pawl spring and shifter pawls.

NOTE: *On 1972 and later models, remove the retaining rings to free the pawls, spacers, and springs from the pawl carrier. To free the shifter forks and finger rollers, first remove the countershaft assembly.*

3. After removing the lever arm shaft, fork shaft, cam follower retainer ring, follower retainer, and follower spring, the shifter forks and finger rollers should come free.

MAINSHAFT AND COUNTERSHAFT DISASSEMBLY

1. Remove from the right crankcase the mainshaft, thrust washer, and the 23 rollers.
2. Remove First gear from the mainshaft using a claw puller if necessary.
3. Pry the Third gear retainer ring from its groove in the mainshaft and replace it.
4. Remove the Third gear washer and Third gear from the mainshaft.
5. With the access cover on an arbor press, press the clutch gear free from its bearing.
6. Remove the First gear washer and Third gear from the countershaft.
7. With a claw puller, remove the drive gear from the countershaft, and remove the gear spacer, Second gear, and the thrust washer.
8. Remove the countershaft low gear and washer.
9. Drift the oiler plug free from inside the access cover.

TRANSMISSION SPROCKET AND SHIFTER MECHANISM INSPECTION

1. Clean all metal parts in a suitable solvent and blow dry.
2. Inspect the mainshaft sprocket for worn or damaged teeth and splines; replace if necessary. Replace the oil seal and gasket if necessary.
3. Replace the gear shifter cam retaining ring. Inspect the shifter cam for worn or grooved thrust points which cause irregular shifting and replace if necessary.
4. Inspect the shifter pawl carrier for grooves or wear at the fingers. Inspect the pawl carrier support for breaks or cracks.
5. Check the bearing for excessive play by loosely assembling the shifter cam, pawl carrier, support, and shims (if applicable). Replace any worn or pitted parts.
6. Replace the pawl carrier springs with 16-coil cadmium plated springs, or fourteen to sixteen coil black phosphatized springs. Spring free-length should be $2\frac{25}{32}$ in. when new.
7. Check pawl spring operation (1970–71 models) by inserting the springs in the carrier holes. Spring free-length should be $1\frac{7}{32}$ in. when new. Replace any worn, grooved, or cracked parts. On 1972 and later models, check pawl and carrier. Free length of spring is 1¾ in.
8. Inspect the finger rollers and shifter forks for warping, wear, or grooves.
9. Check the shifter cam follower and spring for freedom of movement and replace if worn. Free-length of a new spring should be $1\frac{19}{32}$ in.
10. Remove the shifter fork shaft only if it is to be replaced. The shaft is press-fit and aligned at the factory, and therefore should be replaced together with a new cover. Check the shaft for warping or damage by observing shifter fork movement on the shaft. The shaft may only be replaced by pressing out the old and pressing in the new, taking care to keep it perpendicular to the cover face.

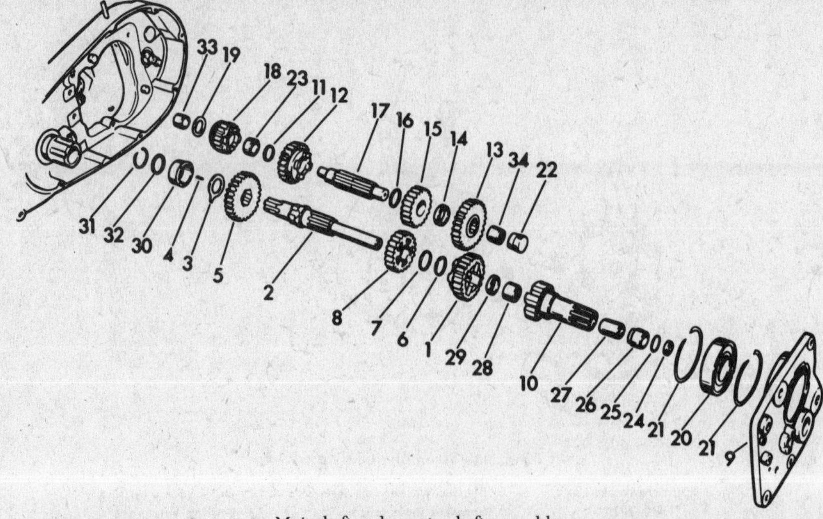

Mainshaft and countershaft assembly

1. Mainshaft second gear
2. Transmission mainshaft
3. Mainshaft thrust washer (variable thickness)
4. Transmission mainshaft roller (23)
5. Mainshaft low gear
6. Mainshaft third gear retainer ring
7. Mainshaft third gear washer
8. Mainshaft third gear
9. Access cover
10. Clutch gear
11. Countershaft low gear washer
12. Countershaft third gear
13. Countershaft drive gear
14. Countershaft gear spacer
15. Countershaft second gear
16. Countershaft second gear thrust washer
17. Transmission countershaft
18. Countershaft low gear
19. Countershaft low gear washer (variable thickness)
20. Mainshaft ball bearing
21. Mainshaft ball bearing snap ring (2)
22. Countershaft oiler plug
23. Countershaft low gear bushing
24. Clutch gear oil seal (1970 only)
25. Clutch hub nut O-ring (1970 only)
26. Clutch gear oil seal extension (1970 only)
27. Clutch gear bushing
28. Clutch gear needle roller bearing
29. Mainshaft thrust washer
30. Mainshaft roller bearing race
31. Mainshaft roller bearing retainer ring
32. Mainshaft roller bearing washer
33. Countershaft bearing—closed end
34. Countershaft bearing—open end

11. Inspect the gear shifter lever arm for warping or damage.
12. Check the bushings for excessive play by inserting and rotating the shaft. Bushings must be pressed in with the gearcase cover and oil seal removed. Drift from the right-side. Remove any high spots with a ½ in. reamer and replace the oil seal.

MAINSHAFT AND COUNTERSHAFT INSPECTION

1. Clean all metal parts in a suitable solvent and blow them dry.
2. Inspect, and replace if necessary, all gears, pinions, and dogs for a worn, chipped, or otherwise damaged condition—especially if the transmission frequently jumped out of gear.
3. Inspect the mainshaft and countershaft for excessive wear on the splines and bearing surfaces, and replace if necessary.
4. Slip the gears into position on their shafts and check for excessive play and replace if necessary. Specifications are listed in the "Transmission Specifications" chart.
5. The low gear bushing is a press-fit. If replaced, check for high spots and ream it until round.
6. Remove the clutch gear oil seal extension with cloth or leather-covered vise grips in order to remove the clutch gear bushing and needle roller bearing.
7. Drift out the clutch gear bushing and drift out the needle roller bearing and thrust washer from the opposite end of the gear.
8. Press a new bushing into the clutch gear shaft, insert the mainshaft and rotate the gear to check for high spots and free-movement. If there is not 0.001–0.002 in. play, ream the bushing to size (H-D Reamer, Part No. 94829-42).
9. Press on the printed side of the needle roller bearing to install the bearing and thrust washer.
10. Seal the oil extension with aluminum paint.
11. Install a new oil seal and O-ring.
12. Test the main shaft and countershaft for alignment with a dial indicator and replace if warped 0.003 in. or more.
13. Check the play between the mainshaft ball bearing, clutch gear, and access cover. Replace if play exceeds specifications listed in "Transmission Specifications."
14. Remove the mainshaft ball bearing snap-ring and press the bearing free on an arbor press from the outside in. If the bearing is drifted out, it should be replaced.
15. Inspect the mainshaft rollers and bearing race and replace if pitted, scored, or worn beyond specifications. Pack with grease before assembly.
16. Remove the race by removing the retaining ring and washer. Heat the case around the bearing and drift from the outside in. Press in a new race until its shoulder seats. Check clearances against those listed in "Transmission Specifications" and replace if necessary. Replace the snap-ring.
17. Check the countershaft needle roller bearings against the proper specifications listed in "Transmission Specifications." Drift free only if replacement is necessary, pressing on the printed side.

The access cover must be $^5/_{64}$ in. from the side.

18. Replace the oiler plug after the shaft clearances are established and replace with the oil hole up.

TRANSMISSION ASSEMBLY

1. Install the cam follower retainer ring and retainer in the access cover.

2. Seat the pawl carrier springs against the pawl carrier support.

1970–71:

3. Assemble the shifter pawls and springs in their respective sockets with the top engaging grooves facing one another.

4. Depress the pawls with a knife blade and assemble the cam, carrier, support, and shims (if applicable).

5. Install the camshaft thrust washer and a new retaining ring, using snap-ring pliers.

6. Depress one pawl at a time with a knife blade and rotate the shifter cam to ensure free cam movement.

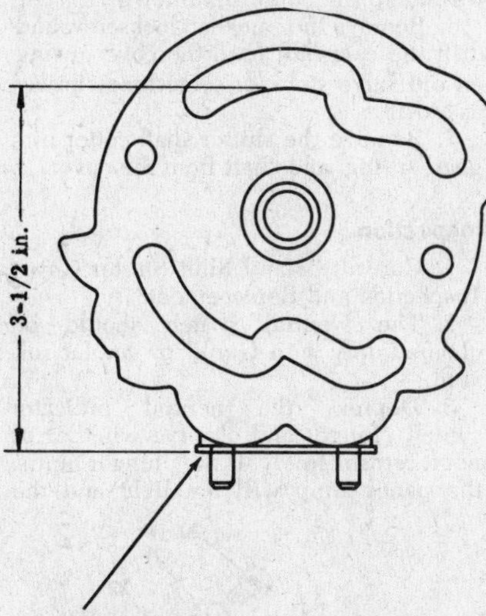

Shimming dimensions for pawl carrier support: rotate cam to 3rd gear position and shim as required using a quantity of 0.010 in. thick shims as necessary to obtain a 3½ in. dimension to the cam surface as shown.

7. Use shims to adjust the height of the cam as shown to ensure proper shifter fork operation.

1972 and later models: Assemble the pawls on the carrier using spacers (one on outside, one underneath) to align the spring hooks and holes. Secure the pawl retaining ring and spring. Depress one pawl at a time while inserting the shifter cam in the pawl carrier. Assemble the carrier into the support so that the carrier ear seats between the springs.

8. Arbor-press the clutch gear into the mainshaft bearing.

9. Assemble the Second gear thrust washer, Second gear, Second gear spacer, and the drive gear on the countershaft, making sure that Second gear rotates freely. Install the assembly in the access cover.

10. Install the mainshaft second gear, countershaft third gear, and shifter forks on the fork shaft with the finger studs pointed toward the access cover and the fork finger in the running groove of the gear. Install the finger rollers.

11. Install the cam follower and follower spring in the follower retainer. Check to make sure that the follower is free in the retainer.

12. Secure the shifting assembly to the access cover with the capscrew and retainer ring while engaging the shifter fork finger rollers in the shifter cam slots.

13. Assemble First gear, Third gear, the Third gear washer, and a new retainer ring on the mainshaft. The ring is easily inserted with Retainer Ring Sleeve (H-D Part No. 96396-52), but snap-ring pliers will also work.

14. Slide Second gear and the clutch gear onto the mainshaft.

15. Place the thinnest, First gear, variable washer against the countershaft shoulder.

16. Slide First gear on the shaft and check the clearance between the faces of it and Third gear. Try different First gear washers until a clearance of 0.038–0.058 in. is obtained. (Washers are available in thicknesses of 0.065, 0.075, 0.085, and 0.100 in.).

17. Assemble all parts to the access cover except for the mainshaft thrust washer, countershaft first gear washer, mainshaft rollers, roller bearing washer, and bearing retainer ring. Shift through the gears several times to ensure proper operation. With the transmission in Neutral, check to see if gear face clearances are between 0.038–0.058 in. Replace the shifter forks if clearance is not obtained.

Mainshaft and Countershaft End-Play

1. Install the thinnest First gear and Third gear variable washers. Temporarily secure the Third gear washer with a dab of heavy grease, with the ear pointing down.

2. With all parts assembled, install the access cover on the crankcase. Take care to align the dowel pins, tap the cover into place with a soft mallet, and secure it with the cover cap screws.

3. Check mainshaft end-play with a dial indicator from the sprocket side of the shaft by shifting the shaft back and forth. Repeat on the countershaft from the access cover side.

4. Wedge a discarded wheel spoke, or something similar, in the countershaft end hole and measure end-play while pulling and pushing on the spoke.

5. End-play for both shafts must be within 0.003–0.009 in. Adjust by installing larger mainshaft thrust and countershaft First gear washers. Washers are available in 0.005 in. gradations from 0.050–0.075 in., and countershaft washers of 0.020, 0.030, and 0.040 in. are also available.

6. Center the lever arm shaft so it will engage the pawl carrier support when the cover is in place. Lightly rotate the shaft to ensure correct engagement before securing the cover.

7. Grease the mainshaft bearing race and assemble the rollers. Secure the roller with the bearing washer and retaining ring.

Mainshaft Sprocket, Starter, and Clutch Assembly Installation

1. Temporarily install the foot-shift lever and place the transmission in Fourth gear.

2. Install the oil seal gasket, seal, retainer, lockwashers, and screws, but do not secure them yet.

3. Temporarily place the sprocket on the mainshaft to correctly position the retainer.

4. Remove the sprocket and secure the screws.

5. Assemble the sprocket, lockwasher, and nut. Secure the washer ear against the nut.

6. Install the rod end and drive chain.

7. Consult the "Starter" section for starter installation procedures.

8. Consult the "Clutch" section for clutch installation procedures.

9. Lubricate the transmission as described in the following section.

Transmission Lubrication

1. Stand the motorcycle upright and remove the oil filler plug from the chaincase top and the oil level plug from the chaincase bottom.

2. Fill the transmission with engine oil until the overflow bégins from the oil level plug hole.

3. Secure both plugs when overflow ceases.

Glide Models

LINKAGE ADJUSTMENT

Hand Shift

Adjust the hand shift if the transmission is moved.

1. Place the transmission in Third gear on four-speed models, and Second gear on three-speed models.

2. Disconnect the shifter rod at the shifter lever.

3. Gently shift the lever back and forth until you feel the spring plunger reach its seat.

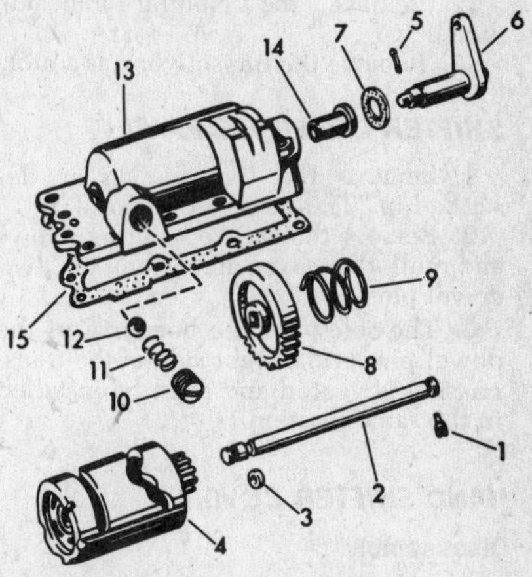

Hand shifter cover assembly

1. Shaft lock screw
2. Shaft
3. Oil seal
4. Shifter cam
5. Cotter pin
6. Shifter lever
7. Leather washer
8. Shifter gear
9. Shifter gear spring
10. Cam plunger cap screw
11. Ball spring
12. Plunger ball
13. Cover
14. Shifter lever bushing
15. Cover gasket

4. Adjust the clevis until the rod can be attached without moving the lever.

Foot Shift

Adjust the shifter rod when the transmission is moved if wear necessitates adjustment.

1. Align the shift lever clamping slot with the foot lever shaft notch (FL only).
2. Disconnect the lever from the rod and adjust the rod end as desired. Secure the locknut and connect the rod and lever (FL, FX to 1973).
3. FX, 1974 and later: remove the retainer clip and adjust the threaded ends on rod.

TRANSMISSION REMOVAL

1. Disconnect the battery ground wire from the negative terminal.
2. Remove the footrest, chain cover compensating sprocket (if applicable, consult "Clutch" section), or shaft nut (nut is removed by striking a 1⅝ in. wrench with a hammer).
3. Remove the chain adjuster mounting bolt and the starter shaft thrust washer (1965 model only).
4. Remove the clutch, clutch hub, drive sprocket, and primary chain as described in the "Clutch" section.
5. Loosen the five transmission mounting bolts and remove the chainguard and oiler.
6. Remove the starter solenoid terminal wires.
7. Remove the battery, carrier, and regulator ground strap from the right-side of the transmission. Remove the right rear footrest bracket.
8. Remove the starter motor bracket and pull the starter motor out of the left-side of the frame. Remove the kick-starter lever (if applicable).
9. Loosen the locknut at the clutch foot control or booster, and turn the rod out until it can be slid free of the clutch release lever.
10. Remove the shifter rod.
11. Disconnect the speedometer cable and housing from the transmission.
12. Remove the Neutral indicator switch.
13. Remove the transmission as a unit.

SHIFTER COVER REMOVAL

1. Remove the transmission as described in "Transmission Removal."
2. Remove the twelve securing screws and pull the cover free from the two dowel pins.
3. The screw for the hole nearest the dowel pin on the right side of the transmission is vented and must be installed in the same location.

HAND SHIFTER COVER

Disassembly

1. Remove the shaft lockscrew and drift the shaft free with a discarded valve stem or something similar.
2. Remove the shifter cam.
3. Remove the shifter lever cotter pin.
4. Pry the shifter gear from the shaft by tapping a screwdriver between the gear and the inside of the cover.
5. Remove the shifter lever and leather washer.
6. Remove the cam plunger capscrew, ball spring, and plunger ball.

Inspection

1. Clean all metal parts in a suitable solvent and blow them dry.
2. Inspect the shifter lever bushing for excessive wear—indicated by excessive lever play—and replace if necessary. Screw a ⅝ in. tap into the bushing. Remove the tap and heat the case to about 300 degrees. Screw in the tap, clamp it in a vise, and tap the cover with a soft mallet until the cover comes free.
3. Inspect the teeth on the shifter gear and cam pinion for wear or damage and replace if necessary.
4. Inspect the plunger ball seat and cam track for excessive wear and replace if the edges are not sharp.
5. The oil seal and cover gasket should be replaced but may be used again if in good condition.

Assembly

1. Hold the shifter gear spring in place inside the cover and place the shifter gear on it so the gear hub is inside the spring. The gear must have the timing mark on the gear tooth facing the shift lever cover port.
2. Slip the leather washer onto the shifter lever and insert the lever through the case and spring so that it meshes with the shifter gear. The lever should be pointed toward the left.
3. Secure the assembly with the lever shaft cotter pin.
4. Insert the cam in the cover so that the pinion gear timing mark aligns with the shift gear mark.
5. Place the oil seal on the camshaft and insert it through the case and cam. Secure it with the shaft lock screw.
6. If cam end-play is greater than 0.0005–0.0065 in., install shims as necessary. If play is too little the cover can be filed as necessary.

FOOT SHIFTER COVER

Disassembly

1. Remove the shifter lever screws, lever, dust shield, and long cover screws.
2. Remove the short cover screw nut from the back of the adaptor plate, withdraw the short cover screw, and remove the pawl carrier cover, gasket, pawl carrier, pawls, pawl springs, and pawl carrier springs.
3. Remove the adaptor plate bracket screw, washer, adaptor plate, and plate gasket.
4. Disconnect the neutral indicator switch from the cover.
5. Bend back the cam follower retainer washer ear to remove the retainer, washer spring, and cam follower.
6. Remove the camshaft lockscrew and drift the camshaft from the cover, using an old valve stem, or something similar, as a drift.
7. Remove the shifter shaft cotter pin, gear, spring, and shaft from the cover.

Inspection

1. Consult "Hand Shift Shifter Cover Inspection and Replacement."
2. The Neutral switch should be cleaned only with Gunk® or similar solvent.
3. Depress the neutral indicator switch plunger and observe whether or not it returns freely. If the plunger binds, the panel lamp will not light and the

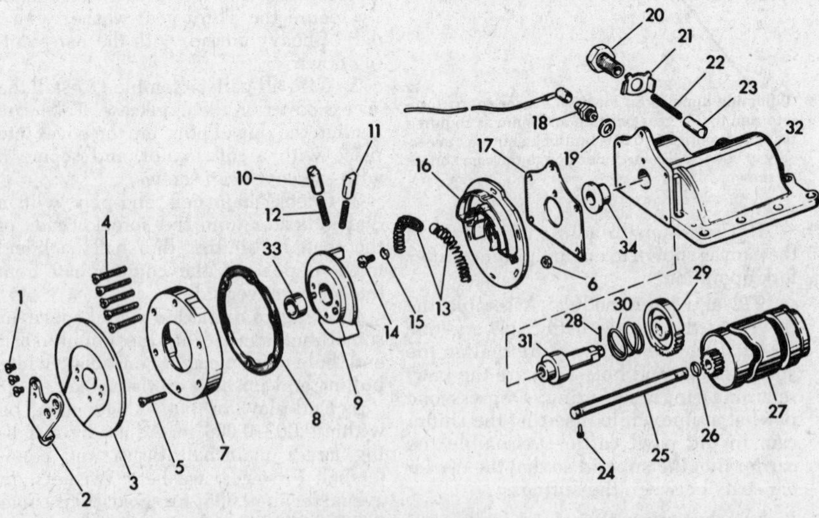

Foot shifter cover assembly

1. Shifter lever screw (3)
2. Shifter lever
3. Dust shield
4. Shifter cover screw (5)
5. Shifter cover screw (short)
6. Cover screw nut
7. Pawl carrier cover
8. Cover gasket
9. Pawl carrier
10. Pawl (right)
11. Pawl (left)
12. Pawl spring (2)
13. Pawl carrier spring (2)
14. Adapter plate bracket screw
15. Adapter plate bracket screw washer
16. Adapter plate
17. Adapter plate gasket
18. Neutral indicator switch
19. Washer
20. Cam follower retainer
21. Cam follower retainer washer
22. Spring
23. Cam follower
24. Cam shaft lock screw
25. Cam shaft
26. Oil seal
27. Shifter cam
28. Cotter pin
29. Shifter gear
30. Shifter gear spring
31. Shifter shaft
32. Shifter cover
33. Pawl carrier bushing
34. Shifter shaft bushing

switch must be replaced. Do not run current through it without the panel lamp neutral indicator in series so the circuit is completed.

4. If the pawl carrier hole has been worn until it is oversized, replace the press-fit pawl carrier bushing.

Assembly

1. Hold the shifter gear spring in the cover and place the shifter gear on it so the gear hub is inside the spring. The gear tooth timing mark must face the cover.

2. Slide the shifter shaft through the cover until it meshes with the gear. The timing mark should be in line with the squared side of the shaft and slightly to the left of the last ratchet tooth on the shaft.

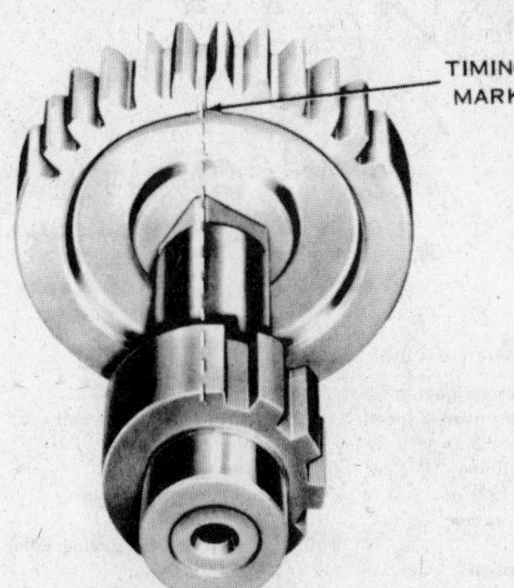

Alignment of shifter gear timing marks

3. Gently tap the shaft and gear together; secure them with the shaft cotter pin.

4. Place the oil seal on the wider of the two camshaft end grooves.

5. Place the shifter cam in the cover and hold it in position where the cam pinion timing mark aligns with the shifter gear timing mark.

6. Secure the cam with the camshaft and secure the camshaft with the lockscrew.

7. Slip in the cam follower and spring and secure them with the retaining washer and retainer.

8. Secure the neutral indicator switch and check to make sure that the plunger contacts the shifter gear.

9. Secure the cover in a vise with the shifter mechanism end pointing up.

10. Place the adaptor plate gasket on the case.

11. Attach the cover screw nut to the back of the adaptor plate with a dab of heavy grease and place the adaptor plate on the gasket.

12. Loosely screw the adaptor plate bracket screw and washer into the hole above the end of the shifter gear.

13. Place the gearshift cam in any gear, other than Neutral, and rock the cam back and forth to be sure that the cam follower is seating properly in one of the indexing notches.

14. Rotate the adaptor plate until the plate timing notch lines up between the two bottom teeth of the shifter gear. Secure it with the adaptor plate bracket screw.

Aligning shifter adaptor plate timing marks

15. Lightly grease the pawl carrier springs and place them in the slots on the adaptor plate.

16. Lightly oil the pawls and check to see that they move freely in the pawl carrier holes.

17. Install the pawl springs and pawls so that the end face notches face each other.

18. Place the pawl carriers on the shifter shaft so that the carrier lug seats between the pawl carrier springs.

19. Lubricate the pawl carrier back.

20. Assemble the cover gasket and cover. Apply Locktite® (H-D Part No. 99619-60) or a suitable thread-sealing compound to the cover screws and insert them. The short screw should seat in the cover screw nut. Secure all screws.

21. Place the dust shield over the pawl carrier dowel pins and set the shifter lever over the dust shield dowl pins. Secure it with the shift lever screws.

Installation

1. Apply sealer to the shifter cover and secure it to the gearbox.

2. Place the assembled shifter cover over the gearbox and secure it with the twelve securing screws. The two longer screws go in holes near the bulge over the shifter gear. The vented screw goes nearest the locating dowel pin on the gearcase right side. Apply a thread sealer to all but the vented screw.

SHIFTER FORK

Removal

1. Remove the shifter cover as described in "Shifter Cover Removal."

2. Disassembly is not necessary if the shifter fork assemblies are not damaged or worn and shifter clutches are not to be replaced.

3. Remove the shaft lockscrew and drift out the shaft.

4. Separate the shifter fork assemblies upon removal; do not mix parts during replacement.

Disassembly

1. Remove the finger rollers.

2. Free the bushing nuts by bending back the washer ears and remove both nuts and washers.

3. Remove the remaining parts, taking note of their positions as an aid in assembly.

Inspection

1. Clean all metal parts in a suitable solvent and blow them dry.

2. Replace bent or worn forks. Do not use forks which have been bent and then straightened.

3. Check the shifter fork bushings for excessive play and replace if necessary. Check new bushings on the shaft and determine if the shaft bushing contact surface is worn.

4. If the bushings bind, they can be lapped by coating the shaft with valve-grinding compound and then spinning the valve in the bushing until movement is free. Clean both parts again thoroughly.

Assembly

1. Assemble in reverse order of disassembly, taking care not to mix any parts. If parts are mixed, it would be better to

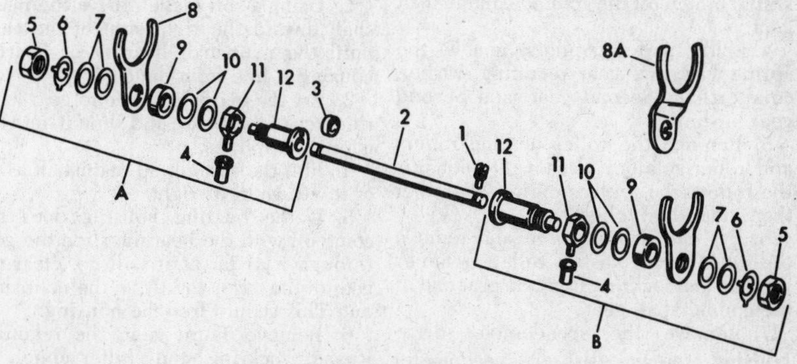

Shifter fork assembly

1. Lock screw
2. Shifter fork shaft
3. Rubber oil seal
4. Shifter finger rollers (2)
5. Nut (2)
6. Lock washer (2)
7. Spacing shim (variable number) (0.007 in.) (0.014 in.)
8. Shifter fork (1 or 2)
8A. Shifter fork (3-speed, reverse only)
9. Standard spacing shim (2)
10. Spacing shim (variable number) (0.007 in.) (0.014 in.)
11. Shifting finger (2)
12. Shifting fork bushing (2)

replace both assemblies than guess which went where.

2. Place Fork Shifter Gauge (H-D Part No. 96384-39) on the shifter cover. Align the tool gauge blocks with the straight cam slots by laying the ⅜ in. gauge rod through both. Secure the blocks with thumb screws.

3. Place the tool on the transmission case so that the shifter finger rollers engage the tool slots.

4. Check that the shifting clutches are centered by inserting a thickness gauge on both sides of the clutch.

5. Increase or decrease the number of variable shims, (0.014 or 0.007 in. shims are available), between the fork and finger to center the clutches.

6. First and Second gears should have 0.080–0.090 in. clearance on both sides.

7. Third and Fourth gears should have 0.100 in. clearance on both sides.

8. Reverse gear should have 0.060–0.070 in clearance between gear teeth.

9. If the gears have engaging dogs, rotate the gears so that the dogs on the gear and clutch overlap by about ⅛ in. before checking clearance.

10. Secure the shaft nut with a thread-sealing compound. Avoid overtightening.

11. Install the forks in the gearbox and secure them with the shaft. The narrowest fork is for the high gear shifter clutch. Secure the shaft lock screw. Install the shifter cover as described in "Shifter Cover Replacement."

Four-speed transmission assembly

1. End cap screw (4)
2. End cap screw washer (4)
3. End cap
4. End cap gasket
5. Countershaft nut
6. Lock washer
7. Lock plate
8A. Countershaft
8B. O-ring
9. Countershaft gear end washer
10. Low gear
10A. Countershaft reverse gear
11. Low gear bushing
12. Low gear bearing washer
13. Shifter clutch
14. Spring lock ring
15. Gear retaining washer
16. Countershaft second gear
16A. Countershaft low gear (3-speed and reverse)
17. Second gear bushing
18. Bearing rollers (22)
19. Roller retainer washer
20. Lock ring
21. Roller thrust washer
22. Roller bearing (22)
23. Retaining washer
24. Lock ring
25. Countershaft gear
25A. Countershaft gear (19-tooth for 3-speed and reverse)
26. Speedometer drive housing screw
27. Washer
28. Speedometer drive unit
29. Drive unit gasket
30. Idler gear shaft
30A. Spacer washer
31. Idler gear
32. Countershaft mounting collar (starter side)
33. Countershaft mounting collar (clutch side)
34. Idler gear bushing
35. Side cover nut and washer (9)
36. Side cover
37. Side cover gasket
38. Side cover upper bushing
39. Side cover lower bushing

FOUR-SPEED GEARBOX DISASSEMBLY

1. Remove the transmission as described in the "Transmission Removal" section.

2. Remove the clutch.

3. Remove the starter assembly.

4. Remove the shifter cover and shifting forks as described in "Shifter Cover Removal" and "Shifter Fork Removal" sections.

Countershaft Disassembly

1. Bend the lockwasher ear away from the countershaft nut and remove both.

2. Drift the countershaft out of the case from left to right.

3. Remove First gear, the First gear bushing, First gear bearing washer, and shifter clutch off the splined countershaft gear.

4. With snap-ring pliers, remove the spring lockring, gear retaining washer, countershaft, Second gear, and Second gear bushing.

5. Remove the roller bearing rollers and roller retainer washer. Do not mix the roller sets; replace entire sets rather than individual rollers.

6. Pry the lockring free and remove the roller thrust washer, rollers, retainer washer, and lockring from the gear end of the countershaft gear.

7. Remove the speedometer drive housing screw, washer, speedometer drive unit, and drive unit gasket.

8. Remove the idler gear shaft, spacer washer, and idler gear on three-speed and reverse-type transmissions. Inserting a ¼–20 tap screw into the shaft will provide a grip for pulling the shaft free. Apply 300° of heat to the case if the shaft will not move.

Mainshaft Disassembly

1. Remove the bearing housing retaining screws, oil deflector, and retaining plate.

2. Using a soft mallet, drive the mainshaft toward the right side of the case, until the mainshaft bearing or bearing housing is free from the case.

3. Pry the mainshaft second gear lockring free of its groove and slide it onto the mainshaft splines.

4. Pull the assembled mainshaft as far as it will go to its right.

5. If the bearing housing does not come off with the bearing, slide the gear through it as far as it will go, clear the gear of the case, and drive the mainshaft out. This should free the housing.

6. Remove Third gear, the retaining washer, lockring, and shifter clutch off the mainshaft and lift them out of the case.

7. Remove the mainshaft through the right-side of the case.

8. If repair is necessary, disassemble the mainshaft gear and bearing assembly.

9. Secure the mainshaft in a copper or wood-jawed vise. Bend the lockwasher ear away from the shaft nut and remove both. Pull the bearing and then the gear from the shaft with a claw puller (H-D Part No. 95635-46) or press them off. Protect the shaft end if a puller is to be used (with H-D Part No. 95636-46).

MAIN DRIVE GEAR

Disassembly

1. Secure the gearbox in a vise or to a work bench. Secure the chain sprocket by laying a length of chain over its teeth and nailing the chain ends to the bench.

2. Bend back the washer ear and remove the locknut (which has a left-hand thread) and washer.

3. Remove the oil deflector and chain sprocket.

4. Push the main drive gear into the case and lift it and the thrust washer out.

5. Remove the 44 rollers and place them where no mix-ups or lost bearings will occur. Bearings must be replaced as an entire set.

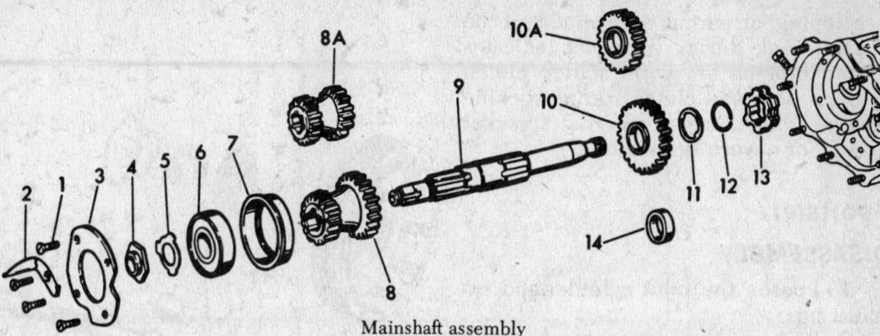

Mainshaft assembly

1. Bearing housing retaining plate screw (4)
2. Oil deflector
3. Retaining plate
4. Ball bearing nut
5. Ball bearing washer
6. Mainshaft bearing
7. Mainshaft bearing housing
8. Low and second gear
8A. Low and reverse gear (hand-shift)
9. Mainshaft
10. Third gear
10A. Mainshaft second gear (hand-shift)
11. Retaining washer
12. Lock ring
13. Shifter clutch
14. Third gear bushing

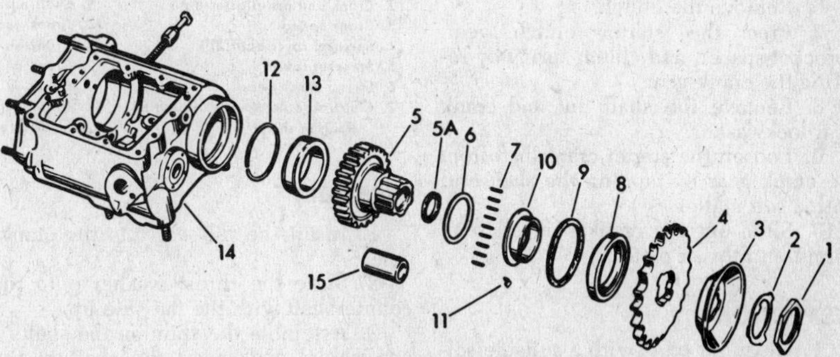

Main drive gear

1. Sprocket lock nut
2. Sprocket lock washer
3. Oil deflector
4. Chain sprocket
5. Main drive gear
5A. Main drive gear shaft seal (1965)
6. Thrust washer
7. Roller bearings (44)
8. Main drive gear oil seal
9. Oil seal cork washer
10. Main drive gear spacer
11. Main drive gear spacer key
12. Bearing race retaining ring
13. Bearing race
14. Gear box
15. Main drive gear bushing

6. Remove the drive gear oil seal, shaft seal, or main drive gear spacer only if worn or damaged.

Inspection

1. Clean all metal parts in a suitable solvent and blow them dry.
2. Inspect all of the gears for damage to the teeth or case hardening and replace if necesssary.
3. Inspect all bushings, bearings, and shafts for wear and excessive play; replace if necessary.
4. The main drive gear bearing race can be pressed in and out. Heating the case to about 300 degrees will facilitate removal. Press a new bearing in until the flange seats on the case. Replace the race retaining ring.
5. Replace the cork washers and oil seals. Apply sealer to the gear end recess when replacing the shaft seal.
6. Replace the shifter clutches and gear engaging dogs for wear or damage, and replace if necessary. Edges should be sharp rather than rounded.
7. Check bearings for smooth operation and proper fit in their races. Specifications are listed in the "Transmission Specifications" chart. Rollers are available in 0.0004 and 0.0008 in. oversizes and must be replaced as a set.

Assembly

1. Assemble the main drive gear oil seal, cork washer, and gear spacer in the case.
2. Install and grease the bearing race and install the rollers.
3. Assemble the main drive gear thrust washer on the main drive gear and slip the gear into the bearing race, taking care not to displace any rollers.
4. Install the main drive gear spacer key in its slot in the outer edge of the gear spacer, with the long section in any gear splineway.
5. Slip the sprocket, with the flat side away from the case, onto the gear splines. Assemble the oil deflector and lockwasher; secure the locknut.
6. Using a dial indicator, check end-play as listed in the "Transmission Specifications" chart.

MAINSHAFT ASSEMBLY

1. Assemble First and Second (or First and Reverse gear depending on the model) gears on the splines, mainshaft bearing housing, bearing, bearing washer, and the bearing nut to the mainshaft.
2. Press the bearing housing over the mainshaft ball bearing, press onto the shaft, and secure with the lockwasher and nut. Bend the washer ear against the nut.
3. Insert the shaft into the gearbox and install the mainshaft Third gear (Second gear on three-speed models), thrust washer, lockring and shifter clutch with the "high" side facing the drive gear.
4. Seat the lockring in its groove on the shaft.
5. Gently tap the shaft assembly into the case with a soft metal hammer or brass drift until the bearing housing flange seats against the case.
6. Install the Reverse idler gear on three-speed models.
7. Assemble and secure the retaining plate, oil deflector, and retaining plate screws.

COUNTERSHAFT ASSEMBLY

1. Insert the lockrings and bearing retainer washers in the countershaft gear.
2. Apply grease to the inside of the countershaft gear and assemble both roller sets.
3. Install the bearing thrust washer in the gear end.
4. Temporarily install the shaft to check bearing end-play and motion. Consult the "Transmission Specifications" chart for necessary information.
5. Apply a dab of heavy grease to the gear end washer and mount it, and the gear, in the case.
6. Check gear end-play by inserting a thickness gauge between the gear and washer. Consult the "Transmission Specifications" chart for proper clearance and adjust with the appropriate number of washers. (0.074, 0.078, 0.082, 0.085, 0.090, 0.095, and 0.100 in. washers are available.) When the correct amount of washers is arrived at, set aside the shaft, gear, and gear end washer.
7. Assemble the Second gear bushing, gear, thrust washer, and gear lockring on the countershaft gear.
8. Assemble the shifter clutch, thrust washer, first gear bushing, and gear on the countershaft gear.
9. Apply a dab of heavy grease to the countershaft gear end washer and place it on end of the gear.
10. Hold the assembly in the case and insert the countershaft. Secure the bearing lockwasher and nut, and bend up an ear of the washer.
11. Install the drive unit gasket, drive unit, washer, and screw.

THREE-SPEED GEARBOX DISASSEMBLY

Procedures are basically the same as outlined for the four-speed box. Refer to the illustrations for parts differences in three-speed.

STARTERS

Clicking noises from the starter gears are an indication of trouble. This will occur with the engine running and the starter crank in its proper position, and is caused by the starter clutch teeth. Tightening down the starter shaft nut on the crank gear camplate will often solve the problem.

Slipping, or partial engagement of the starter crank during its cycle, indicates either broken or worn starter clutch teeth, a damaged clutch spring, sticking of the clutch gear on the sprocket spacer, or a worn brass fitting.

Sportster

DISASSEMBLY

1. Loosen the front cylinder and exhaust pipe.
2. Remove the starter crank clamp bolt and pry the crank free of the shaft.
3. Apply pressure to the end of the starter spring and pry it free of the shaft.
4. Remove the sprocket cover bolts and lightly tap off the cover with a soft mallet while pulling it from the shaft.
5. Push the clutch lever forward and disengage the cable.
6. Remove the clutch.
7. Free the starter clutch gear, sprocket spacer, and clutch spring by rotating the crank gear.
8. Remove the shaft nut and crank gear lockwasher.
9. Loosen the starter crankshaft from the crank gear by tapping the shaft end with a soft mallet.
10. Slide out the crankshaft, oil seal, shims, and thrust plate.

INSPECTION

1. Clean all parts with a suitable solvent, except for the cover gasket if it is to be reused, and blow them dry.
2. Inspect the starter clutch and starter clutch gear for worn or damaged teeth, and replace if necessary.
3. Spin the clutch gear on the spacer and check for binding. Replace any damaged parts.
4. Replace the starter clutch spring if the length is under 1 in., in a free state, or if it is extremely fatigued.
5. Check the starter crankshaft for distortion. Check for excessive wear on the surfaces of the bearing and on the faces of the thrust washer and shaft collar. Replace if necessary.
6. Temporarily mount the following assembly in the left crankcase: crankshaft, oil seal, thrust plate, crank gear, lockwasher, and shaft nut, checking all parts for wear and replacing as necessary.
7. Spin the shaft and measure for excessive end-play with a dial indicator. End-play must be within 0.001–0.007 in. Shims which are 0.007 in. thick are available (H-D Part No. 6802).
8. Inspect the starter crank gear for wear or damage, especially to the ears. The camplate can be replaced independently of the crank gear.
9. Check to make sure that the camplate rivets are all secure.
10. Replace the bushings if excessive end-play is present but the shaft is not worn. Press the old bushing out and the new one in taking care to align the bushing hole with the grease-fitting channel.
11. Only inspect or replace the gear stop pin and washer if the engine is not in the chassis. These parts rarely need service. The pin is a press fit and the washer is secured by peening the pin end.

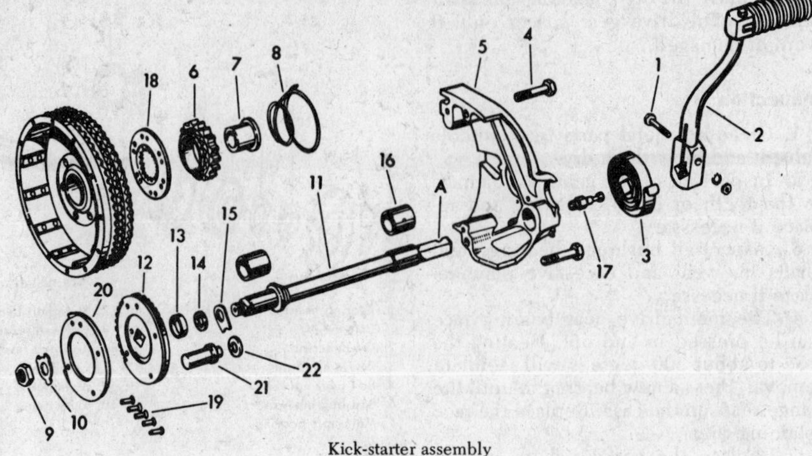

Kick-starter assembly

1. Crank clamp bolt, lock washer
2. Crank and pedal assembly
3. Crank spring
4. Sprocket cover bolt (2)
5. Sprocket cover
6. Starter clutch gear
7. Clutch sprocket spacer available (long or short)
8. Clutch spring
9. Shaft nut
10. Crank gear lock washer
11. Crankshaft
12. Crank gear
13. Crank oil seal
14. Crankshaft shim—0.007 in.
15. Shaft thrust plate
16. Shaft bushing (2)
17. Spring stud
18. Starter clutch
19. Crank gear cam plate rivet (5)
20. Crank gear cam plate
21. Crank gear stop pin
22. Crank gear stop pin washer

ASSEMBLY

1. Insert the oil seal into the crankcase.
2. Slide the thrust washer onto the countershaft with the flat side up.
3. Assemble the shim on the shaft (if applicable) and insert the shaft in the crankcase so that the thrust washer notch lines up with the stop pin.
4. Rotate the crank until the notch on the outer end of the shaft is pointing up.
5. Place the starter gear on the shaft end with the recessed portion of the camplate facing down. The slot should seat against the stop pin. Check to make sure that the thrust washer has not shifted out of place.
6. Install the lockwasher over the shaft so that its prong engages the hole in the crank gear face, and secure it with the flat side of the shaft nut against the washer.
7. Slip the spacer into the starter gear so that the grooved side of the gear bushing seats on the spacer lip.
8. Align the clutch spring small end in the gear bushing groove.
9. Press the starter gear into mesh with the starter clutch, and rotate the crank gear so that the clutch gear and crank gear also mesh. The spring will hold the assembly in place once the cover is installed.
10. Rotate the crank gear to its original position. By taking a strip of metal and drilling holes to match the cover screw securing holes, the strip can be mounted to temporarily hold the spring in position until the cover is mounted.
11. When replacing a sprocket spacer, make sure that you use one of the same length. If new gears are used, the clearance between the teeth must be checked in the following manner:

   a. Measure the distance from the spacer collar to the top of the clutch gear teeth.

   b. Measure the distance from the top of the clutch gear teeth to the sprocket washer.

   c. Subtract the answer of "b" from that of "a" to get the proper clearance.

   d. Use a long spacer if the result is less than 0.040 in. after a small spacer has already been used.

Starter crankshaft installation

1. Starter crankshaft shim—0.007 in.
2. Starter shaft thrust plate
3. Starter crank gear stop pin washer

12. Install the clutch.
13. Secure the clutch cable end in the release lever, and mount and secure the sprocket cover, exhaust pipe, and muffler.
14. Place the crank spring on the shaft end with the spring end pointing upward. Secure the spring on the spring stud by prying with a screwdriver.
15. Mount and secure the starter crank.

Glide Models

DISASSEMBLY

1. Place a drip pan under the transmission.
2. Remove the clutch lever rod from the release lever, cover nuts and washers, and pull the cover and release lever assembly free from the mounting studs.
3. The clutch release bearing should come off with the cover, but may bind on the starter clutch. Do not attempt to pry it from the cover, but it may be pried free from the clutch.
4. Pull the pushrod free of the mainshaft.
5. Secure the crank with a vise or vise grips which are blocked against movement.
6. Bend the lockwasher ear from the crank nut and remove both the nut and the washer.
7. Pull the starter gear with a claw puller or remove the vise and drive the crank free with a soft mallet. Block the crank and cover against swinging when the shaft is free from the gear.
8. Pull the crank out of the cover and the crank spring, thrust washer, crank bushings, and oil seal will all come free.
9. Remove the release lever nut and lockwasher, and pull the release lever free with a claw puller.
10. Remove the release finger and thrust washer by removing the cotter pin and washer; pull the shaft free.

INSPECTION

1. Clean all parts with a suitable solvent and blow them dry.
2. Check play between the starter crankshaft and the cover bushing, and replace if play is excessive. Press new bushings in until they are flush with the outer surface.
3. Replace the oil seal if the transmission was leaking through the starter crank.
4. Check for play in the release lever shaft. Replace the shaft if play is excessive.
5. Inspect the pushrod bearing for wear and replace it if the action is not smooth or is excessively loose.
6. Inspect the crank gear camplate and gear pin for wear. This is all assembled on the starter crank gear and is probably worn if the bushings were worn.

ASSEMBLY

1. Assemble the release lever shaft, lever bushing, release finger, thrust washer, lever bushing, washer, and cotter pin on the starter cover.
2. Press the crank bushing and oil seal in the cover after lightly greasing the seal.
3. Assemble the crank spring and the thrust washer (with beveled side facing spring), and insert the crank after lightly greasing the shaft.
4. Block the crank with a vise and wind the spring by rotating the cover clockwise.
5. With the crank held in normal position, install the crank gear so that the gear will maintain normal crank position.
6. Secure the crank with the lockwasher and nut, bending the washer ear against a flat side of the nut.
7. Install a new gasket on the case studs after applying gasket sealer or silver spray.
8. Install the clutch release bearing into the cover so that the slot in the bearing race engages the clutch release lever finger.
9. Slide the pushrod's narrow end into the bearing.
10. Slide the cover into place making sure the pushrod enters the main shaft.
11. The starter clutch ball plunger and the groove in the release bearing inner race must be aligned.
12. Secure the cover.
13. Fill the case with 1½ pts of oil of the same viscosity as that used in the engine.

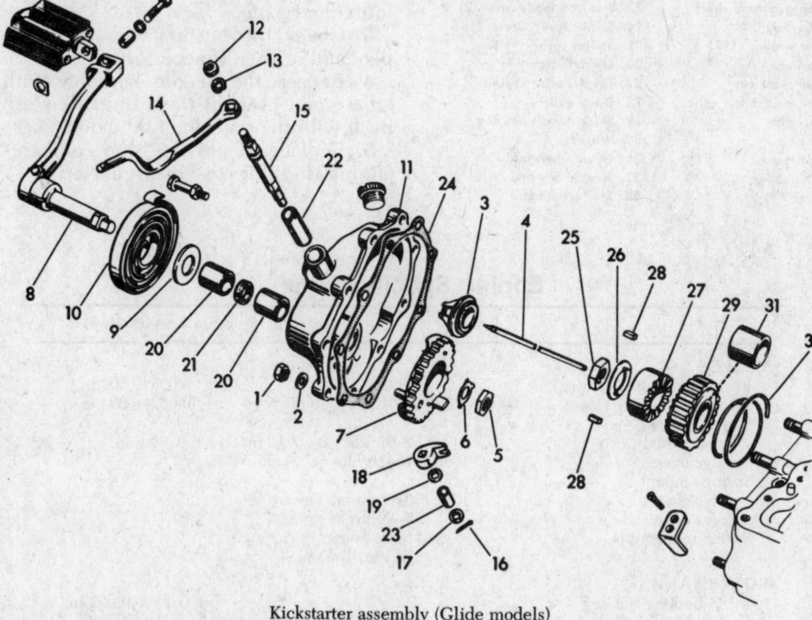

Kickstarter assembly (Glide models)

1. Starter cover nut (9)
2. Plain washer (9)
3. Clutch release bearing
4. Push rod
5. Starter crank nut
6. Eared lock washer
7. Starter gear
8. Crank
9. Thrust washer
10. Starter crank spring
11. Starter cover
12. Release lever nut
13. Lock washer
14. Release lever
15. Release lever shaft
16. Cotter pin
17. Plain washer
18. Release finger
19. Thrust washer
20. Starter crank bushing (2)
21. Oil seal
22. Release lever bushing
23. Release lever bushing
24. Starter cover gasket
25. Starter clutch nut
26. Starter clutch washer
27. Starter clutch
28. Starter clutch key (2)
29. Starter mainshaft gear
30. Starter clutch spring
31. Mainshaft gear bushing

STARTER CLUTCH

Disassembly

1. Remove the starter clutch cover assembly as described in the "Starter Disassembly" section.
2. Bend the lockwasher ear free of the clutch nut and remove both parts.
3. Pull the starter clutch from the mainshaft with Starter Clutch Puller (H-D Part No. 95650-42), or a suitable substitute, taking care not to damage the clutch teeth.
4. Remove the starter clutch keys, mainshaft gear, and clutch spring.

Inspection

1. Clean all parts in a suitable solvent and blow them dry, except for the cover gasket if it is to be reused.
2. Inspect the starter clutch, mainshaft gear, starter gear teeth, mainshaft gear, and starter clutch ratchet teeth. Replace if the teeth are rounded, mushroomed, chipped, or cracked.
3. Examine the mainshaft gear bushing and replace if necessary.

Assembly

Assemble in reverse order of disassembly. Note the following:

1. Replace the gasket if possible. Apply sealer to the case side of the gasket and position it on the case.
2. Rotate the mainshaft gear to ensure free motion and ream the bushing if necessary.
3. Drive the keys into the slots.
4. Secure the starter clutch nut and bend the lockwasher ear against a nut flat side. The top of the starter clutch must never be less than ⅝ in. above edge of the gearbox. If overtightened, the starter clutch may crack, causing damage to the bearing.

Electric Starter Drive

1966 AND LATER SPORTSTER, AND GLIDE MODELS

Harley-Davidson uses a Bendix-type drive assembly. When the starter button is depressed, the solenoid withdraws its plunger, causing the pinion shifter lever to pivot on its base. The arm of the lever rides in the shifter collar and the pivoting action causes the pinion gear to move along the shaft. Rather than a worm sleeve, the shaft itself has special threads

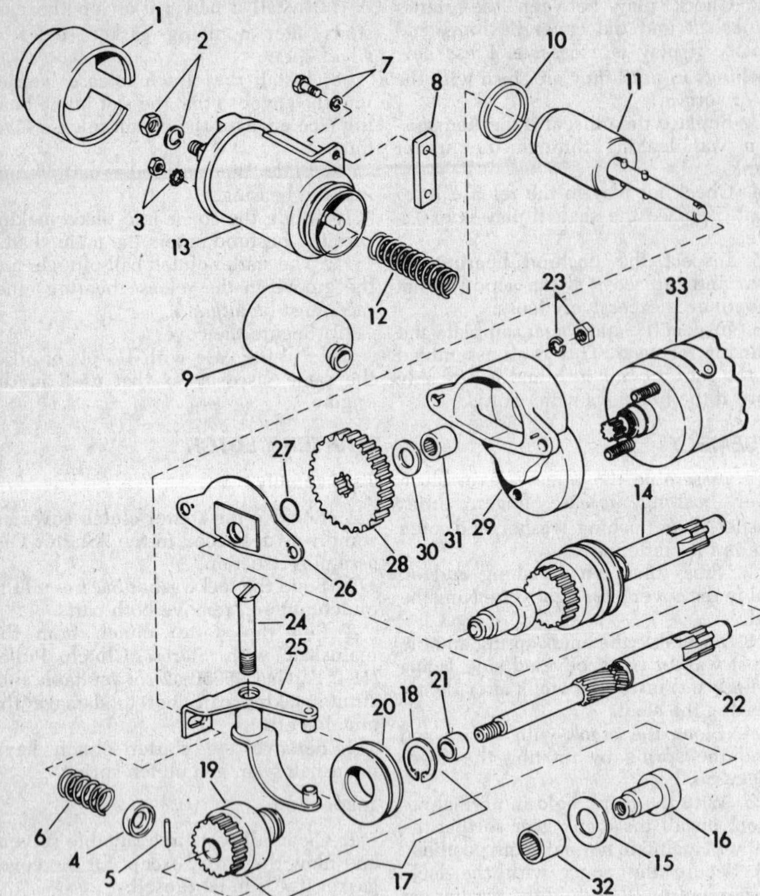

Electric starter shaft, housing, and solenoid

1. Cover
2. Terminal nut and lockwasher (2)
3. Terminal nut and lockwasher
4. Retainer cap
5. Pin
6. Spring
7. Bolt and lockwasher (2)
8. Spacer bar
9. Boot
10. Gasket
11. Plunger
12. Plunger spring
13. Solenoid
14. Pinion gear and shaft assembly
15. Thrust washer (1971 & earlier
16. Pinion shaft nut
17. Pinion and shifter collar assembly
18. Lock ring
19. Pinion gear
20. Shifter collar
21. Spacer
22. Shaft
23. Nut and lockwasher (2)
24. Shifter lever screw
25. Shifter lever
26. Oil deflector
27. Oil deflector O-ring
28. Drive gear
29. Starter shaft housing
30. Washer
31. Needle bearing
32. Needle bearing
33. Starter motor

which are constantly meshed with the threads in the pinion gear.

At the same time the plunger is withdrawn, the solenoid completes the starter motor circuit which rotates the starter shaft. When the pinion gear reaches the collar of the starter shaft nut, it stops and engages the clutch gear. The spiral threads allow the pinion gear to back off if it doesn't mesh properly.

When the button is released, the plunger again shifts the lever so the pinion gear resumes its inoperative position and the starter motor circuit is broken. The clutch gear is a one-way clutch which will allow the starter shaft to spin independently of the engine through a ratcheting action. This means that if you don't release the button after the engine starts, no damage will occur to the starter or the starter drive mechanism.

Solenoid and Starter Drive Shaft Disassembly

1. Disconnect the battery ground wire from the negative terminal post.
2. Remove the nuts and lockwashers from the solenoid terminals and disconnect the wires.
3. Remove the drive housing end cover bolts, lockwashers, and end cover.
4. Press on the solenoid shaft pin retainer cup, and remove the shaft retainer pin and the plunger shaft spring.
5. Remove the solenoid securing bolts, lockwashers, spacer bar, and solenoid assembly.
6. Remove the solenoid boot, plunger, and plunger spring.
7. Remove the pinion shifter lever screw and lift the lever free.
8. Remove the starter drive shaft assembly.
9. Place the drive gear in a wood or copper-lined vise and remove the shaft nut. This must be done with rubber or cloth between the jaws of a vise grip, or something similar, so that nut is not marred or distorted. The nut has a left-hand thread.
10. Slip the pinion gear and shifter collar from the shaft.
11. Using snap-ring pliers, remove the shift collar retaining ring and separate the pinion gear from the shifter collar.
12. Slip the spacer from the shaft.
13. Bushings are a press fit and should be removed only if they are to be replaced.

Solenoid Starter Drive Shaft Inspection and Repair

1. Clean all parts in a suitable solvent and blow them dry.
2. Inspect all parts for excessive wear and replace as necessary. Pay special attention to all gear and pinion teeth. Complete assemblies are available as well as individual parts.
3. Check the bushings for excessive play and replace if necessary.
4. Repack the needle bearings with grease and press-fit them until they are flush with the outside of the housing.
5. Replace, if possible, the collar retaining ring if it has been removed.

Engine Specifications

	Sportster	*Glide Models*
VALVES		
Fit in guide (EX) (loose)	0.0025–0.0045 in.	0.004–0.006 in.
Fit in guide (IN) (loose)	0.0015–0.0035 in.	0.002–0.004 in.
Spring (outer)		
valve closed	52–62 lbs at $1\frac{9}{32}$ in.	
valve open	155–165 lbs at $\frac{15}{16}$ in.	①
Spring (inner)		
valve closed	30–35 lbs at $1\frac{3}{32}$ in.	②
valve open	75–85 lbs at $\frac{3}{4}$ in.	③
Spring free length	$1\frac{1}{2}$ in. (outer) $1\frac{23}{64}$ in. (inner)	
ROCKER ARM		
Fit in bushing (loose)	④	0.0005–0.002 in.
End clearance	0.003–0.004	0.004–0.025 in.
PISTON		
Fit in cylinder (loose)	0.0025–0.003 in.	0.001–0.002 in.
Ring gap	⑤	0.010–0.020 in.
Compression ring side clearance	⑥	0.004–0.005 in.
Oil ring side clearance	0.003–0.005 in.	0.003–0.005 in.
Piston pin fit	Light hand press at 70 degrees Farenheit	
CONNECTING ROD		
Piston pin fit (loose)	0.0008–0.0012 in.	0.0008–0.0012 in.
End play between flywheels	0.006–0.010 in.	⑦
Fit on crank pin	⑧	⑨

Solenoid and Starter Drive Shaft Assembly

Assemble in reverse order of disassembly. Note the following:

1. Lightly lubricate the bearings with heavy grease.
2. Secure the shaft nut with a thread-locking sealer.
3. Spin the assembled shaft in the bearings to check for free movement. This will indicate whether or not the shaft nut was distorted during removal.
4. Stake the starter shaft housing washer.
5. Secure the battery cable and two red wires to the solenoid "top" terminal.

LUBRICATION SYSTEMS

OIL PUMP

Sportster and Glide models have both feed-type and scavenger gear-type pumps incorporated in one pump body.

Oil pumps are long-life units which seldom require repair. Therefore, one should check all related possibilities which might contribute to a "light-on" or "no-pressure" situation before disassembling the pump.

Sportster

OIL PUMP CHECK VALVE DISASSEMBLY

1. Clean the pump surface and its surrounding area thoroughly with a suitable solvent and blow it dry.
2. Disconnect the oil pressure switch wire and remove the switch, oil pump nipple, check valve spring, and ball valve.

OIL PUMP CHECK VALVE INSPECTION

1. Clean all parts in a suitable solvent and blow them dry. Blow out the nipple oil passage and the spring guide.
2. Inspect the nipple and spring for free-motion, wear, and damage, and replace if necessary. Spring free-length should be 1$^{15}/_{64}$ in.
3. Inspect the nipple threads and replace them if they are worn or damaged.
4. Replace the valve balls if they are ringed or are not perfectly smooth.
5. Inspect the ball valve seat for a clean and smooth condition. Slight pitting or striation marks can sometimes be removed by gently tapping with a suitable drift. Replace the pump body if such defects can not be corrected.

OIL PUMP CHECK VALVE ASSEMBLY

1. Assemble in the reverse order of disassembly.
2. All of the parts must be absolutely clean.

Engine Specifications (cont.)

	Sportster	Glide Models
OIL FEED PUMP PRESSURE		
Minimum	6 psi at 20 mph	12–35 psi
TAPPETS		
Guide fit in crankcase (press)	0.0005–0.001 in.	0.002 in. (tight) 0.002 in. (loose)
Fit in guide (loose)	0.0005–0.001 in.	0.001–0.002 in.
Roller fit	0.005–0.001 in.	0.0005–0.001 in.
Roller end clearance	0.008–0.010 in.	0.008–0.010 in.
GEAR CASE		
Intermediate gear shaft in bushing	0.0005–0.001 in.	——
Intermediate (idler) gear on shaft (loose)	——	0.001–0.0015 in.
GEAR CASE		
Cam gear shaft in bushing	0.0005–0.002 in.	0.001–0.0015 in.
Cam gear shaft in needle bearing	0.0005–0.0025 in.	0.0005–0.003 in.
Cam gear shaft end-play	——	0.001–0.005 in.
Cam gear backlash	0.0002–0.005 in.	——
Timer gear end-play	——	0.003–0.007 in.
Idler gear end-play	——	0.003–0.020 in.
Breather gear end-play	——	0.001–0.005 in.
Oil pump driveshaft (crankcase bushing)	——	0.0008–0.0012 in.
FLYWHEEL ASSEMBLY		
Gear shaft nut torque	⑩	⑪
Sprocket shaft nut torque	⑫	⑬
Crankpin nuts torque	150 ft lbs	⑭
Run-out (flywheels) (at rim)	0.003 in. maximum	0.003 in. maximum
Run-out (mainshafts)	0.002 in. maximum	0.001 in. maximum
End-play in crankcase	——	——
SPROCKET SHAFT BEARING		
Cup fit in crankcase (press fit)	0.005–0.0025 in.	0.0015–0.0035 in.
Cone fit on shaft (press fit)	0.0002–0.0012 in.	0.0002–0.0015 in.
End-play	0.001–0.010 in.	0.001–0.006 in.
Shaft fit in bearing (loose)	——	——
Fit in oil return bushing	——	——
PINION SHAFT BEARING		
Shaft fit in roller bearing (loose)	0.0005–0.0015 in.	0.0004–0.0008 in.
Shaft fit in cover bushing (loose)	0.0005–0.0015 in.	0.0005–0.0012 in.

① Spring (outer)
valve closed: 105–115 lbs at 1⅜ in.
valve open: 180–190 lbs at 1 in.
② Spring (inner)
valve closed: 20–30 lbs at 1$^{3}/_{16}$ in.
valve open: 70–80 lbs at $^{57}/_{64}$ in.
③ Spring free length
1$^{31}/_{32}$ in. (outer)
1$^{23}/_{64}$ in. (inner)
④ Fit in bushing (loose)
1971 and earlier: 0.0005–0.002 in.
1972 and later: 0.001–0.0025 in.
⑤ Ring gap
1971 and earlier: 0.010–0.020 in.
1972 and later: 0.015–0.025 in.
⑥ Compression ring side clearance
1971 and earlier: 0.025–0.004 in.
1972 and later: 0.0035–0.005 in.
⑦ End play
between flywheels: 0.005–0.025 in.
⑧ Fit on crankpin: 0.0005–0.001 in.
⑨ Fit on crank pin
1960–1971: 0.0006–0.001 in.
1972 and later: 0.001–0.0015 in.
⑩ Gear shaft nut torque
1971 and earlier: 100 ft lbs
1972 and later: 150 ft lbs
⑪ Gear shaft nut torque
1971 and earlier: 100 ft lbs
1972 and later: 170 ft lbs
⑫ Sprocket shaft nut torque
1971 and earlier: 100 ft lbs
1972 and later: 150 ft lbs
⑬ Sprocket shaft nut torque
1969 and earlier: 100 ft lbs
1970–1971: 170 ft lbs
1972 and later: 400 ft lbs
⑭ Crank pin nuts torque
1971 and earlier: 175 ft lbs
1972 and later: 200 ft lbs

Transmission Specifications

	Sportster	Glide Models
CLUTCH		
Type	①	Dry multiple disc
Capacity (torque)	1900 in./lbs	②
Spring Pressure (total)	③	④
Bearing fit (loose)	0.0005–0.002 in.	0.002–0.003 in.
Clutch release rod reply movement	⅛ in.	⅜–⅝ in.
CHAIN		
Primary (type)	⅜ in. pitch, triple	½ in. pitch, double
Slack	⅝–⅞ in. (cold) ⅜–⅝ in. (hot)	⅝–⅞ in. (cold) ⅜–⅝ in. (hot)
STARTER		
Minimum clearance between starter clutch gear teeth and clutch	0.040 in. (crank in up position)	——
Crankshaft end-play	0.001–0.007 in.	

3. Lightly oil all of the moving parts.
4. Check for free ball action and seating.

OIL PUMP DISASSEMBLY

1. Remove the engine from the frame as described in "Engine Removal."
2. Clean the pump surface and its surrounding areas thoroughly with a suitable solvent and blow it dry.
3. Remove the crankcase stud nuts and the assembled pump. Tap with a hammer on a piece of brass or wood, held on the breather sleeve, to loosen it if necessary.
4. Disassemble the check valve as described in "Oil Pump Check Valve Disassembly."
5. Remove the oil pump body plate and the body plate gasket.
6. Remove the retaining rings with snap-ring pliers (or split-ring if applicable) and slip the scavenger gears free.
7. Remove the breather valve key.
8. Remove the oil pump cover and breather valve assembly.
9. Remove the oil pump and the idler gears.
10. Pry the oil pump seal free.
11. Punch-drive the lockpin free from the oil-pump breather valve gear. Remove the gear from the pump cover only if it is necessary.
12. Remove the breather valve screen.
13. Press the idler gear shaft free only if replacement is necessary.

OIL PUMP INSPECTION

1. Clean all of the parts in a suitable solvent and blow them dry. Blow all passages free.
2. Replace all gaskets, the retaining ring, lockpin, and the oil seal. Homemade gaskets must be avoided since the proper thickness and proper passage holes are essential.
3. Replace all worn or damaged parts.
4. Inspect the pump body for wear or damage.

Transmission Specifications (cont.)

	Sportster	*Glide Models*
GEAR BOX		
Shifter mechanism	Free operation in all positions	—
Cam end-play	—	0.005–0.0065 in.
MAIN AND COUNTERSHAFT GROUPS		
Clutch gear end-play (loose)	0.001–0.002 in.	—
Clutch gear outer bearing (loose)	0.0001–0.0017 in.	—
Clutch gear inner bushing	—	—
Clutch gear ball bearing	0.0001 in. (loose) 0.0009 in. (tight)	—
Low gear bushing (on shaft)	0.0005–0.00016 in.	0.000–0.0015 in. (loose)
(in gear)	—	0.0005–0.0025 in. (loose)
(end-play)	0.004–0.009 in.	—
Low gear end bearing (loose)	—	0.005–0.002 in.
(end-play)	—	0.008–0.012 in.
(in housing)	⑤	—
(on shaft)	⑥	—
(housing in case)	⑦	—
Second gear bushing (on shaft)	0.001–0.0025 in. (loose)	0.000–0.0015 in. (loose)
(in gear)	—	0.0005–0.0025 in. (loose)
(end-play)	—	0.003–0.017 in.
Third gear bushing (on shaft) (loose)	0.002–0.003 in.	0.001–0.002 in.
(in gear)	—	press fit
(end-play)	0.015–0.025 in.	0.000–0.017 in.
Reverse gear and bearing (mainshaft)	—	—
(countershaft)	—	—
MAIN AND COUNTERSHAFT GROUPS		
Reverse gear bushing (on shaft)	—	—
(in gear)	—	—
High gear end bearing (inner)	—	—
Drive gear (on shaft)	0.0005–0.003 in. (loose)	—
roller bearing (loose)	—	0.0005–0.002 in.
inner bearing	—	0.002–0.003 in.
end-play	—	0.003–0.013 in.

① Clutch type
1970 and earlier: dry multiple disc
1971 and later: wet multiple disc

② Clutch capacity
1970 and earlier: 284 ft lbs
1971 and later: 206 ft lbs

③ Spring pressure
1970 and earlier: 150 lbs
1971: 234 lbs
1972 and later: 257 lbs

④ Spring pressure
1970 and earlier: 475 lbs
1971 and later: 315 lbs

⑤ Low gear end bearing in housing
1970 and earlier: snug fit
1971 and later: 0.0015 in. (loose)–0.0001 in. (press)

⑥ Low gear bearing on shaft
1970 and earlier: light press
1971 and later: 0.0001 in. (loose)–0.0010 in. (press)

⑦ Low gear end bearing housing in case
1970 and earlier: light press
1971 and later: 0.0005 in. (loose)–0.0010 in. (press)

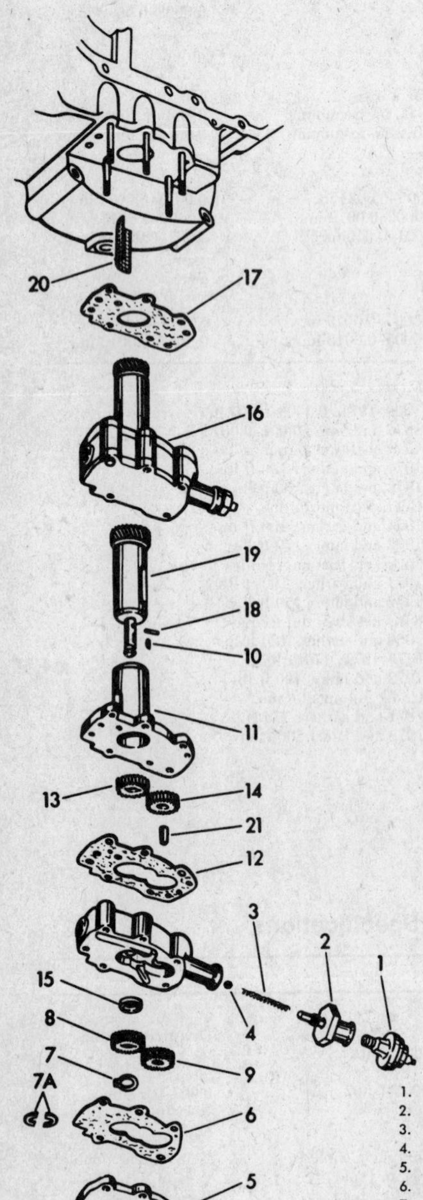

1. Oil pressure switch
2. Oil pump nipple
3. Check valve spring
4. Ball valve
5. Body plate
6. Body plate gasket
7. Retaining ring
7A. Retainer (2) (Half ring)
8. Scavenger pump gear
9. Scavenger pump idler gear
10. Breather valve key
11. Oil pump cover
12. Body cover gasket
13. Pump gear
14. Pump idler gear
15. Oil pump seal
16. Oil pump body
17. Body gasket
18. Drive lock pin
19. Breather valve gear and shaft
20. Crankcase breather valve screen
21. Idler gear shaft

Sportster oil pump

5. Inspect all of the gears for worn or damaged teeth and replace them as necessary.
6. Replace the breather valve key if it is worn or loose.
7. Inspect the breather valve and pump for wear and damage.
8. Check that the valve is a free fit.

OIL PUMP ASSEMBLY

1. Assemble in the reverse order of disassembly.
2. Lightly oil all of the moving parts.
3. Assemble the check valve as described in "Oil Pump Check Valve Assembly."
4. Place the breather valve screen in position and secure it with a daub of grease.
5. Assemble the breather valve in the oil pump cover and secure it with a lock-pin.
6. Press a new scavenger-pump idler gear shaft into the pump body if the old one has been removed.
7. Assemble the pump gears to the pump body.
8. Secure the body gasket using a non-hardening sealer. The gasket must be carefully aligned to permit free oil passage.
9. Assemble the assembled breather valve and cover to the pump body.
10. Place a thin strip of acetate tape over the groove in the breather valve shaft. Install a new oil seal flush into the pump body counterbore with the seal's lip facing the body. Remove the tape.
11. Install the breather valve key and scavenger pump gears, and secure them with a retaining ring (or retainer, whichever is applicable).
12. Install a new body plate gasket using a non-hardening sealer. The gasket may be flattened if necessary by soaking it in water before sealing it.
13. Slide the oil pump and the body plate onto the crankcase studs, and evenly secure the studs.
14. Check for free-motion of the gears. If the gears bind, the pump may be slightly out of alignment. Remedy this by loosening the stud nuts and gently tapping the pump with a soft mallet until the correct alignment is attained.
15. Time the breather valve as follows:
    a. Remove the gearcase cover as described in "Gearcase Disassembly";
    b. Rotate the engine until the flywheel timing mark is aligned in the crankcase view port;
    c. Position the breather gear so the valve hole aligns with the pump body hole;
    d. Shift the breather gear two teeth to the right;
    e. Place the breather screen and pump gasket in position;
    f. Install the pump carefully on the mounting studs and the breather gear will then assume the correct timing position;
    g. Check to be sure that the breather valve hole and the pump body hole are aligned. The flywheel timing mark must still be correctly aligned;
    h. Assemble and secure the gearcase cover and pump.

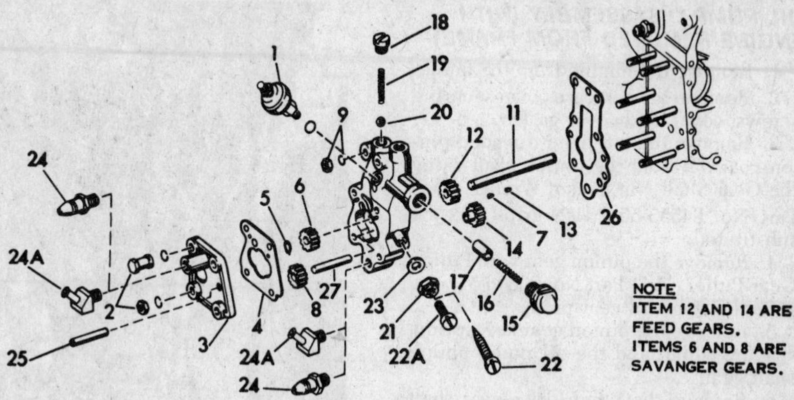

NOTE
ITEM 12 AND 14 ARE FEED GEARS.
ITEMS 6 AND 8 ARE SAVANGER GEARS.

Glide model (1967 and earlier) oil pump assembly

1. Oil pressure switch
2. Cover stud nut or bolt and washer
3. Oil pump cover
4. Cover gasket
5. Lock ring
6. Drive gear
7. Gear key
8. Idler gear
9. Oil pump body mounting stud nuts and washers (2)
10. Oil pump body
11. Oil pump gear drive shaft
12. Drive gear
13. Gear key
14. Idler gear
15. By-pass valve plug
16. By-pass valve spring
17. Check valve spring cover
18. Check valve spring cover screw
19. Check valve spring
20. Check valve ball
21. Chain oiler adjusting screw lock nut
22. Chain oiler adjusting screw
22A. Chain oiler screw (1965–67)
23. Chain oiler adj. screw washer
24A. Oil line nipple (2) (1965)
24B. Oil line nipple (2) (1968)
25. Chain oiler pipe
26. Body gasket
27. Idler gear shaft

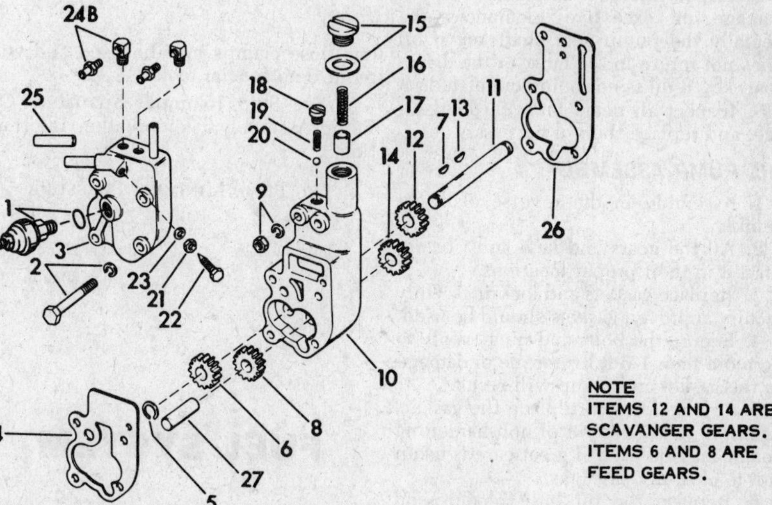

NOTE
ITEMS 12 AND 14 ARE SCAVANGER GEARS.
ITEMS 6 AND 8 ARE FEED GEARS.

Glide model (1968 and later) oil pump assembly

Glide Models

OIL PUMP DISASSEMBLY (WITH ENGINE IN FRAME)

1. Disconnect the oil switch, feed, and scavenger lines from the pump body.
2. Remove the cover stud nuts or bolts and their washers.
3. Slip the oil pump cover and the cover gasket from the gearcase studs.
4. Remove the driveshaft snap-ring with snap-ring pliers, and then remove the drive gear, gear key, and idler gear.
5. Remove the stud nuts which mount the oil pump body and then remove the body.
6. Remove the oil pump gear driveshaft.
7. Remove the scavenger (1968 and later) or the feed (1967 and earlier) drive-gear, gear key, and the scavenger idler gear and key.
8. Remove the by-pass valve plug, spring, and spring sleeve.
9. Remove the check valve cover screw, spring, and ball valve.
10. Loosen the chain oiler adjusting screw locknut (if applicable) and gently seat the adjusting screw while counting the number of turns necessary to seat it. Remove the adjusting screw and washer. The screw must be replaced in the same position during assembly.
11. Remove the chain oiler screw on 1965–67 models.
12. Remove the oil pump nipples.
13. Do not mix any gears or keys.

OIL PUMP DISASSEMBLY (WITH ENGINE REMOVED FROM FRAME)

1. Remove the engine from the frame.
2. Remove the gearcase cover securing screws, cover, and cover gasket.
3. Remove the left-hand threaded pinion gear nut from the pinion shaft using the Gear Shaft Nut Socket Wrench (H-D Part No. 94555-55); vise grips may be substituted.
4. Remove the pinion gear with Pinion Gear Puller (H-D Part No. 96830-51) or a suitable, standard gear puller.
5. Remove the pinion gear key, spring, spacing collar, and the oil pump pinion shaft gear.
6. Remove the pump drive-gear shaft spring-ring, drive gear, and shaft key.
7. Remove the pump body nuts and bolts, then slip the assembled pump and pump gear driveshaft from the gearcase.
8. Disassemble the pump as described in the previous section.

OIL PUMP INSPECTION

1. Clean all of the metal parts in a suitable solvent and blow them dry.
2. Blow all of the passages clear.
3. Inspect the valves and seats for pitting and wear, and replace the pump if its seats are damaged.
4. Inspect the keys and key seats for damage or excessive clearances—especially the pump gear shaft key if oil does not return to the tank, or the driveshaft key if oil is not being circulated.
5. Inspect all gears for wear or damage, and replace them if necessary.

OIL PUMP ASSEMBLY

1. Assemble in the reverse of disassembly.
2. All the gears and keys must be replaced in their proper locations.
3. Replace gaskets and lockrings. Only factory approved gaskets should be used.
4. Secure the bolts and nuts evenly to no more than 4–5 ft lbs torque or damage to the gasket and pump will result.
5. If leaks persist, replace the gaskets again. A small amount of non-hardening sealer may be used if great care is taken not to clog any passages.
6. Replace the oil hose clamps and squeeze them tight. Worm-type automotive hose clamps may be used and will require no special tools.
7. See Step 15 under Sportster "Oil Pump Assembly," for breather information.

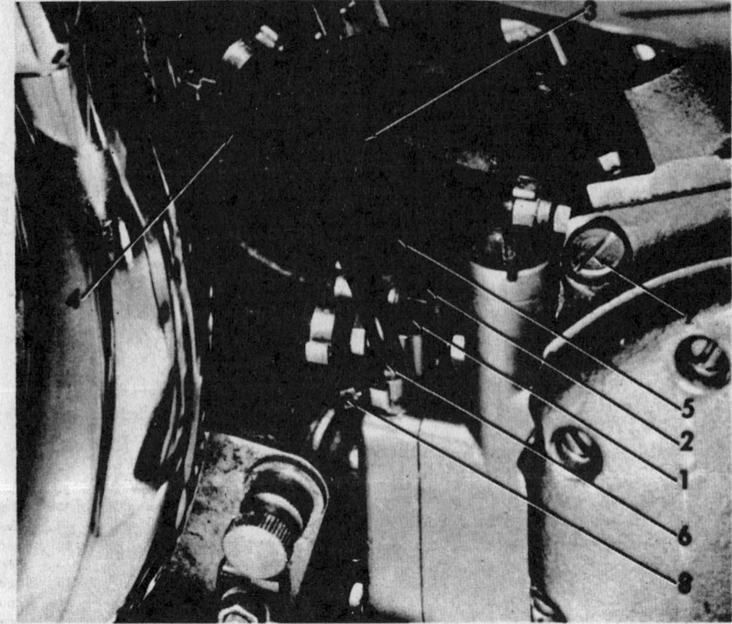

Oil lines (1968 and later)

1. Oil supply line from tank
2. Oil return line to tank
3. Vent line to oil tank
4. Vent line to chain housing
5. Return line from chain housing
6. Front chain oiler line to chain housing
7. Overhead and tappet oil screen plug
8. Rear chain oiler adjusting screw

OIL PUMP MINIMUM PRESSURE	
Sportster	6 psi at 20 mph
Glide models	25 psi at 20 mph
	35 psi at 30 mph

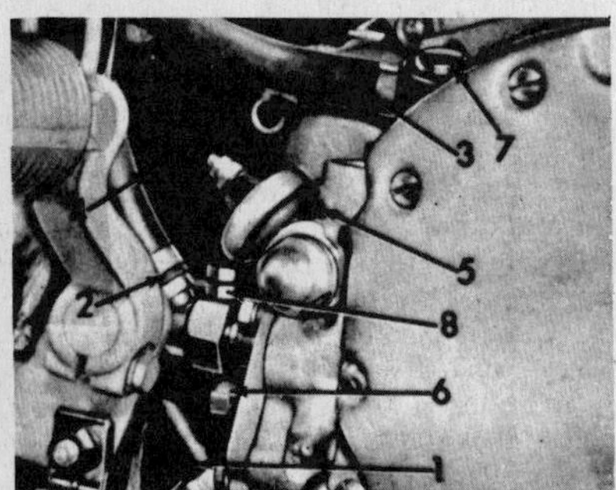

Oil lines (1965–1967)

1. Oil supply line from tank
2. Oil return line to tank
3. Vent line to oil tank
4. Vent line to chain housing
5. Return line from chain housing
6. Front chain oiler line to chain housing
7. Overhead and tappet oil screen plug
8. Rear chain oiler adjusting screw

FUEL SYSTEM

NOTE: *For an operational theory, general inspection, and troubleshooting chart, refer to the "Carburetor" section under "General Information."*

CARBURETOR

Linkert Model DC

The Model DC is a plain, tube-type carburetor with venturi, discharge nozzle, adjustable high- and low-speed needles, and a fixed jet. The only moving parts are the throttle shaft, disc, and float assemblies.

REMOVAL

1. Remove the air cleaner cover, element, and back plate.
2. Disconnect the fuel line at the carburetor.
3. Remove the carburetor bracket (if applicable).
4. Remove the two carburetor securing bolts and pull the carburetor out and off.

DISASSEMBLY

1. Remove the three throttle body screws, lockwashers, body gasket, idle hole body plug, low-speed needle valve, washer, and the needle valve spring from the throttle body.
2. Free the throttle disc from the shaft by removing the throttle shaft screws and lockwashers.
3. Remove the stop screw and spring from the throttle lever, then remove the throttle lever clamping screw from the lever. Remove the spring, washer, and shaft from the throttle body.
4. Remove the carburetor bowl, by tapping it gently, after having removed the four bowl attaching screws.
5. Carefully separate the bowl gasket from the bowl.
6. Free the float by removing the float rod and unscrewing the flat speed nut.
7. Lift the float valve and seat assembly free.
8. Remove the float lever and bracket assembly by removing the float lever screw, lockwasher, and float washer.
9. Remove the support bracket (if applicable), lockwasher, and nut.
10. Removing the bowl nut and gasket reveals the idle tube which should remain in the body. Do not attempt to remove it from the bowl nut, but, if it remains in the body after the bowl nut is removed, it must be removed by tugging gently at the plug end.
11. Remove the nozzle using a screwdriver with a clean, flat head to ensure that no damage is done to the jet orifice.

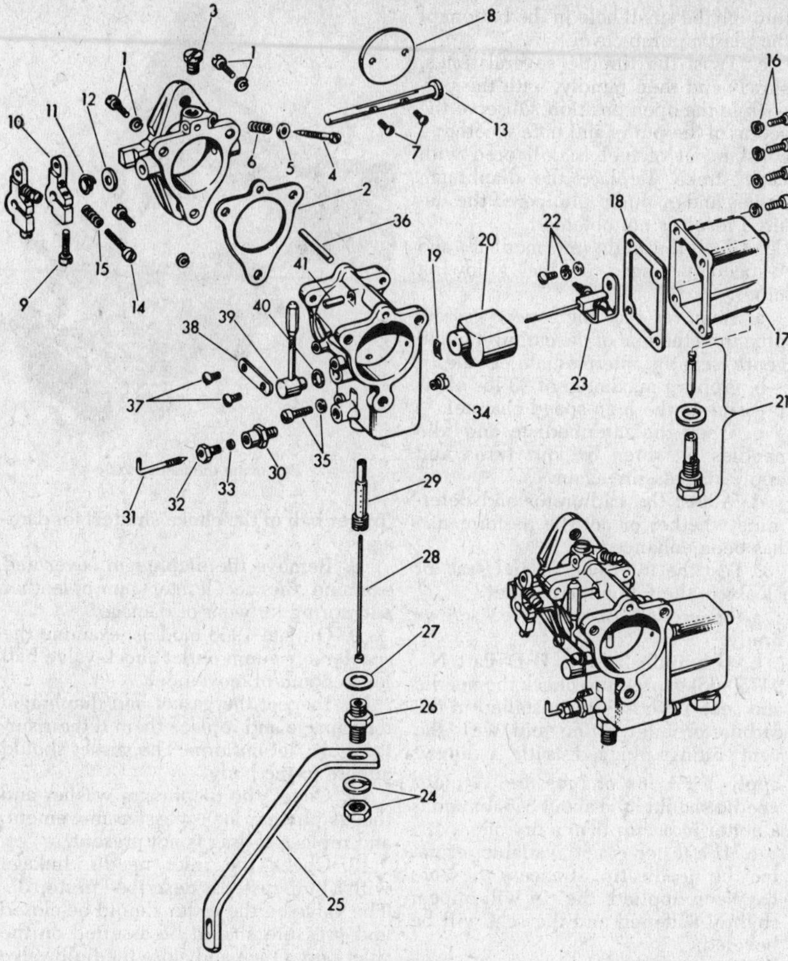

Model DC carburetor assembly

1. Throttle body screw and washer (3)
2. Body gasket
3. Idle hole body plug
4. Low-speed needle valve
5. Low-speed needle valve washer
6. Low-speed needle valve spring
7. Throttle shaft screw (2)
8. Throttle disc
9. Throttle level clamping screw
10. Throttle lever
11. Throttle shaft spring
12. Throttle shaft washer
13. Throttle shaft
14. Throttle lever stop screw
15. Throttle lever stop screw spring
16. Bowl mounting screw (4)
17. Bowl
18. Bowl gasket
19. Float nut
20. Float
21. Float valve and seat
22. Float lever screw and washers
23. Float lever and bracket assembly
24. Support bracket nut and lock washer
25. Support bracket
26. Bowl nut
27. Bowl nut gasket
28. Idle tube assembly
29. Main nozzle
30. High-speed needle valve extension housing
31. High-speed needle valve
32. High-speed needle valve packing nut
33. High-speed needle valve packing
34. Carburetor jet
35. Drain plug and gasket
36. Idle passage tube
37. Throttle shaft screw (2)
38. Vent clamp
39. Vent housing
40. Vent gasket
41. Idle bleed tube

12. Free the high-speed needle valve, packing nut, and packing by removing the high-speed needle valve extension housing.

13. Remove the jet which is located directly across from the high-speed needle valve hole.

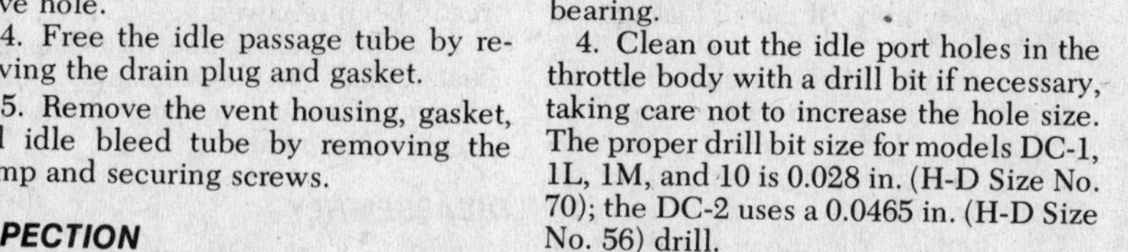

14. Free the idle passage tube by removing the drain plug and gasket.

15. Remove the vent housing, gasket, and idle bleed tube by removing the clamp and securing screws.

INSPECTION

1. Clean all of the parts, other than the gaskets and float, in a carbon and gum-dissolving solution such as Gunk Hydro-Seal® (which is recommended by the factory). Rinse thoroughly and blow them dry.

2. Clear all of the carburetor barrel passages with compressed air. Do not scrape the carbon deposits with any steel instrument.

3. Replace the throttle shaft if there is more than 0.002 in. play noticeable at the bearing.

4. Clean out the idle port holes in the throttle body with a drill bit if necessary, taking care not to increase the hole size. The proper drill bit size for models DC-1, 1L, 1M, and 10 is 0.028 in. (H-D Size No. 70); the DC-2 uses a 0.0465 in. (H-D Size No. 56) drill.

5. Open the idle jet hole with a 0.043 in. drill bit (H-D Size No. 57) and the angular hole which it meets with a 0.0635 in. drill bit (H-D Size No. 52).

6. Clear the nozzle bleed holes with a 0.055 in. drill bit (H-D Size No. 54) and the main passage with a 0.073 in. drill bit (H-D Size No. 17).

7. Clean the high-speed bit needle seat holes with a 0.052 in. drill bit (H-D Size No. 55) for models DC-1, 1L, 1M, 10, 6, 7, and 12. For model DC-2, use a 0.028 in. drill bit (H-D Size No. 70).

8. Check to see that the two vents in the carburetor body are open.

9. Be sure not to enlarge any passages and examine all of the connecting surfaces for possible leaks. Replace any leaky part or any part on which wear has caused excessive clearances.

ASSEMBLY

1. Assemble the vent housing assembly, gasket, idle bleed tube, clamp, and screw in the carburetor body.

2. Slip the tubes into their holes and tap the housing into place.

3. Secure the clamp just tight enough so that the outer ends will touch the body bosses.

4. Assemble the drain plug, gasket, and high-speed jet on the carburetor body.

5. Back out the needle valve before installing this assembly in the main body so that the point will not enter the valve hole when the two units are secured together.

6. Position the needle valve so it doesn't jam into the seat hole and cause damage.

7. Assemble the nozzle.

8. Locate the idle tube in the body hole and press it in until about 1/32 in. extends out from the nozzle hole.

9. Install the bowl nut and gasket; this should hold the idle tube in place.

10. Assemble the float valve and seat assembly, and install the float lever bracket screw loosely so that an adjustment can be made if necessary.

11. Holding the float valve and seat halfway into the bowl, align the lever fingers with the groove in the valve and bring them together while turning the valve into its seat. This must be done with the bowl removed from the body.

12. Invert the bowl and measure the distance from the top of the float rod to the outer edge of the bowl flange which is directly opposite the fuel inlet fitting. at the point where the float valve seats

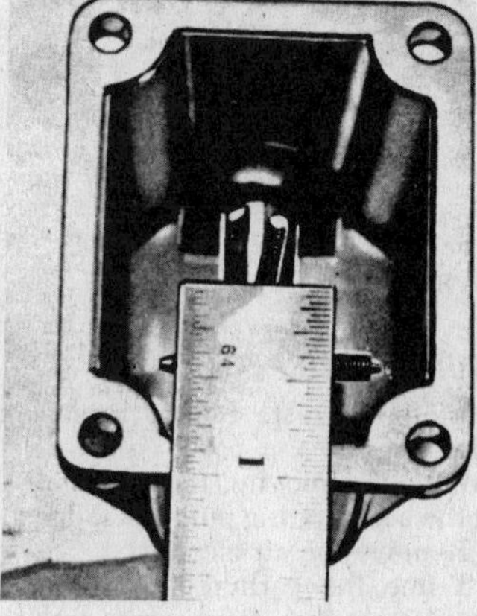

Checking float setting

lightly, the distance should be 1 in. ± 1/64 in.

13. Adjust the slotted float lever bracket until the proper measurement is obtained and then secure the bracket screw.

14. Place the float on the rod with the flat side up and secure it with a speed nut.

15. Mount the bowl to the carburetor main body, taking care not to crush the gasket.

16. Insert the throttle shaft so that the screw seats align with the screw holes on the throttle disc and then loosely mount the throttle disc, with the identification number facing out.

17. Rotate the disc and note whether it binds anywhere. When a position is obtained where movement is free, secure the disc and recheck its movement.

18. Install the throttle lever stop screw and spring.

19. Install the throttle lever, throttle shaft spring, and washer, and position them so that slight end-play exists when the lever is clamped tightly. Place the disc and lever in an open position and secure the throttle lever clamping screw.

20. Install the low-speed needle jet, washer, and spring, taking care not to bevel the seat with excessive pressure.

21. Secure the idle hole body plug.

22. Insert the idle passage tube into the carburetor body with the beveled end out.

23. Assemble the throttle body on the main body, using a new body gasket to ensure proper thickness. Do not use a homemade gasket because the correct thickness is critical.

24. Mount the carburetor and adjust it.

Tillotson Model HD

The model HD is a diaphragm-type carburetor.

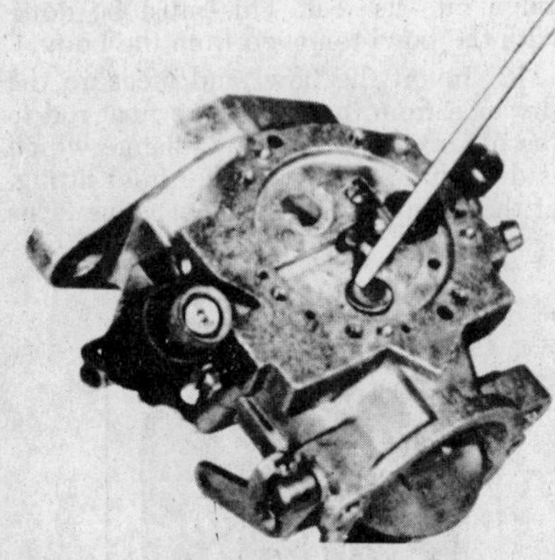

Removing the welch plug

PRELIMINARY INSPECTION

(Complete all tests before replacing any parts.)

1. Without removing the carburetor, inspect the accelerating pump as follows:

a. Remove the air cleaner.

b. Prime the carburetor by gently manipulating the diaphragm with a toothpick which can be inserted through the small hole in the bottom of the plastic pump cover.

c. Twist the throttle several times, slowly and then rapidly, with the petcock in the open position. Observe the action of the pump and note whether a constant jet of fuel is delivered with each stroke. Replace the diaphragm valves and/or pump plunger if the desired result is not obtained.

2. Clean the high, intermediate, and low-speed passages in the following manner:

a. Remove the high-speed screw plug from the rear of the carburetor and gently seat the intermediate needle.

b. Apply a maximum of 90 lbs of air pressure to the high-speed channel.

c. Open the intermediate and idle needles by three or four turns and apply air pressure again.

d. Adjust the carburetor and determine whether or not the performance has been enhanced.

3. Test the inlet needle and seat for air leaks in the following manner:

a. Secure all plastic cover screws firmly.

b. Use Bulb Tester (H-D Part No. 94750-68) to pressure-check the needle and seat. With a tester installed in the carburetor inlet fitting and with the vent fitting plugged with a finger, apply 1–1½ lbs of pressure. A moist needle should hold about 3–5 lbs and is a better indicator than a dry one.

c. If a tester is not available, examine the needle tip. If excess pressure has been applied, the tip will appear slightly flattened and the seat will be beveled.

4. Remove the carburetor and inspect the intermediate adjustment needle and spring for binding which will prevent it from realizing its true seat.

a. Shorten each end of the spring with a grinder and test it for proper seating by applying blue dye to the end of the needle taper. Screw the taper lightly down into its seat and check to see if the blue has been disturbed.

5. Test the main nozzle ball check valve for leakage in the following manner:

a. Seal one end of the main jet port in the venturi with your finger and insert an appropriate size rubber tube into the opposite end of the venturi. Apply alternate vacuum and pressure. Pressure should cause the ball to seat and vacuum pressure should release the ball from the nozzle assembly.

b. Replace the main nozzle check valve assembly if any leakage is present.

c. Remove the welch plug by punching it off center with an appropriate punch. Drift it into the venturi gently, using a soft mallet and an appropriate drift.

d. Replace the new check valve using a drift. Drift (H-D Tool No. 96962-68) is available for these operations.

6. Examine the idle needle and seat for damage.

7. Examine the choke relief disc (upper half of the choke shutter) for damage.

Removing the main nozzle

8. Remove the diaphragm cover and examine the accelerator pump leather and spring for wear or damage.

9. On late 1968 models, examine the accelerator-pump outlet check-valve ball for freedom of movement.

10. Inspect the gasket and diaphragm for damage and replace them if their surfaces are not uniform. The gasket should adhere to the body.

11. Check the diaphragm washer and the diaphragm for excessive movement, and replace if drag is not present.

12. Check the inlet needle linkage with a bulb tester as described in step 3b The valve on the tester should be closed and pressure should be asserted on the inlet port. Open and close the bulb valve about ten times while applying pressure to be sure that it isn't sticking closed.

13. The inlet lever should lie flush with the floor of the carburetor and it must be replaced if it doesn't. If it is not equipped with a shackled needle, substitute with kit No. 27588-66 and torque the seat to 45 in. lbs.

14. Check the economizer ball for proper operation in the following manner:

a. Using a rubber tube of the appropriate size, seal off the economizer welch plug hole and apply mouth pressure both in and out. If the ball does not release each time it is tested, replace it.

b. Inspect the welch plugs by attempting to move them in the body. Since they are a press-fit, they should not move. Replace any leaky or loose plug; never reuse a welch that has already been removed.

c. If the leak is due to a damaged seat, replace the plug and apply a small amount of seal-all or epoxy around the edges of the seat.

DISASSEMBLY

1. Remove the idle and intermediate fuel adjusters.

2. Remove the throttle butterfly mounting screws and the throttle butterfly. Note the position of the butterfly as an aid in reassembly.

3. The throttle shaft assembly may be

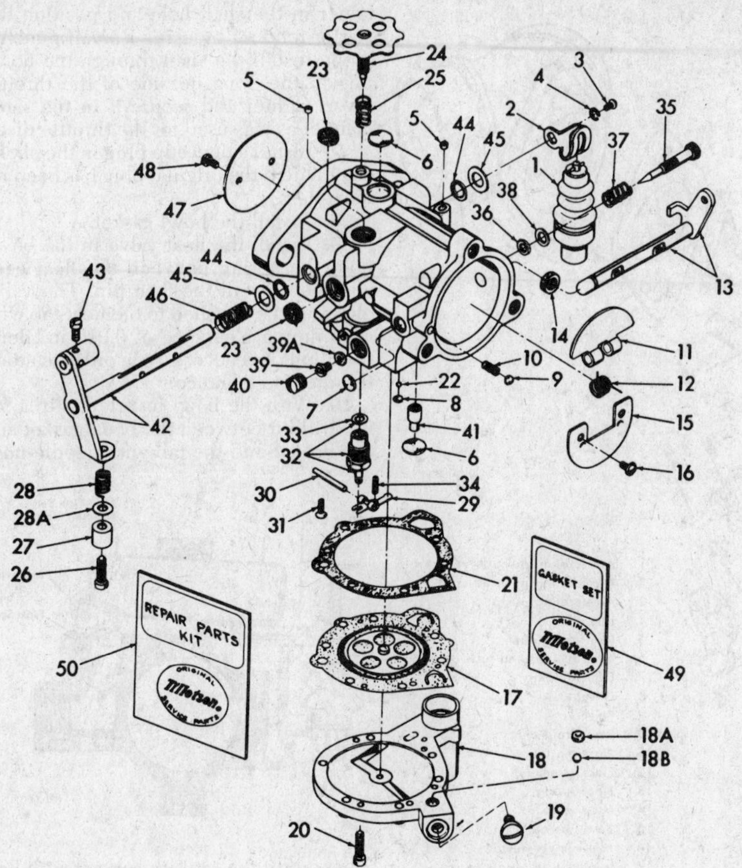

Tillotson model HD carburetor assembly

1. Accelerating pump
2. Accelerating pump lever
3. Accelerating pump lever screw
4. Accelerating pump lever screw L.W.
5. Channel plug (2)
6. Welch plug
7. Welch plug
8. Welch plug
9. Choke shaft friction ball
10. Choke shaft friction spring
11. Choke shutter (top)
12. Choke shutter spring
13. Choke shaft assembly
14. Choke shaft dust seal
15. Choke shutter (bottom)
16. Choke shutter screws
17. Diaphragm
18. Cover
18A. Accelerating pump check ball retainer
18B. Accelerating pump check ball
19. Diaphragm cover plug screw
20. Diaphragm cover screws (6)
21. Diaphragm cover gasket
22. Economizer check ball
23. Fuel filter screen (2)
24. Idle adjustment screw
25. Idle adjustment screw spring
26. Throttle stop screw
27. Throttle stop screw cup
28. Throttle stop screw spring
28A. Throttle stop screw spring washer
29. Inlet control lever
30. Inlet control lever pin
31. Inlet control lever screw
32. Inlet needle and seat
33. Inlet needle seat gasket
34. Inlet control lever tension spring
35. Intermediate adjusting screw
36. Intermediate adjusting screw packing
37. Intermediate adjusting screw spring
38. Intermediate adjusting screw washer
39. Main jet
39A. Main jet gasket
40. Main jet plug screw
41. Main nozzle check valve
42. Throttle shaft assembly
43. Throttle lever wire block screw
44. Dust seal (2)
45. Washer (2)
46. Throttle shaft spring
47. Throttle shutter
48. Throttle shutter screws
49. Gasket overhaul set
50. Overhaul repair kit

slipped out of the body when the retaining screw is removed.

4. Remove the throttle shaft spring, washers, dust seals, accelerating pump assembly, diaphragm cover plug screw, metering diaphragm, and metering diaphragm gasket. Note that the gasket is mounted next to the body.

5. Remove the inlet control lever screw, inlet control lever pin, inlet control lever, and lever control tension spring.

6. Remove the inlet needle, seat, and needle gasket, taking note of proper positioning for replacement.

7. Remove the main jet plug screw, jet, and gasket.

8. Remove the main jet welch plug by drilling a shallow hole off-center with a ⅛ in. drill and then prying it free with a small punch. If you go too deep, the jet will probably be damaged.

9. Remove the remaining three welch plugs in the same manner and the economizer ball will then come free.

10. Remove the choke butterfly securing screws and the lower half of the choke butterfly.

11. Remove the choke shaft and then the upper half of the butterfly, the spring, choke friction ball, and the friction ball spring will all come free.

12. Slide the choke shaft dust seal off the shaft.

INSPECTION

1. Remove all plastic parts and gaskets then clean all of the metal parts in a solvent. Hydroseal solvent is recommended.

2. Blow all passages clear with compressed air. Never use wire to poke the passages free as this causes burrs or increases the port diameters.

3. Inspect all parts for wear and replace any parts which were either found defective in tests or appeared to be excessively worn.

4. If the inlet control lever does not rotate freely on its pin or if the forked end does not firmly engage the needle, it must be replaced.

5. Replace the inlet control lever tension spring if it appears to be stretched or damaged.

6. If the inlet needle point is worn or damaged or if the contact end does not provide a snug fit, they must be replaced.

ASSEMBLY

1. Examine all parts for small particles of dirt which can clog the small passages and blow them clean.

2. Assemble in reverse order of disassembly.

3. Seat the welch plugs with the recommended tool, or with a flat end drift of a diameter slightly smaller than that of the welch. A flat (rather than concave) surface is a good indication of a well-seated plug.

4. Mount the metering spring on the stud on the lever and seat it in the indentation on the body casting.

5. Torque the inlet seat assembly to 40–45 in. lbs and torque the accelerating pump channel plug to 23–28 in lbs.

Bendix Model 16P12

The model 16P12 carburetor is equipped with a dual venturi, an accelerating pump a fixed main jet, an idle stop screw, a low-speed idle screw, and a ring float.

DISASSEMBLY

1. Remove the air cleaner cover, element, and the back plate.

2. Close the petcock and disconnect the fuel line.

3. Disconnect the choke and throttle cables at the carburetor.

4. Remove the accelerating pump lever screw, lever and pump assembly, and remove the piston by rotating the pump lever 90 degrees while compressing the piston shaft spring.

5. Remove the idle tube, tube gasket, main jet and tube assembly, fiber washer, rubber O-ring, float bowl, and bowl drain plug.

6. Press the float pin through the float ears.

7. Lift the float, float spring, and float valve free from the bowl.

8. Remove the bowl gasket.

9. Remove the idle needle, spring throttle stop screw, and spring.

10. Remove the choke disc securing screws and disc.

11. Slide the choke shaft and lever assembly free from the housing and remove the plunger, spring, seal retainer, and seal.

12. Remove the choke shaft cup plug only if replacement is necessary.

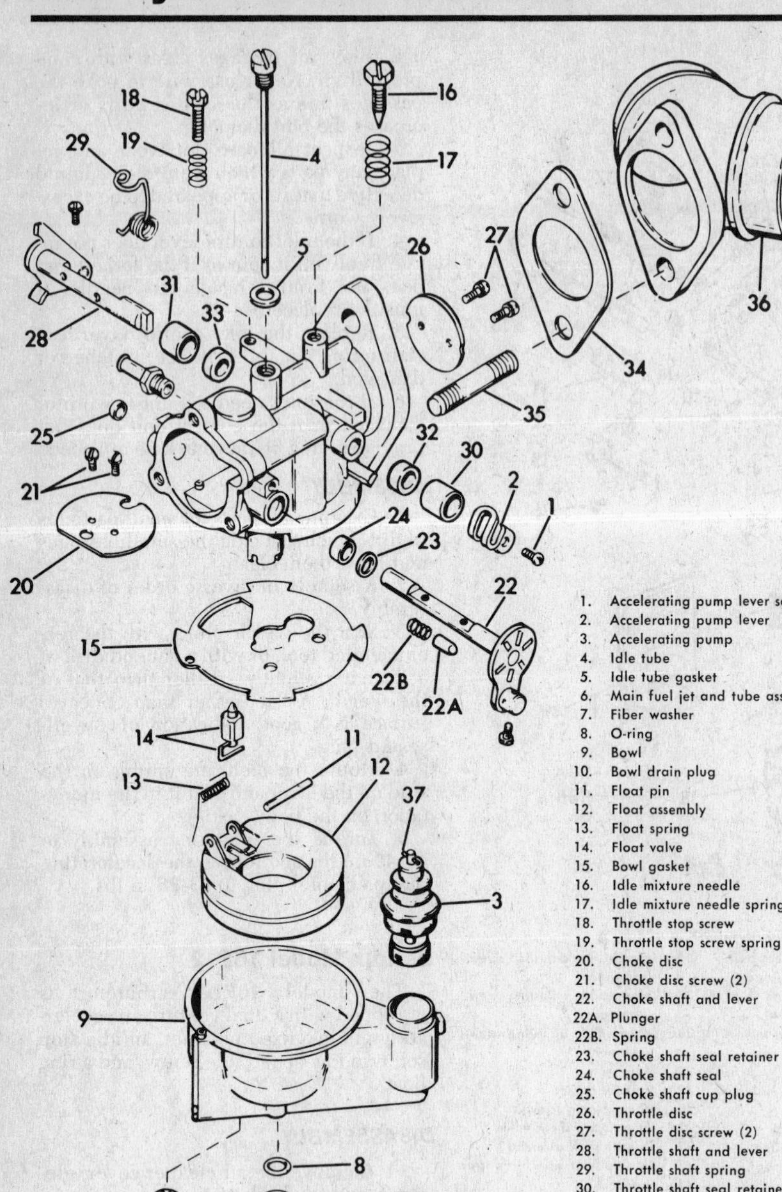

1. Accelerating pump lever screw
2. Accelerating pump lever
3. Accelerating pump
4. Idle tube
5. Idle tube gasket
6. Main fuel jet and tube assembly
7. Fiber washer
8. O-ring
9. Bowl
10. Bowl drain plug
11. Float pin
12. Float assembly
13. Float spring
14. Float valve
15. Bowl gasket
16. Idle mixture needle
17. Idle mixture needle spring
18. Throttle stop screw
19. Throttle stop screw spring
20. Choke disc
21. Choke disc screw (2)
22. Choke shaft and lever

22A. Plunger

22B. Spring

23. Choke shaft seal retainer
24. Choke shaft seal
25. Choke shaft cup plug
26. Throttle disc
27. Throttle disc screw (2)
28. Throttle shaft and lever
29. Throttle shaft spring
30. Throttle shaft seal retainer
31. Throttle shaft seal retainer
32. Throttle shaft seal
33. Throttle shaft seal
34. Manifold gasket
35. Manifold stud (2)
36. Intake manifold
37. Accelerating pump shaft pin

Bendix model 16P12 carburetor assembly

13. Remove the throttle disc securing screws, disc, shaft and lever assembly, and shaft spring.

14. Do not remove either throttle shaft seal retainer unless replacement is necessary.

INSPECTION

1. Clean all metal parts in a carbon and gum-dissolving solution such as Gunk Hydro-Seal® (which is recommended by the factory), rinse thoroughly, and blow them dry.

2. Blow all passages, channels, and jets clear from both directions. Do not try to clear the jets with wire or a drill.

3. Inspect all of the parts for damage, wear, or a pitted condition and replace as necessary.

4. Use all of the parts in the repair kit if such a kit is used.

ASSEMBLY

1. Assemble in reverse order of disassembly.

2. With the throttle return spring in place on the shaft, slip the shaft into the seal retainer and seal.

3. Install the shaft from the nipple side of the carburetor and secure the seal and retainer on the shaft hole boss on the opposite side of the carburetor bore.

4. Install the throttle disc on the flat side of the shaft with disc screws. Operate the shaft rapidly several times to center the disc and then secure the screws.

5. Install the choke shaft seal and retainer in the shaft hole and position the starter retainer by using a small punch.

6. Install the shaft through the housing on the opposite side of the throttle lever. Center and secure it in the same manner as was used for the throttle disc.

7. Install a new cup plug in the choke shaft hole if the original plug has been removed.

8. Install the bowl gasket.

9. Install the float valve in the bowl, hold the spring between the float ears, and then install the float pin. The valve clip must be attached to the float tab with a minimum clearance of 0.010 in. Bend the clip if it is necessary in order to attain the proper clearance.

10. With the bowl inverted, slip a 3/16 in. drill bit between the bowl gasket and the float. Bend the tab with needle-nose pliers until the bit is in contact with both the gasket and the float.

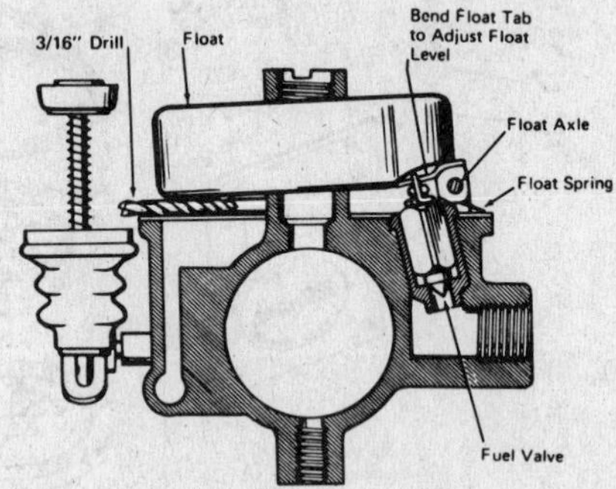

11. Install the throttle stop screw and spring, and turn it in slightly. The no. 2 idle discharge hole must not be uncovered by the throttle disc.

12. Assemble the spring on the idle mixture needle and gently screw it in until it seats, then back it out 1½ turns (72–73) or 2¼ turns (74 and later).

13. Gently place the accelerating pump cup into the pump well and seat the pump boot around the top of the pump boss.

14. Assemble the fiber washer and rubber O-ring on the main jet. The O-ring must seat in the groove near the end of the tube.

15. Check to make sure that the accelerating jet fits properly in the throttle body.

16. With the carburetor inverted and the long end of the spring against the float, install the float bowl. The long end of the spring should seat against the side of the bowl.

17. Loosely install the main jet and secure the drain plug in the bottom of the bowl.

18. Install the idle tube gasket and the tube end in the discharge tube. Secure the idle tube and the main jet.

19. Assemble the accelerating pump lever to the pump and throttle shaft.

Keihin Carburetor

REMOVAL

1. Remove the air cleaner. Disconnect the throttle and choke cables from the carburetor.

2. Remove the mounting nuts and take off the carburetor.

DISASSEMBLY

1. To disassemble the accelerator pump, remove the pump housing (3 screws), remove the spring, diaphragm, and o-rings. Note the spring when removing the housing.
2. Remove the float bowl screws. Take off the float bowl. Remove the float pin securing screw; remove the pin and take out the float. Remove the float needle.
3. Remove the pump rod and boot from the float bowl.
4. Remove the plug over the slow jet. Unscrew the slow and main jets. Take out the main nozzle.
5. Remove the mounting flange o-ring.
6. Remove the throttle lever and spring.
7. Unscrew and remove the throttle stop and low speed mixture screws, which will have springs on them.
8. Remove the brackets, if necessary.
9. The throttle and choke valves are not removeable.

INSPECTION

1. Clean all metal parts in a safe solvent.
2. Check the accelerator pump diaphragm for condition. Replace it if cracked or punctured.
3. Blow the accelerator pump passage clear, which should be done from the side opposite the nozzle.
4. Blow all air and fuel passages clear with compressed air.

ASSEMBLY

1. Assembly is the reverse of disassembly. The use of new o-rings is recommended.
2. Adjust the float level as outlined below.

FLOAT LEVEL ADJUSTMENT

1. There are two adjustments.
2. Check float level with the valve closed. Turn the carburetor upside down and let the float hold the needle against its seat. Measure the distance from the float bowl mating surface to the top surface of the float. It should be 0.55–0.63 in. (14.0–16.0 mm). If adjustment is necessary, bend the lip of the metal tab which secures the float needle.
3. Turn the carburetor to the normal installation position. The float will hang down so that the float valve is full open. Measure the distance between the float bowl mating surface and the bottom of the float. It should be 1.10–1.18 in. (28.0–30.0 mm). If adjustment is necessary, bend the stopper of the metal tab on the float.

INSTALLATION

1. Be sure the mounting flange o-ring is firmly in place. Tighten mounting bolts evenly.
2. Attach cables and check operation. Secure fuel lines, and be sure the overflow tube points away from the engine.

PETCOCK

1974 and Earlier

1. The diaphragm-type petcock, or fuel valve, has two handles. The petcock will pass fuel when the handles are in the vertical position. Turned horizontally, the fuel will be shut off.
2. Shims of a thickness of 0.006 in. (Part No. 616OP) are available in the event that handle movement is too loose.

1975 and Later

1. This petcock has a single handle. "Off," "On," and "Reserve" positions are marked.
2. Disconnect the fuel line and check fuel flow in each position. If operation is faulty, replace the petcock.

ELECTRICAL SYSTEM

CHARGING SYSTEM

Generator-Equipped Models

On DC generator-equipped models, the standard generator used is a two-pole, two-brush unit of conventional construction. Two types of regulator have been used throughout the years, the two-relay type voltage regulator and the three-relay type voltage/current regulator.

TROUBLESHOOTING THE GENERATING SYSTEM

The following is the most direct approach to take in locating the source of generating system difficulties:

1. The following items are indicators of a faulty generating system:
    a. Failure of the generator light to operate.
    b. Repeated or sudden battery discharging.
    c. Excessive battery water evaporation indicating an overcharged state.
2. In testing the generating system, do not commit the following mistakes which will result in damage to the system:

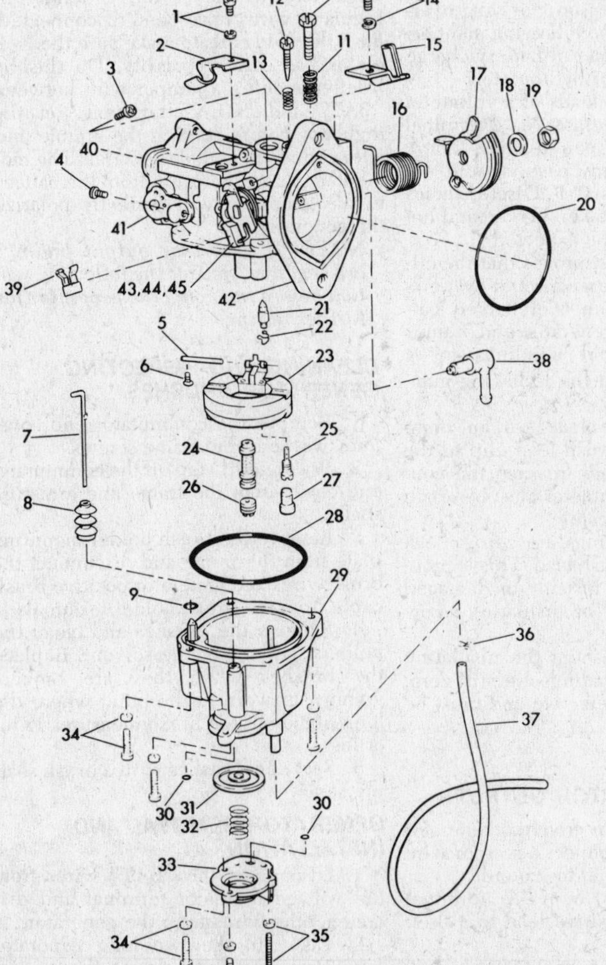

1. Screw & washer
2. Bracket
3. Screw
4. Screw
5. Float pin
6. Screw
7. Rod
8. Boot
9. O-ring
10. Throttle stop screw
11. Spring
12. Low speed mixture screw
13. Spring
14. Screw & washer
15. Bracket
16. Spring
17. Throttle lever
18. Washer
19. Nut
20. O-ring
21. Float needle
22. Clip
23. Float assy.
24. Main nozzle
25. Slow jet
26. Main jet
27. Plug
28. O-ring
29. Float bowl
30. O-ring (2)
31. Diaphragm
32. Spring
33. Housing
34. Screw & washer (5)
35. Screw & washer
36. Clip
37. Hose
38. Fitting
39. Spacer (not standard)
40. Choke plate (not shown)
41. Choke lever
42. Flange
43. Accel. pump lever
44. Rocker arm
45. Rocker arm spring

Keihin carburetor

a. Do not reverse the generator polarity.

b. Do not short or ground any wires unless specifically instructed to do so.

c. Do not operate the engine while the generator output terminal is disconnected.

d. Always connect positive to positive and negative to negative when connecting a charger or booster to the battery.

3. Check for a faulty generator light in the following manner:

a. If the ignition switch is turned off and the light is on, disconnect the generator 1 and 2 leads at their terminals. If the light stays on, check for a short between these two leads. Replace the rectifier bridge if the light goes out. Failure to remedy this situation will result in a discharged battery.

b. If the generator light doesn't go on when the ignition switch is turned on, check for a short between leads 1 and 2. If the light still doesn't come on, reverse the two leads. If the light still hasn't come on, check for an open circuit in the following manner:

(A) Connect the two leads of a voltmeter to ground and the No. 2 generator terminal, and check for a reading. Go on to the next step if a reading is obtained. No reading indicates an open circuit between No. 2 terminal and the battery. Correct this, then see if the light goes on when the ignition is turned on.

(B) Either connect or disconnect both No. 1 and 2 generator leads, turn the ignition switch on, and momentarily ground No. 1 terminal lead only. If the light does not come on, check for a burned out bulb, blown fuse, faulty bulb socket, or an open condition between No. 1 terminal and the ignition switch. Remove the ground from No. 1 terminal if the light comes on, and with No. 1 and 2 terminals connected, ground generator by inserting a screwdriver into the generator test hole.

(C) If the light still hasn't come on, check for open circuits between the wiring harness and the No. 1 terminal, generator brushes, slip rings, and field windings.

(D) If the light came on in the first step and there was a voltmeter reading, replace the regulator.

(E) Consult the next section if the light stays on when the motor is running.

4. Locate the reason for an undercharged battery in the following manner:

a. Make sure the reason the battery keeps going down is not because the accessories have been left on without the engine running.

b. Check the drive belt for proper tension.

c. Check the battery for shorting with a voltmeter or hydrometer indicated by one or more dead cells.

d. Inspect all wiring for loose or poor connections.

e. Connect the leads of a voltmeter from ground to the generator "BAT" terminal, then the No. 1 terminal, then the No. 2 terminal. No reading indicates an open condition between the battery and the voltmeter connection.

5. Check the generator in the following manner if the problem hasn't yet been discovered:

a. Disconnect the battery ground wire, connect an ammeter so the current will pass through it from the generator "BAT" terminal to the lead which was connected to the "BAT" terminal, and reconnect the battery ground wire.

b. Turn on all of the accessories and attach a carbon pile across the battery terminals. Operate the engine until maximum current output is obtained.

c. If generator is good, amperage output will be within 10 percent of output stamped on generator frame. Go back and recheck the previous steps.

d. Ground the generator by inserting a screwdriver through the generator test hole if amperage isn't within 10 percent of its normal rating.

e. Recheck with a carbon pile as described above. If the reading is still not within 10 percent, the regulator must be replaced.

f. Recheck with a carbon pile and overhaul the generator if the reading still isn't within 10 percent of its rated amperage.

6. Locate the reason for an overcharged battery in the following manner:

a. Check the state of battery charge with a voltmeter or hydrometer.

b. Connect the leads of a voltmeter to ground and generator No. 2 terminal to check for an open reading (zero). The voltage, in any case, should not exceed 16.0 volts at 0° F. Discrepancies in measurements taken in cold and hot conditions are to be expected.

7. If the above test proves that the circuit is good and excessive water evaporation still indicates an overcharged battery, separate the generator end frames and check the field windings for a shorted condition in the following manner:

a. Connect the leads of an ohmmeter from the brush lead clip to the end frame and then reverse the connections. The ohmmeter must be set on its lowest range scale.

b. If both readings are zero, check for a grounded brush lead. This is probably caused by a missing or damaged insulating washer or insulating screw sleeve.

c. If, after replacing the insulating elements, both readings are still zero, the regulator is defective and must be replaced.

TESTING GENERATOR OUTPUT

1. Remove the wire from the generator "F" terminal and connect a jumper wire from the "F" terminal to ground.

2. Remove wire(s) from "A" terminal and connect the positive lead to a 0–30 amp ammeter.

3. Run the engine at 2,000 rpm (40 mph in Fourth gear) and briefly connect the negative lead of the ammeter to the positive battery terminal.

NOTE: *Avoid running the engine for long periods with the generator field grounded, and always disconnect the ammeter lead from the battery before stopping the engine so the battery doesn't discharge through the generator.*

CAUTION: *Disconnect the wires from the regulator before grounding the regulator "F" (XLH) or "BT" (XLCH) terminals to check output, or regulator will be damaged.*

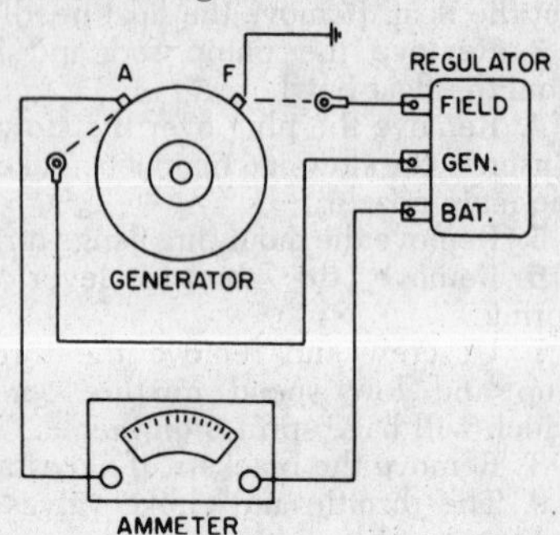

Generator output test

4. If the ammeter reads 10 amps, the generator is good and the trouble is in the voltage regulator or wiring circuit.

5. When installing generators or batteries and whenever the generator or regulator wires have been disconnected, flash the field coils to make sure the generator has correct polarity. Do this by briefly touching a jumper wire between "BAT" and "GEN" terminals on the regulator before starting the engine and after connecting all of the wires. The momentary surge of current from the battery to the generator will correctly polarize the generator.

NOTE: *If generator output findings are negative, consult the following section before removing the generator for further testing.*

CLEANING AND INSPECTING GENERATOR BRUSHES

1. Remove the commutator end cover nuts, washers, and frame screws.

2. Pry or gently tap off the commutator end cover from the frame and armature shaft.

3. Remove the brush holder mounting plate from the frame and disconnect the brush wires and generator positive brush cable from the brush holder terminals.

4. Remove the brushes and clean the holders with a suitable solvent. Replace the brushes when they are broken, gummy, or worn to the point where the longest side of the brush measures ½ in. or less.

5. Seat new brushes with a brush seating stone.

GENERATOR REMOVAL AND INSTALLATION

1. Disconnect the "BAT" wires from the voltage regulator terminal and disconnect the wires from the generator.

2. Take out the two long generator mounting screws and remove the generator from the left-side of the bike.

3. Install the generator in the reverse order of removal.

GENERATOR DISASSEMBLY AND COMPONENT TESTING

Testing Field Coils

An ammeter will react to an overload by sending its needle beyond the range of the calibrated scale. A direct short causes the needle to swing violently to the end of its travel. In both cases, damage will result to the ammeter if contact is not instantly broken. In testing field coils, first make sure there is no short present by making brief contact before securing the test lead. Try to work on a non-conductive surface and never touch the test points together.

The test is made by linking together an ammeter and a battery in series, with the components to be tested connected to leads.

1. Remove or insulate the brushes from armature.

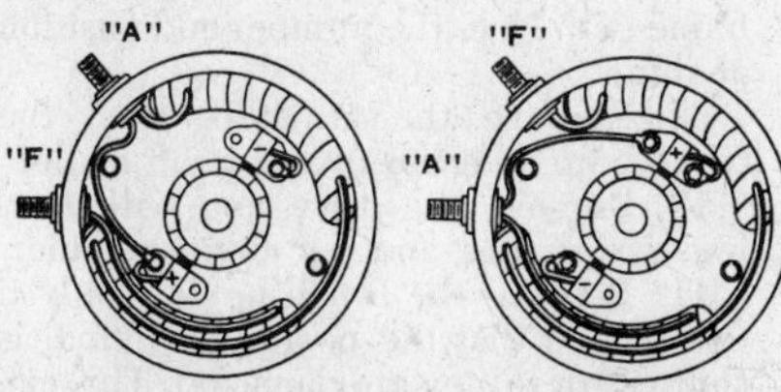

Internal connections of brushes to field terminals

2. Touch one test lead to "F" terminal and ground the other to the generator frame. There should be no reading.
3. Touch one test lead to "A" terminal and ground the other. If there is a reading for either, there is a grounded terminal or else the field coil is grounded to the frame.
4. Check terminal-to-ground contact. No reading means that the terminals are properly insulated. If there was a reading in Steps 2 or 3, but there is not now, the trouble is probably a grounded field coil.
5. Remove the generator drive gear using a gear puller. (H-D puller is Part No. 95715-19A.)
6. Press the armature out of the ball bearings with an arbor press. This can be done by placing the generator frame between the copper jaws of a vice and tapping the gearshaft end with a soft mallet.
7. Disassemble the terminals and remove the field coil leads. Examine all of the terminal components for wear and damage, especially all of the insulators. Replace any that are worn. Assemble all components except the field coil leads.
8. Touch one test lead to the field coil lead and the other to the ground on the generator frame. Check the other coil lead. A reading means that the coil is grounded and that the two coils must be separated by cutting the wire which connects them.
9. Test each field coil as above. A reading means that there is a grounded coil which must be replaced.
10. Test the field coils by touching the test leads to the coil lead terminals. The 6 volt double coils should produce a reading of 0.2 amps; 12 volt double coils should produce a reading of 2.3 amps (1965 models). No reading means an open coil. A higher reading means a shorted coil.
11. Strip back the insulation and scrape the wire clean where the two coil leads are joined. Attach one test lead at this point and the other at either coil lead. The 12 volt coils should produce 4.6 amp (1965 models) readings. Test the other coil lead. No reading means an open coil. A higher reading means a shorted coil. Replace any faulty parts.
12. Touch one test lead to the brush holder mounting plate and the other to the positive (insulated) brush holder. A reading indicates a shorted holder. Clean, check, and replace the plate if necessary.
13. Check the negative brush holder to see that it is securely mounted and well grounded.
14. If the problem has not been located, it is probably the armature.

Testing the Armature

Check for electrical continuity between the armature core and the commutator. If continuity exists, the armature is defective and should be replaced.

Repairing Commutator

The commutator can be turned down on a lathe or sanded with fine "00" sandpaper. Never use emery paper since particles will embed, causing arcing. The mica insulation must be 0.025 in. below the surface of the sections and can be reduced to this point with a hacksaw blade if care is taken to keep the slot bottoms square.

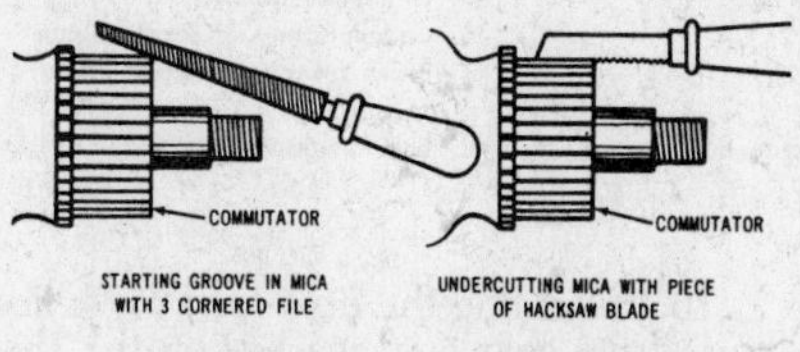

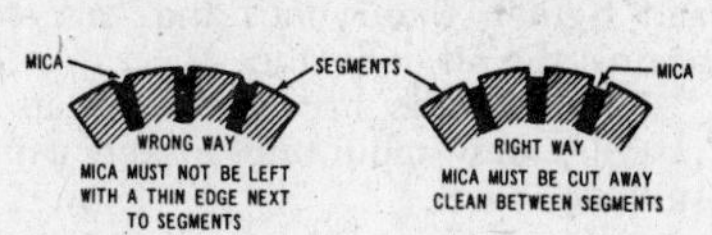

Disassembly

1. Remove the gasket, gear shaft nut, and washer.
2. Remove the drive gear with a gear puller (H-D Part No. 95715-19A) and slip the drive end oil deflector off the shaft.
3. Remove the brush cover strap and the end nuts and washers, then pull the screws out of the frame.
4. Loosen and remove the end cover with a soft mallet.
5. Remove the brush holder mounting plate and securing apparatus.
6. Press the armature out of the bearing with an arbor press, which can be found in any machine shop, or by clamping the generator in a copper-jawed vise and striking the shaft end with a soft mallet.
7. Remove the terminal screws, nuts, washers, insulator, and positive brush cable.
8. Remove the end plate by tapping gently and remove the bearing retainer with needlenose pliers.
9. Press the armature bearing out of drive end plate and remove the bearing retainer.
10. Press the armature oil seal out of the drive end plate from drive-gear side.
11. Remove the two pole screws with a large screwdriver and remove the pole shoes and field coils (only if replacement is necessary).

Inspection

1. Clean all parts except the armature, coils, and brushes in cleaning solvent, and wipe all other components with a cloth soaked in solvent.
2. Inspect all part for excessive wear, especially the insulators, armature windings, coil wrappings, and pole shoe surfaces.
3. Replace the oil seal if the armature looks oily.
4. Replace any part of the brush holder mounting assembly which is bent.
5. Check for excessive play of the armature shaft in the end cover bushing or roller bearing.
6. Bushings can be removed best with a bushing puller (H-D Part No. 97250-58) and an arbor. Be sure that the new bushing seats firmly in the bearing recess in the generator drive end plate.
7. To remove an arbor from the generator case, insert a screwdriver to assist in twisting it out.
8. Roller bearings are removed by pressing and new bearings should be pressed in until the bearing end is flush with the end cover.
9. Replace ball bearings if play is present. Always pack the bearings with a suitable grease.

Assembly

1 Assemble all related parts to the brush holder mounting plate.
2. Place the pole shoes in the field coils and insert into the frame. Tighten the pole shoe screws with a large screwdriver and vise grips until the shoes align themselves in the frame.
3. Place the bearing retainer in the inner groove of the drive end plate and press the bearing in until it finds its seat on the retainer. Compress the bearing retainer with needlenose pliers and secure it in the outer groove.
4. Press the oil seal into the drive end plate.
5. Insert the armature drive end shaft and press it in until it is properly seated.
6. Assemble the "A" terminal coil lead, positive brush cable, terminal screw bushing, bolt clip and terminal insulator on the positive terminal screw.
7. Insert the assembled "A" terminal through the terminal frame hole from inside and secure it with the insulating washer, lockwasher, and terminal screw nut.
8. Assemble the "F" terminal and secure it from the inside out.
9. Slip the frame over the armature,

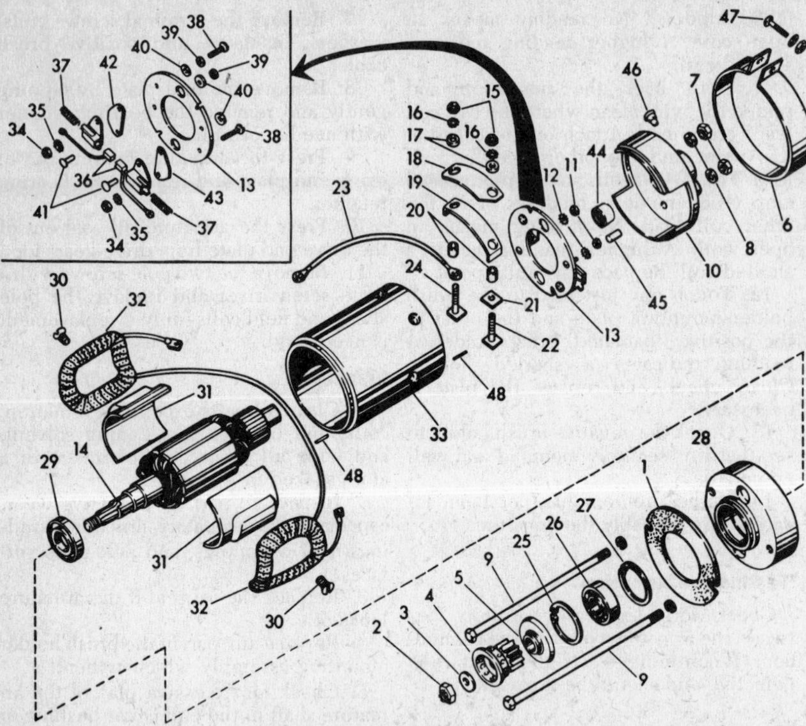

Generator assembly

1. Mounting gasket
2. Gear shaft nut
3. Gear shaft washer
4. Drive gear
5. Drive end oil deflector
6. Brush cover strap
7. Commutator end cover nut (2)
8. Commutator end cover washer (2)
9. Frame screw (2)
10. Commutator end cover
11. Brush cable nut (2)
12. Brush cable washer (2)
13. Brush holder mounting plate
14. Armature
15. Terminal screw nut (2)
16. Terminal screw lockwasher (2)
17. Insulating washer (2)
18. Terminal insulator
19. Terminal bolt clip
20. Terminal screw bushing (2)
21. Bracket insulator
22. Terminal screw (2)
23. Positive brush cable
24. Terminal screw (see item 22)
25. Bearing retainer
26. Armature bearing
27. Bearing retainer
28. Drive end plate
29. Armature oil seal
30. Pole shoe screw
31. Pole shoe (2)
32. Field coil (2)
33. Frame
34. Terminal screw nut (2)
35. Terminal screw lockwasher (2)
36. Brush (2)
37. Brush spring (2)
38. Brush holder plate screw (2)
39. Brush holder plate screw washer (2)
40. Brush holder plate screw washer (3)
41. Brush holder plate rivet (2)
42. Brush holder insulation
43. Brush holder spacer
44. End cover bearing
45. Generator oil wick
46. Commutator end cover oil cup
47. Brush cover screw, lock washer and nut
48. End locating pin (2)

taking care to locate the pin in its hole in the drive end plate.

10. Draw the loose end of the positive brush cable out from the commutator end of the frame.

11. Push the brushes back in their holders to clear the commutator and install the assembled brush mounting plate over the commutator so that the pin lines up with the slot and the brush cable passes through the opposite slot.

12. Secure the positive brush cable and lead to the insulated terminal. Secure the negative brush to the grounded terminal.

13. Place the commutator end cover over the end of the shaft so that the frame pin and notch are aligned.

14. Install the internal lockwashers on the frame screws by feeding them through the generator drive end and secure them from the outside.

15. Check to see if the armature is stuck or if the core strikes the pole shoes, by rotating the shaft. The shaft should turn evenly when pressure is applied. If the core strikes the pole shoes, either the shoes or the generator ends are not properly situated.

16. Assemble the drive end oil deflector, drive gear, and washer on the shaft and tighten them until the gear seats against the oil deflector.

17. Install the brush cover strap and install a new mounting gasket, using a suitable sealer.

FAN COOLED GENERATOR

The fan-cooled generator is basically the same as the standard unit, but is physically larger—capable of generating higher current—and is equipped with a heat-dissipating fan.

Tests concerning this type of generator are the same except that its output is 20 or more amps and the field coils have four leads instead of two. Also, when testing the field coils, the ammeter should read for each coil.

Disassembly

1. Remove the fan housing and associated hardware.

2. Remove the armature shaft nut and washers. Use a gear puller (H-D Part No. 95635-46) to separate the fan from the shaft and remove the key (if applicable).

3. Remove the baffle screws, plate, fan spacer, housing spider, and end plate. Use a gear puller to remove the brush and bearing housing. The bearing should come off with the housing, but leave it there if it doesn't.

4. Remove the terminal screws and the brush and spring assemblies will come out of their holders.

5. If the field coils are to be tested, they are now accessible and no further disassembly is necessary.

6. Drive the clutch spring collar pin out of the collar (Duo-Glide).

7. Remove the clutch spring and drive gear from the armature shaft and use a gear puller to separate the clutch from the shaft. Slip the oil deflector from the shaft.

8. Remove the end frame with a bearing, gasket, oil retainer, and bearing shims (if applicable). This can be done best by loosening the frame screws about ¼ in. and tapping on them to unseat the frame end. Note the number and position of shims.

9. Remove the armature from the frame with an arbor press or soft mallet.

10. Remove the drive end ball bearing, spring ring, and felt grease retainer.

11. Remove the brush holders only if tests prove that the positive terminal is shorted, or if they are damaged. This can be done after the negative brush holder screws and terminal screw nuts are removed.

12. If the pole shoes or field coils are to be replaced, they can be removed by loosening the retaining screws and tapping their heads.

13. Remove the air intake shields.

Inspection

Refer to the preceding "Inspection" section for the standard generator. Procedures are the same.

Assembly

Assemble the generator in reverse order of disassembly. Note the following points:

1. Install the field coils, armature, felt retainer, spring ring, and bearing. Use an arbor press to install the bearing.

2. Install the brush holders on the frame end and fit the frame end over the frame. The end may be drawn on by tightening the frame screws.

3. Route coil leads 1, 2, and 3 through the smaller frame opening, and lead 4 through the larger opening.

4. Run lead 1 behind and around the field coil terminal.

5. Twist leads 1 and 3 together and secure them to the field coil terminal with the terminal screw.

6. Install the positive brush. Twist leads 2 and 4 together and secure them to the positive brush terminal.

7. Assemble the negative brush only when lead 3 is positioned correctly behind the frame screw.

8. Assemble the commutator end of the generator in reverse order of disassembly making sure that the same number of shims are used.

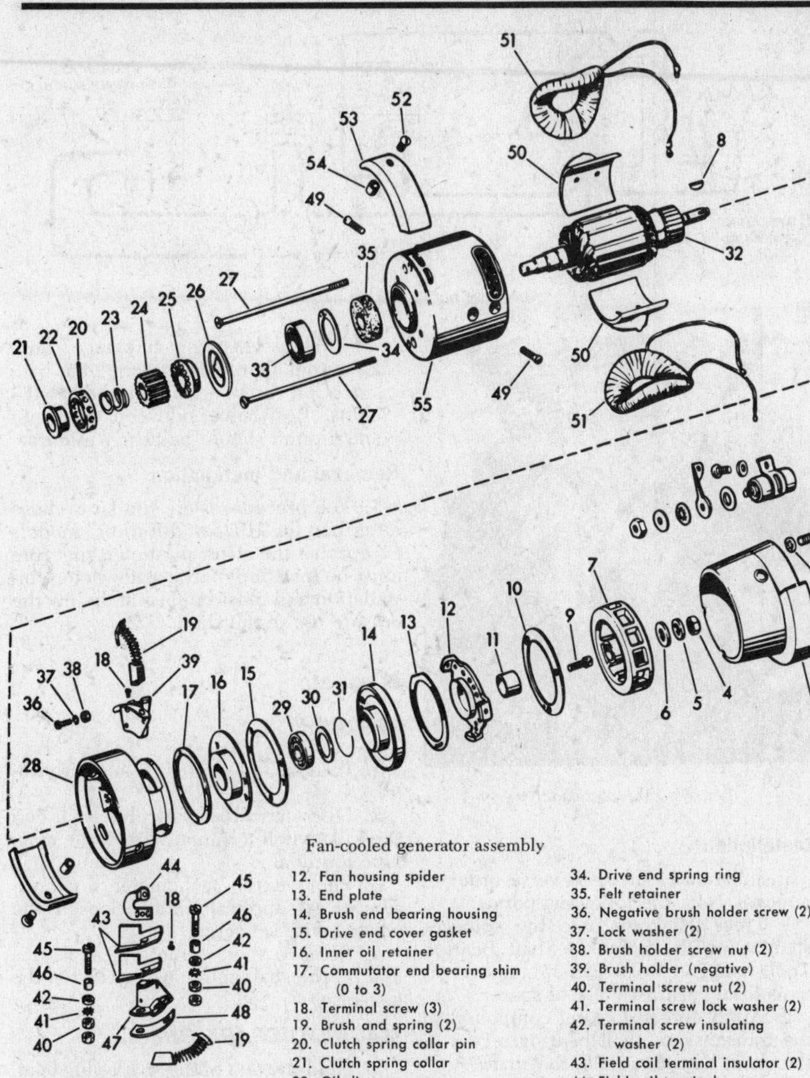

Fan-cooled generator assembly

1. Fan housing screw (3)
2. Internal lock washer (3)
3. Fan housing
4. Armature shaft nut
5. Armature shaft lock washer
6. Armature shaft plain washer
7. Fan
8. Armature shaft key (used 1961 and earlier)
9. Fan baffle plate screw (3)
10. Fan baffle plate
11. Fan spacer
12. Fan housing spider
13. End plate
14. Brush end bearing housing
15. Drive end cover gasket
16. Inner oil retainer
17. Commutator end bearing shim (0 to 3)
18. Terminal screw (3)
19. Brush and spring (2)
20. Clutch spring collar pin
21. Clutch spring collar
22. Oil slinger
23. Clutch spring
24. Drive gear
25. Clutch
26. Drive end oil deflector
27. Frame screw (2)
28. Frame end
29. Armature bearing
30. Armature spacing shim (0.020 in.)
31. Bearing plate spring ring
32. Armature
33. Armature bearing
34. Drive end spring ring
35. Felt retainer
36. Negative brush holder screw (2)
37. Lock washer (2)
38. Brush holder screw nut (2)
39. Brush holder (negative)
40. Terminal screw nut (2)
41. Terminal screw lock washer (2)
42. Terminal screw insulating washer (2)
43. Field coil terminal insulator (2)
44. Field coil terminal
45. Terminal screw (2)
46. Terminal screw bushing (2)
47. Brush holder (positive)
48. Brush holder insulation
49. Pole shoe screw (4)
50. Pole shoe (2)
51. Field coil (2)
52. Air intake shield screw (2)
53. Air intake shield (2)
54. Spacing bushing (2)
55. Generator frame

Regulators

DELCO-REMY

Needed for testing are a voltmeter (20-volt range), and ammeter (30-amp range), and ¼ and 1½ ohm resistors and a 25W variable resistor.

1. Disconnect the wire to the "BAT" terminal of the regulator and connect the ammeter negative lead to the wire, and the positive lead to the regulator terminal.

2. Connect the voltmeter positive lead to the regulator "GEN" terminal and its negative lead to ground on the engine or frame.

3. Disconnect the regulator "F" terminal. Connect the wire to one side of the variable resistor. Connect the other resistor lead to ground. Set the field control knob to the open position.

4. Start and run the engine to 2,000 rpm and turn the resistor control knob until the ammeter reads 10a.

5. If this value is not obtainable, and the voltmeter reads less than 12v, the generator is at fault.

6. If the ammeter reading is obtained or if the voltmeter reading is more than 15v, the regulator is at fault.

7. While adjustment of the regulator is possible (referring to the appropriate Delco-Remy Service Bulletin), replacement is much easier.

BOSCH

Necessary equipment is as described for the Delco-Remy unit.

1. Disconnect the wire from the regulator "B+" terminal.

2. Connect one lead of a 1½ ohm resistor (at least 100W) to the terminal, and connect the other to the positive terminal of an ammeter. Connect the negative ammeter lead to ground.

3. Connect the positive lead of a voltmeter to the regulator "D+" terminal and the negative lead to ground.

4. Disconnect the wire from the regulator "DF" terminal and connect it to one side of the variable resistor. Connect the other resistor lead to ground. Turn the resistor control knob to the open position.

5. Start and run the engine at 2700 rpm. Turn the resistor control knob to the open position.

5. Start and run the engine at 2,700 rpm. Turn the resistor knob slowly towards the "Direct" position until the ammeter reads 10a, then turn it quickly back to open. If the 10a reading is obtained, the regulator is at fault. If the amperage reading is not obtainable and the voltmeter reads less than 12v, the generator is faulty.

6. The regulator is not repairable, and must be replaced in the event of faulty operation.

Alternator-Equipped Models

An alternator is used on 1970 and later Glide models. The alternator consists of twelve coils surrounding a permanently magnetized rotor fitted to the left end of the crankshaft.

1975 AND EARLIER

Observe the following precautions when working on alternator models:

a. Do not run the engine with the battery disconnected;

b. Do not disconnect or ground regulator or rectifier leads while the engine is running;

c. The battery MUST be disconnected if it is being charged on the motorcycle;

d. Reversing battery connections will destroy other electrical components immediately;

e. Do not connect a battery booster to start the engine with a low or dead battery.

Testing

Before testing, check that the battery is in good condition and fully charged. A low or defective battery will invalidate the test results.

Be sure all electrical connections are clean and tight. The regulator module base must be well grounded to the crankcase: be sure the connection is clean and tight.

1. Connect an ammeter in series with the blue wire at the battery. Connect a 250W load rheostat (carbon pile) and voltmeter across the battery. With the rheostat off and the engine running at 3,600 rpm, the voltmeter should read 13.8–15.0 v, at room temperature (75° F). Note that voltage will vary with temperature: the higher the temperature, the higher the relative voltage reading may be.

2. With the engine running at 2,000 rpm, adjust the rheostat until the voltmeter reads 13.0 v. Ammeter reading should be at least 10.5 a. If it is not, proceed as follows:

3. Disconnect the module plug from

the stator plug. With an ohmmeter or 12v continuity light, check connections at female connector. The results should be as follows:

PROBE CONNECTIONS	READING			
	+ Polarity		− Polarity	
	Light	Ohm-meter	Light	Ohm-meter
White to module base (GND)	Off	Infinity	On	3 to 15
White to module base (GND)	Off	Infinity	On	3 to 15
Blue to black	On	3 to 15	Off	Infinity
Red to module base (GND)	Off	Infinity	Off	Infinity

4. If results differ, replace the module. If correct results are obtained, check the stator at the male connector as follows:

Probe Connections	Reading	Replace Stator
White to white	0.3 to 1.0 ohms	0 indicates
White to blue	Both readings	short
White to blue	the same	circuit
Blue to red	1.5 to 2.0 ohms	
Any pin to module base (GND)	Infinity	Any reading indicates short circuit

Removal and Disassembly

1. Remove the left footrest and chain housing cover. If a compensating sprocket is fitted, remove it.
2. Remove the chain adjuster mounting bolt and starter shaft thrust washer.
3. Remove the clutch adjusting screw locknut. Place a metal washer about 1¾ in. diameter with a ⅜ in. hole over the pushrod and fit the locknut.
4. Remove the spring tension adjusting nuts and pull off the clutch outer disc and spring collar assembly.
5. Remove the clutch sprocket and engine sprocket with chain.
6. Remove the three bolts securing the chain housing at the engine sprocket shaft. Loosen the transmission base mounting nuts. Remove the chain housing to transmission mounting bolts.
7. Remove the clutch hub (Tools 94645-41 and 95960-41A). Remove the shaft key. Remove the inner chain guard stud nuts. Disconnect the solenoid wire.
8. Remove the inner chain guard from the mainshaft (Tool 95960-41A). Disconnect the chain oiler hose at the pump. Disconnect remaining hoses at the rear of the chain housing.
9. Remove the sprocket spacer from the shaft. With tool 95960-52A, pull off the alternator rotor.
10. Remove the stator after removing the four screws and disconnecting wiring.

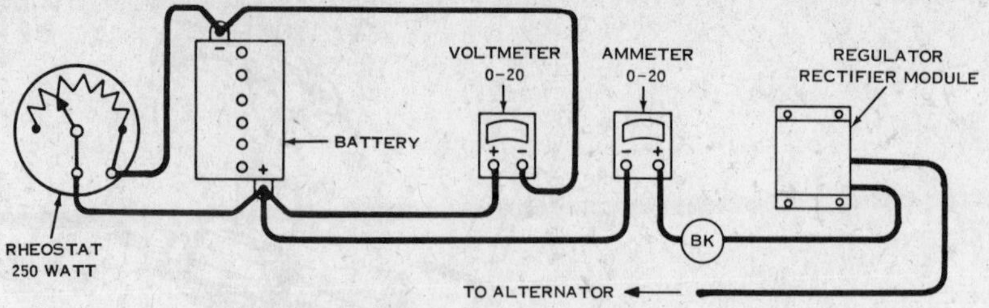

Alternator output test connections

Removing the alternator rotor

Installation

Installation is in the reverse order of removal. Note the following points:

1. Press the rotor onto the sprocket shaft using the Sprocket Shaft Bearing Tool (H-D Part No. 97225-55) until it bottoms firmly against the seal spacer.
2. Apply thread-locking compound to the transmission shaft bearing recess in the chain housing and to the shaft.
3. After the bearing housing is tapped into place, pack the race with grease.
4. Use aluminum paint on the chain housing and transmission surfaces where the two meet.
5. Replace the chain housing O-ring in the engine crankcase groove.
6. Replace the cover gasket.
7. Secure the transmission base mounting nuts only after the engine and transmission are secured to the chain housing.
8. Use a vacuum gauge (H-D Part No. 96950-68) to check the vacuum in the chain housing. With the vent tee hose closed off, the reading should be 20 in. Hg at 1,500 rpm. A lower reading is indicative of an air leak at the gasket, solenoid, starter shaft, or hoses.

1976 MODELS

1. Refer to the section "1975 and Earlier" for preliminary precautions which also apply to this system.

Testing

1. Refer to "1975 and Earlier" for test procedures. They are similar, except for the following points.

a. When checking voltage output (Step 1), the rheostat should be set for 3.5 a. Voltage should be 13.8–15.0v at room temperature.

b. When checking amperage (Step 2), output should be at least 14 a.

c. Coil resistance should be 0.2–0.4 ohms. Resistance between each pin and ground should be nearly infinite.

Removal and Installation

1. The procedures are similar to those described for "1975 and Earlier" models except that the stator plastic magnet ring must be installed on the stator before installation and must be flush or below the outside rim of the shell.

Magneto

REMOVAL

1. Remove the air cleaner and carburetor.
2. Disconnect the spark plug leads and the kill switch terminal wire at the magneto terminal.
3. Remove the tachometer drive assembly (if applicable) and loosen the control wire set screw.
4. Remove the mounting apparatus and lift the shaft and housing clear of the gearcase.

MAGNETO SPARK CHECK

1. Hold the end of the spark plug lead, with the plug cap removed, about ⅛ in. from the spark plug terminal. When the engine is running a blue spark should appear twice in every 360° rotation of the engine between the end of the lead and the plug terminal. If the spark is constant, the engine should not misfire. Do this on both plugs.
2. To test for spark with the engine off but the ignition on, hold the lead not more than ¼ in. from the plug terminal while kicking the engine over. Perform this on both plugs.
3. An easier test method is to remove the plug, reconnect the wire, and ground the plug tip against the cylinder head. Rotate the engine and watch for a blue spark at the plug tip.
4. If no spark is present, the kill button should be checked for a grounded condition before the magneto is removed for service.

DISASSEMBLY AND ASSEMBLY

1. Remove the end capscrews, end cap, and gasket.
2. Remove the spark plug leads. Remove the plug lead terminal by sliding up the lead protector and prying the terminal off with a screwdriver.
3. Remove the condenser mounting screw, washer, breaker arm terminal screw, condenser, and bracket.

4. Remove the point mounting screws, lockwashers, cam fiber and holder, and stationary contact point.

5. Remove the bearing support screws, safety gap (if applicable), and bearing support. Pry the rotor drive and grease retainer washer free, and remove the rotor cam end bearing.

6. Remove the rotor drive-gear pin by filing one end off and then punching it out.

7. Slip the rotor drive-gear from the shaft.

8. Remove the housing screws and slip the housing off the shaft.

9. Remove the O-ring and retainer washer, and drive out the bushing from within the housing (if applicable).

10. Remove the rotor drive and seal outer washer, rotor drive end seal, rotor drive, and grease retainer washer, then force the rotor drive-end snap-ring from the rotor shaft and remove the rotor.

11. Remove the rotor drive-end snap-ring and bearing.

12. Remove the coil bridge set screws, coil, and coil lead springs.

13. Remove the primary ground switch terminal and terminal switch wire.

14. Remove the vent cover screws, cover washers, cover, and screens.

15. Assemble in the reverse order of disassembly, taking care not to severely jar the rotor since this could cause damage.

GROUND SWITCH LOCK

Disassembly

1. Remove the end cap.

2. Remove the retainer clip between the insulating block and housing. This is best done by depressing the retainer clip with a knife, using the key in the switch as a lever, and pulling the key out to exert pressure while turning slightly to pull the lock out of the housing.

3. Remove the ground lock spring and lock ball from the ground-switch insulating block screw hole.

Assembly

1. With the retainer clip on top of the inside switch housing, insert the ground switch lock into the housing.

2. Depress the body retainer clip and push the ground lock switch into the housing, with a knife, so the clip engages the housing.

3. Loosen the condenser screw so the ground switch insulating block screw can be removed.

4. Replace the block screw and switch wire.

5. Replace the lock ball and lock spring.

6. Replace the switch insulating block wire and screw, and tighten the condenser screw.

7. Assemble the magneto in the reverse order of disassembly.

Installation

1. Set the oil seal ring and gasket (if applicable) in place on the gearcase.

2. Mount the magneto adaptor plate.

3. Install the magneto adaptor bolts from inside and tighten the assembly screws.

4. Manual retard magnetos must have the adaptor plates installed together.

5. Insert the rotor shaft into the gearcase and secure the magneto on the adaptor plate.

6. Manual retard magnetos must have the control arm installed before the mounting bolts can be replaced.

CONTACT BREAKERS

Contact Breaker Assembly Removal

1. Before attempting to remove the contact breaker assembly on early models, thoroughly clean the crankcase area around the unit as well as the contact breaker itself. To make sure that no dirt falls into the crankcase, have a clean oil soaked cloth handy to hold around the crankcase as the shaft is withdrawn.

2. On manual advance units, remove the contact breaker cover and cover retainer, then disconnect the spark control wire from the contact breaker cover.

3. On automatic advance units, remove the screw and lockwasher from the contact breaker cover and then remove the cover.

SPORTSTER

1. On 1965 models, remove the nuts and washer which secure the contact breaker base to the stem and remove the base.

2. Remove the two screws and the washer which secure the shaft and housing to the gearcase cover, and lift the shaft and housing free from the gearcase cover.

3. On 1966 automatic-advance types, remove the stem clamp bolts and clamp to free the entire unit clear from the crankcase.

GLIDE MODELS

1. On 1965 automatic-advance types, remove the nuts and washers, then slip the base from the housing. Now the entire unit is free to be lifted from the gearcase housing.

2. On 1966 automatic-advance types, upon removal of the stem clamp nut and clamp, the entire unit is free to be lifted clear of the gearcase cover.

CASE-MOUNTED CONTACT BREAKER

Glide models (1970 and later) and Sportster (1971 and later) have case-mounted breakers.

1. Remove the contact breaker cover and gasket by removing the cover screws.

2. Remove the wire terminal and wire from the breaker points.

3. Remove the contact breaker cam bolt, breaker plate bolts, lockwashers, and washers or screw retainer (whichever is applicable).

4. Remove the breaker assembly and free the contact assembly from the breaker plate by removing the breaker contact screw. Free the condenser lead and flat spring from the breaker contact terminal post. Remove the condenser screw, lockwasher, and condenser.

5. Remove the breaker cam and advance assembly.

6. Free the flyweight spring hooks from the pivot pin grooves and slip the fly-weights from the pivot pins. Springs need not be removed unless replacement is necessary. Flyweight roll pins are a press fit and need not be removed unless replacement is necessary.

Installing Contact Breaker

1965 ELECTRA-GLIDE AUTOMATIC ADVANCE

1. Remove the spark plugs, put the machine in high gear on its center stand, remove the screw plug from the timing inspection hole, and telescope the front push rod.

2. Rotate the engine until the "F" mark on the flywheel is in position.

3. Lubricate the cam end of the shaft and stem assembly, and install the breaker cam on the shaft so that the notches in the cam engage with the fly-weights.

4. Place the breaker base on the stem and shaft assembly and temporarily secure it.

5. The stem and base can only mount correctly in one way due to the stud positions. Check by aligning the base timing marks.

6. Install a new breaker rubber seal.

7. Turn the shaft counterclockwise 60 degrees from the position at which the cam mark and fiber align.

8. Temporarily insert the stem into the gearcase with the timing base marks away from the engine.

9. Align the flywheel timing mark in the fully retarded position.

10. Adjust the gear engagement, one tooth at a time, until the fiber and the cam mark align and secure the assembly to the gearcase.

11. Adjust the ignition timing.

1966 AND LATER ELECTRA-GLIDE AND SPORTSTER AUTOMATIC ADVANCE

1. Remove the spark plugs, put the machine in high gear on its center stand, remove the screw plug from the timing inspection hole, and telescope the front push rod.

2. Rotate the engine until the "Advance timing mark" on the flywheel is in position.

3. Install a new rubber seal.

4. Before installing, turn the shaft to approximately align the cam mark with the fiber follower.

5. Insert the breaker into the gearcase with the cable toward the rear of the engine. This will position the points to the outside of the engine to facilitate adjustment.

6. Align the flywheel timing mark in the center of the inspection hole and observe the position of the cam mark and fiber.

7. Lift the assembly and turn the shaft gear, one tooth at a time, until the

8. Adjust the ignition timing.

1970 AND LATER CASE-MOUNTED CONTACT BREAKER

1. Assemble in the reverse order of disassembly.
2. Lubricate the cam with a light application of high temperature grease during assembly, and thereafter at every 5,000 miles.
3. Seat the advance assembly squarely and firmly on the camshaft end.
4. Adjust the point gap.

STARTING SYSTEM

Troubleshooting

If the engine doesn't start after 30 seconds of operating the starter motor, let the starter cool for no less than two minutes before operating it again.

1. If the starter motor doesn't turn at all, the trouble is either a dead battery or, more likely, a disconnected wire. Check the mounting and wiring connections of the starter first, and then check the battery and return circuits. The solenoid switch should be mounted firmly. All connections must be clean and secure for effective operation.
2. Check the battery for charge by noting the brightness of the headlamp or by using a hydrometer. If the battery is charged and the wiring is good, the problem is either the starter, the switches, or the engine itself.
3. If the battery is charged, the problem may be in the switches. This can be checked by bypassing each switch with a jumper.
4. If the engine oil viscosity is too great, or if the bearings or pistons are too tight, the engine may not turn over. If the engine can be kicked over with the normal amount of effort but the starter won't turn it over (assuming the battery is charged), the starter motor is probably faulty.

Starter Motor

REMOVAL AND INSTALLATION

Sportster

1. Disconnect the cable from the starter motor. Unbolt the clamp from the crankcase.
2. Unscrew the starter motor through-bolts from the starter shaft housing.
3. Remove the starter motor.
4. Installation is the reverse of removal.

Glide Models

1. Disconnect the cable from the starter motor. Remove the nuts securing the starter motor housing to the studs on the chain housing.
2. Remove the starter motor end support plate from the transmission.
3. It may be necessary to loosen and elevate the battery box to provide clearance. Remove the starter motor and shaft housing together.
4. Installation is the reverse of removal.

Delco-Remy Starter Motor

DISASSEMBLY

1. Remove the thru-bolts, nuts, and lockwashers. The bolt which lies nearest the field coil has a vinyl insulating sleeve which must be removed carefully.
2. Remove the commutator end frame and drive end frame. If they don't slide off, tap them gently with a soft mallet.
3. Press or tap the armature from the drive end of the frame.
4. Remove the pole shoe screws, terminal nuts, lockwashers, insulating washers, terminal screw, field coils, and pole shoes.
5. If the brushes are grounded or the holders are defective, remove the brush holders by drilling out the rivets. If done carefully, a cold chisel can be used.
6. Remove the brush springs by turning them clockwise after compressing one side with a screwdriver until the springs leave their seats.
7. Remove the insulated brush by cutting off the lead where it joins the field coil wire.

ASSEMBLY

Refer to the following section on Prestolite starter motors. Procedures are the same.

TESTING THE FRAME AND FIELD ASSEMBLY

1. Test for an open circuit with a test lamp connected to the terminal screw and insulated brush. An open circuit will keep the lamp from lighting.
2. Test for a grounded field circuit with a test lamp lead on the terminal or on each insulated field coil brush, and the other lead grounded to the frame. If the lamp lights, the circuit is grounded.
3. Check each insulated brush holder for a grounded condition by using a test lamp. Replace any for which the lamp lights.
4. Replace the field coils if a short is suspected and note whether performance is enhanced.

TESTING THE ARMATURE

1. Connect a test light or voltmeter between the commutator and armature core.
2. If the light comes on (or the meter responds), the armature coil is grounded and the armature should be replaced.

ARMATURE REPAIR

1. Place the armature in a lathe and turn down the commutator if it is worn, out of round, or if the mica insulation protrudes above the segments. This should only be done by an experienced mechanic.
2. Undercut the mica $1/32$ in. with an undercutting machine or a hacksaw blade. Be sure that the mica surface is flat and even, and is kept free of dirt and copper dust.
3. Lightly sand the commutator with "00" sandpaper to ensure a smooth surface.
4. Examine the bearing, bushing, and thrust washer for damage and wear (i.e., excessive play), and replace if in doubt.
5. Information concerning armature testing may be obtained through Delco-Remy, but replacement is advised over repair.

BRUSH REPLACEMENT AND REPAIR

1. Complete replacement sets are available for brushes, grounded holders, and insulated holders. Minimum acceptable brush length is ¼ in.

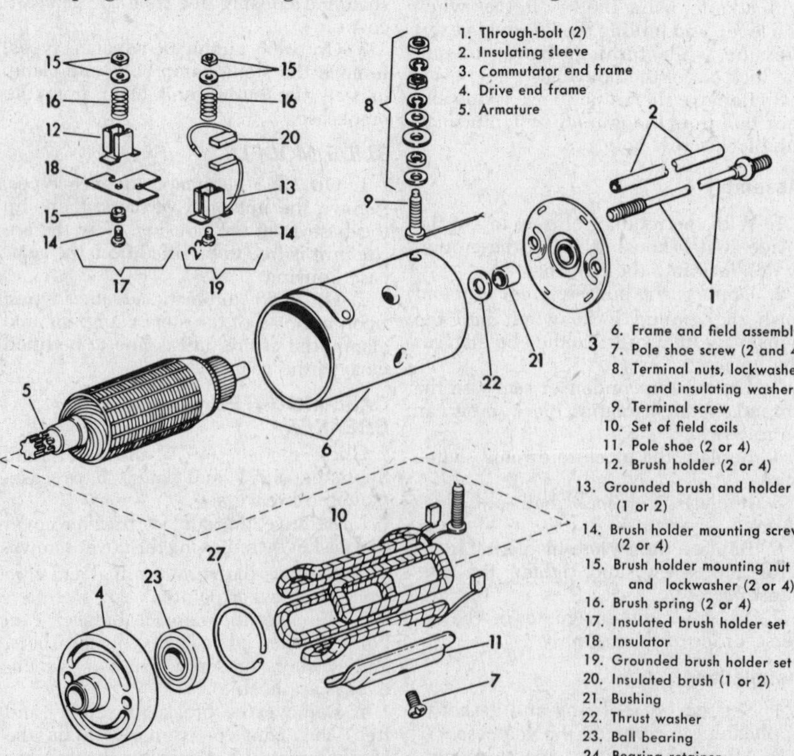

Delco-Remy four-pole starter motor

2. Prepare to replace the insulated brush by cleaning the coil lead end with a file or grinder.

3. Prepare the surface for soldering with rosin flux or use a flux-based solder. Only remove varnish from the leads in the area to be soldered.

4. Solder the coil lead to the back side of the coil, taking care not to use excessive amounts of solder. Solder must never contact the armature. Overheating the brush lead will cause the solder to run onto the wire strands, making the lead inflexible.

5. When replacing the grounded brush, peen the brush holder mounting screws with a hammer so that the nuts won't vibrate loose.

Prestolite Starter Motor

DISASSEMBLY

1. Remove the thru-bolts, washers, lockwashers, and commutator end cover.

2. Insert a tube the diameter of which exceeds that of the commutator. This will keep brushes in place and allow the armature to be replaced without touching the brushes.

3. Remove the armature, drive end cover, and bearing as one assembly. The bearing may have to be pressed out.

TESTING THE FRAME AND FIELD ASSEMBLY

1. Coils can only be tested for an open circuit; any type of coil failure requires replacement of the frame and field assembly.

2. Touch one test lamp lead to the frame and the other to each field coil brush. The lamp should light on each brush; failure to do so indicates an open circuit.

BRUSH REPLACEMENT AND ARMATURE REPAIR

Same as for Delco-Remy starter motor.

ASSEMBLY (ALL MODELS)

1. If the brushes and springs have been released, clamps can be used to hold them in place while reinstalling the armature.

2. Align the end cover mark to the motor terminal.

3. Align the brush holder positioning notch with the motor terminal insulator.

4. Align the commutator end head with the motor terminal.

5. Install the thru-bolts, washers, and lockwashers, and mount entire unit on engine.

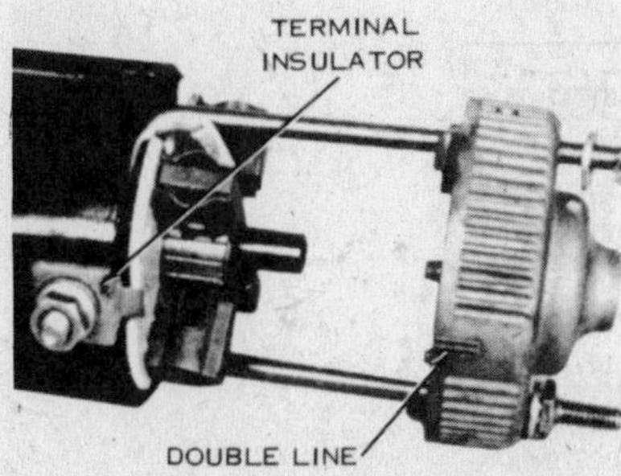

Aligning starter motor cover

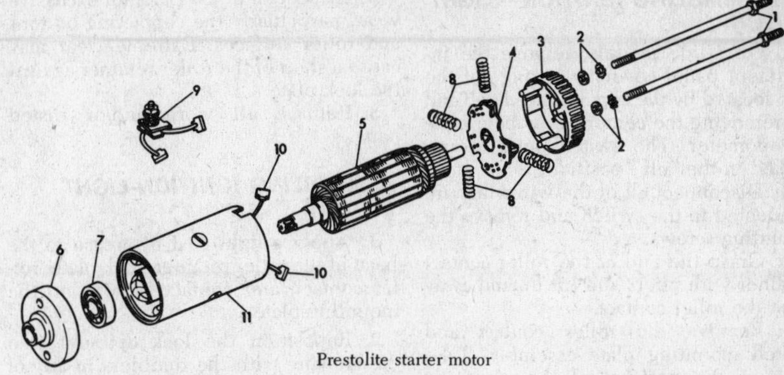

Prestolite starter motor

1. Thru bolt
2. Washer and lockwasher (2)
3. Commutator end cover
4. Brush plate and holder assembly
5. Armature
6. Drive end cover
7. Drive end ball bearing
8. Brush spring (4)
9. Terminal and brush assembly
10. Ground brush (2)
11. Frame and field coil assembly

Hitachi Starter Motor

DISASSEMBLY

1. Remove the cable terminal nut and washers.

2. Remove the nuts and washers from the through-bolts, and take out the bolts.

3. Remove the rear cover screws. Remove the rear cover by tapping it off with a plastic mallet until a screwdriver can be inserted between the armature housing and cover and the cover pried off. Be sure the cable terminal stays in place near the housing.

4. Lift up the brush springs; remove the positive brushes completely (their leads go to the field coils); lift up the negative brushes and use the springs to trap them in their holders, clear of the commutator.

5. Remove the front cover, the armature, and thrust washer(s).

INSPECTION

1. Minimum acceptable brush length is 7/16 in.

2. Check field coil insulation. If necessary, field coils are replaced along with the housing.

3. Check bearing for play and replace if necessary. The rear cover bushing, if defective, is replaced along with the cover itself.

4. Clean commutator surface with No. 00 sandpaper. Mica must undercut commutator segments by 1/32 in.

ASSEMBLY

1. Assembly is basically the reverse of disassembly.

2. Align the mark on the housing with the notch on the front cover.

3. Be sure to align the brush holder with the rear cover screw holes.

4. Tighten through-bolts to 20–25 in. lbs.

SWITCHES

Ignition-Light Switch

This switch is centrally located in the instrument cluster on most models and has three positions plus a center-off position. One click to the right turns on the ignition, a second click to the right is for the ignition and running lights. One click to the left, from the center-off position, is for parking lights only, and, in this and the center-off position, the ignition can be locked off. The key can be removed in any position, on most models, once the ignition has been unlocked.

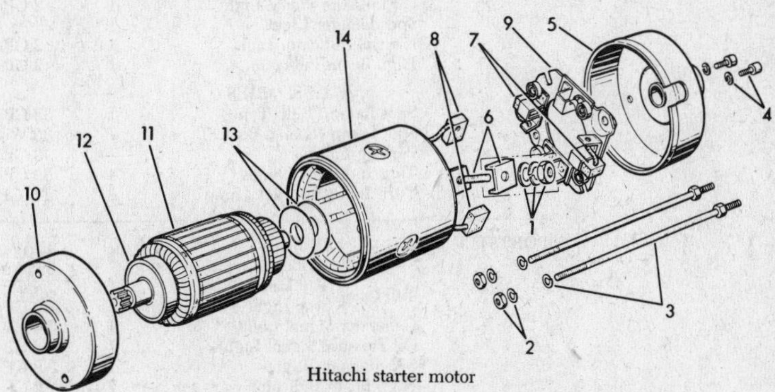

Hitachi starter motor

1. Terminal nut, lockwasher and washer
2. Through-bolt and lockwasher (2)
3. Through-bolt and lockwasher (2)
4. Rear cover screws and lockwashers (2)
5. Rear (commutator end) cover
6. Terminal and insulator
7. Negative brush (2)
8. Positive brush (2)
9. Brush holder assembly
10. Front (drive end) cover
11. Armature
12. Armature ball bearing
13. Thrust washer
14. Frame

DISASSEMBLING IGNITION—LIGHT SWITCH

1. On Glide models, remove the instrument panel cover by prying out the clip located by the trip mileage knob and by removing the center screw below the speedometer. The switch must be unlocked in the "off" position.
2. Disconnect all of the wires that are connected to the switch and remove the mounting screws.
3. Grasp the end of the roller contact retainer with pliers and lift up and away from the roller contact.
4. Remove the roller contact and switch mounting plate assembly. Take note of the position of the mounting plate.
5. The reinforcing plate, contact bar holder, and rubber contact retainer can be removed from the cover by slipping it sideways until one set of tabs clears the slot in the cover, then lifting and sliding in the opposite direction.
6. Remove the switch base and lock plate from the cover. Note that the narrow end of the elongated hole and the lug on the switch cylinder are toward the lock cover hinge.
7. Remove the switch cylinder and cylinder case from the cover. Only remove the cylinder from its case if the lock is faulty. Some models have the cylinder and case as a single unit.

CLEANING AND INSPECTION

1. Wash all parts in solvent and dry them with compressed air.
2. Inspect all of the parts for excessive wear, particularly the contacting buttons and roller surfaces. Extreme wear may cause a short of the roller retainer against the lock plate.
3. Replace all worn and/or rusted parts.

ASSEMBLING IGNITION-LIGHT SWITCH

1. Apply a light coat of grease to the head of the roller retainer, lock plate, roller contact, and contact buttons on the mounting plate.
2. Reposition the lock cylinder into the housing with the tumblers in any of the four registers.
3. Insert the key, while pressing the cylinder into the housing, and turn it to the right until it stops.
4. Remove the key and complete assembly.
5. Complete assembly by using the reverse order of the disassembly procedures.

Solenoid Switch

The solenoid switches open and close the circuits electromagnetically. The 1967 Sportster and all Glide models have switches which can be repaired. There are three connections involved with the solenoid; these are: the control circuit wire, which runs from the starter button to the small terminal stud; the battery cable, which is connected to the largest stud; the starter motor cable, which runs to the large, shorter stud. Proper installation is a must because reversed cables will cause the solenoid coils to remain in circuit and will drain the battery.

When a faulty switch is suspected, tests should be made of the coil windings and the continuity of the circuit through the main switch when the contacts are closed, in the following manner:

1. Connect the positive terminal of a 12 volt battery to coil terminal 1 and the negative lead to coil terminal 2.
2. This should actuate the solenoid and an audible click should be heard. A heavy spark, or no click, indicates either an open or shorted condition and the switch must be replaced.
3. Connect a jumper wire between terminal 1 and the small solenoid terminal that connects to the starter button lead. If the solenoid is heard to operate, but the circuit to the starter motor is still incomplete, the solenoid contacts are probably burnt or eroded.

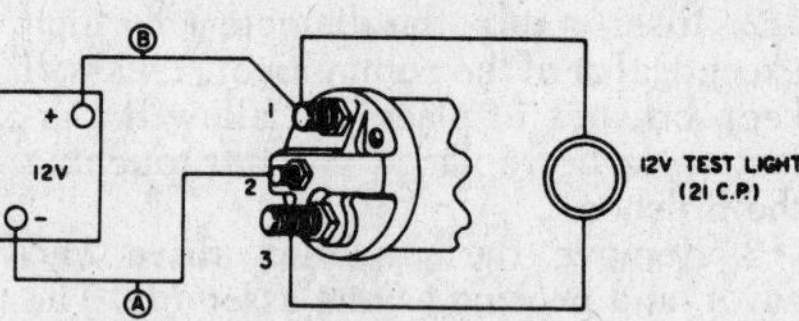

Wiring for testing 1967 Sportster and Electra Glide solenoid

Bulb Chart

Model	Lamp Description	Bulbs Rqd	Candle Power or Wattage 12 V	Harley-Davidson Part Number 12 V
GLIDE MODELS	HEADLAMP	1		67717-64
	Hi Beam		50 Watts	
	Lo Beam		45 Watts	
	TAIL AND STOP LAMP	1		68165-64
	Tail Lamp		4 CP	
	Stop Lamp		32 CP	
	INSTRUMENT PANEL			
	Generator Signal Light	1	2 CP	68462-64
	Oil Pressure Signal Light	1	2 CP	68462-64
	Speedometer Light	1		71090-64
	Neutral Indicator Light	1	2 CP	68462-64
	High Beam Indicator	1	2 CP	68462-64
	ACCESSORIES			
	Spot Lamp (Bulb Type)	1	32 CP	68715-64
	Spot Lamp (Sealed Beam Type)	1	30 Watts	68726-64
	Parking Lamp	—	3 CP	68166-64
	Turn Indicator Lamps	4	32 CP	68572-64A
	Turn Indicator Pilot Lamps	2	1.5 CP	71090-64
SPORTSTER	Headlamp Hi Beam / Lo Beam	1	45 Watts / 35 Watts	67717-65
	Tail Lamp Tail Lamp / Stop Light	1	4 CP / 32 CP	68165-64
	Generator Signal Light	1	4 CP	71092-68
	Oil Pressure Signal Light	1	4 CP	71092-68
	Speedometer Light	1	2 CP	71090-64
	High Beam Indicator	1	2 CP	71092-68
	ACCESSORIES			
	Spot Lamp (Bulb Type)	1	32 CP	68715-64
	Spot Lamp (Sealed Beam Type)	1	30 Watts	68726-64
	Parking Lamp	—	3 CP	68166-64
	Turn Indicator Lamps	4	32 CP	68572-64A
	Turn Indicator Pilot Lamps	2	1.5 CP	71090-64

Delco-Remy Regulator Test Specifications

Delco-Remy Regulators

Regulator Part Number: Harley-Davidson	Regulator Part Number: Manufacturer's Number	For Testing Procedure See Delco-Remy Service Bulletin Number	Regulator Type	Adjustment and Range Amps: Current Regulator Setting	Adjustment and Range (Volts): Cutout Relay Closing Voltage	Adjustment and Range (Volts): Voltage Regulator Setting	Used with Harley-Davidson Generator and Motorcycle Models
74510–64	1119 614	1R 119A	3 Unit Current & Voltage	10 (9.0–11.0)	12.4 (11.8–13.0)	14.3 ° (13.9–14.5) °	Model 64 and later 12V generators (° Upper contact operation. Operation on lower contacts must be 0.1 to 0.3 volt lower)
74510–65	1100 687	1R 262	2 Unit Voltage		12.5 (11.5–13.5)	14.4 ° (13.5–14.9) °	Delcotron Alternator

All 12-Volt Regulators	Current regulator air gap 0.075 in.	Cutout relay air gap and point opening 0.020 in.
	Voltage regulator air gap varies with setting	Voltage regulator point opening 0.016 in.

Bosch Regulators

Harley-Davidson	Manufacturer's Number	Relay Cut-in Voltage	Regulator Voltage: No Load	Regulator Voltage: Load	Used with Harley-Davidson Generator and Motorcycle Models
74511–65	TBA 130–150/12/2	12.4–13.1	13.8–15.4	12.7–14.5 @ 10 amp	1965 Model 65 Generator for 1965–66 Sportster XLH and 1965 and later XLCH

WIRING DIAGRAMS

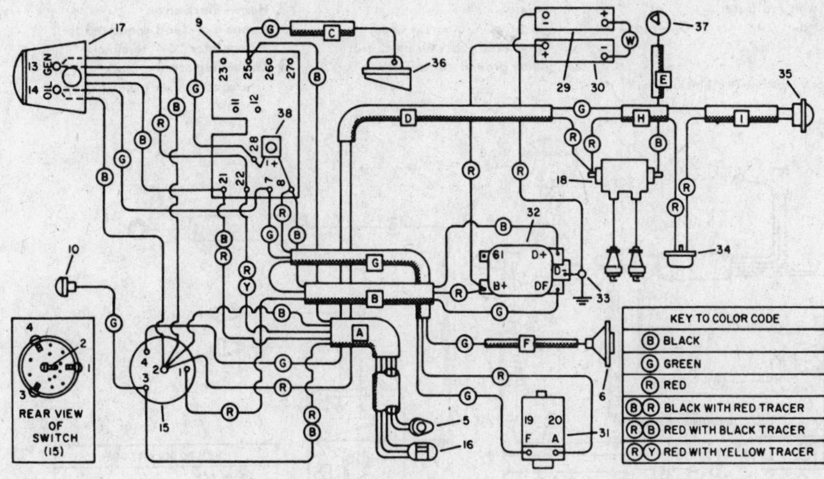

1965–66 Sportster H

A. Handlebars—Red wire with black tracer, black wire with red tracer, red wire with yellow tracer, two black wires
B. Conduit (three wires)—Green, red, and black wires
C. Conduit (one wire)—Green wire
D. Conduit (two wires)—Red and green wires
E. Conduit (one wire)—Black wire
F. Conduit (one wire)—Green wire
G. Conduit (three wires)—One red and two green wires
H. Conduit (two wires)—Black and red wires
5. Horn switch—Two black wires
6. Oil signal light switch—Green wire
7. Terminal—Two green wires
8. Terminal—Black and red wires and rectifier positive terminal
9. Terminal plate
10. Speedometer light—Green wire
11. Terminal—Not used with standard wiring
12. Terminal—Not used with standard wiring
13. Generator signal light—Green and black wires
14. Oil signal light—Green and black wires
15. Ignition-light switch—Terminal #1 red wire; terminal #2 red wire and three black wires; terminal #3 green wire and red wire with black tracer; terminal #4 green wire
16. Headlamp switch—Red wire with black tracer, black wire with red tracer, and red wire with yellow tracer
17. Headlamp—Black and red wires
18. Ignition coil—Three red wires and black wire
19. Generator "F" terminal—Green wire
20. Generator "A" terminal—Red wire
21. Terminal—Black wire with red tracer and black wire
22. Terminal—Red wire with yellow tracer and red wire
23. Terminal—Not used with standard wiring
25. Terminal—Black wire and green wire
26. Terminal—Not used with standard wiring
27. Terminal—Not used with standard wiring
28. Terminal—Green wire and rectifier negative terminal
29. Front battery—Negative terminal black wire; positive terminal white wire
30. Rear battery—Positive terminal red wire; negative terminal white wire
31. Generator—See terminals 19 and 20
32. Regulator—B+ terminal two red wires; DF terminal green wire; D+ terminal black wire; Gnd terminal black wire; G1 terminal not used with standard wiring
33. Terminal, frame screw—Two black wires
34. Stoplight switch—Two red wires
35. Tail lamp—Red and green wires
36. Horn—Green wire
37. Circuit breaker—Two black wires
38. Rectifier—Positive terminal (painted red) to terminal #8 Negative terminal to terminal #28

WIRING DIAGRAMS

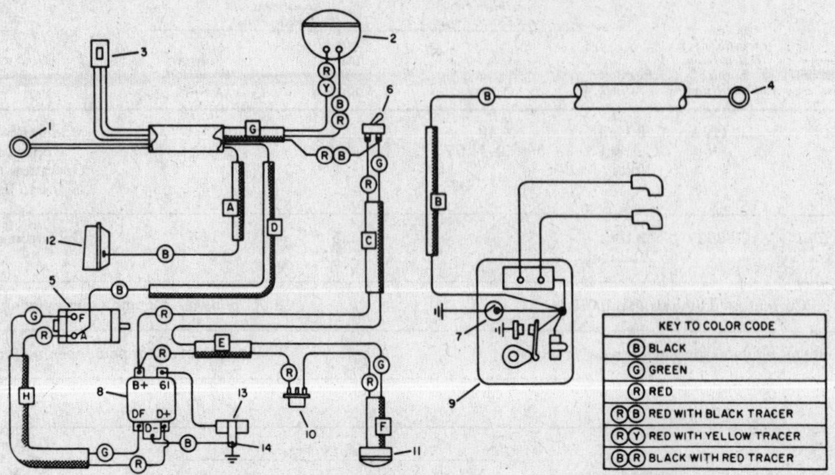

1965 Sportster CH

A. Conduit (one wire)—Black
B. Conduit (one wire)—Black
C. Conduit (two wires)—Red and green
D. Conduit (one wire)—Black
E. Conduit (two wires)—Red and green
F. Conduit (two wires)—Red and green
G. Conduit (three wires) Red wire with black tracer, red wire with yellow tracer, black wire with red tracer
H. Conduit (two wires)—Green and red

1. Horn switch—Two black wires
2. Headlamp—Black wire with red tracer and red wire with yellow tracer
3. Dimmer switch—Red wire with black tracer, red wire with yellow tracer, black wire with red tracer
4. Ignition cut-out switch—Black wire
5. Generator
   "F" terminal—Green wire
   "A" terminal—Red and black wires
6. Light switch—(3 wires)—Red, green and red with black tracer
7. Ignition ground switch lock
8. Voltage regulator—
   "61" terminal—Condenser black wire
   DF terminal—Green wire
   D+terminal—Red wire and condenser wire
   B+ terminal—Two red wires
   Gnd terminal—Black wire
9. Magneto—Black wire
10. Stop light switch—Two red wires
11. Tail and stop lamp—Red and green wires
12. Horn—Black wire
13. Capacitor—Lead connected to regulator "61" terminal
14. Grounding screw—Black wire and condenser ground strap

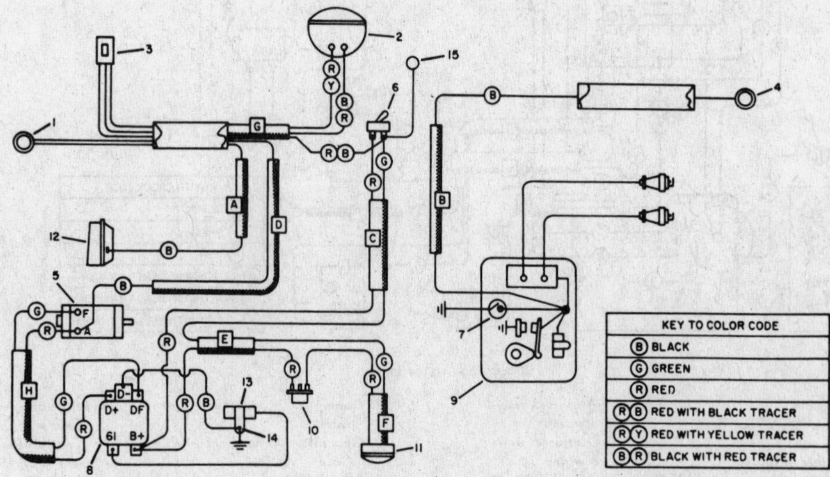

1966 Sportster CH

A. Conduit (one wire)—Black
B. Conduit (one wire)—Black
C. Conduit (two wires) —Red and green
D. Conduit (one wire)—Black
E. Conduit (two wires)—Red and green
F. Conduit (two wires)—Red and green
G. Conduit (three wires)—Red wire with black tracer, red wire with yellow tracer, black wire with red tracer
H. Conduit (two wires)—Green and red

1. Horn switch—Two black wires
2. Headlamp—Black wire with red tracer and red wire with yellow tracer
3. Headlamp dimmer switch—Red wire with black tracer, red wire with yellow tracer, black wire with red tracer
4. Ignition cut-out switch—Black wire
5. Generator
   "F" terminal—Green wire
   "A" terminal—Black wire
6. Light switch—Red, green and red with black tracer wires
7. Ignition ground switch lock
8. Voltage regulator—
   DF terminal—Green wire
   D+ terminal—Red wire and condenser wire
   B+ terminal—Two red wires
   "61" terminal—Black wire
9. Magneto—Black wire
10. Stop light switch—Two red wires
11. Tail and stop lamp—Red and green wires
12. Horn—Black wire
13. Capacitor—Center black wire connected to regulator "61" terminal
14. Grounding screw—Black wire
15. Speedometer lamp

WIRING DIAGRAMS

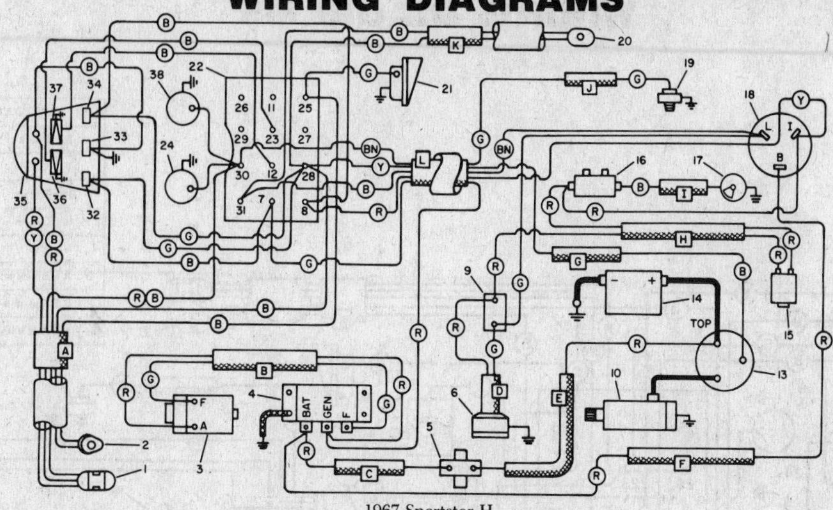

1967 Sportster H

A. Handlebar (five wires)—Red wire with black tracer, black wire with red tracer, red wire with yellow tracer, and 2 black wires
B. Conduit (two wires)—Green and red
C. Conduit (one wire)—Red
D. Conduit (two wires)—Red and green
E. Conduit (one wire)—Red
F. Conduit (one wire)—Red
G. Conduit (one wire)—Black
H. Conduit (two wires)—Red
I. Conduit (one wire)—Black
J. Conduit (one wire)—Green
K. Conduit (two wires)—Black
L. Conduit (five wires)—Brown, yellow, black, red and green

1. Headlamp dimmer switch
2. Horn switch
3. Generator "F" and "A" terminals
4. Regulator
   "BAT" terminal
   "GEN" terminal
   "F" terminal
5. Overload circuit breaker
6. Tail lamp
7. Terminal
8. Terminal
9. Junction terminal board
10. Starter motor
11. Terminal—Not used with standard wiring
12. Terminal
13. Starter solenoid
14. Battery
15. Stoplight switch
16. Ignition coil
17. Circuit breaker
18. Ignition—Light switch
19. Oil signal light switch
20. Starter button
21. Horn
22. Terminal plate
23. Terminal
24. Speedometer light
25. Terminal
26. Terminal—Not used with standard wiring
27. Terminal—Not used with standard wiring
28. Terminal
29. Terminal—Not used with standard wiring
30. Terminal
31. Terminal
32. Oil signal light
33. High beam indicator light
34. Generator indicator light
35. Headlamp
36. Left direction signal pilot lamp
37. Right direction signal pilot lamp
38. Tachometer light

KEY TO COLOR CODE

	B	Black
	Y	Yellow
	BN	Brown
	G	Green
	R	Red
B	R	Black with Red tracer
R	B	Red with Black tracer
R	Y	Red with Yellow tracer

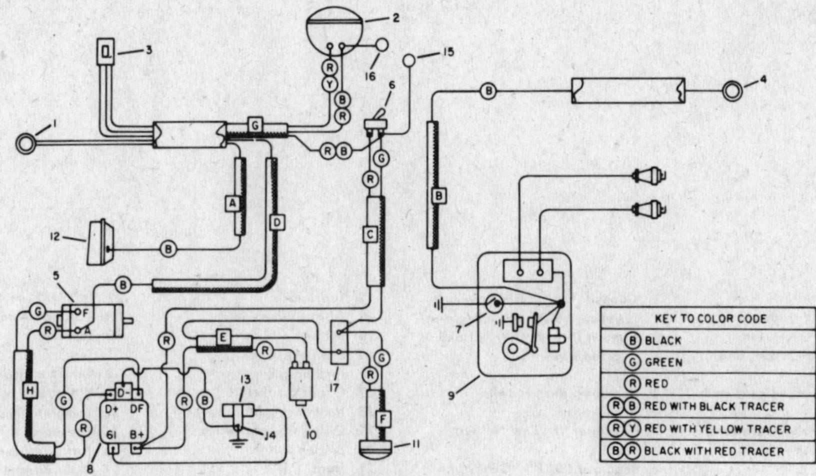

1967–69 Sportster CH

A. Conduit (one wire)—Black
B. Conduit (one wire)—Black
C. Conduit (two wires)—Red and green
D. Conduit (one wire)—Black
E. Conduit (two wires)—Red
F. Conduit (two wires)—Red and green
G. Conduit (three wires)—Red wire with black tracer, red wire with yellow tracer, black wire with red tracer
H. Conduit (two wires)—Green and red

1. Horn switch—Two black wires
2. Headlamp—Black wire with red tracer and red wire with yellow tracer
3. Headlamp dimmer switch—Red wire with black tracer, red wire with yellow tracer, black wire with red tracer
4. Ignition cut-out switch—Black wire
5. Generator
   "F" terminal—Green wire
   "A" terminal—Black wire
6. Light switch—Red, green and red with black tracer wires
7. Ignition ground switch lock
8. Voltage regulator—
   DF terminal—Green wire
   D+ terminal—Red wire and condenser wire
   B+ terminal—Two red wires
   D– terminal—Black wire
9. Magneto—Black wire
10. Stop light switch—Two red wires
11. Tail and stop lamp—Red and green wires
12. Horn—Black wire
13. Capacitor—Black wire connected to regular D– terminal
14. Grounding screw—Black wire
15. Speedometer lamp
16. High beam indicator lamp
17. Terminal strip

WIRING DIAGRAMS

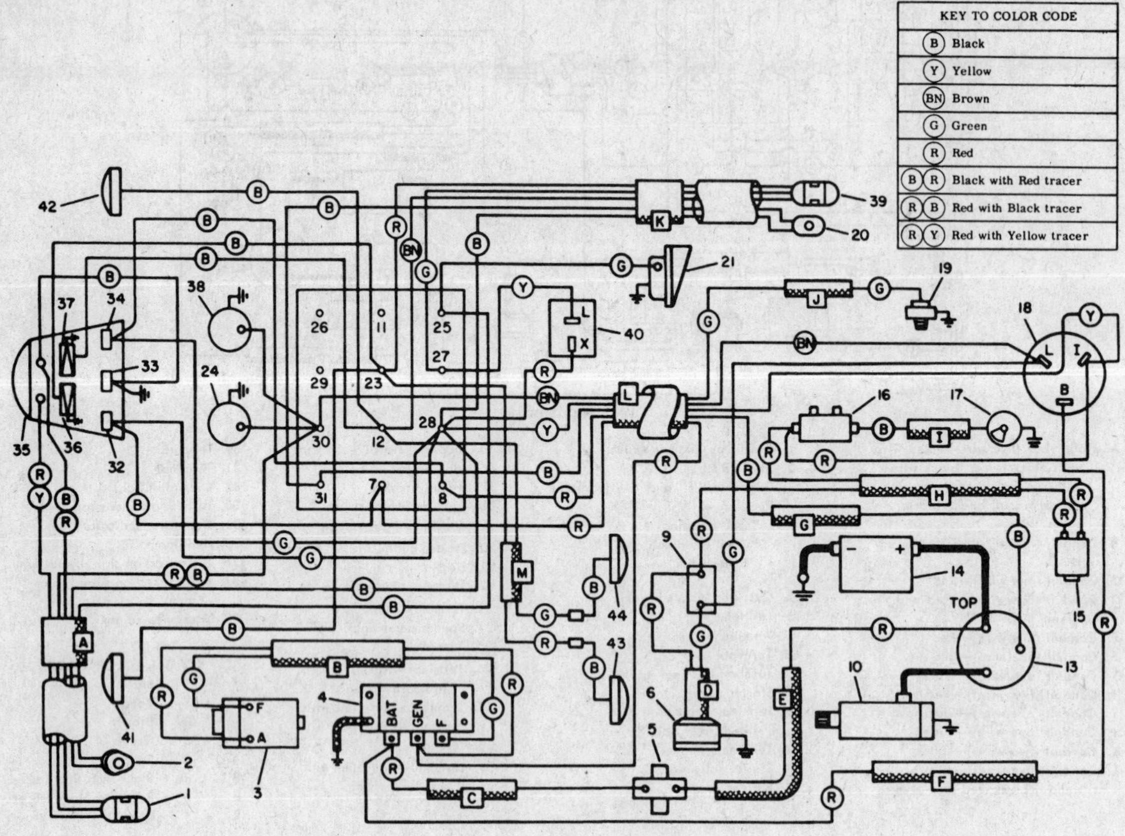

1968–69 Sportster H

A. Handlebar (five wires)—Red wire with black tracer, black wire with red tracer, red wire with yellow tracer, and two black wires
B. Conduit (two wires)—Green and red wires
C. Conduit (one wire)—Red wire
D. Conduit (two wires)—Red and green wires
E. Conduit (one wire)—Red wire
F. Conduit (one wire)—Red wire
G. Conduit (one wire)—Black wire
H. Conduit (two wires)—Red wires
I. Conduit (one wire)—Black wire
J. Conduit (one wire)—Green wire
K. Handlebar (five wires)—Red, brown, green, and two black wires
L. Conduit (five wires)—Brown, yellow, black, red, and green
M. Conduit (two wires)—Red and green wires

1. Headlamp dimmer switch
2. Horn switch
3. Generator "F" and "A" terminals
4. Regulator "BAT", "GEN", and "F" terminals
5. Overload circuit breaker
6. Tail lamp
7. Terminal
8. Terminal
9. Junction terminal board
10. Starter motor
11. Terminal—Not used with standard wiring
12. Terminal
13. Starter solenoid
14. Battery
15. Stoplight switch
16. Ignition coil
17. Circuit breaker
18. Ignition—light switch
19. Oil signal light switch
20. Starter button
21. Horn
22. Terminal plate
23. Terminal
24. Speedometer light
25. Terminal
26. Terminal—Not used with standard wiring
27. Terminal—Not used with standard wiring
28. Terminal
29. Terminal—Not used with standard wiring
30. Terminal
31. Terminal
32. Oil signal light
33. High beam indicator light
34. Generator indicator light
35. Headlamp
36. Left directional signal pilot lamp
37. Right directional signal pilot lamp
38. Tachometer light
39. Direction signal switch
40. Direction signal flasher
41. Left front direction lamp
42. Right front direction lamp
43. Left rear direction lamp
44. Right rear direction lamp

WIRING DIAGRAMS

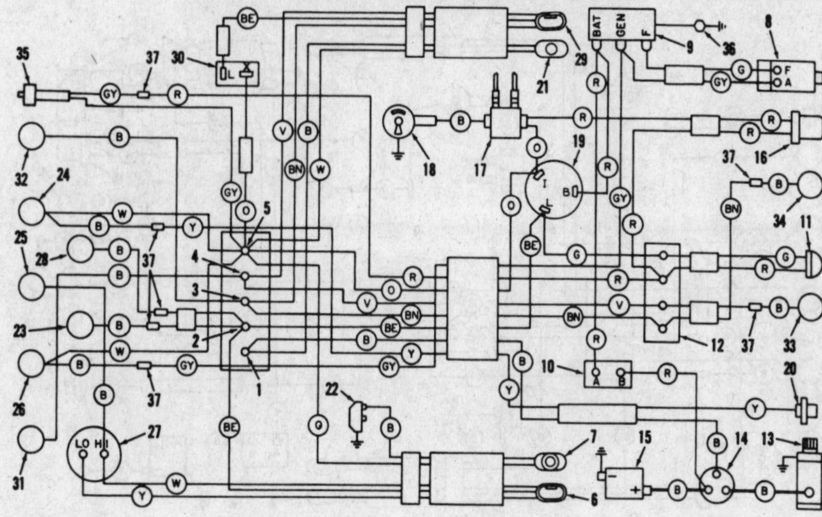

1970–71 XLH

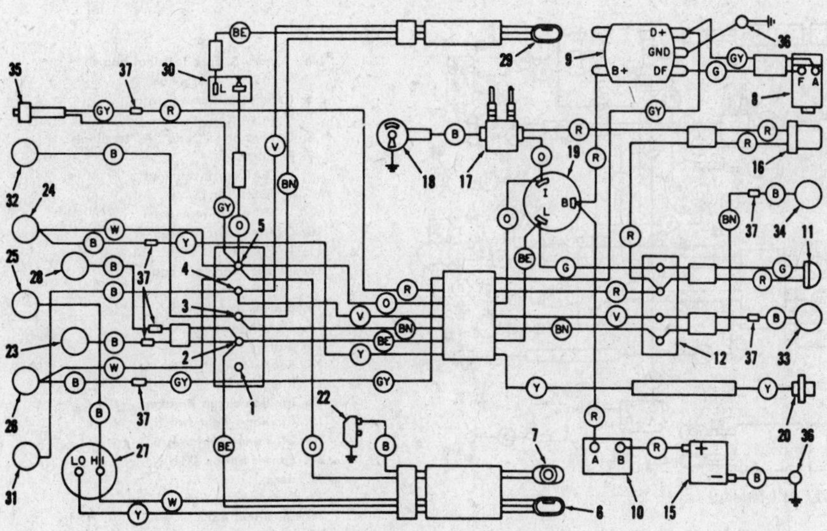

1970–71 XLCH

No's 1. thru 5. Fork terminal board terminals
6. Headlamp dimmer switch
7. Horn switch
8. Generator "F" and "A" terminals
9. Regulator
   "BAT" or B terminal
   "GEN" or D
   "F" or DF terminal
10. Overload circuit breaker
11. Tail lamp
12. Junction terminal board (4 terminals)
13. Starter motor (XLH)
14. Starter solenoid (XLH)
15. Battery
16. Rear stoplight switch
17. Ignition coil
18. Ignition circuit breaker
19. Ignition—light switch
20. Oil signal light switch
21. Starter button (XLH)
22. Horn
23. Speedometer light
24. Oil signal light
25. High beam indicator light
26. Generator indicator light
27. Headlamp
28. Tachometer light
29. Direction signal switch
30. Direction signal flasher
31. Left front direction lamp
32. Right front direction lamp
33. Left rear direction lamp
34. Right rear direction lamp
35. Front stoplight switch
36. Crankcase bolt
37. Connector
38. License lamp
39. Starter relay (XLH)

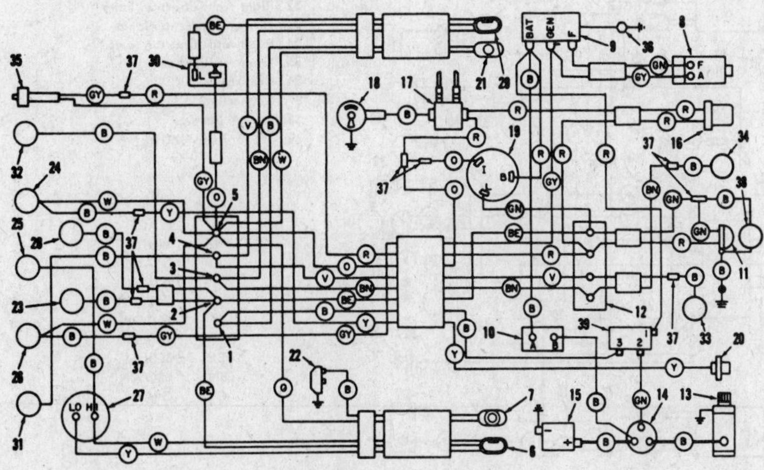

1972 and later XLH (standard seat)

KEY TO COLOR CODE

B	BLACK
W	WHITE
O	ORANGE
R	RED
G	GREEN
Y	YELLOW
V	VIOLET
BE	BLUE
BN	BROWN
GY	GRAY

WIRING DIAGRAMS

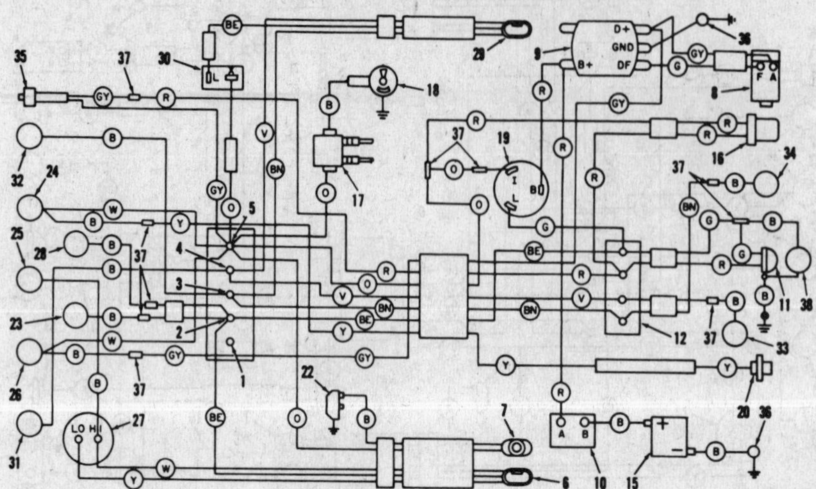

1972 and later XLCH (low seat)

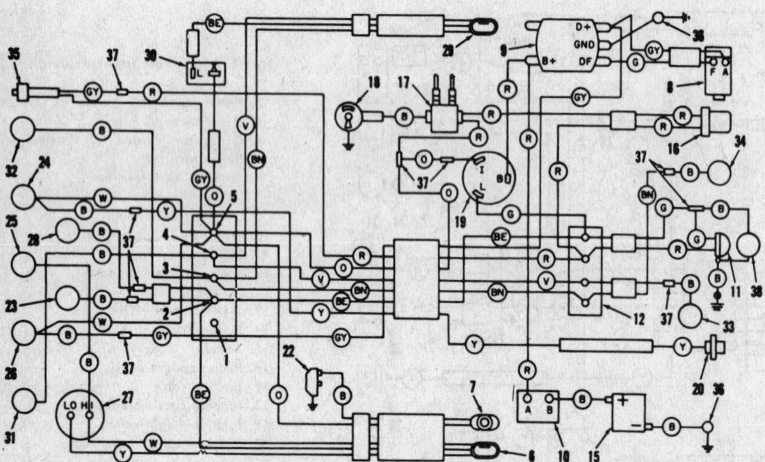

1972 and later XLCH (standard seat)

No's 1. thru 5. Fork terminal board terminals
6. Headlamp dimmer switch
7. Horn switch
8. Generator "F" and "A" terminals
9. Regulator
   "BAT" or B terminal
   "GEN" or D
   "F" or DF terminal
10. Overload circuit breaker
11. Tail lamp
12. Junction terminal board (4 terminals)
13. Starter motor (XLH)
14. Starter solenoid (XLH)
15. Battery
16. Rear stoplight switch
17. Ignition coil
18. Ignition circuit breaker
19. Ignition—light switch
20. Oil signal light switch
21. Starter button (XLH)
22. Horn
23. Speedometer light
24. Oil signal light
25. High beam indicator light
26. Generator indicator light
27. Headlamp
28. Tachometer light
29. Direction signal switch
30. Direction signal flasher
31. Left front direction lamp
32. Right front direction lamp
33. Left rear direction lamp
34. Right rear direction lamp
35. Front stoplight switch
36. Crankcase bolt
37. Connector
38. License lamp
39. Starter relay (XLH)

KEY TO COLOR CODE

B	BLACK
W	WHITE
O	ORANGE
R	RED
G	GREEN
Y	YELLOW
V	VIOLET
BE	BLUE
BN	BROWN
GY	GRAY

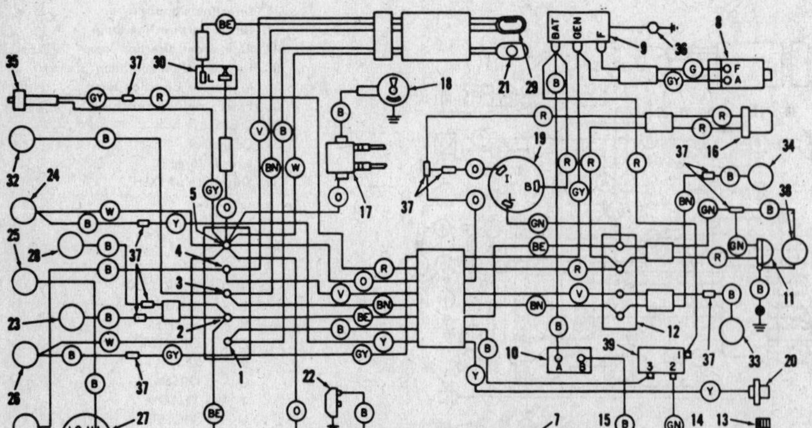

1972 and later XLH (low seat)

WIRING DIAGRAMS

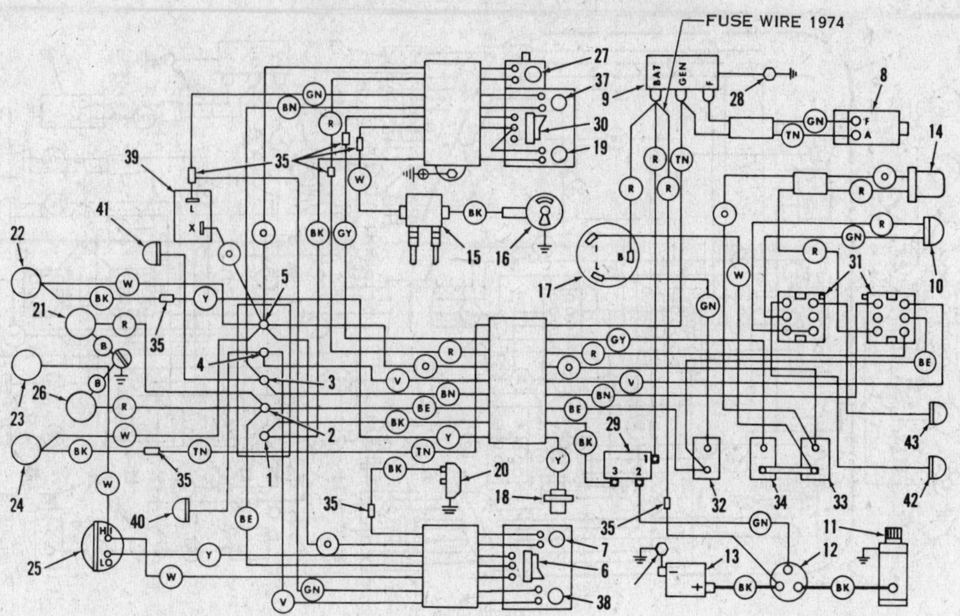

XL (1973–1974)

1. Fork terminal board terminal
2. Fork terminal board terminal
3. Fork terminal board terminal
4. Fork terminal board terminal
5. Fork terminal board terminal
6. Headlamp dimmer switch
7. Horn switch
8. Generator "F" and "A" terminals
9. Regulator
   "BAT" or B+ terminal
   "GEN" or D+
   "F" or DF terminal
10. Tail lamp
11. Starter motor
12. Starter solenoid
13. Battery
14. Rear stoplight switch
15. Ignition coil
16. Ignition breaker (timer)
17. Ignition—light switch
18. Oil signal light switch
19. Starter button
20. Horn
21. Speedometer light
22. Oil signal light
23. High beam indicator light
24. Generator indicator light
25. Headlamp
26. Tachometer light
27. Front stoplight switch
28. Crankcase bolt
29. Starter relay
30. Engine stop switch
31. Rear harness connector
32. Lighting circuit breaker
33. Accessory circuit breaker
34. Ignition circuit breaker
35. Connector
36. Frame bolt
37. Right direction signal switch
38. Left direction signal switch
39. Direction signal flasher
40. Left front direction lamp
41. Right front direction lamp
42. Left rear direction lamp
43. Right rear direction lamp

KEY TO COLOR CODE	
B	BLACK
W	WHITE
O	ORANGE
R	RED
G	GREEN
Y	YELLOW
V	VIOLET
BE	BLUE
BN	BROWN
GY	GRAY
TN	TAN

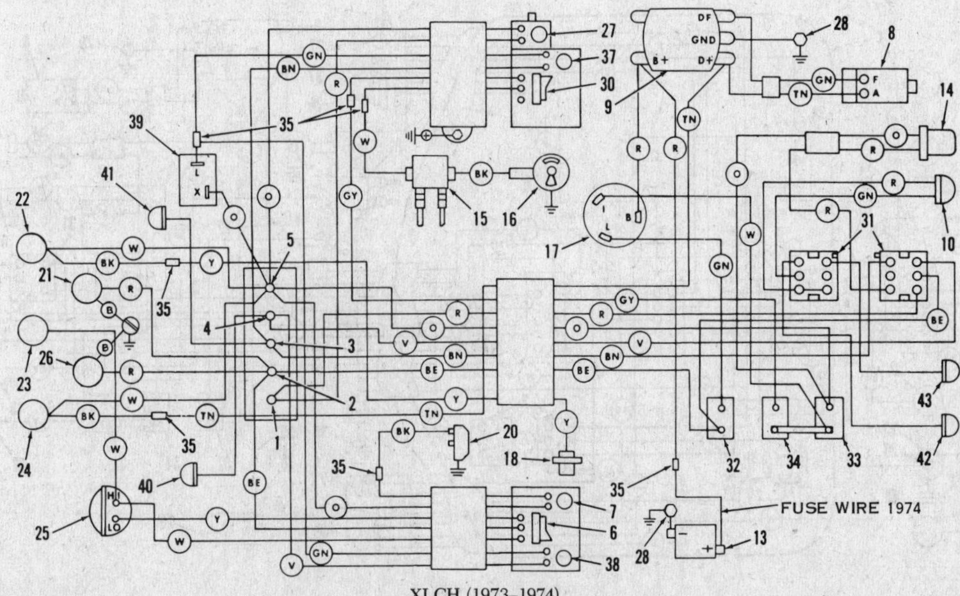

XLCH (1973–1974)

WIRING DIAGRAMS

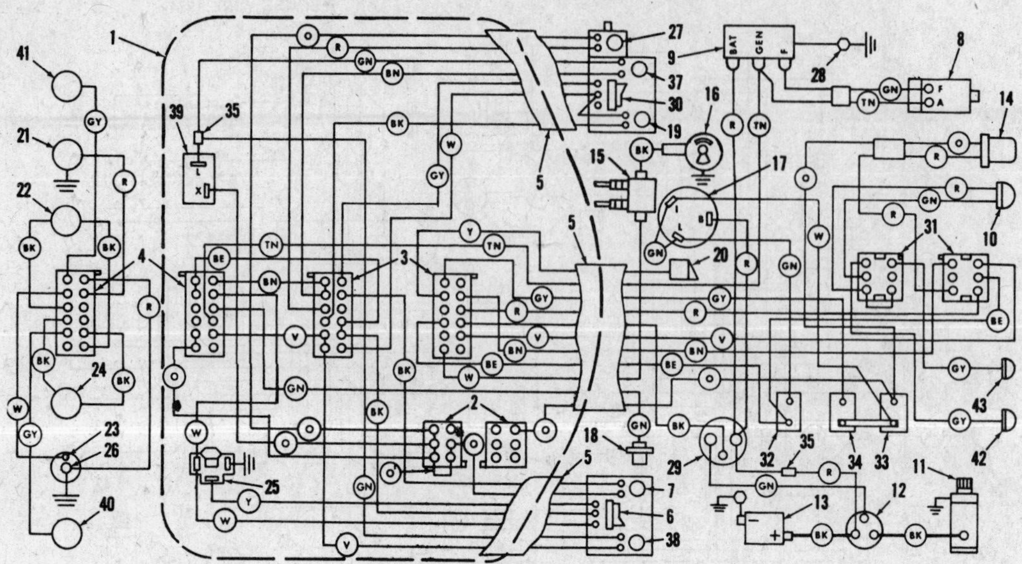

XL (1975–1976)

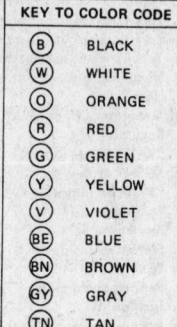

1. Headlamp housing
2. Socket-plug combination
3. Socket-plug combination
4. Socket-plug combination
5. Wiring harness
6. Headlamp dimmer switch
7. Horn switch
8. Generator "F" and "A" terminals
9. Regulator
   "Bat" or B+ terminal
   "Gen" or D+
   "F" or DF terminal
10. Tail lamp
11. Starter motor
12. Starter solenoid
13. Battery
14. Rear stoplight switch
15. Ignition coil
16. Ignition breaker (timer)
17. Ignition—light switch
18. Oil signal light switch
19. Starter button
20. Horn
21. Speedometer light
22. Oil signal light
23. High beam indicator light
24. Generator indicator light
25. Headlamp socket
26. Tachometer light
27. Front stoplight switch
28. Crankcase bolt
29. Starter relay
30. Engine stop switch
31. Rear harness connector
32. Lighting circuit breaker
33. Accessory circuit breaker
34. Ignition circuit breaker
35. Connector
37. Right direction signal switch
38. Left direction signal switch
39. Direction signal flasher
40. Left front direction lamp
41. Right front direction lamp
42. Left rear direction lamp
43. Right rear direction lamp

KEY TO COLOR CODE	
(B)	BLACK
(W)	WHITE
(O)	ORANGE
(R)	RED
(G)	GREEN
(Y)	YELLOW
(V)	VIOLET
(BE)	BLUE
(BN)	BROWN
(GY)	GRAY
(TN)	TAN

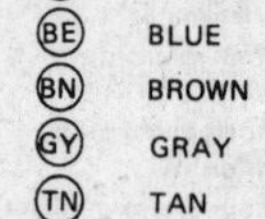

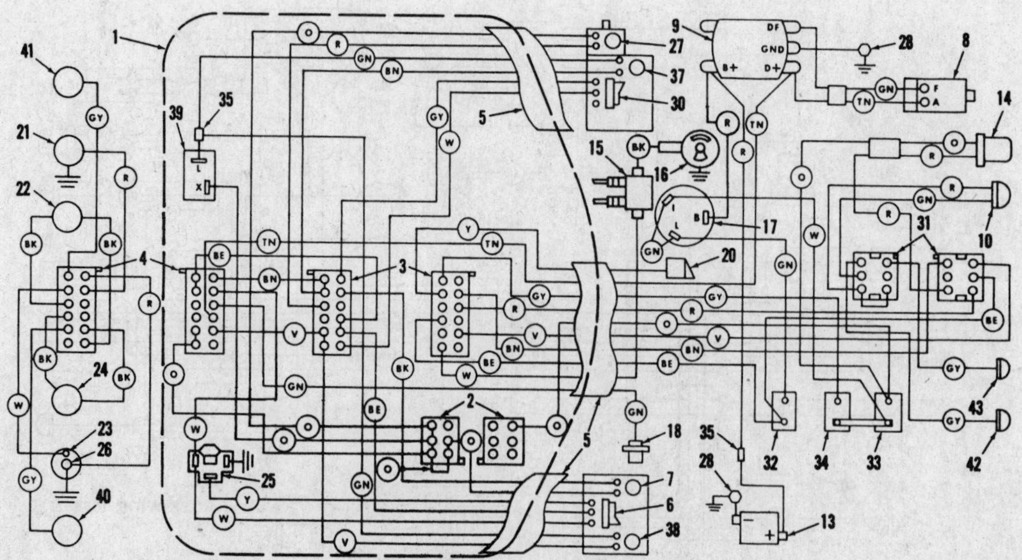

XLCH (1975–1976)

WIRING DIAGRAMS

A. Conduit (four wire)—Red, green, black and yellow
B. Conduit (one wire)—Green
C. Conduit (four wire)—Red, green, yellow and black
D. Left handlebar (loose wires)—red with black tracer, black with red tracer, red with yellow tracer, 2 black wires
E. Right handlebar (loose wires)—2 Black wires
F. Conduit (two wire)—2 Red wires
G. Conduit (one wire)—Yellow
H. Conduit (three wire)—Black, white and yellow
J. Conduit (two wire)—Red and green
K. Conduit (one wire)—Red
L. Conduit (two wire)—Green and red
M. Conduit (one wire)—Black
N. Conduit (one wire)—Black
O. Conduit (one wire)—Black
P. Conduit (two wire)—2 Black wires
Q. Conduit (one wire)—Red

KEY TO COLOR CODE	
R	RED
G	GREEN
B	BLACK
Y	YELLOW
W	WHITE
RB	RED WITH BLACK TRACER
BR	BLACK WITH RED TRACER
RY	RED WITH YELLOW TRACER

1965–67 Electra Glide

LATE 1966 CIRCUIT BREAKER

1. Switch terminal—Switch supply
2. Switch terminal—Headlamp
3. Switch terminal—Not used with standard wiring
4. Switch terminal—Tail lamp
5. Switch terminal—Ignition coil
6. Ignition—Light switch—See terminals 1 through 5
7. Junction terminal
8. Junction terminal
9. Terminal
10. Terminal
11. Terminal—Not used with standard wiring
12. Terminal—Not used with standard wiring
13. Regulator
14. Tail and stop lamp
15. Battery positive terminal
16. Battery negative terminal
17. Oil pressure signal switch
19. Horn switch
20. Terminal—Not used with standard wiring
21. Terminal
22. Terminal
23. Terminal—Not used with standard wiring
24. Terminal
25. Terminal
26. Ignition circuit breaker
27. Stop lamp switch
28. Generator signal light
29. Terminal—Not used with standard wiring
30. Terminal—Not used with standard wiring
31. Terminal
32. Generator "F" terminal
33. Generator "A" terminal
34. Starter solenoid
35. Starter motor
36. Ignition coil
37. Terminal plate
38. Terminal box—See terminals 39 through 43
39. Terminal
40. Terminal
41. Terminal
42. Terminal
43. Terminal
44. Speedometer light
45. Terminal plate top mounting screw (ground)
46. Headlamp
47. Neutral indicator light
48. Neutral switch
49. Starter button
50. Oil signal light
51. Horn
52. Circuit breaker

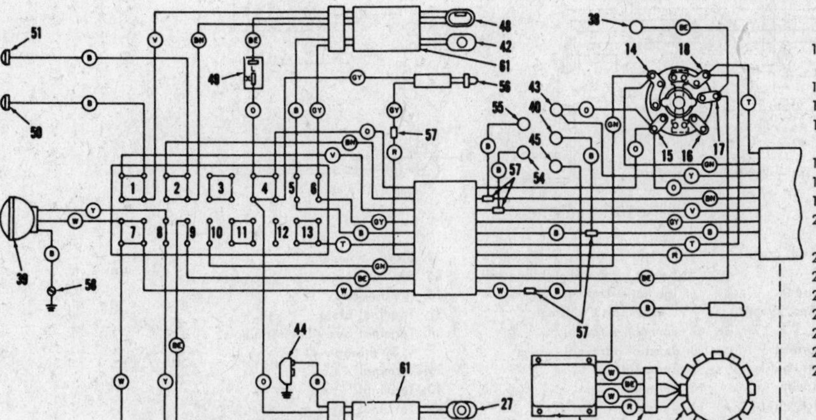

1. to 13. Front terminal board terminals
14. Switch tail lamp terminal
15. Switch ignition terminal
16. Switch terminal (not used with standard wiring)
17. Switch headlamp terminal
18. Switch supply terminal
19. Regulator-rectifier module
20. Alternator to module connector plug
21. Alternator stator
22. Tail and stop lamp
23. Battery positive terminal
24. Battery negative terminal
25. Oil pressure signal switch
26. Handlebar headlamp switch
27. Horn switch

KEY TO COLOR CODE	
B	BLACK
BN	BROWN
G	GREEN
R	RED
W	WHITE
Y	YELLOW
BE	BLUE
V	VIOLET
O	ORANGE
GY	GRAY
T	TAN

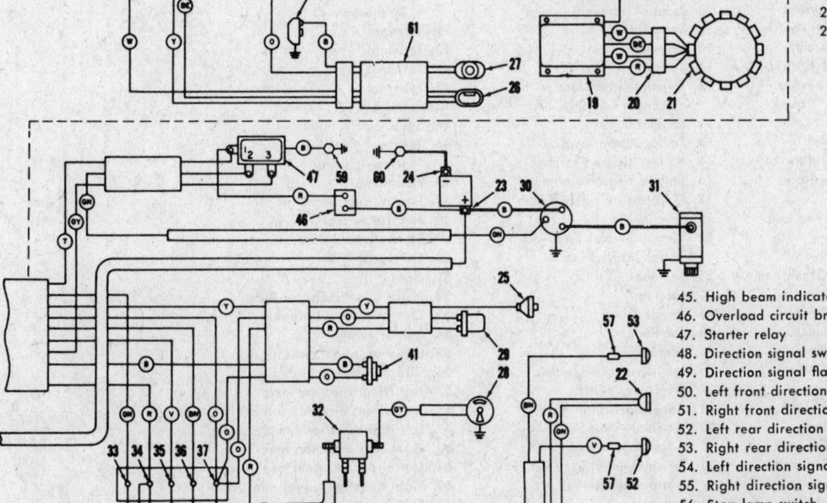

1970 Electra Glide

28. Ignition circuit breaker
29. Stop lamp switch—rear
30. Starter solenoid
31. Starter motor
32. Ignition coil
33. Rear terminal board terminal—top
34. Rear terminal board terminal
35. Rear terminal board terminal
37. Rear terminal board terminal—bottom
38. Speedometer light
39. Headlamp
40. Neutral indicator light
41. Neutral switch
42. Starter button
43. Oil signal light
44. Horn
45. High beam indicator lamp
46. Overload circuit breaker
47. Starter relay
48. Direction signal switch
49. Direction signal flasher
50. Left front direction lamp
51. Right front direction lamp
52. Left rear direction lamp
53. Right rear direction lamp
54. Left direction signal pilot lamp
55. Right direction signal pilot lamp
56. Stop lamp switch—front
57. Connector
58. Terminal board mounting screw
59. Transmission stud
60. Frame lug bolt
61. Handlebar

WIRING DIAGRAMS

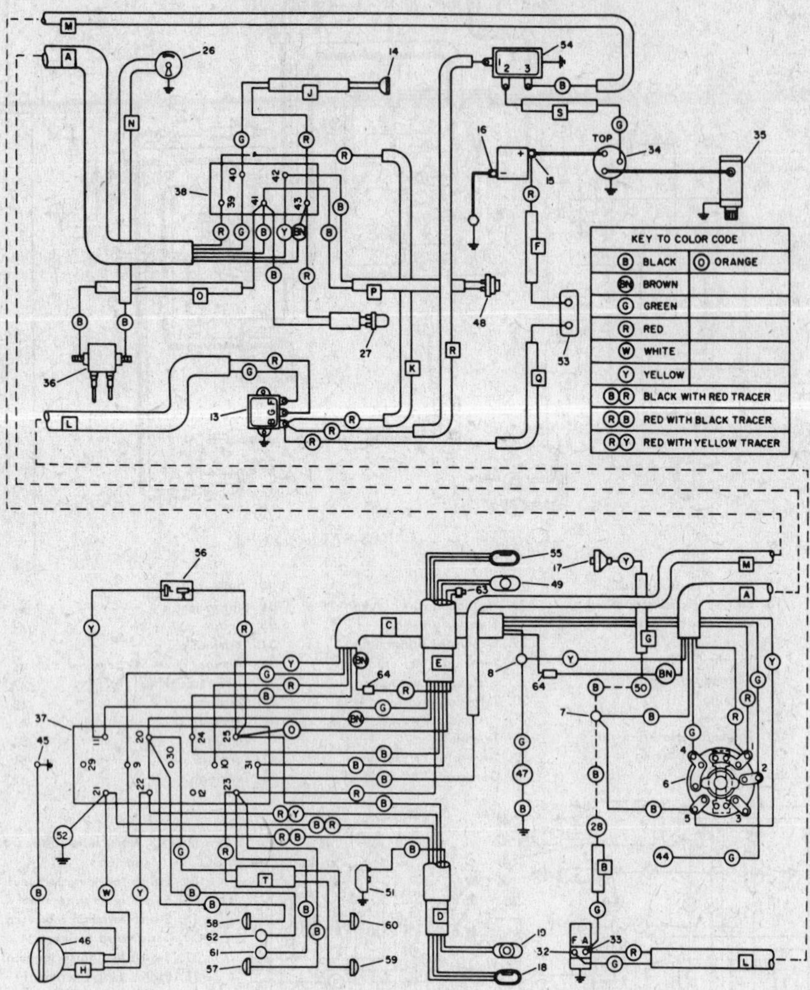

1968–69 Electra Glide

A. Conduit (four wire)—Red, green, black and yellow
B. Conduit (one wire)—Green
C. Conduit (four wire)—Red, green, yellow and black
D. Left handlebar (loose wires)—Red with black tracer, black with red tracer, red with yellow tracer, 2 black wires
E. Right handlebar (loose wires)—Red, green, brown, 2 black wires
F. Conduit (one wire)—Red
G. Conduit (one wire)—Yellow
H. Conduit (three wire)—Black, white and yellow
J. Conduit (two wires)—Red and green
K. Conduit (one wire)—Red
L. Conduit (two wire)—Green and red
M. Conduit (one wire)—Black
N. Conduit (one wire)—Black
O. Conduit (one wire)—Black
P. Conduit (two wire)—2 Black wires
Q. Conduit (one wire)—Red
R. Conduit (one wire)—Red
S. Conduit (one wire)—Green
T. Conduit (two wire)—Red and green

1. Switch terminal—Switch supply
2. Switch terminal—Headlamp
3. Switch terminal—Not used with standard wiring
4. Switch terminal—Tail lamp
5. Switch terminal—Ignition coil
6. Ignition—Light switch—See terminals 1 through 5
7. Junction terminal
8. Junction terminal
9. Terminal
10. Terminal
11. Terminal
12. Terminal—Not used with standard wiring
13. Regulator
14. Tail and stop lamp
15. Battery positive terminal
16. Battery negative terminal
17. Oil pressure signal switch
19. Horn switch
20. Terminal—Not used with standard wiring
21. Terminal
22. Terminal
23. Terminal
24. Terminal
25. Terminal
26. Ignition circuit breaker
27. Stop lamp switch
28. Generator signal light
29. Terminal—Not used with standard wiring
30. Terminal—Not used with standard wiring
31. Terminal
32. Generator "F" terminal
33. Generator "A" terminal
34. Starter solenoid
35. Starter motor
36. Ignition coil
37. Terminal plate
38. Terminal box—See terminals 39 through 43
39. Terminal
40. Terminal
41. Terminal
42. Terminal
43. Terminal
44. Speedometer light
45. Terminal plate top mounting screw (ground)
46. Headlamp
47. Neutral indicator light
48. Neutral switch
49. Starter button
50. Oil signal light
51. Horn
52. Hight beam indicator lamp
53. Overload circuit breaker
54. Starter relay
55. Direction signal switch
56. Direction signal flasher
57. Left front direction lamp
58. Right front direction lamp
59. Left rear direction lamp
60. Right rear direction lamp
61. Left direction signal pilot lamp
62. Right direction signal pilot lamp
63. Stop lamp front switch
64. Connector

WIRING DIAGRAMS

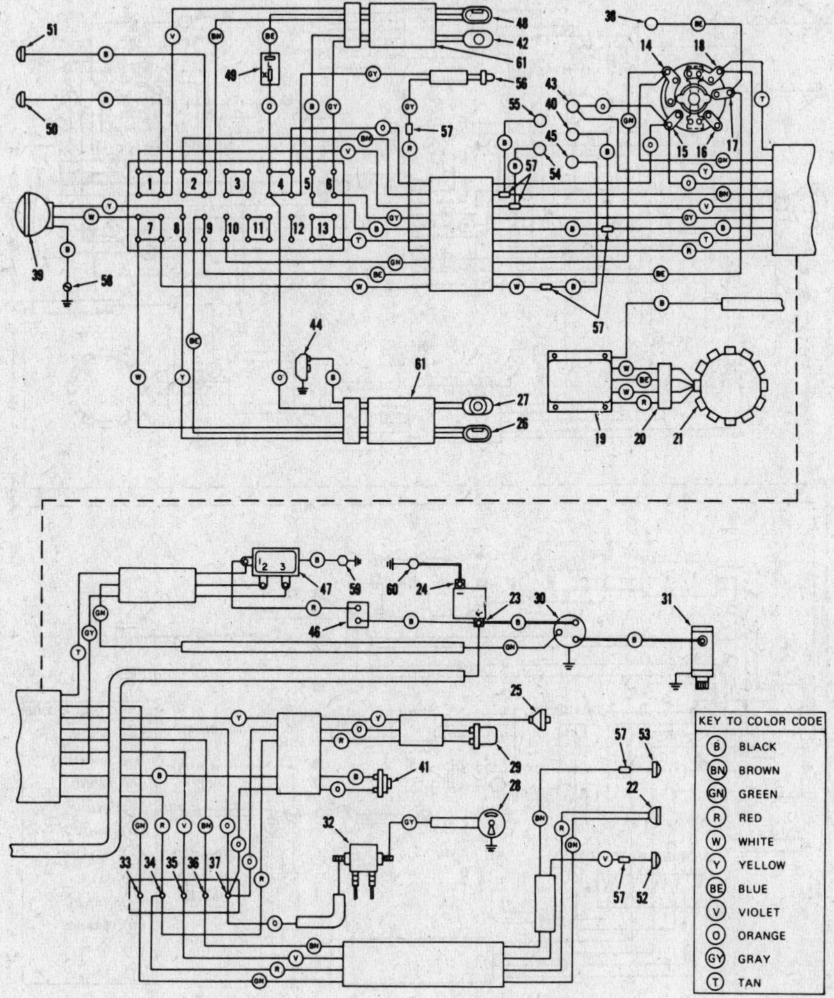

KEY TO COLOR CODE
B BLACK
BN BROWN
GN GREEN
R RED
W WHITE
Y YELLOW
BE BLUE
V VIOLET
O ORANGE
GY GRAY
T TAN

1971 Electra Glide

1. to 13. Front terminal board terminals
14. Switch tail lamp terminal
15. Switch ignition terminal
16. Switch terminal (not used with standard wiring)
17. Switch headlamp terminal
18. Switch supply terminal
19. Regulator-rectifier module
20. Alternator to module connector plug
21. Alternator stator
22. Tail and stop lamp
23. Battery positive terminal
24. Battery negative terminal
25. Oil pressure signal switch
26. Handlebar headlamp switch
27. Horn switch
28. Ignition circuit breaker
29. Stop lamp switch—rear
30. Starter solenoid
31. Starter motor
32. Ignition coil
33. Rear terminal board terminal top
34. Rear terminal board terminal
35. Rear terminal board terminal
37. Rear terminal board terminal—bottom
38. Speedometer light
39. Headlamp
40. Neutral indicator light
41. Neutral switch
42. Starter button
43. Oil signal light
44. Horn
45. High beam indicator lamp
46. Overload circuit breaker
47. Starter relay
48. Direction signal switch
49. Direction signal flasher
50. Left front direction lamp
51. Right front direction lamp
52. Left rear direction lamp
53. Right rear direction lamp
54. Left direction signal pilot lamp
55. Right direction signal pilot lamp
56. Stop lamp switch—front
57. Connector
58. Terminal board mounting screw
59. Transmission stud
60. Frame lug bolt
61. Handlebar

WIRING DIAGRAMS

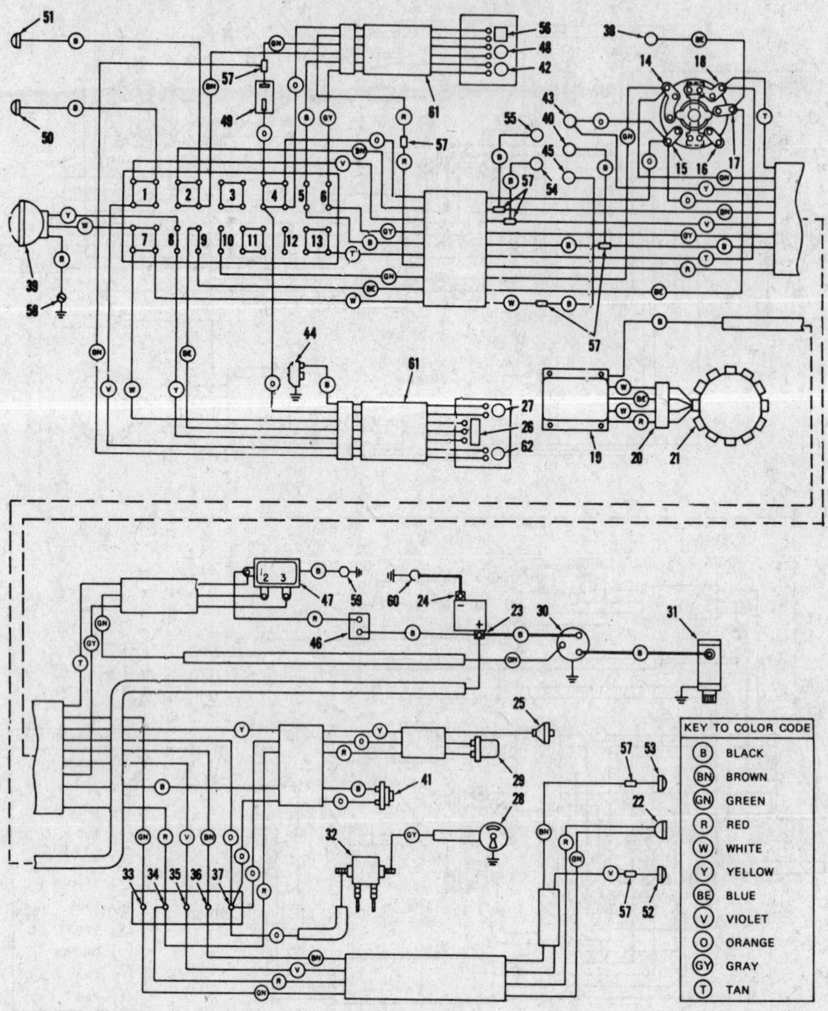

1972 Electra Glide

1. to 13. Front terminal board terminals
14. Switch tail lamp terminal
15. Switch ignition terminal
16. Switch terminal (not used with standard wiring)
17. Switch headlamp terminal
18. Switch supply terminal
19. Regulator-rectifier module
20. Alternator to module connector plug
21. Alternator stator
22. Tail and stop lamp
23. Battery positive terminal
24. Battery negative terminal
25. Oil pressure signal switch
26. Handlebar headlamp switch
27. Horn switch
28. Ignition circuit breaker
29. Stop lamp switch—rear
30. Starter solenoid
31. Starter motor
32. Ignition coil
33. Rear terminal board terminal—top
34. Rear terminal board terminal
35. Rear terminal board terminal
37. Rear terminal board terminal—bottom
38. Speedometer light
39. Headlamp
40. Neutral indicator light
41. Neutral switch
42. Starter button
43. Oil signal light
44. Horn
45. High beam indicator lamp
46. Overload circuit breaker
47. Starter relay
48. Direction signal switch
49. Direction signal flasher
50. Left front direction lamp
51. Right front direction lamp
52. Left rear direction lamp
53. Right rear direction lamp
54. Left direction signal pilot lamp
55. Right direction signal pilot lamp
56. Stop lamp switch—front
57. Connector
58. Terminal board mounting screw
59. Transmission stud
60. Frame lug bolt
61. Handlebar
62. Left direction signal switch

WIRING DIAGRAMS

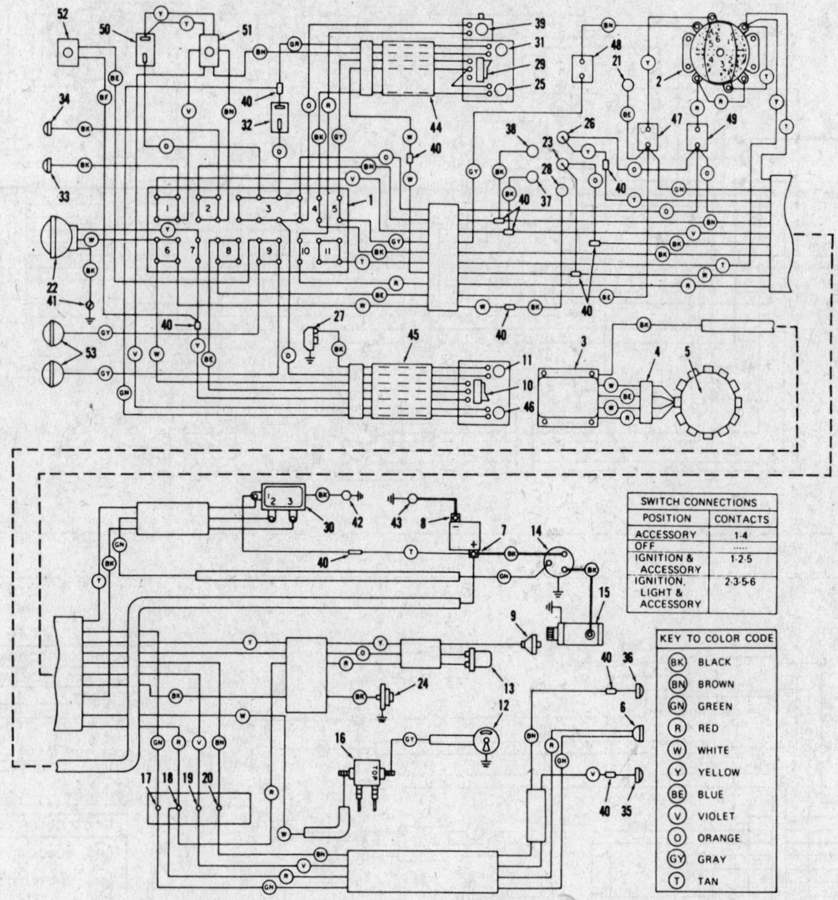

FL/FLH (1973–1974)

1. Front terminal board terminals (1 to 11)
2. Switch terminals (1 to 6)
3. Regulator-rectifier module
4. Alternator to module connector plug
5. Alternator stator
6. Tail and stop lamp
7. Battery positive terminal
8. Battery negative terminal
9. Oil pressure signal switch
10. Headlamp beam switch
11. Horn switch
12. Ignition breaker (timer)
13. Stop lamp switch—rear
14. Starter solenoid
15. Starter motor
16. Ignition coil
17. Rear terminal board terminal—top
18. Rear terminal board terminal
19. Rear terminal board terminal
20. Rear terminal board terminal —bottom
21. Speedometer light
22. Headlamp
23. Neutral indicator light
24. Neutral switch
25. Starter button
26. Oil signal light
27. Horn
28. High beam indicator lamp
29. Engine stop switch
30. Starter relay
31. Right direction signal switch
32. Direction signal flasher
33. Left front direction lamp
34. Right front direction lamp
35. Left rear direction lamp
36. Right rear direction lamp
37. Left direction signal pilot lamp
38. Right direction signal pilot lamp
39. Stop lamp switch—front
40. Connector
41. Terminal board mounting screw
42. Transmission stud
43. Frame lug bolt
44. Right handlebar
45. Left handlebar
46. Left direction signal switch
47. Lighting circuit breaker
48. Ignition circuit breaker
49. Accessories circuit breaker
50. Emergency flasher
51. Emergency flasher switch
52. Passing lamp switch
53. Passing lamp

WIRING DIAGRAMS

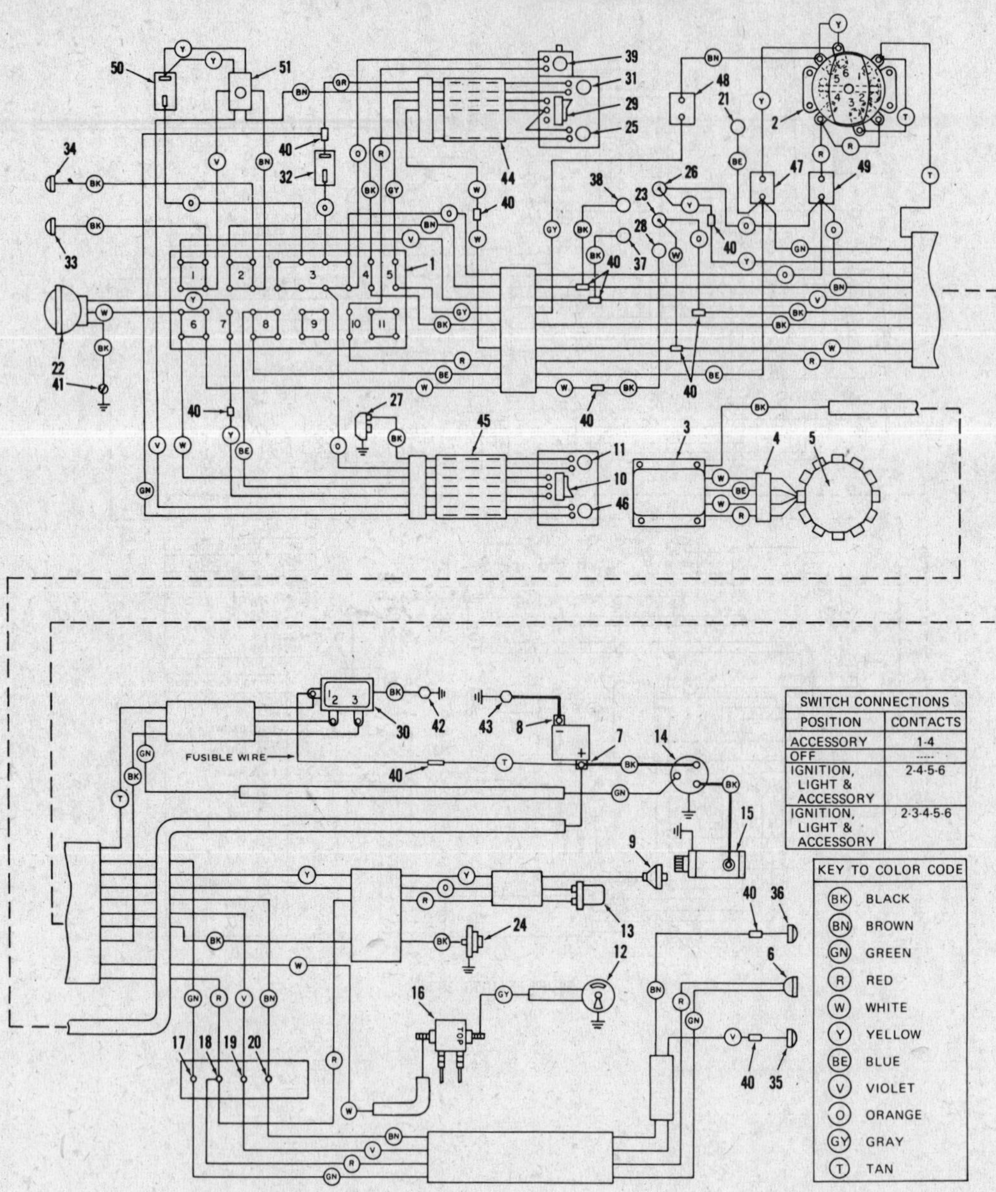

SWITCH CONNECTIONS	
POSITION	CONTACTS
ACCESSORY	1-4
OFF	-----
IGNITION, LIGHT & ACCESSORY	2-4-5-6
IGNITION, LIGHT & ACCESSORY	2-3-4-5-6

FL/FLH (1975)

1. Front terminal board (terminals 1 to 11)
2. Switch (terminals 1 to 6)
3. Regulator-rectifier module
4. Alternator to module connector plug
5. Alternator stator
6. Tail and stop lamp
7. Battery positive terminal
8. Battery negative terminal
9. Oil pressure signal switch
10. Headlamp beam switch
11. Horn switch
12. Ignition breaker (timer)
13. Stop lamp switch—rear
14. Starter solenoid
15. Starter motor
16. Ignition coil
17. Rear terminal board terminal—top
18. Rear terminal board terminal
19. Rear terminal board terminal
20. Rear terminal board terminal—bottom
21. Speedometer light
22. Headlamp
23. Neutral indicator light
24. Neutral switch
25. Starter button
26. Oil signal light
27. Horn
28. High beam indicator lamp
29. Engine stop switch
30. Starter relay
31. Right direction signal switch
32. Direction signal flasher
33. Left front direction lamp
34. Right front direction lamp
35. Left rear direction lamp
36. Right rear direction lamp
37. Left direction signal pilot lamp
38. Right direction signal pilot lamp
39. Stop lamp switch—front
40. Connector
41. Terminal board mounting screw
42. Transmission stud
43. Frame lug bolt
44. Right handlebar
45. Left handlebar
46. Left direction signal switch
47. Lighting circuit breaker
48. Ignition circuit breaker
49. Accessories circuit breaker
50. Emergency flasher
51. Emergency flasher switch

WIRING DIAGRAMS

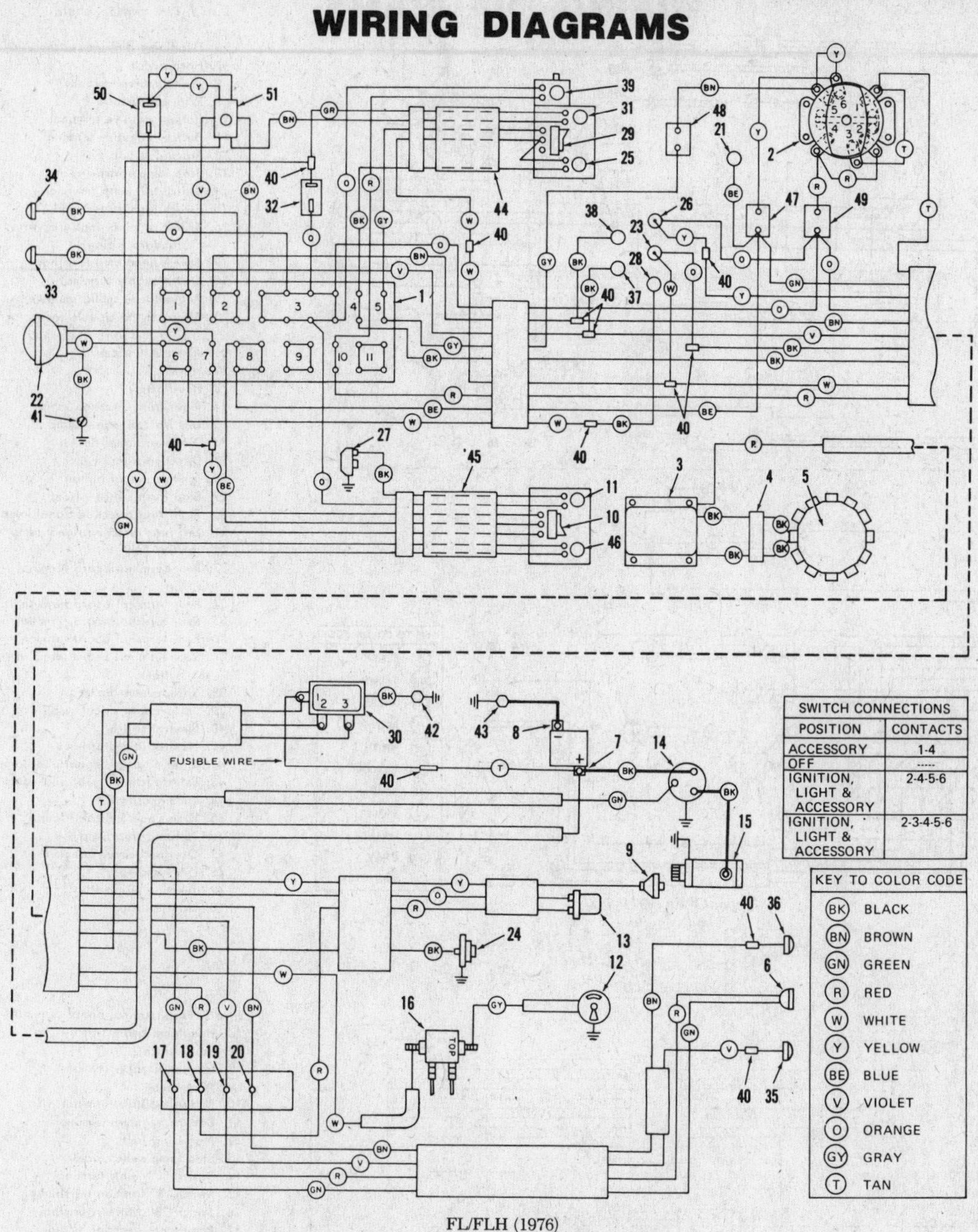

SWITCH CONNECTIONS	
POSITION	CONTACTS
ACCESSORY	1-4
OFF	-----
IGNITION, LIGHT & ACCESSORY	2-4-5-6
IGNITION, LIGHT & ACCESSORY	2-3-4-5-6

FL/FLH (1976)

1. Front terminal board (terminals 1 to 11)
2. Switch (terminals 1 to 6)
3. Regulator-rectifier module
4. Alternator to module connector plug
5. Alternator stator
6. Tail and stop lamp
7. Battery positive terminal
8. Battery negative terminal
9. Oil pressure signal switch
10. Headlamp beam switch
11. Horn switch
12. Ignition breaker (timer)
13. Stop lamp switch—rear
14. Starter solenoid
15. Starter motor
16. Ignition coil
17. Rear terminal board terminal—top
18. Rear terminal board terminal
19. Rear terminal board terminal
20. Rear terminal board terminal—bottom
21. Speedometer light
22. Headlamp
23. Neutral indicator light
24. Neutral switch
25. Starter button
26. Oil signal light
27. Horn
28. High beam indicator lamp
29. Engine stop switch
30. Starter relay
31. Right direction signal switch
32. Direction signal flasher
33. Left front direction lamp
34. Right front direction lamp
35. Left rear direction lamp
36. Right rear direction lamp
37. Left direction signal pilot lamp
38. Right direction signal pilot lamp
39. Stop lamp switch—front
40. Connector
41. Terminal board mounting screw
42. Transmission stud
43. Frame lug bolt
44. Right handlebar
45. Left handlebar
46. Left direction signal switch
47. Lighting circuit breaker
48. Ignition circuit breaker
49. Accessories circuit breaker
50. Emergeny flasher
51. Emergency flasher switch

WIRING DIAGRAMS

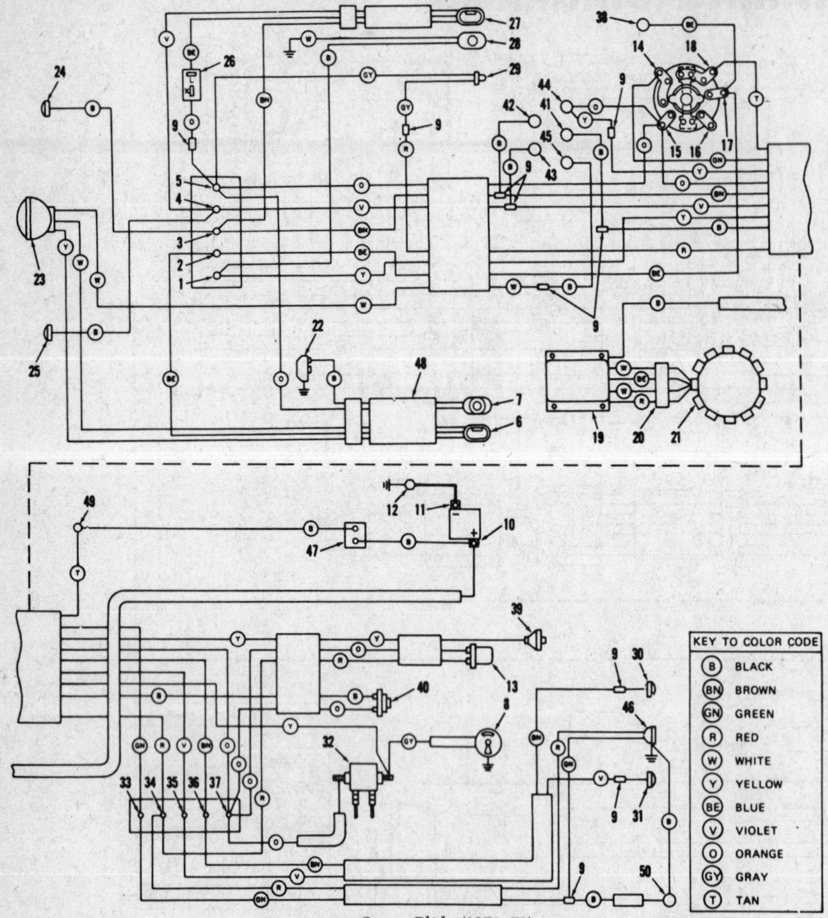

1. to 5. Fork terminal board terminals
6. Headlamp dimmer switch
7. Horn switch
8. Ignition circuit breaker
9. Wire connector
10. Battery positive terminal
11. Battery negative terminal
12. Frame lug bolt
13. Stop lamp switch—rear
14. Switch tail lamp terminal
15. Switch ignition terminal
16. Switch terminal (not used with standard wiring)
17. Switch headlamp terminal
18. Switch supply terminal
19. Regulator—rectifier module
20. Alternator to module connector plug
21. Alternator stator
22. Horn
23. Headlamp
24. Right front direction lamp
25. Left front direction lamp
26. Direction signal flasher
27. Direction signal switch
28. Ignition cutout button
29. Stop lamp switch—front
30. Right rear direction signal lamp
31. Left rear direction signal lamp
32. Ignition coil
33. Rear terminal board terminal—top
34. Rear terminal board terminal
35. Rear terminal board terminal
36. Rear terminal board terminal
37. Rear terminal board terminal—bottom
38. Speedometer light
39. Oil pressure signal switch
40. Neutral switch
41. Neutral indicator light
42. Right direction signal pilot lamp
43. Left direction signal pilot lamp
44. Oil signal lamp
45. High beam indicator lamp
46. Tail and stop lamp
47. Overload circuit breaker
48. Left handlebar
49. Junction terminal
50. License lamp

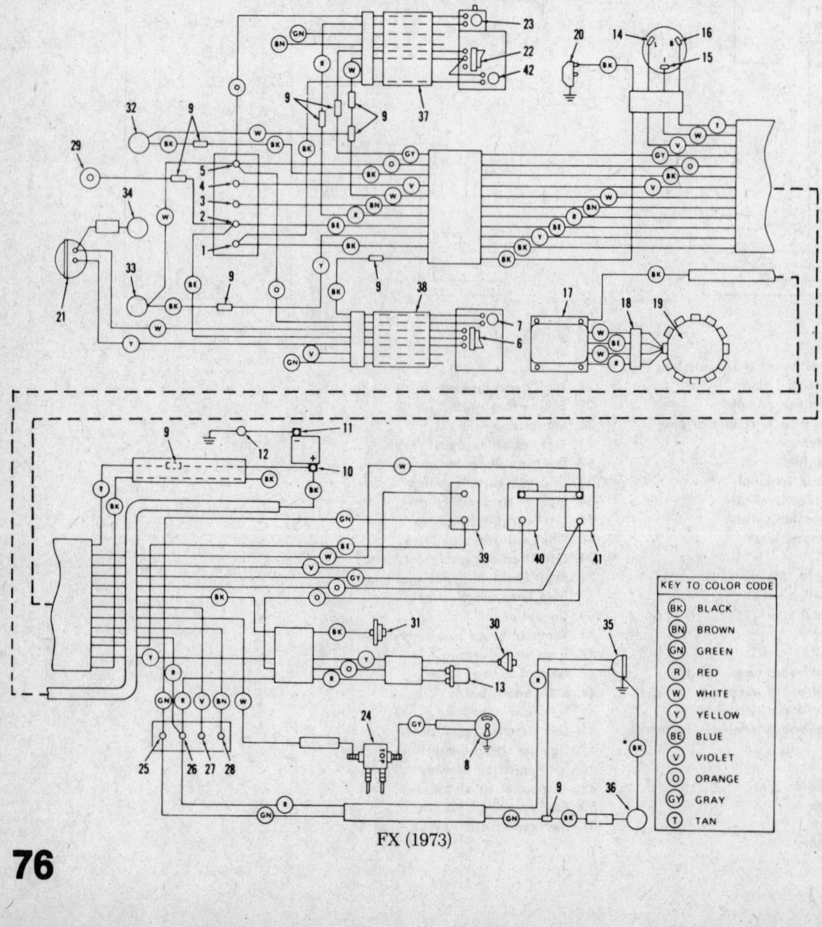

KEY TO COLOR CODE	
B	BLACK
BN	BROWN
GN	GREEN
R	RED
W	WHITE
Y	YELLOW
BE	BLUE
V	VIOLET
O	ORANGE
GY	GRAY
T	TAN

Super Glide (1971–72)

1. to 5. Fork terminal board terminals
6. Headlamp beam switch
7. Horn switch
8. Ignition breaker (timer)
9. Wire connector
10. Battery positive terminal
11. Battery negative terminal
12. Frame lug bolt
13. Stop lamp switch—rear
14. Switch "L" lights terminal
15. Switch "I" ignition terminal
16. Switch "B" battery terminal
17. Regulator—rectifier module
18. Alternator to module connector plug
19. Alternator stator
20. Horn
21. Headlamp
22. Engine stop switch
23. Stop lamp switch—front
24. Ignition coil
25. Rear terminal board terminal—top
26. Rear terminal board terminal
27. Rear terminal board terminal
28. Rear terminal board terminal—bottom
29. Speedometer light
30. Oil pressure signal switch
31. Neutral switch
32. Neutral indicator light
33. Oil signal lamp
34. High beam indicator lamp
35. Tail and stop lamp
36. License lamp
37. Right handlebar
38. Left handlebar
39. Lighting circuit breaker
40. Ignition circuit breaker
41. Accessories circuit breaker
42. Switch

KEY TO COLOR CODE	
BK	BLACK
BN	BROWN
GN	GREEN
R	RED
W	WHITE
Y	YELLOW
BE	BLUE
V	VIOLET
O	ORANGE
GY	GRAY
T	TAN

FX (1973)

WIRING DIAGRAMS

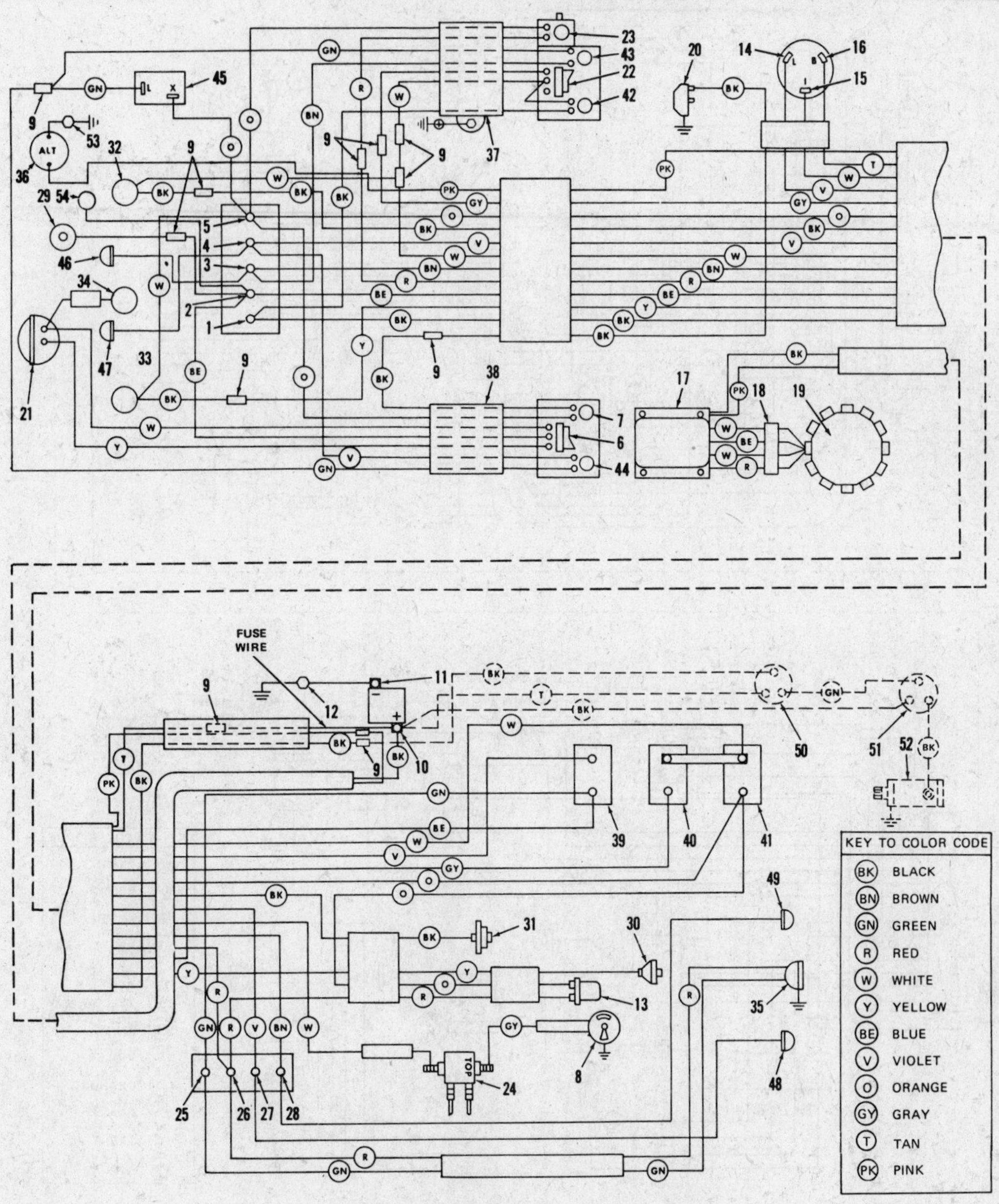

FX/FXE (1974)

1. to 5. Fork terminal board terminals
6. Headlamp beam switch
7. Horn switch
8. Ignition breaker (timer)
9. Wire connector
10. Battery positive terminal
11. Battery negative terminal
12. Frame lug bolt
13. Stop lamp switch—rear
14. Switch "L" lights terminal
15. Switch "I" ignition terminal
16. Switch "B" battery terminal
17. Regulator—recifier module
18. Alternator to module connector plug
19. Alternator stator
20. Horn
21. Headlamp
22. Engine stop switch
23. Stop lamp switch—front
24. Ignition coil
25. Rear terminal board terminal—top
26. Rear terminal board terminal
27. Rear terminal board terminal
28. Rear terminal board terminal—bottom
29. Speedometer light
30. Oil pressure signal switch
31. Neutral switch
32. Neutral indicator light
33. Oil signal lamp
34. High beam indicator lamp
35. Tail and stop lamp
36. Tachometer
37. Right handlebar
38. Left handlebar
39. Lighting circuit breaker
40. Ignition circuit breaker
41. Accessories circuit breaker
42. Switch
43. Right direction signal switch
44. Left direction signal switch
45. Direction signal flasher
46. Left front direction lamp
47. Right front direction lamp
48. Left rear direction lamp
49. Right rear direction lamp
50. Starter relay (FXE only)
51. Starter solenoid (FXE only)
52. Starter motor (FXE only)
53. Handlebar pinch bolt
54. Tachometer light

WIRING DIAGRAMS

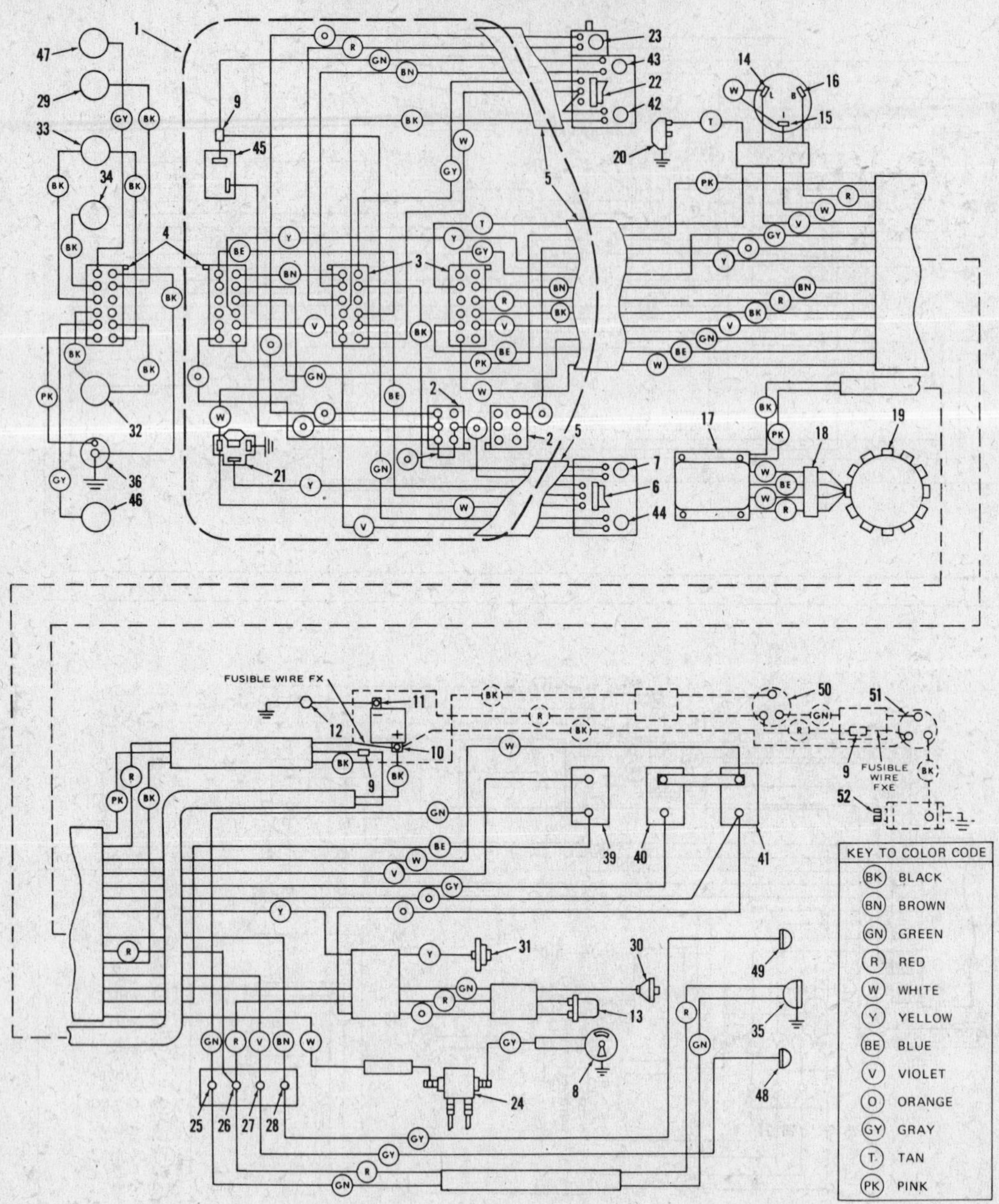

FX/FXE (1975)

1. Headlamp housing
2. Socket-plug combination
3. Socket-plug combination
4. Socket-plug combination
5. Wiring harness
6. Headlamp beam switch
7. Horn switch
8. Ignition breaker (timer)
9. Wire connector
10. Battery positive terminal
11. Battery negative terminal
12. Frame lug bolt
13. Stop lamp switch—rear
14. Switch "L" lights terminal
15. Switch "I" ignition terminal
16. Switch "B" battery terminal
17. Regulator-rectifier module
18. Alternator to module connector plug
19. Alternator stator
20. Horn
21. Headlamp socket
22. Engine stop switch
23. Stop lamp switch—front
24. Ignition coil
25. Rear terminal board terminal—top
26. Rear terminal board terminal
27. Rear terminal board terminal
28. Rear terminal board terminal—bottom
29. Speedometer light
30. Oil pressure signal switch
31. Neutral switch
32. Neutral indicator light
33. Oil signal lamp
34. High beam indicator lamp
35. Tail and stop lamp
36. Tachometer
39. Lighting circuit breaker
40. Ignition circuit breaker
41. Accessories circuit breaker
42. Starter switch
43. Right direction signal switch
44. Left direction signal switch
45. Direction signal flasher
46. Left front direction lamp
47. Right front direction lamp
48. Left rear direction lamp
49. Right rear direction lamp
50. Starter relay (FXE only)
51. Starter solenoid (FXE only)
52. Starter motor (FXE only)

WIRING DIAGRAMS

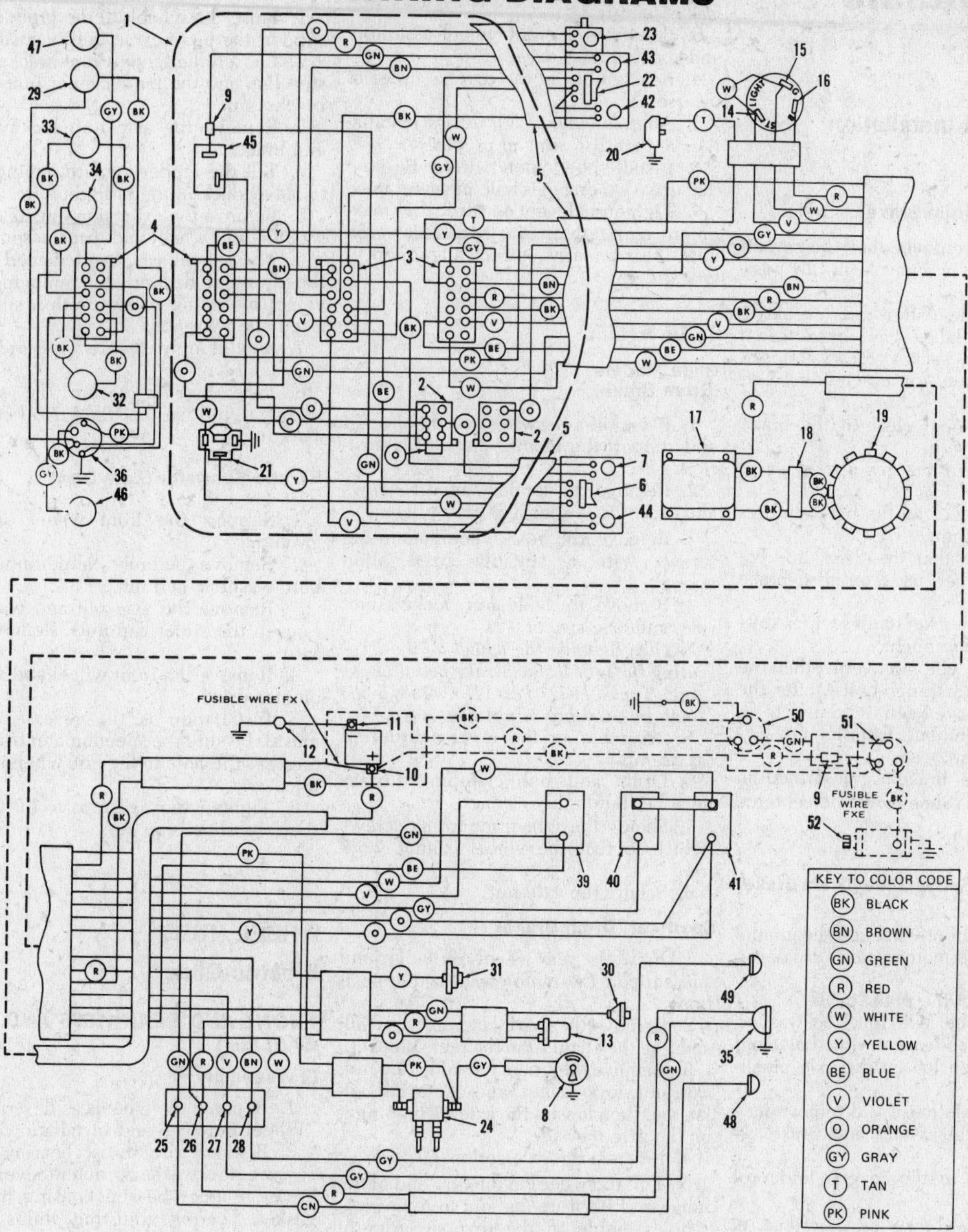

FX/FXE (1976)

1. Headlamp housing
2. Socket-plug combination
3. Socket-plug combination
4. Socket-plug combination
5. Wiring harness
6. Headlamp beam switch
7. Horn switch
8. Ignition breaker (timer)
9. Wire connector
10. Battery positive terminal
11. Battery negative terminal
12. Frame lug bolt
13. Stop lamp switch—rear
14. Switch "ST" lights terminal
15. Switch "G" ignition terminal
16. Switch "B" battery terminal
17. Regulator-rectifier module
18. Alternator to module connector plug
19. Alternator stator
20. Horn
21. Headlamp socket
22. Engine stop switch
23. Stop lamp switch—front
24. Ignition coil
25. Rear terminal board terminal—top
26. Rear terminal board terminal
27. Rear terminal board terminal
28. Rear terminal board terminal—bottom
29. Speedometer light
30. Oil pressure signal switch
31. Neutral switch
32. Neutral indicator light
33. Oil signal lamp
34. High beam indicator lamp
35. Tail and stop lamp
36. Tachometer
39. Lighting circuit breaker
40. Ignition circuit breaker
41. Accessories circuit breaker
42. Starter switch
43. Right direction signal switch
44. Left direction signal switch
45. Direction signal flasher
46. Left front direction lamp
47. Right front direction lamp
48. Left rear direction lamp
49. Right rear direction lamp
50. Starter relay (FXE only)
51. Starter solenoid (FXE only)
52. Starter motor (FXE only)

CHASSIS

WHEELS

Removal and Installation

FRONT WHEEL

Electra-Glide (Drum Brake)

1. Raise the front wheel off the ground and support the motorcycle in this position.
2. Remove the cotter pin (or clevis pin), axle nut, flat washer, bushings (if applicable), and socket screws. Loosen the slider capnuts (or pinch-bolts) and remove the axle.
3. Lift the wheel clear of the brake drum and remove it.
4. Assemble in the reverse order of disassembly.
5. Thoroughly clean the brake linings and the brake drum.
6. Make sure that the disc slips between the caliper pads on disc brake models.
7. Secure the socket screws with a suitably sized allen wrench.
8. Secure the axle nut evenly, then the slider capnuts (or pinch-bolts), after the socket screws have been tightened, to attain proper alignment. Install a new cotter (or clevis pin).
9. Adjust the brake as described in "Maintenance." Shoes must be centered in drum.

Sportster and Super Glide (Drum Brake)

1. Raise the front wheel off the ground and support the motorcycle in this position.
2. Disconnect the brake cable.
3. Remove the axle nut, lockwasher, brake anchor, shoe centering bolt, and lockwasher, then loosen the axle pinch-bolt.
4. Tap the axle loose and remove it.
5. Remove the wheel and brake assembly.
6. Assemble in the reverse order of disassembly.
7. Adjust the brake as described in "Maintenance." Shoes must be centered in drum.

Electra-Glide (Disc Brake)

1. Support the front wheel off the ground.
2. Remove the axle nut cotter pin, axle nut, and washers.
3. Loosen the two fork slider cap nuts and pull out the axle. Remove the wheel.
4. Installation is the reverse of removal. Tighten the axle nut to 50 ft lbs.

FX and Sportster (Early Disc)

1. Raise the front wheel off the ground and support the motorcycle in this position.
2. Remove axle nut and axle nut lock washer. Loosen the slider capnuts. Using a soft hammer, tap the left end of the axle to loosen and start it out. Pull axle out of fork assembly.
3. Remove the front wheel assembly and speedometer drive.
4. Reassemble in the reverse order of disassembly.
5. Align the brake pads during installation so that disc slips in properly.
6. Install speedometer drive. Be sure that drive ear engages hole in wheel hub.
7. Tighten axle nut to 50 ft lbs (maximum) and tighten the two slider capnuts. This ensures correct alignment of fork sliders.

REAR WHEEL

Glide Models (Drum Brake)

1. Raise the rear wheel off the ground and support the motorcycle in this position.
2. Remove the fender support screws and raise the fender flap (if applicable).
3. Remove the rear wheel mounting screws with a suitably sized allen wrench.
4. Remove the axle nut, lockwasher, axle, and axle spacer.

NOTE: *Remove the wheel while actuating the rear brake. Brake Pedal Locking Tool (H-D Part No. 45875-58) may be used but is not necessary.*

5. Assemble in the reverse order of disassembly.
6. Drum and hub clamping surface must be thoroughly cleaned.
7. Secure the wheel mounting screws tightly so that the wheel cannot work free.
8. Secure the axle nut.

Sportster (Drum Brake)

1. Raise the rear wheel off the ground and support the motorcycle in this position.
2. Remove the drive chain master link and free the chain from the rear sprocket.
3. Remove the brake rod adjusting nut, axle nut, lockwasher, and centering collar, and then loosen the axle by tapping it on the axle nut side.
4. Remove the axle and axle spacer.
5. Pull the wheel to the rear end of the frame and lift it up and out to remove.
6. Assemble in the reverse order of disassembly.
7. Adjust the brake as described in "Maintenance."

Disc Brake Models (1973 and Later)

1. Raise rear end of motorcycle off the ground and support in this position.
2. Disconnect rear chain. Remove brake anchor nut and cotter pin. Loosen castle nut.
3. Remove axle nut, lockwasher, axle, and spacer which fit between swing arm and sprocket side of wheel hub. Axle centering spacer fits into rear axle slot in swing arm. Remove wheel assembly.
4. Assemble in the reverse order of disassembly.
5. Tighten axle nut to 50 ft lbs (maximum). Adjust rear chain as described in "Maintenance."

SIDECAR WHEEL

1. Raise the wheel off the ground and support the motorcycle in this position.
2. Loosen the fender front bracket and step lug, and the fender inner brace clip bracket nut.
3. Remove the axle nut, lockwasher, and brace.
4. Tilt the fender forward, taking care to leave slack in the taillight wire.
5. Remove the extension nut, axle nut, washer, and wheel and drum assembly.
6. The wheel can be detached from the drum, if desired, by removing the wheel mounting screws with a suitably sized allen wrench.
7. Assemble in the reverse order of disassembly.
8. Take care to secure the socket screws tightly so that the wheel cannot work free.

FX and Sportster (Late Disc)

1. Support the front wheel off the ground.
2. Remove the brake caliper mounting bolt, washers, and nut.
3. Remove the axle nut and washers. Loosen the slider cap nuts. Remove the axle.
4. Remove the front wheel and speedometer drive.
5. Installation is the reverse of removal. Be sure the speedometer drive ear engages the hole in the hub when installing.
6. Tighten the axle nut to 50 ft lbs., then the slider cap nuts.

WHEEL HUBS

Electric-Glide

FRONT AND REAR (1966 AND EARLIER)

Disassembly

1. Remove the wheels as described in "Wheel Removal and Installation."
2. Remove the thrust bearing cover screws, lockwashers, outer cover, cork grease retainer, bearing housing, housing gasket, bearing adjusting shims, outer thrust washer, bearing sleeve, and inner thrust washer.
3. Remove the bearing assembly and separate for reassembly.
4. Remove the roller retainer thrust washer.
5. Invert the hub and remove the outer roller retainer-spring lockring, retaining washer, hub inner sleeve, cork grease retainer, inner spring lockring, and roller bearing washer.
6. Remove the rollers, retainer, and thrust washer, and separate them for reassembly.

Inspection

1. Clean all parts other than the cork grease retainers, if they are to be reused, in a suitable solvent and blow them dry.
2. Inspect all parts for wear and replace if necessary.
3. Eliminate excessive bearing side-

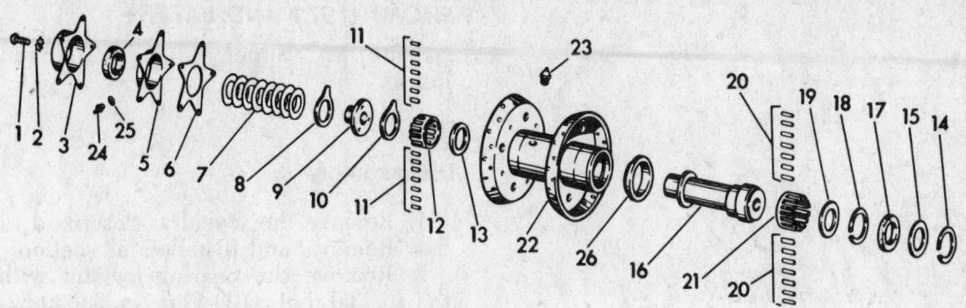

Wheel hub assembly (1966 and earlier)

1. Thrust bearing cover screw (5)
2. Thrust bearing cover screw lockwasher (5)
3. Thrust bearing outer cover
4. Cork grease retainer
5. Thrust bearing housing
6. Thrust bearing housing gasket
7. Thrust bearing adjusting shim (varies) (each 0.002 in. thick)
8. Thrust washer (2) (see item 10)
9. Thrust bearing sleeve
10. Thrust washer (see item 8)
11. Bearing roller (12)
12. Roller retainer
13. Roller retainer thrust washer
14. Roller bearing spring lock ring (2) (see item 18)
15. Retaining washer
16. Hub inner sleeve
17. Cork grease retainer
18. Roller bearing spring lock ring (see item 14)
19. Roller bearing washer
20. Bearing roller (14)
21. Roller retainer
22. Hub shell
23. Grease fitting (2)
24. Grease fitting (see item 23)
25. Plain washer
26. Roller retainer thrust collar

play by adding 0.002 in. adjusting shims until 0.005–0.007 in. clearance is obtained between the thrust bearing sleeve and the thrust bearing outer cover. This measurement must be taken without the cork retainer present.

NOTE: *Bearing assemblies must be replaced as sets.*

4. Fit bearings to eliminate radial play by installing oversize bearing rollers until a clearance of 0.001–0.005 in. is obtained. Rollers are available in 0.0002 in. gradations from 0.001 in. undersize to 0.001 oversize.
5. Replace the snap-rings and cork retainers.

Assembly

1. Assemble in the reverse order of disassembly.
2. Install a washer under the thrust bearing housing grease fitting.
3. Lightly grease the rollers, races, and thrust washers, and inject 1 oz of grease into the hub when it is assembled. Do not overlubricate the hub, since excess grease may get in the brakes.
4. Check bearings for slight play and free-motion.

FRONT AND REAR (1967–1972)

Disassembly

1. Remove the wheels as described in "Wheel Removal and Installation."
2. Remove the wheel mounting socket screws with a suitably sized allen wrench.
3. Remove the brake drum (or brake disc flange) from the hub.
4. Remove the bearing spacer and press the drum bearing, or bearings, free from the hub side with a suitably sized drift.
5. Remove the retainer screws and retainer (late 1970 and later).
6. Remove the left-hand threaded bearing locknut with special tool (H-D Part No. 94630-67) or a suitable substitute, and remove the seal and spacer.
7. Press the hub bearing free with a suitable drift from the drum side.

Inspection

1. Check bearing for wear, rough motion, and excessive looseness of the inner and outer races and replace as necessary.
2. Inspect all of the parts for wear or damage, and replace as necessary.
3. Replace the seal if it is worn, cracked, or damaged, taking special note of the condition of the lip.

Assembly

1. Assemble in the reverse order of disassembly.
2. Pack both sides of the bearings and fill the remaining area in the hub and on the inside bearing of the drum with grease.
3. The drum and hub clamping faces must be completely clean so the wheel cannot work free.

FRONT AND REAR (1973 AND LATER)

Disassembly and Assembly

1. Remove wheel as described in "Wheel Removal and Installation."
2 Remove two lockrings. Remove washers, spacers, oil seal and bearing cones.
3. Remove bearing cups with a bearing puller. Remove spacer from hub.
4. Clean all parts in solvent. Inspect for worn or damaged parts, replace as necessary.
5. Reassemble in reverse order of disassembly.
6. Apply a liberal amount of bearing grease to all bearing cones before assembly.
7. Press oil seal into hub. Lubricate lip of oil seal and install spacer. Bearing end-play should be 0.005 in. to 0.014 in. with an axial load of 100 lbs. applied to bearing cones. If end-play is incorrect, substitute a slightly longer or shorter spacer as necessary.

Super Glide

FRONT (1972 AND EARLIER)

Disassembly

1. Remove the wheel as described in the wheels section "Removal and Installation."
2. Pry the grease retainer free with a pointed instrument.
3. Remove the retaining ring with snap-ring pliers.
4. Gently tap the grease retainer side ball bearing into its seat in the hub. This will cause the spacer to push the other bearing out slightly. Slide the spacer back to the seated bearing.
5. Insert an appropriate sized drift through the seated bearing and drift the opposite bearing out.

Assembly

1. Press the retaining ring side bearing (shielded side out) against its seat in the hub.

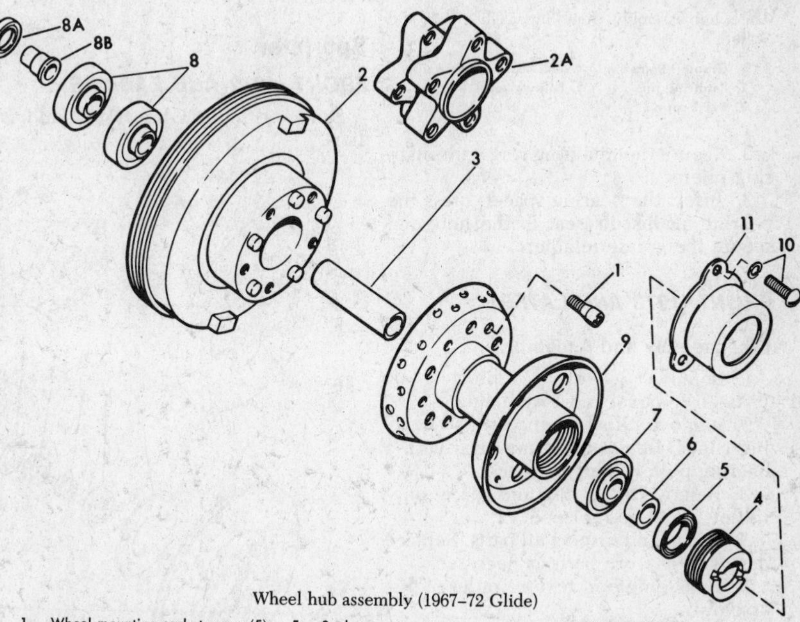

Wheel hub assembly (1967–72 Glide)

1. Wheel mounting socket screw (5)
2. Brake drum (front shown)
2A. Brake disc flange (1972)
3. Bearing spacer
4. Bearing lock nut
5. Seal
6. Spacer
7. Ball bearing
8. Ball bearing (1 front) (2 rear)
8A. Oil seal (1972)
8B. Spacer (1972)
9. Wheel hub
10. Bearing retainer screw (2)
11. Bearing lock nut retainer

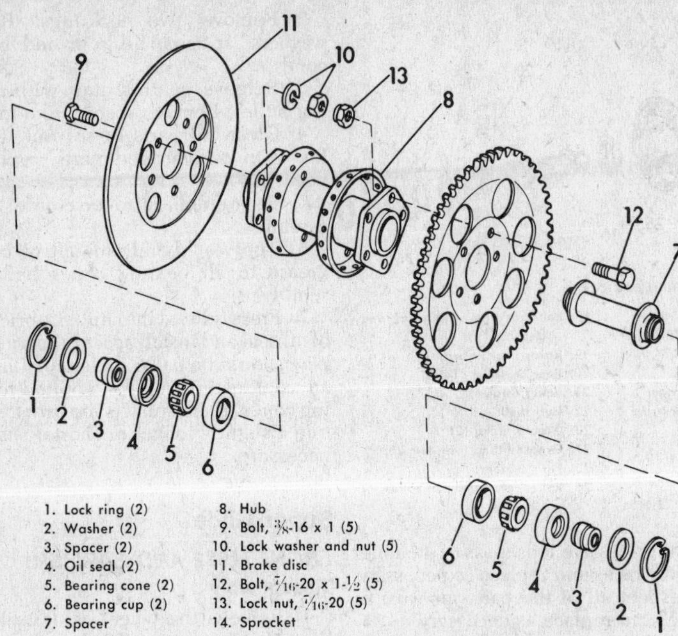

FL/FLH interchangeable wheel, FX rear wheel (1973 and later)

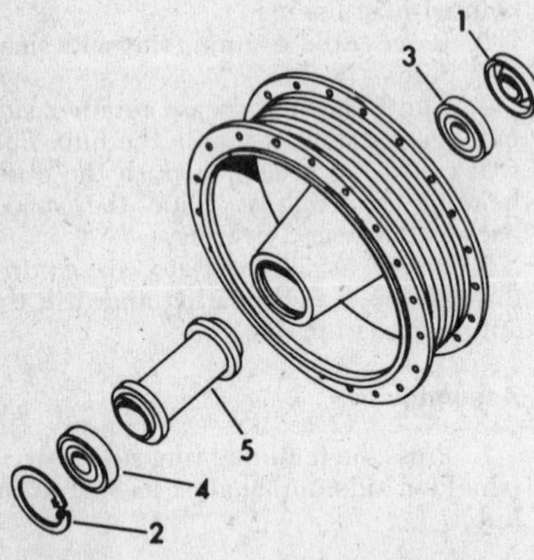

Wheel hub assembly, front (Super Glide 1972 and earlier)

1. Grease retainer
2. Retaining ring
3. Ball bearing
4. Ball bearing (brake side)
5. Bearing spacer

2. Secure the retaining ring with snap-ring pliers.
3. Insert the bearing spacer, press the bearing against its seat in the hub, and secure the grease retainer.

FRONT (1973 AND LATER)

Disassembly and Assembly

1. Remove wheel as directed in "Wheel Removal and Installation."
2. Remove oil seals, spacer, and bearing cones. Remove bearing cups with a bearing puller. Remove spacer.
3. Remove brake disc and spacer only if they are to be replaced.
4. Clean and inspect all parts. Replace damaged or worn parts as necessary.
5. Reassemble in reverse order of disassembly.
6. Apply a liberal amount of bearing grease to all bearing cones before assembly.
7. Press oil seals into hub flush with outer surface. Lubricate lip of oil seal and install spacer. If brake disc and spacer were removed, inspect mating surfaces for flatness and reinstall. Tighten retaining bolts to 35 ft lbs.
8. Install wheel. Inspect bearing end-play, it should be between 0.005 to 0.013 in. If end-play is incorrect, substitute a slightly longer or shorter spacer as necessary.

REAR (1972 AND EARLIER)

Same as "Electra-Glide (1967–1972)."

REAR (1973 AND LATER)

Same as "Electra-Glide (1973 and Later)."

Sportster

FRONT (1972 AND EARLIER)

Same as Super Glide (1972 and Earlier)."

FRONT (1973 AND LATER)

Same as "Super Glide (1973 and Later)."

REAR

Disassembly

1. Remove the wheel as described in the "Removal and Installation" section.
2. Remove the bearing locknut with the special tool (H-D Part No. 94630-67) or a suitable substitute. It will be necessary to break the stakings.
3. Drift the bearing oil seal and the outer spacer free from the opposite side of the hub with a suitable drift.
4. Drift the ball bearing and washer free in the above manner.
5. Remove the bearing spacer.
6. Drift the ball bearing, spacer (or spacer washer), and grease retainer as in the above manner.

Assembly

1. Press the bearing oil seal into the locknut and the outer spacer into the oil seal.
2. Secure the bearing washer, bearing, and assembled locknut to the hub. Stake the locknut in two new places.
3. Insert the bearing spacer in the hub.
4. Press the ball bearing (or unshielded bearing) until it is seated against the bearing spacer.
5. Insert the bearing spacer (or bearing spacer washer) and the grease retainer (or shielded ball bearing).

REAR WHEEL SPROCKET

Drum Brake Models

GLIDE MODELS

1. Remove the wheel as described in the "Replacement and Installation" section for the wheels.
2. Remove the brake drum from the wheel as described in the wheel hub section.
3. Free the sprocket from the drum by chiseling off the heads of all rivets and

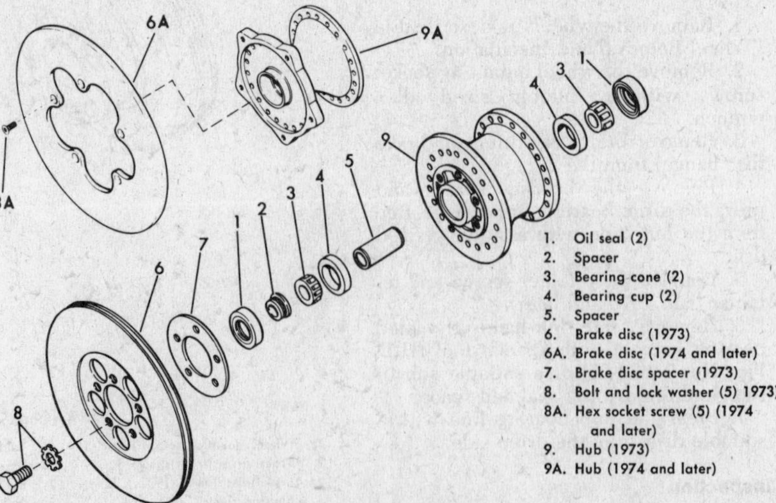

Front hub assembly (FX, 1973 and later)

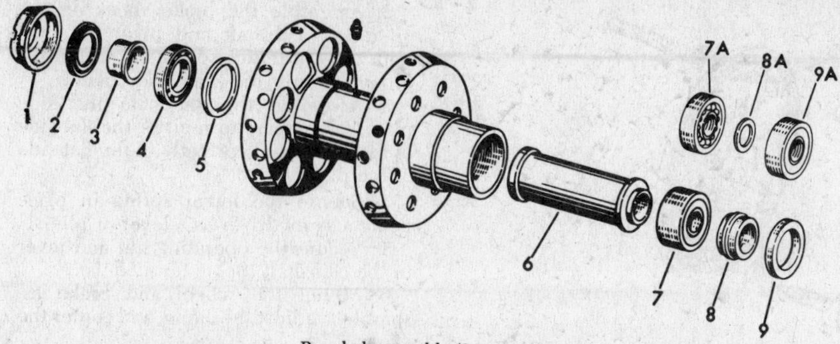

Rear hub assembly (Sportster)

1. Bearing lock nut
2. Bearing oil seal
3. Bearing outer spacer
4. Ball bearing
5. Bearing washer
6. Bearing spacer
7A. Unshielded ball bearing
8A. Bearing spacer washer
9A. Shielded ball bearing

dowel pins from the brake shell side and then by punching them out.

4. If the rivet holes are not worn or elongated and if the drum is still in good condition the rivet holes may be reused. If not, procede as follows:

a. Using a new sprocket as a template (guide), drill a new rivet hole from the brake shell side between the original dowel and the rivet holes. Use a No. 10 drill bit (0.1935 in. diameter) for the 3/16 in. rivets.

b. Drill another hole opposite the first one and secure both with rivets but do not head them.

c. Drill the remaining holes and remove the sprocket.

d. Smooth the drum surface around the rivet holes.

6. Using the sprocket as a template, drill new 3/16 in. dowel holes and smooth off any burrs which may have resulted. The dowel pins must be a press fit.

7. Place the drum on the center support flange of Riveting Jig (H-D Part No. 95600-33B) and carefully align the sprocket on the drum. An appropriate riveting device may be substituted. If substitute rivets are used, make sure that they will provide a strong enough bond.

8. Insert the dowel pins, then the rivets, from the brake shell side in the following manner:

a. Using a hollow driver, drive the sprocket and hub flange together by seating the dowel pins and rivets.

b. Work in opposite pairs to ensure an even seat between the sprocket and hub.

c. Flare the dowel pin and rivet ends with a punch until the heads extend 3/32 in. above the sprocket surface. Use a concave-end punch for the dowel pins and the smaller rivets, and a flat-end punch for the larger diameter rivets.

SPORTSTER

1. See "Glide Models," Steps 1–3.

2. If the original rivet holes are not worn or elliptical, they may be reused. If in poor condition, drill a new set midway between the original dowel and rivet holes.

Use the new sprocket as a template for locating holes.

3. Drill a 9/64 in. hole from the brake shell side.

4. Insert, but do not head, a rivet. Drill another hole directly opposite to the first, inserting a rivet as before.

5. Drill the remaining rivet holes.

6. Remove rivets and sprocket. Deburr the rivet holes.

7. Using the sprocket as a template, drill four new dowel pin holes (3/16 in. dia.). The dowel pins must be a press fit.

8. Position sprocket and drum on riveting jig. Insert and seat the dowel pins first. Then the rivets. Insert the dowel pins and rivets from the brake shell side.

9. Use a hollow driver and seat the dowel pins and rivets driving the sprocket and hub flange together at the same time.

10. Use a concave punch to flare the dowel pin ends. The rivet heads should extend 3/64 in. above the sprocket face.

11. Repeat the procedure for the opposite dowel pins and rivets.

DRIVE CHAIN

REMOVAL AND INSTALLATION

1. Loosen the axle housing frame clamps.

2. Loosen the axle adjusting screw locknuts and shift the axle forward about ½ in.

3. Jack up the right wheel and spin it until either side of the master link is visible through the chainguard slot.

4. Loosely connect the chain links on either side of the master link with mechanic's wire to prevent the chain from running off the sprockets.

5. Remove the master link with Chain Tool (from tool kit—H-D Part No. 95020-38), Shop Tool (H-D Part No. 95021-29) or pry the spring clip from the link with a screwdriver.

6. Attach a new chain to the present chain, or an old chain if chain is to be cleaned, with the master link.

7. Rotate the wheel forward while feeding one chain off the sprockets and the other one on.

8. Attach the loose end of the replacement to the chainguard with a piece of mechanic's wire.

9. Remove the replaced chain and connect the ends of the replacing chain. If a new chain is being mounted, secure it with a new master link, or at least use a new spring clip.

10. Secure the spring clip with Press Tool (H-D Part No. 95020-66) or pry on with a screwdriver.

11. If a second chain is not available, remove the chainguard and feed the chain off from the sprockets by rotating the rear wheel. Replace the chain by putting one end over the rear sprocket. With the transmission in First gear, crank the engine until the chain goes over mainshaft sprocket and secure it with the master link.

12. Adjust the chain as described in "Drive Chain Adjustment."

Determining Chain Wear

1. Lay the chain out on a flat surface.

2. Push the links together, a couple at a time, until all slack has been removed. Measure the overall length.

3. Pull on both ends until the chain is extended to its greatest possible length. Measure the chain again. If the overall length is greater by more than one inch, the chain is excessively worn and must be replaced.

4. This procedure can be used to measure the length of continuous-type primary chains also. Lay the chain on its side to do this and replace if the difference is greater than ⅜ in.

DRUM BRAKES

Front Brake Cable Removal and Installation

1. Remove the wheel and the outer dust cover on Glide models.

2. Remove the clevis clamp nut and clamp.

3. Free the cable from the clevis and pull it free from the upper end of the cable housing (coil).

4. Slide a new cable in from the top of the cover, applying a light coat of grease as it goes in.

5. When installing the side slot cable ferrule in the brake lever, position the slot toward the inside, or down, on the earlier type, with the end slot.

6. Turn the adjusting sleeve clockwise to its stop.

7. Pull the cable from the lower end to remove all slack.

8. With the actuating lever in its lowest position, loop the cable around the clevis and secure it with a clevis clamp and clamp nut.

9. Replace the wheel and dust cover if applicable.

10. Adjust the brake cable.

Front Brake (Drum Brakes)

DISASSEMBLY

Sportster and Super Glide

1. Remove the wheel, with the brake drum, from the fork.

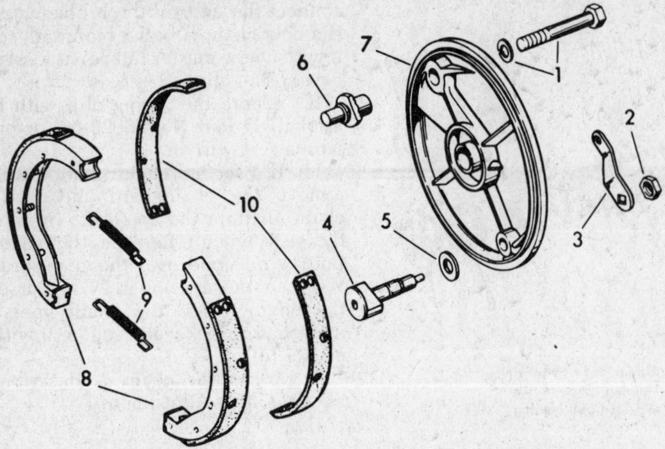

Front brake assembly (Sportster and Super Glide models)

1. Pivot stud screw and washer
2. Operating shaft nut
3. Operating lever
4. Operating shaft
5. Operating shaft washer
6. Shoe pivot stud
7. Brake side plate
8. Brake shoe and lining (2)
9. Brake shoe spring (2)
10. Brake lining (2)

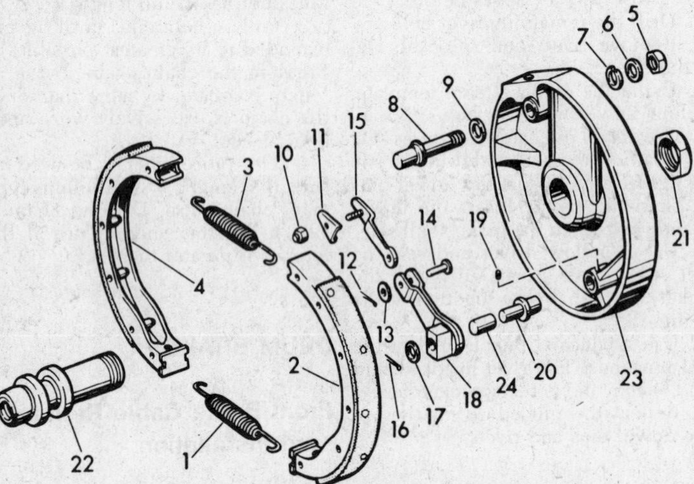

Front brake (1971 and earlier Glide models)

1. Brake shoe spring (2)
2. Brake shoe and lining (2)
3. Brake shoe spring (see item 1)
4. Brake shoe and lining (see item 2)
5. Brake shoe pivot stud nut
6. Pivot stud flat washer
7. Pivot stud lock washer
8. Pivot stud
9. Pivot stud washer
10. Clevis clamp nut
11. Cable clevis clamp
12. Cotter pin
13. Flat washer
14. Cam lever clevis pin
15. Cable clevis
16. Cotter pin
17. Cam lever washer
18. Cam lever
19. Set screw
20. Cam lever stud
21. Axle sleeve nut
22. Front axle sleeve
23. Brake side cover
24. Cam lever bushing

2. Remove the operating shaft nut and lever.
3. Remove, as a unit, the brake shoes, springs, operating shaft, washer, and pivot stud, by tapping with a soft mallet on the operating shaft.
4. Remove the shoes and springs from the pivot stud and operating shaft.

Glide Models

1. Remove the wheel, with the brake drum, from the fork.
2. Remove the dust cover.
3. Remove the shoes and springs by lifting them out and away from the side-cover.
4. Remove the cotter pin, washer, cam lever, lever bushing, set screw, and cam lever stud.

INSPECTION

1. Examine the brake shoes, lining, drum, cam pivot, and the cam for excessive wear, glazing, and embedded particles.
2. Exposed rivets on linings will gouge the drum and must be replaced. Oil-soaked, hard, cracked, or glazed linings must be replaced. Slightly worn linings can be dressed with medium grade sandpaper.
3. Replace the linings with rivets or replace them with ready-lined shoes. Always set the rivets from one end to the other to ensure a smooth, tight fit. Bevel the end of each brake lining.
4. Lightly lubricate the pivot stud (one squirt from a standard grease gun on Sportster grease fittings).
5. Rough up the drum braking surface with emery paper.

ASSEMBLY

1. Assemble in the reverse order of disassembly.
2. Assemble the brake shoes on the operating camshaft and pivot the stud with the top return spring in place in its groove nearest the brake side plate.
3. Assemble the shoes to the side plate, taking care to register the flat side of the pivot stud correctly in the flat side of the plate.
4. Secure the lower spring in place using a screwdriver as a lever or pliers.
5. Secure the operating nut and lever to the camshaft (Sportster models).
6. Mount the wheel and brake assemblies, adjust the cable, and center the shoes.

Rear Brake

DISASSEMBLY

Sportster

1. Remove the wheel from the motorcycle.
2. Free the brake rod from the operating lever by removing the brake rod adjusting nut.
3. Remove the shaft nut and its lockwasher, operating lever, pivot stud nut and its lockwasher, and the locating block.
4. Tap with a soft mallet on operating shaft, and shoes, springs, pivot stud, operating shaft, and washer will all fall away from brake side-plate.
5. The shoes will now come free from the operating shaft and pivot stud.

Glide Models

1. Remove the wheel from the motorcycle.
2. Remove the return spring, anchor spring, and shoes from the side cover.
3. The hold-down leaf springs may now be removed.
4. After removing the cylinder screws and lockwashers, the cylinder will come off from the side-cover.
5. Pry the cylinder boots free and remove the pistons, cups, and springs.

INSPECTION

1. Consult "Front Brake Inspection" for the Sportster and all other models with mechanical rear brakes.
2. Follow the same steps for hydraulic rear brakes but inspect the cylinder and side-cover for signs of leakage.
3. Do not operate the brake pedal with the shoes and springs removed from the back plate.
4. Remove all burrs from the cylinder and piston.
5. If the cylinder is faulty, install a repair kit. Dip the parts in brake fluid and use all of the parts provided. Never use gasoline on any hydraulic parts.

ASSEMBLY

Sportster

1. Assemble in the reverse order of disassembly.
2. Using one spring, mount the shoes on the operating shaft and pivot stud, taking care to seat the spring in its groove on the back plate.

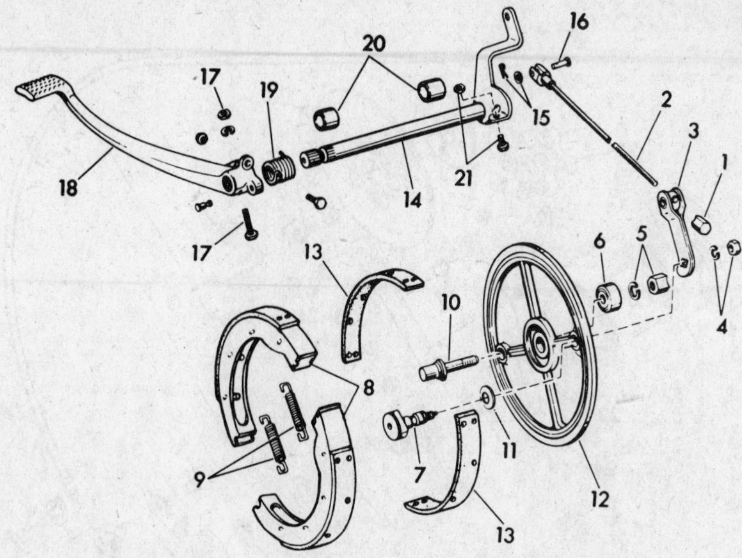

Rear brake and cross-shaft assembly (Sportster, 1974 and earlier)

1. Brake rod adjusting nut
2. Brake rod
3. Brake operating lever
4. Operating shaft nut and lock washer
5. Pivot stud nut and lock washer
6. Locating block
7. Operating shaft
8. Shoe and lining (2)
9. Shoe spring (2)
10. Pivot stud
11. Operating shaft washer
12. Brake side plate
13. Brake lining (2)
14. Cross shaft
15. Rod clevis cotter pin and washer
16. Rod clevis pin
17. Foot lever bolt and nut
18. Foot lever
19. Lever torsion spring
20. Frame brake shaft tube bushing (2)
21. Cross shaft adjusting screw and nut

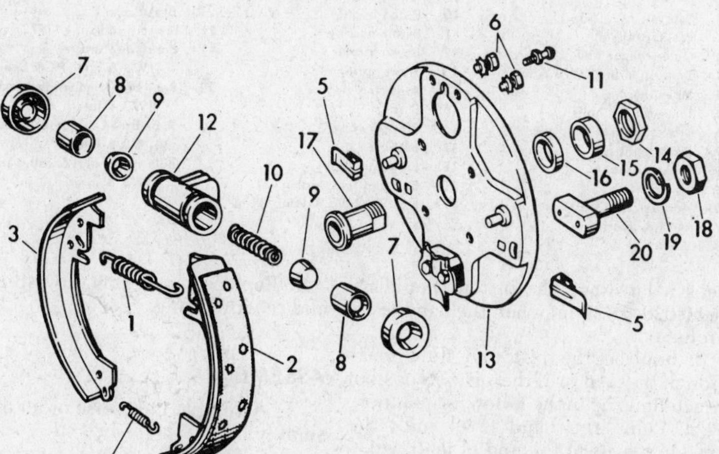

Rear brake assembly (Glide models)

1. Shoe return spring
2. Front brake shoe
3. Rear brake shoe
4. Brake shoe spring
5. Hold-down spring (2)
6. Cylinder screw and lock washer (2 each)
7. Boot (2)
8. Piston (2)
9. Cup (2)
10. Spring
11. Bleeder nipple
12. Wheel cylinder
13. Brake side cover
14. Nut
15. Spacer
16. Collar
17. Brake sleeve
18. Nut
19. Lockwasher
20. Anchor stud

3. Assemble the operating shaft and washer on the side-plate.
4. Mount the locating block, pivot stud nut and lockwasher, operating lever, and the shaft nut and lockwasher on the shaft.
5. Secure the shoes with a second spring. Use a screwdriver as a lever, or pliers to install it.
6. Place the brake rod through the lever ferrule and secure it with an adjusting nut.
7. Assemble the brake and wheel on the motorcycle.
8. Adjust the adjusting rod and center the shoes.

Glide Models

1. Assemble in the reverse order of disassembly.
2. Lightly grease the hold-down leaf springs, and the area on the side plate where the shoes seat during operation.
3. Connect the shoes with the lower return spring, place the assembly on the back plate, and secure it with the upper spring, using a screwdriver as a lever or else with pliers.
4. Place the short hook in the elongated hole on the front shoe (when applicable).
5. On 1965 and later Glide models, the shoes are of different widths and the narrow shoe must be on the rear of the back plate.
6. Assemble the wheel on the motorcycle.
7. Adjust the linkage and center the shoes.

Rear Brake Cross-Shaft Mechanical Brake Models

DISASSEMBLY

1. Disconnect but do not remove the rear chain.
2. Remove the rear cylinder exhaust pipe and muffler.
3. Remove the brake rod, clevis pin, cotter pin, washer, and clevis pin from the lever arm.
4. Back off the pinch-bolt until the foot pedal lever and return spring can be slipped from the shaft.
5. Remove the shaft from the right-side of the machine.

INSPECTION

1. Inspect the shaft and the lever pedal splines, and replace them if they are damaged or worn. Excessive wear will cause the lever to slip on the shaft reducing braking accuracy.
2. Assemble the clevis pin in the rod clevis and check for wear. Replace the pin if it is worn; always replace the cotter pin.
3. Check to see if excessive clearance has developed between the bushings and shaft; replace the bushings if necessary.
4. Bushings can be drifted out from the frame by threading in a ¾–16 in. tap from the outside of each bushing.
5. Press in new bushings, install the shaft, and check to see that the shaft rotates freely.
6. Ream the bushing to the correct size of high spots developed during drifting.

ASSEMBLY

1. Replace bushings if they have been removed.
2. Insert the shaft in the frame tube.
3. Assemble the shaft arm, if it has been removed, and secure it to the brake rod clevis with the pin, washer, and cotter pin.
4. Mount and adjust the chain on the rear sprocket, and assemble the tail pipe and muffler.
5. Set the cross-shaft adjusting screw so that, when it is stopped against the frame, the cross-shaft arm is slightly behind the center of the rear fork pivot bolt. The arm must never be closer than 1½ in. to the inner recess of the transmission sprocket cover.
6. Assemble the brake pedal on the shaft so it lies slightly beneath the foot rest. Adjust the cross-shaft adjusting screw until the pedal is correctly positioned. Always adjust it so the arm moves away from the transmission cover.
7. Secure the cross-shaft bolt locknut.
8. Check the brake pedal adjustment.

DISC BRAKES

Two types of caliper are in use, here referred to as "early" and "late." The early-type caliper was used from 1972 and continues in use on FL/FLH (f&r) and FX (rear).

The early type is easily recognizable since the caliper halves are secured by four through-bolts and it has a symmetrical shape unlike that of the late caliper.

The late-type caliper is used on the front of FX and Sportster models, 1974 and later.

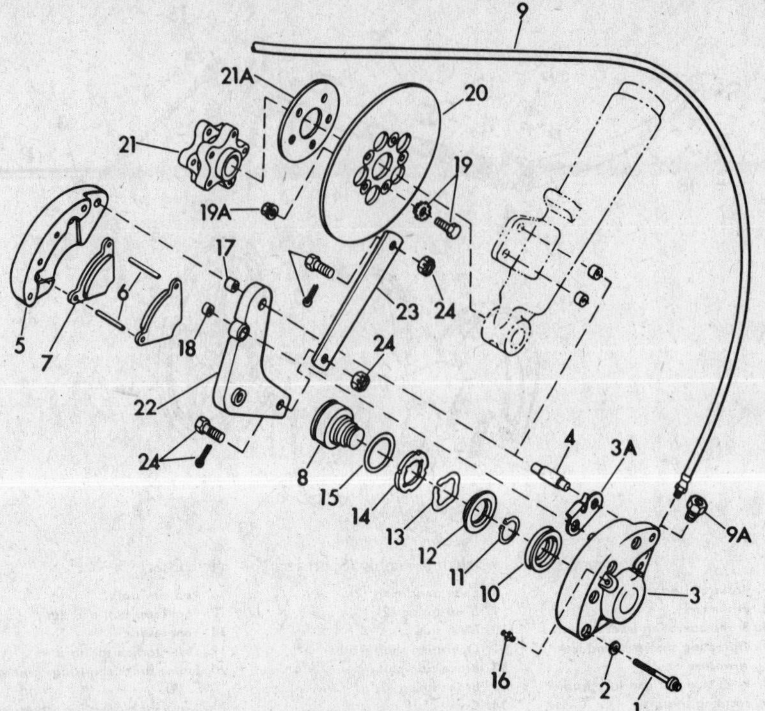

Disc brake assembly (early)

1. Bolt (4)
2. Washer (4)
3. Outer caliper half
3A. Damper spring (1973 & later)
4. Mounting pin
5. Inner caliper half
6. Brake pad mounting pins (2)
7. Brake pads (2)
8. Brake piston
9. Hydraulic line
9A. Adapter (1973 & later FX & Sportster)
10. Piston boot
11. Retaining ring
12. Backing plate
13. Wave spring
14. Adjusting ring
15. O-ring
16. Bleeder valve
17. Bushing
18. Bushing
19. Bolt and lock washer (5)
19A. Nut (5) (1973 & later FL)
20. Brake disc
21. Brake disc flange (1972)
21A. Brake disc spacer (1973 & later FX & Sportster)
22. Rear brake mounting bracket (1973 & later)
23. Rear brake torque arm (1973 & later)
24. Bolt, castle nut, & cotter pin (1973 & later)

Bleeding

1. The brake must be bled anytime a line or cylinder is opened to remove all air.

2. Place a length of plastic tubing of appropriate size over the bleeder nipple and run the tube into a container with about one inch of brake fluid already in it so bubbles will be visible and so no air can get back in the system. Be sure there is no room for leakage around the nipple because brake fluid removes paint.

On front brakes, turn the wheel all the way to the right to get the bleeder valve nearly vertical.

3. Open the bleeder nipple by rotating it counterclockwise about ½ turn.

4. Keep the master cylinder full of fluid at all times to keep air out of the system.

5. Pump the foot pedal or hand lever slowly until no air bubbles come out of the plastic tube.

6. Fill the master cylinder to its original level.

7. Close the bleeder nipple first and then remove the plastic tube.

8. If bubbles keep coming, replace the master cylinder check valve.

9. Do not reuse brake fluid since it is hydrascopic (attracts moisture) and will become moisture-ridden from sitting in the draining container. This will cause spongy brake action.

Caliper (Early)

DISASSEMBLY

WARNING: *Hydraulic brake fluid will damage plastic, paint, and chrome surfaces.*

1. Free the hydraulic line from the hose clamp.

2. Remove the caliper bolts, washers, and outer caliper half.

3. Remove the mounting pin and inner caliper half.

4. Remove the brake pads and pad mounting pins.

5. Inspect the brake pad friction material for excessive wear, damage, or a loose fit, and replace as a set if friction material is less than 1/16 in. thick.

6. Inspect the friction material backing plates for damage or a warped condition and replace them if they are not completely flat.

7. Check the piston retraction with a dial indicator or spin the wheel and check it for drag. The piston should retract 0.020–0.025 in. when the hand lever is released.

8. Replace the piston if fluid leaks through the seal or if the piston does not retract. Replace in the following manner:

a. Pump the hand lever until the piston moves to the end of its travel.

b. Disconnect the hydraulic line or drain the fluid into a clean glass container if the fluid is to be reused.

c. Slide the piston boot away from its groove in the piston and pull the piston free.

d. Remove the retaining ring with snap-ring pliers and slide out the backing plate, wave spring, adjusting ring, and O-ring.

9. Remove the bleeder valve.

10. Clean all of the metal parts in clean brake fluid.

INSPECTION

1. Replace any worn or damaged parts.

2. Replace the outer caliper half if the cylinder bore is scored or damaged.

3. Inspect the brake disc for scoring or warping and replace it if necessary. If the disc is less than 3/16 in. thick, it must be replaced as described in "Brake Disc Removal and Installation."

4. Replace the bushings in the forks slider if they are worn or damaged.

5. Replace the O-ring, adjusting ring, and retaining ring.

ASSEMBLY

1. Assemble in reverse order of disassembly.

2. Immerse the piston, retaining ring, backing plate, wave spring, adjusting ring, piston boot, and O-ring in hydraulic fluid, and assemble in bore.

3. Assemble the piston boot in the caliper bore.

4. Press the piston into the assembled bore until it firmly seats, taking care to avoid scoring the bore.

5. Assemble the bleeder valve on the caliper.

6. Assemble the brake pads and calipers to the fork.

7. Apply a graphite compound to the caliper bolts and torque them to 35 ft lbs.

8. Assemble the hydraulic line, hose clamp, screw, and lockwasher.

9. With the bike standing straight up, fill the reservoir with hydraulic brake fluid to the gasket level.

10. Coat the fittings with a hydraulic sealant if leaks are present (Locktite® is recommended by the factory).

11. Bleed the system as described in "Bleeding Hydraulic System" until any spongy feeling disappears.

Caliper (Late)

DISASSEMBLY

1. Wheel removal is not necessary. Remove the socket head screws which join the caliper halves and separate the halves.
2. Remove the pressure plate with brake pad.
3. Do not remove the piston from the caliper unless the seal leaks or the piston does not operate properly. Remove it, if necessary, by disconnecting and pluging the brake line, removing the rubber boot, and prying out the piston with two screwdrivers.
4. If the friction ring is damaged, remove it from the piston and replace it with a new one.
5. Remove the o-ring from the caliper. Remove the bleeder valve.

INSPECTION

1. Check the brake pads for wear. Replace them, as a set, if either is worn to the indicator groove at the bottom of the pad. Pads are replaced by drilling out the rivets with a $^{9}/_{64}$ in. drill.
2. Check that the pressure plate is flat. If warped, replace it.
3. Check that the caliper bore is free of scoring. If damaged, replace the caliper half.
4. Clean piston and caliper half in clean brake fluid.

ASSEMBLY

1. Assembly is the reverse of disassembly.
2. Lubricate the caliper bore, piston, and o-ring with new brake fluid before inserting piston in bore.
3. Insert the piston squarely into the bore. Rotate it while tapping it into place with a plastic mallet.
4. Be sure both lips of the boot engage their grooves.
5. Push the piston all the way into the bore before assembly.
6. Be sure that all fittings are clean before assembling caliper halves.

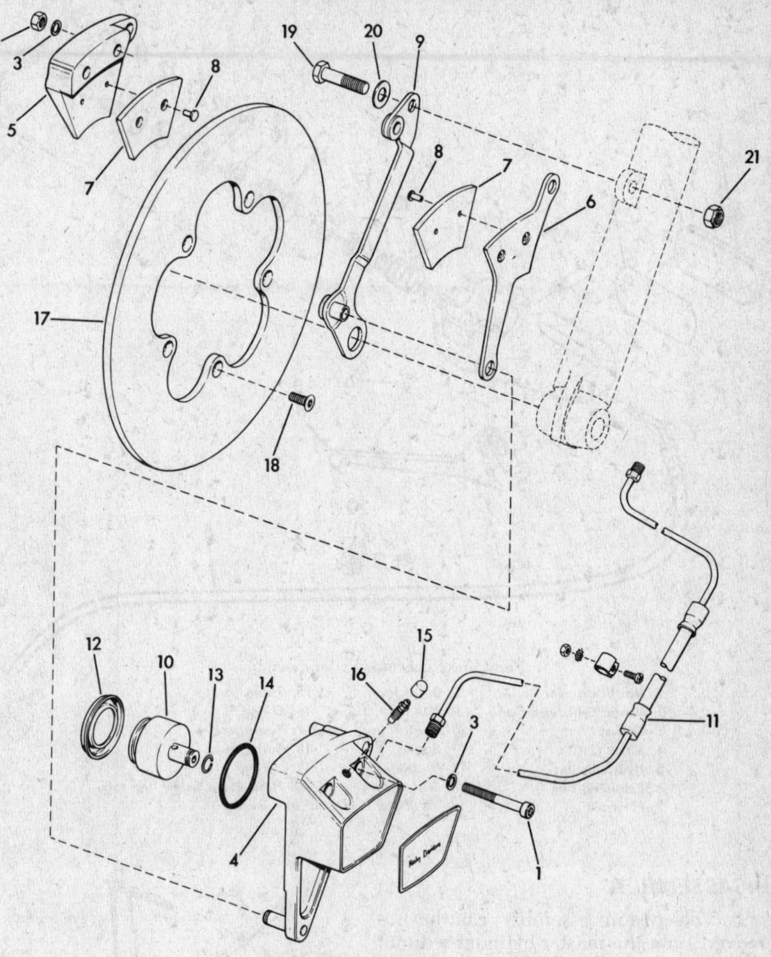

Disc brake assembly (later)

1. Socket head screw (2)
2. Locknut (2)
3. Washer (4)
4. Outer caliper half
5. Inner caliper half
6. Pressure plate
7. Brake pad (2)
8. Rivet (4)
9. Torque arm
10. Piston
11. Hydraulic hose
12. Rubber boot
13. Friction ring
14. O-ring
15. Bleeder valve cap
16. Bleeder valve
17. Brake disc
18. Brake disc mounting screw (5)
19. Torque arm mounting bolt
20. Torque arm mounting bolt washer
21. Torque arm mounting bolt locknut

Brake Disc (Early Type)

REMOVAL AND INSTALLATION

1. Remove the wheel as described in the "Removal and Installation" section.
2. Remove the disc securing bolts and lockwashers.
3. Replace the disc if it is worn to 0.188 in., or less, or if it is warped more than $^{1}/_{32}$ in.
4. Replace the brake disc flange if it is damaged.
5. Reassemble using new lockwashers and torque to 35 ft lbs.
6. Assemble the wheel on motorcycle.

Brake Disc (Late Type)

Procedures are the same as described for the early type disc, except that the disc is secured by five screws instead of bolts. On installation, tighten the screws to 10 ft lbs.

Front Master Cylinder

DISASSEMBLY AND INSPECTION

1. Remove the cover securing screws, cover, and gasket.
2. Disconnect the hydraulic line at the caliper and drain it into a clean glass container if the fluid is to be reused.
3. Disconnect the stoplight wires and remove the handlebar switch assembly.
4. Remove the pivot pin, retaining ring, and pin.
5. Remove the lever, pin, plunger, spring, washers, dust wiper, and retaining ring.
6. Pull the piston, O-ring, piston cup, spring cup, and spring until they are free of the master cylinder.
7. Replace the piston cup and O-ring if they are worn, soft, or swollen.
8. Replace the cylinder walls if they are scratched or grooved.
9. Replace the gasket if it is leaky.
10. Blow the master cylinder vent hole clear.

ASSEMBLY

1. Assemble in the reverse order of disassembly.
2. Use all components of the repair kit if such a kit is to be used.
3. Immerse all internal parts in hydraulic fluid before assembly.
4. Lightly grease the pivot pin and plunger pin before reassembly.
5. Check to see that the relief port in the master cylinder is open when the lever is released.
6. Fill the reservoir to the gasket level with brake fluid.
7. Bleed the system as described in "Bleeding Hydraulic Brake System."
8. Install the gasket with the flat side down and secure the cover.

Rear Master Cylinder

The same master cylinder is used on disc and hydraulic drum brake models.

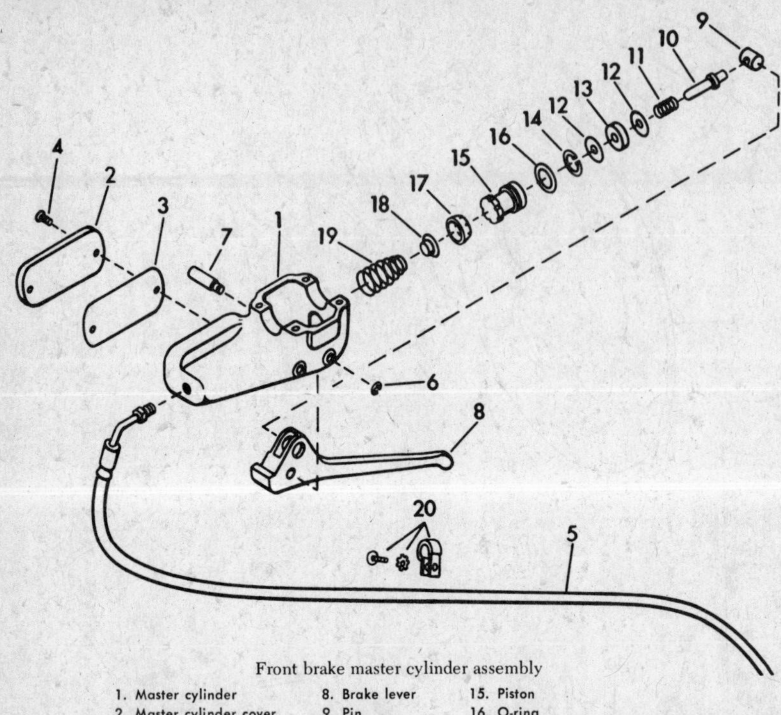

Front brake master cylinder assembly

1. Master cylinder
2. Master cylinder cover
3. Gasket
4. Screw (2)
5. Hydraulic line
6. Retaining ring
7. Pivot pin
8. Brake lever
9. Pin
10. Plunger
11. Spring
12. Washer
13. Dust wiper
14. Retaining ring
15. Piston
16. O-ring
17. Piston cup
18. Spring cup
19. Spring
20. Hose clamp, screw and lockwasher

DISASSEMBLY

1. The piston assembly can be removed from the master cylinder without removing the body from the motorcycle.
2. Remove the rear brake rod clevis pin.
3. Pull out the plunger. Remove the boot, stop wire, stop washer, piston assembly, cup, spring, valve and valve seat (the valve and valve seat are used on 1972 and earlier models only).

INSPECTION

1. Check the rubber parts for damage, cracks, a swollen condition, etc.
2. Check the cylinder walls for scoring.

ASSEMBLY

1. Reverse the disassembly procedure. Lubricate all parts with new brake fluid before assembly.

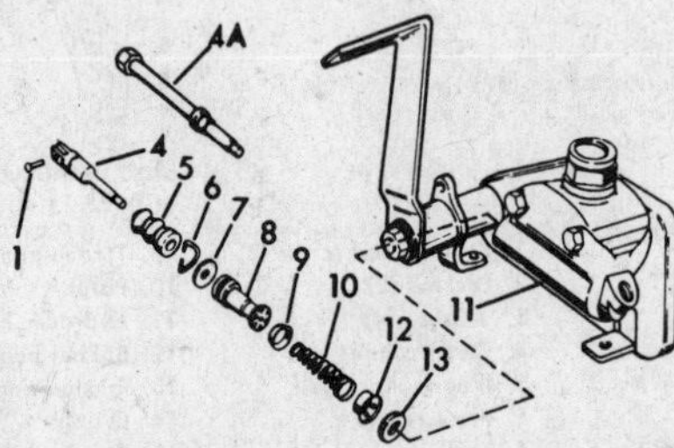

Rear master cylinder assembly (drum and disc brake models)

1. Rod clevis pin
2. Washer
3. Cotter pin
4. Master cylinder plunger
4A. Master cylinder plunger (FX & Sportster 1973 & later)
5. Cylinder boot
6. Stop wire
7. Stop washer
8. Piston assembly
9. Piston assembly
10. Piston return spring
11. Master cylinder
12. Valve (1972 & earlier)
13. Valve seat (1972 & earlier)

FRONT FORK

Fork Slider and Tube Removal

ELECTRA-GLIDE

1. Remove the front wheel as described in the wheels' "Removal and Installation" section.
2. Remove the brake cable clip from the front fender.
3. Remove the axle sleeve nut, pivot stud nut, and brake side-cover and shoe assembly along with the axle sleeve, from the forks.
4. Remove the front fender.
5. Loosen but do not remove the front fork bracket clamping studs.
6. Remove the upper bracket bolts, oil seals, and fork slider and slider tube assemblies from the bottom of the slider covers.

Preliminary Disassembly

1. Remove the headlight cowlings and headlamp.
2. Disconnect all headlight and handle-bar wires at the terminal.
3. Disconnect the throttle and spark cables at the carburetor and the contact breaker.
4. Remove the handlebars.

Disassembly

NON-ADJUSTABLE

1. Remove the fork stem nut, nut lock (if applicable), upper bracket bolts, oil seal, upper bracket cover (if applicable), and handlebar and fork bracket.
2. Using Lock Nut Wrench (H-D Part No. 96219-50) or a suitable substitute, remove the head bearing nut, lift the upper bearing free, and pull the fork free from the bottom of the steering head.
3. Loosen, but do not remove, the fork bracket clamping studs and slip the fork bracket and slider cover assembly free of the fork tubes.
4. Remove the slider tube plugs, drain the oil, and remove the fork springs.
5. Remove the damper valve stud locknut and free the slider tube from the slider.
6. Remove the slider tube snap-ring with snap-ring pliers. Remove the damper tube lower bushing, damper tube bushing gasket, and damper valve stud gasket. Discard and replace all parts other than the tube assembly.

ADJUSTABLE

1. Remove the steering damper adjusting screw, spring cover, spider spring, upper pressure disc, friction washer, anchor plate, friction washer, and lower pressure disc by prying all parts loose when necessary.
2. Remove the fork stem nut, upper bracket bolts and washers, bracket cover and bracket.
3. Using Lock Nut Wrench (H-D Part No. 96219-50) or a suitable substitute, remove the head bearing nut, lift the upper head bearing free, and pull the fork free from the bottom of the steering head.
4. Remove the slider tube plugs.
5. Loosen but do not remove the bracket clamping studs.
6. Continue as described for "Non-Adjustable Glide Models."

Inspection

1. Clean all of the parts in a suitable solvent and blow them dry.
2. Inspect the slider tubes and slider for scratches, grooves, wear, and damage, and replace if necessary. Remove minor faults with a fine oil stone or emery paper.
3. Inspect the valve tube assembly components for pitting, rust, wear, and damage, and replace if necessary.
4. Inspect the slider tube plugs for loose cups or damaged springs and replace if necessary. Oil slots in the cups must be arranged on alternate sides.
5. Inspect the steering head bearings and races for pitting, rough motion, wear,

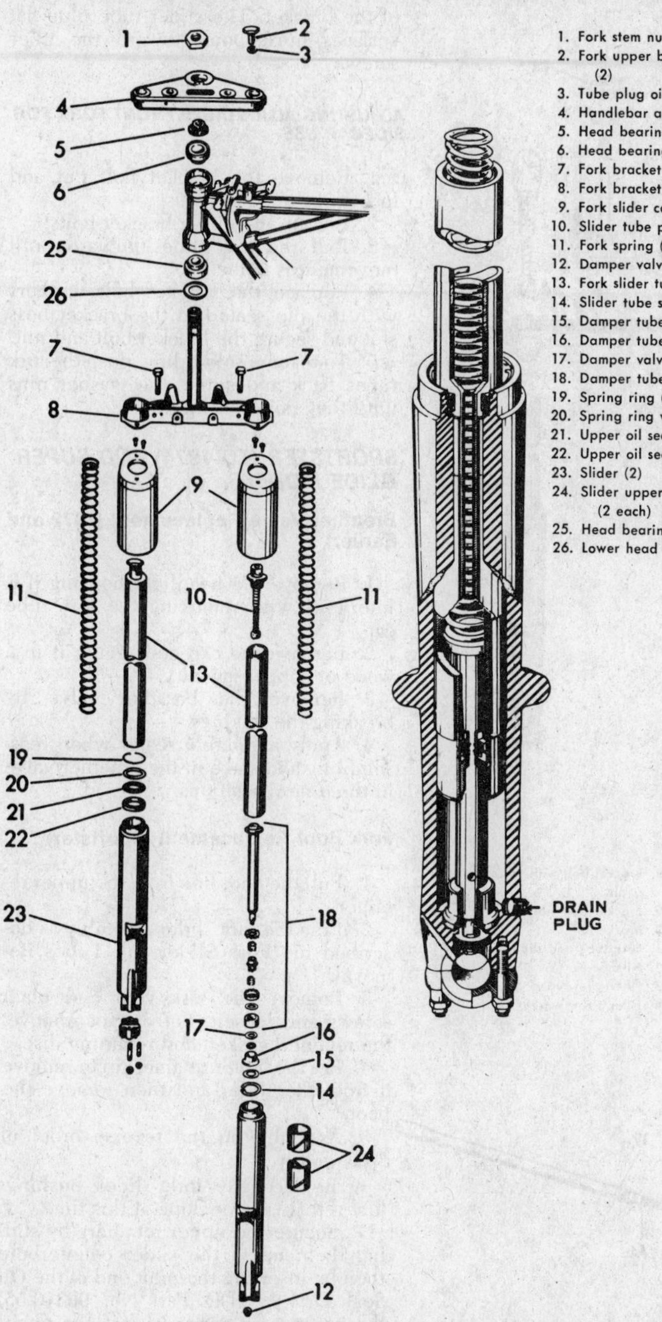

Nonadjustable fork assembly (Glide models)

or damage, and replace in sets whenever necessary.

6. Bearing races can be drifted free with a suitable drift after the head cups are removed. Replace by pressing new races into the head cup and then pressing both into the head frame.

7. Remove both fork slider bushings, if worn, pitted, or damaged, by installing Fork Slider Bushing Puller (H-D Part No. 96255-50) or a suitable substitute. Oil the tool's threads and washer to ease removal. The bushing may be split with a chisel to remove it if care is taken not to damage the slider.

8. Install the new fork slider bushings with Fork Slider Bushing Driver and Guide (H-D Part No. 96285-50) or a suitable drift, or else use a piece of pipe with the slide secured in a copper or wood-jawed vise. If the proper bushing driver is not available, mark the tube where the bushings were originally as an aid in replacing them correctly. Lubricate the bushing and the tube to aid installation. The lower bushing should seat at a position where the second groove of the driver is aligned with the top of the guide. The upper bushing should be $^{1}/_{16}$ in. below the oil seal counterbore.

9. Ream the bushing with Fork Slider Bushing Reamer and Pilots (H-D Part No. 96300-50) or a suitable substitute. Using the long pilot as a guide in the lower bushing, ream the upper bushing by slowly placing the reamer in position while rotating it clockwise. Always continued to rotate the reamer while withdrawing it.

10. Ream the lower bushing with the small pilot as a guide in the same manner as for the upper bushing. Take care not to mar the upper bushing while passing the reamer through it. Pilots can be made from suitably sized lengths of pipe.

Assembly

NON-ADJUSTABLE

1. Install a new upper oil seal and felt washer in a thoroughly cleaned slider. The oil seal may be seated gently in its counterbore with a mallet and Drive (H-D Part No. 96250-50) or a suitable substitute.

2. Install a new spring ring washer and a new spring ring with its gap over the slider top water drain hole.

3. Assemble the damper valve, new upper gasket, lower bushing, and a new lower gasket.

4. Secure a length of 1 in. steel rod vertically in a vise with 13½ in. above the jaws.

5. Place the inverted slider tube over the steel rod and drop the damper valve assembly in upside down.

6. Secure the slider snap-ring in the slider tube notch and check the clearance between the ring and the lower bushing. Insert shims if they are necessary to bring clearance to a maximum of 0.004 in.

7. Slide the slider over the lubricated slider tube and secure the damper valve stud locknut. Check slider motion for binding or drag. Loosen the locknut and rotate the slider 180 degrees before securing it to eliminate binding.

8. Install the assembled fork bracket and slider covers over the slider tubes so $^{5}/_{16}$ in. of tube extends above the top of the bracket and tighten the bracket clamping studs.

9. Fill each tube with Harley-Davidson Fork Oil (oil may be experimented with freely as long as specified quantities are conformed to) or hydraulic fluid, then install the fork springs and secure the slider tube plugs.

10. Secure the lower head bearing guard and a well-packed head bearing on the stem. Install the stem into the steering head.

11. Install a well-packed upper head bearing and secure the head bearing nut until there is slight bearing draw when the head is turned. Back off the nut until the motion is smooth.

12. Install and secure the fork bracket, bracket cover, and slider tube plugs.

13. Loosen the bracket clamping studs and rotate the slider tubes until the tube plug flat sides are to the sides of the forks.

14. Secure the fork stem nut, bracket clamping studs, tube plug oil seals, upper bracket bolts, and handlebar.

15. Complete assembly in the reverse order of disassembly.

ADJUSTABLE

1. Consult "Non-Adjustable Front Fork Assembly."

2. Place the slider tubes in the fork bracket with tubes $5^{1}/_{16}$ in. above the top

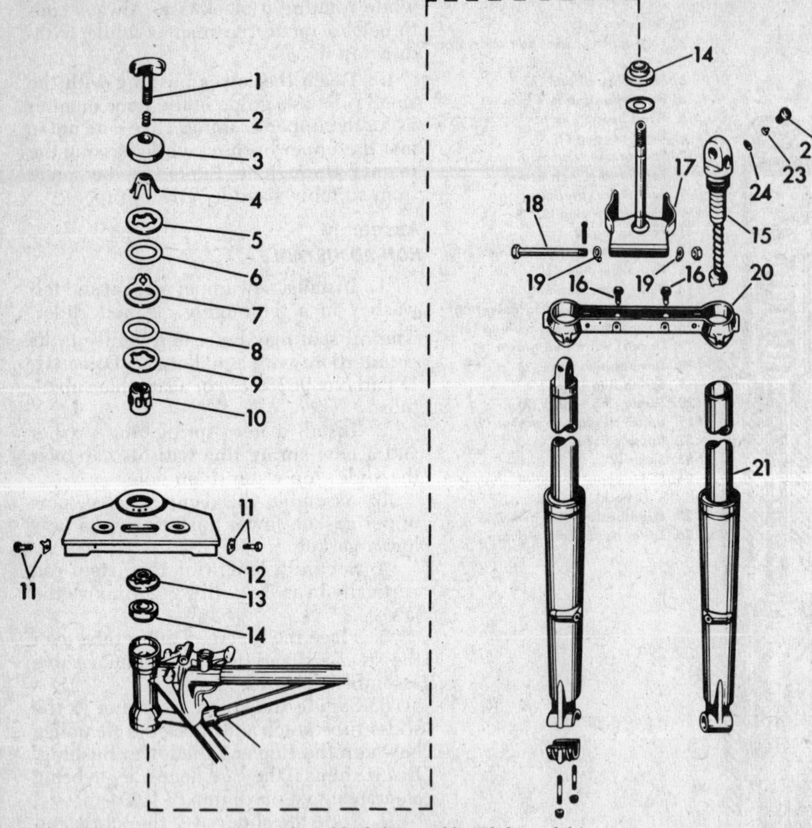

Adjustable fork assembly (Glide models)

1. Steering damper adjusting screw
2. Spring
3. Spider spring cover
4. Spider spring
5. Pressure disc (2)
6. Friction washer (2)
7. Anchor plate
8. Friction washer (see item 6)
9. Pressure disc (see item 5)
10. Fork stem nut
11. Upper bracket bolt and washer (2 each)
12. Upper bracket
13. Head bearing nut
14. Head bearing (2)
15. Slider tube plug (2)
16. Bracket clamping stud (2)
17. Bracket with stem
18. Bracket bolt with nut and cotter pin
19. Bracket bolt washer (2)
20. Bracket
21. Fork tube and slider assembly (2)
22. Filler screw (2)
23. Filler screw valve (2)
24. Filler screw washer (2)

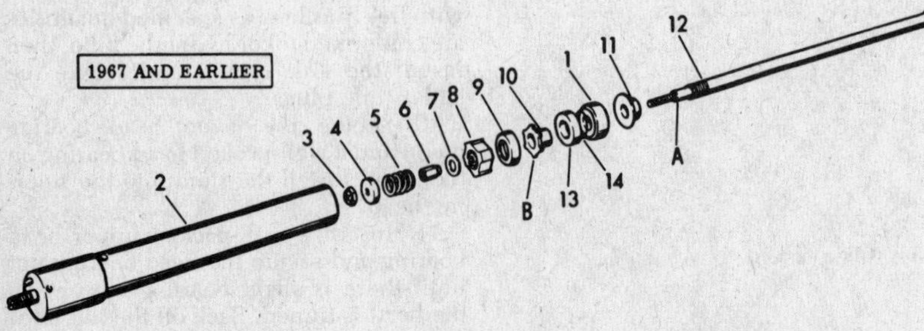

1. Piston stop bushing
2. Shock absorber tube
3. Piston rod nut
4. Recoil valve spring retainer
5. Valve spring
6. Piston spacer
7. Recoil valve washer
8. Piston
9. Piston valve
10. Piston rod stop nut
11. Piston rod guide
12. Piston rod
13. Piston stop collar
14. Piston stop spring

Front fork shock absorbers

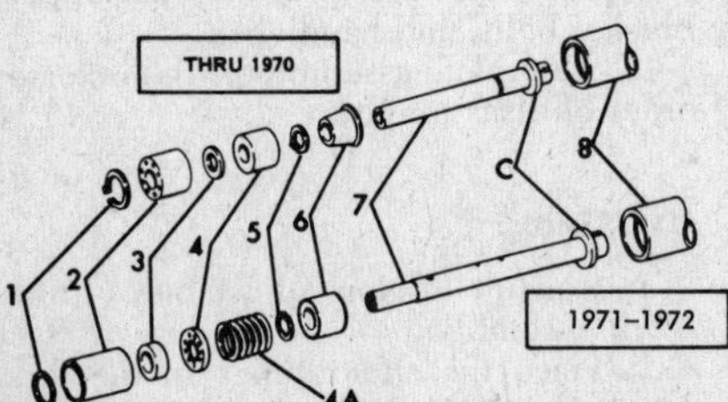

1. Retaining ring
2. Valve body, lower
3. Valve washer
4. Valve body, upper
4A. Spring
5. Piston retaining ring
6. Piston
7. Shock absorber tube
8. Fork tube

of the bracket. The slider tube plug flat surfaces must point toward the filler screw.

ADJUSTING ADJUSTABLE FRONT FORK FOR SIDECAR USE

1. Remove the bracket bolt nut and lockwashers.
2. Loosen the upper bracket bolts.
3. Pull the fork tubes forward until movement is detected.
4. Replace the bracket bolt washers with the pin seated in the bracket boss slot and secure the bracket bolt and nut.
5. To resume solo riding, push the fork tubes back and adjust the washer pins until they point backward.

SPORTSTER (TO 1974) AND SUPER GLIDE MODELS

Breather Valve Replacement (1972 and Earlier)

1. Remove the headlight housing if it interferes with removing the fork tube cap.
2. Remove the cap and secure it in a wood or copper-jawed vise.
3. Remove the breather valve by breaking the stakings.
4. Apply a suitable sealer when reassembling and stake in the breather valve in three new positions.

Fork Boot Replacement (Sportster)

1. Pull the boot free from the upper retainer.
2. Free the fork slider assembly as described in "Fork Slider and Tubes Removal."
3. Remove the fork vent and plain screws and loosen, but do not remove, the retainer, gasket, and retaining disc.
4. Pry the lower retainer lip to remove it from the slider and then remove the boot.
5. Assemble in the reverse order of disassembly.
6. Replace the fork slider bushings first if this is to be done at this time.
7. Secure the upper retainers by sliding them up to the slider counterbore then by inserting the pilot end of the Oil Seal Driver (H-D Part No. 96310-55) through the retainer and into the upper slider bushings. Gently tap the retainer until it is seated. A suitably sized piece of pipe can be used as a drift if the factory tool is not available.

Fork Disassembly

1. Remove the front wheel and brake assembly as described in the "Removal and Installation" for the wheels.
2. Remove the front fender, headlight cowling, and fork tube caps.
3. Loosen, but do not remove, the fork pinch-bolts and free the fork boot from the upper retainer.
4. Slide the fork leg assemblies free from the bottom.
5. Remove the piston rod (or spring) retainer with Wrench (H-D Part No. 94694-52) (on 1972 and earlier models) or a suitable substitute. Models earlier than

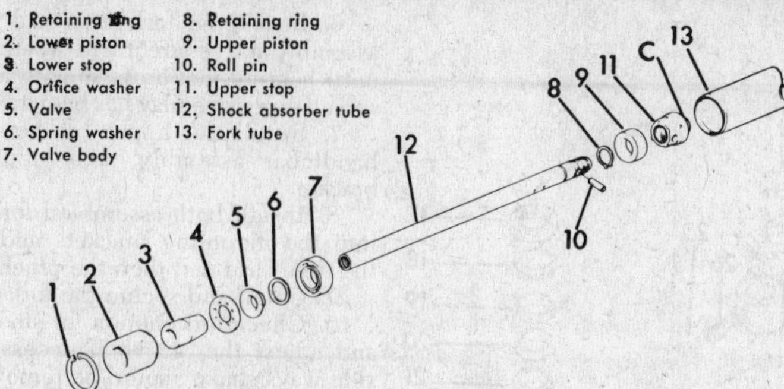

1973 and later FX, Sportster 1973–1974 front shock absorber

1968 require compressing the fork spring, securing the top of the shock absorber with vise grips, and then removing the piston rod retainer.

6. Remove the fork spring and drain plug, and allow the hydraulic fluid or fork oil to drain into a suitable container. Keep hydraulic fluid away from painted surfaces since it can cause corrosive damage.

7. Invert the assembly and remove the tube end bolt and washer by securing the slot in the top of the shock absorber tube with a screwdriver and then turning the end bolt. The shocks will come free on 1967 and earlier models. On 1973 and later models use Socket (H-D Part No. 94556-73) or suitable substitute, with extension on the upper end of shock absorber tube cap to keep it from turning.

8. Free the slider front fork tube and shock absorber assembly.

9. Remove the piston stop bushing with Wrench (H-D Part No. 94691-52) or a suitable substitute and remove from shock absorber tube. Remove the piston rod nut to dismantle the piston rod assembly.

10. Remove the shock absorber retaining ring with snap-ring pliers and slide the lower valve body, washer, upper body, spring (1971 and later), tube, piston, retaining ring, and piston on 1968 and later models. On 1973 and later models, disassemble the shock absorber as follows: Remove retaining ring from fork tube with snap-ring pliers and remove lower piston, lower stop, orifice washer, valve, spring washer, valve body and upper retaining ring. Disassemble upper stop by removing roll pin from shock absorber tube.

11. Remove the headlight assembly and disconnect the speedometer cable at the speedometer head.

12. Remove the stem sleeve end nut and loosen, but do not remove, the upper bracket pinch-bolt.

13. Remove the handlebar and upper fork bracket assembly and lay it aside. It is not necessary to disconnect the cables or wires as long as they do not bend sharply.

14. Remove the upper bracket spacer, stem sleeve, stem and bracket assembly, upper and lower bearing cones and bearings (and separate for reassembly), and head cups (if necessary). Head cups are easily removed by drifting from the opposite end with a suitable drift.

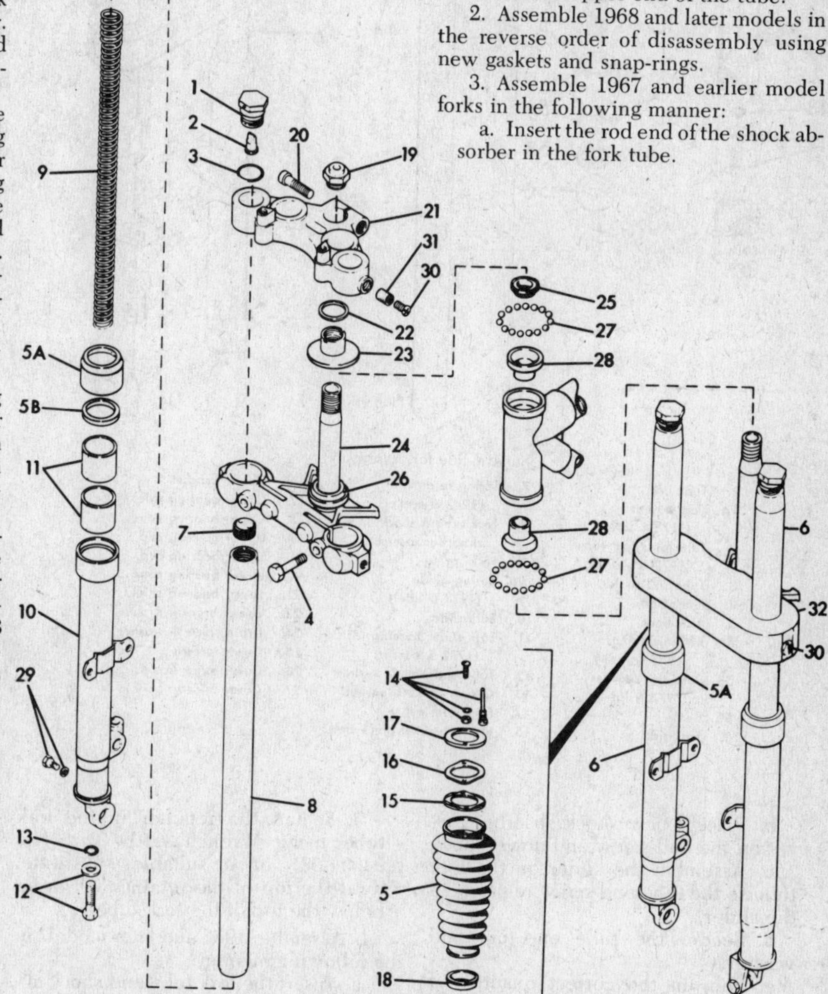

Sportster fork assembly (to 1974)

1. Tube cap
2. Tube breather valve
3. Tube cap seal
4. Pinch bolt
5. Fork boot (1970)
5A. Fork boot (1971)
5B. Seal (1971)
6. Fork side
7. Spring retainer
8. Fork tube and shock absorber assembly
9. Fork spring
10. Fork slider
11. Fork slider bushing (2)
12. Tube end bolt and washer
13. O-ring
14. Vent screw and plain screw (1970)
15. Boot retainer (upper) (1970)
16. Boot gasket (1970)
17. Boot retaining disc (1970)
18. Boot retainer (lower) (1970)
19. Stem sleeve end nut
20. Upper bracket pinch bolt
21. Upper bracket
22. Upper bracket spacer
23. Stem sleeve
24. Stem and bracket assembly
25. Upper bearing cone
26. Lower bearing cone
27. Ball bearings (28)
28. Steering head cups (2)
29. Drain plug and washer
30. Cover screw (2)
31. Insert
32. Cover

INSPECTION

1. Consult the previous section.

ASSEMBLY

1. Assemble 1967 and earlier models in the following manner:

a. Assemble the piston rod guide, piston collar, spring, bushing, and stop nut on the piston rod, with the stop nut face (b) 0.550 in. from the collar (a). Stake around the center of the nut in four new places.

b. Assemble the piston valve, piston, recoil valve washer, piston spacer, valve spring, valve spring retainer, and piston rod nut onto the piston rod.

c. Secure the piston stop bushing in the shock absorber tube with Wrench (H-D Part No. 94691-52) or a suitable substitute, until the top of the bushing is flush with the end of the tube. Stake the bushing by punching through the hole in the upper end of the tube.

2. Assemble 1968 and later models in the reverse order of disassembly using new gaskets and snap-rings.

3. Assemble 1967 and earlier model forks in the following manner:

a. Insert the rod end of the shock absorber in the fork tube.

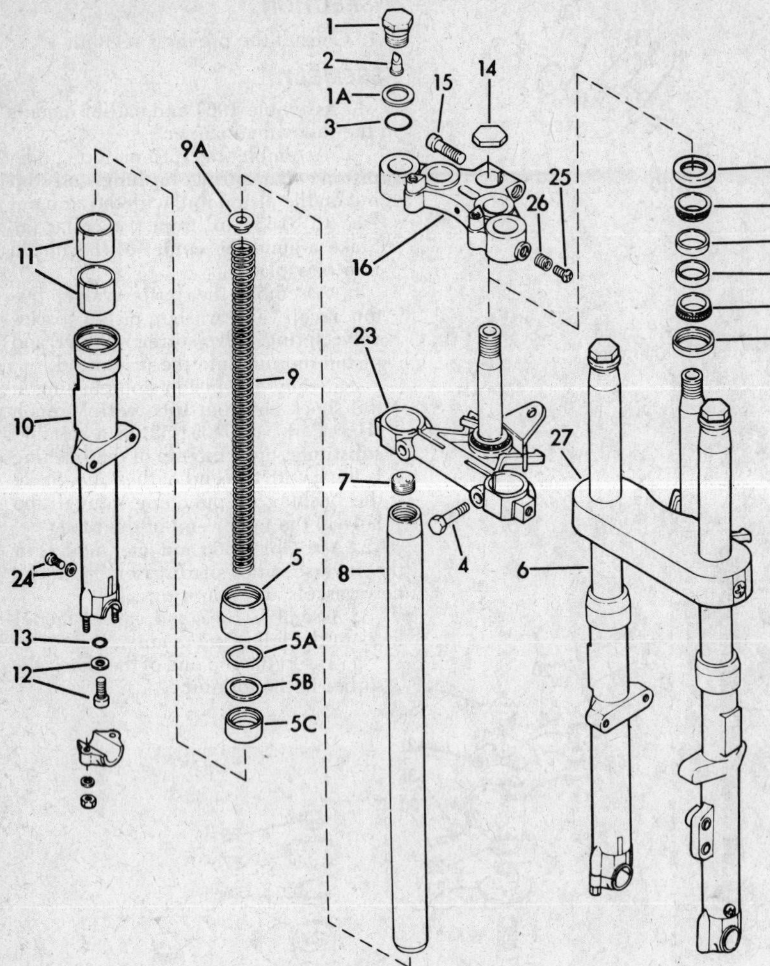

Super Glide fork assembly

1. Tube cap
1A. Cap washer (1973 & later)
2. Tube breather valve (1972 & earlier)
3. Tube cap seal
4. Pinch bolt
5. Fork boot
5A. Retaining ring (1973 & later)
5B. Retaining washer (1973 & later)
5C. Seal
6. Fork side
7. Spring retainer (1972 & earlier)
8. Fork tube & shock absorber assembly
9. Fork spring
9A. Spring guide (1973 & later)
10. Fork slider
11. Fork slider bushing (2) (1972 & earlier)
12. Tube end bolt & washer
13. O-Ring (1972 & earlier)
14. Fork stem nut
15. Upper bracket pinch bolt
16. Upper bracket
17. Upper bearing shield
18. Upper bearing cone
19. Upper bearing cup
20. Lower bearing cup
21. Lower bearing cone
22. Lower bearing shield
23. Lower bracket & stem
24. Drain screw & washer
25. Cover screw
26. Cover screw insert
27. Cover

b. Place a new shock absorber gasket on the end screw and dowel pin.

c. Assemble the slider on the fork tube so the tube end screw registers in the slider.

d. Secure the tube end nut and washer.

e. Pour in the correct quantity of fork oil over the top of the shock absorber rod and into the tube.

f. Insert the fork spring.

g. Screw a $^5/_{16}$ x 24 thread rod (i.e., brake rod) into the end of the shock absorber rod, compress the spring, and grip the flat portions of the rod with vise grips. Remove the threaded rod.

h. Secure the piston rod retainer and remove the grips.

i. Stake the retainer threads through the hole at the top of the absorber rod.

j. Secure the retainer in the fork tube using Wrench (H-D Part No. 94694-52), or a suitable substitute, until the top of the retainer is $^9/_{16}$ in. below the top of the fork tube.

4. Assemble 1968 and later models in the following manner:

a. Insert the fork tube and shock absorber assembly into the slider.

b. Hold the slotted top of the shock absorber rod with a screwdriver and secure a new O-ring and the tube end bolt and washer.

c. Insert a spring retainer ¾ in. below the surface of the fork tube top using Wrench (H-D Part No. 94694-52) or a suitable substitute.

5. Secure the steering head cups, ball bearings, and bearing cones. Bearing cones must be heavily greased.

6. Install the fork stem and bracket assembly and secure it with a stem sleeve until bearing motion is smooth and free and all excessive play has been taken up.

7. Install the upper bracket spacer, handlebar assembly, and upper fork bracket.

8. Install both assembled fork slides into the mounting brackets and secure the tube caps and then the pinch-bolts.

9. Count and secure the fork bolts.

10. Check fork motion for smoothness and adjust the sleeve if necessary. All side-ways shake should be removed.

11. Secure the upper bracket pinch-bolt and nut, and stem the sleeve end.

SPORTSTER (1975 AND LATER)

DISASSEMBLY

1. Remove the front wheel, brake caliper, fender, and headlight bracket.

2. Remove the two cover screws and slide the cover up out of the way to expose the lower bracket.

3. Loosen the lower bracket pinch bolts. Loosen the upper bracket screws.

4. Remove the instruments. Unscrew the tube caps. Pull out the fork legs and drain off the oil.

5. Remove the o-ring from the tube cap, if damaged.

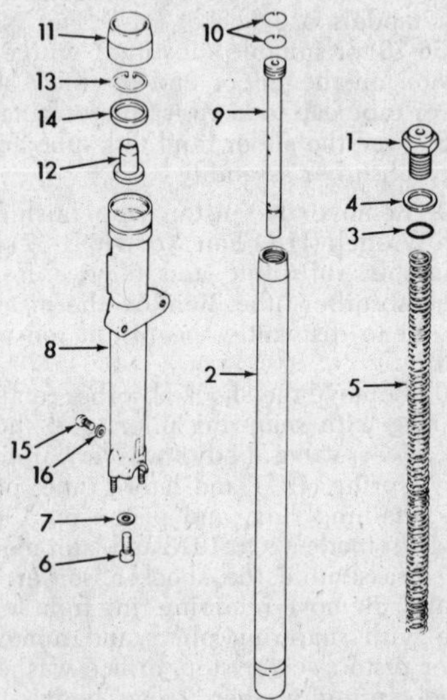

Sportster fork assembly (1975 and later)

1. Tube cap
2. Fork tube
3. O-ring
4. Washer
5. Spring
6. Screw
7. Washer
8. Fork slider
9. Shock absorber tube
10. Wear rings
11. Boot
12. Damper tube sleeve
13. Lock ring
14. Seal
15. Screw
16. Washer

6. Remove the allen bolt from the bottom of the fork slider.

7. Pull the fork slider from the fork tube. Take the shock absorber tube out of the fork tube. Remove the wear rings from the shock absorber, if necessary.

8. Remove the fork boot. Remove the damper tube sleeve from the slider, pulling it carefully past the seal.

9. Remove the slider seal, if necessary, by first removing the lock ring and

prying the seal out. Use new seals if the old ones are removed. The slider may be heated gently to facilitate seal removal.

10. To remove the fork stem and bracket assembly, disconnect the wiring from the panel. Remove the handlebar clamp cover.

11. Remove the headlight and bracket.

12. Remove the fork stem sleeve end nut and loosen the pinch bolt. Remove upper bracket and handlebars from motorcycle.

13. Remove the washer and fork stem sleeve. Free the fork stem and bracket, carefully lowering it from the machine.

INSPECTION

1. New slider seals must be used if the old ones were removed.
2. Check the condition of all o-rings and replace as necessary.
3. Check wear ring condition and replace if damaged or worn.
4. Check that the fork springs are of equal length and not excessively compressed.
5. Check that the oil passage in the lower end of the fork tube is clear.
6. Check condition of steering stem balls and replace balls and races if the balls are rusted or pitted, or the races are indented or worn.

There are 14 balls in each race.

ASSEMBLY

1. Lubricate the bearings and races. Tighten the stem sleeve until movement is smooth and free, but not so free that there is any play.
2. The remainder of the procedure is the reverse of disassembly.

SWING ARM

Disassembly

1. Remove the rear wheel as described in the "Removal and Installation" section for the wheels.

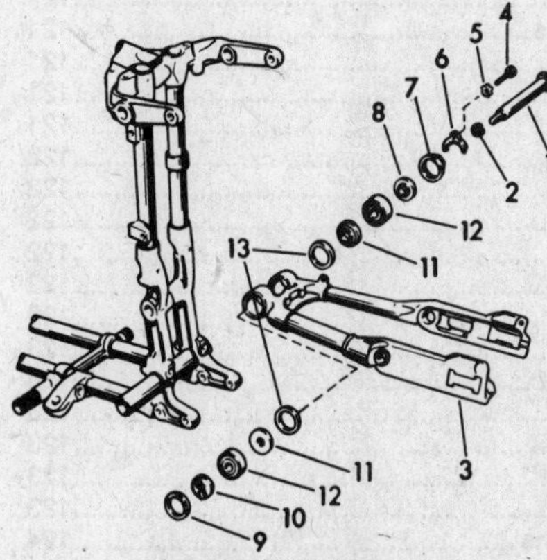

Sportster swing arm

1. Pivot bolt
2. Bearing lock washer
3. Rear fork
4. Bearing screw
5. Shakeproof washer
6. Lockwasher
7. Bearing lock nut—right
8. Outer spacer
9. Bearing lock nut—left
10. Pivot bolt nut
11. Bearing inner spacer (2)
12. Bearing (2)
13. Bearing shield (2)

2. Remove the rear brake assembly and linkage as described in the brake section.
3. Remove the rear shock absorbers as described in "Rear Shock Absorbers."
4. Remove the exhaust pipe and muffler (if necessary).
5. Remove the pivot bolt and rear fork assembly.
6. Remove the bearing screw, washer, lockwasher, right locknut, and outer spacer. Use a punch to remove the left bearing locknut and pivot bolt nut on Sportster models.
7. Press the bearing inner spacer, bearing, and bearing shield from each side of the fork on Sportster models.
8. Press the bearing spacer, seal, and bearing from each side of the fork (Glide models).

Inspection

1. Clean all parts in a suitable solvent and blow them dry.
2. Inspect all parts for wear, pitting, rough bearing motion, or damage, and replace as necessary.
3. Measure the swing arm for correct dimensions.

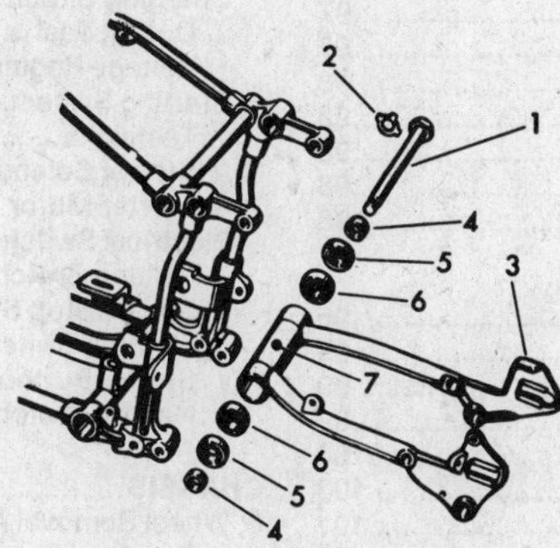

Glide models swing arm assembly

1. Pivot bolt
2. Pivot bolt lock washer
3. Rear fork
4. Pivot bearing spacer (2)
5. Bearing seal
6. Bearing
7. Grease fitting

Assembly

1. Assemble in the reverse order of disassembly.
2. Grease the bearings thoroughly. This must be done every 10,000 miles on Sportsters or it must be greased through the fitting every 2,000 miles on Glide models.
3. Press the bearing shield into the fork from the outside until it is flush with the inside. Insert the bearing with the wide side of the race facing out. Assemble and secure the right bearing locknut and then back it off one full turn. Assemble the pivot bolt nut, then secure the left locknut and stake it in three new places (Sportster models).
4. Apply grease to the bearing seals in the groove between the sealing lips and secure the seals and spacers (Glide models).
5. Preload the bearings in the following manner:
   a. Assemble the pivot bolt.
   b. Weigh the extreme rear end of the fork in a horizontal position, with a spring scale, and note the reading.
   c. Tighten the pivot bolt (Sportster) or the right locknut (Glide models) until bearing drag is increased by one or two pounds above the original reading.
6. Complete reassembly in the reverse order of disassembly.

REAR SHOCK ABSORBERS

Disassembly

1966 AND EARLIER MODELS

1. Remove the cover clamp, top cover mounting stud nuts, stud cover, washer, and rubber bushing.
2. Remove the shock from the mounting studs.
3. Compress the spring until the lower mounting eye can be rotated 90° then remove the shock from the tool (if used).
4. Remove the cam support.
5. Strike the lower mounting eye sharply to free the bumper from the cover flange.
6. Remove the cover and disassemble the lower cam, rotating cam, cam sleeve, dirt seal, and spacer washers.
7. Remove the bumper by extending the absorber piston shaft and the spring-ing bumper.

1967 AND LATER MODELS

1. Remove the mounting stud nuts, upper stud cover, and cup washers.
2. Remove the shock absorber from the mounting studs.
3. Press the stud rubber bushings from the mounting eyes.
4. Remove the retaining ring.
5. Compress the spring until the split key can be removed.
6. Remove the compression tool (if used) and disassemble the remaining items.

Assembly

1966 AND EARLIER MODELS

1. Lightly grease the cam sleeve and cam surface of the adjusting cam.
2. Secure the roller pin in the lower cam and place it on the cam support with the pin and pin slot aligned.
3. Extend the piston rod and assemble the bumper.
4. Assemble the spring in the cover, then the shock in the spring, and strike the upper mounting eye to secure the bumper in the cover flange.
5. Slip the spacer and seal washers into the cover and complete assembly in the reverse order of disassembly.
6. Compress the spring and rotate the lower mounting eye 90° to secure it in the cam support notch.

1967 AND LATER MODELS

1. Lightly grease the cam surfaces.
2. Assemble in the reverse order of disassembly taking care to align the cam faces.
3. Compress the springs and insert the keys and retaining ring (if applicable).

Honda ATC 70-125

INDEX

SERIAL NUMBER LOCATIONS

To avoid confusion when ordering parts, always supply the frame and engine serial numbers.

The frame serial number is stamped onto the left side of the steering head lug.

The engine serial number is stamped onto the lower left side of the crankcase behind the gearshift lever.

MAINTENANCE

NOTE: *Common maintenance procedures are explained in detail in the "General Information" section of this manual.*

LUBRICATION

Checking Oil

1. Oil level should be checked before each ride.
2. A dipstick is fitted to the oil filler cap on the right crankcase cover.
3. Park the machine on a level surface.
4. Start the engine, allow it to idle for several minutes, then shut it off and let it sit for a minute or so.
5. Unscrew and remove the dipstick and wipe it clean.
6. Insert the dipstick, allowing the cap to rest on top of the threads of the hole. Do not screw it in when checking oil level.
7. The oil level should be between the minimum and maximum marks on the dipstick.
8. If level is too low, add enough oil to bring it up to the specified level.

CAUTION: *Do not overfill the crankcase.*

Changing Oil

1. Oil should be changed every 30 operating days if the machine is used under normal operating conditions.
2. At the same time the oil is changed, the oil filter screen and centrifugal filter should be cleaned. See "Oil Filters," below.
3. Oil should be API service rated "SE" or "SF." SAE 20W-40 or 20W-50 can be used when average air temperature is above freezing (32°F). Refer to the "Recommended Lubricants" chart for all temperature oil recommendations.
4. Run the machine until the engine reaches operating temperature.
5. Park the machine on a level surface.
6. Place a container of about 2 qts. capacity beneath the engine.
7. Remove the dipstick.
8. Remove the oil drain plug. Allow the oil to drain for several minutes.
9. With the ignition or kill switch "OFF," turn the engine over with the recoil starter. This will allow more of the oil to drain out.
10. Check the condition of the drain plug washer. Replace it if damaged.
11. Clean the threads of the drain plug. Install the plug and tighten it securely.
12. Clean the oil filters. See below.
13. Add the correct amount and grade of

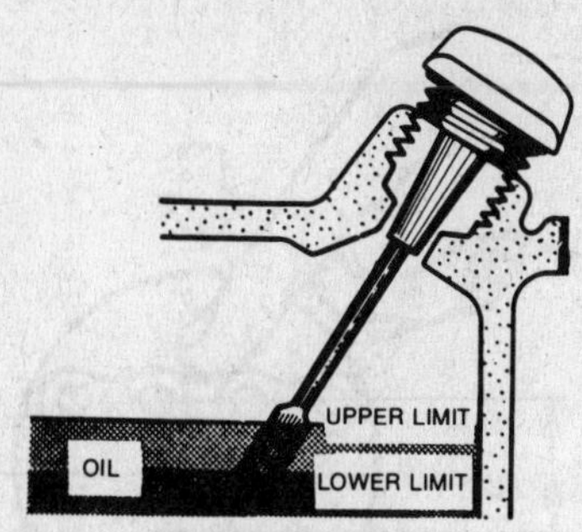

Checking oil level

motor oil. Approximate capacities are as follows. Use the dipstick to check for level:

ATC 70	0.7 qts./0.7L
ATC 90	0.9 qts./0.9L
ATC 110	1.1 qts./1.0L
ATC 125	1.2 qts./1.1L

14. Check oil level as outlined above.
15. Start the engine and let it run for a minute or so. Check for leaks . Recheck level and top up if necessary.

NOTE: *The oil change interval is based on normal operating conditions. If the machine is used under severe conditions (i.e. racing, high-speed riding, stq- and-go commercial use, in dusty environments, cold weather, etc.), changes should be made more frequently. This is especially true if the vehicle is used infrequently such as during the winter months.*

Oil Filters

1. The machines are fitted with a centrifugal filter in the clutch housing. An oil filter screen is located in a slot beneath the clutch.
2. The filters should be cleaned each time the oil is changed, which will be every 30 operating days under normal conditions.
3. Have a clutch outer cover gasket and a crankcase cover gasket on hand. These items should be replaced.
4. Drain the oil as outlined above.
5. Install the drain plug.
6. Place a drip pan beneath the right crankcase cover.
7. On ATC 70 models, remove the right crankcase cover as follows:
   a. Remove the exhaust pipe;
   b. Remove the footpegs;
   c. Remove the carburetor manifold bolts;
   d. Support the engine with a jack or suitable substitute to take the weight off the upper engine mounting bolt. Remove the bolt;
   e. Loosen the lower engine mounting bolt;
   f. Lower the engine;
   g. Remove the right crankcase cover bolts;
   h. Remove the right crankcase cover. If it is stuck, tap it with a plastic mallet to free it.
8. On other models, remove the seat. Remove the rear fender.
9. Remove the starter motor bracket screws, if a starter motor is fitted.
10. Remove the right crankcase cover screws. Remove the cover. If it is stuck, tap it with a plastic mallet to break it free.
11. Remove the ball retainer and clutch cam plate side spring.
12. Remove the oil passage pipe and spring from the center of the clutch.
13. Remove the clutch cam plate.
14. Remove the clutch lever.
15. Remove the clutch outer cover screws. Remove the outer cover and release bearing.
16. Using a clean, lift-free rag, wipe the center of the clutch housing to remove any foreign matter.
17. Install the clutch outer cover and bearing. Using a new cover gasket is recommended.
18. Install the cam plate.
19. Install the clutch lever.
20. Clean the oil passage pipe and spring in a clean solvent, dry them, lubricate lightly and re-install.
21. Install the cam plate side spring and ball retainer, aligning the steel ball with the centerline of the clutch lever.
22. Remove the oil filter screen from its slot below the clutch.
23. Clean the screen in a clean solvent to remove any foreign matter.
24. Check the residue for metal particles. If there are any, it indicates that severe engine wear is taking place. Determine the cause before operating the machine.
25. If the screen cannot be cleaned, or if it is punctured or shows other signs of damage, replace it.

Clutch centrifugal oil filter

26. Install the screen.
27. Check that the two locating dowel pins are in place on the crankcase cover mating survace.
28. Install a new crankcase cover gasket.
29. Install the crankcase cover. Tighten the screws gradually and evenly.
30. Add oil as directed under "Changing Oil," above. Check level. Start the engine and check for leaks.
31. After the machine has been sitting for a minute, make a final level check and top up the crankcase if necessary.

Drive Chain

1. The drive chain can be cleaned and lubricated through the inspection cap on the side of the chain case. Some models may be fitted with a lubrication port on the top rear of the case.
2. Standard chains can be lubricated with commercially available chain lubes or with SAE 80 or 90 oil.

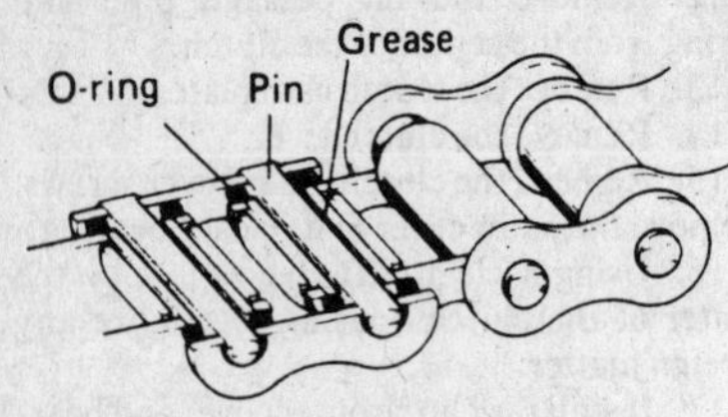

O-ring chain construction

3. Later model ATC 110 and 125 machines are fitted with chains which have rubber O-rings to seal in grease around the pins. These chains should be cleaned only with kerosene. Gasoline and other petroleum-based solvents will damage the O-rings.
4. O-ring chains should be lubricated with SAE 80 or 90 oil or with commercially available chain lubes which are compatible with rubber. Do not use chain lubes unless this is clearly stated on the container.
5. Chain service interval is every 30 operating days.

Chassis Lubrication

1. Chassis lubrication points include wheel and steering head bearings, brake cams and control pivots.
2. Bearings should be lubricated with a good grade of waterproof, medium weight bearing grease. Other points can take general purpose chassis grease.
3. The service interval for these points is every year. See "Chassis" for teardown procedures.
4. Control cables and other sliding surfaces should be lubricated every 30 operating days under normal conditions.

SERVICE CHECKS AND ADJUSTMENTS

Drive Chain

1. The drive chain should have 10-20mm (3/8-3/4 in.) of total up-and-down free-play. This is measured at the chain case inspection hole after removing the rubber cap.
2. Before checking or adjusting the

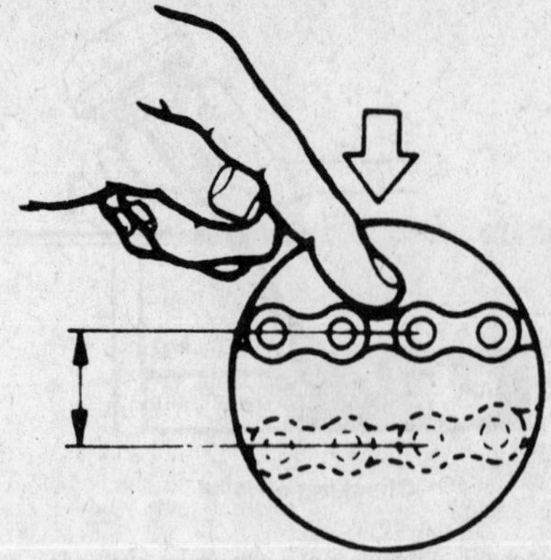
Checking drive chain free-play (10-20 mm/⅜-¾ in.)

chain, the following conditions should be met:
a. The chain should be clean and well lubricated. Dirty chains tend to get tight;
b. The chain should have been checked for tight spots by slowly rotating the wheels and checking for variances in tension. If a tight spot exists, the chain free-play should be adjusted to the proper specification at that point. Note, however, that such a condition is indicative of a worn chain and probably worn sprockets which should be inspected and replaced as soon as possible.
3. Be sure the transmission is in Neutral.
4. Check chain free-play after removing the chain case inspection hole cap.
5. On ATC 125 and late ATC 110 machines, adjust the chain as follows:
a. Loosen the four rear wheel bearing holder bolts.
b. Turn the adjusting nut as required until free- play is correct.
c. Tighten the bearing holder bolts. Proper torque is 36-51 ft. lbs.
d. Recheck chain free-play.
e. Adjust the rear brake.
6. On early ATC 110 models and 70s and 90s, a chain adjustment mechanism is fitted to the chain case. Loosen the locknut or bolt and move the tensioner so that chain free-play is correct. Then tighten the nut or bolt.

Clutch

1. Clutch operation must meet the following standards:
a. The vehicle must go into First gear smoothly without a jolt or stalling;
b. The machine must begin to move smoothly as the throttle is opened and moving performance must not indicate power loss and slippage through the clutch.
2. Under normal operating conditions, the clutch should be adjusted every 30 operating days.
3. Engine must be OFF.
4. Remove the clutch adjuster cap from the right crankcase cover.
5. Loosen the adjusting screw locknut.
6. TUrn the adjusting screw one full turn clockwise.
7. Slowly turn the adjusting screw counterclockwise until resistance is felt.
8. Back the adjusting screw off 1/8 turn clockwise.
9. Hold the adjusting screw in place and tighten the locknut to 14-18 ft. lbs.

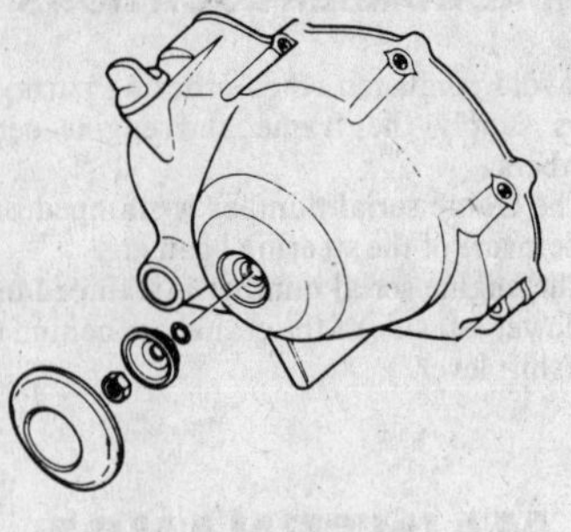
Clutch adjuster

10. Install the cap.
11. Check clutch operation.

Throttle Cable

1. Throttle operation and cable free-play are important safety items which should be attended to without fail. Operation of the throttle should be checked each time before the machine is ridden. The cable adjustment should be checked every 30 operating days.
2. The tip of the throttle lever should move 5-10mm (3/16-3/8 in.) before the throttle slide begins to open.
3. The cable adjuster is fitted to the carburetor end of the cable. Remove the fuel tank and slide back the rubber cover over the adjuster. Loosen the adjuster locknut and turn the adjuster so that cable free-play is correct. Tighten the locknut.
4. On some models, a cable adjuster is fitted to the upper end of the cable as well as to the carburetor end. This adjuster can be used for minor cable adjustments. If two cable adjusters are fitted, use both of them so that neither one approaches the end of its range.
5. With the engine idling, turn the handlebars slowly from lock to lock and listen for any change in engine speed. If this happens, the throttle cable is either too tightly adjusted or is binding somewhere along its routing.
6. Check that the throttle lever returns to the closed position regardless of the position of the handlebars. If it seems to hang up at one point or another, check cable free-play, cable routing and cable and throttle lever lubrication.

Front Brake

1. The tip of the hand lever should have 15-20mm (5/8-3/4 in.) of free movement before the linings contact the drum.
2. Adjust, if necessary, by turning the wing nut at the wheel in until lever free-play is correct.
3. Make minor adjustment, if necessary, with the cable adjuster at the hand lever.

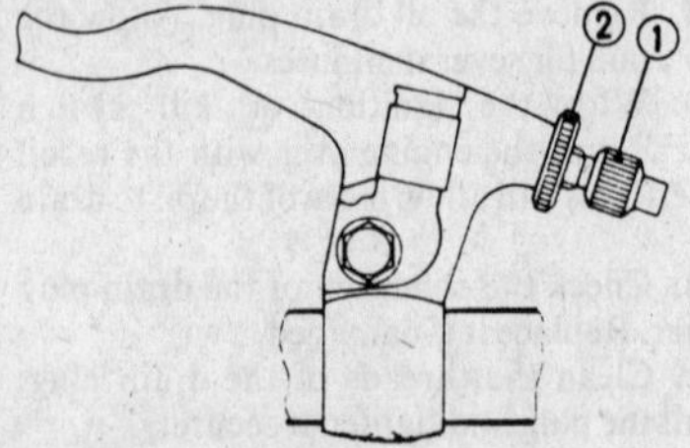

Cable adjuster (1) and locknut (2)

4. Apply the brakes fully and check the wear indicator position relative to the index mark on the brake plate. When the two align, the brake shoes must be replaced.

Rear Brake

ATC 70

1. The tip of the hand lever should have 15-20mm (3/8-3/4 in.) of free movement before the linings contact the drum.

2. Maintain this adjustment with the adjusting nut on the end of the brake rod.

3. Late models are fitted with a wear indicator on the brake plate. If the indicator aligns with the index mark on the brake plate when the brakes are fully applied, the brake shoes must be replaced.

ATC 90/110/125

1. The tip of the rear brake hand lever should have 15-20mm (5/8-3/4 in.) of free movement before the linings contact the drum.

2.-Use the adjuster at the hand lever for minor corrections.

3. Use the adjuster at the foot pedal for major corrections.

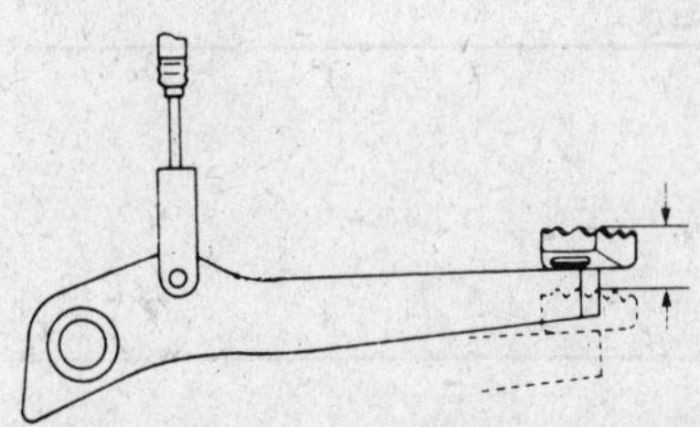

Brake pedal free-play (15-20 mm/⅝-¾ in.)

4. The foot pedal should have 15-20mm (5/8-3/4 in.) of free movement before the linings contact the drum. This free-play is measured at the tip of the pedal.

5. Use the adjuster on the cable at the brake drum to give the correct pedal travel.

CAUTION: *Unless the brake pedal is properly adjusted, the hand lever will not be effective.*

6. When the brakes are fully applied, check the wear indicator on the drum. If the index marks align, replace the brake shoes. See "Chassis."

Tires

1. Periodically check each tire for cuts, embedded matter, excessive tread wear.

2. Tire pressures must be checked when the tires are cold. A special low pressure gauge is needed for accurate readings.

3. Proper tire pressures are as follows:
ATC 70
1970-81 3.0psi
1981-On 2.2 psi
ATC 90/110/125 2.2 psi

CAUTION: *Always maintain tires at the recommended pressures.*

4. If pressure is too low, pump up the tires with a hand-held pump.

CAUTION: *Never apply high pressure air sources to the tire valves. Service station hoses are generally unsuitable for filling these low pressure tires.*

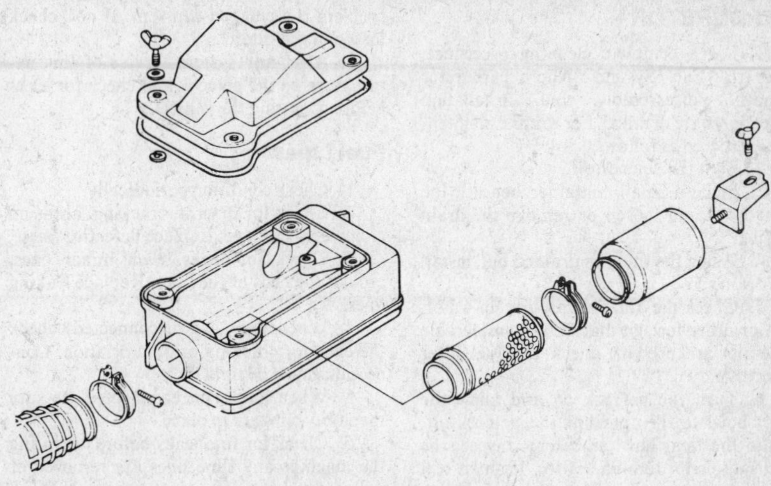

Air cleaner assembly (ATC 125)

Steering Head Bearings

1. Bearing wear and adjustment should be checked periodically.

2. Raise the front end of the machine off the ground by placing a safe, sturdy support beneath the frame.

3. Turn the handlebars slowly from lock to lock.

4. Check for binding, rough rotation and/or bearing noise as the wheel is turned. If any is noted, adjust the bearings as outlined in "Chassis."

5. Grasp the lower end of the forks and attempt to move them back and forth in line with the machine. There must be no play evident. If play is found in the forks, the bearings must be adjusted or replaced. Refer to "Chassis" for procedures.

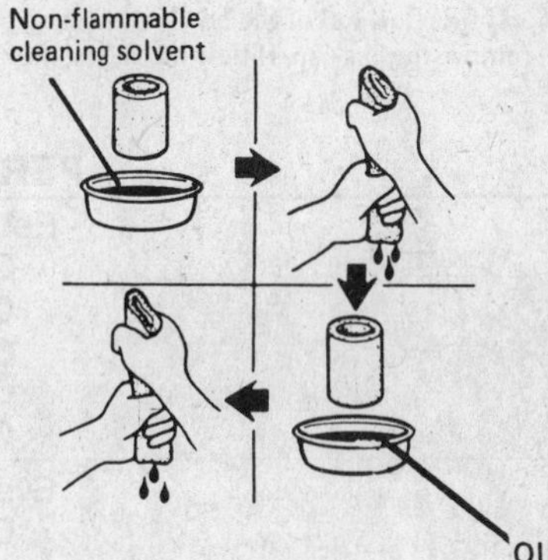

Oiling the air filter element

FUEL SYSTEM

Fuel system maintenance involves cleaning the filter, cleaning or replacing the air filter and cleaning the carburetor. These procedures should be carried out every 30 operating days.

Air Filter

1. Wash the element in a safe, high flash point solvent. Squeeze it to dry thoroughly.

CAUTION: *Do not wring the element out as the pores or fabric may be damaged.*

2. Soak the element in SAE 80 or 90 gear oil. Squeeze off the excess.

3. Fit the element on the frame and insall the assembly in the case.

Fuel Filter

1. The fuel filter is fitted to the carburetor float bowl on some models and behind the petcock on others.

2. Turn the petcock to the off position.

3. Place a rag beneath the carburetor to soak up the small amount of gasoline which will come out.

4. Remove the filter cap from the float bowl or the petcock (two screws).

5. Remove the filter screen.

6. Clean the filter in solvent. If the filter cannot be cleaned or is crushed, punctured or otherwise ineffective, replace it.

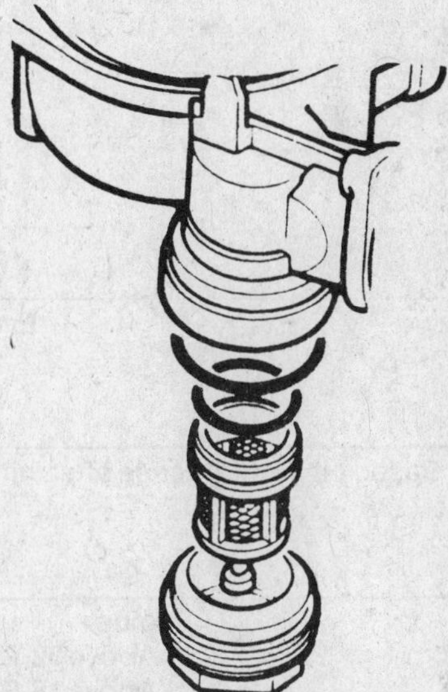

Carburetor float bowl filter

7. If your model has the filter cap, clean the inside of the cap in solvent.

8. Check the condition of the O-ring(s). Replace if knicked, crushed or otherwise damaged, or if leaks are evident.

9. Filter caps should be tightened to 4 ft. lbs.

10. Turn the petcock on and check for leaks before operating the vehicle.

CARBURETOR

1. For a complete cleaning procedure, refer to "Fuel System" where carburetor removal, disassembly and installation procedures are detailed. For routine maintenance, proceed as follows.

2. Shut the petcock off.

3. Place a small container beneath the float bowl and loosen or remove the drain screw.

4. When the fuel has drained out, install the drain screw.

5. Check the drained gasoline for water, dirt or other foreign matter. If considerable amounts are present, check the fuel filter screen.

6. Turn the petcock on and allow the float bowl to fill up. Shut the petcock off. Drain the float bowl as before. Inspect the fuel sample for foreign matter. If any is still present, check the fuel filter. Remove the gas tank and drain off the fuel. Check it for dirt and water. Flush out the tank before installing it.

7. If fuel flow out of the bowl seems sluggish, remove the gas cap. If flow increases, the problem is a clogged cap vent. If not, check for a clogged filter.

8. After any system service of this nature, turn on the petcock and check for leaks before operating the vehicle.

Fuel Lines

1. Check condition periodically.

2. Check for dry rot, cracking, abrasion or accident damage. Replace defective lines.

3. Check for leaks, even minor ones, around the ends of the lines. Replace leaking lines.

4. When lines are disconnected, check the ends for cracking or deterioration. Connections must be tight.

5. When lines are reconnected, be sure the safety clips are in place.

6. Check for fuel leaks before operating the machine any time lines are removed or replaced.

SPARK ARRESTOR

1. The spark arrestor should be decarbonized every 30 operating days. Excessive carbon buildup will cause sluggish performance and possible engine overheating.

2. Park the machine in an open area free of flammable material.

3. On 1985 and later ATC 125 machines, remove the bolt and sealing washer.

4. On other models, remove the spark arrestor bolts and pull it out of the exhaust pipe.

5. On models with a removable spark arrestor, use a wire brush to remove build-up carbon from the unit.

6. On all models, start the engine and, after it reaches operating temperature, rev it several times to blow out the carbon.

CAUTION: *Hot carbon particles may represent a fire hazard if this procedure is carried out in an unsuitable location.*

7. Shut off the engine.

8. After the exhaust system has cooled, replace the arrestor on those machines with a removable unit.

9. On 1985 and later 125s, install the bolt and sealing washer and tighten the bolt to 22-29 ft. lbs.

PERIODIC MAINTENANCE INTERVALS①

Before every ride
- Check engine oil level
- Check tire pressure
- Check throttle operation
- Check brake adjustment
- Check operation of lights, if equipped

Every 30 operating days
- Change engine oil
- Clean oil filters
- Check air filter element
- Check battery level, if equipped
- Clean fuel system
- Lubricate and adjust drive chain
- Adjust clutch
- Decarbonize spark arrestor
- Check tightness of critical fasteners
- Inspect tires for condition
- Adjust cables
- Carry out general chassis lubrication

Every year
- Check condition of fuel lines
- Check brake shoes
- Check wheel and steering head bearings

① Based on normal usage after initial break-in is completed

RECOMMENDED LUBRICANTS

Engine	
Above 32°F	SAE 20W-40, SAE 20W-50, service rated "SE" or "SF"
Above 18°F	SAE 10W-40, service rated "SE" or "SF"
18-85°F	SAE 10W-30, service rated "SE" or "SF"
Below 45°F	SAE 5W, service rated "SE" or "SF"

Drive chain (O-ring)
- SAE 80 or 90 oil
- Commercial chain lubes compatible with rubber

Drive chain (standard)
- Commercial chain lubes
- SAE 80 or 90 oil

RECOMMENDED LUBRICANTS
Air filter SAE 80 or 90 gear oil
Wheel and steering head Bearings Waterproof, medium-weight bearing grease
General lubrication Waterproof, medium-weight chassis grease
Cables Light motor oil Commercial cables lubricants Molybdenum disulphide-based lubricant

TUNE-UP

NOTE: *Common tune-up procedures are explained in detail in the "General Information" section of this manual.*

CAUTION: *All tune-up procedures done with the engine running must be carried out with the machine on level ground in a well-ventilated area. The parking brake should be applied.*

Keep children and other innocents away from hot, running engines. Never leave the vehicle running and unattended.

COMPRESSION TEST

1. A compression check should be made before each tune-up since this will provide a general idea of engine condition.
2. It is necessary to have a gauge with the proper adapter if a screw-in type gauge is used. Plug holes are 10mm and 70cc engines, 12mm on the others. The less expensive "hold-in" type gauge can also be used. Oil the rubber tip to ensure a good seal.
3. The engine must be at operating temperature.
4. Be sure the choke is fully on.
5. Turn the ignition switch "OFF."
6. Fit the gauge. Push the throttle lever wide open and turn the engine over with the recoil starter.
7. The highest gauge reading is the compression.
8. Standard compression is about 175 ±22 psi.
9. Low compression may be caused by valves which are too tightly adjusted, burned or otherwise damaged, worn piston rigns, piston and/or cylinder or other worn engine components.
10. If the compression reading is too low, squirt some motor oil into the cylinder and repeat the test. If the gauge reading is higher, suspect worn rings, piston or cylinder as the cause. If the reading does not increase, suspect problems in the valve train.
11. If the test shows that compression is too high, the problem is likely due to carbon deposits on the piston crown and cylinder. Remove the cylinder head and decarbonize the top end.

CAM CHAIN TENSION

1985 and Later

Cam chain tension is maintained automatically by a spring-loaded plunger operated by oil pressure. No routine adjustment is required.

1984 and Earlier

1. Cam chain adjustment is made with the engine idling. The adjustments can be made in two ways: either with the adjusting screw or with the tensioner bolt.

The adjusting screw locks the spring-loaded tensioner rod in place, and loosening it will allow tension to be automatically taken up.

The tensioner bolt allows the tensioner rod to be moved, compressing the tensioner itself.

The adjusting screw is locatd at the bottom of the left crankcase cover. The tensioner bolt is just below the adjusting screw, beneath a cover bolt.

2. With the engine idling, loosen the adjusting screw locknut and back the screw off (cunterclockwise) about 1 1/2 turns. Tighten the adjusting screw. If chain operation is now quiet, tighten the adjusting screw locknut, since the adjustment is now complete. If chain operation is still noisy, proceed as follows:
3. Remove the tensioner cover bolt. Loosen the adjusting screw locknut and back off the adjusting screw about 1 1/2 turns.
4. Turn the tensioner bolt in or out slowly until proper chain operation is obtained. If the chain chatters, it is too loose and the tensioner bolt should be turned clockwise; if the chain whines, it is too tight, and the tensioner bolt should be turned counterclockwise.
5. When chain operation is quiet, replace the cover bolt, tighten the adjusting screw and the adjusting screw locknut. Adjustment is now complete. Tighten the cover bolt to 14-25 ft. lbs.

VALVE ADJUSTMENT

NOTE: *Valves must be adjusted when the engine is cold.*

1. Remove the spark plug.

Timing inspection hole

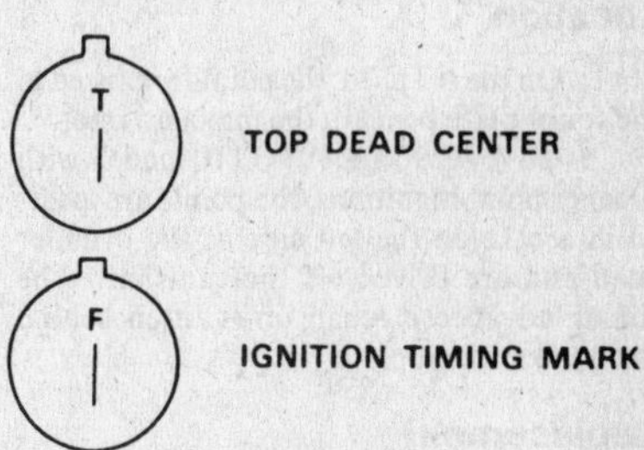

Rotor timing marks

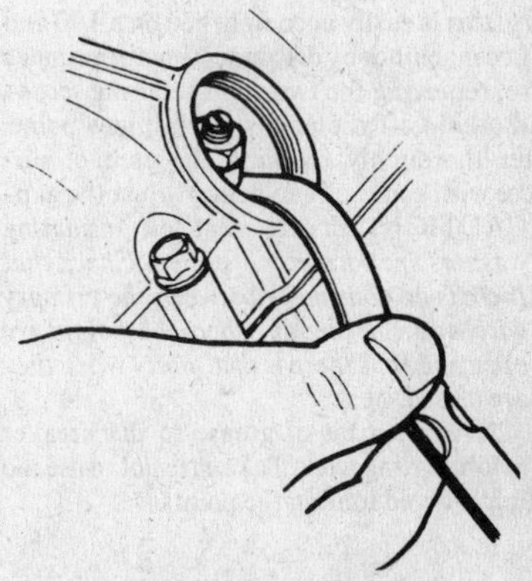

Checking valve clearance

2. Remove the intake and exhaust valve adjuster covers.
3. Remove the timing inspection hole cap on the left crankcase cover, if one is fitted. If not, remove the recoil starter assembly.
4. Turn the engine over slowly while watching the intake rocker arm and the magneto rotor.

NOTE: *The rotor must be turned counterclockwise.*

5. When the intake rocker arm opens the valve and then begins to close it, check the magneto rotor timing marks relative to the timing index mark. When the "T" mark on the rotor aligns with the index mark, stop. The piston should now be at TDC on the compression stroke.
6. Check for rocker arm clearance at the valves. Each rocker arm sh ould have a slight amount of free-play. If they do not, the piston is probably at TDC on the exhaust stroke. Turn the rotor 360°, align the "T" mark and check again.
7. Valve clearances are as follows:

ATC 70, 90: 0.05mm/0.002 in.
ATC 110, 125 0.07mm/0.003 in.
These figures are for both intake and exhaust valves. A feeler gauge blade of the proper

thickness should be a light slip fit between the valve and the adjuster.

8. If adjustment is necessary, loosen the adjuster locknut and turn the adjuster so that the feeler gauge blade is a slip fit. Hold the adjuster in place and tighten the locknut (torque: 11-13 ft. lbs.)

9. After the locknut is tightened, recheck clearance.

10. Install and tighten the adjuster covers to 7-10 ft. lbs.

11. Tighten the spark plug to 9-14 ft. lbs.

CONTACT BREAKER POINTS

Location

1. On the ATC 70, the points are fitted to the stator plate beneath the magneto rotor.

2. On ATC 90 and ATC 110 models with breaker point ingnitions, the points are located in a case on the left side of the cylinder head and are driven off the camshaft. The timing advance mechanism is fitted behind the breaker point plate.

Replacement

ATC 90, 110

1. If replacement of the points is necessary, this is easily accomplished on all 90 and 110cc machines by disconnecting the primary wire, removing the two point securing screws and taking off the points. Install new points after thoroughly cleaning the contact surfaces with a non-oily solvent. Adjust the gap.

CAUTION: *Ensure that all insulating washers are correctly installed. Check that there is no continuity between the primary wire and the engine when the points are open and that there is continuity when they are closed.*

2. Apply a bit of grease to the breaker cam lubricating wick. Take care not to use too much to avoid fouling the points.

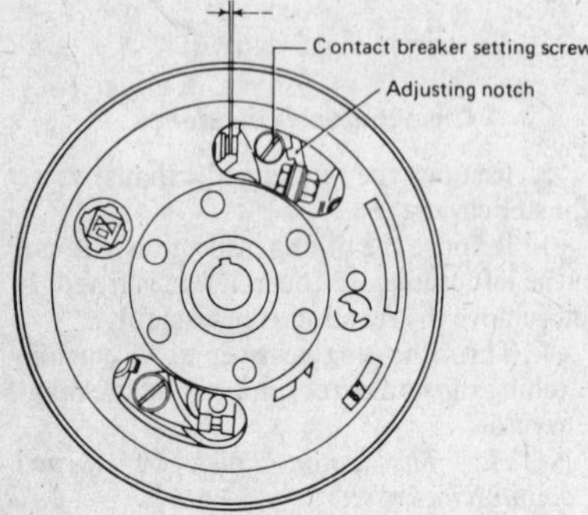

ATC 70 breaker points

ATC 70

1. Remove the recoil starter. Use the special puller to remove the magneto rotor after removing the rotor nut.

NOTE: *The puller has a LEFT-HAND thread.*

2. Disconnect the primary wire; remove the points' securing screw. Install the new point set.

CAUTION: *Ensure that all insulating washers are correctly installed. Check that there is no continuity between the primary wire and the engine when the points are open, and that there is continuity when they are closed.*

3. Apply a bit of grease to the breaker cam lubricating wick. Take care not to apply too much to avoid fouling the points.

4. Install the rotor. Torque the nut to 22-28 ft. lbs.

5. Adjust the point gap. Adjust the ignition timing.

Gapping

Gapping is necessary to compensate for wear of the contact surfaces due to electrical arcing and for wear of the breaker point fiber heel. As the heel wears the points will open later relative to the rotation of the crankshaft, retarding the timing.

Points should be filed (if necessary) and cleaned before gapping.

NOTE: *On ATC 70 machines the ignition timing is adjusted by changing the point gap. Therefore these operations must be carried out at the same time.*

ATC 90/110

1. Remove the points cover.

2. Turn the engine over slowly until the points are open to their maximum gap.

3. With the proper feeler gauge, check the gap. The proper specification for all models is 0.012-0.016 in. (0.3-0.4 mm). The feeler gauge should be a slip fit between a correctly gapped point set.

4. If adjustment is necessary, loosen the two screws which secure the points to the base plate, and use a thin screwdriver at the pry slot provided to bring the gap to the proper specification.

NOTE: *Loosen the screws just enough to allow the points to be moved. If too loose, the points will snap shut instead of holding the adjustment.*

5. Tighten the screws and recheck the gap. It may change slightly when the screws are tightened.

6. If it is not possible to gap the points correctly, the fiber heel is probably worn and the points should be replaced.

ATC 70

1. On this model, adjusting the point gap is the only method of adjusting the ignition timing, so timing should be checked whenever the points are gapped.

2. Remove the recoil starter.

3. Turn the engine over, observing the points through the cutout in the rotor until they are opened to their maximum gap.

4. With a feeler gauge blade, check point gap. Proper gap is 0.012-0.016 in. (0.3-0.4mm).

5. If adjustment is necessary, loosen the point securing screw and use a thin screwdriver at the pry slot provided to bring the gap within the proper specification.

NOTE: *Loosen the securing screw just enough to allow the gap to be adjusted. If it is too loose the points will close completely instead of holding the adjustment.*

6. Tighten the screw and recheck the gap. It may change slightly when the screw is tightened.

7. If it is not possible to correctly gap the points, the fiber heel is evidently badly worn and the point set should be replaced.

IGNITION TIMING

CAUTION: *Running-engine adjustments must be carried out in a well-ventilated area. Be sure the machine is parked on a level surface and that the parking brake is set.*

ATC 70

The timing on these models is accomplished by changing the point gap.

1. Remove the spark plug and the recoil starter.

2. Clean and gap the points to the proper specification as outlined under "Gaping."

3. Hook up the ohmmeter to ground and to the black wire coming from the points.

4. Turn the rotor slowly in the normal direction of rotation (counterclockwise). When the "F" mark on the rotor and the stationary timing mark on the crankcase align, the meter should indicate that the points have just begun to open.

5. If the points open after the "F" mark passes the stationary mark, the timing is too retarded; if they open before the "F" mark aligns, the timing is too advanced.

6. As noted above, ignition timing is corrected by changing the point gap. If the timing was retarded, increase the point gap. If it was advanced, decrease the point gap.

NOTE: *It should be possible to set the timing perfectly while maintaining the point gap within the specification given (0.012-0.016 in 0.3-0.4mm). If the timing marks will not align when the point gap is within this specification, the points must be replaced. Wear of the fiber heel is one cause of this conditions.*

ATC 90/110 (Breaker Points)

1. Remove the recoil starter and the points cover. Remove the spark plug and intake valve cover.

2. Hook the tester up.

3. Turn the engine over so that the engine is just beginning its compression stroke. (The intake valve will go down and come up). Turn the rotor slowly in the normal direction of rotation (counterclockwise). At the instant in which the "F" mark on the rotor aligns with the mark on the crankcase cover, the points should begin to open as indicated by the reaction of the test light or the meter.

4. If the points open before the marks align, the timing is too advanced. If they open after the "F" mark passes the stationary mark, the timing is too retarded.

5. If the timing is not correct, loosen the two philips screws which secure the breaker base plate to the engine. Loosen them just enough to allow the plate to be rotated.

6. Turn the plate using a thin screwdriver applied to the pry slot provided so that the

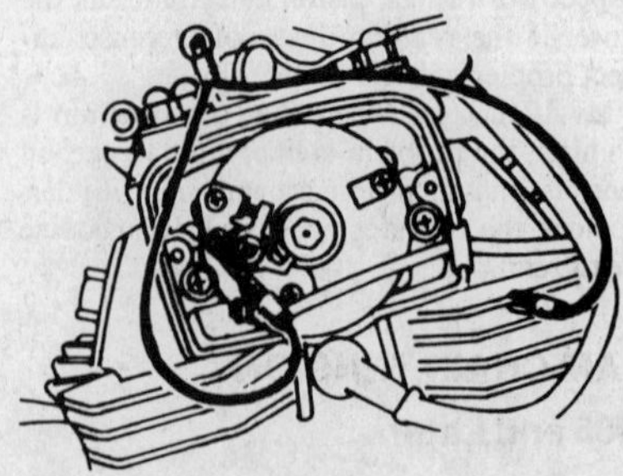

Timing light on breaker point ignition 90 and 110s

points open just as the "F" mark lines up with the stationary mark. If the timing was too advanced, turn the plate counterclockwise. If too retarded, rotate the plate clockwise.

7. Tighten the breaker plate screws and recheck the timing. Sometimes this will cause the plate to move slightly and throw the timing off.

ATC 110/125 (CDI)

1. Remove the timing inspection hole cap on the left crankcase cover.
2. Connect a timing light according to the light manufacturer's instructions.
3. Connect an electronic tachometer if idle speed is not known.
4. Observe the rotor timing marks through the inspection hole while the engine is running.
5. At 1700 rpm (±100 rpm), the "F" mark on the rotor should align with the index mark on the hole.
6. If adjustment is necessary, remove the pulse generator cover on the left side of the cylinder head.
7. Loosen the two base plate screws and turn the plate with a small screwdriver applied to the pry point until the "F" mark aligns with the index mark at 1700 rmp.
8. Tighten the base plate screws. Check that timing is still correct.
9. Shut the engine off.
10. Turn the engine over with the recoil starter until the pulse rotor aligns with the pulse generator.
11. The air gap between the rotor and the pulse generator should be 0.3-0.4mm (0.01-0.02 in.).
12. Adjust by loosening the two small screws which mount the generator to the base plate.

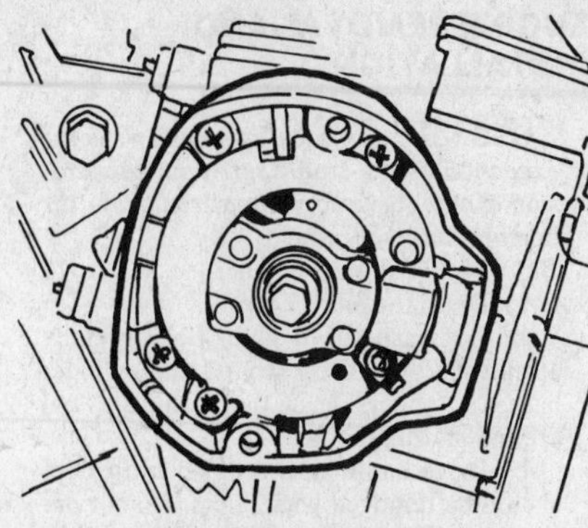

Base plate screws (CDI)

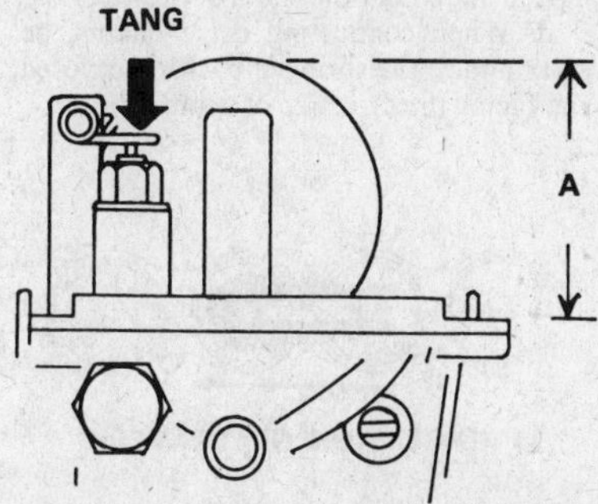

Adjust float level ("A") by bending the tang

13. Install the cover. Install the timing inspection hole cap.

NOTE: *Once set properly, the CDI ignition should not require adjustment. Unless the proper equipment (tach and strobe light) is available, ignition timing should not be attempted.*

CARBURETOR

Float Level

1970-77

1. Remove the carburetor.
2. Remove the float bowl.
3. Remove the float bowl gasket.
4. Float level is defined as the measured distance from the float bowl mating surface (gasket removed) to the top of the float when the float tang is just touching the end of the needle.
5. With the float held in this position, measure the distance from the mating surface to the top of the float. It should be 20.0mm (0.78 in.).
6. If the float level is not within 10% of this value, check for foreign matter on the needle tip or seat. Check for wear of the needle tip. Float needle, seat or both must be replaced if worn or corroded.
7. If the components are in acceptable condition, adjust the float level by bending the float tang up or down.

1978 AND LATER

1. Float level is not adjustable. Generally this item need not be checked until considerable mileage has been covered or fuel system problems arise.
2. Remove the carburetor.
3. Remove the float bowl (2 screws).
4. Remove the float bowl gasket.
5. Float level is defined as the measured distance from the float bowl mating surface (gasket removed) to the top of the float when

TUNE-UP SPECIFICATIONS

VALVE CLEARANCE (INTAKE & EXHAUST)	
ATC 70, 90	0.05mm/0.002 in.
ATC 110, 125	0.07mm/0.003 in.
BREAKER POINT GAP	0.3-0.4mm/0.012-0.016 in.
SPARK PLUG	
OEM	NGK
Type	
ATC 70	
1970-81	C7HS
1982-On	CR7HS
ATC 90	D8HS
ATC 110	
1979-81	D8HA, D8HS
1982-On	DR8ES-L
ATC 125	DR8ES-L
Gap	0.6-0.7mm/0.024-0.028 in.
Torque	9-14 ft lbs.
COMPRESSION	
Standard	175 ± 22 psi
Minimum	128 psi
CARBURETOR	
Idle speed	
ATC 70	1500 ± 100 rpm
ATC 90	1200 ± 100 rpm
ATC 110, 125	1700 ± 100 rpm
Float level	
1970-77	20.0mm/0.78 in.
1978-On	10.7mm/0.42 in.

the float tang is just touching the end of the needle.

6. With the float held in this position, measure the distance from the mating surface to the top of the float. It sh ould be 10.7mm (0.42 in.).

7. If the float level is not within 10% of this value, check for foreign mattr on the needle tip or seat. Check for wear of and needle tip. Float, needle and seat, or all three must be replaced if the level is not correct.

Idle Speed and Mixture

NOTE: *These items must be adjusted when the engine is at operating temperature.*

CAUTION: *Park the machine on a level surface in a well-ventilated area and set the parking brake.*

1. Check that the throttle cable adjustment is correct so that the cable has enough slack to permit the throttle slide to close fully.
2. Screw the pilot in carefully until it is seated, then back it out about 1 1/2 turns.
3. Start the engine and, when it has reached operating temperature, adjust the idle speed as follows:
   ATC 70: 1500 ± 100 rpm
   ATC 90: 1200 ± 100 rpm
   ATC 110, 125: 1700 ± 100 rpm
4. Turn the pilot screw in slowly until the engine stalls, then back it out one full turn.
5. Readjust idle speed, if necessary, to the specification given.

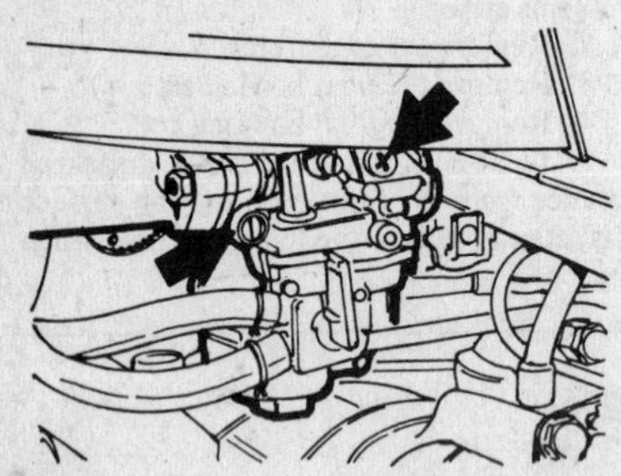

Carburetor pilot (left) and throttle stop (idle) screws

6. Shut the engine off and adjust the throttle cable as outlined in "Maintenance."

NOTE: *If proper idling cannot be obtained using this method, it may be that the fuel system is clogged. Check petcock, filter screen, carburetor, gas cap vent. Other possible causes include a dirty or worn spark plug, a plug which is too cold, improperly adjusted valves or air leaks in the intake system.*

ENGINE AND TRANSMISSION

NOTE: *Engine component removal and installation procedures are given in the following text. Specifications are in the chart at the end of this section. For service procedures and inspection techniques to valves, piston, clutch and other components, refer to "Engine Rebuilding" in the "General Information" section of this manual.*

ENGINE REMOVAL AND INSTALLATION

NOTE: *All engine components with the exception of the crankshaft and transmission can be serviced without removing the engine from the frame.*

Before removing the engine:

a. Drain the oil.

b. Degrease the engine. Be especially attentive to the area around the cylinder base, the underside of the crankcase and around mating surfaces.

c. Drive chain masterlink spring clips should be removed with pliers. Do not pry the clip off with a screwdriver or it will be distorted and will have to be replaced. After disconnecting the chain, install the masterlink on one end of the chain of prevent loss.

d. When connecting drive chains, be certain to fit the spring clip with the closed end facing the direction of chain rotation.

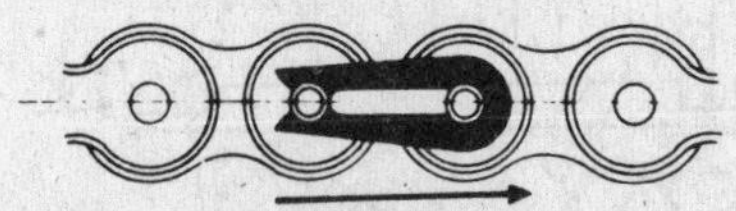

Masterlink spring clip closed end must be installed as shown

ATC 70

1. Remove the skid plate.
2. Remove the chain case.
3. Remove the recoil starter assembly.
4. Remove the exhaust pipe nuts at the cylinder head and the muffler mounting bolts. Remove the exhaust system.
5. Remove the footpeg mounting bar.
6. Remove the carburetor manifold bolts from the cylinder head.
7. Remove the Neutral indicator e-clip. Remove the gearshift lever.
8. Remove the left crankcase cover.
9. Loosen the chain tensioner. Unbolt the engine sprocket.
10. Disconnect the spark plug lead. Loosen the spark plug.
11. Detach the wiring harness from the frame and disconnect the wires at the connectors.
12. Place a jack or other adjustable support beneath the engine.
13. Remove the upper and lower engine mounting bolts.
14. Remove the engine from the left side of the frame.
15. Installation is the reverse of removal. Tighten the engine mounting bolts to 14-18 ft. lbs. Tighten the footpeg bar to 14-18 ft. lbs.

ATC 90/110/125

1. Disconnect the spark plug lead and loosen the plug.
2. Remove the seat and rear fender assembly.
3. On the ATC 125, be sure that the petcock is "OFF" and remove the two screws securing the petcock to the carburetor. Remove the mounting bolt at the rear of the fuel tank and remove the tank.
4. Remove the carburetor manifold bolts from the cylinder head.
5. Disconnect the battery ground (negative) cable from the battery (ATC 125).
6. Disconnect the starter motor cable from the starter motor (ATC 125).
7. Remove the left rear wheel.
8. Remove the skid plate.
9. Remove the chain case axle cover.
10. Remove the chain case.
11. Remove the exhaust pipe nuts from the cylinder head. Remove the muffler mounting bolts. Remove the exhaust system.
12. Remove the footpeg bar.
13. Locate the wiring connectors for points or pulse generator and disconnect.
14. Locate the magento/alternator wiring connectors on the frame and disconnect.
15. Locate the connector of the Neutral indicator wire on the frame and disconnect it.
16. Disconnect the breather tube from the crankcase, if fitted.
17. Disconnect the drive chain.
18. Support the engine by placing a support beneath it.
19. Remove the cylinder head bracket.
20. Remove the rear engine mounting bolts and take the engine out of the left side of the frame.
21. Installation is the reverse of removal. Tighten the cylinder head bracket fasteners to 14-18 ft. lbs. and the rear engine mounting bolts to 22-29 ft. lbs.

TOP END

The following section deals with the removal and installation of the cylinder head, cylinder, piston and related components. Inspection and service procedures are outlined under "Engine Rebuilding" in the "General Information" section of this manual. Specifications are included in the chart at the end of this section.

CAUTION: *When removing cy linder head and cylinder, be sure to note the exact locations of all dowel pins, O-rings and collars on head and cylinder base mating surfaces. Proper installation of these components is critical.*

ATC 70

REMOVAL

1. The engine need not be removed from the frame to remove the cylinder head and cylinder. Remove the exhaust system and the carburetor and manifold from the cylinder.

2. Remove the magneto or alternator rotor cover. Remove the spark plug and the valve adjuster caps. Turn the engine over until the intake valve goes down and comes up, and turn it a bit farther so that the "T"

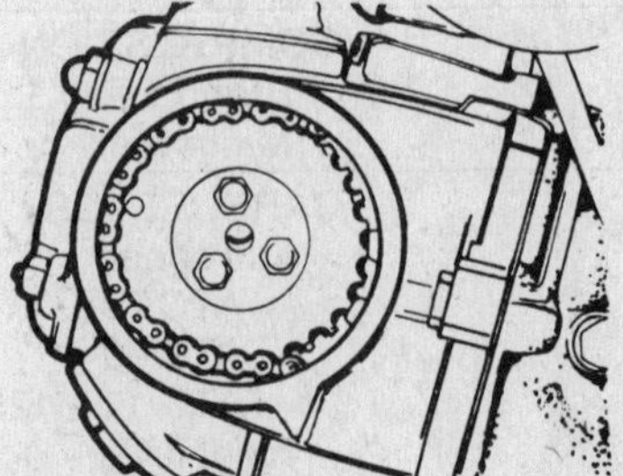

Cam sprocket bolts and sprocket timing mark (arrow) (ATC 70)

mark on the rotor aligns with the stationary index mark.

3. Loosen each cylinder head cover nut 1/4 of a turn at a time until they are loose, then remove them. Note that one or two of the nuts are different and must be installed in the location from which they were removed. On most models, there is one hex nut and three capnuts; an oil sealing washer is fitted beneath the hex nut.

4. Tap the head cover lightly with a plastic mallet to free it if stuck.

5. Remove the bolt from the right side of the cylinder head. This will enable the left side cover to be removed.

6. Remove the two screws on the right side cylinder head cover and remove the cover.

7. Check that the piston is at TDC (the "O" mark on the cam sprocket will be toward the top of the head).

8. Remove the three sprocket mounting bolts, and push in on the camshaft to disengage it from the sprocket. Remove the sprocket after disengaging it from the cam chain.

NOTE: *It may be necessary to hold the camshaft in position while removing the sprocket bolts and this can be done if the engine is in the frame by engaging the transmission except for centrifugal clutch models. If the engine is not in the frame, secure the magneto rotor or the countershaft sprocket.*

9. Remove the cylinder head mounting bolt on the left side of the head. Remove the head, tapping around the mounting surface with a plastic mallet if it is stuck.

10. When the head is removed, remove the two locating pins at the head mating surface and ensure that they are in place when the head is refitted. To remove the rocker arms, thread a suitable bolt into the right side of the rocker arm shafts and pull them out. Keep each rocker arm shaft with its own rocker arm for proper installation. Push the camshaft out of the head.

NOTE: *The cylinder head or cylinder mounting bolt can be used to remove the rocker arm shafts.*

11. Unscrew and remove the cam chain guide roller pin from the left side of the cylinder and remove the guide roller.

12. Remove the cylinder mounting bolt on the left side and pull off the cylinder. Do not allow the piston to strike the studs as it comes out of the cylinder. Check the location of the two hollow dowel pins on the cylinder studs. Remove these and make sure that they are installed when assembling the top end.

13. To remove the piston, remove the wrist pin circlips with needlenose pliers and push out the wrist pin.

NOTE: *Use steady pressure while removing the wrist pin. Support the piston with your other hand. Do not strike or attempt to force out the pin. If it is stuck apply gentle and even heat to the piston crown with a propane torch until the pin is free.*

INSPECTION

Refer to the "Engine Rebuilding" section of "General Information" and to the specifications charts at the end of this section for inspection techniques and service limits, respectively.

INSTALLATION

1. If the piston rings were removed or replaced, be sure that they are installed correctly.

2. Check the profiles of the compression rings. The two rings are not interchangeable. The ring with the plain profile is the top ring and the wedge-shaped ring is the second compression ring.

3. Be sure to install the compression rings with the manufacturer's mark near the end-gap facing upwards.

4. Piston ring end-gaps should be arranged as follows:

a. On models with a one-piece oil ring, arrange end- gaps of the three rings 120° apart around the piston, but not at the very front or rear of the piston or directly above the wrist pin holes.

b. On models with a multi-piece oil ring, end-gaps of the two compression rings and the oil expander should be arranged 120° apart around the piston, but not at the very front or rear of the piston and not directly above the wrist pin holes. The end-gaps of the oil rails should be arranged at about 3/4 in. (20mm) or more - one on either side of the expander end-gap.

5. Install one wrist pin circlip and place the piston on the connecting rod. The triangular mark on the piston crown must be positioned on the *cam chain* side. Insert the wrist pin and the other circlip. Use new circlips and be sure that they are properly seated. Arrange the circlip end-gaps so that they do not align with the cutouts on the piston. Lubricate the wrist pin, rings, and piston skirt with motor oil.

6. Be sure that the O-ring is in place in the crankcase oil passage and the hollow dowel pins are installed on the cam chain side studs. Fit a new cylinder base gasket. Install the cylinder, compressing the rings with your fingers as the piston enters the bore. Feed the cam chain through the cylinder as it is seated. Install and tighten the cylinder mounting bolt.

7. Insall the cam chain guide roller and the roller pin.

8. Install the two hollow pins on the studs: one on the top right stud, the other on the left bottom. Fit the O-rings to the oil passage and to the stud oil passage; fit the head gasket.

9. Install the head, complete with rocker arms and cam, threading the cam chain with its sprocket through, and securing them with a length of wire or a screwdriver.

10. Turn the magneto rotor so that the "T" mark on the rotor is aligned with the index mark on the crankcase. Set the cam sprocket "O" mark at the top of the head. Install and tighten the sprocket bolts to 4-7 ft. lbs. Thread locking compound should be used on these bolts. Lubricate the top end components.

11. The remainder of the procedure is the reverse of disassembly. Note that the cylinder head cover hex nut (on most models) and its copper washer are installed on the lower left stud. Install the head mounting bolt. Tighten the head cover nuts in a cross pattern and in increments of 2-3 ft. lbs. until the proper torque of 6.5-8.7 ft. lbs. is reached. Adjust the cam chain and tappet clearance before starting the engine.

NOTE: *The cylinder head cover may be fitted with an arrow mark. If so, install it so that the arrow points towards the exhaust port (down).*

ATC 90/110/125

REMOVAL

1. The cylinder head, cylinder and piston can be removed with the engine still in the frame.

2. Disconnect the spark plug lead and remove the plug. Remove the valve adjuster caps.

3. Remove the exhaust pipe nuts at the cylinder head.

4. Remove the three muffler mounting bolts.

Cam sprocket bolts (ATC 90-125)

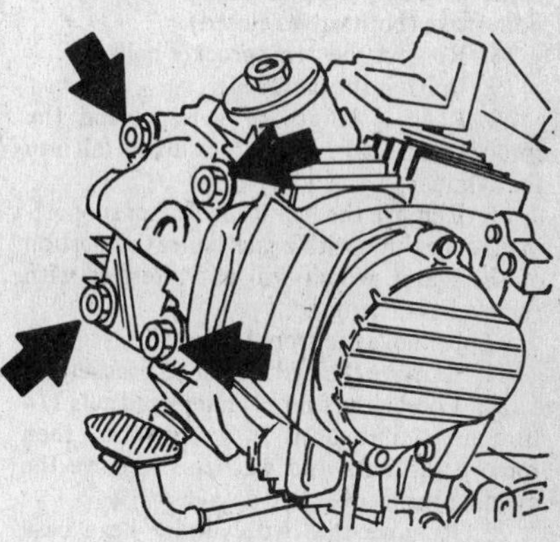

Cylinder head nuts

5. Remove the exhaust system.

6. Remove the manifold bolts on the head and remove the carburetor and manifold.

7. Remove the breaker point or pulse generator cover on the left side of the cylinder head.

8. Disconnect the pulse generator or point wire from the plastic connector on the harness and remove the wire clamp from the cylinder head, if equipped.

9. Remove the base plate screws (2) and remove the base plate.

10. Remove the rotor or advance mechanism bolt.

11. Remove the rotor or advance the mechanism.

12. Remove the pin from the camshaft.

13. Remove the three screws securing the points or generator housing. Remove the housing and gasket from the head.

14. Locate the cam chain tensioner assembly on the left under side of the crankcase.

15. On 1984 and earlier machines, loosen the cam chain locknut and tensioner adjusting screw. On 1985 and later machines, remove the tensioner sealing bolt, washer, tensioner spring and pushrod.

16. Removing the timing inspection hole cap on the left crankcase cover.

17. Use the recoil starter to turn the en-

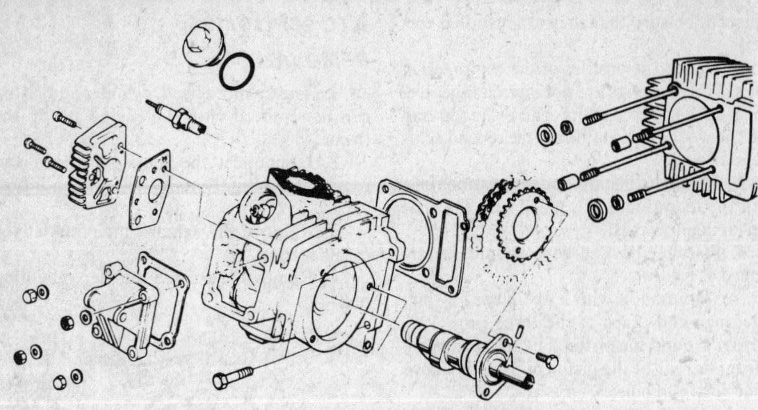

Top end assembly

gine over until the "O" mark on the camshaft sprocket aligns with the index mark on the cylinder head and the magneto rotor "T" mark aligns with the index mark on the inspection hole. The sprocket bolts will be in line with the centerline of the cylinder. This positions the piston at TDC on the compression stroke (both valves closed).

18. Remove the cam sprocket bolts.
19. Pull out the camshaft.
20. Loop a length of wire around the sprocket and chain so that they do not fall into the cylinder.
21. Remove the front wheel after supporting the machine with a jack beneath a portion of the frame which will not interfere with removal of the engine.
22. Remove the front fender.
23. Remove the cylinder head bracket.
24. Loosen the four cylinder head nuts 1/4 turn at a time until they are loose, then remove the nuts and washers. Remove the cylinder head cover and gasket.
25. Remove the two cylinder head base bolts on the left side of the head, if fitted.
26. Remove the head.

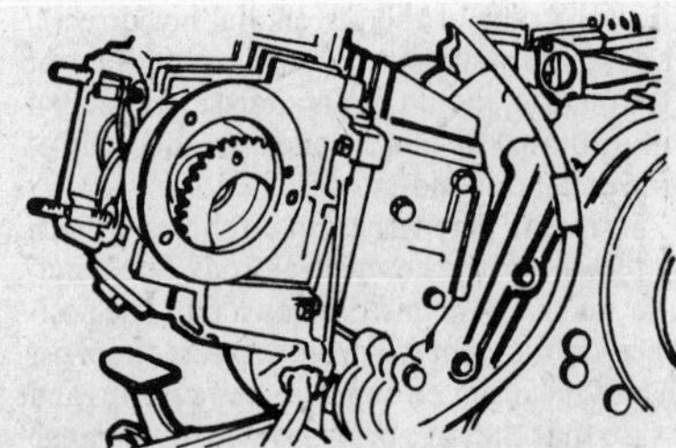

Cylinder head base screws

27. Remove the sprocket from the cam chain.
28. Remove the head gasket.
29. Remove the two cylinder base bolts on the left side of the cylinder, if fitted.
30. Remove the cam chain guide roller bolt from the left side of the cylinder. Remove the roller.
31. Remove the two dowel pins from the cylinder head studs.
32. Remove the O-rings from the cylinder head studs.
33. Carefully pull off the cylinder taking care that the piston does not strike the studs when the cylinder is removed.
34. Remove the cylinder base gasket.
35. Check that the cylinder base dowel pins are in place in the crankcase. If further engine work is contemplated, remove the pins to prevent loss.
36. Stuff a clean, lint-free rag into the crankcase.
37. Remove the piston wrist pin circlips with a needlenose pliers. Push out the wrist pin with a suitable drift. Remove the piston.
38. Remove the four screws and take off the finned cylinder head cover and gasket from the right side of the head.
39. Pull out the rocker arm shafts with a needlenose pliers and remove the rocker arms. Keep each shaft with its own rocker arm and mark them to ensure that they are installed in their original locations during assembly.
40. To remove the valve assemblies, compress the valve springs and remove the keepers.

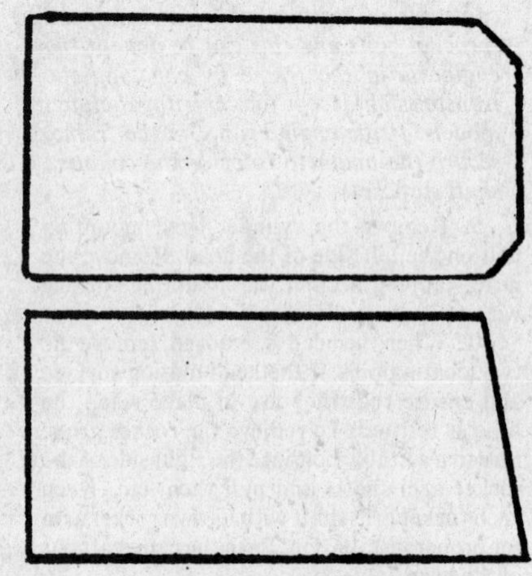

Compression ring profiles

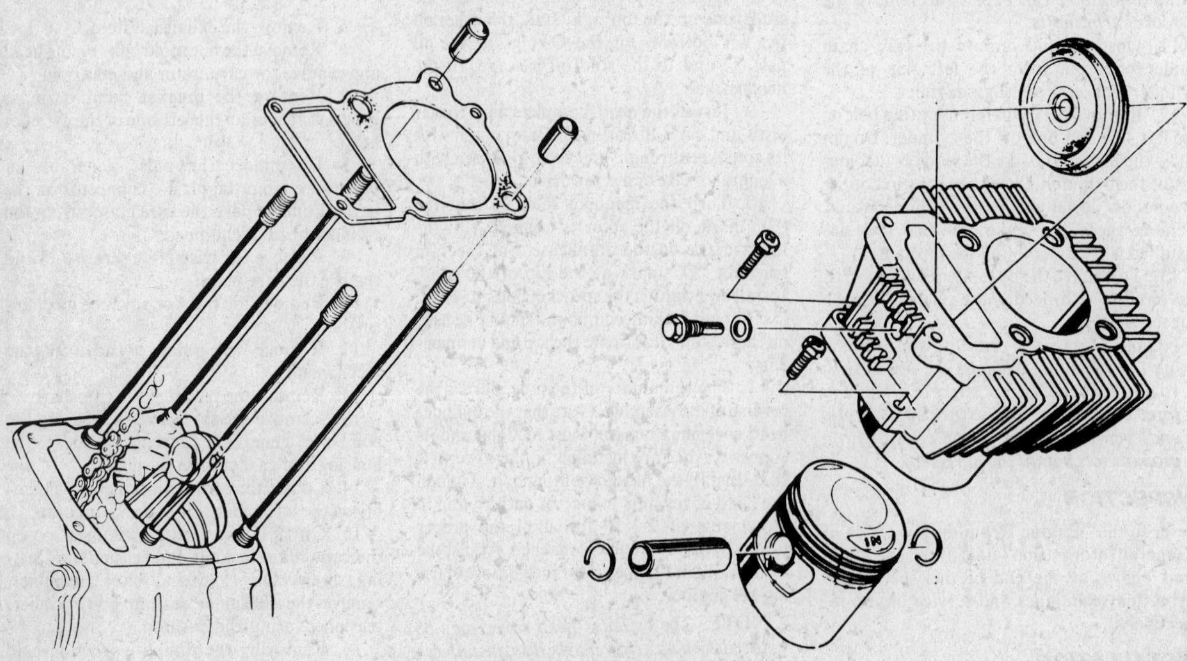

Cylinder and piston assembly

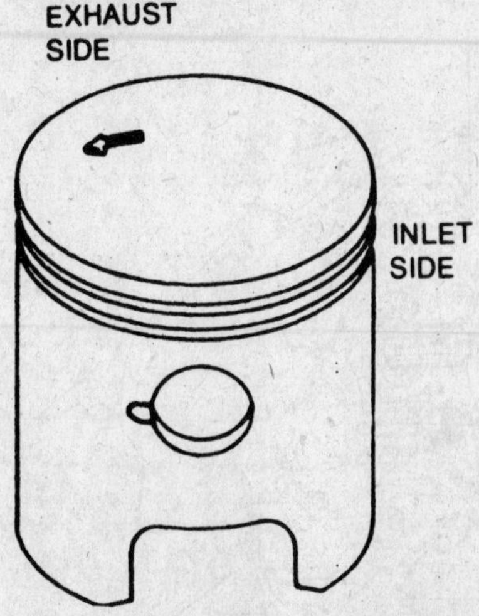

Arrow must point towards the exhaust side (ATC 90-125). On ATC 70s, position piston crown triangle mark on cam chain side

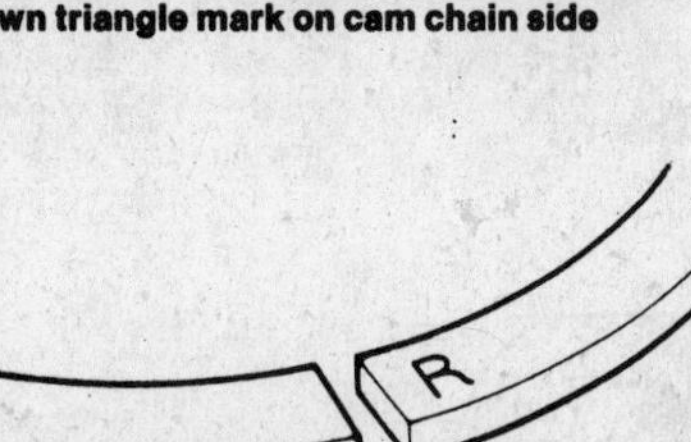

Install rings with manufacturer's mark up

INSPECTION

Refer to the "Engine Rebuilding" section of "General Information" and to the specifications chart in this section for inspection techniques and service limits.

INSTALLATION

1. If the piston rings were removed or replaced, be sure that they are installed correctly.
2. The two compression rings are not interchangeable. The top ring has a plain profile, while the second is wedge-shaped.
3. Be certain to install the compression rings with the manufacturer's mark near the end-gap facing upwards.
4. The piston ring end-gaps should be arranged as follows:
   a. End-gaps of the two compression rings and the oil expander ring should be arranged 120° apart around the piston but not at the very front or rear of the piston and not directly above the wrist pin holes.
   b. The end-gaps of the oil rails should be arranged at about 3/4 in. (20mm) or more on either side of the oil expander ring end-gap.
5. Thoroughly clean the cylinder mating surface.
6. Check that the two dowel pins are in place on the right side cylinder head studs.
7. Use a new cylinder base gasket.
8. Install the piston on the connecting rod so that the "IN" mark on the piston crown is on the intake side.
9. Use new wrist pin circlips. Be sure the circlips are properly seated. The circlip end-gaps should not align with the cut-outs at the wrist pin hole.

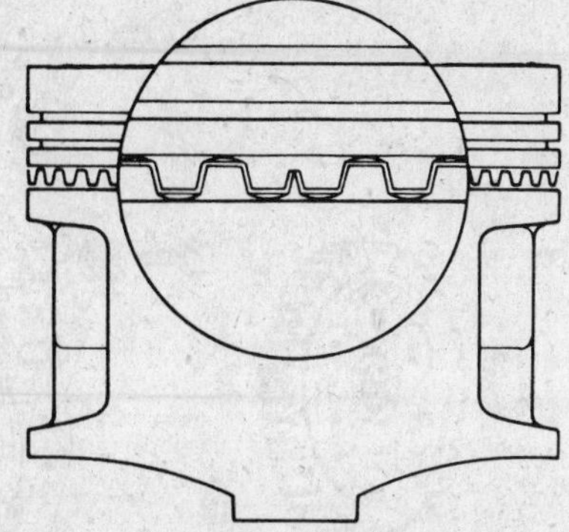

Ends of the oil ring expander must abut, not overlap

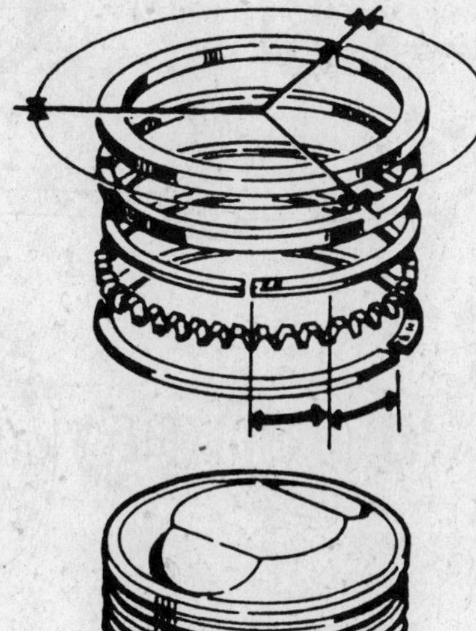

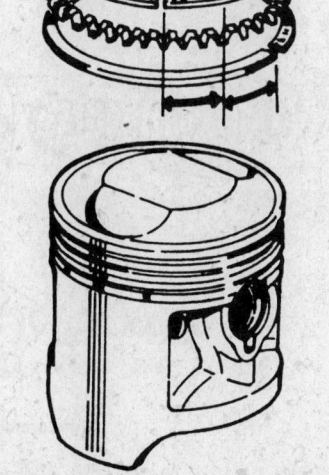

Position ring end gaps around the piston as shown

10. Lubricate the piston and rings. Check that the ring end-gaps are properly aligned.
11. Compress the rings and slide the cylinder over the piston. Pull the cam chain through the cylinder.
12. When the cylinder is seated, install and tighten the cylinder base bolts, if fitted.
13. Fit the cam chain guide roller. Tighten the roller bolt to 7-10 ft. lbs.
14. Use new valve seals when assembling the head.
15. Valve springs are progressively wound. They are installed with the close coils against the head.
16. Lubricate valve stems before inserting them into the guides.
17. After the valve and spring assemblies have been installed, rap the end of each valve smartly with a plastic mallet to ensure that the keepers are properly seated.
18. Lubricate each rocker arm shaft and slip it into place. Use a new gasket beneath the finned. cover.
19. Be sure the dowel pins, O-rings and

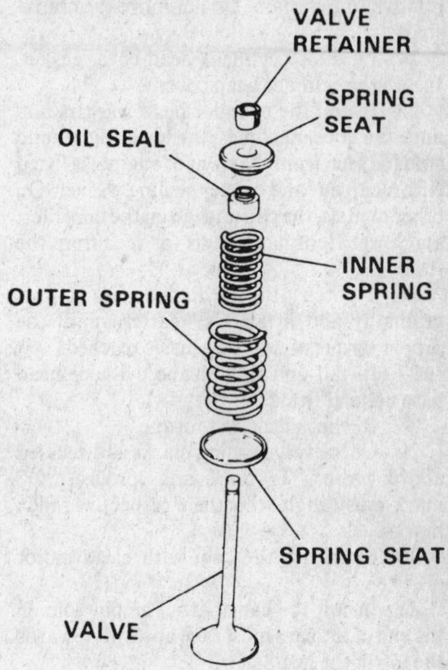

Valve assembly

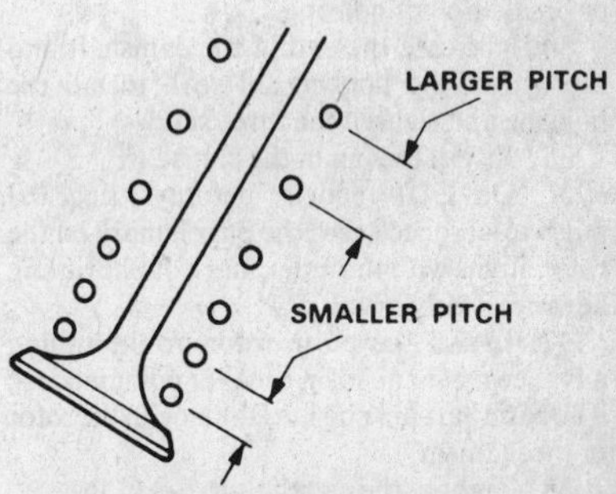

Progressively wound valve springs are fitted with the close coils against the head

collars are in place on the correct cylinder head studes.

20. Use a new cylinder head gasket.
21. Pull the cam chain taut and ensure that it is not jammed or kinked anywhere.

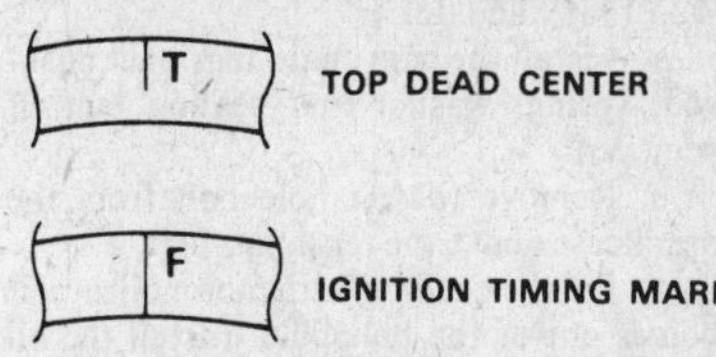

Rotor timing marks

22. Thread the cam sprocket on the chain. Turn the engine so that the magneto rotor "T" mark is aligned with the inspection index mark. The piston will be at TDC. At this point, fit the chain over the cam sprocket so that the "O" mark on the sprocket is at the top of the cylinder head and the sprocket bolt holes are aligned with the centerline of the cylinder.
23. Install the cylinder head. Pull the cam sprocket through. With the rotor "T" mark aligned with the index mark, the "O" mark on the sprocket must align with the index mark on the head. If it does not, move the sprocket

relative to the chain. Do not move the crankshaft.

24. Fit a new cylinder head cover gasket. Install the cylinder head cover.

25. Install the cylinder head washers and nuts. On 90cc machines, the lower right hand stud (as seen from the front of engine) is fitted with a cap nut and copper sealing washer. On other models, the cap nuts go on the upper left and lower right hand studs (as seen from the front).

26. Tighten the cylinder head nuts gradually and in an "X" pattern until the proper torque of 14-16 ft. lbs. is reached.

27. Install and tighten the cylinder head base bolts, if fitted.

28. Recheck head nut torque.

29. Check valve timing marks as discussed above: rotor "T" mark and sprocket "O" mark must align with their respective index marks.

30. Lubricate the cam with clean motor oil.

31. Install the camshaft. The pin hole on the end of the cam must face upwards towards the top of the head.

32. Install the sprocket bolts. Using a non-permanent thread-locking compound is recommended. Torque the bolts to 6-9 ft. lbs.

33. Fit a new gasket behind the generator or breaker point housing.

34.Lubricate the end of the camshaft and the lips of the housing oil seal. Install the housing and tighten the three screws.

35. Install the pin in the camshaft.

36. On CDI models, before fitting the pulse rotor, check that the punch mark on the rotor aligns with the index mark on the timing advance mechanism.

37. Install the pulse rotor or the timing advance mechanism on breaker point models. The camshaft pin engages the slot on the rotor or mechanism.

38. Tighten the cam bolt to 6-9 ft. lbs.

39. Install the base plate assembly.

40. On CDI models, turn the crankshaft so that the "F" mark on the magneto rotor is aligned with the inspection hole index mark.

41. On CDI models, turn the pulse generator base plate so that the pulse generator tooth aligns with the pulse rotor index mark. Tighten the base plate screws.

42. 1985 and later:

a. Install the cam chain tensioner pushrod, spring, washer and sealing bolt, if removed.

b. Remove the oil hole bolt from the crankcase above the tensioner bolt.

c. Fill the pushrod with motor oil until it comes out of the bolt hole. Install the oil hole bolt.

43. Adjust cam chain tension (see "Maintenance.")

44. Turn the engine over slowly with the recoil starter. If resistance is felt, stop immediately and determine the cause. Check that the timing marks all align after one complete engine revolution.

45. Adjust valve clearance as outlined in "Maintenance."

46. The remainder of the procedure is the reverse of removal. Tighten the cylinder head bracket hardware to 14-18 ft. lbs., where applicable.

RIGHT CRANKCASE COVER COMPONENTS

The right crankcase cover contains the clutch, oil pump, primary driven gear and external shift mechanism. All of these components can be serviced without removing the engine from the frame.

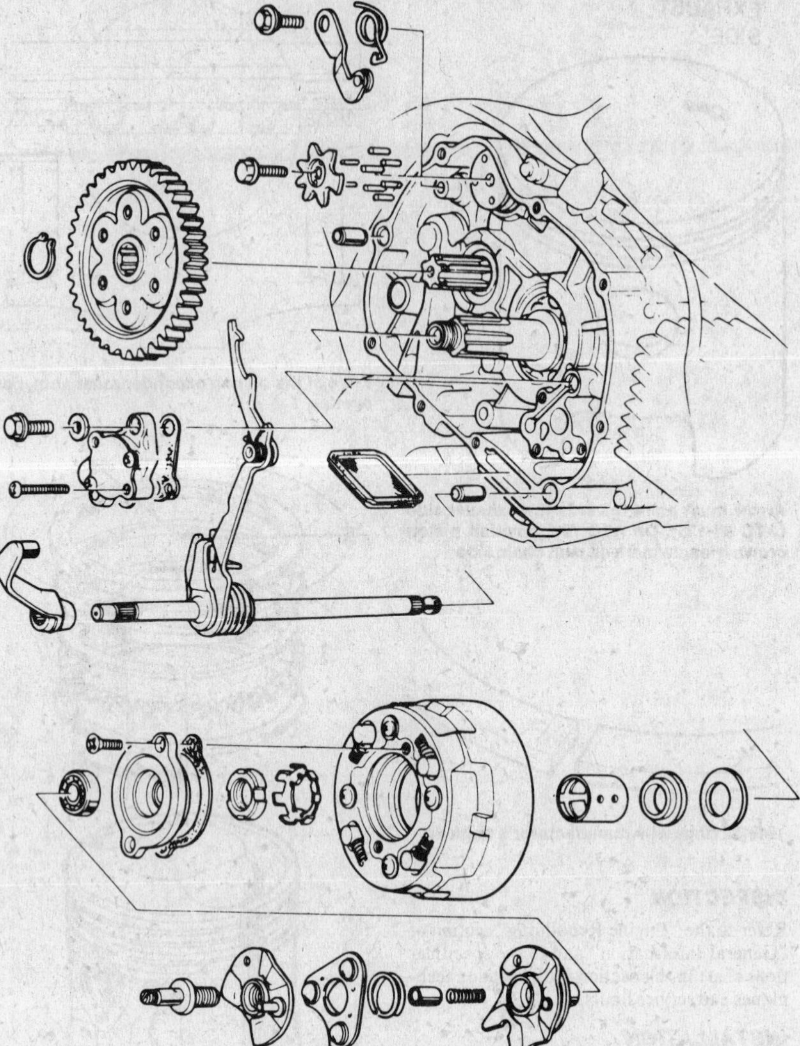

Right crankcase cover components

Primary driven gear circlip

Removal

ATC 70

1. Drain the engine oil.
2. Remove the exhaust pipe.
3. Remove the footpegs.
4. Remove the carburetor manifold bolts from the cylinder head.
5. Support the engine with a jack or suitable substitute to take the weight off the upper engine mounting bolt. Remove the bolt.
6. Loosen the lower engine mounting bolt.
7. Lower the engine until the right crankcase cover is clear of the frame.
8. Place a drip pan beneath the crankcase cover to catch any residual oil which may come out.
9. Remove the cover bolts. Remove the cover. If it is stuck, tap it with a plastic mallet to break it free.
10. Not the locations of the dowel pins on the cover mating surface. Be sure that they are not misplaced.
11. For safety while working, raise the engine and slip the upper engine mounting bolt into place.
12. Remove the components as outlined under "All Models," below.

ATC 90/110/125

1. Remove the seat.
2. Drain the crankcase oil.

3. Place a drip pan beneath the right crankcase cover.
4. Remove the starter motor bracket, if fitted.
5. Remove the crankcase cover screws.
6.Remove the crankcase cover. If it is stuck, tap it with a plastic mallet to break it free.
7. Note the locations of the two locating dowel pins on the mating surface.
8. Remove the components as outlined under "All Models," below.

ALL MODELS

1. Remove the ball retainer and clutch cam plate side spring.
2. Remove the oil passage pipe and spring.
3. Remove the clutch cam plate.
4. Remove the clutch outer cover screws.
5. Remove the release lever.
6. Bend up the locking tap on the clutch nut washer.
7. Remove the clutch nut.
8. Remove the clutch assembly.
9. Remove the clutch center guide.
10. Remove the primary driven gear snap ring.
11. Remove the primary driven gear.
12. To remove the oil pump, remove the hex head bolt and the three pump mounting screws.
13. Remove the gearshift pedal pinch bolt and carefully pull the pedal off the shaft.
14. Clean the exposed splines of the shift shaft to remove any burrs or sharp edges so they won't damage the oil seal.
15. Remove the shift drum stopper bolt and the stopper.
16. Disengage the fingers of the shift arm from the shift drum pins and pull the external shift mechanism out of the case.
17. Remove the shift drum stopper plate, if required.

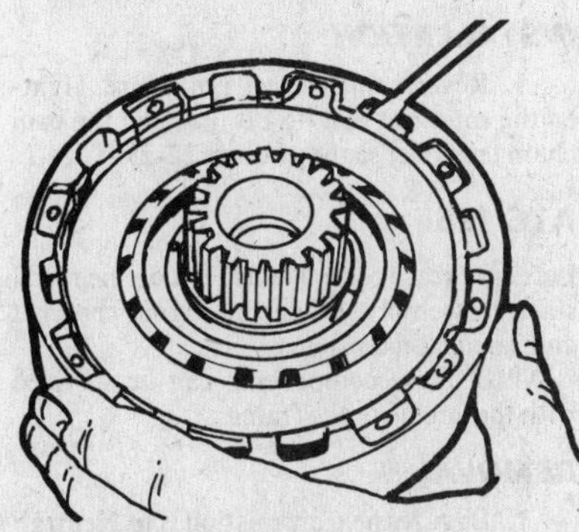
Removing the clutch snap-ring

Inspection

CLUTCH

1. Compress the clutch assembly and remove the large snap-ring on the inner side. Carefully release pressure and separate the components.
2. Remove the snap-ring to separate the primary drive gear from the clutch hub.
3. If further disassembly is required, remove the clutch damper springs from the housing. Remove the four phillips screws from the outer side of the housing and separate the drive plate, clutch springs and housing.

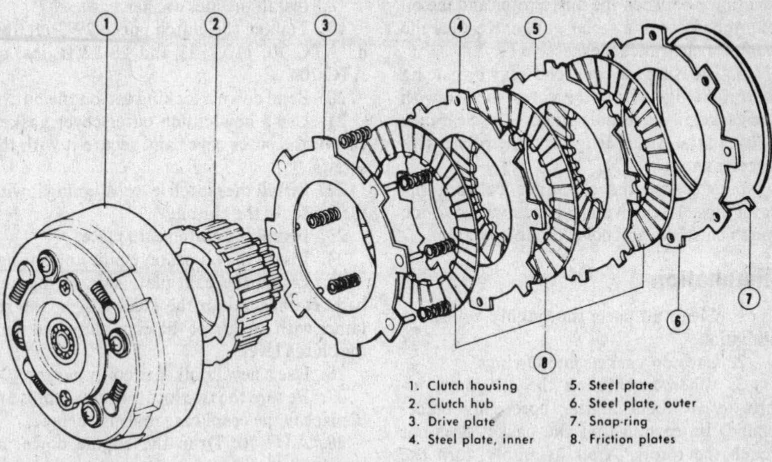

Clutch assembly

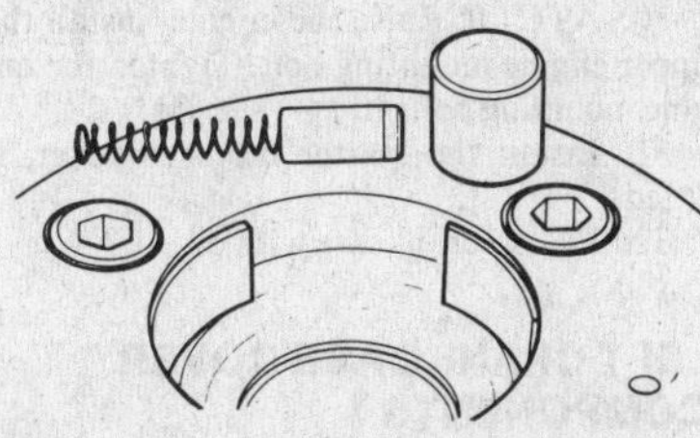
Clutch roller, plunger and spring assembly

4. To complete disassembly, remove the clutch weight stopper ring from the drive plate.
5. Measure clutch spring free length.
6. Check friction plates for worn or damaged friction material. Measure thickness and compare to the given specification.
7. Check steel plates for warpage.
8. Check plate tabs for chipping, wear or other damage.
9. Measure primary gear ID and center guide OD and compare to the specifications.
10. Check gear teeth for pitting, chipping or other damage. Check gears for heat discoloration.

SHIFT MECHANISM

1. Check the splines of the gearshift shaft. If the splines are broken or torn to the extent that it is difficult to properly secure the shift lever, replace the shaft.
2. Check the condition of the shift arm. Be sure that it is not bent. Check that the shift fingers are not bent or worn.

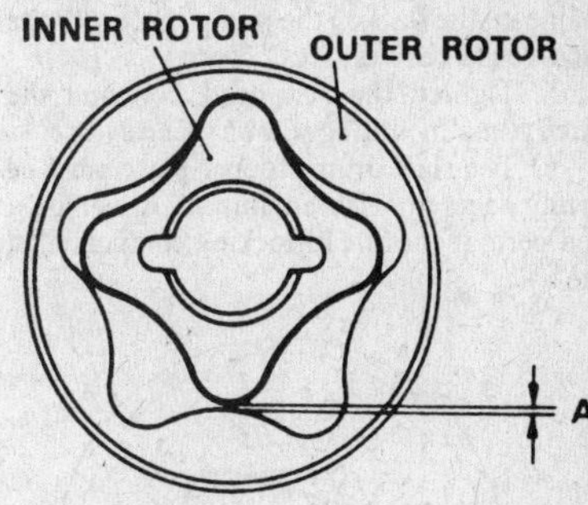

Rotor tip clearance ("A")

3. Check the condition of the springs in the shift linkage, especially the shift lever return spring. If any spring is broken, has lost its tension, or fails to hold its component properly, replace it.
4. Check the condition of the shift drum stopper roller and replace it if worn. The stopper spring should hold the stopper firmly against the stopper plate.
5. Check the stopper plate and pins for wear. Replace if damage.

OIL PUMP

1. Remove the cover screws and remove the cover.
2. Remove the inner and outer rotors.
3. Check all parts for scoring, discoloration or other obvious signs of wear.
4. Install the rotors and measure the

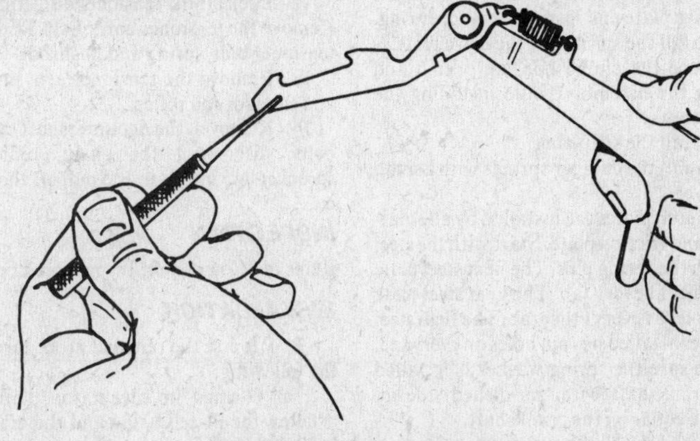
Check shift fingers for damage

clearance between the outer rotor and the oil pump body with a feeler gauge. Replace the pumpt if clearance is excessive.

5. Measure the rotor end-play by placing a straightedge across the cover surface with the gasket in place and measure the clearance between the straightedge and the rotors with a feeler gauge.

6. Measure the clearance between the rotor tips. Excessive clearance will give too much backlash and noisy pump operation.

Installation

1. Clean all parts thoroughly before installation.

2. Use new gaskets and O-rings.

3. When assembling the oil pump, lubricate all metal parts thoroughly beforehand. Be certain that the gasket does not touch the rotors. After assembly, turn the pump by hand. There should be little resistance.

4. Install the pump on the engine. Be sure to line up the flats on the pump shaft with the recess on the driveshaft.

5. Tighten the hex head bolt and the three pump mounting screws securely.

6. The shift drum stopper plate must be firmly secured. Use an impact driver or a non-permanent thread-locking compound on the bolt.

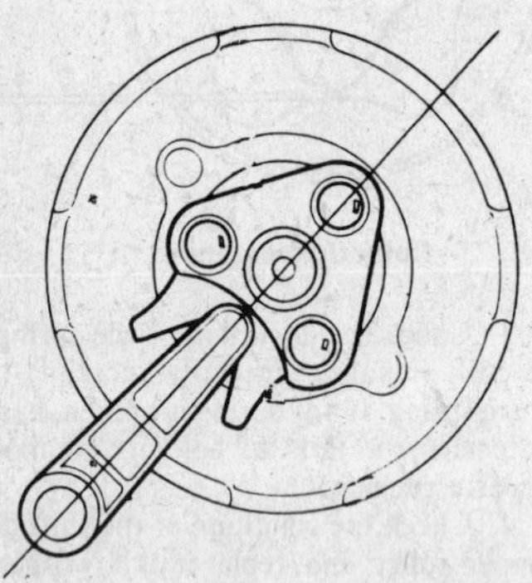

Install the clutch lever as shown

7. Install the external shift mechanism shaft assembly, locating the ends of the return spring on either side of the stopper pin and engaging the fingers of the shift arm with the shift drum pins. Be careful when installing the shaft as there is an oil seal on the left side of the engine.

8. Install the shift drum stopper.

9. Install the primary driven gear.

10 To assemble the clutch, fit the weights on the drive plate and install the stopper ring.

11. Install the springs on the drive plate.

12. Place the clutch housing over it and compress the assembly while installing the phillips screws.

13. Install the snap-ring.

14. Install the damper springs with a small screwdriver.

15. Clutch plates are installed by alternating steel and friction plate. Start with the steel plate with the spring pins. The next steel plate has cut-outs at every tab. The next steel plate has pin holes at every other tab. The final steel plate to be installed has pin holes on every tab.

16. Be sure the spring washer is installed on the crankshaft with the dished side in. Install the collar on the crankshaft.

17. Install the clutch assembly.

18. Install the lockwasher.

19. Tighten the clutch nut to 29-36 ft. lbs. on ATC 90, 110, 125 and 28-33 ft. lbs. on ATC 70s.

20. Bend down a locking tab on the nut.

21. Use a new clutch outer cover gasket. Install the outer cover and secure it with the screws.

22. Install the clutch lever, aligning it with the center of the clutch.

23. Install the clutch cam plate.

24. Install the oil passage pipe and spring.

25. Install the cam plate side spring and ball retainer. Align the steel ball in the retainer with the lug of the cam plate and with the clutch lever.

26. Use a new crankcase cover gasket.

27. Be sure the two locating dowel pins are in place in the crankcase mating surface.

28. ATC 70: Drop the engine down, as before, so that the cover can be installed.

29. Install the cover and tighten the screws evenly.

30. ATC 70: Raise the engine, install the upper engine mounting bolt. Tighten the engine mounting bolts to 14-18 ft. lbs.

31. Install the starter motor bracket, if fitted.

32. Fill the crankcase with oil.

LEFT CRANKCASE COVER COMPONENTS

ATC 70

Left crankcase cover components include the recoil starter, magneto, engine sprocket and cam chain tensioner assembly.

All of these components can be serviced with the engine in the frame.

REMOVAL

1. Drain the oil.
2. Remove the recoil starter assembly.
3. Remove the exhaust pipe.
4. Remove the footpeg bar.
5. Remove the chain case.
6. Remove the E-clip and remove the Neutral indicator.
7. Remove the left crankcase cover.
8. Remove the starter pulley from the rotor.
9. Remove the rotor nut. Using the special puller, remove the rotor.
10. Remove the rotor nut. Using the special puller, remove the rotor.
11. Remove the two screws which secure the coil stator plate. Tap the plate lightly to rotate it, then remove it.
12. Back off the tensioner adjusting screw. Remove the tensioner cover bolt. Remove the tensioner bolt, spring and pushrod.
13. Remove the tensioner arm pivot bolt, and the arm and roller.
14. Remove the countershaft sprocket bolts, disconnect the chain, remove the sprocket locking plate and pull off the sprocket.

INSPECTION

Refer to "Component Inspection," below.

INSTALLATION

1. Reverse the removal procedures. Note the following:

   a. O-rings in the stator plate screw holes, the plate O-ring and the crankshaft oil seal must be replaced.

   b. Tighten the rotor nut to 24-27 ft. lbs. Tighten the starter driven pulley bolts to 6-9 ft. lbs. Tighten the cam chain tensioner sealing bolt to 15-18 ft. lbs. Tighten the engine sprocket plate bolts to 10 ft. lbs.

ATC 90/110

Left crankcase cover components include the recoil starter assembly, magneto, engine sprocket and cam chain tensioner assembly.

All of these components can be serviced with the engine in the frame.

REMOVAL

1. Be sure the transmission is in Neutral.
2. Remove the gearshift lever pinch bolt and carefully pull the lever off its shaft.
3. Remove the three bolts that secure the recoil starter assembly. Remove the recoil starter.
4. Remove the gasket.
5. Remove the starter driven pulley bolts and pulley.
6. Remove the rotor nut and washer.
7. Using the special puller, remove the rotor.
8. Disconnect the magneto wires at the connectors.
9. Remove the stator bolts and take off the stator.
10. If disassembly past this point is required, drain the engine oil.
11. Remove the sub-transmission cover.
12. Remove the sub-transmission gears.
13. Remove the left crankcase cover screws and the cover.
14. Remove the gasket and dowel pins.
15. Remove the cam chain tensioner sealing bolt, spring and pushrod.
16. Disconnect the drive chain to remover the engine sprocket.

INSPECTION

Refer to "Component Inspection", below.

INSTALLATION

1. Reverse the removal procedure. Tighten the rotor nut to 47-54 ft. lbs. and the cam chain tensioner sealing bolt to 22-29 ft. lbs.

ATC 125

Left crankcase components include the recoil starter assembly, magneto, engine sprocket and cam chain tensioner.

All of these components can be serviced with the engine in the frame.

REMOVAL

1. Be sure the transmission is in Neutral.
2. Remove the gearshift lever pinch bolt and carefully pull the lever off its shaft.
3. Remove the recoil starter assembly (3 screws).
4. Remove the gasket.
5. If further disassembly is required.
6. Remove the pulley bolt.
7. Remove the pulley.
8. Remove the air cleaner hose.
9. Disconnect the alternator wires.
10. Remove the Neutral indicator E-clip and washer.
11. Remove the sub-transmission cover bolts.
12. Remove the dowel pins.
13. Remove the gasket.
14. Remove the sub-transmission components.

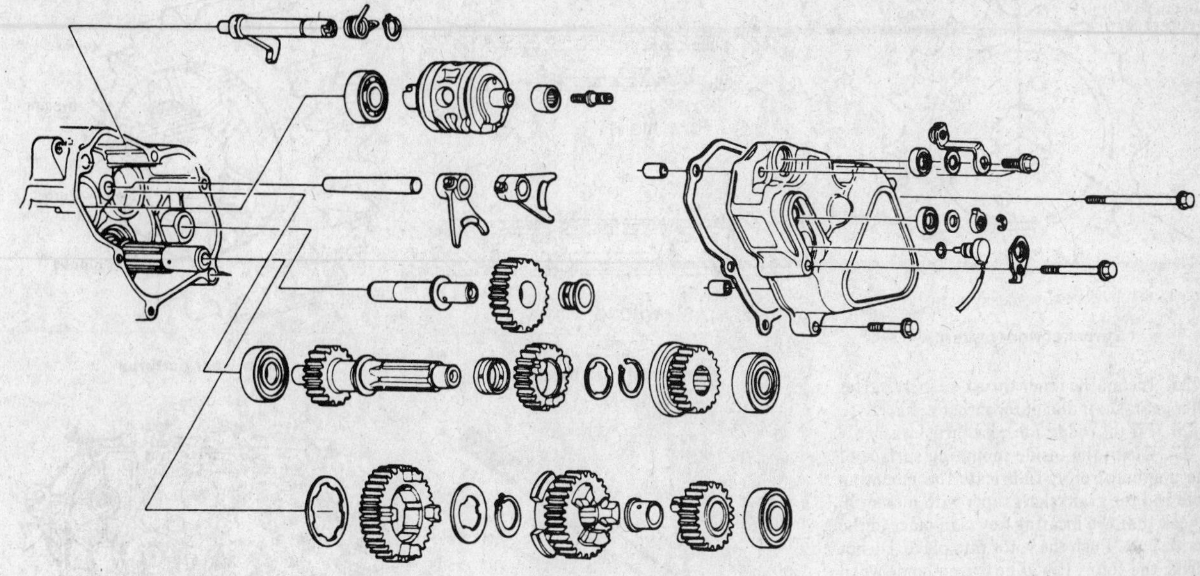
Sub-transmission components

15. Remove the left crankcase cover bolts.
16. Remove the flywheel with a suitable puller.
17. Remove the thrust washers, starter idler gear and shaft.
18. Remove the starter reduction gear washer.
19. Remove the bolt securing the starter driven gear set plate. Remove the plate.
20. Remove the starter driven gear and the needle bearing.
21. Remove the seven bolts securing the left crankcase cover spacer and remove the spacer.
22. Remove the two dowel pins from the crankcase mating surface.
23. Remove the two screws securing the cam chain tensioner guide sprocket set plate. Remove the sprocket.
24. Unscrew and remove the cam chain tensioner oil hole bolt and washer.
25. Remove the tensioner sealing bolt and washer and the spring and pushrod.
26. Disconnect the drive chain at the masterlink.
27. Remove the engine sprocket and bushings.

INSPECTION

Refer to "Component Inspection", below.

INSTALLATION

1. Use new gaskets and O-rings.
2. Clean all metal parts in a safe solvent and dry thoroughly.
3. Lubricate all metal parts with motor oil before assembly.
4. Grease the lips of all seals before installation.
5. Wrap the starter rope around the pulley in a clockwise direction when viewed from the ratchet side of the pulley.
6. Install the recoil spring in the housing, hooking the end of the spring in the place provided.
7. Grease the spring thoroughly.
8. Install the pulley shaft collar.

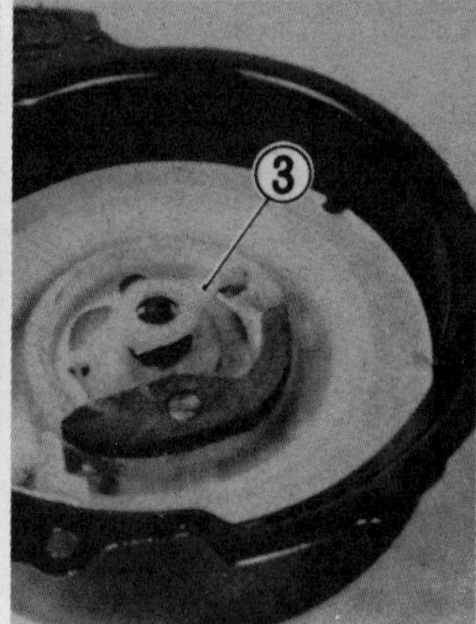

Recoil starter nut (1), ratchet cover (2) and guide (3)

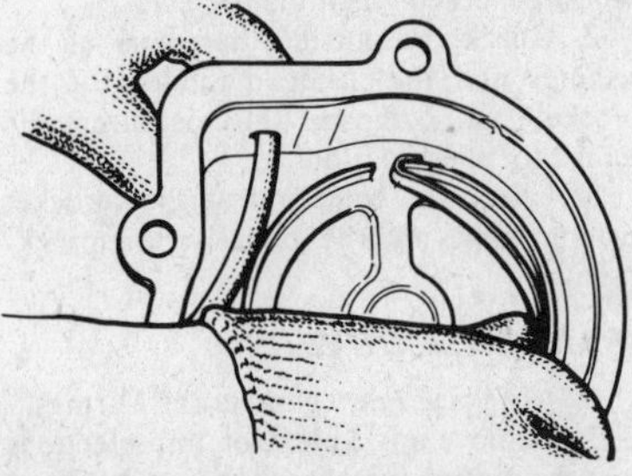
Engage the end of the coil spring into the boss provided

9. Grease the pulley shaft and install the pulley, hooking the end of the spring on the starter housing hook.
10. Turn the pulley two full turns clockwise.
11. Pull the starter rope through the hole and install the handle. Knot the end of the rope. Fit the handle cover.
12. Grease the ratchet and install it on the pulley.
13. Install the spring, spring seat and ratchet guide.
14. Install the cover. Install the cover nut.
15. Check recoil starter operation.
16. Lubricate the engine sprocket bushings and install bushings and sprocket.
17. Connect the drive chain.
18. Install the cam chain guide sprocket and set plate.
19. Fit a new crankcase cover spacer gasket.
20. Check that the two locating dowel pins are in place on the crankcase mating surface.
21. Install the spacer and secure it with the seven bolts. Bolts should be tightened gradually and evenly.
22. Install the starter driven gear spacer on the crankshaft.
23. Install the starter driven gear and needle bearing.
24. Install the driven gear set plate and bolt.

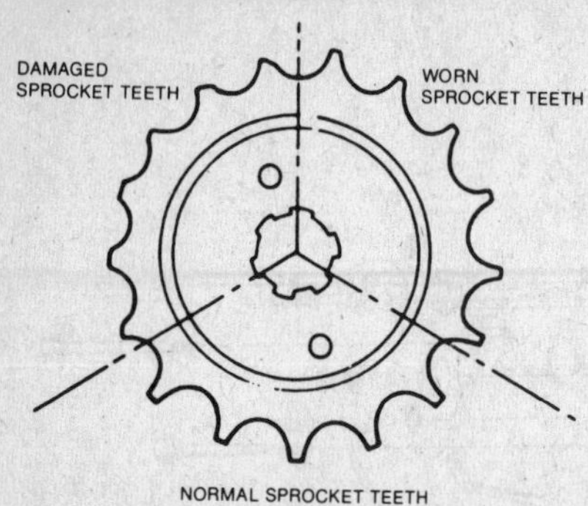

Sprocket wear patterns

Correct oil seal installation

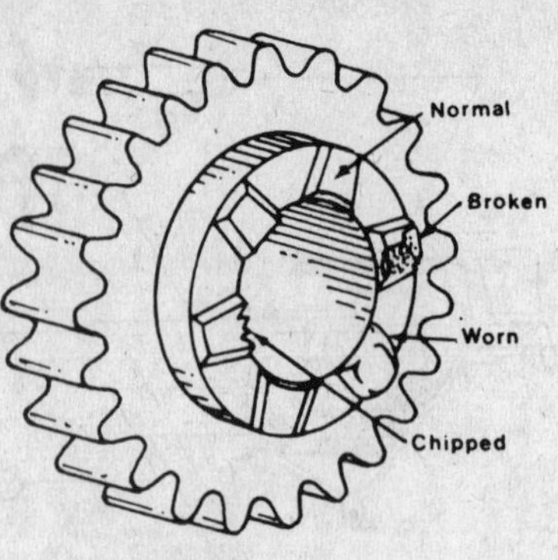

Gear wear patterns

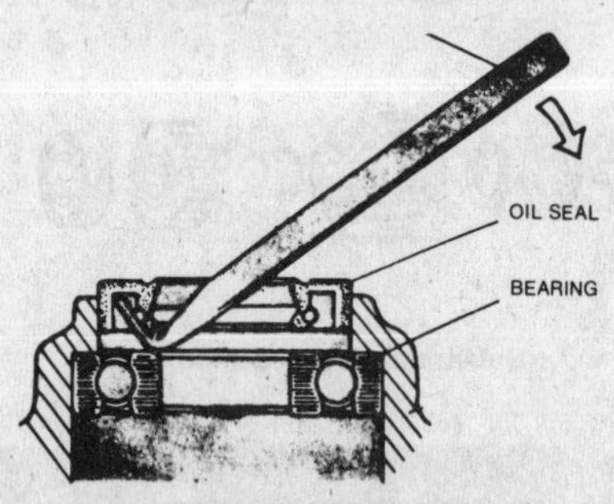

Correct oil seal removal

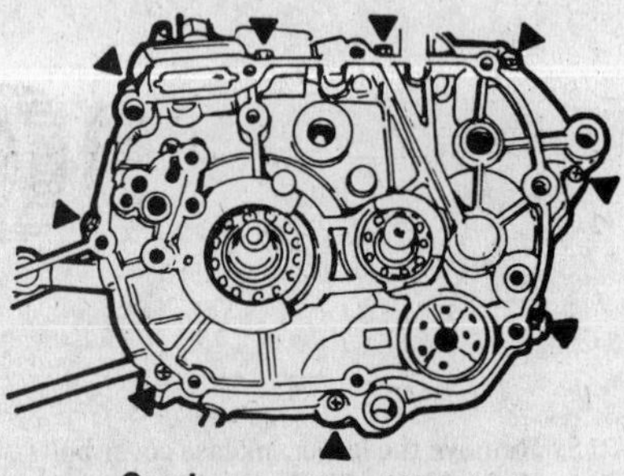

Crankcase screws (ATC 125)

25. Install the inner thrust washer, starter idler gear, shaft and outer thrust washer.
26. Fit the reduction gear thrust washer.
27. Clean the inside mounting surface of the magneto rotor. Lubricate the mounting hole and the crankshaft taper with motor oil. Check that the locating key is in place in the crankshaft. Push the rotor into place. Do not skrike the rotor. It will be driven home when the pulley is installed.
28. Install the left crankcase cover.
29. Grease the oil seal lips and install the pulley, aligning the flats with the groove in the rotor.
30. Install the pulley bolt, washer and O-ring.
31. Tighten the pulley bolt to 29-36 ft. lbs.
32. Install the recoil starter assembly.
33. Install the sub-transmission components.
34. Check that the two locating dowel pins are in place on the cover mating surface.
35. Fit a new cover gasket.
36. Install the sub-transmission cover.
37. Install the neutral indicator washer, indicator and E-clip.
38. The remainder of the procedure is the reverse of disassembly. Do not forget to fill the crankcase with oil before starting the engine.

Component Inspection

RECOIL STARTER

1. Remove the nut (ATC 125) or E-ring (other models) and remove the ratchet cover.
2. Remove the components.
3. Remove the handle cover.
4. Undo the rope knot. Remove the handle.
5. Remove the starter pulley.

CAUTION: *Wear eye protection and use care when removing the pulley. The coil spring may pop out when it is removed.*

6. Check the rope for a frayed or worn condition and replace it if necessary.
7. Check the condition of the coil spring.
8. Check the ratchet components for damage.

MAGNETO

1. Do not drop the rotor as the magnetic properties may be affected. Place it where it will not pick up stray bits of metal.
2. Be sure that the rotor is perfectly clean before installation.
3. For electrical tests, refer to the "Electrical System" section.
4. Check the inside of the rotor and the stator coil core ends for scoring which would indicate that they have been in contact. This condition must be rectified.
5. Check that the stator is secure on its mount.
6. If stator and rotor have been in contact, check the crankshaft bearings. This condition is sometimes caused by bad bearings which allow play in the crankshaft.
7. Check the rotor for cracks, especially around the mounting taper.
8. Check the stator for burned insulation, broken wires or other obvious signs of damage.

ENGINE SPROCKET

1. Check the teeth of the sprocket and ensure that they are not hook-shaped, broken or worn. If wear is evident, the sprocket should be replaced and the chain and rear sprocket checked for similar defects.
2. Check the outside diameters of the bushings and the inside diameters of the sprocket and compare the measurements against the specifications.
3. Check the condition of the sprocket bushing splines and the splines on the sprocket shaft.

CRANKCASE COVERS

1. Always use new gaskets and O-rings.
2. Remove any knicks or imperfections from the mating surfaces with an oilstone or silicon carbide paper.
3. Oil seals can be pried out with a small screwdriver. When installing new seals, press them straight in with a block of wood or the like which will cover the entire seal. Lubricate seal lips before installation.
4. Bearings can be check for condition in place. Remove bearins by taking off any retaining plates. Heat the cover slightly and drive the old bearing(s) out. Installation is the reverse of removal.

GEAR ASSEMBLIES

1. Check the condition of all gear teeth for wear, pitting or cracks. Pay close attention to the base of each tooth since this is wear most damage shows up.
2. Check the engaging dogs on sub-transmission gears.
3. Check dimensions of gears, shafts and shift forks against the specifications given.
4. Check the shaft splines.
5. Check the condition of the shift fork fingers. They should be straight and the tips must be undamaged.
6. Check that the shift fork shaft is not bent.
7. Check all components for heat damage.

LOWER END AND TRANSMISSION

Splitting The Crankcase

1. Remove the engine from the frame.
2. Remove the cylinder head, cylinder and piston.
3. Remove the clutch and gearshift linkage.
4. Remove the recoil starter assembly.
5. Remove the magneto.
6. Remove the cam chain tensioner assembly.
7. Remove the sub-transmission, if equipped.
8. Remove the crankcase screws.
9. Place the engine with the left crankcase down and tap upwards on the right crankcase half with a plastic mallet to separate the case halves.
10. Remove the dowel pins and the gasket.
11. Remove the crankshaft assembly.
12. Remove the gear clusters.

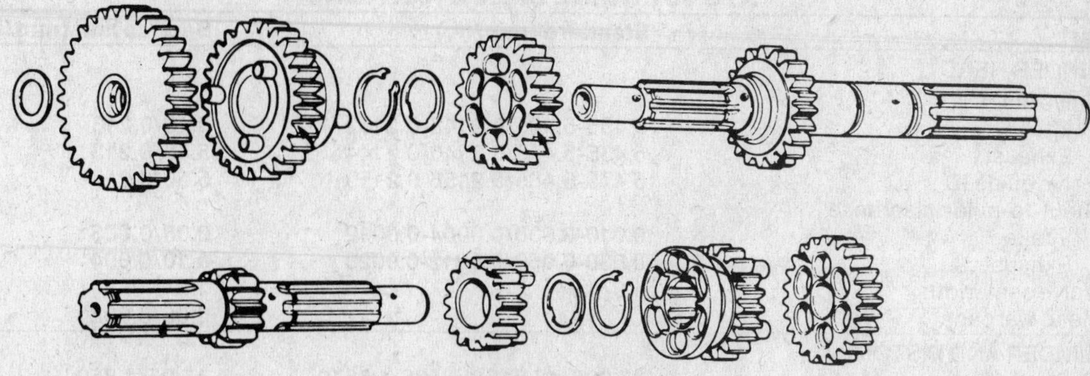

Transmission assembly (ATC 125)

Inspection

CRANKSHAFT

The crankshaft is a pressed-together unit. The connecting rod big end bearing is the caged-needle type. In the event of damage to the con rod, bearing or crankpin, the crankshaft must be replaced as an assembly.

1. Lubricate the big end bearing with oil, and rotate the rod slowly around the crankpin. The movement must be smooth and silent.

2. With a dial gauge, check the up-and-down (radial) movement of the con rod. Compare the reading with the specification given. If rod movement is in excess, of the specifications, the big end bearing is worn and the crankshaft msut be replaced.

3. With a feeler gauge, check the clearance between the con rod big end and the crankshaft flywheel. Compare the measurement with the specification given for axial clearance.

4. Place the crankshaft on a set of V-blocks, and check the crankshaft run-out with a dial gauge. Check both ends of the crank. Compare the run-out reading with the specification given. If excessive, the crank must be replaced.

Crankshaft run-out will be one half of the true indicated reading of the gauge.

CRANKCASES

1. Check for damage to the bearing bosses, especially for stress cracks around the bearing boss.

2. Be sure that both case half mating surfaces are free of any traces of old gasket or gasket material.

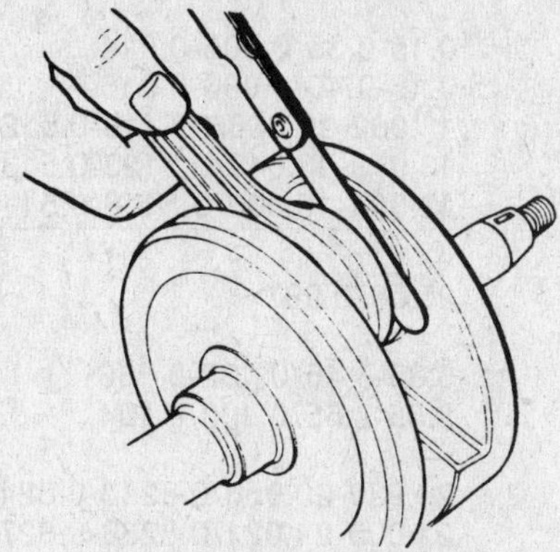

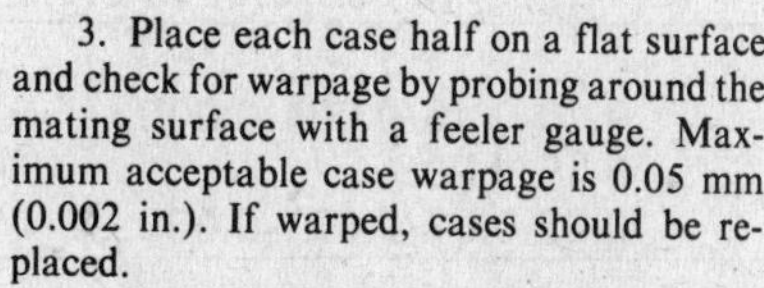

Checking big end side clearance

3. Place each case half on a flat surface and check for warpage by probing around the mating surface with a feeler gauge. Maximum acceptable case warpage is 0.05 mm (0.002 in.). If warped, cases should be replaced.

4. Minor scratches on the mating surfaces can be removed with an oilstone, although it is not permissible to remove much metal.

5. Case halves must be scrupulously clean before assembly. Be sure that all oil passages are clear and that the two dowel pins fitted between the case halves are installed.

TRANSMISSION

1. Check gears, shafts and shift linkage as outlined in the "Engine Rebuilding" section of "General Information."

2. Compare measurements with the specifications in the charts.

NOTE: *Mark shift forks for position before disassembly.*

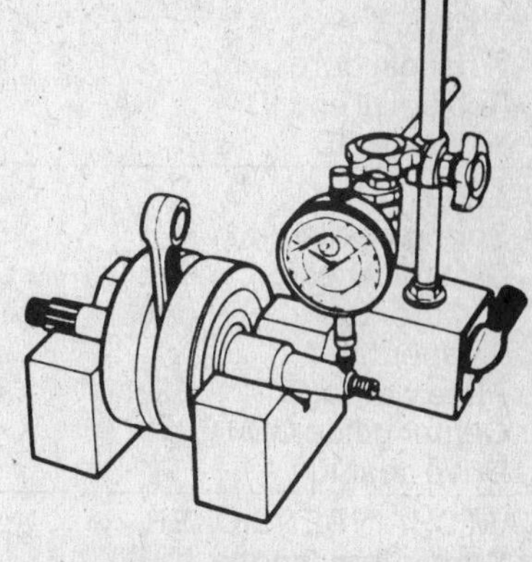

Measuring crankshaft run-out

Crankcase Assembly

1. Reverse the disassembly procedure.
2. Lubricate all components before putting the case halves together.
3. Be sure the crankcase dowel pins and the gasket are properly positioned.
4. Tighten the crankcase screws gradually and evenly.
5. Crankcase screw torque is 5-8 ft. lbs.

ATC 70 ENGINE SPECIFICATIONS

Part	Standard (mm/in.)	Service limi (mm/in.)
CYLINDER HEAD		
Cam lobe height	26.07/1.026	25.69/1.01
Cam bearing clearance	0.010-0.025/0.0004-0.0010	0.05/0.002
Cam side clearance	0.004-0.036/0.0002-0.0014	0.10/0.004
Rocker arm shaft OD	9.978-9.989/0.3928-0.3933	9.91/0.004
Rocker arm ID	10.000-10.015/0.3937-0.3943	10.10/0.398
Valve spring free length		
Inner	25.1/0.99	23.9/0.94
Outer	28.1/1.11	26.9/1.06

ATC 70 ENGINE SPECIFICATIONS

Part	Standard (mm/in.)	Service limi (mm/in.)
CYLINDER HEAD		
Valve stem OD		
Intake	5.455-5.465/0.2148-0.2152	5.40/0.213
Exhaust	5.435-5.445/0.2140-0.2144	5.40/0.213
Valve guide ID	5.475-5.485/0.2156-0.2159	5.50/0.217
Stem-to-guide clearance		
Intake	0.010-0.030/0.0004-0.0012	0.08/0.003
Exhaust	0.030-0.050/0.0012-0.0020	0.10/0.004
Valve seat width	1.0/0.04	1.6/0.06
Head warpage		0.05/0.002
CYLINDER AND PISTON		
Cylinder ID	47.005-47.015/1.8506-1.8510	47.05/1.852
Piston OD	46.98-47.00/1.850-1.8504	46.90/1.847
Ring-to-groove clearance	0.015-0.045/0.0006-0.0018	0.12/0.005
Ring end-gap		
Top, second	0.15-0.35/0.006-0.014	0.5/0.02
Oil	0.15-0.40/0.006-0.016	—
Wrist pin bore	13.002-13.008/0.5119-0.5121	13.06/0.51
Rod small end ID	13.013-13.043/0.5123-0.5135	13.1/0.52
Wrist pin OD	12.994-13.000/0.5116-0.5118	12.98/0.511
CLUTCH		
Spring free length	25.08/0.987	23.1/0.91
Disc thickness		
Outer tab	3.35-3.45/0.132-0.136	3.0/0.12
Inner tab	2.55-2.65/0.100-0.104	2.3/0.09
Plate warpage	—	0.2/0.01
Center guide OD	20.930-20.950/0.8240-0.8248	20.90/0.823
Drive gear ID	21.000-21.021/0.8268-0.8276	21.05/0.829
CAM CHAIN TENSIONER		
Spring free-length	82.8/3.26	77.0/3.0
Pushrod OD	11.985-12.000/0.4718-0.4724	11.94/0.47
OIL PUMP		
Body clearance	0.10-0.15/0.004-0.006	0.20/0.008
Rotor tip clearance	0.15/0.006	0.25/0.010
End clearance	0.02-0.07/0.001-0.003	0.12/0.005
TRANSMISSION		
Gear IDs		
M2, M4, C3	17.016-17.043/0.6699-0.6710	17.10/0.673
C1	17.006-17.018/0.6695-0.6700	17.07/0.672
Mainshaft OD	16.983-16.994/0.6686-0.6691	16.95/0.667
Countershaft OD	16.966-16.984/0.6680-0.6687	16.95/0.667
Shift drum OD	33.950-33.975/1.3366-1.3376	33.93/1.336
Shift fork ID	34.000-34.025/1.3386-1.3396	34.07/1.341
Fork finger thickness	4.86-4.94/0.191-0.195	4.6/0.18
CRANKSHAFT		
Big end side clearance	0.10-0.35/0.004-0.014	0.6/0.02
Big end radial clearance	0-0.012/0-0.0005	0.05/0.002
Run-out	0-0.012/0-0.0005	0.10/0.004

ATC 90 ENGINE SPECIFICATIONS

Part	Standard (mm/in.)	Service limit (mm/in.)
CYLINDER HEAD		
Rocker arm ID	10.00-10.02/0.3937-0.3943	10.1/0.3976
Rocker arm shaft OD	9.972-9.987/0.3926-0.3932	9.92/0.3906
Valve stem OD		
Intake	5.455-5.465/2148-0.2152	5.435/0.2140
Exhaust	5.435-5.445/0.2140-0.2144	5.415/0.2133

ATC 90 ENGINE SPECIFICATIONS

Part	Standard (mm/in.)	Service limit (mm/in.)
CYLINDER HEAD		
Stem-to-guide clearance		
Intake	0.010-0.030/0.0004-0.0012	0.06/0.0024
Exhaust	0.030-0.050/0.0012-0.0020	0.08/0.0032
Valve seat width	0.70-1.20/0.0276-0.0472	1.50/0.059
Valve guide ID	5.475-5.485/0.2156-0.2160	5.525/0.2175
Valve spring free-length		
Inner	26.5/1.043	25.5/1.004
Outer	31.8/1.252	30.6/1.205
CYLINDER AND PISTON		
Cylinder ID	50.00-50.01/1.9685-1.9689	50.1/1.9724
Piston OD	49.97-49.99/1.9674-1.9681	49.9/1.9646
Piston-cylinder clearance	0.025-0.050/0.001-0.002	0.1/0.004
Wrist pin clearance	0.002-0.004/0.0008-0.0016	0.05/0.002
Piston ring-to-groove clearance	0.010-0.045/0.0004-0.0018	0.12/0.0047
Ring end-gap		
Compression	0.15-0.35/0.0059-0.0139	0.5/0.020
Oil	0.15-0.40/0.0059-0.0158	0.50/0.020
CRANKSHAFT		
Big end radial play	0-0.01/0-0.0004	0.05/0.002
Big end side clearance	0.10-0.35/0.0039-0.0138	0.80/0.0315
Run-out	0.03/0.0012	0.10/0.0039
CLUTCH		
Friction disc thickness	2.65-2.75/0.104-0.108	2.25/0.087
Plate warpage	0.10/0.004	0.2/0.008
Spring free-length	27.0/1.063	26.0/1.024
TRANSMISSION		
Shift fork ID	42.00-42.03/1.654-1.655	42.07/1.656
Shift drum OD	41.95-41.98/1.652-1.653	41.93/1.651
Shift fork finger width	5.96-6.04/0.2347-0.2378	5.70/0.2244
Gear backlash	0.084-0.170/0.0033-0.0067	0.25/0.0098
CAM CHAIN TENSIONER		
Spring free-length	82.8/3.26	77.0/3.0
Pushrod OD	11.985-12.000/0.4718-0.4724	11.94/0.47
OIL PUMP		
Body clearance	0.10-0.15/0.004-0.006	0.20/0.008
Rotor tip clearance	0.15/0.006	0.25/0.010
End clearance	0.02-0.07/0.001-0.003	0.12/0.005

ATC 110 ENGINE SPECIFICATIONS①

Part	Standard (mm/in.)	Service limit (mm/in.)
CYLINDER HEAD		
Cam journals		
R	17.927-17.938/0.7058-0.7062	17.90/0.705
L	25.917-25.930/1.0204-1.0209	25.88/1.019
Cam lobe height	24.90-24.98/0.980-0.983	24.6/0.97
Valve spring free-length		
Inner	26.5/1.04	24.0/0.94
Outer	31.8/1.25	28.5/1.12
CYLINDER AND PISTON		
Cylinder ID	52.020-52.030/2.0480-2.0484	52.07/2.050
Piston OD	51.970-51.990/2.0461-2.0468	51.80/2.039
CLUTCH		
Spring free-length	24.5/0.965	23.5/0.925

① Other specifications are the same as the ATC 125

ATC 125 ENGINE SPECIFICATIONS

Part	Standard (mm/in.)	Service limit (mm/in.)
CYLINDER HEAD		
Cam journals		
R	17.934-17.945/0.7060-0.7065	17.90/0.705
L	25.932-25.945/1.0210-1.0215	25.90/1.020
Cam lobe height	24.118-24.278/0.9495-0.9558	23.8/0.94
Rocker arm ID	10.000-10.015/0.3937-0.3943	10.10/0.398
Rocker arm shaft OD	9.972-9.987/0.3926-0.3932	9.92/0.391
Rocker arm-to-shaft clearance	—	0.08/0.003
Cylinder warpage	—	0.10/0.004
Valve spring free length		
Inner	31.1/1.22	29.9/1.18
Outer	35.0/1.38	33.7/1.32
Valve stem OD		
Intake	5.450-5.465/0.2146-0.2152	5.435/0.2139
Exhaust	5.430-5.445/0.2138-0.2144	5.415/0.2132
Valve guide ID	5.475-5.485/0.2157-0.2161	5.525/0.2175
Stem-to-guide clearance		
Intake	0.010-0.035/0.0004-0.0014	0.08/0.003
Exhaust	0.030-0.055/0.0012/0.0022	0.10/0.004
Valve face width	1.2-1.5/0.05-0.06	1.8/0.07
Valve seat width	1.0/0.04	1.6/0.06
Cam bearing ID		
R	18.000-18.018/0.7087-0.7094	18.05/0.711
L	26.000-26.020/1.0236-1.0244	26.05/1.026
Cam journal clearance		
R	—	0.12/0.005
L	—	0.16/0.006
CYLINDER AND PISTON		
Cylinder ID	55.000-55.010/2.1654-2.1657	55.10/2.169
Taper/out-of-round	—	0.05/0.002
Warpage (head mating surface)	—	0.10/0.004
Piston OD	54.955-54.985/2.1636-2.1648	54.90/2.161
Wrist pin bore	15.002-15.008/0.5906-0.5909	15.04/0.592
Wrist pin OD	14.994-15.000/0.5903-0.5906	14.96/0.589
Piston-to-pin clearance	0.002-0.014/0.0001-0.0006	0.02/0.001
Ring-to-groove clearance		
Top	0.015-0.050/0.0006-0.0020	0.12/0.005
Second	0.010-0.045/0.0004-0.0018	0.12/0.005
Ring end-gap		
Top, second	0.10-0.25/0.004-0.010	0.50/0.020
Oil	0.3-0.9/0.01-0.04	—
Rod small end bore	15.016-15.034/0.5912-0.5919	15.05/0.593
CLUTCH		
Spring free-length	21.1/0.83	20.2/0.80
Warpage	—	0.20/0.008
Disc thickness	2.65-2.75/0.104-0.108	2.5/0.10
Drive gear ID	24.000-24.021/0.9449-0.9457	24.10/0.949
Center guide OD	22.00-22.10/0.866-0.870	21.85/0.860
OIL PUMP		
Body clearance	0.15-0.20/0.006-0.008	0.25/0.010
Rotor tip clearance	0.15/0.006	0.20/0.008
CAM CHAIN TENSIONER		
Spring free-length	82.8/3.3	77.0/3.0
Pushrod OD	11.985-12.000/0.4718-0.4724	11.94/0.94
ENGINE SPROCKET		
Bushing OD	21.960-21.993/0.8657-0.8659	21.90/0.862
Sprocket ID	19.992-20.008/0.7870-0.7877	19.94/0.785

ATC 125 ENGINE SPECIFICATIONS

Part	Standard (mm/in.)	Service limit (mm/in.)
CRANKSHAFT		
Run-out	—	0.10/0.004
Big end side clearance	0.15-0.55/0.006-0.022	0.65/0.03
Radial clearance	0.0-0.008/0.0-0.0003	0.05/0.002
Small end ID	15.106-15.034/0.5912-0.5919	15.05/0.593
Crankshaft bearing play		
Axial	0.10-0.35/0.004-0.014	0.8/0.03
Radial	0.003-0.015/0.0001-0.0006	0.05/0.002
TRANSMISSION		
Shift fork ID	42.075-42.100/1.6565-1.6575	42.15/1.659
Shift drum OD	41.950-41.975/1.6516-1.6526	41.8/1.65
Fork/drum clearance	0.118-0.150/0.0046-0.0059	0.155/0.006
Drum groove width	6.10-6.20/0.240-0.244	6.4/0.25
Shift fork finger thickness	5.96-6.04/0.234-0.238	5.70/0.224
Gear ID		
C1	14.000-14.027/0.5512-0.5522	14.10/0.555
M2	18.000-18.018/0.7087-0.7094	18.08/0.712
M4	20.000-20.021/0.7874-0.7882	20.10/0.791
C3	14.000-14.027/0.5512-0.5522	14.10/0.555
Shaft OD		
C1	13.966-13.984/0.5498-0.5506	13.93/0.548
M2	17.966-17.984/0.7073-0.7080	17.93/0.706
C3	19.966-19.984/0.7861-0.7868	19.93/0.785
M4	13.966-13.984/0.5498-0.5506	13.93/0.548

ENGINE TORQUE SPECIFICATIONS

Part	Torque (ft lbs)
ATC 70	
Crankcase screws	5.8-8.0
Cylinder head stud nut	6.5-8.7
Cylinder side bolt	5.8-8.0
Cylinder head side bolt	7.4-10.8
Camshaft sprocket bolts	3.6-6.5
Cylinder head right-side cover	5.1-6.5
Cylinder head left-side cover	5.8-8.7
Valve adjuster locknut	5.1-7.2
Cam chain tensioner pushrod	10.8-18.1
Oil pump	5.8-8.7
Shift drum bolt	6.5-10.8
Shift drum stopper plate	6.5-9.4
Shift drum stopper	7.2-11.6
Clutch hub nut	27.5-32.5
Right crankcase cover	5.8-8.7
Left crankcase cover	5.8-8.0
Alternator/magneto rotor	23.9-27.5
Engine sprocket	6.5-10.8
Oil drain bolt	18.1-25.3
Carburetor	6.5-10.1
Spark plug	9-14
ATC 90/110/125	
Cylinder head nuts	14-16
Cam sprocket bolts	6-9
Cam chain guide roller bolt	7-10
Pulse rotor	6-9
Clutch nut	29-36
Starter driven pulley (125)	29-36
Drum stopper plate bolt	17-20
Carburetor-to-manifold nuts	5-7
Driven sprocket nuts	17-22
Gearshift pedal pinch bolt	9-10
Crankcase screws	5-8

GENERAL TORQUE SPECIFICATIONS①

Part	Torque (ft lbs.)
5 mm screws	2.5-3.6
6 mm screws	5-8
5 mm bolts, nuts	3.5-4.5
6 mm bolts, nuts	6-9
8 mm bolts, nuts	13-18
10 mm bolts, nuts	22-29
12 mm bolts, nuts	36-43
6 mm bolt w/8 mm head	5-8
6 mm flange bolts, nuts	7-10
8 mm flange bolts, nuts	17-22
10 mm flange bolts, nuts	25-33

① Unless otherwise noted

FUEL SYSTEM

GAS TANK

Removal

1. Remove the seat and rear fender.
2. Set the petcock to "Off."
3. Remove the carburetor float bowl drain screw and allow the gas to empty into a suitable container. Dispose of it properly.
4. On models with the petcock on the gas tank, disconnect the fuel line(s) from the carburetor.
5. On models with the petcock on the carburetor, remove the screws which secure the petcock to the carburetor.
6. Detach the rubber band from the rear of the gas tank, or remove the mounting bolt depending on which is fitted.
7. Remove the tank.

Installation

1. Reverse the removal procedure.
2. When installing the tank, be sure to engage the rubber cushions at the front with the seats on the tank.
3. Be sure all fuel line connections are tight.
4. Be certain the petcock is secured.
5. Check for leaks before operating the machine.

CARBURETOR

NOTE: *Removal and installation procedures may vary slightly depending on model and year.*

Removal (All Models)

1. Set the fuel petcock "OFF."
2. Unscrew the carburetor top and pull the throttle slide assembly out. Wrap the assembly in a clean rag and place it out of the way to avoid damage.
3. Remove the choke cable clamp screw, if fitted.
4. Disconnect the choke cable from the carburetor if a cable-operated choke is fitted.
5. Detach the carburetor air vent tube from the clamp on the frame.
6. Loosen the air cleaner clamp screw at the carb intake.
7. Disconnect the overflow line from the carburetor.
8. Remove the manifold bolts from the cylinder head and remove the carbutor complete with manifold.

Disassembly

ATC 70/90

1. If disassembly of the throttle slide components is desired, compress the return spring against the carburetor cap, disengage the cable from the slide, take out the spring clip, needle, and clip.
2. Remove the float bowl petcock filter (if so equipped) by removing the filter plate, O-ring, and filter screen.
3. Remove the float bowl screws or flip up the retainer and separate the float bowl from the carburetor body. Do so carefully, to avoid damage to the floats. Remove and discard the float bowl gasket.

NOTE: *If the bowl is stuck, tap carefully with a plastic mallet to break the seal.*

4. Push out the float pivot pin with a small dowel, and take out the floats. Remove the float needle from its seat. Unscrew the seat itself.
5. Unscrew the main jet.
6. Several types of needle jet (located directly above the main jet) are fitted. Some models have only the jet itself, while others have a jet holder or nozzle with the needle jet located above it. Unscrew the needle jet located above it. Unscrew the needle jet or jet holder if a means is provided (such as a hex head), or simply push the jet holder and/or jet out of the carburetor body with a wooden dowel.
7. Unscrew and remove the pilot jet.
8. Remove the pilot air and throttle stop screws and springs, and the drain knob (if fitted).

ATC 110/125

1. Remove the nuts securing the manifold to the carburetor and separate the components.
2. Unscrew and remove the fuel filter bolt from the float bowl.
3. Remove the fuel filter.
4. Remove the O-ring.
5. Disconnect the air vent tube.
6. Remove the two screws which secure the float bowl. Remove the float bowl carefully. If it is stuck, hold it in place and wrap it with the plastic screwdriver handle to break it free.

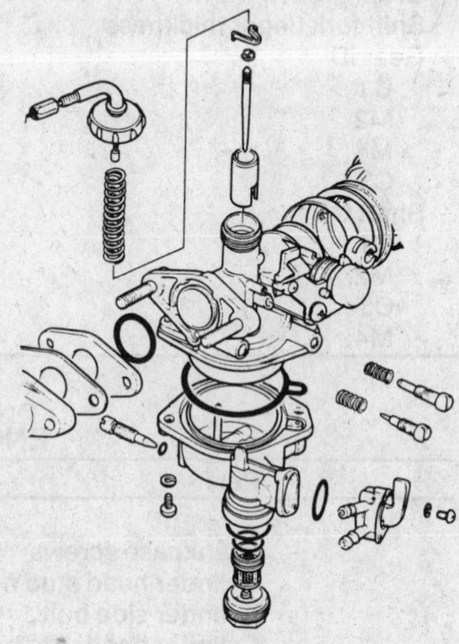

Carburetor assembly (ATC 110/125)

7. Remove the float bowl O-ring.
8. Pull out the float pivot pin.
9. Lift off the float and needle.
10. Unscrew and remove the pilot jet.
11. Remove the main jet from the needle jet holder. Unscrew and remove the needle jet holder. Shake the needle jet out of the carburetor body. If it will not come out, push it out from the top of the carb with a wooden dowel.
12. Turn the pilot screw clockwise while counting the number of turns until it bottoms. Then unscrew and remove it. Be sure to return it to the original setting when assembling.
13. Unscrew and remove the throttle stop screw.
14. Compress the throttle slide spring and disengage the throttle cable from the slide.
15. Remove the needle clip retainer and shake the needle out of the slide. Do not remove the needle clip from the needle.

Inspection (All Models)

NOTE: *Refer to the "General Information" section for carburetor rebuilding techniques.*

1. Clean all metal parts in a clean, safe solvent.
2. Blow air and fuel passages in the carburetor body clear with compressed air.
3. Check the condition of the needle and replace it if it is knicked or scored.
4. Clean all jets with solvent and com-

pressed air. Do not attempt to clean fuel passages with wire or the like, since the calibrated bores may be damaged.

5. Check the float for fuel leakage. Replace it if it is punctured or gas-logged.

6. Check the float needle and needl seat for wear or corrosion. Replace the needle if damage is noted.

7. Clean the fuel filter screen in solvent. If foreign matter cannot be removed, or if the filter is crushed, deformed or punctured, replace it.

Assembly and Installation (All Models)

1. Use new O-rings and gaskets.
2. Install jets carefully and do not overtighten them when installing.
3. Be sure the needle clip is set to the original groove in the needle.
4. Be sure the pilot screw is set to the position it was originally.
5. Tighten manifold bolts to 5-7 ft. lbs.
6. Be sure that all fuel lines are secure before operating the machine. After the carburetor is installed, turn on the fuel petcock and check for leaks.

FUEL PETCOCK

Tank-Mounted

1. On early models, the petcock is mounted on the fuel tank.
2. Set the petcock lever off and disconnect the line(s) from the carburetor.
3. Put the end(s) of the line(s) in a small container and check fuel flow in the "On" and "Reserve" positions.
4. If fuel flow is sluggish, remove the gas cap. If flow increases, the cap vent is clogged. If it does not, the petcock filter is clogged.

Carburetor-Mounted

1. The petcock is mounted on the carburetor float bowl by two screws.
2. To check petcock operation, set it to the "OFF" position, remove the mounting screws and pull it off the float bowl.
3. Place a suitable receptable beneath the petcock and turn it to the "ON" and "RESERVE" positions. If there is no fuel flow, determine the cause.
4. If removing the fuel tank cap increases fuel flow, the problem is a clogged cap vent.
5. If fuel flow is sluggish, remove and clean the gas tank.
6. If fuel flow is questionable, remove the petcock from the lines, being prepared for the gasoline which will come out. If flow from the lines seems normal, replace the petcock.

FUEL LINES

1. Fuel lines should be checked for condition every year.
2. Replace lines that are damaged by abrasion, hardened, cracked or otherwise defective.
3. Be sure that safety clips are fitted to both sides of gas lines.
4. Whenever lines are disconnected or replaced, check for leaks before operating the machine.

ELECTRICAL SYSTEM

Hard starting or misfiring are often caused by ignition system troubles, but since electrical malfunctions are often trickier to pin down than carburetor faults, it is wise to ensure that systems other than the ignition circuit are in serviceable conditon before beginning any work.

1. In the event of hard starting, misfiring or cutting out, first check that all electrical connections are clean, dry and tight.
2. Check the ignition and kill switches for continuity.
3. Check ignition timing accuracy. See "Maintenance."
4. Remove the spark plug. Clean and gap it to 0.6- 0.7mm (0.024-0.028 in.).

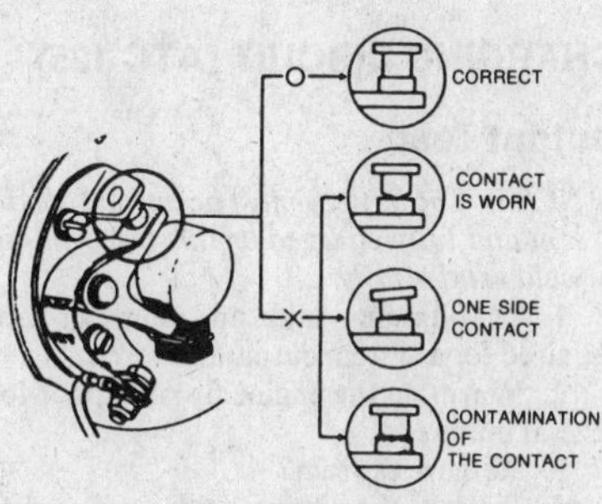

Breaker point condition

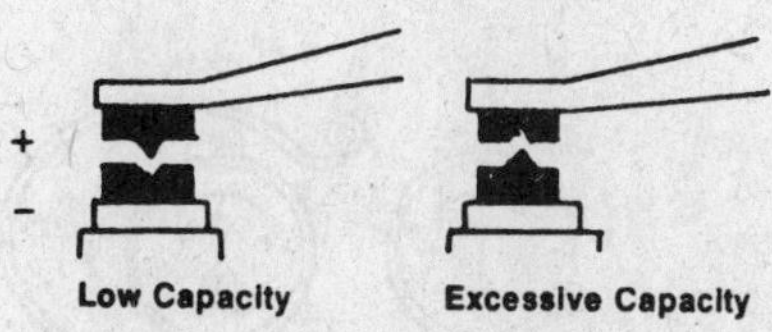

Defective condensers often cause pitting

5. Connect the plug to the cap and ground it against the cylinder head. Turn the engine over with the electric starter. The spark produced should be thick and blue.
6. If there is no spark, or if the spark appears weak and yellow, repeat the test using a piece of metal, such as a nail, inserted into the cap and held about 1/8 in. away from the head. If the spark appears healthy, the plug was the problem.
7. If there is still no spark, or spark is weak, remove the spark plug cap and repeat the test.
8. If there is still no improvement, check the condition of the plug lead. Check for dirt or grease, cracks in the insulation, moisture, etc. If the lead is damaged, it should be replaced. This involves replacing the ignition coil as well.
9. On breaker point-equipped machines, check the point contact surfaces for pitting or wear. Severe pitting is often caused by a defective condenser. Clean and gap the points as outlined in "Maintenance." If this does not solve the problem, inspect main ignition circuit components as outlined below.

Ignition Coil

ATC 70

1. An ohmmeter is required to test the ignition coil.
2. Disconnect the plug lead.
3. Disconnect the primary wire from the coil and check the resistance between the coil's primary wire terminal and ground. It should be about 1.5 ohms.
4. Check resistance between the spark plug cap and the ignition coil's primary wire terminal. It should be 8-9 Ωohms.
5. If either of the measurements are not within specification, replace the ignition coil.
6. Replace the coil if the meter indicates open of shorted coils in either case.

ATC 110/125

1. An ohmmeter is required to test the ignition coil.
2. Disconnect the spark plug lead.
3. Disconnect the primary wire from the coil (black/yellow).
4. Disconnect the green wire from the coil.
5. Remove the coil from the frame.
6. Remove the spark plug cap from the high tension lead.

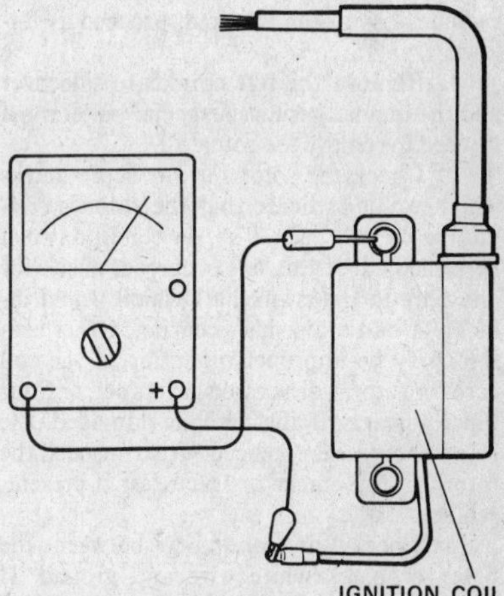

Checking primary winding resistance (ATC 70)

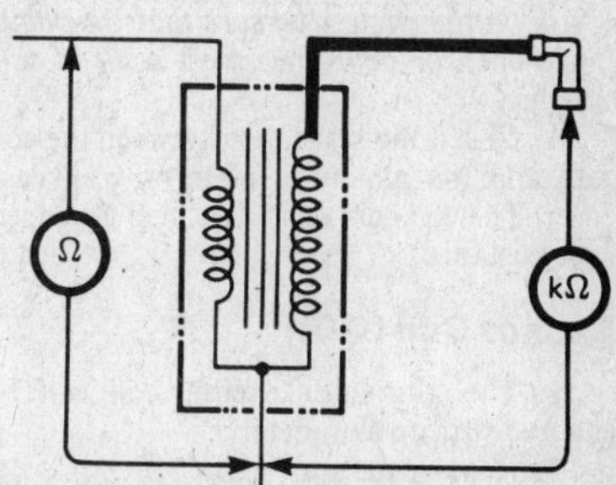

Checking primary and secondary winding resistance (ATC 90-125)

7. Check the resistance across the two low tension leads. It should be about 1.8 ohms or less. If the resistance is not in this range, replace the coil.
8. Check the resistance across the coil terminal to which the green lead was connected and the high tension cable. Resistance should be 4.1 Ωohms. If the reading is not

within this range, the secondary winding is defective and the coil must be replaced.

9. Static resistance tests provide a general clue to coil condition, but cannot detect high voltage insulation leaks. Therefore, even if the resistance readings are acceptable, there is a chance that the coil is defective. Replacing the coil temporarily with one which is known to be good is the only sure check.

Breaker Point Ignition

CONDENSER

1. The condenser can be checked if a capacitance tester is available. Condensers should have a capacitance of approximately 0.25mf. Checking with a "megger" (high-voltage ohmmeter) should yield a resistance of 10M ohms at 1,000v.

2. As noted above, sparking at the points, or points which pit or burn rapidly would indicate a defective condenser. Bad condensers will cause mounds and matching depressions on the points, as illustrated.

MAGNETO

Assuming that all other ignition circuit components have been eliminated as the possible trouble spots, and the ignition and kill switches have been checked, proceed as follows:

1. Remove the left crankcase sidecover and the magneto rotor. A special puller must be used to remove the rotor.

2. Check the rotor for any score marks which would indicate that the rotor is contacting the core ends. If so, the condition must be remedied. If this has occurred, check for any play in the crankshaft which would indicate a bad crankshaft bearing. Other reasons may be improper mounting of the coil cores or rotor, worn crankshaft taper, or rotor taper surface. If the taper is damaged, the rotor should be replaced. Also inspect the rotor for any cracks or fractures. If present, replace.

3. Check for continuity between the black or black/white wire and ground. If continuity does not exist, the primary exciting coil is either broken internally, or is poorly grounded.

NOTE: *If this test is made with the coils still on the engine, be sure that the points are open or held open with a bit of thic paper.*

4. Check the resistance between the coil core and the mounting plate or crankcase cover. The coil core should be well grounded (no resistance).

Excitor Coil (CDI)

1. The alternator excitor coil can be checked with an ohmmeter.

2. Remove the seat.

3. Disconnect the black/red lead at the connector.

4. Check the resistance between the black/red lead and a good ground on the engine. Resistance should be 110-400 ohms.

5. If the reading is not within this range, the alternator stator must be replaced.

Pulse Generator (CDI)

1. The pulse generator is located on the end of the camshaft. The unit can be checked with an ohmmeter.

2. Disconnect the pulse generator wires at the plastic connector. Leads are green and blue/yellow.

3. Resistance across the leads should be 90 ohms.

4. If the reading obtained is not with 10% of the specification, replace the pulse generator.

5. The pulse generator is located beneath the "CDI" cap. It can be removed after the two mounting screws are taken off.

6. If a new pulse generator is fitted, check that the air gap between the pulse rotor and the generator is set at 0.3-0.4mm (0.01-0.02 in.).

CDI Unit

A special tester is needed to check the CDI unit. If all other components in the circuit are found to be serviceable, the CDI unit can be checked most easily by replacing it with one which is known to be in working order.

CHARGING CIRCUIT (ATC 125)

Output Test

NOTE: *The battery must be in good condition and fully charged or this test will not yield valid results.*

1 A voltmeter and an ammeter are required for a system output test.

2. Warm up the engine by running it for several minutes.

3. Remove the seat.

4. Remove the battery holder and cover.

5. Disconnect the red lead at the fuse. Connect the ammeter between the red leads.

6. Connect the voltmeter across the battery terminals.

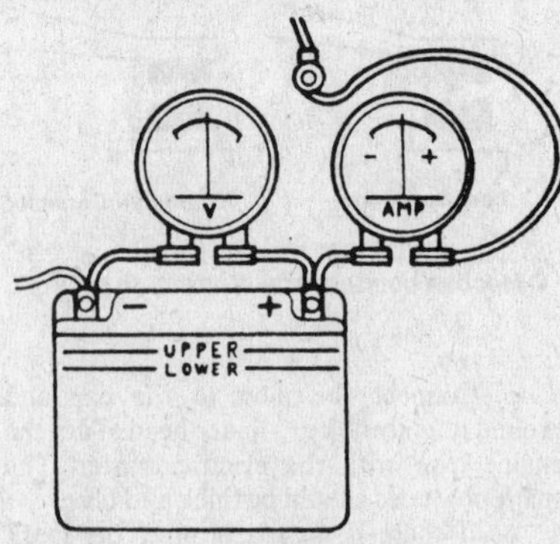

Output test set-up

7. Start the engine and note the readings.

8. The voltmeter should read 14 VDC.

9. The ammeter should read 2.4 a 2,000 rpm and 7.5 a 10,000 rpm.

10. If the readings obtained are not within specification, check the voltage regulator and the alternator charging coil as outlined below.

Voltage Regulator

1. The voltage regulator can be checked either with an ohmmeter or with a self-powered continuity light!

2. Remove the seat.

3. Disconnect the regulator wires at the connector.

4. Regulator leads are yellow, yellow, green, red and black.

5. The check is carried out by testing

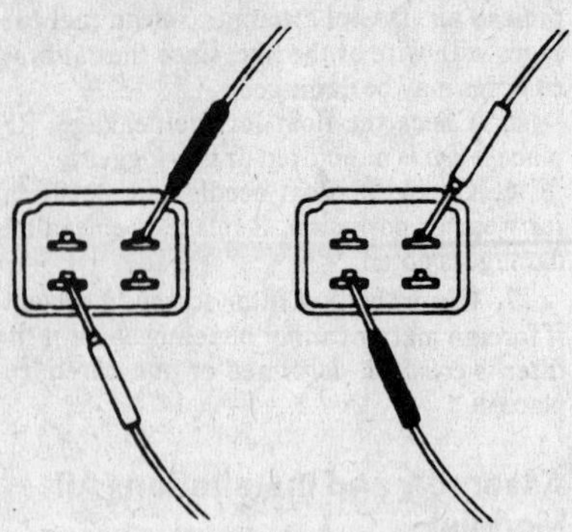

Reversing probe polarity

continuity across each pair of leads, and then reversing the polarity of the meter probes to check for continuity in the opposite direction. (Continuity will be indicated by a reading of 0.2 to 100 ohms depending on the lead involved. "No continuity" will be indicated by an infinite resistance reading.) For each pair of leads there must be continuity in one direction only.

Example: Yellow-green: 1-20 ohms
Green-yellow: Infinity

6. Resistance should be 0.1-1.0 ohms.

7. If the reading is not within this range, replace the alternator stator.

8. Check resistance between each lead and ground on the engine. Resistance must be infinite. Replace the stator if the meter shows any continuity between the wiring and ground.

STARTING SYSTEM (ATC 125)

Testing

1. If, when the starter button is pressed, the starter spins, but the engine does not, the problem is either the starter clutch or the starter motor gears in the left crankcase cover.

2. If the engine turns over very slowly, check the battery for a low state of charge. Check that the engine oil is not too heavy for conditions. If these items are not the problem, suspect a defective starter motor.

3. If nothing at all happens when the starter button is pushed, check all electrical connections in the circuit. Check that the battery is properly charged. Check the ignition switch, starter button switch, neutral switch. Check the starter solenoid. If all of these items are in proper operating condition, check the starter motor.

Starter Solenoid

1. Remove the starter solenoid cover.

2. When the starter button is pressed, their should be an audible "Click" at the solenoid.

3. Disconnect the solenoid high tension leads and the low tension wires at the plastic connector.

4. With an ohmmeter or continuity light, check the resistance of the low tension primary coil (yellow/red and green/red wires). There should be only a few ohms resistance. If this circuit shows an open condition, the solenoid must be replaced.

5. Put 12 VDC across the low tension wires. Check for continuity across the high

tension terminals. There should be no resistance. If the high tension terminals do not show continuity, the solenoid is defective and must be replaced.

Starter Motor

Removal

1. Be certain the ignition switch is "OFF".
2. Disconnect the ground cable at the battery.
3. Remove the exhaust pipe nuts at the cylinder head.
4. Remove the muffler mounting bolts. Remove the exhaust system.
5. Disconnect the high tension lead at the starter motor.
6. Remove the starter motor bracket bolts and the mounting screws and bolts. Remove the starter motor.

DISASSEMBLY

1. Remove the starter motor gear snap-ring.
2. Remove the gear. Remove the inner snap-ring and the thrust washers, if any, behind it. Note the number of washers. They must all be installed when the unit is assembled.
3. Remove the starter motor screws and take off the case end to expose the brushes.
4. Note the number and location of shims on the armature shaft when the cover is taken off.

INSPECTION

1. Electrical tests can be carried out with an ohmmeter or a self-powered test light.
2. Check that continuity exists between each of the commutator segments. If one or more of them is "dead," the motor must be replaced.

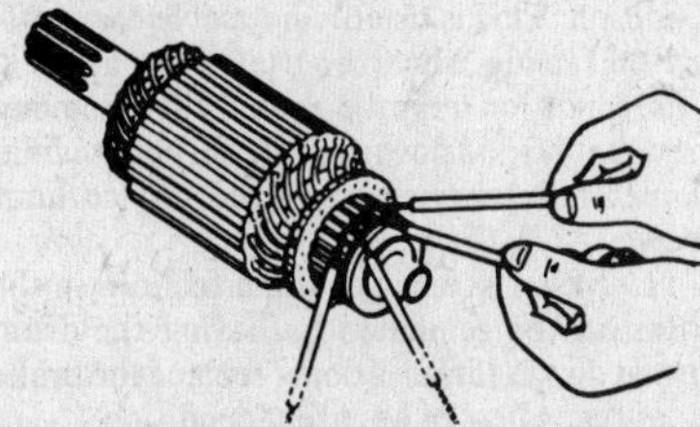

Checking commutator segment continuity

3. Check that there is no continuity between the commutator segments and the armature core. Anything less than infinite resistance here will require replacement of the motor.
4. Check that there is no continuity between the commutator segments and the armature bars.
5. Check that there is no continuity between the brush which is wired to the stator (field) coil and the high tension cable terminal. Lack of continuity here indicates that the field coil is open and the motor must be replaced.
6. Check the commutator segments for signs of wear, scoring or other contact damage.
7. Clean the commutator with a rag and a safe solvent to remove carbon dust and other foreign matter.
8. Check the condition of the carbon

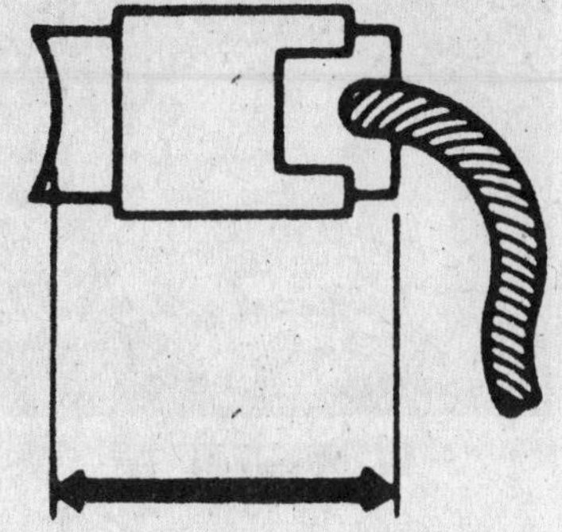

Measure brush length

brushes. Brushes with cracked or oddly worn contact surfaces should be replaced.

9. Measure brush length. Replace them as a set if either measures under 6.5mm (0.26 in.).
10. Check brush spring tension. It should be 410 gr. (14.5 oz.).
11. Check the armature for contact damage as might occur if the armature bars touch the field coils. If any is evident, replace the motor.
12. Discoloration of the commutator segments occuring on two adjacent segments indicates grounded coils. This requires replacement of the motor.
13. Check the condition of the bushings in the end caps. If they are cracked or otherwise damaged, or the armature shows signs of contact damage, the unit must be replaced.

ASSEMBLY

1. Clean all parts thoroughly.
2. Use a small amount of light duty grease to lubricate the bushings in the end caps.

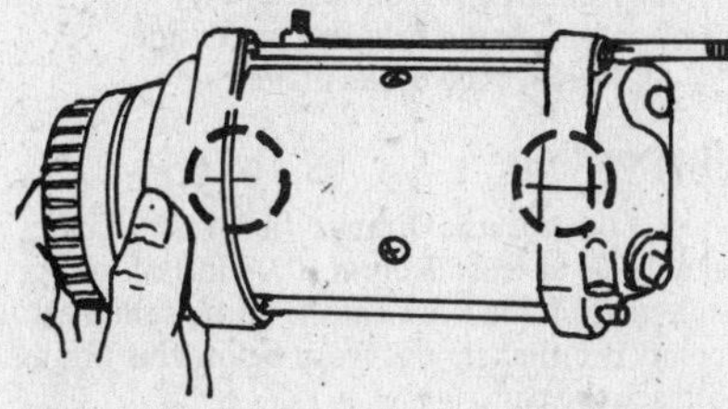

When assembling the starter, align the case marks

3. Be sure that all shims are in place on the brush side of the armature.
4. Be sure that the brush springs are in place and that the brushes are in good contact with the commutator.
5. Check that the brush side end cap O-ring is in good condition.
6. Insert the armature into the case.
7. Install the brush holder with brushes.
8. When assembling the starter motor, align the pin on the brush holder with the notch in the case.
9. Install the rear cover, aligning the slot with the brush holder pin.
10. Align the marks on the motor case and the end covers before tightening the screws.

INSTALLATION

1. Reverse the removal procedure.
2. Lubricate the O-ring before fitting the motor.

ELECTRICAL SWITCHES (ATC 110,125)

Ignition Switch

1. The ignition switch can be checked with an ohmmeter or a self-powered test light.
2. Remove the headlight.
3. Disconnect the ignition switch wires at the connectors (black/white, green, red, black).
4. When the ignition switch is in the "OFF" position, there should be continuity between the black/white and the green leads only.
5. When the ignition switch is in the "ON" position, there should be continuity between the red and the black leads only.
6. If the switch fails either test, replace it.

Engine Stop Switch

1. The switch can be checked with an ohmmeter or self-powered test light.
2. Remove the headlight.
3. Disconnect the stop switch leads at the connectors (green and black/white).
4. When in the "RUN" position, there should be no continuity.
5. In both "OFF" positions, there should be continuity between the green and black/white leads.
6. The switch is a part of the left switch housing which is replaced as an assembly.

Lighting Switch

1. The switch can be checked with an ohmmeter or a self-powered test light.
2. Remove the headlight.
3. Disconnect the switch wires at the plastic connectors (brown, black/brown, white and blue).
4. When the lighting switch is "OFF" there must be no continuity between any of the wires.
5. When the lighting switch is in the "LO" position, there must be continuity between the brown, black/brown and white leads.
6. When the lighting switch is in the "N" position, there must be continuity across all four wires.
7. When the lighting switch is in the "HI" position, there must be continuity between the brown, black/brown and blue leads.
8. If the switch fails any one of these tests, it must be replaced. The switch is a part of the left switch housing which is replaced as an assembly.

Starter Button

1. The button can be checked with an ohmmeter or a self-powered test light.
2. Remove the headlight.
3. Disconnect the green/red and the light green/red button wires at the connectors.
4. There must be continuity across these wires only when the starter button is pushed.
5. If there is always continuity, or if no continuity is indicated when the button is pressed, the switch assembly must be replaced.

Neutral Switch

1. The neutral switch is a part of the starting circuit which will work only if the

switch is closed, indicating that the transmission is in Neutral.

2. The switch can be checked with an ohmmeter or a self-powered test light.
3. Remove the seat.
4. Remove the air cleaner tube.
5. Disconnect the neutral switch wire at the connector (light green/red).
6. Check for continuity between the lead and ground on the engine case. When the transmission is in Neutral, there must be continuity.
7. When the transmission is in any other gear, the switch must be open (no continuity).
8. The switch can be replaced after removing the E- clip which secured it to the sub-transmission cover.

CHASSIS

WHEEL REMOVAL AND INSTALLATION

Front

ATC 70/90

1. Park the machine on a level surface.
2. Apply the parking brake.
3. Remove the axle nut cotter pin. Loosen the axle nut.
4. Raise the front wheel off the ground by placing a sturdy, safe support beneath the frame.
5. Remove the axle nut.
6. Remove the axle. Take out the wheel. Note the spacers on both sides.
7. Installation is the reverse of removal. Be sure the spacers are in place on both sides of the wheel. Tighten the axle nut to 43-58 ft. lbs. Use a new cotter pin.

ATC 110

1. Park the machine on a level surface.
2. Engage the parking brake.
3. Remove the axle nut cotter pins.
4. Loosen the axle nuts.
5. Raise the front of the machine by placing a sturdy, safe support beneath the frame and the front wheel will come out of the forks.
6. Installation is the reverse of removal. Be sure that all spacers are in place on the sides of the wheel. Be sure the axle collars enter the forks. Tighten the two axle nuts evenly until the proper torque of 36-51 ft. lbs. is reached. Use new axle nut cotter pins.

ATC 125

1. Park the machine on a level surface.
2. Engage the parking brake.
3. Disconnect the front brake cable.
4. Remove the axle nut cotter pins.
5. Loosen the axle nuts.
6. Raise the front of the machine by placing a suitable safe support beneath the frame and the front wheel will come out of the forks. Note the spacer on the left side.
7. Installation is the reverse of removal. Note the following:
   a. Be sure the spacer is in place on the left side of the wheel.
   b. Be sure to engage the brake plate with the anchor on the fork leg.
   c. Be sure the axle collars enter the forks on both sides.

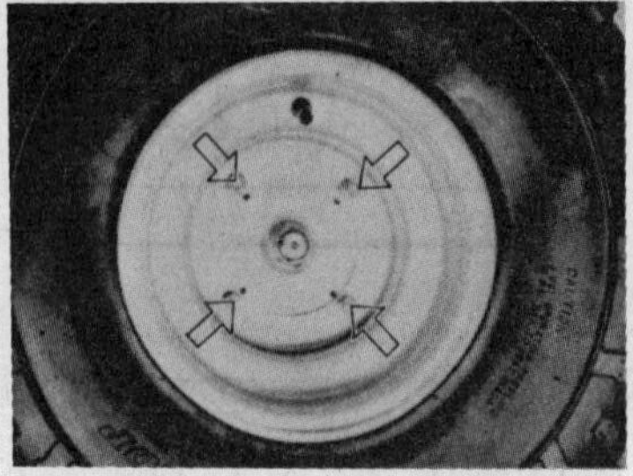

Wheel nuts

   d. Tighten the axle nuts evenly until a torque of 36-51 ft. lbs. is reached.
   e. Use new axle nut cotter pins.

Rear (All Models)

1. Park the machine on a level surface.
2. Engine the parking brake.
3. Loosen each of the wheel nuts or bolts on the wheel you wish to remove.
4. Support the rear wheel(s) off the ground by placing a jack or suitable safety stand beneath the frame.
5. Remove the wheel nuts or bolts.
6. Remove the wheel.
7. To install the wheel, be sure to put it on the hub with the tire valve facing out.
8. Install the wheel nuts or bolts and tighten them in an "X" pattern a bit at a time until the proper torque of 14-18 ft. lbs. is reached.

FRONT BRAKE

Removal

1. Remove the front wheel.
2. Remove the axle nut, brake side.
3. Remove the brake plate.

Inspection

1. Inspect the linings for wear. There should be at least 2.0mm (0.08 in.) of lining material left measured at the lining's thinnest point. If either shoe is worn below this limit, replace the pair.
2. Inspect the linings for scoring or grooves. These may be caused by particles of dirt which enter the drum. If badly scored, the linings should be replaced and the drum inspected closely for the same type of damage.
3. Be sure that the linings are free of any oil or grease. Lubricant-impregnated linings must be replaced.
4. If the linings are in usable condition, rough up the surfaces with coarse sandpaper to break the glaze. Clean them thoroughly afterwards with alcohol or laquer thinner.
5. Clean foreign matter from the brake plate with a rag.

CAUTION: *Brake dust may present a health hazard. Do not blow the brake assemblies clear with a high pressure compressed air source or the particulates may be inhaled.*

6. Inspect the brake drum surface for condition. The drum must be free of scoring or rust.
7. Rust can be removed from the brake drum surface with sandpaper. Polish the surface until it is shiny, then clean it thoroughly.

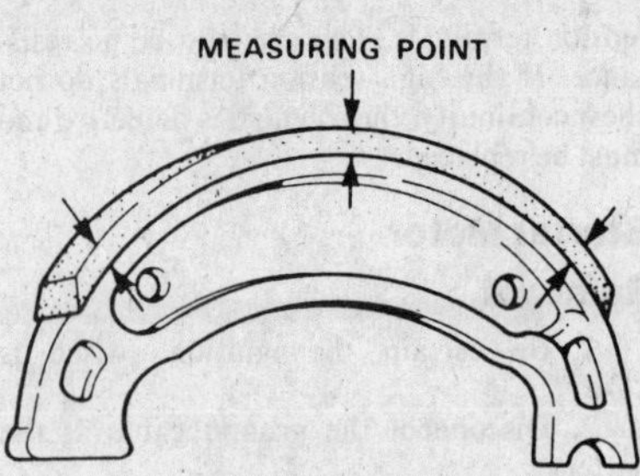

Checking brake lining thickness

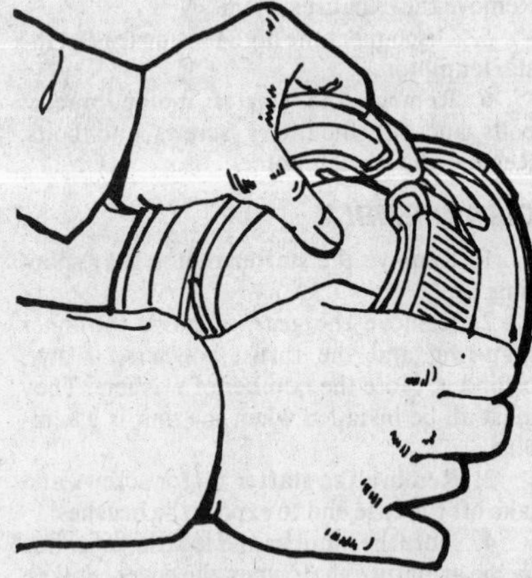

Removing brake shoes from the brake plate

8. Alcohol or laquer thinner can be used to remove dirt or deposits from the drum.
9. Measure the inside diameter of the brake drum. If it measures more than 111mm (4.4 in.), replace it.
10. Measure the diameter of the drum in two directions to check for an out-of-round condition. This is usually noticable as an off-and-on feeling when the brakes are applied. This condition may be remedied by having the drum turned down on a lathe, but the final diameter must not exceed the service limit above.
11. Minor scoring or imperfections in the drum can be remedied by having the drum turned down. If this is done, replace the brake shoes regardless of apparent condition.
12. Check the brake drum rubberr seal for condition and replace it if it is cracked or otherwise damaged.
13. Check the brake drum for cracks or other critical defects.
14. The brake drum is a part of the front wheel hub. To remove it, remove the four mounting nuts. Nuts should be tightened to 14-18 ft. lbs. when installing.
15. Check the wheel bearings in the brake drum. See "Front Wheel Bearings," below.

Disassembly

1. Disconnect the brake cable from the brake lever by removing the adjuster wing nut.
2. Remove the brake lever pinch bolt.
3. Carefully pry the brake lever off the splined cam shaft.
4. Expand the brake shoes by hand and pull them and the return springs off the brake plate by folding them together.
5. Tap the brake cam out of the brake plate taking care not to lose the seals and wear

indicator plate. Note the spring on the inside of the brake plate as well.

6. Clean dirt, brake dust and other foreign matter from the brake plate with a solvent-soaked rag.

7. Check the plate closely for stress cracks or other damage.

8. Check the condition of the brake shoe springs. Replace them if they are rusted, broken, deformed or weakened.

9. Check the brake cam spring and replace it if it is damaged.

10. Check that the brake cam is not bent.

11. Check that the splines on the cam are in good condition.

12. Clean the cam in solvent. Remove rust or corrosion with sandpaper.

13. The cam must turn freely in the brake plate hole. If it does not, determine the cause and remedy it.

14. Check the condition of the grease seals in the brake plate and replace them if damaged. They can be pried out.

Assembly

1. Install the grease seals and spacer in the brake plate if they were removed.

2. Lubricate the brake cam with a good grade of medium-weight chassis grease.

3. Fit the washer and the cam spring on the cam.

4. Insert the cam into the plate. Be sure that the spring end is fitted into the hole in the cam and the other end is hooked over the anchor on the plate.

5. Lubricate the brake shoe pivot with chassis grease.

6. Fit the outer cam grease seal if it is not already in place. Install the wear indicator plate. The tab aligns with the cam cut-out.

7. Install the brake lever, aligning the punch mark on the lever with the punch mark on the end of the cam.

8. Install and tighten the lever pinch bolt.

9. Clean hands thoroughly to avoid contaminating the brake linings.

10. Assemble the shoes and return springs and spread them by hand to fit over the pivot and the cam. Be sure they are properly seated.

11. Work the brake lever by hand and observe operation.

Installation

1. Installation is the reverse of removal.

2. If the brake drum/hub was removed from the wheel, install it and tighten the four nuts in an "X" pattern until a torque of 14-18 ft. lbs. is reached.

3. Grease the wheel bearing seal lips before inserting the axle.

4. Be certain that the axle spacer is in place on the left side of the wheel and that the axle collars are properly positioned when inserting the wheel into the forks.

5. Tighten the axle nuts to 36-51 ft. lbs. and use new cotter pins.

6. Adjust the brake as described in "Maintenance."

FRONT WHEEL BEARINGS

The front wheel bearings are pressed into the wheel hub and can be removed or serviced after the hub is removed from the wheel.

1. Remove the front wheel.

2. Remove the brake plate (ATC 125).

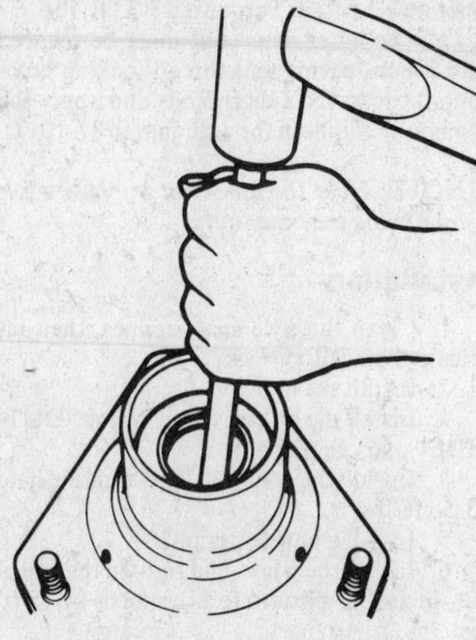

Removing bearings from the hub

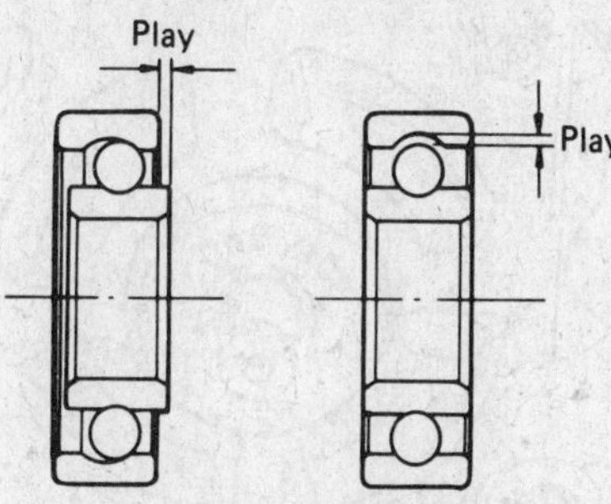

Bearing axial and radial play

3. Remove the hub nuts and take off the hub.

4. Pry out the grease seals on either side.

5. Bearings should be inspected in place, since removal usually damages them.

6. Check each bearing for play of the inner race relative to the outer. Maximum allowable radial (up- and-down) play is 0.05mm (0.002 in.). Maximum axial (in-and-out) play is 0.10mm (0.004 in.). If either bearing exceeds these limits, replace the pair.

7. Check the bearing rotation. If any roughness, binding or noise is noted, replace the set.

8. Remove the bearings by reaching into the hub with a suitable drift and driving out one of them. Remove the spacer. Remove the remaining bearing in the same manner.

9. Lubricate new bearings with a good quality, medium-weight bearing grease. Put a quantity of the lubricant inside the hub as well.

10. Bearings should be driven into the drum until fully seated. A driver large enough to cover the whole bearing should be used so that it can be driven straight in.

11. After the first bearing is installed, fit the spacer, then the other bearing.

12. Press grease seals in carefully.

13. When installing the hub on the wheel, tighten the fasteners in a cross pattern to a torque of 14-18 ft. lbs.

REAR BRAKE

Removal

1. Remove the skid plate.

2. Remove the right rear wheel.

3. Remove the axle nut cotter pin.

4. Remove the axle nut.

5. Remove the hub.

6. On larger models, remove the two brake drum nuts from the axle. Remove the washer if fitted.

7. Remove the brakedrum cover bolts. Remove the cover.

8. Remove the O-ring from the axle, if fitted.

9. Pull off the brake drum.

10. Brake components are now exposed for inspection and service.

Inspection

1. Inspect the linings for wear. There should be at least 2.0mm (0.08 in.) of lining material left at the thinnest point. If either shoe is worn below this limit, replace the pair.

2. Inspect the linings for scoring or grooves. These may be caused by particles of dirt which enter the drum. If badly scored, the linings should be replaced and the drum inspected closely for the same type of damage.

3. Be sure the linings are free of oil and grease. Lubricant-impregnated linings must be replaced.

4. If the linings are in usable condition, rough up the surfaces with sandpaper to break the glaze. Clean them thoroughly afterwards with alcohol or laquer thinner.

5. Clean foreign matter from the brake plate with a rag.

CAUTION: *Brake dust may present a health hazard. Do not blow the brake assembly clear with a high pressure compressed air source or the particulates may be inhaled.*

6. Inspect the brake drum surface for condition. The drum must be free of rust or scoring.

7. Rust can be removed from the drum surface with sandpaper. Polish the surface until it is shiny, then clean it thoroughly.

8. Alcohol or laquer thinner can be used to remove dirt or deposits from the drum.

9. Measure the inside diameter of the drum. Service limits are 111mm (4.4 in.) for ATC 70s up to 1975 131mm (5.2 in.) for ATC 70s after 1975, and 141mm (5.6 in.) for other models.

10. Measure the diameter of the drum in two directions to check for an out-of-round condition. This is usually noticable as an off-and-on feeling when the brakes are applied. This condition may be remedied by having the drum turned down on a lathe, but the final diameter must not exceed the service limit, above.

11. Minor scoring or imperfectons in the drum can be remedied by having the drum turned down. If this is done, replace the brake shoes regardless of apparent condition.

12. Check the splines on the brake drum and those on the axle for condition. If they are worn or show other signs of damage, replace the components.

13. Check the brake drum cover seals and axle O-ring for condition and replace any unserviceable components. If there was evidence of foreign matter inside the brake, the seals should be replaced regardless of apparent condition.

14. Be sure that the drum is free of stress cracks, accident damage, etc.

Disassembly

1. Disconnect the brake rod from the brake lever by removing the adjuster wing nut.
2. Remove the cotter pin and washer from the brake shoe pivot which are fitted to some models.
3. Expand the brake shoes by hand and pull them and the return springs off the brake plate by folding them together.
4. Remove the brake lever pinch bolt.
5. Carefully pry the brake lever off the splined shaft.
6. Remove the wear indicator plate.
7. Tap the brake cam out of the brake plate taking care not to lose any seals which may come out.
8. Clean dirt, brake dust and other foreign matter from the brake plate with a solvent-soaked rag.
9. Check the brake plate closely for stress cracks or other damage.
10. Check the condition of the brake shoe springs. Replace them if they are rusted, broken, deformed or weakened.
11. Check the brake cam spring and replace it if it is damaged.
12. Check that the brake cam is not bent.
13. Check that the splines on the cam are in good condition.
14. Clean the cam in solvent. Remove rust or corrosion with sandpaper.
15. The cam must turn freely in the brake plate hole. If it does not, determine the cause and remedy it.
16. Check the condition of the cam dust seal and the grease seals in the brake plate and replace them if damaged. Grease seals can be pried out.

Assembly

1. Install the grease seals in the brake plate if they were removed.
2. Lubricate the brake cam with a good grade of medium-weight chassis grease.
3. Fit the cam spring on the cam, inserting the end of the spring into the hole in the cam.
4. Install the brake cam. Fit the outer end of the spring over the anchor on the brake plate.
5. Install the dust seal on the outer side of the cam.
6. Lubricate the brake shoe pivot with chassis grease.
7. Install the wear indicator plate, aligning the tab with the cam cut-out.
8. Install the brake lever, aligning the punch mark on the lever with the punch mark on the cam.
9. Install and tighten the lever pinch bolt.
10. Clean hands thoroughly to avoid contaminating the brake linings.
11. Assemble the shoes and return springs and spread them by hand to fit over the pivot and the cam. Be sure they are properly seated. Install the washer and cotter pin, if fitted.
12. Work the brake lever by hand and observe operation.
13. Install the brake drum.
14. Lubricate the axle O-ring and install it, if fitted.
15. Lubricate the center seal of the brake drum cover with grease.
16. Install the cover.
17. Install the washer, if fitted.
18. Install and tighten the brake drum inner nut, if fitted. Torque is 25-33 ft. lbs.
19. The outer drum nut must be secured with a non- permanent thread-looking compound. Clean the axle threads and apply the compound. Tighten the outer nut to 87-101 ft. lbs.

NOTE: *Hold the inner nut in place while tightening the outer nut.*

Installation

1. Clean the axle shaft splines, then lubricate them with grease.
2. Install the hub.
3. Install the hub washer with the "OUTSIDE" mark facing out.
4. Install the axle nut and tighten it to 43-58 ft. lbs.
5. Install a new cotter pin.
6. Install the wheel and tighten the wheel nuts in an "X" pattern to a torque of 14-18 ft. lbs.
7. Connect the rear brake rod and adjust the brake as outlined in "Maintenance."

Install the hub washer with the "OUTSIDE" out

FRONT END

Bearing Adjustment

1. The steering stem bearings are uncaged steel balls. They are adjusted by means of a ring nut beneath the upper triple clamp.
2. To check the bearing adjustment, support the front wheel off the ground. Grasp the fork sliders with both hands.
3. Attempt to move the forks by pulling out on the sliders. If play or movement can be felt, the bearings are too loosely adjusted or worn.
4. Turn the forks slowly from the lock-to-lock. Movement should be smooth, silent, and effortless. If any binding or uneven movement is felt, the balls and the races are either too tightly adjusted, unlubricated, or are worn. If the steering feels uniformly stiff, the bearings are too tightly adjusted. If any noise is noted, the bearings are damaged, or some are missing.
5. With the front wheel off the ground, release the front forks from a few degrees off the centered position. The forks should fall freely to either side of their own weight. If they will not, the bearings are too tightly adjusted, the steering stem is bent, the races are extremely worn, or some of the bearings are missing.
6. Bearings can be adjusted with a hammer and punch or a pin wrench on the adjuster nut under the upper triple clamp after the triple clamp is removed. To do this, remove the handlebars; remove the upper triple clamp fork tube bolts and the steering stem nut and washer. Tap upwards to remove the upper triple clamp.

Upper triple clamp steering stem nut and fork tube bolts (arrows)

7. Tighten or loosen the adjusting nut until operation is as described above.
8. If proper adjustment is not possible, the bearing and races wil probably have to be replaced.
9. On the ATC 70, tighten the steering stem nut to 36-51 ft. lbs. and the fork tube bolts to 29-35 ft. lbs. On other models, tighten the steering stem nut and the fork tube bolts to 36-51 ft. lbs.

Removal

1. Park the machine on a level surface.
2. Apply the parking brake.
3. Support the front end off the ground by placing sturdy, safe supports beneath the frame.
4. Remove the front wheel.
5. Remove the front fender.
6. Remove the handlebars.
7. Remove the headlight, if fitted.
8. Remove the fork tube bolts and the steering stem nut and washer. Tap the upper triple clamp upwards with a mallet to free it if stuck.

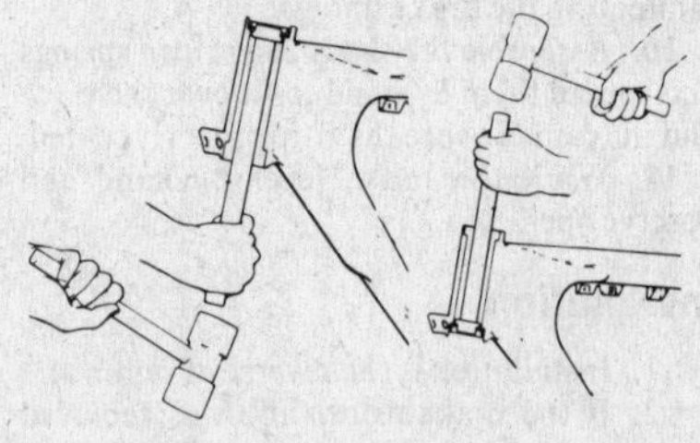

Removing and installing steering stem races in the frame

9. Loosen the steering stem bearing adjuster nut with a pin wrench, then hold the steering stem up while unscreweing the adjuster nut the rest of the way off. Remove the steering stem top cone race and the balls from the top race.
10. Carefully pull the steering stem out from the bottom. Some of the ball bearings from the lower ráce will most likely fall out at this time so be prepared for this. Remove the rest of the balls from the lower race when the stem is removed.
11. Remove the bottom cone race, dust seal, dust seal, and dust seal washer from the steering stem if they are to be replaced. If the steering system has been damaged and is to be replaced, the upper and lower races and balls should also be replaced.

NOTE: *A chisel is usually necessary to remove the lower cone race from the steering stem.*

12. The bearing races in the frame are a press-fit and should not be removed unless replacement is necessary. Inspect them first. If replacement is necessary, the old races can be removed by reaching through the frame lug with a suitable punch and tapping the races out from the inside of the lug.

New races are installed using a suitable sized bushing driver: i.e., one which will drive the race squarely into its seat. Be certain that the race goes straight in.

These races can also be installed using a block of hardwood, of sufficient size to cover the race, in place of a bushing driver.

Inspection

1. Wash the bearings in a suitable solvent.
2. Clean all of the old grease from the bearing race surfaces, the steering stem, and the frame lug.
3. Inspect the bearing race surfaces. They must be clean and smooth. That is, free from any cracks, scoring, indentations, or rust. Run your finger around the bearing race surfaces. Note any roughness or ripples on the race surfaces. If either is damaged, replace both races and balls.
4. Check the balls themselves for rust, pitting, or flat spots. Replace the bearings as a set if any such damage occurs.
5. Check the dust seal for condition and replace if necessay.
6. Check the steering stem for cracks or a bent condition; this is especially important if the bike has been involved in a spill.

Installation

1. Install the dust seal washer, dust seal, and bottom cone race onto the steering stem. Use a good grade of bearing grease to coat the bottom cone race and the top race in the frame lug.
2. Embed the balls into the grease of the top frame race and the bottom cone race. Place a coat of grease on the two remainging races.

NOTE: *There are 21 balls in each race.*

3. When the balls are in place, slip the steering stem through the frame lug and hold it in place, while refitting the top cone race and threading on the adjuster nut.
4. Tighten the adjuster nut, and move the steering stem back-and-forth to work the grease into the bearings, then back off the adjuster nut until the steering stem turns with ease, but has no play.
5. Install the upper triple clamp. Check that the stem moves freely of its own weight from 5°-10° off center; if not check for:
   a. Steering bearings too tight;
   b. Bent steering stem;
   c. Worn races or balls.
6. Install the flat washer, and steering stem nut.
7. Tighten the steering stem nut to 36-51 ft. lbs.
8. Tighten the fork bolts to 29-35 ft. lbs. on the ATC 70 and 36-51 ft. lbs. on the other models.
9. The remainder of the procedure is the reverse of removal.

REAR AXLE

ATC 70

REMOVAL

1. Remove the seat/fender assembly.
2. Remove the skid plate.
3. Place a jack beneath the frame to support the rear wheel off the ground.
4. Remove the rear wheels.
5. Remove the wheel hubs.
6. Remove the chain case.
7. Loosen the tensioner. Disconnect the chain.
8. Remove the rear sprocket.
9. Remove the brake assembly as directed under "Rear Brake," above.
10. Remove the axle.

INSPECTION

1. Inspect components as directed under "Rear Axle" for ATC 90-125 machines, below. Procedures are similar.
2. The bearings can be driven out of their holder after the grease seals on either side are pried out.

INSTALLATION

Reverse the removal procedure.

ATC 90/110/125

REMOVAL

1. Remove the seat.
2. Remove the five skid plate mounting bolts and the skid plate.

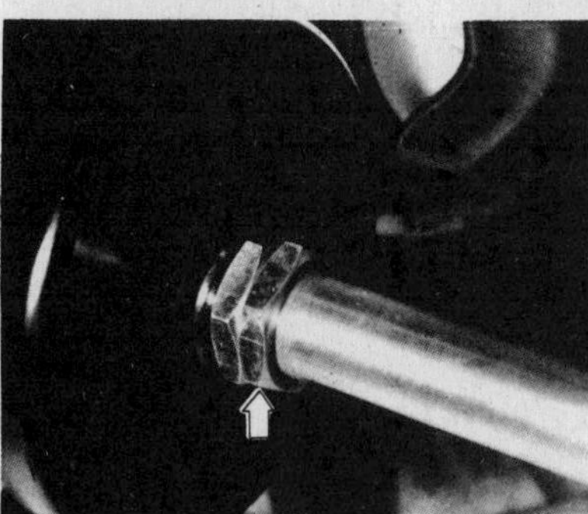

Brake drum nuts

Brake cover bolts

3. Support the rear end of the vehicle with safe, sturdy stands placed beneath the frame.
4. Remove the rear wheel nuts and take off the wheel.
5. Remove the axle nut dust caps, if fitted.
6. Remove the cotter pins.
7. Remove the axle nuts and washers.
8. Pull the hubs off the axle.
9. Disconnect the carburetor overflow tube from the clamps on the chain case.
10. Remove the three bolts securing the seal cover around the rear axle and take off the cover.
11. Remove the chain case mounting bolts.
12. Undo the clamps.
13. Remove the outer chain case half.
14. Back off the rear brake adjuster nut.
15. Loosen the drive chain adjuster nut.
16. Loosen the four bearing holder mounting bolts.
17. Disconnect the drive chain. Be sure to remove the masterlink spring clip with a pliers. Prying the clip off will make it unusable. Put the masterlink on one end of the chain to avoid loss.
18. Remove the two brake drum nuts from the axle.
19. Remove the washer.
20. Remove the brake drum cover bolts.
21. Remove the O-ring from the axle.
22. Pull off the brake drum.
23. Use a plastic mallet to drive the axle out from the right side.
24. Remove the chain case inner half bolts (four). Remove the case half.
25. Remove the rear brake adjuster nut and disconnect the brake rod from the brake lever.
26. Remove the trailer hitch upper mounting bolts
27. Remove the bearing holder from the frame.

INSPECTION

Axle

1. Check sprocket condition.
2. To remove the sprocket, remove the four damper cover nuts, the damper çover and snap-ring.
3. Check the dampers for damage.
4. Check all axle splines for condition.
5. Check axle run-out. When measured in the middle of the axle, the serviceable limit for run-out is 3.0mm (0.12 in.). This is 1/2 of the Total Indicated Reading of the gauge.
6. Check the condition of the O-ring behind the axle flange and replace it if necessary.
7. Assembly is the reverse of disassembly. Grease axle splines before installation. Lubricate the O-ring before fitting it to the axle. Tighten the damper nuts to 17-22 ft. lbs.

Bearing Holder

1. Pry out the grease seals on either side.
2. Bearings should be checked in place, since removal will usually damage them.
3. Check for excessive play of the inner race relative to the outer. Maximum allowable radial (up- and-down) play is 0.05mm (0.002 in.). Maximum allowable axial (in-and-out) play is 0.10mm (0.004 in.).
4. Check the bearings for rough or binding rotation, excessive noise, etc.
5. Replace bearings in sets.
6. Bearings can be removed by driving them out with a hammer and suitable drift. Remove one bearing and take out the spacer and any shims. Drive out the remaining bearing.
7. Pack new bearings with a good grade of medium- weight bearing grease. Place a

quantity of the lubricant in the bearing holder as well.

8. Install bearings with the marked side out.

9. Install the right side bearing first, driving it straight in with a suitably sized bearing driver until it is firmly seated.

10. Install the spacer along with any shims which may be fitted.

11. Install the remaining bearing.

12. Press grease seals straight into the holder.

13. Lubricate the seal lips before assembly.

INSTALLATION

1. Install the bearing holder and fit the four bolts, but do not tighten them yet since the chain must be readjusted.

2. Fit the chain adjuster nut.

3. Connect the brake rod.

4. Install the inner chain case half.

5. Install the axle from the left side of the machine.

6. Check that the brake shoe assemblies are in place.

7. Install the brake drum.

8. Lubricate and install the brake drum O-ring.

9. Lubricate the center seal of the brake drum cover. Install the cover and secure it with the six bolts.

10. Clean the axle threads thoroughly.

11. Fit the washer on the axle.

12. Install the brake drum inner nut and tighten it to 25-33 ft. lbs.

13. The brake drum outer nut must be secured with a non-permanent thread-locking compound. Apply the compound to the threads of the axle, then install the nut.

14. Hold the inner nut in place while the outer is tightened to the proper torque of 87-101 ft. lbs.

15. Connect the drive chain. The closed end of the masterlink spring clip must face the direction of chain rotation.

16. Adjust the chain as outlined in "Maintenance" and tighten the four bearing holder bolts to 51-58 ft. lbs.

17. The remainder of the procedure is the reverse of removal. Note the following:

a. Grease the wheel hub splines before fitting the hubs.

b. Install the hub washers with the "OUTSIDE" mark facing out.

c. Tighten the axle nuts to 36-58 ft. lbs.

d. Use new acle nut cotter pins.

e. Tighten the wheel nuts gradually and in an "X" pattern until the final torgue of 36-43 ft. lbs. is reached.

f. Adjust the rear brake after assembly.

CHASSIS TORQUE SPECIFICATIONS

Part	Torque (ft. lbs.)
ATC 70	
Front axle nut	43-58
Fork tube bolts	29-35
Steering stem nut	36-51
Handlebar clamp bolts	14-18
Lower handlebar clamp nuts	29-35
Drive chain tensioner	18-24
Rear axle nuts	43-58
Rear wheel bolts	14-18
Brake cam holder	5-9
Brake anchor pin	5-9
Rear fender	11-15
Seat	4-7
Rear fender bracket	4-7
Footpeg guard	
8 mm	14-18
10 mm	29-35
Footpegs	14-18
Engine mounting bolts	14-18
Rear wheel hub nuts	14-18
Front wheel hub nuts	14-18
ATC 90, 110, 125	
Front axle nuts	36-51
Fork tube bolts	36-51
Steering stem nut	36-51
Handlebar clamp bolts	13-22
Lower handlebar clamp nuts	29-35
Front wheel hub nuts	14-18
Rear axle nut	43-58
Rear wheel nuts	14-18
Rear wheel hub nuts	14-18
Sprocket damper holder nuts	15-20
Rear brake nuts	
Inner	25-33
Outer	87-101
Bearing holder bolts	36-51

GENERAL TORQUE SPECIFICATIONS①

Part	Torque (ft lbs.)
5 mm screws	2.5-3.6
6 mm screws	5-8
5 mm bolts, nuts	3.5-4.5
6 mm bolts, nuts	6-9
8 mm bolts, nuts	13-18
10 mm bolts, nuts	22-29
12 mm bolts, nuts	36-43
6 mm bolt w/8 mm head	5-8
6 mm flange bolts, nuts	7-10
8 mm flange bolts, nuts	17-22
10 mm flange bolts, nuts	25-33

① Unless otherwise noted

Honda ATC 185/200

MODEL COVERAGE

ATC 185 (1980)
ATC 185S (1981-83)
ATC 200 (1981-85)
ATC 200M (1984-85)

INDEX

SERIAL NUMBER LOCATIONS

To avoid confusion when ordering parts, always supply the frame and engine serial numbers.

The frame serial number is stamped on the left side of the steering head lug.

The engine serial number is stamped onto the lower left side of the crankcase beneath the gearshift lever.

MAINTENANCE

NOTE: *Common maintenance procedures are explained in detail in the "General Information" section of this manual.*

LUBRICATION

Checking Oil

1. Oil level should be checked before each ride.
2. A dipstick is fitted to the oil filler cap on the right crankcase cover.
3. Park the machine on a level surface.
4. Start the machine, allow it to idle for several minutes, then shut it off and let it sit for a minute or so.
5. Unscrew and remove the dipstick and wipe it clean.

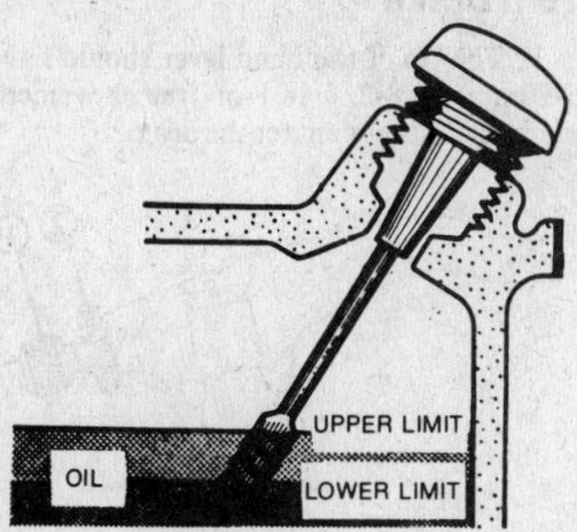

Checking oil level

6. Insert the dipstick, allowing the cap to rest on top of the threads of the hole. Do not screw it in when checking oil level.
7. The oil level should be between the minimum and maximum marks on the dipstick.
8. If level is too low, add enough oil to bring it up to the specified level.

CAUTION: *Do not overfill the crankcase.*

Changing Oil

1. Oil should be changed every 30 operating days or 3 mos. (whichever comes first) if the machine is used under normal conditions.
2. At the same time the oil is changed, the oil filter screen and centrifugal filter should be cleaned. See "Oil Filters," below.
3. Oil should be API service rated "SE" or "SF." SAE 20W-40 or 20W-50 can be used when average air temperature is above freezing (32°F). Refer to the "Recommended Lubricants" chart for all temperature oil recommendations.
4. Run the machine until the engine reaches operating temperature.
5. Park the machine on a level surface.

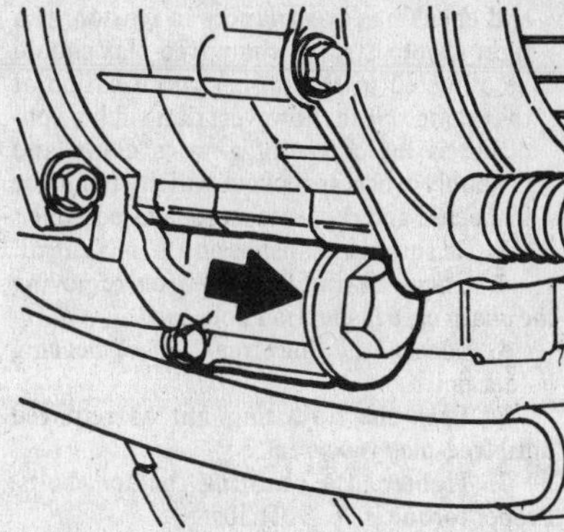

Oil filter screen cap and drain plug

6. Place a container with a capacity of about 2 qts. beneath the engine.
7. Remove the dipstick.
8. Remove the oil filter screen cap on the left side of the engine. Take out the spring and filter screen and allow the oil to drain for several minutes.
9. With the ignition or kill switch "OFF," turn the engine over several times with the recoil starter. This will allow more of the oil to drain out.
10. Check the condition of the filter screen cap o- ring and sealing rubber. Replace them if damaged.
11. Check filter screen condition and clean it thoroughly. See below.
12. Fit the screen, spring and cap. Tighten the cap to 7-11 ft. lbs.
13. Add the correct quantity and grade of oil to the crankcase. Refer to the "Recommended Lubricants" and "Maintenance Data" charts. Crankcase capacities after a routine change are:

    1980 models: 1 qt.

    1981 and later models: 1.4 qts.
14. Check oil level as outlined above.
15. Start the engine and let it run for a minute or so. Check for leaks. Recheck level and top up if necessary.

NOTE: *The oil change interval is based on normal operating conditions. If the machine is used under severe conditions (i.e. racing, high-speed riding, stop-and-go commercial use, in dusty environments, cold weather, etc.), changes should be made more frequently. This is especially true if the vehicle is used infrequently such as during the winter months.*

Oil filter rotor cover bolts

Oil Filters

1. The engine is fitted with an oil filter screen beneath the drain cap on the left side. A centrifugal filter is mounted on the outside of the automatic clutch.
2. The filters should be serviced each time the oil is changed.
3. Have a right crankcase cover gasket on hand before beginning. This item should be replaced.
4. Drain the oil as outlined above.
5. Remove the spring and filter screen from the crankcase.
6. Clean the screen in a clean solvent to remove any foreign matter.
7. Check the residue for metal particles. If there are any, it indicates that severe engine wear is taking place. Determine the cause before operating the machine.
8. If the screen cannot be cleaned, or if it is punctured or shows other signs of damage, replace it.
9. Install the screen.
10. Fit the spring.
11. Install the cap and tighten it to 7-11 ft. lbs.
12. Place a drip pan beneath the right crankcase cover.
13. Remove the cover screws.
14. Remove the cover. If it is stuck, tap it with a plastic mallet to break it free.
15. Remove the oil filter motor cover. It is secured by three bolts.
16. Clean the inside of the cover with a clean rag. Check for metal particulates and other signs which might indicate on-going engine damage.
17. Check the condition of the cover o-ring. Replace it if necessary.
18. Install the cover and tighten the three bolts to 7-10 ft. lbs.
19. Check that the two locating dowel pins are in place on the crankcase cover mating surface.
20. Install a new crankcase cover gasket.
21. Install the crankcase cover. Tighten the screws gradually and evenly.
22. Add oil as directed under "Changing Oil," above. Check level. Start the engine and check for leaks.
23. After the machine has been sitting for a minute. make a final level check and top up the crankcase if necessary.

Drive Chain

185

1. The chain service interval is every 30 operating days.
2. The chain can be lubricated through the inspection hole on the side of the chain case.
3. Chains may be lubricated with commercial sprays designed specifically for motorcycle drive chains or with SAE 80 or 90 gear oil.

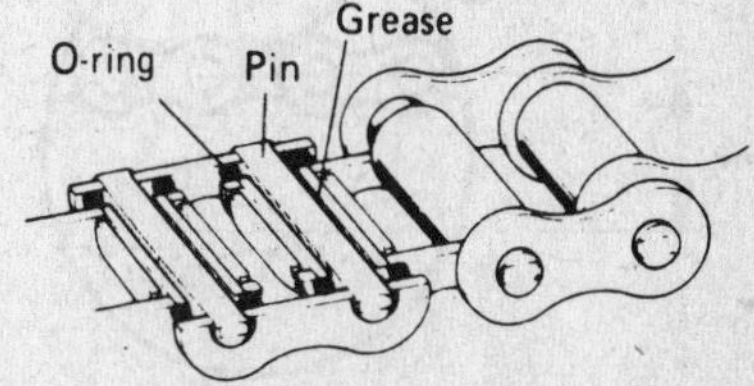

Drive chain o-rings

200

1. The chain service interval is every 30 operating days.

2. The chain can be lubricated through the inspection hole on the side of the chain case.

3. The chain is fitted with rubber O-rings to seal in grease around the pins. It should therefore only be cleaned with kerosene. Gasoline or other petroleum- based solvents will damage the O-rings.

4. The chain should be lubricated with SAE 80 or 90 gear oil or with commercially available spray chain lubes which are compatible with rubber O-ring chains. Do not use chain lubes unless this is clearly stated on the container.

Front Forks

1. Models which are equipped with hydraulic front forks should have the fork oil changed every year. Removal of the fork tubes is required. Removal of the fork tubes is required. Refer to 'Chassis' for procedures.

2. Fork oil capacity is 88cc (3.0 oz.) per leg.

Chassis Lubrication

1. Chassis lubrication points include wheel and steering head bearings, brake cams and brake pedal pivot.

2. Bearings should be lubricated with a good grade of waterproof, medium weight bearing grease. Other points can take general purpose chassis grease.

3. The service interval for these points is every year. See "Chassis" for teardown procedures.

4. Control cables and other sliding surfaces should be lubricated every 30 operating days under normal conditions.

SERVICE CHECKS AND ADJUSTMENTS

Drive Chain

1. The drive chain should have 10-20mm (3/8-3/4 in.) of total up-and-down free-play. This is measured at the chain case inspection hole after removing the rubber cap.

2. Before checking or adjusting the chain, the following conditions should be met:

a. The chain should be clean and well lubricated. Dirty chains tend to get tight;

b. The chain should have been checked for tight spots by slowly rotating the wheels and checking for variances in tension. If a tight spot exists, the chain free-play should be adjusted to the proper specification at that point. Note, however, that such a condition is indicative of a worn chain and probably worn sprockets which should be inspected and replaced as soon as possible.

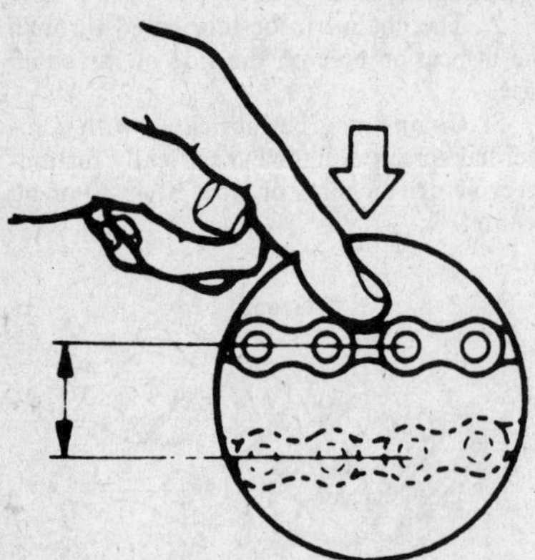

Checking drive chain free-play

3. Be sure the transmission is in Neutral.

4. Chech chain free-play after removing the chain case inspection hole cap.

5. Loosen the four rear wheel bearing holder bolts.

6. Turn the adjusting nut as required until free-play is correct.

7. Tighten the bearing holder bolts. Proper torque is 36-51 ft. lbs.

8. Recheck chain free-play.

9. Adjust the rear brake.

Chain Wear

1. Chain wear can be estimated by measuring the distance between pins after the chain is removed.

2. A clean chain must not exceed 706mm (27.8 in.) between 45 pins. If it does, it must be replaced.

3. New chain 45-pin distance is 699mm (27.5 in.).

4. Before measuring the distance, ensure that the chain is stretched out by hand to the fullest possible length.

Clutch

1. Clutch operation must meet the following standards:

a. The vehicle must go into First gear smoothly without a jolt or stalling;

b. The machine must begin to move smoothly as the throttle is opened and moving performance must not indicate power loss and slippage through the clutch.

2. Under normal operating conditions, the clutch should be adjusted every 30 operating days.

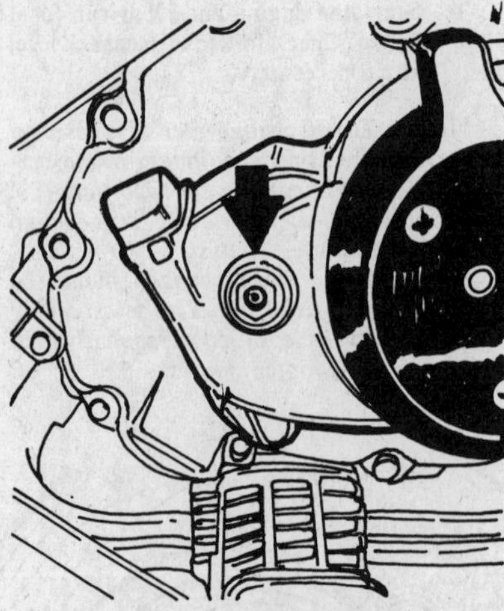

Clutch adjuster

3. Engine must be OFF.

4. Loosen the adjusting screw locknut.

5. Turn the adjusting screw one full turn clockwise.

6. Slowly turn the adjusting screw counterclockwise until resistance is felt.

7. Back the adjusting screw off 1/8 turn clockwise on 1980 models or 1/4 turn on 1981 and later models.

8. Hold the adjusting screw in place and tighten the locknut to 14-18 ft. lbs.

9. Check clutch operation.

Throttle Cable

1. Throttle operation and cable free-play are important safety items which should be attended to without fail. Operation of the throttle should be checked each time before the machine is ridden. The cable adjustment should be checked every 30 operating days.

2. The tip of the throttle lever should move 5-10mm (3/16-3/8 in.) before the throttle slide begins to open.

3. Adjusters are fitted to both ends of the cable. Make minor adjustments with the adjuster at the lever. For major adjustments, use the adjuster on the carburetor. Removal of the gas tank will be necessary. It is better to use the major adjuster once the handlebar adjuster has used up about half of its range.

4. With the engine idling, turn the handlebars slowly from lock to lock and listen for any change in engine speed. If this happens, the throttle cable is either too tightly adjusted or is binding somewhere along its routing.

5. Check that the throttle lever returns to the closed position regardless of the position of the handlebars. If it seems to hang up at one point or another, check cable free-play, cable routing and cable and throttle lever lubrication.

Front Brake

1. The tip of the hand lever should have 15-20mm (5/8-3/4 in.) of free movement before the linings contact the drum.

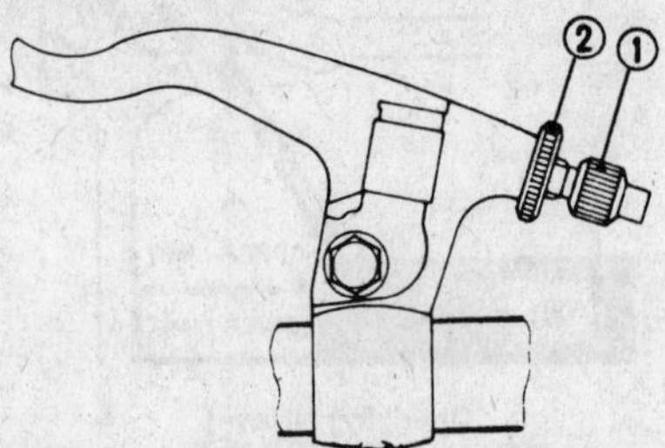

Front brake handlebar adjuster (1) and locknut (2)

2. Make minor adjustments with the cable adjuster at the hand lever, if one is fitted.

3. Other adjustments can be made by turning the adjuster at the wheel in until lever travel is correct.

CAUTION: *Be sure the adjuster cut-out is seated in the brake lever pin.*

4. When the brakes are fully applied, check the wear indicator and the index mark on the brake plate. If the two align, replace the brake shoes. See "Chassis."

Rear Brake

1. The rear brake is controlled by both a hand lever and a foot pedal.

2. At the brake drun, the upper cable is that of the hand lever; the lower cable is connected to the foot pedal.

3. The tip of the rear brake hand lever should have 15-20mm (5/8-3/4 in.) of free movement before the linings contact the drum.

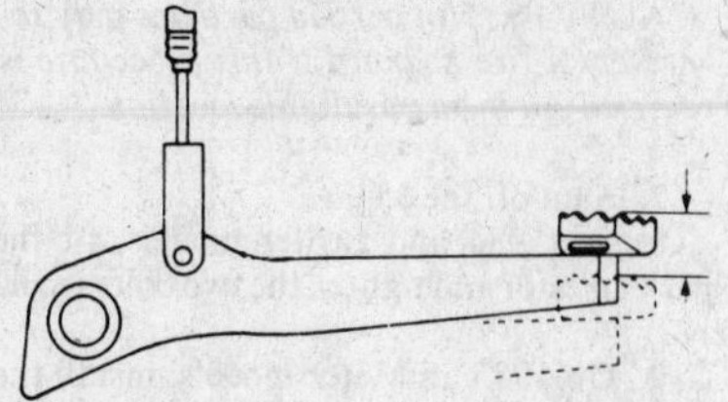
Brake pedal free-play (15-20mm/⅝-¾ in.)

4. Use the cable adjuster on the handlebar, if one is fitted, to make minor adjustments.

5. Use the cable adjuster at the brake to make other adjustments.

CAUTION: *Be sure the adjuster cut-out is seated in the brake lever pin.*

6. The foot pedal should have 15-20mm (5/8-3/4 in.) of free movement before the linings contact the drum. This free-play is measured at the tip of the pedal.

7. Use the adjuster at the brake drum to adjust pedal travel.

CAUTION: *Be sure the adjuster cut-out is seated in the brake lever pin.*

8. Apply the brakes and check the position of the wear indicator relative to the index mark on the brake plate. When the two align, replace the brake shoes. See "Chassis."

Tires

1. Periodically check each tire for cuts, embedded matter, excessive tread wear.

2. Tire pressures must be checked when the tires are cold. A special low pressure gauge is needed for accurate readings.

3. Proper tire pressure is 2.2 psi for both front and rear.

CAUTION: *Always maintain tires at the recommended pressures.*

4. If pressure is too low, pump up the tires with a hand-held pump.

CAUTION: *Never apply high pressure air sources to the tire valves. Service station hoses are generally unsuitable for filling these low pressure tires.*

Steering Head Bearings

1. Bearing wear and adjustment should be checked periodically.

2. Raise the front end of the machine off the ground by placing a safe, sturdy support beneath the frame.

3. Turn the handlbars slowly from lock to lock.

4. Check for binding, rough rotation and/or bearing noise as the wheels are turned. If any is noted, adjust the bearings as outlined in "Chassis".

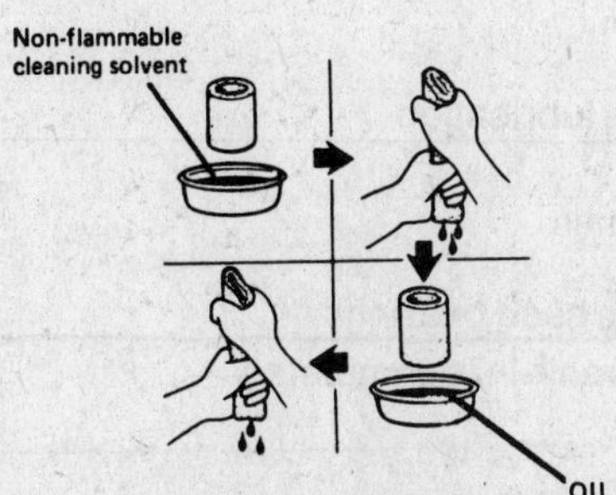

Cleaning the air filter element

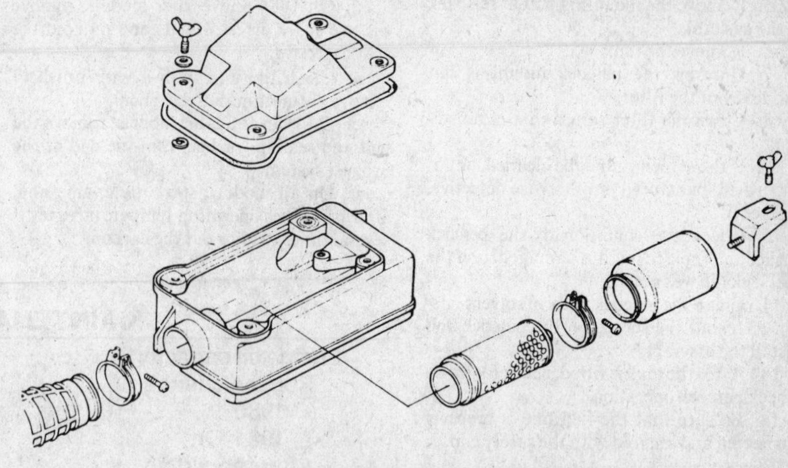
Air filter assembly (typical)

5. Grasp the lower ends of the forks and attempt to move them back and forth in line with the machine. No free-play should be evident. If there is, the bearings must be adjusted. See "Chassis."

FUEL SYSTEM

Fuel system maintenance involves cleaning the fuel filter, cleaning or replacing the air filter and cleaning the carburetor. These procedures should be carried out every 30 operating days.

Air Filter

1980-82

1. Remove the seat.
2. Remove the rear fender on 185 models.
3. Remove the air cleaner case cover.
4. Remove the seal, if fitted.
5. Loosen the air cleaner case hose clamp.
6. Remove the case mounting bolts.
7. Remove the case.
8. Remove the nut from the outside of the case and take out the filter element.
9. Remove the filter element from its holder.
10. On 1980 and 1981 m odels, wash the element in a safe, high flash point solvent. Squeeze it to dry it thoroughly.

CAUTION: *Do not wring the element out as the pores or fabric may be damaged.*

11. On the 1982 models, wash the foam element in a liquid detergent and water solution. Rinse it in clean water and dry by squeezing and allowing it to air dry as long as necessary.

12. On the 1982 models, inspect the paper element incorporated into the holder. Clean it as far as possible by blowing compressed air into the holder to remove loose dirt. The paper element can also be cleaned by washing it in a detergent and water solution if it is very dirty. If the foreign matter is excessive, replace the element.

13. On all models, after cleaning the foam element, soak it in SAE 80 or 90 gear oil and squeeze off the excess.

14. Carefully fit the element back onto the holder and install the assembly.

15. Be sure that all connections are tight.

1983 AND LATER

1. Remove the seat.
2. On 185 models, remove the rear fender.
3. Remove the wing bolts holding the air cleaner case cover. Take off the cover.
4. Loosen the element hose clamp.
5. Remove the element assembly from the case.
6. Remove the retainer or bracket from the back of the element assembly.
7. Remove the filter element from its holder.
8. Wash the element in a safe, high flash point solvent. Squeeze it to dry it thoroughly.

CAUTION: *Do not wring the element out as the pores may be damaged.*

9. After the element is cleaned and dried, soak it in SAE 80 or 90 gear oil and squeeze off the excess.

10. Carefully fit the element back onto the holder and install the assembly.

11. Be sure that all connections are tight.

Fuel Filter

1. The fuel filter screen is fitted to the petcock inside the gas tank.
2. Remove the seat.
3. Be sure the petcock is "OFF."
4. Disconnect the fuel line from the petcock.

Fuel petcock

5. Remove the mounting bolt at the back of the gas tank.
6. Remove the tank.
7. Unscrew the petcock mounting nut and take out the filter.
8. Clean the filter screen in a clean solvent.
9. If the screen cannot be cleaned, or if it is crushed, punctured or otherwise defective, replace it.
10. Check the condition of the petcock gasket and replace it if it is damaged, or if the fuel leakage was noted.
11. Clean the petcock body in solvent.
12. Install the screen on the petcock and install the assembly.
13. After the tank is fitted, check for leaks. Check petcock operation.
14. Be sure that the fuel line is properly connected and secured with the safety clip.

Carburetor

1. For a complete cleaning procedure, refer to "Fuel System" where carburetor removal, disassembly and installation procedures are detailed. For further routine maintenance, proceed as follows.
2. Shut the petcock "OFF."
3. Place a small container beneath the float bowl and loosen the drain screw on the right side of the carburetor.
4. When the fuel has drained out, tighten the drain screw.
5. Check the drained gasoline for water, dirt or other foreign matter. If considerable amounts are present, check the fuel filter screen.
6. Turn the petcock "ON" and allow the float bowl to fill up. Shut the petcock "OFF." Drain the float bowl as before. Inspect the fuel sample for foreign matter. If any is still present, check the fuel filter. Remove the gas tank and drain off the fuel. Check it for dirt and water. Flush out the tank before installing.
7. If fuel flow out of the bowl seems sluggish, remove the gas cap. If flow increases, the problem is a clogged cap vent. If it does not, check for a clogged filter.
8. After any system service of this nature, turn on the petcock and check for leaks before operating the vehicle.

Fuel Lines

1. Check condition periodically.
2. Check for dry rot, cracking, abrasion or accident damage. Replace defective lines.
3. Check for leaks, even minor ones, around the ends of the lines. Replace leaking lines.
4. When lines are disconnected, check the ends for cracking or deterioration. Connections must be tight.
5. When lines are reconnected, be sure the safety clips are in place.
6. Check for fuel leaks before operating the machine any time lines are removed or replaced.

SPARK ARRESTOR

1. The spark arrestor should be decarbonized every 30 operating days. Excessive carbon buildup will cause sluggish performance and possible engine overheating.
2. Park the machine in an open area free of flammable material.
3. On 1984 and earlier models, remove the two spark arrestor bolts and pull out the spark arrestor.
4. Clean the unit with a wire brush to remove any accumulated carbon.
5. On 1985 and later models, remove the bolt and sealing washer from the end of the exhaust system.
6. On all models, start the engine and, after it reaches operating temperature, rev it several times to blow out the carbon.

CAUTION: *Hot carbon particles may represent a fire hazaard if this procedure is carried out in an unsuitable location.*

7. Shut off the engine.
8. On 1984 and earlier models, fit the spark arrestor and tighten the two bolts securely.
9. On 1985 and later models, install the bolt and sealing washer and tighten the bolt to 22-29 ft. lbs.

MAINTENANCE DATA

Engine oil capacity	
Routine change	
1980	1 qt./0.95L
1981-On	1.4 qts./1.3L
After rebuilding	
1980-83	1.43 qts./1.35L
1984-On	1.59 qts./1.50L
Tire pressure (f/r)	2.2 psi
Drive chain free-play	3/8-3/4 in./10-20mm
Fork oil capacity (each leg)	3.0 oz./88cc
Battery	12V, 14ah
Fuel capacity	
1980-83	2.3 gal./8.8L
1984	3.0 gal./11.5L
1984-On	2.8 gal./10.5L
Fuel reserve	
1980-83	0.42 gal./1.6L
1984-On	0.26 gal./1.0L

PERIODIC MAINTENANCE INTERVALS①

Before every ride
- Check engine oil level
- Check tire pressure
- Check throttle operation
- Check brake adjustment
- Check operation of lights

Every 30 operating days
- Change engine oil
- Clean oil filters
- Check air filter element
- Check battery level (if fitted)
- Clean fuel system
- Lubricate and adjust drive chain
- Adjust clutch
- Decarbonize spark arrestor
- Check tightness of critical fasteners
- Inspect tires for condition
- Adjust cables
- Carry out general chassis lubrication

Every year
- Check condition of fuel lines
- Check brake shoes
- Check wheel and steering head bearings

① Based on normal usage after initial break-in is completed

RECOMMENDED LUBRICANTS

Engine	
Above 32°F	SAE 20W-40, SAE 20W-50, service rated "SE" or "SF"
Above 18°F	SAE 10W-40, service rated "SE" or "SF"
18-85°F	SAE 10W-30, service rated "SE" or "SF"
Below 45°F	SAE 5W, service rated "SE" or "SF"
Drive chain	
ATC 185	Commercial lubricant developed specifically for motorcycle drive chains SAE 80 or 90 oil
ATC 200	SAE 80 or 90 oil Commercial chain lube compatible with rubber
Air filter	SAE 80 or 90 gear oil
Hydraulic front forks	ATF
Wheel and steering head bearings	Waterproof, medium-weight bearing grease
General lubrication	Waterproof, medium-weight chassis grease
Cables	Light motor oil Commercial cable lubricants Molybdenum disulphide-based lubricant

TUNE-UP

NOTE: *Common tune-up procedures are explained in detail in the 'General Information' section of this manual.*

WARNING: *All tune-up procedures done with the engine running must be carried out with the machine on level ground in a well-ventilated area. The parking brake should be applied.*

Keep children and other innocents away from hot, running engines. Never leave the vehicle running and unattended.

COMPRESSION TEST

1. A compression check should be made before each tune-up since this will provide a general idea of engine condition.
2. It is necessary to have a gauge with the proper adapter if a screw-in type gauge is used. The plug hole is 12mm. The less expensive "hold-in" type gauge can also be used. Oil the rubber tip to ensure a good seal.
3. The engine must be at operating temperature.
4. Be sure the ignition switch is "OFF."
5. Set the choke fully on.
6. Fit the gauge. Push the throttle lever wide open and turn the engine over with the starter.
7. The highest gauge reading is the compression.
8. Compression should be 156 psi with an acceptable variation of ± 14 psi.
9. Low compression may be caused by valves which are too tightly adjusted, burned or otherwise damaged, worn piston rings, piston and/or cylinder or other worn engine components.
10. If the compression reading is too low, squirt some motor oil into the cylinder and repeat the test. If the gauge reading is higher, suspect worn rings, piston or cylinder as the cause. If the reading does not increase, suspect problems in the valve train.
11. If the test shows that compression is too high, the problem is likely due to carbon deposits on the piston crown and cylinder. Remove the cylinder head and decarbonize the top end.

CAM CHAIN TENSION

1. Cam chain tension should be adjusted every 30 operating days.
2. The tension is adjusted by means of a bolt beneath the rubber cap on the top left side of the crankcase just behind the cylinder.
3. Remove the rubber cap on the asjuster bolt.
4. Start the engine and allow it to idle.
5. Loosen the tensioner adjusting bolt.

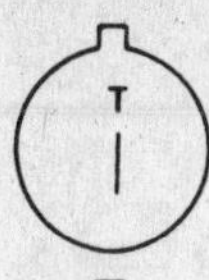

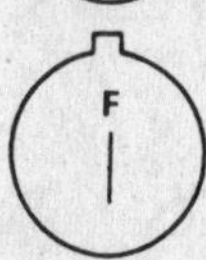

Top dead center and ignition timing rotor marks

Then tighten it to 11-16 ft. lbs. Tension will be set automatically.

CAUTION: *Do not loosen the 6mm hex bolt on top of the adjusting bolt.*

6. Install the rubber cap.

VALVE ADJUSTING

NOTE: *Valve clearance should be checked every 30 operating days. The valves must be checked when the engine is COLD.*

1. Remove the seat.
2. Remove the fuel tank.
3. Remove the spark plug.
4. Remove the intake and exhaust valve adjuster covers.
5. Remove the timing inspection hole cap on the left crankcase cover.
6. Turn the engine over slowly with the recoil starter while watching the intake rocker arm. When the rocker arm opens the valve and then begins to close it, look through the timing inspection hole while continuing to turn the engine over. When the "T" mark on the rotor aligns with the index mark on the hole, stop. The piston should now be positioned at TDC on the compression stroke.
7. Check for rocker arm clearance at the valves. Each rocker arm should have a slight amount of free-play. If they do not, the piston is probably at TDC on the exhaust stroke. Turn the rotor 360°, align the "T" mark and check again.
8. Vallve clearance is 0.05mm (0.002 in.) for both intake and exhaust valves. A feeler gauge blade of this thickness should be a light slip fit between the valve and the adjuster.
9. If adjustment is necessary, loosen the adjuster locknut and turn the adjuster so that the feeler gauge blade is a slip fit. Hold the adjuster in place and tighten the locknut (torque: 11-13 ft. lbs.
10. After the locknut is tightened, recheck clearance.

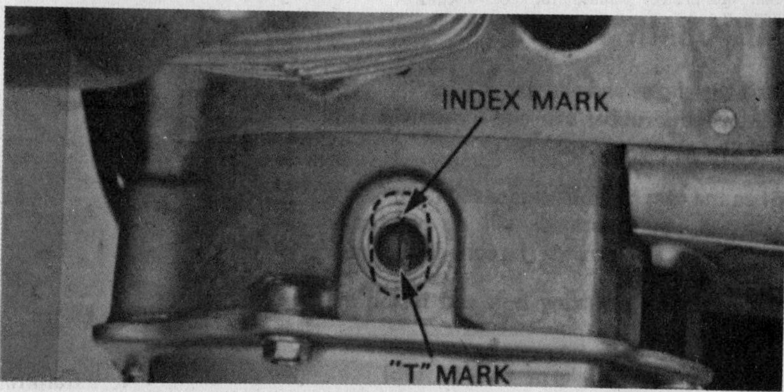

Rotor timing marks

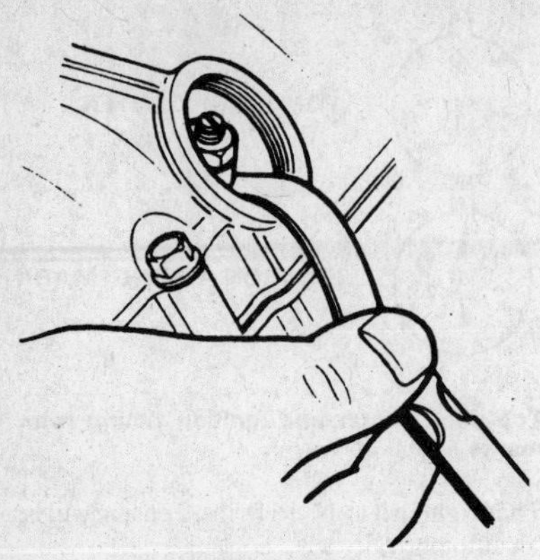

Checking valve clearance

11. Install and tighten the adjuster covers to 7-10 ft. lbs.
12. Tighten the spark plug to 9-14 ft. lbs.
13. Install the timing inspection hole cap, tank, seat.

IGNITION TIMING

CAUTION: *This running-engine adjustment must be carried out in a well-ventilated area. Be sure the vehicle is on a level surface and that the parking brake is set.*

1. Remove the timing inspection hole cap on the left crankcase cover.
2. Connect a timing light according to the light manufacturer's instructions.
3. Connect an electronic tachometer if idle speed is not known.
4. Observe the rotor timing marks through the inspection hole while the engine is running.
5. At 1400 rpm (±100 rpm), the 'F' mark on the rotor should align with the index mark on the hole.
6. If adjustment is necessary, remove the pulse generator cover on the left side of the cylinder head.
7. Loosen the two base plate screws and turn the plate with a small screwdriver applied to the pry point until the "F" mark aligns with the index mark at 1400 rpm.
8. Tighten the base plate screws. Check that timing is still correct.
9. Shut the engine off.
10. Turn the engine over with the recoil starter until the pulse rotor aligns with the pulse generator.
11. The air gap between the rotor and the pulse generator should be 0.3-0.4mm (0.012-0.016 in.).
12. Adjust by loosening the two small screws which mount the generator to the base plate.
13. Install the cover. Install the timing inspection hole cap.

NOTE: *Once set properly, the CDI ignition should not require adjustment. Unless the proper equipment (tach and strobe light) is available, ignition timing should not be meddled with.*

CARBURETOR

Float Level

1. While critical to proper fuel system operation, float level is not generally a routine adjustment. It usually will not need adjustment until considerable mileage has been covered or if fuel system problems arise.
2. Remove the carburetor as outlined in "Fuel System."
3. Remove the float bowl (2 screws).
4. Remove the float bowl gasket.
5. Float level is defined as the measured distance from the float bowl mating surface (gasket removed) to the top of the float when the float tang is just touching the end of the needle.
6. With the float held in this position, measure the distance from the mating surface to the top of the float.
7. Float level specifications are as follows:

   1980-83: 12.5mm/0.49 in.
   1984-On: 14.0mm/0.55 in.
8. If the float level is not within 10% of this value, first check for foreign matter on the tip of the needle and the needle seat. Check the needle tip for wear. Clean or replace components are required. If no dirt or wear is noted, adjust the float level by bending the float tang until the measured level is within specification.

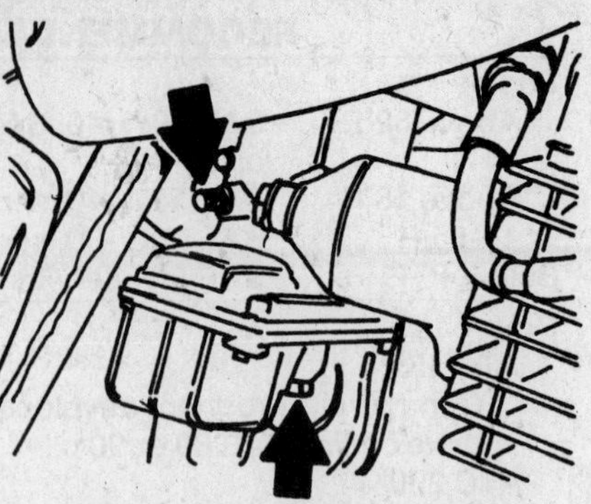

Throttle stop (left) and pilot screws

1. Check that the throttle cable adjustment is correct so that the cable has enough slack to permit the throttle slide to close fully.
2. Screw the pilot in carefully until it is seated, then back it out the following number of turns:

   1983 ATC 185: 1 turn
   1983 ATC 200: 1 1/4 turns
   All others: 2 ±1/8 turns
3. Connect a tachometer to gauge engine speed.
4. Adjust the idle speed with the throttle stop screw until it is 1,400 rpm (±100 rpm).
5. Turn the pilot screw in slowly until the engine stops, then back it out one turn.
6. Start the engine and readjust idle speed, if necessary, so that it is 1,400 ±100 rpm.
7. Shut the engine off and adjust the throttle cable as outlined in "Maintenance."

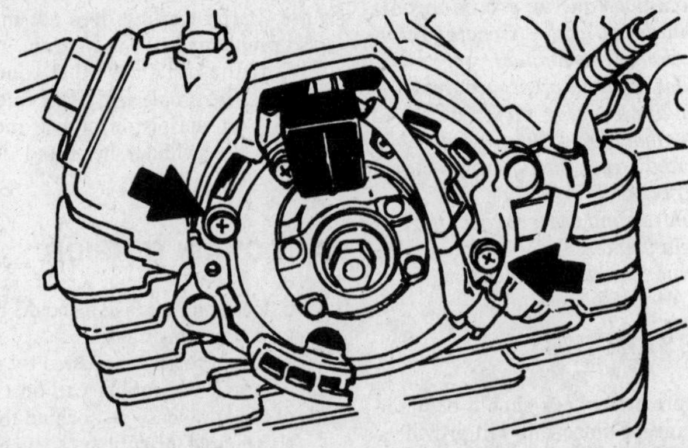

Pulse generator base plate screws

Idle Speed And Mixture

NOTE: *These items must be adjusted when the engine is at operating temperature.*

CAUTION: *Park the machine on a level surface in a well-ventilated area and set the parking brake.*

NOTE: *If proper idling cannot be obtained using this method, it may be that the fuel system is clogged. Check petcock, filter screen, carburetor, gas cap vent. Other possible causes include a dirty or worn spark plug, a plug which is too cold, improperly adjusted valves or air leaks in the intake system.*

TUNE-UP SPECIFICATIONS

VALVE CLEARANCE	
Intake	0.05mm/0.002 in.
Exhaust	0.05mm/0.002 in.

TUNE-UP SPECIFICATIONS

VALVE CLEARANCE	
Intake	0.05mm/0.002 in.
Exhaust	0.05mm/0.002 in.
SPARK PLUG	
OEM	NGK/ND/Champion
Type	①
Gap	0.6-0.7mm/0.024-0.028 in.
Torque	9-14 ft lbs.
IGNITION TIMING	
Initial	10°BTDC ± 2° @ 1400 rpm
Full advance	30°BTDC ± 2° @ 3400 rpm
CARBURETOR	
Idle speed	1400 ± 100 rpm
Pilot screw setting (turns out)	
1983 ATC 185	1
1983 ATC 200	1¼
Other models	2 ± 1/8
Float height	
1980-83	12.5mm/0.49 in.
1984-On	14.0mm/0.55 in.
COMPRESSION	
Standard	156 psi
Allowable variation	14 psi

① 1980-81: D-8EA/X24ES-U/R-6Y
1982-On: DR8ES-L/X24ESR-U/RA6YC

ENGINE AND TRANSMISSION

NOTE: *Engine component removal and installation procedures are given in the following text. Specifications are in the chart at the end of this section. For service procedures and inspection techniques to valves, piston, clutch and other components, refer to "Engine Rebuilding" in the "General Information" section of this manual.*

ENGINE REMOVAL AND INSTALLATION

NOTE: *Removal of the cylinder head, cylinder and piston, as well as service to the crankshaft and transmission, requires removal of the engine from the frame.*

Before removing the engine:

a. Drain the oil.

b. Degrease the engine. Be especially attentive to the area around the cylinder base, the underside of the crankcase and around mating surfaces.

c. Drive chain masterlink spring clips should be removed with pliers. Do not pry the clip off with a screwdriver or it will be distorted and will have to replaced. After disconnecting the chain, install the masterlink on one end of the chain to prevent loss.

d. When connecting drive chains, be certain to fit the spring clip with the closed end facing the direction of chain rotation.

1. Disconnect the spark plug lead and loosen the plug.
2. Remove the seat.
3. Be certain that the petcock is "OFF."
4. Disconnect the fuel line from the carburetor.
5. Remove the mounting bolt at the rear of the tank. Remove the gas tank.
6. Disconnect the ground (negative) cable from the battery if so equipped.
7. Remove the exhaust pipe nuts at the cylinder head. Loosen the clamp bolt(s) at the muffler. Pull off the enhaust pipe.
8. Disconnect the starter motor cable from the starter, if so equipped.
9. Disconnect the crankcase breather tube at the back of the engine.
10. Locate the pulse generator wires at the top of the frame and disconnect them.
11. Locate the alternator wires at the connector(s) on the frame behind the engine and disconnect the wires.
12. Disconnect the choke cable from the carburetor, if so equipped.
13. Unscrew the carburetor cap and pull out the throttle slide assembly. Wrap the assembly in a clean, lint-free cloth and place it out of the way to avoid damage.
14. Loosen the carburetor air cleaner hose clamp. On some models, it may be necessary to remove the right rear fender for access. On others, the clamp screw can be reached through a hole punched in the frame brace.

Install masterlink spring clips with the closed end facing the direction of chain rotation

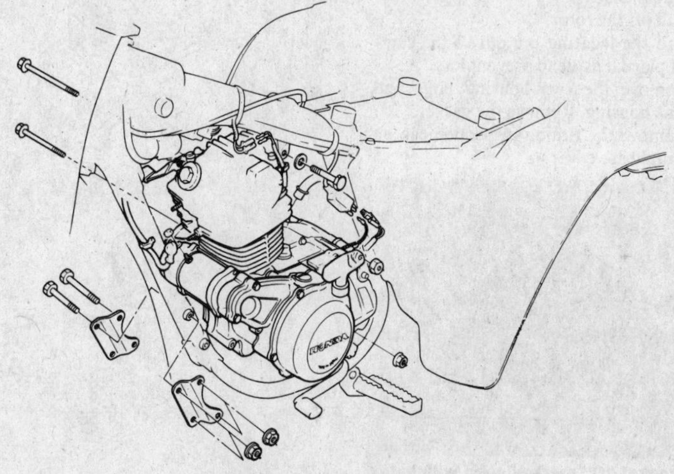

Engine mounting bolt locations

15. Disconnect the carburetor lines.
16. Remove the carburetor mounting nuts. Remove the carburetor.
17. Remove the gearshift lever.
18. Remove the engine sprocket cover.
19. Remove the rear axle seal cover bolts from the chain case.
20. Loosen the chain adjuster nut and the bearing holder bolts and push the rear axle forward to provide slack in the chain.
21. Disconnect the drive chain.
22. Remove the cylinder head frame bolt. Remove the front engine mounting bracket. Remove the rear engine mounting bolts.
23. Remove the engine from the frame.
24. Installation is the reverse of removal. Note the following:
   a. Tighten the cylinder head bolt to 14-18 ft. lbs.
   b. Tighten the front bracket 10mm bolts to 29-35 ft. lbs.
   c. Tighten the front bracket 8mm bolts to 17-20 ft. lbs.
   d. Tighten the rear engine mounting bolts to 29-35 ft. lbs.
   e. Tighten the rear axle bearing holder bolts to 36- 51 ft. lbs.
   f. Be sure to fit the chain masterlink spring clip with the closed end facing the direction of chain rotation.
   g. Fill the crankcase with oil.

TOP END

The following section deals with the removal and installation of the cylinder head, cylinder, piston and related components. Inspection and service procedures are outlined under "Engine Rebuilding" in the "General Information" section of this manual. Specifications are included in the chart at the end of this section.

Removal

1. To remove the cylinder head, cylinder and piston, removal of the engine from the frame is required.
2. Remove the top two pulse cover screws on the left side of the cylinder head and remove the cover.
3. Disconnect the pulse generator wires from the clamp on the cylinder head.
4. Remove the generator mounting plate screws (2) and remove the plate.
5. Remove the pulse rotor bolt from the end of the camshaft.
6. Pull off the rotor.
7. Pull the locating pin out of the camshaft and place it aside to prevent loss.
8. Remove the two housing bolts and remove the housing. Remove the gasket.
9. Remove the timing inspection cap on the left crankcase cover.

Cam sprocket "O" mark aligned with index mark

Cylinder head cap nuts and bolts

10. Remove the rubber cap on the cam chain tensioner and back off the adjuster.
11. Use the recoil starter to turn the engine over untill the "10" mark on the camshaft sprocket aligns with the index mark on the cylinder head and the alternator rotor "T" mark align with the index mark on the inspection hole. The sprocket bolts will be in line with the centerline of the cylinder. This positions the piston at TDC on the compression stroke (both valves closed).
12. Remove the valve adjuster caps. Back off the adjusters.
13. Remove the camshaft sprocket bolts.
14. Disengage the sprocket from the chain and remove it.
15. Remove the camshaft. Loop a length of wire around the chain so that it does not fall into the crankcase.
16. Loosen the four 8mm cylinder head cap nuts and the four 6mm socket head screws 1/4 turn at a time until they are loose, then remove them. Remove the cap nut washers.
17. Remove the cylinder head cover.
18. Remove the camshaft busing on the right side of the engine.

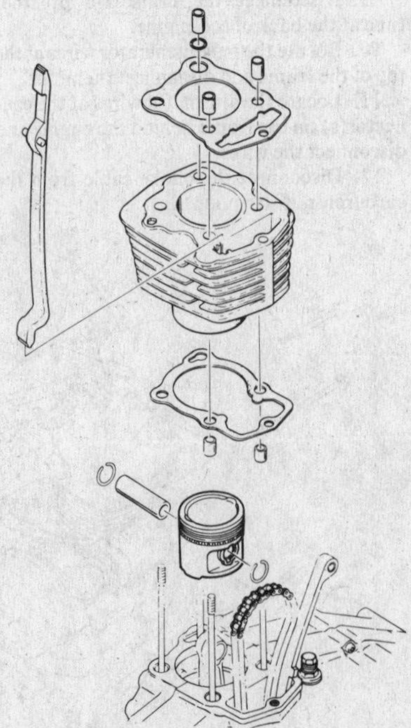

Cylinder assembly

19. Remove the compression release lever from the cover, if necessary, by taking out the guide bolt and pulling out the lever.
20. Remove the carburetor manifold.
21. Remove the cam chain tensioner bolt on the left side of the head.
22. Remove the cylinder head base bolt on the left side of the head.
23. Remove the cylinder head.
24. Remove the head gasket.
25. Note the locations of the three dowel pins and the O-ring on the head mating surface.
26. Remove the cam chain guide.
27. Carefully pull off the cylinder taking care that the piston does not strike the studs when the cylinder is removed.
28. Remove the cylinder base gasket.
29. Check that the cylinder base dowel pins are in place in the crankcase. If further engine work is contemplated, remove the pins to prevent loss.
30. Stuff a clean, lint-free rag into the crankcase.
31. Remove the piston wrist pin circlips with a needlenose pliers. Push out the wrist pin with a suitable drift. Remove the piston.
32. Remove the rocker arm shaft set plate from the side of the head cover.
33. Thread a 6mm bolt into each rocker arm shaft and pull them out. Remove the rocker arms. Keep each shaft with its own rocker arm and mark them to ensure that they are installed in their original locations during assembly.
34. To remove the valve assemblies, compress the valve springs and remove the keepers.

Inspection

Refer to the "Engine Rebuilding" section of "General Information" and to the specifications chart in this section for inspection techniques and service limits.

Installation

1. If the piston rings were removed or replaced, be sure that they are installed correctly.
2. The two compression rings are not interchangeable. The top ring has a plain profile, while the second is wedge-shaped.

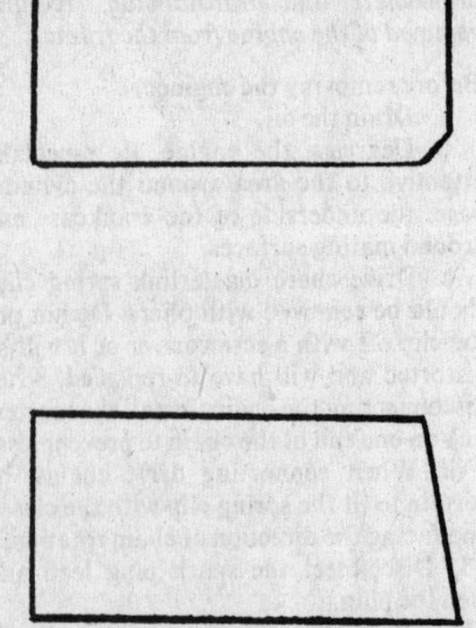

Top and second compression ring profiles

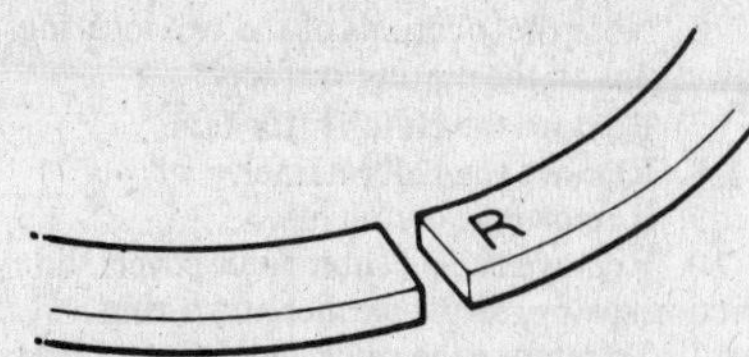

Install rings with the manufacturer's marks up

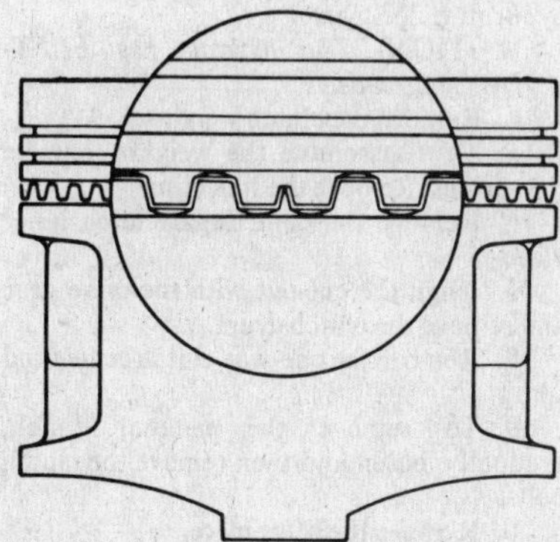

Oil ring expander ends must abut, not overlap

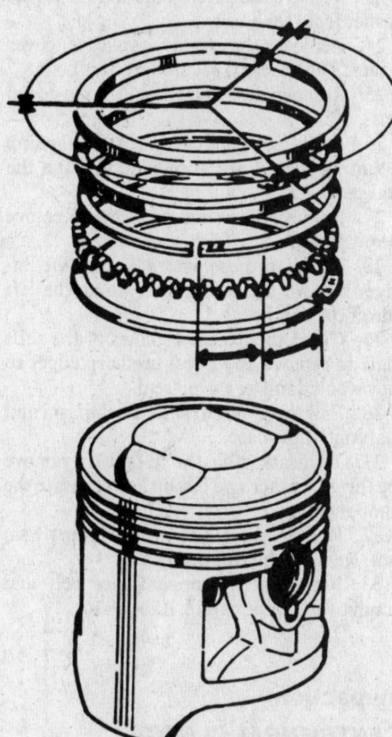

Arrange ring end-gaps around the piston

3. Be certain to install the compression rings with the manufacturer's mark near the end-gap facing upwards.

4. The piston ring end-gaps should be arranged as follows:

a. End-gaps of the two compression rings and the oil expander ring should be arranged 120° apart around the piston but not at the very front or rear of the piston and not directly above the wrist pin holes.

b. The end-gaps of the oil rails should be arranged at about 3/4 in. (20mm) or more on either side of the oil expander ring.

5. Thoroughly clean the cylinder mating surface.

6. Check that the two dowel pins are in place on the left side cylinder head studs.

7. Use a new cylinder base gasket.

8. Install the piston on the connecting rod so that the "IN" mark on the piston crown is on the intake side.

9. Use new wrist pin circlips. Be sure the circlips are properly seated. The circlip end-gaps should not align with the cut-outs at the wrist pin hole.

10. Lubricate the piston and rings. Check that the ring end-gaps are properly aligned.

11. Compress the rings and slide the cylinder over the piston. Pull the cam chain through the cylinder.

12. Install the cam chain guide.

13. Use new valve seals when assembling the head.

14. Valve springs are progressively wound. They are installed with the close coils against the head.

15. Lubricate valve stems before inserting them into the guides.

16. After the valve and spring assemblies have been installed, rap the end of each valve with a plastic mallet to ensure that the keepers are properly seated.

17. Install the cylinder head mating surface dowel pins (3) and O-ring. The dowel pins go on the two left- hand cylinder head studs and the right rear stud. The O-ring is positioned on the right rear stud.

18. Fit a new head gasket.

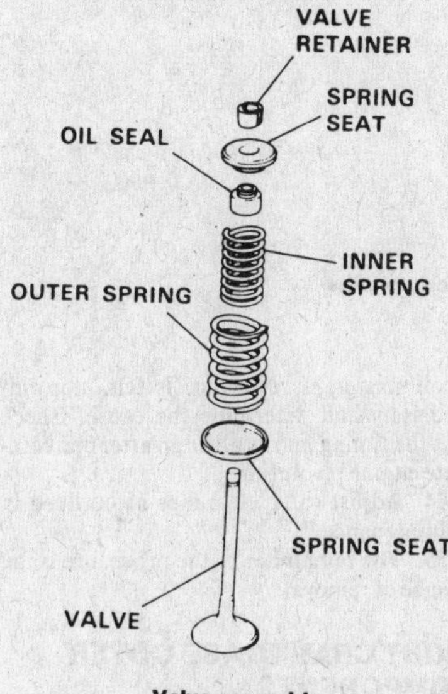

Valve assembly

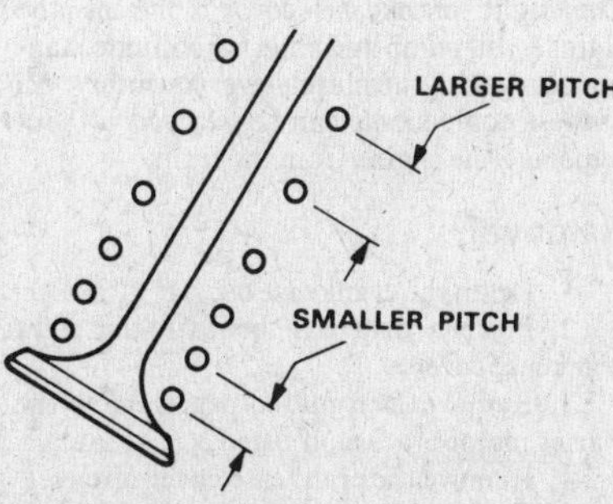

Install springs with the close coils against the head

19. Remove the cam chain tensioner adjuster 6mm bolt.

20. Push down on the tensioner through the bolt hole and tighten the adjuster nut. Install the 6mm bolt.

21. Install the cylinder head.

22. Install and tighten the cylinder head bolt near the left side of the head.

23. Install the tensioner bolt on the left side of the head.

24. Lubricate each rocker arm shaft and slip them into place in the cover. Cut-outs on the shafts must face away from the center of the head.

25. Install the rocker arm shaft set plate.

26. Install the compression release lever thrust washer, spring, washer, and lever. Tighten the set bolt to 4-5 ft. lbs.

27. Check that the two dowel pins are in place on the head cover mating surface.

28. Install the oil hole plug if it was removed.

29. Install the camshaft bushing, inserting the dowel pin into the hole provided.

30. Lubricate cam bearing areas with clean motor oil.

31. Apply liquid sealant to the head cover mating surface.

CAUTION: *Keep the sealant away from cam bearing areas and do not apply it too thickly.*

32. Install the head cover.

33. Install the cap nut washers.

34. Fit the cap nuts and the socket head bolts.

35. Torque the cylinder head bolts and nuts gradually and in a cross pattern beginning with the four nuts and working outwards. Correct fastener torques are:

Bolts: 6-9 ft. lbs.

Cap nuts

1980-81 (ATC 185)	13-14 ft. lbs.
1981 (ATC 200)	14-16 ft. lbs.
Other models	20-22 ft. lbs.

36. Fit the thrust washer onto the camshaft.

37. Lubricate the cam and place it in the head.

38. Pull the cam chain taut and ensure that it is not jammed or kinked anywhere.

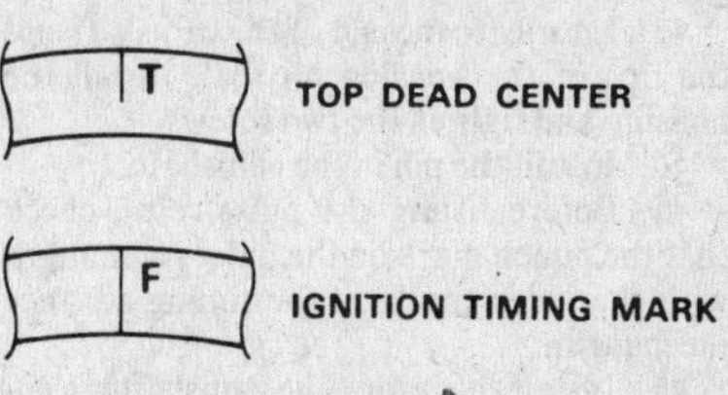

Rotor timing marks

39. Turn the engine, if required, so that the alternator "T" mark aligns with the mark of the timing inspection hole. The piston will be at TDC. At this point, fit the chain over the cam sprocket so that the "O" mark on the sprocket is at the top of the cylinder head and the sprocket bolt holes are aligned with the centerline of the cylinder.

40. Check that the alternator "T" mark is still aligned with the timing mark on the crankcase cover and that the cam sprocket "O" mark aligns with the cylinder head index notch.

41. Install the sprocket bolts. Using a non-permanent thread-locking compound is recommended. Torque the bolts to 6-9 ft. lbs.

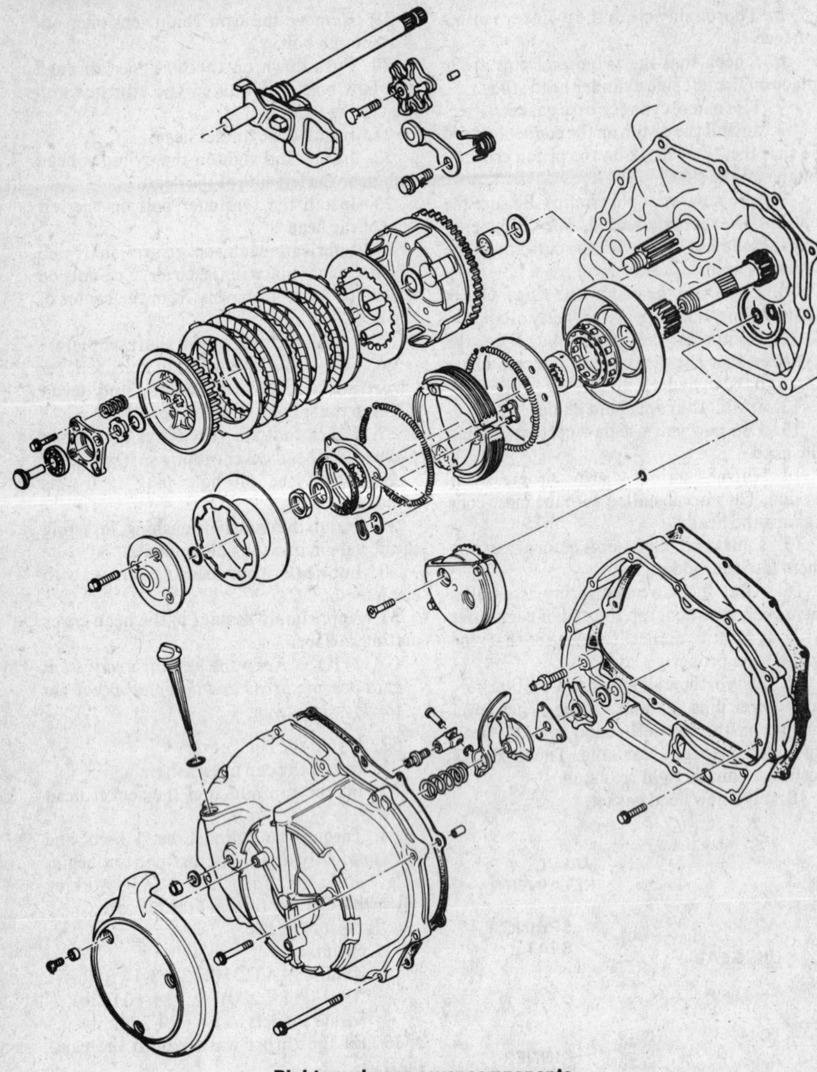

Right crankcase cover components

6. Note the locations of the two locating dowel pins on the mating surface.

7. Remove the clutch lifter cam.

8. Remove the ball retainer.

9. Remove the clutch lifter.

10. Remove the oil filter rotor cover, slide friction spring, thrust washer and o-ring.

11. To remove the centrifugal clutch, first remove the recoil starter.

12. Hold the crankshaft steady with a lever through the starter pulley.

13. Remove the centrifugal clutch locknut by turning clockwise.

CAUTION: *The locknut has LEFT-HAND threads.*

14. Remove the clutch weights.

15. To disassemble the weights, remove the springs. Remove the link clips.

16. Remove the centrifugal clutch inner plate.

17. Align the cut-out with the drive gear and remove the clutch drum.

18. Remove the one-way clutch center and sprag.

19. To remove the manual clutch, gradually loosen and then remove the clutch bolts.

20. Remove the lifter plate.

21. Remove the springs.

22. Remove the clutch locknut. Remove the washer. Remove the clutch assembly.

23. Remove the outer guide and the thrust washer from the shaft.

24. Remove the right crankcase cover spacer. The spacer is secured by four bolts.

25. Remove the gasket and locating dowel pins.

26. Turn the engine over until the oil pump mounting screws are accessible through the gear cover holes.

27. Remove the mounting screws. Remove the oil pump.

28. To remove the external gearshift linkage, remove the gearshift lever on the left side of the engine.

29. Clean the exposed splines of the shift shaft to remove any burrs or sharp edges so they won't damage the oil seal.

30. Pull the external shift mechanism and shaft out of the case.

31. To disassemble the shift shaft, remove the thrust washer and circlip and separate the components.

32. Remove the shift drum stopper arm bolt. Remove the stopper arm.

33. Remove the stopper plate bolt and remove the stopper plate, if required.

42. Fit a new gasket behind the generator housing.

43. Lubricate the end of the camshaft and the lips of the housing oil seal. Install the housing and tighten the two screws.

44. Install the pin in the camshaft.

45. Before fitting the pulse rotor, check that the punch mark on the pulse rotor aligns with the index mark on the timing advance mechanism.

46. Install the rotor. The camshaft pin engages a slot on the rotor.

47. Tighten the rotor bolt to 6-9 ft. lbs.

48. Install the pulse generator base plate assembly.

49. Turn the crankshaft clockwise until the "F" mark on the alternator rotor is aligned with the inspection hole index mark.

50. Turn the pulse generator base plate so that the generator index mark aligns with the pulse rotor index mark. Tighten the base plate screws.

51. Check the air gap between the rotor and generator. It should be 0.3-0.4mm/ 0.012-0.016 in. Adjust by loosening the generator mounting screws and moving the generator.

52. Fill the crankcase with oil.

53. Turn the engine over slowly with the recoil starter. if resistance is felt, stop immediately and determine the cause. Check that the timing marks all align after one complete engine revolution.

54. Adjust valve clearance as outlined in "Maintenance."

55. The remainder of the procedure is the reverse of removal.

RIGHT CRANKCASE COVER COMPONENTS

The right crankcase cover contains the clutches, oil pump and external shift mechanism along with the clutch lever assembly. All of these components can be serviced without removing the engine from the fram.

Removal

1. Drain the crankcase oil.

2. Place a drip pan beneath the right crankcase cover.

3. Remove the right footpeg. Remove the starter motor bracket, if fitted.

4. Remove the crankcase cover screws.

5. Remove the crankcase cover. If it is stuck, tap it with a plastic mallet to break it free.

Inspection

CENTRIFUGAL CLUTCH

1. Measure the thickness of the centrifugal clutch weight linings. Minimum acceptable lining thickness is 4.1mm (0.16 in.). If any measurement is under this specification, replace the weights as a set.

2. Measure the inside diameter of the clutch drum. Replace it if it is over 116.3mm (4.58 in.).

3. Check the inside of the clutch drum for scoring or other signs of unusual wear and replace it if any is noted which cannot be removed with sandpaper or emery cloth. The drum surface must be smooth and featureless- like the surface of a brake drum- to function effectively.

Oil filter rotor cover bolts

Manual clutch spring bolts

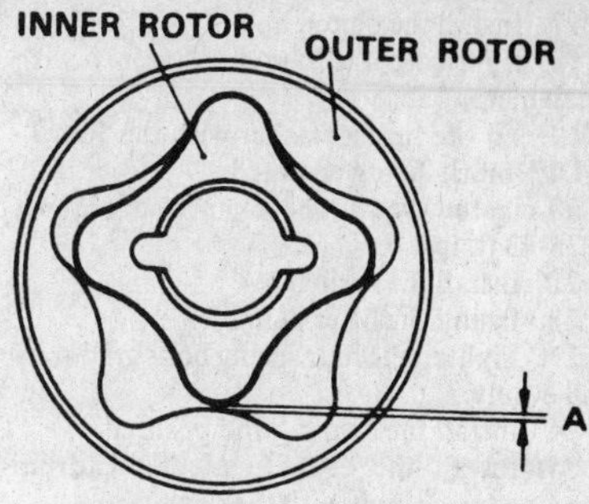

Oil pump rotor tip clearance (A)

4. Check the condition of the gear teeth and replace the drum if they are broken, worn or pitted.

5. Measure the free length of the clutch springs. Replace them if they measure over 282mm (11.1 in.).

6. Check that the clutch weight links are not broken or bent and that the holes in the weights are not elongated.

MANUAL CLUTCH

1. Measure clutch spring free-length. Replace the set if any measures less than 25.0mm (0.98 in.).

2. Check friction plates for worn or damaged friction material. Replace these plates as a set if any one of them is defective. Measure the thickness of each plate. The minimum acceptable sspecification is 2.6mm (0.10 in). Replace the friction plates as a set if any measures less than this.

3. Check the steel plates for discoloration. Check for warpage. The service limit is 0.20mm (0.008 in.).

4. Check plate tabs for chipping, wear or other damage.

5. Measure the inside diameter of the clutch outer guide. Replace it if diameter exceeds 20.05mm (0.79 in.).

6. Check gear teeth for pitting, chipping or other damage. Check gears for heat discoloration.

SHIFT MECHANISM

1. Check the splines of the gearshift shaft. If the splines are broken or torn to the extent that it is difficult to properly secure the shift lever, replace the shaft.

2. Check the condition of the shift arm. Be sure that it is not bent. Check that the shift fingers are not bent or worn.

3. Check the condition of the springs in the shift linkage, especially the shift lever pawl spring. If any spring is broken, has lost its tension or fails to hold its component properly, replace it.

4. Check the condition of the shift drum stopper roller and replace it if worn. The stopper spring should hold the stopper firmly against the stopper plate.

5. Check the stopper plate for wear. Replace if damaged.

OIL PUMP

1. Remove the pump cover screws, the cover and the gasket.

2. Remove the gear cover bolts. Remove the gear cover. Remove the pump driven gear.

3. Remove the inner and outer rotors.

4. Check all parts for scoring, discoloration or other obvious signs of wear.

5. Install the rotors and measure the clearance between the outer rotor and the oil pump body with a feeler gauge. Replace the pump if clearance exceeds 0.40mm (0.016 in.).

6. Measure the rotor end-play by placing a straightedge across the cover surface with the gasket in place and measuring the clearance between the straightedge and the rotors with a feeler gauge. The service limit is 0.25mm (0.010 in.).

7. Measure the clearance between the rotor tips. The service limit is 0.20mm (0.008 in.).

Installation

1. Clean all parts thoroughly before installation.

2. Use new gaskets and O-rings.

3. When assembling the oil pump, lubricate all metal parts thoroughly beforehand. Be certain that the cover gasket does not touch the rotors. After assembly, turn the pump by hand. There should be little resistance.

4. The shift drum stopper plate must be firmly secured. The plate is located by means of a pin and hole. Install the bolt and torque it to 6-9 ft. lbs.

5. Install the stopper arm. Be sure the spring holds the roller against the stopper plate. Tighten the bolt to 7-10 ft. lbs.

6. Assemble the gearshift shaft components on the shaft. The order is: coil spring, shift plate, washer, spring, shift lever, paul spring, washer, circlip, thrust washer.

7. Insert the shift shaft assembly into the crankcase. Be careful when fitting the shaft as there is an oil seal on the left side of the engine. Locate the ends of the pawl spring on either side of the pin.

8. Be sure that both oil pump O-rings are in place on the crankcase.

9. Turn the pump so that the mounting screws are accessible through the cover holes. Install the pump.

10. Install the crankcase spacer locating dowel pins on the mating surface.

11. Install a new spacer gasket.

12. Fit the spacer and tighten the bolts gradually and evenly.

13. Install the manual clutch thrust washer and clutch outer guide on the shaft.

14. Install the clutch housing.

15. Fit the housing thrust washer.

16. Fit a friction plate onto the pressure plate, then alternate steel and friction plates until all are used. Fit the plates into the housing.

17. Install the clutch hub.
18. Lubricate the clutch assembly with clean motor oil.
19. Fit the thrust washer with the "OUTSIDE" mark facing outwards.
20. Install the clutch locknut and torque it to 36-43 ft. lbs.
21. Install the springs.
22. Install the lifter plate.
23. Tighten the four spring bolts gradually and evenly.
24. Install the bearing and pushrod.
25. Install the centrifugal clutch drum aligning the cut-out with the drive gear.
26. Install the one-way clutch sprag.
27. Install the one-way clutch center by turning it counterclockwise.
28. Install the inner plate.
29. Assemble the clutch weights onto the hub with the links and clips.
30. Fit the springs to either side of the weight assembly.
31. Install the weight assembly in the drum.
32. Install the lockwasher.
33. Install the centrifugal clutch locknut.

CAUTION: *The locknut has LEFT-HAND threads.*

34. Tighten the locknut to 76-83 ft. lbs.

NOTE: *If there is a hole machined in the crankshaft, the locknut should be staked in place with a punch after torquing.*

35. Install the oil filter rotor cover gasket.
36. Lubricate and install a new crankshaft o-ring.
37. Install the thrust washer.
38. Install the side friction spring.
39. Fit the rotor cover.

NOTE: *Be sure the friction spring teeth are fitted into the cover groove.*

40. Tighten the rotor cover bolts to 7-10 ft. lbs.
41. Install the clutch ball retainer thrust washer.
42. Install the clutch lifter, engaging the shift assembly arm with the cut-out.
43. Fit the ball retainer.
44. Install lifter cam, aligning the cut-out with the pin in the crankcase.
45. Before installing the right crankcase cover, check that the two locating dowel pins are in place in the mating surface.
46. Fit a new gasket.
47. Install the cover. Tighten the cover bolts gradually and evenly.
48. Tighten the footpeg bolts to 14-18 ft. lbs.
49. Add oil to the crankcase. Check for leaks after the engine has been started.

LEFT CRANKCASE COVER COMPONENTS

Left crankcase cover components include the recoil starter assembly, alternator and engine sprocket.

Removal

1. Be sure that the transmissiion is in Neutral.
2. Remove the gearshift lever pinch bolt and carefully pull the lever off its shaft.
3. Remove the neutral indicator circlip. The indicator is located on the lower rear portion of the recoil starter case. Remove the indicator.
4. Remove the recoil starter assembly (four bolts).
5. Remove the gasket.
6. If further disassembly is required, refer to the section for your model, below.

ATC 200M

1. Drain the engine oil.
2. Remove the pulley bolt.
3. Remove the pulley.
4. Disconnect the alternator wires at the plastic connector on the frame behind the engine.
5. Remove the left crankcase cover (6 bolts.).
6. Remove the thrust washers and the starter motor reduction gears.
7. Remove the flywheel with a suitable puller.
8. Remove the starter reduction gear shaft, thrust washer and gear.
9. Remove the starter driven gear and the needle bearing.

OTHER MODELS

1. Remove the starter driven pulley and the cooling fan by taking out the four bolts.
2. Remove the alternator rotor nut and washer.
3. Remove the rotor with a rotor puller.
4. Remove the engine sprocket cover.
5. Disconnect the alternator wiring at the coupler.
6. Remove the wiring clamp from the engine.
7. Remove the alternator housing bolts. Take off the housing along with the stator.

Inspection

RECOIL STARTER (200M)

1. Remove the ratchet cover nut.
2. Remove the cover.
3. Remove the ratchet, ratchet guide, spring seat and spring.
4. Remove the collar from the pulley shaft.
5. Remove the handle cover.
6. Undo the rope knot. Remove the handle.

Recoil starter ratchet cover nut (1), cover (2) and guide (3) (200M)

7. Remove the starter pulley.

CAUTION: *Wear eye protection and use care when removing the pulley. The coil spring may pop out when it is removed.*

8. Check the rope for a frayed or worn condition and replace it if necessary.
9. Check the condition of the coil spring.
10. Check the ratchet components for damage.

RECOIL STARTER (OTHER MODELS)

1. Remove the circlip.
2. Remove the thrust washer and ratchet cover.
3. Remove the ratchets and ratchet springs.
4. Remove the spring and thrust washer.
5. Remove the handle cover, if fitted.
6. Undo the rope knot. Remove the handle.
7. Release the starter rope slowly.
8. Remove the starter drive pulley by turning it counterclockwise.

CAUTION: *Wear eye protection and use care when removing the pulley. The coil spring may pop out when it is removed.*

9. Check the rope for a frayed condition and replace it if necessary.
10. Check the condition of the coil spring.
11. Check the ratchet components for damage.

ALTERNATOR

1. Do not drop the rotor as the magnetic properties may be affected. Place it where it will not pick up stray bits of metal.
2. Be sure that the rotor is perfectly clean before installation.
3. For electrical tests, refer to the "Electrical System" section.
4. Check the inside of the rotor and the stator coil core ends for scoring which would indicate that they have been in contact. This condition must be rectified.
5. Check that the stator is secure on the crankcase cover spacer. Be sure the mounting bolts are tight.
6. if stator and rotor have been in contact, check the crankshaft bearings. This condition is sometimes caused by bad bearings which allow play in the crankshaft.
7. Check the rotor for cracks, especially around the mounting taper.
8. Check the stator for burned insulation, broken wires or other obvious signs of damage.

STARTER GEARS (200m)

1. Check the starter clutch rollers and springs for damage.
2. Check condition of the starter driven gear needle bearing.
3. Check gear condition. Replace the gears as a set if any one of them is damaged.

CRANKCASE COVERS

1. Always use new gaskets and O-rings.
2. Remove any knicks or imperfections from the mating surfaces with an oilstone or silicon carbide paper.

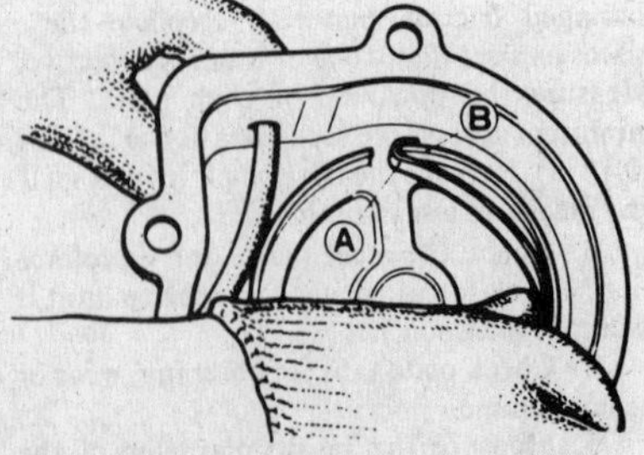

Engage the end of the coil spring (A) on the rib (B)

3. Oil seals can be pried out with a small screwdriver. When installing new seals, press them straight in with a block of wood or the like which will cover the entire seal. Lubricate seal lips before installation.

Installation

1. Use new gaskets and O-rings.
2. Clean all metal parts in a safe solvent and dry thoroughly.
3. Lubricate all metal parts with motor oil before assembly.
4. Grease the lips of all seals before installation.

RECOIL STARTER (200m)

1. Wrap the starter rope around the pulley in a clockwise direction when viewed from the ratchet side of the pulley.
2. Install the recoil spring in the housing, hooking the end of the spring in the place provided.

CAUTION: *Wear eye protection when installing the spring.*

3. Grease the spring thoroughly.
4. Grease the pulley shaft and install the pulley, hooking the end of the spring on the starter housing hook.
5. Turn the pulley two full turns clockwise.
6. Pull the starter rope through the hole and install the handle. Knot the end of the rope. Fit the handle cover.
7. Grease the ratchet and install it on the pulley.
8. Install the spring, spring seat and ratchet guide.
9. Install the cover. Install the cover nut.
10. Check recoil starter operation.

RECOIL STARTER (OTHER MODELS)

1. Thread the starter rope through the center of the pulley.
2. Wrap the rope around the pulley in a clockwise direction as viewed from the ratchet side of the pulley.
3. Grease the pulley shaft.
4. Install the coil spring, hooking the end of the spring in the place provided.

CAUTION: *Wear eye protection when installing the spring.*

5. Grease the spring thoroughly.
6. Install the pulley, turning it clockwise to align the spring end with the starter pulley boss.
7. Turn the pulley two full turns counterclockwise to preload the spring.
8. Route the rope through the hole, install the starter handle and knot the rope.
9. Grease the ratchets.
10. Install the ratchets and springs.
11. Grease and install the thrust washer.
12. Install the spring.
13. Install the ratchet cover, thrust washer and circlip.
14. Check starter operation.

ALTERNATOR/STARTER

1. Installation is the reverse of removal.
2. Be sure that locating dowel pins are in place on mating surfaces.
3. On the 200M, tighten the starter pulley botl to 29-36 ft. lbs.
4. On other models, tighten the rotor nut to 47-54 ft. lbs. Tighten the pulley/fan bolts to 7-10 ft. lbs.
5. Clean the inside mounting surface of the magneto rotor. Lubricate the mounting hole and the crankshaft taper with motor oil. Check that the locating key is in place in the crankshaft. Push the rotor into place. Do not strike the rotor. It will be driven home when the pulley is installed.

LOWER END AND TRANSMISSION

Splitting The Crankcases

1. Remove the engine from the frame.
2. Remove the cylinder head, cylinder and piston.
3. Remove the left and right side crankcase components as outlined above.
4. Remove the left crankcase spacer.
5. Remove the Neutral indicator shaft.
6. Remove the cam chain tensioner adjusting bolt on the top of the crankcase.
7. Remove the cam chain tensioner arm.
8. Remove the tensioner and cam chain.
9. Remove the Neutral Switch.
10. Remove the engine sprocket.
11. Remove the crankcase bolt on the front part of the right side of the engine.
12. Remove the crankcase bolts on the left side of the engine.
13. Place the engine with the left crankcase down and tap upwards on the right crankcase half with a plastic mallet to separate the case halves.
14. Remove the dowel pins and the gasket.
15. Remove the crankshaft assembly.
16. Remove the gear clusters.

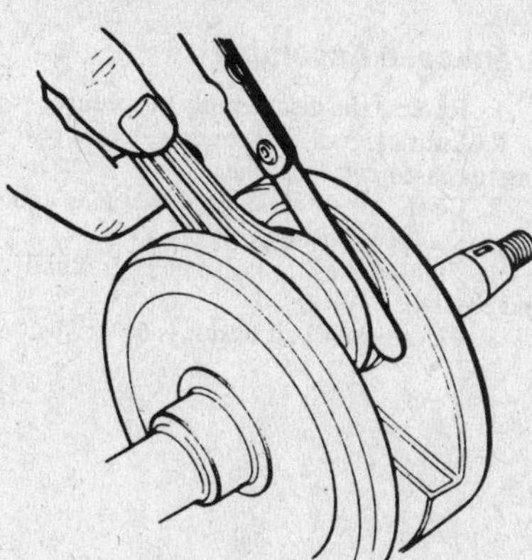

Checking big end side clearance

Inspection

CRANKSHAFT

The crankshaft is a pressed-together unit. The connecting rod big end bearing is the caged-needle type. In the event of damage to the con rod, bearing or crankpin, the crankshaft must be replaced as an assembly.

1. Lubricate the big end bearing with oil, and rotate the rod slowly around the crankpin. The movement must be smooth and silent.
2. With a dial gauge, check the up-and-down (radial) movement of the con rod. Compare the reading with the specification given. If rod movement is in excess of the specifications, the big end bearing is worn and the crankshaft must be replaced.

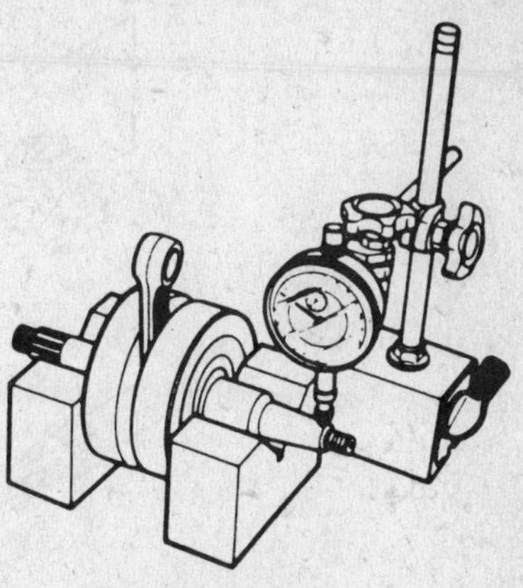

Checking crankshaft run-out

3. With a feeler gauge, check the clearance between the con rod big end and the crankshaft flywheel. Compare the measurement with the specification given for axial clearance.
4. Place the crankshaft on a set of V-blocks, and check the crankshaft run-out with a dial gauge. Check both ends of the crank. Comnpare the run-out reading with the specification given. If excessive, the crank must be replaced.

Crankshaft run-out will be one half of the true indicated reading of the gauge.

CRANKCASES

1. Check for damage to the bearing bosses, especially for stress cracks around the bearing boss.
2. Be sure that both case half mating surfaces are free of any races of old gasket or gasket material.
3. Place each case half on a flat surface and check for warpage by probing around the mating surface with a feeler gauge. Maximum acceptable case warpage is 0.05mm (0.002 in.). If warped, cases should be replaced.

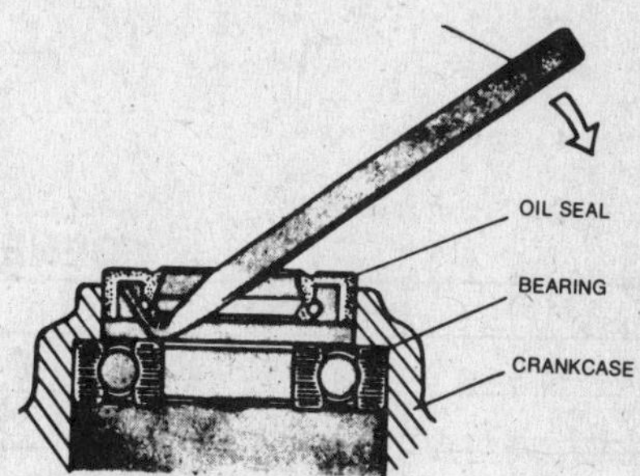

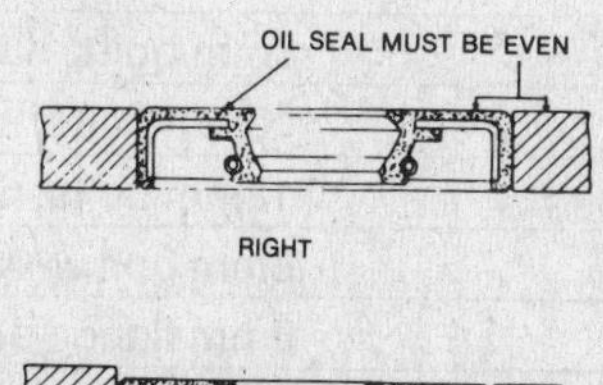

Engine oil seal removal and installation

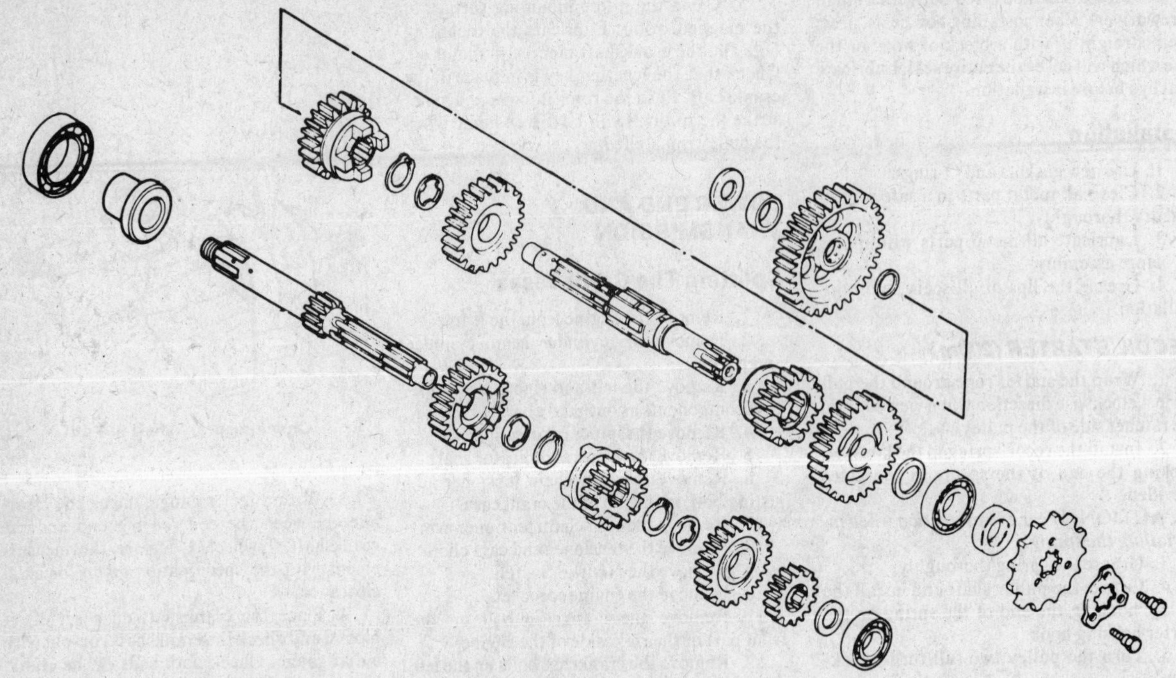

Transmission assembly

4. Minor scratches on the mating surfaces can be removed with an oilstone, although it is not permissible to remove much metal.

5. Case halves must be scrupulosuly clean before assembly. Be sure that all oil passages are clear and that the two dowel pins fitted between the case halves are installed.

TRANSMISSION

1. Check gears, shafts and shift linkage as outlined in the "Engine Rebuilding" section of 'General Information.

2. Compare measurements with the specifications in the charts.

NOTE: *Mark shift forks for position before disassembly.*

Crankcase Assembly

1. Reverse the disassembly procedure.
2. Lubricate all components before putting the case halves together.
3. Be sure the crankcase dowel pins and the gasket are properly positioned.
4. Tighten the crankcase bolts gradually and evenly.
5. FCrankcase bolt torque is 6-9 ft. lbs.

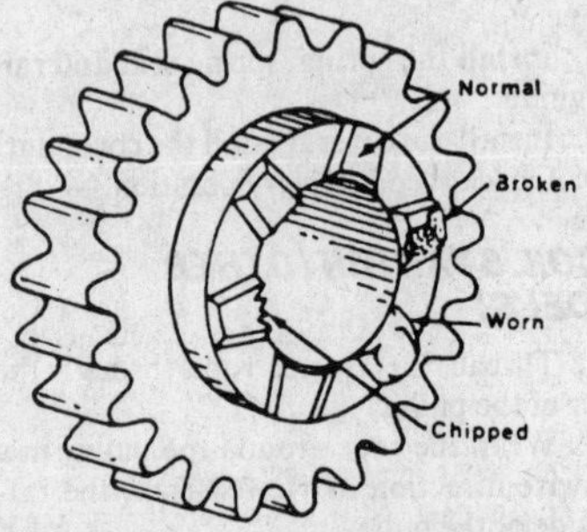

Check gears for damage

GENERAL TORQUE SPECIFICATIONS①

Part	Torque (ft. lbs.)
5mm screws	2.5-3.6
6mm screws	5-8
5mm bolts, nuts	3.5-4.5
6mm bolts, nuts	6-9
8mm bolts, nuts	13-18
10mm bolts, nuts	22-29
12mm bolts, nuts	36-43
6mm bolt w/8 mm head	5-8
6mm flange bolts, nuts	7-10
8mm flange bolts, nuts	17-22
10mm flange bolts, nuts	25-33

① Unless otherwise noted

ENGINE TORQUE SPECIFICATIONS

Part	Torque (ft. lbs.)
Compression release set bolt	4-5
Cylinder head bolts	6-9
Cylinder head cap nuts	
1980-81 (ATC 185)	13-14
1981 (ATC 200)	14-16
Other models	20-22
Camshaft sprocket bolts	6-9
Pulse generator rotor	6-9
Carburetor manifold	6-9
Valve adjuster cover	7-14
Valve adjuster locknut	11-13
Pulse generator cover and housing	3-5
Spark plug	9-14
Oil filter rotor cover	7-10
Manual clutch locknut	36-43
Centrifugal clutch locknut	76-83
Clutch adjusting screw locknut	14-18
Clutch lifter stopper bolt	13-18
Gearshift drum stopper arm bolt	7-10
Gearshift drum stopper plate bolt	6-9
Oil drain cap	7-14
Crankcase bolts	6-9
Cam chain tensioner arm bolt	6-9

ENGINE SPECIFICATIONS

Part	Standard (mm/in.)	Service limit (mm/in.)
CYLINDER HEAD		
Cam lobe height		
Intake	31.379/1.2354	31.199/1.2283
Exhaust	30.978/1.2196	30.798/1.2125
Cam journal OD		
R	19.967-19.980/0.7861-0.7866	19.90/0.784
L	33.957-33.970/1.3370-1.3376	33.90/1.335
Cam bearing ID	33.980-34.075/1.3378-1.3415	34.05/1.341
Camshaft bushing ID	20.005-20.026/0.7876-0.7884	20.05/0.789
Cylinder head warpage	—	0.10/0.004
Rocker arm ID	12.000-12.018/0.4724-0.4730	12.05/0.474
Rocker arm shaft OD	11.977-11.995/0.4715-0.4722	11.93/0.470
Rocker arm-to-shaft clearance	0.005-0.041/0.0002-0.0016	0.08/0.003
Valve spring free-length		
Inner	39.4/1.55	35.5/1.40
Outer	45.5/1.79	41.0/1.61
Valve stem OD		
Intake	5.450-5.465/0.2146-0.2152	5.42/0.213
Exhaust	5.430-5.445/0.2138-0.2144	5.40/0.213
Valve guide ID (In&Ex)	5.475-5.485/0.2156-0.2159	5.50/0.217
Stem-to-guide clearance		
Intake	0.010-0.035/0.0004-0.0014	0.12/0.005
Exhaust	0.030-0.055/0.0012-0.0020	0.14/0.006
Valve face width	1.7/0.07	2.0/0.08
Valve seat width	1.2/0.05	1.5/0.06

ENGINE SPECIFICATIONS

Part	Standard (mm/in.)	Service limit (mm/in.)
CYLINDER AND PISTON		
Cylinder ID		
180	63.000-63.010/2.4803-2.4807	63.10/2.484
200	65.000-65.010/2.559-2.560	65.10/2.563
Taper	—	0.10/0.004
Out-of-round	—	0.10/0.004
Warpage	—	0.10/0.004
Piston OD		
180	62.955-62.985/2.4785-2.4797	62.90/2.476
200	64.95-64.985/2.5573-2.5585	64.90/2.555
Wrist pin bore	15.002-15.008/0.5906-0.5909	15.04/0.592
Wrist pin OD	14.994-15.000/0.5903-.5906	14.96/0.589
Piston-to-pin clearance	0.002-0.014/0.0001-0.0006	0.02/0.001
Ring-to-groove clearance		
Top	0.015-0.050/0.0006-0.0020	0.09/0.004
Second	0.015-0.045/0.0006-0.0018	0.09/0.004
Ring end-gap		
Top, second	0.20-0.40/0.008-0.016	0.50/0.020
Oil	0.30-0.90/0.0012-0.035	—
Piston-to-cylinder clearance	0.015-0.055/0.0006-0.0022	0.10/0.004

Part	Standard (mm/in.)	Service limit (mm/in.)
CLUTCHES		
Manual clutch		
Spring free-length	25.7/1.01	25.0/0.98
Friction plate thickness	2.9-3.0/0.11-0.12	2.6/0.10
Steel plate warpage	—	0.20/0.008
Centrifugal clutch		
Drum ID	116/4.57	116.3/4.58
Weight lining thickness	4.3/0.17	4.1/0.16
Spring free-length	267.5/10.53	282/11.1
Outer guide OD	20.000-20.021/0.7874-0.7882	19.95/0.785
OIL PUMP		
Rotor-to-cover clearance	0.15-0.20/0.006-0.008	0.25/0.010
Rotor tip clearance	0.15/0.006	0.20/0.008
Rotor-to-body clearance	0.30-0.36/0.012-0.014	0.40/0.016
CRANKSHAFT		
Con rod small end ID	15.010-15.028/0.5909-0.5917	15.06/0.593
Big end axial clearance	0.05-0.30/0.002-0.012	0.80/0.032
Big end radial clearance	0-0.008/0-0003	0.05/0.002
Run-out		
Left end	—	0.08/0.003
Right end	—	0.12/0.005
TRANSMISSION		
Shift fork ID	12.00-12.02/0.472-0.473	12.04/0.474
Shift fork finger thickness	4.93-5.00/0.194-0.197	4.50/0.177
Fork shaft OD	11.976-11.994/0.4715-0.4722	11.96/0.471
Gear ID		
C1	16.516-16.534/0.6502-0.6509	16.58/0.653
C3, M4, M5	20.020-20.041/0.7882-0.7890	20.09/0.791
Shaft OD		
C1	16.466-16.484/0.6483-0.6490	16.42/0.646
C2	21.959-21.980/0.8645-0.8654	21.91/0.863
C3, M4, M5	19.959-19.980/0.7858-0.7866	19.91/0.784

FUEL SYSTEM

GAS TANK

Removal

1. Remove the seat.
2. Set the fuel petcock "OFF."
3. Disconnect the fuel line from the petcock.
4. Remove the mounting bolt at the rear of the tank.
5. Remove the tank.

Installation

1. Reverse the removal procedure.
2. When installing the tank, be sure to engage the rubber cushions at the front with the seats on the tank.
3. Be sure that the fuel line at the petcock is pushed on all the way and is secured with the safety clip.
4. Check for leaks before operating the machine.

CARBURETOR

Removal

1. Remove the seat.
2. Remove the fuel tank (see above).
3. Fold up the rubber cover on the carburetor cap, if one is fitted.
4. Unscrew the carburetor cap and pull out the throttle slide assembly. Wrap the assembly in a clean, lint-free rag and place it out of the way to avoid damage.
5. Disconnect the overflow line from the bottom of the float bowl and the vent line from the side of the carburetor.
6. On models with a choke cable, remove the cable clamp screw from the carburetor and disconnect the cable from the lever.
7. Place a rug beneath the float bowl and loosen the drain screw to remove fuel from the bowl.
8. Loosen the air cleaner hose clamp on the air cleaner side of the carb. On some models it may be necessary to remove the right rear fender for access to the clamp screw. On other models, it can be reached through a hole punched in the frame.
9. Remove the carburetor mounting nuts and remove it from the manifold.

Disassembly

1. Remove the maniforld O-ring from the carburetor.
2. Remove the two screws which secure the foloat bowl. Remove the float bowl carefully. If it is stuck, hold it in place and wrap it with the plastic screwdriver handle to break it free.

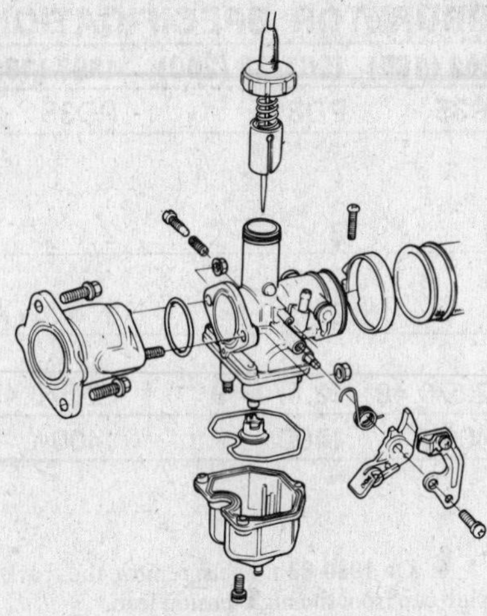

Carburetor assembly

3. Remove the float bowl O-ring.
4. Remove the plastic main jet skirt, if one is fitted.
5. Pull out the float pivot pin.
6. Lift off the float and needle.
7. Unscrew and remove the main jet from the needle jet holder.
8. Unscrew and remove the needle jet holder.
9. Shake the needle jet out of the carburetor body. If it will not come out, push it out from the top of the carb with a wooden dowel.
10. Early models had slow jets pressed into the carb body. These cannot be removed. Late models have screw- in slow jets. These are fitted with a screwdriver slot. Remove the slow jet if a screw-in unit is fitted.
11. Turn the pilot screw clockwise while counting the number of turns until it bottoms. Then unscrew and remove it. Be sure to return it to the original setting when assembling.
12. Unscrew and remove the throttle stop screw.
13. Compress the throttle slide spring and disengage the throttle cable from the slide.
14. Remove the needle clip retainer and shake the needle out of the slide. Do not remove the needle clip from the needle.

Inspection

NOTE: *Refer to the "General Information" section for carburetor rebuilding techniques.*

1. Clean all metal parts in a clean, safe solvent.
2. Blow air and fuel passages in the carburetor body clear with compressed air.
3. Check the condition of the needle and replace it if it is knicked or scored.
4. Clean all jets with solvent and compressed air. Do not attempt to clean fuel passages with wire or the like, since the calibrated bores may be damaged.
5. Check the float for fuel leakage. Replace it if it is punctured or gas-logged.
6. Check the float needle and needle seat for wear or corrosion. Replace the needle if damage is noted.

Assembly and Installation

1. Use new O-rings throughout when assembling.
2. Install jets carefully and do not overtighten them.
3. Be sure the needle clip is set to the original groove in the needle. Refer to the "Carburetor Specifications" chart for needle clip position for specific models.
4. Be sure the pilot screw is set to the position it was originally. Standard settings are given in the "Carburetor Specifications" chart.
5. Tighten the manifold nuts to 5-7 ft. lbs. Be certain to tighten the nuts evenly to avoid wraping the carb flange.
6. Be sure that all fuel lines are secure before operating the machine. After the carburetor is installed, turn on the fuel petcock and check for leaks.

FUEL PETCOCK

1. The petcock is mounted to the gas tank and incorporates a filter screen inside the tank.
2. To check petcock operation, disconnect the fuel line from the carburetor and put the end of the line in a suitable container.
3. Turn the petcock to the "ON" and "RES" positions. If there is no fuel flow, dtermine the cause.
4. If removing the gas cap increases fuel flow, the problem is a clogged vent in the cap.
5. If flow is sluggish or non-existent, remove the gas tank. Unscrew and remove the petcock and check filter condition.

FUEL LINES

1. Fuel lines should be checked for condition every year.
2. Replace lines that are damaged by abrasion, hardened, cracked or otherwise defective.
3. Be sure that safety clips are fitted to both sides of gas lines.
4. Whenever lines are disconnected or replaced, check for leaks before operating the machine.

CARBURETOR SPECIFICATIONS

	1980-81 (185)	1982 (185)	1981-82 (200)	1983 (185)	1983 (200)	1984 and Later (200)
ID	PD35	PD35	PD35	PD35	PD35	PD55
Venturi size (mm/in.)	22/0.9	22/0.9	22/0.9	22/0.9	22/0.9	22/0.9
Main jet	95	100	105	98	95	95

CARBURETOR SPECIFICATIONS

	1980-81 (185)	1982 (185)	1981-82 (200)	1983 (185)	1983 (200)	1984 and Later (200)
ID	PD35	PD35	PD35	PD35	PD35	PD55
Needle clip setting (groove from top)	2	2	2	2	3	3
Pilot screw (turns out)	2	2	2	1	1¼	2
Float level (mm/in.)	12.5/0.49	12.5/0.49	12.5/0.49	12.5/0.49	12.5/0.49	14.0/0.55
Idle speed (rpm)	1400	1400	1400	1400	1400	1400

ELECTRICAL SYSTEM

IGNITION CIRCUIT

Hard starting or misfiring are often caused by ignition system troubles, but since electrical malfunctions are often trickier to pin down than carburetor faults, it is wise to ensure that systems other than the ignition circuit are in serviceable conditon before beginning any work.

1. In the event of hard starting, misfiring or cutting out, first check that all electrical connections are clean, dry and tight.
2. Check the ignition and kill switches for continuity.
3. Check ignition timing accuracy, See "Maintenance."
4. Remove the spark plug. Clean and gap it to 0.6- 0.7mm (0.024-0.028 in.).
5. Connect the plug to the cap and ground it against the cylinder head. Turn the engine over with the electric starter. The spark produced should be thick and blue.
6. If there is no spark, or if the spark appears weak and yellow, repeat the test using a piece of metal, such as a nail, inserted into the cap and held about 1/8 in. away from the head. If the spark appears healthy, the plug was the problem.
7. If there is still no spark, or spark is weak, remove the spark plug cap and repeat the test.
8. If there is still no improvement, check the condition of the plug lead. Check for dirt or grease, cracks in the insulation, moisture, etc. If the lead is damaged, it should be replaced. This involves replacing the ignition coil as well.
9. If all of these components check out, inspect the main ignition circuit components are follows.

Ignition Coil

1. An ohmmeter is required to test the igniton coil.
2. Disconnect the spark plug lead.
3. Remove the seat and gas tank, if necessary, for access to the ignition coil leads and mounting bolts or screws.
4. Disconnect the low tension wires from the coil (green and black/yellow).
5. Remove the mounting hardware and remove the coil from the frame.
6. On 1980-83 models, remove the spark plub cap from the high tension lead.
7. Check primary winding resistance across the terminals to which the green and the black/yellow leads were connected. Readings should be as follows:
   1980-83: 0.2-0.8 ohms
   1984: 0.2-0.4 ohms
   1985-On: 0.16-0.20

   If resistance is not within this range, replace the ignition coil.
8. On 1980-83 models, check the secondary winding by measuring the resistance between the high tension lead (with the spark plug cap removed) and the ignition coil mounting boss above the plug wire. Resistance should be within 10% of the standard specification of 8-15Kohms or the ignition coil should be replaced.
9. On 1984 models, carry out the secondary winding check as described in Step 8. The resistance specifications should be 10-18Kohms with the spark plug cap in place and 3-5 Kohms with the cap and plug wire disconnected from the coil.
10. On 1985 models, secondary winding resistance can be checked by measuring resistance across the spark plug lead and one of the low tension terminals. It should be 7.0-11.2Kohms with the plug cap installed and 3.7-4.5Kohms without it. if the reading is not within 10% of this figure, replace the ignition coil.
11. Static resistance tests provide a general clue to coil condition, but cannot detect high voltage insulation leaks. Therefore, even if the resistance readings are acceptable, there is a chance that the coil is defective. Replacing the coil temporarily with one which is known to be good is the only sure check.

Excitor Coil

1. The alternator excitor coil can be checked with an ohmmeter.
2. Disconnect the black/red lead at the connector behind the engine.
3. Check the resistance between the black/red lead and a goo ground on the engine. Resistance should be 100-400 ohms.
4. If the reading is not within this range, the alternator stator must be replaced.

Pulse Generator

1. The pulse generator is located on the left end of the camshaft. The unit can be checked with an ohmmeter.
2. Locate and disconnect the pulse generator wires at the connector(s). Leads are green and blue/yellow. On some models, it may be necessary to remove the gas tank for access to the connectors.
3. Resistance across the leads should be 20-60 ohms from 1980-83 models and 20-30 ohms for 1984 and later machines.
4. if the reading obtained is not within 10% of the specifications, replace the pulse generator.
5. The pulse generator is located beneath the "CDi" cap on the left side of the cylinder head. It can be removed after the two mounting screws are taken off.
6. If a new pulse generator is fitted, check that the air gap between the pulse rotor and the generator is set at 0.3-0.4mm (0.012-0.016 in.).

CDI Unit

A special tester is needed to check the CDI unit. If all other components in the circuit are found to be serviceable, the CDI unit can be checked most easily by replacing it with one which is know to be in working order.

LIGHTING COIL (EXCEPT 200m)

1. The lighting coil of the alternator can be checked with a continuity tester.
2. Locate the 3-pin connector of the alternator wires behind the engine. Disconnect the wires.
3. Check for continuity between the yellow lead and ground. If there is no continuity, the lighting coil is open and the alternator stator must be replaced.

CHARGING CIRCUIT (200M)

Output Test

NOTE: *The battery must be in good condition and fully charged or this test will not yield valid results.*

1. A voltmeter and an ammeter are required for a system output test.
2. Warm up the engine by running it for several minutes.
3. Remove the seat.
4. Remove the battery holder and cover.
5. Disconnect the red lead at the fuse. Connect the ammeter between the red leads.
6. Connect the voltmeter across the battery terminals.
7. Turn the lignting switch "ON."
8. Start the engine and note the reading.
9. The voltmeter should read 14 VDC.

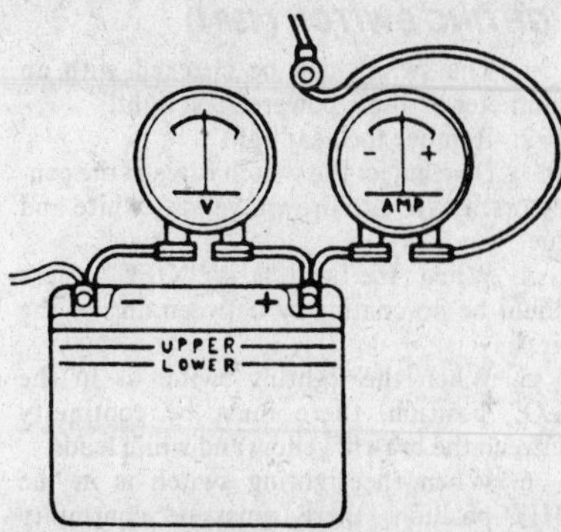

Electrical connections for alternator output test (battery-equipped models)

10. The ammeter should read 4.5a 5,000 rpm.

11. If the readings obtained are not within specifications, check the voltage regulator and the alternator charging coil as outlined below.

Voltage Regulator

1. The voltage regulator can be checked with an ohmmeter.

2. Locate the regulator wires at the 4-pin plastic coupling at the rear of the machine. Leads are red, yellow, yellow and green. Disconnect the wiring.

3. Check continuity in both directions for each pair of leads by refering to the following chart:

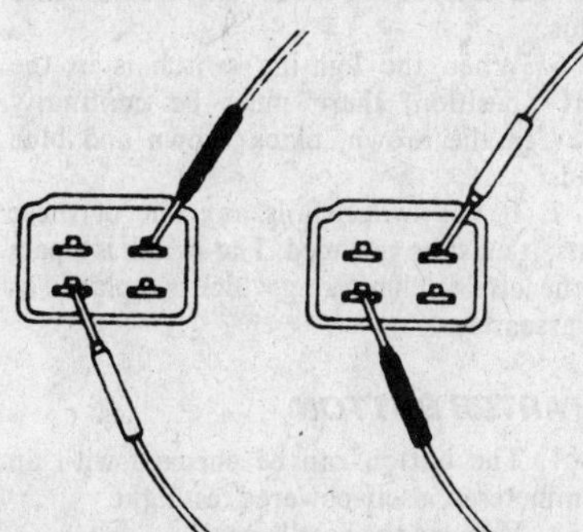

Reversing probe polarity for the voltage regulator test

+Probe	−Probe	Resistance (Kohms)
Red	Yellow	0.1-10
Red	Green	0.2-30
Yellow	Red	Infinity
Yellow	Yellow	1-50
Yellow	Green	0.1-10
Yellow	Red	Infinity
Yellow	Yellow	1-50
Green	Red	Infinity
Green	Yellow	0.5-50

4. If the voltage regulator fails any one of these tests it must be replaced.

5. Remove the regulator by first removing the rear fenders and the tool box. Disconnect the wiring and remove the two mounting bolts.

Charging Coil

1. Use the ohmmeter to check charging coil resistance.

2. Locate the coil wires on the harness behind the engine (leads are yellow and yellow).

3. Disconnect the leads.

4. Check resistance across the two yellow leads on the alternator side of the connector.

5. Resistance should be 0.1-1.0 ohms.

6. If the reading is not within this range, replace the alternator stator.

7. Check resistance between each lead and ground on the engine. Resistance must be infinite. Replace the stator is the meter shows any continuity between the wiring and ground.

STARTING SYSTEM

Testing

1. If, when the starter button is pressed, the starter spins, but the engine does not, the problem is either the starter clutch or the starter motor gears in the left crankcase cover.

2. If the engine turns over very slowly, check the battery for a low state of charge. Check that the engine oil is not too heavy for conditions. If these items are not the problem, suspect a defective starter motor.

3. If nothing at all happens when the starter button is pushed, check all electrical connections in the circuit. Check that the battery is properly charged. Check the ignition switch, starter button switch, neutral switch. Check the starter solenoid. If all of these items are in proper operating condition, check the starter motor.

Starter Solenoid

1. For access to the starter solenoid, remove the rear fenders and the tool box.

2. Remove the starter solenoid cover.

3. When the starter button is pressed, their should be an audible "click" at the solenoid.

4. Disconnect the solenoid high tension leads and the low tension wires at the plastic connector.

5. With an ohmmeter or continuity light, check the resistance of the low tension primary coil (yellow/red and green/red wires). There should be only a few ohms resistance. If this circuit shows an open condition, the solenoid must be replaced.

6. Put 12 VDC acress the low tension wires. Check for continuity across the high tension terminals. There should be no resistance. If the high tension terminals do not show continuity, the solenoid is defective and must be replaced.

Starter Motor

REMOVAL

1. Be certain the ignition switch is "OFF".

2. Disconnect the ground cable at the battery.

3. Remove the exhaust pipe nuts at the cylinder head.

4. Loosen the muffler clamp bolt(s). Remove the exhaust pipe.

5. Disconnect the high tension lead at the starter motor.

6. Remove the starter motor bracket bolts and the mounting bolts. Remove the starter motor.

DISASSEMBLY

1. Remove the starter motor gear snapring.

2. Remove the gear.

3. Remove the case screws and remove the case ends to expose the brushes.

4. Note the location and number of any shims on the armature shaft when the case ends are removed. They must be installed when the unit is assembled.

INSPECTION

1. Electrical tests can be carried out with an ohmmeter or a self-powered test light.

2. Check that continuity exists between each of the commutator segments. If one or more of them is "dead," the motor must be replaced.

3. Check that there is no continuity between the commutator segments and the armature core. Anything less than infinite resistance here will require replacement of the motor.

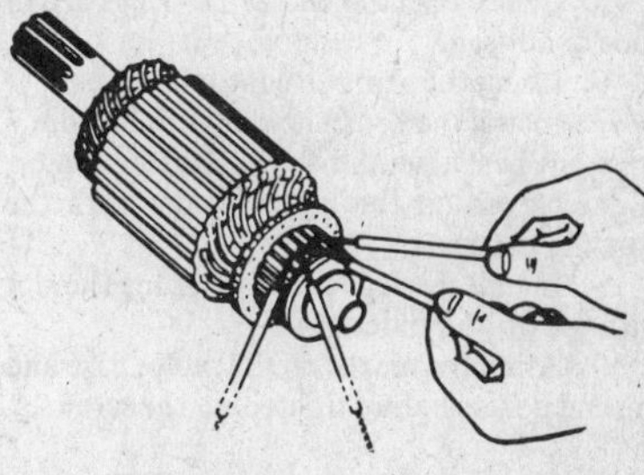

Checking commutator continuity

4. Check that there is no continuity between the commutator segments and the armature bars.

5. Check that there is continuity between the brush which is wired to the stator (field) coil and the high tension cable terminal. Lack of continuity here indicates that the field coil is open and the motor must be replaced.

6. Check the commutator segments for signs of wear, scoring or other contact damage.

7. Clean the commutator with a rag and a safe solvent to remove carbon dust and other foreign matter.

8. Check the condition of the carbon brushes. Brushes with cracked or oddly worn contact surfaces should be replaced.

Starter motor carbon brush free-length

9. Measure brush length. Replace them as a set if either measures under 5.5mm (0.22 in.).

10. Check brush spring tension. It should be 400 gr. (14.1 oz.).

11. Check the armature for contact damage as might occur if the armature bars touch the field coils. If any is evident, replace the motor.

12. Discoloration of the commutator segments occuring on two adjacent segments indicates grounded coils. This requires replacement of the motor.

13. Check the condition of the brushings in the end caps. If they are cracked or otherwise damaged, or the armature shows signs of contact damage, the unit must be replaced.

ASSEMBLY

1. Clean all parts thoroughly.
2. Use a small amount of light duty grease to lubricate the brushings in the end caps.
3. Be sure that all shims are in place on the brush side of the armature.
4. Be sure that the brush springs are in place and that the brushes are in good contact with the commutator.
5. Check that the end cap O-rings are in good condition.
6. Insert the armature into the case.
7. Install the brush holder with brushes.
8. When assembling the starter motor, align the pin on the brush holder with the notch in the case.
9. Install the rear cover, aligning the slot with the brush holder pin.
10. Align the marks on the motor case and the end covers before tightening the screws.

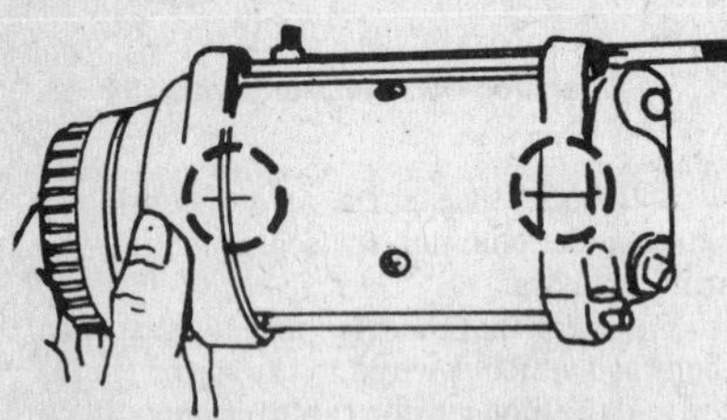

Align case and end-cap marks when assembling the starter

INSTALLATION

1. Reverse the removal procedure.
2. Lubricate the O-ring before fitting the motor.

ELECTRICAL SWITCHES

ATC 185 and 200S

HEADLIGHT/DIMMER SWITCH

1. The headlight/dimmer switch is a three-position unit mounted on the headlight shell.
2. The switch can be checked with an ohmmeter or a self-powered test light.
3. Remove the headlight.
4. Disconnect the switch wires at the connectors. Switch leads are white, yellow, brown and blue.
5. When the switch is "OFF", there should be no continuity between any of the leads.
6. In the "LO" position, continuity should exist between the white, yellow and blue wires.
7. In the "HI" position, continuity should exist between the white, yellow and blue wires.
8. If the switch fails any one of these tests, it must be replaced.

ENGINE STOP SWITCH

1. The engine stop switch, which is located on the right side of the handlebars, can be checked with an ohmmeter or self-powered continuity light. The switch leads are reached through the headlight housing.
2. Remove the headlight.
3. Disconnect the engine stop switch leads at the connectors. Leads are black and green.
4. When the switch is in the "OFF" position, there should be continuity between these leads.
5. When the switch is in the "ON" position, there should be no continuity.

ATC 200M

IGNITION SWITCH (1984)

1. The ignition switch can be checked with an ohmmeter or a self-powered test light.
2. Remove the headlight.
3. Disconnect the switch wires at the connectors (black, green, red and yellow/red).
4. When the switch is in the "OFF" position, there should be continuity between the black and the green wires.
5. When the switch is in the "ON" position, there should be continuity between the red and the yellow/red wires.
6. If the switch fails either tests, replace it.
7. The switch can be accessed by removing the handlebar upper holder and releasing the clips which hold the switch body.

IGNITION SWITCH (1985 AND LATER)

1. The ignition switch can be checked with an ohmmeter or a self-powered test light.
2. Remove the headlight.
3. Disconnect the ignition switch wires at the connectors (black/white, green, red, black).
4. When the ignition switch is in the "OFF" position, there should be continuity between the black/white and the green leads only.
5. When the ignition switch is in the "ON" position, there should be continuity between the red and the black leads only.
6. If the switch fails either test, replace it.
7. The switch can be accessed by removing the handlebar upper holder and releasing the clips which hold the switch body.

ENGINE STOP SWITCH

1. The switch can be checked with an ohmmeter or self-powered test light.
2. Remove the headlight.
3. Disconnect the stop switch leads at the connectors. Switch wires are black and green on 1984 models and black/white and green on the 1985 and later machines.
4. When in the "RUN" position, there should be no continuity.
5. In both "OFF" positions, there should be continuity between the two wires.
6. The switch is a part of the left switch housing which is replaced as an assembly.

LIGHTING SWITCH (1984)

1. The switch can be checked with an ohmmeter or a self-powered test light.
2. Remove the headlight.
3. Disconnect the switch wires at the connectors. Leads are brown, yellow, white and blue.
4. When the switch is "OFF" there should be no continuity between any of the wires.
5. When the lighting switch is in the "LO" position, there must be continuity between the brown, yellow and white leads.
6. When the lighting switch is in the "HI" position, there must be continuity across the brown, yellow and blue leads.
7. If the switch fails any one of these tests, it must be replaced. It is a part of the left switch housing which is replaced as an assembly.

LIGHTING SWITCH (1985 AND LATER)

1. The switch can be checked with an ohmmeter or a self-powered test light.
2. Remove the headlight.
3. Disconnect the switch wires at the plastic connectors (brown, black/brown, white and blue).
4. When the lighting switch is "OFF" there must be no continuity between any of the wires.
5. When the lighting switch is in the "LO" position, there must be continuity between the brown, black/brown and white leads.
6. When the lighting switch is in the "HI" position, there must be continuity between the brown, black/brown and blue leads.
7. If the switch fails any one of these tests, it must be replaced. The switch is a part of the left switch housing which is replaced as an assembly.

STARTER BUTTON

1. The button can be checked with an ohmmeter or a self-powered test light.
2. Remove the headlight.
3. Disconnect the green/red and the light green/red button wires at the connectors.
4. There must be continuity across these wires only when the starter button is pushed.
5. If there is always continuity, or if no continuity is indicated when the button is pressed, the switch assembly must be replaced.

NEUTRAL SWITCH

1. The neutral switch is a part of the starting circuit whicvh will work only if the switch is closed, indicating that the transmission is in Neutral.
2. The switch can be checked with an ohmmeter or a self-powered test light.
3. Locate the neutral switch lead connector on the harness behind the engine.
4. Disconnect the neutral switch wire at the connector (light green/red).
5. Check for continuity between the lead and ground on the engine case. When the transmission is in Neutral, there must be continuity.
6. When the transmission is in any other gear, the switch must be open (no continuity).

SPECIFICATIONS

Headlight	12 V, 45/45W
Taillight	12 V, 5W
Indicator lights	12 V, 3W
Fuse (200M)	
1984	10 A
1985-ON	7 A
Battery (200M)	12 V, 14 ah

CHASSIS

WHEEL REMOVAL AND INSTALLATION

Front (1980-81)

1. Park the machine on a level surface.
2. Engage the parking brake.
3. Disconnect the front brake cable from the brake drum lever by removing the adjusting nut.
4. Remove the cotter pins from each axle nut.
5. Remove the brake anchor bolt cotter pin, if one is fitted.
6. Remove the brake anchor bolt nut.
7. Remove the brake anchor bolt and collar.
8. Loosen the two axle nuts.
9. Raise the front end of the machine by placing a jack beneath the frame and the front wheel assembly will drop out of the forks.

CAUTION: *Keep track of axle nuts, washers, spacers and other mounting hardware.*

10. Installation is the reverse of removal. Note the following points:
    a. Use new cotter pins.
    b. Do not forget to install the brake anchor bolt collar.
    c. Tighten the brake anchor bolt to 15-20 ft. lbs.
    d. Tighten the axle nuts evenly until both are torqued to 36-51 ft. lbs.
    e. Adjust the front brake.

Front (1982)

1. Park the machine on a level surface.
2. Engage the parking brake.
3. Disconnect the front brake cable from the brake drum lever by removing the adjusting nut.
4. Remove the axle nut cotter pins.
5. Loosen both axle nuts.
6. Raise the front end of the machine by placing a jack beneath the frame and the front wheel assembly will drop out of the forks.

CAUTION: *Keep track of axle nuts, washers, spacers and other mounting hardware.*

7. Installation is the reverse of removal. Note the following points:
    a. Use new cotter pins.
    b. Position the wheel assembly between the forks. When lowering the front end down to the wheel, be sure that the brake plate anchor is engaged with the tab ont he right fork leg.
    c. Tighten the axle nust evenly until both are torqued to 36-51 ft. lbs.
    d. Adjust the front brake.

Front (1983 And Later)

1. Park the machine on a level surface.
2. Engage the parking brake.
3. Disconnect the front brake cable from the brake drum lever by removing the adjusting nut.
4. Raise the front wheel off the ground by placing a jack or similar safe, sturdy support beneath the frame.
5. Loosen the four axle cap nuts on the left fork leg.
6. Unscrew and remove the axle.
7. Disengage the brake anchor from the right fork leg.
8. Remove the wheel from the forks.
9. Note the spacer on the right side of the wheel and the collar on the left. Be sure thay are not lost.
10. To install the wheel, check that the axle cap on the left fork leg is properly installed. The "UP" mark stamped on the cap must be in the right position.
11. Check that the spacer on the right side of the wheel is in place. Be sure the collar on the left side is fitted.
12. Position the wheel between the forks.
13. Engage the brake plate anchor with the hole in the right fork leg.
14. Insert the axle and tighten it to 51-80 ft. lbs.
15. Tighten the two upper axle cap nuts first. Then tighten the two lower nuts. Proper torque is 7-10 ft. lbs.
16. Connect and adjust the front brake cable.

Rear (All Models)

1. Park the machine on a level surface.
2. Engage the parking brake.
3. Loosen each of the four wheel nuts on the wheel you wish to remove.
4. Support the rear wheel(s) off the ground by placing a jack or suitable safety stand beneath the frame.
5. Remove the four wheel nuts.
6. Remove the wheel.

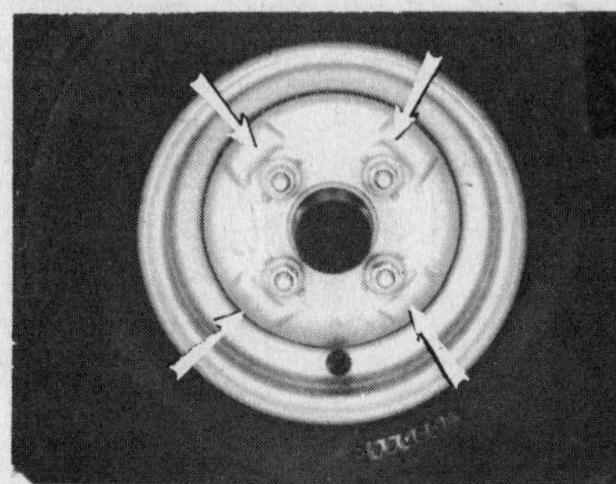

Rear wheel nuts

7. To install the wheel, be sure to put it on the hub with the tire valve facing out.
8. Install the four wheel nuts and tighten them in an "X" pattern a bit at a time until the proper torque of 14-18 ft. lbs. is reached.

FRONT BRAKE

Removal

1. Remove the front wheel.
2. Remove the axle nut on the brake plate side and pull out the axle (1980-82).

CAUTION: *Note the location of all collars, spacers, washers, etc. on the axle.*

3. Remove the brake plate.

Inspection

Brake shoes can be inspected in place on the plate.

1. Inspect the linings for wear. There should be at least 2.0mm (0.08 in.) of lining material left measured at the lining's thinnest point. If either show is worn below this limit, replace the pair.
2. Inspect the linings for scoring or grooves. These may be caused by particles of dirt which enter the drum. If badly scored, the linings should be replaced and the drum inspected closely for the same type of damage.
3. Be sure that the linings are free of and oil or grease. Lubricant-impregnated linings must be replaced.

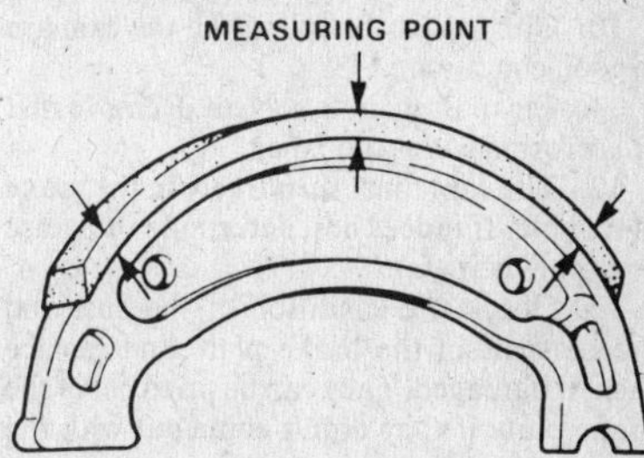

Check brake lining thickness

4. If the linings are in usable condition, rough up the surfaces with coarse sandpaper to break the glaze. Clean them thoroughly afterwards with alcohol or laquer thinner.
5. Clean foreign matter from the brake plate with a rag.

CAUTION: *Brake dust may present a health hazard. Do not blow the brake assemblies clear with a high pressure compressed air source or the particles may be inhaled.*

6. Inspect the brake drum surface for condition. The drum must be free of scoring or rust.
7. Rust can be removed from the brake drum surface with sandpaper. Polish the surface until it is shiny, then clean it thoroughly.
8. Alcohol or laquer thinner can be used to remove dirt or deposits from the drum.
9. Measure the inside diameter of the brake drum. If it measures more than 111mm (4.4 in.), replace it.
10. Measure the diameter of the drum in two directions to check for an out-of-round condition. This is usually noticable as an off-and-on feeling when the brakes are applied. This condition may be remedied by having the drum turned down on a lathe, but the final diameter must not exceed the service limit above.
11. Minor scoring or imperfections in the drum can be remedied by having the drum turned down. If this is done, replace the brake shoes regardless of apparent condition.
12. Check the brake drum rubber seal for condition and replace it if it is cracked or otherwise damaged.
13. Check the brake drum for cracks or other critical defects.

Disassembly

1. Expand the brake shoes by hand and pull them and the return springs off the brake plate by folding the shoes together.
2. Remove the brake lever pinch bolt.
3. Carefully pry the brake lever off the splined cam shaft.
4. Tap the brake cam out of the plate taking care not to lose the thrust washer, wear indicator and any rubber seals which may come out. Note that a return spring is fitted to the cam on some models.
5. Clean dirt, brake dust and other foreign matter from the brake plate with a solvent-soaked rag.
6. Check the plate closely for stress cracks or other damage.
7. Check the condition of the brake shoe springs. Replace them if they are rusted, broken deformed or weakened.
8. Check the condition of the brake cam spring (if equipped) and replace it if it is damaged.
9. Check that the brake cam is not bent.
10. Check that the splines on the cam are in good condition.
11. Clean the cam in solvent. Remove rust or corrosion with sandpaper.
12. The cam must turn freely in the brake plate hole. If it does not, determine the cause and remedy it.
13. Check the condition of the dust and grease seals in the brake plate and replace them if damaged. They can be pried out of the brake plate if they didn't come out with the cam.
14. If the brake drum is damaged, it can be removed by taking out the mounting bolts.

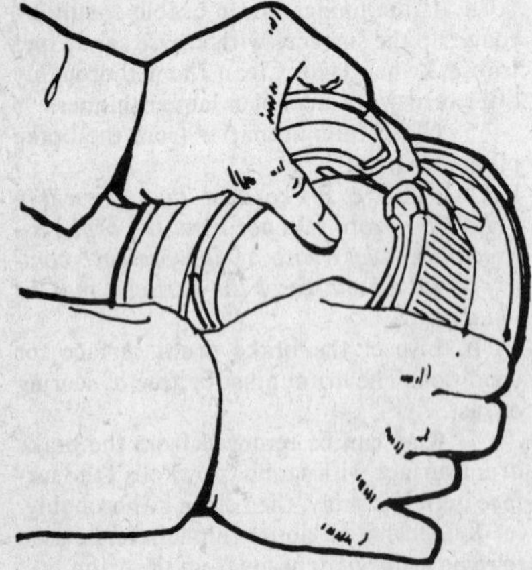

Removing the brake shoes from the plate

Assembly

1. If the brake drum was removed from the hub, install it and tighten the mounting bolts gradually and in a cross pattern to 14-18 ft. lbs. Bend up the locking tabs on late models which have this type of securing device fitted.
2. Install the grease seals in the brake plate if they were removed.
3. Lubricate the brake cam with a good grade of medium-weight chassis grease.
4. Fit the thrust washer and the cam spring on the cam.
5. Insert the cam into the plate. Be sure that the spring end is fitted into the hole in the cam and the other end is hooked over the anchor on the plate.
6. Lubricate the brake shoe pivot with chassis grease.
7. Fit the outer cam dust seal if it is not already in place. Install wear indicator. The tab aligns with the cam cut-out.
8. Install the brake lever, aligning the punch mark on the lever with the punch mark on the end of the cam.
9. Install and tighten the lever pinch bolt.
10. Clean hand throughly to avoid contaminating the brake linings.
11. Assemble the shoes and return springs and spread them by hand to fit over the pivot and the cam. Be sure they are properly seated.
12. Work the brake lever by hand and observe operation.
13. Connect the brake cable and adjust as outlined in "Maintenance" after the wheel is installed.

Installation

1. Clean off the axle shaft.
2. Grease the lips of the wheel bearing seals.
3. Fit the brake drum. Be sure the spacer is in place.
4. Install the axle and axle nut (1980-82).
5. Install the wheel. See above for procedures.

FRONT WHEEL BEARINGS

The front wheel bearings are pressed into the hub and can be inspected and/or serviced after the hub is removed from the wheel.

1. Remove the front wheel.
2. Remove the axle (1980-82). Note the locations of any spacers, collars, washers, etc. Remove axle collars and spacers on both sides of the wheel.
3. Remove the brake plate.
4. Bend down the brake drum bolt locking tabs, if fitted.
5. Remove the brake drum bolts.
6. Remove the brake drum.
7. Remove the wheel hub nuts.
8. Remove the hub from the wheel.
9. Pry out the grease seals on either side.
10. Bearings should be inspected in place, since removal usually damages them.

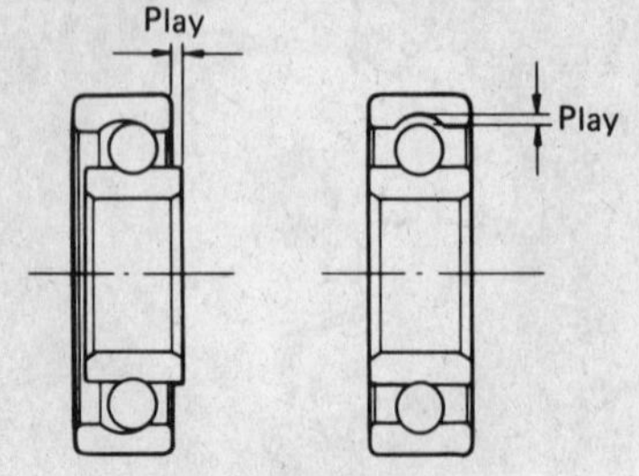

Check wheel bearing play

11. Check each bearing for play of the inner race relative to the outer. Maximum allowable radial (up- and-down) play is 0.05mm (0.002 in.). Maximum allowable axial (in-and-out) play is 0.10mm (0.004 in.). If either bearing exceeds these limits, replace the pair.
12. Check the bearing rotation. If any roughness, binding or noise is noted, replace the set.
13. Remove the bearings by reaching into the hub with a suitable drift and driving out one of them. Remove the spacer. Remove the remaining bearing in the same manner.
14. Lubricate new bearings with a good quality, medium-weight bearing grease. Put a quantity of the lubricant inside the hub as well.
15. Install the left-side bearing first. Drive the bearing straight in until it is seated. A driver large enough to cover the whole bearing should be used.

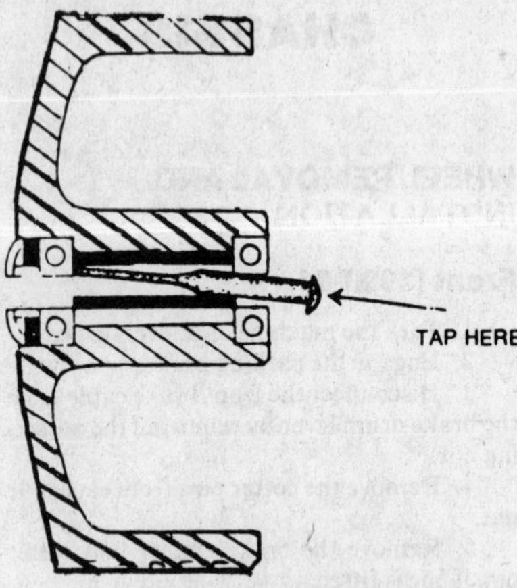

Removing a wheel bearing

16. After the left bearing is installed, install the spacer and the right-side bearing.
17. Use new grease seals. Press seals in carefully until they are flush with the edges of the hub. Grease the seal lips after installation.
18. Check the axle for a bent condition. The maximum acceptable run-out is 0.5mm (0.02 in.), which is 1/2 of the Total Indicated Reading obtained with a dial gauge.
19. When assembling the wheel, tighten the hub nuts gradually and in an "X" pattern until the proper torque of 14-18 ft. lbs. is reached.
20. Tighten brake drum bolts in the same way to 14-18 ft. lbs. Bend up the bolt locking tabs on models equipped with them.
21. On 1983 and later models, ensure that the axle collar is in place on the left side of the wheel before installation.

REAR BRAKE

Removal

1. Remove the right rear wheel.
2. Remove the axle nut cotter pin.
3. Remove the axle nut and washer.
4. Remove the wheel hub.
5. Remove the two brake drum nuts from the axle.
6. Remove the washer from the axle, if so equipped.
7. On models with a sealed rear brake (ATC 200 from 1982, ATC 185 from 1983), remove the brake drum cover bolts. Remove the cover.
8. Pull off the brake drum.
9. Brake components are now exposed for inspection and service.

Inspection

1. Inspect the linings for wear. There should be at least 2.0mm (0.08 in.) of lining

material left at the thinnest point. If either shoe is worn below this limit, replace the pair.

2. Inspect the linings for scoring or grooves. These may be caused by particles of dirt which enter the drum. If badly scored, the linings should be replaced and the drum inspected closely for the same type of damage.

3. Be sure the linings are free of oil and grease. Lubricant-impregnated linings must be replaced.

4. If the lining are in usable condition, rough up the surfaces with sandpaper to break the glaze. Clean them thoroughly afterwards with alcohol or laquer thinner.

5. Clean foreign matter from the brake plate with a rag.

CAUTION: *Brake dust may present a health hazard. Do not blow the brake assembly clear with a high pressure compressed air source or the particulates may be inhaled.*

6. Inspect the brake drum surface for condition. The drum must be free of rust or scoring.

7. Rust can be removed from the drum surface with sandpaper. Polish the surface until it is shiny, then clean it thoroughly.

8. Alcohol or laquer thinner can be used to remove dirt or deposits from the drum.

9. Measure the inside diameter of the drum. If it measures more than 141mm (5.6 in.), replace it.

10. Measure the diameter of the drum in two directions to check for an out-of-round condition. This is usually noticable as an off-and-on feeling when the brakes are applied. This condition may be remedied by having the drum turned down on a lathe, but the final diameter must not exceed the service limit, above.

11. Minor scoring or imperfections in the drum can be remedied by having the drum turned down. If this is done, replace the brake shoes regardless of apparent condition.

12. Check the splines on the brake drum and those on the axle for condition. If they are worn or show other signs of damage, replace the components.

13. Check the brake drum cover seals and axle O-ring for condition and replace any unserviceable components. If there was evidence of foreign matter inside the brake, the seals should be replaced regardless of apparent condition.

14. Be sure that the drum is free of stress cracks, accident damage, etc.

Disassembly

1. Disconnect the brake cables from the brake lever by removing the adjuster nuts.

2. Expand the brake shoes by hand and pull them and the return springs off the brake plate by folding them together.

3. Remove the brake lever pinch bolt.

4. Carefully pry the brake lever off the splined shaft.

5. Remove the wear indicator.

6. Remove the spring from the cam on models with an external return spring.

7. Tap the brake cam out of the brake plate taking care not to lose any seals which may come out.

8. Clean dirt, brake dust and other foreign matter from the brake plate with a solvent-soaked rag.

9. Check the brake plate closely for stress cracks or other damage.

10. Check the condition of the brake shoe springs. Replace them if they are rusted, broken, deformed or weakened.

11. Check the brake cam spring and replace it if it is damaged.

12. Check that the brake cam is not bent.

13. Check that the splines on the cam are in good condition.

14. Clean the cam in solvent. Remove rust or corrosion with sandpaper.

15. The cam must turn freely in the brake plate hole. If it does not, determine the cause and remedy it.

16. Check the condition of the cam dust seal and the grease seals in the brake plate and replace them if damaged. Grease seals can be pried out.

Assembly

1. Install the grease seals in the brake plate if they were removed.

2. Lubricate the brake cam with a good grade of medium-weight chassis grease.

3. Fit the cam spring on the cam, inserting the end of the spring into the hole in the cam (internal return spring).

4. Install the brake cam. Fit the outer end of the spring over the anchor on the brake plate.

5. Install the dust seal on the outer side of the cam.

6. Lubricate the brake shoe pivot with chassis grease.

7. Install the cam return spring (external return spring models).

8. Install the wear indicator plate, aligning the tab with the cam cut-out.

9. Install the brake lever, aligning the punch mark on the lever with the punch mark on the cam. Engage the return spring with the lever hole on external return spring models.

10. Install and tighten the lever pinch bolt.

11. Clean hand thoroughly to avoid contaminating the brake linings.

12. Assemble the shoes and return springs and spread them by hand to fit over the pivot and the cam. Be sure they are properly seated.

13. Work the brake lever by hand and observe operation.

14. Install the brake drum.

15. If the axle was fitted with an O-ring which was removed, lubricate it with grease and install it.

16. On models with sealed brakes, install the cover gasket. Lubricate the center seal of the drum cover with grease. Install the cover. Install and tighten the cover bolts.

17. Install the axle washer, if fitted.

18. Install the brake drum nuts. The outer nut should be secured with a non-permanent thread-locking compound. Torque the inner nut to the specification given, then hold it in place while the outer nut is tightened. Nut torques are as follows:

Inner/outer (1980): 43-58/43 58 ft. lbs.
Inner/outer (1981): 25-33/58-87 ft. lbs.
Inner/outer (1982 ATC 185): 25-33/58-87 ft. lbs.
Inner/outer (1983 ATC 185): 25-33/87-101 ft. lbs.
Inner/outer (1982 and later ATC 200): 25-33/87-101 ft. lbs.

Installation

1. Clean the axle shaft splines, then lubricate them with grease.

2. Install the hub.

3. Install the hub washer with the "OUTSIDE" mark facing out.

4. Install the axle nut and tighten it to 43-58 ft. lbs.

5. Install a new cotter pin.

6. Install the wheel and tighten the wheel nuts in an "X" pattern to a torque of 14-18 ft. lbs.

7. Connect the rear brake cables and adjust the brake as outlined in "Maintenance."

HYDRAULIC FRONT FORKS

Removal

1. Remove the front wheel.

2. Remove the front wheel.

3. Loosen the lower fork tube pinch bolts.

4. Pull each fork tube down and out of the steering stem assembly.

Disassembly

1. Loosen the fork boot clamp and remove the rubber boot.

2. Press down on the fork cap and remove the snap- ring at the top of the fork leg.

CAUTION: *The cap is under spring pressure. Release it gradually after the snap-ring is removed.*

3. Remove the fork cap.

4. Remove the short upper spring, the washer and the longer lower spring.

5. Pour out and discard the fork oil. Purge the fork leg by pumping it several times.

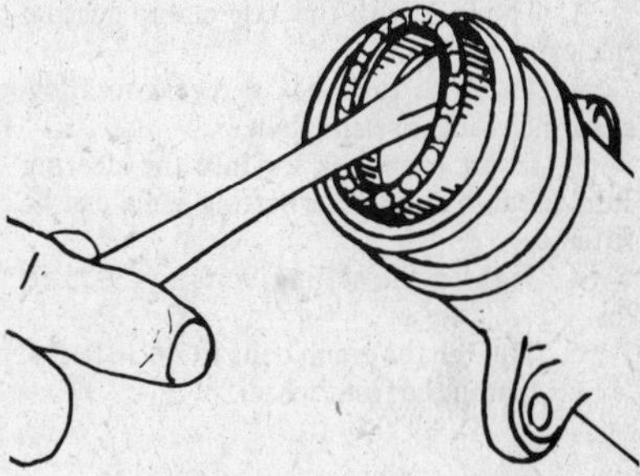

Removing a fork slider oil seal

6. Remove the bolt at the bottom of the fork slider. If the bolt turns but will not thread out, reinstall the springs and cap which may hold the damper in place and allow the slider bolt to be loosened.

7. Remove the damper assembly, rebound spring and oil lock piece.

8. Separate the slider and fork tube.

9. Remove the dust seal from the top of the slider.

10. Remove the slider oil seal snap-ring.

11. Pry out the oil seal. New seals must always be used when assembling.

Inspection

1. Clean all metal parts in a safe solvent.

2. Check fork spring free-length. Fork springs should be replaced as a set (both springs, both fork legs) if any one of them measures less than the serviceable limit. Service limits are 76.1mm (3.00 in.) for the short spring and 230.3mm (8.07 in.) for the long spring.

3. Check the fork tubes for a bent condition, accident damage such as dings,

scratched or corroded plating, etc. Maximum allowable tube run-out is 0.20mm (0.008 in.).

4. Check the condition of the fork cap O-rings and replace if necessary.

Assembly

1. Slip the rebound spring onto the damper.
2. Install the damper assembly into the fork tube.
3. Install the oil lock piece on the end of the damper.
4. Press new oil seals into the top of the sliders. Install the snap-rings. Seals must be driven straight in, not cocked or tilted, and must be seated.
5. Lubricate the seal lips with ATF before installing the sliders.
6. Slip the slider onto the fork tube.
7. Tighten the slider bolt to 11-18 ft. lbs.
8. Install the dust seal.
9. Add 88 cc (3.0 oz.) of ATF to each fork leg.
10. Compress the fork legs and measure the distance from the top of each tube to the oil. It should be 137mm (5.4 in.). Be sure that the level is the same for both fork legs.
11. Install the long fork spring, the seat washer and the short spring.
12. Lubricate the fork cap O-rings. Install the cap, compressing the springs enough to allow the snap-ring to be installed.
13. Install the boot.

Installation

1. The fork with the axle clamp goes on the left.
2. The fork tube has a recess to allow clearance for the setting bolt.
3. Insert each fork leg into the steering stem assembly until the setting bolts can be fitted.
4. Tighten the setting bolts to 29-36 ft. lbs.
5. Tighten the pinch bolts to 29-36 ft. lbs.
6. Install the front wheel.

HANDLEBARS

Removal

1. Remove the headlight from the housing.
2. Disconnect the wiring.
3. Remove the housing mounting bolts. Remove the housing. This is only necessary if the steering stem is to be removed.
4. Remove the electrical wiring clamps on the handlebars.
5. Remove the throttle lever housing.
6. Remove the brake levers.
7. Loosen the choke cable nut and remove the choke cable from the handlebar upper holder (if fitted).
8. Remove the upper holder cover cap, if fitted.
9. Remove the cover screws and cover, if fitted.
10. Remove the handlebar clamps (early models) or holder. Remove the handlebars.

Installation

1. Reverse the removal procedure.
2. The handlebars have punch marks for location. Align the punch marks with the top surface of the holders.
3. Clamps (early models) may have a punch mark near one of the bolt holes. This must face the front of the machine.
4. Tighten the forward clamp or holder bolts first, then the rear bolts.
5. Models using single clamps should have bolts torqued to 5-10 ft. lbs. Models with a one-piece holder should have bolts torqued to 13-22 ft. lbs.
6. Some models have hand lever clamps fitted with a punch mark for location. The punch marks should be up.

STEERING STEM

Removal

1. Remove the headlight.
2. Remove the headlight case.
3. Remove the handlebars.
4. Remove the front wheel.
5. On hydraulic fork models, remove the fork legs.
6. Remove the front fender.
7. Remove the headlight case brackets.
8. Remove the steering stem nut.
9. Remove the bolts above the fork tubes.
10. Remove the upper triple clamp.
11. Holding the steering stem from the bottom, unscrew and remove the bearing adjustment nut.
12. Carefully lower the assembly out of the frame lug, watching that the bearings in the lower race do not drop out.

Inspection

1. Clean bearing balls and races in solvent to remove the old grease.
2. Check the balls for pitting, corrosion and rust, flat spots or other signs of damage. Balls must be replaced in sets.
3. Run a finger around the races and be sure they are smooth and featureless. Ripples, dents, pitted surfaces, etc., mean that the races must be replaced along with the balls.
4. The steering stem lower race can be pried off with a chisel if it resists removal.
5. Frame races can be driven out with a suitable punch by reaching through the frame lug.
6. Drive new frame races into place with a drift. Races must be driven straight in, not cocked or tilted.

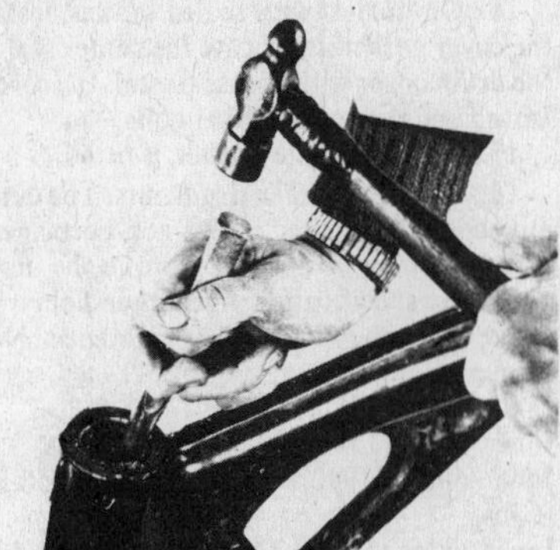

Driving out frame steering head bearing races

Installation

1. Twenty-one (21) balls are used in each race. Be sure all are in place.
2. Smear the steering stem race and the upper frame race with a good grade of waterproof, medium-weight bearing grease.
3. Embed 21 balls in each race.
4. Slip the steering stem assembly up and into the frame, install the top cone race and thread on the adjustment nut. Be sure that the lower race balls do not drop out when installing the steering stem.
5. Tighten the adjustment nut just enough to remove all play from the steering stem, but not so much as to restrict free movement side-to-side. If lateral movement of the assembly is stiff, back the adjustment nut off slightly.
6. The remainder of the procedure is the reverse of removal. Tighten the steering stem nut to 36-51 ft. lbs. On solid forks, tighten the fork tube upper triple clamp bolts to 29-35 ft. lbs. On hydraulic forks, tighten the fork tube upper triple clamp bolts to 36-51 ft. lbs. If the handlebar holder nuts were removed, tighten them to 29-35 ft. lbs.

REAR AXLE

NOTE: *Service procedures will vary slightly depending on model. Later versions have a sealed rear brake system with a number of gaskets and O-rings not incorporated into early machines. Be aware of this in the following procedures.*

Removal

1. Remove the seat.
2. Remove the rear fenders.
3. Remove the skid plate mounting bolts and the skid plate.
4. Support the rear end of the vehicle with safe, sturdy stands placed beneath the frame.
5. Remove the rear wheel nuts and take off the wheels.
6. Remove the axle nut cotter pins.
7. Remove the axle nuts and washers.
8. Pull the hubs off the axle.
9. Disconnect the carburetor overflow tube from the clamps on the chain case, if fitted.
10. Remove the three bolts securing the seal cover around the rear axle and take off the cover.
11. Remove the chain case mounting bolts.
12. Undo the clamps.
13. Remove the outer chain case half.
14. Back off the rear brake adjuster nuts.
15. Loosen the drive chain adjuster nut.
16. Loosen the four bearing holder mounting bolts.
17. Disconnect the drive chain. Be sure to remove the masterlink spring clip with a pliers. Prying the clip off will make it unusable. Put the masterlink on one end of the chain to avoid loss.
18. Remove the two brake drum nuts from the axle.
19. Remove the washer, if equipped.
20. On models with a sealed rear brake system, remove the brake drum cover bolts. Remove the cover. Remove the O-ring from the axle.
21. Pull off the brake drum.
22. Remove the remaining axle O-ring on models with a sealed brake system.
23. Use a plastic mallet to drive the axle out from the right side.

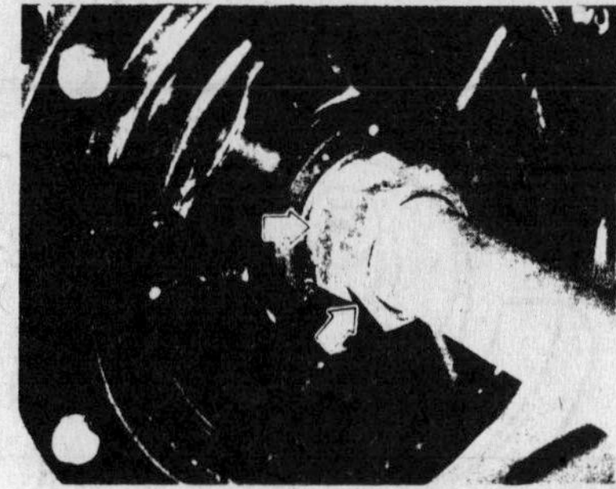
Brake drum nuts

24. Remove the chain slider.
25. Remove the chain case inner half bolts. Remove the case half.
26. Remove the rear brake adjuster nuts and disconnect the cables from the levers.
27. Remove the four rear bearing holder bolts.
28. Remove the bearing holder from the frame.

Inspection

AXLE

1. Check sprocket condition.
2. To remove the sprocket on early models, remove the driven flange bolts and the damper holder bolts.
3. To remove the sprocket on later models, remove the O-ring from the axle. Remove the four damper cover nuts, the damper cover and the snap-ring.
4. Check the dampers for damage.
5. Check all axle splines for condition.
6. Check axle run-out. When measured in the middle of the axle, the serviceable limit for run-out is 3.0mm (0.12 in.). This is 1/2 of the Total Indicated Reading of the gauge.
7. Check the condition of the O-ring behind the axle flange (if fitted) and replace it if necessary.
8. Assembly is the reverse of disassembly. Grease axle splines before installation. Lubricate the O-ring before fitting it to the axle. Tighten the damper nuts to 17-22 ft. lbs. (late models) or the damper bolts to 15-20 ft. lbs. (early models).

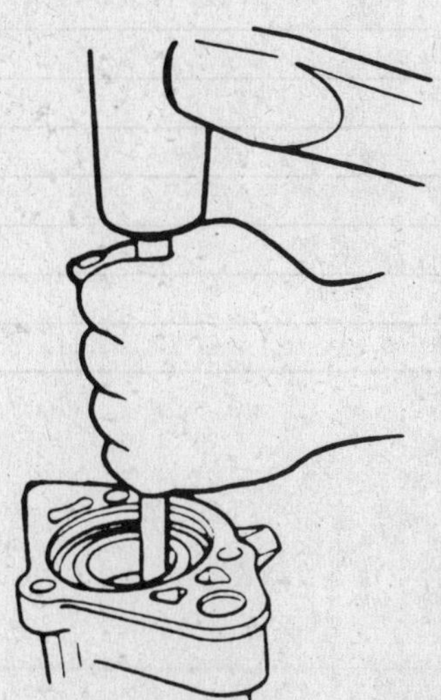
Removing an axle bearing from the holder

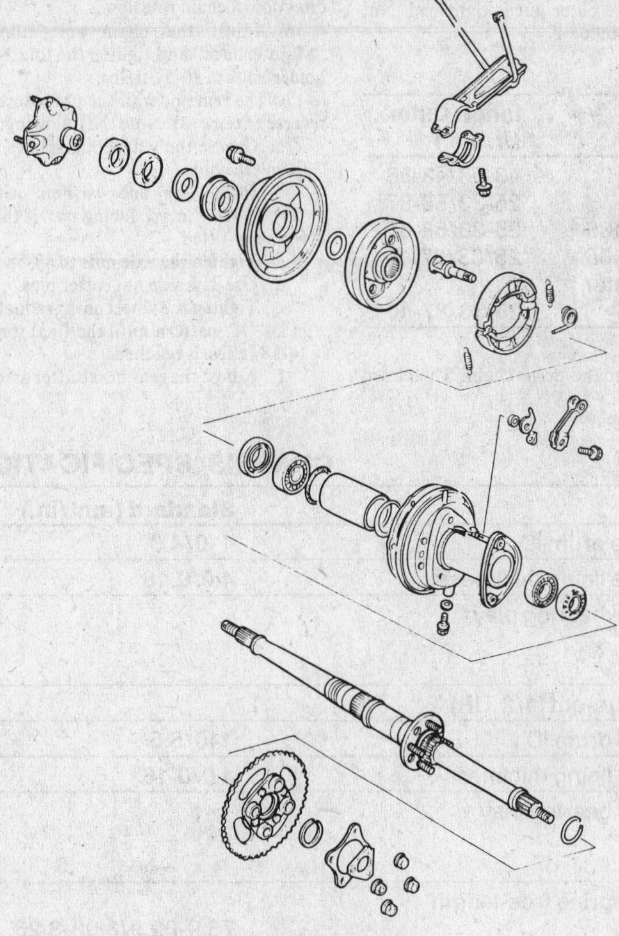
Rear axle assembly

BEARING HOLDER

1. Pry out the grease seals on either side.
2. Remove the bearing O-rings, if fitted.
3. Bearings should be checked in place, since removal will usually damage them.
4. Check for excessive play of the inner race relative to the outer. Maximum allowable radial (up- and-down) play is 0.05mm (0.002 in.). Maximum allowable axial (in-and-out) play is 0.10mm (0.004 in.).
5. Check the bearings for rough or binding rotation, excessive noise, etc.
6. Replace bearings in sets.
7. Bearings can be removed by driving them out with a hammer and suitable drift. Remove one bearing and take out the spacer and any shims. Drive out the remaining bearing.
8. Pack new bearings with a good grade of medium- weight bearing grease. Place a quantity of the lubricant in the bearing holder as well.
9. Install bearings with the marked side out.
10. Install the right side bearing first, driving it straight in with a suitably sized bearing driver until it is firmly seated.
11. Install the spacer along with any shims which may be fitted.
12. Install the remaining bearing.
13. Lubricate and install the bearing O-rings if fitted.
14. Press the grease seals straight into the holder.
15. Lubricate seal lips before installation.

Installation

1. Install the bearing holder and fit the four bolts, but do not tighten them yet since the chain must be readjusted.
2. Fit the chain adjuster nut.
3. Connect the brake cables.
4. Install the inner chain case half.
5. Lubricate and install the left-side axle O-ring.
6. Install the axle from the left side of the machine.
7. Lubricate and install the right-side axle O- ring.
8. Check that the brake shoe assembly is in place.
9. Install the brake drum.
10. Install the brake drum O-ring, if fitted.
11. On models with a sealed brake system, lubricate the center seal of the brake drum cover. Install the cover and secure it with the six bolts.
12. Clean the axle threads thoroughly.
13. Install the axle washer, if fitted.
14. Install the brake drum nuts. The outer nut should be secured with a non-permanent thread-locking compound. Torque the inner

nut to the specification given, then hold it in place while the outer nut is tightened. Nut torques are as follows:

Model year	Inner/Outer (ft. lbs.)
1980	43-58/43-58
1981	25-33/58-87
1982 ATC 185	25-33/58-87
1983 ATC 185	25/33/87-101
1982 and later ATC 200	25-33/87-101

15. Connect the drive chain. The closed end of the masterlink spring clip must face the direction of chain rotation.

16. Adjust the chain as outlined in "Maintenance" and tighten the four bearing holder bolts to 36-51 ft. lbs.

17. The remainder of the procedure is the reverse of removal. Note the following:

a. Grease the wheel hub splines before fitting the hubs.

b. Install the hub washers with the "OUTSIDE" mark facing out, if this type washer is fitted.

c. Tighten the axle nuts to 43-58 ft. lbs.

d. Use new axle nut cotter pins.

e. Tighten the wheel nuts gradually and in an "X" pattern until the final torque of 14-18 ft. lbs. is reached.

f. Adjust the rear brake after assembly.

Install axle nut washers with the mark facing out

CHASSIS SPECIFICATIONS

Part	Standard (mm/in.)	Service limit (mm/in.)
Front brake drum ID	110/4.3	111/4.4
Front brake lining thickness	4.0/0.16	2.0/0.08
Front wheel bearing play		
Axial	—	0.10/0.004
Radial	—	0.05/0.002
Rear axle run-out (1/2 TIR)	—	3.0/0.12
Rear brake drum ID	140/5.5	141/5.6
Rear brake lining thickness	4.0/0.16	2.0/0.08
Rear wheel bearing play		
Axial	—	0.10/0.004
Radial	—	0.05/0.002
Front fork spring free-length		
Short	76.9-82.9/3.03-3.26	76.1/3.00
Long	232.7-238.7/9.16-9.40	230.3/9.07

GENERAL TORQUE SPECIFICATIONS①

Part	Torque (ft. lbs.)
5 mm screws	2.5-3.6
6 mm screws	5-8
5 mm bolts, nuts	3.5-4.5
6 mm bolts, nuts	6-9
8 mm bolts, nuts	13-18
10 mm bolts, nuts	22-29
12 mm bolts, nuts	36-43
6 mm bolt w/8 mm head	5-8
6 mm flange bolts, nuts	7-10
8 mm flange bolts, nuts	17-22
10 mm flange bolts, nuts	25-33

① Unless otherwise noted

CHASSIS TORQUE SPECIFICATIONS

Part	Torque (ft. lbs.)
Front axle nuts (1980-82)	36-51
Front axle (1983 and later)	51-80
Front brake anchor bolt	15-20
Front fork axle cap nuts (1983 and later)	7-10
Rear wheel nuts	14-18
Front wheel hub nuts	14-18
Front brake drum bolts	14-18
Brake drum nuts (inner/outer)	
1980	43-58/43-58*
1981	25-33/58-87*
1982 ATC 185	25-33/58-87*
1983 ATC 185	25-33/87-101*
1982-On ATC 200	25-33/87-101*
Rear axle nuts	43-58
Fork slider bolts	11-18
Fork setting bolts	29-36
Fork pinch bolts	29-36
Handlebar clamp bolts (two)	5-10
Handlebar holder (one-piece)	13-22
Handlebar holder nuts	29-35
Steering stem nut	36-51
Upper triple clamp bolts	
Solid forks	29-35
Hydraulic forks	36-51
Sprocket damper nuts (late models)	17-22
Sprocket damper bolts (early models)	15-20
Bearing holder bolts	36-51
Drive chain slider nuts (early)	5-7
Rear brake adjuster bolt	36-51
Front engine bracket nuts (10mm)	29-35
Front engine bracket nuts (8mm)	17-20
Rear engine bracket nuts	29-35
Cylinder head bracket nut	14-18

*Secure outer nut with non-permanent thread-locking compound

Honda TRX 125

INDEX

GENERAL SPECIFICATIONS

DIMENSIONS	
Overall length	1600mm/63.0 in.
Overall width	980mm/38.6 in.
Overall height	970mm/38.2 in.
Wheelbase	1050mm/41.3 in.
Track (F&R)	710mm/27.9 in.
Seat height	670mm/26.3 in.
Ground clearance	110mm/4.3 in.
ENGINE	
Bore x Stroke	55mm × 52.2mm/2.16 in. × 2.05 in.
Displacement	124cc/7.6 ci
Compression ration	8.8:1
Lubrication system	wet sump
TRANSMISSION	
Type	4-speed, constant mesh
Clutch	Wet, multi-plate automatic
Primary reduction	3.722
Final reduction	3.846 (13/50)
Gear ratios	
SL	3.403
1st	2.462
2nd	1.556
3rd	1.190
4th	0.958
Reverse	4.376
CHASSIS	
Front tire size	20 × 7.00-8
Rear tire size	22 × 11.00-8
Caster	10°
Camber	9°
Trail	38mm/1.50 in.
Dry weight	143.8 kg/316.4 lbs.
Fuel capacity	7.3L/1.9 gal.

SERIAL NUMBER LOCATIONS

To avoid confusion when ordering parts, always supply the frame and engine serial numbers.

The frame serial number is stamped onto the left side bottom frame tube near the footpeg.

The engine serial number is stamped onto the lower left side of the crankcase behind the gearshift lever.

MAINTENANCE

NOTE: *Common maintenance procedures are explained in detail in the "General Information" section of this manual.*

LUBRICATION

Checking Oil

1. Oil level should be checked before each ride.
2. A dipstick is fitted to the oil filler cap on the right crankcase cover.
3. Park the machine on a level surface.
4. Start the engine, allow it to idle for several minutes, then shut it off and let it sit for a minute or so.
5. Unscrew and remove the dipstick and wipe it clean.

Maintain oil level between the dipstick upper and lower level marks (A and B)

6. Insert the dipstick, allowing the cap to rest on top of the threads of the hole. Do not screw it in when checking oil level.
7. The oil level should be between the minimum and maximum marks on the dipstick.
8. If level is too low, add enough oil to bring it up to the specified level.

CAUTION: *Do not overfill the crankcase.*

Changing Oil

1. Oil should be changed every 30 operating days if the machine is used under normal operating conditions.

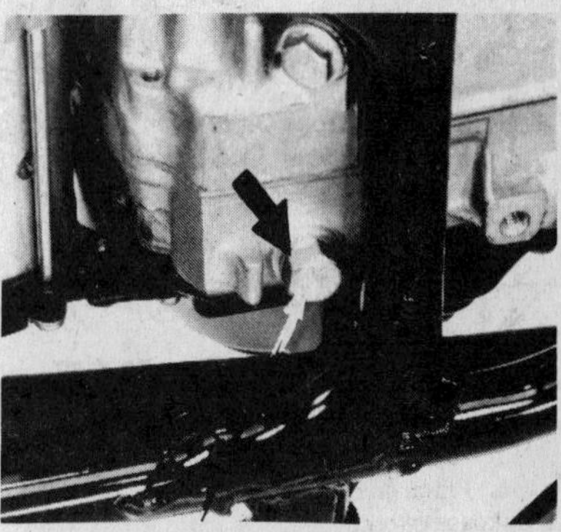

Crankcase drain plug

2. At the same time the oil is changed, the oil filter screen and centrifugal filter should be cleaned. See "Oil Filters," below.
3. Oil should be API service rated "SE" or "SF." SAE 20W-40 or 20W-50 can be used when average air temperature is above freezing (32°F). Refer to the "Recommended Lubricants" chart for all temperature oil recommendations.
4. Run the machine until the engine reaches operating temperature.
5. Park the machine on a level surface.
6. Place a container of over 1 qt. capacity beneath the engine.
7. Remove the dipstick.

8. Remove the oil drain plug. Allow the oil to drain for several minutes.

9. With the ignition or kill switch "OFF," turn the engine over with the recoil starter. This will allow more of the oil to drain out.

10. Check the condition of the drain plug washer. Replace it if damaged.

11. Clean the threads of the drain plug. Install the plug and tighten it securely.

12. Clean the oil filters. See below.

13. Add a little more than a quart of the correct grade of oil. Capacity after a routine change is 1.1 qts. (1 L).

14. Check oil level as outlined above.

15. Start the engine and lit it run for a minute or so. Check for leaks. Recheck level and top up if necessary.

NOTE: *The oil change interval is based on normal operating conditions. If the machine is used under severe conditions (i.e. racing, high-speed riding, stop-and-go commercial use, industy environments, cold weather, etc.), changes should be made more frequently. This is especially true if the vehicle is used infrequently such as during the winter months.*

Oil Filters

1. The machine is fitted with a centrifugal filter in the clutch housing. An oil filter screen is located in a slot beneath the clutch.

2. The filters should be cleaned each time the oil is changed, which will be every 30 operating days under normal conditions.

3. Have clutch outer cover gasket and a crankcase cover gasket onhand. These items should be replaced.

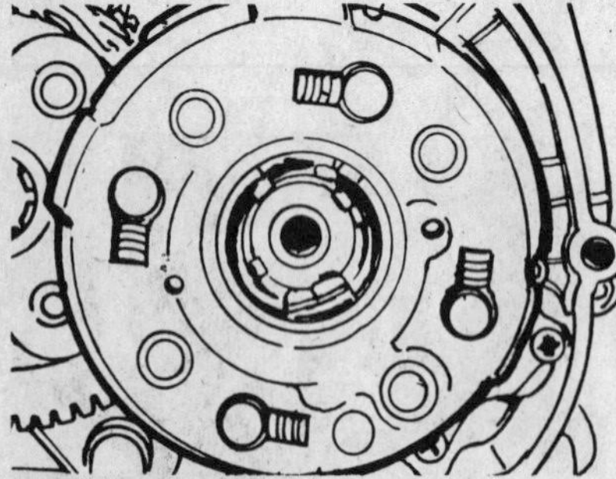

Centrifugal oil filter in clutch housing

4. Drain the oil as outlined below.

5. Install the drain plug.

6. Place a drip pan beneath the right crankcase cover.

7. Remove the starter motor bracket screws.

8. Remove the right crankcase cover screws. Remove the cover. If it is stuck, tap it with a plastic mallet to break it free.

9. Remove the ball retainer and clutch cam plate side spring.

10. Remove the oil passage pipe and spring from the center of the clutch.

11. Remove the clutch cam plate.

12. Remove the clutch lever.

13. Remove the clutch outer cover screws (2).

14. Using a clean, lift-free rag, wipe the center of the clutch housing to remove any foreign matter.

15. Install the clutch outer cover and bearing. Using a new cover gasket is recommended.

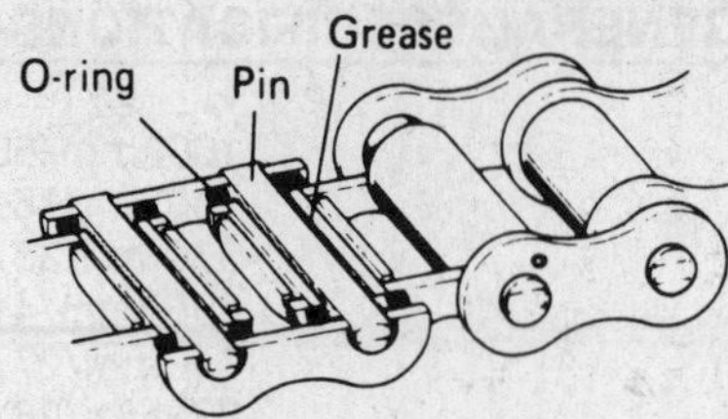

Drive chain construction

16. Install the cam plate.

17. Install the clutch lever.

18. Clean the oil passage pipe and spring in a clean solvent, dry them, lubricate lightly and re-install.

19. Install the cam plate side spring and ball retainer, aligning the steel ball with the centerline of the clutch lever.

20. Remove the oil filter screen from its slot below the clutch.

21. Clean the screen in a clean solvent to remove any foreign matter.

22. Check the residue for metal particles. If there are any, it indicates that severe engine wear is taking place. Determine the cause before operating the machine.

23. If the screen cannot be cleaned, or if it is punctured or shows other signs of damage, replace it.

24. Install the screen.

25. Check that the two locating dowel pins are in place on the crankcase cover mating surface.

26. Install a new crankcase cover gasket.

27. Install the crankcase cover. Tighten the screws gradually and evenly.

28. Add oil as directed under "Changing Oil," above. Check level. Start the engine and check for leaks. Crankcase capacity is 1.1 qts. for a routine change.

29. After the machine has been sitting for a minute, make a final level check and top up the crankcase if necessary.

Drive Chain

1. The drive chain can be cleaned and lubricated through the inspection cap on the side of the chain case or through the lubrication cap on top of the case.

2. The chain is fitted with rubber O-rings to seal in grease around the pins. It should therefore only be cleaned with kerosene. Gasoline or other petroleum- based solvents will damage the O-rings.

3. The chain should be lubricated with motor oil or with commercially available spray chain lubes which are compatible with rubber O-ring chains. Do not use chain lubes unless this is clearly stated on the container.

4. Chain service interval is every 30 operating days.

Chassis Lubrication

1. Chassis lubrication points include wheel and steering head bearings, front suspension kingpins, brake cams and brake pedal pivot.

2. Bearings should be lubricated with a good grade of wataerproof, medium weight bearing grease. Other points can take general purpose chassis grease.

3. The service interval for these points is every year. See "Chassis"for teardown procedures.

4. Control cables and other sliding sur-

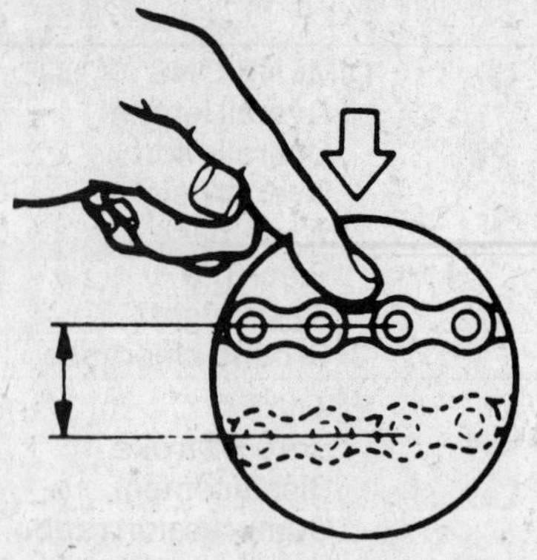

Checking drive chain free-play (3/8-3/4 in.)

faces should be lubricated every 30 operating days undernormal conditions.

SERVICE CHECKS AND ADJUSTMENTS

Drive Chain

1. The drive chain should have 10-20mm (3/8-3/4 in.) of total up-and-down free-play. This is measured at the chain case inspection hole after removing the rubber cap.

2. Before checking or adjusting the chain, the following conditions should be met:

a. The chain should be clean and well lubricated. Dirth chains tend to get tight;

b. The chain should have been checked for tight spots by slowly rotating the wheels and checking for variances in tension. If a tight spot exists, the chain free-play should be adjusted to the proper specification at that point. Note, however, that such a condition is indicative of a worn chain and probably worn sprockets which should be inspected and replaced as soon as possible.

3. Be sure the transmmission is in Neutral.

4. Check chain free-play after removing the chain case inspection hole cap.

5. Loosen the four rear wheel bearing holder bolts.

6. Turn the adjusting nut as required until free-play is correct.

7. Tighten the bearing holder bolts. Proper torque is 51-58 ft. lbs.

8. Recheck chain free-play.

9. Adjust the rear brake.

Chain Wear

1. Chain wear can be estimated by measuring the distance between pins after the chain is removed.

2. A clean chain must not exceed 513mm (20.2 in.) between 41 pins. If it does, it must be replaced.

3. New chain 41-pin distance is 508mm (20.0 in.).

4. Before measuring the distance, ensure that the chain is stretched out by hand to the fullest possible length.

Clutch

1. Clutch operation must meet the following standards:

a. The vehicle must go into First gear smoothly without a jolt or stalling;

b. The machine must begin to move smoothly as the throttle is opened and mov-

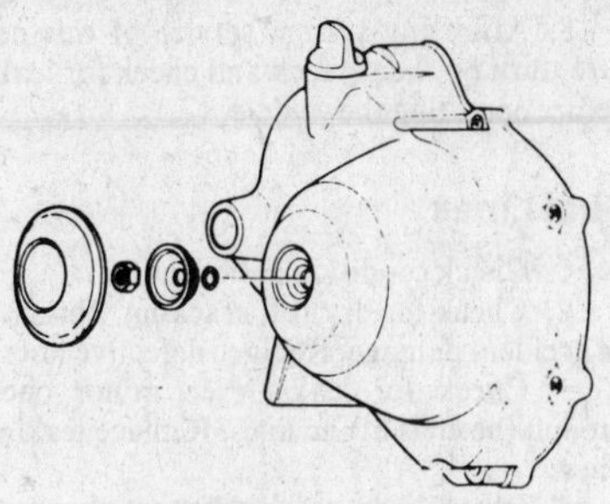
Clutch adjusting screw

ing performance must not indicate power loss and slippage through the clutch.

2. Under normal operating conditions, the clutch should be adjusted every 30 operating days.
3. Engine must be OFF.
4. Remove the clutch adjuster cap from the right crankcase cover.
5. Loosen the adjusting screw locknut.
6. Turn the adjustiing screw one full turn clockwise.
7. Slowly turn the adjusting screw counterclockwise until resistance is felt.
8. Back the adjusting screw off 1/8 turn clockwise.
9. Hold the adjusting screw in place and tighten the locknut to 14-18 ft. lbs.
10. Install the cap.
11. Check clutch operation.

Throttle Cable

1. Throttle operation and cable free-play are important safety items which should be attended to without fail. Operation of the throttle should be checked each time before the machine is ridden. The cable adjustment should be checked every 30 operating days.
2. The tip of the throttle lever should move 5-10mm (3/16-3/8 in.) before the throttle slide begins to open.
3. Adjusters are fitted to both ends of the cable. Make minor adjustments with the adjuster at the lever. For major adjustments, use the adjuster on the carburetor. Removal of the gas tank will be necessary. It is better to use the major adjuster once the handlebar adjuster has used up about half of its range.
4. With the engine idling, turn the handlebars slowly from lock to lock and listen for any change in engine speed. If this happens, the throttle cable is either too tightly adjusted or is binding somewhere along its routing.
5. Check that the throttle lever returns to the closed position regardless of the position of the handlebars. If it seems to hang up at one point or an other, check cable free-play, cable routing and cable and throttle lever lubrication.

Front Brake

1. The tip of the hand lever should have 15-20mm (5/8-3/4 in.) of free movement before the linings contact the drum.
2. Adjust, if necessary, by turning the adjusters at the wheels in until lever free-play is correct.

CAUTION: *turn the adjusters an equal number of turns to ensure equal braking on the two wheels. If proper cable operation cannot be obtained, adjust the primary and secondary cables as outlined in "Chassis."*

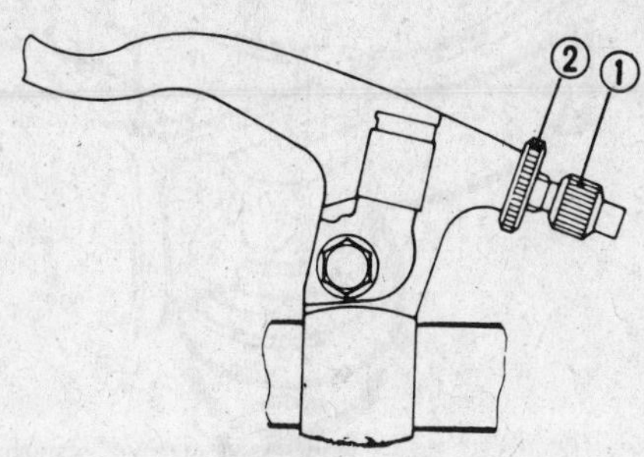

Rear brake adjuster (1) and locknut (2)

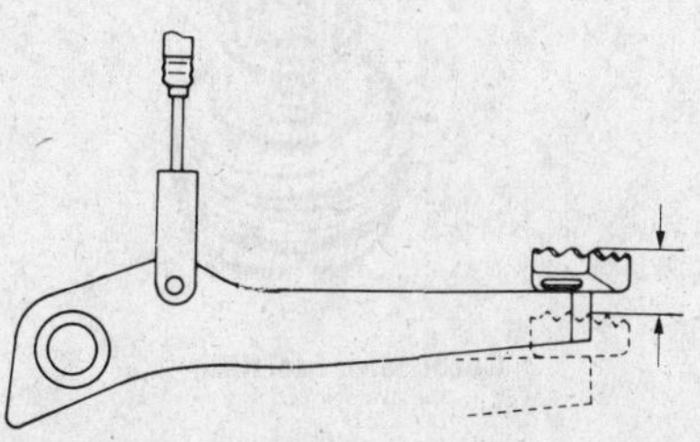
Rear brake pedal should have ⅝-¾ in. of free movement before the linings contact the drum

3. When the brakes are fully applied, check the wear indicators on the drums. If the index marks align, replace the brake shoes. See "Chassis."

Rear Brake

1. The tip of the rear brake hand lever should have 15-20mm (5/8-3/4 in.) of free movement before the linings contact the drum.
2. Use the adjuster at the hand lever for minor corrections.
3. Use the adjuster at the foot pedal for major corrections.
4. The foot pedal should have 15-20mm (5/8-3/4 in.) of free movement before the linings contact the drum. This free-play is measured at the tip of the pedal.
5. use the adjuster on the cable at the brake drum to give the correct pedal travel.

CAUTION: *Unless the brake pedal is properly adjusted, the hand lever will not be effective.*

6. When the brakes are fully applied, check the wear indicator on the drum. If the index marks align, replace the brake shoes. See "Chassis."

Reverse Cable

1. The Reverse lever cable should have 2-4mm (5/64-5/32 in.) of free-play. This is measured between the hand lever and the lever holder.
2. Make the adjustment by using the adjuster at the Reverse lever on the engine.

Tires

1. Periodically check each tire for cuts, embedded matter, excessive tread wear.
2. Tire pressures must be checked when the tires are cold. A special low pressure gauge is needed for accurate readings.
3. Proper tire pressures are 2.9 psi, front and 2.2 psi rear.

CAUTION: *Never apply high pressure air sources to the tire valves. Service station hoses are generally unsuitable for filling these low pressure tires.*

Steering Head Bearings

1. Bearing wear and adjustment should be checked periodically.
2. Raise the front end of the machine off the ground by placing a safe, sturdy support beneath the frame.
3. Turn the handlebars slowly from lock to lock.
4. Check for binding, rough rotation and/or bearing noise as the wheels are turned. If any is noted, adjust the bearings as outlined in "Chassis."

FUEL SYSTEM

Fuel system maintenance involves cleaning the filter, cleaning or replacing the air filter and cleaning the carburetor. These procedures should be carried out every 30 operating days.

Air Filter

1. Remove the seat.
2. Remove the four wing bolts on the air cleaner case cover.
3. Remove the cover.
4. Unscrew and remove the wing bolt at the back of the filter element.

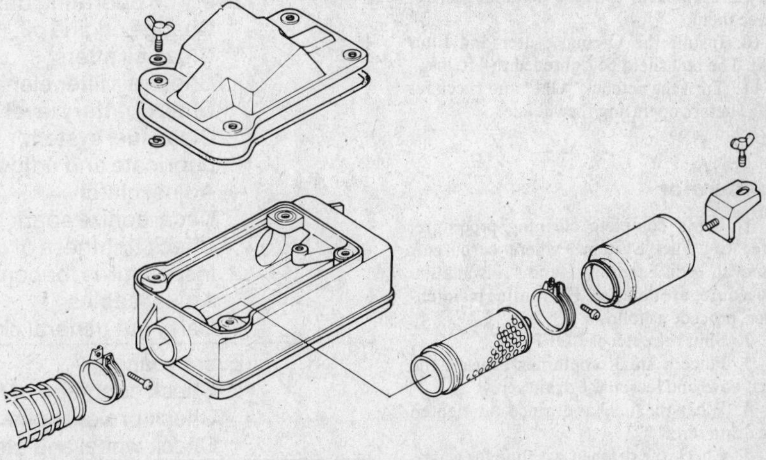
Air filter assembly

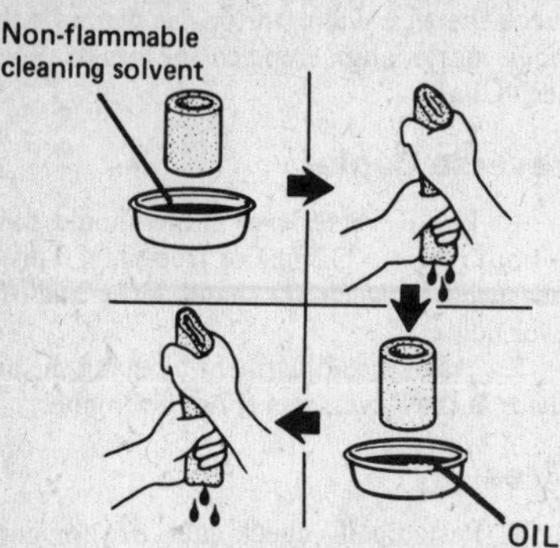

Cleaning and lubricating the filter element

5. Loosen the clamp at the front of the element.
6. Remove the element from the case.
7. Carefully separate the element from its frame.
8. Wash the element in a safe, non-flammable solvent. Squeeze it to dry thoroughly.

CAUTION: *Do not wring the element out as the pores or fabric may be damaged.*

9. Soak the element in SAE 80 or 90 gear oil. Squeeze off the excess.
10. Fit the element on the frame and install the assembly in the case.

Fuel Filter

1. The fuel filter screen is fitted to the carburetor float bowl/petcock.
2. Turn the petcock "OFF."
3. Place a rag beneath the carburetor to soak up the small amount of gasoline which will spill out.
4. Remove the fuel filter bolt.
5. Remove the filter.
6. Remove the filter bolt O-ring if it stayed in the carburetor.
7. Clean the inside of the filter bolt in solvent.
8. Clean the filter in solvent. If the filter cannot be cleaned or is crushed, punctured or otherwise ineffective, replace it.
9. Check the condition of the O-rings. If they are knicked, crushed or damaged, replace them.
10. Install the O-rings, filter and filter bolt. The bolt shold be tightened to 4 ft. lbs.
11. Turn the petcock "ON" and check for leaks before operating the vehicle.

Carburetor

1. For a complete cleaning procedure, refer to "Fuel System" where carburetor removal, disassembly and installation procedures are detailed. For routine maintenance, procede as follows.
2. Shut the petcock "OFF."
3. Place a small container beneath the float bowl and loosen the drain screw.
4. When the fuel has drained out, tighten the drain screw.
5. Check the drained gasoline for water, dirt or other foreign matter. If considerable amounts are present, check the fuel filter screen.
6. Turn the petcock "ON" and allow the float bowl to fill up. Shut the petcock "OFF." Drain the float bowl as before. Inspect the fuel sample for foreign matter. If any is still present, check the fuel filter. Remove the gas tank and drain off the fuel. Check it for dirt and water. Flush out the tank before installing it.
7. If fuel flow out of the bowl seems sluggish, remove the gas cap. If flow increases, the problem is a clogged cap vent. If not, check for a clogged filter.

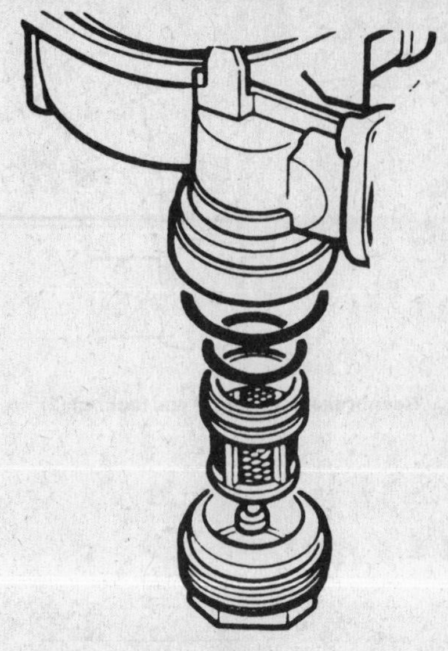

Carburetor fuel filter

8. After any system service of this nature, turn on the petcock and check for leaks before operating the vehicle.

Fuel Lines

1. Check condition periodically.
2. Check for dry rot, cracking, abrasion or accident damage. Replace defective lines.
3. Check for leaks, even minor ones, around the ends of the lines. Replace leaking lines.
4. When lines are disconnected, check the ends for cracking or deterioration. Connections must be tight.
5. When lines are reconnected, be sure the safety clips are in place.
6. Check for fuel leaks before operating the machine any time lines are removed or replaced.

SPARK ARRESTOR

1. The spark arrestor should be decarbonized every 30 operating days. Excessive carbon buildup will cause sluggish performance and possible engine overheating.
2. Park the machine in an open area free of flammable material.
3. Remove the bolt and sealing washer from the end of the spark arrestor.
4. Start the engine and, after it reaches operating temperature, rev it several times to blow out the carbon.

CAUTION: *Hot carbon particles may represent a fire hazard if this procedure is carried out in an unsuitable location.*

5. Shut off the engine. After the exhaust system has cooled, install the bolt and sealing washer and tighten the bolt to 22-29 ft. lbs.

PERIODIC MAINTENANCE INTERVALS①

Before every ride
- Check engine oil level
- Check tire pressure
- Check throttle operation
- Check brake adjustment
- Check operation of lights

Every 30 operating days
- Change engine oil
- Clean oil filters
- Check air filter element
- Check battery level
- Clean fuel system
- Lubricate and adjust drive chain
- Adjust clutch
- Decarbonize spark arrestor
- Check tightness of critical fasteners
- Inspect tires for condition
- Adjust cables
- Carry out general chassis lubrication

Every year
- Check condition of fuel lines
- Check brake shoes
- Check wheel and steering head bearings

①Based on normal usage after initial break-in is completed

RECOMMENDED LUBRICANTS

Engine	
Above 32°F	SAE 20W-40, SAE 20W-50, service rated "SE" or "SF"
Above 18°F	SAE 10W-40, service rated "SE" or "SF"
18-85°F	SAE 10W-30, service rated "SE" or "SF"
Below 45°F	SAE 5W, service rated "SE" or "SF"
Drive chain	
Motor oil	
SAE 80 or 90 oil	
Commercial chain lube compatible with rubber	
Air filter	
SAE 80 or 90 gear oil	
Wheel and steering head Bearings	
Waterproof, medium-weight bearing grease	
Front suspension kingpins	
Waterproof, medium-weight chassis grease	
General lubrication	
Waterproof, medium-weight chassis grease	
Cables	
Light motor oil	
Commercial cables lubricants	
Molybdenum disulphide-based lubricant	

MAINTENANCE DATA

Engine oil capacity	
Routine change	1.1 qts./1.0 L
After rebuilding	1.3 qts./1.2 L
Tire pressure (f/r)	2.9/2.2 psi
Drive chain free-play	3/8-3/4 in./10-20mm
Fuel tank capacity	1.9 gal./7.3 L
Fuel reserve	0.2 gal./0.8 L
Battery	12V, 9ah

TUNE-UP

NOTE: *Common tune-up procedures are explained in detail in the "General Information" section of this manual.*
WARNING: *All tune-up procedures done with the engine running must be carried out with the machine on level ground in a well-ventilated area. The parking brake should be applied.*

Keep children and other innocents away from hot, running engines. Never leave the vehicle running and unattended.

COMPRESSION TEST

1. A compression check should be made before each tune-up since this will provide a general idea of engine condition.
2. It is necessary to have a guage with the proper adapter if a screw-in type gauge is used. The plug hole is 12mm. The less expensive "hold-in" type gauge can also be used. Oil the rubber tip to ensure a good seal.
3. The engine must be at operating temperature.
4. Be sure the choke is off.
5. Turn the ignition switch "ON." Set the kill button "OFF."
6. Fit the gauge. Push the throttle lever wide open and turn the engine over with the electric starter.
7. The highest gauge reading is the compression.
8. Standard compression is 178 ± 22 psi. The minimum acceptable reading is 128 psi.
9. Low compression may be caused by valves which are too tightly adjusted, burned or otherwise damaged, worn pistón rings, piston and/or cylinder or other worn engine components.
10. If the compression reading is too low, squirt some motor oil into the cylinder and repeat the test. If the gauge reading is higher, suspect worn rings, piston or cylinder as the cause. If the reading does not increase, suspect problems in the valve train.
11. If the test shows that compression is too high, the problem is likely due to carbon deposits on the piston crown and cylinder. Remove the cylinder head and decarbonize the top end.

CAM CHAIN TENSION

Cam chain tension is maintained automatically by a spring-loaded plunger operated by oil pressure. No routine adjustment is required.

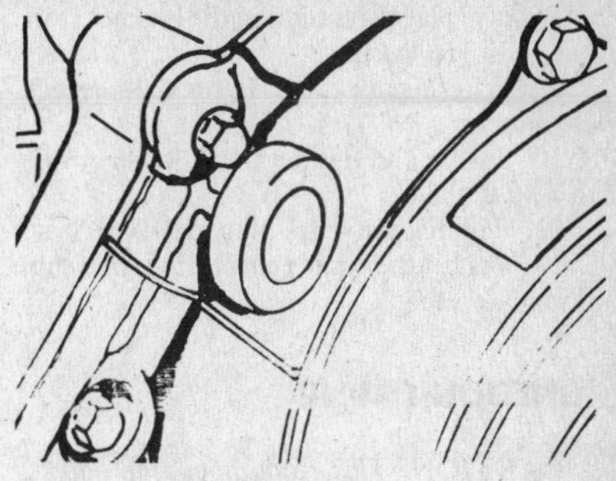

Timing inspection hole

VALVE ADJUSTMENT

NOTE: *Valves must be adjusted when the engine is cold.*

1. Remove the skid plate.
2. Remove the spark plug.
3. Remove the intake and exhaust valve adjuster covers.

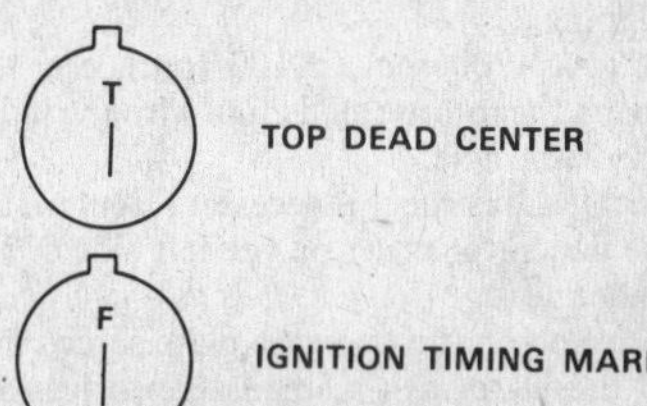

Rotor timing marks

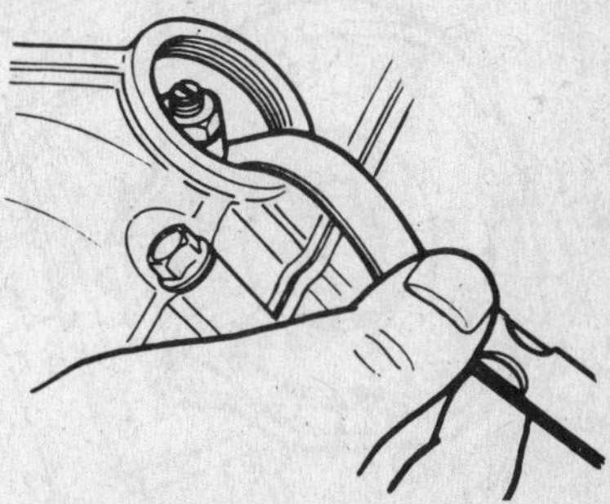

Checking valve clearance

4. Remove the timing inspection hole cap on the left crankcase cover.
5. Turn the engine over slowly with the recoil starter while watching the intake rocker arm. When the rocker arm opens the valve and then begins to close it, look through the timing inspection hole while continuing to turn the engine over. When the "T"mark on the rotor aligns with the index mark on the hole, stop. The piston should now be positioned at TDC on the compression stroke.
6. Check for rocker arm clearance at the valves. Each rocker arm should have a slight amount of free-play. If they do not, the piston is probably at TDC on the exhaust stroke. Turn the rotor 360°, align the "T" mark and check again.
7. Valve clearance is 0.07mm (0.003 in.) for both intake and exhause valves. A feeler gauge blade of this thickness should be a light slip fit between the valve and the adjuster.
8. If adjustment is necessary, loosen the adjuster locknut and turn the adjuster so that the feeler gauge blade is a slip fit. Hold the

adjuster in place and tighten the locknut (torque: 11-13 ft. lbs.).

9. After the locknut is tightened, recheck clearance.

10. Install and tighten the adjuster covers to 7-10 ft. lbs.

11. Tighten the spark plug to 9-14 ft. lbs.

12. Install the timing inspection hole cap, skid plate, etc.

IGNITION TIMING

CAUTION: *This running-engine adjustment must be carried out in a well-ventilated area. Be sure the vehicle is on a level surface and that the parking brake is set.*

1. Remove the timing inspection hole cap on the left crankcase cover.
2. Connect a timing light according to the light manufacturer's instructions.
3. Connect an electronic tachometer if idel speed is not known.
4. Observe the rotor timing marks through the inspection hole while the engine is running.
5. At 1700 rpm (±100 rpm), the "F" mark on the rotor should align with the index mark on the hole.
6. If adjustment is necessary, remove the pulse generator cover on the left side of the cylinder head.
7. Loosen the two base plate screws and turn the plate with a small screwdriver applied to the pry point until the "F" mark aligns with the index mark at 1700 rpm.

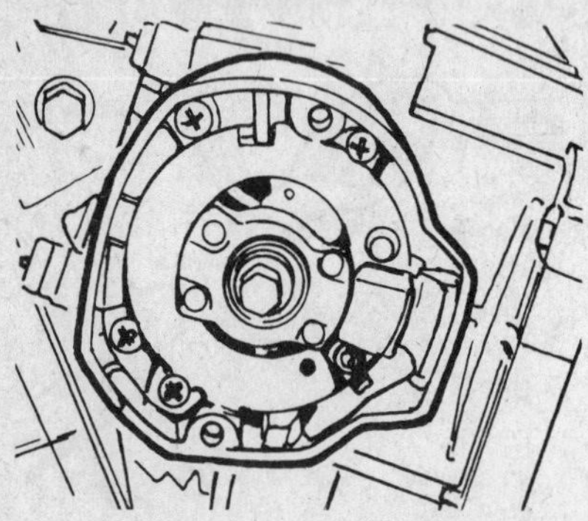

Base plate screws (arrows)

CARBURETOR

Float Level

1. Float level is not adjustable. Generally this item need not be checked until considerable mileage has been covered or fuel system problems arise.
2. Remove the carburetor as outlined in "Fuel System."
3. Remove the float bowl (2 screws).
4. Remove the float bowl gasket.
5. Float level is defined as the measured distance from the float bowl mating surface (gasket removed) to the top of the float when the float tang is just touching the end of the needle.
6. With the float held in this position, measure the distance from the mating surface to the top of the float. It should be 10.7mm (0.42 in.).
7. If the float level is not within 10% of this value, check for foreign matter on the needle tip or seat. Check for wear of and needle tip. Float, needle and seat, or all three must be replaced if the level is not correct.

Idle Speed And Mixture

NOTE: *These items must be adjusted when the engine is at operating temperature.*
CAUTION: *Park the machine on a level surface in a well-ventilated area and set the parking brake.*

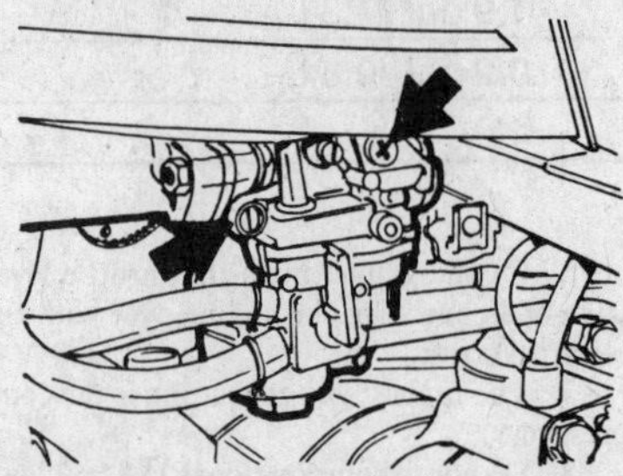

Carburetor pilot screw (left) and throttle stop screw (right)

1. Check that the throttle cable adjustment is correct so that the cable has enough slack to permit the throttle slide to close fully.
2. Screw the pilot in carefully until it is seated, then back it out 1 3/4 turns.
3. When the engine is at operating temperature, turn the throttle stop screw to achieve an idle speed as slow as is possible without stalling.
4. Turn the piliot screw in or out as required until the engine runs smoothly. It should not be necessary to turn the pilot screw more than 1/2 kturn in either direction from the specified setting.
5. Turn the throttle stop screw to achieve an idel speed of 1700 rpm.
6. Shut the engine off and adjust the throttle cable as outlined in "Maintenance."

NOTE: *If proper idling cannot be obtained using this method, it may be that the fuel system is clogged. Check petcock, filter screen, carburetor, gas cap vent. Other possible causes include a dirty or worn spark plug, a plug which is too cold, improperly adjusted valves or air leaks in the intake system.*

TUNE-UP SPECIFICATIONS

VALVE CLEARANCE	
Intake	0.07mm/0.003 in.
Exhaust	0.07mm/0.003 in.
SPARK PLUG	
OEM	NGK/ND/Champion
Type	DR8ES-L X24ESR-U RA6YC
Gap	0.6-0.7mm/0.024-0.028 in.
Torque	9-14 ft lbs.
IGNITION TIMING	
Initial	10° BTDC ± 2° @ 1700 rpm
Full advance	32° BTDC ± 2° @ 3400 rpm
CARBURETOR	
Idle speed	1700 ± 100 rpm
Pilot screw setting	1¾ turns out
Float height	10.7mm/0.42 in.
COMPRESSION	
Standard	178 ± 22 psi
Minimum	128 psi

ENGINE AND TRANSMISSION

NOTE: *Engine component removal and installation procedures are given in the following text. Specifications are in the chart at the end of this section. For service procedures and inspection techniques to valves, piston, clutch and other components, refer to "Engine Rebuilding" in the "General Information"section of this manual.*

ENGINE REMOVAL AND INSTALLATION

NOTE: *All engine components with the exception of the crankshift and transmission can be serviced without removing the engine from the frame.*

Before removing the engine:

a. Drain the oil.

b. Degrease the engine. Be especially attentive to the area around the cylinder base, the underside of the crankcase and around mating surfaces.

c. Drive chain masterlink spring clips should be removed with pliers. Do not pry the clip off with a screwdriver or it will be distorted and will have to be replaced. After disconnecting the chain, install the masterlink on one end of the chain to prevent loss.

d. When connecting drive chains, be certain to fit the spring clip with the closed end facing the direction of chain rotation.

1. Disconnect the spark plug lead and loosen the plug.
2. Remove the seat.
3. Be certain that the petcock is "OFF." Remove the two screws securing the petcock to the carburetor.

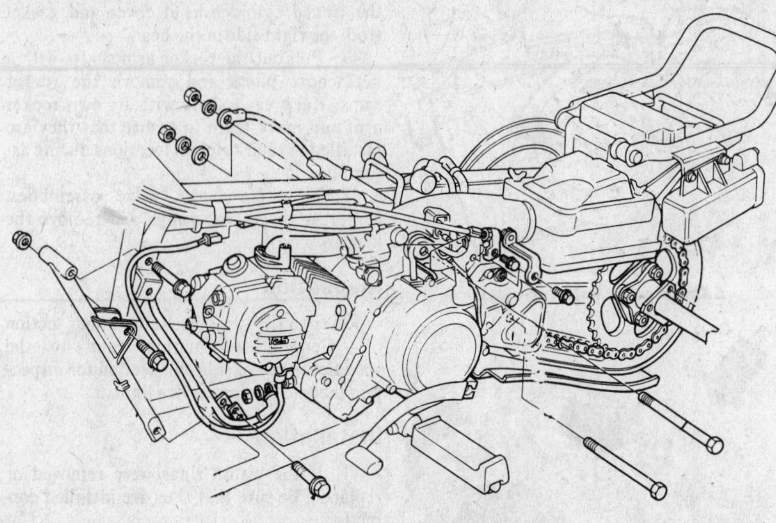
Engine mounting bolts

4. Remove the four nuts securing the front fender assembly to the gas tank.

5. Remove the mounting bolt at the rear of the tank. Remove the gas tank.

6. Disconnect the ground (negative) cable from the battery.

7. Place safety stands beneath the frame and raise the machine so that all four wheels are off the ground.

8. Remove the four wheels.

9. Remove the front carrier and inner fender fasteners. Remove the front fender assembly.

10. Disconnect the starter motor cable from the starter.

11. Locate the pulse generator wire plastic connector at the top frame tube. Disconnect the wiring.

12. Remove the starter motor and pulse generator wiring from the cylinder head and frame clamps.

13. Disconnect the Reverse cable from the lever on the engine.

14. Disconnect the choke cable from the carburetor.

15. Unscrew the carburetor cap and pull out the throttle slide assembly. Wrap the assembly in a clean, lint-free cloth and place it out of the way to avoid damage.

16. Loosen the air cleaner hose clamps and remove the hose.

17. Disconnect carburetor lines.

Closed end of the spring clip must face the direction of chain rotation

18. Remove the manifold bolts and remove the carburetor and manifold from the cylinder head.

19. Disconnect the breather tube from the crankcase behind the cylinder.

20. Disconnect alternator, reverse and neutral switch wires at the plastic connectors on the frame. Free the wiring from the frame clamp.

21. Remove the cotter pin, axle nut and hub of the left side rear wheel.

22. Remove the three seal cover bolts on the chain case.

23. Remove the two chain caase mounting bolts.

24. Remove the exhaust pipe nuts from the cylinder head.

25. Remove the three muffler mounting bolts.

26. Remove the exhaust system.

27. Remove the engine mounting bolt on the cylinder head.

28. Remove the frame downtube bolts.

29. Remove the frame downtube.

30. Remove the two engine mounting bolts at the rear of the engine.

31. Remove the engine from the frame.

32. Installation is the reverse of removal. Note the following:

a. Tighten the front downtube bolts to 29-35 ft. lbs.

b. Tighten the rear engine mounting bolts to 36-43 ft. lbs.

c. Tighten the cylinder head mounting bolt to 22-29 ft. lbs.

d. Tighten the rear axle nut to 43-58 ft. lbs.

e. Tighten the front and rear wheel nuts to 36-43 ft. lbs.

f. Be sure to fit the chain masterlink spring clip with the closed end facing the direction of chain rotation.

g. Fill the crankcase with oil.

TOP END

The following section deals with the removal and installation of the cylinder head, cylinder, piston and related components. Inspection and service procedures are outlined under "Engine Rebuilding" in the "General Information" section of this manual. Specifications are included in the chart at the end of this section.

Removal

1. The cylinder head, cylinder and piston can be removed with the engine still in the frame.

2. Disconnect the spark plug lead and remove the plug.

3. Remove the seat.

4. Be certain that the petcock is "OFF." Remove the two screws securing the petcock to the carburetor.

5. Remove the four nuts securing the front fender assembly to the gas tank.

6. Remove the mounting bolt at the rear of the gas tank. Remove the tank.

7. Support the front wheels off the ground by placing a sturdy, safe support beneath the frame.

8. Remove the front wheels.

9. Remove the front carrier and inner fender fasteners. Remove the front fender assembly.

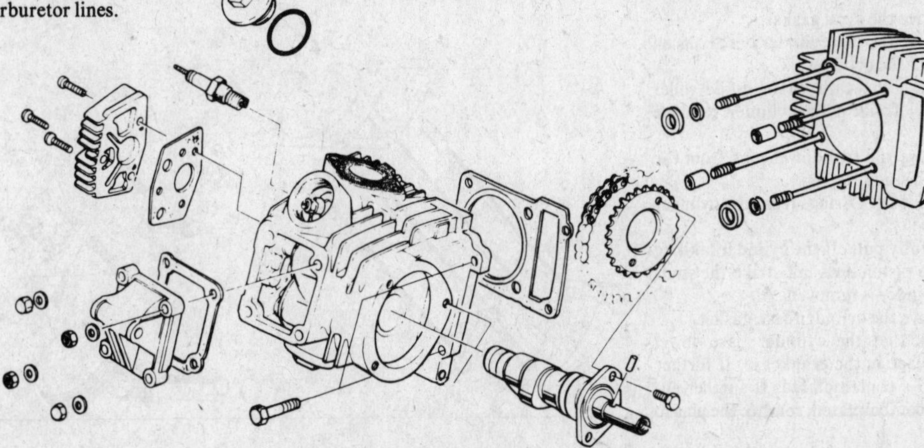
Cylinder head assembly

10. Remove the exhaust pipe nuts at the cylinder head.
11. Remove the three muffler mounting bolts.
12. Remove the exhaust system.
13. Disconnect the choke cable from the carburetor.
14. Disconnect lines from the carburetor.
15. Unscrew the carburetor cap and pull out the throttle slide assembly. Wrap it in a clean, lint-free rag and place it out of the way to avoid damage.
16. Remove the manifold bolts on the head and remove the carburetor and manifold.
17. Drain the engine oil.
18. Remove the pulse generator cover on the left side of the head.
19. Disconnect the pulse generator wire from the plastic connector on the harness and remove the wire clamp from the cylinder head.
20. Remove the generator base plate screws (2) and remove the base plate.
21. Remove the rotor bolt.
22. Remove the rotor.
23. Remove the pin from the camshaft.
24. Remove the three screws securing the generator housing. Remove the housing and gasket from the head.
25. Locate the cam chain tensioner assembly on the left under side of the crankcase.
26. Remove the tensioner sealing bolt, washer, tensioner spring and pushrod.
27. Removing the timing inspection hole cap on the left crankcase cover.
28. Use the recoil starter to turn the engine over until the "O" mark on the camshaft sprocket aligns with the index mark on the cylinder head and the magneto rotor "T" mark aligns with the index mark on the inspection hole. The sprocket bolts will be in line with the centerline of the cylinder. This positions the piston at TDC on the compression stroke (both valves closed).
29. Remove the cam sprocket bolts.
30. Pull out the camshaft.
31. Loop a length of wire around the sprocket and chain so that they do not fall into the cylinder.
32. Loosen the four cylinder head nuts 1/4 turn at a time until they are loose, then remove the nuts and washers. Remove the cylinder head cover and gasket.
33. Remove the two cylinder head base bolts on the left side of the head.
34. Remove the head.
35. Remove the sprocket from the cam chain.
36. Remove the head gasket.
37. Remove the two cylinder base bolts on the left side of the cylinder.
38. Remove the cam chain guide roller bolt from the left side of the cylinder. Remove the roller.
39. Remove the two dowel pins from the cylinder head studs.
40. Remove the O-rings from the cylinder head studs.
41. Carefully pull off the cylinder takikng care that the piston does not strike the studs when the cylinder is removed.
42. Remove the cylinder base gasket.
43. Check that the cylinder base dowel pins are in place in the crankcase. If further engine work is contemplated. If further engine work is contemplated, remove the pins to prevent loss.
44. Stuff a clean, lint-free rag into the crankcase.

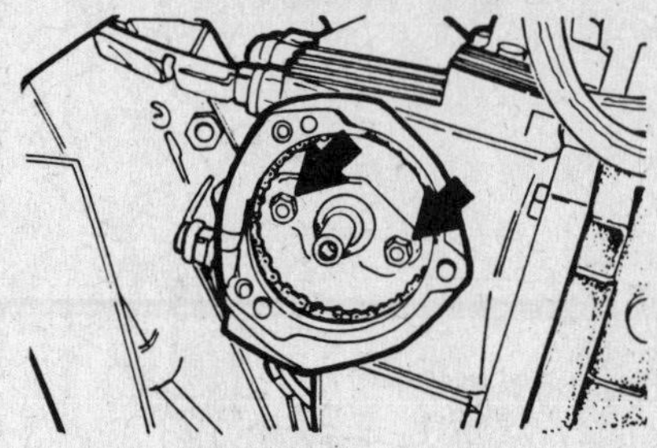

Cam sprocket bolts (arrows)

Cylinder head nuts (arrows)

Cylinder head base bolts (arrows)

45. Remove the piston wrist pin circlips with a needlenose pliers. Push out the wrist pin with a suitable drift. Remove the piston.
46. Remove the four screws and take off the finned cylinder head cover and gasket from the right side of the head.
47. Pull out the rocker arm shafts with a needlenose pliers and remove the rocker arms. Keep each shaft with its own rocker arm and mark them to ensure that they are installed in their original locations during assembly.
48. To remove the valve assemblies, compress the valve springs and remove the keepers.

Inspection

Refer to the "Engine Rebuilding" section of "General Information" and to the specifications chart in this section for inspection techniques and service limits.

Installation

1. If the piston rings were removed or replaced, be sure that they are installed correctly.
2. The two compression rings are not in-

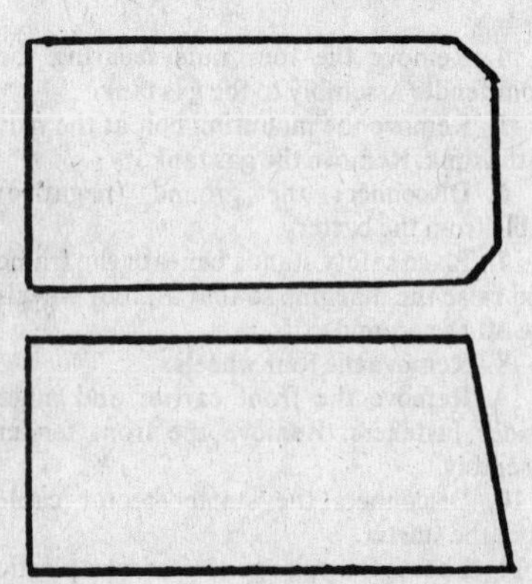

Top and second compression ring profiles

Ring manufacturer's marks must face upwards

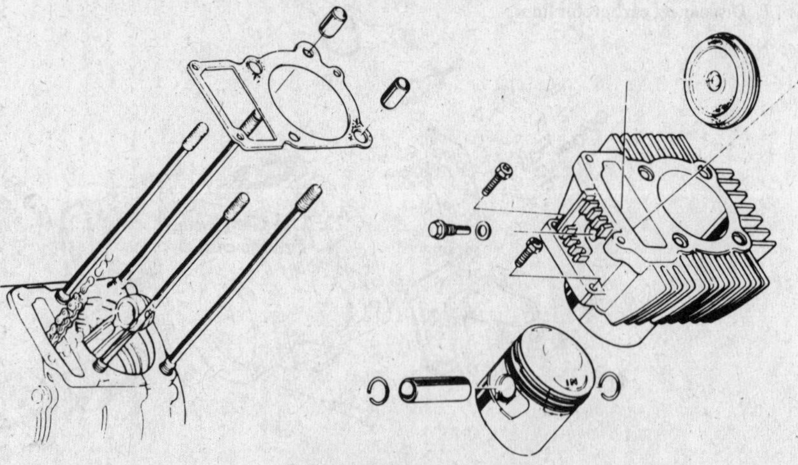

Cylinder and piston assembly

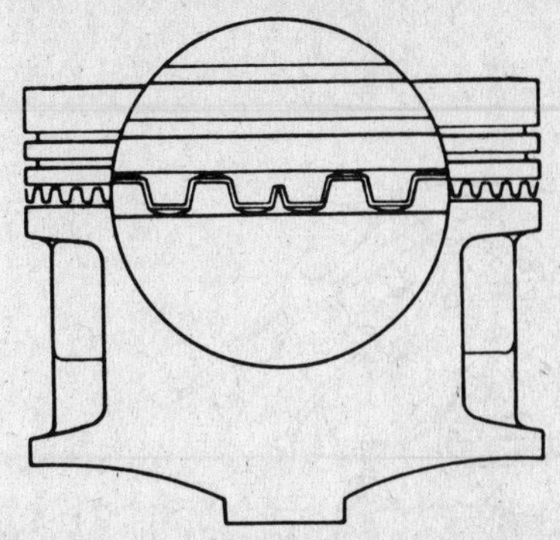

Oil expander ring ends must abut, not overlap

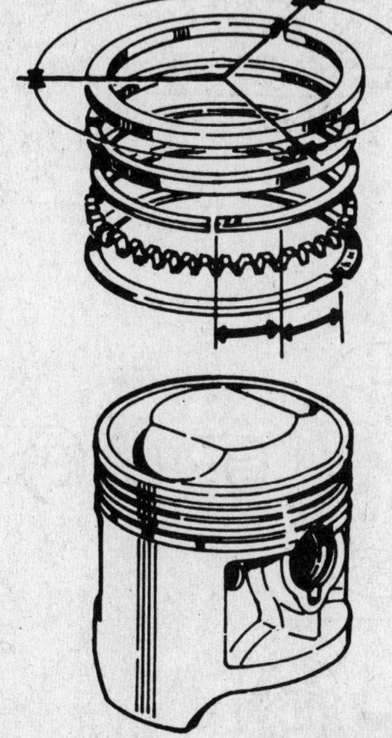

Stagger ring end gaps around the piston

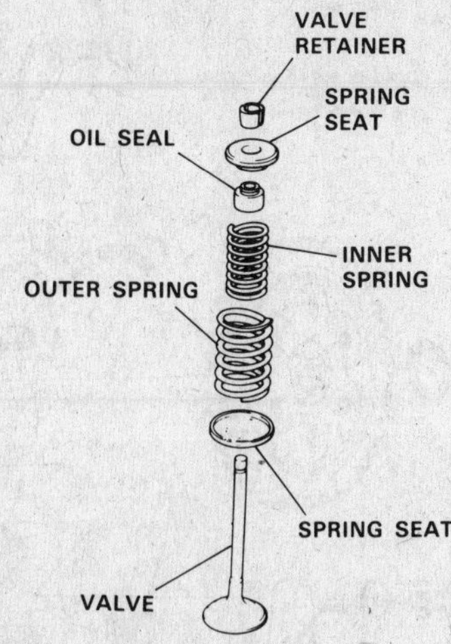

Valve assembly

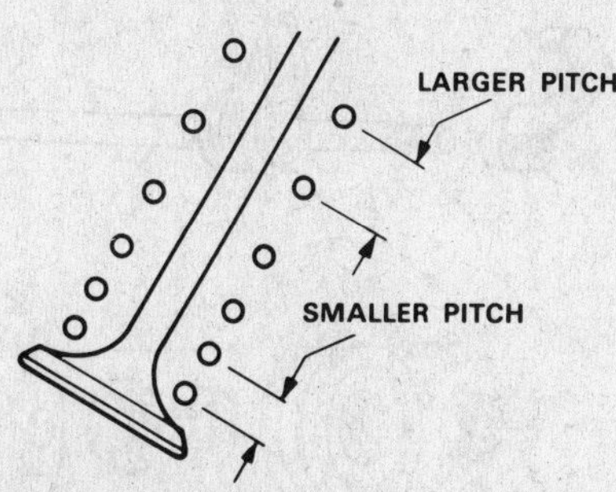

Install valve springs with the close coils against the head

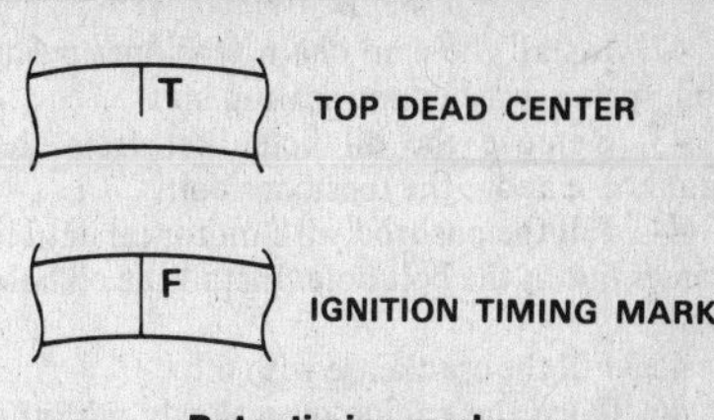

Rotor timing marks

Rotor "T" mark (1) and cam sprocket "O" mark (2) aligned for valve timing

terchangeable. The top ring has a plain profile, while the second is wedge-shaped.

3. Be certain to install the compression rings with the manufacturer's mark near the end-gap facing upwards.

4. The piston ring end-gaps should be arranged as follows:

a. End-gaps of the two compression rings and the oil expander ring should be arranged 120° apart around the piston but not at the very front or rear of the piston and not directly above the wrist pin holes.

b. The end-gaps of the oil rails should be arranged at about 3/4 in. (20mm) or more on either side of the oil expander ring.

5. Thoroughly clean the cylinder mating surface.

6. Check that the two dowel pins are in place on the right side cylinder head studs.

7. Use a new cylinder base gasket.

8. Install the piston on the connecting rod so that the "IN" mark on the piston crown is on the intake side.

9. Use new wrist pin circlips. Be sure the circlips are properly seated. The circlip end-gaps should not align with the cut-outs at the wrist pin hole.

10. Lubricate the piston and rings. Check that the ring end-gaps are properly aligned.

11. Compress the rings and slide the cylinder over the piston. Pull the cam chain through the cylinder.

12. When the cylinder is seated, install and tighten the cylinder base bolts.

13. Fit the cam chain guide roller. Tighten the roller bolt to 7-10 ft. lbs.

14. Use new valve seals when assembling the head.

15. Valve springs are progressively wound. They are installed with the close coils against the head.

16. Lubricate valve stems before inserting them into the guides.

17. After the valve and spring assemblies have been installed, rap the end of each valve smartly with a plastic mallet to ensure that the keepers are properly seated.

18. Lubricate each rocker arm shaft and slip it into place. Use a new gasket beneath the finned cover.

19. Install the dowel pins on the upper right and lower left cylinder head studs (as seen from the front of the engine). Be sure the O-rings and collars are in place on the upper left and lower right studs.

20. Use a new cylinder head gasket.

21. Pull the cam chain taut and ensure that it is not jammed or kinked anywhere.

22. Thread the cam sprocket on the chain. Turn the engine so that the rotor magneto "T" mark is aligned with the inspection index mark. The piston will be at TDC. At this point, fit the chain over the cam sprocket so that the "O" mark on the sprocket is at the top of the cylinder head and the sprocket bolt holes are aligned with the centerline of the cylinder.

23. Install the cylinder head. Pull the cam sprocket through. With the rotor "T" mark aligned with the index mark, the "O" mark on the sprocket must align with the index mark on the head. If it does not, move the sprocket relative to the chain. Do not-move the crankshaft.

24. Fit a new cylinder head cover gasket. Install the cylinder head cover.

25. Install the cylinder head washers and nuts. The cap nuts go on the upper left and lower right studs.

26. Tighten the cylinder head nuts gradually and in an "X" pattern until the proper torque of 14-16 ft. lbs. is reached.

27. Install and tighten the cylinder head base bolts.

28. Recheck head nut torque.

29. Check valve timing marks as discussed above: rotor "T" mark and sprocket "O" mark must align with their respective index marks.

30. Lubricate the cam with clean motor oil.

31. Install the camshift. The pin hole on the end of the cam must face upwards towards the top of the head.

32. Install the sprocket bolts. Using a non-permanent thread-locking compound is recommended. Torque the bolts to 6-9 ft. lbs.

33. Fit a new gasket behind the generator housing.

34. Lubricate the end of the camshaft and the lips of the housing oil seal. Install the housing and tighten the three screws.

35. Install the pin in the camshaft.

36. Before fitting the pulse rotor, check that the punch mark on the pulse rotor aligns with the index mark on the timing advance mechanism.

37. Install the rotor. The camshaft pin engages a slot on the rotor.

38. Tighten the rotor bolt to 6-9 ft. lbs.

39. Install the pulse generator base plate assembly.

40. Turn the crankshaft so that the "F" mark on the magneto rotor is aligned with the inspection hole index mark.

41. Turn the pulse generator base plate so that the pulse generator tooth aligns with the pulse rotor index mark. Tighten the base plate screws.

42. Install the cam chain tensioner pushrod, spring, washer and sealing bolt.
43. Remove the oil hole bolt from the crankcase above the tensioner bolt.
44. Fill the pushrod with motor oil until it comes out of the bolt hole. Install the oil hole bolt.
45. Fill the crankcase with oil.
46. Turn the engine over slowly with the recoil starter. If resistance is felt, stop immediately and determine the cause. Check that the timing marks all align after one complete engine revolution.
47. Adjust valve clearance as outlined in "Maintenance."
48. The remainder of the procedure is the reverse of removal:

Tighten the cylinder head 8mm mounting bolt to 22-29 ft. lbs.

Tighten the frame downtube 10mm bolts to 29-35 ft. lbs.

RIGHT CRANKCASE COVER COMPONENTS

The right crankcase cover contains the clutch, oil pump, primary driven gear and external shift mechanism. All of these components can be serviced without removing the engine from the frame.

Removal

1. Remove the seat.
2. Drain the crankcase oil.
3. Place a drip pan beneath the right crankcase cover.
4. Remove the starter motor bracket.
5. Remove the crankcase cover screws.

Primary driven gear snap-ring (arrow)

6. Remove the crankcase cover. If it is stuck, tap it with a plastic mallet to break it free.
7. Note the locations of the two locating dowel pins on the mating surface.
8. Remove the ball retainer and clutch cam plate side spring.
9. Remove the oil passage pipe and spring.
10. Remove the clutch cam plate.
11. Remove the two clutch outer cover screws. Remove the cover and bearing.
12. Remove the release lever.
13. Bend up the locking tab on the clutch nut washer.
14. Remove the clutch nut.
15. Remove the clutch assembly.
16. Remove the clutch center guide.

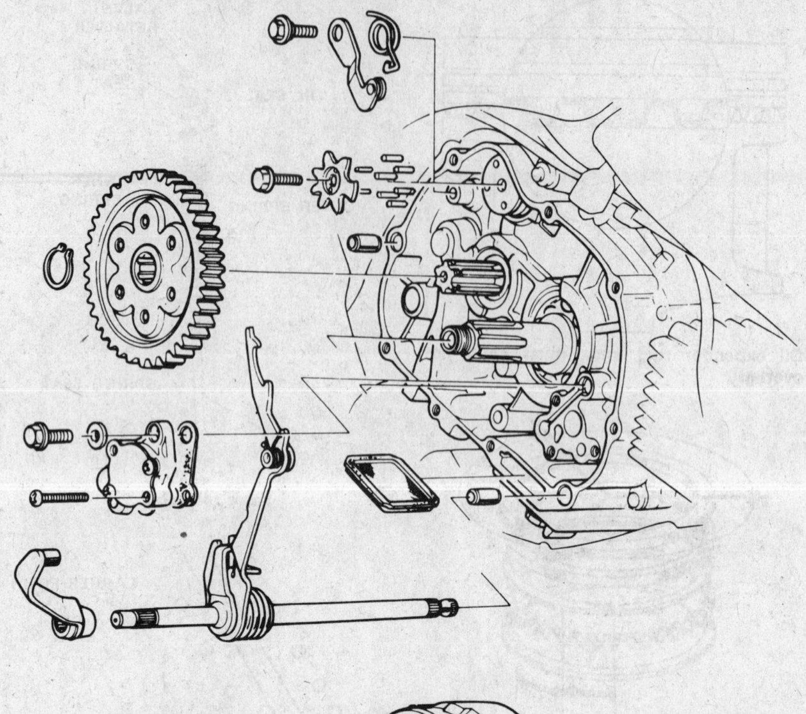

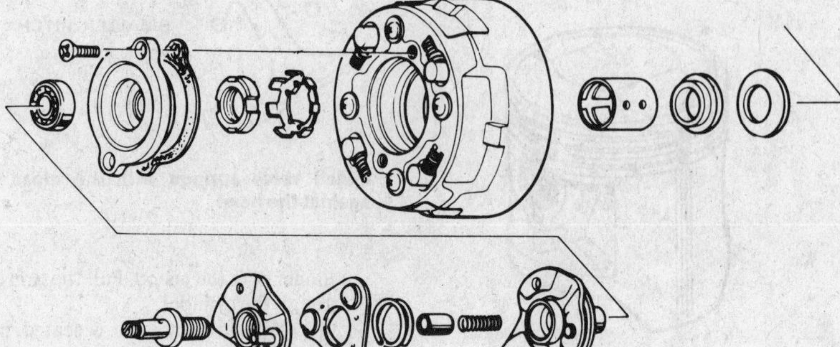

Right crankcase cover components

17. Remove the primary driven gear snap-ring.
18. Remove the primary driven gear.
19. To remove the oil pump, remove the hexhead bolt and the three pump mounting screws.
20. Remove the gearshift pedal pinch bolt and carefully pull the pedal off the shaft.
21. Clean the exposed splines of the shift shaft to remove any burrs or sharp edges so they won't damage the oil seal.
22. Remove the shift drum stopper bolt and the stopper.
23. Disengage the fingers of the shift arm from the shift drum pins and pull the external shift mechanism out of the case.
24. Remove the shift drum stopper plate, if required.

Inspection

CLUTCH

1. Compress the clutch assembly and remove the large snap-ring on the inner side. Carefully release pressure and separate the components.
2. Remove the snap-ring to separate the primary drive gear from the clutch hub.

Removing the clutch snap-ring

3. If further disassembly is required, remove the clutch damper springs from the housing. Remove the four phillips screws from the outer side of the housing and separate the drive plate, clutch springs and housing.
4. To complete disassembly, remove the clutch weight stopper ring from the drive plate.

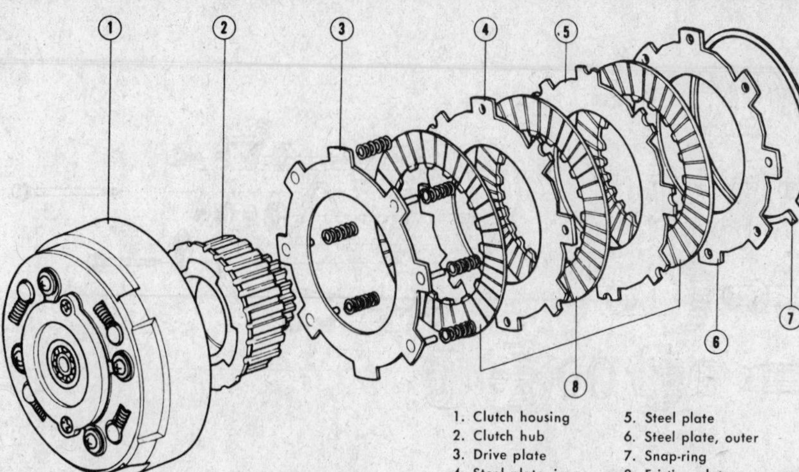

Centrifugal clutch assembly

14. Install the damper springs with a small screwdriver.

15. Clutch plates are installed by alternating steel and friction plate. Start with the steel plate with the spring pins. The next steel plate has cut-outs at every tab. The next steel plate has pin holes at every other tab. The final steel plate to be installed has pin holes on every tab.

16. Be sure the spring washer is installed on the crankshaft with the dished side in. Install the collar on the crankshaft.

17. Install the clutch assembly.

18. Install the lockwasher.

19. Tighten the clutch nut to 29-36 ft. lbs.

20. Bend down a locking tab on the nut.

21. Use a clutch outer cover gasket. Install the outer cover and secure it with the two screws.

5. Measure clutch spring free length.

6. Check friction plates for worn or damaged friction material. Measure thickness and compare to the given specification.

7. Check steel plates for warpage.

8. Check plate tabs for chipping, wear or other damage.

9. Measure primary drive gear ID and center guide OD and compare to the specifications.

10. Check gear teeth for pitting, chipping or other damage. Check gears for heat discoloration.

SHIFT MECHANISM

1. Check the splines of the gearshift shaft. If the splines are broken or torn to the extent that it is difficult to properly secure the shift lever, replace the shaft.

2. Check the condition of the shift arm. Be sure that it is not bent. Check that the shift fingers are not bent or worn.

3. Check the condition of the springs in the shift linkage, especially the shift lever return spring. If any spring is broken, has lost its tension or fails to hold its component properly, replace it.

4. Check the condition of the shift drum stopper roller and replace it if worn. The stopper spring should hold the stopper firmly against the stopper plate.

5. Check the stopper plate and pins for wear. Replace if damaged.

OIL PUMP

1. Remove the cover screws and remove the cover.

2. Remove the inner and outer rotors.

3. Check all parts for scoring, discoloration or other obvious signs of wear.

4. Install the rotors and measure the clearance between the outer rotor and the oil pump body with a feeler gauge. Replace the pump if clearance is excessive.

5. Measure the rotor end-play by placing a straightedge across the cover surface with the gasket in place and measuring the clearance between the straightedge and the rotors with a feeler gauge.

6. Measure the clearance between the rotor tips. Excessive clearance will give too much backlash and noisy pump operation.

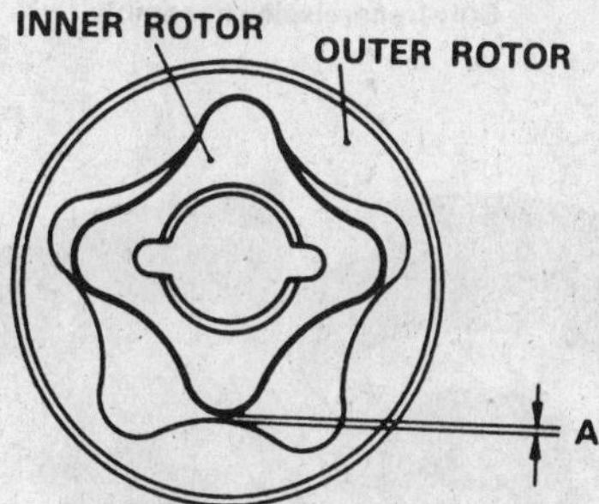

Checking rotor tip clearance

Installation

1. Clean all parts thoroughly before installation.

2. Use new gaskets and O-rings.

3. When assembling the oil pump, lubricate all metal parts thoroughly beforehand. Be certain that the gasket does not touch the rotors. After assembly, turn the pump by hand. There should be little resistance.

4. Install the pump on the engine. Be sure to line up the flats on the pump shaft with the recess on the driveshaft.

5. Tighten the hex head bolt and the three pump mounting screws securely.

6. The shift drum stopper plate must be firmly secured. Use an impact driver or a non-permanent thread-locking compound on the bolt.

7. Install the external shift mechanism shaft assembly, locating the ends of the return spring on either side of the stopper pin and engaging the fingers of the shift arm with the shift drum pins. Be careful when installing the shaft as there is an oil seal on the left side of the engine.

8. Install the shift drum stopper.

9. Install the primary driven gear.

10. To assemble the clutch, fit the weights on the drive plate and install the stopper ring.

11. Install the springs on the drive plate.

12. Place the clutch housing over it and compress the assembly while installing the phillips screws.

13. Install the snap-ring.

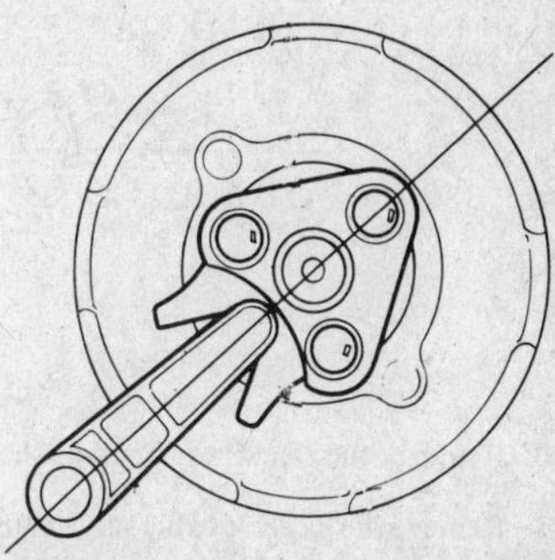

Align the clutch lever as shown

22. Install the clutch lever, aligning it with the center of the clutch.

23. Install the cultch cam plate.

24. Install the oil passage pipe and spring.

25. Install the cam plate side spring and ball retainer. Align the steel ball in the retainer with the lug of the cam plate and with the clutch lever.

26. Use a new crankcase cover gasket.

27. Be sure the two locating dowel pins are in place in the crankcase mating surface.

28. Install the crankcase cover and tighten the screws evenly.

29. Install the starter motor bracket.

30. Fill the crankcase with oil.

LEFT CRANKCASE COVER COMPONENTS

Left crankcase cover components include the recoil starter assembly, magneto, engine sprocket and cam chain tensioner assembly.

All of these components can be serviced with the engine in the frame.

Removal

1. Be sure the transmission is in Neutral.

2. Remove the gearshift lever pinch bolt and carefully pull the lever off its shaft.

3. Remove the recoil starter assembly (3 screws).

4. Remove the gasket.

5. If further disassembly is required, drain the engine oil.

6. Remove the pulley bolt.

7. Remove the pulley.

8. Remove the air cleaner hose.

9. Disconnect the alternator wires and the Reverse switch wire at the connectors.

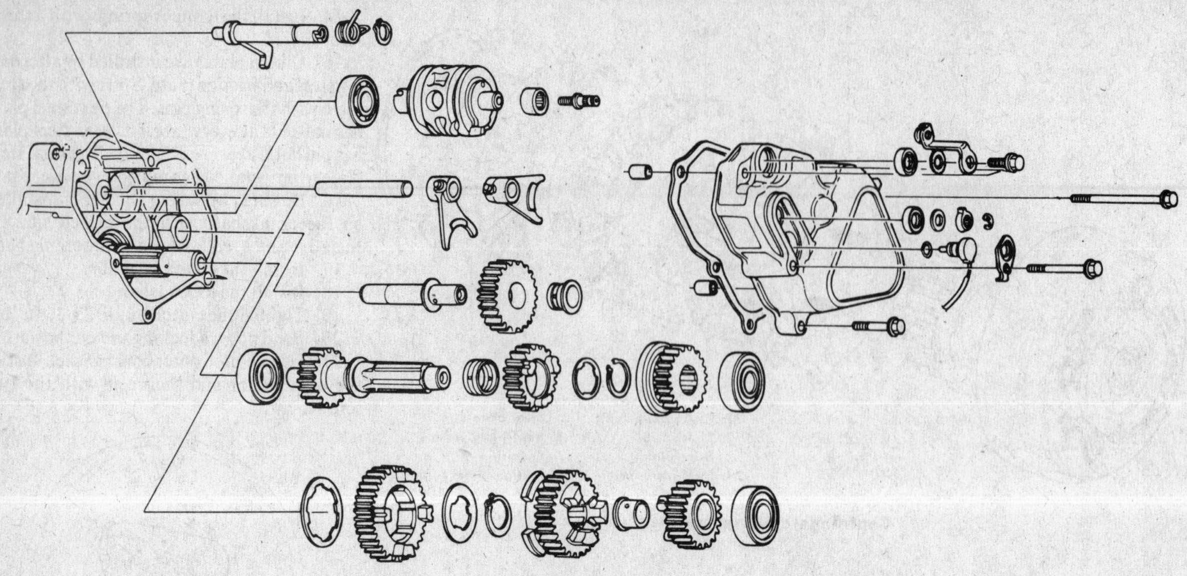

Sub-transmission assembly

10. Remove the Reverse stopper shaft lever.
11. Remove the Reverse cable stay mounting bolt.
12. Remove the Neutral indicator e-clip and washer.
13. Remove the six sub-transmission cover bolts. Remove the cover.
14. Remove the dowel pins.
15. Remove the gasket.
16. Remove the Reverse idle gear.
17. Remove the shift fork shaft. Remove the shift fork.
18. Remove the Reverse drive low gear and the super low gear from the countershaft.
19. Remove the Reverse driven gear with the reduction shaft.
20. Remove the high speed gear snap ring.
21. Remove the high speed gear.
22. Remove the Reverse stopper shaft and sub- transmission shift drum.
23. Remove the left crankcase cover bolts. Remove the cover.
24. Remove the flywheel with a suitable puller.
25. Remove the thrust washers, starter idler gear and shaft.
26. Remove the starter reduction gear washer.
27. Remove the bolt securing the starter driven gear set plate. Remove the plate.
28. Remove the starter driven gear and the needle bearing.
29. Remove the seven bolts securing the left crankcase cover spacer and remove the spacer.
30. Remove the two dowel pins from the crankcase mating surface.
31. Remove the two screws securing the cam chain tensioner guide sprocket set plate. Remove the set plate. Remove the sprocket.
32. Unscrew and remove the cam chain tensioner oil hole bolt and washer.
33. Remove the tensioner sealing bolt and washer and the spring and pushrod.
34. Disconnect the drive chain at the masterlink.
35. Remove the engine sprocket and bushings.

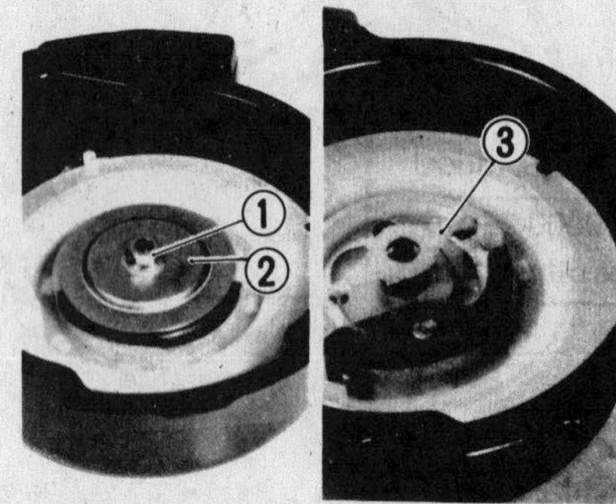

Ratchet cover nut (1), cover (2) and guide (3)

Inspection

RECOIL STARTER

1. Remove the ratchet cover nut.
2. Remove the cover.
3. Remove the ratchet, ratchet guide, spring seat and spring.
4. Remove the collar from the pulley shaft.
5. Remove the handle cover.
6. Undo the rope knot. Remove the handle.
7. Remove the starter pulley.

CAUTION: *Wear eye protection and use care when removing the pulley. The coil spring may pop out when it is removed.*

8. Check the rope for a frayed or worn condition and replace it if necessary.
9. Check the condition of the coil spring.
10. Check the ratachet components for damage.

MAGNETO

1. Do not drop the rotor as the magnetic properties may be affected. Place it where it will not pick up stray bits of metal.
2. Be sure that the rotor is perfectly clean before installation.
3. For electrical tests, refer to the "Electrical System" section.
4. Check the inside of the rotor and the stator coil core ends for scoring which would indicate that they have been in contact. This condition must be rectified.
5. Check that the stator is secure on the crankcase cover spacer. The unit is mounted by three bolts. Be sure they are tight.
6. If stator and rotor have been in contact, check the crankshaft bearings. This condition is sometimes caused by bad bearings which allow play in the crankshaft.
7. Check the rotor for cracks, especially around the mounting taper.
8. Check the stator for burned insulation, broken wires or other obvious signs of damage.

ENGINE SPROCKET

1. Check the teeth of the sprocket and ensure that they are not hook-shaped, broken or worn. If wear is evident, the sprocket should be replaced and the chain and rear sprocket checked for similar defects.

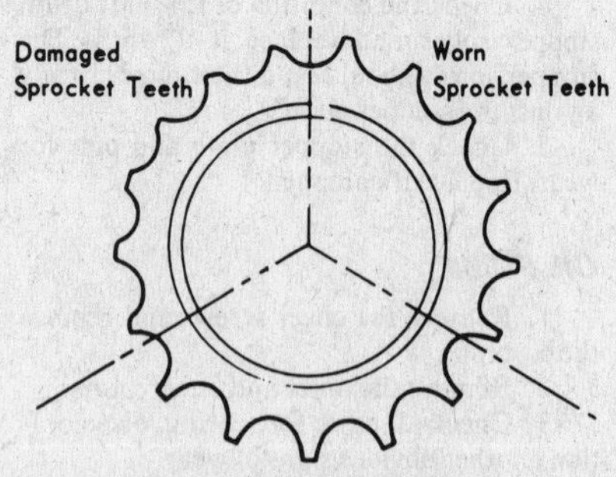

Check sprocket conditon

2. Check the outside diameters of the bushings and the inside diameters of the sprocket and compare the measurements against the specifications.
3. Check the condition of the sprocket bushing splines and the splines on the sprocket shaft.

CRANKCASE COVERS

1. Always use new gaskets and O-rings.
2. Remove any knicks or imperfections from the mating surfaces with an oilstone or silicon carbide paper.
3. Oil seals can be pried out with a small screwdriver. When installing new seals, press them straight in with a block of wood or the like which will cover the entire seal. Lubricate seal lips before installation.
4. Bearings can be check for condition in place. Remove bearings by taking off any retaining plates. Heat the cover slightly and drive the old bearing(s) out. Installation is the reverse of removal.

GEAR ASSEMBLIES

1. Check the condition of all gear teeth for wear, pittting oor cracks. Pay close attention to the base of each tooth since this is wear most damage shows up.
2. Check the engaging dogs on sub-transmmission gears.
3. Check dimensions of gears, shafts and shift forks against the specifications given.
4. Check the shaft splines.
5. Check the condition of the shift fork fingers. They should be straight and the tips must be undamaged.
6. Check that the shift fork shaft is not bent.
7. Check all components for heat damage.

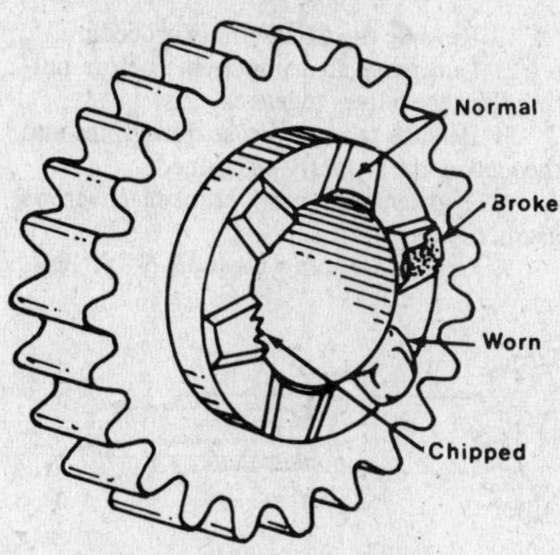

Check gear condition

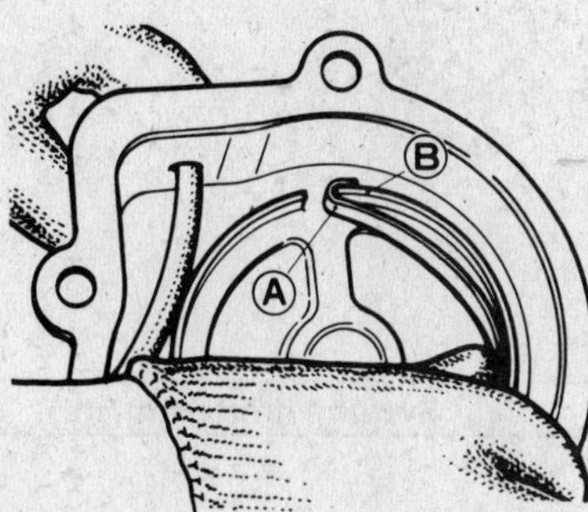

Hook the end of the recoil spring (A) on the rib provided (B)

Installation

1. Use new gaskets and O-rings.
2. Clean all metal parts in a safe solvent and dry thoroughly.
3. Lubricate all metal parts with motor oil before assembly.

Crankcase screws (arrows)

4. Grease the lips of all seals before installation.
5. Wrap the starter rope around the pulley in a clockwise direction when viewed from the ratchet side of the pulley.
6. Install the recoil spring in the housing, hooking the end of the spring in the place provided.

CAUTION: *Wear eye protection when installing the spring.*

7. Grease the spring thoroughly.
8. Install the pulley shaft collar.
9. Grease the pulley shaft and install the pulley, hooking the end of the spring on the starter housing hook.
10. Turn the pulley two full turns clockwise.
11. Pull the starter rope through the hole and install the handle. Knot the end of the rope. Fit the handle cover.
12. Grease the ratchet and install it on the pulley.
13. Install the spring, spring seat and ratchet guide.
14. Install the cover. Install the cover nut.
15. Check recoil starter operation.
16. Lubricate the engine sprocket bushings and install bushings and sprocket.
17. Connect the drive chain.
18. Install the cam chain guide sprocket and set plate.
19. Fit a new crankcase cover spacer gasket.
20. Check that the two locating dowel pins are in place on the crankcase mating surface.
21. Install the spacer and secure it with the seven bolts. Bolts should be tightened gradually and evenly.
22. Install the starter driven gear spacer on the crankshaft.
23. Install the starter driven gear and needle bearing.
24. Install the driven gear set plate and bolt.
25. Install the inner thrust washer, starter idler gear, shaft and outer thrust washer.
26. Fit the reduction gear thrust washer.
27. Clean the inside mounting surface of the magneto rotor. Lubricate the mounting hole and the crankshaft taper with motor oil. Check that the locating key is in place in the crankshaft. Push the rotor into place. Do not strike the rotor. It will be driven home when the pulley is installed.
28. Install the left crankcase cover.
29. Grease the oil seal lips and install the pulley, aligning the flats with the groove in the rotor.
30. Install the pulley bolt, washer and O-ring.
31. Tighten the pulley bolt to 29-36 ft. lbs.
32. Install the recoil starter assembly.
33. Install the reverse idler gear shaft.
34. Install the thrust washer which is located behind the drive sprocket bushing.
35. Fit the high speed gear. Install the thrust washer.
36. Install the high speed gear thrust washer.
37. Fit the Reverse stopper shaft.
38. Pull the Reverse stopper shaft arm and install the shift drum, aligning the groove in the drum with the guide on the Neutral indicator shaft.
39. Install the super low gear driven gear, bushing, thrust washer, snap-ring and Reverse driven gear onto the reduction shaft.
40. Install the Reverse drive low gear bushing.
41. Assemble the reduction shaft assembly, super low gear, Reverse drive low gear and install them. The right shift fork is marked "V6R" and the left shift fork is marked "V6L." These marks face out when the forks are fitted.
42. Install the shift fork shaft.
43. Install the Reverse idler gear and bushing.
44. Check that the two locating dowel pins are in place on the cover mating surface.
45. Fit a new cover gasket.
46. Install the sub-transmission cover.
47. Install the neutral indicator washer, indicator and E-clip.
48. Connect the Reverse cable to the drum stopper shift lever and install the lever with the bolt and washer.
49. The remainder of the procedure is the reverse of disassembly. Do not forget to fill the crankcase with oil before starting the engine.

LOWER END AND TRANSMISSION

Splitting The Crankcases

1. Remove the engine from the frame.
2. Remove the cylinder head, cylinder and piston.
3. Remove the clutch and gearshift linkage.
4. Remove the recoil starter assembly.
5. Remove the magneto.

6. Remove the cam chain tensioner assembly.
7. Remove the sub-transmission.
8. Remove the nine crankcase screws on the right side of the engine.
9. Place the engine with the left crankcase down and tap upwards on the right crankcase half with a plastic mallet to separate the case halves.
10. Remove the dowel pins and the gasket.
11. Remove the crankshaft assembly.
12. Remove the gear clusters.

Inspection

CRANKSHAFT

The crankshaft is a pressed-together unit. The connecting rod big end bearing is the caged-needle type. In the event of damage to the con rod, bearing or crankpin, the crankshaft must be replaced as an assembly.

1. Lubricate the big end bearing with oil, and rotate the rod slowly around the crankpin. The movement must be smooth and silent.
2. With a dial gauge, check the up-and-down (radial) movement of the con rod. Compare the reading with the specification given. If rod movement is in excess of the specifications, the big end bearing is worn and the crankshaft must be replaced.
3. With a feeler gauge, check the clearance between the con rod big end and the crankshaft flywheel. Compare the measurement with the specification given for axial clearance.
4. Place the crankshaft on a set of V-blocks, and check the crankshaft run-out with a dial gauge. Check both ends of the crank. Compare the run-out reading with the specification given. If excessive, the crank must be replaced.

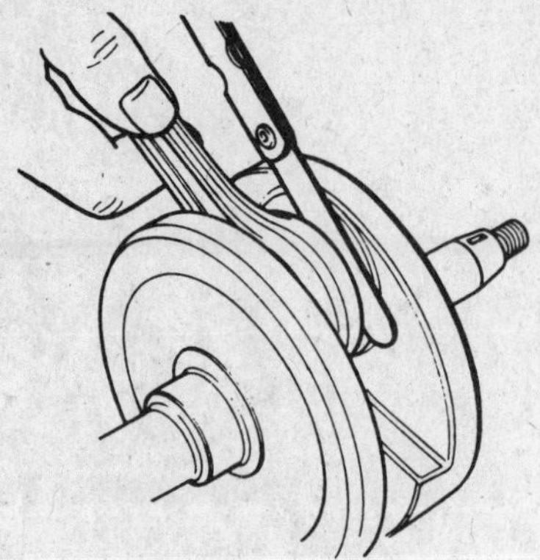

Checking big end side clearance

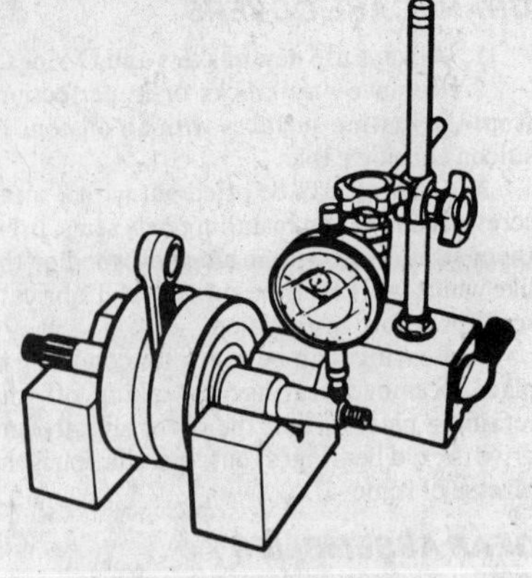

Checking crankshaft run-out

Crankshaft run-out will be one half of the true indicated reading of the gauge.

CRANKCASES

1. Check for damage to the bearing bosses, especially for stress cracks around the bearing boss.
2. Be sure that both case half mating surfaces are free of any traces of old gasket or gasket material.
3. Place each case half on a flat surface and check for warpage by probing around the mating surface with a feeler gauge. Maximum acceptable case warpage is 0.05 mm (0.002 in.). If warped, cases should be replaced.
4. Minor scratches on the mating surfaces can be removed with an oilstone, although it is not permissible to remove much metal.
5. Case halves must be scrupulously clean before assembly. Be sure that all oil passages are clear and that the two dowel pins fitted between the case halves are installed.

TRANSMISSION

1. Check gears, shafts and shift linkage as outlined in the "Engine Rebuilding" section of "General Information".
2. Compare measurements with the specifications in the charts.

NOTE: *Mark shift forks for position before disassembly.*

Crankcase Assembly

1. Reverse the disassembly procedure.
2. Lubricate all components before putting the case halves together.
3. Be sure the crankcase dowel pins and the gasket are properly positioned.
4. Tighten the nine crankcase screws gradually and evenly.
5. Crankcase screw torgue is 5-8 ft. lbs.

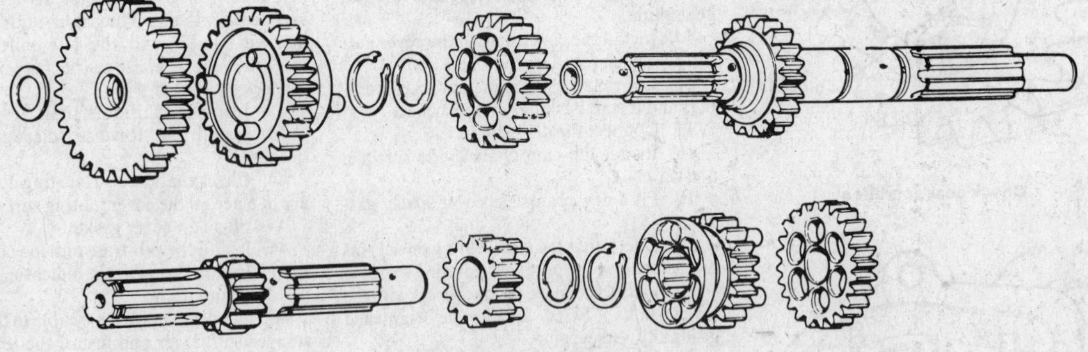

Transmission assembly

ENGINE SPECIFICATIONS

Part	Standard (mm/in.)	Service limit (mm/in.)
CYLINDER HEAD		
Cam journals		
R	17.934-17.945/0.7060-0.7065	17.90/0.705
L	25.932-25.945/1.0210-10215	25.90/1.020
Cam lobe height	24.118-24.278/0.9495-0.9558	23.8/0.94
Rocker arm ID	10.000-10.015/0.3937-0.3943	10.10/0.398
Rocker arm shaft OD	9.972-9.987/0.3926-0.3932	9.92/0.391
Rocker arm-to-shaft clearance	—	0.08/0.003
Cylinder warpage	— —	0.10/0.004

ENGINE SPECIFICATIONS

Part	Standard (mm/in.)	Service limit (mm/in.)
Valve spring free length		
Inner	31.1/1.22	29.9/1.18
Outer	35.0/1.38	33.7/1.32
Valve stem OD		
Intake	5.450-5.465/0.2146-0.2152	5.435/0.2139
Exhaust	5.430-5.445/0.2138-0.2144	5.415/0.2132
Valve guide ID	5.475-5.485/0.2157-0.2161	5.525/0.2175
Stem-to-guide clearance		
Intake	0.010-0.035/0.0004-0.0014	0.08/0.003
Exhaust	0.030-0.055/0.0012-0.0022	0.10/0.004
Valve face width	1.2-1.5/0.05-0.06	1.8/0.07
Valve seat width	1.0/0.04	1.6/0.06
Cam bearing ID		
R	18.000-18.018/0.7087-0.7094	18.05/0.711
L	26.000-26.020/1.0236-1.0244	26.05/1.026
Cam journal clearance		
R	—	0.12/0.005
L	—	0.16/0.006
CYLINDER AND PISTON		
Cylinder ID	55.000-55.010/2.1654-2.1657	55.10/2.169
Taper/out-of-round	—	0.05/0.002
Warpage (head mating surface)	—	0.10/0.004
Piston OD	54.955-54.985/2.1636-2.1648	54.90/2.161
Wrist pin bore	15.002-15.008/0.5906-0.5909	15.04/0.592
Wrist pin OD	14.994-15.000/0.5903-0.5906	14.96/0.589
Piston-to-pin clearance	0.002-0.014/0.0001-0.0006	0.02/0.001
Ring-to-groove clearance		
Top	0.015-0.050/0.0006-0.0020	0.12/0.005
Second	0.010-0.045/0.0004-0.0018	0.12/0.005
Ring end-gap		
Top, second	0.10-0.25/0.004-0.010	0.50/0.020
Oil	0.3-0.9/0.01-0.04	—
Rod small end bore	15.016-15.034/0.5912-0.5919	15.05/0.593
CLUTCH		
Spring free-length	21.1/0.83	20.2/0.80
Warpage	—	0.20/0.008
Disc thickness	2.65-2.75/0.104-0.108	2.5/0.10
Drive gear ID	24.000-24.021/0.9449-0.9457	24.10/0.949
Center guide OD	22.00-22.10/0.866-0.870	21.85/0.860
OIL PUMP		
Body clearance	0.15-0.20/0.006-0.008	0.25/0.010
Rotor tip clearance	0.15/0.006	0.20/0.008
CAM CHAIN TENSIONER		
Spring free-length	82.8/3.3	77.0/3.0
Pushrod OD	11.985-12.000/0.4718-0.4724	11.94/0.94
ENGINE SPROCKET		
Bushing OD	21.960-21.993/0.8657-0.8659	21.90/0.862
Sprocket ID	19.992-20.008/0.7870-0.7877	19.94/0.785
SUB-TRANSMISSION		
Shift fork finger thickness	5.93-6.00/0.233-0.236	5.8/0.23
Shift fork shaft hole ID	10.000-10.015/0.3940-0.3943	10.05/0.413
Shift fork shaft OD	9.972-9.987/0.3926-0.3932	9.95/0.392
Shift drum OD		
R	14.966-14.984/0.5892-0.5899	14.93/0.588
L	11.989-12.000/0.4720-0.4724	11.95/0.470

ENGINE SPECIFICATIONS

Part	Standard (mm/in.)	Service limit (mm/in.)
SUB-TRANSMISSION		
Reverse idle gear		
Bushing ID	15.000-15.018/0.5900-0.5913	15.1/0.59
Gear OD	18.000-18.018/0.7090-0.7094	17.97/0.707
Countershaft end OD		
R	13.966-13.984/0.5498-0.5506	13.93/0.548
L	14.983-14.994/0.5899-0.5905	14.95/0.588
Super low driven gear bushing ID	20.000-20.021/0.7840-0.7882	20.1/0.79
Reduction shaft OD	14.966-14.984/0.5892-0.5899	14.93/0.588
CRANKSHAFT		
Run-out	—	0.10/0.004
Big end side clearance	0.15-0.55/0.006-0.022	0.65/0.03
Radial clearance	0.0-0.008/0.0-0.0003	0.05/0.002
Small end ID	15.106-15.034/0.5912-0.5919	15.05/0.593
Crankshaft bearing play		
Axial	0.10-0.35/0.004-0.014	0.8/0.03
Radial	0.003-0.015/0.0001-0.0006	0.05/0.002
TRANSMISSION		
Shift fork ID	42.075-42.100/1.6565-1.6575	42.15/1.659
Shift drum OD	41.950-41.975/1.6516-1.6526	41.8/1.65
Fork/drum clearance	0.118-0.150/0.0047-0.0059	6.4/0.25
Shift fork finger thickness	5.96-6.04/0.234-0.238	5.70/0.224
Gear ID		
C1	14.000-14.027/0.5512-0.5522	14.10/0.555
M2	18.000-18.018/0.7087-0.7094	18.08/0.712
M4	20.000-20.021/0.7874-0.7882	20.10/0.791
C3	14.000-14.027/0.5512-0.5522	14.10/0.555
Shaft OD		
C1	13.966-13.984/0.5498-0.5506	13.93/0.548
M2	17.966-17.984/0.7073-0.7080	17.93/0.706
C3	19.966-19.984/0.7861-0.7868	19.93/0.785
M4	13.966-13.984/0.5498-0.5506	13.93/0.548

ENGINE TORQUE SPECIFICATIONS

Part	Torque (ft. lbs.)
Cylinder head nuts	14-16
Cam sprocket bolts	6-9
Cam chain guide roller bolt	7-10
Pulse rotor	6-9
Clutch nut	29-36
Starter driven pulley	29-36
Drum stopper plate bolt	17-20
Carburetor-to-manifold nuts	5-7
Driven sprocket nuts	17-22
Gearshift pedal pinch bolt	9-10
Crankcase screws	5-8

GENERAL TORQUE SPECIFICATIONS①

Part	Torque (ft. lbs.)
5mm screws	2.5-3.6
6mm screws	5-8
5mm bolts, nuts	3.5-4.5
6mm bolts, nuts	6-9
8mm bolts, nuts	13-18
10mm bolts, nuts	22-29

GENERAL TORQUE SPECIFICATIONS①

Part	Torque (ft. lbs.)
12mm bolts, nuts	36-43
6mm bolt w/8 mm head	5-8
6mm flange bolts, nuts	7-10
8mm flange bolts, nuts	17-22
10mm flange bolts, nuts	25-33

① Unless otherwise noted

FUEL SYSTEM

GAS TANK

Removal

1. Remove the seat.
2. Set the fuel petcock to "OFF."
3. Remove the carburetor float bowl drain plug and allow the gas to empty into a suitable container. Dispose of it properly.
4. Remove the two screws which secure the fuel petcock to the carburetor.
5. Remove the four nuts which secure the front mudguard assembly to the gas tank.
6. Remove the gas tank mounting bolt at the rear of the tank.
7. Protect the finish of the tank with rags stuffed between tank and mudguard.
8. Pull the tank back and free of the machine.

Installation

1. Reverse the removal procedure.
2. When installing the tank, be sure to engage the rubber cushions at the front with the seats on the tank.
3. Be sure all fuel line connections are tight.
4. Be certain the petcock is secured.
5. Check for leaks before operating the machine.

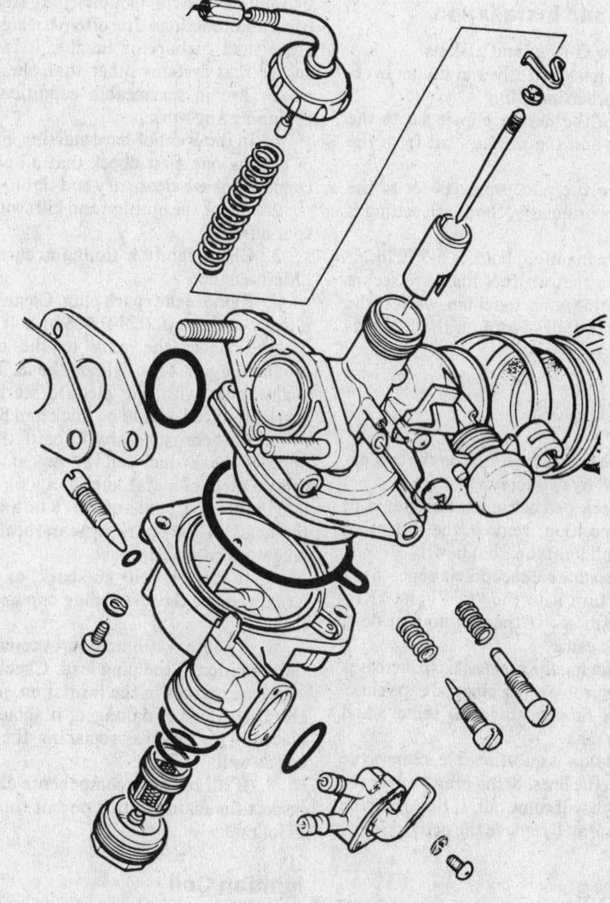

Carburetor assembly

CARBURETOR

Removal

1. Remove the seat.
2. Remove the fuel tank (see above).
3. Unscrew the carburetor top and pull out the throttle slide assembly. Wrap the assembly in a clean rag and place it out of the way to avoid damage.
4. Remove the choke cable clamp screw. Disconnect the choke cable from the carburetor.
5. Detach the carburetor air vent tube from the clamp on the frame.
6. Loosen the air cleaner clamp screw at the carb intake.
7. Disconnect the overflow line from the carburetor.
8. Remove the manifold bolts from the cylinder head and remove the carbutor complete with manifold.

Disassembly

1. Remove the nuts securing the manifold to the carburetor and separate the components.
2. Unscrew and remove the fuel filter bolt from the float bowl.
3. Remove the fuel filter.
4. Remove the O-ring.
5. Disconnect the air vent tube.
6. Remove the two screws which secure the float bowl. Remove the float bowl carefully. If it is stuck, hold it in place and wrap it with the plastic screwdriver handle to break it free.
7. Remove the float bowl O-ring.
8. Pull out the float pivot pin.
9. Lift off the float and needle.
10. Unscrew and remove the pilot jet.
11. Remove the main jet from the needle jet holder. Shake the needle jet out of the carburetor body. If it will not come out, push it out from the top of the carb with a wooden dowel.
12. Turn the pilot screw clockwise while counting the number of turns until it bottoms. Then unscrew and remove it. Be sure to return it to the original setting when assembling.
13. Unscrew and remove the throttle stop screw.
14. Compress the throttle slide spring and disengage the throttle cable from the slide.
15. Remove the needle clip retainer and shake the needle out of the slide. Do not remove the needle clip from the needle.

Inspection

NOTE: *Refer to the "General Information" section for carburetor rebuilding techniques.*

1. Clean all metal parts in a clean, safe solvent.
2. Blow air and fuel passages in the carburetor body clear with compressed air.

3. Check the condition of the needle and replace it if it is knicked or scored.

4. Clean all jets witih solvent and compressed air. Do not attempt to clean fuel passages with wire or the like, since the calibrated bores may be damaged.

5. Check the float for fuel leakage. Replace it if it is punctured or gas-logged.

6. Check the float needle and needle seat for wear or corrosion. Replace the needle if damage is noted.

7. Clean the fuel filter screen in solvent. If foreign matter cannot be removed, or if the filter is crushed, deformed or punctured, replace it.

CARBURETOR SPECIFICATIONS

ID	PB01B
Main jet	95
Slow jet	38
Needle clip setting (groove from top)	3
Float height	10.7 mm (0.42 in.)
Pilot screw (turns out)	1¾
Idle speed (rpm)	1700 ± 100

Assembly and Installation

1. Use new O-rings and gaskets.

2. Install jets carefully and do not overtighten them when installing.

3. Be sure the needle clip is set to the original groove in the needle (3rd from the top).

4. Be sure the pilot screw is set to the position it was originally. Standard setting is 1 3/4 turns out.

5. Tighten manifold bolts to 5-7 ft. lbs.

6. Be sure that all fuel lines are secure before operating the machine. After the carburetor is installed, turn on the fuel petcock and check for leaks.

FUEL PETCOCK

1. The petcock is mounted on the carburetor float bowl by two screws.

2. To check petcock operation, set it to the "OFF" position, remove the mounting screws and pull it off the float bowl.

3. Place a suitable recaptacle beneath the petcock and turn it to the "ON" and "RESERVE" positions. If there is no fuel flow, determine the cause.

4. If removing the fuel tank cap increases fuel flow, the problem is a clogged cap vent.

5. If fuel flow is sluggish, remove and clean the gas tank.

6. If fuel flow is questionable, remove the petcock from the lines, being prepared for the gasoline which will come out. If flow from the lines seems normal, replace the petcock.

FUEL LINES

1. Fuel lines should be checked for condition every year.

2. Replace lines that are damaged by abrasion, hardened, cracked or otherwise defective.

3. Be sure that safety clips are fitted to both sides of gas lines.

4. Whenever lines are disconnected or replaced, check for leaks before operating the machine.

ELECTRICAL SYSTEM

IGNITION CIRCUIT

Hard starting or misfiring are often caused by ignition system troubles, but since electrical malfunctions are often trickier to pin down than carburetor faualts, it is wise to ensure that systems other than the ignition circuit are in serviceable condition before beginning any work.

1. In the event of hard starting, misfiring or cutting out, first check that all electrical connections are clean, dry and tight.

2. Check the ignition and kill switches for continuity.

3. Check ignition timing accuracy. See "Maintenance."

4. Remove the spark plug. Clean and gap it to 0.6- 0.7mm (0.024-0.028 in.).

5. Connect the plug to the cap and ground it against the cylinder head. Turn the engine over with the electric starter. The spark produced should be thick and blue.

6. If there is no spark, or if the spark appears weak and yellow, repeat the test using a piece of metal, such as a nail, inserted into the cap and held about 1/8 in. away from the head. If the spark appears healthy, the plug was the problem.

7. If there is still no spark, or spark is weak, remove the spark plug cap and repeat the test.

8. If there is still no improvement, check the condition of the plug lead. Check for dirt or grease, cracks in the insulation, moisture, etc. If the lead is damaged, it should be replaced. This involves replacing the ignition coil as well.

9. If all of these components check out, inspect the main ignition circuit components as follows.

Ignition Coil

1. An ohmmeter is required to test the ignition coil.

2. Disconnect the spark plug lead.

3. Disconnect the primary wire from the coil (black/yellow).

4. Disconnect the green wire from the coil.

5. Remove the coil from the frame.

6. Remove the spark plug cap from the high tension lead.

7. Check the resistance across the two low tension leads. It should be about 1.8 ohms. If the resistance is not in this range, replace the coil.

8. Check the resistance across the coil terminal to which the green lead was connected and the high tension cable. Resistance should be 4.1 K (± 10%). If the reading is not within this range, the secondary winding is defective and the coil must be replaced.

9. Static resistance tests provide a general clue to coil condition, but cannot detect high voltage installation leaks. Therefore, even if the resistance readings are acceptable, there is a chance that the coil is defective. Replacing the coil temporarily with one which is known to be good is the only sure check.

Excitor Coil

1. The alternator excitor coil can be checked with an ohmm eter.

2. Remove the seat.

3. Disconnect the black/red lead at the connector.

4. Check the resistance between the black/red lead and a good ground on the engine. Resisstance should be 100-400 ohms.

5. If the reading is not within this range, the alternator stator must be replaced.

Pulse Generator

1. The pulse generator is located on the end of the camshaft. The unit can be checked with an ohmmeter.

2. Disconnect the pulse generator wires at the plastic connector. Leads are green and blue/yellow.

3. Resistance across the leads should be 90 ohms.

4. If the reading obtained is not with 10% of the specification, replace the pulse generator.

5. The pulse generator is located beneath the "125 CDI" cap. It can be removed after the two mounting screws are taken off.

6. If a new pulse generator is fitted, check that the air gap between the pulse rotor and the generator is set at 0.3-0.4mm (0.01-0.02 in.).

CDI Unit

A special tester is needed to check the CDI unit. If all other components in the circuit are found to be serviceable, the CDI unit can be checked most easily by replacing it with one which is known to be in working order.

CHARGING CIRCUIT

Output Test

NOTE: *The battery must be in good condition and fully charged or this test will not yield valid results.*

1. A voltmeter and an ammeter are required for a system output test.

2. Warm up the engine by running it for several minutes.

3. Remove the seat.

4. Remove the battery holder and cover.

5. Disconnect the red lead at the fuse. Connect the ammeter between the red leads.

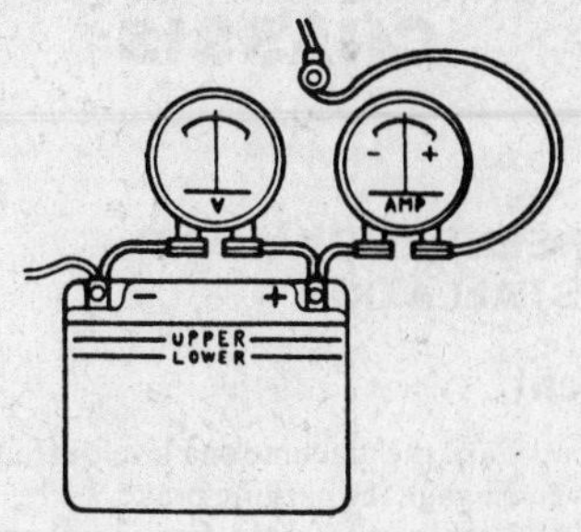

Charging circuit output test connections

6. Connect the voltmeter across the battery terminals.

7. Start the engine and note the readings.

8. The voltmeter should read 14 VDC.

9. The ammeter should read 2.4 a @ 2,000 rpm and 7.5 a @ 10,000 rpm.

10. If the readings obtained are not within specification, check the voltage regulator and the alternator charging coil as outlined below.

Voltage Regulator

1. The voltage regulator can be checked either with an ohmmeter or with a self-powered continuity light.

2. Remove the seat.

3. Disconnect the regulator wires at the connector.

4. Regulator leads are yellow, yellow, green, red and black.

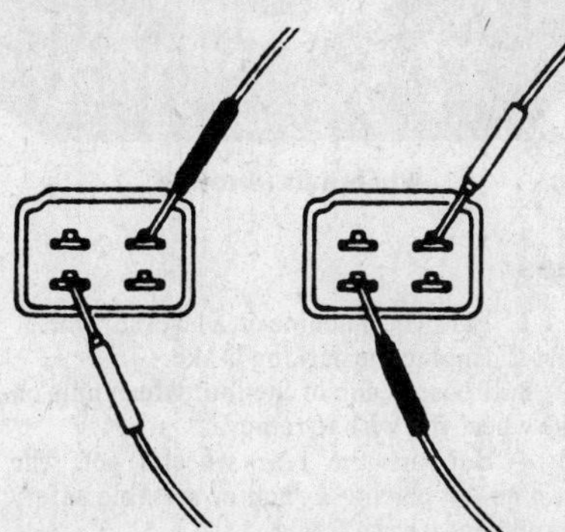
Reversing test probe polarity for regulator testing

5. The check is carried out by testing continuity across each pair of leads, and then reversing the polarity of the meter probes to check for continuity in the opposite direction. (Continuity will be indicated by a reading of 0.2 to 100 ohms depending on the lead involved. "No continuity" will be indicated by an infinite resistance reading.) For each pair of leads there must be continuity in one direction only.
Example: Yellow-green: 1-20 ohms
Green-yellow: Infinity.

6. If any of the tests show a pair of leads has continuity in both, or in neither direction, replace the voltage regulator.

Charging Coil

1. Use an ohmmeter to check charging coil resistance.

2. Remove the seat.

3. Remove the air cleaner hose.

4. Disconnect the alternator charging coil wires at the plastic connector. The wires are yellow and yellow.

5. Check resistance across the two yellow leads on the alternator side of the connector.

6. Resistance should be 0.1-1.0 ohms.

7. If the reading is not within this range, replace the alternator stator.

8. Check resistance between each lead and ground on the engine. Resistance must be infinite. Replace the stator is the meter shows any continuity between the wiring and ground.

STARTING SYSTEM

Testing

1. If, when the starter button is pressed, the starter spins, but the engine does not, the problem is either the starter clutch or the starter motor gears in the left crankcase cover.

2. If the engine turns over very slowly, check the battery for a low state of charge. Check that the engine oil is not too heavy for conditions. If these items are not the problem, suspect a defective starter motor.

3. If nothing at all happens when the starter button is pushed, check all electrical connections in the circuit. Check that the battery is properly charged. Check the ignition switch, starter button switch, neutral switch. Check the starter solenoid. If all of these items are in proper operating condition, check the starter motor.

Starter Solenoid

1. Remove the starter solenoid cover.

2. When the starter button is pressed, their should be an audible "click" at the solenoid.

3. Disconnect the solenoid high tension leads and the low tension wires at the plastic connector.

4. With an ohmmeter or continuity light, check the resistance of the low tension primary coil (yellow/red and green/red wires). There should be only a few ohms resistance. If this circuit shows an open condition, the solenoid must be replaced.

5. Put 12 VDC across the low tension wires. Check for continuity across the high tension terminals. There should be no resistance. If the high tension terminals do not show continuity, the solenoid is defective and must be replaced.

Starter Motor

REMOVAL

1. Be certain the ignition switch if "OFF".

2. Disconnect the ground cable at the battery.

3. Remove the exhaust pipe nuts at the cylinder head.

4. Remove the muffler mounting bolts. Remove the exhaust system.

5. Disconnect the high tension lead at the starter motor.

6. Remove the starter motor bracket bolts and the mounting screws and bolts. Remove the starter motor.

DISASSEMBLY

1. Remove the starter motor gear snap-ring.

2. Remove the gear. Remove the inner snap-ring and the thrust washers, if any, behind it. Note the number of washers. They must all be installed when the unit is assembled.

3. Remove the starter motor screws and take off the case end to expose the brushes.

4. Note the number and location of shims on the armature shaft when the cover is taken off.

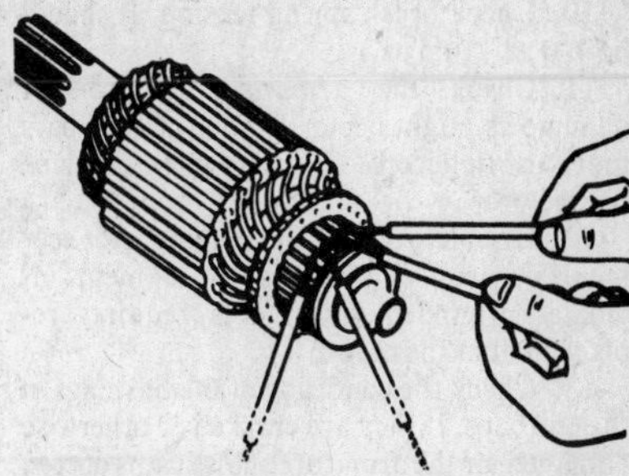
Checking commutator segment continuity

INSPECTION

1. Electrical tests can be carried out with an ohmmeter or a self-powered test light.

2. Check that continuity exists between each of the commutator segments. If one or more of them is "dead," the motor must be replaced.

3. Check that there is no continuity between the commutator segments and the armature core. Anything less than infinite resistance here will require replacement of the motor.

4. Check that there is no continuity between the commutator segments and the armature bars.

Minimum allowable brush length is 6.5 mm (0.26 in.)

5. Check that there is continuity between the brush which is wired to the stator (field) coil and the high tension cable terminal. Lack of continuity here indicates that the field coil is open and the motor must be replaced.

6. Check the commutator segments for signs of wear, scoring or other contact damage.

7. Clean the commutator with a rag and a safe solvent to remove carbon dust and other foreign matter.

8. Check the condition of the carbon brushes. Brushes with cracked or oddly worn contact surfaces should be replaced.

9. Measure brush length. Replace them as a set if either measures under 6.5mm (0.26 in.).

10. Check brush spring tension. It should be 410 gr. (14.5 oz.).

11. Check the armature for contact damage as might occur if the armature bars touch the field coils. If any is evident, replace the motor.

12. Discoloration of the commutator segments occuring on two adjacent segments indicates grounded coils. This requires replacement of the motor.

13. Check the condition of the bushings in the end caps. If they are cracked or otherwise damaged, or the armature shows signs of contact damage, the unit must be replaced.

ASSEMBLY

1. Clean all parts thoroughly.
2. Use a small amount of light duty grease to lubricate the bushings in the end caps.
3. Be sure that all shims are in place on the brush side of the armature.
4. Be sure that the brush springs are in place and that the brushes are in good contact with the commutator.
5. Check that the brush side end cap O-ring is in good condition.
6. Insert the armature into the case.
7. Install the brush holder with brushes.
8. When assembling the starter motor, align the pin on the brush holder with the notch in the case.

Align case and end-cover marks when assembling the starter motor

9. Instsall the rear cover, aligning the slot with the brush holder pin.
10. Align the marks on the motor case and the end covers before tightening the screws.

INSTALLATION

1. Reverse the removal procedure.
2. Lubricate the O-ring before fitting the motor.

ELECTRICAL SWITCHES

Ignition Switch

1. The ignition switch can be checked with an ohmmeter or a self-powered test light.
2. Remove the headlight.
3. Disconnect the ignition switch wires at the connectors (black/white, green, red, black).
4. When the ignition switch is in the "OFF" position, there should be continuity between the black/white and the green leads only.
5. When the ignition switch is in the "ON" position, there should be continuity between the red and the black leads only.
6. If the switch fails either test, replace it.

Engine Stop Switch

1. The switch can be checked with an ohmmeter or self-powered test light.
2. Remove the headlight.
3. Disconnect the stop switch leads at the connectors (green and black/white).
4. When in the "RUN" position, there should be no continuity.
5. In both "OFF" positions, there should be continuity between the green and black/white leads.
6. The switch is a part of the left switch housing which is placed as an assembly.

Lighting Switch

1. The switch can be checked with an ohmmeter or a self-powered test light.
2. Remove the headlight.
3. Disconnect the switch wires at the plastic connectors (brown, black/brown, white and blue).
4. When the lighting switch is "OFF" there must be no continuity between any of the wires.
5. When the lighting switch is in the "LO" position, there must be continuity between the brown, black/brown and white leads.
6. When the lighting switch is in the "N" position, there must be continuity across all four wires.
7. When the lighting switch is in the "HI" position, there must be continuity between the brown, black/brown and blue leads.
8. If the switch fails any one of these tests, it must be replaced. The switch is a part of the left switch housing which is replaced as an assembly.

Starter Button

1. The button can be checked with an ohmmeter or a self-powered test light.
2. Remove the headlight.
3. Disconnect the green/red and the light green/red button wires at the connectors.
4. There must be continuity across these wires only when the starter button is pushed.
5. If there is always continuity, or if no continuity is indicated when the button is pressed, the switch assembly must be replaced.

Neutral Switch

1. The neutral switch is a part of the starting circuit which will work only if the switch is closed, indicating that the transmission is in Neutral.
2. The switch can be checked with an ohmmeter or a self-powered test light.
3. Remove the seat.
4. Remove the air cleaner tube.
5. Disconnect the neutral switch wire at the connector (light green/red).
6. Check for continuity between the lead and ground on the engine case. When the transmission is in Neutral, there must be continuity.
7. When the transmission is in any other gear, the switch must be open (no continuity).
8. The switch can be replaced after removing the E- clip which secured it to the sub-transmission cover.

Specifications
- Headlight 12 V, 45/45W
- Taillight 12 V, 5W
- Indicator lights 12 V, 3W
- Fuse 7A
- Battery 12 V, 9ah

CHASSIS

WHEEL REMOVAL AND INSTALLATION

Front

1. Park the machine ona level surface.
2. Engage the parking brake.
3. Loosen each of the four wheel nuts on the wheel you wish to remove.
4. Support the front wheel(s) off the ground by placing a jack or suitable safety stand beneath the frame.
5. Remove the four wheel nuts.
6. Remove the wheel.
7. To install the wheel, be sure to put it on the hub with the tire valve facing out.
8. Install the four wheel nuts and tighten them in an "X" pattern a bit at a time until the proper torque of 36-43 ft. lbs. is reached.

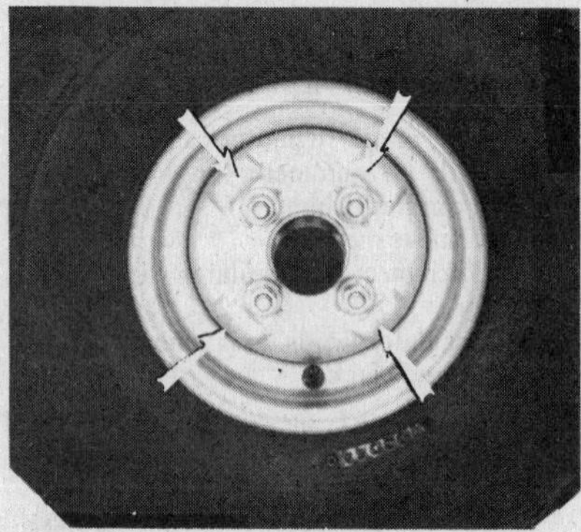

Wheel nuts (arrows)

Rear

1. Park the machine on a level surface.
2. Engine the parking brake.
3. Loosen each of the four wheel nuts on the wheel you wish to remove.
4. Support the rear wheel(s) off the ground by placing a jack or suitable safety stand beneath the frame.
5. Remove the four wheel nuts.
6. Remove the wheel.
7. To instsall the wheel, be sure to put it on the hub with the tire valve facing out.
8. Install the four wheel nuts and tighten them in an "X" pattern a bit at a time until the proper torque of 36-43 ft. lbs. is reached.

FRONT BRAKE

Removal

1. Remove the front wheel.
2. Back off the brake adjuster wing nut, counting the number of turns so that adjustment can be equalized when reassembling.
3. Remove the axle nut cotter pin.
4. Remove the axle nut.
5. Remove the brake drum.

Inspection

Brake shoes can be inspected in place on the plate.

1. Inspect the linings for wear. There should be at least 2.0mm (0.08 in.) of lining

Front wheel axle nut (arrow)

material left measured at the lining's thinnest point. If either shoe is worn below this limit, replace the pair.

NOTE: *If linings on one wheel are worn, both front brakes should be replaced to ensure equal performance.*

2. Inspect the linings for scoring or grooves. These may be caused by particles of dirt which enter the drum. If badly scored, the linings should be replaced and the drum inspected closely for the same type of damage.

3. Be sure that the linings are free of and oil and grease. Lubricant-impregnated linings must be replaced.

4. If the linings are in usable condition, rough up the surfaces with coarse sandpaper to break the glaze. Clean them thoroughly afterwards with alcohol or laquer thinner.

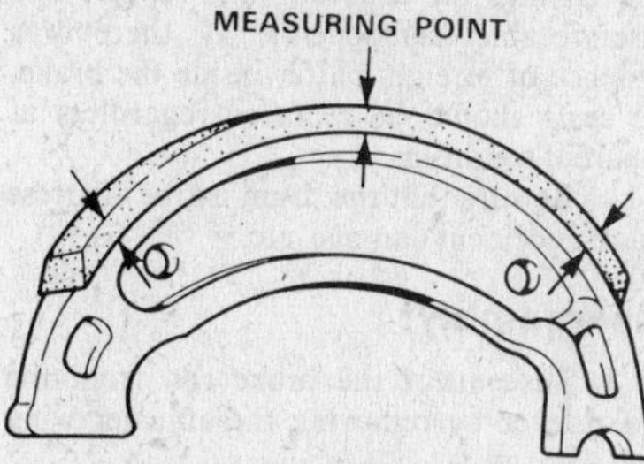

Checking brake lining thickness

5. Clean foreign matter from the brake plate with a rag.

CAUTION: *Brake dust may present a health hazard. Do not blow the brake assemblies clear with a high pressure compressed air source or the particulates may be inhaled.*

6. Inspect the brake drum surface for condition. The drum must be free of scoring or rust.

7. Rust can be removed from the brake drum surface with sandpaper. Polish the surface until it is shiny, then clean it thoroughly.

8. Alcohol or laquer thinner can be used to remove dirt or deposits from the drum.

9. Measure the inside diameter of the brake drum. If it measures more than 111mm (4.4 in.), replace it.

10. Measure the diameter of the drum in two directions to check for an out-of-round condition. This is usually noticable as an off-and-on feeling when the brakes are applied. This condition may be remedied by having the drum turned down on a lathe, but the final diameter must not exceed the service limit above.

11. Minor scoring or imperfections in the drum can be remedied by having the drum turned down. If this is done, replace the brake shoes regardless of apparent condition.

12. Check the brake drum rubber seal for condition and replace it if it is cracked or otherwise damaged.

13. Check the brake drum for cracks or other critical defects.

14. Check the wheel bearings in the brake drum. See "Front Wheel Bearings," below.

Disassembly

1. Disconnect the brake cable from the brake lever by removing the adjuster wing nut.
2. Remove the brake lever pinch bolt.
3. Carefully pry the brake lever off the splined cam shaft.
4. Expand the brake shoes by hand and pull them and the return springs off the brake plate by folding them together.
5. Tap the brake cam out of the brake plate taking care not to lose the seals and wear indicator plate. Note the spring on the inside of the brake plate as well.

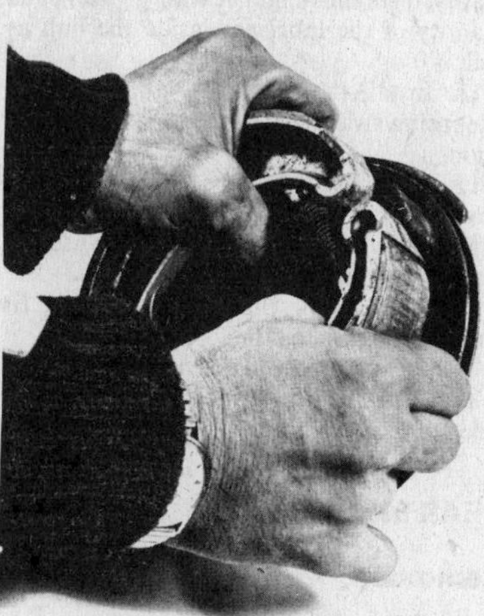

Removing the brake shoes from the plate

6. Clean dirt, brake dust and other foreign matter from the brakeplate with a solvent-soaked rag.
7. Check the plate closely for stress cracks or other damage.
8. Check the condition of the brake shoe springs. Replace them if they are rusted, broken, deformed or weakened.
9. Check the brake cam spring and replace it if it is damaged.
10. Check that the brake cam is not bent.
11. Check that the splines on the cam are in good condition.
12. Clean the cam in solvent. Remove rust or corrosion with sandpaper.
13. The cam must turn freely in the brake plate hole. If it does not, determine the cause and remedy it.
14. Check the condition of the grease seals in the brake plate and replace them if damaged. They can be pried out.

Assembly

1. Install the grease seals and spacer in the brake if they were removed.
2. Lubricate the brake cam with a good grade of medium-weight chassis grease.
3. Fit the washer and the cam spring on the cam.
4. Insert the cam into the plate. Be sure that the spring end is fitted into the hole in the cam and the other end is hooked over the anchor on the plate.
5. Lubricate the brake shoe pivot with chassis grease.
6. Fit the outer cam grease seal if it is not already in place. Install the wear indicator plate. The tab aligns with the cam cut-out.
7. Install the brake lever, aligning the punch mark on the end of the cam.
8. Install and tighten the lever pinch bolt.
9. Clean hand thoroughly to avoid contaminating the brake linings.
10. Assemble the shoes and return springs and spread them by hand to fit over the pivot and the cam. Be sure they are properly seated.
11. Work the brake lever by hand and observe operation.
12. Connect the brake cable and adjust as outlined in "Maintenance" after the brake drum is installed.

Installation

1. Clean off the axle shaft.
2. Grease the lips of the wheel bearing seals.
3. Fit the brake drum. Be sure the spacer is in place.
4. Install the axle nut. Tighten it to 51-65 ft. lbs.
5. Install a new axle cotter pin.
6. Install the wheel. Check for free rotation. Adjust the brakes as outlined in "Maintenance."

FRONT BRAKE CABLE

Removal

1. Remove the front wheels.
2. Remove the front fender mounting bolts at the fuel tank.
3. Remove the inner fenders.
4. Remove the carrier mounting bolts.
5. Remove the front fender.
6. Unscrew the wing nut adjusters and disconnect both secondary brake cables from the brake brake levers at the wheels.
7. Disconnect the brake cables from the frame clamps and brackets.
8. Remove the junction box mounting bolts.
9. Remove the three rear plate screws.
10. Remove the junction box from the cable/sprocket assembly.
11. Remove the plastic guide.
12. Remove the junction E-clip.
13. Remove the sprocket pin and sprocket.
14. Disconnect the upper cable from the hand lever.

Installation

1. Assembly is the reverse of disassembly.
2. Use a good grade of chassis grease and lubricate the chain, sprocket, sprocket pin and guide. Apply grease to the inside of the junction box as well.
3. Be sure the rubber cable seals are in place in the junction box.
4. Connect the primary cable to the hand lever.

5. Connect the secondary cables to the brake levers at the wheels.

6. Install the wheels.

7. Adjust the cable assembly as described below.

Adjustment

1. The primary cable adjuster at the junction box should be screwed all the way into the box.

2. Turn the adjuster wing nuts at the wheels in by equal amounts until both ends of the chain in the junction box are equal distances from the ends of the secondary cables.

3. Continue turning the adjuster wing nuts until the ends of the chain are as close as possible to the ends of the secondary cables.

4. Turn the adjuster nuts by equal amounts until both front wheels are locked.

5. Turn the primary cable adjuster on top of the junction box out until there is no free-play at the hand lever. Turn the adjuster out another 2 1/2 turns. Tighten the locknut and slip the dust cover into place.

6. Loosen both adjuster wing nuts by equal amounts until their levers have 2.8-3.3mm (0.11-0.13 in.) of free-play before the linings contact the drums.

7. Check that the hand lever has 15-20mm (5/8-3/4 in.) of free-play measured at the tip of the lever. Use the wing nuts to make this final adjustment. Be sure to turn both by equal amounts.

8. Install the rear plate, box mounting bolts, etc.

9. Check brake operation before riding. If the vehicle pulls to one side when the front brake is applied, repeat the adjustment procedure.

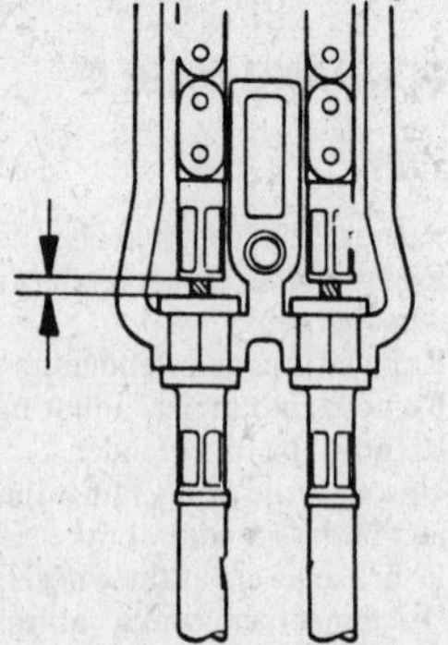

Equalize gap between chain ends and cables

FRONT WHEEL BEARINGS

The front wheel bearings are fitted to the brake drums and can be removed and/or serviced after the brake drums are taken off.

1. Remove the front wheel(s).

2. Remove the axle nut cap. Remove the axle nut cotter pin. Remove the axle nut.

3. Remove the brake drum.

4. Remove the spacer from the drum.

5. Pry out the grease seals on either side.

6. Bearings should be inspected in place, since removal usually damages them.

7. Check each bearing for play of the inner race relative to the outer. Maximum allowable radial (up- and-down) play is 0.05mm (0.002 in.). Maximum allowable axial (in-and-out) play is 0.10mm (0.004 in.).

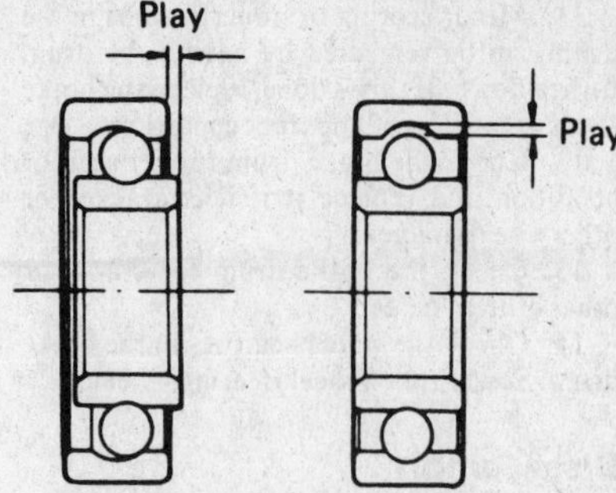

Bearing axial (left) and radial (right) play

If either bearing exceeds these limits, replace the pair.

8. Check the bearing rotation. If any roughness, binding or noise is noted, replace the set.

9. Remove the bearings by reaching into the hub with a suitable drift and driving out one of them. Remove the spacer. Remove the remaining bearing in the same manner.

10. Lubricate new bearings with a good quality, medium-weight bearing grease. Put a quantity of the lubricant inside the hub as well.

11. Install the bearings with the sealed side facing away from the center of the brake drum.

12. Bearings should be driven into the drum until fully seated. A driver large enough to cover the whole bearing should be used so that it can be driven straight in.

13. After the first bearing is installed, fit the spacer, then the other bearing.

14. Press grease seals in carefully.

15. When refitting the drum, tighten the axle nut to 51-65 ft. lbs. Use a new cotter pin.

REAR BRAKE

Removal

1. Remove the right rear wheel.
2. Remove the axle nut dust cap.
3. Remove the cotter pin.
4. Remove the axle nut and washer.
5. Remove the wheel hub.
6. Remove the two brake drum nuts from the axle.
7. Remove the washer.
8. Remove the brake drum cover bolts. Remove the cover.
9. Remove the O-ring from the axle.
10. Pull of the brake drum.
11. Brake components are now exposed for inspection and service.

Inspection

1. Inspect the linings for wear. There should be at least 2.0mm (0.08 in.) of lining material left at the thinnest point. If either shoe is worn below this limit, replace the pair.

2. Inspect the linings for scoring or grooves. These may be caused by particles of dirt which enter the drum. If badly scored, the linings should be replaced and the drum inspected closely for the same type of damage.

3. Be sure the linings are free of oil and grease. Lubricant-impregnated linings must be replaced.

4. If the linings are in usable condition, rough up the surfaces with sandpaper to break the glaze. Clean them thoroughly afterwards with alcohol or laquer thinner.

5. Clean foreign matter from the brake plate with a rag.

CAUTION: *Brake dust may present a health hazard. Do not blow the brake assembly clear with a high pressure compressed air source or the particulates may be inhaled.*

6. Inspect the brake drum surface for condition. The drum must be free of rust or scoring.

7. Rust can be removed from the drum surface with sandpaper. Polish the surface until it is shiny, then clean it thoroughly.

8. Alcohol or laquer thinner can be used to remove dirt or deposits from the drum.

9. Measure the inside diameter of the drum. If it measures more than 141mm (5.6 in.), replace it.

10. Measure the diameter of the drum in two directions to check for an out-of-round condition. This is usually noticable as an off-and-on feeling when the brakes are applied. This condition may be remedied by having the drum turned down on a lathe, but the final diameter must not exceed the service limit, above.

11. Minor scoring or imperfections in the drum can be remedied by having the drum turned down. If this is done, replace the brake shoes regardless of apparent condition.

12. Check the splines on the brake drum and those on the axle for condition. If they are worn or show other signs of damage, replace the components.

13. Check the brake drum cover seals and axle O-rings for condition and replace any unserviceable components. If there was evidence of foreign matter inside the brake, the seals should be replaced regardless of apparent condition.

14. Be sure that the drum is free of stress cracks, accident damage, etc.

Disassembly

1. Disconnect the brake rod from the brake lever by removing the adjuster wing nut.

2. Expand the brake shoes by hand and pull them and the return springs off the brake plate by folding them together.

3. Remove the brake lever pinch bolt.

4. Carefully pry the brake lever off the splined shaft.

5. Remove the wear indicator plate.

6. Tap the brake cam out of the brake plate taking care not to lose any seals which may come out.

7. Clean dirt, brake dust and other foreign matter from the brake plate with a solvent-soaked rag.

8. Check the brake plate closely for stress cracks or other damage.

9. Check the condition of the brake shoe springs. Replace them if they are rusted, broken, deformed or weakened.

10. Check the brake cam spring and replace it if it is damaged.

11. Check that the brake cam is not bent.

12. Check that the splines on the cam are in good condition.

13. Clean the cam in solvent. Remove rust or corrosion with sandpaper.

14. The cam must turn freely in the brake plate hole. If it does not, determine the cause and remedy it.

15. Check the condition of the cam dust

seal and the grease seals in the brake plate and replace them if damaged. Grease seals can be pried out.

Assembly

1. Install the grease seals in the brake plate if they were removed.
2. Lubricate the brake cam with a good grade of medium-weight chassis grease.
3. Fit the cam spring on the cam, inserting the end of the spring into the hole in the cam.
4. Install the brake cam. Fit the outer end of the spring over the anchor on the brake plate.
5. Install the dust seal on the outer side of the cam.
6. Lubricate the brake shoe pivot with chassis grease.
7. Install the wear indicator plate, aligning the tab with the cam cut-out.
8. Install the brake lever, aligning the punch mark on the lever with the punch mark on the cam.
9. Install and tighten the lever pinch bolt.
10. Clean hands thoroughly to avoid contaminating the brake linings.
11. Assemble the shoes and return springs and spread them by hand to fit over the pivot and the cam. Be sure they are properly seated.
12. Work the brake lever by hand and observe operation.
13. Install the brake drum.
14. Lubricate the axle O-ring and install it.
15. Lubricate the center seal of the brake drum cover with grease.
16. Install the cover.
17. Install the washer.
18. Install and tighten the brake drum inner nut. Torque is 25-33 ft. lbs.
19. The outer drum must be secured with a non- permanent thread-locking compound. Clean the axle threads and apply the compound. Tighten the outer nut to 87-101 ft. lbs.

NOTE: *Hold the inner nut in place while tightening the outer nut.*

Installation

1. Clean the axle shaft splines, then lubricate them with grease.
2. Install the hub.
3. Install the hub washer with the "OUTSIDE" mark facing out.
4. Install the axle nut and tighten it to 36-58 ft. lbs.
5. Install a new cotter pin.
6. Install the wheel and tighten the wheel nuts in an "X" pattern to a torque of 36-43 ft. lbs.
7. Install the dust cap.
8. Connect the rear brake rod and adjust the brake as outlined in "Maintenance."

FRONT END

Removal

1. Park the machine on a level surface.
2. Apply the parking brake.
3. Support the front end off the ground by placing sturdy, safe supports beneath the frame.
4. Remove the front wheels.
5. Remove the skid plate (four bolts).
6. Remove the tie-rods by pulling out the cotter pins and removing the tie-rod nuts at the steering shaft and the steering knuckles.
7. Disconnect the brake cables from the brake levers.
8. Remove the axle nut cotter pin. Remove the axle nut. Pull off the brake drum.
9. Remove the kingpin bolt cotter pin.
10. Remove the kingpin bolt castellated nut.
11. Remove the kingpin bolt.
12. Remove the brake plate/axle assembly.
13. Remove the dust collars, dust seals and the kingpin from the front tube.
14. To remove the front tube, bend up the locking tabs and remove the four tube mounting bolts.

Inspection

TIE-RODS

1. Check the tie-rods for accident damage, a bent condition, etc.
2. Inspect the rubber seals for deterioration, cracks or tears.
3. If the tie-rod is disassembled, be sure to fit the ball joint with the "L" mark on the steering shaft side of the rod. Ball joints must be threaded onto the rods as far as possible.

KINGPIN

1. Clean the kingpin in solvent.
2. Measure the outside diameters of the kingpin at the bearing surfaces. If diameter measures less than 17.9mm (0.70 in.), replace it.
3. Measure the inside diameters of the kingpin bushings. Maximum acceptable diameter is 18.2mm (0.72 in.). If the measurement exceeds this figure, replace the bushings.
4. The bushings can be removed from the frame by driving them out with a hammer and drift. They are installed in like manner.
5. Check condition of the dust seals and replace them if damaged.

Installation

1. Clean all parts thoroughly before installing them.
2. Use new cotter pins where they are fitted.
3. If the front tube was removed, install it and tighten the mounting bolts to 58-72 ft. lbs. Bend down the washer locking tabs.
4. Lubricate the kingpins with a good grade of chassis grease and insert them into the bushings.
5. Grease the lips of the dust seals and install the seals and collars.
6. Install the brake plate assembly.
7. Fit the kingpin bolt. Tighten the nut to 36-43 ft. lbs. I nstall a new cotter pin.
8. Install the tie-rods, noting that the "L" marked ball joint goes on the steering shaft side (the flat machined into the rod is closer to the wheel).
9. Tighten the tie-rod castellated nuts to 25-31 ft. lbs.
10. If the tie-rods were disassembled, or if new ones were installed, adjust toe-in as outlined below.

Toe-In Adjustment

1. Park the machine on a level surface.
2. Position the front wheels straight ahead.
3. Mark the center of each front tire at the forward most part of the tire. Measure the distance between the marks.
4. Roll the machine forward until the two marks are 180° from their original position. Measure this distance.
5. Subtract the first measurement from the second. The result is the toe-in. It should be 10-20mm (3/8-3/4 in.).
6. To adjust toe-in, loosen the two lock nuts on each tie-rod and use a wrench on the machined flat of each rod to turn it until toe-in is correct.

NOTE: *Be sure to turn each rod by equal amounts.*

7. Tighten the lock nuts to 25-31 ft. lbs.
8. Recheck toe-in.
9. Measure the distance from the center of each tire to the steering shaft. The distances must be equal on both sides.

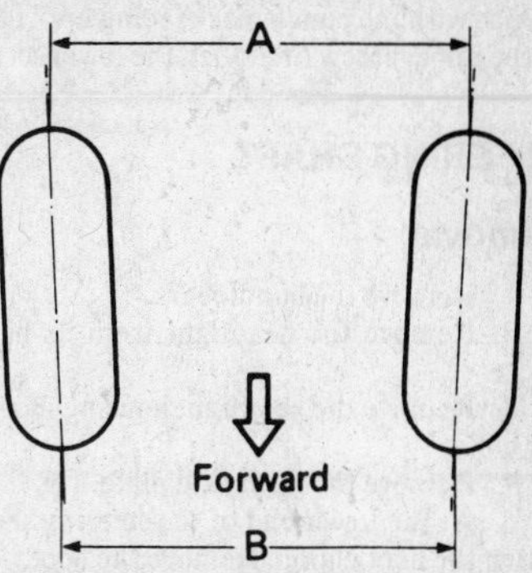

Toe-in is derived by subtracting distance "B" from "A" (10-20mm [3/8-3/4 in.])

Steering Stopper Adjustment

Early models may have adjustable steering stopper bolts secured by locknuts. Clearance between the tie- rod and the front wheel rim should be 4-6mm (3/8-5/8 in.) on both sides when the wheels are fully turned. Adjust by loosening the lock nut and turning the stopper bolt as required.

HANDLEBARS

Removal

1. Remove the wiring clamps from the handlebars.
2. Remove the throttle lever housing.
3. Remove the left and right brake lever holders.
4. Remove the switch housing on the left side.
5. Loosen the choke cable nut. Detach the choke cable from the handlebar upper holder.
6. Remove the rubber cover.
7. Remove the handlebar holder (four bolts).
8. Remove the handlebars.

Installation

1. When fitting the bars, align the punch mark on the bars with the top surface of the handlebar holders.
2. Install the holder and tighten the four bolts to 17-22 ft. lbs. Front bolts should be secured first, then the two rear bolts.
3. The rest of the procedure is the reverse of removal. Install the brake lever holder

clamps with the punch mark facing up. Tighten the upper screw first, then the lower screw.

STEERING SHAFT

Removal

1. Remove the handlebars.
2. Remove the headlight from its housing.
3. Remove the headlight housing mounting bolts.
4. Remove the front skid plate.
5. At the lower end of the steering shaft, loosen the boot clamp. Remove the boot.
6. Remove the cotter pin.
7. Remove the steering shaft nut and washer.

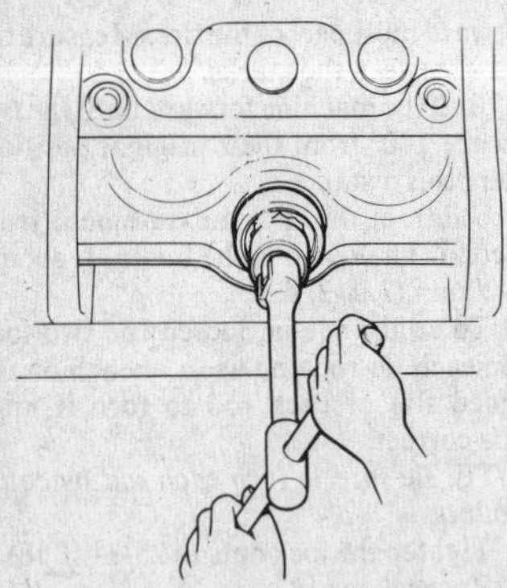

Removing the steering shaft nut

8. Disconnect the tie-rods from the steering knuckle.
9. Dirve out the steering shaft.
10. Remove the headlight bracket.
11. Remove the steering collar.

Inspection

1. Check the shaft for a bent condition and replace it if damaged in this way. Do not attempt to straighten a bent shaft.
2. Measure the outside diameter of the shaft where the collar is positioned. It should be no less than 25.3mm (0.99 in.), or the shaft should be replaced.
3. Measure the inside and outside diameters of the collar. Service limits are 25.7mm (1.01 in.) and 35.0mm (1.37 in.) respectively.
4. Replacement of the lower steering stem bearing requires a special tool to remove the locknut. Locknut torque is 29-43 ft. lbs.

Installation

1. Reverse the removal procedure.
2. Use a good grade of chassis grease on the steering shaft bearing, collar and shaft surfaces.
3. If the handlebar lower holders were removed, torque nuts to 29-35 ft. lbs.
4. When fitting the shaft, align the punch marks on the shaft and steering knuckle.
5. Fit the O-ring to the lower ends of the shaft.
6. Tighten the lower nut to 36-51 ft. lbs.

REAR AXLE

Removal

1. Remove the seat.

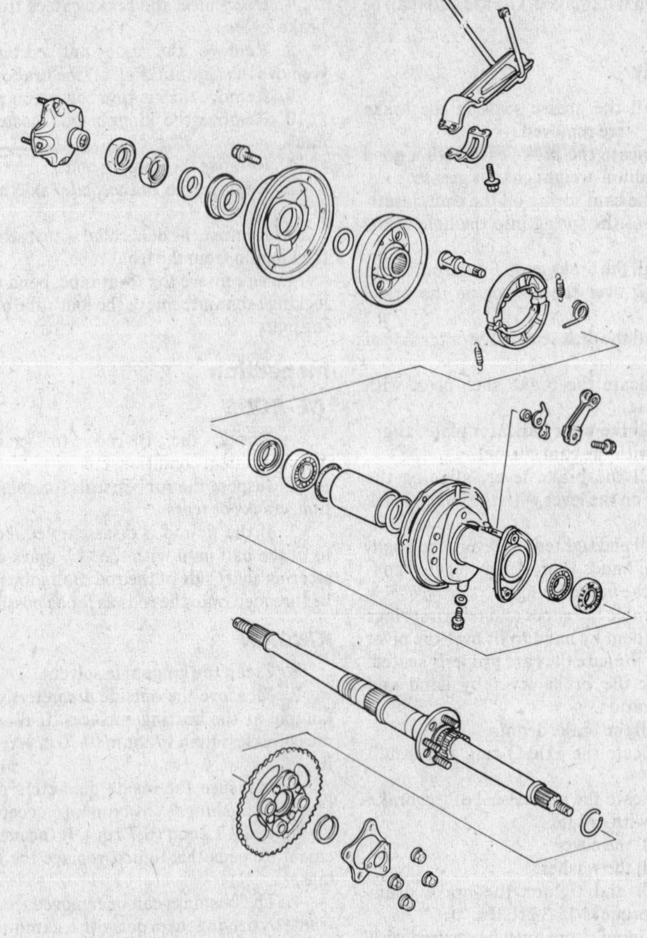

Rear axle assembly

Brake drum nuts (arrows)

2. Remove the five skid plate mounting bolts and the skid plate.
3. Support the rear end of the vehicle with safe, sturdy stands placed beneath the frame.
4. Remove the rear wheel nuts and take off the wheels.
5. Remove the axle nut dust caps.
6. Remove the cotter pins.
7. Remove the axle nuts and washers.
8. Pull the hubs off the axle.
9. Disconnect the carburetor overflow tube from the clamps on the chain case.
10. Remove the three bolts securing the seal cover around the real axle and take off the cover.
11. Remove the chain case mounting bolts.
12. Undo the clamps.
13. Remove the chain case mounting bolts.
14. Back off the rear brake adjuster nut.
15. Loosen the drive chain adjuster nut.
16. Loosen the four bearing holder mounting bolts.
17. Disconnect the drive chain. Be sure to remove the masterlink spring clip with a pliers. Prying the clip off will make it unusable. Put the masterlink on one end of the chain to avoid loss.
18. Remove the two brake drum nuts from the axle.
19. Remove the washer.
20. Remove the brake drum cover bolts. Remove the cover.
21. Remove the O-ring from the axle.
22. Pull off the brake drum.
23. Use a plastic mallet to drive the axle out from the right side.
24. Remove the chain case inner half bolts (four). Remove the case half.
25. Remove the rear brake adjuster nut and disconnect the brake rod from the brake level.
26. Remove the trailer hitch upper mounting bolts.
27. Remove the bearing holder from the frame.

Inspection

AXLE

1. Check sprocket condition.
2. To remove the sprocket, remove the four damper cover nuts, the damper cover and snap-ring.
3. Check the dampers for damage.
4. Check all axle splines for condition.
5. Check axle run-out. When measured in the middle of the axle, the serviceable limit for run-out is 3.0mm (0.12 in.). This is 1/2 of the Total Indicated Reading of the gauge.
6. Check the condition of the O-ring behind the axle flange and replace it if necessary.
7. Assesmbly is the reverse of disassembly. Greasse axle splines before installation. Lubricate the O-ring before fitting it to the axle. Tighten the damper nuts to 17-22 ft. lbs.

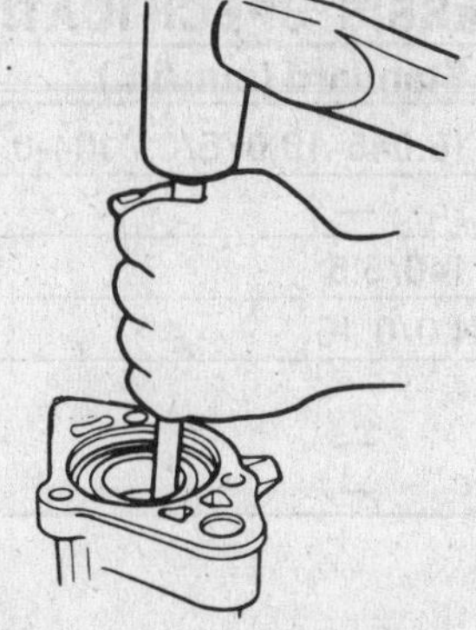

Removing a rear axle bearing from the holder

Axle nut washer must be installed with the mark facing "OUTSIDE"

BEARING HOLDER

1. Remove the trailer hitch from the bearing holder.
2. Pry out the grease seals on either side.
3. Bearings should be checked in place, since removal will usually damage them.
4. Check for excessive play of the inner race relataive to the outer. Maximum allowable radial (up- and-down) play is 0.05mm (0.002 in.). Maximum allowable axial (in-and-out) play is 0.1mm (0.004 in.).
5. Check the bearings for rough or binding rotation, excessive noice, etc.
6. Replace bearings in sets.
7. Bearings can be removed by driving them out with a hammer and suitable drift. Remove one bearing and take out the spacer and any shims. Drive out the remaining bearing.
8. Pack new bearings with a good grade of medium-weight bearing grease. Place a quantity of the lubricant in the bearing holder as well.
9. Install bearings with the marked side out.
10. Install the right side bearing first, driving it straight in with a suitably sized bearing driver until it is firmly seated.
11. Install the spacer along with any shims which may be fitted.
12. Install the remaining bearing.
13. Press grease seals straight into the holder.
14. Lubricate the seal lips before assembly.

Installation

1. If the trailer hitch was removed from the bearing holder, install it and tighten the bolts slightly. The hitch clamp goes on the under side of the holder (the same side as the drain bolt).
2. Install the bearing holder and fit the four bolts, but do not tighten them yet since the chain must be readjusted.
3. Fit the chain adjuster nut.
4. Connect the brake rod.
5. Fit the trailer hitch to the rear carrier stay and tighten all trailer hitch mounting hardware.
6. Install the inner chain case half.
7. Install the axle from the left side of the machine.
8. Check that the brake shoe assemblies are in place.
9. Install the brake drum.
10. Lubricate and instaall the brake drum O-ring.
11. Lubricate the center seal of the brake drum cover. Install the cover and secure it with the six bolts.
12. Clean the axle threads thoroughly.
13. Fit the washer on the axle.
14. Install the brake drum inner nut and tighten it to 25-33 ft. lbs.
15. The brake drum outer nut must be secured with a non-permanent thread-locking compound. Apply the compound to the threads of the axle, then install the nut.
16. Hold the inner nut in place while the outer is tightened to the proper torque of 87-101 ft. lbs.
17. Connect the drive chain. The closed end of the masterlink spring clip must face the direction of chain rotation.
18. Adjust the chain as outlined in "Maintenance" and tighten the four bearing holder bolts to 51-58 ft. lbs.
19. The remainder of the procedure is the reverse of removal. Note the following:
    a. Grease the wheel hub splines before fitting the hubs.
    b. Install the hub washers with the "OUTSIDE" mark facing out.
    c. Tighten the axle nuts to 36-58 ft. lbs.
    d. Use new axle nut cotter pins.
    e. Tighten the wheel nuts gradually and in an "X" pattern until the final torque of 36-43 ft. lbs. is reached.
    f. Adjust the rear brake after assembly.

CHASSIS SPECIFICATIONS

Part	Standard (mm/in.)	Service limit (mm/in.)
Front brake drum ID	110/4.3	111/4.4
Front brake lining thickness	4.0/0.16	2.0/0.08
Front wheel bearing play		
Axial	—	0.10/0.004
Radial	—	0.05/0.002
Steering shaft OD	25.35-25.40/0.998-0.999	25.3/0.99
Steering collar		
ID	25.2-25.6/0.99-1.00	25.7/1.01
OD	35.1-35.5/1.38-1.39	35.0/1.37
Kingpin OD	17.966-17.984/0.7073-0.7080	17.9/0.70

CHASSIS SPECIFICATIONS

Part	Standard (mm/in.)	Service limit (mm/in.)
Kingpin bushing ID	18.045-18.075/0.7104-0.7112	18.17/0.715
Rear axle run-out (1/2 TIR)	—	3.0/0.12
Rear brake drum ID	140/5.5	141/5.6
Rear brake lining thickness	4.0/0.16	2.0/0.08
Rear wheel bearing play		
Axial	—	0.10/0.004
Radial	—	0.05/0.002

CHASSIS TORQUE SPECIFICATIONS

Part	Torque (ft. lbs.)
Steering shaft nut	36-51
Handlebar upper holder bolts	17-22
Handlebar lower holder nut	29-35
Wheel nuts (front & rear)	36-43
Front axle nuts	51-65
Brake drum nut	
Inner	25-33
Outer	87-101*
Foot pegs (before Frame No. 007407)	17-22
Foot pegs (Frame No. 007407 and later)	25-33
Front engine mounting bolts (10 mm)	29-35
Front engine mounting bolt (8 mm)	22-29
Engine rear mounting bracket	36-43
Drive chain guide	5-8
Mud guards	5-7
Rear axle nuts	36-58
Bearing holder bolts	51-58
Lower steering bearing locknut	29-43
Front tube mounting bolts	58-72
Tie-rod lock nuts	25-31
Kingpin bolts	36-43
Tie-rod mounting nuts	25-31
Sprocket damper nuts	17-22

*Use a non-permanent thread-locking compound

GENERAL TORQUE SPECIFICATIONS ①

Part	Torque (ft. lbs.)
5mm screws	2.5-3.6
6mm screws	5-8
5mm bolts, nuts	3.5-4.5
6mm bolts, nuts	6-9
8mm bolts, nuts	13-18
10mm bolts, nuts	22-29
12mm bolts, nuts	36-43
6mm bolt w/8 mm head	5-8
6mm flange bolts, nuts	7-10
8mm flange bolts, nuts	17-22
10mm flange bolts, nuts	25-33

① Unless otherwise noted

Honda Four-Stroke Singles

MODEL COVERAGE

Z50A	CT70H	C90	CB100, K1-K3	CL125S
C65/M	SL70	CD90	CL100/S	SL125
S65	XR75	CT90	SL100	TL125, K1-K2
C70/M	S90	SL90	CB125S/S1/S2	TL125 (76)
CL70	CL90/LK	ST90	CD125S	CB125S (76)

INDEX

NOTE: See supplement to this section for 1982 and later information.

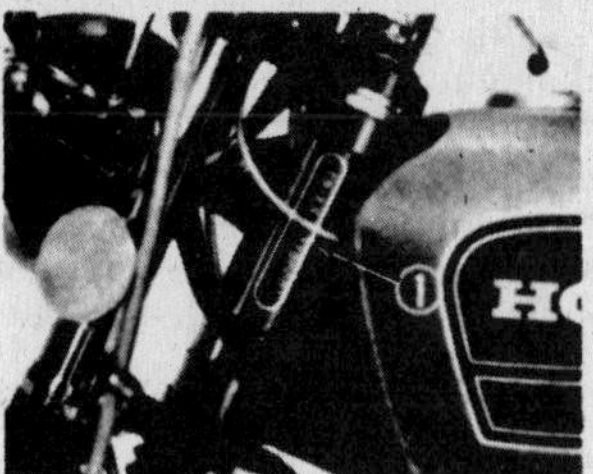

Frame serial number location

Frame serial number location

Engine serial number location

MAINTENANCE

NOTE: *Common maintenance procedures are explained in detail in "General Information."*

OIL CHANGES AND LUBRICATION

Checking Oil

On all models the oil level is checked by means of the dipstick incorporated into the filler cap. The filler cap is located in the right crankcase cover. To check the oil:

1. Start the engine and allow it to warm up for a few minutes.
2. Hold the motorcycle upright on level ground, remove the dipstick and wipe it clean.
3. Reinsert the dipstick, allowing the dipstick cap to rest on the top of the threads of its hole. The oil level should be between the maximum and minimum marks on the dipstick.

If the level is below the minimum mark on the dipstick, add enough oil through the hole to bring the level up to the maximum mark.

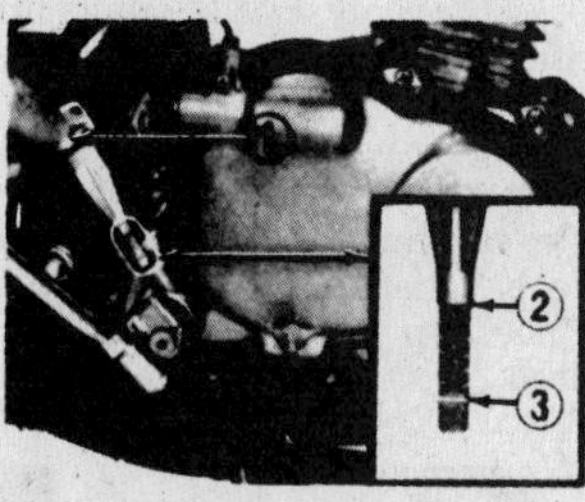

Engine oil level must be maintained between the upper (2) and lower (3) dipstick level marks

Changing Oil

1. Change the engine oil every 1,500 miles, or on machines without a speedometer, every 30 operating days or every 3 months. Use high detergent motor oil service rated "SE" only.

NOTE: *The oil change interval is based on normal operating conditions. If the motorcycle is used under severe conditions (i.e., racing, high-speed operation, stop-and-go riding, dusty conditions, operation in cold weather, etc.), changes should be made more frequently. This is also true if the machine is used infrequently especially during winter months.*

2. Run the engine until it is at normal operating temperature. Oil must always be changed when the engine is warm.
3. Remove the dipstick, and place a pan beneath the engine to catch the oil. Remove the drain plug and allow the oil to drain for several minutes. Kick the engine over a few times with the kick-starter to remove any oil remaining in the delivery system.
4. Replace the drain plug and tighten it securely.
5. Remove and clean the filter, if applicable, as outlined below.
6. Fill the sump with the correct amount and grade of oil. Refer to the charts at the end of this section. Run the engine for a minute or so, then shut it off and let it sit for one minute and check the oil level; add oil as necessary until the level is correct.

NOTE: *The use of oil additives is not recommended, as they may cause clutch slippage.*

Oil Filter

Two types of oil filter are used: a filter screen and a centrifugal filter. The centrifugal oil filter is located on the right-side of the crankshaft on the XR75 and 100/125 cc machines, or in the clutch on other models.

50–90 cc models have the filter screen in the crankcase under the right crankcase cover, while on the 100/125 cc bikes, the filter screen is beneath a cap on the left-side of the crankcase sump.

On 100/125 cc models, the filter screen is easily accessible, and should therefore be cleaned at every oil change. The screen on other models and the centrifugal filter on all models is reached after removing the right crankcase cover, and service should be performed at every 6,000 miles or 1 year intervals.

OIL FILTER SCREEN

100/125 cc Models

1. Drain the oil as previously described.

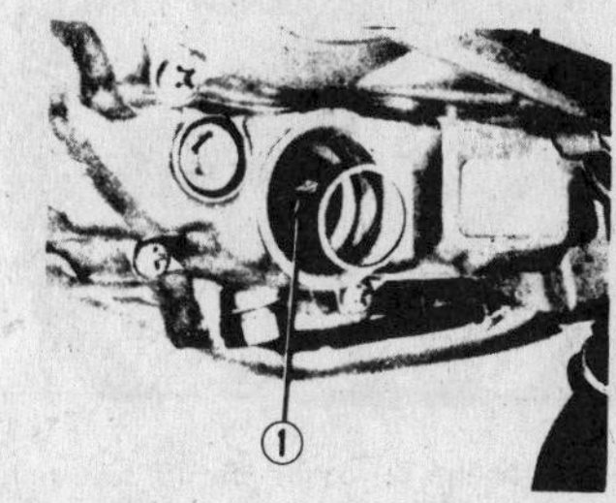

Oil filter screen location (100/125)

2. Remove the oil filter screen cap. Take out the spring and the filter screen.
3. Wash the screen in solvent; remove any trapped particles; blow dry.
4. Check the screen for punctures or a crushed condition; replace it if necessary. Install the screen, spring, and cap. Tighten firmly.

50–90 cc Models

Service the filter screen at the same time as the centrifugal oil filter. This involves removing the right crankcase cover. See below.

CENTRIFUGAL OIL FILTER

All Models

1. Drain the oil as previously described.
2. Remove the skid plate, if fitted.
3. Remove the kick-starter lever and footpeg(s). Disconnect the tach and clutch cables if these are connected to the cover.
4. Loosen the rear brake adjusting nut so that the brake pedal can be depressed enough to allow the crankcase cover to clear.
5. Place a pan beneath the right crankcase cover. Loosen the cover screws with an impact driver and remove them. Tap the cover gently with a plastic mallet if necessary to free it, and remove the cover.
6. On 100/125 cc models, and the XR75, remove the centrifugal oil filter rotor cover.
7. On 50–90 cc models, remove the clutch housing cover.
8. Clean any metal particles out of the filter with a clean rag. Install the filter cover.

Models which have the clutch on the crankshaft have the centrifugal oil filter located in the clutch center beneath the housing cover (2)

9. On 50–90 cc models, remove the filter screen and clean it in solvent. Check it for punctures and replace it if damaged.

Be sure to line up the tabs (3) on the filter cap with the slots (4) in the rotor (2) (100/125)

10. Before installing the crankcase cover, check the condition of the gasket, and replace it if nicked or damaged.

Front Forks

1. Fork oil should be changed every 6,000 miles or every 12 months.

2. ATF is recommended for all forks, although any quality oil designed for motorcycle forks is acceptable.

Motor oils of varying viscosities (10W-40, 20W, 30W) can also be used.

Various type of oils may not be compatible, however. If you are going to change the *type* of fork oil, it is best to flush the fork legs with a solvent before adding the new type oil. Do not use gasoline, as this may damage rubber parts.

3. To drain the fork oil, remove the drain plug at the lower portion of one of the fork sliders. Pump the slider up and down several times until all the old oil is expelled. Then turn the forks all the way to the right to completely drain the right fork leg, or to the left for the left fork leg. Check the condition of the drain plug gasket. Replace it if necessary. Refit and tighten the drain plug.

4. Repeat the procedure with the other fork leg.

Fork filler caps

5. Support the front wheel off the ground. Remove the fork filler cap from each fork leg. The handlebar clamps may have to be removed and the handlebars pulled back to allow access to the fork caps. Loosening the upper triple clamp pinch-bolts (if fitted) may make removal easier. **On TL125K2 and later models, remove the rubber cap, press down on the plug with a phillips screwdriver, remove the snap-ring and take out the plug.**

6. Add the correct quantity of oil to each fork leg. Capacities for each model are given in the "Maintenance Data" **chart at the end of this section.**

Chassis Lubrication

1. The swing arm pivot on some models is fitted with a grease nipple. This item should be lubricated with a good grade of chassis grease every 3,000 miles. Grease should be applied until some of it shows at either end of the swing arm.

2. Wheel and steering head bearings are lubricated with bearing grease. This should be done every 6,000 miles. Refer to the "Chassis" section for procedures.

SERVICE CHECKS AND ADJUSTMENTS

Drive Chain

1. The chain should have about ¾ in. (20 mm) of total up-and-down free-play measured in the middle of the lower chain run.

Chain free-play is measured in the middle of the lower chain run and is the total up-and-down movement of the chain

2. Before checking or adjusting the chain slack, the following conditions should be met:

a. A support should be placed under the engine if necessary, so that the rear wheel is off the ground;

b. The transmission should be placed in Neutral;

c. The chain should be clean and well lubricated;

d. The chain should have been checked for any tight spots by slowly rotating the wheel and checking for variances in the chain tension. If a tight spot exists, the chain tension should be adjusted to the prescribed free-play at the tight spot. Note, however, that such a condition is indicative of a worn chain and probably sprockets which should be replaced as soon as possible.

3. To adjust the chain, first back off the rear brake adjuster nut.

4. Remove the axle nut cotter pin and loosen the axle nut several turns.

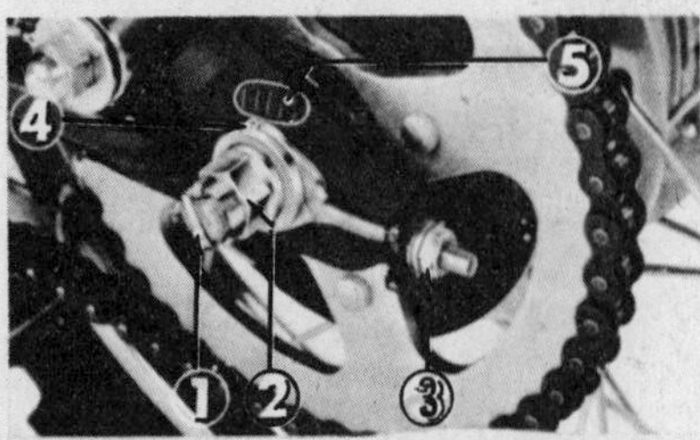

Chain adjustment: (1) cotter pin; (2) axle nut; (3) adjuster nuts; (4) adjuster alignment mark; (5) swing arm alignment marks

5. Turn each of the adjuster nuts by equal amounts until the chain tension is approximately correct.

6. Check wheel alignment by means of the aligning marks inscribed on both sides of the swing arm. Be sure that both adjusters are lined up with the same mark on each side.

7. On the TL125, the chain is adjusted by means of eccentric plates. After loosening the axle nut, turn each plate the correct number of serrations until chain tension is correct.

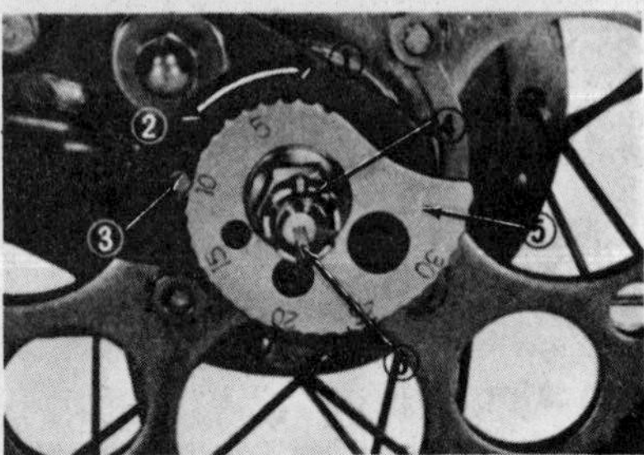

Chain adjuster, TL125: (1 and 2) direction of adjuster plate movement; (3) stud; (4) axle nut; (5) eccentric adjusting plates; (6) cotter pin

If the plates are difficult to move, either pull the wheel back by hand to move the plates off the stud, or tap the side of the tire with your hand while moving the eccentric adjusting plates.

8. Tighten the axle nut and check the chain tension. Then check that the chain has proper tension with the weight of a rider on the machine. Correct if necessary. Tighten the axle nut to the proper torque. Fit a new cotter pin.

Centrifugal Clutch

1. Models such as the Z50, ST/CT90, CT70, C70M, and several others utilize a centrifugal clutch. No adjustment is necessary if: a) the motorcycle goes smoothly into First gear without a jolt or stalling; b) the motorcycle begins to move as the throttle is opened and moving performance is satisfactory, and c) the clutch does not slip when the kick-starter is operated.

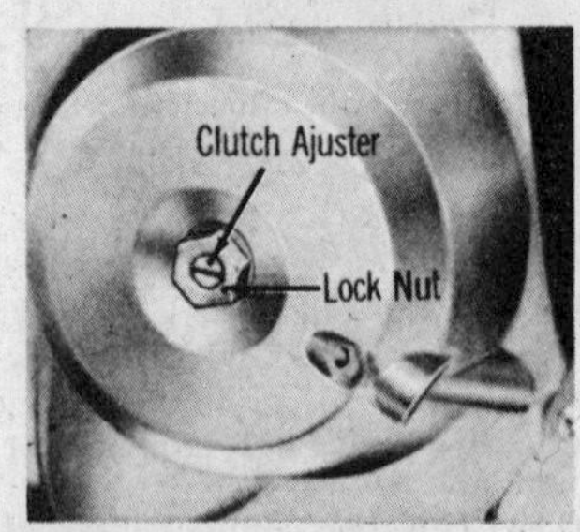

Centrifugal clutch adjuster

2. If adjustment is necessary, loosen the clutch adjusting screw locknut located on the right crankcase cover. Turn the adjusting screw about one turn clockwise (right). Then slowly turn the adjusting screw counterclockwise until resistance is felt. Stop, and turn the screw clockwise about ⅛–¼ turn, and tighten the locknut. Check clutch operation.

Manual Clutch

1. There are two adjusters on the clutch cable. Cable free-play should be maintained at 10–20 mm (0.4–0.8 in.) of hand lever movement measured at the end of the lever.

Use the adjuster at the hand lever for routine adjustments; the one at the engine end can be used for major adjustments.

2. After adjusting the cable to the proper specification, clutch operation should be correct. Gears should be easily engaged (without excessive noise), Neutral should be found easily, and the bike should not have a tendency to creep when in gear with the clutch disengaged. If any of these symptoms are noted, or if clutch slippage is evident, adjust the clutch as follows:

SL70, CT70H, CL70, S65

1. Remove the clutch adjuster cover plate on the right crankcase cover. Run down the cable adjuster at the handlebar to give a good deal of cable free-play.

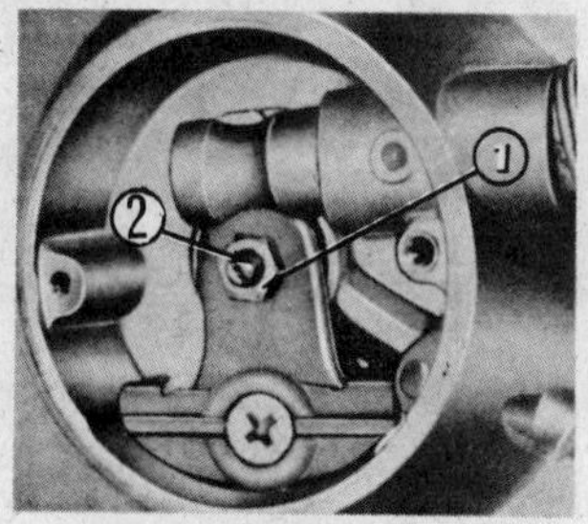

Manual clutch adjusting screw (2) and locknut (1) (70 cc)

2. Loosen the adjusting screw locknut, and turn the screw clockwise until resistance is felt. Then back it off ⅛–¼ turn to the left. Tighten the locknut; adjust the cable free-play as previously outlined. Check clutch operation.

S90, CL90/L, SL90, TL125, 100/125 (1976 AND LATER)

Clutch adjustment is made by adjusting the cable. Use the handlebar or lower end cable adjuster to keep free-play to 10–20 mm (0.4–0.8 in.)

100/125 MODELS, (1975 AND EARLIER), XR75

1. The clutch is adjusted by means of an adjusting screw on the right crankcase cover.

2. If adjustment is necessary, run down the cable adjuster on the handlebar until there is excess play in the cable. Loosen the adjusting screw locknut.

3. On later models, the clutch lever at the engine and the crankcase are fitted with marks. Turn the adjusting screw in or out so that the crankcase mark is aligned with the centerline of the clutch lever, as illustrated. Then tighten the adjusting screw locknut, and set the cable to to the proper free-play.

4. On earlier models, turn the adjusting screw counterclockwise until resistance is felt; stop, and turn the adjusting

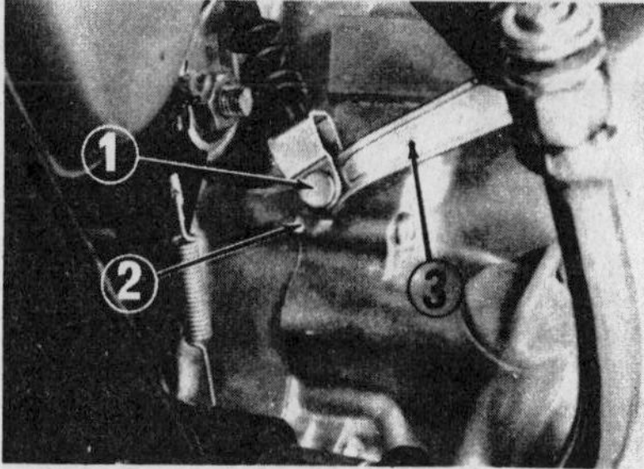

On late model 100–125 cc (to 1975), use the adjuster to align the centerline of the clutch lever (1) with the crankcase mark (2)

screw ⅛–¼ turn clockwise, and tighten the locknut. Set the cable free-play to the proper specification.

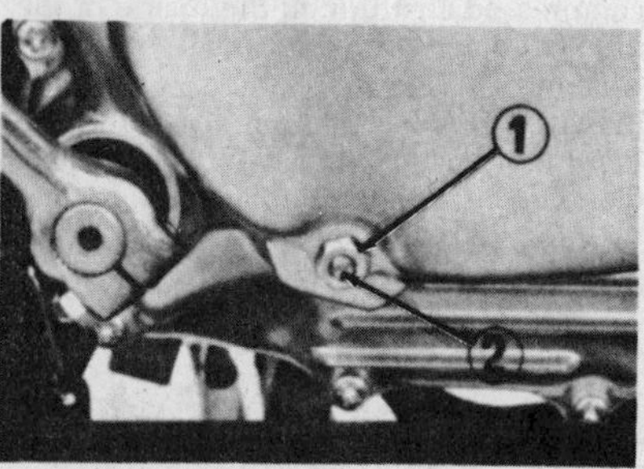

Clutch adjuster location (100–125 cc) (1975 and earlier)

5. Check clutch operation with the forks turned fully to one side or the other. Be sure that the cable is not kinked or sharply bent anywhere along its route.

Throttle Cable

The throttle cable should be adjusted *after* the idle speed. This procedure is given in the "Tune-Up" section.

The throttle cable should have enough free-play to allow 10–15° of twist-grip rotation before the throttle slide begins to lift.

1. The throttle cable can be adjusted with either the adjuster near the twist-grip, or the adjuster located on the top of the carburetor, beneath the rubber boot. Most have adjusters in both these locations. It is preferable to turn each adjuster out a little way, rather than have one turned out to near its limit.

Front Brake (Drum)

1. Use the adjuster nut at the lower end of the cable or the cable adjuster on the brake plate (depending on model) to allow the handlebar lever to move 20–30 mm (0.8–1.2 in.) before the linings contact the drum. This movement is measured at the tip of the lever.

2. Maintain the adjustment as the linings wear by using the cable adjuster at the handlebar lever.

Front Brake (Disc)

1. The handlebar lever should have 20–30 mm (0.8–1.2 in.) of free-play before the pads contact the disc.

2. The brake cable is self-adjusting; if service is necessary refer to the "Chassis" section.

Rear Brake

1. Use the adjusting nut on the end of the brake rod so that the brake pedal has about 25 mm (1 in.) of travel before the shoes contact the drum.

2. On models which have an auxiliary rear brake lever on the left handlebar, use the brake cable adjuster at the lower end of the cable so that the hand lever will move 20–30 mm (0.8–1.2 in.) before the linings contact the drum.

Note that the two brake adjustments (pedal and lever) are accomplished independently, but adjusting one necessitates adjusting the other.

Brake Wear

1. On disc brakes, the pads are equipped with red wear limit marks; they must be replaced as a set when worn to the red line.

2. Some late models are equipped with brake wear indicator marks on the brake lever and plate. If the marks line up when the brake is fully applied, inspect or replace the brake shoes.

3. When the brake is fully applied, the angle formed by the brake plate lever and the cable or rod should not be greater than 90°. If it is, and brake adjustment is correct, it is probable that the linings are worn to the point of replacement.

Brake Light Switch

The switch should be checked for operation after the brakes are adjusted. The rear brake light switch is adjustable and is mounted in a slotted bracket and secured by locknuts. Moving the switch up on the bracket allows the brake light to turn on sooner. Moving it down allows the light to turn on later. Generally, the brake light should come on just as the linings contact the drum.

Steering Stem Bearings

The steering stem bearings should be checked periodically and adjusted if necessary. Refer to the "Chassis" section.

Grasp the fork sliders (with the front wheel supported off the ground) and pull them straight out. No play should be felt. If play is evident or if the bearings bind or make noise when the forks are turned, adjustment and lubrication are needed.

FUEL SYSTEM

1. Fuel system maintenance involves cleaning the petcock and filter, cleaning or replacing the air cleaner, and cleaning the carburetor.

2. The carburetor should be removed, disassembled, and cleaned every 3,000 miles. The procedures are outlined in the **"Fuel Systems" section.**

3. The petcock should be serviced every 3,000 miles. On models with a sediment bowl or a carburetor-mounted petcock, shut off the fuel, unscrew the sediment bowl or cover plate and take out the O-ring and filter screen. Clean the parts in solvent and inspect the screen for

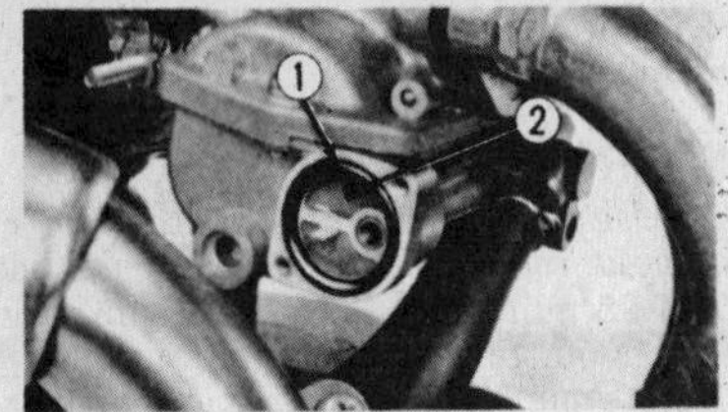

On some models, the O-ring and screen (1 and 2) are located in the carburetor itself

holes or other defects; replace it with a new one if damaged in any way. Inspect the O-ring for any cuts or cracks and replace it if necessary. After installing the parts, turn on the fuel and check for leaks.

Some models require that the petcock be removed to clean the filter screen. In this case, drain the gas tank, disconnect the fuel lines, and unscrew and remove the petcock. Clean the filter. Check the condition of the rubber petcock washer. After installation, check for leaks.

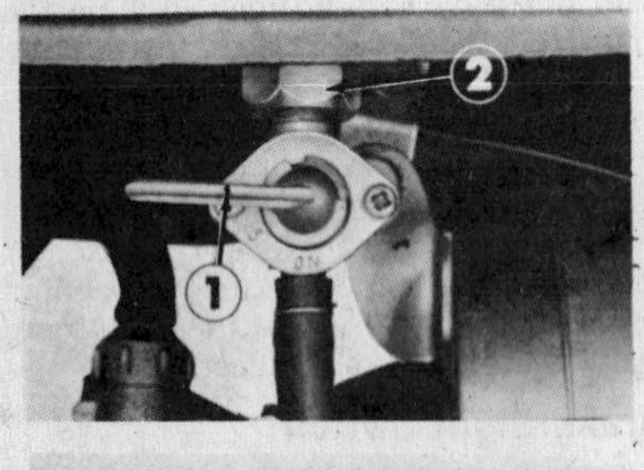

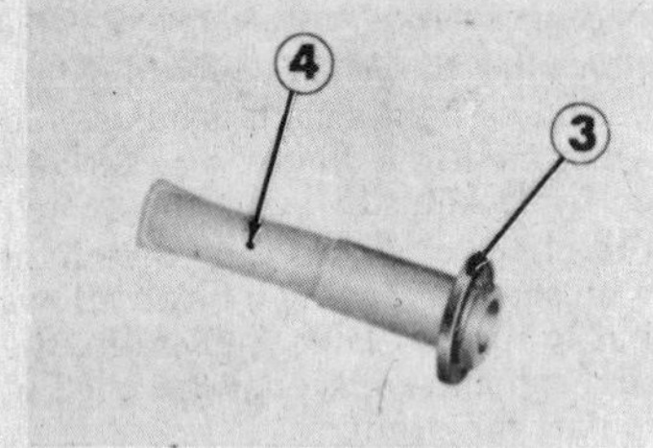

Petcock (1), securing nut (2); the O-ring and filter screen (3 and 4) are located on the petcock intake pipe

Air Cleaner Service

1. Newer models are equipped with a foam-type filter element. After removing the element, wash it in solvent (such as kerosene) and wring dry. Then soak the element in SAE 10W-30 oil and wring off the excess. Reinstall.

Filter maintenance should be carried out at least every 1,500 miles, or 30 operating days, but more often if the machine is operated in dusty areas.

Air cleaner securing nuts (1), and spring clamp (2) (100-125 cc)

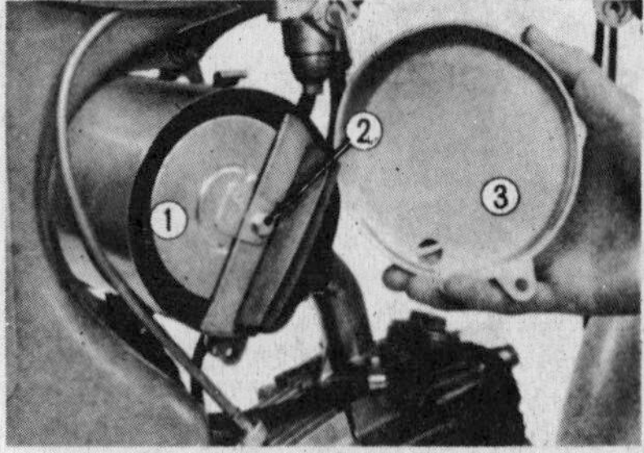

Air cleaner element (1), securing bolt (2), and cover plate (3) (90 cc)

2. Older models have a paper element. The filter element is serviced by brushing off the outside with a stiff brush to loosen any accumulated dirt. Then apply compressed air through the inside of the filter to remove the deposits.

Note that this method is only partially effective. It is recommended that the element be replaced after two or three such cleaning operations. Replacing the paper element with the newer foam-type if possible is recommended.

DECARBONIZATION

1. Models equipped with spark arrestors should have this item serviced every 1,500 miles or every 30 operating days. Excessive carbon buildup in the spark arrestor will cause sluggish performance and possible engine overheating.

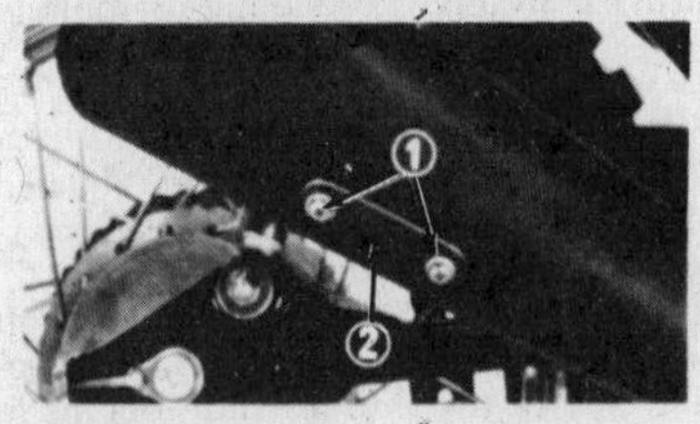

Spark arrestor cover plate (2) and securing screws (1) (XR75 shown)

2. Models may be equipped with a simple spark arrestor cover plate, or a removable baffle at the end of the muffler, or both, depending on the type of exhaust system fitted (see the illustrations).

3. Spark arrestor maintenance should be done when the engine is cold.

Spark arrestor (2) and securing bolt (1) (ST90 shown)

4. On models with only a spark arrestor cover plate, remove the cover screws and the cover. Start the engine, allow it to warm up, and rev it about 20 times to clean out the arrestor port. Check the condition of the cover plate gasket, and fit a new one if damaged.

5. On models with a removable baffle, remove the securing bolt at the end of the exhaust pipe. Grasp the spark arrestor with large pliers and pull it out.

Heat the spark arrestor with a propane torch until it is quite hot. Grasping the arrestor with large pliers, tap it against a wooden block to knock off carbon particles. When it cools, remove the rest of the deposits with a stiff wire brush and solvent.

Before replacing the arrestor, start the engine and rev it several times to remove any carbon built up in the muffler.

6. On models with both a cover plate and a removable arrestor, perform both Steps (4 and 5).

NOTE: *These procedures must be carried out out-doors in an area away from combustible materials.*

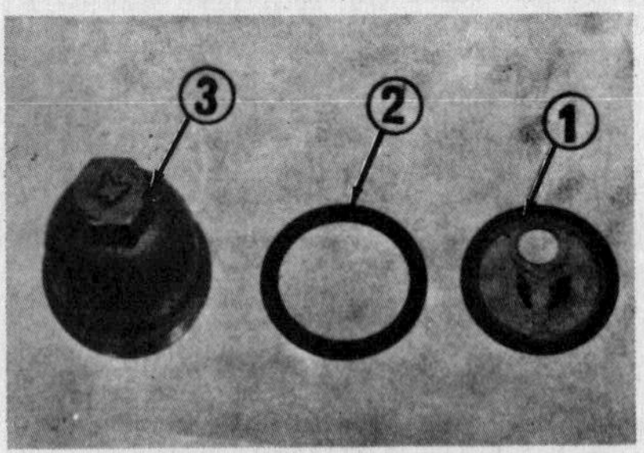

Petcock components: (1) filter screen; (2) O-ring; (3) sediment bowl

HEADLIGHT ADJUSTMENT

Set the machine about 25 feet away from and perpendicular to a wall, preferably of a color which reflects light well.

Headlight mounting bolts (1), lateral adjusting screw (2), and rim mounting screws (3)

The machine should be off the stand, and with a rider putting his weight on the machine as in operation. Start the engine and switch on the high beam. The headlight high beam should be parallel to the ground, and should hit the wall directly in front of the machine.

Vertical adjustment is made by loosening the two headlight mounting bolts slightly and pivoting the headlight up or down.

Lateral adjustment is made by means of the screw on the right-side of the headlight. Turning the screw clockwise will move the beam to the left and vice versa.

Recommended Lubricants

Engine
High-detergent motor oil, service rated "SE"

All temperatures:	SAE 10W-40 SAE 10W-30
Above 59° F	SAE 20-50 SAE 30
32–59° F	SAE 20/20W
Below 32° F	SAE 10W

Front Forks
ATF
SAE 10W-40
SAE 30
SAE 20

Air Filter (foam type)
SAE 10W-30

Wheel and Steering Head Bearings
High-quality bearing grease

Grease Fittings
High-quality chassis grease

Cables and General Lubrication
Molybdenum disulfide or graphite-based lubricants
SAE 20 or 30 oil

Drive Chain
Lubricant designed specifically for motorcycle drive chains

Periodic Maintenance *

Weekly
- Check engine oil level
- Tire pressure (cold)
- Spokes for tightness
- Battery electrolyte level
- Tightness of critical nuts and bolts
- Chain adjustment

Every 200 miles
- Lubricate and adjust drive chain

Every 1500 miles
- Change engine oil
- Clean and inspect air filter element
- Decarbonize spark arrestor

Every 2000 miles
- Clean and lubricate drive chain

Every 3000 miles
- Clean and gap spark plug
- Check points and ignition timing
- Check valve adjustment
- Check cam chain tension
- Check clutch
- Check carburetor settings
- Clean fuel filter and sediment bowl
- Grease fittings
- Lubricate controls and cables

Every 6000 miles
- Clean centrifugal and screen oil filters
- Change front fork oil
- Adjust steering head bearings

* Mileage based upon normal usage after break-in is complete

Maintenance Data

	Gas Tank (gal)	Engine Oil (qt/l)	Front Forks @ Leg (oz/cc)	Tire Pressure① Front/Rear (psi)
50, 65, 70 cc Engines				
Z50A	1.0	0.8/0.8	—	14/14
C65/M	1.2	0.8/0.8	—	24/30
S65	1.7	0.8/0.8	—	24/30
C70/M	1.2	0.7/0.7	—	25/28
CL70	1.6	0.7/0.7	3.4/100	25/28
CT70, K1	0.66	0.7/0.7	—	18/21
CT70K2-on	0.65	0.7/0.7	3.4/100	17/20
CT70H, K1	0.66	0.7/0.7	—	18/21
CT70H K2-on	0.66	0.7/0.7	3.4/100	18/21
SL70	1.3	0.7/0.7	3.7/110	20/23
XR75	0.8	0.9/0.9	3.7/110	17/20
90 cc Engines				
S90	1.8	0.9/0.9	4.4–4.7/130–140	26/29
CL90/L	2.0	0.9/0.9	4.4–4.7/130–140	26/29
CD90	1.8	0.9/0.9	—	26/29
C90	1.5	0.9/0.9	—	26/29
CT90	1.7	0.9/0.9	—	26/29
CT90 from Frame No. 000001A-on	1.6	0.9/0.9	4.4–4.7/130–140	26/28
SL90	2.2	0.9/0.9	6.1–6.5/180–190	26/29
ST90	0.7	1.0/1.0	3.6–3.7/105–110	18/24
100, 125 cc Engines				
CB100, K1-K2	2.0	1.1/1.0	4.4–4.7/130–140	26/29
CB100K3	2.0	1.1/1.0	3.6–3.7/105–110	26/32
CL100/S	2.0	1.1/1.0	4.4–4.7/130–140	26/28
SL100	2.0	1.1/1.0	6.1–6.5/180–190	26/28
SL100 K2-on	1.8	1.1/1.0	4.6–4.9/135–145	26/28
CB125S, CD125S	2.0	1.1/1.0	4.4–4.7/130–140	26/28
CB125S1/S2	2.0	1.1/1.0	4.1–4.4/120–130	26/28
CB125 (76)	2.5	1.1/1.0	3.6–3.7/105–110	26/32
CL125S	2.0	1.1/1.0	4.1–4.4/120–130	26/28
SL125, K1	1.8	1.1/1.0	6.1–6.5/180–190	26/28
SL125 K2-on	1.8	1.1/1.0	4.9–5.3/145–155	26/28
TL125	1.2	1.1/1.0	4.4–4.7/130–140	7–21

① Add 2 psi front, 4–6 psi rear, when carrying a passenger or for high-speed operation

— Not applicable

Battery Specifications

Model	Yuasa Battery	Voltage	Amp Hrs	Continuous Charging Rate (amps)
Z50A K1	B60-6	6	2	0.2
S65, C65	MBC1-6A	6	2	0.2
C70M	6N11-2D	6	11	1.1
CL70	6N5.5-1D-1	6	5.5	0.5
CT70/H	B60-6A	6	2	0.2
CT70 K1 CT70H K1	B60-6	6	2	0.2
SL70	B60-6A	6	2	0.2
SL70 K1	B60-6	6	2	0.2
CT90	B37-6A	6	5.5	0.5
S90	6N6-1B	6	6	0.6
CL90	6N6-1B	6	6	0.6
SL90	B37-6A	6	5.5	0.5
ST90	B37-6A	6	5.5	0.5
CB/CL/SL100	6N6-3B	6	6	0.6
CD/CB/CL/SL125 (All)	6N6-3B	6	6	0.6

TUNE-UP

NOTE: *Common tune-up procedures are explained in detail in "General Information."*

CAM CHAIN ADJUSTMENT

NOTE: *Early models under 100 cc had an automatically tensioned cam chain. No adjustment is necessary. For other models, refer to the appropriate heading below.*

100/125 cc Engines

1975 AND EARLIER

1. The cam chain adjuster and locknut are located on the top of the crankcase behind and to the left of the cylinder, beneath a rubber cap.
2. With the engine idling, note the indication of chain noise. Chattering will indicate that the chain is too loose; whining means that it is too tight.
3. With the engine idling, loosen the adjuster locknut. Turn the adjuster clockwise about half a turn so that it is loose; then turn it counterclockwise to take up slack in a loose chain.
4. Turn the adjuster until resistance is felt. The chain should be operating quietly at this point. It should not be necessary to turn the adjuster very much to achieve adjustment.

Cam chain adjuster (2) and locknut (1) (100–125, to 1975)

5. Tighten the adjuster locknut.
6. If the adjuster was turned too far, the chain will be too tight and will begin to whine. In this case, repeat the adjustment procedure until quiet operation is obtained.

(1976 AND LATER)

1. The cam chain adjuster is located behind and to the left of the cylinder, beneath a rubber cap.
2. With the engine idling, loosen the large adjusting bolt, then retighten. Tension will be set automatically.

NOTE: *A 6 x 10 mm bolt is fitted to the top of the adjusting bolt. Do not loosen this bolt.*

50-90 cc Engines (Except XR75)

Some early models such as the Z50-K2 have an automatic tensioner; no adjustment is necessary. For other models, proceed as follows:

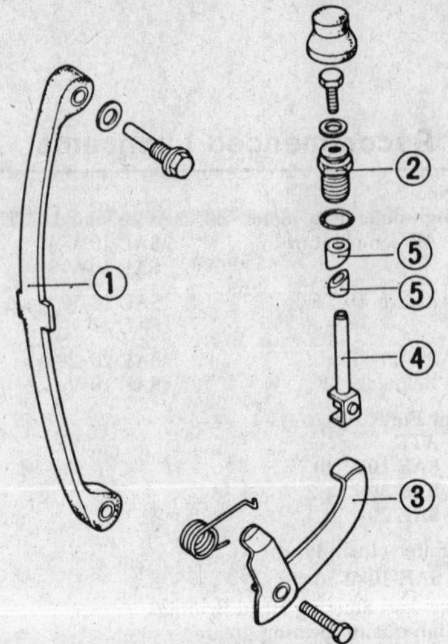

Cam chain adjuster (100–125, 76)

1. Cam chain tensioner
2. Adjusting bolt
3. Tensioner arm
4. Set bar
5. Collars

1. Cam chain adjustment is made with the engine idling. The adjustments can be made in two ways: either with the adjusting screw or with the tensioner bolt.

The adjusting screw locks the spring-loaded tensioner rod in place, and loosening it will allow tension to be automatically taken up.

The tensioner bolt allows the tensioner rod to be moved, compressing the tensioner itself.

Locknut (1), adjusting screw (2), and tensioner cover bolt (4) (50-70 cc)

The adjusting screw is located at the bottom of the left crankcase cover. The tensioner bolt is just below the adjusting screw, beneath a cover bolt.

2. With the engine idling, loosen the adjusting screw locknut and back the screw off (counterclockwise) about ½ turn. Tighten the adjusting screw. If chain operation is now quiet, tighten the adjusting screw locknut, since the adjustment is now complete. If chain operation is still noisy, proceed as follows:
3. Remove the tensioner cover bolt. Loosen the adjusting screw locknut and back off the adjusting screw about ½ turn.
4. Turn the tensioner bolt in or out slowly until proper chain operation is obtained. If the chain chatters, it is too loose and the tensioner bolt should be turned clockwise; if the chain whines, it is too

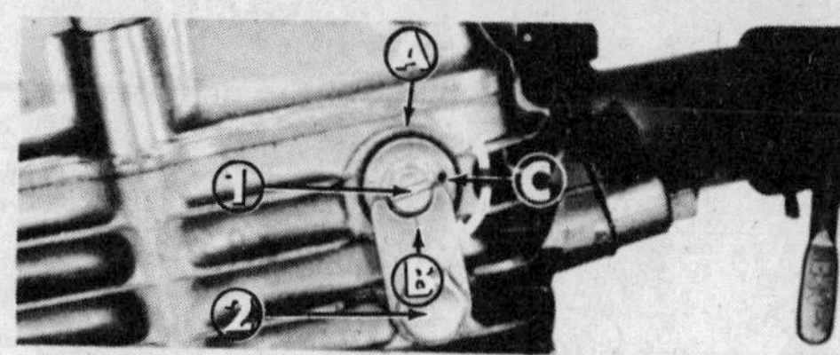

Cam chain adjuster plate bolt (2), chain adjuster (1); median position (C) (XR75)

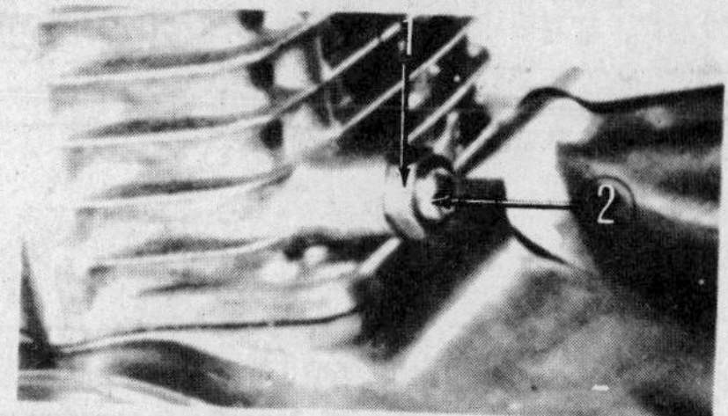

Cam chain tensioner (2) and locknut (1) (XR75)

tight, and the tensioner bolt should be turned counterclockwise.

5. When chain operation is quiet, replace the cover bolt, tighten the adjusting screw and the adjusting screw locknut. Adjustment is now complete.

XR75

1. Adjust the cam chain if operation is noisy. The adjuster is located at the top left-side of the cylinder head.

2. Adjust the cam chain with the engine idling. Loosen the chain adjuster plate bolt. If the chain chatters, turn the adjuster clockwise to take up excess slack. If the chain whines, turn the adjuster counterclockwise to increase slack.

NOTE: *Do not attempt to turn the adjuster more than 90° from the median position.*

3. When chain operation is quiet, tighten the plate bolt.

4. If turning the adjuster fully to position "B" in the illustration fails to quiet a loose chain, proceed as follows:

5. Shut off the engine. Remove the magneto cover, spark plug, and head cover. Turn the engine over (counterclockwise) until the intake valve goes down and comes up. Continue turning the engine over until the "T" mark on the rotor is aligned with the index mark on the crankcase cover. The piston is now at top dead center on the compression stroke.

6. The cam chain tensioner is located at the bottom rear of the cylinder.

Loosen the adjuster plate bolt, and turn the adjuster so that the punch mark lines up with position "C" as shown in the illustration. This is the middle of the adjustment range.

7. Holding the piston at TDC, loosen the tensioner locknut. Back the tensioner off about ½ turn, then tighten it. Secure the locknut.

8. Start the engine and make any adjustment to the cam chain necessary using the adjuster on the head as before.

VALVE ADJUSTMENT

All Models

NOTE: *Valves must be adjusted when the engine is cold.*

1. Remove the alternator or magneto rotor cover or inspection cap.

2. 100/125 and XR75: Remove the gas tank.

3. Remove the intake and exhaust valve caps, or the head cover on the XR75.

4. Remove the spark plug.

5. Turn the engine over slowly in the normal direction of rotation (the rotor will turn counterclockwise) while observing the intake valve. When the valve goes down and begins to come up, continue turning the engine over until the "T" mark on the rotor lines up with the timing index mark on the crankcase cover.

Piston top dead center occurs when the "T" mark on the rotor aligns with the index mark on the crankcase cover (1) (100-125 cc shown)

6. The piston should now be at top dead center on the compression stroke with both valves closed. Check for clearance at the valves. Each should have a slight amount of free-play. If they do not, the piston is at TDC on the exhaust stroke. Turn the rotor 360° and check again.

7. Valve clearance for all models is 0.002 in. (0.05 mm) for both intake and exhaust valves.

Adjusting the valve clearance: loosen the adjuster locknut (1) and turn the adjuster (2) until the feeler gauge (3) is a slip fit between the adjuster and the valve

8. If adjustment is necessary, loosen the adjuster locknut and turn the adjuster to effect proper adjustment. Tighten the locknut.

NOTE: *The adjustment may change when the locknut is tightened. Hold the adjuster steady while securing the nut. Recheck the clearance afterward.*

9. Repeat the procedure at the other valve.

CONTACT BREAKER POINTS

Location

1. On battery ignition 90, 100, and 125 cc machines and the magneto-ignition TL125, the points are located in a case on the left-side of the cylinder head, and are operated off the camshaft. The timing advance mechanism is fitted behind the breaker point plate.

2. On 50–70 cc machines, the points are fitted to the stator plate beneath the magneto rotor. The timing advance mechanism is fitted to the rotor, on those models which have one.

Replacement

1. If replacement of the points is necessary, this is easily accomplished on all 90–125 cc bikes by disconnecting the primary wire, removing the two point securing screws and taking off the points. Install the new points after thoroughly cleaning off the contact surfaces with a non-oily solvent, and adjust the gap.

2. On 50–70 cc machines, remove the left crankcase cover. Use the special puller to remove the magneto rotor after removing the rotor nut. Disconnect the primary wire, remove the points securing screw. Install the new point set and reset the gap. Check the ignition timing.

CAUTION: *Ensure that all insulating washers are correctly installed. Check that there is no continuity between the primary wire and the engine when the points are open, and that there is continuity when they are closed.*

3. Apply a bit of grease to the breaker cam lubricating wick. Take care not to apply too much to avoid fouling the points.

Gapping

Gapping is necessary to compensate for wear of the contact surfaces due to electrical arcing and for wear of the breaker point fiber heel. As the heel wears the points will open later relative to the rotation of the crankshaft, retarding the timing.

Points should be filed (if necessary) and cleaned before gapping.

NOTE: *On 50–70 cc machines the ignition timing is adjusted by changing the point gap. Therefore these operations must be carried out at the same time.*

Tune-Up Specifications

	Z50A	C65/M	S65
IGNITION			
Standard spark plug (NGK)	C6H	C7HS	C7HS
Spark plug gap (in./mm)	0.024–0.028/0.6–0.7	0.024–0.028/0.6–0.7	0.024–0.028/0.6–0.7
Breaker point gap (in./mm)	0.012–0.016/0.3–0.4	0.012–0.016/0.3–0.4	0.012–0.016/0.3–0.4
VALVE CLEARANCE			
Intake (in./mm)	0.002/0.05	0.002/0.05	0.002/0.05
Exhaust (in./mm)	0.002/0.05	0.002/0.05	0.002/0.05
CARBURETOR			
Pilot air screw (turns out)	1⅜	1¼	1½
Float level (in./mm)	0.7/18①	0.69/17.5	0.8/19.5
Idle speed (rpm)	1400	1000–1200	1000–1200
CRANKING COMPRESSION (psi)	170	170	170

	C70	C70M	CL70
IGNITION			
Standard spark plug (NGK)	C7HS	C7HS	C7HS
Spark plug gap (in./mm)	0.024–0.028/0.6–0.7	0.024–0.028/0.6–0.7	0.024–0.028/0.6–0.7
Breaker point gap (in./mm)	0.012–0.016/0.3–0.4	0.012–0.016/0.3–0.4	0.012–0.016/0.3–0.4
VALVE CLEARANCE			
Intake (in./mm)	0.002/0.05	0.002/0.05	0.002/0.05
Exhaust (in./mm)	0.002/0.05	0.002/0.05	0.002/0.05
CARBURETOR			
Pilot air screw (turns out)	1½	1⅛	1⅛
Float level (in./mm)	0.60/15.5	0.60/15.5	0.3/7.0
Idle speed (rpm)	1200	1200	1300
CRANKING COMPRESSION (psi)	170	170	170

	CT70/H	SL70	XR75
IGNITION			
Standard spark plug (NGK)	C7HS	C7HS	C7HS
Spark plug gap (in./mm)	0.024–0.028/0.6–0.7	0.024–0.028/0.6–0.7	0.024–0.028/0.6–0.7
Breaker point gap (in./mm)	0.012–0.016/0.3–0.4	0.012–0.016/0.3–0.4	0.012–0.016/0.3–0.4
VALVE CLEARANCE			
Intake (in./mm)	0.002/0.05	0.002/0.05	0.002/0.05
Exhaust (in./mm)	0.002/0.05	0.002/0.05	0.002/0.05

① K3-on—0.65/16.5

90–125 CC

1. Remove the points cover.
2. Turn the engine over slowly until the points are open to their maximum gap.
3. With the proper feeler gauge, check the gap. The proper specification for all models is 0.012–0.016 in. (0.3–0.4 mm).

To adjust the point gap, loosen the two screws (1), and lever the points with a screwdriver at (2) (90-125 cc)

4. If adjustment is necessary, loosen the two screws which secure the points to the base plate, and use a thin screwdriver at the pry slot provided to bring the gap to the proper specification.

   NOTE: *Loosen the screws just enough to allow the points to be moved. If too loose, the points will snap shut instead of holding the adjustment.*
5. Tighten the screws and recheck the gap. It may change slightly when the screws are tightened.
6. If it is not possible to gap the points correctly, the fiber heel is evidently worn, and the point set should be replaced.

50–70CC

1. On these models, adjusting the point gap is the only method of adjusting the ignition timing, so the timing should be checked whenever the points are gapped.
2. Remove the rotor cover.
3. Turn the engine over, observing the points through the cutout in the rotor until they are opened to their maximum gap.
4. With the proper feeler gauge blade, check the gap. Proper gap for all models is 0.012–0.016 in. (0.3–0.4 mm).
5. If adjustment is necessary, loosen the point securing screw, and use a thin screwdriver at the pry slot provided to bring the gap to within the proper specification.

   NOTE: *Loosen the securing screw just enough to allow the gap to be adjusted.*

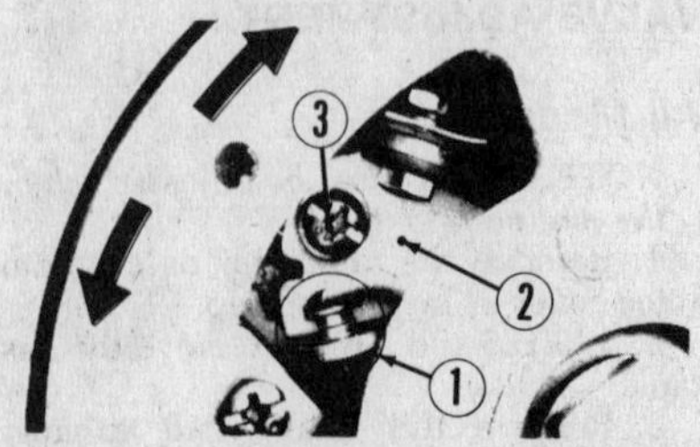

The point securing screw (3) is loosened slightly to change the point gap on most 50-70 cc models

Tune-Up Specifications (cont.)

	CT70/H	*SL70*	*XR75*
CARBURETOR			
Pilot air screw (turns out)	1¾	1½	1¼
Float level (in./mm)	0.78/20.0	0.28/7.0	0.83/21.0
Idle speed (rpm)	1300	1500	1400
CRANKING COMPRESSION (psi)	170	170	170
	S90	*CL90/L*	*CD90*
IGNITION			
Standard spark plug (NGK)	D6HS	D6HS	D6HS
Spark plug gap (in./mm)	0.024–0.028/0.6–0.7	0.024–0.028/0.6–0.7	0.024–0.028/0.6–0.7
Breaker point gap (in./mm)	0.012–0.016/0.3–0.4	0.012–0.016/0.3–0.4	0.012–0.016/0.3–0.4
VALVE CLEARANCE			
Intake (in./mm)	0.002/0.05	0.002/0.05	0.002/0.05
Exhaust (in./mm)	0.002/0.05	0.002/0.05	0.002/0.05
CARBURETOR			
Pilot air screw (turns out)	1¼	1½	1¼
Float level (in./mm)	②	0.78/19.5	0.83/21.0
Idle speed (rpm)	1250–1350	1250–1350	1250–1350
CRANKING COMPRESSION (psi)	170	170	170
	C90	*CT90*	*CT90 (from Frame No. 000001A)*
IGNITION			
Standard spark plug (NGK)	D6HS	D8HS	D8HS
Spark plug gap (in./mm)	0.024–0.028/0.6–0.7	0.024–0.028/0.6–0.7	0.024–0.028/0.6–0.7
Breaker point gap (in./mm)	0.012–0.016/0.3–0.4	0.012–0.016/0.3–0.4	0.012–0.016/0.3–0.4
VALVE CLEARANCE			
Intake (in./mm)	0.002/0.05	0.002/0.05	0.002/0.05
Exhaust (in./mm)	0.002/0.05	0.002/0.05	0.002/0.05
CARBURETOR			
Pilot air screw (turns out)	1	1½	1⅛
Float level (in./mm)	0.83/21.0	0.83/21.0	③
Idle speed (rpm)	1400–1600	1400–1600	1400–1600
CRANKING COMPRESSION (psi)	170	170	170

② Keihin—0.78/19.5
Mikuni—0.95/24.0

③ CT90—0.85/21.5
K1—0.94/23.5

If it is too loose the points will close completely instead of holding the adjustment.

6. Tighten the screw and recheck the gap. It may change slightly when the screw is tightened.
7. If it is not possible to correctly gap the points, the fiber heel is evidently badly worn and the point set should be replaced.

IGNITION TIMING

Dynamic Timing

ALL MODELS

1. Remove the magneto or alternator rotor cover so that the timing marks are visible.
2. Hook up the timing light according to the manufacturer's instructions. Most lights use the vehicle's own battery as a power source.
3. Start the engine, aiming the light on the rotor. Note the following:
   a. At idle, the "F" mark on the rotor should line up with the timing indicator on the crankcase cover;
   b. As the revolutions increase, the "F" mark should be seen to move in a direction opposite that of crankshaft rotation (except on Z50 and CT70 models which do not have timing advance mechanisms);
   c. Finally, at full advance (about 3,000 rpm and above on most models), the twin rotor marks must line up with the timing indicator mark on the crankcase cover.

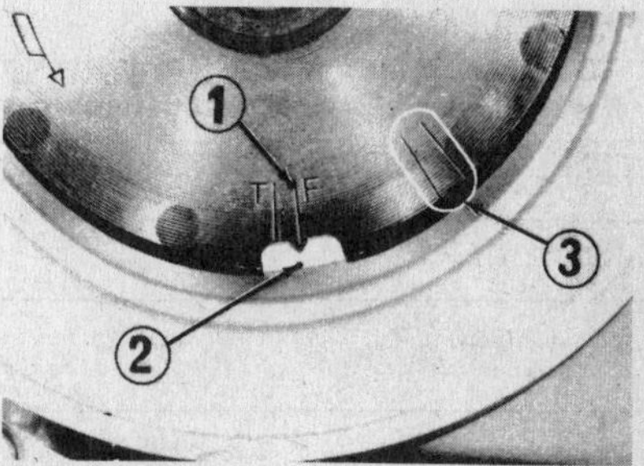

The "F" mark (1) is the firing point with the timing not advanced. The two slash marks (3) indicate the full advance firing point. (2) is the stationary timing mark

4. The full advance reading is the most important. If the rotor and crankcase marks do not align, proceed as follows:
5. 90–125 cc models: remove the points cover. Loosen the two screws which secure the breaker base plate just enough to allow the plate to be turned. Using a thin screwdriver applied at the pry point provided, rotate the plate in the direction necessary so that the timing marks align.

Rotating the plate clockwise advances the timing; rotating it counterclockwise retards the timing.

Tighten the breaker plate screws and recheck the timing.

6. 50–70 cc models: Timing is adjusted by changing the point gap. Set the point

Tune-Up Specifications (cont.)

	CT90 (K2-on)	SL90	ST90
IGNITION			
Standard spark plug (NGK)	D8HS	D8HS	D6HS
Spark plug gap (in./mm)	0.024–0.028/0.6–0.7	0.024–0.028/0.6–0.7	0.024–0.028/0.6–0.7
Breaker point gap (in./mm)	0.012–0.016/0.3–0.4	0.012–0.016/0.3–0.4	0.012–0.016/0.3–0.4
VALVE CLEARANCE			
Intake (in./mm)	0.002/0.05	0.002/0.05	0.002/0.05
Exhaust (in./mm)	0.002/0.05	0.002/0.05	0.002/0.05
CARBURETOR			
Pilot air screw (turns out)	1	1¼	1½
Float level (in./mm)	0.78/20.0	0.2/5.0	0.83/21.0
Idle speed (rpm)	1300	1300	1200–1300
CRANKING COMPRESSION (psi)	170	170	170
	CD/CB/CL/ SL-100/125	TL125(To 75)	TL 125 (76)
IGNITION			
Standard spark plug (NGK)	D8ESL	D8ESL	D8ESL
Spark plug gap (in./mm)	0.024–0.028/0.6–0.7	0.024–0.028/0.6–0.7	0.024–0.028/0.6–0.7
Breaker point gap (in./mm)	0.012–0.016/0.3–04	0.012–0.016/0.3–04	0.012–0.016/0.3–04
VALVE CLEARANCE			
Intake (in./mm)	0.002/0.05	0.002/0.05	0.002/0.05
Exhaust (in./mm)	0.002/0.05	0.002/0.05	0.002/0.05
CARBURETOR			
Pilot air screw (turns out)	1½	¾–1	1
Float level (in./mm)	0.95/24.0	0.85/21.5	0.95/24.0
Idle speed (rpm)	1200–1300	1300	1300
CRANKING COMPRESSION (psi)	170	170	170

To adjust the ignition timing, loosen the two screws (1), and rotate the base plate (2) (90-125 cc)

gap to the proper value (0.012–0.016 in./0.3–0.4 mm) as previously outlined. If the strobe light indicates that the timing is not incorrect, increase or decrease the point gap until it is.

NOTE: *Increasing the point gap advances the timing; decreasing it retards the timing. The point gap must still remain within the limits given. If it is not possible to correct the timing while retaining the proper gap, the points must be replaced.*

Static Timing

90–125 CC MODELS

1. Remove the alternator rotor cover and the points cover. Remove the spark plug and intake valve cover.

2. Hook the tester up. Remember that if a light is used on the magneto ignition TL125, the black/white points wire must be disconnected.

3. Turn the engine over so that the engine is just beginning its compression stroke. (The intake valve will go down and come up). Turn the rotor slowly in the normal direction of rotation (counterclockwise). At the instant in which the "F" mark on the rotor aligns with the mark on the crankcase cover, the points should begin to open as indicated by the reaction of the test light or the meter.

4. If the points open before the marks align, the timing is too advanced. If they open after the "F" mark passes the stationary mark, the timing is too retarded.

5. If the timing is not correct, loosen the two phillips screws which secure the breaker base plate to the engine. Loosen them just enough to allow the plate to be rotated.

6. Turn the plate using a thin screwdriver applied to the pry slot provided so that the points open just as the "F" mark lines up with the stationary mark. If the timing was too advanced, turn the plate counterclockwise. If too retarded, rotate the plate clockwise.

7. Tighten the breaker plate screws and recheck the timing. Sometimes this will cause the plate to move slightly and throw the timing off.

50–70CC MODELS

The timing on these models is accomplished by changing the point gap.

1. Remove the spark plug and the magneto rotor cover.

2. Clean and gap the points to the proper specification as outlined under "Gapping."

3. Hook up the ohmmeter to ground and to the black wire coming from the points.

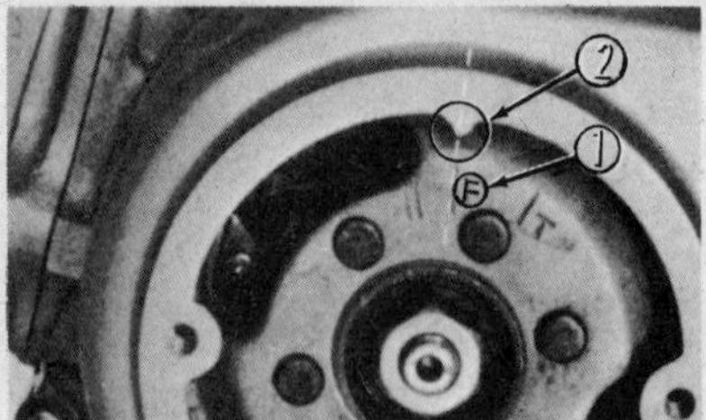

The points should just begin to open when the "F" mark on the rotor aligns with the stationary timing mark (50-70 cc)

4. Turn the rotor slowly in the normal direction of rotation (counterclockwise). When the "F" mark on the rotor and the stationary timing mark on the crankcase align, the meter should indicate that the points have just begun to open.

5. If the points open after the "F" mark passes the stationary mark, the timing is too retarded; if they open before the "F" mark aligns, the timing is too advanced.

6. As noted above, ignition timing is corrected by changing the point gap. If the timing was retarded, increase the point gap. If it was advanced, decrease the point gap.

NOTE: *It should be possible to set the timing perfectly while maintaining the point gap within the specification given (0.012–0.016 in. 0.3–0.4 mm). If the timing marks will not align when the point gap is within this specification, the points must be replaced. Wear of the fiber heel is one cause of this condition.*

CARBURETOR

Adjusting Float Level

Generally, float level will not need adjustment unless the carburetor has been disassembled, fuel delivery problems have been noted, or considerable mileage has been covered.

1. Remove the carburetor from the motorcycle as outlined in the "Fuel Systems" section.
2. Remove the float bowl. Remove the float bowl gasket.
3. Float level is defined as the measured distance from the float bowl mating surface on the carburetor body (gasket removed) to the top of the floats, when the tang of the float arm is just touching the end of the float needle. A special gauge is available to check the float level although a vernier caliper can also be used.
4. With the carburetor upside down, gradually lower the floats until the tang of the float arm just touches the end of the float needle. The tang should not depress the needle, but just contact it. Measure the distance from the carburetor body to the top of the floats. Compare the reading with the proper float level for your machine as given in the "Tune-Up Specifications" chart at the end of this section.

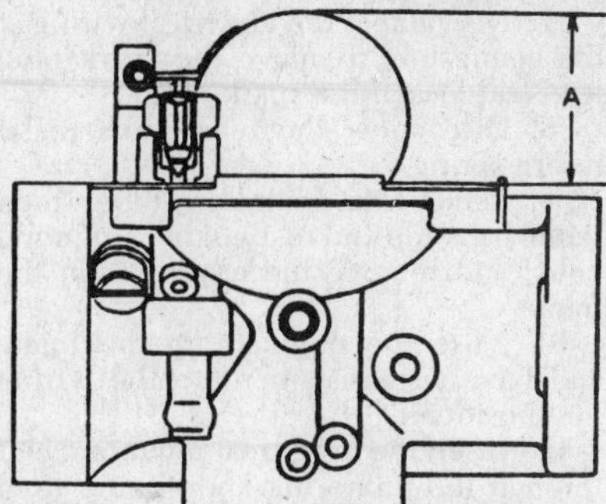

Float level is the distance "A" from the float bowl gasket surface (gasket removed) to the top of the floats

5. If adjustment is necessary, bend the float arm tang *only* to raise or lower the float level.
6. Float level will not be correct if the needle is worn, or if there is foreign matter on the needle seat. Refer to "Carburetor" for more information.

Idle Speed and Mixture

NOTE: *These items must be adjusted when the engine is at operating temperature.*

1. Ensure that the throttle cable adjustment is approximately correct so that the cable has enough slack to allow the throttle slide to be fully closed.
2. Screw the pilot air screw in (carefully) until it bottoms lightly, then turn it out the number of turns shown in the "Tune-Up Specifications" chart at the end of this section.
3. Start the engine. When operating temperature is reached, adjust the throttle stop screw so that the engine idles as slowly as possible. Then turn the pilot air screw in or out until the engine runs smoothly. It should not be necessary to vary the air screw more than one half turn in either direction from the given setting.

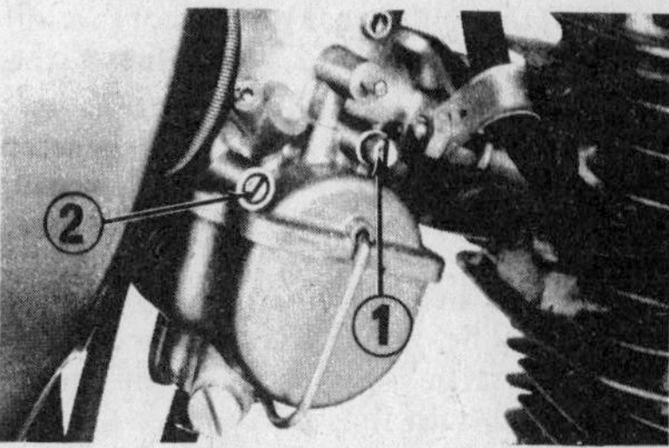

Throttle stop (1) and pilot air (2) screws

4. Adjust the throttle stop screw so that the engine idles at the desired rpm.

NOTE: *If proper idling cannot be obtained using this method, it may be that the fuel system is clogged with dirt (check petcock, filter, carburetor), the plug is bad or too cold, the valves are improperly adjusted, or there is an air leak somewhere in the system.*

5. After adjusting the idle speed and mixture, adjust the throttle cable as outlined in the "Maintenance" section.

ENGINE AND TRANSMISSION

Removal and installation procedures are given below. Specifications are in the charts at the end of this section. For service procedures of common engine components such as cylinder head, pistons, clutch, etc., refer to the "Engine Rebuilding" section in "General Information."

ENGINE REMOVAL AND INSTALLATION

The following notes apply to all models:

1. Drain the oil before removing the engine.
2. Degreasing and thoroughly cleaning the engine before removal is highly recommended. Be especially attentive to the cylinder base and the underside of the crankcase, and around mating surfaces.
3. On models which have the fuel petcock incorporated into the carburetor, use a C-clamp to pinch off the fuel line before removing the carburetor from the cylinder head.
4. When disconnecting the final drive chain, use pliers to remove the masterlink spring clip. Do not pry the clip off with a screwdriver or it will be distorted and then must be replaced. After disconnecting the chain, install the masterlink on one end of the chain to prevent loss.

NOTE: *On models with a full coverage chaincase, wire the ends of the chain together and attach them to a point on the frame so that the chain doesn't fall into the chaincase.*

5. Upon installation, install the spring clip with the closed end facing the direction of chain rotation.

100/125 cc Models

1. Remove the exhaust pipe and muffler. Remove the seat and the gas tank.
2. Remove the rider footpegs (except TL125) by removing the step bar bolted to the lower frame members.
3. Run down the clutch cable adjuster(s) and disconnect the cable from the lever on the engine.
4. Unbolt the carburetor from the engine, and hang it well out of the way to avoid possible damage.
5. Remove the left and right frame sidecovers. Disconnect the alternator leads at the plastic connector. Remove the spark plug cap. Loosen the spark plug. Disconnect the ignition primary wire at the connector near the ignition coil.
6. Disconnect the tach cable at the engine (if fitted).
7. Remove the gearshift lever pinch-bolt and carefully pull the shift lever off the splined shaft. Back off the rear brake adjuster.
8. Remove the left rear crankcase cover. Disconnect the chain.
9. Back off the rear brake adjuster nut to allow a good bit of movement in the brake pedal.
10. Remove the front engine mounting nuts and bolts and remove the mounting plates. Remove the top and rear mounting bolts; remove the engine from the frame.

Engine mounting bolt locations

11. Installation is the reverse of the removal procedure. After the engine is fitted into the frame, use a screwdriver

through the top mounting bracket to support the engine until the other mounting bolts are fitted.

12. Exhaust system nuts and bolts must be tightened gradually.

ST90

1. Remove the right shock absorber, and remove the muffler along with the rear brackets.
2. Disconnect the spark plug lead and loosen the plug.
3. Unbolt the carburetor from the cylinder head.
4. Remove the rear portion of the left crankcase cover, and disconnect the drive chain.
5. Disconnect the electrical wiring at the plastic connectors. Disengage the carburetor drain tube from the engine clamp.
6. Have an assistant support the motorcycle. The front downtubes (sub-frame) must be removed and the side-stand along with it.

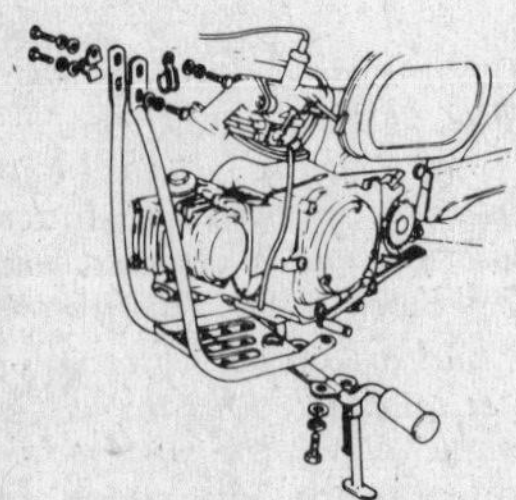

Sub-frame and footpeg assembly (ST90)

7. Remove the footpeg step bar.
8. Remove the sub-frame.
9. Remove the nuts on the rear engine mounting bolts. Support the engine so that it will not fall, and pull out the rear mounting bolts.

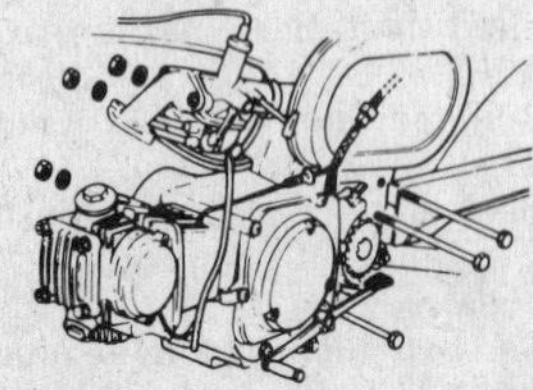

Engine mounting bolts (ST90)

10. Remove the engine from the frame.
11. Before installing the engine, bolt the step bar to it. The remainder of installation is the reverse of removal.

CT90, C90

1. Remove the front fender (CT90) (early models).
2. Remove the frame tube cover (CT90). Remove the fairing (C90).
3. Remove the footpeg step bar.
4. Remove the rear portion of the left crankcase cover and disconnect the drive chain (C90). On the CT90, disconnect the chain and disengage it from the countershaft sprocket.
5. Remove the muffler.
6. Unbolt the carburetor manifold from the cylinder head.
7. Disconnect the electrical wiring at the connectors. Remove the spark plug lead and loosen the spark plug.
8. Disconnect the rear brake pedal return spring.
9. Remove the front downtubes, then remove the top and rear engine mounting bolts, and remove the engine from the frame.
10. Raise the engine into the frame and have an assistant route the wiring into position.
12. Insert the lower rear mounting bolt through the frame lug and engine from the left-side, then pivot the engine up and install the remaining bolts.
13. The remainder of installation is the reverse of the removal procedure.

SL90

1. Remove the exhaust system.
2. Remove the rear portion of the left crankcase cover, and disconnect the drive chain.
3. Run down the clutch cable adjusters, and disconnect the cable from the engine lever.
4. Remove the spark plug lead and loosen the spark plug.
5. Disconnect the carburetor manifold from the cylinder head.
6. Remove the gearshift and kick-starter lever pinch-bolts, and carefully pull these levers off their shafts.
7. Remove the left sidecover and disconnect the electrical wires at the connectors.
8. Remove the four bolts for the top rear engine mounting plates.
9. Remove the bottom engine mounting bolts and remove the engine from the frame.
10. Installation is the reverse of the removal procedure.

S90, CL90/L, CD90

1. Remove the rider footpeg step bar.
2. Remove the exhaust system.
3. Remove the rear portion of the left crankcase cover and disconnect the drive chain.
4. Run down the cable adjusters and disconnect the clutch cable from the lever at the engine.
5. Disconnect the spark plug lead and loosen the spark plug.
6. Unbolt the carburetor manifold from the cylinder head.
7. Remove the battery cover and disconnect the battery leads. Disconnect the alternator leads at the connector.
8. Unhook the brake pedal spring.
9. Remove the top and rear engine mounting bolts and remove the engine from the frame.
10. Installation is basically the reverse of the removal procedure. Note the following points:
    a. Block up the engine under the frame;
    b. Route the wiring harness up to the battery box and suspend the engine from the frame by inserting a screwdriver into a frame and engine mounting point;
    c. Insert the engine mounting bolts from the left-side, then secure and torque the mounting nuts;
    d. Connect the brake pedal return spring to the lower mounting bolt;
    e. Connect all the wiring harness leads;
    f. Connect the battery leads to the battery terminals, push the wires up into the top of the battery box, install the battery, taking care not to pinch any of the wires, and route the battery overflow tube down through the bottom of the battery box;
    g. Connect the clutch cable to the release lever;
    h. Install the intake manifold to the cylinder head, taking care to correctly position the O-ring between the manifold and the cylinder head;
    i. Attach the high-tension lead to the spark plug. The lead should be secured by the clip under the right-side intake manifold mounting bolt;
    j. Install the muffler assembly.

XR75

1. Remove the muffler.
2. Unbolt the carburetor manifold from the cylinder head.
3. Loosen the adjusters on the clutch cable and disconnect the cable from the lever on the engine.
4. Remove the spark plug cap and loosen the spark plug.
5. Remove the left-side crankcase cover. Disconnect the drive chain.
6. Disconnect the magneto wire at the connector.
7. Loosen all of the mounting bolt nuts.
8. Remove the front mounting bolts and mounting plates. While supporting the engine with one hand, remove the upper rear mounting bolt.
9. Let the engine swing forward; then remove the lower rear bolt.
10. Installation is the reverse of removal.

Lower rear engine mounting bolt (XR75)

SL70

1. Remove the seat by loosening the shock absorber capnuts and pulling it off. Disconnect the fuel line at the petcock and fold back the rubber mounting at the rear of the gas tank. Pull the gas tank back and off the machine.
2. Remove the frame sidecovers. Disconnect and remove the battery. Remove the tool box. Remove the chain guard. Remove the gearshift lever and the kick-starter lever.
3. Remove the engine left-side cover. Use an impact driver to loosen the phillips screws to avoid damage.
4. Disconnect the drive chain.
5. Remove the exhaust system after

unbolting the muffler from the frame and the exhaust pipe from the cylinder head.

6. Loosen the carburetor air cleaner hose clamp screw, remove the air cleaner case mounting bolts, and remove the case.

7. Unscrew the carburetor cap and pull out the slide assembly. Tape the slide out of the way to avoid damage. Remove the manifold bolts at the cylinder and take away the manifold and carburetor as a unit. Plug the cylinder intake port with a clean piece of rag to keep foreign matter out.

8. Disconnect the electrical wiring at the plastic coupler. Remove the spark plug cap. Loosen the plug.

9. Disconnect the clutch cable at the engine.

10. Remove the two engine mounting plate bolts on the right engine mounting plate. Remove the long engine mounting bolts (two). The lower bolt is removed by loosening it from the left-side. Remove the right-side engine mounting plate.

11. Protect the frame tubes with a covering of some sort. Remove the engine by moving it forward in the frame, then swing the back of the engine out to the right and take the engine out of the frame.

12. Installation is the reverse of the above. Tighten engine mounting bolts to 15–22 ft lbs.

13. When installing the muffler, check the gasket for damage and replace it if necessary. Tighten the muffler bolt and the cylinder mounting nuts gradually.

CL70

1. Remove the gearshift lever pinch-bolt, and carefully pull the lever off the splined shaft.
2. Remove the footpeg step bar.
3. Remove the rear portion of the left crankcase cover and disconnect the drive chain.
4. Remove the exhaust system.
5. Unbolt the carburetor intake manifold from the cylinder head.
6. Run down the clutch cable adjusters and disconnect the cable from the engine lever.
7. Disconnect the spark plug lead and loosen the plug.
8. Remove the battery cover and disconnect the wiring at the connector.
9. Disconnect the rear brake pedal return spring from the pedal.
10. Remove the engine mounting bolts and nuts and remove the engine from the frame.
11. Installation is the reverse of removal.

CT70/H

1. Remove the engine bash plate (two bolts).
2. Remove the exhaust system which is secured at the cylinder head and two places on the frame.
3. Remove the spark plug.
4. Unscrew the carburetor cap, pull out the slide assembly, and arrange it so that it is out of the way and won't be damaged when the engine is removed.
5. Remove the four bolts which secure the crankcase protector downtubes to the frame near the steering head.
6. Remove the chain guard. Remove the left crankcase cover. Disconnect the drive chain.
7. Remove the two bolts beneath the engine which secure the skid plate portion of the crankcase protector, and remove it.
8. Remove the step bar (two bolts).
9. Disconnect the rear brake pedal return spring at its top mount.
10. Remove the carburetor intake manifold from the cylinder head.
11. Remove the two engine mounting bolts, and remove the engine.
12. Installation is the reverse of removal.

C65/M, C70/M, S65

1. Remove the air cleaner assembly (except S65).
2. Remove the fairing (if applicable).
3. Remove the exhaust system.
4. Remove the footpeg step bar.
5. Remove the tool box.
6. Unbolt the carburetor (C models) or the manifold (S65) from the cylinder head.
7. Run down the clutch cable adjuster and disconnect the cable from the engine lever.
8. Remove the pinch-bolts and take off the gearshift and kick-starter levers.
9. Remove the left-side crankcase cover. Disconnect the drive chain.
10. Remove the spark plug. Detach the spark plug lead from the clip on the right sidecover. Disconnect the starter motor lead and the electrical wiring.
11. Disconnect the rear brake pedal return spring and stoplight switch spring.
12. Support the engine while removing the rear mounting bolts; remove the engine from the frame.
13. Installation is the reverse of removal.

Z50

1. Remove the exhaust system.
2. Unscrew the carburetor cap, and pull out the throttle slide assembly. Secure it out of the way to avoid damage.
3. Remove the lead and loosen the spark plug.
4. Disconnect the magneto wiring at the plastic connector.
5. Disconnect the fuel line from the carburetor.
6. Remove the left crankcase cover. Disconnect the drive chain.
7. Remove the two engine mounting bolts while supporting the engine; remove the engine from the frame.
8. Installation is the reverse of removal.

TOP END

The following section deals with the removal and installation of the cylinder head, cylinder, piston, and related components. Inspection and service procedures for these and other common engine components are outlined in the "Engine Rebuilding" section in "General Information." Specifications for individual models are given in the charts at the end of this section.

100/125 cc Models (1975 and Earlier)

REMOVAL

1. Removal of the top end necessitates removing the engine from the frame. Refer to the "Engine Removal and Installation" procedures.
2. Remove the breaker point cover. Scribe a line across the breaker plate to the engine to preserve ignition timing. Remove the two breaker plate screws and remove the plate. Remove the valve adjusting hole caps and loosen the adjusters.
3. Remove the bolt which secures the breaker cam. Pull the breaker cam and spark advance assembly off the camshaft.
4. Remove the two screws which hold the breaker point housing to the engine. Use an impact driver to loosen these screws. Remove the housing.
5. Loosen the cam chain adjuster screw locknut (on the crankcase) and unscrew the tensioner screw a few turns. Place a clean rag beneath the cam sprocket, and carefully remove the sprocket bolts. Remove the sprocket.

Sprocket bolts (1), cam chain (2), camshaft (3), and sprocket (4)

Loop a piece of wire around the cam chain and secure it to any fixed point to prevent the chain from falling into the crankcase.

6. Pull out the camshaft. Note that the camshaft will have to be turned to allow the intake and exhaust lobes to clear the opening through which the cam is removed. Perform this operation carefully. Hold the chain out of the way as the cam is removed.
7. Remove the cam chain tensioner mounting bolt in the head and detach the tensioner from its seat in the head.

Prying the tensioner (2) out of its seat with a screwdriver (1)

8. Remove the cylinder head bolt beneath the breaker point housing. Remove the four capnuts on top of the cylinder head. Remove the cylinder head.

Cam chain tensioner mounting bolt (1), tensioner (2), cylinder head (3), and cylinder head capnuts (4)

9. Remove the cam chain guide from the cylinder. Lift the cylinder up on its studs until there is enough room to stuff a clean rag between the cylinder and the crankcase. This will catch any foreign matter or pieces of broken ring which might fall into the cases when the cylinder is removed.

10. After removing the cylinder, remove the piston wrist pin circlips with needlenose pliers. Push out the wrist pin with a suitable drift.

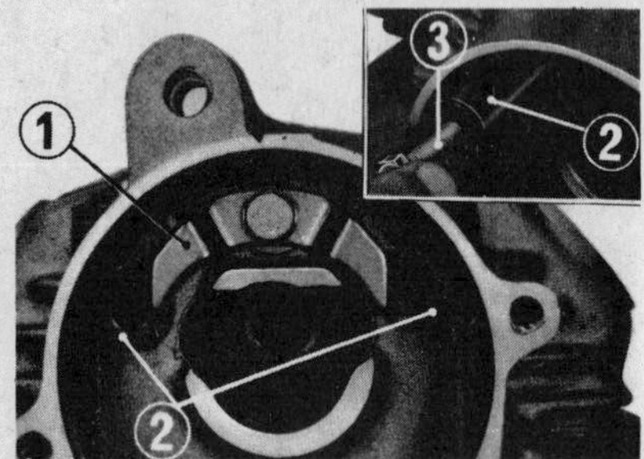

Remove the bolt which secures the rocker arm shaft retaining plate (1) and pull out the shafts (2) with a puller bolt (3) 6 mm thread diameter

11. To remove the rocker arms from the cylinder head, first remove the rocker arm shaft retaining plate. Thread a 6 mm bolt into the rocker arm shafts and pull them out of the head (the cylinder head bolt is 6 mm and can be used for this operation). Mark each rocker arm and shaft for position and keep the pairs together so that each rocker arm can be installed on its proper shaft.

INSTALLATION

1. Install one wrist pin circlip and place the piston on the connecting rod noting that the "IN" stamped on the crown must be located on the intake port side or that the arrow points toward the exhaust port.

Install the wrist pin and the other circlip.

NOTE: *Always use new circlips; install them so that the end-gaps do not align with the cutouts on the piston.*

Arrange the ring end-gaps so that they are 120° apart, but none should be perpendicular to or parallel with the wrist pin. Lubricate the piston and rings with motor oil.

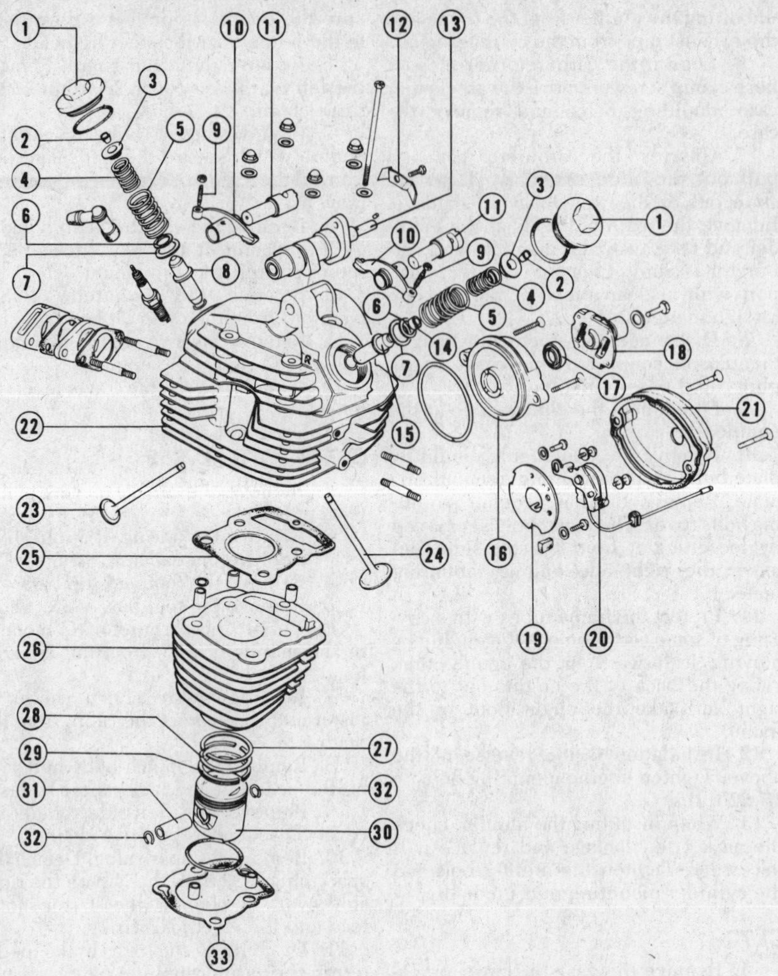

Top end assembly (100–125 cc, 1975 and earlier)

1. Valve adjusting cap
2. Valve spring keeper
3. Valve spring retainer
4. Inner valve spring
5. Outer valve spring
6. Inner spring seat
7. Outer spring seat
8. Valve guide
9. Adjusting screw
10. Rocker arm
11. Rocker arm shaft
12. Rocker arm shaft retainer plate
13. Camshaft
14. Valve seal
15. Valve guide
16. Contact breaker housing
17. Oil seal
18. Spark advance mechanism
19. Breaker plate
20. Breaker points
21. Breaker cover
22. Cylinder head
23. Exhaust valve
24. Intake valve
25. Cylinder head gasket
26. Cylinder
27. Top compression ring
28. Bottom compression ring
29. Oil ring
30. Piston
31. Wrist pin
32. Wrist pin circlip
33. Cylinder base gasket

2. Fit the cylinder base gasket. Make sure that all O-rings and locating pins are installed and lower the cylinder over the piston, compressing the rings with your fingers as the piston enters the bore. Pull the cam chain up through the cylinder. Install the cam chain guide.

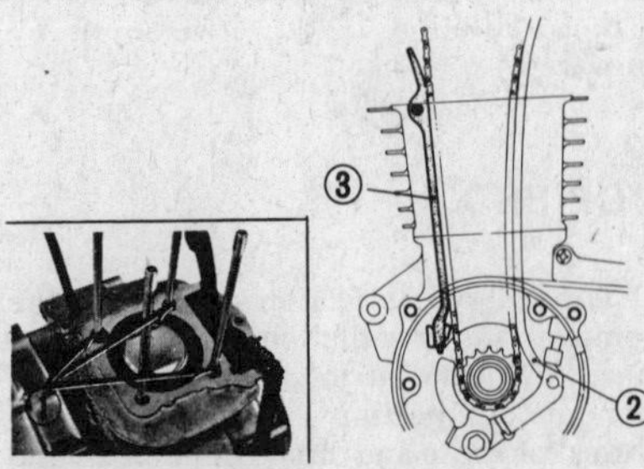

Cylinder locating pins (1), cam chain tensioner (2), and chain guide (3)

3. Assemble the rocker arms in the head if removed. Fit a head gasket, and install the head. Pull the cam chain through and tie it aside. Fit the cam chain tensioner into its seat and install the tensioner mounting bolts.

4. Tighten the cylinder head capnuts and bolt in a cross pattern and in gradual increments until the proper torque of 13–14.5 ft lbs is reached.

5. Lubricate and install the camshaft. Arrange the cam so that the locating pin for the spark advance mechanism points upward.

6. Remove the alternator rotor cover and turn the crankshaft so that the "T" mark on the rotor is aligned with the mark on the stator. The piston is now at top dead center. Install the cam sprocket on the camshaft, looping the cam chain over it, so that the "0" mark on the sprocket is aligned with the mark on the top of the cylinder head. Be sure that the rotor "T" mark is still aligned. Fit the

camshaft sprocket bolts and tighten them to 6–9 ft lbs. These bolts should be secured with thread locking compound. The valve timing is now adjusted.

The "O" mark on the cam sprocket (2) must align with the mark (3) on the head with the piston positioned at TDC

7. The remainder of the procedure is the reverse of disassembly. Be sure to engage the slot in the timing advance mechanism with the pin in the camshaft. Adjust the cam chain, check ignition timing, etc., before starting the engine. Check cylinder head torque after the engine has been run and cooled off.

100/125 cc Models

(1976 AND LATER)

1. The cylinder head on 1976 models has been modified to a two-piece type instead of the original single-piece casting. The head is now fitting with a cover secured by four allen bolts.

This change has been made to the following units: CB100E-1300001, CB125S-1300001 and subsequent.

2. Removal, disassembly, and installation of the top end components is performed in the same manner as for the 1975 and earlier engines. It is not necessary to remove the cylinder head cover in order to remove the camshaft or rocker arms. Its removal, however, may facilitate removal of valves and inspection of cam bearings.

3. Refer to 100/125 cc (1975 and Earlier) for procedures.

Specifications for the 125cc engine (1976) have been changed. Be sure to refer to the correct chart at the end of this section.

4. When assembling, be sure the oil seal rubber near the right-side cam bearing is in place. Use gasket sealer on the cylinder head cover mating surface.

90 cc Models

REMOVAL

1. The cylinder head, cylinder, and piston may be removed with the engine still in the frame.

2. Remove the exhaust system and the carburetor manifold from the cylinder head.

3. Remove the valve adjustment caps; remove the breaker point cover.

4. Disconnect the point wire. Mark the position of the breaker plate relative to the point housing to facilitate ignition timing upon assembly. Remove the breaker plate screws and pull off the plate.

5. Remove the bolt from the end of the camshaft. Pull off the timing advance mechanism.

6. Remove the dowel pin from the camshaft. Remove the three phillips screws which secure the point housing to the head and remove the housing and its gasket.

Remove the camshaft dowel pin (2); then remove the three screws and the point housing

7. Rotate the engine so that the "0" mark on the cam sprocket aligns with the notch on the cylinder head. The sprocket bolts will be in line with the centerline of the cylinder.

Position the piston at TDC on the compression stroke before removing the head by aligning the sprocket "O" mark with the top of the head. The sprocket bolts (1) will align with the cylinder centerline as illustrated.

The piston is now at top dead center on the compression stroke.

8. Remove the two cam sprocket bolts.

CAUTION: *The cylinder head nuts must remain tightened when removing the sprocket bolts.*

9. Remove the camshaft. Take out the sprocket.

10. Loosen each of the four cylinder

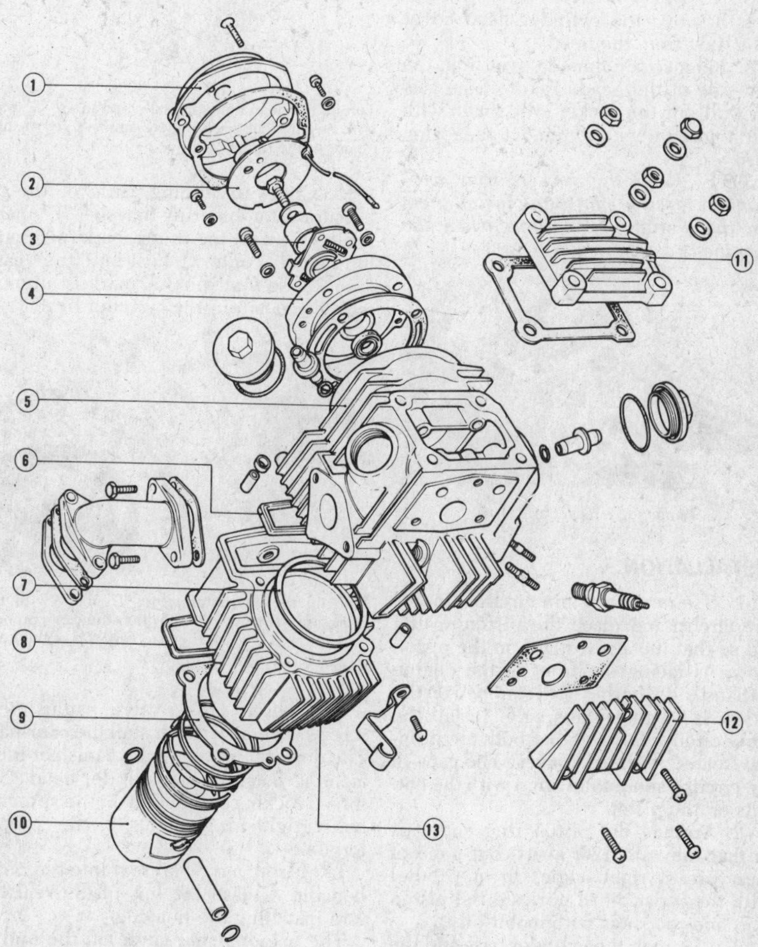

Top end assembly (90 cc)

1. Point cover
2. Breaker points
3. Timing advance
4. Point housing
5. Cylinder head
6. Cam chain chamber gasket
7. Head gasket
8. Cam chain chamber gasket (lower)
9. Cylinder base gasket
10. Piston
11. Cylinder head cover
12. Head cover, right-side
13. Cylinder

head nuts ¼ turn at a time in an "X" pattern until they are loose; then remove them. Lift off the cylinder head. Remove the gasket.

11. Remove the cam chain guide roller pin from the left-side of the cylinder.

12. Slowly pull off the cylinder, taking care that the piston does not strike the engine when the cylinder is removed.

13. After removing the cylinder, remove the piston wrist pin circlips with a needlenose pliers. Push out the wrist pin with a suitable drift.

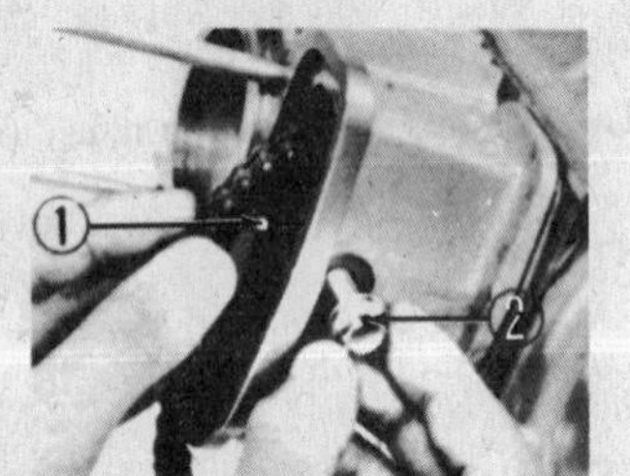

Remove the cam chain roller pin (2) and the roller (1)

14. Remove the cylinder head cover and gasket from the head.

15. Remove the finned cover from the right-side of the head. Take off the gasket. Pull out the rocker arm shafts with needlenose pliers, and remove the rocker arms.

NOTE: *Keep the rocker arms with their respective shafts and install them in their original locations when the engine is assembled.*

Removing a rocker arm shaft

INSTALLATION

1. Use new wrist pin circlips. Install one circlip and place the piston on the rod so that the arrow mark on the piston crown is facing the front of the engine (exhaust side) or the "IN" stamped on the crown is on the intake side. Install the other circlip. Be sure that both are properly seated in their grooves. The gaps in the circlips should not align with the cutouts on the piston.

2. Arrange the piston ring end-gaps so that they are 120° apart, but none of them are at right angles to or parallel with the wrist pin. Lubricate the piston skirt and the rings with motor oil.

3. Clean off the cylinder base and the crankcase mating surface. Fit a new base gasket and a cam chain chamber gasket.

4. After ensuring that any cylinder guide pins or O-rings are in place, install the cylinder. As the cylinder is moved down on the studs, pull the cam chain through. Compress the piston rings carefully as the piston enters the bore. Place the piston at top dead center.

5. Install the cam chain guide roller and pin.

6. Assemble the cylinder head, refitting the rocker arms and shafts, the right-side cover and the top cover. Use new cover gaskets. Rocker arm shafts should be lubricated before installation.

7. Fit a new head gasket and upper cam chain chamber gasket. Fit the cam sprocket to the chain.

8. Install the head, drawing the cam sprocket up through the head as it is installed. Loop a length of wire through the sprocket and wire it to the head to keep it in place while torquing the head nuts.

9. Install and tighten the head nuts, noting that the lower left-hand nut is a capnut fitted with a copper washer.

Tighten the nuts in gradual increments in an "X" pattern until a final torque of 13–16 ft lbs is reached.

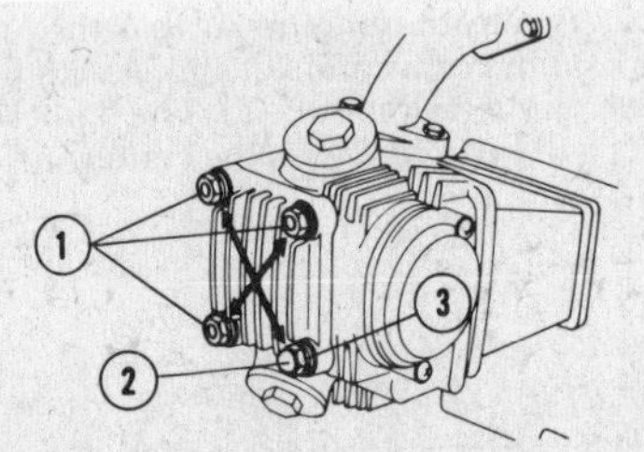

Torque the head nuts gradually and in an "X" pattern; be sure that the capnut (2) and copper washer (3) are in the right place

10. Check the timing marks on the alternator rotor ensuring that the "T" mark is aligned with the index mark (piston at top dead center). Position the cam sprocket so that the "0" mark is aligned with the notch in the cylinder head.

Line up the alternator rotor "T" mark with the crankcase mark (2), then position the cam sprocket so that the "O" mark is at the very top of the head (1) and aligned with the notch

11. Loosen the valve adjustment screws several turns. Install the camshaft. The dowel pin hole in the camshaft must face the notch in the cylinder head. Use thread locking compound on the sprocket bolts, tightening them to the proper torque.

12. Install a new oil seal into the point housing. Grease the lips of the seal before installing the housing.

The use of a seal guide on the end of the camshaft is recommended to avoid damaging the lips of the seal when the housing is installed. (Tool No. 07043-1280100).

13. Install the housing, using a new gasket behind it. Install the dowel pin on the camshaft. Fit the spark advance mechanism, cam bolt, etc. The remainder of installation is the reverse of removal. Adjust the cam chain, valves, and ignition timing, and recheck these after a few miles of operation.

50–70 cc Models (Except XR75)

REMOVAL

1. The engine need not be removed from the frame to remove the cylinder head and cylinder. Remove the exhaust system and the carburetor and manifold from the cylinder.

2. Remove the magneto or alternator rotor cover. Remove the spark plug and the valve adjuster caps. Turn the engine over until the intake valve goes down and comes up, and turn it a bit farther so that the "T" mark on the rotor aligns with the stationary index mark.

The piston is now at top dead center on the compression stroke (both valves closed).

3. Loosen each cylinder head cover nut ¼ of a turn at a time until they are loose, then remove them. Note that one or two of the nuts are different and must be installed in the location from which they were removed.

On most models, there is one hex nut and three capnuts; an oil sealing washer is fitted beneath the hex nut.

4. Tap the head cover lightly with a plastic mallet to free it if stuck.

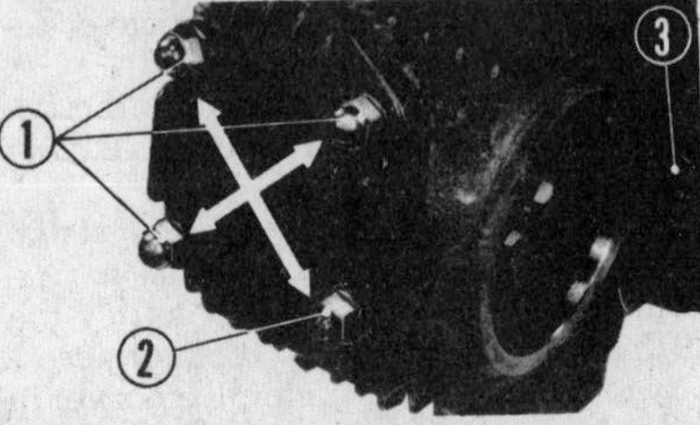

Remove the three capnuts (1); and the hex nut (2), to remove the cylinder head cover. Remove the head bolt (3) before attempting to remove the head (50-70 cc)

5. Remove the bolt from the right-side of the cylinder head. This will enable the left-side cover to be removed.

6. Remove the two screws on the right-side cylinder head cover and remove the cover.

7. Check that the piston is at TDC (the "0" mark on the cam sprocket will be toward the top of the head).

8. Remove the three sprocket mounting bolts, and push in on the camshaft to disengage it from the sprocket. Remove the sprocket after disengaging it from the cam chain.

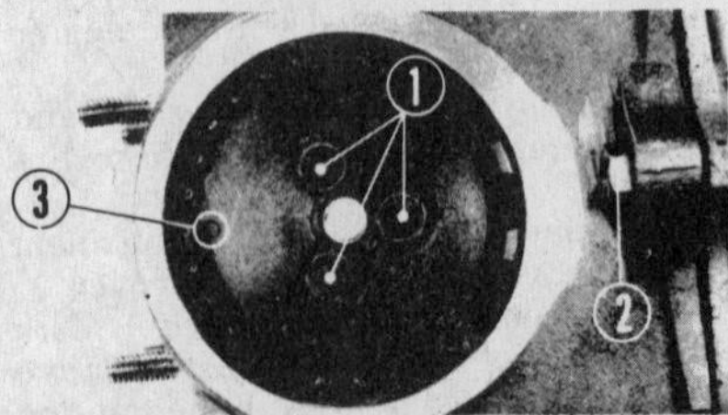

Align the sprocket mark (3) with the top of the head before removing the sprocket bolts (1)

NOTE: *It may be necessary to hold the camshaft in position while removing the sprocket bolts and this can be done if the engine is in the frame by engaging the transmission except for centrifugal clutch models. If the engine is not in the frame, secure the magneto rotor or the countershaft sprocket.*

9. Remove the cylinder head mounting bolt on the left-side of the head. Remove the head, tapping around the mounting surface with a plastic mallet if it is stuck.

10. When the head is removed, remove the two locating pins at the head mating surface and ensure that they are in place when the head is refitted. To

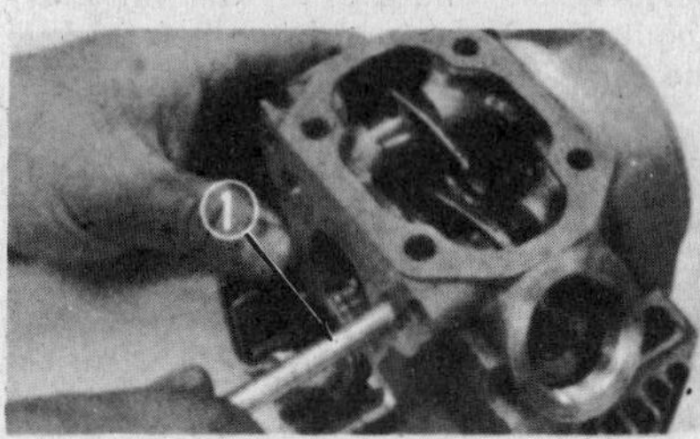

Removing the rocker arm shaft with a 6 mm puller bolt

remove the rocker arms, thread a 6 mm bolt into the right-side of the rocker arm shafts and pull them out. Keep each rocker arm shaft with its own rocker arm for proper installation. Push the camshaft out of the head.

NOTE: *The cylinder head or cylinder mounting bolt can be used to remove the rocker arm shafts.*

11. Unscrew and remove the cam chain guide roller pin from the left-side of the cylinder and remove the guide roller.

Removing the cam chain guide roller pin (1)

12. Remove the cylinder mounting bolt on the left-side and pull off the cylinder. Do not allow the piston to strike the studs as it comes out of the cylinder. Check the location of the two hollow dowel pins on the cylinder studs. Remove these and make sure that they are installed when assembling the top end.

13. To remove the piston, remove the wrist pin circlips with needlenose pliers and push out the wrist pin.

NOTE: *Use steady pressure while removing the wrist pin. Support the piston with your other hand. Do not strike or attempt to force out the pin.*

INSTALLATION

1. Install one wrist pin circlip and place the piston on the connecting rod. The triangular mark on the piston crown must be positioned on the *cam chain* side. Insert the wrist pin and the other circlip. Use new circlips and be sure that they are properly seated. Arrange the circlip end-gaps so that they do not align with the cutouts on the piston. Arrange the piston rings so that the end-gaps are 120° apart, but are not perpendicular to or parallel with the wrist pin. Lubricate the wrist pin, rings, and piston skirt with motor oil.

2. Be sure that the O-ring is in place in the crankcase oil passage and the hollow dowel pins are installed on the cam chain side studs. Fit a new cylinder base gasket. Install the cylinder, compressing the rings with your fingers as the piston enters the bore. Feed the cam chain through the cylinder as it is seated. Install and tighten the cylinder mounting bolt.

3. Install the cam chain guide roller and the roller pin.

4. Install the two hollow pins on the studs: one on the top right stud, the other on the left bottom. Fit the O-rings to the oil passage and to the stud oil passage; fit the head gasket.

5. Install the head, complete with rocker arms and cam, threading the cam chain with its sprocket through, and securing them with a length of wire or a screwdriver.

6. Turn the magneto rotor so that the "T" mark on the rotor is aligned with the index mark on the crankcase. Set the cam sprocket "0" mark at the top of the head. Install and tighten the sprocket bolts to 4–7 ft lbs. Thread locking compound should be used on these bolts. Lubricate the top end components.

7. The remainder of the procedure is the reverse of disassembly. Note that the cylinder head cover hex nut (on most models) and its copper washer are installed on the lower left stud. Install the head mounting bolt. Tighten the head cover nuts in a cross pattern and in increments of 2–3 ft lbs until the proper torque of 6.5–8.7 ft lbs is reached. Adjust the cam chain and tappet clearance before starting the engine.

XR75

REMOVAL

1. The top end can be removed with the engine in the frame. Remove the gas tank, exhaust system, carburetor, and manifold.

2. Remove the magneto rotor cover. Remove the spark plug.

3. Remove the cylinder head cover.

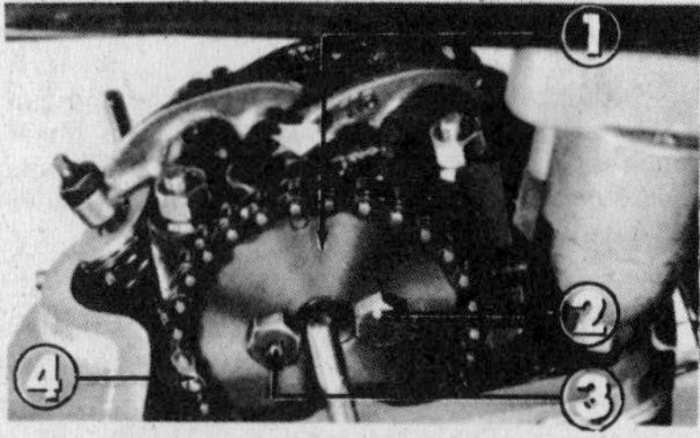

Cam sprocket positioned for removal. Note "O" mark on the sprocket (1) and the cam housing mark (arrow). Sprocket bolts (2 and 3) are not interchangeable.

4. Turn the engine over until the "0" mark on the cam sprocket is aligned with the mark on the cam housing. Unscrew and remove the two cam sprocket bolts.

NOTE: *The bolts are not interchangeable. Mark the location of each so that they can be installed in their original locations.*

5. Remove the cam sprocket. Loop a length of wire around the chain and secure it so that it doesn't fall into the cylinder.

6. Remove the three hex nuts and one capnut and take off the camshaft housing complete with cam and rocker arms.

Remove the camshaft housing (1) after removing the four nuts circled

7. Thread an 8 mm bolt into the rocker arm shafts and pull them out. Mark each and the rocker arms for proper installation. Remove the cam.

8. Remove the cam chain tensioner set plate bolt from the cylinder head. Pull out the tensioner adjuster.

9. Remove the cylinder head. If stuck, strike carefully with a plastic mallet. When removing the head, be sure that the cam chain does not fall into the crankcase.

Note the location of the dowel pins and O-rings on the head-cylinder mating surface. Be sure that they are correctly installed when assembling the engine.

10. Remove the cam chain guide. It can be pulled out of the cylinder. Loosen the cam chain tensioner bolt.

11. Remove the cylinder. When the cylinder is lifted off the crankcase, stuff a clean rag between the cylinder and case to catch any pieces of broken ring, dirt, etc.

Note the location of any dowel pins or O-rings between the cylinder and the case. These must be in their proper locations when assembling the engine.

12. Remove the wrist pin circlips with needlenose pliers.

NOTE: *Keep the rag in place while doing this.*

13. Push out the wrist pin. If the pin resists removal, the piston crown may be heated gently with a propane torch.

CAUTION: *Never strike the wrist pin to remove it. Use steady pressure only. Support the piston with one hand while the wrist pin is removed.*

INSTALLATION

1. The piston must be installed so that the "IN" marking on the crown is on the intake side. Use new wrist pin circlips.

Circlips should be firmly seated in their grooves. The open ends should not align with the piston cutout.

2. Arrange the piston rings so that the end-gaps of the two compression rings and the oil ring expander are 120° apart. Arrange the end-gaps of the two oil rails about 45° on either side of the expander end-gap.

None of the ring end-gaps should be perpendicular to or parellel with the wrist pin.

3. A new cylinder base gasket must be used. Be sure that any dowel pins or O-rings are in place before installing the cylinder.

4. Lubricate the piston assembly with motor oil before fitting the cylinder. Pull the cam chain through the cylinder as it is installed. Install the chain guide.

5. Use a new head gasket. Install the head, making sure that any dowel pins or O-rings are in place.

6. Install the cam housing, cam, and rocker arms in the head. Turn the cam so that both valves are closed. Clean the threads of the cylinder studs, and oil them lightly. Fit the cam housing nuts, and tighten them in a cross pattern until the correct torque (5.8–8.7 ft lbs) is reached.

7. Remove the rotor cover. Turn the engine over until the "T" mark on the rotor aligns with the index mark.

8. Install the cam sprocket so that the "0" mark on the sprocket aligns with the mark on the cam housing.

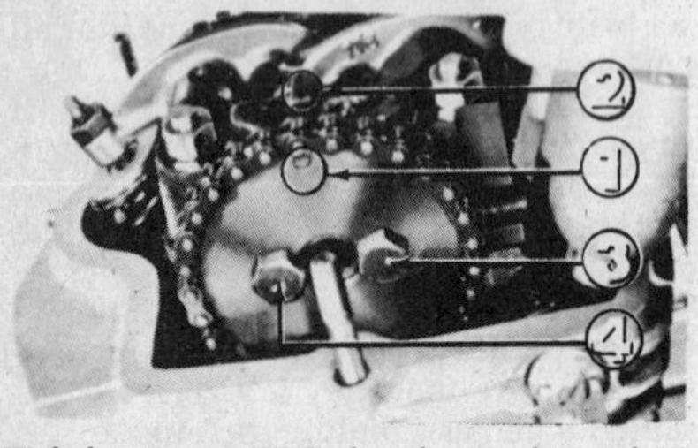

With the piston at TDC, align the sprocket mark (1) with the housing mark (2), then install the bolts (3 and 4)

9. Fit the sprocket bolts, noting their proper locations. Use thread locking compound on these bolts. Torque to 5.8–8.7 ft lbs.

10. The remainder of the procedure is the reverse of removal. Adjust the cam chain and valve clearance before starting the engine.

TOP END SERVICE

Service and inspection procedures for the components in the top end are outlined in the "Engine Rebuilding" section in "General Information," while specifications for individual models are given in the specifications charts at the end of this section; however, note the following:

1. Early model 100s (up to Frame No. 200000) were equipped with straight-wound valve springs. If the later progressively-wound springs are fitted as a replacement, they must be replaced in sets.

2. Some models use stellite-tipped valves. Attempting to resurface the valve stem will wear away the hardened stellite surface.

Progressively-wound valve springs are installed with the close coils against the head

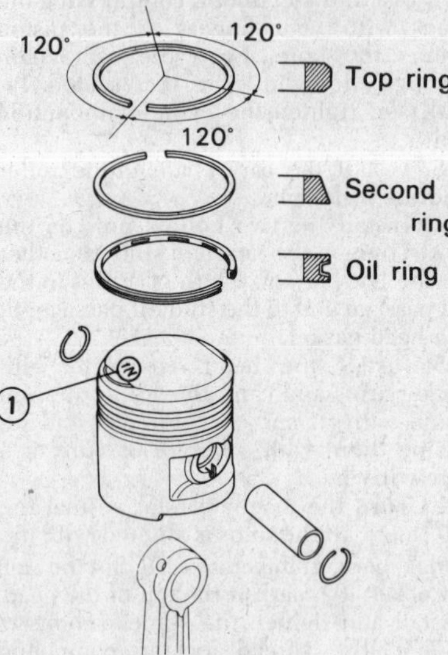

Ring end-gaps should be spaced 120° apart. The piston must be installed so that the "IN" mark is toward the intake side on the head. Note the difference between the top and bottom compression rings.

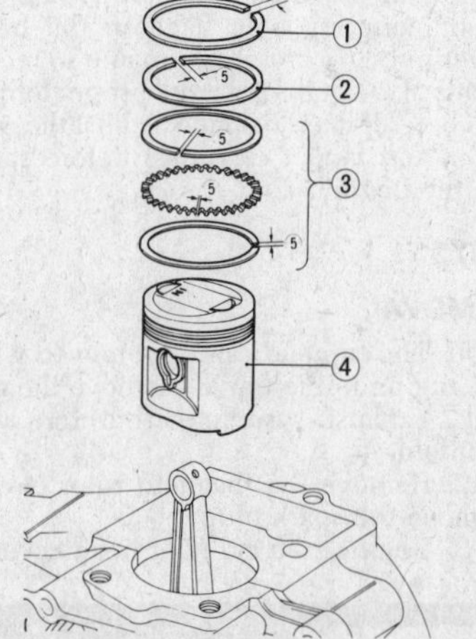

On models with multi-piece oil rings, the end-gap of the expander should be 120° from the lower compression ring, and the two oil rail end-gaps should be about 45° on either side of the expander end-gap

3. Before installing the rings on the piston, first note that the two compression rings are not interchangeable in most cases. The wedge-shaped ring is the lower compression ring.

Also note that rings must always be installed so that the manufacturer's mark (the small letter near the end-gap) faces *up* when the rings are in place.

4. If two-rail oil rings are used, install one rail on the piston below the oil ring groove. Install the oil rail expander in the groove, than move the lower rail into the groove. Install the upper oil rail.

5. Arrange the ring end-gaps 120° apart, but do not position any end-gap at the very front or the very back of the piston (perpendicular to the wrist pin), or directly above the wrist pin holes.

If a two-rail oil ring is used, position the end-gap of the oil ring expander 120° from the lower compression ring, then position the end-gaps of the oil rails about 45° (20–30 mm) on either side of the expander end-gap.

CRANKCASE COVER COMPONENTS

Right Crankcase Cover Components

100–125 CC MODELS

Clutch, oil pump and filter, and the gearshift mechanism are accessible after removing the right crankcase cover. To remove the kick-starter, it is necessary to split the cases. Refer to "Lower End and Transmission."

Removal and Installation

1. Drain the oil. Remove the exhaust system and the right footpeg. Remove the kick-starter lever. Disconnect the clutch cable, and the tach cable, if fitted. Remove the right crankcase cover.

2. Remove the oil filter rotor cap (three screws). Remove the rotor nut. A special wrench is needed to remove the nut. Remove the rotor.

3. Remove the oil pump gear cover. Remove the oil pump gear and shaft. The oil pump is secured by two bolts. Remove them and remove the pump.

Removing the oil filter rotor nut with the special wrench (2). Note the clutch holder (3). (100-125 cc)

Oil pump gear (1) and shaft (2)

Oil pump (2) and securing bolts (1)

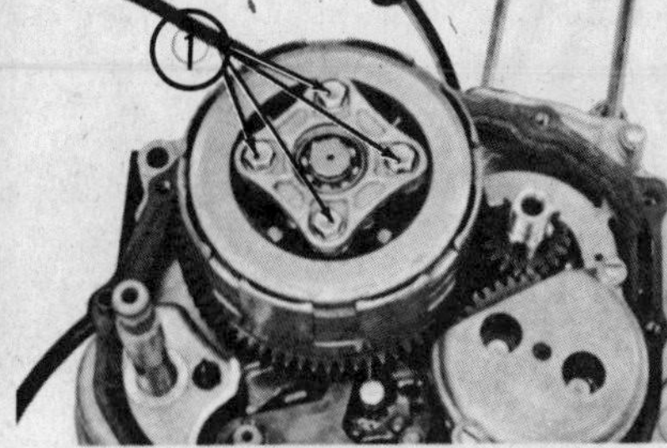

Clutch lifter plate bolts (1)

Removing the shift plate circlip (2)

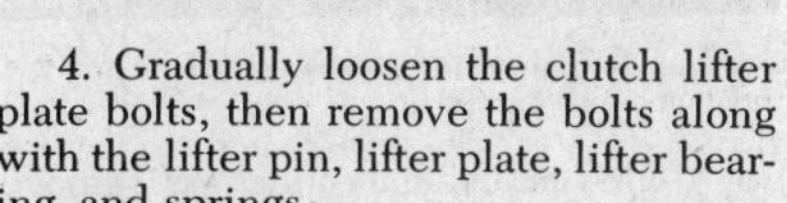

Remove the gearshift drum stopper and spring (1 and 2) and stopper plate (3)

4. Gradually loosen the clutch lifter plate bolts, then remove the bolts along with the lifter pin, lifter plate, lifter bearing, and springs.

5. Remove the crankshaft primary gear. Remove the clutch hub snap-ring, housing as a unit. The clutch lever in the right cover on TL125 and 100/125(76) can be removed after removal of the cotter pin. Be sure the spring is correctly installed.

6. To remove the gearshift linkage, remove the circlip on the shift shaft and remove the shift plate from the shaft.

7. Remove the gearshift drum stopper and spring. Remove the shift drum stopper plate. Both of these parts are secured by single bolts.

8. Remove the gearshift lever (left-side). Pull the gearshift shaft out from the right-side.

9. Refer to "Component Inspection," which follows.

10. Assembly is the reverse of the above. Note the following points:

a. The stopper plate is equipped with a locating pin hole. Match it with the pin in the shift drum. Install the gearshift shaft so that the ends of the shaft return spring are located on either side of the boss on the crankcase;

b. Tighten the clutch lifter plate bolts progressively until a torque of 5.6–8.7 ft lbs is reached;

c. Before installing the oil pump, be sure that the O-rings are installed;

d. When installing the oil filter, note that the rotor washer is marked for proper installation. The "outside" side of the washer must face out. Tighten the rotor nut to 29–36 ft lbs.

90CC MODELS

Clutch, oil pump, primary driven gear, and the gearshift mechanism are accessible after removing the right-side cover. To remove the kick-starter mechanism, it

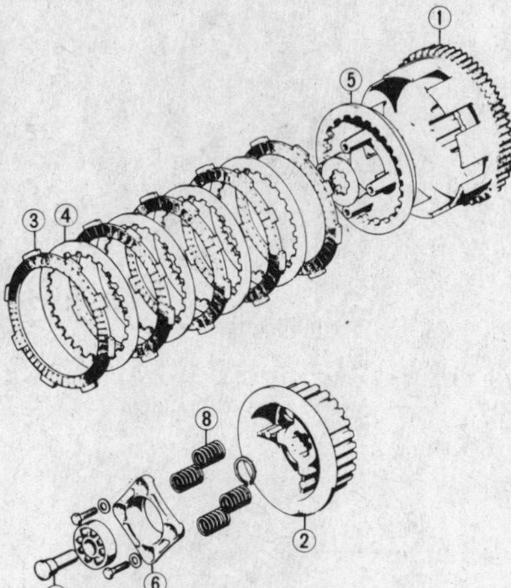

Clutch assembly (100-125 cc)

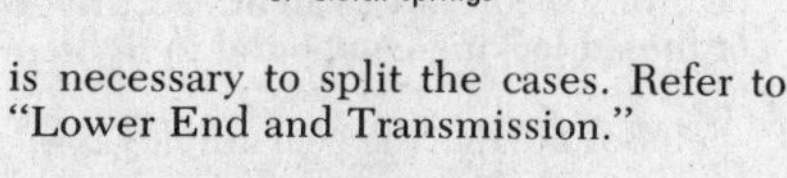

1. Clutch housing
2. Clutch hub
3. Friction plate
4. Steel plate
5. Pressure plate
6. Lifter plate
7. Lifter pin
8. Clutch springs

is necessary to split the cases. Refer to "Lower End and Transmission."

Removal and Installation

1. Drain the oil. Disconnect the clutch cable from the lever at the engine (if fitted).

2. On models with a tubular sub-frame (ST/CT models), remove the footpegs and the sub-frame.

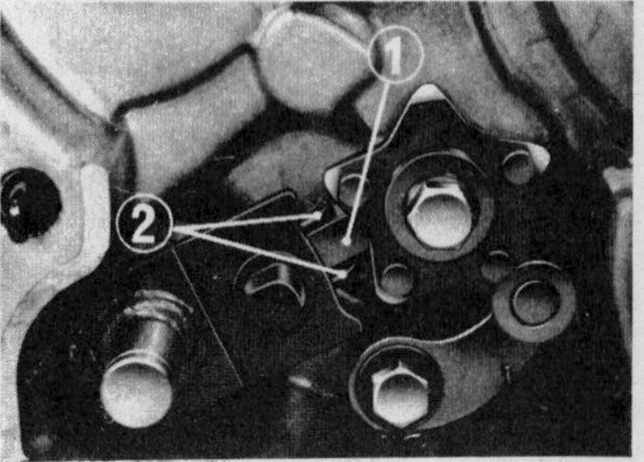

Upon assembly, be sure that the ends of the return spring (2) are installed on either side of the crankcase boss (1)

Clutch housing (2) and cover (1) (90 cc)

3. Slack off the rear brake adjuster nut several turns. Remove the pinch-bolt and pull off the kick-starter.

4. Remove the clutch cover plate. Remove the right crankcase cover. Remove and discard the cover gasket.

5. On centrifugal clutches, remove the clutch lifter lever and the lifter.

6. Remove the clutch housing cover usually secured by two phillips screws.

7. Bend down the tab on the clutch

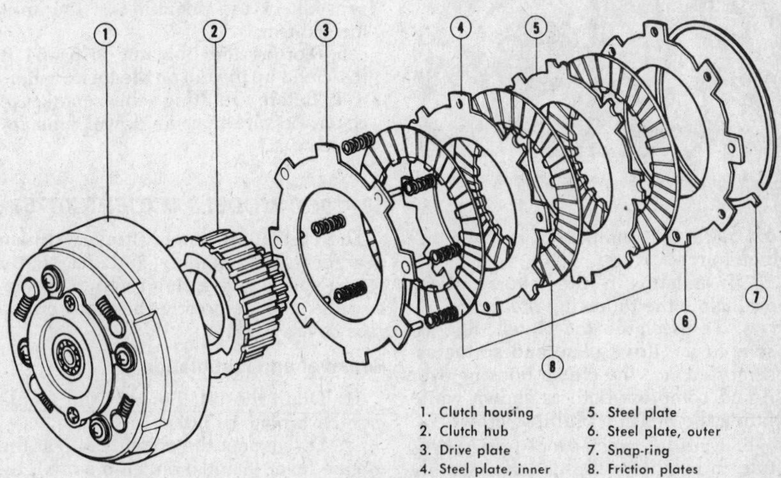

1. Clutch housing
2. Clutch hub
3. Drive plate
4. Steel plate, inner
5. Steel plate
6. Steel plate, outer
7. Snap-ring
8. Friction plates

Centrifugal clutch components

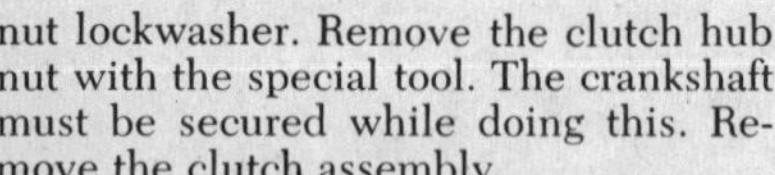
Primary driven gear (2), snap-ring (1), oil pump (3), securing screws (4), hex bolt (6), and pump cover screws (5)

nut lockwasher. Remove the clutch hub nut with the special tool. The crankshaft must be secured while doing this. Remove the clutch assembly.

8. If disassembly of the clutch is required, compress it using the special Honda tool, or compress the assembly is a soft-faced vise. Remove the large snap-ring on the inner side. Carefully remove the clutch from the vise or tool (it is under spring pressure when compressed), and separate the components: steel and friction plates, free springs (centrifugal clutch), clutch hub, and gears.

If further disassembly is desired, remove the clutch damper springs in the clutch housing. Remove the phillips screws from the outer side of the housing and separate drive plate, clutch springs, and housing.

To complete disassembly, remove the clutch weight stopper ring from the drive plate.

9. Remove the oil pump by removing the hex bolt and three phillips screws. Remove the oil filter screen.

10. Remove the snap-ring to remove the large primary driven gear.

11. Remove the pinch-bolt and pull the foot gearshift lever off the splined shift shaft. Remove the shift drum stopper. Disengage the fingers of the shift arm from the shift drum pins and pull the shift shaft assembly out of the case. Remove the phillips screw and the shift drum stopper plate (if desired).

Shift drum stopper (1), stopper plate (2), and shift arm (3)

12. Refer to "Component Inspection," which follows.

13. Installation is the reverse of removal. Note the following points:

a. To assemble the clutch, first assemble the drive plate and spring assembly. Place the clutch housing over it and compress both as shown while fitting the housing phillips screws;

b. Use the special tool or a substitute to compress the clutch assembly while the snap-ring is fitted;

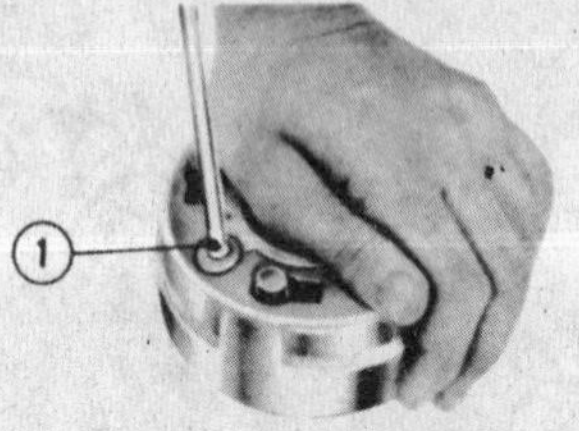

Assembling the clutch

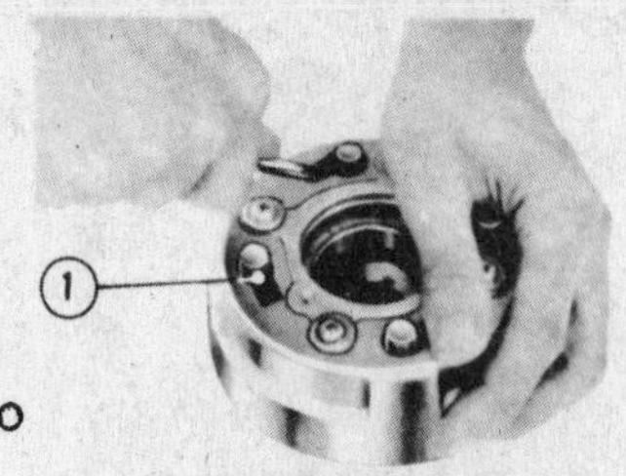

Installing the damper springs

c. Install the damper springs with a screwdriver as illustrated;

d. The shift drum stopper plate must be firmly secured. Use an impact driver or thread locking compound to tighten it;

e. Be sure that the gearshift lever return spring pin is secured in the crankcase. Install the gearshift shaft assembly, locating the ends of the return spring on either side of the stopper pin and engaging the fingers of the shift arm with the shift drum pins;

f. Install the shift drum stopper, so that the roller bears against one of the detents of the shift drum stopper plate;

g. Check the operation of the shift mechanism;

h. Torque the hub nut to 54–64 ft lbs. Bend up the tab on the lockwasher;

i. Before refitting the crankcase cover, be sure that the dowel pins are in place.

50–70CC MODELS (EXCEPT XR75)

The clutch, oil pump, primary driven gear, gearshift assembly, and kick-starter return spring and spring retainer are accessible after removing the right crankcase cover.

Removal and Installation

1. Drain the oil. Remove the crankcase bash plate (if fitted).

2. Disconnect the clutch cable at the engine lever (manual clutch models); remove the kick-starter lever.

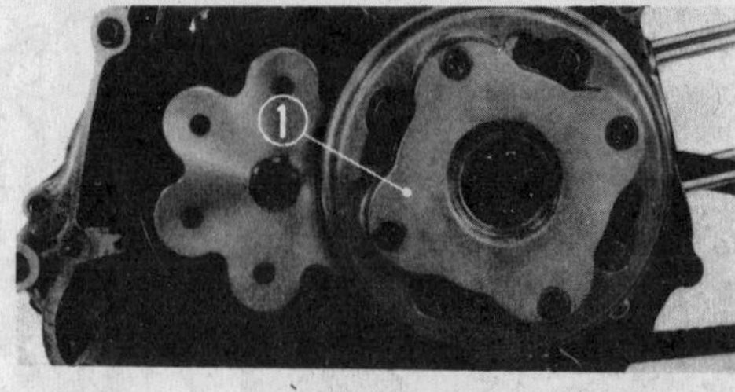

Clutch cover (50-70 cc)

3. Take out the screws and remove the right crankcase cover.

NOTE: *On most models the cover screws are of different lengths; note their locations to install properly. Note the dowel pins between the case and cover.*

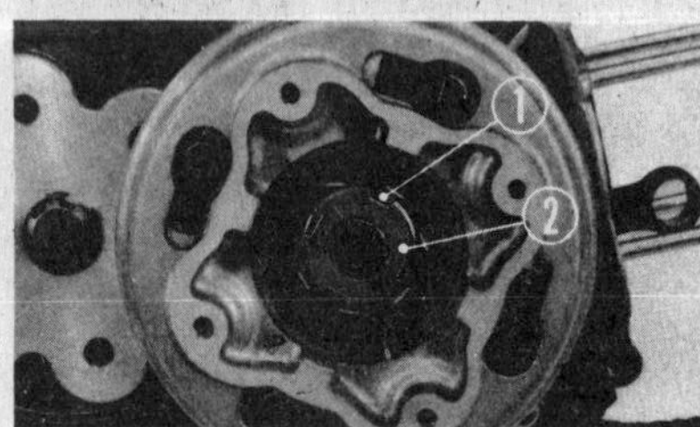

Bend up the tab of the lockwasher (1) to remove the clutch hub nut (2)

4. On centrifugal clutches, remove the clutch lifter lever and the lifter.

5. Remove the clutch housing cover.

6. Bend down the tab on the clutch nut lockwasher. Remove the clutch hub nut with the special wrench. The crankshaft must be secured while doing this.

Remove the clutch assembly from the crankshaft.

7. If disassembly of the clutch is desired, compress it using the special Honda tool, or compress the assembly in a soft-faced vise. Remove the large snap-ring on the inner side. Carefully remove the clutch from the vise or tool (it is under spring pressure when compressed) and separate the components: steel and friction plates, free springs (centrifugal clutch), clutch hub, and gears.

If further disassembly is desired (centrifugal clutches), remove the clutch damper springs in the housing. Remove the phillips screws from the outer side of the housing and separate the drive plate, clutch springs, and housing.

8. Remove the three oil pump mounting screws to remove the oil pump. Remove the filter screeen.

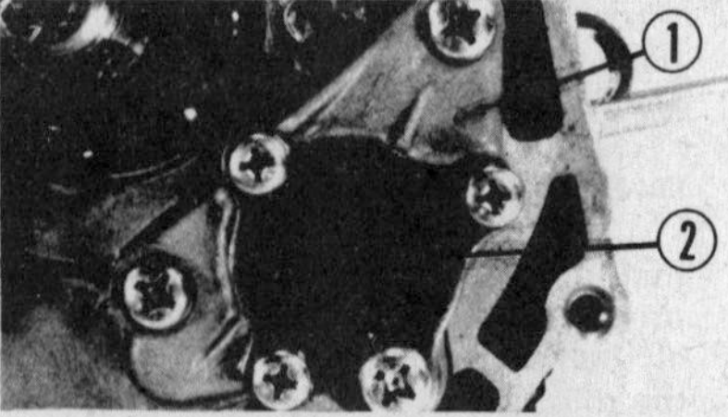

Oil pump (1) and cover (2)

9. Remove the circlip to remove the large primary driven gear. Remove the circlip from the kick-starter shaft. Detach the kick-starter return spring from the

crankcase, and remove the spring and retainer.

10. Remove the shift drum stopper and spring. Remove the gearshift lever from the left-side of the engine. Loosen the shift drum stopper plate screw, disengage the fingers of the shift arm from the shift drum dowel pins, and pull the gearshift shaft out of the crankcases.

Right crankcase cover components (SL70 shown)

1. Kick-starter spring retainer
2. Kick-starter shaft
3. Return spring
4. Shift drum stopper plate
5. Shift arm
6. Shift drum stopper

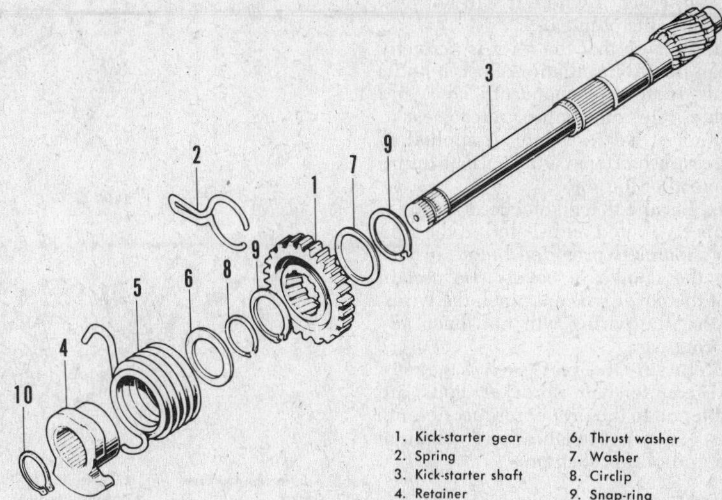

1. Kick-starter gear
2. Spring
3. Kick-starter shaft
4. Retainer
5. Return spring
6. Thrust washer
7. Washer
8. Circlip
9. Snap-ring
10. Circlip

Kick-starter components (50-70 cc)

11. Refer to "Component Inspection," following.

12. Installation is the reverse of removal. Note the following points:

a. The shift drum stopper plate screw should be secured with thread locking compound or an impact driver;

b. Be sure that the gearshift lever return spring pin is secured in the crankcase. Install the gearshift shaft assembly, locating the ends of the return spring on either side of the stopper pin and engaging the fingers of the shift arm with the shift drum pins;

c. Install the shift drum stopper, so that the roller bears against one of the detents of the shift drum stopper plate;

d. Check the operation of the shift mechanism;

e. Install the kick-starter return spring and spring retainer. One end of the spring should engage the crankcase, and the pawl on the retainer should rest against the stopper boss of the crankcase. Install the kick-starter shaft circlip;

f. The collar installed on the crankshaft behind the clutch is fitted with the larger diameter side toward the engine. The clutch should be assembled before fitting it to the crankshaft;

g. Tighten the clutch nut to 27.5-32.5 ft lbs, and bend down the tab on the lockwasher;

h. When fitting the cover, be sure that the dowel pins are in place and the screws are correctly located. They are of different lengths.

XR75

Removal and Installation

1. Drain the oil. Remove the exhaust pipe. Remove the kick-starter arm. Disconnect the clutch cable from the lever at the engine.

2. Remove the skid plate and footpeg.

3. Remove the right crankcase cover screws and tap lightly on the cover with a plastic mallet to free it if necessary.

4. Remove the oil filter screen.

5. Remove the centrifugal oil filter rotor cover (three screws), and remove the rotor nut with the special wrench. Keep the crankshaft from turning by jamming the primary gear with a block of hardwood, or by engaging the transmission and applying the rear brake.

6. Remove the rotor and the primary gear.

7. Remove the oil pump gear cover, then the pump assembly.

8. Remove the clutch lifter plate bolts, loosening them evenly. Remove the clutch lifter plate and springs.

9. Remove the circlip from the clutch shaft, and take out the clutch hub and plates as an assembly.

10. Remove the splined washer and the clutch housing.

11. Remove the shift drum stopper. Remove the stopper plate.

12. Remove the gearshift lever from the left-side of the engine. Pull out the shifter return spring and shaft from the right-side. Do not lose the small shifter damper spring.

13. Refer to "Component Inspection," following.

14. Assembly is the reverse of the above.

Note the following points:

a. Check the stopper and stopper plate for proper operation after tightening the bolts;

b. Be sure to fit the splined washer to the clutch shaft after installing the housing;

c. The oil pump O-rings and gasket should be replaced with new ones. The gasket must not contact the rotor. Do not forget to install the tach gear thrust washer;

d. Tighten the clutch bolts gradually and evenly. Adjust the clutch after assembly.

Left Crankcase Cover Components

The left crankcase cover contains the alternator or magneto, the countershaft sprocket, and the cam chain tensioner on some models.

All components can be removed for service with the engine in the frame.

Certain precautions should be observed when handling these components:

a. The rotor must be removed with a special puller. Do not attempt to pry the rotor off the tapered crankshaft;

b. Do not heat or strike the rotor as this may affect its magnetic properties;

Clutch lifter plate (2) and bolts (1)

Shift drum stopper (1) and stopper plate (2)

c. Do not drop the rotor once it is removed. Place it where it will not pick up stray bits of metal;

d. Be sure that the rotor is perfectly clean before installation. Push it on its shaft (note the woodruff key) and tighten the rotor bolt or nut to seat it. Do not strike it. Some oil applied to the crankshaft taper will facilitate future removal of the rotor;

e. Be sure that all electrical wiring is properly routed and seated in the rubber grommets provided before installing the crankcase covers. Be certain that the cover will not pinch the wires, or that the wiring will not touch any moving part;

f. Be sure that parts such as the rotor and countershaft sprocket bolts are tightened to the proper torque. Refer to the "Torque Specifications" chart at the end of this section.

100–125 cc Models

REMOVAL AND INSTALLATION

1. Drain the oil. Remove the alternator wiring at the plastic coupler. Remove the gearshift lever.
2. Remove the alternator rotor cover. Remove the countershaft sprocket cover. Disconnect the neutral switch wire if fitted. Remove the forward section of the left crankcase cover.
3. Remove the screws securing the alternator stator. Secure the rotor, and remove the rotor bolt. Using the special puller, remove the rotor.
4. Early models: remove the cam chain tensioner arm pivot bolt, and take out the tensioner components.

Cam chain tensioner bolt (1), arm (2), adjusting bolt (3) (early type, 100-125 cc)

5. Remove the countershaft sprocket bolts, disconnect the chain, remove the sprocket locking plate, and pull off the sprocket.
6. Refer to "Component Inspection," following.

Alternator wiring grommet (1) and neutral switch wire routing

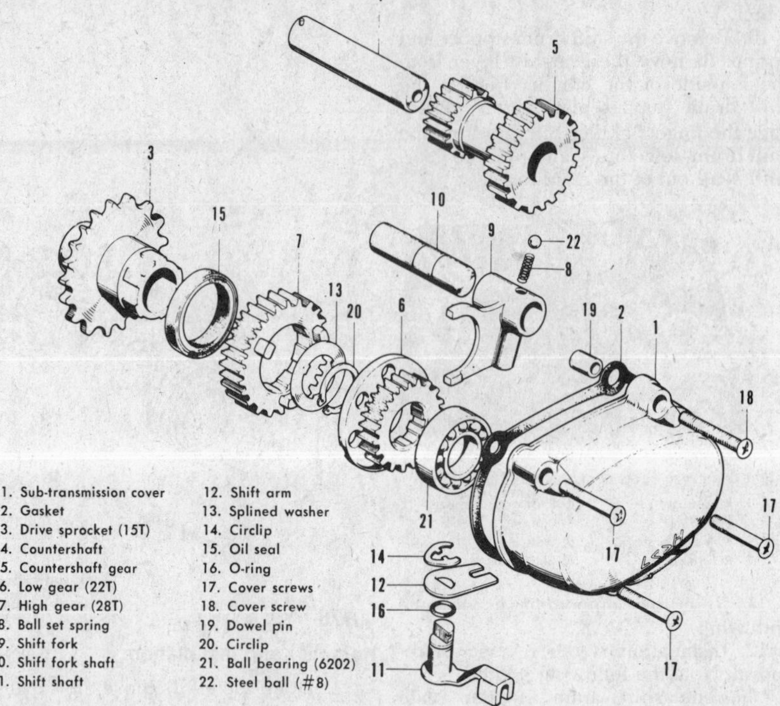

Sub-transmission components (CT90)

7. Installation is the reverse of the above. Be sure that the O-ring is installed around the alternator stator. Be sure that the alternator wiring is correctly routed before installing the cover.

90 cc Models

REMOVAL AND INSTALLATION

1. Drain the oil. Disconnect the alternator wiring at the connector. Disconnect the neutral switch wire, if fitted.
2. Remove the rotor cover. Remove the gearshift lever.
3. CT90: Remove the sub-transmission cover. Remove the sub-transmission Low gear, counter gear and shaft, shift fork and shaft. Remove the circlip, splined washer, and sub-trans High gear.
4. Other models: Remove the countershaft sprocket cover.
5. All: Remove the left crankcase cover.
6. Remove the screws which secure the alternator stator.

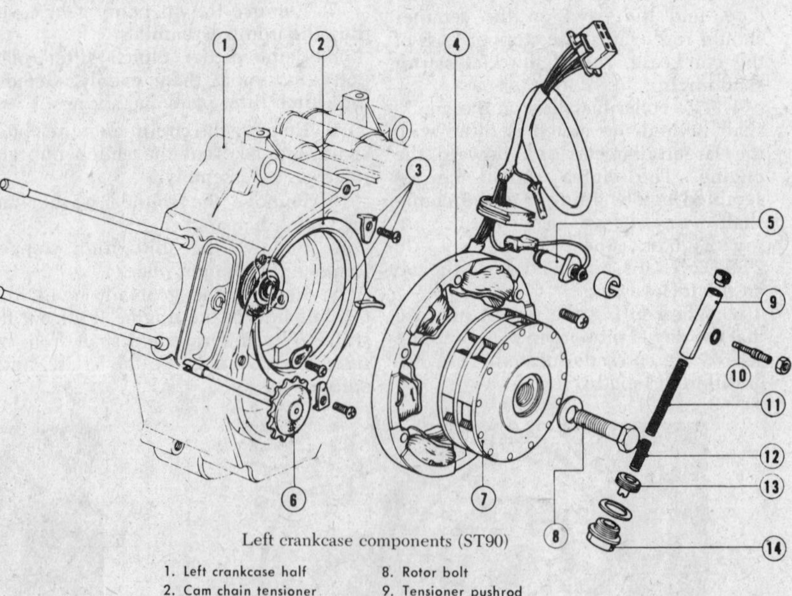

Left crankcase components (ST90)

1. Left crankcase half
2. Cam chain tensioner
3. Retaining plates
4. Alternator stator
5. Neutral switch
6. Cam chain guide roller
7. Alternator rotor
8. Rotor bolt
9. Tensioner pushrod
10. Adjusting bolt
11. Tensioner spring, main
12. Tensioner spring, secondary
13. Tensioner bolt
14. Cover bolt

7. Remove the alternator rotor bolt. Using the special tool, remove the rotor.
8. Back off the cam chain tensioner adjusting screw. Remove the tensioner cover bolt. Remove the tensioner bolt, spring and pushrod.
9. Remove the tensioner sprocket.
10. To remove the tensioner and roller, the top end assembly must be removed. Refer to that section. Remove the cam chain, then the three screws which hold the tensioner retaining plates.
11. Remove the countershaft sprocket bolts, disconnect the chain, remove the sprocket locking plate, and pull off the sprocket. CT90: The sprocket can be removed after disconnecting the chain.
12. Refer to "Component Inspection," following.
13. Installation is the reverse of the above.

50-70cc Models

REMOVAL AND INSTALLATION

1. Drain the oil. Disconnect the alternator or magneto wiring at the connector. Disconnect the neutral switch wire, if fitted. Remove the gearshift lever.
2. Remove the rotor nut. Using the special puller, remove the rotor.
3. Remove the rotor nut. Using the special puller, remove the rotor.
4. Remove the two screws which secure the coil stator plate. Tap the plate lightly to rotate it, then remove it.

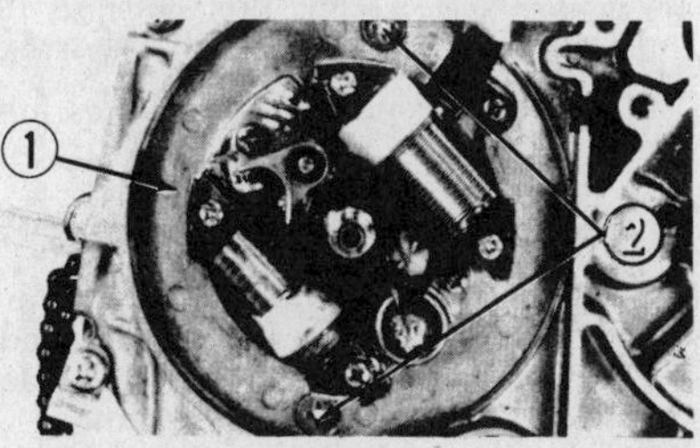

Magneto stator plate (1) and securing screws (2) (50-70 cc)

5. Back off the tensioner adjusting screw. Remove the tensioner cover bolt. Remove the tensioner bolt, spring, and pushrod.
6. Remove the tensioner arm pivot bolt, and the arm and roller.
7. Remove the countershaft sprocket bolts, disconnect the chain, remove the sprocket locking plate, and pull off the sprocket.

NOTE: *On models with a full-coverage chain guard, wire the ends of the chain together to keep them from falling into the chaincase.*

8. Refer to "Component Inspection," following.
9. Installation is the reverse of the above. Note that the O-rings in the stator plate screw holes, the plate O-ring and the crankshaft oil seal must be in place.

Component Inspection

NOTE: *Where necessary, refer to the specifications charts at the end of this section for wear limits and tolerances.*

CLUTCH

Clutch component inspection procedures are outlined in "Engine Rebuilding." Specifications for individual models are given in the charts at the end of this section.

GEARSHIFT LINKAGE

Note those procedures applicable to the type of shift linkage fitted to your model.

1. Check the splines on the gearshift shaft. If the splines are broken or torn to such an extent that it is difficult to properly secure the shift lever, replace the shaft.
2. 50–90 cc: Check the condition of the shift arm. Be sure that it is not bent. Check that the shift fingers are not bent or worn.

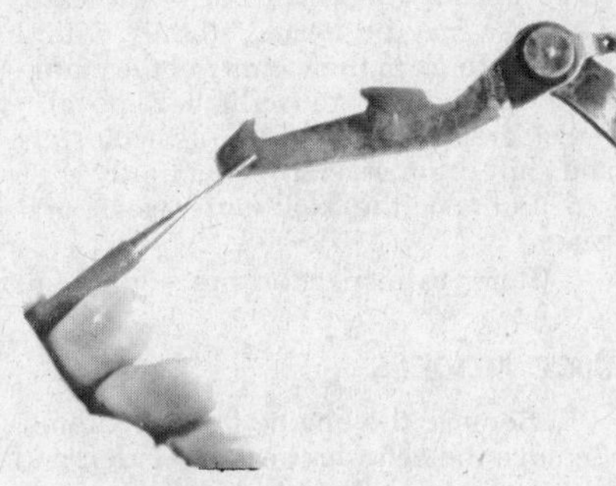

Check the shift arm fingers for damage

3. Check the condition of the springs in the shift linkage, especially the shift lever return spring. If any spring has lost its tension, or fails to hold its component properly, replace it.
4. 100–125 cc: Check the inner surfaces of the shift plate for wear caused by contact with the shift drum stopper plate pins. Replace the shift plate or stopper plate if wear is evident.
5. Check the condition of the shift drum stopper roller and replace it if worn. The stopper spring should hold the stopper firmly against the stopper plate.
6. Check the shift drum stopper plate and pins for wear. Replace if damaged.

KICK-STARTER

50–70 cc Models

1. Check the splines on the kick-starter shaft and replace the shaft if they are torn or will not secure the starter lever properly.
2. Check that the return spring retainer is not chipped and that its splines are not damaged.
3. The kick-starter return spring must be able to return the kick-starter lever to its stop and hold it there. If weakened or broken, replace it.

Other kick-starter components are accessible only after splitting the crankcases. Refer to that section.

OIL PUMP

Test procedures can be found in the **"Lubrication Systems" section.** When installing the pump or related parts, new O-rings and gaskets should always be used.

ALTERNATOR

1. For electrical tests, refer to the **"Electrical Systems" section.**
2. Check the rotor and stator for signs of wear. If there has been contact between the rotor and the stator assembly, this condition must be rectified. In addition, the components should be tested to make sure that they still operate properly. Check the stator for foreign matter on the poles, burnt wiring, damaged insulation, etc.
3. Check that the stator assembly is securely mounted, and properly aligned. If the rotor has contacted the stator, check for play in the crankshaft. This condition may sometimes be caused by a bad crank bearing.
4. Remove any rust or corrosion from the crankshaft taper. Check the woodruff key for step-wear.
5. Check that the rotor has little or no run-out as it turns. If run-out exists, determine the cause.
6. If scoring on either the rotor or the stator components is severe, the part(s) should be replaced.

MAGNETO

1. For electrical tests, refer to the **"Electrical Systems" section.**
2. Check the inside of the rotor and the coil core ends for scoring which would indicate that they have been in contact. This condition must be rectified.
3. Check that the coils are securely mounted to the stator plate. Check that the plate is securely mounted. If the stator coils and rotor have been in contact, check for play in the crankshaft. This condition is sometimes caused by a bad crank bearing.
4. Check the rotor for cracks, especially on the tapered mount. Check that the timing advance mechanism (if fitted) functions properly. When the breaker cam is turned, the springs should have enough tension to return it to its original position easily.
5. Check the coils for broken or burned wiring, bad insulation, etc.

COUNTERSHAFT SPROCKET

1. Check the teeth of the sprocket and ensure that they are not hook-shaped, broken, or worn. If any wear is in evidence, the sprocket should be replaced, and the chain and rear wheel sprocket closely inspected for condition.
2. Check the rotational play of the sprocket on the countershaft. The sprocket splines should not show signs of wear. Replace the sprocket if it is not a firm fit on the shaft.

CRANKCASE COVERS

1. Always use new crankcase cover gaskets where they are fitted.
2. Remove any nicks or imperfections from the mating surfaces with an oilstone or silicon carbide paper.
3. Oil seals, where fitted, can be pried out. When fitting new seals, press them in with a block of wood or something similar which will cover the whole seal.

Press seals straight in until seated. Grease the seal lips before installation.

4. On some models, clutch lifter levers are fitted into the right crankcase cover. The levers can be pulled out after removing the pin which secures them to check the O-ring and spring.

5. Crankcase covers may be fitted with one or more hollow locating pins. These must be installed before the cover is fitted.

SUB-TRANSMISSION (CT90)

1. Check the condition of all the gear teeth for wear, pitting, or cracks. Pay close attention to the base of each tooth, since this is where most damage shows up.

2. Check the engaging dogs on the sub-trans High gear for wear or chipping. Inspect the corresponding holes in the Low gear as well.

3. Check the splines on the gears and the countershaft sprocket for wear or damage.

4. Check the condition of the shift fork fingers. They should be straight and the tips must be undamaged. To remove the shift fork shaft, pull it out. Note the steel ball and spring which locates the fork on the shaft.

Check the shaft for wear or discoloration. Be sure that the bore of the fork is without score marks.

To install the shaft into the fork, insert the spring and ball, and use a thin screwdriver through the hole in the fork to push down the ball so that the shaft can be inserted.

5. Check the condition of the countershaft ball bearing. Rotation of the bearing must be smooth and without binding. If necessary to remove the bearing, heat the cover slightly and tap out the bearing.

6. If leakage is noted from the sub-trans shift lever, remove the securing clip on the inside of the cover, and pull out the shift lever. Replace the O-ring on the shift lever shaft.

7. Installation is the reverse of removal. Use a new cover gasket. Be sure that the locating pin is in place for the upper right-hand cover screw. Note that this screw is threaded for its entire length.

LOWER END AND TRANSMISSION

Splitting the Crankcases

100–125 CC MODELS

1. Remove the engine from the frame. Remove the cylinder head, cylinder, and piston. Remove the left and right-side covers and the components therein. Refer to the preceding sections for procedures.

2. Loosen the screws securing the crankcase halves (one screw is in the right case, the remaining 10 are in the left), with an impact driver. Remove the screws. Separate the case halves. The crank and transmission will remain in the right case half.

Crankcase screws (100-125 cc)

NOTE: *If the cases are stuck, they may be freed by tapping very gently with a plastic mallet. Do not strike the crankshaft or transmission shafts.*

3. Remove the case gasket. Exercising care, tap the crankshaft out of the case. The case may be heated slightly with a propane torch in the vicinity of the crankshaft bearing boss to facilitate removal.

4. Carefully remove the gear clusters and shift drum assembly as a unit.

5. Pull out the kick-starter shaft and gears.

6. Refer to inspection procedures following.

90CC MODELS

1. Remove the engine from the frame. Remove the cylinder head, cylinder, and piston. Remove the left and right crankcase covers and remove the alternator stator and rotor, the countershaft sprocket, clutch, primary driven gear, gearshift shaft, cam chain, etc. Refer to the preceding sections for procedures. The oil pump need not be removed.

2. Remove the shift drum bolt on the left case half. Remove the screws in the right crankcase half. Tap around the mating surface with a plastic mallet and separate the case halves. Remove the case gasket.

The crankshaft and gear assemblies will remain in the left case half.

Gearshift drum bolt (1) (90 cc)

CAUTION: *Do not strike the ends of the crank or transmission shafts to separate the cases.*

3. Remove the kick-starter shaft from the right case half (new type) or left half (older type).

4. Remove the crankshaft from the left case half. The case may be heated gently with a propane torch in the vicinity of the bearing boss to facilitate removal.

5. Remove the gear clusters and shift drum.

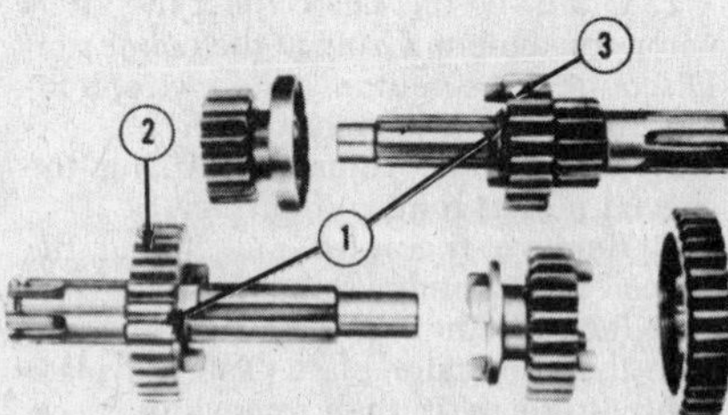

Transmission components (ST90): snap-ring (1); countershaft Third gear (2); mainshaft High gear

6. Refer to inspection procedures following.

50–70CC MODELS (EXCEPT XR75)

1. Remove the engine from the frame. Remove the cylinder head, cylinder, and piston. Remove the left and right-side covers and the components therein.

Refer to the preceding sections for procedures.

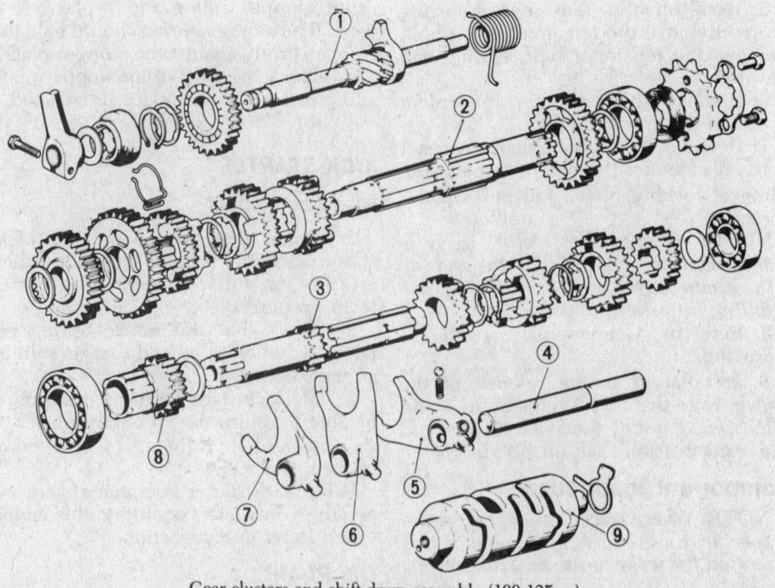

Gear clusters and shift drum assembly (100-125 cc)

1. Kick-starter shaft
2. Countershaft
3. Mainshaft
4. Shift fork shaft
5. Left shift fork
6. Center shift fork
7. Right shift fork
8. Kick-starter gear
9. Shift drum

Tensioner arm pivot bolt (1) and arm (2) (50-70 cc)

2. Unscrew and remove the cam chain tensioner pushrod bolt, and remove the pushrod assembly. Remove the tensioner arm pivot bolt, and remove the arm and roller assembly.

3. Remove the shift drum bolt beneath the rubber plug on the left crankcase half. Remove the eight crankcase screws on the left case half.

The screws are of three different lengths. Note their location as they are removed.

4. Separate the cases. The crank and transmission will remain in the left half.

NOTE: *If the cases are stuck, they may be freed by tapping very gently with a plastic mallet. Do not strike the crankshaft or transmission shafts.*

5. Remove the case gasket. Pull out the kick-starter shaft assembly.

6. With care, tap the crankshaft out of the case. The case may be heated slightly with a propane torch in the vicinity of the crankshaft bearing boss to facilitate removal.

7. Very carefully remove the gear clusters and shift drum assembly as a unit.

8. Refer to the inspection procedures following.

XR75

1. Remove the engine from the frame.

2. Remove the top end assembly: **cylinder head, cylinder, and piston.**

3. Remove the oil filter rotor and the oil pump. Remove the clutch, gearshift linkage, stopper arm and plate, magneto, and countershaft sprocket.

Refer to the preceding sections for procedures.

4. Remove the two phillips screws at the upper left and lower right of the right crankcase half.

Right crankcase half (1) and securing screws (2) (XR75)

5. Split the cases by tapping around the mating surface with a plastic mallet. The crankshaft and gear clusters will remain in the left crankcase half.

6. Detach the kick-starter return spring from the crankcase and pull out the kick-starter shaft assembly.

7. Remove the cam chain from the crank sprocket and take out the crankshaft. The left case may be heated slightly with a propane torch in the vicinity of the crankshaft bearing boss to facilitate removal.

Crankshaft (1), shift fork shaft (2), shift fork (3), and shift drum (4)

8. Remove the shift fork shaft and the two shift forks. Remove the shift drum.

9. Remove the main- and countershafts and their gears as a unit.

10. Refer to the inspection procedures following.

Transmission

Inspection procedures for the transmission are outlined in "Engine Rebuilding."

Kick-Starter

1. Check the splines on the kick-starter shaft and replace the shaft if they are damaged to the extent that they will not secure the kick-starter lever properly.

2. If the kick-starter gear has a plain bore, check that it is not galled or worn. If the gear has a splined bore, check that the splines are in good condition, and that the gear does not have excessive backlash on its shaft.

3. Check the condition of the gear teeth. On models with the ratchet-type kick-starter, the teeth on the side of the kick-starter gear are critical. If chipped or worn, the gear should be replaced.

4. Check the condition of the teeth on the ratchet gear and replace the gear if they are worn.

5. Check that the gear splines on the kick-starter shaft (where fitted) are in good condition. Check that the kick-starter shaft stopper or spring retainer and the stopper on the crankcase are not worn or chipped. If a stopper bolt is fitted, be sure that it is firmly secured in the case.

6. Check that the kick-starter shaft return spring is able to hold the kick-starter lever firmly in place. If the lever fails to return to its proper position, replace the return spring.

7. Check the retainer spring fitted to ratchet-type starters and replace it if bent or otherwise damaged.

Crankshaft

The crankshaft is a pressed-together unit. The connecting rod big end bearing is the caged-needle type. In the event of damage to the con rod, bearing or crankpin, the crankshaft must be replaced as an assembly.

1. Lubricate the big end bearing with oil, and rotate the rod slowly around the crankpin. The movement must be smooth and silent.

2. With a dial gauge, check the up-and-down (radial) movement of the con rod. Compare the reading with the specification given. If rod movement is in excess of the specifications, the big end bearing is worn and the crankshaft must be replaced.

3. With a feeler gauge, check the clearance between the con rod big end and the crankshaft flywheel. Compare the measurement with the specification given for axial clearance.

Checking big end side clearance (2) with a feeler gauge (1)

4. Place the crankshaft on a set of V-blocks, and check the crankshaft run-out with a dial gauge. Check both ends of the crank. Compare the run-out reading with the specification given for your model. If excessive, the crank must be replaced.

Crankshaft run-out will be one half of the true indicated reading of the gauge.

Crankcases

1. Check for damage to the bearing bosses, especially for stress cracks around the bearing boss.

2. Be sure that both case half mating surfaces are free of any traces of old gasket or gasket material.

3. Place each case half on a flat surface and check for warpage by probing around the mating surface with a feeler gauge. Maximum acceptable case warpage is 0.05 mm (0.002 in.). If warped, cases should be replaced.

4. Minor scratches on the mating surfaces can be removed with an oilstone, although it is not permissible to remove much metal.

5. Case halves must be scrupulously clean before assembly. Be sure that all oil passages are clear and that any dowel pins fitted between the case halves are installed.

Crankcase Assembly

100–125 CC MODELS

1. Assemble the shift drum mechanism if it was disassembled. The left gearshift fork is secured by a spring-loaded ball. To install, insert the spring and the ball into the shift fork, push the ball down with a thin screwdriver, and slip in the shaft.

2. Install the components into the case in the reverse of the removal procedure. Note the following points:

a. Install the crankshaft into the case by pushing it straight in until the bearing is seated. Do not strike the end of the crankshaft to install it;

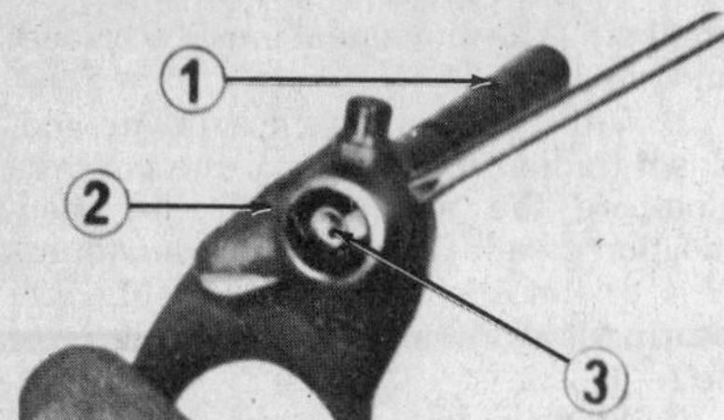

Installing the shift fork shaft (1) in the fork (2) by compressing the ball and spring (3) with a thin phillips screwdriver (100-125 cc)

b. Install the gear clusters first, then the shift drum. Position the shift drum so that the neutral switch rotor would be parallel with the cylinder. This is equivalent to Neutral. Noting the locating marks on the shift forks, install the right, center, and left forks, in that order, engaging the cam follower pin of each fork with the proper groove in the shift drum. Then install the shift fork shaft;

c. Install the kick-starter shaft. Be sure that the return spring is seated in the crankcase. The retainer spring must protrude through the hole in the crankcase as illustrated;

d. Lubricate all bearings with motor oil;

The neutral switch rotor (4) on the shift drum (3) should be parallel with the cylinder (about 10° from vertical) when installing the shift forks (100-125 cc)

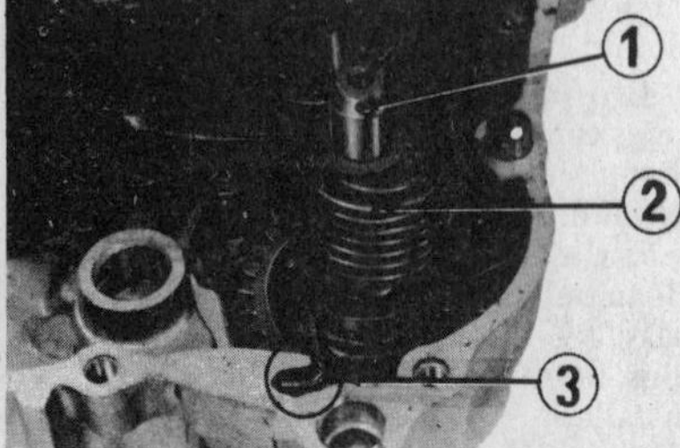

When installing the kick-starter assembly (1), be sure that the end of the return spring (2), is fitted into the cutout in the case (3)

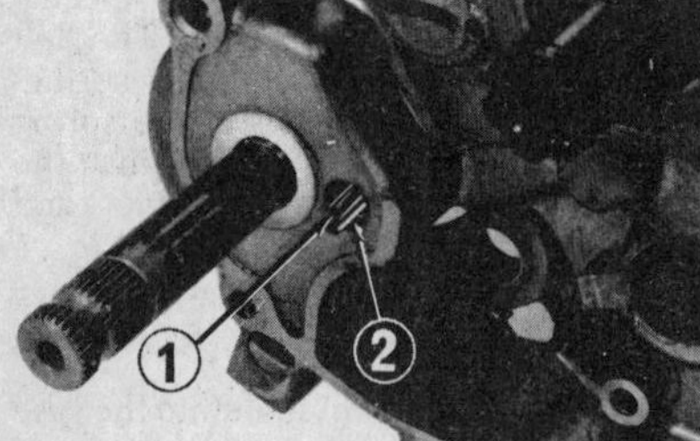

The end of the retainer spring protrudes through the hole in the case

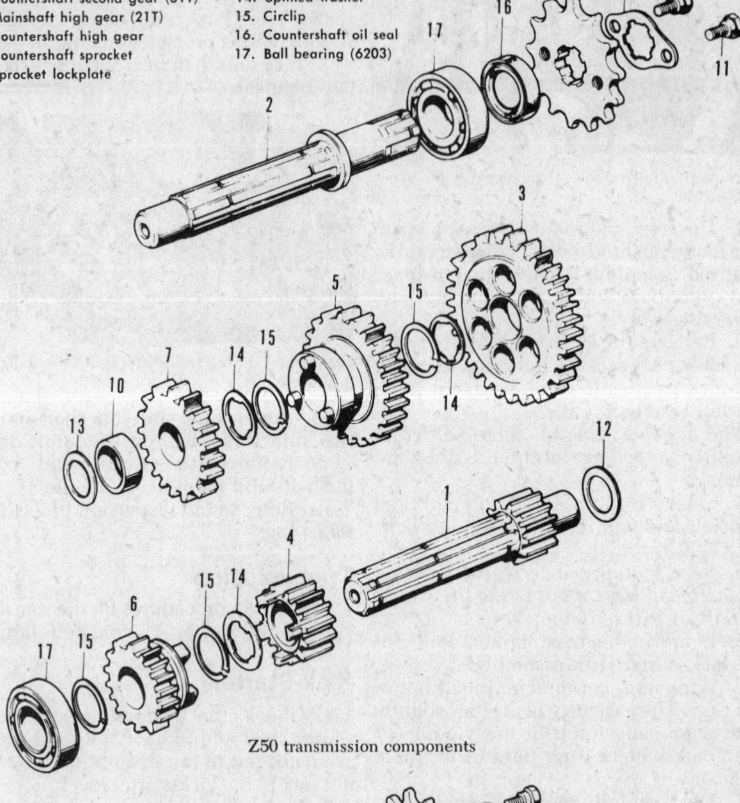

Z50 transmission components

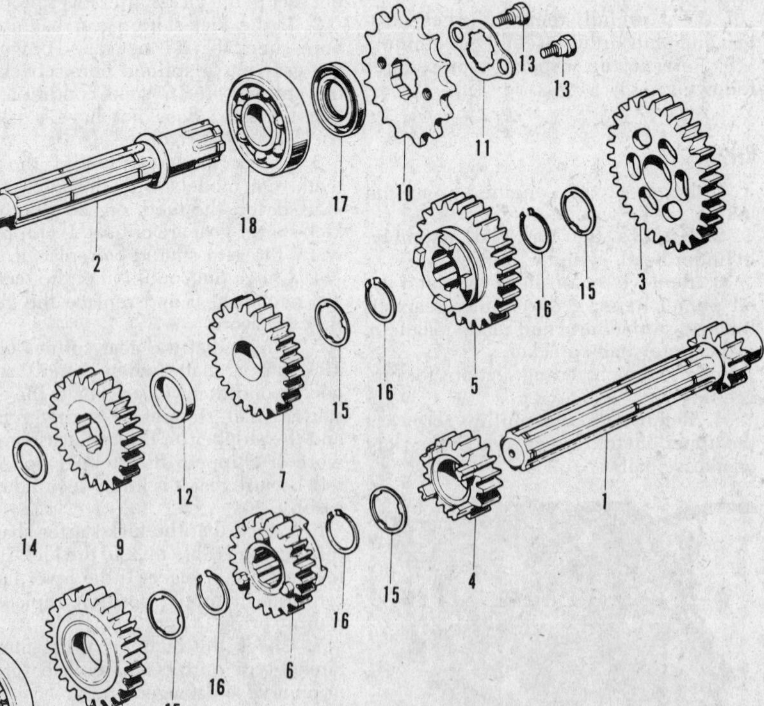
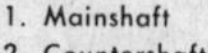
SL70 transmission components

e. Fit a new gasket. Ensuring that the transmission is in Neutral, assemble the case halves. Do not force the cases together. Install the crankcase screws and tighten them in a cross pattern, to about 8 ft lbs;

NOTE: *Do not use the screws to mate the cases. This should be accomplished before they are tightened.*

f. Check for free rotation of the crankshaft and the gears, and operation of the kick-starter and shifter.

90cc MODELS

1. Assemble the shift drum mechanism if it was disassembled. Slide the forks onto the shift drum, install the pins, and fit the securing clips.
2. Assemble the shift drum assembly and the gear clusters and insert them into the left crankcase half. On newer models, the kick-starter shaft is inserted into the right crankcase half, the left half on older machines.

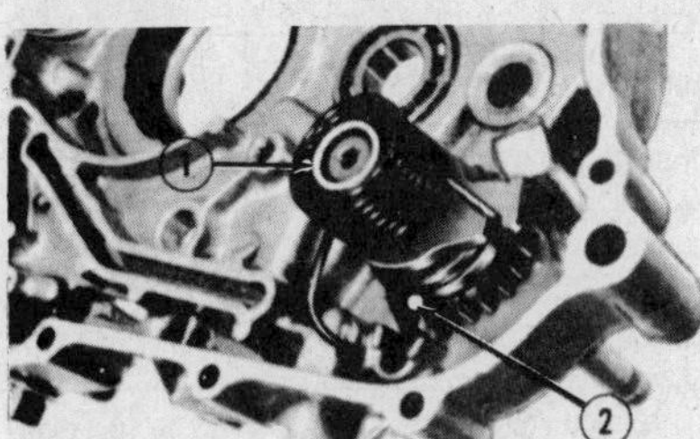

Kick-starter components (late models, 90 cc)

3. Install the crankshaft in the left case half, after heating the case as on removal. Do not strike the crankshaft to seat the bearing.
4. Lubricate all interior components with motor oil.
5. Be sure that the mating surface dowel pins are in place. Fit a new gasket. Mate the case halves. Do not force or strike the cases to bring them together.
6. Fit the case screws and the shift drum bolt.
7. Check for smooth rotation of the crank and correct operation of the shifter mechanism.

50-70CC MODELS (EXCEPT XR75)

1. Assemble the shift drum mechanism if it was disassembled. Slide the forks onto the shift drum, install the pins, and fit the securing clips.

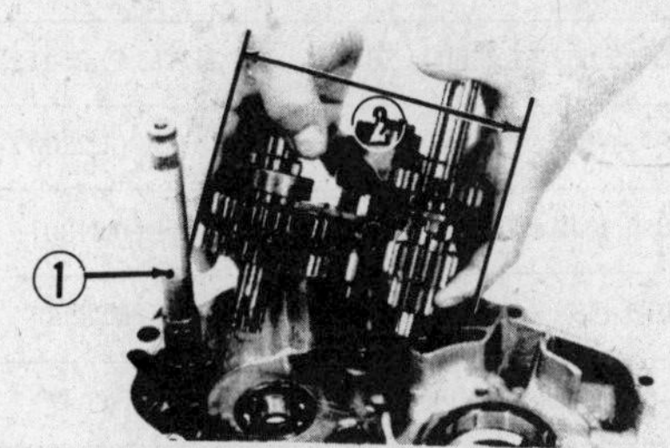

Installing the gear clusters (50-70 cc)

2. Assemble the shift drum assembly and the gear clusters and insert them into the left crankcase half. Insert the kick-starter assembly.
3. Install the crankshaft in the left case half, after heating the case as on removal.

Engine and Transmission Specifications

125 cc Models (1975 and Earlier)

		Standard mm (in.)	Serviceable Limit mm (in.)
ENGINE			
Cylinder bore diameter (standard)		56.00–56.01 (2.2047–2.2051)	56.10 (2.2086)
Piston OD (standard)		55.74–55.76 (2.1945–2.1953)	55.65 (2.1810)
Piston-cylinder clearance		0.025–0.05 (0.001–0.002)	0.1 (0.004)
Wrist pin hole ID		15.002–15.008 (0.5906–0.5909)	15.04 (0.5921)
Wrist pin OD		14.994–15.000 (0.5903–0.5906)	14.96 (0.5890)
Piston ring side clearance	Top	0.025–0.055 (0.0010–0.0022)	0.09 (0.0035)
	2nd	0.015–0.045 (0.0006–0.0018)	0.09 (0.0035)
Piston ring end-gap	Top	0.15–0.35 (0.0059–0.0138)	0.5 (0.0197)
	2nd	0.15–0.35 (0.0059–0.0138)	0.5 (0.0197)
	Oil	0.30–0.90 (0.0118–0.0354)	—
Connecting rod big end bearing clearance		0–0.008 (0–0.0003)	0.05 (0.0020)
Connecting rod big end side clearance		0.05–0.30 (0.0020–0.0118)	0.8 (0.0315)
Crankshaft run-out	Left-side	0.02 (0.0008) max	0.05 (0.0020)
	Right-side	0.015 (0.0006) max	0.05 (0.0020)
Rocker arm-to-shaft clearance		0.016–0.052 (0.0006–0.0021)	0.08 (0.0032)
Cam height	In	31.906 (1.2561)	31.776 (1.2510)
	Ex	31.496 (1.2400)	31.366 (1.2349)
Valve stem OD	In	5.450–5.465 (0.2146–0.2175)	5.41 (0.2130)
	Ex	5.430–5.445 (0.2138–0.2167)	5.39 (0.2122)
Valve stem-to-guide clearance	In	0.01–0.035 (0.0004–0.0014)	0.12 (0.0047)
	Ex	0.03–0.055 (0.0012–0.0022)	0.14 (0.0055)
Valve seat width		0.7 (0.028)	1.5 (0.059)
Valve spring free-length	Inner	36.55 (1.4390)	33.2 (1.3071)
	Outer	41.6 (1.6378)	37.5 (1.4764)
TRANSMISSION			
Clutch friction disc thickness		2.9–3.0 (0.1142–0.1181)	2.6 (0.1024)
Clutch plate warpage		0.1 (0.0039) max	0.2 (0.0079)
Clutch spring free-length		35.5 (1.3976)	32 (1.260)
Shift fork ID		12.000–12.018 (0.4724–0.4732)	12.05 (0.4744)
Shift fork shaft OD		11.976–11.994 (0.4715–0.4722)	11.96 (0.4709)
Shift fork finger width		4.93–5.00 (0.1941–0.1969)	4.7 (0.1859)
Kick-starter gear ID		24.900–24.921 (0.9803–0.9811)	24.94 (0.9819)
Transmission gear backlash		NA	0.2 (0.008)

Do not strike the crankshaft to seat the bearing.

4. Lubricate all interior components with motor oil.

5. Be sure that the mating surface dowel pins are in place. Fit a new gasket. Mate the case halves. Do not force or strike the cases to bring them together.

6. Fit the case screws. Note that the case screws are of different lengths. Tighten the case screws in a cross pattern to about 8 ft lbs. Do not tighten the screws unless the cases are mated. Do not use the screws to mate the cases.

7. Hold the shift drum against the case and install the shift drum bolt.

8. Check for smooth rotation of the crank and proper operation of the shift mechanism and kick-starter.

XR75

1. Install the gear clusters together in the left crankcase half.

2. Install the shift drum insuring that the neutral switch rotor on the drum points toward the neutral switch on the case.

3. Install the center gearshift fork, engaging it first with the mainshaft Third gear and then with the groove in the shift drum.

4. Install the right gearshift fork engaging it with the countershaft Second gear and the shift drum. Install the shift fork shaft. Check gear rotation.

Installing the shift fork shaft (1) (XR75)

5. Install the kick-starter shaft, engaging the end of the return spring with the crankcase lug. Install the kick-starter pedal onto the shaft, and use it to rotate the shaft until the kick-starter spring retainer can be pushed down into the recess in the case.

6. Loop the cam chain through the cutout in the left case, then install the crankshaft. The case bearing boss may be heated slightly as on removal to facilitate installation of the crank.

Rotate the shaft as shown until the spring retainer (2) can be pushed down into the recess (3). The other end of the return spring must be engaged as shown (1).

7. Lubricate all interior components with motor oil.

125 cc Models (1976) ①

		Standard mm (in.)	Serviceable Limit mm (in.)
ENGINE			
Cylinder bore diameter (standard)		56.50–56.51 (2.2244–2.2247)	56.60 (2.2283)
Piston OD (standard)		56.46–56.48 (2.2228–2.2236)	56.35 (2.2184)
Crankshaft run-out Left and right sides		0.02 (0.0008)	0.05 (0.0020)
Valve spring free-length	Inner	39.2 (1.5433)	35.2 (1.3858)
	Outer	44.85 (1.7658)	40.5 (1.5945)

① For all other 1976 engine specifications, refer to "125 CC Models (1975 and Earlier)."

100 cc Models

ENGINE			
Cylinder bore diameter (standard)		50.50–50.51 (1.9881–1.9885)	50.56 (1.9906)
Piston OD (standard)		50.47–50.49 (1.9870–1.9878)	50.38 (1.9835)
Piston-cylinder clearance		0.025–0.05 (0.001–0.002)	0.1 (0.004)
Wrist pin hole ID		14.002–14.008 (0.5513–0.5515)	14.04 (0.5528)
Wrist pin OD		13.994–14.000 (0.5509–0.5512)	13.96 (0.5496)
Piston ring side clearance	Top	0.015–0.045 (0.0006–0.0018)	0.09 (0.0035)
	2nd	0.015–0.045 (0.0006–0.0018)	0.09 (0.0035)
	Oil	0.015–0.045 (0.0006–0.0018)	0.09 (0.0035)
Piston ring end-gap	Top	0.15–0.35 (0.0059–0.0138)	0.5 (0.0197)
	2nd	0.15–0.35 (0.0059–0.0138)	0.5 (0.0197
	Oil	0.15–0.35 (0.0059–0.0138)	0.5 (0.0197)
Connecting rod big end bearing clearance		0–0.008 (0–0.0003)	0.05 (0.0020)
Connecting rod big end side clearance		0.05–0.30 (0.0020–0.0118)	0.8 (0.0315)
Crankshaft run-out	Left-side	0.02 (0.0008) max	0.05 (0.0020)
	Right-side	0.015 (0.0006) max	0.05 (0.0020)
Rocker arm-to-shaft clearance		0.016–0.052 (0.0006–0.0021)	0.08 (0.0032)
Cam height	In	31.903–32.063 (1.2560–1.2623)	31.853 (1.2541)
	Ex	31.039–31.199 (1.2220–1.2273)	30.989 (1.2200)
Valve stem OD	In	5.450–5.465 (0.2146–0.2175)	5.41 (0.2130)
	Ex	5.430–5.445 (0.2138–0.2167)	5.39 (0.2122)
Valve stem-to-guide clearance	In	0.01–0.035 (0.0004–0.0014)	0.12 (0.0047)
	Ex	0.03–0.055 (0.0012–0.0022)	0.14 (0.0055)
Valve seat width		0.75 (0.0295)	1.5 (0.059)
Valve spring free-length	Inner	33.5 (1.3189)	30.2 (1.1890)
	Outer	40.9 (1.6102)	36.8 (1.4488)

8. Install the two dowel pins on the case mating surface, fit a new gasket and install the other case half.

9. Be sure that the cases are mated all the way around (do not force the cases together), then install and tighten the two case screws.

10. Check for smooth crankshaft rotation and for proper operation of the shifter and kick-starter.

NOTE: *When mating the cases, be sure that each shaft and the end of the kick-starter retainer spring enter their holes in the right case.*

Engine Torque Specifications

100–125 cc Models

Part	Torque (ft lbs)
Cylinder head	11.5–14.5
Spark advance mechanism bolt	5.8–8.7
Cam sprocket	5.8–8.7
Cylinder mounting bolt	8.7–13.0
Alternator rotor	18.8–23.2
Alternator stator	5.8–8.7
Crankcase cover screws	5.8–8.7
Cam chain tensioner arm	5.8–8.7
Oil filter rotor	29.0–36.0
Oil pump gear cover	2.9–4.4
Oil pump body	5.6–8.7
Clutch spring bolts	5.6–8.7
Gearshift drum stopper bolt	5.6–8.7
Gearshift drum stopper plate	5.6–8.7
50–90 cc Models	
Crankcase screws	5.8–8.0
Cylinder head stud nut	6.5–8.7
Cylinder side bolt	5.8–8.0
Cylinder head side bolt	7.4–10.8
Camshaft sprocket bolts	3.6–6.5
Cylinder head right-side cover	5.1–6.5
Cylinder head left-side cover	5.8–8.7
Valve adjuster locknut	5.1–7.2
Cam chain tensioner pushrod	10.8–18.1
Oil pump	5.8–8.7
Shift drum bolt	6.5–10.8
Shift drum stopper plate	6.5–9.4
Shift drum stopper	7.2–11.6
Clutch hub nut	27.5–32.5
Right crankcase cover	5.8–8.7
Left crankcase cover	5.8–8.0
Alternator/magneto rotor	23.9–27.5
Countershaft sprocket	6.5–10.8
Oil drain bolt	18.1–25.3
Carburetor	6.5–10.1
Spark plug	8.0–10.8
XR75	
Crankcase screws	5.1–8.7
Crankcase cover screws	5.1–8.7
Cylinder head cover	5.8–8.7
Camshaft holder	5.8–8.7
Camshaft sprocket	7.3–11.6
Carburetor manifold	5.8–8.7
Magneto rotor	21.7–27.5
Oil filter rotor	25.3–32.6
Tappet adjuster locknut	5.1–8.0
Engine drain plug	14.5–21.7

General Torque Specifications ①

Part	Torque (ft lbs)
5 mm machine screws	2.2–2.9
6 mm machine screws	5.0–7.2
6 mm hex bolts	5.8–8.7
8 mm hex bolts	13.0–18.1
10 mm hex bolts	21.7–28.9
6 mm flange bolts	7.2–10.1
8 mm flange bolts	17.4–21.7
10 mm flange bolts	21.7–28.9

① Unless otherwise specified

100 cc Models

		Standard mm (in.)	Serviceable Limit mm (in.)
TRANSMISSION			
Clutch friction disc thickness		2.9–3.0 (0.1142–0.1181)	2.6 (0.1024)
Clutch plate warpage		0.1 (0.0039) max	0.2 (0.0079)
Clutch spring free-length		35.5 (1.3976)	32 (1.260)
Shift fork ID		12.000–12.018 (0.4724–0.4732)	12.05 (0.4744)
Shift fork shaft OD		11.976–11.994 (0.4715–0.4722)	11.96 (0.4709)
Shift fork width		4.93–5.00 (0.1941–0.1969)	4.7 (0.1859)
Kick-starter gear ID		24.900–24.921 (0.9808–0.9811)	24.94 (0.9819)
Transmission gear backlash		—	0.2 (0.008)
90 cc Models			
ENGINE			
Cylinder bore diameter (standard)		50.0–50.01 (1.9685–1.9689)	50.1 (1.9724)
Piston OD (standard)		49.97–49.99 (1.9674–1.9681)	49.9 (1.9646)
Piston-cylinder clearance		0.025–0.05 (0.001–0.002)	0.1 (0.004)
Wrist pin hole clearance		0.002–0.004 (0.0008–0.0006)	0.05 (0.002)
Piston ring side clearance		0.01–0.045 (0.0004–0.0018)	0.12 (0.0047)
Piston ring end-gap			
Compression rings		0.15–0.35 (0.0059–0.0139)	0.5 (0.020)
Oil ring		0.15–0.40 (0.0059–0.0158)	0.50 (0.020)
Connecting rod big end clearance		0–0.01 (0–0.0004)	0.05 (0.002)
Connecting rod big end side clearance		0.10–0.35 (0.0039–0.0138)	0.80 (0.0315)
Crankshaft run-out		0.03 (0.0012) max	0.10 (0.0039)
Rocker arm ID		10.00–10.02 (0.3937–0.3943)	10.1 (0.3976)
Rocker arm shaft OD		9.972–9.987 (0.3926–0.3932)	9.92 (0.3906)
Valve stem OD	In	5.455–5.465 (0.2148–0.2152)	5.435 (0.2140)
	Ex	5.435–5.445 (0.2140–0.2144)	5.415 (0.2133)
Valve stem-guide clearance	In	0.010–0.030 (0.0004–0.0012)	0.06 (0.0024)
	Ex	0.030–0.050 (0.0012–0.0020)	0.08 (0.0032)
Valve seat width		0.70–1.20 (0.0276–0.0472)	1.50 (0.059)
Valve guide ID		5.475–5.485 (0.2156–0.2160)	5.525 (0.2175)
Valve spring free-length	Inner	26.5 (1.0433)	25.5 (1.0039)
	Outer	31.8 (1.2520)	30.6 (1.2047)
TRANSMISSION			
Clutch friction disc thickness Manual clutch		2.8–2.9 (0.110–0.114)	2.4 (0.094)
Centrifugal clutch		2.65–2.75 (0.104–0.108)	2.25 (0.087)

LUBRICATION SYSTEM

OIL PUMP SERVICE

50-90 cc Models

1. Remove the right crankcase cover and clutch assembly as described in the "Engine and Transmission" chapter.
2. Remove the three mounting screws and/or bolt from the oil pump, and remove the oil pump assembly.

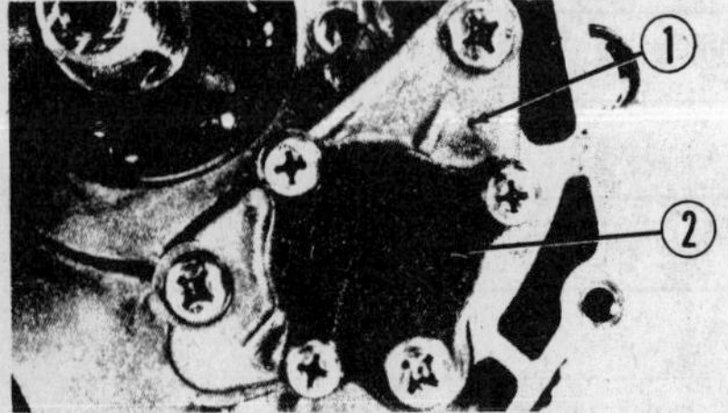

Oil pump (1) and cover (2) (50-90 cc)

3. Remove the cover screws and remove the cover. Remove the inner and outer rotors, and inspect for obvious damage.
4. Install the rotors and measure the clearance between the outer rotor and the oil pump body with a feeler gauge. Replace the pump if clearance is excessive.

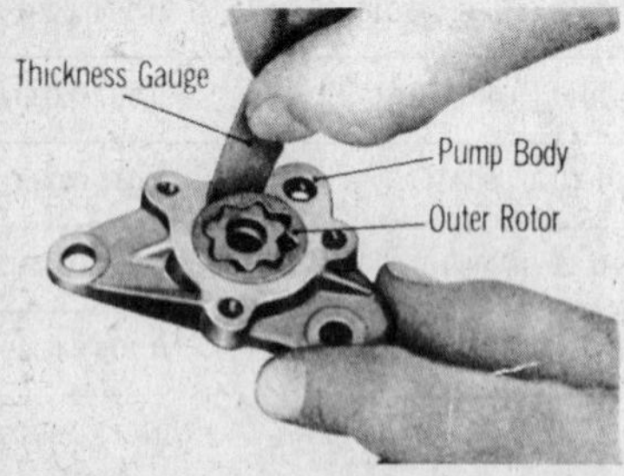

Measuring outer rotor-to-pump body clearance

5. Measure the rotor end-play by placing a straightedge across the cover surface with the gasket in place and measuring the clearance between the straightedge and the rotors with a feeler gauge.

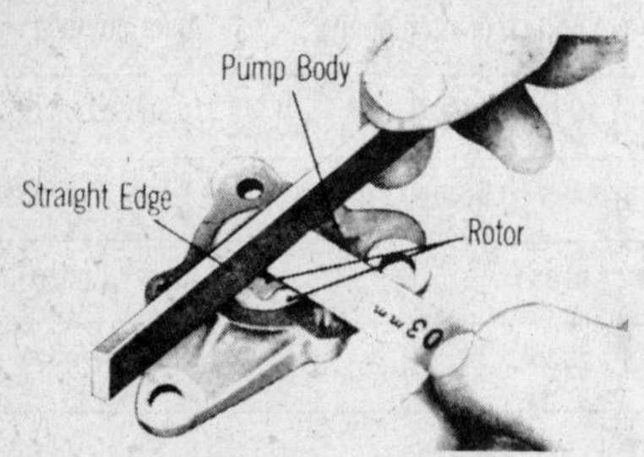

Checking rotor end-play

6. Measure the clearance between the rotors with a feeler gauge. Excessive clearance will cause excessive backlash

90 cc Models

		Standard mm (in.)	Serviceable Limit mm (in.)
TRANSMISSION			
Clutch plate warpage		0.10 (0.004) max	0.2 (0.008)
Clutch spring free-length Manual clutch		26.8 (1.0551)	25.8 (1.032)
Centrifugal clutch		27.0 (1.063)	26.0 (1.024)
Shift fork ID		42.0–42.025 (1.6535–1.6545)	42.065 (1.6561)
Shift drum OD		41.950–41.975 (1.6516–1.6522)	41.93 (1.6508)
Shift fork finger width		5.96–6.04 (0.2347–0.2378)	5.70 (0.2244)
Transmission gear backlash		0.084–0.170 (0.0033–0.0067)	0.25 (0.00984)

70 cc Models

		Standard mm (in.)	Serviceable Limit mm (in.)
ENGINE			
Cylinder bore diameter (standard)		47.00–47.01 (1.8504–1.8508)	47.1 (1.8540)
Piston OD (standard)		46.98–46.99 (1.8497–1.850)	46.9 (1.8465)
Piston-cylinder clearance		0.025–0.050 (0.001–0.002)	0.1 (0.004)
Piston ring side clearance			
Compression rings		0.015–0.045 (0.0006–0.0018)	0.1 (0.004)
Oil ring		0.010–0.045 (0.0004–0.0018)	0.1 (0.004)
Piston ring end-gap			
Compression rings		0.15–0.35 (0.006–0.014)	0.5 (0.020)
Oil ring		0.15–0.40 (0.006–0.016)	0.5 (0.020)
Valve seat width		1.0–1.3 (0.040–0.051)	2.0 (0.080)
Valve guide ID		5.475–5.485 (0.2156–0.2159)	5.525 (0.2175)
Valve stem OD	In	5.455–5.465 (0.2148–0.2187)	5.40 (0.2126)
	Ex	5.435–5.445 (0.2070–0.2109)	5.38 (0.2048)
Valve stem-guide clearance	In	0.01–0.03 (0.0004–0.0012)	0.08 (0.0032)
	Ex	0.03–0.05 (0.0012–0.002)	0.1 (0.004)
Valve spring free-length	Outer	28.1 (1.106)	26.9 (1.059)
	Inner	25.1 (0.988)	23.9 (0.941)
Connecting rod big end axial clearance		0.1–0.35 (0.004–0.0138)	0.8 (0.0315)
Connecting rod big end radial clearance		0.01–0.012 (0.0004–0.0005)	0.05 (0.002)
TRANSMISSION			
Clutch friction disc thickness		3.50 (0.138)	3.10 (0.122)
Clutch plate warpage		——	0.15 (0.006)
Clutch spring free-length			
Manual clutch		20.0 (0.79)	19.0 (0.75)
Centrifugal clutch		21.4 (0.84)	20.4 (0.80)

and noisy pump operation. Replace the pump if clearance is excessive.

7. Assemble the pump using a new cover gasket. The gasket must not touch the rotors. Try to turn the pump by hand, it should turn freely with little resistance.

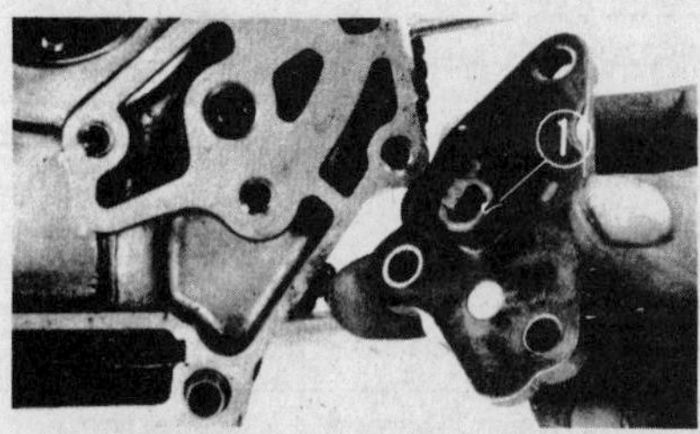

Be sure that the driving tab of the pump is properly fitted into its slot upon installation

8. Install the pump on the engine. Be sure to line up the tab on the pump drive with the slot in the pump driveshaft.

XR75, 100–125 cc Models

1. Drain the crankcase. Remove the exhaust system. Remove the kick-starter.
2. Disconnect the clutch cable from the right-side cover. Remove the skid plate and step bar (if fitted).
3. Remove the right crankcase cover.
4. Remove the oil filter rotor cover.
5. Using the special wrench, remove the rotor nut.

NOTE: *To stop the crankshaft from turning, engage the transmission and apply the rear brake or use a block of wood jammed between the primary gear and the clutch gear.*

6. Remove the oil pump gear cover.

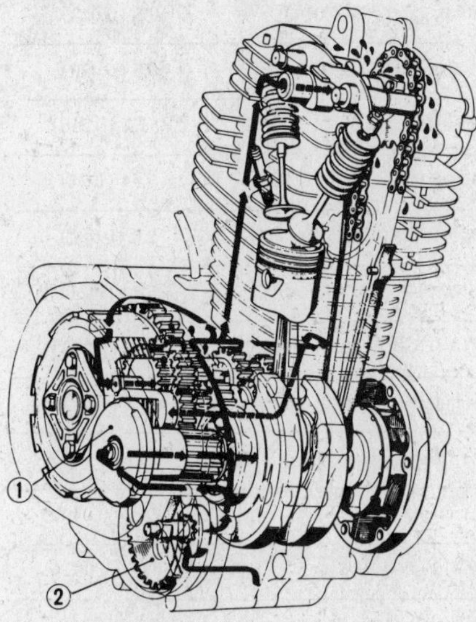

Lubrication system (100–125 cc)

7. Remove the oil pump drive gear and shaft. Note the thrust washer on the end of the shaft.
8. Remove the two pump mounting bolts and remove the oil pump.
9. Remove the two screws from the cover on the back of the oil pump, and remove the cover.
10. Remove the two rotors and inspect

70 cc Models

TRANSMISSION		Standard mm (in.)	Serviceable Limit mm (in.)
Shift drum diameter		33.95–33.98 (1.3366–1.3377)	33.9 (1.335)
Shift fork ID		34.0–34.03 (1.3385–1.3395)	34.2 (1.347)
Shift fork finger width	Right	5.5–6.3 (0.217–0.248)	5.3 (0.209)
	Left	4.5–5.3 (0.177–0.209)	4.3 (0.169)
Transmission gear backlash		0.09–0.18 (0.0035–0.0070)	0.25 (0.010)

XR75

ENGINE			
Cam height	In	27.677–27.717 (1.0896–1.0972)	27.5 (1.0827)
	Ex	27.540–27.586 (1.0833–1.0861)	27.36 (1.0772)
Rocker arm-to-shaft clearance		0.013–0.037 (0.0005–0.0015)	0.1 (0.0039)
Valve seat width		1.0 (0.0394)	1.5 (0.0591)
Valve stem OD	In	5.450–5.465 (0.2146–0.2152)	5.42 (0.2134)
	Ex	5.430–5.445 (0.2138–0.2144)	5.40 (0.2126)
Valve-to-valve guide clearance	In	0.01–0.035 (0.0004–0.0014)	0.08 (0.0031)
	Ex	0.03–0.055 (0.0012–0.0022)	0.1 (0.0039)

XR75

ENGINE			
Valve spring free-length	Inner	28.05 (1.1043)	27.0 (1.0630)
	Outer	33.8 (1.3307)	32.7 (1.2874)
Cylinder bore (standard)		47.0–47.01 (1.8504–1.8508)	47.1 (1.8543)
Piston OD (standard)		46.97–46.99 (1.8492–1.8500)	46.80 (1.8425)
Cylinder-piston clearance		0.025–0.050 (0.001–0.002)	0.1 (0.004)
Wrist pin hole diameter		13.002–13.008 (0.5119–0.5121)	13.06 (0.5142)
Wrist pin OD		12.994–13.00 (0.5116–0.5118)	12.9 (0.5079)
Piston ring side clearance	Compression	0.015–0.045 (0.0006–0.0018)	0.15 (0.0059)
	Oil	0	0.15 (0.0059)
Piston ring end-gap	Compression	0.15–0.35 (0.0059–0.0138)	0.5 (0.0197)
	Oil	0.3–0.9 (0.012–0.035)	0.5 (0.0197)
TRANSMISSION			
Friction disc thickness		2.8–2.9 (0.1102–0.1142)	2.5 (0.0984)
Clutch plate warpage		0.1 (0.0039) max	0.2 (0.0079)
Clutch spring free-length		27.3 (1.0748)	25.3 (0.9961)
Cam chain guide wear		—	1.0 (0.0394)
Cam chain tensioner wear		—	1.0 (0.0394)

Removing the oil pump drive gear (1) and shaft (2) (100-125 cc and XR75)

Pump (2) and mounting bolts (1)

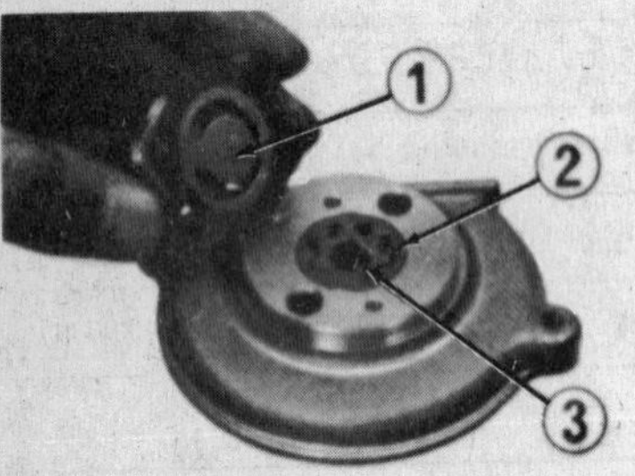

Pump cover (1), outer rotor (2), and inner rotor (3)

them for any obvious damage such as chipped teeth.

11. Check the outer rotor-to-pump body clearance and compare the reading with the proper specification. Replace the pump if clearance is excessive.

12. Check the inner rotor-to-outer rotor clearance, and compare the reading against the proper specification. Replace the pump if the clearance is excessive.

13. When installing the pump, always use a new pump gasket. Be sure that the gasket does not contact the rotor.

14. Install the two rotors, and replace the pump cover. Line up the lug on the cover with the notch of the pump body.

15. Install the oil pump driveshaft into the pump. Line up the cutout on the driveshaft with the inner rotor.

16. Place the two O-rings in position in the lower crankcase and replace the pump, drive gear, and gear cover.

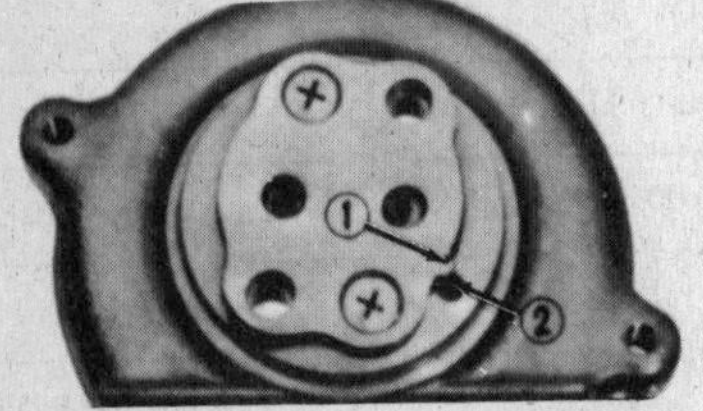

When fitting the cover, note that the lug of the cover should align with the notch of the pump body

XR75

		Standard mm (in.)	Serviceable Limit mm (in.)
TRANSMISSION			
Shift fork finger width		4.93–5.0 (0.1941–0.1969)	4.5 (0.1772)
Shift fork bore diameter		12.00–12.018 (0.4724–0.4731)	12.05 (0.4726)
Shift fork guide OD		11.976–11.994 (0.4715–0.4722)	11.9 (0.4685)
Shift fork guide pin-to-drum groove clearance		0.05–0.2 (0.0020–0.0079)	0.3 (0.0118)
Gear backlash	Low	0.085–0.169 (0.0033–0.0067)	—
	Second	0.089–0.179 (0.0035–0.0070)	0.2 (0.0079)
Gear backlash	Third and Fourth	0.084–0.170 (0.0033–0.0067)	—

65 cc Models

ENGINE			
Cylinder bore diameter (standard)		44.0 (1.734)	44.1 (1.738)
Piston OD (standard)		43.5 (1.714)	42.5 (1.708)
Piston-cylinder clearance		0.025–0.050 (0.001–0.002)	0.1 (0.004)
Piston ring side clearance	Compression	0.015–0.045 (0.0006–0.0018)	0.12 (0.005)
	Oil	0.010–0.045 (0.0004–0.0018)	0.12 (0.005)
Piston ring end-gap	Compression	0.15–0.35 (0.006–0.014)	0.5 (0.020)
	Oil	0.1–0.35 (0.004–0.014)	0.5 (0.020)
Valve guide ID		5.5 (0.217)	5.53 (0.218)
Valve seat		5.5 (0.217)	5.44 (0.214)
Valve stem diameter	In	1.0–1.3 (0.040–0.051)	2.0 (0.080)
	Ex	5.5 (0.217)	5.44 (0.214)
Valve stem-guide clearance	In	0.010–0.030 (0.0004–0.0012)	0.06 (0.0023)
	Ex	0.030–0.050 (0.0012–0.0020)	0.08 (0.0032)
Valve spring free-length	Outer	27.4 (1.080)	26.2 (1.030)
	Inner	25.1 (0.990)	23.9 (0.940)
Connecting rod big end radial clearance		0–0.012 (0–0.0005)	0.05 (0.002)
Connecting rod big end axial clearance		0.10–0.35 (0.004–0.014)	0.6 (0.024)
Crankshaft run-out		0.015 (0.0006)	0.05 (0.002)
TRANSMISSION			
Friction disc thickness		3.5 (0.138)	3.1 (0.122)
Plate warpage		—	0.15 (0.006)
Clutch spring free-length		19.2 (0.756)	18.2 (0.717)

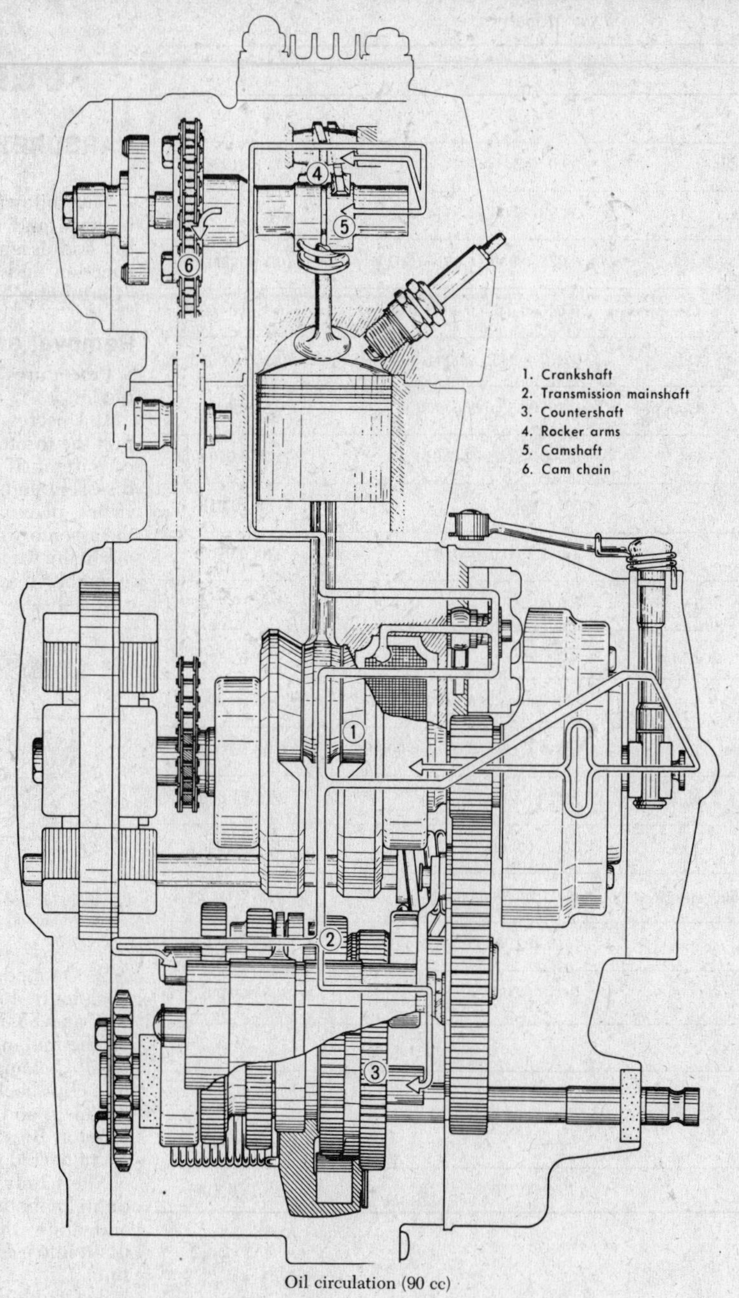

Oil circulation (90 cc)

Oil Pump Specifications

Model	Standard	Serviceable Limit
	50–90 cc	
Rotor-pump body clearance (mm/in.)	0.10–0.15/0.004–0.006	0.20/0.0079
Rotor-top of body clearance (mm/in.)	0.02–0.07/0.008–0.027	0.12/0.0047
Rotor-rotor clearance (mm/in.)	0.02–0.07/0.008–0.027	0.12/0.0047
	XR75	
Rotor-pump body clearance (mm/in.)	0.15/0.0059	0.20/0.0079

Model	Standard	Serviceable Limit
Rotor-rotor clearance (mm/in.)	0.15/0.0059	0.20/0.0079
	100–125 cc	
Rotor-pump body clearance (mm/in.)	0.15–0.20/0.006–0.008	0.25/0.01
Rotor-rotor clearance (mm/in.)	0.15/0.006	0.20/0.0079

50 cc Models

		Standard mm (in.)	Serviceable Limit mm (in.)
ENGINE			
Cylinder bore diameter (standard)		39.0 (1.54)	39.1 (1.55)
Piston diameter (standard)		39.98–39.00 (1.534–1.535)	38.88 (1.530)
Piston-cylinder clearance		0.025–0.050 (0.001–0.002)	0.1 (0.004)
Piston ring side clearance	Compression	0.015–0.045 (0.0006–0.0018)	0.12 (0.005)
	Oil	0.010–0.045 (0.0004–0.0018)	0.12 (0.005)
Piston ring end-gap	Compression	0.15–0.35 (0.006–0.014)	0.5 (0.020)
	Oil	0.1–0.35 (0.004–0.014)	0.5 (0.020)
Valve guide ID		5.5 (0.217)	5.53 (0.218)
Valve seat		1.0–1.3 (0.040–0.051)	2.0 (0.080)
Valve stem diameter	In	5.5 (0.217)	5.44 (0.214)
	Ex	5.5 (0.217)	5.44 (0.214)
Valve stem-guide clearance	In	0.010–0.030 (0.0004–0.0012)	0.06 (0.0023)
	Ex	0.030–0.050 (0.0012–0.0020)	0.08 (0.0032)
Valve spring free-length	Outer	28.1 (1.106)	26.9 (1.060)
	Inner	25.1 (0.990)	23.9 (0.940)
Connecting rod big end radial clearance		0–0.012 (0–0.0005)	0.05 (0.002)
Connecting rod big end axial clearance		0.10–0.35 (0.004–0.014)	0.6 (0.024)
Crankshaft run-out		0.015 (0.0006)	0.05 (0.002)
TRANSMISSION			
Friction disc thickness		3.5 (0.138)	3.1 (0.122)
Plate warpage		—	0.15 (0.006)
Clutch spring free-length		19.6 (0.772)	18.2 (0.717)

NA Not available

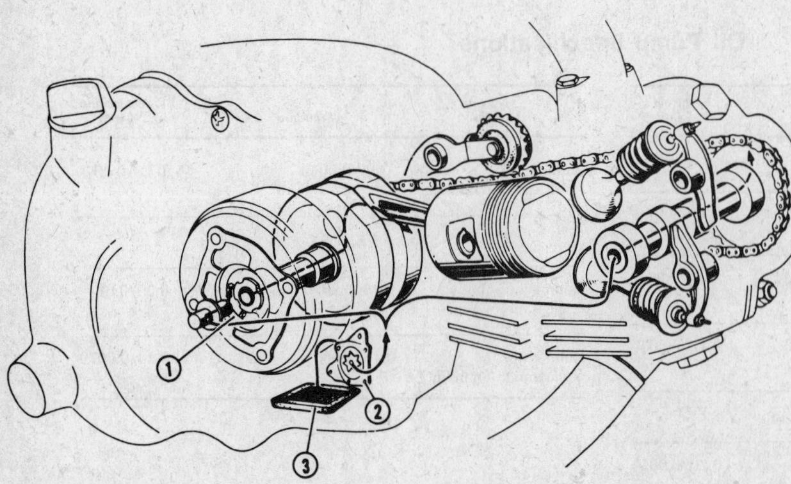

50-70 cc lubricating system: (1), centrifugal oil filter; (2), oil pump; (3), filter screen

FUEL SYSTEM

CARBURETOR

The following section deals with the removal and installation, and disassembly and assembly of the carburetor. Inspection and service is outlined under "Carburetor" in "General Information."

Removal and Installation

Procedures will vary depending on model.

1. Unscrew the carburetor cap and pull the throttle slide assembly out of the carburetor. If the slide assembly is to be disassembled, see the procedure below. If not, place a small plastic bag around the assembly to keep out dirt, and place it out of the way. Note that mishandling the assembly may necessitiate replacement of the slide or needle.

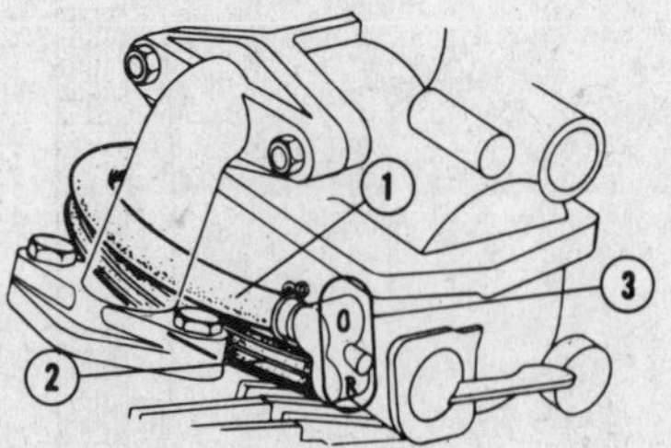

The main (1) and reserve (2) fuel lines must be correctly connected

2. On models which have the fuel petcock located on the carburetor float bowl (CT and ST models for example), pinch off the fuel main and reserve lines with a small C-clamp or the like; move the fuel line clips back up the line and disconnect the main and reserve lines from the carburetor. Be sure to note where each line is connected before disconnecting them.

Alternately, loosen the carburetor drain knob, turn the petcock to "reserve" and allow the contents of the tank to drain into a container by way of the drain line.

3. On other models, check that the fuel is shut off, and disconnect the fuel line from the carburetor.
4. Remove the float bowl drain plug (if fitted) and drain off any gas in the float bowl. Disconnect any overflow or breather tubes.
5. Loosen the carburetor or manifold mounting nuts a bit at a time until loose, then remove them.
6. Loosen the air cleaner hose clamp or band. Remove the carburetor.
7. Installation is the reverse of the above, but the following points should be noted:
   a. Be sure that the carburetor mounting flange O-ring is installed in its groove before fitting the carburetor;
   b. When tightening the carburetor or manifold flange nuts, do so evenly to prevent warpage;
   c. On models with a carburetor mounted petcock, note that the petcock

pipes are marked. Be sure to connect the correct line to the pipes;

d. Lubricate the throttle slide if desired with a molybdenum or graphite lubricant. Insert it into the carburetor with the slide cutaway facing away from the engine. Be sure that the slot in the slide is engaged with the tab in the carburetor body;

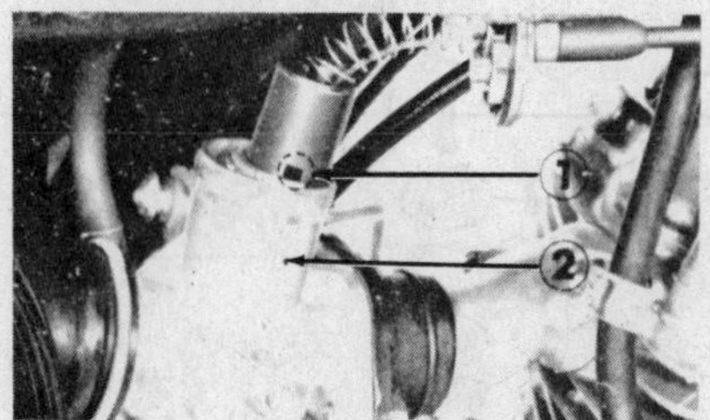

When fitting the slide, note that the slot in the slide (1) is engaged with the tab in the carb body

e. Be sure that the slide goes in easily, and especially that the needle enters the needle jet. Do not push or force the slide into place. If resistance is noted, it is probable that the needle is cocked to one side and is not entering the jet;

f. Tighten the carburetor cap and check throttle operation. The slide must move freely up and down.

Disassembly

1. If disassembly of the throttle slide components is desired, compress the return spring against the carburetor cap, disengage the cable from the slide, take out the spring clip, needle, and clip.

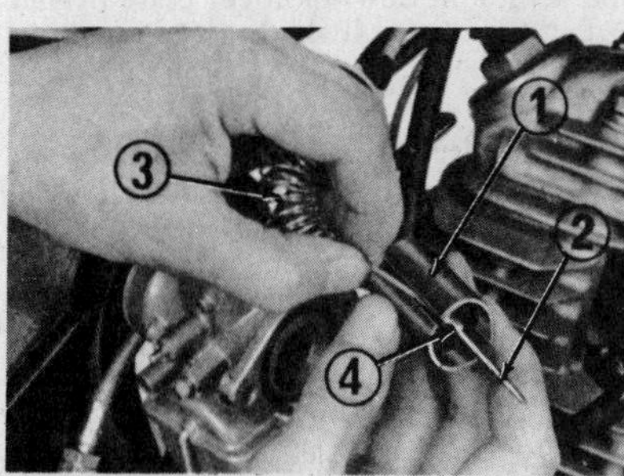

To disassemble the throttle slide, compress the return spring (3) and slip the cable end (4) out of the slide

2. Remove the float bowl petcock filter (if so equipped) by removing the filter plate, O-ring, and filter screen.

Carburetor-mounted petcock components: (1), filter screen; (2), lever

3. Remove the float bowl screws or flip up the retainer and separate the float bowl from the carburetor body. Do so carefully, to avoid damage to the floats. Remove and discard the float bowl gasket.

NOTE: *If the bowl is stuck, tap carefully with a plastic mallet to break the seal.*

4. Push out the float pivot pin with a small dowel, and take out the floats. Remove the float needle from its seat. Unscrew the seat itself.

5. Unscrew the main jet.

6. Several types of needle jet (located directly above the main jet) are fitted. Some models have only the jet itself, while others have a jet holder or nozzle with the needle jet located above it. Unscrew the needle jet or jet holder if a means is provided (such as a hex head), or simply push the jet holder and/or jet out of the carburetor body with a wooden dowel.

Main jet (1), pilot jet (2), floats (3), float needle (4)

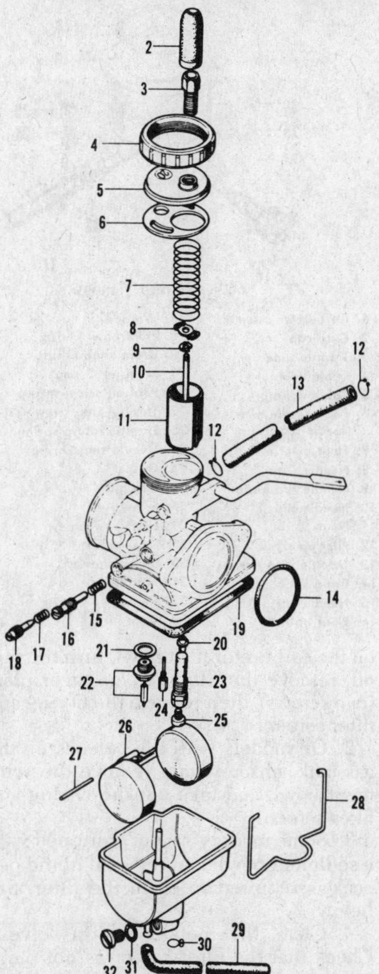

7. Unscrew and remove the pilot jet.

8. Remove the pilot air and throttle stop screws and springs, and the drain knob (if fitted).

Assembly

Assembly is basically the reverse of the above, but note the following points:

1. Float bowl gaskets and manifold and needle jet O-rings (where fitted) should always be replaced with new ones. Other O-rings or fiber gaskets should be carefully inspected and replaced if less than perfect in condition. Check O-rings for tears or cracks, fiber gaskets for crushed condition.

2. Exercise care when installing jets. Install the needle jet, holder if fitted, main jet, pilot jet, and float needle seat.

Some models have an O-ring on the needle jet which must be in place.

CAUTION: *Do not overtighten the jets as they are made of soft brass which is easily damaged.*

3. Install the float needle into its seat. Hold the floats in place and install the pivot pin.

4. Assemble the throttle slide.

5. Install the pilot air screw, turning it in until lightly seated, then backing it out the proper number of turns as listed in the chart at the end of this chapter.

6. After completing assembly, install the carburetor on its manifold. If the carburetor bolts to the manifold, make sure that the bolts or nuts are tightened evenly, but not overtightened.

7. Check for fuel or air leaks; make final adjustments to the throttle stop and pilot air screws.

Atomizer Plate

An atomizer plate has been fitted to the intake manifold on some 1976 models. The plate needs no service or maintenance, but if removed, it must be installed in the correct way. Refer to the illustration of the unit.

1. Carburetor assembly
2. Cable boot
3. Cable adjuster
4. Cap ring
5. Cap
6. Cap plate
7. Throttle slide return spring
8. Clip plate
9. Needle clip
10. Needle
11. Throttle slide
12. Circlip
13. Feed line
14. Manifold O-ring
15. Holder spring
16. Throttle stop screw
17. Holder spring
18. Pilot air screw
19. Float bowl gasket
20. Needle jet
21. Float needle seat gasket
22. Float needle and seat
23. Main nozzle, needle jet holder
24. Pilot jet
25. Main jet
26. Float assembly
27. Pivot pin
28. Float bowl retainer
29. Overflow line
30. Circlip
31. Gasket
32. Drain plug

Carburetor assembly (100-125 cc)

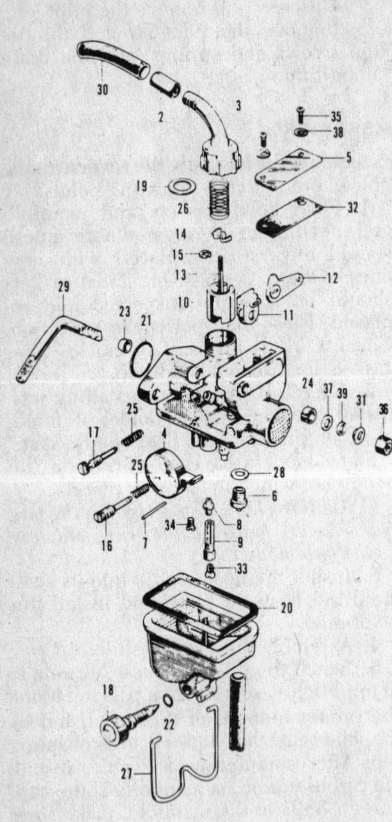

Z50 carburetor (early)

1. Carburetor assembly
2. Cable adjuster
3. Cap
4. Float
5. Choke cover
6. Float needle seat
7. Pivot pin
8. Needle jet
9. Main nozzle, needle jet holder
10. Throttle slide
11. Choke valve
12. Choke arm
13. Needle
14. Needle clip plate
15. Clip
16. Pilot air screw
17. Throttle stop screw
18. Drain knob
19. Washer
20. Float bowl gasket
21. Manifold O-ring
22. Drain knob O-ring
23. Seal
24. Seal seat
25. Holder spring
26. Throttle return spring
27. Float bowl retainer
28. Needle seat gasket
29. Choke lever
30. Cable boot
31. Washer
32. Choke cover gasket
33. Main jet
34. Pilot jet
35. Screw
36. Mounting nut
37. Washer
38. Lockwasher
39. Lockwasher

Z50 carburetor (later)

1. Carburetor assembly
2. Carb cap
3. Throttle slide
4. Cable boot
5. Cable adjuster
6. Float needle and needle seat
7. Float pivot pin
8. Needle
9. Needle clip plate
10. Needle clip
11. Float
12. Pilot air screw
13. Throttle stop screw
14. Drain knob
15. Needle jet
16. Float bowl
17. Washer
18. Float bowl O-ring
19. Drain knob O-ring
20. Main jet O-ring
21. Pilot air screw spring
22. Throttle stop screw spring
23. Throttle return spring
24. Needle seat O-ring
25. Gasket
26. Clip plate
27. Screw
28. Float bowl screw
29. Lockwasher
30. Lockwasher
31. Fuel line
32. Circlip
33. Main jet

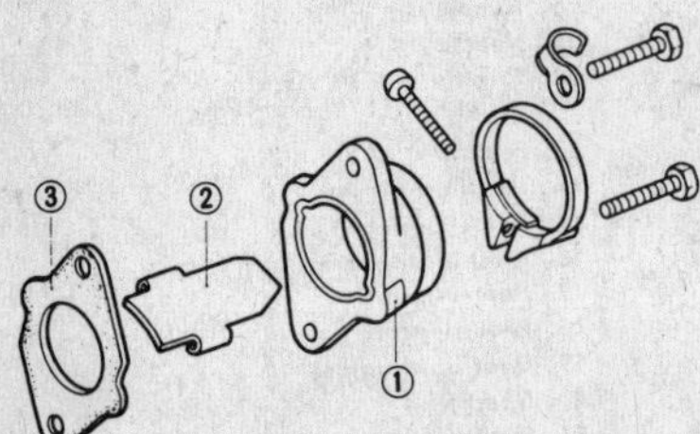

Manifold (1), atomizer plate (2), gasket (3). (1976 models)

FUEL PETCOCK AND LINES

Cleaning

1. On models with the petcock located on the carburetor float bowl, turn the fuel off, remove the filter screen cover plate (two screws), then remove the O-ring and filter screen.

2. On models with the petcock on the gas tank, unscrew and remove the sediment bowl, and take out the O-ring and filter screen.

3. Some models are not equipped with a sediment bowl, and removal of the petcock is required to clean the filter. See below.

4. Clean the metal parts in solvent. Check that the filter screen is not punctured, and that the O-ring is not torn or otherwise damaged.

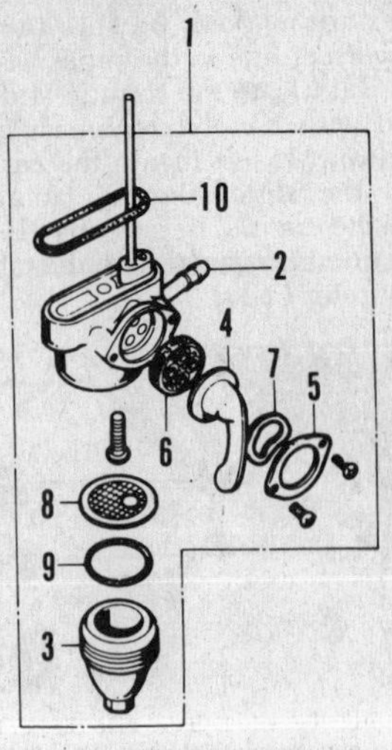

Petcock components

1. Petcock assembly
2. Petcock body
3. Sediment bowl
4. Petcock lever
5. Lever plate
6. Gasket
7. Spring
8. Filter
9. O-ring for sediment bowl
10. O-ring for petcock body

5. Run a little gasoline through the petcock to flush out any dirt. Catch the gas in a suitable container. Turning the petcock to "Reserve" for a few seconds should remove the better part of any water or dirt in the bottom of the gas tank.

6. Check petcock operation in all operations. There must be no fuel flow when the petcock lever is turned to the "stop" position.

7. Replace the filter screen, O-ring, and sediment bowl or cover plate in that order. Check for leaks before operating the motorcycle.

Disassembly

At somewhat more extended intervals, the petcock should be removed from the gas tank or carburetor and cleaned.

1. Drain the gas tank completely. Disconnect the fuel line(s) from the petcock.

2. On petcocks which have sediment bowls, remove the bowl, O-ring and filter screen.

3. Remove the phillips screws beneath the filter screen and remove the petcock from the gas tank.

4. On tank-mounted petcocks without a sediment bowl, unscrew the nut which secures the petcock to the tank and remove the petcock. Remove the filter screen and rubber gasket.

5. Remove the two screws from the fuel lever setting plate, and remove the setting plate, lever spring, lever, and gasket.

Inspection

1. Clean all metal parts in solvent and blow dry. Clean the filter screens thoroughly, or replace if there is evidence of punctures or damage.

2. Inspect the O-rings for damage and replace if any is noted, or if leakage was evident in the petcock. Check any gaskets for crushed or cracked condition. Inspect the lever spring for cracks or fatigue.

3. Inspect the fuel lines for cracks or

abrasion damage. Replace if any sort of fault is noted.

Assembly

1. Install the fuel valve gasket, lever, spring, and setting plate. Secure with the two screws.

2. Be sure that the petcock O-ring (if fitted) is properly seated, or that the gasket is in place.

3. Install the petcock on the tank. Fit the sediment bowl filter, O-ring, and bowl if applicable. Check for leaks.

4. Be sure that all fuel lines are firmly secured at their connections and that the safety circlips are in place.

ELECTRICAL SYSTEMS

IGNITION CIRCUIT

Hard starting or misfiring are often caused by ignition system troubles, but since electrical malfunctions are often trickier to pin down than carburetor faults, it is wise to ensure that systems other than the ignition are in serviceable condition before beginning any work.

1. In the event of hard starting, misfiring, or cutting out, first check that all electrical connections are clean and tight. If the machine will not start at all, check the fuse (near the battery) first.

2. On battery ignition machines, check the charge of the battery and recharge or replace it as necessary. Be sure that the battery terminals are clean and the connections secured tightly.

3. Check the ignition and kill switches for continuity.

4. Check the ignition timing for accuracy.

5. Remove the spark plug, clean it thoroughly, or replace it with a new one; gap the plug to 0.6–0.7 mm (0.024–0.028 in.). Connect it to its cap, and ground it against the cylinder head. Kick the engine over briskly. The spark produced should be thick and blue.

6. If there is no spark, or if the spark is weak and yellow, repeat the test using a piece of metal, such as a nail, inserted into the spark plug cap and held about ⅛ in. away from the cylinder. If the spark is healthy, the problem was the spark plug; if not, check the condition of the points. Inspect, clean, and gap the points or replace them if they are badly pitted or worn. **If excessive arcing or sparking at the points is noted while the machine is running, the problem may be the condenser. A defective condenser will also cause new points to wear out quickly.** new points to wear out quickly.

7. If the problem is not in the points or the spark plug, the spark plug cap should be checked. Noise suppressor caps are fitted, which are designed to eliminate radio interference and provide a hotter spark by means of a resistor in the cap. Sometimes the resistor breaks down, and the cap then becomes an open circuit. Remove the cap from the spark

Carburetor Specifications

Model	*Z50*	*065/M*	*S65*	*C70*	*C70M*
Main jet	50	72	85	75	75
Air jet	100	150	150	150	150
Air screw (turns out)	1⅛	1¼	1½	1½	1⅛
Throttle slide	2.0	2.0	1.5	2.5	2.5
Pilot jet	38	35	38	35	35
Float level (in./mm)	0.7/18①	0.69/17.5	0.8/19.5	0.6/15.5	0.6/15.5

① K3-on—0.65/16.5

Model	*CL70*	*CT70/H*	*SL70*	*XR75*	*S90*
Main jet	72	60	68	100	85
Air jet	90	150	90	NA	150
Air screw (turns out)	1⅛	1¾	1½	1¼	1¼
Throttle slide	2.5	2.5	NA	NA	2.5
Pilot jet	38	35	40	38	38
Float level (in./mm)	0.3/7.0	0.78/20.0	0.28/7.0	0.83/21.0	②

② Keihin—0.78/19.5
Mikuni—0.95/24.0

Model	*CL90/L*	*CD90*	*C90*	*CT90*	*CT90 (from Frame No. 000001A)*
Main jet	85	90	75	72	80
Air jet	150	150	120	120	120
Air screw (turns out)	1½	1¼	1	1½	1⅛
Throttle slide	2.5	2.5	2.0	2.0	2.5
Pilot jet	35	40	40	40	38
Float level (in./mm)	0.78/19.5	0.83/21.0	0.83/21.0	0.83/21.0	③

③ CT90—0.85/21.5
K1—0.94/23.5

Model	*CT90(K2-on)*	*100 (to 75)*	*100(76)*	*125(To 75)*	*125(76)*	*TL125(76)*
Main jet	80	110	105	105	110	92
Air jet	120	100	100	100	100	100
Air screw (turns out)	1	1½	1½	1½	1½	1
Throttle slide	2.5	2.5	2.5	NA	NA	NA
Needle clip (groove from top)	NA	NA	2	NA	2	2
Pilot jet	38	38	38	38	45	35
Float level (in./mm)	0.78/20.0	0.95/24.0	0.95/24.0	0.95/24.0④	0.95/24.0	0.95/24.0

④TL125:0.85/21.5

NA Not available

plug lead, and ground the end of the lead against the cylinder head. If a fat, blue spark is produced when the engine is kicked over, the problem was the cap. Replace it with a new one.

8. If the cap checks out okay, carefully inspect the cable itself. Check for dirt or grease, cuts or cracks in the insulation, moisture, etc. If the lead is damaged, it must be replaced. This also involves replacing the coil.

9. If the trouble has not been pinpointed, the ignition coil windings should be checked for continuity, using an ohmmeter.

a. On battery ignition machines, disconnect the two low-tension coil leads and check for continuity between them. This is a check of the primary winding. If there is no continuity, replace the coil;

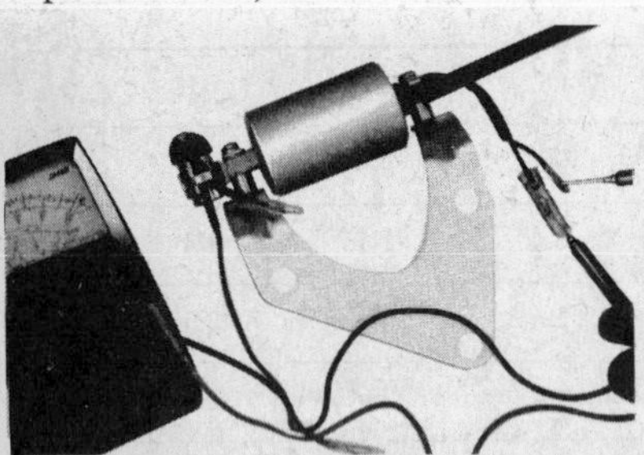

Checking ignition coil primary winding continuity (battery ignition)

b. On magneto ignition machines, check the primary winding by checking for continuity between the coil's low-tension wire (black or black/white) and the coil mounting plate. If continuity does not exist, replace the coil;

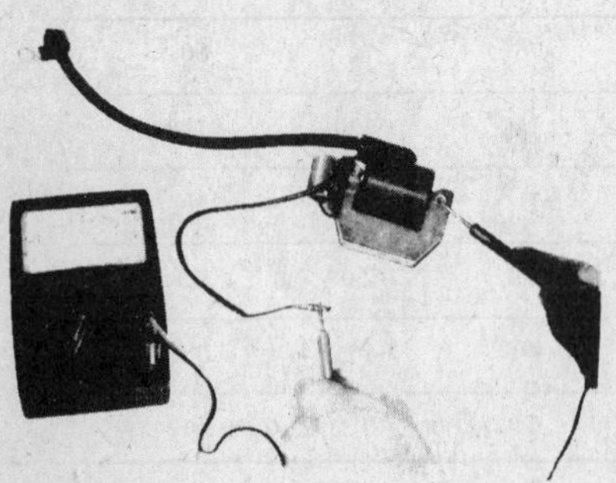

Checking primary winding continuity (magneto ignition)

c. On battery ignition machines, check for continuity across the coil's blue low-tension lead and the high-tension (spark plug) lead. Resistance may be very high (5–10,000 ohms), but continuity must exist. This checks the secondary winding;

d. On magneto ignition machines, check for continuity across the high-tension lead and the coil mounting bracket. If there is no continuity, replace the coil.

Even if continuity is present in the coil windings, it is possible that the coil is still defective. Replacing the coil temporarily with one which is known to be serviceable is recommended.

10. The condenser can be checked. If a capacitance tester is available. Condensers should have a capacitance of approximately 0.25mf. Checking with a "megger" (high-voltage ohmmeter) should yield a resistance of 10M ohms at 1,000v.

On battery ignition machines, the checks above cover all ignition circuit components and the trouble should be evident. On magneto ignition bikes, the magneto itself must be checked if the cause of the problem has not yet been determined.

Assuming that all other ignition circuit components have been eliminated as the possible trouble spots, and the ignition and kill switches have been checked, proceed as follows:

1. Remove the left crankcase sidecover and the magneto rotor. A special puller must be used to remove the rotor.

2. Check the rotor for any score marks which would indicate that the rotor is contacting the core ends. If so, the condition must be remedied. If this has occurred, check for any play in the crankshaft which would indicate a bad crankshaft bearing. Other reasons may be improper mounting of the coil cores or rotor, worn crankshaft taper, or rotor taper surface. If the taper is damaged, the rotor should be replaced. Also inspect the rotor for any cracks or fractures. If present, replace.

3. Check for continuity between the black or black/white wire and ground. If continuity does not exist, the primary exciting coil is either broken internally, or is poorly grounded.

NOTE: *If this test is made with the coils still on the engine, be sure that the points are open or held open with a bit of thick paper.*

4. Check the resistance between the coil core and the mounting plate or crankcase cover. The coil core should be well grounded (no resistance).

CHARGING CIRCUIT

Battery Ignition Models

1. In the event that the battery overcharges, check the condition of the battery itself. A shorted or defective battery is the most likely cause.

2. If the battery discharges quickly, or fails to hold a charge, check the battery, rectifier, and alternator.

RECTIFIER

An ohmeter or a continuity tester is used to check the rectifier. Do not use a megger.

1. Disconnect the rectifier leads at the plastic connector. There are four leads wired to the connector. This rectifier is the full-wave type, consisting of four diodes wired as shown in the illustration. To check the rectifier, you will be checking each diode in turn to ensure that current will flow through each in one direction only. Current flow in both directions, or no current flow in either direction through a diode indicates that it is defective.

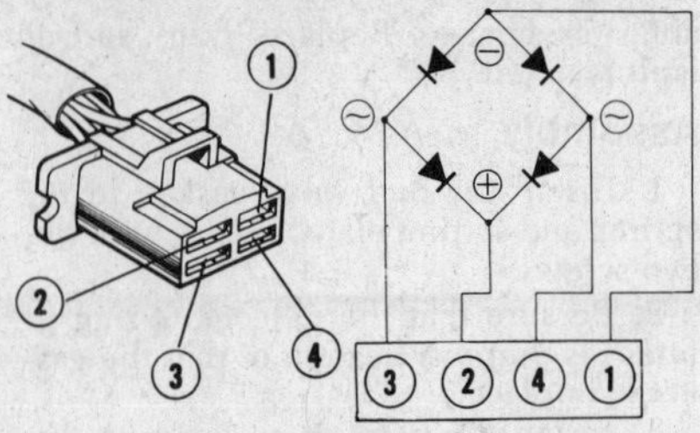

Full-wave rectifier leads

1. Green
2. Red/White
3. Yellow
4. Pink

2. Connect the negative lead of the tester to the green wire, and the positive lead to the yellow, red/white, and pink wires in turn.

In each case, note whether or not there is continuity.

NOTE: *On an ohmmeter, "continuity" will be indicated by a resistance of 5–40 ohms. "No continuity" by a resistance of 100 or more ohms.*

3. Now reverse the tester connections, connecting the positive tester lead to the green wire, and the negative to each of the others in turn.

In every case, the reaction of the tester must be the opposite of the first test: i.e., if the first test showed continuity between two leads, reversing the tester connections must show no continuity.

Continuity in both directions, or lack of continuity in both directions for any given pair of wires is indicative of a defective rectifier.

ALTERNATOR

1. A dynamic test may be carried out if a voltmeter and ammeter are available. The battery must be fully charged. Hook up the voltmeter across the battery terminals, and the ammeter to the positive terminal of the battery and to the red/white lead, as shown.

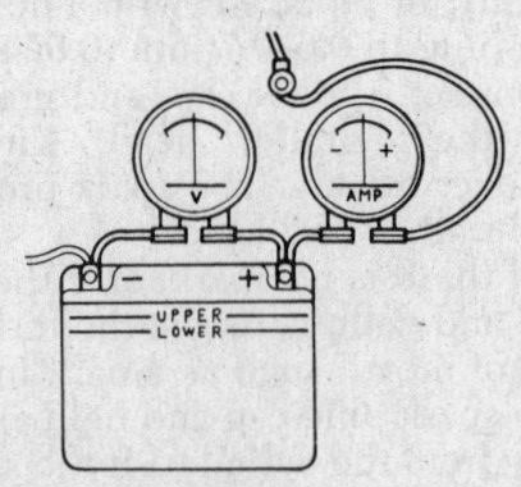

Voltmeter and ammeter connections to check alternator output

2. Start the engine and note the voltmeter and ammeter readings at the given rpm and compare them to those given in the "Alternator Output" chart for your machine. If the readings are not within the proper specifications, the stator coil should be removed from the machine and checked for continuity as outlined below.

3. Check for continuity between all three stator leads. Continuity must exist, or the stator assembly has a broken wire and it must be replaced.

4. Check for continuity between the yellow lead and the stator core. If continuity exists, there is a short, and the stator must be replaced.

Alternator Output

Lights	Beginning of Charging	5000 rpm
	90 cc	
Off	6.8v, 1000 rpm	7.8v/1.3a
High beam	6.8v, 3500 rpm	7.2v/0.2a
Low beam	6.8v, 2200 rpm	7.8v/1.3a
	100 cc	
Off	6.8v, 1000 rpm	7.8v/1.3a
High beam	6.8v, 3500 rpm	7.8v/1.3a
Low beam	6.8v, 2200 rpm	7.2v/1.3a
	125 cc	
Off	6.8v, 1000 rpm	7.9v/1.7a
Low beam	6.8v, 2000 rpm	7.8v/1.3a

Magneto/Alternator Models

1. Rectifiers are fitted to models which have batteries. In the event that the battery overcharges, it is probable that the battery itself is faulty.

2. If the battery fails to hold a charge or discharges quickly, check the battery itself, then the rectifier and magneto lighting coil.

RECTIFIER

1. The rectifier is a simple half-wave unit which has two leads (red/white and green). To check the rectifier, disconnect these leads, and connect a test light or ohmmeter across the rectifier terminals. Note whether or not continuity exists. Now reverse the leads and note whether or not there is continuity.

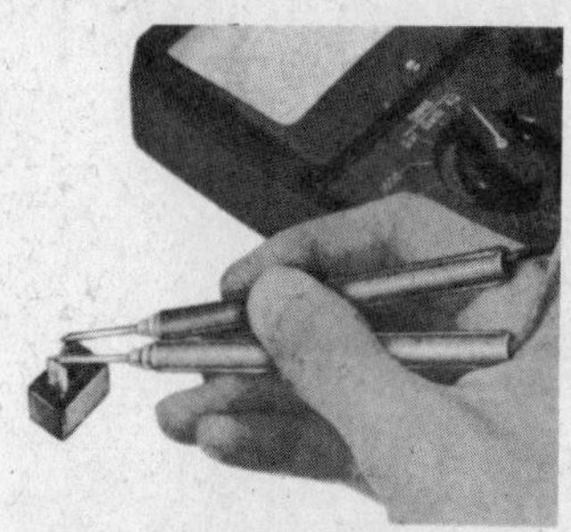

Checking the half-wave rectifier

2. There must be continuity in one direction only. If there is continuity in both directions or neither direction, the rectifier is defective. If an ohmmeter is used, resistance should be 5–40 ohms in the forward direction (continuity) and about 600 ohms for the reverse.

ALTERNATOR

1. To check the lighting coil, use an ohmmeter or continuity light.

2. Disconnect the alternator wiring at the plastic connector. Check for continuity between the green lead and ground on the engine case. Check for continuity between the yellow lead and ground. Check for continuity between the green and the yellow leads. Continuity must exist in all three cases or the lighting coil must be replaced.

3. If lights are dim on models which have no battery, suspect the magneto/alternator coil. Check for burned wiring, scored coil core ends, etc. Make continuity checks as in Step 2.

If the coil seems satisfactory, the rotor magnets may have become weakened. Replace the rotor if this has happened.

Checking for continuity between alternator leads

STARTING SYSTEM

The starting system consists of the starter motor and clutch, the solenoid, and the handlebar-mounted starter switch. When the button is pressed, the electrical circuit to the solenoid is closed and the solenoid is activated, sending the battery current directly to the starter motor. The starting system is quite reliable and it is unlikely that you will experience any major problems.

Testing

1. If the starter will not operate, switch on the headlight and observe its intensity. If it is dim when the starter is not being operated, check the battery connections and recharge the battery. If the headlight doesn't light, check the fuse, and the battery connections, and check the electrical continuity of the wire between the ignition switch and the battery.

2. If the headlight is bright, press the starter button momentarily and watch the light. If it remains bright, touch a screwdriver blade between the two starter solenoid terminals. If the starter operates, connect a test light between the small yellow/red wire on the solenoid and ground. If the test light comes on as the button is pushed, the solenoid is faulty. If it does not light, look for defective wiring between the starter button and the ignition switch, or simply a burned out starter button switch. If the starter does not operate and the headlight dims as the main solenoid terminals are bridged, the starter motor is faulty. If the headlight does not dim, look for a bad connection at the starter.

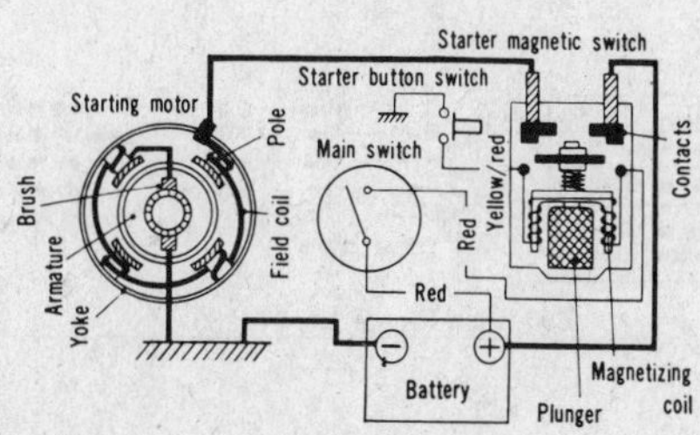

Electric starter wiring diagram

3. If the starter motor operates freely, but will not turn the engine over, the starter clutch is not operating (a rare occurrence). To remove the clutch it will be necessary to first take off the left-side crankcase cover and remove the alternator rotor. If the overrunning clutch is defective and the starter keeps spinning after the engine starts, it must be repaired immediately to prevent serious damage to the starter assembly.

Starter Motor Service

1. Check for electrical continuity between the commutator and armature core using a multimeter or test light and battery. If continuity exists, the armature coil is grounded and the armature or complete starter motor should be replaced.

2. Check continuity between the brush wired to the stator (field) coil and the starter motor cable terminal. Lack of continuity indicates that an open circuit exists in the stator coil and the starter motor unit should be replaced.

3. Examine the carbon brushes for damage to the contact surfaces and measure their length. Replace the brushes as a set if they are damaged in any way or if they measure less than 0.3 in. (7.5 mm).

4. Brush spring tension should be determined with a small spring scale. Replace the springs if they exert less than 0.8 lbs of tension.

5. Polish the commutator with fine emery cloth and blow it off thoroughly before installing it. Check the following components for excessive wear and damage: clutch spring and rollers; bearings; bushings; oil seal; reduction gears; and the sprockets. Replace all parts as necessary if worn or damaged. When reassembling the starter clutch, apply a thin coat of silicone grease to the rollers.

Starter Solenoid Service

The solenoid is an electromagnetic switch which closes and completes the circuit between the starter and the battery when activated by the starter button. The solenoid is a necessary addition to the starting circuit because the starter button switch is not capable of handling the amperage load required to operate the starter, and because mounting a heavy-duty switch on the handlebar, with the large cable needed to handle the load, is impractical.

If the solenoid does not work, check the continuity of the primary coil by connecting a multimeter or test light and battery to the two small solenoid leads. Lack of continuity indicates an open circuit and the solenoid must be replaced. If the primary coil winding is continuous, disassemble the solenoid and clean the contact points with emery paper or a small file. The points, after long use, have a tendency to become pitted or burned due to the large current passing across them. Be sure to disconnect the battery before disconnecting the cables from the solenoid when it is to be removed. Replace the solenoid if cleaning the points fails to repair it.

WIRING DIAGRAMS

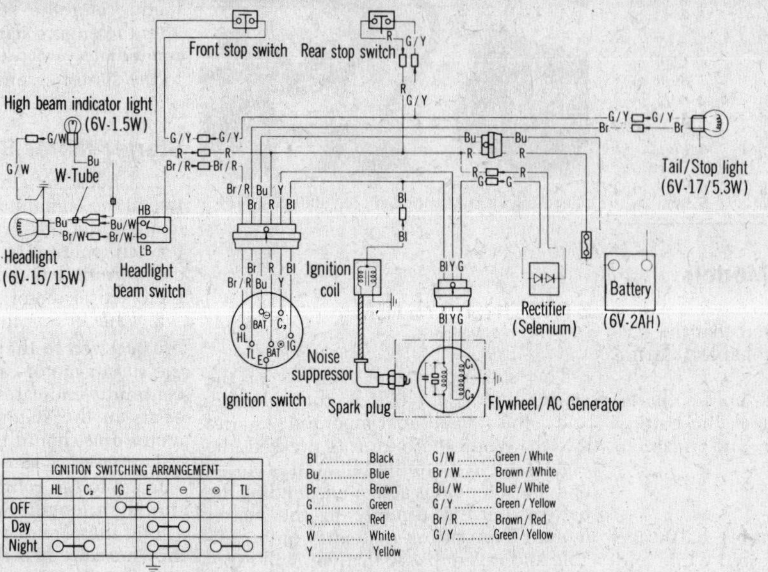

IGNITION SWITCHING ARRANGEMENT							
	HL	C_2	IG	E	⊖	⊗	TL
OFF			○	○			
Day				○	○		
Night	○	○		○	○	○	○

Z50 (from Frame No. 120001)

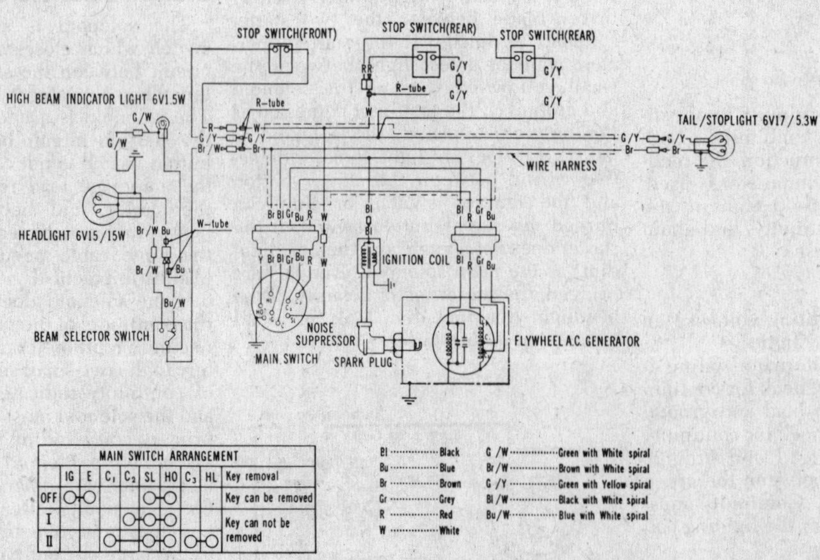

MAIN SWITCH ARRANGEMENT									
	IG	E	C_1	C_2	SL	HO	C_3	HL	Key removal
OFF	○	○			○	○			Key can be removed
I				○	○	○			Key can not be removed
II			○		○	○	○	○	

Z50 (from Frame No. 270236)

WIRING DIAGRAMS

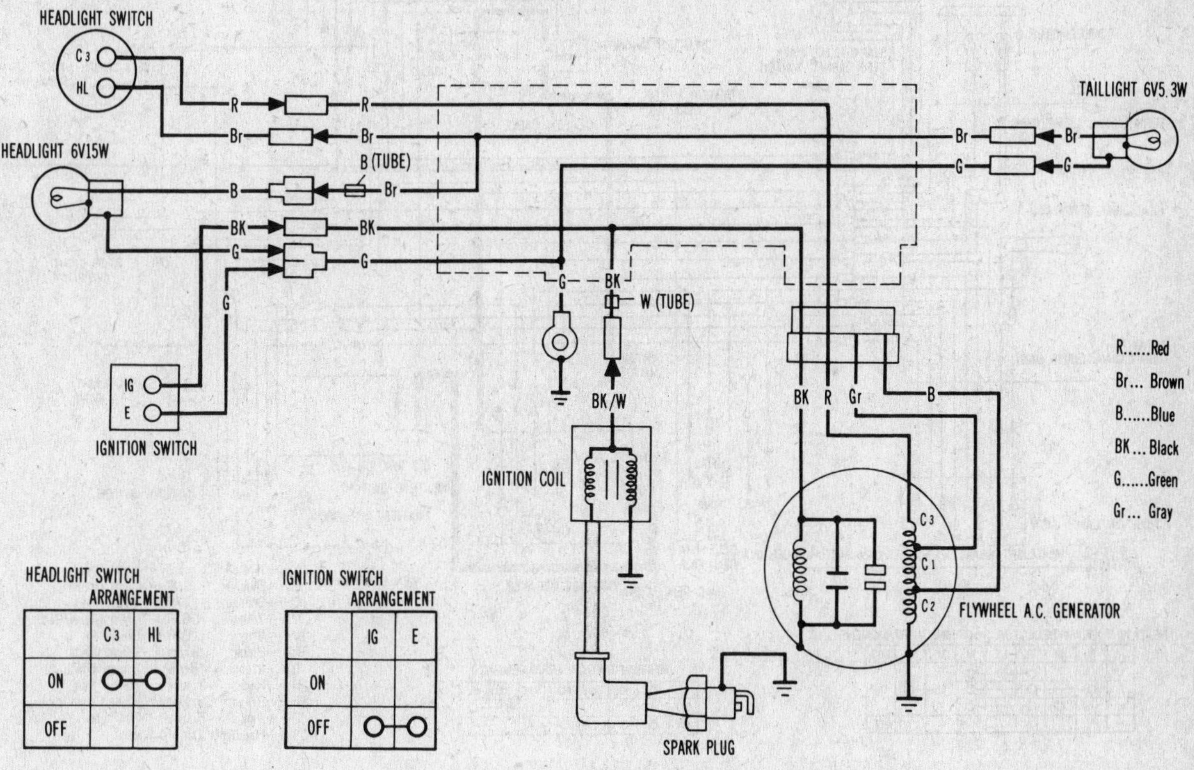

Z50 K4-on

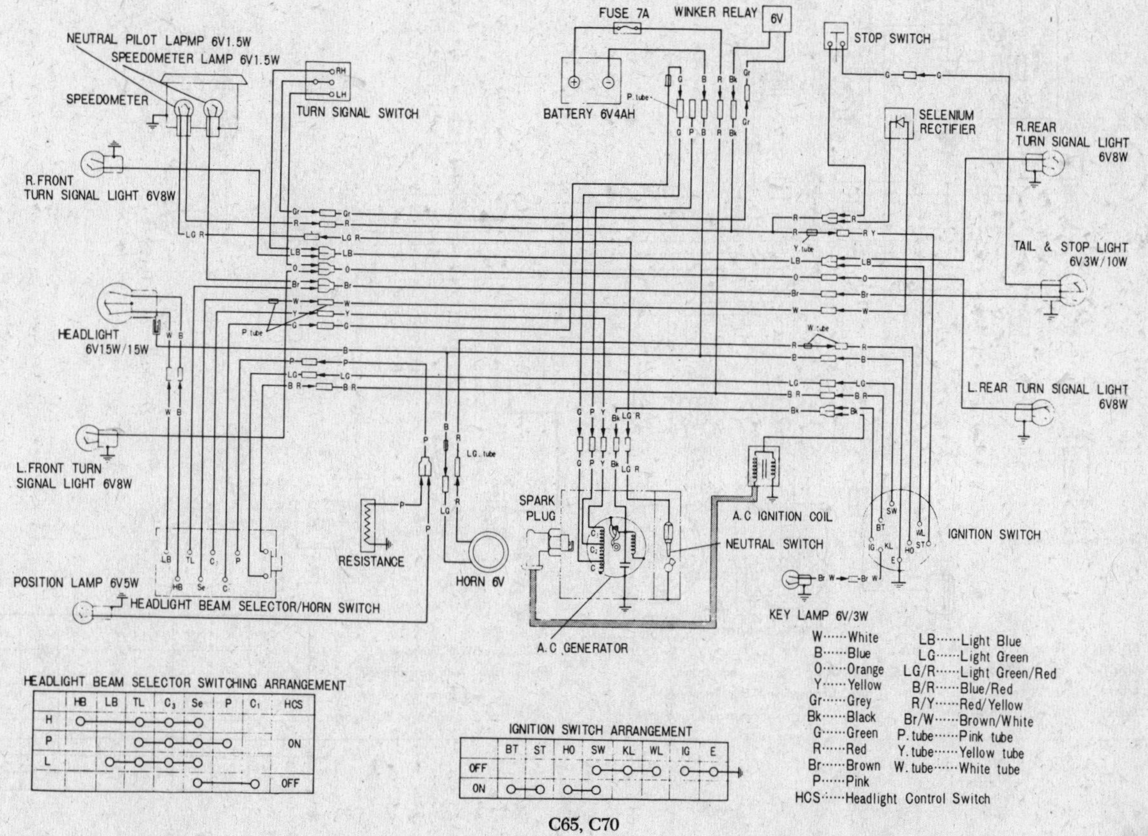

C65, C70

WIRING DIAGRAMS

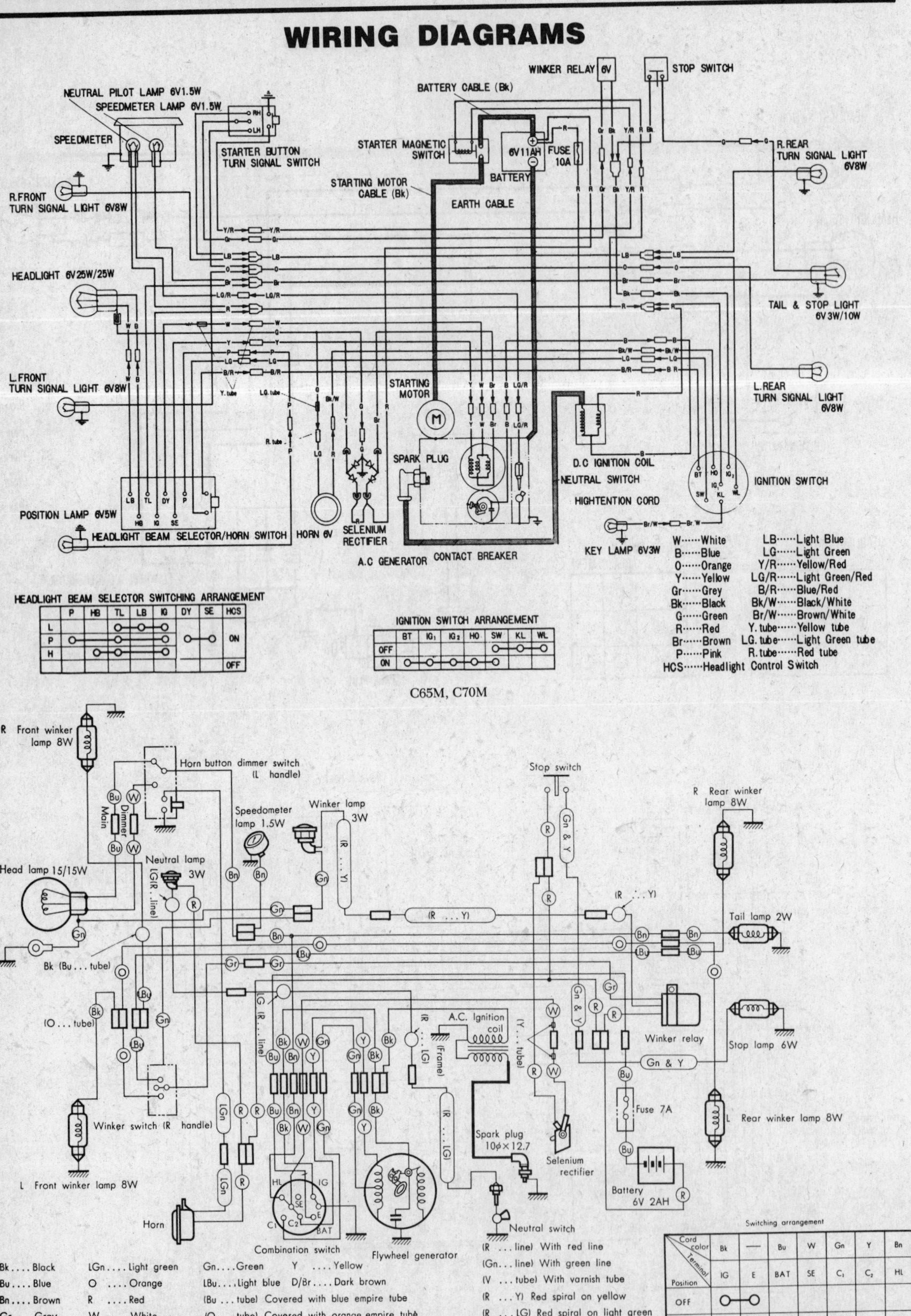

C65M, C70M

S65

WIRING DIAGRAMS

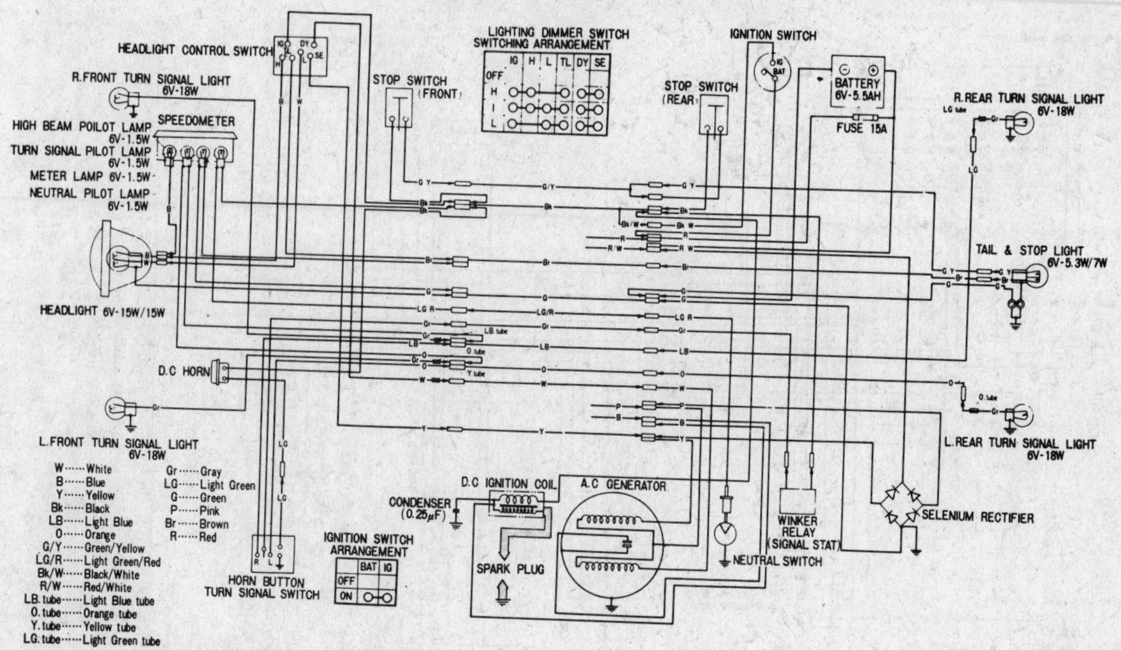

CL70

Wiring Diagram

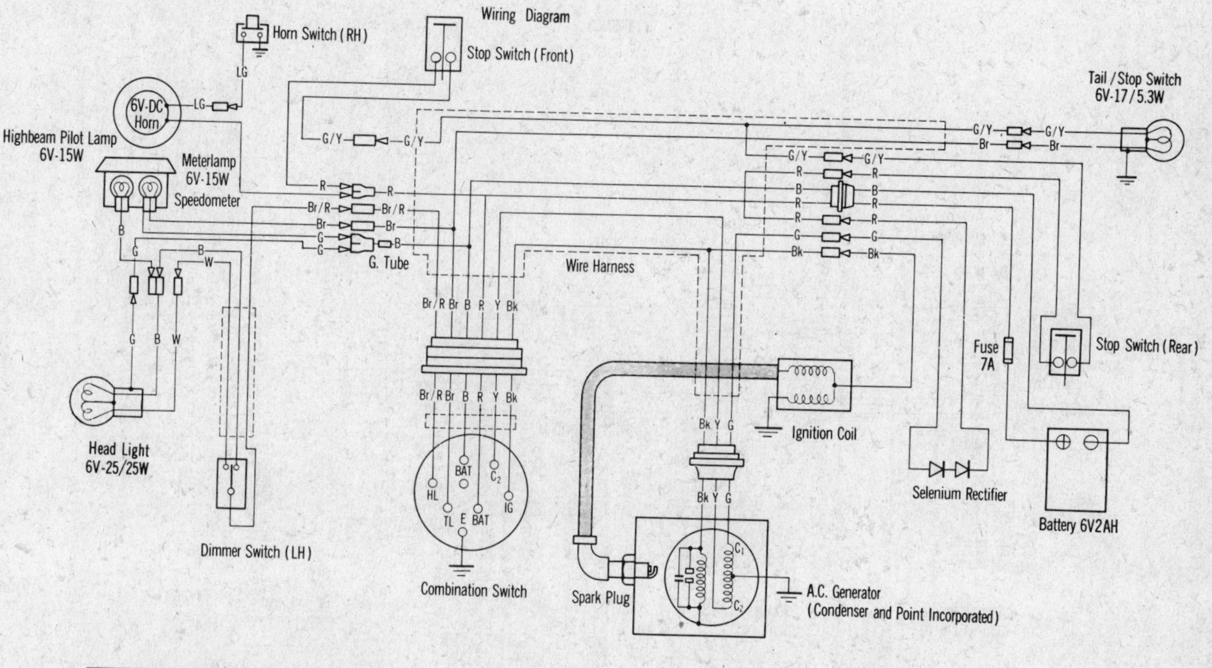

Combination Switching diagram							
	HL	C2	IG	E	BAT ⊖	BAT ⊕	TL
OFF			O—	—O			
I				O—	—O		
II	O—	—O		O—	—O	O—	—O
Cord Color	BR/R	Y	BK		B	R	R

W .... White
B .... Blue
O .... Orange
Y .... Yellow
Gr .... Grey
Bk .... Black
G .... Green
R .... Red
Br .... Brown
P .... Pink
HCS .... Headlight Control Switch
LB .... Light Blue
LG .... Light Green
Y/R .... Yellow/Red
LG/R .... Light Green/Red
B/R .... Blue/Red
Bk/W .... Black/White
Br/W .... Brown/White
Y. Tube .... Yellow Tube
LG. Tube .... Light Green Tube
R. Tube .... Red Tube

CT70

WIRING DIAGRAMS

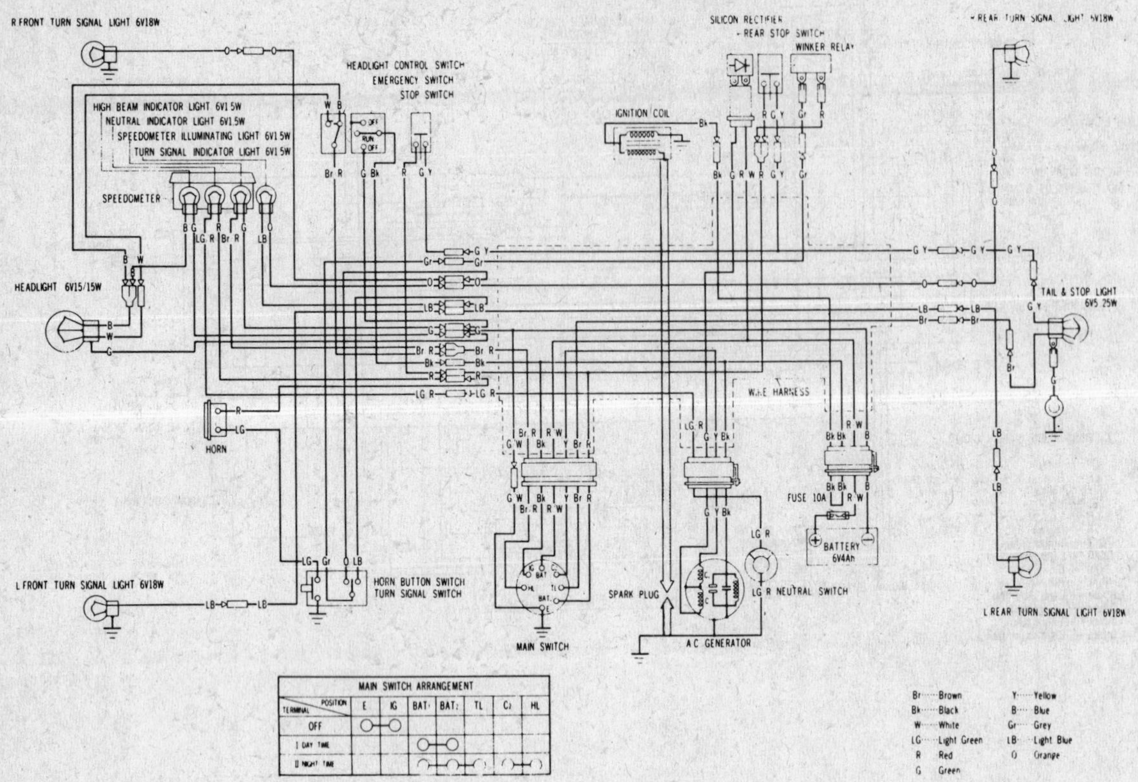

CT70K3

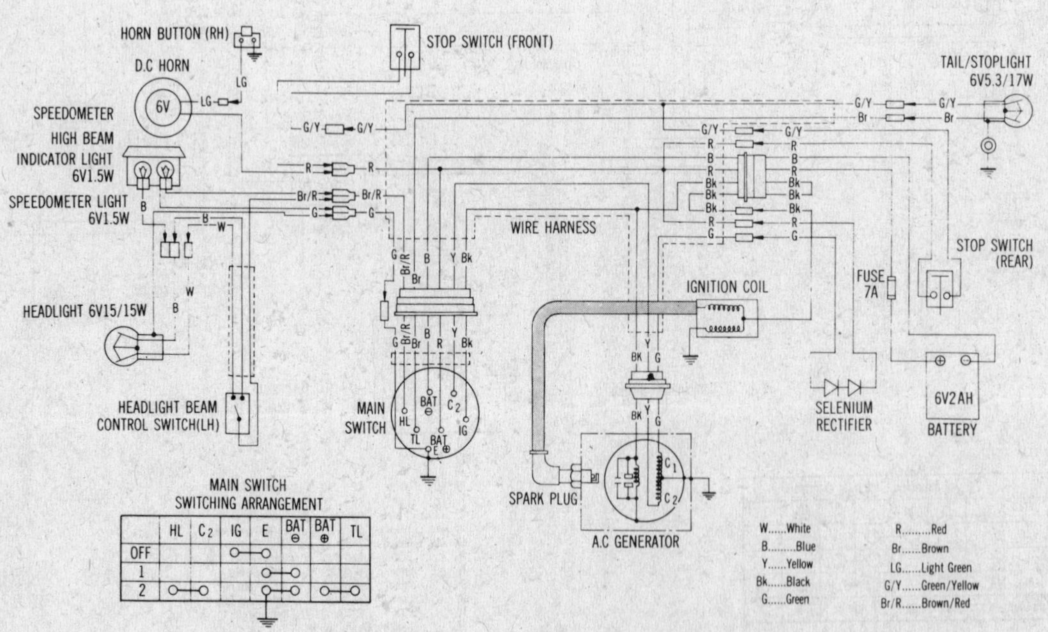

CT70H

WIRING DIAGRAMS

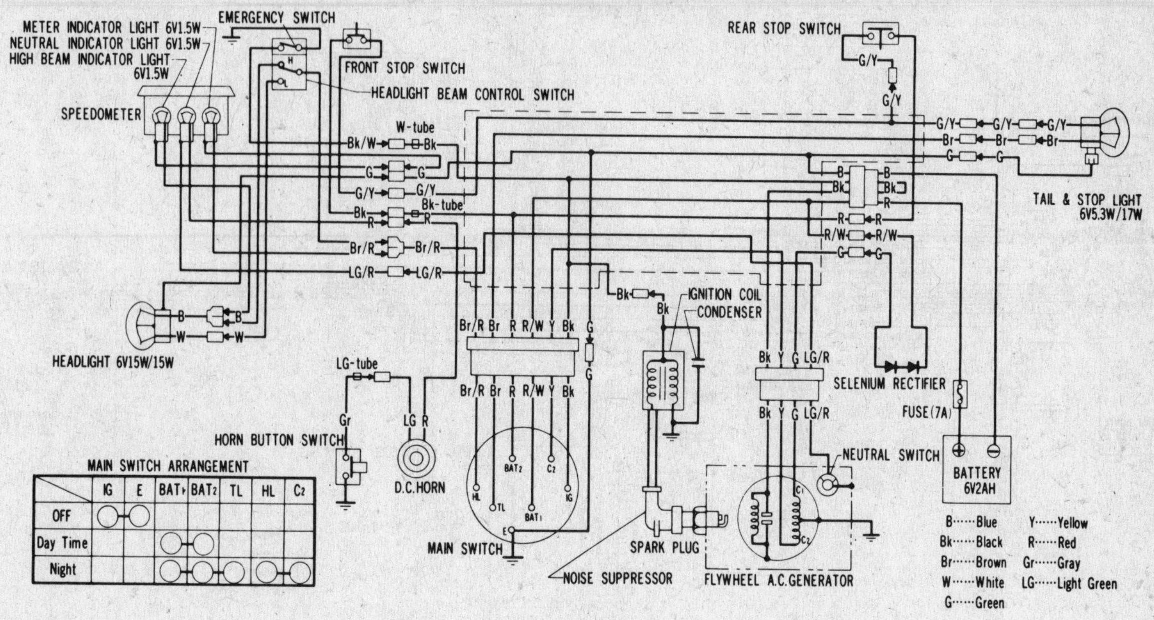

SL70

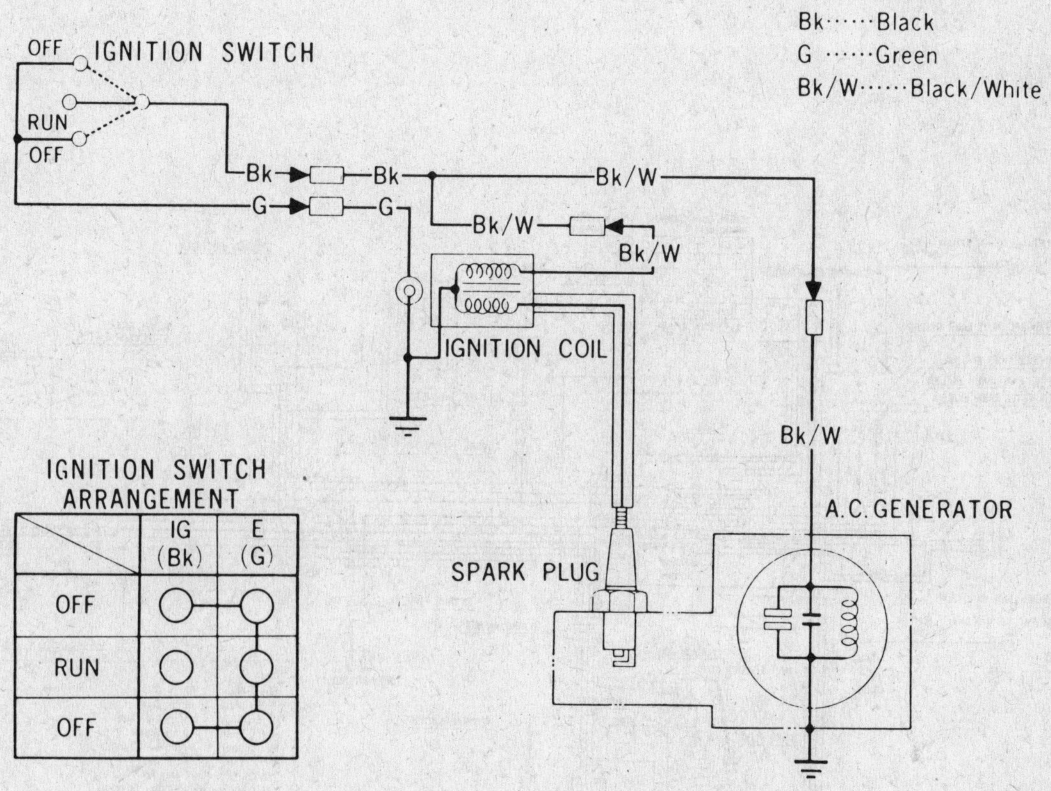

XR75

WIRING DIAGRAMS

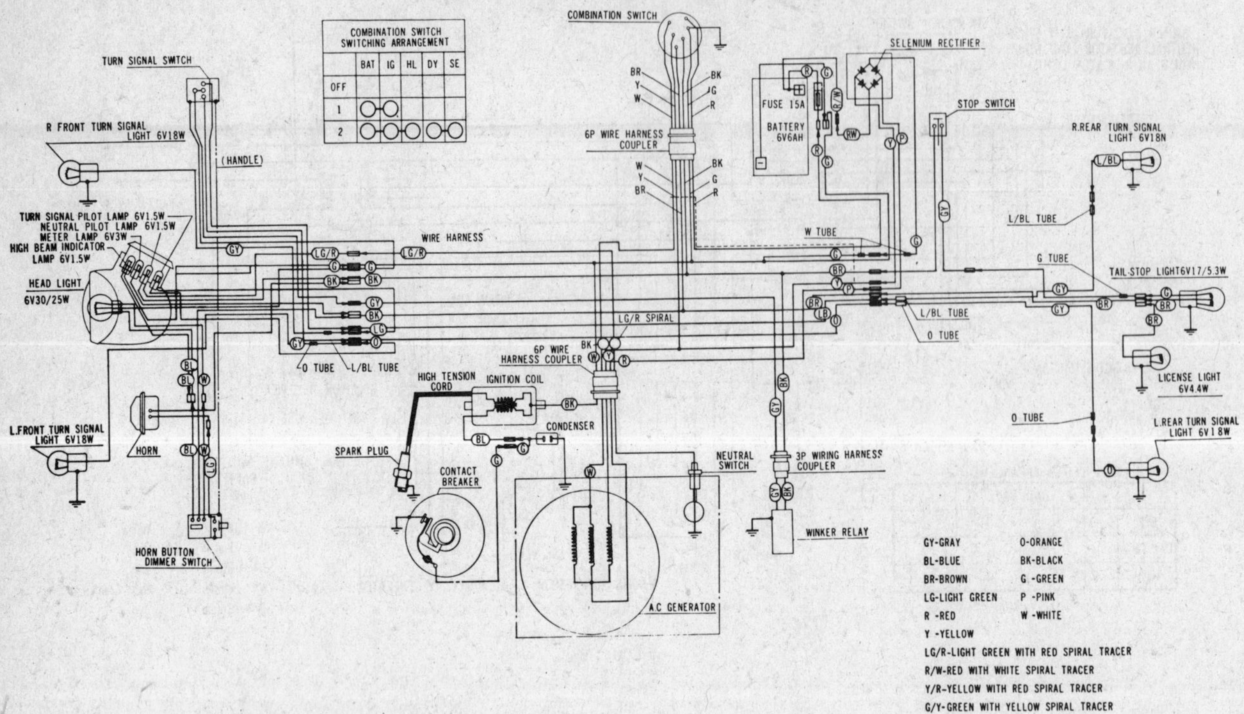

S90

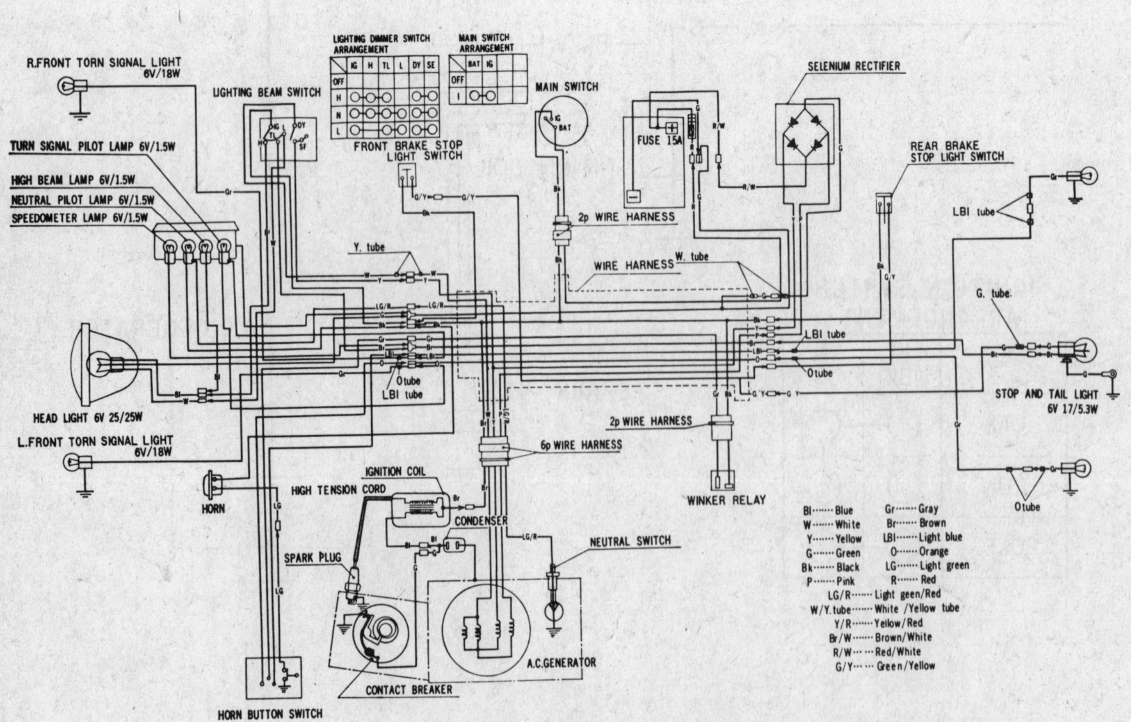

CL90/L

WIRING DIAGRAMS

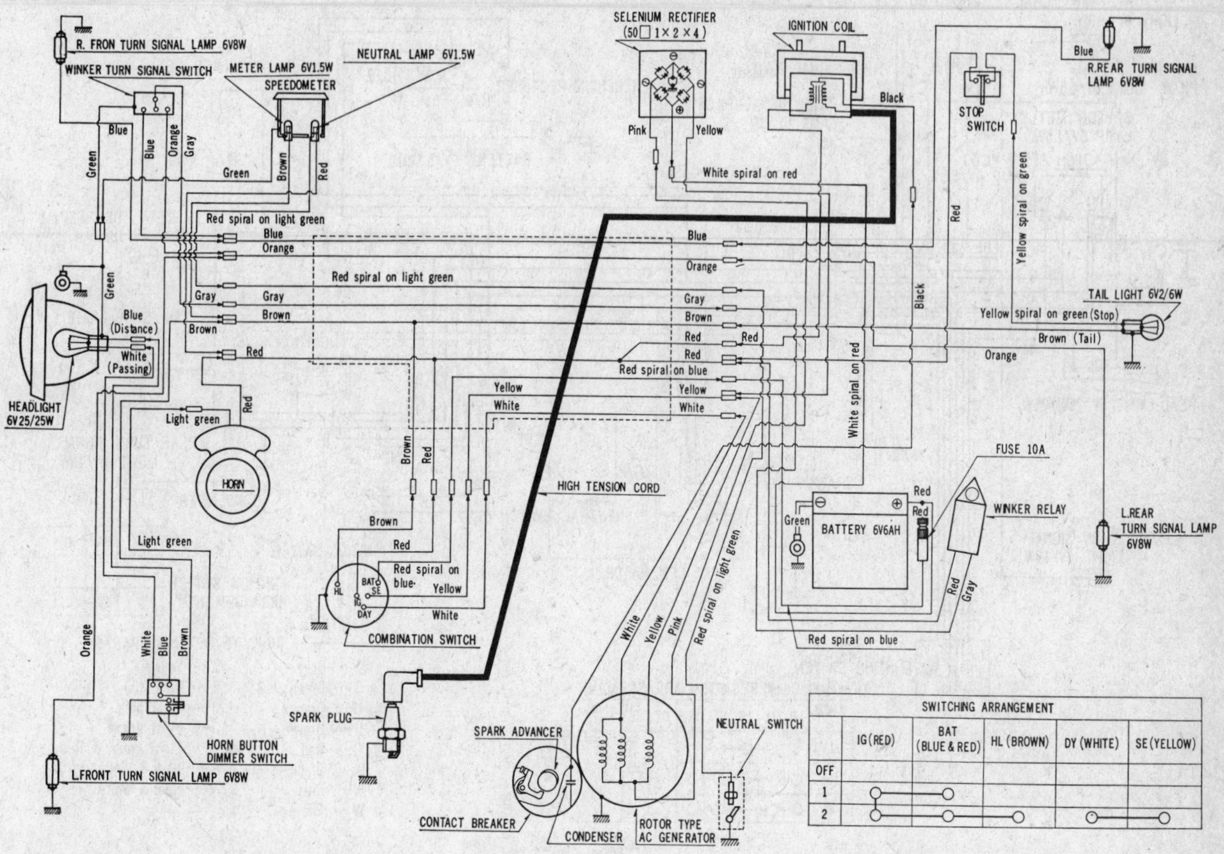

SWITCHING ARRANGEMENT					
	IG (RED)	BAT (BLUE & RED)	HL (BROWN)	DY (WHITE)	SE (YELLOW)
OFF					
1	○	○			
2	○	○	○	○	○

CD90

G······Green
R······Red
B······Brown
O······Orange
P······Pink
GR······Gray

W······White
Y······Yellow
BL······Blue
LG······Light green
LBL······Light blue

LG/R······Light green with red spiral tracer
W/Y······White with yellow spiral tracer
B/R······Brown with red spiral tracer
G/Y······Green with yellow spiral tracer
R/W······Red with white spiral tracer
BL/R······Blue with red spiral tracer
BL/Y······Blue with yellow spiral tracer

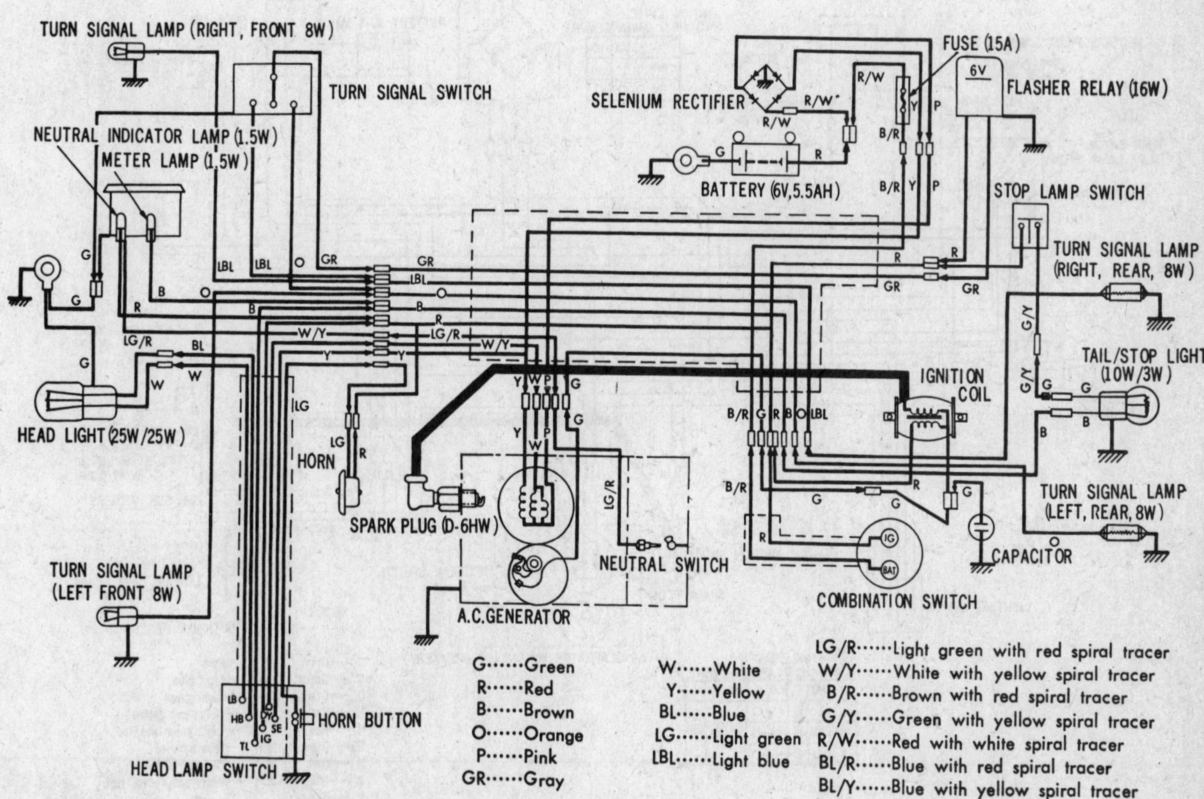

C90

WIRING DIAGRAMS

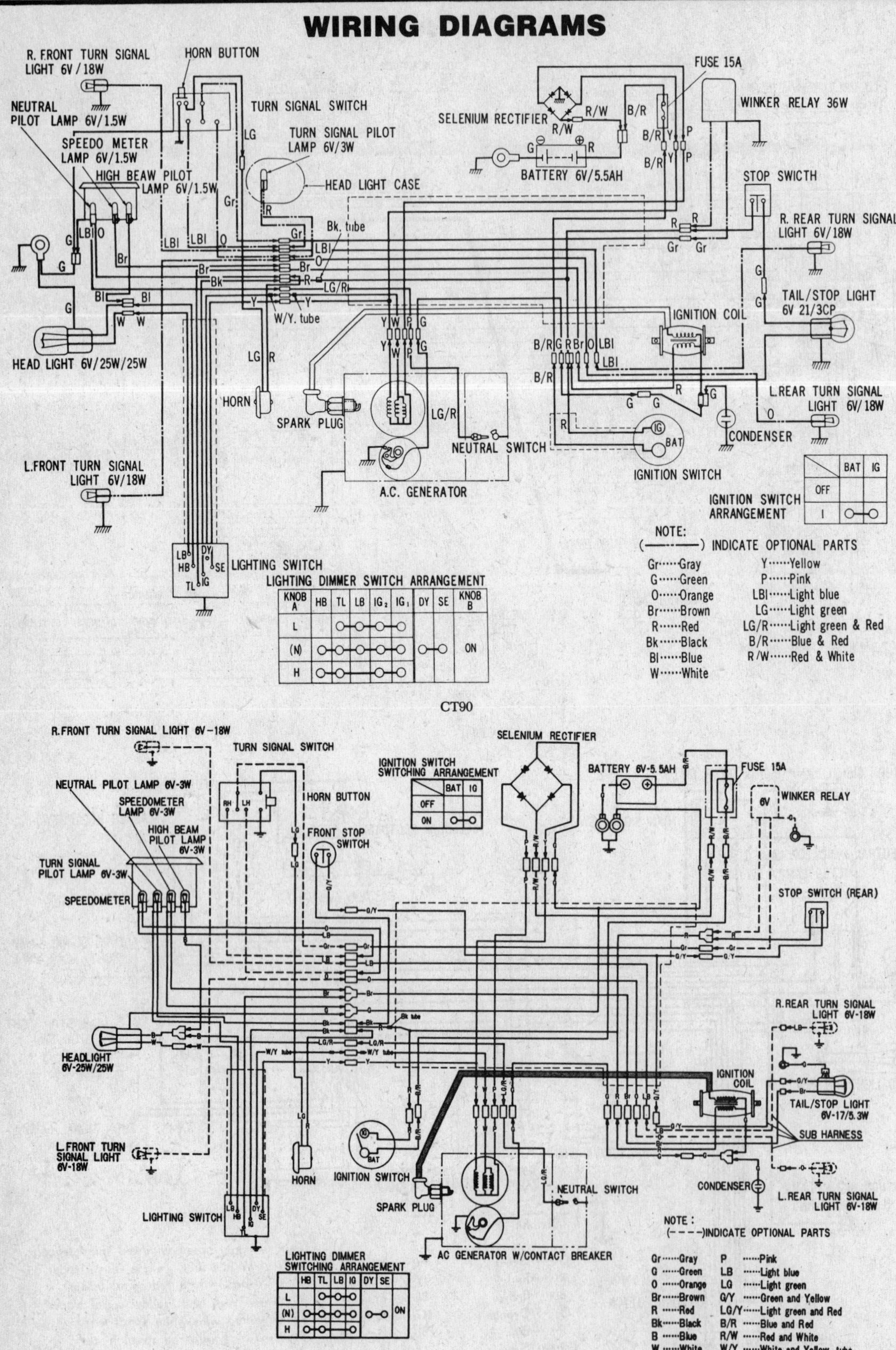

CT90 (from Frame No. 000001A)

WIRING DIAGRAMS

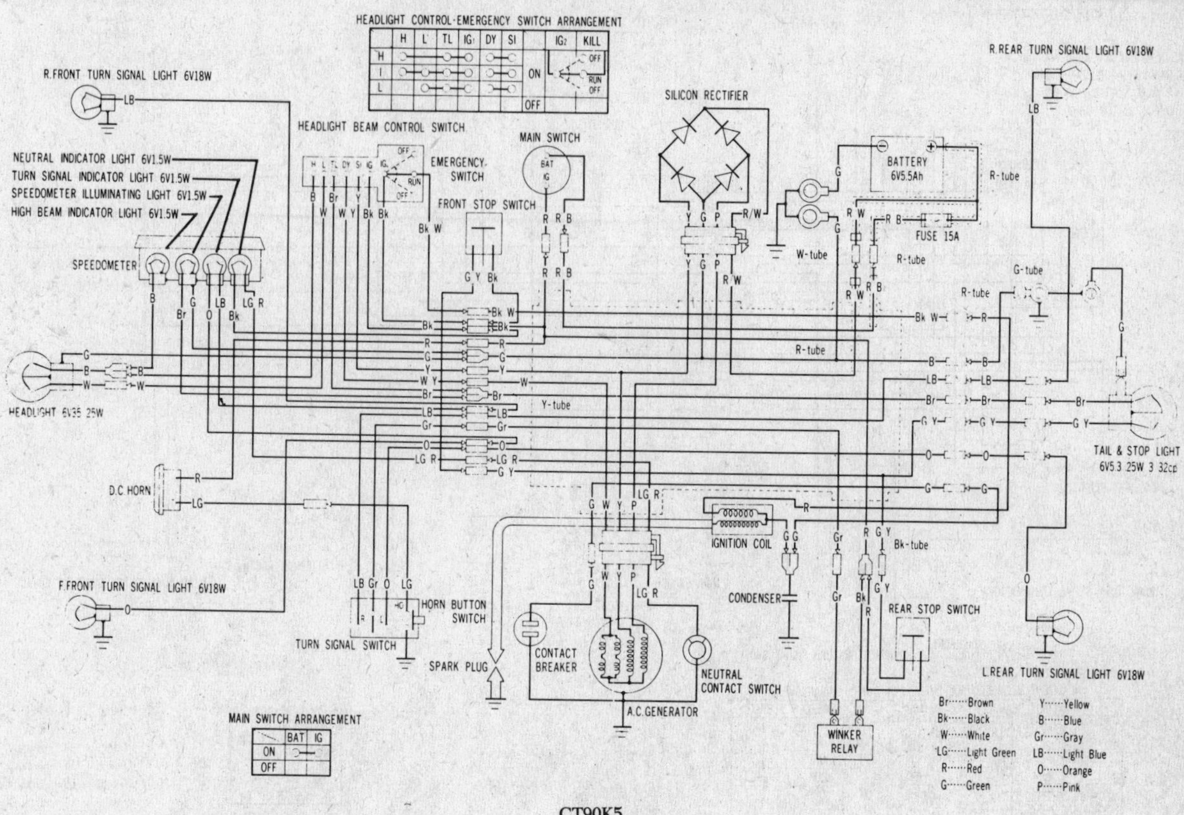

CT90K5

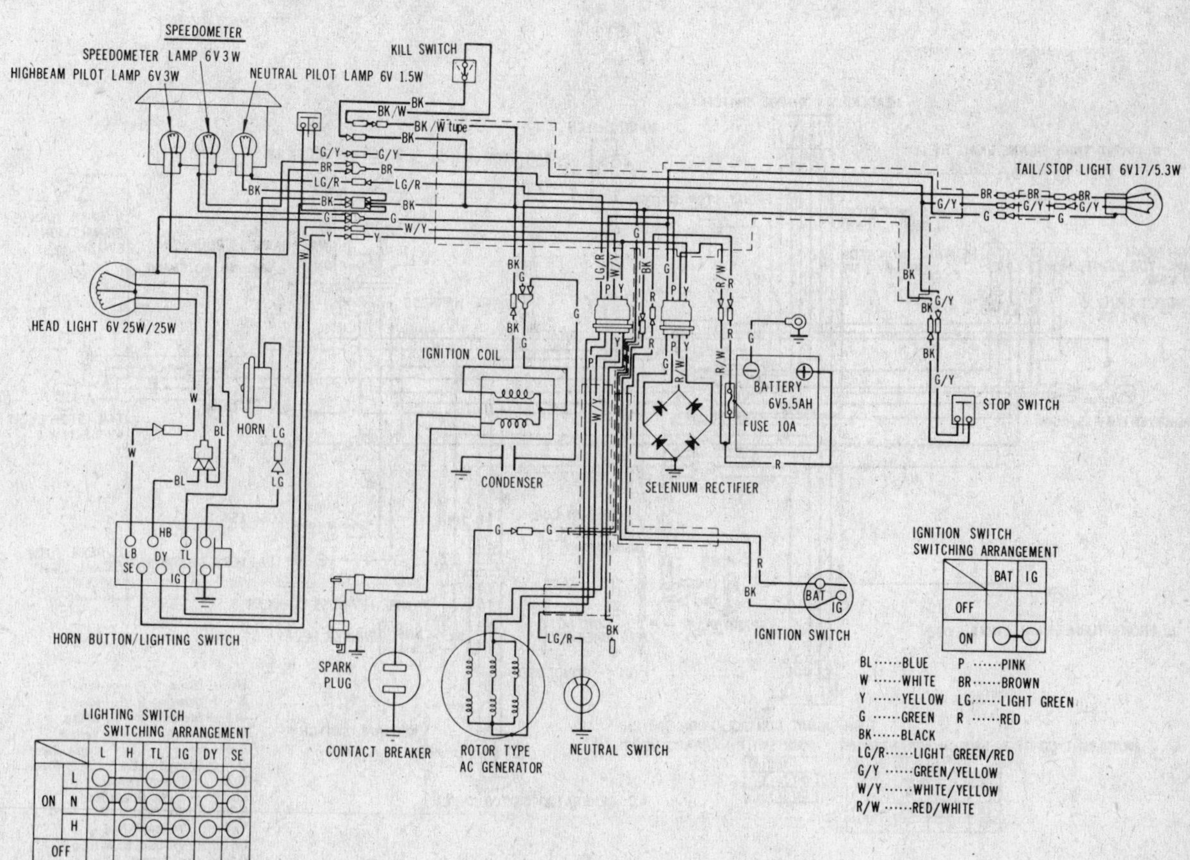

SL90

WIRING DIAGRAMS

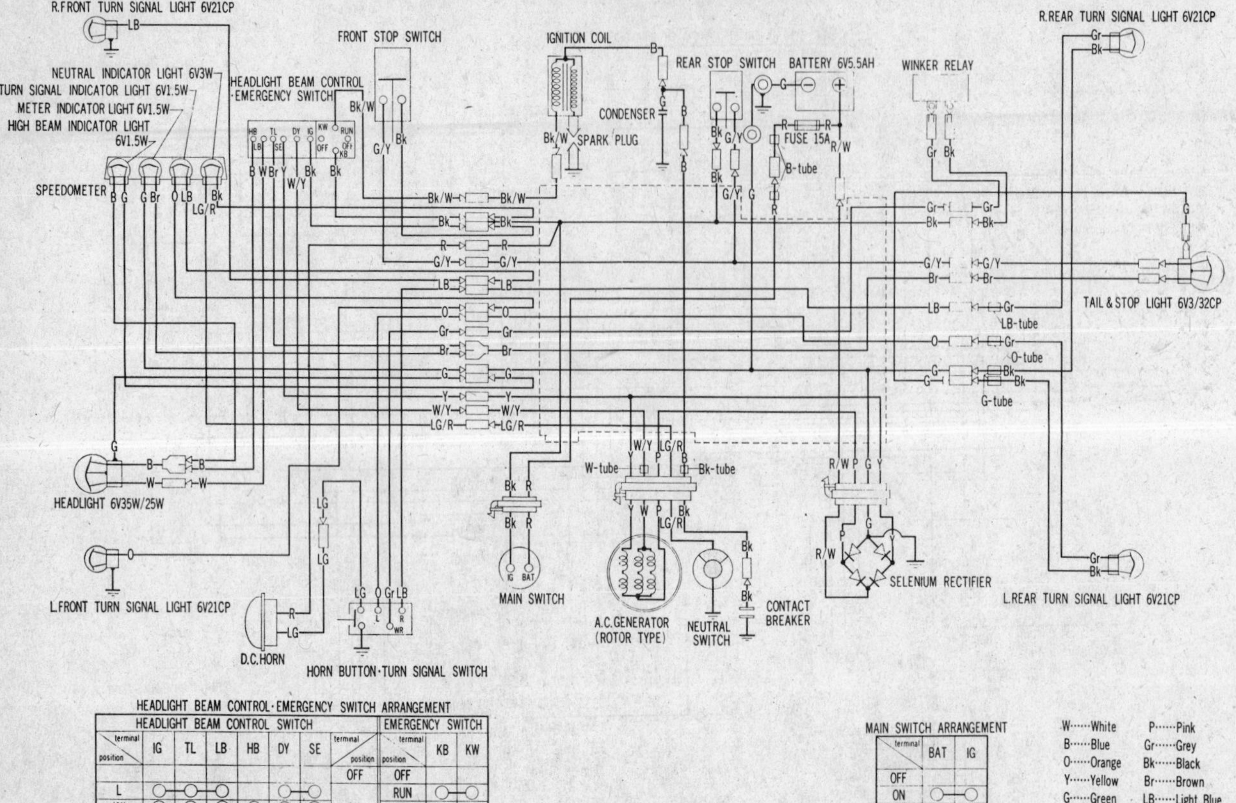

ST90

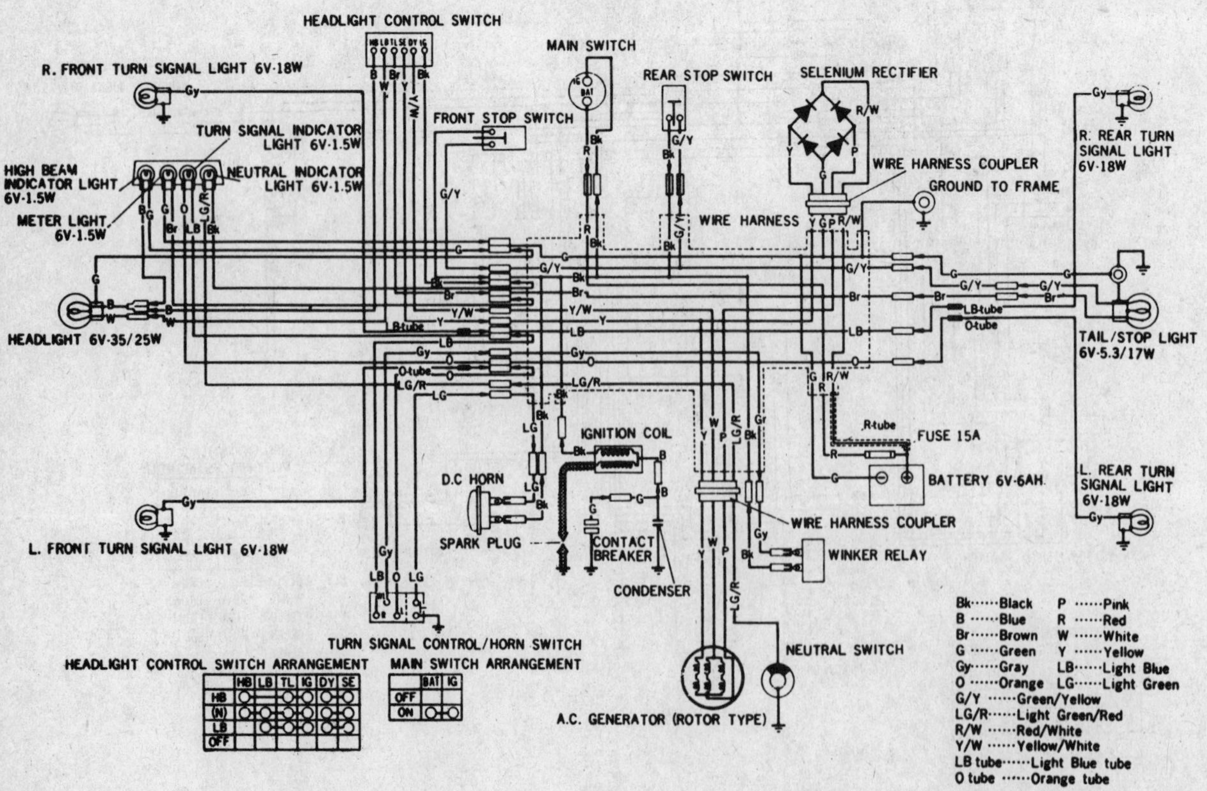

CB100

WIRING DIAGRAMS

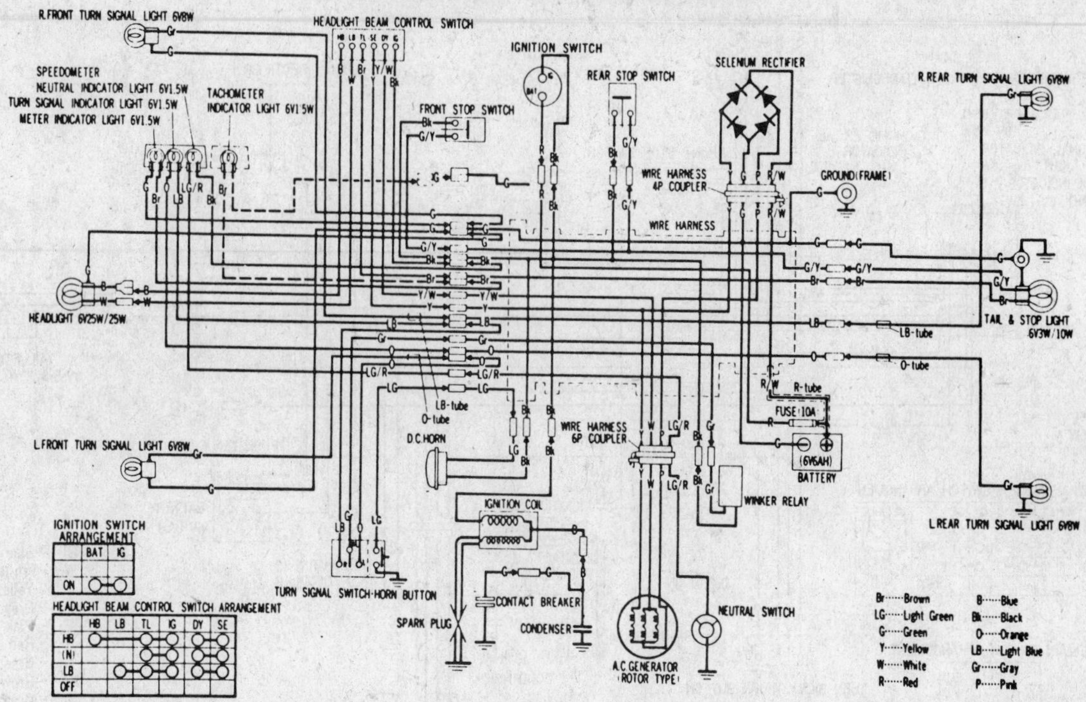

CB100K3

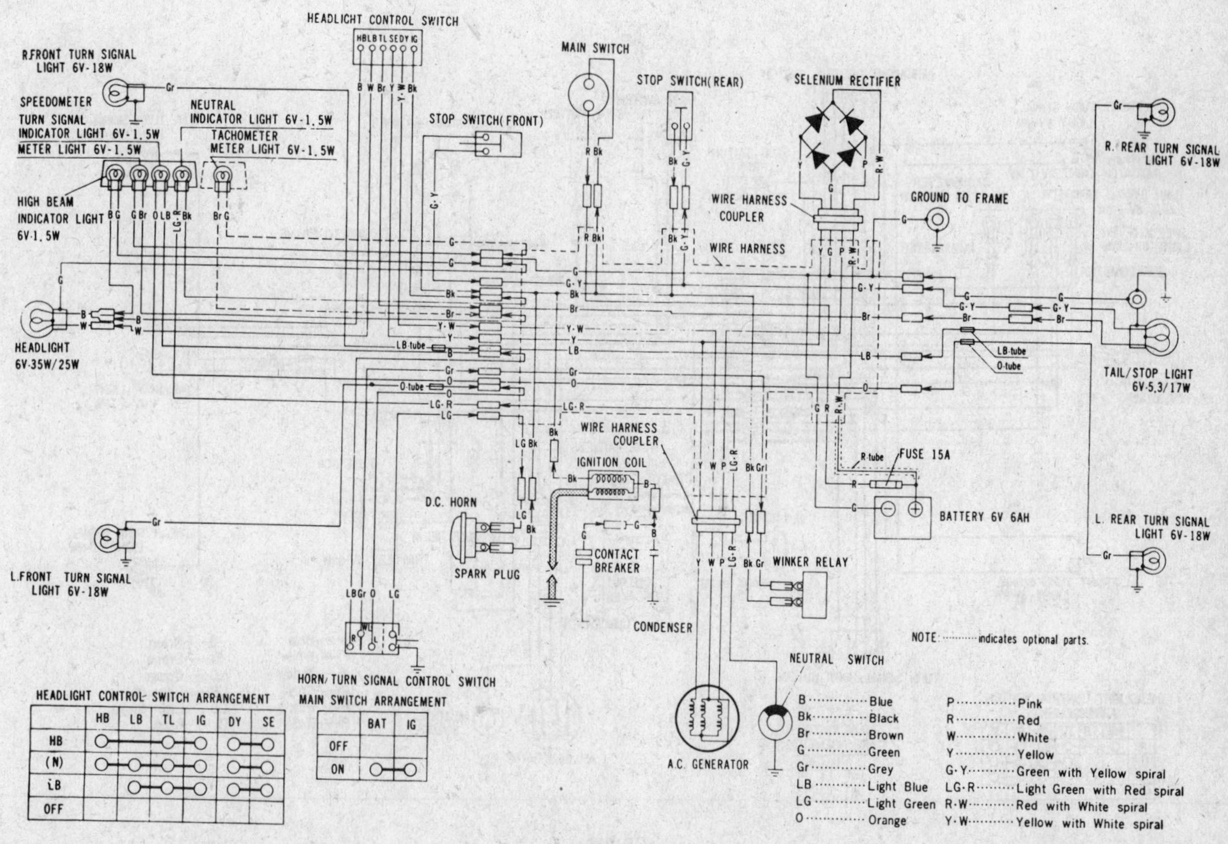

CL100/CL100S

WIRING DIAGRAMS

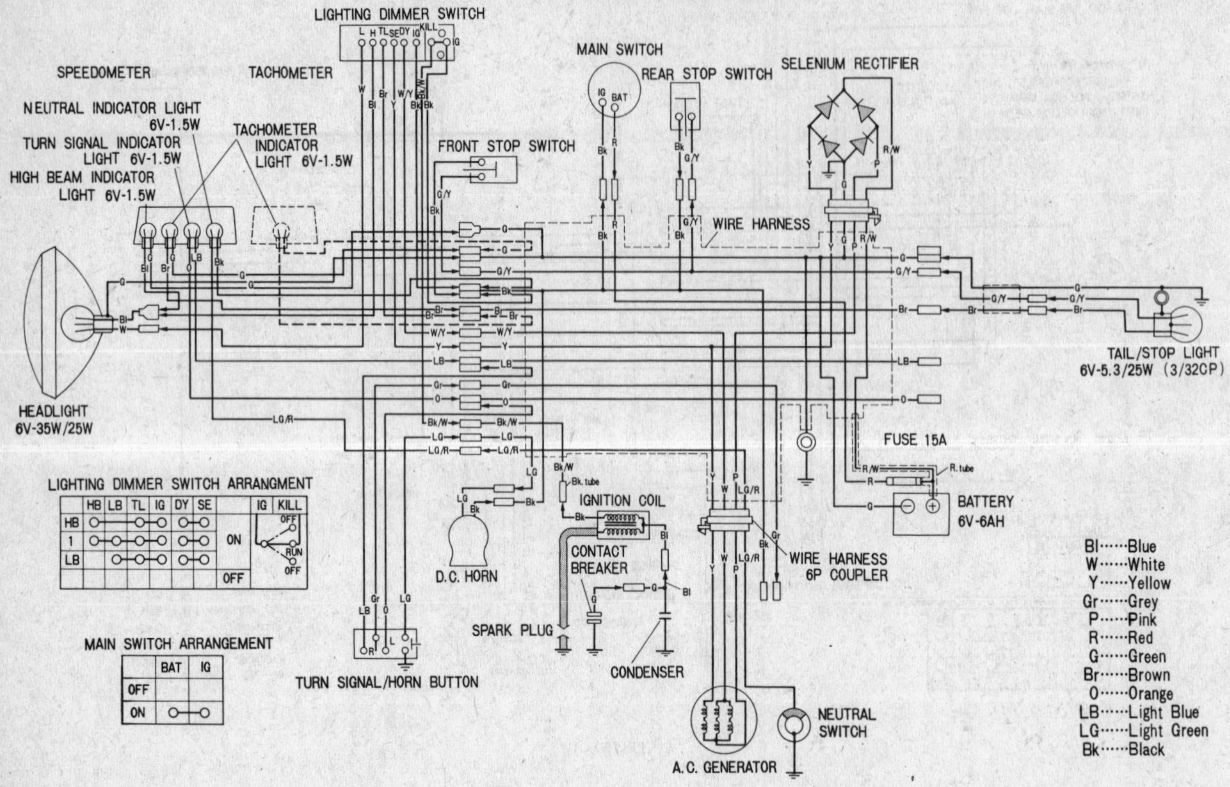

SL100

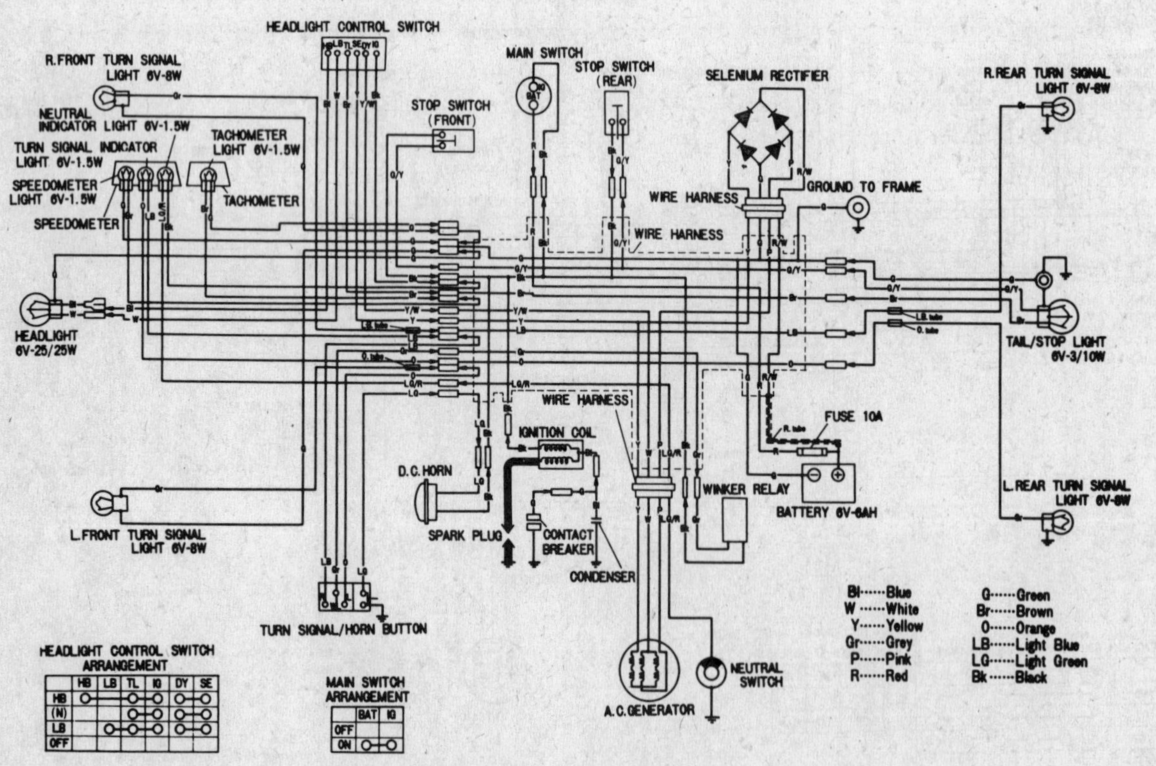

CB125S

WIRING DIAGRAMS

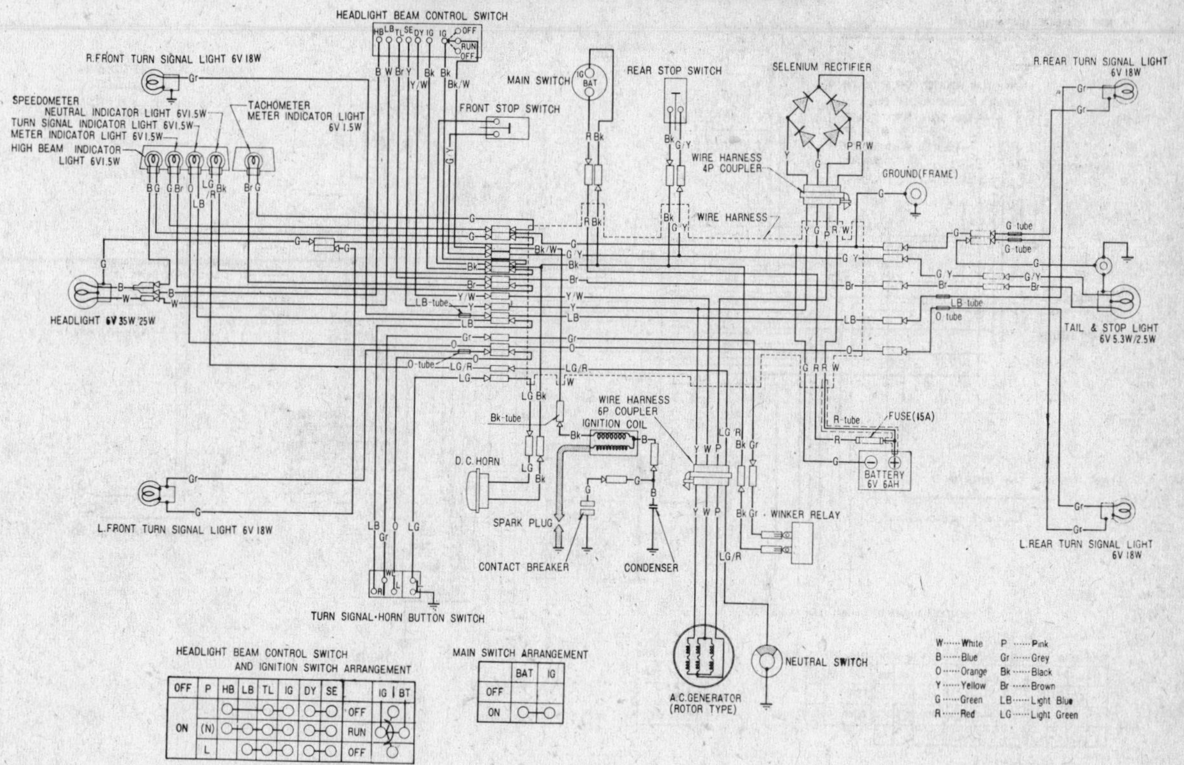

CB125S1

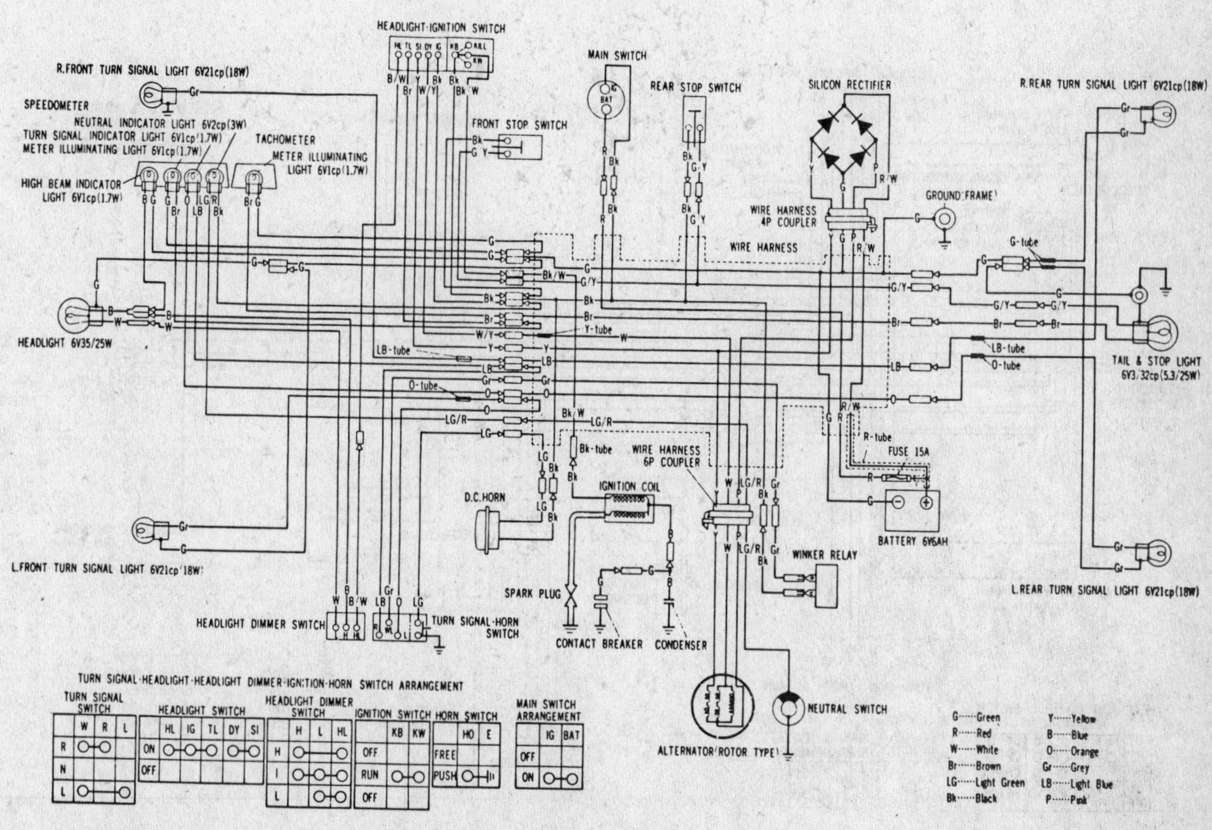

CB12552

WIRING DIAGRAMS

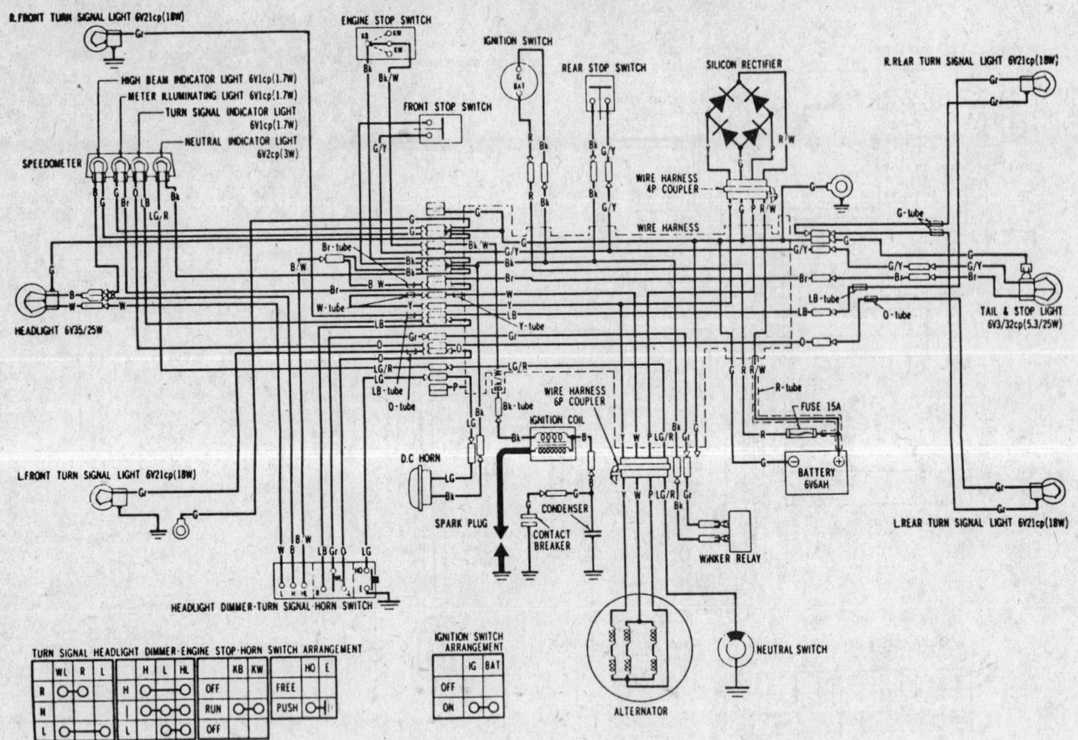

CB125S(76)

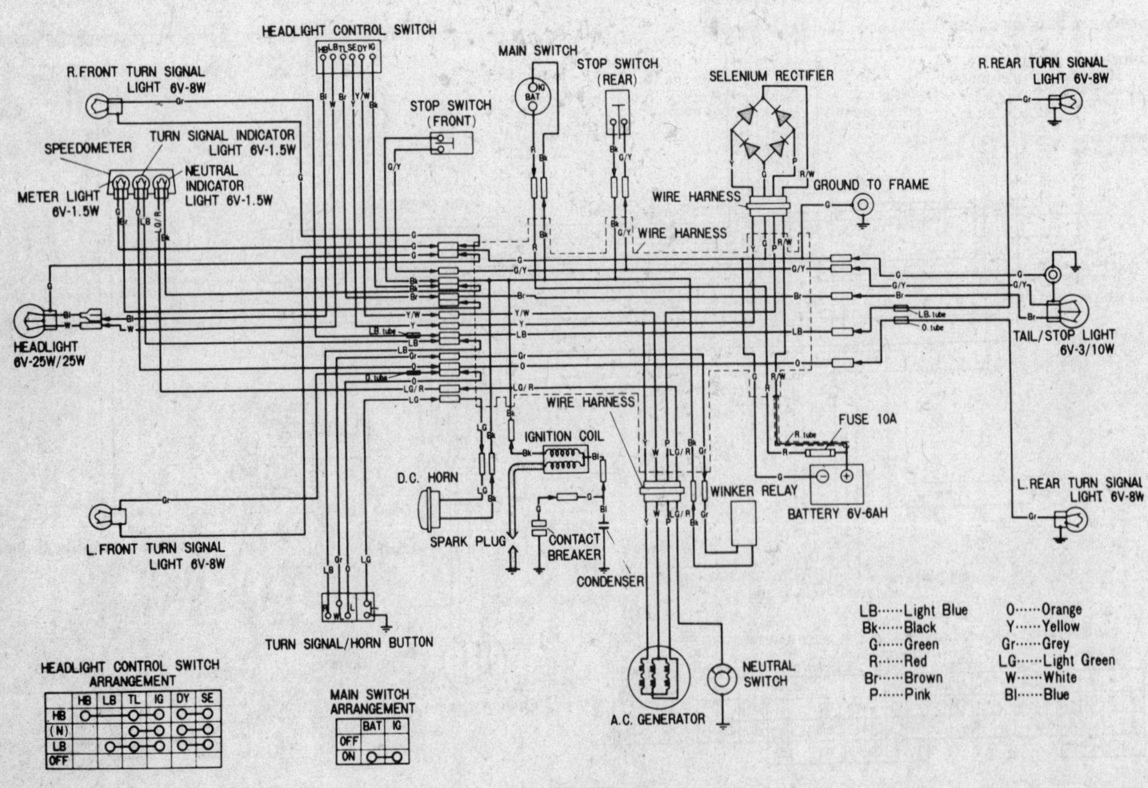

CD125S

WIRING DIAGRAMS

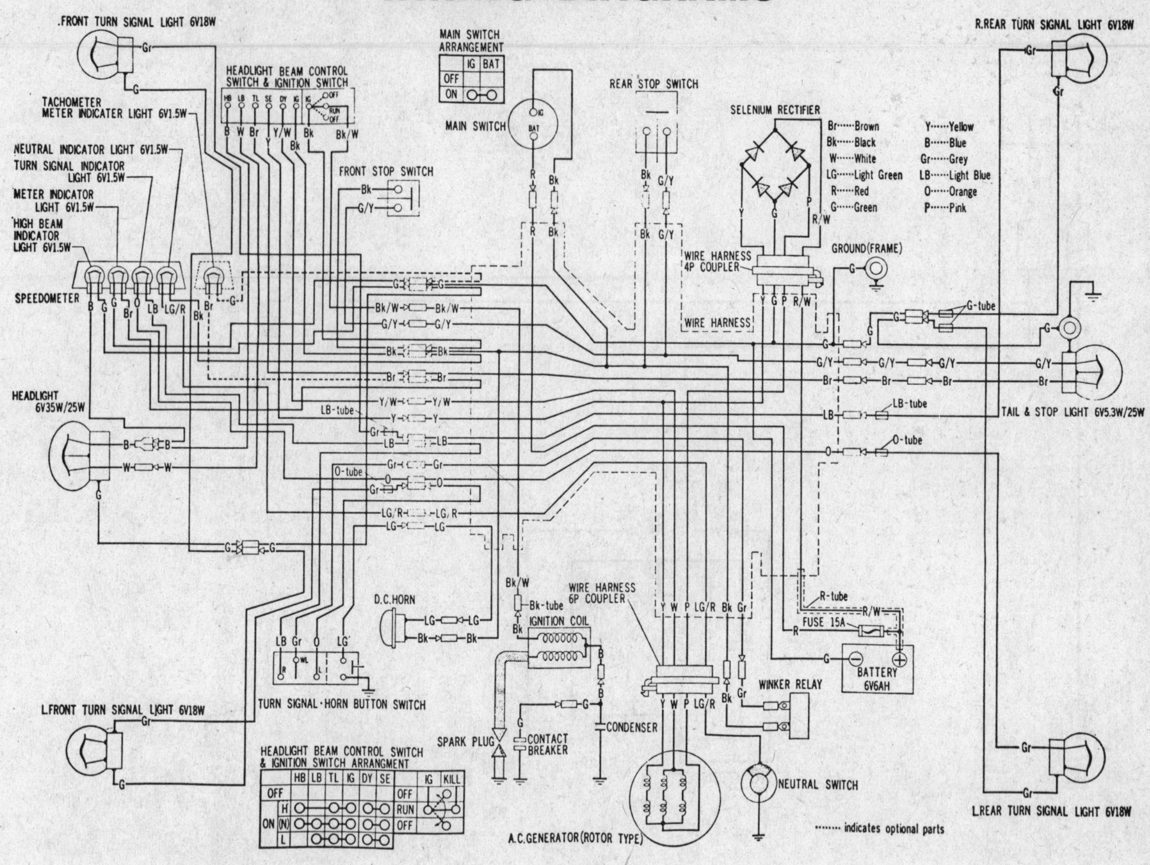

CL125S

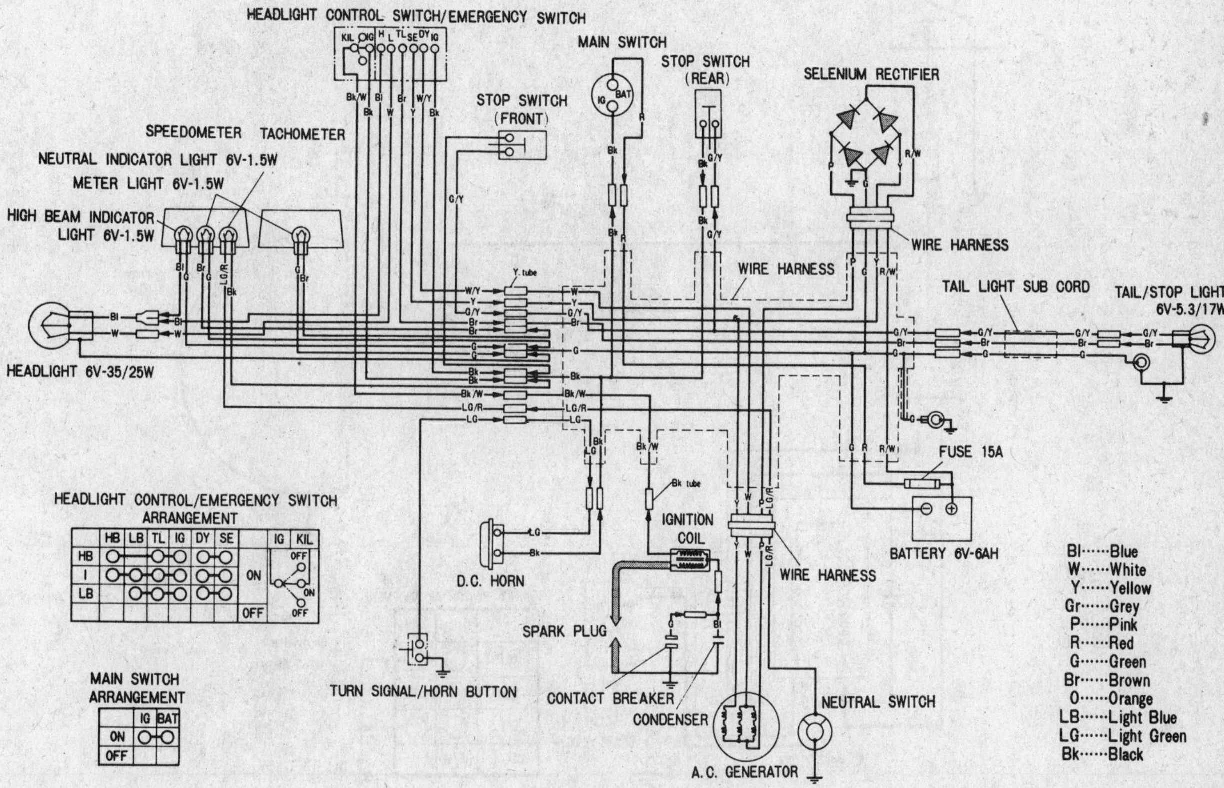

SL125

WIRING DIAGRAMS

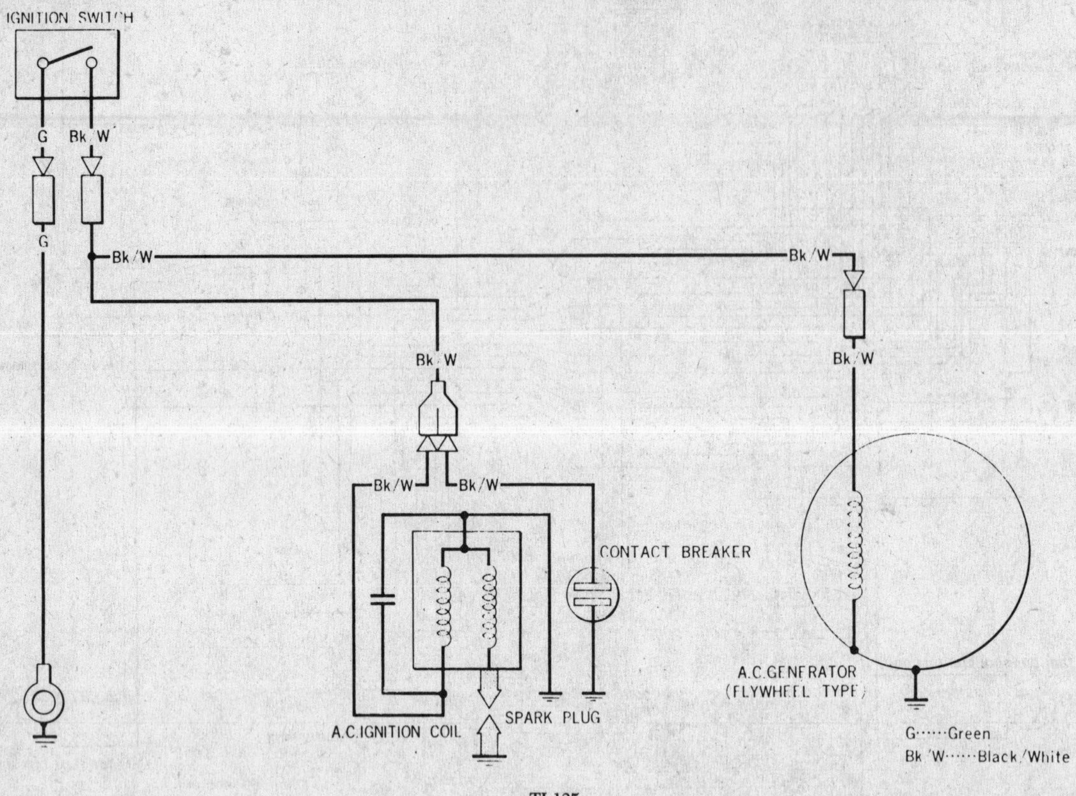

TL125

IGNITION SWITCH

Gr

Gr

Bk/W

Bk/W

Bk/W

Bk/W

Bk/W

A.C.GENERATOR (FLYWHEEL TYPE)

CONTACT BREAKER

AC IGNITION COIL

SPARK PLUG

IGNITION SWITCH ARRANGEMENT

	IG	E
OFF		
RUN		
OFF		
COLOR	Bk/W	

Gr······Grey
Bk······Black
W······White

TL125K2

WIRING DIAGRAMS

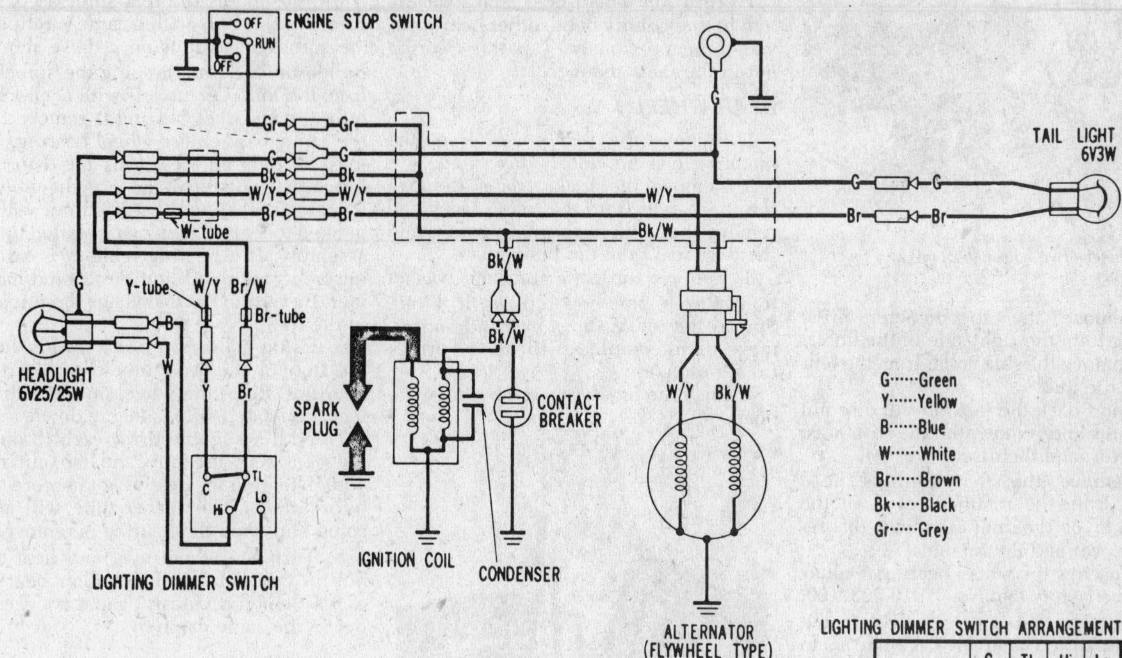

TL125(76)

LIGHTING DIMMER SWITCH ARRANGEMENT

		C	TL	Hi	Lo
OFF					
ON	Hi	O	O	O	
	Lo	O	O	—	O

CHASSIS

WHEELS

Removal and Installation

FRONT WHEEL

1. Support the front wheel off the ground by placing a crate or another suitable object beneath the engine.

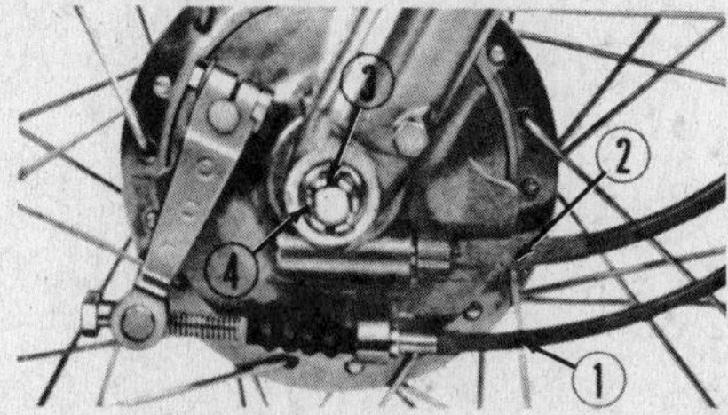

To remove the front wheel disconnect the brake cable (1), speedometer cable (2), and remove the cotter pin (3), and the axle nut (4)

2. Disconnect the front brake cable (drum brakes) and the speedometer cable at the front wheel.
3. Remove the front axle nut and pull out the axle. The wheel is now free to be removed.
4. Remove the front brake assembly (drum brakes) by pulling the front brake plate from the hub.
5. Installation is in the reverse order of removal. Be sure to locate the tab on the left fork leg into the slot in the brake plate.

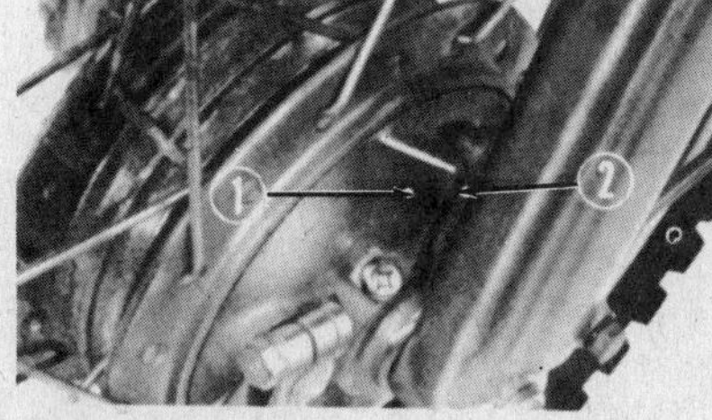

When installing the front wheel, the tab (2) must be fitted into the slot (1)

REAR WHEEL

1. Place the motorcycle on its center stand, or find some way to block the rear wheel up so that it can spin freely.
2. Remove the cotter pin, securing nut, lockwasher, and flat washer from the brake anchor at the brake plate.
3. Remove the cotter pin and axle nut from the left-side of the axle.
4. Remove the rear brake adjusting nut from the end of the brake cable and disconnect the cable from the brake lever.
5. Remove the masterlink from the drive chain. Place the masterlink on the end of the chain for safekeeping.
6. Pull the axle out from the right-side and remove the wheel assembly from the swing arm.

NOTE: *Place the wheel spacers on the axle in the order that they are removed, and screw the axle nut on the axle for safekeeping.*

7. To install the wheel:
Hold the wheel in place and slip the axle in place from the right-side. Be sure that the spacers are in their correct locations. Place both ends of the chain on the rear sprocket and install the masterlink with the open end of the spring clip facing opposite the direction of rotation.
8. Engage the brake anchor with the brake plate and secure with the flat washer, lockwasher, and the nut. Install a new cotter pin in the brake anchor bolt.
9. Turn the axle nut on finger-tight. Adjust the drive chain slack; the slack, measured midway between the sprockets, should be about ¾ in.
10. Slip the brake cable through the fitting in the brake lever and install the adjusting nut. Adjust the cable so that the brake pedal has 1 in. free-play before the brake shoes contact the drum.
11. Tighten the axle nut to the proper torque, which can be found in the "Chassis Torque Specifications" chart at the end of this section. Then back the nut off until a slot in the axle nut is lined up with a hole in the axle. Secure the axle nut in place with a new cotter pin.

Wheel Disassembly

FRONT WHEEL

Disc Brake

1. Remove the front wheel from the motorcycle as described previously.

CAUTION: *Do not operate the brake lever when the front wheel is removed. To do so will advance the ratchet adjuster to a point where the disc will not fit between the pads when the wheel is installed. If this should happen, the caliper will have to be disassembled and the adjusting screw in the brake arm loosened. Refer to the "Front Disc Brake" following.*

Speedometer drive housing (1), retainer cover (2), and retainer (3)

2. Remove the speedometer drive housing from the right-side of the hub.

3. Remove the side collar from the left-side of the hub.

4. Bend back the tabs on the disc nut lockplates and remove the the disc nuts, lockplates, and the disc.

5. Remove the four phillips head screws from the retainer cover on the right-side of the hub. Remove the retainer cover and the retainer.

6. Unscrew the wheel bearing retainer using the factory tool No. 07910-3230100. If the factory tool is not available use a blunt punch and hammer. Take care not to distort the retainer or damage the threads in the hub. Replace the oil seal in the retainer if the lips are damaged.

7. To remove the wheel bearings use a blunt punch and hammer. Remove the bearing in the left-side of the hub first. Reach through the center of the hub and tap the inside of the bearing evenly around its circumference to remove it. Be sure that the bearing does not become cocked to one side on removal. After the first bearing has been removed, remove the spacer tube from the center of the hub. Remove the second bearing using a block of wood large enough to cover the entire bearing. If the bearings resist removal, gently heat the bearing bosses in the hub with a propane torch and then try to tap them out.

Drum Brake

1. Remove the front wheel from the motorcycle as previously described.

2. Remove the brake plate. Remove the cotter pin and washer from the upper brake pivot (if fitted). Spread the brake shoes by hand until they will clear the brake cam, remove the shoes complete with the brake springs from the plate.

3. Remove the pinch-bolt from the brake lever and remove the lever, return spring, flat washer, and dust seal. Push the brake cam out of the brake plate.

4. Remove the wheel spacer from the right-side of the hub. Remove the oil seals from the right-side of the hub and the inside of the brake plate. These seals can be pried out with a hooked tool as new seals should always be used on reassembly. However take care not to score the hub surface.

5. Using a propane torch, gently heat the area around one of the bearings. Turn the wheel assembly over, placing it on a bench so that the heated side faces down.

6. With a suitable drift and hammer, tap out the bearing. The spacer tube will also come out after the bearing is removed.

7. Turn the wheel over, and heat the hub in the vicinity of the other bearing as was done previously. Tap this bearing out in the same manner.

REAR WHEEL

1. Remove the rear wheel from the motorcycle as previously described.

2. Remove the brake plate. Remove the pinch-bolt from the brake lever and remove the brake lever, flat washer, and the dust seal from the brake plate.

3. Remove the cotter pin and washer from the upper brake pivot if fitted. Spread the brake shoes by hand and remove them complete with their springs from the plate.

4. Push the brake cam out of the brake plate.

Removing the sprocket circlip

5. To service the wheel bearings the rear sprocket will have to be removed. On most models the rear sprocket is secured to the hub with a large circlip. If the sprocket has nuts on it these should be loosened before tapping the sprocket from the hub. On models with a sprocket hub, the sprocket bearing is removed in the same manner as a wheel bearing. On most models an oil seal is fitted to the hub on the outside of the left wheel bearing; this seal should be pried out with a hooked tool and a new one installed upon assembly. If a bearing retainer is fitted, unscrew it with a blunt punch and hammer. Be careful not to damage the threads in the hub.

6. Using a propane torch gently heat the hub in the area around one of the bearings. Place the wheel on a bench so that the heated side is facing down.

7. With a suitable drift reach through the center of the hub and tap out the wheel bearing, be careful not to score the hub surface. The spacer tube will also come out when the bearing is removed.

8. Turn the wheel over and heat the hub in the vicinity of the other bearing as was done previously. Tap this bearing out in the same manner.

Inspection

ALL MODELS

Brakes

1. Clean all parts thoroughly in a suitable solvent, making a special effort to remove the dust and built-up dirt from the brake plate.

2. Inspect the shoes for wear. There should be at least 2.0 mm (0.08 in.) of lin-

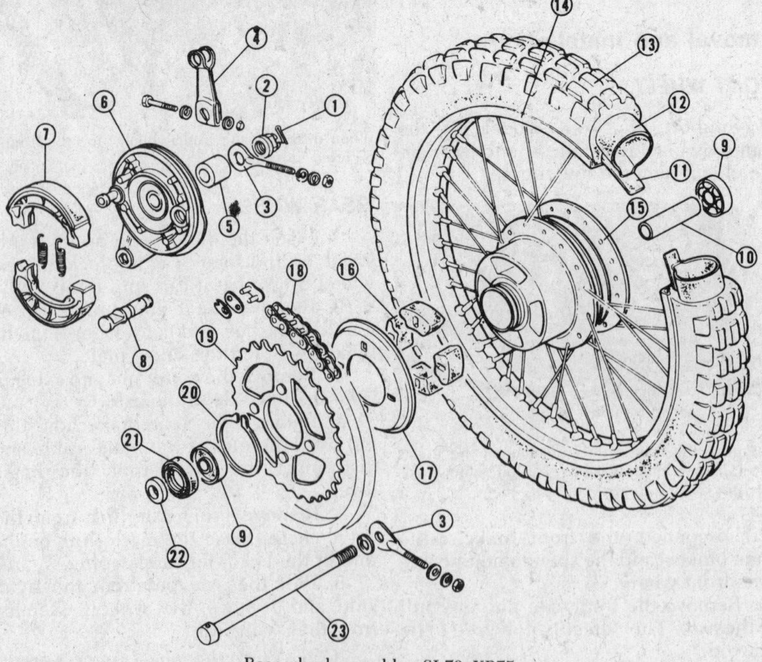
Rear wheel assembly—SL70, XR75

1. Cotter pin
2. Axle nut
3. Chain adjuster
4. Brake lever
5. Axle spacer
6. Brake plate
7. Brake shoe
8. Brake cam
9. Wheel bearing
10. Bearing spacer
11. Rim band
12. Tube
13. Tire
14. Rim
15. Hub
16. Rubber damper
17. Damper cover
18. Chain
19. Rear sprocket
20. Circlip
21. Oil seal
22. Axle spacer
23. Axle

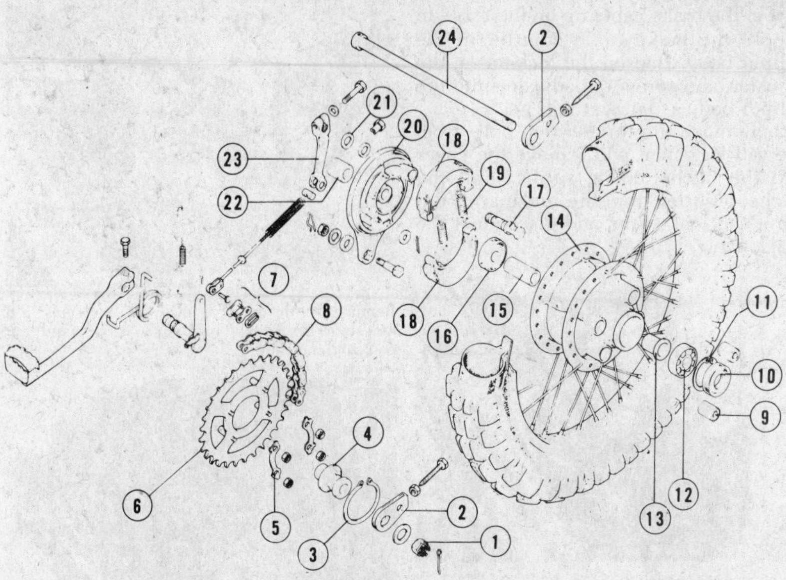

Rear wheel assembly—100, 125 cc models

1. Axle nut
2. Chain adjuster
3. Snap-ring
4. Spacer
5. Lockwasher
6. Sprocket
7. Masterlink
8. Chain
9. Rubber damper
10. Oil seal
11. Snap-ring
12. Wheel bearing
13. Axle spacer
14. Hub
15. Bearing spacer
16. Wheel bearing
17. Brake cam
18. Brake shoe
19. Brake return spring
20. Brake plate
21. Brake cam dust seal
22. Spacer
23. Brake lever
24. Axle

ing material left (measured at the lining's thinnest point) or the shoes must be replaced.

3. Inspect the linings for scoring or grooves. These may be caused by particles of dirt which enter the drum. If badly scored, the shoes should be replaced and the drum inspected closely for the same type of damage.

Be sure that the linings are free of any oil or grease. Impregnated linings must be replaced.

4. If the linings are in usable condition, rough up the surface with coarse sandpaper. Then, clean the linings with alcohol, or lacquer thinner. Clean the brake drum with the same solvent.

5. Check that the brake lever pinch-bolt is not bent. Replace it if this has occurred. Replace the brake lever if the splines are worn or broken.

6. Inspect the splines on the brake cam. These should be in good condition. The cam must rotate freely in the brake plate passage. If it does not do so, use a fine grade of sandpaper on both the cam and the surface of the passage.

7. Check the condition of the brake springs. Replace them if weakened, rusted, or deformed.

8. Check the brake plate for cracks or fractures.

Brake Drums

1. Upon disassembly of the hub, inspect the brake drum surface for condition. The drums must be clean and free of score marks or rust.

2. Rust can be removed from the drum surface with sandpaper. Polish the surface until it is shiny, then clean it thoroughly.

3. Alcohol or lacquer thinner can be used to remove dirt or deposits from the drum.

4. The drum should be checked for concentricity. An out-of-round condition is usually noticeable as an on-off-on feeling when the brake is applied while riding. With the wheel assembly mounted on the machine, spin the wheel while applying the brake very lightly. The rubbing noise of the brake against the drum should be heard for the entire revolution of the wheel.

5. An out-of-round condition and most scoring can be removed by having the drum turned on a lathe. This operation should be entrusted to a qualified specialist with the proper equipment. Usually, the tire and wheel bearings will have to be removed so that the wheel can be chucked in the lathe. If the rim needs to be trued, have this done before any work on the drum is performed, as the action of the spokes while truing the rim may further aggravate the drum warpage.

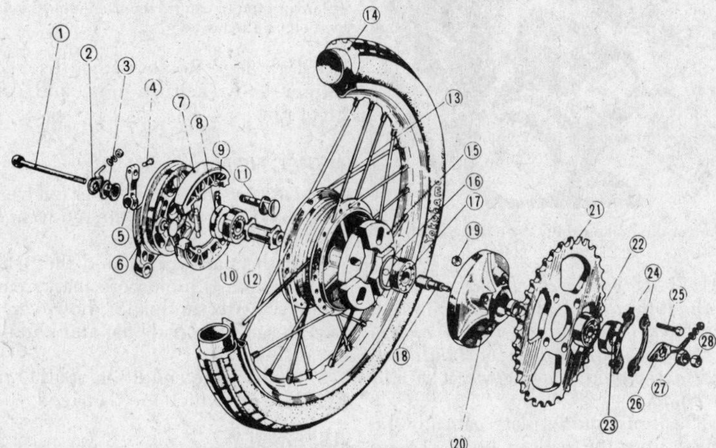

Rear wheel assembly—90 cc models

1. Axle
2. Chain adjuster
3. Side collar
4. Bolt
5. Brake lever
6. Brake plate
7. Brake shoe
8. Oil seal
9. Brake spring
10. Wheel bearing (6301)
11. Brake cam
12. Bearing spacer tube
13. Hub
14. Tire
15. Rubber dampers
16. O-ring
17. Wheel bearing (6301)
18. Axle sleeve
19. Nut
20. Sprocket hub
21. Rear sprocket
22. Hub bearing (6203Z)
23. Oil seal
24. Lockplate
25. Sprocket bolt
26. Chain adjuster
27. Axle sleeve nut
28. Axle nut

Cushion Hub

When the sprocket and the drive flange are removed, check the condition of the rubber dampers in the hub. Replace them if they are worn, cracked, or hardened. The dampers must not allow the drive flange to move more than ½ in. in the hub. This reading is taken by placing the flange in the hub and noting the total movement of the rim of the flange relative to the rim of the hub in the plane of wheel rotation. If movement exceeds ½ in., the dampers should be replaced.

Wheel Bearings

1. Clean the bearings, and spacer tube in a suitable solvent, removing all of the old grease. Clean out the hub as well.

2. Check the bearing bosses in the hub for scuffs, cracks, or distortion. If they are in any way damaged, the hub must be replaced.

3. Check the condition of the spacer tube, and replace if damaged.

4. Bearing condition is very important. Check the balls themselves for pitting, wear, or rust.

5. Apply a few drops of light oil to the bearing and spin it. The bearing must rotate smoothly and freely. Any roughness or binding in rotation will necessitate new bearings.

6. Place the bearing on a flat surface. Place your fingers on the outer bearing race to hold it steady. Attempt to move the inner race back and forth. In a good bearing, the race will spin, but not move in any other direction. If it does, the bearing must be replaced.

7. Note that the bearings must be replaced in pairs.

Wheel Assembly

ALL MODELS

Assembly is in the reverse order of disassembly; however, note the following points:

1. Obtain a good grade of wheel bearing grease to lubricate the wheel bearings.

2. Pack the wheel bearings until they are completely filled.

3. Drive one of the bearings into its seat. Put a quantity of wheel bearing grease into the hub. Install the retainer if so equipped. Install the spacer tube and drive the other bearing into its seat. The sealed surface of the bearing must face the outside of the hub, where applicable.

Bearings should be installed with a block of hardwood as a drift. Do not strike the inner race of the bearing when installing it. Tap around the outer race until the bearing is straight in the hub, then drive it straight in.

NOTE: *When a bearing retainer is fitted, the bearing with the retainer should be installed first. Then install and tighten the retainer, spacer tube, and the other bearing.*

4. Replace all of the oil seals with new ones. Like the bearings, the seals should be pressed straight in.

5. Coat the surface of the brake cam with chassis grease before installing it into the brake plate.

6. Lubricate the brake shoe pivot points with chassis grease. Take care not to allow any grease to come into contact with the surface of the brake shoes or drums.

7. Line up the slots in the speedometer gear with the slots in the wheel hub.

8. Install the brake lever on the brake cam so that the punch marks on the brake lever and the brake cam are lined up.

When installing the brake levers, note that the punch mark on the lever (1) must align with that on the brake cam (2)

Front Disc Brake

DISASSEMBLY

1. Slide the rubber boot on the lower part of the brake cable up on the cable to expose the brake cable adjuster in the caliper body. Loosen the locknut on the adjuster, and screw the adjuster into the caliper body as far as it will go.

2. Remove the three 6 mm bolts from the caliper cover, and remove the cover and the ratchet fixing spring. Pull the ratchet adjuster from the brake arm. Remove the brake arm, and disconnect the brake cable.

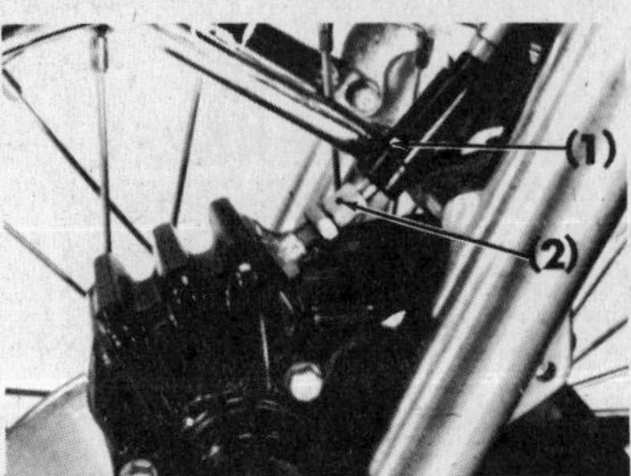

Slide the rubber boot (1) up to expose the cable adjuster (2)

Remove the caliper cover bolts (2), and remove the cover from the caliper body (1)

Disconnect the brake cable (1) from the brake arm (2)

CAUTION: *Cover the brake arm in a clean cloth or a plastic bag to prevent dirt from entering the inside of the mechanism. The brake arm should not be disassembled; if defective, it should be replaced.*

3. The thrust guide plate can now be removed from the caliper body. To remove the disc pads, screw one of the caliper cover bolts (6 mm) into the threaded hole in the back of pad A (the pad to the outside of the disc). Using the bolt, pull the pad out of the caliper. Remove the front wheel as described at the beginning of this section. Pad B (pad to the inside of the disc) can be removed by pushing on the lockpin on the back of the caliper body. Remove the pad from the left-side of the caliper.

4. Remove the two 6 mm and one 8 mm caliper mounting bolts from the left fork leg. Remove the disc cover, caliper body, caliper joint, and caliper pivot pin.

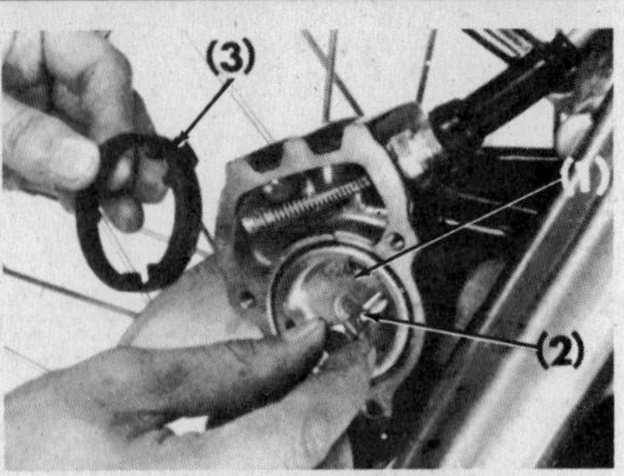

Remove the thrust guide plate (3), and screw a 6 mm screw (2), into the back of pad A (1), to pull the pad from the caliper

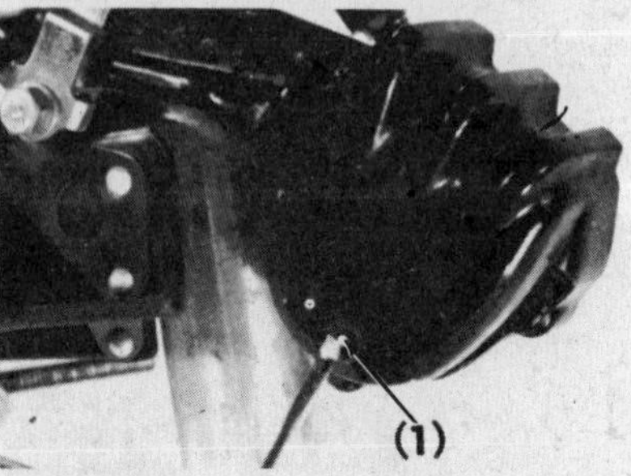

Push on the lockpin (1) to remove pad B from the caliper

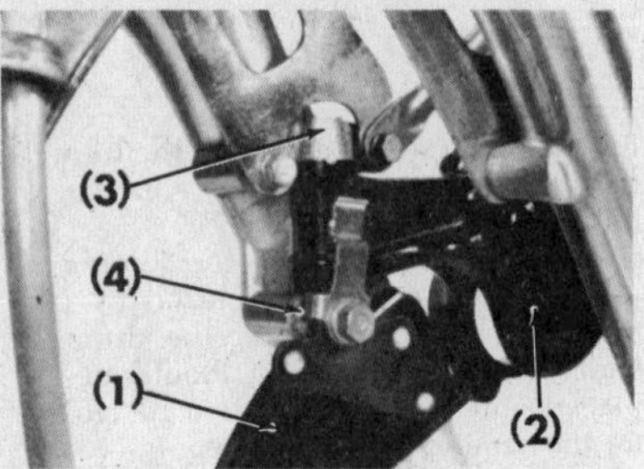

Disc cover (1), caliper (2), caliper joint (3), and caliper pivot pin (4), can be removed after the mounting bolts are removed

INSPECTION

1. Inspect the brake pads for wear. If either pad is worn past the red wear limit line, replace both pads.

2. If the pads are scored they should be replaced. Minor score marks can be removed with sandpaper; however, take care to sand the pads flat and parallel to the disc surface.

3. Inspect the condition of all O-rings. Replace any which are damaged.

ASSEMBLY

1. Install an O-ring on the caliper pivot pin and apply some chassis grease to the pin. Slip the pin through the caliper and install the remaining O-ring on the top of the pin. Slip the caliper joint over the end of the pin. Install the caliper assembly to the left fork leg, locating the disc cover to the lower (8 mm) mounting bolt. Be sure that the pivot pin is installed correctly and that the lockplate is in place on the lower mounting bolt.

2. Place a small amount of silicon grease (KS62M) on the back of pad B, and

Upon assembly be sure that the pivot pin (1), is installed correctly

install pad B into the right-side of the caliper, locating the lockpin through the hole in the back of the caliper.

3. Install the front wheel.

4. Place a new O-ring on pad A and coat the entire circumference of the pad with a thin layer of silicon grease (KS62M). Install the pad into the caliper aligning the punch marks on the pad and the caliper body as the pad is installed.

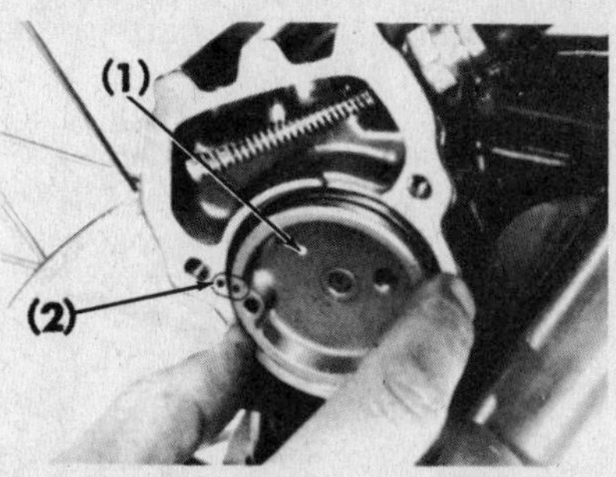

When installing pad A (1), be sure that the punch marks (2), on the pad and the caliper align

5. Install the thrust plate guide into the caliper. Connect the brake cable to the brake arm. With a small screwdriver, turn the adjusting screw in the center of the brake arm counterclockwise until resistance is felt. The adjusting screw should turn freely. Install the brake arm.

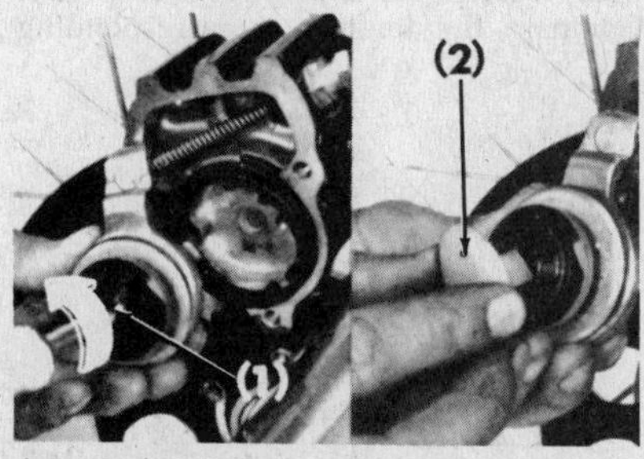

Turn the adjusting screw (1) counterclockwise until resistance is felt, then install the ratchet adjuster (2) into the brake arm

6. Install the ratchet adjuster, locating it into the slot in the adjusting screw. Install a new caliper cover gasket, the caliper cover, and ratchet fixing spring. Secure the cover with the three cover bolts.

7. Screw the adjusting bolt out of the caliper body all the way. Then screw in the adjuster until there is slack in the cable. From this position turn the adjuster out another 2 to 3 turns.

8. Operate the hand lever about 10 times. The lever should automatically adjust itself to the proper free-play of 20–30 mm (0.8–1.2 in.) measured at the tip of the lever.

9. After adjustment is correct, slip the rubber boot over the cable adjuster. Raise the front wheel off the ground and check that the wheel spins freely.

PAD REPLACEMENT

1. The procedures for removing and installing the pads for replacement are given under "Front Disc Brake—Disassembly" and "Assembly." However, Step 4 under "Disassembly," and Step 1 under "Assembly" can be omitted.

CABLE REPLACEMENT

1. Remove the cover from the left-side of the caliper. Screw the cable adjuster into the caliper body as far as possible. Remove the brake arm with the ratchet adjuster in place and disconnect the cable from the brake arm. Screw the adjuster out of the caliper body and remove the cable from the caliper.

2. Remove the rubber boot from the hand lever, disconnect the cable from the lever, and remove the cable.

3. Connect the new cable to the hand lever and replace the rubber boot.

4. Screw the cable adjuster on the new cable all of the way into the caliper body. Connect the cable end to the brake arm and install the brake arm into the caliper body. Install the caliper cover. Turn the cable adjuster out of the caliper until there is no slack in the cable and then turn the adjuster out another 2 to 3 turns.

5. Operate the hand lever about 10 times. The lever should automatically adjust itself to the proper free-play of 20–30 mm (0.8–1.2 in.), measured at the tip of the lever.

BRAKE DISC SERVICE

The brake disc normally requires no service of any kind. However, if the disc becomes scored for any reason, it should be replaced and a new set of pads should be installed. A badly scored disc will reduce the effectiveness of the brake and shorten pad life considerably. If the front brake lever oscillates or fluctuates when the brake is applied at speed, the indication is that the brake disc is warped or bent. Check the run-out of the disc with a dial indicator and replace it if run-out exceeds 0.012 in. (0.3 mm). To replace the disc:

1. Remove the front wheel.

2. Bend back the locktabs, unscrew the six nuts, and remove the disc from the hub.

3. Mount the new disc on the hub and tighten the nuts evenly, using new locktabs to secure the nuts.

4. Examine the brake pads and replace them if they are close to the limit of wear or have worn in an unusual pattern.

FRONT FORKS

Removal

MINI-TRAIL FORK

The mini-trail fork does not contain oil.

1. Remove the front wheel.

2. Remove the front fender.

3. Remove the bolt at the top of each fork leg and the steering stem nut.

4. The fork leg can be removed from each side after unscrewing the front fork guide cap with a chain wrench.

ALL OTHER MODELS

1. Loosen the fork filler caps located at the top of each fork leg.

2. Support the front wheel off the ground by placing a crate or another suitable object beneath the engine.

3. Remove the front wheel. Remove the fender.

4. Loosen the pinch-bolts on the upper and lower triple clamps, and remove the fork legs one at a time by pulling them straight down. If the fork legs resist removal, spread the lower triple clamp with a wedge and tap the fork leg out with a soft faced mallet.

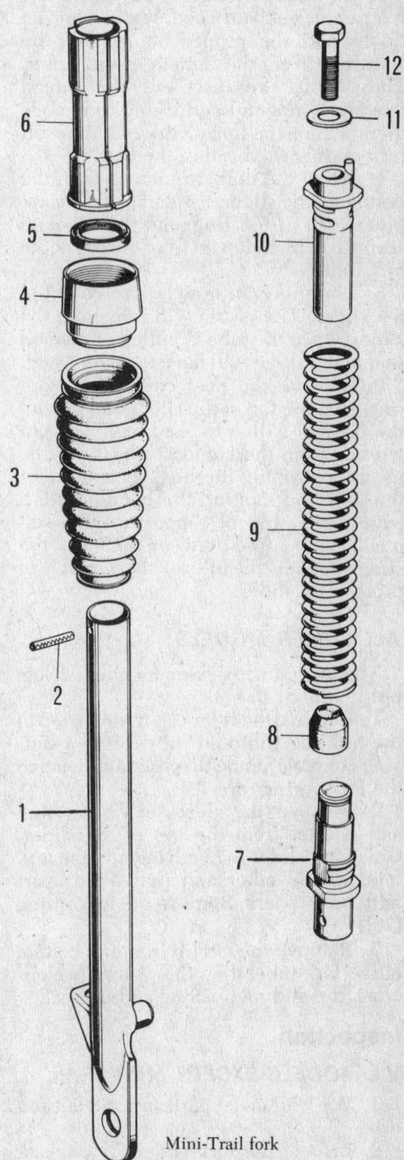

Mini-Trail fork

1. Fork slider
2. Pin
3. Boot
4. Fork guide cap
5. Dust seal
6. Fork guide pipe
7. Lower holder
8. Piston
9. Fork spring
10. Upper holder
11. Washer
12. Fork cap bolt

Disassembly

MINI-TRAIL FORK

1. Fix the fork assembly in a vise by the upper holder. Strike the spring with a drift to remove it from the upper holder. Do not damage the upper holder as this is done.
2. Separate the spring from the lower holder in the same manner as above.
3. Using a small drift, push out the pin which secures the under holder and piston to the fork slide pipe.

TL125

The procedure is given for one fork leg, but it applies to both.

1. Remove the filler cap from the top of the fork tube and pour the oil into a suitable container to be disposed of.
2. Remove the spring(s) from the top of the tube.
3. Turn the fork upside-down and rest it on a block of hardwood. With an impact driver and the proper bit remove the allen bolt from the bottom of the slider. These bolts are installed with thread locking compound and trying to remove them without an impact driver will result in rounding the head of the bolt.
4. When the bolt is removed from the bottom of the slider, the damper rod complete with piston ring, and the rebound spring can be removed from the top of the fork tube.
5. The tube can now be pulled out of the slider. The piston will remain in the slider. Once the tube is pulled out the oil seal in the slider will have to be replaced.
6. Remove the dust cover and snap-ring from the top of the slider and pry out the oil seal with a hooked tool. The pin wrench from the Honda tool kit may be used by slipping the hooked end under the seal and tapping the handle with a hammer. A strip of copper or other soft metal can be used between the top of the slider and the handle of the wrench to protect the slider.

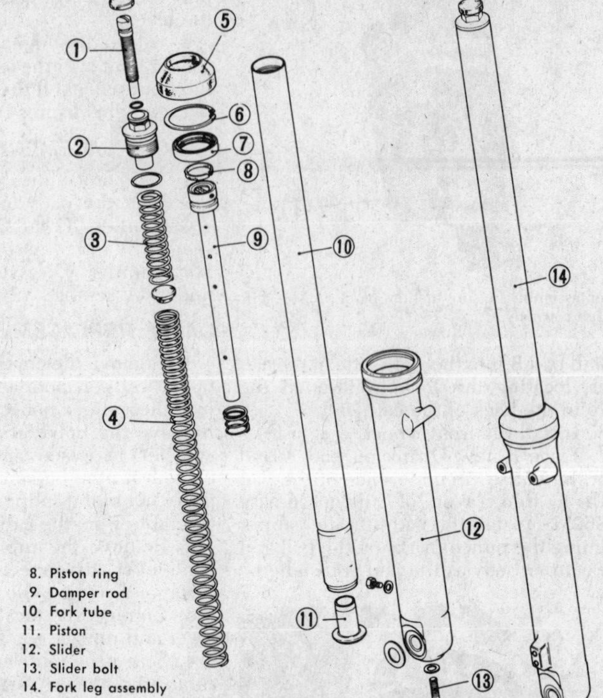

1. Spring adjuster
2. Fork filler cap
3. Fork spring, short
4. Fork spring, long
5. Dust cover
6. Snap-ring
7. Oil seal
8. Piston ring
9. Damper rod
10. Fork tube
11. Piston
12. Slider
13. Slider bolt
14. Fork leg assembly

TL125 front fork

ALL OTHER MODELS

The procedure is given for one fork leg, but it applies to both.

1. Remove the filler cap from the top of the fork leg and pour the oil into a suitable container to be disposed of. Remove the fork spring (pre-76).
2. Remove the dust seal, snap-ring, and washer from the top of the slider. Grasp the slider in one hand and the fork tube in the other and pull them apart with a sharp jerk. Remove the fork spring (76).
3. Remove the circlip from the bottom of the fork tube, then the piston, two circlips, the sliding bushing and oil seal.

Inspection

ALL MODELS EXCEPT MINI-TRAIL

1. Wash all metal parts in a solvent and dry.
2. Inspect the fork slider for cracked, broken, or distorted axle brackets, worn inner bore surfaces, damaged threads, or dents which have affected the inner bore. Replace the slider if defective in any of the above ways.
3. Inspect the fork tubes for condition: the chrome plating must be intact throughout. Check for damaged threads, and worn or scuffed inner or outer surfaces. Check the tubes for straightness. This is done by placing the tubes in a set of V-blocks and checking the run-out with a dial gauge. If the tube is bent more than 0.060 in. as indicated by the gauge, it must be replaced.
4. TL125 only: Inspect the piston ring for wear or scoring.
5. Check the filler cap O-ring for cracks or any other signs of wear; replace it if damaged.
6. Check the general condition of the fork springs. Replace any which are badly rusted, have collapsed coils, etc. Compare the lengths of corresponding

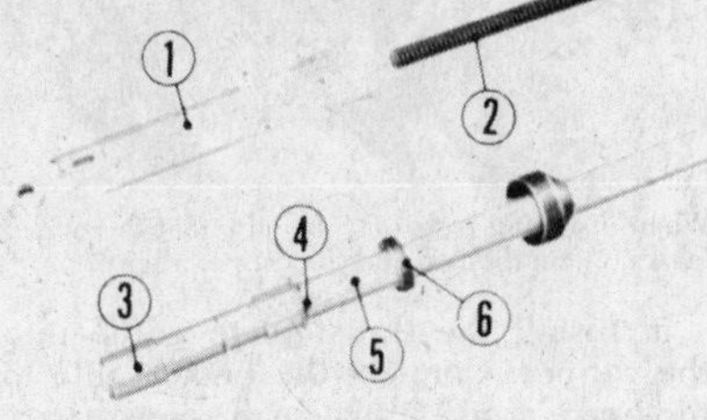

Internal fork spring components: fork slider (1), spring (2), piston (3), sliding bushing (4), fork tube (5), slider oil seal (6)

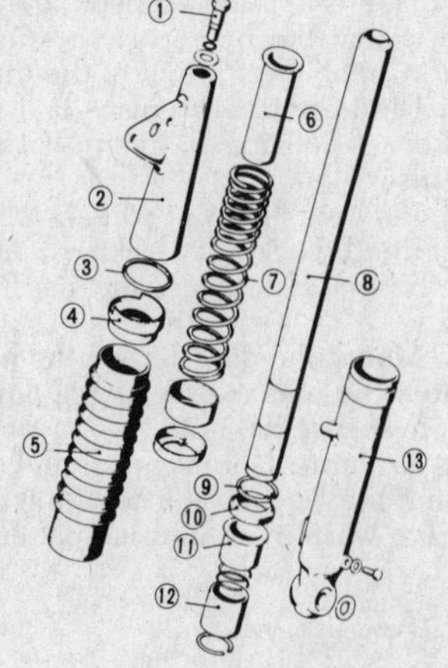

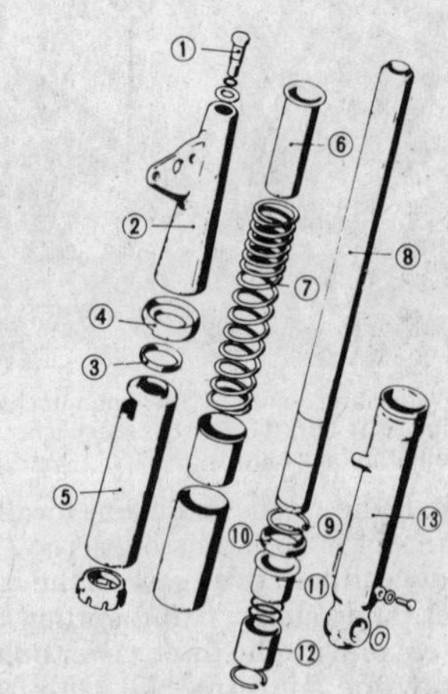

Slider bushing fork used on most models

1. Filler cap
2. Headlight brackets
3. Gasket
4. Bezel ring
5. Fork boot or cover
6. Spring guide
7. Fork spring
8. Fork tube
9. Circlip
10. Oil seal
11. Slider bushing
12. Piston
13. Fork slider

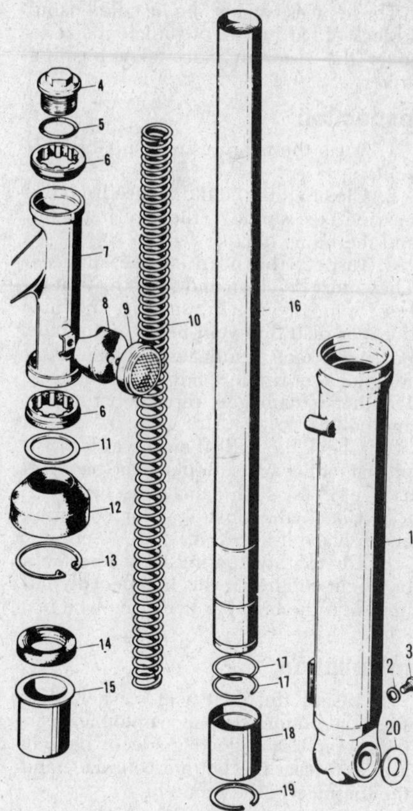

Internal fork—spring type

1. Fork slider
2. Gasket
3. Drain plug
4. Filler cap
5. O-ring
6. Cushion
7. Headlight bracket
8. Reflector base
9. Reflector
10. Fork spring
11. Washer
12. Dust seal
13. Circlip
14. Oil seal
15. Slider bushing
16. Fork tube
17. Circlips
18. Piston
19. Circlip
20. Axle washer

springs. They should be of approximately equal length. If the springs differ in length by more than ¼ in., both springs should be replaced.

7. All except TL125: Inspect the inside surfaces of the piston and sliding bushing for signs of wear or score marks. Replace as necessary. Place the sliding bushing on the fork tube and check for excessive play. The bushing should be a close fit.

8. Coat all parts with ATF before assembly. New oil seals must always be used.

MINI-TRAIL FORK

1. With the fork assembled, compress the fork and check for proper operation. Note any noise and correct the condition causing it.

2. Compare the free-length of the springs. If the springs differ in length by more than ¼ in., both should be replaced.

Assembly

TL125

1. Be sure that the piston is in the slider. Lubricate the new oil seal with ATF and install it into the top of the slider. Place a block of hardwood over the seal and drive it straight into the slider as far as possible. Then place the old seal on top of the new one and drive them in until the new one clears the snap-ring groove in the slider. Take out the old seal. Be sure that the new seal is straight in the slider. The distance from the top of the oil seal to the snap-ring groove should be the same all around the seal. Install the snap-ring. Lubricate the lips of the seal.

2. Install the rebound spring and damper rod in the fork tube. Carefully install the slider on the tube. Replace the fork springs and cap temporarily. Turn the fork upside down and install the bolt in the bottom of the slider. The threads of this bolt should be coated with thread locking compound.

3. Fit the drain plugs; be sure to install the gaskets.

4. Remove the cap and fill the forks with the proper amount of ATF. Note that the amount added to rebuilt forks will be slightly more than for a normal fork oil change.

5. Refit the fork tubes through the triple clamps. The top of the fork tube should be even with the top of the upper triple clamp.

6. Tighten the pinch-bolts on the lower triple clamp, and then tighten the fork filler caps and the pinch-bolts on the upper triple clamp, in that order.

7. Fit the front wheel and check the operation of the forks.

8. Adjust the forks by means of the adjusting screws at the top. Turning the screws in will stiffen the suspension and vice versa.

MINI-TRAIL FORK

1. Assembly is in the reverse order of the disassembly, however, note the following points:

a. When the fork leg is assembled, the locating pin on the upper holder must be perpendicular to the axle mounting lug on the slide pipe;

b. Secure the upper holder and piston to the fork slide pipe with the pin. Coat the upper and lower holders with a thin coat of grease and install the spring;

c. Fit the forks to the steering stem, noting that the locating pin on the top of the fork leg must fit into the slot in the top of the steering fork.

ALL OTHER MODELS

1. Install a new oil seal on the fork tube. Be sure to lubricate the seal with ATF before placing it on the tube.

2. Install the sliding bushing on the tube with the flange on the bushing facing the top of the tube. Install the two circlips, piston, and bottom circlip. All of the circlips must be a snug fit on the fork tube; if not replace them. Slide the fork spring into the tube from the bottom.

3. Place the fork tube into the slider and drive the oil seal into its seat in the top of the slider. Replace the washer, snap-ring, and dust seal.

4. Fill the fork leg with the proper amount of ATF. Replace the top washer, O-ring, and filler cap.

Leading Link Type Forks

DISASSEMBLY

1. Remove the front wheel.

2. Remove the 6 mm lockpin and the 7 mm locknut, then remove the front cushion joint washer and joint rubber. The front cushion and suspension arm can be removed as a unit by removing the front arm pivot bolt and the hex bolt.

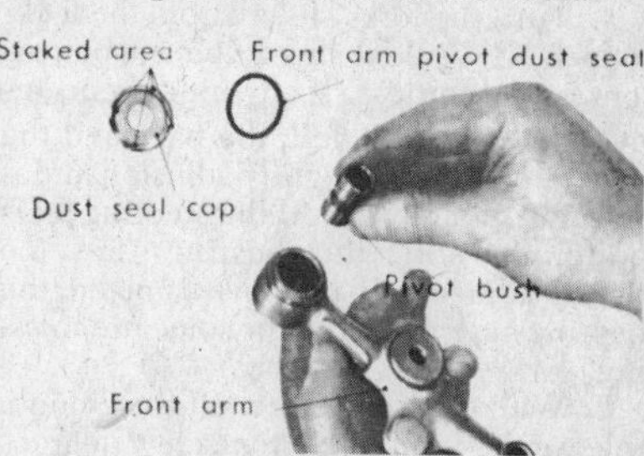

Pivot dust seal

3. Remove the front arm rebound stopper by removing the 8 mm hex nut and bolt.

4. Separate the front cushion and the front suspension arm by removing the 8 mm hex nut and the front cushion lower securing bolt. Take care not to loose the front cushion lower dust seal cap, seal, and spacer collar. The dust seal can be removed by unlocking the staking.

5. The suspension unit is now ready to be dismantled. The lower portion of the cushion is a sealed unit which cannot be rebuilt, and which must be replaced if weak or damaged. Disassemble the cushion by removing the locknut and spring. The spring guide, seat, stopper rubber, and outer collar are now free to be removed.

INSPECTION

1. Clean all parts in a suitable solvent and blow them dry. The dust seals should be replaced as a matter of course.

2. Inspect the damper unit for oil leaks, warpage, or inefficient damping characteristics, and replace them if necessary.

3. Inspect the suspension and fork components for a worn or damaged condition and replace them as necessary. If the fork legs are bent slightly they can usually be straightened.

4. Measure the free-length of the spring and replace it if collapsed, worn, or damaged.

ASSEMBLY

1. Assembly is basically the reverse order of disassembly.

2. Lubricate the suspension arm with grease and apply engine oil to the dust seal.

3. Lubricate the assembly when the assembly process is complete, by applying grease through the grease fitting using an automotive type grease gun.

STEERING STEM ASSEMBLY

Bearing Adjustment

1. The steering stem bearings are un-

caged #6 steel balls. They are adjusted by means of a ring nut beneath the upper triple clamp.

2. To check the bearing adjustment, support the front wheel off the ground. Grasp the fork sliders with both hands.

3. Attempt to move the forks by pulling out on the sliders. If play or movement can be felt, the bearings are too loosely adjusted or worn.

4. Turn the forks slowly from the lock-to-lock. Movement should be smooth, silent, and effortless. If any binding or uneven movement is felt, the balls and the races are either too tightly adjusted, unlubricated, or are worn. If the steering feels uniformly stiff, the bearings are too tightly adjusted. If any noise is noted, the bearings are damaged, or some are missing.

5. With the front wheel off the ground, release the front forks from a few degrees off the centered position. The forks should fall freely to either side of their own weight. If they will not, the bearings are too tightly adjusted, the steering stem is bent, the races are extremely worn, or some of the bearings are missing.

6. Bearings can be adjusted with a hammer and punch or a pin wrench on the adjuster nut under the upper triple clamp after the triple clamp is removed. To do this, remove the handlebars; on CT/ST90 models remove the handlebar clamp lever by removing the cotter pin and nut from the bottom of the clamp under the lower triple clamp, and remove the handlebars. Remove the fork filler caps, loosen the two or three triple clamp pinch-bolts (if fitted) and remove the steering stem nut. Tap the underside of the triple clamp upward to remove it.

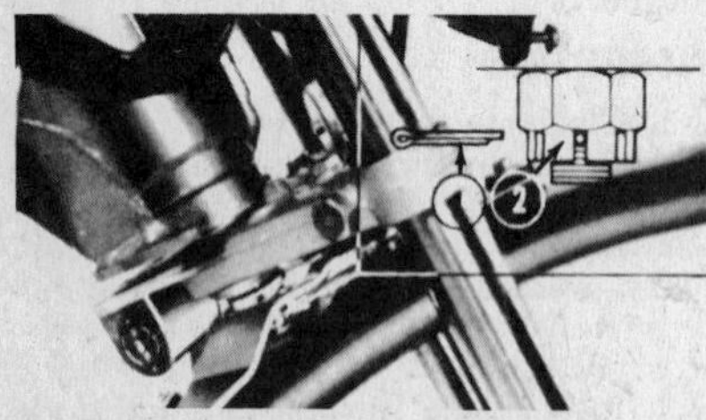

On CT/ST90 models, remove the handlebar clamp lever by removing the cotter pin (1) and the nut (2)

7. Tighten or loosen the adjusting nut a little at a time until the steering stem adjustment conforms to that outlined above.

8. If proper adjustment is not possible, the bearings and races will probably need to be replaced.

Removal

1. Remove the front wheel, fender forks, fuel tank, handlebars, and the handlebar clamp on ST90 models.

2. Disconnect the speedometer and tachometer cables from the instruments (if fitted). Remove the headlight lens and disconnect the wire harness. Remove the headlight shell, speedometer, and tachometer.

3. Loosen the upper triple clamp pinch-bolts (if fitted). Remove the steering stem nut and washer. Tap the upper triple clamp upward with a plastic mallet to remove it.

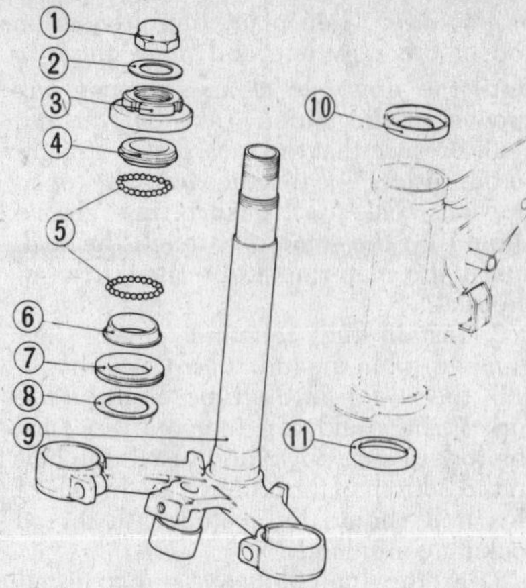

Typical steering stem assembly

1. Steering stem nut
2. Washer
3. Bearing adjuster nut
4. Upper race
5. Ball bearings
6. Lower race
7. Dust seal
8. Washer
9. Lower triple clamp and steering stem
10. Upper frame race
11. Lower frame race

4. Loosen the steering stem bearing adjuster nut with a pin wrench, then hold the steering stem up while unscrewing the adjuster nut the rest of the way off. Remove the steering stem top cone race and the balls from the top race.

5. Carefully pull the steering stem out from the bottom. Some of the ball bearings from the lower race will most likely fall out at this time so be prepared for this. Remove the rest of the balls from the lower race when the stem is removed.

6. Remove the bottom cone race, dust seal, and dust seal washer from the steering stem if they are to be replaced. If the steering stem has been damaged and is to be replaced, the upper and lower races and balls should also be replaced.

NOTE: *A chisel is usually necessary to remove the lower cone race from the steering stem.*

7. The bearing races in the frame are a press-fit and should not be removed unless replacement is necessary. Inspect them first. If replacement is necessary, the old races can be removed by reaching through the frame lug with a suitable punch and tapping the races out from the inside of the lug.

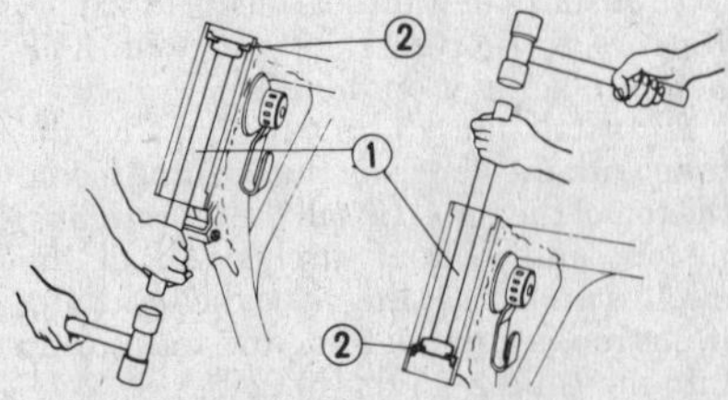

Using a bearing driver (1) to remove the bearing races in the frame

New races are installed using a suitable sized bushing driver: i.e., one which will drive the race squarely into its seat. Be certain that the race goes straight in.

These races can also be installed using a block of hardwood, of sufficient size to cover the race, in place of a bushing driver.

Inspection

1. Wash the bearings in a suitable solvent.

2. Clean all of the old grease from the bearing race surfaces, the steering stem, and the frame lug.

3. Inspect the bearing race surfaces. They must be clean and smooth. That is, free from any cracks, scoring, indentations, or rust. Run your finger around the bearing race surfaces. Note any roughness or ripples on the race surfaces. If either is damaged, replace both races and balls.

4. Check the balls themselves for rust, pitting, or flat spots. Replace the bearings as a set if any such damage occurs.

5. Check the dust seal for condition and replace if necessary.

6. Check the steering stem for cracks or a bent condition; this is especially important if the bike has been involved in a spill.

Installation

1. Install the dust seal washer, dust seal, and bottom cone race onto the steering stem. Use a good grade of bearing grease to coat the bottom cone race and the top race in the frame lug.

2. Embed the balls into the grease of the top frame race and the bottom cone race. Place a coat of grease on the two remaining races.

3. When the balls are in place, slip the steering stem through the frame lug and hold it in place, while refitting the top cone race and threading on the adjuster nut.

4. Tighten the adjuster nut, and move the steering stem back-and-forth to work the grease into the bearings, then back off the adjuster nut until the steering stem turns with ease, but has no play.

5. Install the upper triple clamp and fork tubes. Check that the stem moves freely of its own weight from 5°–10° off center; if not check for:
   a. Steering bearings too tight;
   b. Bent steering stem;
   c. Worn races or balls.

6. Install the flat washer, and steering stem nut.

7. Install the front wheel, front fender, headlight bracket, handlebars, and fuel tank.

REAR SHOCKS

No service to the rear shocks is possible. In the event of oil leaks, bent or broken plunger shaft, dented or otherwise damaged case, the shock absorber must be replaced.

If the shock absorbers are somewhat old, and one fails in the course of normal usage (such as an oil leak) it would be wise to replace both shocks to ensure equal damping characteristics.

To check a shock which is removed from the machine, place the bottom end on the ground and use the weight of your body to compress it as much as possible. Release the shock and note its rebound behavior. If the shock returns quickly at first, then slowly returns to its normal length, it is serviceable. If it returns to its normal length all at once, it should be replaced.

SWING ARM

Inspection

1. Disconnect the drive chain. Remove the rear wheel.
2. Remove the shock absorbers and chain guard.
3. Measure the distance between the top and bottom shock absorber mounts on both sides. The two measurements must be identical, or the swing arm will have to be replaced.
4. Check that the rear wheel mounting plates are parallel.

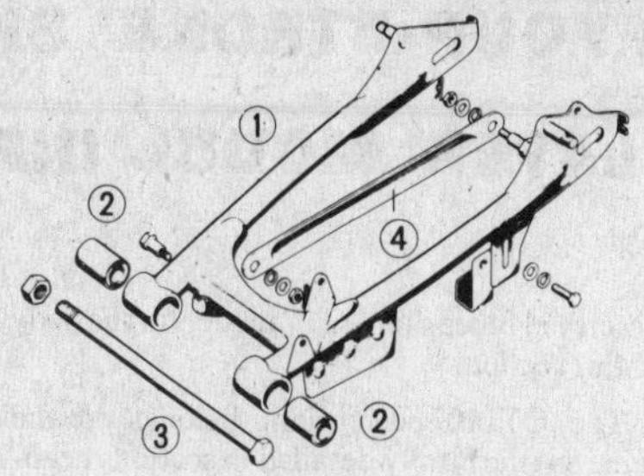

Typical swing arm assembly

1. Swing arm
2. Bushing
3. Pivot bolt
4. Brake anchor

5. Grasp the legs of the swing arm and attempt to move it from side-to-side. Any noticeable side-play will indicate that the swing arm bushings need replacement.

The swing arm is most likely to be damaged if the machine is operated for any length of time with a broken or otherwise defective shock absorber.

Removal and Installation

1. Proceed as above. Then remove the swing arm pivot bolt nut, and pull the pivot bolt out from the right-side.
2. Remove the swing arm by pulling it straight back.
3. The swing arm should be inspected for cracks or fractures, especially around the welds.

After removal of the swing arm, the dust seals (if fitted), and bushings can be replaced. This should be done every 10,000 miles, or more often depending on how the machine is used, or if the bushings are worn (see "Inspection").

4. Remove the bushing(s), tapping them out with a hammer and punch. Once the bushings are removed, they should be replaced.
5. Lubricate new bushings with a good chassis grease. Press the bushings into the swing arm, then install the swing arm collar if fitted.
6. Install the swing arm on the machine. Grease and install the pivot bolt. After tightening the swing arm pivot bolt nut, move the swing arm up and down to ensure that movement is smooth and effortless.

Chassis Specifications

Part	Standard Specification mm (in.)	Serviceable Limit mm (in.)
Brake lining thickness	—	2.0 (0.079)
Axle bend (front and rear)	0.05 (0.002) max	0.2 (0.0079)
Wheel bearings		
axial play	0.05 (0.002)	0.2 (0.0079)
radial play	0.003–0.018 (0.0001–0.0007)	0.035 (0.0014)
Rim run-out	0.5 (0.020) max	2.0 (0.079)
Disc brake (125) disc run-out	—	0.3 (0.012)

Chassis Torque Specifications

Part	Torque (ft lbs)
90–125 cc	
Front axle nut	25.3–36.2
Rear axle nut	29.0–43.4
Swing arm pivot nut	25.3–36.2
Engine mounting bolts	14.5–21.7
Handlebar clamps	5.6–8.7
Steering stem nut	43.4–57.9
Triple clamp pinch-bolts	18.1–21.7
Rear shock mounting bolt	18.1–21.7
Rear shock mounting nut	21.7–29.0
Rear brake anchor	7.3–14.7
Rear sprocket nuts	14.5–21.7
Brake plate lever pinch-bolts	
(front)	5.6–8.0
(rear)	5.6–7.3
50–70 cc	
Axle nuts (front and rear)	29.0–39.8
Engine mounting bolts	14.5–21.7
Fork filler caps	25.4–32.6
Triple clamp pinch-bolts	14.5–21.7
Rear shock mounts	14.5–21.7
Swing arm pivot nut	25.4–32.6
Steering stem nut	43.4–65.1
Rear brake anchor	7.3–14.5
Handlebar clamp	5.9–8.7

General Torque Specifications

Part	Torque (ft lbs)
6 mm machine screws	5.0–7.2
6 mm hex bolts	5.8–8.7
8 mm hex bolts	13.0–18.1
10 mm hex bolts	21.7–28.9
6 mm flange bolts	7.2–10.1
8 mm flange bolts	17.4–21.7
10 mm flange bolts	21.7–28.9

① Unless otherwise specified

HONDA FOUR-STROKE SINGLES

1982 AND LATER MODEL INFORMATION

CB125S

Late model CB125 machines are identical to those described in the body of this section for models "1976 and Later" with the exception of the Capacitor Discharge Ignition which replaces the breaker points previously used.

Ignition timing is carried out in the same way: by rotating the base plate on which the pulse generator is mounted until the rotor "F" mark aligns with the timing indicator at idle or the full advance marks align with the indicator at 3,000 rpm and above.

CT110

The running gear of the CT110 is the same as described for earlier "CT" models in the body of this section.

The CT110 powerplant belongs to the same engine family detailed in sections headed "90cc models" although a number of refinements have been made.

Exact procedures for this engine are outlined in the ATC70-125 section under the "110/125" heading.

Important differences are outlines below.

Engine Oil

Quantity: 1.1 qts./1.0 L during routine change.

Grade: SAE 10W-40 or equivalent service rated "SE" or "SF".

Tune-Up Specifications

Spark plug: DR8HS

Plug gap: 0.6-0.7mm/0.024-0.028 in.

Valve clearance: 0.07mm/0.003 in.

Compression: 178 ± 22 psi

Idle speed: 1300 rpm

Carburetor float level: 10.7mm/0.43 in.

Ignition timing: Remove the timing inspection cap on the front of the left crankcase cover. At idle, the "F" mark on the rotor should align with the timing index mark. Adjustments can be made by rotating the pulse generator base plate.

ENGINE AND TRANSMISSION SPECIFICATIONS

110 cc Models

	Standard (mm/in.)	Serviceable limit (mm/in.)
CYLINDER HEAD		
Cam journal OD		
R	17.927-17.938/0.7058-0.7062	17.90/0.705
L	25.9/7-25.930/1.0204-1.0209	25.88/1.019
Cam lobe height	24.90-24.98/0.980-0.983	24.6/0.97
Rocker arm ID	10.000-10.015/0.3937-0.3943	10.10/0.398
Rocker arm shaft OD	9.972-9.987/0.3926-0.3932	9.92/0.391
Rocker arm-to-shaft clearance	—	0.08/0.003
Cylinder head warpage	—	0.10/0.004
Valve spring free-length		
Inner	26.5/1.04	24.0/0.94
Outer	31.8/1.25	28.5/1.12
Valve stem OD		
Intake	5.455-5.465/0.2148-0.2152	5.44/0.214
Exhaust	5.430-5.445/0.2138-0.2144	5.41/0.213
Valve guide ID (In&Ex)	5.475-5.485/0.2157-0.2161	5.53/0.218
Stem-to-guide clearance		
Intake	—	0.08/0.003
Exhaust	—	0.10/0.004
Valve face width	1.2-1.5/0.05-0.06	1.8/0.07
Valve seat width	1.0/0.04	1.6/0.06
Cam hole ID		
R	18.000-18.018/0.7087-0.7094	18.05/0.711
L	26.000-26.020/1.0236-1.0244	26.05/1.026
Cam bearing clearance		
R	—	0.12/0.005
L	—	0.16/0.006

ENGINE AND TRANSMISSION SPECIFICATIONS

110 cc Models

	Standard (mm/in.)	Serviceable limit (mm/in.)
CYLINDER AND PISTON		
Cylinder ID	52.020-52.030/2.0480-2.0484	52.07/2.050
Taper	—	0.05/0.002
Out-of-round	—	0.05/0.002
Piston OD	51.970-51.990/2.0461-2.0468	5.180/2.039
Wrist pin bore	15.002-15.008/0.5906-0.5909	15.04/0.592
Wrist pin OD	14.994-15.000/0.5903-0.5906	14.96/0.589
Piston-to-pin clearance	0.002-0.014/0.0001-0.0006	0.02/0.001
Ring-to-groove clearance		
Top	0.015-0.050/0.006-0.0020	0.12/0.005
Second	0.010-0.045/0.0004-0.0018	0.12/0.005
Ring end-gap		
Top, second	0.10-0.25/0.004-0.010	0.50/0.02
Oil	0.30-0.90/0.012-0.035	—
Con rod small end ID	15.016-15.034/0.5912-0.5919	15.05/0.593
TRANSMISSION		
Sub-transmission		
Idle shaft OD	13.000-13.011/0.5118-0.5122	12.95/0.510
Drive sprocket bushing A		
OD	21.960-21.993/0.8646-0.8659	21.90/0.862
ID	19.992-20.025/0.7871-0.7884	19.94/0.785
Shift fork ID	42.000-42.025/1.6535-1.6545	42.1/1.66
Shift drum OD	41.950-41.975/1.6516-1.6526	41.8/1.65
Fork-to-drum clearance	0.025-0.075/0.0010-0.0030	0.10/0.004
Drum groove width	6.1-6.2/0.240-0.244	6.4/0.25
Fork finger width	5.96-6.04/0.234-0.238	5.70/0.224
Gear ID		
C1, C3	14.000-14.027/0.5512-0.5522	14.10/0.555
M2	18.000-18.018/0.7087-0.7094	18.08/0.712
M4	20.000-20.021/0.7874-0.7882	20.10/0.791
Shaft OD		
C1, M4	13.966-13.984/0.5498-0.5506	13.93/0.548
M2	17.966-17.984/0.7073-0.7080	17.93/0.706
C3	19.966-19.984/0.7861-0.7868	19.93/0.785
Drive sprocket bushing B		
ID	19.992-20.025/0.7871-0.7884	19.94/0.785
OD	21.960/21.993/0.8646-0.8659	21.90/0.862
CRANKSHAFT		
Run-out	—	0.10/0.004
Con rod big end side clearance	0.05-0.30/0.002-0.012	0.8/0.03
Con rod small end radial clearance	0-0.008/0-0.0003	0.05/0.002

Honda 125-200 Twins

MODEL COVERAGE

SS125	SL175
CL125	CB200
CB175	CL200
CL175	CB200T

INDEX

General Specifications

	CB125 (from serial no. 4,000,001)	CL125 (from serial no. 4,000,001)	SS125 (from serial no. 2,000,001)	CB175 (from serial no. 4,000,001)	CL175 (from serial no. 4,000,001)	SL175	CB200	CL200
ENGINE								
Displacement (cc)	124	124	124	174	174	174	198	198
Bore and stroke (mm)	44 x 41	44 x 41	44 x 41	52 x 41	52 x 41	52 x 41	55.5 x 41.0	55.5 x 41.0
Compression ratio	9.4 : 1	9.4 : 1	9.4 : 1	9.0 : 1	9.0 : 1	9.0 : 1	9.0 : 1	9.0 : 1
Carburetor (Keihin)	(2) 18mm	(2) 18mm	NA	(2) 20mm	(2) 22mm	NA	(2) 18mm	(2) 18mm
Weight (lb)	77.2	68.4	75.0	88.2	82.7	NA	NA	NA
DRIVE TRAIN								
Clutch type	wet, multi-plate	wet, multi-plate	wet, multi-plate	wet, multi-plate	wet, multi-plate	wet, multi-plate	wet, multi-plate	wet, multi-plate
Gear ratios:								
1st	2.692	2.615	2.615	2.769	2.769	2.769	2.796	2.796
2nd	1.667	1.611	1.611	1.882	1.882	1.882	1.882	1.882
3rd	1.286	1.190	1.190	1.450	1.450	1.450	1.450	1.450
4th	1.043	0.880	0.880	1.173	1.173	1.173	1.174	1.174
5th	0.880	——	——	1.000	1.000	1.000	0.960	0.960
Primary reduction	3.875	3.875	3.875	3.700	3.700	3.700	3.700	3.700
Final reduction	3.133	3.133	3.071	2.375	2.470	2.687	2.333	2.333
CHASSIS								
Weight (lb)	262	254	265	280	274	262.4	291	291
Wheelbase (in.)	50.4	50.4	50.4	50.4	50.8	51.6	50.8	50.4
Tire size (in.):								
front	2.50 x 18	2.75 x 18	3.00 x 17	2.75 x 18	3.00 x 19	3.00 x 19	2.75 x 18	2.75 x 18
rear	2.75 x 18	3.00 x 18	3.00 x 17	3.00 x 18	3.00 x 18	3.50 x 17	3.00 x 18	3.00 x 18
Overall length (in.)	77.9	76.0	78.0	78.4	78.3	78.5	76.2	77.4
Overall width (in.)	29.3	31.9	29.5	29.3	32.3	30.7	28.3	32.5
Overall height (in.)	40.9	40.6	40.2	40.9	42.5	42.9	41.7	42.1
Ground clearance (in.)	5.5	6.1	5.5	6.6	7.8	NA	6.1	7.1
ELECTRICAL SYSTEM								
Ignition	battery and coil	battery and coil	battery and coil	battery and coil	battery and coil	battery and coil	battery and coil	battery and coil
Starting system	electric and kick	electric and kick	electric and kick	electric and kick	electric and kick	kick	electric and kick	electric and kick

NA Not available
—— Not applicable

MAINTENANCE

NOTE: *Common maintenance procedures are explained in detail in "General Information."*

LUBRICATION

Checking Oil Level

The oil level is checked with the dipstick incorporated into the filler cap. The filler cap is located in the right crankcase cover. To check the oil level:

1. Start the engine and allow it to warm up for a few minutes.
2. With the motorcycle on the center stand on level ground, remove the dipstick and wipe it clean.
3. Reinsert the dipstick, allowing it to rest on the top of the threads of its hole. The oil level should be between the maximum and the minimum marks on the dipstick. If the level is below the minimum mark, add enough oil through the filler hole to bring the level up to the maximum mark.

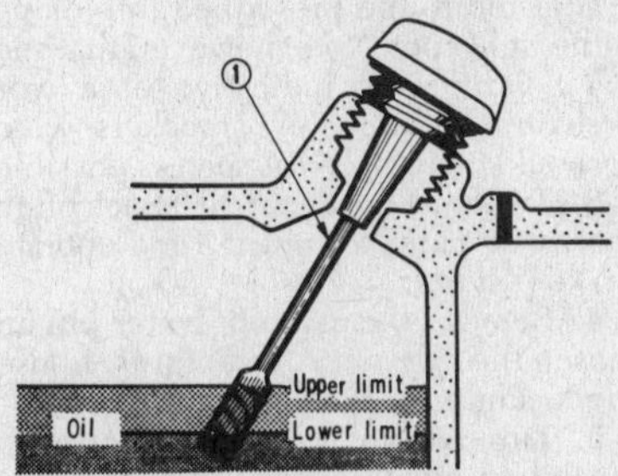

When checking oil level, the dipstick should rest on the threads as shown

CAUTION: *Do not overfill.*

Changing Oil

Oil should be changed every 1,500 miles or at three-month intervals, whichever comes first.

Use oil with a service rating of "SE" only. SAE 10W-30 or SAE 10W-40 may be used at most temperatures. For temperature extremes, refer to the "Recommended Lubricants" chart at the end of this section.

1. Allow the engine to run for a few minutes until it is close to operating temperature.
2. Remove the dipstick, then place a pan under the engine to catch the oil. Remove the drain plug from the sump, and allow the oil to drain for a minute or two, then kick the engine over a few times with the kick-starter (be sure that the key is off) to remove any oil remaining in the delivery system.
3. Refit the drain plug and add oil according to the "Maintenance Data" chart. Run the engine for a minute or two, then shut if off; wait one minute and check the oil level. Add oil as necessary to bring the level up to the maximum mark on the dipstick.

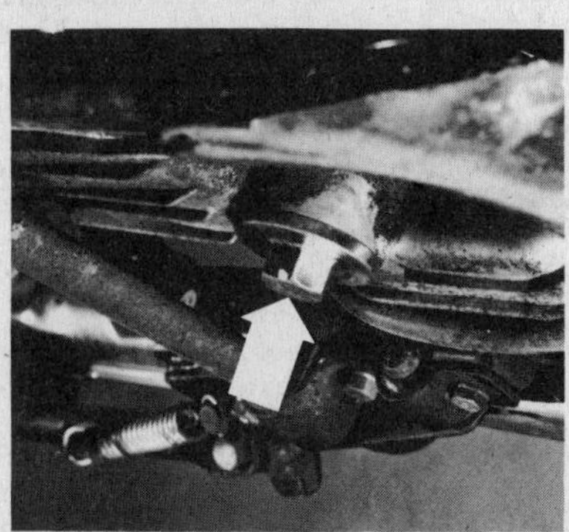
Drain plug location (arrow)

Oil Filter

All models use two oil filters. The centrifugal oil filter mounted on the right end of the crankshaft should be cleaned every 6,000 miles or every 12 months. The oil filter screen located at the bottom of the oil pump should be cleaned and inspected at more extended intervals. The centrifugal oil filter on 125 and 175 models can be cleaned through the access cover plate on the right crankcase cover. The centrifugal filter on 200 models and the filter screen on all models can only be cleaned after removing the right crankcase cover.

1. Clean the filter in conjunction with an oil change. Drain the oil as previously described and install the drain plug but do not fill with oil at this time.
2. 125, 175 models: Remove the three screws from the access cover plate on the right crankcase cover and remove the cover plate.
3. 200 models: Remove the right muffler (CB models), and the kick-starter lever. Remove the two screws from the chrome access cover on the right crankcase cover and disconnect the clutch cable. Place a pan beneath the right crankcase cover. Loosen the cover screws with an impact driver and remove them. Tap the cover gently with a plastic mallet if necessary to free it, and remove the cover.

Loosen the rear brake adjusting nut so that the brake pedal can be depressed enough to allow the crankcase cover to clear.

4. Remove the screw from the center of the filter cap. Remove the cap with a pliers.
5. Clean the inside of the filter rotor with a clean rag and solvent.
6. Clean the filter cap and cover plate (125, 175) and dry thoroughly. Inspect the

Remove the cap, and clean out the rotor (1) and filter screen (2) (200)

O-ring on the filter cap and replace it if damaged in any way.

7. Inspect the oil guide in the cover plate (125, 175) or in the right crankcase cover (200). The guide should be free to move in and out and have sufficient spring force behind it to hold it against the filter cap.

8. 200 models: The filter screen can be pulled off of the bottom of the oil pump. Clean the filter screen in clean solvent and blow dry. Inspect the screen mesh for any puncture holes, if any are noted the screen should be replaced.

9. 125, 175 models: Install the filter cap with the vanes located in the grooves on the inside of the filter housing, and secure with the screw.

10. 200 models: Install the filter cap with the tab on the filter cap aligned with the mark on the filter rotor, secure in place with the 6 mm screw.

On 200 models, align the tab on the filter cap (2) with the punch mark on the filter rotor (1)

11. 125, 175 models: Install the cover plate using a new O-ring if necessary.

NOTE: *When installing the cover plate on 125 and 175 models be sure that the oil passages in the cover plate and the right crankcase cover line up.*

12. 200 models: Install the right crankcase cover. Before installing the cover, check the condition of the gasket, and replace it if nicked or damaged. Install the kick-starter lever making sure to line up the punch marks on the shaft and the lever, if marks are fitted.

13. Fill the crankcase with oil.

Front Forks

1. Fork oil should be changed every 6,000 miles or every 12 months.

2. Refer to the "Recommended Lubricants" chart for the correct oil for your model.

3. To drain the fork oil, remove the drain plug at the lower portion of one of the fork sliders. Allow the oil to drain for several minutes into a suitable container, then pump the forks up and down several times. After most of the oil is expelled, turn the forks all the way to the right to completely drain the right fork leg, or all the way to the left for the left fork leg. Check the condition of the drain plug gasket. Replace it if necessary. Refit the drain plug and tighten it securely.

4. Repeat the procedure with the other fork leg.

Fork drain plug (arrow)

Fork filler cap (arrow)

5. Support the front wheel off the ground. Remove the fork filler cap from the top of each fork leg; it may be necessary to remove the handlebar holders and place the handlebars out of the way. Loosening the upper triple clamp pinch-bolts may make removal easier. On models with internal fork springs, the front end of the motorcycle can be lowered to force the springs out of the fork tubes. Either move the spring to one side or remove the spring altogether (if possible) to aid filling the forks.

6. Add the correct amount of oil to each fork leg. Capacities for each model are given in the "Maintenance Data" chart.

7. Inspect the condition of the fork filler cap O-ring, and replace it if it is torn or cracked. Fit the caps and tighten them securely. Tighten the handlebars and pinch-bolts if they were loosened. Allow a moment for the oil to settle in the forks before operation.

Chassis Lubrication

1. The swing arm pivot on some models is fitted with a grease nipple. This item should be lubricated with a good grade of chassis grease every 3,000 miles. Grease should be applied until some of it shows at either end of the swing arm.

2. Wheel and steering head bearings are lubricated with bearing grease. This should be done every 6,000 miles. Refer to the "Chassis" section.

SERVICE CHECKS AND ADJUSTMENTS

Drive Chain

1. The chain should have about ¾ in. (20 mm) of total up-and-down free-play measured in the middle of the lower chain run.

The chain should have the illustrated amount of free-play

2. Before checking or adjusting the chain slack, the following conditions should be met:

a. A support should be placed under the engine if necessary so that the rear wheel is off the ground;

b. The transmission should be placed in Neutral;

c. The chain should be cold, clean, and well lubricated;

d. The chain should have been checked for any tight spots by slowly rotating the wheel and checking for variances in the chain tension. If a tight spot exists, the chain tension should be adjusted to the prescribed free-play at the tight spot. Note, however, that such a condition is indicative of a worn chain and probably sprockets which should be replaced as soon as possible.

3. To adjust the chain, first back off the rear brake adjuster nut if a rod-operated brake is fitted.

4. Remove the axle nut cotter pin and loosen the axle nut several turns. Loosen the locknuts on the chain adjusters.

5. Turn each of the adjuster bolts in or out by an equal amount until the chain tension is approximately correct.

6. Check wheel alignment by means of the aligning marks inscribed on both sides of the swing arm. Be sure that both adjusters are lined up with the same mark on each side.

Chain adjuster bolt (arrow) and alignment marks (triangle)

7. Tighten the axle nut and check the chain tension. Then check the tension with the weight of a rider on the machine; there must still be at least ½ in. of slack. Correct if necessary. Tighten the axle nut to the proper torque and fit a new cotter pin. Tighten the locknuts on the chain adjusters.

Clutch

There are two adjusters on the clutch cable. Cable free-play should be maintained at 10–20 mm (0.4–0.8 in.) of hand lever movement measured at the end of the lever as illustrated.

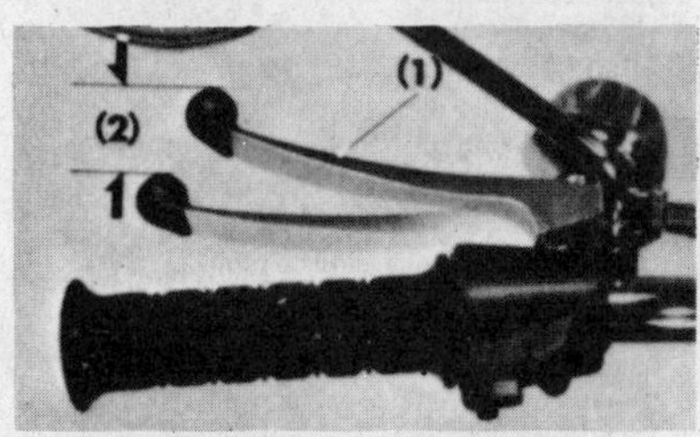

Clutch lever free-play (2) should be maintained at 10–20 mm (0.4–0.8 in.), measured at the tip of the lever

Use the adjuster at the hand lever for routine adjustments; the one at the engine can be used for major adjustments.

The clutch release mechanism should be adjusted every 3,000 miles or 6 months, or whenever the clutch begins to drag or slip and satisfactory operation cannot be obtained by adjusting free-play at the lever. At the time of adjustment, lubricate the grease fitting (125, 175); one or two shots of the grease gun should be sufficient.

1. Screw the cable adjuster at the clutch lever all the way into the lever housing (increasing lever free-play).
2. Back off the locknut and turn the cable adjuster at the engine case into the case (increasing cable free-play to maximum).
3. 200 models: Remove the two screws from the chrome access cover on the right crankcase cover, and remove the cover.
4. Loosen the clutch adjuster locknut (200) or bolt (125, 175), and turn the adjuster clockwise until resistance is felt.

Clutch adjuster locknut and adjusting screw (200)

On 125, 175 models, loosen the lockbolt (1) and turn the adjuster (2) to adjust the clutch

Then turn the adjuster in the opposite direction (counterclockwise) about ⅛–¼ turn on 125, 175 models and ¼–½ turn on 200 models and tighten the locknut (200) or bolt (125, 175).

5. Unscrew the lower cable adjuster out of the engine case until the proper free-play of 10–20 mm (0.4–0.8 in.) is obtained measured at the tip of the lever. Tighten the locknut. Minor adjustments can be made with the adjuster at the clutch lever.

Throttle Cable

The throttle cable free-play should be adjusted *after* the idle speed. This procedure is given in the "Tune-Up." The standard throttle cable free-play is 10–15° of grip rotation for all models. The cable should be well lubricated before attempting to adjust the free-play.

1. Cable free-play is adjusted with the adjuster near the twist-grip. Loosen the locknut on the adjuster and screw the adjuster in or out until free-play is correct. Tighten the locknut.
2. Check that the cable operates smoothly and maintains some free-play when the handlebars are cut all the way to the right or left.

Front Drum Brake

1. Use the cable adjuster on the brake plate to allow about 20–30 mm (0.8–1.2 in.) of handlebar lever free-play before the shoes contact the drum. This free-play is measured at the tip of the lever.
2. This free-play can be maintained as the shoes wear by using the adjuster at the handlebar lever.

Front Disc Brake

1. The handlebar lever should have 20–30 mm (0.8–1.2 in.) of free-play before

Front brake cable adjuster (2) and locknut (1). Turning the adjuster in direction "A" will take up excess lever free-play.

the pads contact the disc.

2. The brake cable is self-adjusting; if service is necessary refer to "Chassis."

Rear Brake

Use the adjusting nut on the end of the brake rod so that the brake pedal has 1 in. of free-play before the shoes contact the drum. The pedal height can be adjusted with the brake pedal stopper bolt.

Brake Light Switch

The switches should be checked for operation after the brakes are adjusted. The rear brake light switch is mounted in a slotted bracket and secured by locknuts. Moving the switch up on the bracket allows the brake light to turn on sooner. Moving it down allows the light to turn on later. Do not turn the switch to adjust it as the wires will become twisted and may break. Generally, the brake light should come on just as the linings contact the drum.

The front switch is not adjustable.

Rear brake light switch

Steering Stem Bearings

The steering stem bearings should be checked periodically and adjusted if necessary. Refer to the "Chassis" section.

Fuel System

1. Fuel system maintenance involves cleaning the petcock and filter, cleaning or replacing the air cleaner, and cleaning the carburetors.
2. The carburetors should be removed, disassembled, and cleaned every 4,000 miles. The procedures are outlined in the "Fuel Systems" section.
3. The petcock should be serviced every 3,000 miles. Shut the fuel off, then unscrew and remove the petcock sediment bowl. Take out the O-ring and fuel

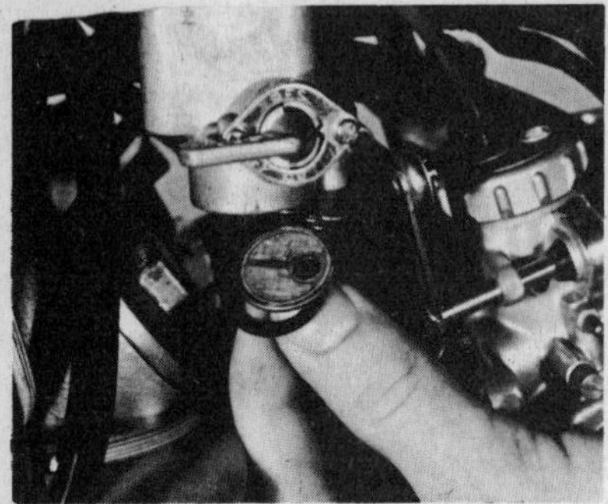

Removing the O-ring and filter screen

filter screen. Clean the parts in solvent and inspect the screen for any holes or other defects, replace it if it is damaged in any way. Inspect the O-ring for any cuts or cracks and replace it if necessary. Reinstall the filter screen, O-ring, and sediment bowl. Turn the fuel on and check for leaks.

Air Cleaner Service

The air cleaner should be serviced or replaced every 1,500 miles or more often depending on conditions.

ALL MODELS EXCEPT SL175

Removal

1. Open the seat. On CL models the exhaust system must be removed. Remove the right and left sidecovers.
2. Loosen the air cleaner connecting band. Remove the nut from the center of the air cleaner case, and remove the case.
3. Remove the two element mounting bolts and remove the element.

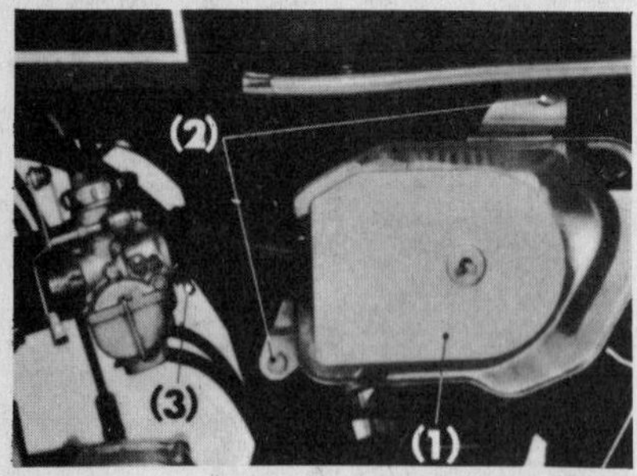

To remove the element (1), remove the mounting bolts (2)

Cleaning

1. Tap the air cleaner to remove any loose dirt. Blow compressed air through the element from the inside out.
2. Inspect the element and connecting tube for any holes; replace any air cleaner found defective. An oil-impregnated element or one which cannot be cleaned sufficently should also be replaced.
3. Inspect the area where the element is bonded to the mounting plate. If the bonding is cracked or separated replace the element.

Installation

1. Installation is in the reverse order of removal.
2. After installing the air cleaners, start the engine and check for any air leaks.

SL175

Removal

1. Remove the plastic sidecovers from both sides.

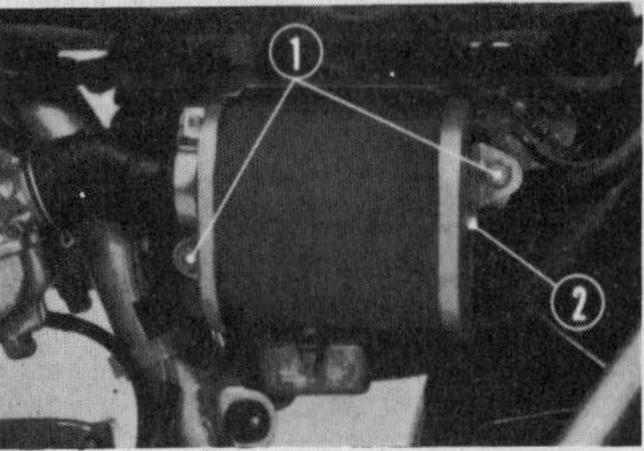

SL175 element mounting bolts (1 and 2).

2. Remove the two mounting bolts, and loosen the connecting band holding the carburetor inlet tube to the carburetor. Remove the air cleaner.
3. Remove the bolt from the center of the back of the air cleaner and remove the element.

Cleaning

1. Once the air cleaner element is removed, it should be cleaned in a clean solvent such as kerosene.
2. When the air cleaner element has dried thoroughly, soak it in clean motor oil SAE 30W until it is fully saturated then wring off the excess oil.
3. Inspect the element for any damage, such as holes or a damaged case. Replace any air cleaner found defective.

Installation

1. Installation is in the reverse order of removal.
2. Start the engine and check for any air leaks. Any air leaks should be corrected as they can cause a lean mixture resulting in possible engine damage.

Headlight Adjustment

1. Set the machine about 25 feet away from and perpendicular to a wall, preferably of a color which reflects light well.

The machine should be off the stand, and with a rider putting his weight on the machine as in operation.

2. Switch on the high beam. The headlight high beam should be parallel to the ground and should hit the wall directly in front of the machine.
3. Vertical adjustment is made by loosening the two headlight shell mounting bolts slightly and pivoting the shell up or down.
4. Lateral adjustment is accomplished by means of the screw on the right-side of the headlight. Turning the screw clockwise will move the beam to the left; turning it counterclockwise will move it to the right.

Recommended Lubricants

Engine	General—All Temperatures SAE 10W-30 SAE 10W-40 Alternate SAE 30 SAE 20 or 20W SAE 10W	 Above 59° F 32°–59° F Below 32° F
Forks	ATF SAE 10W-30	
Control Cables	10W-30 motor oil Graphite-base lubricant	
Tach, Speedo Cables	Light-duty, lithium-base grease	
Wheel Bearings	Waterproof, medium-weight bearing grease	
Steering Head Bearings	Waterproof, medium-weight bearing grease	

Periodic Maintenance Intervals ①

Daily
- Chain slack
- Cable adjustments
- Brake adjustment

Weekly
- Battery fluid level
- Spoke condition
- Oil level
- Tire pressure

Every 1500 miles
- Change engine oil
- Adjust drive chain

Every 3,000 miles
- Clean, gap, or replace spark plugs
- Check and adjust clutch
- Clean or replace air filter
- Check ignition timing
- Clean, gap, or replace breaker points
- Clean fuel petcock
- Check carburetor operation
- Adjust cam chain tensioner
- Adjust valve clearance
- Lubricate cables and twist-grip
- Inspect fuel lines
- Inspect chain and sprocket condition
- Lubricate breaker point pad

Every 4,000 miles
- Grease speedometer drive mechanism
- Overhaul carburetors
- Inspect rims and run-out

Every 6,000 miles
- Clean oil filter
- Lubricate wheel bearings
- Lubricate steering head bearings
- Inspect brake shoes
- Change fork oil

① Based on normal use after break-in is complete

Battery Specifications

Model	*Yuasa No.*	*JIS No.*	*Voltage*	*Amp/Hrs*	*Cont Charging Rate (amps)*
SS125A CL125A	B54-6	—	6	12	1.2
CB175 CL175	MBW3-12C	12N9-4B	12	9	0.9
SL175	B101-12	12N5-4B	12	5	0.5
CB200 CL200	MBW3-12C	12N9-4B	12	9	0.9

Maintenance Data

	SS125	CL125	CB175	CL175	SL175	CB/CL200
Engine oil capacity (qt)	1.25	1.25	1.6	1.6	1.6	1.8
Fuel tank capacity (gal)	2.2	2.5	2.3	2.4	2.4	2.4
Front fork capacity (cc/oz) When changing	135/4.5	135/4.5	135/4.5②	135/4.5②	175/5.8	115–118/3.9–4.0
After disassembly	145/4.8	145/4.8	145/4.8③	145/4.8③	185/6.1	128–132/4.3–4.5
Tire pressure (psi)① Front	26	26	26	26	26	26
Rear	28	28	28	28	28	28

① Add 6 psi to the rear tire for two-up or extended high-speed operation.

② Late models: 115–118/3.9–4.0

③ Late models: 128–132/4.3–4.5

TUNE-UP

NOTE: *Common tune-up procedures are explained in detail in "General Information."*

CAM CHAIN ADJUSTMENT

175, 200

1. Remove the alternator cover.
2. Using a wrench on the alternator bolt, rotate the alternator rotor counterclockwise so that the "T" mark on the rotor is aligned with the timing index mark on the stator.

Rotor positioned at top dead center ("T" mark aligned)

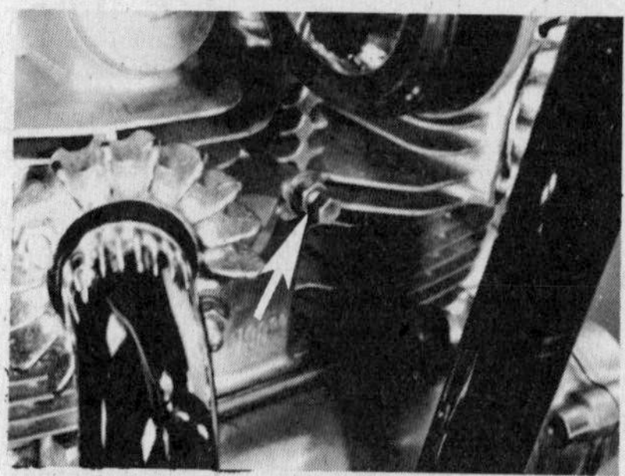

Cam chain adjuster bolt (arrow)

3. Loosen the locknut on the tensioner setting bolt and back the setting bolt out three or four turns. The tensioner will automatically apply the correct amount of tension on the chain.
4. Tighten the setting bolt to a torque of 2–3.5 ft lbs, then tighten the locknut.

125

1. Remove the alternator rotor cover.
2. Remove the left-side intake valve cover.
3. Turn the alternator rotor clockwise (the opposite direction of normal rotation) until the left intake valve opens fully (spring compressed) and begins to close.
4. Turn the alternator rotor counterclockwise until the left intake valve barely moves.
5. Loosen the locknut on the cam chain adjuster bolt and turn the adjuster bolt (left-hand thread) clockwise so that the tension is removed from the chain. Now turn the adjuster screw counterclockwise until resistance is just felt. Tighten the locknut while holding the adjuster screw from turning.

   CAUTION: *Do not over tighten the adjuster screw past the point where resistance is noticed or the tensioner and the chain will suffer premature wear.*

VALVE ADJUSTMENT

NOTE: *Valves must be adjusted when the engine is cold.*

1. Remove the alternator cover.
2. Remove the four valve tappet covers. The fuel tank can be removed for easy access to the tappet adjusters.
3. Remove both spark plugs.
4. Turn the crankshaft, using the rotor bolt, until the "T" mark on the alternator rotor is aligned with the timing index mark on the stator.
5. With the crankshaft in this position both cylinders will be at top dead center (TDC), however, one cylinder will be on its compression stroke and the other on its exhaust stroke. To determine which cylinder is on compression, check to see which pair of valves (intake and exhaust) are fully closed, in which case there will be clearance at both rocker arms. The valves for the cylinder which is on its compression stroke are correctly positioned for adjustment.
6. The correct valve clearance for both valves is 0.05 mm (0.002 in.). Slip the correct feeler gauge between the valve stem and the rocker arm adjuster. The feeler gauge should be a slip-fit (a slight drag), in a correctly adjusted valve.

Checking valve clearance

7. If adjustment is necessary, loosen the adjuster locknut and turn the adjuster to effect adjustment. Tighten the locknut.

   NOTE: *The adjustment may change when the locknut is tightened. Hold the adjuster steady while securing the locknut. Recheck the clearance afterwards.*
8. Turn the rotor one full turn (360°) counterclockwise and line up the "T" mark with the timing index mark again. In this position the other cylinder will be on its compression stroke and both valves should be closed. Adjust the valve clearance as described in Steps 6 and 7 above.

CONTACT BREAKER POINTS

Location

The points are located in a case on the left-side of the cylinder head, and are operated off the camshaft. The timing advance mechanism is fitted on the camshaft behind the breaker point base plate.

Replacement

1. If replacement of the points is necessary, this is easily accomplished by disconnecting the primary wire, removing the two point securing screws, and taking off the points. Install the new points after thoroughly cleaning off the contact surfaces with a non-oily solvent, and adjust the gap. If a breaker plate assembly is purchased, simply disconnect the pri-

mary wire from the wiring harness and remove the two breaker base plate screws. Install the new breaker base plate and connect the primary wire. Clean the surfaces of the points and adjust the gap. Whenever the points are replaced, the ignition timing will have to be set.

2. Apply a bit of grease to the breaker cam lubricating wick. Take care not to apply too much to avoid fouling the points.

Gapping

Points should be filed (if necessary) and cleaned before gapping.

1. Remove the alternator cover, and points cover.
2. Using the rotor bolt, turn the engine over until the points are open to their maximum gap.
3. With the proper feeler gauge, check the gap. The proper specification for all models is 0.3–0.4 mm (0.012–0.016 in.).
4. If adjustment is necessary, loosen the two screws which secure the points to the base plate and open or close the points to bring the gap to the proper specification.

NOTE: *Loosen the screws just enough to allow the points to be moved. If too loose, the points will snap shut instead of holding the adjustment.*

Points securing screws used to adjust point gap

5. Tighten the screws and recheck the gap.
6. If it is not possible to gap the points correctly, the fiber heel is evidently worn; the set of points should be replaced.

Lubrication

1. On all models it is necessary to lubricate the cam follower fiber heel and the pivot point of the contact breaker occasionally.
2. A small dab of grease (high melting point, if possible) should be applied to the lubricator wick so that the lubricator can distribute it onto the breaker cam. A drop of engine oil should be applied to the pivot point.
3. In both cases it is imperative that care be taken to keep the lubricant away from the points contact surface.
4. The lubricating wick should be adjusted so that it just contacts the breaker cam.
5. If the wick is missing the grease can be applied sparingly to the cam itself.

IGNITION TIMING

NOTE: *Points must be cleaned and gapped before checking timing. Dirty points will cause inaccurate readings.*

Dynamic Timing

1. Remove the alternator cover so that the timing marks are visible.

NOTE: *A white grease pencil or some paint can be used on the rotor and stator timing indicator marks to increase their visibility under the strobe light.*

2. Hook up the timing light to either cylinder according to the manufacturer's instructions.
3. Start the engine, aiming the light on the rotor. Note the following:
   a. At idle, the "F" mark on the rotor should line up with the timing index mark on the stator;
   b. As the revolutions increase, the "F" mark should be seen to move in a direction opposite that of the crankshaft rotation;
   c. Finally, at full advance (about 4,000 rpm and above), the twin rotor marks must line up with the timing index mark.

Full spark advance timing marks aligned with pointer

4. The full advance reading is the most important. If the twin marks on the rotor and the timing index mark do not align, proceed as follows:
5. Loosen the two screws which secure the breaker base plate just enough to allow the plate to be turned. Rotate the base plate in the direction necessary so that the timing marks align.

Rotating the base plate clockwise advances the timing; rotating the plate counterclockwise retards the timing.

Tighten the base plate screws and recheck the timing.

If proper ignition timing is not possible, replace the points, since the fiber heel is probably worn.

Breaker base plate screws

Static Timing

1. Remove the points cover, and the alternator cover.
2. Remove the spark plugs and hook up the tester as described previously.
3. Turn the engine over slowly in the normal direction of rotation (counterclockwise). At the instant in which the "F" mark on the rotor aligns with the index mark on the stator, the points should begin to open as indicated by the reaction of the test light or meter.

"F" mark aligned with the pointer

4. If the points open before the marks align, the timing is too advanced, If the points open after the "F" mark passes the index mark, the timing is too retarded.
5. If the timing is not correct, set the "F" mark so that it is aligned with the index mark. Loosen the two screws which secure the breaker base plate and rotate the plate until the light or the meter indicates that the points have just opened. Tighten the base plate screws and recheck the timing.

CARBURETOR

Three adjustments to be made to the carburetor are the float level, the idle mixture, and the idle speed. For the first of these, the carburetor must be removed from the motorcycle.

Adjusting Float Level

Generally, float level will not need adjustment unless the carburetor has been disassembled, fuel delivery problems have been noted, or considerable mileage has been covered.

1. Remove the carburetor from the motorcycle as outlined in the "Fuel Systems" section.
2. Remove the float bowl. Remove the float bowl gasket.
3. Float level is defined as the measured distance from the float bowl mating surface on the carburetor body (gasket removed) to the top of the floats, when the tang of the float arm is just touching the end of the float needle. A special gauge is available at Honda dealers to check the float level although a vernier caliper can also be used.

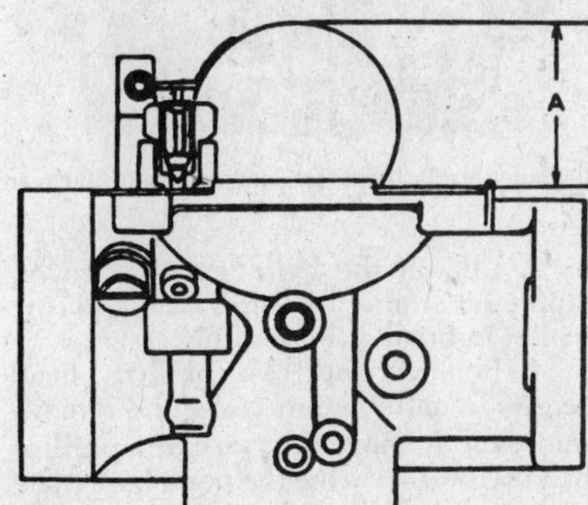

Float level is the distance "A" from the float bowl gasket surface (gasket removed) to the top of the floats

4. With the carburetor held upside down, gradually lower the float until the tang of the float arm just touches the end of the float needle. The tang should not depress the needle, but just contacts it. Measure the distance from the top of the float. Compare the reading with the proper float level for your machine.
5. If adjustment is necessary, bend the float arm tang *only* to raise or lower the float level.
6. Float level will not be correct if the needle is worn, or if there is foreign matter on the needle seat.

Idle Speed and Mixture

NOTE: *These items must be adjusted when the engine is at operating temperature.*

1. Ensure that the throttle cable adjustment is approximately correct so that the cable has enough slack to allow the throttle slides to be fully closed.

2. Screw the pilot screws in carefully until they bottom lightly, then back them out the number of turns shown in the "Tune-Up Specifications" chart.

Carburetor pilot screw (left) and throttle stop screw

3. Start the engine. When operating temperature is reached, adjust the throttle stop screws so that the engine idles smoothly at about 1200 rpm.

4. Place a hand behind each muffler to ensure that both cylinders are running evenly. If the idle speed and mixture adjustment screws are misadjusted, one cylinder may "lead" the other. Adjust the throttle stop screws, if necessary, so that both cylinders are running evenly.

5. Adjust each pilot screw so that the engine runs as smoothly as possible. It should not be necessary to vary the pilot screw setting more than ½ turn from the standard given.

NOTE: *If proper idling cannot be obtained using this method, it may be that the fuel system is clogged with dirt (check petcock, filter, carburetor), the plug is bad or too cold, the valves are improperly adjusted, or there is an air leak somewhere in the system.*

6. Check that the two carburetors are synchronized.

Carburetor Synchronization

1. Remove the air cleaner assembly.
2. Twist the throttle fully open to lift up the slides.

3. Position a mirror behind the carburetors or reach into the carburetor bores with the thumb and index finger of one hand.

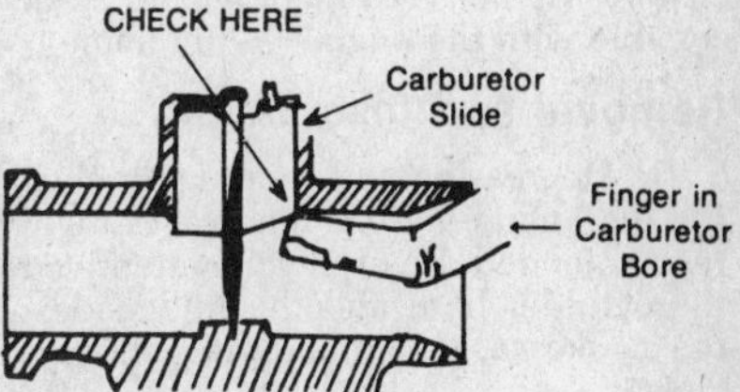

Check for carburetor synchronization by ensuring that both slides clear the carburetor bores at the same time

4. Slowly close the throttle and watch, or feel, the slides as they are being lowered; they should enter their respective bores simultaneously.

5. If the slide positions are unequal, raise or lower one to match the other by turning the adjuster at the top of the carburetor.

6. Another check is to place a finger on each carburetor slide when the throttle is fully closed, then move the twist-grip very slightly. Both slides should begin to lift at the same time. Adjust as described above if necessary.

7. After adjusting the idle speed and synchronizing the throttle slides, adjust the throttle cable free-play.

Tune-Up Specifications

	125	*175*	*200*
Spark Plug, standard (NGK/ND)	D-8HS/X24FS	D-8HS/X24FS	D-8ES-L/X24ES
Spark Plug Gap (in./mm)	0.0240.028/0.6–0.7	0.024–0.028/0.6–0.7	0.024–0.028/0.6–0.7
Breaker Point Gap (in./mm)	0.012–0.016/0.3–0.4	0.012–0.016/0.3–0.4	0.012–0.016/0.3–0.4
Valve Clearance			
Intake (in./mm)	0.002/0.05	0.002/0.05	0.002/0.05
Exhaust (in./mm)	0.002/0.05	0.002/0.05	0.002/0.05
Carburetor Adjustments			
Pilot Air Screw (turns out)	1⅛ ± ⅛	①	②
Idle Speed (rpm)	1200	1200	1200
Float Level (in./mm)	0.82/21	0.82/21	0.82/21
Compression Pressure (psi)	142	170	170

① CB/CL 175: ⅞ ± ⅛
SL 175: 1⅛ ± ⅛

② CB200: 1¼ ± ⅛
CL200: ⅝ ± ⅛

ENGINE AND TRANSMISSION

NOTE: *For engine component inspection procedures and techniques, refer to "Engine Rebuilding" in the General Information section.*

Engine Service

1. To remove the cylinder head, barrels, and pistons, the engine must be removed from the frame.

2. Crankcase cover components: oil pump, clutch, gearshift mechanism, alternator, countershaft sprocket, and the cam chain tensioner (125 models), are all accessible with the engine in the frame.

Removal and Installation

1. Degreasing and thoroughly cleaning the engine before removal is highly recommended. Be especially attentive to the cylinder base and the underside of the crankcase, and around the mating surfaces.

2. Drain the oil from the sump, and reinstall the drain plug.

3. Turn the fuel petcock to the off position and disconnect the fuel lines from the petcock. Disconnect the balance line from the tank and remove the tank.

NOTE: *To safely remove the tank, either drain it completely prior to removal, or obtain a four inch length of fuel line and two small clamps. Attach one of the clamps to the fuel tank's balance line. Disconnect the lines; fit the spare length of fuel line to the fitting on the tank with the other clamp already attached. This will prevent fuel from spilling out of the tank when the fuel line is disconnected for removal.*

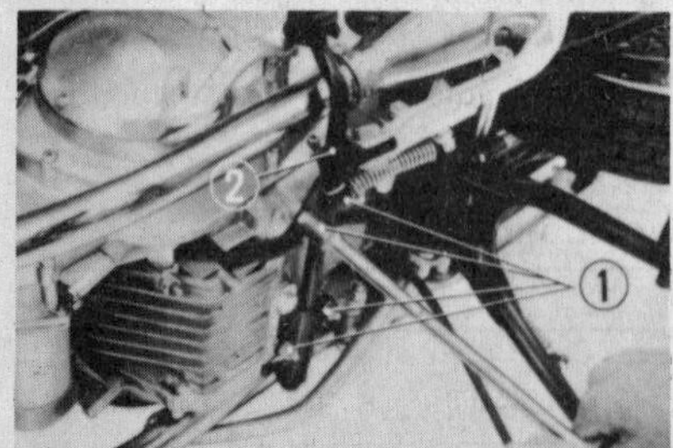

Step-bar mounting bolts (1) and step-bar (2) (125)

4. Remove the step-bar, and the exhaust system. On 125 models, remove the brake pedal spring and the stoplight switch spring.

5. Open the seat and remove the battery. When disconnecting the battery always disconnect the negative terminal first.

6. If an electric starter is fitted, disconnect the starter motor cable from the selenoid.

7. Unscrew the carburetor caps and pull the throttle slide assembly out of the carburetor.

8. Disconnect the choke rod from the left carburetor. Loosen the band securing the air cleaner to the carburetor. Unbolt the intake manifold from the cylinder head and remove the intake manifold and the carburetors.

9. Remove the three phillips head screws from the left rear crankcase cover, and remove the cover.

10. Disconnect the drive chain.

Disconnecting the clutch cable (1) from the release mechanism (2) (125, 175)

11. 125, 175 models: Disconnect the clutch cable from the clutch release mechanism on the left-side of the engine.

12. 200 models: Remove the chrome cover from the right crankcase cover. Screw the clutch adjuster at the right crankcase cover in to allow some freeplay in the cable. Disconnect the cable from the release mechanism.

13. Remove the cover on the right-side of the cylinder head. Remove the phillips head set screw and disconnect the tachometer cable from the engine.

14. Disconnect the alternator leads from the wiring harness at the plastic connector. Disconnect the point primary wire from the wiring harness.

15. Disconnect the spark plug leads, and loosen the plugs.

16. Remove the nuts from the engine mounting bolts, 4 on 125 models, 9 on 175, 200 models. Remove the mounting bolts being careful not to damage the threads on the bolts, then lift the engine out of the frame.

Engine mounting bolts (175)

17. Installation is in the reverse order of the removal procedures, however, note the following points:

a. Install the battery ground cable to the rear upper mounting bolt. Scrape any paint or rust from the frame under the cable to ensure a good ground;

b. When connecting the battery, connect the positive terminal first. Route the battery overflow tube so that it will release any overflow (sulfuric acid) well below the frame and swing arm;

c. Install the throttle slide into the carburetor with the cutaway of the slide facing the air cleaner;

d. Install the masterlink spring clip with the closed end facing the direction of chain rotation.

CYLINDER HEAD

Removal

175, 200

1. Remove the engine from the frame.

2. Loosen the eight 8 mm capnuts and the head bolt gradually and evenly in an X pattern about ¼ turn at a time until they are all loose, then remove them.

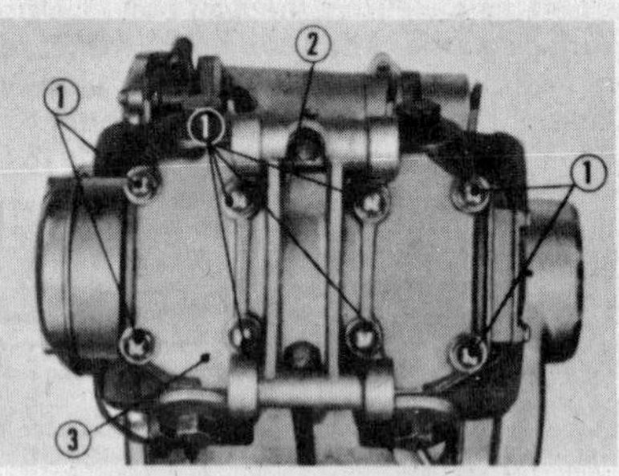

Cylinder head capnuts (1), bolt (2), and head cover (3)

3. Lift off the cylinder head cover, tapping it around the sides with a plastic mallet to break it loose if necessary.

4. Remove the two phillips head screws from the points cover and remove the cover. Remove the two 5 mm phillips head screws securing the point base plate to the point side housing, and remove the base plate. Remove the 6 mm bolt and flat washer from the end of the camshaft. Remove the spark advance unit from the end of the camshaft. Be careful when removing the spark advance unit that the breaker cam (point cam) is not pulled from the unit. If the cam is removed be sure to install it in the correct direction, it is possible to install the cam 180° off making proper ignition timing impossible.

Spark advance unit (1) and point base (2)

5. Remove the three screws from the alternator cover on the right-side of the engine and remove the cover. Remove the valve adjuster caps.

6. Loosen the cam chain tensioner set bolt.

7. 175 only: Using the alternator rotor turn the engine over until the cam chain masterlink is at the top of the cam sprocket. The "T" mark on the alternator rotor should be aligned with the timing index mark on the stator. Stuff a clean rag into the cylinder head around the cam sprocket and remove the cam chain masterlink. Tie a piece of wire or string to each end of the cam chain. At this point the cylinder head can be removed. If the head is stuck, tap around the base of the head with a plastic mallet to free it, take care not to break the cooling fins.

The following procedures refer only to 200 models.

8. Remove the four phillips head screws from the side housing on either side of the cylinder head. Using the alternator rotor bolt turn the engine over until the "T" mark on the alternator rotor is aligned with the timing index mark on the stator, in this position one of the cylinders will be at top dead center (TDC) of its compression stroke. The intake and exhaust valves for this cylinder will be closed (clearance between the rocker arms and the cam). Remove the side housing on that side. Screw a 6 mm bolt into each of the rocker arm shafts, and pull them from the head. Remove the rocker arms. Temporarily install the side housing, but do not install the securing screws.

Using a 6 mm bolt (2) to remove the rocker arm shaft (1) and rocker arm (3) (200)

9. Turn the alternator rotor bolt one complete turn (360°) counterclockwise, this will position the other cylinder at TDC of its compression stroke. Remove the rocker arm shafts and the rocker arms, then install the side housing in the same fashion as before.

10. Turn the engine over with the rotor bolt so that one of the cam sprocket bolts is at the top of the sprocket, remove the bolt. Turn the alternator rotor one complete turn counterclockwise and remove the remaining sprocket bolt. Both the side housings can now be removed. Remove the dowel pin from the right-side of the cam.

11. Lift the cam chain off the sprocket and lift the cam and the sprocket out the top of the cylinder head from the right-side. Wrap a piece of stiff wire around the cam chain so that it does not fall down in to the crankcase. The cylinder head can now be lifted off. If the head resists removal tap around the bottom with a plastic mallet to free it, however, take care not to break the cooling fins.

Lift off the chain (3) and remove the sprocket and cam (1 and 2)

125 MODELS

1. Remove the engine from the frame as described previously.
2. Remove the side covers from the sides of the cylinder head. Remove the two screws which secure the breaker point plate to the head and remove the plate. Remove the bolt from the left-side of the camshaft and pull the spark advancer unit off the cam.

The chain masterlink will be close to the sprocket "0" mark. To remove the sprocket, remove the bolts (2 and 3).

3. Remove three screws from the point base and remove the point base.
4. Rotate the engine so that the cam chain masterlink is located at the top of the cam sprocket.
5. Remove the two bolts which secure the cam sprocket to the camshaft. Remove the sprocket.

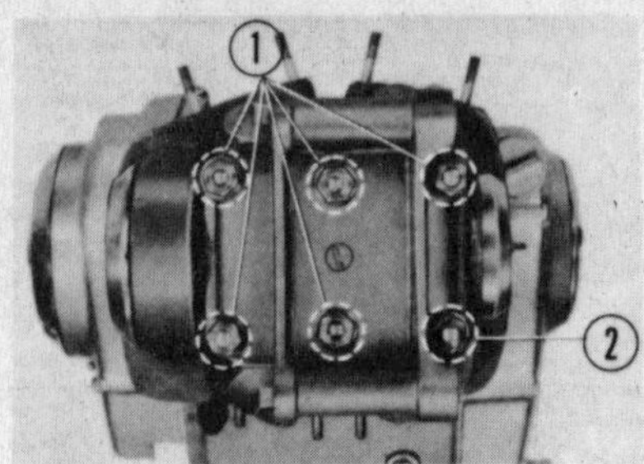

Cylinder head nuts (1) and capnut (2)

6. Remove the masterlink from the cam chain. Take care not to drop the masterlink into the cam chain passage. Fasten a piece of stiff wire onto each end of the cam chain, this will facilitate installation of the cam chain apon assembly.
7. Loosen the 6 head nuts gradually and evenly in an X pattern until they are all loose and then remove them and the breather cover.
8. Lift off the cylinder head, tapping around the base of the head with a plastic mallet if necessary to break the seal.

Disassembly

Disassembly of the head involves removing the camshaft, rocker arms, cam chain tensioner (175) and the valves on the 125, 175 models while on 200 models, only the cam chain tensioner and the valves remain in the head after the head is removed. Note, however, that the combustion chamber should be decarbonized and the sealing ability of the valves checked for all models before the valves are removed. Refer to the following inspection section for these procedures.

1. 175, 200 models: Remove the cam chain tensioner set bolt, and remove the tensioner push-bar and the tensioner spring.
2. 175 models: Loosen the valve adjusters so that there is clearance between the rocker arms and the cam. Remove the four screws from the right and left cylinder head side housings. Remove the side housings tapping them on the side with a plastic mallet if necessary. Pull the rocker arm shafts out of the head and remove the rocker arms. The cam can be lifted out of the head from the top.

Remove the rocker arm shafts (1) (175)

Remove the bolt (2) from the set plate (1) and remove the rocker arms (3) (125)

Removing the rocker arm shafts (1)

3. 125 models: Loosen the valve adjusters so that there is clearance at the rocker arms. Remove the bolt from the rocker arm shaft set plate and remove the plate. Pull the rocker arm shafts out of the head. Remove the rocker arms. Slide the camshaft out of the left-side of the head.
4. The valves can be removed after compressing the springs with a valve spring compressor and removing the

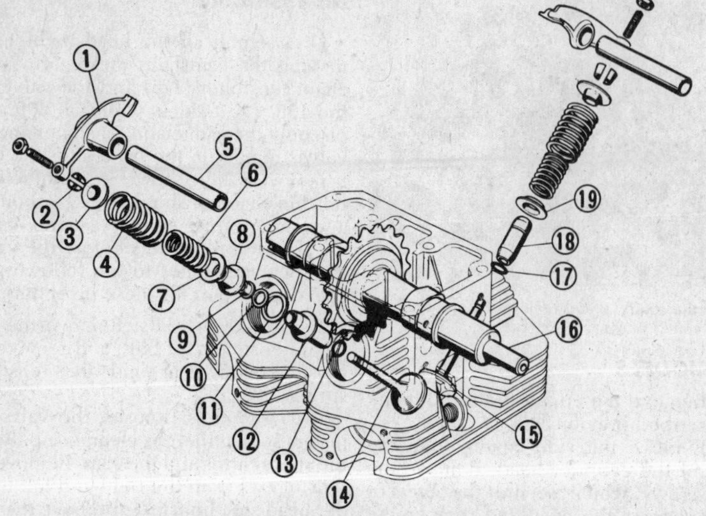

Cylinder head assembly (175). Other models are similar.

1. Rocker arm
2. Valve keeper
3. Spring retainer
4. Valve spring (outer)
5. Rocker arm shaft
6. Valve spring (inner)
7. Inner seal
8. Valve stem seal cap
9. Valve seal
10. Rubber cushion
11. Spring seal
12. Intake valve guide
13. O-ring
14. Exhaust valve
15. Intake valve
16. Camshaft
17. Guide clip
18. Intake valve guide
19. Spring seat

valve spring keepers. Remove the keepers, valve spring retainers, valve springs, and the spring seats. Where fitted, the valve seals should be removed from the guide and replaced with a new one upon assembly. All parts removed should be marked so that they can be installed in the same location they were removed from; this is especially important for the valves.

Inspection

Specifications are given in the charts at the end of this section.

CYLINDER HEAD

1. Maximum allowable mating surface warpage is 0.05 mm (0.002 in.).

2. 175, 200 models: Inspect the cam chain tensioner push bar and replace it if it is bent. Remove any burrs from the push bar with a file. Measure the free-length of the tensioner spring. If the spring is less than 80 mm (3.15 in.) in length, it should be replaced. Check the end of the set bolt and if it is deformed, the bolt should be replaced; this is a sign that the bolt has been overtightened.

VALVES

1. Valve seat width should be about 1.0 mm (0.04 in.) all the way around.

2. Valve faces and tips have a stellite surface. Refacing or grinding the tip are not recommended. Replace unsatisfactory valves.

3. If the valve guides are to be replaced, they should be driven out from the combustion chamber side with a proper size valve guide driver, and replaced with an oversized guide. After the guide is installed the inside bore should be reamed to the proper size.

NOTE: *The valve seats are cut at an angle relative to the valve guide (45°), therefore, whenever the guides are replaced the valve seats should be refaced with a valve seat grinder to the specifications shown in the accompanying illustration, and the valves lapped into the new seats.*

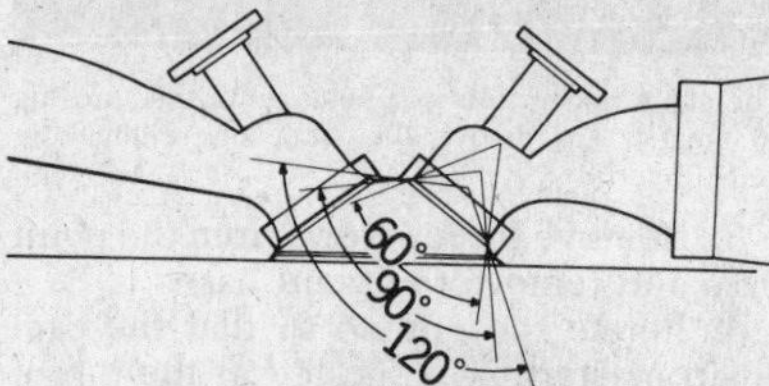

Specifications for valve seat angle (200)

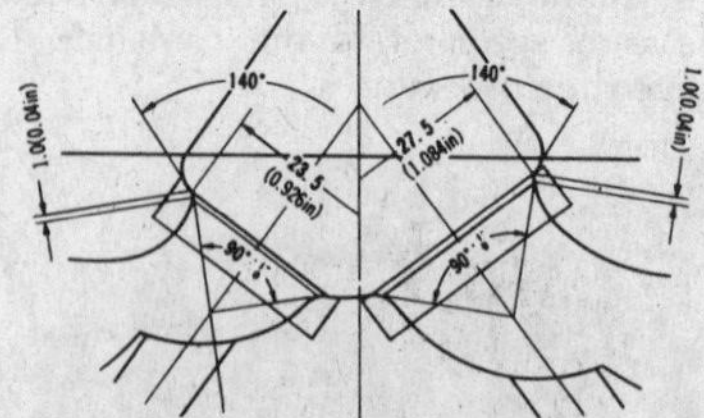

Specifications for valve seat angle (175)

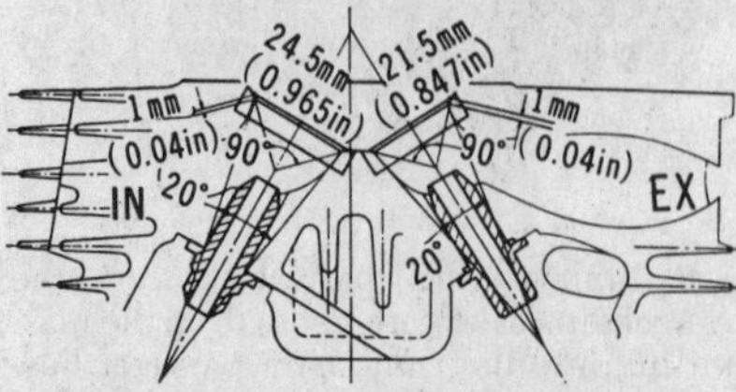

Specifications for valve seat angle (125)

Assembly

1. All parts should be coated with clean motor oil or one of the newer assembly lubricants before installing them.

2. Install the valve into its guide after coating the stem with oil. Install the spring seat, and oil seal (if fitted). Install the inner and outer valve springs with the close coils facing down (toward the head); the springs are progressively wound. Install the upper spring seat. Compress the springs with a valve spring compressor so that the keeper may be installed. Do not compress the springs more than is necessary to install the keepers. To do so may damage the valve guide or the oil seal (if fitted).

When installing the valve springs, be sure that the close coils are closest to the head

3. 125, 175: Install the camshaft into the head so that the "O" mark on the cam sprocket is at the top. It will be necessary to hold the cam sprocket in place on the 125 so that the cam can be installed properly. The two cam sprocket bolts are different types; be sure that the sprocket is positioned correctly and the bolts installed in the proper holes. Install the rocker arms and the rocker arm shafts and the set plate (125). On 125 models, once the cam is correctly positioned the sprocket can be removed.

4. 175, 200 models: Install the cam chain tensioner spring onto the push bar, then install the push bar into the head. Push the tensioner into the head as much as possible and tighten the set bolt.

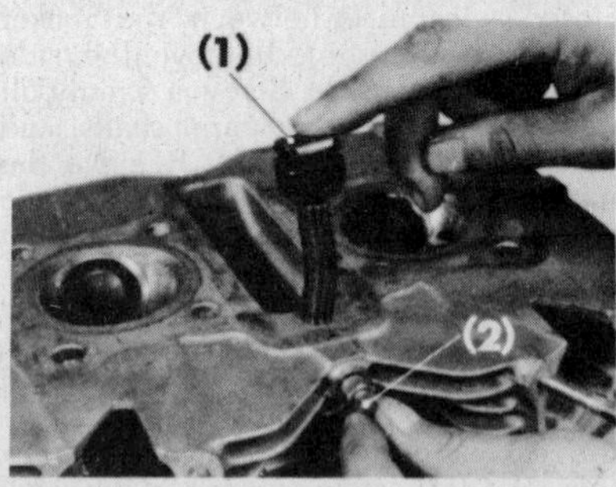

Push the cam chain tensioner push bar in as far as possible and tighten the set bolt (175, 200)

Installation

200

1. Install a new head gasket onto the top of the cylinder. Be sure that the mating surface of the cylinder and the head are clean and free of any scratches.

2. Install a guide pin to each of the outside cylinder studs (four total) and an O-ring to each of the outside rear studs.

3. Turn the crankshaft so that the "T" mark on the alternator rotor is aligned with the timing index mark on the stator. Hold the cam chain up when turning the crankshaft so it will not be jammed around the sprocket on the crankshaft. Be sure that the cam chain tensioner is pushed into the head as far as it will go. Install the head routing the cam chain

through the center. Slip a rod through the chain to keep it from falling down into the cylinder until the cam is to be installed.

4. Install the cam chain sprocket so that the aligning marks on the sprocket are parallel to the cylinder head mating surface.

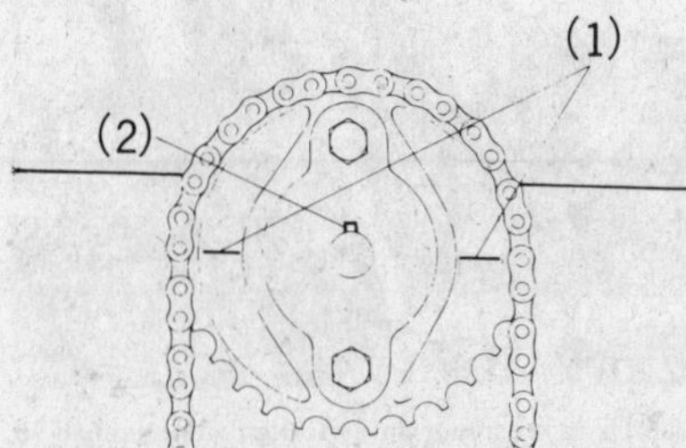

Install the sprocket so that the aligning marks (1) on the sprocket are parallel to the mating surface. The pin for the advance unit (2) must be vertical when the cam is installed

5. Install the camshaft into the cam sprocket with the locating pin for the spark advancer pointing up. Install the two cam sprocket bolts into the cam, and torque to 12–16 ft lbs.

NOTE: *The two cam bolts are special bolts and should not be confused with a standard 6 mm bolt. It is recommended that these bolts be replaced with new ones once removed, and installed with a thread locking compound.*

6. Install the rocker arms and the rocker arm shafts. Install the cylinder head side housing using new gaskets beneath them. Do not forget to prelube the camshaft bearings and the rocker arms and shafts.

7. Loosen the cam chain tensioner set bolt and recheck the valve timing. When the "T" mark on the alternator rotor is aligned with the timing index mark on the stator, the aligning marks on the camshaft sprocket MUST be perfectly parallel to the cylinder head mating surface. If the marks are not parallel, remove the camshaft and reset the timing.

8. If the timing is correct, install the breather cover gasket and the breather cover. Install the cylinder head nuts noting that the condenser is mounted on the right center rear stud. Tighten the head nuts in the order shown in the accompanying illustration a few ft lbs at a time until all the nuts are torqued to 13–16 ft lbs.

Cylinder head tightening sequence (200)

9. Adjust the valve clearance and the ignition timing.

175

1. Install a new head gasket to the top of the cylinder. Install a guide pin onto each of the outside studs (4 total). Install an O-ring onto the rear outside guide pins.

2. Slip the cam chain through the cam chain passage in the head and lower the head onto the top of the cylinder.

3. Using the alternator rotor bolt, turn the engine over so that the "T" mark on the rotor is aligned with the timing index mark on the stator. When rotating the crankshaft, hold the cam chain up so that it does not jam up around the crankshaft sprocket. When the crankshaft is in position, position the chain so that both sides are equal length.

4. Install the cam so that the "O" mark on the sprocket is at the top of the sprocket (in a line with the crankshaft and camshaft), and connect the cam chain. When installing the masterlink spring clip, the open end of the spring clip MUST face the opposite direction of chain rotation. The cam rotates counterclockwise when viewed from the left side.

With the "T" mark on the rotor aligned with the index mark, the "O" mark on the cam sprocket should be vertical as shown. Then install the cam chain masterlink (175)

NOTE: *It would be a good practice to replace the cam chain masterlink once removed as a broken cam chain will usually cause quite extensive damage to the engine.*

5. Install the rocker arms, rocker arm shafts, and the cylinder head side housings. New gaskets should be used under the side housings. The rocker arms should be installed onto the same shafts that they were removed from.

6. Release the cam chain tensioner set bolt, the chain will automatically adjust itself. Tighten the set bolt and locknut. Recheck the valve timing. If the "O" mark on the cam sprocket is not at top dead center of the cam sprocket with the "T" mark on the alternator rotor is aligned with the timing index mark on the stator, the valve timing will have to be reset.

If the timing is correct, the breather cover gasket and the breather cover can be installed. Tighten the head nuts in the order shown in the accompanying illustration. Tighten the bolts in increments of a few ft lbs until they are all tightened to the proper torque of 11.5–14.5 ft lbs.

7. Adjust the ignition timing and the valve clearance

Cylinder head tightening sequence (175)

125

1. Install a new head gasket on the top of the cylinder.

2. Turn the crankshaft so that the "T" mark on the alternator is in line with the timing index mark on the stator. Install the head while routing the cam chain through the passage in the head. Connect the cam chain with the masterlink; be sure that the open end of the masterlink spring clip is facing the opposite the direction of chain rotation (the cam turns counterclockwise when viewed from the left).

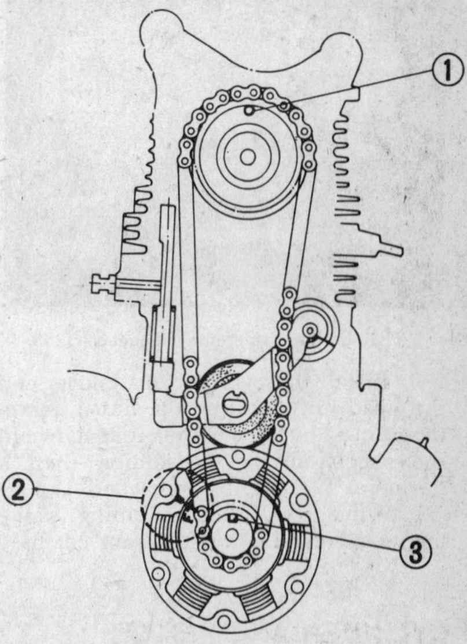

Valve timing index marks: 1, sprocket mark; 2, index mark and "T" mark; 3, crankshaft keyway. When the cam chain is joined, the marks must align as shown

3. Install the sprocket so that the "O" mark is at the top of the sprocket (in line with a line drawn from the crankshaft through the camshaft), when the "T" mark on the rotor is aligned with the timing index mark.

When the "T" mark on the alternator rotor is aligned with the index mark, the "O" mark on the sprocket (2) must align with the mark (1) of the cylinder head

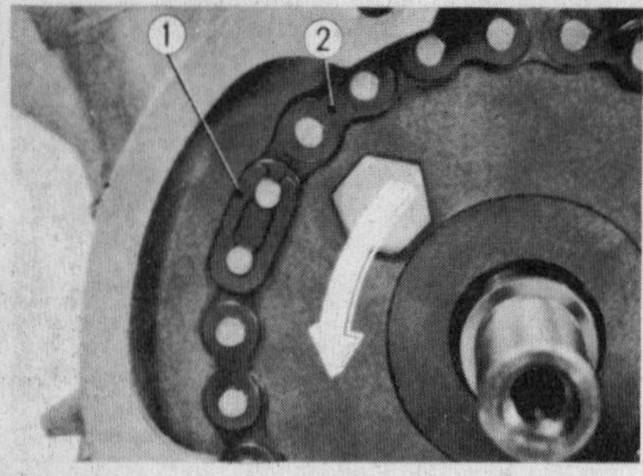

Be sure to install the cam chain masterlink with the closed end facing the direction of chain rotation (125)

4. Install the two cam bolts; note that the two bolts are different types and their installation should not be reversed. It would be a good idea to replace these bolts with new ones and install them with thread locking compound. Torque the cam bolts to 11.5–15 ft lbs.

5. Install the point base. Install the spark advancer locating the slot in the back of the advancer to the pin on the cam; secure the place with a 6 mm bolt. Install the breaker points.

Cylinder head tightening sequence (125)

6. Install the cylinder head cover and the head nuts. Torque the nut in increments of a few ft lbs in the order shown in the accompanying illustration until a torque of 12–15 ft lbs is reached.

7. Adjust the ignition timing, valve tappet clearance, and the cam chain.

CYLINDER AND PISTON

Removal

1. Remove the cylinder head.

2. Lift off the head gasket. If the head gasket is blown (a piece missing) or shows signs of leakage, inspect the cylinder head closely for warpage in this area.

3. Remove the cylinder hold-down bolt(s) located at the rear of the cylinder, or on the left-side of the cylinder (125).

4. Using the alternator rotor bolt, turn the crankshaft until the pistons are at the top of their strokes. Lift the cylinder up until the bottom of the pistons can be seen at the bottom of the cylinder, then stuff a clean rag around each of the connecting rods. This will prevent the rods from falling against the crankcase when the cylinders are removed and also keep foreign matter from entering the crankcase.

NOTE: *If the cylinder resists removal, tap around the bottom of the cylinder with a plastic mallet. When doing this be careful that the cooling fins are not damaged as will happen if they are struck at an angle. Never attempt to remove the cylinder by prying against the cooling fins.*

Cylinder bolt (1) (175, 200)

Cylinder bolts (1) (125)

5. With the rag still in place around the connecting rods, remove the wrist pin circlips. The easiest way to remove the circlips is with a pair of needlenose pliers. First rotate the circlip until the opening is near the cutout in the piston. Grasp the circlip near the end-gap and twist in while pulling out. The circlips should never be reused once removed.

6. Push the wrist pin out of the piston by hand if possible. If the pin resists removal, gently head the piston crown with a propane torch and try to push out the pin. Take care when heating the piston not to overheat it; this may distort it. If the pin still resists removal, the factory tool will have to be used. This tool has a band that fits around the piston and a screw device which is screwed in to push out the pin.

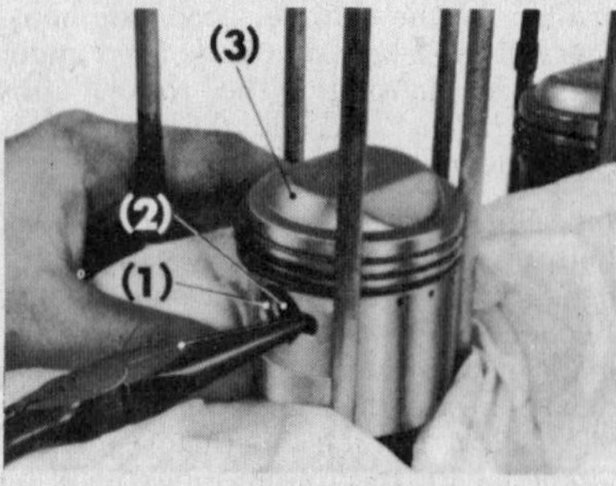

Removing the wrist pin circlips

CAUTION: *Never attempt to remove the wrist pin by tapping it out, as the connecting rod or the big end bearing will be damaged in the attempt.*

7. When the wrist pin is removed, the piston can be lifted from the connecting rod. As soon as the piston is removed it should be marked so that it can be installed in the proper cylinder.

8. 175, 200: Remove the two bolts securing the cam chain guide roller to the upper crankcase, and remove the roller assembly. Remove the cylinder base gasket. To remove the pivot pin from the tensioner arm, remove the circlip from either side and slip the pin out.

Cam chain tensioner guide roller components (175, 200)

1. Bolt
2. Snap-ring
3. Pivot arm
4. Chain tensioner roller
5. Guide roller

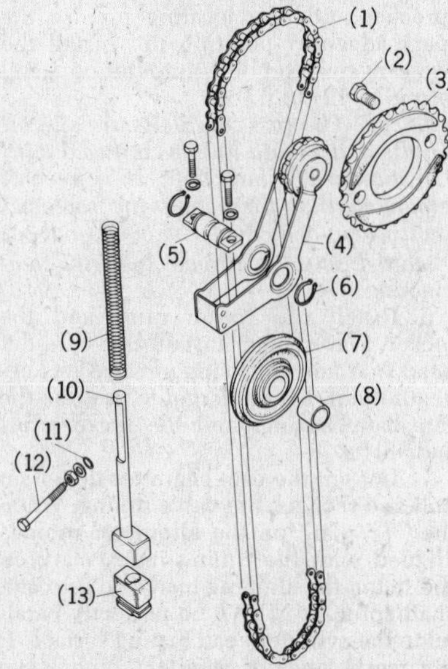

Cam chain tensioner components (175, 200)

1. Cam chain
2. Knock bolt
3. Cam sprocket
4. Chain tensioner
5. Pivot arm
6. Snap-ring
7. Guide roller
8. Collar
9. Tensioner spring
10. Push bar
11. O-ring
12. Setting bolt
13. Tensioner push rubber

Inspection

1. The piston and bore specifications in the "Engine Specifications" chart are for standard pistons. Oversize pistons have the oversize stamped on the piston crown. Oversize pistons are available in four oversizes from Honda (0.25, 0.50, 0.75, and 1.0 mm). New pistons come with the wrist pin and rings. If an oversize piston is needed due to a worn bore or worn or damaged pistons, obtain the piston first then have the cylinder bored so that the piston-to-cylinder wall clearance is 0.025–0.050 mm (0.001–0.002 in.).

2. If only piston rings are to be replaced with rings of the same size (standard with standard or oversize with the same oversize), the cylinders must be honed and the ridge at the top of the cyl-

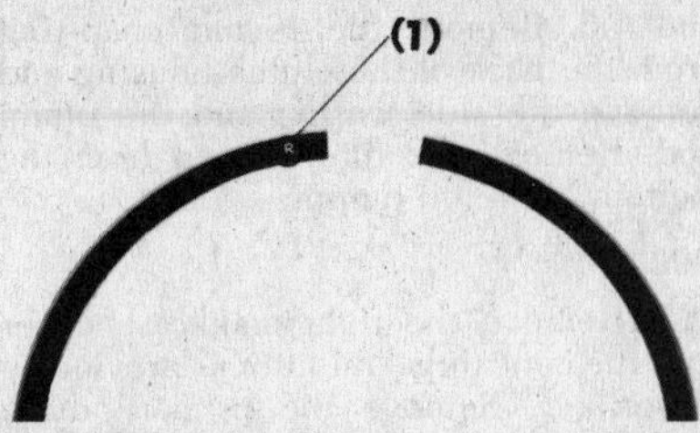

When the ring is installed, the manufacturer's mark (1) must be installed facing upward

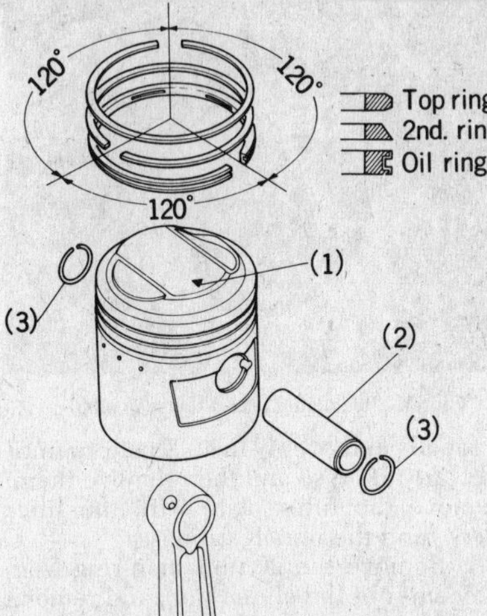

Piston and ring installation. The mark on the piston crown (1) should point toward the front of the engine. Circlip (3) end-gaps should not align with the cutouts on the piston.

inder removed. The ridge at the top of the cylinder is the upper limit of the top ring's travel. The top ring will wear so that it is mated perfectly with the ridge, however, a new ring will hit the ridge and collapse the piston. Honing the cylinder will aid in seating the new rings.

3. When rings are installed on the pistons, the manufacturer's mark must face *up;* ring end-gaps should be spaced 120° apart around the piston, with no end-gap directly at the front or rear of the piston or directly above the wrist pin.

If a multi-piece oil ring is fitted, position the end gap of the expander 120° from that of the lower compression ring, and the end-gaps of the oil rails 20–30 mm (0.8–1.2 in.) on either side of the expander end-gap.

Installation

1. Install a new wrist pin circlip into the left-side of the right piston and into the right-side of the left piston. If the piston has an arrow stamped on the top, install the piston so that the arrow is pointing to the front of the engine (exhaust side). If the piston has "IN" stamped on the top, install the piston so that the mark is to the rear (intake side) of the engine.

When installing the wrist pin circlips, be sure that the end-gap of the circlip is either at the top or the bottom of the circlip groove and that it is properly seated in the groove.

2. Install the bushing into the cam chain guide roller (200). Hold the guide roller in place in the tensioner arm and slip the pivot pin through the tensioner

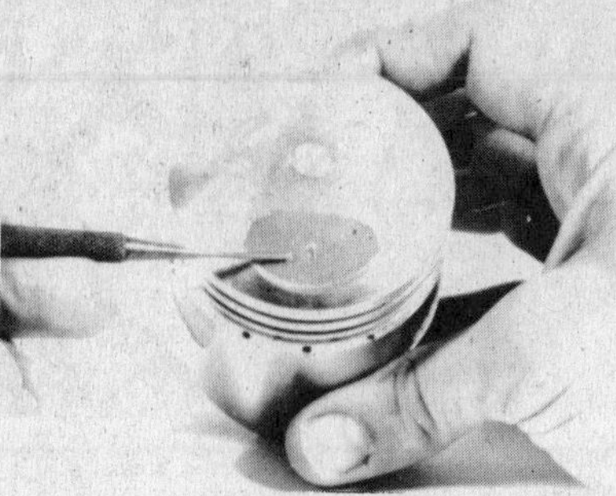

The arrow on the piston crown must point toward the front (exhaust side) of the engine

arm and guide roller. Secure the pivot pin in place with the two circlips.

3. Install the tensioner arm assembly between the cylinders with the small roller toward the rear of the engine. Install the two mounting bolts and lockwashers. Torque the bolts to 7–9 ft lbs.

4. Install a new cylinder base gasket and two locating pins to the upper crankcase mating surface.

5. Position the piston on the connecting rod so that the wrist pin holes line up with the connecting rod small end, and install the wrist pin after coating it with oil. Place a cloth under each piston to cover the hole in the crankcase and install the remaining circlip. Be sure that the circlip end-gap is either at the top or bottom of its groove.

6. Pull the cam chain up so that it runs on either side of the tensioner arm pivot pin.

7. Position the pistons at the top of their stroke. If piston bases are available, install them under the pistons, and position the pistons so that they are resting on the base. Coat the piston skirt and rings with clean motor oil; also coat the cylinder walls. Slide the cylinders down over the cylinder studs and pull the cam chain up between the cylinders. If a ring compressor is available, install it on the pistons. If not, have an assistant compress the rings as the cylinders are lowered over the pistons. Make sure that the ring end-gaps are still spaced 120° apart, and that the locating pins are installed in the upper crankcase. Install the cylinder hold-down bolt.
stalled in the upper crankcase. Install the cylinder hold-down bolt.

8. Install the locating pins in the top of the cylinder. Coat the head gasket with a thin coat of oil and position it on the cylinder.

9. Install the cylinder head.

CRANKCASE COVER COMPONENTS

The following sections deal with removal, installation, and inspection procedures for those components located beneath the left and right crankcase covers.

These parts can be serviced with the engine in the frame.

Note the following points:

1. Always drain the oil before removing the right or left front crankcase covers.

2. Any oil seals fitted to the covers (such as kick-starter or gearshift shaft seals) should be carefully checked each time the cover is removed. If the lips of the seal are torn or damaged, or if the seal leaks, remove it by prying it out of the cover with a small screwdriver or hooked tool. Take care not to use the cover itself as a leverage point without protecting it from possible damage.

To install a new seal, press it in with a block of wood which will cover the entire seal. Be sure that the seal is driven straight in until flush with the outer surface of the case, and not cocked to one side. Grease the lips of the seal before inserting any shaft into it. Where the seal must pass over splines on a shaft, ensure that there are no sharp edges from damaged splines which may tear the seal.

3. It is necessary to remove the centrifugal oil filter before the clutch housing can be removed. This requires a special wrench.

Right Crankcase Cover

The right crankcase cover houses the centrifugal oil filter, the clutch, oil pump, external shifter mechanism, and the primary drive.

REMOVAL AND INSTALLATION

1. Remove the oil filler cap and drain the oil.

2. Remove the kick-starter pinch-bolt and pull the kick-starter off its shaft.

3. On CB models, remove the right exhaust pipe.

4. 200 models: Remove the clutch cover and disconnect the clutch cable.

5. Remove the mounting screws and remove the crankcase cover noting the location of any locating pins.

6. Installation is in the reverse order of removal, however, note the following points:

a. Install a new cover gasket;

b. Be sure that the two locating pins are in place between the cover and the crankcase;

c. Inspect the kick-starter shaft seal in the cover. If the lips are torn or damaged the seal should be replaced before installation.

Centrifugal Oil Filter

REMOVAL AND INSTALLATION

1. The oil filter can be removed through the access cover in the right crankcase cover on 125, 175 models. On 200 models, the right crankcase cover must be removed.

2. Remove the screw from the center of the filter cap and pull the cap off the filter housing by screwing an 8 mm bolt into the center, or by using a pliers.

3. Bend back the locktabs from the filter nut in the center of the filter housing. Hold the crankshaft from turning while removing the filter nut with special wrench (Tool No. 07916-2830000). Once the nut is removed the filter housing can be removed from the crankshaft.

4. To install the filter, slide the filter housing onto the end of the crankshaft. Install the tab washer into the filter housing so that the slot in the large tab is

Removing the oil filter cap (1) retaining screw (2)

located over a set of splines inside the filter housing. Install the filter nut with the chamfered side toward the engine, and bend the tabs of the tab washer into the slots in the filter nut.

5. Install the filter cap into the filter housing, noting that the vanes on the cap must fit into the splines in the filter housing. Before installing the filter cap, be sure that the O-ring is in place on the cap, and that it is in good condition.

Clutch and Primary Drive

REMOVAL

125, 175

1. Remove the right crankcase cover and the centrifugal oil filter as described previously. Remove the outside primary gear.

2. Remove the four clutch spring bolts. These bolts should be loosened gradually and evenly in an X pattern to avoid distorting the pressure plate. Remove the spring retainer plate, the clutch springs, the pressure plate, and the pressure plate lifter.

3. Remove the friction and steel clutch

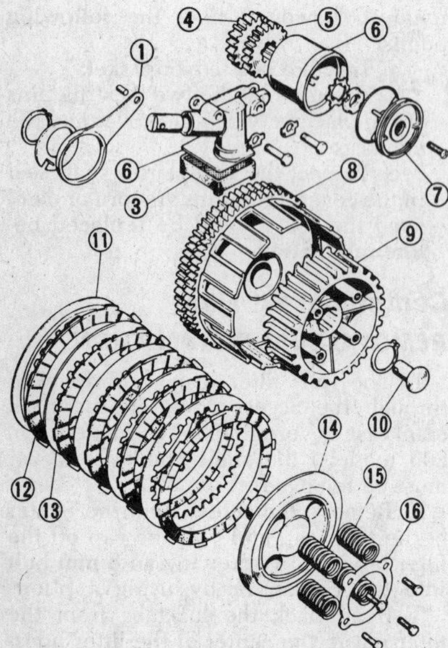

Clutch assembly (125, 175)

1. Pump rod
2. Pump body
3. Filter screen
4. Primary drive gear (inside)
5. Primary drive gear (outside)
6. Filter housing
7. Filter cap
8. Clutch housing
9. Clutch hub
10. Lifter
11. Hub plate
12. Friction plate
13. Steel plate
14. Pressure plate
15. Clutch spring
16. Spring retainer

Outside primary gear (1) and clutch pressure plate bolts (2)

Removing the clutch hub snap-ring

Oil pump mounting bolts (1)

To remove the piston (3), push out the pin (2); to remove the rod from the clutch housing, remove the snap-ring (1)

plates, note that the steel plate at the rear of the hub is a special plate and must be installed first upon assembly. Remove the 20 mm snap-ring from the center of the clutch hub and remove the hub.

4. Bend back the tabs securing the oil pump mounting bolts, and remove the bolts. The clutch housing and the oil pump assembly can now be removed together.

5. Remove the inside primary gear from the end of the crankshaft. Remove the clutch pushrod from the center of the mainshaft. It may be necessary to apply the clutch lever so that the pushrod will protrude from the mainshaft.

6. Remove the oil pump from the pump rod. Push the pin out of the oil pump piston and remove the piston from the rod. Remove the 26 mm snap-ring from the back of the clutch housing and remove the side washer and the pump rod. Remove the filter screen from the bottom of the oil pump.

200

1. Remove the right crankcase cover and the centrifugal oil filter as previously described. Remove the primary drive gear from the end of the crankshaft.

2. Loosen the four lifter plate bolts

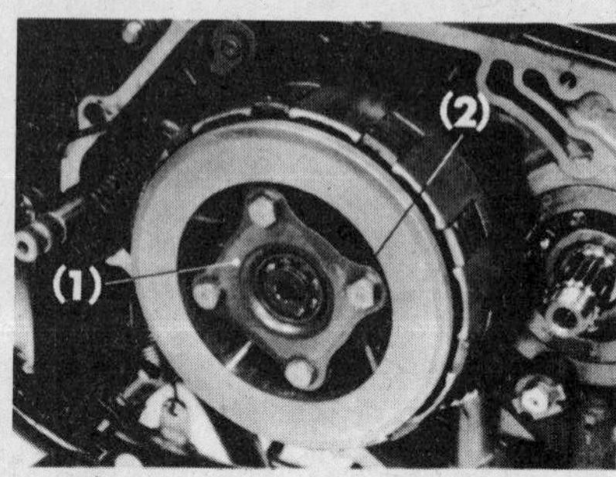

Clutch lifter plate (1) and bolts (2) (200)

gradually and evenly in an X pattern until they are all loose and then remove them. Remove the lifter plate with the lifter piece, and the clutch springs.

3. Remove the 20 mm snap-ring from the center of the clutch hub, and remove the hub together with the clutch plates and the pressure plate.

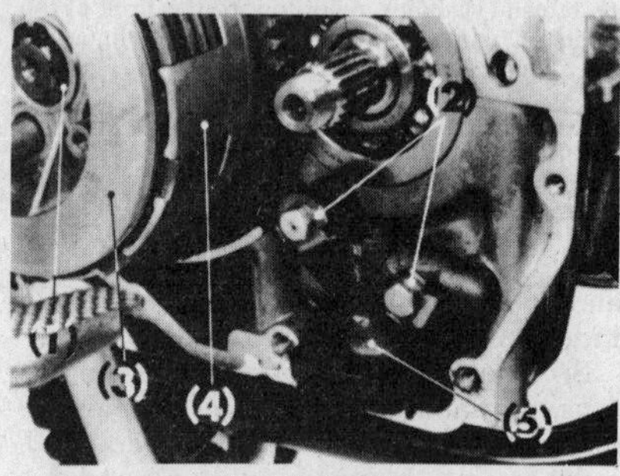

To remove the clutch assembly, remove the snap-ring (1) and oil pump bolts (2)

4. To remove the plates from the hub, first lift off the 5 friction plates and the 4 steel plates between them. Remove the 92 mm set ring from the hub and lift off the hub plate, the clutch disc spring, and the clutch disc spring seat.

5. Remove the two bolts securing the oil pump in place, and remove the clutch housing together with the oil pump.

6. Pull the pump from the pump rod. Push the pin out of the oil pump piston and remove the piston. Remove the snap-

Clutch housing and oil pump components: 1, snap-ring; 2, side washer; 3, pump rod; 4, pin; 5, piston

ring from the back of the clutch hub, and remove the pump rod side washer, and the pump rod.

INSPECTION

Refer to the specifications charts at the end of this section for clutch dimensions.

Refer to "Lubrication System" for oil pump inspection procedures.

INSTALLATION

125, 175

1. Slip the pushrod into the center of the mainshaft. Be sure that the domed end of the rod is on the clutch side.
2. Install the inside primary gear onto the end of the crankshaft.
3. Install the oil pump connecting rod to the back of the clutch housing, install the side washer. Fit the tab on the side washer into the hole in the clutch housing, and secure in place with the snap-ring. Fit the oil pump piston to the connecting rod and install the piston pin. Oil the piston and insert it into the bore of the oil pump.
4. Install the clutch housing and the oil pump at the same time. Use a new gasket behind the oil pump. Mount the oil pump with the two mounting bolts and bend the side of the lockplates up against the flats on the head of the bolts. Be sure that the lockplates are secured to the oil pump by the large tab on the bottom. Use new lockplates if necessary.
5. Install the clutch hub on the mainshaft and secure with a snap-ring. Install the pushrod and the pressure plate lifter. Install the special steel plate onto the hub first, then install a friction plate, steel plate, and so on until all of the plates are installed. The top plate should be a friction plate.
6. Install the pressure plate, clutch springs, spring retainer plate, and bolts. Tighten the bolts gradually and evenly in an X pattern until they are tight.

When installing the primary gears, line up the punch marks (1)

7. Install the remaining primary drive gear so that the punch mark on the gear is aligned with the punch mark on the inside gear, then install the centrifugal oil filter. When installing the oil filter locknut, be sure that the chamfered side is facing the engine.
8. Install the right crankcase cover.

200

1. Install the clutch pushrod into the center of the mainshaft so that the domed end is facing the clutch.
2. Install the oil pump connecting rod to the back of the clutch housing, install the side washer. Fit the tab on the side washer into the hole in the clutch housing, and secure in place with the snap-ring. Fit the oil pump piston to the connecting rod and install the piston pin. Oil the piston and insert it into the bore of the oil pump.
3. Install the clutch housing and the oil pump at the same time. Use a new gasket behind the oil pump. Mount the oil pump with the two mounting bolts and bend the side of the lockplates up against the flats on the head of the bolts. Be sure that the lockplates are secured to the oil pump by the large tab on the bottom. Use new lockplates if necessary.
4. Install the primary gear onto the end of the crankshaft.

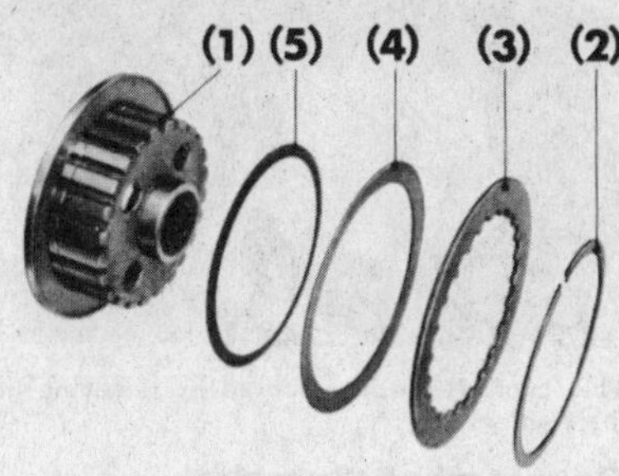

Clutch components: 1, clutch hub; 2, set-ring; 3, hub plate; 4, disc spring; 5, disc spring seat (200)

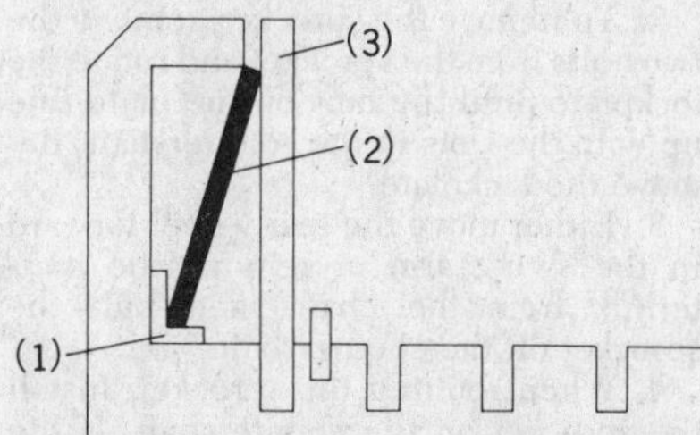

Clutch disc spring seat (1), clutch disc spring (2), and clutch hub plate (3) installed on hub

5. Install the clutch disc spring seat, clutch disc spring, the hub steel plate, and the 92 mm set ring onto the hub as shown in the accompanying illustration. Install a friction plate, a steel plate, and so on until all of the plates are in place, the top plate should be a friction plate. Install the pressure plate to the rear of the hub.
6. Install the hub assembly into the clutch housing, and secure it in place with the snap-ring.
7. Install the clutch springs into the hub. Install the spring retainer plate and the bolts. Tighten the bolts gradually and evenly in an X pattern.
8. Install the centrifugal oil filter onto the end of the crankshaft. When installing the oil filter locknut be sure that the chamfered side is facing the engine.
9. Install the right crankcase cover and adjust the clutch.

Shifter Mechanism

REMOVAL

1. Remove the right crankcase cover and the clutch as previously described.
2. Remove the shift lever and the left rear crankcase cover. Remove the circlip from the shifter shaft on the left-side.

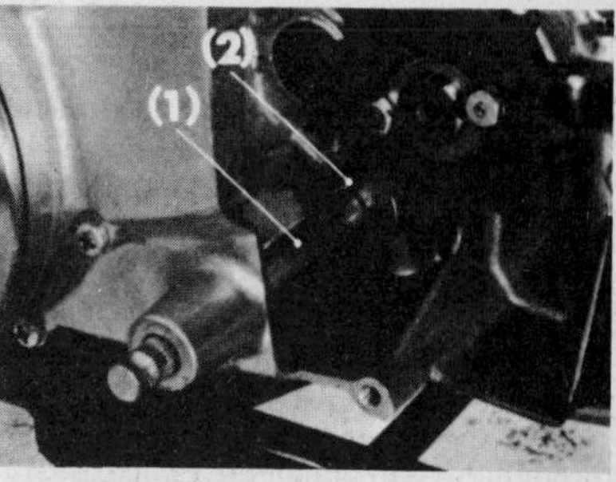

Remove the circlip (2) from the shifter shaft (1) to remove the shaft

3. Pull the shift arm down to disengage the fingers from the shift drum and pull the shaft out from the right-side.
4. Remove the nut from the drum stopper stud and remove the drum stopper, drum stopper spring, drum stopper collar, neutral stopper, stopper arm plate, and neutral stopper spring.

Shift arm (1), shift drum (2), shift shaft (3)

Shift drum stopper (1) and neutral stopper (2)

INSPECTION

1. Check that the drum stopper collar has not been crushed. If this has happened, replace it.
2. Check the splines on the gearshift shaft. If the splines are broken or torn to such an extent that it is difficult to properly secure the shift lever, replace the shaft.
3. Check the shift arm. Be sure that it is not bent. Check that the fingers of the shift arm are not worn or bent.
4. Check the condition of the springs in the shift linkage, especially the shift lever return spring. If any spring has lost its tension, or fails to hold its component properly, it must be replaced.
5. Check that the return spring pin is secure in the case.

INSTALLATION

1. Install the neutral stopper spring, stopper arm plate, neutral stopper, drum stopper collar, drum stopper spring, and the drum stopper onto the drum stopper stud. Install the flat washer and the nut. Check the drum stopper and the neutral stopper are free to move. If not, the nut is too tight or the drum stopper collar is crushed.
2. Coat the shift shaft with a light coat of grease and slip it through the right-side of the engine. As the shaft comes through the left-side of the crankcase, install the snap-ring on the shaft. Ensure that the fingers of the shift arm are in contact with the pins in the shift drum.
3. Refit the clutch and the right crankcase cover. On 200 models, be sure to adjust the clutch before operation.

Left Crankcase Cover

The left crankcase cover houses the alternator, starter clutch, neutral switch, countershaft sprocket, and the clutch release mechanism (125, 175).

REMOVAL AND INSTALLATION

1. Remove the pinch-bolt from the shift lever and pull the lever off its shaft.
2. Remove the three mounting screws from the rear cover and remove the cover. Note the location of any locating pins.

Disconnect the neutral switch lead (1) and remove the cable clamp (2)

3. Before removing the front cover, drain the engine oil or remove the battery and tilt the motorcycle at about a 45° angle to the right. Remove the three stator cover mounting screws. Remove the stator cover.
4. Disconnect the alternator wiring from the wiring harness. Disconnect the lead from the neutral switch. Remove the cable clamp from the alternator leads.
5. Remove the mounting screws from the front cover and remove the cover. On 125, 175 models, disconnect the clutch cable from the release mechanism.

NOTE: *On 125, 175 models, be sure not to lose the steel ball from the clutch release mechanism when the cover is removed.*

6. The stator can be removed from the cover once the three mounting screws are removed.
7. To install the covers, attach the stator to the front cover with the three mounting screws. Use a new gasket under the front cover. Be sure to install the two locating pins under each cover.

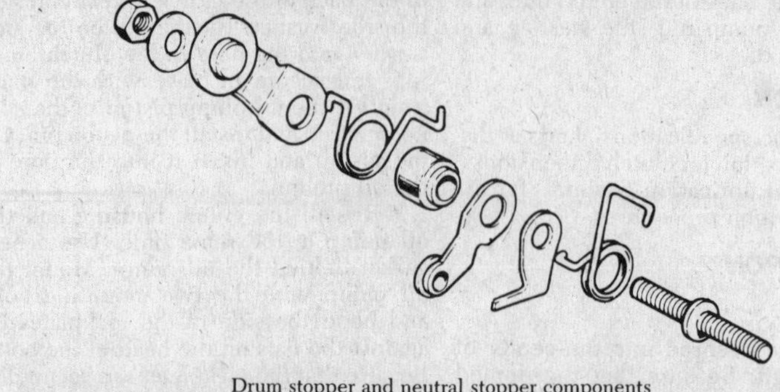

Drum stopper and neutral stopper components

The stator (1) can be removed by removing the three screws (2)

Countershaft Sprocket

1. Remove the left rear crankcase cover as described previously.
2. To remove the sprocket, remove the two bolts from the sprocket and rotate the lockplate until the tabs on the plate line up with the slots in the countershaft. Remove the lockplate.
3. Either move the rear wheel forward in the swing arm or remove the masterlink from the chain, and pull the sprocket off the countershaft.
4. When refitting the sprocket, install the sprocket on the countershaft. If the masterlink has not been removed, refit the chain to the sprocket before installing the sprocket to the countershaft. Install the lockplate on the countershaft and rotate it until the holes in the sprocket line up with the holes in the lockplate. Install the two bolts and torque to 5.8–8.7 ft lbs.

Alternator and Starter Assembly

REMOVAL

1. Remove the crankcase covers and stator as described previously.
2. Remove the rotor bolt while holding the engine from turning over.
3. Remove the alternator rotor using the factory tool (Tool No. 07933-2160000). The starter clutch is removed with the alternator rotor.
4. Remove the woodruff key from the taper on the crankshaft.
5. The starter clutch can be removed from the back of the rotor after removing the three phillips head screws. Remove the clutch side plate.
6. The starter motor chain can be removed (after removing the sprocket setting plate), by pulling off both sprockets and the chain at the same time.
7. Unbolt the starter motor from the front of the engine, disconnecting the starter motor cable at the motor, and remove the motor tapping the shaft lightly with a plastic mallet if necessary.

Removing the starter clutch screws from the alternator rotor

INSPECTION

1. For further inspection of the alternator rotor, stator, and starting motor, refer to "Electrical System."
2. Check that the rollers in the starter clutch are free to move. Also check that they all have the same amount of spring tension on them. If any spring feels weak in relation to the others, replace it by removing the roller, spring cap, and spring. Replace the spring and install the cap and roller.
3. Inspect the clutch housing for any cracks. If found defective, it must be replaced.
4. Inspect the surface of the starter sprocket where the rollers contact it. If badly scored, the sprocket and the rollers should be replaced.
5. Inspect the condition of the sprocket teeth. If they are hooked or appear to be worn badly, replace both sprockets and the chain.

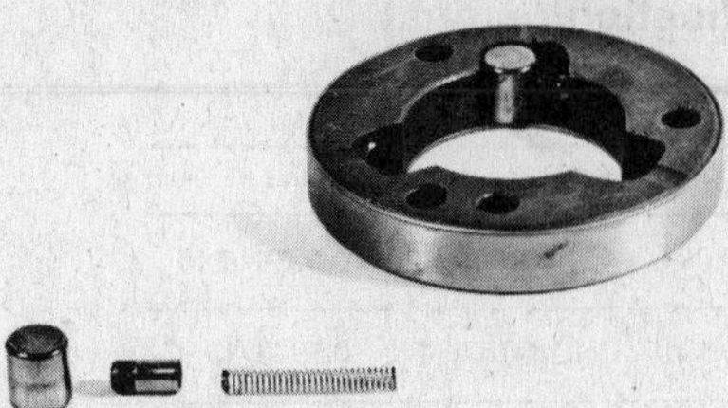

Starter clutch components

INSTALLATION

1. Mount the starter motor on the front of the engine with the two mounting screws.
2. Install the starter motor chain and the two sprockets at the same time. Install the starter sprocket setting plate.
3. Mount the starter clutch on the rotor with the three screws. Be sure to install the side plate between the rotor and the clutch.
4. Install the woodruff key in the crankshaft and install the rotor lining up the slot in the rotor with the key in the crankshaft. Draw the rotor down on the crankshaft with the rotor bolt, never strike the rotor as this may affect the magnets.
5. Install the stator in the crankcase cover, then install the cover using a new gasket. Check that the rotor does not come in contact with the stator as the engine turns over. Install the stator cover and the rear cover.

CRANKCASE COMPONENTS

To service the kick-starter, transmission, or the crankshaft, the crankcases will have to be separated. To service the kick-starter and transmission, the left and right crankcase covers and the components beneath them will have to be removed. Service to the crankshaft also necessitates the disassembly of the top end as the cam chain must be removed with the crankshaft (200) or disconnected (125, 175).

Splitting the Crankcases

1. Remove the engine from the frame.
2. If the crankshaft is to be serviced, disassemble the top end as outlined previously.
3. Remove the right and left crankcase covers and the components beneath them.

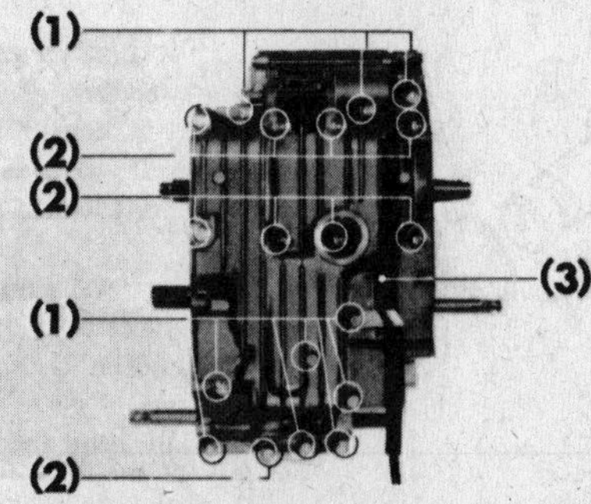

Lower crankcase bolts: 1, 6 mm; 2, 8 mm; 3, starter motor cable

Engine Specifications

200

Component	*Standard (in./mm)*	*Wear Limit (in./mm)*
Rocker arm-to-shaft clearance	0.0005–0.0017/0.013–0.043	0.004/0.1
Cam height Intake	0.9865/25.058	0.9803/24.9
Exhaust	0.9792/24.872	0.9724/24.7
Valve seat width	0.0394–0.0551/1.0–1.4	0.0709/1.8
Valve-to-guide clearance Intake	0.0006–0.0014/0.015–0.035	0.0032/0.08
Exhaust	0.0013–0.0022/0.033–0.055	0.0039/0.1
Valve spring free-length Inner	1.3091/33.25	1.2598/32.0
Outer	1.3799/35.05	1.3583/34.5
Valve stem OD Intake	0.2157–0.2161/5.48–5.49	0.2134/5.42
Exhaust	0.2150–0.2154/5.46–5.472	0.2126/5.40
Cylinder ID (standard)	2.1850–2.1834/55.50–55.51	2.1890/55.6
(max)		2.2290/56.6
Piston skirt OD	2.1839–2.1846/55.47–55.49	2.1819/56.42
Wrist pin OD	0.5903–0.5906/14.994–15.000	0.5866/14.9
Wrist pin hole ID	0.5906–0.5909/15.002–15.008	0.5925/15.05
Piston ring side clearance Top	0.0016–0.0030/0.04–0.075	0.0059/0.15
Second	0.0010–0.0024/0.025–0.06	0.0059/0.15
Oil	0.0006–0.0018/0.015–0.045	0.0059/0.15
Piston ring end-gap	0.0059–0.0138/0.15–0.35	0.0295/0.75
Oil pump bore-to-plunger clearance	0.0010–0.0025/0.025–0.063	0.0067/0.17
Pump rod-to-clutch housing clearance	0.0010–0.0030/0.025–0.075	0.0059/0.15
Friction disc thickness	0.1150–0.1213/2.92–3.08	0.1024/2.6
Clutch steel plate warpage	0.0039/0.1	0.0079/0.2
Clutch spring free-length	1.1126/28.26	1.0512/26.7
Shift fork finger thickness	0.2110–0.2142/5.36–5.44	0.1969/5.0
Shift fork ID	1.3386–1.3396/34.000–34.025	1.3415/34.075
Shift drum OD	1.3366–1.3376/33.950–33.975	1.3346/33.9
Shift fork guide pin clearance in shift drum	0.0035–0.0070/0.11–0.179	0.0197/0.5
Transmission gear backlash 1st, 2nd, 3rd	0.0035–0.0070/0.089–0.179	0.0079/0.2
4th, 5th	0.0037–0.0074/0.094–0.188	0.0079/0.2

Upper crankcase bolts (125 shown)

NOTE: *Loosen the oil filter nut and the rotor bolt before removing the clutch.*

4. Turn the engine upside down and remove the nine 6 mm bolts and nine 8 mm bolts from the lower crankcase. One of these bolts can be reached through the drain plug opening. Remove any mounting bolts from the upper crankcase. Remove the lower crankcase half, tapping around the mating surface with a plastic mallet to free the case half if stuck. The crankshaft and the transmission will remain in the upper half.

Kick-Starter

REMOVAL

1. Split the crankcases as described previously.
2. Remove the return spring from the kick-starter shaft on the outside of the lower crankcase.
3. Remove the circlip from the inside of the shaft and remove the components from the shaft. Slip the shaft out of the case.

INSPECTION

1. Inspect the splines on the end of the kick-starter shaft. If they are damaged to the extent that the kick-starter lever cannot be properly fastened, the kick-starter shaft should be replaced.
2. Check the condition of all circlips. Replace any which are distorted.
3. Inspect the condition of the springs, replacing any which are weak or broken.

The friction spring should be seated properly in the gear

4. Check that the kick gear rotates freely on the shaft gear. If the gear binds, it should be repaired or replaced.

INSTALLATION

1. Install the shaft into the lower crankcase half. Install the components on the shaft as shown in the accompanying illustration. Hold the shaft so that the

Engine Specifications (cont.)

200

Component	Standard (in./mm)	Wear Limit (in./mm)
Crankshaft run-out (at center)	0.0008/0.02	0.0059/0.15
Connecting rod small end ID	0.5912–0.5919/15.016–15.034	0.5933/15.07
Connecting rod big end side clearance	0.0028–0.0130/0.07–0.33	0.0236/0.6

175

Component	Standard (in./mm)	Wear Limit (in./mm)
Rocker arm-to-shaft clearance	0.0005–0.0017/0.013–0.043	0.004/0.1
Cam height Intake	0.9865/25.06	0.9802/24.90
Exhaust	0.9790/24.87	0.9668/24.70
Valve seat width	0.028–0.039/0.7–1.0	0.0709/1.8
Valve-to-guide clearance Intake	0.0006–0.0014/0.015–0.035	0.0032/0.08
Exhaust	0.0013–0.0022/0.033–0.055	0.0039/0.1
Valve spring free-length Inner	1.1890/30.2	1.0984/27.9
Outer	1.2520/31.8	1.2047/30.6
Valve stem OD Intake	0.2157–0.2161/5.48–5.49	0.2134/5.42
Exhaust	0.2149–0.2153/5.46–5.47	0.2126/5.40
Cylinder ID (standard)	2.0472–2.0476/52.00–52.01	2.0512/52.1
(max)	——	2.1299/54.1
Piston skirt OD (standard)	2.0452–2.0471/51.95–51.97	2.0433/51.90

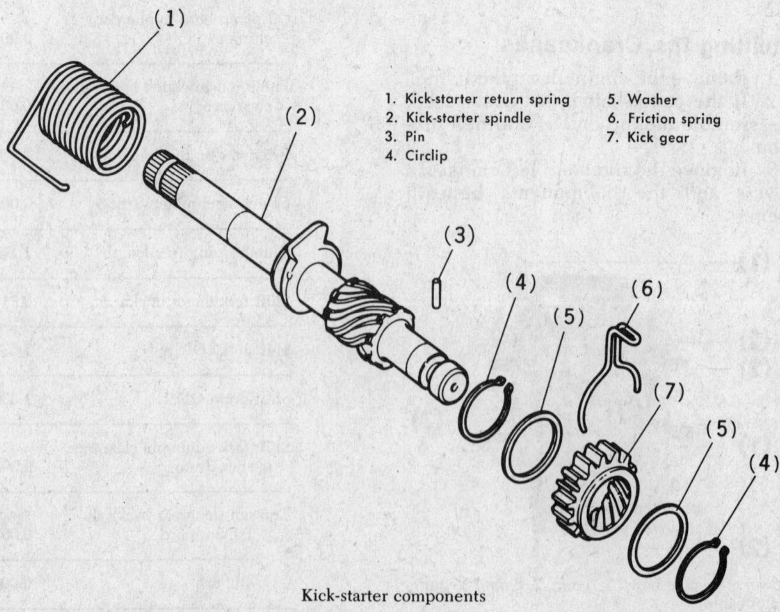

Kick-starter components

stop on the shaft is against the stop in the lower crankcase when installing the internal components. Be sure that the friction spring is seated properly in the crankcase.

When installing the kick-starter shaft (1), be sure that the friction spring (2) is located in the recess in the crankcase (3)

Transmission

REMOVAL

1. Split the crankcases as described previously. The transmission shafts can be lifted out of the top case.

Mainshaft (1) and countershaft (2)

2. Remove the neutral switch rotor and the drum stopper from the shift drum. Remove the bearing set plate from the right side of the upper crankcase. Remove the guide pin clips and the guide pins from the shift forks. Mark the location of each shift fork (left, center, and right; or, left and right on four-speed transmissions), and slide the shift drum out of the case from the right-side.

Removing the bearing set plate (1) to remove the shift drum

3. The transmission gears can be removed from their shafts after removing the circlips which secure them. All components should be carefully laid out in the order in which they are removed so that they can be installed in their proper locations.

Engine Specifications (cont.)

175

Component	Standard (in./mm)	Wear Limit (in./mm)
Cylinder taper (max)	0.0002/0.005	0.0020/0.05
Cylinder out-of-round (max)	0.0002/0.005	0.0020/0.05
Piston ring groove width Top, Second	0.047–0.048/1.205–1.220	0.0512/1.3
Oil	0.098–0.099/2.50–2.52	0.1024/2.6
Ring thickness Top	0.046–0.0464/1.165–1.180	0.0443/1.125
Second	0.046–0.047/1.175–1.190	0.0447/1.135
Oil	0.097–0.098/2.475–2.490	0.0957/2.43
Ring end-gap (all)	0.006–0.016/0.15–0.40	0.0315/0.8
Ring side clearance Top, Second	0.0006–0.0018/0.015–0.045	0.004/0.1
Oil	0.0004–0.0018/0.01–0.045	0.004/0.1
Wrist pin hole ID	0.5118–0.5120/13.000–13.006	0.5128/13.05
Piston-to-cylinder clearance	0.0004–0.0020/0.01–0.05	0.004/0.1
Oil pump bore-to-plunger clearance	0.0010–0.0025/0.025–0.063	0.0067/0.17
Pump rod-to-clutch housing clearance	0.0010–0.0030/0.025–0.075	0.0059/0.15
Clutch friction disc Thickness	0.115–0.121/2.92–3.08	0.0984/2.5
Warpage	less than 0.0079/0.2	0.0196/0.5
Clutch steel plate Thickness	0.118/3.0	0.114/2.9
Warpage	—	0.0196/0.5
Clutch spring free-length	1.2224/31.05	1.1929/30.3
Cam chain tensioner spring free-length	3.268/83	3.1496/80
Shift drum groove	0.240–0.244/6.1–6.2	0.256/6.4
Mainshaft-to-mainshaft gear clearance 2nd	0.0006–0.0018/0.016–0.045	0.004/0.1
5th	0.0004–0.0018/0.011–0.045	0.004/0.1
Countershaft-to-countershaft gear clearance 3rd, 4th	0.0004–0.0010/0.009–0.025	0.004/0.1
1st	0.0006–0.0018/0.016–0.045	0.004/0.1
Transmission shaft bearing clearance (630HS) Axial clearance	less than 0.002/0.05	0.004/0.1
Radial clearance	0.0004–0.0010/0.01–0.025	0.002/0.05

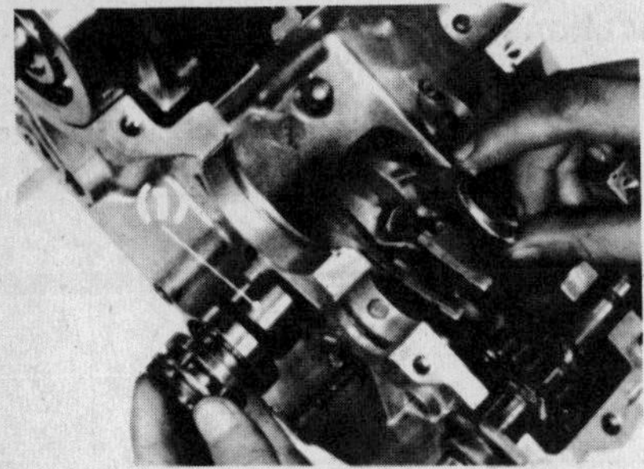

Remove the shift drum (1) and shift forks

INSTALLATION

1. Slip the shift drum into the upper crankcase; as the drum enters the case, install the shift forks. Be sure that the forks are installed in the same position from which they were removed. Install the neutral switch to the end of the shift drum.

2. Install the bearing set plate and the neutral stopper and drum stopper. Position the shift drum in the neutral position as seen by the neutral switch.

3. Assemble the mainshaft and the countershaft. Install the transmission shafts in the upper case. Be sure that the shift forks are fitted to the proper gears. Be sure that the bearings are fitted to the set ring or the locating pins. When properly fitted the bearings should sit flush in the case.

4. The remainder of assembly is in the reverse order of removal.

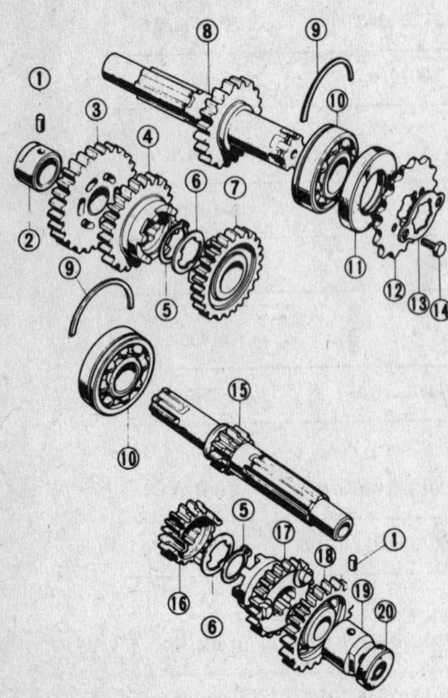

Transmission (4-speed)

1. Locating pin
2. Bushing
3. Countershaft first gear
4. Countershaft second gear
5. Circlip
6. Thrust washer
7. Countershaft third gear
8. Countershaft
9. Bearing set ring
10. Ball bearing
11. Oil seal
12. Countershaft sprocket
13. Lockplate
14. Bolt
15. Mainshaft
16. Mainshaft second gear
17. Mainshaft third gear
18. Mainshaft fourth gear
19. Bushing
20. Oil seal

Engine Specifications

125

Component	Standard (in./mm)	Wear Limit (in./mm)
Rocker arm-to-shaft clearance	0.0005–0.0017/0.013–0.043	0.004/0.1
Cam height Intake	0.9865/25.06	0.9802/24.90
Exhaust	0.9790/24.87	0.9668/24.70
Valve seat width	0.028–0.039/0.7–1.0	0.0709/1.8
Valve-to-guide clearance Intake	0.0006–0.0014/0.015–0.035	0.0032/0.08
Exhaust	0.0013–0.0022/0.033–0.055	0.0039/0.1
Valve spring free-length Inner	1.1890/30.2	1.0984/27.9
Outer	1.2520/31.8	1.2047/30.6
Valve stem OD Intake	0.2157–0.2161/5.48–5.49	0.2134/5.42
Exhaust	0.2149–0.2153/5.46–5.47	0.2126/5.40
Wrist pin hole ID	0.5118–0.5120/13.000–13.006	0.5128/13.05
Piston-to-cylinder clearance	0.0004–0.0020/0.01–0.05	0.004/0.1
Cylinder ID (standard)	1.7323–1.7327/44.0–44.01	1.7361/44.1
(max)	—	
Cylinder taper (max)	0.0002/0.005	0.0020/0.05
Cylinder out-of-round (max)	0.0002/0.005	0.0020/0.05
Piston ring groove width Top, Second	0.047–0.048/1.205–1.220	0.0512/1.3
Oil	0.098–0.099/2.50–2.52	0.1024/2.6
Ring thickness Top	0.046–0.0464/1.165–1.180	0.0443/1.125
Second	0.046–0.047/1.175–1.190	0.0447/1.135
Oil	0.097–0.098/2.475–2.490	0.0957/2.43
Ring end-gap (all)	0.006–0.016/0.15–0.40	0.0315/0.8
Ring side clearance Top, Second	0.0006–0.0018/0.015–0.045	0.004/0.1
Oil	0.0004–0.0018/0.01–0.045	0.004/0.1
Oil pump bore-to-plunger clearance	0.0010–0.0025/0.025–0.063	0.0067/0.17
Pump rod-to-clutch housing clearance	0.0010–0.0030/0.025–0.075	0.0059/0.15
Clutch friction disc Thickness	0.115–0.121/2.92–3.08	0.0984/2.5
Warpage	less than 0.0079/0.2	0.0196/0.5

When refitting the transmission shafts, be sure that the pins or set rings are in place and the bearings are seated properly

Engine Specifications (cont.)

125

Component	Standard (in./mm)	Wear Limit (in./mm)
Clutch steel plate Thickness	0.118/3.0	0.114/2.9
Warpage	—	0.0196/0.5
Clutch spring free-length	1.2224/31.05	1.1929/30.3
Cam chain tensioner spring free-length	3.268/83	3.1496/80
Shift drum groove	0.240–0.244/6.1–6.2	0.256/6.4
Mainshaft-to-mainshaft gear clearance 2nd	0.0006–0.0018/0.016–0.045	0.004/0.1
5th	0.0004–0.0018/0.011–0.045	0.004/0.1
Countershaft-to-countershaft gear clearance 3rd, 4th	0.0004–0.0010/0.009–0.025	0.004/0.1
1st	0.0006–0.0018/0.016–0.045	0.004/0.1
Transmission shaft bearing clearance (6304HS) Axial clearance	less than 0.002/0.05	0.004/0.1
Radial clearance	0.0004–0.0010/0.01–0.025	0.002/0.05

Crankshaft

REMOVAL

1. Remove the top end and split the cases as described previously.
2. The crankshaft can be lifted out of the upper crankcase. On 200 models, the cam chain is removed with the crankshaft

CAUTION: *Do no lose the main bearing locating pins when the crankshaft is removed.*

INSPECTION

1. Mount the crankshaft center main bearings in a set of V-blocks, and measure the run-out of the crankshaft with a dial gauge. Measurements should be taken at either end of the crankshaft and on each of the flywheels. If the run-out exceeds the service limit, the crankshaft should be replaced.

Removing the crankshaft. Note bearing locating pins.

Measuring crankshaft run-out

2. With the crankshaft supported at both ends, mount a dial gauge to the top of each main bearing in turn. Attempt to move the outer race up and down. The measurement on the dial gauge is the total radial clearance. If the clearance exceeds the service limit, the crankshaft should be replaced.
3. With the crankshaft firmly supported, fix a dial gauge to the bottom of the connecting rod, and measure the up and down play. The dial gauge will indicate the amount of radial clearance. If the clearance exceeds the service limit, the crankshaft should be replaced.
4. Using a feeler gauge, measure the side clearance of the connecting rod. If the side clearance is beyond the service limit, replace the crankshaft.
5. With an inside micrometer, measure the bore of the connecting rod small end. If the bore is found to exceed the service limit, the connecting rod and the crankshaft should be replaced.
6. Rotate each of the main bearings. They should be smooth and silent. If rough or noisy, they should be replaced.

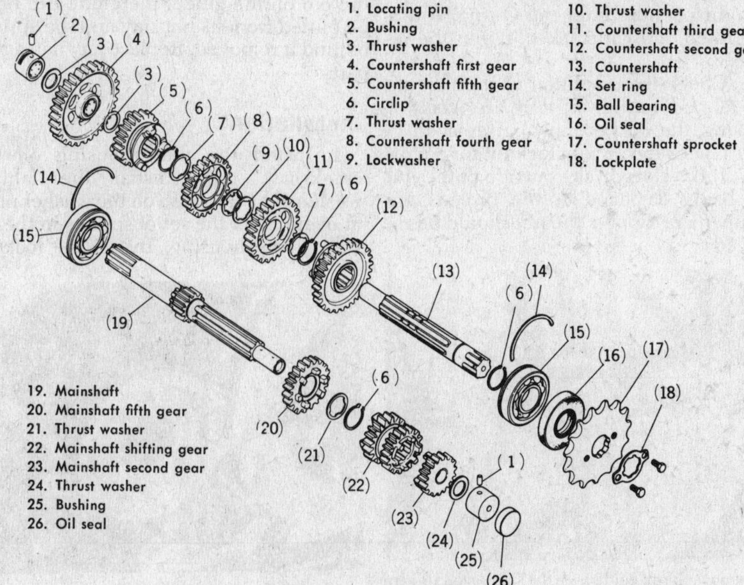

Transmission (5-speed)

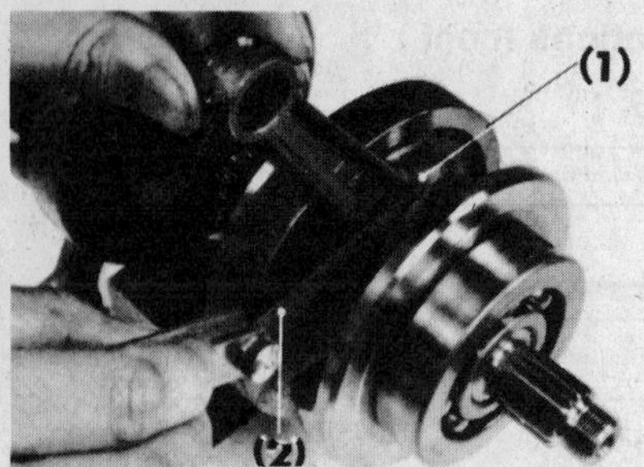

Measuring connecting rod side clearance

The aligning marks on the crank bearings should be flush with the crankcase surface so that the locating pins will fit properly into the bearings

INSTALLATION

1. Fit the cam chain to the sprocket on the crankshaft.
2. Fit the crankshaft into place. Be sure that the bearing locating pins are properly seated in the upper crankcase half. The aligning marks on the bearing should be flush with the crankcase mating surface.
3. Assemble the crankcases and the top end.

Assembling the Crankcases

1. The crankcase mating surface must be clean and free of any scratches. Minor repairs can be made with an oilstone.
2. Apply a thin coat of sealing compound to the crankcase mating surface. Be careful not to get any of the sealer on the bearings or inside surface of the crankcase.
3. Install the lower case. Make sure that the cases mate properly before installing the crankcase bolts. If they do not, check that all of the bearing locating pins are in place.
4. Install the crankcase bolts and tighten them evenly and gradually in an "X" pattern, starting from the inside and working out.
5. Install the crankcase cover components and the top end as described previously.

Engine Torque Specifications 175/200

Item	*Thread Dia (mm)*	*Torque (ft lbs)*
Cylinder head nuts	8	13.0–16.0
Cylinder head bolt	6	6.5–10.1
Crankcase cover	6	5.1–8.0
Crankcase	8	14.5–18.8
	6	5.1–8.0
Intake manifold	6	5.8–8.7
Cam sprocket (200)	7	12.3–16.6
Alternator rotor	10	25.3–32.5
Tappet locknut	5	5.1–8.0
125		
Cylinder head nuts	8	11.6–13.8
Cankcase cover	6	5.1–8.0
Alternator rotor	—	11.6–15.2
Crankcase	8	14.5–18.0
	6	5.1–8.0
Tappet locknut	5	5.1–8.0
Cylnder base nuts	6	6.5–10.1

General Torque Specifications①

Part	*Torque (ft lbs)*
6 mm machine screws	5.0–7.2
6 mm hex bolts	5.8–8.7
8 mm hex bolts	13.0–18.1
10 mm hex bolts	21.7–28.9
6 mm flange bolts	7.2–10.1
8 mm flange bolts	17.4–21.7
10 mm	21.7–28.9

① Unless otherwise specified

LUBRICATION SYSTEM

These Honda twins are of the wet sump type. All models have a plunger-type pump driven from the clutch housing by way of a connecting rod. Before entering the pump, the oil passes through an oil filter screen to remove any large particles. Before being pumped to the cylinder head, the oil is further filtered through a centrifugal oil filter before being pumped under pressure to the crankshaft assembly and the transmission shafts.

CENTRIFUGAL OIL FILTER

Removal

1. Remove the right crankcase cover.
2. Remove the 6 mm screw from the center of the filter cap. Screw an 8 mm screw into the cap and pull the cap out of the housing using the screw, or remove it with a pliers.
3. Hold the crankshaft from turning by either placing the transmission in gear and applying the rear brake or by wedging a soft (copper or brass) bar between the primary gears. Bend back the locktabs on the tabbed washer and remove the special 16 mm locknut using the factory tool (Tool No. 07961-2830000). Remove the tabbed washer and the filter housing.

Inspection

1. Clean all parts in a clean solvent and allow to dry.
2. Inspect the condition of the filter capscrew. If the head is rounded or if the threads are stripped, it should be replaced.
3. Inspect the filter cap O-ring. If it is deformed, torn, or cracked, it must be replaced.
4. Check the condition of the tabs on the tabbed washer. If they are weak or missing, the washer must be replaced.
5. Check the 16 mm locknut for condition. If the slots on the outside of the nut are badly damaged or the threads are chipped or stripped, the nut should be replaced.
6. Inspect the oil guide in the right crankcase cover (200) or in the filter cover plate (125, 175). It should be free to move in and out. Push the guide in, it should have enough spring force behind it to push it out. To remove the guide, line up the opening on the retaining circlip with the tab on the guide, the guide can now be pulled from its housing and the spring behind it removed. Replace any damaged parts.

Installation

1. Install the filter housing on the crankshaft, then install the tabbed washer. The large tab on the washer must fit over one of the set of splines in the inside of the housing. Install the locknut

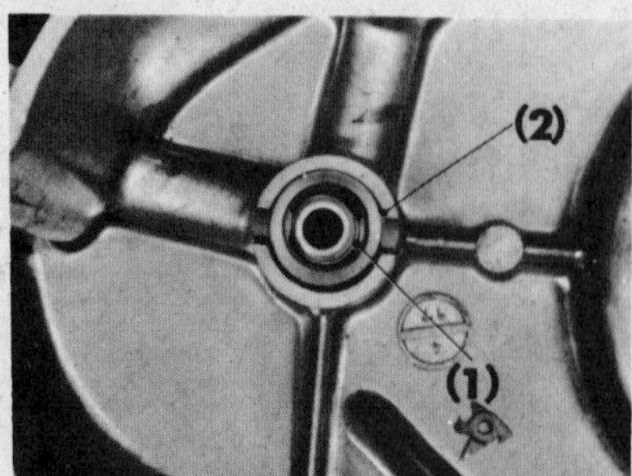

To remove the oil guide from the side cover, line up the slot in the retaining circlip (1) with the tab in the inside of the guide (2)

On 200 models, line up the tab on the filter cap (2) with the mark on the filter housing (1)

with the chamfered side facing the engine, and tighten with the factory tool (Tool No. 07961-2830000).

2. Install the filter cap using a new O-ring if necessary, and secure in place with a 6 x 20 mm screw. The vanes on the filter cap must fit into the splines in the filter housing. On 200 models, the tab on the cap must align with the mark on the housing.

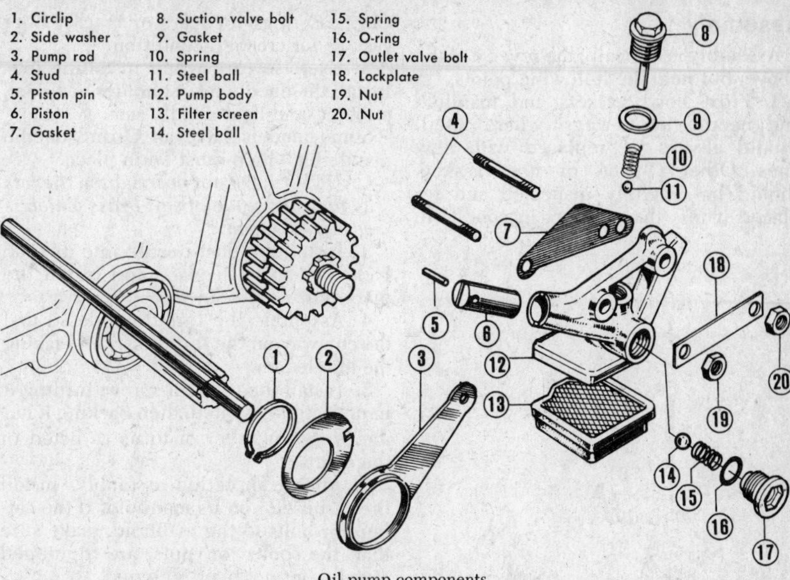

Oil pump components

OIL PUMP AND FILTER SCREEN

The oil pump and filter screen are removed and installed with the clutch housing. Refer to "Engine and Transmission."

Inspection

1. Calculate the clearance between the oil pump connecting rod and the clutch housing. The standard clearance is 0.001–0.003 in. (0.025–0.075 mm). If the clearance exceeds 0.006 in. (0.15 mm), replace parts as necessary to bring the clearance to the standard specification.

2. Calculate the clearance between the pump piston and the pump bore. The standard clearance is 0.001–0.0025 in. (0.025–0.063 mm). If the clearance exceeds 0.007 in. (0.17 mm), the pump assembly (pump, piston, and rod) should be replaced as a unit.

3. Make a visual inspection of the piston and bore in the oil pump. If either is scored, replace the pump as an assembly.

4. 125, 175 models: On most models the ball valves can be removed for inspection by removing the valve cap, washer, spring, and ball. Inspect the ball for any signs of wear. If the ball is worn, replace the pump as an assembly.

5. 200 models: The pump operation can be checked after assembly. Start the engine and allow it to warm up until it will idle with the choke off. Loosen the left rear head capnut; if the pump is operating properly, oil should begin to seep out the gasket surface. After checking operation, torque the head nut to 13–16 ft lbs.

6. Remove the filter screen from the bottom of the pump and wash in clean solvent. Inspect the screen for any puncture marks. If the screen mesh is broken to any extent, the screen must be replaced.

7. Check the oil pump gasket for condition. If defective in any way, it must be replaced. It is recommended that the gasket be replaced regardless of apparent condition.

8. Inspect the condition of the mounting bolt or nut lockplate and replace it if the tabs are fatigued.

Oil Pump Specifications

Plunger-to-housing calculated clearance:	
nominal—in.	0.001–0.0025
mm	0.025–0.063
maximum—in.	0.0067
mm	0.17
Oil pump capacity:	
nominal—cc/min @ rpm	3,600 @ 10,000
minimum—cc/min @ rpm	3,400 @ 10,000

FUEL SYSTEM

CARBURETOR

Removal and Installation

1. Unscrew the carburetor cap and pull the throttle slide assembly out of the carburetor. If the slide assembly is to be disassembled, see the procedure below. If not, place a small plastic bag around the assembly to keep out dirt, and place it out of the way. Note that mishandling the assembly may necessitate replacement of the slide or needle.

2. Check that the fuel petcock is shut off, and disconnect the fuel line from the carburetor.

3. Remove the float bowl drain plug, and drain off any gas in the float bowl. Disconnect any overflow or breather tubes.

4. Loosen the carburetor or the manifold mounting nuts or bolts, then remove them.

5. Loosen the air cleaner hose clamp or band. Remove the carburetor.

6. Installation is in the reverse of the above, but note the following points:

a. Be sure that the carburetor mounting flange O-ring is installed in its groove before fitting the carburetor.

b. When tightening the carburetor or manifold flange nuts, do so evenly to prevent warpage.

c. Lubricate the throttle slide if desired with a molybdenum or graphite lubricant. Insert it into the carburetor with the slide cutaway facing away from the engine. Be sure that the slot in the slide is engaged with the tab in the carburetor body;

d. Be sure that the slide goes in easily, and especially that the needle enters the needle jet. Do not push or force the slide into place. If resistance is noted, it is probable that the needle is cocked to one side and is not entering the jet;

e. Tighten the carburetor cap and check throttle operation. The slide must move freely up and down.

Disassembly

1. If disassembly of the throttle slide components is desired, compress the return spring against the carburetor cap, disengage the cable from the slide, take out the spring clip, needle, and needle clip. If the clip must be removed from the needle, note which groove it is located in so that it can be installed in the same location unless tuning changes are to be made.

2. Flip up the retainer on the float bowl and separate the float bowl from the carburetor body. Do so carefully, to avoid damage to the floats. Remove and discard the float bowl gasket.

NOTE: *If the float bowl is stuck, tap carefully with a plastic mallet to break the seal.*

3. Push out the float pivot pin with a small dowel, and take out the floats. Remove the float needle from its seat. Unscrew the seat itself.

4. Unscrew the main jet.

5. Unscrew the jet holder and push the needle jet out from the top of the carburetor using a small wooden dowel.

6. Unscrew and remove the pilot jet.

7. Remove the pilot air and throttle stop screws and springs.

Assembly

Assembly is basically the reverse of the above, but note the following points:

1. Float bowl gaskets and manifold and needle jet O-rings (where fitted) should always be replaced with new ones. Other O-rings or fiber gaskets should be carefully inspected and replaced if less than perfect in condition. Check O-rings for tears or cracks; fiber gaskets for crushed condition.

2. Exercise care when installing jets. Install the needle jet, jet holder, main jet, pilot jet, and float needle seat.

Some models have an O-ring on the needle jet which must be in place.

CAUTION: *Do not overtighten the jets as they are made of soft brass which is easily damaged.*

3. Install the float needle into its seat. Hold the floats in place and install the pivot pin.

4. Assemble the throttle slide so that the cutaway on the throttle slide is facing the air cleaner.

5. Install the pilot air screw, turning it in until lightly seated, then backing it out the proper number of turns as listed in the chart.

6. After completing assembly, install the carburetor on its manifold. If the carburetor bolts to the manifold, make sure that the bolts or nuts are tightened evenly, but not overtightened.

7. Check for fuel or air leaks; make final adjustments to the throttle stop and pilot air screws.

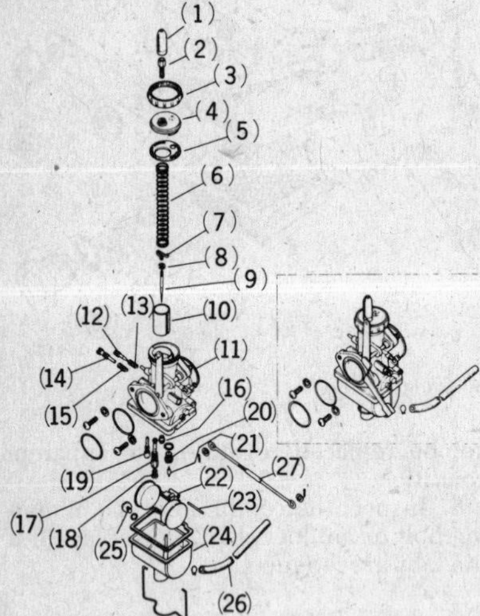

Carburetor assembly (200)

1. Adjuster cap
2. Adjuster
3. Cap ring
4. Cap
5. Gasket
6. Slide return spring
7. Needle clip plate
8. Needle clip
9. Needle
10. Throttle slide
11. Carburetor body
12. Pilot air screw
13. Spring
14. Throttle stop screw
15. Spring
16. Needle jet
17. Needle jet holder
18. Main jet
19. Pilot jet
20. Float needle seat
21. Float needle
22. Float
23. Float pivot pin
24. Float bowl
25. Drain plug
26. Overflow tube
27. Choke rod

FUEL PETCOCK AND LINES

Cleaning

1. Unscrew and remove the sediment bowl, take out the O-ring, and filter screen.

2. Clean the metal parts in solvent. Check that the filter screen is not punctured, and that the O-ring is not torn or otherwise damaged.

3. Run a little gas through the petcock to flush out any dirt. Catch the gas in a suitable container. Turning the petcock to "Reserve" for a few seconds should remove the better part of any water or dirt in the bottom of the fuel tank.

4. Check petcock operation in all positions. There must be no fuel flow when the petcock lever is turned to the "Stop" position.

5. Install the filter screen, O-ring, and sediment bowl in that order. Check for leaks before operating the motorcycle.

Disassembly

At somewhat extended intervals, the petcock should be removed from the fuel tank and cleaned.

1. Drain the fuel tank completely. Disconnect the fuel lines from the petcock. Remove the sediment bowl, O-ring, and filter screen.

2. Unscrew the nut which holds the petcock to the fuel tank (200 models), or remove the phillips head screw from the inside of the petcock above the filter screen (125, 175), and remove the petcock.

3. Remove the two screws from the fuel lever setting plate, and remove the setting plate, lever spring, lever, and gasket.

Assembly

1. Install the fuel valve gasket, lever, lever spring, and setting plate. Secure with the two screws.

2. Be sure that the petcock O-ring or gasket is in place and install the petcock on the fuel tank. Install the sediment bowl filter screen, O-ring, and sediment bowl.

3. Be sure that the fuel lines are firmly secured at their connections and the safety circlips are in place.

Carburetor Specifications

	CB200	*CL200*	*CB175*	*CL175*	*SL175*	*SS125*	*CL125*	*CB125*
Pilot air screw (turns out)	1¼ ± ⅛	⅝ ± ⅛	⅞ ± ⅛	⅞ ± ⅛	1⅛ ± ⅛	1⅛ ± ⅛	1⅛ ± ⅛	1⅛ ± ⅛
Jet needle (groove from top)	3	3	NA	NA	NA	NA	NA	NA
Float level (mm/in.)	21/0.82	21/0.82	21/0.82	21/0.82	21/0.82	21/0.82	21/0.82	21/0.82
Pilot jet	38	35	38	38	38	35	35	35
Air jet	NA	NA	150	100	150	100	150	150
Main jet	88	95	98	90	92	95	92	92

NA Not available

Float bowl components

1. Pilot jet
2. Main jet
3. Float
4. Float arm
5. Float pivot pin

ELECTRICAL SYSTEM

The same basic type of electrical system is used on all models covered in this manual.

Ignition is by means of battery-and-coil, the battery also being used to power the lights and accessories.

Battery charging is accomplished by means of an alternator with a permanently-magnetized rotor. Alternator output (AC) is changed to direct current (DC) by the rectifier and this current charges the battery. On late model 175s and the 200, a voltage regulator is fitted to ground excess alternator output.

IGNITION CIRCUIT TESTS

The ignition circuit consists of the battery, a set of breaker points, condenser, ignition coil, spark plug leads and caps, and the spark plugs.

One set of points is used along with a single ignition coil. Both plugs fire at the same time, although only one cylinder is on the compression stroke at a time. Therefore, there is a waste spark at one cylinder each time the engine fires.

The contact breaker set is mounted on a plate and is opened and closed by a breaker cam on the left-side of the camshaft. The ignition coil and condenser are mounted beneath the gas tank.

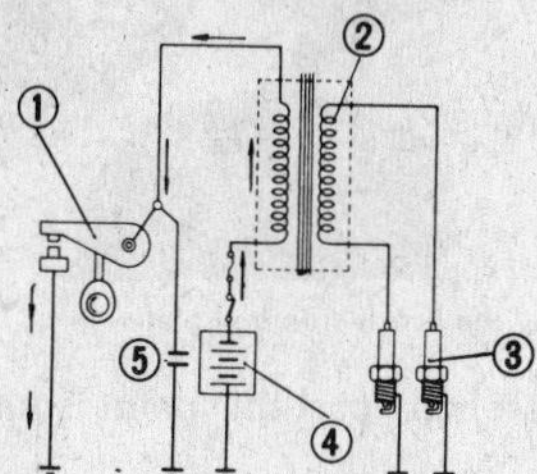

Ignition circuit: 1, breaker points; 2, coil; 3, spark plugs; 4, battery; 5, condensers

1. Noise suppressor spark plug caps are fitted, which are designed to eliminate radio interference and provide a hotter spark by means of a resistor in the cap.

Sometimes the resistor breaks down, and the cap then becomes an open circuit. Remove the cap from the plug lead, and hold the lead about ⅛ in. away from the cylinder head, while kicking over the engine. If a good spark is now evident, the cap was at fault. Replace both caps if one was defective.

2. If new points have just been installed, a no-spark condition can be caused by improperly installed or damaged insulating washers on the points primary wire terminal.

3. The ignition coil windings should be checked for continuity, using an ohmmeter.

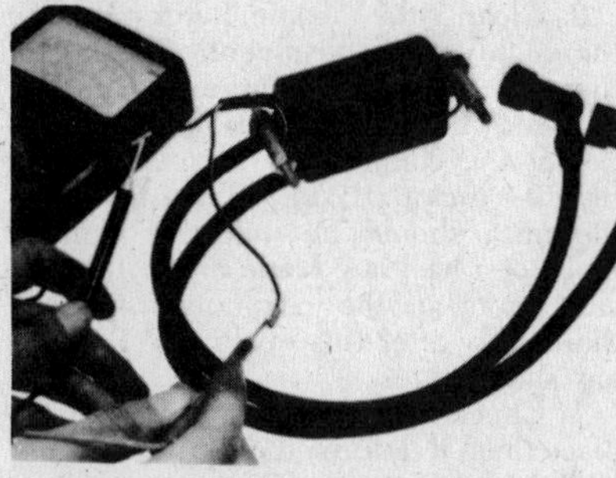

Checking the ignition coil primary winding for continuity

a. Disconnect the two low-tension coil leads and check for continuity between them. This is a check of the primary winding. If there is no continuity, replace the coil since the winding is broken internally;

b. Check for continuity across the two high tension (spark plug) leads. Resistance should be very high, but continuity must exist. If resistance is low or infinite, the secondary winding insulation is breaking down or the winding is broken. The coil must be replaced in either case.

If the condition of the coil is still questionable, replacing it temporarily with one known to be good is recommended.

4. The condenser can be checked if a capacitance tester is available. Condensers should have a capacitance of approximately 0.3 mf. Checking with a

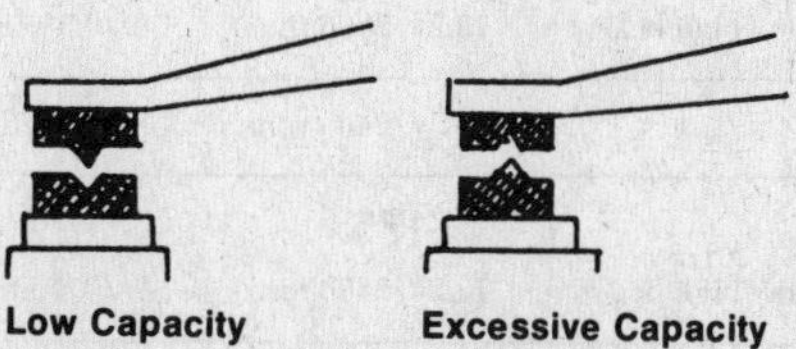

A defective condenser will cause mounds and matching depressions on the point contact surfaces

"megger" (high-voltage ohmmeter) should yield a resistance of 10m ohms or better at 1,000v. Replace the condenser if it fails either test.

NOTE: *After testing, ground the condenser lead against the case to discharge it.*

As noted above, sparking at the points, or points which pit or burn rapidly would indicate a defective condenser. Bad condensers will cause mounds and matching depressions on the points, as illustrated.

5. If the trouble is a misfire, and the tests above do not pinpoint the problem, check the condition and operation of the automatic timing advance unit.

CHARGING CIRCUIT TESTS

The charging circuit consists of the alternator, rectifier, a voltage regulator (where applicable), and the battery.

1. In the event that the battery overcharges, check the battery itself, and the voltage regulator.

2. If the battery discharges quickly, or fails to hold a charge, check the battery, the regulator, rectifier, and alternator.

Voltage Regulator

A bad voltage regulator may cause the battery to go dead, or may overcharge it

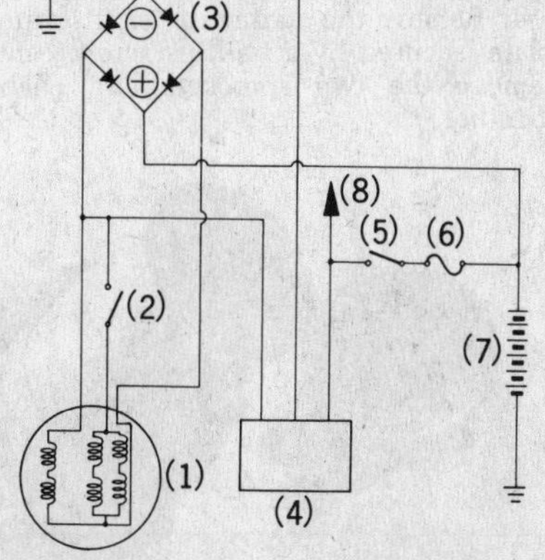

Charging circuit: 1, alternator; 2, headlight switch; 3, rectifier; 4, voltage regulator; 5, main switch; 6, fuse; 7, battery; 8, load

causing electrolyte loss, short light bulb life, etc. The regulator is located beneath the battery box, and is rubber mounted. It can be tested with an ohmmeter, continuity tester, or ammeter.

1. If the battery goes dead, disconnect the three regulator leads (yellow, green, and black).

2. With an ohmmeter or continuity light, check for continuity between the yellow lead and the green lead. Check for continuity between the yellow lead and ground.

There must not be continuity in either case. If there is, the regulator must be replaced.

3. If an ammeter is available, connect it in series with the battery positive wire. Start and run the engine at more than 2,000 rpm. If the ammeter indicates that the battery is discharging, disconnect the regulator yellow lead and repeat the test. If the battery now shows that it is receiving a charge, the regulator must be replaced. If no change is noted, proceed with the rectifier and alternator tests which follow.

4. If the battery overcharges, check as follows:

Assuming that the battery is in good condition and *fully* charged, start the engine and connect a good voltmeter across the battery terminals. Run the engine at 4,000 rpm. The voltage across the battery should increase to between 14–15 volts, but not more. If the meter reads more than 15 volts, the regulator must be replaced.

NOTE: *This test will not be valid unless the battery is fully charged. To check this, run the engine until the voltage stabilizes, then disconnect the regulator black lead. If the voltage increases, the results of the test were valid.*

5. When mounting the regulator, be sure that the rubber dampers are in place. The regulator could be damaged by excess vibration.

Rectifier

The rectifier is located behind that battery or under the battery case.

The rectifier should be checked in the

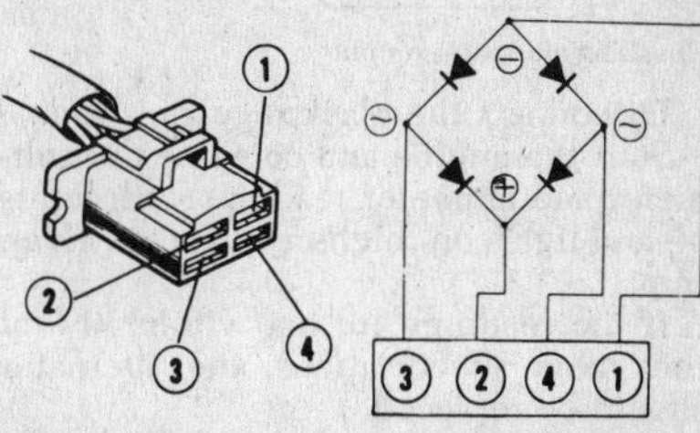

Rectifier leads: 1, green; 2, red/white; 3, yellow; 4, pink

event of insufficient battery charging. Tests can be carried out with a continuity light or a standard (low-voltage) ohmmeter.

CAUTION: *Do not apply high-voltage to the rectifier.*

1. Disconnect the leads and remove the rectifier from the machine.

2. The test involves testing current flow through the rectifier in both directions. The rectifier consists of four

diodes. When in working condition, a diode will pass current in one direction only.

If the diode passes current in both directions, or in neither direction, it is defective. If any of the diodes are defective, the rectifier must be replaced.

3. Connect the negative lead of the tester to the green wire, and the positive lead to the yellow, red/white, and pink wires in turn.

In each case, note whether or not there is continuity.

NOTE: *On an ohmmeter, "continuity" will be indicated by a resistance of 5–40 ohms. "No continuity" by a resistance of 100 or more ohms.*

4. Now reverse the tester connections, connecting the positive tester lead to the green wire, and the negative to each of the others in turn.

In every case, the reaction of the tester must be the opposite of the first test: i.e., if the first test showed continuity between two leads, reversing the tester connections must show no continuity.

Current flow in both, or in neither, directions for any two leads indicates that the rectifier is defective and must be replaced.

Alternator

The alternator should be checked in the event of low or no battery charging not attributable to the other components.

1. A dynamic output test can be carried out if a voltmeter and ammeter are available. The battery *must* be fully charged or the test may be invalid.

Hook up the voltmeter across the battery terminals, disconnect the battery red/white lead and connect it to the ammeter. Connect the other side of the ammeter to the battery positive terminal.

Checking alternator output

Disconnect the black regulator lead.

Start the engine and compare the voltmeter and ammeter readings with lights off and lights on (high-beam) at the given rpm.

If the readings are not within 10% of the given specifications, the alternator should be replaced.

NOTE: *The alternator should not be excessively hot when this test is carried out.*

2. Using an ohmmeter or continuity tester, a static stator test can be carried out.

Disconnect the alternator wiring at the plastic connector.

3. Check for continuity between the white, the yellow, and the pink leads. Continuity must exist, or the stator assembly has a broken wire and it must be replaced.

4. Check for continuity between the yellow lead and the stator core. If continuity exists, there is a short, and the stator must be replaced.

5. Check for cracked or melted insulation or scored or burned coil core ends.

Alternator Output

Headlight Switch	*Charging Begins*	*5000 rpm*
	200	
On (high beam)	13.2v/2800 rpm	14v/0.5 amp
Off	14.2v/2400 rpm	14v/0.5 amp
	175	
On (high beam)	13.2v/2800 rpm	14v/0.8 amp
On (low beam)	13.2v/2200 rpm	14v/1.5 amp
Off	13.2/2400 rpm	14v/1.8 amp
	125	
On (high beam)	13.2v/2000 rpm	1.7–2.5 amp
Off	13.2/1300 rpm	1.7–2.5 amp

STARTER MOTOR

1. If the starter motor spins when the button is pushed, but the engine does not, the starter clutch is defective. Refer to "Engine and Transmission," for starter clutch removal and inspection procedures.

2. If the warning lights dim when the starter button is pushed, but the engine and starter do not turn over, the battery may be too low, or the starter may be defective.

3. If nothing happens when the starter button is pushed, either the starter solenoid is defective, or there is a loose wire in the electric starter circuit.

Removal and Disassembly

1. Disconnect the lead at the starter motor.

2. Remove the alternator cover, both sections of the left crankcase cover, and disconnect the neutral switch lead.

3. Remove the alternator rotor.

4. Remove the starter sprocket setting plate (secured by a phillips screw), and remove the two sprockets and chain together.

Removing the output side end plate

5. Remove the two screws which secure the starter motor, and tap the starter out of the case.

6. To disassemble the starter, remove the two long phillips screws and remove the end plates.

NOTE: *Exercise caution when removing the output side end plate as this contains the reduction gears.*

7. Disconnect the starter carbon brush leads (2) and remove the brush mounting plate.

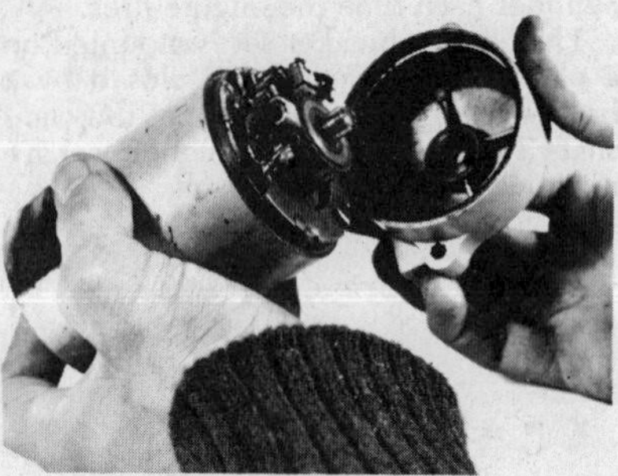

Removing the brush side end plate

Disassembly past this point is not necessary.

Inspection

1. Use an ohmmeter or continuity tester to check the starter motor.

2. Check for continuity between each of the commutator segments. There must be continuity between all of them. If there is a dead spot, the starter must be replaced.

3. Check for continuity between the armature core and the commutator; there must be none. If continuity exists, the starter must be replaced.

4. Check for continuity between the starter lead terminal and the brush leads. Continuity must exist or the starter must be replaced.

5. Measure the length of each carbon brush. Replace them if either is less than 5 mm (0.2 in.). Standard (new) brush length is 11.0–12.5 mm (0.4–0.5 in.). Replace any brush which is pitted or cracked.

6. Clean the commutator surface thoroughly with a solvent. Check that there is no scoring on the commutator surface. The mica insulation should undercut the commutator segments by at least 0.3 mm (0.012 in.). If less than this, the mica should be undercut using a piece of a hacksaw blade or the like. Be sure to clean the commutator surface thoroughly after this operation. Remove any sharp edges.

7. Check the brush springs and replace them if deformed or if they will not hold the brush firmly against the commutator.

Assembly and Installation

1. Reverse the above procedures. Be sure that the output side O-rings are in place.

2. After assembling the starter, check that the armature will turn without excessive binding.

Starter Solenoid

1. The starter solenoid can be checked by disconnecting the high-tension lead from the starter motor, and pushing the starter button. The solenoid should click when the button is pushed.

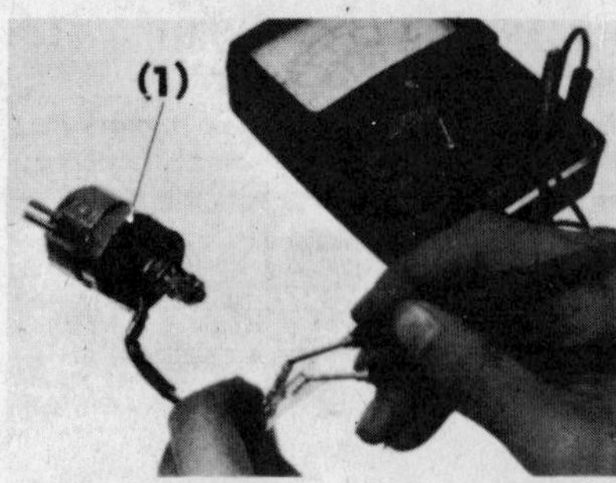

Checking for continuity across the solenoid primary leads

2. If it does not, use an ohmmeter or continuity light to check for continuity across the solenoid's primary leads (black and yellow/red). If continuity does not exist, replace the solenoid.

3. Connect a fully charged 12-volt battery to the primary leads, then check for continuity across the high-tension leads. If there is no continuity, replace the solenoid.

ELECTRICAL SWITCHES

All electrical switches are easily checked with an ohmmeter or self-powered continuity light after disconnecting the switch leads at the plastic connectors.

NOTE: *Wire color codes may differ on some older models.*

Ignition Switch

1. With the key turned to the first position, check for continuity between the black and red leads. If continuity does not exist, replace the switch.

2. With the key in the first position, continuity must exist between the brown and the brown/white leads.

3. With the key in the second position, continuity must exist between the red and brown leads.

Brake Light Switches

1. Check for continuity across the front brake light switch terminals (black and green/yellow). Continuity should occur when the brake lever has moved 10–20 mm (0.4–0.8 in.), measured at the tip of the lever.

2. Check for continuity between the black and green/yellow leads to check the rear brake light switch. Continuity should occur when the brake pedal has moved about 25 mm (1 in.). This switch is adjustable.

Kill Button

1. The kill button should show no continuity between the black and the black/white leads when in either "off" position. When in the "run" position, there must be continuity.

Neutral Switch

1. Remove the left crankcase cover. With the transmission in Neutral, check for continuity between the switch and the crankcase. There should be continuity.

Checking neutral switch operation

2. When the transmission is in gear, there should be no continuity.

Horn

1. If the horn will not function, connect a 12-volt battery directly to the horn terminals. If the horn does not sound, it is defective.

2. If the horn does sound, check the horn button by disconnecting the light green lead in the headlight and check for continuity between the lead and ground, which should be present when the horn button is pushed.

Headlight Switch

EXCEPT 200T

1. When the switch is "off," there should be no continuity between the leads except the brown/white and white leads on 200 cc models.

2. When the switch is in the high-beam position (H), there should be continuity between the yellow/white and the yellow leads, and between the black, blue, and brown/white leads.

3. When the switch is in the low-beam position (L), there must be continuity between the yellow/white and yellow leads, and between the black, white, and brown/white leads.

200T

There is no headlight switch; the dimmer switch is fitted to the left handlebar.

To check the dimmer: in the "Lo" position, continuity should exist between the white and black/white leads. In the "Hi" position, continuity should exist between the black/white and black leads.

Turn Signal Switch

1. When the left-hand turn signal is activated, there will be continuity between the gray lead and the orange lead.

2. When the right-hand switch is activated, continuity will exist between the gray lead and the light blue lead.

Starter Button

1. If nothing happens when the starter button is pushed, and the solenoid seems correct, check the starter button.

200T

a. Disconnect the starter button leads. When the button is free, continuity should exist between the black and black/white leads;

b. When the button is depressed, continuity should exist between the black and yellow/red leads.

NOTE: *The starter button shuts off the headlight when the starter button is pushed.*

OTHER MODELS

a. Disconnect the yellow/red starter button lead. Check for continuity between the yellow/red switch lead and ground. Continuity should exist only when the starter button is pushed.

NOTE: *After separating the starter button housing, spray the button contacts with electrical connector cleaner.*

WIRING DIAGRAMS

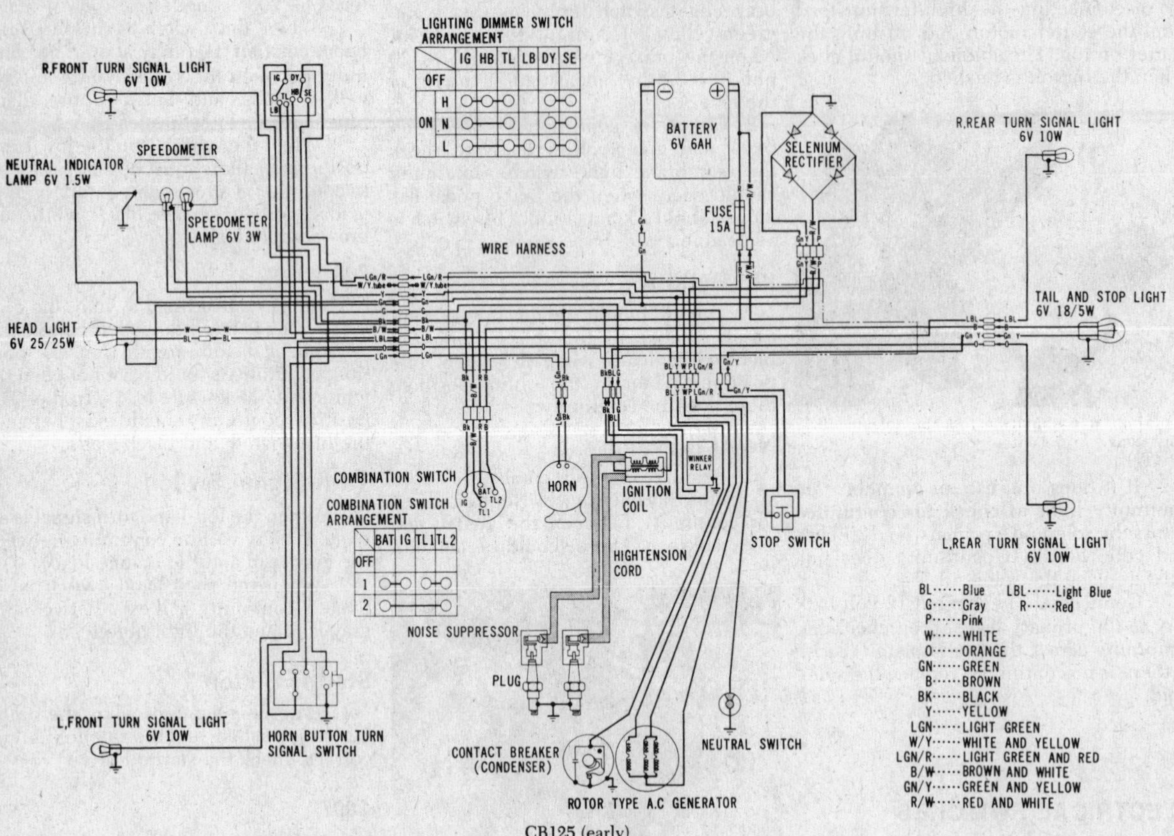

CB125 (early)

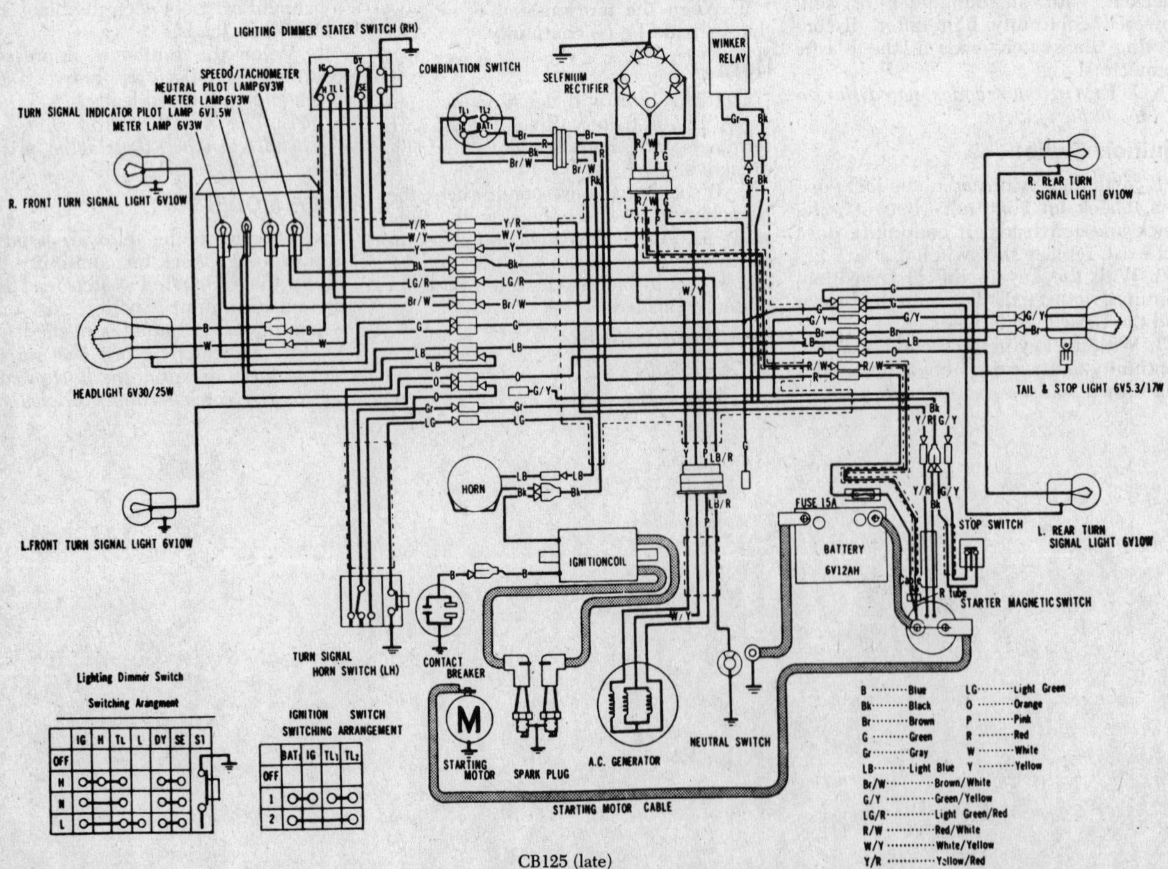

CB125 (late)

WIRING DIAGRAMS

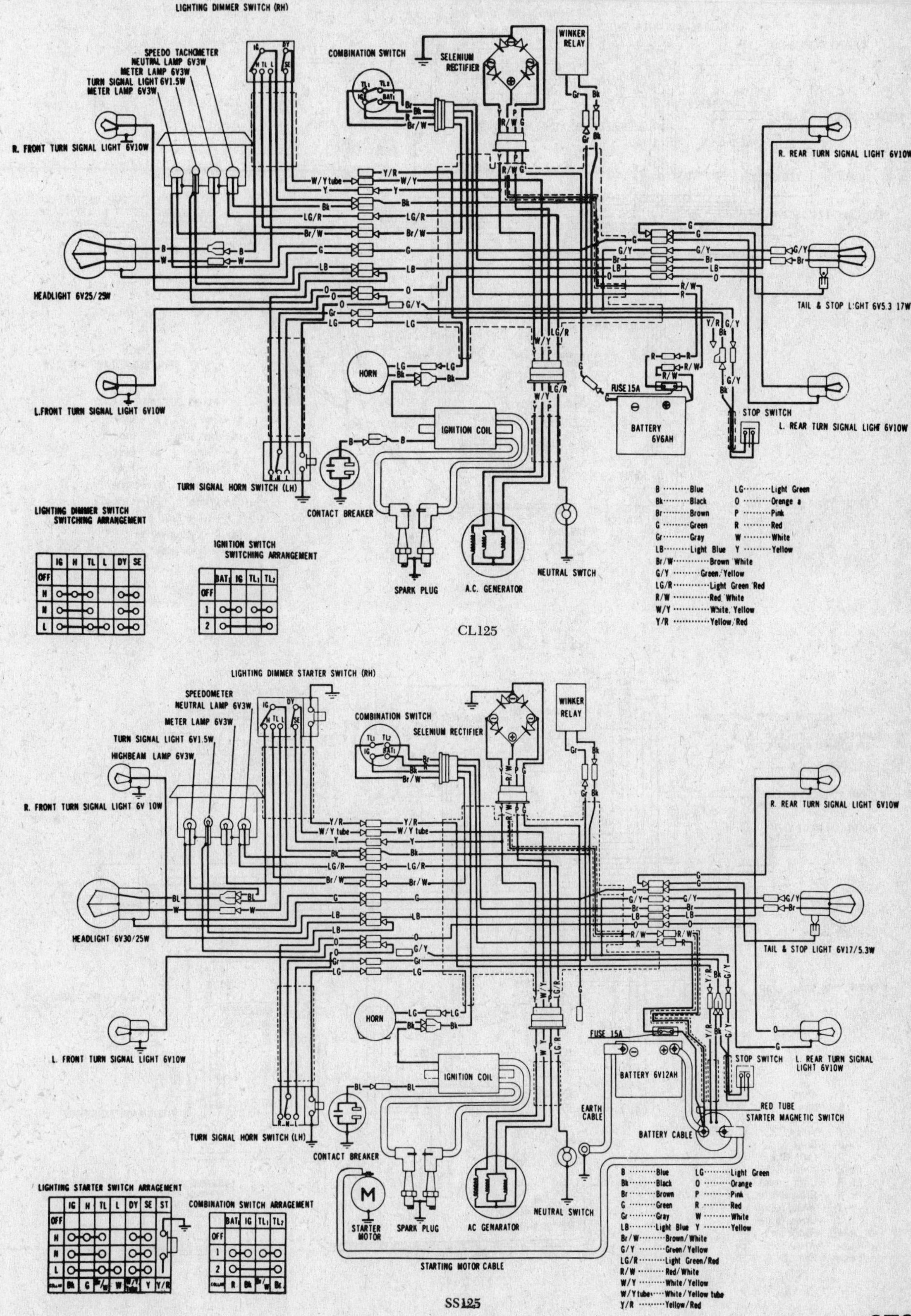

CL125

SS125

WIRING DIAGRAMS

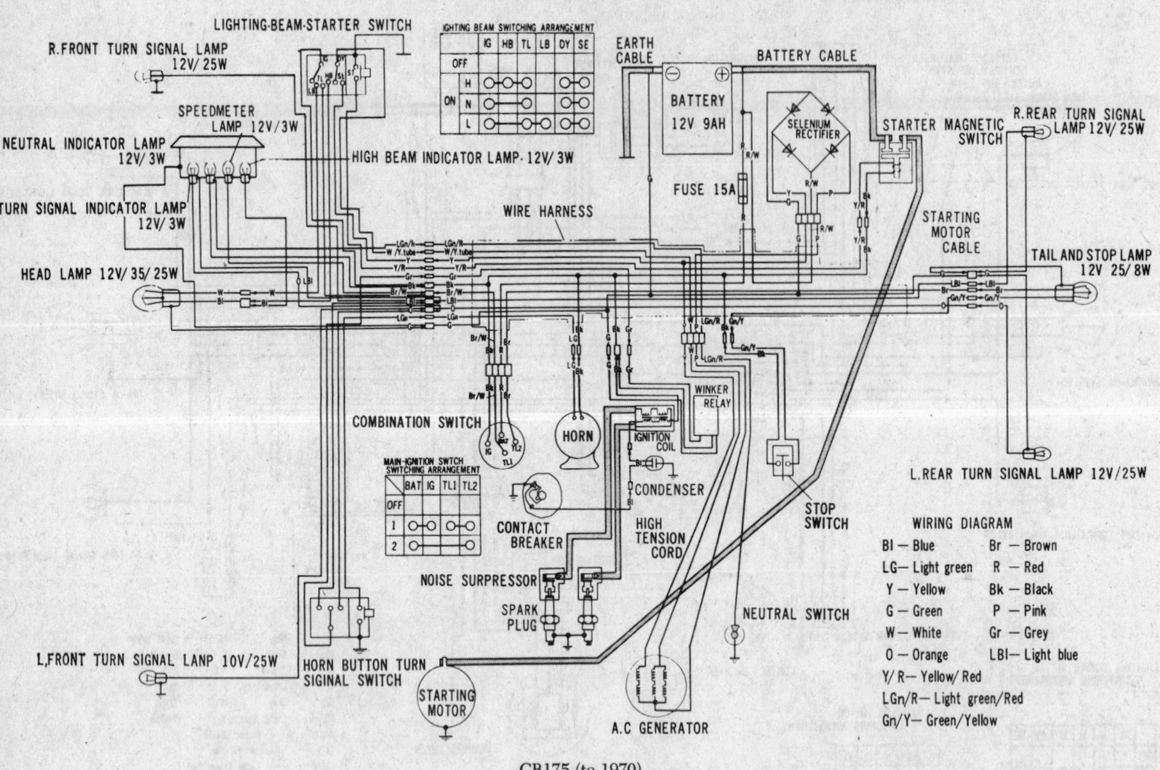

CB175 (to 1970)

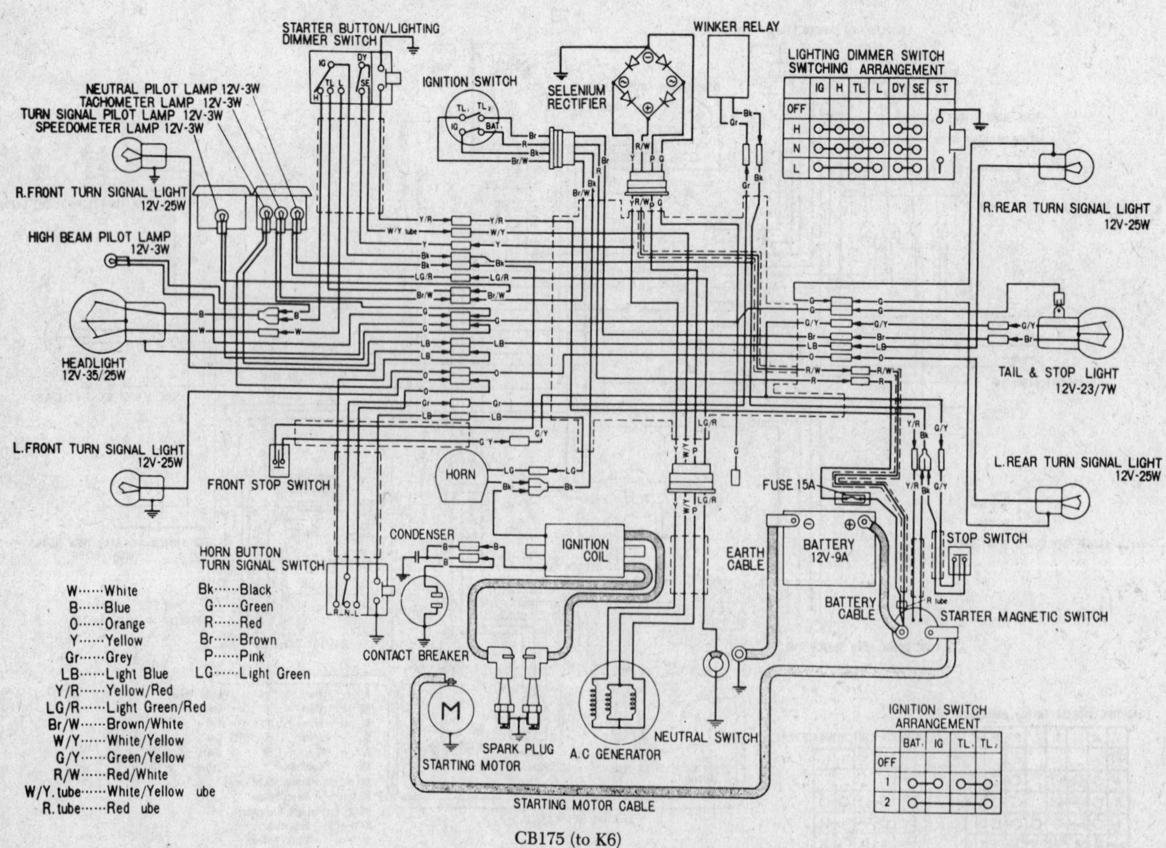

CB175 (to K6)

WIRING DIAGRAMS

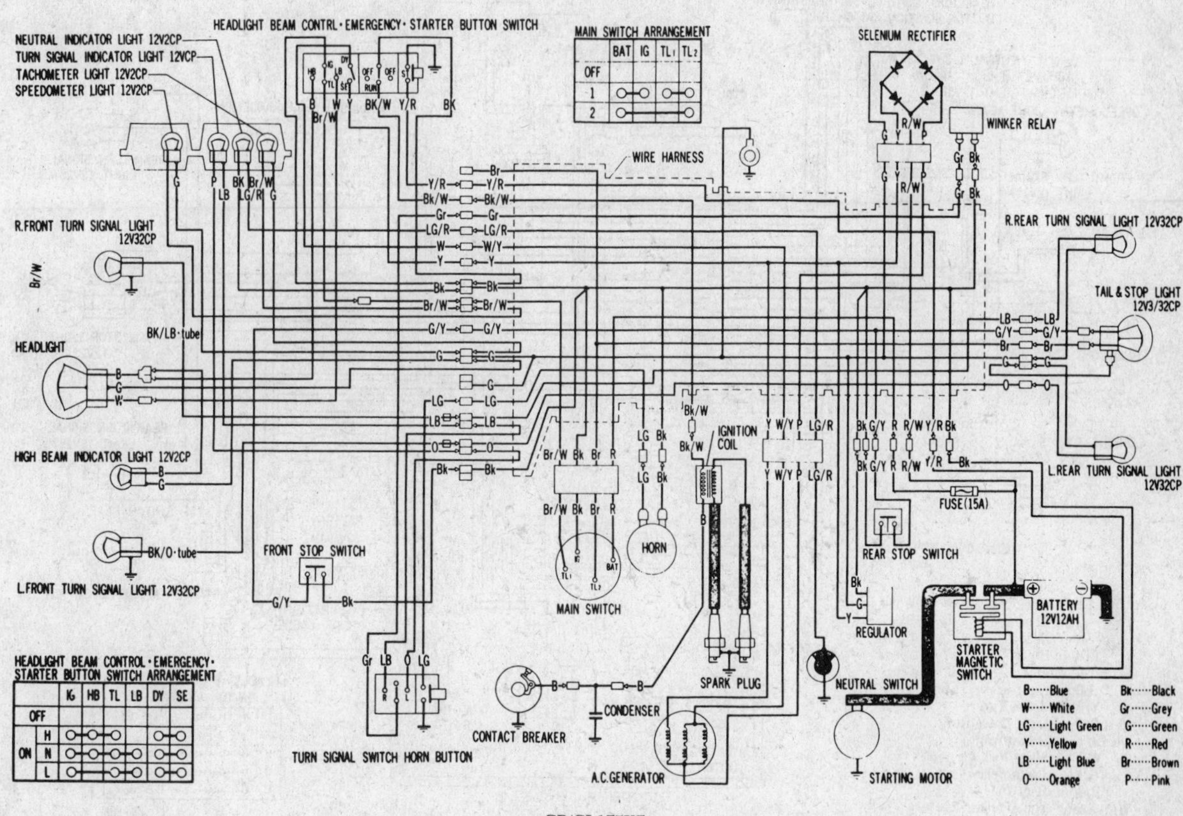

CB/CL175K7

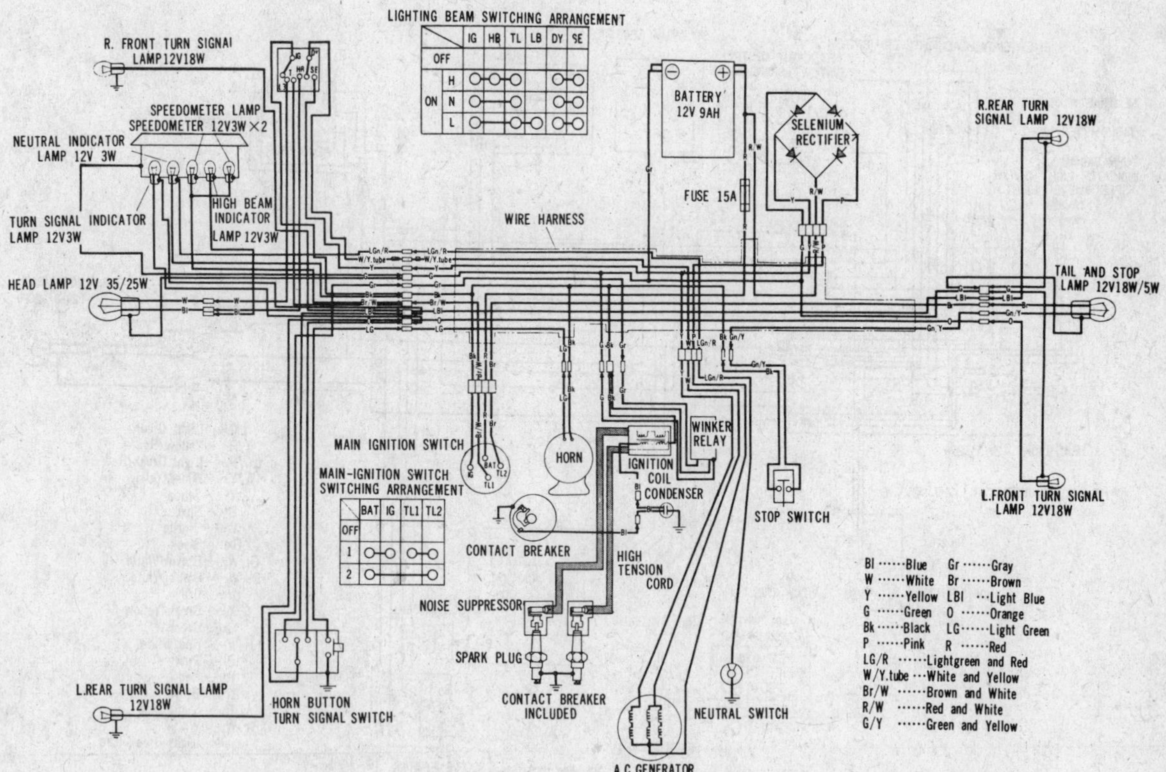

CL 175 (to 1970)

WIRING DIAGRAMS

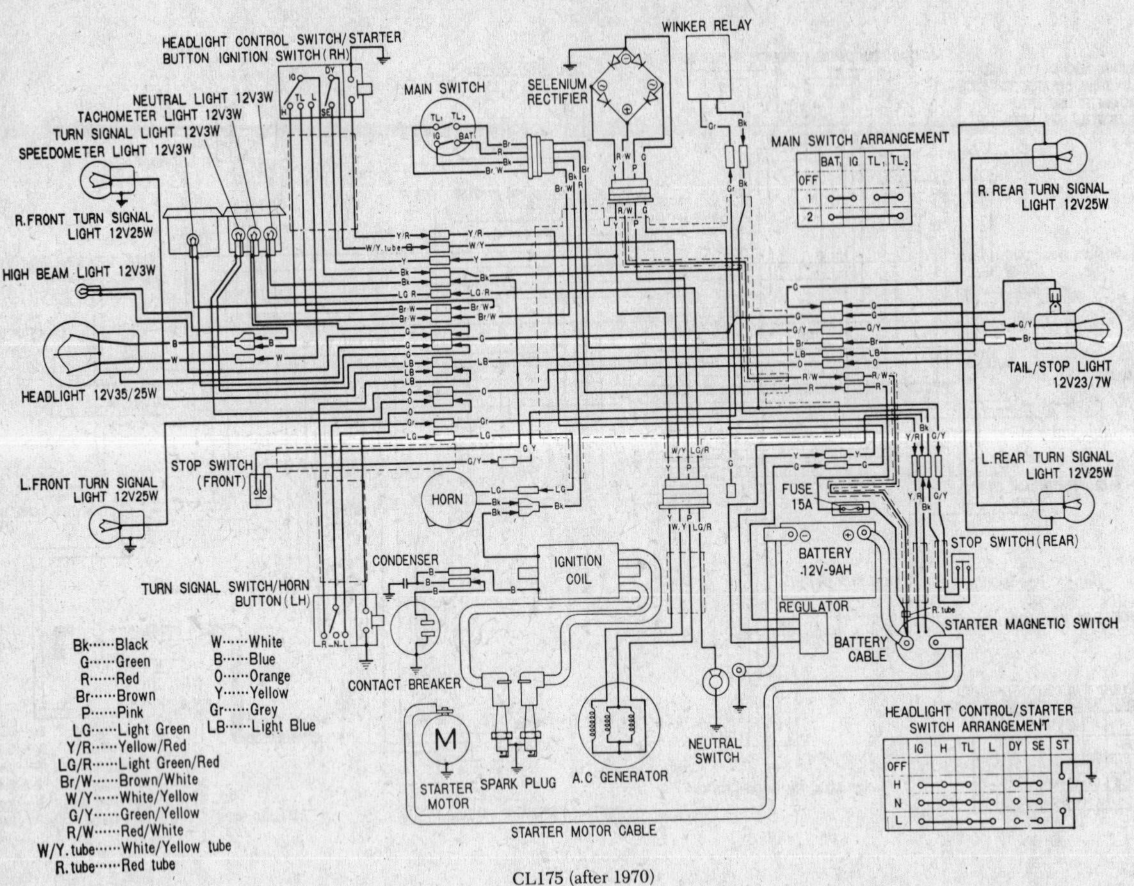

CL175 (after 1970)

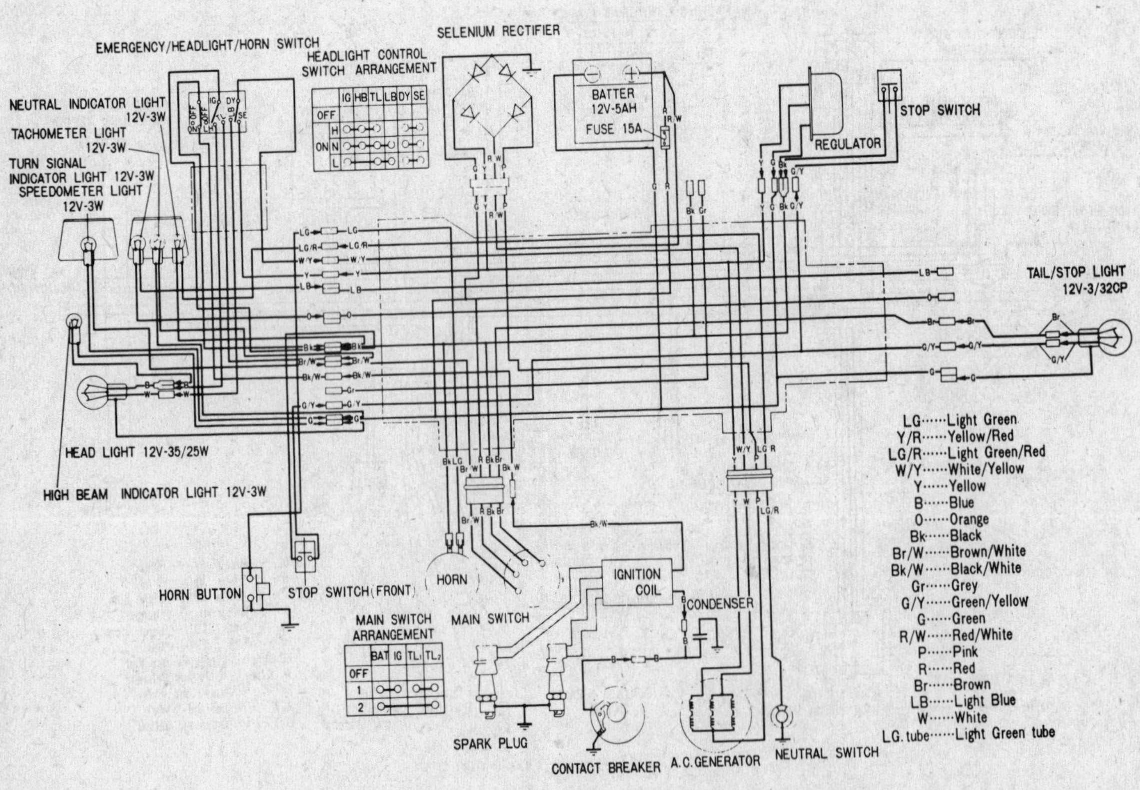

SL175

WIRING DIAGRAMS

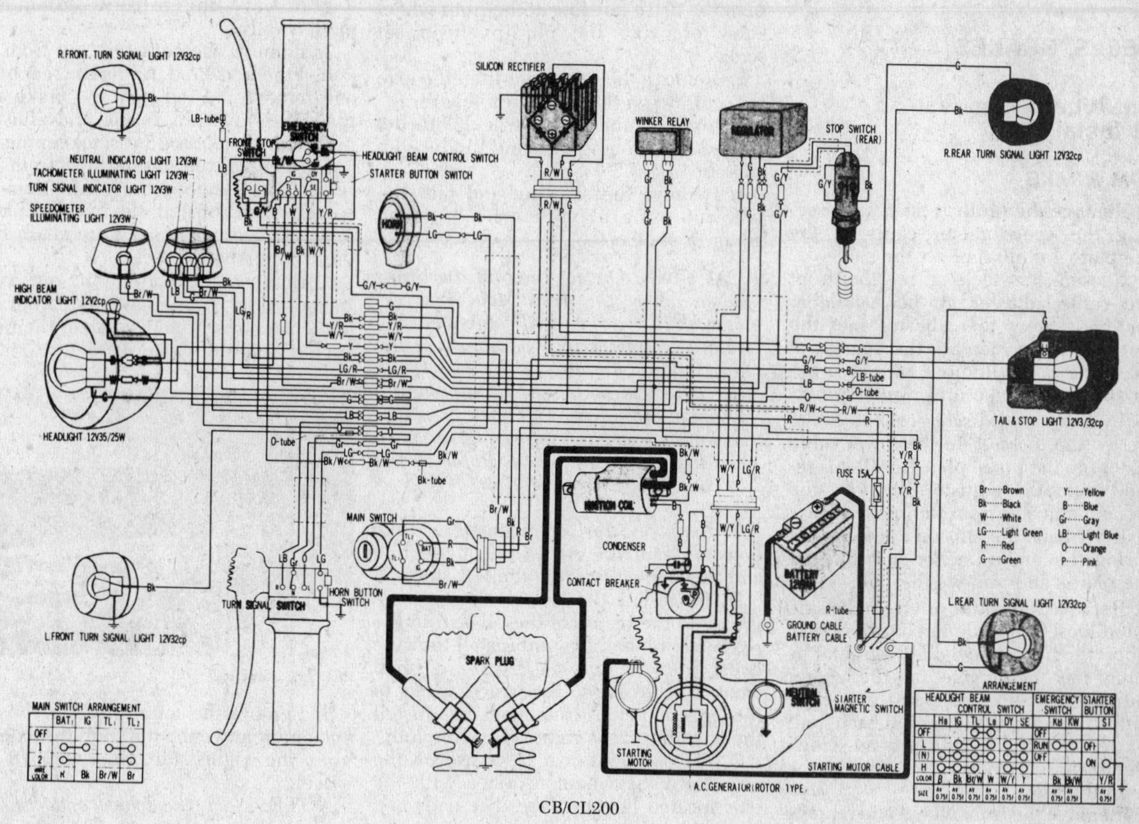

CB/CL200

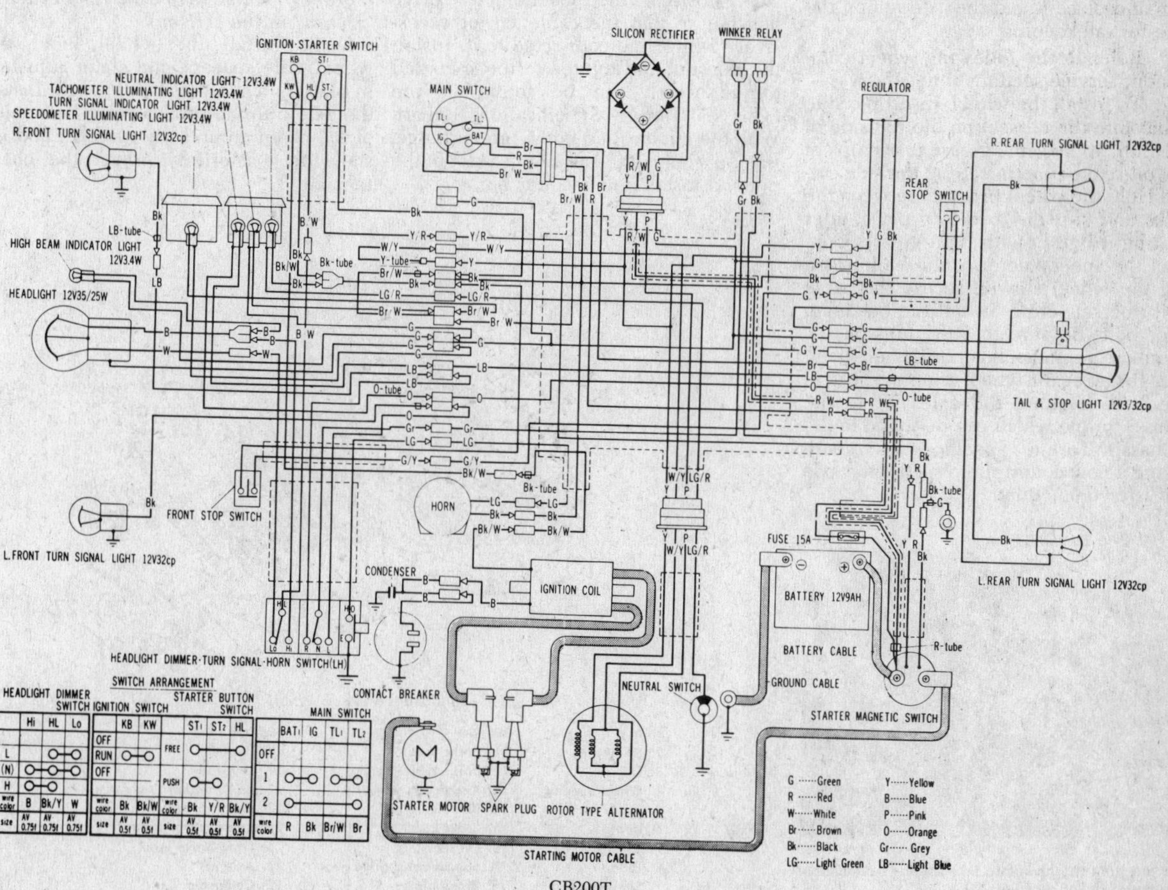

CB200T

CHASSIS

WHEELS, BRAKES

Front Wheel Removal and Installation

DRUM BRAKE

1. Remove the phillips head screw securing the speedometer cable to the brake plate and disconnect the cable.
2. Loosen the locknut on the front brake cable adjuster at the handlebar lever, and screw the adjuster into the lever housing to increase the amount of slack in the cable. Remove the cotter pin from the front brake arm, pull the arm back by hand, and disconnect the cable. Unscrew the locknut on the lower cable adjuster (on the brake plate), until it is removed from the adjuster. Remove the cable and adjuster from the brake plate.
3. Bend back the tabs on the lockplate securing the brake anchor bolt (on the brake plate), and remove the bolt.
4. Remove the cotter pin from the axle nut and loosen the axle nut a turn or two. Support the front wheel off the ground by placing the motorcycle on the center stand and installing a support under the engine. Remove the axle nut, and pull the axle out using a phillips head screwdriver or similar tool inserted through the hole in the axle.
5. Remove the front wheel and remove the side collar from the left-side of the hub and place it and the axle nut on the axle for safekeeping.
6. Refer to the following wheel component service sections if necessary.
7. To install the wheel, insert the side collar into the oil seal on the left-side of the hub, apply some grease to the lips of the oil seal before installing the side collar. Hold the wheel in place between the forks and slip the axle into place, after coating it lightly with light grease. Connect the speedometer cable while rotating the wheel slowly, secure the cable with the set screw. Install the brake anchor bolt. Be sure that the tabs on the lockplate are in good condition and bend the tabs up against the flats on the head of the bolt. Tighten the axle nut to the proper torque which can be found in the "Chassis Torque Specifications" chart. Using a new cotter pin to secure the axle nut is recommended.

Be sure that the lockplate tabs (2) are bent against the flat of the anchor bolt (3)

DISC BRAKE

1. Disconnect the speedometer cable from the drive housing at the front wheel after removing the phillips head set screw.
2. Remove the cotter pin from the axle nut and loosen the axle nut a few turns.
3. Support the front wheel off the ground by placing a stand under the engine.
4. Remove the axle nut and pull the axle out using a phillips head screwdriver or similar tool.

CAUTION: *Do not operate the brake lever when the front wheel is removed. To do so will advance the ratchet adjuster to a point where the disc will not fit between the pads when the wheel is installed. If this should happen, the caliper will have to be disassembled and the adjusting screw in the brake arm loosened. Refer to the "Front Disc Brake" section.*

5. Remove the speedometer drive housing from the right-side of the hub and the side collar from the left-side.
6. To install the wheel, apply some grease to the inside of the oil seal in the right-side of the hub, and install the side collar into the oil seal. Apply a small amount of grease to the inside works of the speedometer drive housing, install the housing on the right-side of the hub.
7. Place a light coat of grease on the axle, hold the wheel in place with the disc located between the disc pads and slip the axle into place from the right-side. Position the speedometer drive housing so that the cable is not excessively bent when connected to it. Install the axle nut and tighten to the specified torque which can be found in the "Chassis Torque Specifications" chart. With the nut torqued in the proper range, line up a hole in the axle with a slot in the nut and install a new cotter pin.

Rear Wheel Removal and Installation

1. Remove the exhaust system (CB models only).
2. Remove the adjusting nut from the end of the brake rod. Apply the rear brake and remove the rod from the brake arm. Place the clevis pin, spring, and adjusting nut on the brake rod for safekeeping.
3. Remove the masterlink from the rear chain. Remove the chain from the sprocket and install the masterlink on one end. Do not remove the chain from the countershaft sprocket.
4. Remove the cotter pin, nut, plain washer, and rubber washer from the brake anchor bolt and separate the brake anchor from the brake plate.

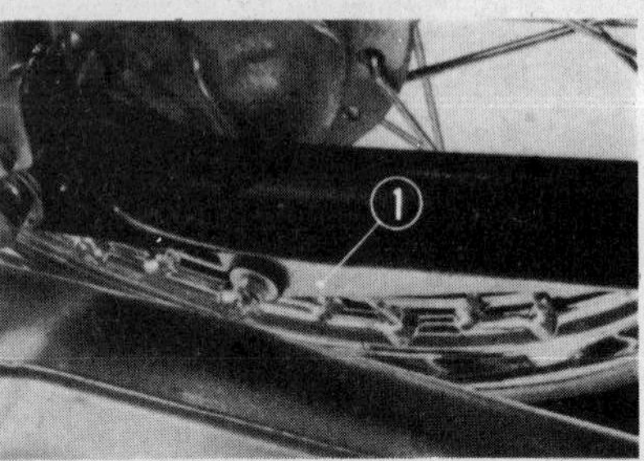

Rear brake anchor

5. Remove the cotter pin from the axle nut, and remove the nut. Pull the axle out from the right side, and remove the wheel.

NOTE: *Place the wheel spacers, and the chain adjusters on the axle in the order in which they were removed and screw on the axle nut.*

6. To install the wheel, hold the wheel, axle spacers, and chain adjusters in place and slip the axle through. Install the axle nut hand-tight. Wrap both ends of the chain around the sprocket and install the masterlink. Adjust the chain tension.

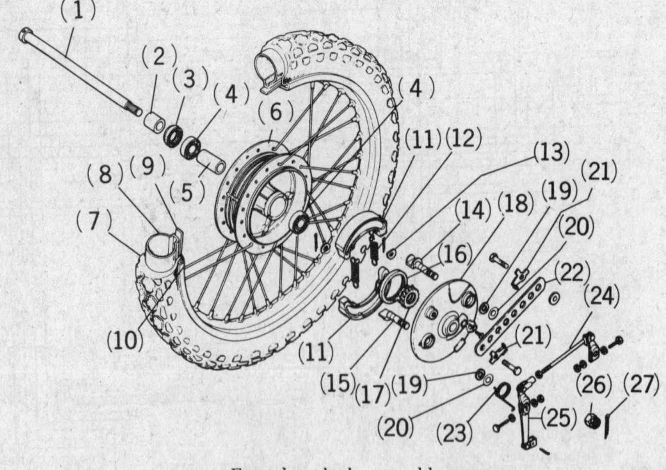

Front drum brake assembly

1. Axle
2. Side collar
3. Oil seal
4. Wheel bearing
5. Spacer
6. Hub
7. Tire
8. Tube
9. Rim band
10. Rim
11. Brake shoe
12. Brake return spring
13. Anchor pin washer
14. Brake cam
15. Brake cam
16. Oil seal
17. Speedometer drive gear
18. Brake plate
19. Dust seal
20. Washer
21. Lockwasher
22. Brake anchor
23. Brake arm return spring
24. Brake rod and rear lever
25. Front brake lever
26. Axle nut
27 Cotter pin

7. Engage the brake anchor to the brake plate and install the rubber washer, plain washer, and the nut. Secure the nut with a new cotter pin.

8. Slip the clevis pin into the brake arm and insert the brake rod through it. Screw on the adjuster nut until the brake lever has about 1 in. (25 mm) free-play. Tighten the axle nut.

Wheel Bearings

Removal of the wheel bearings necessitates removing the hub oil seals. These must be replaced with new ones upon reassembly.

REMOVAL

1. Remove the wheel and take out the brake plate (drum brakes). On disc brake wheels, remove the speedometer drive mechanism.

2. Drum brake wheels: On rear wheels, remove the circlip securing the sprocket to the hub and tap the sprocket off. Remove the oil seal from the side of the hub opposite the brake plate, and the snap-ring from beneath the oil seal. On front wheels, remove the oil seal from the right-side of the hub.

3. Disc brake wheels: Remove the four screws from the right-side of the hub and remove the speedometer drive retainer, retainer cover, and the O-ring. Unscrew the bearing retainer from the left-side of the hub being careful not to damage it. The oil seal can be removed from the retainer for replacement if damaged.

4. To remove the wheel bearings use a blunt punch and hammer. Remove the bearing in the left-side of the hub first. Reach through the center of the hub and tap the inside of the bearing evenly around its circumference to remove it. Be sure that the bearing does not become cocked to one side on removal. After the first bearing has been removed, remove the spacer tube from the center of the hub. Remove the second bearing using a driver large enough to cover the inside race of the bearing. A round piece of hardwood can be used. If the bearings resist removal, gently heat the bearing bosses in the hub with a propane torch and then try to tap them out.

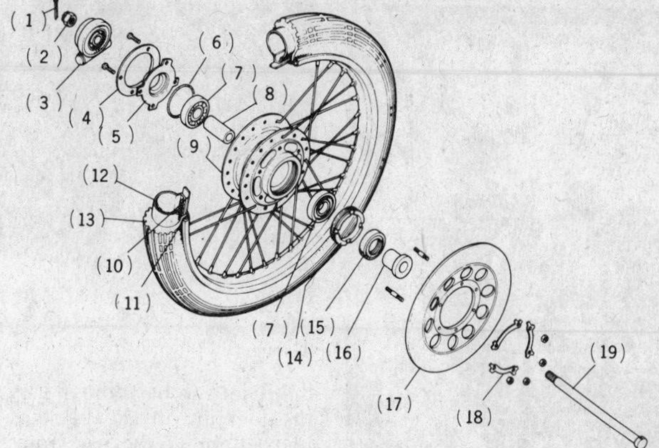

Front disc brake assembly

1. Cotter pin
2. Axle nut
3. Speedometer drive box
4. Retainer cover
5. Retainer
6. O-ring
7. Wheel bearing
8. Spacer
9. Hub
10. Rim band
11. Rim
12. Tube
13. Tire
14. Wheel bearing retainer
15. Oil seal
16. Side collar
17. Brake disc
18. Lockwashers
19. Axle

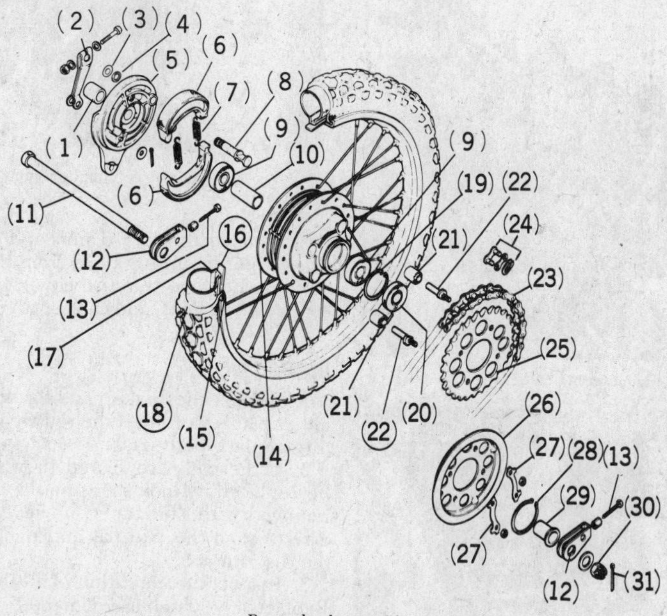

Rear wheel assembly

1. Side collar
2. Brake lever
3. Washer
4. Dust seal
5. Brake plate
6. Brake shoe
7. Return spring
8. Brake cam
9. Wheel bearing
10. Spacer
11. Axle
12. Chain adjuster
13. Adjuster bolt
14. Hub
15. Rim
16. Rim band
17. Tube
18. Tire
19. Snap-ring
20. Oil seal
21. Damper rubbers
22. Sprocket bolt
23. Drive chain
24. Masterlink
25. Rear sprocket
26. Side plate
27. Lockwasher
28. Snap-ring
29. Side collar
30. Axle nut
31. Cotter pin

INSTALLATION

Assembly is in the reverse order of disassembly; however, note the following points:

1. Obtain a good grade of wheel bearing grease (such as Lithium or Moly) to lubricate the wheel bearings.

2. Pack the wheel bearings until they are completely filled.

3. Apply some grease to the inside of the hub and drive one of the wheel bearings into its seat. Install the retainer or snap-ring if so equipped. Install the spacer tube and drive the other bearing into its seat. The sealed surface of the wheel bearings must face the outside of the hub.

NOTE: *When a bearing retainer is fitted, the bearing closest to the retainer should be installed first. Then install and tighten the retainer, spacer and the other bearing.*

4. Install any oil seals. Be sure that they are driven straight into their seats. Coat the lips of the seals with grease before installing the axle.

Front Disc Brake

DISASSEMBLY

1. Slide the rubber boot on the lower part of the brake cable up on the cable to expose the brake cable adjuster in the caliper body. Loosen the locknut on the adjuster, and screw the adjuster into the caliper body as far as it will go.

2. Remove the three 6 mm bolts from the caliper cover, and remove the cover and the ratchet fixing spring. Pull the ratchet adjuster from the brake arm. Remove the brake arm, and disconnect the brake cable.

CAUTION: *Cover the brake arm in a clean cloth or a plastic bag to prevent dirt from entering the inside of the mechanism. The brake arm should not be disassembled; if defective, it should be replaced.*

3. The thrust guide plate can now be removed from the caliper body. To remove the disc pads, screw one of the cali-

Disc brake cable adjuster

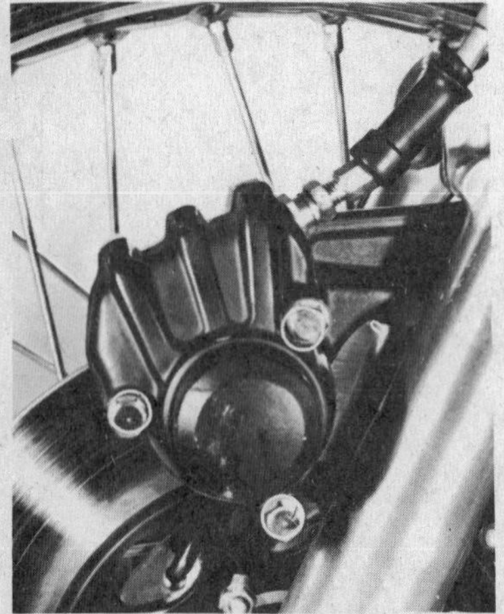
Caliper cover mounting bolts

Disconnect the cable (1) from the brake arm (2)

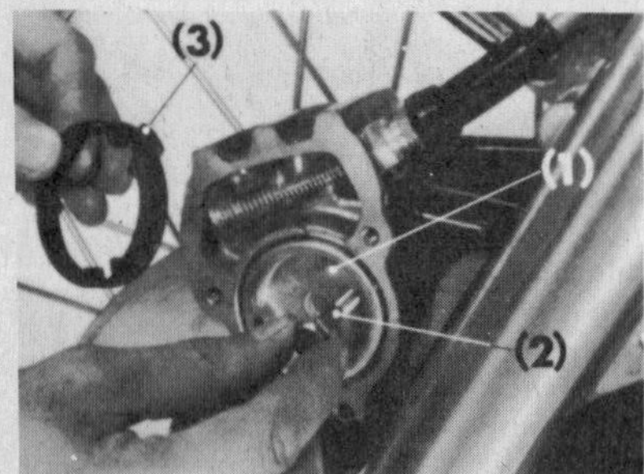

Remove the thrust guide plate (3), and use a 6 mm bolt (2) to withdraw pad (1)

per cover bolts (6 mm) into the threaded hole in the back of pad A (the pad to the outside of the disc). Using the bolt, pull the pad out of the caliper. Remove the front wheel. Pad B (pad to the inside of

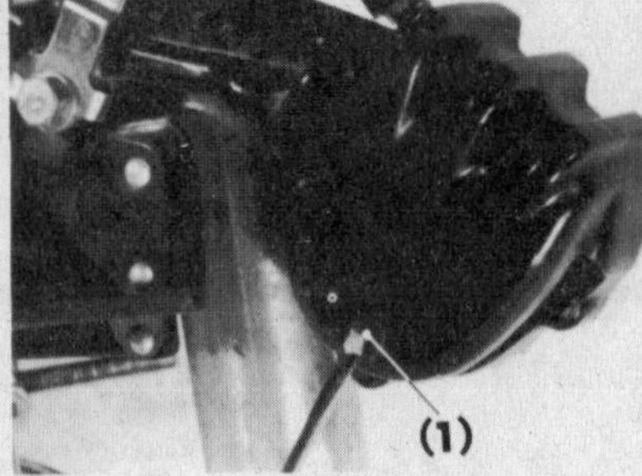

Remove pad B by pushing on lockpin (1)

the disc) can be removed by pushing on the lockpin on the back of the caliper body. Remove the pad from the left-side of the caliper.

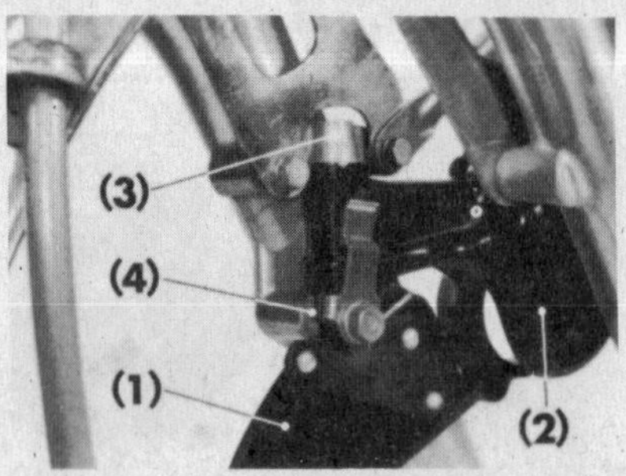

Disc cover (1), caliper body (2), caliper joint (3), caliper pivot pin (4)

4. Remove the two 6 mm and one 8 mm caliper mounting bolts from the left fork leg. Remove the disc cover, caliper body, caliper joint, and caliper pivot pin.

INSPECTION

1. Inspect the brake pads for wear. If either pad is worn past the red wear limit line, replace both pads.

2. If the pads are scored they should be replaced. Minor score marks can be removed with sandpaper; however, take care to sand the pad flat and parallel to the disc surface.

3. Inspect the condition of all O-rings. Replace any which are damaged.

ASSEMBLY

1. Install an O-ring on the caliper pivot pin and apply some chassis grease to the pin. Slip the pin through the caliper and install the remaining O-ring on the top of the pin. Slip the caliper joint over the end of the pin. Install the caliper assembly to the left fork leg, locating the disc cover to the lower (8 mm) mounting bolt. Be sure that the pivot pin is installed correctly and that the lockplate is in place on the lower mounting bolt.

2. Place a small amount of silicon grease (KS62M) on the back of pad B, and install pad B into the right-side of the caliper, locating the lockpin through the hole in the back of the caliper.

3. Install the front wheel.

4. Place a new O-ring on pad A and coat the entire circumference of the pad with a thin layer of silicon grease (KS62M). Install the pad into the caliper aligning the punch marks on the pad and the caliper body as the pad is installed.

Be sure that the caliper pivot pin (1) is installed correctly

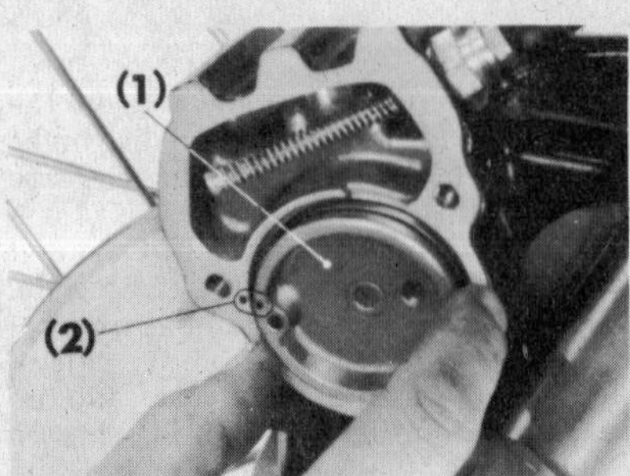

When installing pad "A" (1), line up the punch marks (2)

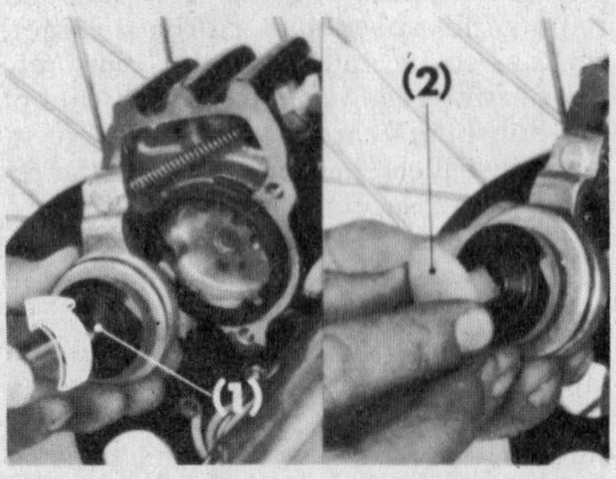

Turn the adjusting screw (1) counterclockwise until resistance is felt. Install the ratchet adjuster (2)

5. Install the thrust plate guide into the caliper. Connect the brake cable to the brake arm. With a small screwdriver, turn the adjusting screw in the center of the brake arm counterclockwise until resistance is felt. The adjusting screw should turn freely. Install the brake arm.

6. Install the ratchet adjuster, locating it into the slot in the adjusting screw. Install a new caliper cover gasket, the caliper cover, and ratchet fixing spring. Secure the cover with the three cover bolts.

7. Screw the adjusting bolt out of the caliper body all the way. Then screw in the adjuster until there is slack in the cable. From this position turn the adjuster out another 2 to 3 turns.

8. Operate the hand lever about 10 times. The lever should automatically adjust itself to the proper free-play of 20–30 mm (0.8–1.2 in.), measured at the tip of the lever.

9. After adjustment is correct, slip the rubber boot over the cable adjuster. Raise the front wheel off the ground and check that the wheel spins freely.

PAD REPLACEMENT

1. The procedures for removing and installing the pads for replacement are given under "Front Disc Brake—Disassembly" and "Assembly." However,

Step 4 "Disassembly," and Step 1 under "Assembly" can be omitted.

CABLE REPLACEMENT

1. Remove the cover from the left-side of the caliper. Screw the cable adjuster into the caliper body as far as possible. Remove the brake arm with the ratchet adjuster in place and disconnect the cable from the brake arm. Screw the adjuster out of the caliper body and remove the cable from the caliper.
2. Remove the rubber boot from the hand lever, disconnect the cable from the lever, and remove the cable.
3. Connect the new cable to the hand lever and replace the rubber boot.
4. Screw the cable adjuster on the new cable all of the way into the caliper body. Connect the cable end to the brake arm and install the brake arm into the caliper body. Install the caliper cover. Turn the cable adjuster out of the caliper until there is no slack in the cable and then turn the adjuster out another 2 to 3 turns.
5. Operate the hand lever about 10 times. The lever should automatically adjust itself to the proper free-play of 20–30 mm (0.8–1.2 in.), measured at the tip of the lever.

BRAKE DISC

The brake disc normally requires no service of any kind. However, if the disc becomes scored for any reason, it should be replaced and a new set of pads should be installed. A badly scored disc will reduce the effectiveness of the brake and shorten pad life considerably. If the front brake lever oscillates or fluctuates when the brake is applied at speed, the indication is that the brake disc is warped or bent. Check the runout of the disc with a dial indicator and replace it if run-out exceeds 0.012 in. (0.3mm). To replace the disc:

1. Remove the front wheel.
2. Bend back the locktabs, unscrew the six nuts, and remove the disc from the hub.
3. Mount the new disc on the hub and tighten the nuts evenly, using new locktabs to secure the nuts.
4. Examine the brake pads and replace them if they are close to the limit of wear or have worn in an unusual pattern.

Drum Brake Service

All models use a single-leading shoe rear brake, while, with the exception of the CB200, a single or twin-leading shoe is used on the front brake. Hondas use brakes in which the lining is bonded to the shoe. Lining and shoe, therefore, are purchased and replaced as a single unit.

1. Brakes can be inspected in place on the brake plate.
2. Inspect the lining for wear. There should be at least 0.06 in. (1.5 mm) of lining left at the thinnest point, or the linings must be replaced.
3. Inspect the linings for scoring or grooves. These may be caused by particles of dirt which have entered the drum. If badly scored, the shoes should be replaced. If scoring of the shoes is evident, it would be wise to inspect the brake drum for the same type of damage.

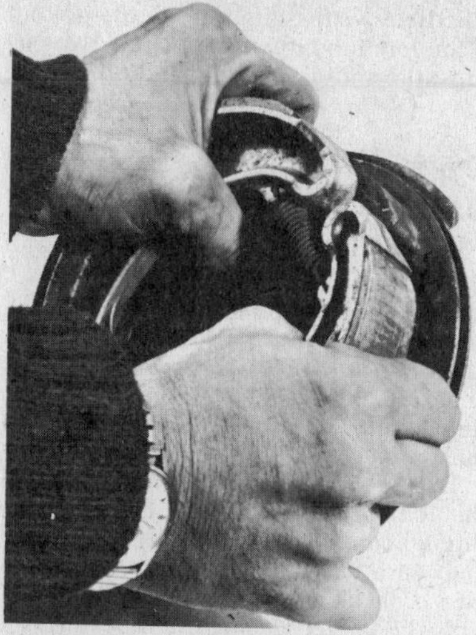

Removing brake shoes from the plate

Be sure that there is no oil or grease present on the linings. Oil-impregnated linings must be replaced. If the linings do show this condition, determine the source of the lubricant: defective wheel bearing oil seals, excessive chain lube, etc.

4 If the linings are usable, rough up the surface with sandpaper. Then clean the linings thoroughly with alcohol or lacquer thinner. Clean the brake drum with the same solvent.

5. To disassemble the brake plate, simply grasp each shoe and fold them toward the center of the brake plate as shown. They may be installed using the same method.
6. Remove the brake springs. Remove the brake lever pinch-bolt(s) and pull the lever(s) off the splined brake camshaft(s).

NOTE: *The plurals refer to twin-leading shoe brakes.*

7. Push the brake cam(s) out of the plate from the outside using hand pressure or by tapping with a plastic mallet. Note the presence of any shims on the cam(s) and be sure they are in place when the brake plate is reassembled. Remove the dust seal(s) from the brake plate.
8. Check that the brake lever pinch-bolts are not bent. This can easily happen if they are overtightened. Replace any bolts in this condition. Inspect the brake lever splines and replace the lever(s) if these are worn or torn.
9. Inspect the splines on the brake cam(s). These should be in good condition. Check that they can rotate freely in the brake plate passage. If it will not, use a fine grade of sandpaper on the camshaft and the surface of the brake plate passage.
10. Clean the cam(s) thoroughly in a solvent to remove any old grease, rust or corrosion. Use sandpaper or emery cloth to polish the cams. Clean off any residue; before reassembly, smear the cams with chassis grease.
11. Inspect the brake plate for cracks or fractures, and replace it if necessary.
12. On twin-leading shoe brakes, the brake plate linkage should be checked for wear, especially on high mileage machines, and replaced if necessary.
13. Check the condition of the brake springs, noting any twisted or fatigued hooks. Replace any broken, rusted, or old springs with new ones.
14. Clean all parts thoroughly with a suitable solvent, making a special effort to remove the dust and built-up dirt from the backing plate.
15. When reassembling the hub, note the following points:
    a. Ensure that the brake cams are lubricated with chassis grease and that any shims which were on the cams are in place;
    b. The use of new dust seals is recommended;
    c. Lubricate the brake shoe pivot points with a little grease;
    d. Install the shoes as on removal. Hook them together with the springs, and fold them down over the brake cam(s) and pivot(s);
    e. Install the brake lever(s) so that the punch mark on the lever is in line with the punch mark on the brake cam, if fitted.

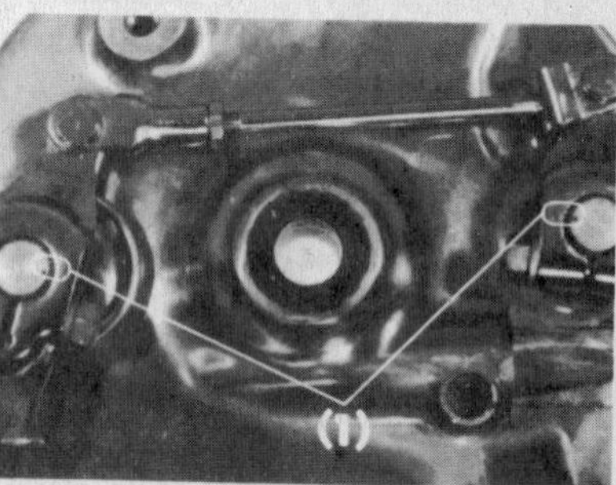

When installing the brake rod, line up the punch marks (1)

FRONT FORKS

Removal

1. Loosen the fork filler caps at the top of each fork leg. If the upper triple clamp is not fitted with fork leg pinch-bolts, the filler caps will have to be removed.
2. Support the front wheel off the ground by placing a stand under the engine. Remove the front wheel.
3. On disc brake models, remove the caliper from the left fork leg.
4. Remove the front fender.
5. Loosen the lower triple clamp pinch-bolts. Loosen the upper triple clamp pinch-bolts (if fitted). Spread the lower triple clamp with a small wedge and pull the fork legs out from the bottom one at a time.

Disassembly

CB/CL200, 175K7

The procedure is given for one fork leg, but it applies to both.

1. Remove the filler cap from the top of the fork tube and pour the oil into a suitable container to be disposed of.
2. Remove the spring(s) from the top of the tube.

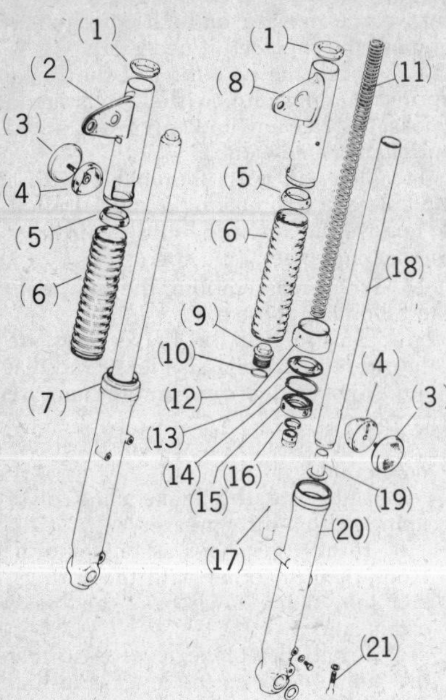

CB/CL200, 175K7

1. Upper cushion
2. Headlight bracket
3. Reflector
4. Reflector base
5. Lower cushion
6. Fork boot
7. Fork leg assembly
8. Headlight bracket
9. Fork filler cap
10. O-ring
11. Fork spring
12. Slider cover
13. Dust seal
14. Snap-ring
15. Fork seal
16. Piston ring
17. Damper rod
18. Fork tube
19. Piston
20. Slider
21. Allen bolt

3. Turn the fork upside-down and rest it on a block of hard wood. With an impact driver and the proper bit remove the allen bolt from the bottom of the slider. These bolts are installed with thread locking compound and trying to remove them without an impact driver will result in rounding the head of the bolt.

When the bolt is removed from the bottom of the slider, the damper rod complete with piston ring, and the rebound spring can be removed from the top of the fork tube.

5. The tube can now be pulled out of the slider. The piston will remain in the slider. Once the tube is pulled out the oil seal in the slider will have to be replaced.

6. Remove the dust cover and snap-ring from the top of the slider and pry out the oil seal with a hooked tool. The pin wrench from the Honda tool kit may be used by slipping the hooked end under the seal and tapping the handle with a hammer. A strip of copper or other soft metal can be used between the top of the slider and the handle of the wrench to protect the slider.

ALL OTHER MODELS

The procedure is given for one fork leg, but it applies to both.

1. Remove the filler cap from the top of the fork leg and pour the oil into a suitable container to be disposed of. Remove the fork spring.

2. Remove the dust seal, snap-ring, and washer from the top of the slider. Grasp the slider in one hand and the fork tube in the other and pull them apart with a sharp jerk.

3. Remove the circlip from the bottom of the fork tube, then the piston, two circlips, the sliding bushing and oil seal.

Inspection

ALL MODELS

1. Wash all metal parts in a solvent and dry.

2. Inspect the fork slider for cracked, broken, or distorted axle brackets, worn inner bore surfaces, damaged threads, or dents which have affected the inner bore. Replace the slider if defective in any of the above ways.

3. Inspect the fork tubes for condition: the chrome plating must be intact throughout. Check for damaged threads, and worn or scuffed inner or outer surfaces. Check the tubes for straightness. This is done by placing the tubes in a set of V-blocks and checking the run-out with a dial gauge. If the tube is bent more than 0.060 in. as indicated by the gauge, it must be replaced.

4. 200, late 175: Inspect the piston ring for scoring or wear.

5. Check the filler cap O-ring for cracks or any other signs of wear. Replace it if damaged.

6. Check the general condition of the fork springs. Replace any which are badly rusted, have collapsed coils, etc. Compare the lengths of corresponding springs. They should be of approximately equal length. If the springs differ in length by more than 1/4 in., both springs should be replaced.

7. Inspect the inside surfaces of the piston and sliding bushing for signs of wear or score marks. Replace as necessary. Place the sliding bushing on the fork tube and check for excessive play. The bushing should be a close fit.

8. Coat all parts with ATF before assembly. New oil seals must always be used.

Assembly

200, LATE 175

1. Be sure that the piston is in the slider. Lubricate the new oil seal with ATF and install it into the top of the slider. Place a block of hard wood over the seal and drive it straight into the slider as far as possible. Then place the old seal on top of the new one and drive them in until the new one clears the snap-ring groove in the slider. Take out the old seal. Be sure that the new seal is straight in the slider. The distance from the top of the oil seal to the snap-ring groove should be the same all around the seal. Install the snap-ring. Lubricate the lips of the seal.

2. Install the rebound spring and damper rod in the fork tube. Carefully install the slider on the tube. Replace the fork springs and cap temporarily. Turn the fork upside down and install the bolt in the bottom of the slider. The threads of this bolt should be coated with thread locking compound.

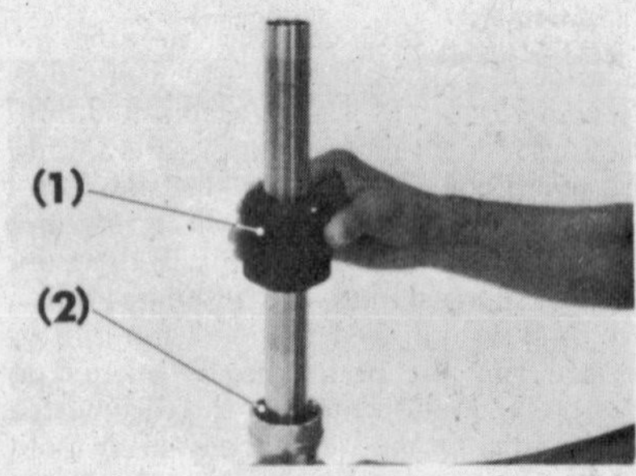

Installing a fork slider seal with the driver (1)

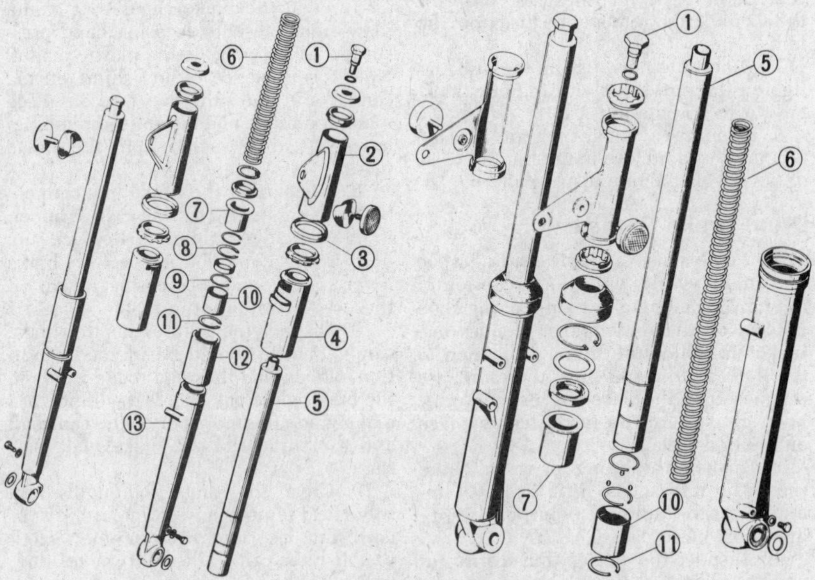

CB/CL125 and CB/CL/SL175

1. Filler cap
2. Headlight bracket
3. Bezel ring
4. Fork cover
5. Fork tube
6. Fork spring
7. Slider bushing
8. Stopper ring, valve
9. Stopper ring, piston
10. Piston
11. Piston circlip
12. Fork cover cap
13. Fork slider

3. Fit the drain plugs; be sure to install the gaskets.

4. Remove the cap and fill the forks with the proper amount of ATF. Note that the amount added to rebuilt forks will be slightly more than for a normal fork oil change.

ALL OTHER MODELS

1. Install a new oil seal on the fork tube. Be sure to lubricate the seal with ATF before placing it on the tube.

2. Install the sliding bushing on the tube with the flange on the bushing facing the top of the tube. Install the two circlips, piston, and bottom circlip. All of the circlips must be a snug fit on the fork tube; if not replace them. Slide the fork spring into the tube from the bottom.

3. Place the fork tube into the slider and drive the oil seal into its seat in the top of the slider. Replace the washer, snap-ring, and dust seal.

4. Fill the fork leg with the proper amount of oil. Replace the top washer, O-ring, and filler cap.

Installation

ALL MODELS

1. Refit the fork tubes through the triple clamps. The top of the fork tube should be even with the top of the upper triple clamp.

2. Tighten the pinch-bolts on the lower triple clamp, and then tighten the fork filler caps and the pinch-bolts on the upper triple clamp, in that order.

3. Fit the front wheel and check the operation of the forks.

STEERING STEM ASSEMBLY

Bearing Adjustment

On models equipped with a friction steering damper, the damper should be loosened (counterclockwise) as much as possible so that it does not interfere with the bearing movement while checking or adjusting the bearing. If an oil damper is fitted, remove it from the steering stem.

1. The steering stem bearings are uncaged #8 balls. They are adjusted by means of a ring nut beneath the upper triple clamp.

2. To check bearing adjustment, support the front wheel off the ground. Grasp the tip of the front fender, place your other hand beneath the lower triple clamp at the frame lug.

3. Attempt to move the forks by pulling up on the tip of the fender. If play or movement can be felt at the lower triple clamp, the bearings are adjusted too loosely or are worn.

4. Turn the forks slowly from lock-to-lock. Movement should be smooth, silent, and effortless. If any binding or uneven movement is felt, the balls and races are either too tightly adjusted or they are worn. If the steering feels uniformly stiff, the bearings are too tightly adjusted. If any noise is noted, the bearings are damaged or some are missing.

Adjusting steering head bearings

5. With the front wheel off the ground, release the front forks from a few degrees off the centered position. The forks should fall freely to either side of their own weight. If they will not, the bearings are too tightly adjusted, the steering stem is bent, the races are extremely worn, or some of the bearings are missing.

6. To adjust the bearings, remove the front wheel, front forks, handlebars, and the upper triple clamp. The bearings are adjusted by means of the adjuster nut under the upper triple clamp.

7. Tighten or loosen the adjuster nut a little at a time until the steering stem adjustment conforms to that outlined above. Temporarily install the forks, upper triple clamp, and the steering stem nut to check the adjustment.

8. If proper adjustment is not possible, the bearings and races will probably need to be replaced.

Disassembly

1. Remove the front wheel, front forks, and handlebars. If a friction steering damper is fitted, remove it by removing the two cotter pins from under the lower triple clamp, and unscrewing the damper rod and removing the friction plates. If an oil shock damper is fitted, unbolt it from the lower triple clamp.

2. Unscrew the steering stem nut and disconnect the speedometer and tachometer cables from their instruments. Remove the upper triple clamp.

3. Disconnect the wiring inside the headlight shell, and remove the headlight shell and the fork ears.

4. Loosen the steering stem adjuster nut with a pin wrench, then hold the steering stem up while unscrewing the adjuster nut the rest of the way off. Remove the steering stem top cone race and the ball bearings from the top race.

5. Carefully pull the steering stem out from the bottom. Some of the ball bearings from the lower race will probably fall out at this time so be prepared for this.

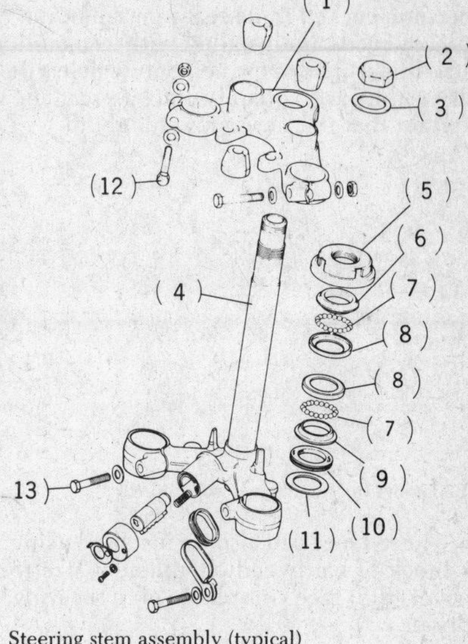

Steering stem assembly (typical)

1. Upper triple clamp
2. Steering stem nut
3. Washer
4. Steering stem
5. Bearing adjuster nut
6. Top cone race
7. Steering head bearing balls
8. Frame races
9. Lower cone race
10. Dust seal
11. Washer
12. Upper triple clamp pinch-bolt
13. Lower triple clamp pinch-bolt

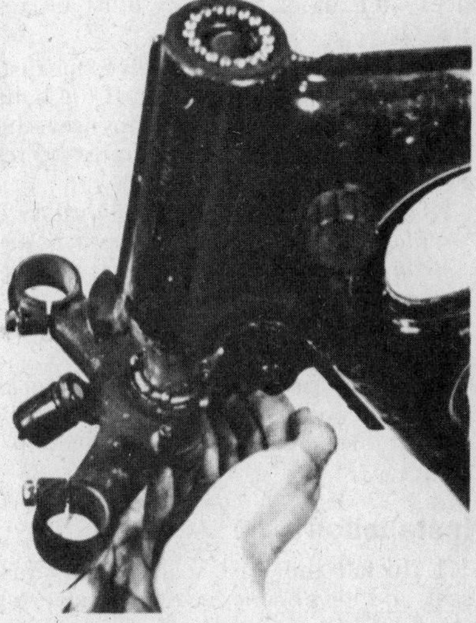

Removing the steering stem

6. Remove the bottom cone race, dust seal, and dust seal washer from the steering stem if they are to be replaced. These will have to be pried off with a chisel, therefore only remove them if necessary.

7. The bearing races in the frame lug are a press-fit and should not be removed unless replacement is necessary. If replacement is necessary, the old races can be removed by reaching through the frame lug with a suitable punch and tapping the race evenly around its circumference to remove it from the inside of the

frame lug. Be sure that the race does not become cocked in its seat upon removal.

New races are installed with a suitable sized bearing driver: i.e., one which will drive the race squarely into its seat. Be certain that the race goes straight in.

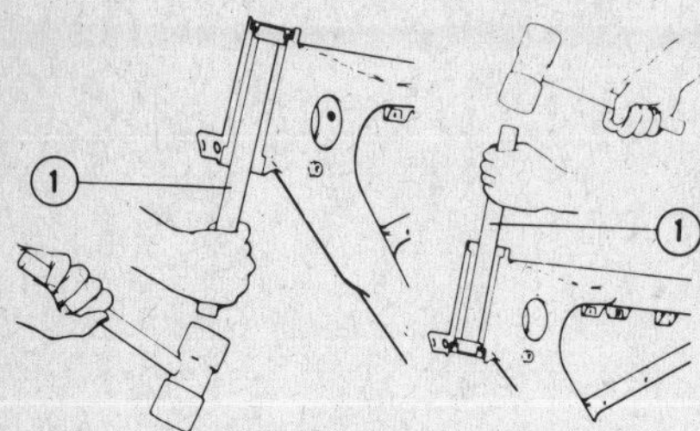

Removing the frame races with a drift

These races can also be installed using a block of hardwood of sufficient size to cover the race in place of a bearing driver.

Inspection

1. Wash the ball bearings in a suitable solvent.
2. Clean all of the old grease from the bearing race surfaces, steering stem, and frame lug.
3. Inspect the bearing race surfaces. They must be clean and smooth. That is free from any cracks, scoring, rust, or indentations. Run your finger around each of the bearing races. Note any roughness or ripples on the race surface. If any imperfections are noted, both the sets of races and all of the balls must be replaced.
4. Check the balls themselves for rust, pitting, scoring, or flat spots. If the balls are found to be defective in any way, the balls and both sets of races must be replaced.

NOTE: *Balls and races must always be replaced in a set as worn races will destroy new balls and worn balls will destroy new races.*

5. Check the dust seal for condition and replace if torn or cracked.
6. Check the steering stem for cracks or a bent condition; this is especially important if the bike has been involved in a spill.

Installation

1. Install the dust seal washer, dust seal, and lower cone race on the steering stem. Use a good grade of bearing grease to coat the bottom cone race and the upper race in the frame lug.
2. Embed 18 balls into the grease of each race.
3. When the balls are in place, slip the steering stem through the frame lug and hold it in place while refitting the top cone race and threading on the adjuster nut.
4. Tighten the adjuster nut all of the way by hand, rotating the steering stem to work the grease into the balls.
5. Tighten the adjuster nut until the steering stem turns freely, but has no play.
6. Install the fork tubes, headlight assembly, and upper triple clamp, flat washer, and steering stem nut. Check that the stem moves freely of its own weight from 5°–10° off center; if not, check for:
   a. Steering bearing too tight;
   b. Bent steering stem;
   c. Worn races or balls.
7. Install the front fender, front wheel, and handlebars.

REAR SHOCK ABSORBERS

The damper unit of the rear shock absorbers cannot be serviced; therefore, if defective, the unit must be replaced.

If the shock absorbers are somewhat old, and one fails in the course of normal usage, it would be a good idea to replace both shocks to ensure equal damping characteristics.

CAUTION: *Do not attempt to disassemble the damper unit of the rear shocks. These contain gas under high pressure.*

To check a shock which is removed from the machine, place the bottom end on the ground and use the weight of your body to compress it as much as possible. Release the shock and note the rebound behavior. If the shock returns quickly at first, then slowly returns to the normal length, it is serviceable. If it returns to its normal length all at once, it should be replaced.

SWING ARM

All Models

INSPECTION

1. Disconnect the chain. Remove the rear wheel and sprocket assembly.
2. Remove the shock absorbers and chain guard.
3. Measure the distance between the top and bottom shock absorber mounts on both sides. The two measurements must be identical, or the swing arm will have to be replaced or fixed.
4. Check that the rear wheel mounting plates are parallel.
5. Grasp the legs of the swing arm and attempt to move it from side-to-side. Any
6. Lubricate the new bushings and both the inside and outside of the inner collar with a good chassis grease. Press in

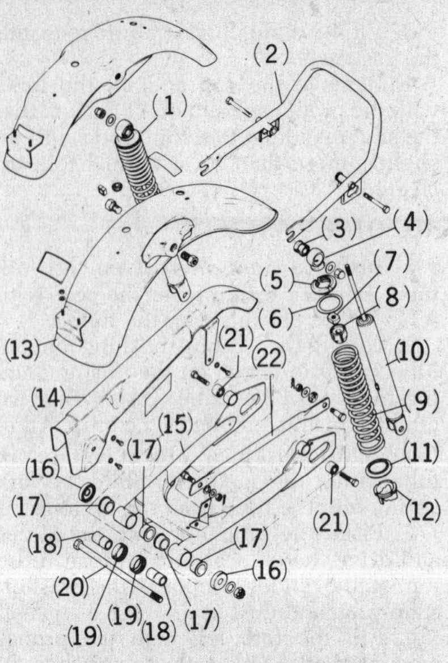

Rear suspension assembly (200 shown)

1. Rear shock absorber
2. Handle
3. Rubber bush
4. Upper eye
5. Split collars
6. Spring seat
7. Locknut
8. Stopper rubber
9. Spring
10. Damper
11. Lower spring seat
12. Spring adjuster
13. Rear fender
14. Chain guard
15. Swing arm
16. Dust seal
17. Bushing
18. Collar
19. Dust seal
20. Pivot bolt
21. Rubber bushing
22. Brake anchor

one bushing, refit the inner collar and install the other bushing.

7. Install the swing arm on the machine. After tightening the swing arm pivot shaft nut, move the swing arm up and down to ensure that movement is smooth and effortless.

noticeable side-play will indicate that the swing arm bushings and center collars need replacement.

The swing arm is most likely to be damaged if the machine is operated for any length of time with a broken or otherwise defective shock absorber.

REMOVAL AND INSTALLATION

1. Proceed as above. Then unscrew the swing arm pivot bolt nut, and pull out the pivot bolt.
2. Remove the swing arm.
3. The swing arm should be inspected for cracks or fractures, especially around the welds.
4. After removing the swing arm, the dust seals and the swing arm bushings can be replaced. This should be done every 10,000 miles or more often depending on how the machine is used, or if the bushings are worn.
5. Using a small drift, push the center collar out of the swing arm. Remove the bushings, tapping them out with a long drift and hammer. Once the bushings are removed, they should be replaced.

Chassis Specifications

200

Item	Standard (mm/in.)	Service Limit (mm/in.)
Brake disc face run-out	0.05/0.002	0.20/0.008
Brake disc bend	0.05/0.002	0.3/0.12
Brake disc thickness	4.9–5.1/0.019–0.20	4.0/0.158
Front brake lining thickness	4.5–4.7/0.177–0.185	2.0/0.079
Front brake drum ID	160–160.3/6.299–6.311	161.0/6.339
Wheel rim run-out	0.5/0.02	2.0/0.079
Wheel bearing axial play	0.05/0.002	0.1/0.004
Wheel bearing radial play	0.03/0.001	0.05/0.002
Axle run-out	0.01/0.0004	0.2/0.008
Rear brake lining thickness	4.5–4.7/0.177–0.185	1.5/0.06
Rear brake drum ID	140.0–140.3/5.512–5.524	141.0/5.551
Fork spring free-length	453.7/17.862	445.0/17.52
Rear spring free-length	196.7/7.745	185.0/7.284
Swing arm bushing-to-center collar clearance	0.04–0.125/0.0016–0.005	0.3/0.012
Swing arm bushing ID	20.00–20.05/0.787–0.789	20.2/0.795
Fork slider ID	31.00–31.04/1.220–1.222	31.14/1.226
Fork tube OD	30.925–30.950/1.217–1.218	30.90/1.217

175

Item	Standard (mm/in.)	Service Limit (mm/in.)
Front brake lining thickness	5.0/0.197	4.0/0.158
Front brake drum ID	158.8–160/6.291–6.299	162.0/6.378
Wheel rim run-out	0.5/0.02	2.0/0.079
Wheel bearing axial play	0.05/0.002	0.1/0.004
Wheel bearing radial play	0.03/0.001	0.05/0.002
Axle run-out	0.01/0.0004	0.2/0.008
Rear brake lining thickness	4.5–4.8/0.177–0.189	4.0/0.158
Rear brake drum ID	139.8–140/5.504–5.512	142.0/5.59
Fork spring free-length	409.3/16.114	376.0/14.803
Sliding bushing OD	35.425–35.450/1.395–1.396	35.4/1.394
Rear spring free-length①	188.3/7.413	174.0/6.35
Rear spring free-length②	216.6/8.527	200.0/7.374
Swing arm pivot bolt-to-bushing clearance	0.1–0.3/0.004–0.012	0.5/0.02

125

Item	Standard (mm/in.)	Service Limit (mm/in.)
Front brake lining thickness	4.5–4.8/0.177–0.189	2.0/0.079
Front brake drum ID	139.3–139.5/5.43–5.44	140.3/5.46
Wheel rim run-out	0.5/0.02	2.0/0.079
Wheel bearing axial play	0.05/0.002	0.1/0.004
Wheel bearing radial play	0.03/0.001	0.05/0.002
Axle run-out	0.01/0.004	0.2/0.008
Rear brake lining thickness	4.5–4.8/0.177–0.189	1.5/0.06
Rear brake drum ID	129.3–129.5/5.09–5.10	130.3/5.18
Fork spring free-length		
CB125	414.8/16.33	384/15.1
CL/SS125	418.4/16.47	388.0/15.03
Rear spring free-length	203.3/8.0	180.0/7.08
Swing arm bushing ID	12.1–12.3/0.48	12.5/0.49
Swing arm pivot bolt OD	12.0/0.47	——
Swing arm pivot bolt max allow bend	0.02/0.0008	0.05/0.002

① CB/CL models
② SL models

Chassis Torque Specifications

200

Item	Torque (ft lbs)
Front axle nut	44–58
Rear axle nut	51–65
Swing arm pivot bolt	44–50
Steering stem nut	58–72
Triple clamp pinch-bolts	13–18
Handlebar clamps	13–18
Spokes	1–2
Engine mounting bolts	13–18
Brake anchor nut	6–7
Rear shocks	18–25
Step bar	13–18

175

Item	Torque (ft lbs)
Front axle nut	50–65
Rear axle nut	50–65
Swing arm pivot bolt	36–44
Engine mounting bolt	22–29
Handlebar clamps	7–9
Steering stem nut	65–87
Rear shock mounting bolt	14–25
Brake anchor bolts	11–18
Step bar	11–18

125

Item	Torque (ft lbs)
Front axle nut	51–72
Rear axle nut	72–79
Steering stem nut	72–87
Spokes	1–2
Rear shock mounting bolts	15–25
Engine mounting bolts	
Upper	15–22
Lower	22–29
Brake anchor bolts	10–18
Handlebar clamps	10–18

General Torque Specifications①

Part	Torque (ft lbs)
6 mm machine screws	5.0–7.2
6 mm hex bolts	5.8–8.7
8 mm hex bolts	13.0–18.1
10 mm hex bolts	21.7–28.9
6 mm flange bolts	7.2–10.1
8 mm flange bolts	17.4–21.7
10 mm	21.7–28.9

① Unless otherwise specified

Honda 350-360 Twins

MODEL COVERAGE

CB350	SL350	CL360
CB350G	CB360	CB360T
CL350	CB360G	CJ360T

INDEX

MAINTENANCE

NOTE: *Common maintenance procedures are explained in detail in "General Information."*

LUBRICATION

Checking Oil Level

When the motorcycle is on the center stand on level ground, the oil level should be between the maximum and minimum marks on the dipstick with the filler cap resting on the top of the threads of its hole.

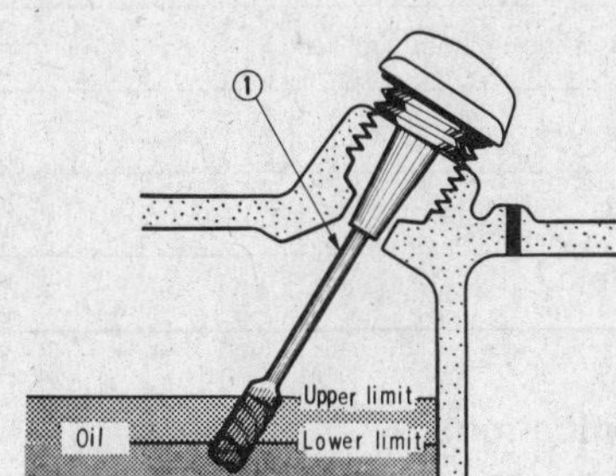

Maintain oil level between upper and lower dipstick marks. Note that the dipstick must rest on the top of the threads when checking

Changing Oil

The oil should be changed every 1,000 miles after the break-in period. The oil should be changed when warm.

1. Remove the oil filler cap, and the drain plug. After allowing a minute for the oil to drain, kick the engine over a few times with the kick-starter (be sure that the key is off) to remove any oil in the delivery system.
2. Refit the drain plug and add 1½ qts of the correct grade of oil. Run the engine for a minute or two, then shut it off; wait one minutes and check the oil level. Add oil as necessary to bring the level up to the maximum mark on the dipstick.

Oil Filter

A centrifugal oil filter is used on all models. As the oil passes through the spinning filter, dirt particles are forced to the outside of the filter housing and the clean oil passes through the center of the filter into the right crankcase cover. The filter should be cleaned every 6,000 miles or 12 months.

1. Clean the oil filter in conjunction with an oil change. Drain the oil, but do not reinstall the drain plug.
2. 350 models only: Remove the three screws from the circular cover plate on the right crankcase cover. Remove the cover. Pry slots are provided for a small screwdriver.
3. 360 models only: Remove the right step bar, kick-starter lever, and right crankcase cover.
4. Remove the circlip from the oil filter. Screw a 6 mm (crankcase cover) screw into the center of the filter cap; this will pull the cap off.

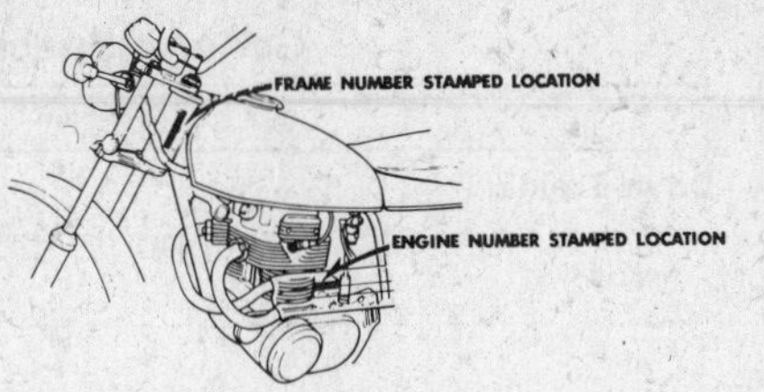

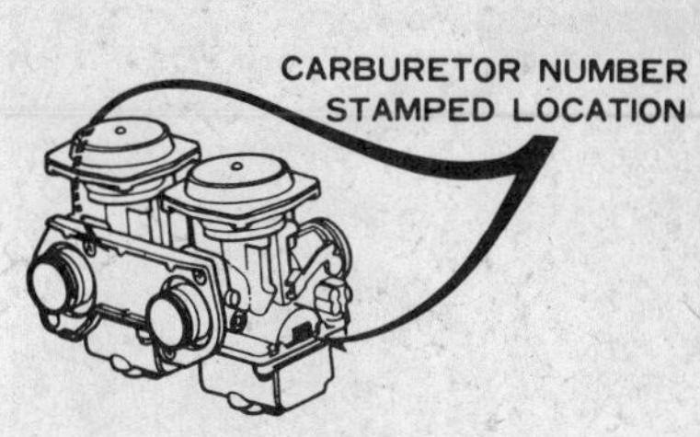

General Specifications CB/CL350

	CB350-to K3	*CB350 K4-on*	*CL350-to K3*	*CL350 K4-on*
Engine				
Displacement (cc)	325			
Bore and stroke (mm/in.)	60 x 50.6/2.52 x 1.992			
Compression ratio	9.5 : 1			
Carburetion (Keihin)	28 mm CV type			
Weight (lbs)	115.5	115.0	115.5	114.7
Valve train	Chain-driven, overhead camshaft			
Chassis				
Type	Semi-double cradle			
Suspension				
Front	Telescopic fork			
Rear	Swing arm—De Carbon shocks			
Tire size				
Front	3.00 x 18		3.00 x 19	
Rear	3.50 x 18		3.50 x 18	
Wheelbase (mm/in.)	1320/52			
Weight (kg/lb)	160/352.8	168.5/371.5	157/345.4	169/372.6
Overall length (mm/in.)	2010/79.2		2020/79.5	2025/79.7
Overall width (mm/in.)	775/30.5	776/30.2	830/32.7	
Overall height (mm/in.)	1075/42.3	1085/42.7	1090/42.9	
Ground clearance (mm/in.)	150/5.9	145/5.7	180/7.1	160/6.3
Drive Train				
Clutch type	Wet, multi-plate type			
Gear ratios:				
1st	2.353			
2nd	1.636			
3rd	1.269			
4th	0.036			
5th	0.900			

Removing the filter rotor snap-ring

The filter cap can be removed by threading a 6 mm (crankcase cover) screw into it

5. Clean the inside of the filter housing with a clean rag and solvent.

6. Clean the filter cap and cover plate (350) and dry thoroughly. Inspect the O-ring on the filter cap and replace it if damaged in any way.

Inspect the oil guide in the cover plate (350) or in the right crankcase cover (360). The guide should be free to move

Checking oil guide operation

in and out, and have sufficient spring force behind it to hold it against the filter cap.

7. Install the filter cap with the vanes located in the grooves on the inside of the

General Specifications (cont.)

	CB350-to K3	*CB350 K4-on*	*CL350-to K3*	*CL350 K4-on*
Drive Train				
Gear ratios:				
6th	—			
Primary reduction	3.714			
Final reduction	2.250		2.375	
Electrical System				
Ignition	Battery and coil			
Starting system	Starter motor and kick			
Charging system	Alternator			
Battery (volt/amp hrs)	12/12			
Regulator	Pointless			

General Specifications SL350

	SL350	*SL350 K1-K2*
Engine		
Displacement (cc)	325	325
Bore and stroke (mm/in.)	60 x 50.6/2.52 x 1.992	
Compression ratio	9.5 : 1	9.5 : 1
Carburetion (Keihin)	28 mm CV	PW 24
Weight (lbs)	115	103.5
Valve train	Chain-driven, overhead camshaft	
Chassis		
Type	Semi-double, cradle	Double cradle
Suspension		
Front	Telescopic fork	
Rear	Swing arm—De Carbon shocks	
Tire size		
Front	3.25 x 19	3.00 x 21
Rear	4.00 x 18	4.00 x 18
Wheelbase (mm/in.)	1390/54.72	1400/55.1
Weight (kg/lb)	139/306.5	148/326
Overall length (mm/in.)	2110/83.07	2165/85.2
Overall width (mm/in.)	840/33.07	870/34.3
Overall height (mm/in.)	1145/45.08	1175/46.3
Ground clearance (mm/in.)	210/8.3	230/9.1

filter housing, and secure with the circlip.

8. On 350 models, install the cover plate using a new O-ring or gasket if necessary.

NOTE: *When installing the filter cover plate on 350 models be sure that the oil holes in the cover plate and the right crankcase cover line up.*

9. On 360 models, install the right crankcase cover, kick-starter lever, and right step bar.

Front Forks

1. ATF is recommended for the front forks. If slightly stiffer damping characteristics are desired, use SAE 20 or SAE 30 oil.

2. Fork oil should be changed every 3,000 miles or once every 6 months.

3. To drain the fork oil, remove the drain plug at the lower portion of one of the fork sliders. Allow the oil to drain for several minutes into a suitable container, then pump the forks up and down several times. After most of the oil is expelled, turn the forks all the way to the right to completely drain the right fork leg, or all the way to the left for the left fork leg. Check the condition of the drain plug gasket. Replace it if necessary. Refit the drain plug and tighten it securely.

4. Repeat the procedure with the other fork leg.

5. Support the front wheel off the ground. Remove the fork filler caps from the top of each fork leg; it may be necessary to remove the handlebar holders and place the handlebars out of the way. Loosening the upper triple clamp pinchbolts (if fitted) may make removal easier. On models with internal fork springs, the front end of the motorcycle can be lowered to force the springs out of the fork tubes. Either move the spring to one side or remove it altogether to aid filling the forks.

6. Add the correct amount of ATF to each fork leg. Capacities for each model are given in the "Maintenance Data" chart at the end of this section.

Chassis Lubrication

1. The swing arm pivot is fitted with two grease nipples on most models. These should be lubricated with a good grade of chassis grease every 3,000 miles. Grease should be applied until some of it shows at either end of the swing arm.

2. Wheel and steering head bearings are lubricated with bearing grease. This should be done every 6,000 miles.

Late models have the swing arm grease fitting in the middle of the swing arm. Lubricate it in the same manner as the earlier type.

SERVICE CHECKS AND ADJUSTMENTS

Drive Chain

1. The chain should have about ¾ in. (20 mm) of total up-and-down free-play measured in the middle of the lower chain run.

General Specifications (cont.)

	SL350	*SL350 K1-K2*
Drive Train		
Clutch type	Wet, multi-plate type	
Gear ratios:		
1st	2.353	2.866
2nd	1.636	1.800
3rd	1.280	1.333
4th	1.036	1.035
5th	0.900	0.870
6th	—	—
Primary reduction	3.714	3.714
Final reduction	2.500	2.625
Electrical System		
Ignition	Battery and coil	Battery and coil
Starting system	Starter motor and kick	Kick
Charging system	Alternator	
Battery (volt/amp hrs)	12/12	12/5
Regulator	Pointless	

General Specifications CB/CL360, CJ360

	CB360	*CL360*	*CJ360*
Engine			
Displacement (cc)	356		
Bore and Stroke (mm/in.)	67 x 50.6/2.638 x 1.992		
Compression ratio	9.3 : 1		
Carburetion (Keihin)	28 mm CV type		
Weight (lbs)	348	350	351
Valve train	Chain-driven, overhead camshaft		
Chassis			
Type	Semi-double cradle		
Suspension			
Front	Telescopic fork		
Rear	Swing arm—De Carbon shocks		
Tire size			
Front	3.00 x 18	3.00 x 18	3.00 x 18
Rear	3.50 x 18	3.50 x 18	3.50 x 18

Check chain free-play in the middle of the lower chain run

2. Before checking or adjusting the chain slack, the following conditions should be met:

a. The motorcycle should be placed on the center stand so that the rear wheel is off the ground;

b. The transmission should be placed in Neutral;

c. The chain should be clean and well-lubricated;

d. The chain should have been checked for any tight spots by slowly rotating the wheel and checking for variances in the chain tension at different points. If a tight spot exists, the chain tension should be adjusted to the prescribed free-play at the tight spot. Note, however, that such a condition is indicative of a worn chain and probably sprockets which should be replaced as soon as possible.

3. To adjust the chain, first back off the rear brake adjuster nut if a rod-operated brake is fitted.

4. Remove the axle nut cotter pin and loosen the axle nut several turns. Loosen the locknut on each chain adjuster bolt.

5. Turn each of the adjuster bolts in or out by equal amounts until the chain tension is approximately correct.

Adjusting chain free-play. Be sure that the adjuster (circle) indicates the same aligning mark on each side of the swing arm.

6. Check wheel alignment by means of the aligning marks inscribed on both sides of the swing arm. Be sure that both adjusters are lined up with the same mark on each side. If not, turn one of the adjuster bolts in or out so that alignment is achieved.

7. Tighten the axle nut and check the chain tension. The chain tension should also be checked with the weight of a rider sitting on the motorcycle when it is off the center stand; the chain should still have at least ½ in. of free-play. Correct if necessary. After adjustment is correct, torque the axle nut to the proper torque, 72 ft lbs. Fit a new cotter pin and tighten the adjuster locknuts.

General Specifications (cont.)

	CB360	*CL360*	*CJ360*
Chassis			
Wheelbase (mm/in.)	1345/53.0	1345/53.0	1375/54.1
Weight (kg/lbs)	162/357	162/357	162/357
Overall length (mm/in.)	2040/80.3	2040/80.3	2075/81.7
Overall width (mm/in.)	775/30.5	820/32.3	790/31.1
Overall height (mm/in.)	1125/44.3	1115/43.9	1110/43.7
Ground clearance (mm/in.)	160/6.3	160/6.3	160/6.3
Drive Train			
Clutch type		Wet, multi plate type	
Gear ratios:			
1st		2.500	2.438
2nd		1.750	1.667
3rd		1.375	1.375
4th		1.111	1.111
5th		0.965	0.965
6th		0.866	—
Primary reduction		3.714	3.714
Final reduction		2.125	2.063
Electrical System			
Ignition		Battery and coil	
Starting system		Starter motor and kick	Kick
Charging system		Alternator	
Battery (volt/amp hrs)		12/12	12/9
Regulator		Pointless	

— Not applicable
NA Not available

Clutch

Two adjustments are made to the clutch: cable adjustment and pushrod adjustment. Usually the pushrod need not be adjusted unless the clutch malfunctions. Cable adjustment must always be maintained at the proper specification.

Before adjusting the clutch, apply a few shots of chassis grease to the adjuster grease fitting and operate the clutch lever a few times to distribute the grease. The clutch cable should also be well-lubricated.

1. The clutch lever should be able to be moved 10–20 mm (0.4–0.8 in.) measured at the tip of the lever before the clutch begins to disengage. If clutch operation is not satisfactory after this adjustment is made, proceed as follows:

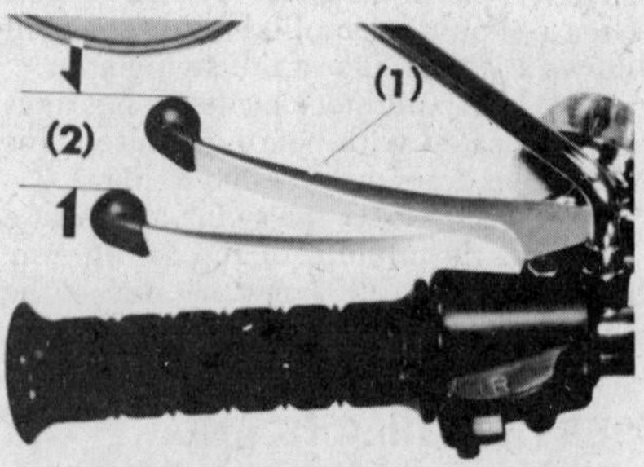

Clutch cable free-play is measured at the tip of the clutch lever

2. Loosen the locknut on the handlebar adjuster and screw the adjuster into the lever housing to give as much slack in the cable as possible.

Adjusting the clutch

3. Loosen the locknut on the cable adjuster located at the top of the left rear crankcase cover, and screw the adjuster into the crankcase cover.
4. Loosen the locknut on the pushrod adjuster located on the left rear crankcase cover. Screw the adjusting screw counterclockwise until a noticeable resistance is felt, then turn the adjusting screw clockwise ¼ turn. Tighten the locknut.
5. Back the cable adjuster on the crankcase out until there is approximately 10–20 mm (0.4–0.8 in.) of free-play measured at the tip of the lever. Tighten the locknut.
6. Minor adjustments can be made at the handlebar adjuster.
7. Use the handlebar adjuster to maintain the correct amount of free-play.

Throttle Cable

The throttle cable free-play should be adjusted *after* the idle speed. The standard throttle cable free-play is 10–15° of grip rotation for all models. The cable should be well lubricated before attempting to adjust free-play.

360 MODELS

1. Loosen the locknut on the cable adjuster located near the twist-grip and screw the adjuster in to give the maximum amount of free-play.
2. Loosen the locknut on the lower adjuster. Turn the adjuster until there is approximately 10–15° of play at the twist-grip, then tighten the locknut.
3. Fine adjustment is accomplished with the adjuster near the twist-grip. Be sure to tighten all locknuts when the adjustment is correct. Check cable operation and free-play when the handlebars are cut hard right or left. If it changes, either the cable is too tightly adjusted or is binding somewhere.

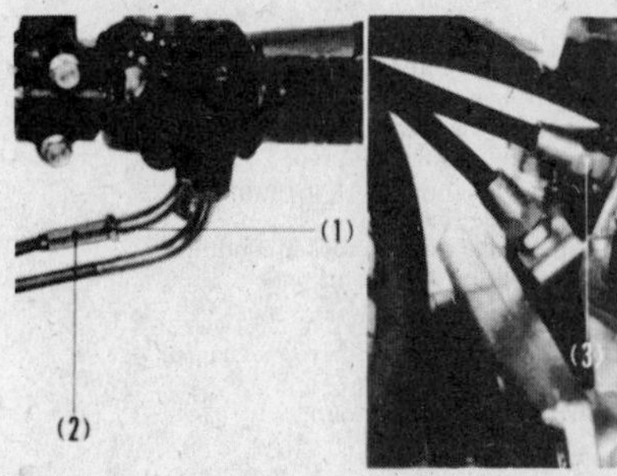

Throttle cable adjusters (2 and 3) and locknut (1) (360)

350 MODELS

1. Cable free-play is adjusted with the adjuster near the twist-grip. Loosen the locknut on the adjuster and screw the adjuster in or out until free-play is correct. Tighten the locknut.
2. Check that the cable operates smoothly and maintains some free-play when the handlebars are cut all the way to the right or left. If the idle speed changes when this is done, the cable is either too tightly adjusted, or it is binding somewhere along its routing.

Front Drum Brake

1. Use the cable adjuster on the brake plate to allow about 20–30 mm (0.8–1.2 in.) of handlebar lever free-play before the shoes contact the drum. This free-play is measured at the tip of the lever.
2. This free-play can be maintained as the shoes wear by using the adjuster at the handlebar lever.

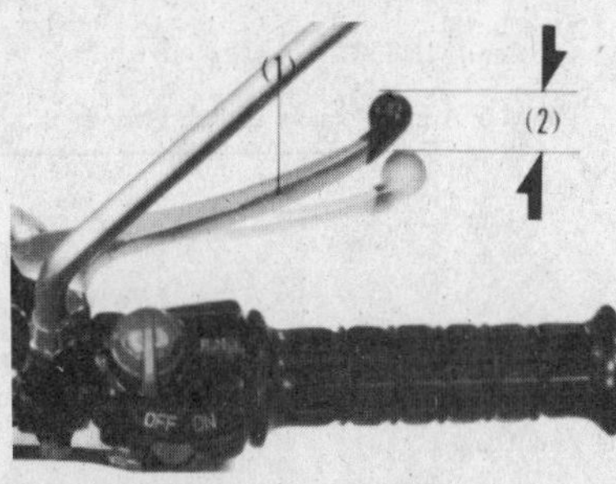

On front drum brakes, the brake lever should have about 1 in. of movement (measured at the end of the level) before the linings contact the drum

Disc Brake

Disc brakes need no attention other than a periodic check of the fluid level and pad wear.

Maintain brake fluid level at the level line

1. After removing the reservoir cap and rubber diaphragm, check to see if the fluid is up to the level mark on the inside of the master cylinder. If the level is below the level mark, add enough DOT 3 brake fluid to bring the level up to the mark. Reinstall the diaphragm and the cap, and tighten securely.
2. Check the brake pad wear, and replace the pads in a set if either one is worn past the red limit line.

Rear Brake

Use the adjusting nut on the end of the cable or rod so that the brake pedal has 1 in. of free-play before the shoes contact the drum. The pedal height can be adjusted with the stopper bolt.

Check pedal free-play with a rider on the machine.

Brake Light Switch

The switches should be checked for operation after the brakes are adjusted. The rear brake light switch is mounted in a slotted bracket and secured by locknuts. Moving the switch up on the bracket allows the brake light to turn on sooner. Moving it down allows the light to turn on later. Do not turn the switch to adjust it as the wires will become twisted and may break. Generally, the brake light should come on just as the linings contact the drum. The front brake light switch is not adjustable and must be replaced if defective.

Steering Stem Bearings

The steering stem bearings should be checked periodically and adjusted if necessary. Refer to the "Chassis" section.

FUEL SYSTEM

1. Fuel system maintenance involves cleaning the petcock and filter, cleaning or replacing the air cleaner, and cleaning the carburetors.
2. The carburetors should be removed, disassembled, and cleaned every 4,000 miles.

Removing the filter screen and O-ring

3. The petcock should be serviced every 3,000 miles. Shut the fuel off, then unscrew and remove the petcock sediment bowl. Take out the O-ring and fuel filter screen. Clean the parts in solvent and inspect the screen for any holes or other defects, replace it if it is damaged in any way. Inspect the O-ring for any cuts or cracks and replace it if necessary. Reinstall the filter screen, O-ring, and sediment bowl. Turn the fuel on and check for leaks.

AIR CLEANER SERVICE

The air cleaner should be serviced or replaced every 1,500 miles or more often depending on conditions.

All Except SL350K1-K2

REMOVAL

1. Open the seat. On CL models the

exhaust system must be removed. Remove the right and left sidecovers.

2. Loosen the air cleaner connecting band. Remove the bolt running through the center of the air cleaners, and the air cleaner element mounting bolt.

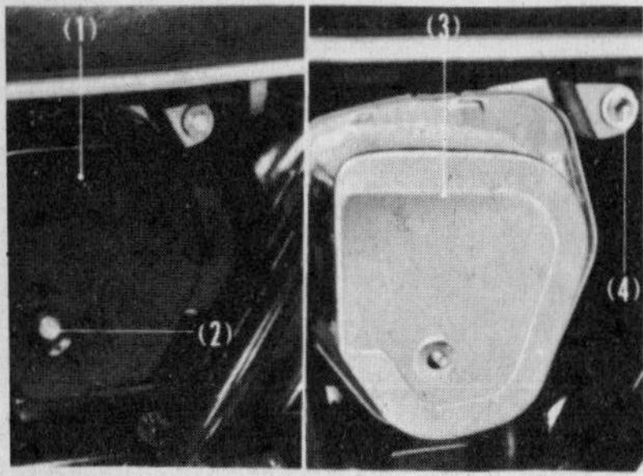

Air cleaner cover (1), cover mounting bolt (2), element (3), and element mounting bolt (4)

3. Remove the air cleaner cover and the air cleaner element.

CLEANING

1. Tap the air cleaner to remove any loose dirt. Blow compressed air through the element from the inside out.

2. Inspect the element and connecting tube for any holes; replace any air cleaner found defective. An oil-impregnated element or one which cannot be cleaned sufficiently should also be replaced.

3. Inspect the area where the element is bonded to the mounting plate. If the bonding is cracked or separated replace the element.

INSTALLATION

1. Installation is in the reverse order of removal.

2. After installing the air cleaners, start the engine and check for any air leaks.

SL 350K1-K2

REMOVAL

1. Remove the plastic sidecovers from both sides.

2. Remove the two mounting bolts, and loosen the connecting tube band. Remove the air cleaner.

3. Remove the bolt from the center of the back of the air cleaner and remove the element.

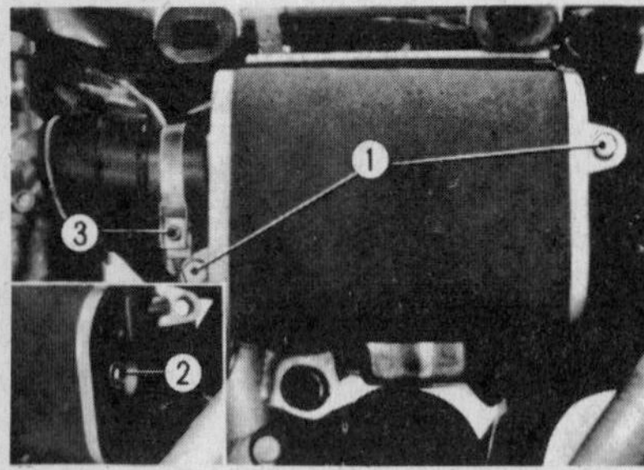

Foam-type element (SL models): air cleaner mounts (1), element mount (2), carburetor clamp screw (3)

CLEANING

1. Once the air cleaner element is removed, it should be cleaned in a clean solvent such as kerosene.

2. When the air cleaner element has dried thoroughly, soak it in gear oil SAE 90 until it is fully saturated then wring off the excess oil.

3. Inspect the element for any damage, such as holes or a damaged case. Replace any air cleaner found defective.

INSTALLATION

1. Installation is in the reverse order of removal.

2. Start the engine and check for any air leaks. Any air leaks should be corrected as they can cause a lean mixture resulting in possible engine damage.

Recommended Lubricants

Engine	General—All Temperatures	
	SAE 10W-30	
	SAE 10W-40	
	Alternate	
	SAE 30	Above 59° F
	SAE 20 or 20W	32°–59° F
	SAE 10W	Below 32° F
Forks	ATF	
	SAE 30W	
Control Cables	10W-30 motor oil	
	Graphite-base lubricant	
Tach, Speedo Cables	Light-duty, lithium-base grease	
Wheel Bearings	Waterproof, medium-weight bearing grease	
Steering Head Bearings	Waterproof, medium-weight bearing grease	
Swing Arm Pivot and Clutch Fitting	Waterproof, medium-weight chassis grease	

Maintenance Data

	CB350	*CL350*	*SL350*	*CB360*	*CL360*	*CJ360*
Fuel Tank (gal)	3.2	2.4	2.4	2.7	2.4	3.7
Crankcase						
After Disassembly (qt)	2.1	2.1	2.1	2.1	2.1	2.1
When Changing (qt)	1.6	1.6	1.6	1.6	1.6	1.6
Forks						
After Disassembly (cc/oz)	①	②	185/6.5	160/5.4	160/5.4	140/4.7
When Changing (cc/oz)			170/6.25	135/4.6	135/4.6	125/4.2
Tire pressure						
Front (psi)	26	26	22	26	26	25
Rear (psi) ③	29	29	22	28	28	28

① CB350 to K3—200/6.75
185/6.5
CB350K4 and later—160/5.4
135/4.6

② CL350 to K3—200/6.75
185/6.5
CL350K4 and later—160/5.4
135/4.6

③ 36 psi for two-up or extended high speed operation

Periodic Maintenance Intervals

Daily
- Chain slack
- Cable adjustments
- Brake adjustment

Weekly
- Battery fluid level
- Spoke condition
- Oil level
- Tire pressure

Every 1,000 miles
- Change engine oil
- Check disc brake fluid
- Adjust drive chain

Every 3,000 miles
- Clean, gap, or replace spark plugs
- Check and adjust clutch
- Clean or replace air filter
- Check ignition timing
- Clean, gap, or replace breaker points
- Clean fuel petcock
- Check carburetor operation
- Adjust cam chain tensioner
- Adjust valve clearance
- Lubricate swing arm pivot
- Lubricate cables and twist-grip
- Inspect fuel lines
- Inspect chain and sprocket condition
- Lubricate breaker point pads

Every 4,000 miles
- Grease speedometer drive mechanism
- Overhaul carburetors
- Inspect rims for run-out

Every 6,000 miles
- Clean oil filter
- Lubricate wheel bearings
- Lubricate steering head bearings
- Inspect brake shoes
- Change fork oil

Every 8,000 miles
- Flush and renew disc brake fluid

TUNE-UP

NOTE: *Common tune-up procedures are explained in detail in "General Information."*

CAM CHAIN ADJUSTMENT

NOTE: *Early 350 models were equipped with an automatically-adjusting, hydraulic-type cam chain tensioner. No adjustment is possible. These early units can be replaced with the improved adjustable units found on later models with no internal engine modification.*

350 Models

1. Remove the left exhaust valve cover and the alternator cover. Remove the spark plugs.

2. Turn the engine over counterclockwise using the rotor bolt until the left exhaust valve just begins to open, then turn the engine in the opposite direction (clockwise) to 90° after the top dead center (ATDC) for the left cylinder. Refer to the accompanying illustration.

3. Loosen the locknut on the tensioner setting bolt and back the setting bolt out a few turns, the tensioner will automatically adjust itself. Tighten the setting bolt and locknut.

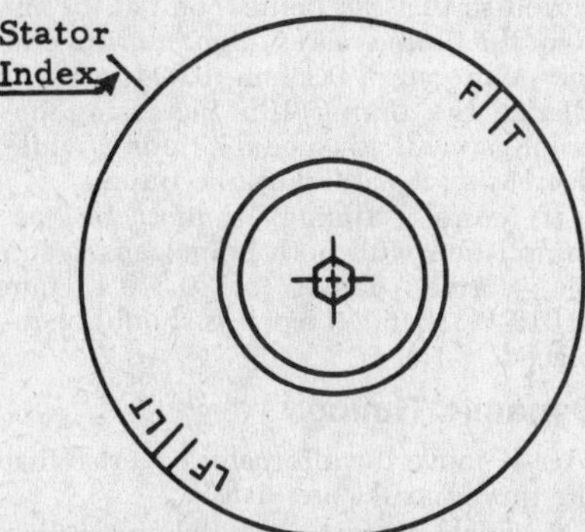

The engine is properly set up for cam chain adjustment when the left piston is 90° past TDC of its compression stroke, as indicated by the action of the valves and the position of the alternator rotor marks

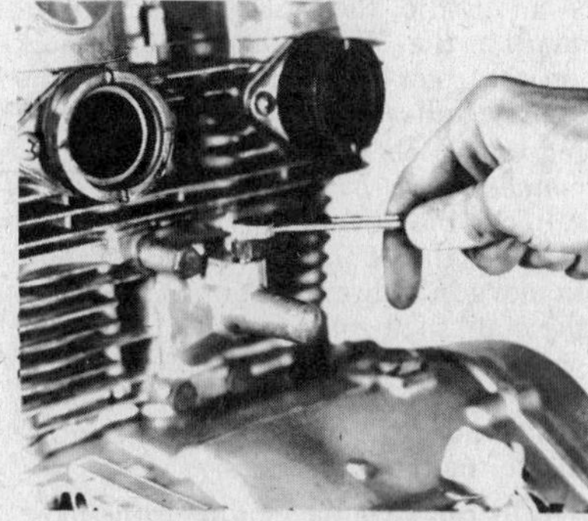

Adjusting the cam chain (350)

360 Models

1. Remove the stator cover and the left cylinder valve tappet covers. Remove the spark plugs. Using the rotor bolt, turn the crankshaft counterclockwise while watching the left cylinder intake tappet; when the tappet descends all the way and then starts to rise, line up the "LT" mark on the rotor with the index mark on the stator. In this position the left cylinder is at top dead center (TDC) of the compression stroke. Turn the crankshaft another 90° (counterclockwise). The valves should all be closed in this position. This is the only position that the cam chain tensioner may be adjusted in.

Cam chain setting bolt (1), locknut (2), and plunger cap (3) (360)

2. Loosen the setting bolt locknut and back the setting bolt out a few turns, the tension will automatically be adjusted. Tighten the setting bolt and the locknut.

3. If after performing the adjustment outlined above, the cam chain still is excessively noisy, perform the adjustment as described below.

NOTE: *When listening for cam chain noise the valves should be adjusted properly so that tappet noise will not be confused with cam chain noise.*

4. Start the engine and as soon as the engine will idle with the choke off, perform the adjustment by removing the plunger cap. Loosen the setting bolt locknut and back out the setting bolt a few turns. Push the tensioner plunger in with a screwdriver until the cam chain is silent and, while maintaining pressure with the screwdriver, tighten the setting bolt and locknut. Do not use more pressure on the plunger than is necessary, as this will overtighten the chain and cause rapid wear of the cam chain and the tensioner components. Install the plunger cap.

VALVE ADJUSTMENT

NOTE: *Valves must be adjusted when engine is cold.*

350 Models

1. Remove the alternator cover, intake and exhaust valve caps, and the point and tach drive housing covers.

2. Remove the spark plugs.

3. Turn the engine over slowly in the normal direction of rotation (the rotor will turn counterclockwise) while observing the left intake valve. When the valve goes down and begins to come up, continue turning the engine over until the "LT" mark on the rotor lines up with the timing index mark on the stator.

4. The left piston should now be at top dead center (TDC) of the compression stroke with both valves closed. Check for clearance at both valves for the left cylinder. Each should have a slight amount of free-play. If they do not, the piston is at TDC on the exhaust stroke. Turn the rotor 360° and check again.

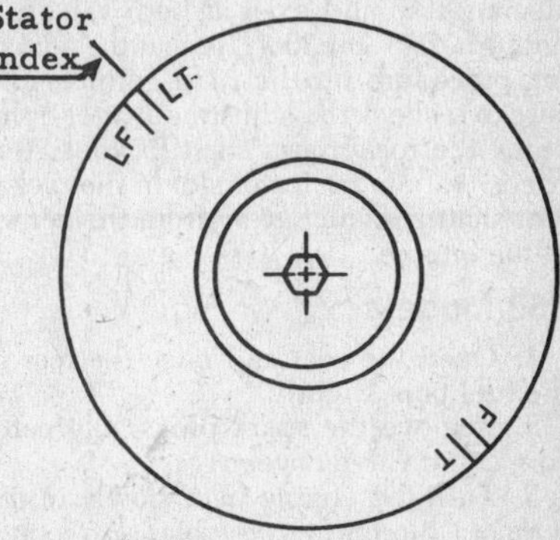

Alternator rotor marks indicating that the left cylinder is at top dead center

5. Valve clearance is 0.05 mm (0.002 in.) for the intake valves and 0.1 mm (0.004 in.) for the exhaust valves.

6. If adjustment is necessary, loosen the locknut on the rocker arm shaft (in the point and tach drive housings) and turn the rocker arm shaft until the adjustment is correct. Tighten the locknut and recheck the adjustment.

Adjusting the valves (350)

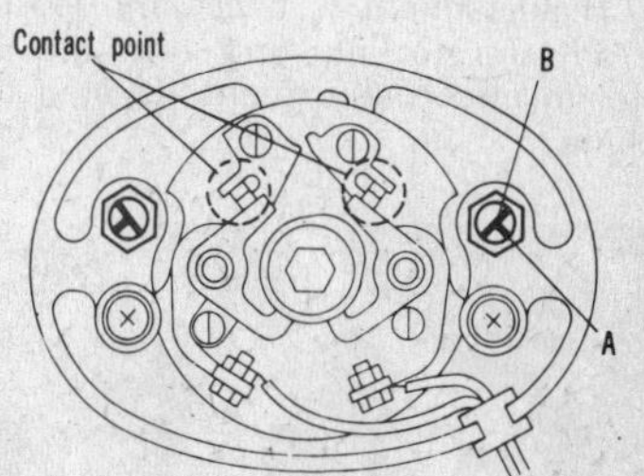

The index marks (A) on the rocker arm shafts (B) must be pointing away from the center of the cylinder head (350)

NOTE: *Each rocker arm shaft has an indicator slot. This slot must face the front of the engine on the exhaust valves and to the rear of the engine on the intake valves.*

7. After completing the adjustment of the left cylinder turn the rotor counterclockwise 180° and align the "T" mark on the rotor with the timing index mark on the stator. The right piston should be at TDC of the compression stroke and clearance should exist at both valves; if not turn the rotor 360°. Repeat the adjusting procedure for the right cylinder. Be sure to recheck the adjustment after tightening the rocker arm shaft locknut. Also check that the indicator slot in the rocker arm shaft is facing away from the center of the engine.

360 Models

1. Open the seat and raise the rear of the fuel tank slightly.
2. Remove the spark plugs, alternator cover, and valve covers.
3. Turn the engine over slowly in the normal direction of rotation (counterclockwise) while observing the left intake valve. When the valve goes down and then starts to rise, continue turning the engine over until the "LT" mark on the rotor lines up with the timing index mark on the stator.

Left cylinder at top dead center when the rotor (1) and stator index mark (2) are aligned (360)

4. The left piston should now be at top dead center (TDC) on the compression stroke with both valves closed. Each valve should have a slight amount of freeplay. If they do not, the piston is at TDC on the exhaust stroke. Turn the rotor 360° and check again.
5. The correct valve clearance is 0.05 mm (0.002 in.) for the intake valves and 0.08 mm (0.003 in.) for the exhaust valves.
6. If adjustment is necessary, loosen the adjuster locknut and turn the adjuster to effect adjustment. Tighten the locknut.

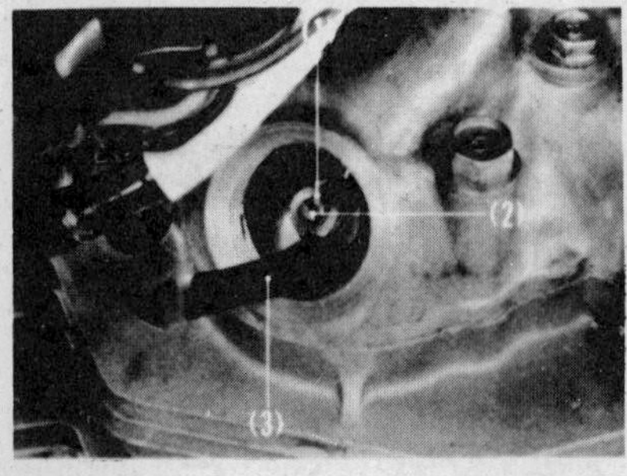

Adjusting the valves: adjuster locknut (1), adjusting screw (2), and feeler gauge (3) (360)

NOTE: *The adjustment may change when the locknut is tightened. Hold the adjuster steady while securing the locknut. Reckeck the clearance afterwards.*

7. Turn the rotor 180° counterclockwise and line up the "T" mark on the rotor with the timing index mark on the stator. In this position both valves for the right cylinder should be closed. Adjust the valve clearance as described for the left cylinder above.

CONTACT BREAKER POINTS

Location

1. The points are located in a case on the left-side of the cylinder head, and are operated off the camshaft. The timing advance mechanism is fitted behind the breaker point base plate.

Replacement

1. If replacement of the points is necessary, this is easily accomplished by disconnecting the primary wire from the points, removing the two point securing screws, and taking off the points. Install the new points after thoroughly cleaning off the contact surfaces with a non-oily solvent, and adjust the gap. If a breaker plate assembly is purchased simply disconnect the yellow and blue point wires from the wiring harness and remove the two breaker plate screws. Install the new breaker plate and connect the primary wires. Clean the surfaces of the points and adjust the gap. Whenever the points are replaced, the ignition timing will have to be set.

Breaker plate screws (1), point securing screws (3 and 4), pry point (2) (360)

2. Apply a bit of grease to the breaker cam lubricating wick. Take care not to apply too much to avoid fouling the points.

Gapping

Points should be filed (if necessary) and cleaned before gapping.

1. Remove the alternator cover, and points cover.
2. Using the rotor bolt, turn the engine over until one set of points is open to their maximum gap.
3. With the proper feeler gauge, check the gap. The proper specification for all models is 0.3–0.4 mm (0.012–0.016 in.). The feeler gauge should be a slip fit between the points if they are correctly gapped.
4. If adjustment is necessary, loosen the two screws which secure the points to the base plate, and use a thin screwdriver at the pry slot provided to bring the gap to the proper specification.

NOTE: *Loosen the screws just enough to allow the points to be moved. If too loose, the points will snap shut instead of holding the adjustment.*

5. Tighten the screws and recheck the gap. It may change slightly when the screws are tightened.
6. Repeat the procedure for the other set of points.
7. If it is not possible to gap the points correctly, the fiber heel is evidently worn; the set of points should be replaced.

IGNITION TIMING

The method of adjusting the timing is the same regardless of the type of equipment used. The *left* cylinder is set *first* and timing is adjusted by moving the base plate. The points on the left-side of the base plate are those for the left cylinder. After the left cylinder is correctly timed, the right cylinder can be checked, and adjusted if necessary. To adjust the right cylinder timing, the point gap is varied so that the points open at the instant the timing marks align. A change in the point gap of 0.1 mm (0.004 in.) will change the timing 10°. Increasing the point gap will advance the timing, while decreasing it will retard the timing.

If correct timing cannot be accomplished with both point gaps set in the correct range of 0.3–0.4 mm (0.012–0.016 in.), the points should be replaced.

Dynamic Timing

1. Remove the alternator cover so that the timing marks are visible.
2. Hook up the timing light according to the manufacturer's instructions. Most lights use the vehicle's own battery as a power source.
3. Start the engine, aiming the light on the rotor. Note the following:
   a. At idle, the "LF" (left cylinder) mark or the "F" (right cylinder) mark on the rotor should line up with the timing indicator on the stator, depending on which plug the strobe light is connected to;
   b. As the revolutions increase, the "LF" or the "F" mark should be seen to move in a direction opposite that of the crankshaft rotation;
   c. Finally, at full advance (about 3,200 rpm and above), the twin rotor marks must line up with the timing indicator mark on the stator.
4. The full advance reading is the most important. If the rotor marks and the stator indicator do not align, proceed as follows:
5. Time the *left* cylinder *first*. Remove the points cover. Loosen the two screws which secure the breaker base plate just

Rotor timing marks: (1) firing point; (2) stator index; (3) full advance firing point

enough to allow the plate to be turned. Using a thin screwdriver applied at the pry point provided, rotate the plate in the direction necessary so that the timing marks align.

Rotating the plate clockwise advances the timing; rotating the plate counterclockwise retards the timing.

Tighten the base plate screws and recheck the timing.

6. Connect the timing light to the right cylinder and check the timing as for the left cylinder this time using the "F" mark on the rotor.

If the right cylinder timing is incorrect, loosen the two screws which secure the right-side points to the base plate. Open or close the point gap so that the timing marks align as the points open.

7. After the ignition timing is set, recheck the point gaps. Both must still be within the proper specification (0.3–0.4 mm/0.012–0.016 in.).

If either gap is not within this value, increase or decrease it as necessary so that it is. Increase or decrease the other point gap by the same amount. Both must be within the given range.

After making any adjustment to the point gap, the timing will have to be readjusted.

If the gaps have been changed by equal amounts, it will only be necessary to adjust the timing by moving the base plate.

If proper ignition timing is not possible, replace both sets of points, since the fiber heels are probably worn.

Static Timing

1. Remove the alternator cover, points cover, and the left intake valve cover.

2. Remove the spark plugs and hook up the tester.

3. Turn the engine over so that the left cylinder is on the compression stroke (the left intake valve will go down and come up). Turn the engine over slowly in the normal direction of rotation (counterclockwise). At the instant in which the "LF" mark on the rotor aligns with the index mark on the stator, the points should begin to open as indicated by the reaction of the test light or the meter.

4. If the points open before the marks align, the timing is too advanced. If they open after the "LF" mark passes the index, the timing is too retarded.

5. If the timing is not correct, set the "LF" mark so that it is aligned with the index mark on the compression stroke. Loosen the two screws which secure the breaker base plate and rotate the plate until the light or meter indicates that the points have just opened. Tighten the base plate screws and recheck the timing.

6. After completing the timing for the left cylinder, connect the light or meter to the points for the right cylinder. Turn the rotor 180° counterclockwise until the "F" mark aligns with the index mark; at this point the right set of points should just open. If the timing is incorrect, align the "F" mark with the index mark and increase or decrease the point gap so that the points just open as indicated by the light or meter. Refer to steps 6 and 7 under "Dynamic Timing," above. Tighten the set screws and recheck the timing and the point gap for both cylinders. Note that both gaps must still be within specifications.

CARBURETOR

Adjusting Float Level

1. Remove the carburetor from the motorcycle.

2. Remove the float bowl. Remove the float bowl gasket.

3. Float level is defined as the measured distance from the float bowl mating surface on the carburetor body (gasket removed) to the top of the floats, when the tang of the float arm is just touching the end of the float needle. A special gauge is available to check the float level although a vernier caliper can also be used.

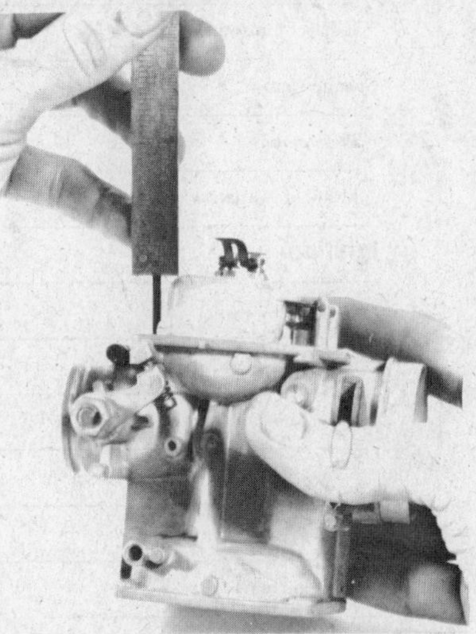

Checking float level

4. With the carburetor held at about a 45° angle, gradually lower the floats until the tang of the float arm just touches the end of the float needle. The tang should not depress the needle, but just contact it. Measure the distance from the carburetor body to the top of the floats. Compare the reading with the proper float level for your machine as given in the "Carburetor Specifications" chart.

5. If the adjustment is necessary, bend only the float arm tang to raise or lower the float level.

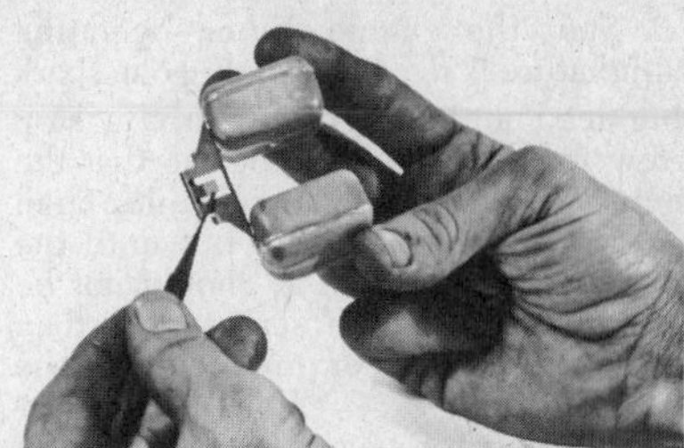

Bend the float tang to adjust float level

6. Float level will not be correct if the needle is worn, or if there is foreign matter on the needle seat.

Idle Speed and Mixture

NOTE: *These items must be adjusted when the engine is at operating temperature.*

350 MODELS

1. Ensure that the throttle cable adjustment is approximately correct so that the cable has enough slack to allow the throttle plates or slides (SL 350) to be fully closed.

2. Screw the pilot screw in carefully until it bottoms lightly, then turn it out the number of turns shown in the "Tune-Up Specifications" chart.

Setting the pilot screw

Adjusting the throttle stop screw (350)

3. Start the engine. When operating temperature is reached, unplug one spark plug lead and adjust the throttle stop screw for the other cylinder so that the engine idles as slowly as possible. Then turn the pilot screw in or out until the engine runs smoothly. It should not be necessary to vary the screw more than one half turn in either direction from the given setting.

4. Connect the spark plug lead and run the engine a few moments to allow the engine to clear out. Repeat Step 3 (above) for the other cylinder.

5. Connect both plug leads again and turn each throttle stop screw out by equal amounts until the proper idle is reached.

6. Check that the two carburetors are synchronized by opening and closing the throttle while watching the throttle stop screws. Both screws must begin to move at the same time when the throttle is opened. If one begins to move before the other, use the cable adjusters on the carburetors so that the movement of the stop screws is synchronized.

7. Snap the throttle open and closed several times to make sure that synchronization is maintained.

8. Adjust the throttle cable free-play using the adjuster near the twist-grip so that the throttle has 10–15° of free rotation before the stop screws begin to move.

360 MODELS

1. Turn each pilot screw in carefully until it bottoms lightly, then turn each out 1 turn. Using the throttle stop screw, set the idle at 1,200 rpm. Turning the screw in will increase the idle speed.

2. Turn the pilot screw for one cylinder in or out until the highest idle speed is reached. Perform this operation for the remaining cylinder. Reset the idle speed with the throttle stop screw if necessary.

Throttle stop screw (1) (360)

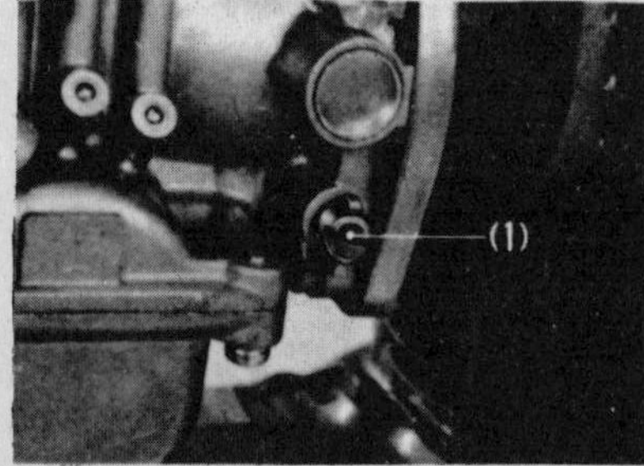

Pilot screw (1) (360)

Vacuum gauge plug (1) (360)

3. If after performing the above operations the correct idle speed cannot be obtained or the exhaust pipe backpressure differs between the two cylinders, synchronize the carburetors as described below.

4. Remove the fuel tank and connect it to the carburetors with longer fuel lines. The fuel tank must be higher than the level of the carburetors. Remove the plugs from the carburetors and install vacuum gauges in their place.

5. Start the engine and note the reading on the gauges. The difference in vacuum between the two cylinders should be less than 2 cm Hg, and both should be within the range of 16–24 cm Hg.

6. If the difference in vacuum between the two carburetors is greater than 2 cm Hg, loosen the locknut on the adjusting screw and turn the adjusting screw in or out until both carburetors are within 2 cm Hg of each other. When the adjustment is complete tighten the locknut and rev the engine up a few times. Recheck the gauges and readjust if necessary.

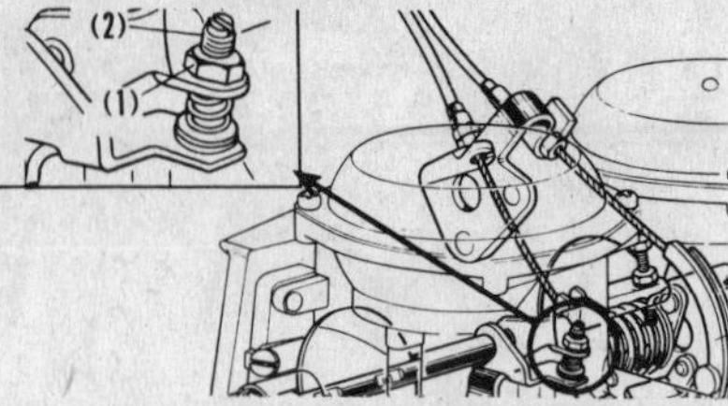

Adjusting screw (2) and locknut (1)

7. If the carburetors cannot be adjusted so that they are within 2 cm Hg of each other or if either carburetor is out of the range of 16–24 cm Hg, check the following:

a. Air leaks around intake manifold or air cleaner;
b. Ignition timing;
c. Tappet clearance;
d. Compression pressure;
e. Spark plug gap and condition;
f. Punctured carburetor diaphragm.

8. Repeat Steps 1 and 2 to adjust the pilot screw and idle speed.

Tune-Up Specifications

	350	360
Engine		
Valve Clearance (cold)		
Intake (in./mm)	0.002/0.05	0.002/0.05
Exhaust (in./mm)	0.004/0.10	0.003/0.08
Compression		
Pressure (psi)	170	170
Maximum variation (psi)	15	15
Ignition		
Spark plugs		
Standard makes *	NCK/ND	NGK/ND
Type: standard	B8ES/W24ES	B8ES/W24ES
cold	B9ES/W27E	B9ES/W27E
hot	B7ES/W22ES	B7ES/W22ES
Gap (in./mm)	0.028–0.032/0.7–0.8	0.028–0.032/0.7–0.8
Point gap (in./mm)	0.012–0.016/0.3–0.4	0.012–0.016/0.3–0.4
Maximum advance (deg @ rpm) **	27°–33° @ 3000	NA
Carburetion		
Idle speed (rpm)	1100	1200
Pilot screw opening	¾–1	1
Vacuum range, (in./cm Hg)	—	6.2–9.5/16–24
Uniformity (in./cm Hg)	—	0.78/2.0

* Other reputable makes are also acceptable. Be sure to select plugs of the proper heat range, reach, and diameter.
** Includes initial (static) advance

— Not applicable
NA Not available

ENGINE AND TRANSMISSION

NOTE: *Common service and inspection procedures for engine components such as pistons, valve assemblies, etc., are given in the "Engine Rebuilding" section under General Information. Specifications for Honda 350/360 engines are given in the charts at the end of this section.*

ENGINE REMOVAL AND INSTALLATION

350

1. Remove the oil filler cap and drain the oil. When the oil is completely drained refit the filler cap and drain plug.
2. Remove the exhaust system.
3. Open the seat and remove the battery. When disconnecting the battery always disconnect the negative terminal first; this will prevent shorting the battery to the frame when disconnecting the positive terminal.
4. Disconnect the starter motor cable (if fitted) from the solenoid.
5. Turn the fuel petcock to the off position and disconnect the fuel lines. Use two small C-clamps to pinch off the fuel balance tube and a spare piece of fuel line. Disconnect the balance tube from one side of the fuel tank, and plug the open side of the tank with the spare piece of pinched fuel line. Remove the tank from its rear mount by pulling back on the rubber strap while lifting up the rear of the tank. Pull the tank up and back to remove it from the front mounts.
6. Disconnect the alternator leads from the wiring harness at the connector. Disconnect the yellow and blue breaker point leads from their connectors.
7. Remove the rear horn mounting bolt and loosen the front bolt, tilt the horn out of the way, as shown.
8. Disconnect the tachometer cable from the engine after removing the phillips head set screw.
9. Remove the stepbar (except SL models) and gearshifter. Remove the four screws from the countershaft sprocket cover and remove the cover with the clutch cable still attached. Take care not to lose the steel ball from the clutch release mechanism when removing the cover.
10. Remove the masterlink from the drive chain. Install the masterlink on one end of the chain for safekeeping.
11. Disconnect the brake rod from the brake pedal, remove the brake pedal pivot bolt, and the brake pedal.
12. Loosen the connecting bands holding the carburetors to the intake manifold and the air cleaners. Disconnect the choke band from the right carburetor. Remove the carburetors and disconnect the throttle cables. On SL models with direct control type carburetors, place the throttle slides in a plastic bag secured with a rubber band around the cable.

Top engine mount (350)

Spacer location (350)

13. Disconnect the spark plug leads. Loosen the spark plugs.
14. Remove the three bolts from the top engine mount and remove the two mounting plates.
15. Remove the nuts from the lower engine mounting bolts. Remove the starter motor cable from the rear mounting bolts and remove all of the mounting bolts. Note that the battery negative cable will be completely disconnected when the nut is removed from the upper rear mount. It should be removed and placed in a safe place.
16. Remove the engine, lifting it out of the right-side of the frame.
17. Installation is the reverse of the removal procedures; however, note the following points:
    a. The starter motor cable is held in place by two clamps fastened to the rear engine mounting bolts;
    b. The battery negative cable is fastened to the upper rear mounting bolt on the right-side. Be sure to clean all dirt and paint from the frame so that the cable may make a good ground;
    c. A spacer is fitted between the frame and the engine on the left front mount (CB, CL models);
    d. When connecting the drive chain be sure that the opening in the masterlink spring clip is facing the opposite direction of chain rotation;
    e. Install the mounting bolts from the right-side of the frame and the nuts from the left;
    f. Check that the steel ball is still in place in the clutch release mechanism when installing the countershaft sprocket cover;
    g. Adjust the throttle cables, rear brake, valve clearance, and ignition timing. Be sure that the drain plug is tightened and fill the sump with oil.

360

1. Remove the oil filler cap and drain the engine oil. When the oil has completely drained, refit the filler cap and the drain plug hand-tight.
2. Open the seat and remove the battery. When disconnecting the battery always disconnect the negative terminal first, this will prevent shorting the battery to the frame when disconnecting the positive terminal.
3. Disconnect the starter motor cable from the solenoid.
4. Turn the fuel petcock to the off

Battery negative cable (arrow) and lower engine mounting bolts

position and disconnect the fuel lines from the petcock and remove the fuel tank.

5. Disconnect the yellow and blue breaker point leads from their connectors under the fuel tank.

6. Disconnect the tachometer cable from the engine after first removing the phillips head set screw.

7. Remove the exhaust system.

8. Remove the gearshifter pinch-bolt and pull the gearshifter from the shifter shaft. Remove the four screws from the countershaft sprocket cover and remove the cover with the clutch cable attached. Take care not to lose the steel ball from inside the clutch release mechanism when the cover is removed.

9. Remove the two bolts from the countershaft sprocket. Turn the countershaft sprocket lockplate until the tabs on the inside of the lockplate line up with the slots on the countershaft, and remove the lockplate. Remove the countershaft sprocket and the chain from the countershaft.

10. Loosen the connecting bands holding the carburetors to the intake manifold and the air cleaner. Pull the carburetors straight back until they are free of the intake manifold and remove them from the left-side. Disconnect the throttle cables from the carburetors.

11. Disconnect the alternator wiring from the wiring harness at the connector between the air cleaners. Remove the spark plug leads from the spark plugs.

12. Disconnect the brake rod from the rear brake pedal. On CL models, remove the pinch-bolt from the pedal and pull the pedal off the shaft. On CB models, remove the bolt from the end of the pivot shaft and remove the shaft and the pedal.

13. Remove the three bolts from the upper engine mount and remove the two mounting plates.

14. Remove the two bolts from the mounting plate at the upper right mount and the through-bolt. Remove the mounting plate.

15. Remove the four front mounting bolts, three from the right-side and one from the left-side.

16. Remove the nuts from the lower rear mounting bolt and remove the bolt and the foot pegs.

17. Remove the engine from the right-side.

18. Installation is the reverse of the removal procedures. Note the following points:

a. Install the engine in the frame from the right-side;

b. Install the mounting bolts and plates as shown;

c. The battery negative terminal is fastened to the upper rear engine mounting through-bolt. Scrape any rust or paint from the mounting plate before attaching the cable; this will ensure a good ground;

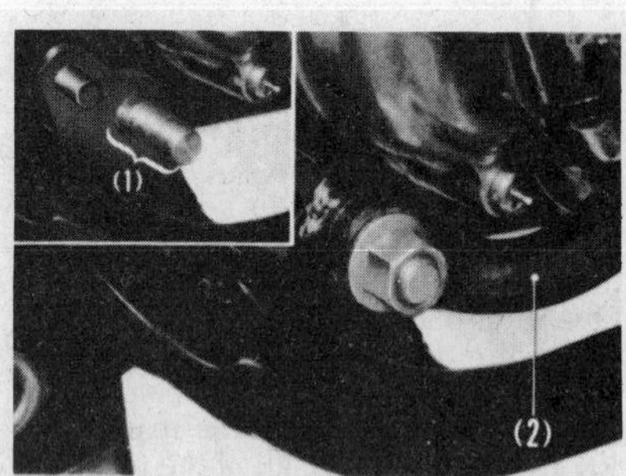

The lower mounting bolt (1) should be threaded equally into each nut; footpeg (2)

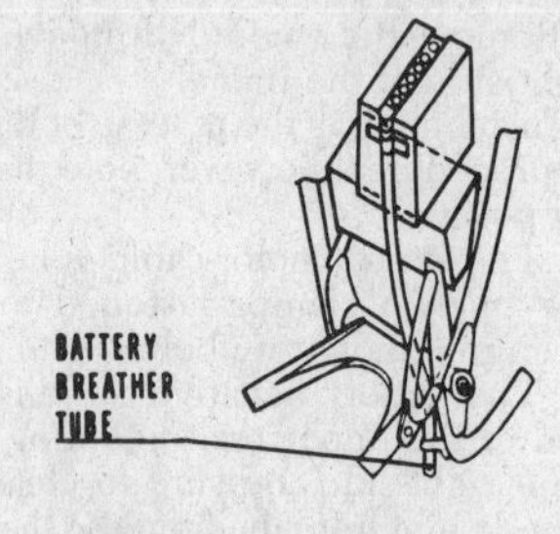

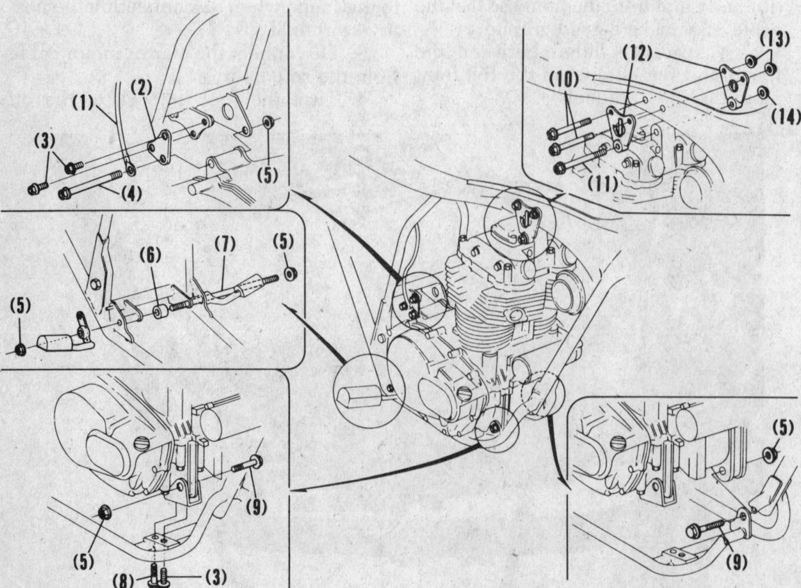

Engine mounting bolt and plate locations (360)

d. The lower rear mounting bolt should be threaded equally into each nut;

e. Connect the starter motor cable, and route the battery overflow tube as shown;

f. Before installing the countershaft sprocket cover, make sure that the steel ball is in place in the clutch release mechanism;

g. When connecting the fuel lines to the petcock, the right carburetor is connected to the rear outlet on the petcock and the left carburetor is connected to the forward outlet;

TOP END OVERHAUL

Disassembly

350

1. Remove the engine from the frame as described previously.

2. Remove the chrome covers from the point and tach drive housings. Remove the three phillips head securing screws from the alternator stator cover and remove the cover. Remove the spark plugs.

3. Remove the breaker plate after removing the two phillips head securing screws and disconnecting the yellow and blue leads from the wiring harness. The plate can be marked in relation to the point housing before removal for approximate setting of the ignition timing upon reassembly.

4. Remove the breaker cam bolt and washer from the left-side of the cam. Remove the spark advance unit from the left end of the camshaft; do this by looping a piece of string behind the unit and pulling it off the camshaft.

Rocker arm shaft locknuts and tach drive housing mounting screws

CAUTION: *Note that if the* point cam *is removed from the advance unit it must be installed correctly with the weights fully open; it is possible to install the point cam 180° off, making proper ignition timing impossible.*

5. Loosen the eight cylinder head cap nuts 1/4 turn at a time in an "X" pattern until they are all loose, then remove them and the washers beneath them. Remove the top cover, cover gasket, breather plate, and breather plate gasket from the cylinder studs.

6. Remove the four cam chain tensioner mounting bolts and remove the cam chain tensioner and gasket.

7. Using the rotor bolt, turn the engine over until all of the valves are closed. Remove the four locknuts and washers from the eccentric rocker arm shafts (note that these are special washers). Remove the four phillips head screws from the point and tach drive housings, and remove the housings, tapping around the sides with a plastic mallet if necessary to free them. Remove and discard the gasket.

Mark the location of each rocker arm and shaft

8. Remove the rocker arm shafts and the rocker arms marking their position so that they can be installed in their original position upon reassembly.

9. Temporarily install the point and tach drive housings, but do not install the mounting screws. Using the rotor bolt, turn the engine over until the "LT" mark on the rotor is approximately 10° after TDC of the exhaust stroke (the exhaust lobe of the left cylinder should be facing the front of the engine) and remove the cam sprocket alignment bolt. Turn the crankshaft 360° so that the remaining cam sprocket bolt (shouldered sprocket setting bolt) can be removed.

10. Remove the point and tach drive housings. Slip the cam out from the right-side of the cam case with the "L" mark on the cam sprocket and the alignment pin for the spark advance unit facing up. Slip a screwdriver through the sprocket to prevent it from falling through the head.

Removing the camshaft

11. Remove the four phillips head screws from the cam case and remove the cam case and gasket.

12. Remove the two head set bolts located near the spark plug holes and lift the head and head gasket off. Note the location of any dowel pins.

13. To remove the cylinders, hold the cam chain up and position the pistons so that they are at the same level. Lift off the cylinders, tapping around the base of the cylinder with a plastic mallet if necessary. Do not allow the pistons to fall against the crankcase.

CAUTION: *The cam chain tensioner roller located between the cylinders is held in place with two rubber pads. Once the cylinders are removed these are easily dropped into the crankcase.*

14. Carefully remove the cylinder base gasket and lift out the rubber pads from the cam chain tensioner roller with needlenose pliers. Slip out the roller pin and remove the tensioner roller assembly.

Removing the tensioner roller assembly

15. Stuff a clean lint-free cloth into the crankcase under the pistons. Remove the circlip from the outside of each piston and push the wrist pin out from the inside. Remove the pistons and mark their location on the inside of the skirt.

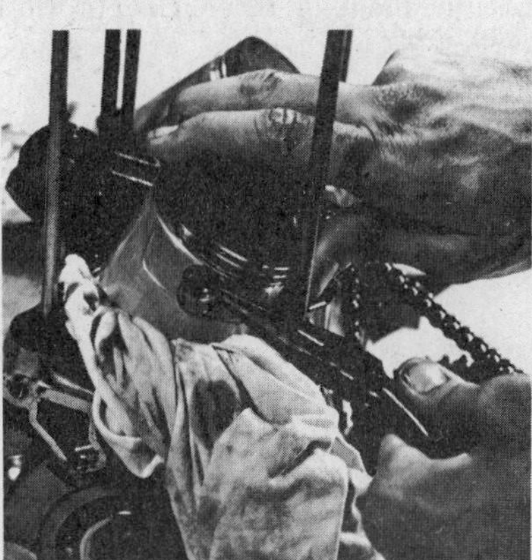

Removing a wrist pin circlip

360

The top end can be disassembled for inspection and service with the engine in the frame.

1. Open the seat and remove the fuel tank.

2. Remove the upper engine mounting plates after removing the three mounting bolts.

3. Remove the two phillips head screws from the point cover and remove the cover. Remove the breaker plate after removing the two securing screws and disconnecting the yellow and blue leads from the wiring harness.

4. Remove the spark advance unit from the end of the camshaft. This can be done by looping a piece of string around behind the advance unit and pulling the string. Note that the point cam is a part of the advancer unit, if the point cam is removed from the unit be sure that it is installed correctly. The point cam can be installed 180° off, making correct ignition timing impossible.

5. Remove the breather cover after removing the four mounting bolts.

6. Remove the spark plugs.

7. Disconnect the tachometer cable from the cylinder head cover after removing the phillips head set screw. Remove the tappet caps from the cylinder head cover.

8. Remove the three phillips head screws from the alternator stator cover and remove the cover. While watching the intake tappet for the left cylinder, turn the engine over with the rotor bolt until the intake tappet goes all of the way down and then rises. Continue turning the crankshaft until the "LT" mark on the rotor is 90° past the index mark on the stator. In this position the left cylinder should be 90° after top dead center (ATDC) of the compression stroke, and all of the valves should be closed.

9. Loosen the 14 cylinder head cover mounting bolts (6-6 mm, 8-8 mm) gradually and evenly in an "X" pattern until they are all loose (two are inside the breather cover), and then remove them. Remove the cylinder head cover working it out the left-side. Be sure not to lose the two dowel pins located between the cylinder head and the cylinder head cover. To inspect the rocker arms and the rocker arm shafts they will have to be removed from the cylinder head cover. To remove the rocker arm shafts from the right-side, unscrew the cap bolt from the cover and screw a 6 mm screw into the end of the shaft. Using the screw, pull the shaft out

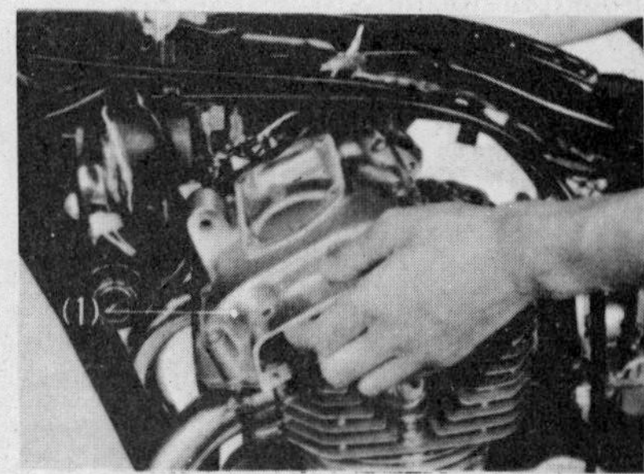

Removing the cylinder head cover (360)

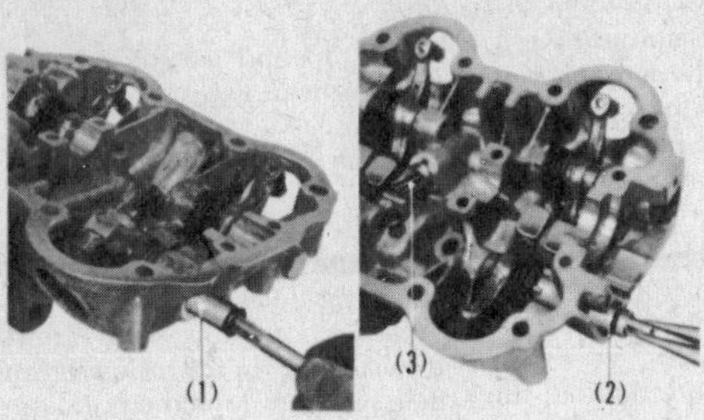

Removing the rocker arm shafts (360)

Removing the tensioner holder (3) and tensioner slipper (4)

of the cover, the rocker arm and side spring can now be removed. To remove the rocker arm shafts from the left-side, pry out the rubber plug from the cover and pull the shafts out with a pair of needlenose pliers, remove the rocker arm and side spring.

10. Remove the cam chain tensioner holder from the top of the cylinder head. Remove the tensioner slipper.

11. Using the rotor bolt, turn the engine over until one of the cam sprocket bolts is at the top of the sprocket, remove the bolt. Turn the crankshaft one complete turn (360°) and remove the remaining bolt.

12. Slip the cam chain off the sprocket and remove the cam and sprocket together. Take care not to let the thrust washers on the right-side of the cam fall into the engine. Slip a screwdriver through the chain to prevent if from falling through the head.

13. Remove the exhaust system and carburetors.

14. Remove the two 6 mm bolts located near either spark plug hole, then loosen the eight cylinder head nuts gradually and evenly in an "X" pattern until they are all loose, then remove them. Lift the head up and off the cylinder studs, tapping it around the bottom with a rubber mallet to break it loose if necessary. Remove the head gasket and the four dowel pins. If the cylinders are to remain in place, slip a screwdriver through the cam chain to prevent it from falling through the cylinders.

15. Hold the cam chain up and position the pistons so that they are the same level in the cylinders. Lift the cylinders up and off the studs. Catch the pistons as the cylinders are removed so that they do not become damaged from hitting the crankcase. Remove the cylinder base gasket and the two dowel pins and stuff a clean lint-free cloth into the crankcase around the pistons.

16. Remove the wrist pin circlip from the outside of each piston, and push the wrist pin out from the inside.

Inspection

1. 350 models: The minimum outside diameter of the rocker arm shaft is 12.90 mm (0.508 in.).

2. 360 models: The rocker arm shaft-to-rocker arm clearance should not exceed 0.1 mm (0.0039 in.).

3. Before installing the rings on the piston, first note that the two compression rings are not interchangeable. The

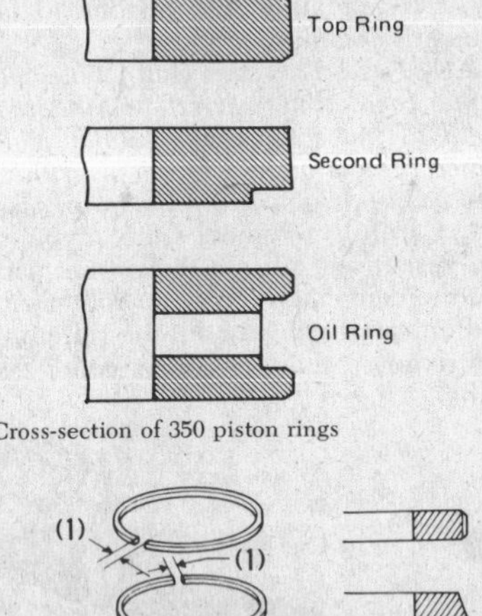

Cross-section of 350 piston rings

When installing the rings, space the end-gaps 120° apart (1); ring cross-sections show proper installation of 360 cc rings

lower compression ring is wedge-shaped (360) or stepped (350).

Also note that rings must be installed with the manufacturer's mark (the small letter near the end-gap) facing up when the rings are in place.

Assembly

350

1. Install a new wrist pin circlip into the left-side of the right piston and into the right-side of the left piston. The arrow stamped on the piston crown must face the front of the engine (exhaust side).

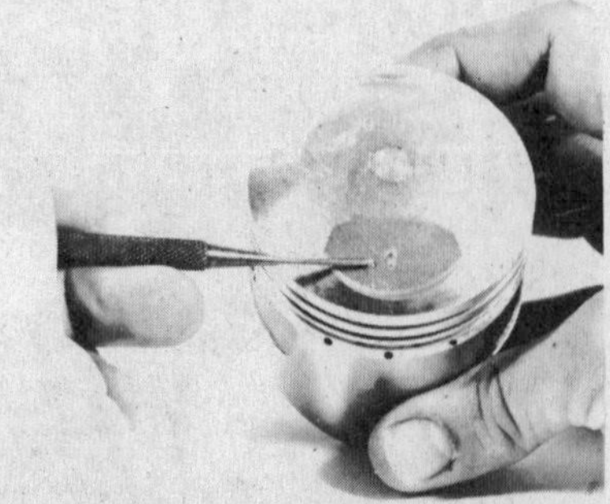
The arrow on the piston crown must point toward the exhaust port (350 shown)

2. Position the piston on the connecting rod so that the wrist pin holes line up with the connecting rod small end, and install the wrist pin after coating it with oil. Place a cloth under each piston to cover the hole in the crankcase, and install the remaining circlip.

3. Install the lower cam chain roller into the cam chain, and then slip the tensioner over the cam chain and roller, then insert the roller pin through the center of the roller. Fit the tensioner assembly in place between the cylinders with the cutouts in the roller pin facing up. Apply a drop of gasket cement to the bottom of each of the rubber inserts and place an insert in each side of the roller pin.

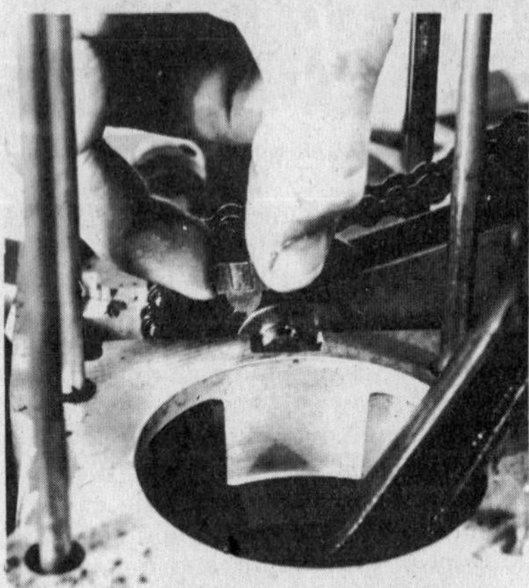
Installing the rubber roller pin inserts

4. Carefully install the cylinder base gasket, when routing the cam chain through the center of the gasket do not lift the tensioner out of place as the rubber inserts may fall into the crankcase.

5. Position the pistons at the same level. Coat the piston skirt and rings with clean motor oil, also oil the cylinder walls. Slide the cylinders down over the cylinder studs and onto the pistons while an assistant compresses the rings as they enter the bore. Make sure that the ring end-gaps are still spaced 120° apart and the two dowel pins are located to the outside front studs.

6. Using a piece of hooked wire, pull the cam chain up from between the cylinders. Install the cam chain sprocket into the cam chain so the "L" mark on the sprocket is on the left-side.

7. Make sure that the arrow on each piston is facing the front of the engine and the two dowel pins are located to the

outside front studs. Install the head gasket placing a thin coat of oil on both sides of the gasket to ensure a good seal. Place the cylinder head into position and install the two 6 mm bolts, but do not tighten them to the proper torque until after the head is torqued properly.

8. Place the cam case gasket into position. Install the dowel pins on the outside rear studs and install the cam case. Tighten the four 6 mm mounting screws to 4.3–5.3 ft lbs in an "X" pattern a little at a time. Recheck the torque after the head is installed and torqued.

Installing the cam case while pulling the chain through

9. While holding the cam chain up, turn the engine over with the rotor bolt until the "LT" mark is aligned with the index mark on the stator. With the engine in this position, position the cam chain sprocket so that the "L" mark is at the top. The flat surface on the sprocket rubber damper should be parallel to the cam case mating surface.

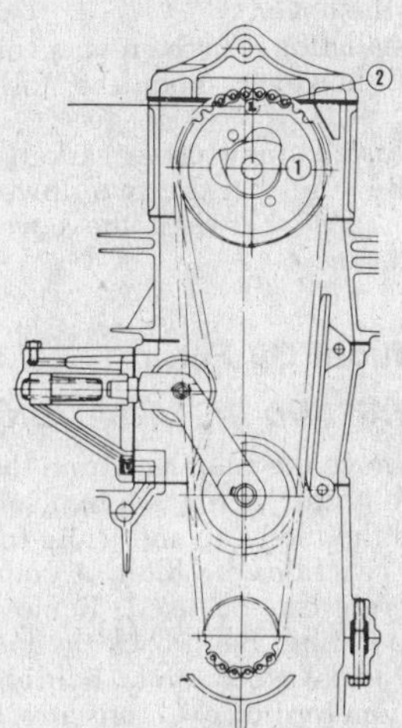

Correct valve timing: the "LT" mark on the alternator rotor is aligned with the stator index mark and the flat surface of the sprocket (1) rubber should be parallel with the upper surface of the cam case (2)

10. Slip the cam into the cam case and through the sprocket. When installing the cam, the spark advance aligning pin should be on the top of the cam. When

Install the camshaft through the right-side of the cam case

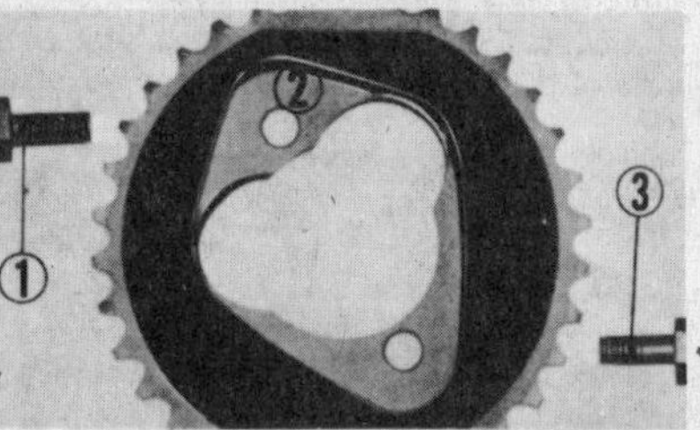

Sprocket setting bolt (1), sprocket (2), and alignment bolt (3)

the cam is in place, install the cam sprocket setting bolt. There are two different sprocket bolts; their installation must not be reversed. The sprocket setting bolt is threaded full length and should be installed in the top of the sprocket when the "L" mark is up. Hold the cam up and turn the crankshaft 360°, this will position the sprocket so that the sprocket alignment bolt may be installed (this is a shouldered bolt).

NOTE: *These bolts should be replaced with new ones once removed. They should also be coated with thread locking compound before installing them.*

11. Install the rocker arm and shafts making sure that they are installed in their original positions. The cam lobes should all be facing down for easy installation of the rockers. Install the tach drive and point housings making sure to coat the inside of the bearings before installing them on the cam. Do not use force to install the housings, hand-pressure is all that is necessary if the cam is in the right position (all lobes facing down; 90° after TDC compression stroke left cylinder).

12. With clearance between all four rocker arms and the cam, set a dial gauge to the side of the cam sprocket and measure the cam side clearance. If the clearance is greater than 1.0 mm (0.04 in.), remove one of the side housings and install thrust washers until the clearance is within the standard specification of 0.2–0.6 mm (0.008–0.024 in.). Thrust washers are available from Honda in 0.1 and 0.2 mm sizes. Again check the side clearance with the side housing installed and properly torqued. Note that the side clearance can only be measured with both housings properly torqued.

13. Install the spark advance unit, locating the pin on the camshaft to the slot in the advance unit. Install the breaker points making sure that there is a flat washer on each of the securing screws.

Engage the pin on the cam with the slot in the timing advance mechanism

14. Push the tensioner pushrod into the tensioner housing and lock it there with the set bolt. Mount the tensioner in position on the rear of the cylinders with the four mounting bolts. Release the set bolt and the tensioner will automatically adjust itself. Tighten the set bolt and the locknut.

Cylinder head nut torquing sequence (350)

15. Install the breather plate gasket, breather plate, top cover gasket and top cover. Install a washer and capnut on each of the cylinder studs and tighten them gradually and evenly in an "X" pattern, starting from the inside and working out until the proper torque of 13–14.5 ft lbs is reached.

16. The remainder of assembly is in the reverse order of the removal procedures.

360

1. Install a new wrist pin circlip into the left-side of the right piston and into the right-side of the left piston. The arrow stamped into the piston crown must face the front of the engine (exhaust side).

2. Position the piston over the connecting rod so that the wrist pin holes are in line with the connecting rod small end. Coat the wrist pin with clean engine oil and insert it into the piston until it is centered between the wrist pin circlip grooves. Install the remaining circlips making sure that they are firmly seated in

the grooves.

NOTE: *Placing a clean rag under the pistons when installing the circlips will prevent the circlips from falling into the crankcase in the event of a mishap.*

3. Install the cylinder base gasket and the two dowel pins. The dowel pins are located at the front of the engine around the outside cylinder studs.

4. Position the pistons at the same level and coat the piston skirt and rings with clean engine oil, also coat the cylinder walls with oil. Slide the cylinders down over the studs and onto the pistons while an assistant compresses the rings as they enter the bore. Make sure that the ring end-gaps are still spaced 120° apart and that no end-gap is located to the front or rear (90° from the wrist pin) of the cylinder.

Installing camshaft thrust washers (2) to adjust side-play (3)

5. Using a hooked piece of wire, pull the cam chain out from between the cylinders.

6. Before installing the head, check the camshaft side clearance. This is done by placing the cam in the head with a dial gauge fixed to one end and measuring the amount the cam can be moved sideways. If not within the standard specification 0.07–0.3 mm (0.003–0.012 in.), correct by installing thrust washers to the right-side of the cam. Thrust washers are available in two sizes: 1.0 and 1.1 mm.

7. Install the head gasket placing a light coat of oil on each side to ensure a good seal. Install a dowel pin to each of the four outside studs, and lower the head into position while pulling the cam chain through the center of the head.

8. Hold the cam chain up and turn the crankshaft until the "LT" mark on the rotor is aligned with the index mark on the stator. With the crankshaft in this position install the cam sprocket so that the aligning marks on the sprocket are facing the left-side of the engine and are parallel to the cylinder head mating surface. Install the camshaft making sure that the thrust washers are in place on the right-side of the cam. Rotate the cam until the holes in the sprocket and cam align and install one of the securing bolts. Turn the crankshaft 360° and install the remaining sprocket securing bolt. Rotate the crankshaft 360° to the "LT" mark and check that the aligning marks on the cam sprocket are still parallel to the head mating surface.

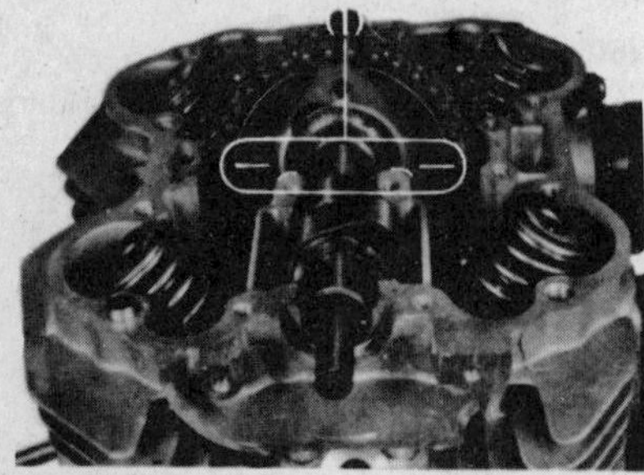
After aligning the "LT" mark on the alternator rotor, install the cam sprocket so that the aligning marks (1) are parallel to the cylinder head mating surface

NOTE: *Coat the cam bolts with thread locking compound before installing them.*

9. Install the cam chain guide to the front of the cylinder head. Install the tensioner slipper and the tensioner holder to the rear of the cylinder head. The narrow side of the holder must face the cam sprocket. Install the oil seal on the left-side of the camshaft.

Installing the cam chain tensioner holder

10. Torque the head nuts in the pattern shown in the accompanying illustration. Torque 10 mm nuts to 21.7–24.6 ft lbs and 6 mm bolts to 5.1–8.0 ft lbs. The bolts should be clean and lightly oiled to obtain accurate readings.

11. Using the rotor bolt, turn the engine over until all of the cam lobes are facing down. Pour oil over the cam, fill the oil baths with oil, and coat the cam bearings. Place a thin coat of sealing agent on the mating surface of the cylinder head cover. Take care that the sealer does not come in contact with the bearing surfaces.

Cylinder head tightening sequence

12. Install the cylinder head cover and tighten the bolts evenly and gradually, in the pattern shown in the accompanying illustration, until the proper torque is reached. Note that a cable clamp is fitted to the rear outside bolt on either side, and that bolts numbered 3, 5 in the illustration are fitted with a washer.

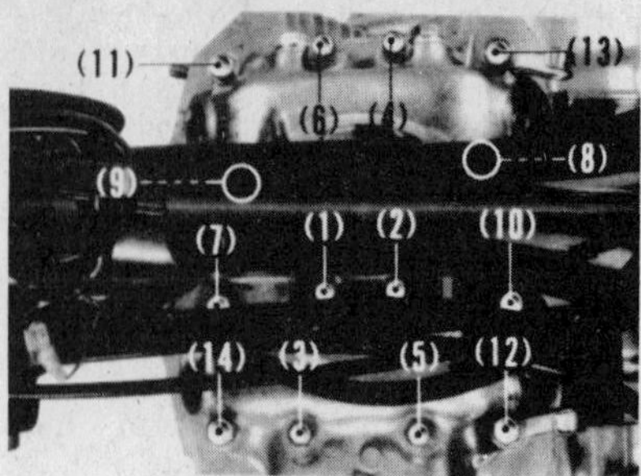

Cylinder head cover tightening sequence

13. Install the spark advance unit on the end of the cam noting that the pin on the cam is fitted in the slot in the advance unit. Install the contact breaker points.

14. Adjust the cam chain tension, tappet clearance, ignition timing, and point gap.

CRANKCASE COVER COMPONENTS

Right Crankcase Cover

REMOVAL AND INSTALLATION

1. Remove the oil filler cap, the drain plug, and drain the engine oil.
2. Remove the kick-starter pinch-bolt and pull the kick-starter off its shaft.
3. Remove the right exhaust pipe (CB models).
4. Remove the right footpeg (360 models).
5. Remove the cover mounting screws (12 on 360 models, 10 on 350 models) and remove the cover.
6. Installation is in the reverse order of removal, however, note the following points:
   a. Install a new cover gasket;
   b. Be sure that the two dowel pins are in place between the cover and the crankcase.

Centrifugal Oil Filter

REMOVAL AND INSTALLATION

1. Remove the snap-ring from the centrifugal oil filter. Screw a 6 mm screw or bolt into the filter cap and using the bolt pull the cap from the filter. A crankcase cover screw can be used. Remove the filter cap O-ring. Bend back the locktabs on the lockwasher and, holding the engine from turning over, unscrew the 16 mm locknut from the inside of the oil filter using the special Honda Tool No. 07916-283000 for 360 models, or Tool No. 07086-28301 for 350 models. Remove the oil filter housing, lockwasher, and spring washer.
2. To install the filter, install the filter housing on the end of the crankshaft. Install the cone shaped washer with the side marked "OUTSIDE" facing away

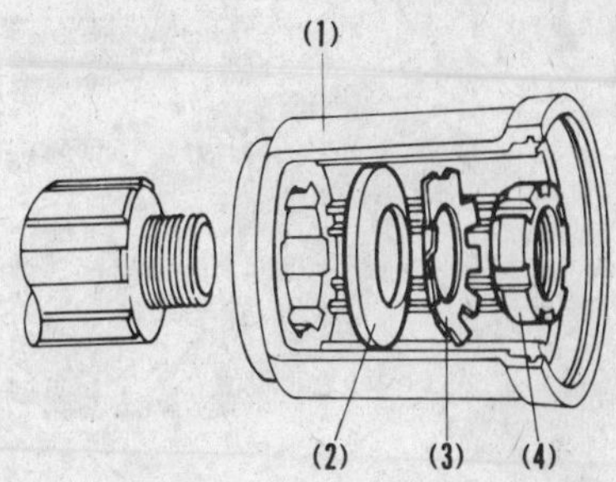

Oil filter housing (1), spring washer (2), lockwasher (3), and filter nut (4)

from the engine. Install the tabbed lockwasher, fitting the slot in the large tab over a set of splines in the filter housing. This will keep the washer from turning. Install the filter locknut onto the crankshaft and tighten with the factory tool, then bend the tabs on the washer into the slots in the filter nut.

3. Install the filter cap noting that the vanes on the cap must fit into the slots in the filter housing. Secure the cap in place with a snap-ring; be sure that the snap-ring is firmly seated.

Clutch and Primary Drive

REMOVAL AND INSTALLATION

1. Remove the right crankcase cover.

Removing the clutch pressure plate

2. Remove the four clutch spring bolts, washers, and the clutch springs. Remove the clutch pressure plate, the lifter, and the pushrod.

Removing the clutch hub snap-ring

Removing the clutch hub

3. Remove the friction and steel clutch plates. Remove the 25 mm snap-ring from the center of the clutch hub and remove the hub. Remove the stop ring and remove the steel plate from the hub.

4. Remove the centrifugal oil filter as described previously. On 350 models, remove the outside primary gear. On 360 models, remove the oil pump idler gear and shaft.

5. 350 models: Bend back the locktabs on the oil pump set plate, and remove the three mounting bolts.

6. The clutch housing can now be removed. On 350 models, the oil pump is removed with the clutch housing. The primary gear on 360 models and the inside primary gear on 350 models can now be removed.

Removing the oil pump connecting rod

On 350 models to remove the oil pump connecting rod from the clutch housing, remove the snap-ring then lift off the side washer and the connecting rod. The piston can be removed from the connecting rod by pushing the piston pin out with a small drift.

7. To install the clutch, install the primary gear to the end of the crankshaft. 350 models have two primary gears, install only the spacer and inside one at this time in that order.

8. 350 models: Install the oil pump connecting rod to the back of the clutch housing, install the side washer, fit the tab on the side washer into the hole in the clutch housing, and secure in place with the snap-ring. Fit the oil pump piston to the connecting rod and install the piston pin. Oil the piston and insert it into the bore in the oil pump. Install the clutch housing and the oil pump at the same time. Use a new gasket behind the oil pump.

9. Install the clutch housing (and oil pump on 350 models) slip the clutch pushrod through the center of the mainshaft. On 350 models, mount the oil pump with the three mounting bolts and

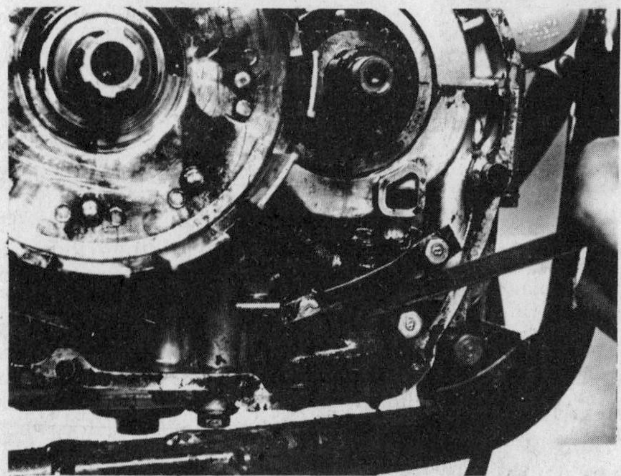
Bending down the oil filter locktabs

Removing the clutch housing and oil pump together (350)

Special steel plate (1), clutch hub (2), and stop-ring (3) (360)

bend the sides of the lockplate up against the flats on the heads of the bolts. Use a new lockplate if necessary.

10. Install the special steel plate on the clutch hub and secure in place with the stop ring.

11. Install the clutch hub on the mainshaft and secure with a snap-ring. Install the clutch plates starting with a friction plate and then a steel plate and so on until all the plates are in place. The top plate should be a friction plate.

12. Fit the pressure plate lifter to the center of the clutch hub, then install the pressure plate, clutch springs, washers, and bolts. Tighten the bolts gradually and evenly in an "X" pattern until they are tight.

13. Install the remaining primary gear on 350 models, then install the centrifugal oil filter. On 360 models, install the oil pump idler gear and shaft.

Installing the pressure plate lifter

Oil Pump and Filter Screen

REMOVAL AND INSTALLATION

1. On 350 models, the oil pump and filter screen are removed and installed with the clutch housing. Refer to the preceding "Clutch Removal and Installation" section.

2. The following steps refer only to 360 models.

3. Remove the right crankcase cover as described previously.

4. Remove the idler gear and shaft.

5. Remove the three mounting bolts from the oil filter screen and remove the screen. Remove the two remaining mounting bolts from the oil pump and remove the pump.

6. Complete inspection procedures for the oil pump and filter screen can be found in "Lubrication System."

Removing the idler gear (2) and shaft (1) (360)

Oil filter screen (1) and mounting bolts (2 and 3) (360)

Oil pump (1) and mounting bolts (2) (360)

Oil pump O-rings (1) (360)

7. Install the oil pump and filter screen in the reverse order of removal, however, note that the two O-rings behind the pump must be in good condition. If in doubt as to their condition, replace them with new ones.

Shifter Mechanism

REMOVAL AND INSTALLATION

1. Remove the right crankcase cover and clutch as described previously.

2. Remove the shift lever pinch-bolt and pull the shift lever off the shift shaft.

Removing the shift arm

Shift drum stopper (360)

and install the mounting bolts. Do not overtighten the bolts. Coat the shift shaft with a light coat of grease and slip it through the right-side of the engine. Ensure that the fingers of the shift arm are in contact with the pins in the shift drum.

5. Refit the clutch and the right crankcase cover.

Left Crankcase Cover

REMOVAL AND INSTALLATION

1. Remove the pinch-bolt from the shift lever and pull the lever off its shaft.

2. Remove the four mounting screws from the rear cover and remove the cover.

NOTE: *Take care not to lose the steel ball from the clutch release mechanism when the cover is removed.*

3. Disconnect the clutch cable from the clutch release mechanism inside the cover.

4. Before removing the front cover, drain the engine oil. Remove three stator cover mounting screws. Remove the stator cover.

5. Disconnect the alternator wiring from the wiring harness. On 360 models, remove the carburetor to reach the connector. Disconnect the neutral switch lead from the neutral switch.

6. Remove the crankcase cover. The stator can be removed from the cover once the three mounting screws are removed.

7. To install the covers, attach the stator to the front cover with the three mounting screws. Use a new gasket under the front cover. Be sure to install the two dowel pins under each cover.

Clutch Release Mechanism

1. To remove the clutch release mechanism from the cover, unscrew the ad-

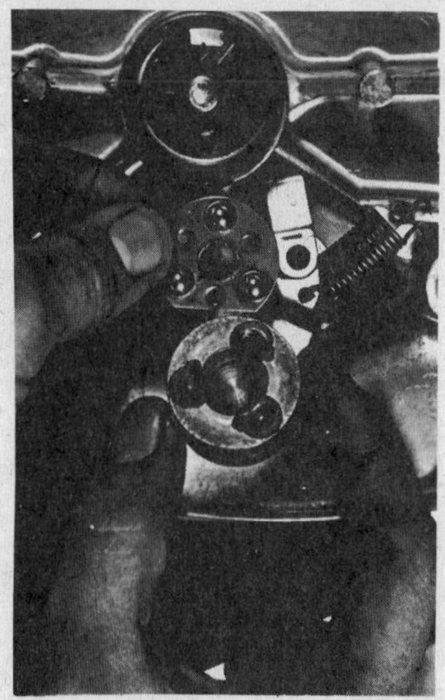

Clutch release mechanism

juster locknut from the adjuster screw. Unhook the return spring from the inside of the cover and the release mechanism can be removed from the case.

2. Clean all of the parts in solvent.

3. Inspect the adjuster screw for damaged threads. Inspect the clutch adjusting cam and release lever for wear from the ball retainer.

4. Check the dust seal for condition. If it is cracked or torn or shows signs of age, it should be replaced.

5. Clean the boss in the case with solvent.

6. Grease all parts before installing them into the case. Be sure to install the flat washer under the adjuster locknut.

Countershaft Sprocket

1. Remove the left rear crankcase cover as described previously.

2. To remove the sprocket, remove the two bolts from the sprocket and rotate the lockplate until the tabs on the plate line up with the slots in the countershaft. Remove the lockplate.

3. Either move the rear wheel forward in the swing arm or remove the masterlink from the chain, and pull the sprocket off the countershaft.

4. When refitting the sprocket, install the sprocket on the countershaft. If the masterlink has not been removed, refit the chain to the sprocket before installing the sprocket to the countershaft. Install the lockplate on the countershaft and rotate it until the holes in the sprocket line up with the holes in the lockplate. Install the two bolts and torque to 5.8–8.7 ft lbs.

Alternator and Starter Assembly

REMOVAL

1. Remove the crankcase covers and stator as described previously.

2. Remove the rotor bolt while holding the engine from turning over.

3. Remove the alternator rotor using the factory rotor puller. In most cases the rear axle can be used in place of the puller; screw the axle into the center of the rotor until it is firmly seated. Slip a rod through the hole in the head of the axle and tap the rod with a hammer. If the rotor resists removal, use the factory puller. The starter clutch is removed with the rotor.

4. Remove the woodruff key from the taper on the crankshaft.

5. The starter clutch can be removed from the back of the rotor after removing the three phillips head screws. Remove the clutch side plate.

6. The starter motor chain can be removed by pulling off both sprockets and the chain at the same time.

7. Unbolt the starter motor from the front of the engine, disconnecting the starter motor cable at the motor, and remove the motor tapping the shaft lightly with a plastic mallet if necessary.

INSPECTION

1. For further inspection of the alternator rotor, stator, and starting motor, refer to "Electrical System."

2. Check that the rollers in the starter clutch are free to move. Also check that they all have the same amount of spring tension on them. If any spring feels weak in relation to the others, replace it by removing the roller, spring cap, and spring. Replace the spring and install the cap and roller.

Removing the rotor with the rear axle

Check condition of the starter clutch and rollers

Removing the starter sprockets and chain

Removing the sprocket lockplate

Removing the rotor bolt

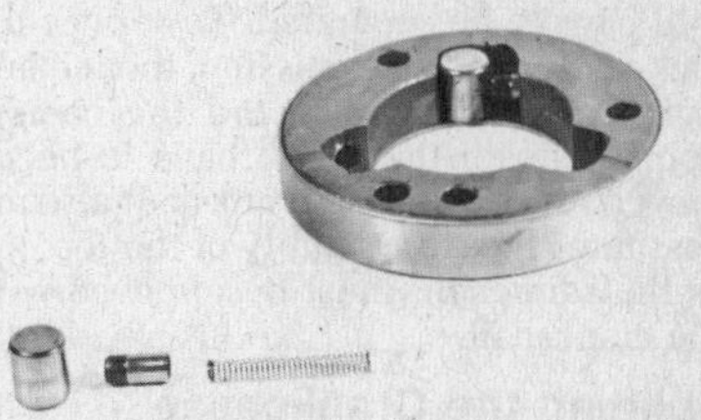

Starter clutch components

3. Inspect the clutch housing for any cracks. If found defective, it must be replaced.

4. Inspect the surface of the starter sprocket where the rollers contact it. If badly scored, the sprocket and the rollers should be replaced.

5. Inspect the condition of the sprocket teeth. If they are hooked or appear to be worn badly, replace both sprockets and the chain.

INSTALLATION

1. Mount the starter motor on the front of the engine with the two mounting bolts.

2. Install the starter motor chain and the two sprockets at the same time. Install the starter sprocket setting plate.

Be sure that the starter sprocket set plate is secured

3. Mount the starter clutch on the rotor with the three screws. Be sure to install the side plate between the rotor and the clutch.

4. Install the woodruff key in the crankshaft and install the rotor lining up the slot in the rotor with the key in the crankshaft. Draw the rotor down on the crankshaft with the rotor bolt, never strike the rotor as this may affect the magnets.

5. Install the stator in the crankcase cover, then install the cover using a new gasket. Check that the rotor does not come in contact with the stator as the engine turns over. Install the stator cover and the rear cover.

CRANKCASE COMPONENTS

To service the kick-starter, transmission, or the crankshaft, the crankcases will have to be separated. To service the kick-starter and transmission, the left and right crankcase covers and the components beneath them will have to be removed. Service to the crankshaft also necessitates the disassembly of the top end as the cam chain must be removed with the crankshaft.

Splitting the Crankcases

1. Remove the engine from the frame.

2. If the crankshaft is to be serviced, disassemble the top end as outlined previously.

3. Remove the right and left crankcase covers and the components beneath them.

NOTE: *Loosen the oil filter nut and the rotor bolt before removing the clutch.*

4. Remove the neutral stop bolt from the upper case after bending back the locktab. Remove the spring and ball beneath the bolt.

5. Remove the crankcase bolt(s) from the upper crankcase (1 on 360 models, 2 on 350 models). Turn the engine upside down and remove the remaining crankcase bolts from the lower crankcase. Remove the lower crankcase half, tapping around the mating surface with a plastic mallet to free the case half, if stuck. The crankshaft and the transmission will remain in the upper half.

Removing the shift drum neutral stop bolt

Top crankcase bolts

Kick-Starter

REMOVAL

1. Split the crankcases as described previously.

2. Remove the washer, circlip, and return spring from the kick-starter shaft on the outside of the lower crankcase.

3. Remove the circlip from the inside of the shaft and remove the components from the shaft. Slip the shaft out of the case.

INSTALLATION

1. Install the shaft into the lower crankcase half. Install the components on the shaft as shown in the accompanying illustration. Hold the shaft so that the stop on the shaft is against the stop in the lower crankcase when installing the internal components. Be sure that the ratchet guide plate (360 models) or the friction spring (350 models) is seated properly in the crankcase.

Removing the kick-starter circlip (350)

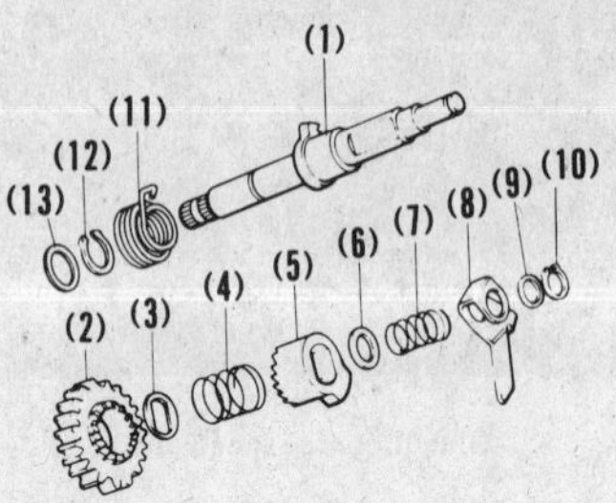

Kick-starter components (360): install in order shown

1. Kick-starter shaft
2. Kick-starter gear
3. Washer
4. Spring
5. Ratchet gear
6. Shim
7. Spring
8. Ratchet guide plate
9. Shim
10. Circlip
11. Return spring
12. Circlip
13. Shim

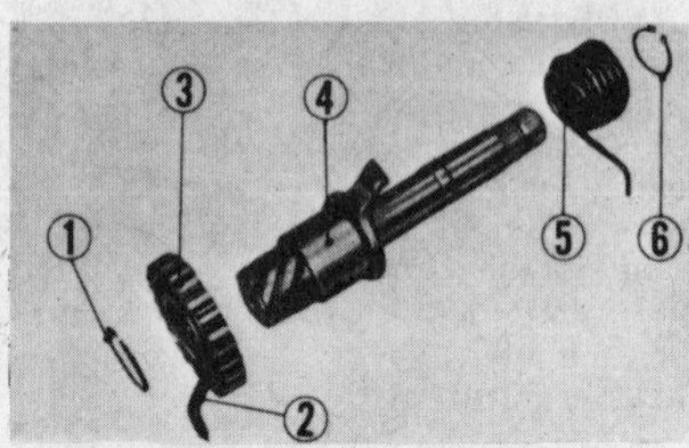

Kick-starter (CB/CL350)

1. Circlip
2. Friction spring
3. Kick-starter gear
4. Kick-starter shaft
5. Return spring
6. Circlip

Be sure that the friction spring is seated properly in the crankcase (350)

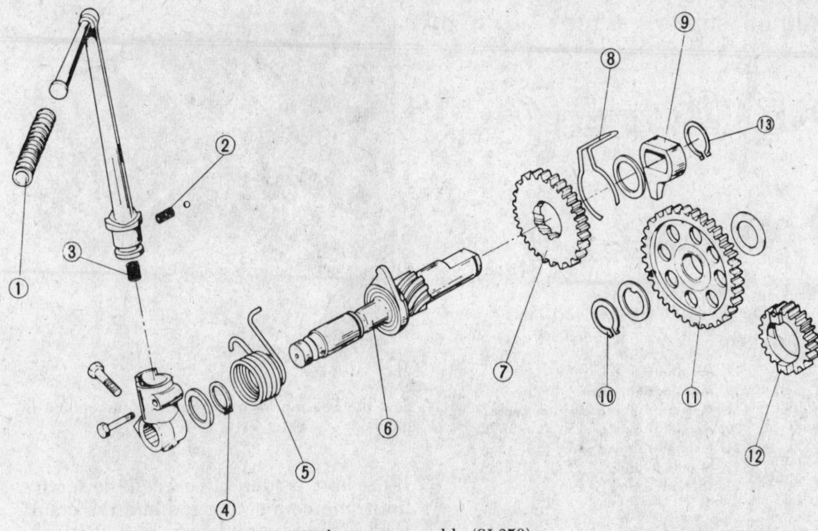

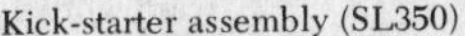

Kick-starter assembly (SL350)

1. Rubber
2. Starter lever spring
3. Starter knuckle spring
4. Circlip
5. Return spring
6. Kick-starter shaft
7. Kick-starter gear
8. Friction spring
9. Shaft stopper
10. Circlip
11. Idler gear
12. Driven gear
13. Circlip

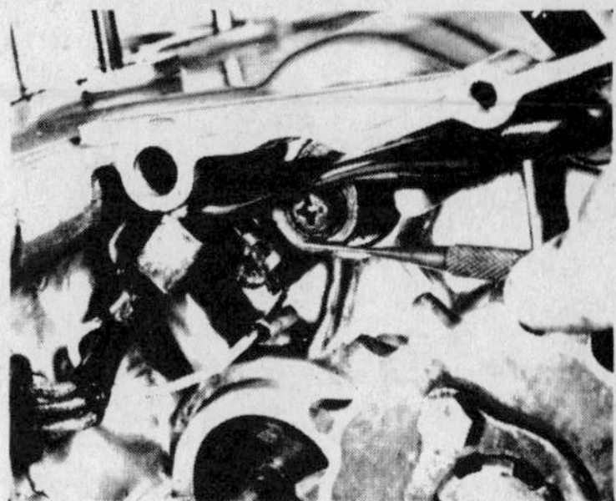

Neutral switch rotor in neutral position

Transmission

REMOVAL

1. Split the crankcases as described previously. The transmission shafts can be lifted out of the top case.

2. 350 models: Remove the neutral switch rotor and the drum stopper from the shift drum. Remove the guide pin clips and the guide pins from the shift forks. Mark the location of each shift fork (left, center, and right) and slide the shift drum out of the case from the right-side.

3. 360 models: Remove the shift drum stopper and stopper spring. Remove the shift fork guide shaft after marking the location of the two shift forks (left or right), remove the forks taking care not to lose their guide pins. Remove the guide pin clip and guide pin from the remaining shift fork and slide the drum out the right-side of the case.

4. The transmission gears can be removed from their shafts after removing the circlips which secure them. All components should be carefully laid out in the order in which they are removed so that they can be installed in their proper locations.

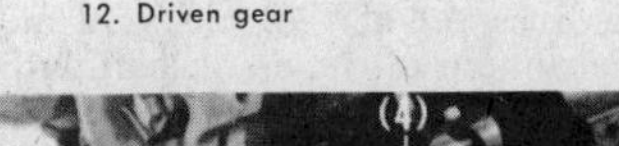

Removing the shift fork shaft (3), and shift forks (4), drum stopper and spring (1 and 2) also shown

Removing the neutral switch rotor

Removing the shift drum

INSTALLATION

1. Slip the shift drum into the upper crankcase; as the drum enters the case, install the shift fork(s). Be sure that the fork(s) are installed in the same position from which they were removed. Install the neutral switch to the end of the shift drum.

2. Position the shift drum in the neutral position (as seen by the neutral switch) and install the neutral stopper ball, spring, lockplate, and bolt. Bend the lockplate up against the flat on the head of the bolt.

3. 360 models: Install the shift fork shaft, inserting it through the shift forks as it enters the case. Install the guide pins and check that they fit into the grooves in the shift drum.

4. Assemble the mainshaft and the countershaft as shown in the accompanying illustration. Install the transmission shafts in the upper case. Be sure that the shift forks are fitted to the proper gears.

Be sure that the bearings are fitted to the set ring or the locating pins. When properly fitted the bearings should sit flush in the case.

5. The remainder of assembly is in the reverse order of removal.

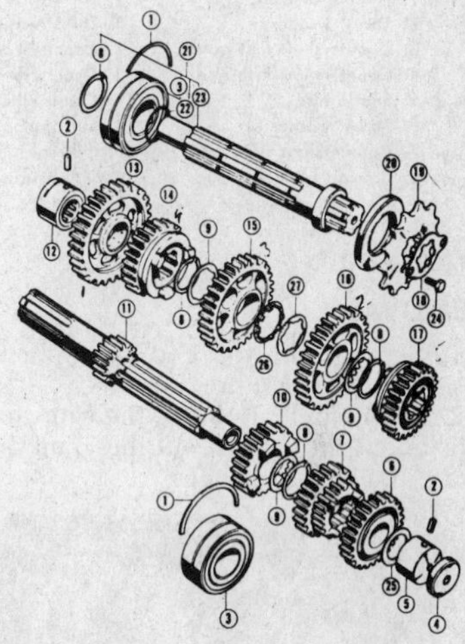

Transmission assembly (350)

1. Set ring
2. Dowel pin
3. Ball bearing
4. Oil seal
5. Needle bearing
6. Mainshaft fifth gear
7. Mainshaft second and third gear
8. Circlip
9. Thrust washer
10. Mainshaft fourth gear
11. Mainshaft
12. Needle bearing
13. Countershaft first gear
14. Countershaft fourth gear
15. Countershaft third gear
16. Countershaft second gear
17. Countershaft fifth gear
18. Lockplate
19. Countershaft sprocket
20. Oil seal
21. Countershaft (complete)
22. O-ring
23. Countershaft
24. Bolt
25. Thrust washer
26. Lockwasher
27. Thrust washer

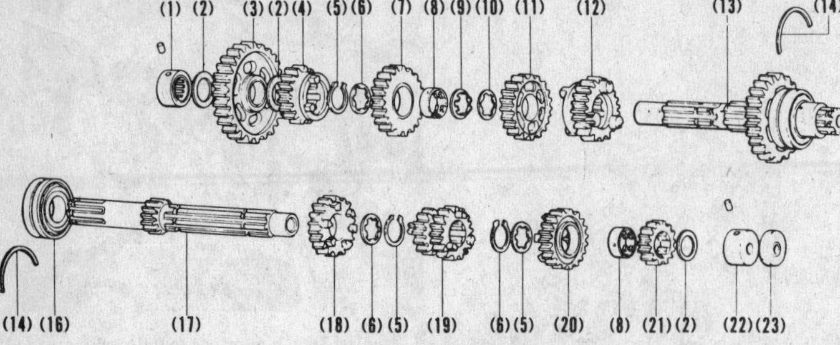

Transmission assembly (360)

1. Needle bearing
2. Thrust washer
3. Countershaft first gear
4. Countershaft fifth gear
5. Snap-ring
6. Thrust washer
7. Countershaft third gear
8. Splined bushing
9. Lockwasher
10. Thrust washer
11. Countershaft fourth gear
12. Countershaft sixth gear
13. Countershaft
14. Set ring
15. Oil seal
16. Ball bearing
17. Mainshaft
18. Mainshaft fifth gear
19. Mainshaft third and fourth gears
20. Mainshaft sixth gear
21. Mainshaft second gear
22. Needle bearing
23. Oil seal

Crankshaft

REMOVAL

1. Remove the top end and split the cases as described previously.

2. 360 models: Remove the cam chain tensioner arm and lift out the crankshaft and cam chain together.

Cam chain tensioner arm (1) (360)

3. 350 models: Loosen the four main bearing cap bolts gradually and evenly until they are all loose and then remove them. Lift the crankshaft and cam chain out of the case together.

CAUTION: *Do not lose the main bearing locating pins when the crankshaft is removed.*

INSPECTION

1. Mount the crankshaft center main bearings in a set of V-blocks, and measure the run-out of the crankshaft with a dial gauge. Measurements should be taken at either end of the crankshaft and on each of the flywheels. If the run-out exceeds the service limit, the crankshaft should be replaced.

2. With the crankshaft supported at both ends, mount a dial gauge to the top of each main bearing in turn. Attempt to move the outer race up and down. The measurement on the dial gauge is the total radial clearance. If the clearance exceeds the service limit, the crankshaft should be replaced.

3. With the crankshaft firmly supported, fix a dial gauge to the bottom of the connecting rod, and measure the up and down play. The dial gauge will indicate the amount of radial clearance of the rod bearing. If the clearance exceeds the service limit, the crankshaft should be replaced.

4. Using a feeler gauge, measure the side clearance of the connecting rod. If the side clearance is beyond the service limit, replace the crankshaft.

5. With an inside micrometer, measure the bore of the connecting rod small end.

Seat the bearing locating pins into the cut-out in the case

If the bore is found to exceed the service limit, the connecting rod and the crankshaft should be replaced.

6. Rotate each of the main bearings. They should be smooth and silent. If rough or noisy, they should be replaced.

INSTALLATION

1. Fit the cam chain to the sprocket on the crankshaft.

2. Fit the crankshaft into place. Be sure that the bearing locating pins are properly seated in the upper crankcase half.

3. 360 models: Install the cam chain tensioner arm.

4. Install the main bearing cap (350) and tighten the four bolts gradually and evenly in an "X" pattern until the proper torque of 15.9–17.4 ft lbs is reached.

5. Assemble the crankcases and the top end.

360 Cam Chain Tensioner

The cam chain tensioner can be removed from the lower case by loosening the setting bolt and pulling the tensioner push bar and springs from the inside. When installing the tensioner push bar, the mark on the pad must face up. Push the push bar in to compress the springs and tighten the setting bolt.

Removing the crankshaft

Checking crankshaft run-out

Mark (2) on tensioner push bar (1) must face upward (360)

Assembling the Crankcases

1. The crankcase mating surface must be clean and free of any scratches. Minor repairs can be made with an oilstone.

2. Apply a thin coat of sealing compound to the crankcase mating surface. Be careful not to get any of the sealer on the bearings or inside surface of the crankcase.

3. Install the lower case. Make sure that the cases mate properly before installing the crankcase bolts. If they do not, check that all of the bearing locating pins are in place.

4. Install the crankcase bolts and tighten them evenly and gradually in an "X" pattern, starting from the inside and working out.

5. Install the crankcase cover components and the top end as described previously.

LUBRICATION SYSTEM

CENTRIFUGAL OIL FILTER

Removal

1. Remove the right crankcase cover.
2. Remove the snap-ring from the filter cap. Screw a 6 mm screw into the center of the cap and, using the screw, pull off the cap.
3. Hold the crankshaft from turning by placing the transmission in gear and applying the rear brake. Bend back the tabs on the lockwasher and remove the special 16 mm locknut using the factory tool (Tool No. 07916-2830000). Remove the tabbed lockwasher, and the filter housing.

Inspection

1. Clean all parts in clean solvent and allow to dry.
2. Inspect the snap-ring. It should be replaced if it is distorted or is a loose fit in the filter housing.
3. Inspect the filter cap O-ring. If it is deformed, torn, or cracked, it must be replaced.

4. Check the 16 mm locknut for condition. If the slots on the outside of the nut are badly damaged or the threads are chipped or stripped, the nut should be re-

Engine Specifications 350

Item	Standard (mm/in.)	Service Limit (mm/in.)
Camshaft side clearance	0.2–0.6/0.008–0.024	1.0/0.04
Camshaft lobe diameter	36.858–36.898/1.451–1.453	36.68/1.444
Camshaft journal diameter	21.939–21.960/0.864–0.865	21.92/0.863
Camshaft bearing ID	22.00–22.021/0.866–0.867	20.05/0.868
Rocker arm shaft diameter	12.950–12.986/0.510–0.511	12.90/0.508
Max head warpage	—	0.05/0.002
Valve seat width	1.0–1.3/0.040–0.051	2.0/0.08
Valve-to-valve guide clearance		
Intake	0.01–0.035/0.0004–0.0014	0.08/0.0031
Exhaust	0.03–0.055/0.0012–0.0022	0.09/0.0035
Valve stem diameter		
Intake	6.975–6.990/0.2746–0.2752	6.955/0.2738
Exhaust	6.955–6.970/0.2738–0.2744	6.935/0.2730
Valve spring free-length		
Outer spring	49.0/1.929	47.8/1.882
Inner spring	39.8/1.567	39.3/1.547
Cylinder bore	64.01–64.02/2.5201–2.5205	64.1/2.524
Max cylinder taper	0.005/0.0002	0.05/0.002
Out-of-round	0.005/0.0002	0.05/0.002
Piston diameter	63.97–63.99/2.5185–2.5193	63.9/2.51
Piston ring side clearance		
Top ring	0.030–0.060/0.0012–0.0024	0.18/0.007
Second ring	0.015–0.045/0.0006–0.0018	0.165/0.0065
Oil ring	0.010–0.045/0.0004–0.0018	0.170/0.0067
Ring end-gap	0.2–0.4/0.008–0.016	0.8/0.032
Piston ring thickness		
Top ring	1.460–1.475/0.057–0.058	1.435/0.0564
Second ring	1.457–1.490/0.058–0.059	1.435/0.0564
Oil ring	2.475–2.490/0.097–0.098	2.430/0.096
Wrist pin hole diameter	15.002–15.008/0.5906–0.5909	15.08/0.5937
Wrist pin diameter	14.994–15.000/0.590–0.5906	14.96/0.5889
Oil pump bore	16.000–16.018/0.630–0.631	16.1/0.634
Oil pump piston diameter	15.955–15.970/0.628–0.629	15.930/0.627

Engine Specifications (cont.) 350

Item	Standard (mm/in.)	Service Limit (mm/in.)
Clutch		
Friction disc thickness	2.62–2.78/0.031–0.110	2.3/0.906
Steel plate warpage	0.15/0.006	0.3/0.012
Spring free-length	31.9/1.258	30.5/1.20
Crankshaft run-out		
Shaft	0.02/0.0008	0.15/0.006
Counterweight	0.10/0.004	0.3/0.012
Main bearing radial play	0.012–0.020/0.0005–0.0008	0.05/0.002
Connecting rod		
Big end radial play	0.004–0.012/0.0002–0.0005	0.05/0.002
Big end side clearance	0.07–0.33/0.0028–0.0130	0.60/0.023
Small end bore	15.016–15.034/0.591–0.592	15.07/0.593
Transmission gear backlash		
1st, 2nd	0.044–0.133/0.0017–0.0052	0.2/0.008
3rd, 4th, 5th	0.046–0.14/0.0018–0.0055	0.2/0.008
Gear-to-shaft clearance		
M4, M5	0.02–0.062/0.0008–0.0024	0.1/0.0039
C1	0.02–0.054/0.000–0.002	0.1/0.0039
C2, C3	0.04–0.084/0.0016–0.002	0.1/0.0047
Shift fork thickness		
A (fitted to C4, C5)	4.93–5.0/0.94–0.197	4.6/0.181
B (fitted to M2, M3)	6.93–6.0/0.233–0.236	5.6/0.22
Fork bore diameter	40.0–40.025/1.575–1.576	40.075/1.577
Gearshift drum OD	39.95–39.975/1.5689–1.5738	39.9/1.571

Engine Specifications 360

Item	Standard (mm/in.)	Service Limit (mm/in.)
Camshaft side clearance	0.07–0.3/0.0028–0.012	Must be within standards
Camshaft lobe diameter		
Intake	40.314/1.587	40.1/1.579
Exhaust	40.339/1.588	40.1/1.579
Rocker arm-to-shaft clearance	0.016–0.061/0.0006–0.0024	0.1/0.004
Max head warpage	——	0.3/0.012
Value seat width	1.0–1.3/0.04–0.05	2.0/0.08

Filter cap O-ring

placed.

5. Check the condition of the tabs on the lockwasher, if they are weak or missing, the washer must be replaced.

6. Inspect the condition of the cone-shaped washer. If the washer appears to be flat, it should be replaced.

Installation

1. Install the filter housing on the crankshaft, then install the cone-shaped washer lockwasher, and locknut.

NOTE: *On 360 models and late model 350s, one side of the cone-shaped washer is marked "OUTSIDE." This side must face away from the engine. If the washer is not marked, the convex side should face away from the engine. It is recommended that this washer be replaced with a new one whenever it is removed. When installing the tab lockwasher, the slot in the large tab must fit over the splines inside the filter housing.*

When installing the locknut, be sure that the chamfered side is facing the engine.

2. Tighten the locknut to 32.6–39.7 ft lbs for 360 models and 21.7–23.1 ft lbs for 350 models. Bend the tabs on the lockwasher into the slots in the filter nut.

3. Install the filter cap and O-ring. Be sure that the vanes of the filter cap are fitted into the slots in the filter housing. Be sure that the circlip is firmly seated.

OIL PUMP AND FILTER SCREEN

350 Models

On 350 models, the oil pump and filter screen are removed and installed with the clutch housing. Refer to the "Engine and Transmission" section.

INSPECTION

NOTE: *CB/CL350K3,K4 and SL350K1,K2 were equipped with a larger oil pump than the early models. A new pump assembly can be installed on the early models to provide better lubrication. However, if this is done, be sure to install new crankcase cover gaskets, as they were also modified. The new pump can be identified by the alloy pump body and steel piston. The*

Engine Specifications (cont.)
360

Item	Standard (mm/in.)	Service Limit (mm/in.)
Valve-to-valve guide clearance		
Intake	0.01–0.035/0.0004–0.0014	0.08/0.003
Exhaust	0.03–0.05/0.0012–0.0020	0.09/0.0035
Valve stem diameter		
Intake	6.975–6.990/0.2746–0.2752	6.955/0.2738
Exhaust	6.955–6.970/0.2738–0.2744	6.935/0.2730
Valve spring free-length		
Outer spring	49.0/1.93	47.8/1.88
Inner spring	39.8/1.56	39.3/1.57
Cylinder		
Bore	67.01–67.02/2.6382–2.6386	67.1/2.6417
Max taper	0.005/0.0002	0.05/0.002
Out-of-round	0.005/0.0002	0.05/0.002
Piston diameter	66.97–66.99/2.6366–2.6374	66.85/2.6319
Piston ring side clearance		
Top ring	0.02–0.06/0.0008–0.0024	0.15/0.0059
Second ring	0.02–0.06/0.0008–0.0016	0.15/0.0059
Oil ring	0.010–0.045/0.0004–0.0018	0.15/0.0059
Piston ring end-gap		
Top ring	0.2–0.4/0.0079–0.0157	0.8/0.0315
Second ring	0.15–0.35/0.0059–0.0138	0.75/0.0295
Oil ring	0.2–0.4/0.0079–0.0157	0.8/0.0315
Wrist pin hole diameter	16.002–16.008/0.6300–0.6302	16.05/0.6319
Wrist pin diameter	15.994–16.00/0.6297–0.6299	15.9/0.6260
Oil pump		
Outer rotor-to-pump body clearance	0.15–0.21/0.0059–0.0083	0.35/0.0138
Radial clearance of outer rotor	0.02–0.08/0.0008–0.0032	0.1/0.0039
Clutch		
Friction disc thickness	2.62–2.78/0.1031–0.1095	2.3/0.9055
Steel plate warpage	0.1/0.0039	0.2/0.0079
Spring free-length	31.25/1.2305	29.7/1.1693
Crankshaft run-out		
Shaft	0.05/0.002	Below 0.1/0.0039
Counterweight	0.1/0.004	Below 0.1/0.0039

Early and late model oil pumps

early pump body was a steel casting with an alloy piston. Note that if this modification is made the entire pump assembly must be changed.

1. Inspect the bore in the oil pump. If it is scored, the pump housing and piston should be replaced.

2. Check the condition of the pump piston. If it is scored, it should be replaced.

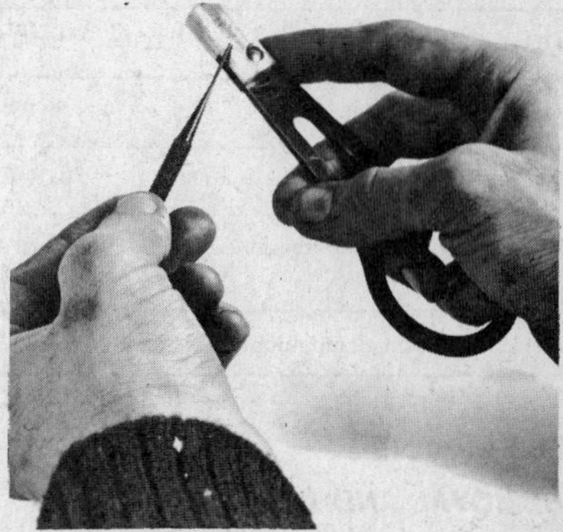

Check the pump piston for scoring (350)

3. CB/CL350,K1,K2/SL350: If a micrometer is available, measure the diameter of the pump piston. If found to be less than 15.930 mm (0.627 in.), the piston should be replaced.

4. CB/CL350,K1,K2/SL350: With an inside micrometer, measure the pump bore if found to be larger than 16.1 mm (0.634 in.), the pump housing and piston should be replaced.

5. Remove the suction valve bolt from the top of the pump (if fitted), and the steel ball beneath it. If the ball shows signs of wear, the pump should be replaced.

6. Remove the filter screen from the bottom of the pump and wash in clean solvent. Inspect the screen for any puncture marks. If the screen mesh is broken to any extent, the screen must be replaced.

7. Check the oil pump gasket for condition. If defective in any way, it must be replaced. It is recommended that this gasket be replaced regardless of apparent condition.

8. Inspect the condition of the mounting bolt lockplate and replace it if the tabs are fatigued.

Engine Specifications (cont.)
360

Item	Standard (mm/in.)	Service Limit (mm/in.)
Connecting rod		
Big end radial play	0.004–0.012/0.0002–0.0005	0.05/0.0020
Big end side clearance	0.07–0.33/0.0028–0.0130	0.60/0.0236
Small end ID	15.016–15.034/0.5912–0.5919	15.07/0.5933
Gearshift fork-to-drum		
clearance (A and B)	0.05–0.22/0.0020–0.0087	0.3/0.118
ID of gearshift fork		
Fork A	13.000–13.018/0.5118–0.5125	12.95/0.5098
Fork B	40.000–40.025/1.5748–1.5758	40.075/1.0798
Shift fork width		
Fork A and B	5.93–6.00/0.2335–0.2362	5.5/0.2165
OD of shift fork guide shaft	12.957–12.984/0.5101–0.5112	12.9/0.5079
OD of gearshift drum	39.950–39.975/1.5374–1.5384	39.9/1.5709
Kick-starter pinion-to-shaft clearance	0.04–0.082/0.0016–0.0032	0.1/0.004
Thickness of cam chain tensioner slipper (at center)	4.0/0.1575	3.0/0.1181
Thickness of cam chain guide (at center)	6.1–6.3/0.2402–0.2480	5.0/0.1969

360 Models

REMOVAL AND INSTALLATION

1. Remove the right crankcase cover. Refer to Chapter 4 if necessary.
2. Remove the idler gear and shaft.
3. Remove the three mounting bolts from the oil filter screen, and remove the screen. Remove the two remaining mounting bolts from the oil pump and remove the pump.
4. Install the oil pump and filter in the reverse order of removal, however, note that the two O-rings behind the pump must be in good condition. If in doubt as to their condition, replace them with new ones.

DISASSEMBLY

To disassemble the pump, remove the three phillips head screws from the rear of the pump and pull the pump halves apart.

NOTE: *It is not recommended that the pump be disassembled. If the pump is suspected of being defective, it should be replaced as a unit rather than making an effort to repair it.*

INSPECTION

1. Inspect the condition of the oil pump drive gear and idler gear. If any teeth are chipped, broken, or missing, replace the gears and inspect the primary gear for the same damage.
2. Measure the clearance between the two rotors. If the clearance exceeds the service limit, replace the pump.
3. Measure the side clearance of the rotors. If the side clearance exceeds the service limit given at the end of this chapter, replace the pump.

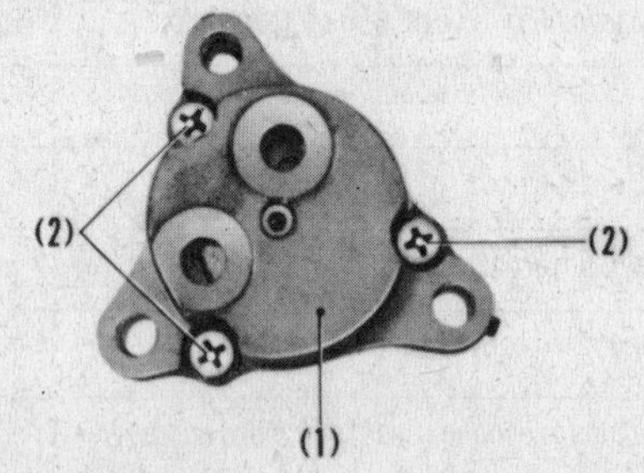

Disassemble the pump (1) by removing the three screws (2) (360)

Engine Torque Specifications

Item	Thread Diameter (mm)	Torque (ft lbs)
350		
Crankcase cover screws	6	5–8
Cam case screws	6	4.5–5.2
Cylinder head nuts	8	13–14.5
Cylinder head screws	6	5–8
Oil filter locknut	16	22–23
Main bearing cap bolts	8	16–17.5
Alternator mounting bolt	8	16–17.5
Crankcase mounting bolts	6	7–9
360		
Crankcase cover screws	6	5–8
Cylinder head bolts	6	5–8
	10	22–25
Camshaft sprocket bolts	7	13–15
Alternator mounting bolt	8	22–25
Oil filter locknut	16	32–39
Crankcase mounting bolts	6	7–9

FUEL SYSTEM

CARBURETOR

For an operational theory, general inspection procedures and a carburetor troubleshooting chart, refer to the "Carburetor" section under "General Information."

Direct-Control Type

REMOVAL AND INSTALLATION

1. Unscrew the carburetor cap and pull the throttle slide assembly out of the carburetor. If the slide assembly is to be disassembled, see the procedure below. If not, place a small plastic bag around the assembly to keep dirt out, and place it out of the way. Note that mishandling the assembly may necessitate replacement of the slide or needle.
2. Turn the fuel supply off at the petcock, and disconnect the fuel line from the carburetor.
3. Remove the float bowl drain plug, and drain off any gas in the float bowl. Disconnect any overflow or breather tubes.
4. Loosen the intake manifold and air cleaner connecting bands. Remove the carburetor.
5. Installation is in the reverse order of the above, but the following points should be noted:
   a. Lubricate the throttle slide if desired with a molybdenum or graphite lubricant. Insert it into the carburetor with the slide cutaway facing the air cleaner. Be sure that the slot in the

Oil Pump Specifications
CB/CL350, K1, K2/SL350

Item	Standard Value (mm/in.)	Service Limit (mm/in.)
Oil pump bore diameter	16.000–16.018/0.630–0.631	16.1/0.634
Oil pump piston diameter	15.955–15.970/0.628–0.629	15.930/0.627
CB/CL/CJ360		
Oil pump outer rotor-to-pump body clearance	0.15–0.21/0.0059–0.0083	0.35/0.0138
Radial clearance of oil pump outer rotor	0.02–0.08/0.0008–0.0032	0.1/0.0039

slide is engaged with the tab in the carburetor body;

b. Be sure that the slide goes in easily, and especially that the needle enters the needle jet. Do not push or force the slide into place. If resistance is noted, it is probable that the needle is cocked to one side and is not entering the needle jet;

c. Tighten the carburetor cap and check throttle operation. The slide must move freely up and down. The throttle return spring must have enough tension to snap the slide to its fully closed position if the throttle is opened and released;

d. Connect the fuel line from the right carburetor to the rear outlet on the petcock, and the fuel line from the left carburetor to the front outlet on the petcock. Secure the fuel lines in place with a spring clip;

e. Turn the fuel on and check for leaks. Start the engine and check for air leaks around the intake manifold and the air cleaner.

DISASSEMBLY

1. If disassembly of the throttle slide components is desired, compress the return spring against the carburetor cap, disengage the cable from the slide, take out the spring clip, needle and clip.
2. With the carburetor upside down, flip up the retainer and separate the float bowl from the carburetor body. Do so carefully to avoid damage to the float.
3. Push out the float pivot pin with a small drift, and remove the float. Remove the float needle from its seat. Unscrew the seat itself.
4. Using a small screwdriver, remove the main jet, pilot jet, pilot air screw, and throttle stop screw.
5. Unscrew the main jet holder using the correct size wrench. The needle jet can now be removed from above the main jet holder.

ASSEMBLY

Assembly is basically the reverse of the disassembly procedures, but note the following points:

1. Float bowl gaskets and jet O-rings should always be replaced with new ones. Other O-rings and fiber gaskets should be carefully inspected and replaced if less than perfect in condition. Check O-rings for tears and cracks; fiber gaskets for a crushed condition.
2. Exercise care when installing jets, they are made of soft brass and are easily damaged if overtightened. Install the needle jet, main jet holder, main jet, pilot jet, and float needle seat.
3. Install the float needle into its seat. Hold the floats in place and install the pivot pin. Install the float bowl.
4. Assemble the throttle slide.
5. Install the pilot air screw, turning it in until lightly seated, then backing it out the proper number of turns as listed in the chart at the end of this section.
6. After completing assembly, install the carburetor on its manifold.
7. Check for fuel or air leaks; make final adjustments to the throttle stop and pilot air screws.

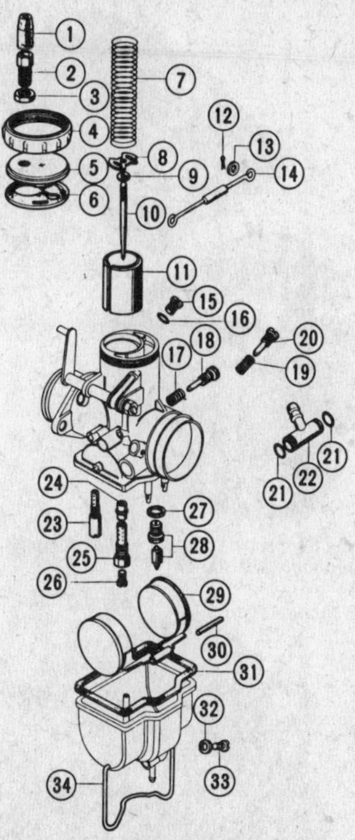

SL350 carburetor

1. Rubber cap
2. Cable adjuster
3. Locknut
4. Cap
5. Top
6. Rubber gasket
7. Slide return spring
8. Needle retaining clip
9. C-clip
10. Needle
11. Slide
12. Cotter pin
13. Float washer
14. Choke linkage rod
15. Plug
16. Flat washer
17. Air screw spring
18. Air screw
19. Throttle stop screw spring
20. Throttle stop screw
21. O-ring
22. T-connector
23. Low speed jet
24. Main jet tube
25. Main jet holder
26. Main jet
27. Flat washer
28. Needle and seat assembly
29. Float
30. Float hinge pin
31. Float bowl gasket
32. Flat washer
33. Drain plug
34. Float bowl clip

Constant-Velocity Type

REMOVAL AND INSTALLATION

350 Models

1. Turn off the fuel supply at the petcock and drain the float bowls. Disconnect the fuel lines at the petcock. Remove the fuel tank.
2. CL Models: Remove the exhaust system.
3. Remove the plastic sidecovers and the air cleaners.
4. Loosen the connecting bands which hold the carburetors to the intake manifold. Remove the left carburetor from the intake manifold and loosen the choke band pinch-bolt, and slip the band off the shaft. Remove the cable stay and disconnect the cable from the throttle lever. Remove the right carburetor and disconnect the throttle cable in the same manner.
5. Installation is in the reverse order of the above, however, note the following points:

a. Connect the throttle cables before mounting the carburetors;

b. Mount the right carburetor first, then connect the choke band as the left carburetor is installed;

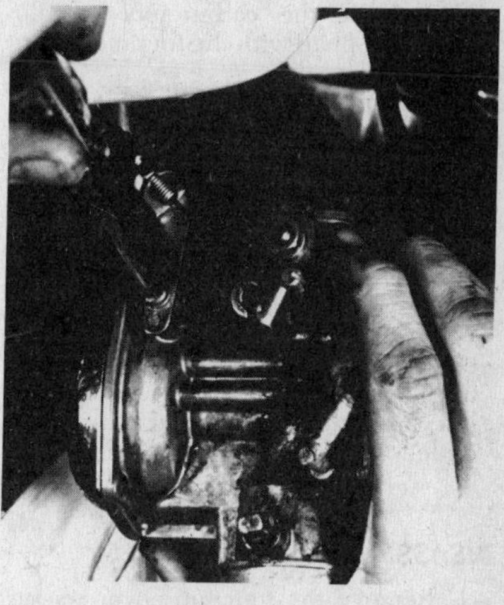

Removing the cable adjuster bracket (350)

c. Connect the fuel line from the right carburetor to the rear outlet on the petcock, and the fuel line from the left carburetor to the front outlet. Secure the fuel lines in place with a spring clip;

d. Turn the fuel on and check for leaks. Start the engine and check for air leaks around the intake manifold and air cleaner.

360 Models

1. Turn the fuel supply off at the petcock and drain the float bowls. Disconnect the fuel lines at the petcock and remove the fuel tank.
2. CL Models: Remove the exhaust system.
3. Loosen the connecting bands which secure the carburetors to the intake manifold and air cleaner. Pull the carburetors back toward the air cleaners until they are free of the intake manifold, then remove them by lowering them out from the left-side.
4. Disconnect the throttle cables from the cable stay. Loosen the choke band pinch-bolt and remove the choke band from the left carburetor.
5. Remove the carburetors from the mounting plate after removing the four mounting screws.
6. Installation is in the reverse order of the above, but note the following points:

a. Connect the choke band to both carburetors, tighten the pinch-bolt and bend the locktab up against the nut on the pinch-bolt;

b. Set the throttle lever to the stop screw and install the coil spring as shown in the accompanying illustration;

Set the throttle lever to the stop screw (1) and install the spring (2)

c. Mount the carburetors on the mounting plate with the four mounting screws;

d. Connect the throttle cables with the throttles fully closed. The closing cable is connected to the lower cable stay and the opening cable is connected to the top cable stay. Mount the carburetor assembly on the engine. Adjust the cables and secure them in place with the locknuts;

e. Connect the fuel lines to the petcock. The right carburetor is connected to the rear outlet on the petcock, the left carburetor is connected to the front outlet.

DISASSEMBLY (ALL MODELS)

1. Remove the four top cover screws and remove the top cover. Very carefully lift out the return spring and the throttle slide. If the needle is to be removed from the slide, unscrew the needle holder (360 models) or remove the spring retainer (350 models), and remove the needle.

2. Turn the carburetor upside down and remove the four float bowl screws and carefully remove the float bowl.

3. Remove the primary and secondary main jets. On 350 models, these are held in place with a retainer, while on 360 models, they unscrew.

4. Using a small drift, push out the float pivot pin and remove the float. Note that on 360 models, the float needle is removed with the float; on 350 models, the float needle can be lifted from the needle seat.

5. 360 models: Using a small wrench, unscrew the jet holder from the carburetor body, and push the needle jet out from the inside of the carburetor. The main nozzle located in front of the needle jet can also be pushed out of the carburetor body.

Removing the top cover

Removing the primary and secondary main jets and spring retainer (350 shown)

Removing the float needle

Removing the pilot jet

Removing the main nozzle

6. Unscrew the pilot jet from the carburetor.

7. 350 models: Using a small wooden dowel, push the needle jet and main nozzle out of the carburetor.

8. Remove the phillips head set screw from the float needle seat stay and remove the needle seat by lifting it out.

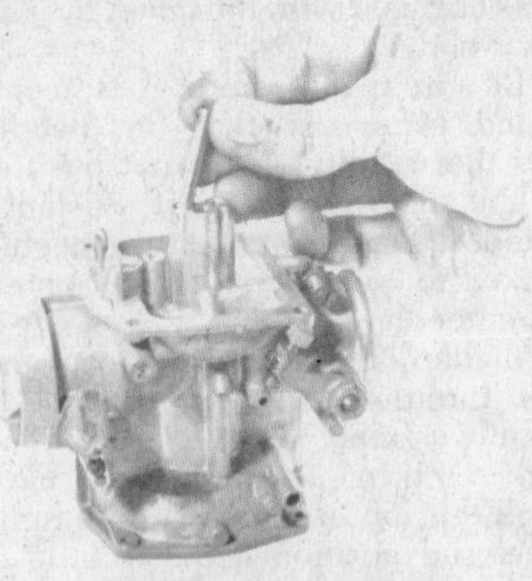

Removing the needle jet

Removing the needle seat

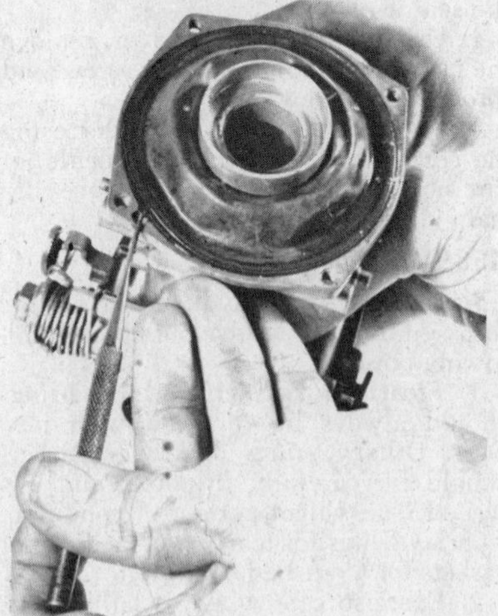

Fit the tab on the diaphragm into the slot in the body

9. Unscrew the pilot screw.

ASSEMBLY (ALL MODELS)

Assembly is basically the reverse of the disassembly procedures, but note the following points:

1. Float bowl gaskets and jet O-rings should always be replaced with new ones. Other O-rings and fiber gaskets should be carefully inspected and replaced if less than perfect in condition. Check O-rings for tears and cracks; fiber gaskets for a crushed condition.

2. Exercise care when installing jets, they are made of soft brass and are easily damaged.

3. Install the pilot screw, turning it in until lightly seated, then back it out the proper number of turns as listed in the chart at the end of this section.

4. Fit the tab on the diaphragm into the slot in the body.

5. Tighten the float bowl and top cover screws evenly and in an "X" pattern in order to prevent distortion.

FUEL PETCOCK AND LINES

Cleaning

1. Unscrew and remove the sediment bowl, take out the O-ring, and filter screen.

2. Clean the metal parts in solvent. Check that the filter screen is not punctured, and that the O-ring is not torn or otherwise damaged.

3. Run a little gas through the petcock to flush out any dirt. Catch the gas in a suitable container. Turning the petcock to "Reserve" for a few seconds should remove the better part of any water or dirt in the bottom of the fuel tank.

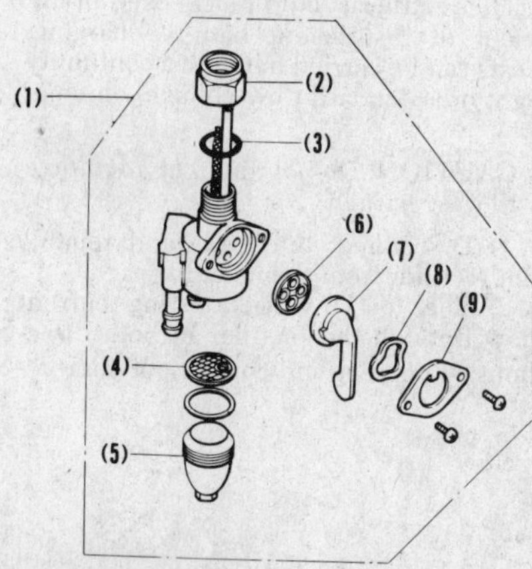

Petcock components

1. Petcock assembly
2. Nut
3. O-ring
4. Filter screen
5. Sediment bowl
6. Lever gasket
7. Lever
8. Lever spring
9. Set plate

Carburetor Specifications

Item	*CB/CL350 Engine No. 1000001–1045164*	*CB/CL350 Engine No. 1045165–1065278*	*CB/CL350 Engine No. 1065279–and later*	*SL350*	*CB/CJ360*	*CL360*
Setting Mark	350-A	3-C	3-D	A	745B	747B
Venturi Bore	28 mm	28 mm	28 mm	24 mm	28 mm	28 mm
Main Jet primary	#60	#70	#70	#120	#68	#68
secondary	#115	#110	#105	——	#68	#68
Air Jet primary	#50	#150	#150	#150	#150	#150
secondary	#50	#50	#50	——	#50	#50
Pilot Air Jet	#90	#90	#90	——	#85	#85
Needle Jet	——	——	——	2.515 mm	——	——
Slide Cutaway	——	——	——	2.5	——	——
Pilot Jet	#38	#35	#35	#40	#35	#35
Pilot Screw (turns out)	¾ ± ⅛	1 ± ⅛	1 ± ⅛	1 ± ⅛	1	1
Float Level (mm/in.)	19/0.75	21/0.83	26/1.05	26/1.05①	18.5/0.73	18.5/0.73

① SL350 K1-K2—25/0.98

—— Not applicable

4. Check petcock operation in all positions. There must be no fuel flow when the petcock lever is turned to the "Stop" position.

5. Install the filter screen, O-ring, and sediment bowl in that order. Check for leaks before operating the motorcycle.

Disassembly

At somewhat extended intervals, the petcock should be removed from the fuel tank and cleaned.

1. Drain the fuel tank completely. Disconnect the fuel lines from the petcock. Remove the sediment bowl, O-ring, and filter screen.

2. Unscrew the nut which holds the petcock to the fuel tank, and remove the petcock.

3. Remove the two screws from the fuel lever setting plate, and remove the setting plate, lever spring, lever, and gasket.

Assembly

1. Install the fuel valve gasket, lever, lever spring, and setting plate. Secure with the two screws.

2. Be sure that the petcock O-ring or gasket is in place and install the petcock on the fuel tank. Install the sediment bowl filter screen, O-ring, and sediment bowl.

3. Be sure that the fuel lines are firmly secured at their connections and the safety circlips are in place.

ELECTRICAL SYSTEM

IGNITION CIRCUIT

1. Troubleshooting the ignition system is made somewhat easier by the fact that the components for the two cylinders are completely independent.

2. If there is a no-spark condition at *both* cylinders, the trouble will be in the battery, fuse, or wiring connections. Check the 15A fuse (located near the battery) first. If this fuse is blown, none of the electrical components will function.

If the fuse is satisfactory, check the battery state-of-charge. Although a low battery may not operate the electric starter, it does not require a very high state-of-charge to spark the plugs, turning the engine over with the kick-starter.

Check the battery terminal connections, then the ignition circuit connections, ignition switch, etc.

3. In the event of hard starting, misfiring, or cutting out, first check the carburetors. Be sure that the fault is electrical before replacing any components. Be sure that all connections are clean, dry, and tight. Wiring plugs and connectors often accumulate dirt or water, and sometimes work loose. Check these first, then proceed as follows:

4. In the event of the above troubles, or a no-spark condition at one cylinder, the plug, plug cap, lead, coil, condenser, or points for that cylinder may be defective.

5. Remove the spark plug, clean it thoroughly, or replace it with a new one; gap the plug to 0.7–0.8 mm (0.028–0.032 in.). Connect it to its cap, and ground it against the cylinder head. Kick the engine over briskly. The spark produced should be thick and blue.

6. If there is no spark, or if the spark is weak and yellow, repeat the test using a piece of metal, such as a nail, inserted into the spark plug cap and held about ⅛

in. away from the cylinder. If the spark is healthy, the problem was the spark plug; if not, check the condition of the points. Inspect, clean, and gap the points or replace them if they are badly pitted or worn. If excessive arcing or sparking at the points is noted while the machine is running, the problem may be the condenser. A defective condenser will also cause new points to wear out quickly.

If new points have just been installed, a no-spark condition can be caused by damaged or improperly installed insulating washers on the points wire terminal.

7. If the problem is not in the points or the spark plug, the spark plug cap should be checked. Noise suppressor caps are fitted, which are designed to eliminate radio interference and provide a hotter spark by means of a resistor in the cap. Sometimes the resistor breaks down, and the cap then becomes an open circuit. Remove the cap from the spark plug lead, and ground the end of the lead against the cylinder head. If a fat, blue spark is produced when the engine is kicked over, the problem was the cap. Replace it with a new one.

8. If the cap checks out okay, carefully inspect the cable itself. Check for dirt or grease, cuts or cracks in the insulation, moisture, etc. If the lead is damaged, it must be replaced. This also involves replacing the coil.

9. If the trouble has not been pinpointed, the ignition coil windings should be checked for continuity, using an ohmmeter.

a. Disconnect the two low-tension coil leads (blue or yellow and black/white) and check for continuity between them. This is a check of the primary winding. If there is no continuity, replace the coil;

b. Check for continuity across the coil's blue or yellow low-tension lead and the high-tension (spark plug) lead. Resistance may be very high, but continuity must exist. This checks the secondary winding.

Even if continuity is present in the coil windings, it is possible that the coil is still defective. Replacing the coil temporarily with one which is known to be serviceable is recommended.

10. The condenser can be checked if a capacitance tester is available. Condensers should have a capacitance of approximately 0.25 mf. Checking with a "megger" (high-voltage ohmmeter) should yield a resistance of 5m ohms or better at 1,000v. Replace the condenser if it fails either test.

NOTE: *After testing, ground the condenser lead against the case to discharge it.*

As noted above, sparking at the points, or points which pit or burn rapidly would indicate a defective condenser. Bad condensers will cause mounds and matching depressions on the points.

11. If the trouble is a misfire, and the tests above do not pinpoint the problem, check the condition and operation of the automatic timing advance unit

CHARGING CIRCUIT

Voltage Regulator

A bad voltage regulator may cause the battery to go dead, or may overcharge it causing electrolyte loss, short light bulb life, etc. The regulator is located beneath the battery box, and is rubber mounted. It can be tested with an ohmmeter, continuity tester, or ammeter.

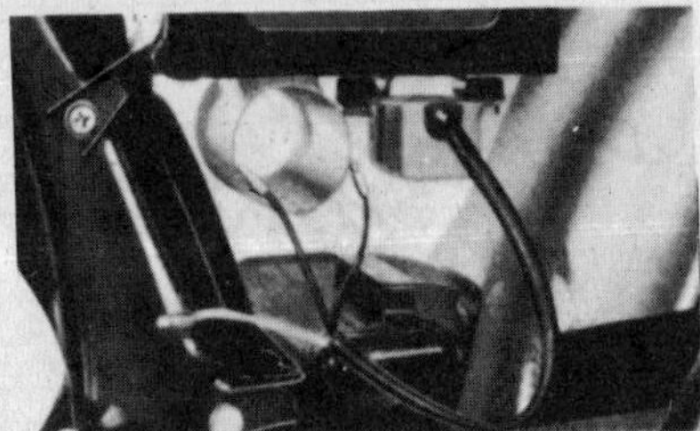

Voltage regulator location

1. If the battery goes dead, disconnect the three regulator leads (yellow, green, and black).

2. With an ohmmeter or continuity light, check for continuity between the yellow lead and the green lead. Check for continuity between the yellow lead and the motorcycle frame.

There must not be continuity in either case. If there is, the regulator must be replaced.

3. If an ammeter is available, connect it in series with the battery positive wire. Start and run the engine at more than 2,000 rpm. If the ammeter indicates that the battery is discharging, disconnect the regulator yellow lead and repeat the test. If the battery now shows that it is receiving a charge, the regulator must be replaced. If no change is noted, proceed with the rectifier and alternator tests which follow.

4. If the battery overcharges, check as follows:

Assuming that the battery is in good condition and *fully* charged, start the engine and connect a good voltmeter across the battery terminals. Run the engine at 4,000 rpm. The voltage across the battery should increase to between 14–15 volts, but not more. If the meter reads more than 15 volts, the regulator must be replaced.

NOTE: *This test will not be valid unless the battery is fully charged. To check this, run the engine until the voltage stabilizes, then disconnect the regulator black lead. If the voltage increases, the results of the test were valid.*

5. When mounting the regulator, be sure that the rubber dampers are in place. The regulator could be damaged by excess vibration.

Rectifier

The rectifier is located behind the battery (350) or under the battery case.

The rectifier should be checked in the event of insufficient battery charging. Tests can be carried out with a continuity light or a standard (low-voltage) ohmmeter.

CAUTION: *Do not apply high-voltage to the rectifier.*

1. Disconnect the leads and remove the rectifier from the machine.

2. The test involves testing current flow through the rectifier in both directions. The rectifier consists of four

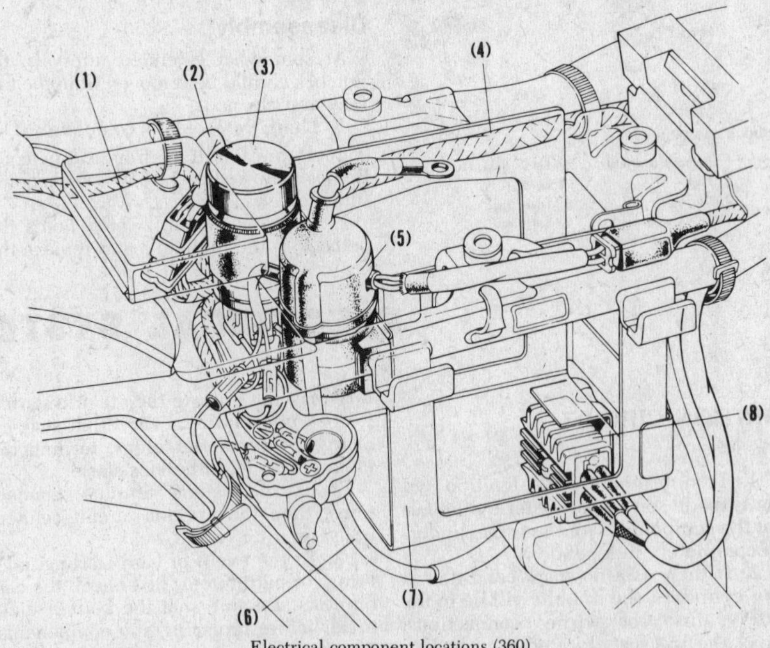

Electrical component locations (360)

1. Fuse box
2. Fuse box leads
3. Flasher relay
4. Wiring harness
5. Starter switch
6. Starter motor cable
7. Battery case
8. Rectifier

diodes. When in working condition, a diode will pass current in one direction only.

If the diode passes current in both directions, or in neither direction, it is defective. If any of the diodes is defective, the rectifier must be replaced.

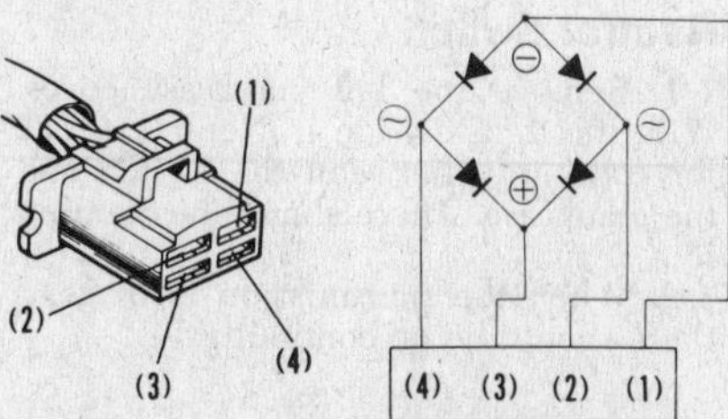

Rectifier wires: (1) green, (2) red/white, (3) yellow, (4) pink

3. Connect the negative lead of the tester to the green wire, and the positive lead to the yellow, red/white, and pink wires in turn.

In each case, note whether or not there is continuity.

NOTE: *On an ohmmeter, "continuity" will be indicated by a resistance of 5–40 ohms. "No continuity" by a resistance of 100 or more ohms.*

4. Now reverse the tester connections, connecting the positive tester lead to the

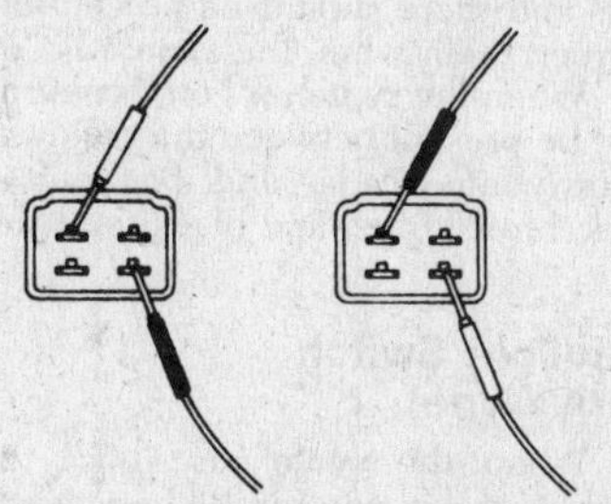

Rectifier is checked by reversing the connections and checking for current flow

green wire, and the negative to each of the others in turn.

In every case, the reaction of the tester must be the opposite of the first test: i.e., if the first test showed continuity between two leads, reversing the tester connections must show no continuity.

Current flow in both, or in neither direction, for any two leads indicates that the rectifier must be replaced.

Alternator

The alternator should be checked in the event of low or no battery charging not attributable to the other components.

1. A dynamic output test can be carried out if a voltmeter and ammeter are available. The battery *must* be fully charged or the test may be invalid.

Hook up the voltmeter across the battery terminals, disconnect the battery red/white lead and connect it to the ammeter. Connect the other side of the ammeter to the battery positive terminal.

Disconnect the black regulator lead.

Start the engine and compare the voltmeter and ammeter readings with lights off and lights on (high-beam) at the given

Alternator Charging Specifications

	350	360
Beginning of Charging (12.6v)		
lights off	under 1400 rpm	under 1550 rpm
high-beam on	under 2000 rpm	under 2100 rpm
5000 rpm		
lights off	14.8v/1.5–2.5A	14.8v/1.2A (min)
high-beam on	14.8v/1.2–2.5A	14.8v/1.2A (min)
10,000 rpm		
lights off	15.5v/4A (max)	15.5v/4A (max)
high-beam on	15.5v/4A (max)	15.5v/4A (max)

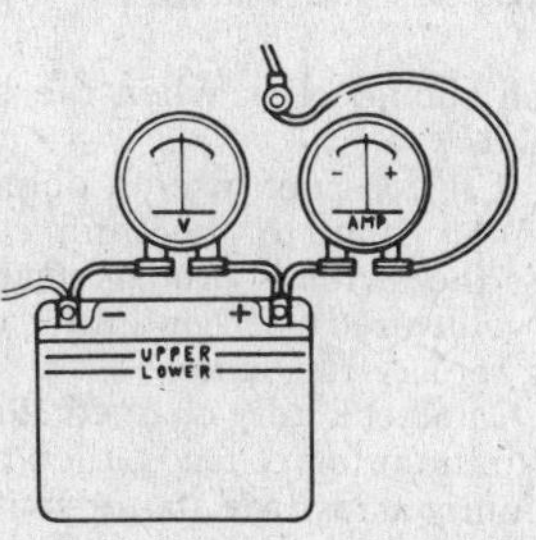

Alternator output set-up

rpm.

If the readings are not within 10% of the given specifications, the alternator should be replaced.

NOTE: *The alternator should not be excessively hot when this test is carried out.*

2. Using an ohmmeter or continuity tester, a static stator test can be carried out.

Disconnect the alternator wiring at the plastic connector.

Check for continuity between the white, the yellow, and the pink leads. Continuity must exist, or the stator assembly has a broken wire and it must be replaced.

Check for continuity between the yellow lead and the stator core. If continuity exists, there is a short, and the stator must be replaced.

Checking stator continuity

STARTER MOTOR

1. If the starter motor spins when the button is pushed, but the engine does not, the starter clutch is defective. Refer to "Engine and Transmission," for starter clutch removal and inspection procedures.

2. If the warning lights dim when the starter button is pushed, but the engine and starter do not turn over, the battery may be too low, or the starter may be defective.

3. If nothing happens when the starter button is pushed, either the starter solenoid is defective, or there is a loose wire in the electric starter circuit.

Removal and Disassembly

1. Disconnect the lead at the starter motor.

2. Remove the alternator cover, both sections of the left crankcase cover, and disconnect the neutral switch lead.

3. Remove the alternator rotor, using either the special puller, or the rear axle

4. Remove the starter sprocket setting plate (secured by a phillips screw), and remove the two sprockets and chain together.

5. Remove the two screws which secure the starter motor, and tap the starter out of the case.

6. To disassemble the starter, remove the two long phillips screws and remove the end plates.

Disconnecting the brush leads

NOTE: *Exercise caution when removing the output side end plate as this contains the reduction gears.*

7. Disconnect the starter carbon brush leads (2) and remove the brush mounting plate.

Disassembly past this point is not necessary.

Inspection

1. Use an ohmmeter or continuity tester to check the starter motor.

2. Check for continuity between each of the commutator segments. There must be continuity between all of them. If there is a dead spot, the starter must be replaced.

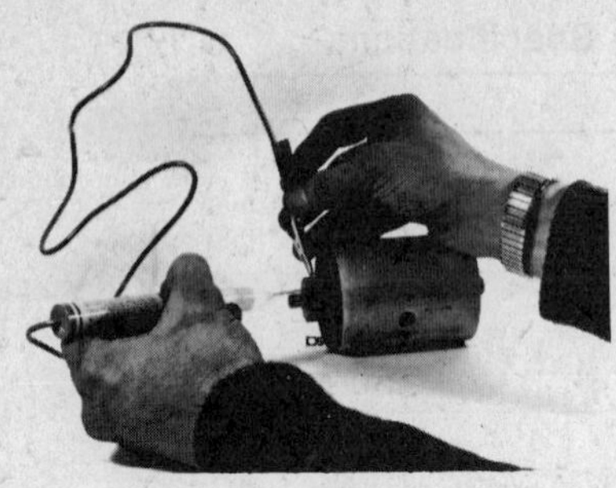

Checking for continuity between each of the commutator segments

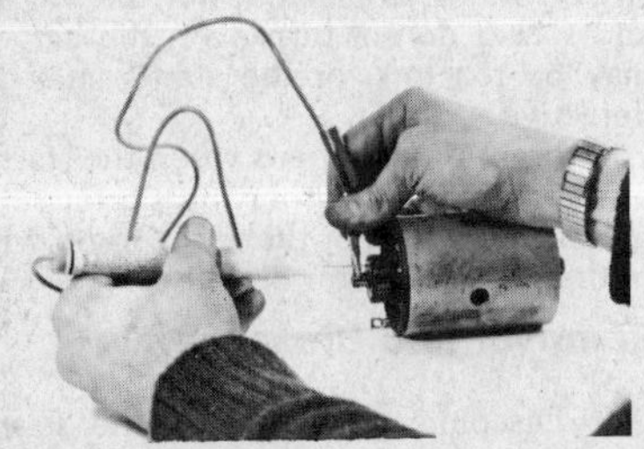

Checking for continuity between the commutator and the armature core

3. Check for continuity between the armature core and the commutator; there must be none. If continuity exists, the starter must be replaced.
4. Check for continuity between the starter lead terminal and the brush leads. Continuity must exist or the starter must be replaced.
5. Measure the length of each carbon brush. Replace them if either is less than 7.5 mm (0.3 in.).

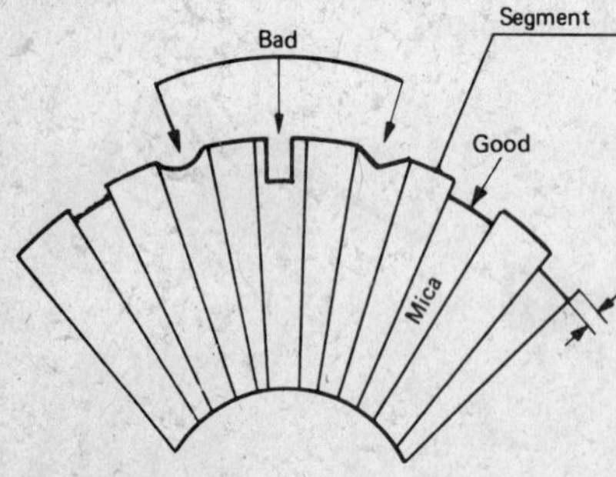

Commutator groove condition

6. Clean the commutator surface thoroughly with a solvent. Check that there is no scoring on the commutator surface. The mica insulation should undercut the commutator segments by at least 0.3 mm (0.012 in.). If less than this, the mica should be undercut using a piece of a hacksaw blade or the like. Be sure to clean the commutator surface thoroughly after this operation. Remove any sharp edges.

Assembly and Installation

1. Reverse the above procedures. Be sure that the output side O-rings are in place.

2. After assembling the starter, check that the armature will turn without excessive binding.

Starter Solenoid

1. The starter switch (or solenoid) can be checked by disconnecting the high-tension lead from the starter motor, and pushing the starter button. The starter switch should click when the button is pushed.

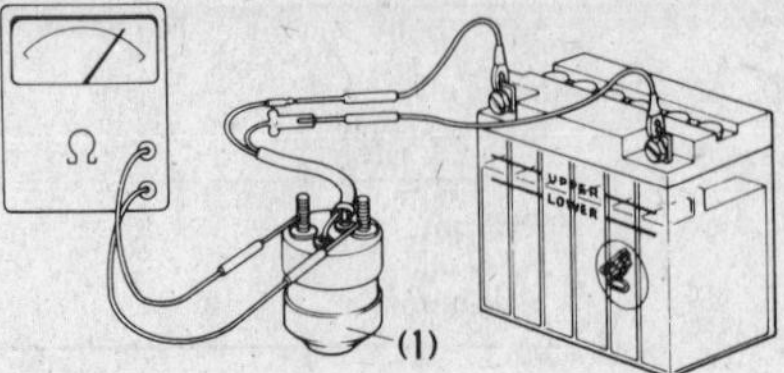

Checking the starter switch (1)

2. If it does not, use an ohmmeter or continuity light to check for continuity across the switch's primary leads (black and yellow/red). If continuity does not exist, replace the switch.
3. Connect a fully charged 12-volt battery to the primary leads, then check for continuity across the starter switch high-tension leads as illustrated. If there is no continuity, replace the switch.

ELECTRICAL SWITCHES

All electrical switches are easily checked with an ohmmeter or self-powered continuity light after disconnecting the switch leads at the plastic connectors.

Ignition Switch

1. With the key turned to the first position, check for continuity between the black and red leads. If continuity does not exist, replace the switch.
2. With the key in the first position, continuity must exist between the brown and the brown/white leads.

3. With the key in the second position, continuity must exist between the red and brown leads.

Clutch Switch

1. Late models have a clutch starter switch incorporated into the clutch lever holder to prevent operation of the electric starter when in gear with the clutch engaged.
2. Check for continuity between the green and green/red switch leads. Continuity should exist only when the clutch is disengaged.

Brake Light Switches

1. Check for continuity across the front brake light switch terminals. Continuity should occur when the brake lever has moved 5–10 mm (0.2–0.4 in.), measured at the tip of the lever.
2. Check for continuity between the black and green/yellow leads to check the rear brake light switch. Continuity should occur when the brake pedal has moved about 25 mm (1 in.). This switch is adjustable.

Kill Button

1. The kill button should show no continuity between the black and the black/white leads when in either "off" position. When in the "run" position, there must be continuity.

Neutral Switch

1. Remove the left crankcase cover. With the transmission in Neutral, check for continuity between the switch and the crankcase. There should be continuity.
2. When the transmission is in gear, there should be no continuity.

Horn

1. If the horn will not function, connect a 12-volt battery directly to the horn terminals. If the horn does not sound it is defective.
2. If the horn does sound, check the horn button by disconnecting the light green lead and check for continuity between the lead and ground, which should be present when the horn button is pushed.

Headlight Switch (Late-Type)

1. There are five headlight switch leads and there should be no continuity between them when the switch is "off."
2. When the switch is "on," continuity must be present between the yellow and yellow/white leads, and between the black, brown/blue, and black/red leads.

Headlight Switch (Early Type)

1. When the switch is "off," there should not be continuity between the leads.

2. When the switch is in the high-beam position (H), there should be continuity between the yellow/white and the yellow leads and between the black, blue, and brown/white leads.
3. When the switch is in the low-beam (L) position, there must be continuity between the yellow/white and yellow leads, and between the black, white, and brown/white leads.

Dimmer Switch

On late models with a separate dimmer switch on the left handlebar:
1. In the high position, there must be continuity between black/yellow and blue wires.
2. In the low-beam position, there must be continuity between the black/yellow and the white wires.

Turn Signal Switch

1. When the left-hand turn signal is activated, there will be continuity between the gray lead and the orange lead.
2. When the right-hand switch is activated, continuity will exist between the gray lead and the light blue lead.

WIRING DIAGRAMS

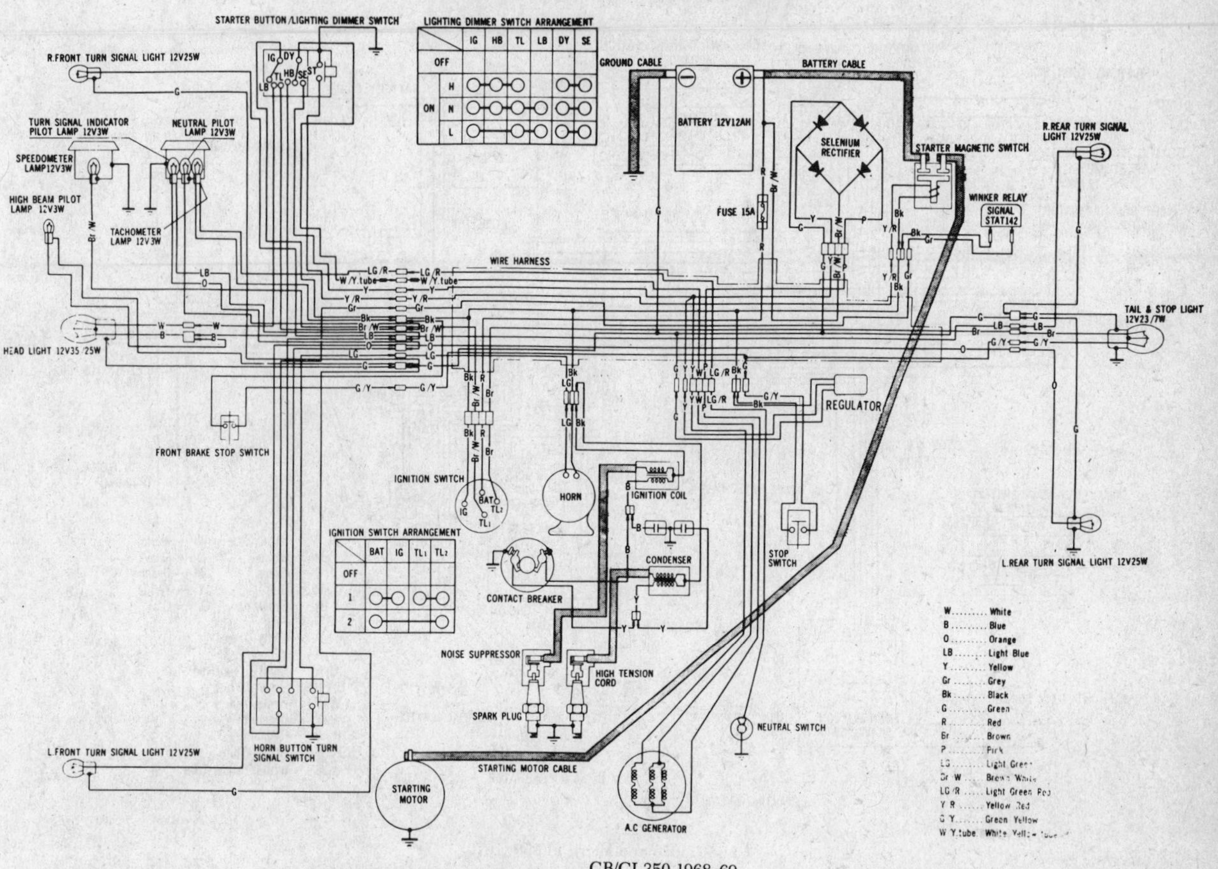

CB/CL350 1968–69

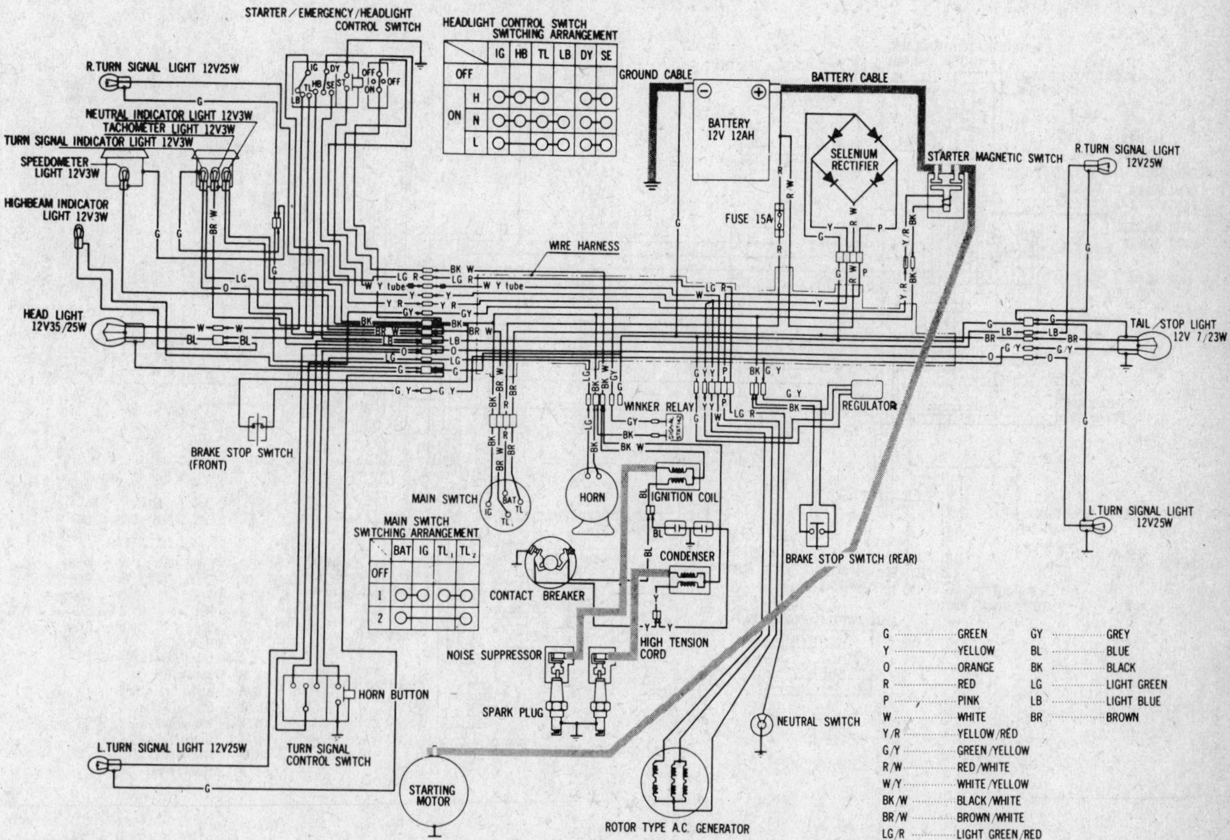

CB350 1970 and later

WIRING DIAGRAMS

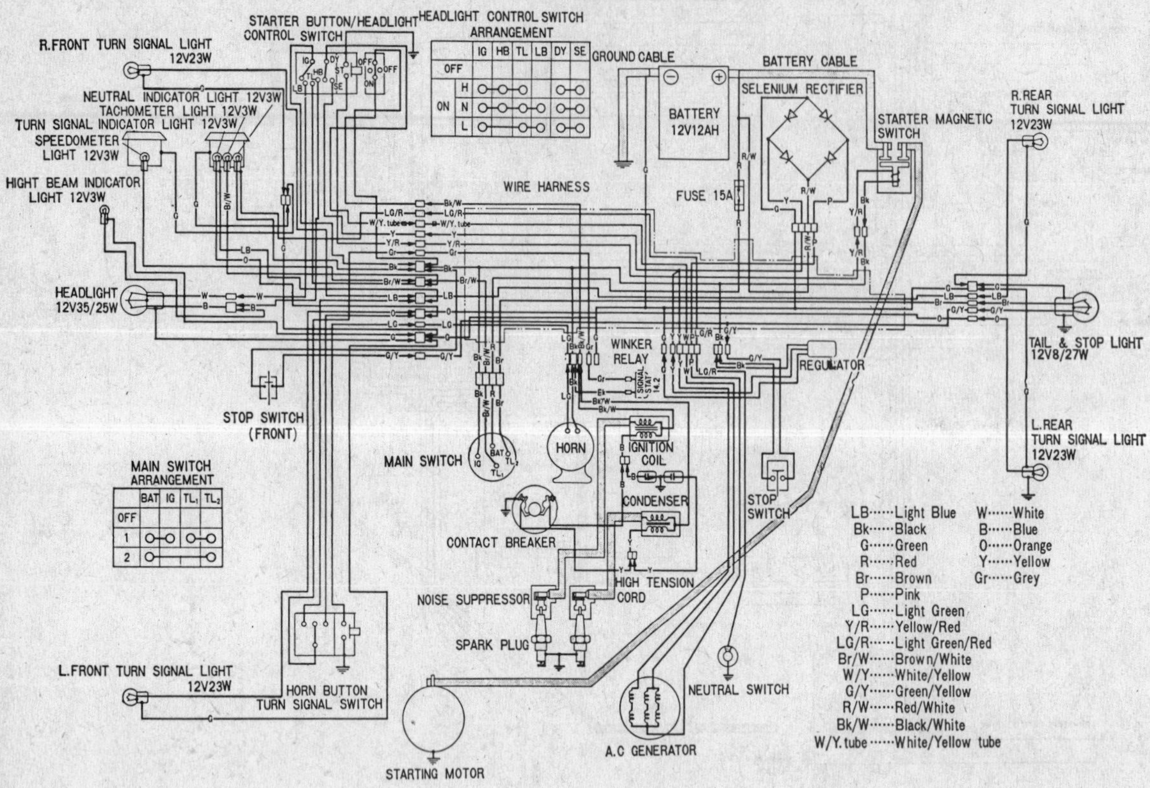

CL350 (1970 and later); SL350 (1970)

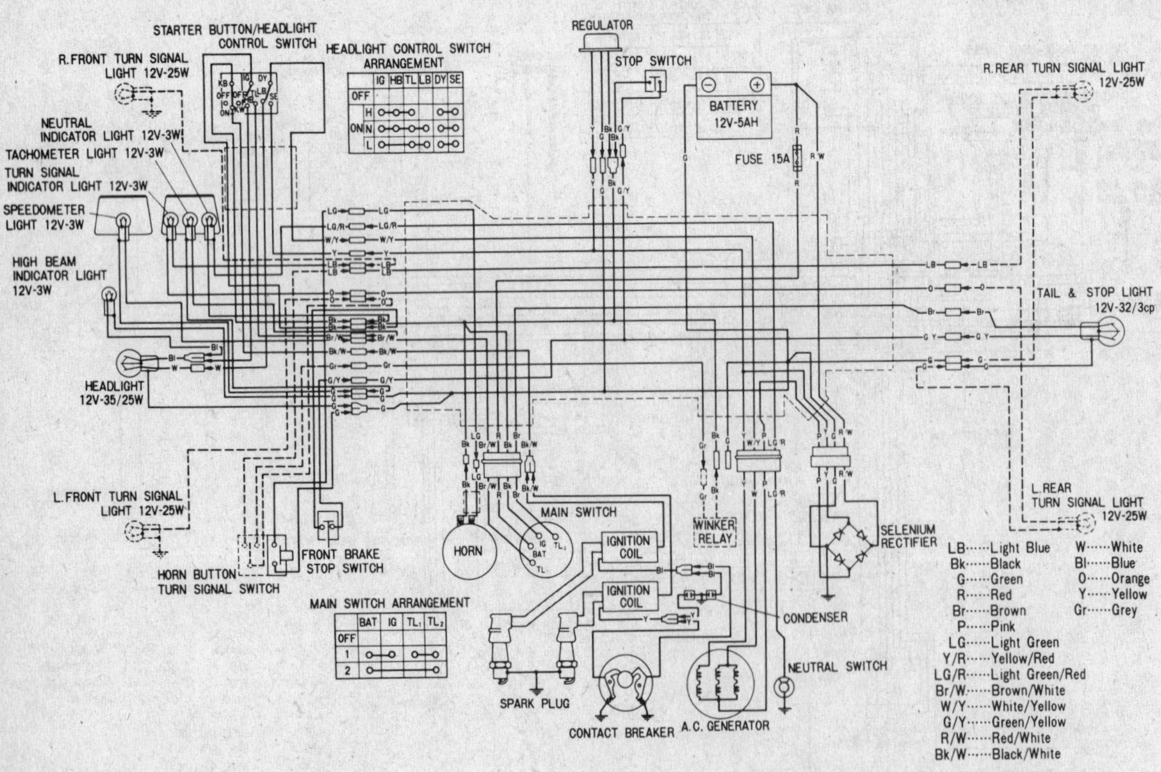

SL350K1/K2

WIRING DIAGRAMS

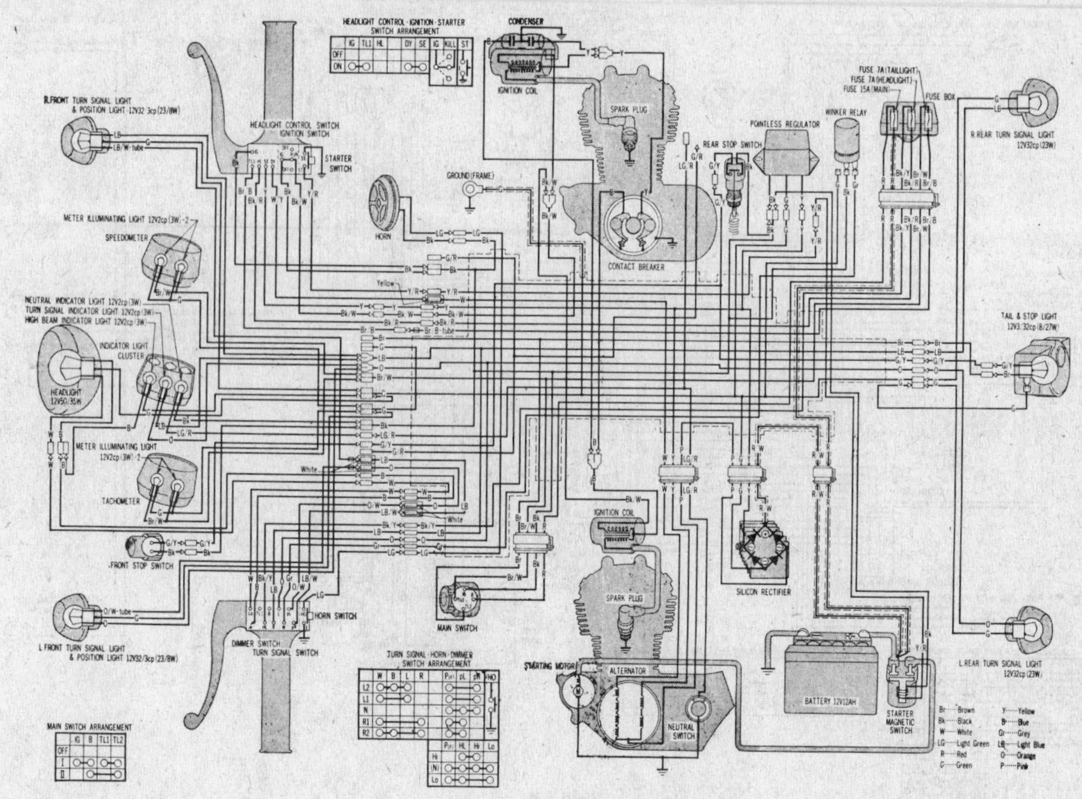

CB/CL360

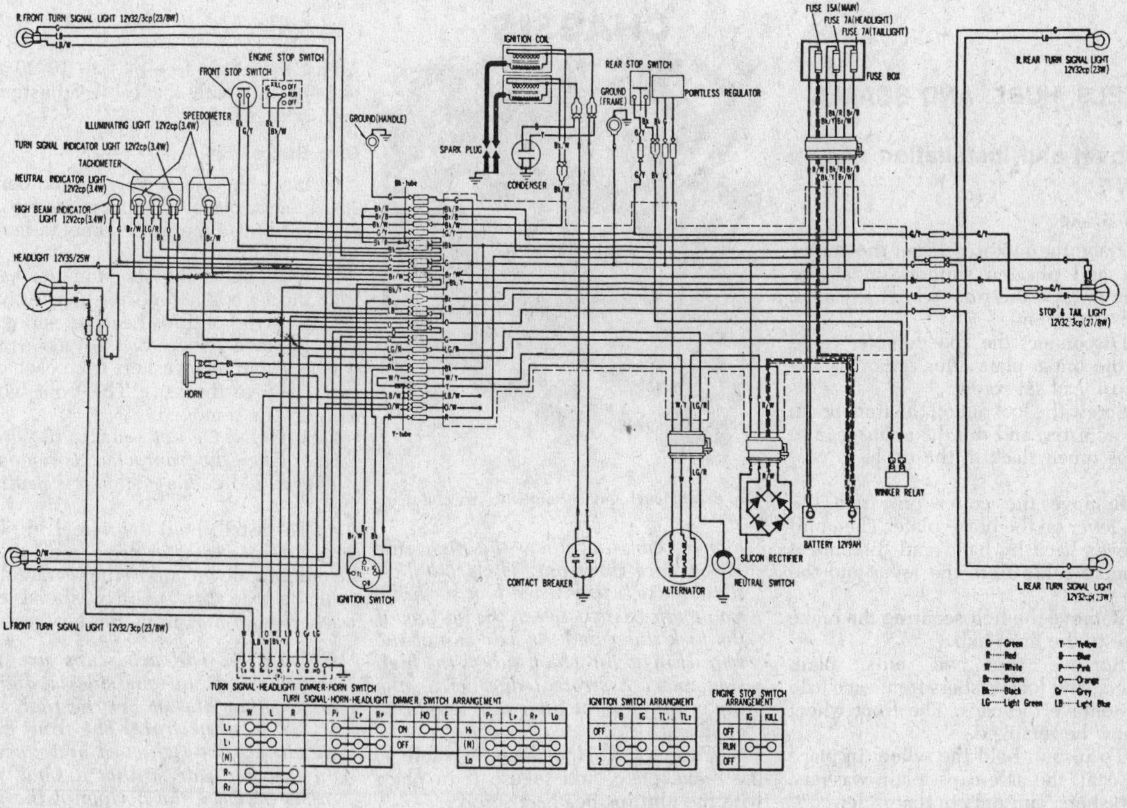

CJ360T

WIRING DIAGRAMS

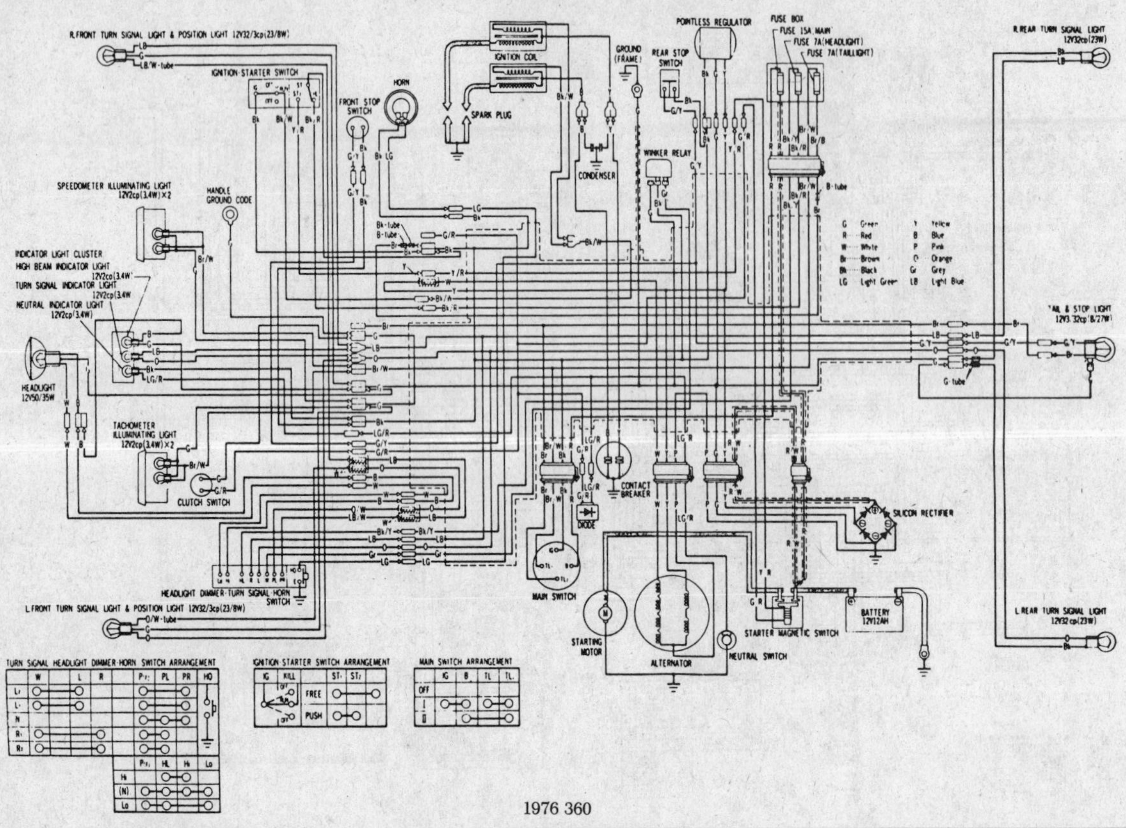

1976 360

CHASSIS

WHEELS, HUBS, AND BRAKES

Removal and Installation

FRONT

Drum Brake

1. Place the motorcycle on the center stand, and place a support under the engine to raise the front wheel at least 2 in. off the ground.
2. Disconnect the speedometer cable from the brake plate after removing the phillips head set screw.
3. Screw the locknut off the front brake cable adjuster, and run the adjuster in to give as much slack in the cable as possible.
4. Remove the cotter pin from the brake lever on the brake plate. Then pull the lever back by hand and disconnect the brake cable from the lever and the brake plate.
5. Remove the bolt securing the brake anchor to the front hub.
6. Remove the two nuts, plain washers, and lockwashers from each axle cap. Remove the caps. The front wheel can now be removed.
7. To install, hold the wheel in place and install the axle caps, plain washers, lockwashers, and nuts in that order.

CAUTION: *The axle caps are machined unevenly (one side is slightly higher than the other) the high side MUST face the front. The front bolt should also be tightened first so that a small gap exists between the bottom of the fork slider and the axle cap at the rear. If in doubt which side is the high side, place a straightedge across the top of the cap, the high side should be apparent.*

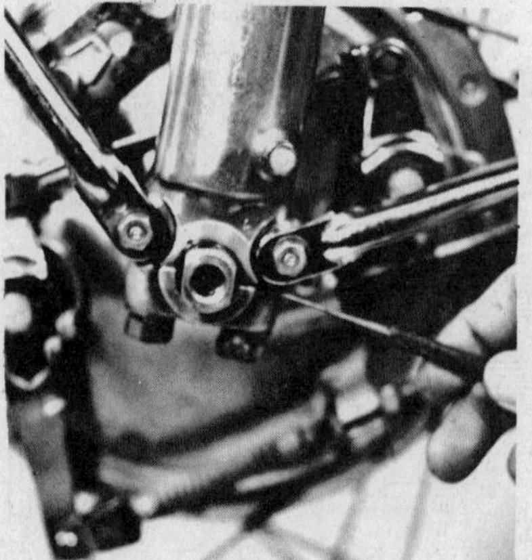

Cap should touch fork at front with space at rear

8. Connect the speedometer cable to the brake plate, and secure it in place with the phillips head set screw.
9. Bolt the brake anchor to the brake plate. Connect the brake cable to the brake lever and then to the brake plate.

Adjust the cable free-play to 10–20 mm (0.6–0.8 in.) with the cable adjuster on the brake plate.

Disc Brake

1. Place the motorcycle on the center stand, and place a support under the engine to raise the front wheel at least 2 in. off the ground.
2. Disconnect the speedometer cable from the speedometer drive housing after removing the phillips head set screw.
3. Remove the two nuts, plain washers, and lockwashers from each axle cap. Remove the caps. The front wheel can now be removed.

CAUTION: *Do not squeeze the brake lever when the front wheel is removed. This will force the piston in the caliper out.*

4. To install, hold the wheel in place with the speedometer drive housing facing slightly down and to the rear, and install the axle caps, plain washers, lockwashers, and nuts in that order.

CAUTION: *The axle caps are machined unevenly (one side is slightly higher than the other) the high side MUST face the front. The front bolts should also be tightened first starting on the disc side so that a small gap exists between the bottom of the fork slider and the axle cap at the rear. If in doubt which side is the high side, place a straightedge across the top of the cap, the high side should be apparent.*

5. Connect the speedometer cable to the speedometer drive housing, and secure it in place with the phillips head set screw.

REAR

1. Place the motorcycle on its center stand so that the rear wheel is off the ground.
2. Remove the mufflers (CB models only), or remove the lower shock mounting bolts so the axle drops below the mufflers.
3. Remove the cotter pin, nut, lockwasher, and plain washer from the brake anchor bolt, and separate the brake anchor from the brake plate.
4. Remove the rear brake adjusting nut, depress the brake pedal, and separate the brake rod from the brake lever. Place the clevis pin, spring, and adjusting nut on the brake rod for safekeeping.

Disconnecting the rear brake anchor at the brake plate

5. Remove the cotter pin from the rear axle nut. Remove the axle nut and flat washer.
6. Remove the masterlink from the drive chain. Place the masterlink on the end of the chain for safekeeping. If the chain doesn't have a masterlink, loosen the chain adjuster locknuts and run the adjusters in. Move the wheel forward in the swing arm and slip the drive chain off the rear sprocket once the axle is removed. This can be done for either type of chain and does not require removal of the masterlink.
7. Pull the axle out from the right-side and remove the wheel assembly from the swing arm.

NOTE: *Place the wheel spacers on the axle in the order that they are removed, and screw the axle nut on the axle for safekeeping.*

8. To install the wheel: wrap the drive chain around the rear sprocket. Hold the wheel in place and slip the axle in place from the right-side. Be sure that the wheel spacers are in their correct locations. If the masterlink was removed, place both ends of the chain on the rear sprocket and install the masterlink as shown with the open end of the spring clip facing opposite the direction of rotation.

9. Turn the axle nut on finger-tight. Adjust the drive chain slack; the slack, measured midway between the sprockets, should be about ¾ in. Refer to "Maintenance."
10. Secure the brake anchor to the brake plate with a plain washer, lockwasher, nut, and a new cotter pin in that order.

DIRECTION OF TRAVEL

Install the spring clip with the closed end facing the direction of chain travel

11. Slip the brake cable or brake rod through the fitting in the brake lever and screw on the adjusting nut. Adjust the cable so that the brake pedal has 1 in. of free-play before the brake shoes contact the drum.
12. Tighten the axle nut to the proper torque. The proper torque for your model can be found in the "Chassis Torque Specifications" chart at the end of this section. Then back the nut off until a slot in the axle nut is lined up with a hole in the axle. Secure the axle nut in place with a new cotter pin.

Drum Brake Service

All models use a single-leading shoe rear brake, while, a twin-leading shoe is used on the front. Hondas use brakes in which the lining is bonded to the brake shoe. Lining and shoe, therefore, are purchased and replaced as a single unit.

1. Remove the wheel from the motorcycle. On the front wheel, unscrew the axle. Remove the brake plate from the hub.
2. Brakes can be inspected on the brake plate.
3. Inspect the lining for wear. There should be at least 0.1 in. (2.5 mm) of lining material left (measured at the linings thinnest point) or the shoes must be replaced.
4. Inspect the linings for grooves or scoring. These may be caused by particles of dirt which have entered the drum. If badly scored, the shoes should be replaced. If scoring of the shoes is evident, the drum should be inspected for the same type of damage.

Be sure that there is no oil or grease present on the linings. Oil-impregnated linings must be replaced. If the linings show this condition, determine the source of the lubricant: defective wheel bearing oil seals, excessive chain lube, etc.

5. If the linings are usable, rough up the surface with coarse sandpaper. Then clean the linings with alcohol or laquer thinner. Clean the brake drum with the same solvent.
6. To disassemble the brake plate, remove the cotter pin(s) and washer(s) from the brake pivot(s). Grasp each shoe and fold them toward the center of the brake plate. They may be installed in the same manner.
7. Remove the brake springs. Remove the brake lever pinch-bolt(s) and pull the lever(s) off the splined brake cam(s).

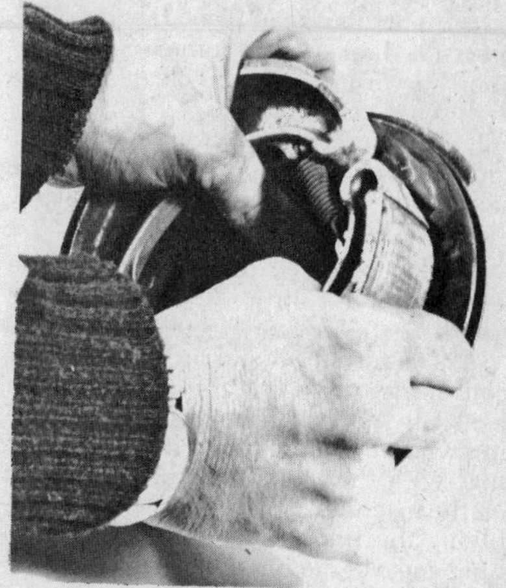

Removing the shoes from the plate

NOTE: *The plurals refer to the twin-leading shoe brakes.*

8. Push the brake cam(s) out of the brake plate from the outside using hand-pressure or if necessary by tapping with a plastic mallet. Remove the plain washer and dust seals from the brake plate.
9. Check that the brake lever pinch-bolts are not bent. This can easily happen if they are overtightened. Replace any bolts in this condition. Inspect the brake lever splines and replace the lever(s) if these are worn or stripped.
10. Inspect the splines on the brake cam(s). These should be in good condition. Check that the brake cam(s) are not bent and that they can rotate freely in the brake plate passage. If it will not, use a fine grade of sandpaper on the camshafts and the surface of the brake plate passage.
11. Clean the cam(s) thoroughly in a solvent to remove any old grease, rust, or corrosion. Use sandpaper or emery cloth to polish the cams. Clean off any residue; before reassembly, smear the cams with chassis grease.
12. Inspect the brake plate for cracks or fractures, and replace it if necessary.
13. Check the condition of the brake springs, noting any twisted or fatigued hooks. Replace any broken, rusted, or old springs with new ones.
14. Clean all parts thoroughly with a suitable solvent, making a special effort to remove the dust and built-up dirt from the backing plate.
15. When reassembling the hub, note the following points:
    a. Ensure that the brake cams are lubricated with chassis grease;
    b. The use of new dust seals is recommended;
    c. Lubricate the brake shoe pivot points with a little grease;
    d. Install the shoes as on removal. Hook them together with the springs, and fold them down over the brake cam(s) and pivot(s). Install new cotter pins to the pivot points;
    e. When installing the brake lever on the brake cam, be sure that the punch marks on the lever and cam align.

BRAKE DRUMS

1. Upon disassembly of the hub, inspect the brake drum surface for condition. The drums must be clean and free from score marks or rust.
2. Rust can be removed from the drum surface with sandpaper. Polish the surface until it is shiny, then clean it thoroughly.
3. Alcohol or lacquer thinner can be used to remove dirt or deposits from the drum.
4. The drum should be checked for concentricity. An out-of-round condition is usually noticeable as an on-off-on feeling when the brake is applied while riding. With the wheel assembly mounted on the machine, spin the wheel while applying the brake very lightly. The rubbing noise of the brakes against the drum should be heard for the entire revolution of the wheel.
5. An out-of-round condition and most scoring can be removed by having the drum turned on a lathe.

Disc Brake Service

When handling disc brake fluid, observe the following cautions:

a. Brake fluid absorbs moisture very quickly, and then becomes useless. Therefore, never use fluid from an old or unsealed container;

b. Brake fluid will quickly damage paint. Place a protective cover on the gas tank;

c. Use only DOT #3 brake fluid.

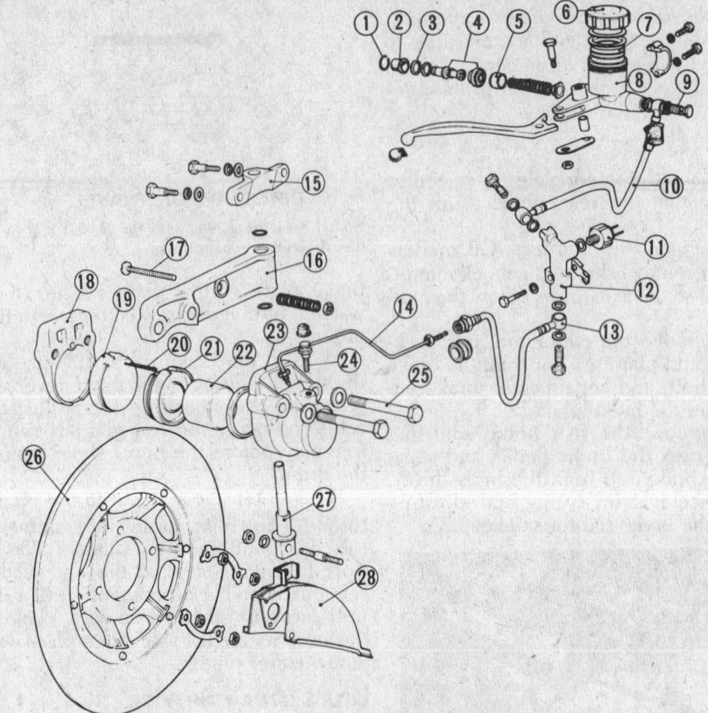

Front disc brake components

1. Boot clip
2. Boot
3. Internal circlip
4. Piston
5. Primary cup
6. Oil cup cap
7. Diaphragm
8. Master cylinder
9. Oil bolt
10. Front brake hose
11. Stop switch
12. 3-way joint
13. Front brake hose
14. Front brake pipe
15. Caliper holder joint
16. Caliper holder
17. Caliper adjust bolt
18. Caliper half (inner)
19. Pad (inner)
20. Cotter pin
21. Pad (outer)
22. Piston
23. Caliper half (outer)
24. Bleeder valve
25. Caliper securing bolts
26. Front brake disc
27. Caliper holder
28. Disc cover

FLUSHING

The brake system should be flushed out every 8,000 miles, or once a year.

1. Attach a length of vinyl tube, about 4 mm in diameter, to the bleed screw on the brake caliper and put the other end into a small container.
2. Remove the master cylinder cap, and the diaphragm. Loosen the bleed screw about ½ turn. Pull the brake lever slowly to the handgrip, then tighten the bleed screw. Release the lever. Repeat until the master cylinder is almost empty.
3. Add new brake fluid to the master cylinder and continue squeezing and releasing the brake lever slowly until the new fluid begins to come out of the vinyl tube. Bleed the system as outlined below.

BLEEDING

1. Needed for this operation are a torque wrench, a small cup, and a vinyl tube with an inside diameter of 4 mm.
2. Be sure that the reservoir is topped up. After checking the reservoir level, replace the diaphragm and cap.
3. Connect the vinyl tube to the bleed screw on the caliper, making sure that it is a tight fit; then insert the other end of the tube into a small container with several inches of brake fluid in it. Be sure that the end of the tube is below the level of the fluid in the container.
4. Apply the brake lever *slowly* several times, then hold it ON.
5. While holding the brake lever on, loosen the bleed screw. The brake lever will be pulled toward the handgrip. Close the bleed screw BEFORE the lever bottoms out on the handgrip.
6. Repeat the procedure until the fluid issuing from the lower end of the tube is completely free of air bubbles.

NOTE: *During the operation, keep a check on the reservoir fluid level, maintaining it near its normal position.*

7. Tighten the bleed screw to 4.5–6.7 ft lbs.
8. Top up the reservoir to the level line.

PAD REPLACEMENT

1. Both pads should be replaced as a set when either pad is worn past the red limit line.

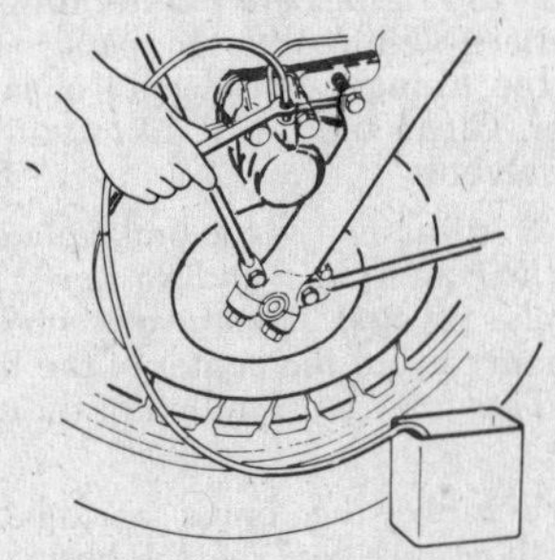

Bleeding the disc brake

2. Disconnect the brake line from caliper A and cover the open end with the rubber bleeder cap, which will keep out dirt or foreign matter.

To remove the caliper halves for replacement of the pads, disconnect the brake line (1), remove the setting bolts (2), and remove the caliper halves (3 and 4)

3. Loosen the caliper setting bolts about ¼ turn.
4. Remove the front wheel. Now the caliper setting bolts can be removed, and the two caliper halves can be separated from the caliper pivot arm.
5. To remove pad B (the pad closest to the wheel) from caliper B, remove the cotter pin from the top of the pad.
6. To remove pad A (piston pad) from Caliper A, hold the caliper with the pad facing down, and tap the caliper lightly on top. The pad should fall out.

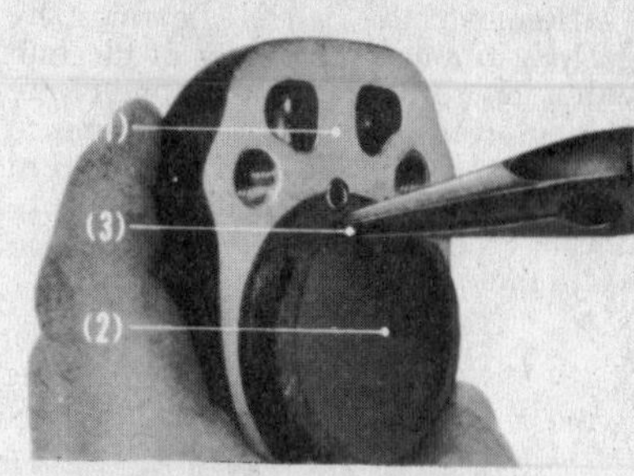

To remove pad B (2) from caliper B (1), first remove cotter pin (3)

7. When installing pads, apply a small amount of silicon grease to the sides of the pad, and to the center of the back of the pad.

CAUTION: *Avoid getting any grease or oil on the braking surface of the pad.*

8. Install pad B into Caliper B and secure with a new cotter pin. Install pad A into caliper A with the slot in the pad facing the top of the caliper.

9. Install the two caliper halves to the caliper pivot arm and tighten the two setting bolts.

NOTE: *Fitting new pads in the place of a set which were considerably worn will cause the fluid level to rise. The excess fluid will be forced out of the inlet passage when the front wheel is mounted and the piston is forced back into the caliper.*

10. Install the front wheel taking care to locate the disc between the pads. It may be necessary to turn the caliper adjusting screw clockwise to fit the wheel. The piston pad may have to be forced back in the caliper. With the wheel in place connect the brake line and check that the setting bolts are tightened to the proper torque of 9–12 ft lbs. Adjust the caliper and bleed the system.

NOTE: *After installing new pads, avoid hard application of the brake for at least 50 miles.*

CALIPER ADJUSTMENT

1. The caliper should be adjusted whenever the pads are replaced.
2. Place the motorcycle on the center stand, and place a support under the engine to raise the front wheel off the ground.

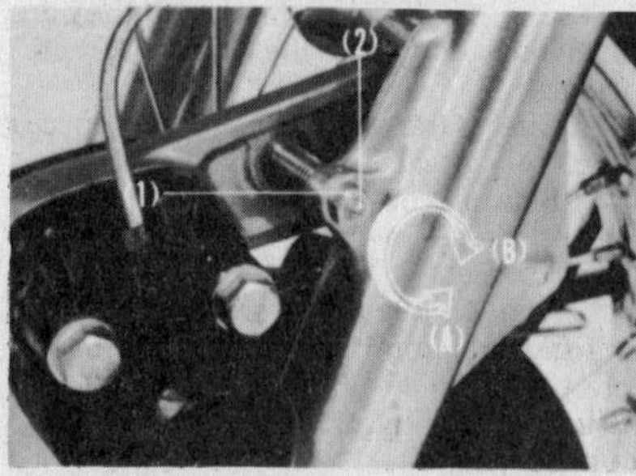

Caliper adjusting screw (1), and locknut (2)

3. Using a 10 mm socket, loosen the adjuster screw locknut. With a small screwdriver turn the adjusting screw clockwise until the wheel rotates freely, then rotate the adjusting screw counterclockwise until the fixed pad (pad B) just contacts the disc.
4. Turn the adjusting screw another ½–1 turn clockwise so that there is a small clearance between pad B and the disc. Tighten the locknut.

CALIPER REMOVAL AND DISASSEMBLY

NOTE: *A compressed air supply will be necessary to remove the piston from the caliper.*

1. Remove the front wheel.
2. Disconnect the hydraulic brake line from the caliper, and fit the rubber cap from the bleeder valve onto the end of the brake line to prevent dirt from entering the system.
3. Remove the caliper adjusting screw locknut from the adjusting screw and unscrew the adjusting screw from the right-side. Remove the adjusting screw spring.

Caliper mounting bolts (1 and 2), and adjusting screw (3)

4. Remove the three mounting bolts which secure the caliper pivot arm to the left fork slider. Remove the mud guard and the caliper assembly. The pivot shaft can be pulled from the pivot arm.

NOTE: *The two caliper halves can be removed from the pivot arm and disassembled without removing the pivot arm or the front wheel. To remove the caliper halves in this manner, see the section under "Pad Replacement."*

5. To disassemble the caliper, remove the two setting bolts from the caliper and separate the two caliper halves from the caliper pivot arm. Remove the two pads as described under "Pad Replacement."
6. Remove the piston from caliper A by blowing compressed air into the fluid inlet passage.
7. The piston seal can be removed from caliper A using a wood or plastic tool. However, note that if the cylinder walls are scored while removing the seal, the caliper half will have to be replaced.

CALIPER INSPECTION

1. Check pad wear. If either pad is worn past the red limit line, replace both pads as a set.
2. Measure the inside diameter of the caliper cylinder bore and the outside diameter of the piston. Compare the measured value with the service limit given at the end of this section; if either part is worn beyond its service limit, it must be replaced.
3. Check the bore in caliper A for scoring. If scoring is evident, the caliper half should be replaced.
4. Check the piston for scoring; replace it if scoring is evident.
5. Check the pivot shaft for wear, also check the pivot arm for wear at the pivot points. Replace as necessary.
6. Check the condition of the two pivot shaft O-rings. If they are torn or cracked they should be replaced with new ones.

CALIPER ASSEMBLY AND INSTALLATION

Since it is imperative that no dirt or foreign matter be allowed to enter the hydraulic system, assembly should take place in a clean area preferably on a sheet of white paper.

Clean and lubricate all internal brake parts with fresh DOT 3 brake fluid before assembly.

Use only genuine Honda replacement parts when replacing any parts in the brake system.

1. Install the pivot shaft into the pivot arm. Be sure to apply some grease to the pivot points. Note that an O-ring is fitted to either side of the pivot arm.
2. Mount the pivot arm to the left fork slider with the three mounting bolts. Install the adjusting screw, spring, and locknut.
3. Install the piston seal into the caliper using a wood or plastic tool. Take care not to score the cylinder bore. Installing a new seal is recommended.
4. Install the piston into the caliper half, then install the piston pad. Install the fixed pad to caliper B and secure it with a new cotter pin.
5. Install the two caliper halves to the pivot arm, and torque the setting bolts to 9–12 ft lbs.
6. Mount the front wheel. Bleed the brake as described under "Bleeding". Adjust the caliper as described under "Caliper Adjustment".

BRAKE DISC

1. Check the disc for run-out by securing a dial gauge to the fork slider. If the run-out is 0.3 mm (0.0118 in.) or more, remove the disc and check it for warpage. Maximum warpage is 0.3 mm (0.0118 in.) If the disc is not warped, suspect the wheel bearings.
2. Measure the thickness of the disc. Minimum allowable thickness is 6.0 mm (0.236 in.)
3. To remove the disc, remove the front wheel, bend down the locking tabs on the disc securing nuts, and remove the nuts.
4. When installing the disc, care should be taken to tighten the bolts evenly and gradually until the proper torque of 13–16.6 ft lbs is reached. Ensure that the locking tabs are bent up against the flats on the disc bolts.

Master Cylinder

REMOVAL AND DISASSEMBLY

NOTE: *Be very careful when removing and replacing the master cylinder or refilling the reservoir. Brake fluid can remove paint or damage plastic in seconds and therefore should be handled with care.*

1. Place a cloth underneath the connection to absorb any spilled fluid and disconnect the brake line from the master cylinder. Cover the open end of the brake line with a plastic bag secured with a rubber band to prevent dirt from entering the brake system.

2. Remove the two mounting bolts and remove the master cylinder from the handlebar. Unscrew the reservoir cap and discard the brake fluid.

3. Remove the brake lever by unscrewing the pivot bolt.

4. Carefully remove the boot and 18 mm snap-ring.

5. Remove the piston, check valve, return spring, and primary cup by blowing compressed air into the brake line fitting or by carefully pushing it out with a wooden dowel.

Removing snap-ring (2), with snap-ring pliers (1)

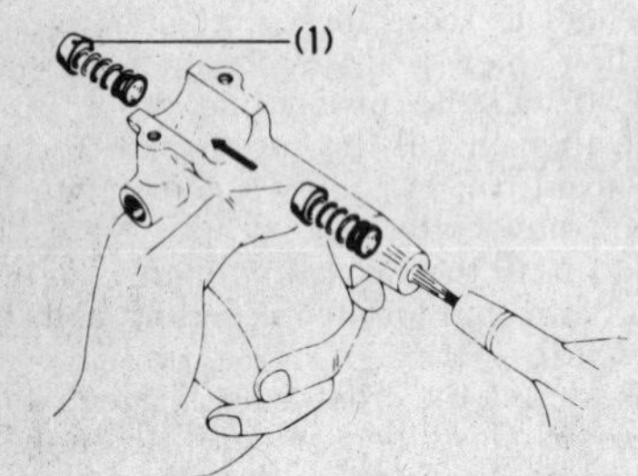

Removing the primary cup (1) with compressed air

INSPECTION

1. Clean all components in clean brake fluid.

2. Check the master cylinder bore for signs of wear, grooves, scoring, etc.

3. Check the piston for scoring or grooves.

4. Replace the primary cup with a new item each time it is removed.

5. Replace any rubber items which show signs of wear or age, cracks, brittle condition, etc.

ASSEMBLY AND INSTALLATION

1. Coat all internal brake parts with fresh brake fluid, including the bore in the master cylinder.

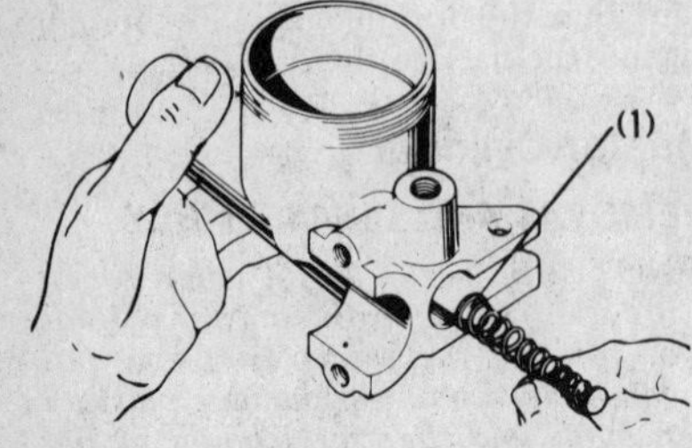

Installing check valve (1)

2. Install the return spring to the check valve and install them into the master cylinder. Be sure that the check valve is facing the correct direction.

3. Install the primary cup after lubricating it with fresh brake fluid.

NOTE: *Make sure that the primary cup does not turn sideways during installation.*

4. Install the piston assembly and 18 mm snap-ring. Install the boot and brake lever.

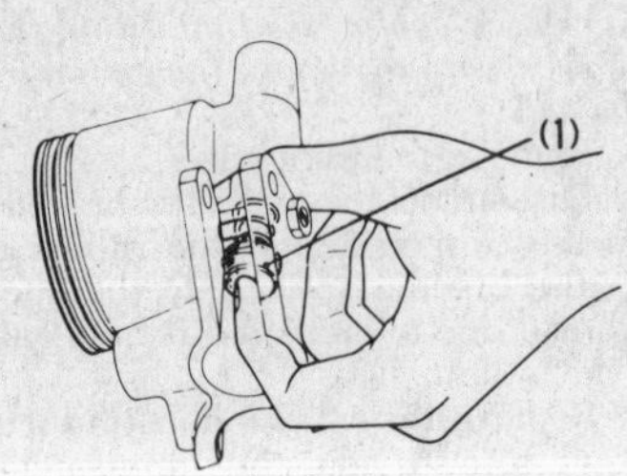

Installing primary cup (1)

5. Mount the master cylinder on the handlebar. Connect the brake line and torque the banjo bolt to 24–29 ft lbs. Fill the reservoir with fresh brake fluid and bleed the system as previously described.

NOTE: *Be sure that there is a joint washer on either side of the brake line where it is bolted to the master cylinder.*

Wheel Bearings

Removal of the wheel bearings necessitates removing the hub oil seals. These must be replaced with new ones upon reassembly.

DISASSEMBLY

1. Remove the wheel. For the front wheel remove the axle, side collar, and brake plate (drum brakes), or the speedometer drive housing (disc brakes). On the rear wheel, remove the brake plate and any side collars.

2. Remove any dust covers, or dust seals. Unscrew the bearing retainer, if fitted (all rear wheels; sprocket side and disc brake, disc side).

Removing bearing retainer (350 shown)

3. Pry out the oil seal. An oil seal is fitted to the disc side on disc brake wheels and on the side opposite the brake plate on wheels fitted with a drum brake. Use a small screwdriver, or, preferably, an elbow-shaped tool to remove the oil seal.

4. Remove the wheel bearings by reaching through the center of the hub with a long drift and tapping one of the bearings evenly around its circumference until it is removed. Be careful not to turn the bearing sideways in its seat on removal as there is danger of causing damage to the hub.

Removing wheel bearing

5. When either bearing is removed, the spacer tube can be remove from the hub. After removing the spacer tube, remove the other bearing in the same manner as the first.

NOTE: *On some models, especially high mileage machines, the hub should be heated gently with a propane torch in the vicinity of the bearing bosses to facilitate removal.*

INSPECTION

1. Clean the bearings and spacer tube in a suitable solvent, removing all of the old grease. At this point, it would be wise to clean out the hub as well.

2. Check the bearing bosses in the hub for scuffs, cracks, or distortion. If they are in any way damaged, the hub must be replaced.

3. Check the condition of the spacer tube, and replace it if damaged.

4. Bearing condition is very important. Check the balls themselves for pitting, wear, or rust.

5. Apply a few drops of light oil to the bearing and spin it. The bearing must rotate smoothly and freely. Any roughness or binding in rotation will necessitate a new bearing.

6. Note that the bearings must be replaced in pairs.

ASSEMBLY

Assembly is in the reverse order of disassembly; however, note the following points:

1. Obtain a good grade of wheel bearing grease (such as Lithium or Moly) to lubricate the wheel bearings.
2. Pack the wheel bearings until they are completely filled.
3. Place a small amount of wheel bearing grease to the inside of the hub and drive one of the bearings into its seat. Install the retainer if so equipped. Install the spacer tube and drive the other bearing into its seat. The sealed surface of the bearing must face the outside of the hub.

NOTE: *When a bearing retainer is fitted, the bearing closest to the retainer should be installed first. Then install and tighten the retainer, spacer tube, and the other bearing.*

4. Replace all of the oil seals with new ones.

FRONT FORKS

Removal and Disassembly

Two basic types of front forks are used: internal or external fork springs.

1. Remove the front wheel and fender.
2. On disc brake models remove the three caliper mounting bolts and adjusting screw from the left fork slider, and lift the caliper away from the fork leg.

CAUTION: *Do not allow the caliper to hang by the brake line. Tie it out of the way with some string or wire.*

3. Loosen the fork filler caps as they may be difficult to remove once the fork leg is removed from the motorcycle.
4. On 360 models, remove the emblem from the lower triple clamp.
5. Loosen the pinch-bolts on the upper triple clamp (if fitted) and then loosen the pinch-bolts on the lower triple clamp. Remove the fork legs one at a time by pulling them down.

NOTE: *From this point disassembly and inspection refers to one fork leg, but applies to both.*

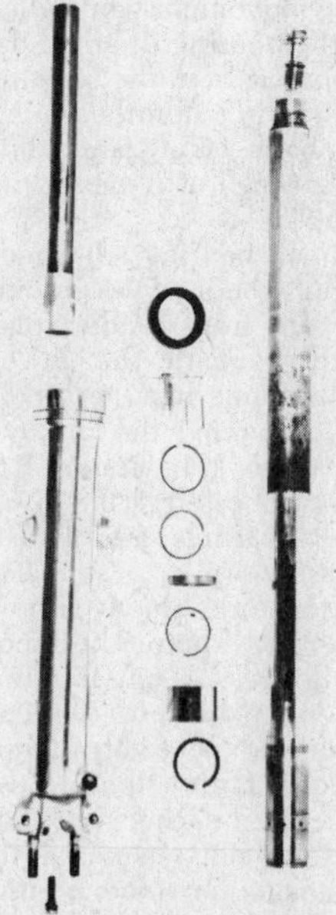

Early model 350 front forks

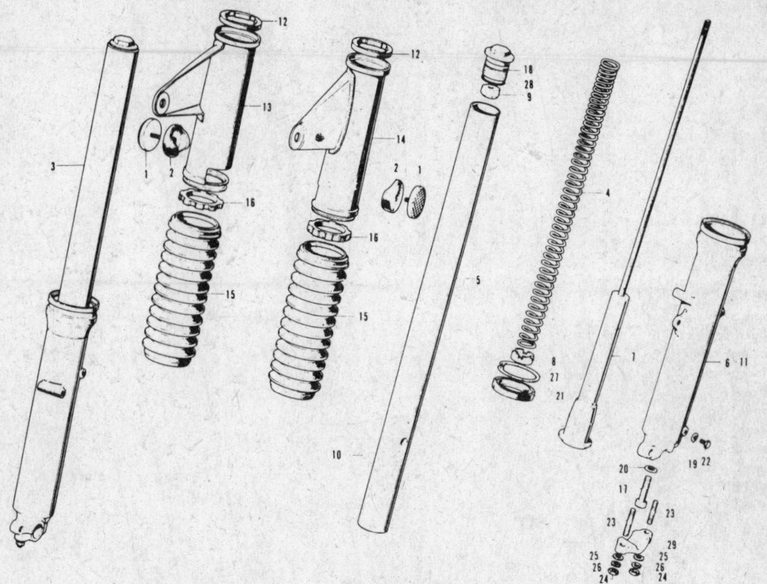

Late model 350 front forks (CL shown)

1. Reflector
2. Reflector base
3. Fork leg (right)
4. Fork spring
5. Fork tube
6. Fork slider
7. Damper
8. Spring seat
9. Damper rod nut
10. Fork assembly (left)
11. Fork slider
12. Bush
13. Headlight mount (right)
14. Headlight mount (left)
15. Fork boot
16. Bush
17. Fork slider allen bolt
18. Fork filler cap
19. Drain plug washer
20. Allen bolt washer
21. Oil seal
22. Drain plug
23. Axle cap stud
24. Axle capnut
25. Washer
26. Lockwasher
27. Circlip
28. O-ring
29. Axle cap

6. Remove the fork filler bolt from the top of the fork leg. Remove the spring (350 to K3, 360) and invert the fork over a container to drain off the oil.
7. Remove the rubber boot (if fitted). With an inpact driver remove the screw from the bottom of the slider. Remove the circlip at the top of the slider, and separate the slider from the fork tube.
8. New oil seals should always be used once the slider has been separated from the tube. Pry out the old seal with a screwdriver, but be careful not to score the slider surface.
9. On early model forks with the damper components on the fork tube: remove the circlip at the bottom of the fork tube and take off the damper components. Use a new circlip upon assembly.

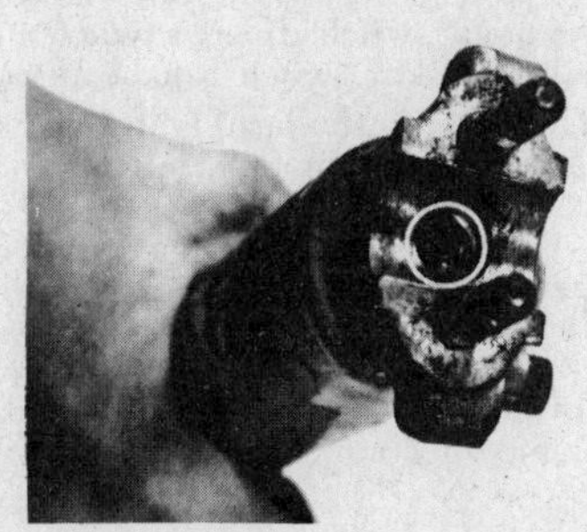

Slider screw must be removed with an impact driver

Inspection

1. Inspect the fork tubes for bends as might have been incurred in an accident. Replacement is recommended rather than attempting to straighten bent fork tubes.
2. Check that the surface of the tube on which the slider components move are smooth and free of rust or scoring. Minor rusting should be removed with fine emery cloth.
3. Check the spring condition; check that the spring heights are equal and that they are within the length specifications given at the end of this section. If either spring is compressed more than 0.25 in., both should be replaced.
4. Check that the damper rod (where fitted) is straight and that all damper components are clean.
5. On early-type forks, check the slider bushing for scoring or wear, and replace it if damaged.
6. Replace the fork filler cap O-rings if they are not in good condition.
7. Clean all metal parts thoroughly in a solvent and lubricate them lightly with fork oil before assembly.

Assembly and Installation

Assembly is in the reverse order of disassembly. Note the following points.

1. On the early-type forks the oil seal must be placed on the fork tube before the damper components, and then inserted in the slider with the fork tube.
2. On the later model forks the oil seal can be driven into the slider before the fork tube is inserted. Use the old seal on top of the new one to drive it in, then remove the old seal.
3. Refit the circlip, being sure that it is properly seated. The use of a new circlip is recommended.

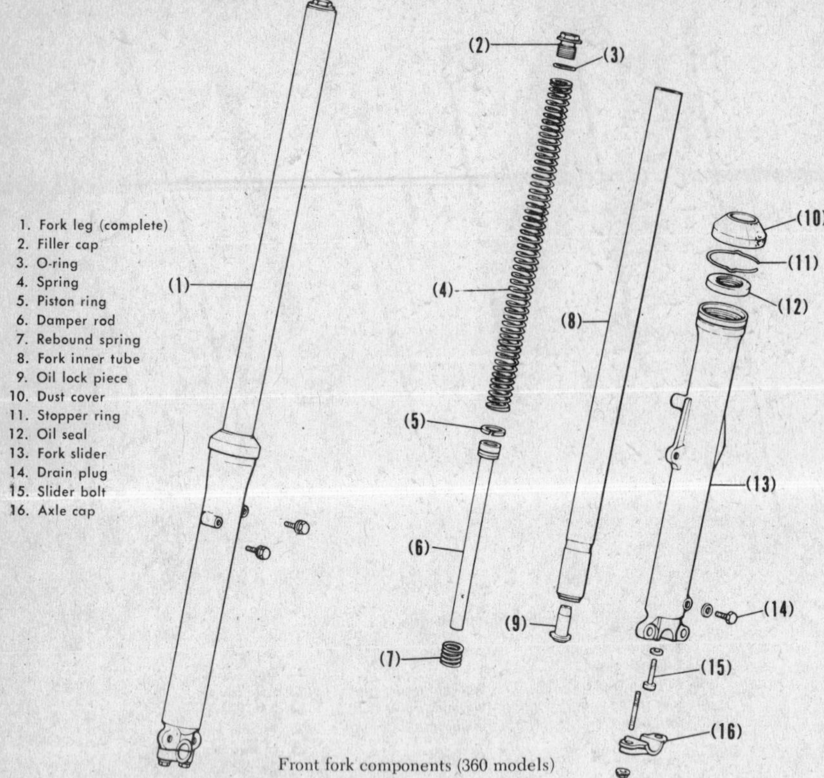

Front fork components (360 models)

4. Fill the forks with the correct grade and quantity of oil and install the filler caps. Install the fork legs into the triple clamps. Tighten the lower triple clamp pinch-bolts and then check that the filler cap is tight. Tighten the upper triple clamp bolts (if fitted).

5. Adjust the brake caliper (if fitted) after assembly is complete.

HANDLEBAR

Disassembly

1. On models with a disc brake remove the master cylinder by unscrewing the two clamp bolts.

2. Disconnect the front brake cable (drum brakes) at the lower end by loosening the locknut on the cable adjuster on the brake plate. Screw the adjuster in to increase the amount of cable free-play. Remove the cotter pin from the brake lever and pull the lever back by hand, slip the cable end pin up and out of the brake lever.

3. Remove the brake (drum brake) and clutch cables from the handlebars by loosening the adjuster locknut and screwing the adjuster into the lever housing. Line up the slots in the adjuster screw and the locknut with the slot in the lever housing. Pull the lever back to the handlebar and pull the cable sheath out of the adjuster as the lever is released. Remove the cable end pin from the lever.

4. To disconnect the clutch cable from the lower end, remove the gearshift lever and chain cover. Screw the adjuster on the chain cover in to increase the amount of cable free-play. Disconnect the cable from the clutch release mechanism in the chain cover.

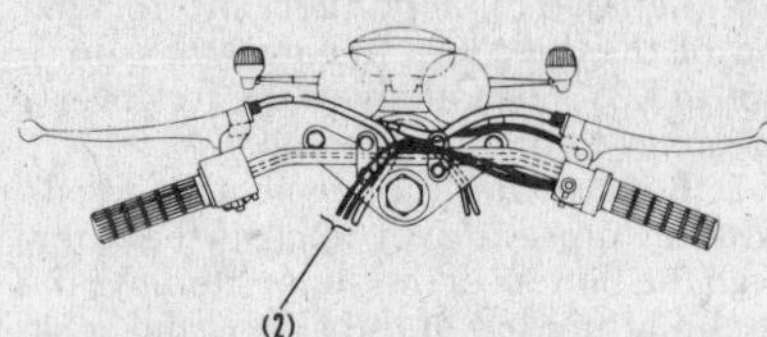

Route the throttle cables (2), as shown

5. To remove the throttle cable(s) from the twist-grip, unscrew the phillips head screws from the bottom of the throttle cable housing. Lift up the top of the housing and disconnect the throttle cable(s) from the twist-grip. To replace the cable(s), disconnect the cable from the carburetor and route the new cable as shown.

6. The electrical wiring for the horn, starter motor switch, dimmer switch, turn signals, and kill switch can be disconnected either in the headlight shell (350 models) or under the fuel tank (360 models).

7. Remove the handlebars by unscrewing the four bolts from the handlebar holders (two bolts on each holder). Mark the front of each holder before it is removed so that they can be installed in the same direction.

Inspection

1. Check the handlebar for a bent condition. It is recommended that a bent handlebar be replaced as straightened handlebars will be weakened and may break under extreme use.

2. Check that the brake, clutch, and throttle cables are not frayed at the ends. Replace any cable in this condition.

3. Check that the cables move freely in their sheaths. Replace any cable with a bent or kinked sheath.

Assembly

1. Install the electrical switches on the handlebar pulling the wires through the center of the handlebars using a lead of wire or string fastened to the longest wire.

2. Mount the handlebars on the upper triple clamp, and install the handlebar holders, with the punch mark on the handlebars aligned with the top of the lower holder.

CAUTION: *The handlebar holders are machined unevenly (one side is slightly higher than the other); the high side must face the front. The high side (front) on some models can be identified by a punch mark on the top of the holder. If in doubt which side is the high side, place the holder on a straightedge, the high side should be apparent.*

Tighten the front bolt first, so that the upper and lower holder are touching in the front and a small gap is left at the rear.

3. Connect the cables to the controls. When installing the twist-grip into the housing, be sure that the cable tensioner is correctly installed.

4. The remainder of assembly is in the reverse order of disassembly.

5. Check the operation of all controls before riding the motorcycle.

STEERING STEM ASSEMBLY

Bearing Adjustment

On models equipped with a friction steering damper, the damper should be loosened (counterclockwise) as much as possible so that it does not interfere with the bearing movement while checking or adjusting the bearing. If an oil damper is fitted, remove it from the steering stem.

1. The steering stem bearings are uncaged #8 balls. They are adjusted by means of a ring nut beneath the upper triple clamp.

2. To check bearing adjustment, support the front wheel off the ground. Grasp the tip of the front fender, place your other hand beneath the lower triple clamp at the frame lug.

3. Attempt to move the fork by pulling up on the tip of the fender. If play or movement can be felt at the lower triple clamp, the bearings are adjusted too loosely or are worn.

4. Turn the forks slowly from lock-to-lock. Movement should be smooth, silent, and effortless. If any binding or uneven movement is felt, the balls and races are either too tightly adjusted or they are worn. If the steering feels uniformly stiff, the bearings are too tightly adjusted. If any noise is noted, the bearings are damaged or some are missing.

5. With the front wheel off the ground, release the front forks from a few degrees

off the centered position. The fork should fall freely to either side of their own weight. If they will not, the bearings are too tightly adjusted, the steering stem is bent, the races are extremely worn, or some of the bearings are missing.

Adjusting the steering bearings with the Honda pin wrench

6. To adjust the bearings, remove the front wheel, front forks, handlebars, and the upper triple clamp. The bearings are adjusted by means of the adjuster nut under the upper triple clamp.

7. Tighten or loosen the adjuster nut a little at a time until the steering stem adjustment conforms to that outlined above. Temporarily install the forks, upper triple clamp, and the steering stem nut to check the adjustment.

8. If proper adjustment is not possible, the bearings and races will probably need to be replaced.

Removal

1. Remove the front wheel, front forks, and handlebars. If a friction steering damper is fitted, remove it by removing the two cotter pins from under the lower triple clamp, and unscrewing the damper rod and removing the friction plates. If an oil shock damper is fitted, unbolt it from the lower triple clamp.

2. Unscrew the steering stem nut and disconnect the speedometer and tachometer cables from their instruments. Remove the upper triple clamp.

3. Disconnect the wiring inside the headlight shell, and remove the headlight shell and the fork ears.

4. Loosen the steering stem adjuster nut with a pin wrench, then hold the steering stem up while unscrewing the adjuster nut the rest of the way off. Remove the steering stem top cone race and the ball bearings from the top race.

5. Carefully pull the steering stem out from the bottom. Some of the ball bearings from the lower race will probably fall out at this time so be prepared for this.

6. Remove the bottom cone race, dust seal, and dust seal washer from the steering stem if they are to be replaced. These will have to be pried off with a chisel, therefore only remove them if necessary.

7. The bearing races in the frame lug are a press-fit and should not be removed

Removing the adjuster nut

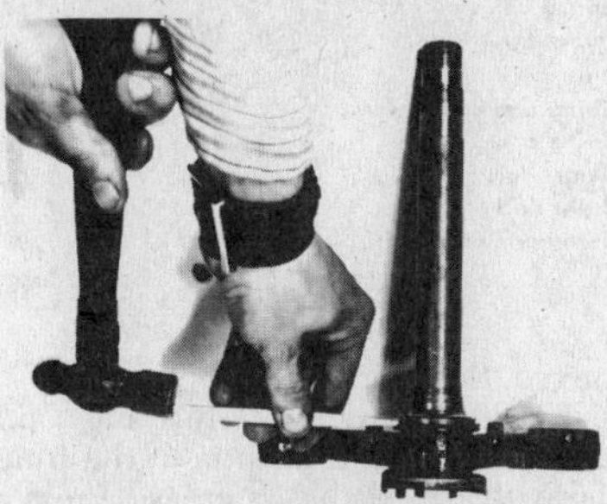

Removing the lower cone race

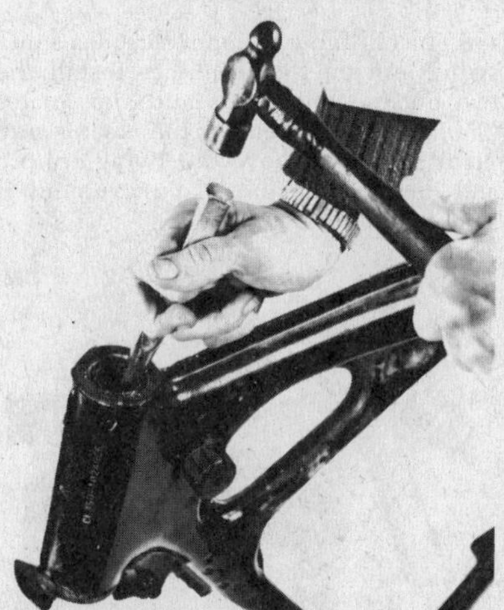

Removing the bearing races in the frame lug with a hammer and punch

unless replacement is necessary. If replacement is necessary, the old races can be removed by reaching through the frame lug with a suitable punch and tapping the race evenly around its circumference to remove it from the inside of the frame lug. Be sure that the race does not become cocked in its seat upon removal.

New races are installed with a suitable sized bearing driver: i.e., one which will drive the race squarely into its seat. Be certain that the race goes straight in.

These races can also be installed using a block of hard wood of sufficient size to cover the race in place of a bearing driver.

Inspection

1. Wash the ball bearings in a suitable solvent.

2. Clean all of the old grease from the bearing race surfaces, steering stem, and frame lug.

3. Inspect the bearing race surfaces. They must be clean and smooth. That is free from any cracks, scoring, rust, or indentations. Run your finger around each of the bearing races. Note any roughness or ripples on the race surface. If any imperfections are noted, both the sets of races and all of the balls must be replaced.

4. Check the balls themselves for rust, pitting, scoring, or flat spots. If the balls are found to be defective in any way, the balls and both sets of races must be replaced.

NOTE: *Balls and races must always be replaced in a set as worn races will destroy new balls and worn balls will destroy new races.*

5. Check the dust seal for condition and replace if torn or cracked.

6. Check the steering stem for cracks or a bent condition; this is especially important if the bike has been involved in a spill.

Installation

1. Install the dust seal washer, dust seal, and lower cone race on the steering stem. Use a good grade of bearing grease to coat the bottom cone race and the upper race in the frame lug.

2. Embed 18 balls into the grease of the top frame lug and 19 balls into the grease of the lower cone race.

3. When the balls are in place, slip the steering stem through the frame lug and hold it in place while refitting the top cone race and threading on the adjuster nut.

4. Tighten the adjuster nut all of the way by hand, rotating the steering stem to work the grease into the balls.

5. Tighten the adjuster nut until the steering stem turns freely, but has no play.

6. Install the fork tubes, headlight assembly, and upper triple clamp, flat washer, and steering stem nut. Check that the stem moves freely to the steering lock of its own weight when released from 5°–10° off center; if not check for:

a. Steering bearings too tight;
b. Bent steering stem;
c. Worn races or balls.

7. Install the front fender, front wheel, and handlebars.

REAR SHOCK ABSORBERS

No service to the rear shock is possible. In the event of oil leaks, bent or broken plunger shaft, dented or otherwise damaged case, the shock absorber must be replaced.

If the shock absorbers are somewhat old, and one fails in the course of normal usage, it would be a good idea to replace both shocks to insure equal damping characteristics.

CAUTION: *Do not attempt to disassemble the rear shocks. Gas is under high pressure.*

To check a shock which is removed from the machine, place the bottom end on the ground and use the weight of your body to compress it as much as possible. Release one shock and note the rebound behavior. If the shock returns quickly at first, then slowly returns to the normal length, it is serviceable. If it returns to its normal length all at once, it should be replaced.

SWING ARM

All Models

INSPECTION

1. Disconnect the chain. Remove the rear wheel and sprocket assembly.

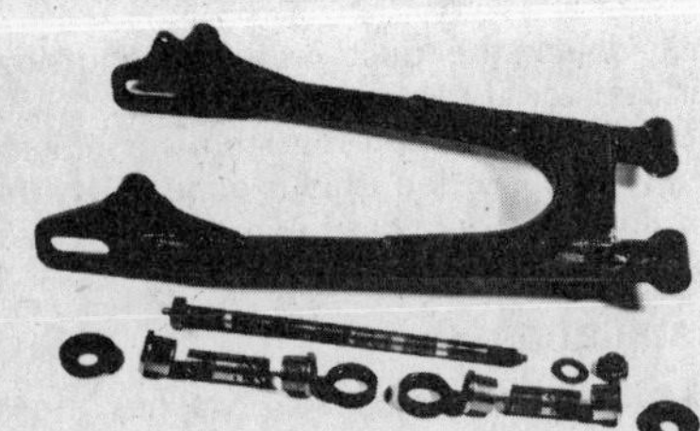

Swing arm components (350)

2. Remove the shock absorbers and chain guard.
3. Measure the distance between the top and bottom shock absorber mounts on both sides. The two measurements must be identical, or the swing arm will have to be replaced or fixed.
4. Check that the rear wheel mounting plates are parallel.
5. Grasp the legs of the swing arm and attempt to move it from side-to-side. Any noticeable side-play will indicate that the swing arm bushings in the frame need replacement.

The swing arm is most likely to be damaged if the machine is operated for any length of time with a broken or otherwise defective shock absorber.

REMOVAL AND INSTALLATION

1. 360 models: Proceed as above. Then unscrew the swing arm pivot bolt nut, and pull out the pivot bolt.
2. 350 models: Proceed as above. Then remove the shifter linkage. Remove two 6 mm bolts and one 8 mm bolt from each of the side plates. Remove the nut from the pivot bolt and remove the pivot bolt and the two side plates.
3. Remove the swing arm.
4. The swing arm should be inspected for cracks or fractures, especially around the welds.
5. After removing the swing arm, the dust seals and the swing arm bushings and center collars can be replaced. This should be done every 10,000 miles or more often depending on how the machine is used, or if the bushings are worn.
6. Using a small drift, push the center collar out of the swing arm. Remove the bushings, tapping them out with a long drift and hammer. Once the bushings are removed, they should be replaced.
7. Lubricate the new bushings and both the inside and outside of the inner collar with a good chassis grease. Press in one bushing, refit the inner collar and install the other bushing.
8. Install the two inner dust seals and swing arm on the machine. Install the two outside dust seals and side plates (350). After tightening the swing arm pivot shaft nut, move the swing arm up and down to ensure that movement is smooth and effortless.

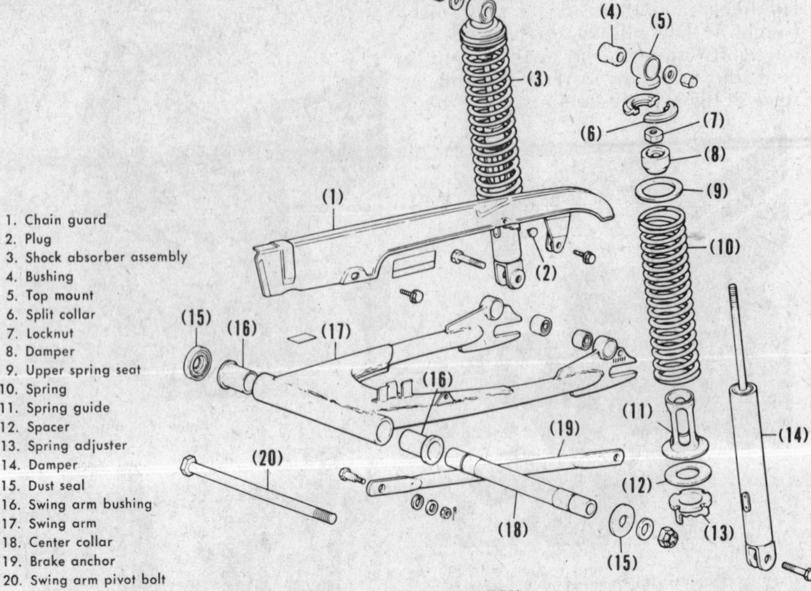

Swing arm components (360)

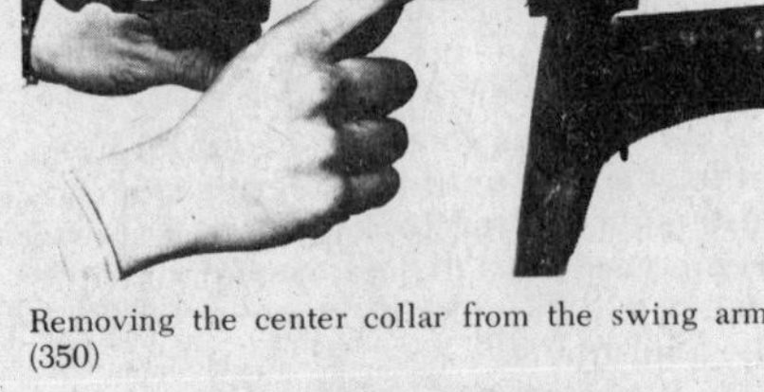

Removing the center collar from the swing arm (350)

Removing the swing arm bushings (350 shown)

Disc Brake Torque Specifications

Component	*Thread Diameter (mm)*	*Torque (ft lbs)*
Master cylinder banjo bolts	—	24.6–28.9
Front brake disc nuts	8	13.0–16.6
Brake line joint	6	5.8–7.2
Brake hose joint	—	4.3–7.2
Master cylinder bolt	6	5.7–7.2
Caliper mounting bolts	—	24.6–28.9

Disc Brake Specifications

Measurement	*Standard (in./mm)*	*Service Limit (in./mm)*
ID of caliper cylinder	1.5032–1.5039/38.18–38.20	1.5045/38.215
OD of caliper piston	1.5006–1.5032/38.115–38.18	1.5002/38.105
ID of master cylinder	0.5512–0.5529/14.000–14.043	0.5534/14.055
OD of master cylinder piston	0.5495–0.5506/13.957–13.984	0.5488/13.940
Thickness of disc	0.2717–0.2795/6.9–7.1	0.2362/6.0
Disc run-out	0.002/0.05	0.0118/0.3
Pad-to-disc clearance	0.002/0.05	0.006/0.15

Chassis Specifications

	CB/CL350 K1, K2, K3, SL350	CB/CL350 K4-on	SL350, K1, K2	CB/CL/CJ360
Wheels				
Rim run-out max (in./mm)	0.08/2.0	0.08/2.0	0.08/2.0	0.08/2.0
Wheel Bearings				
Front Axial run-out max (in./mm)	0.004/0.1	0.004/0.1	0.004/0.1	0.004/0.1
Radial run-out max (in./mm)	0.002/0.05	0.002/0.05	0.002/0.05	0.002/0.5
Rear Axial run-out max (in./mm)	0.004/0.1	0.004/0.1	0.004/0.1	0.004/0.1
Radial run-out max (in./mm)	0.002/0.05	0.002/0.05	0.002/0.05	0.002/0.05
Brakes				
Front drum brake Drum ID max (in./mm)	7.17/182	7.17/182	7.17/182	7.17/182
Lining thickness min (in./mm)	0.1/2.5	0.1/2.5	0.1/2.5	0.1/2.5
Lever free-play (in./mm)	0.8/20	0.8/20	0.8/20	0.8/20
Rear drum brake Drum ID max (in./mm)	6.38/162	6.38/162	6.38/162	6.338/161
Lining thickness min (in./mm)	0.1/2.5	0.1/2.5	0.1/2.5	0.1/2.5
Pedal free-play (in./mm)	1/25	1/25	1/25	1/25
Front Suspension				
Spring free-length min (in./mm)	7.72/196	16.378/416	NA	18.425/468.0
Tilt max (deg)	2.5	2.5	2.5	2.5
Sliding bushing OD (in./mm)	1.472/37.385	—	—	—
Damper piston OD min (in./mm)	—	1.2944/32.875	1.2944/32.875	NA
Slider ID max (in./mm)	1.484/37.680	1.3063/33.18	1.3063/33.18	1.3047/33.139
Rear Suspension				
Suspension travel (in./mm)	NA	3.6/91.0	NA	3.1/77.6
Spring free-length min (in./mm)	6.902/175.3	7.480/190	8.54/217	8.1732/207.6
tilt max (deg)	2.5	2.5	2.5	2.5
Swing arm pivot bushing ID max (in./mm)	0.795/20.18	0.795/20.18	0.795/20.18	0.8543/21.7

— Not applicable NA Not available

Chass Torque Specifications 360

Component	Thread Diameter (mm)	Torque (ft lbs)
Front brake anchor	10	13–18
Steering stem nut	24	50–65
Upper triple clamp-to-front forks	8	13–17
Handlebar holder	8	13–18
Lower triple clamp-to-front forks	8	13–18
Spokes Front wheel Rear wheel	—	1.1–1.5
Swing arm pivot bolt	14	39–50
Front axle nut	12	40–47
Front fork axle caps	8	19–24
Engine mounting bolts	8 10	19–24 29–40
Rear axle nut	16	58–72
Rear sprocket nuts	10	44–50
Rear brake lever pinch-bolt	8	13–18
Rear brake anchor	8	13–18
Rear suspension	10	22–29
Foot rest	10	29–39
Gearshift and kick-starter levers	6	6–7
Seat band	6	6–7

350

Component	Thread Diameter (mm)	Torque (ft lbs)
Front brake anchor	10	13–18
Steering stem nut	24	58–87
Upper triple clamp pinch-bolts	8	13–17
Lower triple clamp pinch-bolts	8	13–18
Fork filler cap	16	50–58
Front fork axle caps	8	13–18
Front axle nut	12	40–47
Handlebar holder	8	13–18
Engine mounting bolts	10	25–32
Swing arm pivot nut	14	40–50
Upper rear shock mount	10	25–32
Lower rear shock mount	10	25–32
Rear axle nut	16	58–72

Honda 450-500 Twins

MODEL COVERAGE

CB450
CB450K1-K7
CL450
CL450K1-K6
CB500T

INDEX

General Specifications

Model	CB 450 (1966–67)	CB 450 (1968–69)	CL 450 (1968–69)	CB 450K3	CL450K3
ENGINE					
Displacement (cc/cu in.)	444/27.1	444/27.1	444/27.1	444/27.1	444/27.1
Bore and stroke (mm)	70 x 57.8	70 x 57.8	70 x 57.8	70 x 57.8	70 x 57.8
Compression ratio	8.5 : 1	9.0 : 1	9.0 : 1	9.0 : 1	9.0 : 1
Carburetion (Keihin)	(2) 36 mm CV	(2) 36 mm CV	(2) 36 mm CV	(2) 36 mm CV	(2) 36 mm CV
Torque (ft lb) @ rpm	27.6 @ 7,250	28 @ 7,500	29 @ 7,000	28 @ 7,500	29 @ 7,000
Weight (lb)	146.6	137.8	137.8	137.8	137.8
DRIVE TRAIN					
Clutch type	wet, multi-plate	wet, multi-plate	wet, multi-plate	wet, multi-plate	wet, multi-plate
Gear ratios:					
1st	2.411	2.412	2.412	2.412	2.412
2nd	1.400	1.636	1.636	1.636	1.636
3rd	1.034	1.269	1.269	1.269	1.269
4th	0.903	1.000	1.000	1.000	1.000
5th	——	0.844	0.844	0.844	0.844
Primary reduction	3.304	3.304	3.304	3.304	3.304
Final reduction	2.333	2.333	2.333	2.333	2.333
CHASSIS					
Weight (lb)	412	412	401	430	414.5
Wheelbase (in.)	53.2	54.0	54.0	54.3	54.0
Tire size (in.)					
front	3.25 x 18	3.25 x 18	3.25 x 19	3.25 x 19	3.25 x 19
rear	3.50 x 18	3.50 x 18	3.50 x 18	3.50 x 18	3.50 x 18
Overall length (in.)	82.0	83.0	84.5	82.7	82.0
Overall width (in.)	30.2	30.5	32.5	31.5	34.4
Overall height (in.)	53.2	43.0	43.5	44.9	45.5
Ground clearance (in.)	5.4	5.5	6.0	5.3	5.3
ELECTRICAL SYSTEM					
Ignition	battery and coil	battery and coil	battery and coil	battery and coil	battery and coil
Starting system	electric and kick	electric and kick	electric and kick	electric and kick	electric and kick
Charging system:					
battery (volts/amp hrs)	12/12	12/12	12/12	12/12	12/12
alternator	rotor type	rotor type	rotor type	rotor type	rotor type
regulator	——	non-adjustable silicon type	non-adjustable silicon type	non-adjustable silicon type	non-adjustable silicon type

Model	CB 450K4 and K5	CL 450K4–K5	CL 450K6	CB 450K6–K7	CB 500T
ENGINE					
Displacement (cc/cu in.)	444/27.1	444/27.1	444/27.1	444/27.1	498/30.4
Bore and stroke (mm)	70 x 57.8	70 x 57.8	70 x 57.8	70 x 57.8	70 x 64.8
Compression ratio	9.0 : 1	9.0 : 1	9.0 : 1	9.0 : 1	8.5 : 1
Carburetion (Keihin)	(2) 36 mm CV	(2) 36 mm CV	(2) 36 mm CV	(2) 36 mm CV	(2) 36 mm CV
Torque (ft lb) @ rpm	28 @ 7,500	29 @ 7,000	29 @ 7,000	28 @ 7,500	NA
Weight (lb)	137.8	137.8	137.8	137.8	139.0
DRIVE TRAIN					
Clutch type	wet, multi-plate	wet, multi-plate	wet, multi-plate	wet, multi-plate	wet, multi-plate
Gear ratios:					
1st	2.412	2.412	2.412	2.412	2.277
2nd	1.636	1.636	1.636	1.636	1.521
3rd	1.269	1.269	1.269	1.269	1.230
4th	1.000	1.000	1.000	1.000	1.000
5th	0.844	0.844	0.844	0.844	0.844
Primary reduction	3.304	3.304	3.304	3.304	3.304
Final reduction	2.333	2.333	2.333	2.333	2.200
CHASSIS					
Weight (lb)	430	414.5	406	410	425
Wheelbase (in.)	54.3	54.0	54.1	54.1	55.5
Tire size (in.)					
front	3.25 x 19	3.25 x 19	3.25 x 19	3.25 x 19	3.25 x 19
rear	3.50 x 18	3.50 x 18	3.50 x 18	3.50 x 18	3.75 x 18
Overall length (in.)	82.7	82.0	83.3	83.3	84.3
Overall width (in.)	30.5	32.7	33.9	32.7	32.9
Overall height (in.)	42.3	42.9	42.9	45.3	44.7
Ground clearance (in.)	5.7	7.1	7.1	5.7	NA
ELECTRICAL SYSTEM					
Ignition	battery and coil	battery and coil	battery and coil	battery and coil	battery and coil
Starting system	electric and kick	electric and kick	electric and kick	electric and kick	electric and kick
Charging system:					
battery (volts/amp hrs)	12/12	12/12	12/12	12/12	12/12
alternator	rotor type	rotor type	rotor type	rotor type	rotor type
regulator	non-adjustable silicon type	non-adjustable silicon type	non-adjustable silicon type	non-adjustable silicon type	non-adjustable

NA Not available

Serial Number Locations

On all models, the frame number is located on the left-side of the steering head lug.

The engine serial number is located on the left-side of the engine, on top of the crankcase. These numbers should be used when ordering replacement parts for the engine or frame to ensure that the replacement part is identical to the part originally installed.

NOTE: *Beginning in 1967, Honda (and many other manufacturers) began using nuts and bolts manufactured to the ISO metric standard rather than the earlier JIS standard that had been widely used in Japan. ISO and JIS hardware is interchangeable in some sizes; however, the thread pitch in a few of the common sizes used has been changed and, in these cases, the hardware is not interchangeable. Note also that, except for the 10 mm size (6 mm diameter thread), the width (across flats) of size ISO nuts and bolts (relative to the thread diameter), has been reduced from that of JIS hardware. Early ISO parts are identified by an embossed dot on the bolt head or nut.*

Interchangeability Chart

Thread Diameter	*Width Across Flats*		*Thread Pitch*	
	ISO	*JIS*	*ISO*	*JIS*
3 mm	5.5	6	0.5	0.6
4 mm	7	8	0.7	0.75
5 mm	8	9	0.8	0.9
6 mm	10	10	1.0	1.0
8 mm	12	14	1.25	1.25
10 mm	14	17	1.25	1.25
12 mm	17	19	1.25	1.5
14 mm	19	21	1.5	1.5
16 mm	22	23	1.5	1.5
18 mm	24	26	1.5	1.5
20 mm	27	29	1.5	1.5

MAINTENANCE

NOTE: *Common maintenance procedures are explained in detail in "General Information."*

LUBRICATION

Checking Oil Level

The oil level is checked with the dipstick incorporated into the filler cap. The filler cap is located in the right crankcase cover. To check the oil level:

1. Start the engine and allow it to warm up for a few minutes.
2. With the motorcycle on the center stand on level ground, remove the dipstick and wipe it clean.
3. Reinsert the dipstick, allowing the filler cap to rest on the top of the threads of its hole. The oil level should be between the maximum and minimum marks on the dipstick. If the level is below the minimum mark, add enough oil to bring the level up to the maximum mark.

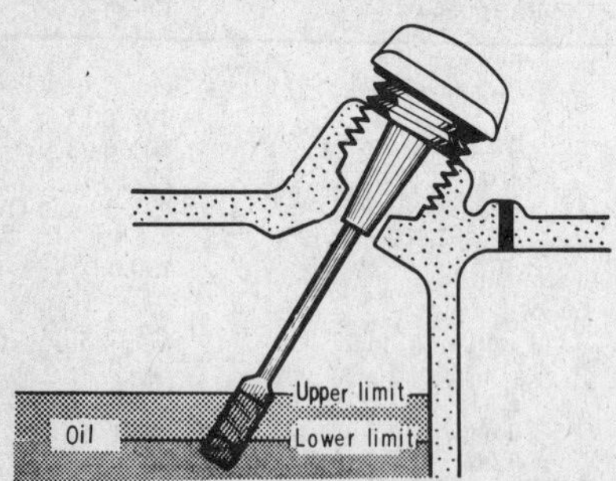

The dipstick should rest on the top thread of its hole when checking oil level

CAUTION: *Do not overfill.*

Changing Oil

The oil change interval is 1500 miles or 3 months.

Use oil with a service rating of "SE" only. SAE 10W–30 or SAE 10W–40 may be used at all temperatures. For temperature extremes, refer to the "Recommended Lubricants" chart at the end of this section.

1 Allow the engine to run for a few minutes until it is close to operating temperature.
2. Remove the drain plug from the sump, and allow the oil to drain for a minute or two, then kick the engine over a few times with the kick-starter (be sure that the key is off) to remove any oil remaining in the delivery system.

Oil Filter

A centrifugal oil filter is used on all models. The filter should be cleaned every 6,000 miles or 12 months.

1. Clean the oil filter in conjunction with an oil change. Drain the oil, but do not reinstall the drain plug.
2. Remove the three screws from the circular cover plate on the right crankcase cover. Remove the cover.
3. Remove the circlip from the oil filter. Screw a 6 mm (crankcase cover) screw into the center of the filter cap; this will pull the cap off.

Filter cover removed

Removing the filter cap

4. Clean the inside of the filter housing with a clean rag and solvent.
5. Clean the filter cap and cover plate and dry thoroughly. Inspect the O-ring on the filter cap and replace it if damaged in any way.
6. Inspect the oil guide in the cover plate. The guide should be free to move in and out and have sufficient spring force behind it to hold it against the filter cap.
7. Install the filter-cap with the vanes located in the grooves on the inside of the filter housing, and secure with the circlip.
8. Install the cover plate using a new O-ring if necessary.

Front Forks

1. ATF is recommended for the front forks. If slightly stiffer damping characteristics are desired, use SAE 20 or SAE 30 oil.
2. Fork oil should be changed every 6,000 miles or once every year.
3. To drain the fork oil, remove the drain plug at the lower portion of one of the fork sliders. Allow the oil to drain for several minutes into a suitable container, then pump the forks up and down several times. After most of the oil is expelled, turn the forks all the way to the right to completely drain the right fork leg, or all the way to the left for the left fork leg. Check the condition of the drain plug gasket. Replace it if necessary. Refit the drain plug and tighten it securely.

Fork drain plug

Fork filler cap

Chain slack should be about ¾ in. measured at the middle of the lower chain run

4. Repeat the procedure with the other fork leg. Look at the old oil, if it contains water or inordinate amounts of dirt, the fork seals should be replaced.

5. Support the front wheel off the ground by placing a suitable jack beneath the engine. Remove the handlebar clamp bolts and move the bars aside if necessary. Remove the filler cap from the top of each fork leg. On models with internal fork springs, either move the spring to one side or take it out altogether to facilitate adding oil.

6. Add the correct amount of ATF to each fork leg. Capacities for each model are given in the "Maintenance Data" chart at the end of this section.

7. Inspect the condition of the fork filler cap O-ring, and replace it if it is torn or cracked. Fit the caps and tighten them securely. Tighten the handlebars front bolts first and pinch-bolts if they were loosened. Allow a moment for the oil to settle in the forks before operation.

Chassis Lubrication

1. The swing arm pivot is fitted with a grease nipple. This is on the end of the pivot bolt (450) or on the swing arm itself (500T). This item should be lubricated with a good grade of chassis grease every 3,000 miles. Grease should be applied until some of it shows at either end of the swing arm.

2. Wheel and steering head bearings are lubricated with bearing grease. This should be done every 6,000 miles. Refer to the "Chassis" section for procedures.

SERVICE CHECKS AND ADJUSTMENTS

Drive Chain

1. The chain should have about ¾ in. (20 mm) of total up-and-down free-play measured in the middle of the lower chain run.

2. Before checking or adjusting the chain slack, the following conditions should be met:

a. The motorcycle should be placed on the center stand so that the rear wheel is off the ground;

b. The transmission should be placed in Neutral;

c. The chain should be clean and well-lubricated;

d. The chain should have been checked for any tight spots by slowly rotating the wheel and checking for variances in the chain tension at different points. If a tight spot exists, the chain tension should be adjusted to the prescribed free-play at the tight spot. Note, however, that such a condition is indicative of a worn chain and probably sprockets which should be replaced as soon as possible.

3. To adjust the chain, first back off the rear brake adjuster nut.

4. Remove the axle nut cotter pin and loosen the axle nut several turns. Loosen the locknut on each chain adjuster bolt.

5. Turn each of the adjuster bolts in or out by equal amounts until the chain tension is approximately correct.

6. Check wheel alignment by means of the aligning marks inscribed on both sides of the swing arm. Be sure that both adjusters are lined up with the same mark on each side. If not, turn one of the adjuster bolts in or out so that alignment is achieved.

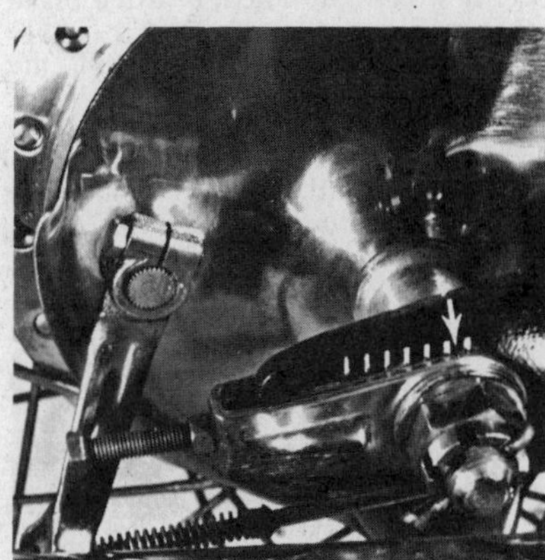
When adjusting the chain, be sure that the index mark on the adjuster aligns with the same swing arm mark on both sides

7. Tighten the axle nut and check the chain tension. The chain tension should also be checked with the weight of a rider sitting on the motorcycle when it is off the center stand; the chain should still have at least ½ in. of free-play. Correct if necessary. After adjustment is correct, torque the axle nut to 60–72 ft lbs.

Fit a new cotter pin and tighten the adjuster locknuts. Readjust the rear brake.

Clutch

Use the cable adjuster at the engine or at the handlebar to maintain the correct amount of cable slack. The clutch lever should be able to be moved 10–20 mm (0.4–0.8 in.) measured at the tip of the lever before the clutch begins to disengage.

If clutch operation is not satisfactory after making this adjustment, proceed as follows:

1. Apply a few shots of chassis grease to the clutch adjuster grease fitting and operate the clutch several times to distribute the grease. Make sure that the cable itself is well lubricated.

2. If either of the cable adjusters is close to the end of its adjustment range, back off its locknut and turn it in several turns.

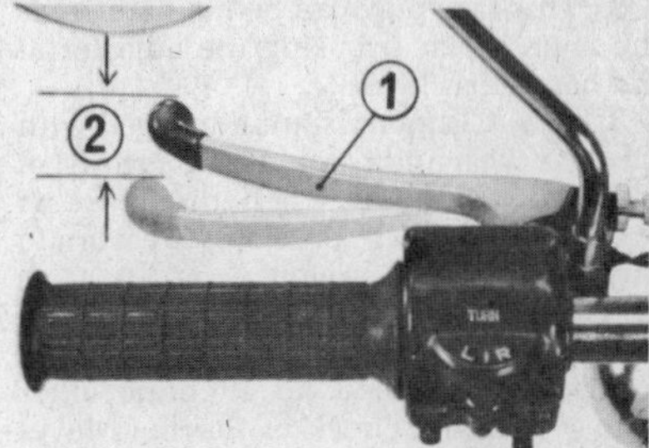

The clutch lever should have 10–20 mm (0.4–0.8 in.) of free movement (2) before the clutch begins to disengage

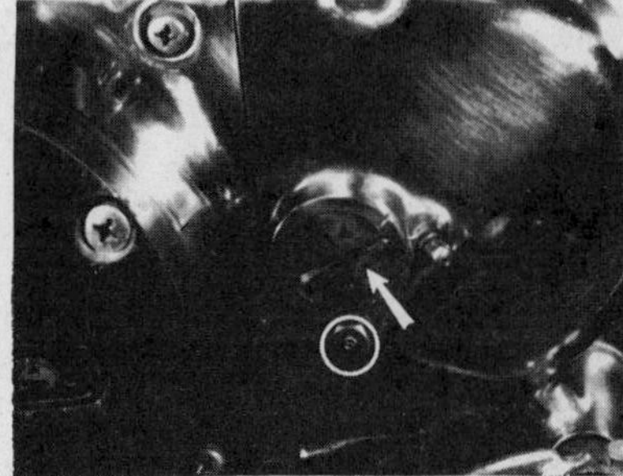
After loosening the bolt (circle), turn the adjuster (arrow) to effect proper lever free-play

3. Loosen the clutch adjuster lockbolt on the left crankcase cover. Turn the adjuster as needed to effect proper lever free-play. Turning the adjuster clockwise will decrease free-play; turning the adjuster counterclockwise will increase the free-play.

4. Tighten the lockbolt; use either of the cable adjusters, if necessary, for fine adjustment. Be sure that the cable adjuster locknuts are secured.

Throttle Cable

The throttle cable free-play should be adjusted *after* the idle speed. This procedure is given in the "Tune-Up" section. The standard throttle cable free-play is 10–15° of grip rotation for all models.

1. Cable free-play is adjusted with the adjuster near the twist-grip. Loosen the locknut on the adjuster and screw the adjuster in or out until freeplay is correct. Tighten the locknut.

Front Drum Brake

1. Use the cable adjuster on the brake plate to allow about 20–30 mm (0.8–1.2 in.) of handlebar lever free-play before the shoes contact the drum. This free-play is measured at the tip of the lever.

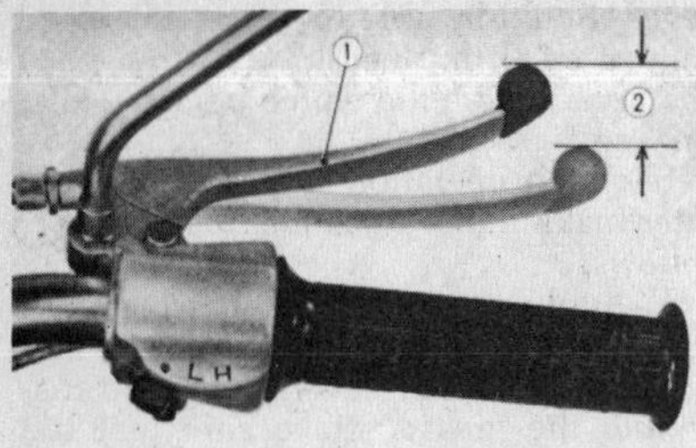

The front brake lever should have 20–30 mm (0.8–1.2 in.) of movement (2) before the linings or pads are fully applied

2. This free-play can be maintained as the shoes wear by using the adjuster at the handlebar lever.

3. Late CL models are equipped with a brake wear indicator. If the arrows of the indicator align when the brake is fully applied, the brake shoes are worn to the point of replacement.

Disc Brake

Disc brakes need no attention other than a periodic check of the fluid level and pad wear:

1. After removing the reservoir cap and rubber diaphragm, check to see if the fluid is up to the level mark on the inside of the master cylinder. If the level is below the level mark, add enough DOT 3 brake fluid to bring the level up to the mark. Reinstall the diaphragm and the cap, and tighten securely.

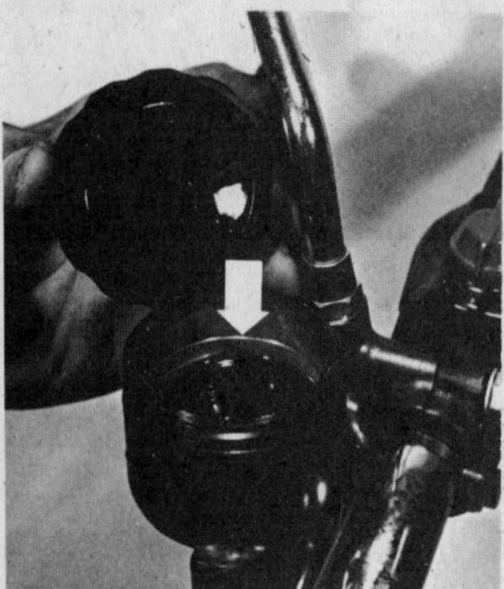
Maintain the brake fluid level at the level line (arrow)

NOTE: *The fluid level will drop slightly as the pads wear.*

2. Check the brake pad wear, and replace the pads in a set if either one is worn past the red limit line (1972 and later).

On pre-1972 brakes, check the clearance between the front of the caliper and the disc. Replace both pads if clearance is less than 0.06 in. (1.5 mm).

Refer to the "Chassis" section for brake system service procedures.

3. If the brake lever feels spongy, bleed the system. This procedure can also be found in the "Chassis" section.

4. Early disc brake models are equipped with an adjusting screw on the handlebar lever bracket. After loosening the adjuster locknut, turn the adjuster to allow 20–30 mm (0.8–1.2 in.) of lever travel (measured at the tip of the lever) before the pads are fully forced against the disc. This adjustment usually will not need to be reset once lever travel is correct. If the lever travel becomes excessive and the brake pads are satisfactory, suspect air in the brake lines.

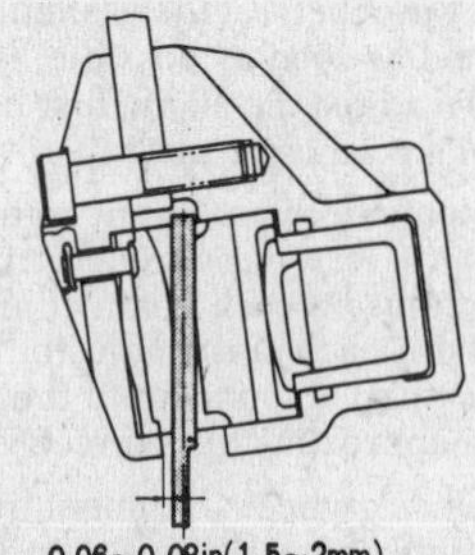

Brake pad wear check (early models)

CALIPER ADJUSTMENT

The caliper must be adjusted whenever new pads are fitted, or if the brake seems to drag.

1. Raise the front wheel off the ground.

2. Loosen the adjusting screw locknut and turn the adjusting screw *counterclockwise* until the pads contact the disc. A slight drag will be noted when spinning the wheel.

Brake caliper adjustment screw

3. Turn the adjusting screw *clockwise* until the wheel spins freely; then turn the adjusting screw ½ turn more in the same direction and tighten the locknut.

4. Check that the wheel turns freely without drag. Check for proper brake operation.

Rear Brake

1. Use the adjusting nut on the end of the rod so that the brake pedal has 1 in. (25 mm) of movement before the shoes contact the drum. Check movement with the weight of the rider on the machine.

2. Late models are equipped with a brake wear indicator. If the arrows of the indicator align when the brake is fully applied, the brake shoes are worn to the point of replacement.

3. The pedal height may be adjusted for rider comfort by means of the stopper bolt provided. Adjust the brake after adjusting the pedal height.

Brake Light Switch

The switches should be checked for operation after the brakes are adjusted. The rear brake light switch is mounted in a slotted bracket and secured by locknuts. Moving the switch up on the bracket allows the brake light to turn on sooner. Moving it down allows the light to turn on later.

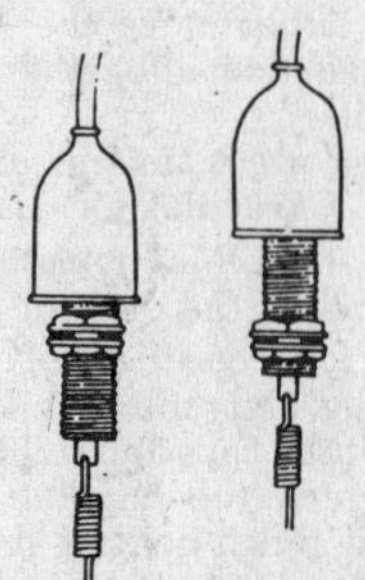

Do not turn the switch itself for adjustment. Turn the locknuts only, or the wires will become twisted and may break.

Generally, the brake light should come on just as the linings contact the drum.

Headlight Adjustment

1. Set the machine about 25 feet away from and perpendicular to a wall, preferably of a color which reflects light well.

The machine should be off the stand, and with a rider putting his weight on the machine as in operation.

2. Switch on the high beam. The headlight high beam should be parallel to the ground and should hit the wall directly in front of the machine.

3. Vertical adjustment is made by loosening the two headlight shell mounting bolts slightly and pivoting the shell up or down.

4. Lateral adjustment is accomplished by means of the screw on the right-side of the headlight. Turning the screw clockwise will move the beam to the left; turning it counterclockwise will move it to the right.

Steering Stem Bearings

The steering stem bearings should be checked periodically and adjusted if necessary. Refer to the "Chassis" section.

FUEL SYSTEM

1. Fuel system maintenance involves cleaning the petcock and filter, cleaning or replacing the air cleaner, and cleaning the carburetors.

2. The carburetors should be removed, disassembled, and cleaned every 6,000 miles. Refer to "Fuel System.

3. The petcock should be serviced every 3,000 miles.

450: Shut off the fuel; unscrew the petcock sediment bowl. Take out the O-ring and fuel filter screen. Clean the parts in solvent and inspect the screen for any holes or other defects. Replace it if damaged. Inspect the O-ring for any cuts or cracks. Reinstall the screen, O-ring, and bowl. Turn on the fuel and check for leaks.

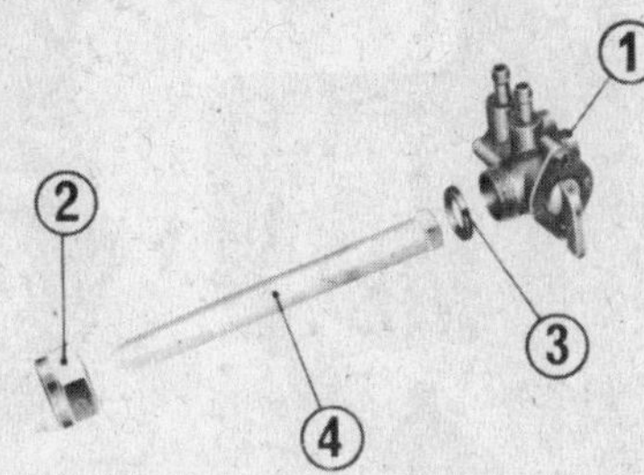

Petcock components (500T)

1. Petcock body
2. Nut
3. O-ring
4. Filter screen

500T: The petcock filter screen is inside the gas tank. Disconnect the fuel lines, remove the tank from the machine, and drain off the gas. Unscrew the securing nut and carefully take out the petcock. Remove the securing nut and filter from the petcock. Wash the filter in solvent to remove any foreign matter. Replace the filter if it is badly clogged or punctured. Check the condition of the gasket and replace it if crushed or nicked. Installation is the reverse of the above. Be sure that the fuel lines are secured to the petcock with safety clips. Check for leaks before operation.

Air Cleaner Service

The paper element air cleaner should be cleaned every 3,000 miles and replaced every 6,000 miles, under normal conditions.

REMOVAL

500T

1. Remove the left and right side-covers.

2. Remove the air cleaner covers.

3. Loosen the air cleaner hose clamps. Remove the element securing bolts, and take out the elements.

450

1. Open the seat. On CL models, the exhaust system must be removed.

2. Remove the left and right side-covers.

3. Loosen the air cleaner hose clamps. Remove the air cleaner-to-frame securing bolt. Remove the bolt running through the center of the air cleaner elements.

4. Remove the covers and the air cleaner elements.

SERVICE

1. Brush off heavy deposits of dirt with a brush. Apply compressed air through the inside of the elements to blow off any remaining deposits.

2. Since this method will be only partially successful, replacement of the elements every 6,000 miles is recommended.

3. Inspect the element and connecting tube for any damage; replace any air cleaner found defective. An oil-impregnated element or one which cannot be cleaned sufficiently should also be replaced.

4. Inspect the area where the element is bonded to the mounting plate. If the bonding is cracked or separated, replace the element.

INSTALLATION

1. Check all rubber parts for deterioration and replace if necessary.

2. Be sure that the air cleaners are properly installed and that all connections are properly fitted and secured to prevent leaks.

Breather Element

The 500T is fitted with a crankcase rebreather. After removing the air cleaner elements, remove the bolt which secures the breather cover, and remove the cover and drain tube.

Bolt (1), breather cover (2), and drain tube (3) (500T)

Remove the breather element from the air cleaner box. Clean the element in a clean solvent and dry thoroughly. Soak it in engine oil or gear oil (80 or 90W) and squeeze off the excess.

Check that the breather drain tube is clear; squeeze the end to remove any oil or water; clean out the inside of the breather case.

Install all components in the reverse of removal.

Periodic Maintenance Intervals ①

Daily
- Brake adjustment
- Engine oil level
- Cable adjustments
- Chain slack
- Lights

Weekly
- Battery fluid level
- Spokes for tightness
- Tire pressure (cold)

Every 1500 miles
- Change engine oil
- Check disc brake fluid level

Every 2000 miles
- Clean final drive chain

Every 3000 miles
- Clean and gap or replace spark plugs
- Clean and gap breaker points
- Check ignition timing
- Adjust valve clearance
- Adjust cam chain tensioner
- Lubricate breaker point cam
- Service all grease fittings
- Clean fuel petcock
- Lubricate controls and cables
- Clean air cleaner elements
- Clean breather elements (500T)
- Inspect condition of chain and sprockets
- Check condition of all fuel lines
- Check carburetor operation
- Check brake pads for wear

Every 6000 miles
- Clean oil filter
- Change fork oil
- Replace air cleaner elements
- Adjust steering head bearings

Every 12000 miles
- Flush and renew disc brake fluid
- Repack wheel and steering head bearings

① Based on normal usage after break-in is complete.

Maintenance Data

	CB450 ('66–'67)	CB/CL450 ('68–'69)	CB/CL450 ('70–'71)	CB/CL450 ('72–'74)	CB500T
Crankcase (qts)	3.0	3.0	3.0	3.0	3.0
Front Forks (cc/oz)					
When changing	210/7.1	270/9.2	210/7.1	140/4.8	165–180/5.6–6.3
After rebuilding	230/7.8	290/9.9	225/7.7	160/5.4	185–200/6.3–6.8
Tire Pressure (psi)					
Normal					
Front	26	26	26	28	26
Rear	28	28	28	28	28
High-speed or w/passenger					
Front	26	26	26	28	28
Rear	34	34	34	34	36
Battery					
Yuasa No.	12N12A-4A	12N12A-4A	12N12A-4A	12N12A-4A	12N12A-4A
Voltage	12	12	12	12	12
Continuous charging rate (amps)	1.2	1.2	1.2	1.2	1.2

Recommended Lubricants

Engine
General—All Temperatures
SAE 10W-30, service rating "SE"
SAE 10W-40, service rating "SE"
Alternate

SAE 30	Above 59° F
SAE 20 or 20W	32°–59° F
SAE 10W	Below 32° F

Forks
ATF
SAE 30W, SAE 20W

Control Cables
10W-30 motor oil
Graphite-base lubricant
Molybdenum disulphide-base lubricant

Tach, Speedo Cables
Light-duty, lithium-base grease

Wheel Bearings
Waterproof, medium-weight bearing grease

Steering Head Bearings
Waterproof, medium-weight bearing grease

Grease Fittings
Waterproof, medium-weight chassis grease

TUNE-UP

NOTE: *Common tune-up procedures are explained in detail in "General Information."*

CAM CHAIN ADJUSTMENT

1. The cam chain tensioner is located behind the cylinders and consists of a aluminum housing and a spring-loaded tensioner rod which is held in place by a lockbolt.

2. To adjust the cam chain, turn the engine over with the kick-starter; loosen the lock bolt nut, and back the bolt off one or two turns. The proper chain tension will be set automatically.

3. Tighten the bolt to secure the tensioner rod, then tighten the locknut.

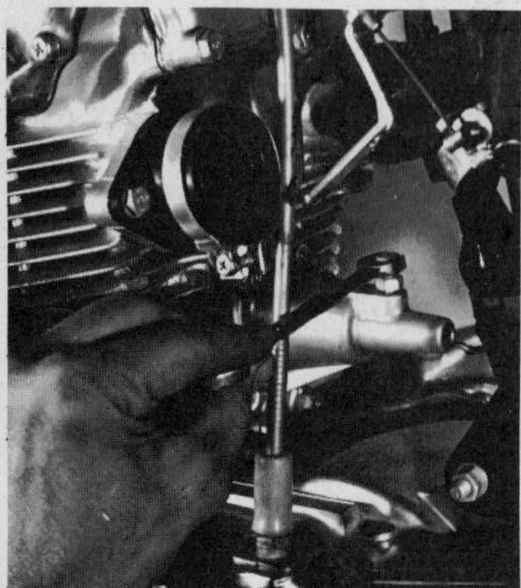

Adjusting cam chain tension

Alternate Method

1. Loosen the locknut and tensioner bolt.

2. Insert a piece of stiff wire, such as a straightened paper clip, into the tail section of the tensioner housing and hold it gently against the end of the tensioner rod (on early 450s, the rod protrudes from the housing).

Checking cam chain tensioner rod movement

3. Turn the engine over slowly in the normal direction of rotation. You will be able to feel the tensioner rod move back and forth as chain tension varies.

4. Do this several times and note that point at which the rod is farthest in. Stop the engine at this point. Tighten the tensioner bolt and locknut.

CAUTION: *Never push on the tensioner rod to force it in; do not hold the rod in place while tightening the bolt. All tension must be supplied by the tensioner spring.*

VALVE ADJUSTMENT

NOTE: *The valves must be adjusted when the engine is cold.*

1. Lift the seat. Shut off the fuel, disconnect the line(s) at the petcock, and remove the gas tank. Remove the carburetors.

2. Remove the intake and exhaust cam covers at the rear and front of the cylinder head.

3. Remove the alternator rotor cover. Remove the spark plugs.

4. Valve adjustment is made by turning the cam follower shafts which are eccentric. Clearance is measured between the camshaft lobe and the cam follower pad.

"LT" rotor mark aligned for left cylinder valve clearance setting

If the index marks are aligned, turn the engine 360° to adjust the valves

Valve clearance is measured between the lobe and the cam follower pad

Clearance for all valves is 0.03 mm (0.0012 in.).

5. Turn the alternator rotor in the normal direction of rotation (counterclockwise) until the "LT" mark on the rotor aligns with the stator index mark. If the index marks of the intake and exhaust cams are aligned with the marks on the bearing holders on the right ends of the cam, turn the alternator rotor 360°. The left cylinder is now at top dead center on the compression stroke.

6. Check the clearance of the valves for the left cylinder. If clearance is correct, a feeler gauge of 0.03 mm/0.0012 in. will be a light drag fit between the cam lobe and the cam follower pad.

7. If adjustment is necessary, loosen the locknut and turn the cam follower shaft as necessary to effect proper clearance.

Do not turn the shaft more than 180°.

8. Tighten the shaft locknut, and recheck the clearance.

9. Turn the alternator rotor 180° so that the "T" mark on the rotor aligns with the stator index mark and check that the right cylinder is at TDC on the compression stroke. Check valve clearances and make adjustments as outlined in Steps 6–8.

10. Valve clearance is *decreased* by turning the shafts in the following directions:

The index marks on the cam follower shafts must point away from the center of the head

Left-side	EX—turn counterclockwise IN—turn clockwise
Right-side	IN—turn counterclockwise EX—turn clockwise

To increase clearance, reverse the above directions.

CONTACT BREAKER POINTS

Location

1. The points are located in a case on the left-side of the cylinder head, and are operated off the exhaust camshaft. The timing advance mechanism is fitted behind the breaker point base plate.

Replacement

1. If replacement of the points is necessary, this is easily accomplished by disconnecting the primary wire, removing the two point securing screws, and taking off the points. Install the new points after thoroughly cleaning off the contact surfaces with a non-oily solvent, and adjust the gap. If a breaker plate assembly is purchased, simply disconnect the yellow and blue point wires from the wiring harness and remove the two breaker plate screws. Install the new breaker plate and connect the primary wires. Clean the surfaces of the points and adjust the gap. Whenever the points are replaced, the ignition timing will have to be set.

2. Apply a bit of grease to the breaker cam lubricating wick. Take care not to apply too much to avoid fouling the points.

Remove mounting screws and disconnect primary wire (circles) for point removal

Gapping

Points should be filed (if necessary) and cleaned before gapping.

1. Remove the points cover.
2. Using the rotor bolt, turn the engine over until one set of points is open to their maximum gap.
3. With the proper feeler gauge, check the gap. The proper specification for all models is 0.3–0.4 mm (0.012–0.016 in.).

Loosen the two screws (arrows) to adjust the point gap

4. If adjustment is necessary, loosen the two screws which secure the points to the base plate, and use a thin screwdriver at the pry slot provided to bring the gap to the proper specification.

NOTE: *Loosen the screws just enough to allow the points to be moved. If too loose, the points will snap shut instead of holding the adjustment.*

5. Tighten the screws and recheck the gap. It may change slightly when the screws are tightened.
6. Repeat the procedure for the other set of points.
7. If it is not possible to gap the points correctly, the fiber heel is evidently worn; the set of points should be replaced.

Lubrication

1. On all models it is necessary to lubricate the cam follower fiber heel and the pivot point of the contact breaker occasionally. This minimizes wear and ensures that the timing will remain accurate for a longer period. A worn heel will retard the timing.
2. A small dab of grease (high melting point, if possible) should be applied to the lubricator wick so that the lubricator can distribute it onto the breaker cam. A drop of engine oil should be applied to the pivot point.
3. In both cases it is imperative that care be taken to keep the lubricant away from the points contact surface.
4. The lubricating wick should be adjusted so that it just contacts the breaker cam.
5. If the wick is missing the grease can be applied sparingly to the cam itself.

IGNITION TIMING

NOTE: *Points must be cleaned and gapped before checking timing. Dirty points will cause inaccurate readings.*

The method of adjusting the timing is the same regardless of the type of equipment used. The *left* cylinder is set *first* and timing is adjusted by moving the base plate. After the left cylinder is correctly timed, the right cylinder can be checked, and adjusted if necessary. To adjust the right cylinder timing, the point gap is varied so that the points open at the instant the timing marks align. A change in the point gap of 0.1 mm (0.004 in.) will change the timing 10°. Increasing the point gap will advance the timing, while decreasing it will retard the timing.

If correct timing cannot be accomplished with both point gaps set in the correct range of 0.3–0.4 mm (0.012–0.016 in.), the points should be replaced.

Dynamic Timing

1. Remove the alternator cover so that the timing marks are visible, and remove the points cover.

NOTE: *A white grease pencil or some paint can be used on the rotor and stator timing indicator marks to increase their visibility under the strobe light.*

2. Hook up the timing light according to the manufacturer's instructions. Most lights use the vehicle's own battery as a power source.
3. Start the engine, set the idle at 1,100 rpm, aiming the light on the rotor. Note the following:
   a. At idle, the "LF" (left cylinder) mark or the "F" (right cylinder) mark on the rotor should line up with the timing indicator on the stator, depending on which plug the strobe right is connected to;
   b. As the revolutions increase past 1,800 rpm, the "LF" or the "F" mark should be seen to move in a direction opposite that of the crankshaft rotation;
   c. Finally, at full advance (about 3,200 rpm and above), the twin rotor marks must line up with the timing indicator mark on the stator.
4. The full advance reading is the most important. If the rotor marks and the stator indicator do not align, proceed as follows:
5. Time the *left* cylinder *first.* Loosen the two screws which secure the breaker base plate just enough to allow the plate to be turned. Using a thin screwdriver applied at the pry point provided, rotate

Left cylinder timing when fully advanced

the plate in the direction necessary so that the timing marks align.

Rotating the plate clockwise advances the timing; rotating the plate counterclockwise retards the timing.

Adjust ignition timing by loosening the screws (arrows) and rotating the plate with a screwdriver applied to the pry point (circle)

Tighten the base plate screws and recheck the timing.

6. Connect the timing light to the right cylinder and check the timing as for the left cylinder this time using the "F" mark on the rotor.

If the right cylinder timing is incorrect, loosen the two screws which secure the right cylinder's points to the base plate.

NOTE: *The point set on the right of the breakerplate is for the right cylinder.*

Open or close the point gap so that the timing marks align as the points open, but keep the point gap within 0.3–0.4 mm (0.012–0.016 in.).

7. After the ignition timing is set, recheck the point gaps. Both must still be within the proper specification (0.3–0.4 mm/0.012–0.016 in.).

If either gap is not within this value, increase or decrease it as necessary so that it is. Increase or decrease the other point gap by the same amount. Both must be within the given range.

After making any adjustment to the point gap, the timing will have to be readjusted.

If the gaps have been changed by equal amounts, it will only be necessary to adjust the timing by moving the base plate.

If proper ignition timing is not possible, replace both sets of points, since the fiber heels are probably worn.

Static Timing

1. Remove the alternator cover, points cover, and the intake cam cover.

2. Remove the spark plugs and hook up the tester.

NOTE: *The point set on the left of the breaker plate is for the left cylinder.*

3. Turn the engine over so that the left cylinder is on the compression stroke (the left intake valve will go down and come up). Turn the engine over slowly in the normal direction of rotation (counterclockwise). At the instant in which the "LF" mark on the rotor aligns with the index mark on the stator, the left points should begin to open as indicated by the reaction of the test light or the meter.

4. If the points open before the marks align, the timing is too advanced. If they open after the "LF" mark passes the index, the timing is too retarded.

5. If the timing is not correct, set the "LF" mark so that it is aligned with the index mark with the piston on its compression stroke. Loosen the two screws which secure the breaker base plate and rotate the plate until the light or meter indicates that the points have just opened. Tighten the base plate screws and recheck the timing.

6. After completing the timing for the left cylinder, connect the light or meter to the points for the right cylinder. Turn the rotor 180° counterclockwise until the "F" mark aligns with the index mark; at this point the right set of points should just open. If the timing is incorrect, align the "F" mark with the index mark and increase or decrease the point gap so that the points just open as indicated by the light or meter. Refer to Steps 6 and 7 under "Dynamic Timing," above. Tighten the set screws and recheck the timing and the point gap for both cylinders. Note that both gaps must still be within specifications.

CARBURETORS

Three adjustments to be made to the carburetors are the float level, the idle mixture, and the idle speed. For the first of these, the carburetors must be removed from the motorcycle.

Adjusting Float Level

Generally, float level will not need adjustment unless the carburetor has been disassembled, fuel delivery problems have been noted, or considerable mileage has been covered.

1. Remove the carburetors from the motorcycle as outlined in the "Fuel Systems" section.

2. Remove the float bowl. Remove the float bowl gasket.

3. Float level is defined as the measured distance from the float bowl mating surface on the carburetor body (gasket removed) to the top of the float, when the tang of the float is just touching the end of the float needle. A special gauge is available to check the float level although a vernier caliper can also be used.

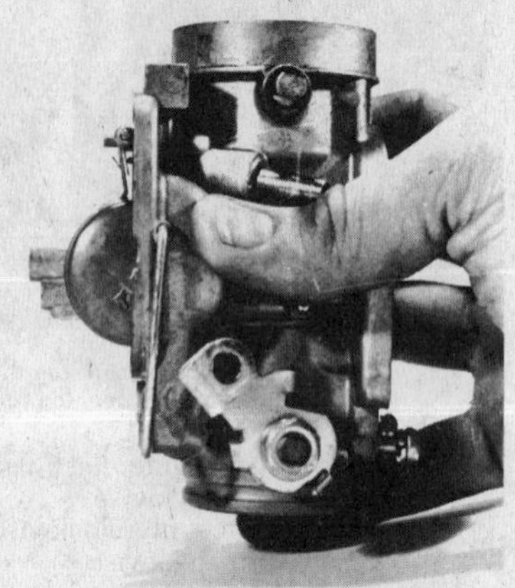

Checking float level

4. With the carburetor held as shown, measure the distance from the float bowl mating surface to the top of the float when the float tang is just touching, but not depressing, the float needle.

Correct float level for all models is 20.0 mm (0.79 in.).

5. If the adjustment is necessary, bend the float tang *only* to raise or lower the float level.

Be sure that both carburetors are set to the same float level.

6. Float level will not be correct if the needle is worn, or if there is foreign matter on the needle seat.

Idle Speed and Mixture

NOTE: *These items must be adjusted when the engine is at operating temperature.*

450 AND 500T

1. Remove the caps from the pilot screws (500T).

2. Check that the throttle cable has enough slack so that the throttle plates are not held open by their cables. Check by starting the engine and turning each stop screw out by about one turn. If idle speed does not decrease, the plate(s) are being held open by the cable(s).

Carburetor throttle stop (arrow) and pilot (circle) screws

3. Turn the pilot screws in very carefully until they are lightly seated, then back each one out one turn for the 450, or 1½ turns for the 500T.

4. Set the idle speed to about 1,200 rpm, turning the stop screw for each carburetor by equal amounts if adjustment is necessary to achieve proper idle speed.

5. Disconnect one spark plug lead. Adjust the stop screw for the other cylinder so that the engine runs on one cylinder as slowly as possible. Turn the pilot screw in or out until the engine runs smoothly. It should not be necessary to turn the pilot screw more than one-half turn in either direction from the standard setting.

6. Connect the other spark plug lead, rev the engine a few times to clean out the engine, and then repeat this procedure with the other cylinder.

7. When both carburetors have been set, connect both plug leads. Engine idle speed will be high, so turn each stop screw out by equal amounts so that an idle of 1,100 rpm is obtained.

8. Check that the two carburetors are synchronized by opening and closing the throttle while watching the throttle stop screws. Both screws must begin to move at the same time when the throttle is opened. If one begins to move before the other, use the cable adjusters on the carburetors so that the movement of the stop screws is synchronized.

This cable adjuster is used to synchronize the throttle plates

9. Snap the throttle open and closed several times to make sure that synchronization is maintained.

10. Adjust the throttle cable free-play using the adjuster near the twist-grip so that the throttle has 10–15° of free rotation before the stop screws begin to move.

11. Install the pilot screw caps on the 500T so that the stop is pointed downward.

500T ONLY

The 500T is equipped with vacuum gauge fittings to adjust idle speed and mixture if such gauges are available.

1. Raise the gas tank as far as possible using longer fuel lines from the petcock to the carburetors.

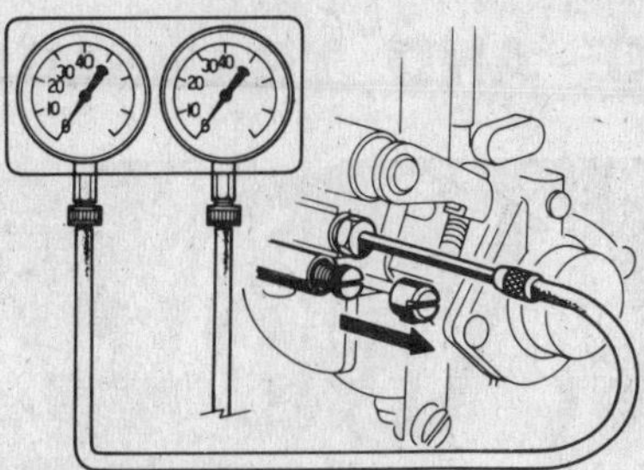

Vacuum gauge installed on carburetor (500T)

2. Remove the vacuum gauge plugs from the carburetors and fit the vacuum lines (Tool No. 07510–3000200) and vacuum gauges (Tool No. 07504–3000100).

3. Loosen the cable adjuster locknuts and turn the adjusters in to allow a good amount of play in the cables.

4. Remove the caps from the carburetor pilot screws. Turn each screw in carefully until it bottoms, then turn each out 1½ turns.

5. With the engine idling, adjust the throttle stop screws to yield an idle speed of 1,100 rpm.

6. The vacuum gauges should show equal readings. Normal vacuum is 200–240 mm Hg. The two cylinders must be within 20 mm Hg of each other. Turn either or both of the throttle stop screws until both gauges give the same reading.

7. Turn the pilot screw on either carburetor in or out until the highest rpm is reached. It should not be necessary to turn the pilot screw more than ½ turn from the standard setting. Repeat the procedure with the other carburetor.

8. Readjust the vacuum readings and idle speed with the throttle stop screws if necessary.

9. Install the caps to the pilot screws with the stops pointed downward.

10. Synchronize the carburetors and adjust the cables as outlined in Steps 8–10, above.

Be sure that all cable adjuster locknuts are tightened. When original fuel lines are installed, be sure that all connections are tight.

11. If the carburetors cannot be adjusted so that they are within 20 mm Hg of each other or if either is not within the 200–240 mm Hg range, check the following:

a. Air leaks around the intake manifold or air cleaner;
b. Ignition timing;
c. Tappet clearance;
d. Compression pressure;
e. Spark plug gap and condition of plugs.

Tune-Up Specifications

	450	*500T*
VALVE CLEARANCE (mm/in.)		
Intake	0.03/0.0012	0.03/0.0012
Exhaust	0.03/0.0012	0.03/0.0012
COMPRESSION (psi)		
Normal	180	180
Max allowable variance (low/high)	160/213	160/213
Max allowable variance between cylinders	15	15
IGNITION SYSTEM		
Point gap (mm/in.)	0.3–0.4/0.012–0.016	0.3–0.4/0.012–0.016
Spark plug (NCK/ND)	B8ES/W24ES	B8ES/W24ES
Plug gap (mm/in.)	0.7–0.8/0.028–0.032	0.7–0.8/0.028–0.032
CARBURETOR		
Pilot screw (turns out)	1	1½
Idle speed (rpm)	1100	1100
Float level (mm/in.)	20.0/0.79	20.0/0.79
Vacuum at idle (mm/in. Hg)	——	200–240/7.8–9.4
Max allowable variation between cylinders (mm/in. Hg)	——	20/0.78

—— Not applicable

ENGINE AND TRANSMISSION

NOTE: *For engine component inspection techniques and procedures, refer to "Engine Rebuilding" in the General Information section.*

Engine Service

1. To remove the cylinder head, barrels, and pistons, the engine must be removed from the frame.

2. Crankcase cover components: oil pump, clutch, gearshift mechanism, alternator, and countershaft sprocket, are all accessible with the engine in the frame.

3. To remove the cylinder head, a special tool is needed to break the endless cam chain. A special tool is also needed to press on a new masterlink plate when joining the chain. Disassembly should never be attempted unless these tools and a new masterlink are available.

4. Read each procedure carefully before beginning so that replacement items such as gaskets, O-rings, etc., can be purchased beforehand.

ENGINE REMOVAL AND INSTALLATION

450

1. Drain the oil.

2. Turn the fuel tap off, disconnect the fuel lines and the balance line, and remove the gas tank.

To safely remove the tank, either drain it completely prior to removal, or obtain a four inch length of fuel line and two small clamps. Attach one clamp to the fuel tank's balance line. Disconnect the line; fit the spare length of fuel line to the tank fitting with the clamp already attached. This will prevent fuel from spilling out since the balance line must be disconnected for removal.

3. Remove the exhaust system.

4. Remove the air filters, disconnect the choke band from the left carb, loosen the carburetor-to-intake manifold clamps, and remove the carburetors.

5. Remove the cable adjuster holder from each carburetor. Place the carburetors in a safe location.

6. Remove the footpeg and shift lever, and take off the left-side rear crankcase cover. Use an impact driver to remove the cover screws. Disconnect the clutch cable at the cover. Separate the chain at the masterlink. If an endless-type chain is fitted, loosen the rear brake adjuster, back off the rear axle chain adjusters, move the wheel forward as far as possible, and take the chain off the sprocket.

7. Disconnect the engine electrical leads (alternator, neutral switch, and points) at the connectors.

8. Disconnect the wires from the spark plugs and tuck them up out of the way. Loosen the spark plugs.

9. Disconnect the starter motor cable from the starter solenoid and disconnect the tachometer cable from the cylinder

Engine mounting bolts

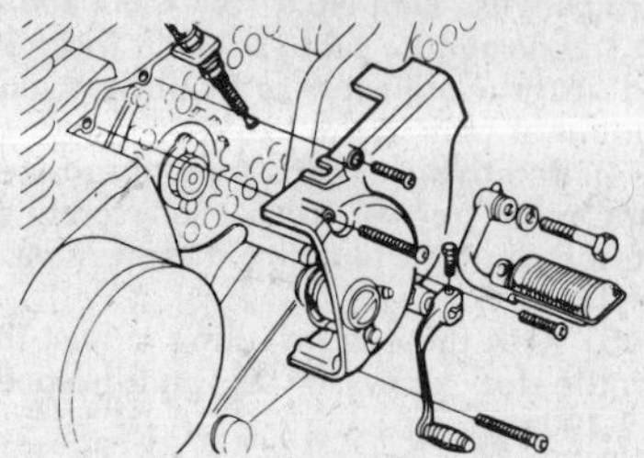

Left rear crankcase cover removal

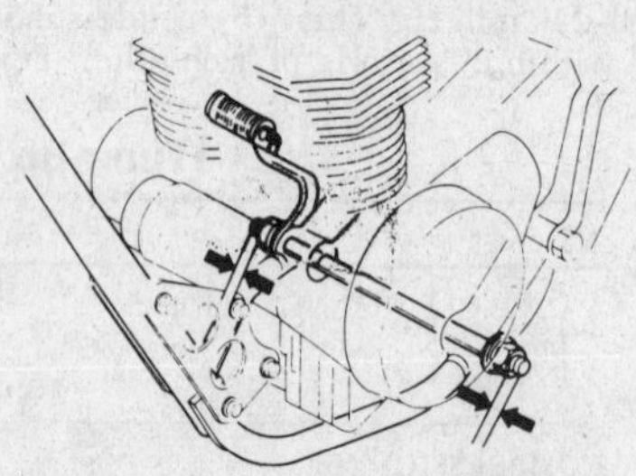

About the same number of threads should protrude from each side

head. Disconnect the head breather tube. Remove the horn to prevent accidental damage.

10. Unscrew the engine mounting bolts and remove the engine from the left side.

Installation is a reversal of the removal procedure. Note the following points:

1. Do not forget to connect the battery ground cable when installing the engine mounting bolts. The cable connection must be clean and tight.

2. The chain master link clip should be installed so that the closed end faces the direction of forward rotation.

3. Make sure that the steel ball has been installed in the clutch release lever before reinstalling the crankcase cover.

4. Coat the threads of the cover screws with a lubricant or anti-seize compound and use an impact driver to secure them.

500T

1. Lift the seat, disconnect the fuel lines from the gas tank petcock, and remove the tank.

2. Remove the exhaust pipes and mufflers. This is done by removing the clamps at the cylinder head, removing the balance box bolts, removing the passenger footrests, and taking off the exhaust system as a unit.

3. Remove the tach cable from the head.

4. Disconnect the spark plug leads. Loosen the spark plugs.

5. Remove the left and right air cleaner covers. Loosen the clamps at the carburetors and the air cleaner bolts and remove the elements. Disconnect the choke band at one carburetor. Disconnect any overflow lines from the carburetors. Loosen the clamps at the manifold and remove the carburetors. Remove the throttle cable adjuster holder from each carburetor. Put the carburetors in a safe place.

6. Disconnect the starter motor cable at the solenoid.

7. Disconnect the alternator switch, and points wires at the connectors.

8. Loosen the rear brake adjuster as much as possible. Remove the axle nut cotter pin and loosen the axle nut several turns. Loosen the chain adjuster bolt locknut and screw out the adjuster bolt. Push the wheel forward as far as possible.

9. Remove the left rider footpeg. Remove the gearshift lever (carefully) from its splined shaft. Remove the rear portion of the left crankcase cover. Use an impact driver to remove the cover screws.

10. Remove the countershaft sprocket protector. Unbolt the sprocket lockplate, and slide the sprocket off its shaft.

11. Remove the horn and electrical wiring box.

12. Remove the engine mounting plates and bolts. Remove the engine from the frame.

Installation is the reverse of the above. Note the following points:

1. When installing the rider footpegs, the nuts should be tightened equally so that approximately the same number of stud threads protrude on each side.

2. Be sure that the battery ground cable connection is clean and tight.

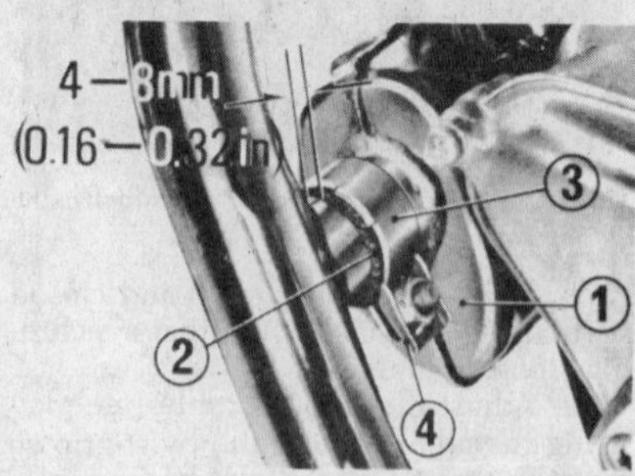

Balance chamber (1); gasket (2); clamp (3); bolt (4)

3. Use a lubricant or anti-seize compound on the crankcase cover screws and tighten them with an impact driver.

4. When refitting the exhaust system, be sure that the balance chamber gaskets are in place, flush with the ends of the chamber.

Clearance between the chamber ends and the exhaust pipes should be 4–8 mm (0.16–0.32 in.).

CYLINDER HEAD

Removal

NOTE: *A special chain breaker/installation tool is needed to properly remove and install the head.*

1. Remove the engine from the frame.
2. Remove the eight bolts and take off the cam covers. Remove the gaskets if they adhere to the head. These gaskets must be replaced with new ones upon reassembly.
3. Remove the spark plugs; remove the alternator cover. Back off the cam chain tensioner bolt.

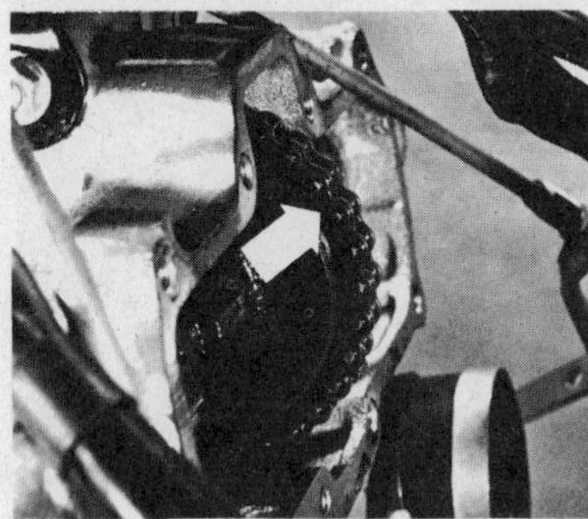

The cam chain masterlink has indentations on the rivets

4. Turn the engine over until the special masterlink on the cam chain is accessible on the intake side of the engine.
5. Wire up the cam chain on the lower side of the masterlink and below the exhaust cam sprocket so the ends will not slip into the engine when the masterlink is removed.
6. Use the chain breaker (Honda Tool No. 07968–2830100) to separate the chain at the masterlink.

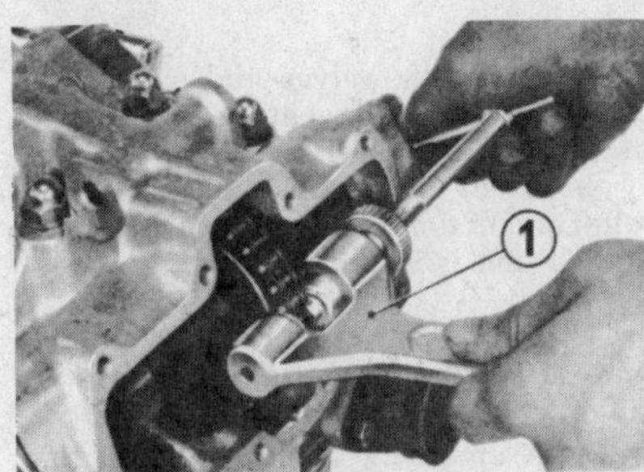

Separating the cam chain

7. Remove the eight cylinder head capnuts. These nuts should be loosened a little at a time and in a cross pattern. Loosen the outer four first, then the inner four; when all are loose, remove them from the studs.
8. Remove the cylinder head. If the head is stuck, tap around the mating surface with a plastic mallet, being cautious of the fins.
9. Remove the head gasket.
10. Attach the two ends of the cam chain to fixed points on the crankcase with pieces of wire to keep them from falling into the crankcase.
11. Note the hollow dowel pins on the cylinder-head mating surface. These must be in place on the two right-hand studs and the forward left-hand stud upon assembly.

Disassembly

1. Remove the front and rear cam chain guide rollers from the head by removing the four bolts.

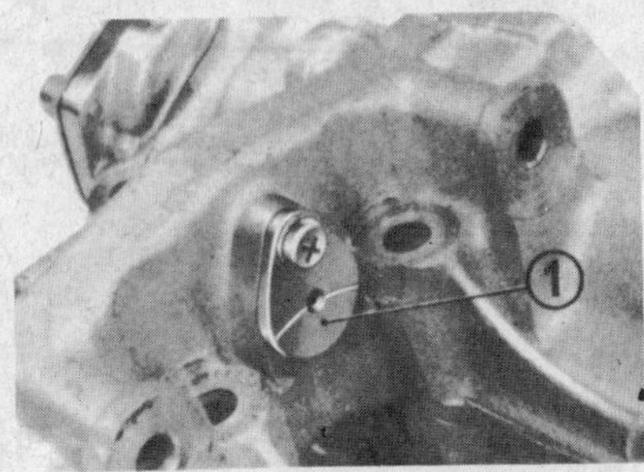

Upper chain guide roller pin (1)

2. Remove the screw securing the upper chain guide roller pin. Remove the pin and roller.
3. Remove the locknuts from the cam follower shafts on the right and left-sides of the intake camshaft. Remove the right and left covers. Remove the intake camshaft.

CAUTION: *Note the camshaft shims. They must be installed to take up sideplay.*

4. Remove the locknut from the tachometer drive side exhaust cam follower shaft. Remove the tachometer drive box and driveshaft from the head.
5. Remove the breaker point cover. Remove the locknut from the cam follower shaft. Scribe a line across the breaker point plate to the head to approximate ignition timing for assembly. Remove the two screws and remove the breaker plate complete with points. Remove the breaker cam bolt and pull off the timing advance assembly.
6. Remove the points housing after removing the securing screws. Remove the exhaust camshaft.
7. Pull out the cam follower shafts and the cam followers.

NOTE: *Keep each cam follower with its respective shaft. Also note the position of each follower and shaft in the head. Components must be installed in their original locations.*

8. Loosen the bolt on one of the torsion bar holders, backing it off several

Removing the cam follower shaft (1) and cam follower (2)

Torsion bar holder (1) and special tool (2)

turns. Use the special tool (Tool No. 07973–2830001) to turn the torsion bar holder in the direction marked on the end of the bar to take the tension off the bolt. Then remove the bolt. Pull out the torsion bar; remove the outer arm. Repeat the procedure with the remaining torsion bars.

NOTE: *As other torsion bar components are removed, keep each assembly together. All components must be installed in their original locations. Torsion bars should not be interchanged between cams or sides.*

9. To remove the valves, remove the valve keepers and spring retainer.
10. Inspect valve guides for condition before attempting removal. If replacement is necessary, remove the bolt securing the guide stopper. Remove the seal. Drive the guide out of the head with either the Honda tool (No. 07942-2830000) or a like substitute.
11. The exhaust cam right-side cover houses the tachometer drive mechanism. If removal is necessary, remove the phillips screw which secures the cable fitting; remove the bolt from the rear of the cover; remove the driveshaft and driven shaft.

All washers and seals in this assembly should be replaced with new ones upon assembly.

Valve keepers (1); spring retainer (2); and valve (3)

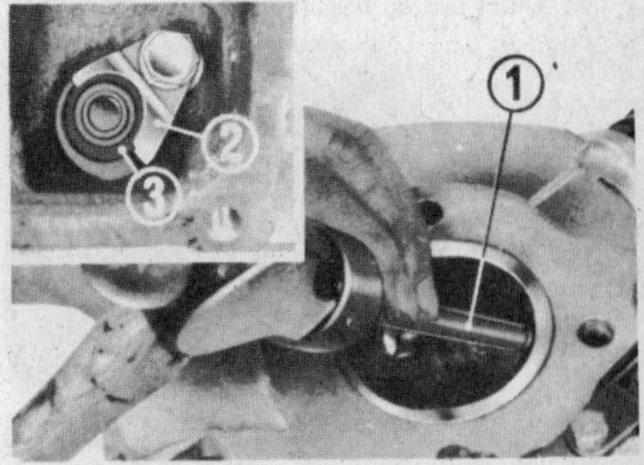

Removing a valve guide (1); valve guide stopper (2); and seal (3)

Inspection

For specifications of the top end components, refer to the charts at the end of this section.

CAMSHAFT

In addition to the usual checks, camshaft side-play must be checked.

1. Install each camshaft, along with its shims; lubricate, install, and secure the end covers. Check each camshaft for free rotation. Check each for side-play. Side-play must be within 0.05–0.35 mm (0.002–0.014 in.). If it is not, remove or substitute the proper camshaft shims.

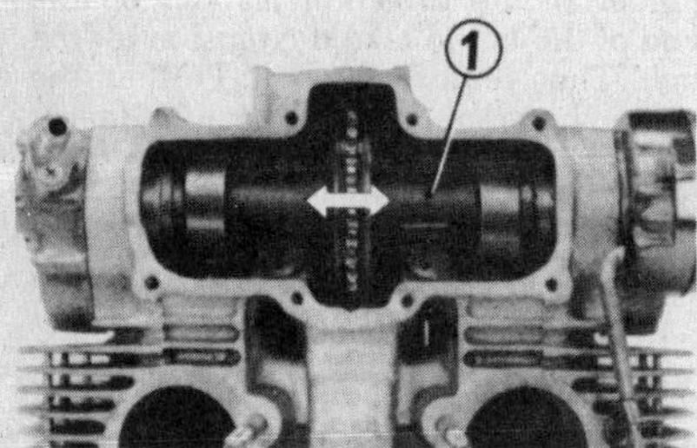

Checking cam side play

TORSION BARS

1. Check the condition of the torsion bar and outer arm assembly. The splines must be in very good condition. If either the arm or the bar show signs of heat damage or discoloration, replace them.
2. Check the tension of the torsion bar before reassembly. With the valve assembly in place, attach a torque wrench to the torsion bar holder and read the amount of force required to preload the torsion bar so that the bolt can be installed. This reading will yield the seated pressure of the valve which should be about 44–55 in. lbs. If tension is below 44 in. lbs, either replace the torsion bars or fit a thicker valve spring retainer.

If replacing the torsion bars, replace all as a set. If tension is satisfactory, do *not* fit a thicker retainer. Standard thickness is 7.0 mm. Service retainer thickness is 7.7 mm.

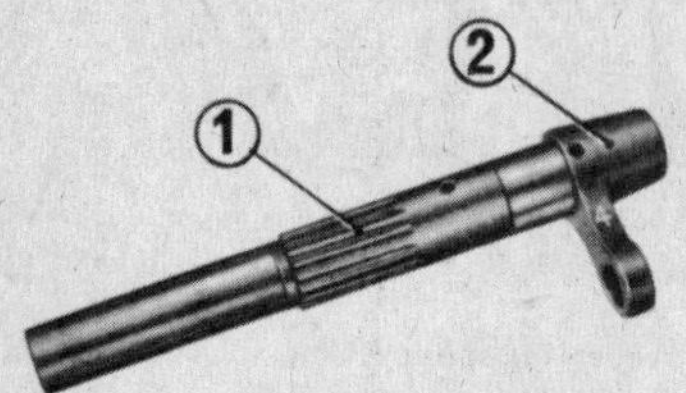

Outer torsion bar (1) and holder (2)

Checking torsion bar tension with a torque wrench (2) and adapter (1)

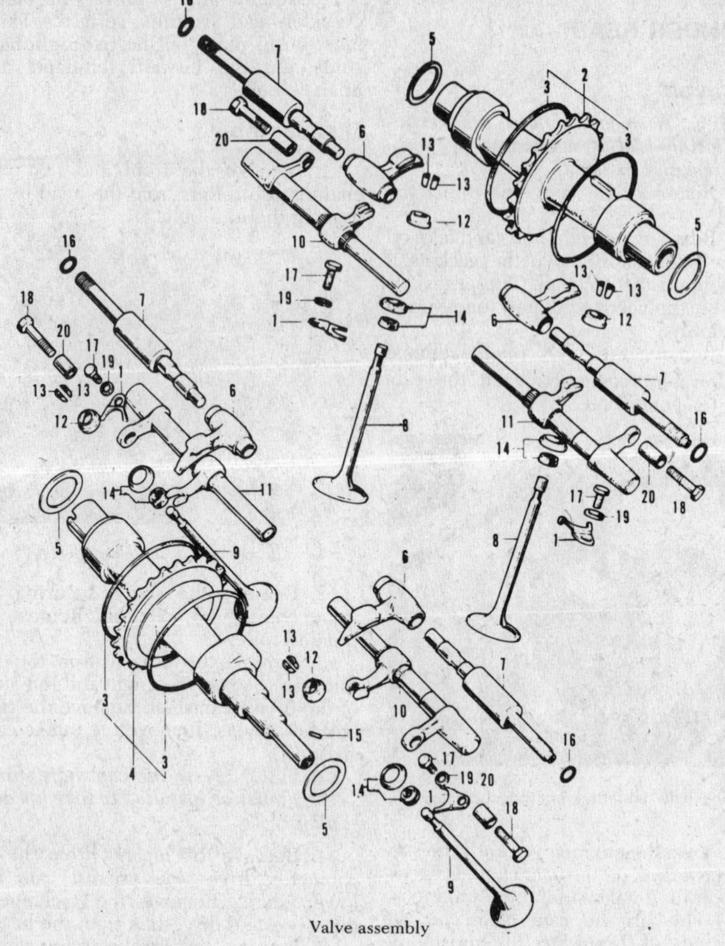

Valve assembly

1. Valve guide retainer
2. Camshaft, intake
3. O-ring
4. Camshaft, exhaust
5. Camshaft spacer
6. Cam follower
7. Cam follower shaft
8. Intake valve
9. Exhaust valve
10. Torsion bar assembly, L-EX, R-IN
11. Torsion bar assembly, R-EX, L-IN
12. Valve spring retainer
13. Valve keepers
14. Valve seal
15. Camshaft pin
16. O-ring
17. Bolt
18. Outer arm bolt
19. Lockwasher
20. Dowel pin

VALVES

Valves have stellite tips and edges. Machining or grinding the tips or edges of the head is not recommended.

Assembly

1. Install valve guides (if removed) using the guide driver (Tool No. 07942–1180100). Ream the guide after installation with Tool No. 07984–5900000. Be sure that the guide O-rings are installed.

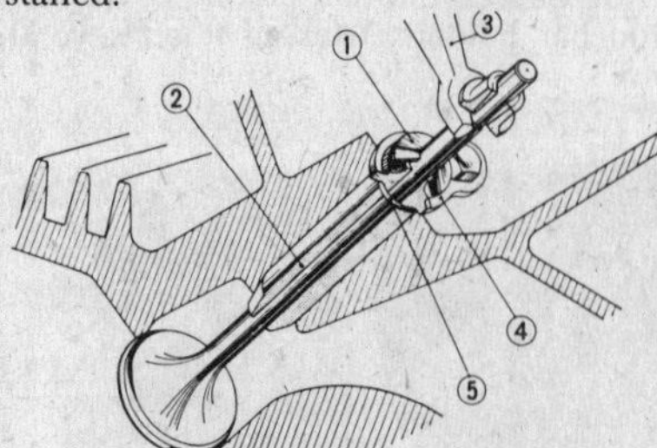

Valve assembly

1. Valve seal
2. Valve guide
3. Torsion bar
4. Valve guide keeper
5. Valve

2. Install the valves and check seat width. If necessary, recut the seat and lap in the valves.
3. Install the upper cam chain guide roller and fit the roller pin ensuring that a new O-ring is installed in the groove of the pin.
4. Fit the valve guide stopper and seal. Install the outer arm, the valve, retainer, and valve keepers.
5. Assemble the torsion bar. Note that the torsion bars are marked "EX-L/IN-R" or "EX-R/IN-L"; be sure that each one is correctly installed.

Installing the torsion bar assembly (1) and outer arm (2)

6. Fit the torsion bar holder dowel pin; install the torsion bar and holder, then turn the bar in the direction marked so that the holder bolt can be installed and secured.

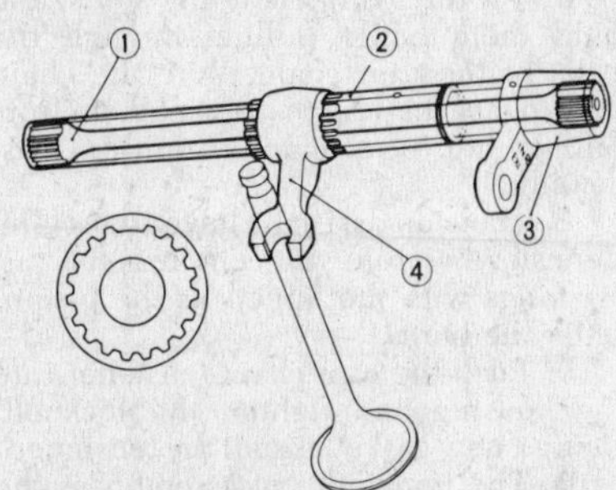

Valve spring assembly: 1, torsion bar; 2, torsion bar outer; 3, holder; 4, outer arm

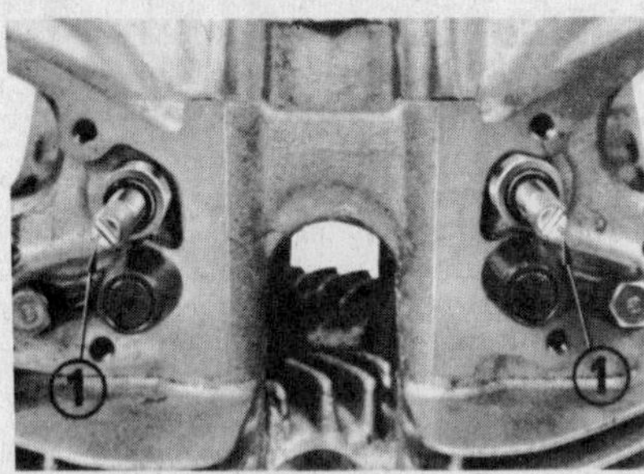

Cam follower shaft index marks (1) must point away from the center of the head

7. Lubricate the cam followers and shafts and install them. Note the small mark on the end of each cam follower shaft. This mark must point away from the center of the cylinder head and approximately 45° down from the horizontal when the shafts are installed.

8. Lubricate and install the intake cam and shims. Fit the cam covers. Be sure that cam side clearance is correct.

9. Lubricate and install the exhaust camshaft and shims. Lubricate the lips of the oil seal; install the breaker point housing. Install the tach drive box and driveshaft aligning the tabs on the drive gear with the slots in the camshaft. Check cam side-play as previously outlined.

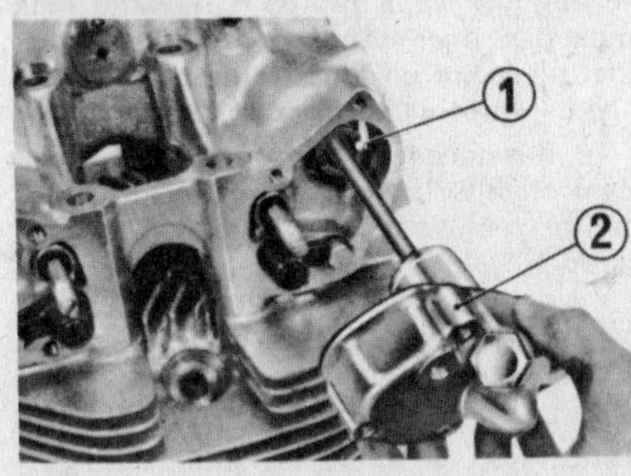

When installing the tach drive box (2), align the tabs on the drive gear with the slots in the cam (1)

10. Install the timing advance mechanism, aligning the slot in the mechanism with the pin in the camshaft.

11. Fit the breaker plate, complete with points, and align the scribed timing mark if you made one. Check the ignition timing after assembly has been completed.

12. Install, but do not tighten, the cam follower shaft locknuts. Valves must be adjusted after assembly is completed.

Installation

1. Fit a new head gasket to the cylinder and check that the dowel pins and O-rings are in place in the cylinder.

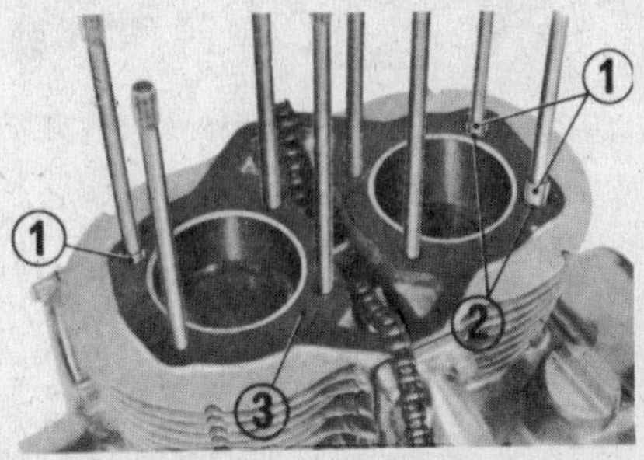

Be sure that the hollow dowel pins and O-rings (1 and 2) are in place before fitting the head gasket (3)

2. Install the head, pulling the cam chain up through it as it is moved down on the studs.

NOTE: *The stud threads should be cleaned and oiled lightly to ensure correct torque readings when securing the head.*

3. Fit the capnuts to the studs. Note that the nuts have special washers fitted beneath them for oil sealing.

4. Tighten the capnuts in increments of a few ft lbs until the proper torque of 25.3 ft lbs is reached. Note that the nuts must be tightened in a cross pattern beginning with the center nuts.

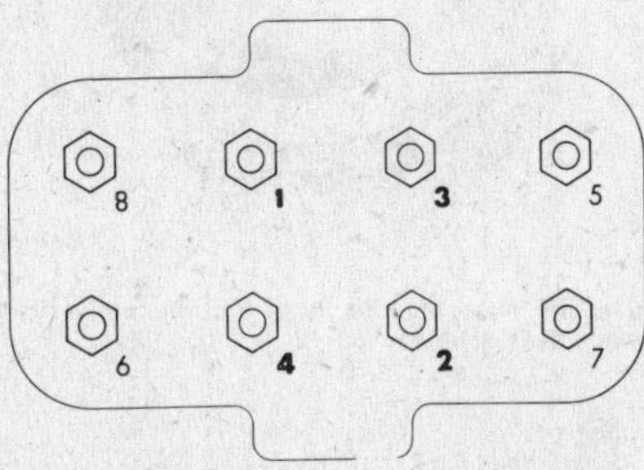

Cylinder head nut tightening order

5. Turn the engine over so that the "LT" mark on the alternator rotor is aligned with the timing mark. Turn the camshafts so that the index mark on the right-side of each camshaft is aligned with the mark on the cam cover bearing.

Align the cam marks with the index marks on the right side-covers

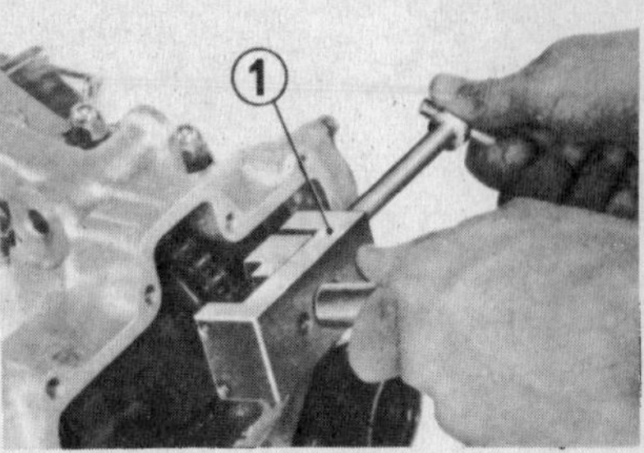

Installing the cam chain master link with the special tool (1)

6. Route the cam chain over the cam and under the idler sprocket. Use the cam chain installation tool (No. 07968–2830200) to install a new masterlink. Joining the chain on the intake side is easiest.

7. The remaining steps are in the reverse of disassembly. Be sure to adjust the cam chain and valves before operation.

CYLINDER AND PISTON

Removal

1. Remove the engine from the frame; remove the cylinder head. Remove the cam chain tensioner.

2. Lift up the cylinder so that it is several inches out of the crankcase. If the cylinder resists removal, tap around the base with a plastic mallet to free it.

3. Stuff a clean rag between the bottom of the cylinder and the crankcase to protect the pistons and catch any pieces of broken piston ring when the pistons come out of the bore.

4. Remove the cylinder from the studs. Note the hollow dowel pins at the cylinder-crankcase mating surface.

5. Remove the piston wrist pin circlips with a needlenose pliers. Discard old circlips; new ones must be used on assembly.

6. Push out the wrist pin and remove the piston from the connecting rod.

CAUTION: *Push the wrist pin out with a blunt drift using steady pressure. Do not attempt to strike or impact the drift to remove the pin or the rod will be bent. If the wrist pin resists removal, heat the piston crown gently and evenly with a propane torch until the pin can be pushed out.*

Remove the other piston in the same manner.

7. Remove the cylinder base gasket.

Inspection

1. Oversize pistons are available in four oversizes in increments of 0.25 mm. Pistons come complete with rings, wrist pin, and circlips. The size is stamped on the piston crown. When fitting new pistons, set piston-to-cylinder wall clearance to 0.025–0.050 mm (0.001–0.002 in.)

2. Check the connecting rods for a bent condition. This can be accomplished with two small rectangular blocks of metal of equal thickness. Insert the wrist pins into the rods, and position

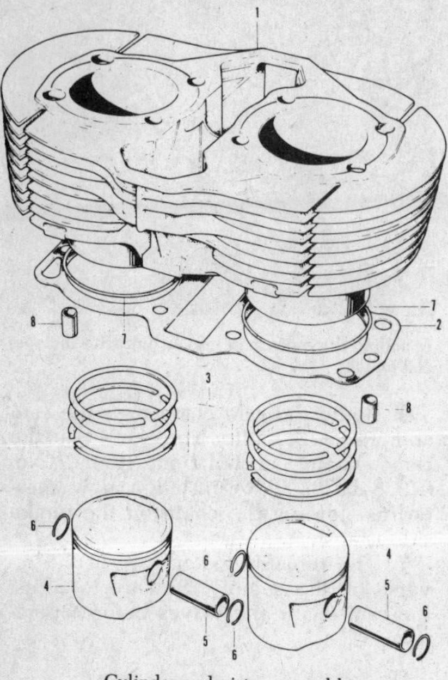

Cylinder and piston assembly

1. Cylinders
2. Cylinder base gasket
3. Piston rings
4. Pistons
5. Wrist pins
6. Wrist pin circlips
7. O-ring
8. Dowel pins

the pieces of metal beneath them on either side of the rods and resting on the crankcase. Rotate the engine so that the wrist pin rests on the blocks. Both sides of the wrist pin must contact the metal blocks or the rod is bent, and must be replaced along with the crankshaft.

3. Be sure that all oil passages in the cylinder are clear. Check the condition of the cam chain tensioner guide rollers. Replace them if the rubber is chipped, grooved, or otherwise damaged.

4. Replace the cylinder base O-ring. Check that any dowel pins or O-rings fitted to the cylinder are in their proper places before installation.

Installation

1. Before installing the rings on the piston, first note that the two compression rings are not interchangeable. The ring with beveled edges is the upper compression ring.

Also note that rings must always be installed so that the manufacturer's mark (the small letter near the end-gap) faces *up* when the rings are in place.

2. Install one rail on the piston below the oil ring groove. Install the oil rail expander in the groove, then move the lower rail into the groove. Install the upper oil rail. Install the two compression rings noting the difference between the upper and lower ones.

3. Arrange the ring end-gaps 120° apart, but do not position any end-gap of the compression rings or the oil rail expander at the very front or the very back of the piston (perpendicular or parallel to the wrist pin).

Position the end-gap of the oil ring expander 120° from the lower compression ring, then position the end-gaps of the oil rails about 45° (20-30 mm) on either side of the expander end-gap.

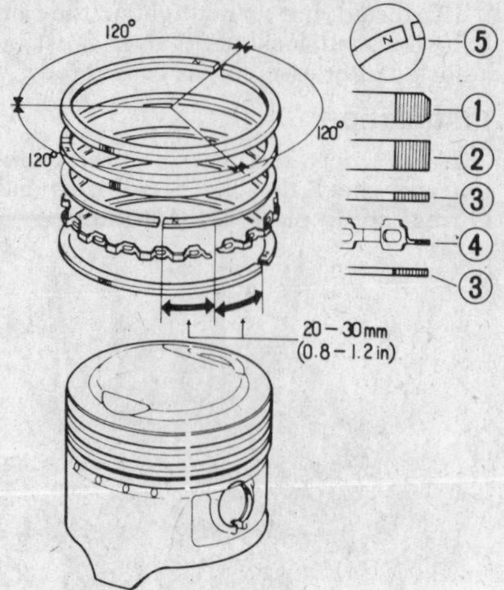

Piston ring installation. Be sure that rings are installed in the proper grooves (1–4) with the mark facing upward (5) and the end-gaps staggered 120° apart

4. Install one wrist pin circlip and place the piston on the connecting rod. "IN" is marked on the piston crown and must be positioned on the intake side. Oil the wrist pin and insert it. Install the other circlip.

NOTE: *Be sure to use new circlips.*

The "IN" mark must be located on the intake side when the piston is installed

When fitting the circlip, be sure that the end-gap and the cut-out in the piston do NOT align

Be sure that the circlips are properly seated. The end-gap of the circlips should point downward or positioned so that they do not align with the cutout of the wrist pin hole.

5. Check that the dowel pins are in place in the crankcase. Fit a new cylinder base gasket after any gasket compound or remains of the old gasket are removed from the crankcase mating surface.

6. Check that the piston rings are properly aligned. Lubricate the piston skirts and rings with motor oil.

7. Fit the cylinders to the studs, and hold them while pulling through the ends of the cam chain. Wire the chain ends out of the way to prevent them from falling into the engine during reassembly.

8. Have an assistant lower the cylinders slowly while you compress the piston rings with the fingers as the pistons enter the bores.

9. Push the cam chain tensioner into the housing and tighten the lockbolt. Using a new gasket, install the tensioner.

10. The remainder of assembly is the reverse of the removal procedure.

CRANKCASE COVER COMPONENTS

The following sections deal with removal, installation, and inspection procedures for those components located beneath the left and right crankcase covers.

These parts can be serviced with the engine in the frame.

Note the following points:

1. Always drain the oil before removing the right or left front crankcase covers. Place a drip pan beneath the cover before breaking the seal to catch any residue. If the cover resists removal, tap the top and sides with a plastic mallet to free it.

2. The kick-starter shaft oil seal in the right cover should be carefully checked each time the cover is removed. If the lips of the seal are torn or damaged, or if the seal leaks, remove it by prying it out of the cover with a small screwdriver or hooked tool. Take care not to use the cover itself as a leverage point without protecting it from possible damage.

To install a new seal, press it in with a block of wood which will cover the entire seal. Be sure that the seal is driven straight in until flush with the outer surface of the case, and not cocked to one side. Grease the lips of the seal before inserting any shaft into it. Where the seal must pass over splines on a shaft, ensure that there are no sharp edges from damaged splines which may tear the seal.

3. It is necessary to remove the centrifugal oil filter before the clutch housing can be removed. This requires a special wrench.

Right Crankcase Cover Components

The right crankcase cover houses the centrifugal oil filter, the clutch and primary drive, the oil pump and the gearshift linkage as well as the kick-starter return spring.

Right Crankcase Cover

REMOVAL AND INSTALLATION

1. Drain the engine oil.

2. Remove the right exhaust pipe and muffler (except CL models). Remove the footpeg stepbar.

3. Remove the kick-starter lever pinch-bolt and carefully pull the kick-starter off its splined shaft.
4. Remove the cover screws with an impact driver. Remove the cover. If stuck, tap around the mating surface with a plastic mallet. Be sure that a drip pan is beneath the cover to catch any remaining oil.
5. Installation is the reverse of the above. Note the following points:
   a. Remove all traces of old gasket or gasket compound from the mating surfaces. Remove any nicks or imperfections from the mating surfaces of the cover and crankcase with an oilstone;
   b. Use a new cover gasket;
   c. Be sure that the two dowel pins are in place between the cover and the crankcase before assembly;
   d. Lubricate the lips of the kick-starter shaft oil seal before installing the cover;
   e. When refitting the kick-starter lever, align the punch mark on the lever with that on the shaft;
   f. Tighten the cover screws in a cross pattern; then secure with an impact driver.

Centrifugal Oil Filter

REMOVAL AND INSTALLATION

1. Remove the crankcase cover.
2. Remove the snap-ring from the centrifugal oil filter. Screw a 6 mm screw or bolt into the filter cap and pull off the filter cap. A crankcase cover screw is 6 mm and can be used.
3. Bend back the tabs on the lock-washer, and, holding the engine so that it does not turn over, remove the nut from the inside of the filter rotor using special Honda tool No. 07196-6390000 (500T) or No. 07086-28301 (450).
4. Remove the rotor. Clean it thoroughly in a solvent.

Removing the oil filter rotor (2) with the special wrench (1)

5. Installation is the reverse of the above. Replace the cap's O-ring if it is not in perfect condition. Be sure that the rotor spring washer is installed with the "OUTSIDE" marked side out. Then fit the lockwasher, secure the nut tightening it to about 35 ft lbs, and bend down the lockwasher tabs.

6. Push the filter cap into place noting that the vanes on the cap fit into the slots in the rotor. Be sure that the snap-ring is firmly seated.

Clutch and Primary Drive, Oil Pump

REMOVAL

The clutch housing and the oil pump must be removed together.

1. Remove the right crankcase cover.
2. Remove the centrifugal oil filter assembly.
3. Remove the clutch pressure plate bolts, washers, and clutch springs. Remove the pressure plate.
4. Remove the steel and friction plates from the clutch housing.
5. Remove the snap-ring which secures the clutch hub and remove the hub. Remove the clutch pushrod.

Removing the clutch plates

Removing the clutch housing (1) and oil pump (2) together

6. Remove the oil pump bolts; take off the clutch housing and the oil pump together. When the clutch housing is clear of its shaft, remove the oil pump plunger from the oil pump.
7. To remove the pump plunger and connecting rod from the housing, remove the circlip.
8. Remove the primary gear from the crankshaft.

INSPECTION

1. For oil pump specifications, refer to "Lubrication System."
2. Clutch housing-to-plate tab backlash should not exceed 0.8 mm (0.032 in.)

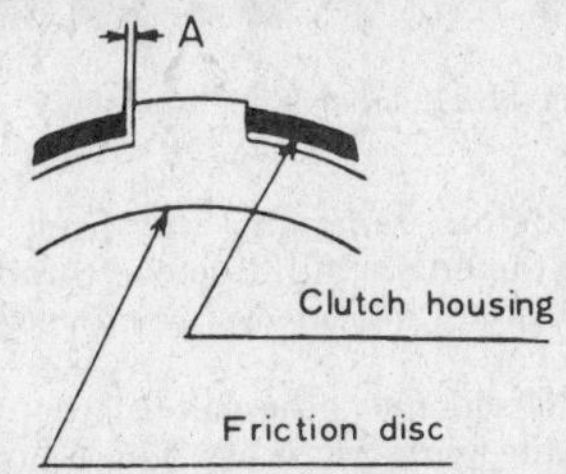

Excessive clearance (A) between the clutch housing and the friction plates will cause clutch backlash

or the plates or housing should be replaced.

3. The clutch hub should be a close fit on its shaft. If the splines of the hub appear to be damaged, or if there is an excess of rotational movement (greater than 0.12 mm/0.005 in.), replace the hub.

INSTALLATION

1. Installation is the reverse of the removal procedure.
2. Assemble the oil pump connecting rod to the clutch housing. The shouldered side of the rod faces away from the housing. Install the side washer, fitting the tab on the side washer into the hole in the housing. Install the snap-ring.
3. Put the primary gear on the crankshaft.
4. Clean the oil pump thoroughly in a solvent. After it is completely dry, fill the pump with motor oil. Clean and install the pump filter.
5. Ensure that the hollow dowel pin fitted behind the oil pump is in place. Fit the pump plunger into the pump and install the clutch housing and oil pump.

Snap-ring (1), side washer (2), plunger pin (3), and connecting rod (4)

Align the pressure plate arrow (1) with one of the cut-out splines on the hub (2)

6. Fit the clutch hub, snap-ring, plates, pushrod, pressure plate, springs, washers, and bolts. Where the pressure plate is marked with an arrow, align the arrow with one of the hub cut-out splines. Tighten the pressure plate bolts gradually in a cross pattern.
7. Install the centrifugal oil filter.

Shift Mechanism

REMOVAL

The shifter shaft is fitted with an oil seal where it comes out of the left-side of the crankcase below the countershaft sprocket. If the seal leaks, it can be replaced after removal of the shifter shaft.

1. Remove the exhaust system (except CL models).
2. Remove the footpeg assembly.
3. Drain the engine oil

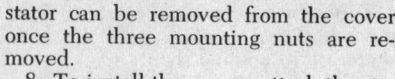

To remove the shift shaft (1), remove the snap-ring (2)

Gearshift arm (1); shift drum (2); shift shaft (3)

Neutral stopper (1); shift drum stopper (2)

4. Remove the right crankcase cover. Remove the centrifugal oil filter, clutch, and oil pump.
5. Remove the gearshift pedal.
6. Remove the rear section of the left crankcase cover.
7. Remove the snap-ring and washer from the left-side of the gearshift shaft.
8. Disengage the fingers of the shift arm from the shift drum and pull the shift arm assembly out of the crankcase.
9. Remove the nut securing the shift drum stopper and neutral stopper. Remove the stopper assembly.

10. If the shifter shaft oil seal leaks, pry it out of the crankcase. Install a new seal, driving it squarely into the case with a block of wood large enough to cover the entire seal. Grease the lips of the seal thoroughly before inserting the shifter shaft.

INSTALLATION

1. Installation is the reverse of removal.

2. Be sure that the gearshift return spring paws are positioned on either side of the pin.

3. Check gearshifting before reassembly is complete.

Shifter return spring pin (1); return spring (2); shift shaft (3)

Shift drum stopper (1) and neutral stopper (2)

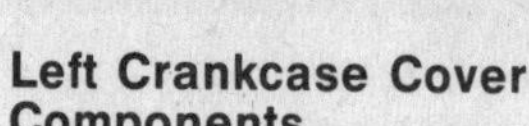

Left Crankcase Cover Components

The left crankcase cover houses the alternator, starter clutch, neutral switch, countershaft sprocket, and the clutch release mechanism.

Left Crankcase Cover

REMOVAL AND INSTALLATION

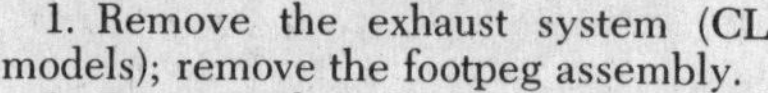

1. Remove the exhaust system (CL models); remove the footpeg assembly.
2. Remove the pinch-bolt from the shift lever and pull the lever off its shaft.
3. Remove the four mounting screws from the rear cover and remove the cover.

NOTE: *Take care not to lose the steel ball from the clutch release mechanism when the cover is removed.*

4. Disconnect the clutch cable from the clutch release mechanism inside the cover.

Clutch cable (1); lockbolt (2); fixing piece (3); lifter (4)

5. Before removing the front cover, drain the engine oil. Remove three stator cover mounting screws. Remove the stator cover.
6. Disconnect the alternator wiring from the wiring harness. Disconnect the neutral switch lead from the neutral switch.
7. Remove the crankcase cover. The stator can be removed from the cover once the three mounting nuts are removed.
8. To install the covers, attach the stator to the front cover. Use a new gasket. Be sure to install the dowel pins under the cover.

Clutch Release Mechanism

1. To remove the clutch release mechanism, unscrew the adjuster lockbolt from the crankcase cover. Unhook the return spring from the inside of the cover and the release mechanism can be removed from the case.

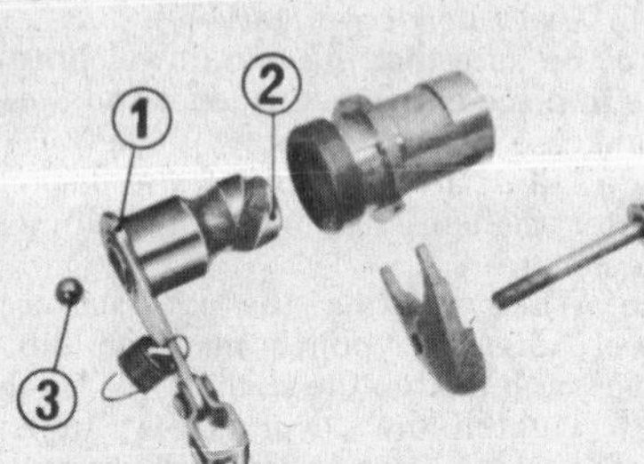
Clutch lifter (1); threads (2); steel ball (3)

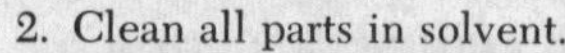

2. Clean all parts in solvent.
3. Inspect the adjuster and lifter for damaged threads.
4. Check the dust seal for condition. If it is cracked or torn, or shows signs of age, replace it.
5. Clean the boss in the case with solvent.
6. Thoroughly grease the mechanism before installation.

Countershaft Sprocket

REMOVAL AND INSTALLATION

1. Remove the footpeg assembly and the left rear crankcase cover. Remove the sprocket protector plate if fitted.
2. To remove the sprocket, remove the two bolts from the sprocket and rotate the lockplate until the tabs on the plate line up with the slots in the countershaft. Remove the lockplate.
3. Either move the rear wheel forward in the swing arm or remove the masterlink from the chain, and pull the sprocket off the countershaft.
4. When refitting the sprocket, if the masterlink has not been removed, refit the chain to the sprocket before installing the sprocket to the countershaft. Install the lockplate on the countershaft and rotate it until the holes in the sprocket line up with the holes in the lockplate. Install the two bolts and torque to 5.8–8.7 ft lbs.

Alternator and Starter Assembly

REMOVAL

1. Remove the crankcase covers and stator as previously described.
2. Remove the rotor bolt.
3. Remove the alternator rotor using the factory rotor puller. The starter clutch is removed with the rotor.
4. Remove the woodruff key from the crankshaft taper.
5. The starter clutch can be removed

Removing the starter clutch screws

from the back of the rotor after removing the three phillips head screws. Remove the starter clutch side plate.

6. The starter motor chain can be removed by removing the sprocket retaining plate and pulling off both sprockets and the chain together.

7. Disconnect the starter motor cable at the motor; unbolt the motor from the engine, and remove the motor, tapping the shaft lightly with a plastic mallet.

INSPECTION

1. For electrical tests of the alternator rotor, stator, and starting motor, refer to "Electrical System."

2. Check that the rollers in the starter clutch are free to move. Also check that they all have the same amount of spring tension on them. If any spring feels weak in relation to the others, replace it by removing the roller, spring cap, and spring. Replace the spring and install the cap and roller.

3. Inspect the starter clutch housing for any cracks. If found defective, it must be replaced.

4. Inspect the surface of the starter sprocket where the rollers contact it. If badly scored, the sprocket and the rollers should be replaced.

5. Inspect the condition of the sprocket teeth. If they are hooked or appear to be worn badly, replace both sprockets and the chain.

6. Check the rotor and stator for signs of wear. If there has been contact between the rotor and the stator assembly, this condition must be rectified. In addition, the components should be tested to make sure that they still operate properly. Check the stator for foreign matter on the poles, burnt wiring, damaged insulation, etc.

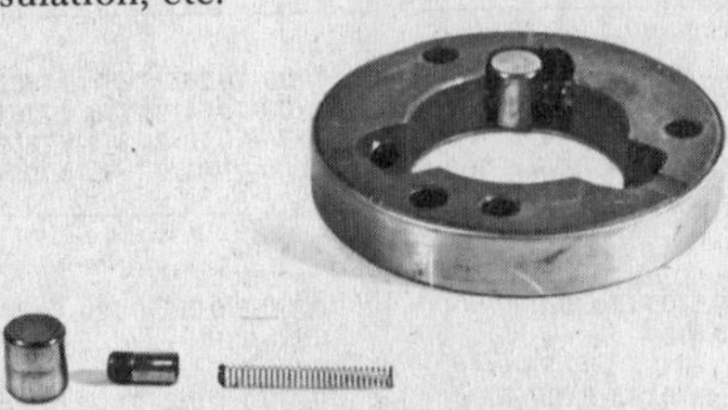

Starter clutch components

7. Check that the stator assembly is securely mounted, and properly aligned. If the rotor has contacted the stator, check for play in the crankshaft. This condition may sometimes be caused by a bad crank bearing.

8. Remove any rust or corrosion from the crankshaft taper. Check the woodruff key for step-wear.

9. Check that the rotor has little or no run-out as it turns. If run-out exists, determine the cause.

10. If scoring on either the rotor or the stator components is severe, the part(s) should be replaced.

INSTALLATION

1. Mount the starter motor on the front of the engine with the two mounting bolts.

2. Install the starter motor chain and the two sprockets at the same time. Install the starter sprocket retaining plate.

3. Mount the starter clutch on the rotor with the three screws. Be sure to install the side plate between the rotor and the clutch.

4. Install the woodruff key in the crankshaft and install the rotor lining up the slot in the rotor with the key in the crankshaft. Draw the rotor down on the crankshaft with the rotor bolt; never strike the rotor as this may affect the magnets.

5. Install the stator in the crankcase cover, then install the cover using a new gasket. Check that the rotor does not come in contact with the stator as the engine turns over. Install the stator cover and the rear cover.

LOWER END AND TRANSMISSION

The following section deals with service to the transmission, shift drum assembly, kick-starter, and crankshaft.

Engine removal is required. If only the transmission needs service, the top end may remain in place. If removal of the crankshaft is required, the top end assembly must be removed first.

Splitting the Crankcases

1. Remove the engine from the frame.

2. Remove the left and right crankcase covers and the components therein: alternator and starter, starter sprockets, countershaft sprocket, centrifugal oil filter, clutch, oil pump and primary gear, gearshift shaft, drum stoppers, etc. Refer to the preceding sections for procedures.

3. Remove the kick-starter shaft return spring.

4. If the crankshaft must be removed, remove the cylinder head, cylinder, and pistons.

5. Remove the crankcase bolts on the top case half. Turn the engine over so that the crankcase bolts on the lower case half are accessible.

6. Remove the crankcase bolts. Remove the lower crankcase half. If it is stuck, tap the front and back of the lower

Crankcase bolts: (1) 6 mm; (2) 8 mm

case at the mating surface with a plastic mallet to free it.

7. To remove the crankshaft, remove the center main bearing cap bolts. Remove the bearing cap, noting that the cap should be reinstalled with the correct side facing forward. The cap is marked for location ("F" for forward) on late models.

Removing the center main bearing cap

8. Carefully lift out the crankshaft.

9. Inspection of the transmission gears should be made with the gears in place. If removal is necessary, carefully lift out the gear clusters and shafts complete. Do not disassemble the shafts unless necessary. All circlips must be replaced once they are removed. Lay out each bearing, gear, thrust washer, and circlip in the order removed.

10. 4-speed: To remove the shift drum, remove the shift fork pin clip from each shift fork. Use a magnetic-tipped screwdriver or the like to remove each guide

Mainshaft (1); countershaft (2)

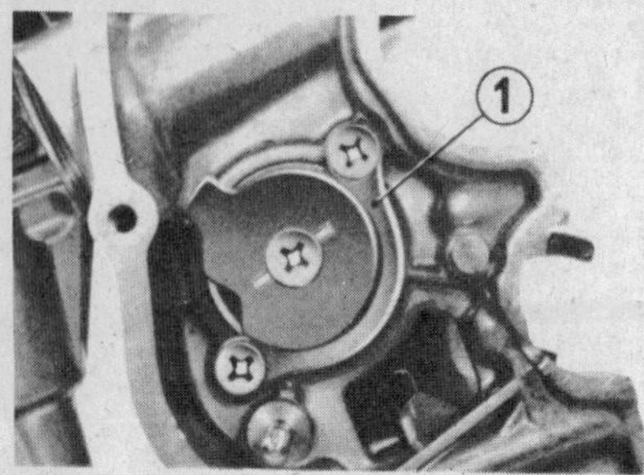

Shift drum bearing retaining plate (1)

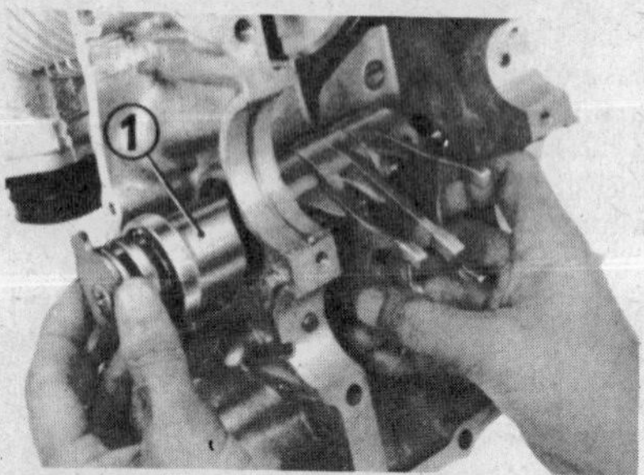

Removing the shift drum (1)

Kick-starter lockplate (1), bolt (2), shaft (3)

pin. Remove the neutral stopper plunger bolt from the top of the upper case half. Remove the shift drum from the right-side and remove the shift forks.

11. 5-speed: To remove the shift drum, remove the shift drum bearing retainer plate. Remove the guide pin clip from each shift fork; remove the guide pin from each shift fork, drawing them out with a magnetic-tipped screwdriver or the like. Pull out the shift drum. Remove the forks.

12. To remove the kick-starter assembly, remove the return spring. Remove the circlip from the shaft. Bend down the locking tabs on the kick-starter shaft bolt and pull out the shaft. Remove the kick-starter gear and friction spring.

Component Inspection

CRANKCASES

1. Clean the top and bottom cases thoroughly in a solvent, taking care to remove all traces of metal particles, sludge, etc.

2. Carefully inspect the mating surfaces. Remove all traces of gasket compound. Remove any nicks or burrs on the mating surfaces with an oilstone.

3. Check that the bearing locating pins for the crankshaft and transmission shafts are not pushed into the case. Check that all bearing locating half-rings are in place

Engine and Transmission Specifications

	500T	*450*
Camshaft Journal OD (mm/in.)		
standard	21.97–21.98/0.865–0.866	21.97–21.98/0.865–0.866
service limit	21.92/0.862	21.92/0.862
Cam Lobe Height (mm/in.)		
Intake and Exhaust		
standard	4.69–4.73/0.185–0.186	4.69–4.73/0.185–0.186
service limit	4.65/0.183	4.65/0.183
Camshaft Run-Out (mm/in.)	0.01/0.0004	0.01/0.0004
Cylinder Head Cam Bearing ID (mm/in.)		
standard	22.00–22.02/0.866–0.867	22.00–22.02/0.866–0.867
service limit	22.05/0.868	22.05/0.868
Cam Side Clearance (mm/in.)		
standard	0.05–0.35/0.002–0.014	0.05–0.35/0.002–0.014
service limit	0.4/0.016	0.4/0.016
Cam Follower ID (mm/in.)		
standard	10.20–10.22/0.402	10.20–10.22/0.402
service limit	10.28/0.405	10.28/0.405
Valve Guide ID (mm/in.)		
Intake and Exhaust		
standard	7.00–7.01/0.2756–0.2760	7.00–7.01/0.2756–0.2760
service limit	7.05/0.2776	70.5/0.2776
Valve Stem OD (mm/in.)		
Intake		
standard	6.97–6.99/0.275	6.97–6.99/0.275
service limit	6.96/0.274	6.96/0.274
Exhaust		
standard	6.97–6.98/0.274–0.275	6.97–6.98/0.274–0.275
service limit	6.95/0.274	6.95/0.274
Valve-to-Guide Clearance (mm/in.)		
Intake		
standard	0.01–0.03/0.0004–0.0012	0.01–0.03/0.0004–0.0012
service limit	0.08/0.003	0.08/0.003
Exhaust		
standard	0.03–0.05/0.0012–0.0020	0.03–0.05/0.0012–0.0020
service limit	0.10/0.004	0.10/0.004
Valve Stem Run-Out (mm/in.)		
standard	—	—
service limit	0.02/0.0008	0.02/0.0008
Valve Seat Width (mm/in.)		
standard	1.0–1.3/0.039–0.051	1.0–1.3/0.039–0.051
service limit	2.0/0.79	2.0/0.79
Cylinder Bore (standard) (mm/in.)		
standard	70.00–70.01/2.756	70.00–70.01/2.756
service limit	70.11/2.760	70.11/2.760
Piston (standard) OD (mm/in.)		
standard	69.95–69.97/2.754–2.755	69.95–69.97/2.754–2.755
service limit	69.87/2.751	69.87/2.751
Piston-to-Cylinder Clearance (mm/in.)		
standard	0.025–0.050/0.001–0.002	0.025–0.050/0.001–0.002
service limit	0.1/0.004	0.1/0.004
Wrist Pin Hole ID (mm/in.)		
standard	17.00/0.669	17.00/0.669
service limit	17.1/0.673	17.1/0.673
Wrist Pin Diameter (mm/in.)		
standard	16.99–17.00/0.669	16.00–17.00/0.669
service limit	16.95/0.667	16.97/0.667
Cylinder Taper (mm/in.)		
standard	—	—
service limit	0.05/0.002	0.05/0.002
Cylinder Ovality (mm/in.)		
standard	—	—
service limit	0.05/0.002	0.05/0.002
Piston Oversizes (mm/in.)		
0.25	70.25–70.26/2.7657–2.7662	70.25–70.26/2.7657–2.7662
0.50	70.50–70.51/2.7756–2.7761	70.50–70.51/2.7756–2.7761
0.75	70.75–70.76/2.7854–2.7859	70.75–70.76/2.7854–2.7859
1.00	71.00–71.01/2.7953–2.7958	71.00–71.01/2.7953–2.7958
Piston Ring End-Gap (mm/in.)		
Top		
standard	0.3–0.5/0.012–0.020	0.3–0.5/0.012–0.020
service limit	0.8/0.031	0.8/0.031
Second		
standard	0.3–0.5/0.012–0.020	0.3–0.5/0.012–0.020
service limit	0.8/0.031	0.8/0.031

in their grooves.

CRANKSHAFT

1. Lubricate each of the crank bearings with motor oil and rotate them slowly. Bearing rotation must be smooth, effortless, and quiet; otherwise, the bearing(s) may be damaged.
2. Check the bearings for discoloration or obvious damage. The race on the outer crank bearings may be removed to check the rollers. The right-side race is secured by a circlip.
3. If a dial gauge is available, mount the crank in a set of V-blocks and check for run-out at both ends. Maximum allowable run-out is 0.1 mm (0.004 in.). This figure (run-out) will be ½ of the true indicated reading of the gauge.

Checking crankshaft run-out

4. Lubricate the big end bearing of each rod and slowly rotate the rod around the crankpin. Any noise or halting in the bearing movement may indicate that it is defective. Any vertical play indicates a worn bearing.
5. Use a feeler gauge to measure the side clearance between the rod big end and the flywheel. Standard clearance is 0.07–0.33 mm (0.0028–0.013 in.). Maximum allowable clearance is 0.5 mm (0.020 in.). Clearance in excess of this necessitates replacement of the rod and bearing.
6. Measure the radial clearance of each big end bearing by mounting a dial indicator on it and moving it up and down. Standard clearance is 0.008 mm (0.0003 in.) or less. The serviceable limit is 0.05 mm (0.002 in.). If clearance exceeds this amount, the con rod bearings must be replaced.

Checking main bearing radial clearance

7. Measure the inside diameter of the small end. Replace the rod if diameter exceeds 17.07 mm (0.672 in.).
8. Check the radial clearance of each crankshaft bearing with the dial gauge mounted directly on top of the bearing.

Engine and Transmission Specifications

	500T	450
Oil		
standard	0.2–0.4/0.008–0.016	0.2–0.4/0.008–0.016
service limit	0.8/0.031	0.8/0.031
Piston Ring Side Clearance (mm/in.)		
Top		
standard	0.04–0.07/0.0016–0.0028	0.04–0.07/0.0016–0.0028
service limit	0.15/0.006	0.15/0.006
Second		
standard	0.020–0.045/0.0008–0.0018	0.020–0.045/0.0008–0.0018
service limit	0.15/0.006	0.15/0.006
Oil (one-piece type)		
standard	—	0.01/0.0004
service limit	—	0.1/0.004
Crankshaft Run-Out (mm/in.)		
standard	0.02/0.0008	0.02/0.0008
service limit	0.1/0.004	0.1/0.004
Con Rod Big End Bearing Clearance (mm/in.)		
standard	0–0.008/0–0.0003	0–0.008/0.0003
service limit	0.05/0.002	0.05/0.002
Big End Side Clearance (mm/in.)		
standard	0.07–0.33/0.0028–0.0130	0.07–0.33/0.0028–0.0130
service limit	0.5/0.02	0.5/0.02
Connecting Rod Small End ID (mm/in.)		
standard	17.016–17.034/0.6699–0.6706	17.016–17.034/0.6699–0.6706
service limit	17.07/0.6721	17.07/0.6721
Main Bearing Radial Clearance (mm/in.)		
standard	0.006–0.014/0.0002–0.0005	0.006–0.014/0.0002–0.0005
service limit	0.03/0.001	0.03/0.001
Oil Pump Con Rod-to-Clutch Clearance (mm/in.)		
standard	0.025–0.075/0.0010–0.0030	0.025–0.075/0.0010–0.0030
service limit	0.15/0.006	0.15/0.006
Oil Pump Plunger OD (mm/in.)		
standard	18.955–18.970/0.746–0.748	18.955–18.870/0.746–0.748
service limit	18.93/0.745	18.93/0.745
Oil Pump Cylinder ID (mm/in.)		
standard	19.00–19.01/0.748	19.00–19.01/0.748
service limit	19.10/0.752	19.10/0.752
Clutch Friction Plate Thickness (mm/in.)		
standard	3.42–3.58/0.135–0.141	3.42–3.58/0.135–0.141
service limit	3.1/0.12	3.1/0.12
Clutch Plate Warpage (mm/in.)		
standard	0.15/0.006	0.15/0.006
service limit	0.35/0.014	0.35/0.014
Clutch Spring Free-Length (mm/in.)		
standard	38.0/1.50	37.3/1.47
service limit	37.3/1.47	39.4/1.55
Clutch Hub Backlash (mm/in.)		
standard	0.02–0.06/0.0008–0.0024	0.02–0.06/0.0008–0.0024
service limit	0.12/0.005	0.12/0.005
Transmission-Gear-Gear Backlash (mm/in.)		
standard	—	—
service limit	0.2/0.008	0.2/0.008
Mainshaft—4th Gear Clearance (mm/in.)		
standard	0.02–0.06/0.0008–0.0024	0.02–0.062/0.0008–0.0024
service limit	0.15/0.006	0.15/0.006
Mainshaft—5th Gear Clearance (mm/in.)		
standard	0.02–0.05/0.0008–0.0021	0.02–0.054/0.0008–0.0021
service limit	0.13/0.005	0.13/0.005
Countershaft—1st Gear Clearance (mm/in.)		
standard	0.02–0.05/0.0008–0.0021	0.02–0.054/0.0008–0.0021
service limit	0.10/0.004	0.10/0.004
Countershaft—2nd/3rd Gear Clearance (mm/in.)		
standard	0.004–0.08/0.0016–0.0032	0.04–0.08/0.0016–0.0032
service limit	0.18/0.007	0.18/0.007
Transmission Gear-to-Shaft Clearance (mm/in.)		
standard	—	—
service limit	0.15/0.006	0.15/0.006
Gearshift Drum OD (mm/in.)		
standard	34.95–34.98/1.376–1.377	—
service limit	34.9/1.37	—

Standard radial (up and down) clearance is 0.014 mm (0.0005 in.). Replace all the bearings if the clearance of any exceeds 0.03 mm (0.0012 in.).

NOTE: *Special presses and jigs are necessary to disassemble or align the crankshaft. If they are not available, the crankshaft will have to be replaced in the event of damage to the rods or center main bearings.*

KICK-STARTER

1. Inspect the splines on the end of the kick-starter shaft. If they are damaged to the extent that the kick-starter lever cannot be fastened tightly to the shaft, replace it.
2. Check the condition of the circlip. Replace it if deformed or weakened.
3. Check the condition of the kick-starter return spring. If the spring cannot return the shaft quickly and hold it firmly against its stop, it should be replaced.
4. Check the friction spring for deformation.
5. Check the curved splines on the shaft and the corresponding splines on the kick-starter gear. The gear must move smoothly on the shaft. If it binds or sticks or if it can become cocked, replace the gear and shaft.
6. Check the kick-starter gear for broken or worn teeth. Replace it if damaged.

Assembling the Cases

In every case the bearings should be cleansed by squirting clean oil through them to carry away any particles of foreign matter. Bearing rotation must be perfectly smooth. If the rotation is halting, this is a sign that some particles are trapped in the bearing.

1. Fit the kick-starter shaft assembly, using a new lockwasher for the bolt. The friction spring fits into the groove in the upper case half.
2. The shift forks are marked for position: "R," "C," and "L."

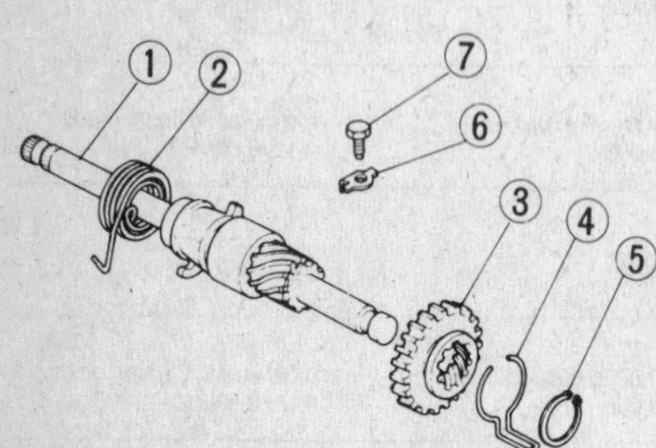

Kick-starter shaft assembly

1. Kick-starter shaft
2. Return spring
3. Kick-starter gear
4. Friction spring
5. Snap-ring
6. Lockwasher
7. Bolt

Fit the friction spring (2) into the groove (1) in the case

Engine and Transmission Specifications (cont.)

	500T	450
Gearshift Fork ID (mm/in.)		
standard	34.0/1.34	34.0/1.34
service limit	34.1/1.343	34.1/1.343
Shift Fork Finger Thickness (mm/in.)		
L&R		
standard	4.9–5.0/0.194–0.197	4.9–5.0/0.194–0.197
service limit	4.6/0.181	4.6/0.181
Center		
standard	5.9–6.0/0.233–0.236	5.6/0.221

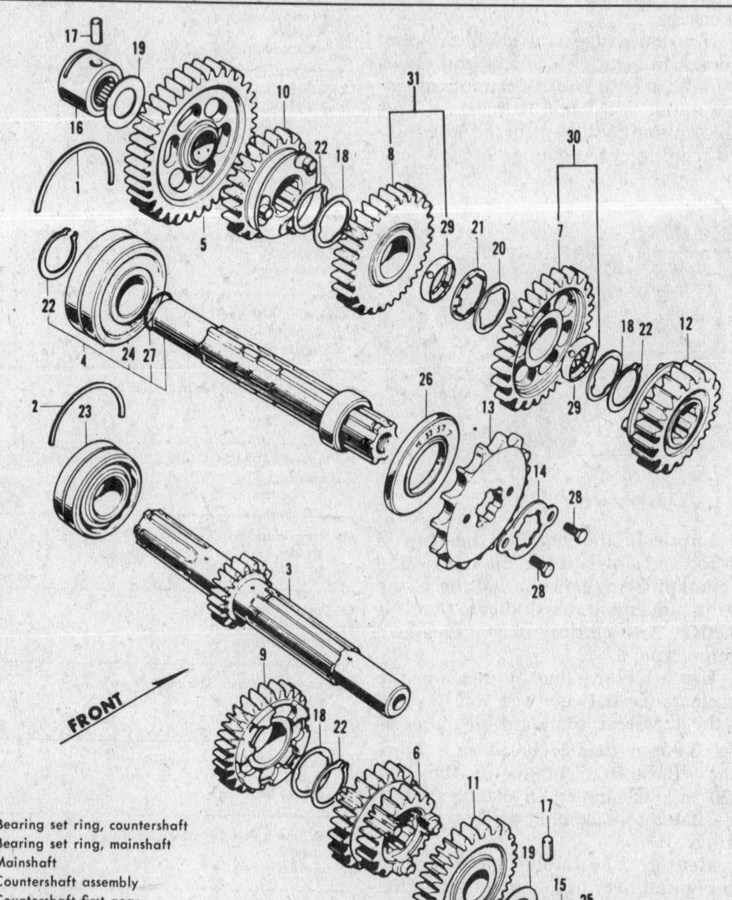

Transmission assembly

1. Bearing set ring, countershaft
2. Bearing set ring, mainshaft
3. Mainshaft
4. Countershaft assembly
5. Countershaft first gear
6. Mainshaft 2d, 3rd gears
7. Countershaft 2d gear
8. Countershaft 3rd gear
9. Mainshaft 4th gear
10. Countershaft 4th gear
11. Mainshaft 5th gear
12. Countershaft 5th gear
13. Countershaft sprocket
14. Sprocket lockplate
15. Mainshaft needle bearing
16. Countershaft needle bearing
17. Bearing locating pins
18. Thrust washer, splined
19. Thrust washer
20. Thrust washer, splined
21. Lockwasher
22. Snap-ring
23. Mainshaft ball bearing
24. Countershaft ball bearing
25. Mainshaft oil seal
26. Countershaft oil seal
27. O-ring
28. Sprocket lockbolts
29. Splined bush
30. Countershaft 2d gear w/bush
31. Countershaft 3rd gear w/bush

Shift forks installed: (1) right, (2) center, (3) left (5-speed)

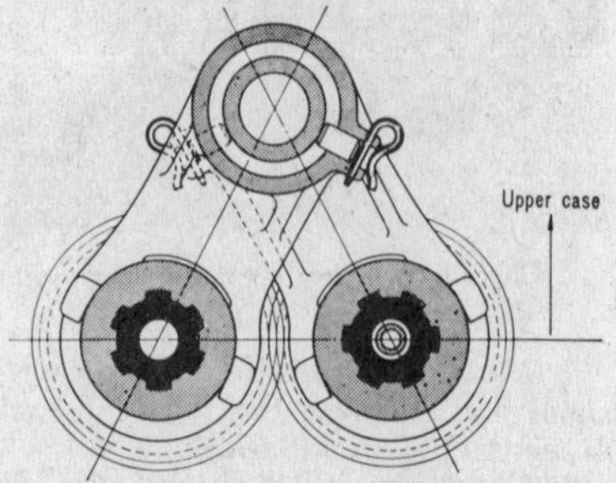

Shift forks installed (4-speed)

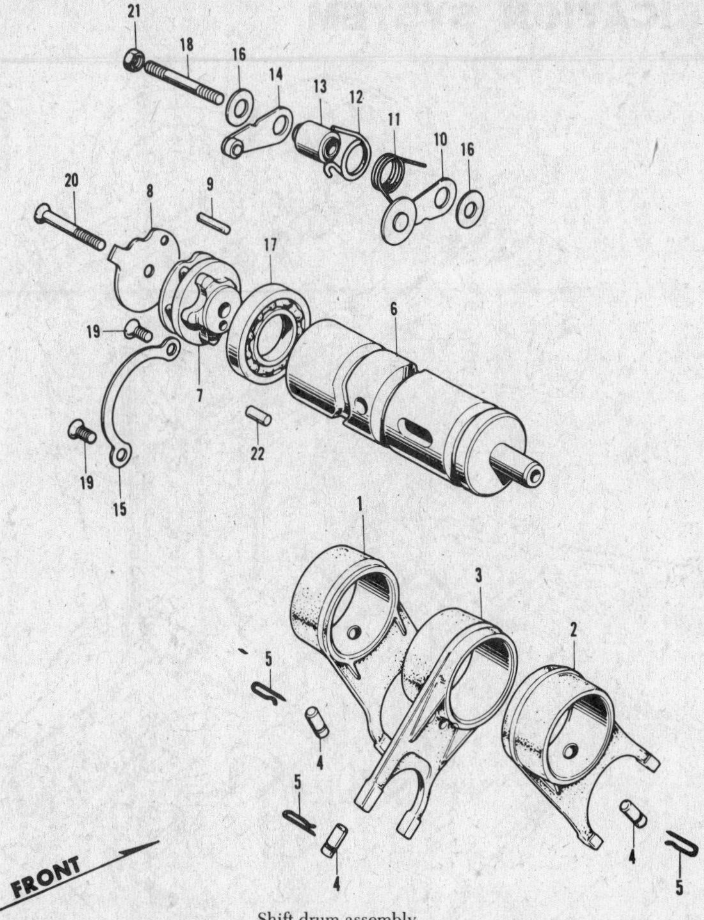

Shift drum assembly

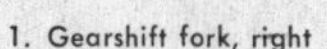

1. Gearshift fork, right
2. Gearshift fork, left
3. Gearshift fork, center
4. Gearshift fork guide pins
5. Guide pin clips
6. Shift drum
7. Shift drum stopper plate
8. Stopper cam
9. Shift drum pins
10. Shift drum stopper
11. Stopper spring
12. Neutral stopper spring
13. Stopper collar
14. Neutral stopper
15. Bearing retainer plate
16. Washer
17. Ball bearing
18. Stud
19. Retainer screws
20. Stopper screw
21. Stud nut
22. Dowel pin

3. Install the shift drum, slipping it through the shift forks. Insert the guide pins, and the guide pin clips. Refer to the illustrations showing correct pin clip positions. Install the bearing retainer plate (5-speed), or the neutral stopper plunger (4-speed). Lubricate the shift drum assembly.

4. Carefully fit the crankshaft into the case. Note the bearing locating pins and the corresponding slots. Each of the bearings must be properly seated. There is no need to force the bearings into place. Line up the locators and install the crank. Lubricate the crank bearings with clean motor oil.

Fit the center main bearing cap, proper end forward, and tighten the bolts in a cross pattern to 18–25 ft lbs.

5. Install the gear clusters, engaging the shift forks with their proper gears as the clusters are fitted.

Crank bearings are fitted with pins which must be seated in the cut-outs in the crankcase

Where applicable, the main bearing cap must be installed with the arrow pointing toward the front of the engine

Be sure that the shaft bearings are properly located either by the locating pins or the locating rings. The needle bearing with the oil groove is installed on the countershaft, and the bearing without the groove on the mainshaft (unloaded sides).

6. Lubricate the transmission gears and bearings and check for smooth operation.

7. Fit a new countershaft oil seal and mainshaft oil seal.

8. Apply gasket compound to the mating surface of the upper case. An excess of compound will run down into the cases when they are mated.

9. Check that the oil passage dowel pins are in place on the left-side of the upper case. Fit the lower case. Install the bolts and tighten them in a cross pattern starting with those closest to the center. The cases should be mated all the way around prior to tightening the bolts. Do not attempt to force the cases together.

10. The remainder of the procedure is the reverse of disassembly.

Be sure that the locating pins and rings for the transmission shaft bearings are in place

Engine Torque Specifications

Part	Torque (ft lbs)
Cylinder head nuts—500T:	33–40
450:	20–22
Spark plugs	18–21
Centrifugal oil filter nut	33–40
Alternator rotor bolt	22–25
Screws	
5 mm	2.5–3.6
6 mm	5.1–8.0
Bolts/Nuts①	
5 mm	3.3–4.3
6 mm	5.6–8.7
8 mm	13.0–18.1
10 mm	22–29
12 mm	36–43
6 mm flange bolt	7.3–10.1
8 mm flange bolt	17–21
10 mm flange bolt	22–29

① Unless otherwise noted. Refers to thread diameter, not head size.

LUBRICATION SYSTEM

Honda 450 and 500 models have the same type of lubrication system: a wet-sump engine with plunger oil pump.

The oil pump consists of a body incorporating steel ball(s) as check valves, and a plunger whose movement in the housing alternately sucks in and pumps out oil. The plunger is driven by a connecting rod off the clutch housing.

Oil in the crankcase is sucked up by the oil pump, passing through a wire mesh filter screen to remove any large bits of foreign matter before it enters the pump body. From the pump, the oil is

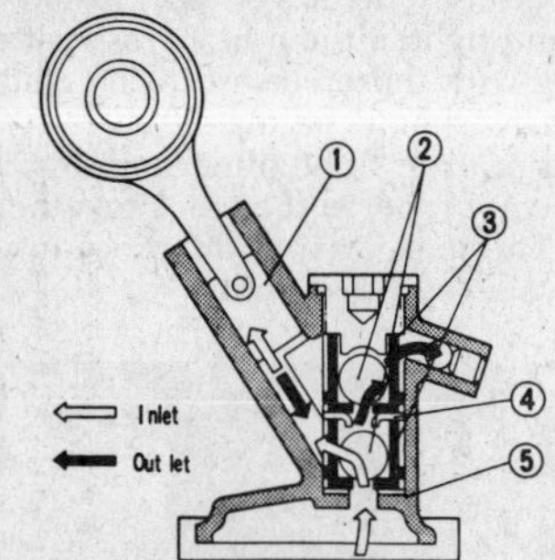

Cross-section of 450 oil pump

1. Plunger
2. Steel ball
3. Ball seat
4. Ball stopper
5. Rubber seat

passed through a centrifugal oil filter mounted on the crankshaft. The rotation of the centrifugal oil filter rotor forces any particles in the oil against the rotor walls while the clean oil passes out and is forced through the crankcase, to lubricate the pistons and lower end, and up along the cylinder studs to lubricate the cams and valve gear.

Additional oil is pumped through the transmission shafts, all of it eventually returning to the crankcase sump where the cycle is repeated.

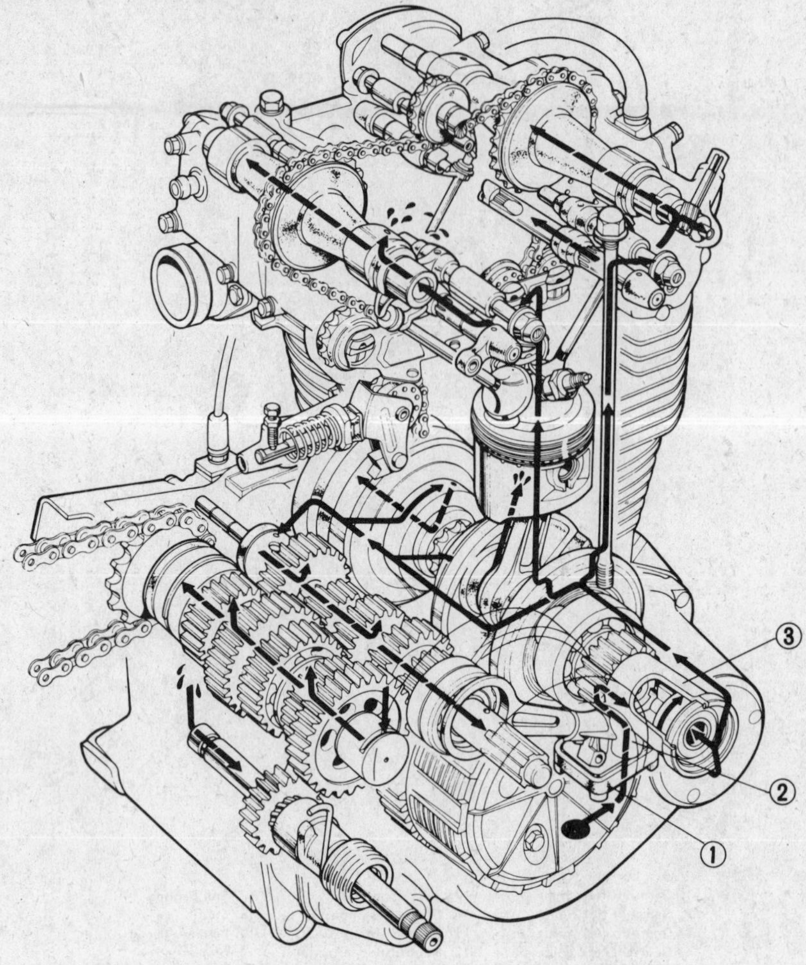

Lubrication system: (1) pump filter screen, (2) oil pump, (3) centrifugal oil filter

OIL PUMP

The oil pump was changed beginning with K3-model 450s. The early-type uses a steel body and an alloy plunger. The later-type pump has an alloy body with a steel plunger.

In addition, the later pump has a bore some 3 mm larger than the earlier type. The new pump can be fitted to older machines with no modifications.

Removal

To remove the oil pump, drain the oil, remove the right exhaust system (CB models), the right crankcase cover, and the centrifugal oil filter; the clutch and oil pump are removed together.

Inspection

1. Clean the centrifugal oil filter rotor in solvent.
2. Check that the oil guide piece on the centrifugal filter cover can move freely.

New style oil pump (left) has an alloy body and steel plunger

3. The O-ring on the cover must be in good condition. If it is not, replace it.
4. Remove the filter screen from the bottom of the oil pump and clean it thoroughly in solvent and blow dry.
5. Clean the oil pump body in clean motor oil.
6. Check the pump plunger and the bore of the pump for scoring or wear marks. Replace pump and plunger if any

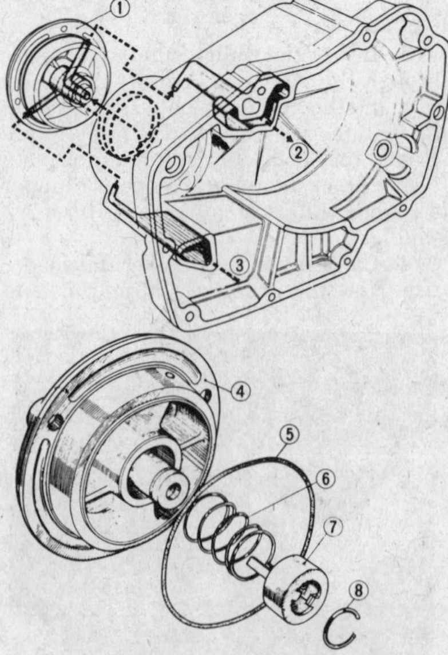

Centrifugal oil filter cover assembly

1. Oil filter cover
2. Oil passage to crankcase
3. Oil passage from sump
4. Oil filter cover
5. O-ring
6. Oil guide spring
7. Oil guide
8. Stop-ring

defects are noted on the plunger or the pump bore.

7. With a micrometer, measure the diameter of the plunger and the diameter of the pump bore, and subtract the two values.

Standard clearances are 0.030–0.054 mm/0.0010–0.0030 in. (500) and 0.02–0.063 mm/0.0010–0.0025 in. (450).

Replace both plunger and body if clearance exceeds 0.2 mm/0.0079 in. (500) or 0.17 mm/0.0067 in. (450).

8. Remove the snap-ring from the clutch housing and remove the connecting rod and thrust washer.

9. To remove the plunger from the rod, push out the pin.

Check the clearance between the rod (2) and the clutch housing (1)

10. Check the inner surface of the connecting rod big end for wear or galling, and the rod mounting area on the clutch housing as well.

11. Measure the inside diameter of the rod big end and the outside diameter of the clutch housing area and compare the two measurements.

Standard clearance between the two is 0.025–0.075 mm/0.0010–0.0030 in.

Replace rod or housing if clearance exceeds 0.15 mm (0.0059 in.)

12. Late models: Shake the oil pump and listen for the rattle of the check valve ball(s). The ball(s) must be free in the pump body.

13. On some early models, the pump can be disassembled for cleaning or inspection by removing the pump ball stopper plug at the top. This should not be undertaken, however, except in the event of pump failure, in which case the pump will have to be replaced anyway.

Installation

1. Apply a quantity of clean motor oil to the pump bore before installation.

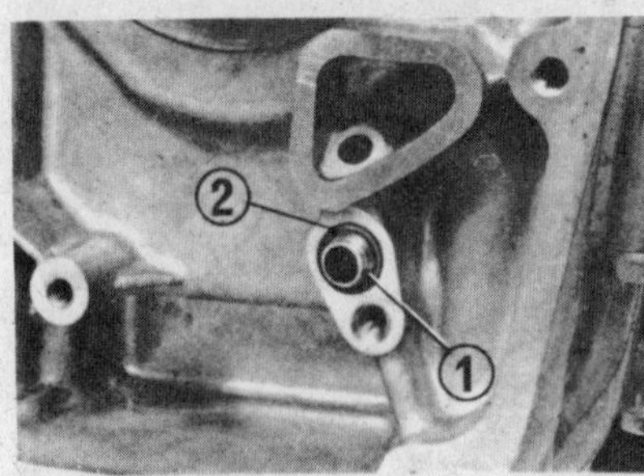

Be sure that the hollow dowel pin (1) and O-ring (2) are in place behind the pump

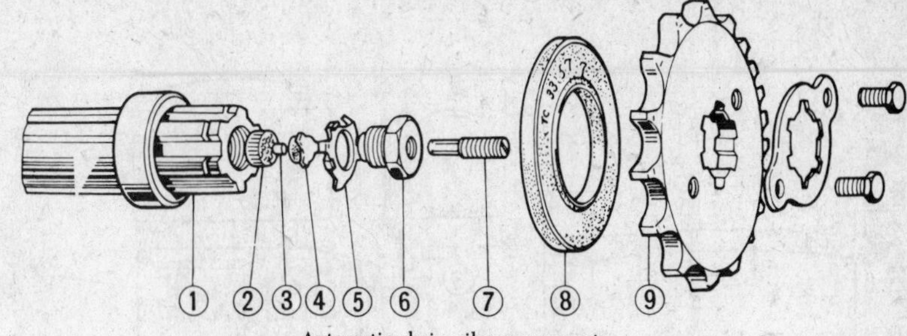

Automatic chain oiler components

1. Countershaft
2. Oil plug
3. Oil stopper
4. Rubber orifice
5. Lockwasher
6. Oiler plug
7. Adjusting screw
8. Oil seal
9. Countershaft sprocket

2. Be sure that the hollow dowel pin is in place behind the pump in the crankcase, and that a new O-ring has been fitted to the pin.

3. Install components as directed in "Engine and Transmission."

4. After installation is completed and the correct quantity of oil added, kick the engine over several times with the kickstarter (ignition off) before starting the engine.

5. Allow the engine to idle for a minute or so, then loosen the two cylinder head capnuts on the right-side of the head.

If oil seeps out, the pump is operating properly.

Tighten the head nuts to 33–40 ft lbs (500) or 20–22 ft lbs (450).

CHAIN OILER

Some models are equipped with an automatic chain oiling device incorporated into the sprocket side of the countershaft. The oiler is fitted with an adjusting screw to meter the amount of oil which passes through.

The screw may be turned in (clockwise) to decrease or shut off the flow of oil; turning it counterclockwise will increase the oil flow.

Maximum oiling is achieved when the screw is turned three turns out from closed.

FUEL SYSTEM

Air Cut-Valve

The carburetors on the 500T are fitted with a diaphragm-operated air cut-valve.

The purpose of the valve is to prevent popping in the mufflers when the throttle is suddenly closed.

When the throttle plate is closed after high-speed operation, the amount of fuel supplied to the engine is limited by the idle circuit's pilot screw. Due to the fact that the engine is still turning rapidly after the throttle is shut off, a high vacuum is created on the engine side of the throttle plate. This results in an excess of air being drawn into the engine through the slow jet.

This lean mixture may be too unbalanced to burn in the combustion chamber, so that the unburned or partially burned gases accumulate in the exhaust pipes and muffler. After the engine has turned over a number of times, the amount of fuel passing through may eventually make this mixture in the exhaust system rich enough to ignite which causes a popping in the exhaust system.

To prevent this, an air cut-valve is fitted to the slow jet. The valve takes advantage of the high vacuum condition noted above. When this condition occurs, the spring-loaded diaphragm of the valve is activated by the high vacuum and moves to obstruct the amount of air passing through the slow jet. The valve allows only a small amount of the air to pass into the carburetor intake, effectively richening the mixture so that combustion occurs in the engine, rather than in the exhaust pipes.

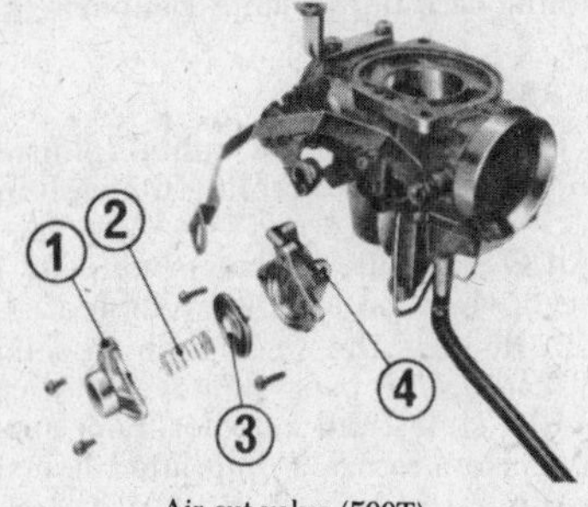

Air cut-valve (500T)

1. Cover
2. Spring
3. Diaphragm
4. Air cut-valve body

Blow-By Gas Circulator

The 500T is equipped with a recirculation system for crankcase gases. The gases are forced out of the head by the downward movement of the pistons. They are ejected into a breather box located between the two air cleaners.

A breather element separates any oil from the crankcases gases, and the oil is fed back into the crankcases. The gases are fed to the air cleaners where they join fresh air from the outside, and then are burned in the combustion chamber.

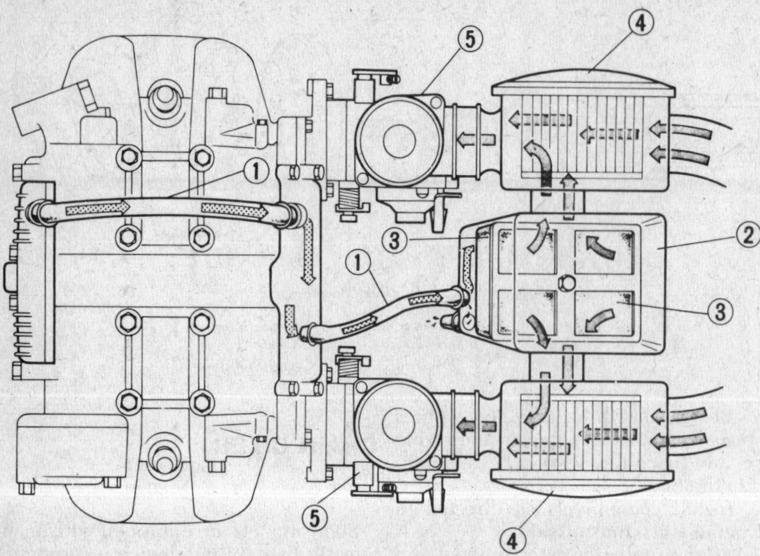

Induction and recirculation system (500T)

Removing the carburetor cap

Removing the float pivot pin

CARBURETORS

Removal

1. On CL models, remove the exhaust system.
2. Remove the left and right sidecovers.
3. Shut off the fuel petcock; disconnect the lines from the petcock. Disconnect the overflow lines from the float bowls.

Carburetor clamp screws (circles)

4. Lift the seat and remove the gas tank.

To safely remove the tank on 450 models, either drain it completely prior to removal, or obtain a four in. length of fuel line and two small clamps. Attach one clamp to the fuel tank's balance line. Disconnect the line; fit the spare length of fuel line to the tank fitting with the clamp already attached. This will prevent fuel from spilling out of the tank when the balance line is disconnected for removal.

5. Drain the carburetor float bowls, catching the gasoline in a suitable receptacle.

CAUTION: *Do not allow gasoline to spill on a hot engine.*

6. Loosen the clamps which secure the

Cable adjuster holder screws

carburetors to the air cleaner and manifold hoses. Remove the air cleaners.

7. Disconnect the choke band from the left carburetor.
8. Pull off one of the carburetors; unscrew the cable adjuster holder from the carburetor body. Disconnect the cable from the throttle plate. Remove the remaining carb in the same manner.

Disassembly

1. Have carburetor rebuild kits on hand before disassembling the carburetors.

All O-rings and gaskets should be replaced when the unit is assembled.

2. Remove the screws which secure the carburetor cap. Remove the cap, throttle slide, and needle. Four-speed 450s have a return spring fitted beneath the cap.
3. Remove the throttle slide gasket from the carburetor body.
4. Pry up the float bowl retainer and

Removing the main jet

remove the float bowl. Do this carefully. If it is stuck, hold the carburetor *and* float bowl firmly and tap the bowl with a plastic mallet.

5. Pull out the pivot pin and remove the float. Unscrew and remove the main jet and the needle jet holder. Remove the needle jet.
6. Unscrew and remove the pilot jet and the slow jet.

Removing the needle jet holder

Removing the float needle

7. Remove the float needle. Unscrew the needle seat.

8. Remove the pilot screw cap (if fitted), and remove the pilot screw and spring. Use a small hooked wire to remove the pilot screw washer and O-ring.

9. 500T: Remove the two screws which secure the air cut-valve. If disassembly of the valve is required, remove the two screws which secure the valve cap; carefully remove the spring and diaphragm.

10. If disassembly of the throttle slide is required, remove the needle set screw and separate the needle and slide.

Assembly

Assembly is basically the reverse of the disassembly procedure. Note the following points:

1. Always use new gaskets and O-rings.

2. Exercise care when installing jets—they are made of soft brass and are easily damaged if overtightened.

3. If the throttle slide and needle have been disassembled, first check that both needle clips are installed in the third groove from the top. Install the needle in the slide and secure the set screw.

4. When installing the pilot screw, first assemble the spring, washer, and O-ring; screw it in very gently until it is seated,

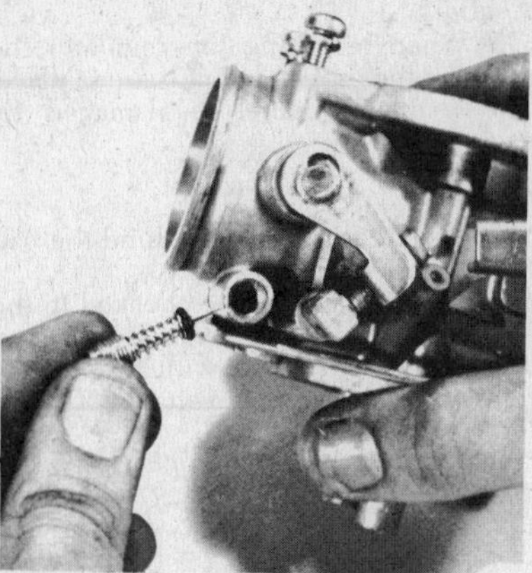

Installing the pilot screw

then back it off 1 turn (450) or 1½ turns (500T).

5. When installing the throttle slide into the carb body, engage the tab with the slot in the slide.

Installation

1. Reverse the removal procedure to install the carburetors.

2. Be sure that all connections are tight. Check that fuel lines are secured with clips, and are not contacting the carburetors except at the connections.

3. Check that the choke band is connected. Be sure that both carburetors are vertical. Check cable adjustments.

4. Before operation, turn on the fuel and check for leaks.

Carburetor Specifications

	450	*500T*
Setting Number	14H	751A
Main Jet	130	145
Slow Jet	38	80
Pilot Jet	38	NA
Needle (groove from top)	3	3
Pilot Screw (turns open)	1	1½
Float Level (mm/in.)	20.0/0.79	20.0/0.79

NA Not available

ELECTRICAL SYSTEM

NOTE: *The following precautions should be observed when carrying out electrical system tests.*

1. Be positive that battery connections are not reversed. This will burn out the rectifier almost immediately.

2. Be certain that all electrical connections are noted before disconnecting them, so that they may be reconnected properly.

3. If the battery is being charged in the motorcycle, the battery terminals *must* be disconnected, or the voltage regulator may be damaged.

4. Never disconnect the battery while the engine is running.

5. Check battery condition first, before carrying out any other charging system checks.

IGNITION CIRCUIT TESTS

1. Noise suppressor spark plug caps are fitted, which are designed to eliminate radio interference by means of a resistor in the cap. Sometimes the resistor breaks down, and the cap then becomes an open circuit. Remove the cap from the spark plug lead, and ground the end of the lead against the cylinder head. If a fat, blue spark is produced when the engine is kicked over, the problem was the cap. Replace it with a new one.

2. The ignition coil windings should be checked for continuity, using an ohmmeter.

a. Disconnect the two low-tension coil leads (blue or yellow and black or black/white), and check for continuity between them. This is a check of the primary winding. If there is no continuity, replace the coil;

b. Check for continuity across the black or black/white low-tension lead

Testing the ignition coil primary winding for continuity

and the high-tension (spark plug) lead. Resistance may be very high, but continuity must exist. This checks the secondary winding;

c. Even if continuity is present in the coil windings, it is possible that the coil is still defective. Replacing the coil temporarily with one which is known to be serviceable is recommended.

10. The condenser can be checked if a capacitance tester is available. Condensers should have a capacitance of approximately 0.24 mf. Checking with a "megger" (high-voltage ohmmeter) should yield a resistance of 10M ohms or better at 1,000v. Replace the condensers if they fail either test.

NOTE: *After testing, ground the condenser lead against the case to discharge it.*

As noted above, sparking at the points, or points which pit or burn rapidly would

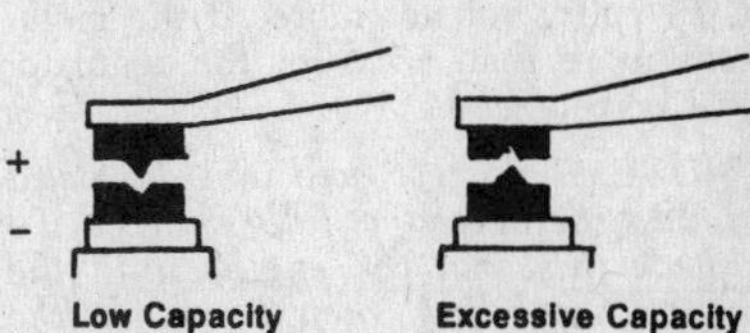

Mounds and pits on contact breaker surfaces caused by a defective condenser

indicate a defective condenser. Bad condensers will cause mounds and matching depressions on the points.

11. If the trouble is a misfire, and the tests above do not pinpoint the problem, check the condition and operation of the automatic timing advance unit.

CHARGING CIRCUIT

1. In the event that the battery overcharges, check the battery itself, and the voltage regulator.

2. If the battery discharges quickly, or fails to hold a charge, check the battery, the regulator, rectifier, and alternator.

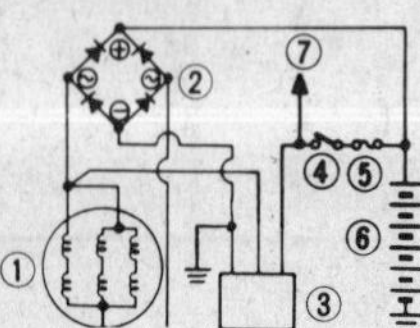

Charging circuit components

Voltage Regulator

A bad voltage regulator may cause the battery to go dead, or may overcharge it causing electrolyte loss, short light bulb life, etc.

The regulator is located beneath the battery box, and is rubber mounted. It can be tested with an ohmmeter, continuity tester, or ammeter.

1. If the battery goes dead, disconnect the three regulator leads (yellow, green, and black).

2. With an ohmmeter or continuity light, check for continuity between the yellow lead and the green lead. Check for continuity between the yellow lead and the motorcycle frame.

There must not be continuity in either case. If there is, the regulator must be replaced.

3. If an ammeter is available, connect it in series with the battery positive wire. Connect the regulator leads. Start and run the engine at more than 2,000 rpm. If the ammeter indicates that the battery is discharging, disconnect the regulator yellow lead and repeat the test. If the battery now shows that it is receiving a charge, the regulator must be replaced. If no change is noted, proceed with the rectifier and alternator tests which follow.

4. If the battery overcharges, check as follows:

Assuming that the battery is in good condition and *fully* charged, start the engine and connect a good voltmeter across the battery terminals. Run the engine at 4,000 rpm. The voltage across the battery should increase to between 14–15 volts, but not more. If the meter reads more than 15 volts, the regulator must be replaced.

NOTE: *This test will not be valid unless the battery is fully charged. To check this, run the engine until the voltage stabilizes, then disconnect the regulator black lead. If the voltage increases, the results of the test were valid.*

5. When mounting the regulator, be sure that the rubber dampers are in place. The regulator could be damaged by excess vibration.

Rectifier

The rectifier is located behind the battery or under the battery case.

The rectifier should be checked in the event of insufficient battery charging. Tests can be carried out with a continuity light or a standard (low-voltage) ohmmeter.

CAUTION: *Do not apply high-voltage to the rectifier.*

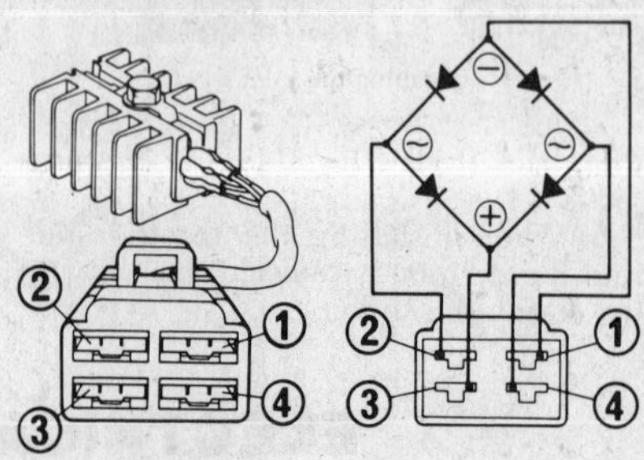

Rectifier leads: (1) green; (2) red/white; (3) yellow; (4) pink

1. Disconnect the leads and remove the rectifier from the machine.

2. The test involves testing current flow through the rectifier in both directions. The rectifier consists of four diodes. When in working condition, a diode will pass current in one direction only.

If the diode passes current in both directions, or in neither direction, it is defective. If any of the diodes is defective, the rectifier must be replaced.

3. Connect the negative lead of the tester to the green wire, and the positive lead to the yellow, red/white, and pink wires in turn.

In each case, note whether or not there is continuity.

NOTE: *On an ohmmeter, "continuity" will be indicated by a resistance of 5–40 ohms. "No continuity," by a resistance of 100 or more ohms.*

4. Now reverse the tester connections, connecting the positive tester lead to the green wire, and the negative to each of the others in turn.

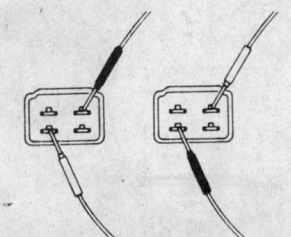

Reversing tester connections to check rectifier

In every case, the reaction of the tester must be the opposite of the first test: i.e., if the first test showed continuity between two leads, reversing the tester connections must show no continuity.

Continuity in both directions, or lack of continuity in both directions for any given pair of wires is indicative of a defective rectifier.

Alternator

The alternator should be checked in the event of low or no battery charging not attributable to the other components.

1. A dynamic output test can be carried out if a voltmeter (500T) and ammeter (450 and 500T) are available. The battery *must* be fully charged or the test may be invalid.

Hook up the voltmeter across the battery terminals (500T), disconnect the battery red/white lead, and connect it the ammeter. Connect the other side of the ammeter to the battery positive terminal.

Disconnect the black regulator lead.

Start the engine and compare the voltmeter and ammeter readings with lights off and lights on at the given rpm as shown in the "Alternator Output" chart.

If the readings are not within 10% of the given specifications, the alternator should be replaced.

NOTE: *The alternator should not be excessively hot when this test is carried out.*

2. Using an ohmmeter or continuity tester, a static stator test can be carried out.

Disconnect the alternator wiring at the plastic connector.

3. Check for continuity between the white, the yellow, and the pink leads. Continuity must exist, or the stator assembly has a broken wire and it must be replaced.

Alternator Output

	Lights Off	*Lights On (Low Beam)*	*Lights On (Hight Beam)*
450			
Beginning of Charging (rpm)	1000	1500	1800
Charging Current (amps)			
3000 rpm	3.5	2.1	1.1
5000 rpm	4.5	2.9	1.9
10,000 rpm	5.7	4.0	3.2
500			
Beginning of Charging (rpm)	—	—	2800
Charging Current/Battery Voltage			
5000 rpm	—	—	1.2a/15.5v
8000 rpm	—	—	3.5a/15.5v

4. Check for continuity between the yellow lead and the stator core. If continuity exists, there is a short, and the stator must be replaced.

5. Check for broken or cracked insulation or scored or burned coil core ends.

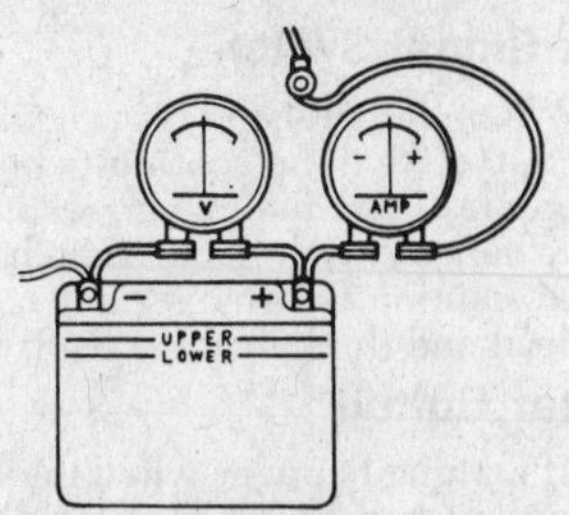

Voltmeter and ammeter set up for alternator output test

STARTER MOTOR

1. If the starter motor spins when the button is pushed, but the engine does not, the starter clutch is defective. Refer to "Engine and Transmission," for starter clutch removal and inspection procedures.

2. If the warning lights dim when the starter button is pushed, but the engine and starter do not turn over, the battery may be too low, or the starter may be defective.

3. If nothing happens when the starter button is pushed, either the starter solenoid is defective, or there is a loose wire in the electric starter circuit.

Removal and Disassembly

1. Disconnect the lead at the starter motor.

2. Remove the alternator cover, both sections of the left crankcase cover, and disconnect the neutral switch lead.

3. Remove the alternator rotor, using either the special puller.

4. Remove the starter sprocket setting plate (secured by a phillips screw), and remove the two sprockets and chain together.

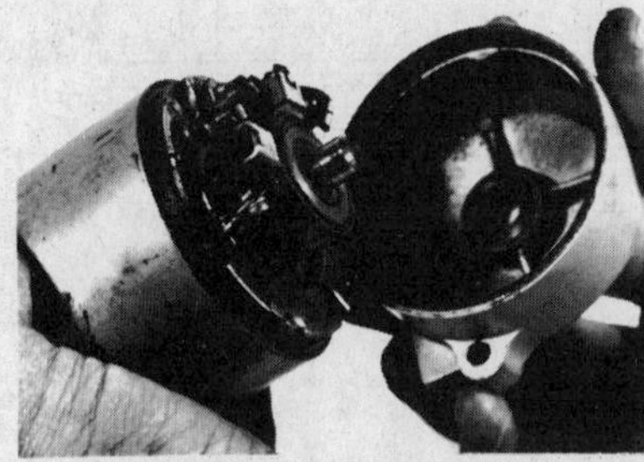

Starter motor end plate removal

5. Remove the two screws which secure the starter motor, and tap the starter out of the case.

6. To disassemble the starter, remove the two long phillips screws and remove the end plates.

NOTE: *Exercise caution when removing the output side end plate as this contains the reduction gears.*

7. Disconnect the starter carbon brush leads (2) and remove the brush mounting plate.

Disassembly past this point is not necessary.

Inspection

1. Use an ohmmeter or continuity tester to check the starter motor.

2. Check for continuity between each of the commutator segments. There must be continuity between all of them. If there is a dead spot, the starter must be replaced.

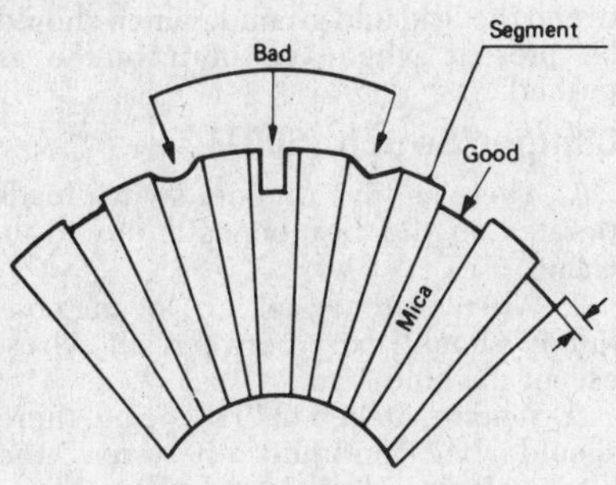

States of commutator condition

3. Check for continuity between the armature core and the commutator; there must be none. If continuity exists, the starter must be replaced.

4. Check for continuity between the starter lead terminal and the brushes. Continuity must exist or the starter must be replaced.

5. Measure the length of each carbon brush. Replace them if either is less than 5 mm (0.2 in.). Standard brush length (new) is 11.0–12.5 mm (0.43–0.49 in.). Replace any brush which is pitted or cracked.

6. Clean the commutator surface thoroughly with a solvent. Check that there is no scoring on the commutator surface. The mica insulation should undercut the commutator segments by at least 0.3 mm (0.012 in.). If less than this, the mica should be undercut by a qualified specialist.

7. Check the condition of the brush springs and replace them if deformed or if they will not hold the brush firmly against the commutator.

Assembly and Installation

1. Reverse the above procedures. Be sure that the output side O-rings are in place.

2. After assembling the starter, check that the armature will turn without excessive binding.

Solenoid

1. The starter solenoid can be checked by disconnecting the high-tension lead from the starter motor, and pushing the starter button. The starter switch should click when the button is pushed.

2. If it does not, use an ohmmeter or continuity light to check for continuity across the switch's primary leads (black and yellow/red 450, or yellow/red and green/red, 500T). If continuity does not exist, replace the switch.

3. Connect a fully charged 12-volt battery to the primary leads, then check for

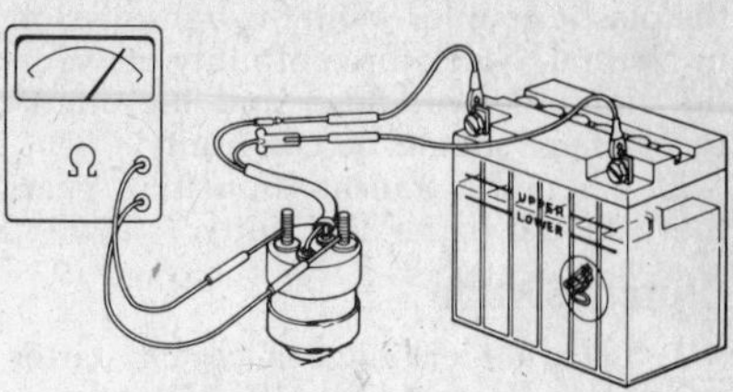

Testing the starter solenoid

continuity across the starter switch high-tension leads. If there is no continuity, replace the switch.

ELECTRICAL SWITCHES

All electrical switches are easily checked with an ohmmeter or self-powered continuity light after disconnecting the switch leads at the plastic connectors.

Ignition Switch

1. With the key turned to the first position, check for continuity between the black and red leads. If continuity does not exist, replace the switch.

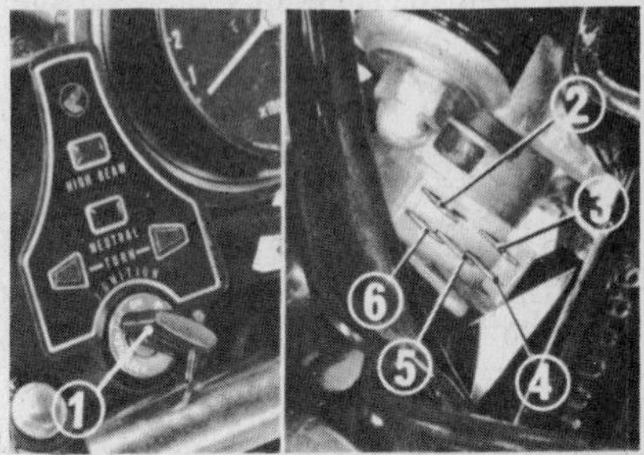

Ignition switch connections (500T)

1. Ignition switch
2. Brown
3. Brown/white
4. Brown
5. Red
6. Black

2. With the key in the first position, continuity must exist between the brown and the brown/white leads.

3. With the key in the second or "Park" position, continuity must exist between the red and brown leads.

Brake Light Switches

1. Check for continuity across the front brake light switch terminals. Continuity should occur when the brake lever has moved about 1 in. (25 mm), measured at the tip of the lever.

2. Check for continuity between the black and green/yellow leads to check the rear brake light switch. Continuity should occur when the brake pedal has moved about 25 mm (1 in.). This switch is adjustable.

Kill Button

1. The kill button should show no continuity between the black and the black/white leads when in either "off" position. When in the "run" position, there must be continuity.

Neutral Switch

1. Disconnect the alternator wiring at

the plastic coupler. With the transmission in Neutral, check for continuity between the lightgreen/red lead and the crankcase. There should be continuity.

2. When the transmission is in gear, there should be no continuity.

Clutch Switch

1. Late models have a clutch starter switch incorporated into the clutch lever holder to prevent operation of the electric starter when in gear with the clutch engaged. The lead connectors are in the headlight shell.

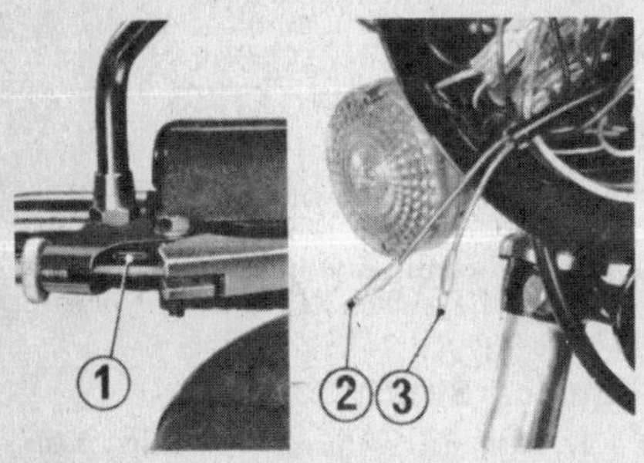

Clutch switch (1) and green and green/red clutch switch leads (2 and 3) (500T)

2. Check for continuity between the green and green/red switch leads. Continuity should exist only when the clutch is disengaged.

Silicon Diode

1. The diode is a part of the electric starter interlock circuit.

2. Check for continuity across the diode with an ohmmeter in the high reading range. Current must flow in one direction only. Current flow (continuity) in both or neither direction is indicative of a defective diode.

Horn

1. If the horn will not function, connect a 12-volt battery directly to the horn terminals. If the horn does not sound, it is defective.

2. If the horn does sound, check the horn button by disconnecting the light green lead and check for continuity between the lead and ground, which should be present when the horn button is pushed.

Dimmer Switch (500T)

1. There are five dimmer switch leads (located in the box beneath the triple clamp).

2. When switched to "Lo" beam, continuity should exist between all wires, except the blue lead.

3. When switched to "Hi" beam, there should be continuity between the black/yellow and the blue leads only.

4. When in the median position between "Lo" and "Hi" there should be continuity between all leads.

Headlight Switch (450)

1. The headlight switch lead connectors are inside the headlight shell.

2. When the headlight is switched off, there will be no continuity between the leads.

3. When the headlight is switched to "Lo" beam, there will be continuity between the yellow and white leads and between the black, brown/white, and white leads.

4. In the "Hi" beam position, there will be continuity between the, yellow and white leads and between the black, blue, and brown/white leads.

Turn Signal Switch

1. When the left-hand turn signal is activated, there will be continuity between the gray lead and the orange lead.

2. When the right-hand switch is activated, continuity will exist between the gray lead and the light blue lead.

Starter Button

1. If nothing happens when the starter button is pushed, and the solenoid seems functional, check the starter button.

500T

a. Disconnect the starter button leads. When the button is free, continuity should exist between the black and black/red leads;

b. When the button is depressed, continuity should exist between the black and yellow/red leads.

NOTE: *The black/red lead shuts off the headlight when the starter button is pushed. This lead has an inline 7A fuse in the fuse box.*

450

a. Disconnect the yellow/red starter button lead. Check for continuity between the yellow/red switch lead and ground. Continuity should exist *only* when the starter button is pushed.

NOTE: *After separating the starter button housing, spray the button contacts with electrical connector cleaner.*

WIRING DIAGRAMS

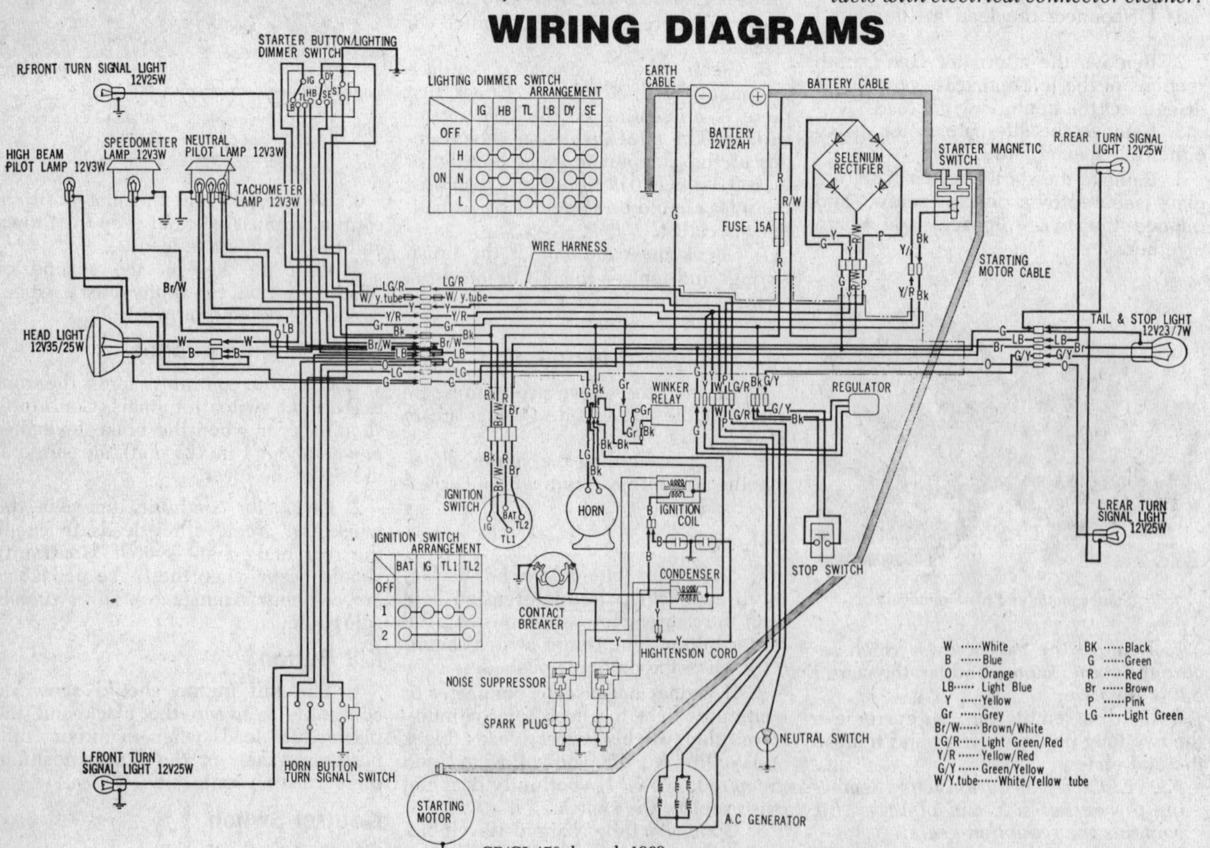

CB/CL450 through 1969

WIRING DIAGRAMS

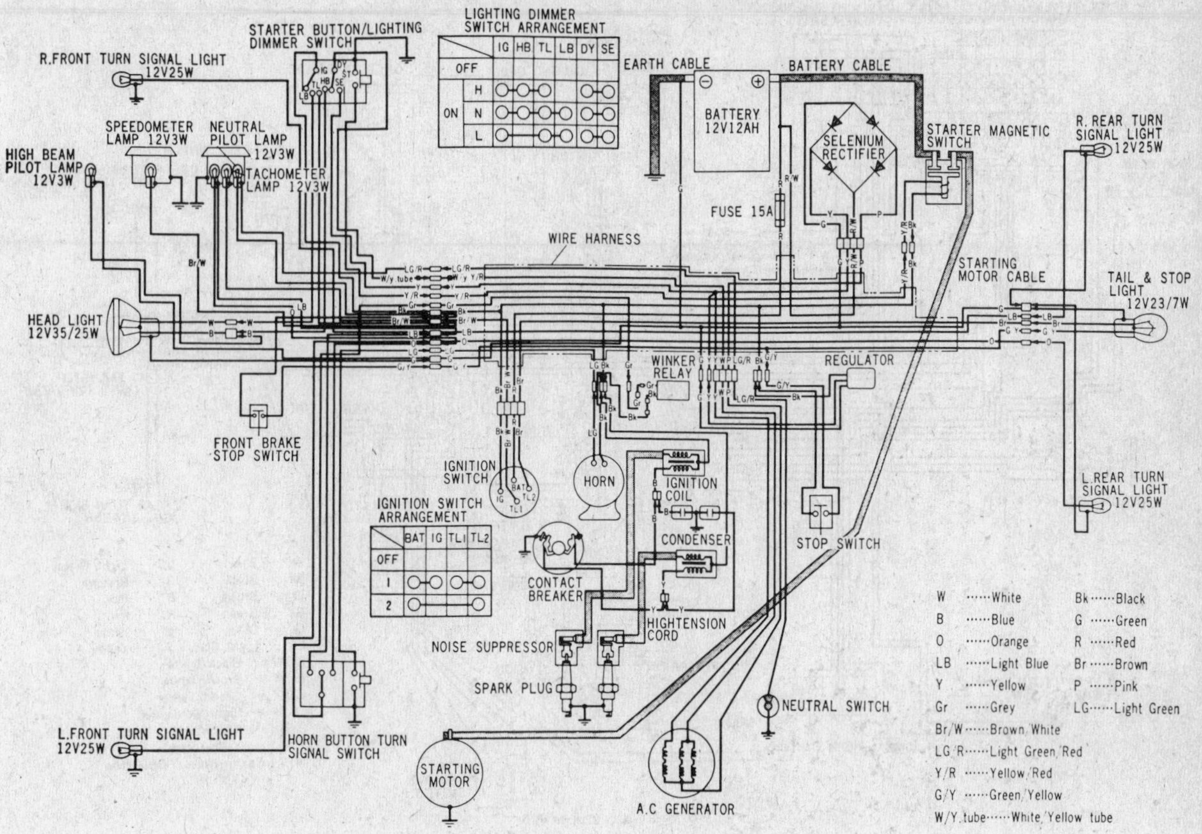

	IG	HB	TL	LB	DY	SE
OFF						
ON H	O	O	O		O	O
ON N	O	O	O	O	O	O
ON L	O		O	O	O	O

	BAT	IG	TL1	TL2
OFF				
1	O	O	O	O
2	O			O

W ······White
B ······Blue
O ······Orange
LB ······Light Blue
Y ······Yellow
Gr ······Grey
Br/W······Brown White
LG/R······Light Green/Red
Y/R ······Yellow/Red
G/Y ······Green/Yellow
W/Y. tube······White/Yellow tube
Bk······Black
G ······Green
R ······Red
Br ······Brown
P ······Pink
LG······Light Green

CB/CL450 with front brake light switch through 1969

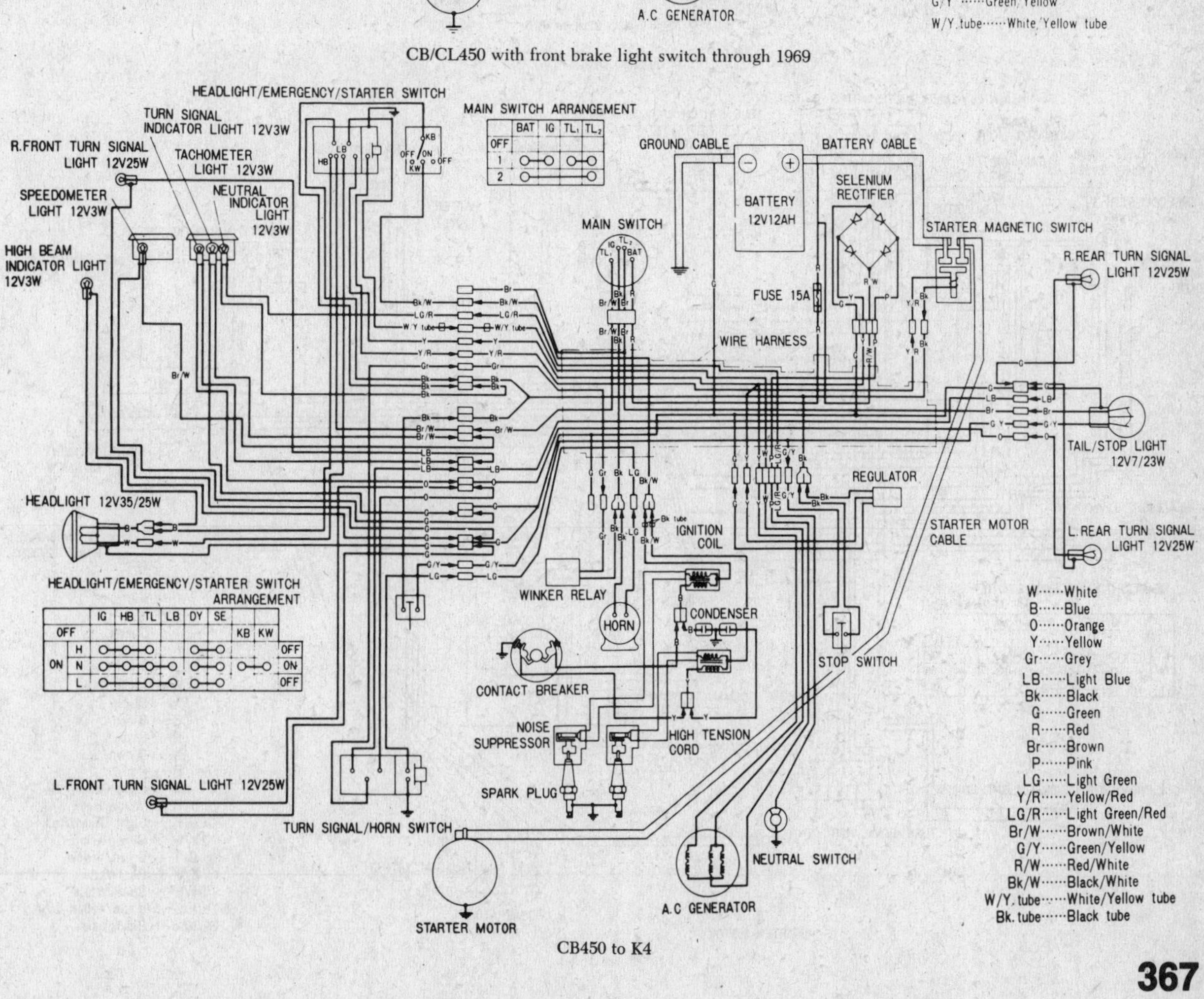

	BAT	IG	TL_1	TL_2
OFF				
1	O	O	O	O
2	O			O

		IG	HB	TL	LB	DY	SE	KB	KW	
OFF										
ON	H	O	O	O		O	O			OFF
ON	N	O	O	O	O	O	O	O	O	ON
ON	L	O		O	O	O	O			OFF

W······White
B······Blue
O······Orange
Y······Yellow
Gr······Grey
LB······Light Blue
Bk······Black
G······Green
R······Red
Br······Brown
P······Pink
LG······Light Green
Y/R······Yellow/Red
LG/R······Light Green/Red
Br/W······Brown/White
G/Y······Green/Yellow
R/W······Red/White
Bk/W······Black/White
W/Y. tube······White/Yellow tube
Bk. tube······Black tube

CB450 to K4

WIRING DIAGRAMS

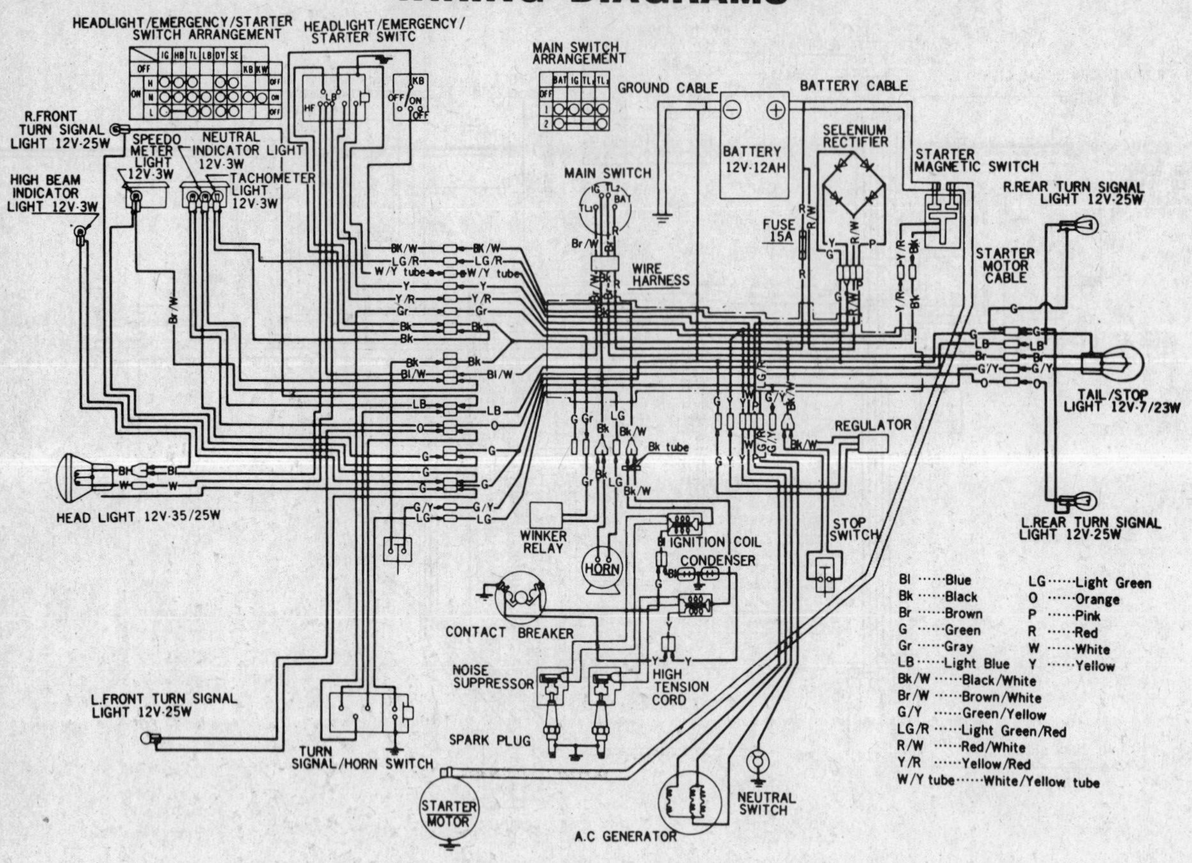

CL450 to K4

HEADLIGHT/EMERGENCY/STARTER SWITCH
TURN SIGNAL INDICATOR LIGHT 12V3W
R.FRONT TURN SIGNAL LIGHT 12V32W
TACHOMETER LIGHT 12V3W
SPEEDOMETER LIGHT 12V3W
NEUTRAL INDICATOR LIGHT 12V3W
HIGH BEAM INDICATOR LIGHT 12V3W
MAIN SWITCH ARRANGEMENT
GROUND CABLE
BATTERY CABLE
BATTERY 12V12AH
SELENIUM RECTIFIER
STARTER MAGNETIC SWITCH
MAIN SWITCH
FUSE 15A
WIRE HARNESS
R.REAR TURN SIGNAL LIGHT 12V32W
TAIL/STOP LIGHT 12V3/32W
REGULATOR
HEADLIGHT 12V50/40W
IGNITION COIL
STARTER MOTOR CABLE
L.REAR TURN SIGNAL LIGHT 12V32W
HEADLIGHT/EMERGENCY/STARTER SWITCH ARRANGEMENT
WINKER RELAY
HORN
CONDENSER
CONTACT BREAKER
STOP SWITCH
NOISE SUPPRESSOR
HIGH TENSION CORD
SPARK PLUG
L.FRONT TURN SIGNAL LIGHT 12V32W
TURN SIGNAL/HORN SWITCH
NEUTRAL UWITCH
A.C GENERATOR
STARTER MOTOR

W······White
B······Blue
O······Orange
Y······Yellow
Gr······Grey
LB······Light Blue
Bk······Black
G······Green
R······Red
Br······Brown
P······Pink
LG······Light Green
Y/R······Yellow/Red
LG/R······Light Green/Red
Br/W······Brown/White
G/Y······Green/Yellow
R/W······Red/White
Bk/W······Black/White
W/Y. tube······White/Yellow tube
Bk. tube······Black tube

CB/CL450 K5

WIRING DIAGRAMS

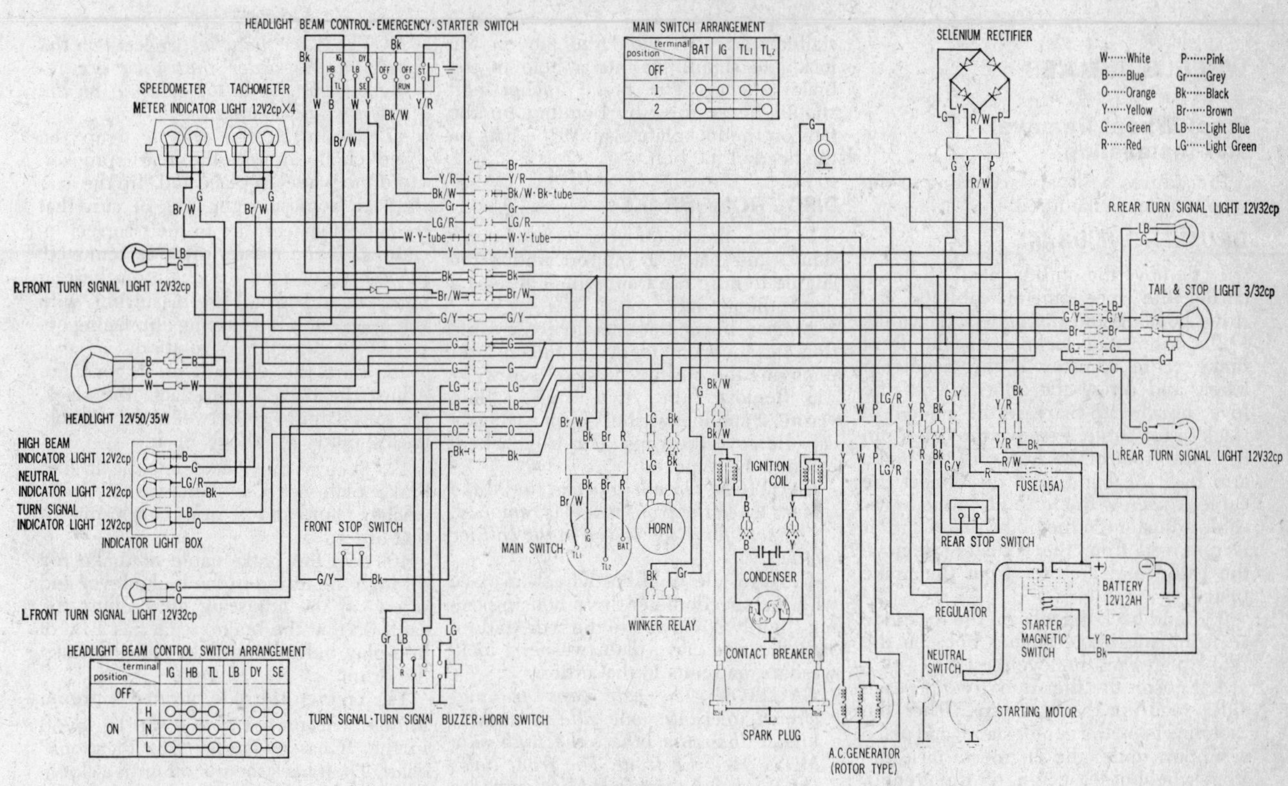

CB/CL450 K6-on

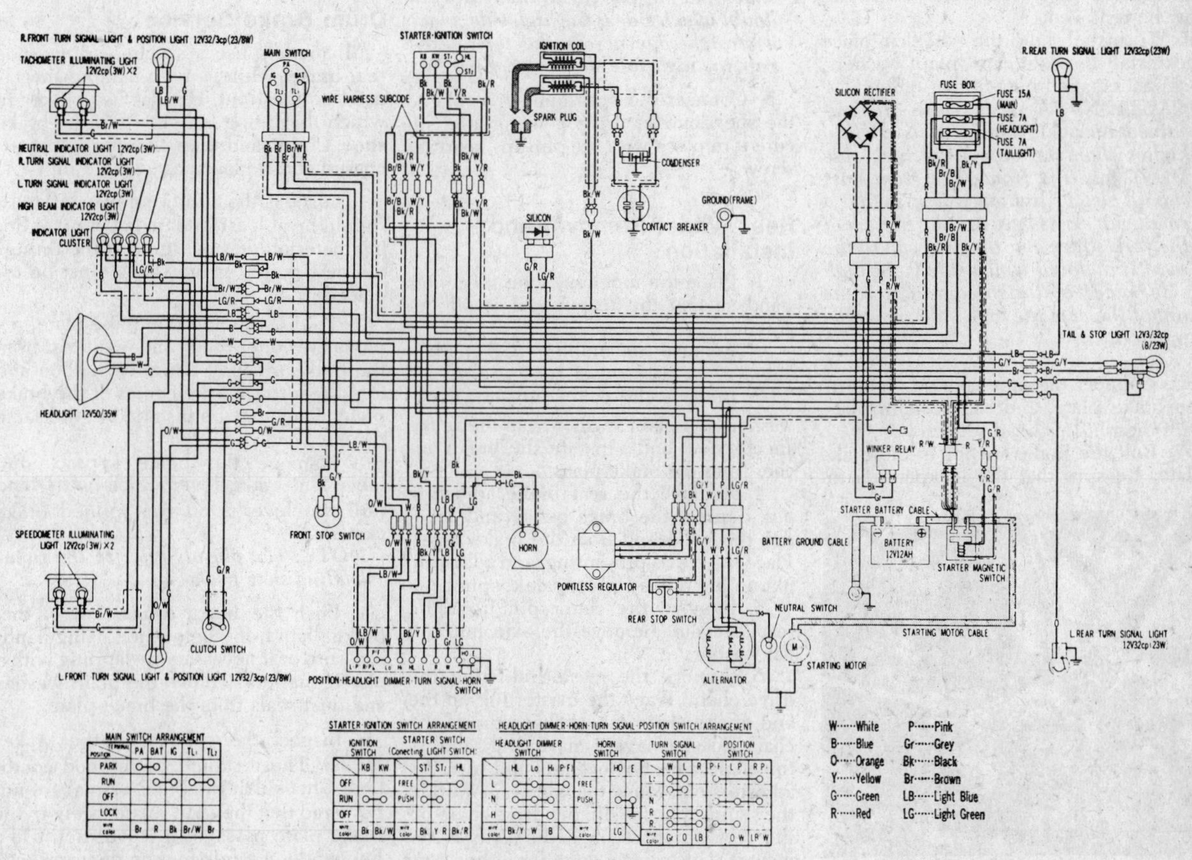

CB500T

CHASSIS

WHEELS, BRAKES

Front Wheel Removal and Installation

Procedures will vary according to the type of front brake fitted.

DRUM FRONT BRAKE

1. Remove the phillips head screw securing the speedometer cable to the drive housing and disconnect the cable.
2. Loosen the locknut on the front brake cable adjuster at the handlebar lever, and screw the adjuster into the lever housing to increase the amount of slack in the cable. Remove the cotter pin from the front brake arm, pull the brake arm back by hand, and disconnect the cable. Unscrew the locknut on the lower cable adjuster (on the brake plate) until it is removed from the adjuster. Remove the cable and adjuster from the brake plate.
3. Bend back the tabs on the lockplate securing the brake anchor bolt (on the brake plate) and remove the bolt.
4. Loosen the four nuts (two on each side) securing the axle caps. Place the motorcycle on the center stand, and place a support under the engine to raise the front wheel at least 2 in. off the ground. Remove the two nuts, lockwashers, and plain washers from each of the axle caps. Remove the caps. The front wheel can now be removed.
5. To install, hold the wheel in place and install the axle caps, plain washers, lockwashers, and nuts in that order.

 CAUTION: *The axle caps are machined unevenly (one side is slightly higher than the other) the high side MUST face the front. The front nuts should also be tightened first so that a small gap exists between the bottom of the fork slider and the axle cap to the rear. If in doubt which side is the high side, place a straightedge across the top of the cap, the high side should be apparent.*

6. Connect the speedometer cable to the brake plate, and secure it in place with the phillips head set screw.
7. Bolt the brake anchor to the brake plate. Be sure that the lockplate is installed correctly, the large tab on the lockplate should fit into a hole in the brake anchor. The brake anchor bolt should be secured by bending up the tabs on the lockplate against the flats on the head of the bolt.

The gap between the axle cap and the fork must be at the rear of the fork

DISC FRONT BRAKE

1. Place the motorcycle on the center stand, and place a support under the engine to raise the front wheel at least 2 in. off the ground.
2. Disconnect the speedometer cable from the speedometer drive housing after removing the phillips head set screw.
3. Remove the two nuts, plain washers, and lockwashers from each axle cap. Remove the caps. The front wheel can now be removed.

 CAUTION: *Do not squeeze the brake lever when the front wheel is removed. This will force the piston in the caliper out.*

4. To install, hold the wheel in place with the speedometer drive housing facing slightly down and to the rear, and install the axle caps, plain washers, lockwashers, and nuts in that order.

 CAUTION: *The axle caps are machined unevenly (one side is slightly higher than the other) the high side MUST face the front. The front bolts should also be tightened first starting on the disc side so that a small gap exists between the bottom of the fork slider and the axle cap at the rear. If in doubt which side is the high side, place a straightedge across the top of the cap, the high side should be apparent.*

5. Connect the speedometer cable to the speedometer drive housing, and secure it in place with the phillips head set screw.

Rear Wheel Removal and Installation

1. Place the motorcycle on its center stand so that the rear wheel is off the ground.
2. Remove the mufflers (CB models only).
3. Remove the cotter pin, nut, lockwasher, and plain washer from the brake anchor bolt, and separate the brake anchor from the brake plate.
4. Remove the rear brake adjusting nut, depress the brake pedal, and separate the brake rod from the brake lever. Place the clevis pin, spring, and adjusting nut on the brake rod for safekeeping.
5. Remove the cotter pin from the rear axle nut. Remove the axle nut and flat washer.
6. Remove the masterlink from the drive chain. Place the masterlink on the end of the chain for safekeeping. If the chain doesn't have a masterlink, loosen the chain adjuster locknuts and turn the adjusters out. Move the wheel forward in the swing arm and slip the drive chain off the rear sprocket once the axle is removed. This can be done for either type of chain and does not require removal of the masterlink.

 NOTE: *Place the wheel spacers on the axle in the order that they are removed, and screw the axle nut on the axle for safekeeping.*

7. To install the wheel: wrap the drive chain around the rear sprocket. Hold the wheel in place and slip the axle in place from the right-side. Be sure that the wheel spacers are in their correct locations. If the masterlink was removed, place both ends of the chain on the rear sprocket and install the masterlink with the open end of the spring clip facing opposite the direction of rotation.
8. Turn the axle nut on finger-tight. Adjust the drive chain slack; the slack, measured midway between the sprockets, should be about ¾ in.
9. Secure the brake anchor to the brake plate with a plain washer, lockwasher, nut, and a new cotter pin in that order.
10. Slip the brake cable or brake rod through the fitting in the brake lever and screw on the adjusting nut. Adjust the cable so that the brake pedal has 1 in. of free-play before the brake shoes contact the drum.
11. Tighten the axle nut to the proper torque. The proper torque can be found in the "Chassis Torque Specifications" chart. Then back the nut off until a slot in the axle nut is lined up with a hole in the axle. Secure the axle nut in place with a new cotter pin.

Drum Brake Service

All models use a single-leading shoe rear brake, while, a twin-leading shoe is used on the front. Hondas use brakes in which the lining is bonded to the brake shoe. Lining and shoe, therefore, are purchased and replaced as a single unit.

1. Inspect the lining for wear. There should be at least 0.08 in. (2.0 mm) of lining material left (measured at the linings thinnest point) or the shoes must be replaced.
2. To disassemble the brake plate, remove the cotter pin(s) and washer(s) from the brake pivot(s). Grasp each shoe and fold them toward the center of the brake plate. They may be installed in the same manner.
3. Remove the brake springs. Remove the brake lever pinch-bolt(s) and pull the lever(s) off the splined brake cam(s).

 NOTE: *The plurals refer to the twin-leading shoe brakes.*

4. Push the brake cam(s) out of the brake plate from the outside using hand-pressure or if necessary by tapping with a plastic mallet. Remove the plain washer and dust seals from the brake plate.
5. Inspect the splines on the brake cam(s). These should be in good condition. Check that the brake cam(s) are not bent and that they can rotate freely in the brake plate passage. If it will not, use a fine grade of sandpaper on the camshafts and the surface of the brake plate passage.

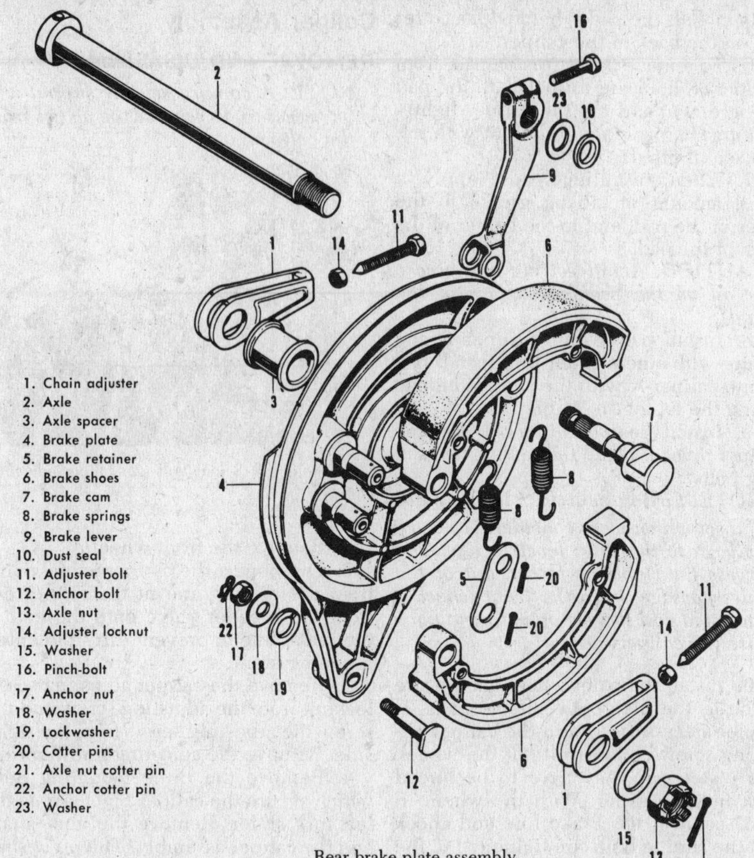

Rear brake plate assembly

6. Clean the cam(s) thoroughly in a solvent to remove any old grease, rust, or corrosion. Use sandpaper or emery cloth to polish the cams. Clean off any residue; before reassembly, smear the cams with chassis grease.

7. On twin-leading shoe brakes, the brake plate linkage should be checked. The connecting rod is secured to each brake lever by a clevis pin and cotter pin. These pins can be removed after the cotter pins are taken off. They should be checked for wear, especially on high mileage machines, and replaced if necessary.

8. When reassembling the brake plate, note the following points:

a. Ensure that the brake cams are lubricated with chassis grease;

b. The use of new dust seals is recommended;

c. Lubricate the brake shoe pivot points with a little grease;

d. Install the shoes as on removal. Hook them together with the springs, and fold them down over the brake cam(s) and pivot(s). Install new cotter pins to the pivot points;

e. When installing the brake lever on the brake cam, be sure that the punch marks on the lever and cam align, if they are there.

Disc Brake Service

When handling disc brake fluid, observe the following cautions:

a. Brake fluid absorbs moisture very quickly, and then becomes useless. Therefore, never use fluid from an old or unsealed container;

b. Brake fluid will quickly damage paint. Place a protective cover on the gas tank;

c. Use only DOT #3 brake fluid.

FLUSHING

The brake system should be flushed out every 8,000 miles, or once a year.

1. Attach a length of vinyl tube to the bleed screw on the brake caliper and put the other end into a small container.

2. Remove the master cylinder cap, and the diaphragm. Loosen the bleed screw about ½ turn. Pull the brake lever slowly to the handgrip, then tighten the bleed screw. Release the lever. Repeat until the master cylinder is almost empty.

3. Add new brake fluid to the master cylinder and continue squeezing and releasing the brake lever slowly until the new fluid begins to come out of the vinyl tube. Bleed the system as outlined below.

BLEEDING

1. Needed for this operation are a torque wrench, a small cup, and a vinyl tube.

2. Be sure that the reservoir is topped up. After checking the reservoir level, replace the diaphragm and cap.

3. Connect the vinyl tube to the bleed screw on the caliper, making sure that it is a tight fit; then insert the other end of the tube into a small container with several inches of brake fluid in it. Be sure

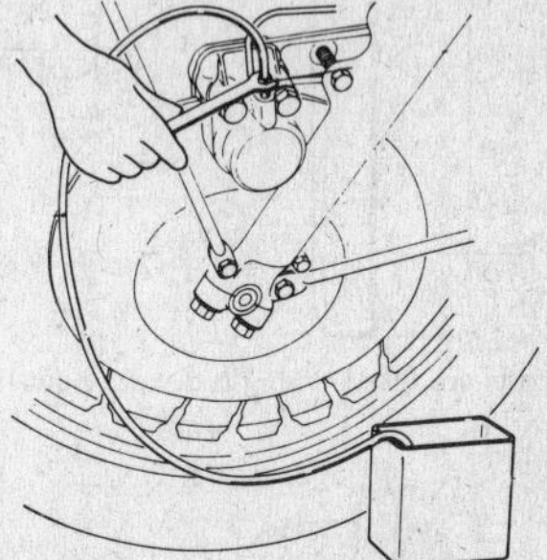

Bleeding the disc brake

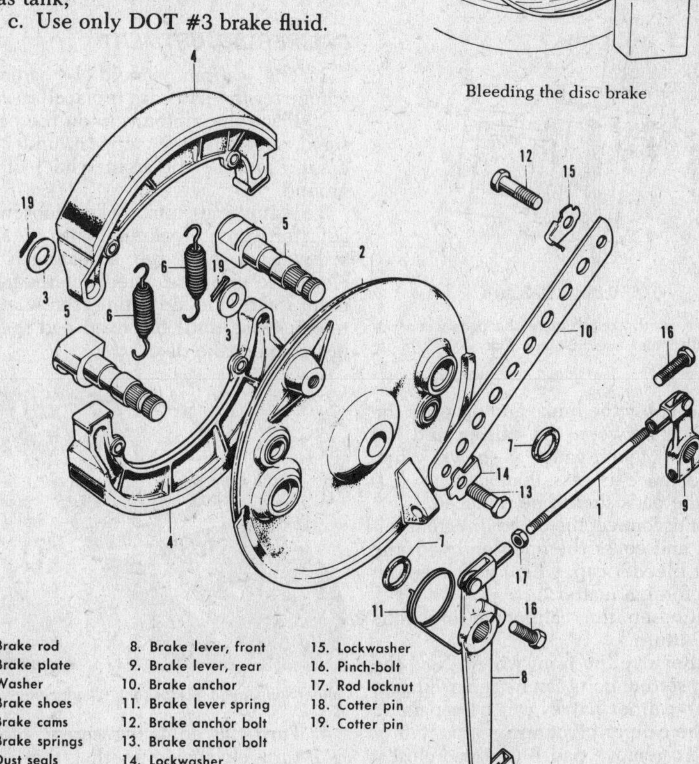

Front drum brake assembly

that the end of the tube is below the level of the fluid in the container.

4. Apply the brake lever *slowly* several times, then hold it ON.

5. While holding the brake lever on, loosen the bleed screw. The brake lever will be pulled toward the handgrip. Close the bleed screw BEFORE the lever bottoms out on the handgrip.

6. Repeat the procedure until the fluid issuing from the lower end of the tube is completely free of air bubbles.

NOTE: *During the operation, keep a check on the reservoir fluid level, maintaining it near its normal position.*

7. Tighten the bleed screw to 4.5–6.7 ft lbs.

8. Top up the reservoir to the level line.

PAD REPLACEMENT

1. Both pads should be replaced as a set when either pad is worn past the red limit line.

The brake pads that came as standard equipment on the early disc brake models (pre-Ks), were not marked with a limit line. To determine pad wear on these

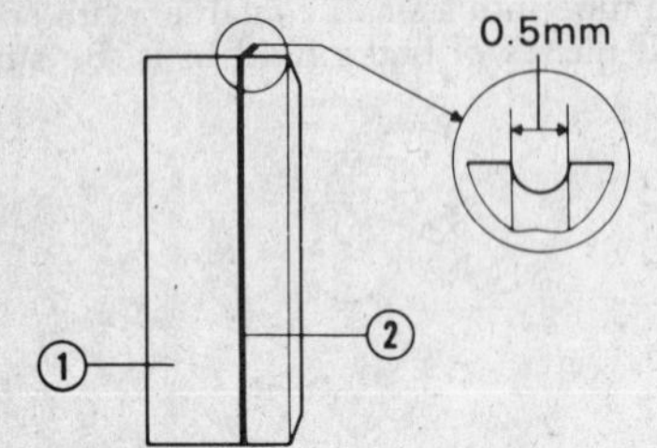

Brake pads are fitted with a red wear limit line (2)

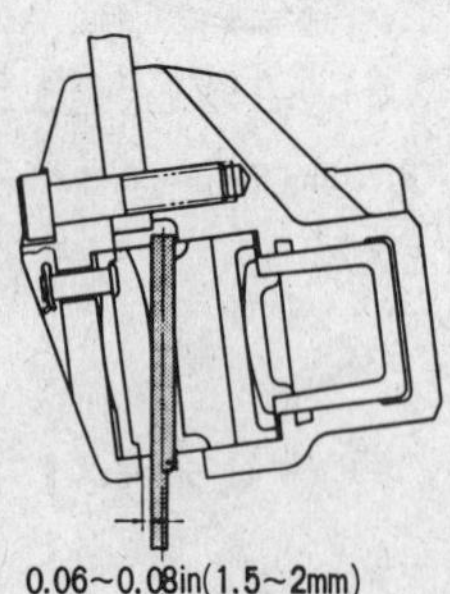

On older disc brakes, replace the pads when caliper-to-disc clearance is less than 0.06–0.08 in. (1.5–2.0 mm)

models, apply the brake and measure the clearance between the caliper and the disc with a feeler gauge as shown. When the clearance is less than 0.08 in. (2.0 mm), the pads should be replaced.

2. Disconnect the brake line from caliper A and cover the open end with the rubber bleeder cap, which will keep out dirt or foreign matter.

3. Loosen the caliper setting bolts about ¼ turn.

4. Remove the front wheel. Now the caliper setting bolts can be removed, and the two caliper halves can be separated from the caliper pivot arm.

5. To remove pad B (the pad closest to the wheel) from caliper B, remove the cotter pin from the top of the pad. On early models the pad is held with a cotter pin on the back of the caliper.

6. To remove pad A (piston pad) from Caliper A, hold the caliper with the pad facing down, and tap the caliper lightly on top. The pad should fall out with the pad seat if fitted.

7. When installing pads, apply a small amount of silicon grease to the sides of the pad, and to the center of the back of the pad.

CAUTION: *Avoid getting any grease or oil on the braking surface of the pad.*

8. Install pad B into Caliper B and secure with a new cotter pin. Install pad A into caliper A with the slot in the pad facing the top of the caliper.

9. Install the two caliper halves to the caliper pivot arm and tighten the two setting bolts.

NOTE: *Fitting new pads in the place of a set which were considerably worn will cause the fluid level to rise. The excess fluid will be forced out of the inlet passage when the front wheel is mounted and the piston is forced back into the caliper.*

10. Install the front wheel taking care to locate the disc between the pads. It may be necessary to turn the caliper adjusting screw clockwise to fit the wheel. The piston pad may have to be forced back in the caliper. With the wheel in place connect the brake line and check that the setting bolts are tightened to the proper torque of 9–12 ft lbs. Adjust the caliper and bleed the system.

NOTE: *After installing new pads, avoid hard application of the brake for at least 50 miles.*

CALIPER ADJUSTMENT

1. The caliper should be adjusted whenever the pads are replaced.

2. Place the motorcycle on the center stand, and place a support under the engine to raise the front wheel off the ground.

3. Using a 10 mm socket, loosen the adjuster screw locknut. With a small screwdriver turn the adjusting screw clockwise until the wheel rotates freely, then rotate the adjusting screw counterclockwise until the fixed pad (pad B) just contacts the disc.

Caliper adjustment: (1) locknut, (2) adjusting screw

4. Turn the adjusting screw another ½–1 turn clockwise so that there is a small clearance between pad B and the disc. Tighten the locknut.

Caliper Assembly

REMOVAL AND DISASSEMBLY

NOTE: *A compressed air supply will be necessary to remove the piston from the caliper.*

6 mm bolts (1), 8 mm bolt (2), caliper adjusting screw (3)

1. Remove the front wheel.

2. Disconnect the hydraulic brake line from the caliper, and fit the rubber cap from the bleeder valve onto the end of the brake line to prevent dirt from entering the system.

3. Remove the caliper adjusting screw locknut from the adjusting screw and unscrew the adjusting screw from the right-side. Remove the adjusting screw spring.

4. Remove the three mounting bolts which secure the caliper pivot arm to the left fork slider. Remove the mud guard and the caliper assembly. The pivot shaft can be pulled from the pivot arm.

NOTE: *The two caliper halves can be removed from the pivot arm and disassembled without removing the pivot arm or the front wheel. To remove the caliper halves in this manner, see the section under "Pad Replacement."*

5. To disassemble the caliper, remove the two setting bolts from the caliper and separate the two caliper halves from the caliper pivot arm. Remove the two pads as described under "Pad Replacement."

6. Remove the piston from caliper A by blowing compressed air into the fluid inlet passage.

7. The piston seal can be removed from caliper A using a wood or plastic tool. However, note that if the cylinder walls are scored while removing the seal, the caliper half will have to be replaced.

INSPECTION

1. Check pad wear. If either pad is worn past the red limit line, it must be replaced. If no red line is present inspect the pads as described under "Pad Replacement."

2. Measure the inside diameter of the caliper cylinder bore and the outside diameter of the piston. Compare the measured value with the service limit given at the end of this section; if either part is worn beyond its service limit, it must be replaced.

3. Check the bore in caliper A for scoring. If scoring is evident, the caliper half should be replaced.

4. Check the piston for scoring; replace it if scoring is evident.

5. Check the pivot shaft for wear, also check the pivot arm for wear at the pivot

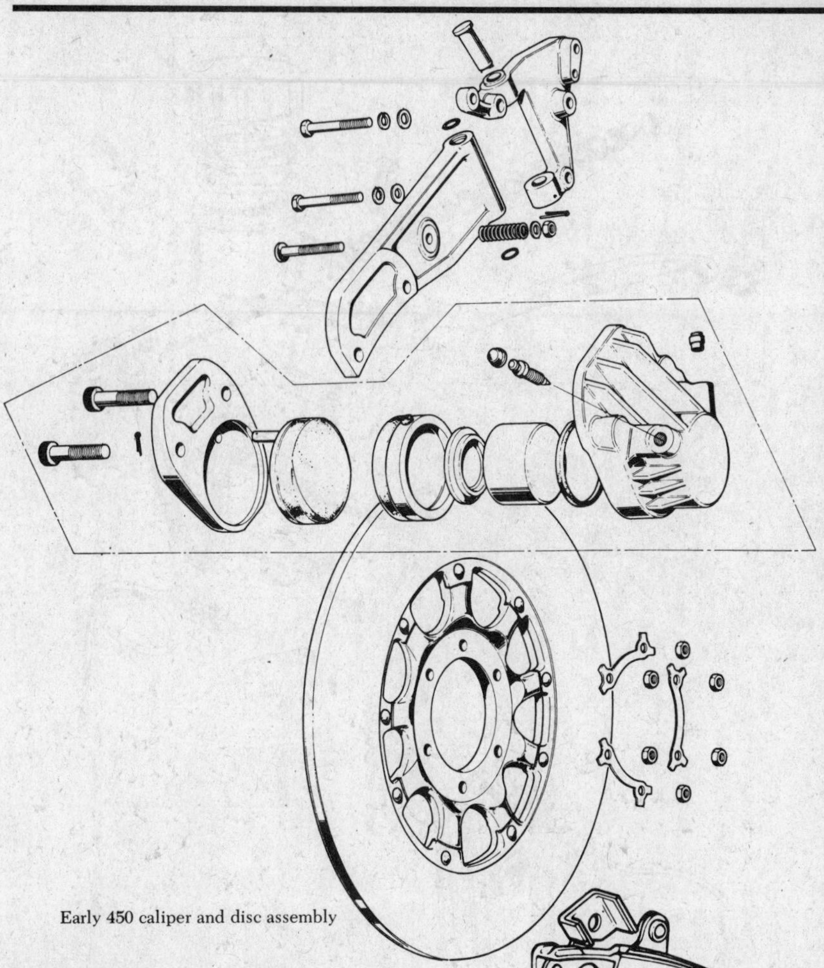

Early 450 caliper and disc assembly

points. Replace as necessary.

6. Check the condition of the two pivot shaft O-rings. If they are torn or cracked they should be replaced with new ones.

ASSEMBLY AND INSTALLATION

Since it is imperative that no dirt or foreign matter be allowed to enter the hydraulic system, assembly should take place in a clean area preferably on a sheet of white paper.

Clean and lubricate all internal brake parts with fresh DOT 3 brake fluid before assembly.

Use only "Genuine Honda Parts" when replacing any parts in the brake system.

1. Install the pivot shaft into the pivot arm. Be sure to apply some grease to the pivot points. Note that an O-ring is fitted to either side of the pivot arm.
2. Mount the pivot arm to the left fork slider with the three mounting bolts. Install the adjusting screw, spring, and locknut.
3. Install the piston seal into the caliper using a wood or plastic tool. Take care not to score the cylinder bore. Installing a new seal is recommended.
4. Install the piston into the caliper half, then install the piston pad. Install the fixed pad to caliper B and secure it with a new cotter pin.
5. Install the two caliper halves to the pivot arm, and torque the setting bolts to 9–12 ft lbs.
6. Mount the front wheel. Bleed the brake as described under "Bleeding" Adjust the caliper as described under "Caliper Adjustment".

Brake Disc

1. Check the disc for warpage by attaching a dial gauge to the fork slider and its indicator on the side of the disc. Maximum warpage is 0.3 mm (0.012 in.).

Check for run-out by placing the dial gauge indicator on the edge of the disc. Maximum allowable run-out is 0.05 mm (0.002 in.).

If either measurement exceeds these service limits, emove the disc from the wheel and recheck warpage. If it exceeds the specification, replace it; if it does not, suspect worn wheel bearings.

Excessive run-out can also be caused by worn bolt holes or bolts. Worn bolt holes will necessitate replacement of the disc.

2. Measure the thickness of the disc. Minimum allowable thickness is 6.0 mm (0.236 in.)
3. To remove the disc, remove the front wheel, bend down the locking tabs on the disc securing nuts, and remove the nuts.
4. When installing the disc, care should be taken to tighten the bolts evenly and gradually until the proper torque of 13–16.6 ft lbs is reached. Ensure that the locking tabs are bent up against the flats on the disc bolts.

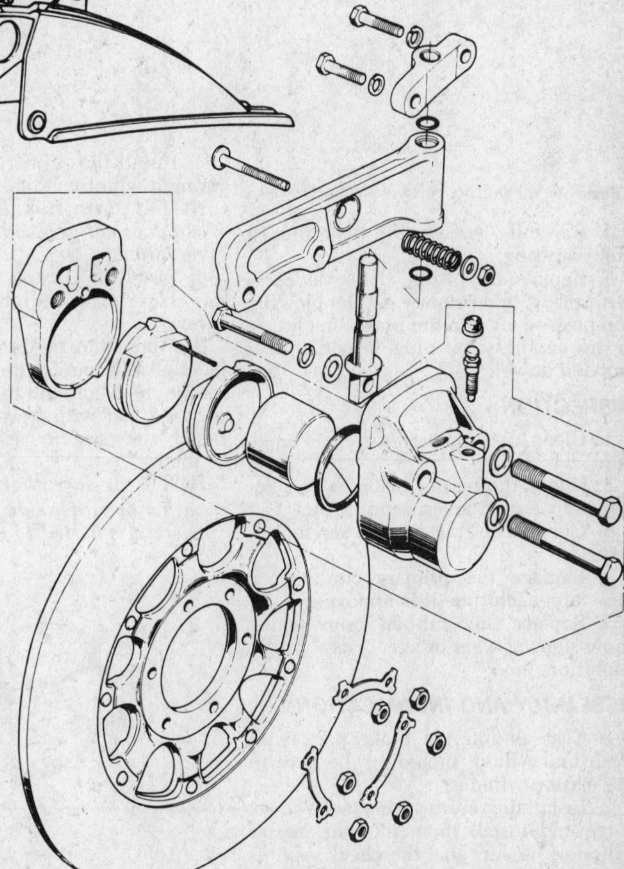

Late 450 and 500T caliper and disc assembly

Master Cylinder

REMOVAL AND DISASSEMBLY

NOTE: *Be very careful when removing and replacing the master cylinder or refilling the reservoir. Brake fluid can remove paint or damage plastic in seconds and therefore should be handled with care.*

1. Place a cloth underneath the connection to absorb any spilled fluid and disconnect the brake line from the master cylinder. Cover the open end of the brake line with a plastic bag secured with a rubber band to prevent dirt from entering the brake system.
2. Remove the two mounting bolts and remove the master cylinder from the handlebar. Unscrew the reservoir cap and discard the brake fluid.
3. Remove the brake lever by unscrewing the pivot bolt.

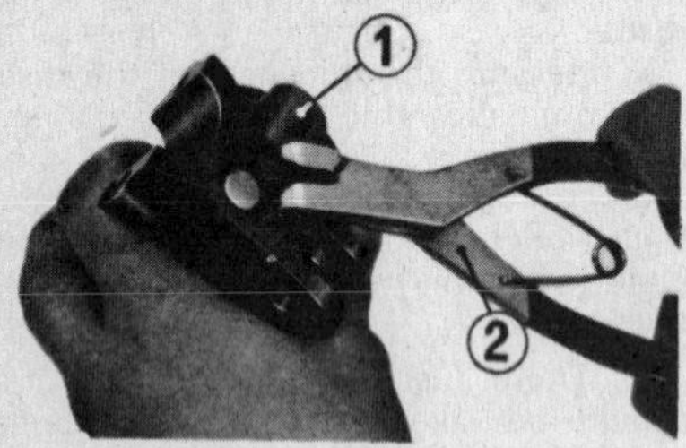

Removing the master cylinder snap-ring

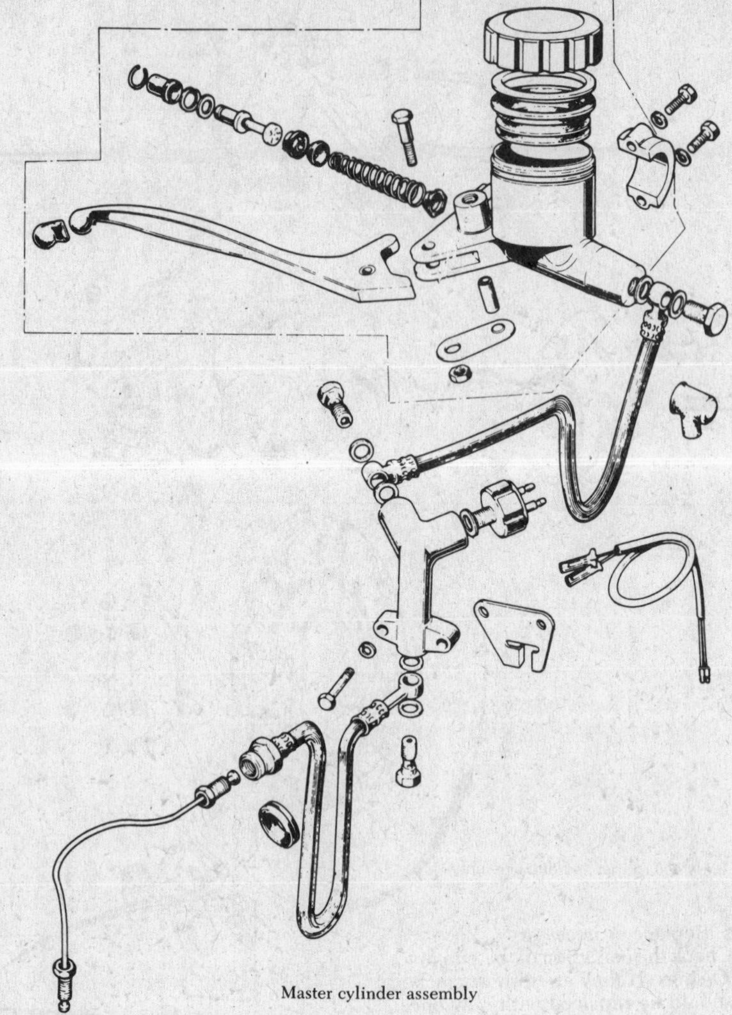
Master cylinder assembly

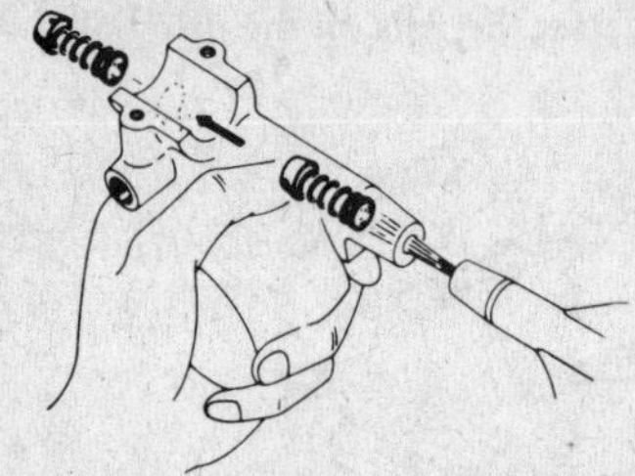
Removing the primary cup with compressed air

4. Carefully remove the boot and 18 mm snap-ring.
5. Remove the piston, check valve, return spring, and primary cup by blowing compressed air into the brake line fitting or by carefully pushing it out with a wooden dowel.

INSPECTION

1. Clean all components in clean brake fluid.
2. Check the master cylinder bore for signs of wear, grooves, scoring, etc.
3. Check the piston for scoring or grooves.
4. Replace the primary cup with a new item each time it is removed.
5. Replace any rubber items which show signs of wear or age, cracks, brittle condition, etc.

ASSEMBLY AND INSTALLATION

1. Coat all internal brake parts with fresh brake fluid, including the bore in the master cylinder.
2. Install the return spring to the check valve and install them into the master cylinder. Be sure that the check valve is facing the correct direction.
3. Install the primary cup after lubricating it with fresh brake fluid.

NOTE: *Make sure that the primary cup does not turn sideways during installation.*

4. Install the piston assembly and 18 mm snap-ring. Install the boot and brake lever.
5. Mount the master cylinder on the handlebar. Connect the brake line and torque the banjo bolt to 24–29 ft lbs. Fill the reservoir with fresh brake fluid and bleed the system as previously described.

NOTE: *Be sure that there is a joint washer on either side of the brake line where it is bolted to the master cylinder.*

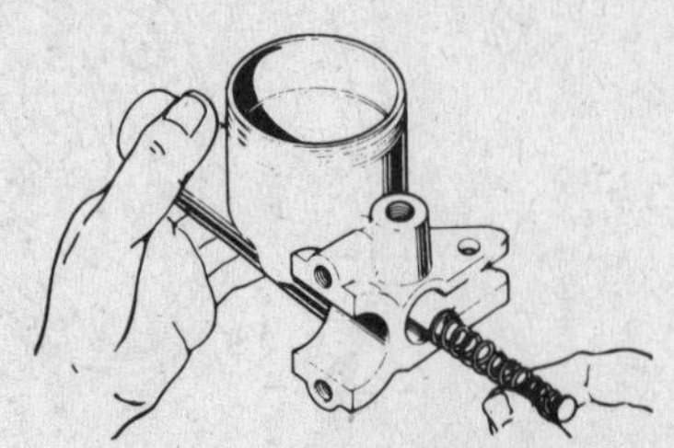
Installing the return spring

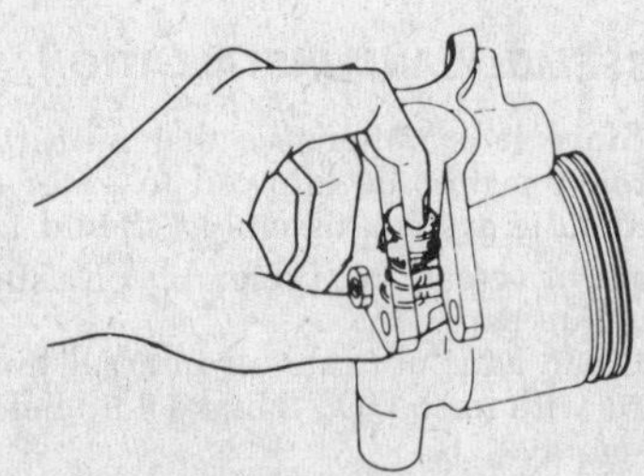
Installing the primary cup

Wheel Bearings

Removal of the wheel bearings necessitates removing the hub oil seals on some wheels. These must be replaced with new ones upon reassembly.

DISASSEMBLY

1. Remove the wheel. For the front wheel remove the axle, spacer, and brake plate (drum brakes), or the speedometer drive housing (disc brakes). On the rear wheel, remove the brake plate and any spacers.
2. Remove any dust covers, or dust seals. Unscrew the bearing retainer, if fitted (all rear wheels, sprocket side and disc brake, disc side).
3. Pry out the oil seal. An oil seal is fitted to the disc side on disc brake wheels.

Use a small screwdriver, or, preferably, an elbow-shaped tool to remove the oil seal.

4. Remove the wheel bearings by reaching through the center of the hub with a long drift and tapping one of the bearings evenly around its circumference until it is removed. Be careful not to turn the bearing sideways in its seat on removal as there is danger of causing damage to the hub.

5. When either bearing is removed, the spacer tube can be removed from the hub. After removing the spacer tube, remove the other bearing in the same manner as the first.

NOTE: *On some models, especially high mileage machines, the hub should be heated gently with a propane torch in the vicinity of the bearing bosses to facilitate removal.*

ASSEMBLY

Assembly is in the reverse order of disassembly; however, note the following points:

1. Obtain a good grade of wheel bearing grease to lubricate the wheel bearings.

2. Pack the wheel bearings until they are completely filled.

3. Place a small amount of wheel bearing grease to the inside of the hub and drive one of the bearings into its seat. Install the retainer if so equipped. Install the spacer tube and drive the other bearing into its seat. The sealed surface of the bearing must face the outside of the hub.

NOTE: *When a bearing retainer is fitted, the bearing closest to the retainer should be installed first. Then install and tighten the retainer, spacer tube, and the other bearing.*

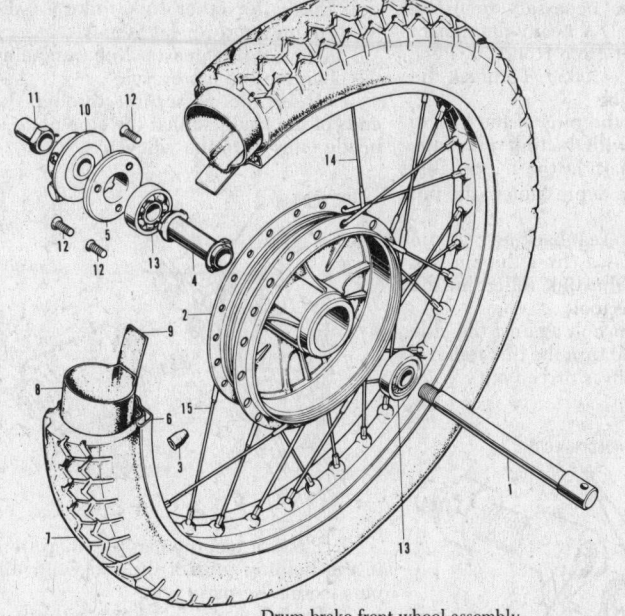

1. Axle
2. Brake hub
3. Balance weight
4. Spacer
5. Bearing retainer
6. Rim
7. Tire
8. Tube
9. Rim band
10. Speedometer drive
11. Axle nut
12. Retainer screws
13. Wheel bearing
14. Inner spoke
15. Outer spoke

Drum brake front wheel assembly

4. Replace all of the oil seals with new ones.

FINAL DRIVE

Chain Removal and Installation

1970 and Earlier Models

The chain can be separated and pulled off the sprockets after the master link has been removed. Threading the chain back onto the countershaft sprocket is made easier if you have an old length of chain lying around that you can hook onto the chain on the bike as it is removed. Leave the old chain draped over the sprocket so that you can hook the good chain back onto it and pull it over the sprocket when you are ready to reinstall it. Be sure to install the master link clip with the closed end facing in the direction of forward rotation of the chain.

1971 and Later Models

To remove the endless chain used on

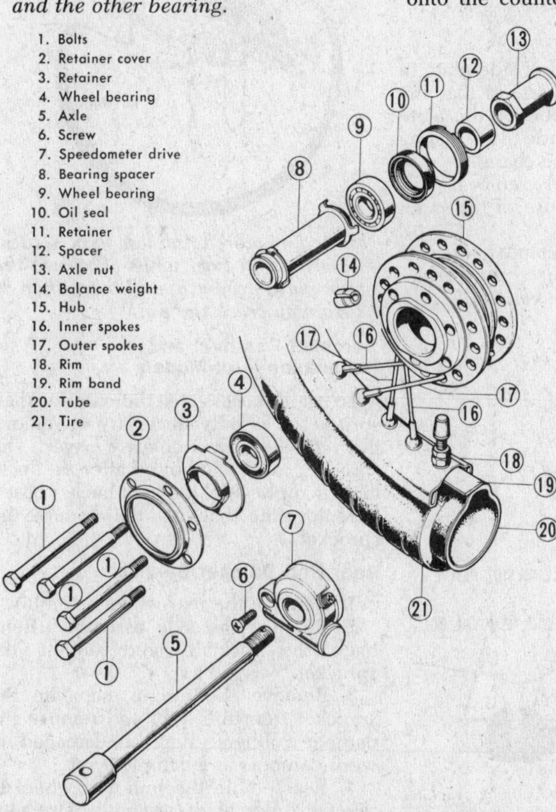

Disc brake wheel assembly

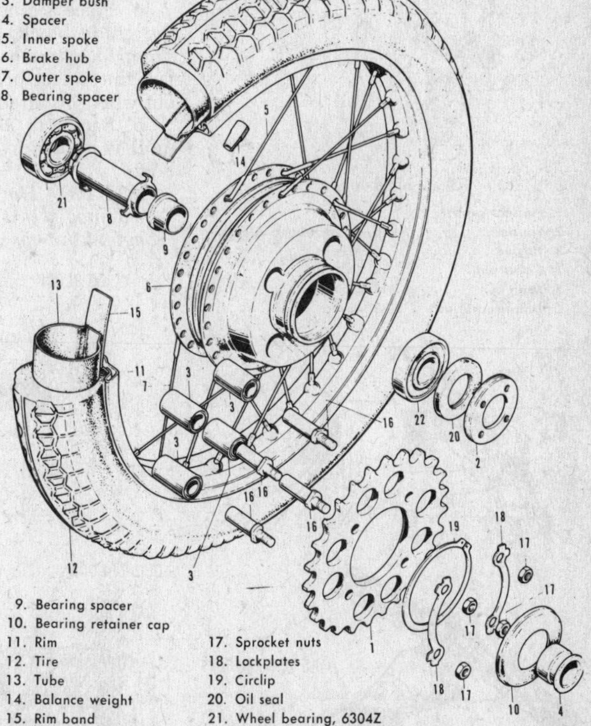

Rear wheel assembly

these models it is necessary to use a chain breaking tool. A heavy-duty chain breaker is available from Honda dealers, part number 07062–30050. To break the chain using this tool:

1. Grind or file the pins of the link to be removed flush with the link side plate. Do not cut the chain at the master link (identifiable by the depression in the pin centers).

2. Swing the pin seat backing plate on the chain breaker away from the pin seat and place one of the link rollers in the holding lugs of the tool.

3. Seat the main bolt against the side plate of the link and turn the link removal bolt in until the pin is driven out.

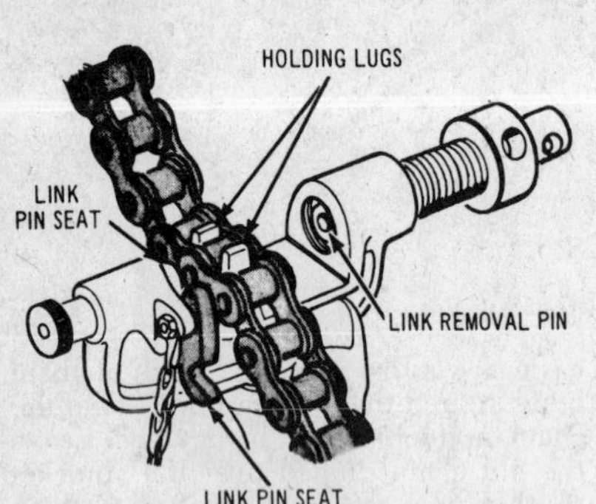

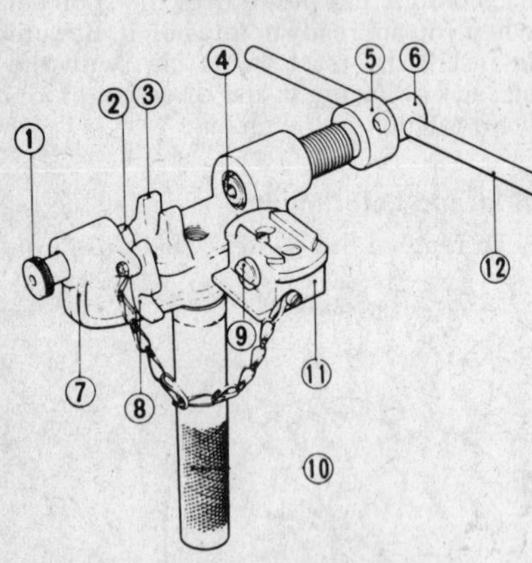

Chain breaker

1. Pin seat knob
2. Pin seat
3. Holder
4. Cotter pin
5. Main bolt
6. Link removal bolt
7. Body
8. Pin seat backing plate
9. Wedge
10. Grip
11. Guide
12. Lever

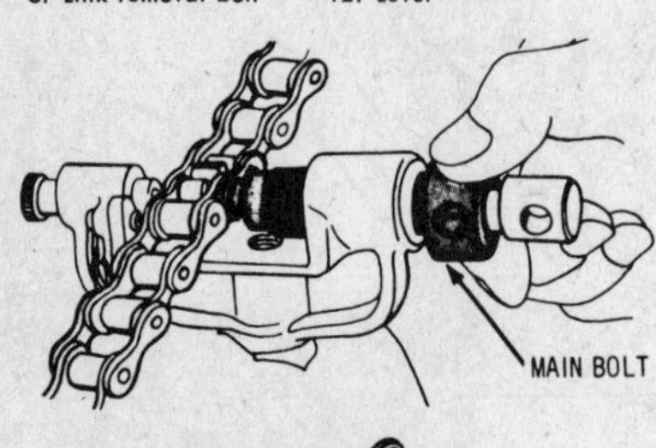

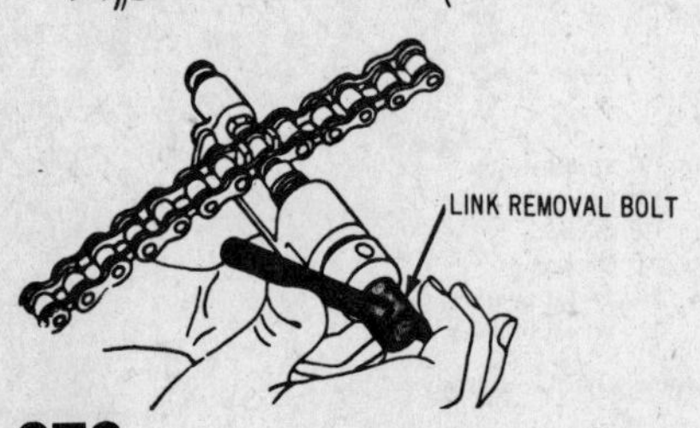

4. Place the other link roller in the holding lugs and repeat Step 3.

To install a new master link (replacing the chain on the motorcycle):

1. Insert the master link through the ends of the chain so that the side plate is inside (closest to the wheel).

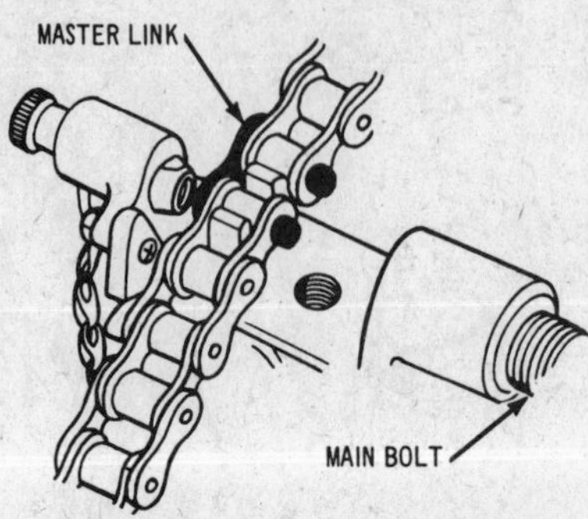

2. Place one of the master link rollers in the holding lugs of the tool with the pins facing the main bolt.

3. Push the pin seat knob in until it contacts the pin and swing the pin seat backing plate over to lock the pin seat in position.

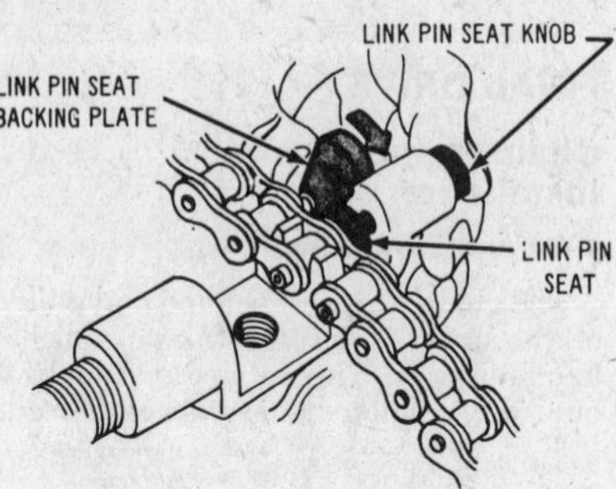

4. Place the master link side plate in the guide block, as shown, so that the stamped letters or numbers on the plate face the surface of the guide block (facing out when installed on the chain).

5. Back out the link removal bolt until it is behind the nose of the main bolt.

CAUTION: *The link removal bolt will be damaged if it is allowed to protrude beyond the nose of the main bolt.*

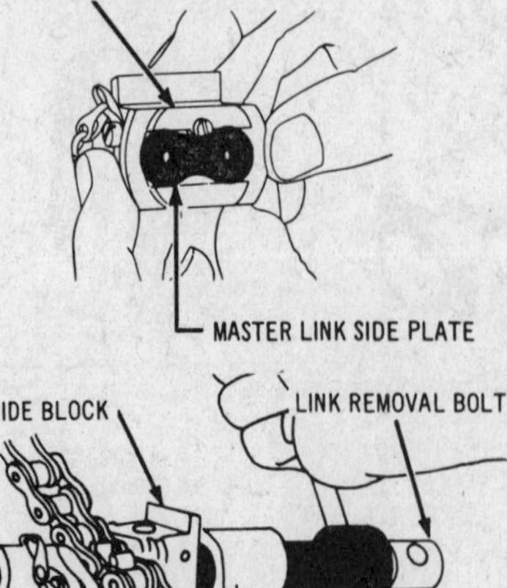

6. Place the guide block in the tool with the master link side plate against the pins. Make sure that the pins are aligned with the holes in the side plate.

7. Turn the main bolt in until the pins pass through the plate and seat against the recess in the guide block.

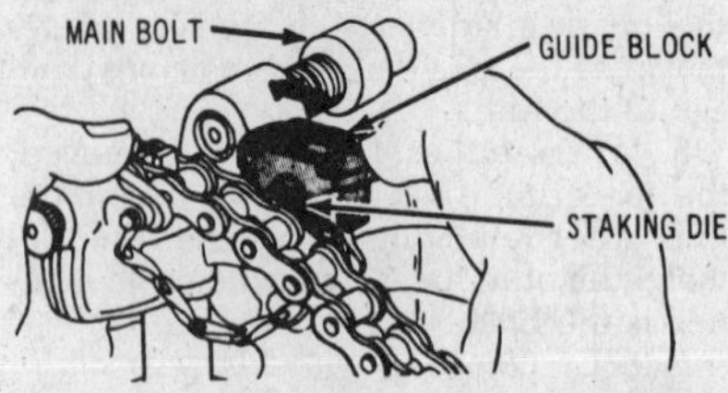

8. Reposition the guide block so that the staking die faces the pin and the protruding shoulder of the guide block is below the side plate.

9. Turn the main bolt in until the staking die contacts the pin and check to make sure that the die is centered across the pin.

10. Turn the main bolt in an additional ¾ turn to stake the pin. Repeat Steps 8–10 for the other master link pin. Examine both pins to amke sure that they are properly staked.

CAUTION: *The main bolt must be turned no more or no less than ¾ turn. Less than ¾ turn will not secure the side plate properly, and more than ¾ turn may crack the pin.*

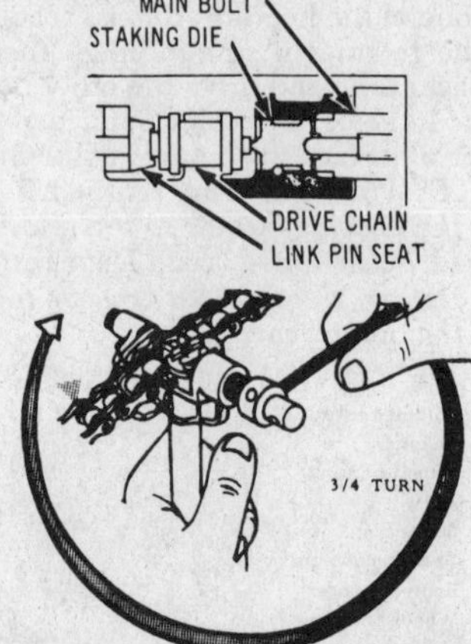

Sprocket Removal and Installation—All Models

To gain access to the countershaft sprocket it is only necessary to remove the left-side rear crankcase cover. The sprocket can be unbolted after the locktabs (if applicable) are bent back. Loosen or remove the chain and then remove the sprocket.

Rear Hub Damper Service

1. Remove the rear wheel assembly.

2. Remove the axle assembly. Bend back the locktabs and unbolt the sprocket.

3. Remove the circlip, separate the sprocket from the hub, and remove the damper rubbers. Replace damaged or worn dampers as a complete set.

4. Reassemble the hub and wheel in reverse order of disassembly. Use new locktabs to secure the sprocket nuts.

HANDLEBAR

Disassembly

1. On models with a disc front brake, remove the master cylinder by unscrewing the two clamp bolts.

2. On models with a drum front brake, disconnect the brake cable at the lower end by loosening the locknut on the cable adjuster on the brake plate. Screw the adjusting nut back while holding the cable with a pair of pliers, this will increase the amount of free-play in the cable. Remove the cotter pin from the brake arm and pull the arm back by hand, slip the cable end pin down and out of the brake arm.

3. Remove the brake (drum brakes) and clutch cables from the handlebars by loosening the adjuster locknut and screwing the adjuster into the lever housing. Line up the slots in the adjuster and locknut with the slot in the lever housing. Pull the lever back to the handlebar and pull the cable sheath out of the adjuster as the lever is released. Remove the cable end pin from the lever.

4. To disconnect the clutch cable at the lower end, remove the gearshift lever and left rear crankcase cover. Screw the adjuster on the crankcase cover in to increase the amount of cable free-play. Disconnect the cable from the clutch release mechanism in the crankcase cover.

5. To remove the throttle cable from the twist-grip, unscrew the phillips head screws from the bottom of the lever housing. Lift up the top of the housing and disconnect the cable from the twist-grip. To replace the cable first note how it is routed, disconnect the cables from the carburetors, and route the new one in the same way as the one which was removed.

6. The electrical wiring for the horn, starter motor switch, dimmer switch, turn signals, kill switch, and the headlight switch (450 only) can be disconnected in the headlight shell (450 models) or in the wiring box on the frame downtube (500 models).

7. Remove the handlebars by unscrewing the four bolts from the handlebar holders (two bolts on each holder). Mark the front of the holders before they are removed so that they can be installed in the same direction.

8. If the lever housings are to be removed, do not pull the wiring out of the handlebars using the housing as this is likely to pull the wires out of the housing. Pull on the wires while feeding the wires in the other side.

Assembly

1. Install the electrical switches on the handlebar pulling the wires through the center of the handlebars using a lead of wire or string fastened to the longest wire.

2. Mount the handlebars on the upper triple clamp, and install the handlebar holders, with the punch mark on the handlebars aligned with the top of the lower holder.

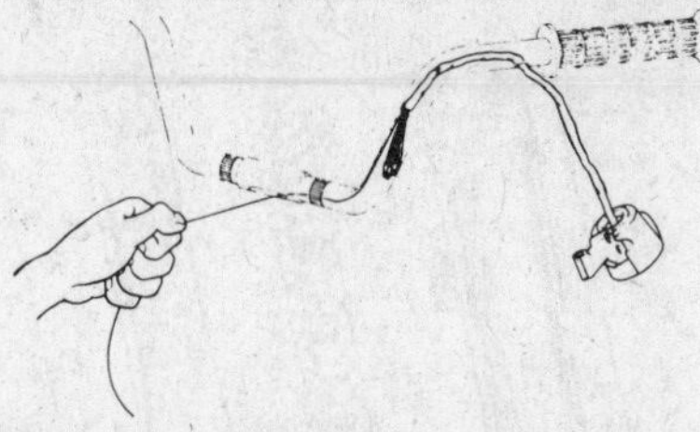

Routing electrical wires through the handlebars

CAUTION: *The handlebar holders are machined unevenly (one side is slightly higher than the other); the high side must face the front. The high side (front) on some models can be identified by a punch mark on the top of the holder. If in doubt which side is the high side, place the holder on a straightedge, the high side should be apparent.*

The gap of the handlebar clamps should be toward the rear of the machine. The front of the clamp is fitted with a punch mark on recent models.

Tighten the front bolt first, so that the upper and lower holder are touching in the front and a small gap is left at the rear.

3. Connect the cables to the controls. When installing the twist-grip into the housing, be sure that the cable tensioner is correctly installed.

4. The remainder of assembly is in the reverse order ot disassembly.

5. Check the operation of all controls before riding the motorcycle.

FRONT FORKS

There are several types of forks fitted to the 450 models. Early models had a sliding bushing fork with an external fork spring. Later models used a sliding bushing fork with an internal fork spring. The K5 and later models used a damper rod type fork. The removal and installation procedures are the same regardless of the type of fork fitted. Refer to the exploded view of your type fork when performing the disassembly and assembly procedures.

Removal and Installation

1. Remove the front wheel, fender, and caliper (disc brake) or brake anchor (drum brake).

2. Loosen the fork filler caps as they may be hard to loosen after the fork leg is removed. On early 450 4-speed models, the caps will have to be removed before the fork leg can pass through the upper triple clamp.

3. Loosen the pinch-bolts on the upper and lower triple clamps, and remove the fork legs, one at a time, by pulling them straight out from the bottom. Removal can be facilitated by spreading the lower triple clamp with a wedge if necessary.

4. To install the fork leg, slip it in place in the upper and lower triple clamps. On 450 4-speed models, tighten the filler caps to pull the fork into position in the upper triple clamp. On other 450 models, position the fork legs so that the top of the fork tube is flush with the top of the upper triple clamp. On the 500, the chamfered edge of the fork tube should be flush with the triple clamp surface. Tighten the lower triple clamp pinch-bolts, the filler caps, and the upper triple clamp pinch-bolts (if fitted), in that order.

Fork upper and lower triple clamp pinch-bolts (1) and filler cap (2)

The chamfered edge of the fork tube should align with the top surface of the triple clamp (500T)

5. Install the fender and the caliper or brake anchor. Install the front wheel and check the forks for proper operation. Be sure that the brake anchor bolts are properly secured with the tabs on the lockplates. Install the axle caps with the high side toward the front, and tighten the front nuts first. Adjust the brake caliper (disc brake), after assembly is complete.

Overhaul

CB450 (4-SPEED MODELS)

1. Drain the oil from the fork either from the drain plug or out the top of the fork tube. If draining the oil out the top, removing the drain plug to let air in will result in faster draining.

2. Unscrew the fork seal housing from the fork slider. If the factory tool is not available, wrap the housing in a piece of

old inner tube and fasten a hose clamp tightly around it. Grasp the fitting on the hose clamp with a pair of vise-grips, and using the vise-grips turn the fork seal housing off.

3. After the fork seal housing is unscrewed from the slider, the slider can be removed. The two fork springs and the spring seat can be removed from the bottom of the fork tube.

4. To remove the damper components from the fork tube, remove the bottom stop-ring, piston, damper valve, damper valve stop-ring, slider bushing stop-ring, and the slider bushing.

5. If the fork seal is to be replaced, remove the seal housing from the fork tube. Pry out the fork seal retainer, and the fork seal. If the fork seal is removed from the fork tube, the seal *must* be replaced. Replacing the seal as preventive maintenance when ever the fork leg is disassembled is recommended.

6. For inspection of the components of the fork leg refer to the inspection section in the following text.

7. Assembly is in the reverse order of disassembly. Install the fork seal into the fork seal housing, and replace the seal retainer. Coat the lips of the seal with fork oil before installing the housing on the fork tube. The housing should be installed from the bottom of the fork leg.

8. Coat all parts in clean fork oil before installing them on the fork tube. Install the slider bushing, slider bushing stop-ring, damper valve stop-ring, damper valve, piston, and the bottom snap-ring.

9. Install the springs in the fork tube in the order and direction that they were removed. Be sure to install the spring seat with a washer on either side between the springs.

10. Install the fork tube into the slider. Fill the fork leg with the proper amount and type of oil. Refer to the "Recommended Lubricants" and "Maintenance Data" charts at the end of "Maintenance."

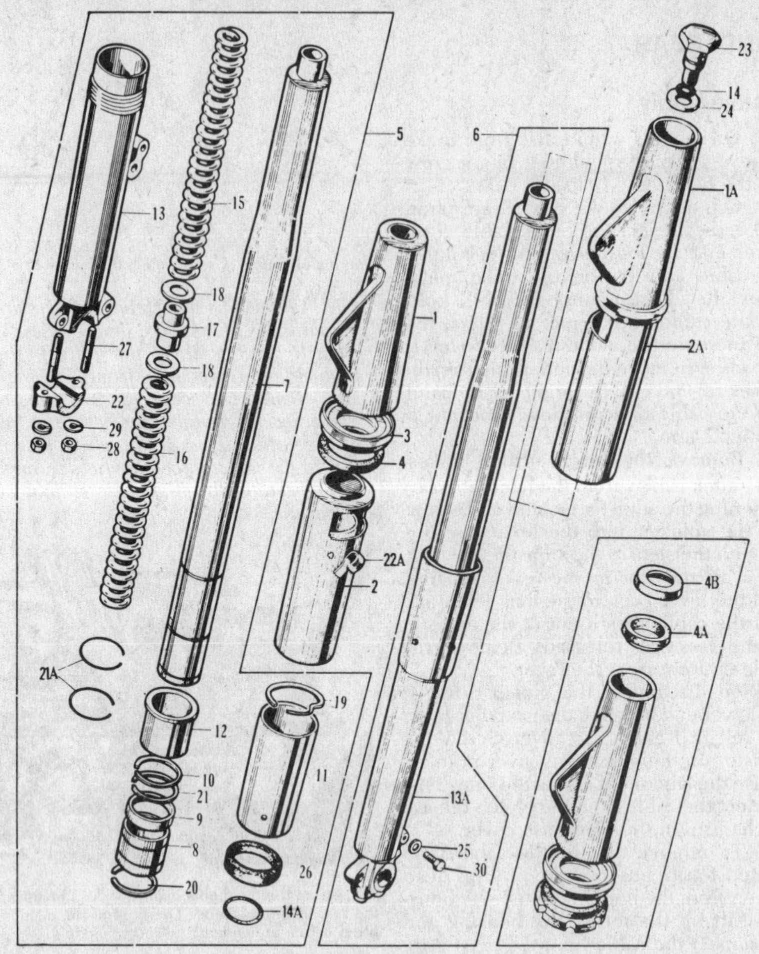

Front fork assembly (4-speed)

1.	Headlight bracket, right	11.	Fork seal housing	21.	Stopper ring
1A.	Headlight bracket, left	12.	Slider bushing	21A.	Piston stop-rings
2, 2A.	Fork cover	13.	Fork slider, right	22.	Axle cap
3.	Bezel ring	13A.	Fork slider, left	22A.	Speedometer cable clip
4.	Cover seat	14.	Filler bolt O-ring	23.	Filler cap
4A.	Cover seat	14A.	Oil seal O-ring	24.	Washer
4B.	Bezel ring	15.	Upper fork spring	25.	Gasket
5.	Fork leg assembly, right	16.	Lower fork spring	26.	Oil seal
6.	Fork leg assembly, left	17.	Spring seat	27.	Axle cap studs
7.	Fork tube	18.	Washer	28.	Nut
8.	Piston	19.	Oil seal retainer	29.	Lockwasher
9.	Damper valve	20.	Stopper ring	30.	Drain bolt
10.	Stopper ring				

450 (*BEFORE 1972*)

1. Remove the fork filler cap from the top of the fork leg. Remove the spring and invert the fork over a container to drain off the oil.

2. Remove the rubber boot (if fitted). With an impact driver remove the bolt from the bottom of the slider. Remove the circlip at the top of the slider, and separate the slider from the fork tube.

3. New oil seals should always be used once the slider has been separated from the tube. Pry out the old seal with a screwdriver, but be careful not to score the slider surface.

4. Remove the circlip from the bottom of the fork leg and remove the damper components.

5. For inspection of the fork components, refer to the "Inspection" section in the following text.

6. To assemble the fork, coat the lips of the oil seal with fork oil and slip the seal on the fork tube from the bottom.

7. Install the damper components in the reverse order in which they were removed. Refer to the exploded view of your fork leg.

8. Coat the threads of the allen bolt with thread locking compound before installing it with an impact driver.

Removing the fork slider circlip

450 (*1972 AND LATER*)

1. Remove the fork filler caps and the piston rod locknuts.

2. Pull the spring out of the tube and invert the fork leg assembly over a suitable container to drain the oil.

3. Pull the rubber boot off the leg if it remained attached when the leg was removed. Remove the circlip at the top of the fork slider, and separate the fork leg and slider.

4. Pry the seal out of the fork slider, taking care not to damage the inside surface.

5. The damper assembly can be removed from the slider after unscrewing

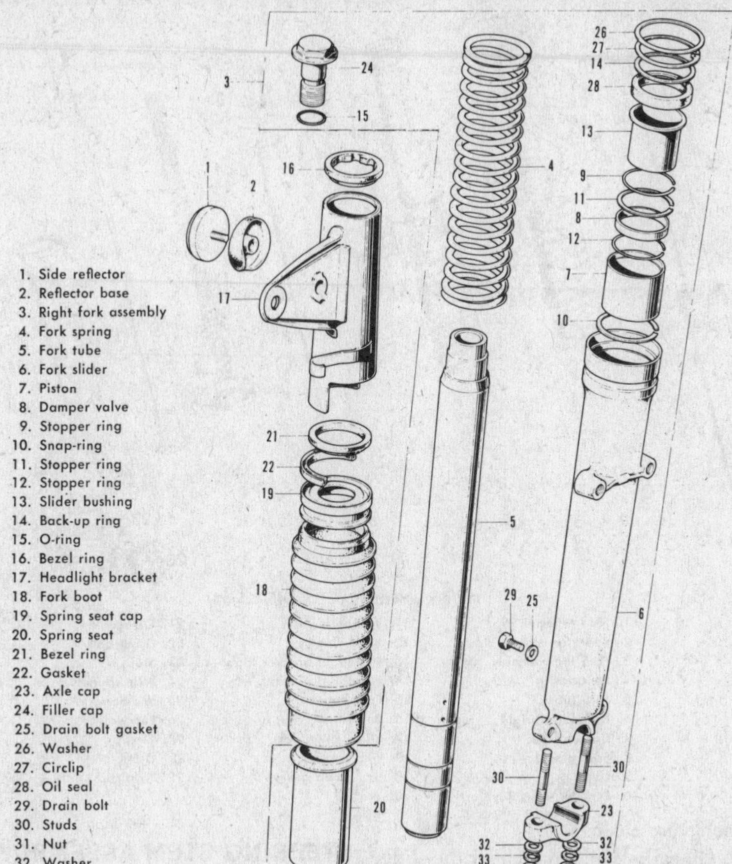

Front fork assembly (CB450K1-K2/CL450K1-K4)

the allen bolt that is recessed into the bottom.

6. Refer to the following "Inspection" section for inspection of the fork leg components.

7. To assemble the fork leg, coat the lips of the oil seal with grease and drive it into the top of the slider. Be sure that it is driven in far enough to allow the circlip to be refitted. If necessary, the old oil seal can be used to drive in the new one.

Separating the fork slider from the fork leg

8. Install the damper assembly into the slider and tighten the allen bolt with an impact driver. The threads of the allen bolt should be coated with thread locking compound before installing it.

9. Install the fork tube into the slider and refit the slider circlip.

10. Fill the fork leg with the proper amount and type of oil. Refer to the "Maintenance Data" chart at the end of "Maintenance." Tighten the filler caps after installation.

500T

The procedure is given for one fork leg but applies to both.

1. Remove the filler cap from the top of the fork leg and pour the oil into a suitable container to be disposed of. The fork spring will come out when the fork leg is turned upside down and can be removed at this time.

2. Turn the fork leg upside down and rest it on a block of hard wood. With an impact driver and the proper bit, remove the allen bolt from the bottom of the slider.

NOTE: *These bolts are installed with thread locking compound and trying to remove them without an impact driver will result in rounding the head of the bolt.*

3. When the bolt is removed from the bottom of the slider, the damper rod complete with piston ring, and the rebound spring can be removed by taking them out from the top of the fork leg.

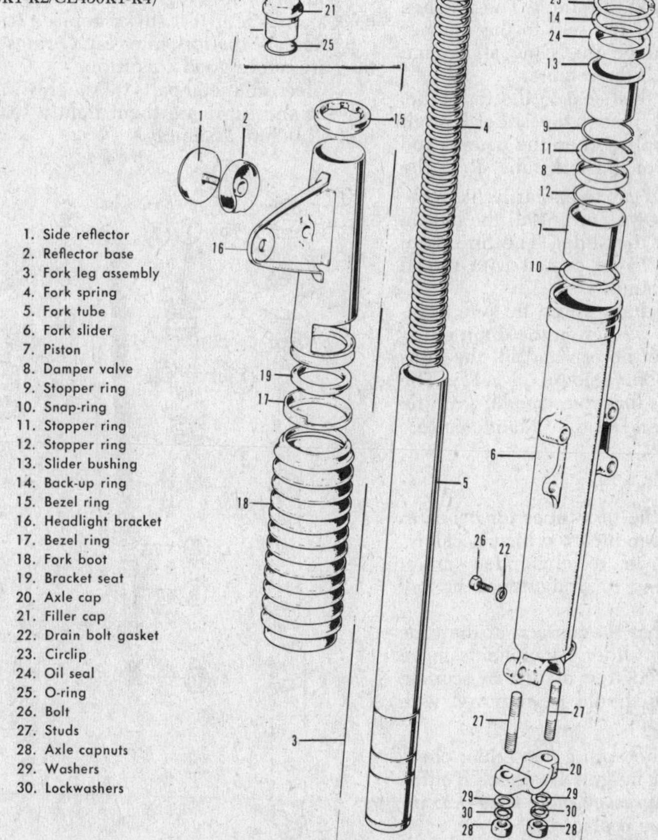

Front fork assembly (CB450K3-K4)

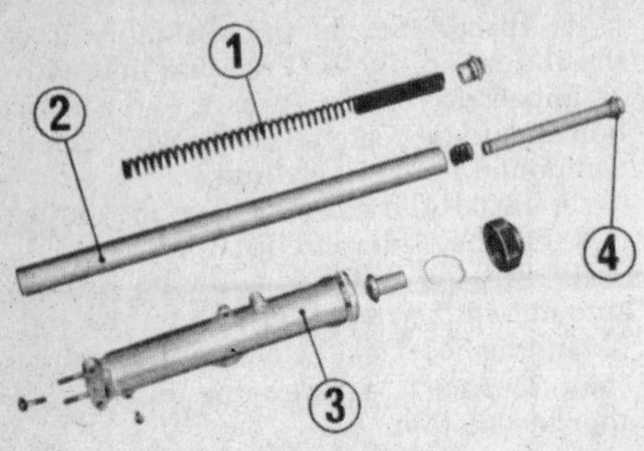

Fork components (CB500T)

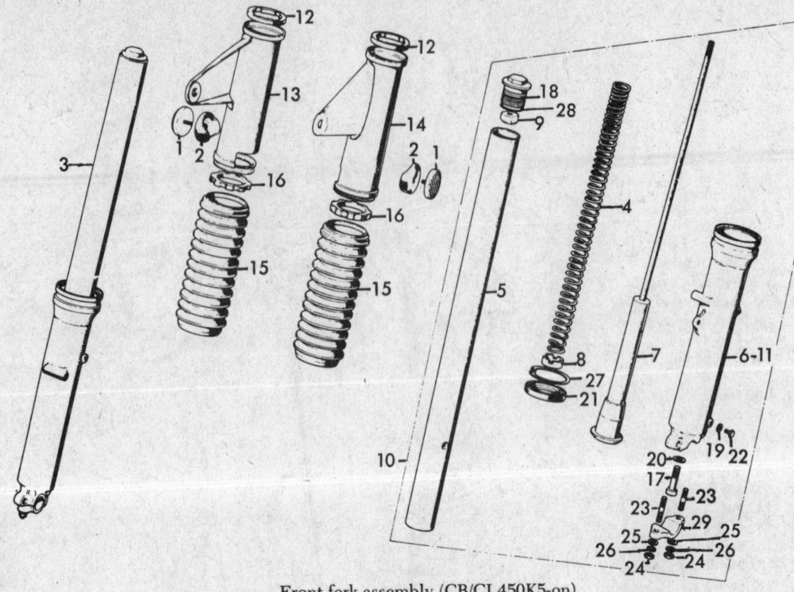

Front fork assembly (CB/CL450K5-on)

1. Side reflector
2. Reflector base
3. Fork leg assembly, right
4. Fork spring
5. Fork tube
6. Fork slider, right
7. Damper rod
8. Spring seat
9. Locknut
10. Fork leg assembly, left
11. Fork slider, left
12. Bezel ring
13. Headlight bracket, right
14. Headlight bracket, left
15. Fork boots
16. Bezel ring
17. Slider allen bolt
18. Filler cap
19. Drain bolt gasket
20. Washer
21. Oil seal
22. Drain bolt
23. Studs
24. Axle capnuts
25. Washer
26. Lockwasher
27. Circlip
28. O-ring
29. Axle cap

4. The inner tube can now be pulled out of the slider. Once the inner tube is pulled out of the slider, the oil seal in the slider will have to be replaced.

5. Remove the dust cover and retainer from the top of the slider and pry out the oil seal with a hooked tool. The pin wrench from the Honda tool kit may be used by slipping the hooked end under the seal and tapping on the handle with a hammer. A strip of copper or soft metal can be placed between the top of the slider and the wrench to protect the slider.

6. For inspection procedures, refer to the following "Inspection" section.

7. To assemble the fork leg, lubricate the oil seal with ATF and install it in the top of the slider. Place a block of hard wood over the seal and drive it into the slider as far as possible. Then place the old oil seal on top of the new one and drive them in until the new seal clears the snap-ring groove in the slider. Take out the old seal. Be sure that the new seal is straight in the slider. The distance from the top of the seal to the retainer groove should be the same all around the seal. Install the retainer.

8. Fit the dust seal to the fork tube, then carefully install the slider. Install the rebound spring then the damper rod from the top of the fork tube. Refit the fork spring and cap temporarily. Turn the fork upside down and install the bolt in the bottom of the slider. The threads of this bolt should be coated with thread locking compound.

9. Fit the drain plugs; be sure to install a copper washer on the drain plug.

10. Remove the cap and fill the forks with the proper amount of ATF. The specifications for your model can be found at the end of the "Maintenance." Refit the cap.

Inspection

1. Inspect the fork tubes for bends as might have been incurred in an accident. Replacement is recommended rather than attempting to straighten bent fork tubes.

2. Check that the surface of the tube on which the slider components move are smooth and free of rust or scoring. Minor rusting should be removed with fine emery cloth.

3. Check the spring condition; check that the spring heights are equal. If either spring is compressed more than 0.25 in., both should be replaced.

4. Check that the damper rod (where fitted) is straight and that all damper components are clean.

5. On early-type forks, check the slider bushing for scoring or wear, and replace it if damaged. The bushing must be a close fit on the fork leg. If it can be rocked back and forth or if it sticks, replace it.

6. Replace the fork filler cap O-rings if they are not in good condition.

7. Clean all metal parts thoroughly in a solvent and lubricate them lightly with fork oil before assembly.

STEERING STEM ASSEMBLY

Bearing Adjustment

On models equipped with a friction steering damper, the damper should be loosened (counterclockwise) as much as possible so that it does not interfere with the bearing movement while checking or adjusting the bearing.

1. The steering stem bearings are uncaged #8 balls or ¼ in. balls. They are adjusted by means of a ring nut beneath the upper triple clamp.

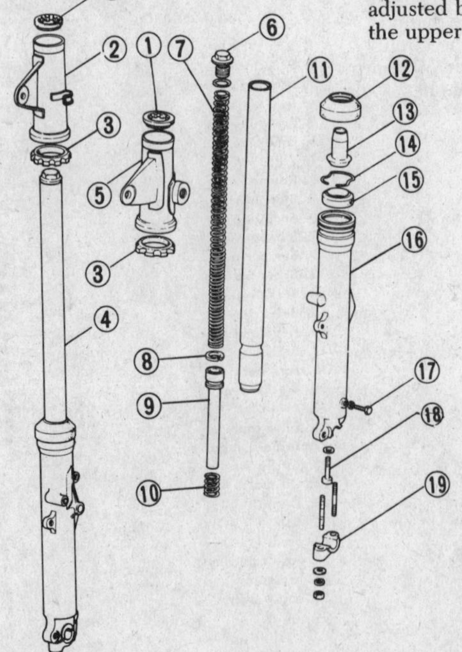

1. Bracket seat
2. Headlight bracket, right
3. Bracket seat
4. Fork leg assembly, right
5. Headlight bracket, left
6. Filler cap
7. Fork spring
8. Piston ring
9. Damper rod
10. Rebound spring
11. Fork tube
12. Dust cap
13. Oil lock piece
14. Oil seal stopper
15. Oil seal
16. Fork slider
17. Drain bolt
18. Slider bolt
19. Axle cap

Front fork assembly (CB500T)

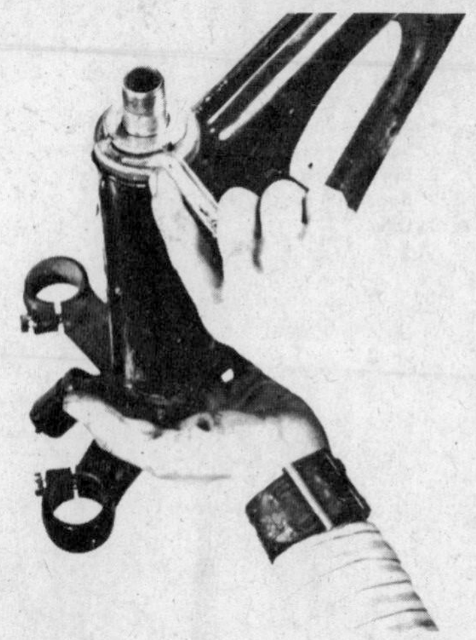
Adjusting the steering head bearings

2. To check bearing adjustment, support the front wheel off the ground. Grasp the tip of the front fender, place your other hand beneath the lower triple clamp at the frame lug.

3. Attempt to move the fork by pulling up on the tip of the fender. If play or movement can be felt at the lower triple clamp, the bearings are adjusted too loosely or are worn.

4. Turn the forks slowly from lock-to-lock. Movement should be smooth, silent, and effortless. If any binding or uneven movement is felt, the balls and races are either too tightly adjusted or they are worn. If the steering feels uniformly stiff, the bearings are too tightly adjusted. If any noise is noted, the bearings are damaged or some are missing.

5. With the front wheel off the ground, release the front forks from a few degrees off the centered position. The fork should fall freely to either side of their own weight. If they will not, the bearings are too tightly adjusted, the steering stem is bent, the races are extremely worn, or some of the bearings are missing.

6. To adjust the bearings, remove the upper triple clamp. The bearings are adjusted by means of the adjuster nut under the upper triple clamp.

7. Tighten or loosen the adjuster nut a little at a time until the steering stem adjustment conforms to that outlined above.

8. If proper adjustment is not possible, the bearings and races will probably need to be replaced.

Disassembly

1. Remove the front wheel, front forks, and handlebars. If a friction steering damper is fitted, remove it by removing the two cotter pins from under the lower triple clamp, and unscrewing the damper rod and removing the friction plates.

2. Loosen the rear pinch-bolt on the triple clamp. Unscrew the steering stem nut and disconnect the speedometer and tachometer cables from their instruments. Remove the upper triple clamp.

3. Disconnect the wiring inside the headlight shell, and remove the headlight shell and the fork ears.

4. Loosen the steering stem adjuster nut with a pin wrench, then hold the steering stem up while unscrewing the adjuster nut the rest of the way off. Remove the steering stem top cone race and the ball bearings from the top race.

5. Carefully pull the steering stem out from the bottom. Some of the ball bearings from the lower race will probably fall out at this time so be prepared for this.

6. Remove the bottom cone race, dust seal, and dust seal washer from the steering stem if they are to be replaced. These will have to be pried off with a chisel, therefore only remove them if necessary.

7. The bearing races in the frame lug are a press-fit and should not be removed unless replacement is necessary. If replacement is necessary, the old races can be removed by reaching through the frame lug with a suitable punch and tapping the race evenly around its circumference to remove it from the inside of the frame lug. Be sure that the race does not become cocked in its seat upon removal.

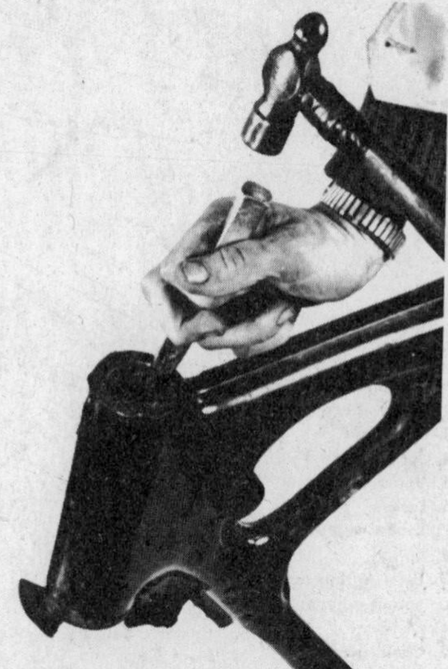
Removing the lower frame race

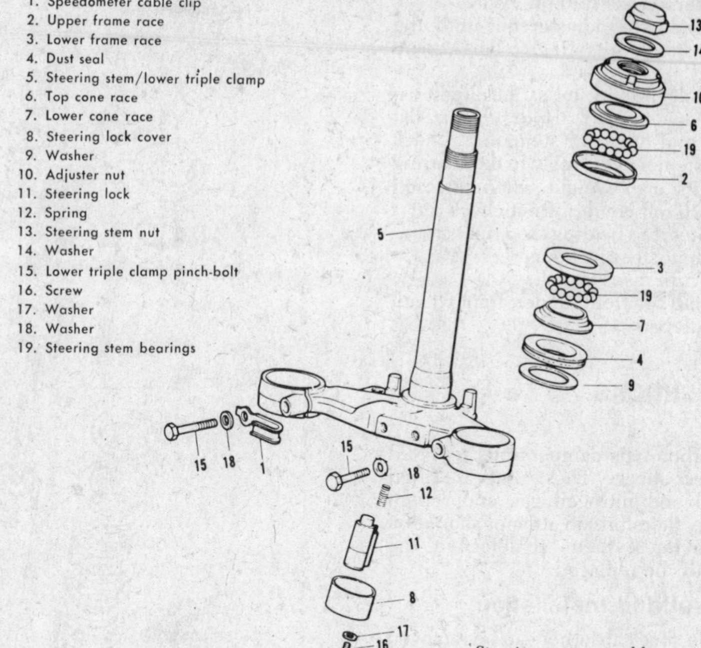

Steering stem assembly

New races are installed with a suitable sized bearing driver: i.e., one which will drive the race squarely into its seat. Be certain that the race goes straight in.

These races can also be installed using a block of hard wood of sufficient size to cover the race in place of a bearing driver.

Inspection

1. Inspect the bearing race surfaces. They must be clean and smooth. That is free from any cracks, scoring, rust, or indentations. Run your finger around each of the bearing races. Note any roughness or ripples on the race surface. If any imperfections are noted, both the sets of races and all of the balls must be replaced.

2. Check the balls themselves for rust, pitting, scoring, or flat spots. If the balls are found to be defective in any way, the balls and both sets of races must be replaced.

NOTE: *Balls and races must always be replaced in a set as worn races will destroy new balls and worn balls will destroy new races.*

Installation

1. Install the dust seal washer, dust seal, and lower cone race on the steering stem. Use a good grade of bearing grease to coat the bottom cone race and the upper race in the frame lug.

2. Embed 18 balls into the grease of the top frame lug and 19 balls into the steering stem through the frame lug and hold it in place while refitting the top cone race and threading on the adjuster nut.

4. Tighten the adjuster nut all of the way by hand, rotating the steering stem

to work the grease into the balls.

5. Tighten the adjuster nut until the steering stem turns freely, but has no play.

6. Install the fork tubes, headlight assembly, and upper triple clamp, flat washer, and steering stem nut. Check that the stem moves freely to the steering lock of its own weight when released from 5°–10° off center; if not check for:

a. Steering bearings too tight;
b. Bent steering stem;
c. Worn races or balls.

7. Install the front fender, front wheel, and handlebars.

REAR SHOCKS

DeCarbon type damper units are fitted to the rear shocks. These units are filled with oil and nitrogen gas under high pressure, therefore no attempt should be made to repair them. If defective, the units must be replaced.

Removal and Installation

1. The shock absorber can be removed after the upper and lower mounting bolts and the lift bar on the right-side are removed.

2. To remove the spring, first set the spring adjustment cam on the softest position. Then compress the spring either using a spring compressor (Tool No. 07958–3290000) or by hand and have an assistant remove the spring retainers.

3. Measure the free-length of the spring, if less than 7.7 in. (195 mm) (450) or 8.1 in. (205 mm) (500T), the springs should be replaced.

4. Assembly is the reverse of disassembly. Progressively wound springs are installed with the close coils at the bottom of the shock.

5. Install the shock on the machine and check that it does not bind in operation.

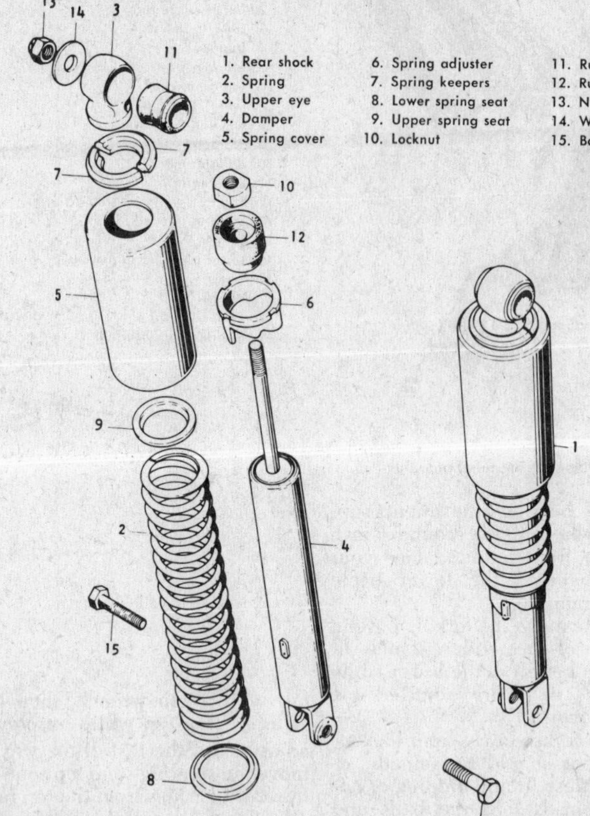

Rear shock absorber assembly

SWING ARM

Inspection

1. Remove the exhaust system (CB models).

2. Remove the rear wheel, shock absorbers, and chain guard.

3. Measure the distance between the top and bottom shock absorber mounts on both sides. The two measurements must be identical, or the swing arm will have to be replaced.

4. Check that the rear wheel mounting plates are parallel.

5. Grasp the legs of the swing arm and attempt to move it from side-to-side. Any noticeable side-play will indicate that the swing arm bushings need replacement.

The swing arm is most likely to be damaged if the machine is operated for any length of time with a broken or otherwise defective shock absorber.

Removal and Installation

1. Proceed as above. Then remove the swing arm pivot bolt nut, and pull the pivot bolt out from the right-side.

2. Remove the swing arm by pulling it straight back.

3. The swing arm should be inspected for cracks or fractures, especially around the welds.

After removal of the swing arm, the dust seals and bushings can be replaced. This should be done every 10,000 miles, or more often depending on how the machine is used, or if the bushings are worn (see "Inspection").

4. Remove the bushings, tapping them out with a hammer and punch. Once the bushings are removed, they should be replaced.

5. Lubricate new bushings with a good chassis grease. Press the bushings into the swing arm, then lubricate and install the swing arm collar.

6. Install the swing arm on the machine. Grease and install the pivot bolt. After tightening the swing arm pivot bolt nut, move the swing arm up and down to ensure that movement is smooth and effortless.

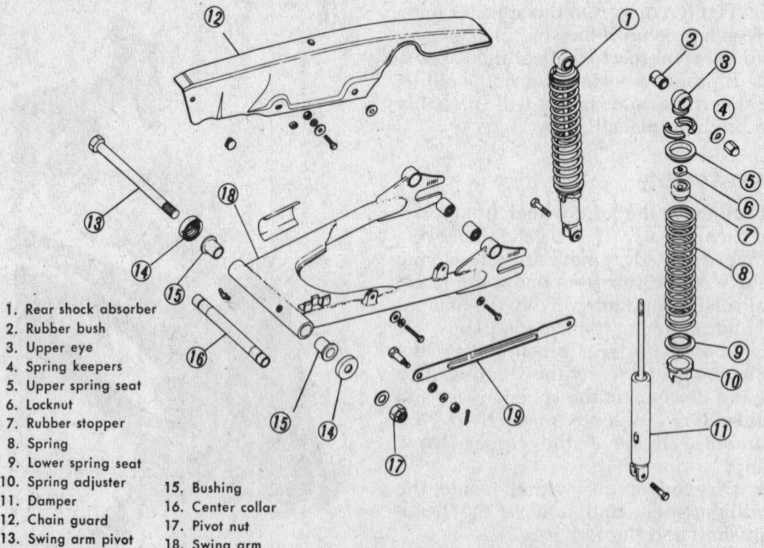

Swing arm assembly (CB500T)

Removing the swing arm pivot bolt

Chassis Torque Specifications 450

Component	Thread Diameter (mm)	Torque (ft lbs)
Front brake anchor	10	13–20
Steering stem nut	24	65–87
Upper triple clamp-to-front forks	8	18–25
Handlebar clamps	8	18–25
Lower triple clamp-to-front forks	10	18–25
Spokes Front wheel Rear wheel	——	1.1–1.5
Swing arm pivot bolt	14	51–65
Front axle nut	12	54–61
Front fork axle caps	8	13–20
Engine mounting bolts	8 10	13–20 29–58
Rear axle nut	18	58–87
Rear sprocket nuts	10	25–58
Rear brake lever pinch-bolt	8	13–18
Rear brake anchor	8	15–20
Rear suspension	10	29–58
Foot rest	10	29–58
Gearshift lever	6	6–7
Seat band	6	6–7

Chassis Torque Specifications 500T

Component	Thread Diameter (mm)	Torque (ft lbs)
Steering stem nut	24	50–65
Upper triple clamp-to-front forks	8	18–25

Chassis Torque Specifications 500T

Component	Thread Diameter (mm)	Torque (ft lbs)
Handlebar clamps	8	18–25
Lower triple clamp-to-front forks	10	21–29
Spokes Front wheel Rear wheel	——	1.1–1.5
Swing arm pivot bolt	14	72–94
Front axle nut	12	40–47
Front fork axle caps	8	13–20
Engine mounting bolts	8 10	13–20 29–58
Rear axle nut	18	58–72
Rear sprocket nuts	10	21–29
Rear brake lever pinch-bolt	8	13–18
Rear brake anchor	8	13–18
Rear suspension	10	29–58
Gearshift pinch-bolt	6	6–7

Disc Brake Torque Specifications

Component	Thread Diameter (mm)	Torque (ft lbs)
Master cylinder banjo bolts	——	24.6–28.9
Front brake disc nuts	8	13.0–16.6
Brake line joint	6	5.8–7.2
Brake hose joint	——	4.3–7.2
Master cylinder bolt	6	5.7–7.2
Caliper mounting bolts	——	24.6–28.9

Chassis Specifications

	450	500
WHEELS Rim run-out (max) (in./mm)	0.08/2.0	0.08/2.0
BEARINGS Axial run-out (max) (in./mm) Radial run-out (max) (in./mm)	0.004/0.1 0.002/0.05	0.004/0.1 0.002/0.05
BRAKES Rear drum ID (max) (in./mm) Lining thickness (min) (in./mm)	7.13/181 0.079/2.0	7.13/181 0.079/2.0
FRONT SUSPENSION Spring free-length (min) (in./mm) Tilt (max) (deg)	① 1.5	17.3/440 1.5
REAR SUSPENSION Spring free-length (min) (in./mm)	②	8.1/205
AXLES Bend (max) (in./mm)	0.008/0.2	0.008/0.2

① 450—7.5/191
K1–K2—8.1/205
K5–K7—16.7/425

② Early models—7.85/199
K3–K4—7.5/195
K5–on—8.1/205

Disc Brake Specifications

Measurement	Standard (in./mm)	Service Limit (in./mm)
ID of caliper cylinder	1.5032–1.5039/38.18–38.20	1.5045/38.215
OD of caliper piston	1.5006–1.5032/38.115–38.18	1.5002/38.105
ID of master cylinder	0.5512–0.5529/14.000–14.043	0.5534/14.055
OD of master cylinder piston	0.5495–0.5506/13.957–13.984	0.5488/13.940
Thickness of disc	0.2717–0.2795/6.9–7.1	0.2362/6.0
Disc run-out	0.002/0.05	0.0118/0.3
Pad-to-disc clearance	0.002/0.05	0.006/0.15

Honda Hawk/Nighthawk Twins

MODEL COVERAGE

CB 400 T, T1, T2
CB 400 A
CM 400 T
CM 400 A
CM 400 E
CB 450 T
CB 450 SC, Nighthawk
CM 450 A, C, E

INDEX

Engine serial number location

Frame serial number location

MAINTENANCE

NOTE: *Common maintenance procedures are explained in detail in the "General Information" section.*

LUBRICATION
Motor Oil

Honda four-stroke oil is recommended for all temperatures. SAE 10W-40 or 20W-50 can also be used. Use only motor oil with an "SE" or "SF" service rating.

When the air temperature is consistently below 15°C (59°F), use SAE 10W-30, service rating "SE" or "SF."

CHECKING OIL LEVEL

1. A dipstick is provided to check the oil level. The oil should be checked after the engine has been running for at least a couple of minutes.
2. The motorcycle should be parked on level ground and put on the centerstand.
3. Unscrew and remove the dipstick and wipe it off. Reinsert the dipstick, allowing it to rest on the treads of the hole. Oil level should be between the maximum and minimum marks on the stick. If the oil level is too low, add enough oil to bring the level up to between the marks. Do not overfill the crankcase.

CHANGING OIL

1. The recommended oil change interval after break-in is 1,800 miles or every year, whichever comes first.

Let the dipstick rest on the hole threads when checking oil level

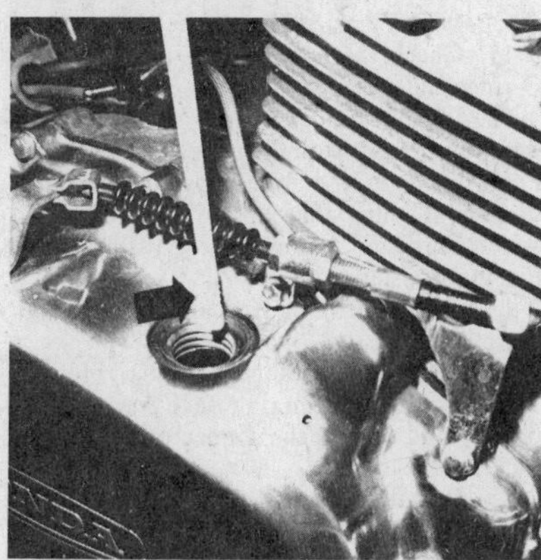
Maintain the oil level between the marks

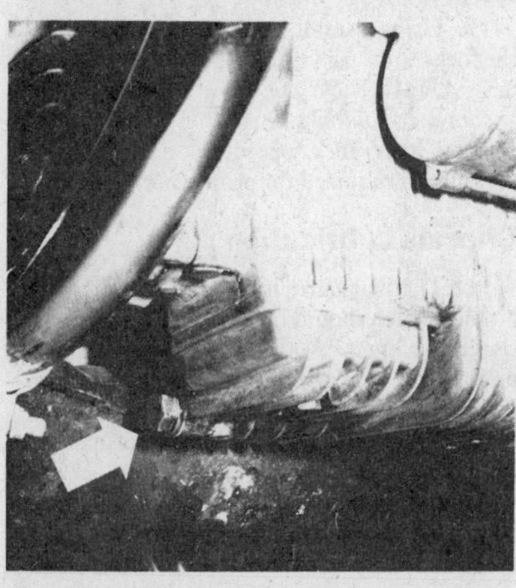
Oil drain plug

2. Oil should be changed when the engine is warm. This ensures more complete draining and makes it more likely that the oil will carry off any particulate matter with it.
3. Remove the dipstick. Place a suitable container (at least 3 qt capacity) beneath the engine and remove the drain plug. Allow the oil to drain off for several minutes. Kick the engine over with the kickstarter (be sure that the ignition is switched off) to remove any remaining oil.

Check the drain plug gasket. Replace it if it is damaged. Install the plug and tighten it to 18–25 ft lbs.

4. Remove the oil filter bolt and filter element if it is to be replaced. The filter should be replaced at every other oil change.

Refer to the following section for the filter replacement procedure.

5. Add approximately 2.6 qts. (2.5 l) of the recommended grade and viscosity of oil to the crankcase. If the filter is not being changed, add a bit less. At any rate, final level determination must be made with the dipstick in the manner outlined under "Checking Oil Level," above.
6. Start the engine and let it run for a few minutes. Then shut it off and check the oil level with the dipstick. Add additional oil, if necessary, to bring the oil level up to the upper level mark.

OIL FILTER

1. The disposable filter element should be changed at every other oil change: every 3,600 miles or every year, whichever comes first.
2. Drain the oil as outlined above.
3. Remove the oil filter bolt and let down the bolt and filter case along with the filter. Have a suitable receptacle placed beneath the case to catch any oil which may drip out.
4. A spring and a washer are fitted below the filter element. Do not loose them.
5. Clean the filter bolt and case in a solvent which is safe for rubber. Note that the filter bolt and case both have sealing o-rings.
6. Be sure that the filter bolt oil passages are clear and the by-pass valve inside operates properly.
7. Check the condition of the filter bolt and filter case o-rings. If they show signs of deterioration, cracking, or tears, replace them.
8. Clean the case mating surface on the crankcase thoroughly. Lightly oil the filter bolt o-ring and the case o-ring.
9. Install the filter bolt into the case, then fit the spring, the washer, and the new filter element.
10. Install the filter assembly.

Oil filter components

Tighten the filter bolt to 20-23 ft lbs.

CAUTION: *Do not overtighten the filter bolt, or future removal may be extremely difficult. A torque wrench is very important.*

11. Refill the engine with the proper grade and quantity of oil as outlined above. Start the engine and let it run for several minutes. Check for leaks.

NOTE: *When the filter case is removed it should be carefully checked for cracks or other damage around the filter bolt boss. If there is any such damage noted here, replace the case. This sort of thing may happen if the filter bolt is overtightened.*

FILTER SCREEN

The oil pump pick-up pipe in the sump is fitted with a coarse mesh filter screen. This screen, however, is only accessible after splitting the crankcases, and is therefore not a routine maintenance item.

Whenever the cases are split, the screen should be removed from the pipe and cleaned in solvent. Foreign matter can be removed with a relatively soft brush.

FRONT FORKS (STANDARD)

The front forks are hydraulically damped units which use ATF to accomplish their function. The ATF is semi-permanent and need only be replaced when the forks are rebuilt. No drain plugs are fitted to the fork sliders, so changing the fluid is not a routine operation.

FRONT FORKS (AIR-ASSISTED)

Air-assisted forks have drain plugs on the fork sliders. Although no maintenance interval is recommended by the factory, the procedure for changing the oil is given below to be used at the discretion of the service person.

1. Support the front wheel off the ground. Be certain that the motorcycle is securely and safely supported.
2. Remove the dust caps from the fork valve stems.
3. Slowly bleed off the air pressure in each fork leg by pressing the needle valve.

CAUTION: *Release pressure slowly.*

4. CB450SC: remove the cover plate between the gauges and the handlebars.
5. Other models: protecting the gas tank finish with a heavy cloth, remove the handlebars by removing the upper clamp bolts. Rest the assembly on the gas tank.
6. Disconnect the air hose from the fittings.
7. Unscrew and remove the fittings from the fork cap assemblies. Unscrew and remove the fork caps.

CAUTION: *The caps are under spring pressure. Remove them slowly and with caution.*

8. Remove the drain screw from each fork slider in turn and allow the fluid to drain for several minutes. Then install the screws and tighten them securely.
9. Remove the upper fork spring from each leg to facilitate adding oil. Note that the spring spacer may come out with the spring. Take care that it is not lost.
10. Fill each fork leg with Dexron ATF. Quantities are:

CB450SC: 6.3 oz./185cc
CM450A, C: 6.9 oz./205cc
CM400A, C, T, CB450T: 5.8 oz./172cc
CB400T: 5.9 oz./175cc

11. Check the condition of the fork cap O-rings and replace them if necessary.
12. Install the fork spring spacers if they were removed. Install the upper fork springs. Push down on the fork caps to start the threads. Tighten the caps to 12-22 ft. lbs. When tightening, take air hose fitting position into consideration.
13. lightly lubricate the air hose O-ring seals.
14. Install the air connector and tighten to 3-5 ft. lbs. Connect the air hose to the cap (3-5 ft. lbs.) and then to the connector (11-14 ft. lbs.).
15. Install the handlebars, aligning the punch mark with the clamp.
16. Tighten the forwardmost handlebar clamp bolts first and then the rear clamp bolts (13-18 ft. lbs.).
17. Using a small, hand-held air pump, fill the forks to 11 psi (±3 psi).

CAUTION: *Do not use a compressed air source to fill forks.*

18. Check fork operation and readjust pressure as required for proper performance.

Chassis Lubrication

1. The swing arm is fitted with two grease nipples which should be lubricated with chassis grease every 3,600 miles. Apply grease until it shows at both ends of the swing arm pivot.
2. Wheel and steering head bearings are lubricated with bearing grease, the service interval being 10,800 miles. Refer to "Chassis," for procedures.

Swing arm grease fitting, left side

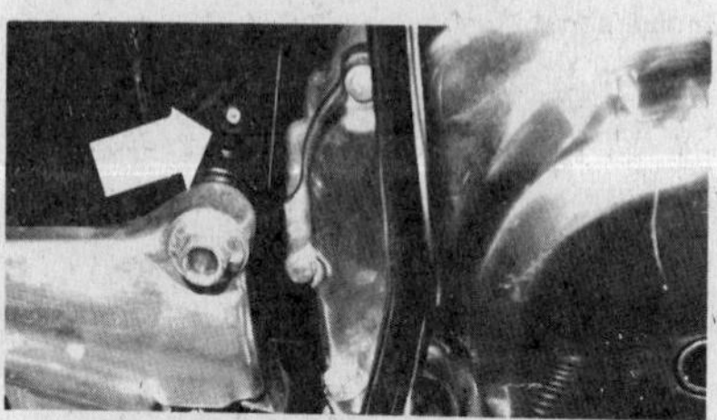

Swing arm grease fitting, right side

SERVICE CHECKS AND ADJUSTMENTS

Drive Chain

1. The chain should have about 20 mm/0.75 in. of total up-and-down free-play measured in the middle of the lower chain run.
2. Before checking or adjusting the chain slack, the following conditions should be met:

Chain adjuster bolt (arrow)

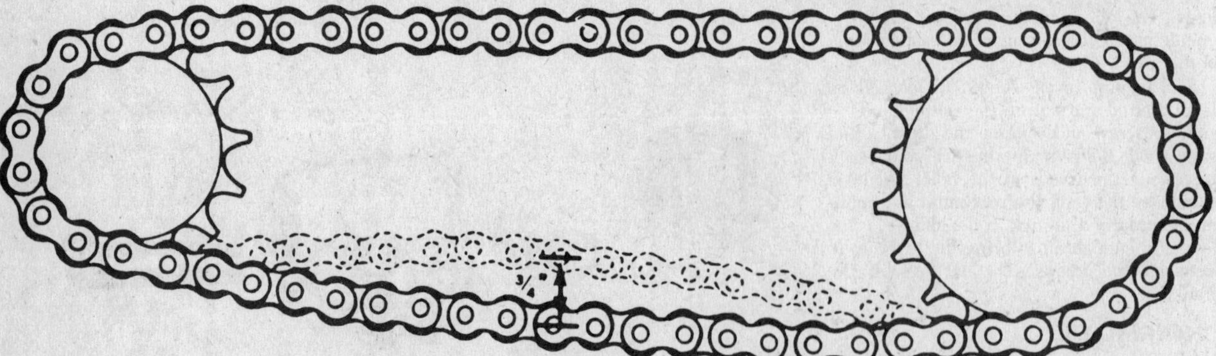

Chain play should be measured in the middle of the lower run

a. The motorcycle should be placed on both wheels with a rider sitting with his weight on the seat.

b. The transmission should be placed in neutral;

c. The chain should be clean and well-lubricated;

d. The chain should have been checked for any tight spots by slowly rotating the wheel and checking for variances in the chain tension at different points. If a tight spot exists, the chain tension should be adjusted to the prescribed free-play at the tight spot. Note, however, that such a condition is indicative of a worn chain and probably worn sprockets, which should be replaced as soon as possible.

3. To adjust the chain, first back off the rear brake adjuster not on drum rear brakes.

4. Remove the axle nut cotter pin (if fitted) and loosen the axle nut several turns. Loosen the locknut on each chain adjuster bolt.

5. Turn each of the adjuster bolts in or out by equal amounts until the chain tension is approximately correct.

6. Check wheel alignment by means of the aligning marks inscribed on both sides of the swing arm. Be sure that both adjusters are lined up with the same mark on each side. If not, turn one of the adjuster bolts in or out so that alignment is achieved.

7. Tighten the axle nut and adjuster bolt nuts and check the chain tension. Correct if necessary. After adjustment is correct, torque the axle nut to 58-72 ft lbs.

Fit a new cotter pin (if equipped). Readjust the rear brake on drum brake models.

CAUTION: *Chain wear indicators are fitted to the adjusters on most models. The chain must be replaced when the indicator red zone aligns with the end of the swing arm (see illustration). When replacing the chain, sprocket condition must be checked as well.*

Clutch (Manual Transmission)

1. Cable adjustment must always be maintained at the proper specification. If the cable has insufficient free-play, the clutch will slip and rapidly burn out. If it has too much play, the clutch will not completely disengage, resulting in hard shifting and creeping at stops.

2. Use the cable adjuster at the handlebar to maintain the correct amount of cable slack. The clutch hand lever should be able to be moved 2-3 mm/0.08-0.12 in. measured between the lever and the lever holder before the clutch begins to disengage.

This will be approximately 10-20 mm/3/8-3/4 in. of free movement measured at the ball end of the clutch hand lever.

Do not screw the adjuster at the hand lever out so far that you can see more than 8 mm/0.3 in. of the adjuster threads between the adjuster socket and the circular locknut. If proper clutch adjustment cannot be obtained in this manner, proceed as follows:

3. Screw the adjuster at the hand lever in as far as possible. Use the adjuster on the engine to get the hand lever free-play as close to the correct value as possible. Then

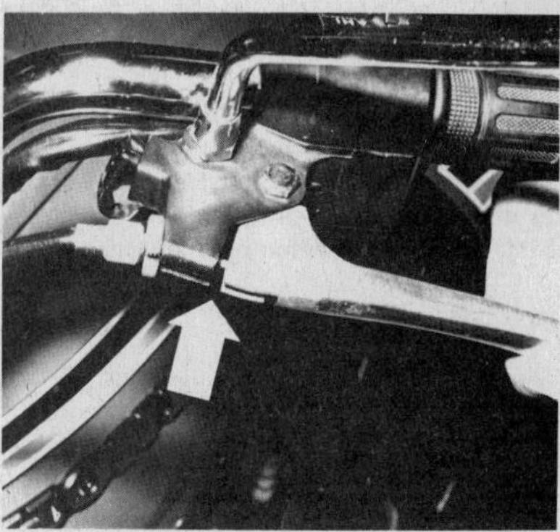

Gap (arrow) should be 2–3 mm/0.08–0.12 in. before the clutch begins to disengage

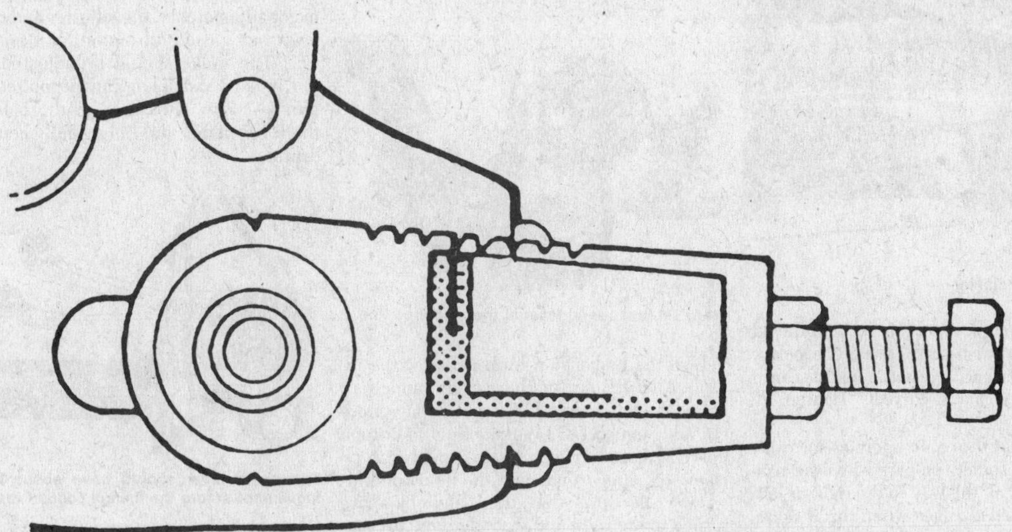

Replace chain and sprockets when the red zone aligns with the end of the swing arm.

Lower clutch cable adjuster

make any minor adjustments with the adjuster at the hand lever.

4. If correct cable adjustment does not result in correct clutch operation, the clutch itself should be disassembled and inspected.

Throttle Cables

The throttle cable free-play should be adjusted *after* the idle speed. This procedure is given in the "Tune-Up" section. The standard throttle cable free-play is 10–15° (2–6 mm/0.08–0.24 in.) of grip rotation for all models. The cable should be well lubricated before attempting to adjust free-play.

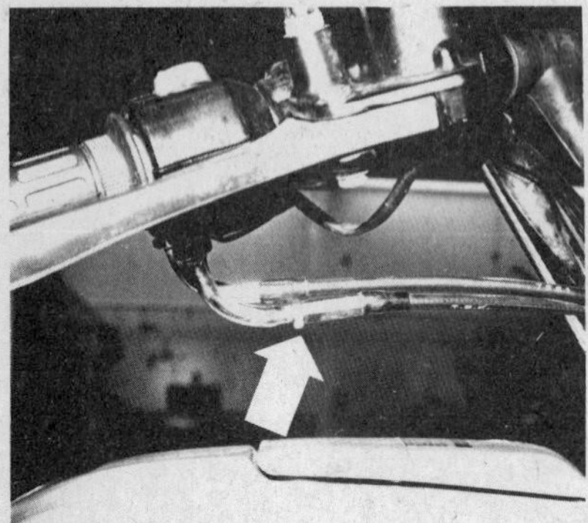

Throttle cable adjuster

1. Cable free-play is adjusted with the adjuster near the twist-grip. Loosen the locknut on the adjuster and screw the adjuster in or out until free-play is correct. Tighten the locknut.

2. Check that the cable operates smoothly and maintains some free-play when the handlebars are cut all the way to the right or left. If the idle speed changes when this is done, the cable is either too tightly adjusted, or it is binding somewhere along its routing.

3. Major throttle cable adjustments can be made at the cable adjuster near the carburetors. Run the adjuster at the handlebar in as far as possible first, then make the proper adjustment with the lower adjuster. Make any necessary fine adjustments with the adjuster at the twist-grip.

Lower throttle cable adjuster

Brakes

FRONT DISC

Disc brakes need little attention other than a periodic check of the fluid level and pad wear.

Late models have a see-through reservoir so that fluid level may be checked at a glance. The handlebars should be turned all the way to the right for a level check.

Earlier models have a level line inscribed on the inside of the brake fluid reservoir.

a. Clean the area around the reservoir with a clean rag to remove any dirt or grime.

b. Turn the handlebars all the way to the right.

c. Remove the master cylinder reservoir cap and diaphragm.

CAUTION: *Brake fluid will remove paint. Cover the gas tank with a protective cloth to avoid possible damage.*

d. Check the brake fluid line relative to the level line inscribed on the inside of the reservoir. The fluid level should be at or near the upper level mark.

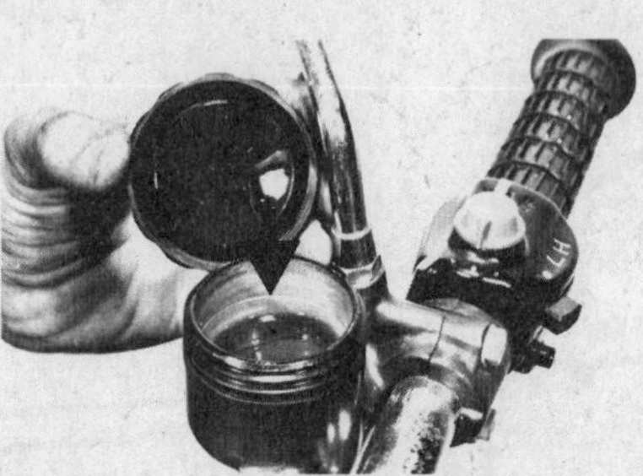

Maintain brake fluid level at the inscribed line

1. If the brake fluid level is below the inscribed level line on the earlier models or below the line marked "Lower" on late models, add enough DOT 3 brake fluid to bring it up. The reservoir cap on late models can be taken off after removing the four phillips screws. Be sure that the handlebars are turned to the right and that adequate precautions are taken in the event of brake fluid spillage.

NOTE: *Do not mix brands of brake fluid. Do not add fluid from an old or unsealed container. Brake fluid is hydroscopic—it absorbs moisture and quickly becomes useless when exposed to air for any length of time.*

2. The fluid level may drop slightly as the pads wear. If the level was significantly below the level line, carefully inspect the system for leaks.

CAUTION: *Do not operate the brake lever with the reservoir cap removed.*

3. Install the diaphragm and cap and tighten it securely. Check brake operation.

4. Remove the caliper inspection cap if fitted and check pad wear. The pads should be replaced as a set if either is worn to or near the red limit line inscribed on them. Refer to "Chassis," for pad replacement and brake system service procedures.

Brake pad inspection slot

5. If the brake lever feels spongy, or if brake effectiveness has been reduced, the possible cause is air bubbles in the line. To remedy this, bleed the system. This procedure can also be found in "Chassis."

6. Although hand lever travel is not adjustable, it should generally yield about 1 in. of movement (measured at the ball end of the hand lever) before it stops firmly. Excessive travel may be due to excessively worn pads, low fluid level, or air in the lines.

FRONT DRUM

The front drum brake is a twin-leading shoe unit. Two cable adjusters are fitted. The lower adjuster (at the brake plate) is used for major adjustments, the adjuster and the hand lever being used for minor adjustments.

1. The brake should be adjusted so that the brake hand lever can be pulled 20–30 mm/¾–1¼ in. measured at the ball end of the lever before the linings fully contact the drum.

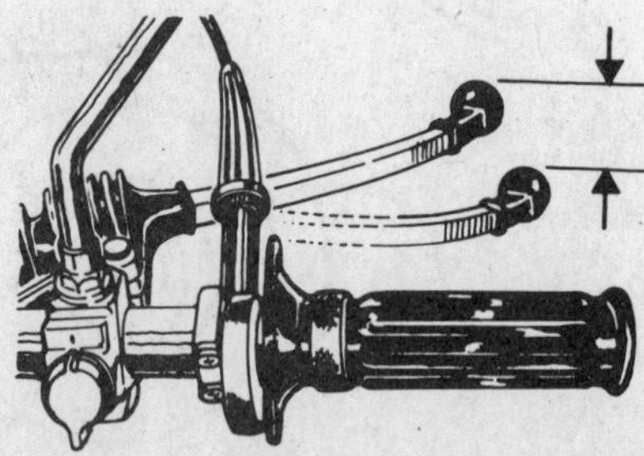

The brake lever should have about 1 inch of movement before the linings contact the drum

2. To adjust the brake, loosen the locknut(s) and turn the adjuster(s) in the proper direction.

3. Check brake lining wear by applying the brake lever fully and inspecting the position of the wear indicator pointer on the hub.

When the arrow and slash mark align with the brake fully applied, the linings should be checked for wear and will probably need replacement.

4. When the hand lever is released, check that the brakes fully retract and that the wheel turns freely. If it does not, either the cable is binding in the sheath due to dirt or corrosion, or else the brake shoe return springs are weak. Lubricate the cable thoroughly as described in this chapter and check again before disassembling the hub.

Adjusting the brake at the brake plate

5. The brake rod is adjustable, but is preset and need not be attended to unless the entire brake assembly is taken apart. Refer to "Chassis," in the event of unsatisfactory brake operation for complete service procedures.

REAR DRUM

1. Check brake pedal height first. If the pedal is not in a comfortable position for you, back off the adjuster nut on the end of the brake rod. Loosen the pedal height stopper bolt locknut, and turn the bolt in or out to adjust the pedal to the desired rest position. Standard pedal position has the upper surface of the pedal about 10 mm/0.4 in. below the upper side of the footpeg rubber. Readjust the brake and the brake light switch.

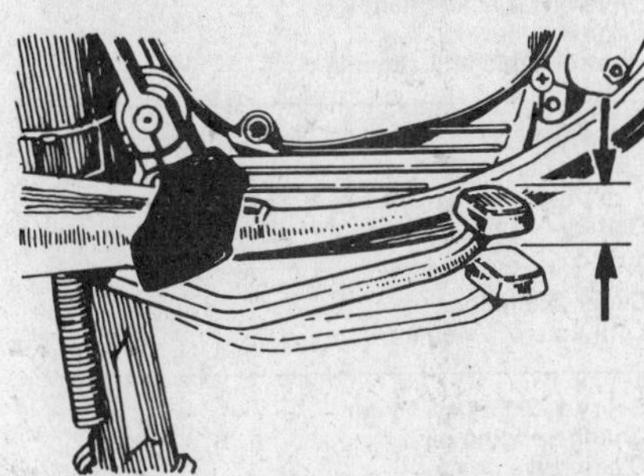
The brake pedal should have about 1 inch of movement before the linings contact the drum

Rear brake adjusting nut

2. The brake pedal should have 20–30 mm/¾–1¼ in. of free movement before the linings fully contact the drum.

Since the rear brake is rod-operated, this free movement should be checked with the motorcycle *off* the stands and a rider sitting on the seat.

Use the adjusting nut on the end of the brake rod to make the adjustment. Be sure that the nut is turned in full increments. It has a cut-out which must be seated in the clevis pin it bears against.

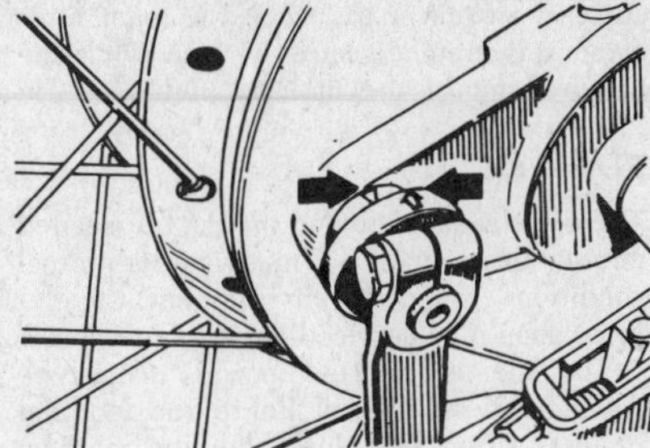
Brake wear indicator marks

3. With the rear wheel off the ground, check for free rotation after the brake is released. If the brakes drag, check the brake pedal linkage for sticking. Use motor oil to lubricate pivot points. If all else fails, suspect the brake shoe return springs.

4. Adjust the rear brake light switch (see below).

5. When the rear brake is fully applied, check the wear indicator. If the arrow on the lever aligns with the slash mark when the brake is fully applied, the linings are probably worn to the point of replacement.

PARKING BRAKE (400/450A)

1. Adjust the brake pedal height and pedal free-play as outlined above.

2. The parking brake hand lever should have no more than 5 mm/0.2 in. of free movement. To adjust, use the adjusters at either end of the cable.

Major adjustments should be made at the lower end of the parking brake cable, while minor adjustments should be made at the hand lever.

Note that screwing the adjusters out of their holders will reduce lever free-play and vice-versa.

Brake Light Switches

The switches should be checked for operation after the brakes are adjusted. The rear brake light switch and adjuster nut are mounted on a slotted bracket. The rear switch is adjusted by holding the switch and turning the adjuster nut to effect adjustment. Moving the switch up on the bracket allows the brake light to turn on sooner. Moving it down allows the light to turn on later. Do not turn the switch to effect adjustment as the wires will become twisted and may break.

The front disc brake switch is activated by the hand lever. This switch is not adjustable; if defective, it must be replaced.

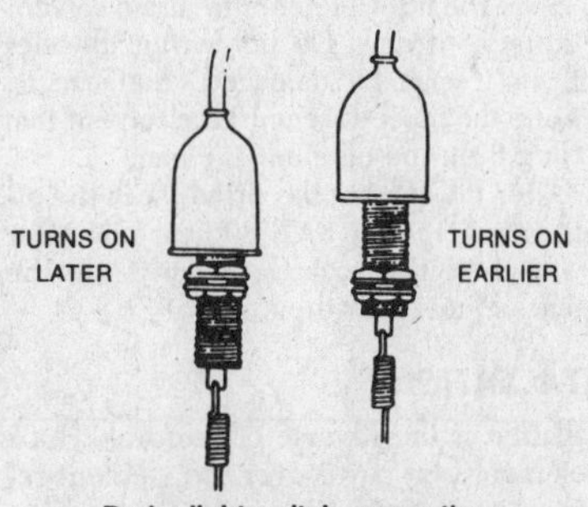

Brake light switch connections

The front drum brake switch is not adjustable.

Brake light switches should be activated as soon as the lever or pedal moves about ½ in.

If the switches fail to operate properly, refer to "Electrical System" for testing procedures.

Side Stand

The rubber pad on the end of the side stand should be replaced whenever it is worn to the indicated wear limit line. An arrow marks the line.

Replace when worn to the limit line

Headlight Adjustment

1. Set the machine about 25 feet away from the perpendicular to a wall, preferably of a color which reflects light well.

Lateral and vertical headlight adjustments

The machine should be off the stand, and with a rider putting his weight on the machine as in operation.

2. Switch on the high beam. The headlight high beam should be parallel to the ground and should hit the wall directly in front of the machine.

3. Vertical adjustment is made by loosening the two headlight shell mounting bolts slightly and pivoting the shell up or down.

4. Lateral adjustment is accomplished by means of the screw on the right side of the headlight. Turning the screw clockwise will move the beam to the left; turning it counterclockwise will move it to the right.

Air Forks

Air forks should be checked for pressure. It should be 11 plus or minus 3 psi for each leg.

Balancer Chain Adjustment

The balancer chain should be adjusted every 10,800 miles.

1. Drain the engine oil.
2. Disconnect the clutch cable and the tachometer cables from the right crankcase cover, if fitted.
3. Remove the right crankcase cover. Refer to "Engine and Transmission," for detailed procedures.
4. Loosen the 8 mm nut. Chain tension will be set automatically. Tighten the nut to 15–18 ft lbs.

Balancer chain adjustment nut (arrow)

5. Check that the stopper plate has not moved to the end of its adjustment range. If the plate is touching the 8 mm nut stud, remove the 8 mm and 10 mm nuts and the stopper plate. Install the stopper plate one or more splines out of the original position. Install the 10 mm nut and tighten it to 22–25 ft lbs. Install the 8 mm nut and secure it to 15–18 ft lbs.

NOTE: *If the punch mark on the shaft is below a horizontal line through the shaft center after this is done, the balancer chain must be replaced. Refer to chapter 4.*

FUEL SYSTEM

Petcock

1. Remove the fuel tank from the motorcycle.
2. Drain the gasoline.
3. Unscrew the locknut and remove the petcock. The fuel filter is fitted to the petcock intake pipe and is inside the gas tank.
4. Clean the fuel filter in a solvent. Remove any foreign matter from the mesh with a soft brush. If the mesh is badly clogged and cannot be cleaned, or if it is punctured, replace it with a new one.
5. Check the condition of the sealing washer and replace it if it is damaged.
6. Installation is the reverse of removal. Tighten the petcock locknut to 15–18 ft lbs.

CAUTION: *Do not overtighten the locknut.*

7. After installation, check for leaks before operating the motorcycle.

Be sure that the fuel line is properly installed and secured with the safety clip.

Carburetors

Every 3,600 miles, the carburetors should be removed and cleaned. Removal of the units together is required.

Air Cleaner

The air cleaner element may be either a wet porous-foam type or a dry paper filter. They are easy to tell apart, since the foam filter element is stretched across a frame, while the paper element is a cylindrical unit.

FOAM FILTER

The air cleaner element should be cleaned and re-oiled every 3,600 miles, under normal conditions. In a dusty environment, the element should be serviced even more often.

The element is the porous foam-type which relies upon an oil film to trap and hold foreign matter. Therefore, the filter must be serviced properly in order to do its job.

REMOVAL

1. Remove the seat.
2. Unscrew and remove the three phillips screws from the air cleaner cover and remove the cover.
3. Take out the filter element.

Removing the filter element

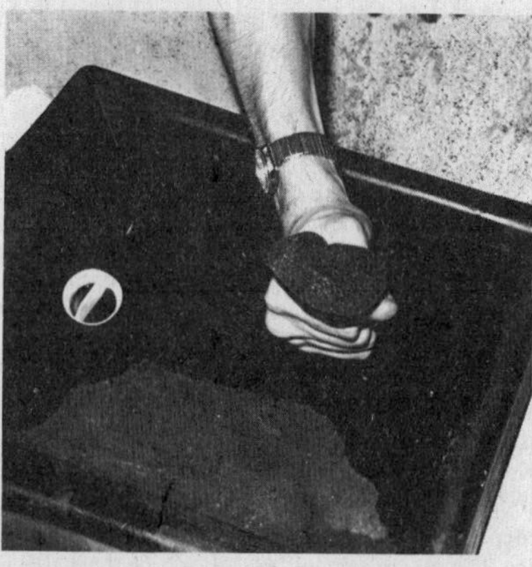

Squeeze the element, do not wring it out

SERVICE

1. Soak the filter element in a safe solvent and squeeze it dry. Do not wring the element, or it may be damaged. Squeeze it. Continue the procedure until the solvent that is wrung from the element is clean.
2. After the solvent has dried, soak the element in SAE 90 or SAE 80 gear oil. After allowing the oil to soak thoroughly into the element, squeeze off the excess.

INSTALLATION

Installation is the reverse of removal. Hook the element case pawls over the element retainer.

PAPER FILTER

The paper filter should be cleaned about every 3,600 miles under normal conditions, and replaced every 7,200 miles. The filter element is removed and installed in the manner described for the foam filter, above. Service, however, is limited to blowing out as much of the accumulated dust and dirt as possible with compressed air applied to the inside of the filter. Since this is not a very effective method, the element should be replaced after one such cleaning regardless of apparent condition.

Crankcase Ventilation System

A breather tube is connected to the cylinder head which carries crankcase vapors to the air cleaner case instead of having them exhausted into the atmosphere. The vapors are recycled, entering the carburetors along with fresh air. Any oil vapor is trapped in the breather chamber at the bottom of the air cleaner case, and condensing oil is drained off.

The system needs no maintenance other than a check to see that the connections are tight, and the hoses not rotted or cracked.

Periodic Maintenance Intervals ①

Before each ride
Safety items (lights, brakes, horn)
Drive chain adjustment
Engine oil level
Control cable adjustments

Weekly
Engine oil level
Tire pressures (check when cold)
Battery electrolyte level

Every 200 miles
Lubricate drive chain

Every 1,800 miles/1 year
Change engine oil
Clean drive chain

Every 3,600 miles/1 year
Replace oil filter
Clean air filter
Check spark plugs
Check valve adjustment
Control operation
Adjust cam chain tension
Check carburetor adjustments
Check carburetor synchronization
Check brake fluid level (disc brake)
Check brake pad/lining wear (all brakes)
Check brake operation
Headlight adjustment
Clutch/drum brake lever free-play
Check wheel bearings
Check rim run-out and spoke tension
Lubricate swing arm
Lubricate control cables
Lubricate tach and speedometer cables

Every 7,200 miles
Replace spark plugs
Check steering head bearings
Replace paper air filter element

Every 10,800 miles/2 years
Adjust balancer chain tension
Flush and refill disc brake system
Repack wheel and steering head bearings

① Based on normal usage after initial service and break-in are completed.

TUNE-UP

NOTE: *Common tune-up procedures are explained in detail in the "General Information" section.*

CAUTION: *All tune-up procedures made with the engine running must be carried out with the machine on the centerstand on firm, level ground, and in a well-ventilated area.*

On automatic transmission models, the parking brake should always be applied when carrying out any procedure of this nature.

Always be sure to keep children and other innocents away from hot, running engines. Never leave the motorcycle running and unattended.

CAM CHAIN ADJUSTMENT

Cam chain adjustment should be carried out when the engine is at operating temperature.

Recommended Lubricants

	Engine Honda Four-stroke oil SAE 10W-40, service-rated "SE" or "SF" SAE 20W-40, service-rated "SE" or "SF" SAE 20W-50, service-rated "SE" or "SF" SAE 10W-30, service-rated "SE" or "SF" for low-temperature use
	Front Forks ATF
	Disc Brake Fluid DOT 3 standard hydraulic disc brake fluid
	Control cables Light weight motor oil Graphite-based lubricant Molybdenum-disulphide-based lubricant
	Tach, speedometer cables Light duty grease
	Throttle twist grip Light duty grease
	Grease fittings Waterproof, medium-weight chassis grease Multi-purpose Type NLGI No. 2
	Wheel and steering head bearings Waterproof, medium-weight bearing grease (check suitability for disc brake wheel where applicable)
	Drive chain Good quality lubricant developed and sold specifically for motorcycle drive chains
	Foam Air Filter Element SAE 90 gear oil SAE 80 gear oil

MAINTENANCE DATA (400)

Component	CB 400T (78-80)	CB 400A (78-80)	CM 400T/A (79-80)	CM 400E (80)	CB/CM 400T (81)	CM 400A/E (81)
Fuel capacity (gal/l)	3.7/14 (Type I) 3.4/13 (Type II)	3.4/13 —	2.6/10 —	3.7/14 —	3.4/13 (CB) 2.6/10 (CM)	2.6/10 (A) 3.7/14 (E)
Fuel reserve (gal/l)	0.8/8.0 (Type I) 0.75/2.8 (Type II)	0.75/2.8 —	0.8/3.0 —	0.9/3.4 —	0.8/3.0 (CB) 0.45/1.7 (CM)	0.45/1.7 (A) 0.9/3.5 (E)
Oil capacity (qts/l)	2.6/2.5①	2.6/2.5①	2.6/2.5①	2.6/2.5①	2.6/2.5①	2.6/2.5①
Front forks (oz./cc) (each leg)	4.9/140	4.9/140	4.9/140	4.6/135	②	②
Tire pressures (psi)						
Solo (f/r)	24/32	24/32	24/28	24/28	28/28	28/28
Two-up or extended high speed (f/r)	24/36	24/36	24/36	24/36	28/36	28/36
Battery						
Voltage (v)	12	12	12	12	12	12
Capacity (ah)	9 (Type I) 12 (Type II)	12 —	12 —	12 —	12 —	12 —
Continuous charging rate (amps)	0.9 (Type I) 1.2 (Type II)	1.2	1.2	1.2	1.2	1.2
Drive chain slack (mm/in.)	20/0.75	20/0.75	20/0.75	20/0.75	20/0.75	20/0.75
Drum brake lever/pedal free-play (mm/in.)	25/1	25/1	25/1	25/1	25/1	25/1

① At routine change. After engine rebuild, add 3.2 qts/3.0 l on "T" and "E" models, 3.5 qts/3.3 l on "A" models.

② CB 400T: 5.9/175 at routine change
6.4/190 when rebuilding

CM 400T/A: 5.8/172 at routine change
6.3/187 when rebuilding

CM 400E: 4.6/135

MAINTENANCE DATA (450)

Component	CM 450A/C	CM 450E	CB 450T	CB 450SC
Fuel capacity (gal/l)	3.4/13	3.4/13	3.4/13	3.2/12
Fuel reserve (gal/l)	0.5/2.0	0.5/2.0	0.5/2.0	0.5/2.0
Oil capacity (qts/l)	2.6/2.5①	2.6/2.5①	2.6/2.5①	2.6/2.5①
Front forks (oz./cc) (each leg)	6.9/205②	na	5.8/172②	6.3/185②
Tire pressures (psi)				
Solo (f/r)	28/28	24/28	28/28	28/28
Two-up or extended high speed (f/r)	28/36	24/36	28/36	28/36
Battery				
Voltage (v)	12	12	12	12
Capacity (ah)	12	12	12	12
Continuous charging rate (amps)	1.2	1.2	1.2	1.2
Drive chain slack (mm/in.)	20/0.75	20/0.75	20/0.75	20/0.75
Drum brake lever/pedal free-play (mm/in.)	25/1	25/1	25/1	25/1

① At routine change. After engine rebuild, add 3.5 qts/3.3 l.

② At routine change. Add 0.5 oz./15 cc more when rebuilding.

Cam chain adjuster (arrow)

1. With the engine idling, loosen the cam chain tensioner locknut and back it off one or two turns. The cam chain tensioner is located behind the cylinders.

2. Tighten the locknut. Cam chain tension is now automatically set.

VALVE ADJUSTMENT

NOTE: *Valves must be adjusted when the engine is cold.*

1. Remove the seat.

2. Turn the petcock to the "OFF" position, disconnect the fuel line from the petcock, disconnect the fuel line from the petcock, and remove the gas tank.

3. Remove the left crankcase cover. Have a drip pan beneath the cover ready to catch any motor oil which may drip out.

4. Remove the oil cylinder head cover (two bolts).

5. Turn the engine over until the "T" mark on the alternator rotor aligns with the index mark on the crankcase. This will place one of the pistons at Top Dead Center on the compression stroke, which means that all valves for that cylinder will be closed.

Jiggle the rocker arms to find which cylinder is at this position. There should be some slight movement in the rocker arms for that cylinder which is on the compression stroke, and it is that one which must be checked and/or adjusted.

"T" (top dead center) mark aligned with stator index

Checking for play at a closed valve

6. Slip a feeler gauge blade of the proper thickness in between the top of the valve and the rocker arm adjusting screw to check the clearance.

Clearances for all models are as follows:
Intake: 0.10 mm/0.004 in.
Exhaust: 0.14 mm/0.006 in.

If the clearance is correct, a feeler gauge blade of the proper thickness will be a light slip fit between the rocker arm adjuster and the valve.

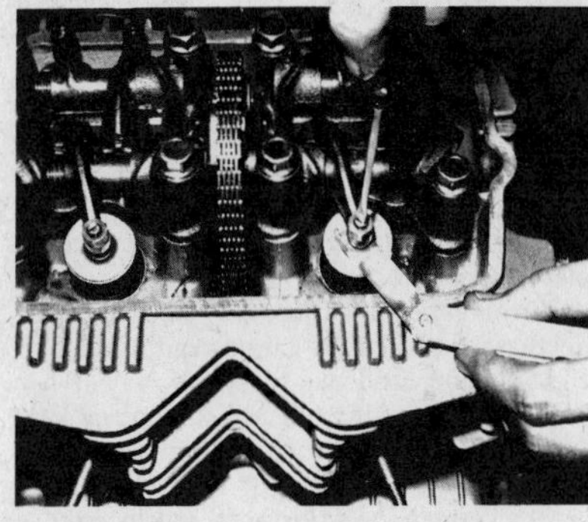

Adjusting the valve clearance

7. Adjust the clearance, if necessary, by loosening the adjuster locknut, and turning the adjuster so that there is just a slight drag on the feeler gauge blade when it is pulled through. Hold the adjusting screw in this position, and tighten the locknut. You may note that the clearance tends to be reduced when the locknut is tightened no matter how carefully you attempt to hold the adjusting screw stationary. This is normal. Compensate by letting your original setting be slightly on the loose side, so that tightening the adjusting screw locknut will bring the clearance to within the proper specification.

8. After the valves for one cylinder have been checked, rotate the alternator rotor one full turn (360°) and once again align the "T" mark with the index mark. The remaining cylinder will now be at TDC on the compression stroke, and the valves for that cylinder can be checked or adjusted in the same manner.

IGNITION TIMING

The CDI ignition system fitted to Hawk models is not adjustable, and the unit needs no routine maintenance.

An ignition timing check need only be carried out if performance is not satisfactory. An automative-type strobe light is needed. Timing is checked at idle and "full advance," which is over 5,000 rpm.

If the timing is not correct, it must be caused by a defect in the CDI unit.

1. Park the motorcycle on the centerstand in a well-ventilated area.

2. Remove the left crankcase cover. Have a drip pan ready beneath the cover to catch the little motor oil which may escape when the cover is removed.

3. Hook up the strobe light according to the manufacturer's instructions. Pick-up can be from either cylinder. Fit a tachometer on models not equipped with one.

4. The procedure varies slightly from this point, depending on whether the machine is an automatic or not.

5. On all except "A" models, start the engine and allow it to idle (1,200 rpm or lower), while aiming the strobe light at the alternator rotor marks. At this speed, the "F" mark on the rotor should align with the stationary index mark on the crankcase.

"F" mark (idle firing point)

Full advance firing point aligned with stator index mark

6. Increase the speed to 5,350 rpm or higher. At this speed, the full advance marks should align with the index marks. The full advance marks are two parallel lines on the rotor. The index mark should be centered between them.

7. On the "A" models, start the engine, and allow it to idle with the transmission in *neutral.* Idle speed should be 1,250 rpm or lower. At this point, the "FN" mark on the alternator rotor should align with the stationary index mark on the crankcase.

8. Shift the transmission into "1" or "2". The "F" mark on the rotor should now be aligned with the index mark.

9. Refer to Step 6, above for a full advance timing check.

CARBURETORS

Carburetor adjustments to be made during a tune-up include setting float level, synchronization, idle speed and mixture, and fast idle adjustment.

Adjusting Float Level

1. Float level is a measure of the amount of gasoline which will be in the float bowls during operation. While it is a critical specification, it will not normally need readjustment once properly set. Float level, therefore, need not be checked at every tune-up, but should be attended to from time to time.

2. Remove the carburetors.

3. Remove the float bowls. With the carburetor(s) positioned with the engine side down, lower the float until the float arm just touches but does not depress the tip of the float needle. Float level is the measured distance from the bottom of the float to the float bowl mating surface.

4. Proper float level for all models is 15.5

Measuring float height (H)

mm/0.61 in. Adjust, if necessary, by pushing out the float pivot pin, removing the floats, and bending the float arm tang. Bending the tang towards the carburetor body will increase the float level measurement and vice-versa.

5. Both carburetors must have the same float level. Measure both before changing either. Note that the measured float level will be inaccurate if the float needle tip is worn or if there is foreign matter on the needle seat.

Synchronization

Carburetor synchronization means nothing more than adjusting the linkage so that both butterfly valves begin to open at the same time and open the same amount. This prevents one carburetor from "leading" the other, with the resultant consequences of reduced performance, increased engine strain, and so on.

Vacuum gauges are necessary to properly synchronize the carburetors although a rough approximation can be made, if necessary, by visually aligning the butterflies (see below).

The butterflies are synchronized by means of a single screw located between the two carburetors. Turning the screw simultaneously closes one butterfly while opening the other.

NOTE: *Be sure that the throttle cable is properly adjusted before attempting this operation.*

1. Run the engine until normal operating temperature is reached.
2. Park the motorcycle on the centerstand in a well ventilated area.
3. Remove the seat.
4. Turn the petcock to the "OFF" position, disconnect the fuel line at the petcock, and remove the gas tank.
5. Using a long fuel line, place the gas tank where the seat used to be and secure it with a strap. Fit the fuel line so that gas can flow to the carburetors.
6. Install the vacuum gauges. The vacuum gauges fittings are located at the top of each manifold. Threaded plugs must be removed first.
7. Start the engine and allow it to idle at 1,200 rpm. Note the vacuum gauge reading. Both gauges should read 200-240 mm Hg/8.0-9.6 in Hg at idle.

Vacuum gauge fitting (arrow)

Synchronizer screw (arrow)

8. The two carburetors should be at least within 40 mm/0.16 in. Hg. If they are not, locate the adjusting screw between them. Loosen the locknut, and turn the screw so that the vacuum readings for both units are as close as possible.

Turning the adjusting screw *clockwise* will decrease the vacuum gauge reading on the right cylinder, and vice-versa.

Note that turning the adjusting screw will affect the readings on *both* gauges, so make adjustments carefully.

9. Tighten the adjusting screw locknut.
10. Rev the engine a few times, then let it idle. Check that the butterflies are still properly synchronized.
11. After returning all components to their normal positions, readjust the idle speed, if necessary.

NOTE: *If idle vacuum is not within the proper range to start with, check engine compression, valve adjustment, spark plug condition, and look for any mechanical faults such as a leaking head gasket, air leak at the manifold, etc.*

Remember that raising the rpm lowers *the vacuum reading, and vice-versa.*

12. If vacuum gauges are not available, a rough method of synchronizing the carburetors may be carried out. Remove the carburetors as a unit from the motorcycle. Look into the engine side of the carburetors and note the relative positions of the edges of the butterflies in relation to the small by-pass passages in the bottom of the bores. Both butterflies should be in the same position relative to these by-pass holes.

Idle Speed and Mixture

NOTE: *Adjust the idle speed AFTER synchronization.*

Idle speed and mixture adjustments must be carried out when the engine is at operating temperature.

1. Start and run the engine until it is at operating temperature.
2. Park the motorcycle on the centerstand in a well ventilated area. Automatic models must be in neutral, as must manual transmission machines.
3. Each carburetor is fitted with a pilot screw to control the idle mixture. The screws are located near the float bowls on the engine side of the carburetors.

On 1980 and later models, these screws are fitted with plastic limiter caps. These caps should not be removed, nor should adjustment of the screws outside the range allowed by the caps be attempted. To do so may violate clean air ordinances.

Adjustment as described in Step 4 should only be necessary if the carburetors have been disassembled for cleaning or rebuilding.

4. Turn each screw in *carefully* until it is

Pilot screw (arrow)

Throttle stop screw (arrow)

seated, then back each one out the following number of turns:

CB 400T (78-79): 1½
CB 400A (78-79): 1¾
CB/CM 400T/E (80-81): 2 (pre-set)
CB/CM 400A (80-81): 2¼ (pre-set)
CM 450A: 2¾ (pre-set)
Other 450's: 2¼ (pre-set)

5. Start the engine, and use the throttle stop screw between the carburetors so that the idle speed is 1,200-1,250 rpm.

NOTE: *Be sure that the throttle cable has sufficient free-play before attempting to adjust the idle speed.*

6. Rev the engine a few times and then ensure that idle returns to normal.

Fast Idle

Fast idle speed should be 2,000-3,000 rpm. If adjustment is necessary, remove the carburetors, back off the throttle stop screw and close the butterfly. Adjust the fast idle lever so that the clearance between the fast idle lever and the throttle drum is about 1.2 mm/0.047 in.

Stall Speed Check (400/450A)

1. Park the motorcycle on the centerstand in a well ventilated area.
2. Apply the parking brake, after ensuring that it is working properly.
3. Start the engine and allow it to run until the rpm stabilizes.
4. Connect a tachometer and shift the transmission into 1st. Hold down the rear brake pedal, and open the throttle slowly.
5. Stall speed should be 3,550-3,850 rpm.
6. Repeat the test with the transmission in 2d.

CAUTION: *Do not keep the throttle open for more than 10 seconds at a time. Use* both *brakes to stall the engine.*

7. If the stall speed is less than 3,400 rpm in either gears, or both, refer to the "Troubleshooting" charts at the end of the "Engine and Transmission" section for possible causes.

TUNE-UP SPECIFICATIONS

Item	CB/CM 400T/E	CB/CM 400A	CM 450A	CB/CM 450T/E/C/SC
Compression				
Cranking pressure (psi)	185	185	185	185
Maximum allowable variation (psi)	15	15	15	15
Valve clearance				
Intake (mm/in.)	0.10/0.004	0.10/0.004	0.10/0.004	0.10/0.004
Exhaust (mm/in.)	0.14/0.006	0.14/0.006	0.14/0.006	0.14/0.006
Ignition				
Type	CDI	CDI	CDI	CDI
Advance at idle (deg BTDC)	15@1,200 rpm	7.5@1,250 rpm	7.5@1,250 rpm	15@1,200 rpm
Full advance (deg BTDC)	43@4,500 rpm	43@4,500 rpm	43@4,500 rpm	43@4,500 rpm
Idle advance in gear (deg BTDC)	—	7.5@1,250 rpm	7.5@1,250 rpm	—
Spark plugs (OEM)	NGK/ND	NGK/ND	NGK/ND	NGK/ND
Spark plug type (NGK/ND)	D-8EA/X24ES-U	D-8EA/X24ES-U	③	③
Plug gap (mm/in.)	0.6-0.7/0.024-0.028	0.6-0.7/0.024-0.028	④	④
Carburetion				
Throttle free-play (mm/in.)	2-6/0.08-0.24	2-6/0.08-0.24	2-6/0.08-0.24	2-6/0.08-0.24
Idle speed (hot rpm)	1,200	1,250	1,250	1,200
Fast idle (rpm)	2,500	2,000	2,000	2,500
Pilot screw settings (turns out)	①	②	2¾	2¼
Synchronization vacuum (mm Hg)	200-240	200-240	200-240	200-240
Allowable vacuum variation (mm Hg)	40	40	40	40
Float level (mm/in.)	15.5/0.61	15.5/0.61	15.5/0.61	15.5/0.61

① 1978-79: 1½
1980-81: 2 (pre-set)

② 1978-79: 1¾
1980: 2¼ (pre-set)

③ 1982: DR-8ES-L/X24ESR-U
1983: DPR-8EA/X24EPR-U9

④ 1982: 0.6-0.7/0.024-0.028
1983: 0.8-0.9/0.032-0.035

ENGINE AND TRANSMISSION

NOTE: *For engine component inspection techniques and procedures, refer to "Engine Rebuilding" in the General Information section.*

Engine Service

1. The cylinder head, barrels, and pistons can be removed with the engine in the frame.
2. Crankcase cover components such as the clutch, oil pump, alternator, etc., can also be serviced without removing the engine.
3. Service to the crankshaft, transmission, and gear shift components requires removal of the engine.
4. Read each procedure carefully before beginning so that replacement items such as gaskets, O-rings, etc., can be purchased before-hand.

CAUTION: *When disassembling the top end of the engine, be sure to note the location of all dowel pins and O-rings. These components are critical to operation of the lubrication system and are easy to misplace when components are being removed or installed.*

ENGINE

Removal and Installation

Engine removal is necessary to service lower end components (crankshaft, connecting rods, transmission, etc.), as well as the shift mechanism and kickstarter.

1. Clean and degrease the engine thoroughly before removal. This will minimize the chances of foreign matter getting into the

crankcases during the disassembly procedure.

2. Drain the engine oil.

3. Remove the seat and frame side covers.

4. Remove the gas tank.

5. Remove the gearshift lever pinch bolt, and carefully pull the gearshift lever from the splined shaft.

6. Remove the left crankcase cover.

7. Remove the exhaust system. Loosening the muffler and muffler chamber clamp bolts will facilitate removal.

8. Remove the drive chain masterlink and pull off the chain. Reinstall the masterlink and spring clip on one end of the chain to avoid loss.

9. Remove the chain protector.

10. Disconnect the alternator wiring coupler beneath the left side cover.

11. Remove the tachometer cable securing bolt from the crankcase and disconnect the tachometer cable from the engine, if fitted.

12. Disconnect the clutch cable from the engine, if fitted.

13. Disconnect the starter motor cable from the starter motor, if fitted.

14. Disconnect the crankcase breather tube from the cylinder head cover.

15. Disconnect the spark plug caps and loosen or remove the spark plugs.

16. Disconnect the neutral switch and oil pressure switch wires at the connectors behind the right side cover.

On 400A models, remove the oil pressure switch protector at the right front of the crankcase. Disconnect the wire lead from the switch. Disconnect the transmission indicator leads behind the right crankcase cover.

17. Loosen the carburetor-to-manifold clamp screws.

18. Remove the right-side rider's footpeg.

19. Remove the kickstarter pinch bolt and carefully pull the kickstarter from the splined shaft.

20. Place a scissors jack or the like beneath the engine to support its weight while the engine mounting bolts are being removed.

21. Remove the engine mounting bolts at the front of the engine.

22. Remove the head steady bolts and the mounting plates.

23. Remove the rear engine mounting bolts and remove the engine from the frame.

NOTE: *Use the jack to lift the engine slightly as necessary to take the weight off the bolts as they are removed. Do not attempt to drive bolts out or the threads may be ruined. Be prepared for any eventuality when the last of the mounting bolts is removed.*

24. Installation is basically the reverse of removal. Note the following points:

a. Tighten the front lower (10 mm) mounting bolts to 33-43 ft lbs, and the front upper (8 mm) mounting bolts to 15-22 ft lbs.

b. Tighten the 10 mm head steady bolt to 33-43 ft lbs, and the 8 mm head steady bolts on the frame to 15-22 ft lbs. The 8 mm head steady plate bolts on the head itself should be secured to 13-18 ft lbs.

c. Tighten the rear engine mounting bolts to 33-43 ft lbs.

d. The upper rear mounting bolt secures the battery ground cable to the frame; be sure that it is connected.

e. Be sure that all wiring cables are properly routed and protected by their grommets where applicable.

f. Adjust cable free-play and drive chain tension after installation.

g. Be sure to check crankcase oil level before starting the engine.

TOP END

The top end components (cylinder head, camshaft, pistons) can be serviced without removing the engine from the frame.

Cylinder Head Removal

The cylinder head can be removed without the use of special tools. A valve spring compressor will, of course, be required to remove and install the valves properly. A torque wrench will be required to install the cylinder head.

1. Remove the gas tank.

2. Remove the exhaust system. Removal will be facilitated by loosening the muffler and muffler camber clamp bolts.

3. Remove the gearshift lever pinch bolt and carefully pull the gearshift lever from its splined shaft. Remove the left crankcase cover.

4. Loosen the carburetor-to-manifold clamp screws and detach the carburetors from the cylinder head.

5. Remove the cylinder head steady mounting bolts and plates. Disconnect the spark plug caps and remove the spark plugs.

6. Remove the cam chain tensioner bolt.

7. Remove the cylinder head cover. On 450 models, disconnect the oil lines at the rocker arm assemblies. Hold the line fittings with a wrench when loosening the bolts to avoid damage. Disconnect the line from the cylinder head and crankcase and remove the oil pipe assembly. Note the locations of all seals and washers.

Removing the cam chain tensioner bolt

Cylinder head bolts (arrows)

Removing the cylinder head bolts and rocker arm assemblies

NOTE: *The front cylinder head bolts are longer than those at the rear. Do not confuse them.*

NOTE: *The head should not be removed when the engine is hot due to the possibility of warpage.*

8. Gradually, and in a cross pattern, loosen each of the eight cylinder head bolts. Then remove them.

If the engine is in the frame, use the access holes provided in the upper frame member to remove the center bolts.

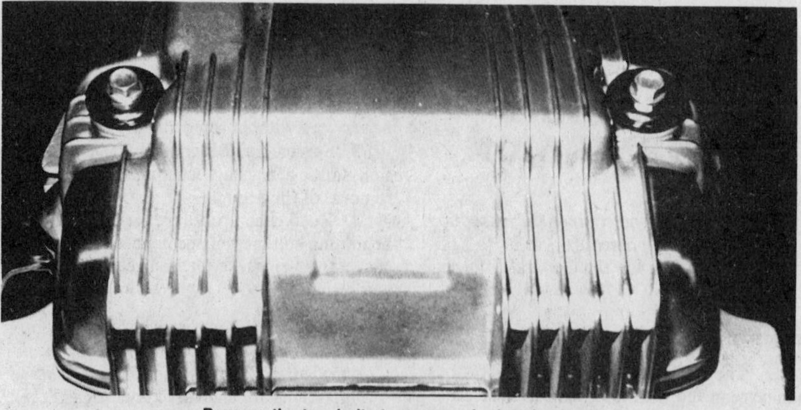

Remove the two bolts to remove the head cover

Removing the rocker arm shafts

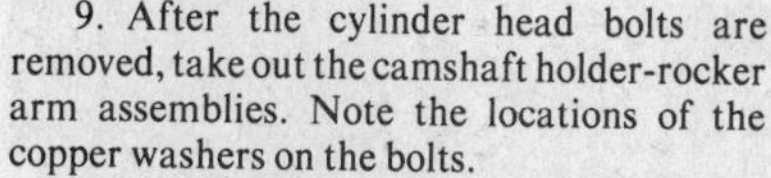

9. After the cylinder head bolts are removed, take out the camshaft holder-rocker arm assemblies. Note the locations of the copper washers on the bolts.

10. Pull out the rocker arm shafts to separate the rocker arms from the camshaft holders. Note the coil springs in the assembly. Be sure to mark each part before removal so that it can be installed in its original location.

11. Use a wrench on the alternator rotor nut and slowly turn the engine over until each of the camshaft sprocket bolts becomes accessible. Remove each bolt, taking extreme care that they do not fall into the crankcases.

12. Detach the cam chain from the camshaft sprocket. Pull the cam out to the right side of the engine.

NOTE: *For proper installation, note that the left side of the camshaft is notched.*

13. Loop a length of wire around the cam chain and secure it so that it does not fall into the crankcase.

14. Remove the cylinder head. If the head is stuck, use a large screwdriver and pry it free of the cylinders. Apply the screwdriver to the special ribbed points only.

15. Note the locations of the oil passage dowel pins and O-rings of the cylinder head mating surface. Be sure that they are in place. They may adhere to the head and fall out unnoticed later on.

Removing the rocker arms and springs

Cam sprocket bolt

16. Remove the cylinder head gasket. A new one must be used when the head is installed.

Removing the camshaft

Removing the cylinder head

Cylinder and Piston Removal

1. Remove the cylinder head as outlined above.

2. Remove the cam chain tensioner clip and pin, taking extreme care that they do not fall into the crankcase.

3. Remove the cam chain tensioner lock-

Cylinder dowel pin and O-ring locations (arrows)

Removing the cam chain tensioner clip

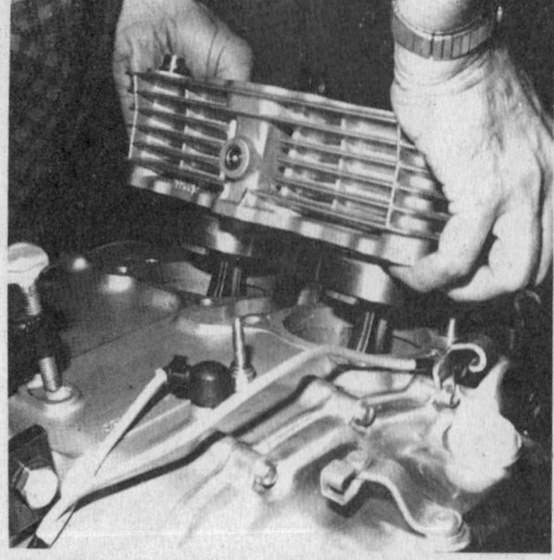
Removing the cylinders

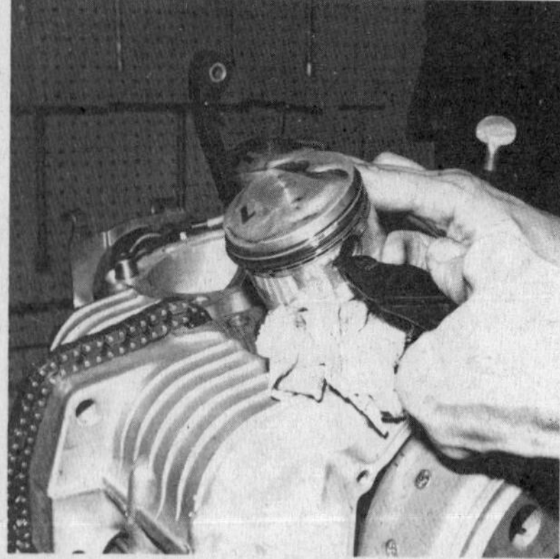
Removing a wrist pin circlip

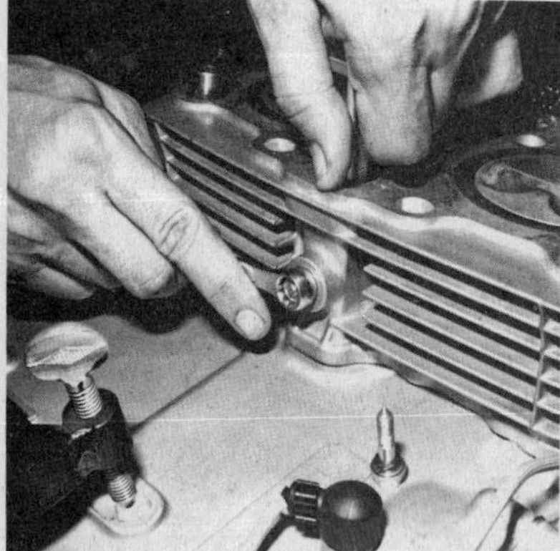
Removing the tensioner locknut

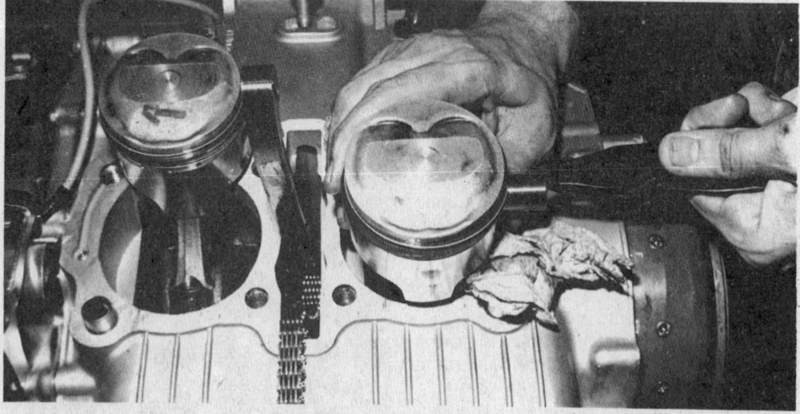
Pulling out a wrist pin

nut, washer, and o-ring. Remove the tensioner base and cam chain guide.

4. Lift the cylinder a few inches off its seat and stuff a clean, lint-free rag or rags beneath the pistons. This is to prevent any foreign matter or pieces of broken piston ring from falling into the crankcase when the cylinders are removed.

5. Lift the cylinder straight up and free of the pistons.

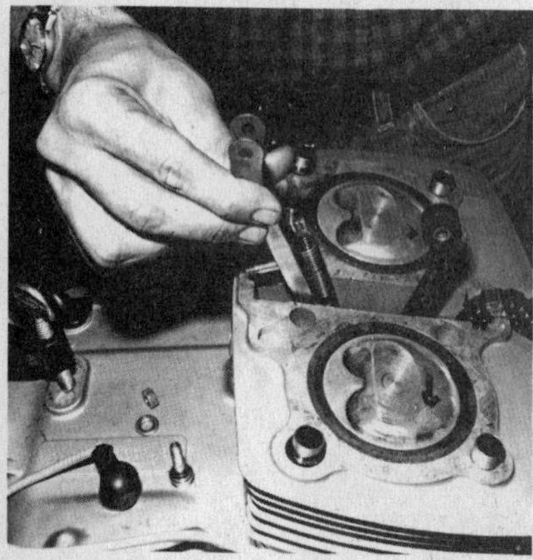
Removing the tensioner base

6. With a needle-nosed pliers, remove the wrist pin circlips from the pistons. Push out the piston wrist pins and remove the pistons from the rods.

Support the piston with one hand while pushing out the wrist pin to minimize chances of bending the rod. Push the pin out with steady pressure. Do *not* use an impact method. If the wrist pins resist removal, heat the piston crown gently and evenly with a propane torch until the pins can be easily pushed out.

Disgard the wrist pin circlips. New circlips must be used on assembly.

7. Mark each piston so that it can be installed in its original cylinder on reassembly.

8. Take note of the location of the oil passage dowel pins and o-rings on the cylinder-crankcase mating surface. Be sure that all are in their proper locations. Sometimes they may adhere to the cylinder when it is removed and fall out later.

9. Remove the cylinder base gasket. A new one must be used on assembly.

Inspection

CAMSHAFT

1. Check the cam lobes for flaking of the hardened surface, or blue discoloration, as well as the more obvious scoring, and replace the cam if any of these signs of damage are noted. Blue discoloration is often caused by overheating or lack of oil. In this event, all other components such as bearing surfaces should be checked for wear. Check the lubrication system for clogged passages, and the condition of the oil pump as well.

2. With a micrometer, measure the height of each cam lobe and compare your reading with the proper specification. They are as follows:

Intake 37.008–37.208 mm/1.457–1.465 in.

Exhaust 37.040–37.240 mm/1.458–1.466 in.

Replace the camshaft if any of the lobes measures less than 36.9 mm/1.45 in.

3. Mount the camshaft in a set of v-blocks and measure the run-out with a dial gauge. Replace the cam if the run-out exceeds 0.10 mm/0.004 in.

4. Make a visual inspection of the cam journals and the cam bearing surfaces on the cylinder head and holders. If any scoring or damage is noted, replace the cam or the head and holders as necessary. These surfaces should be perfectly smooth and free of parallel scratch or score marks as might be caused by impurities in the oil. If in doubt as to the condition of the bearings, measure the journals with a micrometer and the bearings with Plastigauge.

5. To measure the cam bearing clearance with Plastigauge, first clean the cam journals and bearing surfaces of any oil. Install the cam, applying a strip of Plastigauge to the top of the journal. Loosen the valve adjusters if the rocker arms are still installed in the cam holders. Install the cam holders and tighten the securing bolts gradually and in a cross pattern to 22–24 ft lbs.

NOTE: *Do not turn the camshaft during this operation.*

6. Remove the camshaft holders and measure the width of the plastic strip with the gauge provided. The cam, cam holders, and cylinder head should be replaced when the clearance exceeds the following limits:

end bearings 0.20 mm/0.008 in.

center bearings 0.23 mm/0.009 in.

These are the bearing clearance replacement limits. Standard bearing clearances are as follows:

end bearings 0.040–0.141 mm/0.0016–0.0056 in.

center bearings 0.090–0.191 mm/0.0035–0.0075 in.

ROCKER ARMS AND SHAFTS

1. Check the condition of the rocker arm bores and the corresponding areas of the respective shafts. These areas must be free of scoring, discoloration, or other signs of wear or damage. The surfaces should be smooth and featureless. Run a finger along each shaft and see if any step wear is evident. If the parts show signs of wear, replace them.

2. If possible, measure the inside diameter of each rocker arm bore. Standard diameter is 12.000–12.018 mm/0.4724–0.4731 in. Replace the rocker arm if the diameter is greater than 12.03 mm/0.474 in.

3. Measure the diameter of each rocker arm shaft at three places along its length. Standard shaft diameter is 11.966–11.984 mm/0.4711–0.4718 in. Replace the shaft if the measured diameter is less than 11.95 mm/0.470 in.

4. If a micrometer is not available, clean each rocker arm and shaft thoroughly, oil the shaft lightly, and insert it into the arm. Check for play. There should not be any. If you can feel play here, replace both the shaft and rocker arm.

5. Check the cam contacting pad of each rocker arm for pitting or wear. Replace the arm if wear is evident.

6. Check the condition of the valve tappet. Replace the tappet if the end is chipped or looks hammered.

7. Clean each rocker arm thoroughly in a clean solvent and be sure that the oil passage in each is clear.

8. If an inside micrometer is available, check the inside diameter of the rocker arm shaft holders. There should be little wear here because the rocker arm shaft turn very little, if at all. Standard holder inside diameter is 12.000–12.027 mm/0.4724–0.4735 in. The holder should be replaced if the measured diameter exceeds 12.05 mm/–.474 in.

CYLINDER HEAD

1. Remove the cylinder head gasket from the cylinder head if it has adhered to the surface. If it is stuck, scrape the gasket off with a putty knife or the like. Be careful not to scratch the head mating surface. Remove all elements of the gasket. Stubborn bits of gasket can be more easily removed if they are soaked in a safe solvent.

2. Place a straightedge across the cylinder head surface in all possible directions and check for warpage by attempting to slip feeler gauge blades between the straightedge and the head. Maximum allowable head warpage is 0.10 mm/0.004 in. If the measured warpage exceeds this figure, the head should be milled to restore a flat mating surface.

A check of the head for warpage is especially important if the machine has blown a head gasket, or there is evidence of oil leaks from the head mating surface.

3. Use a wire brush fitting on a power drill to decarbonize the combustion chambers. The valves should be left in place as this is done, as it minimizes the chances of causing damage to the valve seats.

VALVE ASSEMBLY

Before removing the valves, check their sealing ability by pouring a small quantity of gasoline into each port and allowing the head to sit for about five minutes. If the valves are properly seating, leakage into the combustion chamber will be minimal.

1. To remove the valves, and install them properly, a suitable C-clamp is necessary. Compress the valve springs and remove the keepers, retainers, springs, seals, and spring seats. Inspect the valves, guides, springs, and valve seats in the following manner. Keep each assembly separate so that every piece can be installed in its original location. New valve seals must always be used on assembly.

2. If considerable mileage has been covered, the valve springs should be replaced as a matter of course. Always replace valve springs as a set.

Measure the free-length of each valve spring with a vernier caliper. If any of the springs is less than the service limit, the springs should all be replaced.

NOTE: *Intake and Exhaust valve springs are not interchangeable. Keep the assemblies separate and mark them for installation in their original locations.*

Valve spring service limits are as follows:

Intake inner 35.5 mm/1.40 in.
Intake outer 49.0 mm/1.93 in.
Exhaust inner 39.5 mm/1.56 in.
Exhaust outer 49.5 mm/1.95 in.

Replace the springs as a set if any one of them is found to be less than that length. Standard valve spring lengths are as follows:

Intake inner 36.6 mm/1.44 in.
Intake outer 50.6 mm/1.99 in.
Exhaust inner 40.8 mm/1.61 in.
Exhaust outer 51.1 mm/2.01 in.

Note that these are the standard lengths for new springs, and will not usually be found on the installed springs.

3. Each valve must be free to move up and down in its guide with little resistance. Any sticking or binding as the valve is moved in the guide will indicate that the valve stem or guide is in poor condition.

4. Inspect the valve, paying close attention to the edges of the valve head for pitting, burnt or broken edges, excessive carbon build-up, etc. A certain amount of carbon and lead deposits on the valve face and the top of the exhaust valve are inevitable. Heavy deposits should be carefully scraped off with a dull knife, or a wire wheel, and the valve finished up with very fine emery cloth.

Do not touch the valve seating area during these operations.

If the valve has burnt or broken edges, it must be replaced.

5. Check the end of the valve stem for indented wear caused by the valve adjuster. Although rare, it may occur after long mileage. Since an indentation here will make proper valve adjustments impossible, the valve should be replaced.

NOTE: *The tips and edges of the valves are stellite-coated. Machining for any reason is not recommended. In case of wear, replace the valve.*

6. Carbon deposits should not extend too far up along the valve stem. This would indicate a worn or cracked valve guide.

7. Wet, oily deposits on the back of the valve head is indicative of a worn guide or bad seal. Less severe wear to these components show up as brown oil stains on the valve stem.

8. Holding a valve in your fingers, spin it while observing the head. A wobble is indicative of a bent valve. If a dial gauge is available, check the run-out of the head. Replace the valve if run-out exceeds 0.03 mm (0.0012 in.). Run-out is the total indicated dial gauge reading.

Attempt to rotate the valve by hand when it is fully inserted into the guide. If the valve will not rotate easily, or if it sticks as it is turned, it is probably bent.

9. A quick check of the operational worthiness of a valve and guide can be accomplished by dipping the valve stem in oil and inserting it into its guide. Place a finger over the other end of the guide. Pull the valve a little way out of the guide and release it. The valve should be drawn back into the guide by suction if the components are in serviceable condition.

10. Measure the diameter of each valve at least three places along its length. Compare the smallest of the reading obtained with the valve service limit specifications.

Intake valves must be replaced if any of the three measurements is less than 5.44 mm/0.214 in. Service limit for the exhaust valves is 6.54 mm/0.257 in.

11. If an inside micrometer is available, measure the inside diameter of each valve guide. The guides should be lightly reamed with special stock sized reamers Nos. 07984-2000000 for the intakes and 07984-6110000 for the exhausts. This is to remove any carbon build-up and insure and accurate measurement.

Guides should be replaced if the inside diameters measure in excess of 5.60 mm/0.220 in. for the intake guides, and 6.70 mm/0.264 in. for the exhaust guides.

12. Subtract the measured valve stem diameters from the valve guide diameters for each valve-guide set. Maximum allowable valve-to-guide clearance is 0.10 mm/0.004 in.

If the clearance thus calculated exceeds this amount, either the valve, the guide, or both must be replaced.

It may be possible to bring the valve-to-guide clearance to within the proper specification by replacing the valve alone. Diameters of new valves are as follows:

Intake 5.455–5.470 mm/0.2148–0.2154 in.

Exhaust 6.555–6.570 mm/0.2580–0.2587 in.

If the use of a new valve does not reduce the clearance to within the service limit, the guide must be replaced.

NOTE: *The valve seats should be recut and the valves lapped in any time the guide is replaced.*

13. To replace a valve guide, heat the cylinder head in an oven to a temperature of 212° F (100° C). Drive out the old guide(s) with a suitable drift. If the old guide was cracked or belled out by an engine catastrophe such as a valve hitting a piston, it may be necessary to chisel off the protruding (lower) end of the guide to facilitate removal. This will make it less likely that the guide bore in the head will be enlarged or scuffed during the removal procedure. While the head is still hot, drive in the new guide(s) until fully seated.

NOTE: *When replacing valve guides, use the special oversized guides.*

14. Ream newly installed guides with intake guide reamer 07984-2000000 or exhaust guide reamer 07984-6110000. Flush the guide thoroughly afterwards to remove any metal particles.

15. After installing new guides, the valve seat should be recut and the valve lapped in.

16. Check the width of the valve seat in the head. It should be about 1.1-1.3 mm/0.04-0.05 in. all the way around. If the seat is narrower or wider than this, if the width varies, or if the seat or the valve edges are pitted, the seat should be recut and the valve lapped in.

NOTE: *Valve springs are progressively wound. When installing them, be sure they are fitted with the close coils towards the cylinder head.*

Intake and exhaust valve springs are not interchangeable. The exhaust springs are longer. Be sure that they are not interchanged.

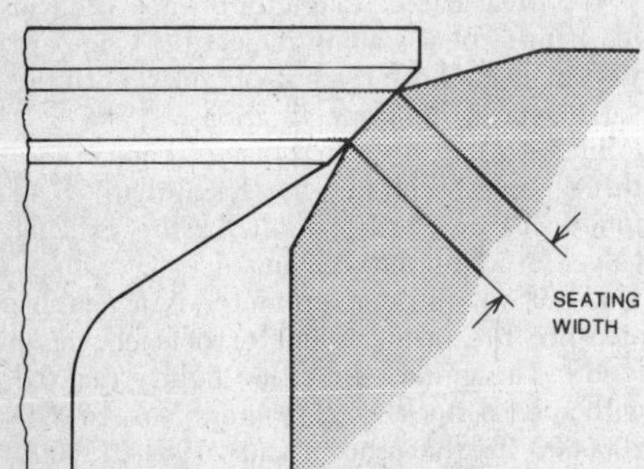

Valve seat width measurement point

Springs are installed with the close coils (arrows) towards the head

SEAT CUTTING

1. Use a machinist's dye to check the width and position of the valve seat. Apply the dye to the valve's beveled seating area and a very small amount of grinding compound to the valve seat in the head. Spin the valve back and forth against the seat for several seconds, then remove the grinding compound and inspect the pattern of the seat, from which the dye will have been removed.

2. The valve seat should be about 1.1-1.3 mm/0.04-0.05 in. wide and even in width all around the valve. The maximum acceptable seat width is 2.0 mm/0.08 in.

3. If the seat is uniform in width but is too wide, use a flat cutter, then a 30° cutter to reduce the seat width to within specification.

4. If the seat is centered on the valve face, but is too narrow, use a 45° cutter to increase the width to the proper specification.

5. If the seat is too narrow, and is towards the top edge of the face, first use a flat cutter, and then the 45° cutter.

6. If the seat is too narrow and positioned towards the bottom edge of the face, use a 30° cutter first, then a 45° cutter.

LAPPING

1. Valves should be lapped into their seats if the leakage test shows poor sealing, if the seat has been recut, if the valve edges or seat in the head are pitted, if the motorcycle has covered considerable mileage, or if new valves or guides are fitted.

Lapping a valve

2. Clean off all carbon build-up on the surface of the combustion chamber. Place three small dabs of valve lapping paste around the circumference of the valve head and place the valve into the guide.

3. If you have a lapping tool, use it as the manufacturer directs. Usually the tool will turn the valve back and forth while rotating it around the seat at the same time. Do not use excessive pressure during the operation.

If you do not have such a tool, a piece of thick fuel line placed over the valve stem works just as well. Turn the valve back and forth and rotate it to a new position every few seconds.

NOTE: *Check the condition of the valve face and seat frequently. When a smooth, even finish is evident, stop lapping. Excessive lapping may lead to a pocketed valve.*

4. Remove the valve and clean it thoroughly. Remove any traces of lapping compound from the seat and the combustion chamber. Swab out the guide with a cotton swab soaked in a solvent. Squirt a little oil into the guide so that it may carry away any particles inside.

CYLINDERS AND PISTONS

1. Make a visual inspection of the cylinder bore, noting any imperfections. The cylinder walls should be uniformly smooth.

2. With an inside micrometer, measure the diameter of each bore at the top, middle, and bottom. Make measurements in two directions, 90° apart, both parallel and perpendicular to the piston wrist pins.

If the difference between the high and lower measurement in any one direction (taper) is greater than 0.05 mm (0.002 in.), or if the difference between two measurements at any point on the cylinder (out-of-round) exceeds 0.01 mm (0.0004 in.), the cylinders should be bored to the next oversize and fitted with new pistons.

On 400 models, standard cylinder bore diameter is 70.50-70.51mm/2.775-2.776 in. If any of the six measurements yields a reading in excess of 70.60mm/2.78 in., both cylinders should be bored to the first oversize and the proper oversize piston fitted.

On 450 models, the nominal diameter is 75.00-75.01mm/2.9530 in. The wear limit is 75.10mm/2.957 in.

3. Make a visual inspection of the pistons. Scoring, scuffing, or seizure marks on the piston skirts may be removed with a fine grade of emery or crocus cloth if they are not too severe. Sanding should be done in a cross-hatch pattern. If the damage is severe (more than about ½ in. wide), the pistons should be replaced.

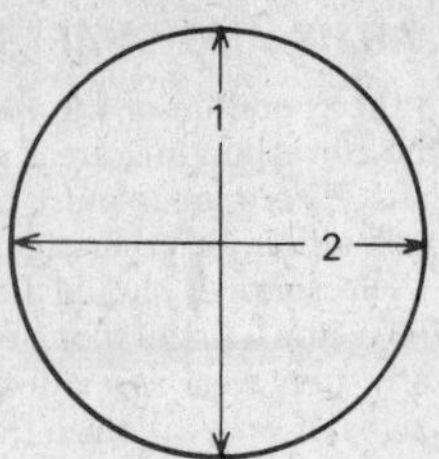

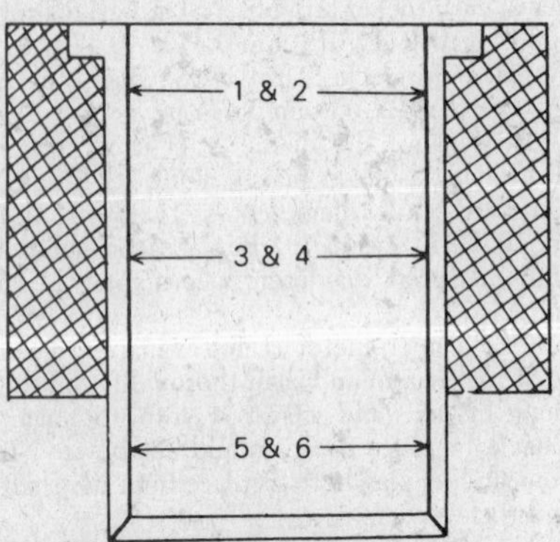

Cylinder measurement points

Measuring the piston diameter

4. The rings must be free to remove in the piston grooves. If they cannot, either they are carbon clogged (which necessitates replacing the rings and cleaning out the grooves), or metal has been pushed into the grooves by a piston seizure. In this event, pistons and rings must be replaced. Carbon-clogged rings are almost always broken when an attempt is made to remove or free them, so be prepared to buy a new set.

5. Measure the diameter of each piston about 7mm from the bottom edge of the skirt and perpendicular to the wrist pin.

Standard piston diameter for 400 models is 70.47-70.49mm/2.774-2.775 in. If either piston measures less than 70.40mm/2.772 in., replace both.

Standard piston diameter for 450 models is 74.73-74.74mm/2.942-2.943 in. The wear limit is 74.65mm/2.939 in.

6. Compare the largest of the six cylinder bore measurements with the piston diameter measurement. If the difference exceeds 0.10 mm/0.004 in., the pistons should be replaced with the next oversize and the cylinders bored to the proper diameter.

NOTE: *Oversize pistons have the oversize stamped on the piston crown. Oversize pistons are available in four oversizes from Honda (0.25, 0.50, 0.75, and 1.0 mm).*

New pistons come with the wrist pin and rings. If an oversize piston is needed due to a worn bore or worn or damaged pistons, obtain the piston first then take the piston and cylinders to your dealer or machine shop and have the cylinder bored so that the piston-to-cylinder wall clearance is 0.025-0.050 mm (0.001-0.002 in.).

7. Check the condition of the wrist pins. If the pins are blued or show indications of step-wear, they should be replaced. Usually, step-wear can be detected by running a fingernail along the length of the wrist pin. A more conclusive method is to measure the diameter of the pin at three places along its length and compare the readings.

On 400 models, standard wrist pin diameter is 16.994-17.000mm/0.6690-0.6693 in. The pins should be replaced if the measured diameter is less than 16.98mm/0.669 in.

On 450 models, standard wrist pin diameter is 17.994-18.000mm/0.7084-0.7087 in. Pins should be replaced if the measured diameter is less than 17.98mm/0.708 in.

8. Insert each wrist pin into its piston and check for play of the pin in the piston hole. There must be none. The pin must be a fairly tight fit. If the pin is easily inserted and can be turned or moved vertically with no effort, the pistons and pins should be replaced.

If an inside micrometer is available, measure the diameters of the wrist pin holes.

On the 400, standard hole diameter is 17.002-17.008mm/0.694-0.6696 in. The piston must be replaced if the hole measures 17.04mm/0.671 in. or more. On the 450, standard hole diameter is 18.002-18.008mm/0.7084-0.7087 in. The piston must be replaced if the hole measures 18.04mm/0.710 in. or more.

9. Maximum allowable piston-to-wrist pin clearance is 0.004 mm/0.0016 in. The value for your engine is obtained by comparing the measurements of the piston hole and that of the ends of the wrist pins.

10. Lightly oil each wrist pin and insert it into its connecting rod. Check for vertical play. There must be none. If play exists, or if the rod small end is discolored or the bore inner surface is scored or otherwise damaged, the rod and/or pin should be replaced.

On 400 models, standard small end bore diameter is 17.016-17.034 in. The rod must be replaced if diameter exceeds 17.06mm/0.672 in.

On 450 models, standard small end bore diameter is 18.016-18.034mm/0.7093-0.7100 in. The replacement limit is 18.06mm/0.732 in.

11. Check the connecting rods for a bent condition. This can be accomplished with two small rectangular blocks of metal of equal thickness. Insert the wrist pins into the rods, and position the pieces of metal beneath them on either side of the rods and resting on the crankcase. Rotate the engine so that the wrist pin rests on the blocks. Both sides of the wrist pin must contact the metal blocks, or the rod is bent and must be replaced.

12. Before installation, decarbonize the piston crowns. Remove any carbon from the ring grooves with a piece of broken ring or a very thin screwdriver. Be careful not to scratch the grooves.

Carefully check the cylinder, cleaning the bore thoroughly. If considerable mileage has been covered, honing the cylinders and fitting new rings is recommended. If the cylinders are honed, make a strenuous effort to clean them thoroughly afterwards, preferably with very hot soapy water and a stiff brush. This is to remove any abrasive particles deposited by the hone in the course of the operation.

Remove any traces of gasket material from the cylinder base and head mating surface.

13. Be sure that all oil passages in the cylinder are clear. Check the condition of the cam chain tensioner guides and replace them if damaged.

14. Replace the cylinder base O-rings. Check that any O-rings and the important dowel pins fitted to the cylinders are in their proper locations before installation.

15. Check the upper surface of the cylinders for warpage by laying a straightedge across them in several directions, and trying to slip feeler gauge blades between the cylinder block and the straightedge. Maximum allowable warpage is 0.10 mm/0.004 in. If a feeler gauge blade thicker than this will fit between the block and the straightedge, the block should be resurfaced.

This check is especially important in the event of a blown head gasket or oil leakage between the cylinder head and the cylinders.

PISTON RINGS

Two checks to be made on the piston rings are side clearance and end-gap. These checks should be made on both new and used rings.

1. Piston ring side clearance is applicable to compression rings only and it is checked with the rings installed on the piston. Insert a feeler gauge blade between the ring and the ring groove and check that the clearance is within the proper specification. They are as follows.

For the top compression ring, the standard side clearance is 0.03-0.06 mm/0.001-0.002 in. and the service limit is 0.10 mm/0.004 in.

For the seond compression ring, the standard clearance is 0.25-0.055 mm/0.0009-0.0022 in., and the service limit is 0.10 mm/0.004 in.

If the measured side clearance is greater than the service limit given, pistons or rings should be replaced. In actuality, a side clearance which is too small is also a defect, since the rings must be free to move around the piston. Sometimes a piston seizure will cause piston material to be pushed into the ring lands thus freezing the rings.

If the clearance is too large, the rings or grooves are worn. Check that the grooves are not carboned up. If new rings do not bring the side clearance to within the proper specification, pistons and rings should be replaced.

2. To remove the rings from the piston, use a ring spreader. Decarbonize the ring grooves.

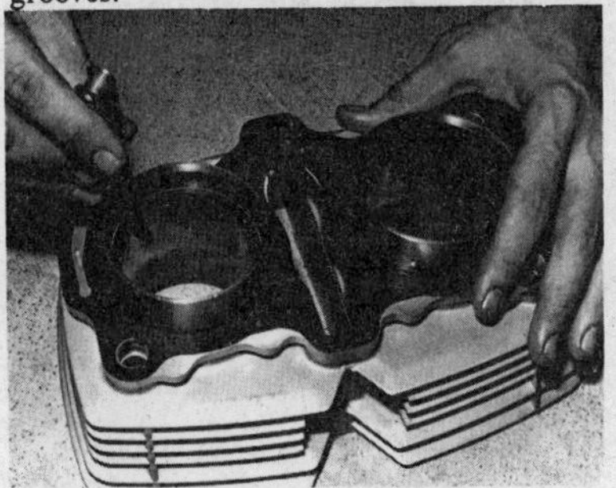

Measuring ring end-gap

Filing ring ends

3. To check the ring end-gap, ensure first that the cylinder bore is not excessively worn. Place each ring, in turn, into the bottom of its cylinder and push it in an inch or more using the piston skirt to align the ring in the bore. Measure the end-gap with a feeler gauge. If the end-gap is larger than the service limit, the rings must be replaced. If the measured end-gap of new rings is too large, the cylinder is worn and should be bored to the next oversize.

On 400 models, standard end-gap for the two compression rings is 0.2-0.4mm/0.008-0.016 in. The service limit is 0.60mm/0.024 in. On 450 models, standard end-gap for the two compression rings is 0.10-0.30mm/0.004-0.012 in. The service limit is 0.50mm/0.020 in.

For the oil scraper rails, the standard end-gap is 0.2-0.9 mm/0.008-0.035 in., and the replacement limit is 1.10 mm/0.043 in.

If new rings are fitted and the end-gap is too small, the ring ends must be filed. Hold the ring steady as illustrated, closing the ends over a thin, fine file. Do not squeeze the ring, as this is the easiest way to break it. A few strokes of the file will increase the end-gap.

Always install rings so that the letter near the end-gap faces up

CAUTION: *Do not make more than a few strokes before checking the end-gap again. It is easy to remove too much metal.*

Do not allow the file to slip out of the ring, as this risks breaking it.

4. Roll each ring around its own groove and ensure that this can be done easily. If a ring sticks or binds in the groove, the pistons must be replaced.

Cylinder and Piston Installation

1. When installing piston rings, note that all rings are installed with the manufacturer's mark (the small letter near the end-gap) facing *up*.

TOP

SECOND

OIL

Ring profiles. The top ring is chrome-plated

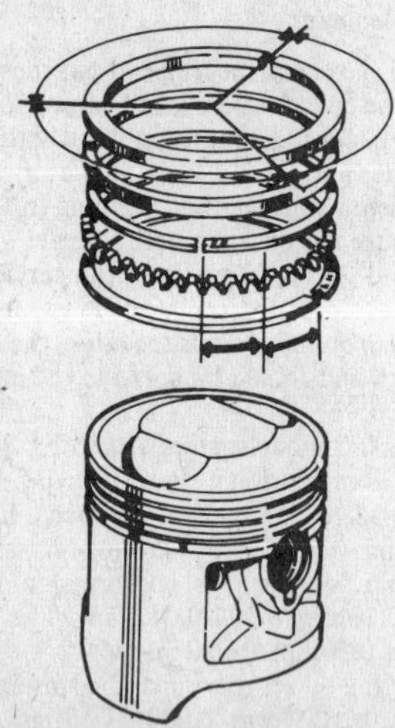

Ring end-gap positions with three piece oil ring

2. To install the three-piece oil ring, install one rail on the piston below the oil ring groove, fit the expander, then move the rail into place. Install the top rail. Note the illustration of the ring profiles. The top ring is chrome-plated.

3. Use a ring expander to install the rings to reduce the chance of breaking them.

Be sure to install the pistons with the "EX" mark on the exhaust side

Be sure that the circlip end-gap and piston cut-out (arrows) do not align

4. Ring end-gaps must be staggered around the piston so that they do not overlap. Position the end-gaps as shown in the illustration. Note that none of the end-gaps are positioned at the very front or sides of the piston.

5. Install the pistons on their connecting rods so that the "EX" marks on the crown face the front (exhaust side) of the engine.

NOTE: *Be sure to use new wrist pin circlips.*

6. Slip the wrist pins into place, heating the piston crown as on removal if necessary. Install the wrist pin circlips with a needle-nosed pliers. Be sure each circlips is firmly seated in its groove and arranged so that the circlip end-gap and the cut-out in the piston do *not* align.

7. Lubricate the rings and piston skirts with clean motor oil.

8. Install the dowel pins and oil control orifices in their proper locations.

9. Install the cylinders base gasket. Check that the cam chain is properly engaged with the crankshaft sprocket.

10. Install the cylinder, routing the cam chain up through its passage as the cylinders are lowered. Compress the piston rings with your fingers as the pistons enter the bores. Be sure the cylinders are firmly seated.

11. Install the cam chain guide.

12. Install the O-ring on the tensioner base bolt and fit the base onto the cylinder. Tighten the locknut with the tensioner base pulled up fully.

13. Install the tensioner on the tensioner base with the pin and clip.

CAUTION: *Stuff a clean rag into the cylinder cut-out to reduce the chances of dropping the pin or clip into the crankcases.*

Cylinder dowel pins and orifices (arrows)

Cylinder Head Installation

1. If the valves were removed from the head, install them now, using the spring compressor as on removal.
After the valves are installed, strike the end of each one with a plastic mallet to ensure that the keepers are properly seated.

2. Assemble the rocker arms and shafts and the cam holders, ensuring that each component is in its original location.

3. Install the dowel pins in the cylinder mating surface. Fit a new head gasket. Loosen the cam chain tensioner locknut and pull the tensioner up as far as possible. Tighten the locknut.

4. Install the cylinder head. Install the cam chain tensioner bolt, collar, and O-ring.

5. Pull the cam chain up through the cylinder head cut-out and secure it.

Method of fitting the cylinders without ring compressors

Fitting the cam chain guide

Rocker arm holder locating dowel pins (arrows)

Install the cam sprocket so that the index marks face the left side of the engine and the camshaft so that the notch on the end is also on the left

Align the "T" mark with the index mark for valve timing

The sprocket index marks (arrows) must be flush with the head mating surface when the alternator "T" mark is aligned

6. Thoroughly lubricate the cam bearings in the head. Place the cam sprocket alongside the cam chain and slip the camshaft through both of them. The notch on the end of the cam goes towards the left side of the engine.

Be sure that the sprocket is fitted with the timing marks towards the left side of the engine.

7. Turn the alternator rotor so that the "T" mark on the rotor is aligned with the stationary index mark.

8. Align the timing marks on the cam chain sprocket so that they are aligned with the head cover mating surface. Fit the cam chain over the sprocket, making sure that neither the crankshaft nor the sprocket are moved out of this alignment.

9. Turn the camshaft to align the sprocket bolt holes with the sprocket holes. When the rotor and sprocket marks are correctly aligned, the notch on the end of the cam should point straight up.

10. Using a non-permanent threadlocking compound on the cam sprocket bolts, install the bolts and tighten them to 13-16 ft lbs.

After installation, check that the valve timing marks on the alternator rotor and the cam sprocket can still be properly aligned.

11. Fit the oil passage dowel pins to their proper locations in the head. They are located at the four corners.

12. Lubricate the cam journals and lobes with fresh motor oil.

13. Install the cam holder and rocker arm assemblies.

14. Install the cylinder head bolts. Note that the four center bolts are fitted with copper washers. The front bolts are longer than the rear ones.

NOTE: *On 1980 and later models, the two inner cylinder head bolts on the left side are fitted with rubber oil seals. Be sure that these bolts are properly located.*

15. Tighten the head bolts gradually and in a cross pattern a few ft lbs at a time until the proper torque is reached.

Cylinder head bolts should be tightened to 22-24 ft lbs.

Tighten the four bolts in the center first, then the others.

NOTE: *Be sure that the head bolt threads are cleaned thoroughly before installation. Otherwise, the torque reading may be misleading.*

16. Install the external oil pipe assembly fitted to 450 models. Check that all seals and sealing washers are in place and properly installed. When tightening the oil line fitting bolts, be sure that the lines are not crimped. Hold them steady with a wrench as the bolts are secured.

17. Fill the cam lobe lubrication pockets with clean, fresh motor oil, and lube the rocker arm assemblies as well.

18. Adjust the cam chain tension, valve clearance, etc.

19. Install a new cylinder head cover gasket, then fit the cover itself, tightening the bolts to 6-9 ft lbs.

20. If the carburetor manifolds have been removed from the head, install them with the narrow end down. Ensure that the manifold O-rings are in good condition before installation. They must be properly seated in the groove.

CRANKCASE COVER COMPONENTS

Clutch (Manual Transmission)

NOTE: *A special tool is needed to remove the clutch hub nut.*

REMOVAL

1. Drain the oil.
2. Disconnect the tachometer cable from the crankcase cover, if fitted.
3. Run in the clutch cable adjusters, and disconnect the clutch cable from the lever on the crankcase cover.
4. Remove the right-side rider's footpeg.
5. Remove the kickstarter pinch bolt and carefully pull the lever from its splined shaft.
6. Remove the crankcase cover screws, and take off the cover. If the cover is stuck, carefully tap around the sides with a plastic mallet to break it free.
7. If removal of the clutch lever is desired, remove the clutch lifter, then the lever circlip and spring. Pull out the lever, noting the O-ring oil seal.
8. Gradually, and in a cross pattern, loosen the clutch lifter plate bolts until they are free.
9. Remove the bolts, lifter plate, and the clutch springs.
10. Prevent the engine from turning over by engaging the transmission and applying the rear brake, or a similar method.

Remove the clutch hub nut with the special tool. Remove the washer. Take the

Removing the clutch bolts (arrows) gradually and in a cross pattern

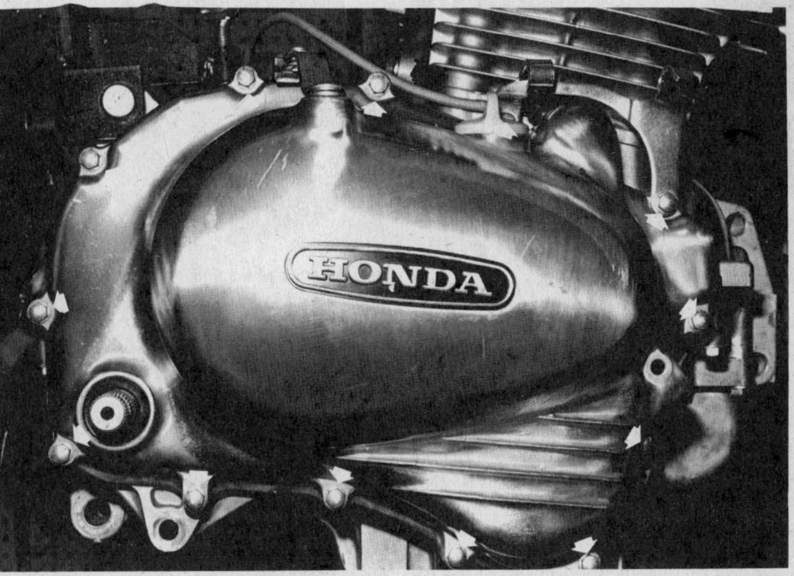

Right crankcase cover screws (arrows)

Right crankcase cover components

The outermost friction plate is different from the others

Removing the clutch plates

Removing the clutch springs

Removing the clutch thrust washer

The clutch hub nut must be removed with a special tool

Removing the clutch hub

clutch assembly out as a unit. Note the thrust washer on the shaft behind the clutch.

11. Remove the clutch plates from the clutch housing. Do not mix up the friction plates. The outermost friction plate is different (thicker) than the others.

INSPECTION

1. Check the condition of the kick-start shaft oil seal. If it leaks, or if the lips show signs of damage, pry the old seal out with a small screwdriver. Press the new seal straight into the cover. Apply some oil or grease to the seal lips before installation.

2. Check the condition of the clutch cover mating surface. Remove any burrs or imperfections with an oilstone.

3. Check the condition of the clutch lifter plate bearing. Oil the bearing and rotate it slowly. Rotation should be smooth, effortless, and noiseless. If the bearing sticks or binds, replace it.

Place the bearing on a flat surface and hold the outer race securely in place. Attempt to move the inner race back and forth. There should be no play. If any movement of the inner race is noted, replace the bearing. The bearing should also be replaced in the event of obvious damage, such as dented balls, scored races, or blue discoloration.

4. Measure the clearance between the clutch hub and the plain steel plate. It should be 0.1–0.5 mm/0.004–0.020 in. If the measurement is in excess of this limit, the spring should be replaced. This can be accomplished after the set ring is removed from the clutch hub.

5. Measure the free length of each clutch spring with a vernier caliper. Standard spring free length is 42.75 mm/1.683 in. The springs should be replaced as a set if any of them measures less than 41.25 mm/1.624 in.

6. Check the condition of the clutch friction plates. Replace the plates as a set if any of them show signs of damage to the friction material, excessive warpage, or damage to the engaging tabs.

7. Measure the thickness of each friction plate with a vernier caliper.

The standard thickness of the outermost friction plate is 3.0 mm/0.118 in. This plate should be replaced if the measured thickness is less than 2.60 mm/0.102 in.

The standard thickness of the other friction plates is 2.7 mm/0.106 in. Replace these plates as a set if any of them measures less than 2.30 mm/0.090 in.

8. Check the steel plates for scoring or blue discoloration and replace them if they are damaged.

9. Check each steel plate for warpage by

placing them on a flat surface, such as a piece of glass, and attempting to slip a feeler gauge blade between the plate and the surface. Maximum acceptable plate warpage is 0.20 mm/0.008 in. Replace any plate which is warped more than this amount.

10. Check the friction plate tabs for wear or damage. Check the clutch housing for indented wear caused by the tabs. Remove any burrs or grooves with a file or an oilstone. If the damage is severe, or grooves cannot be removed without removing a large amount of metal, replace the components.

11. Check the corresponding splines of the clutch hub and steel plates for indented wear. Remove any imperfections with a file or an oilstone.

12. Check the condition of the clutch housing gear teeth. Note any pitting or chipping. Check the primary gear teeth as well. If damage to either is noted, replace both. Since the gear teeth are hardened, damage is unlikely. Any wear to the teeth will be most evident at the very base of the teeth. Once the hardened surface wears off, wear of the remaining metal will be very rapid.

13. Check the clutch housing bushing for scoring or blue discoloration, and replace it if damaged. Check the outside diameter of the bushing and the inside diameter of the clutch housing.

The clutch housing bushing has a standard outside diameter of 32.950–32.975 mm/1.297–1.298 in. Replace the bushing if the measured diameter is less than 32.90 mm/1.295 in.

The clutch housing has a standard diameter of 33.000–33.025 mm/1.299–1.300 in. The housing should be replaced if the diameter measured is larger than 33.07 mm/1.302 in.

INSTALLATION

Installation is basically the reverse of removal. Note the following points.

1. If the clutch disc spring was removed, fit it by installing the spring seat, spring, the steel plate, and the set ring onto the clutch hub.

NOTE: *Be sure that the set ring is firmly seated in its groove.*

2. Assemble the clutch plates into the housing. Install the pressure plate first, then a friction plate. Alternate steel and friction plates until all are installed.

NOTE: *The last friction plate to be installed is the thickest of the lot.*

3. Install the clutch hub. Turn it slightly in either direction to align the splines with the plates. Be sure it is properly seated.

4. Be sure that the thrust washer is installed on the clutch shaft.

5. Install the bushing on the clutch shaft.

6. Install the clutch assembly.

7. Securing the engine sprocket so that the engine does not turn over, fit the clutch hub washer (the "Outside" stamped on the washer must face you as you install it), then the hub nut with the chamfered side facing the engine. Use the special tool to tighten the hub nut to 33–36 ft lbs.

8. Fit the clutch springs, lifter plate, and bolts. Tighten the bolts gradually, and in a cross pattern until they are secured.

9. If the clutch lever in the right crankcase cover was removed, install the o-ring,

Be sure to install the hub washer with the "Outside" facing outwards

then the lever, spring and circlip. Be sure that the circlip is properly seated.

10. Rotate the lever about 120° from the straight down position, until the holes in the lever and crankcase cover align, then fit the lifter.

11. Fit a new cover gasket, and install the cover. Tighten the bolts gradually and in a cross pattern. Adjust the clutch after the assembly is completed.

Torque Converter (Automatic Transmission)

NOTE: *Refer to the "Troubleshooting" at the end of "Engine and Transmission" before attempting to service the torque converter.*

REMOVAL

1. Removal of the right crankcase cover is not necessary if only the torque converter is to be removed.

2. Drain the oil from the crankcase.

3. Remove the torque converter case bolts. Remove the case. If it is stuck, tap it gently with a plastic mallet to free it. Do not strike it with great force. The case is located with dowel pins.

4. Pry the torque converter off its shaft with a screwdriver applied to the groove on the edge of the torque converter. Place a rag between the screwdriver and the crankcase mating surface to avoid damaging the gasket or the crankcase.

5. Remove the needle bearings from the shaft.

6. Note the location of the check valve which will protrude slightly from the crankcase to the right of the torque converter. The valve is spring loaded. Do not loose it.

INSPECTION

1. Be sure that all of the oil passages in the torque converter case are clear.

2. Measure the inside diameter of the converter case where the end of the shaft rides. Standard diameter is 13.000–13.018 mm/0.512.0–0.513 in. The replacement limit is 13.04 mm/0.513 in.

3. Check the condition of the bearing in the converter case. Bearing rotation should be smooth and effortless. If the bearing sticks or binds when it is rotated, or if it shows obvious signs of ball damage or blue discoloration, replace it. The bearing can be replaced by heating the case gently and evenly with a propane torch, or better yet, in an oven, and knocking the bearing out. Install the new bearing before the case cools. Be sure that it is pressed in as far as possible.

4. Measure the diameter of the torque converter shaft at its very end. Standard diameter is 12.966–12.984 mm/0.510–0.511 in. The shaft must be replaced if the measured diameter is less than 12.96 mm/0.510 in.

5. Compare the two measured diameters—that of the shaft end and the case inside diameter. The maximum allowable clearance is 0.08 mm/0.003 in.

6. Check the condition of the needle bearings. The rollers should be smooth and featureless. Note any pitting, discoloration, or flat spots. Note damage to the cages, and to the shaft surfaces that the rollers ride on. Replace the bearings if they are damaged.

7. Measure the diameter of the converter shaft in the area on which the needle bearings ride. Standard shaft diameter at this point is 24.974–24.993 mm/0.983–0.984 in. The shaft should be replaced if the measured diameter is 24.97 mm/0.983 in.

8. Check the torque converter seal ring for wear or damage, and replace it if necessary.

9. Pull out the check valve and spring from the crankcase. Check the check valve for scoring or wear and replace it if necessary. Measure the spring free length with a vernier caliper. Standard free length is 18.5 mm/0.73 in. The spring should be replaced if the measured length is less than 16.7 mm/0.66 in.

INSTALLATION

Installation is the reverse of removal. Note the following points.

1. Lubricate the needle bearings with clean motor oil, and install them on the shaft.

2. Install the torque converter by carefully engaging the primary drive and driven gears while holding the converter in place.

3. Set the transmission in gear, then rotate the rear wheel to align the splines of the torque converter and the converter shaft.

4. Engage the kickstarter driven gear on

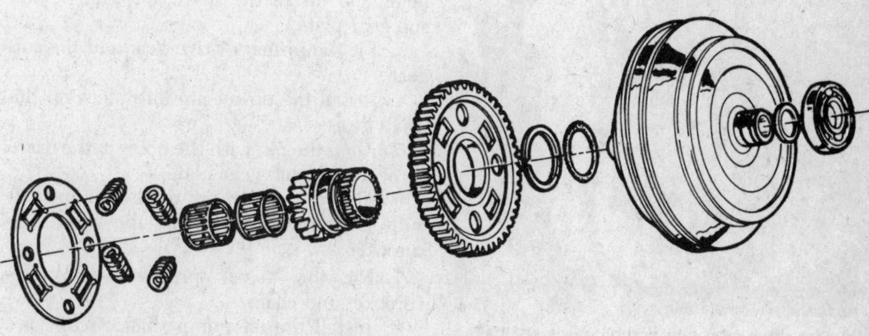

Torque converter assembly

the back of the torque converter with the kickstarter idler gear by operating the kickstarter lever slowly.

5. After installing the case gasket, be sure that the two dowel pins and the check valve are in place. Then install the case.

Right Crankcase Cover ("A" Models)

REMOVAL

1. Remove the torque converter as outlined above.
2. Remove the right-side rider's footpeg.
3. Remove the kickstarter pinch bolt and carefully pull the kickstarter from its splined shaft.
4. Remove the crankcase cover bolts. Remove the crankcase cover. If the cover sticks, carefully tap around its circumference with a plastic mallet to free it.

INSPECTION

1. Check the kickstarter shaft oil seal in the case. If the lips are torn, or if the seal leaks in operation, pry it out with a small screwdriver. Drive the new seal straight in. Remove any burrs from the kickstarter shaft and oil the seal lips before installation to ensure that no damage is done on installation.
2. Check the o-ring on the crankcase cover mating surface and replace it if it is knicked or crushed.
3. Check the crankcase cover mating surface for knicks or other damage. Slight imperfections can be removed with an oilstone.

INSTALLATION

Installation is the reverse of removal. Note the following points.

1. Use a new crankcase cover gasket, if the old one is damaged in any way.
2. Be sure that the two dowel pins are in place before fitting the cover.
3. Tighten the crankcase cover bolts gradually and evenly in a cross pattern until all are secured.

Primary Drive Gear (Manual Transmission)

REMOVAL

1. Remove the right crankcase cover.
2. Stop the engine from turning, and remove the primary drive gear bolt. Remove the oil pump drive gear circlip.
3. Pull off the chain and sprockets together.
4. Remove the primary drive gear.

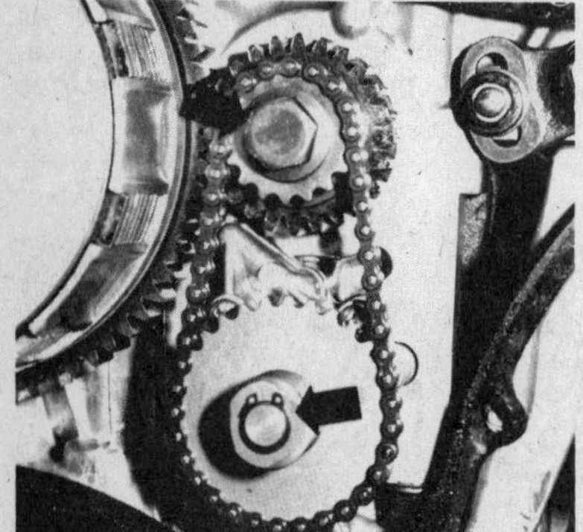

Primary drive gear bolt and oil pump shaft snap ring (arrows)

Removing the oil pump drive chain and sprockets

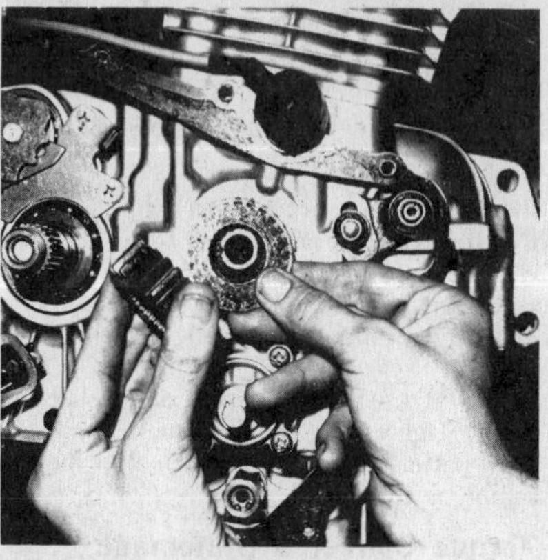

Removing the primary gear

INSTALLATION

1. Installation is the reverse of removal. Note that the oil pump sprocket is located by a pin on the oil pump shaft.
2. Note the thrust washer behind the primary drive gear. Tighten the primary gear bolt to 33–36 ft lbs.

Primary Drive Gear ("A" Models)

REMOVAL

1. Remove the right crankcase cover (see above).
2. Stop the engine from turning over, and remove the primary drive gear bolt.
3. Remove the oil pump drive sprocket circlip.
4. Remove the chain and sprockets together. Remove the sub gear spring, plate, the primary drive gear, and the thrust washer.

INSTALLATION

1. Installation is the reverse of removal. Be sure that the thrust washer is fitted onto the crankshaft with the chamfered inside diameter facing the engine.
2. Install the sub gear spring on the oil pump drive sprocket. Align the dowel pin holes and install the drive sprocket on the sub gear plate.
3. Fit the primary drive gear and the sub gear.
4. Install the dowel pin into place on the drive gear.
5. Align the pin with the holes in the drive sprocket and sub gear plate.
6. Align the dowel pin on the pump shaft with the dowel groove in the oil pump sprocket.
7. Fit the drive sprocket, oil pump sprocket and chain.
8. Install the oil pump shaft circlip, and ensure that it is properly seated.
9. Tighten the primary drive gear bolt to 33–36 ft lbs.

Oil Pump (All Models)

Refer to "Lubrication System," for oil pump removal, inspection, and installation.

Primary Driven Gear ("A" Models)

The primary driven gear, along with the kickstarter driven gear, are fitted to the back of the torque converter.

REMOVAL

1. Remove the torque converter. Refer to the section above.
2. Remove the four 6 mm bolts which secure the primary driven gear to the torque converter. Remove the side plate, damper springs, and the primary driven gear.

INSPECTION

1. Check the condition of the primary driven gear teeth. Look for chipped or worn teeth, and for pitting especially at the base of the teeth. Replace the gear if any damage is noted.
2. Measure the free length of each of the damper springs. Standard free length is 18.0 mm/0.71 in. The springs should be replaced as a set if any of them measures less than 16.0 mm/0.63 in.

INSTALLATION

Installation is the reverse of removal. Be sure that the damper springs are properly seated.

External Gearshift Mechanism (Manual Transmission)

REMOVAL

1. Remove the right side crankcase cover. Remove the clutch assembly. Refer to the preceding sections.
2. Remove the pinch bolt from the gearshift lever on the left side of the engine, and carefully pull the lever from its splined shaft.
3. Disengage the fingers of the shift arm from the shift drum pins and pull out the external gearshift mechanism.
4. Unbolt and remove the shift drum stopper arm.
5. Remove the shift drum stopper plate bolt, take off the stopper plate, the shift drum pins, and the collar.

External gear shift linkage

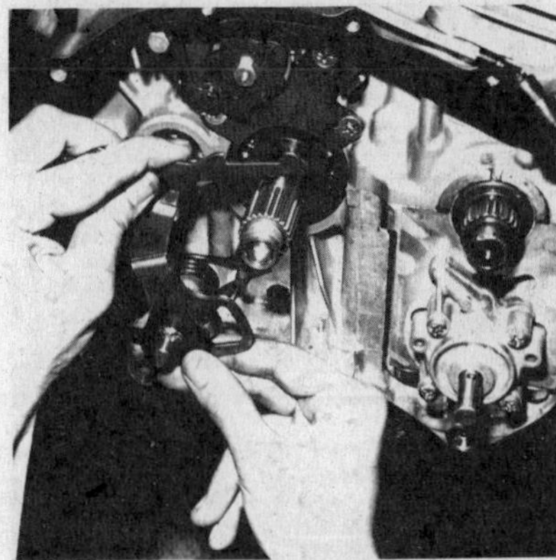

Removing the shift arm

Shift drum stopper arm bolt (white arrow) and stopper plate bolt (black arrow)

INSPECTION

1. Check the shift drum pins for damage. Replace any that are broken or chipped.
2. Check the splines on the gearshift shaft. If the splines are broken or torn to such an extent that it is difficult to properly secure the shift lever, replace the shaft. Make sure that the gearshift shaft is not bent.
3. Check the shift arm. Be sure that it is not bent. Check that the fingers of the shift arm are not worn or bent.
4. Check the condition of the springs in the shift linkage, especially the shift lever return spring. If any spring has lost its tension, or if it fails to hold its component properly, it must be replaced.

INSTALLATION

Installation is the reverse of removal. Be sure that the shift shaft return spring pawls are properly seated.

Use a non-permanent thread-locking compound on the threads of the shift drum stopper plate bolt. Tighten the bolt to 6–9 ft lbs.

Linkage/Kickstarter ("A" Models)

REMOVAL

1. Remove the torque converter. Remove the right side crankcase cover. Refer to the preceding sections.
2. The kickstarter friction disc assembly is fitted to the right side crankcase cover. To remove it, remove the circlip, and take off the friction disc and spring.
3. Remove the kickstarter gear from its shaft.
4. Remove the coil ring, thrust washer, idler gear, needle bearing, and countershaft collar from the shaft. Keep these components arranged in the order of removal, so that they can be easily reinstalled.

Be sure that the return spring is firmly seated

5. Remove the gearshift lever on the left side of the engine. Be sure not to damage the shaft splines when pulling the lever off.
6. Remove the gearshift arm spring.
7. Remove the kickstarter inhibitor arm and the thrust washer.
8. Pull out the gearshift shaft.
9. Remove the kickstarter stopper plate.
10. Pull out the kickstarter shaft.
11. Remove the kickstarter ratchet, spring, washer, collar, and starter spring.
12. Remove the shift drum stopper bolt and stopper assembly.
13. Remove the shift drum cam plate bolt and the cam plate. Remove the drum center.

INSPECTION

1. Check the condition of the kickstarter friction disc. Measure the depth of the oil groove. It should be no more than 0.1 mm/0.004 in. If the depth exceeds this limit, turn the friction disc around when installing it so that the other side is exposed to wear.
2. Check the condition of the teeth of all the gears. If any teeth are chipped or worn, or if there is pitting or the hardened surface has been worn away, replace that gear and the one with which it meshes.
3. Check the condition of the splines on the kickstarter shaft, and replace the shaft if they are torn or otherwise damaged.
4. Measure the inside diameter of the kickstarter gear. Standard diameter is 18.500–18.521 mm/0.7283–0.7292 in. Replace the gear if the inside diameter measures more than 18.54 mm/0.730 in.
5. Measure the diameter of the kickstarter shaft at that point on which the gear rides. Standard shaft diameter is 18.459–18.480 mm/0.7267–0.7276 in. The shaft should be replaced if the measured diameter is less than 18.44 mm/0.726 in.
6. Check the condition of all springs in the assembly, and replace them if they are broken, deformed, or show a lack of tension.
7. Check the condition of the shift arm fingers, and replace the arm if the fingers are chipped or worn, or if the arm is bent.
8. Check the condition of the needle bearing. Look for flatened or damaged rollers, blue discoloration, damaged roller cage, etc. Replace the needle bearing if any damage is noted.
9. Check the inner splines of the ratchet for the kickstarter shaft. Inspect the corresponding splines on the shaft. Replace either component if any damage is noted. The ratchet should be a good close fit on the shaft.
10. The kickstarter return spring should be checked. Replace it if it is broken, or if it no longer posses sufficient tension to hold the kickstarter lever securely against its stop.

INSTALLATION

Installation is the reverse of removal. Note the following points.

1. Install the gearshift drum center and the cam plate. Note that both are located by pins.
2. Install the drum stopper assembly. Use a non-permanent thread-locking compound on the threads of the stopper bolt. Secure the bolt to 6–9 ft lbs.
3. Install the kickstarter spring and collar onto the shaft.
4. Install the ratchet spring and ratchet on the shaft by aligning the punch marks on the ratchet and the shaft.
5. Install the thrust washer on the inner side of the kickstarter shaft and install it.
6. Engage the hook on the kickstarter return spring on the boss provided.
7. Install the kickstarter stopper plate so that the ratchet lug contacts the stopper plate by rotating the shaft with the kickstarter lever.
8. Install the gearshift shaft.
9. Install the kickstarter inhibition arm and the thrust washer.
10. Install the collar and needle bearing. While pressing the inhibitor arm into place on the shaft, install the kickstarter idler gear. Secure the idler gear with the thrust washer and coil ring.
11. Install the kickstarter gear.

Alternator (All Models)

REMOVAL

NOTE: *A special puller is needed to remove the alternator rotor.*

1. Remove the gearshift lever pinch bolt, and carefully pull the lever off its splined shaft to avoid damage to the splines.
2. Remove the left side crankcase cover.
3. Engage the transmission and apply the

Removing the alternator rotor bolt

Removing the rotor with the special puller

Alternator stator assembly

Removing the three phillips screws (arrows) to remove the stator. Do not touch the white painted screws

rear brake to prevent the engine from turning over on "T" and "E" models, or use the special holder which fits the alternator rotor. Remove the rotor bolt.

4. Use the special puller to remove the alternator rotor.

5. To remove the stator, disconnect the stator wiring from the connector behind the left side cover. Remove the three phillips screws which secure the stator.

CAUTION: *Do not loosen the two painted screws. This will affect ignition timing.*

INSTALLATION

1. Install the stator. It might be safe to use some non-permanent thread-locking compound on the stator mounting screws. Route the wiring properly, being sure that the grommet and clamp are doing their job.

2. Be sure that the alternator rotor woodruf key is in place, and push the rotor onto the crankshaft as far as possible after aligning the slot in the rotor with the key.

3. Install and tighten the rotor bolt torquing it to 70–90 ft lbs.

4. The remainder of the installation procedure is the reverse of removal.

Engine Sprocket (All Models)

REMOVAL

1. Remove the gearshift lever pinch bolt and carefully pull the lever from its splined shaft.

2. Remove the left crankcase cover bolts and remove the cover.

3. Loosen the two engine sprocket bolts.

4. Disconnect the rear drive chain at the masterlink.

5. Remove the engine sprocket bolts, turn the locking plate slightly to remove it from the shaft, then take off the engine sprocket.

INSTALLATION

Installation is the reverse of removal. Use a non-permanent thread-locking compound on the engine sprocket bolts and tighten them securely.

LOWER END AND TRANSMISSION

Splitting the Crankcases (Manual Transmission)

Splitting the crankcases is necessary to service the crankshaft balancer, crankshaft, connecting rods, transmission, kickstarter assembly, and internal gearshift mechanism.

1. Remove the engine from the frame.

2. Remove the left and right side crankcase covers and the components therein: clutch, alternator, engine sprocket, primary drive gear assembly, oil pump, external shift mechanism, etc.

3. If the crankshaft or connecting rods are going to be serviced, the top end components must be removed. If the transmission is the problem, these components can remain in place.

4. Remove the starter motor.

5. Turn the engine upside down. Gradually, and in a cross pattern, loosen each of the crankcase bolts.

6. Remove the lower case half. All of the components will remain in the upper case half, except for the kickstarter shaft assembly.

If the crankcase half is stuck, first ensure that all of the bolts have been removed. Tap gently around the edges of the lower case half with a plastic mallet to break it free.

There is a dowel pin at the rear of the engine which will remain in the lower case half. Do not loose it. Another, at the front of

Starter motor mounting bolts (arrows)

Lower crankcase half bolts

the engine, should remain in the upper case half. Note the o-ring locations as well.

CB 400A, CM 400A

Splitting the crankcases is necessary to service the crankshaft balancer, crankshaft, connecting rods, transmission, and internal gearshift mechanism.

1. Remove the engine from the frame.

2. Remove the left and right side crankcase covers.

3. To service the crankshaft and/or connecting rods, remove the top end components, oil pump chain, kickstarter idler gear, kickstarter gear, inhibitor arm, and the alternator. Refer to the appropriate sections above.

To service the crankshaft balancer only, the top end components may remain in place.

If only the transmission is to be serviced, the top end components may remain in place, and it is only necessary to remove the alternator and the kickstarter components.

4. Remove the oil pressure switch.

5. Turn the engine over. Remove the starter motor.

6. Remove the crankcase bolts. These should be loosened gradually and in a cross pattern to prevent possible warpage of the cases. Lift off the lower crankcase half. The major components will remain in the upper case half, with the exception of the kickstarter shaft assembly.

Note the location of the dowel pins and o-rings which will remain in the upper case half. Be sure that they are in position before assembly.

Case Assembly (All Models)

1. Be sure that the crankcase mating surface is clean and free of all traces of old gasket compound. Minor scratches or burrs can be removed with an oilstone, although care must be taken that the surface is not grooved when doing this.

2. Lubricate all bearing surfaces with motor oil.

3. Be sure that the crankshaft and transmission shafts are properly seated. The transmission shaft bearings are located with set rings or dowel pins. Be sure the shift forks are engaged with their gears.

4. Be sure that all dowel pins between the cases are in place.

5. Apply a thin coat of a liquid gasket compound to the case mating surface. Install the

lower case half. After ensuring that it is properly seated, install the crankcase bolts and tighten them gradually and in a cross pattern.

Tighten the 8 mm bolt to 15–22 ft lbs.

Tighten the 6 mm bolts to 7–10 ft lbs.

Transmission/Gear Shift Assembly (5-Speed)

REMOVAL

1. Before removing the gears from the crankcase, check the backlash of each set of meshing gears. This is done with a dial gauge by locking one gear in place and attempting to move the meshing gear relative to it.

Standard backlash is 0.045–0.140 mm/0.0018–0.0055 in.

Any set of gears whose measured backlash exceeds 0.20 mm/0.008 in. should be replaced.

Checking gear backlash

2. With the transmission shafts in place, remove the bearing holder and the rear balancer chain guide. Put the transmission in neutral if it is not there already. Measure the clearance between each set of gear dogs and the adjacent gear with a feeler gauge. Maximum allowable clearance is 0.30 mm/0.12 in. If the measured clearance exceeds this specification, replace the gears in question.

3. Remove the transmission shafts from the crankcase. Remove the oil oriface and dowel pin to prevent loss.

4. Remove the bearing stopper plate for the shift drum.

5. Mark the shift forks for location before removal. Remove the shift drum. Remove the shift fork shaft, shift forks, and guide pin.

6. Remove the snap-ring which secures the kickstarter shaft assembly. Remove the shaft and gear.

The kickstarter shaft components can be removed from the shaft.

INSPECTION

1. If disassembly of the gear shafts is required, be sure to lay out each piece in the order in which it is removed to facilitate reassembly.

2. Flush the transmission shaft bearings with clean motor oil and check operation. Bearing rotation must be smooth, effortless, and quiet. There must be no play between the inner and outer bearing races. If damage is noted, replace the bearings as a set.

3. Check the gear teeth for damage, wear, or pitting. Pay close attention to the very base of the teeth. Gears are surfacedhardened, and if this hardened layer is damaged, what is left will not last long. Check the engaging dogs and/or dog slots on each gear for chipping or wear. Check that splined gears are a good fit on their shaft (neither too loose nor too tight) and that the splines on the shafts and on the gears are in good condition. Check that gears with plain bores can rotate freely but are not too loose on their shafts. Check all parts for damage due to overheating or lack of lubricant.

NOTE: *Gears should always be replaced in pairs.*

4. The "Mainshaft" is the shaft to which the clutch is fitted. The "Countershaft" is the one with the engine sprocket on it.

Check the inside of the bores of the gears with plain holes in the middle. The bore surfaces should be smooth and featureless. If scoring is noted, replace the gear. If an inside micrometer is available, measure the inside diameters of these gears, and compare your readings to the following service limits:

For the mainshaft 4th and 5th gears, the maximum allowable inside diameters is 25.10 mm/0.988 in.

The mainshaft 4th gear is the second one from the clutch. The 5th gear is the fourth from the clutch.

For the countershaft 3rd gear, the maximum allowable bore diameter is 25.10 mm/0.988 in. This gear is located third from the engine sprocket.

For the countershaft 1st gear, bore diameter is 24.10 mm/0.949 in. This gear is fifth from the engine sprocket.

Replace any gear whose bore diameter exceeds these limits.

5. Check the inside and outside diameters of the countershaft 1st gear bushing. Maximum allowable inside diameter is 20.06 mm/0.790 in. Minimum allowable outside diameter is 23.95 mm/0.943 in.

Replace the bushing if it is not within specification, or if it is scored. The standard diameters for a new bushing are 20.020–20.041 mm/0.7882–0.7890 in. for the inside diameter, and 23.984–24.005 mm/0.9443–0.9451 in. for the outside diameter.

6. Measure the diameters of the main and countershafts at those areas on which the gears ride. Service limits are as follows:

At the middle of the mainshaft, the diameter should be no less than 24.93 mm/0.981 in.

At the very end of the countershaft, opposite the engine sprocket, the minimum allowable diameter is 19.96 mm/0.786 in.

At the middle of the countershaft, the diameter should be no less than 24.93 mm/0.981 in.

7. Compare the measurements of the gear bores and the shaft diameters. No gear should have more than 0.15 mm/0.006 in. of clearance where it rides on the shaft.

8. Measure the diameter of the shift drum where it rides in the crankcase. Standard diameter is 34.950–34.975 mm/1.3760–1.3770 in. The shift drum should be replaced if the measured diameter is less than 34.90 mm/1.374 in.

9. Measure the inside diameter of the crankcase where the shift drum rides. The standard case inside diameter is 35.000–35.025 mm/1.3780–1.3789 in. The crankcase should be replaced if the hole measures more than 35.05 mm/1.380 in.

10. Carefully inspect the shift fork shaft for damage or signs of wear. Roll the shaft along a flat surface to ensure that it is not bent. Replace it if it is.

11. Measure the diameter of the shift fork shaft at three places along its length. Standard shaft diameter is 12.966–12.984 mm/0.5105–0.5112 in.

Replace the shaft if the measured diameter is less than 12.95 mm/0.510 in.

12. Check each shift fork for damage or wear. The shift fork fingers should be in good condition. Replace the forks if the fingers are chipped or show other signs of wear. Measure the width of each finger with a micrometer. Standard thickness is 5.93–6.00 mm/0.233–0.236 in. The shift forks should be replaced if the thickness measured is less than 5.50 mm/0.217 in.

13. Measure the inside diameter of each shift fork if an inside micrometer is available. The standard bore diameter is 13.000–13.018 mm/0.5118–0.5125 in.

Replace any shift fork whose bore diameter exceeds 13.05 mm/0.514 in.

14. Check the kickstarter gear for obvious signs of damage such as wear or pitting of the teeth, worn or chipped ratchet teeth (on the sides of the gear), or wear or scoring of the bore. Replace it if necessary.

15. Measure the bore of the kickstarter gear. Standard bore diameter is 18.500–18.521 mm/0.7283–0.7292 in. Replace the gear if the bore diameter exceeds 18.54 mm/0.730 in.

16. Measure the diameter of the kickstarter shaft in the area on which the gear rides.

The standard shaft diameter at this point is 18.459–18.480 mm/0.7267–0.7276 in. Replace the shaft if the measured diameter is less than 18.44 mm/0.726 in.

17. Lubricate the shift drum bearing with some motor oil and rotate it to check operation. Bearing rotation should be smooth and effortless. Check the bearing for blue discoloration, damaged balls, and so on. Replace it as necessary.

18. Check the condition of the shift fork pins. Replace them if they are worn as might be indicated by a shiny appearance.

19. Check the corresponding shift fork pin grooves on the shift drum. Look for signs of excessive wear, and replace the drum if this is noted. Wear at this point is unlikely, except in extreme instances.

20. Check the condition of the kickstarter ratchet gear. Replace the gear if there is wear of the ratchet teeth, the internal splines, or the stopper arm.

INSTALLATION

1. Clean all of the components in a solvent and dry them thoroughly. After they are dry, lubricate them with clean motor oil.

2. Assemble the kickstarter shaft components. When installing the ratchet gear, be sure to align the punch mark on the side of the gear with the punch mark on the shaft. This is to locate the stopper arm.

3. Install the kickstarter shaft assembly in the lower crankcase half. Fit the snap ring. Be sure that it is firmly seated.

4. Install the shift drum. Fit the guide pins to the shift forks, and position them so that the shift fork shaft can be installed.

5. Install the shift drum bearing stopper plate. The plate is secured with three phillips

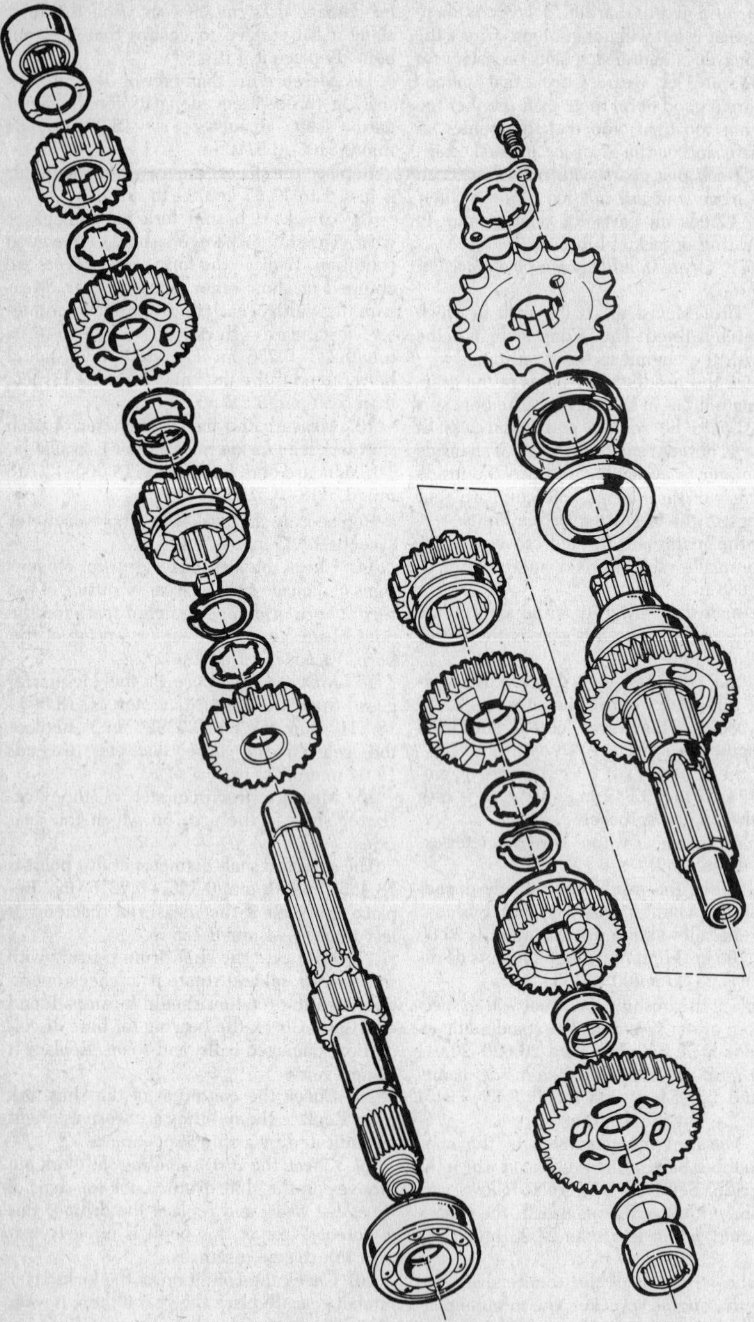
Transmission assembly (5-speed)

head screws which must be securely tightened, and then peened to lock them in place.

6. Assemble the transmission shaft assemblies. Be sure to use new circlips. Lubricate the bearings with motor oil before installation.

7. Be sure that the oil oriface and the bearing locator dowel pin are in place in the upper crankcase half before installing the transmission shafts.

8. Fit the mainshaft, aligning the marks on the needle bearing race with the crankcase mating surface.

9. Install the countershaft. Align the marks on the needle bearing race in the same manner as for the mainshaft, noting also that this bearing must fit over a locating dowel pin.

Be sure that both shafts are properly seated before installing the lower case half. Failure to do so may result in the dowel pin being pushed into the case. Then new crankcases will be needed.

10. Install the balancer chain guide.

11. Install the bearing holder. Be sure that the dowel pins are in place. Tighten the bolts as follows:

10 mm: 24–27 ft lbs.

6 mm: 7–10 ft lbs.

Torquing should be done gradually and in a cross pattern.

Transmission/Gear Shift Assembly (6-Speed)

Working and inspection procedures for the 6-speed transmission are basically the same as for the 5-speed outlined above, although the specifications differ. Service limits for the 6-speed transmission are as follows:

1. Maximum allowable backlash between any two gears is 0.20 mm/0.008 in.

2. Gear inside diameter (max) is 25.10 mm/0.988 in. for the mainshaft 5th, countershaft 3rd, and countershaft 4th gears.

Gear inside diameter for the mainshaft 6th gear is 28.10 mm/1.106 in. and for the countershaft 1st it is 24.10 mm/0.949 in.

3. Gear bushing outside diameter for the mainshaft 6th gear is 27.93 mm/1.100 in., and for the countershaft 1st gear it is 23.95 mm/0.943 in.

4. Gear bushing inside diameter for the countershaft 1st gear is 20.10 mm/0.791 in.

5. Mainshaft outside diameter is 24.93 mm/0.981 in.

6. Countershaft outside diameter at the countershaft 3rd and 4th gears is 24.93 mm/0.981 in. and at the countershaft 1st gear it is 19.95 mm/0.785 in.

7. Gear-to-shaft clearance for the mainshaft 5th, countershaft 3rd and countershaft 4th gears is 0.10 mm/0.004 in.

8. Gear-to-bushing clearance is 0.10 mm/0.004 in. for the mainshaft 6th gear and 0.07 mm/0.003 in. for the countershaft 1st gear.

9. Shift fork finger thickness is 5.85 mm/0.230 in. for the mainshaft 3rd and 4.85 mm/0.191 in. for countershaft 5th and 6th.

10. Shift fork inside diameter is 13.05 mm/0.514 in.

Refer to the 5-speed section for details of the inspection procedure if necessary.

Transmission/Gear Shift Assembly ("A" Models)

NOTE: *Before suspecting the 400A of trouble, be sure to refer to the "Troubleshooting" charts at the end of "Engine and Transmission" for diagnostic help. This may help to pinpoint the exact source of the trouble.*

REMOVAL

1. Remove the engine from the frame.
2. Separate the crankcase halves.
3. Check the backlash of each pair of meshing gears. This is done with a dial indicator. Lock one gear in place, and position the indicator to register movement of the other gear.

Standard backlash is 0.045–0.140 mm/0.0018–0.0055 in. Replace any set of gears which show more than 0.20 mm/0.008 in. of backlash.

4. With the transmission in Neutral measure the gear dog clearances with a feeler gauge. Replacement limit is 0.3 mm/0.012 in.

5. After these checks have been carried out, continue the disassembly procedure by removing the shift drum stopper plate. Remove the main and countershafts.

6. Remove the stator from the mainshaft. Remove the needle roller bearing and the ball bearings.

7. To disassemble the countershaft, remove the oil seal, needle bearing, and 2d gear. Lay the parts out in the order removed to facilitate reassembly.

8. Carefully remove the clip, gearshifter, and the steel balls.

NOTE: *There are 45 of the steel balls. Do not lose any.*

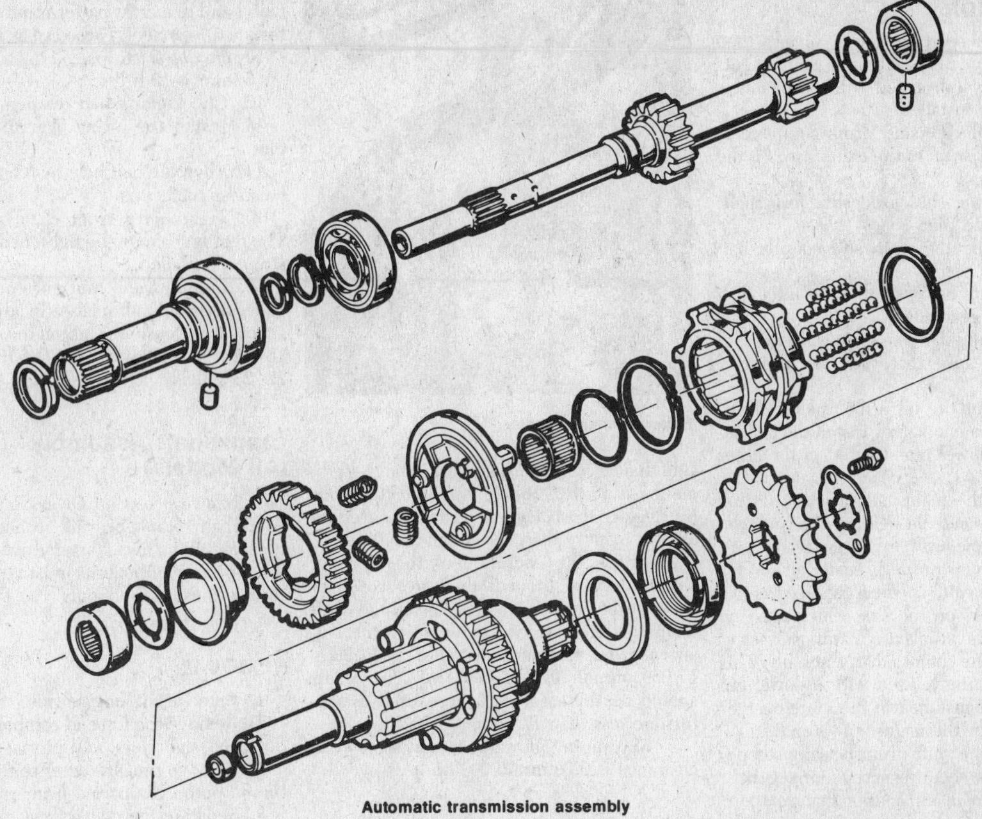

Automatic transmission assembly

9. Remove the gear center, damper springs, and shifter plate from the 2d gear.

10. Remove the change switch from the right side of the upper crankcase half.

11. Remove the gearshift fork shaft and the shift fork. Remove the shift drum.

12. Remove the bearings, spacer, and neutral switch cam from the drum.

INSPECTION

1. Check the condition of the kickstarter shaft splines, and replace the shaft if they are damaged or torn.

2. Check the condition of the kickstarter gear. Note any damage to the teeth or wear or chipping of the ratchet teeth on the side of the gear. Replace it as necessary.

3. Measure the diameter of the kickstarter shaft at that point on which the gear rides. Standard shaft diameter is 18.459–18.480 mm/0.7267–0.7276 in. Replace the shaft if the diameter measures less than 18.44 mm/0.726 in.

4. Measure the inside diameter of the gear bore. Standard diameter is 18.500–18.521 mm/0.7283–0.7292 in. Replace the gear if the measured diameter is more than 18.54 mm/0.730 in.

5. Oil the mainshaft and stator shaft bearings lightly and check their operation. Bearing movement should be smooth and effortless. If the bearing sticks or binds, or if there exist obvious signs of damage to the balls or discoloration, replace the bearing(s).

6. Check the seal rings on the shafts for wear or damage and replace as necessary.

7. Measure the diameter of the mainshaft. Standard diameter is 15.966–15.984 mm/0.6286–0.6293 in. Replace the shaft if the measured diameter is less than 15.95 mm/0.628 in.

8. Measure the inside diameter of the stator shaft bushing. Standard bushing diameter is 16.000–16.018 mm/0.6299–0.6306 in. The bushing must be replaced if the measured diameter exceeds 16.05 mm/0.632 in.

9. Check the gearshifter balls for dented or pitted condition, and replace them as a set if any are unserviceable.

10. Measure the outside diameter of the countershaft. The standard diameter is 19.980–19.993 mm/0.7866–0.7871 in. at the narrow portion of the shaft and 24.994–25.007 mm/0.9840–0.9845 in. at the step. Replacement limits are 19.95 mm/0.785 in. and 24.97/0.983 in. respectively.

11. Measure the gearshifter groove width. The standard width is 6.10–6.18 mm/0.240–0.243 in. Replace the gearshifter if the width exceeds 6.4 mm/0.25 in.

12. Check the gearshifter assembly needle bearings for discoloration, flattened or pitted rollers, damaged cages, etc. Replace them as necessary, as a set.

13. Measure the gear center inside diameter. Standard diameter is 30.014–30.027 mm/1.1817–1.1822 in. If the gear center bore is scored, or if the inside diameter exceeds 30.04 mm/1.183 in., replace it.

14. Inspect the gearshifter and shifter plate dogs for chipping or wear, and replace them if any is noticed.

15. Measure the free length of each of the gear damper springs. Stock free length is 13.9–14.7 mm/0.547–0.579 in. Replace the springs as a set if the measured free length of any one of them is less than 13.3 mm/0.52 in.

16. Check the condition of the 2d gear teeth, and replace the gear if any of the teeth are chipped or damaged, or if there is pitting or wear of the hardened gear surfaces. Pay special attention to the area at the very base of the teeth.

17. Check the condition of the gear shift fork shaft. Roll the shaft along a flat surface to ensure that it is not bent. Replace it if it is. Measure the diameter of the shaft at three places along its length. Standard shaft diameter is 12.973–12.984 mm/0.5107–0.5112 in. The shaft should be replaced if any of the three measurements is less than 12.97 mm/0.510. The shaft should also be checked for step wear and replaced accordingly.

18. Check the condition of the shift fork fingers, and replace the fork if the fingers are cracked or chipped or show obvious signs of wear. Measure the finger width. Standard width is 5.9–6.0 mm/0.232–0.236 in. The fork should be replaced if the measured width is less than 5.8 mm/0.228 in.

19. Check the condition of the shift fork roller pin. The pin should be replaced if it is worn, or if the diameter is less than 5.93 mm/0.233 in.

20. Check the inside and outside diameters of the pin roller. Replace the roller if the outside diameter measures less than 9.8 mm/0.386 in., or the inside diameter more than 6.15 mm/0.242 in.

21. Inspect the shift drum bearings. Replace the bearings as a set if either of them shows signs of discoloration, dented or pitted balls, rough rotation, play of the outer bearing race, etc.

22. Measure the guide groove width on the shift drum. Standard width is 10.05–10.15 mm/0.396–0.400 in. Replace the drum if the measured width exceeds 10.4 mm/0.41 in.

INSTALLATION

1. Clean all parts in a safe solvent, then dry thoroughly. Be sure that all components are thoroughly lubricated with clean motor oil as they are installed.
2. Assemble the shift drum components and install the drum in the crankcase. Fit the change switch.
3. Install the shift fork, shift fork shaft, guide roller and pin.
4. Assemble the main and countershaft assemblies.
5. Install five (5) steel balls into each groove of the gearshifter.
6. Install the damper springs into the 2d gear, making sure that they are properly seated.
7. Blow out the oil orifice in the mainshaft seat of the crankcase. Install the orifice, and the two dowel pins located in the other shaft seats.
8. Install the mainshaft carefully, fitting the hole in the needle bearing race into the dowel pin previously mentioned. Be sure that the bearing is properly seated or serious damage may result. The bearing race has two reference marks on the side which must be aligned with the crankcase mating surface.
9. Install the countershaft assembly. This also has a bearing located with a dowel pin which must be installed in the same manner as described for the mainshaft (Step 8).
10. Install the shift drum bearing stopper plate. Peen the securing screws for security.
11. Check main and countershaft rotation.
12. The remainder of the procedure is the reverse of removal. Be sure that all components, especially the bearings, are well lubricated before installing the lower crankcase half.

Crankshaft Balancer (All Models)

REMOVAL

1. Remove the engine from the frame.
2. Split the crankcases. If the balancer alone is to be serviced, the top end components can remain in place. If crankshaft or connecting rod service is the ultimate aim, the top end must be removed. Refer to the preceding sections for operating procedures.
3. Remove the oil filter screen.
4. Remove the bearing holder bolts.
5. Remove the front chain guide.
6. Take out the rear balancer shaft and the balancer.
7. Remove the oil orifice. Remove the rear chain guide. Remove the cam chain tensioner.
8. Remove the 8 mm and 10 mm nuts and the balancer stopper plate.
9. Remove the balancer clip and spring. Remove the front balancer shaft and the chain.
10. Remove the circlip and side plate from the balancer. Remove the sprockets and damper rubbers.

INSPECTION

1. Check the damper rubbers for damage such as cracks or a crushed condition. Replace them as a set if they do not appear to be in serviceable condition.
2. Check the inside diameter of the balançers for scoring. Replace it if the surface is not smooth and featureless. Measure the inside diameter of the balancers. Standard diameter is 18.010–18.028 mm/0.7090–0.7098 in. Replace the balancers if the measured diameter is more than 18.04 mm/0.710 in.
3. Check the condition of the balancer shafts. Replace them if they are scored or show other visible damage. Check the shaft diameters at those points on which the balancers ride. Standard diameter is 17.966–17.984 mm/0.7073–0.7080 in. The shafts should be replaced if the measured diameters are less than 17.95 mm/0.707 in.
4. Maximum allowable balancer-to-shaft clearance is 0.08 mm/0.003 in.

Balancer chain adjuster

INSTALLATION

NOTE: *Clean all metal parts in a safe solvent, then dry thoroughly. Be sure that all bearing surfaces are lubricated with motor oil or assembly lubricant before installation.*

1. Fit the damper rubbers to the balancers.
2. Install the sprockets, noting that the side with the spacer faces the balancer.

Be sure to align the marks on the balancer and sprocket.

3. Assemble the front balancer, chain, and shaft.
4. Position the punch mark on the end of the shaft at 10 o'clock and install the spring. Rotate the shaft to 6 o'clock. Install the stopper plate with the stud bolt centered in the plate groove. Tighten the 10 mm nut temporarily.
5. Rotate the stopper plate clockwise as far as possible. Tighten the 8 mm nut.
6. Install the cam chain tensioner. Assemble the rear chain guide and oil orifice.
7. Align the front balancer "TC" mark and the crankshaft aligning mark with the crankcase mating surface. Install the chain so that the rear balancer "TH" mark is also aligned with the crankcase mating surface.
8. Check that the dowel pins and bearing inserts are in place in the bearing holder. Install the rear balancer in the bearing holder by inserting the shaft.
9. Fit the front chain guide.
10. Install the bearing holder. With the front balancer "TC" mark aligned with the crankcase mating surface, check that the rear balancer "TH" mark is aligned with the bearing holder shoulder and that the crankweight mark is flush with the crankcase mating surface.
11. Tighten the bearing holder bolts gradually, and in a cross pattern, until the proper torque is reached. These are as follows:

10 mm: 24–27 ft lbs.
6 mm: 7–10 ft lbs.

12. Check crankshaft rotation.
13. Install the o-ring over the oil screen pipe.
14. Align the bolt hole by rotating the rear balancer shaft.
15. Tighten the front chain guide bolts. The rear bolt should be tightened with the oil strainer installed.
16. Loosen the 8 mm nut on the stopper plate. This will automatically adjust the balancer chain tension. Tighten the 8 mm nut to 15–18 ft lbs. Then tighten the 10 mm nut to 22–25 ft lbs.

Crankshaft Assembly (All Models)

The following section covers service to the crankshaft, crank bearing, connecting rods, starter clutch, and starter drive. Note that the top end components must be removed to service these components.

REMOVAL

1. Remove the engine from the frame.
2. Remove the top end components: cylinder head, cylinders, and pistons.
3. Remove the alternator stator and rotor, the oil pump chain, and primary drive.
4. Separate the crankcases.
5. Remove the bearing holder and the balancer assembly. Refer to the preceding section.
6. Before removing the crank assembly, check the connecting rod side clearance. Big end clearance (between the rod and the crank flywheel), can be measured with a feeler gauge blade. Standard clearance is 0.05–0.25 mm/0.002–0.010 in. The rods should be replaced if the measured clearance exceeds 0.35 mm/0.14 in.
7. Unbolt and remove the connecting rods. Mark the rods "L" or "R" so that they will be installed on their correct crankpin during assembly. Also, do not interchange caps between rods, or reverse the position of the cap relative to its own rod. Note that the oil holes at the base of the connecting rods point towards the rear of the engine. It is imperative that they be installed correctly.

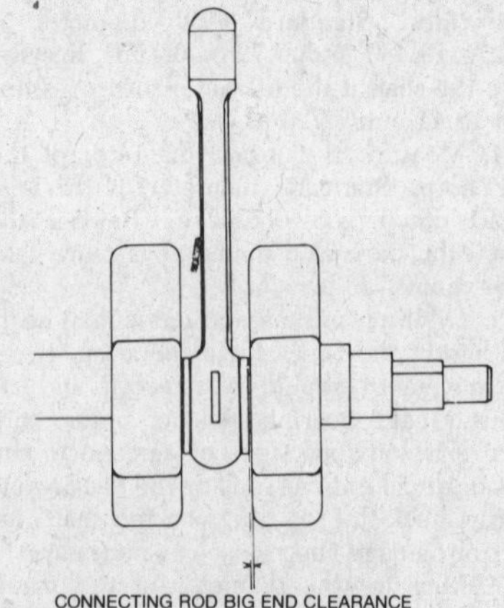

Check con rod big end clearance

8. To remove the crankshaft from the case, simply lit it out, being careful that the chains do not catch on anything.

9. To remove the starter clutch from the crankshaft, a special tool is needed (No. 07703-0010200). Remove the oil seal, the starter drive gear, the "torx" bolts, and finally the starter clutch.

INSPECTION

1. Check the starter clutch for cracks. Check the roller condition and replace them if obvious signs of wear are evident.

2. Check the condition of the starter drive gear teeth, and replace the gear if any are chipped or broken. Measure the outside diameter of the drive gear. Standard diameter is 54.170–54.200 mm/2.1327–2.1339 in. Replace the gear if the diameter measures less than 54.15 mm/2.132 in.

3. Check crankshaft run-out. Mount the crankshaft in a set of v-blocks, and afix a dial indicator to the center main bearing journal. Rotate the crank and check run-out. If it exceeds 0.05 mm/0.002 in., the crank must be replaced.

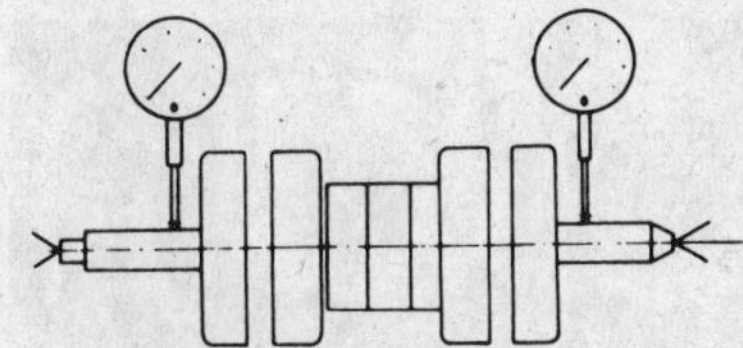

Checking crankshaft run-out

4. To remove the starter idler gear, remove the securing bolt and pull out the shaft. Check the gear for wear or damage in the normal manner. Measure the bore of the gear. If it exceeds 16.05 mm/0.632 in., the gear should be replaced.

Check the shaft for scoring or step-wear, and replace it if necessary. The shaft diameter should not be less than 15.95 mm/0.628 in.

The maximum allowable clearance between the shaft and the gear is 0.1 mm/0.004 in.

5. Standard connecting rod bearing clearance is 0.020–0.044 mm/0.0008–0.0017 in. Check this clearance with plastigauge. Con rod bolts should be torqued to 18–21 ft lbs during this procedure. If the clearance exceeds 0.08 mm/0.003 in., new bearing inserts are required.

6. Make a visual inspection of the con rod journals on the crankshaft. These journals should be absolutely free of score marks or other signs of wear. If very minor scoring is evident, it should be removed with emery tape. Since the journal surfaces are very hard, however, anything more than minor scoring will require extensive service work. Con rod bearings must also be smooth and featureless. Even seemingly minor marks, usually visible as parallel lines on the bearing surface, will require replacement.

7. Con rod bearing replacements are color coded. First, check the bearing insert ID mark on the side of the rod cap. Then check the crackpin diameter ID mark on the bottom edge of the outermost flywheels. The last number is the crankpin code.

Find the proper bearing insert according to the following chart:

Crankpin Code

Connecting Rod ID	1	2	3
1	E (Yellow)	D (Green)	C (Brown)
2	D (Green)	C (Brown)	B (Black)
3	C (Brown)	B (Black)	A (Blue)

Bearing insert thicknesses are as follows:
A (Blue): 1.502–1.506 mm
B (Black): 1.498–1.502 mm
C (Brown): 1.494–1.498 mm
D (Green): 1.490–1.494 mm
E (Yellow): 1.486–1.490 mm

8. Check main bearing clearance with plastigauge.

Standard clearance is 0.020–0.044 mm/0.0008–0.0017 in. Maximum allowable clearance is 0.08 mm/0.0003 in. If the bearing inserts or journals show signs of wear or score marks which cannot be easily removed with emery tape, the bearing inserts must be replaced.

9. Bearing insert replacements are color coded. To determine the correct insert to use, proceed as follows.

Check the bearing holder insert ID letter stamped on the bearing holder for each bearing. They are arranged from left to right for the left, center, and right journals respectively.

Then check the letter code for the crank journal ID. These are stamped on the outer flywheels just above the con rod journal codes.

Determine the correct bearing insert by referring to the following chart:

Journal Code

Holder Code	A	B	C
A	E (Yellow)	D (Green)	C (Brown)
B	D (Green)	C (Brown)	B (Black)
C	C (Brown)	B (Black)	A (Green)

Bearing insert thicknesses are as follows:
A (Blue): 1.502–1.506 mm
B (Black): 1.498–1.502 mm
C (Brown): 1.494–1.498 mm
D (Green): 1.490–1.494 mm
E (Yellow): 1.486–1.490 mm

INSTALLATION

1. Install the springs, plungers, and rollers to the starter clutch. Oil the assembly lightly.

2. Fit the starter clutch to the crankshaft, aligning the dowel pin which locates the clutch.

Tighten the "torx" bolts to 9–10 ft lbs.

NOTE: *Use a non-permanent thread-locking compound on the bolt threads.*

3. Install the starter gear.

Engine Torque Specifications

Part	Torque (ft lbs)
Cylinder head cover bolt	6–9
Tappet adjuster nut	9–12
Cylinder head bolt	22–24
Cam sprocket bolts	13–16
Spark plugs	11–14
Primary drive gear bolt	33–36
Clutch hub nut	33–36
Balancer Nuts	
8 mm	15–18
10 mm	22–25
Alternator rotor bolt	70–90
Crankshaft bearing holder (10 mm)	24–27
Connecting rod nuts	18–21
Oil filter	20–23
Oil drain plug	18–25
Exhaust pipe flange	6–9

Standard Torque Specifications ①

Bolt/Nut	Torque (ft lbs)
5 mm bolt/nut/screw	3–4
6 mm	6–9
8 mm	13–18
10 mm	22–29
12 mm	36–43
6 mm screw	5–8
6 mm flanged	7–10
8 mm flanged	14–22
10 mm flanged	22–29

① Unless otherwise noted.

If the starter idler gear has been removed, install the o-ring on the idler gear shaft, and fit the shaft and gear into the case. Align the bolt hole in the shaft with the hole in the case by rotating the shaft with a screwdriver. Tighten the bolt securely.

4. Fit a new oil seal on the end of the crankshaft. Lubricate the lips and edges of the seal to ease installation.

5. Install the cam chain.

6. Lubricate the crank journals and the connecting rod journals with motor oil or an assembly lubricant.

7. Install the connecting rods. Be sure that each con rod cap is matched with its proper rod and is properly installed on that rod. Match up the rod and cap ID numbers. nstall the rods on the crankpins so that the oil holes in the rods point towards the rear of the engine.

Tighten the con rod bolts to 18–21 ft lbs. These bolts should be tightened gradually and evenly.

8. Install the bearing holder as outlined under "Balancer" removal and installation, above. Tighten the fasteners as follows:

10 mm:24–27 ft lbs.
6 mm: 7–10 ft lbs.

9. Be sure that the cam chain is properly fitted on the sprocket.

Transmission Troubleshooting (CB/CM 400A)

Problem	Possible Causes	Inspection/Remedy
Engine does not stall during stall test	Lack of oil	Check level.
	Converter regulator valve missing	See text.
	Regulator valve stuck open	Clean or replace.
	Clogged oil passages	Bow clear.
	Oil pump defective	Replace.

Transmission Troubleshooting (CB/CM 400A) (cont.)

Problem	Possible Causes	Inspection/Remedy
	Broken oil pump chain	Replace.
	Damaged primary drive gear	Replace.
	Damaged oil pump sprocket	Replace.
	Torque converter pump flange or boss or rivet damaged	Replace.
Engine does not stall in one gear during stall test	Gearshifter place or shifter dog damaged	Replace. Refer to Chapter 4.
Motorcycle will not run in 1st and will not stall	Damaged 1st gear	Replace. Refer to Chapter 4.
	Damaged 1st gear shifter plate or dog	Replace.
Motorcycle will not run in 2nd and will not stall	Damaged 2d gear	Replace.
	Damaged 2d gear shifter plate or dog	Replace.
Motorcycle will not run in 2nd, does stall, but will not start	Burned or seized 2d gear	Replace.
Stall speed too high with hard starting or poor performance	Clogged oil orifice	Clean.
	Pressure regulator valve stuck	Clean or replace.
	Weakened or damaged regulator valve spring	Replace.
Stall speed normal, but engine is hard to start or has poor performance	Burnt or seized gear or bearing on main or countershaft	Check shafts and gear assemblies.
Stall speed too low or fluctuating with hard starting or poor acceleration	Seized or damaged primary drive gear	Replace.
	Seized or damaged primary driven gear	Replace.
	Damaged stator shaft, gear, or bearing	Replace.
	Converter cam slipping	Replace.
	Damaged cam or roller spring	Replace.
Poor high-speed acceleration, but normal stall speed	Engine oil level too high	Fill to correct level.
	Free-wheeling cam seized	Replace.
Poor acceleration with stall speed too low or fluctuating	Damaged free-wheeling cam or roller spring	Replace.

Oil pump drive chain and sprockets

Oil pump mounting screws (arrows)

LUBRICATION SYSTEM

OIL PUMP

Removal

"T" AND "E" MODELS

1. Drain the oil from the crankcase.
2. Disconnect the tachometer cable from the right crankcase cover, if fitted.
3. Run down the clutch cable adjusters, and disconnect the clutch cable from the lever on the right crankcase cover.
4. Remove the right side rider's footpeg.
5. Remove the kickstarter lever pinch bolt, and carefully pull the lever from its splined shaft.
6. Remove the right crankcase cover bolts and remove the cover. If it is stuck, tap around the sides gently with a plastic mallet to free it.
7. Prevent the engine from turning over by placing the transmission in gear and applying the rear brake. Remove the primary gear bolt.
8. Remove the circlip from the oil pump shaft. Remove the sprockets and chain.
9. Remove the mounting screws and take off the oil pump.

"A" Models

1. Drain the oil from the crankcase.
2. Remove the torque converter case bolts. Remove the case. If it is stuck, tap it gently with a plastic mallet to free it. Do not strike it with great force. The case is located with dowel pins.
3. Pry the torque converter off its shaft with a screwdriver applied to the groove on the edge of the converter. Place a rag between the screwdriver and the crankcase mating surface to avoid damaging the gasket or crankcase.
4. Remove the right-side rider's footpeg.
5. Remove the kickstarter pinch bolt and carefully pull the lever from its splined shaft.
6. Remove the crankcase cover bolts. Remove the crankcase cover. If it is stuck, carefully tap around its circumference with a plastic mallet to free it.
7. Stop the engine from turning over and remove the primary gear bolt. Remove the circlip from the oil pump shaft. Remove the sprockets and chain together.
8. Remove the mounting screws and take out the oil pump.

Inspection

ALL MODELS

1. Remove the oil pump gasket.
2. Remove the two phillips screws which secure the back of the pump and take off the back. Remove the thrust washer from the shaft.
3. Remove the pin from the oil pump

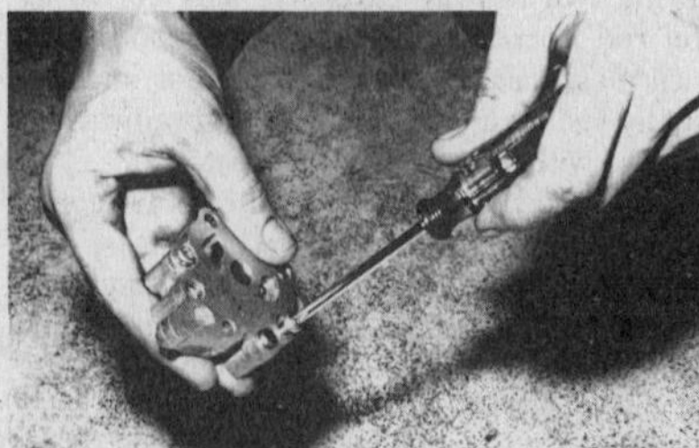
Pump cover screw removal

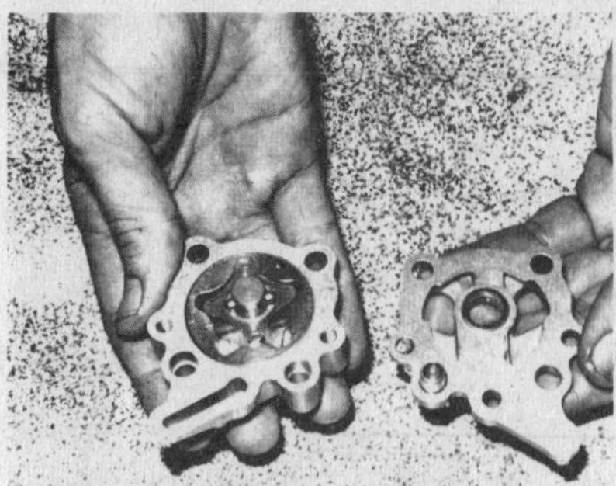

Separating the pump and cover. Do not loose the shaft shim

shaft. Pull out the shaft. Remove the inner and outer rotors from the pump body.

4. Measure the clearance between the tip of the inner rotor and the outer rotor. If the measured clearance exceeds 0.10 mm/0.004 in., replace both rotors.

5. Measure the clearance between the outer rotor and the pump body. If the clearance exceeds 0.35 mm/0.014 in., replace the rotors and pump body.

6. Place a straightedge across the back of the oil pump and measure the side clearance between the rotors and the straightedge. If the clearance exceeds 0.10 mm/0.004 in., replace the assembly.

Installation

ALL MODELS

1. Clean all parts thoroughly in a safe solvent and dry thoroughly. Lubricate all parts with fresh motor oil during the assembly procedure.

2. Install the pin which drives the inner rotor into the shaft if it has been removed.

3. Install the inner and outer rotors onto the drive shaft. Note that the punch marks on the rotors should face the same direction.

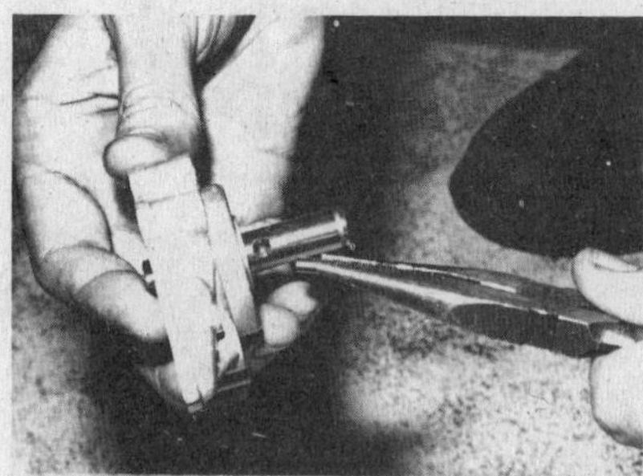

Removing the drive shaft pin

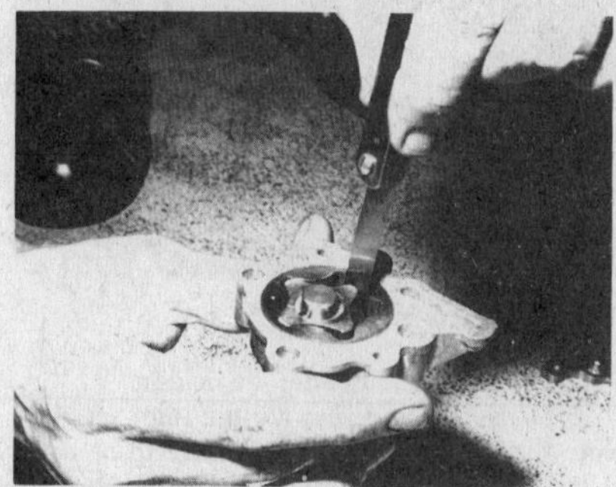

Measuring inner rotor-to-outer rotor clearance

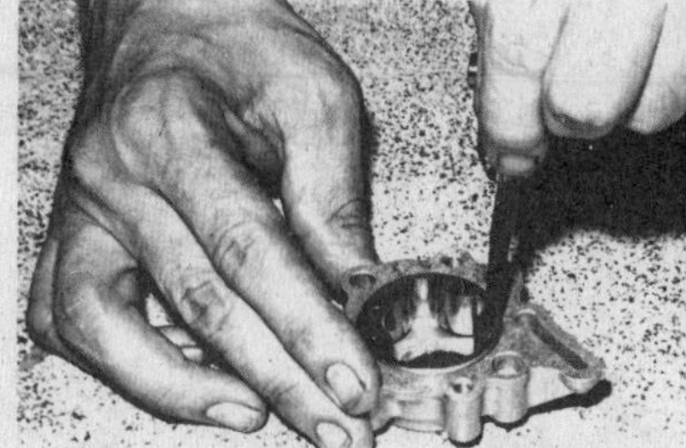

Checking outer rotor-to-pump body clearance

Measuring rotor side clearance

4. Install the assembly in the pump body. Lubricate it thoroughly.

5. Fit the shaft thrust washer. Install the two dowel pins. Install the back of the pump and secure it with the two phillips screws.

6. Use a new oil pump gasket and install the pump on the engine.

7. Check that the pump rotates freely and does not bind or stick when the shaft is turned.

8. Install the sprockets and chain. Tighten the primary drive gear bolt 33–36 ft lbs.

9. The remainder of the assembly procedure is the reverse of removal.

OIL PRESSURE RELIEF VALVE

1978–79

The oil pressure relief valve is located directly below the oil pump and is threaded into the crankcase. Failure is unlikely. The valve consists of a housing and spring-loaded plunger.

To inspect the valve, unscrew the housing from the crankcase. Remove the snap-ring, and take out the spring seat, spring, and plunger. Clean all parts thoroughly in a safe solvent.

Check the spring for a broken or collapsed condition. Check the plunger for wear or scoring. Check the inside of the housing as well. Replace the assembly if any part looks unserviceable.

Clean all parts thoroughly in a solvent. Make sure that any dirt or other foreign matter is removed. Dry the components thoroughly, then install in the reverse of the disassembly procedure.

1980 On

The oil pressure relief valve for these models is the same unit described above, but it is located inside the crankcase and can only be removed once the cases have been split. Refer to the "Engine and Transmission" section for this procedure.

OIL PRESSURE SWITCH

The oil pressure warning light should go on when the ignition is switched on, and should go out immediately when the engine is started.

If the light fails to go on when the ignition is turned on, check the bulb. If the bulb is satisfactory, check the wiring between the bulb and the switch.

If the warning light fails to go *off* when the engine is started, or comes on when riding, stop the engine *immediately*. Check the oil level with the dipstick. If the oil level is satisfactory, lack of oil pressure may be due to pump failure, a bearing failure, or a blockage in an oil passage.

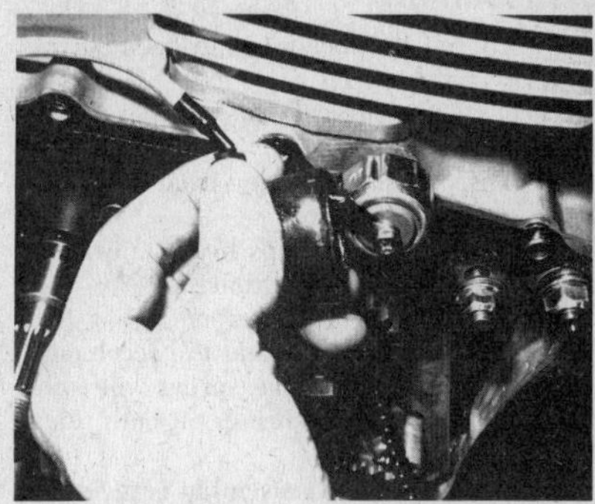

Oil pressure switch

Oil Pump Specifications

Inner rotor-to-outer rotor clearance (max)	0.10 mm/0.004 in.
Outer rotor-to-body clearance (max)	0.35 mm/0.014 in.
Rotor side clearance (max)	0.10 mm/0.004 in.
Relief valve blow off point	56.9–75.4 psi

Oil pump components

FUEL SYSTEM

CARBURETORS

All models use similar CV carburetors, although venturi size and jets may differ from model to model. Models from 1980 on are also equipped with an accelerator pump on the left-side carburetor which is fitted to the bottom of the float bowl.

Removal

The carburetors must be removed as an assembly.

1. Turn the petcock to the "off" position, disconnect the fuel line from the petcock. Remove the gas tank.

Disconnect the overflow tubes from the bottoms of the float bowls.

2. Loosen the screws which secure the carburetor straps at the manifold and the air cleaner.
3. Pull the carburetors back while pushing down until they are free of the intake manifold spigots.
4. Back off the locknuts on the throttle cable adjusters and disconnect the throttle cables from the levers.
5. Remove the choke cable clamp and disconnect the choke cable.
6. Remove the carburetors from the motorcycle.

Disassembly

1. Loosen the locknut, and back off the butterfly synchronization screw.

NOTE: *The slides will have to be synchronized after assembly.*

2. Disconnect the spring from the choke lever.
3. Remove the phillips head screws and take off the rear and the front stays.
4. Separate the carburetors, noting that the fuel connecting pipe and the accelerator pump pipe and the choke spring will come loose. The pipes have o-rings on both sides. Do not loosen them.

From this point, disassembly is given for one carburetor, but applies to both.

5. Unscrew and remove the carburetor tops. Take out the spring, and the throttle slide assembly with jet needle.

The jet needle can be removed from the throttle slide after taking off the full open stopper and unscrewing the needle set screw.

6. Remove the seal ring from the top of the carburetor body.
7. Remove the air jet cover.

Removing the carburetor cap screws

Removing the cap and spring

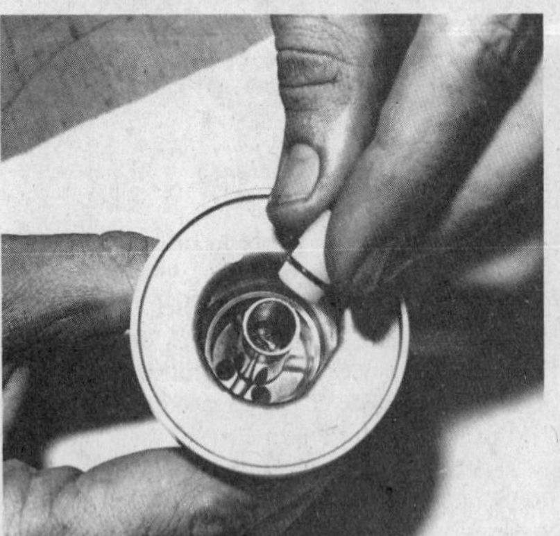

Removing the needle cover

Removing the air jet cover

8. On 1980 and later models, unscrew and remove the accelerator pump cover at the bottom front of the left-side carburetor's float bowl. Remove the spring. Carefully remove the pump diaphragm and rod assembly.

On all models, remove the float bowl screws and very carefully take off the float bowl. If the bowl is stuck, hold it and the carb body together with one hand and rap the side of the bowl with a plastic screwdriver handle or the like to break it loose. Be careful. Carburetor components are quite fragile.

9. Unscrew and remove the primary and secondary main jets.
10. Remove the slow jet plug.

NOTE: *The slow jet itself is a press-fit in the carburetor body and cannot be removed.*

11. Remove the primary nozzle which is beneath the primary main jet.

Float bowl screws (arrows)

Removing the pilot screw

Removing the secondary main jet

Removing the primary nozzle

12. Remove the needle jet holder.
13. Unscrew and remove the pilot screw. Note that the pilot screw will have to be adjusted during reassembly. Note the spring and o-ring on the jet.

Removing the needle jet

Diaphragm assembly

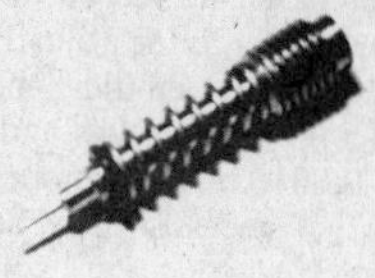

Pilot screw assembly

Pushing out the float pivot pin

Diaphragm screws (arrows)

Taking out the floats and needle

14. Use a needle-nosed pliers to pull out the float pin. Remove the floats. Remove the float needle.

15. Remove the air cut-off valve cover and take out the spring. Remove the diaphragm very carefully and take out the O-ring as well.

Inspection

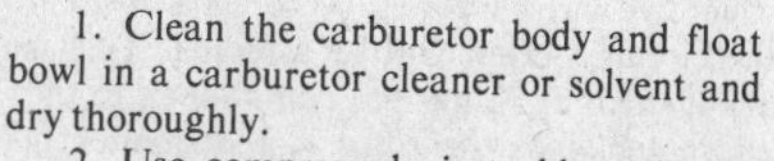

1. Clean the carburetor body and float bowl in a carburetor cleaner or solvent and dry thoroughly.
2. Use compressed air to blow air and fuel passages clear.
3. Clean all fuel jets in the same manner. CAUTION: *Do not insert anything into the jet passages to clear them; use air pressure only.*
4. Inspect the carburetor body for any vibration or stress cracks.
5. Check the condition of the throttle slide. Smooth movement of the slide on the carburetor body is imperative. If the slide sticks or binds at any point from full closed to wide open, replace it.
6. Inspect the needle jet and the needle. The needle must be free of nicks or score marks along its tapered portion. More often, however, these components will need to be replaced because of normal wear.

Assembly

Assembly is bsically the reverse of the disassembly procedure. Note the following points:

1. Always use new gaskets and O-rings.
2. Exercise care when installing jets—they are made of soft brass and are easily damaged if overtightened.
3. Be sure that the float pivot pin is properly seated, and that the floats pivot freely.
4. Tighten the float bowl screws slowly and evenly. Be sure that the O-ring is seated in its groove before installing the float bowl.
5. When installing the pilot screw, place the O-ring and the spring on the screw, then turn it in very carefully until it is seated. Then back the screw off the following number of turns:
   - CB/CM 400T, 400E (1978-79): 1½
   - CB/CM 400T, 400E (1980-81): 2
   - CB 400A (1978-79): 1¾
   - CB/CM 400A (1980-81): 2¼
   - CM 450A: 2¾
   - Other 450's: 2¼
6. When joining the two carburetors together, be sure that the O-rings are in place on either side of the fuel pipes. Fit the pipe into the carbs carefully to avoid damage to the O-rings.
7. Do not forget the choke relief spring.

Accelerator Pump Adjustment

On 1980 and later models, adjust the accelerator pump as follows:

CARBURETOR SPECIFICATIONS

	CB/CM 400T (78-79)	CB/CM 400A (78-79)	CM 400T (80)	CM 400A (80)	CB 400T (80-81)	CM 400E (80-81)	CB/CM 450T/ E/C/SC	CM 450A
Type	CV	CB	CV	CV	CV	CV	CV	CV
Venturi diameter (mm/in.)	32/1.28	28/1.10	30/1.18	28/1.10	30/1.18	30/1.18	30/1.18	28/1.10
Setting mark	VB 21A	VB 24A	VB 22A	VB 24C	VB 22B	VB 22E	VB 24G-N	VB 24E
Pilot screw (turns out)	1½	1¾	2	2¼	2	2	2¼	2¾
Float level (mm/in.)	15.5/0.61	15.5/0.61	15.5/0.61	15.5/0.61	15.5/0.61	15.5/0.61	15.5/0.61	15.5/0.61
Idle speed (rpm)	1,200	1,250	1,200	1,250	1,200	1,200	1,200	1,250
Fast idle (rpm)	2,500	2,000	2,500	2,000	2,500	2,500	2,500	2,000
Idle vacuum (mm Hg)	200-240	200-240	200-240	200-240	200-240	200-240	200-240	200-240

1. Loosen the throttle stop screw until the throttle plates are fully closed.

2. Check the clearance between the accelerator pump rod and the adjusting arm.

This clearance should be 0-0.04 mm/0-0.0016 in. CM models and 0.01-0.04 mm/0.0004-0.0016 in. for B models.

3. Adjust, if necessary, by bending the adjusting arm.

4. Check the clearance between the adjusting arm and the stopper on the carburetor body. It should be 7.0 mm/0.28 in. for manual transmission models and 8.9 mm/0.36 in. for the automatics.

Adjust, if necessary, by bending the adjusting arm.

Installation

Installation is the reverse of removal. Note the following points:

1. Do not interchange the "pull" and "push" throttle cables. The "pull" cable is closest to the engine.

2. Be sure that the carburetors are firmly seated in the manifold spigots.

3. Be sure that the air cleaner tubes are not twisted or folded up so as to block the carburetor intakes.

4. Adjust the throttle cables, butterfly synchronization, idle and fast idle adjustments.

5. Be sure that all fuel line connections are tight and secured with the safety clips. Before operation, turn on the fuel and check for leaks.

Replace any tubes which are torn or dry-rotted.

AIR CLEANER CASE

The blow-by gas circulator, whose purpose and operation is described above, is incorporated into the air cleaner case. Although service should never be necessary, removal of the system is as follows:

1. Remove the fuel tank.
2. Remove the rear wheel.
3. Remove the left and right rear shock absorbers.
4. Remove the rear fender.
5. Remove the battery.
6. Disconnect the breather tube (at top) and drain tube (at the bottom) from the air cleaner case.
7. Loosen the carburetor clamp screws at the air cleaner tubes.
8. Remove the three air cleaner case mounting bolts and take out the case.
9. Installation is the reverse of removal. Be sure that all tube connections are tight.

ELECTRICAL SYSTEM

CHARGING SYSTEM

System Tests

ALTERNATOR OUTPUT

A DC voltmeter, ammeter, and a fully charged battery in good condition are needed to ensure accurate results for this test.

The test should be carried out when the engine is at operating temperature.

Alternator output set-up

NOTE: *Be sure that the battery is fully charged and in good condition, otherwise the test results will not be valid.*

1. Disconnect the black wire coming from the rectifier/regulator unit.

2. Disconnect the battery positive terminal lead. Connect the ammeter between the battery positive terminal and the red lead coming from the battery.

3. Connect the DC voltmeter to the battery positive terminal and to a good ground.

4. Turn the lights on to high beam and start the engine. Note the meter readings.

5. Charging should start at about 1,200 rpm.

At 5,000 rpm, the voltmeter should read 14.5 volts, and the ammeter at least 5 amps.

6. If both meters do not read close to these standards, the system has a malfunction. If too low, the alternator rectifier, or regulator may be at fault.

ALTERNATOR

The alternator is the easiest component in the charging system to test, and therefore it should be checked first. The alternator has three coils of wires in the stator assembly which are wired in series. If there is a break in the circuit, output will be affected. This is about the only thing that can happen to the alternator since the rotor is a permanently magnetized unit and trouble with it is unlikely.

To check the alternator, a simple continuity light or an ohmmeter can be used.

Disconnect the stator wiring at the connector. Check for continuity between each of the three yellow leads in turn. There must be continuity in each case. If there is not, the stator assembly must be replaced.

Check for continuity between each yellow lead and a ground such as the engine cases, or stator core. There must be none. If continuity is evident here, there is a short in the stator, and the unit must be replaced.

NOTE: *It is not necessary to remove the stator from the engine to carry out these tests. Further, it is preferable to check the unit at operating temperature, since circuit failure may be evident only when the unit gets hot.*

REGULATOR

A DC voltmeter is used to check the regulator.

With all heads connected, connect the voltmeter across the battery terminals, and start the engine. Running the engine to at least 5,000 rpm, note the meter reading.

If the voltmeter exceeds 15.0 volts, the regulator is defective and should be replaced.

If the voltmeter reads less than 14.0 volts, the trouble is either the regulator or the rectifier. The units must be replaced together in any event.

NOTE: *As above, this test requires a fully charged battery in good condition in order to be valid.*

RECTIFIER

The rectifier should be checked in the event of insufficient battery charging. Tests can be carried out with a continuity light or a standard (low-voltage) ohmmeter.

CAUTION: *Do not apply high-voltage to the rectifier.*

1. Disconnect the leads and remove the rectifier from the machine.

2. The test involves testing current flow through the rectifier in both directions. The rectifier consists of six diodes. When in working condition, a diode will pass current in one direction only.

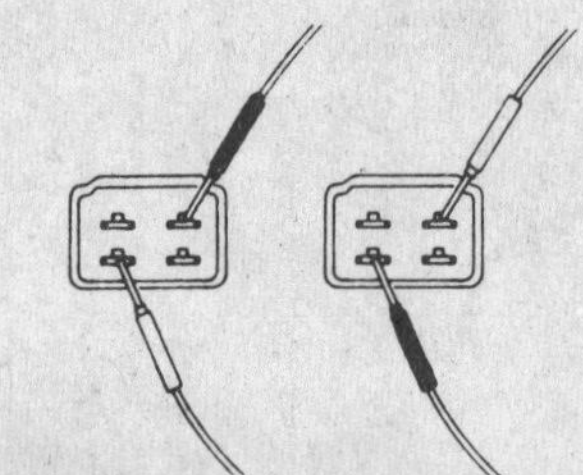

Reverse connections to check the rectifier

Electrical components beneath left side cover

If the diode passes current in both directions, or in neither direction, it is defective. If any of the diodes is defective, the rectifier must be replaced.

3. Check the continuity between the green lead and each of the yellow leads in turn. Reverse the tester leads and repeat the test.

Between the green lead and each yellow lead, there should be continuity in one direction only. If you are using an ohmmeter, "continuity" will be 5-40 ohms. "No continuity" should be at least 2,000 ohms.

For each pair of wires, the tester should show continuity in one direction, but not when the tester leads are reversed. If there is continuity in both directions, or in neither, the unit must be replaced.

4. Check continuity between the red/white lead and each of the yellow leads in the same manner. The same results should be obtained.

5. If the rectifier fails any test, it must be replaced.

IGNITION SYSTEM

The Honda Hawks use a solid-state Capacitor Discharge Ignition system which consists of an ignition coil, sending unit, and signal generating coil.

Special equipment must be used to check the system components. Therefore, these tests must be left to a Honda dealer.

STARTING SYSTEM

The starting system consists of the starter motor and clutch, the solenoid, and the handlebar-mounted starter switch. When the button is pressed, the electrical circuit to the solenoid is closed and the solenoid is activated, sending the battery current directly to the starter motor. The starting system is quite reliable and it is unlikely that any major problems will arise.

Testing

1. If the starter motor spins when the button is pushed, but the engine does not, the starter clutch is defective.

Starter solenoid

2. If the warning lights dim when the starter button is pushed, but the engine and starter do not turn over, the battery may be too low, or the starter may be defective.

3. If nothing happens when the starter button is pushed, either the starter solenoid is defective, or there is a loose wire in the electric starter circuit.

4. If a "click" is heard when the starter button is pushed, but nothing else happens, either the battery is too low to operate the starter motor, or there is a bad connection in the high tension cables from the battery to the solenoid or from the solenoid to the motor.

5. Bad connections are the most likely source of trouble. If one is suspected, disconnect the starter motor cable from the battery and from the solenoid.

CAUTION: *Disconnect the battery side first.*

6. Clean the copper eyelets with sandpaper until they are shiny. Before this cable is refitted, do the same to the cable from the solenoid to the starter motor.

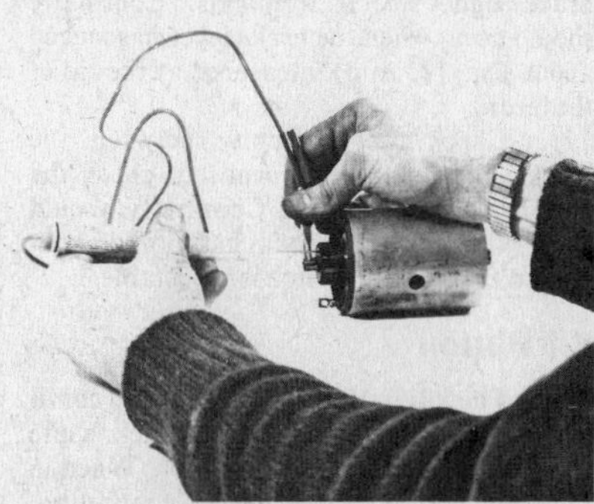

Checking for continuity between the commutator and armature core

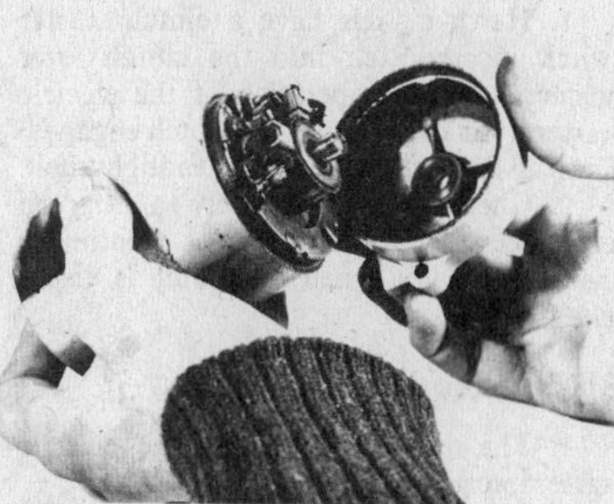

Removing the starter motor cover

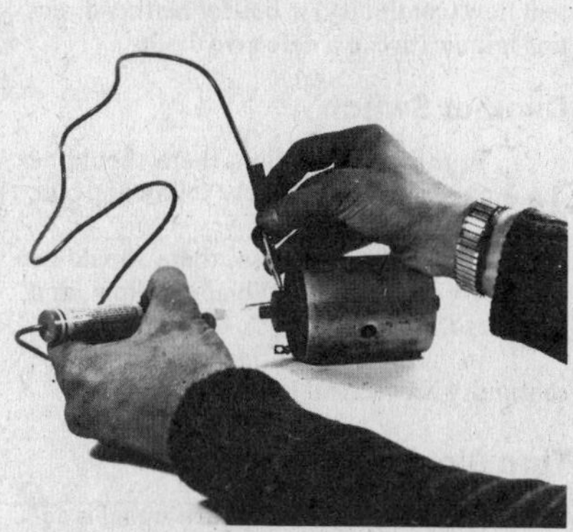

Checking resistance between each commutator segment

Starter Motor

REMOVAL AND INSTALLATION

1. Disconnect the starter motor cable from the battery positive terminal.

2. Disconnect the starter motor cable from the starter motor.

3. Remove the oil pressure switch protector on models so equipped. Disconnect the switch wire, and remove the switch.

4. Remove the mounting bolts and take out the starter motor.

5. To disassemble the starter motor, remove the two long case screws. Carefully remove the case cover with the mounting bolt holes.

6. When assembling the motor, be sure to align the match marks on the case and the two covers.

INSPECTION

1. Check electrical continuity between the commutator and armature core using a multitester or test light and battery. If continuity exists, the armature coil is grounded and the complete starter motor unit must be replaced.

2. Check for continuity between all of the commutator segments. Continuity must exist in each case.

3. Check continuity between the brush that is wired to the stator coil and the starter motor cable. Lack of continuity indicates an open circuit in the stator coil, and the starter motor unit should be replaced.

4. Examine the carbon brushes for damage to the contact surfaces and measure their length. Replace the brushes as a set if either one measures less than 5.5 mm (0.22 in.), or if they are damaged in any way.

5. Brush spring tension should be measured with a small pull-scale. Replace the springs if they have weakened to less than 0.4 kg (0.8 lb) tension.

6. The mica undercut of the commutator should be maintained at 0.3 mm (0.012 in.). Any carbon deposits should be cleaned out of the commutator grooves, and a piece of hacksaw blade or the like used to increase the undercut depth if necessary. Refer to the illustration.

7. Polish the commutator with fine emery cloth and then clean it thoroughly before installing.

Starter Solenoid

1. If the battery is in reasonably good condition, and nothing at all happens when the starter button is pushed, check the solenoid.

2. Disconnect the starter cable at the starter motor. When the button is pushed, there should be an audible "click" which indicates that the solenoid is opening.

3. If further testing is necessary, remove the solenoid from the machine.

CAUTION: *Be sure to disconnect the cables at the battery before disconnecting the solenoid terminals.*

Connect a fully charged 12-volt battery across the solenoid low-tension leads and check for continuity across the high-tension terminals with an ohmmeter or self-contained test light. If there is no continuity, replace or repair the solenoid.

4. Check for continuity across the low-tension terminals with an ohmmeter or self-

powered test light. If there is none, the primary winding of the solenoid is broken, and the unit must be replaced.

5. The primary cause of solenoid malfunction is pitting and/or burning of the contact points inside. It may be possible to restore a solenoid to serviceable condition by taking it apart and dressing the points with a file or emery paper. If this doesn't work, replace it.

6. If starter trouble began just after the starter button housing was disassembled or moved for any reason, check the connections at the switch as they may have come adrift.

ELECTRICAL SWITCHES

Most electrical switches can be easily checked with an ohmmeter or a self-powered low voltage test light. In most cases, the switch is nothing more than a mechanically activated "gate" which must pass or not pass current as needed. Therefore, continuity, or the lack of it, at the right time is what you will be checking for.

Oil Pressure Switch

1. The oil pressure warning light should come on when the ignition is switched on, and go off as soon as the engine starts.

2. If the light does not come on, check the bulb first.

3. If the bulb is good, disconnect the blue/red lead from the switch. Check for continuity between the switch and the engine. There should be continuity when the engine is *off*, and no continuity when the engine is running.

4. Ground the blue/red lead coming from the wiring harness to the engine with a short length of jumper wire. With the ignition on and the engine off, the warning light should go on. If it does not, the wire is broken somewhere between the bulb and the switch.

Neutral Switch

1. The neutral indicator light should go on when the ignition is switched on, and go out when a gear is engaged.

2. If the indicator light will not go on, check the bulb first.

3. Disconnect the light green/red lead from the neutral switch on the engine. Check the continuity between the switch itself and the engine. There should be continuity when the transmission is in neutral, no continuity when a gear is engaged. If the switch does not behave in this manner, replace it.

Horn

1. If the horn will not function, disconnect the two leads and connect a 12-volt battery directly to the horn terminals. The light green wire is the positive side. If the horn does not sound, it is defective.

2. If the horn does sound, disconnect the light green lead and connect a voltmeter or simple test light (12-volt bulb) between the lead and a good ground. You should get battery voltage when the horn button is pushed. If not, the horn button may be defective.

3. Check that there is continuity between the horn's black lead and ground on the frame. If not, the lead is broken.

Ignition Switch

1. With the key turned to the first position, check for continuity between the black and red leads. If continuity does not exist, replace the switch.

2. With the key in the first position, continuity must exist between the brown and the brown/white leads.

3. With the key in the second or "Park" position, continuity must exist between the red and brown leads.

4. When the ignition switch is in the "Off" position, there must be continuity between the black/white and green leads.

5. In the "Park" position, there must be continuity between the black/white and green leads.

Brake Light Switches

If neither hand lever or brake pedal will activate the brake light, suspect the bulb.

To check the individual switches, proceed as follows:

1. Check for continuity across the front brake light switch terminals. Continuity should occur when the brake lever has moved about 1 in. (25 mm), measured at the tip of the lever.

2. Check for continuity between the black and green/yellow leads to check the rear brake light switch. Continuity should occur when the brake pedal has moved about 25 mm (1 in.). This switch is adjustable.

Kill Button

1. The kill button should show no continuity between the black and the black/white leads when in either "off" position. When in the "run" position, there must be continuity.

Clutch Switch

1. Hawk models have a clutch starter switch incorporated into the clutch lever holder to prevent operation of the electric starter when in gear with the clutch engaged. The lead connectors are in the headlight shell.

2. Check for continuity betwen the green and green/red switch leads. Continuity should exist only when the clutch is disengaged.

Silicon Diode

1. The diode is a part of the electric starter interlock circuit.

2. Check for continuity across the diode with an ohmmeter in the high reading range. Current must flow in one direction only. Current flow (continuity) in both or neither direction is indicative of a defective diode.

Dimmer Switch

1. In the "Hi" position, there should be continuity between the black/yellow and blue leads.

2. In the "Lo" position, there should be continuity between the black/yellow and white leads.

3. In the median position, there should be continuity between all leads.

Turn Signal Switch

1. When the right-hand turn signal is activated, there should be continuity between the green lead and the light blue lead and between the brown/white lead and the orange/white lead.

2. In the neutral position, there should be continuity between the brown/white, light blue/white, and orange/white leads, but none between the others.

3. In the left-hand position, there should be continuity between the green lead and the orange lead and between the brown/white and light blue/white leads.

Starter Button

1. If nothing happens when the starter button is pushed, refer to "Starting System," "Testing," above. If the solenoid is operable and the connections are clean and tight, check the starter button.

2. Disconnect the starter button leads. When the button is free, continuity should exist between the black and the black/red leads.

3. When the button is depressed, continuity should exist between the black and yellow/red leads.

NOTE: *The black/red lead shuts off the headlight when the starter button is pushed.*

This lead has a 7 amp fuse in the fuse box.

CHASSIS

FRONT WHEEL ASSEMBLY

Removal and Installation

DRUM BRAKE

1. Support the front wheel several inches off the ground by placing a scissors jack, safety stand, etc., beneath the engine.

CAUTION: *Be certain that the motorcycle is firmly supported and that placement of the jack does not cause instability.*

2. Remove the phillips screw and disconnect the speedometer cable from the brake plate.

3. Run in the brake cable adjusters and disconnect the brake cable from the lever on the brake plate.

4. Remove the brake anchor securing bolt from the fork slider.

5. Remove the axle nut cotter pin, and remove the axle nut. If the axle turns, use a wrench on the flats provided to secure it.

6. Unscrew and remove the axle cap nuts and remove the axle cap.

7. Pull out the front axle, and remove the wheel.

8. Installation is the reverse of removal.

9. Insert the axle from the right side of the wheel while holding it in place in the fork.

NOTE: *After the wheel is in place, turn the brake plate, if necessary, so that the brake anchor bolt holes in the slider and the anchor align. It will be difficult to turn the plate after the axle nut is tightened.*

10. Use a wrench on the flats provided on the right side of the axle to hold it in place, and tighten the axle nut to 36-58 ft lbs. Be sure to turn the axle nut so that the cotter pin can be fitted. Use a new cotter pin.

11. Install the axle cap so that the arrow stamped on it faces towards the *front*.

Tighten the forwardmost axle cap nut *first* to 13-18 ft lbs, then tighten the rear nut.

12. Install the speedometer cable. Turn the wheel slowly while inserting the cable to be sure it is firmly seated. Fit the screw.

13. Secure the brake anchor bolt. Install the brake cable and adjust the brake.

DISC BRAKE (SINGLE PISTON)

1. Support the front wheel several inches off the ground by placing a scissors jack, safety stand, etc., beneath the engine.

CAUTION: *Be certain that the motorcycle is firmly supported and that placement of the jack does not cause instability.*

2. Remove the phillips screw and disconnect the speedometer cable from the drive box.

3. Remove the axle nut cotter pin and the axle nut. If the axle turns, use a wrench on the flats provided to secure it.

4. Unscrew and remove the axle cap nuts and remove the axle cap.

5. Push the axle out to the right. Pull the wheel forward until the disc clears the caliper and remove it.

6. Installation is the reverse of removal.

7. Carefully install the wheel so that the disc enters the caliper correctly.

8. Insert the axle from the right side of the motorcycle.

9. Fit the axle cap. Note that the arrow on the cap must face towards the front of the motorcycle (gap towards rear). Install the axle cap nuts. They will be tightened later.

10. Position the speedometer drive so that, when the cable is connected, it will not be excessively bent. The socket in the drive box should be about 90° from the forks.

11. Install the axle nut. Hold the axle in place with a wrench on the flats provided and tighten the nut to 36-58 ft. lbs. Be sure that the nut is positioned so that the cotter pin can be inserted. Using a new cotter pin is recommended as a good safety practice.

12. Tighten the axle cap nuts. The front nut must be tightened first, then the rear nut. There must be a gap between the cap and the slider at the rear. Proper torque is 13-18 ft. lbs.

Be sure that the axle cap is installed so that the gap (arrow) is at the rear

Axle nut and speedometer cable securing screw (arrows)

Front axle flat (arrow)

13. Install the speedometer cable, turning the wheel slowly while inserting the cable to be sure it is properly engaged. Fit the securing screw.

14. Check operation of the front brake before riding.

DISC BRAKE (DUAL PISTON)

1. Support the front wheel several inches off the ground by placing a scissors jack, safety stand, or the like, beneath the engine.

CAUTION: *Be certain that the motorcycle is firmly supported and that placement of the stand does not cause instability.*

2. Remove the caliper from the caliper bracket. Tie it up to avoid damage to the brake line.

3. Remove the axle nut cotter pin, if fitted. Unscrew and remove the axle nut.

4. Remove the axle cap nuts (right side) and remove the cap.

5. Unscrew the speedometer cable set screw and pull the cable out of the drive box.

6. Pull the axle out to the right and lower the wheel until it clears the forks.

7. Installation is the reverse of removal. Proceed as follows:

8. Position the wheel in the forks and insert the axle.

9. Install the axle cap, positioning it so that the arrow points toward the front of the motorcycle (the gap between cap and slider must be towards the rear). Install the cap washers and nuts. They will be tightened later.

10. Position the speedometer drive box so that the cable will not be excessively bent when it is connected. The cable fitting should be about 90° from the forks.

11. Tighten the axle nut to 36-58 ft. lbs. It will be necessary to hold the axle flats with a wrench while the nut is tightened. Install the nut so that the cotter pin, if fitted, can be inserted. Using a new cotter pin is recommended.

12. Tighten the *front* axle cap nut first, then the rear axle cap nut. Proper torque is 13-18 ft. lbs. There must be a gap at the rear of the cap if installation is correct.

13. Install the speedometer cable while slowly rotating the wheel and tighten the set screw.

14. Install the caliper and tighten the mounting hardware. Proper torques are:

Upper bolt or nut: 18-24 ft. lbs.

Lower bolt: 14-18 ft. lbs.

15. Check the brake for proper operation before riding the motorcycle.

REAR WHEEL ASSEMBLY

Removal and Installation

1. Park the motorcycle on the centerstand.

2. Back off the rear brake adjuster nut and disconnect the brake rod from the pin in the brake lever. Put these parts in a place where they will not be lost.

3. Remove the cotter pin, if fitted, the nut, and disconnect the brake anchor from the brake plate.

4. Disconnect the drive chain at the masterlink. Always remove the spring clip with a pair of blunt-nosed pliers. Do not attempt to pry it off with a screwdriver, or it may be distorted.

5. Back off the brake adjuster bolts' locknuts, and loosen the adjuster bolts.

6. Remove the rear axle not cotter pin and take off the axle nut.

7. Pull out the axle and remove the wheel.

8. Installation is the reverse of removal. Note the following points.

9. The long spacer goes on the right side of the wheel.

10. Be sure that the brake anchor nut is tightened to 13-18 ft lbs. Fit the cotter pin. Using a new one is recommended.

11. Be sure to install the masterlink spring clip with the closed side facing the direction of

Rear brake anchor nut (arrow)

Install masterlink spring clips so that the closed end is facing the direction of chain rotation

only brake fluid conforming to DOT 3 specifications. Any brand meeting this requirement is acceptable. The brake fluid container of all reputable brands will be plainly marked with the standards the fluid meets or exceeds.

NOTE: *It is sometimes helpful to let the cycle sit for several hours before bleeding the system. Pulling and tapping on the lines will help expel any air bubbles trapped in the system. If you find that you can't get the system bled properly and the master cylinder has been dry for awhile, the seals inside the cylinder may have become dried and cracked. In this case rebuild the master cylinder.*

1. Top up the reservoir with brake fluid and replace the cap to keep dirt and moisture out and the fluid in. Cover the gas tank with a thick cloth to avoid damage due to spilled brake fluid.

2. Attach one end of a small diameter rubber hose to the bleed valve on the caliper, and place the other end in a jar which contains several inches of clean, new brake fluid. Be sure that the end of the hose is submerged in this fluid. Arrange the hose so that it loops upward after leaving the bleed valve, and see that it has no kinks or sharp bends.

3. Pump the brake lever rapidly several times until some resistance is felt and, holding the lever against the resistance, open the bleed valve about one-half turn. When the lever bottoms, close the valve (do not overtighten) and then release the lever.

4. Repeat the operation until no more air is released out of the hose and the brake lever is firm in operation. Check the fluid level in the reservoir often to make sure that it doesn't go dry and draw more air into the system. Do not reuse fluid that has been pumped out of the system. Do not use fluid that has been stored for more than a few weeks after the seal on its container has been opened, as brake fluid will absorb moisture from the air and may corrode the master cylinder and caliper.

5. Refill the reservoir to the level mark when through (but do not overfill). Avoid overtightening the cap or fluid will weep around the cap edge.

Pad Replacement

1978-1980

Pads should be replaced as a set when either of them is worn to the red limit line.

1. Remove the caliper cover.
2. Take out the pad pin securing clip.
3. Push the caliper as far as possible to the right.
4. Pull out the pad pins with a pair of needle-nosed pliers. Take out the old pads.

Brake pad pins (arrows)

5. Slip in the new pads. Note that the pad shim is installed on the inner (wheel) side of the caliper.
6. Insert the pad pins. The holes in the pins must face outwards.
7. Install the pin clip into the pin holes. Fit the cover.

NOTE: *Try to avoid hard application of the brake for about fifty miles after fitting new pads to give them a chance to seat properly.*

1981 (EARLY)

Pads should be replaced as a set when either of them is worn to the red limit line.

1. Remove the brake pad pin retainer.
2. Push the caliper as far as possible towards the wheel.
3. Remove the pins. Take out the brake pads.
4. Insert the new pads, pad pins, and pin retainer. Tighten the retainer to 6-9 ft. lbs.

NOTE: *Try to avoid hard application of the brake for about fifty miles after fitting new pads to give them a chance to seat properly.*

1981 AND LATER (DUAL PISTON)

Pads should be replaced as a set when either of them is worn to the red limit line. On dual piston calipers, the caliper must be removed from the fork slider to replace the brake pads.

1. Remove the two bolts or bolt and nut securing the caliper to the caliper bracket.
2. Remove the pin retainer bolt. Remove the pin retainer.
3. Remove the pad pins and the brake pads.
4. Push in the pistons to allow the pads to be installed. Install the anti-rattle spring.
5. Install the outboard pad and hold it in place with one pin. Install the other pad and push the pin through it.
6. Hold the pads against the anti-rattle spring and insert the remaining pin.
7. Install the pin retainer. Be sure it is completely seated in the groove.
8. Install the pin retainer bolt.
9. Position the caliper on the caliper bracket. Lightly lubricate the upper pivot bolt with silicone grease.
10. Tighten the caliper mounting hardware to the following specifications:

Upper bolt or nut: 18-24 ft. lbs.
Lower bolt: 14-18 ft. lbs.

NOTE: *Avoid hard application of the brake for about fifty miles after fitting new pads to give them a chance to seat properly.*

Caliper (1978-80)

REMOVAL

1. Attach a length of plastic hose to the caliper bleed nipple, placing the other end of the hose into a container. Loosen the bleed nipple and pump the brake hand lever until the system is drained of fluid.
2. Disconnect the brake line from the caliper, wrapping the end with a small plastic bag or the like to prevent fluid leakage.
3. Remove the caliper cover. Remove the clip. Pull out the pad pins with a needle-nosed pliers, and take out the pads and shim.

Caliper bolts (arrows)

4. Loosen the two caliper shaft bolts evenly. Push them in while unscrewing them. Remove the caliper half.
5. Remove the speedometer cable clamp. Remove the carrier with the other caliper half.

DISASSEMBLY

1. Remove the piston in the following manner. Cover the inner side of the caliper half with a clean rag. Apply low air pressure to the caliper fluid line hole to force the piston out.
2. Push the lip of the fluid seal into the caliper half to unseat it, then remove it. The seal must be replaced with a new one on assembly.
3. Unscrew the caliper shaft bolts by hand and remove them. Separate the carrier and the other caliper half. Note the rubber boots.

INSPECTION

1. Clean all parts in new brake fluid. Do not use gasoline or other solvents.
2. All rubber parts should be replaced with new ones once the caliper has been disassembled.
3. Check the piston for scoring or other obvious signs of wear, and replace it if damage is noted. Check the caliper bore as well.
4. Measure the piston diameter. Standard diameter is 38.115-38.180 mm/1.5006-1.5031 in. The piston should be replaced if the measured diameter is less than 38.105 mm/1.5002 in.
5. Measure the inside diameter of the caliper bore. Standard diameter is 38.180-38.200 mm/1.5031-1.5039 in. The caliper half should be replaced if the bore diameter measures in excess of 38.215 mm/1.5045 in.

ASSEMBLY AND INSTALLATION

1. Clean all parts in clean brake fluid. As noted, all rubber parts should be replaced.
2. Coat the piston fluid seal with silicon grease or clean brake fluid and carefully install it in the caliper half. Be sure that it is firmly seated in its groove.
3. Smear a little brake fluid on the sides of the piston and install it in the caliper half noting that the dished side of the piston must face the brake pads. Install the piston boot.
4. Coat the caliper shaft bolt O-rings with clean brake fluid and install them on the shafts.
5. Assemble the caliper half, carrier, and caliper bolts. Be sure that the boots are properly seated in the shaft grooves.
6. Fit the caliper half and carrier assembly onto the fork slider. Install the other caliper half. Tighten the caliper shaft bolts to 22-29 ft lbs. The bolts must be tightened gradually and evenly.
7. The remainder of the procedure is the reverse of removal. Install the pads. Install the brake line. Fill the system with fluid. Bleed the line as outlined in the preceding section.

Caliper (1981 And Earlier)

REMOVAL

1. Drain the brake line and disconnect the brake line from the caliper. See Steps 1-2 under "Caliper (1978-80)", above.

2. Remove the pad pin retainer, pad pins, and pads.

3. Remove the caliper mounting bolt, the caliper shaft, and take off the caliper.

DISASSEMBLY

1. Remove the boots and collar of the mounting bolt sleeve.

2. Remove the pad spring.

3. Stuff a clean rag into the caliper and position it so that the pistons will be forced out away from you. Apply low air pressure to the fluid inlet to push out the pistons.

CAUTION: *Do not use high pressure.*

4. Remove the pistons. Pry out the fluid seals taking care that the piston bores are not scratched as you do this. New seals must always be used on assembly.

INSPECTION

1. Clean all metal parts in new brake fluid. Do not use gasoline or other solvents.

2. All rubber parts should be replaced with new ones once the caliper has been disassembled.

3. Check the pistons for scoring or other obvious signs of wear, and replace them if damage is evident. Check the caliper bores as well.

4. Measure the piston diameters. Standard diameter is 30.20 mm/1.189 in. The piston(s) should be replaced if diameter is less than 30.14 mm/1.187 in.

Pistons should be replaced as a set.

5. Clean out the caliper bores with clean brake fluid. Measure the inside diameter of each bore. Standard diameter is 30.23 mm/1.190 in. Replace the caliper if either bore measures greater than 30.29 mm/1.193 in.

ASSEMBLY AND INSTALLATION

1. Clean all parts in clean, new brake fluid.

2. Use new fluid seals and coat them with fresh brake fluid or silicon grease. Install the seals being sure that they are properly seated in their grooves.

3. Coat the pistons with fresh brake fluid and carefully insert them in the bores with the dished end on the brake pad side.

4. Install the collar and boots being sure that the boots are properly seated.

5. Install the pad spring.

6. Smear the caliper shaft with brake fluid or silicon grease. Install the caliper on the carrier. Tighten the caliper shaft to 18-22 ft. lbs. Tighten the caliper mounting bolt to 14-18 ft. lbs.

7. Make sure that the caliper shaft boot is properly seated in the shaft groove.

8. Connect the brake line, install the pads, refill and bleed the system as outlined in the above sections.

Caliper (Late 1981 And Later)

REMOVAL

1. Attach a length of plastic hose to the caliper bleed nipple, placing the other end of the hose in a container. Loosen the nipple and pump the brake lever until the system is drained of fluid.

2. Disconnect the brake line from the caliper. Wrap the end of the line in a plastic bag or the like to prevent fluid leakage.

3. Loosen the caliper bracket bolts (or bolt and nut-two types of mounting may be encountered).

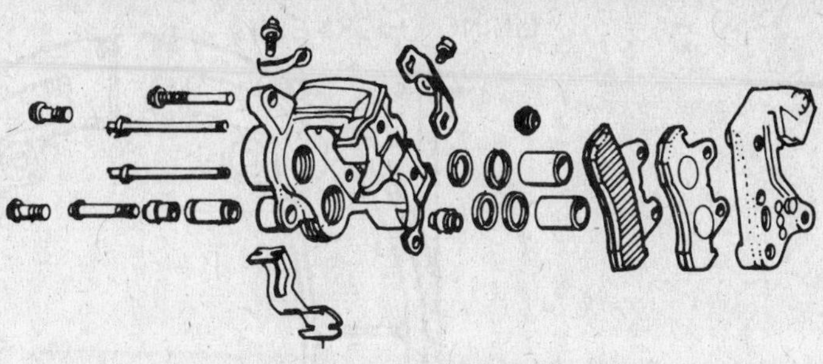

Dual Piston Caliper (1981-On)

4. Remove the bracket bolts securing the caliper to the fork slider and remove the assembly.

DISASSEMBLY

1. Remove the pin retainer bolt.

2. Remove the pin retainer, pins and pads.

3. Stuff a rag into the caliper to catch the pistons.

4. Position the caliper so that the pistons will be pointing away from you when they come out.

5. Apply *low pressure* compressed air to the brake line hole in the caliper to force the pistons out of their bores.

6. Pry out the piston boots and seals.

INSPECTION

1. Clean all metal parts in clean brake fluid. Do not use gasoline or other solvents.

2. All rubber parts must be replaced with new ones.

3. Check the pistons for wear or signs of scoring. Check the piston bores as well. Metal surfaces must be smooth and featureless. Scoring on either pistons or caliper bores will usually make it necessary to replace both parts.

4. If a piston is frozen in the caliper, replace the caliper.

ASSEMBLY AND INSTALLATION

1. Clean all metal parts in clean brake fluid. As noted, all rubber parts must be replaced.

2. Lubricate all rubber parts with new, clean brake fluid as they are assembled. Coat pistons with the fluid as they are inserted into their bores.

3. Be sure that seals and boots are completely seated in their grooves.

4. Tighten the caliper bracket mounts as follows:

Upper pivot bolt or nut: 18-24 ft. lbs.
Lower mounting bolt: 14-18 ft. lbs.

5. Tighten the caliper bracket-to-slider mounting bolts to 22-29 ft. lbs.

Brake Disc

REMOVAL

1. Remove the front wheel. Refer to the preceding section.

2. Unbolt and remove the brake disc.

INSPECTION

1. The brake disc usually requires no service. However, if the disc becomes scored for any reason, it should be replaced and a new set of pads should be installed. A badly scored disc will reduce the effectiveness of the brake and shorten pad life considerably. If the front brake lever oscillates or fluctuates when the brake is applied at speed, it is possible that the disc is warped.

2. Check the disc run-out with a dial gauge. If run-out exceeds 0.3 mm/0.012 in., the disc must be replaced.

3. Check the thickness of the disc at several places. Standard thickness is 4.9-5.1 mm/0.19-0.20 in. If the thickness measures less than 4.0 mm/0.16 in., the disc should be replaced.

INSTALLATION

Installation is the reverse of removal. Tighten the disc mounting bolts to 20-24 ft lbs.

Master Cylinder

REMOVAL AND DISASSEMBLY

NOTE: Be very careful when removing and replacing the master cylinder or refilling the reservoir. Brake fluid can remove paint or damage plastic in seconds and therefore should be handled with care.

1. Place a cloth underneath the connection to absorb any spilled fluid and disconnect the brake line from the master cylinder. Cover the open end of the brake line with a plastic bag secured with a rubber band to prevent dirt from entering the brake system.

2. Remove the two mounting bolts and remove the master cylinder from the handlebar. Unscrew the reservoir cap and discard the brake fluid.

3. Remove the brake lever by unscrewing the pivot bolt.

4. Carefully remove the boot and 18 mm snap-ring.

5. Remove the piston, check valve, return spring, and primary cup by blowing compressed air into the brake line fitting or by carefully pushing it out with a wooden dowel.

INSPECTION

1. Clean all components in clean brake fluid.

2. Check the master cylinder bore for signs of wear, grooves, scoring, etc.

3. Check the piston for scoring or grooves.

4. Replace the primary cup with a new item each time it is removed.

5. Replace any rubber items which show signs of wear or age, cracks, brittle condition, etc.

6. With a micrometer, check the diameter of the piston. Standard diameter is 13.957-13.984 mm/0.5495-0.5506 in.

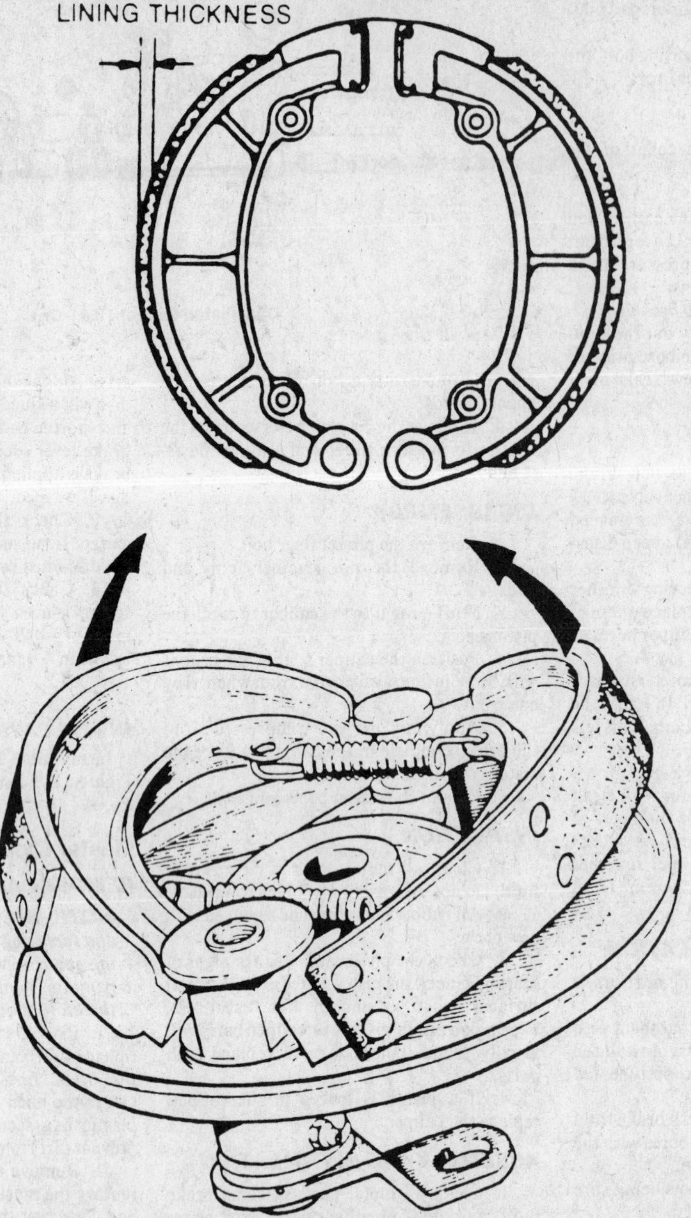

Removing the brake shoes

The piston assembly should be replaced if the measured diameter is less than 13.940 mm/0.5488 in.

7. If possible, check the inner diameter of the master cylinder bore. Standard inside diameter is 14.000-14.043 mm/0.5512-0.5529 in. The assembly should be replaced if the measured diameter is larger than 14.055 mm/0.5533 in.

ASSEMBLY AND INSTALLATION

1. Coat all internal brake parts with fresh brake fluid, including the bore in the master cylinder.

2. Install the return spring to the check valve and install them into the master cylinder. Be sure that the check valve is facing the correct direction.

3. Install the primary cup after lubricating it with fresh brake fluid.

NOTE: *Make sure that the primary cup does not turn sideways during installation.*

4. Install the piston assembly and 18 mm snap-ring. Install the boot and brake lever.

5. Mount the master cylinder on the handlebar. Connect the brake line and torque the banjo bolt to 24-29 ft lbs. Fill the reservoir with fresh brake fluid and bleed the system as previously described.

NOTE: *Be sure that there is a joint washer on either side of the brake line where it is bolted to the master cylinder.*

DRUM BRAKE SERVICE

1. Remove the wheel from the motorcycle. On the front wheel, unscrew the axle. Remove the brake plate from the hub.

2. Brakes can be inspected on the brake plate.

3. Inspect the lining for wear. There should be at least 0.08 in. (2.0 mm) of lining material left (measured at the linings thinnest point) or the shoes must be replaced.

4. Inspect the linings for grooves or scoring. These may be caused by particles of dirt which have entered the drum. If badly scored, the shoes should be replaced. If scoring of the shoes is evident, the drum should be inspected for the same type of damage.

Be sure that there is no oil or grease present on the linings. Oil-impregnated linings must be replaced. If the linings show this condition, determine the source of the lubricant: defective wheel bearing oil seals, excessive chain lube, etc.

5. If the linings are usable, rough up the surface with coarse sandpaper. Then clean the linings with alcohol or lacquer thinner. Clean the brake drum with the same solvent.

6. To disassemble the brake plate, remove the cotter pin(s) and washer(s) from the brake pivot(s). Grasp each shoe and fold

them toward the center of the brake plate. They may be installed in the same manner.

7. Remove the brake springs. Remove the brake lever pinch-bolt(s) and pull the lever(s) off the splined brake cam(s). Note that the levers are marked for position on the cam(s) with punch marks.

NOTE: *The plurals refer to the twin-leading shoe brakes.*

8. Push the brake cam(s) out of the brake plate from the outside using hand-pressure or if necessary by tapping with a plastic mallet. Remove the plain washer and dust seals from the brake plate.

9. Check that the brake lever pinchbolts are not bent. This can easily happen if they are overtightened. Replace any bolts in this condition. Inspect the brake lever splines and replace the lever(s) if these are worn or stripped.

10. Inspect the splines on the brake cam(s). These should be in good condition. Check that the brake cam(s) are not bent and that they can rotate freely in the brake plate passage. If it will not, use a fine grade of sandpaper on the camshafts and the surface of the brake plate passage.

11. Clean the cam(s) thoroughly in a solvent to remove any old grease, rust, or corrosion. Use sandpaper or emery cloth to polish the cams. Clean off any residue; before reassembly, smear the cams with chassis grease.

12. Inspect the brake plate for cracks or fractures, and replace it if necessary.

13. On twin-leading shoe brakes, the brake plate linkage should be checked. The connecting rod is secured to each brake lever by a clevis pin and cotter pin. These pins can be removed after the cotter pins are taken off. They should be checked for wear, especially on high mileage machines, and replaced if necessary.

14. Check the condition of the brake springs, noting any twisted or fatigued hooks. Replace any broken, rusted, or old springs with new ones.

15. Clean all parts thoroughly with a suitable solvent, making a special effort to remove the dust and built-up dirt from the backing plate.

16. When reassembling the hub, note the following points:

a. Ensure that the brake cams are lubricated with chassis grease;

b. The use of new dust seals is recommended;

c. Lubricate the brake shoe pivot points with a little grease;

d. Install the shoes as on removal. Hook them together with the springs, and fold them down over the brake cam(s) and pivot(s). Install new cotter pins to the pivot points;

e. When installing the brake lever on the brake cam, be sure that the punch marks on the lever and cam align.

Brake Drums

1. Upon disassembly of the hub, inspect the brake drum surface for condition. The drums must be clean and free from score marks or rust.

2. Rust can be removed from the drum surface with sandpaper. Polish the surface until it is shiny, then clean it thoroughly.

3. Alcohol or lacquer thinner can be used to remove dirt or deposits from the drum.

4. The drum should be checked for concentricity. An out-of-round condition is usually noticeable as an on-off-on feeling when the brake is applied while riding. With the wheel assembly mounted on the machine, spin the wheel while applying the brake very lightly. The rubbing noise of the brakes against the drum should be heard for the entire revolution of the wheel.

5. An out-of-round condition and most scoring can be removed by having the drum turned on a lathe. This operation should be entrusted to a qualified specialist with the proper equipment. Usually, the tire and wheel bearings will have to be removed so that the wheel can be chucked to the lathe. If the rim needs to be trued, have this done before any work on the drum is performed, as the action of the spokes while truing the rim may further aggravate the drum warpage.

6. With a large vernier caliper, measure the inside diameter of the brake drums.

The service limit for the front drum is 181.0 mm/7.13 in., while for the rear it is 141.0/5.55 in.

Replace the drum if the measured diameter exceeds the service limit.

Brake Linkage Adjustment

The brake linkage which connects the two brake levers on twin-leading shoe front brakes (Type I) usually needs no readjustment once set, so that this step will not be necessary unless the linkage itself has been disassembled for some reason.

If it has, proceed as follows:

1. Disconnect the brake rod from the rear lever on the brake plate by removing the cotter pin and taking out the clevis pin.

2. Loosen the locknut on the brake rod near the front brake lever.

3. Adjust the brake cable so that the hand lever moves about 1 in. (measured at the ball end of the lever) before the brake shoe which is still connected contacts the brake drum fully.

4. Have an assistant hold the brake hand lever in the "full on" position as outlined in Step 3.

5. With your thumb, or the heel of your palm, push the rear brake lever forward as far as possible until the brake shoe contacts the drum.

At this point, the clevis pin holes on the brake rod should align with the hole in the brake lever you are pushing. If the holes do not align, lengthen or shorten the brake rod by screwing the rod in or out until alignment is achieved. Refit the clevis pin and cotter pin.

FRONT FORKS (STANDARD)

Removal

1. Remove the front wheel as outlined above.

2. Unbolt the brake caliper (on disc brake models) from the fork slider. It is not necessary to disconnect the brake line or disassemble the caliper. Unbolt the brake line clamp.

3. Remove the front fender.

4. Remove the fork crown bolts at the top of each fork leg.

5. Loosen the lower triple clamp pinch bolts for each fork leg.

6. Pull the fork legs down until free of the triple clamps. It may be necessary to twist the legs while pulling down on them.

Disassembly

1. Secure the upper end of the fork leg in a vise. Be careful not to knick the chrome or crush the fork tube. Protect it with a heavy rag or use a wood-faced vise.

2. Unscrew the spring bolt at the top of the fork leg. A 14 mm allen wrench is used.

Unscrew the bolt carefully. It is spring-loaded and may pop out when fully loosened.

3. Take out the spring seat. Remove the fork spring.

4. Turn the fork leg upside down and drain off the fork fluid.

5. Remove the slider bolt from the very bottom of the slider. The slider should be secured in a vise, protected against damage in the same manner as the fork tube, above.

Fork slider allen bolt

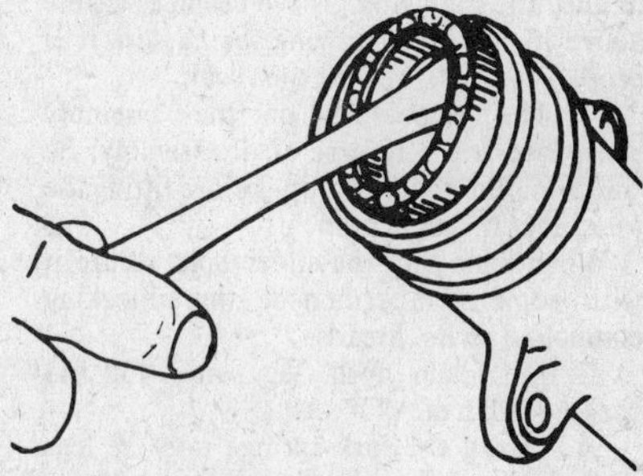

Prying out a front fork oil seal

If the bolt turns, but will not come loose, the piston inside is probably turning. In this case, temporarily reinstall the fork spring and spring bolt, which should serve to hold the piston while the bolt is unscrewed.

6. Separate the slider from the fork tube. Remove the rebound spring, oil lock piece, and piston assembly.

7. Remove the dust seal from the top of the slider.

8. Remove the oil seal snap-ring. Pry out the oil seal with a small screwdriver or elbow-shaped tool. Protect the top edge of the slider while prying with a heavy rag. New seals must always be used on assembly.

Inspection

1. Inspect the fork tubes for bends such as might have been incurred in an accident. If a dial indicator is available, check the run-out of each fork tube. Maximum allowable bend-

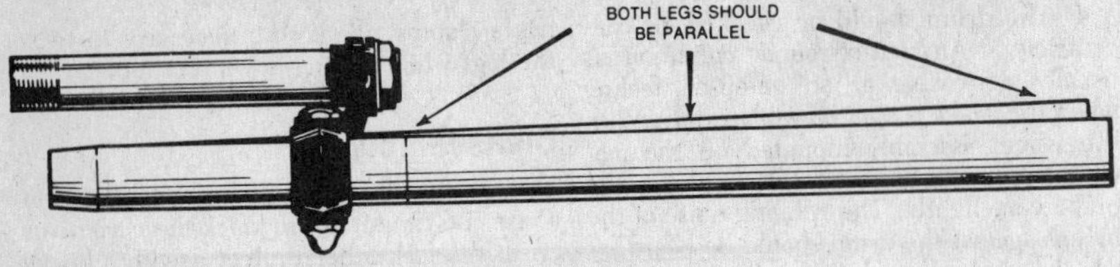
BOTH LEGS SHOULD BE PARALLEL

Check for bent fork legs

ing is 0.2 mm/0.008 in. This value is ½ of the total indicated reading of the gauge.

If the tubes are just slightly bent, it may be possible to straighten them with a large press. Severely bent tubes, however, or those which are dented or kinked, must be replaced.

2. The chrome plating on the fork tubes must be in perfect condition in the area along which the slider oil seal rides. If the plating is chipped or flaking, the seal will leak. Damage to the plating requires replacement of the tube.

3. Compare the spring heights of the fork springs for each fork leg. If either spring is shorter than 480.0 mm/18.9 in., both should be replaced.

4. Check the piston assembly for scoring or wear. Be sure that all the bleed holes are clear.

5. Clean all metal components in a safe solvent and dry them thoroughly.

Assembly

1. Install new oil seals into the sliders. The seals should be installed with a suitably sized driver or large socket which must be large enough to cover the whole seal and thus drive it straight in. Do not cock or twist the seal when pressing it in. It can easily become warped and therefore useless. Drive the seal in until the snap-ring groove becomes visible above it. Fit the snap-ring, being sure it is properly seated, then the dust seal.

2. The remainder of the assembly procedure is the reverse of disassembly. Be sure to oil the slider seal lips before fitting the fork tubes through them.

When installing the slider bolt, secure it with some non-permanent thread-locking compound on its threads.

3. Fill each fork leg with 137-143 cc/4.6-4.8 oz. of ATF.

4. Install the fork springs into the legs with the narrow ends of the springs *down*. Install the spring seat and 14 mm bolt.

Installation

1. Slide each fork leg up through the triple clamps until the top edge of the leg is flush with the top of the upper triple clamp.

2. Install and tighten the fork crown bolts to 51-65 ft lbs.

3. Tighten the lower triple clamp pinch bolts to 13-18 ft lbs.

4. The remainder of the procedure is obvious. Torque caliper mounting bolts to 22-29 ft lbs.

FRONT FORKS (AIR-TYPE)

The following procedure applies to 1981 and later models fitted with air forks.

CAUTION: *The fork caps are under air and spring pressure. Be sure that the system is depressurized before beginning work. Eye and face protection is recommended.*

Removal

1. Remove the front wheel as outlined above.

2. Remove the brake caliper. It is not necessary to disconnect the brake line from the caliper.

3. Remove the front fender.

4. Depressurize the forks.

5. Disconnect the air hose from the fork caps.

6. Loosen the fork cap bolts.

7. Remove the nameplate on the lower triple clamp.

8. Loosen the upper and lower triple clamp pinch bolts. Pull each fork leg down and remove them from the machine.

Disassembly

1. Remove the fork cap bolt.

CAUTION: *The cap is under spring pressure. Exercise caution when taking it off.*

2. Remove the two springs and washer from the fork tube.

3. Secure the fork slider in a vise, protecting the finish by wrapping it in a rag. Remove the bolt from the bottom of the slider. If the bolt cannot be broken loose, temporarily install the springs and cap bolt to hold it and then loosen the slider bolt.

4. Drain the ATF. Remove the piston and rebound spring.

5. Remove the dust seal from the top of the slider. Remove the snap-ring beneath the dust seal.

6. Use a magnet to remove the back-up plate. Pull the fork tube out of the slider until resistance is felt. Then move it up and down until the fork seal comes free of the slider.

7. Remove the oil seal, back-up ring, and slider bushing from the fork tube. Remove the oil lock piece inside the slider.

Inspection

Refer to the "Inspection" section for standard front forks, above. Fork spring free lengths for air forks are as follows:

Short spring: 235 mm/9.25 in. for the CB 400T and CB 450T; 232 mm/9.13 in. for the CM 400A, C, T, CM 450A, C, SC.

Long spring: 335 mm/13.19 in. for the CB 400T and CB 450T; 306 mm/12.06 in. for the CM 400A, C, T, CM450A, C, SC.

These are the service limits. Replace the springs in both fork legs if any measures less than these specifications.

Measure the diameter of the fork tubes in the area of slider operation and replace if less than 32.90 mm/1.295 in.

Check the fork bushings for wear or scoring. Replace them if scoring is excessive, or if the copper bushing base is visible on more than ¾ of the bushing surface.

Assembly

1. Clean all metal parts in a safe solvent. Clean the bushings in ATF. Use new fork slider seals.

2. Install the bushings on the fork tubes. Insert the oil lock piece. Install the rebound spring and piston.

3. Use a non-permanent thread-locking compound on the slider bolt. Tighten it to 11-18 ft. lbs.

4. Insert the fork tube into the slider. Fit the slider bushing and back-up ring. Use an old bushing or the like to drive the new one into place.

5. Lubricate the lips of the slider seal with ATF and slip the seal along the fork tube. Note that the seal is installed with the marked side *up*. Drive the seal into the slider until the snap-ring groove is visible. Install the back-up plate, snap-ring, and dust cover.

6. Pour the proper quantity of ATF into each fork leg. Refer to the "Maintenance Data" charts, above, for quantities.

7. Install the long spring, washer, short spring. Fit the cap bolt.

Installation

1. Slide the fork tube into the triple clamps. On the CM 400 and CM 450A, C and T, position the end of the tube 3 mm/0.12 in. above the top of the upper triple clamp. On other models, make it flush.

2. Tighten the upper triple clamp pinch bolts to 7-9 ft. lbs. Tighten the lower triple clamp bolts to 13-18 ft. lbs.

3. Tighten the fork caps to 11-22 ft. lbs.

4. Grease the air line fitting O-rings. Tighten the hose to 3-5 ft. lbs. to the right fork cap. Install the air hose connector on the left fork cap. Tighten it to 3-5 ft. lbs. Tighten the air hose to 11-14 ft. lbs. on the left fork cap.

5. Pressurize the forks to 11 psi.

CAUTION: *Use a hand-pump only. Do not use a compressed air source. Do not exceed the recommended pressure.*

6. Apply the front brake and pump the forks up and down several times. Place the bike on the center stand and check the air pressure. Adjust if necessary.

STEERING STEM ASSEMBLY

Bearing Adjustment

1. The steering stem bearings are uncaged ¼-in. balls. They are adjusted by means of a ring nut beneath the upper triple clamp.

2. To check bearing adjustment, support the front wheel off the ground. Grasp the tip of the front fender and place your other hand beneath the lower triple clamp at the frame lug.

3. Attempt to move the fork by pulling up on the tip of the fender. If play or movement can be felt at the lower triple clamp, the bearings are adjusted too loosely or are worn. An alternate method is to grasp the fork sliders and attempt to move them back and forth in line with the motorcycle. No play should be noted.

4. Turn the forks slowly from lock-to-lock. Movement should be smooth, silent, and effortless. If any binding or uneven movement is felt, the balls and races are either too tightly adjusted or they are worn. If the steering feels uniformly stiff, the bearings are

too tightly adjusted. If any noise is noted, the bearings are damaged or some are missing.

5. With the front wheel off the ground, release the front forks from a few degrees off the centered position. The fork should fall freely to either side of their own weight. If they will not, the bearings are too tightly adjusted, the steering stem is bent, the races are extremely worn, or some of the bearings are missing.

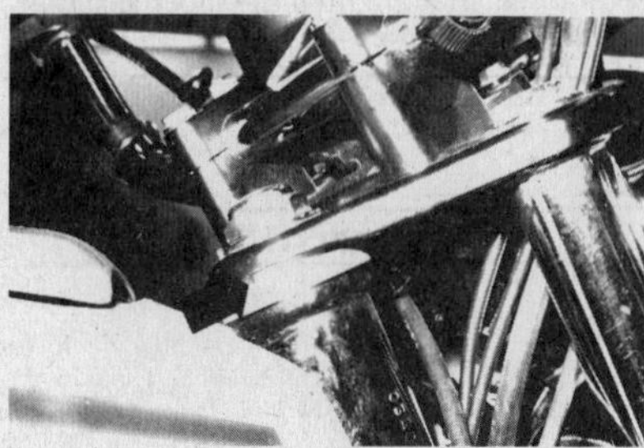

Steering head bearing adjusting nut (arrow)

6. The bearings are adjusted by means of the adjuster nut under the upper triple clamp.

7. Tighten or loosen the adjuster nut a little at a time until the steering stem adjustment conforms to that outlined above.

8. If proper adjustment is not possible, the bearings and races will probably need to be replaced.

Removal

1. Jack the front wheel off the ground.
2. Remove the gas tank to provide working clearance.
3. Remove the front wheel, brake caliper on disc brake models, and the front fender.
4. Remove the headlight shell.
5. Unbolt the instruments.
6. Remove the handlebars.
7. Unscrew and remove the steering stem nut.
8. Remove the fork crown bolts. Remove the fork covers.
9. Loosen the lower triple clamp pinch bolts and remove the fork legs.
10. Loosen the steering stem adjuster nut with a pin wrench, then hold the steering stem up while unscrewing the adjuster nut the rest of the way off.

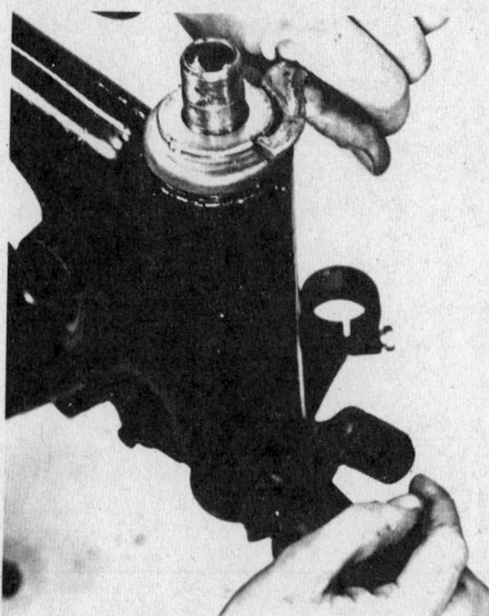

Removing the adjusting nut

Remove the top cone race and the ball bearings from the top race.

11. Carefully pull the steering stem out from the bottom. Some of the ball bearings from the lower race will probably fall out at this time so be prepared for this.
12. Remove the bottom cone race, dust seal, and dust seal washer from the steering stem if they are to be replaced. These will have to be pried off with a chisel, therefore only remove them if necessary.
13. The bearing races in the frame lug are a press-fit and should not be removed unless replacement is necessary. If replacement is necessary, the old races can be removed by reaching through the frame lug with a suitable punch and tapping the race evenly around its circumference to remove it from the inside of the frame lug. Be sure that the race does not become cocked in its seat upon removal.

New races are installed with suitable sized bearing driver: i.e., one which will drive the race squarely into its seat. Be certain that the race goes straight in.

These races can also be installed using a block of hard wood of sufficient size to cover the race in place of a bearing driver.

Inspection

1. Wash the ball bearings in a suitable solvent.
2. Clean all of the old grease from the bearing race surfaces, steering stem, and frame lug.
3. Inspect the bearing race surfaces. They must be clean and smooth. That is free from any cracks, scoring, rust, or indentations. Run your finger around each of the bearing races. Note any roughness or ripples on the race surface. If any imperfections are noted, both the sets of races and all of the balls must be replaced.
4. Check the balls themselves for rust, pitting, scoring, or flat spots. If the balls are found to be defective in any way, the balls and both sets of races must be replaced.

NOTE: *Balls and races must always be replaced in a set as worn races will destroy new balls and worn balls will destroy new races.*

5. Check the dust seal for condition and replace if torn or cracked.
6. Check the steering stem for cracks or a bent condition; this is especially important if the bike has been involved in a spill.

Installation

1. Install the dust seal washer, dust seal, and lower cone race on the steering stem. Use a good grade of bearing grease to coat the bottom cone race and the upper race in the frame lug.
2. Embed 18 balls into the grease of the top frame lug and 19 balls into the grease of the lower cone race.
3. When the balls are in place, slip the steering stem through the frame lug and hold it in place while refitting the top cone race and threading on the adjuster nut.
4. Tighten the adjuster nut all of the way by hand, rotating the steering stem to work the grease into the balls.
5. Tighten the adjuster nut until the steering stem turns freely, but has no play.
6. Install the fork tubes, headlight assembly, and upper triple clamp, flat washer, and steering stem nut. Tighten the steering stem nut to 65–87 ft lbs. Cehck that the stem moves freely to the steering lock of its own weight when released from 5°–10° off center; if not check for:
   a. Steering bearings too tight;
   b. Bent steering stem;
   c. Worn races or balls.
7. Install the front fender, front wheel, and handlebars.

SWING ARM

Inspection

1. Remove the chain guard.
2. Remove the rear wheel assembly. Remove the shock absorbers, removing the top bolt first on each one.
3. Measure the distance between the top and bottom shock absorber mounts on both sides. The two measurements must be identical, or the swing arm will have to be replaced.
4. Check that the rear wheel mounting plates are parallel.
5. Grasp the legs of the swing arm and attempt to move it from side-to-side. Any noticeable side-play will indicate that the swing arm bushings need replacement.

The swing arm is most likely to be damaged if the machine is operated for any length of time with a broken or otherwise defective shock absorber.

Removal and Installation

1. Proceed as above. Then remove the swing arm pivot bolt nut, and pull the pivot bolt out from the right-side.

Swing arm pivot nut

2. Remove the swing arm by pulling it straight back.
3. The swing arm should be inspected for cracks or fractures, especially around the welds.

After removal of the swing arm, the dust seals sleeves and bushings can be replaced.

4. With a small punch and hammer, drive out the sleeve on each side of the swing arm. Remove the bushings, tapping them out with a long drift and hammer. Once the bushings are removed, they should be replaced.
5. Lubricate the new bushings and both inside and outside of the sleeves with a good grade of chassis grease. Press in one bushing, refit the sleeve, and install the other bushing.
6. Use some grease to hold the dust seals in place on both sides of the bushings.
7. Install the swing arm. Insert the pivot shaft from the right side. Install and tighten the pivot shaft nut.

Correct pivot shaft nut torque is 40–51 ft lbs.

After tightening the nut, move the swing arm up and down to ensure that movement is smooth and effortless.

REAR SHOCK ABSORBERS

No service to the rear shock is possible. In the event of oil leaks, bent or broken plunger shaft, dented or otherwise damaged case, the shock absorber must be replaced.

If the shock absorbers are somewhat old, and one fails in the course of normal usage, it would be a good idea to replace both shocks to insure equal damping characteristics.

Shock absorbers can be removed from the motorcycle by removing the two mounting bolts, top bolt first.

To check a shock which is removed from the machine, place the bottom end on the ground and use the weight of your body to compress it as much as possible. Release one shock and note the rebound behavior. If the shock returns quickly at first, then slowly returns to the normal length, it is serviceable. If it returns to its normal length all at once, it should be replaced.

CAUTION: *A special spring compressor is necessary to remove the damper assembly from the spring. This work should be left to a specialist.*

On installation, tighten the shock absorber mounting bolts to 22–29 ft lbs.

CHASSIS TORQUE SPECIFICATIONS

Part	Torque (ft lbs)
Steering stem nut	65-87
Caliper mounting bolts (1978-80)	22-29
Caliper mounting bolt (1981-On)	14-18
Caliper shaft (1981-On)	18-24
Caliper bracket (1981-On)	22-29
Fork crown bolts (standard forks)	51-65
Fork caps (air forks)	11-22
Lower triple clamp pinch bolts	13-18
Upper triple clamp pinch bolts	7-9
Air fittings	3-5
Air hose	11-14
Front axle nut	36-58
Rear axle nut	51-72
Swing arm shaft nut	40-51
Rear shock absorber bolts	22-29
Front axle cap nuts	13-18
Foot peg mounting bolts	40-47
Rear brake anchor nut	11-17
Brake disc bolts	20-24
Rear sprocket nuts	43-51
Engine mounting, 10 mm flange	33-43

Honda 350-650 Fours

MODEL COVERAGE

CB 350 F, F1
CB 400 F
CB 500, K1-K2
CB 550, K1-K2
CB 550 K
CB 550 F
CB 650/C

INDEX

GENERAL INFORMATION

SERIAL NUMBER LOCATION

In order to prevent possible confusion when purchasing parts, always refer to the engine and frame serial numbers. The frame number is stamped on the left side of the steering lug, while the engine number is behind the cylinders on the top left side of the crankcase.

MAINTENANCE

NOTE: *Common maintenance procedures are explained in detail in the "General Information" section.*

LUBRICATION

Motor Oil

For use in all temperatures, Honda recommends SAE 10W-40 motor oil service rating "SE" or "SF."

Straight grades can also be used according to ambient air temperatures as given in the "Recommended Lubricants" chart at the end of this section.

Checking Oil Level

1. Allow the engine to run for several minutes before checking the oil level.
2. With the machine parked on the center stand on level ground, and with the engine shut off, unscrew and remove the dipstick and wipe it clean. Reinsert the dipstick, allowing it to rest on the threads of its hole. Do not screw it in. Remove it and check the level. It should be between the upper and lower level marks inscribed on the dipstick. If it is at or near the lower mark, add enough oil to bring the level up to the upper mark, but do not overfill the crankcase.

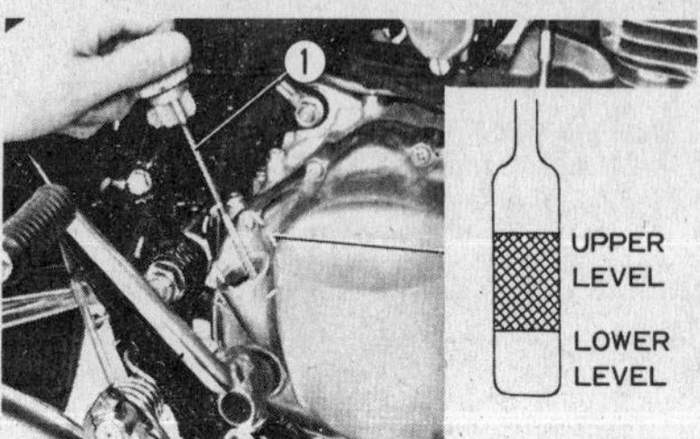

Dipstick upper and lower level marks

Changing Oil

1. The recommended oil change interval is 1,500 miles, or three months, whichever comes first.
2. Oil should be changed when the engine is warm. This ensures more complete draining and makes it more likely that the oil will carry off any particulate matter with it.
3. Remove the dipstick. Unscrew and remove the crankcase drain plug, allowing the oil to drain for several minutes into a suitable container. Kick the engine over several times with the kickstarter (ignition switched *off*) to remove any old oil remaining in the system.

Oil drain plug (1) and oil filter bolt (2) (350/400)

4. Check the condition of the drain plug gasket. Install the plug, and tighten it to about 25 ft lbs.

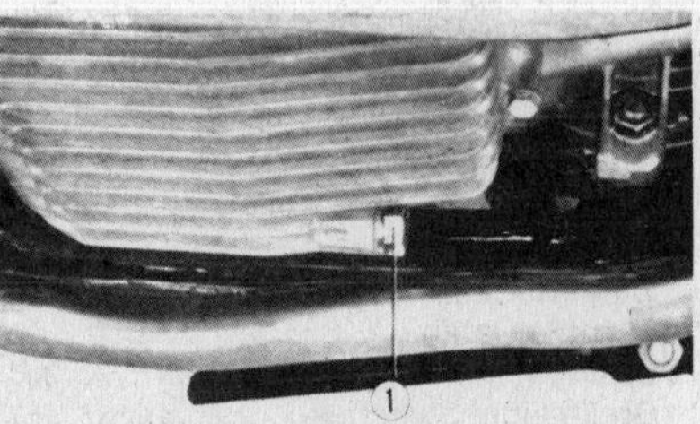

Oil drain plug (1) (500/550)

5. If the oil filter is to be replaced, refer to "Oil Filter," below.
6. SAE 10W-40 oil is recommended for all models and can be used at any temperature. If the average air temperature is above 59° F (15° C), SAE 20W-50 oil can also be used.

General Specifications

	CB350F	*CB400F*	*CB500*	*CB550*	*CB650*
ENGINE					
Type	Four-cylinder, single overhead camshaft, air-cooled				
Displacement (cc/ci)	347/21.1	408/24.9	498/30.38	544/33.19	627/38.2
Bore x Stroke (mm/in.)	47.0 x 50.0/1.850 x 1.969	51.0 x 50.0/2.008 x 1.969	56.0 x 50.6/2.205 x 1.992	58.5 x 50.6/2.302 x 1.992	59.8 x 55.8/2.354 x 2.197
Compression Ratio	9.3 : 1	9.4 : 1	9.0 : 1	9.0 : 1	9.0 : 1
Carburetion	(4) 21 mm Keihin	(4) 21 mm Keihin	(4) 22 mm Keihin	(4) 22 mm Keihin	(4) 26 mm Keihin
Lubrication	wet sump	wet sump	wet sump	wet sump	wet sump
DRIVE TRAIN					
Clutch	wet, multi-plate	wet, multi-plate	wet, multi-plate	wet, multi-plate	wet, multi-plate
Primary Reduction	3.423	3.423	2.000	3.062	2.737
Final Reduction	2.235	2.235	2.000 (17/34)	2.176 (17/37)	2.500 (16/40)
Transmission Ratios (overall)					
1st	2.733	2.733	2.353	2.353	2.500
2d	1.850	1.800	1.636	1.636	1.722
3rd	1.416	1.375	1.269	1.269	1.333
4th	1.148	1.111	1.036	1.036	1.074
5th	0.965	0.965	0.900	0.900	0.885
6th	—	0.866	—	—	—
CHASSIS					
Dry Weight (kg/lbs)	170/375	170/375	183/404	192/423	196/431
Frame Type	semi-double cradle	semi-double cradle	full double cradle	full double cradle	full double cradle
Wheelbase (mm/in.)	1355/53.3	1355/53.3	1405/55.5	1405/55.5	1430/56.3
Tire Size:					
front	3.00 x 18	3.00 x 18	①	3.25 x 19	3.50H19
rear	3.50 x 18	3.50 x 18	3.50 x 18	3.75 x 18	4.50H17
Overall Length (mm/in.)	2060/81.1	2040/80.3	②	2120/83.5	2170/85.4
Overall Width (mm/in.)	780/30.7	780/30.7	825/32.5	825/32.5	850/33.5
Overall Height (mm/in.)	1090/42.9	1080/42.5	1115/44.0	1115/44.0	1175/46.3
Ground Clearance (mm/in.)	155/6.1	150/5.9	165/6.5	160/6.3	160/6.3
ELECTRICAL SYSTEM					
Ignition	battery and coil	battery and coil	battery and coil	battery and coil	transistor
Starting	electric and kick	electric and kick	electric and kick	electric and kick	electric
Charging	alternator	alternator	alternator	alternator	alternator
Regulator	dual-contact	dual-contact	dual-contact	dual-contact	solid-state
Battery (volts/amp hours)	12/12	12/12	12/12	12/12	12/12
Alternator	three-phase excited field	three-prase excited field	three-phase excited field	three-phase excited field	three-phase excited field

① CB500: 3.15 x 19
CB500K1-K2: 3.25 x 19

② CB500: 2105/83.0
CB500K1-K2: 2120/83.5

7. Add about 3 qts of oil to the crankcase. Start the engine and allow it to run for several minutes, then shut it off and check the oil level. Add oil, as necessary, to bring the level up to the upper mark on the dipstick. Crankcase capacities are as follows:

CB350/400	3.7 qts.
CB500/550/650	3.2 qts.

Oil Filter

1. The oil filter element should be replaced at every other oil change, or at 3000 mile/6 month intervals.

Oil filter assembly

1. Oil filter cover
2. O-ring
3. Spring
4. Washer
5. Oil filter element
6. Oil filter center bolt

2. After removing the crankcase drain plug and allowing the oil to run off, remove the oil filter housing bolt, placing a drip pan or suitable substitute beneath the housing to catch any oil in the filter housing.
3. Take out the old filter, washer, and spring. Clean the housing. Check the condition of the housing O-ring.
4. Wipe off the mating surface on the crankcase with a clean rag. Oil the O-ring lightly with clean oil.
5. Slipping the filter housing bolt into place, fit the spring and washer, then the new filter element. Install the housing, tightening the housing bolt to 20–24 ft lbs.

CAUTION: *Do not overtighten the housing bolt. If this is done, it will not only be difficult to remove, but it may crack the housing in the area around the bolt hole. If the bolt is difficult to remove, be sure to inspect the housing closely around the bolt hold for small cracks.*

6. Add oil to the crankcase as outlined under "Changing Oil," above.

Filter Screen

1. All models are equipped with a filter screen in the sump which should be cleaned and inspected at 6,000-mile or 12-month intervals.

Oil strainer screen

2. After draining the sump, unbolt and remove the oil pan.
3. Withdraw the screen from the oil pump, and clean it in a safe solvent, brushing off foreign matter if necessary. Inspect the screen mesh for holes, and replace it if any are noted.

When refitting the filter screen, align the slot in the strainer with the crankcase rib.

4. When installing the pan, a new gasket should be used. After refilling the system with oil, start the engine and check for leaks around the oil pan mating surface.

Front Forks

350/500

1. ATF is recommended for all forks. Special types of oil designed specifically for motorcycle forks can also be used, although care must be taken to flush the forks thoroughly when changing types or brands of fork fluid, since some may not be compatible with others.

Do not use gasoline to flush forks.

2. Fork oil should be changed every 6,000 miles or 12 months.
3. Place a container beneath one of the fork sliders and remove the drain plug. Pump the slider up and down until all the oil is expelled. Examine the plug gasket, then refit the plug. Repeat the procedure with the other slider.

Fork slider drain plug (1)

4. Examine the drained oil. If it contains water or is exceptionally dirty, it may be that the fork gaitors or dust covers are damaged and allowing foreign matter to get past. This will also damage fork seals quickly. Check that the gaitors or dust covers are properly secured and replace them if cracked, ripped, or otherwise damaged.
5. Remove the handlebar clamp bolts and move the bars to one side or the other to allow access to the fork filler caps.
6. The fork filler caps are threaded into the fork tubes, and are also connected to the fork damper rod. Removal will be facilitated by first loosening the upper triple clamp pinch bolts. Next, compress the front forks either by placing a block beneath the front wheel, or by parking the machine on the side stand, rather than the center stand.
7. Remove *one* of the fork filler caps which should rise out of the fork tube if the forks are sufficiently compressed.

CAUTION: *Do not remove both filler caps simultaneously unless the front wheel is supported off the ground, or the forks will collapse.*

8. Add the proper grade and quantity of ATF to the fork tube. Capacities are:

350	105cc/3.6 oz.
500	145cc/4.9 oz.

9. Inspect the filler cap O-rings for condition. Oil them lightly before refitting the cap(s).
10. Allow the forks to extend so that the damper is drawn back into the fork tube. Secure the filler cap. Tighten the upper triple clamp pinch bolt.

Fork filler caps (1)

11. Repeat the procedure with the remaining fork leg.
12. Secure the handlebars, tightening the forwardmost bolts first.
13. After several miles of operation, check the area around the fork slider seals for leaks or seepage. Even a minimal amount would necessitate replacement of the seals. A coating of grime building up in this area over a period of time is also indicative of ineffective seals.

400/550/650 (Except Air Shocks)

1. ATF is recommended for all forks. Special types of oil designed specifically for motorcycle forks can also be used, although care must be taken to flush the forks thoroughly when changing types or brands of fork fluid, since some may not be compatible with others.

Do not use gasoline to flush forks.

2. Fork oil should be changed every 6,000 miles or 12 months.
3. Place a container beneath one of the fork sliders and remove the drain plug. Pump the slider up and down until all the oil is expelled. Examine the plug gasket, then refit the plug. Repeat the procedure with the other slider.
4. Examine the drained oil. If it contains water or is exceptionally dirty, it may be that the fork gaitors or dust covers are damaged and allowing foreign matter to get past. This will also damage fork seals quickly. Check that the gaitors or dust covers are properly secured and replace them if cracked, ripped, or otherwise damaged.
5. Support the front wheel off the ground by placing a scissors jack or similar device beneath the engine.

CAUTION: *Do not remove the fork filler caps without supporting the front wheel in this manner.*

6. Remove the handlebar clamp bolts and move the bars to one side or the other to allow access to the fork filler caps.
7. Loosen the upper triple clamp pinch bolts to facilitate removal of the filler caps. Remove the fork filler caps. The caps are under spring tension, so care should be exercised when removing them.
8. Add the proper grade and quantity of oil to each fork leg. For a routine oil change, these quantities are:

400/650	145–150 cc/4.8–4.9 oz.
550	170–175 cc/5.8–5.9 oz.

9. Inspect the filler cap O-rings for condition. Oil them lightly before refitting the caps. Install the caps and tighten them securely. Tighten the upper triple clamp pinch bolts.
10. Secure the handlebars, tightening the forwardmost bolts first.
11. After several miles of operation, check the area around the fork slider seals for leaks

or seepage. Even a minimal amount would necessitate replacement of the seals. A coating of grime building up in this area over a period of time is also indicative of ineffective seals.

Chain slack should be measured at the middle of the lower run

Chassis Lubrication

1. The swing arm pivot is fitted with one or two grease nipples which should be lubricated with chassis grease every 3,000 miles. On most models the nipples are on the ends of the swing arm pivot shaft, while the latest designs have a single nipple in the middle of the swing arm.

2. Wheel and steering head bearings are lubricated with bearing grease, the service interval being 12,000 miles or 24 months.

Swing arm grease nipple (1)

SERVICE CHECKS AND ADJUSTMENTS

Drive Chain

1. The chain should have about ¾ in. (20 mm) of total up-and-down free-play measured in the middle of the lower chain run.

2. Before checking or adjusting the chain slack, the following conditions should be met:

a. The motorcycle should be placed on the center stand so that the rear wheel is off the ground;

b. The transmission should be placed in neutral;

c. The chain should be clean and well-lubricated;

d. The chain should have been checked for any tight spots by slowly rotating the wheel and checking for variances in the chain tension at different points. If a tight spot exists, the chain tension should be adjusted to the prescribed free-play at the tight spot. Note, however, that such a condition is indicative of a worn chain and probably worn sprockets which should be replaced as soon as possible.

3. To adjust the chain, first back off the rear brake adjuster nut.

4. Remove the axle nut cotter pin and loosen the axle nut several turns. Loosen the locknut on each chain adjuster bolt.

5. Turn each of the adjuster bolts in or out by equal amounts until the chain tension is approximately corrected.

6. Check wheel alignment by means of the aligning marks inscribed on both sides of the swing arm. Be sure that both adjusters are lined up with the same mark on each side. If not, turn one of the adjuster bolts in or out so that alignment is achieved.

7. Tighten the axle nut and adjuster bolt nuts and check the chain tension. The chain tension should also be checked with the weight of a rider sitting on the motorcycle when it is off the center stand; the chain should still have at least ½ in. of free-play. Correct if necessary. After adjustment is correct, torque the axle nut to 60–72 ft lbs.

Fit a new cotter pin. Readjust the rear brake.

Clutch

1. Cable adjustment must always be maintained at the proper specification. If the cable has insufficient free-play, the clutch will slip and rapidly burn out. If it has too much play, the clutch will not compltely disengage, resulting in hard shifting and creeping at stops.

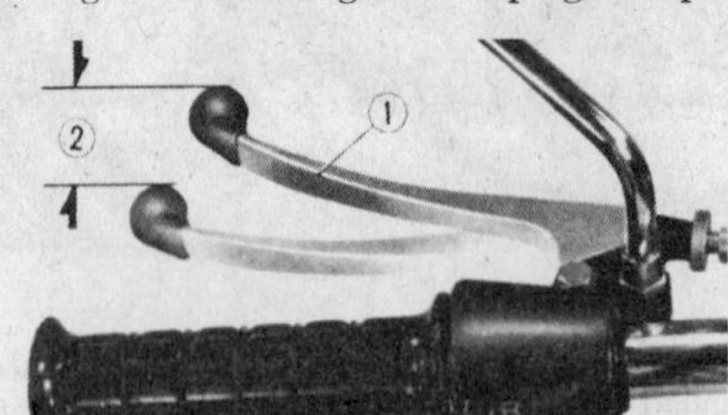
Measure free-play (2) at the end of the lever

2. Use the cable adjuster at the handlebar or engine to maintain the correct amount of cable slack. The clutch hand lever should be able to be moved 10–20 mm (0.4–0.8 in.) measured at the tip of the lever before the clutch begins to disengage.

If clutch operation is not satisfactory after making this adjustment, proceed as follows:

350/550 Models

1. Using the cable adjuster at the engine, align the clutch lever and the right crankcase index marks as illustrated.

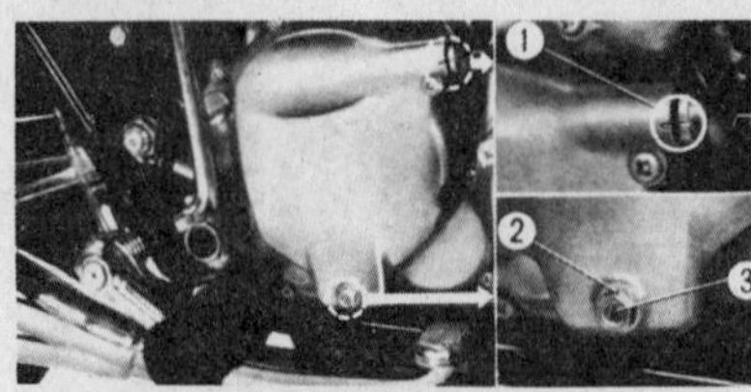
Line up the marks (1), loosen the locknut (2), and rotate the adjuster (3) (350)

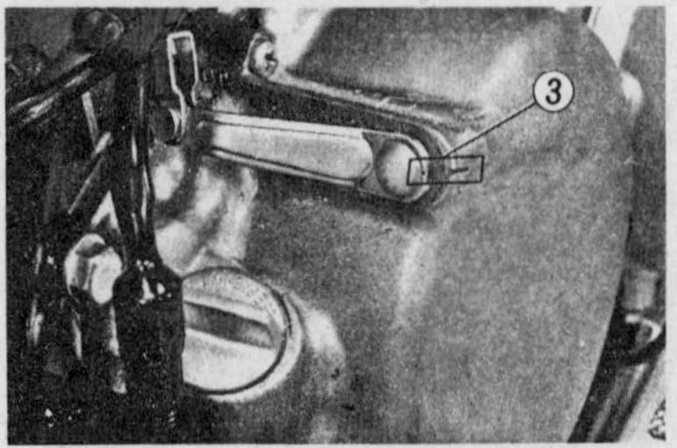
Clutch lever alignment marks (550)

2. Loosen the clutch adjuster locknut. Turn the adjuster counterclockwise until resistance is felt, then back it off about ¼ turn and tighten the locknut.

3. Use the cable adjusters so that the hand lever has the prescribed amount of free-play.

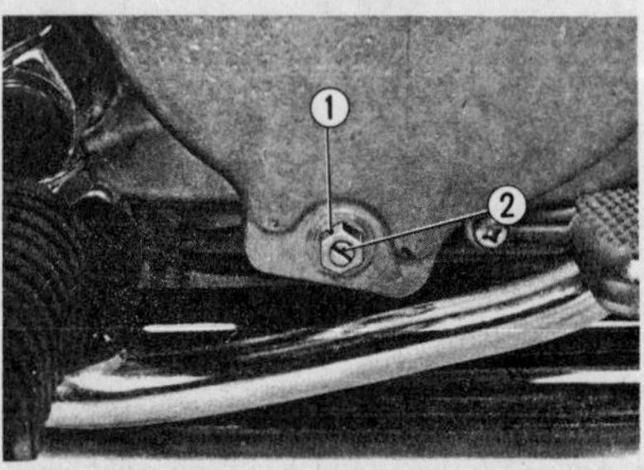
Clutch adjuster locknut (1) and adjuster (2) (550)

400 Models

1. Loosen the locknut, and screw the cable adjuster at the hand lever all of the way into the lever bracket.

2. Loosen the locknut, and screw the adjuster at the clutch housing all of the way into the housing to increase cable free-play to the maximum.

3. Remove the clutch cover from the clutch housing. Loosen the locknut on the clutch adjuster, and turn the adjuster in (clockwise) until a slight resistance is felt. From the point where resistance is first felt back the adjuster out (counterclockwise) ¼–½ turn, and tighten the locknut.

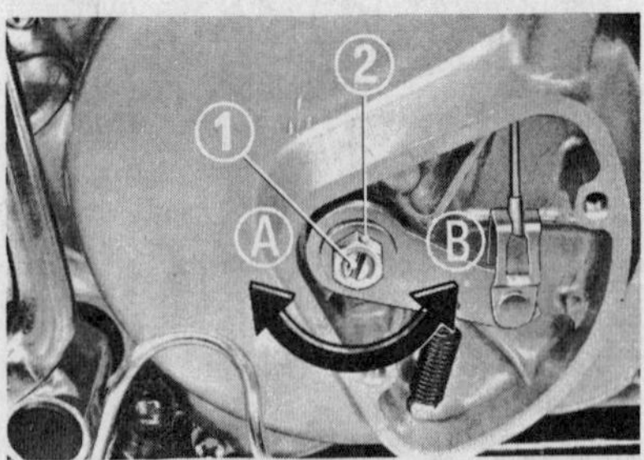

Clutch adjuster (1) and locknut (2) (400)

4. Using the cable adjuster at the clutch housing, adjust the cable so that there is about ¾ in. of free-play at the end of the hand lever. Use the adjuster at the hand lever to bring the cable free-play into specification.

500 Models

1. Loosen the locknut, and screw the cable adjuster at the hand lever all of the way into the lever bracket.

2. Loosen the locknut, and screw the adjuster at the engine into the housing to increase cable free-play to the maximum.

3. Loosen the clutch adjuster lockbolt and,

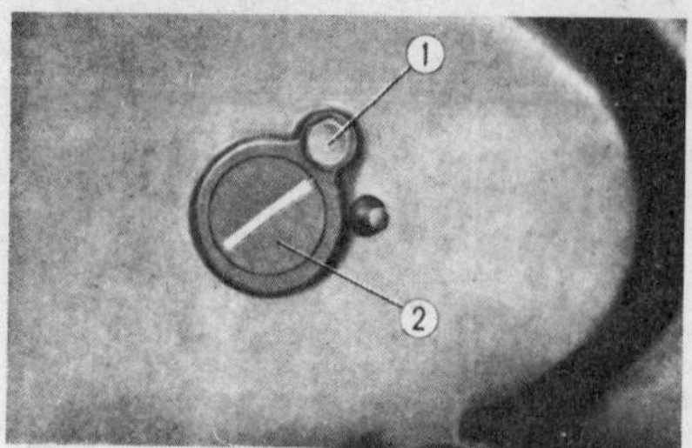
Clutch adjuster (2) and lockbolt (1)

using a large screwdriver, turn the adjuster clockwise until a slight resistance is felt. At this point, turn the adjusting screw counterclockwise approximately ⅛ in. and tighten the lockbolt.

4. Turn the cable adjuster at the engine out so that there is about ½ in. of free-play measured at the end of the lever, and tighten the locknut. Use the cable adjuster at the hand lever to bring the cable free-play into specification.

650 Models

1. Loosen the locknut on the cable adjuster at the engine and screw the adjuster all the way in to obtain maximum cable free-play.
2. Remove the clutch adjuster cover.
3. Loosen the clutch adjuster locknut. Turn the adjuster screw in (clockwise) until a slight resistance is felt, then back it off ¾ turn and hold it there while the locknut is secured.
4. Use the cable adjuster at the engine to give the proper amount of cable free-play.

Throttle Cable

1. The throttle cable is fitted with an adjuster at the twist-grip. The twist-grip should be able to be rotated approximately 10–15° before the throttle slides begin to open. This is equivalent to about 2–4 mm (0.08–0.16 in.) of cable free-play.

Cable adjuster (1) and locknut (2) location

2. Use the cable adjuster at the handlebar to make and maintain this adjustment. To check that the cable has sufficient slack, start the engine and turn the forks slowly from lock-to-lock. Idle speed must not increase. If it does, it indicates that the cable has insufficient free-play, is incorrectly routed, or is binding at some point.

Front Brake (350–550)

The front disc brake needs no routine maintenance other than a periodic check of fluid level and pad wear. If the brakes drag or lack power, adjustment of the caliper may be necessary, an operation which should also be done when new pads are fitted.

Brake fluid level line (1)

1. Position the front wheel so that it points straight ahead. After removing the master cylinder reservoir cap and diaphragm, check to see if the brake fluid level is up to the mark inscribed on the inside of the reservoir. Fluid level will drop slightly as the pads wear. If the fluid is below the level mark, add enough DOT 3 brake fluid to bring the level up to the mark. Reinstall the diaphragm and the cap, and tighten it securely.

CAUTION: *Do not use brake fluid from an old or unsealed container.*

2. Check the brake pads for wear and replace both of them if either is worn to the red limit line inscribed around the pads.

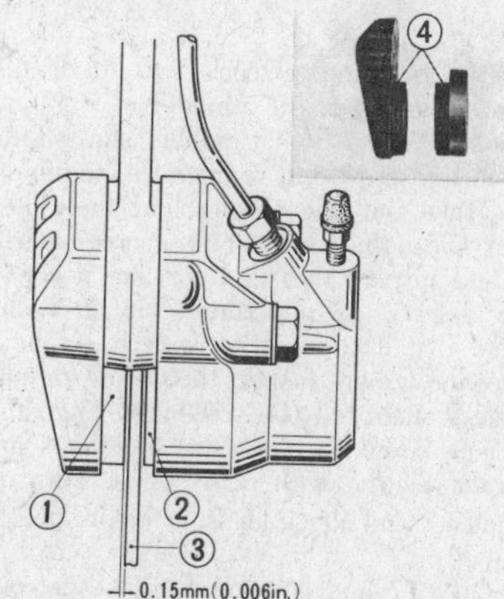

Replace the pads when worn to the red limit line (4)

1. Inner pad
2. Outer pad
3. Brake disc
4. Wear limit indicator

3. The brake lever should have 2–5 mm (0.08–0.2 in.) of free-play. If the lever has excessive travel and/or a mushy feel, the system should be bled.

Brake system service procedures such as pad replacement and bleeding are outlined in the "Chassis" section.

CALIPER ADJUSTMENT

The caliper must be adjusted whenever new pads are fitted, or if the brake seems to drag.

1. Raise the front wheel off the ground.
2. Clearance between the innermost pad and the brake disc should be 0.15 mm (0.006 in.).
3. To make the adjustment, loosen the adjusting screw locknut and turn the adjusting screw *counterclockwise* until the innermost pad contacts the disc. A slight drag on the front wheel will be noted when spinning the wheel.
4. Turn the adjusting screw *clockwise* until the wheel spins freely; then turn the adjusting screw ½ turn more in the same direction and tighten the locknut.
5. Check that the wheel turns freely without drag. Check for proper brake operation.

Brake caliper adjusting screw and locknut (1 and 2)

6. Brakes which drag constantly after application and which cannot be cured with proper caliper adjustment may be caused by sticking or seizure of the caliper bracket on its pivot. Free movement of the caliper is necessary for proper operation of the brake. This can be inhibited by dirt or other foreign matter between the pivot and caliper bracket. If the wheel will not turn freely after the brake is applied, try striking the caliper with the heel of your hand. If this frees the wheel, it is probable that the swinging bracket is becoming stuck. A penetrating fluid or parts lubricant applied to the bracket pivot will often remedy this problem.

Front Brake (650)

1. Turn the handlebars so that the brake fluid reservoir is parallel to the ground for an accurate check of the fluid level.
2. Maintain the fluid level between the upper and lower level marks.

Fluid level will drop slightly as the pads wear. If too much is added, fitting new pads may necessitate draining some of the fluid.

Use DOT 3 brake fluid only. Do not use fluid from an old or unsealed container.

3. Check the pads for wear and replace both of them if either is worn to the red limit line visible through the inspection slot on top of the caliper.

Rear Brake

1. Brake lining wear on newer models can be determined by means of the wear indicator pointer fitted to the brake lever on the hub. If the pointer lines up with the red slash mark when the brake pedal is fully applied, the linings are worn as far as possible for effective braking and should now be replaced.

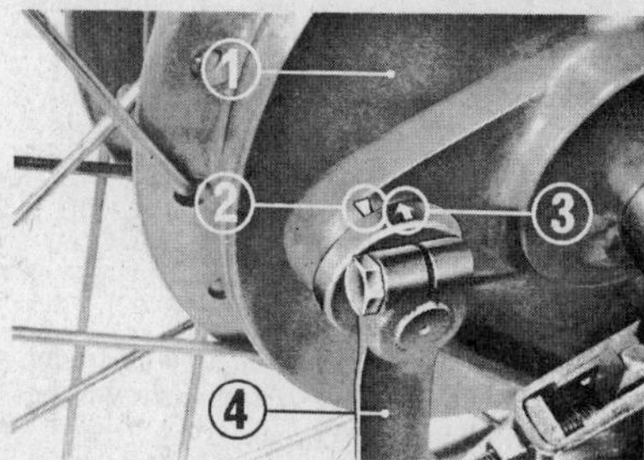
Brake wear indicator; replace the linings if the arrow and mark align when the brake is fully applied

2. On older models, observe the angle formed by the brake lever on the hub and the brake rod when the brake is fully applied. When the lever and rod form an angle greater than 90°, the shoes should be checked for wear as they probably are worn to the point of needing replacement.

3. The rear brake should be adjusted so

that there is approximately 25 mm (1 in.) of free-play at the pedal before the linings contact the drum. Adjust by turning the hex nut on the brake rod. When adjustment has been made, be sure that the nut is seated properly on the brake lever pin. Also, check the operation of the brake light switch.

4. Brake pedal position may be adjusted to suit individual taste by backing off the brake adjusting nut, loosening the pedal height adjusting bolt locknut, and turning the bolt until pedal position is satisfactory. Thereafter, adjust pedal free-play and the brake light switch.

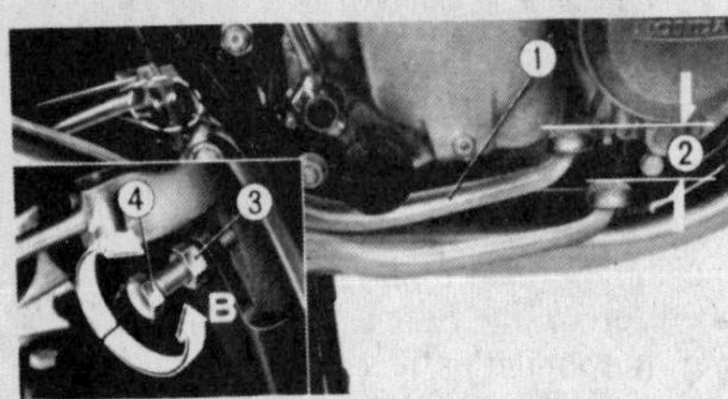

Rear brake pedal free-play (2). Pedal height can be adjusted by loosening the locknut (3) and rotating the adjusting bolt (4)

Brake Light Switches

The switches should be checked for operation after the brakes are adjusted. The rear brake light switch is mounted in a slotted bracket and secured by locknuts. Moving the switch up on the bracket allows the brake light to turn on sooner. Moving it down allows the light to turn on later.

Brake light switch; turning the locknut in direction A will allow the light to come on sooner

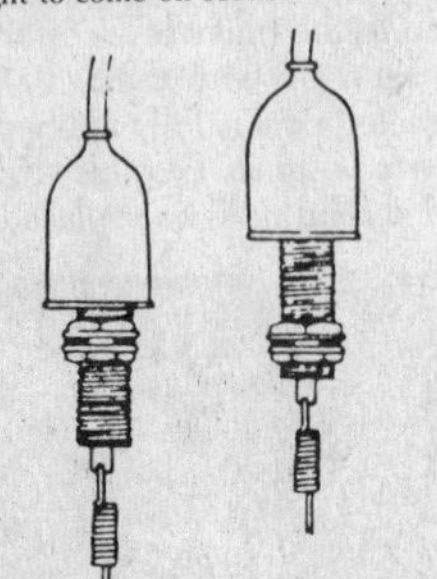

Do not turn the switch itself for adjustment. Turn the locknuts only, or the wires will become twisted and may break.

Generally, the brake light should come on just as the linings contact the drum.

The front brake light switch is activated by fluid pressure and is not adjustable. If it fails, check the switch as outlined in "Electrical Systems," chapter 7.

Headlight Adjustment

1. Set the machine about 25 feet away from and perpendicular to a wall, preferably of a color which reflects light well.

The machine should be off the stand, and with a rider putting his weight on the machine as in operation.

2. Switch on the high beam. The headlight high beam should be parallel to the ground and should hit the wall directly in front of the machine.

3. Vertical adjustment is made by loosening the two headlight shell mounting bolts slightly and pivoting the shell up or down.

4. Lateral adjustment is accomplished by means of the screw on the right-side of the headlight. Turning the screw clockwise will move the beam to the left; turning it counterclockwise will move it to the right.

FUEL SYSTEM

Fuel system maintenance involves cleaning the petcock fuel filter screen, cleaning or replacing the air cleaner, cleaning the carburetors, and cleaning the breather element (if fitted).

Normal service interval is 3,000 miles. Every 6,000 miles, the air cleaner element should be replaced.

Petcock

1. Two types of petcock are fitted, the change occurring on 1975 models.

2. On 1974 and earlier models, shut off the fuel, and unscrew and remove the sediment bowl. Take out the O-ring and fuel filter screen. Clean the bowl and filter screen in solvent and inspect the filter for any holes or other defects. If punctured, or so badly clogged that it cannot be properly cleaned, replace the screen. Inspect the O-ring for cuts or cracks. Reinstall the screen, O-ring, and sediment bowl. Be sure the fuel lines are properly secured with safety clips. Turn on the petcock and check for leaks before operation.

3. On 1975 and later models, the petcock filter screen is inside the gas tank. Shut off the fuel flow, and disconnect the lines from the petcock. Disconnect the fuel tank overflow line if fitted. Remove the gas tank and drain off the gas. Unscrew the securing nut and carefully take out the petcock. Remove the filter screen and securing nut from the petcock. Wash the filter in solvent to remove any foreign matter. Replace the filter element if it is badly clogged or if punctured. Check the condition of the gasket and replace it if it is crushed or nicked.

Installation is the reverse of removal. Be sure that the fuel lines are properly secured to the petcock with safety clips. Check for leaks before operation.

Petcock assembly

1. Sediment bowl
2. O-ring
3. Fuel filter
4. 6 mm screws
5. Petcock body
6. Gasket
7. Lever
8. Spring
9. Set plate
10. Screws

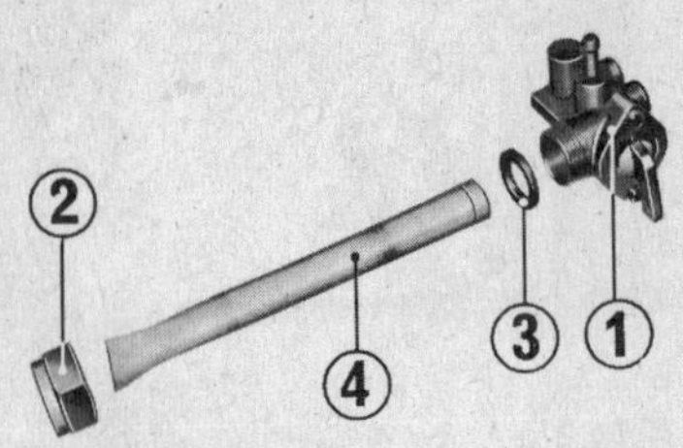

Petcock assembly (1975 and later) 1: petcock body; 2: nut; 3: o-ring; 4: filter screen

Air Filter (350–550)

1. Lift the seat and remove the tool tray and air cleaner cover.

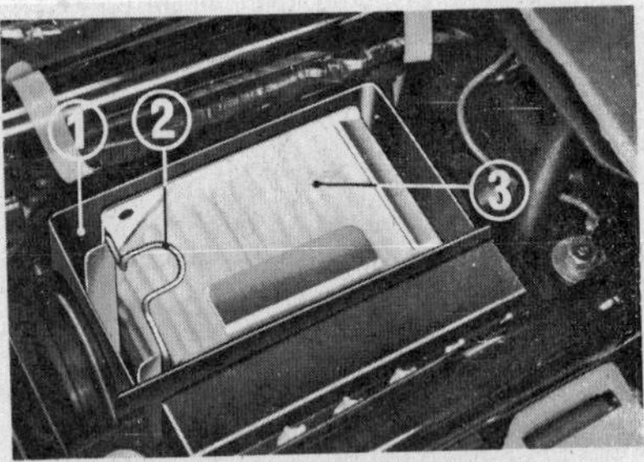

Case (1), set spring (2), filter element (3)

2. Pull out the spring clip. The filter element can now be withdrawn.

3. Tap the element lightly to remove any loose dirt, or use a reasonably soft brush to remove deposits. Blow out remaining dirt by applying compressed air to the inside of the element, if feasible.

4. Since cleaning paper elements is only partially effective, the unit should be replaced with a new one every 6,000 miles, or more often if used in a dusty environment.

Air Filter (650)

1. Remove the left side cover.

2. Remove the two air cleaner cover screws and take out the element.

3. Tap the element lightly to remove any loose dirt, or use a reasonably soft brush to remove deposits. Blow out remaining dirt with compressed air, if available.

4. Since cleaning dry paper elements in this fashion is only partially effective, the air cleaner element should be replaced with a new one every 6,000 miles, or more often if used in a dusty environment.

Breather Element

1. CB400 and 550 models are fitted with a crankcase rebreather system which directs crankcase fumes into the air cleaner box. A breather element separates water and oil from the air and allows them to drain off.

2. The breather element is accessible after removing the air cleaner element. Remove the element cover and take out the element.

3. Wash the element in a safe solvent and dry it thoroughly.

4. Check that the breather drain tube is clear. Squeeze the end to remove any oil or water; clean the inside of the breather case.

5. Install components in the reverse of removal.

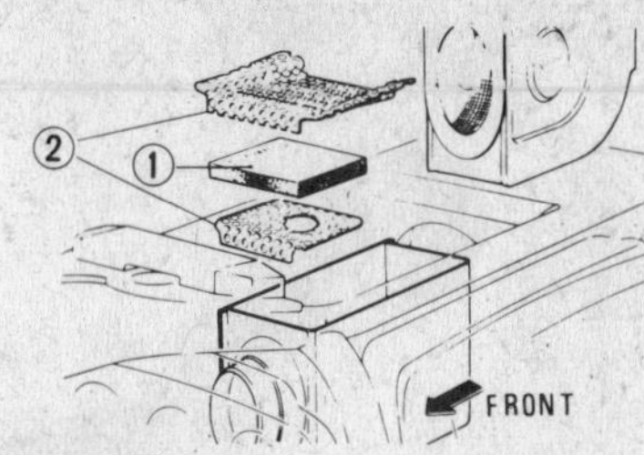

Breather assembly (400)

6. On the CB650, a collection tube for condensed crankcase vapors is equipped with a transparent section. The plug should be removed and residue drained off when it is visible.

Carburetors

1. Cleaning of the carburetor float bowl and jets should be accomplished every 3,000 miles.

2. For this operation, removal of the carburetors from the motorcycle as an assembly is recommended. Refer to "Fuel Systems," for procedures.

Recommended Lubricants

Engine
- General, all temperatures: SAE 10W-40, service rating "SE" or "SF"
- Alternates: Above 59° F: SAE 30, SAE 20W-50
  - 32° F to 59° F: SAE 20 or 20W
  - Below 32° F: SAE 10W

Front forks
- ATF
- SAE 10W-30
- SAE 20W
- SAE 30W

Disc brakes
- DOT 3 standard brake fluid

Control cables
- Light motor oil
- Graphite-based lubricant
- Molybdenum-disulphide-based lubricant

Tach, speedometer cables; throttle twist-grip
- Light duty grease

Wheel and steering head bearings
- Waterproof, medium-weight bearing grease

Grease fittings
- Waterproof, medium-weight chassis grease

Drive chain
- Lubricant developed specifically for motorcycle drive chains

Periodic Maintenance Intervals ①

Before each ride
- Safety items
- Operation of lights
- Chain adjustment
- Control cable adjustment

Weekly
- Engine oil level
- Tire pressure (check when cold)
- Battery electrolyte level

Every 200 miles
- Lubricate chain

Every 500 miles
- Check tightness of critical fasteners

Every 1,500 miles/3 months
- Change engine oil

Every 2,000 miles
- Clean and lubricate chain

Every 3,000 miles/6 months
- Change oil filter
- Service all grease fittings
- Clean breather element (if fitted)
- Clean air filter element
- Lubricate breaker cam felt
- Clean fuel petcock screen
- Lubricate all controls and cables
- Check disc brake fluid level
- Check brake pads or shoes for wear
- Check operation of brake controls
- Check clutch operation
- Check condition of chain and sprockets
- Check condition of fuel lines
- Clean and check carburetor operation
- Check spokes for tightness
- Check swing arm bushings
- Clean and gap or replace spark plugs
- Clean and gap breaker points
- Check ignition timing
- Adjust valve clearance
- Adjust cam chain tensioner

Every 6,000 miles/12 months
- Clean oil filter screen
- Change fork oil
- Replace air filter element
- Adjust steering head bearings

Every 12,000 miles/24 months
- Flush and refill disc brake fluid
- Repack wheel and steering head bearings

① Based on normal usage after initial service and break-in are completed

TUNE-UP

NOTE: *Common tune-up procedures are explained in detail in the "General Information" section.*

COMPRESSION TEST

1. A compression check should be made before each tune-up since this will provide a general idea of engine condition.

2. It is necessary to have a gauge with a flexible hose and the proper screw-in adapter (plug holes are 12 mm).

3. The engine should be at operating temperature when checking compression.

4. Remove all of the spark plugs and fit the gauge to one of the plug holes.

5. Close the choke and hold the throttle wide open while spinning the engine with the starter motor. Note the compression reading and repeat the test with the remaining cylinders.

6. Compression may vary according to gauge tolerance and several other factors. However, it should normally be between 140 and 170 psi. All cylinders must be within 15 psi of this range and of each other.

CAM CHAIN ADJUSTMENT

CB650

1. Remove the pulser generator cover (right side).

2. Be sure that the ignition is *off* and the transmission is in neutral.

3. Loosen the cam chain tensioner locknut located between cylinders Nos. 2 & 3 at the rear of the cylinder block.

4. Slowly turn the engine over in the normal direction of rotation (clockwise viewed from the right side of the engine) using a wrench on the crankshaft special nut. While doing this, retighten the tensioner locknut. Chain tension will be set automatically.

Other Models

1. Raise the seat, disconnect the fuel lines, and remove the gas tank.

2. Remove the points cover. Remove the valve adjuster caps from the No. 1 (left outside) cylinder, and remove all four spark plugs to make it easier to turn the engine over.

Maintenance Data

	CB350	CB400F	CB500	CB550, 550F (1974–76)	CB550, 550F (1977–78)	CB650
Oil capacity (l/qts)	3.5/3.7	3.5/3.7	3.0/3.2	3.0/3.2	3.2/3.4	3.0/3.2
Front forks (cc/oz)						
Routine change	105/3.0	145–150/4.8–4.9	140/4.7	170–175/5.8–5.9	③	150/4.9
After rebuilding	125/4.2	160–165/5.6–5.8	160/5.4	185–190/6.3–6.5	160–165/5.6–5.8	170/5.8
Tire pressure (psi)						
Solo (front/rear)	26/28	26/28	①	25/28	25/28	28/32
Two-up or extended high speed (front/rear)	26/36	26/36	②	28/36	28/36	28/40
Battery						
Voltage/Output (v/ah)	12/12	12/12	12/12	12/12	12/12	12/12
Continuous charging rate (amps)	1.2	1.2	1.2	1.2	1.2	1.2

① CB500: 26/29
CB500K1-K2: 29/29
② CB500: 26/34
CB500K1-K2: 29/34
③ CB550K: 150–155/5.1–5.2
CB550F: 145–150/4.8–4.9

3. Using a wrench on the special nut provided for this purpose on the end of the breaker cam shaft, turn the engine over in the normal direction of rotation (clockwise as viewed from the right side) until the "T" (top dead center) mark for cylinders Nos. 1 and 4 ("1.4") aligns with the timing index mark.

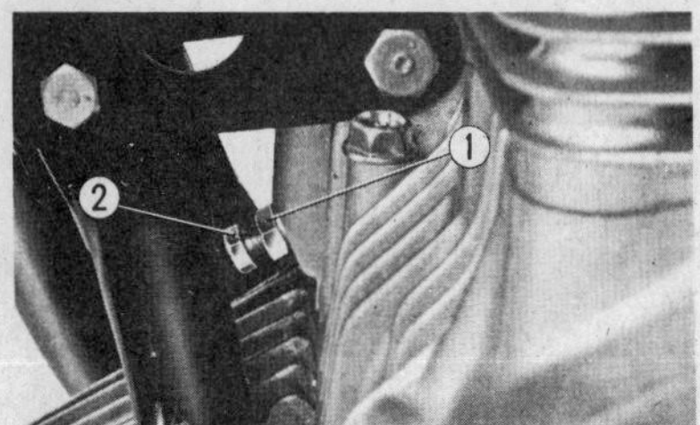

Cam chain locknut (1) and tensioner bolt (2) (350/400)

4. Check that there is clearance at both valves for the No. 1 cylinder. If not, turn the crankshaft one complete revolution (360°) until the marks again align, and check the valves. To be effective, the chain adjustment must be performed when the No. 1 cylinder is on the compression stroke.

5. After the crankshaft has been properly positioned, continue to turn it clockwise until the spring peg on the timing advancer is just to the right of the timing index mark. In this position, cylinders 1 and 4 will be at 15° ATDC (after top dead center) and the adjustment can be performed.

CAUTION: *Do not rotate the crankshaft counterclockwise* (opposite the direction of normal rotation) *if you have turned it too far. Instead, rotate it clockwise through two revolutions so that the No. 1 piston will again be on the compression stroke and you can position the spring peg just to the right of the timing mark without having to turn the crankshaft back. Otherwise all of the slack may not be taken out of the chain.*

6. 350/400: The cam chain adjuster is located on the front of the engine. After positioning the engine as outlined above, loosen the locknut and back out the adjuster bolt until you can turn it with your fingers. At this point the bolt has released pressure on the

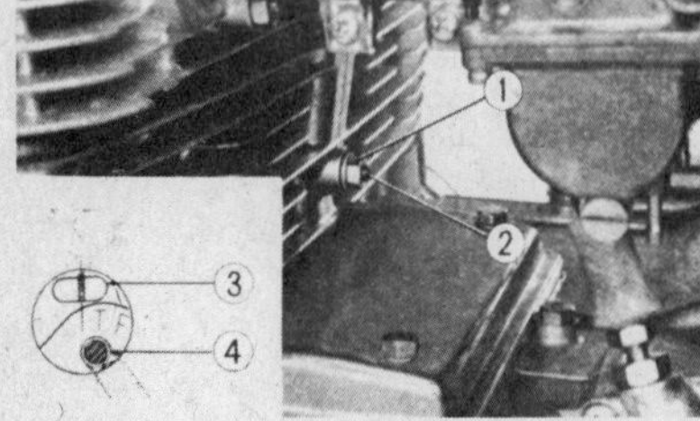

Cam chain adjuster (500)

1. Locknut 3. Timing mark
2. Adjuster 4. Spring peg

tensioner rod which has moved in automatically to take up the slack. Tighten the bolt to 5.9–7.2 ft lbs, then tighten the locknut.

7. 500/550: After positioning the crankshaft as outlined above, loosen the tensioner locknut and the proper chain tension will be obtained automatically. Tighten the locknut.

VALVE ADJUSTMENT

NOTE: *Valves must be adjusted when the engine is* cold.

In the following procedure, the cylinders are numbered 1 through 4, going from left to right from the point of view of a rider sitting on the machine. The firing order is 1-2-4-3.

1. Disconnect the fuel lines from the petcock, raise the seat, and remove the gas tank.

2. Unscrew and remove the valve adjuster caps from each cylinder. On the CB650, remove the adjustment covers and the breather cover. Remove the breaker points or pulser generator cover (right side). Remove the spark plugs.

3. Using a wrench on the special nut on the end of the crankshaft, turn the engine over in the normal direction of rotation (clockwise) and observe the valves of the No. 1 (left outside) cylinder. When the intake valve opens and then closes, the piston is approaching top dead center (TDC) on the compression stroke. Continue to turn the crankshaft slowly while observing the timing marks on the timing advancer. When the "T" 1.4 mark aligns with the index mark, check for clearance at both valves for the No. 1 cylinder. If there is clearance here, the crankshaft is properly positioned with the No. 1 cylinder at TDC on the compression stroke, and the valves can be adjusted according to the following procedure. If there is not clearance at both valves, the piston is at TDC on the *exhaust* stroke and the engine must be turned through one complete revolution until the "T" 1.4 mark again comes into alignment.

Rotate the engine with a wrench on the special nut (1) until the "T1.4" mark (2) and the index mark (3) line up

4. When the engine is properly set up as outlined in step 3, half the valves can be adjusted. These are the valves identified as "A" in the following chart:

(Looking down on the engine, from the rider's position.) Right side

	No. 1 Cyl	*No. 2 Cyl*	*No. 3 Cyl*	*No. 4 Cyl*
Exhaust Valves	A	A	B	B
Intake Valves	A	B	A	B

5. Valve clearances are as follows:

	350/400	*500/550/650*
Intake (mm/in.)	0.05/0.002	0.05/0.002
Exhaust (mm/in.)	0.05/0.002	0.08/0.003

The clearances are measured between the valve stem and the adjusting screw. If the valve clearance is correct, a feeler gauge blade of this thickness will be a light slip fit. That is, there should be some resistance when pulling the blade through the valve, but not a considerable amount.

6. If the clearance is too large or too small, loosen the valve adjuster locknut and turn the adjuster so that a slip fit is obtained. Hold the adjuster in position and tighten the locknut securely (350/400: 5–8 ft. lbs.; 500/550/650: 8–11 ft. lbs.). Recheck clearance after tightening the nut.

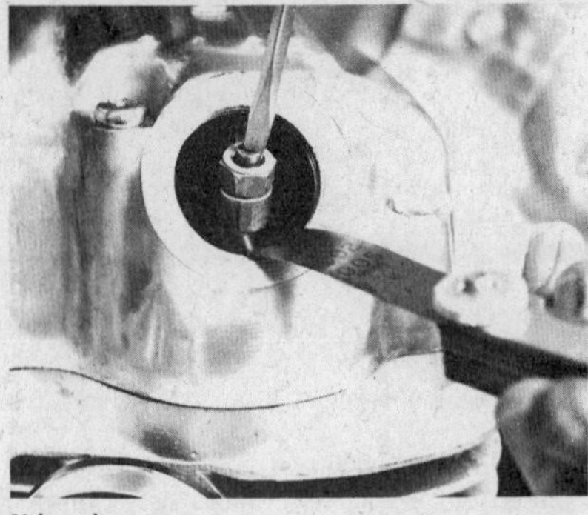
Valve adjustment

7. After all of the "A" valves are adjusted, turn the crankshaft one complete revolution (360°) until the "T" 1.4 mark again aligns with the index mark. In this position, the No. 4 (right outside) cylinder should be at TDC on the compression stroke (check for clearance at both valves) and the valves marked "B" can now be adjusted.

NOTE: *When the engine is at operating temperature, the valves should be very quiet. Ticking from properly adjusted valves is sometimes due to the valve stem becoming indented by the valve adjuster screw. This should be confined to older machines, since the valve ends are stellite-coated. Indentations on the valve stem will give a false feeler gauge reading: the clearance will be too large. Valves can be checked by visual inspection by unscrewing the adjuster.*

While more annoying than harmful, the only safe remedy for this situation is replacement of the valves.

CONTACT BREAKER POINTS

Location

The points and condensers are located on the right end of the crankshaft beneath the chromed points cover. The timing advance mechanism is fitted onto the crankshaft behind the breaker point base plate.

Replacement

1. Points sets are available complete with condensers already mounted on the breaker plate. Removal is accomplished by removing the small-6 mm bolt on the end of the breaker cam and taking off the large nut used to turn the engine over. This large nut is keyed to its shaft, not threaded. Next, disconnect the primary wires at the connectors. Carefully pull the wires through, noting the proper routing. Remove the three screws which secure the breaker plate. When the new plate is fitted, position it so that the securing screws are approximately centered in their slots, and adjust the point gaps and the ignition timing.

2. If the points are purchased separately, disconnect the primary wire at each point set, remove the securing screw, and remove the old points.

When installing new points, note that the

proper installation of the insulating washers at the primary terminal is critical. If improperly installed, no spark will occur. There is a small insulating tube which fits around the terminal bolt and two insulating washers, one immediately on either side of the terminal bracket. All connectors (condenser, primary wire, points spring) are made on the outer sides of three washers (i.e., no connector must touch the bracket, which is a ground).

3. New points may have a protective coating on the contact surfaces to prevent oxidation. Clean off these surfaces with a non-oily solvent before attempting to start the machine.

4. If the motorcycle will not start immediately after installation of new points, check that the primary wire connections are tight, that the insulating washers at the primary terminal are properly installed, and that the contact surfaces are thoroughly cleaned.

5. Condensers are easily replaced after disconnecting the lead at the primary terminal and removing the screw which secures the condenser to the base plate.

Gapping

FEELER GAUGE METHOD

Periodic gapping is necessary to compensate for erosion of the contact surfaces due to electrical arcing and for wear of the fiber heel. As the heel wears, the points will open later relative to the rotation of the crankshaft, thus retarding the timing slightly.

Points should be filed (if necessary) and cleaned before gapping.

1. Remove the points cover.
2. Using the special nut, turn the engine over until one of the two sets of points is fully open.
3. With the proper feeler gauge blade, check the gap. The proper specification is 0.3–0.4 mm (0.012–0.016 in.), and the blade should be a slip fit between the points if the gap is correct.

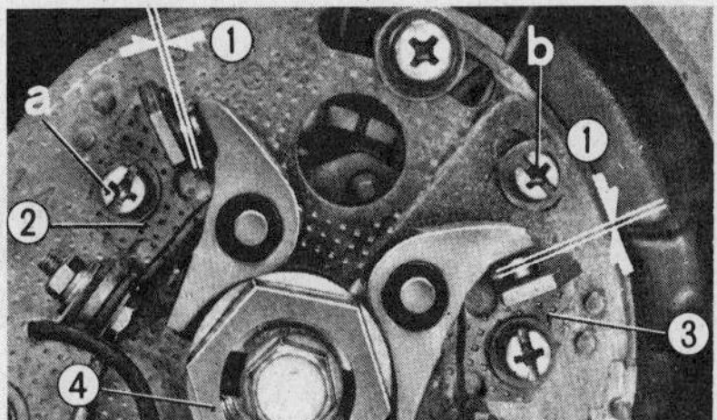

Loosen screws "a" and "b" to adjust point gap (1)

4. If adjustment is necessary, loosen the screw which secures the point set to its plate, and use a small screwdriver at the pry point provided to adjust the gap.

CAUTION: *Loosen the screw just enough to allow the points to be moved. If loosened too much, the points will snap shut instead of holding the gap.*

5. Tighten the screw and recheck the gap. It may change slightly when the screw is tightened.
6. Repeat the procedure with the remaining points set. Try to adjust both sets so that the feeler gauge blade has the same "feel" in both sets. This will help to ensure accurate timing.
7. If it is not possible to gap the points correctly, the fiber heel is evidently worn; the points should then be replaced.

DWELL METER METHOD

Point gap can also be adjusted with the aid of a dwell meter if one is available. "Dwell" is the amount of time the points are closed relative to crankshaft revolution and is expressed in degrees.

The adjustment is made with the engine idling, the meter connections being: positive lead to the primary wire terminal, and negative lead to the engine (ground).

With the meter set to the "8 cylinder" range, the proper dwell specification will be 23.75°; if set to the "4 cylinder scale, it will be 47.5°.

Increasing the point gap will decrease the dwell reading, and vice-versa.

Lubrication

1. On all models it is necessary to occasionally lubricate the cam follower fiber heel and the pivot point of the contact breaker. This minimizes wear and ensures that the timing will remain accurate for a longer period. A worn heel will retard the timing.
2. A small dab of grease (high melting point, if possible) should be applied to the lubricator wick so that the lubricator can distribute it onto the breaker cam. A drop of engine oil should be applied to the pivot point.
3. In both cases it is imperative that care be taken to keep the lubricant away from the points contact surface.
4. The lubricating wick should be adjusted so that it just contacts the breaker cam.

BREAKER POINT IGNITION TIMING

The timing advance mechanism behind the breaker plate is fitted with marks which indicate piston position when they are aligned with the stationary timing mark (visible through the inspection hole in the breaker plate). There are two sets of marks, identified 1.4 and 2.3 to indicate which cylinders they represent.

The timing marks on the advance mechanism are interpreted as follows: "T" indicates top dead center, "F" is the fixed advanced firing point, which is when the plug fires before the automatic timing advancer comes into play and is about 10° BTDC. An additional pair of marks indicates the full advance firing point, which is 33°–36° BTDC above 2500 rpm.

Observing the breaker plate, note that the points set on the left are marked "1.4." They control the timing for those two cylinders, and are secured to the large base plate. The righthand points, marked "2.3," are mounted on a smaller moveable plate. Therefore, cylinders 1 and 4 are set first, and the timing for this pair is adjusted by rotating the entire base

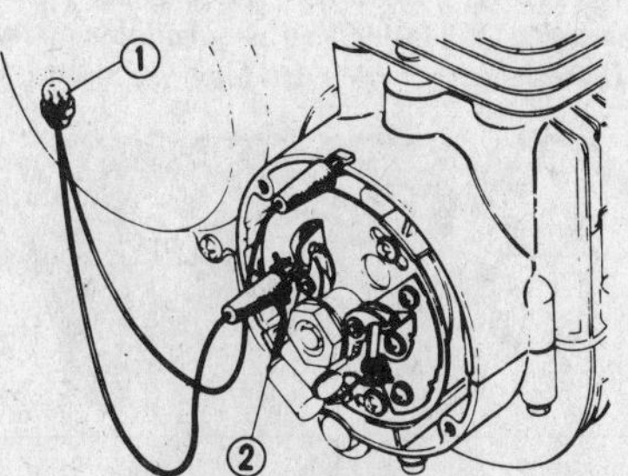

Ignition timing setup with test light (1) connected to the breaker points (2)

plate. Obviously, this will affect the timing of the remaining cylinders. The latter are adjusted, if necessary, by moving only the points themselves as they have slotted fittings for this purpose.

Dynamic Timing

1. Clean and gap both sets of points as described previously.
2. Hook up the strobe light according to the directions of the light's manufacturer to pick up the impulses from the No. 1 (left outside) cylinder.
3. Start the engine and adjust the idle, if necessary, to the recommended idle speed.
4. Aim the light at the timing marks visible through the inspection hole in the points base plate. At idle, the "F" mark should align with the timing index mark.

Before the timing advance mechanism comes into play, the "F" mark (1) should align with the timing index mark (2)

5. To check ignition timing at full advance, increase the engine speed until the motor is turning 2,500–3,000 rpm. At this point, the timing index mark should be between the two full advance marks scribed into the timing advance mechanism.

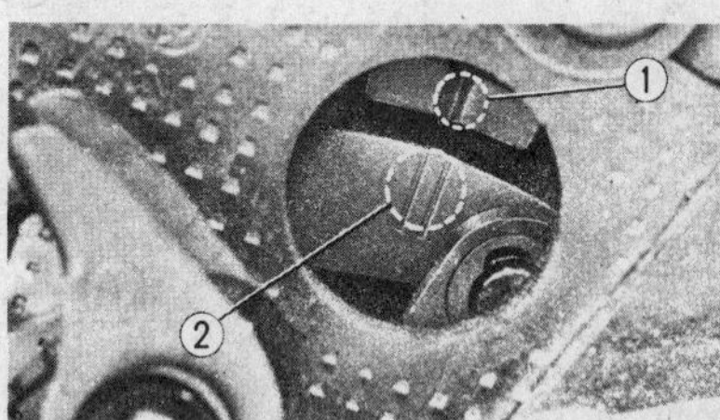

Full advanced timing marks (2) aligned with index mark (1)

6. If adjustment is necessary, carefully loosen the three base plate screws and rotate the plate so that the proper marks align at the specified rpm. Establishing this alignment at full advance is recommended. Tighten the base plate screws.
7. Repeat the procedure, this time having the strobe light pick up cylinder No. 2. If adjustment is necessary, loosen the two screws which secure points set 2.3 to its plate, and

Loosen screws "c" and rotate the breaker plate (1) to adjust the ignition timing for the Nos. 1 and 4 cylinders

use a small screwdriver at the pry point provided to move the set so that proper mark alignment is achieved. Tighten the screws.

8. If it is not possible to achieve full advance alignment without moving the base plate or points set 2.3 all the way to the end of their range of allowable travel, it is possible that the points are either incorrectly gapped, or that they are worn to the point where they must be replaced.

Static Timing

1. Connect one of the test light or tester leads to the primary wire terminal for the points set "1.4." Ground the other lead to the engine.

2. If the test device is not self-powered, turn the ignition switch *on* and be sure the kill switch is in the "on" position as well.

3. Turn the engine over in the normal direction of rotation until the "F" mark for cylinders 1 and 4 align with the timing index mark. The test instrument should react at the instant these marks align, indicating that the points have opened. If they do not, loosen the three base plate screws and rotate the base plate so that the points just open when these timing marks are in alignment. Moving the base plate clockwise will retard the timing; counterclockwise will advance it.

Cylinders 1 and 4 are now correctly timed. Tighten the base plate screws and recheck.

4. Repeat the procedure with points set 2.3. If adjustment is necessary, loosen the two screws which secure these points to their mounting plate and use a small screwdriver at the pry point provided. Tighten the screws and recheck the timing.

Troubleshooting

1. If the static method is used, the reaction of the test light or meter should be positive when the points open. If the instrument seems to hesitate before indicating that the points are open, if may be because of defective condensers or dirty or pitted points surfaces.

2. If it is necessary to move the base plate or the points plate to the extreme end of the adjustment range to effect proper timing, the points or points heel is probably worn to the limit, and the set should be replaced.

Breaker cam (1) and shaft (2)

3. If the dynamic method is used, the various timing marks should hold their positions steadily at given rpms. If they seem to move erratically, check the condition of the timing advance mechanism behind the base plate. Check for weak or broken springs or stiff movement of the advancer weights. When the breaker cam is turned so that the weights move outwards, and then is released, it should return to the original position. If it does not, the springs are too weak and must be replaced. Try penetrating oil to ease movement of the mechanism if it is stiff. If this fails, replace the mechanism.

When installing the advancer unit, make sure that the pin is fitted into the locating hole.

TRANSISTOR IGNITION TIMING

Dynamic Timing

1. Remove the pulser generator cover (right side).

2. Connect a strobe light to cylinder No. 1 or No. 4.

3. Start the engine and allow it to idle at about 1,050 rpm while aiming the timing light through the cutout in the pulser generator plate.

4. At this engine speed, the "1.4 F-I" mark should line up with the stationary index mark.

5. At 2,725 rpm and higher, the full advance marks should align with the stationary timing mark.

6. If the marks do not align, loosen the three large phillips screws which secure the base plate, and rotate the plate until the proper alignment is achieved.

Static Timing

1. Rotate the crankshaft clockwise until the "1.4 S-F" mark aligns with the stationary timing mark.

2. At this point, the tooth on the rotor should align with the narrow projection of the 1.4 pulser generator (on the left).

3. If adjustment is necessary, loosen the three base plate screws and rotate the plate so that this alignment is made.

CARBURETORS

Carburetor adjustments to be made during a tune-up procedure include checking float level; idle speed, and mixture; carburetor synchronization; and travel limit adjustments.

Adjusting Float Level

1. Float level is a measure of the amount of gasoline which will be in the float bowls during operation. While it is a critical specification, it will not normally need readjustment once properly set. Float level, therefore, need not be checked at every tune-up, but should be attended to from time to time.

2. Remove the carburetors.

3. Remove the float bowls and the float bowl gaskets. With the carburetors positioned horizontally, lower the float until the float tang just touches the tip of the float needle and seats the needle. Float level is the measured distance from the bottom of the float to the float bowl mating surface.

NOTE: *A special float level gauge (part number 07144-99998) is available from Honda dealers which will facilitate this task.*

Adjusting float (1) height with the factory tool (2)

4. Compare the measured float level with the following standard values:

350/400	21 mm/0.83 in.
500/550	22 mm/0.87 in.
650	12.5 mm/0.50 in.

5. All carburetors must have the same float level. Measure all before changing any. Adjust, if necessary, by removing the float assembly and carefully bending the float arm tang. Bending the tang towards the carburetor body will increase the float level measurement and vice-versa.

6. Note that the measured float level will be inaccurate if the needle tip is worn, or if there is foreign matter on the needle seat.

Synchronization and Idle Adjustment (350–550)

NOTE: *These adjustments must be made when the engine is at operating temperature. Other tune-up operations (valve adjustment, ignition timing, etc.) should be performed first.*

1. To gain access to the slide adjusting screws, raise the rear of the gas tank as far as possible and support it in this position. It may be necessary to fit longer fuel lines temporarily so that the tank can be raised higher. Be sure that there is an adequate fuel supply.

2. Turn each pilot screw in until it is lightly seated, then back each out *one* turn on 350, 500 and 550 machines, and *two* turns on 400s.

3. 350/400: Adjust the idle speed screw so that the measured distance from the cable holder to the cable fitting (see illustration) is 56 mm (2.21 in.).

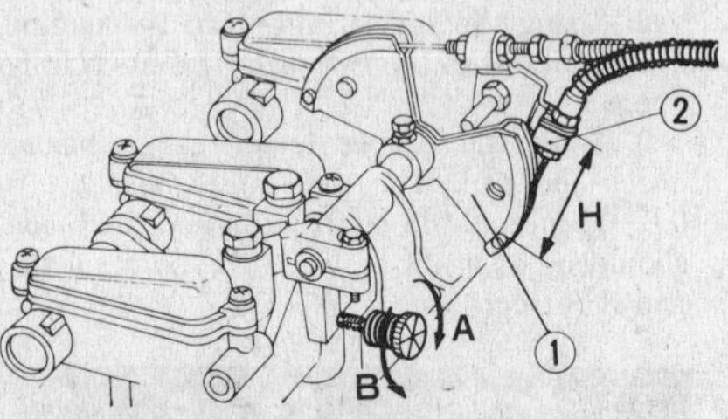

Adjust the idle speed screw so that "H" is 56 mm (2.21 in.) (350/400)

4. 500/550: Adjust the idle speed screw so that the measured distance between the cable holder and the throttle lever is 49 mm (1.94 in.). Refer to the illustration.

5. Install the vacuum gauge hoses to the intake manifolds.

6. Start the engine and check the vacuum readings for each cylinder. Each should be between 16–24 cm Hg and all cylinders must be within 3 cm Hg of each other.

7. To adjust the vacuum, loosen the locknut and turn the adjusting screw clockwise to increase the vacuum reading and coun-

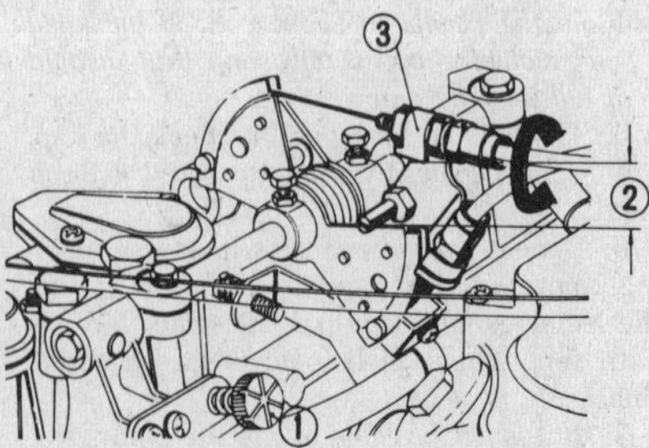

Adjust the idle speed screw (1) so that distance (2) is 49 mm (1.94 in.)

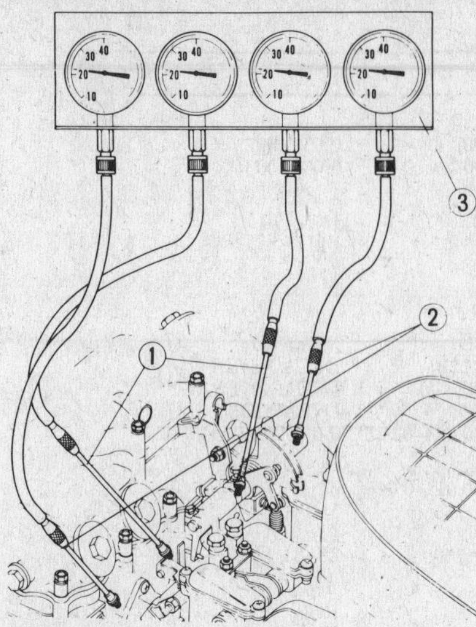

Vacuum gauge connections

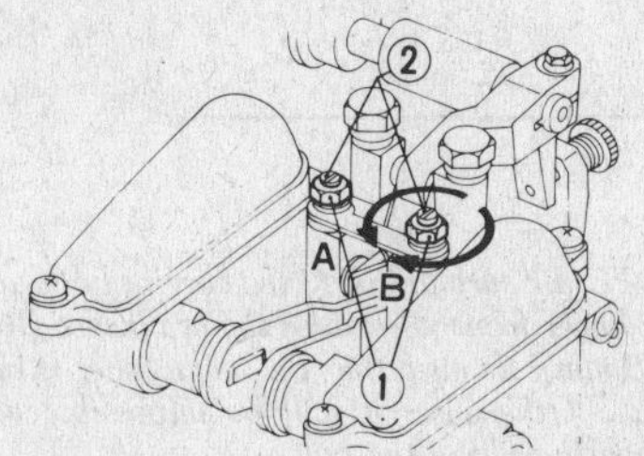

Vacuum adjusting screw locknuts (1) and screws (2)

terclockwise to decrease it. Try to maintain the same idle speed during adjustment.

NOTE: *Provision is made on some vacuum gauges for dampening needle movement if the needle tends to oscillate over a wide range. Do not overdampen the needles. A fluctuation of about one gradation on the scale is acceptable.*

8. After the desired settings have been obtained, snap the throttle open and shut a few times and recheck the vacuum readings after the engine has settled down. Readjust any carburetor(s) that show a lack of uniformity.

CAUTION: *Do not allow the engine to overheat by idling it for more than about five minutes while stationary. A household electric window fan can be used to provide a stream of air over the engine to keep it cool while making these adjustments.*

9. If the vacuum reading is less than 15 cm Hg for any carburetor, check the valve clearances, compression, ignition timing, and check for air leaks at the carburetor and intake manifold.

10. After all four carburetors have been synchronized, adjust the pilot screws to obtain the maximum idle speed consistent with smoothness. It should not be necessary to vary the pilot screws settings more than ¼ turn from the standard given settings (Step 2).

11. Adjust the idle speed to 1200 rpm (350, 400) or 1,000 rpm (500, 550) with the idle speed screw.

12. Remove the vacuum gauge tubes and tighten the intake manifold plugs securely.

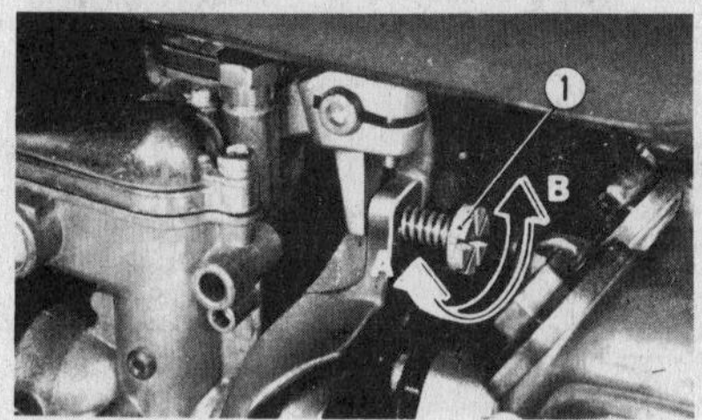

Idle speed screw (1)

Synchronization and Idle Adjustment (650)

These adjustments should be made with the engine at operating temperature.

1. Park the motorcycle on the centerstand in a well-ventilated area. Be sure that the transmission is in neutral.

CAUTION: *Be sure that the work area is properly ventilated. Do not allow the engine to idle for more than a few minutes to avoid overheating the engine.*

2. Remove the side covers. Raise the seat. Remove the gas tank. Use long fuel lines to allow fuel flow to the carburetors while the tank is secured out of the way. Tank should be positioned higher than is normal.

3. Install the vacuum gauge(s).

4. Remove the carburetor tops.

5. Start the engine and check vacuum readings at 1,050 rpm.

Difference between the carburetors should be 60 mmHg (2.4 in. Hg) or less.

6. Equalize the readings, if necessary, by loosening the locknuts and turning the adjusting screws.

Note that the No. 2 carburetor is not adjusted. It is the standard against which the other readings are to be compared.

7. After adjustment, gun the engine once or twice and recheck the vacuum readings.

8. Use the idle adjustment screw to set idle at 1,050 rpm.

Fast Idle Adjustment (350/400)

1. This adjustment is made after the carburetor slides have been synchronized. The engine should be at operating temperature.

2. Open (i.e. disengage) the choke lever fully and check the clearance between the link plate and the adjusting screw. It should be 0–0.3 mm (0–0.012 in.). Adjust the clearance, if necessary, by loosening the locknut and turning the adjusting screw.

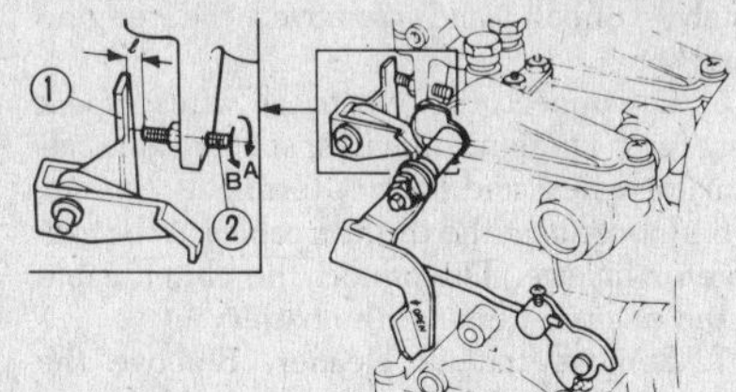

Fast idle adjustment

3. Start the engine. Slowly raise and lower the choke lever until maximum idle speed is obtained. It should be 3,500–4,500 rpm. Readjust the screw if necessary so that this idle is obtained.

Fast Idle Adjustment (650)

NOTE: *This adjustment must be made when the engine is cold.*

1. Pull out the choke knob and start the engine. Fast idle speed should be 2,000 plus or minus 700 rpm.

2. To adjust, shut off the engine and remove the gas gank.

3. Turn the fast idle adjusting screw until it touches the cam surface.

4. Push the choke knob in and turn the adjusting screw in 2½ turns.

5. Recheck fast idle speed.

Choke Adjustment (650)

1. Remove the gas tank.

2. Check that the choke lever is fully closed when the knob is pulled all the way out.

3. Make adjustments by loosening the choke cable clamp and moving the cable as required. Tighten the clamp holding the choke lever fully closed.

Throttle Cable Adjustment

PLAY ADJUSTMENT

1. Back off the cable adjuster at the handlebar to increase cable play. Leave a small amount of adjustment range so that final, small adjustments can be made.

After loosening the locknuts (2), rotate the adjuster (1) clockwise to increase play or counterclockwise (3) to decrease it

2. Loosen the cable adjuster locknut at the carburetors and turn the adjuster until there is about 10–15° of rotation of the twistgrip before the slides begin to lift. Retighten the locknut.

NOTE: *The throttle lever should hit the eccentric pin when the twistgrip is forced to the fully closed position. If the lever will not hit the pin, replace the return cable.*

3. Make any fine adjustments necessary with the adjuster at the twistgrip. With the engine idling, turn the forks slowly from lock-to-lock. Any variation in the idle speed indicates that the cable is too tightly adjusted, is kinked, or is binding somewhere.

OVERTRAVEL LIMIT ADJUSTMENT

Loosen the locknut and turn the eccentric pin until clearance between the throttle lever and the pin is 2.0–2.1 mm (0.080–0.83 in.) for the 350/400 or 2–3 mm (0.08–0.12 in.) for the 500/550.

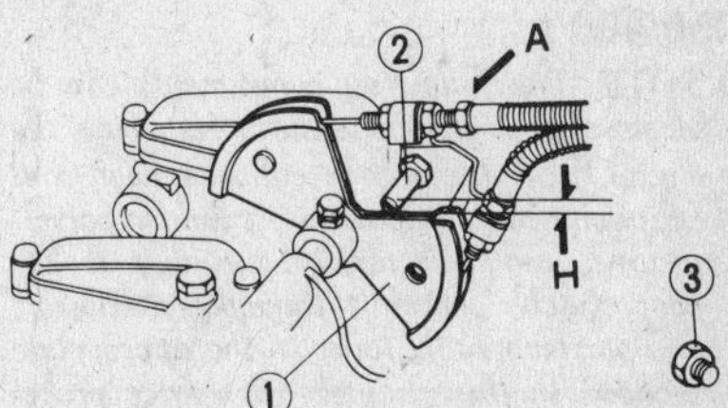

After loosening the locknut (3), rotate the eccentric pin (2) until the clearance between the pin and lever (1) is correct

Tune-Up Specifications

	350	400	500 550	650
VALVE CLEARANCE (cold)				
Intake (mm/in.)	0.05/0.002	0.05/0.002	0.05/0.002	0.05/0.002
Exhaust (mm/in.)	0.05/0.002	0.05/0.002	0.08/0.003	0.08/0.003
COMPRESSION (hot)				
Standard (psi)	157–170	157–170	157–170	157–170
Minimum (psi)	140	140	140	140
Maximum allowable variation (psi)	15	15	15	15
SPARK PLUGS				
Standard makes	NGK/ND	NGK/ND	NGK/ND	NGK/ND ①
Standard plug	D8ESL/X24ES	D8ESL/X24ES	D7ES/X22ES	D8EA/X24ES-U ①
Cold (NGK)	D10E	D10E	D8E, D8ES	D9EA/X27ES-U
Hot (NGK)	D8E, D7ES	D8E, D7ES	D7E	D7EA/X22ES-U ①
Gap (mm/in.)	0.6–0.7/0.024–0.028	0.7–0.8/0.028–0.032	0.6–0.7/0.024–0.028	0.6–0.7/0.024–0.028
IGNITION				
Point gap (mm/in.)	0.3–0.4/0.012–0.016	0.3–0.4/0.012–0.016	0.3–0.4/0.012–0.016	na
Static advance (degrees BTDC)	5	5	5	5
Maximum advance (degrees BTDC)	28–31 @ 2500 rpm	28–31 @ 2500 rpm	28–31 @ 2500 rpm	28–31 © 2700 rpm
CARBURETION				
Idle speed (rpm)	1200	1200	1000	1050
Pilot screw (turns out)	7/8 ± 3/8	2 ± 1/2	1 ± 1/4	1 5/8
Synchronization vacuum range (cm/in. Hg)	16–24/6.2–9.5	16–24/6.2–9.5	16–24/6.2–9.5	16–24/6.2–9.5
Uniformity (cm/in. Hg)	3.0/1.2	3.0/1.2	3.0/1.2	6.0/2.4
Float level (mm/in.)	21/0.83	21/0.83	22/0.87	12.5/0.50

① Late models may use resistor plugs: "DR8", "ESR-U", etc.

FULL THROTTLE LIMIT ADJUSTMENT

Adjust the throttle lever stop screw so that the carburetor slides can be pulled up 0–1.0 mm (0–0.04 in.) above the top of the carburetor bore before the throttle lever contacts the stop screw.

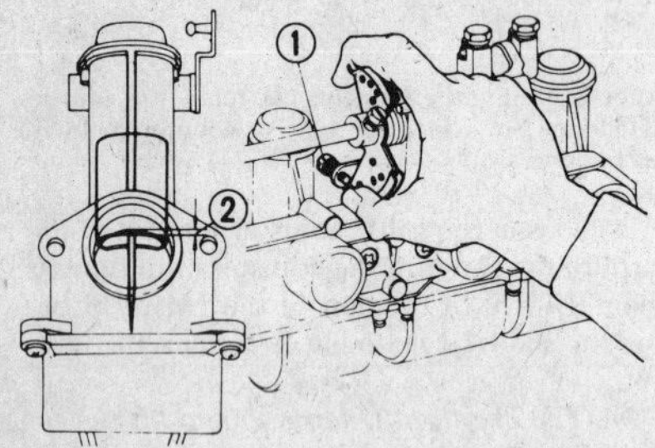

Adjust the stop screw (1) until the correct clearance (2) is arrived at

ENGINE AND TRANSMISSION

NOTE: *Common engine rebuilding techniques and procedures are explained in detail in the "General Information" section.*

ENGINE REMOVAL AND INSTALLATION

350/400

NOTE: *The following components can be serviced or replaced without removing the engine from the frame: cylinder head and cylinder head components, cylinder barrel, pistons, cam chain tensioner guide and slipper, clutch, gearshift linkage, alternator, and starter motor. Refer to the appropriate sections in this chapter for service procedures.*

1. Remove the drain plug and drain off the oil. Remove the oil filter.

2. Disconnect the fuel lines and remove the gas tank. Remove the footpegs (passenger's), and the exhaust system.

3. Remove the pinch-bolt and pull the gearshift lever off its shaft. Remove the rear portion of the left crankcase cover.

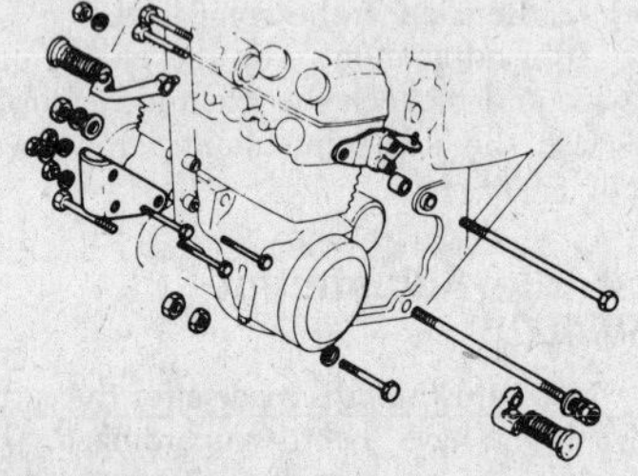

Engine mounting bolts (350/400)

4. Disconnect the final drive chain; alternately, unbolt and remove the engine sprocket.

5. Disconnect the electrical wires: spark plug caps, ignition coil wires, starter cable, alternator wires, and battery terminals.

6. Disconnect the throttle cables at the carburetor linkage. Disconnect the clutch cable at the engine. Remove the battery.

7. Remove the air cleaner. Remove the carburetors.

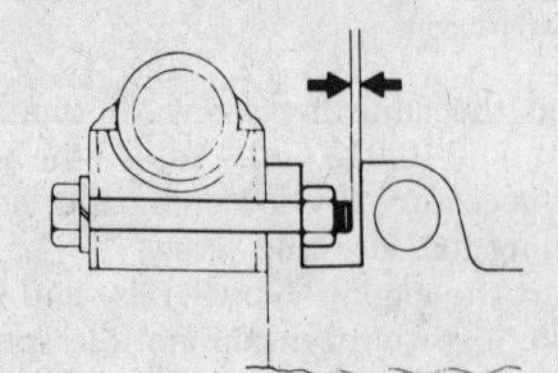

Front mounting bolt clearance is close; lockwasher must be in place

8. Remove the engine mounting bolts, mounting plates, and remove the engine from the frame.

a. Installation is the reverse of the above.

NOTE: Be sure to install the correct bolts at the lower front portion of the crankcase (10 x 75 mm). Be sure that the lockwasher is in place. Otherwise, it will be impossible to properly tighten the bolt.

b. Tighten the engine mounting bolts to 22–29 ft lbs.

500/550

NOTE: *The following components can be serviced or replaced without removing the engine from the frame: cylinder head and cylinder head components, cylinder barrel, pistons, cam chain tensioner, clutch, gearshift linkage, alternator, and starter motor. Refer to the appropriate sections in this chapter for service procedures.*

1. Turn the fuel tap off, disconnect the fuel lines, and remove the tank.

2. Unscrew the drain plug and filter housing bolt, and drain the oil.

3. Unbolt and remove all four exhaust pipes and mufflers.

4. Remove the wires from the spark plugs and disconnect the ground cable at the battery terminal.

5. Remove the 5 mm screw and withdraw the tachometer cable from the tachometer drive at the cylinder head.

6. Raise the seat and remove the air filter element. Unscrew the three bolts and remove the air filter housing.

7. Disconnect the throttle cables from the throttle linkage at the carburetors.

8. Loosen the air filter intake clamp and

Carburetor mounting clamps (1 and 2)

intake manifold tube clamp at each carburetor. Remove the carburetors as a unit.

9. Disconnect the starter motor cable from the solenoid and the alternator output wire at the connector near the battery.

10. Remove the shift lever. Unbolt and remove the starter motor cover and left crankcase cover. Disconnect the clutch cable from the release mechanism.

Disconnect the starter cable (1) and the magnetic switch (2), then disconnect the generator leads (3)

11. Remove the countershaft sprocket and drive chain. Disconnect the contact breaker point leads (yellow and blue) at the connectors.

12. Remove the engine mounting bolts and plates as illustrated. Raise the rear of the engine slightly and remove it from the right-side of the frame.

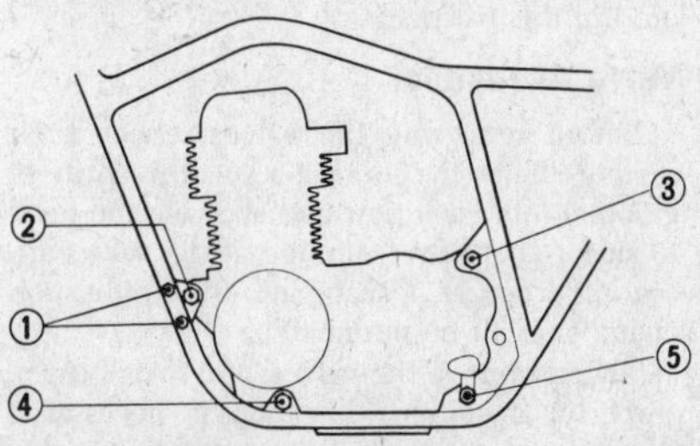

Left-side engine mounting points

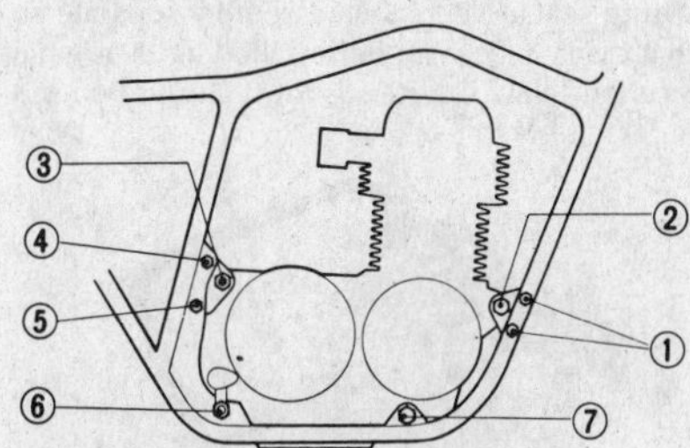

Right-side engine mounting points

Installation is in reverse order of removal. The following points should be noted:

a. Tighten engine bolts to 22–29 ft lbs and mounting plate bolts to 13–18 ft lbs.

b. Do not neglect to connect the battery ground cable to the rear engine mount bolt as the bolt is installed.

c. Route the starter motor and alternator cables behind the frame tube.

d. Make sure that the muffler connecting clamps are in place on each pair of mufflers.

e. When installation is complete, refill the engine with oil. Adjust the clutch, drive chain, and carburetors.

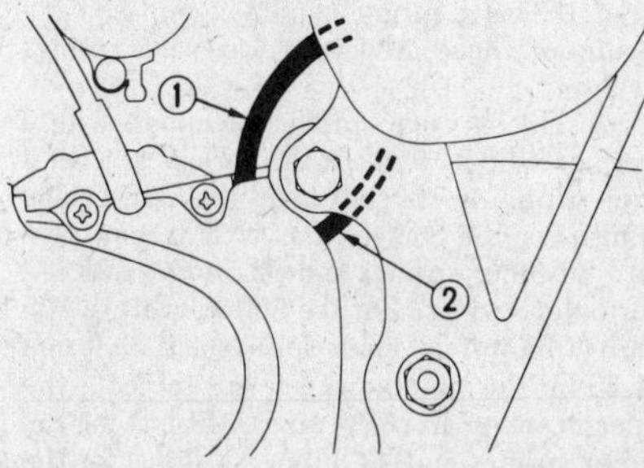

Generator (1) and starter (2) cables correctly routed

650

NOTE: *The following components can be serviced or replaced without removing the engine from the frame: cylinder head, cylinders, pistons, cam chain tensioner, clutch, gearshift linkage, alternator, and starter motor.*

1. Drain the engine oil.
2. Remove the gas tank and the two side covers.
3. Disconnect the starter cable at the solenoid. Disconnect the ignition wiring coupler.
4. Disconnect the crankcase breather tube from the cover.
5. Remove the carburetor assembly.
6. Disconnect the tach cable from the head. Disconnect the spark plug caps.
7. Disconnect the clutch cable at the engine. Remove the rear brake pedal.
8. Remove the right side rider's footpeg. Remove the brakelight switch.
9. Remove the exhaust system complete.
10. Disconnect the alternator, neutral, and oil pressure wires at the couplers.
11. Remove the gearshift lever. Remove the left rear crankcase cover.
12. Loosen the rear axle nut, back the adjusting bolts off and push the wheel forward as far as possible. Unbolt and remove the engine sprocket and chain.
13. Remove the oil filter.
14. Place a jack beneath the engine to take the stress of the mounting bolts and remove the mounting bolts and engine bracket bolts. Remove the engine from the right side of the frame.
15. Installation is the reverse of removal. Check that mounting bolt torque is correct:

8 mm flange bolt/nut: 19–23 ft. lbs.
10 mm flange bolt/nut: 22–29 ft. lbs.
12 mm flange bolt/nut: 58–72 ft. lbs.

TOP END

NOTE: *Specifications not given in the following text may be found in the "Engine Specifications" charts at the end of this section.*

Cylinder Head Removal

350/400

1. Remove the fuel tank, ignition coils, and breather cover, then disconnect the tachometer cable at the cylinder head.

2. Remove the eight tappet access caps, loosen the rocker arm adjusting screws, and remove the cylinder head cover. Remove the rocker arm shafts from the cover by removing the cap nuts, screwing a 10 mm (1.25 mm pitch) bolt into the shaft, and pulling it out. Mark each shaft and rocker arm for location.

3. Remove the exhaust system, spark plugs, and cam chain tensioner holder, then remove the tensioner holder and slipper.

Removing a rocker arm shaft (1) with a puller bolt (2)

4. Remove the point cover, then rotate the crankshaft, by means of a suitable wrench on the special nut, until one of the cam sprocket bolts is vertical to the cylinder head, and remove the bolt. Rotate the crankshaft 180° and remove the remaining sprocket bolt.

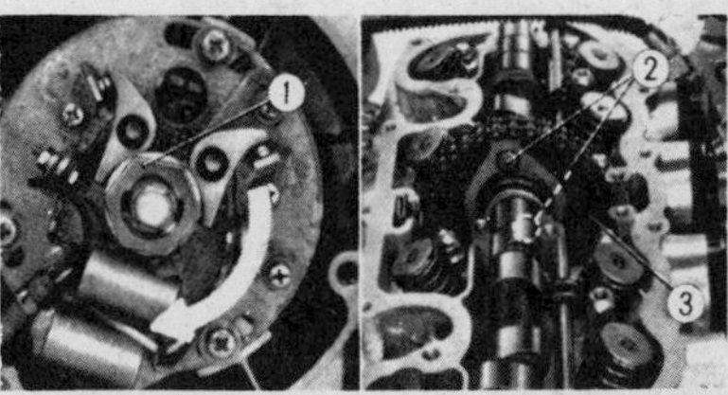

Use the special nut (1) to rotate the crankshaft until the cam sprocket mounting bolts (2) are positioned as shown (350/400)

Lift the chain (1) off the sprocket (3) with a screwdriver (2) before removing the cam (4) (350/400)

5. Lift the cam chain to avoid scratching the camshaft, then slip the camshaft out from the right.

NOTE: *Loop a piece of wire around the chain to prevent it from falling into the crankcase.*

6. Remove the air cleaner element, loosen the air cleaner chamber retaining screw, and remove the carburetor assembly.

7. Remove the cylinder head securing bolts in a crisscross pattern as illustrated, remove the cam chain guide, and lift off the cylinder head, striking it with a soft mallet to loosen it if necessary.

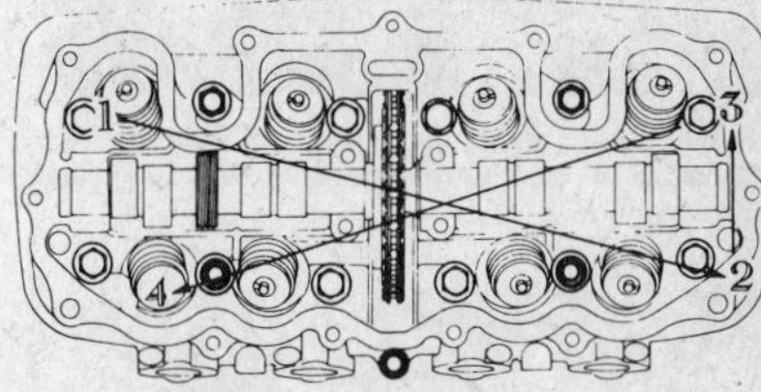

Head bolt loosening sequence (350/400)

500/550

1. Turn the fuel tap off and disconnect the fuel lines. Remove the fuel tank.
2. Unbolt and remove all four exhaust pipes and mufflers.
3. Disconnect the tachometer cable from the tachometer drive at the cylinder head.
4. Remove the wires from the spark plugs.

Take out the six screws and remove the breather cover.

Breather cover (1) mounting screw location (500 and 550)

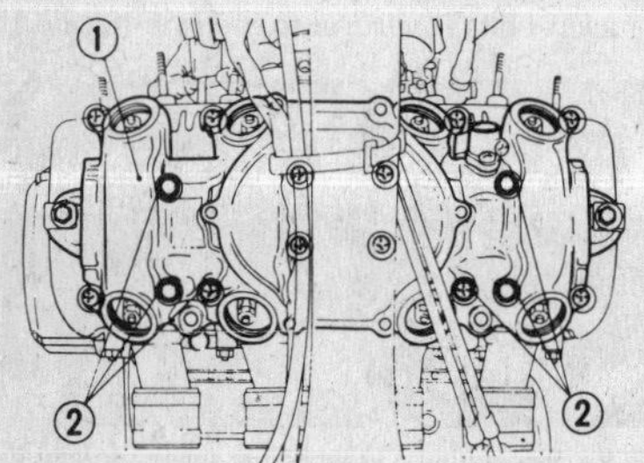

Keep the copper washers (2) separate for reinstallation when installing the cover (1) (500 and 550)

5. Remove the valve adjuster access caps, the left and right sidecovers, and the cover set plate. Gradually and uniformly (to prevent distortion) loosen the 12 screws and six bolts which secure the camshaft cover.

6. Loosen the adjuster locknut on the cam chain adjuster and turn the screw fully clockwise (about ¼ turn), then retighten the locknut. In this position, the cam chain is relieved of tension.

7. Remove the two camshaft sprocket mounting bolts and carefully withdraw the camshaft through the sprocket towards the right-side of the engine. Lift off the cam chain and remove the sprocket.

8. Remove the carburetors and unscrew the cam chain tensioner mounting bolts. The 12 cylinder head nuts and two flange bolts can now be removed and the cylinder head can be lifted off the engine. It is important that the bolts and nuts are loosened gradually and evenly in a cross pattern.

After unbolting the sprocket bolts (4) from the cam (3), loop a piece of wire around the chain (500 and 550) to secure it

Removing a rocker arm shaft (1) with a puller bolt (2)

9. To remove the rocker arms, remove the rocker arm shaft end bolts. Screw a 6 mm bolt into the shaft and pull it out. Mark each rocker arm and shaft for location after removal.

650

1. Remove the gas tank. Disconnect the tach cable on the head. Disconnect the breather tube. Pull off the plug caps. Remove the spark plugs.

2. Remove the breather cover and the adjuster covers. Remove the carburetors and the exhaust system.

3. Gradually, and in a cross pattern, loosen and remove the head cover bolts. Remove the cover.

4. Remove the pulser generator cover. Use a wrench on the special nut to turn the engine over until one of the two camshaft sprocket bolts is accessible. Remove the bolt. Turn the engine over and remove the remaining bolt.

5. Move the sprocket off the shoulder of the cam. Loop a length of safety wire around the sprocket and chain to keep them from falling into the engine when the cam is removed. Detach the chain from the sprocket. Remove the camshaft.

6. Remove the cam chain tensioner set bolt. Remove the six rubber seals.

7. Remove the 14 cylinder head bolts. Remove the head.

8. Remove the head gasket. Note the location of dowel pins and O-rings which are fitted between the head and the cylinder block.

9. To remove the rocker arms, remove the rocker arm shaft cotter pin nuts. Drive the pins out. Remove the rocker arm shaft cap bolts.

10. Thread a 6 mm bolt into the rocker arm shaft and pull the shaft out.

Inspection

ALL MODELS

Cylinder Head

1. Clean any traces of gasket material from the cylinder head mating surface. Place a straightedge across the mating surface and check for warpage by attempting to slip a feeler gauge blade between the head and the straight edge. Standard head warpage is about 0.05 mm (0.002 in.) and maximum allowable warpage is 0.3 mm (0.012 in.). At this point the head should be milled to restore a flat mating surface.

2. Use a wire brush fitting on a power drill to decarbonize the combustion chambers. The valves should be left in place when this is done, as it minimizes the chance of causing damage to the valve seats.

Camshaft

1. Check the condition of the cam bearings in the head and the cylinder head cover. Bearing surfaces must be smooth and free of scoring or marks of wear. If imperfections are noted, it is necessary to replace the head and the head cover.

2. Check the journal surfaces of the camshaft for similar signs of wear and replace the cam if the journal and surfaces are scored.

3. Measure the height of each cam lobe and compare your reading against the standard specification. Replace the camshaft if the lobe height is less than 28.00 mm (1.1024 in.) (intake and exhaust) on the 350/400, or 34.85 mm (1.3720 in.) (intake), 34.45 mm (1.3563 in.) (exhaust) on the 500/550. For the 650, service limits are 35.6 mm (1.40 in.) for the intake and 35.3 mm (1.39 in.) for the exhaust.

4. Visually inspect the lobes for pitting and replace the cam if this condition is noted.

5. Measure camshaft run-out, as illustrated, using a dial indicator. Maximum acceptable run-out is 0.1 mm (0.004 in.). Replace the cam if run-out exceeds this limit.

Rocker Arms

1. Check each rocker arm for pitting of the cam contact pad and replace any if damage is noted.

2. Check the fit of each rocker arm on its shaft. Rocker arm-to-shaft clearance can be as great as 0.1 mm (0.004 in.) (maximum).

3. Check each rocker arm shaft for scoring or wear of the rocker arm contact area. Replace any damage shaft. Inspect the rocker arm bores in like manner.

4. Check the shafts for a bent condition and replace them if so damaged. Check the arms and shafts for blue discoloration which is a sign of overheating usually caused by lack of lubrication; replace the arms and shafts if discolored in this manner.

Valve Assembly

Before removing the valves, check their sealing ability by pouring a small quantity of gasoline into each port and allowing the head to sit for about five minutes. If the valves are seating properly, leakage into the combustion chambers will be minimal.

1. To remove the valves, and install them properly, a suitable C-clamp is necessary. Compress the valve springs, and remove the split collars, retainers, springs, seals, and spring seats. Keep each assembly separate so that every piece can be installed in its original location. New valve seals must always be used on assembly.

Using a valve spring compresser (1) to remove the springs

Inspect the valves, guides, springs, and valve seats in the following manner.

2. If considerable mileage has been covered, the valve springs should be replaced as a matter of course. Always replace valve springs as a set.

3. Check valve spring free-length with a vernier caliper. Replace the springs as a set if any spring is shorter than the serviceable limit. For the 350/400 this is 27.0 mm (1.06 in.) for inner springs and 32.5 mm (1.28 in.) for outer springs. For the 500/550 this is 34.5 mm (1.35 in.) for inner springs and 39.0 mm (1.53 in.) for outer springs. For the 650, the specifications are 37.9 mm (1.49 in.) for the inner springs and 43.3 mm (1.70 in.) for the outer.

4. Each valve must be free to move up and down in its guide with little resistance. Any sticking or binding as the valve is moved in the guide will indicate that the valve stem or guide is in poor condition.

5. Inspect the valve, paying close attention to the edges of the valve head for pitting, burnt or broken edges, excessive carbon build-up, etc. A certain amount of carbon and lead deposits on the valve face and the top of the exhaust valve are inevitable. Heavy deposits should be carefully scraped off with a dull knife, or a wire wheel, and the valve finished up with very fine emery cloth.

Do not touch the valve seating area during these operations.

If the valve has burnt or broken edges, it must be replaced.

6. Check the end of the valve stem for indented wear caused by the valve adjuster. Although rare, it may occur after long mileage. Since an indentation here will make proper valve adjustments impossible, the valve should be replaced.

NOTE: *The tips and edges of the valves are stellite-coated. Machining for any reason is not recommended. In case of wear, replace the valve.*

7. Carbon deposits should not extend too far up along the valve stem. This would indicate a worn or cracked valve guide.

8. Wet, oily deposits on the back of the valve head is indicative of a worn guide or bad seal. Less severe wear to these components show up as brown oil stains on the valve stem.

9. Holding a valve in your fingers, spin it while observing the head. A wobble is indicative of a bent valve. If a dial gauge is available, check the run-out of the head. Replace the valve if run-out exceeds 0.05 mm (0.002 in.). Run-out is the total indicated dial gauge reading.

Attempt to rotate the valve by hand when it is fully inserted into the guide. If the valve will not rotate easily, or if it sticks as it is turned, it is probably bent.

10. Check valve-to-stem clearance and compare to the specification given. There are two ways of doing this. The first is to measure the diameter of the valve stem and the diameter of the inside of the guide and subtract the difference. Another way, somewhat easier, is to insert the valve into the guide, holding it about ½ in. off the seat, and check the total amount of allowable movement in two directions using a dial gauge. Maximum allowable clearances are as follows. For the 350/400, 0.3 mm (0.0118 in.) for both the intake and exhaust valves. For the 500/550/650, 0.08 mm (0.0031 in.) for the intake valves, and 0.10 mm (0.0039 in.) for the exhaust.

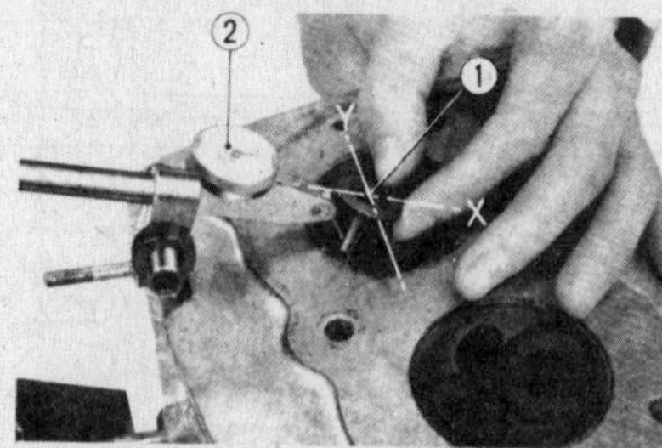

Checking valve-to-valve guide clearance with a dial indicator

If the measured clearances exceed these amounts, replace both valve and guide.

A quick check of the operational worthiness of a valve and guide can be accomplished by dipping the valve stem in oil and inserting it into its guide. Place a finger over the other end of the guide. Pull the valve a little way out of the guide and release it. The valve should be drawn back into the guide by suction if the components are inserviceable condition.

11. To remove valve guides, use a suitable drift.

Heating the head in an oven will facilitate removal and installation. Be sure the guides are fully seated.

After installing a guide, it must be reamed to the proper size. Use the proper Honda

Using a drift (1) to remove a valve guide

reamer for the application. Alternately, ream the valve guides to give clearances of 0.01–0.03 mm (0.0004–0.0012 in.) for the intake guides, and 0.03–0.05 (0.0012–0.0020 in.) for the exhaust guides.

12. After installing new guides, the valve seat should be recut and the valves lapped in. Valve seat angle is 45°. Valve seat width 0.7–1.5 mm (0.03–0.06 in.) for 350/400 models, and 1.0–1.5 mm (0.04–0.06 in.) for the 500/550/650.

Cylinder Head Installation

ALL MODELS

1. Use new valve guide oil seals.

2. Valve springs may be progressively wound. Always install such springs so that the close coils are next to the head. The tops of the springs may be marked with paint.

On 650s, rocker arm shaft cotter pins should be torqued to 7–10 ft. lbs.

Progressively wound springs are installed with the close coils (arrows) towards the head

3. Install the cylinder head gasket, two dowel pins, and two O-rings on the cylinder. Mount the cylinder head on the cylinder while pulling the cam chain through the center of the head. Hold the chain from dropping down using a screwdriver as before. Tighten the head nuts gradually, in the sequence shown, to a final torque value of 14.5–16.5 ft. lbs. for all except the 650 which is 17–22 ft. lbs. After the nuts have been properly torqued, install and tighten the two 6 mm flange bolts (50/550/650) to 7–10 ft. lbs.

CAUTION: *Take care not to drop any hardware into the crankcase.*

On the 650, loosen the cam chain tensioner locknut and pull up on the tensioner.

Gasket (1) dowel pin (2) and O-ring (3) locations

Tighten the locknut. This will give the cam chain maximum slack to make cam installation easier.

4. Hold the cam chain and cam chain sprocket together and install the camshaft

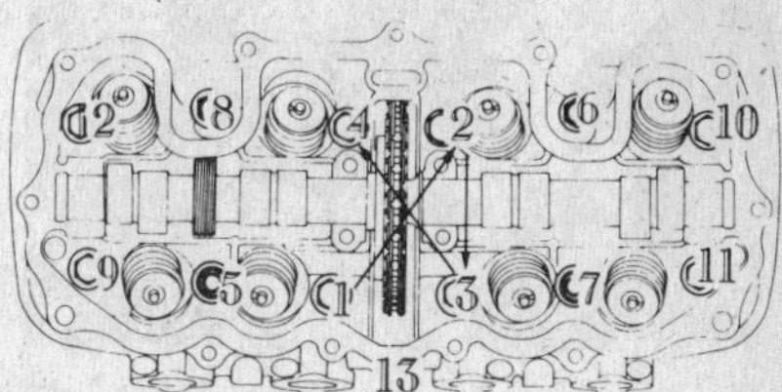

Head nut tightening sequence (350/400)

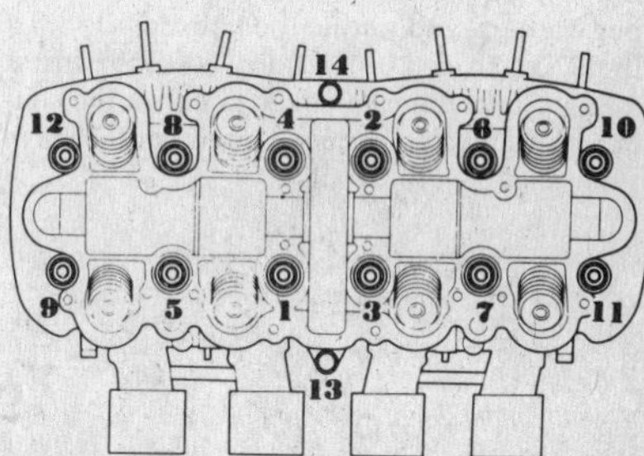

Head bolt tightening sequence (500/550/650)

through them from the right-side of the engine. The cam notch must be on the right. To set the valve timing properly, remove the ignition points cover and rotate the engine clockwise until the T(1.4) mark on the ignition advance unit aligns with the timing mark.

a. 350/400: Turn the cam sprocket until the lines on the sprocket are aligned with the cylinder head surface, as shown. Align the cam so it can be bolted to the sprocket.

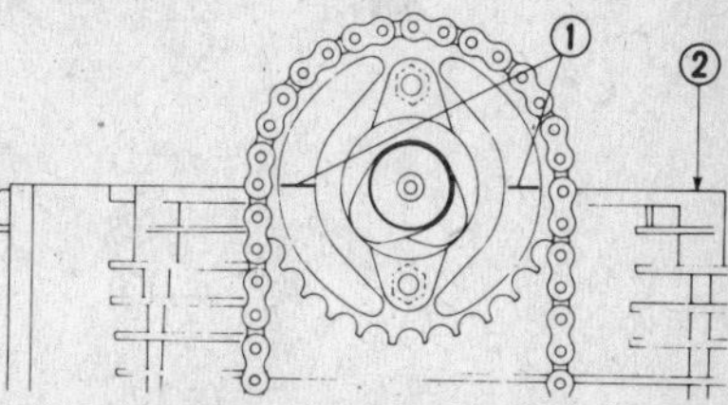

Align the index lines (1) with the head surface (2) (350/400)

b. 500/550/650: Turn the camshaft until the center of the notch on the camshaft is aligned with the cylinder head surface, as shown. The notch must face the front of the engine.

Place the chain over the sprocket, and bolt the sprocket to the camshaft.

5. Install the carb assembly on the head. Install the two dowel pins and six rubber seals as shown. Install the camshaft cover gasket,

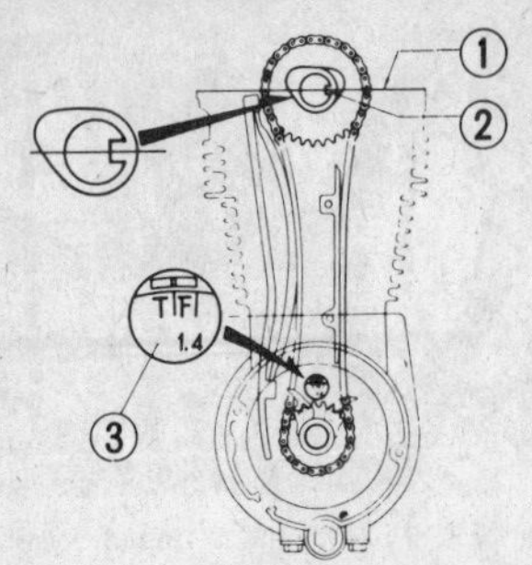

When the "T" mark (3) is lined up with the index mark, the notch (2) must face the front of the engine and align with the cylinder head surface (500/550/650)

Dowel pins (1) and sealing rubbers (2) installed

refit the cover; do not forget to refit the copper washers, and torque the bolts to 5.1–8.0 ft lbs (350/400) or 6.0–8.5 ft lbs (500/550). Insert a finger into the cam cover to check the contact of each valve adjuster screw on the valve stem end. See illustration.

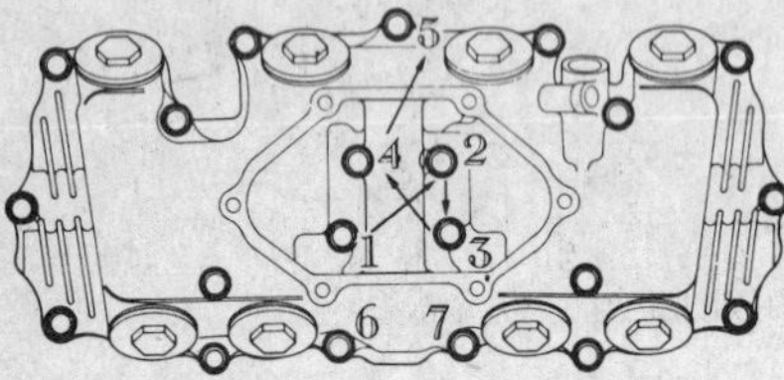

Head cover bolt tightening sequence (350/400)

The valve tappet adjusting screw is not properly contacting the valve.

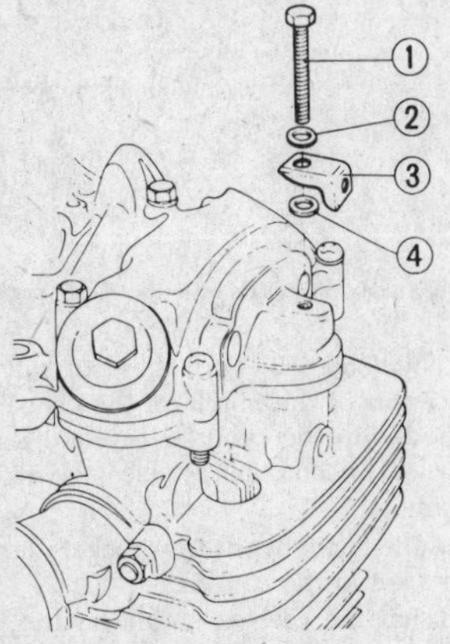

The 6 mm screw (1) secures the copper washer (2), set plate (3), and the aluminum washer (4)

6. Install the small cam cover side setplate with the chrome washer on top and the aluminum washer on the bottom. Install O-rings on the dowel pins of the left and right-side covers and mount them on the head. Install the breather cover.

NOTE: *Spark plug wire clips should face forward on both sides.*

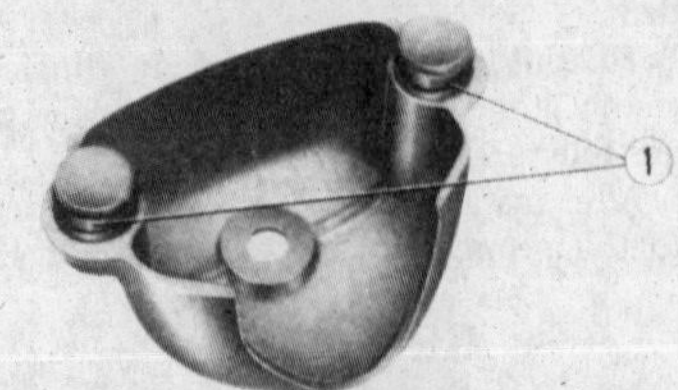

O-ring location

7. Reverse the disassembly procedure for the remaining components.

Cylinder and Piston Removal

ALL MODELS

1. Remove the cylinder head.
2. On the 350/400, remove the cam chain tensioner guide. Back off the chain tensioner locknut. Unbolt the tensioner holder and remove the cam chain tensioner.
3. On 500/550 models, raise the cam chain guide slightly, and turn it 90° and lift it out. Back off the cam chain tensioner locknut, raise the cylinder barrels about 1 in. and lift out the chain tensioner assembly.
4. On the 650, remove the cam chain tensioner locknut. Remove the tensioner and chain guide.

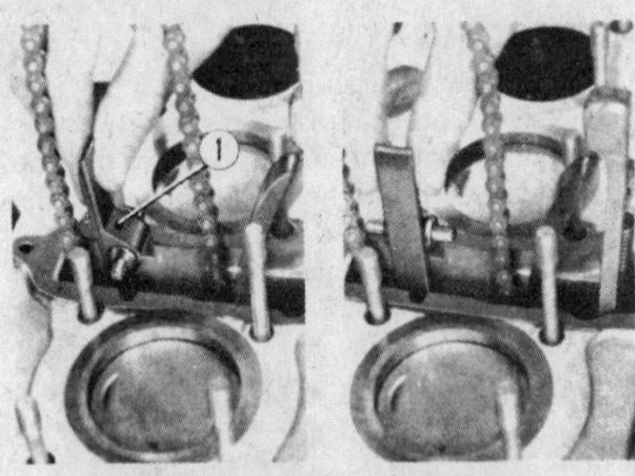

Lift up the chain guide and turn it 90° to remove it

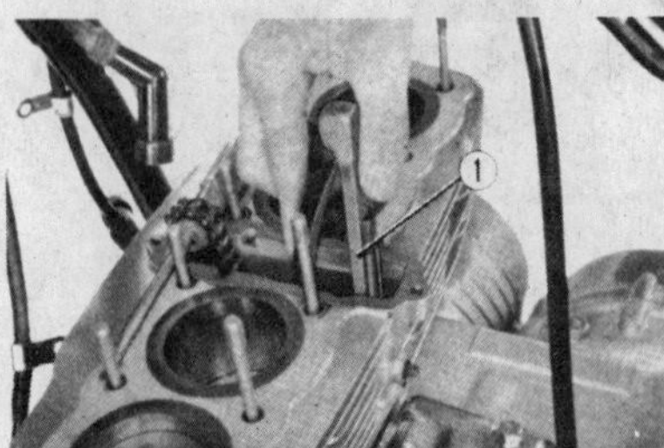

Removing the cam chain tensioner

5. Carefully raise the cylinder assembly. If it is stuck, tap lightly on the sides with a plastic mallet to break it loose. If a pry groove is fitted, use a screwdriver to break the cylinders loose, as illustrated. When the cylinder is lifted away, be careful that the pistons do not fall against the case as they come out of their bores.
6. Remove the wrist pin circlips from the pistons.

Carefully pry at the groove (2) to remove the cylinder (1)

CAUTION: *Do not allow the circlips to fall into the crankcase. To avoid having to split the cases to retrieve a clip, cover the crankcase openings with a cloth.*

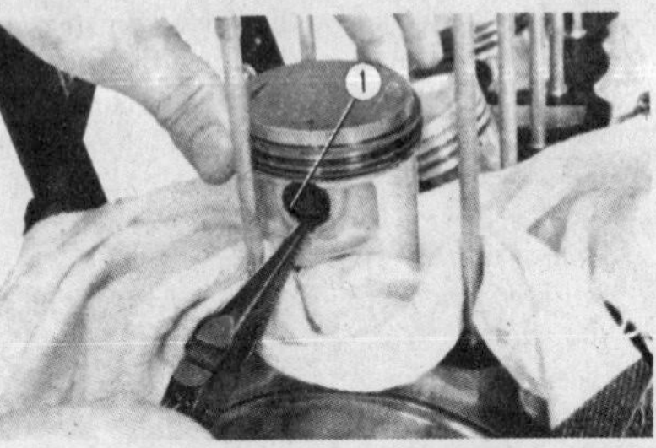

Removing the piston wrist pin circlip (1)

7. Grasp the piston with one hand and push out the wrist pin with a suitable drift. If the piston will not come out, the piston crown may be heated, evenly and gently, with a propane torch. If the pin still resists, it is advisable to use the shop wrist pin removal tool. This consists of a steel band or bands which fit around the piston while the attached screw device is used to push out the pin.

CAUTION: *Never strike the wrist pin or attempt to use brute force to drive it out. The connecting rod may be bent in the attempt.*

Inspection

1. Make a visual inspection of the cylinder bore, noting any imperfections. The cylinder walls should be uniformly smooth.
2. With an inside micrometer, measure the diameter of each bore at the top, middle, and bottom. Make measurements in two directions, 90° apart, both parallel and perpendicular to the piston wrist pins. If any measurement exceeds the serviceable limit given in the specifications charts at the end of this chapter, or if the difference between the high and low measurement in any given direction is greater than 0.05 mm (0.002 in.), the cylinders should be bored out to the next oversize.

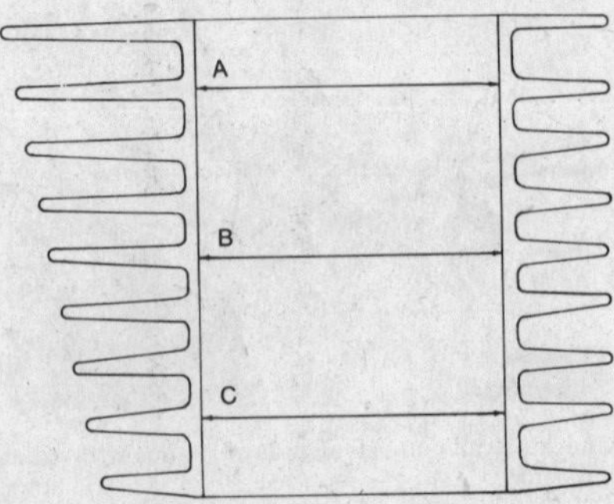

Measure cylinder diameter in two directions at each of the three points shown

Maximum allowable difference between the cylinders is 0.1 mm (0.004 in.).

3. Make a visual inspection of the pistons. Scoring, scuffing, or seizure marks on the piston skirts may be removed with a fine grade of emery or crocus cloth if they are not too severe. Sanding should be done in a cross-hatch pattern. If the damage is severe (more than about ½ in. wide), the pistons should be replaced.

4. The rings must be free to move in the piston grooves. If they cannot, either they are carbon clogged (which necessitates replacing the rings and cleaning out the grooves), or metal has been pushed into the grooves by a piston seizure. In this event, pistons and rings must be replaced. Carbon-clogged rings are almost always broken when an attempt is made to remove or free them, so be prepared to buy a new set.

5. Measure the diameter of the pistons at the bottom of the skirt perpendicular to the wrist pin. If any measures less than the serviceable limit given in the charts at the ends of this section, the pistons should be replaced. If this has occurred, the cylinders are probably worn as well, and the solution is to have them bored out to the next oversize.

NOTE: *New pistons come with the wrist pin and rings. If oversized pistons are needed due to a worn bore or worn or damaged piston, obtain the pistons first, then have your dealer or a machine shop bore the cylinders to the proper size. This is obtained by measuring the diameter of the new pistons and boring the cylinders to that size plug the piston-to-cylinder clearance of 0.025–0.050 mm (0.001–0.002 in.).*

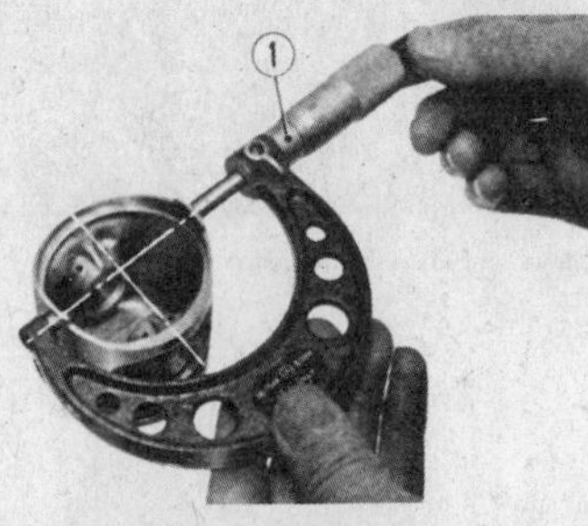

Measuring the piston diameter with a micrometer

There are four piston oversizes available in increments of 0.25 mm. The size is stamped on the piston crown.

6. If an inside micrometer is available, measure the inside diameter of the wrist pin holes and compare the reading with the specification given in the charts at the end of this chapter. The wrist pins should be a light push fit into the holes. If they are too loose, the pistons should be replaced.

7. Check the condition of the wrist pins. Measure the diameter of the pins at three places along their length and compare the diameter to the service specification. Replace the pins if the diameter is less than the serviceable limit, or if the pins are discolored from overheating.

8. The wrist pins ride directly on the connecting rod small ends. Measure the inside diameter of the small ends and compare the reading with the specifications given. If larger than the serviceable limit, the rod must be replaced.

9. Be sure that all oil passages in the cylinder are clear. Check the condition of the cam chain tensioner guides and replace them if damaged.

10. Replace the cylinder base O-rings. Check that any O-rings and the important dowel pins fitted to the cylinders are in their proper locations before installation.

PISTON RINGS

Two checks to be made on the piston rings are side clearance and end-gap. These checks should be made on both new and used rings.

1. Piston ring side clearance for compression rings and one-piece oil rings is checked with the rings installed on the piston. Insert a feeler gauge blade between the ring and the ring groove and check that the clearance is within the specification given for your machine. If the clearance is too large, the rings or grooves are worn. If too small, metal may have been pushed into the grooves due to a piston seizure. Check that the grooves are not just carboned up. If new rings do not bring the clearance to the proper value, the pistons must be replaced.

2. To remove the rings from the piston, use a ring spreader. Decarbonize the ring grooves.

3. To check the ring end-gap, ensure first that the cylinder bore is not excessively worn. Place each ring, in turn, into the bottom of its cylinder and push it in an inch or more using the piston skirt to align the ring in the bore. Measure the end-gap with a feeler gauge. If the end-gap is larger than the service limit, the rings must be replaced. If the measured end-gap of new rings is too large, the cylinder is worn and should be bored to the next oversize.

If new rings are fitted and the end-gap is too small, the ring ends must be filed. Hold the ring steady, closing the ends over a thin, fine file. Do not squeeze the ring, as this is the easiest way to break it. A few strokes of the file will increase the end-gap.

CAUTION: *Do not make more than a few strokes before checking the end-gap again. It is easy to remove too much metal.*

Do not allow the file to slip out of the ring, as this risks breaking it.

4. Roll each ring around its own groove and ensure that this can be done easily. If a ring sticks or binds in the groove, the pistons must be replaced.

Cylinder and Piston Installation

1. When installing piston rings, note that all rings are installed with the manufacturer's mark (the small letter near the end-gap) facing *up*.

NOTE: *The compression rings are not interchangeable. Refer to the illustrations showing the ring profiles.*

Install rings so that the manufacturer's mark faces up (arrow)

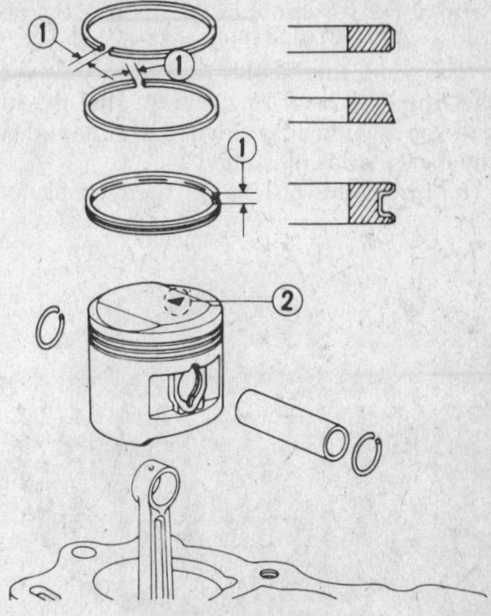

Make sure that the ring gaps (1) are staggered and the mark (2) is facing the exhaust side

2. To install the three-piece oil ring, install one rail on the piston below the oil ring groove, fit the expander, then move the rail into place. Install the top rail.

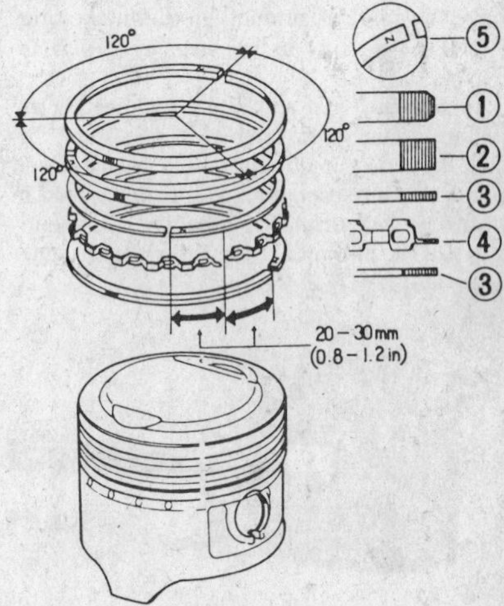

Installation of piston rings

3. Use a ring expander to install the rings to reduce the chance of breaking them.

4. Ring end-gaps must be staggered around the piston so that they do not overlap. If a one-piece oil ring is used, space the end-gaps about 120° apart, but do not position any of

Ring end-gap positions (three-piece oil ring)

them at the very front or very rear of the piston, or directly over the wrist pin hole.

The same thing holds true of models with the three-piece oil ring, except that the rail end-gaps should be positioned to either side of the expander as illustrated.

5. Install the pistons on their connecting

Install the pistons on the rods so that the arrows face the front of the engine

rods so that the arrow marks on the crown point towards the front (exhaust side) of the engine. Pistons marked with "IN" should have this mark positioned on the intake side.

NOTE: *Be sure to use new wrist pin circlips.*

6. Slip the wrist pins into place, heating the piston crown as on removal if necessary. Install the wrist pin circlips with a needle-nosed pliers. Be sure each circlips is firmly seated in its groove and arranged so that the circlip end-gap and the cut-out in the piston do *not* align.

Install the wrist pin circlips so the end-gap and cut-out (arrows) do not align

7. Lubricate the rings and piston skirts with clean motor oil.

8. Install the cylinder base gasket and the two dowel pins (oriface valve) and O-rings on the crankcase.

NOTE: *Blow compressed air through the dowel pin holes before installation to make sure they are not clogged.*

9. Rotate the engine until No. 2 and 3 pistons are at Top Dead Center and place a piston base (Honda part number 07033-33301 for the 350/400, or, for the others, 07033-

Gasket (1) dowel pins (2) and O-ring (3) placement is critical

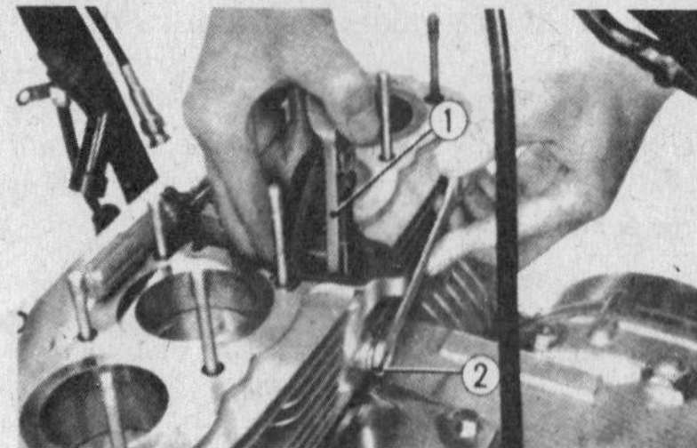

Installing the tensioner (1) and locknut (2)

55102) under the pistons to hold them in position. (A block of wood cut to suitable size works just as well). Compress the rings on No. 2 and 3 pistons and slide the cylinder down over them. Rotate the engine until No. 1 and 4 pistons contact the base of the cylinder (taking care not to pull No. 2 and 3 pistons out of their bores), compress the rings, and slide the cylinder against the crankcase, raise the cam chain through the center of the cylinder and put a screwdriver through the center of it to keep it from dropping down. Also, with the cylinder about one in. from the crankcase, install the cam chain tensioner in the cylinder. Hold the tensioner down by hand and install the O-ring and washer, and tighten the lock-

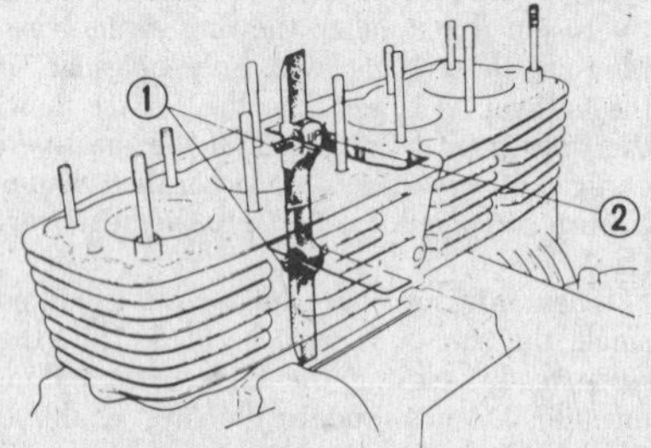

Chain guide pins (1) and "up" mark (2)

nut. Install the cam chain guide into the cylinder as illustrated so the "UP" mark is correctly positioned (500/550).

NOTE *If the cylinder studs are to be replaced, a special stud wrench (Honda part number 07779-99902) should be used because the studs are secured with thread-locking compound. When installing new studs, thoroughly clean the stud holes, apply thread-locking compound, and torque the studs to 15–16 ft lbs.*

CRANKCASE COVER COMPONENTS

The following sections deal with the removal, inspection, and installation of those components found beneath the left and right crankcase covers. These include the clutch, breaker points, and alternator. These components can be serviced with the engine in the frame.

Clutch

DISASSEMBLY

350/550

1. Drain the oil from the sump.

2. Remove the kick-start lever and the right-side footrest.

3. Take out the screws and pull off the right-side rear crankcase (clutch) cover.

Clutch pushrod (1), bolts (2) and pushrod plate (3)

4. Remove the clutch lifter rod from the center of the mainshaft.

5. Remove the four bolts from the lifter plate evenly and remove the lifter plate, and clutch springs.

6. Remove the 25 mm snap-ring from the mainshaft in the center of the clutch hub, and pull the clutch assembly off the mainshaft.

7. Remove the clutch hub, discs, and plates from the clutch housing. On 350 models the hub can be further disassembled by removing the 92 mm set ring, special plate, clutch disc spring, and disc spring seat.

If it is desired to remove the release or adjuster mechanisms:

8. Remove the cotter pin from the clutch lever inside the right crankcase cover. Withdraw the clutch lever from the case.

Removing the clutch circlip

Remove the set ring (1) to further disassemble the clutch hub (2)

Removing the clutch hub (1) and plates (2) from the housing (3) and pressure plate (4)

9. Remove the locknut and washer from the clutch adjuster, and withdraw the clutch adjusting lever from the case.

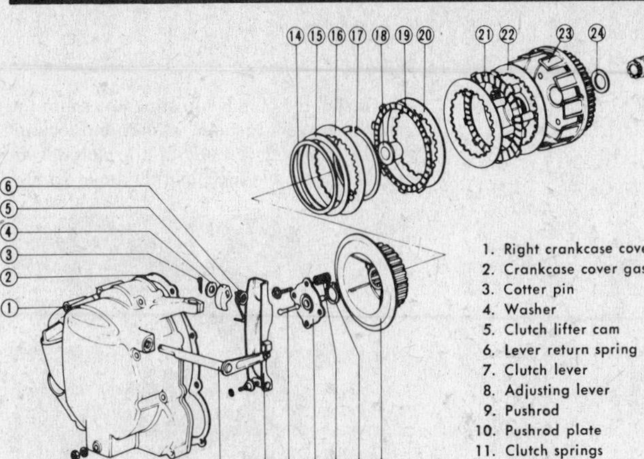

Clutch assembly (350)

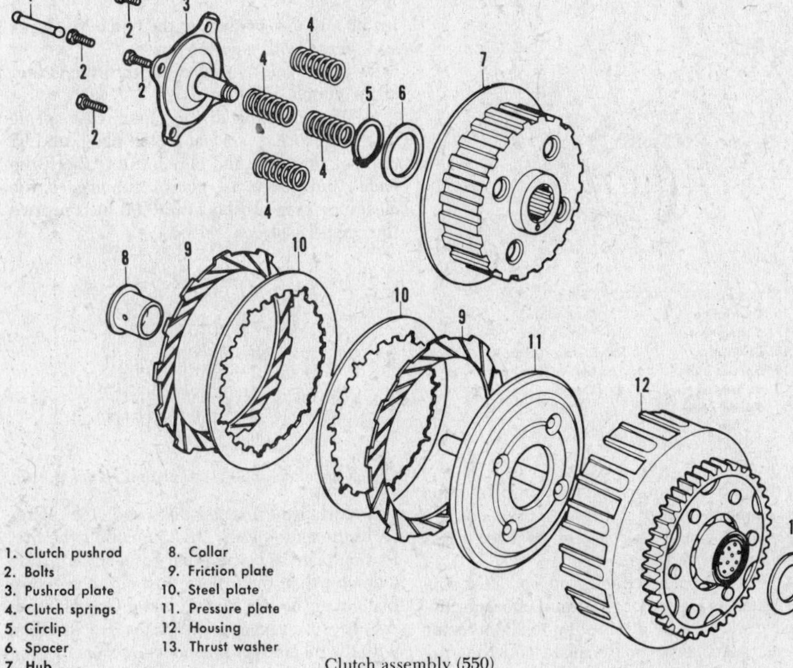

Clutch assembly (550)

400

1. Drain the oil from the sump.
2. Remove the kick-start lever, and the right footrest. Remove the rear brake adjusting nut from the brake rod.
3. Remove the two screws securing the release mechanism cover plate to the right crankcase cover and remove the cover plate.
4. Disconnect the clutch cable from the release lever. If necessary, screw the cable adjuster into the crankcase cover to allow more free-play in the cable.

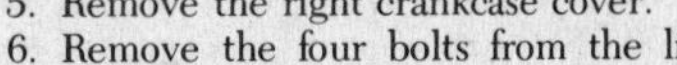

5. Remove the right crankcase cover.
6. Remove the four bolts from the lifter plate evenly and remove the lifter plate, and clutch springs.
7. Remove the special locknut from the center of the clutch hub using the special tool (Tool number 07916-6390000) after bending back the tabs on the lockwasher. Remove the clutch assembly.
8. Remove the hub and plates from the clutch housing. Lift the steel plates and the friction discs from the clutch hub. The hub can be further disassembled by removing the 92 mm set ring, special plate, clutch disc spring, and the disc spring seat.

If it is desired to remove the release or adjuster mechanism from the crankcase cover:

9. Remove the locknut from the clutch adjusting screw, and remove the release lever and lever spring. Remove the clutch cam plate, ball retainer, clutch lifter, and adjusting screw from the inside of the cover.

Locknut (1), tab washer (2) and lockwasher (3)

Clutch hub (1) and set ring (2)

500

1. Drain the engine oil.
2. Remove the kick-start lever.
3. Take out the screws and pull off the right-side rear crankcase (clutch) cover.
4. Unscrew the four pressure-plate mounting bolts and remove the plate and four springs. Remove the release piston.

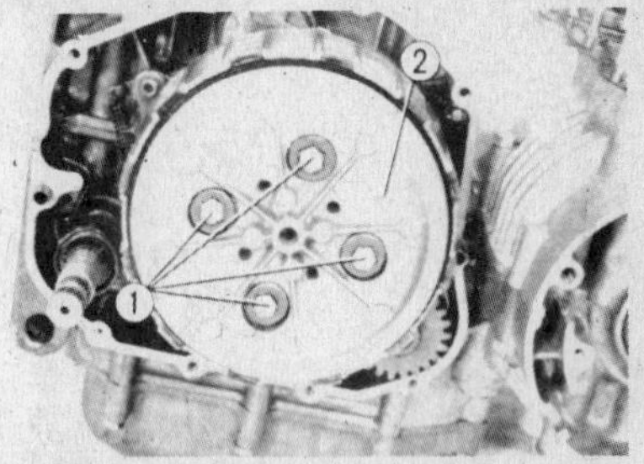

Remove the pressure plate mounting bolts (1)

Removing the snap-ring (1) which secures the clutch hub (2)

5. Remove the large circlip and shims (if any). Pull the clutch hub assembly off the mainshaft.
6. Remove the clutch center section, discs, and plates from the clutch housing.

If it is desired to remove the release or adjuster mechanisms:

7. Remove the left-side, rear crankcase cover and disconnect the clutch cable from the release lever.

Removing the release mechanism (1)

8. Unscrew the clutch adjuster lockbolt and remove the adjuster from the left crankcase cover. Pull the release rod out of the crankcase.

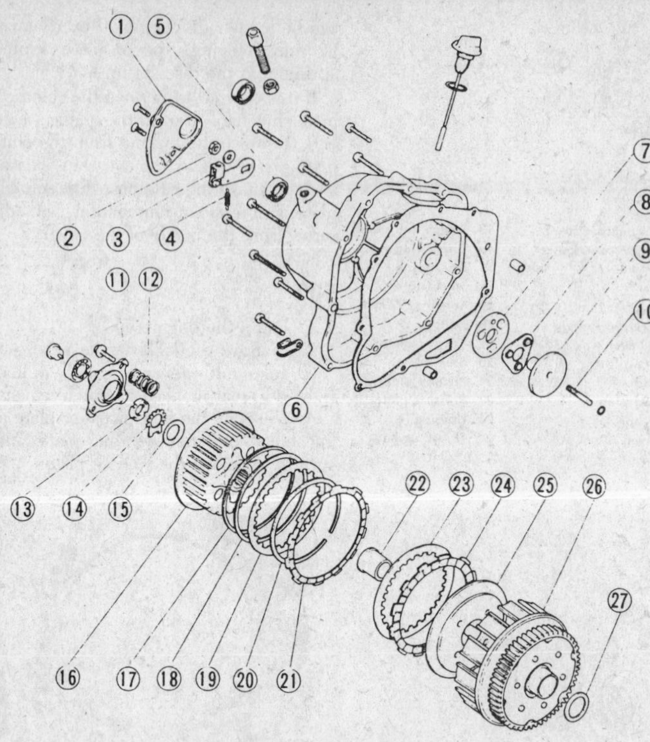

Clutch assembly (400)

1. Clutch cover
2. Locknut
3. Release lever
4. Spring
5. Oil seal
6. Right crankcase cover
7. Cam plate
8. Ball retainer
9. Lifter
10. Adjusting screw
11. Lifter Plate
12. Clutch spring
13. Locknut
14. Tab washer
15. Lockwasher
16. Clutch hub
17. Spring seat
18. Disc spring
19. Special plate
20. 92 mm set ring
21. Friction disc
22. Collar
23. Steel plate
24. Friction disc
25. Pressure plate
26. Clutch housing
27. Thrust washer

650

1. Drain the engine oil.

2. Remove the right side rider's footpeg. Disconnect the clutch cable at the clutch cover.

3. Remove the clutch cover.

4. If dissassembly of the clutch lifter is desired, remove the adjusting screw, adjusting arm, and lifter shaft.

5. Remove the lifter guide, bearing, and bearing retainer from the clutch.

6. Remove the clutch spring bolts, loosening them gradually. Remove the lifter plate and springs.

7. Put the transmission in gear and apply the rear brake so that the engine will not turn over. Use the special clutch hub nut socket to remove the hub nut.

8. Remove the clutch assembly from its shaft.

INSPECTION

1. Check the condition of the kick-start-shaft oil seal. If it leaks, or if the lips show signs of damage, pry the old seal out with a small screwdriver. Press the new seal straight into the cover. Apply some oil or grease to the seal lips before installation.

2. Check the condition of the clutch cover mating surface. Remove any burrs or imperfections with an oilstone.

3. Measure the thickness of the friction plates with a vernier caliper and replace them as a set if any is less than the serviceable limit which is 2.3 mm (0.091 in.) for the 350/400, and 550, and 3.0 mm (0.11 in.) for the 500. On the 650, the outermost friction plate has a replacement limit of 2.4 mm (0.09 in.) while the others should be replaced as a set if less than 3.2 mm (0.13 in).

4. Place the steel clutch plates on a flat surface, such as a piece of glass, and check for excessive warpage by attempting to slip a feeler gauge blade between the plate and the surface. Replace the steel and friction plates as a set if warpage exceeds 0.2 mm (0.008 in.) for the 350/400 or 0.3 mm (0.011 in.) for the 500/550/650.

5. Measure the free length of each clutch spring and replace them as a set if any is less than the serviceable limit which is 34.0 mm (1.34 in.) for the 350, 29.8 mm (1.71 in.) for the 400, 30.5 mm (1.20 in.) for the 500, and 35.4 mm (1.39 in.) for the 550 and 650.

Be sure that the springs are tightened evenly on assembly.

6. Check the friction plate tabs for wear or damage. Check the clutch housing for indented wear caused by the tabs. Remove any burrs with a file or oilstone.

7. Check the corresponding splines of the clutch hub and steel plates for indented wear.

8. Check the condition of the lifter plate bearing, if fitted. Rotation must be smooth, noiseless, and effortless. Replace the bearing if rotation is rough, the races loose, or rotation noisy.

9. On the 650, measure the outside diameter of the clutch bushing and the inside diameter of the clutch hub. The former should be at least 29.94 mm (1.18 in.), the latter no more than 30.05 mm (1.18 in.).

ASSEMBLY

350/550

1. Install the clutch adjusting lever into the crankcase cover. Install a washer and locknut onto the adjusting screw. Slip the clutch lever into the case while installing the lever spring.

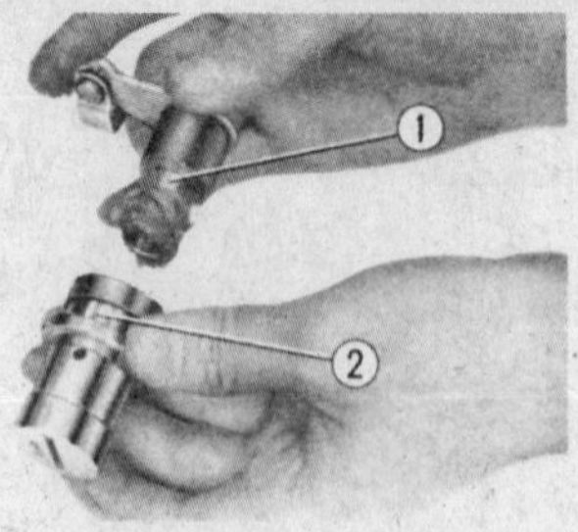

Installing the lifter (1) in the adjuster (2)

Install a 10 mm washer on the end of the lever and secure with a cotter pin.

2. Install the 25 mm collar into the center of the clutch housing.

3. 350 only: Install the clutch disc spring seat, disc spring, special clutch plate, and 92 mm set ring onto the clutch hub. Check the clutch hub-to-special plate clearance. If the clearance exceeds 0.5 mm (0.02 in.), replace the special plate.

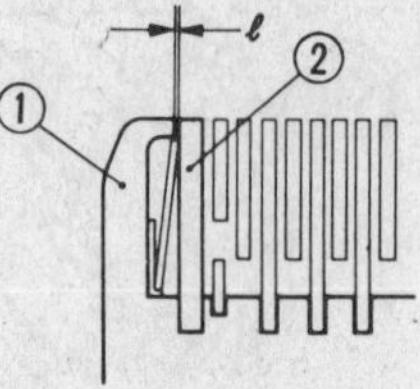

Check the clutch hub (1) to plate (2) clearance (b)

4. Install the friction discs and steel plates on to the clutch hub. On 350 models the first friction plate to be installed has a larger inside diameter than the others. Install the pressure plate over the last friction plate. On 550 models, be sure the friction plates are installed with the oil grooves positioned as shown in the illustration.

5. Install the hub assembly into the clutch housing. Install the 25 mm thrust washer on the mainshaft, then install the clutch assembly on the mainshaft, and secure with a 25 mm snap-ring.

6. 550 only: Check end-play of the clutch assembly with a dial indicator, and if end-play exceeds 0.1 mm (0.004 in.), a shim should be installed behind the circlip. Shims are available in thicknesses of 0.1, 0.3, and 0.5 mm.

7. Install the clutch springs, lifter plate, and lifter rod.

8. Install the clutch cover, and adjust the clutch.

400

1. Install the clutch cam plate, ball retainer, clutch lifter, and adjusting screw into the inside of the crankcase cover. Install the release lever, lever spring, and locknut on the adjusting screw.

2. Install the disc spring seat, disc spring, and the special clutch plate on the hub and secure with a 92 mm set ring.

Check the clutch hub-to-special plate clearance. If the clearance exceeds 0.5 mm (0.02 in.) replace the special plate.

3. Install the remaining plates and friction discs on the hub. Note that the first friction disc installed on the hub has a larger inside diameter than the other friction discs.

4. When all of the plates and discs are installed, fit the pressure plate over the top friction disc.

5. Fit the center collar to the clutch housing. Install the thrust washer on the mainshaft, and install the clutch housing.

6. Install the hub assembly into the clutch housing. Secure the hub on the shaft with a lockwasher, tab washer, and special locknut. The large tab on the tab washer should fit over the lug on the hub. Bend at least one of the tabs of the tab washer into a slot in the locknut.

7. Install the clutch springs, and lifter plate. Install the four clutch bolts.

8. The remainder of assembly is the reverse of disassembly.

500

1. Install the release rod into the crankcase so that the round end is toward the right-side.

2. Apply grease to the clutch release, assemble it into the adjuster, and install it in the left crankcase cover. Tighten the lockbolt and connect the clutch cable to the release lever.

3. Install the steel ball into the clutch release and mount the left crankcase cover on the engine.

4. Coat the friction discs with fresh engine oil and assemble the discs and plates onto the center section. Install the center section in the clutch housing. Don't forget the thrust washer. Be sure the friction discs are installed with the oil grooves positioned as shown in the illustration.

NOTE: *Beginning with engine number CB 550E-1018728, modified clutch discs and plates have been used. Earlier engines suffering from clutch slip may be modified with these parts, as they are interchangeable.*

5. Install the clutch assembly on the mainshaft and lock it in place with the circlip. Check end-play of the clutch assembly with a dial indicator, and if end-play exceeds 0.004 in. (0.1 mm), a shim should be installed behind the circlip. Shims are available in thicknesses of 0.1, 0.3, and 0.5 mm.

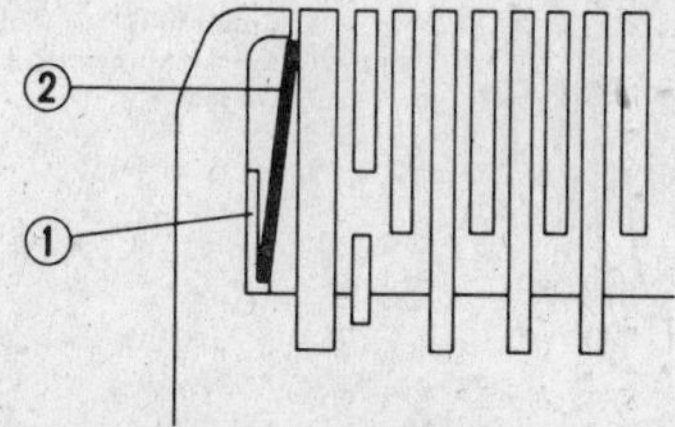

Make sure that the disc spring seat (1) and disc spring (2) are properly seated

End-play can be taken up with a shim (3) behind the circlip (2); (1) is the clutch collar

6. Slip the release piston into the mainshaft and install the pressure plate, with springs on the clutch housing.

7. Install the crankcase (clutch) cover using a new gasket.

8. Refill the engine with oil, and adjust the clutch.

650

1. Assembly is the reverse of disassembly. Be sure that the thrust washer is fitted to the shaft behind the clutch.

2. Be sure that the hub nut washer is installed with the "Outside" facing outwards.

3. Tighten the hub nut to 34–38 ft. lbs.

4. Install the lifter plate with the cupped side facing outwards.

5. Pre-lube the clutch assembly.

Ignition Timing Assembly

REMOVAL

1. Remove the breaker points cover. Disconnect the two leads behind the engine.

2. Remove the small bolt which secures the special nut used to turn the engine over.

3. Remove the three screws which secure the breaker plate and remove it.

4. Pull off the timing advance mechanism as a unit, taking care not to take apart the mechanism and breaker cam.

Inspection

1. For inspection of points, condensers, etc., refer to "General Information."

2. The timing advance mechanism movement must be free. When the breaker cam is turned so that the weights move out to the fully extended position, releasing the cam should result in its returning to the original location. If it will not, try penetrating oil or the like to ease movement. Check for weak springs. Replace the unit if proper action cannot be obtained.

INSTALLATION

Installation is the reverse of removal. Note that the timing advance mechanism is located with a pin on the crankshaft.

Alternator

REMOVAL

1. Remove the alternator cover.

2. Remove the alternator rotor mounting bolt.

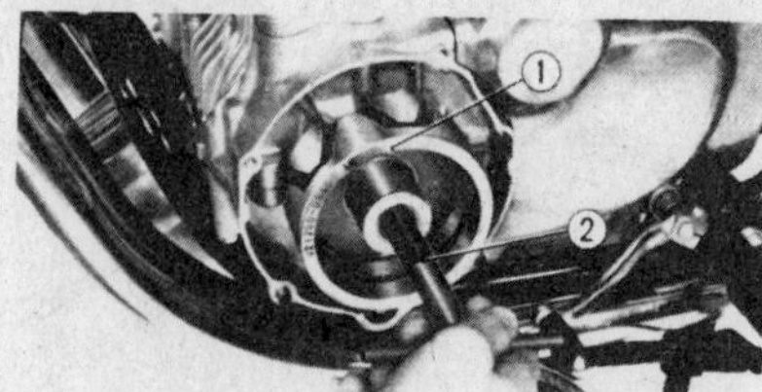

Removing the rotor (1) with the special puller (2) (350/400)

3. The rotor is a push-fit onto the tapered crankshaft. Remove the rotor with the special tool (number 07011-33301 for the 350/400 or 07011-21601 for the 500/550 or 07733-0020001 for the 650).

INSPECTION

Refer to "Electrical System," for alternator tests.

INSTALLATION

Tighten the rotor bolt to 22–29 ft. lbs. for the 350/400 or 29–30 ft. lbs. for the 500/550 and 36–43 ft. lbs. for the 650.

LOWER END

Disassembly

350/400

1. Drain the oil from the sump and oil filter, then remove the engine from the frame as directed in the "Engine Removal and Installation" section.

2. Disassemble the top end as described in the "Top End" section.

3. Remove the alternator rotor using a suitable rotor puller (Honda part number 07011-33301).

4. Remove the right crankcase cover, clutch and gearshift spindle, then disassemble the positive stopper, gearshift drum stopper, and the neutral stopper arm.

Removing the shift spindle (350/400)

Remove the positive stopper (1), shift drum stopper (2), and neutral stopper arm (3) (350/400)

5. Remove the contact breaker and automatic advance mechanism.

6. Invert the engine and remove the oil pan and oil pump assembly.

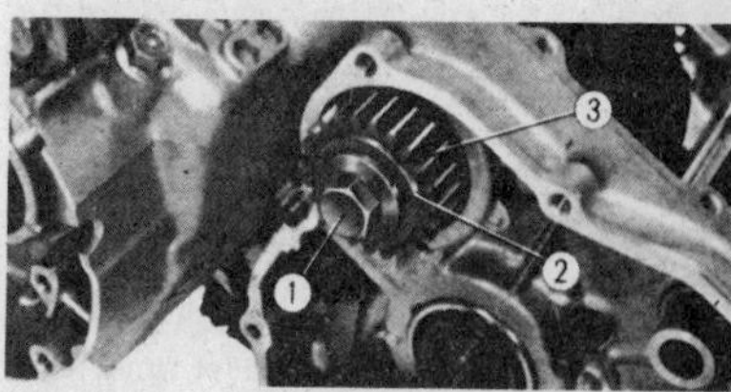

Remove the 12 mm bolt (1) in order to remove the lockwasher (2) and secondary drive gear (3) (350/400)

Removing the primary shaft (1) (350/400)

7. Remove the 12 mm bolt from the end of the primary shaft, slide the secondary drive gear off the primary shaft, then slip the primary shaft out to the right.

8. Remove the internal circlip (52 mm), the ball bearing, and the 25 mm collar as illustrated.

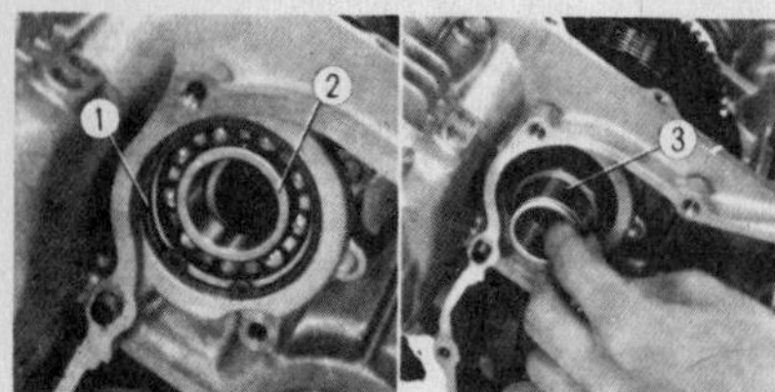

Remove the internal circlip (1) and bearing (2), then remove the collar (3) (350/400)

9. Evenly loosen the bolts from the lower crankcase working in a criss-cross pattern from the inside out, then gently tap the cases with a soft mallet to separate them.

10. Remove the transmission and shifter components if necessary. The gear assemblies should be removed simultaneously.

500/550

1. Remove the engine from the frame and remove the cylinder head, cylinder barrel, and pistons as described in the preceding section on top end overhaul.

2. Take off the alternator cover and remove the rotor using, if possible, a rotor puller (Honda part number 07011-21601).

3. Remove the ignition points cover and unscrew the 6 mm bolt at the end of the breaker cam. Remove the hexagonal washer. Take out the three phillips head screws and remove the complete breaker plate assembly.

4. Remove the clutch unit as described under "Clutch."

5. Remove the shift lever. Withdraw the shift linkage from the right-side of the engine while holding the shift arm down.

6. Take off the starter cover and remove the starter motor.

7. Place the engine upside down, preferably on a large piece of cardboard. Unscrew the ten bolts, and remove the oil pan and oil pump pick-up.

8. Unscrew the ten 8 mm lower crankcase bolts, gradually, in reverse order of the tightening sequence. Remove the thirteen 6 mm bolts from the lower crankcase.

9. Turn the engine over again so that it is resting on the lower crankcase in its normal position and remove the three 8 mm and three 6 mm bolts.

10. Separate the crankcase halves by tapping with a rubber mallet and lifting the upper crankcase away. Lift the transmission mainshaft and countershaft assemblies out of the case. Do not lose the bearing set rings.

NOTE: *Be very careful not to mar the mating surfaces of the crankcase halves during handling or when removing old gasket cement.*

Bearing set plate location (1) (500 and 550)

11. Unscrew the two bolts and remove the transmission primary shaft bearing set plate. Remove the circlip and pull out the primary shaft using tool number 07009-32301 or a suitable gear puller. Lift out the starter clutch and primary sprocket assembly.

Removing the primary shaft (1) with a puller (2) (500 and 550)

12. Lift out the crankshaft. Unbolt the connecting rod bearings caps, remove the rods, and slip the cam and primary chains off the crankshaft. Mark or tag the rods so that they may be installed in their original positions.

650

1. Remove the engine from the frame. Remove the oil filter, oil pan, and strainer.

2. Remove the cylinder head, cylinders, and pistons.

3. Remove the clutch. Remove the gearshift linkage.

4. Remove the alternator rotor, pulser generator, spark advance mechanism, and starter motor.

5. Remove the upper crankcase bolts. Turn the engine over and remove the lower crankcase bolts. Bolts should be loosened gradually and in a cross pattern to eliminate the chances of warpage.

6. Remove the primary shaft circlip. Use a gear puller to remove the primary drive gear. Remove the bearing stopper plate.

7. Disconnect the primary chain tensioner spring.

8. Remove the primary shaft. This must be done with a slide-hammer or similar tool.

9. Separate the crankcase halves. The crankshaft and transmission will remain in the upper case half.

Inspection

Check the crankshaft run-out by placing the ends of the crankshaft in V-blocks and rotating the shaft while taking a reading with a dial indicator at the center journal. Replace the crankshaft if run-out exceeds 0.05 mm (0.0019 in.). (Run-out equals one-half the dial indicator reading.)

Checking crankshaft (2) run-out with a dial indicator (1)

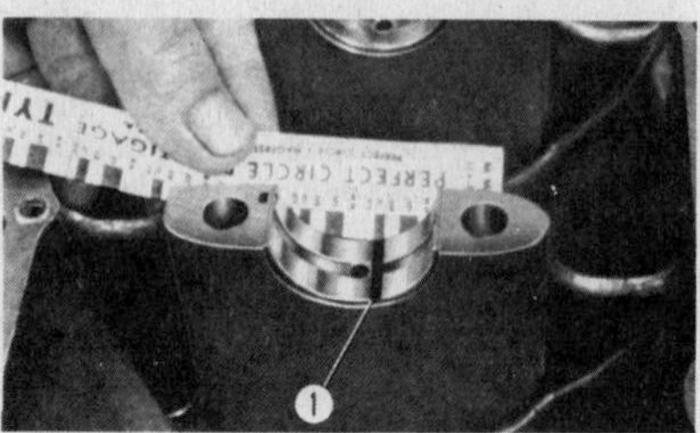

Using plastigauge (1) to obtain the bearing clearance

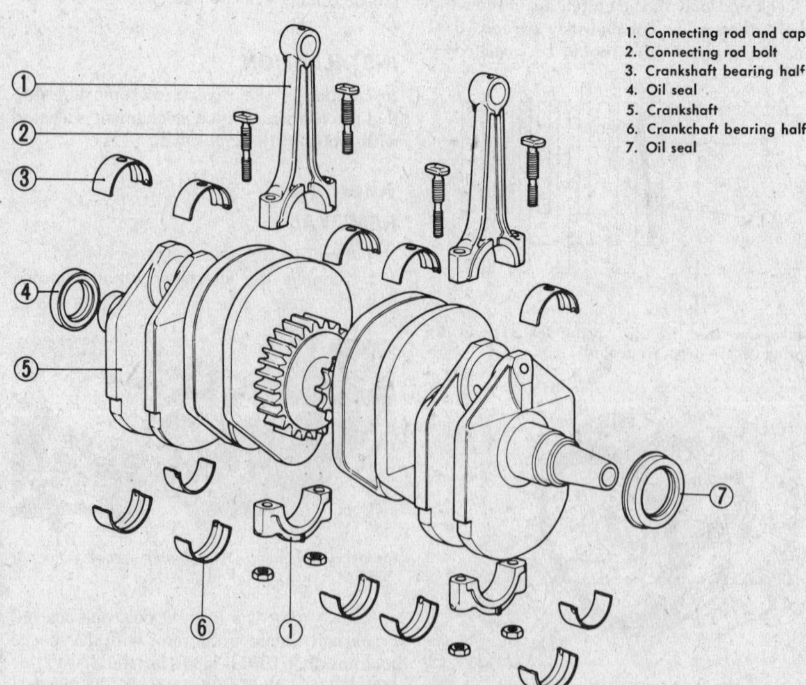

Crankshaft assembly (350/400)

MAIN BEARINGS

Inspect the bearing journals for scoring and damage. Measure the journal diameter in several places to check for ovality and taper. Maximum acceptable variation of journal diameter is 0.05 mm (0.0019 in.).

Journal wear can be checked using a material such as plastigauge. Cut strips of plastigauge to fit across each bearing, install the crankshaft and lower crankcase, and torque the ten 8 mm lower crankcase bolts in the correct sequence to 15 ft lbs. Do not turn the crankshaft and measure the plastigauge with the scale provided. If clearance exceeds 0.08 mm (0.0032 in.), the bearings should be replaced. Bearings that are damaged in any way should not be reused.

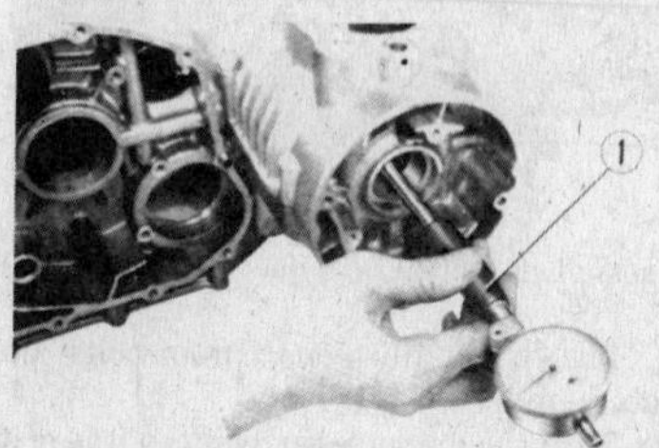

Checking bearing seat diameter with a dial gauge (1)

MAIN BEARING SELECTION

If the main bearings are to be replaced, two measurements must be made: inside diameter of the bearing seats and crankshaft journal diameter. To check bearing seat diameter, assemble the upper and lower crankcases with the ten bolts, as described above. Measure the seats with an inside dial indicator in the vertical direction and select from the following code letters according to measurements obtained for each bearing seat.

Code Letter Size Chart (Bearing Seat Diameter)

500/550/650

Seat Diameter	*Code*
1.4173–1.4176 in./ 36.000–36.008 mm	A
1.4176–1.4179 in./ 36.008–36.016 mm	B
1.4179–1.4182 in./ 36.016–36.024 mm	C

350/400

Seat Diameter	*Code*
1.3780–1.3783 in./ 35.000–35.008 mm	A
1.3783–1.3786 in. 35.008–35.016 mm	B
1.3786–1.3789 in./ 35.016–35.024 mm	C

Next, measure the crankshaft bearing journal diameters with a micrometer and select one of the following two code numbers for each journal.

Code Number Size Chart (Journal Diameter)

500/550/650

Journal Diameter	*Code*
1.2987–1.2992 in./ 32.99–33.00 mm	1
1.2983–1.2987 in./ 32.98–32.99 mm	2

350/400

Journal Diameter	*Code*
1.2586–1.2590 in./ 31.97–31.98 mm	1
1.2590–1.2594 in./ 31.98–31.99 mm	2
1.2594–1.2598 in./ 31.99–32.00 mm	3

Use the codes obtained to pick out the proper bearings from the bearing selection chart.

Bearing Selection Chart

500/550/650

		Code Number	
		1	*2*
Code Letters	A	D yellow	C green
	B	C green	B brown
	C	B brown	A black

350/400

		Code Number		
		1	*2*	*3*
Code Letters	A	B brown	C green	D yellow
	B	A black	B brown	C green
	C	AA blue	A black	B brown

CONNECTING RODS AND BEARINGS

ROD BEARING SELECTION

Connecting rod bearings need not be replaced unless the bearing shells show signs of wear and/or damage, or if there is excessive clearance between the bearing and crankpin. To check the clearance, cut a strip of plastigauge and place it across the bearing shell, as when checking main bearing clearance. Install the rod bearing cap and torque the nuts to 15 ft lbs. Do not turn the crankshaft or move the connecting rod. Remove the bearing cap and measure the plastigauge with the scale. Maximum acceptable clearance is 0.08 mm (0.0032 in.).

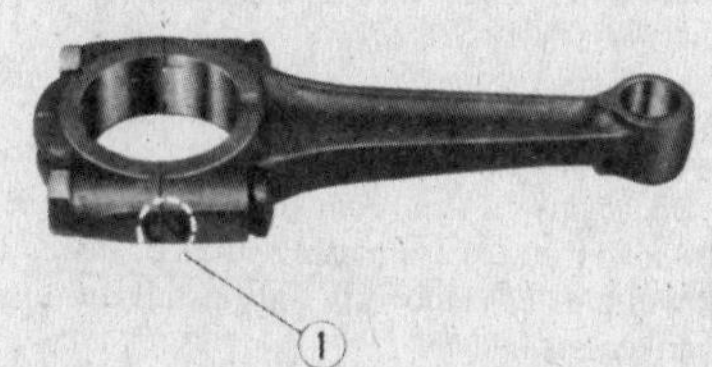

Con rod bearing code number

If the rod bearings are to be replaced, measure the diameter of the crankpin and select from the following bearing code letters.

Code Letter Size Chart (Crankpin Diameter)

500/550/650

Crankpin Diameter	*Code*
1.3775–1.3780 in./ 34.99–35.00 mm	A
1.3771–1.3775 in./ 34.98–34.99 mm	B

350/400

Crankpin Diameter	*Code*
1.2586–1.2590 in./ 31.97–31.98 mm	A
1.2590–1.2594 in./ 31.98–31.99 mm	B
1.2594–1.2598 in./ 31.99–32.00 mm	C

Now using the code letter obtained above and the code *number* stamped on the connecting rod, select the proper bearings from this chart.

Bearing Selection Chart

500/550/650

		Code Letter	
		A	*B*
Code Number	1	D yellow	C green
	2	C green	B brown
	3	B brown	A black

350/400

		Code Letter		
		A	*B*	*C*
Code Number	1	C green	D yellow	E red
	2	B brown	C green	D yellow
	3	A black	B brown	C green

CONNECTING ROD REPLACEMENT

1. Measure the con rod side clearance. Clearance for the 350/400 must not exceed 0.15 mm (0.0059 in.); clearance for the 500/550/650 must not exceed 0.35 mm (0.0138 in.).
2. Measure the inside diameter of the con rod small ends. Bushing diameter should be no greater than 13.1 mm (0.516 in.) for the 350/400; 15.07 mm (0.593 in.) for the 500, 550, and 650.

Checking connecting rod side clearance with a feeler gauge (1)

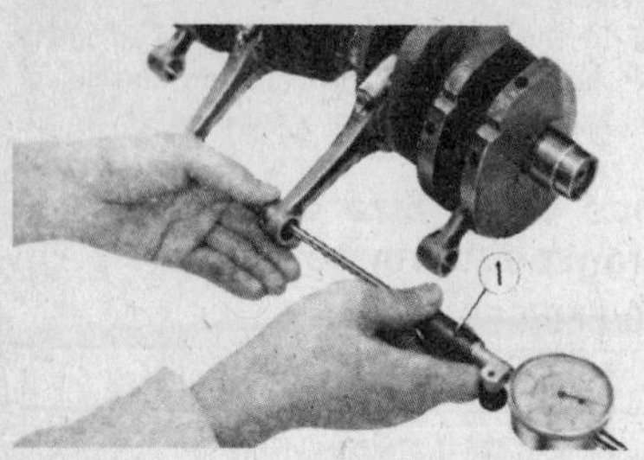
Measuring the connecting rod small end diameter with a dial gauge (1)

3. If either of the above measurements is greater than the limits given, the rod should be replaced.

4. A replacement con rod of the same weight as the original should be selected. Rod weight can be determined by the code *letter*

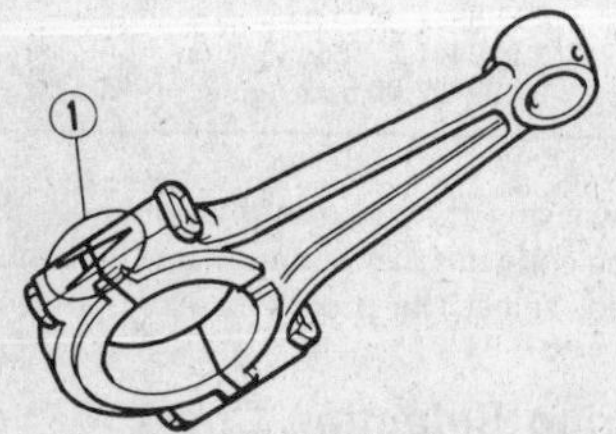
Weight code letter location (1)

stamped on the big end of the rod. When replacing all four rods, ensure that the weight variation between them does not exceed five grams.

NOTE: *Rod weight includes the con rod cap and bolts, but does not include the bearing inserts.*

Rods marked "A" or "B" are replaced with rods marked "B."

Rods marked "C," "D," or "E" are replaced with rods marked "D."

"F" and "G" rods are replaced with "F"-marked rods.

ASSEMBLY

350/400

1. Assembly is basically in the reverse order of disassembly. Rods must be fitted to the crank with the tang facing the exhaust side of the engine. Make sure that all components are thoroughly clean, and coat all bearing surfaces with a suitable lubricant. New gaskets, oil seals, and O-rings should be used.

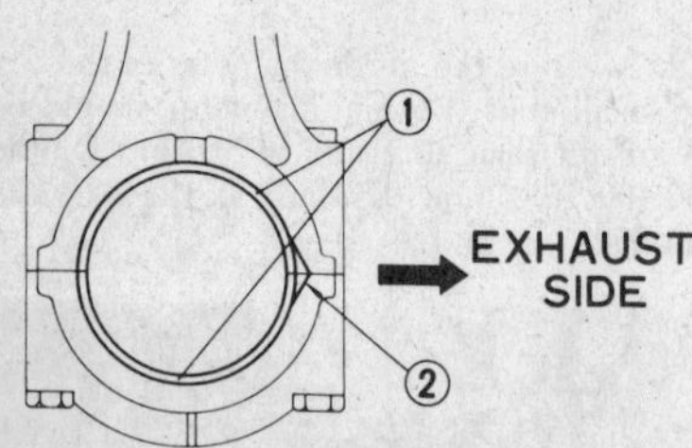

Be sure the rods are correctly installed on the crankshaft

2. When installing the cam chain tensioner push bar, do so with the mark facing upward. Depress the bar by hand and lock it in place with the adjusting bolt and locknut.

3. Install the primary chain guide with its recessed mark facing the transmission.

Install the primary chain guide (1) with the mark (2) facing up (350/400)

4. Apply a uniformly thin coat of a suitable liquid gasket compound to the crankcase mating surfaces, taking care not to foul any bearing surfaces.

5. Check that all dowel pins are properly installed before fitting the case halves together.

Crankcase bolt tightening sequence (350/400)

6. Secure the ten bolts on the crankcase in the order shown, torquing them to 16.6–18.1 ft lbs (2.3–2.5 kg/m).

500/550

1. Position the main bearing shells in the crankcase halves and coat them with engine oil.

2. Install the primary and cam chains on the crankshaft and intall the connecting rods, in their original positions, tightening the nuts to 15 ft lbs. Note that the rods must be installed on the crank so that the bearing insert keys face the front of the engine. Place the crankshaft assembly in the upper crankcase.

3. Install the primary chain around the starter clutch and, holding the starter gear and clutch in position, drive the primary shaft in from right to left. Be careful not to damage the needle bearings in the starter gear hub and do not forget to install the circlip. Install the mainshaft and countershaft gear assemblies, taking care to position the bearing set rings and dowel pins correctly.

Installing the starter clutch (1) and gear (2) on the primary shaft (3) (500/550)

4. Install the bearing set plate with the two 6 mm retaining bolts.

5. Apply a *thin* coat of gasket cement to the lower crankcase mating surface, install the dowel pins (if removed), and install the upper crankcase.

6. Hold the crankcases together tightly and turn the engine upside down. Install the ten 8 mm bolts and torque them, in the sequence shown, to 17–18 ft lbs.

NOTE: *Position the two bolts with "9" stamped on the bolt head as shown in the tightening sequence.*

Crankcase bolt tightening sequence (500 and 550)

7. Install the thirteen 6 mm bolts and torque them to 8 ft lbs.

8. Turn the engine over again so it is resting on the bottom crankcase and install the three 6 mm and three 8 mm bolts. Position the two 8 mm bolts marked "8" on the bolt head as indicated in the illustration.

6 mm (1) and 8 mm (2) bolt positions (500 and 550)

9. Install the oil pump pick-up and mount the oil pan with the ten 6 mm bolts.

10. Install the starter motor.

11. Install the shift linkage, as removed, and install the shift lever.

12. Mount the clutch assembly in accordance with procedures given in the section on clutch service.

13. Place the ignition advance dowel pin in the hole in the crankshaft and mount the oil pan with the ten 6 mm screws. Install the special washer with the 6 mm bolt in the breaker cam.

14. Install the alternator rotor and tighten the bolt to 30 ft lbs. Install the alternator cover.

650

1. Prelube the con rod bearings and fit each rod onto its proper crankpin.

NOTE: *The code number on each rod must face the front of the engine.*

Tighten the rod bolts gradually and evenly to 17–20 ft. lbs.

2. Clean the crankcase mating surfaces thoroughly.

3. Apply a non-permanent liquid sealant to the mating surface of the lower crankcase.

CAUTION: *Keep the sealant clear of oil passages and bearings.*

4. Pre-lube the crank bearings.

5. Be sure that the transmission shaft bearings and oil seal are properly seated.

6. Position the primary chain and damper assembly. Assemble the crankcase halves.

7. Drive the primary shaft in with a plastic mallet.

8. Install the bearing stopper plate, pri-

mary drive gear, and circlip. Connect the tensioner spring.

9. Tighten the crankcase bolts gradually and in a cross pattern.

8 mm bolts: 16–19 ft. lbs.
6 mm bolts: 7–10 ft. lbs.

NOTE: *Crankshaft bolts should be lubricated with moly grease.*

TRANSMISSION

Shifter Mechanism

DISASSEMBLY

350/400

NOTE: *For convenience sake, Honda breaks the shifter mechanism down into two sub-groups. Group "A" components can be serviced with the engine still mounted in the frame. Group "B" components can only be serviced once the engine has been dismantled.*

GROUP A

1. Run the engine until normal operating temperature is reached, then drain the sump. Place the transmission in the Neutral position.
2. Remove the right-side footrest, the kickstarter pedal, the shift lever, the right-side crankcase cover, and the gear shift spindle.

Removing the gearshift spindle

3. Remove the positive stopper, the gear shift drum stopper, and the neutral stopper arm.

Positive stopper (1), drum stopper (2), and neutral stopper arm (3)

4. Remove the contact breaker cover, base plate assembly, and advance mechanism.
5. Remove the oil pump, then remove the secondary drive gear from the primary shaft after removing the 12 mm bolt.

Remove the 12 mm bolt (1) and lockwasher (2) to remove the secondary drive gear (3)

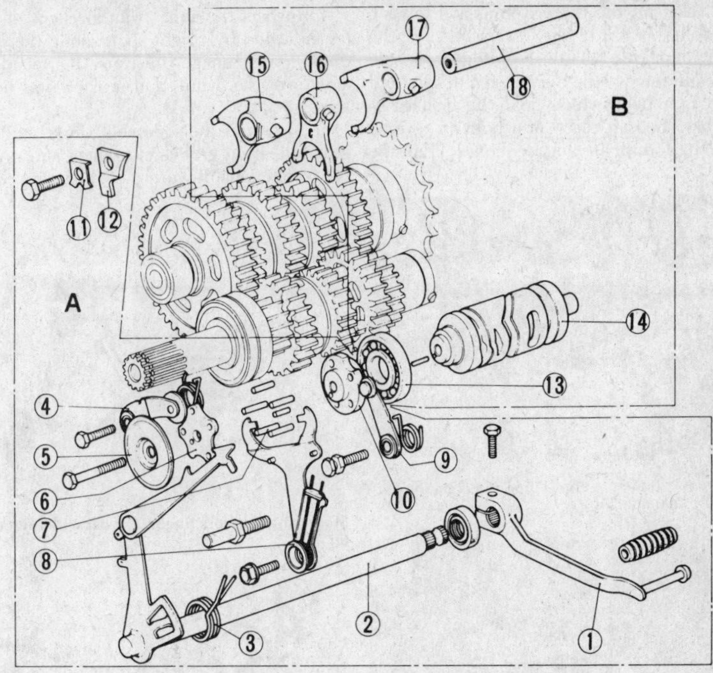

Shifter mechanism (350/400)

Group A (On-vehicle operations)	Group B (Engine removal required)
1. Gearshift pedal	10. Gearshift drum center
2. Gearshift spindle	11. Lockwasher, 8 mm
3. Return spring	12. Guide shaft set place
4. Gearshift drum stopper	13. Ball bearing
5. Gearshift side plate	14. Gearshift drum
6. Drum stopper plate	15. Gearshift fork (right)
7. Rollers (6)	16. Gearshift fork (center)
8. Positive stopper	17. Gearshift fork (left)
9. Neutral stopper arm	18. Shift fork guide shaft

GROUP B

1. Remove the engine from the frame as directed in the "Engine Removal and Installation" section, then perform all of the steps listed in the preceding section.

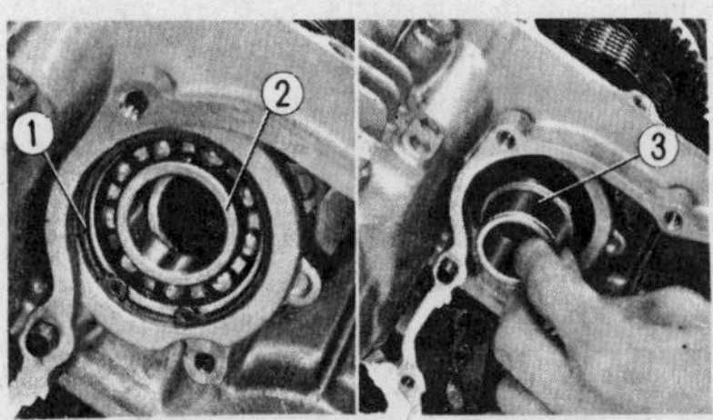

Remove the circlip (1) and bearing (2) to remove the collar (3)

2. Pull the primary shaft out through the right-side of the case.
3. Remove the internal circlip, ball bearing, and collar as illustrated.
4. Evenly remove the crankcase securing bolts, then tap on the case halves with a soft mallet, and remove the lower crankcase.

Removing the shift fork guide shaft (1) and drum (2) (350/400)

5. Remove the transmission mainshaft and countershaft at the same time.
6. Remove the gearshift set plate, then remove the shift fork guide shaft and gearshift drum.

500/550

1. Remove the engine.
2. Remove the clutch assembly as described in the previous section.
3. Remove the shift lever. Depress the gearshift arm and withdraw the linkage from the right side.
4. Unscrew the shift-drum limit bolt and remove the limit arm. Take out the camplate retaining screw and remove the camplate.

External shift mechanism (500 and 550)

1. Shift drum stopper	5. Bearing set plate
2. Stopper bolt	6. Oil guide plate securing screw
3. Neutral stopper	7. Oil guide plate
4. Neutral stopper bolt	8. Cam plate

5. Take out the three 8 mm, and three 6 mm bolts on top of the rear section of the upper crankcase. Turn the engine upside down and remove the thirteen 6 mm bolts and ten 8 mm bolts which hold the crankcases together. Loosen the 8 mm bolts in reverse order of the tightening sequence. Tap the lower crankcase with a rubber mallet to break the seal and lift it off the engine.

Remove the guide pin clip (1) and pin (2) to free the drum (3) (500 and 550)

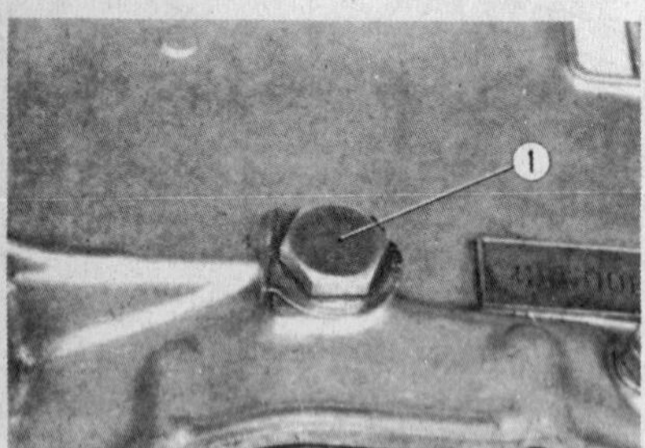

Shift drum guide screw (1) (500 and 550)

6. Remove the neutral switch from the shift drum.

7. Unscrew the shift-drum guide screw from the upper crankcase and remove the spring, spring cap, and ball.

8. Lift the transmission mainshaft and countershaft assemblies out of the crankcase, taking care not to lose the bearing set rings. Remove the shift fork guide pin clips and pins, and pull the shift drum out of the crankcase.

650

1. Separate the crankcase halves as described in the previous section.

2. To remove the shift drum, remove the drum bearing stopper plate. Remove the cam plate and the shift drum center.

3. Remove the neutral switch.

4. Remove the shift fork shaft and forks. Remove the shift drum and bearing.

5. Remove the shift fork set pin clip. Remove the shift fork set pin and fork.

INSPECTION

All Models

1. Clean all components thoroughly in a suitable solvent, then blow dry.

2. Inspect the shift fork fingers for signs of wear or damage, measure the width of each fork finger, and the inside diameter of each fork, and replace any components worn past their serviceable limits.

3. Inspect the shift fork guide shaft for signs of wear or damage, measure the outside diameter of the shaft, and replace it if worn past its serviceable limit.

4. Inspect the shift drum for signs of wear (as indicated by bright spots along the drum grooves) or damage, measure the outside diameter of the drum, and replace it as necessary.

5. Measure the gearshift fork guide-to-gearshift drum groove clearance, and replace the components if worn past their serviceable limits.

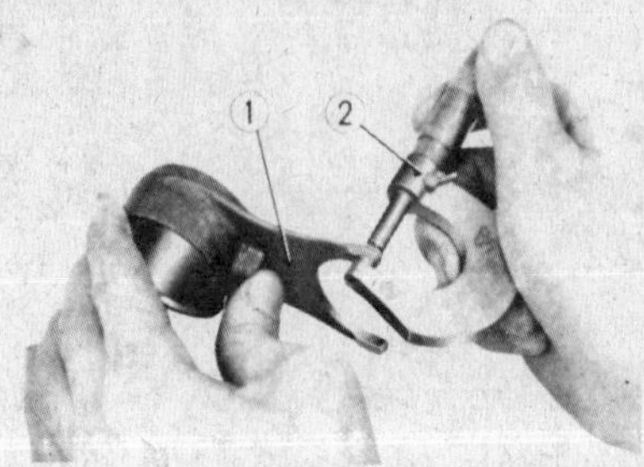

Measuring shift fork finger (1) wear with a micrometer

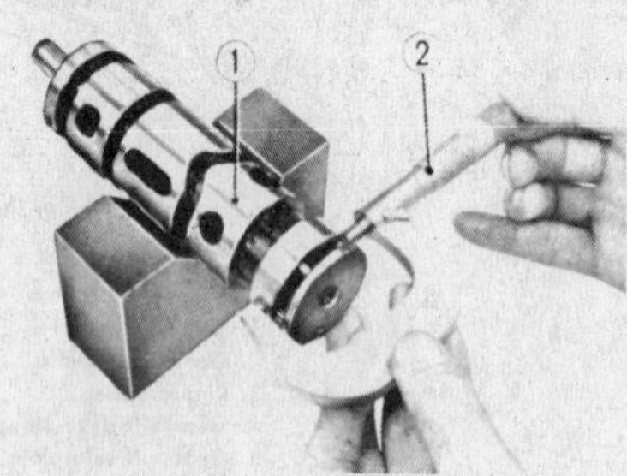

Measuring the shift drum (1) with a micrometer

ASSEMBLY

350/400

1. Install the shift drum and gears in the Neutral position.

2. Install the guide set plate, securing it by bending the lockwasher locking tab against the flat of the bolt.

3. Install the shift forks in their respective positions. Note that the forks are marked, "R," "C," and "L" for identification.

4. Make sure that the shift drum stopper, neutral stopper, and positive stopper are in their proper positions and that they work properly.

Guide set plate (1) lockwasher (2) and bolt (3) installed (350/400)

Shift forks installed (350/400)

5. Rotate the spindle to check for proper operation.

6. Install the transmission components as directed in the "Transmission" section.

7. Assemble the case halves together as directed in the "Lower End" section.

500/550

NOTE: *Modified shift-drum limit assemblies (making Neutral selection easier) are used from engine number CB 500E-1018728. Old and new parts are interchangeable. The new parts are available, along with the clutch plates mentioned in the clutch service section, in kit form, from Honda dealers so that earlier models can be updated.*

1. Place the shift forks in the crankcase as shown and install the shift drum.

2. Insert the guide pins into the forks and secure them with the clips. Be sure that the clips are installed in the proper direction. Refer to the accompanying illustration.

Shift drum (3), forks (2) and guide pin clips (1) installed (500 and 550)

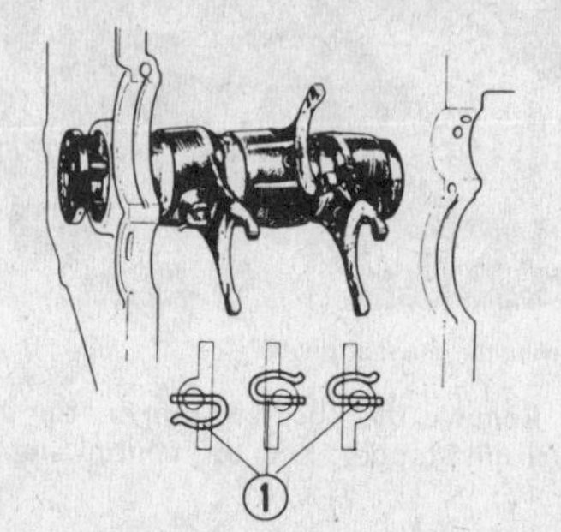

Installing the guide pin clips (1) as indicated (500 and 550)

3. Align the counterbored section of the shift drum with the guide screw hole and install the steel ball, spring cap, and spring. Install the O-ring and locktab, and tighten the guide screw. Lock the guide screw in position with the locktab.

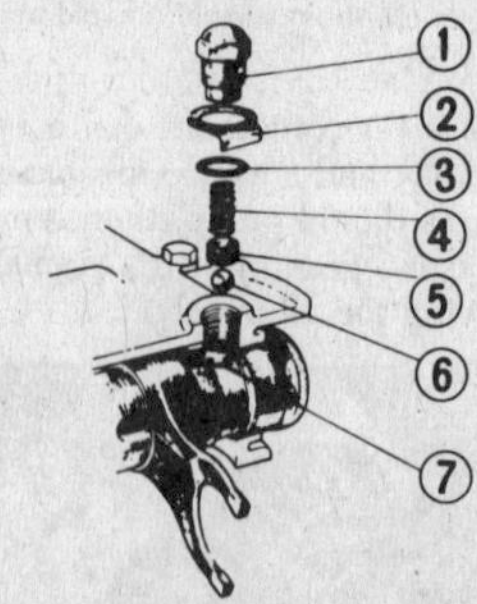

Guide screw assembly (500 and 550)

1. Guide screw cap
2. Lockwasher
3. O-ring
4. Spring
5. Spring cap
6. Ball
7. Detent

4. Align the neutral switch with the groove in the shift drum and lock in place with the 6 mm screw.

5. Replace the transmission mainshaft and countershaft assemblies in the upper crankcase, taking care to locate the bearing settings and dowel pins properly, and apply a thin coat of gasket cement to the crankcase mating surface. Carefully join the crankcase halves and install the ten 8 mm bolts. Tighten the bolts, in the correct sequence, to 17–18 ft lbs. Install and tighten the thirteen 6 mm bolts to 8 ft lbs. (Refer to "Lower End.")

Bearing set rings (1) and dowel pins (2) installed (500 and 550)

Installing the cam plate (2) on the pin (1) (500 and 550)

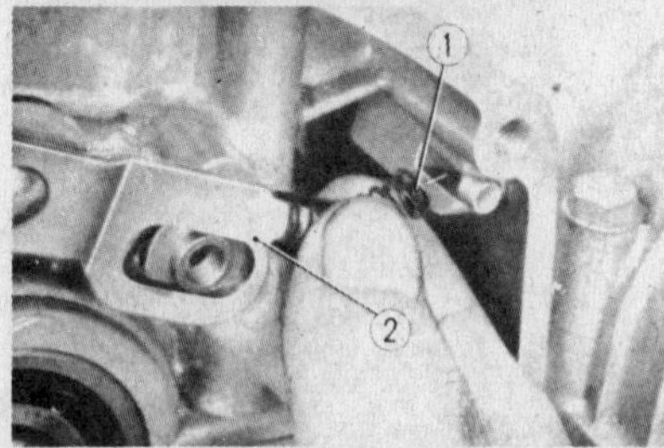

Installing the spring (1) on the stopper (2) (500 and 550)

NOTE: *Position the two 8 mm bolts with "9" stamped on the bolt head as shown in the tightening sequence.*

6. Turn the engine up so that it is resting on the lower crankcase and install the three 8 mm and three 6 mm bolts through the upper crankcase. Position the two 8 mm bolts marked "8" on the bolt head as indicated in the illustration.

7. Install the camplate on the shift drum, making sure that the pin in the drum and hole in the complate are aligned. Coat the threads of the retaining screw with the thread-locking compound before installing.

8. Place the spring on the end of the shift drum limit arm and install the end of the spring into the crankcase groove. Install and tighten the limit bolt, and make sure that the arm operates smoothly. If there is excessive vertical movement, the arm should be replaced.

9. Install the shift linkage and shift arm, and make sure that the arm operates smoothly in both directions. Install the shift lever.

10. Fit the clutch on the engine and reinstall the engine in the frame. Do not forget to refill the engine with oil.

650

Installation is basically the reverse of removal. Be sure to align the hole in the needle bearings with the dowel pins by aligning the marks flush with the crankcase surface. Align the ball bearing groove with the set ring.

Push the countershaft oil seal in until the oil seal lip is completely seated.

Transmission, Primary and and Kick-Starter

DISASSEMBLY

350/400

1. Follow all the steps listed in the "Shifter Mechanism" section.

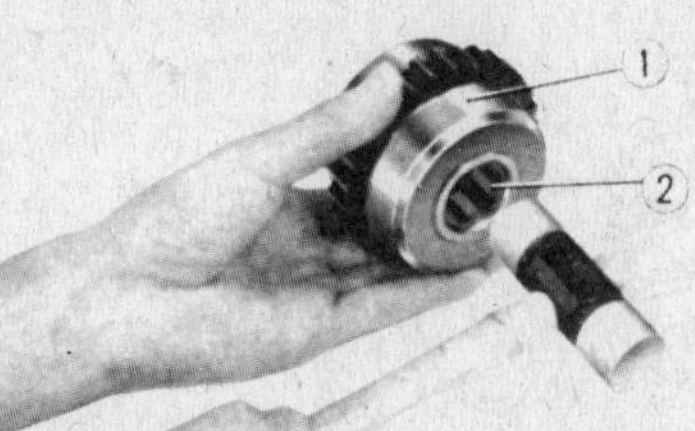

Removing the primary drive sprocket (1) from the hub (2) (350/400)

2. Remove the primary driven sprocket and the starter driven gear, then remove the driven sprocket hub from the primary driven sprocket, and remove the hub rubber dampers.

3. Disassemble the transmission shafts assemblies as necessary, keeping the components separate for assembly in their original positions.

500/550

1. Follow Steps 1, 2, and 5 in the preceding section on shifter mechanism disassembly.

2. Lift the transmission mainshaft and countershaft assemblies out of the crankcase. Do not lose the bearing set rings.

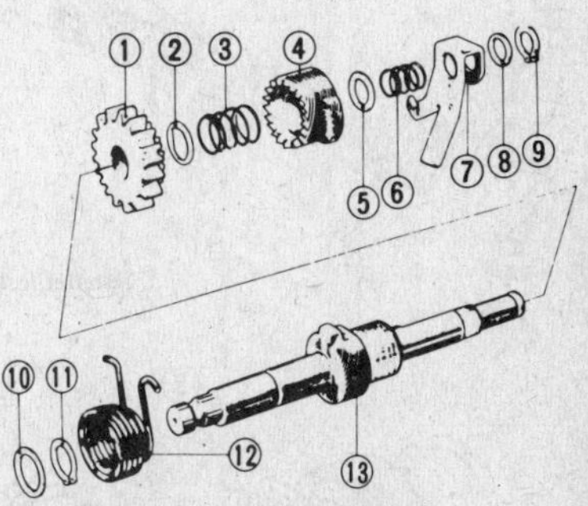

Kick-starter assembly (500 and 550)

1. Kick-starter gear
2. Thrust washer
3. Set spring
4. Ratchet gear
5. Thrust washer
6. Spring
7. Stopper
8. Thrust washer
9. Snap-ring
10. Thrust washer
11. Snap-ring
12. Return spring
13. Kick-starter shaft

3. To remove the kick-start gear and shaft, first remove the 18 mm circlip and return spring from the end of the shaft. Remove the 12 mm circlip from the end of the shaft inside the case and withdraw the shaft from the lower crankcase.

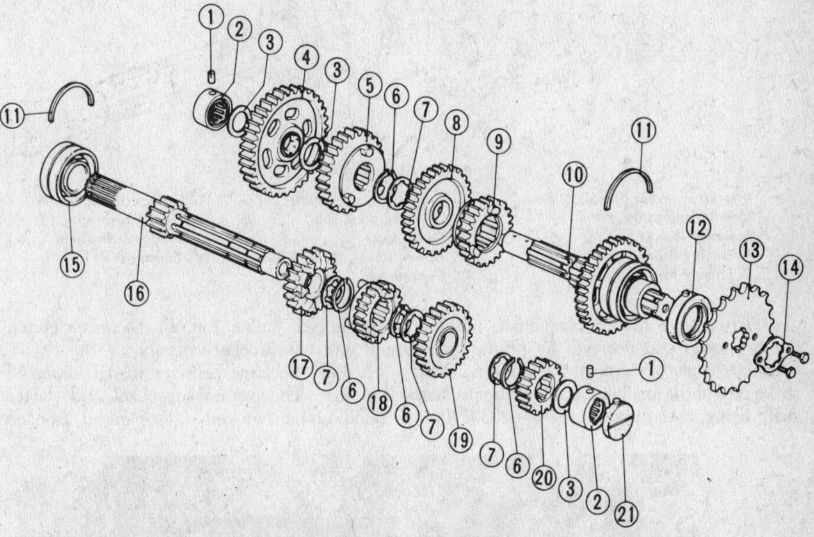

Transmission assembly (350/400)

1. Gearshift fork guide pins (two), 6 mm
2. Needle bearings (two), 20 mm
3. Thrust washers (three), 20 mm
4. Countershaft low gear, 41 T
5. Countershaft fourth gear, 31 T
6. Circlips (four), 25 mm
7. Thrust washers (four)
8. Countershaft third gear, 34 T
9. Countershaft top gear, 28 T
10. Countershaft, 37 T
11. Bearing set rings (two), 52 mm
12. Oil seal
13. Drive sprocket, 17 T
14. Drive sprocket fixing plate
15. Ball bearing
16. Mainshaft
17. Mainshaft fourth gear, 27 T
18. Mainshaft third gear, 24 T
19. Mainshaft top gear, 29 T
20. Mainshaft second gear, 20 T
21. Oil seal

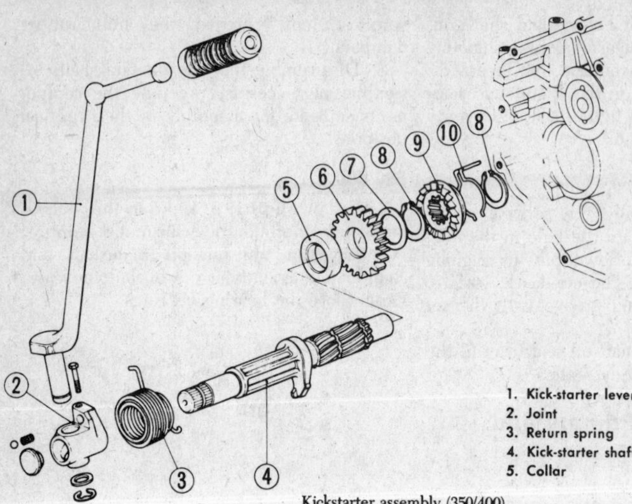

Kickstarter assembly (350/400)

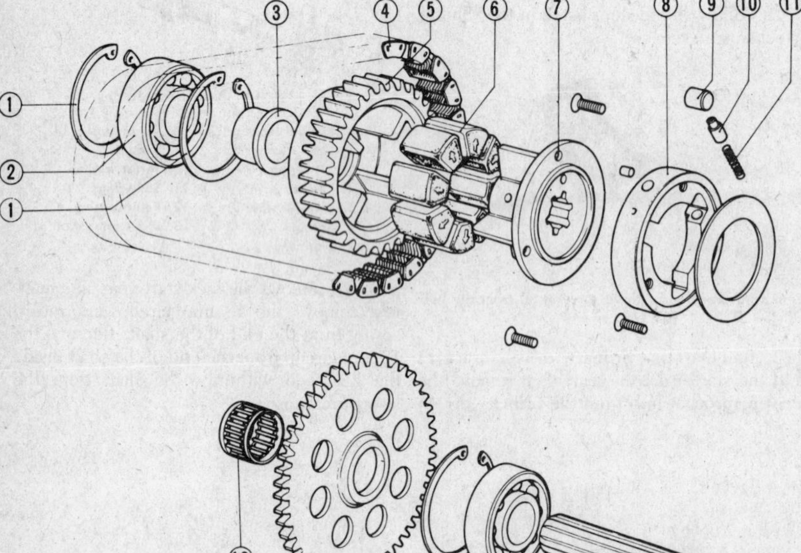
Primary shaft assembly

1. Internal circlips (three), 52 mm
2. Ball bearings (two)
3. Collar 25 x 21.8
4. Primary drive chain
5. Primary driven sprocket
6. Rubber dampers (eight)
7. Driven sprocket hub
8. Clutch outer
9. Rollers (three), 10.2 x 9.5
10. Caps (three)
11. Springs (three)
12. Needle bearing
13. Starter driven gear
14. Primary shaft

4. To remove the primary shaft, unscrew the two bolts and remove the primary shaft bearing set plate. Remove the 20 mm circlip at the end of the shaft and pull out the primary shaft using tool number 07009–32301 or a suitable gear puller. Lift out the starter clutch and primary sprocket assembly.

5. Pull the large primary shaft bearing off the shaft. The primary sprocket and starter clutch can be removed and separated after the primary sprocket circlip and the three 6 mm screws have been removed.

Remove the return spring (2) after removing the snap-ring (1) (500 and 550)

Remove the snap-ring (1) and then the kick-starter shaft (2) (500 and 550)

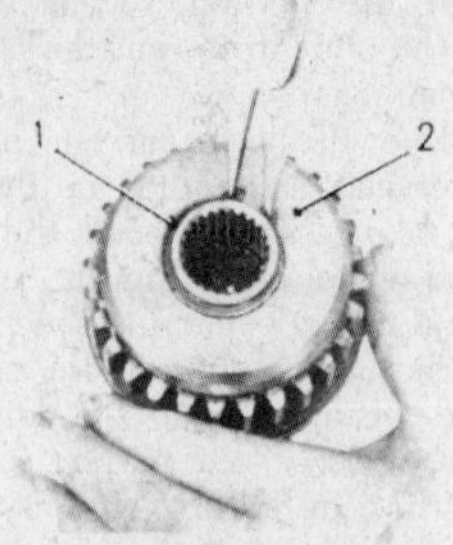
Removing the snap-ring (1) from the primary driven sprocket (2) (500 and 550)

650

Disassembly of the transmission is straightforward. Be sure to lay out the components in the proper order as they are removed.

INSPECTION

All Models

1. Set the mainshaft and countershaft gear assemblies into the crankcase and measure backlash. Maximum acceptable backlash is 0.2 mm (0.008 in.) for all gear sets. Replace gears (mating pairs) on both shafts that exceed the limits. Inspect the dogs and replace any gears with damaged or excessively worn dogs.

Measuring backlash with a dial gauge (1)

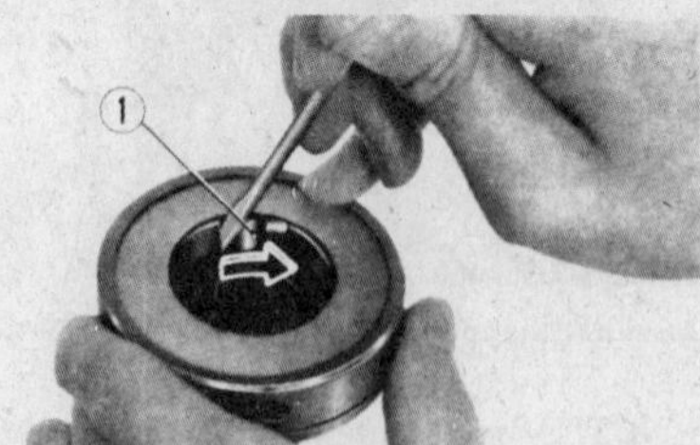
Checking the starter clutch rollers (1)

Check the ball bearings for excessive play and make sure that the gears slide smoothly on the shaft splines.

2. Examine the damper rubbers in the pri-

Check the sprocket (1) rubbers (2) for damage

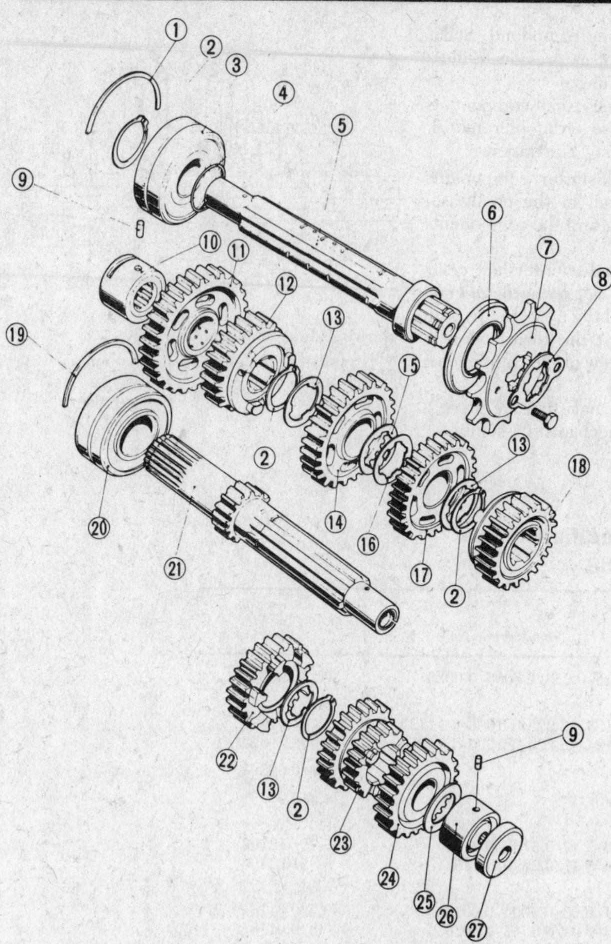

Transmission assembly (500 and 550)

1. Bearing set ring
2. Circlip
3. Ball bearing
4. O-ring
5. Countershaft
6. Oil seal
7. Countershaft sprocket
8. Sprocket mounting plate
9. Shift fork pin
10. Needle bearing
11. Countershaft first gear, 40 T
12. Countershaft fourth gear, 29 T
13. Thrust washer
14. Countershaft third gear, 33 T
15. Lockwasher
16. Thrust washer
17. Countershaft second gear, 36 T
18. Countershaft fifth gear, 27 T
19. Bearing set ring
20. Ball bearing
21. Mainshaft
22. Mainshaft fourth gear, 28 T
23. Mainshaft second and third gears, 22 and 26 T
24. Mainshaft fifth gear, 30 T
25. Thrust washer
26. Needle bearing
27. Oil seal

mary sprocket and replace them if they do not appear to be in perfect condition.

3. If it is necessary to replace the starter clutch needle bearing assembly or to replace other components, the housing can be removed after the three phillips head screws have been taken out.

ASSEMBLY

350/400

1. Assembly is in the reverse order of disassembly. New circlips and seals should be used, and all components should be liberally coated with a suitable assembly lubricant.

2. Note the following when installing the kickstarter assembly;

a. The hair pin section of the starter pinion friction spring is inserted into the crankcase stopper groove.

b. Hook the "A" end of the starter spring as shown, then install the kick starter assembly. The "B" end of the spring should be hooked onto the crankcase rib as illustrated.

Installing the kickstarter return spring (350/400)

c. Make sure that the starter pinion gear is properly meshed with Low gear.

3. Note the following when assembling the mainshaft assembly;

a. Install the ball bearing with the bearing set ring installed in its groove.

b. Install the needle bearing so that its guide pin fits in the guide pin hole.

c. Install the oil seal so that its dowel fits into the pin hole in the upper crankcase half.

4. Note the following when assembling the countershaft assembly;

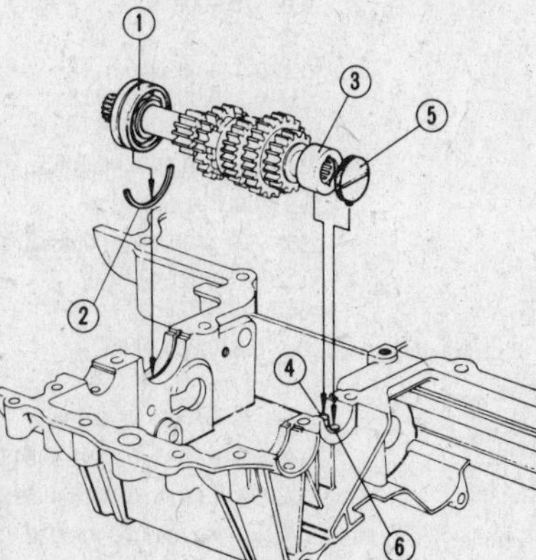

Installing the mainshaft assembly (350/400)

1. Ball bearing
2. Bearing set ring
3. Needle bearing
4. Guide pin
5. Oil seal
6. Seal pin hole

a. When installing the needle bearing, make sure that the crankcase guide pin is seated in its pin hole.

b. Install the ball bearing with its ring groove fitted onto the ring installed in the upper case half.

c. Install the oil seal so that its pin is seated in the pin hole in the upper case.

d. After both shafts are installed in the case, check the transmission for smooth operation by rotating the crankshaft.

5. If the clutch outer body has been disassembled, stake each of the three flat screws, as illustrated, after screwing them in.

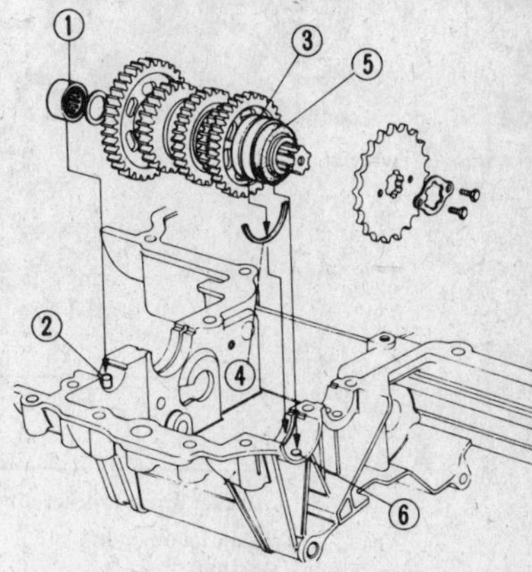

Installing the countershaft assembly (350/400)

1. Needle bearing
2. Guide pin
3. Ball bearing
4. Bearing set ring
5. Oil seal
6. Oil seal pin hole

Peen the three screws (1) if they have been removed (350/400)

Installing the primary shaft and collar (350/400)

6. Insert the primary shaft through the right-side of the case after the case halves have been assembled, but not secured, then install the collar.

7. The primary shaft ball bearing will have to be driven into place with a suitable drift, and then secured with the 25 mm internal circlip.

Installing the bearing (1) and circlip (2) (350/400)

8. Secure the case halves as directed in the "Lower End" section.

9. Install the primary shaft lockwasher so that the word "OUTSIDE" faces outward.

500/550/650

1. Assemble the starter clutch housing and clutch hub, coating the threads of the three screws with thread-locking compound. Stake the screws with a punch, as previously illustrated, to prevent loosening.

Lockwasher (1) correctly installed

2. Assemble the primary shaft components onto the shaft in reverse order of removal. Refer to the accompanying illustration.

e. Assemble the kick-starter components onto the shaft and install in the crankcase. Refer to the exploded view of the components for order of assembly.

4. If the mainshaft and countershaft gears have been removed, *do not reuse the old circlips*. Take care to install the new circlips with the smooth edge against the thrust washer. Refer to the exploded view of the components for order of assembly.

5. Follow Steps 5, 6, and 10 in the preceding section on shifter mechanism assembly.

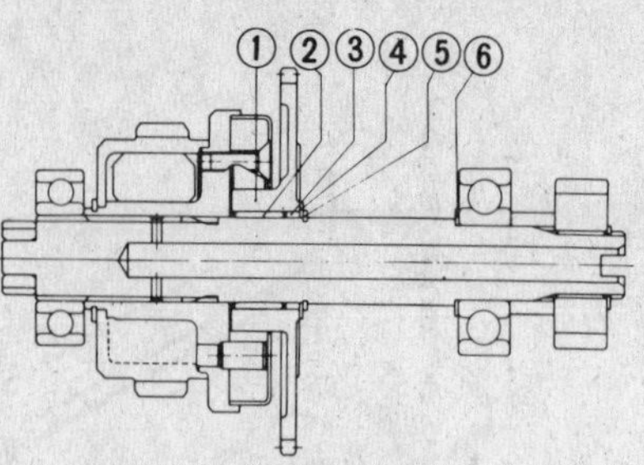

Primary shaft assembly (500 and 550)

1. Starter clutch gear
2. Needle bearing
3. Spacer
4. Thrust washer
5. Snap-ring
6. Thrust washer

Engine Specifications
350

	Standard (mm/in.)	Serviceable Limit (mm/in.)
Rocker arm-to-rocker arm shaft clearance	0.016–0.052/0.0006–0.0020	0.1/0.0039
Cam lobe height		
Intake	28.185–28.225/1.1096–1.1112	28.0/1.1024
Exhaust	28.184–28.224/1.1096–1.1111	28.0/1.1024
Camshaft center journal runout	——	0.1/0.0039
Valve seat width	0.7/0.03	1.5/0.06
Valve stem O. D.		
Intake	5.48–5.49/0.2158–0.2161	5.35/0.2106
Exhaust	5.46–5.47/0.2150–0.2154	5.35/0.2106
Valve-to-valve guide clearance		
Intake	0.01–0.03/0.0004–0.0012	0.3/0.0118
Exhaust	0.03–0.05/0.0012–0.0020	0.3/0.0118
Valve spring preload		
Inner	19.2/13.0–14.6 kg (0.7559/28.665–32.1930 lbs)	——
Outer	23.7/32.0–32.4 kg (0.9330/70.560–71.4420 lbs)	——
Valve spring free length		
Inner	29.0/1.1417	27.0/1.0630
Outer	34.5/1.3583	32.5/1.2795
Cylinder head warpage	——	0.3/0.0118
Cylinder diameter	47.00–47.01/1.8504–1.8508	47.1/1.8543
Piston diameter	46.97–46.99/1.8492–1.8500	46.85/1.8445
Piston pin hole I. D.	13.002–13.008/0.5119–0.5121	13.05/0.5138
Piston pin O. D.	12.994–13.00/0.5116–0.5118	12.9/0.5079
Piston ring-to-piston ring groove clearance		
Top ring	0.03–0.055/0.0012–0.0022	0.15/0.0059
Second ring	0.015–0.045/0.0006–0.0018	0.15/0.0059
Oil ring (one piece)	0.015/0.0006	0.15/0.0059
Piston ring end gap		
Top ring	0.1–0.3/0.0039–0.0118	0.7/0.0276
Second ring	0.1–0.3/0.0039–0.0118	0.7/0.0276
Oil ring (one piece)	0.1–0.3/0.0039–0.0118	0.7/0.0276
Clutch friction disc thickness	2.62–2.78/0.1032–0.1095	2.3/0.0906
Clutch plate warpage	0.1/0.0039, max	0.2/0.0079
Clutch spring preload	25.0/19.3–20.7 kg (0.9842/42.557–45.643 lbs)	——
Clutch spring free length	35.5/1.3976	34.0/1.3386
Clutch center-to-clutch plate B clearance	0.1–0.5/0.004–0.02	Beyond assembly standard
Gear shift fork finger width	5.93–6.00/0.2335–0.2362	5.5/0.2165
Gear shift guide shaft O. D.	12.957–12.984/0.5101–0.5112	12.9/0.5079
Gear shift fork I. D.	13.000–13.018/0.5118–0.5125	12.95/0.5098
Kick starter pinion-to shaft clearance	0.04–0.082/0.0016–0.0032	0.1/0.004
Gear shift fork dowel-to-drum groove clearance	0.05–0.22/0.0020–0.0087	0.3/0.0118
Transmission gear backlash		
1st and 2nd	0.044–0.134/0.0017–0.0053	0.2/0.0079
3rd, 4th and 5th	0.046–0.142/0.0018–0.0056	0.2/0.0079

Engine Specifications
400

	Standard (mm/in.)	Serviceable Limit (mm/in.)
Transmission gear-to-shaft clearance		
Countershaft 1st	0.04–0.074/0.0016–0.0029	0.2/0.0079
Other gears	0.04–0.081/0.0016–0.0032	0.2/0.0079
Cam chain tensioner slipper thickness (center)	4.0/0.1575	3.0/0.118, max
Cam chain guide thickness	6.1–6.3/0.2402–0.2480	5.0/0.197
Crankshaft runout (center)	0.03/0.0012, max	0.05/0.0020
Crankshaft journal clearance	0.018–0.048/0.0007–0.0019	0.08/0.0032
Connecting rod small end I. D.	13.012–13.033/0.5123–0.5131	13.10/0.5158
Connecting rod big end side clearance	0.02–0.07/0.0008–0.0028	0.15/0.0059
Connecting rod big end-to-crankshaft journal clearance	0.018–0.048/0.0007–0.0019	0.08/0.0032
Primary chain guide thickness (center)	6.0–6.3/0.236–0.248	5.0/0.197
Rocker arm-to-rocker arm shaft clearance	0.016–0.052/0.0006–0.0020	0.1/0.0039
Cam lobe height		
Intake	28.185–28.225/1.1096–1.1112	28.0/1.1024
Exhaust	28.184–28.224/1.1096–1.1111	28.0/1.1024
Camshaft center journal runout	——	0.1/0.0039
Valve seat width	0.7/0.03	1.5/0.06
Valve stem O. D.		
Intake	5.48–5.49/0.2158–0.2161	5.35/0.2106
Exhaust	5.48–5.49/0.2158–0.2161	5.35/0.2106
Valve-to-valve guide clearance		
Intake	0.01–0.03/0.0004–0.0012	0.3/0.0118
Exhaust	0.01–0.03/0.0004–0.0012	0.3/0.0118
Valve spring preload		
Inner	19.2/13.0–14.6 kg (0.7559/28.665–32.1930 lbs)	——
Outer	23.7/32.0–32.4 kg (0.9330/70.560–71.4420 lbs)	——
Valve spring free length		
Inner	29.0/1.1417	27.0/1.0630
Outer	34.5/1.3583	32.5/1.2795
Cylinder head warpage	——	0.3/0.0118
Cylinder diameter	51.00–51.01/2.0079–2.0083	51.1/2.0118
Piston diameter	50.97–50.99/2.0067–2.0075	50.85/2.0020
Piston pin hole I.D.	13.002–13.008/0.5119–0.5121	13.05/0.5138
Piston pin O.D.	12.994–13.00/0.5116–0.5118	12.9/0.5079
Piston ring-to-piston ring groove clearance		
Top ring	0.025–0.055/0.0010–0.0022	0.15/0.0059
Second ring	0.015–0.045/0.0006–0.018	0.15/0.0059
Piston ring end gap		
Top ring	0.15–0.35/0.0059–0.0138	0.7/0.0276
Second ring	0.15–0.35/0.0059–0.0138	0.7/0.0276
Oil ring	0.2–0.5/0.0079–0.0197	0.9/0.0035
Clutch friction disc thickness	2.62–2.78/0.1032–0.1095	2.3/0.0906
Clutch plate warpage	0.1/0.0039 max	0.2/0.0079
Clutch spring free length	31.25/1.2303	29.75/1.1712
Clutch center-to-clutch plate B clearance	0.1–0.5/0.004–0.02	Beyond assembly standard
Gearshift fork finger width	5.93–6.00/0.2335–0.2362	5.5/0.2165
Gearshift guide shaft O.D.	12.957–12.984/0.5101–0.5112	12.9/0.5079
Gearshift fork I.D.	13.000–13.018/0.5118–0.5125	12.95/0.5098
Kick starter pinion-to-shaft clearance	0.04–0.082/0.0016–0.0032	0.1/0.004
Gearshift fork dowel-to-drum groove clearance	0.05–0.22/0.0020–0.0087	0.3/0.0118
Transmission gear backlash	——	0.2/0.0079
Transmission gear-to-shaft clearance		
Countershaft 1st	0.04–0.074/0.0016–0.0029	0.2/0.0079
Other gears	0.04–0.081/0.0016–0.0032	0.2/0.0079
Cam chain tensioner slipper thickness (center)	4.0/0.1575	3.0/0.118 max
Cam chain guide thickness	6.1–6.3/0.2402–0.2480	5.0/0.197
Crankshaft runout (center)	0.03/0.0012 max	0.05/0.0020
Crankshaft journal clearance	0.018–0.048/0.0007–0.0019	0.08/0.0032
Connecting rod small end I.D.	13.012–13.033/0.5123–0.5131	13.10/0.5158
Connecting rod big end side clearance	0.02–0.07/0.0008–0.0028	0.15/0.0059
Connecting rod big end-to-crankshaft journal clearance	0.018–0.048/0.0007–0.0019	0.08/0.0032
Primary chain guide thickness (center)	6.0–6.3/0.236–0.248	5.0/0.197

Engine Specifications (cont.)

500

	Standard (mm in.)	Serviceable Limit (mm/in.)
Camshaft runout	——	0.1/0.004
Cam lobe height		
Intake	34.93–34.97/1.3742–1.3768	35.85/1.4075
Exhaust	34.53–34.57/1.3595–1.3610	34.45/1.3563
Valve seat width	1.0–1.5/0.04–0.06	1.5/0.06
Valve face runout	——	0.05/0.009
Valve stem O.D.		
Intake	5.450–5.465/0.2145–0.2150	——
Exhaust	5.430–5.445/0.2137–0.2142	——
Valve-to-valve guide clearance		
Intake	0.010–0.035/0.00039–0.00137	0.080/0.0031
Exhaust	0.030–0.050/0.0011–0.0019	0.10/0.0039
Valve spring free length		
Inner	35.7/1.40	34.5/1.35
Outer	40.4/1.59	39.0/1.53
Cylinder head warpage	——	0.3/0.011
Cylinder diameter	56.00–56.01/2.204–2.205	56.1/2.208
Piston diameter	55.97–55.99/2.203–2.204	55.85/2.198
Piston pin hole I.D.	——	15.08/0.593
Piston ring-to-groove clearance		
Top	0.040–0.075/0.0015–0.0029	0.18/0.007
Second	0.025–0.060/0.0009–0.0023	0.15/0.005
Oil	0.020–0.055/0.0007–0.0021	0.15/0.005
Piston ring end-gap	0.15–0.35/0.005–0.013	0.7/0.027
Clutch friction disc thickness	3.3/0.13	3.0/0.11
Clutch plate warpage	——	0.3/0.011
Clutch spring free length	31.9/1.25	30.5/1.20
Gearshift drum O.D.	39.950–39.975/1.5728–1.5738	39.9/1.5709
Gearshift fork I.D.	40.00–40.025/1.5748–1.5757	40.075/1.5797
Gearshift fork finger width		
Center	5.93–6.00/0.233–0.236	5.60/0.220
Right and Left	4.93–5.00/0.194–0.197	4.60/0.181
Gear backlash		
1st, 2d, 3rd	0.044–0.133/0.0017–0.0051	0.2/0.0078
4th, 5th	0.046–0.140/0.0018–0.0055	0.2/0.0078
Crankshaft journal clearance	0.020–0.046/0.00079–0.00181	0.080–0.0031
Crankshaft runout	——	0.05/0.0019
Crankshaft journal ovality	——	0.05/0.0019
Connecting rod big end clearance	0.020–0.046/0.00079–0.00181	0.08/0.0031
Connecting rod side clearance	0.12–0.27/0.0047–0.0106	0.35/0.0138
Connecting rod small end I.D.	15.016–15.034/0.5911–0.5918	15.07/0.5930

550

	Standard (mm/in.)	Serviceable Limit (mm/in.)
Camshaft runout	——	0.1/0.004
Cam lobe height		
Intake	34.93–34.97/1.3742–1.3768	35.85/1.4075
Exhaust	34.53–34.57/1.3595–1.3610	34.45/1.3563
Valve seat width	1.0–1.5/0.04–0.06	1.5/0.06
Valve face runout	——	0.05/0.009
Valve stem O.D.		
Intake	5.450–5.465/0.2145–0.2150	——
Exhaust	5.430–5.445/0.2137–0.2142	——
Valve-to-valve guide clearance		
Intake	0.020–0.045/0.00079–0.00177	0.080/0.0031
Exhaust	0.030–0.050/0.0011–0.0019	0.10/0.0039
Valve spring free length		
Inner	35.7/1.40	34.5/1.35
Outer	40.4/1.59	39.0/1.53
Cylinder head warpage	——	0.3/0.011
Cylinder diameter	58.50–58.51/2.303–2.304	58.6/2.307
Piston diameter	58.47–58.49/2.300–2.301	58.35/2.302
Piston pin hole I.D.	——	15.08/0.593

Engine Specifications (cont.)

550

	Standard (mm/in.)	Serviceable Limit (mm/in.)
Piston ring-to-groove clearance		
Top	0.040–0.075/0.0015–0.0029	0.18/0.007
Second	0.025–0.060/0.0009–0.0023	0.15/0.005
Oil	——	——
Piston ring end-gap		
compression	0.15–0.35/0.005–0.013	0.7/0.027
oil	0.3–0.9/0.01–0.035	1.1/0.043
Clutch friction disc thickness	2.6/0.12	2.3/0.09
Clutch plate warpage	——	0.3/0.011
Clutch spring free length	36.8–1.45	35.4/1.39
Gearshift drum O.D.	39.950–39.975/1.5728–1.5738	39.9/1.5709
Gearshift fork I.D.	40.00–40.025/1.5748–1.5757	40.075/1.5797
Gearshift fork finger width		
Center	5.93–6.00/0.233–0.236	5.60/0.220
Right and Left	4.93–5.00/0.194–0.197	4.60/0.181
Gear backlash		
1st, 2d, 3rd	0.044–0.133/0.0017–0.0051	0.2/0.0078
4th, 5th	0.046–0.140/0.0018–0.0055	0.2/0.0078
Crankshaft journal clearance	0.020–0.046/0.00079–0.00181	0.080/0.0031
Crankshaft runout	——	0.05/0.0019
Crankshaft journal ovality	——	0.05/0.0019
Connecting rod big end clearance	0.020–0.046/0.00079–0.00181	0.08/0.0031
Connecting rod side clearance	0.12–0.27/0.0047–0.0106	0.35/0.0138
Connecting rod small end I.D.	15.016–15.034/0.5911–0.5918	15.07/0.5930

650

	Standard (mm/in.)	Serviceable Limit (mm/in.)
Cam lobe height		
Intake	35.627–35.787/1.4026–1.4089	35.6/1.40
Exhaust	35.314–35.474/1.3903–1.3966	35.3/1.39
Camshaft run-out	—	0.1/0.004
End clearance	0.035–0.050/0.0013–0.0020	0.1/0.004
Bearing clearance	0.160–0.202/0.0063–0.0080	0.21/0.008
Rocker arm inside diameter	12.000–12.018/0.4724–0.4731	12.05/0.474
Rocker arm shaft diameter	11.973–11.984/0.4714–0.4718	11.94/0.470
Valve stem diameter		
Intake	5.475–5.490/0.2156–0.2161	5.47/0.215
Exhaust	5.455–5.470/0.2148–0.2154	5.45/0.214
Valve guide inside diameter	5.500–5.515/0.2165–0.2171	5.55/0.219
Valve stem-to-guide clearance		
Intake	0.010–0.040/0.0004–0.0016	0.08/0.003
Exhaust	0.030–0.050/0.0012–0.0020	0.10/0.004
Valve stem runout	—	0.05/0.002
Valve seat width	1.2/0.05	1.5/0.06
Valve spring free length		
Inner	39.2/1.54	37.9/1.49
Outer	44.8/1.77	43.3/1.70
Cylinder diameter	59.800–59.810/2.3543–2.3547	59.90/2.358
Piston diameter	59.77–59.79/2.353–2.354	59.65/2.348
Piston-cylinder clearance		0.10/0.004
Ring-to-groove clearance		
Top, Second	0.015–0.045	0.15/0.006
Ring end-gap		
Top, Second	0.10–0.30/0.004–0.012	0.7/0.028
Oil	0.3–0.9/0.012–0.035	1.1/0.043
Wrist pin hole diameter	15.002–15.008/0.5906–5909	15.08/0.594
Wrist pin diameter	14.994–15.000/0.5903–0.5906	14.98/0.590
Small end inside diameter	15.016–15.034/0.5912–0.5919	15.07/0.593
Cam chain tensioner spring	81.0 mm/7 kg	81.0 mm/5 kg

Engine Specifications (cont.) 650

	Standard (mm in.)	Serviceable Limit (mm/in.)
Clutch spring free-length	36.8/1.45	35.4/1.39
Disc thickness		
A	3.42–3.58/0.135–0.141	3.2/0.13
B	2.62–2.78/0.103–0.109	2.4/0.09
Plate warpage	—	0.3/0.012
Clutch hub ID	29.990–30.005/1.1807–1.1813	30.05/1.183
Clutch bushing OD	29.959–29.980/1.1795–1.1803	29.94/1.179
Con rod big end side clearance	0.12–0.27/0.005–0.011	0.35/0.014
Crankshaft run-out	—	0.05/0.002
Big end bearing clearance	0.018–0.047/0.0007–0.0019	0.08/0.003
Main bearing clearance	0.020–0.048/0.0008–0.0019	0.08/0.003
Cam chain length	184.87–184.90/7.279–7.280	186.4/7.34
Primary chain length	114.15–114.40/4.494–4.504	115.5/4.55
Transmission backlash		
1st, 2d, 3rd	0.044–0.133/0.0017–0.0052	0.20/0.008
4th, 5th	0.046–0.140/0.0018–0.0055	0.20/0.008
Gear inside diameter		
M4, C2, C3	25.020–25.041/0.9850–0.9859	25.06/0.987
M5	23.000–23.033/0.9055–0.9068	23.06/0.908
C1	24.000–24.033/0.9449–0.9462	24.06/0.947
Gear bushings		
M5 OD	22.984–22.993/0.9849–0.9052	22.96/0.904
M5 ID, C1 ID	20.010–20.030/0.8665–0.7886	20.07/0.790
C1 OD	23.984–23.993/0.9443–0.9446	23.95/0.943
Mainshaft OD		
at M4	24.959–24.980/0.9826–0.9835	24.93/0.981
at M5	19.987–20.000/0.7869–0.7874	19.93/0.785
Countershaft OD		
at C1	19.987–20.000/0.7869–0.7874	19.93/0.785
at C2, C3	24.959–24.980/0.9826–0.9835	24.93/0.981
Gear-to-bushing or shaft clearance	—	0.10/0.004
Shift fork claw thickness	5.93–6.00/0.233–0.236	5.6/0.22
Shift fork inside diameter		
center	38.000–38.025/1.4961–1.4970	38.075/1.499
l & r	13.000–13.018/0.5118–51.25	13.04/0.513
Shift fork shaft diameter	12.966–12.984/0.5104–0.5112	12.90/0.508
Shift drum diameter	37.950–37.975/1.4941–1.4951	37.90/1.492

Engine Specifications 500/550

Part	Torque (ft lbs)
Tappet adjusting nut	8.0–10.8
Cam sprocket bolt, 7 x 12	10.1–10.8
Cylinder head nut, 8 mm	14.5–16.6
Alternator rotor bolt	28.9–30.3
Starting clutch screw, 6 x 18 cross flat head screw	14.5–17.3
Upper crankcase bolts, 8 x 100 Flange hex bolt	14.5–18.1
Upper crankcase bolts, 8 x 145 hex bolt	16.6–18.0
Lower crankcase bolts, 8 x 100 hex bolt	14.5–18.1
Connecting rod nuts	14.5–15.9
Oil pump screw, 6 x 35 cross flat head screw	5.7–8.6
Clutch bolts, 6 x 45 hex bolt	5.7–8.6
Spark advancer bolt, 6 x 55 Flange hex bolt	8.0–10.8
Tachometer gear holder screw, 6 x 16 cross flat head screw	7.2–10.0
Exhaust pipe flange nut, 6 mm	5.7–8.6
Oil pressure switch	10.8–14.5
Gear shift lever bolt, 6 x 20 hex bolt	5.7–7.2
Oil filter bolt	19.5–23.8
Spark plugs	8.6–11.6
Oil drain bolt	25.3–28.9
Clutch spring, 6 x 20 hex bolt	7.2–10.1
Tappet hole cap	7.2–10.1
Oil path cap	7.2–10.1
Gear shift return spring, 8 mm bolt	14.5–21.7
Drive sprocket	

Engine Torque Specifications 650

Part	Torque (ft. lbs.)
Breather cover	6–9
Tach gear holder	6–9
Cylinder head cover	6–9
Valve adjusting nut	9–12
Rocker arm shaft cotter pin	7–10
Rocker arm shaft cap bolt	6–9
Cylinder head bolts	
8 mm	17–22
6 mm	7–10
Spark plugs	9–12
Cam sprocket bolts	16–19
Cam chain tensioner	7–10
Crankcase bolts	16–19
Oil gallery cap	7–10
Alternator rotor	36–43
Spark advancer	6–9
Connecting rods	17–20
Starter clutch	9–12
Clutch hub nut	34–38
Oil filter case	20–24
Oil pressure switch	7–15
Neutral switch rotor	4–7
Primary chain tensioner	7–10
Primary chain nozzle	6–9
Gearshift return pin	17–20
Throttle cable adjusting locknut	4–6

Engine Torque Specifications 350/400

Part	Torque (ft lbs)
Crankcase and crankcase covers	5.1–8.0
Cylinder head	14.5
Carburetor manifold-to-cylinder head	5.1–8.0
Cam sprocket	11.6–14.5
Alternator rotor	21.7–29.0
Primary drive gear	21.7–29.0
Tappet adjusting nut	5.1–8.0
Upper and lower crankcases	15.2–18.9
Cylinder head cover	5.1–8.0
Connecting rod	14.5–15.2

LUBRICATION SYSTEM

OIL PUMP

Removal and Installation

The oil pump can be removed without moving the engine from the frame. The procedure is as follows:

1. Drain the engine oil.
2. Remove the starter motor cover (500/550).
3. Remove the shift lever and left footrest.
4. Remove the left crankcase cover. A hammer-driven impact wrench will aid in re-

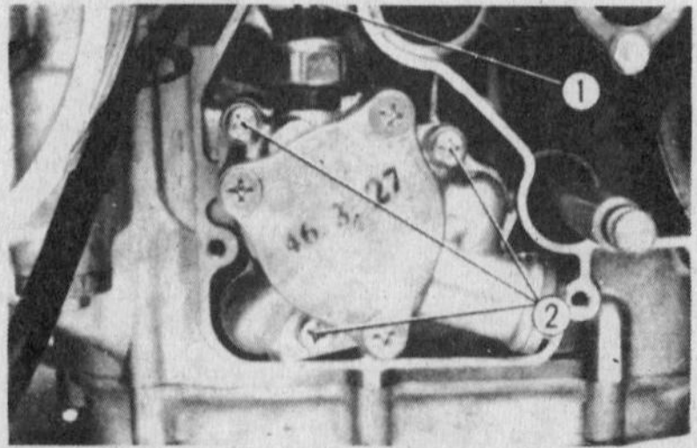

Oil pump mounting bolts (1 and 2)

moving the screws without damaging the heads.

5. Disconnect the wire from the pressure switch, located on top of the pump.

6. Remove the pump mounting bolts and withdraw the pump.

Installation is in reverse order of removal. The following points should be observed:

1. Use new gaskets and O-rings.
2. Do not forget to refill the engine with oil.

Oil Pump Service

DISASSEMBLY

1. Remove the cap and withdraw the relief valve and spring.

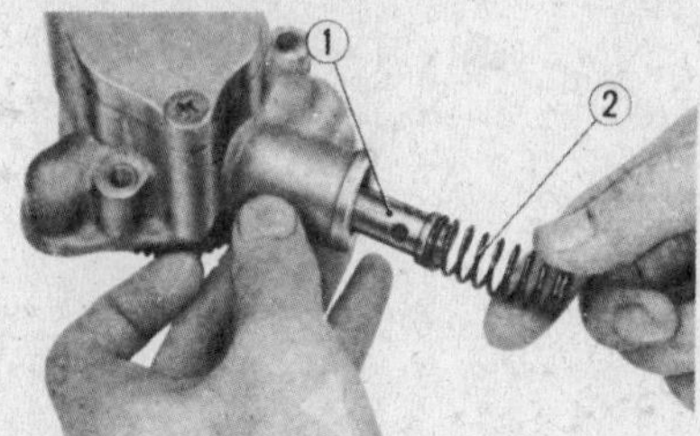

Removing the relief valve (1) and spring (2)

2. Remove the three screws and the side-cover, exposing the rotors. Withdraw the rotors and mark them as shown (if not already marked).

3. Remove the drive pin and withdraw the drive gearshaft.

4. Unscrew the pressure switch from the pump body.

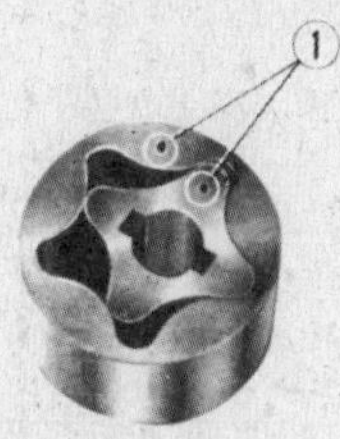

Rotor marks must be aligned when installing rotors

INSPECTION

1. Measure the clearance between the inner and outer rotors, as illustrated. Replace both rotors if clearance exceeds 0.3 mm (0.0118 in.) (350/400) or 0.35 mm (0.013 in.) (500/550) or 0.15 mm (0.006 in.) (650).

2. Measure the clearance between the outer rotor and housing. If clearance exceeds 0.35 mm (0.013 in.), the complete pump should be replaced.

3. Examine all components for damage and stress cracks.

4. Examine the relief valve for wear and replace if necessary. It is a good idea to replace the spring at this time to be sure of maintaining proper oil pressure.

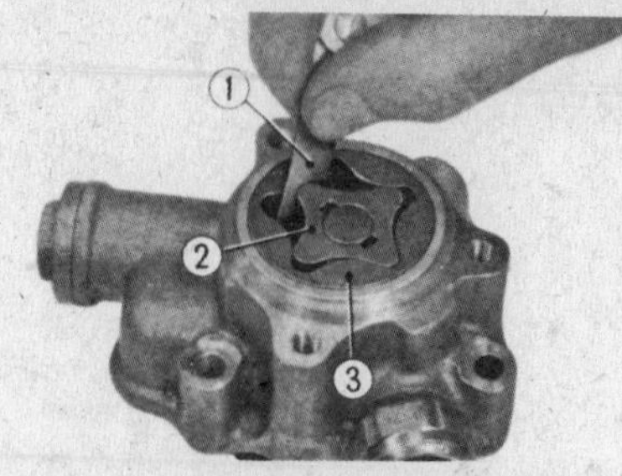

Measuring clearance between the inner (2) and outer (3) rotors with a feeler gauge (1)

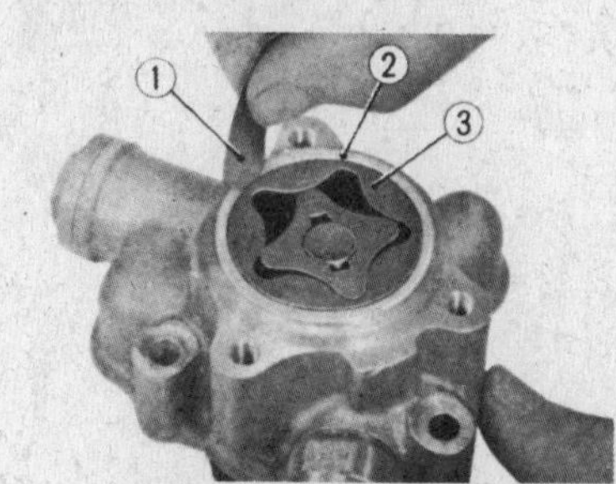

Checking clearance between the pump body housing (2) and the outer rotor (3) with a feeler gauge (1)

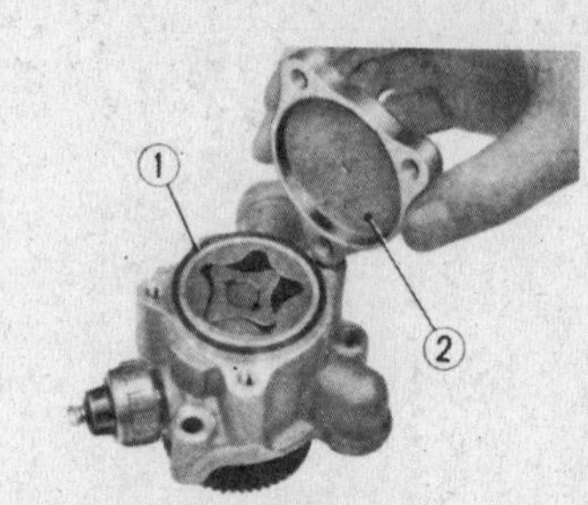

Replace the O-ring (1) before installing the cover (2)

Install the O-ring collar (1) and the O-rings (2 and 3) before bolting up the pump

ASSEMBLY

Assemble in the reverse order of disassembly.

1. Do not reuse old O-rings.
2. Lubricate all moving parts with oil before installing.
3. Be sure that the drive pin is securely installed in the shaft.
4. When installing the rotors, make sure that the mark in the side of each faces in the same direction. The rotors may be installed with the marks facing either toward or away from the side cover.
5. Use extreme care when installing the pressure-relief valve cap. *Overtightening will cause the cap to fracture.* Tighten to 7.5–10 ft lbs.

FUEL SYSTEM

NOTE: *Carburetor operation and inspection procedures are explained in detail in the "General Information" section.*

CARBURETORS

All Models (1971–80)

REMOVAL AND INSTALLATION

1. Remove the fuel tank.
2. Raise the seat and remove the air filter element. Unbolt and remove the air filter housing.
3. Disconnect the throttle cables from the carburetor linkage.
4. Loosen the air filter intake clamp at each carburetor.
5. Loosen the carburetor-to-intake tube clamps and withdraw the carburetors toward the rear.

Installation is in reverse order of removal. The following points should be noted:

1. Make sure that the carburetors are securely clamped to the intake tubes. Use new clamps if necessary.
2. Check carburetor adjustment and synchronization after installation as described in "Tune-Up."

Oil Pump Specifications

	350/400		500/550		650	
	Standard (mm/in.)	*Serviceable Limit (mm/in.)*	*Standard (mm/in.)*	*Serviceable Limit (mm/in.)*	*Standard (mm/in.)*	*Serviceable Limit (mm/in.)*
Rotor-to-rotor clearance						
Main pump	0.15/0.0059	0.3/0.0118	na	0.35/0.013	na	0.15/0.006
Auxiliary pump	0.15/0.0059	0.3/0.0118	na	0.35/0.013	na	0.15/0.006
Outer rotor-to-pump body clearance						
Main pump	0.06–0.12/0.0024–0.0047	0.35/0.013	na	0.35/0.013	na	0.35/0.013
Auxiliary pump	0.15–0.20/0.0059–0.0079	0.35/0.013	na	0.35/0.013	na	0.35/0.013

na: not available

DISASSEMBLY

1. Remove the throttle return spring. Be careful not to damage the spring hook.
2. Unscrew the nuts and remove the dust plate, as illustrated.
3. Remove the adjuster holders from the linkage arms.
4. Unbolt and separate the carburetors from the mounting plate.
5. Separate the carburetors. Do not misplace the connecting tubes.

Removing the throttle return spring (1)

Remove the nuts (1) and dust plate (2), then loosen the capnuts (3)

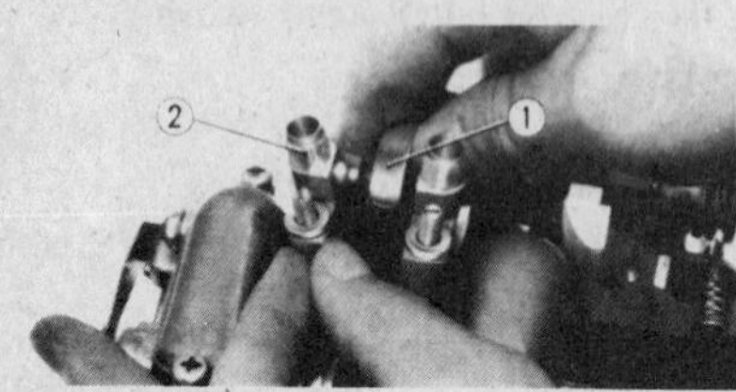

Remove the link arm (1) from the adjuster holders (2)

Remove the adjuster screw (1) from the adjuster holders (2)

Bend back the lockwasher (1) locking tabs, then remove the bolts (2 and 3)

NOTE: *Disassembly procedure from this point on is given for one carburetor, but applies to all four. Keep each carburetor and its components separate from the others; do not interchange parts between carburetors.*

6. Remove the two screws and lift off the carburetor cap.

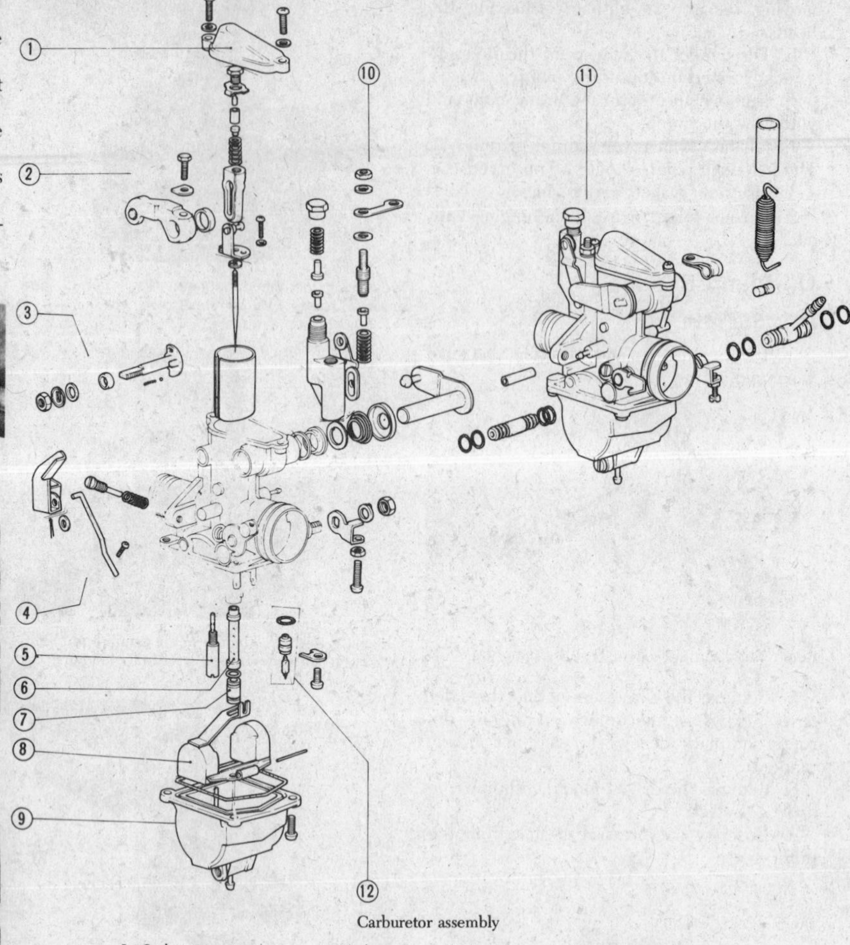

Carburetor assembly

1. Carburetor cap
2. Throttle slide linkage
3. Choke arm
4. Choke rod
5. Pilot jet
6. Needle jet
7. Main jet
8. Floats
9. Float bowl
10. Adjuster holder
11. Carburetor (complete)
12. Float needle and seat

7. Position the throttle slide to full-open and bend back the two locktabs.
8. Remove the bolt from the shaft end and remove the linkage arm in direction "A" using a screwdriver.
9. Loosen the bolt on the throttle slide about one-half turn and pry the linkage arm loose.
10. Remove the two screws and rotate the slide plate one-quarter turn in either direction to align the tab on the plate with the groove in the shaft. Remove the plate.
11. Remove the jet needle from the throttle slide.
12. Remove the float bowl.
13. Remove the leaf spring and unscrew the main jet.
14. Pull out the float hinge pin and remove the float.

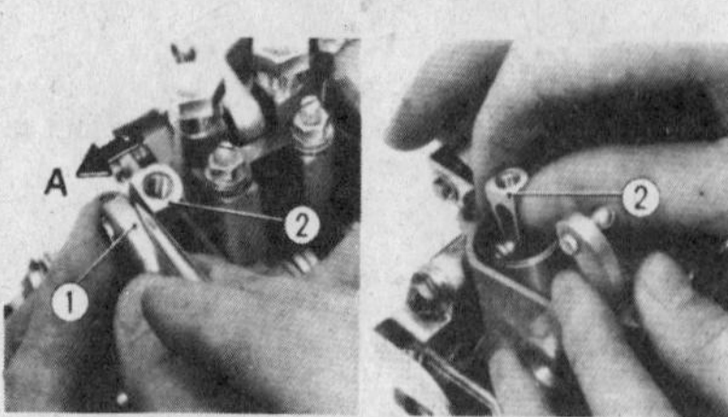

Removing the link arm (1) and throttle shaft (2)

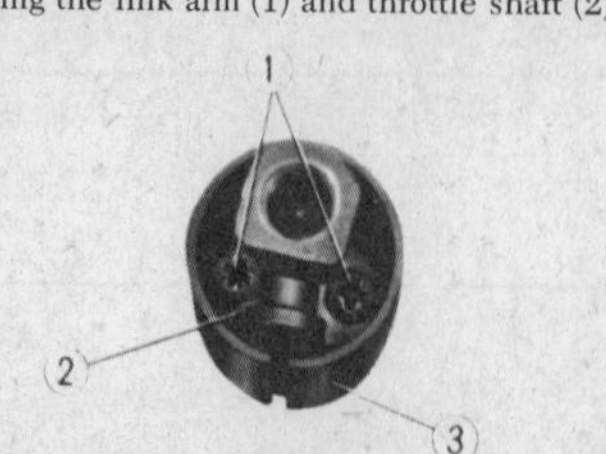

Remove the screws (1) and turn the plate (2) 90° to separate it from the slide (3)

Remove the leaf spring (1), main jet (2), and pilot jet (3)

Remove the float arm pin (1), then remove the float (2)

Remove the clip plate (1) and needle seat and needle (2)

15. Remove the screw and clip plate, and withdraw the float needle and seat.

16. Remove the main jet tube, low-speed jet, and air screw.

CLEANING

Clean all metal parts in a solvent or carburetor cleaner. Use compressed air to dry parts. Blow all fuel jets clear. Never insert anything into the jet bores to clear them if clogged.

INSPECTION

1. Check the throttle slide surfaces for scoring or signs of wear. The slide should be smooth. The movement of the slide in the carburetor body should be very easy.
2. Examine the jet needle for wear along the tapered portion as indicated by bright spots or unevenness of the taper. Also check the needle for nicks, and replace it if any damage is noted. Be sure that the needle clip is repositioned in the original groove if removed.
3. After many miles the needle and needle jet should be replaced, as these parts are subject to wear. Wear of these components may show up as a rich running condition in the mid-throttle range. If the needle seems worn, it would be best to replace the needle jet as well.
4. Check the float needle for wear of the tip or foreign matter and replace if necessary. Check the needle seat for corrosion or foreign matter. Clean off the seat if only dirty. Corroded needle seats should be replaced.
5. If brass floats are fitted, check the floats for punctures by shaking them close to the ear and listening for any gas inside. Replace any float assembly with this condition.
6. Check the carburetor body and the float bowl for stress cracks.
7. Inspect the pilot air screws. The taper of the screws should be very even. Replace if the screw tip is blunted.

Assembly

Assembly is the reverse of the disassembly procedure. The following points should be noted:

1. Use new gaskets and O-rings.
2. The float should be positioned so that when the float arm just touches the end of the float needle, the distance from the top of the floats to the float bowl mating surface on the carburetor is 12.5 mm (0.5 in.) on the 650, 21 mm (0.83 in.) on the 350/400 or 22 mm (0.89 in.) on the 500/550. Bend the float arm in the desired direction if adjustment is necessary. Make sure that the floats are even. Note that this measurement must be made without the float bowl gasket in place.

NOTE: *A special float level gauge (part number 07144-99998) is available from Honda dealers.*

3. Do not overtighten the jets when installing them in the carburetor body.
4. Make sure that the jet needle is installed in the same position as when it was removed. Changing needle position in the slide will affect running at mid-range throttle openings.

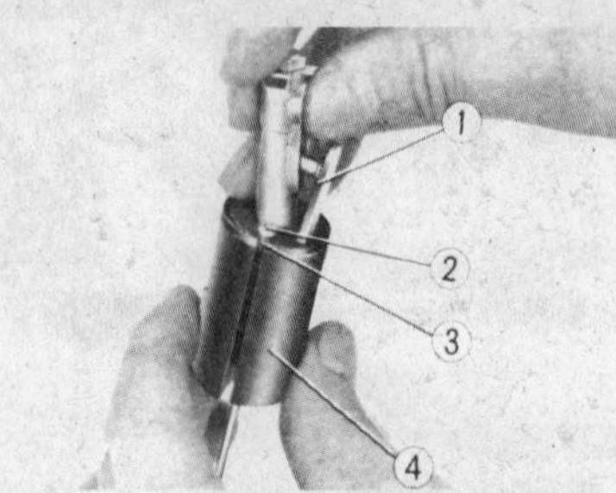

Install the spring washers (3), then position the plate (1) and push it down. Rotate the plate 90° toward the link arm and secure it with the mounting screws (2)

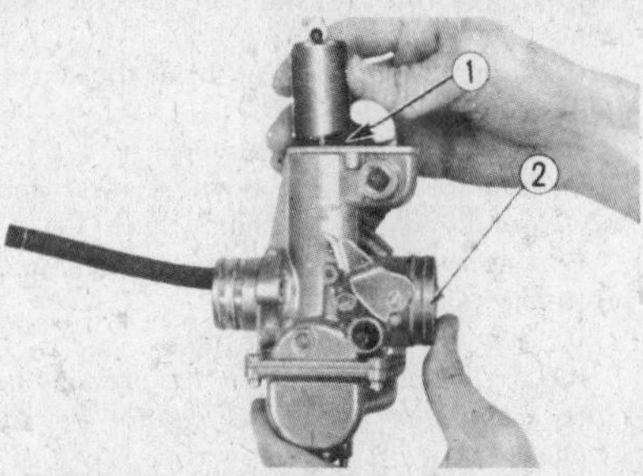

Make sure that the cutaway section (1) of the slide is toward the choke valve (2)

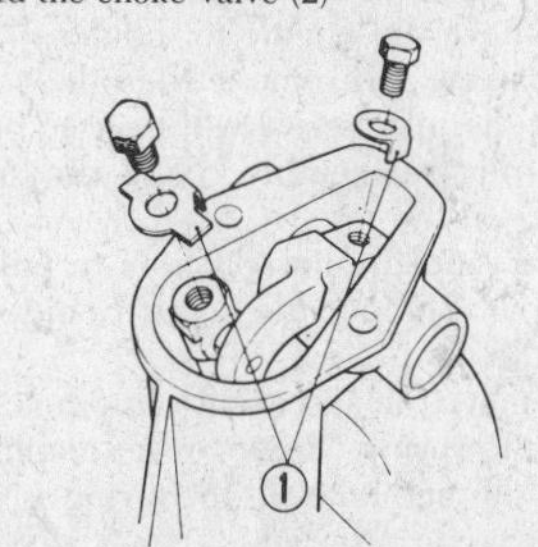

Install the locktabs (1) as shown

Secure the spring (1) with the capnut (2) on the adjuster holders

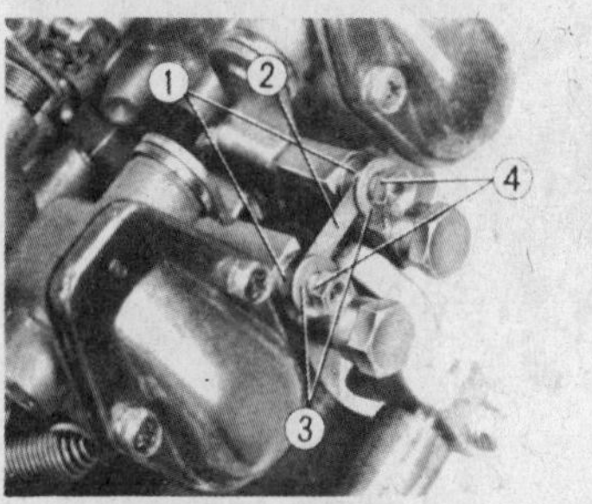

Install the washers (1), dust plate (2), washers (3), and nuts (4) in that order

5. To install the adjuster holder (if removed), first insert the spring and spring seat. Open the throttle slide about halfway and install the holder onto the shaft while holding the spring seat down with a thin screwdriver.
6. Install the locktabs as shown.
7. Do not forget the spring under the capnut on the adjuster holders.
8. Install the special washers and dust plate as shown.

Fuel line routing (350/400)

Fuel line routing (500/550)

9. Route the fuel lines as shown.
10. Open the throttle lever until it contacts the stop screw. The throttle slide-to-bore clearance should be 0–1.0 mm (0–0.04 in.). Adjust the clearance, if necessary, by turning the stop screw.

1981 Models

REMOVAL AND INSTALLATION

NOTE: *The carburetors must be removed as an assembly.*

1. Turn the petcock "off," disconnect the fuel line at the carburetor.
2. Remove the left and right side covers.
3. Remove the air cleaner assembly.
4. Loosen the carburetor manifold clamps. Remove the carburetors as an assembly. Disconnect the choke and throttle cables.

CAUTION: *Remember that the carburetors are full of gasoline. Drain the float bowls into a suitable container by loosening the drain screws.*

5. Installation is the reverse of removal. Note the following points:
   a. Do not interchange the "pull" and "push" throttle cables. The "pull" cable is closest to the engine.
   b. Be sure that the carburetors are firmly seated in the manifold spigots.
   c. Be sure that the air cleaner tubes are not twisted or folded up so as to block the carburetor intakes.
   d. Adjust the throttle cables, butterfly synchronization, idle and fast idle adjustments.

e. Be sure that all fuel line connections are tight and secured with the safety clips. Before operation, turn on the fuel and check for leaks.

DISASSEMBLY

1. Loosen the locknut, and back off the butterfly synchronization screw.

NOTE: *The slides will have to be synchronized after assembly.*

2. Disconnect the spring from the choke lever.

3. Remove the phillips head screws and take off the rear and the front stays.

4. Separate the carburetors, noting that the fuel connecting pipe and the choke spring will come loose. The pipe has o-rings on both sides. Do not lose them.

From this point, disassembly is given for one carburetor, but applies to both.

5. Unscrew and remove the carburetor tops. Take out the spring, and the throttle slide assembly with jet needle.

The jet needle can be removed from the throttle slide after taking off the full open stopper and unscrewing the needle set screw.

Removing the needle jet

Removing the cap and spring

Float bowl screws (arrows)

Removing the secondary main jet

6. Remove the seal ring from the top of the carburetor body.

7. Remove the air jet cover.

8. Remove the float bowl screws, and very carefully take off the float bowl.

9. Unscrew and remove the primary and secondary main jets.

10. Remove the slow jet plug.

NOTE: *The slow jet itself is a press-fit in the carburetor body and cannot be removed.*

11. Remove the primary nozzle which is beneath the primary main jet.

12. Remove the needle jet holder.

13. Unscrew and remove the pilot screw. Note that the pilot screw will have to be adjusted during reassembly. Note the spring and o-ring on the jet.

14. Use a needle-nosed pliers to pull out the float pin. Remove the floats. Remove the float needle.

15. Remove the air cut-off valve cover and take out the spring. Remove the diaphragm very carefully and take out the o-ring as well.

INSPECTION

1. Clean the carburetor body and float bowl in a carburetor cleaner or solvent and dry thoroughly.

2. Use compressed air to blow air and fuel passages clear.

3. Clean all fuel jets in the same manner.

CAUTION: *Do not insert anything into the jet passages to clear them; use air pressure only.*

4. Inspect the carburetor body for any vibration or stress cracks.

5. Check the condition of the throttle slide. Smooth movement of the slide on the carburetor body is imperative. If the slide sticks or binds at any point from full closed to wide open, replace it.

Pushing out the float pivot pin

6. Inspect the needle jet and the needle. The needle must be free of nicks or score marks along its tapered portion. More often, however, these components will need to be replaced because of normal wear. As the throttle slide moves up and down while the machine is in operation, the needle is rubbing against the jet. Eventually, these components will wear enough to cause a noticeable rich running condition in the mid-throttle range. If this occurs, both the needle and the jet should be replaced. If the components are more than four years old, new ones should be fitted before attempting to tune the carburetor, or taking remedial action to correct a rich condition.

7. Check the throttle slide for scoring. Replace it if any is noted.

8. Inspect the tip of the float needle and the needle seat for dirt or corrosion. Check the needle tip for wear. If worn, the needle should be replaced.

If there is any corrosion or deposits evident on the needle seat, the deposits must be removed, or the parts replaced.

NOTE: *Do not attempt to clean the needle or needle seat by lapping one against the other.*

To check the efficiency of the float needle valve, proceed as follows:

a. With the carburetor assembled except for the float bowl, connect it to its fuel line;

b. Place a number of dry rags beneath the carburetor, and hold it upright (in its normal operating position) with one hand;

c. With the other hand, gently raise the float assembly until the float needle is seated. Have an assistant turn the fuel petcock on:

d. If the needle and seat are in good condition and forming a good seal, no gasoline will flow out of the carburetor;

e. If a leak is noted, replace the needle and seat.

CAUTION: *While performing this test, be sure that adequate precautions are taken in the event of spilling.*

The float level should be checked prior to assembly. Refer to chapter 3.

9. Check that the tapered portion of the pilot screw is smooth and clean. Replace it if it is crushed or blunted.

10. Inspect the float bowl for a warped gasket surface, or stress cracks (especially around the screw holes).

11. Check the air cut-valve diaphragm for condition. Replace it if ripped or punctured.

ASSEMBLY

Assembly is basically the reverse of the disassembly procedure. Note the following points:

1. Always use new gaskets and O-rings.

2. Exercise care when installing jets—they are made of soft brass and are easily damaged if overtightened.

3. Be sure that the float pivot pin is properly seated, and that the floats pivot freely.

4. Tighten the float bowl screws slowly and evenly. Be sure that the O-ring is seated in its groove before installing the float bowl.

5. When joining the two carburetors together, be sure that the o-rings are in place on either end of the fuel pipe. Fit the pipe

into the carbs carefully to avoid damage to the o-rings.

6. Do not forget the choke relief spring.

CARBURETOR SEPARATION

Although almost all routine work can be performed with the carburetors attached together, the units may have to come apart. If this is desired, proceed as follows:

1. Unhook the choke relief spring from the shaft arm between carburetors Nos. 3 and 4.
2. Loosen the synchronization screw locknuts. Turn the synchronization screws in until they seat and note the number of turns so that they can be roughly repositioned when assembling. Then back the screws out until there is no tension.
3. Remove the rear bracket which is held to each carburetor by two screws.
4. Remove the front bracket.
5. Separate the carburetors between units Nos. 2 and 4. Pull them straight apart to avoid damage to the lines.
6. File the staked ends of the choke valve screws. Remove the screws. They must be replaced with new ones on assembly.
7. Remove the fuel line holder from the No. 1 carb. Separate the carbs. Be careful to pull them straight apart to avoid damage to the fuel and air lines.
8. After noting the spring position, remove the choke relief spring from the choke linkage. Remove the choke shaft.

NOTE: *The choke shaft, valves, and screws cannot be reused.*

9. Remove the cotter pin from the accelerator pump rod. Remove the plain washers, spring and collar.
10. Remove the fast idle adjusting arm bolt.
11. Remove the fast idle adjusting arm and springs.
12. Remove the accelerator pump rod. Drive out the throttle linkage retaining pin. Remove the throttle linkage.
13. Assembly is basically the reverse of disassembly. Note the following points:
    a. assemble one pair of carbs at a time;
    b. use new o-rings on the fuel line joints;
    c. lubricate the o-rings with a bit of grease before assembly;
    d. install the fuel line, accelerator pump joint and air vent pipes on the No. 3 unit. Install the choke dust tube. Loosen the synchronization adjusting screw until there is no tension. Insert the No. 3 unit throttle link between the plain washers. Assemble carburetors Nos. 3 and 4.

    NOTE: *The large washer should be positioned on the spring side.*

    e. assemble carburetors Nos. 1 and 2 in the same manner;
    f. insert new choke shafts and assemble the linkage;
    g. install the front bracket screws, but do not tighten them;
    h. place the carbs on a flat surface with the float bowls facing up. Press them together and tighten the screws evenly by tightening the left side screw on each carburetor first, then going back and securing the right side screw on each one. Tighten the screws gradually to 3–4 ft. lbs.

    NOTE: *After securing the screws, check for smooth choke shaft operation. Recheck alignment if operation is not satisfactory.*

    i. fit the rear bracket using the same procedure. Tighten the rear bracket screws to 2–3 ft. lbs.
    j. install the thrust springs between No. 1 and 2 and between Nos. 3 and 4 throttle linkages;
    k. turn each synchronization adjusting screw to its original position as noted during disassembly:
    l. adjust the throttles so that the distance between the by-pass hole and the throttle plate is the same for each unit;
    m. open the throttle slightly, then release. Be sure that the throttle linkage is smooth and free of binding;
    n. hook the choke relief spring to the choke shaft between units 3 and 4. Install the choke valves, but do not tighten the screws; be sure that choke valve operation is smooth, then tighten the valve screws to 5–11 ft. lbs. Fold the tabs on the lockwasher up. Recheck choke and throttle operation.

FUEL PETCOCK

REMOVAL, CLEANING, AND INSPECTION

1974 and Earlier Models

1. Turn the petcock lever to "stop" and disconnect the fuel lines.
2. Raise the seat, and raise and support the rear of the gas tank.
3. Unscrew the sediment bowl from the petcock, being careful of the gasoline which will also spill out.
4. Remove the O-ring and filter.
5. Remove the two screws which secure the petcock body to the gas tank, and remove the petcock.
6. Clean all components in gasoline and dry; then inspect for damage.
7. When assembling the petcock, it is advisible to use new gaskets and O-rings.

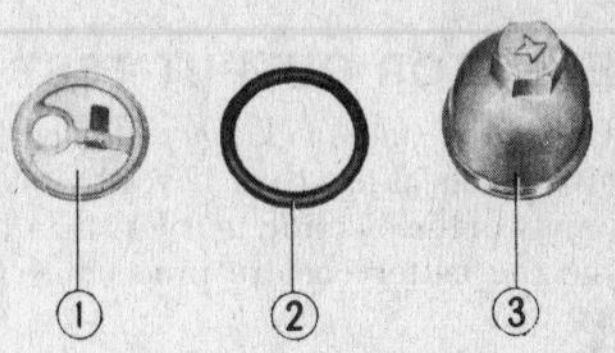

Fuel petcock filter screen (1), O-ring (2) and sediment bowl (3)

8. After installing the petcock, check for proper gas flow as well as leaks.

1975 and Later Models

The petcock filter screen is inside the gas tank.

1. Disconnect the fuel lines from the petcock. Remove the tank from the machine, and drain off the gas.

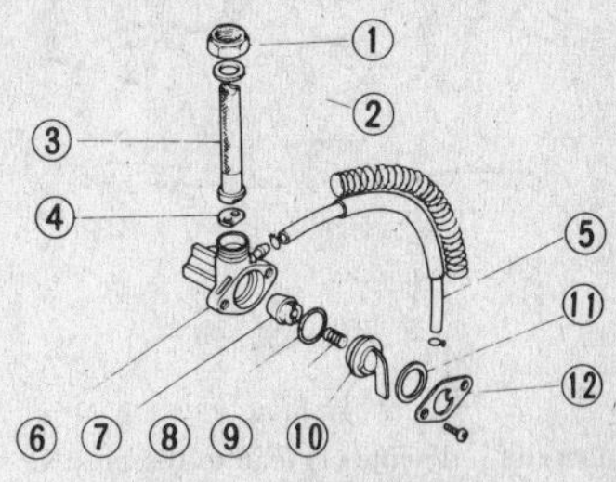

1975 and later petcock

1. Nut
2. Gasket
3. Filter screen
4. Seat
5. Fuel line
6. Petcock body
7. Valve
8. O-ring
9. Spring
10. Lever
11. Washer
12. Plate

2. Unscrew the securing nut and carefully take out the petcock. Remove the securing nut and filter from the petcock.
3. Wash the filter in a solvent. Replace the filter if it is punctured or badly clogged. Check the condition of the gasket and replace it if it is crushed or nicked.

Carburetor Specifications

	350	400	500	550	650 (79–80)	650 (81)
Type	Keihin	Keihin	Keihin	Keihin	Keihin	Keihin
Bore diameter (mm/in.)	21/0.82	21/0.82	22/0.89	22/0.89	26/1.02	na
Main jet	75	75	100	100	90	120
Pilot jet	35	40	40	38	na	na ①
Slide cutaway	2.5	2.5	2.5	2.5	na	na
Needle clip position (groove from top)	3	3	3	3	na	na
Pilot screw setting (turns out)	⅞± ⅜	2± ½	1± ⅛	1± ⅛	preset	preset
Air jet	na	na	150	150	na	100
Float level (mm/in.)	21/0.83	21/0.83	22/0.87	22/0.87	12.5/0.5	15.5/0.61

na: not available ① Nighthawk: 118

ELECTRICAL SYSTEMS

ALTERNATOR OUTPUT TEST

1. Check the state of charge of the battery. If battery voltage is less than 12 volts, or if specific gravity of the electrolyte is less than 1.26, recharge the battery before proceeding with the test.

2. The test is performed using an ammeter and a voltmeter. Connect the ammeter as follows: disconnect the positive (+) battery cable and connect it to the positive side of the ammeter; connect the negative (−) side of the ammeter to the positive battery terminal. Connect the voltmeter as follows: connect the positive side of the ammeter to the positive battery cable, and ground the negative voltmeter lead on the engine.

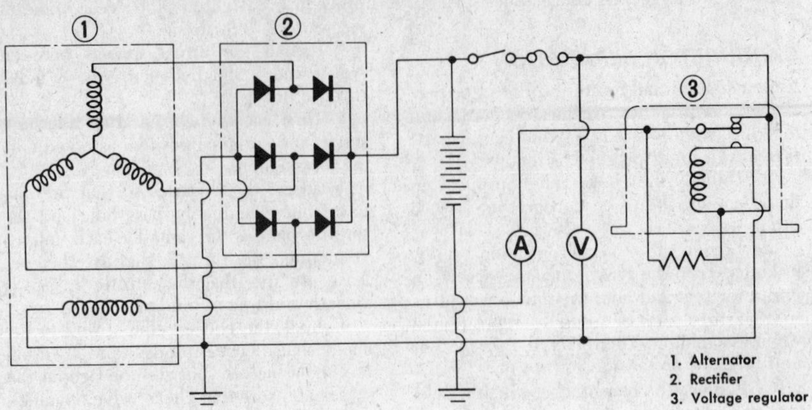

Regulator test (350/400)

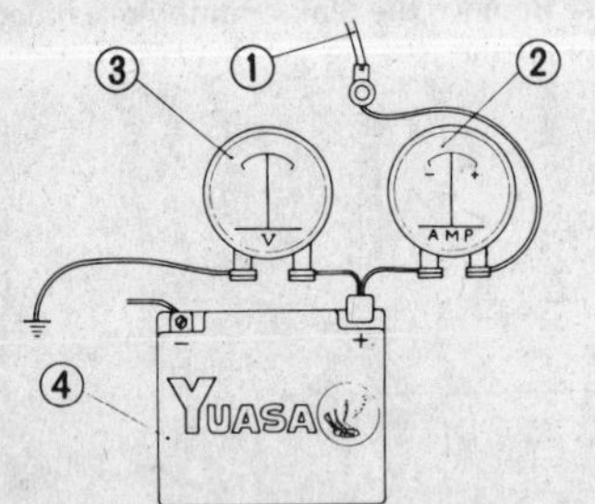
Connect the red/white (1) lead to the positive side of the ammeter (2), and connect the voltmeter (3) to the positive battery (4) terminal and ground

1. Red/white lead
2. Ammeter
3. Voltmeter
4. Battery

3. Start the engine and check the amperage and voltage output of the alternator under both day riding (lights off) and night riding (lights on) conditions. If the readings obtained are noticeably greater or smaller than those in the accompanying table, adjust the regulator. Slight variation is acceptable due to the effect of the state of charge of the battery upon alternator output. If alternator output is satisfactory but the battery has discharged during use, refer to the section on testing the rectifier.

NOTE: *The 650 is tested with the headlight on "High" beam. The readings should show initial charging beginning at 1,650 rpm and should indicate a minimum of zero amps/14 volts at 5,000 rpm.*

REGULATOR ADJUSTMENT

350/400

NOTE: *Perform the following tests with a fully charged battery.*

1. Connect a DC voltmeter from the regulator ignition terminal to ground, then disconnect the white lead from the field terminal (F), and connect an ammeter between the lead and the terminal.

2. Take a field current reading with the engine idling, and compare it with the Mode I limits given in the accompanying chart. If the value found exceeds the value given, either the regulator or alternator field coil is defective.

Mode	*Field Current*	*Voltage*
I (idle)	2.4–2.6A	to 13.2V
II	1.2–1.3A	13.5–14.5V
III	0–1.2A	14.0–15.0V

3. Slowly increase the engine speed until the ammeter needle deflects to read half the Mode I value, and compare the reading at the moment of deflection with the Mode II value given in the accompanying chart.

4. Increase the engine speed to at least 4,000 rpm, and note the maximum voltage reading. The field current and voltage should agree with the Mode III value given in the chart. If the field current doesn't decrease as voltage increases, the regulator is defective. If the field current and voltage values do not agree with those given in the chart, the regulator should be adjusted. If the voltage is in excess of 15.0V, the system is overcharging.

5. Armature and angle gap are adjusted simultaneously by bending the holder until gaps of 0.012 in. (0.3 mm) 0.08 in. (0.2 mm) respectively are attained.

6. Adjust the point gap by bending the lower point bracket until a gap of 0.018 in. (0.45 mm) is attained.

7. Correct the voltage readings by bending the adjusting arm *up* to increase the charging voltage, or *down* to decrease it.

Adjusting gap by bending the adjusting arm

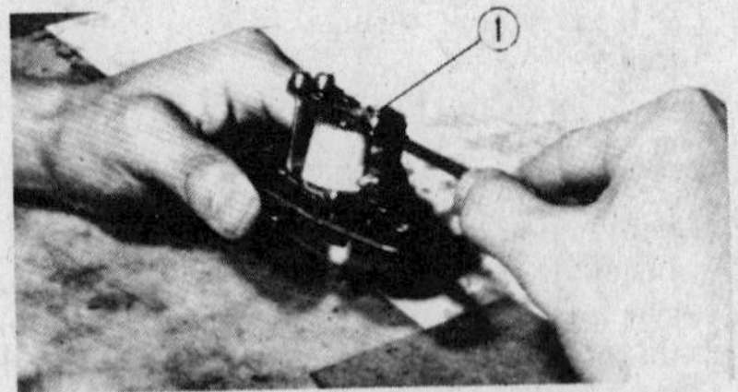
Checking clearance between the top point (1) and the lower one

Alternator Output (350/400)

Engine rpm	1000	2000	3000	4000	5000	6000	7000	8000
Charging current (amps)								
Night riding (headlight on)	1.6	1.9	2.0	1.8	1.6	1.5	1.4	1.4
Day riding (headlight off)	—	—	4	2.6	2.0	1.6	1.4	1.4
Battery terminal voltage	12.5	14.2	15	15	15	15	15	15

Alternator Output (500/550)

Engine rpm	1000	2000	3000	4000	5000	6000	7000	8000
Charging current (amps)								
Day riding (headlight off)	6.5	0	2.4	1.3	1.0	1.0	0.8	0.6
Night riding (headlight on)	2–3	1	1	1	1	1	1	1
Battery terminal voltage	12	12.4	13.2	14.5	14.5	14.5	14.5	14.5

500/550

NOTE: *Perform the following tests with a fully charged battery.*

1. Disconnect the three wires at the regulator, marking them so that they can be replaced on the same terminals. Take out the two mounting bolts and remove the regulator unit.

2. Remove the two screws and take off the regulator cover.

3. Examine the condition of both sets of contact points. If dirty or pitted, they may be cleaned up with fine emery paper.

4. Measure the core gap with a feeler gauge. If the gap does not measure within 0.024–0.040 in. (0.6–1.0 mm), loosen the

Regulator adjusting points

A. Core gap — 1. Core gap adjusting screw
B. Point gap — 2. Point gap adjusting screw
3. Moveable contact

core gap adjusting screw and move the point body up or down as required.

5. Measure the gap of the upper point set in the same manner. The points should be gapped at 0.008 in. (0.2 mm). To adjust the gap, loosen the adjusting screw and move the lower contact up or down as required.

6. Temporarily install the regulator with one of the mounting bolts, leaving the cover off. Connect the three wires.

7. Loosen the voltage adjusting screw locknut. If the alternator output test showed insufficient output, turn the voltage adjusting screw clockwise about one-quarter turn. If the test showed output to be excessive, turn the screw counterclockwise about one-quarter turn. Tighten the locknut and rerun the alternator output test. Readjust the screw as necessary to obtain satisfactory alternator output.

8. If alternator output is unstable or excessive after the regulator has been adjusted properly, chances are that the regulator is faulty. If alternator output is insufficient and

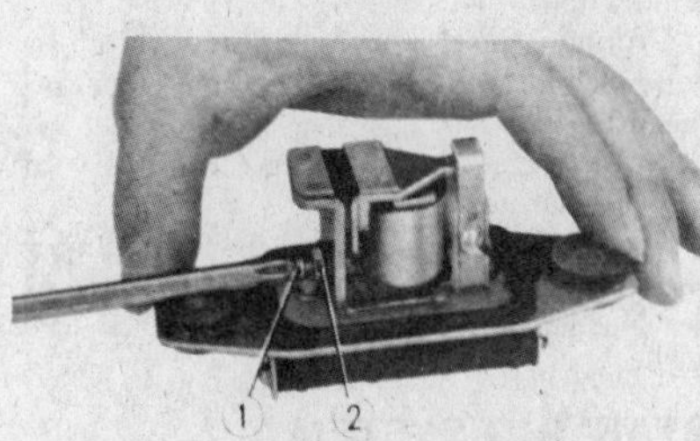

Loosen the locknut (2) and rotate the adjusting screw (1) to correct voltage

cannot be brought up to specification through regulator adjustment, the alternator itself should be suspected. Before proceeding any further, make sure that the battery is producing at least 12 volts at the terminals, and that none of the cells are dead or have a noticeably lower specific gravity than the rest. If the battery checks out all right, replace the regulator or check into the alternator (refer to the "Alternator Service" section), as indicated.

TESTING THE RECTIFIER

Except 650

If alternator output is satisfactory but the battery discharges as the engine is running, it is quite possible that the rectifier is not functioning properly. (This is assuming, of course, that the battery is not old and tired or has one or more bad cells.) Before removing and testing the rectifier, make sure that it is solidly mounted on the frame. The rectifier is grounded through its mounting and will not operate without a good ground.

CAUTION: *Do not loosen or tighten the nut that holds the rectifier unit together, as this will adversely affect operation of the rectifier.*

1. To test the rectifier, first pull apart the plastic connector, unscrew the mounting nut, and remove the rectifier unit. Inside the rectifier are six diodes which, if functioning properly, will allow electricity to pass in only one direction.

2. Check the diodes, using either a multimeter or a test light and the motorcycle battery. If the test light and battery are to be used, simply run a length of wire off one of the battery terminals and connect one of the test light leads to the other terminal. The two free wire ends will be used to check electrical continuity of the diodes.

3. Connect one of the leads to pin number 4 in the connector block and touch the other lead to pins 1, 2, and 3, in turn. Now, reverse the leads and repeat the procedure. The test light should light (or the meter needle respond) in one direction only.

4. If all is well so far, connect one of the leads to pin 5 and touch the other to pins 1, 2, and 3 again. Reverse the leads, as before, and repeat.

5. Continuity in both directions or in neither direction (when reversing the leads) indicates a defective diode, in which case the rectifier unit must be replaced.

NOTE: *On an ohmmeter, "continuity" will be indicated by a resistance of 5–40 ohms. "No continuity," by a resistance of 100 or more ohms.*

The diodes are quite susceptible to failure from excessive heat and electrical overload. Observe the following precautions to avoid rectifier failure:

a. Do not use high-voltage test equipment to test the rectifier diodes.

b. Do not run the engine at high rpm with the rectifier "P" terminal disconnected, or else the high voltage that is produced will damage the rectifier.

c. Do not quick-charge the battery (high-output charging equipment) without first disconnecting one of the battery cables.

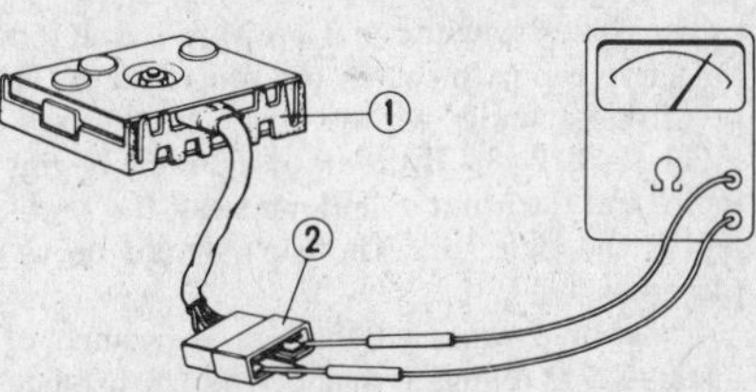

Rectifier (1) with coupler (2) attached to tester

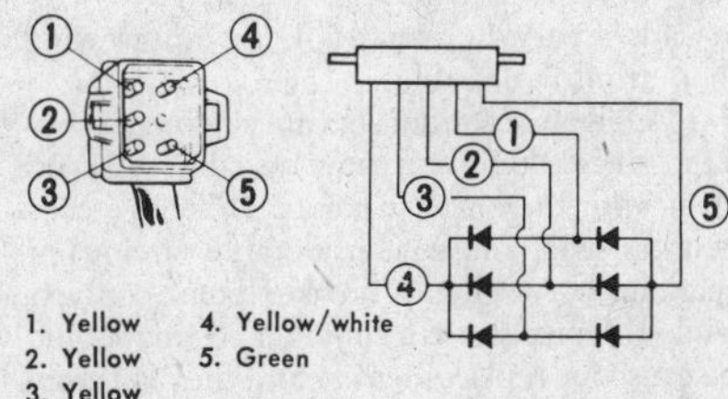

1. Yellow — 4. Yellow/white
2. Yellow — 5. Green
3. Yellow

Schematic diagram of rectifier showing connector pin arrangement

REGULATOR/RECTIFIER (650)

1979–1980

Testing for the unit regulator/rectifier is done with an ohmmeter.

Resistance between green and any yellow lead should be 5–40 ohms.

Resistance in the reverse direction should be at least 2,000 ohms.

Resistance between the red/white lead and any yellow lead should be 5–40 ohms.

Reversing the probes should yield at least 2,000 ohms.

1981

Regulator and rectifier are tested separately. Refer to the following charts.

Rectifier

(−) \ (+)	*Red/White*	*Green*	*Yellow 1*	*Yellow 2*	*Yellow 3*
Red/White		∞	∞	∞	∞
Green	0.5–50		0.5–50	0.5–50	0.5–50
Yellow 1	0.5–50	∞		∞	∞
Yellow 2	0.5–50	∞	∞		∞
Yellow 3	0.5–50	∞	∞	∞	

Regulator

(−) \ (+)	*Black*	*White*	*Green*
Black		1–30	0.5–20
White	0.5–30		1–50
Green	0.5–20	0.5–30	

Unit: kΩ

Alternator service

Remove the alternator cover and the components will be accessible for testing.

Field Coil Test (650)

Carbon brushes are marked with scribed lines. When wear reaches these lines, the brushes must be replaced.

Field coil resistance should be a few ohms.

Field Coil Test (Except 650)

Check continuity between the two field coil leads (white and green) using a multi-tester or a test light and the battery. If there is continuity, the field coil is satisfactory. Standard field coil resistance is 4.9 ohms, ± 10 percent. The field coil can be removed from the cover by simply taking out the three mounting screws under the plate on the outside of the cover.

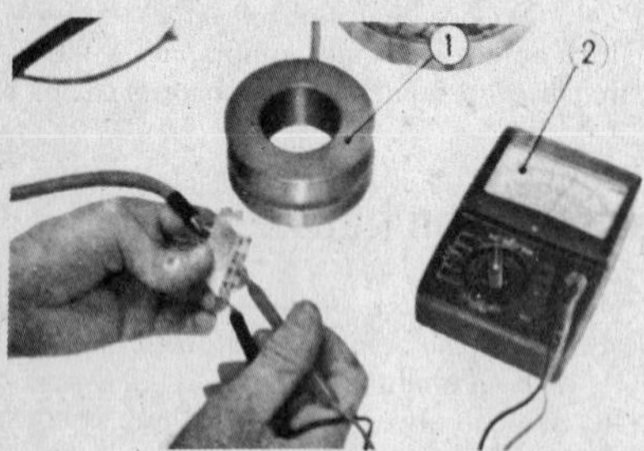

Testing the field coil (1) leads with a multi-tester (2)

Stator Coil Test (All)

Check for continuity between the three stator coil leads (yellow) in the same manner as the field coil test. If there is continuity, the stator coil is satisfactory. Standard stator resistance is 0.61–0.69 ohm for the 350/400, 0.32–0.38 ohm for the 500/550 and 0.41–0.51 ohms for the 650. To remove the stator from the cover, simply take out the three mounting screws.

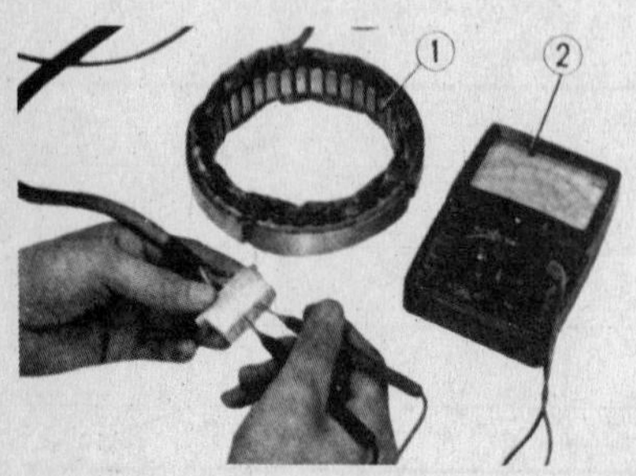

Testing the stator coil leads (1) with a multi-tester (2)

Rotor (All)

The alternator rotor need not be removed at this time. If it must be taken off, pull it off the crankshaft after the retaining bolt has been removed, using Honda tool number 07011–33301 (350/400) or 07933–2160000 (500/550) to avoid damage to the rotor or crankshaft taper. When reinstalling the rotor, tighten the retaining nut to 29 ft lbs (350/400) or 30 ft. lbs. (500/550), or 36–43 ft. lbs. (650).

BREAKER POINT IGNITION SYSTEM

The ignition system consists of the battery, breaker points, coils, condensers, spark plug caps, and spark plugs.

There are two sets of breaker points and two ignition coils. Each coil fires two cylinders. They are paired Nos. 1 and 4, and Nos. 2 and 3.

1. In the event of failure of the ignition system, first check the fuses; if all are in working order, check that the snap connectors for the coils and breaker points are all clean and tight.
2. If these items are all in working order, the problem may be isolated to the coils, condensers, or plug caps.
3. If only one cylinder fails to fire, and the problem is not a loose connection or defective spark plug, suspect the plug cap. The caps are fitted with a resistor to prevent radio interference while in operation, and heat and vibration may cause the value of this resistor to increase considerably, even to becoming an open circuit.

The easiest way to see if a misfire is due to a defective cap is to switch the plug lead of the non-firing cylinder with its corresponding cylinder (1–4, 2–3). If the dead cylinder begins to fire and the other cylinder ceases, the problem is the plug cap. The caps should be replaced as a set.

Functional caps will have a resistance of 5,000–7,500 ohms. Usually, when resistance reaches about 9,000 ohms, the plug for that cap will no longer fire.

Caps are easily removable by unscrewing them from their cables.

4. Defective condensers are seldom a problem, since these are now usually replaced along with the breaker points. Defective condensers will cause considerable arcing or sparking between the breaker point contacts while the machine is running, and this should be cause for replacement before they fail completely. Badly burned or pitted points contact surfaces can also be caused by defective condensers, as well as by improper adjustment. If the points are in bad condition, replace them and the condensers as well.
5. Condenser capacity can be checked with electrical test equipment (if available) in place on the machine provided that the condenser is first disconnected from the primary terminal. Capacitance should be 0.22 MFD (350/400) or 0.24 MFD (500/550). The resistance of the condensers should be in excess of 10 MΩ. A variation of 10% in either reading is allowable.

NOTE: *Be sure that the breaker points for the condenser being tested are open during the test.*

6. If the condensers are not suspect, check the ignition coils. Coils should be checked for continuity of the windings. First disconnect the blue and the black/white leads from the left coil and check for continuity between these leads. If there is none, the coil must be replaced.

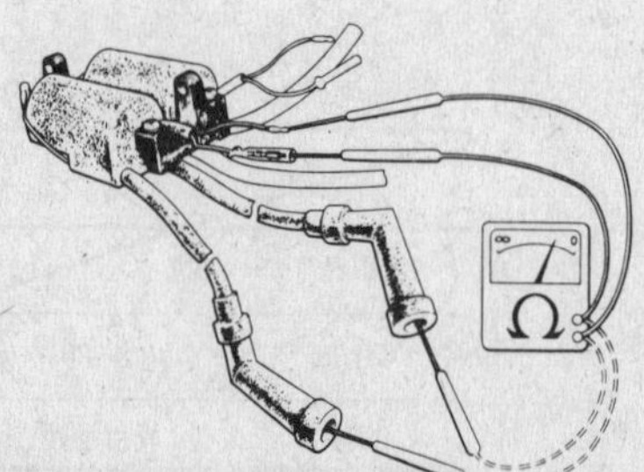

Testing the ignition coil for continuity

For the other coil, carry out the same test between the yellow and the black/white leads.

Check for continuity on the high-tension side of each coil. Disconnect the two spark plug leads of one of the coils and check the continuity between them. If none exists, replace the coil. Repeat the test with the other coil. Remember you will be checking continuity between plug leads 1 and 4 and leads 2 and 3.

7. Coils are secured to the frame with two bolts and are easily removed if defective by disconnecting the wires, and removing the bolts after the gas tank is taken off.

TRANSISTOR IGNITION

Pulser Generator

Check the coil resistance after disconnecting the wiring coupler beneath the right side cover.

Resistance between the yellow and the yellow/white leads should be 530 plus or minus 50 ohms. This is for cylinder Nos. 2 & 3.

Resistance for cylinder Nos. 1 and 4 is checked between the blue and the bue/white leads. It should have the same value.

Spark Unit

Disconnect the wires at the pulser generator.

Attach the positive probe of a voltmeter to the blue/yellow terminal or the yellow/white terminal of the 6-prong connector. Ground the negative meter probe. Turn on the ignition switch.

Ground each terminal (blue/white or yellow/white of the 4-prong connector intermittently.

The voltage should change from 12 v to zero in each test.

The blue/white terminal is for cylinder Nos. 1 and 4. The yellow/white is for cylinder Nos. 2 and 3.

STARTING SYSTEM

The starting system consists of the starter motor and clutch, the solenoid, and the handlebar-mounted starter switch. When the button is pressed, the electrical circuit to the solenoid is closed and the solenoid is activated, sending the battery current directly to the starter motor. The starting system is quite reliable and it is unlikely that any major problems will arise.

Testing

The following two paragraphs are applicable to machines with a switch, a by-pass is incorporated to kill the headlight when the starter is used.

If the starter will not operate, switch on the headlight and observe its intensity. If it is dim when the starter is not being operated, check the battery connections and recharge the battery. If the headlight doesn't light, check the fuse, the battery connections, the ignition switch and its connections, and check the continuity of the wire between the ignition switch and the battery.

If the headlight is bright, press the starter button momentarily and watch the light. If it remains bright, touch a screwdriver blade between the two starter solenoid terminals. If the starter operates, connect a test light between the small yellow/red wire on the solenoid and ground. If the test light comes on as the button is pushed, the solenoid is faulty. If it does not light, look for defective wiring between the starter button and solenoid or between the starter button and ignition switch, or simply a burned out starter button switch. If the starter does not operate and the headlight dims as the main solenoid terminals are bridged, the starter motor is faulty. If the headlight does not dim, look for a bad connection at the starter.

If the starter motor operates freely but will not turn the engine over, the starter clutch is not functioning (a rare occurrence). To remove the starter clutch it is necessary to remove the engine and split the cases. Refer to the section on transmission and primary drive service in chapter 4 for removal and installation procedures.

Starter Motor Service

REMOVAL AND INSTALLATION

1. Disconnect the cable from the positive battery terminal.
2. Disconnect the starter motor cable from the solenoid.
3. Remove the starter motor cover and the left-side crankcase cover.
4. Unscrew the two starter motor mounting bolts and lift the starter out.
5. Installation is in reverse order of removal.

INSPECTION

1. Take out the two screws and remove the starter side cover.
2. Check electrical continuity between the communtator and armature core, using a multi-tester or test light and battery. If continuity exists, the armature coil is grounded and the armature or complete starter motor unit should be replaced.
3. Check for continuity between all of the commutator segments. Continuity must exist in each case.
4. Check continuity between the brush that is wired to the stator coil and the starter motor cable. Lack of continuity indicates an open circuit in the stator coil and the starter motor unit should be replaced.
5. Examine the carbon brushes for damage to the contact surfaces and measure their length. Replace the brushes as a set if either one measures less than 5.5 mm (0.22 in.), or if they are damaged in any way.
6. Brush spring tension should be measured with a small pull-scale. Replace the springs if they have weakened to less than 0.4 kg (0.8 lb) tension.
7. The mica undercut of the commutator should be maintained at 0.3 mm (0.12 in.). Any carbon deposits should be cleaned out of the commutator grooves, and a piece of hacksaw blade or the like used to increase the undercut depth if necessary. Refer to the illustration.

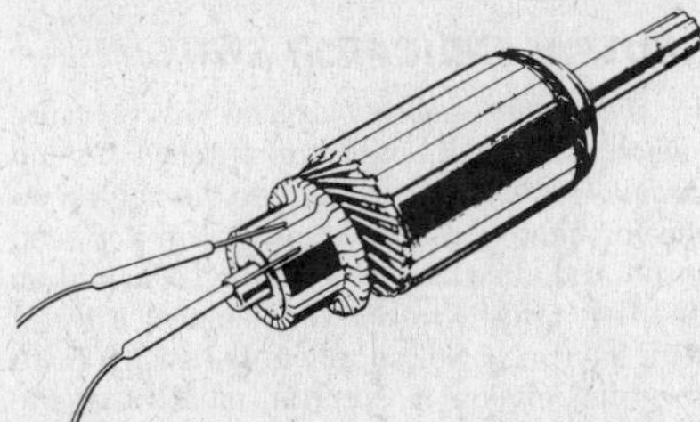

Checking for continuity between commutator segments

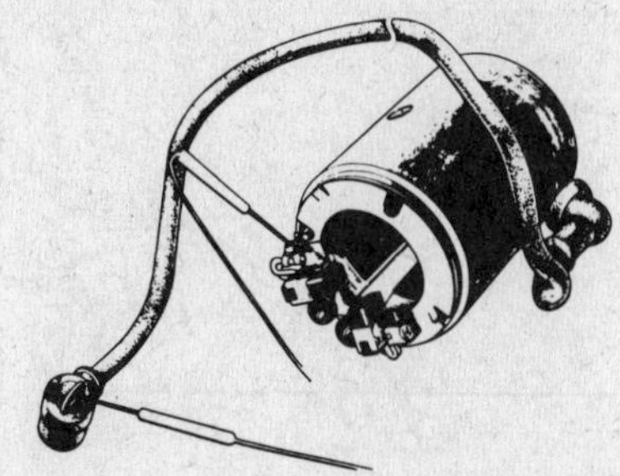

Testing the stator coil for continuity

Brush (1) and brush mounting screw (2) locations

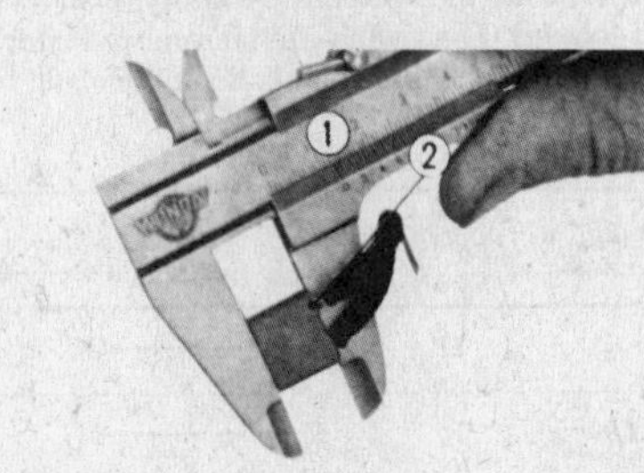

Measuring brush (2) length with vernier calipers (1)

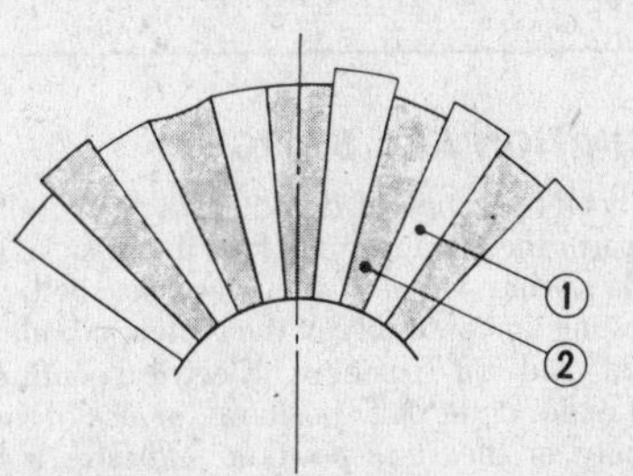

The mica (2) should undercut the commutator (1) by 0.012 in. (0.3 mm)

8. Polish the commutator with fine emery cloth and then clean it thoroughly before installing.

Starter Solenoid

1. If the battery is in reasonably good condition, and nothing at all happens when the starter button is pushed, check the solenoid.
2. Disconnect the starter cable at the starter motor. When the button is pushed, there should be an audible "click" which indicates that the solenoid is opening.
3. If further testing is necessary, remove the solenoid from the machine.

CAUTION: *Be sure to disconnect the cables at the battery before disconnecting the solenoid terminals.*

Connect a fully charged 12-volt battery across the solenoid low-tension leads and check for continuity across the high-tension terminals with an ohmmeter or self-contained test light. If there is no continuity, replace or repair the solenoid.

4. Check for continuity across the low-tension terminals with an ohmmeter or self-powered test light. If there is none, the primary winding of the solenoid is broken, and the unit must be replaced.

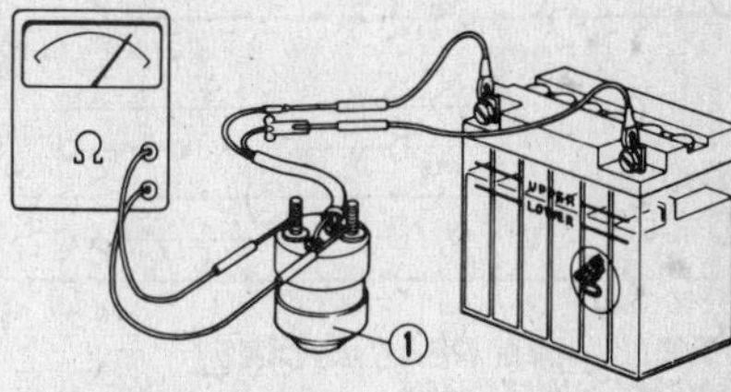

Testing the solenoid (1)

5. The primary cause of solenoid malfunction is pitting and/or burning of the contact points inside. It may be possible to restore a solenoid to serviceable condition by taking it apart and dressing the points with a file or emery paper. If this doesn't work, replace it.
6. If starter trouble began just after the starter button housing was dissembled or moved for any reason, check the connections at the switch as they may have come adrift.

ELECTRICAL COMPONENTS

Turn Signal Flasher

If none of the turn signals will flash, chances are that the turn signal flasher has failed. A Signal-Stat 142 flasher is used on the Fours and is located near the battery.

NOTE: *The flasher must be properly grounded to operate.*

Switches

TESTING AND REPLACEMENT PROCEDURES

The operation of any switch can be checked using a multi-tester or test light to determine the electrical continuity of the switch in its different positions. Follow the procedures given below for testing the individual switches. If, during any test, you find that electricity is available at the switch but the switch won't work, make sure that it is not simply a bad ground that is sabotaging it before you buy a replacement. Removal and installation procedures are given after the testing information, as it is not necessary to remove the switches in order to check them.

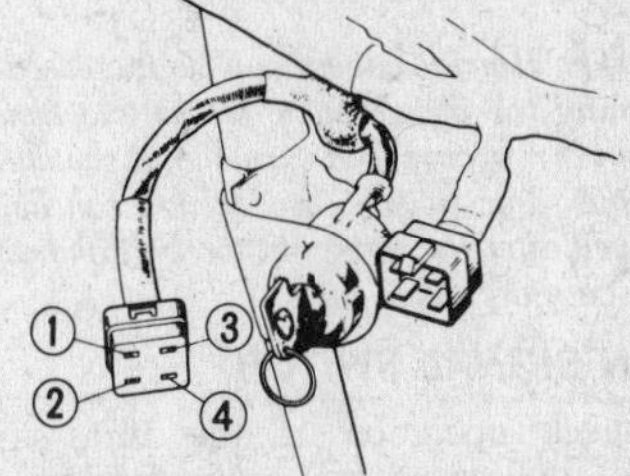

Main switch continuity test connections

IGNITION (MAIN) SWITCH

Pull the ignition switch connector apart and check continuity of the switch in its three positions using the accompanying chart as a guide. If any part of the test shows the switch to be faulty, the switch should be replaced.

The switch can be removed after the retaining nut has been unscrewed.

		BAT	IG	TL 1	TL 2
Wire Color		Red	Black	Brown/White	Brown
Key position	OFF				
	1	O	O	O	O
	2	O			O

FRONT AND REAR BRAKE LIGHT SWITCHES

The front brake light switch is located between the fork legs just under the headlight. To check its operation, connect the two test leads to the switch terminals, leaving the switch wires connected, and operate the front brake lever. If the tester does not show continuity as the brake is applied (ignition on), check to see if there is electricity at the switch power supply lead (black wire). If there is, replace the brake light switch. If there is not, check the continuity of the black wire between its connections at the brake light switch and ignition switch to determine if there is a loose connector, a short circuit, or a break in the wire.

The front brake light switch can be removed by pulling off the wires and unscrewing it. It may be necessary to bleed the brake after installation.

The rear switch may be tested in the same manner as the front switch. Make sure that it is not simply improperly adjusted and that the spring is strong enough to actuate it. Adjustment can be made by turning the large nut on the switch.

HORN BUTTON AND HORN

If the horn is not working, check to see if it is receiving electricity by connecting the tester between the light green wire at the horn and a good ground (such as the engine crankcase). Turn on the ignition and press the horn button. If the tester responds, the horn is faulty or is not properly grounded. If the tester does not respond, connect the tester lead to the light green wire in the headlight shell and press the horn button again (ignition on). If there is still no electricity available, replace the horn button. If there is electricity at the headlight shell but not at the horn, check the green wire for loose connections or a short circuit between the headlight and horn.

NOTE: *Horn loudness can be increased by turning the adjusting screw in (clockwise). The horn button and turn signal switch are in the same switch case, which can be removed after the screws in the bottom half of the case are taken out.*

TURN SIGNAL SWITCH

To check operation of the turn signal switch, pull apart the connectors for the orange, gray, and blue wires in the headlight shell. Check continuity of the switch in its three positions with a multitester or test light and battery, using the accompanying chart as a guide. (Be sure to connect the tester to the three wire ends leading to the switch, not the turn signal bulbs.) If any part of the test shows the switch to be faulty, it should be replaced.

Knob	Blue Lead	Gray Lead	Orange Lead
R	O	O	
OFF (center)			
L		O	O

To remove the switch, take out the screws at the bottom of the switch case and separate the upper and lower halves of the switch.

LIGHTING SWITCH

To check operation of the lighting switch, pull apart the connectors for the black, blue, brown/white, and white leads in the headlight shell. Check continuity of the switch in its different positions, using the accompanying chart as a guide. (Be sure to connect the tester to the three wire ends leading to the switch, not the lights. The brown/white wire is for the highbeam indicator light.) If any part of the test shows the switch to be faulty, it should be replaced. The switch can be removed after the screws in the bottom half of the case have been taken out.

Wire Color		IG Black	HB Blue	TL Brown/White	LB White
	H	O	O	O	
ON	P	O		O	
	L	O		O	O
OFF					

IGNITION KILL SWITCH

Check operation of the kill switch by pulling apart the connectors for the black and black/white wires in the headlight shell, and testing for continuity of the switch in both the "on" and "off" positions. Electrical continuity in either of the "off" positions, or *lack* of continuity in the "on" position, indicates a bad switch. (Be sure to connect the tester to the wire ends leading to the switch, and not to the ignition coil and ground.)

Ignition Kill Switch		
Wire Color	Black	Black/White
ON	O	O
OFF		

The switch can be removed after the screws in the bottom half of the case have been taken out.

STARTER BUTTON

Check operation of the starter button by connecting the tester between the yellow/red wire in the headlight shell and ground. Lack of continuity with the button depressed indicates a bad switch.

Starter Switch		
Wire Color	Ground	Yellow/Red
ON	O	O
OFF		

The switch can be removed after the screws in the bottom half of the case have been taken out.

OIL PRESSURE SWITCH

When oil pressure drops below approximately 4.3 psi on the 350/400, or 7 psi on the 500/550, the oil pressure switch closes, completing the ground circuit of the oil pressure warning light which will then light up. There is no power supplied to the oil pressure switch and it must be tested using equipment with its own power source such as a multimeter or test light and battery. Connect the meter leads to the oil pressure switch lead and to ground. If the tester does not respond, the switch has not closed and is defective. (The engine must not be running or else oil pressure will be too high to allow the switch to close.)

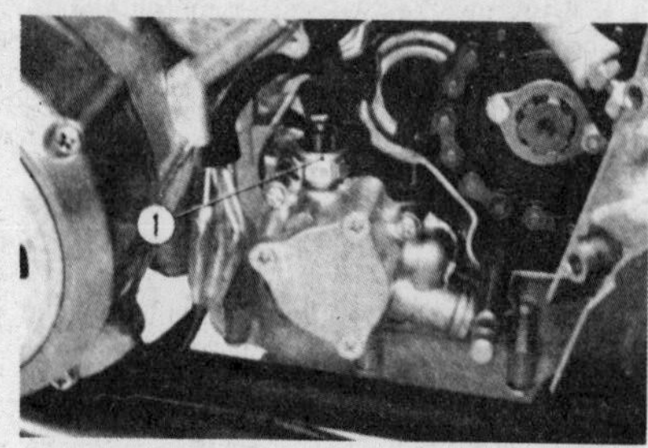

Oil pressure control switch location

The oil pressure switch is located on top of the oil pump. To remove, simply unscrew the switch unit after the lead has been disconnected.

NEUTRAL INDICATOR SWITCH

In the same manner as the oil pressure switch, the neutral indicator switch closes and completes the ground circuit to the neutral indicator light when the transmission is placed in neutral, at which time the light should go on. If it refuses to do this, connect a tester with its own power supply to the switch (with the transmission in Neutral) means that the switch should be replaced.

The switch is located on the left-side of the upper crankcase.

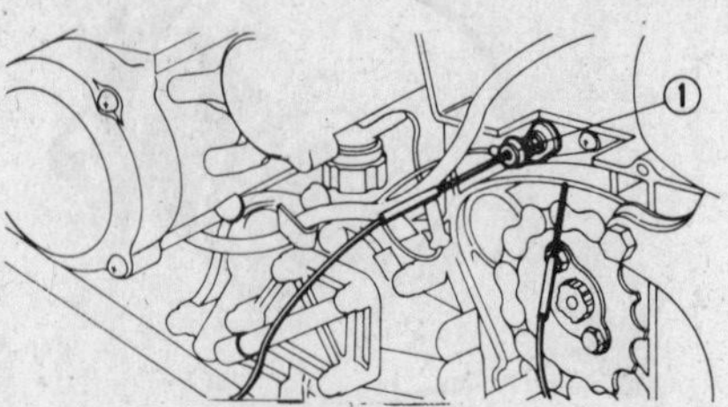

Neutral indicator switch location

WIRING DIAGRAMS

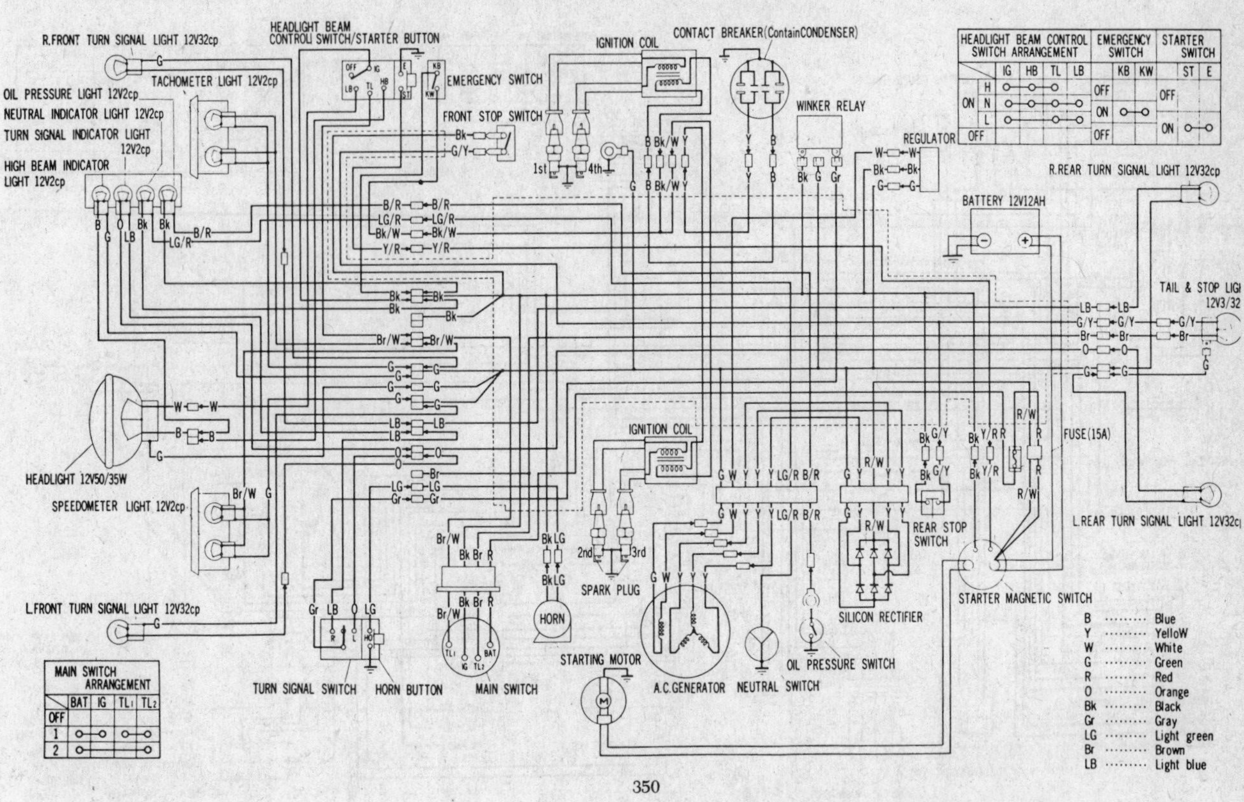

HEADLIGHT BEAM CONTROL SWITCH ARRANGEMENT		IG	HB	TL	LB
ON	H	o	o	o	
	N	o		o	o
	L	o		o	o
OFF					

EMERGENCY SWITCH	KB	KW
OFF		
ON	o	o
OFF		

STARTER SWITCH	ST	E
OFF		
ON	o	o

MAIN SWITCH ARRANGEMENT	BAT	IG	TL1	TL2
OFF				
1	o	o	o	o
2	o			o

350

R.FRONT TURN SIGNAL LIGHT & POSITION LIGHT 12V32 3cp 23 8W
IGNITION-STARTER SWITCH
SPEEDOMETER ILLUMINATING LIGHT 12V2cp 3.4W
MAIN SWITCH
INDICATOR LIGHT CLUSTER
R.TURN SIGNAL INDICATOR LIGHT 12V2cp 3.4W
HIGH BEAM INDICATOR LIGHT 12V2cp 3.4W
L.TURN SIGNAL INDICATOR LIGHT 12V2cp 3.4W
NEUTRAL INDICATOR LIGHT 12V2cp 3.4W
OIL PRESSURE INDICATOR LIGHT 12V2cp 3.4W
HEADLIGHT 12V50 35W
TACHOMETER ILLUMINATING LIGHT 12V2cp 3.4W
CLUTCH SWITCH
HEADLIGHT DIMMER TURN SIGNAL-HORN SWITCH
L.FRONT TURN SIGNAL LIGHT & POSITION LIGHT 12V32/3cp 23/8W
HORN
IGNITION COIL
SPARK PLUG
FRONT STOP SWITCH
CONTACT BREAKER & CONDENSER
GROUND (FRAME)
REAR STOP SWITCH
WINKER RELAY
SILICON RECTIFIER
FUSE BOX
FUSE 15A MAIN
FUSE 7A HEADLIGHT
FUSE 7A TAIL LIGHT
R.REAR TURN SIGNAL LIGHT 12V32cp(23W)
TAIL & STOP LIGHT 12V3/32cp 8/27W
POINTLESS REGULATOR
SILICON RECTIFIER
STARTING MOTOR
ALTERNATOR
OIL PRESSURE SWITCH
NEUTRAL SWITCH
STARTER MAGNETIC SWITCH
BATTERY 12V12AH
L.REAR TURN SIGNAL LIGHT 12V32cp 23W
TURN SIGNAL-HORN-HEADLIGHT DIMMER SWITCH ARRANGEMENT
MAIN SWITCH ARRANGEMENT
IGNITION-STARTER SWITCH ARRANGEMENT

G Green
R Red
W White
Br Brown
Bk Black
LG Light Green
Y Yellow
B Blue
O Orange
Gr Grey
LB Light Blue

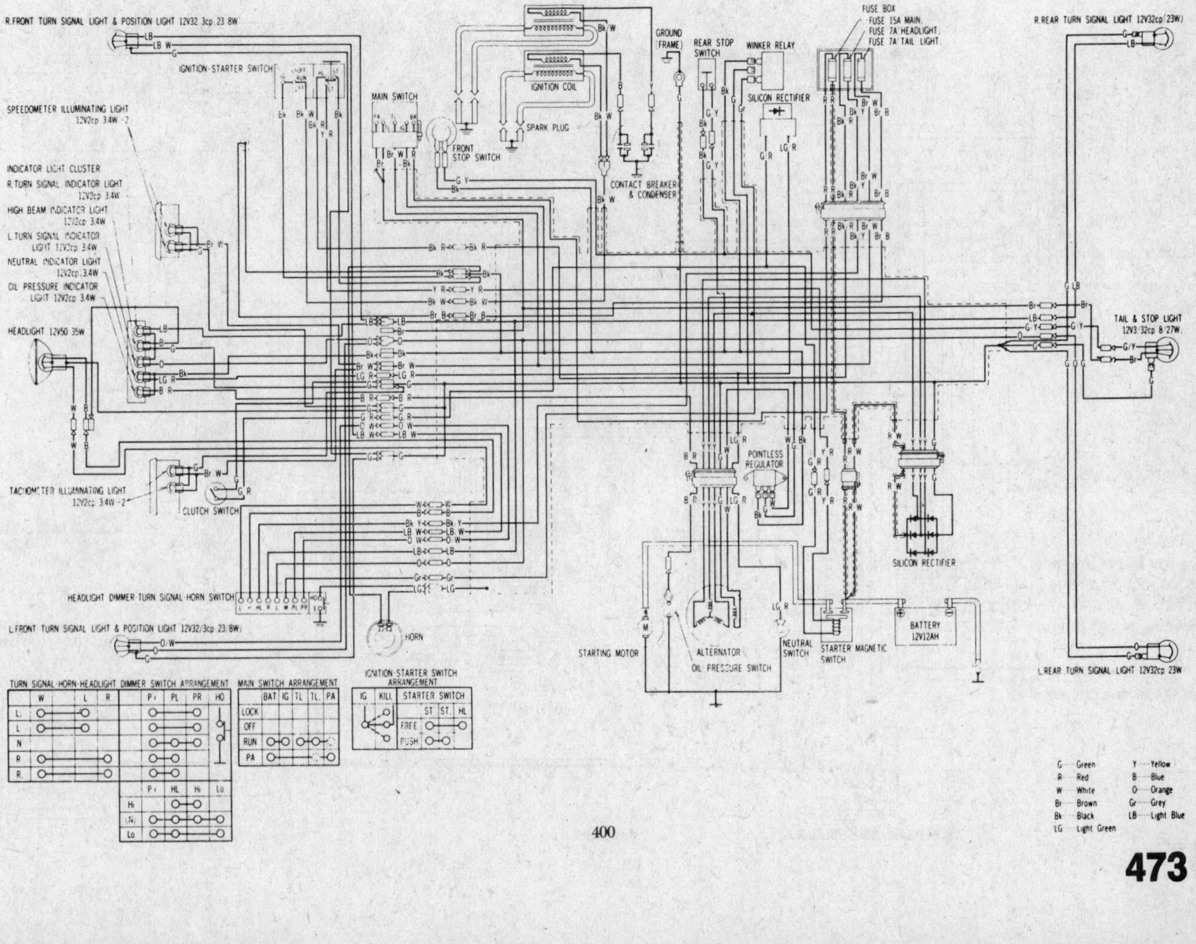

400

WIRING DIAGRAMS

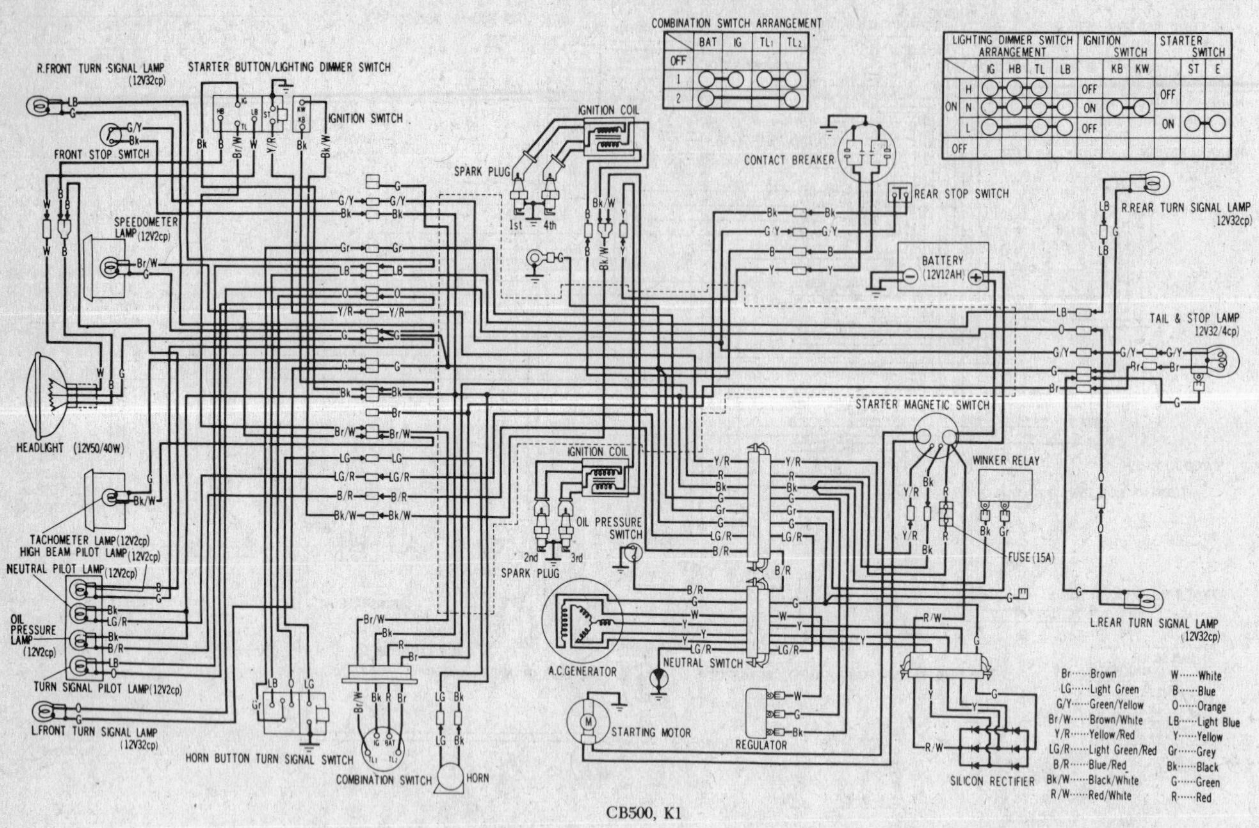

CB500, K1

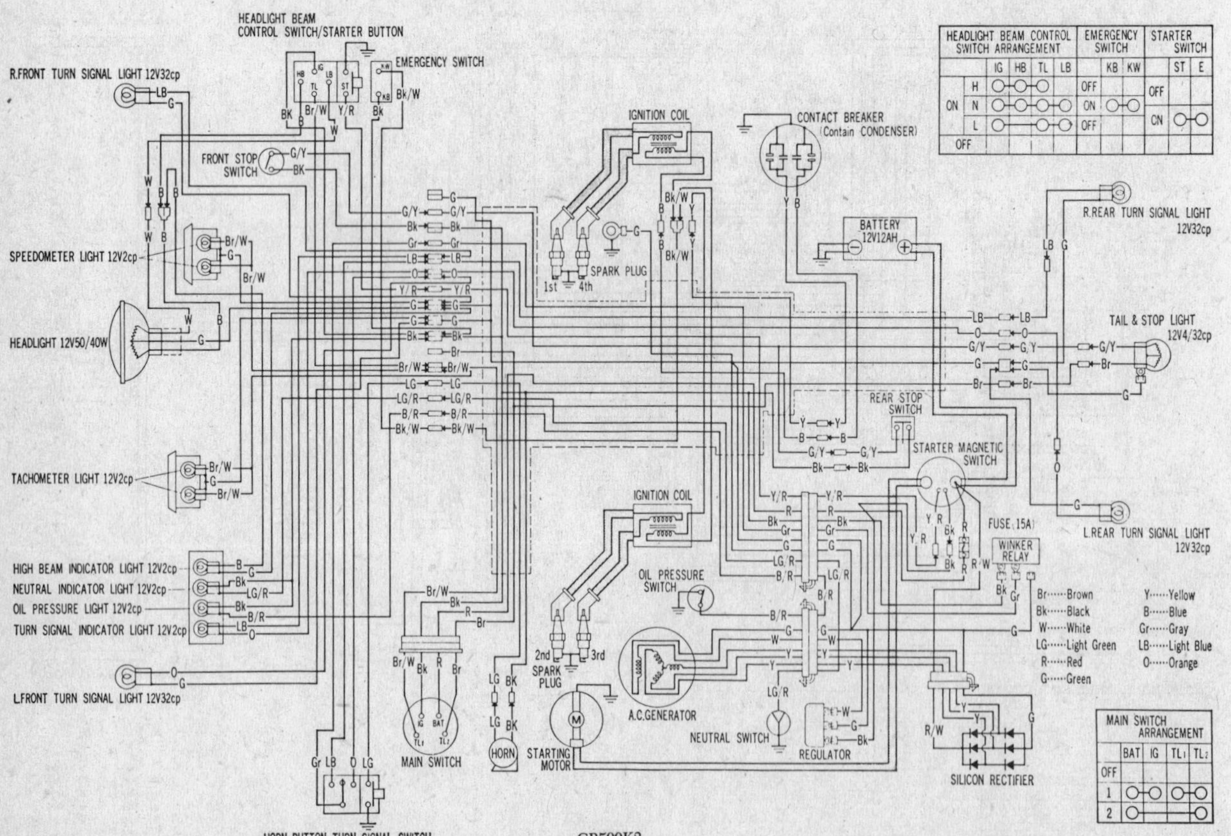

CB500K2

WIRING DIAGRAMS

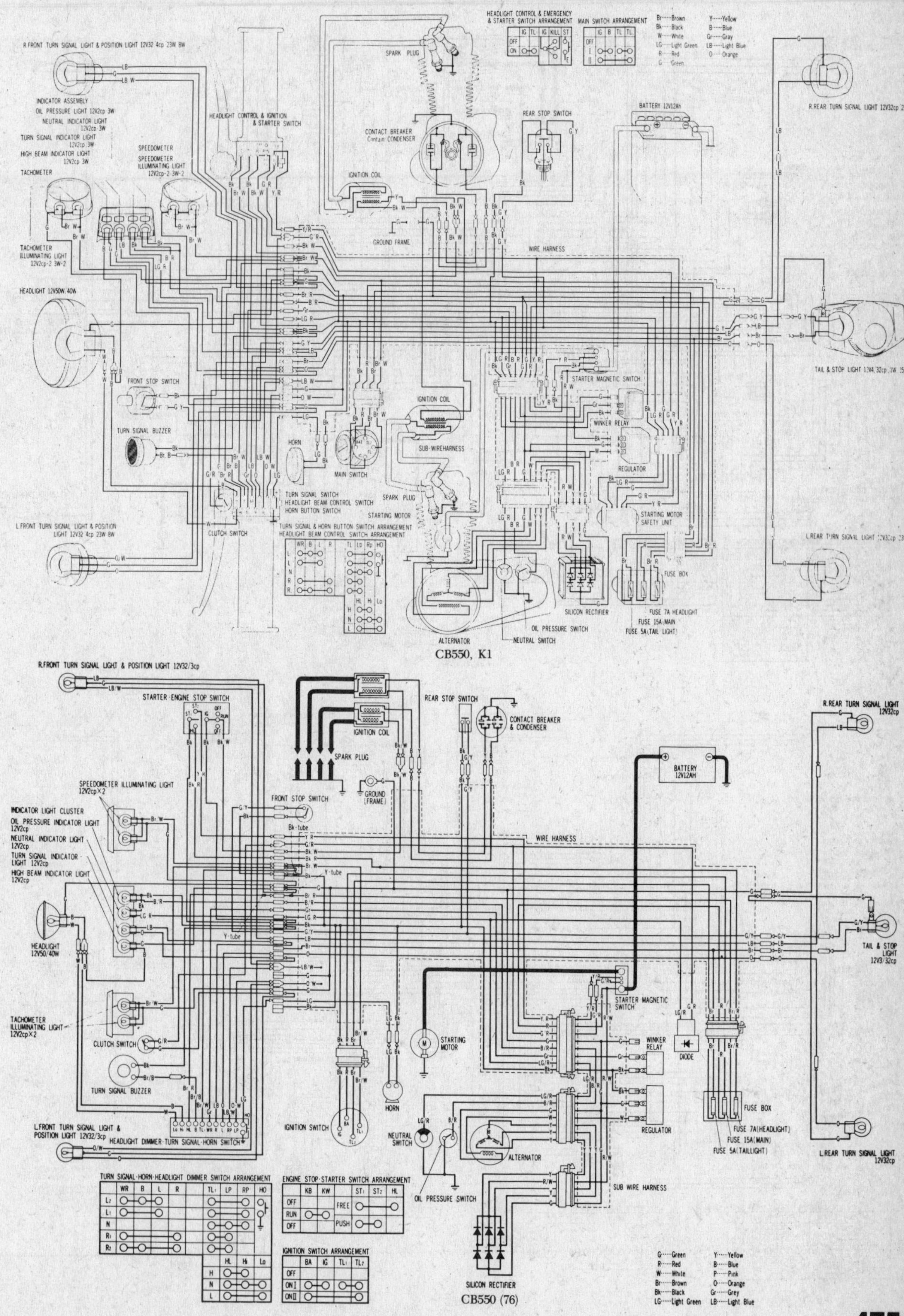

CB550, K1

CB550 (76)

WIRING DIAGRAMS

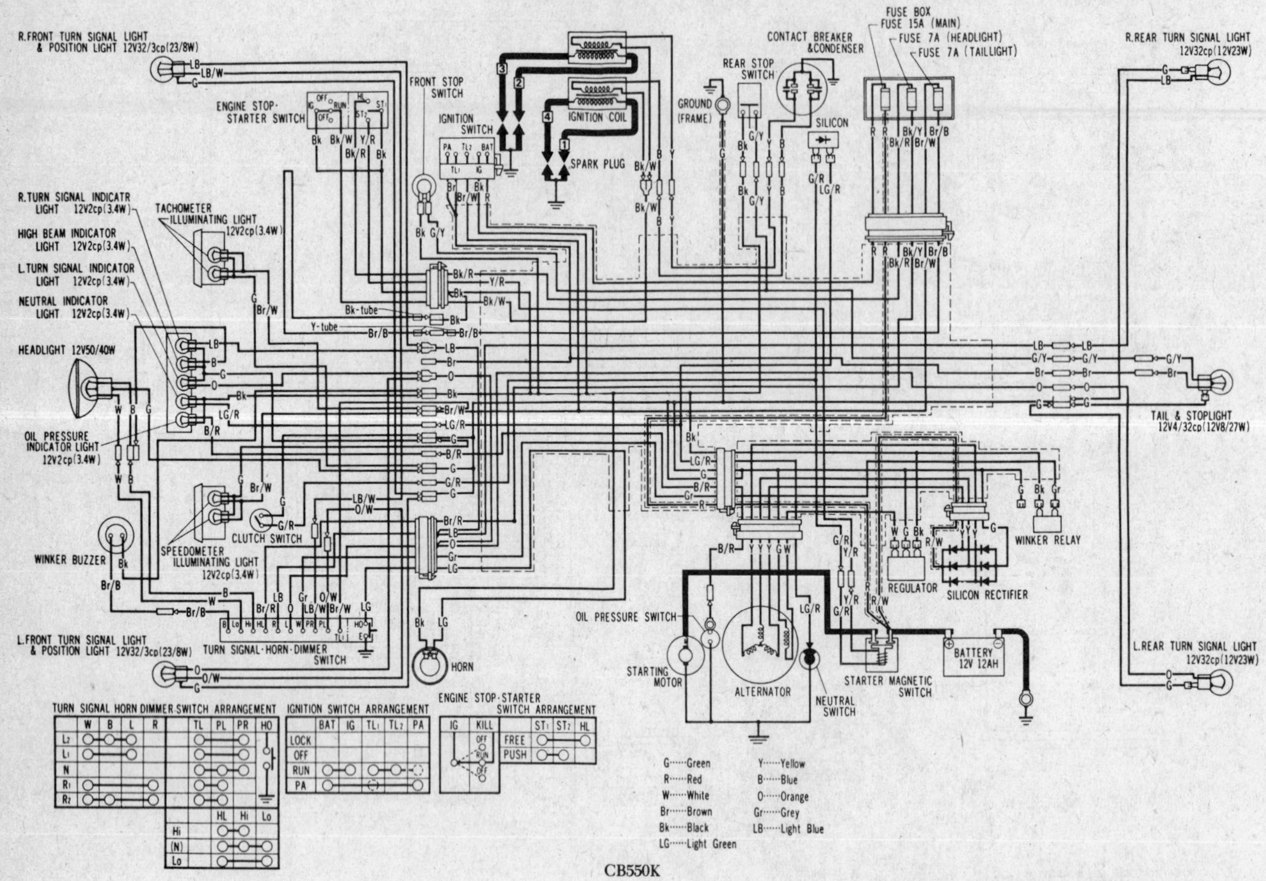

R.FRONT TURN SIGNAL LIGHT & POSITION LIGHT 12V32/3cp(23/8W)
ENGINE STOP-STARTER SWITCH
FRONT STOP SWITCH
IGNITION SWITCH
IGNITION COIL
SPARK PLUG
GROUND (FRAME)
REAR STOP SWITCH
CONTACT BREAKER &CONDENSER
FUSE BOX
FUSE 15A (MAIN)
FUSE 7A (HEADLIGHT)
FUSE 7A (TAILLIGHT)
SILICON
R.REAR TURN SIGNAL LIGHT 12V32cp(12V23W)
R.TURN SIGNAL INDICATR LIGHT 12V2cp(3.4W)
TACHOMETER ILLUMINATING LIGHT 12V2cp(3.4W)
HIGH BEAM INDICATOR LIGHT 12V2cp(3.4W)
L.TURN SIGNAL INDICATOR LIGHT 12V2cp(3.4W)
NEUTRAL INDICATOR LIGHT 12V2cp(3.4W)
HEADLIGHT 12V50/40W
Bk-tube
Y-tube
OIL PRESSURE INDICATOR LIGHT 12V2cp(3.4W)
TAIL & STOPLIGHT 12V4/32cp(12V8/27W)
WINKER BUZZER
SPEEDOMETER ILLUMINATING LIGHT 12V2cp(3.4W)
CLUTCH SWITCH
WINKER RELAY
REGULATOR
SILICON RECTIFIER
OIL PRESSURE SWITCH
STARTING MOTOR
ALTERNATOR
NEUTRAL SWITCH
STARTER MAGNETIC SWITCH
BATTERY 12V 12AH
L.FRONT TURN SIGNAL LIGHT & POSITION LIGHT 12V32/3cp(23/8W)
TURN SIGNAL-HORN-DIMMER SWITCH
HORN
L.REAR TURN SIGNAL LIGHT 12V32cp(12V23W)
TURN SIGNAL HORN DIMMER SWITCH ARRANGEMENT
IGNITION SWITCH ARRANGEMENT
ENGINE STOP-STARTER SWITCH ARRANGEMENT
G······Green
R······Red
W······White
Br······Brown
Bk······Black
LG······Light Green
Y······Yellow
B······Blue
O······Orange
Gr······Grey
LB······Light Blue

CB550K

R.FRONT TURN SIGNAL LIGHT & POSITION LIGHT 12V32.3cp 23 8W
CONTACT BREAKER & CONDENSER
FUSE BOX
FUSE 15A MAIN
FUSE 7A HEADLIGHT
FUSE 7A TAILLIGHT
R.REAR TURN SIGNAL LIGHT 12V32cp 23W
GROUND FRAME
REAR STOP SWITCH
ENGINE STOP-STARTER SWITCH
FRONT STOP SWITCH
IGNITION SWITCH
IGNITION COIL
SPARK PLUG
SILICON RECTIFIER
SPEEDOMETER ILLUMINATING LIGHT 12V2cp 3.4W ×2
INDICATOR LIGHT CLUSTER
R.TURN SIGNAL INDICATOR LIGHT 12V2cp 3.4W
HIGH BEAM INDICATOR LIGHT 12V2cp 3.4W
L.TURN SIGNAL INDICATOR LIGHT 12V2cp(3.4W)
NEUTRAL INDICATOR LIGHT 12V2cp(3.4W)
OIL PRESSURE INDICATOR LIGHT 12V2cp(3.4W)
G······Green
R······Red
W······White
Br······Brown
Bk······Black
LG······Light Green
Y······Yellow
B······Blue
P······Pink
O······Orange
Gr······Grey
LB······Light Blue
Bk-tube
Y-tube
TAIL & STOP LIGHT 12V4/32cp(8/27W
HEADLIGHT 12V50/40W
TURN SIGNAL BUZZER
CLUTCH SWITCH
TACHOMETER ILLUMINATING LIGHT 12V2cp 3.4W ×2
WINKER RELAY
SILICON RECTIFIER
POINTLESS REGULATOR
HEADLIGHT DIMMER-TURN SIGNAL-HORN SWITCH
L.FRONT TURN SIGNAL LIGHT & POSITION LIGHT 12V32/3cp(23/8W)
HORN
STARTING MOTOR
ALTERNATOR
OIL PRESSURE SWITCH
NEUTRAL SWITCH
STARTER MAGNETIC SWITCH
BATTERY 12V12AH
L.REAR TURN SIGNAL LIGHT 12V32cp 23W
TURN SIGNAL-HORN-HEADLIGHT DIMMER SWITCH ARRANGEMENT
IGNITION SWITCH ARRANGEMENT
ENGINE STOP-STARTER SWITCH ARRANGEMENT

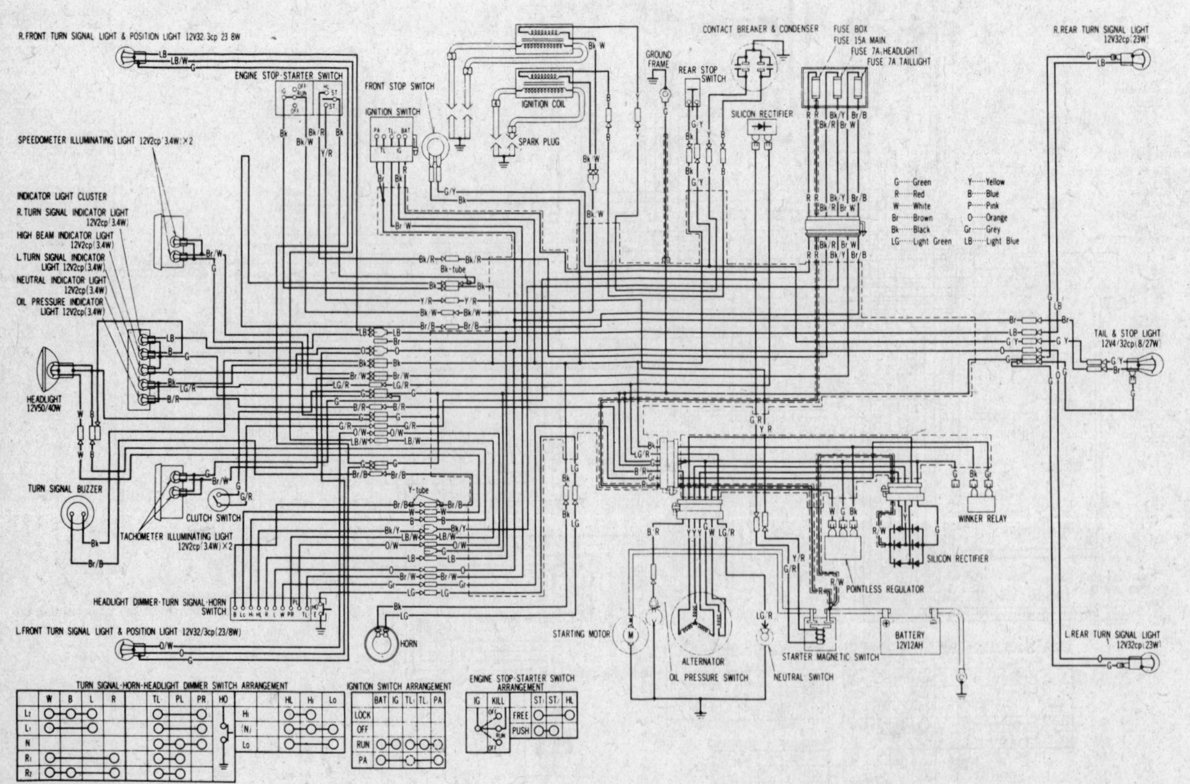

CB550F

WIRING DIAGRAMS

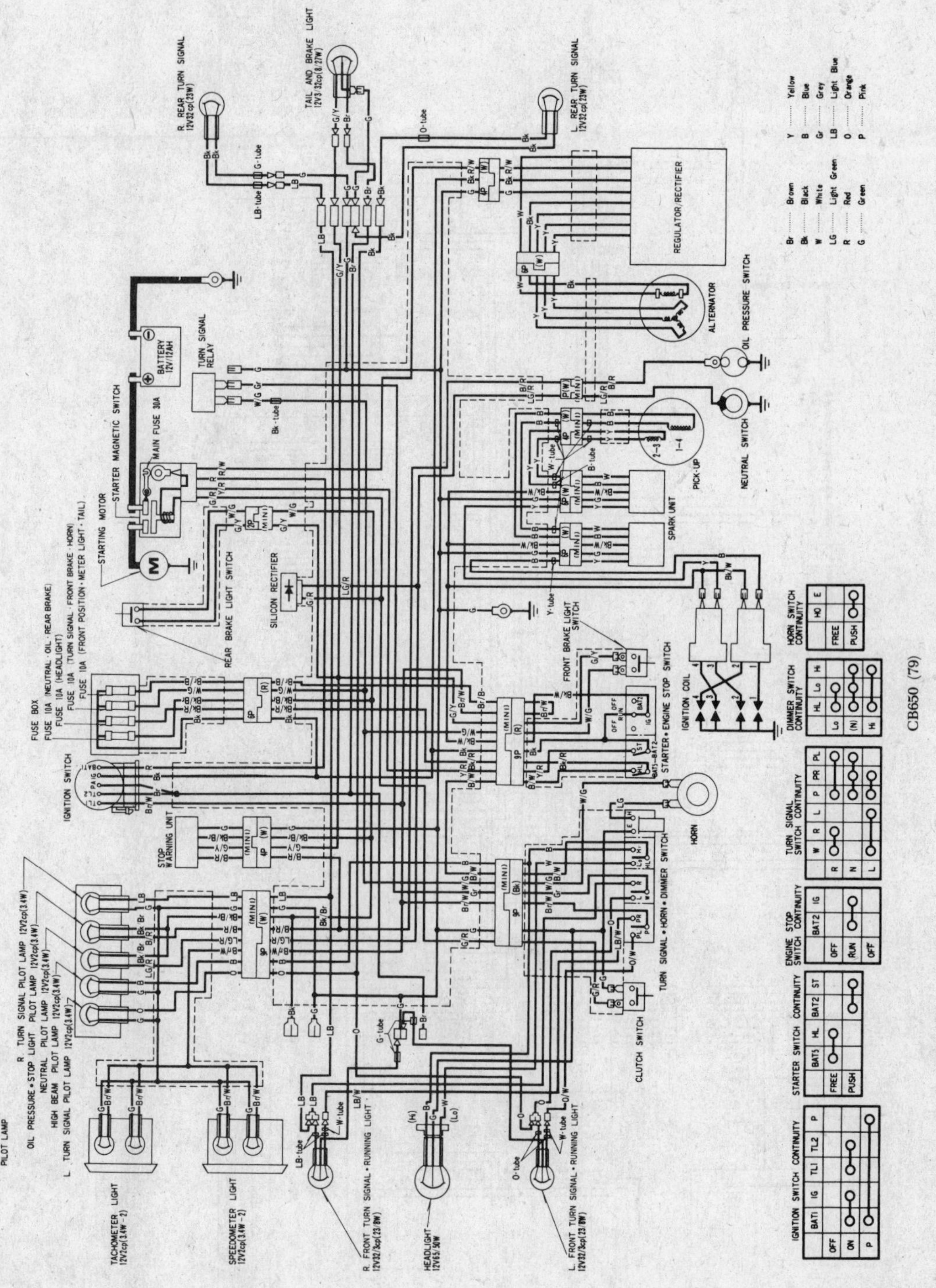

CB650 ('79)

WIRING DIAGRAMS

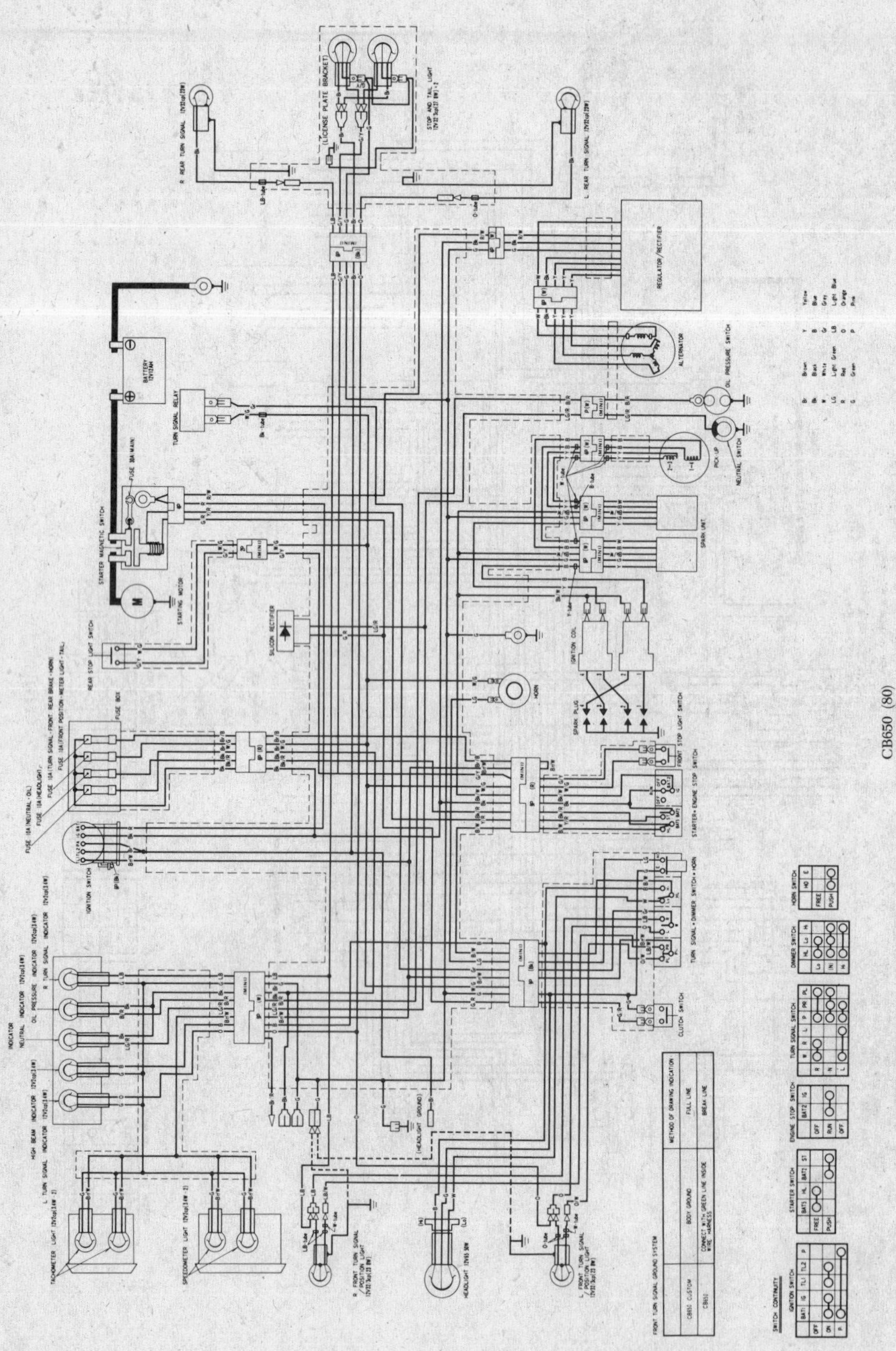

WIRING DIAGRAMS

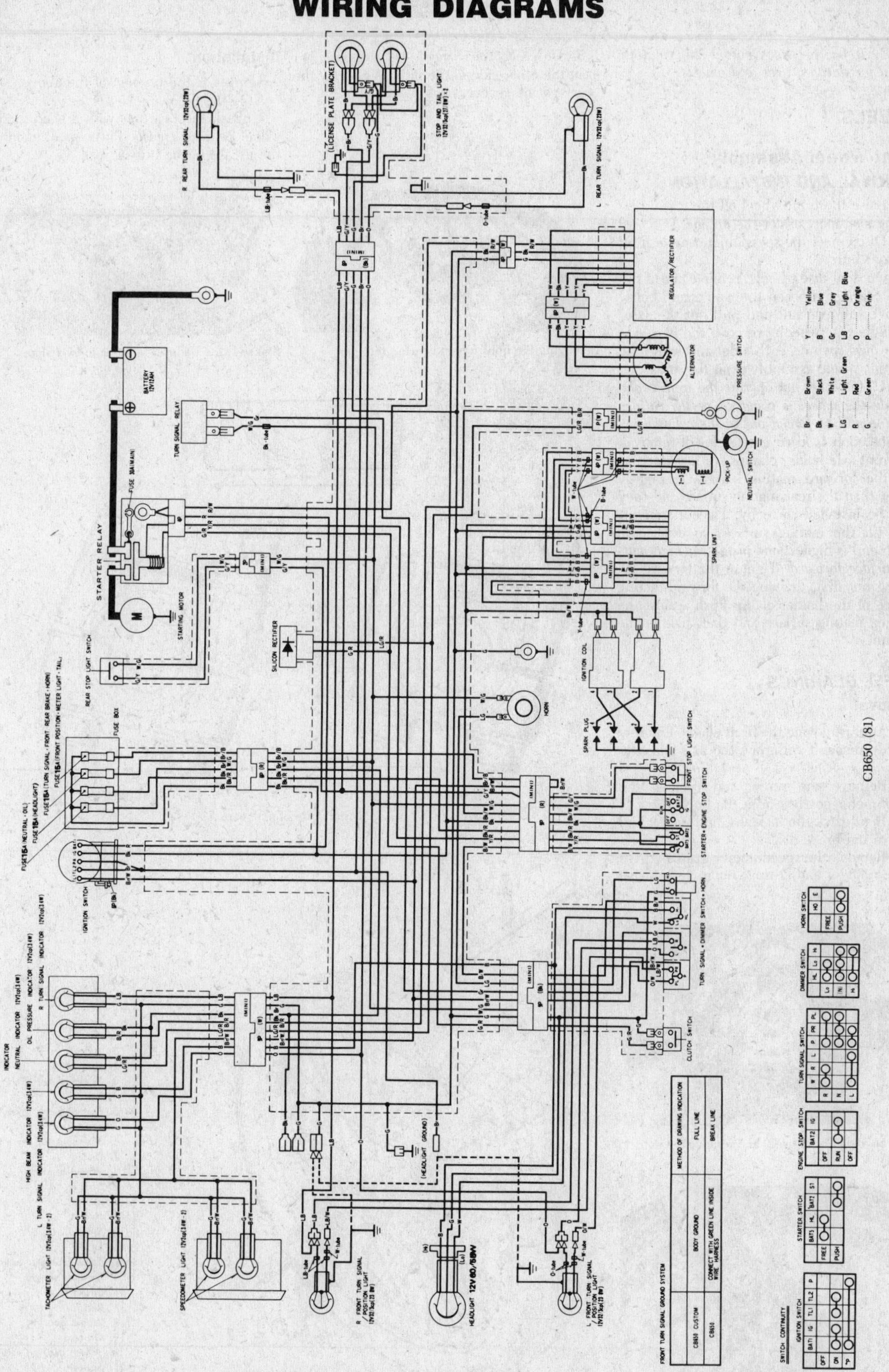

CHASSIS

NOTE: *Refer to the General Information section for data on tires and wheels.*

WHEELS

Front Wheel Assembly

REMOVAL AND INSTALLATION

1. Raise the front wheel off the ground by placing a support under the engine.
2. Disconnect the speedometer cable from the front hub.
3. On dual-disc wheels, remove one of the brake calipers. Loosen the axle clamp bolts. Remove the axle nut and pull out the axle. On single-disc wheels, remove the four axle clamp nuts (two on each side) and withdraw the front wheel assembly from the forks.

CAUTION: *Do not operate the front brake while the wheel is removed or the caliper piston will be forced out of the cylinder.*

Installation is in reverse order of removal. The front axle holder clamps are machined so that the forward mating surface is slightly higher than the rear mating surface and they must be installed correctly. Place a straightedge on the mating surfaces to determine which end is higher, and *install the high mating surface forward.* Tighten the forward retaining nut first, drawing the forward mating surface of the holder clamp flush against the fork leg mating surface and then tighten the rear nut.

WHEEL BEARINGS

Removal

1. After removing the front wheel, unscrew the axle nut and withdraw the axle and axle collar.
2. Remove the screw and remove the speedometer gearbox from the hub.
3. Bend back the locktabs, and unbolt and remove the brake disc.
4. Remove the speedometer gearbox drive flange retainer and O-ring. Remove the drive flange.

Bend back the locktabs (2) and remove the nuts (1) to remove the disc

Using a bearing driver (1) to install a bearing

5. Unscrew the wheel bearing retainer from the other side of the hub. Withdraw the bearings and spacer.

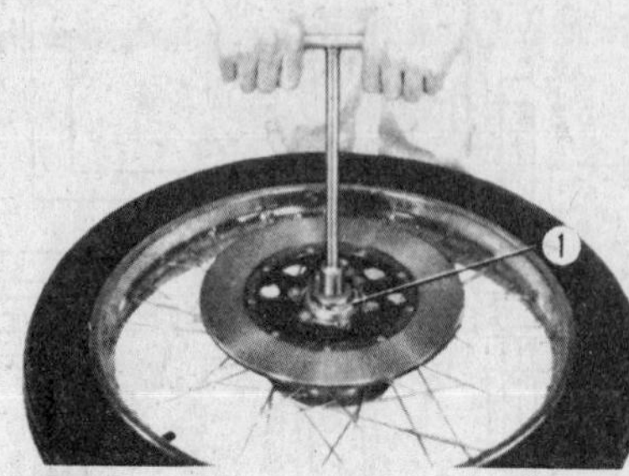

Removing the front wheel bearing retainer

Installation

Assembly is the reverse of the above.

Note the following:

1. Pack the bearings with a good grade of wheel bearing grease. Put a small handful of the grease in the hub as well.

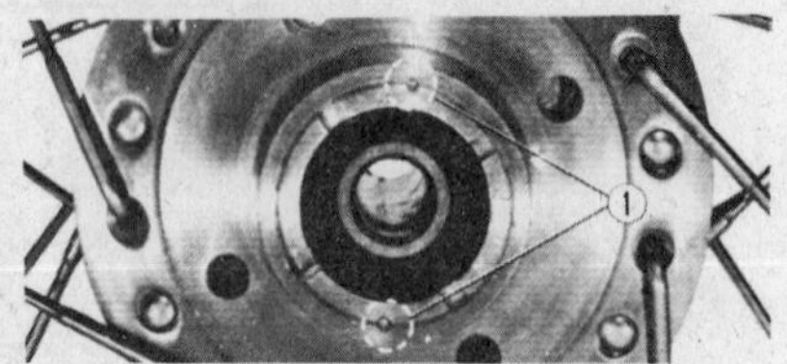

Stake (1) the bearing retainer in two places

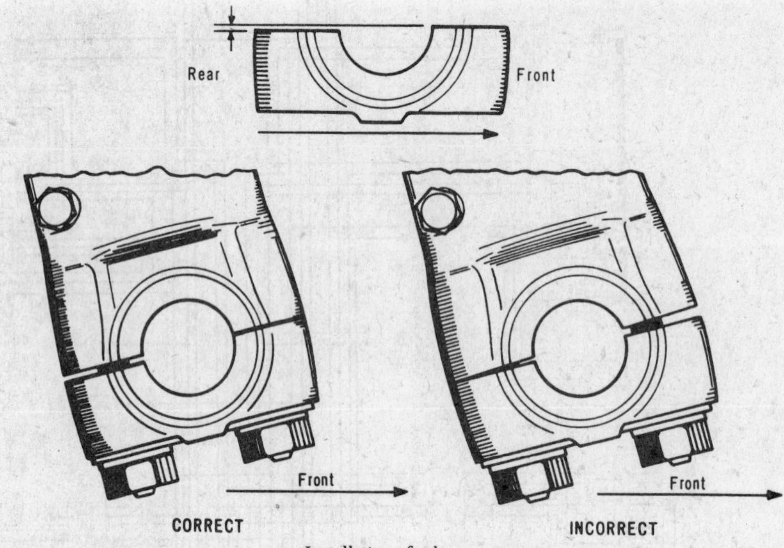

Installation of axle caps

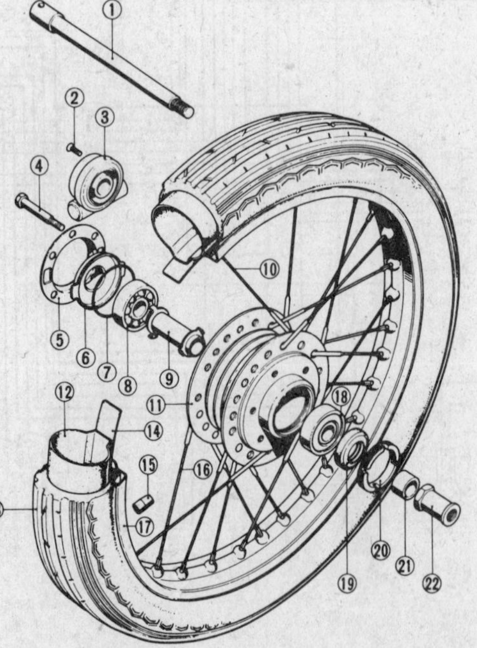

1. Axle
2. Screw
3. Speedometer drive
4. Bolt
5. Speedometer drive flange retainer
6. Speedometer drive flange
7. O-ring
8. Wheel bearing
9. Spacer
10. Spoke
11. Hub
12. Tube
13. Tire
14. Tube protector band
15. Balance weight
16. Spoke
17. Rim
18. Wheel bearing
19. Oil seal
20. Wheel bearing retainer
21. Spacer
22. Axle nut

Front wheel assembly (500)

2. Do not forget to install the spacer in the hub before installing the bearing.

3. Bearings may be driven into place using the Honda service tool or a suitable substitute such as the front axle.

4. Use a new oil seal and lubricate it with oil to make installation into the bearing retainer easier.

Install the O-ring (2) before fitting the speedometer drive cover (1)

Bend up the locking tab of the tongued washers (1)

5. Stake the bearing retainer in two places after it is installed.

6. Do not forget to replace the O-ring behind the speedometer drive flange.

7. On dual-disc wheels, tighten the axle nut to 40–47 ft. lbs. Tighten the caliper mounting bolts to 22–29 ft. lbs.

Measure the gap between the left disc and the left caliper holder. It should be 0.7 mm/ 0.028 in. If it isn't, pull the left fork slider out until the gap is correct, then tighten the axle pinch bolt to 11–18 ft. lbs.

Rear Wheel Assembly

REMOVAL AND INSTALLATION

1. Place the machine on the center stand. On 350 and 500 models, remove the mufflers.

2. Remove the rear brake adjuster nut and separate the brake rod from the lever.

3. Disconnect the brake anchor from the hub by removing the lockpin and unscrewing the nut and bolt.

4. Loosen the chain adjuster bolt on both sides. Remove the cotter pin and loosen the axle nut.

Rear wheel axle mounting and chain adjusters (500)

1. Cotter pin
2. Axle nut
3. Adjuster bolt
4. Adjuster bolt locknut
5. Swing arm pinch-bolt
6. Stopper

5. Push the wheel forward and lift the chain off the rear sprocket.

6. Remove the lockbolts and chain adjuster stop plates. Withdraw the wheel rearward from the swing arm.

Installation is in reverse order of removal. Adjust the chain so that there is ½–¾ in. slack at the midpoint of the run. Brake pedal freeplay should be 1 in. (25 mm). Tighten the axle nut to 58–72 ft lbs.

WHEEL BEARINGS

Removal

1. After removing the rear wheel, remove the axle from the hub.

2. On 350/400 models, remove the hub circlip and tap the sprocket assembly out of the hub.

Removing the sprocket from the hub (350/400)

3. On 500/550 models, bend down the locktabs and remove the sprocket nuts to take off the sprocket.

4. On 650 models, loosen the sprocket nuts, remove the flange from the hub, and tap the assembly out of the hub.

5. Unscrew the bearing retainer and drive the bearings out of the hub.

NOTE: *On 500/550 models, the bearing retainer has a left-hand thread.*

Installation

Reverse the removal procedure. Note the following:

1. Pack the bearings with wheel bearing grease. Place a small handful in the hub as well.

2. Do not forget the bearing spacer.

3. The bearings may be driven into place with the Honda tool or a suitable substitute.

4. Use a threat-locking compound on the bearing retainer.

BRAKES

Front Disc (350–550)

PAD REPLACEMENT

1. Check the pads for wear by noting the red wear indicator line inscribed on them. Replace the pads as a set when either is worn close to this red line.

2. Remove the front wheel. Remove the two bolts from the side of the caliper and remove the right-side caliper half.

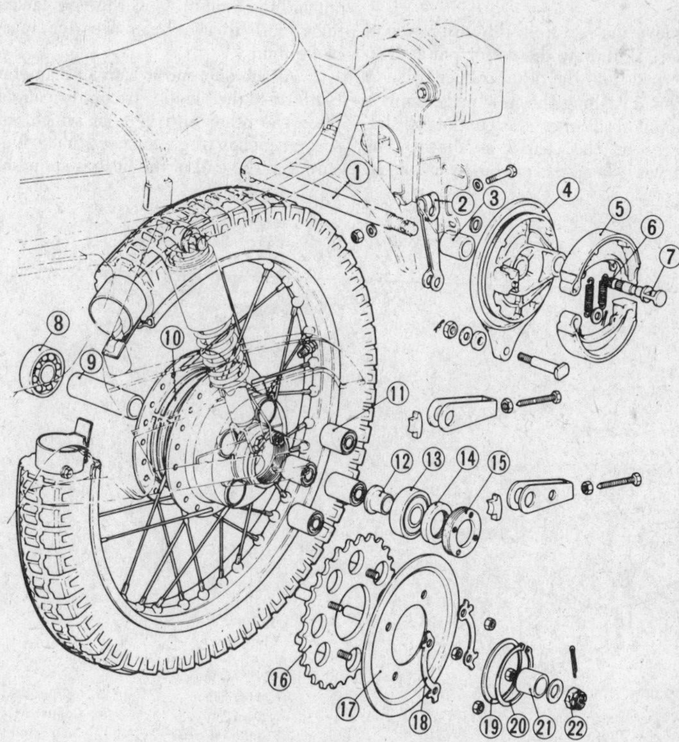

Rear wheel and brake assembly (350/400)

1. Rear axle
2. Brake arm
3. Collar
4. Brake backing plate
5. Brake shoe
6. Brake shoe spring
7. Brake cam
8. Wheel bearing
9. Spacer
10. Hub
11. Damper
12. Spacer
13. Wheel bearing
14. Dust seal
15. Bearing retainer
16. Rear sprocket
17. Sprocket plate
18. Lockwasher
19. Washer
20. Circlip
21. Spacer
22. Axle nut

Remove the caliper bolts (1) to separate the caliper halves

Removing the piston side pad (2) from the caliper half (1)

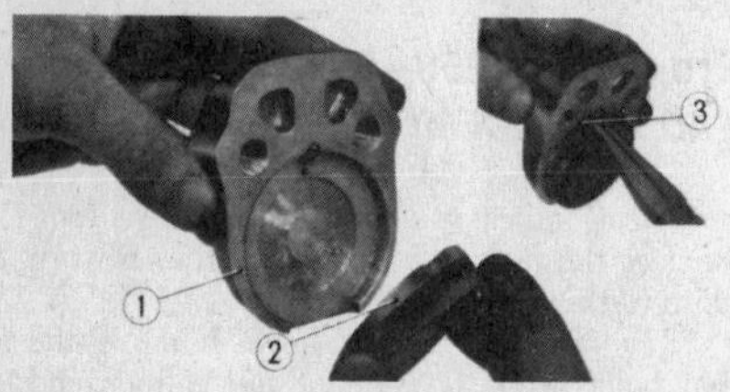

The cotter pin (3) holds the fixed pad (2) in the caliper half (1)

3. Remove the pad from the piston side of the caliper. Withdraw the cotter pin and remove the pad from the other caliper half.

4. Before installing the new pads, apply a small amount of silicone grease to the pad sliding surfaces on the caliper as shown. The grease serves to keep pad operation smooth by

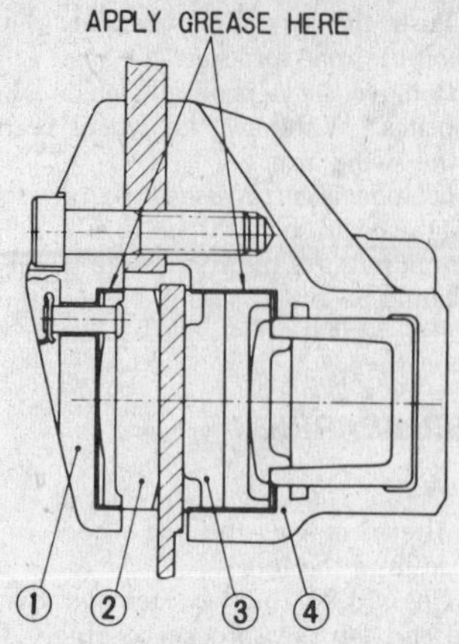

When fitting pads (2 and 3) into the caliper halves (1 and 4), lightly grease the assemblies as shown

repelling dust and water as well as providing lubrication. Use grease sparingly and do not allow it to contact the pad friction material.

5. Install the new pads in the caliper halves and bolt the caliper together.

6. Install the front wheel, and adjust the caliper as outlined in the "Maintenance" chapter. Avoid hard application of the brake for about fifty miles to aid seating of the pads.

BLEEDING

1. Top up the reservoir with brake fluid and replace the cap to keep dirt and moisture out and the fluid in. Cover the gas tank with a thick cloth to avoid damage due to spilled brake fluid.

2. Attach one end of a small diameter rubber hose to the bleed valve on the caliper, and place the other end in a jar which contains several inches of clean, new brake fluid. Be sure that the end of the hose is submerged in this fluid. Arrange the hose so that it loops upward after leaving the bleed valve, and see that it has no kinks or sharp bends.

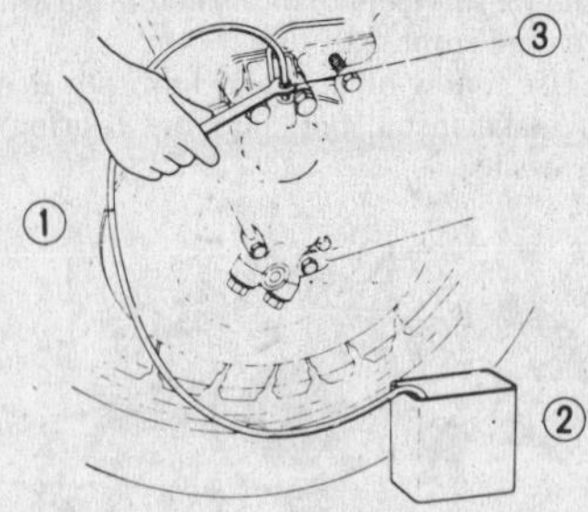

Attach a bleeder hose (1) to the bleed valve (3), and run the hose into a container (2), immersing the hose end in clean brake fluid

3. Pump the brake lever rapidly several times until some resistance is felt and, holding the lever against the resistance, open the bleed valve about one-half turn. When the lever bottoms, close the valve (do not overtighten) and then release the lever.

4. Repeat this operation until no more air is released out of the hose and the brake lever is firm in operation. Check the fluid level in the reservoir often to make sure that it doesn't go dry and draw more air into the system. Do not reuse fluid that has been pumped out of the system. Do not use fluid that has been stored for more than a few weeks after the seal on its container has been opened, as brake fluid will absorb moisture from the air and may corrode the master cylinder and caliper. Be sure to refill the reservoir to the level mark (do not overfill) when through. Avoid overtightening the cap or fluid will weep around the cap edge.

CALIPER

Leakage of brake fluid from around the caliper piston indicates that the caliper assembly is worn or damaged and the cause should be investigated immediately. To remove, inspect, and rebuild the caliper assembly:

1. Remove the front wheel.
2. Unscrew the hydraulic line connection at the caliper and catch the fluid that drains from the line in a suitable container and dispose of it. (Do not reuse old brake fluid.)
3. Unscrew the three caliper mounting

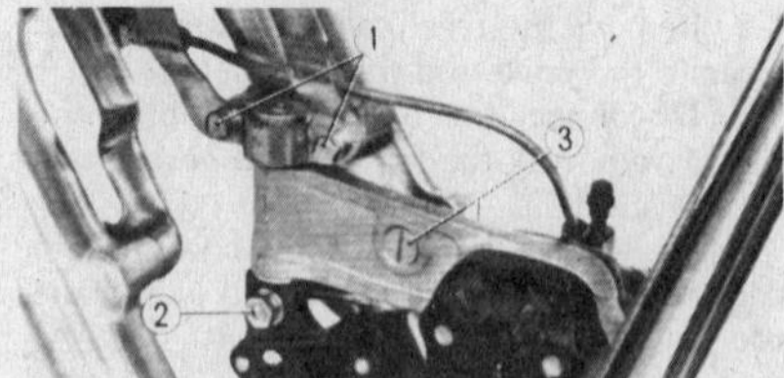

Caliper mounting bolts (1 and 2) and adjusting screw (3) locations

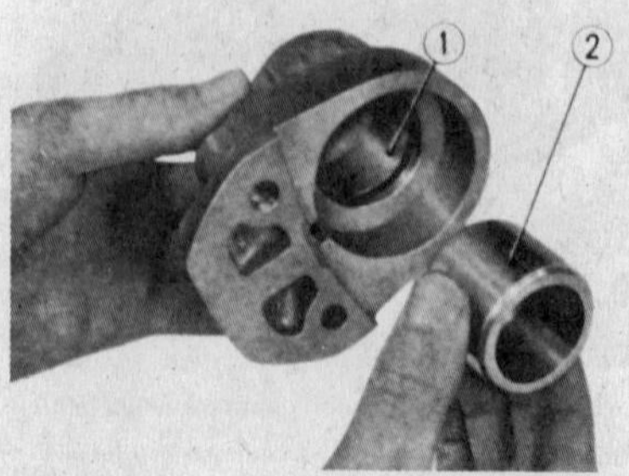

Removing the piston (2) from the caliper half (1)

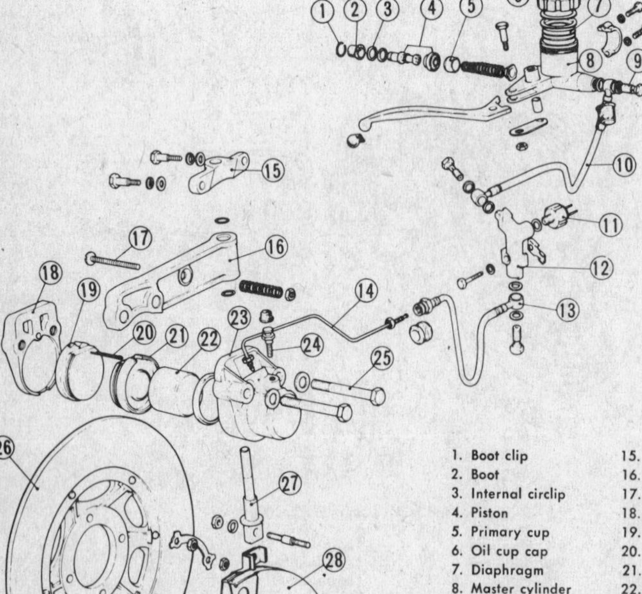

1. Boot clip
2. Boot
3. Internal circlip
4. Piston
5. Primary cup
6. Oil cup cap
7. Diaphragm
8. Master cylinder
9. Oil bolt
10. Front brake hose
11. Stop switch
12. 3-way joint
13. Front brake hose
14. Front brake pipe
15. Caliper holder joint
16. Caliper holder
17. Caliper adjust bolt
18. Caliper half (inner)
19. Pad (inner)
20. Cotter pin
21. Pad (outer)
22. Piston
23. Caliper half (outer)
24. Bleeder valve
25. Caliper securing bolts
26. Front brake disc
27. Caliper holder
28. Disc cover

Disc brake assembly

bolts at the left fork leg and remove the caliper.

4. Remove the two bolts and separate the caliper halves.

5. Remove the pad seat from the caliper piston and withdraw the piston.

6. Remove the seal from the cylinder using a plastic or wood instrument to avoid damaging the bore.

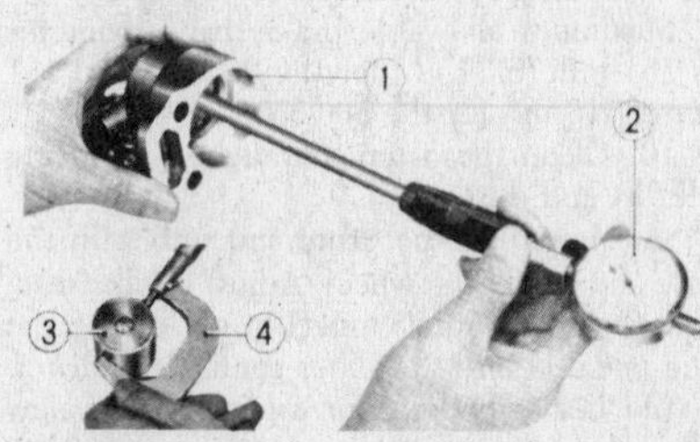

Measuring the piston bore (1) and piston (3) with micrometer (2 and 4)

7. Examine the cylinder bore and piston surface for scoring and pitting, and replace if damaged. Cylinder bore diameter should not exceed 38.215 mm (1.504 in.) and piston diameter should not be less than 38.105 mm (1.500 in.). Maximum calculated clearance between the piston and cylinder is 0.115 mm (0.0045 in.). Replace parts as necessary. Clean all components and dry with compressed air.

8. Use a new seal in the cylinder bore and lubricate it thoroughly with fresh brake fluid before installing. Make sure that it is seated properly in its groove.

9. Lubricate the piston with brake fluid and install it in the cylinder. Be careful not to twist the seal or force it out of the groove. Install the pad seat on the piston.

10. Reinstall the brake pads in the caliper halves. Use new pads if the old ones have been in contact with brake fluid.

11. Bolt the caliper halves together and remount the caliper assembly on the fork leg.

12. Connect the hydraulic line and replace the front wheel.

13. Bleed and adjust the brake. Refer to the appropriate headings in this section.

MASTER CYLINDER

Brake fluild leakage around the brake lever and excessive lever travel (after bleeding the brake to make sure that there is no air trapped in the hydraulic system) are indications of master cylinder malfunction. The rebuilding procedure is as follows.

NOTE: *Be very careful, when removing and replacing the master cylinder, in filling the reservoir. Brake fluid can damage paint and plastic, and extreme care should be exercised in its handling. Wipe up any spills immediately.*

1. Place a cloth underneath the connection to absorb any spilled fluid and disconnect the brake hose from the master cylinder.

2. Unscrew the clamp bolts and remove the master cylinder from the handlebar. Unscrew the reservoir cap and discard the brake fluid.

3. Remove the rubber boot. Remove the snap-ring and withdraw the washer, piston, secondary cup, primary cup, spring and check valve.

4. Check the cylinder bore for scoring and pitting, and measure the wear using a dial indicator. Bore diameter should not exceed 14.055 mm (0.553 in.). Replace the master cylinder assembly if damaged or worn.

5. Clean all components in solvent and dry with compressed air.

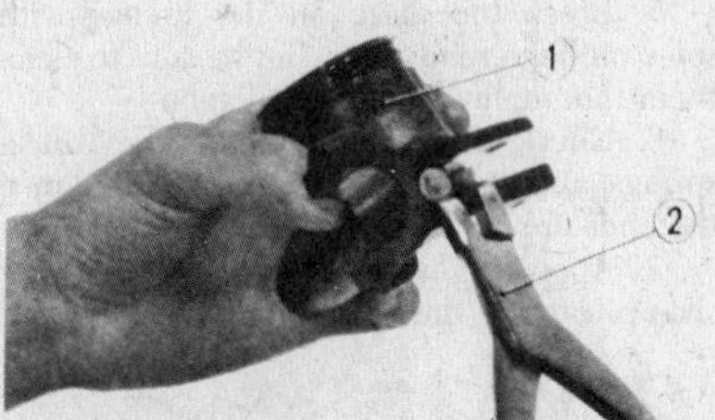

Removing the snap-ring from the master cylinder (1) with snap-ring pliers (2)

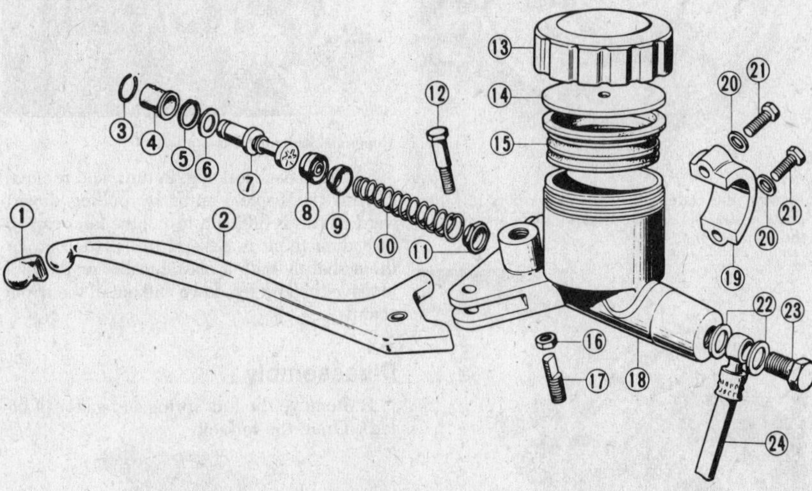

Master cylinder assembly

1. **Lever cap**
2. **Brake lever**
3. **Retainer washer**
4. **Boot**
5. **Internal circlip**
6. **Washer**
7. **Piston**
8. **Secondary cup**
9. **Primary cup**
10. **Spring**
11. **Check valve**
12. **Pivot bolt**
13. **Reservoir cap**
14. **Cap washer**
15. **Diaphragm**
16. **Master cylinder body**
17. **Clamp**
18. **Spring washer**
19. **Bolt**
20. **Joint washers**
21. **Bolt**
22. **Brake hose**

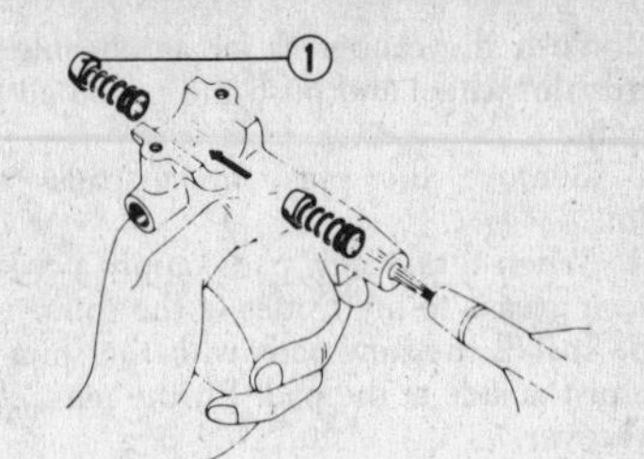

The primary cup (1) can be blown out with compressed air

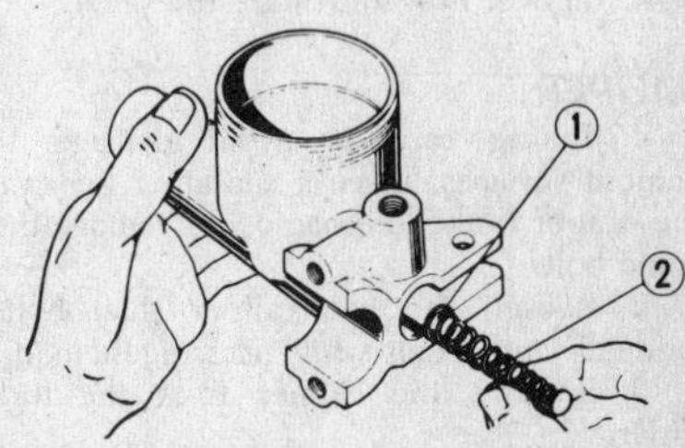

Removing the check valve (1) and return spring (2)

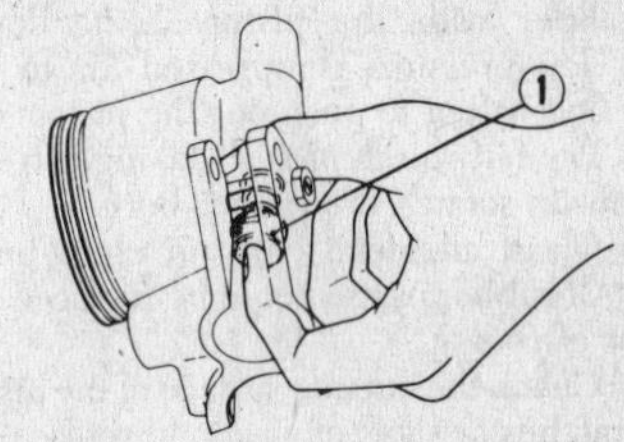

Seating the primary cup (1) during assembly

6. Use a new seal and lubricate it with fresh brake fluid. Install the components in the bore as removed.

7. Mount the master cylinder on the handlebar and connect the brake hose. Do not forget to install the two washers at the connection.

8. Fill the reservoir to the level mark with brake fluid and bleed the brake. (Use brake fluid conforming to DOT 3 specification.)

Disc

The brake disc normally requires no service of any kind. However, if the disc becomes scored for any reason, it should be replaced and a new set of pads should be installed. A badly scored disc will reduce the effectiveness of the brake and shorten pad life considerably. If the front brake lever oscillates or fluctuates when the brake is applied at speed, the indication is that the brake disc is warped or bent. Check the run-out of the disc with a dial indicator and replace it if run-out exceeds 0.3 mm (0.012 in.). To replace the disc:

1. Remove the front wheel.
2. Bend back the locktabs, unscrew the six nuts, and remove the disc from the hub.
3. Mount the new disc on the hub and tighten the nuts evenly, using new locktabs to secure the nuts.
4. Examine the brake pads and replace them if they are close to the limit of wear or have worn in an unusual pattern.

Front Disc (CB650)

PAD REPLACEMENT

1. Remove the caliper cover. Take out the clip.

2. Push the caliper as far as possible towards the wheel and push the piston all the way in.

3. Remove the pins, brake pads, and shim.

4. When fitting new pads, apply a coat of silicon grease to both sides of the shim.

5. Install the new pads with the shim on the piston side of the pad. Fit the pins, clip, and cover.

BLEEDING

See "Bleeding," under "Front Disc (350-550)," above. Procedures are the same.

CALIPER

1. Taking care to avoid damage to painted surfaces, place a container beneath the caliper brake line banjo and remove the banjo bolt.

2. Loosen the two caliper shaft bolts gradually and evenly while pressing them in.

3. Remove the caliper from the fork slider.

4. Remove the piston boot.

5. Place a rag over the piston and hold the caliper with the piston facing down. Apply low-pressure compressed air to the banjo bolt fitting to push out the piston.

6. Pry out the fluid seal, taking extreme care not to scratch the caliper bore.

7. Clean all metal parts in clean brake fluid. All rubber parts should be replaced as a matter of course.

8. Check the outside surface of the piston for scratches or signs of wear and replace it if the piston surface is not perfect. Measure the OD of the piston. If it is under 42.800 mm (1.6850 in.) replace it.

9. Check the caliper bore for similar damage. Make sure that the fluid seal groove is perfectly clear of foreign matter. Measure the inside diameter of the caliper bore. If it is more than 42.940 mm (1.6905 in.), replace it.

10. Assembly is the reverse of disassembly. Use all new rubber parts. Be sure to lubricate the piston and seal with medium grade high temperature silicon grease or some new brake fluid before assembly.

Be sure that the fluid seal is firmly seated in its groove.

Be sure to install the piston with the boot lip facing out.

Tighten the caliper shaft bolts to 22–29 ft. lbs.

NOTE: *On some models the upper caliper bolt has a rubber seal and is marked for location.*

CALIPER CARRIER

The caliper carrier will remain on the fork slider when the caliper halves are removed. When rebuilding the system, remove the two carrier bolts and separate the components. Clean all metal parts in clean brake fluid. Replace the caliper shaft o-rings and boots. Lubricate the o-rings with silicon grease or new brake fluid before assembly. When assembling, be sure that the boots are seated in the caliper shaft grooves. Tighten the carrier bolts to 22–29 ft. lbs.

MASTER CYLINDER

The master cylinder components are the same as described for the "Front Disc (350-550)," above. Refer to that section.

DISC

Replace the disc if measured thickness is less than 6.0 mm (0.24 in.) at any point, or if the disc surface is warped, scored, or otherwise damaged.

Rear Drum

Rear brake lining wear on newer models can be determined by means of the wear indicator pointer fitted to the brake lever on the hub. If the pointer lines up with the red slash mark when the brake pedal is fully depressed, the linings are worn beyond use and should be replaced.

On older models, observe the angle formed by the brake lever on the hub and the brake rod when the brake is fully applied. When the lever and rod form an angle greater than 90°, the shoes should be replaced. The replacement procedure is as follows:

1. Remove the rear wheel.

2. Unscrew the axle nut and withdraw the axle. Separate the backing plate from the brake drum.

3. Remove the cotter pin and washer from each brake shoe pivot and lift the shoe away from the backing plate. Minimum acceptable lining thickness at any point is 2.0 mm (0.08 in.) for the 500/550/650 and for the 350/400 it is 2.5 mm (0.1 in.)

4. Check the linings for scoring or embedded foreign matter, and replace them if necessary. Oil or grease-impregnated linings should also be replaced.

5. Break the glaze on the linings with some medium sandpaper, but be sure to clean them thoroughly before installation.

6. Check the condition of the brake springs, and replace them if badly rusted or if the ends are deformed.

7. Apply a *light* coat of grease to the brake shoe pivots and the actuating cam. Install the springs and shoes as on removal, using new cotter pins.

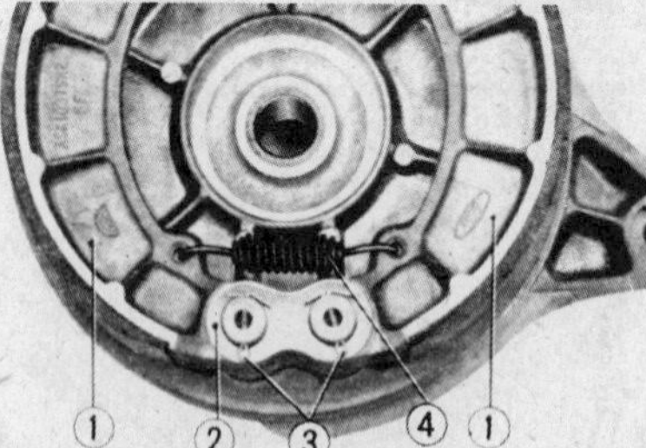

Remove the cotter pins (3) and washers (2), then fold the shoes (1) off the backing plate and remove the springs (4)

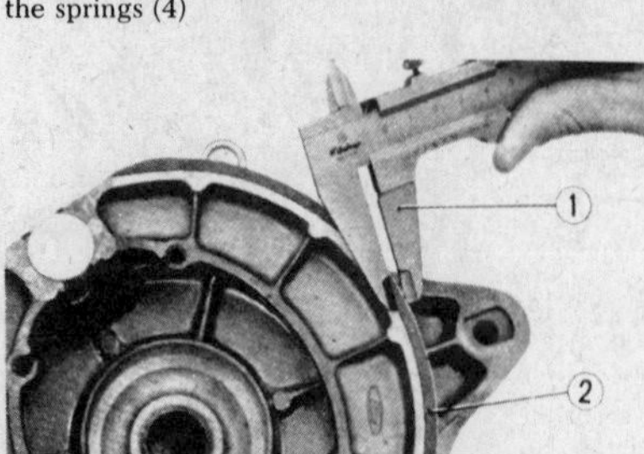

Measuring shoe material (2) with a vernier caliper (1)

8. Inspect the condition of the brake drum surfaces. There should be no scoring. If scored, the drum can sometimes be salvaged by having it turned down on a lathe. Refer work of this nature to a qualified machinist.

9. Measure the inside diameter of the drum in two directions, perpendicular to each other. A difference in the two readings indicates that the drum is warped. This condition is sometimes felt in an "off-on-off" feeling when applying the rear brake, and it, too, may be remedied by turning down the drum.

Maximum allowable brake drum diameter is 161 mm (6.34 in.) for the 350/400 and 181 mm (7.13 in.) for the 500/550.

10. Clean the drum thoroughly, removing all dirt and dust.

11. Assemble the drum and hub with the axle and install the wheel. Adjust the brake so that there is about 25 mm (1 in.) of free-play at the pedal before the shoes contact the drum. Avoid heavy braking for a few miles if new shoes have been fitted.

FRONT FORKS (STANDARD)

Removal

1. Support the front wheel off the ground. Remove the front wheel and fender.

2. Remove the caliper from the fork slider. CAUTION: *Do not allow the caliper to hang by the brake hose. Tie it out of the way with string or wire.*

3. Remove the fork filler cap at the top of each fork leg.

NOTE: *It may be necessary to remove the handlebars to do so, but the controls may be left connected, and the bars gently laid to one side when the mounting bolts are removed.*

4. Loosen the upper and lower triple clamp pinch bolts.

Upper and lower triple clamp bolts

5. Grasp each fork leg, in turn, and remove it from the triple clamps by pulling downward. If this is difficult, install the filler cap(s), threading them in several turns, then strike them sharply with a plastic mallet or the like to drive the fork leg down and out of the triple clamps.

Disassembly

1. Remove the fork spring and gaitor (if fitted). Drain the fork oil.

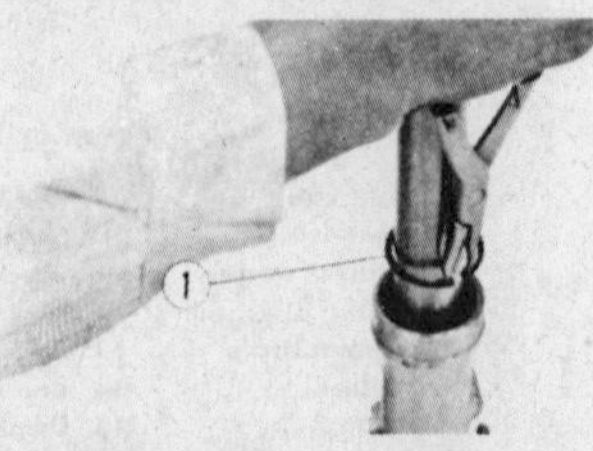

Removing the fork slider circlip

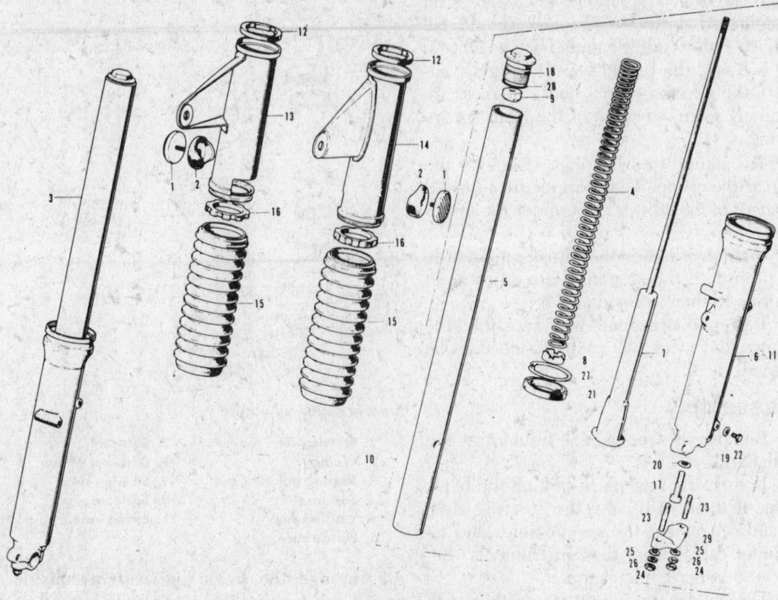

Front fork assembly (350/500)

1. Reflector
2. Reflector base
3. Fork leg (right)
4. Fork spring
5. Fork tube
6. Fork slider
7. Damper
8. Spring seat
9. Damper rod nut
10. Fork assembly (left)
11. Fork slider
12. Bush
13. Headlight mount (right)
14. Headlight mount (left)
15. Fork boot
16. Bush
17. Fork slider allen bolt
18. Fork filler cap
19. Drain plug washer
20. Allen bolt washer
21. Oil seal
22. Drain plug
23. Axle cap stud
24. Axle capnut
25. Washer
26. Lockwasher
27. Circlip
28. O-ring
29. Axle cap

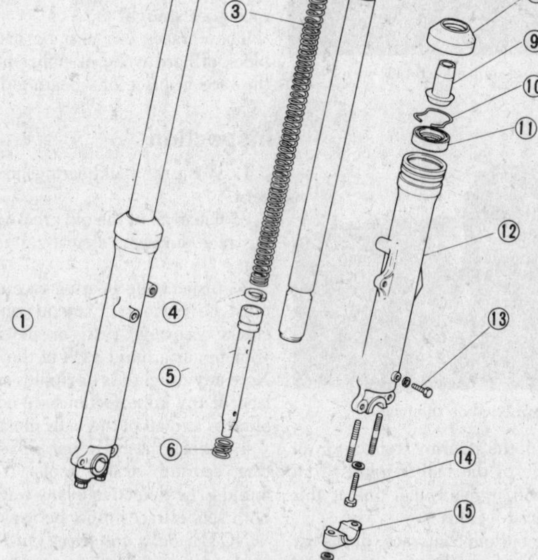

Front fork assembly (400/550/650)

1. Fork leg
2. Filler cap
3. Fork spring
4. Piston ring
5. Damper
6. Rebound spring
7. Fork tube
8. Dust cap
9. Oil lock piece
10. Circlip
11. Oil seal
12. Fork slider
13. Drain plug
14. Allen bolt
15. Axle cap

2. Remove the fork slider dust seal, if fitted. Remove the slider oil seal circlip.

3. Remove the allen bolt at the bottom of the slider and separate the fork components.

4. The slider oil seal will remain in the slider. Oil seals must always be replaced when the forks are disassembled. Pry out the old seal with a screwdriver or a hooked tool, protecting the lip of the slider with a piece of wood or soft metal pad beneath your lever. Drive new seals straight in until seated. An old seal can be used to drive in the new seals. Be sure the seals are driven straight in and not cocked or tilted. Seals should be driven in just far enough to allow fitting the circlip.

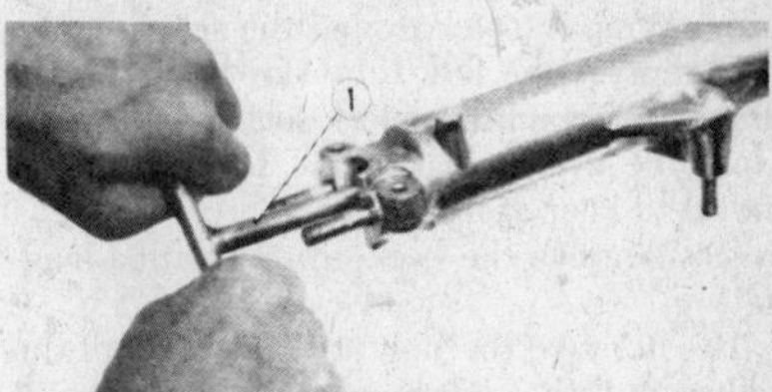

Removing the slider allen bolt

Oil the lips of seals before assembly.

Assembly

Assembly is the reverse of disassembly. On 400/550/650 forks, be sure that the rebound spring is in place.

Installation

1. Install each fork leg into the triple clamp and align the top of each fork tube with the surface of the upper triple clamp.

2. Tighten the upper triple clamp pinch bolts, the lower triple clamp bolts, and fill the forks with the correct grade and quantity of oil.

3. The remainder of the procedure is the reverse of removal.

AIR FORKS

WARNING: *1981 models are equipped with air forks. Special precautions are necessary when attempting to service these forks:*

1. Always wear hand and eye protection. Fork caps are under air and spring pressure.

2. Always depressurize the forks before attempting to disassemble them.

Removal

1. Depressurize the forks and disconnect the air hose from the right hose connector.

2. Disconnect the air hose from the left front fork.

3. Remove the front wheel, brake caliper(s), and front fender.

4. Loosen the triple clamp pinch bolts. Pull out each fork tube in turn.

Disassembly

CAUTION: *Fork caps are under spring pressure.*

1. Remove the air valve from the fork cap.

2. Install special plugs H/C 095806 and P/N M 2280-999-95806.

3. Secure the fork tube in a soft-faced vise and remove the fork cap remembering that it is under spring pressure.

4. Remove the fork spring.

5. Remove the dust seal, snap-ring, and back-up plate.

6. Remove the cap, tool, and seal. Pour off the fork fluid.

7. Extend the fork tube as far as possible. Pour ATF into the fork tube up to the bottom of the threads and install the fork tube cap.

8. Place the seal driver over the fork tube. Wrap a towel around the seal area.

Compress the fork tube slowly with a hydraulic press until the fork seal is forced out. Hold the driver against the seal during removal to keep it from tilting.

9. Remove the back-up ring with a magnet.

10. Remove the bolt at the bottom of the slider. Pull the slider and fork tube apart. It may be necessary to work the components apart due to the seal which is pressed into the slider.

Inspection

1. Replace the fork springs as a set if either measures less than 473.7 mm (1865 in.) on the CB650 or 542.7 mm (21.37 in.) on the CB650C.

2. Minimum acceptable fork tube diameter measured in the area on which the slider rides is 34.90 mm (1.374 in.).

3. Replace the bushing if the copper layer shows over more than ¾ of the total surface.

Assembly and Installation

Reverse the removal procedures. Note the following points.

a. Install the snap-ring with the radiused edge facing down.

b. Fork capacities are as follows:

CB650	210 cc (7.1 oz)
CB650C	245 cc (8.3 oz)

c. Torque the fork tube cap to 11–22 ft. lbs.

d. After the installation, fill each tube to 10–16 psi.

NOTE: *Use air only in the forks.*

STEERING STEM ASSEMBLY

Bearing Adjustment

1. The steering stem bearings are uncaged #8 balls or ¼-in. balls. They are adjusted by means of a ring nut beneath the upper triple clamp.

2. To check bearing adjustment, support the front wheel off the ground. Grasp the tip of the front fender and place your other hand beneath the lower triple clamp at the frame lug.

3. Attempt to move the fork by pulling up on the tip of the fender. If play or movement can be felt at the lower triple clamp, the bearings are adjusted too loosely or are worn.

An alternate method is to grasp the fork sliders and attempt to move them back and forth in line with the motorcycle. No play should be noted.

4. Turn the forks slowly from lock-to-lock. Movement should be smooth, silent, and effortless. If any binding or uneven movement is felt, the balls and races are either too tightly adjusted or they are worn. If the steering feels uniformly stiff, the bearings are too tightly adjusted. If any noise is noted, the bearings are damaged or some are missing.

5. With the front wheel off the ground, release the front forks from a few degrees off the centered position. The fork should fall freely to either side of their own weight. If they will not, the bearings are too tightly adjusted, the steering stem is bent, the races are extremely worn, or some of the bearings are missing.

6. To adjust the bearings, remove the upper triple clamp. The bearings are adjusted by means of the adjuster nut under the upper triple clamp.

7. Tighten or loosen the adjuster nut a little at a time until the steering stem adjustment conforms to that outlined above.

8. If proper adjustment is not possible, the bearings and races will probably need to be replaced.

Disassembly

1. Remove the front wheel, front forks, and handlebars.

2. Loosen the rear pinch-bolt on the triple clamp, if fitted. Unscrew the steering stem nut and disconnect the speedometer and tachometer cables from their instruments. Remove the upper triple clamp.

3. Disconnect the wiring inside the headlight shell and remove the head-light shell and the fork ears.

4. Loosen the steering stem adjuster nut with a pin wrench, then hold the steering stem up while unscrewing the adjuster nut the rest of the way off. Remove the steering stem top cone race and the ball bearings from the top race.

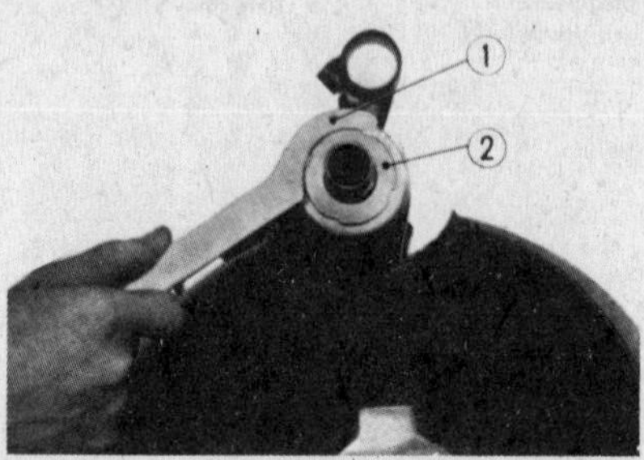

Removing the steering stem adjuster (2) with a hook wrench (1)

Top bearings (1) positioned on the race

5. Carefully pull the steering stem out from the bottom. Some of the ball bearings from the lower race will probably fall out at this time so be prepared for this.

6. Remove the bottom cone race, dust seal, and dust seal washer from the steering stem if they are to be replaced. These will have to be pried off with a chisel; therefore only remove them if necessary.

7. The bearing races in the frame lug are a press-fit and should not be removed unless replacement is necessary. If replacement is necessary, the old races can be removed by reaching through the frame lug with a suitable punch and tapping the race evenly around its circumference to remove it from the inside of the frame lug. Be sure that the race does not become cocked in its seat upon removal.

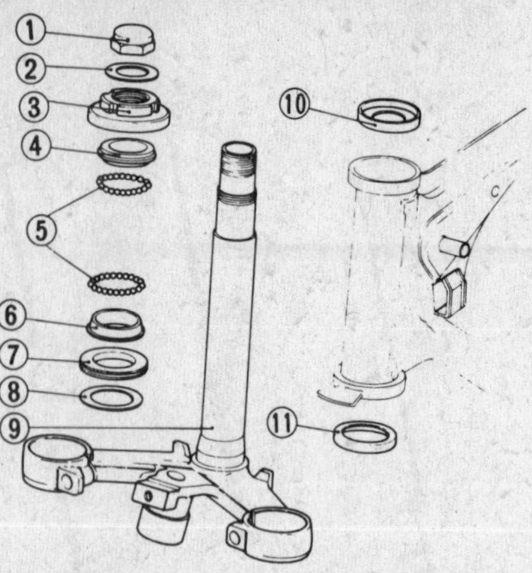

Steering stem assembly

1. Steering stem top nut
2. Washer
3. Bearing adjusting nut
4. Top race
5. Ball bearings
6. Bottom race
7. Dust seal
8. Dust seal washer
9. Steering stem
10. Top race
11. Bottom race

New races are installed with a suitably sized bearing driver, i.e., one which will drive the race squarely into its seat. Be certain that the race goes straight in.

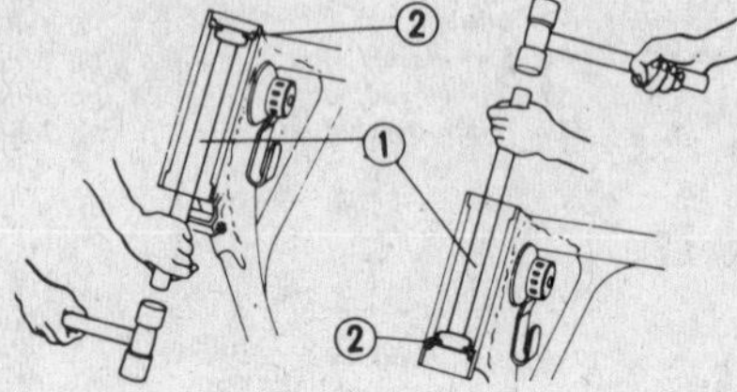

Using a drift (1) to drive out races (2)

These races can also be installed using a block of hard wood of sufficient size to cover the race in place of a bearing driver.

Inspection

1. Wash the ball bearings in a suitable solvent.

2. Clean all of the old grease from the bearing race surfaces, steering stem, and frame lug.

3. Inspect the bearing race surfaces. They must be clean and smooth and free of any cracks, scoring, rust, or indentations. Run your finger around each of the bearing races. Note any roughness or ripples on the race surface. If any imperfections are noted, both sets of races and all of the balls must be replaced.

4. Check the balls themselves for rust, pitting, scoring, or flat spots. If the balls are found to be defective in any way, the balls and both sets of races must be replaced.

NOTE: *Balls and races must always be replaced in a set because worn races will destroy new balls and worn balls will destroy new races.*

5. Check the dust seal for condition and replace if torn or cracked.

6. Check the steering stem for cracks or a bent condition; this is especially important if the bike has been involved in a spill.

Installation

1. Install the dust seal washer, dust seal, and lower cone race on the steering stem. Use a good grade of bearing grease to coat the bottom cone race and the upper race in the frame lug.
2. On the 350/400, install 19 balls in the upper race and 18 in the lower. On the 500/550/650, fit 18 balls into the upper race, and 19 in the lower.
3. When the balls are in place, slip the steering stem through the frame lug and hold it in place while refitting the top cone race and threading on the adjuster nut.
4. Tighten the adjuster nut all the way by hand, rotating the steering stem to work the grease into the balls.
5. Tighten the adjuster nut until the steering stem turns freely, but has no play.
6. Install the fork tubes, headlight assembly, and upper triple clamp, flat washer, and steering stem nut. Check that the stem moves freely to the steering lock of its own weight when released from 5°–10° off center; if not check for:
   a. Steering bearings too tight;
   b. Bent steering stem;
   c. Worn races or balls.
7. Install the front fender, front wheel, and handlebars.

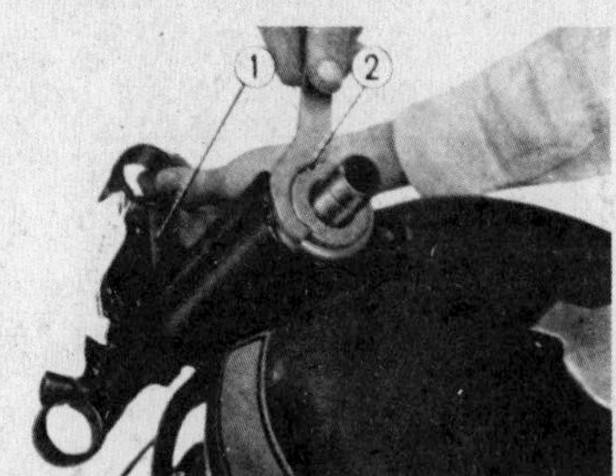

Tightening down on the stem adjusting nut (2) while checking for smooth motion of the stem (1)

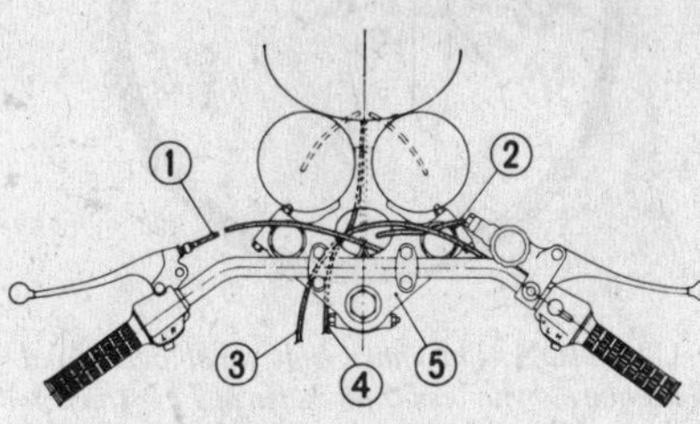

Correct routing for the cables and wiring

1. Clutch cable
2. Brake hose
3. Throttle cable
4. Wiring harness
5. Upper triple clamp

REAR SHOCKS

Rear shocks are sealed units which cannot be disassembled or repaired. If a shock is damaged due to accident or if it leaks oil, it must be replaced. Shock absorbers are best replaced in sets.

Removal and Installation

1. The shock absorbers can be removed after their upper and lower fasteners are taken off.
2. To remove the spring, first set the cam ring on the softest position. Then compress the spring by hand or with the aid of the special tool and remove the spring retainers.

SWING ARM

Inspection

1. Remove the muffler(s).
2. Remove the rear wheel, shock absorbers, and chain guard.
3. Measure the distance between the top and bottom shock absorber mounts on both sides. The two measurements must be identical, or the swing arm will have to be replaced.
4. Check that the rear wheel mounting plates are parallel.
5. Grasp the legs of the swing arm and attempt to move it from side to side. Any noticeable side-play will indicate that the swing arm bushings need replacement.

The swing arm is most likely to be damaged if the machine is operated for any length of time with a broken or otherwise defective shock absorber.

Removal and Installation

1. Proceed as above. Then remove the swing arm pivot bolt nut and pull the pivot bolt out from the right side.
2. Remove the swing arm by pulling it straight back.
3. The swing arm should be inspected for cracks or fractures, especially around the welds.

After removal of the swing arm, the dust seals and bushings can be replaced. This should be done every 10,000 miles or more often depending on how the machine is used, or if the bushings are worn (see "Inspection," above).

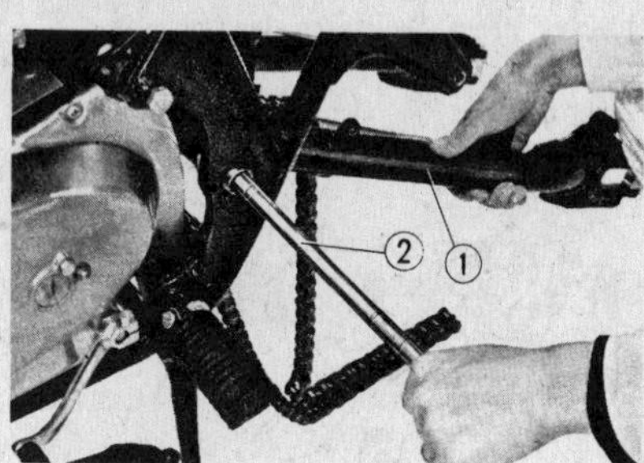

Removing the swing arm spindle (2)

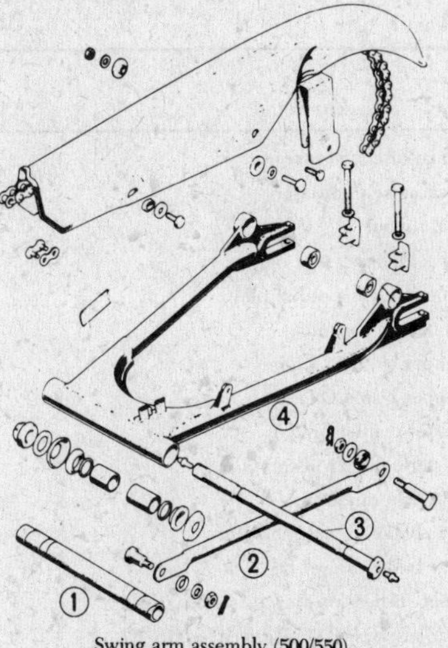

Swing arm assembly (500/550)

1. Collar
2. Brake anchor
3. Spindle
4. Swing arm

4. Remove the bushings, tapping them out with a hammer and punch. Once the bushings are removed, they should be replaced.
5. Lubricate new bushings with a good chassis grease. Press the bushings into the swing arm, then lubricate and install the swing arm collar.
6. Clean out the pivot bolt (500/550) and ensure that all grease passages are clear. Install the swing arm on the machine. Grease and install the pivot bolt. After tightening the swing arm pivot bolt nut, move the swing arm up and down to ensure that movement is smooth and effortless.

FINAL DRIVE

Chain Removal and Installation

MASTERLINK CHAINS

The chain can be separated and pulled off the sprockets after the master link has been removed. Threading the chain back onto the countershaft sprocket is made easier if you have an old length of chain lying around that you can hook onto the chain on the bike as it is removed. Leave the old chain draped over the sprocket so that you can hook the good chain back onto it and pull it over the sprocket when you are ready to reinstall it. Be sure to install the master link clip with the closed end facing in the direction of forward rotation of the chain.

DIRECTION OF TRAVEL

Always install the spring clip with the closed end facing the direction of chain rotation

ENDLESS CHAINS

To remove the endless chain it is necessary to use a chain breaking tool. A heavy-duty chain breaker is available from Honda dealers, part number 07062–30050. To break the chain using this tool:

1. Grind or file the pins of the link to be removed flush with the link side plate. Break

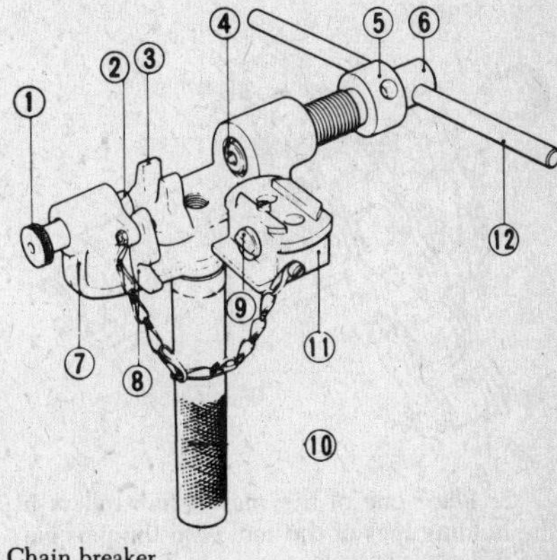

Chain breaker

1. Pin seat knob
2. Pin seat
3. Holder
4. Cotter pin
5. Main bolt
6. Link removal bolt
7. Body
8. Pin seat backing plate
9. Wedge
10. Grip
11. Guide
12. Lever

the chain at the master link (identifiable by the depression in the pin centers).

2. Swing the pin seat backing plate on the chain breaker away from the pin seat and place one of the link rollers in the holding lugs of the tool.

3. Seat the main bolt against the side plate of the link and turn the link removal bolt in until the pin is driven out.

4. Place the other link roller in the holding lugs and repeat step 3.

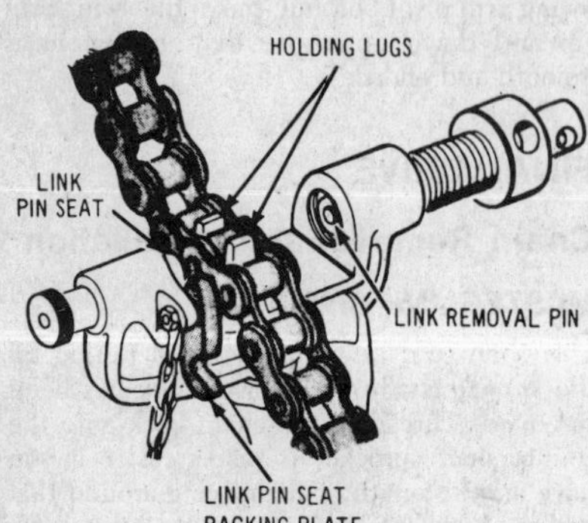

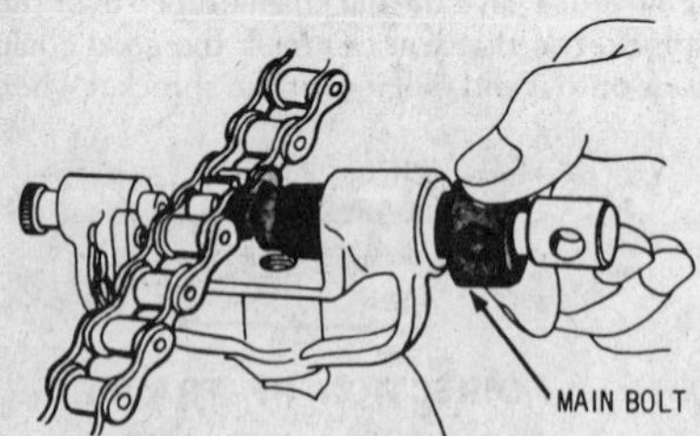

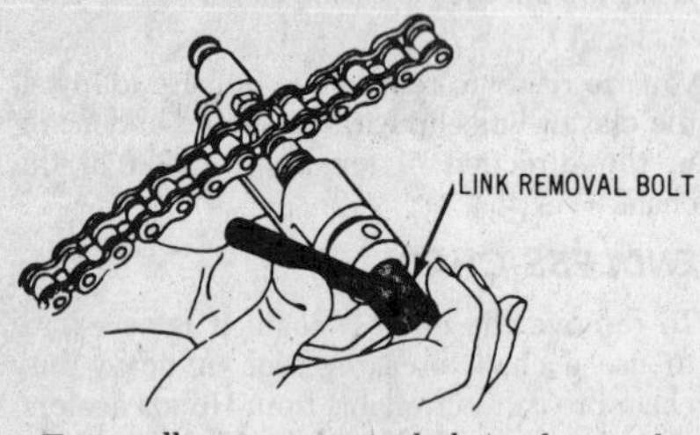

To install a new master link (replacing the chain on the motorcycle):

1. Insert the master link through the ends of the chain so that the side plate is inside (closest to the wheel).

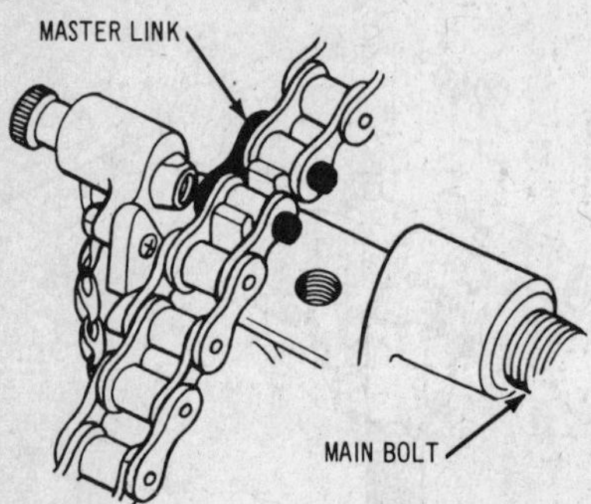

2. Place one of the master link rollers in the holding lugs of the tool with the pins facing the main bolt.

3. Push the pin seat knob in until it contacts the pin and swing the pin seat backing plate over to lock the pin seat in position.

4. Place the master link side plate in the guide block, as shown, so that the stamped

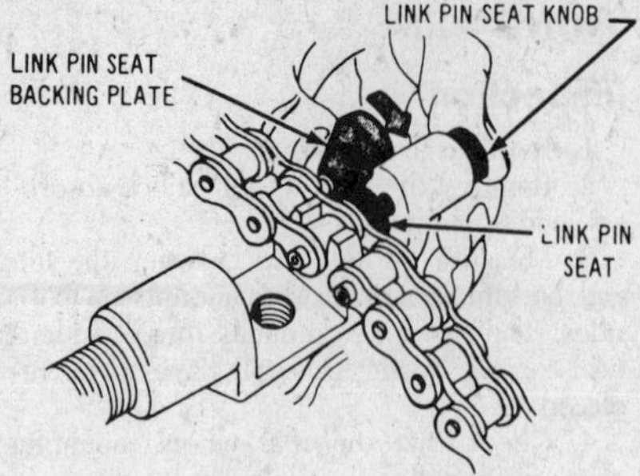

letters or numbers on the plate face the surface of the guide block (facing out when installed on the chain).

5. Back out the link removal bolt until it is behind the nose of the main bolt.

CAUTION: *The link removal bolt will be damaged if it is allowed to protrude beyond the nose of the main bolt.*

6. Place the guide block in the tool with the master link side plate against the pins. Make sure that the pins are aligned with the holes in the side plate.

7. Turn in the main bolt until the pins

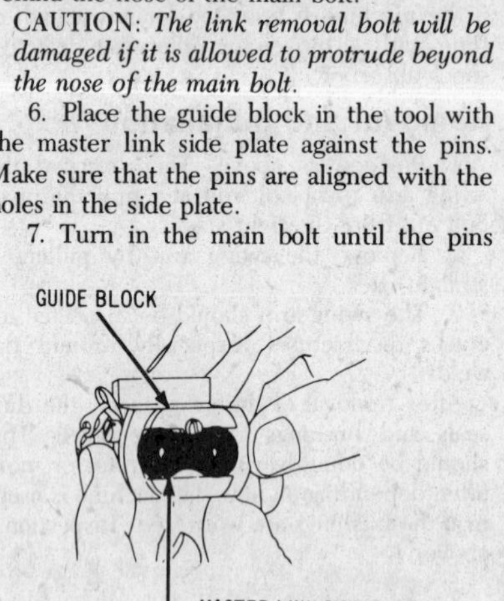

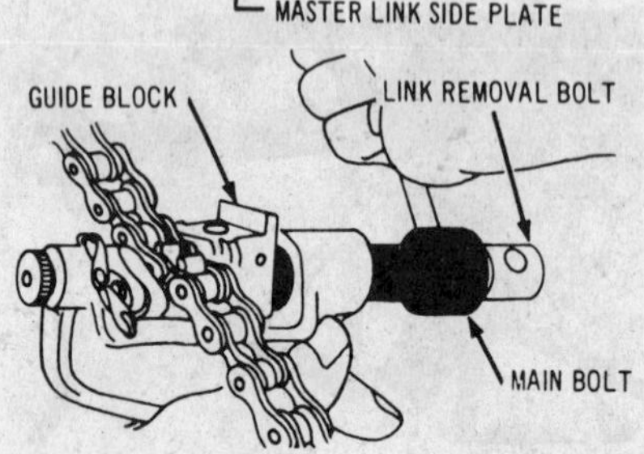

pass through the plate and seat against the recess in the guide block.

8. Reposition the guide block so that the staking die faces the pin and the protruding shoulder of the guide block is below the side plate.

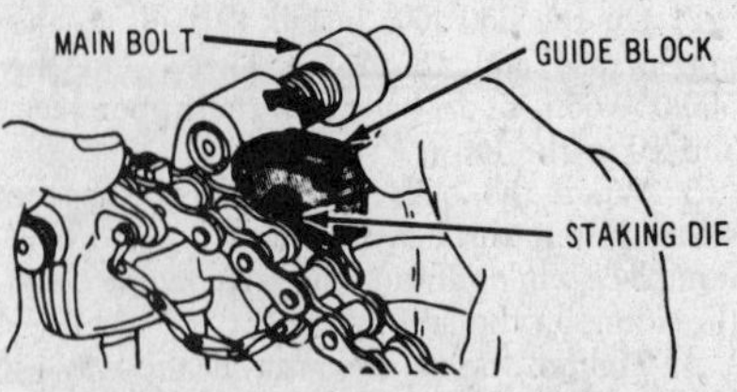

9. Turn in the main bolt until the staking die contacts the pin. Check to make sure that the die is centered across the pin.

10. Turn in the main bolt an additional ¾ turn to stake the pin. Repeat steps 8–10 for the other master link pin. Examine both pins to make sure that they are properly staked.

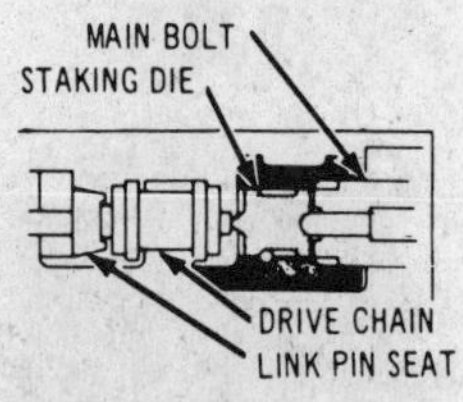

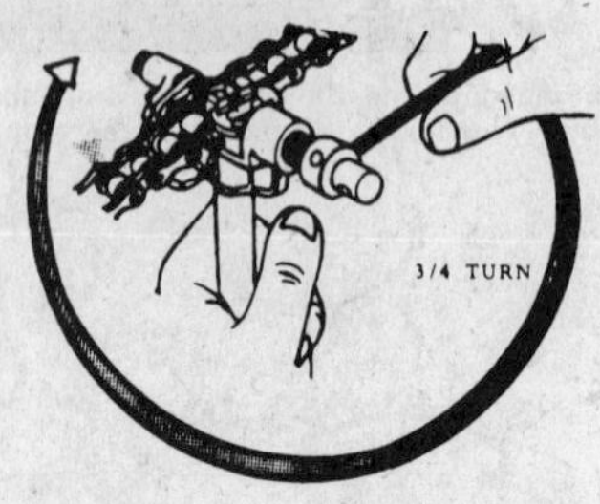

CAUTION: *The main bolt must be turned no more or no less than ¾ turn. Less than ¾ turn will not secure the side plate properly, and more than ¾ turn may crack the pin.*

Chassis Specifications
350/400

	Standard (mm/in.)	*Serviceable Limit (mm/in.)*
Brake disc face runout	0.3/0.0118, max	0.3/0.0118, min
Brake disc thickness	6.9–7.1/0.2717–0.2795	—
Rim runout	0.5/0.0197, max	2.0/0.079
Wheel bearing end play	0.07/0.0028, max	0.1/0.0039
Wheel bearing radial play	0.03/0.0012, max	0.05/0.0020
Front axle runout	0.01/0.0004	0.2/0.0079
Caliper cylinder I.D.	38.18–38.20/1.5032–1.5039	38.215/1.5045
Caliper piston O.D.	38.115–38.480/1.5006–1.5150	38.105/1.5002
Master cylinder I.D.	14.00–14.043/0.5512–0.5529	14.055/0.5533
Master cylinder piston O.D.	13.957–13.984/0.5495–0.5505	13.940/0.5488
Rear axle runout	0.01/0.0004	0.2/0.0079
Rear brake lining thickness	4.9–5.0/0.1929–0.1969	2.5/0.0984
Rear brake drum I.D.	160.0–160.3/6.2992–6.3110	161/6.3386
Front suspension spring free length	①	②
Rear suspension spring free length	③	190/7.480
Swing arm pivot bushing-to-center collar clearance	0.1–0.3/0.0039–0.0118	0.5/0.02
Swing arm bushing I.D.	21.5–21.552/0.8465–0.8485	21.70/0.8543

Chassis Specifications (cont.)

350/400

	Standard (mm/in.)	Serviceable Limit (mm/in.)
Center collar O.D.	21.427–21.460/0.8436–0.8449	21.35/0.8406
Front fork slider I.D.	33.000–33.039/1.2992–1.3007	33.18/1.3063
Front fork tube O.D.	32.90–32.98/1.2952–1.2984	32.875/1.2944

① 350: 426.5/16.80 400: 478.6/18.84 ② 350: 416/16.39 400: 450/17.72 ③ 350: 195.8/7.71 400: 210.4/8.28

500/550

	Standard (mm/in.)	Serviceable Limit (mm/in.)
Brake disc face runout	0.3/0.118, max	0.3/0.118
Rim runout	0.5/0.020	2.0/0.08
Wheel bearing end play (TIR)	0.07/0.028	0.1/0.004
Wheel bearing radial play (TIR)	0.03/0.0012	0.05/0.002
Axle runout	0.01/0.0004	0.2/0.008
Caliper cylinder I.D.	38.18–38.20/1.5031–1.5039	38.215/1.504
Caliper piston O.D.	38.115–38.48/1.5006–1.5150	38.105/1.5002
Master cylinder I.D.	14.00–14.043/0.5512–0.5529	14.055/0.5533
Master cylinder piston O.D.	13.957–13.984/0.5495–0.5505	13.940/0.5488
Rear brake lining thickness	5.0/0.20	2.0/0.08
Rear brake drum I.D.	179.8–180.0/7.079–7.087	181.0/7.125
Front suspension spring free length	451.7/17.78	425.0/16.73
Rear shocks spring free length	210.4/8.283	205/8.070
Swing arm bushing I.D.	21.448–21.5/0.844–0.846	21.8/0.858
Center collar O.D.	21.427–21.46/0.843–0.844	21.4/0.842

Chassis Torque Specifications

350/400

Component	Thread dia (mm)	Torque (ft lbs)
Steering stem nut	24	57.9–86.9
Upper triple clamp-to-front forks	8	13.1–16.7
Handlebar holder	8	13.1–16.7
Lower triple clamp-to-front forks	8	13.1–16.7
Spokes	—	
Front wheel	—	1.9–2.2
Rear wheel	—	1.5–1.9
Swing arm pivot bolt	14	39.8–50.7
Front wheel axle nut	12	32.6–39.8
Front fork axle caps	8	13.1–16.7
Engine mounting bolts	10	21.7–29.0
Master cylinder banjo bolts	—	24.6–28.9

350/400

Component	Thread dia (mm)	Torque (ft lbs)
Front brake disc nuts	8	13.0–16.6
Brake line joint	6	5.8–7.2
Brake hose joint	—	4.3–7.2
Master cylinder bolt	6	5.7–7.2
Caliper mounting bolts	—	24.6–28.9
Rear wheel axle nut	16	57.9–72.4
Rear sprocket nuts	10	21.7–29.0
Rear brake arm pinch-bolt	6	5.9–7.3
Rear brake anchor	8	13.1–16.7
Rear suspension	10	21.7–29.0
Step bar	12	32.6–39.8
Gearshift and kick-starter levers	6	5.9–7.3
Seat band	6	5.9–7.3

500/550

Component	Torque (ft lbs)
Rear brake pedal bolt (8 x 32 hex)	13.0–18.1
Step bar nut (12 mm)	36.2–43.4
Engine mounting bolt	21.7–28.9
Engine mounting plate	13.0–18.1
Swing arm pivot nut (14 mm)	39.8–50.6
Rear shock upper nut (10 mm capnut)	21.7–28.9
Rear shock lower bolt (10 x 32 hex)	21.7–28.9
Master cylinder banjo bolts	24.6–28.9
Brake stop switch	24.6–28.9
Front brake disc nuts (8 mm)	13.0–16.6
Brake line joint (6 x 28 hex)	5.8–7.2
Brake hose joint	4.3–7.2
Master cylinder bolt (6 x 28 hex)	5.7–7.2
Caliper mounting bolts	24.6–28.9
Fork filler caps	39.8–47.0
Steering stem nut	57.9–86.7
Steering stem bolt (10 x 40 hex)	21.7–28.9

500/550

Component	Torque (ft lbs)
Rear axle nut	57.8–72.3
Front axle cap nuts (8 mm)	13.0–16.6
Handlebar holder bolt (8 x 40 hex)	13.0–16.6
Front axle nut	39.8–47.0
Rear brake anchor bolt and nut (8 mm)	13.0–16.6
Upper triple clamp pinch-bolt (8 x 56 hex)	13.0–16.6
Drive chain adjuster bolt and nut (8 mm hex)	10.8–14.5
Rear axle adjuster stopper bolt (750)	13.0–16.6
Center stand pivot bolt (8 x 40 hex)	10.8–14.5
Passenger peg nuts	32.5–43.4
Caliper joint pin	13.0–18.1
Lower triple clamp pinch-bolt	21.7–28.9
Rear sprocket nuts	21.7–28.9

Chassis Specifications (cont.)
650

	Standard (mm/in.)	Serviceable Limit (mm/in.)
Axle runout	—	0.2 (0.01)
Rim runout	—	2.0 (0.08)
Fork-spring free-length		
Standard forks	501.7 (19.8)	492.7 (19.4)
CB650 air forks	488.4 (19.23)	473.7 (18.65)
CB650C air forks	559.5 (22.03)	542.7 (21.37)
Fork tube bend	—	0.2 (0.01)
Fork slider ID (standard)	35.042–35.104 (1.3796–1.3820)	35.15 (1.384)
Fork tube OD (standard)	34.930–34.950 (1.3752–1.3760)	34.90 (1.374)
Fork tube OD (air fork)	34.975–34.950 (1.3770–1.3760)	34.90 (1.37)
Rear shock spring free-length	224.7 (8.8)	220.6 (8.7)
Swing arm bushing ID	21.500–21.552 (0.8465–0.8485)	21.7 (0.854)
Swing arm collar OD	21.427–21.460 (0.8436–0.8449)	21.4 (0.843)
Rear brake lining thickness	5.0 (0.197)	2.0 (0.08)
Rear brake drum ID	180.0–180.3 (7.09–7.10)	181.0 (7.1)
Front brake disc thickness	6.9–7.1 (0.27–0.28)	6.0 (0.24)
Disc run-out	—	0.3 (0.01)
Master cylinder ID	14.000–14.043 (0.5512–0.5529)	14.055 (0.5533)
Master cylinder piston OD	13.957–13.984 (0.5495–0.5506)	13.945 (0.5490)
Caliper piston OD	42.815–42.820 (1.6856–1.6858)	42.800 (1.6850)
Caliper bore ID	42.850–42.926 (1.6870–1.6000)	42.940 (1.6905)

General Torque Specifications ①

Component	Torque (ft lbs)
Hex bolt, 6 mm	5.7–8.6
Hex bolt, 8 mm	
Engine	14.5–17.3
Frame	10.8–16.6
Phillips head screws	5.7–8.6

① Use only if torque for specific nuts and bolts is not given in preceeding charts

Chassis Torque Specifications
650

Component	Torque (ft. lbs.)
Steering stem nut	58–87
Handlebar	20–23
Upper triple clamp	7–9
Fork cap bolt	15–22
Steering stem	22–29
Front axle holder	13–18
Front axle nut	40–48
Front brake disc	20–24
Brake line fittings	18–25
Caliper carrier	22–29
Caliper	22–29
Rear axle	58–72
Rear sprocket	58–72
Swing arm pivot nut	43–51
Rear brake anchor	13–18
Rear shocks	22–29
Engine mounting bolts	
10 mm	22–29
12 mm	58–72
8 mm	19–23
Footpegs	22–29
Gearshift lever	6–9

Supplement

1982 AND LATER MODEL INFORMATION

Front Forks

Note the following capacities for 1982 and later forks:

650 S-Models: 10.2 oz./320cc
Nighthawk: 6.5 oz./190cc

Quantities listed are for each leg at routine change.

Front Brakes

Service procedures for master cylinder and caliper are as described in the main section, although specifications differ. They are as follows:

Part	Serviceable limit
Caliper bore ID	
Nighthawk	27.08 mm/1.066 in.
Other models	30.1 mm/1.193 in.
Piston OD	
Nighthawk	26.9 mm/1.060 in.
Other models	30.1 mm/1.187 in.
Disc Thickness	
Nighthawk	4.0 mm/0.16 in.
Other models	6.0 mm/0.24 in.

Fuel Petcock

The petcock used on these models has a sediment bowl and filter screen above it and is very similar to the type described under "1974 and Earlier" in the main section.

Honda 750/900 Fours

MODEL COVERAGE

CB750 1969
CB750 K1-K5 1970-1975
CB750 1976
CB750 K 1977-1978
CB750 F 1975-1978
CB750 A 1976-1978
CB750 K 1979-1981
CB750 K LTD 1979-1981
CB750 F 1979-1981
CB750 C 1980-1981
CB900 C/F 1980-1981

INDEX

GENERAL INFORMATION

SERIAL NUMBER LOCATION

In order to prevent possible confusion when purchasing parts, always refer to the engine and frame serial numbers. The frame number is stamped on the right side of the steering lug, while the engine number is behind the cylinders on the top right side of the crankcase.

Engine serial number location

MAINTENANCE

NOTE: *Common maintenance procedures are explained in detail in the "General Information" section.*

LUBRICATION

Motor Oil

For use in all temperatures, Honda recommends SAE 10W-40 motor oil, service rating "SE" or "SF."

1969–78

1. Due to the dry-sump lubrication system, if the machine has been sitting idle for more than a few hours the engine must be run for several minutes before the oil is checked.
2. The motorcycle should be parked on the center stand on level ground.
3. Check the oil level with the dipstick that is part of the oil tank cap. The level should be between the upper and lower marks inscribed on the dipstick. If the oil level is below the lower level mark, top it up with the proper grade of oil to bring the level to the upper mark.

Frame serial number location

Upper and lower oil level marks

The dipstick must rest on top of the threads for an accurate reading

General Specifications

Component	CB750 (69)—CB750K1	CB750K2—CB750 (76)	CB750K (77–78)
ENGINE			
Type	air-cooled, in-line 4-cylinder, OHC		
Displacement (cc/ci)	736/44.9	736/44.9	736/44.9
Bore x stroke (in./mm)	2.401 x 2.480/61 x 63	2.401 x 2.480/61 x 63	2.401 x 2.480/61 x 63
Compression ratio	9.0 : 1	9.0 : 1	9.2 : 1
Carburetion	(4) 28 mm Keihin	(4) 28 mm Keihin	(4) 28 mm Keihin
Lubrication	dry sump	dry sump	dry sump
TRANSMISSION			
Clutch	wet, multi-plate	wet, multi-plate	wet, multi-plate
Primary reduction	1.708	1.708	1.985
Gear ratios (overall)			
1st	2.500	2.500	2.500
2nd	1.708	1.708	1.708
3rd	1.333	1.333	1.333
4th	1.097	1.097	1.133
5th	0.939	0.939	0.969
Final reduction (f/r sprocket teeth)	2.667 (18/48)	2.667 (18/48)	2.824 (17/48)
CHASSIS			
Dry weight (lbs/kg)	479/218	479/218	508/230
Frame	full double cradle	full double cradle	full double cradle
Wheelbase (in./mm)	57.3/1455	57.3/1455	58.9/1519
Overall length (in./mm)	85.0/2160	85.6/2175	89.8/2280
Overall width (in./mm)	34.8/885	34.3/870	34.6/879
Overall height (in./mm)	45.5/1155	46.1/1170	45.7/1160
Ground Clearance (in./mm)	5.5/140	5.5/140	5.9/150
Tire size			
front	3.25 x 19	3.25 x 19	3.50 x 19
rear	4.00 x 18	4.00 x 18	4.50 x 17
ELECTRICAL SYSTEM			
Ignition	battery and coil	battery and coil	battery and coil
Starting system	electric and kick	electric and kick	electric and kick
Charging system	alternator	alternator	alternator
Battery (volts/ah)	12/14	12/14	12/14
Alternator	12 v/0.21 kW @ 5000 rpm	12 v/0.21 kW @ 5000 rpm	12 v/0.21 kW @ 5000 rpm
Regulator	dual-contact type		

Component	CB750F	CB750A	CB750K (79–81)
ENGINE			
Type	air-cooled, in-line 4-cylinder, OHC		
Displacement (cc/ci)	736/44.9	736/44.9	749/45.7
Bore x stroke (in./mm)	2.401 x 2.480/61 x 63	2.401 x 2.480/61 x 63	2.440 x 2.440/62 x 62
Compression ratio	9.2 : 1	8.6 : 1	9.0 : 1
Carburetion	(4) 28 mm Keihin	(4) 24 mm Keihin	(4) 30 mm Keihin
Lubrication	dry sump	wet sump	wet sump
TRANSMISSION			
Clutch	wet, multi-plate	automatic	wet, multi-plate
Primary reduction	1.985	1.351	2.382
Gear ratios (overall)			
1st	2.500	2.263 (L)	2.533
2nd	1.708	1.520 (D)	1.789
3rd	1.333	na	1.391
4th	1.133	na	1.160
5th	0.969	na	0.964
Final reduction (f/r sprocket teeth)	2.824 (17/48)	2.824 (17/48)	2.533 (15/38)
CHASSIS			
Dry weight (lbs/kg)	499/227	531/241	512/233
Frame	full double cradle	full double cradle	full double cradle
Wheelbase (in./mm)	57.9/1470	58.3/1480	59.8/1520
Overall length (in./mm)	86.6/2200	88.6/2250	87.4/2200
Overall width (in./mm)	33.9/860	34.1/865	34.6/880
Overall height (in./mm)	45.7/1160	46.7/1185	45.7/1160
Ground Clearance (in./mm)	5.3/135	5.3/135	5.9/150
Tire size			
front	3.25 x 19	3.50 x 19	3.50 x 19
rear	4.00 x 18	4.50 x 17	4.25 x 18
ELECTRICAL SYSTEM			
Ignition	battery and coil	battery and coil	transisterized
Starting system	electric and kick	electric and kick	electric
Charging system	alternator	alternator	alternator
Battery (volts/ah)	12/14	12/20	12/14
Alternator	12 v/0.21 kW @ 5000 rpm	12 v/0.29 kW @ 5000 rpm	12 v/0.26 kW @ 5000 rpm
Regulator	dual-contact type		transisterized

750A

1. The 750A has a wet-sump lubrication system, all of the oil being contained in the crankcases.

2. Allow the engine to run for several minutes before checking the oil level.

3. With the machine parked on the center stand on level ground, and with the engine shut off, unscrew and remove the dipstick and wipe it clean. Reinsert the dipstick, allowing it to rest on the threads of its hole. Do not screw it in. Remove it and check the level. It should be between the upper and lower level marks inscribed on the dipstick. If it is at or near the lower mark, add enough oil to bring the level up to the upper mark, but do not overfill the crankcase.

1979 AND LATER

1. These models have a wet-sump lubrication system, all of the oil being contained in the crankcases.

2. Allow the engine to run for several minutes before checking the oil level.

3. With the machine parked on the center stand on level ground, and with the engine shut off, unscrew and remove the dipstick and wipe it clean. Reinsert the dipstick, allowing it to rest on the threads of its hole. Do not screw it in. Remove it and check the level. It should be between the upper and lower marks inscribed on the dipstick. If it is at or near the lower mark, add enough oil to bring the level up to the upper mark, but do not overfill the crankcase.

Wet-sump dipstick level marks

Changing Oil

NOTE: *Manual transmission models 1969–1978 have a dry-sump lubrication system.*
1979–1981 models have a wet-sump system, as does the 750A.

1. The recommended oil change interval is 1,500 miles or 3 months for manual transmission models 1969–1978, 3,000 miles or 6 months for the 750A, and 4,000 miles or 1 year for 1979–1981 models.

Time and mileage intervals are both important and the oil should be changed at whichever occurs first.

These intervals are based on normal motorcycle usage *after* initial break-in is completed.

2. Oil should be changed when the engine is warm. This ensures more complete draining and makes it more likely that the oil will carry off any particulate matter with it.

3. On dry-sump models, remove the oil tank cover, raise the seat (if necessary), and remove the tank filler cap. Remove the tank drain plug, draining the oil into a suitable container (at least 4-qt capacity). After drain-

General Specifications (cont.)

Component	CB750K LTD, C	CB750F (79–81)	CB900C/F
ENGINE			
Type	air-cooled, in-line 4-cylinder, OHC		
Displacement (cc/ci)	749/45.7	749/45.7	902/55
Bore x stroke (in./mm)	2.440 x 2.440/62 x 62	2.440 x 2.440/62 x 62	2.540 x 2.720/64.5 x 69.0
Compression ratio	9.0 : 1	9.0 : 1	8.8 : 1
Carburetion	(4) 30 mm Keihin	(4) 30 mm Keihin	(9) 32 mm Keihin
Lubrication	wet sump	wet sump	wet sump
TRANSMISSION			
Clutch	wet, multi-plate	wet, multi-plate	wet, multi-plate
Primary reduction	2.382	2.382	2.041
Gear ratios (overall)			
1st	2.533	2.533	2.375
2nd	1.789	1.789	1.789
3rd	1.391	1.391	1.391
4th	1.160	1.160	1.160
5th	0.964	0.964	0.964
Final reduction (f/r sprocket teeth)	2.533 (15/38)	2.533 (15/38)	3.091 (11/34)
CHASSIS			
Dry weight (lbs/kg)	516/234	507/230	571/259
Frame	full double cradle	full double cradle	full double cradle
Wheelbase (in./mm)	59.8/1520	59.8/1520	62.2/1580
Overall length (in./mm)	90.2/2290	86.4/2195	90.9/2310
Overall width (in./mm)	34.6/880	34.1/865	36.0/915
Overall height (in./mm)	45.7/1160	44.9/1140	46.1/1170
Ground Clearance (in./mm)	5.7/145	5.5/140	5.9/150
Tire size			
front	3.50 x 19	3.25 x 19	110/90-19-62H
rear	4.50 x 17 ①	4.00 x 18	130/90-16-67H
ELECTRICAL SYSTEM			
Ignition	transistorized	transistorized	transistorized
Starting system	electric	electric	electric
Charging system	alternator	alternator	alternator
Battery (volts/ah)	12/14	12/14	12/14
Alternator	12 v/0.26 kW @ 5000 rpm	12 v/0.26 kW @ 5000 rpm	12v/0.26 kW @ 5000 rpm
Regulator	transistorized	transistorized	transistorized

na: not applicable
①C: x 16

ing is completed, check the condition of the drain plug gasket, replacing it if necessary; then install the plug and tighten it securely (torque to about 25 ft. lbs.). Remove the crankcase drain plug, allowing this oil supply to drain for several minutes. Kick the engine over several times with the kickstarter to remove any oil in the delivery system. Install the plug and tighten it to about 25 ft. lbs.

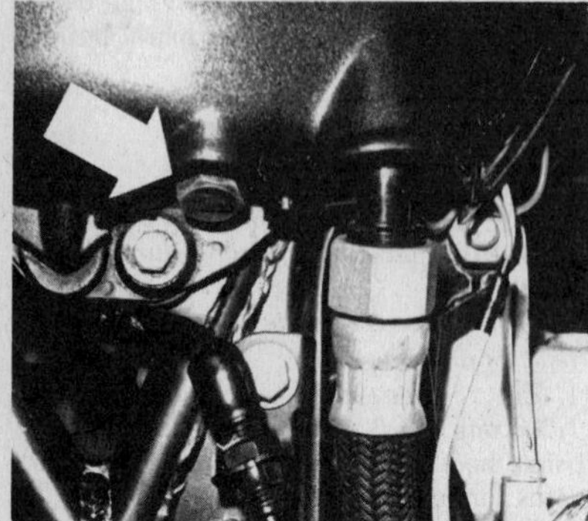
Oil tank drain plug

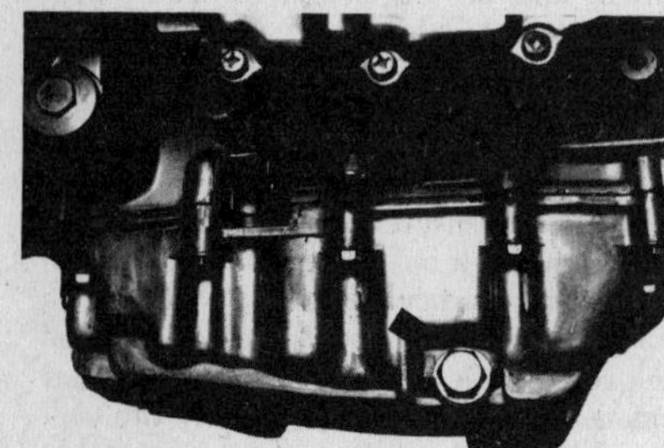
750A crankcase drain plug

4. On 750A and 1979–1981 models, all of the oil is contained in the crankcases, and it can all be removed after the drain plug is taken out. Your container should be able to hold more than 4 qts. Check the condition of the drain plug gasket, and install the plug, tightening to 25–33 ft. lbs. on the 750A and 25–29 ft. lbs. on 1979–1981 machines.

5. If the oil filter is to be replaced, see "Oil Filter," below.

6. On the 750A, add about 4.2 qts (4.0 l) of SAE 10W-40 oil to the engine. Secure the filler cap and allow the engine to run for several minutes. After shutting it off, check the oil level and top up if necessary.

7. On all other 1969–1978 models, add about 2.6 qts (2.5 l) of SAE 10W-40 motor oil to the tank. Start the engine and allow it to run for several minutes. Then shut it off and check the oil level. It will be necessary to add additional oil until the level is at the top dipstick mark. System capacity is 3.7 qts. (3.5 l).

8. On 1979–1981 motorcycles, add about 3.7 qts. (3.5 l) of SAE 10W-40 motor oil, or equivalent. Tighten the dipstick, start the engine and let it run for a minute or so. After shutting it off, check the oil level and top up if necessary.

Oil Filter

1. The filter element should be changed at every oil change on the 1979–1981 models and the 750A, at every other oil change on 1969–1978 models.

2. After removing the crankcase drain plug and allowing the oil to run off, remove the oil filter housing bolt, placing a drip pan or suitable substitute beneath the housing to catch any oil in the filter housing.

3. Take out the old filter, washer, and spring. Clean the housing. Check the condition of the housing o-ring.

4. Wipe off the mating surface on the crankcase with a clean rag. Oil the o-ring lightly with clean oil.

5. Slipping the filter housing bolt into place, fit the spring and washer, then the

Removing the filter from the housing

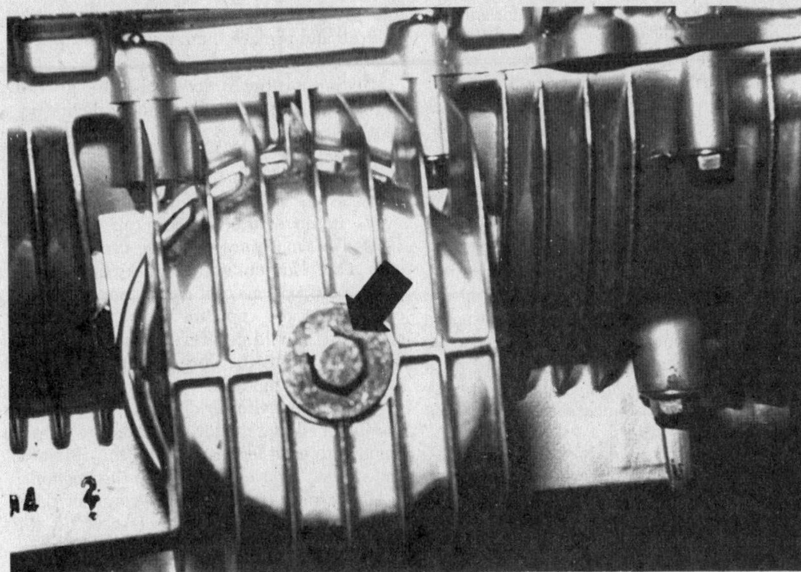

Oil filter bolt

new filter element. Install the housing, tightening the housing bolt to 20–24 ft. lbs.

CAUTION: *Do not overtighten the housing bolt. If this is done, it will not only be difficult to remove, but it may crack the housing in the area around the bolt hole. If the bolt is difficult to remove, be sure to inspect the housing closely around the bolt hole for small cracks.*

6. Add oil to the crankcase or oil tank as outlined under "Changing Oil" above.

Arrows indicate holes for bolts which have copper washers

Filter Screen

1. All models are equipped with a filter screen in the sump which should be cleaned and inspected at 12,000-mile or 24-month intervals.
2. After draining the sump, unbolt and remove the oil pan.

On 1979–1981 models, note the locations of the three pan bolt copper washers which are located on the right side.

3. Withdraw the screen from the oil pump, and clean it in a safe solvent, brushing off foreign matter if necesary. Inspect the screen mesh for holes, and replace it if any are noted.
4. When installing the pan, a new gasket should be used. After refilling the system with oil, start the engine and check for leaks around the oil pan mating surface.

Note that after pan rmoval, the engine may require more oil than after a routine change.

Oil pan bolts should be torqued to 7–10 ft. lbs.

Oil Path Body (1979 and Later)

The oil path body should be checked when the filter screen is serviced. Remove the oil path body after the screen. Check it for cracks or other damage. Replace it if any is noted.

Note: All replacement oil path bodies have an oil flow restriction and can be installed even if the original part does not.

Oil Pressure (1969–78)

Oil pressure should be checked every 6,000 miles or 12 months. A gauge may be connected at the oil gallery access hole at the right side of the engine after the plug has been removed. Honda service tools No. 07068-30001 (adapter) and No. 07065-30001 (pressure gauge) may be used. The gauge should register 50–64 psi when the engine is warm (oil temperature 140–160°F) and running at 3,000 rpm. If the oil is cold, a higher reading will be obtained.

If oil pressure is unsatisfactory, determine and correct the fault. Refer to chapter 5, "Lubrication Systems," for additional information.

Oil Pressure (1979 and Later)

Oil pressure should be checked every 6,000 miles or 12 months. Honda service tools No. 07506-3000000 (oil pressure gauge) and No. 07510-4220100 (adapter) may be used. The gauge is attached to the oil pressure switch hole behind the cylinders.

Check the pressure when the engine is at operating temperature (about 176°F/80°C). At 7,000 rpm, pressure should be 71 psi. If the oil is cold, a higher reading will be obtained.

If oil pressure is unsatisfactory, determine

Crankcase filter screen

Oil pressure sensor and gallery plug (1969–1978)

Oil pressure sensor and pressure gauge fitting (1979–1981)

the reason and correct the fault before further operation of the motorcycle. Refer to "Lubrication Systems," for additional information.

Use a liquid sealant on the threads of the oil pressure switch when reinstalling it. Check that the oil pressure light operates properly.

Transmission Oil Pressure (750A)

A test of the transmission oil pressure is undertaken in the event of trouble. Refer to "Engine and Transmission."

Subtransmission Oil

A level plug is fitted to enable a quick check of the subtransmission oil level.

1. Park the motorcycle on the center stand on a level surface.
2. Shift the subtransmission into "Low."
3. Remove the cover.
4. Remove the level plug. The oil should be level with the lower threads of the plug hole. In other words, oil should just begin to ooze out.

Add SAE 80 hypoid gear oil if the level is low.

5. To change the oil, proceed as above. Remove the drain bolt and the filler cap.
6. Fit the drain bolt after several minutes have elapsed.

NOTE: *Draining will be much quicker if the engine is at operating temperature.*

7. Tighten the drain bolt to 12–14 ft. lbs.
8. Add about 20.4 oz. (600 cc) of SAE 80 hypoid gear oil to the subtransmission. Check the level as before.

Rear Drive Box

1. To check the oil level in the rear drive box, park the machine on the center stand on a level surface.
2. Remove the level plug/filler. The oil should be just level with the bottom threads of the hole, or just ready to ooze out. Add SAE 90 hypoid gear oil for temperatures above 40°F or SAE 80 for temperatures below this.
3. To change the oil, remove the drain bolt and allow the oil to drain for several minutes. Draining will be quicker if the engine is at operating temperature.
4. After refitting the drain bolt, add 5.1 oz. (150 cc) of the proper oil grade. Check level as before.

Front Forks (1969–80)

1. ATF oil is recommended for all forks after 1972, SAE 10W-30 oil for forks 1972 and earlier. If slightly stiffer damping characteristics are desired, SAE 20 or SAE 30 oil can also be used. Special types of oil designed specifically for motorcycle forks can also be used, although care must be taken to flush the forks thoroughly when changing types or brands of fork fluid, since some may be incompatible with others.
2. Fork oil should be changed every 6,000 miles or 12 months on all 1969–1978 models except the 750A, whose recom-

Front fork oil drain plug

Fork filler cap

mended interval is 12,000 miles or 24 months. Models 1979–1980 should have this service done at 4,000 miles or 12 month intervals.

3. Place a container beneath one of the fork sliders and remove the drain plug. Pump the slider up and down until all the oil is expelled. Examine the plug gasket, then refit the plug. Repeat the procedure with the other slider.
4. Examine the drained oil. If it contains water or is exceptionally dirty, it may be that the fork gaitors or dust covers are damaged and allowing foreign matter to get past. This will also damage fork seals quickly. Check that the gaitors or dust covers are properly secured and replace them if cracked, ripped, or otherwise damaged.
5. Support the front wheel off the ground by placing a scissors jack or similar device beneath the engine.
6. Remove the handlebar clamp bolts and move the bars to one side or the other to allow access to the fork filler caps.
7. Remove the rubber cap plugs on 1979–1980 machines. Remove the fork filler caps. Often loosening the upper triple clamp pinch bolts will make it easier to remove the caps. Since the caps are under spring tension, care should be exercised when removing them. Note the spring seats below the caps on some models.
8. Remove the fork springs to facilitate the job of adding the fork oil. Add the proper amount to each leg, as given in the "Maintenance Data" chart at the end of this section.
9. Inspect the filler cap o-rings for damage and replace them if necessary. Fit the springs, seats (if fitted), and caps, tightening them securely.

Proper filler cap torque is 40–47 ft. lbs. (1969–1978) or 15–22 ft. lbs. (1979–1980). Tighten the triple clamp pinch bolts if they were loosened. Secure the handlebars, tightening the forwardmost bolts first.

10. After several miles of operation, check the area around the fork slider seals for leaks or seepage. Even a minimal amount of seepage will require replacement of the seals. A coating of grime building up in this area over a period of time is also indicative of ineffective seals.

Air Forks (1981)

No routine oil changes are necessary on these forks. Refer to "Chassis" for service procedures.

Drive Chain

1977–81 MODELS

These models are fitted with a chain which has rubber o-rings between the plates to aid lubricant retention.

The chain should be lubricated about every 300 miles, or sooner if it appears to be dry. For lubrication, use SAE 80 or 90 weight gear oil only. Do not use commercial chain lubricants, as they may contain additives which will damage the rubber o-rings.

About every 2,000 miles, the chain should be cleaned with kerosine.

The chain o-rings can be damaged by steam cleaning, high-pressure spray, and certain solvents. Keep this in mind when cleaning the motorcycle.

1976 AND EARLIER MODELS

Chains for these models are serviced in the usual manner. Refer to the "General Information" section under "Maintenance."

On models with a chain oiler incorporated into the engine sprocket shaft, adjust the oiler as follows:

1. Remove the engine sprocket cover and wipe the sprocket and chain clean.
2. Ride the bike for a minute or two at about 50–60 mph, then stop and check the oil output to the chain. Normal output will yield a chain which is wet with oil, but the lubricant should not be found on the tire or rim.

3. To increase chain oil flow, turn the adjusting screw counterclockwise about ¼ turn, and recheck. To decrease the oil feed, turn the screw clockwise about ¼ turn and recheck.

4. Maximum output is obtained when the adjusting screw is turned out about three turns from the seated position.

It is recommended that the chain be lubricated periodically with a good brand of motorcycle chain lubricant in any case, since motor oil is not the best chain lubricant.

Chain play should be measured in the middle of the lower run

Chassis Lubrication

1. The swing arm pivot is fitted with one or two grease nipples which should be lubricated with chassis grease every 3,000 miles. On most models the nipples are on the ends of the swing arm pivot shaft, while the latest designs have a single nipple in the middle of the swing arm.

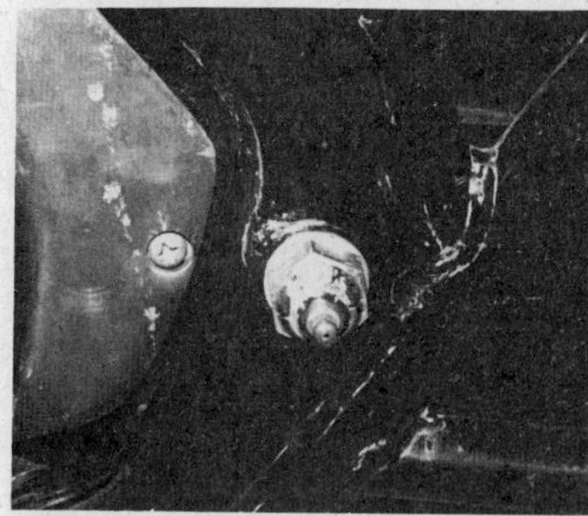

Swing arm grease fitting (early)

2. Wheel and steering head bearings are lubricated with bearing grease, the service interval being 12,000 miles or 24 months. Refer to "Chassis," for procedures.

Drive Shaft Coupling

Shaft-drive models have a grease fitting located on the rear drive box.

Use lithium-based chassis grease to lubricate the coupling every 8,000 miles.

Swing arm grease fitting (late)

SERVICE CHECKS AND ADJUSTMENTS

Drive Chain

1. The chain should have about 20mm (¾ in.) of total up-and-down free-play measured in the middle of the lower chain run.

2. Before checking or adjusting the chain slack, the following conditions should be met:

a. The motorcycle should be placed on the center stand so that the rear wheel is off the ground;

b. The transmission should be placed in neutral;

c. The chain should be clean and well-lubricated;

d. The chain should have been checked for any tight spots by slowly rotating the wheel and checking for variances in the chain tension at different points. If a tight spot exists, the chain tension should be adjusted to the prescribed free-play at the tight spot. Note, however, that such a condition is indicative of a worn chain and probably worn sprockets, which should be replaced as soon as possible.

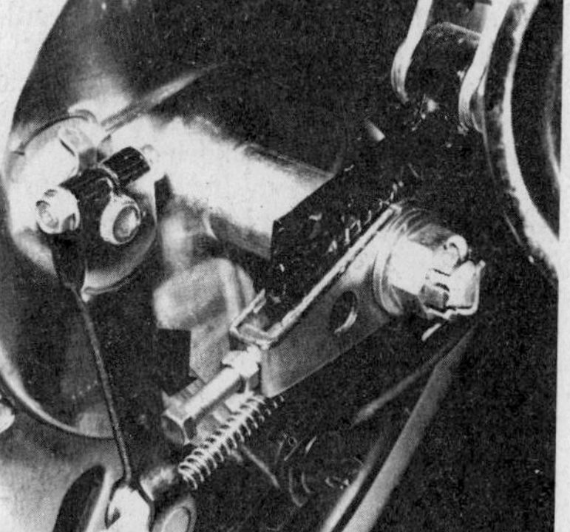

Chain adjuster bolt (arrow)

3. To adjust the chain, first back off the rear brake adjuster nut on drum rear brakes.

4. Remove the axle nut cotter pin and loosen the axle nut several turns. Loosen the locknut on each chain adjuster bolt.

5. Turn each of the adjuster bolts in or out by equal amounts until the chain tension is approximately correct.

6. Check wheel alignment by means of the aligning marks inscribed on both sides of the swing arm. Be sure that both adjusters are lined up with the same mark on each side. If not, turn one of the adjuster bolts in or out so that alignment is achieved.

7. Tighten the axle nut and adjuster bolt nuts and check the chain tension. The chain tension should also be checked with the weight of a rider sitting on the motorcycle when it is off the center stand; the chin should still have at least ½ in. of free-play. Correct if necessary. After adjustment is correct, torque the axle nut to 60–72 ft. lbs.

Fit a new cotter pin. Readjust the rear brake on drum brake models.

will wear out a set of sprockets in short order.

8. 1977 and later models have a plate on the chain adjuster which indicates the replacement limit for the chain. This should be done when the edge of the red zone aligns with the rear of the swing arm.

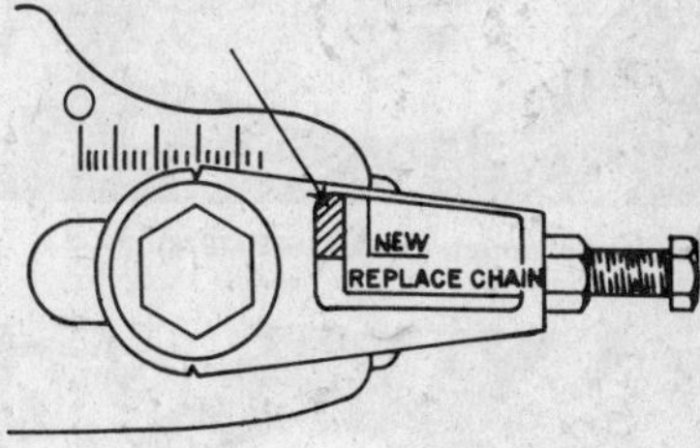

Clutch

750

1. Cable adjustment must always be maintained at the proper specification. If the cable has insufficient free-play, the clutch will slip and rapidly burn out. If it has too much play, the clutch will not completely disengage, resulting in hard shifting and creeping at stops.

2. Use the cable adjuster at the handlebar or engine to maintain the correct amount of cable slack. The clutch hand lever should be

able to be moved 2–3mm (0.08–0.12 in.) measured between the clutch lever and the lever holder before the clutch begins to disengage.

It should not be necessary to screw the cable adjuster at the handlebar out very far to make and to maintain this adjustment. If it is necessary to screw the handlebar adjuster out so that more than about 8 mm (0.3 in.) of thread are showing, screw it *in* several turns, and proceed to make the cable adjustment with the adjuster at the lower end of the cable. Use the handlebar adjuster for fine adjustment.

If clutch operation is not satisfactory after properly adjusting the cable, the problem may be in the clutch itself.

First make sure that the cable is properly lubricated and free to move in the sheath. Lack of lubrication, dirt, or rust in the cable can cause it to bind or otherwise impair operation.

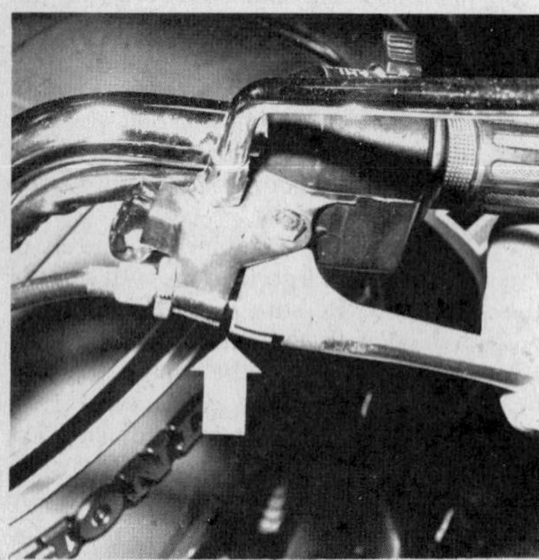

Point at which cable free-play is measured

Clutch adjustment screw (1969–1978)

Clutch adjustment screw (1979–1980)

To adjust the clutch, proceed as follows:

3. Screw the cable adjuster at the lever all the way in, thus increasing cable free-play. Back off the locknut and turn the cable adjuster at the engine in as well.

4. Remove the clutch housing cover plate (1969–1978) or the clutch lifter cap (1979–1981).

Loosen the clutch adjusting screw locknut.

5. Turn the adjusting screw clockwise until a slight resistance is felt, then turn it counterclockwise ¼ turn (1969–1978) or ¾ turn (1979–1981). Holding the screw in this position, tighten the locknut.

6. Turn the cable adjuster at the engine out until there is about 13 mm (0.5 in.) of free-play in the hand lever. Tighten the locknut on the engine cable adjuster.

7. Make any further minor adjustments with the adjuster at the hand lever,

900

1. Adjust the clutch cable in the same way as described for 750 models outlined above.

2. Adjust the clutch in the manner described for the 750 (Step 5, above), but back the adjusting screw off 1½ turns for the 900.

Throttle Cable

1969–1978

1. The throttle cable is fitted with an adjuster at the twist-grip. The twist-grip should be able to be rotated approximately 10–15° (2–4 mm [0.08–0.16 in.]) before the throttle slides begin to open.

2. Use the cable adjuster at the handlebar to make and maintain this adjustment. To check that the cable has sufficient slack, start the engine and turn the forks slowly from lock-to-lock. Idle speed must not increase. If it does, it indicates that the cable has insufficient free-play, is incorrectly routed, or is binding at some point.

3. For complete throttle cable and linkage adjustments, refer to chapter 3, "Tune-Up."

4. For major cable adjustments, use the adjuster(s) at the carburetors.

Throttle cable adjuster

1979 AND LATER

1. The throttle cable is fitted with an adjuster at the twist-grip. The twist-grip should be able to be rotated approximately 2–6 mm (0.08–0.24 in.) before the butterflies in the carburetors begin to open.

2. Use the cable adjuster at the handlebar to make and to maintain this adjustment. To check that the cable has sufficient slack, start the engine and turn the forks slowly from lock-to-lock. Idle speed must not increase. If it does, this indicates that the cable has insufficient free-play, is incorrectly routed, or is binding at some point, perhaps due to a kink or dirt or corrosion inside the sheath.

NOTE: *The accelerator pump may flood the engine if the twist-grip is operated several times in succession.*

3. For complete throttle cable and linkage adjustments, refer to "Tune-Up."

4. For major cable adjustments, use the adjuster(s) at the carburetors.

Brakes

FRONT DISC

Disc brakes need no attention other than a periodic check of fluid level and pad wear:

1. On late models with a see-through reservoir, fluid level can be checked at a glance. Turn the handlebars so that the fluid level is parallel to the ground for an accurate check.

If the level is near the lower mark, add enough DOT 3 brake fluid to bring it up to normal.

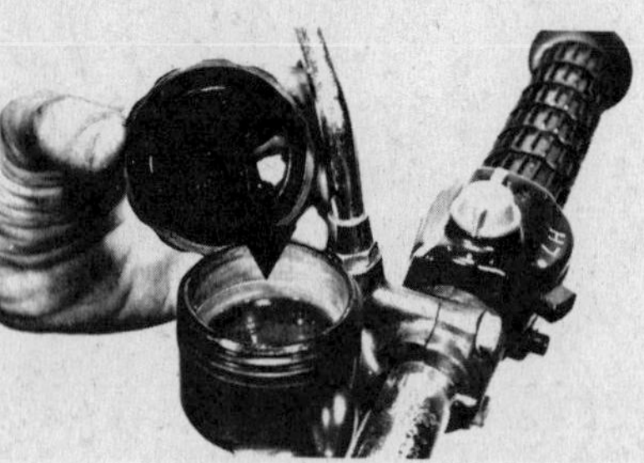

Maintain brake fluid level at the inscribed line

NOTE: *Brake fluid is hydroscopic. It absorbs moisture. Therefore, do not use fluid from an old or unsealed container. Exercise extreme care in handling the brake fluid.*

CAUTION: *Clean the reservoir thoroughly with a rag before removing the cap. Turn the handlebars fully to the right before the cap is removed to avoid spillage. Cover the tank with a cloth. Brake fluid removes paint.*

2. On earlier models, the reservoir cap and diaphragm beneath it must be removed to check the fluid level. Clean around the reservoir with a rag to remove any dirt before removing the cap.

If the level is below the line inscribed on the inside of the reservoir, add enough DOT 3 brake fluid to bring the level up to the mark. Reinstall the diaphragm and cap and tighten it securely.

If the cap is overtightened, the reservoir may weep fluid.

NOTE: *Read the "Note" and "Caution" in Step 1, above.*

CAUTION: *Fluid level may drop slightly as the pads wear. But if the drop is significant, it may indicate a system leak. Check the system thoroughly in any case noting any dirt or sludge build-up at hose junctions, near rubber boots, around the caliper piston(s), etc.*

3. Check the brake pad wear, and replace the pads in a set if either one is worn to the red limit line (1972 and later). On pre-1972 brakes, check the clearance between the front of the caliper and the disc. Replace both

Fluid level lines are inscribed on the master cylinder reservoir

pads if clearance is less than 1.5 mm (0.06 in.).

Refer to "Chassis," for brake system service procedures.

4. If the brake lever feels spongy, bleed the system. This procedure can also be found in "Chassis."

5. Early models are equipped with an adjusting screw on the handlebar lever bracket. After loosening the adjuster locknut, turn the adjuster to allow ¼ to ½ in. of lever travel (measured at the tip of the lever) before the pads are fully forced against the disc. This adjustment usually will not need to be reset once lever travel is correct. If the lever travel becomes excessive and the brake pads are satisfactory, suspect air in the brake lines.

Warning: Do not operate the brake lever with reservoir cap or caliper pads removed.

Caliper Adjustment

Early model swinging-type brake calipers (see illustration) should be adjusted whenever new pads are fitted, or if the brake seems to drag or causes a squeaking as the wheel turns.

1. Raise the front wheel off the ground.
2. Loosen the adjusting screw locknut and turn the adjusting screw *counterclockwise* until the innermost pad contacts the disc. A slight drag will be noted when spinning the wheel.
3. Turn the adjusting screw *clockwise* until the wheel spins freely; then turn the adjusting screw ½ turn more in the same direction and tighten the locknut.
4. Check that the wheel turns freely without drag. Check for proper brake operation.
5. Brakes which drag constantly after application and which cannot be cured with proper caliper adjustment may be caused by sticking or seizure of the caliper bracket on its pivot. Free movement of the caliper is necessary for proper operation of the brake. This can be inhibited by dirt or other foreign matter between the pivot and caliper bracket. If the wheel will not turn freely after the brake is applied, try striking the caliper with the heel of your hand. If this frees the wheel, it is probable that the swinging bracket is becoming stuck. A penetrating fluid or parts lubricant applied to the bracket pivot will often remedy this problem.

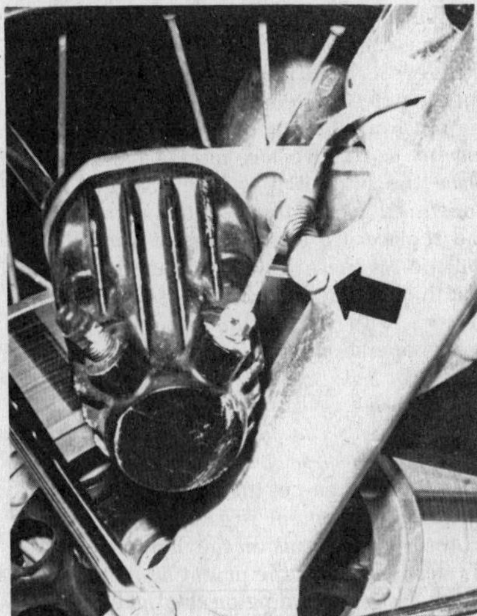

Caliper adjusting screw

REAR DISC

NOTE: *Read the "Notes" and "Cautions" under "Front Disc," above, regarding the use and handling of brake fluid.*

1. The transparent master cylinder allows inspection of the fluid level without removing the reservoir cap. If the fluid level is below the level mark, remove the cap and diaphragm and add enough DOT 3 brake fluid to bring the level up to the proper level. Clean the reservoir off with a rag before removing the cap to keep out dirt. Reinstall the diaphragm and cap and tighten it securely.

If the cap is overtightened, the reservoir may seep fluid.

Rear master cylinder level lines

CAUTION: *Do not operate the brake pedal with the cap removed.*

2. A brake wear indicator is fitted to the rear caliper, so that pad wear can be checked easily after removing the cover. If either pad is worn to the red mark on the caliper, replace the pads as a set.

3. On 1978 and earlier models, pedal height can be adjusted to suit personal preference by loosening the brake rod locknut, removing the cotter pin and clevis pin from the rod, and then turning the clevis. Lengthening the rod will raise the pedal, and vice-versa. Maintain adequate clearance between the brake pedal arm and the bottom of the footpeg.

4. On 1979 and 1980 models, pedal height should be adjusted so that the top of the pedal is about 7 mm (0.25 in.) above the top of the footpeg rubber. This adjustment can be made by turning the adjuster locknut until it is loose, then turning the adjuster until proper pedal height is obtained. Tighten the locknut.

5. If brake pedal height is changed, check the operation of the brake light switch.

REAR DRUM

1. Brake lining wear on newer models can be determined by means of the wear indicator pointer fitted to the brake lever on the hub. If the pointer lines up with the red slash mark when the brake pedal is fully applied, the linings are worn as far as possible for effective braking and should now be replaced.

2. On older models, observe the angle formed by the brake lever on the hub and the brake rod when the brake is fully applied. When the lever and rod from an angle greater than 90°, the shoes should be checked for wear as they probably are worn to the point of needing replacement.

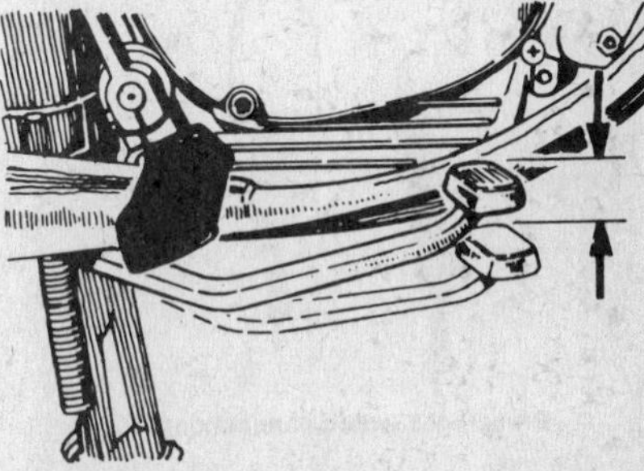

The brake pedal should have about 1 inch of movement before the linings contact the drum

Rear brake adjusting nut

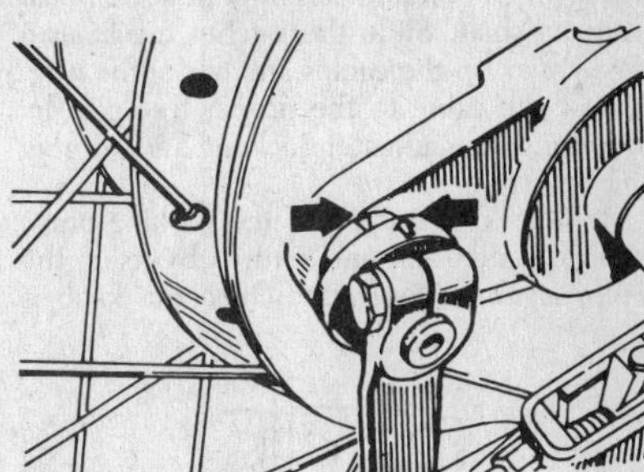

Brake wear indicator marks

3. The rear brake should be adjusted so that there is approximately 25 mm (1.0 in.) free-play at the pedal before the linings contact the drum. Adjust by turning the hex nut on the brake rod. When adjustment has been made, be sure that the nut is seated properly on the brake lever pin. Also, check the operation of the brake light switch.

4. Brake pedal position may be adjusted to suit individual taste by backing off the brake adjusting nut, loosening the pedal height adjusting bolt locknut, and turning the bolt until pedal position is satisfactory. Thereafter, adjust pedal free-play and the brake light swich.

Brake Light Switches

The switches should be checked for operation after the brakes are adjusted. The rear brake light switch and adjuster nut are mounted on a slotted bracket. The rear switch is adjusted by holding the switch and turning the adjuster.

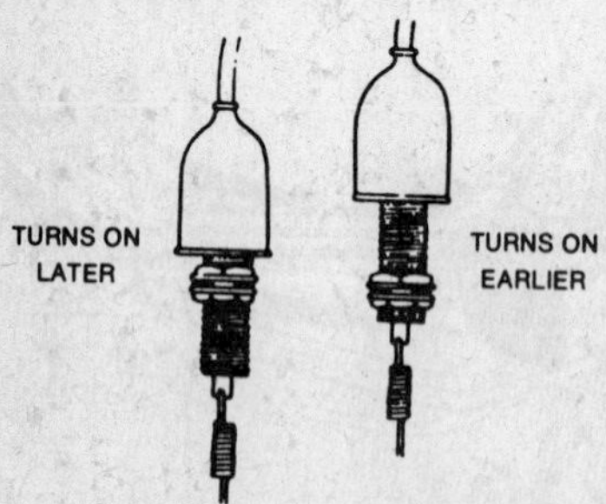

Brake light switch connections

Moving the switch upon the bracket allows the brake light to turn on sooner. Moving it down allows the light to turn on later. Do not turn the switch to effect adjustment as the wires will become twisted and may break. Generally, the brake light should come on just as the linings contact the drum or just as the brake begins to operate in the case of disc rear brakes.

The front switch is activated by the pressure of the brake fluid in the brake line. This switch is not adjustable; if defective, it must be replaced.

Parking Brake (750A)

1. The parking brake cable should have 2 mm (0.08 in.) of free-play.

2. To adjust the cable, remove the brake pedal pinch bolt and carefully pull the pedal from its shaft. Slide the ratchet mechanism dust cover up the cables and out of the way. Adjust the cable to the proper free-play by loosening the adjuster locknut and turning the adjuster.

3. Check operation. If the parking brake knob is pulled out and returns by itself, the cable is much too tight. Once the knob is pulled, the brake pedal should lock after being depressed about 20 mm (0.8 in.). If it will not lock, check the condition of the ratchet pawls (refer to chapter 8, "Chassis").

4. Be sure that the ratchet mechanism bears against the parking brake light switch. The switch should be fully screwed into the mechanism housing.

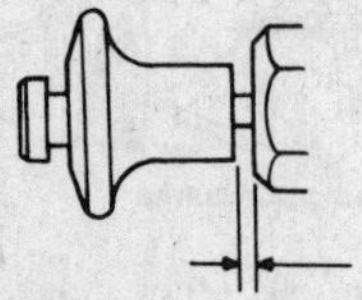

The parking brake cable should have about 2 mm (0.08 in.) of free-play

Neutral Return Rod (750A)

1. The shift lever must return to the "N" (neutral) position each time the side stand is lowered. Routine adjustment should not be necessary, but if the shift lever will not return to "N," proceed as follows:

2. Park the bike on the center stand. Retract the side stand and shift the transmission into the "D" (drive) position.

3. Loosen the return rod locknut, and turn the rod in a clockwise direction when viewed from the rear of the machine. When it stops, rotate it one turn in the opposite direction and tighten the locknut.

4. Check operation by setting the side stand down. The stand should bear against its stop, and the transmission must shift into "N."

5. If adjustment will not yield proper operation, check the return rod spring for a weak or partially collapsed condition and replace it if necessary.

Headlight Adjustment

1. Set the machine about 25 feet away from the perpendicular to a wall, preferably of a color which reflects light well.

The machine should be off the stand, and with a rider putting his weight on the machine as in operation.

2. Switch on the high beam. The headlight high beam should be parallel to the ground and should hit the wall directly in front of the machine.

3. Vertical adjustment is made by loosening the two headlight shell mounting bolts slightly and pivoting the shell up or down.

Vertical and lateral headlight adjustment points

4. Lateral adjustment is accomplished by means of the screw on the right side of the headlight. On 1969–1978 models, turning the screw clockwise will move the beam to the left; turning it counterclockwise will move it to the right.

On 1979–1981 models, turning the screw clockwise will move the beam to the right, and vice-versa.

FUEL SYSTEM

Fuel system maintenance involves cleaning the petcock and fuel filter screen, cleaning or replacing the air cleaner, cleaning the carburetors, and cleaning the breather element or tube (if so equipped).

On 1969–1978 models, the normal service interval is 3,000 miles. Every 6,000 miles, the air cleaner element should be replaced.

On 1979–1981 models, the normal service interval is 4,000 miles. The air cleaner element should be replaced every 8,000 miles.

Petcock

1. Two types of petcock are fitted, the change occuring on 1975 models.

2. On 1974 and earlier models, shut off the fuel and unscrew and remove the sediment bowl. Take out the o-ring and the fuel filter screen. Clean the bowl and filter screen in solvent and inspect the filter for any holes or other defects. If punctured, or so badly clogged that it cannot be properly cleaned, replace the screen. Inspect the o-ring for cuts or cracks. Reinstall the screen, o-ring, and sediment bowl. Turn on the petcock and check for leaks before operation.

Petcock filter screen and o-ring

3. In 1975 and later models, the petcock filter screen is inside the gas tank. Shut off the fuel flow and disconnect the fuel lines. Remove the gas tank and drain off the gas. Unscrew its securing nut and carefully take out the petcock. Remove the filter and securing nut from the petcock. Wash the filter in solvent to remove any foreign matter. Replace the filter if it is badly clogged or if punctured. Check the condition of the gasket and replace it if it is crushed or nicked. Installation is the reversal of removal. Be sure that the fuel lines are properly secured to the petcock with safety clips. Check for leaks before operation.

Air Filter

1969–78

1. Remove one of the side covers. Access to the filter element is gained by removing either the wing-nuts on the underside of the air cleaner case or the mounting bolts on top of the case, depending on the model.

2. Remove the lower half of the case and take out the filter element.

3. Tap the element lightly to remove any loose dirt, or use a reasonably soft brush to remove deposits. Blow out remaining dirt by applying compressed air to the inside of the element, if feasible.

Air cleaner box wing nuts (1969–1978)

4. Since cleaning paper elements is only partially effective, the unit should be replaced with a new one every 6,000 miles, or more often if used in a dusty environment.

1979 AND LATER

1. Remove the left side cover.
2. Remove the two air cleaner cover screws and take off the cover.
3. Pull out the air cleaner element set spring and remove the element.
4. Tap the element lightly to remove any loose dirt, or use a reasonably soft brush to remove deposits. Blow out remaining dirt by applying compressed air to the inside of the element, if feasible.
5. Since cleaning paper elements is only partially effective, the unit should be replaced with a new one every 8,000 miles, or more often if used in a dusty environment. If in doubt, and the element seems excessively dirty, replacement is recommended.
6. Installation is the reverse of removal.

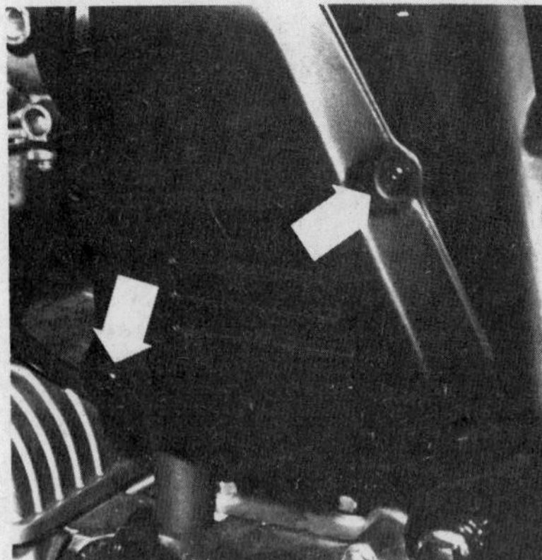

Air cleaner box screws (1979–1980)

Breather Element

1. A crankcase rebreather is fitted to late models before 1979. The breather is accessible after raising the seat.
2. Remove the breather case mounting bolt and disconnect the lines.
3. Remove the two case screws and separate the components: case cover, cover gasket, spring, retaining plate, and breather element.
4. Wash the element in a safe solvent and dry thoroughly. Refit the components in the reverse of the removal procedure.

Breather Tube

1. Models 1979–1981 are fitted with a plugged breather tube which must be drained at the fuel system service interval.
2. Remove the drain plug and allow the deposits to drain into a small container. When refitting the plug, be sure that it is pushed all the way into the tube.

Breather tube location

Recommended Lubricants

Engine
- General, all temperatures: SAE 10W-40, service rating "SE" or "SF"
- Above 60°F (15°C): SAE 30
- 15° to 60°F (−10° to 15°C): SAE 20 or 20W
- Above 15°F (−10°C): SAE 20W-50, service rating "SE" or "SF"
- Below 32°F (0°C): SAE 10W

Subtransmission
- SAE 80 Hypoid gear oil

Front forks
- ATF (1973 and later)
- SAE 10W-30 (1972 and earlier)
- SAE 20W
- SAE 30W

Rear drive box
- Above 40°F : SAE 90
- Below 40°F : SAE 80

Disc brakes
- DOT 3 standard brake fluid

Control cables
- Light motor oil
- Graphite-based lubricant
- Molybdenum-disulphide-based lubricant

Tach, speedometer cables; throttle twist-grip
- Light duty grease

Wheel and steering head bearings
- Waterproof, medium-weight bearing grease

Grease fittings
- Waterproof, medium-weight chassis grease

Drive chain
- 1969–1976: Lubricant developed specifically for motorcycle drive chains
- 1977–1981. SAE 80 or 90 gear oil

Periodic Maintenance Intervals ①

Before each ride
- Safety items
- Operation of lights
- Chain adjustment
- Control cable adjustment

Weekly
- Engine oil level
- Tire pressure (check when cold)
- Battery electrolyte level

Every 200 miles
- Lubricate chain (1976 and earlier)

Every 500 miles
- Check tightness of critical fasteners
- Lubricate chain (1977 models)

Every 1,500 miles/3 months
- Change engine oil (1969–1978 except 750A)

Every 2,000 miles
- Clean and lubricate drive chain

Every 3,000 miles/6 months
- Change engine oil (750A)
- Change oil filter (1969–1978)
- Service all grease fittings
- Clean breather element (if fitted)
- Clean air filter element (1969–1978)
- Lubricate breaker cam felt
- Clean fuel petcock screen
- Lubricate all controls and cables
- Check disc brake fluid level
- Check brake pads or shoes for wear
- Check operation of brake controls
- Check clutch operation
- Check condition of chain and sprockets
- Check condition of fuel lines
- Clean and check carburetor operation
- Check spokes for tightness
- Check swing arm bushings
- Clean and gap or replace spark plugs
- Clean and gap breaker points
- Check ignition timing
- Adjust valve clearance
- Adjust cam chain tensioner

Every 4,000 miles/12 months
- Change engine oil (1979–1981)
- Change oil filter (1979–1981)
- Change fork oil (1979–1981)
- Clean air filter element (1979–1981)

Every 6,000 miles/12 months
- Check parking brake (750A)
- Change fork oil (1969–1978 except 750A)
- Replace air filter element (1969–1978)
- Adjust steering head bearings
- Check oil pressure

Every 8,000 miles
- Replace air filter element (1979–1981)
- Lubricate drive shaft coupling (900)

Every 12,000 miles/24 months
- Flush and refill disc brake system
- Clean oil filter screen
- Change fork oil (750A)
- Repack wheel and steering head bearings

Every 24,000 miles/48 months
- Change subtransmission oil (900)
- Change drive box oil (900)

①Based on normal usage after initial service and break-in are completed.

Maintenance Data

Item	*750 and K-Models (K1-K2) (1969–1972)*	*750 K-Models (1973–1978)*	*750F (1975–1978)*	*750A*	*750K/F (1979–1981)*	*900C/F*
Fuel capacity (gal)	4.5	①	4.3	5.1	5.3	4.4
Oil capacity (qt)	3.7 ③	3.7 ③	3.7 ③	②	⑥	⑧
Front forks (cc/oz)						
Routine change	200–210/ 6.8–7.1	145/4.9	145/4.9	145/4.9	155/5.2	—
After rebuilding	220–230/ 7.5–7.8	155–160/ 5.3–5.4	155–160/ 5.3–5.4	155–160/ 5.3–5.4	173–178/ 5.8–6.0	280/9.5
Tire pressure (psi)						
Solo (front/rear)	28/28	④	32/40	25/32	28/32	32/32
Two-up or extended high speed (front/rear)	32/34	⑤	32/42	28/36	28/40	32/40
Battery						
Voltage/output (v/ah)	12/14	12/14	12/14	12/20	12/14	12/14
Continuous charging rate (amps)	1.4	1.4	1.4	2.0	1.4	1.4
Oil pressure (psi)						
Warm engine @ 3000 rpm	50–64	50–64	50–64	50–64	⑦	⑦

①1973–1976: 4.5
1977: 5.0
②Routine charge: 4.2
After rebuilding: 5.8
③Oil tank capacity at upper dipstick mark: 2.1 qt. Sump and oil filter hold remaining 1.6 qt
④1973–1975: 28/30
1976–1978: 28/28
⑤1973–1975: 32/34
1976–1978: 32/40
⑥Routine change: 3.7
After rebuilding: 4.7
⑦71 psi @ 7000 rpm
⑧Routine change: 3.7
After rebuilding: 4.8
Subtransmission: 20.4 oz/600 cc
Rear drive box: 5.10 oz/150 cc

NOTE: *The breather tube should be drained more frequently if the motorcycle is used in the rain or often at wide open throttle.*

Carburetors

1. Although major overhaul of the carburetors requires their removal as a unit, the float bowl and jets can be cleaned with the units in place.

2. Make sure the petcock is shut off. Drain the fuel from the carburetor float bowls.

3. On most models, the foat bowls are secured with a retaining clip. When flipped up, carefully lower the float bowl until it is clear of the floats. On late models, the float bowls are secured by phillips screws. Observe the same cautions when removing them.

4. Unscrew the pilot jet. With a suitable socket, unscrew and remove the main jet holder, which will come out with the main jet and emulsion tube. On 1979–1981 models, the primary main jet comes out with a screwdriver. Blow the jets clear, then install. Clean any residue out of the float bowl. When installing, be sure to position the bowl carefully to avoid damage to the floats. If secured by screws, tighten them gradually and evenly.

TUNE-UP

NOTE: *Common tune-up procedures are explained in detail in the "General Information" section.*

Twin-cam models (1979–80) require feeler gauges, a micrometer, and a special tool to hold down the valve spring for valve clearance adjustments.

For ignition timing on 1969–78 models, marks are provided to determine piston position, but a test light or ohmmeter is necessary to determine when the points open. If the dynamic timing method is used, an automotive-type strobe light is needed. The strobe light can be used to check the timing both at idle and at full advance, and therefore this method is considered the most accurate way of setting the timing.

1979–81 models feature a transistorized breakless ignition system. Timing should be checked with a strobe light. There is a static timing check possible, but the results will not be as accurate.

CAUTION: *Due to the automatic transmission, all running engine adjustments to the 750A must be carried out with the rear wheel firmly supported off the ground, the transmission in neutral, and the parking brake applied, unless specifically stated otherwise.*

Many adjustments call for the use of a tachometer, which is not fitted to the 750A. An automotive tach-dwell unit makes a satisfactory substitute. Readings must be adjusted. Engine rpm will be *twice* that shown on the 4-cylinder scale of an automotive tach-dwell meter, or *four times* that shown on the 8-cylinder scale.

COMPRESSION TEST

1. A compression check should be made before each tune-up since this will provide a general idea of engine condition.

2. It is necessary to have a gauge with a flexible hose and the proper screw-in adapter (plug holes are 12 mm).

3. The engine should be at operating temperature when checking compression.

4. Remove all of the spark plugs and fit the gauge to one of the plug holes.

5. Close the choke and hold the throttle wide open while spinning the engine with the starter motor. Note the compression reading and repeat the test with the remaining cylinders.

6. Compression may vary according to gauge tolerance and several other factors. However, it should normally be between 140 and 170 psi. All cylinders must be within 15 psi of this range and of each other.

CAM CHAIN ADJUSTMENT

1969–78

1. Disconnect the fuel lines from the petcock, raise the seat, and remove the gas tank.

2. Remove the points cover. Remove the valve adjuster caps from the No. 1 (left outside) cylinder, and remove all four spark plugs.

3. Using a wrench on the special nut provided for this purpose on the end of the breaker cam shaft, turn the engine over in the normal direction of rotation (clockwise as seem from the right side) until the "T" (top dead center) mark for cylinders Nos. 1 and 4 align with the timing index mark (1.4).

4. Check that there is clearance at both valves for the No. 1 cylinder. If not, turn the crankshaft one complete revolution (360°)

Cam chain adjustment bolt (1969–1978)

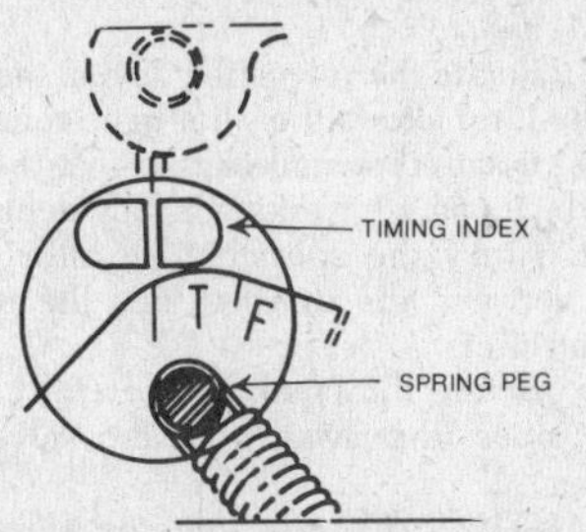

Crankshaft position for cam chain adjustment (1969–1978)

until the marks again align, and check the valves. To be effective, the chain adjustment must be performed when the No. 1 cylinder is on the compression stroke.

5. After the crankshaft has been properly positioned, continue to turn it clockwise until the spring peg on the timing advancer is just to the right of the timing index mark. In this position, cylinders 1 and 4 will be at 15° ATDC (after top dead center) and the adjustment can be performed.

CAUTION: *Do not rotate the crankshaft counterclockwise (opposite the direction of normal rotation) if you have turned it too far. Instead, rotate it clockwise through two revolutions so that the No. 1 piston will again be on the compression stroke and you can position the spring peg just to the right of the timing mark without having to turn the crankshaft back. Otherwise all of the slack may not be taken out of the chain.*

6. After positioning the crankshaft as outlined, loosen the cam chain tensioner bolt locknut and back out the bolt until you can turn it with your fingers. At this point, the tensioner bolt has released the tensioner rod, which is spring-loaded and which will move in automatically to take up the chain slack. Then tighten the tensioner bolt to 5.9–7.2 ft lbs and secure the locknut.

1979 and Later

The cam chain adjustment is made with the engine running. Read the procedure carefully first to cut down on the time the engine will have to idle.

1. Start the engine and let it idle.
2. Loosen the front cam chain tensioner bolt locknut. Turn the bolt out ½ turn. Tighten the bolt and secure the locknut.

Front cam chain adjustment bolt (1978–1981)

Rear cam chain tensioner bolts (1978–1981)

3. There are two cam chain tensioner locknuts behind the cylinders. Loosen both locknuts ½ turn, then tighten each one.

Cam chain tension will be set automatically when the bolt and locknuts are first loosened, then secured.

VALVE ADJUSTMENT

1969–78

In the following procedure, the cylinders are numbered 1 through 4, going from left to right from the point of view of a rider sitting on the machine. The firing order is 1-2-4-3.

NOTE: *Valves must be adjusted when the engine is COLD.*

1. Disconnect the fuel lines from the petcock, raise the seat, and remove the gas tank.
2. Unscrew and remove the valve adjuster caps from each cylinder. Remove the points cover. Remove the spark plugs.
3. Using a wrench on the special nut on the end of the contact breaker shaft, turn the engine over in the normal direction of rota-

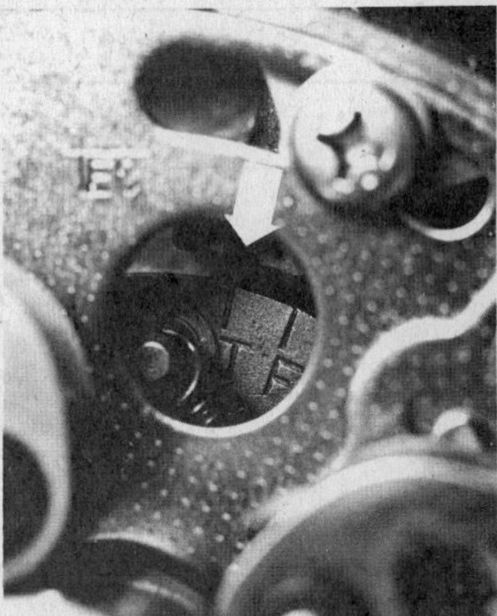

Crankshaft position for valve adjustment: cylinders 1 & 4 at TDC

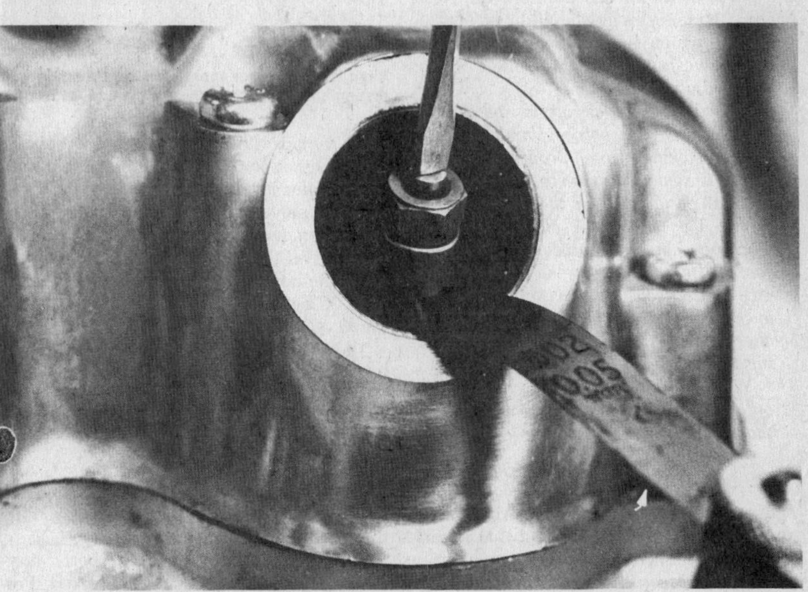

Adjusting valve clearance

tion (clockwise) and observe the valves of the No. 1 (left outside) cylinder. When the intake valve opens and then closes, the piston is approaching top dead center (TDC) on the compression stroke. Continue to turn the crankshaft slowly while observing the timing marks on the timing advancer. When the "T" 1.4 mark aligns with the index mark, check for clearance at both valves for the No. 1 cylinder. If there is clearance here, the crankshaft is properly positioned with the No. 1 cylinder at TDC on the compression stroke, and the valves can be adjusted according to the following procedure. If there is not clearance at both valves, the piston is at TDC on the *exhaust* stroke and the engine must be turned through one complete revolution until the "T" 1.4 mark again comes into alignment.

4. When the engine is properly set up as outlined in step 3, half the valves can be adjusted. These are the valves identified as "A" in the following chart:

(Looking down on the engine, from the rider's position.) Right side

Valves	*No. 1 Cyl*	*No. 2 Cyl*	*No. 3 Cyl*	*No. 4 Cyl*
Exhaust Valves	A	A	B	B
Intake Valves	A	B	A	B

5. Valve clearances are 0.05 mm (0.002 in.) (intake) and 0.08 mm (0.003 in.) (exhaust) measured between the valve stem and the adjusting screw. If the valve clearance is correct, a feeler gauge blade of this thickness will be a light slip fit. That is, there should be some resistance when pulling the blade through the valve, but not a considerable amount.

6. If the clearance is too large or too small, loosen the valve adjuster locknut and turn the adjuster so that a slip fit is obtained. Hold the adjuster in position and tighten the locknut securely (11–12 ft lbs). Recheck clearance after tightening the nut.

7. After all of the "A" valves are adjusted, turn the crankshaft one complete revolution (360°) until the "T" 1.4 mark again aligns with the index mark. In this position, the No. 4 (right outside) cylinder should be at TDC on the compression stroke (check for clearance at both valves) and the valves marked "B" can now be adjusted.

NOTE: *When the engine is at operating temperature, the valves should be very quiet. Ticking from properly adjusted valves is sometimes due to the valve stem becoming indented by the valve adjuster screw. This should be confined to older machines, since the valve ends are stellite-coated. Indentations on the valve stem will give a false feeler gauge reading: the clearance will be too large. Valves can be checked by visual inspection by unscrewing the adjuster.*

While more annoying than harmful, the only safe remedy for this situation is replacement of the valves.

1979 and Later

Valve clearance can be *checked* with an ordinary feeler gauge. If *adjustment* is necessary, however, a micrometer and special valve lifter holder, as well as a selection of shims, will be necessary.

CAUTION: *We recommend that this operation be left to persons with the required tools and experience.*

CHECKING CLEARANCE

NOTE: *Valve clearance must be checked when the engine is COLD.*

1. Lean the motorcycle to the left to drain as much oil as possible from the head.

2. Remove the side covers. Raise the seat.

Checking valve clearance

Align the cam index mark with the cylinder head mating surface before checking valve clearance

3. Remove the gas tank.

4. Disconnect the tachometer cable from the cylinder head cover.

5. Remove the spark plug caps.

6. Remove the cylinder head cover bolts and take off the cover.

7. Remove the alternator cover.

8. Clearance for all valves is 0.08 mm/0.003 in.

The acceptable clearance range is 0.06–0.13 mm/0.002–0.005 in.

This clearance is measured by inserting a feeler gauge blade of the proper thickness between the cam lobe and the valve lifter shim.

A feeler gauge blade which is the proper thickness gives a light drag when pulled through the actual clearance.

The crankshaft must be properly positioned before the clearance is checked. Proceed as follows:

9. Rotate the crankshaft clockwise when viewed from the right side of the engine and align the index mark on the right side of the exhaust camshaft with the front cylinder head mating surface.

Check and record the clearances of the *exhaust* valves for Cylinder Nos. 1 and 3.

NOTE: *Cylinders are numbered consecutively 1 through 4 with No. 1 being on the left from the point of view of a rider.*

10. Rotate the crankshaft clockwise 180° (the cams will turn 90°).

Check and record the clearances of the *intake* valves for Cylinder Nos. 1 and 3.

11. Rotate the crankshaft clockwise 180°.

Check and record the clearances of the *exhaust* valves for Cylinder Nos. 2 and 4.

12. Rotate the crankshaft 180° clockwise.

Check and record the clearances of the *intake* valves for Cylinder Nos. 2 and 4.

13. If adjustment of any valve is necessary, proceed to the next section.

ADJUSTING CLEARANCE

1. If the measured valve clearance is not within specification (0.06–0.13 mm/0.002–0.005 in.), continue to insert feeler gauge blades between the cam and valve lifter shim to find the actual clearance. The feeler gauge blade should be a light drag when pulled through.

Record the actual clearance.

NOTE: *Valve adjustment shims are available in 0.05 mm increments from 2.30 to 3.50 mm.*

2. Rotate the valve lifter so that the notch on the lifter allows the shim to be removed.

3. Rotate the crankshaft so that the valve on which you are working is fully depressed.

4. Insert the special valve lifter holder tool between the camshaft and the two adjacent lifters.

5. Rotate the crankshaft carefully so the cam lobes turn away from the valve lifter holder.

CAUTION: *Be sure that the other camshaft does not begin to open the valves for the cylinder you are adjusting. They could hit the valves which the special tool is holding open.*

6. Remove the installed shim with a tweezers. Measure and record the thickness of this shim with a micrometer.

Turn the tappet around, if necessary, to remove the shim

Removing the adjustment shim while the valve is held open by the special tool

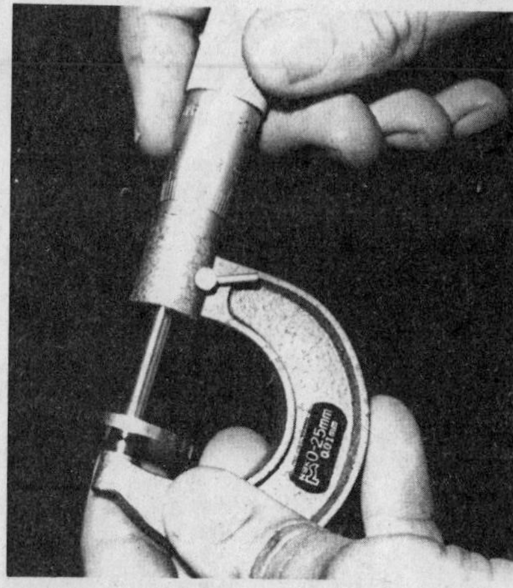

Measuring shim thickness

7. Refer to the valve shim selection chart.

The measured clearances run down the left side of the chart. The shim just removed can be found across the top of the chart.

To find the correct replacement shim, find the spot where the two readings meet. The shaded columns in the chart will serve as an example.

NOTE: *The thickest available shim is 3.5 mm. If a thicker shim is required to acheive the specification, there is evidently a good deal of carbon on the valve seats. A complete valve job is recommended.*

8. When the correct replacement shim is obtained, measure its thickness just to be sure.

9. Insert the new shim. Carefully turn the crankshaft so that the cam lobes will hold the valves you are adjusting fully open.

CAUTION: *Again, do not allow the lobes of the other cam to open the valves on the cylinder you are working on.*

10. Remove the special tool.

11. Rotate the crankshaft several times to seat the new shim. Recheck the clearance.

CONTACT BREAKER POINTS

Location

The points and condensers are located on the right end of the crankshaft beneath the chromed points cover. The timing advance mechanism is fitted onto the crankshaft behind the breaker point base plate.

Replacement

1. Points sets are available complete with condensers already mounted on the breaker plate. Removal is accomplished by removing the small 6-mm nut on the end of the breaker cam and taking off the large nut used to turn the engine over. This large nut is keyed to its shaft, not threaded. Next, disconnect the primary wires at the connectors behind the engine. Carefully pull the wires through, noting the proper routing. Remove the three screws which secure the breaker plate. When the new plate is fitted, position it so that the securing screws are approximately centered in their slots, and adjust the point gaps and the ignition timing.

2. If the points are purchased separately, disconnect the primary wire at each point set, remove the securing screw, and remove the old points. When installing new points, note that the proper installation of the insulating washers at the primary terminal is critical. If improperly installed, no spark will occur. There is a small insulating tube which fits around the terminal bolt and two insulating washers, one immediately on either side of the terminal bracket. All connectors (condenser, primary wire, points spring) are made on the outer sides of these washers (i.e., no connector must touch the bracket, which is a ground).

3. New points may have a protective coating on the contact surfaces to prevent oxidation. Clean off these surfaces with a non-oily solvent before attempting to start the machine.

VALVE SHIM SELECTION CHART   STANDARD VALVE CLEARANCE = $0.08^{+0.05}_{-0.02}$ mm

VALVE CLEARANCE mm / PRESENT SHIM SIZE mm (SHIM mm)	2.30	2.35	2.40	2.45	**2.50** (EX)	2.55	2.60	2.65	2.70	2.75	2.80	2.85	2.90	2.95	3.00	3.05	3.10	3.15	3.20	3.25	3.30	3.35	3.40	3.45	3.50
0.01–0.05		2.30	2.35	2.40	**2.45**	2.50	2.55	2.60	2.65	2.70	2.75	2.80	2.85	2.90	2.95	3.00	3.05	3.10	3.15	3.20	3.25	3.30	3.35	3.40	3.45
0.06–0.13	SPECIFIED CLEARANCE														NO CHANGE REQUIRED										
EX **0.14–0.16**	**2.35**	**2.40**	**2.45**	**2.50**	**2.55**	2.60	2.65	2.70	2.75	2.80	2.85	2.90	2.95	3.00	3.05	3.10	3.15	3.20	3.25	3.30	3.35	3.40	3.45	3.50	
0.17–0.21	2.40	2.45	2.50	2.55	2.60	2.65	2.70	2.75	2.80	2.85	2.90	2.95	3.00	3.05	3.10	3.15	3.20	3.25	3.30	3.35	3.40	3.45	3.50		
0.22–0.26	2.45	2.50	2.55	2.60	2.65	2.70	2.75	2.80	2.85	2.90	2.95	3.00	3.05	3.10	3.15	3.20	3.25	3.30	3.35	3.40	3.45	3.50			
0.27–0.31	2.50	2.55	2.60	2.65	2.70	2.75	2.80	2.85	2.90	2.95	3.00	3.05	3.10	3.15	3.20	3.25	3.30	3.35	3.40	3.45	3.50				
0.32–0.36	2.55	2.60	2.65	2.70	2.75	2.80	2.85	2.90	2.95	3.00	3.05	3.10	3.15	3.20	3.25	3.30	3.35	3.40	3.45	3.50					
0.37–0.41	2.60	2.65	2.70	2.75	2.80	2.85	2.90	2.95	3.00	3.05	3.10	3.15	3.20	3.25	3.30	3.35	3.40	3.45	3.00						
0.42–0.46	2.65	2.70	2.75	2.80	2.85	2.90	2.95	3.00	3.05	3.10	3.15	3.20	3.25	3.30	3.35	3.40	3.45	3.50							
0.47–0.51	2.70	2.75	2.80	2.85	2.90	2.95	3.00	3.05	3.10	3.15	3.20	3.25	3.30	3.35	3.40	3.45	3.50								
0.52–0.56	2.75	2.80	2.85	2.90	2.95	3.00	3.05	3.10	3.15	3.20	3.25	3.30	3.35	3.40	3.45	3.50									
0.57–0.61	2.80	2.85	2.90	2.95	3.00	3.05	3.10	3.15	3.20	3.25	3.30	3.35	3.40	3.45	3.50										
0.62–0.66	2.85	2.90	2.95	3.00	3.05	3.10	3.15	3.20	3.25	3.30	3.35	3.40	3.45	3.50											
0.67–0.71	2.90	2.95	3.00	3.05	3.10	3.15	3.20	3.25	3.30	3.35	3.40	3.45	3.50												
0.72–0.76	2.95	3.00	3.05	3.10	3.15	3.20	3.25	3.30	3.35	3.40	3.45	3.50													
0.77–0.81	3.00	3.05	3.10	3.15	3.20	3.25	3.30	3.35	3.40	3.45	3.50														
0.82–0.86	3.05	3.10	3.15	3.20	3.25	3.30	3.35	3.40	3.45	3.50															
0.87–0.91	3.10	3.15	3.20	3.25	3.30	3.35	3.40	3.45	3.50																
0.92–0.96	3.15	3.20	3.25	3.30	3.35	3.40	3.45	3.50																	
0.97–1.01	3.20	3.25	3.00	3.35	3.40	3.45	3.50																		
1.02–1.06	3.25	3.30	3.35	3.40	3.45	3.50																			
1.07–1.11	3.30	3.35	3.40	3.45	3.50																				
1.12–1.16	3.35	3.40	3.45	3.50																					
1.17–1.21	3.40	3.45	3.50																						
1.22–1.26	3.45	3.50																							
1.27–1.31	3.50																								

To remove the points, disconnect the primary wires (small arrows) and remove the securing screws (larger arrows)

Point wire connectors

4. If the motorcycle will not start immediately after installation of new points, check that the primary wire connections behind the engine are tight, that the insulating washers at the primary terminal are properly installed, and that the contact surfaces are thoroughly cleaned.

5. Condensers are easily replaced after disconnecting the lead at the primary terminal and removing the screw which secures the condenser to the base plate.

Gapping

Feeler Gauge Method

Periodic gapping is necessary to compensate for erosion of the contact surfaces due to electrical arcing and for wear of the fiber heel. As the heel wears, the points will open later relative to the rotaiton of the crankshaft, thus retarding the timing slightly.

Points should be filed (if necessary) and cleaned before gapping.

1. Remove the points cover.
2. Using the special nut, turn the engine over until one of the two sets of points is fully open.
3. With the proper feeler gauge blade, check the gap. The proper specification is 0.3–0.4 mm (0.012–0.016 in.), and the blade should be a slip fit between the points if the gap is correct.
4. If adjustment is necessary, loosen the screw which secures the point set to its plate, and use a small screwdriver at the pry point provided to adjust the gap.

CAUTION: *Loosen the screw just enough to allow the points to be moved. If loosened too much, the points will snap shut instead of holding the gap.*

5. Tighten the screw and recheck the gap. It may change slightly when the screw is tightened.
6. Repeat the procedure with the remaining points set. Try to adjust both sets so that the feeler gauge blade has the same "feel" in both sets. This will help to ensure accurate timing.

Checking point gap. Loosen the securing screws (arrows) to adjust the gap

7. If it is not possible to gap the points correctly, the fiber heel is evidently worn; the points should then be replaced.

DWELL METER METHOD

Point gap can also be adjusted with the aid of a dwell meter if one is available. "Dwell" is the amount of time the points are closed relative to crankshaft revolution and is expressed in degrees.

The adjustment is made with the engine idling, the positive meter connections lead to the primary wire terminal, and negative lead to the engine (ground).

With the meter set to the "8 cylinder" range, the proper dwell specification will be 23.75°; if set to the "4 cylinder" range, it will be 47.5°.

Increasing the point gap will decrease the dwell reading, and vice-versa.

Lubrication

1. On all models it is necessary to occasionally lubricate the cam follower fiber heel and the pivot point of the contact breaker. This minimizes wear and ensures that the timing will remain accurate for a longer period. A worn heel will retard the timing.
2. A small dab of grease (high melting point, if possible) should be applied to the lubricator wick so that the lubricator can distribute it onto the breaker cam. A drop of engine oil should be applied to the pivot point.
3. In both cases it is imperative that care be taken to keep the lubricant away from the points contact surface.
4. The lubricating wick should be adjusted so that it just contacts the breaker cam.

IGNITION TIMING

1969–78

The timing advance mechanism behind the breaker plate is fitted with marks which indicate piston position when they are aligned with the stationary timing mark (visible through the inspection hole in the breaker plate). There are two sets of marks, identified 1.4 and 2.3 to indicate which cylinders they represent.

The timing marks on the advance mechanism are interpreted as follows: "T" indicates top dead center, "F" is the fixed advanced firing point, which is when the plug fires

Automatic advance mechanism timing marks

before the automatic timing advancer comes into play and is about 10° BTDC. An additional pair of marks indicates the full advance firing point, which is 33°–36° BTDC above 2500 rpm.

NOTE: *Points must be cleaned and gapped before checking timing. Dirty points will cause inaccurate readings.*

Observing the breaker plate, note that the points set on the left are marked "1.4." They control the timing for those two cylinders, and are secured to the large base plate. The righthand points, marked "2.3," are mounted on a smaller moveable plate. Therefore, cylinders 1 and 4 are set first, and the timing for this pair is adjusted by rotating the entire base plate. Obviously, this will affect the timing of the remaining cylinders. The latter are adjusted, if necessary, by moving only the points themselves as they have slotted fittings for this purpose.

Loosen the three screws (larger arrows) and rotate the braker plate to adjust the timing for cylinders 1 & 4. Loosen the two screws (smaller arrows) and move the breaker points to adjust the timing for cylinders 2 & 3

DYNAMIC TIMING

1. Clean and gap both sets of points as described previously.
2. Hook up the strobe light according to the directions of the light's manufacturer to pick up the impulses from the No. 1 (left outside) cylinder.
3. Start the engine and adjust the idle, if necessary, to the recommended idle speed.
4. Aim the light at the timing marks visible through the inspection hole in the points base plate. At idle, the "F" mark should align with the timing index mark.
5. To check ignition timing at full advance, increase the engine speed until the motor is turning 2,500–3,000 rpm. At this point, the timing index mark should be between the two full advance marks scribed into the timing advance mechanism.
6. If adjustment is necessary, carefully loosen the three base plate screws and rotate the plate so that the proper marks align at the specified rpm. Establishing this alignment at full advance is recommended. Tighten the base plate screws.
7. Repeat the procedure, this time having the strobe light pick up cylinder No. 2. If adjustment is necessary, loosen the two screws which secure points set 2.3 to its plate, and use a small screwdriver at the pry point provided to move the set so that proper mark alignment is achieved. Tighten the screws.
8. If it is not possible to achieve full advance alignment without moving the base plate or points set 2.3 all the way to the end of their range of allowable travel, it is possible that the points are either incorrectly gapped, or that they are worn to the point where they must be replaced.
9. If other troubles are encountered, see "Troubleshooting" below.

Full advance firing point aligned with timing mark (breaker plate removed for clarity)

STATIC TIMING

1. Connect one of the test light or tester leads to the primary wire terminal for the points set "1.4." Ground the other lead to the engine.
2. If the test device is not self-powered, turn the ignition switch *on* and be sure the kill switch is in the "on" position as well.
3. Turn the engine over in the normal direction of rotation until the "F" mark or cylinders 1 and 4 align with the timing index mark. The test instrument should react at the instant these marks align, indicating that the points have opened. If they do not, loosen the three base plate screws and rotate the base plate so that the points just open when these timing marks are in alignment. Moving the base plate clockwise will retard the timing; counterclockwise will advance it.

Cylinders 1 and 4 are now correctly timed. Tighten the base plate screws and recheck.

4. Repeat the procedure with points set 2.3. If adjustment is necessary, loosen the two screws which secure these points to their mounting plate and use a small screwdriver at the pry point provided. Tighten the screws and recheck the timing.

Fixed advance (F) mark aligned with timing mark

Checking the operation of the automatic timing advance mechanism

TROUBLESHOOTING

1. If the static method is used, the reaction of the test light or meter should be positive when the points open. If the instrument seems to hesitate before indicating that the points are open, it may be because of defective condensers or dirty or pitted points surfaces.
2. If it is necessary to move the base plate or the points plate to the extreme end of the adjustment range to effect proper timing, the points or points heel is probably worn to the limit, and the set should be replaced.
3. If the dynamic method is used, the various timing marks should hold their positions steadily to given rpms. If they seem to

move erratically, check the condition of the timing advance mechanism behind the base plate. Check for weak or broken springs or stiff movement of the advancer weights. When the breaker cam is turned so that the weights move outwards, and then is released, it should return to the original position. If it does not, the springs are too weak and must be replaced. Try penetrating oil or a spray parts easer to ease movement of the mechanism if it is stiff. If this fails, replace the mechanism.

4. If the advancer shaft is bent, which will be noticeable as the engine is turned over, remove the advance mechanism and bend the shaft so that total run-out is no more than 0.1 mm (0.004 in.). To remove the advancer mechanism, pull it off by grasping the plate, not the breaker cam. If the cam disengages from the plate, it is possible to reinstall it incorrectly.

When installing the advancer unit, make sure that the pin is fitted into the locating hole.

Timing marks and timing adjustment bolts

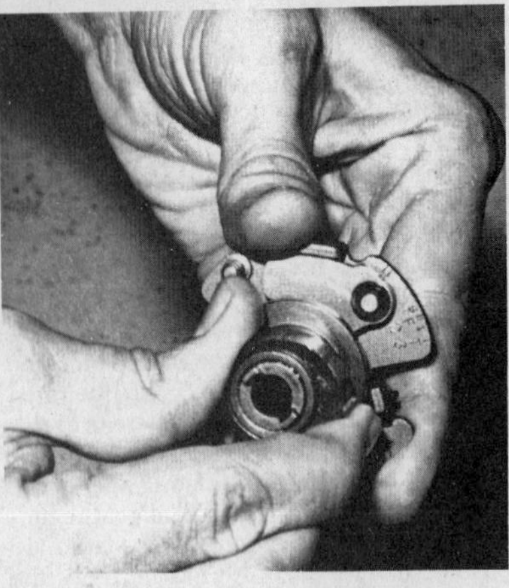

Checking advance mechanism operation

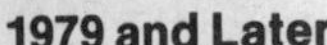

1979 and Later

The ignition system on these models is transistorized, and should therefore be trouble-free. Once set properly, the timing should not need readjustment.

An automotive timing light is the only accurate method of checking the timing. It allows the timing to be checked at idle as well as at full advance. There is, however, a crude static method (given below), but the accuracy of this check is problematical.

It is recommended to either use a strobe light or leave the timing alone.

1. Park the motorcycle on the centerstand in a well-ventilated area. Remove the pulser generator cover (left side).

Pulser generator cover screws

2. Connect the strobe light to the No. 1 (left) cylinder.

3. Start the engine and allow it to idle at about 1,000 rpm.

4. Check the timing marks through the window in the base plate. At about 1,000 rpm, the "1.4 F-I" mark on the timing advance mechanism should align with the index mark.

5. If the marks do not align, loosen the two large phillips screws or bolts at the top and bottom of the base plate just a bit, and turn the plate so that the marks are lined up. Tighten the two screws securely and recheck the timing.

Turning the plate clockwise will advance the timing, while counterclockwise rotation will retard it.

6. Full advance timing is not acheived until 6,000 rpm. Since engine damage may result on an unloaded engine at 8,000 rpm, the full advance check should only be carried out by someone with experience.

7. The full advance timing marks are two slash marks which, as noted, should align with the timing index mark at 6,000 rpm. If idle timing is correct, but full advance timing is not, the only trouble can be the timing advance mechanism. See "Troubleshooting," below.

Full advance marks aligned with index mark

Static timing alignment (arrow)

8. The static timing method is simple. Remove the generator cover. Rotate the crankshaft counterclockwise and align the "1.4 S-F" mark with the timing index mark. If the timing is correct, the narrow projection of the "1.4" pulser generator (the one of the left) will align with the rotor tooth. Adjustment is made by loosening the two large phillips screws or bolts at the top and bottom of the base plate and rotating the plate so that alignment is accomplished.

NOTE: *Either No. 1 or No. 4 cylinder must be on the firing stroke when the check is made. If alignment is not obvious, rotate the crankshaft 360° and recheck.*

TROUBLESHOOTING

Due to the nature of the system, any malfunction as regards spark or lack of same must be due to electrical causes.

If the timing marks align at idle speed, but not a full advance, the trouble is probably the timing advance mechanism located behind the pulser base plate.

The various timing marks should hold their positions steadily at any given rpm. If they seem to move erratically, this is also probably due to the advance mechanism.

After removing the pulser base plate, check the timing advance mechanism for weak or broken springs or stiff movement of the advancer weights. When the breaker cam is turned so that the weights move outwards, and then is released, it should return to the original position. If it does not, the springs are too weak and must be replaced. Try penetrating oil or a spray parts easer to ease movement of the mechanism if it is stiff. If this fails, replace the mechanism.

CARBURETORS

Carburetor adjustments to be made during a tune-up procedure include checking float level, idle speed, and mixture; carburetor synchronization; and travel limit adjustments.

CAUTION: *These adjustments should be made only in a well-ventilated area.*

To avoid engine damage due to an overheated engine, read the procedures several times before beginning. A large household window fan, positioned near the front of the engine, may help to keep engine temperature down during these adjustments.

Adjusting Float Level

Float level is a measure of the amount of gasoline which will be in the float bowls during operation. While it is a critical specification, it will not normally need readjustment once properly set. Float level, therefore, need not be checked at every tune-up, but should be attended to from time to time.

1. Remove the carburetors as outlined in "Fuel Systems."
2. Remove the float bowls. With the carburetor(s) positioned horizontally, lower the float until the float arm just touches the tip of the float needle. Float level is the measured distance from the bottom of the float to the float bowl mating surface.

Measuring float height (H)

Increase float height by bending the tang towards (B); decrease it by bending towards (A)

NOTE: *A special float level gauge (part No. 07144-99998) is available to facilitate this task.*

3. Compare the measured float level with the standard value given in the "Tune-Up Specifications" chart at the end of this section. Adjust, if necessary, by removing the float assembly and carefully bending the float arm tang. Bending the tang towards the carburetor body will increase the float level measurement, and vice-versa.
4. All carburetors must have the same float level. Measure all before changing any. Note that the measured float level will be inaccurate if the float needle tip is worn, or if there is foreign matter on the needle seat.

750 Pre-K Models

IDLE SPEED, MIXTURE, SYNCHRONIZATION

NOTE: *The following adjustments must be made when the engine is at operating temperature. Other tune-up operations (valve adjustment, ignition timing, etc.) should be performed first.*

1. Remove the air cleaner box and the gas tank.
2. Engage the choke. Check the clearance between the choke valve and the carburetor body for each unit. If the clearance is greater than 0.5 mm (0.02 in.), adjust by means of the variable length rods which connect the choke valves. After this adjustment, disengage the choke.
3. Adjust the throttle stops screws on each carburetor so that the "T" marks on the screws align with the index marks on the carburetor bodies.
4. Adjust each of the short throttle cables so that each has 1–2 mm (0.04–0.08 in.) of free-play before the slide(s) begin to lift. Use the cable adjuster atop each carburetor to make this adjustment, and try to adjust each carburetor so that the free-play of all the cables are as near to one another as possible.
5. Gently turn in the pilot screw on each carburetor until it is seated, then back each out one full turn.
6. Install the air cleaner and gas tank. At this point it would be helpful if the rear of the tank were proppeed up. The use of longer fuel lines will be necessary. Be sure the tank has a good supply of fuel.

For the following adjustments the engine must be fully warmed up.

7. Attach the vacuum gauge fittings to each of the carburetors. Start the engine and adjust the idle speed, if necessary, to 850–950 rpm by turning the throttle stop screws out in small equal increments. The gauges should read about 20–22 cm Hg. Lowering the idle speed will increase the vacuum and vice-versa. All cylinders must be within 3.0 cm (1.2 in.) Hg of each other. Use the throttle stop screws to equalize the pressure, if necessary.

NOTE: *Some vacuum gauges are equipped with adjustable dampers to eliminate needle oscillation. Do not overdampen the needles. A fluctuation of about 1 graduation of the scale is acceptable.*

8. If the pressure is below 15 cm (0.59 in.) Hg, check for sticking or improperly adjusted valves, lack of free-play in the throttle cable(s), loose spark plug(s), or air leaks at the manifolds.
9. Turn each pilot screw alternately in either direction about ⅛ turn at a time (pausing for a few seconds after each change) to determine the point at which the highest engine rpm is reached. It should not be necessary to turn the screws *out* more than 1 turn, nor *in* more than ½ turn from the standard setting. If it is, check the following:
   a. If the screw must be turned more than 1 additional turn out: clogged air passage, worn or damaged air screw taper, loose pilot jet, or float level set too high.
   b. If the screw must be turned more than ½ turn in: obstructed pilot jet or jet passage, worn or damaged pilot air screw seat, too low a float level.
10. Synchronize the throttle slides as follows: hold the throttle open about ¼ of the twist-grip rotation for about 30 seconds. All cylinders should show the same vacuum gauge reading within 3.0 cm (1.2 in.) Hg.

Correct any variation by means of the cable adjusters atop each carburetor. Increase the vacuum gauge reading by screwing the adjuster *in* and vice versa.

11. After all the cylinders have been equalized, snap the throttle open and shut a few times and recheck the adjustment. Be sure the cable adjuster locknuts are secured and the rubber caps refitted.
12. Adjust throttle cable free-play at the twist-grip, if necessary. Turn the forks slowly from side to side with the engine running to ensure that engine speed doesn't change, which would indicate badly adjusted or kinked cables.

NOTE: *During this procedure, do not allow the engine to overheat by idling for long periods of time while stationary. An ordinary household window fan can be used to blow air over the engine if the adjustment time takes longer than about five minutes.*

750K1–K5, 750 (76), 750F (75–76)

These adjustments must be made when the engine is at operating temperature. Other tune-up operations (valve adjustment, ignition timing, etc.) should be performed first.

SYNCHRONIZATION

1. Raise the rear of the fuel tank as far as the fuel lines will allow and support the tank in this position. It may be helpful to temporarily fit longer fuel lines so that the tank can be raised higher.
2. Slide the rubber boots on the carburetor tops back on the linkage arms.

Throttle idle adjusting screw, pilot screw (right) and vacuum gauge fitting (center)

Throttle rod adjustment nut

3. Connect the vacuum gauge tubes to the carburetors.

4. Start the engine and adjust the idle speed with the throttle stop screws to about 1,000 rpm.

5. Loosen the adjuster nut locknuts and turn the adjuster nuts until all carburetors are indicating uniformly (within 3.0 cm Hg) between 16–24 cm Hg. Turning the adjuster nuts clockwise increases vacuum, and counterclockwise decreases vacuum. Try not to increase the idle speed while making adjustments.

NOTE: *Some vacuum gauges are equipped with adjustable dampers to eliminate needle oscillation. Do not overdampen the needle. A fluctuation of about one gradation on the scale is acceptable.*

CAUTION: *Do not allow the engine to overheat by idling it for long periods while stationary. A household electric window fan can be used to provide a flow of air over the engine to prevent overheating when adjustment time exceeds more than about five minutes.*

6. After adjustment has been made, check to see that at least one thread on each throttle rod protrudes above the locknuts. If not, turn all four adjuster nuts in an equal amount until at least one thread on each throttle rod is exposed, reset the idle speed with the throttle stop screw, and recheck the vacuum readings.

7. Snap the throttle open several times to verify synchronization before tightening the locknuts.

CAUTION: *When tightening the locknuts, hold the adjuster nut in position with a wrench to prevent the torque from being transferred through the throttle rod and twisting it off. Tighten the locknuts to 11–17 in. lbs, or about 1 ft. lb. Do not overtighten.*

8. When refitting the rubber boots, make sure that the bottom rim is fully seated in the groove at the base of the adjuster linkage. It is a good idea at this time to open the throttle wide to expose the throttle rods and lubricate the rods and adjuster linkage with silicone grease. *Do not use a petroleum-based lubricant.* The throttle shaft pivots may be lubricated with motor oil.

IDLE ADJUSTMENT

Adjust the carburetor pilot screws so that the maximum vacuum draw is obtained, consistent with engine smoothness. Standard pilot screw adjustment range is ¾–1¼ turns from the fully closed position. Readjust the throttle stop screw, if necessary, to reduce idle speed to about 1,000 rpm. Recheck vacuum uniformity and idle smoothness. Remove the vacuum gauge tubes and tighten the carburetor plugs firmly.

THROTTLE CABLE ADJUSTMENT

Play Adjustment

1. Back off the cable adjuster at the handlebar to increase cable play. Leave a small amount of adjustment range available so that final, small adjustments can be made.

2. Loosen the cable locknut at the carburetor end and turn the adjuster until there is about 3–4 mm (0.12–0.17 in.) play at the throttle grip. Retighten the locknut.

NOTE: *The throttle lever should hit the eccentric pin when the throttle grip is forced to the fully closed position. If the lever will not hit the pin, replace the return cable.*

Clearance is measured between the eccentric pin (arrow) and the lever

3. Make any desired final cable play adjustment at the handlebar adjuster.

Overtravel Limit Adjustment

Simply loosen the locknut and turn the eccentric pin, as shown, until clearance between the pin and the throttle lever is 2–3 mm (0.08–0.12 in.).

Full Throttle Limit Adjustment

Adjust the throttle lever stop screw so that there is a distance of 32.5–33.0 mm (1.28–1.29 in.) between the carburetor top and the bottom of the adjuster linkage with the throttle fully open, as shown.

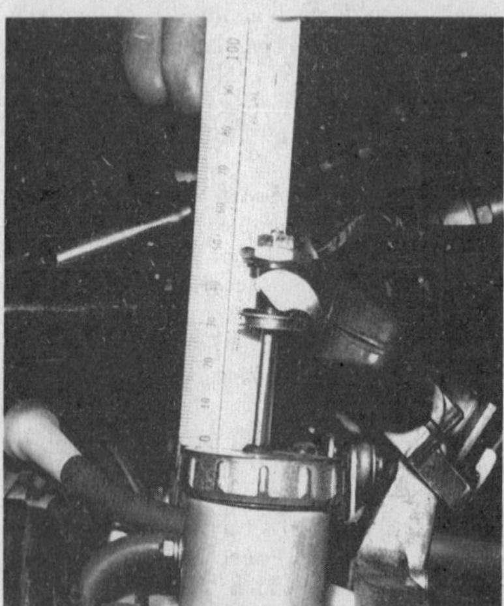

Checking full throttle limit adjustment

Throttle Rod and Linkage Lubrication

Lubricate the throttle rods and seals, and the linkage pivot points, as shown in the illustration. If this does not restore smooth throttle operation, the carburetor tops should be removed, the throttle components thoroughly cleaned and dried, and the throttle rod guides and seals lubricated with silicone grease. *Do not use a petroleum-based grease.*

750A

The following operations should be accomplished with the engine at operating temperature, except for setting the fast idle, which is performed on a cold engine. Other tune-up operations (valve adjustments, ignition timing, etc.) should be performed first.

SYNCHRONIZATION

1. Remove the gas tank, supporting it out of the way and higher than the carburetors so that access to the carburetor caps is simplified. Fit longer fuel lines so that the carburetors can be supplied. Connect the vacuum gauges. Connect the tachometer.

2. Start the engine and allow it to idle. Readings of all four gauges should be the same.

3. If vacuum gauge readings differ, remove the caps from the carburetors for cylinders Nos. 1, 3, and 4. The No. 1 cylinder is on the left from the rider's point of view.

4. Loosen the locknuts and turn the adjusters so that each carburetor yields the same vacuum reading as No. 2.

5. Adjust idle speed.

IDLE ADJUSTMENT

1. Engine must be at operating temperature. With the tachometer connected, adjust the throttle stop screw to yield an idle speed of 1,000 rpm. Transmission should be in "N."

2. With the machine on the center stand and the parking brake engaged, gently turn in the pilot screws until seated, then back off until the highest idle speed is reached, which should be about 1¼± ¾ turn from the seated position.

3. Readjust the throttle stop screw to give an idle speed of 1,000 rpm.

Linkage lubrication points

4. Shift the transmission into "L" or "D." If idle speed drops, adjust the throttle opener.

THROTTLE OPENER

1. The engine must be at operating temperature, on the center stand, and with the parking brake engaged. Connect a tachometer. Raise the rear of the gas tank to allow access to the adjusting screw.

2. With the transmission in "N," adjust idle speed to 1,000 rpm using the throttle stop screw.

3. Shift into "L" or "D." If idle speed varies, bring it back to 1,000 rpm using the throttle adjusting screw. Refer to the illustration. Shift into neutral and recheck the idle speed.

FAST IDLE

1. Fast idle speed is 3,000–4,000 rpm. Adjustment is made on a cold engine.

2. To adjust, pull the choke lever fully open. Turn the fast idle screw in until it just contacts the choke cam.

3. Release the choke and turn the fast idle screw an additional 2½ turns. Tighten the locknut.

4. Start the engine (cold), engage the choke and check idle speed.

ACCELERATOR PUMP

1. Two adjustments are necessary: the pump-rod-to-pump-arm clearance, and the pump-arm-to-carburetor-stay clearance.

2. With the throttle closed, check clearance between the pump rod and the pump arm (A). It should be 0.6–0.8 mm (0.024–0.032 in.). Adjust, if necessary, by bending the pump arm tongue very carefully.

Accelerator pump adjustments: A, pump rod and pump arm; B, pump arm and carburetor stay

3. With the throttle closed, check the clearance between the pump arm and the carburetor stay (B). It should be 10.0–10.5 mm (0.39–0.41 in.). Adjust, if necessary, by carefully bending the pump arm.

750K, 750F (1977–78)

These models are fitted with the newer type of carburetor similar to those of the 750A, and synchronization and idle speed adjustments are performed in the same manner with the obvious exception that all adjustments are made with the transmission in neutral with no need to worry about idle speed in gear. Also, there is no fast idle adjustment. Refer to the "750A" section for procedures.

750K, 750F (1979 AND LATER)/ 900C/F

These adjustments must be made when the engine is at operating temperature. Other tune-up operations (valve adjustment, ignition timing, etc.) should be performed first.

IDLE ADJUSTMENT

The pilot screws are pre-set. No adjustment is necessary unless the carburetors have been disassembled.

If adjustment is necessary, proceed as follows.

1. Turn each pilot screw in until it is lightly seated, then back each one out the following number of turns depending on the carburetors fitted:

VB42A: 1½ turns
VB42C: 1¾ turns

CAUTION: *Take care when screwing the pilot screws in. Damage to the tips may result if they are overtightened.*

2. When the engine is at operating temperature, adjust the idle speed with the throttle stop screw. Idle speed is 900–1,100 rpm.

3. Turn each pilot screw out ½ turn. If engine speed increases by 50 rpm or more, turn each screw out an additional ½ turn.

4. Readjust the idle speed with the throttle stop screw.

5. Turn the pilot screw for the No. 1 carburetor *in* until engine speed drops by 50 rpm.

Throttle idle adjusting screw

6. At this point, turn the No. 1 carburetor pilot screw *out* by ⅜ turn on VB42A units or ¾ turn on VB42C models.

7. Readjust idle speed with the throttle stop screws.

8. Repeat Steps 6 and 7 on the other carburetors.

9. Make final idle adjustment with the throttle stop screw so that the machine idles at 900–1,100 rpm.

SYNCHRONIZATION

A set of vacuum gauges is needed for carburetor synchronization. In addition, longer fuel lines will be needed, since the gas tank must be removed to allow access to the adjustment screws.

1. Remove the side covers and raise the seat.

2. Disconnect the fuel line and remove the gas tank. Connect the longer fuel line, and position the tank so that it is out of the way of the adjusting screws, but can still feed gasoline to the carburetors.

CAUTION: *Be sure that the gas tank is properly secured.*

3. Remove the plugs on the manifolds and install the vacuum gauge adaptors.

4. Start the engine. Set idle speed to 900–1,100 rpm.

5. All carburetors should give vacuum gauge readings within 2.4 in. Hg (6.0 mm Hg) of each other.

6. The No. 2 carburetor cannot be adjusted. The reading for this carburetor must be taken as the standard, and all others adjusted to it.

7. To equalize vacuum readings, loosen the adjusting screw locknuts, and turn the screws so that the vacuum for all four carburetors is as close as possible. Tighten the locknuts.

8. Rev the engine a few times and recheck vacuum readings. Readjust the idle speed if necessary.

Vacuum source on manifold

Idle speed screw

Carburetor synchronization screw

FAST IDLE

Fast idle should be 1,500–2,500 rpm. This reading is taken when the engine is *cold*.

1. Close the throttles and open the choke valve. Measure the clearance between the throttle link and the fast idle adjusting arm pin.

It should be 0.7–1.0 mm/0.03–0.04 in.

2. Adjust the fast idle, if necessary, by opening and closing the fork end of the fast idle adjusting arm.

ACCELERATOR PUMP

1. Measure the clearance between the accelerator pump rod and adjusting arm with the throttles closed. It should be 0–0.04 mm/0–0.0016 in.

2. This adjustment is made by bending the adjusting arm.

3. Measure the clearance between the adjusting arm and the stopper on the carburetor body. Clearance should be 3.1–3.3 mm/0.12–0.13 in. Adjust by bending the adjusting arm.

ENGINE AND TRANSMISSION

NOTE: *Engine rebuilding techniques and procedures are explained in detail in the "General Information" section.*

NOTE: *Be sure that bolt and nut threads are clean and undamaged before torquing. Torque readings apply to clean, dry threads unless otherwise noted.*

Engine Service

1. To remove the cylinder head, barrels, and pistons, the engine must be removed from the frame, on all models except the 750A. On 1979–81 models, the cams can be removed and installed with the engine still in the frame.

2. Crankcase cover components: oil pump, clutch, gearshift mechanism, alternator, and countershaft sprocket, are all accessible with the engine in the frame. Be sure to note the locations of oil guide pins and o-rings in the crankcase covers, cylinder head, and cylinder.

3. Read each procedure carefully before beginning so that replacement items such as

Tune-Up Specifications

Item	750, K-Models and F 1969–1978	750A	750K, 750F 1979–1981	900C/F
COMPRESSION				
Cranking pressure (psi)	140–170	140–170	156–184	142–198
Max allowable variation (psi)	15	15	15	15
VALVE CLEARANCE				
Intake (mm/in.)	0.05/0.002	0.05/0.002	0.08/0.003	0.08/0.003
Exhaust (mm/in.)	0.08/0.003	0.08/0.003	0.08/0.003	0.08/0.003
IGNITION				
Spark plugs				
OEM	NGK/ND	NGK/ND	NGK/ND	NGK/ND
Standard	D-8ES-L/X24ES	D-8ES-L/X24ES	D-8EA/X24ES-U	D-9EA/X27ES-U
Cold	D-8ES, D-10E	D-8ES, D-10E	D-7EA/X22ES-U	—
Hot	D-8E, D-7ES	D-8E, D-7ES	D-9EA/X27ES-U	D-8EA/X24ES-U
Spark plug gap (mm/in.)	0.6–0.7/0.024–0.028	0.6–0.7/0.024–0.028	0.6–0.7/0.024–0.028	0.6–0.7/0.024–0.028
Point gap (mm/in.)	0.3–0.4/0.012–0.016	0.3–0.4/0.012–0.016	na	na
Dwell (degrees)	①	①	na	na
Ignition timing				
Static (degrees BTDC)	10	10	10	10
Maximum (degrees BTDC @ 2500 rpm)	33–36	33–36	③	⑤
CARBURETION				
Idle speed (rpm)	950–1,000	950–1,000	900–1,100	1,000
Fast idle (rpm)	na	3,000–4,000	1,500–2,500	1,000–2,500
Pilot screw (turns out)	1 ± ½	1¼	④	na
Vacuum range (cm/in. Hg)	16–24/6.2–9.5	16–24/6.2–9.5	na	na
Uniformity (cm/in. Hg)	3.0/1.2	3.0/1.2	6.0/2.4	6.0/2.4
Float level (mm/in.)	②	14.5/0.57	15.5/0.61	15.5/0.61

① If read on a dwell meter "4 cyl" scale: 47.5°. On an "8 cyl" scale: 23.75°.
② 1969–1976: 26.0/1.02
1977–1978: 14.5/0.57
③ 40° @ 6,000 rpm
36° @ 7,400 rpm
④ VB42A: 1½
VB42C: 1¾
⑤ 38°30′ @ 3,200 rpm
na: not applicable

gaskets, o-rings, etc., can be purchased beforehand.

ENGINE REMOVAL AND INSTALLATION

1969–78 (Except 750A)

The following components can be serviced or replaced without removing the engine from the frame: oil pump, clutch, alternator, starter drive, cam chain tensioner, and gearshift linkage.

1. Turn the fuel tap off, disconnect the fuel lines, and remove the tank.
2. Drain the oil from the crankcase and oil tank, and remove the oil filter.
3. Remove the exhaust system.
4. Disconnect the tachometer cable from the cylinder head and remove the wires from the spark plugs.
5. Unscrew the carburetor caps and withdraw the slides (early models) or disconnect the throttle cables from the carburetor linkage (K1 and later).
6. Remove the air filter housing, disconnect the carburetors from the intake tubes, and remove the carburetors as an assembly.
7. Remove the kick-start lever and the clutch housing cover. Disconnect the clutch cable from the clutch lever.
8. Disconnect the brake-light switch spring and remove the brake pedal and footpeg.
9. Unbolt the two oil lines from the engine and remove the oil tank. Disconnect the oil tank breather line from the upper crankcase.
10. Remove the shift lever and take off the engine sprocket (rear crankcase) cover. Loosen the rear axle nut and drive chain adjusters so that the wheel can be moved forward and the chain can be lifted off the rear wheel sprocket. Remove the engine sprocket.
11. Disconnect the positive battery cable, then disconnect the starter motor cable at the solenoid, the alternator lead at the connector near the battery, and the brake light switch lead at the upper, right-side, rear motor mount.
12. Remove the engine mount bolts, as illustrated. Raise the rear of the engine and lift it out from the right side of the frame.

Installation is in reverse order of removal. The following points should be noted:

a. Be sure to connect the battery ground strap to the upper, rear engine-mount bolt as the bolt is installed.

b. Torque all mounting bolts to the proper specification. Refer to the "Torque Specifications" chart at the end of this section.

c. Take care to connect the scavenge and delivery oil lines in their original positions.

d. Make sure that the muffler connecting clamps are in place on each pair of mufflers.

e. When installation is complete, refill the engine with oil. Adjust the clutch, drive chain, and carburetors.

750A

It is possible to remove the cylinder head, barrels, and pistons without removing the engine from the frame. The alternator, torque converter, oil pump, transmission oil pump, and shift mechanism are also accessible.

1. Drain the oil. Shut off the fuel petcock, disconnect the fuel lines, and remove the gas tank.
2. Remove the left and right side covers. Remove the air cleaner box. Disconnect the carburetor overflow tubes. Disconnect the throttle cables and choke cable. Loosen the carburetor clamps and remove them together.
3. Disconnect the spark plug leads from the plugs.
4. Remove the rear brake pedal, the left and right footpegs, the shift lever, and the right-side passenger peg.
5. Remove the exhaust system.
6. Disconnect the wiring at the connectors on the right-side.
7. Disconnect the neutral return arm and the wiring connectors on the left side. Remove the engine sprocket cover. Loosen the rear wheel axle nut, back off the chain adjusters, and move the wheel forward. Unbolt and remove the engine sprocket.
8. Remove the oil filter and housing. Remove the oil pan and remove the oil screen from the engine oil pump.
9. Remove the engine mounting bolts and take the engine out from the left side of the machine.

Installation is the reverse of removal. Note the following points:

a. Be sure the battery negative cable is properly attached to its mounting bolt.

b. Tighten engine mounting bolts to the proper torque:

10 mm: 22–29 ft. lbs.
12 mm: 40–47 ft. lbs.

c. Check engine oil level, chain tension, etc., before starting the engine.

750 (1979 and Later)

1. Drain the oil. Remove the side covers. Raise the seat and disconnect the overflow tube.
2. Disconnect the fuel line at the fuel tank, and remove the tank.
3. Remove the air cleaner box and the carburetors.
4. Disconnect the wiring at the plastic connectors.
5. Remove the exhaust system.
6. Disconnect the spark plug caps from the plugs. Disconnect the tach cable at the head.
7. Push the rear wheel forward as much as possible after loosening the rear axle nut and folding down the chain adjusters. Remove the left rear crankcase cover. Unbolt and remove the engine sprocket along with the chain.
8. Remove the rear brake pedal. Remove the rider footpegs. Remove the gearshift lever. Disconnect the clutch cable at the engine.
9. Place a jack beneath the engine and raise it just slightly to get the engine weight off the mounting bolts. Remove the engine mounting bolts and plates and move the engine out of the frame towards the right side.

Installation is the reverse of removal. Note the following points:

Tighten engine mounting bolts to the proper torque values:

8 mm flange bolt/nut: 13–18 ft. lbs.
10 mm flange bolt/nut: 22–29 ft. lbs.
12 mm flange bolt/nut: 40–47 ft. lbs.

Tighten the engine sprocket bolt to 24–27 ft. lbs.

Be sure that all wires and cables are properly arranged and secured by clamps or cable ties where applicable.

After installation, adjust the throttle and clutch cables, choke cable, and drive chain tension.

900

1. Drain the oil. Remove the left and right side covers.
2. Remove the gas tank and seat.
3. Remove the side stand.
4. Remove the exhaust system.
5. Disconnect the oil cooler hoses from the engine.
6. Remove the air cleaner assembly and the carburetors.
7. Disconnect the tach cable at the engine. Disconnect the spark plug caps.
8. Disconnect the wiring at the couplers. Disconnect the starter motor cable and the battery negative cable.
9. Remove the brake pedal. Remove the brake pedal bracket lower mounting bolt and loosen the upper bolt.
10. Remove the clutch cable holder.
11. Remove the rear wheel. Remove the final drive gear. Move the swing arm boot back and disengage the drive shaft from the engine.
12. Place a jack beneath the engine to take the weight off the mounting bolts. Remove the mounting bolts and brackets and take the engine out of the frame from the left side.
13. Installation is the reverse of removal. Note the following torque settings:

8 mm: 14–17 ft. lbs.
10 mm: 25–33 ft. lbs.

TOP END

Cylinder Head Removal (1969–78)

1. Remove the engine from the frame. This is not necessary on 750A models provided that the gas tank, carburetors, and exhaust system are removed. Remove the spark plugs.
2. Take out the three bolts and remove the breather cover. Remove the starter motor cover.
3. Remove the cam cover screws and take off the cover, tapping the sides carefully with a plastic mallet to break it free, if necessary.
4. Remove the keeper bolts from each rocker arm shaft after the engine has been turned so that the two valves for the shaft you are removing are *closed*. After the bolts are removed, the shaft should be able to be pushed out easily. If this is not possible, turn the engine over slowly until the shafts are free.

NOTE: *Rocker arms and rocker arm shafts should be marked for location so that they*

Valve cover screws

Top end components

Rocker arm shaft bolts

can be reinstalled in their original locations.

5. Turn the engine over to align the valve timing marks at the right end of the camshaft with the cam bearing cap joint, as illustrated. Unbolt and remove the cam bearing caps.

Note that each cap is coded with a mark stamped on the cap and the cam holder which indicates the proper location of each cap, and the proper direction it is to be installed. Caps must be installed in their original locations and in the proper direction since they are line-reamed at the factory after being bolted together in this way.

6. Remove the two cam sprocket bolts. Remove the cam chain tensioner from the cylinder.

7. Disengage the cam sprocket from the camshaft and the chain from the sprocket. Carefully remove the camshaft, turning it this way and that so that the lobes clear the sprocket.

NOTE: *Wire the chain out of the way. Do not allow excess slack in the chain or it may slip off its sprocket on the crankshaft. If this happens, it will be necessary to split the cases to retrack the chain.*

8. Remove the cam holders.

Align the cam timing marks before unbolting the cam caps

Removing the camshaft

9. Remove the four rubber caps which cover cylinder head bolts. Remove these bolts and the set bolts at the rear and front of the head.

10. Gradually loosen the 16 main cylinder head nuts, starting with the outermost nuts

Removing a rocker arm

Cylinder head nuts

Cam cover bolts

first. Lift off the cylinder head. Be sure to secure the cam chain so it doesn't fall into the cylinder.

Cylinder Head Removal (1979 and Later)

NOTE: *The camshafts may be removed and replaced with the engine still in the frame. Removal of the cylinder head, however, requires engine removal. If removal of the cams only is required, follow the procedure starting at Step 2.*

1. Remove the engine from the frame.
2. Remove the cylinder head cover bolts and the cylinder head cover.
3. Remove the oil line alongside the cam chain guide. Remove the chain guide as well.
4. The camshaft holders are marked "A" to "E" on the exhaust side and "F" to "L" on the intake side. Note the marks. Proper installation is critical. When installing, the arrow marks must face forward.
5. Remove the camshaft holders "B," "C," "H," and "J."
6. Remove the oil reservoir caps and the *rear* cam chain guide attaching plate.
7. Remove the dowel pins.
8. Loosen the front cam chain tensioner locknut and bolt. Press the cam chain tensioner down, then retighten the lockbolt and nut. This will get a lot of the tension out of the chain.
9. Loosen the rear chain tensioner adjusting locknut. Pull the rear cam chain tensioner up to reduce chain tension and tighten the adjusting locknut.
10. Remove the pulser generator cover. Turn the crankshaft counterclockwise until the "1.4T" mark on the rotor aligns with the index mark.
11. Make sure that the intake *and* exhaust cam lobes for cylinder No. 1 or No. 4 both face the spark plug. If not, turn the engine 360° so that this condition is met.
12. Remove camshaft holders "G" and "K." Remove holders "F" and "L." Remove the dowel pins.
13. Remove the intake camshaft.
14. Remove the accessible exhaust cam sprocket bolt. Turn the crankshaft counterclockwise until the other cam sprocket bolt can be removed. Remove the "D" and gear camshaft holders. Remove holders "A" and "E."
15. Remove the exhaust cam. Remove the dowel pins.
16. Loop a piece of wire around the cam chain to keep it from falling into the crankcase. Remove the cam sprocket.
17. Valve adjusting shims and lifters can now be removed. Be sure to mark all components for position before removal.
18. Remove the oil line at the rear of the cylinders.
19. Remove the two rear cam chain tensioner locknuts.
20. Remove the two cam chain housing bolts.
21. Remove the 12 cylinder head cap nuts.

NOTE: *Loosen the bolts gradually and in a cross pattern to prevent head warpage.*

22. Remove the cylinder head. Remove the head gasket, dowel pins at the sides, and the cam chain guide. Be sure to secure the

Top end oil line

cam chain so that it doesn't fall into the cylinder.

Cylinder and Piston Removal (All Models)

1. 1979–81: Remove the bolt from the lower front cylinder base.

2. Carefully lift the cylinder unit away from the crankcase. If it can't be raised easily, tap the sides *lightly* with a rubber mallet to break the seal.

3. 1979–81: Remove the cam chain tensioner. 1969–78: remove the two cam chain tensioner rubber mounts from the crankcase and lift out the tensioner roller assembly. The guide roller can be removed from the tensioner by pushing the roller pin.

4. 1969–78: remove the cam chain guide pin from the bottom of the cylinder and withdraw the guide assembly.

5. All: remove the wrist pin circlips from the pistons.

CAUTION: *Do not allow the circlips to fall into the crankcase. To avoid having to split the cases to retrieve a clip, cover the crankcase openings with a cloth.*

Discard the circlips once they have been removed. New circlips must be used on assembly.

6. Remove the wrist pins from the pistons and mark the pistons, inside the skirt, so they can be replaced in their original bores.

The wrist pin should be pushed out while supporting the piston with one hand. Never strike or attempt to drift out a wrist pin, or the connecting rod may be bent. If the wrist pins resist removal, heat the piston crown(s) gently with a propane torch or the like until the pins can be pushed out easily.

Inspection

CAMSHAFT

1. On 1969–1978 models, to check camshaft bearings wear, install the camshaft holder on the cylinder head and install the bearing caps on the holder. Check the marks on the holder and caps to ensure that the caps are installed in their original positions. Torque the capnuts and bolts to 8 ft. lbs. Measure the inside diameter of one of the bearings with an inside micrometer in both the horizontal and vertical directions and then calculate the average value. Next, measure the diameter of the corresponding, camshaft journal and compute the bearing clearance. Repeat this operation for the remaining camshaft bearings. Replace the holder and caps as a set if clearance of any bearing exceeds 0.21 mm (0.0083 in.).

NOTE: *Bearing clearance may also be measured using a material such as plastigauge.*

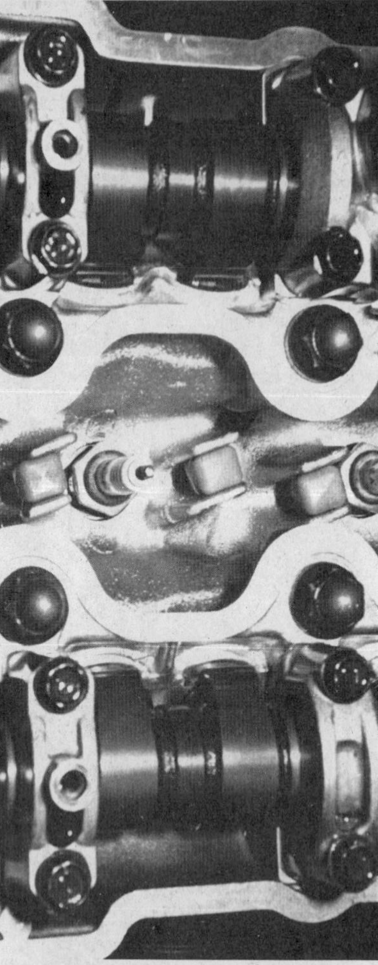

Make sure that the intake and exhaust lobes for cylinder No. 1 or 4 face the spark plug

Check the cam bearing for signs of scoring or wear

Measuring the camshaft journal diameter

2. On 1979–1981 models, the cam bearing clearance should be checked with plastigauge.

Remove the adjusting shims and valve lifters. Be sure to mark each part for reassembly. Remove any oil residue from the journals. Put a strip of plastigauge on each journal, then install the holders. Be sure that each holder is fitted on the proper journal, and that the arrow faces the front of the engine. Holders are marked "A" to "E" for the exhaust and "F" to "L" for the intake cams respectively, from left to right side of the engine. Tighten the holders in a cross pattern to 9–12 ft. lbs. Service limits are as follows:

A, E, F, L:	0.13 mm (0.0051 in.)
D, G, K, gear:	0.16 mm (0.0063 in.)
B, C, H, J:	0.19 mm (0.0075 in.)

If the clearance of any of the journals exceeds specifications, replace the camshaft and recheck. If clearance is still too high, the head must be replaced.

NOTE: *Holders and head are replaced at the same time.*

3. Examine the camshaft lobes for scoring and wear. If the lobes are visibly imperfect, the camshaft should be replaced. The lobes should present a bright, shiny, and unmarked surface. Measure the cam height as illustrated ("A" in the illustration). Minimum acceptable measurements are given in the specification chart at the end of this section.

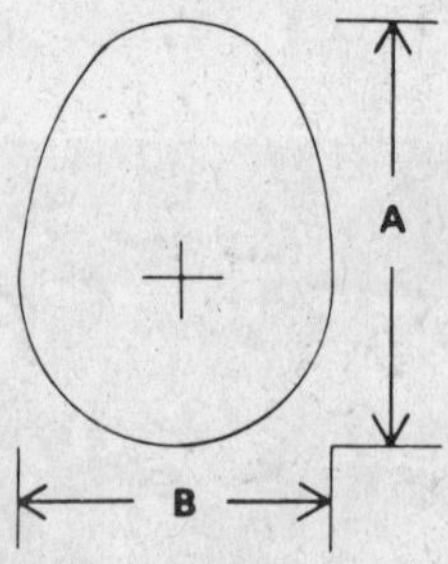

Cam lobe height (A) and base circle diameter (B)

On 1969–1978 models, the base circle diameter of each cam lobe should be not less than 27.93 mm (1.099 in.). The base circle measurement ("B" in the illustration) is taken in a plane perpendicular to the cam height measurement, through the camshaft centerline. Replace the camshaft if the base circle measurements are not within specification.

4. Check camshaft run-out using a dial indicator while rotating the camshaft. To obtain an accurate reading, the ends of the camshaft should be supported in machined V-blocks. Camshaft run-out must not exceed 0.1 mm (0.004 in.), true indicated reading.

ROCKER ARMS AND SHAFTS (1969–1978)

1. Measure the inside diameter of the rocker arm supports and measure the diameter of the rocker arm shaft in the area of bearing contact. If calculated clearance exceeds 0.11 mm (0.0044 in.), replace parts as necessary to reduce clearance to within the limit. Check the fit of the rocker arms on the shafts and replace the arms and/or shafts if play is excessive.

2. Check the condition of the rocker arm bores and the corresponding areas of the shafts. Note any blue discoloration which might be due to excessive heat or lack of lubrication. Replace the rocker arms and shafts if this condition exists, or if there are obvious signs of damage, such as scoring.

CYLINDER HEAD

1. Clean any traces of head gasket material from the cylinder head mating surface. Place a straight edge across the mating surface and check for warpage by attempting to slip feeler gauge blades between the head and straight edge. Standard head warpage is about 0.05 mm (0.002 in.), and maximum allowable warpage is 0.1 mm (0.004 in.). At this point, the head should be milled to restore a flat mating surface.

2. Use a wire brush fitting on a power drill to decarbonize the combustion chambers. The valves should be left in place as this is done, as it minimizes the chance of causing damage to the valve seats.

VALVE ASSEMBLY

1. To remove the valves, and install them properly, a suitable C-clamp is necessary. Compress the valve springs and remove the split collars, retainers, springs, seals, and spring seats. Inspect the valves, guides, springs, and valve seats in the following manner. Keep each assembly separate so that every piece can be installed in its original location. New valve seals must always be used on assembly.

2. If considerable mileage has been covered, the valve springs should be replaced as a matter of course. Always replace the valve springs as a complete set.

Check valve spring free-length with a micrometer. Replace the springs if any is below the following service limits.

1969–1978 (inner): 37.0 mm (1.457 in.)
(outer): 40.0 mm (1.575 in.)
1979–81 (inner): 39.8 mm (1.57 in.)
(outer): 42.5 mm (1.67 in.)

3. Each valve must be free to move up and down in its guide with little resistance. Any sticking or binding as the valve is moved in the guide will indicate that the valve stem or guide is in poor condition.

4. Inspect the valve, paying close attention to the edges of the valve head for pitting, burnt or broken edges, excessive carbon buid-up, etc. A certain amount of carbon and lead deposits on the valve face and the top of the exhaust valve are inevitable. Heavy deposits should be carefully scraped off with a dull knife, or a wire wheel, and the valve finished up with very fine emery cloth.

Do not touch the valve seating area during these operations.

If the valve has burnt or broken edges, it must be replaced.

5. On 1969–1978, models, check the end of the valve stem for indented wear caused by the valve adjuster. Although rare, it may occur after long mileage. Since an indentation here will make proper valve adjustments impossible, the valve should be replaced.

NOTE: *The tips and edges of the valves are stellite-coated. Machining for any reason is not recommended. In case of wear, replace the valve.*

6. Carbon deposits should not extend too far up along the valve stem. This would indicate a worn or cracked valve guide.

7. Wet, oily deposits on the back of the valve head is indicative of a worn guide or bad seal. Less severe wear to these components show up as brown oil stains on the valve stem.

8. Holding a valve in your fingers, spin it while observing the head. A wobble is indicative of a bent valve. If a dial gauge is available, check the run-out of the head. Replace the valve if run-out exceeds 0.05 mm (0.002 in.). Run-out is the total indicated dial gauge reading.

Attempt to rotate the valve by hand when it is fully inserted into the guide. If the valve will not rotate easily, or if it sticks as it is turned, it is probably bent.

9. Check valve-to-stem clearance and compare to the specification given. There are two ways of doing this. The first is to measure the diameter of the valve stem and the diameter of the inside of the guide and subtract the difference. Another way, somewhat easier, is to insert the valve into the guide, holding it about ½ in. off the seat, and check the total amount of allowable movement in two directions using a dial gauge.

NOTE: *Ream the valve guides to remove any carbon deposits before checking clearance. Maximum allowable clearances are as follows:*

1969–1978 (intake): 0.08 mm (0.003 in.)
(exhaust): 0.1 mm (0.004 in.)
1979–1981 (intake): 0.07 mm (0.003 in.)
(exhaust): 0.09 mm (0.004 in.)

10. On 1979–1981 models, valve stem diameter should be measured at three places along the length of the valve. Serviceable limits are 5.47 mm (0.215 in.) for the intake valves, and 5.44 mm (0.214 in.) for the exhaust valves. Serviceable limits for the guides are 5.54 mm (0.218 in) for the intake guides, and for the exhaust guides.

11. If the valve-to-guide clearance is too high, the guides are probably the component which needs replacement. If replacement of the guides does not bring the clearance to within specification, replace the valves as well.

NOTE: *After installing new guides, the valve seat should be recut and the valves lapped in.*

A quick check of the operational worthiness of a valve and guide can be accomplished by dipping the valve stem in oil and inserting it into its guide. Place a finger over the other end of the guide. Pull the valve a little way out of the guide and release it. The valve should be drawn back into the guide by suction if the components are in serviceable condition.

12. To remove valve guides, use a suitable drift, or Honda tool No. 07046-30001. Heating the head in an oven will facilitate removal and installation. Be sure the set rings are in place on the guides before installation. Be sure the guides are fully seated.

After installing a new guide, it must be reamed to the proper size. On 1969–1978 models, this should be 6.60–6.61 mm (0.2598–0.2602 in.). On 1979–1981 models, the proper inside diameter is 5.50–5.52 mm (0.2165–5.52 mm (0.2165–0.2171 in.).

13. Check the width of the valve seat and the valve seating area. Valve seat width should be 1.0/1.3 mm (0.039–0.051 in.). The seat should be recut if the width exceeds 1.5 mm (0.06 in.).

14. Check the sides of the valve lifters, and replace any which show scoring or unusual signs of wear. Measure the diameter of each lifter if a micrometer is available. Replace any which measures less than 27.96 mm (1.101 in.).

15. Measure the inside diameter of the valve lifter bores. If the bores measure more than 28.04 mm (1.104 in.) in diameter, the head should be replaced.

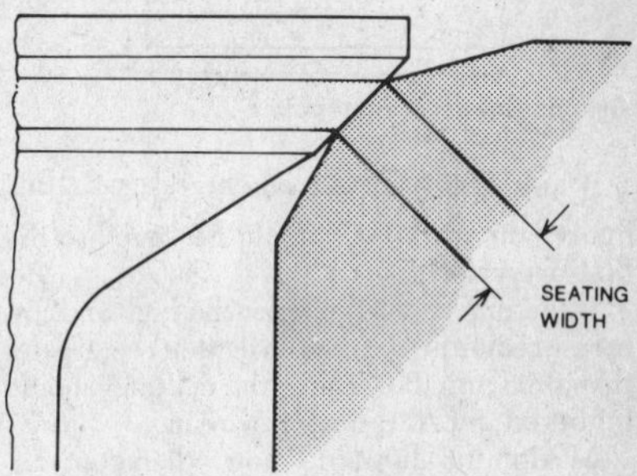

Valve seat width measurement point

Springs are installed with the close coils (arrows) towards the head

NOTE: *Valve springs are progressively wound. When installing them, be sure they are fitted with the close coils towards the cylinder head. Some models have the tops of the springs painted white.*

CYLINDERS AND PISTONS

1. Make a visual inspection of the cylinder bore, noting any imperfections. The cylinder walls should be uniformly smooth.

2. With an inside micrometer, measure the diameter of each bore at the top, middle, and bottom. Make measurements in two directions, 90° apart, both parallel and perpendicular to the piston wrist pins.

Maximum allowable cylinder bore diameters are as follows (standard bore):

750, 1969–1978: 61.1 mm (2.406 in.)
750, 1979–1981: 62.1 mm (2.445 in.)
900, 1980–1981: 64.60 mm (2.543 in.)

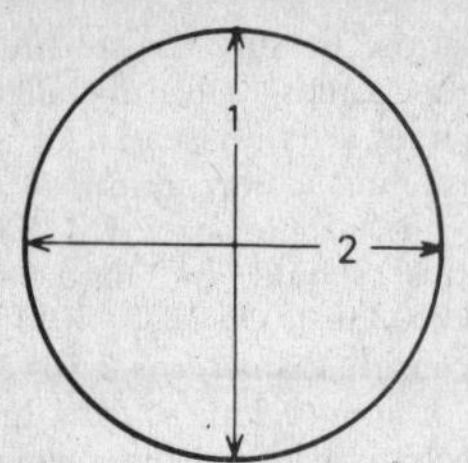

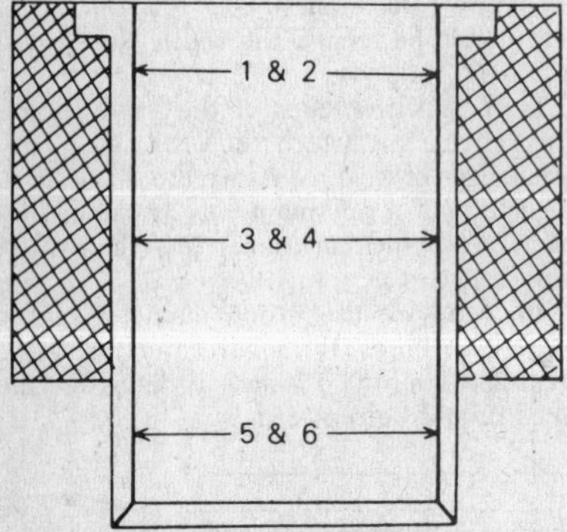

Cylinder measurement points

If any of the measurements exceeds this figure, the cylinders should be bored to the first oversize.

If the difference between the high and low measurements in any direction is greater than 0.05 mm (0.002 in.), the cylinder should be bored out to the next oversize.

Maximum allowable bore diameter difference between cylinders is 0.1 mm (0.004 in.)

3. Make a visual inspection of the pistons. Scoring, scuffing, or seizure marks on the piston shirts may be removed with a fine grade of emery or crocus cloth if they are not too severe. Sanding should be done in a cross-hatch pattern. If the damage is severe (more than about ½ in. wide), the pistons should be replaced.

4. The rings must be free to move in the piston grooves. If they cannot, either they are carbon clogged (which necessitates replacing the rings and cleaning out the grooves), or metal has been pushed into the grooves by a piston seizure. In this event, pistons and rings must be replaced. Carbon-clogged rings are almost always broken when an attempt is made to remove or free them, so be prepared to buy a new set.

5. Measure the diameter of the pistons about 10 mm (0.4 in.) from the bottom of the skirt perpendicular to the wrist pin. Replacement limits for standard size pistons are as follows:

750, 1969–1978: 60.85 mm (2.3957 in.)
750, 1979–1981: 61.90 mm (2.4370 in.)
900, 1980–1981: 64.40 mm (2.535 in.)

NOTE: *New pistons come with the wrist pin and rings. If oversized pistons are needed due to a worn bore or worn or damaged piston, obtain the pistons first, then have your dealer or a machine shop bore the cylinders to the proper size. This is obtained by measuring the diameter of the new pistons and boring the cylinder to that size plus the piston-to-cylinder clearance of 0.025–0.050 mm (0.001–0.002 in.).*

There are four piston oversizes available in increments of 0.25 mm. The size is stamped on the piston crown.

6. If an inside micrometer is available, measure the inside diameter of the wrist pin holes. The wrist pins should be a light push fit into the holes. If too loose, the pistons should be replaced.

Maximum allowable wrist pin hole diameter is as follows:

750, 1969–1978: 15.08 mm (0.5937 in.)
750, 1979–1981: 15.05 mm (0.5930 in.)
900, 1980–1981: 15.05 mm (0.5930 in.)

7. Check the condition of the wrist pins. Measure the diameter of the pins at three places along their length and compare the diameter to the service specification. The minimum allowable wrist pin diameter is as follows:

750, 1969–1978: 14.96 mm (0.589 in.)
750, 1979–1981: 14.98 mm (0.590 in.)
900, 1980–1981: 14.98 mm (0.590 in.)

Replace the wrist pins if any of the measurements is under this limit, or if they are discolored from overheating.

8. The wrist pins ride directly on the connecting rod small ends. Measure the inside diameters of the small ends and compare to the service limits:

All models: 15.07 mm (0.5933 in.)

If the meaurements are larger than these limits, the rod(s) must be replaced.

9. Although not as conclusive as a direct measurement, the condition of the wrist pins and small ends can be checked by inserting the pins and checking for vertical movement. There should be none. If there is noticeable movement in the pins, either the pins or the rods, or both, are in need of replacement. If the rod small ends are discolored or scored, the rods should be replaced.

10. Check the connecting rods for a bent condition. This can be accomplished with two small rectangular blocks of metal of equal thickness. Insert the wrist pins into the rods, and position the pieces of metal beneath them on either side of the rods and resting on the crankcase. Rotate the engine so that the wrist pin rests on the blocks. Both sides of the wrist pin must contact the metal blocks, or the rod is bent and must be replaced.

11. Before installation, decarbonize the piston crowns. Remove any carbon from the ring grooves with a piece of broken ring or a very thin screwdriver. Be careful not to scratch the grooves.

Carefully check the cylinder, cleaning the bores thoroughly. If considerable mileage has been covered, honing the cylinders and fitting new rings is recommended. If the cylinders are honed, make a strenuous effort to clean them thoroughly afterwards, preferably with very hot soapy water and a stiff brush. This is to remove any abrasive particles deposited by the hone in the course of the operation.

Remove any traces of gasket material from the cylinder base and the head mating surface.

12. Be sure that all oil passages in the cylinder are clear. Check the condition of the cam chain tensioner guides and replace them if damaged.

13. Replace the cylinder base o-rings. Check that any o-rings and the important dowel pins fitted to the cylinders are in their proper locations before installation.

PISTON RINGS

Two checks to be made on the piston rings are side clearance and end-gap. These checks should be made on both new and used rings.

1. Piston ring side clearance for compression rings and one-piece oil rings is checked with the rings installed on the piston. Insert a feeler guage blade between the ring and the ring groove and check that the clearance is within the specification given for your machine in the "Engine Specifications" chart at the end of this section. If the clearance is too large, the rings or grooves are worn. If too small, metal may have been pushed into the grooves due to a piston seizure. Check that the grooves are not just carboned up. If new rings do not bring the clearance to the proper value, the pistons must be replaced.

2. To remove the rings from the piston, use a ring spreader as illustrated. They are available at most auto stores. Decarbonize the ring grooves.

3. To check the ring end-gap, ensure first that the cylinder bore is not excessively worn. Place each ring, in turn, into the bottom of its cylinder and push it in an inch or more using the piston skirt to align the ring in the bore. Measure the end-gap with a feeler gauge. If the end-gap is larger than the service limit, the rings must be replaced. If the measured end-gap of new rings is too large, the cylinder is worn and should be bored to the next oversize.

If new rings are fitted and the end-gap is too small, the ring ends must be filed. Hold the ring steady as illustrated, closing the ends over a thin, fine file. Do not squeeze the ring, as this is the easiest way to break it. A few strokes of the file will increase the end-gap.

Removing rings with a ring expander

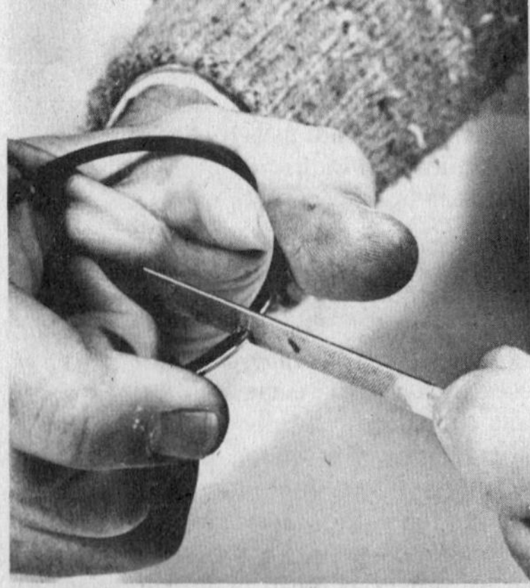

Filing ring ends

CAUTION: *Do not make more than a few strokes before checking the end-gap again. It is easy to remove too much metal.*

Do not allow the file to slip out of the ring, as this risks breaking it.

4. Roll each ring around its own groove and ensure that this can be done easily. If a ring sticks or binds in the groove, the pistons must be replaced.

Cylinder and Piston Installation (All Models)

1. When installing piston rings, note that all rings are installed with the manufacturer's mark (the small letter near the end-gap) facing *up*.

NOTE: *The compression rings are not interchangeable. The upper compression ring has beveled edges and is chrome-plated, while the lower one has a square or angled cross-section.*

2. To install the three-piece oil ring, install one rail on the piston below the oil ring groove, fit the expander, then move the rail into place. Install the top rail.

Always install rings so that the letter near the end-gap faces up

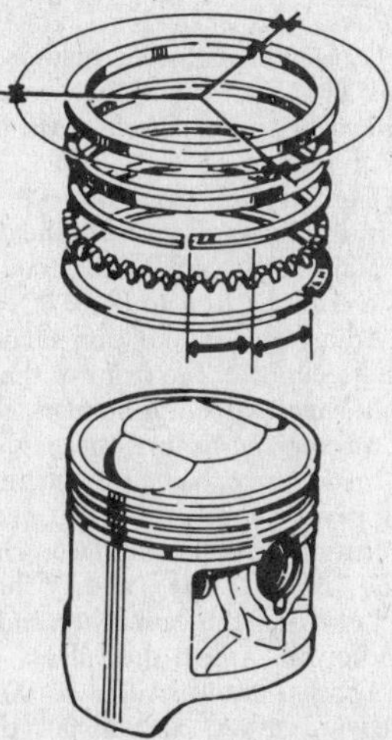

Ring end-gap positions with three piece oil ring

3. Use a ring expander to install the rings to reduce the chance of breaking them.

4. Ring end-gaps must be staggered around the piston so that they do not overlap. If a one-piece oil ring is used, space the end-gaps about 120° apart, but do not position any of them at the very front or very rear of the piston, or directly over the wrist pin hole.

The same thing holds true of models with the three-piece oil ring, except that the rail end-gaps should be positioned to either side of the expander as illustrated.

5. Install the pistons on their connecting rods so that the arrow marks on the crown face the front (exhaust side) of the engine on 1969–1978 models. On 1979–1981 models, install the pistons so that the"IN" marks are towards the rear.

NOTE: *Be sure to use new wrist pin circlips.*

6. Slip the wrist pins into place, heating the piston crown as on removal if necessary. Install the wrist pin circlips with a needle-nosed pliers. Be sure each circlips is firmly seated in its groove and arranged so that the circlip end-gap and the cut-out in the piston do *not* align.

7. Lubricate the rings and piston skirts with clean motor oil.

8. Install o-rings and dowel pins on the crankcase mating surface. On 1969–1978 models, the o-rings go to the rear centermost studs, while the dowel pins are located on the front outside studs. Location is critical. Install the cylinder base gasket. On 1979–1981 models, the dowel pins go behind cylinders Nos. 1 and 4.

To install three-piece oil rings, fit the first rail below the ring groove, install the expander, then the top rail

Stagger oil ring end-gaps (arrows)

9. Route the cam chain through the chain tensioner roller, mount the roller assembly on the upper crankcase, and install the rubber mounts. Make sure that the chain guide is positioned correctly in the cylinder.

10. Rotate the engine until No. 2 and 3 pistons are at top dead center, and place a piston base under the pistons to hold them in position. (A block of wood cut to suitable size works just as well.) Compress the rings on No. 2 and 3 pistons and slide the cylinder barrel down over them. Rotate the engine until No. 1 and 4 pistons contact the base of the cylinder (taking care not to pull No. 2 and 3 pistons out of their bores). Compress the rings and slide the cylinder over the pistons. Before seating the cylinder against the crankcase, raise the cam chain through the center of the cylinder and put a screwdriver through the center of it to keep it from dropping down, or attach a piece of mechanic's wire to the chain and pull it up.

Install the pistons so that the arrows face the front of the engine

When fitting the wrist pin circlips, the piston cut-out and circlip end-gaps should not align

Cylinder Head Installation (1969–78)

1. Install the o-rings and dowel pins on the cylinder. The o-rings are located at the rear centermost studs while the dowel pins go to the front outside ones.

NOTE: *On 1974 and later models, each set of four studs between cylinders 1 and 2 and between 3 and 4 are fitted with a collar and oil seal between the cylinder and cylinder head.*

Install the head gasket.

2. Mount the cylinder head on the cylinder while pulling the cam chain through the center of the head. Hold the chain to keep it from dropping into the crankcase, using a screwdriver or a length of wire.

3. Install the cylinder head fasteners and tighten them gradually and evenly in the sequence shown. Tighten the 6-mm bolts to 8 ft. lbs. and the 8-mm nuts to 15–18 ft. lbs. This tightening is done in a cross pattern starting at the middle of the head and working outwards.

NOTE: *Cylinder studs should be clean and dry for an accurate torque reading.*

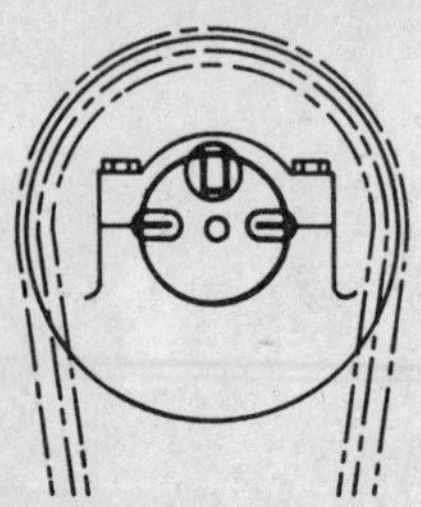

When the "T" mark for cylinder 1 & 4 are aligned with the index mark, install the cam with the cut-out at the top and the two slash marks aligned with the cam cap mating surface as shown

Install the cam bearing caps so that the marks (arrows) match up

4. To set the valve timing properly, remove the ignition points cover and rotate the engine clockwise until the "T" mark (for No. 1 and 4 pistons) aligns with the index timing mark (top dead center). Install the camshaft holders onto the head, hold the cam chain and sprocket together, and install the camshaft. Rotate the camshaft until the marks at the end of the shaft are aligned with the bearing cap joint, as illustrated. The groove must be toward the top. Place the cam chain over the sprocket, bolt the sprocket onto the camshaft, tighten the sprocket bolts to 12–15 ft. lbs., and install the bearing caps. Make sure that the caps are replaced in their original positions (note the matching marks on cap and holder), and tighten the cap nuts and bolts to 7–9 ft. lbs.

5. Install the rocker arms and rocker arm shafts, tightening the shaft retaining bolts to 6–9 ft. lbs. Make sure that the rocker arms are installed in their original positions. Loosen the cam chain tensioner locknut and adjuster bolt, and install the tensioner on the rear of the cylinder.

Lubricate all top-end components with clear engine oil.

6. Adjust the valve clearance in accordance with procedures described in chapter 3, and install the camshaft cover.

NOTE: *Before the cover is installed, take out the tachometer drive-gear limit bolt, coat the threads with threadlock compound, and tighten the bolt firmly to prevent the possibility of it loosening from heat and vibration.*

7. Fit the breather cover and install the engine in the frame. Perform a complete tune-up. Do not neglect to adjust the cam chain tension and refill the engine with oil.

Cylinder Head Installation (1979 and Later)

1. Tighten the two cam chain tensioner locknuts at the rear of the cylinder block.

2. Loosen the lower adjusting locknut and pull the tensioner up. Retighten the locknut.

Exhaust cam punch marks aligned with cylinder head mating surface (arrows)

Cam caps must be installed so that the arrows on them point towards the front of the engine

3. Install the dowel pins, head gasket, and cam chain guide.

4. Install the cylinder head assembly.

5. Tighten the cap nuts gradually and in a cross pattern starting in the center and working outwards. Tighten the nuts a few ft. lbs. at a time until the proper torque of 26–29 ft. lbs. is reached.

NOTE: *Cylinder studs should be clean and dry for an accurate torque reading.*

6. Lubricate the cam chain housing bolts with molybdenum disulphide or the like and install them.

7. Install the oil line. The banjo bolt with the larger oil orifice hole on the side is installed at the *top*.

8. Lubricate the camshaft bearings with an assembly lube.

9. Turn the crankshaft counterclockwise until the "1.4 T" mark aligns with the index mark.

10. Pull the cam chain tensioner up as far as possible.

11. Place the intake cam chain over the exhaust cam sprocket, aligning the sprocket punch marks with the cylinder head mating surface.

12. Insert the exhaust camshaft through the sprocket and the exhaust cam chain, positioning the cam lobes for the No. 1 (left) cylinder towards the spark plug.

13. Engage the exhaust cam chain with the sprocket. Install cam holders "A" and "E" loosely. Fit one of the cam sprocket bolts.

NOTE: *The arrow marks on the cam holders point towards the front of the engine.*

14. Install the cam holder "D" and the tach gear holder. Be sure to position the cam so that the flange fits into holder "D".

15. Turn the crankshaft counterclockwise 360° and install the other camshaft sprocket bolt. Tighten the bolt to 13–15 ft. lbs. Turn the crankshaft around again and tighten the first sprocket bolt to 13–15 ft. lbs.

16. Tighten the cam holder bolts in a cross pattern to 9–12 ft. lbs.

17. Adjust the front cam chain with the locknuts on the rear of the cylinder.

18. Make sure that the "1.4T" mark on the crankshaft aligns with the index mark. Make sure that the cam lobes for cylinder No. 1 face the spark plug. Check that punch marks on the exhaust cam sprocket are aligned with the cylinder head mating surface.

When these conditions are met, engage the intake cam chain with the intake cam sprocket aligning the sprocket punch marks with the cylinder head in the same manner as for the other sprocket.

19. Install the intake cam, positioning the cam lobes for the No. 1 cylinder towards the spark plugs. Install, but do not fully tighten, a cam sprocket bolt.

NOTE: *If the sprocket was not removed from the camshaft, install the assembly together.*

20. Loosely install cam holders "F" and "L." Install "G" and "K." Be sure to position the cam so that its flange fits into the slot in the "K" holder.

21. Tighten the cam sprocket bolts to 13–15 ft. lbs. as was done with the other two.

22. Tighten the cam holder bolts gradually and in a cross pattern to 9–12 ft. lbs.

23. Adjust the intake cam chain tension with the locknut at the front of the engine.

24. Recheck valve timing mark alignments before attempting to turn the engine over.

25. Install the exhaust cam chain guide attaching plate and oil reservoir caps.

26. Install the oil line and cam chain guide with the "B," "C," "H," and "J" holders.

27. Lubricate the cam lobes and bearings with motor oil. Adjust the valves.

28. Apply a liquid sealant to the cylinder head cover gasket, and install the cover. Tighten the bolts to 6–9 ft. lbs.

29. The remainder of the procedure is the reverse of disassembly.

CRANKCASE COVER COMPONENTS MANUAL TRANSMISSION MODELS

The following sections deal with the removal, inspection, and installation of those components found beneath the left and right crankcase covers. These include the clutch, breaker points, alternator, starter drive, and shift mechanism. These components can be serviced with the engine in the frame.

Clutch (1969–78)

REMOVAL

1. Drain the oil from the crankcase. Place a drip pan beneath the clutch cover to catch any residue remaining in the clutch case when the cover is removed.
2. Remove the kick-start lever.
3. Remove the clutch cover plate. Disconnect the cable from the release lever. Detach the cable from the clutch cover.
4. Remove the clutch case cover screws and take off the cover. If it is stuck, tap lightly on the top and sides to break it free. Pull the cover off carefully, taking care that the kickstart shaft oil seal does not contact the shaft splines any more than is necessary.
5. Unscrew the four clutch lifter plate bolts, threading them out gradually and evenly. Remove the bolts, plate, and springs.
6. Unscrew the clutch hub nut. A Honda special tool is available for this job (No. 07916-2830000), but a socket of about the right size can be modified to fit the clutch hub nut if you are handy.

Remove the tongued washer and lockwasher. Remove the clutch hub.

Clutch spring bolts

Clutch hub nut removal requires a special socket

7. Remove the outermost friction plate and stopper ring. Remove the friction plates and steel plates.
8. Remove the clutch washer, pressure plate, and clutch housing.

INSPECTION

1. Check the condition of the kick-start shaft oil seal. If it leaks, or if the lips show signs of damage, pry the old seal out with a small screwdriver. Press the new seal straight into the cover. Apply some oil or grease to the seal lips before installation.

Removing the clutch plates

2. Check the condition of the clutch cover mating surface. Remove any burrs or imperfections with an oilstone.
3. Measure the thickness of the friction plates, and replace them if they are less than 3.1 mm (0.122 in.) thick.
4. Place the steel clutch plates on a flat surface, such as a piece of glass, and check for excessive warpage by attempting to slip a feeler gauge blade between the surface and the plate. Replace the steel and friction plates as a set if warpage exceeds 0.3 mm (0.012 in.).
5. Measure the free-length of each clutch spring and replace them as a set if any are found to be less than 30.5 mm (1.2 in.) long, or if their length varies. If the latter is true, be sure that all of the bolts are evenly tightened on assembly.
6. Check the friction plate tabs for wear or damage. Check the clutch housing for indented wear caused by the tabs. Remove any burrs with a file or oilstone.
7. Check the corresponding splines of the clutch hub and steel plates for indented wear.
8. Check the condition of the lifter plate bearing. Rotation must be smooth, noiseless, and effortless. Replace the bearing if rotation is rough, the races loose, or rotation noisy.

ASSEMBLY

1. Install the clutch housing and spline washer on the mainshaft.
2. Install the pressure plate and install the friction and steel plates alternately, beginning with a friction plate, until all are in place. Install the stopper ring, then the outer (smaller diameter) friction plate.
3. Install the clutch hub, spring washer, lockwasher, and nut. Tighten the hub nut to 33–36 ft. lbs.
4. Install the clutch springs and lifter plate assembly, tightening the spring bolts gradually and evenly. The remainder of the procedure is the reverse of removal.
5. Adjust the clutch and the clutch cable after assembly is completed.

Clutch (1979 and Later)

REMOVAL

NOTE: *Removal of the clutch hub nut requires a special tool.*

1. Drain the oil from the crankcases.
2. Run the clutch cable adjuster at the handlebar in all the way, and then disconnect the cable from the lever at the engine.
3. Remove the rear brake pedal pinch bolt and carefully pull the pedal from its splined shaft.
4. Remove the clutch cover. Place a drip pan beneath the cover before removal to catch any oil remaining in the clutch case. Remove the clutch cover gasket and dowel pins.
5. Remove the clutch lifter shaft and adjusting arm, if desired.
6. Gradually, and in a cross pattern, loosen the six clutch spring bolts and remove the lifter plate and springs.
7. Temporarily refit the brake pedal.

Clutch spring bolts

Removing the pressure plate

A special socket is required to remove the clutch hub nut

Place the transmission gear, apply the rear brake, and remove the clutch hub nut with the special tool after bending down the tab on the lockwasher.

8. Remove the clutch assembly. There is a shim on the clutch shaft behind the assembly.

9. Remove the clutch hub. Remove the clutch steel plates and friction plates.

Removing the clutch plates

NOTE: *Keep the plates in order. They are not interchangeable. Note the locations of the washer and collar.*

INSPECTION

1. Check the condition of the clutch cover mating surface. Remove any burrs or imperfections with an oilstone.

2. Measure the thickness of the friction plates, and replace them if they are less than 3.4 mm (0.13 in.) thick.

3. Place the steel clutch plates on a flat surface, such as a piece of glass, and check for excessive warpage by attempting to slip a feeler gauge blade between the surface and the plate. Replace the steel and friction plates as a set if warpage exceeds 0.3 mm (0.012 in.).

4. Measure the free-length of each clutch spring and replace them as a set if any are found to be less than 32.8 mm (1.3 in.) long, or if their length varies. If the latter is true, be sure that all of the bolts are evenly tightened on assembly.

5. Check the friction plate tabs for wear or damage. Check the clutch housing for indented wear caused by the tabs. Remove any burrs with a file or oilstone.

6. Check the corresponding splines of the clutch hub and steel plates for indented wear.

7. Check the condition of the lifter plate bearing. Rotation must be smooth, noiseless, and effortless. Replace the bearing if rotation is rough, the races loose, or rotation noisy.

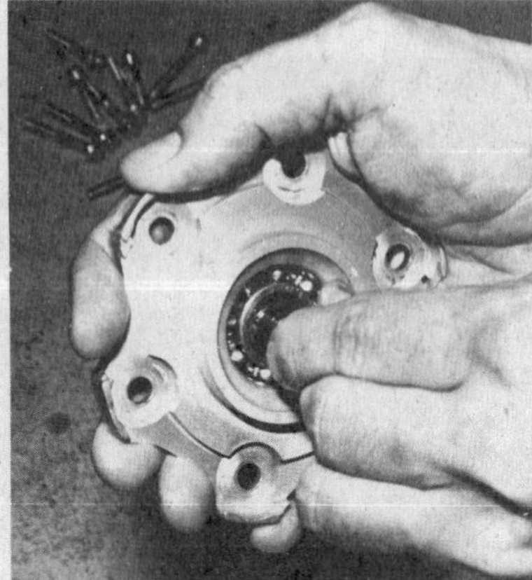

Checking the pressure plate bearing for play

8. Check the condition of the clutch hub shaft splines. The hub must be a good snug fit on its shaft. If it is very loose, or if the hub splines show signs of wear or damage, replace it.

9. Check the pressure plate for cracks.

10. Check the condition of the clutch housing gear teeth. If any damage is noted replace the housing. Check the condition of the primary drive gear as well. Refer to the following section.

11. Check the clutch housing bearings for condition. If either of the bearings shows discoloration or damaged rollers or cages, replace both of them.

ASSEMBLY

1. Install the clutch shaft shim behind the clutch housing. Lubricate the housing bearings, then install the housing.

2. Fit the washer on the outside of the housing, then the collar.

3. Install the pressure plate.

4. Install one of the ordinary friction plates, then alternate steel and friction plates until all are installed. The *next to last* steel plate to be installed is different from the others. The *last* friction plate has slanted grooves and must be installed properly. Note the illustration.

5. Fit the clutch hub.

6. Lubricate the entire assembly with clean engine oil.

7. Install the clutch hub nut washer. "OUTSIDE" is marked on the washer, and it must be correctly installed.

8. Position the lockwasher correctly. Install and tighten the hub nut. Proper torque is 33–40 ft. lbs. Secure the engine as on removal to tighten the nut.

Bend up the tab on the lockwasher.

9. Install the lifter plate, springs, and spring bolts. Tighten the bolts gradually and in a cross pattern until all are secured.

10. If the shaft and adjuster in the clutch cover have been removed, be sure to lubricate the lifter shaft hole with an assembly lube before installation.

11. Be sure to use a new clutch case gasket and that the dowel pins are in place.

The next-to-last steel plate is different from the others

Be sure that the last friction plate is correctly installed. The grooves must be positioned as shown

Be sure to install the washer with the "Outside' mark facing outwards

Primary Drive Gear (1979–81)

REMOVAL

1. Remove the clutch assembly as outlined above.
2. Hold the primary gear with the special holder.
3. Loosen the gear bolt.
4. Remove the bolt, lockwasher, collar, and drive gear.

INSPECTION

Check the gear for wear and replace it if it shows worn or chipped teeth. Check for pitting of the gear teeth. This will be most obvious near the base of the teeth.

INSTALLATION

1. Install the drive gear with the larger gear facing outwards. Install the collar, aligning the hole in the collar with the pin in the drive gear.
2. Tighten the gear bolt to 60–72 ft. lbs.

Primary drive gear

Ignition Timing Assembly (1969–78)

REMOVAL

1. Remove the breaker points cover. Disconnect the two leads behind the engine.
2. Remove the small nut which secures the special nut used to turn the engine over.
3. Remove the three screws which secure the breaker plate and remove it.
4. Pull off the timing advance mechanism as a unit, taking care not to take apart the mechanism and breaker cam.
5. Remove the advancer shaft.

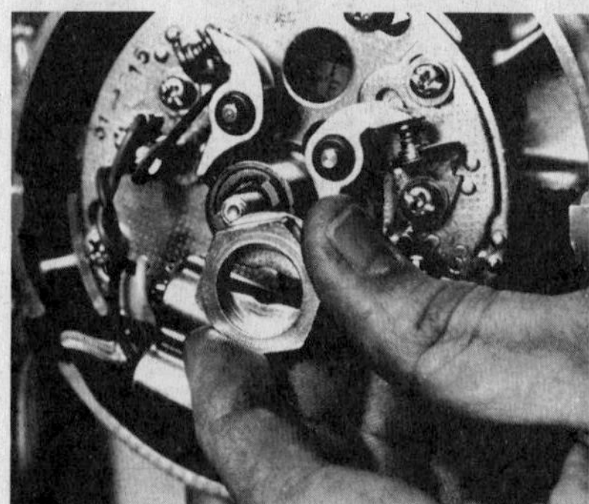

Removing the special nut

INSPECTION

1. The timing advance mechanism movement must be free. When the breaker cam is turned so that the weights move out to the fully extended position, releasing the cam should result in its returning to the original location. If it will not, try penetrating oil or the like to ease movement. Check for weak springs. Replace the unit if proper action cannot be obtained.
2. Check that the advancer shaft is not bent. Straighten or replace it if it is.

Removing the timing advance mechanism

INSTALLATION

Installation is the reverse of removal. Note that the timing advance mechanism is located with a pin on the crankshaft.

Ignition Timing Assembly (1979 and Later)

REMOVAL

1. Remove the pulser generator cover.
2. Remove the left rear crankcase cover.
3. Scribe a line across the crankcase and the timing base plate to approximate timing.
4. Remove the two large phillips screws and remove the timing base plate and pulser generators.
5. Hold the crank steady by putting a wrench on the spacer, and remove spark advancer bolt. Remove the spark advance mechanism.

Timing advance mechanism

INSPECTION

1. The timing advance mechanism movement must be free. When the breaker cam is turned so that the weights move out to the fully extended position, releasing the cam should result in the cam's returning to the original position. If it will not, try penetrating oil or the like to ease movement. Check for weak springs. Replace the unit if proper action cannot be obtained.

INSTALLATION

Installation is the reverse of removal. Note that the timing advance mechanism is located with a pin. The spacer must be aligned as well.

Tighten the advance mechanism bolt to 24–27 ft. lbs.

Locating pin must be noted when installing the mechanism

Alternator/Starter Drive (1969–78)

REMOVAL

1. Remove the crankcase drain plug and drain off the oil.
2. Remove the alternator cover.
3. Remove the alternator rotor mounting bolt. The rotor is a push-fit onto the tapered crankshaft. Remove the rotor with special tool No. 07933-3000000 or a suitable substitute.
4. Remove the starter clutch gear and the starter reduction gear.

Alternator cover screws

INSPECTION

1. Refer to "Electrical System," for alternator tests.
2. Check the condition of the starter drive gears and replace them if the teeth are worn or broken.
3. The starter clutch should be replaced if defective, a condition indicated if the starter motor, but not the engine, turns over when the starter button is pushed.

Alternator rotor

INSTALLATION

Installation is the reverse of removal. Tighten the rotor bolt to 58–65 ft. lbs.

Alternator (1979 and Later)

REMOVAL

1. Remove the right side frame side cover. Disconnect the alternator wiring coupler.
2. Remove the alternator cover (3 bolts).
3. Remove the stator from the cover, if desired, by removing the five phillips screws.
4. Shift the transmission into gear and apply the rear brake. Remove the alternator rotor bolt.
5. Use the special alternator rotor puller to remove the rotor.

CAUTION: *Do not strike the rotor. Do not put the rotor anywhere it might pick up metal particles.*

Alternator components

Removing the rotor bolt

INSPECTION

1. Refer to "Electrical System" for electrical tests.
2. Check the length of each carbon brush. If worn to the scribed wear limit line, replace them.

Brushes can be removed by removing the mounting screws.

INSTALLATION

Installation is the reverse of removal. Tighten the rotor bolt to 58–72 ft. lbs.

Starter Drive (1979 and Later)

REMOVAL

1. Remove the left front crankcase cover. Remove the spark advance mechanism after removing the mounting bolt.
2. Remove the starter clutch assembly.
3. Remove the starter driven gear and shaft.

INSPECTION

1. Clean all components thoroughly in a safe solvent.

Starter drive components

2. Check the rollers for smooth operation. Check for wear, and replace them if any signs of it are evident.
3. Check the gear teeth for a chipped, worn, or pitted condition. Replace both gears if either is worn.
4. Check the outside diameter of the large starter drive gear. Replace it if it is less than 42.3 mm (1.66 in.).

INSTALLATION

1. Installation is the reverse of removal. Note the following points:
   a. tighten the starter clutch lockbolts to 19–22 ft. lbs.
   b. be sure to align the timing advance mechanism with its hole. The spacer needs alignment as well. Tighten the advance lockbolt to 24–27 ft. lbs.

Gearshift Mechanism (1969–78)

REMOVAL

1. After loosening the pinch bolt, carefully pull the gearshift lever off the splined shaft.
2. Drain the oil from the crankcase; then place a drip pan beneath the gearshift mechanism cover to catch any residue remaining.
3. Remove the screws which secure the rear section of the left crankcase cover and pull off the cover, taking care that the gearshift lever shaft oil seal is not damaged on the threads of the shaft.

If the cover resists removal, tap the top and side with a plastic mallet to break it loose.

4. Disengage the fingers of the shift arm from the shift drum and pull out the arm.
5. Remove the two 6-mm bolts and take off the shift drum stopper and the shifter positive stopper.

INSPECTION

1. Check the fingers of the shift arm for wear or bent condition.
2. Check that all pins are properly located in the shift drum.
3. Check that the shift arm spring and stopper springs have proper tension and are not weak or broken.
4. Check the condition of the cover oil seal, and replace it if it leaks or the lips show signs of damage by prying it out with a small screwdriver. Press the new seal straight in. Grease the seal lips before installation.

INSTALLATION

Installation is the reverse of the removal procedure.

Gearshift Mechanism (1979 and Later)

REMOVAL

1. Drain the engine oil.
2. Remove the shift lever pinch bolt and very carefully pull the lever from its splined shaft.
3. Remove the rear brake pedal.
4. Run the clutch cable adjuster at the handlebar all the way in, and disconnect the cable from the lever at the engine.
5. Place a drip pan beneath the clutch cover, and remove it.
6. Remove the clutch assembly (see above).
7. Pull out the gearshift assembly.
8. Remove the shift drum stopper arm bolt and spring.
9. Remove the roller stopper plate bolt and the plate.
10. Remove the bearing stopper plate if

Gearshift mechanism

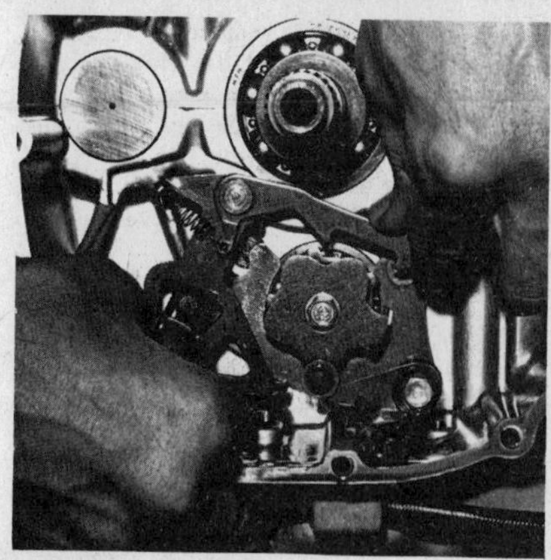

Removing the shift shaft

the bearing is going to be removed (engine disassembly required).

INSPECTION

1. Check the fingers of the shift arm for wear or a bent condition.
2. Check that all pins are properly located in the shift drum.
3. Check that the shift arm spring and stopper springs have proper tension and are not weak, corroded, or broken.
4. Check the condition of the left crankcase cover oil seal, and replace it if it leaks or the lips show signs of damage. Pry it out with a small screwdriver. Press the new seal straight in. Grease the seal lips before installation.

INSTALLATION

1. Install the bearing collar if it has been removed.
2. If the bearing retainer plate was removed, use a non-permanent thread-locking compound on the screw threads.
3. Install the roller stopper pins, plate, and bolt. Tighten it securely.
4. Install the drum stopper arm, bolt, and return spring.
5. Install the gearshift spindle assembly.
6. Rotate the spindle and check for smooth operation.
7. The remainder of the procedure is the reverse of disassembly.

Subtransmission

DISASSEMBLY

1. Remove the rider footpegs.
2. Remove the exhaust pipe heat shield. Remove the gear selector pedal and arm.
3. Drain the subtransmission oil. Remove the cover.
4. Remove the circlip, the washer, and the cotters.
5. Remove the smaller reduction drive gear and collar.
6. Remove the shift drum, shift fork, and shifter with splined collar.
7. Remove the collar and the larger reduction drive gear and washer.
8. Remove the shift drum stopper arm and spring. Remove the o-ring.
9. To remove the spring-loaded reduction driven gear a special tool must be used.

CAUTION: *Do not attempt to remove this gear without the special tool.*

10. Compress the reduction driven gear with the special tool and remove the cotters. Carefully release the tool noting that the gear will spring off unless the tool is backed off gradually.
11. Remove the dowel pins, reduction driven gear, damper lifter, spring, and spring seat.

INSPECTION

1. Check all gears for the usual signs of wear.
2. Check the components against the following specifications:

Drive gear ID: 31.04 mm (1.222 in.)
Gear collar OD: 30.94 mm (1.218 in.)
Driven gear ID: 25.04 mm (0.982 in.)
Driven gear shaft OD: 24.95 mm (0.982 in.)
Shift fork finger thickness: 5.7 mm (0.224 in.)

If any component fails to meet these service limits, it must be replaced.

ASSEMBLY

Assembly is the reverse of removal. Install the drive gears so that the "OUT" mark stamped on each gear does face the proper way.

When fitting the drive gear collar, be sure to align the collar and countershaft oil holes.

CRANKCASE COVER COMPONENTS (AUTOMATIC TRANSMISSION MODELS)

Torque Converter

REMOVAL

1. Drain the oil.
2. Remove the rear brake pedal and the right-side footpeg.

Removing the torque converter case cap. Note the check valve (arrow)

3. Remove the chromed protector cover.
4. Remove the torque converter case cap. Note the spring-loaded check valve behind the cap.
5. Remove the securing screws and take off the torque converter case. Note the oil guide pins at the case joint.
6. To remove the converter assembly as a unit, a special tool must be used.
7. To disassemble the converter, remove the securing bolts and separate the components.
8. Disassemble the stator, if so desired, by removing the snap-rings. Carefully separate the components noting their positions.

INSPECTION

1. Check the inside surfaces of the case cap for scoring or wear. Check the bushing for wear or excessive cap-to-bushing clearance.
2. Check the valve spring for a weakened condition.
3. Check the stator hub outside diameter. Replace it if less than 39.9 mm (1.571 in.). Inside diameter service limit is 26.1 mm (1.028 in.).
4. Check the thickness of the stator side plates and replace them if less than 5.9 mm (0.232 in.).
5. Check thickness of the thrust washers and replace them if less than 1.9 mm (0.075 in.).
6. With the stator assembled and positioned on its shaft, it should be possible to turn the one-way clutch in the counterclockwise direction only.
7. Check the torque converter cover bushing diameter. Serviceable limit is 13.0 mm (0.512 in.).

INSTALLATION

Installation is the reverse of removal. Tighten turbine bolts to 9–12 ft. lbs., and thoroughly lubricate all parts during assembly.

Ignition Timing Assembly

Refer to "Crankcase Cover Components: Manual Transmission," above; procedures are identical.

Alternator/Starter Drive

Refer to "Crankcase Cover Components: Manual Transmission," above; procedures are identical. Tighten the rotor bolt to 72–87 ft. lbs.

Oil Pump

REMOVAL

1. Drain the oil. Place a drip pan beneath the left crankcase cover to catch any residue.
2. Remove the left-side footpeg, kick-start rubber, gearshift lever, and the neutral return arm.
3. Remove the screws securing the rear portion of the left crankcase cover. If the cover resists removal, tap gently with a plastic mallet to free it.
4. Remove the three screws and take off the left case. Unbolt and remove the oil pump.

INSPECTION

Refer to "Lubrication Systems," for oil pump inspection procedures.

INSTALLATION

Installation is the reverse of removal.

Shifter Mechanism

REMOVAL

1. Drain the oil. Place a drip pan beneath the left crankcase cover to catch any residue.
2. Remove the left-side footpeg, gearshift and neutral return levers, and kick-start rubber.
3. Remove the screws securing the rear portion of the left crankcase cover. If the cover resists removal, tap gently with a plas-

Gearshift case securing screws (arrows)

Oil pump fastening bolts

tic mallet to free it. Pull the cover straight out to avoid damage to the oil seals.

4. Remove the ratchet guide nut. Remove the gearshift inner piece, taking care that the spring-loaded pawls do not fly off.

5. Remove the neutral keeping spindle and the shift spindle.

6. Remove the shift stoppers and the gearshift outer piece.

7. Remove the manual valve and plate.

INSPECTION

1. Check all parts for wear.
2. Check the shift pawls for chipping or wear.
3. Check that the springs have sufficient tension.

INSTALLATION

Installation is the reverse of removal.

Be sure that the springs are preloaded for tension. Also make sure that the arm of the neutral return arm is set under the pin of the manual valve.

Left crankcase cover components

LOWER END (1969–78)

Working procedures for the lower end are similar for all models. The primary difference lies in the procedure for the removal of the crankcase cover components in the automatic versus the manual transmission machines.

Disassembly

1. Remove the oil filter case. Remove the engine from the frame following the procedure outlined at the beginning of this chapter.

2. Referring to the preceding sections, remove the clutch or torque converter case, breaker point assembly and shaft, alternator and starter drive, shifter mechanism, and oil pump (automatic).

It is not necessary to remove the clutch or torque converter if only the crankshaft is going to be serviced. Conversely, service work to the transmission does not require removal of the alternator rotor.

3. Remove the bearing retainer for the transmission countershaft bearing (manual transmission).

4. Remove the starter motor cover. Remove the top end components: cam chain tensioner, head, cylinders, and pistons.

5. Remove the oil pan.

6. Remove all of the upper crankcase bolts. Turn the engine over and remove the lower crankcase bolts. Separate the crankcase halves.

Lower crankcase bolts (750A). Note bolts accessible after removing oil pan (arrows)

7. Lift out the mainshaft (manual transmission) or primary shaft (automatic), and disengage the primary chain. Lift out the shaft.

INSPECTION

Check crankshaft run-out by supporting the ends of the crankshaft in V-blocks and rotating it slowly while reading with a dial gauge at the center journal. If run-out exceeds 0.05 mm (0.002 in.), the crankshaft should be replaced.

Run-out in this case is one-half of the total indicated dial gauge reading.

MAIN BEARINGS

1. Journal wear can be checked using a material such as plastigauge. Cut strips of plastigauge to fit across each bearing, install the crankshaft and lower crankcase, and torque the 8-mm lower crankcase bolts in the correct sequence to 15 ft. lbs. Do not turn the crankshaft. Unbolt the case, lift out the crankshaft, and measure the plastigauge with the scale provided. If clearance exceeds 0.08 mm (0.0032 in.), the bearings should be replaced. Do not reuse bearings that are damaged in any way.

Standard bearing clearance is 0.020–0.046 mm (0.008–0.0018 in.).

2. Inspect the journals for scoring and damage. Measure the journal diameter in several places to check for ovality and taper.

Checking crankshaft run-out with a dial gauge

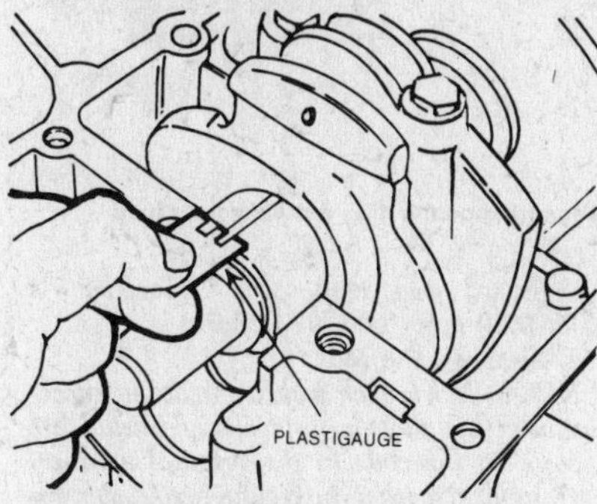

Measuring the main bearing oil clearance

Maximum acceptable variation of journal diameter is 0.05 mm (0.002 in.).

NOTE: *When the bearing halves are installed in the crankcases, the tops of the bearings should protrude 0.068–0.98 mm (0.0027–0.0039 in.). above the crankcase flanges.*

Main Bearing Selection

1. In most cases, the original bearing inserts can be replaced with new bearings of the same size. Size identification is made by the color code on the end surface of each bearing. Simply replace each main bearing insert with one of the same color.

2. It may be desirable, however, to measure the diameter of the crankshaft journals so that journal wear (if any) can be taken into account when selecting bearing size. In this case, it will be necessary to convert journal sizes into code letters so that the appropriate bearings can be selected. After the diameter of each journal has been measured, refer to the following chart for journal size codes.

JOURNAL DIAMETER CODE CHART

Journal Diameter	Code
36.000–35.995 mm	A
35.995–35.990 mm	B
35.990–35.985 mm	C

NOTE: *The original (new) crankshaft journal size codes, which you may want to refer to, can be found stamped on the side of the crankshaft weight adjacent to the primary drive sprocket. (See the illustration.) However, on very early engines (up to engine number CB 750E-1015587), Japanese symbols were used instead of letters for journal size coding. Disregard these symbols and rely on your own journal diameter measurements.*

Crankshaft journal size codes are interpreted as follows: J L - A A B B C

J Code designation for crankshaft journal.
L Indicates that the journals are designated from the left side of the crankshaft.
A Indicates that A is the size code of the left end crankshaft journal.
A Indicates that A is the size code of the second journal from the left end.
B Indicates that B is the size code of the third journal from the left end.
B Indicates that B is the size code of the fourth journal from the left end.
C Indicates that C is the size code of the right end crankshaft journal.

Note that the code given above is only an example of a typical code, and that others will differ.

3. After the journal size codes have been determined, locate the main bearing seat diameter code, which is stamped on the lower crankcase as shown in the accompanying illustration. For reference purposes, the code letters convert as follows:

BEARING SEAT DIAMETER CODE CHART

Seat Diameter	Code
39.000–39.008 mm	A
39.008–39.016 mm	B
39.016–39.024 mm	C

4. Finally, using the journal and seat diameter code letters you have arrived at for each bearing, select the proper bearing color codes.

BEARING SELECTION CHART

Seat Code	Journal Code A	B	C
A	yellow	yellow	green
B	green	green	brown
C	brown	brown	black

CONNECTING RODS AND BEARINGS

NOTE: *Mark the location of each rod before removal.*

Rod Bearing Selection

1. To check rod-bearing-to-crankpin clearance, cut a strip of plastigauge and place it across the bearing shell, as when checking main bearing clearance. Install the rod bearing cap and tighten the nuts to 14.5 ft. lbs. Do not turn the crankshaft or move the connecting rod. Remove the cap and measure the plastigauge with the scale. Maximum acceptable clearance is 0.08 mm (0.0032 in.). If clearance exceeds this amount, the bearings should be replaced. Standard clearance is 0.020–0.046 mm (0.008–0.0018 in.).

2. In most cases the original bearings can be replaced with new bearings of the same size. Size identification is made by the color code on the end surface of each bearing. Simply replace each rod bearing with one of the same color.

It may be desirable, however, to measure the diameter of the crankpins so that wear can be taken into account when selecting bearing size. In this case it will be necessary to convert crankpin sizes into code numbers so that the appropriate bearings can be selected, in the same manner as main bearing selection. After the diameter of each crankpin has been measured, refer to the following chart for crankpin size codes.

CRANKPIN DIAMETER CODE CHART

Crankpin Diameter	Code
36.000–35.995 mm	3
35.995–35.990 mm	4
35.990–35.985 mm	5

3. After the crankpin size codes have been determined, locate the rod bearing seat diameter code, stamped on the side of the connecting rod big end.

For reference purposes, the seat diameter code numbers convert as follows:

BEARING SEAT DIAMETER CODE CHART

Seat Diameter	Code
39.000–39.008 mm	1
39.008–39.016 mm	2
39.016–39.024 mm	3

4. Finally, using the crankpin and seat diameter code numbers you have arrived at for each bearing, select the proper bearing color.

BEARING SELECTION CHART

Seat Code	Crankpin Code 3	4	5
1	yellow	yellow	green
2	green	green	brown
3	brown	brown	black

Connecting Rod Replacement

If a connecting rod is to be replaced, a replacement of the same weight code as the original should be selected. Rod weight can be determined by the code letter stamped on the rod bearing cap. When replacing all four rods, ensure that the weight codes are the same. Rod weight includes the bearing cap and bolts, but does not include the bearing shells.

NOTE: *Prior to engine number CB 750E-1017739, Japanese symbols were used for the rod weight code. The connecting rods used in engines produced after this engine number use letter codes, and the machined surfaces on either side of the big end are slightly redesigned. The old and new type rods are interchangeable; however, when replacing an old-type rod with a new-type, always select one having a weight code of A, regardless of the symbol that appears on the old rod.*

Assembly

1. Fit the cam and primary drive chains onto the crankshaft and install the connecting rods in their original positions, as marked. Tighten the rod bolts to 15 ft. lbs. Lubricate the bearings and install the crankshaft in the upper crankcase.

2. Fit the primary chain over the transmission mainshaft or primary shaft sprocket and install the shaft on the upper crankcase.

Make sure that the shaft bearing set rings are positioned in the bearing seats before installing the shaft.

3. Install the oil collar, o-ring, and two dowel pins on the upper crankcase. Thoroughly clean both crankcase mating surfaces and apply a thin, even coat of gasket cement to only one of the surfaces.

4. Carefully fit the lower crankcase half on the upper one. Install and tighten the ten 8-mm lower crankcase mounting bolts to 17–18 ft. lbs. Next, install the 6-mm mounting bolts and tighten to 8 ft. lbs.

Be sure to tighten the bolts gradually and in the order shown (cross pattern).

5. Turn the engine right-side up and install the upper crankcase mounting bolts; torque them to the same specification.

6. The remainder of the procedure is the reverse of removal. Refer to the individual sections for component installation.

LOWER END (1979 AND LATER)

Disassembly

1. Remove the oil filter case. Remove the engine from the frame following the procedures outlined at the beginning of this section.

2. Referring to the preceding sections, remove the clutch case, pulser generator assembly, alternator, starter drive, and shift mechanism. Remove the subtransmission (900).

It is not necessary to remove the clutch if only the crankshaft is going to be serviced. Conversely, service work to the transmission does not require removal of the alternator rotor.

3. Remove the bearing retainer for the countershaft bearing (behind the shift assembly).

4. Remove the starter motor cover. Remove the top end components: head, cylinders, and pistons.

5. Remove the oil pan. Remove the oil strainer.

6. Remove the upper crankcase bolts. There are 8 of them, all located behind the cylinders.

7. Turn the engine over and remove all of the lower crankcase bolts. There are 24.

8. Separate the crankcase halves. If they seem stuck, first check that all of the fasteners have been removed. Next, tap around the crankcase mating surfaces with a plastic mallet.

CAUTION: *Do not attempt to pry the crankcases apart.*

The crank and transmission shafts will remain in the upper case half.

The internal gearshift mechanism will come away with the lower crankcase half.

9. Lift out the primary shaft and disengage the chain. Lift out the crankshaft assembly. Remove the transmission shafts.

Inspection

Check crankshaft run-out by supporting the ends of the crankshaft in v-blocks and rotating it slowly while reading with a dial gauge at the center journal. If run-out exceeds 0.05 mm (0.002 in.), the crankshaft should be replaced.

Run-out in this case is one-half of the total indicated dial gauge reading.

CAM CHAIN

1. Place the cam chain over the intake cam sprockets. Secure one sprocket, pull at the other with about 29 lbs. tension.

2. Measure the chain length. If it exceeds 311.8 mm (12.28 in.), the cam chain should be replaced.

PRIMARY CHAIN

Refer to "Manual Transmission, 1979–1981," below.

PRIMARY CHAIN TENSIONER

1. Remove the spring and plunger.

2. Remove the nut, oil line, and tensioner fluid valve.

3. Remove the slipper assembly.

4. Check the holes in the oil lines and plunger for blockage.

5. Clean all parts with a safe solvent.

6. Check the slipper for damage or excessive wear, and replace if necessary.

6. Installation is the reverse of removal.

MAIN BEARINGS

1. Journal wear can be checked using plastigauge. Cut strips of plastigauge to fit across each bearing after cleaning all the oil residue from the bearing surface. Be sure that the material is not placed across the bearing holes. Install the main bearing inserts on the journals of the lower crankcase half and tighten the crankcase bolts gradually and in a cross pattern to the following torques:

crankshaft 8 mm bolts	15–18 ft. lbs.
crankshaft 8 mm bolts	15–18 ft. lbs.
6 mm bolts	7–10 ft. lbs.
10 mm bolts	33–36 ft. lbs.

Remove the lower crankcase half and check the bearing clearance.

Crankshaft bearing serviceable limit is 0.08 mm (0.003 in.). If clearance exceeds this limit, the bearing inserts should be replaced. Always replace inserts as a set, even if only one is over specification.

Standard bearing clearance is 0.020–0.060 mm (0.00080.0024 in.).

2. Inspect the journals for scoring or other visible signs of wear. Measure the journal diameter in several directions to check for ovality and taper. Maximum acceptable variation out-of-round of the journals is 0.05 mm (0.002 in.).

3. To find the correct main bearing insert first find the crankcase inside diameter code numbers which are stamped on the back of the upper crankcase half. The letters "A", "B," and "C" indicate crankcase journal inside diameters from left to right.

4. Next, check the crank journal outside diameter codes stamped on the crank flywheels. These, too, will be coded "A," "B," and "C."

5. Refer to the following chart to determine the correct bearing insert replacement:

CONNECTING RODS AND BEARINGS

1. With the rods installed on the crank, check side clearance between the rod cap and the crank flywheel with a feeler gauge. Serviceable limit is 0.3 mm (0.01 in.).

Measuring connecting rod side clearance

Standard big end side clearance is 0.05–0.20 mm (0.002–0.008 in.).

2. Remove the rods.

NOTE: *Mark each rod for location, direction of installation, and always install the caps on the rods in the original manner. Caps are neither interchangeable nor reversible.*

3. Check each of the rod bearing inserts for scoring. The inserts should be featureless. If scoring or signs of wear are noted, the inserts should be replaced.

4. Check the condition of the crankshaft journals. They should be very shiny, and have a flawless surface. If scored, the journals may have to be turned down on a lathe.

5. Connecting rod bearing inserts are color-coded according to size. First determine whether clearance is excessive by using plastigauge to determine bearing clearance. Lay a strip of the material across the journal. Fit the rod, being sure it is installed on the correct journal, in the proper direction, and that the bearing cap is facing the original direction. Tighten the cap to 22–25 ft. lbs.

NOTE: *Be sure not to turn the rod when the plastigauge is in place.*

6. Maximum acceptable rod clearance is 0.08 mm (0.003 in.).

Standard clearance is 0.020–0.060 mm (0.008–0.0024 in.).

7. If the measurement shows that the rod bearings need replacement, proceed as follows:

Check the crankpin outside diameter code stamped on the flywheels of the crank.

Both codes will be "1," "2," or "3."

Refer to the chart to determine the correct color bearing insert replacement:

8. When fitting new bearing inserts, be sure to align the oil hole in the bearing insert with the hole in the connecting rod.

			Main Journal O.D. Code		
			A	*B*	*C*
			35.992–36.000 mm	*35.984–35.992 mm*	*35.975–35.984 mm*
Case I.D. Code	A	39.000–39.008 mm	D (Yellow)	C (Green)	B (Brown)
	B	39.008–39.016 mm	C (Green)	B (Brown)	A (Black)
	C	39.016–39.024 mm	B (Brown)	A (Black)	E (Blue)

Connecting Rod I.D. Code		Crankpin O.D. Code 1 35.992–36.000 mm	2 35.984–35.992 mm	3 35.975–35.984 mm
1	39.000–39.008 mm	E (Yellow)	D (Green)	C (Brown)
2	39.008–39.016 mm	D (Green)	C (Brown)	B (Black)
3	39.016–39.024 mm	C (Brown)	B (Black)	A (Blue)

9. Be sure to lubricate the rod bearings thoroughly before assembly.

CONECTING ROD REPLACEMENT

If a connecting rod itself is to be replaced, a replacement of the same weight code as the original should be selected. Rod weight can be determined by the code letter stamped on the rod big end. Factory-fitted rods are stamped "A" to "G." Replacement rods are stamped "B," "D," and "F." Replacements are to be made as follows:

Factory code	Replacement code
A, B	B
C, D, E	D
F, G	F

Assembly

1. When fitting the rods to the crankpins, be sure that the rods are fitted to the original locations, that the caps are correctly installed, and that the oil hole in the rod points towards the *rear* of the engine.
2. Tighten the rod caps to 22–25 ft. lbs.

Cap bolts should be tightened gradually and evenly. Check that the rod can turn freely after each tightening sequence.

NOTE: *Be sure that the rod bearings are well lubricated before installation.*

3. Be sure that the crankcase mating surfaces are clean and free of any old gasket compound.
4. Apply a liquid gasket sealant to the lower crankcase half mating surface.

CAUTION: *Keep the sealant away from main bearings.*

5. Fit the cases together being sure that they mate all the way around. Do not force the cases together. Be sure that the shift forks are fitted into the gear grooves when assembling.
6. Tighten the crankcase bolts gradually and evenly beginning at the center of the crank and working outwards. Proper torques are as follows:

crankshaft 8 mm bolts	15–18 ft. lbs.
crankcase 8 mm bolts	15–18 ft. lbs.
6 mm bolts	7–10 ft. lbs.
10 mm bolts	33–36 ft. lbs.

Crankshaft bolts should be clean and well lubricated for accurate torque readings.

Be sure that the washers are in place beneath the crank bolts.

7. Tighten the upper crankcase half bolts starting at the front.

MANUAL TRANSMISSION (1969–78)

Primary Drive and Kick-Start Mechanism

PRIMARY DRIVE CHAIN INSPECTION

An automatic primary chain tensioner is incorporated to reduce chain vibration, wear, and noise. However, it is possible for the chain to stretch beyond the range of the tensioner, resulting in excessive primary drive noise. Chain wear can be checked without disassembling the engine. Proceed as follows:

1. Drain the oil from the crankcase.
2. Unscrew the ten oil pan mounting bolts and drop the pan.
3. Measure the distance between the chain tensioner bracket and the oil pan mounting flange with a vernier caliper, as shown. The chain should be replaced if the measurement exceeds 70 mm (2.76 in.).
4. Examine the tensioner roller and replace it if damaged or noticeably worn.

DISASSEMBLY

Disassembly of the primary drive or kickstart mechanism entails splitting the crankcases. The crankcases can be separated *without* disassembling the top end components, however, unless replacement of the primary chain is necessary. Refer to the "Lower End" section, above.

Primary Drive

To remove the primary drive chain, simply lift the crankshaft out of the case and slip the chain off. If necessary, the mainshaft chain sprocket can be removed from the shaft and replaced. However, if the crankshaft sprocket is worn or damaged, the crankshaft itself must be replaced.

Kick-Start Mechanism

1. To disassemble the kick-start mechanism, first remove the kick-start shaft retaining pin and withdraw the shaft. Remove the gear assembly and return spring. Finally, take off the ratchet spring and remove the kick-start pawl.
2. Check to make sure that the gear turns smoothly in one direction and locks in the other. The kick-start shaft diameter should not measure less than 19.93 mm (0.785 in.), and the inside diameter of the gear (shaft bore) should not exceed 20.08 mm (0.790 in.). Replace parts as necessary.
3. Install the gear, kick-start flange, and return spring together in the lower crankcase. Hook the end of the spring on the case and force the flange down with a screwdriver to hook it on the pin. Install the kick-start shaft and shaft retaining pin.

ASSEMBLY

Reassemble the engine in accordance with the assembly procedures given in the "Lower End" section, above. Install the engine in the frame and refill the engine with oil. Before starting the engine, crank it over with the starter (with the kill switch off) until oil pressure is developed.

Gear Set and Shifter Mechanism

DISASSEMBLY

1. Remove the engine from the frame, following procedures outlined in the beginning of this chapter. Remove the crankcase cover components according to the procedures given above.
2. Remove the countershaft bearing retainer.
3. Remove the upper crankcase mounting bolts. Turn the engine over and remove the lower crankcase bolts; separate the cases.

NOTE: *It is not necessary to remove the top end components to service the gear set or shifter mechanism.*

4. Lift out the complete mainshaft and disengage the primary chain. Remove the final driveshaft oil guide and lift out the driveshaft.
5. Pull out the shift fork shaft and remove the forks.
6. Unscrew the neutral detent (stopper) bolt, remove the plunger, and remove the shift drum from the crankcase.
7. Remove the outer (left-side) countershaft ball bearing, slide the countershaft fifth gear off the shaft, and lift out the countershaft assembly.
8. The inner (right-side) countershaft is necessary. The bearing should be removed with a slide-hammer type puller (Honda No. 07048-30025). Gently heating the case may facilitate removal.

Inspection

NOTE: *Do not disassemble the gear set unless inspection shows that replacement of individual gears is necessary. Gear shaft circlips are not reusable and must be replaced with new ones whenever the gear set is taken apart.*

If the gear set is disassembled, carefully lay out each piece in the order it is removed to facilitate reassembly.

1. Flush the transmission shaft bearings with clean motor oil and check operation. Bearing rotation must be smooth, effortless, and quiet. There must be no play between the inner and outer bearing races. If damage is noted, replace the bearings as a set.
2. Install the countershaft and mainshaft assemblies in the crankcase and measure gear backlash with a dial gauge. "Backlash" is the amount of movement noticeable in a gear when the gear with which it meshes is locked in place. Maximum acceptable backlash is 0.20 mm (0.008 in.) for all five sets. Replace any set of gears over this limit.

Note that gears are always replaced in pairs.

3. Check the gear teeth for damage, wear, or pitting. Pay close attention to the very

base of the teeth. Gears are surface-hardened, and if this hardened layer is damaged, what is left will not last long. Check the engaging dogs and/or dog slots on each gear for chipping or wear. Check that splined gears are a good fit on their shaft (neither too loose nor too tight) and that the splines on the shafts and on the gears are in good condition. Check that gears with plain bores can rotate freely but are not too loose on their shafts. Check all parts for damage due to overheating or lack of lubricant.

4. Compute gear-to-shaft clearance (bushing clearance) of gears C_1, C_2, C_3, M_4, and M_5 by measuring the shaft diameter and comparing it to the inside diameter of the gears. Maximum acceptable clearance is 0.18 mm (0.007 in.). Replace the gear, bush, or shaft if any gear has clearance in excess of this amount.

5. Measure the thickness of the shift fork fingers. Replace any fork whose fingers measure less than 6.1 mm (0.24 in.) thick.

6. Measure the diameter of the shift drum guide pin on each shift fork. Minimum acceptable diameter is 6.6 mm (0.26 in.). Replace the fork if pin diameter is less than this.

7. Check the inside diameter of each fork. Maximum acceptable inside diameter is 13.04 mm (0.513 in.). Check shift fork shaft diameter at several places along its length. The fork must not be less than 12.9 mm (0.508 in.) thick at any place or replacement is in order. Roll the shaft along a flat surface and check that it is not bent. If it is, straighten or replace the shaft.

8. Examine the shift drum cam grooves for damage and wear. Measure the diameter of the drum. Replace it if the drum is worn to less than 11.95 mm (0.515 in.) on the right side, or 35.92 mm (1.414 in.) on the left side.

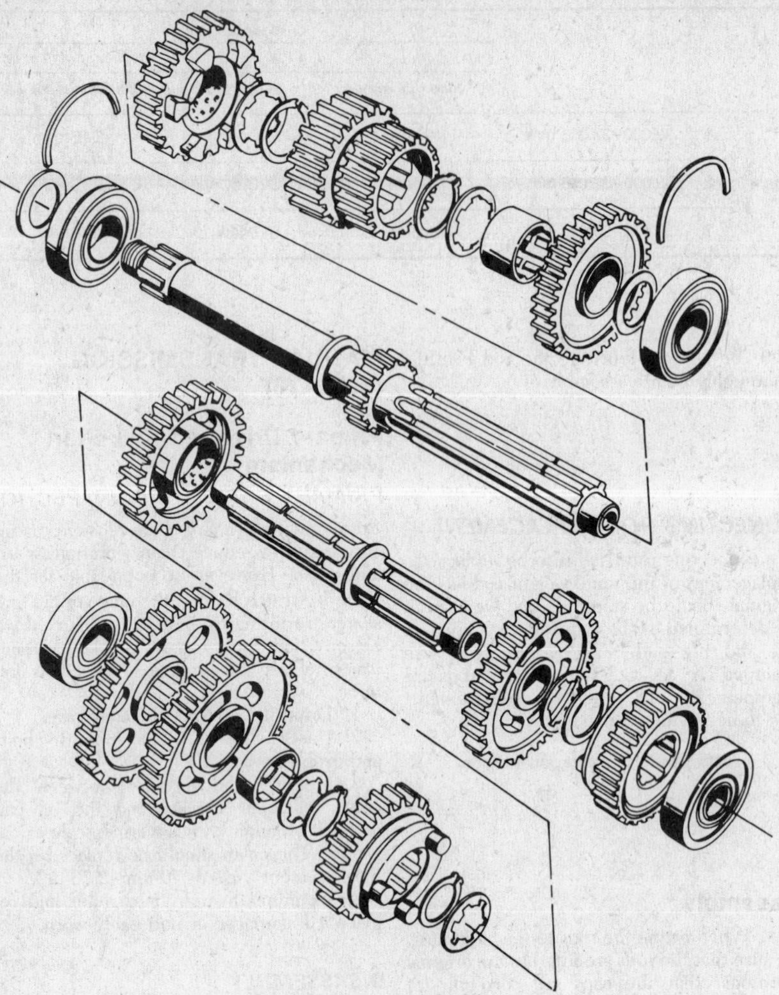

Transmission assembly (1969–1978)

Assembly

1. Assemble the gear set components onto their shafts. Use *new* circlips. Fit the circlips with the smooth edge against the thrust washers.

2. Install the right-side countershaft bearing in the case if it was removed. Installation will be facilitated by chilling the bearing for several hours before installation. Alternately, heat the case gently.

3. Install the countershaft with gears in place. Fit the countershaft fifth gear onto the shaft, then the left-side bearing.

4. Install the shift drum and neutral plunger. Neutral position on the shift drum is at the depression on the drum.

5. Install the shift forks with the forks marked "R" and "L" fitted to the grooves in the countershaft fourth and fifth (C4 and C5) gears, respectively. The fork marked "C" is fitted to the mainshaft second and third gear unit. The pins at the back of the shift forks should be located in the shift drum cam grooves. Install the fork shaft into the case and through the forks.

6. Place the bearing set ring in the bearing seat and install the final driveshaft assembly in the upper crankcase. Install the final driveshaft oil guide.

7. Mount the primary chain on the mainshaft sprocket and lower the mainshaft assembly into place. Do not forget to position the bearing set rings in the bearing seats before installing the mainshaft. Make sure that the transmission is in neutral before assembling the cases.

8. The remainder of assembly is the reverse of disassembly. Be sure to tighten the crankcase bolts to the proper torque in the proper order. For specifications and illustrations, refer to the assembly procedure in the "Lower End" section, above.

MANUAL TRANSMISSION (1979 AND LATER)

Primary Chain

1. Place the primary chain over the primary driven gears. Secure one gear, apply 79 ft. lbs. of torque to the other.

2. Measure the chain length. If the primary chain measures more than 131.1 mm (5.16 in.) in length, replace it.

Primary Shaft

1. The components of the shaft can be removed after removing the primary drive gear lockbolt.

2. Check for scoring of the shaft surfaces and damage to the splines. Replace the shaft if such wear is noted.

3. Check the gears for chipped, worn, or pitted teeth. If any damage is noted, replace the gear and the gear with which it meshes.

4. Check the gear bearings for looseness, noisy rotation, or visible damage to the balls. Replace as a set if either is damaged.

Gear Set

NOTE: *Do not disassemble the gear set unless inspection shows that replacement of individual gears is necessary. Gear shaft circlips are not reusable and must be replaced with new ones whenever the gear set is taken apart.*

If the gear set is disassembled, carefully lay out each piece in the order it is removed to facilitate reassembly.

1. Flush the transmission shaft bearings with clean motor oil and check operation. Bearing rotation must be smooth, effortless, and quiet. There must be no play between the inner and outer bearing races. If damage or wear is evident, replace the bearings as a set.

2. Install the countershaft and mainshaft assemblies in the crankcase and measure gear backlash with a dial gauge. "Backlash" is the amount of movement noticeable in a gear when the gear with which it meshes is locked in place. Maximum acceptable backlash is 0.12 mm (0.005 in.) for all gear pairs of the 750. Standard backlash for the 750 is 0.024–0.074 mm (0.0009–0.0029 in.). For the 900, maximum acceptable backlash is 0.15 mm (0.006 in.). The standard backlash is 0.023–0.117 mm (0.0009–0.0046 in.).

Note that gears are always replaced in pairs.

3. Check the gear teeth for wear, damage, or pitting. Pay close attention to the very base of the teeth. Gears are surface-hardened, and if this hardened layer is damaged or worn away, what is left will not last long. Check the engaging dogs and/or dog slots on each gear for chipping or wear. Check that splined gears are a good fit on their shaft (neither too loose nor too tight) and that the splines on the shafts and on the gears are in good condition. Check that the gears with plain bores can rotate freely, but are not too loose on their shafts. Check all parts for damage due to overheating or lack of lubrication. This is indicated many times by bluish discoloration of the components.

4. Check the gear inside diameter of the mainshaft 4th and 5th gears and the countershaft 1st and 3rd gears. Compare the reading to the serviceable limit given in the specifications chart at the end of this section.

5. Check the outside diameter of the mainshaft 5th gear and countershaft 1st gear. Check the inside diameter of the countershaft 1st gear.

Compare the measurements to the specifications given at the end of this section.

6. Measure the mainshaft outside diameter at the spot on which the mainshaft 4th gear rides. If less than 27.93 mm (1.10 in.), replace the mainshaft.

7. Measure the diameter of the countershaft at the places where the countershaft 1st gear bushing and the countershaft 3rd gear ride. Compare to the specifications at the end of the section.

8. Compare the gear to shaft or bushing to shaft clearances. It should not exceed 0.10 mm (0.004 in.) for mainshaft 4th gear to shaft, countershaft 1st to its bushing, countershaft 1st bushing to its shaft, or countershaft 3rd to the shaft. It should not exceed 0.12 mm (0.005 in.) for the mainshaft 5th gear to its bushing.

Shift Drum

1. To remove the shift drum assembly from the case half, remove the bearing stopper plate. Take out the shift fork shaft and the shift forks. Remove the shift drum.

2. Measure the thickness of the shift fork fingers. Replace any fork whose fingers measure less than 6.1 mm (0.24 in.) thick.

3. Check each fork for wear or chipping of the guide pin and replace if the pin is not in good condition.

4. Check the inside diameter of each fork. Maximum acceptable inside diameter is 13.04 mm (0.513 in.). Check shift fork shaft diameter at several places along its length. The fork must not be less than 12.9 mm (0.508 in.) thick at any spot or replacement is in order.

Roll the shaft along a flat surface and check that it is not bent. If it is, straighten or replace it.

5. Examine the shift drum pin grooves for damage and wear.

6. Installation is the reverse of removal. Note that the shift forks are not interchangeable. Be sure to use a non-permanent thread-locking compound on the shift drum bearing retainer screw threads. The shift fork shaft should be a fairly snug fit in the shaft holes in the case. Check for wear or burrs in these holes.

Transmission Assembly

1. If the gear sets have been removed from the shafts, use *new* shaft circlips. Fit the circlips with the smooth edge against the thrust washers.

2. The mainshaft bearing is press-fit on its shaft and should be driven on with a special tool or a suitable drift.

3. Be sure to align the oil holes in any gears or bushings with the oil holes in the respective shaft.

The mainshaft 5th gear bushing has such an oil hole as does the countershaft 5th gear.

4. Be sure that the set rings are in place on the loaded sides of the transmission shafts. Be sure that the dowel pin is in place in the case to locate the counter shaft.

5. Countershaft oil seal must be 40 x 62 x 13.5-2 *only*.

6. When fitting the shafts, be sure that they are properly seated and located by the set rings and dowel pin. Make sure that the oil seal lip is seated in the groove.

7. Check the crankcase oil oriface for a clogged condition before assembly.

The remainder of the procedure is the reverse of disassembly.

Refer to "Crankcase Assembly," above.

AUTOMATIC TRANSMISSION

Transmission Oil Pressure

1. The transmission oil pressure can be checked by means of an oil pressure gauge and gauge fitting (tool No. 07510-3930100). The crankcase is equipped with a pressure gauge fitting on the left side bottom.

2. Park the machine on the center stand and apply the parking brake.

3. Warm the engine until operating temperature is reached. Shut off the engine and connect the pressure gauge.

4. Restart the engine. With the transmission in neutral and the engine idling at 1,500 rpm, oil pressure should be 57–114 psi.

CAUTION: *Do not rev up the engine with the gauge attached.*

5. If the pressure is not within specification, refer to the chart, "Transmission Troubleshooting: Automatic Transmission" in chapter 9.

Stall Speed Test

Before attempting this test, observe the following precautions:

a. Do not let the test last for more than 10 seconds per test.

b. Do not shift gears at any engine speed above idle.

c. No oil pressure gauge must be connected.

d. The engine must be at operating temperature.

1. Park the motorcycle on the center stand with the rear wheel supported firmly off the ground and the parking brake set.

2. Connect a tachometer.

3. When the engine is at operating temperature, shift into low. Open the throttle. The engine should stall out at 2,500–2,900 rpm.

If stall speed is not within this specification, refer to the chart, "Transmission Troubleshooting: Automatic Transmission" in chapter 9.

4. Shift into drive, and repeat the test.

Regulator Valve

The regulator valve should be trouble-free, and removal should not be attempted unless the automatic transmission troubleshooting chart in chapter 9 indicates that a malfunction is probable.

REMOVAL

1. Drain the oil.

2. Remove the oil pan. Remove the oil screen.

3. Unbolt and remove the distribution plate. Unbolt and remove the regulator valve.

INSPECTION

Disassembly of the valve is not possible. Check by substituting a new valve.

INSTALLATION

Installation is the reverse of removal. Use a new drain plug washer, and tighten the drain plug to 25–33 ft. lbs.

Gear Set/Clutches

REMOVAL

1. Remove the engine from the frame. Remove the oil filter case.

2. Remove the side cover components: torque converter, breaker point assembly, left-side case with shifter mechanism, and oil pump.

It is not necessary to disturb the top end components.

3. Remove the upper crankcase bolts; turn the engine over and remove the lower crankcase bolts. Separate the crankcase halves.

4. Lift out the primary shaft and disengage the Hy-Vo drive chain. Lift out the mainshaft and countershaft.

NOTE: *Do not disassemble the transmission shafts unless it is necessary. Gears can be visually inspected in place.*

INSPECTION

1. Check the condition of the gears, noting any wear to the teeth, cracks, or scoring. Replace any damaged gears, and the corresponding gear with which the damaged gear meshes.

2. Check the transmission shafts for scoring or wear.

3. Check the shaft and gear ball and needle bearings. Bearings must be free of discoloration, and must have effortless, quiet movement. For ball bearings, there should be no axial or radial play of the inner race relative to the outer.

If any bearing is worn or damaged, replace the set.

4. Taking care that the friction disc is not damaged in the process, measure the clearance between the clutch end plate and the top friction disc using a feeler gauge blade. If the measured distance is not within 0.5–0.8 mm (0.020–0.032 in.), replace the end plate.

End plates are fitted with a code number which indicates their thickness. New plates are available in six thicknesses according to the following table:

Code No.	Thickness (mm in.)
1	1.8/0.071
2	2.1/0.083
3	2.4/0.095
4	2.7/0.106
no mark	3.0/0.118
6	3.3/0.130

5. Applying compressed air to the oil passage at the back of the clutch, check that the clutch engages, and disengages when the pressure is removed. If it does not, check the clutch piston.

6. To disassemble the clutch, a special tool is necessary to compress the assembly while the snap-ring is removed.

CAUTION: *It is not safe to attempt disassembly without the special tool.*

7. Fit the assembled clutch to the tool and compress the return spring.

8. Remove the small snap-ring. Remove the large snap-ring and separate the clutch components, noting their locations to avoid interchanging the positions of the various parts.

9. Apply compressed air to an oil passage at the rear of the clutch to force out the clutch piston.

10. Check the free length of the clutch return spring. Replace it if shorter than 36.0 mm (1.42 in.). Standard length is 39.7 mm (1.56 in.).

11. Check the thickness of the clutch friction discs and replace them as a set if any is thinner than 1.9 mm (0.075 in.). Standard thickness is 1.95–2.05 mm (0.077–0.081 in.).

12. Check the thickness of the steel plates. Standard thickness and serviceable limits are the same for the friction discs (step 11).

13. Be sure all oil passages are clear. Inspect the check valve for loose rivets.

14. Assembly is the reverse of disassembly. Lubricate the clutch piston before installation and rotate it while pressing down to install it. Be sure the piston is fully seated.

Install the oil seal rings so that their endgaps are 180° apart.

15. If new plates have been fitted, check disc-to-top plate clearance as in step 4.

INSTALLATION

Installation is the reverse of removal. Thoroughly lubricate all parts with motor oil.

Tighten the crankcase mounting bolts in a cross pattern to the proper torque:

8 mm 15–18 ft. lbs.
6 mm 7–10 ft. lbs.

Engine Specifications
5-Speed, 1969 –1978

Part	Standard (mm/in.)	Serviceable Limit (mm/in.)
CYLINDER HEAD		
Valve run-out	—	0.05/0.002
Valve guide bore	6.60–6.61/0.2598–0.2602	6.64/0.2614
Valve stem/guide clearance		
Intake	0.010–0.030/0.0004–0.0012	0.080/0.0031
Exhaust	0.040–0.060/0.0016–0.0024	0.10/0.0039
Valve spring free-length		
Inner	38.1/1.50	37.0/1.457
Outer	41.2/1.62	40.0/1.575
Cam valve lift		
Intake	7.98–8.02/0.314–0.316	—
Exhaust	7.48–7.52/0.295–0.296	—
Cam height		
Intake	—	35.86/1.411
Exhaust	—	35.36/1.392
Cam base circle diameter	27.98–28.02/1.102–1.103	27.93/1.100
Cam run-out	—	0.1/0.004
Cam bearing diameter	22.02–22.04/0.867–0.868	22.0/0.870
Rocker arm inside diameter	12.00–12.02/0.472–0.473	12.05/0.474
Rocker arm shaft diameter	11.97–11.98/0.471–0.472	11.94/0.470
Rocker arm-to-shaft clearance	—	0.11/0.0044
CYLINDERS, PISTONS, RINGS		
Cylinder bore	61.01–61.02/2.4020–2.4024	61.1/2.4055
Taper and ovality	—	0.05/0.002
Piston diameter	60.97–60.99/2.4002–2.4009	60.85/2.3957
Wrist pin hole diameter	15.00–15.01/0.5906–0.5909	15.08/0.5937
Wrist pin diameter	14.99–15.00/0.5903–0.5906	14.96/0.589
Available piston oversizes	0.25, 0.50, 0.75, 1.00 mm	—
Ring end-gap		
Compression	0.2–0.4/0.008–0.016	0.7/0.028
Oil (one piece)	0.1–0.3/0.004–0.0012	0.7/0.028
Ring side clearance		
Top compression	0.04–0.07/0.0015–0.0028	0.18/0.007
Second compression	0.025–0.055/0.001–0.002	0.17/0.0065
Oil (one piece)	0.010–0.040/0.0004–0.0012	0.11/0.0044
CRANKSHAFT AND CONNECTING RODS		
Crankshaft journal diameter	35.99–36.00/1.4169–1.4173	35.94/1.415
Taper and ovality	—	0.05/0.002
Bearing clearance	0.020–0.046/0.0008–0.0018	0.08/0.0032
Crankpin diameter	35.99–36.00/1.4169–1.4173	35.94/1.415
Con rod bearing clearance	0.020–0.046/0.0008–0.0018	0.08/0.0032
Wrist pin bushing diameter	15.016–15.034/0.5912–0.5919	15.07/0.5933
CLUTCH		
Friction plate thickness	3.42–3.58/0.135–0.141	3.1/0.122
Plate warpage	—	0.03/0.012
Spring free-length	31.94/1.258	30.5/1.201
Spring tension (lb. @ in.)	215–227 @ 0.98	199 @ 0.98
TRANSMISSION		
Shift drum diameter		
Right side	—	11.95/0.515
Left side	—	35.92/1.414
Shift fork inside diameter	—	13.04/0.513
Shift fork finger width	—	6.10/0.240
Gear backlash	0.044–0.140/0.0018–0.0055	0.20/0.008

Engine Specifications 750A

Part	Standard (mm/in.)	Serviceable Limit (mm/in.)
CYLINDER HEAD		
Valve run-out	—	0.05/0.002
Valve guide bore	6.60–6.61/0.2598–0.2602	6.64/0.2614
Valve stem/guide clearance		
Intake	0.01–0.03/0.0004–0.0012	0.08/0.0031
Exhaust	0.04–0.06/0.0016–0.0024	0.10/0.0039
Valve spring free-length		
Inner	38.1/1.50	37.0/1.457
Outer	41.2/1.62	40.0/1.575
Cam height		
Intake	35.314/1.3903	35.24/1.3874
Exhaust	34.893/1.3737	34.82/1.3709
Cam run-out	—	0.1/0.004
Cam journal diameter		
Center	21.789–21.810/0.8578–0.8587	21.74/0.8559
Ends	21.939–21.960/0.8637–0.8646	21.89/0.8618
Cam bearing diameter	22.02–22.04/0.8669–0.8678	22.00/0.866
Rocker arm inside diameter	12.00–12.02/0.472–0.473	12.05/0.474
Rocker arm shaft diameter	11.97–11.98/0.471–0.472	11.94/0.470
Rocker arm-to-shaft clearance	—	0.11/0.0044
CYLINDERS, PISTONS, RINGS		
Cylinder bore	61.01–61.02/2.4020–2.4024	61.1/2.4055
Taper and ovality	—	0.05/0.002
Piston diameter	60.97–60.99/2.4002–2.4009	60.85/2.3957
Wrist pin hole diameter	15.00–15.01/0.5906–0.5909	15.08/0.5937
Wrist pin diameter	14.99–15.00/0.5903–0.5906	14.96/0.589
Available piston oversizes	0.25, 0.50, 0.75, 1.00 mm	—
Ring end-gap		
Compression	0.2–0.4/0.008–0.016	0.7/0.028
Oil (one piece)	0.1–0.3/0.004–0.0012	0.7/0.028
Ring side clearance		
Top compression	0.04–0.07/0.0015–0.0028	0.18/0.007
Second compression	0.025–0.055/0.001–0.002	0.17/0.0065
Oil (one piece)	0.010–0.040/0.0004–0.0012	0.11/0.0044
CRANKSHAFT AND CONNECTING RODS		
Crankshaft journal diameter	35.99–36.00/1.4169–1.4173	35.94/1.415
Taper and ovality	—	0.05/0.002
Bearing clearance	0.020–0.046/0.0008–0.0018	0.08/0.0032
Crankpin diameter	35.99–36.00/1.4169–1.4173	35.94/1.415
Con rod bearing clearance	0.020–0.046/0.0008–0.0018	0.08/0.0032
Wrist pin bushing diameter	15.016–15.034/0.5912–0.5919	15.07/0.5933
TORQUE CONVERTER		
Stator hub outside diameter	39.957–39.991/1.5738–1.5745	39.9/1.571
Stator hub inside diameter	26.000–26.033/1.0236–1.0249	26.1/1.028
Stator side plate thickness	5.95–6.00/0.2343–0.2362	5.9/0.232
TC cover bushing inside diameter	13.000–13.018/0.5120–0.5125	13.0/0.512
Thrust washer thickness		
27 x 54 x 2	1.95–2.05/0.0768–0.0807	1.9/0.075
38 x 66 x 2	1.95–2.00/0.0768–0.0787	1.9/0.075
Oil pressure relief valve-to-body clearance	0.025–0.070/0.001–0.0028	0.1/0.004
CLUTCH		
Initial clearance	0.5–0.8/0.020–0.032	—
Return spring free-length	39.7/1.563	36.0/1.42
Friction plate thickness	1.95–2.05/0.0768–0.0807	1.9/0.075
Steel plate thickness	1.95–2.05/0.0768–0.0807	1.9/0.075

Engine Specifications 750, 1979–1981

Part	Standard (mm/in.)	Serviceable Limit (mm/in.)
CYLINDER HEAD		
Valve run-out	—	0.05/0.002
Valve guide bore	5.500–5.515/0.2165–0.2171	5.54/0.218
Valve stem dia.		
Intake	5.475–5.490/0.2156–0.2161	5.47/0.215
Exhaust	5.455–5.470/0.2148–0.2154	5.44/0.214
Valve stem/guide clearance		
Intake	—	0.07/0.003
Exhaust	—	0.09/0.004
Valve spring free-length		
Inner	40.7/1.60	39.8/1.57
Outer	43.9/1.73	42.5/1.67
Cam height		
Intake	37.000–37.160/1.4567–1.4630	36.9/1.45
Exhaust	37.500–37.660/1.4763–1.4827	37.4/1.47

Engine Specifications
750, 1979–1981 (cont.)

Part	Standard (mm/in.)	Serviceable Limit (mm/in.)
CYLINDER HEAD		
Cam bearing clearance		
A,F,E,L	0.040–0.082/0.0016–0.0032	0.13/0.0051
Gear holder, G	0.062–0.109/0.0024–0.0043	0.16/0.0063
B, H, C,J	0.065–0.139/0.0033–0.0055	0.19/0.0075
D,K	0.062–0.109/0.0024–0.0043	0.16/0.0063
Cam run-out	—	0.05/0.002
Valve lifter outside diameter	27.972–27.993/1.1013–1.1021	27.96/1.101
Valve lifter bore	28.000–28.016/1.1024–1.1030	28.04/1.104
Lifter-to-head clearance	—	0.07/0.003
CYLINDERS, PISTONS, RINGS		
Cylinder bore	62.000–62.010/2.4409–2.4413	62.10/2.445
Warpage	—	0.10/0.004
Ring side clearance		
Top	0.030–0.065/0.0012–0.0026	0.09/0.004
Second	0.025–0.055/0.0010–0.0022	0.09/0.004
Ring end-gap		
Top, second	0.10–0.30/0.004–0.012	0.5/0.020
Oil	0.3–0.9/0.012–0.035	1.1/0.043
Piston diameter	61.95–61.98/2.439–2.440	61.90/2.437
Wrist pin bore	15.002–15.008/0.5906–0.5909	15.05/0.593
Rod small end diameter	15.016–15.034/0.5912–0.5919	15.07/0.593
Wrist pin diameter	14.994–15.000/0.5903–0.5906	14.98/0.590
Piston-to-pin clearance	—	0.04/0.002
Piston-to-cylinder clearance	—	0.10/0.004
CRANKSHAFT AND CONNECTING RODS		
Big end side clearance	0.05–0.20/0.002–0.008	0.3/0.01
Run-out	—	0.05/0.002
Crankpin bearing clearance	0.020–0.060/0.0008–0.0024	0.08/0.003
Crank journal bearing clearance	0.020–0.060/0.0008–0.0024	0.08/0.003
Journal taper and ovality	—	0.05/0.002
Cam chain length	309.05–309.35/12.167–12.179	311.8/12.28
Primary chain length	129.78–129.98/5.109–5.117	131.1/5.16
CLUTCH		
Spring free-length	34.2/1.35	32.8/1.29
Plate warpage	—	0.3/0.012
Disc thickness	3.72–3.88/0.146–0.153	3.4/0.13
TRANSMISSION		
Shift fork inside diameter	13.000–13.018/0.5118–0.5125	13.04/0.513
Finger thickness	6.43–6.50/0.253–0.256	6.1/0.24
Shift fork shaft diameter	12.966–12.985/0.5104–0.5112	12.90/0.508
Backlash	0.024–0.074/0.0009–0.0029	0.12/0.005
Gear inside diameter		
M4, C3	28.020–28.041/1.1031–1.1040	28.06/1.105
M5	31.025–31.050/1.2215–1.2224	31.07/1.223
C1	25.000–25.021/0.9843–0.9851	25.06/0.987
Shaft diameters		
at M4	27.959–27.980/1.1007–1.1016	27.93/1.100
at C1 bushing	21.987–22.000/0.8656–0.8661	21.93/0.863
at C3	27.959–27.980/1.1007–1.1016	27.93/1.100
Clearances		
M4 to shaft	—	0.10/0.004
M5 to bushing	—	0.12/0.005
C1 to bushing	—	0.10/0.004
C1 bushing to shaft	—	0.10/0.004
C3 to shaft	—	0.10/0.004

Engine Specifications
900, 1980–1981

Part	Standard (mm/in.)	Serviceable Limit (mm/in.)
CYLINDER HEAD		
Cam lobe height		
Intake	37.420–37.580/1.4732–1.4795	37.3/1.47
Exhaust	37.920–38.080/1.4929–1.4992	37.8/1.49
Cam bearing clearance		
A,F,E,L	0.040–0.082/0.0016–0.0032	0.13/0.005
Gear holder, G, D, K	0.062–0.109/0.0024–0.0043	0.16/0.006
B,H,C,J	0.085–0.139/0.0033–0.0055	0.19/0.008

Engine Specifications
900, 1980–1981 (cont.)

Part	Standard (mm/in.)	Serviceable Limit (mm/in.)
CYLINDER HEAD		
Camshaft run-out	—	0.1/0.004
Side clearance	0.05–0.25/0.002–0.10	0.4/0.02
Valve lifter OD	27.972–27.993/1.1013–1.1021	27.96/1.101
Valve lifter bore ID	28.010–28.026/1.1028–1.1034	28.035/1.1037
Lifter-to-cylinder head	—	0.07/0.003
Valve spring free-length		
Outer	43.9/1.73	42.5/1.67
Inner	40.7/1.60	39.8/1.57
Valve stem diameter		
Intake	5.475–5.490/0.2156–0.2161	5.47/0.215
Exhaust	5.455–5.470/0.2148–0.2154	5.45/0.215
Valve guide ID (IN and EX)	5.500–5.515/0.2165–0.2171	5.54/0.218
Valve-to-guide clearance		
Intake	0.010–0.040/0.004–0.0016	0.07/0.003
Exhaust	0.030–0.060/0.0012–0.0024	0.09/0.004
Valve seat width	1.0/0.004	1.5/0.06
Cylinder head warpage	—	0.10/0.004
Cam chain length	175.70–175.92/6.917–6.926	177.3/6.97
CYLINDERS, PISTONS, RINGS		
Cylinder bore diameter	64.500–64.510/2.5393–2.5397	64.60/2.543
Piston diameter	64.46–64.49/2.538–2.539	64.40/2.535
Piston wrist pin bore	15.002–15.008/0.5906–0.5909	15.05/0.593
Con rod small end ID	15.016–15.034/0.5912–0.5919	15.076/0.5935
Wrist pin diameter	14.994–15.000/0.5903–0.5906	14.98/0.590
Piston-to-pin clearance	0.002–0.0014/0.0001–0.0006	0.04/0.002
Cylinder-to-piston clearance	0.01–0.05/0.0004–0.002	0.10/0.004
Wrist pin-to-rod clearance	0.016–0.040/0.0006–0.0016	0.060/0.0024
Piston ring-to-groove clearance		
Top and second	0.015–0.045/0.0006–0.0018	0.09/0.004
Piston ring end-gap		
Compression rings	0.15–0.30/0.006–0.012	0.5/0.02
Oil rails	0.30–0.90/0.012–0.035	1.1/0.04
CLUTCH		
Clutch spring free-length	35.3/1.39	33.9/1.33
Disc thickness	3.72–3.88/0.146–0.153	3.4/0.13
Plate warpage	—	0.30/0.012
CRANKSHAFT AND CONNECTING RODS		
Big end side clearance	0.05–0.20/0.002–0.008	0.3/0.01
Run-out	—	0.05/0.002
Crankpin bearing clearance	0.020–0.060/0.0008–0.0024	0.08/0.003
Crank journal bearing clearance	0.020–0.060/0.0008–0.0024	0.08/0.003
Journal taper and ovality	—	0.05/0.002
Cam chain length	309.05–309.35/12.167–12.179	311.8/12.28
Primary chain length	129.78–129.98/5.109–5.117	131.1/5.16
TRANSMISSION		
Backlash		
1st, 2d	0.021–0.110/0.0008–0.0043	0.15/0.006
3rd, 4th, 5th	0.023–0.117/0.0009–0.0046	0.15/0.006
Shift fork ID	13.000–13.018/0.5118–0.5125	13.04/0.513
Shift fork finger thickness	6.43–6.50/0.253–0.256	6.1/0.24
Shift fork shaft diameter	12.966–12.985/0.5104–0.5112	12.90/0.508
Gear inside diameter		
M4, C3	28.010–28.041/1.1031–1.1040	28.06/1.105
M5	31.025–31.050/1.2215–1.2224	31.07/1.223
Cl	25.000–25.021/0.9843–0.9851	25.06/0.987
Shaft diameters		
at M4	27.959–27.980/1.1007–1.1016	27.93/1.100
at C1 bushing	21.987–22.000/0.8656–0.8661	21.93/0.863
at C3	27.959–27.980/1.1007–1.1016	27.93/1.100
Clearances		
M4 to shaft	—	0.10/0.004
M5 to bushing	—	0.12/0.005
C1 to bushing	—	0.10/0.004
C1 bushing to shaft	—	0.10/0.004
C3 to shaft	—	0.10/0.004
SUBTRANSMISSION		
Reduction drive gear ID	31.000–31.025/1.220–1.221	31.04/1.222
Drive gear collar OD	30.950–30.975/1.218–1.219	30.94/1.218
Reduction driven gear ID	25.000–25.021/0.984–0.985	25.04/0.986
Final drive gear shaft OD	24.959–24.980/0.982–0.983	24.95/0.982
Damper spring free-length	107.7/4.24	—
Drive gear backlash	0.08–0.18/0.003–0.007	0.25/0.010
Shift fork finger thickness	6.00–6.10/0.236–0.240	5.7/0.22
Reduction gear backlash	0.072–0.143/0.003–0.006	0.20/0.008

Torque Specifications 1969–1978

Part	Manual Transmission (ft. lbs.)	750A (ft. lbs.)
Alternator rotor bolt	58–65	72–87
Cam bearing cap nuts	7–9	7–9
Cam cover	6–8	6–8
Camshaft sprocket bolts	12–14	13–16
Clutch hub nut	33–36	—
Torque converter turbine set bolt	—	9–12
Connecting rod cap nuts	15–16	15–16
Crankcase bolts (8 mm)	16–18	16–18
Crankcase bolts (6 mm)	8	8
Cylinder head nuts	15–18	15–18
Cylinder head bolts (6 mm)	8	8
Cylinder studs	15–16	15–16
Drain plug	25–29	25–33
Exhaust flange nuts (6 mm)	6–9	6–9
Gearshift return spring	15–22	—
Oil gallery cap	7–10	7–10
Oil filter bolt	22–24	22–24
Oil pressure switch	11–15	11–15
Oil pump bolts	6–7	6–7
Shift pivot bolt	—	17–20
Shift lever bolt	6–7	6–7
Spark advancer bolt	6–9	6–9
Spark plugs	12	12
Starter clutch screws	15–17	17–20
Tachometer gear holder screws	7–10	—
Tappet adjuster locknut	11–12	8–11
Tappet cap	7–10	7–10

Torque Specifications 1979–1981

Part	Torque (ft. lbs.)
Cylinder head cover	6–9
Cam holder	9–12
Cylinder head	26–29
Cam sprocket bolts	13–15
Spark plugs	9–12
Crankcase 8 mm	15–18
Alternator rotor bolt	58–72
Primary shaft	58–72
Mainshaft	28–30
Drive (engine) sprocket	24–27
Con rod nuts	22–25
Oil filter bolt	20–23
Oil pressure switch	11–14
Neutral switch	11–14
Oil drain plug	25–29
Oil pipe banjos	15–18
Spark advancer bolt	24–27
Starter clutch	19–22

General Torque Specifications ①

Fastener	Torque (ft. lbs.)
6-mm hex bolt/nut	6–9
6-mm flange bolt	7–10
8-mm hex bolt/nut	13–16
8-mm flange bolt	17–22
10-mm hex bolt/nut	22–29

①unless otherwise noted

LUBRICATION SYSTEM

CHECKING OIL PRESSURE

1969–78

1. Oil pressure can be checked after removing the oil gallery cap on the right side of the engine and fitting pressure gauge adapter (No. 07510-3000000) and gauge (No. 07506-3000000).

2. At engine operating temperature (oil temperature 140°F/60°C) oil pressure should be 50–64 psi (3.5–4.5 kg/sq cm) at 3,000 rpm.

1979 and Later

Oil pressure can be checked after removing the oil pressure switch behind the cylinders. Use Honda service tools No. 07506-3000000 (oil pressure gauge) and No. 07510-4220100 (adapter).

Check the pressure when the engine is at operating temperature (about 176°F/80°C). At 7,000 rpm, oil pressure should be 71 psi. If the oil is cold, pressure may be somewhat higher.

ENGINE OIL PUMP SERVICE

1969–78 (Except 750A)

REMOVAL AND INSTALLATION

The oil pump can be removed without removing the engine from the frame. The procedure is as follows:

1. Drain the crankcase oil.
2. Remove the crankcase sump (oil pan).
3. Remove the three oil pump mounting bolts and withdraw the pump.

Installation is in reverse order orf removal. Observe the following points:

a. Use new gaskets and o-rings.

b. Do not forget to install the three oil guide pins and o-rings when installing the pump.

c. Refill the engine with oil.

DISASSEMBLY

1. Remove the three side cover mounting bolts from the oil pump.
2. Remove the left cover (opposite the oil pump drive gear) and remove the inner and outer delivery rotors.
3. Remove the dowel pin from the drive gearshaft and withdraw the shaft.
4. Remove the inner and outer scavenge rotors.
5. Remove the metal oil strainer from the bottom of the pump. Remove the four bolts at the pump base and separate the rotor housing from the pump body.
6. Remove the check valve cap bolts and remove the cap. Withdraw the check valve and spring.
7. Unscrew the oil pressure relief valve cap and withdraw the valve and spring.

INSPECTION

1. Clean the oil strainer in solvent and replace it if damaged in any way.
2. Examine the side covers, rotor housing, and pump body for damage and stress cracks.
3. Assemble each outer rotor, in turn, into the housing and measure the clearance between the rotor and housing. Clearance should not exceed 0.35 mm (0.014 in.).
4. Install each inner rotor, in turn, into its matching outer rotor and measure clearance between the inner rotor tips and the outer rotor, as illustrated. Clearance should not exceed 0.35 mm (0.014 in.).
5. If the clearance limit is exceeded in steps 3 or 4 above, the housing and rotors should be measured for wear and should be replaced as necessary. Rotors should be replaced in sets (inner and outer) only.
6. Measure the diameter of the check valve and check valve cylinder bore. Measurements should be within the limits given in the "Oil Pump Specifications" chart at the end of this chapter. The calculated clearance between the valve and bore should not exceed 0.17 mm (0.0067 in.). Replace the valve and/or oil pump body if worn beyond specification.
7. Check the oil pressure relief valve and bore in the same manner as above (step 6). Calculated clearance should not exceed 0.10 mm (0.0039 in.).
8. Check rotor end-play by measuring the thickness of each outer rotor, in turn, and subtracting this from the measured depth of the corresponding rotor housing. Calculated endplay at either side of the pump should not exceed 0.12 mm (0.0047 in.). Replace the rotor housing or rotors as necessary (refer to "Oil Pump Specifications").

ASSEMBLY

Assembly is in reverse order of disassembly. The following points should be noted:

a. Oil pump rotors are fitted with punch marks and should be installed so that both punch marks face the same direction.

b. Do not reuse old o-rings.

c. Lubricate all moving parts with fresh oil before installing.

d. Be sure that the drive pins are securely installed in the drive gearshaft.

e. After the pump is assembled, turn the drive gear by hand to make sure that the pump operates smoothly.

f. Before installing the pump in the crankcase, immerse it in oil and turn the drive gear until the pump is filled.

750A

REMOVAL AND INSTALLATION

The oil pump can be removed without removing the engine from the frame.

1. Drain the oil.
2. Remove the gearshift lever, kick-start rubber, and left-side footpeg.
3. Remove the rear portion of the left-side crankcase cover. Have a drip pan ready beneath the cover to catch any oil residue.
4. Remove the left side case. Unbolt and remove the oil pump.

The oil distribution plate and regulator valve, as well as the filter screen, are accessible after the oil pan is removed. Refer to chapter 4.

Installation is the reverse of removal. Note the following points:

a. Use a new case gasket.

b. Be sure the pump internals are thoroughly lubricated before installation.

c. Tighten the oil pump bolts securely.

DISASSEMBLY

1. Remove the two bolts which hold the oil pump cases together and separate the case halves, removing the pump cover. Remove the pump body after taking out the shaft pin.

2. Remove the inner rotor, outer rotor, and the remaining pump shaft pin. Withdraw the shaft.

INSPECTION

1. Clean all components thoroughly.

Check the clearances for both sets of rotors as follows:

2. Measure the clearance between the outer rotor and the oil pump body. It should be 0.15–0.22 mm (0.0059–0.0087 in.). Replace the pump if clearance is over 0.35 mm (0.0138 in.).

3. Measure the clearance between the tips of the inner rotor and the outer rotor. The standard value is 0.15 mm (0.0059 in.). Replace the pump if clearance exceeds 0.20 mm (0.0079 in.).

4. Place a straightedge across the rotors and body and measure the clearance between the rotor surface and the straightedge. Standard clearance is 0.02–0.06 mm (0.0008–0.0024 in.). Replace the pump if the clearance is more than 0.08 mm (0.0031 in.).

Measuring clearance between the outer rotor and the pump body

Measuring inner rotor to outer rotor clearance

Checking clearance between the rotors and the pump body

ASSEMBLY

Assembly is the reverse of disassembly. Be sure the internals are well lubricated.

Oil pump rotors are fitted with punch marks and they should be installed so that both marks face the same direction.

1979 and Later

REMOVAL AND INSTALLATION

It is possible to remove the oil pump without removing the engine from the frame.

Oil pump mounting bolts (arrows)

1. Remove the rider footpegs. Remove the gearshift lever.

2. Remove the left rear crankcase cover.

3. Remove the oil pump cover (6 bolts).

4. Remove the oil pump by removing the 4 bolts (do not remove the phillips screws at this point).

5. Installation is the reverse of removal. Lubricate the pump internals by filling it with motor oil. Use a new pump gasket. When installing the pump, engage the gears carefully. Be sure that the dowel pin in the lower right-hand corner is fitted.

6. After the pump cover is installed, be sure that the neutral switch wire is properly arranged and secured with its clamp.

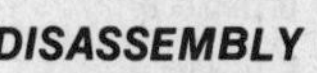

DISASSEMBLY

1. Remove the two phillips screws which secure the pump body cover.

2. Remove the inner and outer rotors. Remove the drive pin and shaft.

NOTE: *The rotors are punch-marked to indicate position. Note the direction of the punch marks, and be sure that the rotors are installed the same way they came out.*

INSPECTION

1. Clean all parts thoroughly.

2. Measure the clearance between the inner and outer rotors. Clearance should not exceed 0.15 mm (0.006 in.) on 750 models or 0.20 mm (0.008 in.) for 900s. If the measurements exceed these service limits, replace the rotors.

3. Check the clearance between the outer rotor and the pump body. If clearance exceeds 0.35 mm (0.014 in.), either the pump body or the rotors will have to be replaced. This specification applies to both 750 and 900 models.

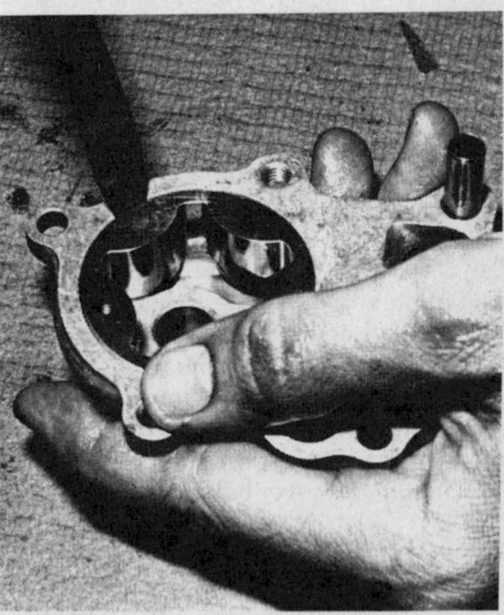

Measuring outer rotor to body clearance

4. Place a straightedge across the pump body and rotors and measure the rotor-to-housing clearance by attempting to slip a feeler gauge blade between the straightedge and the rotors. If clearance exceeds 0.1 mm (0.004 in.), replace the rotors or the pump body.

NOTE: *The rotors are always replaced in sets.*

ASSEMBLY

1. Clean all parts thoroughly, and lubricate the internal parts with clean motor oil.

2. Install the outer rotor into the pump body. Note the position of the rotor punch mark.

3. Install the drive shaft.

4. Insert the pin into the drive shaft.

5. Install the inner rotor, aligning the slots in the rotor with the pin on the drive shaft.

6. Fit the body cover. Tighten the screws securely.

SUBTRANSMISSION OIL PUMP

Removal

1. Remove the rider footpegs.

2. Remove the exhaust pipe heat shield. Remove the selector lever and the selector arm.

3. Drain the subtransmission oil.

4. Remove the cover.

5. Remove the shift drum.

6. Remove the o-ring.

7. Heat the case gently and evenly in the area around the bearing. Tap the bearing out with a plastic mallet.

8. Remove the circlip and take out the oil pump assembly.

Inspection

1. Clean the filter screen in place with compressed air.

NOTE: *Do not attempt removal of the filter screen.*

2. Clean all parts in clean motor oil.
3. Check bearing rotation in the usual manner.

Installation

1. Lubricate all parts with clean motor oil. Be sure that the components are free of foreign matter.
2. Install the pump assembly, aligning the oil pump boss with the cover groove.
3. Install the circlip. Drive the bearing into place.
4. Lubricate the bearing with fresh SAE 80 oil.
5. Install the shaft drum.
6. Turn the rear wheel or drive gear by hand so that the slot in the drive gear shaft collar is vertical. Install the case cover with the oil pump drive shaft boss aligned with the collar slot and new o-ring.

CAUTION: *The cover must be installed carefully and without the use of force. If installation is not easy, check the location of the shift drum and shift fork.*

7. Tighten the cover bolts to 22–25 ft. lbs.

FUEL SYSTEM

NOTE: *For carburetor theory and operational description, refer to the "General Information" section.*

CARBURETORS

CB750 Pre-K1

NOTE: *The procedure dscribed below applies to the early carburetor assembly with four short individual cables controlling the throttle slides*

REMOVAL AND INSTALLATION

1. Remove the fuel tank. Drain the carburetor float.
2. Unscrew the cap from the top of each carburetor and carefully withdraw the slides.
3. Loosen the air filter connecting clamp at each carburetor and remove the air filter housing so that the carburetors can be moved back.
4. Loosen the carburetor-to-intake tube mounting clamps and remove the carburetors as a unit.

Installation is in reverse order of removal. The following points should be noted:

a. Make sure that the carburetors are securely clamped to the intake tubes. If necessary, replace the clamps.

b. When reinstalling the slides in the carburetors, take special care not to damage the needles when dropping them into the jet tubes. The tab in the slide bore must engage the slot in the slide. Tighten the caps firmly by hand after the slides have been installed.

c. Check carburetor adjustment and synchronization after installation. Check for smooth throttle operation.

DISASSEMBLY

NOTE: *Disassembly procedure is given for one carburetor but applies to all four. Keep each carburetor and its components separate from the others; do not interchange parts between carburetors.*

1. Disconnect the carburetor slide from the throttle cable by compressing the spring and feeding the inner cable into the slide so that the cable end can be disengaged from the retaining slot.
2. Disconnect the choke linkage and remove the screws holding the carburetors to the mounting plate. Remove all four carburetors and separate them. Do not misplace the connecting tube.
3. Release the float bowl by swiveling back the retaining clip.
4. Tap out the float hinge pin using a small diameter rod or drift. Remove the float and lift the float needle out of the valve seat. Unscrew the seat from the carburetor body.
5. Using a small screwdriver, remove the main jet, pilot jet, and pilot air screw. The main jet and jet holder can be taken out as one piece if desired.
6. Unscrew the main jet holder is not already removed.

CLEANING

Clean all metal parts in a solvent or carburetor cleaner which is safe for plastic parts. Use compressed air to dry parts. Blow all fuel jets clear. Never insert anything into the jet bores to clear them if clogged.

ASSEMBLY

Assembly is the reverse of the disassembly procedure. The following points should be noted:

a. Use new gaskets and o-rings.

b. The float should be positioned so that when the float arm just touches the tip of the float needle, the distance from the top of the float to the float bowl mating surface on the carburetor is 26 mm (1.02 in.). Bend the float arm in the desired direction if adjustment is necessary.

NOTE: *A special float level gauge (part No. 07144-99998) is available from Honda dealers.*

c. Do not overtighten the jets when installing them in the carburetor body.

d. Make sure that the jet needle is installed in the same position as when removed. Changing needle position in the slide will affect running at mid-range throttle openings.

e. Check for smooth operation of the chokes after the linkage has been connected. If a clearance greater than 0.5 mm (0.02 in.) exists between the choke valve and throttle bore with the choke fully

Oil Pump Specifications

	Standard (mm/in.)	Serviceable Limit (mm/in.)
1969–1978 (Except 750A)		
Rotor housing diameter	40.65–40.68/1.600–1.602	40.85/1.608
Rotor housing depth		
Delivery side	18.02–18.04/0.7095–0.7102	18.07/0.711
Scavenge side	12.02–12.04/0.4732–0.4740	12.07/0.474
Rotor diameter	40.53–40.56/1.589–1.600	40.50/1.595
Rotor thickness		
Delivery side	17.98–18.00/0.7079–0.7087	17.95/0.707
Scavenge side	11.98–12.00/0.4717–0.4724	11.95/0.471
Check valve diameter	17.93–17.95/0.7059–0.7067	17.91/0.705
Check valve cylinder bore	18.00–18.03/0.7087–0.7097	18.08/0.712
Relief valve diameter	11.957–11.984/0.4707–0.4718	11.93/0.450
Relief valve cylinder bore	11.973–12.000/0.4714–0.4724	12.03/0.474
Rotor tip clearance	—	0.35/0.014
Rotor-to-housing clearance	—	0.35/0.014
750A		
Outer rotor-to-body clearance	0.15–0.22/0.0059–0.0087	0.35/0.0138
Rotor tip clearance	0.15/0.0059	0.20/0.0079
Rotor-surface-to-body clearance	0.02–0.06/0.0008–0.0024	0.08/0.0031
Relief-valve-to-body clearance	0.025–0.070/0.001–0.0028	0.1/0.004
750, 1979–1981		
Outer rotor-to-body clearance	—	0.35/0.0138
Rotor tip clearance	—	0.15/0.006
Rotor surface-to-body clearance	—	0.1/0.004
900		
Outer rotor-to-body clearance	0.15–0.22/0.059–0.087	0.35/0.014
Rotor tip clearance	0.15/0.059	0.20/0.008
Rotor surface-to-body clearance	0.02–0.07/0.008–0.028	0.10/0.004

closed, the adjusting rod should be lengthened or shortened as required.

NOTE: *The carburetors on the CB 750 (pre-K1 models) were modified during the production run, and all early models without the modifications are entitled to have this update performed by the dealer, regardless of whether or not the machine is out of warranty or was purchased used. An examination of the caps will reveal whether or not the carburetors incorporate the modifications. The original caps are 11.5 mm (0.45 in.) high and the modified caps are 14.5 mm (0.57 in.) high.*

CB750K1-K5, CB750 (1976), CB750F (1975–76)

REMOVAL AND INSTALLATION

Carburetors should be removed as an entire assembly.

1. Remove the gas tank. Remove the side covers. Remove the air cleaner box. Drain the gas from the float bowls.
2. Disconnect the overflow lines from the carburetors.
3. Disengage the carburetor cables from the pulley and the adjusters from their holders.
4. Loosen the carburetor manifold screws.
5. Pull off the carburetors.

To remove the carburetors, disconnect the choke linkage and remove the two phillips screws (arrows)

Back off the throttle rod nuts to disengage the carburetor from the linkage

6. To remove individual carburetors, disconnect the return springs, and remove the cotter pin which secures the choke linkage pin.
7. Fold back the rubber boot on the carburetor top. Back off the adjuster nuts. Remove the two phillips screws at the carburetor fold.

Installation is the reverse of removal. Synchronization of the carburetors is necessary.

DISASSEMBLY

1. Unscrew and remove the carburetor cap and take out the slide assembly. To remove the needle, take out the two small phillips screws inside the carburetor slide.
2. Flip back the float bowl retaining clip. Remove the float bowl.
3. Unscrew and remove the main jet holder with the main jet. Unscrew and remove the pilot jet.
4. Push out the float pivot pin and remove the float bulbs.
5. Remove the float needle.
6. Unscrew and remove the needle seat.
7. Turn the carburetor over and take out the needle jet, pushing it out from the top if necessary.
8. Unscrew and remove the pilot screw.

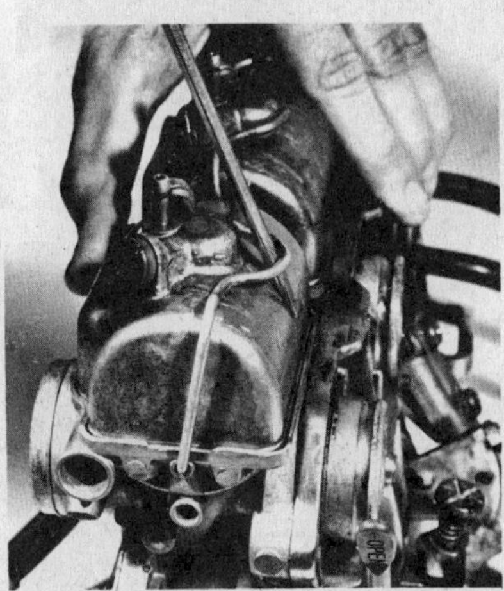

Removing the float bowl

Removing the main jet and holder

CLEANING

Since the carburetor may have inserted plastic parts, use only a parts cleaner which will not harm plastic.

Use compressed air to dry the parts. Blow all fuel and air passages clear. Never insert anything into jet bores to clear them if they are clogged.

Removing the floats

ASSEMBLY

Assembly is the reverse of the disassembly procedure. The following points should be noted:

1. Use new gaskets and o-rings.
2. The float should be positioned so that when the float arm just touches the tip of the float needle, the distance from the top of the float to the float bowl mating surface on the carburetor is 26.0 mm (1.02 in.). Bend the float arm in the desired direction if adjustment is necessary.

   NOTE: *A special float level gauge (part No. 07144-99998) is available from Honda dealers.*
3. Do not overtighten the jets when installing them in the carburetor body.
4. Make sure that the jet needle is installed in the same position as when removed. Changing needle position in the slide will affect running at mid-range throttle openings.
5. Check for smooth operation of the chokes after the linkage has been connected. If a clearance greater than 0.5 mm (0.02 in.) exists between the choke valve and throttle bore with the choke fully closed, the adjusting rod should be lengthened or shortened as required.

CB750A, CB750K (77), CB750F (77)

REMOVAL AND INSTALLATION

Carburetors must be removed as an entire assembly.

1. Remove the gas tank. Remove the side covers. Remove the air cleaner box. Drain the float bowls.
2. Disconnect the overflow lines from the carburetors.
3. Disengage the carburetor cables from the pulley and the adjusters from their holders.
4. Loosen the carburetor manifold screws.
5. Pull off the carburetors.

Installation is the reverse of removal.

DISASSEMBLY

1. Remove the float bowl screws and take off the float bowl.
2. Unscrew and remove the main jet, jet holder, and pilot jet.

3. Push out the float pivot pin and remove the float bulbs to which the float needle is attached.
4. Remove the needle jet.
5. To disassemble the carburetors completely, remove the two screws which secure the choke plate at each carburetor mouth.
6. Remove the top from each carburetor. Remove the brace which holds them together. Remove the shaft securing screw

Float bowl securing screws (arrows)

(accessible after removing the tops). Disconnect the balance tubes. Slide the carburetors off the throttle shaft.

CLEANING

Clean the carburetor in a solvent which is safe for plastic parts.

Use compressed air to blow parts dry. Blow all air and fuel passages clear. Never insert anything into the jet bores to clear them if clogged.

ASSEMBLY

Assembly is the reverse of disassembly. Float level is 14.5 mm (0.571 in.).

CB750K,F,C (1979 AND LATER) and CB900

REMOVAL AND INSTALLATION

NOTE: *The carburetors must be removed as an assembly.*

1. Turn the petcock "off," disconnect the fuel line at the carburetor.
2. Remove the left and right side covers.
3. Loosen the air cleaner clamps. Move the air cleaner as far as possible to the rear.
4. Loosen the carburetor manifold clamps. Remove the carburetors as an assembly. Disconnect the choke and throttle cables.

CAUTION: *Remember that the carburetors are full of gasoline. Drain the float bowls into a suitable container by loosening the drain screws.*

5. Installation is the reverse of removal. Note the following points:

a. Do not interchange the "pull" and "push" throttle cables. The "pull" cable is closest to the engine.

b. Be sure that the carburetors are firmly seated in the manifold spigots.

c. Be sure that the air cleaner tubes are not twisted or folded up so as to block the carburetor intakes.

d. Adjust the throttle cables, butterfly synchronization, idle and fast idle adjustments.

e. Be sure that all fuel line connections are tight and secured with the safety clips. Before operation, turn on the fuel and check for leaks.

DISASSEMBLY

1. Loosen the locknut, and back off the butterfly synchronization screw.

NOTE: *The slides will have to be synchronized after assembly.*

2. Disconnect the spring from the choke lever.
3. Remove the phillips head screws and take off the rear and the front stays.
4. Separate the carburetors, noting that

Removing the cap and spring

Float bowl screws (arrows)

the fuel connecting pipe and the choke spring will come loose. The pipe has o-rings on both sides. Do not lose them.

From this point, disassembly is given for one carburetor, but applies to both.

5. Unscrew and remove the carburetor tops. Take out the spring, and the throttle slide assembly with jet needle.

The jet needle can be removed from the throttle slide after taking off the full open stopper and unscrewing the needle set screw.

6. Remove the seal ring from the top of the carburetor body.
7. Remove the air jet cover.
8. Remove the float bowl screws, and very carefully take off the float bowl.
9. Unscrew and remove the primary and secondary main jets.
10. Remove the slow jet plug.

Removing the secondary main jet

Removing the needle jet

Pushing out the float pivot pin

NOTE: *The slow jet itself is a press-fit in the carburetor body and cannot be removed.*

11. Remove the primary nozzle which is beneath the primary main jet.
12. Remove the needle jet holder.
13. Unscrew and remove the pilot screw. Note that the pilot screw will have to be adjusted during reassembly. Note the spring and o-ring on the jet.
14. Use a needle-nosed pliers to pull out the float pin. Remove the floats. Remove the float needle.
15. Remove the air cut-off valve cover and take out the spring. Remove the diaphragm very carefully and take out the o-ring as well.

ASSEMBLY

Assembly is basically the reverse of the disassembly procedure. Note the following points:

1. Always use new gaskets and O-rings.

2. Exercise care when installing jets—they are made of soft brass and are easily damaged if overtightened.

3. Be sure that the float pivot pin is properly seated, and that the floats pivot freely.

4. Tighten the float bowl screws slowly and evenly. Be sure that the O-ring is seated in its groove before installing the float bowl.

5. When installing the pilot screw, place the o-ring and the spring on the screw, then turn it in very carefully until it is seated. Then back the screw off the number of turns indicated in the "Carburetor Specifications" chart.

6. When joining the two carburetors together, be sure that the o-rings are in place on either end of the fuel pipe. Fit the pipe into the carbs carefully to avoid damage to the o-rings.

7. Do not forget the choke relief spring.

Carburetor Separation

Although almost all routine work can be performed with the carburetors attached together, the units may have to come apart. If this is desired, proceed as follows:

1. Unhook the choke relief spring from the shaft arm between carburetors Nos. 3 and 4.

2. Loosen the synchronization screw locknuts. Turn the synchronization screws in until they seat and note the number of turns so that they can be roughly repositioned when assembling. Then back the screws out until there is no tension.

3. Remove the rear bracket which is held to each carburetor by two screws.

4. Remove the front bracket.

5. Separate the carburetors between units Nos. 2 and 4. Pull them straight apart to avoid damage to the lines.

6. File the staked ends of the choke valve screws. Remove the screws. They must be replaced with new ones on assembly.

7. Remove the fuel line holder from the No. 1 carb. Separate the carbs. Be careful to pull them straight apart to avoid damage to the fuel and air lines.

8. After noting the spring position, remove the choke relief spring from the choke linkage. Remove the choke shaft.

NOTE: *The choke shaft, valves, and screws cannot be reused.*

9. Remove the cotter pin from the accelerator pump rod. Remove the plain washers, spring and collar.

10. Remove the fast idle adjusting arm bolt.

11. Remove the fast idle adjusting arm and springs.

12. Remove the accelerator pump rod. Drive out the throttle linkage retaining pin. Remove the throttle linkage.

13. Assembly is basically the reverse of disassembly. Note the following points:

a. assemble one pair of carbs at a time;

b. use new o-rings on the fuel line joints;

c. lubricate the o-rings with a bit of grease before assembly;

d. install the fuel line, accelerator pump joint and air vent pipes on the No. 3 unit. Install the choke dust tube. Loosen the synchronization adjusting screw until there is no tension. Insert the No. 3 unit throttle link between the plain washers. Assemble carburetors Nos. 3 and 4.

NOTE: *The large washer should be positioned on the spring side.*

e. assemble carburetors Nos. 1 and 2 in the same manner;

f. insert new choke shafts and assemble the linkage;

g. install the front bracket screws, but do not tighten them;

h. place the carbs on a flat surface with the float bowls facing up. Press them together and tighten the screws evenly by tightening the left side screw on each carburetor first, then going back and securing the right side screw on each one. Tighten the screws gradually to 3–4 ft. lbs.

NOTE: *After securing the screws, check for smooth choke shaft operation. Recheck alignment if operation is not satisfactory.*

i. fit the rear bracket using the same procedure. Tighten the rear bracket screws to 2–3 ft. lbs.

j. install the thrust springs between No. 1 and 2 and between Nos. 3 and 4 throttle linkages;

k. turn each synchronization adjusting screw to its original position as noted during disassembly:

l. adjust the throttles so that the distance between the by-pass hole and the throttle plate is the same for each unit;

m. open the throttle slightly, then release. Be sure that the throttle linkage is smooth and free of binding;

n. hook the choke relief spring to the choke shaft between units 3 and 4. Install the choke valves, but do not tighten the screws; be sure that choke valve operation is smooth, then tighten the valve screws to 5–11 ft. lbs. Fold the tabs on the lockwasher up. Recheck choke and throttle operation.

FUEL PETCOCK

Removal, Cleaning, and Inspection

1974 AND EARLIER MODELS

1. Turn the petcock lever to "stop" and disconnect the fuel lines.

2. Raise the seat, and raise and support the rear of the gas tank.

3. Unscrew the sediment bowl from the petcock, being careful of the gasoline which will also spill out.

4. Remove the o-ring and filter.

5. Remove the two screws which secure the petcock body to the gas tank, and remove the petcock.

6. Clean all components in gasoline and dry; then inspect for damage.

7. When assembling the petcock, it is advisable to use new gaskets and o-rings.

8. After installing the petcock, check for proper gas flow as well as leaks.

1975 AND LATER MODELS

The petcock filter screen is inside the gas tank.

Carburetor Specifications

Item	*1969*	*1970–1976 K-Models*	*750F (1975–1978)*	*750A*	*1977–1978 K-Models*	*1979–1981 All 750s*	*900*
Type	(4) Keihin	(4) Keihin	(4) Keihin	(4) Keihin	(4) Keihin	(4) CV	(4) CV
Bore diameter (mm/in.)	28/1.1	28/1.1	28/1.1	24/0.94	24/0.94	30/1.18	32/1.3
Main jet	120	①	105	102	102	68/102 ②	68/105
Pilot jet	40	40	40	38	38	na	na
Slide cutaway	2.5	2.5	2.5	na	na	na	na
Jet needle (mm/in.)	7.6 × 3.8/ 0.30 × 0.15	7.6 × 3.8/ 0.30 × 0.15	na	na	na	na	na
Needle clip position (grooves from top)	3	3	3	3	3	na	na
Pilot screw setting (turns out)	1 ± 1/8	1 ± 1/8	1 ± 3/8	1¼	1¼	③	④
Float level (mm/in.)	26.0/1.02	26.0/1.02	26.0/1.02	14.5/0.57	14.5/0.57	15.5/0.61	15.5/0.61

①K1-K2: 120
K3: 110
K4-76: 105
②CB750F: 68/98
③VB42A: 1½
VB42C: 1¾
na: not available
④1980: 2
1981: 2½

1. Disconnect the fuel lines from the petcock. Remove the tank from the machine, and drain off the gas.

2. Unscrew the securing nut and carefully take out the petcock. Remove the securing nut and filter from the petcock.

3. Wash the filter in a solvent. Replace the filter if it is punctured or badly clogged. Check the condition of the gasket and replace it if it is crushed or nicked.

Installation is the reverse of removal. Be sure that the fuel lines are secured to the petcock with the safety clips. Check for leaks before operating the motorcycle.

ELECTRICAL SYSTEM

CHARGING SYSTEM, 1969–78

Alternator Output Test

1. Check the state of charge of the battery. If battery voltage is less than 12 volts, or if specific gravity of the electrolyte is less than 1.260 (fully charged), recharge the battery before proceeding with the test.

2. The test is performed using an ammeter and a voltmeter. Connect the ammeter as follows: disconnect the positive (+) battery cable and connect it to the positive side of the ammeter; connect the negative (−) side of the ammeter to the positive battery terminal. Connect the voltmeter as follows: connect the positive side of the ammeter to the positive battery cable, and ground the negative voltmeter lead on the engine.

3. Start the engine and check the amperage and voltage output of the alternator under both day riding (lights off) and night riding (lights on) conditions, assuming it is possible to shut off the headlight on your model. If the readings obtained are noticeably greater or smaller than those in the accompanying table, adjust the regulator. Slight variation is acceptable due to the effect of the state of charge of the battery upon alternator output. If alternator output is satisfactory but the battery has discharged during use, refer to the section on testing the rectifier.

Alternator output set-up

Regulator Adjustment

1. Disconnect the three wires at the regulator, marking them so that they can be replaced on the same terminals. Take out the two mounting bolts and remove the regulator unit.

2. Remove the two screws and take off the regulator cover.

3. Examine the condition of both sets of contact points. If dirty or pitted, they may be cleaned up with fine emery paper.

4. Measure the core gap with a feeler gauge. If the gap does not measure within 0.6–1.0 mm (0.024–0.040 in.), loosen the core gap adjusting screw and move the point body up or down as required.

5. Measure the gap of the upper point set in the same manner. The points should be gapped at 0.3–0.4 mm (0.012–0.016 in.). To adjust the gap, loosen the adjusting screw and move the lower contact up or down as required.

6. Temporarily install the regulator with one of the mounting bolts, leaving the cover off. Connect the three wires.

7. Loosen the voltage adjusting screw locknut. If the alternator output test showed insufficient output, turn the voltage adjusting screw clockwise about ¼ turn. If the test showed output to be excessive, turn the screw counterclockwise about ¼ turn. Tighten the locknut and rerun the alternator output test. Readjust the screw as necessary to obtain satisfactory alternator output.

8. If alternator output is unstable or excessive after the regulator has been adjusted properly, chances are that the regulator is faulty. If alternator output is insufficient and cannot be brought up to specification through regulator adjustment, the alternator itself should be suspected. Before proceeding any further, make sure that the battery is producing at least 12 volts at the terminals, and that none of the cells are dead or have a noticeably lower specific gravity than the rest. If the battery checks out alright, replace the regulator or check into the alternator (refer to the "Alternator Service" section), as indicated.

Testing the Rectifier

If alternator output is satisfactory but the battery discharges as the engine is running, it is quite possible that the rectifier is not functioning properly. (This is assuming, of course, that the battery is not old and tired or has one or more bad cells.) Before removing and testing the rectifier, make sure that it is solidly mounted on the frame. The rectifier is grounded through its mounting and will not operate without a good ground.

CAUTION: *Do not loosen or tighten the nut that holds the rectifier unit together, as this will adversely affect operation of the rectifier.*

1. To test the rectifier, first pull apart the plastic connector, unscrew the mounting nut, and remove the rectifier unit. Inside the rectifier are six diodes which, if functioning properly, will allow electricity to pass in only one direction.

2. Check the diodes, using either a multimeter or a test light and the motorcycle battery. If the test light and battery are to be used, simply run a length of wire off one of the battery terminals and connect one of the test light leads to the other terminal. The two free wire ends will be used to check electrical continuity of the diodes.

3. Connect one of the leads to pin green in the connector block and touch the other lead to each yellow lead in turn. Now, reverse the leads and repeat the procedure. The test light should light (or the meter needle respond) in one direction only.

4. If all is well so far, connect one of the leads to red/white and touch the other to each yellow again. Reverse the leads, as before, and repeat.

5. Continuity in both directions or in neither direction (when reversing the leads) indicates a defective diode, in which case the rectifier unit must be replaced.

NOTE: *On an ohmmeter, "continuity" will be indicated by a resistance of 5–40 ohms. "No continuity," by a resistance of 2000 or more ohms.*

The diodes are quite susceptible to failure from excessive heat and electrical overload. Observe the following precautions to avoid rectifier failure:

a. Do not use high-voltage test equipment to test the rectifier diodes.

b. Do not run the engine at high rpm with the rectifier "P" terminal disconnected, or else the high voltage that is produced will damage the rectifier.

c. Do not quick-change the battery (high-output charging equipment) without first disconnecting one of the battery cables.

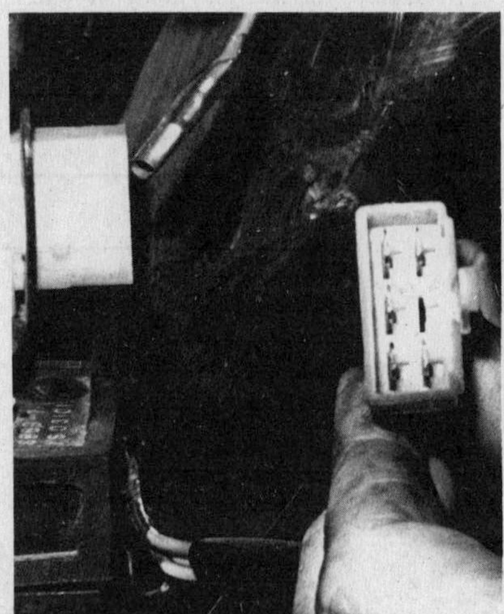
Rectifier connector

Alternator Output

Engine rpm	*1000*	*2000*	*3000*	*4000*	*5000*	*6000*	*7000*	*8000*
Day riding (headlight off)	6.5	0	2.4	1.3	1.0	1.0	0.8	0.6
Night riding (headlight on)	2–3	1	1	1	1	1	1	1
Battery terminal voltage	12	12.4	13.2	14.5	14.5	14.5	14.5	14.5

Alternator Service

Removing the alternator cover will allow access to the alternator components for testing purposes.

The field coil and the alternator stator will remain in the cover. To remove the stator, remove the four screws inside the cover. To take out the field coil, remove the three screws visible on the outside of the cover.

FIELD COIL

1. Check for continuity between each field coil lead and the core, using an ohmmeter or test light. If there is continuity between the leads and core, the coil is grounded and must be replaced.
2. Check for continuity between the two leads themselves. Continuity must exist or the coil is open and must be replaced.

Resistance of the field coil should be on the order of 7.2 ohms for 5-speed models, and 4.1 ohms for the 750A. If significantly less than this (within 10%), replace the coil.

Alternator field coil (white arrow) and stator (black arrow)

STATOR COIL

1. Check for continuity between pairs of yellow stator coil leads. Continuity must exist in all cases. If there is an open circuit, the stator must be replaced.
2. Check the resistance of the stator coils (between yellow leads). It should be about 0.2 ohms for 5-speed models, and 0.48 ohms for the 750A.
3. Check for continuity between each coil lead and the coil body. There must be none, or replacement is in order.

ROTOR

The rotor can be left in place unless replacement is necessary.

NOTE: *On some 750s, the rotor has a tendency to slip on the crankshaft taper as the engine is running, decreasing alternator output and causing the battery to discharge. To prevent this, the crankshaft and rotor tapers must be absolutely clean and smooth before installing the rotor, and the retaining nut must be tightened to specification. If the slipping persists, apply a thin layer of valve lapping compound to the crankshaft taper and install the rotor over it. This will lock the rotor firmly on the crankshaft after the retaining nut is tightened.*

CHARGING SYSTEM

Alternator Output Test

Refer to the alternator output test procedures given for earlier models, above.

With the headlight on "high beam," initial battery charging should begin at 1,700 rpm.

At 5,000 rpm, there should be a minimum of 8 amps/14.0 volts.

If readings are not satisfactory, check the alternator circuits as described below, and the regulator/rectifier unit. Unlike the previous system, the regulator is not adjustable.

Testing the Rectifier

Refer to "Testing the Rectifier" for the earlier models, above. Procedures and results should be the same. Be sure to observe all of the appropriate cautions.

Testing the Regulator

A check of the voltage regulator can be carried out if the alternator does not keep the battery charged. The regulator, however, cannot be adjusted. If defective, it must be replaced.

1. Connect a DC voltmeter across the battery. Start the engine and run it up to about 2,000 rpm.
2. Battery voltage should be in the neighborhood of 14–15 volts.

NOTE: *The battery must be in good condition and fully charged to ensure an accurate reading.*

3. If the reading is not satisfactory, proceed as follows.
4. Connect two 12-v motorcycle batteries in series (positive to negative terminals). Be sure that they are in good condition and fully charged.
5. Connect a variable resistor, capable of at least 100 ohms across the batteries with a 50 ohm resistor between. Connect a DC voltmeter across the batteries.
6. Connect the battery leads to the green and the black regulator leads at the 4-p connector. Apply a test light to the black and the white regulator leads at the 6-p connector. Adjust the variable resistor until the voltmeter reads 14–15 volts. At this point, the test light should go out.

If the test light does not go out, or if it will not light at all, replace the regulator.

Alternator Service

Removing the alternator cover will allow access to the alternator components for testing purposes.

The alternator stator and the brush holder will remain in the cover. To remove them, remove the two brush holder screws and the three stator coil screws.

ROTOR

1. Clean the rotor with a rag to remove any metal particles or foreign matter. To remove the rotor, place the transmission in gear and apply the rear brake. Remove the rotor bolt. Remove the rotor with the special puller.
2. When installing the rotor, first be sure that the crankshaft taper is clean. Push the rotor on by hand. Do not hammer it on or strike it.
3. Tighten the rotor bolt to 58–72 ft. lbs.

Removing the alternator rotor bolt

BRUSHES

1. Replace the alternator brushes when they are worn to the scribed limit line.
2. Clean the brushes with a bit of gasoline if they are dirty.
3. Clean the brush tracks on the rotor in the same manner.

Check brush length. Limit line is marked on the brushes

STATOR COILS

1. Check for continuity between pairs of the yellow stator coil wires. Continuity must exist in all cases. If there is an open circuit, the stator must be replaced.
2. Check the resistance of the stator coils (across pairs of yellow wires). Resistance should be 0.41–0.51 ohms in each case. If the resistance is too high or too low, replace the stator.
3. Check for continuity between each yellow lead and the stator body. There must be none, or replacement is in order.
4. Resistance between the black and white terminals should be 10–12 ohms.

FIELD COIL

The field coil is within the rotor. There should be 3.6–4.4 ohms restance between the brush tracks on the rotor. If resistance is very high, replace the rotor.

IGNITION SYSTEM, 1969–78

The ignition system consists of the battery, breaker points, coils, condensers, spark plug caps, and spark plugs.

There are two sets of breaker points and two ignition coils. Each coil fires two cylinders. They are paired No. 1 and 4, and No. 2 and 3.

1. In the event of failure of the ignition system, first check the fuses; if all are in working order, check that the snap connectors for the coils and breaker points are all clean and tight.

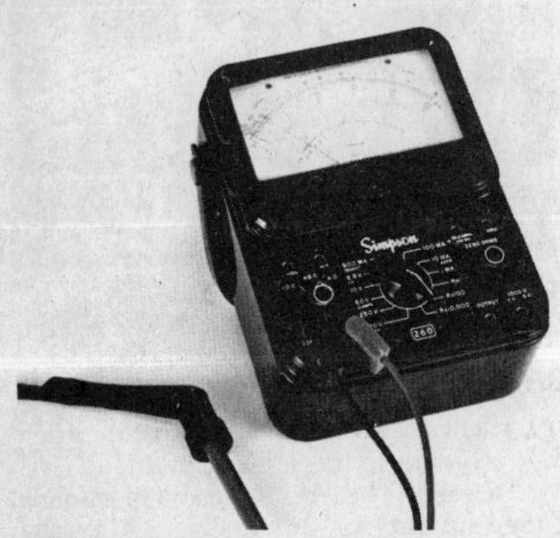

Checking spark plug cap resistance

2. Inspect the breaker points, plugs, and battery. If these items are all in working order, the problem may be isolated to the coils, condensers, or plug caps.

3. If only one cylinder fails to fire, and the problem is not a loose connection or defective spark plug, suspect the plug cap. The caps are fitted with a resistor to prevent radio interference while in operation, and heat and vibration may cause the value of this resistor to increase considerably, even to becoming an open circuit.

The easiest way to see if a misfire is due to a defective cap is to switch the plug lead of the non-firing cylinder with its corresponding cylinder (1–4, 2–3). If the dead cylinder begins to fire and the other cylinder ceases, the problem is the plug cap. The caps should be replaced as a set.

Functional caps will have a resistance of 5,000–7,500 ohms. Usually, when resistance reaches about 9,000 ohms, the plug for that cap will no longer fire.

Caps are easily removable by unscrewing them from their cables.

4. Defective condensers are seldom a problem, since these are now usually replaced along with the breaker points. Defective condensers will cause considerable arcing or sparking between the breaker point contacts while the machine is running, and this should be cause for replacement before they fail completely. Badly burned or pitted point contact surfaces can also be caused by defective condensers, as well as by improper adjustment. If the points are in bad condition, replace them and the condensers as well.

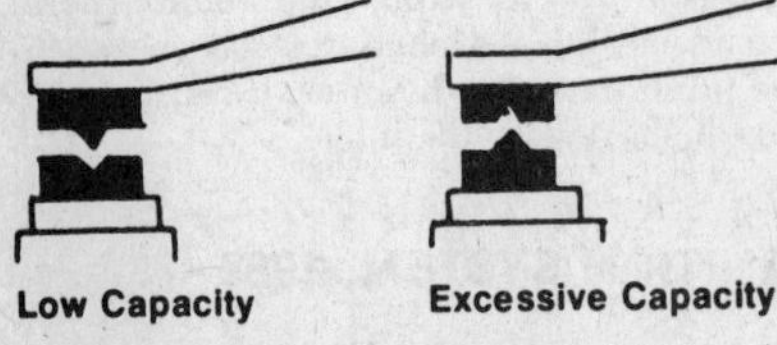

A defective condenser will cause mounds and matching depressions on the point contact surfaces

5. Condenser capacity can be checked with electrical test equipment (if available) in place on the machine, provided the condenser is first disconnected from the primary terminal. Capacitance should be 0.24 MFD. The resistance of the condensers should be in excess of 10 MΩ. A variation of 10% in either reading is allowable.

6. If the condensers are not suspect, check the ignition coils. Coils should be checked for continuity of the windings. First disconnect the blue and the black/white leads from the left coil and check for continuity between these leads. If there is none, the coil must be replaced.

For the other coil, carry out the same test between the yellow and the black/white leads.

Check for continuity on the high-tension side of each coil. Disconnect the two spark plug leads of one of the coils and check the continuity between them. If none exists, replace the coil. Repeat the test with the other coil. Remember you will be checking continuity between plug leads 1 and 4 and leads 2 and 3.

7. Coils are secured to the frame with two bolts and are easily removed, if defective, by disconnecting the wires and removing the bolts after the gas tank is taken off.

IGNITION SYSTEM, 1979 AND LATER

The transistorized ignition system encompasses the battery, pulser generator, spark unit, ignition coils, and the spark plugs and caps.

The coils are paired so that cylinders 1–4 and 2–3 fire at the same time. They will probably not fire alone unless there is a high tension leak in the system. Therefore, there will probably be lack of spark at two cylinders at a time.

1. In the event of spark failure, first suspect the spark plugs or caps. Refer to "Ignition System, 1969–1978," Steps 1, 3, and 7.

2. Remove the spark plugs. Connect the caps and lay the plugs on the cylinder head to act as a ground. Remove the generator cover and touch a screwdriver across the rotor and the pulser generator steel core. Repeat several times. There should be a good spark at the plug.

3. Check pulser coil resistance with an ohmmeter after disconnecting the pulsers at the connector beneath the left side cover.

Resistance should be 480–590 ohms at 68°F/20°C. If it is not within this range, replace the pulser coil.

4. To check the spark unit, disconnect the 6-p connector for cylinders 1–4 or the 4-p connector for cylinders 2–3 (top and second from the top respectively) beneath the left side cover.

Attach the positive lead of a DC voltmeter to the blue/with white tube terminal of the 6-p connector or the yellow/with white tube of the 4-p connector. Attach the negative meter lead to ground.

Turn on the ignition switch. Use a jumper wire to ground the blue or yellow terminal intermittently. Voltage should vary from 12 v to 0 v as this is done.

If it does not, replace the spark unit.

STARTING SYSTEM

The starting system consists of the starter motor and clutch, the solenoid, and the handlebar-mounted starter switch. When the button is pressed, the electrical circuit to the solenoid is closed and the solenoid is activated, sending the battery current directly to the starter motor. The starting system is quite reliable and it is unlikely that any major problems will arise.

Testing

The following two paragraphs are applicable to machines with a headlight switch. On models without a switch, a by-pass is incorporated to kill the headlight when the starter is used.

If the starter will not operate, switch on the headlight and observe its intensity. If it is dim when the starter is not being operated, check the battery connections and recharge the battery. If the headlight doesn't light, check the fuse, the battery connections, the ignition switch and its connections, and check the continuity of the wire between the ignition switch and the battery.

If the headlight is bright, press the starter button momentarily and watch the light. If it remains bright, touch a screwdriver blade between the two starter solenoid terminals. If the starter operates, connect a test light between the small yellow/red wire on the solenoid and ground. If the test light comes on as the button is pushed, the solenoid is faulty. If it does not light, look for defective wiring between the starter button and solenoid or between the starter button and ignition switch, or simply a burned out starter button switch. If the starter does not operate and the headlight dims as the main solenoid terminals are bridged, the starter motor is faulty. If the headlight does not dim, look for a bad connection at the starter.

If the starter motor operates freely but will not turn the engine over, the starter clutch is not functioning (a rare occurrence). To remove the starter clutch on the 750, it is necessary only to remove the alternator cover and pull off the rotor to gain access to the clutch.

Starter Motor Service

REMOVAL AND INSTALLATION

1. Disconnect the cable from the positive battery terminal.

2. Disconnect the starter motor cable from the solenoid.

3. Remove the starter motor cover and the left-side crankcase cover.

4. Unscrew the two starter motor mounting bolts and lift the starter out.

5. Installation is in reverse order of removal.

INSPECTION

1. Take out the two screws and remove the starter side cover.

2. Check electrical continuity between the commutator and armature core using a multitester or test light and battery. If continuity exists, the armature coil is grounded and the complete starter motor unit must be replaced.

3. Check for continuity between all of the

commutator segments. Continuity must exist in each case.

4. Check continuity between the brush that is wired to the stator coil and the starter motor cable. Lack of continuity indicates an open circuit in the stator coil, and the starter motor unit should be replaced.

Starter mounting bolts

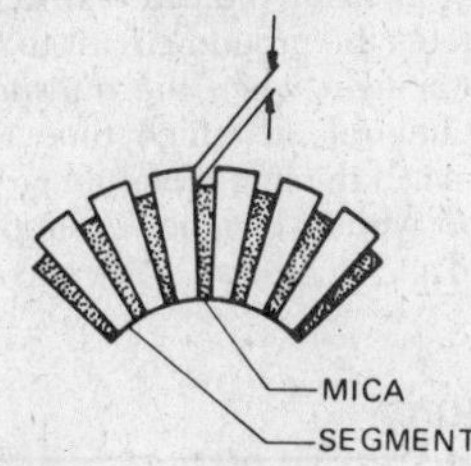

Mica undercut

5. Examine the carbon brushes for damage to the contact surfaces and measure their length. Replace the brushes as a set if either one measures less than 5.5 mm (0.22 in.) for 1978 or earlier, or 7.5 mm (0.30 in.) for 1979–1981, or if they are damaged in any way.

6. Brush spring tension should be measured with a small pull-scale. Replace the springs if they have weakened to less than 0.4 kg (0.8 lb) tension for pre-1979 models or 0.6 kg (0.9 lb) on 1979–1981 machines.

7. The mica undercut of the commutator should be maintained at 0.3 mm (0.012 in.). Any carbon deposits should be cleaned out of the commutator grooves, and a piece of hacksaw blade or the like used to increase the undercut depth if necessary. Refer to the illustration.

8. Polish the commutator with fine emery cloth and then clean it thoroughly before installing.

Starter Solenoid

1. If the battery is in reasonably good condition, and nothing at all happens when the starter button is pushed, check the solenoid.

2. Disconnect the starter cable at the starter motor. When the button is pushed, there should be an audible "click" which indicates that the solenoid is opening.

3. If further testing is necessary, remove the solenoid from the machine.

CAUTION: *Be sure to disconnect the cables at the battery before disconnecting the solenoid terminals.*

Connect a fully charged 12-volt battery across the solenoid low-tension leads and check for continuity across the high-tension terminals with an ohmmeter or self-contained test light. If there is no continuity, replace or repair the solenoid.

4. Check for continuity across the low-tension terminals with an ohmmeter or self-powered test light. If there is none, the primary winding of the solenoid is broken, and the unit must be replaced.

5. The primary cause of solenoid malfunction is pitting and/or burning of the contact points inside. It may be possible to restore a solenoid to serviceable condition by taking it apart and dressing the points with a file or emery paper. If this doesn't work, replace it.

6. If starter trouble began just after the starter button housing was disassembled or moved for any reason, check the connections at the switch as they may have come adrift.

ELECTRICAL COMPONENTS

Turn Signal Flasher

If none of the turn signals will flash, chances are that the turn signal flasher has failed. A Signal-Stat 142 flasher is used on the 750 and is located near the battery.

NOTE: *The flasher must be properly grounded to operate.*

Switches

TESTING AND REPLACEMENT PROCEDURES

The operation of any switch can be checked using a multi-tester or test light to determine the electrical continuity of the switch in its different positions. Follow the procedures given below for testing the individual switches. If, during any test, you find that electricity is available at the switch but the switch won't work, make sure that it is not simply a bad ground that is sabotaging it before you buy a replacement. Removal and installation procedures are given after the testing information, as it is not necessary to remove the switches in order to check them.

IGNITION (MAIN) SWITCH

1969–1978

Pull the ignition switch connector apart and check continuity of the switch in its three positions, using the accompanying chart as a guide. If any part of the test shows the switch to be faulty, the switch should be replaced.

The switch can be removed after the retaining nut has been unscrewed.

		BAT	*IG*	*TL 1*	*TL 2*
Wire Color		*Red*	*Black*	*Brown/White*	*Brown*
Key position	OFF				
	1	O———	———O	O———	———O
	2	O———	———	———	———O

1979 and Later

After disconnecting the coupler at the switch, check for continuity. The terminals may be identified as follows:

TL2 and TL1 are paired above the other three terminals;

The three terminals are IG, BAT, and P respectively.

In the "P" key position, there should only be continuity between the BAT terminal and P.

In the "ON" position, there should be continuity between BAT and IG and between TL1 and TL2 only.

In the other key positions, there should be no continuity between any of the terminals.

FRONT AND REAR BRAKE LIGHT SWITCHES

The front brake light switch is located between the fork legs just under the headlight. To check its operation, connect the two test leads to the switch terminals, leaving the switch wires connected, and operate the front brake lever. If the tester does not show continuity as the brake is applied (ignition on), check to see if there is electricity at the switch power supply lead (black wire). If there is, replace the brake light switch. If there is not, check the continuity of the black wire between its connections at the brake light switch and ignition switch to determine if there is a loose connector, a short circuit, or a break in the wire.

The front brake light switch can be removed by pulling off the wires and unscrewing it. It may be necessary to bleed the brake after installation.

The rear switch may be tested in the same manner as the front switch. Make sure that it is not simply improperly adjusted and that the spring is strong enough to actuate it. Adjustment can be made by turning the large nut on the switch.

HORN BUTTON AND HORN

If the horn is not working, check to see if it is receiving electricity by connecting the tester between the light green wire at the horn and a good ground (such as the engine crankcase). Turn on the ignition and press the horn button. If the tester responds, the horn is faulty or is not properly grounded. If the tester does not respond, connect the tester lead to the light green wire and press the horn button again (ignition on). If there is still no electricity available, replace the horn button. If there is electricity at the headlight shell but not at the horn, check the green wire for loose connections or a short circuit between the headlight and horn.

NOTE: *Horn loudness can be increased by turning the adjusting screw in (clockwise). The horn button and turn signal switch are in the same switch case, which can be removed after the screws in the bottom half of the case are taken out.*

TURN SIGNAL SWITCH

1969–1978

To check operation of the turn signal switch, pull apart the connectors for the orange, gray, and blue wires. Check continuity of the switch in its three positions with a multi-tester or test light and battery, using the accompanying chart as a guide. (Be sure to connect the tester to the three wire ends leading to the switch, not the turn signal bulbs.) If any part of the test shows the switch to be faulty, it should be replaced.

Knob	Blue Lead	Gray Lead	Orange Lead
R	○	○	
OFF (center)			
L		○	○

To remove the switch, take out the screws at the bottom of the switch case and separate the upper and lower halves of the switch.

1979–1981

Test procedures are similar to those described for earlier models, above. "R" should give continuity between blue and gray; "L" should give it between gray and orange, as above. In addition, "R" should give continuity between brown/white and orange/white; "L" should give continuity between brown/white and blue/white; "OFF" should give continuity between brown/white, orange/white, and blue/white.

LIGHTING SWITCH

1969–1978

To check operation of the lighting switcl pull apart the connectors for the black, blue brown/white, and white leads. Check cont nuity of the switch in its different positions using the accompanying chart as a guide. (B sure to connect the tester to the three wir ends leading to the switch, not the lights The brown/white wire is for the highbeam ir

Wire Color		IG Black	HB Blue	TL Brown/White	LE Whi
	H	○	○	○	
ON	P	○		○	
	L	○		○	○
OFF					

dicator light.) If any part of the test shows the switch to be faulty, it should be replaced. The switch can be removed after the screws in the bottom half of the case have been taken out.

1979 and Later

"HI" should give continuity between blue/white and blue;

"N" between blue/white, blue, and white;

"LO" between blue/white and white

IGNITION KILL SWITCH

Check operation of the kill switch by pulling apart the connectors for the black and black/white wires in the headlight shell, and testing for continuity of the switch in both the on and off positions. Electrical continuity in either of the off positions, or *lack* of continuity in the on position, indicates a bad switch. (Be sure to connect the tester to the wire ends leading to the switch, and not to the ignition coil and ground.)

Ignition Kill Switch

Wire Color	Black	Black/White
ON	○	○
OFF		

The switch can be removed after the screws in the bottom half of the case have been taken out.

STARTER BUTTON

Check operation of the starter button by connecting the tester between the yellow/red wire and ground. Lack of continuity with the button depressed indicates a bad switch.

Starter Switch

Wire Color	Ground	Yellow/Red
ON	○	○
OFF		

The switch can be removed after the screws in the bottom half of the case have been taken out.

OIL PRESSURE SWITCH

When oil pressure drops below approximately 7 psi, the oil pressure switch closes, completing the ground circuit of the oil pressure warning light which will then light up. There is no power supplied to the oil pressure switch, so it must be tested using equipment with its own power source such as a multimeter or test light and battery. Connect the meter leads to the oil pressure switch lead and to ground. If the tester does not respond, the switch has not closed and is defective. (The engine must not be running or else oil pressure will be too high to allow the switch to close.)

The oil pressure switch is located on top of the crankcase (just behind the cylinders). To remove, simply unscrew the switch unit after the lead has been disconnected.

NEUTRAL INDICATOR SWITCH

In the same manner as the oil pressure switch, the neutral indicator switch closes and completes the ground circuit to the neutral indicator light when the transmission is placed in neutral, at which time the light should go on. If the light does not go on, connect a tester with its own power supply to the switch lead and to ground. Lack of continuity

Electrical Specifications

Model:	*CB750 (5-speed) 1969–1978*	*CB750A*	*CB750, CB900 1979–1981*
ALTERNATOR			
Type		3-phase excited field	
Battery voltage (volts)	12	12	12
Output (kW @ 5000 rpm/volts-amps)	0.210/12–13	0.290/14.5–18	0.260/14–15
Polarity	negative ground	negative ground	negative ground
Stator coil resistance (ohms)	0.2	0.48	0.48
Field coil resistance (ohms)	7.2	4.1	4.0
REGULATOR			
Type	dual contact mechanical	dual contact mechanical	solid-state
Model (Hitachi)	TL12-38	TL12-38	—
Core gap (mm/in.)	0.6–1.0/0.024–0.040	0.6–1.0/0.024–0.040	na
Point gap (mm/in.)	0.3–0.4/0.012–0.016	0.3–0.4/0.012–0.016	na
RECTIFIER			
Type	6-diode, full-wave	6-diode, full-wave	6-diode, full-wave
Model (Hitachi)	SB6B-7	SB6B-7	—
Output (volts/amps)	12/15	12/15	12/15
BATTERY			
Model (Yusa)	B64-12	Y50-N18L-A2	YB14L-A2
Voltage (v)	12	12	12
Capacity (amp hrs)	14	20	14
Electrolyte specific gravity (68° F)	1.260–1.280	1.270–1.290	1.280
Charging rate (amps/hr)	1.4	2.0	1.4
STARTER MOTOR			
Output (kW)	0.6	0.6	0.6
Rated operation (max)	30 seconds continuous	30 seconds continuous	30 seconds continuous
Carbon brush length (mm/in.)			
Standard	12–13/0.47–0.51	12–13/0.47–0.51	12–13/0.47–0.51
Serviceable limit	5.5/0.22	5.5/0.22	7.5/0.30
Brush spring tension (gr)	500–600	500–600	560
Mica undercut (minimum mm/in.)	0.3/0.012	0.3/0.012	0.3/0.012
Draw under load (v/amps)	8.5/120	8.5/120	8.5/120
Stall load (v/amps)	5.0/280	5.0/280	5.0/280
Solenoid operating voltage (v)	7.5	7.0	7.0
LIGHTS			
Headlight	12v-50/40W (SAE 6012)	12v-50/40W (SAE 6012)	12v-65/50W
Tail/stoplight	12v-7/25W (SAE 1157)	12v-7/25W (SAE 1157)	12v-8/27W (2) (SAE 1157)
Turn signals			
Front	12v-32cp (SAE 1034)	12v-32cp (SAE 1034)	12v-23/8W
Rear	12v-32cp (SAE 1073)	12v-32cp (SAE 1073)	12v-23W
Meter lights	12v-2cp (SAE 57)	12v-2cp (SAE 57)	12v-2cp (SAE 57)
Position light	12v-3cp	12v-3cp	12v-3cp
FUSES			
Main (amps) ①	15	15	30
Headlight (amps)	7	7	10
Taillight, meter lights (amps) ①	5	5	10

①K3 and later

(with the transmission in neutral) means that the switch should be replaced.

The switch is located at the underside of the engine on 1969–1978 models, and near the engine sprocket on more recent machines.

CLUTCH SWITCH

On late models which incorporate a clutch safety switch, disconnect the leads at the clutch.

There should be continuity when the clutch is pulled in.

To remove the switch, disconnect the wiring, remove the clutch lever, and remove the switch.

The switch has a small protrusion which must point towards the handlebar when it is installed.

CHASSIS

WHEELS

Front Wheel Assembly

REMOVAL AND INSTALLATION

Single Disc

1. Raise the front wheel off the ground by placing a support under the engine.
2. Disconnect the speedometer cable from the front hub.

Be sure that the axle cap is installed so that the gap (arrow) is at the rear

3. Remove the four axle clamp nuts (two on each side) and withdraw the front wheel assembly from the forks.

CAUTION: *Do not operate the front brake while the wheel is removed or the caliper piston will be forced out of the cylinder.*

Installation is in reverse order of removal.

Note that the front axle holder clamps are machined so that the forward mating surface is slightly higher than the rear mating surface. They must be installed correctly. Place a straightedge on the mating surfaces to determine which end is higher, and *install the high mating surface forward.* On late models, install the clamps so that the "F" mark is at the front. Tighten the forward retaining nut first, drawing the forward mating surface of the holder clamp flush against the fork leg mating surface and then tighten the rear nut. Proper torque is 13–18 ft. lbs. for both nuts.

Twin Disc

1. Support the front wheel off the ground by placing a support beneath the engine.
2. Disconnect the speedometer cable.
3. Unbolt and remove one of the brake calipers from the fork sliders. It is not necessary to disconnect the brake lines, but a piece of cardboard or the like can be inserted between the brake pads to prevent their closing together.

CAUTION: *Do not operate the brake lever while the calipers are removed.*

4. Remove the four axle clamp nuts (two on each side), take off the clamps, and take out the wheel.

Installation is the reverse of removal. Be sure that the axle clamps are installed correctly: they are machined unevenly, and the higher side must be installed towards the front of the motorcycle. Tighten the nut for the high side first.

On late models, "F" is marked on the axle clamps and this must be installed towards the front of the fork. Proper torque is 13–18 ft. lbs.

Wheel Bearings

REMOVAL

1. After removing the front wheel, unscrew the axle nut and withdraw the axle and axle collar.
2. Remove the screw and remove the speedometer gearbox from the hub.
3. Bend back the locktabs and unbolt and remove the brake disc.
4. Remove the speedometer gearbox drive flange retainer. Remove the drive flange.
5. Unscrew the wheel bearing retainer from the other side of the hub. Withdraw the bearings and spacer.

Bearings are usually driven out with a hammer and drift. Once removed, however, bearings should be replaced with new ones. Check bearing condition in place if possible.

INSTALLATION

Assembly is the reverse of the above.

Note the following points:

a. Pack the bearings with a good grade of wheel bearing grease. Put a small handful of the grease in the hub as well.

Removing a wheel bearing

b. Do not forget to install the spacer in the hub before installing the bearing.

c. Bearings may be driven into place using Honda service tool No. 07048-30001 or a suitable substitute.

d. Use a new oil seal and lubricate it with oil to make installation into the bearing retainer easier.

e. Stake the bearing retainer in two places after it is installed.

NOTE: *The front hub on the CB 750 (1970 and later) is narrower than on the CB 750 (1969). In addition, the speedometer drive flange and flange retainer and the brake disc mounting bolts are changed to fit the narrower hub. It is important that the correct disc mounting bolts are used (if removed) or the disc will not be securely mounted.*

Rear Wheel Assembly

REMOVAL AND INSTALLATION

Rear Drum Brake

1. Place the bike on the center stand.
2. Remove the rear brake adjusting nut and separate the brake rod from the lever.
3. Disconnect the brake anchor from the hub by removing the lockpin and unscrewing the nut and bolt.
4. Loosen the chain adjuster locknuts and back the bolts out.
5. Remove the cotter pin and loosen the axle nut. Turn the adjusters downwwrd.
6. Remove the lockbolts and chain adjuster stop plates. Push the wheel forward and lift the chain off the rear sprocket. Withdraw the wheel rearward from the swing arm.

Installation is in reverse order of removal. Tighten the axle nut to 58–72 ft. lbs.

Rear Disc Brake (Chain Drive)

1. Loosen the locknut on the chain adjusters and back the adjusters out. Remove the cotter pin from the rear axle, and remove the axle nut.
2. Slide the wheel forward in the swing arm and lift the chain off the sprocket. The wheel can now be removed.

NOTE: *Do not apply the rear brake with the wheel removed, as the piston may be forced out of the caliper.*

3. When installing, tighten the rear axle nut to 58–72 ft. lbs.

Rear Disc Brake (Shaft Drive)

1. Park the machine on the center stand.
2. Remove the axle nut cotter pin and remove the axle nut.
3. Loosen the axle pinch bolt and pull out the axle. Note washer location.
4. Raise the brake caliper. Pull the wheel to the left to disengage the drive flange and remove it from the machine.

NOTE: *Do not apply the rear brake with the rear wheel removed, as the caliper piston may pop out.*

5. When installing, grease the drive flange. Tighten the axle nut to 58–72 ft. lbs., and the axle pinch bolt to 17–21 ft. lbs.

Wheel Bearings

REMOVAL

1. After removing the rear wheel, remove the axle and brake plate from drum brake models.

2. Tap the sprocket and sprocket plate out of the hub with a soft drift or block of wood.

3. Unscrew the bearing retainer(s) and drive the bearings out of the hub.

4. The bearing in the sprocket hub can be removed in the same manner.

INSTALLATION

Reverse the removal procedure. Note the following points:

a. Pack the bearings with wheel bearing grease. Place a small handful in the hub as well.

b. Do not forget the bearing spacer.

c. The bearings may be driven into place with Honda tool No. 07048-30001 or a suitable substitute.

d. Use a thread-locking compound on the bearing retainer(s).

e. Apply a small quantity of grease to the friction surfaces of the flange and wheel hub.

FRONT BRAKE SERVICE

Single Disc, 1969–1978

Before attempting work on the hydraulic disc brake system, note the following points:

a. Never use brake fluid from an old or an unsealed container. Brake fluid is hydroscopic—it absorbs moisture—and therefore quickly becomes useless unless kept in a sealed environment.

b. Never reuse brake fluid which has been flushed from the system.

c. The system uses DOT 3 brake fluid. This standard is marked on the can. Do not use any other type. Do not mix types or brands of brake fluid, as they may not be compatible.

d. When handling brake fluid, cover all painted parts (such as the gas tank) which may be accidentally damaged by spillage. Brake fluid will remove paint in short order.

e. Keep brake fluid away from the pads and disc surfaces. If there is contact, clean them off immediately with a non-oily solvent. If pads cannot be cleaned, replace them.

f. With the exception of the pads and disc, all internal caliper and master cylinder parts should be cleaned in new brake fluid *only*. Do not attempt to clean these parts in solvents of any type.

g. Any time any of the brake line connections have been loosened or disconnected, the system must be bled to remove air. Refer to the section below.

PAD REPLACEMENT

1. To determine pad wear on the CB 750 (1969) and 750K1, measure the clearance between the caliper and the disc with a feeler gauge as shown. When the clearance is less than 2.0 mm (0.08 in.), the pads should be replaced.

2. On other models, check the pads for wear by noting the red wear indicator line. Replace the pads when they are worn close to this red line.

3. Remove the front wheel. Remove the two bolts from the side of the caliper and remove the right-side caliper half.

4. Remove the pad from the piston side of the caliper. Withdraw the cotter pin and remove the pad from the other caliper half.

5. Before installing the new pads, apply a small amount of silicone grease to the pad sliding surfaces on the caliper as shown. The

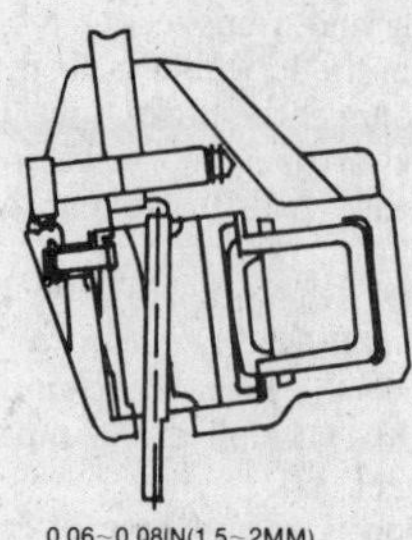

Checking pad wear on early (1969–1970) models

grease serves to keep pad operation smooth by repelling dust and water as well as providing lubrication. Use grease sparingly and do not allow it to contact the pad friction material.

6. Install the new pads in the caliper halves and bolt the caliper together.

7. Install the front wheel and adjust the brake as explained in the following section. Avoid heavy braking until at least 50 miles have been covered.

ADJUSTMENT

1. Loosen the caliper adjuster bolt locknut and turn the bolt until the inside pad (closest to the wheel) lightly contacts the disc.

2. Turn the adjuster bolt in the opposite direction about ¼–½ turn and tighten the locknut.

3. On the very early models, provision is made for adjustment of brake lever free-play at the lever. Loosen the locknut and turn the adjuster screw until ¼–½ in. free-play is obtained at the end of the lever. Retighten the locknut to 13–17 ft. lbs. The lever is not adjustable on the other models.

CALIPER

Leakage of brake fluid from around the caliper piston indicates that the caliper assembly is worn or damaged, and the cause should be investigated immediately. To remove, inspect, and rebuild the caliper assembly:

1. Remove the front wheel.

2. Unscrew the hydraulic line connection at the caliper and catch the fluid that drains from the line in a suitable container and dispose of it. (Do not reuse old brake fluid.)

3. Unscrew the three caliper mounting bolts at the left fork leg and remove the caliper.

4. Remove the two bolts and separate the caliper halves.

5. Remove the pad seat from the caliper piston and withdraw the piston.

6. Remove the seal from the cylinder and replace if damaged. Cylinder bore diameter should not exceed 38.22 mm (1.504 in.) and piston diameter should not be less than 38.11 mm (1.500 in.). Maximum calculated clearance between the piston and cylinder is 0.115 mm (0.0045 in.). Replace parts as necessary. Clean all components and dry with compressed air.

7. Use a new seal in the cylinder bore and lubricate in throughly with fresh brake fluid before installing. Make sure that it is seated properly in its groove.

8. Lubricate the piston with brake fluid and install it in the cylinder. Be careful not to twist the seal or force it out of the groove. Install the pad seat on the piston.

9. Reinstall the brake pads in the caliper halves. Use new pads if the old ones have been in contact with brake fluid.

10. Bolt the caliper halves together and remount the caliper assembly on the fork leg.

11. Connect the hydraulic line and replace the front wheel.

12. Bleed and adjust the brake (refer to the appropriate headings in this section).

MASTER CYLINDER

Brake fluid leakage around the brake lever and excessive lever travel (after bleeding the brake to make sure that there is no air trapped in the hydraulic system) are indications of master cylinder malfunction. The rebuilding procedure is as follows.

CAUTION: *Be very careful, when removing and replacing the master cylinder, in filling the reservoir. Brake fluid can damage paint and plastic, and extreme care should be exercised in its handling. Wipe up any spills immediately.*

1. Place a cloth underneath the connection to absorb any spilled fluid and disconnect the brake hose from the master cylinder.

2. Unscrew the clamp bolts and remove the master cylinder from the handlebar. Unscrew the reservoir cap and discard the brake fluid.

3. Remove the rubber boot. Remove the snap-ring and withdraw the washer, piston, secondary cup, primary cup, spring, and check valve.

4. Check the cylinder bore for scoring and pitting, and measure the wear using a dial indicator. Bore diameter should not exceed 14.06 mm (0.553 in.). Replace the master cylinder assembly if damaged or worn.

5. Check the piston diameter. Minimum allowable diameter is 13.94 mm (0.549 in.).

6. Clean all components in solvent and dry with compressed air.

7. Use a new seal and lubricate it with fresh brake fluid. Install the components in the bore as removed.

8. Mount the master cylinder on the handlebar and connect the brake hose. Do not forget to install the two washers at the connection.

9. Fill the reservoir to the level mark with brake fluid and bleed the brake. (Use DOT 3 brake fluid.)

BLEEDING

1. Top up the reservoir with brake fluid and replace the cap to keep dirt and moisture out and the fluid in. Cover the gas tank with a thick cloth to avoid damage due to spilled brake fluid.

2. Attach one end of a small diameter rubber hose to the bleed valve on the caliper, and place the other end in a jar which contains several inches of clean, new brake fluid. Be sure that the end of the hose is submerged in this fluid. Arrange the hose so that it loops upward after leaving the bleed valve, and see that it has no kinks or sharp bends.

3. Pump the brake lever rapidly several times until some resistance is felt and, holding the lever against the resistance, open the bleed valve about one-half turn. When the

Bleeding the brake system

lever bottoms, close the valve (do not overtighten) and then release the lever.

4. Repeat this operation until no more air is released out of the hose and the brake lever is firm in operation. Check the fluid level in the reservoir often to make sure that it doesn't go dry and draw more air into the system. Do not reuse fluid that has been pumped out of the system. Do not use fluid that has been stored for more than a few weeks after the seal on its container has been opened, as brake fluid will absorb moisture from the air and may corrode the master cylinder and caliper.

5. Refill the reservoir to the level mark when through (but do not overfill). Avoid overtightening the cap or fluid will weep around the cap edge.

DISC SERVICE

The brake disc normally requires no service of any kind. However, if the disc becomes scored for any reason, it should be replaced and a new set of pads should be installed. A badly scored disc will reduce the effectiveness of the brake and shorten pad life considerably. If the front brake lever oscillates or fluctuates when the brake is applied at speed, the indication is that the brake disc is warped or bent. Check the run-out of the disc with a dial indicator and replace it if run-out exceeds 0.3 mm (0.012 in.). To replace the disc:

1. Remove the wheel.
2. Bend back the locktabs (if fitted), unscrew the nuts, and remove the disc from the hub.
3. Mount the new disc on the hub and tighten the nuts evenly, using new locktabs (if fitted) or thread-locking compound to secure the nuts.
4. Examine the brake pads and replace them if they are close to the limit of wear or have worn in an unusual pattern.

Twin Disc, 1977–1978

The CB750F (77–78) is equipped with two brake calipers. The calipers are the same as these found on the rear of 1977–1978 models equipped with a rear disc brake. Refer to "Rear Brake Service, Disc Brake Models," below.

When bleeding the system, bleed the caliper furthest from the master cylinder (left side) first.

Single Disc, 1979 and Later

PAD REPLACEMENT

1. Remove the caliper cover. Take out the clip.
2. Push the caliper as far as possible towards the wheel and push the piston all the way in.
3. Remove the pins, brake pads, and shim.
4. When fitting the new pads, apply a coat of silicon grease to both sides of the shim.
5. Install the new pads with the shim on the piston side of the pad. Fit the pins, clip, and cover.

CALIPER

1. Taking care to avoid damage to painted surfaces, place a container beneath the caliper brake line banjo, and remove the banjo bolt.
2. Loosen the two caliper shaft bolts gradually and evenly while pressing them in.
3. Remove the caliper from the fork slider.
4. Remove the piston boot.
5. Place a rag over the piston and hold the caliper with the piston facing down. Apply low-pressure compressed air to the banjo bolt fitting to push out the piston.
6. Pry out the fluid seal with a small screwdriver or the like, taking extreme care not to scratch the caliper bore.
7. Clean all metal parts in clean brake fluid. All rubber parts should be replaced as a matter of course.
8. Check the piston outside surface for scratches or signs of wear, and replace it if the surface is not perfect. Measure the OD of the piston. If it is under 42.765 mm (1.6837 in.), replace it.
9. Check the caliper bore for like damage. Make sure that the fluid seal groove is perfectly clear of foreign matter. Measure the ID of the caliper bore. If it is more than 42.915 mm (1.6896 in.), replace it.
10. Assembly is the reverse of disassembly. Use all new rubber parts. Be sure to lubricate the piston and seal with medium grade hi-temperature silicon grease or some new brake fluid before assembly.

Be sure that the fluid seal is firmly seated in its groove.

Be sure to install the piston with the boot lip facing out.

Tighten the caliper shaft bolts to 22–29 ft. lbs.

Caliper mounting bolts

Measuring piston diameter

CALIPER CARRIER

The caliper carrier will remain on the fork slider when the caliper halves are removed. When rebuilding the system, remove the two carrier bolts and separate the components. Clean all metal parts in clean brake fluid. Replace the caliper shaft o-rings and boots. Lubricate the o-rings with silicon grease or new brake fluid before assembly. When assembling, be sure that the boots are seated in the caliper shaft grooves. Tighten the carrier bolts to 22–29 ft. lbs.

MASTER CYLINDER

The master cylinder components are the same as described for the "Single Disc, 1969–1978." Refer to that section, above.

DISC

Replace the disc if measured thickness is less than 6.0 mm (0.24 in.) at any point, or if the disc surface is warped, scored, or otherwise damaged.

BLEEDING

Bleeding procedures are carried out in the same manner as outlined for the "Single Disc, 1969–1978," above. Refer to that section.

Twin Disc, 1979–81

PAD REPLACEMENT

1. Remove the two caliper allen head bolts. Remove the caliper from the carrier.
2. Remove both brake pads and the shim.
3. Install the new brake pads and the shim. Install the shim with the arrow facing upwards.
4. When fitting the caliper, tighten the two allen bolts gradually and evenly to 11–14 ft. lbs.

CALIPER

Working procedures are the same as for "Single Disc, 1979–80," above. Specifications differ.

Caliper piston replacement limit is less than 38.09 mm (1.500 in.).

Caliper bore replacement limit is 38.24 mm (1.506 in.).

MASTER CYLINDER

Procedures are the same as for the master cylinder under "Single Disc, 1969–1978," above. Specifications differ.

Master cylinder bore diameter should be no more than 15.925 mm (0.6270 in.).

Master cylinder piston diameter should be no less than 15.815 mm (0.6226 in.).

DISC

Replace the disc if the thickness at any point is under 4.0 mm (0.16 in.), or if the disc is scored or warped.

BLEEDING

Refer to the "Single Disc, 1969–78," section for bleeding procedures.

REAR BRAKE SERVICE

Disc Brake, 1977–78

PAD REPLACEMENT

1. Remove the 5-mm bolt from the top of the caliper and lift up the pad cover.
2. Push down on the pad set spring and withdraw the two pad pins from the right caliper half.
3. Remove the two brake pads from the top of the caliper. If the same brake pads are to be reused, mark the pads so that they can be installed in the caliper half from which they were removed so that the direction of rotation will not be reversed.
4. To install new pads, drop them in place. Press the set spring down and insert the two pad pins in place through the pads. Be sure that the set spring is hooked on the narrow section of the pins.
5. Replace the pad cover and secure with the 5-mm bolt.

CALIPER

Removal

1. Remove the banjo bolt from the caliper and disconnect the brake line. Allow the fluid to drain from the line into a suitable container. Wipe up any spilled fluid immediately. Place a plastic bag around the end of the line and banjo bolt to prevent dirt from entering the system.
2. If the caliper is to be disassembled, loosen the two caliper set bolts at this time as they may be difficult to loosen once the caliper is removed.
3. Disconnect the brake anchor from the front of the caliper.
4. Remove the axle and lift off the caliper as an assembly.

Disassembly

1. Remove the 5-mm bolt from the top of the caliper. Remove the wear indicator cover and the pad cover.
2. With an 8-mm allen wrench remove the caliper set bolts and separate the two caliper halves.
3. Remove the o-ring from between the caliper halves.
4. Lift out the set spring, pads, and pad pins.
5. Remove the securing clip from the dust seal and remove the dust seal.
6. To remove the piston, apply compressed air to the inlet hole. Be careful to catch the piston as it is forced out.
7. Remove the piston seal, being careful not to scratch the cylinder bore. This seal should be replaced with a new one once removed.

Inspection

1. The bore of the caliper should be between 38.18–38.20 mm (1.5031–1.5039 in.). If the bore exceeds 38.215 mm (1.5045 in.) for either cylinder, both caliper halves should be replaced.
2. The piston outside diameter should be between 38.115–38.480 mm (1.5006–1.5150 in.). If either piston is smaller than 38.105 mm (1.5002 in.) the piston should be replaced.

Assembly

1. Install the piston seal into the groove in the caliper half.
2. Place a thin coat of silicon grease on the bore of the caliper and the piston seal.
3. Install the pistons and dust seals.
4. Install the pads, pad pins, and set spring. Install a new o-ring in the fluid passage between the two caliper halves, and bolt the caliper halves together. Tighten the bolts to 18–21 ft. lbs.
5. Install the pad cover and the wear indicator cover and secure with a 5-mm bolt.

Installation

1. Hold the caliper in place and install the axle.
2. Connect the brake anchor and brake line. Be sure that there is a washer on either side of the banjo fitting.
3. Bleed the system.

MASTER CYLINDER

Removal

1. Disconnect the rear brake line from the caliper by removing the banjo bolt. Take care not to lose the washers fitted to either side of the brake line fitting. Drain the master cylinder into a suitable container by pumping the brake pedal.
2. Remove the cotter pin from the brake rod pin, then remove the brake rod pin.
3. Remove the two mounting bolts and lift off the master cylinder.

Disassembly

1. Loosen the 8-mm not on the push rod and remove the brake rod joint from the end of the rod. Remove the 8-mm bolt and pull off the rubber boot.
2. Remove the snap-ring from the bottom of the master cylinder and pull out the brake rod.
3. Remove the piston and secondary cup assembly from the bottom of the cylinder.
4. Remove the primary cup, spring, and check valve.
5. Remove the master cylinder cap and diaphragm.

On early CB750F models up to frame No. CB750F-1010687, the master cylinder had a separate oil reservoir. On later models the reservoir is integrated with the master cylinder body. To remove the reservoir from the early models:

6. Remove the two screws located in the bottom of the reservoir and lift out the bottom plate.
7. Lift off the reservoir and o-ring.

Inspection

1. The bore of the master cylinder should be between 14.000–14.043 mm (0.5512–0.5529 in.). If the bore exceeds 14.055 mm (0.5533 in.), the master cylinder should be replaced.
2. The outside diameter of the piston should be between 13.957–13.980 mm (0.549–0.550 in.). If the piston is smaller than 13.940 mm (0.548 in.), the piston should be replaced.
3. Inspect the seals. If any are hard or scored, they should be replaced.

Assembly

1. Coat all parts of the master cylinder, including the bore, in clean brake fluid before installing them.
2. Install the check valve on the end of the spring, and be sure that it is facing the proper direction. Install the spring and check valve into the cylinder.
3. Install the primary cup so that the cupped side is facing the spring.
4. Install the piston and secondary cup. Install the piston so that the secondary cup is towards the bottom of the master cylinder. The lips of the secondary should face the top of the cylinder.
5. Install the 18-mm snap-ring, push rod, rubber boot, 8-mm nut, and brake rod joint.

Installation

1. Hold the master cylinder in place and install the two mounting bolts.
2. Connect the brake rod joint to the brake shaft with the brake rod pin and secure with a new cotter pin.
3. Connect the brake line to the rear caliper. Be sure to install a washer on both sides of the fitting.
4. Fill the master cylinder with new DOT 3 brake fluid and bleed the system.

BRAKE PEDAL HEIGHT

The height of the brake pedal can be adjusted by screwing the brake rod joint up or down on the master cylinder push rod.

1. Loosen the brake rod joint locknut.
2. Separate the brake rod joint from the pedal shaft by removing the brake rod pin.
3. Turn the brake rod joint either up or down to effect adjustment.
4. The clearance between the brake pedal and the footrest should be at least 5 mm (0.19 in.).
5. When adjustment is correct, connect the brake rod joint to the brake shaft with the brake rod pin, and secure in place with a new cotter pin.

BLEEDING

Refer to the section on bleeding the front brake, above.

DISC SERVICE

Service to the front and rear disc are the same. Refer to the "Disc Service" section for front wheel, above.

Disc Brake, 1979 and Later

This rear disc brake is the same as the front twin disc system described above. Refer to those sections.

Rear disc thickness should be no less than 6.0 mm (0.24 in.).

Drum Brake Models

BRAKE SHOE REPLACEMENT

Rear brake lining wear on newer models can be determined by means of the wear indicator pointer fitted to the brake lever on the hub. If the pointer lines up with the red slash mark when the brake pedal is fully depressed, the linings are worn beyond use and should be replaced.

On older models, observe the angle formed by the brake lever on the hub and the brake rod when the brake is fully applied. When the lever and rod form an angle greater than 90°, the shoes should be replaced. The replacement procedure is as follows:

1. Remove the rear wheel.
2. Unscrew the axle nut and withdraw the axle. Separate the backing plate from the brake drum.
3. Remove the cotter pin and washer from each brake shoe pivot and lift the shoe away from the backing plate. Minimum acceptable lining thickness at any point is 2.0 mm (0.08 in.) for all models.
4. Check the linings for scoring or embedded foreign matter, and replace them if necessary. Oil or grease-impregnated linings should also be replaced.

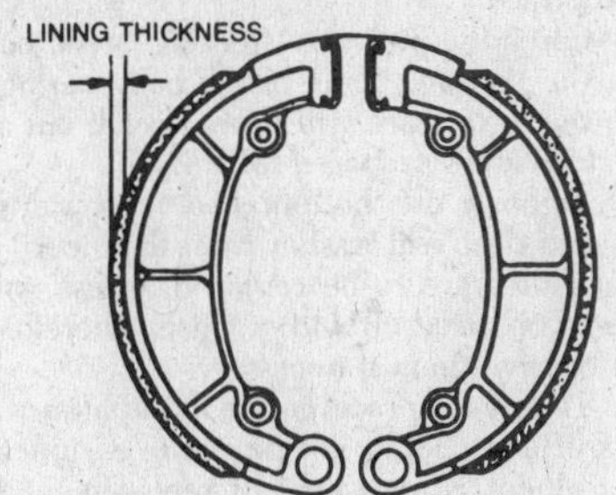

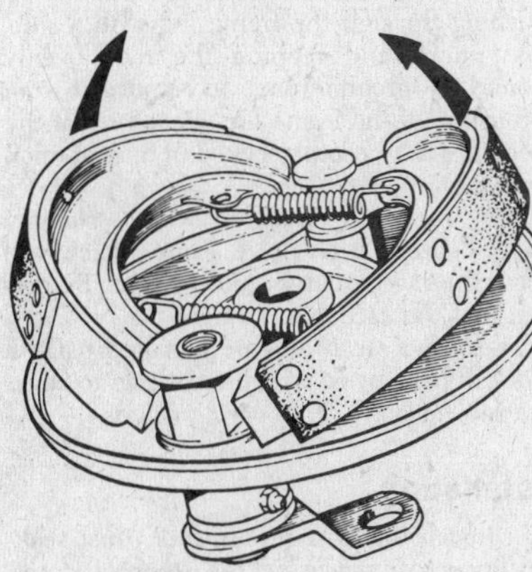

Removing the brake shoes

5. Break the glaze on the linings with some medium sandpaper, but be sure to clean them thoroughly before installation.
6. Check the condition of the brake springs, and replace them if badly rusted or if the ends are deformed.
7. Apply a *light* coat of grease to the brake shoe pivots and the actuating cam. Install the springs and shoes as on removal, using new cotter pins.
8. Inspect the condition of the brake drum surfaces. There should be no scoring. If scored, the drum can sometimes be salvaged by having it turned down on a lathe. Refer work of this nature to a qualified machinist.
9. Measure the inside diameter of the drum in two directions, perpendicular to each other. Maximum allowable diameter is stamped on the drum. A difference in the two readings indicates that the drum is warped. This condition is sometimes felt in an "off-on-off" feeling when applying the rear brake, and it, too, may be remedied by turning down the drum.
10. Clean the drum thoroughly, removing all dirt and dust.
11. Assemble the drum and hub and the axle and install the wheel. Adjust the brake so that there is about 25.0 mm (1.0 in.) of freeplay at the pedal before the shoes contact the drum. Avoid heavy braking for a few miles if new shoes have been fitted.

Parking Brake (750A)

DISASSEMBLY

1. Remove the rear brake lever by removing the pinch bolt and carefully pulling the lever from its splined shaft.
2. Slide the ratchet mechanism dust cover up along the cables and out of the way.
3. Unscrew the parking brake switch. Disconnect the parking brake cable from the ratchet lever and unscrew the adjuster from the ratchet base.
4. Remove the rear brake joint, the circlip and washer, ratchet case lever and pawls, and the return spring.

INSPECTION

1. Clean all parts in solvent to remove old grease.
2. Check the spring for tension. Make sure the spring ends are in good condition.
3. Check the ratchet case for wear of the teeth and inspect the pawls for wear as well. Replace the assembly if the teeth or pawls are chipped or worn.

ASSEMBLY

1. Grease the ratchet assembly shaft and the inside of the ratchet case with a good grade of chassis grease.
2. Assembly is the reverse of disassembly. Be sure that the return spring is properly anchored. Screw the switch in all the way. Adjust the cable to 2 mm (0.08 in.) of freeplay as outlined in chapter 2, "Maintenance."

FRONT FORKS (STANDARD)

Removal

1. Support the front wheel off the ground. Remove the front wheel and fender.
2. Remove the caliper(s) from the fork slider.

CAUTION: *Do not allow the caliper(s) to hang by the brake hose. Tie them out of the way with string or wire.*

3. Remove the fork filler cap at the top of each fork leg.

NOTE: *It may be necessary to remove the handlebars to do so, but the controls may be left connected, and the bars gently laid to one side when the mounting bolts are removed.*

4. Loosen the upper and lower triple clamp pinch bolts.
5. Grasp each fork leg, in turn, and remove it from the triple clamps by pulling downward. If this is difficult, install the filler cap(s), threading them in several turns, then strike them sharply with a plastic mallet or the like to drive the fork leg down and out of the triple clamps.

Disassembly

1. Remove the fork spring and gaitor (if fitted). Drain the fork oil.
2. Remove the fork slider dust seal, if fitted. Remove the slider oil seal circlip. On K2 and earlier models the slider can be removed at this point.
3. Remove the allen bolt at the bottom of the slider (K3 and later) and separate the fork components.
4. On 1973 and later models, the slider oil seal will remain in the slider. Oil seals must always be replaced with the forks are disassembled. Pry out the old seal with a screwdriver or a hooked tool, protecting the lip of the slider with a piece of wood or soft metal pad beneath your lever. Drive new seals straight in until seated. An old seal can be used to drive in the new seals. Be sure the seals are driven straight in and not cocked or tilted. Seals should be driven in just far enough to allow fitting the circlip.
5. On 1972 and earlier models, the seal will remain on the fork leg with the other fork components once the slider is removed. Take off the components after removing the snapring at the bottom of the fork leg, and then those above the damper piston.

Oil the lips of seals before assembly.

Inspection

1. Inspect the fork tubes for bends such as might have been incurred in an accident. Replacement is recommended rather than attempting to straighten bent fork tubes.
2. Check that the surface of the tube on which the slider components move is smooth and free of rust or scoring. Minor rusting should be removed with fine emery cloth.

On K3 and later fork tubes, the chrome plating must be in perfect condition. If it is peeled or damaged, the fork tube must be replaced if oil leaks occur.

3. Check the spring condition. Make sure the spring heights are equal and that they are within the lengths specified in the "Chassis Specifications" chart.
4. Check that the damper rod (where fitted) is straight, and that all damper components are clean.
5. Check the slider bushing and the damper piston for scoring or wear, and replace them if damaged (K2 and earlier models).
6. Replace the fork filler cap o-rings if they are not in good condition.
7. Clean all metal parts thoroughly in a solvent and lubricate them lightly with fork oil before assembly.

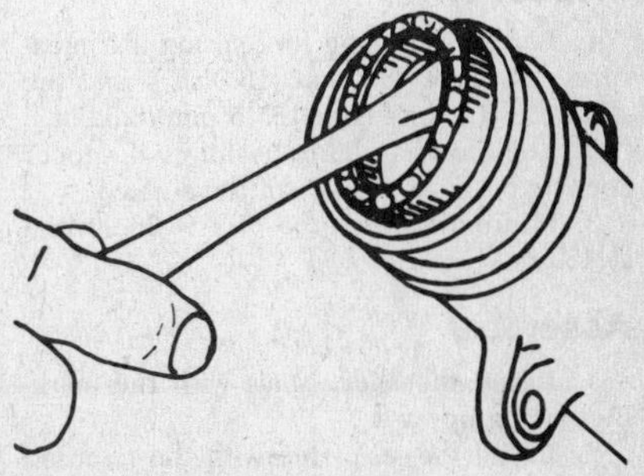

Prying out a front fork oil seal

Assembly

Assembly is the reverse of disassembly. Note the following points:

a. On K2 and earlier forks, lubricate the components thoroughly and assemble them on the fork tube. Slip on the fork slider and use a seal driver or a suitable substitute to seat the seal. Fit the circlip.

b. On K3 and later forks, be sure the rebound spring is in place.

Installation

1. Install each fork leg into the triple clamp and align the top of each fork tube with the surface of the upper triple clamp.
2. Tighten the upper triple clamp pinch bolts, the lower triple clamp bolts, and fill the forks with the recommended grade and quantity of oil (see chapter 2, "Mainte- quantity of oil.
3. The remainder of the procedure is the reverse of removal.

FRONT FORKS (AIR TYPE)

Removal

1. Remove the handlebars.
2. Disconnect the air hose and remove the connector from the right fork tube.
3. Disconnect the air hose from the left fork.
4. Remove the upper triple clamp.
5. Remove the headlight.
6. Remove the front wheel.
7. Loosen the lower triple clamp pinch bolts and pull the fork legs out of the triple clamp.

Disassembly

CAUTION: *Depressurize the fork tubes before attempting disassembly. The fork caps are under both air and spring pressure. Use caution when removing them.*

1. Fork seal replacement does not require separating tube and slider.
2. Depressurize the fork leg and remove the valve stem and hose connector. Install the special plugs into the cap.
3. Remove the caps.
4. Remove the oil seal dust cover and snap-ring. Use a magnet to take out the back-up plate.
5. Extend the fork leg. Fill the leg with ATF and fit the cap.
6. Compress the fork leg until the seal is forced out.
7. Remove the fork slider bolt and pull the slider and fork leg apart until they separate.

Inspection

1. Replace the long fork spring if it measures less than 429 mm (16.9 in.), and the shorter if it is less than 165.5 mm (6.52 in.).
2. Replace the slider bushings if copper appears on more than ¾ of the surface.
3. Minimum fork tube OD is 36.90 mm (1.453 in.).

Assembly

1. Install the slider seals with the markings facing upwards.
2. Install the snap-ring with the radiused side facing down.
3. Fill each fork leg with 280 cc (9.5 oz) of ATF.
4. Tighten the cap bolts to 11–22 ft. lbs.
5. Standard air pressure is 11–16 psi.

CAUTION: *Use a hand-operated air pump only to fill fork tubes.*

Installation

Reverse the removal procedures.

Torques:

Steering stem nut: 58–87 ft. lbs.
Upper triple clamp pinch bolts: 7–9 ft. lbs.
Lower triple clamp pinch bolts: 33–40 ft. lbs.

STEERING STEM ASSEMBLY

Bearing Adjustment

1. On 1969–1978 models, the steering stem bearings are uncaged #8 or ¼ in. balls. They are adjusted by means of a ring nut beneath the upper triple clamp.

On 1979–1981 models, a set of tapered roller bearings is used.

2. To check bearing adjustment, support the front wheel off the ground. Grasp the tip of the front fender and place your other hand beneath the lower triple clamp at the frame lug.
3. Attempt to move the fork by pulling up on the tip of the fender. If play or movement can be felt at the lower triple clamp, the bearings are adjusted too loosely or are worn. An alternate method is to grasp the fork sliders and attempt to move them back and forth in line with the motorcycle. No play should be noted.
4. Turn the forks slowly from lock-to-lock. Movement should be smooth, silent, and effortless. If any binding or uneven movement is felt, the balls and races are either too tightly adjusted or they are worn. If the steering feels uniformly stiff, the bearings are too tightly adjusted. If any noise is noted, the bearings are damaged or some are missing.

The bearings are adjusted by means of the adjuster nut

5. With the front wheel off the ground, release the front forks from a few degrees off the centered position. The fork should fall freely to either side of their own weight. If they will not, the bearings are too tightly adjusted, the steering stem is bent, the races are extremely worn, or some of the bearings are missing.
6. To adjust the bearings, remove the upper triple clamp. The bearings are adjusted by means of the adjuster nut under the upper triple clamp.
7. Tighten or loosen the adjuster nut a little at a time until the steering stem adjustment conforms to that outlined above.
8. If proper adjustment is not possible, the bearings and races will probably need to be replaced.

Disassembly

1. Remove the front wheel, front forks, and handlebars.
2. Loosen the rear pinch-bolt on the triple clamp. Unscrew the steering stem nut and disconnect the speedometer and tachometer cables from their instruments. Remove the upper triple clamp.
3. Disconnect the wiring inside the headlight shell and remove the headlight shell and the fork ears.
4. Loosen the steering stem adjuster nut with a pin wrench, then hold the steering stem up while unscrewing the adjuster nut the rest of the way off. Remove the steering stem top cone race and the ball bearings from the top race.
5. Carefully pull the steering stem out from the bottom. Some of the ball bearings from the lower race will probably fall out at this time so be prepared for this.
6. Remove the bottom cone race, dust seal, and dust seal washer from the steering stem if they are to be replaced. These will have to be pried off with a chisel; therefore only remove them if necessary.
7. The bearing races in the frame lug are a press-fit and should not be removed unless replacement is necessary. If replacement is necessary, the old races can be removed by reaching through the frame lug with a suitable punch and tapping the race evenly around its circumference to remove it from the inside of the frame lug. Be sure that the race does not become cocked in its seat upon removal.

New races are installed with a suitably sized bearing driver, i.e., one which will drive the race squarely into its seat. Be certain that the race goes straight in.

These races can also be installed using a block of hard wood of sufficient size to cover the race in place of a bearing driver.

Installation

1. Install the dust seal washer, dust seal, and lower cone race on the steering stem. Use a good grade of bearing grease to coat the bottom cone race and the upper race in the frame lug.
2. Embed 18 balls into the grease of the top frame lug and 19 balls into the grease of the lower cone race.
3. When the balls are in place, slip the steering stem through the frame lug and hold it in place while refitting the top cone race and threading on the adjuster nut.
4. Tighten the adjuster nut all the way by hand, rotating the steering stem to work the grease into the balls.
5. Tighten the adjuster nut until the steering stem turns freely, but has no play.
6. Install the fork tubes, headlight assembly, and upper triple clamp, flat washer, and steering stem nut. Check that the stem moves freely to the steering lock of its own weight when released from 5°–10° off center; if not check for:

a. Steering bearings too tight;
b. Bent steering stem;
c. Worn races or balls.

7. Install the front fender, front wheel, and handlebars. Route the cables and controls as illustrated.

REAR SHOCKS (STANDARD)

Removal and Installation

1. The shock absorbers can be removed after their upper and lower fasteners are taken off.
2. To remove the spring, first set the cam ring on the softest position. Then compress the spring by hand or with the aid of special tool No. 07959-3290000 and remove the spring retainers.
3. Measure the free length of the springs. They should be about 216 mm (8.5 in.) on 1969–1978 models, and 237 mm (9.5 in.) on 1979–1980 machines. Replace both if either measures less than this amount.
4. Check the springs for straightness. Replace them if tilt exceeds 2.5°.

REAR SHOCKS (AIR TYPE)

Removal and Installation

1. Remove the left side cover.
2. Remove the air valve cap. Disconnect the switch wire.
3. Remove the three-way joint mounting nut.
4. Disconnect the air hoses from the three-way joint.
5. Remove the upper and lower shock mounts and remove the shock.
6. Grease air fitting o-rings before installation to ensure a good seal.
7. Tighten shock mounts to 22–29 ft. lbs.

Disassembly

CAUTION: *Wear face and eye protection.*

1. Disconnect the air hose from the shock.
2. Remove the boot.
3. Remove the seal circlip and back-up plate. Drain off as much oil as possible.
4. Place the bottom mount in a soft-face vise. Replace the boot and hold the top of the shock by it. Apply compressed air to the air fitting to force out the seal.

CAUTION: *Do not use excessive air pressure. Take adequate precautions to prepare for fluid spillage. Do not hold the bottom of the shock.*

Assembly

1. Oil capacity is 365 cc (12.5 oz.) of ATF per shock.
2. Install the circlip with the sharp edge facing upwards.
3. Air pressure should be 28–64 psi.

SWING ARM (CHAIN DRIVE)

Inspection

1. Remove the muffler(s).
2. Remove the rear wheel, shock absorbers, and chain guard.
3. Measure the distance between the top and bottom shock absorber mounts on both sides. The two measurements must be identical, or the swing arm will have to be replaced.
4. Check that the rear wheel mounting plates are parallel.
5. Grasp the legs of the swing arm and attempt to move it from side to side. Any noticeable side-play will indicate that the swing arm bushings need replacement.

The swing arm is most likely to be damaged if the machine is operated for any length of time with a broken or otherwise defective shock absorber.

Removal and Installation

1. Proceed as above. Then remove the swing arm pivot bolt nut and pull the pivot bolt out from the right side.
2. Remove the swing arm by pulling it straight back.
3. The swing arm should be inspected for cracks or fractures, especially around the welds.

After removal of the swing arm, the dust seals and bushings can be replaced. This should be done every 10,000 miles or more often depending on how the machine is used, or if the bushings are worn (see "Inspection," above).

4. Remove the bushings, tapping them out with a hammer and punch. Once the bushings are removed, they should be replaced.
5. Lubricate new bushings with a good chassis grease. Press the bushings into the swing arm, then lubricate and install the swing arm collar.
6. Clean out the pivot bolt and ensure that all grease passages are clear. Install the swing arm on the machine. Grease and install the pivot bolt. After tightening the swing arm pivot bolt nut, move the swing arm up and down to ensure that movement is smooth and effortless.

SWING ARM (SHAFT DRIVE)

Removal

1. Remove the rear wheel.
2. Remove the lower shock mount bolts.
3. Disconnect the brake hose from the swing arm.
4. Remove the cotter pin and the rear brake caliper. Remove the final drive gear.
5. Remove the left swing arm pivot cap. Loosen the locknut and remove the swing arm pivot adjusting bolt.
6. Remove the right swing arm pivot cap and the pivot bolt.
7. Remove the swing arm.

Installation

1. Grease bearings and swing arm pivots before installation.
2. Tighten the pivot bolt to 36–51 ft. lbs. Tighten the adjusting bolts to 12–14 ft. lbs.
3. Check swing arm operation. Recheck adjusting bolt torque. Tighten locknut to 36–51 ft. lbs.

CHAIN FINAL DRIVE

Chain Inspection

The chain should be regularly inspected for wear and damage in the following manner:

1. Place the bike on the center stand and thoroughly lubricate the chain.
2. Measure the amount of slack at the middle of the chain run, and, if slack exceeds 1.5 in., adjust the chain. Refer to chapter 2.
3. Turn the wheel slowly and examine the chain for:
   a) damaged rollers
   b) loose pins,
   c) rusted links,
   d) binding or kinked links.

Replace the chain if the rollers are damaged or the pins are loose, or if rusted or binding links cannot be worked free with lubrication

Sprocket Inspection

Check the sprockets for broken or worn teeth. Worn sprocket teeth have a hooked, asymetrical appearance. If the side of the sprocket is worn, the indication is that the sprockets are misaligned. In any case of wear or damage, the sprocket should be replaced. Remember that worn sprockets can ruin a good chain, and vice versa. Do not hesitate to replace the chain and both sprockets, if need be, to avoid costly and dangerous chain failure.

Chain Removal and Installation

MASTER LINK CHAINS

The chain can be separated and pulled off the sprockets after the master link has been removed. Threading the chain back onto the countershaft sprocket is made easier if you have an old enough chain lying around that you can hook onto the chain on the bike as it is removed. Leave the old chain draped over the sprocket so that you can hook the good chain back onto it and pull it over the sprocket when you are ready to reinstall it. Be sure to install the master link clip with the closed end facing in the direction of forward rotation of the chain.

ENDLESS CHAINS

To remove the endless chain it is necessary to use a chain breaking tool. A heavy-duty chain breaker is available from Honda dealers, part No. 07062-30050. To break the chain using this tool:

1. Grind or file the pins of the link to be removed flush with the link side plate. Break the chain at the master link (identifiable by the depression in the pin centers).
2. Swing the pin seat backing plate on the chain breaker away from the pin seat and place one of the link rollers in the holding lugs of the tool.
3. Seat the main bolt against the side plate of the link and turn the link removal bolt in until the pin is driven out.
4. Place the other link roller in the holding lugs and repeat step 3.

To install a new master link (replacing the chain on the motorcycle):

1. Insert the master link through the ends of the chain so that the side plate is inside (closest to the wheel).
2. Place one of the master link rollers in the holding lugs of the tool with the pins facing the main bolt.
3. Push the pin seat knob in until it contacts the pin and swing the pin seat backing plate over to lock the pin seat in position.
4. Place the master link side plate in the guide block, so that the stamped letters or numbers on the plate face the surface of the

Chassis Torque Specifications

Component	Torque (ft. lbs.)
Rear brake pedal bolt (8 x 32 hex)	13–18
Step bar nut (12 mm)	36–43
Engine mounting bolt	22–29
Engine mounting plate	13–18
Swing arm pivot nut (14 mm)	40–51
Rear shock upper nut (10 mm cap nut)	14–22
Rear shock lower bolt (10 x 32 hex)	22–29
Master cylinder banjo bolts	25–29
Brake stop switch	25–29
Front brake disc nuts (8 mm)	13–17
Brake line joint (6 x 28 hex)	6–7
Brake hose joint	4–7
Master cylinder bolt (6 x 28 hex)	6–7
Caliper mounting bolts	25–29
Fork filler caps	40–47
Steering stem nut	58–87
Steering stem bolt (10 x 40 hex)	22–29
Rear axle nut	58–72
Front axle cap nuts (8 mm)	13–18
Handlebar holder bolt (8 x 40 hex)	13–17
Front axle nut	40–47
Rear brake anchor bolt and nut (8 mm)	13–17
Upper triple clamp pinch-bolt (8 x 56 hex)	13–17
Drive chain adjuster bolt and nut (8 mm hex)	11–15
Rear axle adjuster stopper bolt	13–17
Center stand pivot bolt (8 x 40 hex)	11–15
Passenger peg nuts	33–43
Caliper joint pin	13–18
Lower triple clamp pinch-bolt	22–29
Rear sprocket nuts	22–29

General Torque Specifications ①

Fastener	Torque (ft lbs)
6-mm hex bolt/nut	6–9
6-mm flange bolt	7–10
8-mm hex bolt/nut	18
8-mm flange bolt	17–22
10-mm hex bolt/nut	22–29

①unless otherwise noted

Brake Specifications 1969–78

Component	Single Disc (mm/in.)
FRONT DISC BRAKE (EXCEPT 77–78F)	
Disc thickness	
Standard	7.0/0.275
Minimum	5.5/0.217
Disc run-out	
Standard	0.1/0.004
Maximum	0.3/0.012
Master cylinder bore diameter	
Maximum	14.06/0.553
Piston diameter	
Minimum	13.94/0.549
Caliper bore diameter	
Maximum	38.22/1.504
Caliper piston diameter	
Minimum	38.11/1.500
Caliper-to-disc clearance	
Minimum	0.15/0.006
REAR DISC BRAKE and 750F FRONT BRAKE (77–78)	
Disc run-out (mm/in.)	
Standard	0.1/0.004
Maximum	0.3/0.012
Master cylinder bore diameter	
Standard	14.000–14.043/ 0.5512–0.5529
Maximum	14.055/0.5533
Piston diameter	
Standard	13.957–13.980/ 0.549–0.550
Minimum	13.940/0.548
Caliper bore diameter	
Standard	38.18–38.20/ 1.5031–1.5039
Maximum	38.215/1.5045
Caliper piston diameter	
Standard	38.115–38.480/ 1.5006–1.5150
Minimum	38.105/1.5002
DRUM BRAKE	
Drum diameter	
Maximum	183.0/7.21
Lining thickness	
Minimum	2.0/0.08

Brake Specifications 1979–81

Component	Single Disc (mm/in.)	Twin Disc (mm/in.)
FRONT DISC		
Disc Thickness		
Standard	7.0/0.28	5.0/0.20
Minimum	6.0/0.24	4.0/0.16
Run-out		
Standard	—	—
Maximum	0.3/0.012	0.3/0.012
Master cylinder bore diameter		
Maximum	14.06/0.553	15.925/0.6270
Master cylinder piston diameter		
Minimum	13.94/0.549	15.815/0.6226
Caliper bore diameter		
Maximum	42.92/1.690	38.24/1.506
Caliper piston diameter		
Minimum	42.77/1.684	38.09/1.500
REAR DISC		
Disc run-out		
Serviceable limit	—	0.3/0.012
Master cylinder bore diameter		
Standard	—	14.000–14.043/ 0.5512–0.5529
Maximum	—	14.055/0.5533
Master cylinder piston diameter		
Standard	—	13.957–13.980/ 0.549–0.550
Minimum	—	13.940/0.548
Caliper bore diameter		
Standard	—	38.18–38.23/ 1.5031–1.5051
Maximum	—	38.24/1.506
Caliper piston diameter		
Standard	—	38.098–38.148/ 1.4999–1.5019
Maximum	—	38.09/1.500
REAR DRUM		
Drum diameter		
Maximum	181/7.1	—
Lining thickness		
Minimum	2.0/0.08	—

guide block (facing out when installed on the chain).

5. Back out the link removal bolt until it is behind the nose of the main bolt.

CAUTION: *The link removal bolt will be damaged if it is allowed to protrude beyond the nose of the main bolt.*

6. Place the guide block in the tool with the master link side plate against the pins. Make sure that the pins are aligned with the holes in the side plate.

7. Turn in the main bolt until the pins pass through the plate and seat against the recess in the guide block.

8. Reposition the guide block so that the staking die faces the pin and the protruding shoulder of the guide block is below the side plate.

9. Turn in the main bolt until the staking die contacts the pin. Check to make sure that the die is centered across the pin.

10. Turn in the main bolt an additional ¾ turn to stake the pin. Repeat steps 8–10 for the other master link pin. Examine both pins to make sure that they are properly staked.

CAUTION: *The main bolt must be turned no more or no less than ¾ turn. Less than ¾ turn will not secure the side plate properly, and more than ¾ turn may crack the pin.*

Sprocket Removal and Installation

To gain access to the engine sprocket it is only necessary to remove the left-side rear crankcase cover. The sprocket can be unbolted after the locktabs (if applicable) are bent back. Loosen or remove the chain and then remove the sprocket.

Rear Hub Damper Service

1. Remove the rear wheel assembly and withdraw the axle.
2. Remove the sprocket and final drive flange. The sprocket may be separated from the flange by bending down the locktabs and removing the sprocket nuts.
3. Replace worn or cracked damper rubbers. When refitting damper rubbers, lubricate them thoroughly with a soapy solution or dishwashing liquid to facilitate insertion into the hub.

Chassis Specifications

Item	1969–1972	1973–1978	1979–1981
WHEELS			
Rim run-out (mm/in.)			
Standard	0.5/0.02	0.5/0.02	0.5/0.02
Serviceable limit	2.0/0.08	2.0/0.08	2.0/0.08
Wheel bearing run-out (mm/in.)			
Axial	0.1/0.004	0.1/0.004	0.1/0.004
Radial	0.05/0.002	0.05/0.002	0.05/0.002
FRONT FORKS (STANDARD)			
Spring free-length (mm/in.)			
Minimum	460/18.11	480/18.9	493/19.4
Slider inside diameter (mm/in.)			
Standard	—	35.07–35.10/1.381–1.382	35.04–35.10/1.380–1.382
Maximum	39.68/1.559	35.25/1.388	35.15/1.384

Kawasaki KLT 110/160

MODEL COVERAGE

KLT 110-A1
KLT 110-A2
KLT 160-A1

INDEX

GENERAL SPECIFICATIONS

	KLT 110	KLT 160
ENGINE		
Type	4-stroke, SOHC	4-stroke, SOHC
Bore × Stroke (mm/in.)	51.0 × 50.6/2.01 × 1.99	61.0 × 52.4/2.40 × 2.06
Displacement (cc/ci)	103/6.2	153/9.3
Compression ratio	8.2:1	9.5:1
Carburetor	Keihin PC18	Mikuni VM22SS
Ignition system	CDI	CDI
Starting system	Rope	Rope
Lubrication	Wet sump	Wet sump
TRANSMISSION		
Clutch	Centrifugal	Centrifugal
Primary reduction	3.619 (76/21)	3.695 (85/23)
Transmission type	5-speed, constant mesh	5-speed, constant mesh
Gear ratios		
1st	3.307 (43/13)	3.076 (40/13)
2nd	2.111 (38/18)	1.842 (35/19)
3rd	1.545 (34/22)	1.304 (30/23)
4th	1.285 (27/21)	1.076 (28/26)
5th	1.111 (30/27)	0.928 (26/28)
Reverse	—	3.384 (28/13 × 33/21)
Final drive	Chain	Shaft
Final reduction	4.166 (50/12)	3.712 (21/18 × 35/11)
Overall reduction	16.754 (5th gear)	12.738 (5th gear)
DIMENSIONS		
Overall length (mm/in.)	1700/66.9	1730/68.1
Overall width (mm/in.)	975/38.4	1000/39.4
Overall height (mm/in.)	970/38.2	1000/39.4
Wheelbase (mm/in.)	1075/42.3	1110/43.7
Ground clearance (mm/in.)	130/5.1	135/5.3
Seat height (mm/in.)	705/27.8	695/27.4
Dry weight (kg/lbs.)	109/240	124/273
Turning radius (min.) (m/ft.)	1.8/5.9	1.7/5.6
Fuel tank capacity (1/gal.)	9.5/2.5	9.5/2.5
FRAME		
Type	Tubular, single cradle	Tubular, semi-double cradle
Caster	19.5°	23°
Trail (mm/in.)	10/0.39	17/0.70
Track (mm/in.)	700/27.6	740/29.1
Front tire	22 × 11.00-8	21 × 9.00-8
Rear tires	22 × 11.00-8	22 × 11.00-8
Brakes (f/r)	Drum	Drum

MAINTENANCE

NOTE: *Common maintenance procedures are explained in detail in the "General Information" section of this manual.*

LUBRICATION

Motor Oil

1. Use motor oil service rated "SE" or "SF."

2. For all-temperature use, the following grades are recommended: SAE 10W-40, 10W-50, 20W-40 or 20W-50.

Checking Oil Level

1. Oil level should be checked every time before riding the machine.

2. A sight glass for checking oil level is fitted to the right crankcase cover.

3. Be sure the machine is parked on a level surface to ensure an accurate reading.

4. Level should be checked after the engine has been running for a few minutes. Shut it off and let the oil settle for a minute or so.

5. Oil level should be between the upper and lower level marks inscribed on the crankcase. If the level is too low, add just enough lubricant of the correct grade to bring it up between the marks. Do not overfill.

Oil level sight glass (A) and level marks (B)

Changing Oil

1. The oil should be changed every 30 days when the machine is in regular use.

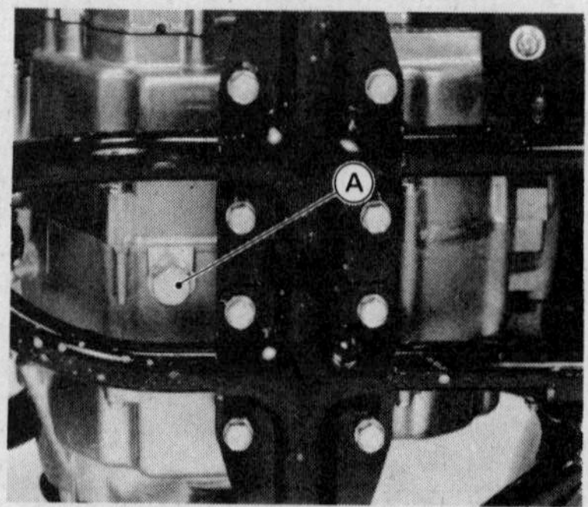

Oil drain plug (A) (110)

2. Oil should be drained when the engine is at operating temperature. This ensures more complete draining and makes it more likely that the oil will carry off any particulates with it.

3. Park the machine on a level surface.

4. Place a suitable container (about 2 qts. capacity) beneath the drain plug.

5. Remove the drain plug and allow the oil to drain for several minutes.

6. Clean the drain plug in a safe solvent. Check gasket condition. Replace it if damaged.

7. After the oil has drained completely, install the drain plug. Tighten it to 22 ft. lbs. on 110 models and 58 ft. lbs. on 160 models.

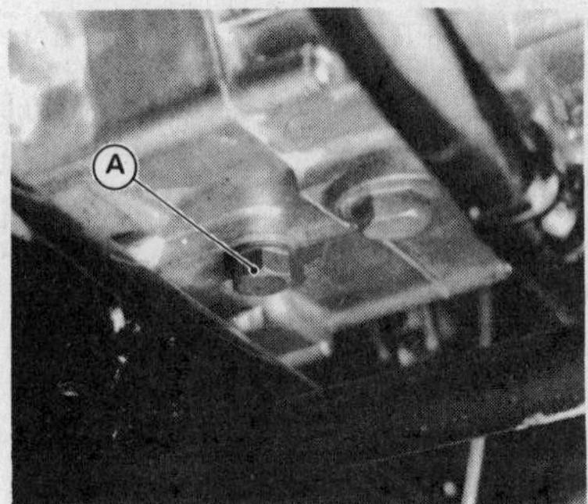

Oil drain plug (A) and filter screen plug (160)

8. If the filter screen is to be cleaned, see below. This procedure should be carried out at every third oil change (90 days).

9. Remove the crankcase filler cap and add the correct quantity and grade of oil.

10. Crankcase capacities are:
KLT 110: 1.2 qts. (1.1 L)
KLT 160: 1.8 qts. (1.7 L)
These are approximations. Determine the exact amount of oil to be added by watching the sight glass.

11. When the sight glass indicates that oil level is correct, install the filler cap, start the engine and allow it to run for several minutes. Check for leaks. Shut the engine off and recheck the level after a minute or so.

Filter Screen

KLT 110

1. The engine is fitted with an oil filter screen inside the right crankcase cover. The screen should be cleaned every third oil change, or after every 90 days of operation.

2. Have a new crankcase cover gasket on hand.

3. Drain the oil as outlined above.

4. Place a drip pan beneath the right crankcase cover.

Filter screen (A)(110)

5. Disconnect the oil line at the front of the cover.

6. Remove the crankcase cover screws.

7. Remove the crankcase cover. If it is stuck, tap around the top and bottom with a plastic mallet to free it.

8. Remove the cover gasket.

9. Remove the filter screen.

10. Clean the screen in a safe solvent. Remove all foreign matter.

11. Check the debris for metal particles. If any are present, severe engine wear is taking place. Determine the cause. This may be due to a leaking air filter, insufficient engine oil, etc.

12. If the screen is punctured or cannot be cleaned effectively, replace it.

13. Install the screen.

14. Clean the gasket surface thoroughly, removing all traces of old gasket material.

15. Install the new gasket.

16. Check that the two cover dowel pins are in place. Check that the clutch release lever and clutch bearing are in place.

17. Install the crankcase cover.

18. Tighten the cover screws evenly.

19. Fill the crankcase with the proper quantity and grade of oil. Check level with the sight glass. Run the engine for several minutes and check for leaks.

KLT 160

1. The engine is fitted with a filter screen in a plug located near the oil drain plug.

2. The screen should be cleaned at every third oil change, or after every 90 days.

3. Drain the oil as outlined above.

4. Remove the filter screen bolt near the drain bolt.

5. Clean the filter screen in a clean, safe solvent. Remove all foreign matter.

6. Check the debris for metal particles. If any are present, severe engine wear is taking place. This may be due to a leaking air filter, insufficient engine oil, etc or other, more serious, problems.

7. If the screen is punctured or cannot be cleaned effectively, replace it.

8. Inspect the plug gasket and replace it if damaged.

9. Install the plug and tighten it to 58 ft. lbs.

10. Fill the crankcase with the proper grade and quantity of oil. Check level with the sight glass. Run the engine for several minutes and check for leaks.

Final Gear Case

1. SAE 10W-40 motor oil, service rated "SE" or "SF" is recommended.

2. Gear case capacity is 0.2 qts. (0.2 L).

3. The gear case oil should be changed once a year under conditions of normal use.

Final gear case filler plug (A), and level plug (B)

CHECKING OIL LEVEL

1. Park the machine on a level surface.

2. Remove the level plug from the gear case. Oil should just begin to come out of the level hole. If it does not, add just enough SAE 10W-40 SF motor oil so that the oil starts to come out.

3. Check the condition of the level plug gasket and replace it if it is crushed or otherwise damaged.

4. Tighten the level plug to about 7 ft. lbs.

CHANGING OIL

1. Run the machine until operating temperature is reached.

2. Park the machine on a level surface.

3. Place a drip pan beneath the final gear case.

4. Remove the filler plug. Remove the gear case drain plug. Allow the oil to drain for several minutes.

5. Clean the drain plug thoroughly in a safe solvent. Check gasket condition. Using a new gasket is recommended.

6. Install the drain plug. Tighten it to 22 ft. lbs.

Final gear case drain plug (A)

7. Inspect the drained oil for metal particles. If present, it indicates that the drive train is undergoing severe wear. The cause should be determined before the machine is operated any more.

8. Fill the gear case with about 0.2 qts of SAE 10W-40 motor oil, service rated SF.

9. Remove the level plug. Add more oil, if necessary, until oil just begins to seep out of the level hole.

10. Install the level plug and the filler plug. The level plug should be tightened to about 7 ft. lbs. The filler plug should be tightened to 22 ft. lbs.

CAUTION: *Check that none of the drained oil has gotten on the tire. If it has, wipe it off.*

Front Forks

1. Oil in hydraulic-type front forks should be changed every 90 days.

2. Forks use SAE 5W-20 motor oil.

3. The change procedure involves removing each fork leg and dumping the fluid out. This procedure is given in the "Chassis" section under "Hydraulic Front Forks."

Drive Chain (KLT 110)

1. The drive chain is fitted with rubber O-rings between the chain plates to seal in lubricant and keep out dirt. Therefore, the chain should be lubricated only with oil (SAE 90 is recommended). Do not use commercial chain lubricants or petroleum-based solvents as they may damage the O-rings.

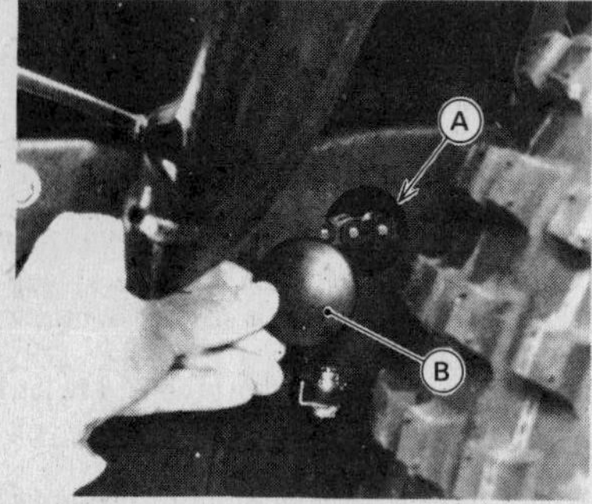

Chain case inspection hole (A) and cap (B)

2. Remove the rubber inspection cap from the chain case and check chain condition. If it is dirty, it should be removed and thoroughly cleaned before lubrication. Refer to "Rear Axle" in the "Chassis" section for removal and installation procedures.

3. Support the rear wheels off the ground.

4. Slowly rotate the real wheels while brushing SAE 90 oil onto the chain. Be sure that the lubricant is applied to both the inner and outer plates.

5. After the chain has been thoroughly lubricated, adjust slack as outlined under "Service Checks and Adjustments", below.

General Lubrication

1. General lubrication points include control cables, control lever pivots and joints, brake cams, the propeller shaft joint (KLT 160), wheel and steering bearings and the throttle lever housing.

2. The service interval will depend on how the machine is used. Cables, levers and chassis pivots should be lubricated about every 30 days of use under normal operating conditions. Wheel and steering bearings should be attended to about every 90 days of use.

3. Refer to the "Chassis" section for procedures to reach wheel and steering bearings.

SERVICE CHECKS AND ADJUSTMENTS

Drive Chain (KLT 110)

1. The drive chain should have 0.4-1.0 in. (10-25mm) of total up and down slack when measured at the inspection hole on the chain case.

2. Before checking or adjusting chain slack, the following conditions must be met:

Chain adjuster locknut (A) and axle mounting bolts (B)

a. The rear wheels of the machine should be supported off the ground.

b. The chain must be clean and well lubricated.

c. The chain should have been checked for tight spots by slowly rotating the rear wheels and checking tension at several points. If a tight spot exists, the chain should be adjusted to the proper slack at the tight spot. Note, however, that such a condition indicates that chain, sprockets or both are worn and should be inspected and probably replaced as soon as possible.

3. If total up-and-down chain slack at the inspection hole is not within the 0.4-1.0 in. (10-25mm) range, refer to the illustration and procede as follows.

4. Loosen the chain adjuster locknut (A).

5. Loosen the four axle mounting bolts (B).

6. Turn the adjuster locknut clockwise (as seen from the back of the machine) to tighten a slack chain. To provide more slack to a tight chain, turn the locknut counterclockwise and push the axle forward.

7. When slack is correct, tighten the four axle mounting bolts (torque is 43 ft. lbs.). Tighten the adjuster locknut (43 ft. lbs.).

8. Recheck chain slack. Repeat the procedure if it is not within specification.

Clutch

KLT 110

1. The clutch should be adjusted after every 10 days of operation.

2. Remove the clutch adjusting screw rubber cap on the right crankcase cover.

3. Loosen the adjusting screw locknut.

4. Back the adjusting screw off (CCW) a bit, then turn it clockwise until resistance is felt.

Clutch adjusting screw (A) and locknut (B) (110)

5. Hold the adjusting screw in this position and tighten the locknut.

6. Install the rubber cap.

Clutch adjusting screw (A) and locknut (B) (160)

KLT 160

1. The clutch should be adjusted after every 10 days of operation.

2. Remove the clutch adjusting screw rubber cap on the right crankcase cover below the oil filler cap.

3. Loosen the adjusting screw locknut.

4. Turn the adjusting screw clockwise until resistance is felt. Stop.

5. Turn the adjusting screw counterclockwise until resistance is felt.

6. Hold the adjusting screw in this position and tighten the locknut.

7. Install the rubber cap.

Throttle Cable

1. Throttle cable free-play should be checked about every 10 days of operation.

2. The throttle cable has adjusters at the hand lever and at the carburetor. Either can be used for adjustment.

3. The throttle lever should be able to move 2-3mm (0.08-0.12 in.) before the throttle slide starts to open.

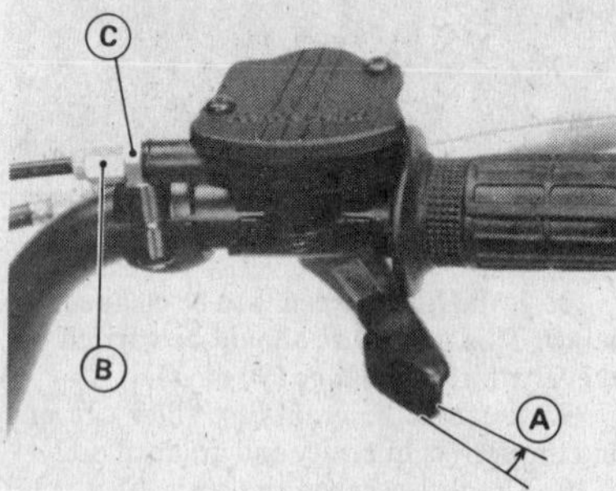

Throttle lever free-play (A), adjuster (B) and locknut (C)

4. To make this adjustment, slide back the rubber adjuster cover. Loosen the adjuster locknut and turn the adjuster in or out until lever free-play is correct. Tighten the adjuster locknut and put the cover back in place.

5. Let the engine idle and turn the handlebars slowly from lock-to-lock. Idle speed must not change. If it does, the cable is either too tightly adjusted, or is binding somewhere along its route. Determine the cause before operating the machine.

CAUTION: *Throttle cable adjustment is an important safety item.*

Front Brake

KLT 110-A1

1. The brake cable adjuster is fitted to the drum end of the cable.

2. When the brake hand lever is applied, the gap between the hand lever and the lever holder should be 4-5mm (0.16-0.20 in.) before the linings contact the drum.

3. To make this adjustment, turn the adjusting screw at the lower end of the cable.

4. Check that the brake wear indicator stays within the "Usable Range" when the brake is fully applied. If it does not, the brake shoes must be replaced.

5. After adjusting the cable, support the front wheel off the ground and spin the tire. There should be no noise indicating dragging brakes. Apply the brake hand lever several times and ensure that the brakes release each

time. If they do not, determine the cause and remedy the condition. Possible causes include a binding cable due to dirt, corrosion or incorrect routing, worn or damaged brake return springs or a corroded or damaged brake cam.

6. When the brake hand lever is fully applied, the angle formed by the lever at the drum and the cable should be 80-90° for maximum brake effectiveness. If not within this specification, it is possible to remove the lever from the splined shaft and reposition it so that the angle is correct.

CAUTION: *Do not change the position of the brake wear indicator.*

KLT 110- A2, KLT 160

1. Brake cable adjusters are fitted to the hand lever bracket and to the brake drum. Use the upper adjuster for minor brake adjustments. When it starts to pass about half of its adjustment range, use the adjuster at the drum.

2. When the brake hand lever is applied, the gap between the hand lever and the lever holder should be 4-5mm (0.16-0.20 in.) before the linings contact the drum.

3. Make minor adjustments with the adjuster at the hand lever. Loosen the adjuster locknut and screw the adjuster in or out until the gap is correct, then tighten the locknut.

4. For major adjustments, or when the handlebar adjuster has used up more than half of its usable range, use the adjuster at the drum.

5. Loosen the upper adjuster locknut and turn the adjuster in all the way. Tighten the locknut.

6. Back off the drum adjuster mounting nuts and slide the adjuster on its bracket so that hand lever free movement is 4-5mm (0.16-0.20 in.).

7. Tighten the mounting nuts. Recheck adjustment and make minor corrects, if required, with the hand lever adjuster.

8. After adjusting the cable, support the front wheel off the ground and spin the tire. There should be no noise indicating dragging brakes. Apply the lever several times and ensure the brakes release each time. If they do not, determine the cause and remedy the condition. Possible causes include a cable binding due to dirt, corrosion or incorrect routing, worn or damaged brake return springs or corroded or damaged brake cam.

Rear Brake

1. The rear brake is controlled by both a hand lever and a foot pedal. Both lever and pedal must be adjusted at the same time.

2. The brake pedal on KLT 160 models is adjustable for position. To position the pedal, back off the rod adjuster, loosen the stop bolt locknut and turn the stop bolt so that the pedal at- rest position is comfortable for the operator. Adjust the pedal travel as outlined in the following steps.

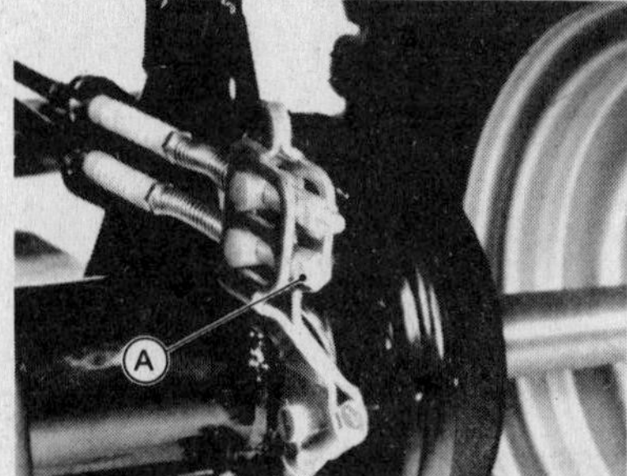

Brake pedal adjuster (A)

3. Adjust the brake pedal first. The pedal should have about 25mm (1 in.) of free movement before the linings contact the drum. Adjust by means of the adjuster on the end of the rod or cable at the rear brake drum.

4. To adjust the hand lever, adjusters are fitted to the hand lever bracket and to the end of the cable at the brake drum.

5. Use the hand lever adjuster for minor adjustments. When it starts to pass about half of its adjustment range, use the adjuster at the brake drum end of the cable.

6. The hand lever should have 4-5mm (0.16-0.20 in.) of free movement before the linings contact the drum. This distance is measured between the hand lever and the lever holder.

Brake hand lever adjuster (A)

7. To adjust at the handlebar, loosen the adjuster locknut and turn the adjuster in or out until free play is correct. Tighten the locknut.

8. To adjust at the drum, first screw the handlebar adjuster all the way in.

9. Turn the adjuster at the brake drum until hand lever free play is correct. Make minor corrections, if required, with the adjuster at the handlebar.

10. After adjusting both the brake pedal and the brake hand lever, support the rear wheels off the ground and check operation. Spin the wheels and apply both pedal and lever several times. Ensure that the brakes release fully after every application. There should be no noise to indicate dragging. If there is, determine the cause and remedy the condition. Possible causes include weak or damaged brake return springs, a corroded or damaged brake cam, an unlubricated or corroded brake cable, pedal or lever pivot or incorrectly routed cable.

Steering Stem

1. Steering stem bearing adjustment should be checked every 90 days of operation.

2. To check bearing adjustment, support the front wheel off the ground. Grasp the lower ends of the fork tubes and attempt to move the forks back and forth in line with the machine. There should be no detectable movement. If there is, bearings must be adjusted.

3. Turn the forks slowly from lock-to-lock, again with the front wheel off the ground. Movement should be smooth, silent and effortless. If any binding or uneven movement is felt, the balls and races are

Checking steering stem bearing adjustment

either too tightly adjusted or are worn. If the steering feels uniformly stiff, the bearings are too tightly adjusted. If any noise is noted, the bearings are damaged and/or some are missing.

4. With the front wheel off the ground, release the forks from a position a few degrees to either side of the centered position. They should fall freely to the lock of their own accord. If they do not, the bearings are too tightly adjusted, the steering stem is bent, the races are worn or some of the bearings are missing.

5. Remove the gas tank.

6. Remove the upper triple clamp rubber cover.

7. Loosen the upper triple clamp bolts above the fork tubes.

8. Loosen the steering stem bolt.

Steering stem bearing adjuster nut (A)

9. Use a pin wrench to turn the adjuster nut beneath the upper triple clamp until bearing action conforms to behavior described above—i.e., no play and smooth movement. Do not turn the adjuster nut more than 1/8 turn at a time.

10. When bearing movement is correct, tighten the bolts above the fork tubes (22 ft. lbs.) and the steering stem bolt (40 ft. lbs.).

11. Recheck bearing operation.

NOTE: *If correct bearing operation cannot be achieved, or if it is necessary to turn the adjuster nut more than two turns, suspect worn or damaged bearings and/or races. See "Chassis" for disassembly instructions.*

FUEL SYSTEM

Fuel system maintenance involves cleaning the air filter element, cleaning the fuel petcock screens and cleaning the carburetor float bowl. The air filter element should be cleaned every 10 days of use. The petcock and carburetor should be attended to every 90 days of use.

Air Filter

REMOVAL

1. Remove the seat.
2. Remove the air cleaner cover which is secured by two screws.
3. Lift the air cleaner element with holder straight up and out.

Air cleaner cover screws (A)

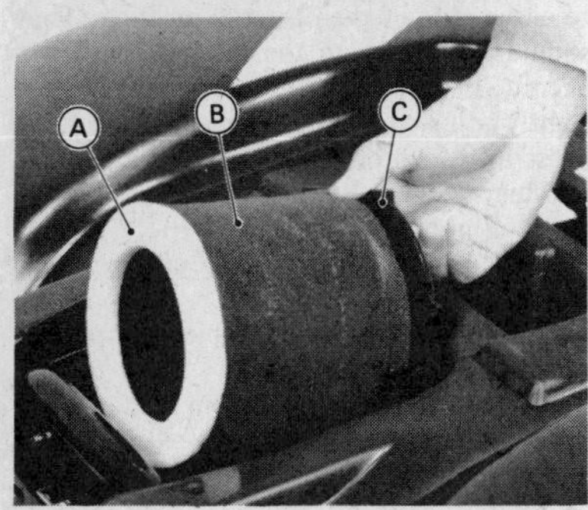

Filter element gasket (A), element (B) and holder (C)

SERVICE

1. Carefully remove the air cleaner element from the frame.
2. In a well-ventilated area, clean the element in a safe solvent.
CAUTION: *Low flash point solvents such as gasoline should not be used as they present a safety hazard.*
3. Squeeze the element to dry it. Do not wring it out as the pores may be damaged or the element itself may be ripped.
4. When all dirt has been purged, dry the element thoroughly.
5. Inspect element condition. If it cannot be cleaned effectively, or if the fabric is worn, torn or otherwise damaged, the element should be replaced.
6. Soak the element in clean SAE 30 motor oil or a commercial air cleaner oil. Squeeze out the excess.

INSTALLATION

1. Pull the element back over the frame.
2. Install the element holder in the air cleaner case engaging the lower end in the slot provided.
3. Grease the element gasket with a light- weight general purpose grease.
4. Slip the element into the case with the gasket side towards the engine. Be sure it is fully seated.
5. Fit the air cleaner cover with the intake tube towards the rear of the machine.
6. Be sure to hook the lip on the front edge of the cover under the forward edge of the case.
7. Secure the cover screws.

Petcock

1. The fuel petcock is fitted with filter screens on the pipes inside the fuel tank. The petcock should be removed and the screens cleaned after every 90 operating days.
2. The procedure involves removing the fuel tank. Refer to "Fuel Systems" for procedures.

Carburetor

1. Although a thorough cleaning of the carburetor necessitates its removal from the machine, water and foreign matter can be removed from the float bowl by unscrewing the float bowl drain plug and allowing the gasoline to drain into a suitable container.
CAUTION: *Be sure to do this in a well-ventilated area a safe distance from sparks or open flames.*

Carburetor float bowl drain plug (A)

Fuel petcock filter screens (A)

2. Check the drained gasoline for foreign matter, water, etc. If there seems to be a fair amount of it, check that the air filter is clean and properly installed.
3. Turn the petcock to the "RES" position with the drain plug unscrewed and watch the gasoline which drains out. If it has more foreign matter in it, the tank should be removed and purged and the petcock filter screens should be cleaned.
4. If flow from the carburetor float bowl seems sluggish, a clogged filter or clogged fuel cap vent may be the problem. Check the fuel system and clean it thoroughly. Refer to "Fuel Systems" for procedures.

MAINTENANCE DATA

	KLT 110	KLT 160
Fuel tank capacity (gal/L)	2.5/9.5	2.5/9.5
Engine oil capacity (qts./L)	1.2/1.1	1.8/1.7
Final gear case (qts./L)	—	0.2/0.2
Hydraulic forks (oz./cc each leg)	3.0/88①	3.0/88①
Tire pressure (psi)		
Front	2	3
Rear	2	2
Chain slack (mm/in.)	25/1.0	—

① Total capacity

TUNE-UP

NOTE: *Common tune-up procedures are explained in detail in the "General Information" section.*

COMPRESSION TEST

1. A compression test should be performed before and after a complete tune-up, as it will provide clues to the general mechanical condition of the engine.
2. A hold-in type gauge can be used if it is so constructed that clearance is not a problem. If a screw-in type gauge is used, a 12mm adapter is required to fit the spark plug hole.
3. Run the engine until it is at operating temperature.
4. Disconnect the spark plug lead and remove the plug.
5. Fit the compression gauge. Hold the throttle wide open while cranking the engine and note the compression reading. The highest reading is the measurement to be considered.

NOTE: *The KLT 160 is equipped with an automatic compression release which will make a dramatic difference in compression readings. The ACR may also be a cause of compression problems. Be aware of this before troubleshooting for a possible engine problem.*

6. Standard compression for the KLT 110 is 164-192 psi. The minimum acceptable reading is 125 psi and the maximum acceptable reading is 192 psi.
7. Standard compression for the KLT 160 is 14-43 psi. This is due to the operation of the ACR and is not true engine compression.
8. If the compression reading is too high, it is likely that the piston crown and/or combustion chamber is carboned up. The cylinder head should be removed and the head and piston decarbonized. On the KLT 160, a higher-than- normal compression reading may also indicate a defective ACR. The unit should be removed and inspected before further work is done. Refer to "Top End" in the "Engine And Transmission" section.
9. If the compression is too low, squirt some motor oil into the cylinder and repeat the test. If the compression reading increases, suspect a worn piston, cylinder and/or rings. If it does not increase, suspect worn, damaged or poorly adjusted valves, leaking seats, etc. Low compression may also be due to a defective ACR on the KLT 160. The unit should be removed and inspected before further work is done. Refer to "Top End" in the "Engine And Transmission" section.
10. Other causes of low compression include a warped head and/or blown head gasket. The compression will not increase when oil is added to the cylinder if this is the problem.

CAM CHAIN TENSIONER

Cam chain tension is maintained automatically. No routine adjustments are required as long as the tensioner is functioning properly. See "Engine And Transmission" under "Top End" for tensioner removal and inspection.

PERIODIC MAINTENANCE INTERVALS①

Before each ride
- Safety items
- Operation of lights
- Chain adjustment (KLT 110)
- Throttle operation
- Brake operation
- Engine oil level
- Tire pressure (check when cold)

Every 10 days of operation
- Brake wear
- Control cable adjustments
- Tightness of critical fasteners
- Clutch adjustment
- Air filter cleaning

Every 30 days of operation
- Change engine oil
- General lubrication

Every 90 days of operation
- Clean oil filter screen
- Clean carburetor and petcock
- Grease propeller shaft joint (KLT 160)
- Change fork oil (hydraulic forks)
- Lubricate wheel and steering head bearings
- Grease brake cams

Every year
- Change final gear case oil (KLT 160)
- Clean spark arrestor

① Based on normal usage after initial service and break-in are completed.

RECOMMENDED LUBRICANTS

Engine
- SAE 10W-40, service rating "SE" or "SF"
- SAE 10W-50, service rating "SE" or "SF"
- SAE 20W-40, service rating "SE" or "SF"
- SAE 20W-50, service rating "SE" or "SF"

Final Gear Case
- SAE 10W-40, service rating "SE" or "SF"

Front Forks (Hydraulic)
- SAE 5W-20

Drive Chain (KLT 110)
- SAE 90 oil

Air Filter Element
- SAE 30

Control cables
- Light motor oil
- Graphite-based lubricant
- Molybdenum disulphide-based lubricant
- Commercial motorcycle cable lubes

VALVE ADJUSTMENT

Checking Clearance

NOTE: *Valve clearance must be checked when the engine is COLD.*

1. Remove the seat. See "Chassis."
2. Remove the gas tank. See "Fuel Systems."
3. Remove the spark plug.
4. Remove the intake and exhaust valve covers.
5. Remove the timing inspection plug on top of the left crankcase cover.
6. Remove the recoil starter case.
7. Use a wrench on the bolt or nut on the end of the crankshaft and carefully turn the engine over in a counterclockwise direction until the intake valve opens and closes.
8. Continue turning the engine in the same direction while watching the magneto rotor through the inspection hole.

Timing indicator (A), "T" mark (B) and inspection plug (C)

9. When the "T" mark on the rotor aligns with the indicator, stop and hold the engine in this position. The piston is now at TDC on the compression stroke, both valves are closed and adjustment can be checked.
10. Check for clearance at both valves by attempting to move the rocker arms with your fingers. If one seems tight, it may be that the piston is at TDC on the exhaust stroke. In this case, repeat the procedure until you are sure that both valves are closed.

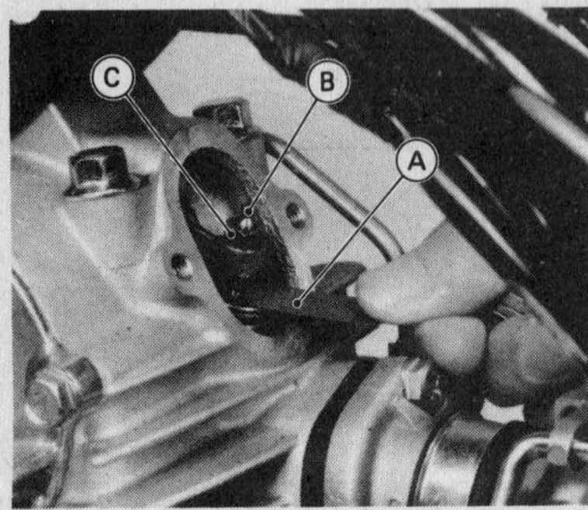

Checking valve clearance: feeler gauge (A), adjuster (B), locknut (C)

11. Valve clearances are as follows:
    KLT 110:
    Intake: 0.12-0.17mm/0.005-0.007 in.
    Exhaust: 0.12-0.17mm/0.005-0.007 in.
    KLT 160:
    Intake: 0.12-0.17mm/0.005-0.007 in.
    Exhaust: 0.18-0.23mm/0.007-0.009 in.
12. A feeler gauge blade of the thickness shown above should be a slip fit between the adjuster and stem of a correctly adjusted valve. If the blade is too loose or too tight, adjust the valves as outlined below.

Adjusting Clearance

1. Check clearance as outlined above.
2. Loosen the valve adjuster locknut and turn the adjuster so that a feeler gauge blade of the correct thickness is a light slip fit between adjuster and valve stem.
3. Hold the adjuster in place and tighten the locknut.
4. Recheck clearance. Often it will change when the adjuster locknut is tightened.

IGNITION TIMING

1. Ignition timing requires a stroboscopic timing light and a tachometer.
2. Timing can be checked by removing the timing inspection plug on the left crankcase cover and noting the alignment of the magneto rotor timing marks with the indicator. The "F" mark should align below 1500 rpm for the 110 and 1350 rpm for the 160. The advance mark should align at 4000 rpm and above for the 110 and at 5000 rpm and above for the 160.

Ignition timing: indicator (A), "F" mark (B), advance mark (C) and inspection plug (D)

3. Timing is not adjustable, however, and if the proper alignments are not made, the CDI unit must be replaced. Refer to "Electrical Systems."

CARBURETOR

Carburetor adjustments to be made during a tune-up include float level, idle speed and mixture.

Adjusting Float Level

1. Float level is a measure of the amount of gasoline that remains in the carburetor during operation. While it is a critical specification, it will not normally need readjustment once properly set. Float level, therefore, need not be adjusted at every tune-up, but should be attended to from time to time.
2. If a fuel level gauge is available, service fuel level can be obtained without removing the carburetor from the machine. Service fuel levels are as follows:
   KLT 110: 2.5 ± 1mm (0.10 ± 0.04 in.)
   KLT 160: 5.0 ± 1mm (0.20 ± 0.04 in.)
3. To adjust float height, remove the carburetor (see "Fuel Systems".)
4. Remove the float bowl.
5. Remove the float bowl gasket.
6. Carefully lower the float until the tang just touches the tip of the float needle.
7. The distance from the float bowl mating surface to the top of the float is the float height. It should be:
   KLT 110: 20mm (0.8 in.)
   KLT 160: 33.3mm (1.3 in.)
8. If the measurement is not correct, remove the float and bend the tang so the float height is brought within specification.

NOTE: *The float height adjustment will be incorrect if the float needle is worn or if there is foreign matter on the needle or needle seat.*

Idle Speed And Mixture

NOTE: *The following adjustments should be performed when the engine is at operating temperature. Other adjustments (valves, air cleaner, etc.) should be done first.*

Pilot screw (A)(110)

RECOMMENDED LUBRICANTS

Wheel and steering stem bearings	Waterproof, medium-weight bearing grease
Throttle lever housing	Waterproof, light duty grease
General chassis lubrication	Waterproof, medium-weight chassis grease

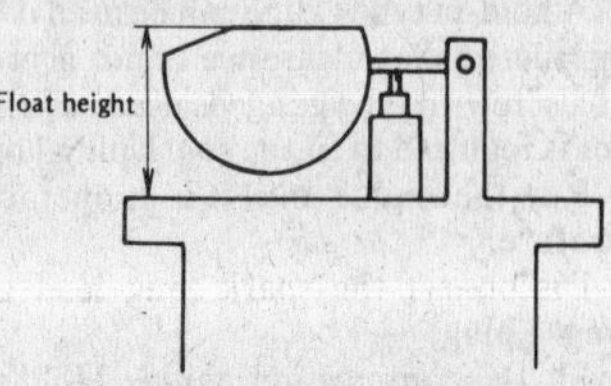

Carburetor float height

Throttle stop screw (A)(110)

Pilot screw (A)(160)

1. Locate the pilot screw on the side of the carburetor.

Throttle stop screw (A)(160)

2. Turn the screw in carefully until it is lightly seated, then back it out the following number of turns:

KLT 110: 1-3/8

KLT 160: 1-1/4

CAUTION: *Do not overtighten the screw or the calibrated tip will be damaged.*

3. Locate the throttle stop screw.

4. Turn the screw as required until the engine is running at the lowest smooth idle speed.

SPARK ARRESTOR CLEANING

1. The spark arrestor should be decarbonized every year.

Spark arrestor (B) and mounting bolt (A)

2. Remove the bolt that secures the spark arrestor in the muffler.

3. Pull out the spark arrestor.

4. In an open, well-ventilated area clear of flammable materials, start the engine.

5. When operating temperature is reached, rev the engine while tapping the muffler with a plastic mallet. This will dislodge built-up carbon particles.

CAUTION: *This procedure must be carried out in a safe area. Hot carbon particles are a fire hazard.*

6. Shut off the engine.

7. Scrape carbon build-up from the arrestor.

8. Install the arrestor and secure it with the bolt.

TUNE-UP SPECIFICATIONS

	KLT 110	KLT 160
SPARK PLUG		
Type	D-7EA	D-8EA
COMPRESSION		
Standard (psi)	164-192	14-43 ①
Minimum (psi)	125	14
Maximum (psi)	192	43
VALVE CLEARANCE		
Intake (mm/in.)	0.12-0.17/0.005-0.007	0.12-0.17/0.005-0.007
Exhaust (mm/in.)	0.12-0.17/0.005-0.007	0.18-0.23/0.007-0.009
IGNITION TIMING		
Retarded	10° @ 1500 rpm	10° @ 1350 rpm
Full advance	35° @ 4000 rpm	35° @ 4600 rpm
CARBURETOR		
Float height (mm/in.)	20/0.8	33.3/1.3
Service fuel level (mm/in.)	2.5 ± 1/0.10 ± 0.04	5.0 ± 1/0.20 ± 0.04
Pilot screw (turns out)	1⅜	1¼

① ACR-affected

ENGINE AND TRANSMISSION

NOTE: *Engine rebuilding techniques and procedures are explained in detail in the "General Information" section of this manual.*

ENGINE REMOVAL AND INSTALLATION

KLT 110

1. Drain the engine oil.
2. Remove the seat.

Engine mounting bolts (A) and bracket bolts (B) (110)

3. Remove the rear fender.

4. Remove the gas tank. See "Fuel Systems."

5. Remove the carburetor. See "Fuel Systems."

6. Remove the air cleaner case.

7. Loosen the muffler clamp on the exhaust pipe. Remove the muffler bracket bolts on the frame. Remove the nuts securing the exhaust pipe at the cylinder head. Remove the exhaust system.

8. Remove the three screws from the engine sprocket cover on the left side of the engine. Remove the sprocket cover.

9. Back off the chain adjuster nut at the

rear axle and push the axle forward to increase chain slack.

10. Remove the engine sprocket circlip from the shaft.

Engine mounting bolts (A) and bracket bolts (B) (110)

11. Pull off the engine sprocket and chain.

12. Remove the securing hardware and take off the upper half of the chain case.

13. Remove the shift lever from its shaft.

14. Disconnect the lead from the spark plug.

15. Disconnect the magneto wiring at the plastic connectors.

16. Remove the chain guard (just to the rear of the engine sprocket).

17. Remove the engine mounting bolts and bracket bolts at the front and rear of the engine and at the cylinder head. See illustrations.

18. Installation is the reverse of removal. Tighten the cylinder head mounting bolt and bracket bolts to 13 ft. lbs. Tighten the front and rear bracket bolts to 13 ft. lbs. and the front and rear engine mounting bolts to 22 ft. lbs.

19. The engine sprocket must be installed with the number facing outward. If the sprocket collar was removed from the mainshaft, a new O-ring should be used. Install the collar with the bevelled side in.

20. Do not forget to refill the crankcase with motor oil.

KLT 160

1. Drain the engine oil.
2. Remove the seat.
3. Remove the rear fender.
4. Remove the gas tank. Refer to "Fuel Systems."
5. Remove the carburetor. See "Fuel Systems."
6. Loosen the muffler clamp. Remove the two muffler bracket bolts. Remove the exhaust pipe nuts at the cylinder head. Remove the exhaust system.

Engine mounting bolts (A) and bracket bolts (B) (160)

Engine mounting bolts (A) and bracket bolts (B) (160)

7. Remove the pinch bolt and pull the shift lever from its shaft.

8. Disconnect the lead from the spark plug.

9. Disconnect the magneto wiring at the plastic connectors on the frame behind the engine.

10. Loosen the propeller shaft clamp screws.

11. Remove the engine mounting bolts and the bracket bolts.

12. Pull the engine forward to clear the rear mounting brackets and then out to the right side of the frame.

13. Installation is the reverse of removal. Note the following.

14. Lubricate the propeller shaft joints with bearing grease.

15. Be sure the joint spring is installed on the pinion gear nut.

16. Turn the rear wheel to align the joint splines and the pinion gear splines.

17. Tighten the engine mounting bolts at the front and rear of the engine to 22 ft. lbs. Tighten the bracket bolts and the mounting bolt at the cylinder head to 15 ft. lbs.

18. Be sure to refill the crankcase with motor oil before attempting to start the engine.

TOP END

KLT 110

REMOVAL

The top end components (cylinder head, cylinder and piston) can be removed without removing the engine from the frame.

1. Remove the seat.
2. Remove the gas tank. Remove the carburetor. See "Fuel Systems" for procedures.
3. Loosen the muffler clamp. Remove the muffler bracket bolts. Remove the exhaust pipe nuts at the cylinder head. Remove the exhaust system.
4. Remove the recoil starter assembly.
5. Remove the two bolts and take off the camshaft sprocket cover. Pry slots are provided under the bolt hole bosses.
6. Use a wrench on the magneto rotor nut to turn the engine over until the slash mark on the cam sprocket aligns with the pointer on the top of the cylinder head.
7. Remove the cam chain tensioner in the following manner:

a. Remove the lock bolt from the top of the cam chain tensioner.

b. Screw in a longer bolt of the same dimensions (6mm dia./1.0mm pitch). Tighten the bolt securely to hold the pushrod in place.

c. Remove the tensioner mounting bolts and take off the tensioner.

CAUTION: *Do not turn the engine over with the tensioner removed or damage may result.*

8. Remove the cam sprocket bolts.
9. Pull the sprocket off the cam and disengage it from the chain.
10. Loop a length of wire through the chain and secure it to prevent the chain from falling into the cylinder.
11. Disconnect the lead from the spark plug.
12. Loosen the spark plug.
13. Remove the cylinder head mounting brackets.
14. Remove the cylinder head oil pipe banjo bolts at the head and the crankcase.
15. Remove the oil pipe mounting screws and remove the pipe.
16. Remove the 6mm cylinder head bolts near the cam sprocket housing.
17. Remove the 8mm cylinder head bolts on the top of the head.
18. Lift the cylinder head from the cylinder and remove it.
19. Note the locations of the dowel pins on the cylinder head/cylinder mating surface.
20. Remove the head gasket.
21. To remove the cylinder, lift it up while turning the front cam chain guide.
22. Note the location of the dowel pins on the crankcase mating surface.
23. Remove the wrist pin circlips and push out the wrist pin to remove the piston.
24. Remove the cylinder base gasket.

DISASSEMBLY

1. Remove the valve adjuster caps from the head.

Align pointer (A) and sprocket slash mark (B) prior to cylinder head removal

Cylinder head 8 mm bolts (A) and 6 mm bolts (B)

Valve adjuster caps (A) and rocker arm shaft retainer (B)

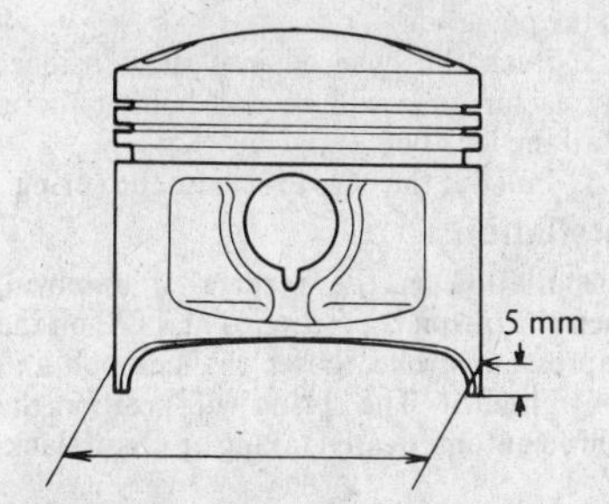

Measure piston diameter 5 mm above the edge of the skirt

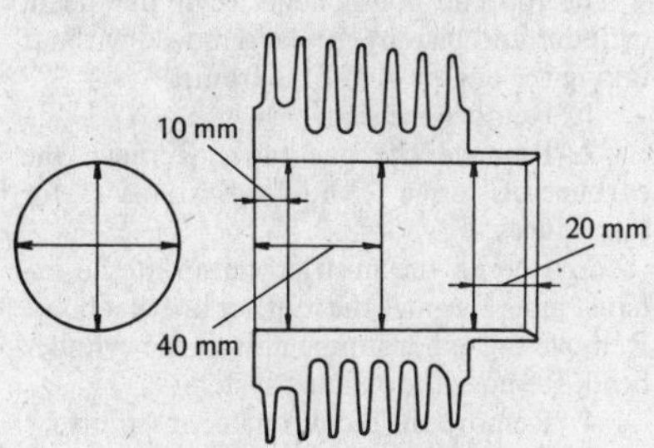

Cylinder bore measurement points

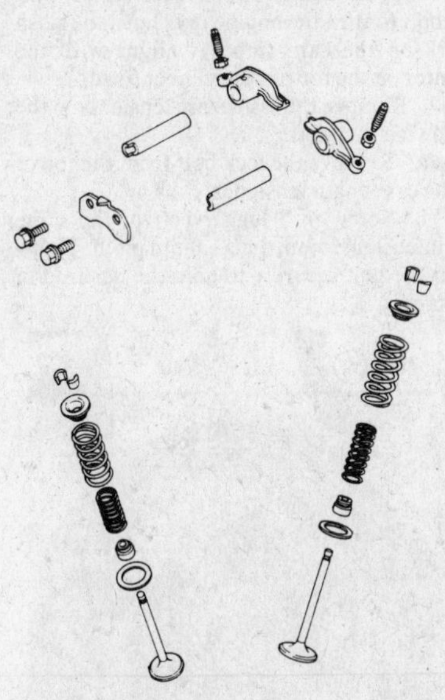
Valve train

2. Remove the two bolts which secure the rocker arm shaft retainer.

3. Pull the rocket arm shafts out of the head and remove the rocker arms.

NOTE: *Keep all assemblies together so that they may be reinstalled in their original locations.*

4. Remove the camshaft by pulling it straight out of the head.

5. Check the valves for leakage. If service is required, compress the valve springs and remove the valve keepers. Remove the spring retainer, springs, spring seat and valve on each side.

6. Remove the valve seals from the guides by prying off the seal clip and pulling off the seal.

INSPECTION

Refer to the "Engine Rebuilding" section of "General Information" for standard inspection techniques and procedures. Compare component condition against the standard values and service limits given in the "Engine Specifications" chart.

Note the following points:

1. To determine piston and cylinder wear and clearance, measure the piston diameter 5mm above the edge of the skirt. Measure the cylinder diameter 10mm from the top, 40mm from the top and 20mm from the bottom of the bore.

2. Oversized pistons are available in 0.5 and 1.0mm. The sizes are stamped on the piston crown.

ASSEMBLY

1. Use new seals and gaskets.

2. Clean the ends of the valve guides.

3. Lubricate the inside of each valve seal and slip it over the end of the guide. Push down until the seal is seated in the guide groove.

4. Lubricate the valve stems with engine-assembly lube before inserting them in the guides.

5. Check valve springs. Progressively wound springs must be installed with the close coils against the head.

NOTE: *If you are reusing the original valve train components, ensure that they are all installed in their original locations.*

6. Lubricate the camshaft with clean motor oil. Insert the camshaft into the head with the cam lobes point down.

7. Lubricate and install the rocker arm shafts slipping them into the rocker arm on each side. Be sure the cutaways face the center of the head.

8. Install and secure the rocker arm shaft retainer.

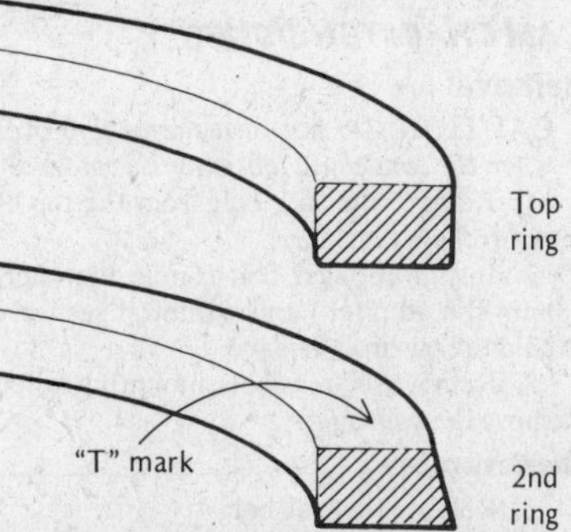

Top and 2nd compression ring profiles. "T" mark must face up when rings are fitted

INSTALLATION

1. Install the oil ring expander on the piston and then the two oil rails. The rails are interchangeable. Be sure that the expander ring ends butt together.

2. Check the compression ring profiles. The lower compression ring is wedge-shaped; the top compression ring has a plain profile. Be sure to install each in the proper groove.

3. Compression rings are to be fitted with the manufacturer's mark (near the end-gap) facing up.

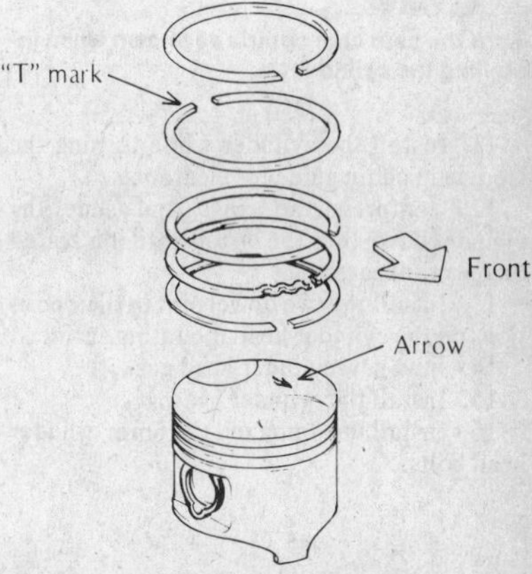

Ring end-gaps must be positioned as shown. Arrow on piston crown must point towards the exhaust port

4. When installing the piston on the connecting rod, be sure the arrow on the piston crown points towards the exhaust port.

5. After pushing the wrist pin into place, install the circlips.

NOTE: *New circlips must be used. Never reuse old circlips.*

6. Be sure the circlips are well seated. When installing them, do not compress them any more than is necessary to effect installation.

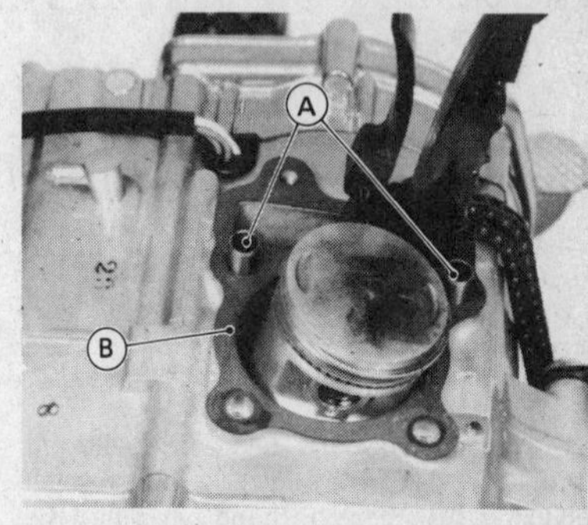

Be sure the dowel pins (A) and cylinder base gasket (B) are in place

7. Arrange the piston ring end-gaps around the piston so that the end-gap of the top ring and the oil expander ring face the front of the engine and the end-gap of the lower compression ring faces the rear of the engine. The end-gaps of the two oil rails should be positioned about 30° on either side of the expander end-gap.

8. Lubricate the rings and piston skirt with fresh motor oil.

9. Be sure the two dowel pins are in place in the crankcase.

10. Use a new cylinder base gasket.

Turn the cam chain guide as shown when installing the cylinder

11. Install the cylinder while turning the front cam chain guide for clearance.

12. Compress the rings and slide the cylinder down over the piston until it is seated on the crankcase.

13. Install the two dowel pins in their positions on the cylinder head mounting surface.

14. Fit a new cylinder head gasket.

15. Install the cylinder head.

16. Install the 8mm and the 6mm cylinder head bolts.

Cylinder head gasket (A) and dowel pins (B)

Cylinder head bolt tightening sequence

17. The 8mm bolts must be tightened gradually and in a cross pattern. Tighten each bolt to 8 ft. lbs., then go around again until the final torque of 16 ft. lbs. is reached.

18. Tighten the two 6mm bolts to 7.3 ft. lbs.

19. Remove the timing inspection plug on top of the left crankcase cover.

20. Check that the "T" mark on the magneto rotor is aligned with the pointer. If not, put some tension on the cam chain so that it will not get caught on anything and turn the rotor slowly until the "T" mark is aligned.

21. Check that the camshaft is positioned with the lobes downward as it was installed.

22. Pull the cam chain taut without moving the crankshaft. Engage the cam sprocket with the chain and install it on the cam so that the slash mark on the sprocket aligns with the pointer at the top of the head. Do not turn the crankshaft to make this alignment. If necessary, move the sprocket after disengaging it from the chain. For valve timing to be correct, the magneto rotor "T" mark must be aligned with the pointer at the crankcase and the sprocket slash mark must be aligned with the pointer at the top of the head.

23. Install the two cam sprocket bolts. The bolts should be secured with a non-permanent thread-locking compound and tightened to 8.7 ft. lbs.

Position the piston at TDC on the compression stroke: pointer (A) and "T" mark (B) must align when seen through the inspection plug hole (C)

Align cylinder head pointer (A) and cam sprocket slash mark (B)

24. Bolt the cam chain tensioner into place. Remove the long bolt which was fitted when the unit was removed and install the stock bolt in its place.

25. Turn the engine over slowly with a wrench on the magneto rotor nut and ensure that the timing marks align after a crankshaft revolution. If any resistance is felt when turning the engine over, stop immediately and determine the cause. If the sprocket is not correctly timed, the valves may strike the piston.

26. The remainder of the procedure is the reverse of disassembly.

CAM CHAIN TENSIONER

Removal

CAUTION: *Do not turn the engine over when the cam chain tensioner is removed.*

1. Remove the lock bolt from the top of the cam chain tensioner.
2. Install a longer bolt (6mm diameter, 1.0mm thread pitch) and tighten it securely to hold the pushrod in place.
3. Remove the tensioner mounting bolts. Remove the tensioner.

Disassembly

1. Remove the lock bolt.
2. Pull out the pushrod. Note the ball and retainer assembly and spring.
3. Remove the ball and retainer assembly and spring from the pushrod.

Inspection

1. Clean all parts in solvent.
2. Check the pushrod for scoring.
3. Lubricate the pushrod and move it in and out of the tensioner body. Movement must be perfectly smooth. The assembly must be replaced if the pushrod sticks or binds when moved.

Assembly

1. Lubricate the internals before assembly.
2. Slip the spring over the end of the pushrod and compress it so that the hole in the pushrod is clear.
3. Insert a piece of wire into the pushrod hole to hold the spring in place.
4. Insert the ball and retainer assembly into the pushrod.
5. Push the pushrod into the tensioner body as far as it will go and hold it there. Install the lock bolt.
6. Pull out the wire to release the spring.

Installation

Installation is the reverse of removal. When the piston is positioned at TDC on the compression stroke, loosen the lock bolt and then tighten it. The spring will position the pushrod automatically, taking up chain slack.

KLT 160

REMOVAL

The top end components (cylinder head, cylinder and piston) can be removed without taking the engine out of the frame.

1. Remove the seat.
2. Remove the gas tank. Remove the carburetor. See "Fuel Systems" for procedures.
3. Loosen the muffler clamp at the exhaust pipe. Remove the muffler bracket bolts. Remove the exhaust pipe nuts at the cylinder head. Remove the exhaust system.
4. Remove the recoil starter assembly.
5. Remove the two screws and take off the camshaft sprocket cover. Pry slots are provided under the screw hole bosses.
6. Use a wrench on the recoil starter pulley bolt to turn the engine over until the slash mark on the cam sprocket aligns with the pointer on the top of the cylinder head.
7. Remove the cam chain tensioner in the following manner:
    a. Remove the lock bolt from the top of the cam chain tensioner.
    b. Screw in a longer bolt of the same dimensions: 6mm dia./1.0mm pitch. Tighten the bolt securely to hold the pushrod in place.

Align pointer (A) and cam sprocket slash mark (B) before removing the cylinder head

c. Remove the tensioner mounting bolts and take off the tensioner.

CAUTION: *Do not turn the engine over with the tensioner removed or damage may result.*

8. Holding the crankshaft with a wrench on the recoil starter pulley bolt, remove the cam sprocket bolt.
9. Pull the sprocket off the cam and disengage it from the chain.
10. Loop a length of wire through the chain and secure it to prevent the chain from falling into the cylinder.
11. Disconnect the lead from the spark plug.
12. Loosen the spark plug.
13. Remove the cylinder head mounting brackets.
14. Remove the cylinder head oil pipe banjo bolts at the head and the crankcase.
15. Remove the oil pipe.
16. Remove the 6mm cylinder head bolts near the cam sprocket housing.
17. Remove the 8mm cylinder head bolts on the top of the head.

Cylinder head 8 mm bolts (A) and 6 mm bolts (B)

18. Lift the cylinder head from the cylinder and remove it.
19. Note the locations of the dowel pins on the cylinder head/cylinder mating surface.
20. Remove the head gasket.
21. To remove the cylinder, lift it up while feeding the cam chain through until the piston comes out.
22. Note the locations of the dowel pins on the crankcase mating surface.
23. Remove the wrist pin circlips and push out the wrist pin to remove the piston.
24. Remove the cylinder base gasket.

DISASSEMBLY

1. Remove the valve adjuster caps from the head.
2. Remove the two screws which secure the rocker arm shaft retainer. Remove the retainer.

Valve adjuster caps (A) and rocker arm shaft retainer (B)

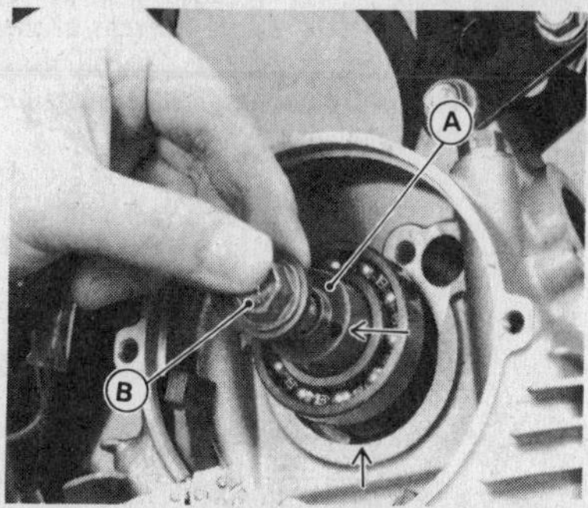

Removing the camshaft (A) with the sprocket bolt (B). Position the cam as shown (arrows) so that lobes will clear

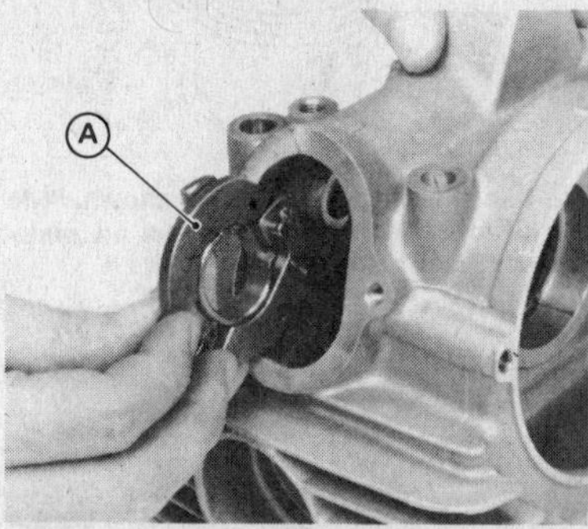

Removing the automatic compression release

3. To remove the rocker arm shafts, thread the cam sprocket bolt into each of them in turn and pull them out of the head. Remove the rocker arms.

NOTE: *Keep all assemblies together so that they may be reinstalled in their original locations.*

4. Remove the camshaft from the head in the following manner:

a. Thread the cam sprocket bolt into the camshaft.

b. Turn the cam so that the intake lobe (on the left side of the engine) points downward.

c. Pull out the cam and bearing assembly.

5. Remove the automatic compression release from the cylinder head.
6. Check the valves for leakage. If service is required, compress the valve springs and remove the valve keepers. Remove the spring retainer, springs, spring seat and valve on each side.
7. Remove the valve seals from the guides by prying off the seal clip and pulling off the seal.

INSPECTION

Refer to the "Engine Rebuilding" section of "General Information" for standard inspection techniques and procedures. Compare component condition against the standard values and service limits given in the "Engine Specifications" chart. Note the following points:

1. Check the automatic compression release unit by cleaning it in a solvent and lubricating it lightly with motor oil. Check the condition of the spring. Replace it if deformed or otherwise damaged. Check that the weights move smoothly. If they do not, or if the release pin is damaged, the ACR must be replaced.
2. To determine piston and cylinder wear and clearance, measure the piston diameter 5mm above the edge of the skirt. Measure the cylinder diameter 10mm from the top, 40mm from the top and 20mm from the bottom of the bore.
3. Oversized pistons are available in 0.5 and 1.0mm. The sizes are stamped on the piston crown.

ASSEMBLY

1. Use new seals and gaskets.
2. Clean the ends of the valve guides.
3. Lubricate the inside of each valve seal and slip it over the end of the guide. Push down until the seal is seated in the guide groove.
4. Lubricate the valve stems with engine-assembly lube before inserting them in the guides.
5. Slip the ACR into the head if it was removed before installing the valve spring assemblies.
6. Progressively wound valve springs must be installed with the close coils against the head.

NOTE: *If you are reusing the original valve train components, ensure that they are all installed in their original locations.*

Install the ACR (A) so that the cam dowel pin (B) fits into the notch (C)

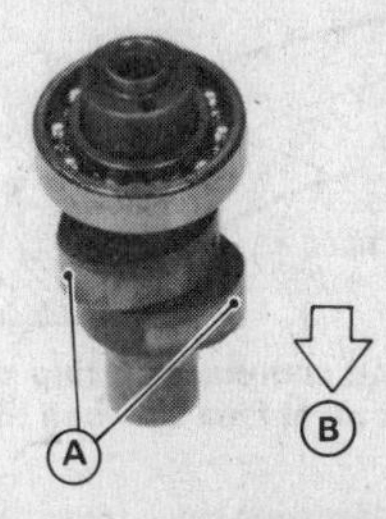

When installing the cam, the lobes (A) must point down (B); the pin hole (arrow) must be in the lowest position

7. Lubricate the camshaft and bearing before installation.

8. Hold the ACR in place and insert the cam into the head with the intake lobe pointing down.

9. Rotate the cam until the dowel pin engages the notch on the ACR, then push the cam into place.

10. Turn the camshaft so that the lobes point down. The pin hole in the end of the cam will be in the lowest position.

11. Lubricate the rocker arm shafts.

12. Hold the rocker arms in place and insert the shafts. The cutaways must face the center of the head.

13. Install and secure the rocker arm shaft retainer. The chamfered edge of the retainer faces the front of the engine.

INSTALLATION

1. Install the oil ring expander on the piston and then the two oil rails. The rails are interchangeable. Be sure that the expander ring ends butt together.

2. Check the compression ring profiles. The lower compression ring is wedge-shaped; the top compression ring has a plain profile. Be sure to install each in the proper groove.

Oil expander ring ends must not overlap (A)

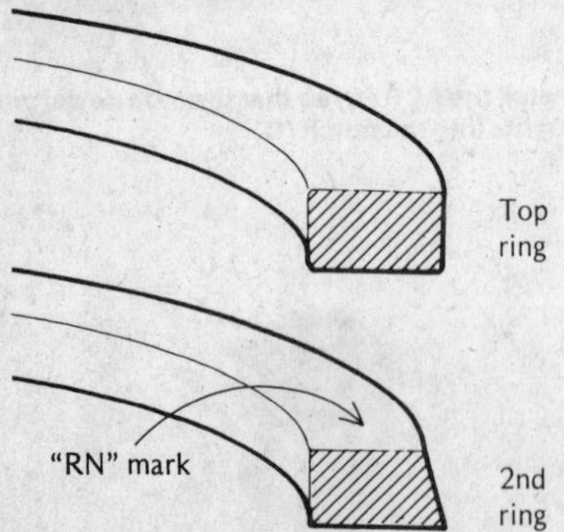

Top and 2nd compression ring profiles; the "RN" mark must face up when the rings are fitted

3. Compression rings are to be fitted with the manufacturer's mark (near the end-gap) facing up.

4. When installing the piston on the connecting rod, be sure the arrow on the piston crown points towards the exhaust port.

5. After pushing the wrist pin into place, install the circlips.

NOTE: *New circlips must be used. Never reuse old circlips.*

6. Be sure the circlips are well seated. When installing them, do not compress them any more than is necessary to effect installation.

7. Arrange the piston ring end-gaps around the piston so that the end-gap of the top ring and the oil expander ring face the front of the engine and the end-gap of the lower compression ring faces the rear of the engine. The end-gaps of the two oil rails should be positioned about 30° on either side of the expander end-gap.

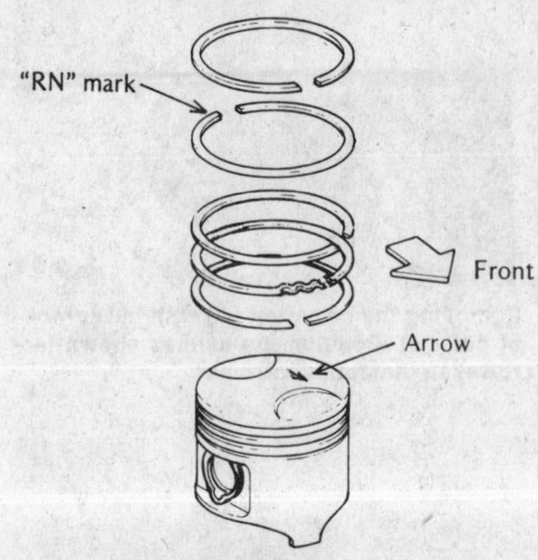

Position the ring end-gaps as shown. "RN" marks must face up and arrow on piston crown must face the exhaust port

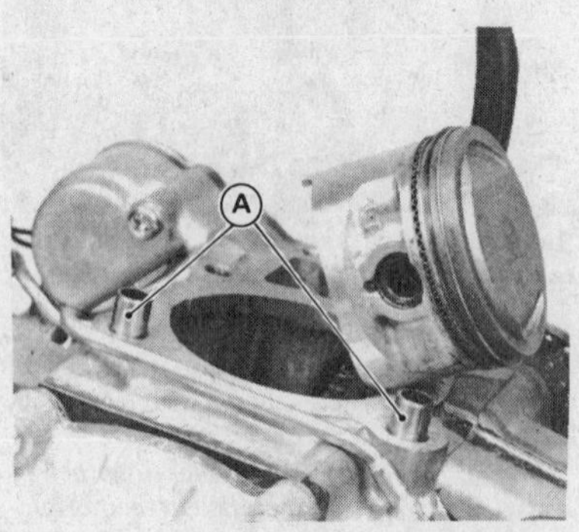

Be sure the cylinder dowel pins (A) are in place

8. Lubricate the rings and piston skirt with fresh motor oil.

9. Be sure the two dowel pins are in place in the crankcase.

10. Use a new cylinder base gasket.

11. Install the cylinder while pulling the cam chain through.

12. Compress the rings and slide the cylinder down over the piston until it is seated on the crankcase.

Cylinder head gasket (A) and dowel pins (B)

13. Install the two dowel pins in their positions on the cylinder head mounting surface.

14. Fit a new cylinder head gasket.

15. Install the cylinder head.

16. Install the 8mm and the 6mm cylinder head bolts. The bolt threads should be lubricated with motor oil before installation.

Cylinder head bolt tightening sequence

17. The cylinder head bolts must be tightened gradually and in a cross pattern.

Tighten the 8mm bolts to 9.4 ft. lbs. and the 6mm bolts to 4.3 ft. lbs. on the first time around, then do it again until the final torque of 18 ft. lbs. for the 8mm bolts and 7.3 ft. lbs. for the 6mm bolts is reached.

18. Remove the timing inspection plug on the left crankcase cover.

Pointer "A" and "T" mark (B) must align when viewed through the inspection plug (C) when the cam spocket is being fitted

19. Check that the "T" mark on the magneto rotor is aligned with the pointer. If it is not, put some tension on the cam chain so that it will not get caught on anything and turn the rotor slowly until the "T" mark is aligned.

20. Check that the camshaft is positioned with the lobes downward as it was installed.

21. Pull the cam chain taut without moving the crankshaft. Engage the cam sprocket with the chain and install it on the cam so that the slash mark on the sprocket aligns with the pointer at the top of the head. Do not turn the crankshaft to make this alignment. If necessary, move the sprocket after disengaging it from the chain. For valve timing to be correct, the magneto rotor "T" mark must align with the pointer at the crankcase and the sprocket slash mark must be aligned with the pointer at the top of the head.

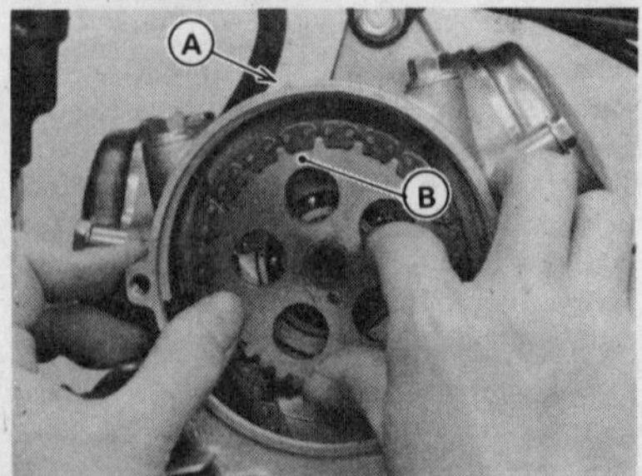

Pointer (A) and cam sprocket slash mark (B) must align for valve timing to be correct

22. Be sure that the cam timing pin and the sprocket hole are aligned.

23. Lubricate the threads of the sprocket bolt and tighten it to 22 ft. lbs. Hold the crankshaft with a wrench on the recoil starter pulley bolt while the cam sprocket nut is tightened.

24. Bolt the cam chain tensioner into place. Remove the long bolt which was fitted when the unit was removed and install the stock bolt in its place.

25. Turn the engine over slowly with a wrench on the recoil starter pulley bolt and ensure that the timing marks align after a crankshaft revolution. If any resistance is felt when turning the engine over, stop immediately and determine the cause. If the sprocket is not correctly timed, the valves may strike the piston.

26. The remainder of the procedure is the reverse of removal.

CAM CHAIN TENSIONER

Removal

CAUTION: *Do not turn the engine over when the cam chain tensioner is removed.*

1. Remove the lock bolt from the top of the cam chain tensioner.
2. Install a longer bolt (6mm diameter, 1.0mm thread pitch) and tighten it securely to hold the pushrod in place.
3. Remove the tensioner mounting bolts. Remove the tensioner.

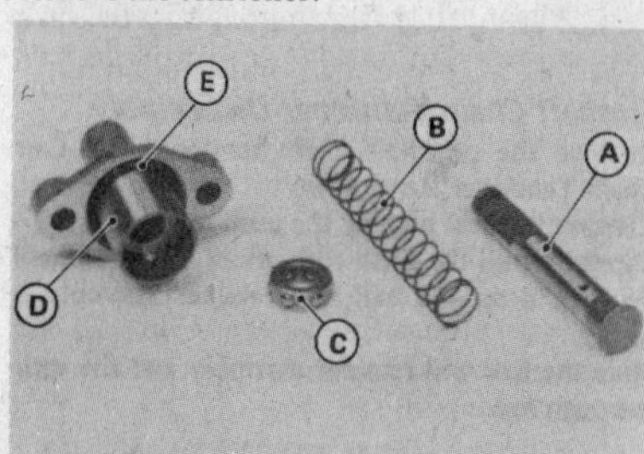

Cam chain tensioner components: pushrod (A), spring (B), ball and retainer assembly (C), body (D) and o-ring (E)

Disassembly

1. Remove the lock bolt.
2. Pull out the pushrod. Note the ball and retainer assembly and spring.
3. Remove the ball and retainer assembly and spring from the pushrod.

Inspection

1. Clean all parts in solvent.
2. Check the pushrod for scoring.
3. Lubricate the pushrod and move it in and out of the tensioner body. Movement must be perfectly smooth. The assembly must be replaced if the pushrod sticks or binds when moved.

Assembly

1. Lubricate the internals before assembly.
2. Slip the spring over the end of the pushrod and compress it so that the hole in the pushrod is accessible.
3. Insert a piece of wire into the pushrod hole to hold the spring in place.
4. Insert the ball retainer assembly into the pushrod.
5. Push the pushrod into the tensioner as far as it will go and hold it there. Insert the lock bolt.
6. Pull out the wire to release the spring.

Installation

Installation is the reverse of removal. When the piston is positioned at TDC on the compression stroke, loosen the lock bolt and then tighten it. The spring will position the pushrod automatically, taking up chain slack.

CRANKCASE COVER COMPONENTS

KLT 110

RECOIL STARTER

Removal

1. Remove the three screws securing the recoil starter assembly to the crankcase cover.
2. Remove the assembly.
3. Remove the four bolts to remove the starter pulley.

Recoil starter case screws (A)

Disassembly

1. Remove the e-ring and thrust washer from the reel shaft.
2. Remove the cover.
3. Remove the spring and thrust washer.
4. Remove the pawls and springs.
5. Pull the rope out about 1 1/2 ft. until the reel notch is near the rope hole. Clamp the rope so that it cannot retract with locking pliers.
6. Remove the handle cap.
7. Pull the rope out of the handle and untie the knot.
8. Remove the handle.
9. Hold the reel with one hand and unlatch the locking pliers from the rope.
10. Allow the reel to wind the rope in slowly.

CAUTION: *The coil spring is under tension. If it is to be removed, take adequate safety precautions to prevent personal injury.*

11. Check that the reel tension is released. Turn it 1/4 turn CCW past the rest position and slowly lift it straight up and out of the housing. Watch the coil spring beneath it. There must be no tension felt on the reel while it is removed. If there is, push it back into place and move it back and forth until it feels free.
12. To remove the coil spring, place the housing face down on a bench and strike the bench with a plastic mallet to knock the spring loose.

CAUTION: *Strike the bench, not the housing.*

Inspection

1. Clean metal parts in a safe solvent.
2. Check the pawls for chipping or excessive wear. Replace them if damaged.
3. Inspect the rope for fraying or wear.
4. Inspect all springs for rust, weakness, distortion or other signs of wear and replace them if necessary.

Assembly

1. Grease the coil spring.
2. Wear gloves to prevent injury while installing the coil spring.
3. Install the coil spring in the housing, hooking the outer end of the spring onto the tab in the housing.

Wind the rope around the reel in a clockwise direction (A)

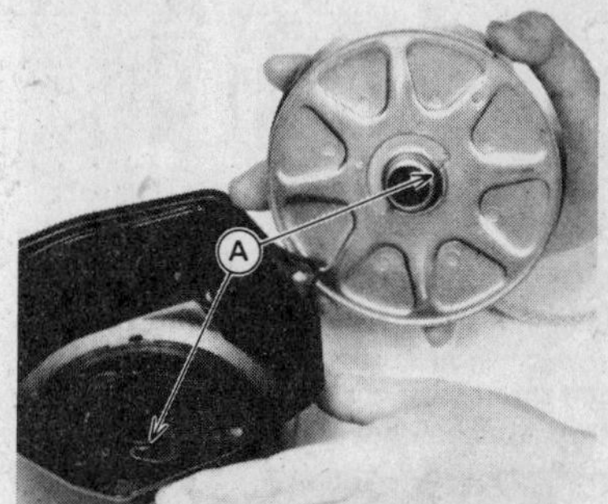

Engage the tab on the reel with the inner hook on the coil spring (A)

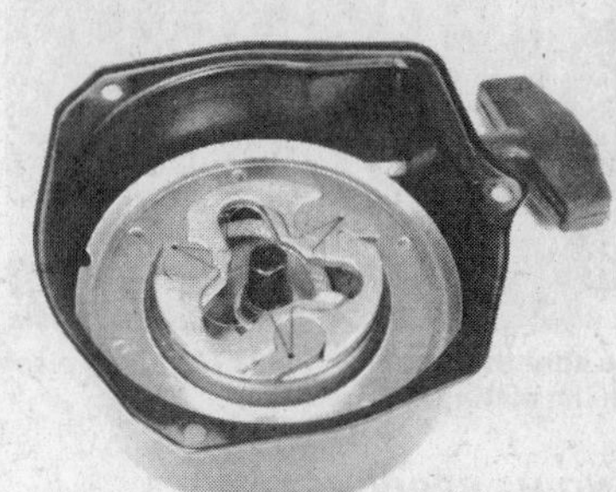

Install pawls and springs as shown

4. Wind the rope around the reel in a clockwise direction.
5. Insert the reel in the housing, turning it so that the tab on the reel engages the inner hook on the coil spring.
6. Rotate the reel two full turns clockwise to preload the coil spring.
7. Be sure the pawls and springs are installed as shown.
8. The remainder of the procedure is the reverse of disassembly.

Installation

1. Use a non-permanent thread-locking compound on the pulley bolts and tighten them securely.
2. Install the assembled housing and tighten the three screws.

LEFT CRANKCASE COVER

Removal

1. Remove the recoil starter.
2. Remove the pulley from the magneto flywheel.
3. Place a drip pan beneath the left side of the engine to catch any oil which may come out when the cover is removed.
4. Remove the neutral indicator switch on the rear part of the crankcase cover.
5. Remove the shift lever pinch bolt and carefully pull the shift lever off the shaft.
6. Remove the left crankcase cover screws and take off the cover.

Installation

1. Use a new cover gasket.
2. Be sure that the two locating dowel pins are in place on the cover mating surface.
3. Check oil level after installation and top up if necessary.

Left crankcase cover (A), neutral indicator switch (B) and shift lever pinch bolt (C)

Be sure the two dowel pins (A) are in place on the mating surface (B)

ENGINE SPROCKET

Removal

1. Remove the engine sprocket cover (three screws).
2. Remove the circlip from the transmission mainshaft.
3. Pull the sprocket off the shaft. If necessary, increase chain slack by backing off the chain adjuster and pushing the axle forward.
4. Remove the transmission shaft collar.
5. Remove the O-ring from the shaft.

Inspection

See "General Information" for generic sprocket inspection. Diameter across the base of the teeth must be at least 40.4mm (1.59 in.).

Installation

1. Use a new mainshaft O-ring and lubricate it before installing it on the shaft.
2. Install the collar with the bevelled side facing the engine.
3. Engage the sprocket with the chain. The sprocket must be fitted so that the side stamped with the number faces out.
4. Install the cover.

Install the collar with the bevelled side (A) facing the engine

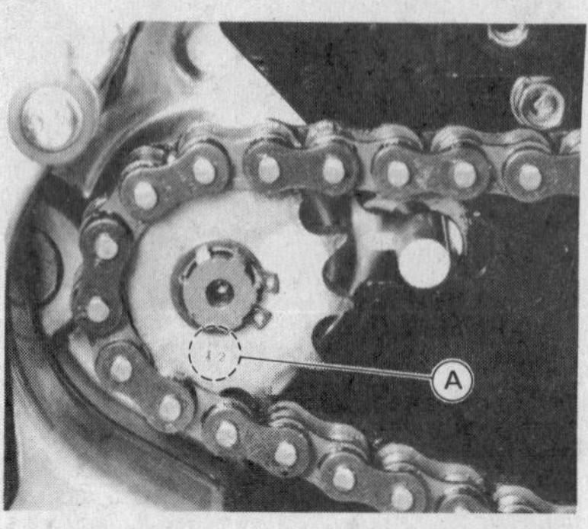

Sprocket numbers (A) must face outward

MAGNETO

Removal

1. Remove the recoil starter housing.
2. Remove the pulley from the rotor.
3. Remove the left crankcase cover.
4. Secure the magneto rotor and remove the nut.
5. Pull the rotor off the shaft with the special tool.

CAUTION: *Do not strike the rotor to knock it loose or the magnetic properties may be impaired.*

6. Remove the pin from the crankshaft.
7. Disconnect the magneto wiring at the plastic connectors.

Stator screws (A)

8. Remove the three stator mounting screws.
9. Remove the stator.
10. Remove the gasket.

Clean surfaces (C); align pin (A) and slot (B) before installation

8. Remove the three stator mounting screws.
9. Remove the stator.
10. Remove the gasket.

Inspection

1. See "Electrical System" for system tests.
2. Check the physical condition of all components.
3. Check the stator oil seal for torn or otherwise damaged lips.

Installation

1. Clean all parts thoroughly. Be sure there is no foreign matter on the crankshaft or on the inside of the magneto rotor.
2. Use a new stator gasket.
3. Lubricate the lips of the stator oil seal before installation.
4. Tighten the stator mounting screws securely.
5. Insert the wiring grommet into the cutout in the crankcase and route the wires as they were originally.
6. Clean off the crankshaft taper.
7. Insert the pin into the taper slot.
8. Push the magneto rotor into place.

CAUTION: *Do not strike the rotor to force it home. Be certain that the pin is not knocked out when the rotor is installed.*

9. Tighten the rotor nut to 31 ft. lbs.

CLUTCH

Removal

1. Drain the engine oil. Place a drip pan beneath the right crankcase cover.
2. Remove the screw holding the oil pipe to the right crankcase cover.
3. Remove the right crankcase cover screws. Remove the cover. Tap the cover with a plastic mallet to break it free if it is stuck. The clutch release assembly will come away with the cover.
4. Pull out the clutch release lever.
5. Remove the clutch pusher plate by removing the three mounting screws and flatwashers.
6. Remove the bushings with collars and pusher pins.
7. Holding the clutch in place, remove the housing nut and washer.
8. Remove the clutch assembly and collar from the crankshaft.

Disassembly

1. Hold the large retainer to keep it from flying free and remove it.

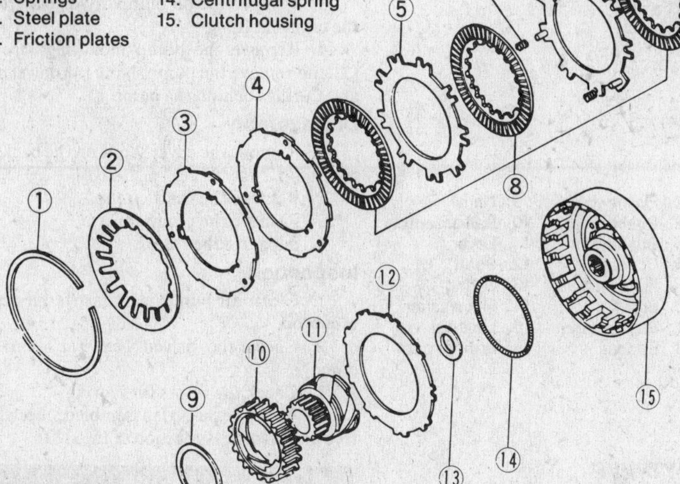

Clutch assembly

Engage the teeth of the spring with the teeth of the top steel plate

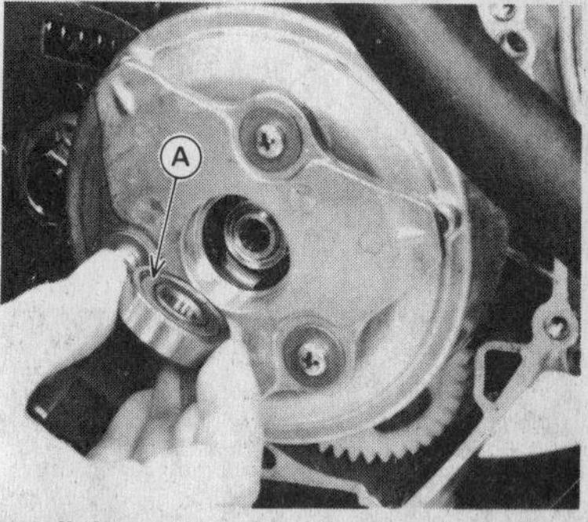
Install the pusher plate bearing so that the sealed side (A) faces in

Clutch pusher plate (A)

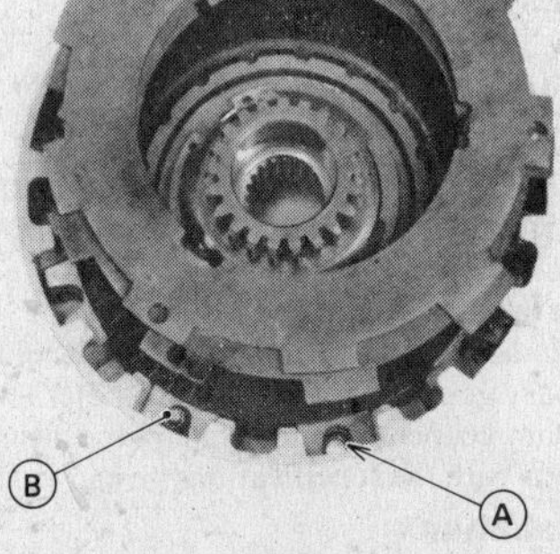
Steel plate with press-fit pins (B) must be installed in the clutch housing (A) as shown

Clutch release lever must align with the center of the clutch

2. Separate the clutch components.

3. Remove the circlip from the primary gear and separate the gear from the clutch hub.

Inspection

1. Clean all metal parts in a solvent and dry thoroughly.

2. Refer to the "General Information" section of this manual under "Engine Rebuilding" for clutch inspection techniques and procedures.

3. Friction plate thickness limit is 2.6mm (0.10 in.).

4. Plate warpage limit is 0.3mm (0.012 in.).

5. Check the clutch housing grooves for wear. If notches are worn into the housing from the steel plates, the housing should be replaced.

6. Check the housing groove where the centrifugal spring bears against the housing. If worn, replace the housing.

7. Check the spring for wear.

8. Check the clutch hub splines for damage due to the movement of the friction plates. Check the grooves of the hub for wear. Replace the hub if damage is evident.

Assembly

1. Lubricate the plates with motor oil before assembly.

Fit last two steel plates so that holes align with pins

2. Refer to the exploded view of the clutch as a guide to assembly.

3. The steel plate with the press-fitted pins must be installed in the clutch housing as shown.

4. The last two steel plates must be installed so that the holes on the plates align with the pins on the middle steel plate.

5. Engage the teeth of the spring with the teeth of the top steel plate.

6. When all components are assembled, compress the clutch and install the large retainer into the groove.

Be sure the dowel pins (A) are in place; check that the filter screen (B), bearing (C) and release lever (D) are in place before fitting the cover

Installation

1. Tighten the housing nut to 46 ft. lbs.

2. Be sure the bearing in the clutch pusher plate is installed with the sealed side in.

3. The clutch release lever must point towards the center of the clutch.

4. Be sure the dowel pins are in place in the right crankcase cover mating surface.

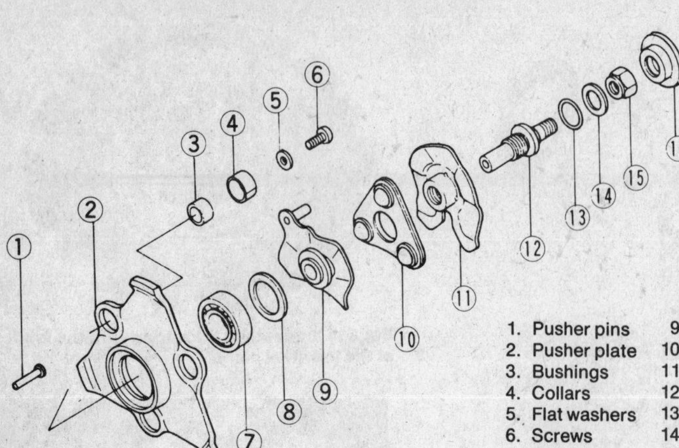

1.	Pusher pins	9.	Cam
2.	Pusher plate	10.	Ball assembly
3.	Bushings	11.	Lever
4.	Collars	12.	Shaft
5.	Flat washers	13.	O-ring
6.	Screws	14.	Flat washer
7.	Ball bearing	15.	Locknut
8.	Spacer	16.	Rubber cap

Clutch release assembly

Clutch release lever boss must engage the notch on the release cam (A)

5. Check clutch release assembly installation if it was removed. See below.
6. Use a new crankcase cover gasket.
7. When fitting the cover, fit the clutch release lever boss into the notch on the release cam.
8. Attach the oil pipe to the crankcase cover.
9. Fill the engine with oil.
10. Adjust the clutch as outlined in "Maintenance."

CLUTCH RELEASE

Removal

1. Remove the right crankcase cover.
2. Remove the clutch release cam, ball assembly and lever from the right crankcase cover.
3. Remove the rubber adjuster cap from the outside of the crankcase cover.
4. Unscrew the adjuster locknut. Remove the washer and O-ring.
5. Remove the release shaft.

Inspection

1. Clean all metal parts in solvent.
2. Check parts for wear.

Installation

1. Lubricate components before installation.
2. Reverse the removal procedure. Adjust the clutch as outlined in "Maintenance."
3. Refer to the exploded view as a guide to component installation.

PRIMARY DRIVE

Removal

1. The primary gear is a part of the clutch assembly and is removed along with it.
2. To remove the secondary gear, lock the gear train and remove the nut.
3. Remove the gear.
4. Remove the collar behind the gear.

Inspection

1. Check the gear teeth for wear, pitting and other damage. Minor imperfections can be removed with an oilstone. If damage is more extensive, replace the gear(s).
2. Measure the inside diameter of the primary gear and the outside diameter of the primary gear collar and compare the measurements with the specifications given.

Installation

1. Reverse the removal procedure.
2. Tighten the secondary gear nut to 53 ft. lbs.

Oil pump mounting screws (A)

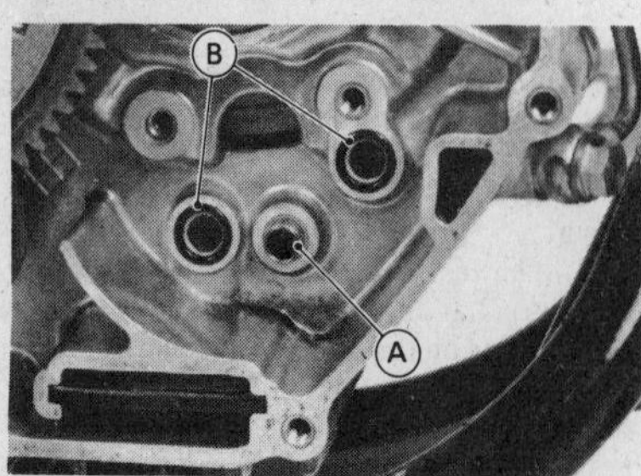

Dowel pin (A) and o-rings (B) must be in place behind the pump

OIL PUMP

Removal

1. Remove the right crankcase cover.
2. Remove the clutch.
3. Remove the oil pump drive gear from the crankshaft.
4. Remove the pump mounting screws (3) and remove the pump. Note the dowel pin and O-rings behind the pump.

Disassembly

1. Remove the cover screw on the back of the pump.
2. Remove the shaft circlip.
3. Remove the pump cover.
4. Separate the rotors.

Inspection

1. Clean all pump metal parts in clean motor oil.
2. Check the driven gear for wear or damage.
3. Check the rotors for scoring.
4. After the pump is assembled, check for free and effortless rotation of the shaft.

Pump drive gear must be installed with the marked side out (A) and the groove (B) engaged with the crankshaft pin (C)

Assembly and Installation

1. Lubricate all pump parts with clean motor oil before assembly.
2. Fill the pump with clean motor oil before installation.
3. Be sure the dowel pin and O-rings positioned behind the pump are in place.
4. Tighten the mounting screws securely.
5. Install the pump drive gear with the marked side out and the groove engaging the crankshaft pin.

Removing the external shift mechanism

EXTERNAL SHIFT MECHANISM

Removal

1. Remove the right crankcase cover.
2. Remove the gearshift lever (left side).
3. Remove the left crankcase cover.

4. Remove the footpegs.
5. Remove the secondary gear.
6. Thoroughly clean off and deburr the gearshift lever splines on the left side of the gearshift shaft to prevent damage to the oil seal when the shaft is pulled through.
7. Disengage the shift fingers from the shift drum. Pull the external shift assembly out to the right side of the engine.
8. Disconnect the shift drum position lever spring from the lever.
9. Remove the lever bolt and take off the lever.

Inspection

1. Check the shaft for a bent condition.
2. Check the gearshift shaft splines for damage.

Shift drum position lever (A)

3. Check the shift arm fingers for a bent condition.
4. Check the pawl spring for weakness or deformity.
5. Check the shift drum position lever spring for condition.
6. Check the shift arm spring for condition.
7. Check that the pawl spring pin in the crankcase is tight.

Installation

1. Check that the shift drum position lever moves freely after its bolt is tightened.
2. Lubricate the shift shaft lightly with oil before installation to avoid damage to the oil seal on the left side.
3. Position the pawl spring arms on either side of the pin when installing it.
4. The remainder of the procedure is the reverse of removal.

KLT 160

RECOIL STARTER

Removal

1. Remove the six screws securing the recoil starter case to the crankcase cover.

Position the pawl spring arms (A) on either side of the pin

Recoil starter case screws

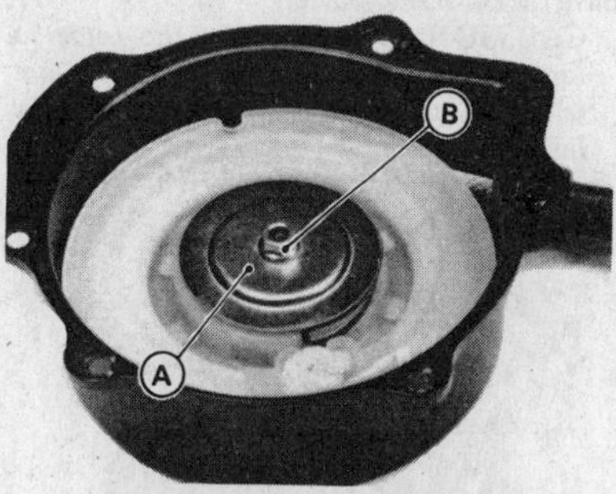

Ratchet cover (A) and nut (B)

2. Remove the assembly.
3. Remove the starter pulley bolt.
4. Remove the pulley.

Disassembly

1. Remove the ratchet cover nut.
2. Remove the ratchet cover.
3. Remove the recoil guide, cover, shaft and spring.
4. Remove the pawl.
5. Pull the rope out about 1 1/2 ft. and clamp it with locking pliers so that it will not retract.
6. Remove the handle cap.
7. Pull the rope out of the handle and untie the knot.
8. Remove the handle.
9. Hold the reel with one hand and unlatch the locking pliers from the rope.
10. Allow the reel to wind the rope in slowly.

CAUTION: *The coil spring is under tension. If it is to be removed, take adequate safety precautions to prevent personal injury.*

11. Check that the reel tension is released. Turn it 1/4 turn CCW past the rest position and slowly lift it straight up and out of the housing. Watch the coil spring beneath it. There must be no tension felt on the reel while it is removed. If there is, push it back into place and move it back and forth until is feels free.
12. To remove the coil spring, place the housing face down on a bench and strike the bench with a plastic mallet to knock the spring loose.

CAUTION: *Strike the bench, not the housing.*

Inspection

1. Clean metal parts in a safe solvent.
2. Check the pawl for chipping or excessive wear. Replace it if damaged.
3. Inspect the rope for fraying or wear.
4. Inspect the springs for rust, weakness, distortion or other signs of wear and replace them if necessary.

Assembly

1. Grease the coil spring.
2. Wear gloves to prevent injury while installing the coil spring.
3. Install the coil spring in the housing, hooking the outer end of the spring onto the tab in the housing.
4. Wind the rope around the reel in a clockwise direction.
5. Insert the reel in the housing, turning it so that the tab on the reel engages the inner hook on the coil spring.
6. Rotate the reel two full turns clockwise to preload the coil spring.
7. Be sure the pawl and recoil guide are installed as shown.

Wind the rope around the reel as shown (A)

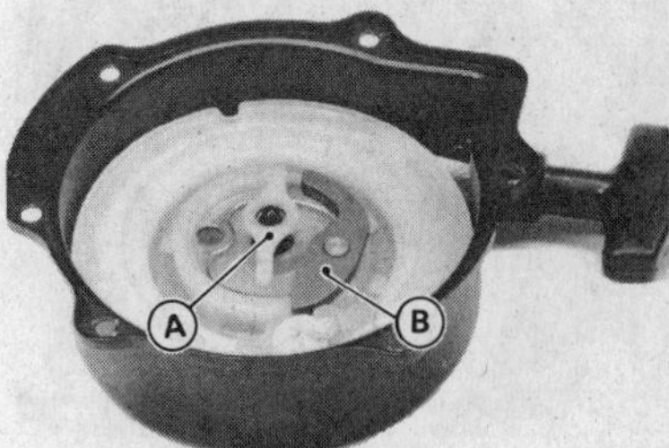

Be sure the recoil guide (A) and the pawl (B) are installed as shown

8. The remainder of the procedure is the reverse of disassembly.
9. Tighten the ratchet cover nut to 8.7 ft. lbs.

Installation

1. Align the pulley keyway with the key in the crankshaft and install the pulley.
2. Tighten the pulley bolt to 43 ft. lbs.

LEFT CRANKCASE COVER

Removal

1. Remove the recoil starter.
2. Remove the pulley from the crankshaft.
3. Disconnect the magneto wires from the harness at the plastic connectors.
4. Place a drip pan beneath the left side of the engine to catch any oil which may come out when the cover is removed.
5. Remove the neutral indicator switch on the gear case cover.
6. Remove the gear case cover.
7. Remove the reverse lever bolt and take off the reverse lever.
8. Remove the six left crankcase cover screws and take off the cover.

Gear case cover (A) and neutral indicator switch (B)

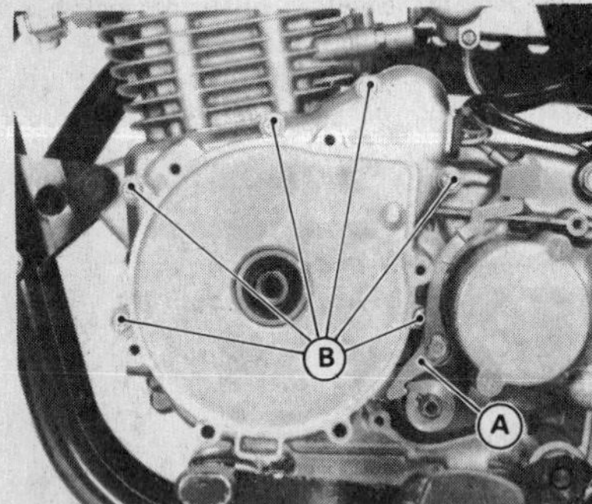

Reverse lever (A) and crankcase cover screws (B)

Be sure dowel pins (A) are in place before fitting the cover

Installation

1. Use a new cover gasket.
2. Be sure the dowel pins are in place on the cover mating surface.
3. Check oil level after installation and top up if necessary.

MAGNETO

Removal

1. Remove the recoil starter housing.
2. Remove the pulley from the crankshaft.
3. Remove the left crankcase cover.
4. Remove the magneto rotor from the crankshaft with the puller.

CAUTION: *Do not strike the rotor to knock it loose or the magnetic properties may be impaired.*

5. Remove the woodruff key from the crankshaft.
6. To remove the stator from the crankcase cover, remove the screw and take off the wiring holder.
7. Remove the three stator mounting screws and take off the stator.

Inspection

1. See "Electrical System" for system tests.
2. Check the physical condition of all components.

Installation

1. Clean all parts thoroughly. Be sure there is no foreign matter on the crankshaft or on the inside of the rotor or stator.
2. Tighten the stator mounting screws securely.
3. Be sure that wiring is protected and correctly arranged.
4. Clean off the crankshaft taper.
5. Check that the woodruff key is in place in the crankshaft slot.
6. Align the keyway with the key and push the rotor into place.

CAUTION: *Do not strike the rotor to force it home. Be certain the key is not knocked out of place when the rotor is installed.*

7. Pulley bolt torque is 43 ft. lbs.

Stator mounting screws (A)

Clean areas (C); align slot (B) and key (A) before fitting the rotor

REVERSE LEVER

Removal

1. Unscrew the neutral indicator mounting screw and remove the washer and indicator.
2. Remove the gear case screws.
3. Remove the gear case.
4. Remove the reverse lever pivot bolt and take off the lever and spring.
5. Remove the shift drum stopper from the end of the drum.
6. Remove the dowel pin.

Inspection

1. Check the lever for a bent condition.
2. Check spring condition.

Installation

1. Reverse the removal procedure.

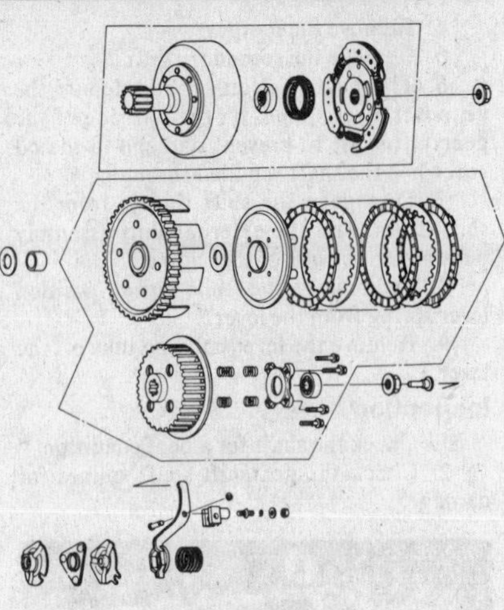
Clutch assembly

2. Check that the lever moves smoothly after the bolt is tightened.

CLUTCHES

Removal

1. Drain the engine oil.
2. Place a drip pan beneath the right crankcase cover.
3. Remove the right crankcase cover screws. Remove the cover. If it is stuck, tap it with a plastic mallet until free. The clutch release assembly will come away with the cover.

Removing the primary clutch housing (B) with a gear puller (A)

Remove the inner race (B) from the one-way clutch (C) by turning it clockwise (A)

4. Remove the recoil starter housing.
5. Stop the engine from turning over with a device on the recoil starter pulley.
6. Remove the primary clutch hub nut.
7. Loosen the secondary clutch spring bolts.

8. Remove the primary clutch housing from the crankshaft with a gear puller.
9. Remove the primary clutch hub assembly.
10. Remove the inner race by turning it clockwise.
11. Remove the one-way clutch.
12. Remove the pusher and ball bearing from the secondary clutch spring plate.
13. Unscrew the secondary clutch spring bolts evenly.
14. Remove the spring plate.
15. Remove the clutch springs.
16. Secure the secondary clutch hub, remove the hub nut.
17. Remove the hub.
18. Remove the clutch plate assembly and clutch wheel.
19. Remove the secondary clutch housing and sleeve. Note that there are flat washers on both ends of the sleeve.

Inspection

1. Clean all metal parts in a solvent and dry thoroughly.
2. Refer to the "Engine Rebuilding" section of "General Information" for clutch inspection techniques and procedures.
3. Secondary clutch wear limits are:
Friction plate min. thickness: 2.4mm (0.095 in.)

Secure the secondary clutch hub with a holder (A) and remove the nut (B)

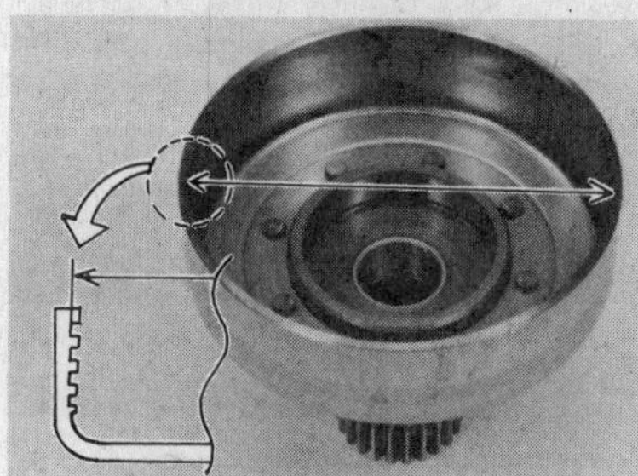

Measure the inside diameter of the primary clutch housing; check for wear of the grooves

Measure primary clutch shoe lining groove depth

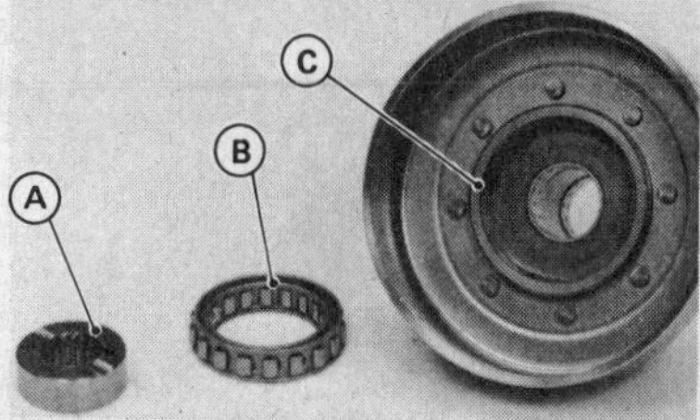

Inner race (A), one-way clutch (B), outer race (C)

Align the marks on the clutch wheel and hub (A)

Plate warpage (max.): 0.3mm (0.012 in.)
Clutch spring free length: 23.5mm (0.93 in.)

4. Measure the inside diameter of the primary clutch housing at several places. If any measurement exceeds 116.5mm (4.59 in.), replace it.
5. Check the primary clutch shoe lining for damage.
6. Measure the shoe groove depth and replace the shoes as a set if any of the measurements are under 0.5mm (0.02 in.).
7. Check the one-way clutch, inner race and outer race for damage.

Installation

1. Lubricate secondary clutch plates with motor oil before installation.
2. Refer to the exploded view of the clutches as a guide to assembly.
3. Assemble the secondary clutch hub by installing a friction plate and then alternating steel and friction plates.
4. Install the clutch wheel, aligning the marks on the wheel and the hub.
5. Install the spring plate with springs and bolts, but do not tighten the bolts fully.
6. Install the clutch housing on its shaft.
7. Install the partially assembled clutch hub onto the shaft turning the shaft gear by hand so that the shaft splines will mesh with the hub splines.
8. Remove the clutch spring plate assembly.
9. Oil the threads and the seating surface of the clutch hub nut.
10. Install the hub nut and tighten it to 14.5 ft. lbs.
11. Install the spring plate assembly.
12. Tighten the spring bolts gradually and evenly. Bolt final torque is to be done after the primary clutch is fitted. While tightening, ensure that the clutch wheel splines engage the hub splines. There should be a gap between the wheel and clutch housing and no play in the plates.
13. Fit the one-way clutch into the primary clutch housing by first fitting the projection on the cage into the groove on the housing.

When the clutch is installed, there should be a gap (C) between the wheel (B) and the housing (A)

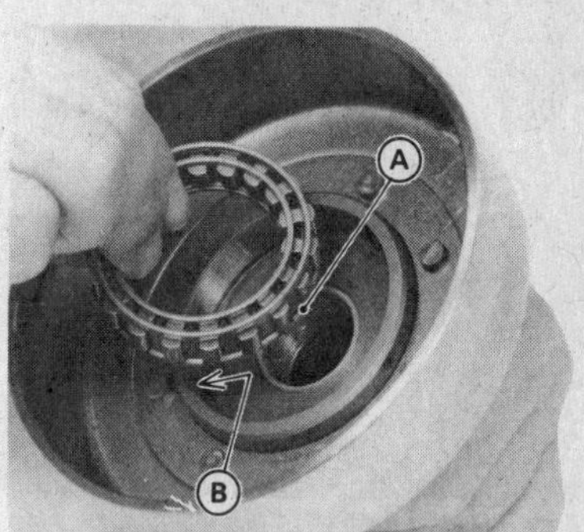

Fit the projection on the cage (A) into the groove on the housing (B)

14. Install the primary clutch hub assembly on the crankshaft.
15. Lubricate the hub nut threads and seating surface.
16. Install the primary clutch hub nut and tighten it to 14.5 ft. lbs.
17. Tighten the secondary clutch spring bolts to 11 ft. lbs. Be sure to tighten the bolts in a cross pattern.
18. Grease the secondary clutch pusher and install it.
19. Remove all old gasket from the right crankcase cover mating surface.
20. Install the clutch release cams and ball assembly. Note that the projection on the ball assembly must face in.
21. Be sure the locating dowel pins are in place on the crankcase mating surface.

CLUTCH RELEASE

Removal

1. Remove the right crankcase cover.
2. Remove the clutch release adjusting screw plug from the outside of the cover.

Grease the secondary clutch pusher (A) before installation

The projection (A) on the ball assembly must face in

Measure the inside diameter of the primary gear

Pump cover screw (A) and shaft circlip (B)

Be sure dowel pins (A) are installed; be sure the clutch release is properly seated

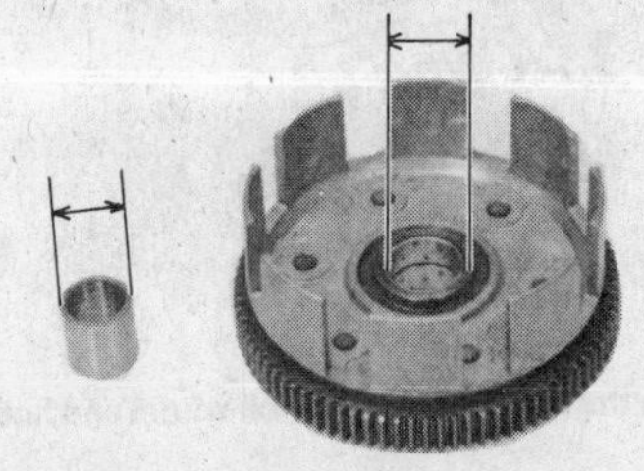
Measure the inside diameter of the secondary gear and the outside diameter of the secondary gear collar

3. Remove the triangular cover from the crankcase cover.

4. Unscrew and remove the locknut and adjusting screw.

5. Remove the flat washer and O-ring.

6. Remove the clutch release lever and spring from the right engine cover.

7. Remove the E- ring and pull the clevis pin from the clutch release lever clevis.

8. Pull the release cams and ball assembly from the shift shaft.

Inspection

1. Clean all metal parts in solvent.
2. Check parts for wear.

Installation

1. Lubricate components before installation.

2. Reverse the removal procedure. Adjust the clutch as outlined in "Maintenance."

3. Refer to the exploded view as a guide to installation.

PRIMARY DRIVE

Removal

1. The primary and secondary gears are a part of the primary and secondary clutch assemblies, respectively, and are removed/installed along with the clutches.

Checking primary (A) and secondary (B) gear backlash

Inspection

1. Check gear backlash with both clutches installed on their shafts.

2. Maximum allowable backlash is 0.14mm (0.006 in.). If the measurement exceeds this specification, both gears should be replaced.

3. Check the gear teeth for wear, pitting and other damage. Minor imperfections can be removed with an oilstone. If damage is more extensive, replace the gear(s).

4. Measure the inside diameter of the primary gear and the diameter of the crankshaft on the area on which the primary gear rides. Compare the measurements to the specifications. Replace worn parts as required.

5. Measure the inside diameter of the secondary gear and the outside diameter of the secondary gear collar. Compare the measurements obtained against the specifications. Replace worn parts as required.

Installation

1. See "Installation" under "Clutches", above.

Oil pump mounting screws (A) and drive gear (B)

OIL PUMP

Removal

1. Remove the right crankcase cover.
2. Remove the primary clutch.
3. Remove the oil pump mounting screws (3) and remove the pump. Note the dowel pin and O-rings behind the pump.
4. If removal of the drive gear is required, the secondary clutch must be removed.

Disassembly

1. Remove the pump cover screw on the back of the pump.
2. Remove the shaft circlip.
3. Remove the pump cover.
4. Separate the rotors.

Inspection

1. Clean all pump metal parts in clean motor oil.
2. Check the driven gear for wear or damage.
3. Check the rotors for scoring.
4. After the pump is assembled, check for free rotation of the shaft.

Engage the pump drive gear cutout (A) with the pin (B)

Be sure the dowel pin (A) and o-rings (B) are in place behind the oil pump

Assembly and Installation

1. Lubricate all pump parts with clean motor oil before assembly.
2. Fill the pump with clean motor oil before installation.
3. Be sure the dowel pin and O-rings positioned behind the pump are in place.
4. If the drive gear was removed, be sure to engage the cutout in the back of the gear with the crankshaft pin.
5. Tighten the pump mounting screws securely.

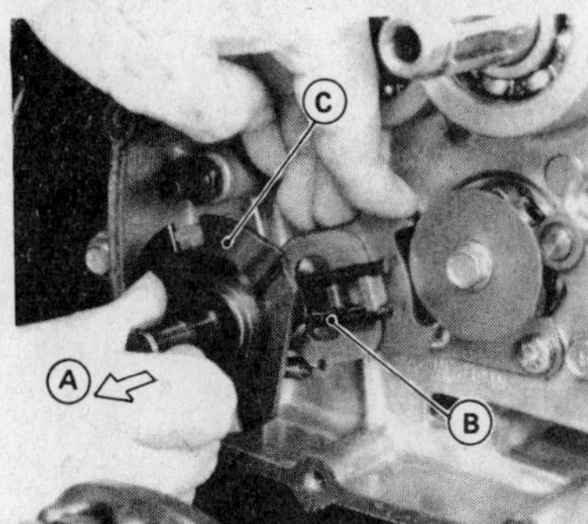

Removing the external shift mechanism (C) and return spring (B)

Shift drum positioning lever (A)

EXTERNAL SHIFT MECHANISM

Removal

1. Remove the right crankcase cover.
2. Remove the cluches.
3. Remove the clutch release cam and ball assembly.
4. Remove the gearshift lever (left side).
5. Thoroughly clean off and deburr the gearshift lever splines on the left side of the gearshift shaft to prevent damage to the oil seal when the shaft is pulled through.
6. Disengage the shift fingers from the shift drum. Pull the external shift assembly out to the right side of the engine.
7. Disconnect the shift drum positioning lever spring from the lever.
8. Remove the lever bolt and take off the lever.

Inspection

1. Check the shaft for a bent condition.
2. Check the gearshift shaft splines for damage.
3. Check that the ends of the shift fingers are not chipped. Check the shift drum pins.
4. Check the springs for weakness or deformity.
5. Check that the pins in the crankcase are tight.

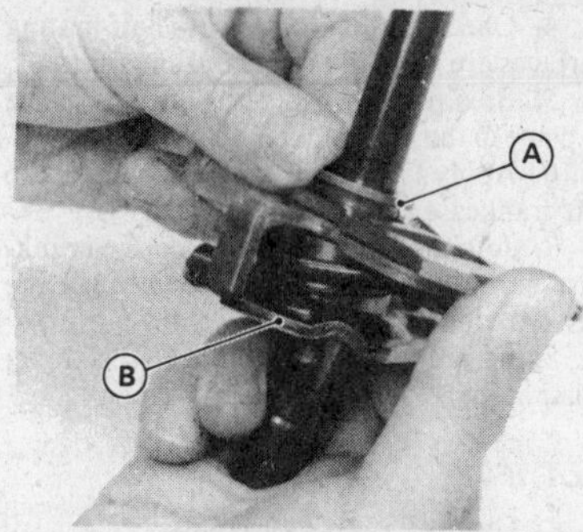

Be sure the shift arm collar (A) and the clutch release cam (B) are in place before installing the mechanism

Installation

1. Check that the shift drum position lever moves freely after its bolt is tightened.
2. Lubricate the shift shaft lightly with oil before installation to avoid damage to the oil seal on the left side.
3. Be sure the shift arm collar and clutch release cam are in place.
4. Position the spring arms on either side of the pin when the assembly is installed.
5. The remainder of the procedure is the reverse of removal.

LOWER END AND TRANSMISSION

Splitting The Crankcases

KLT 110

1. Remove the engine from the frame.
2. Remove the top end components.
3. Remove the crankcase cover components: recoil starter, magneto rotor and stator, engine sprocket, clutch and drive gears, oil pump, external shift mechanism, etc.

Crankcase screws (110)

Crankcase screws (160)

4. Remove the crankcase screws.
5. Separate the case halves by prying carefully at the slots provided.
6. The crankshaft and transmission will remain in the left crankcase half.

KLT 160

1. Remove the engine from the frame.
2. Remove the top end components.
3. Remove the crankcase cover components: recoil starter, magneto, clutches, drive gears, oil pump, external shift mechanism, reverse lever and front bevel gears.
4. Remove the pickup coil.
5. Remove the oil pipe banjo bolts. Remove the oil pipe mounting screw and take off the pipe.
6. Remove the crankcase screws and separate the case halves.

Inspection

Refer to the "Engine Rebuilding" section under "General Information" for lower end and transmission component inspection procedures. Compare measurements against those given in the "Engine Specifications" charts.

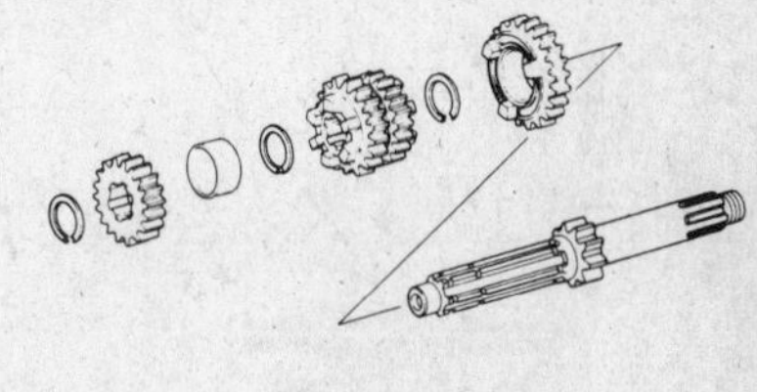

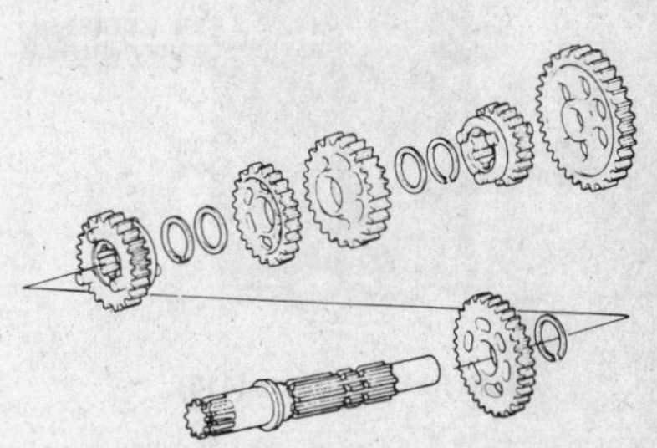

Gear cluster (110)

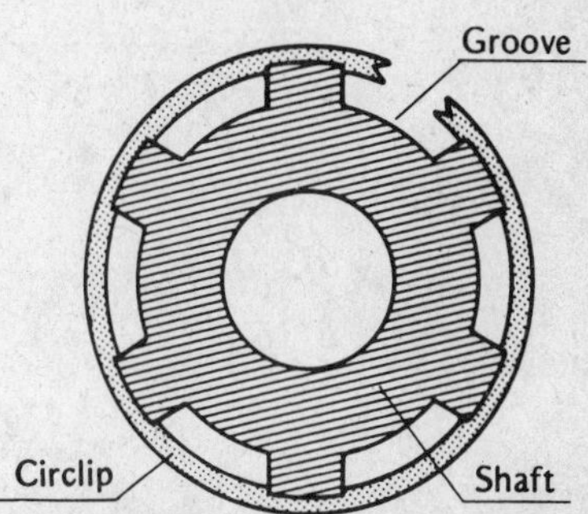

Install transmission shaft circlips as shown

Crankcase Assembly

KLT 110

1. Clean all parts thoroughly.
2. Be sure transmission shaft circlips are installed as shown in the illustration.
3. Lubricate the crankshaft and transmission components before assembling the cases.

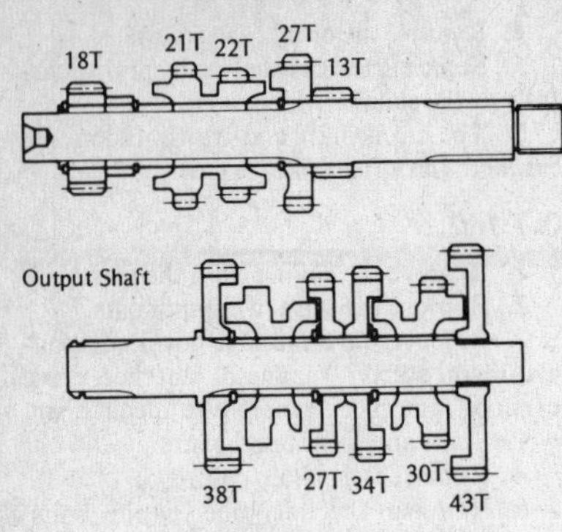

Gear positions (110)

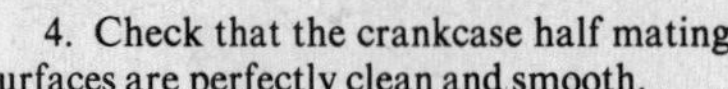

4. Check that the crankcase half mating surfaces are perfectly clean and smooth.
5. Be sure the two locating dowel pins are in place in the left crankcase half.
6. Apply a liquid gasket compound to the left crankcase half mating surface.
7. Join the halves and tighten the crankcase screws gradually and evenly until the cases are joined.
8. Check for free rotation of the transmission shafts and the crankshaft.

KLT 160

1. Clean all parts thoroughly.
2. Lubricate the crankshaft and transmission components before assembling the cases.
3. Be sure that transmission shaft circlips are installed as shown in the illustration.
4. Check that the crankcase half mating surfaces are perfectly smooth and clean.
5. Be sure the two locating dowel pins are in place in the right case half.
6. Apply a liquid gasket compound to the right crankcase half mating surface.
7. Join the halves and tighten the crankcase screws gradually and evenly until the cases are joined.
8. Check for free rotation of the transmission shafts and the crankshaft.

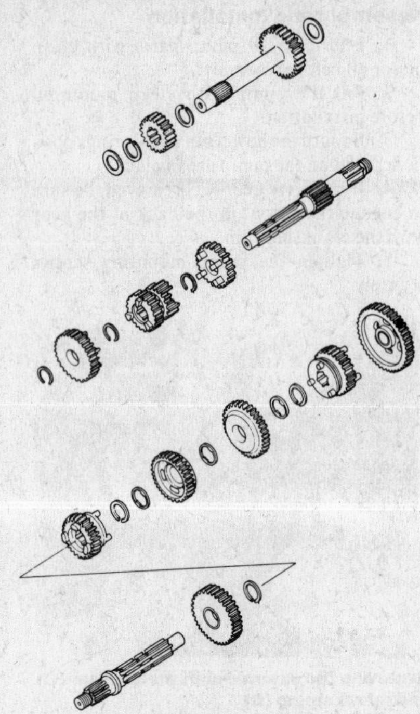

Gear cluster (160)

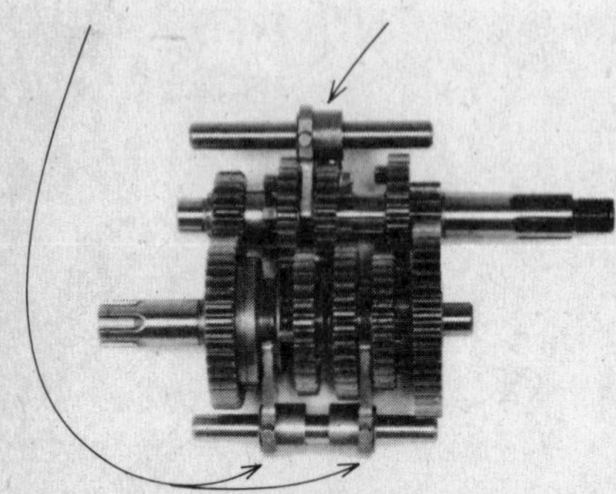

Shift fork positions (110)

Be sure the crankcase dowel pins (A) are in place

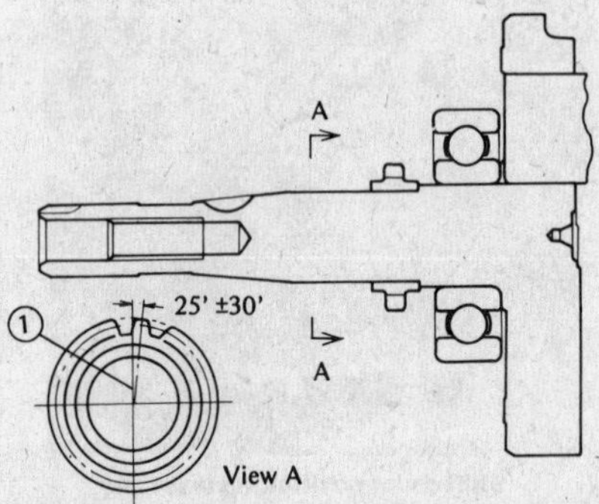

Install the cam chain sprocket on the crank as shown (1)

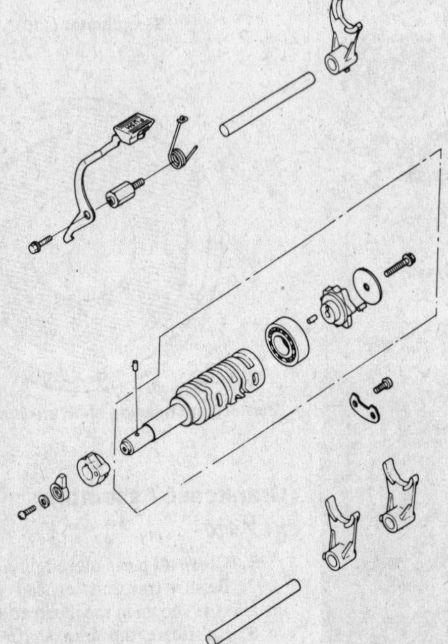

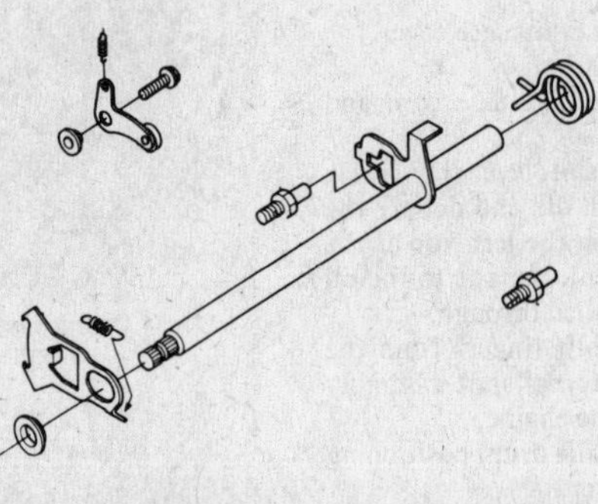

Shift assembly (160)

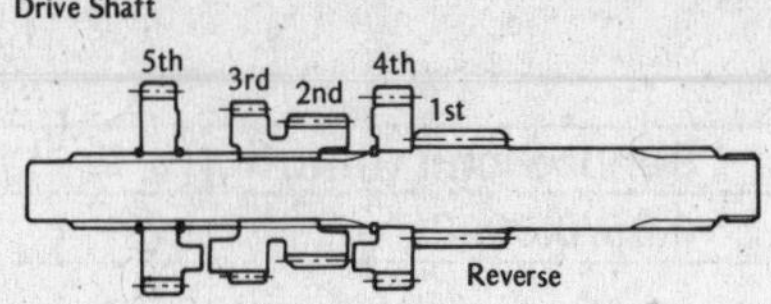

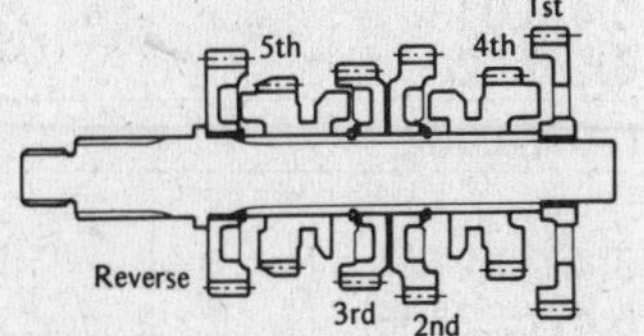

Gear positions (160)

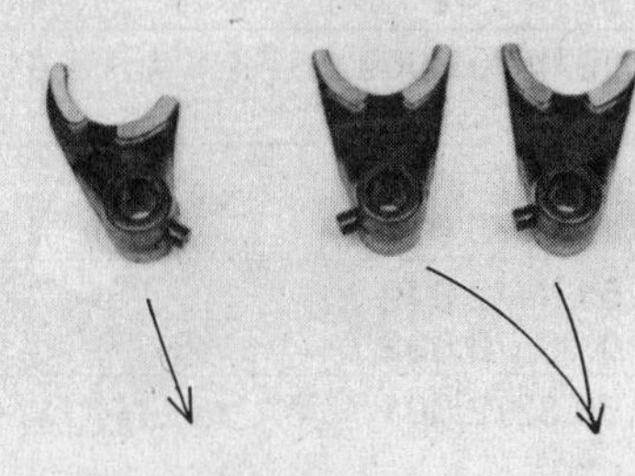

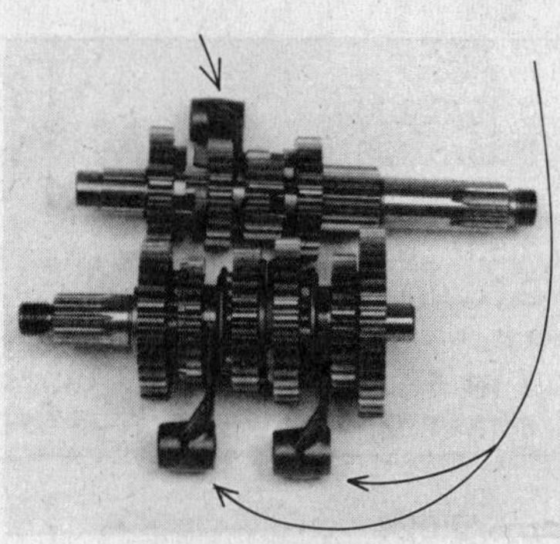

Shift fork positions (160)

Be sure the crankcase dowel pins (A) are in place

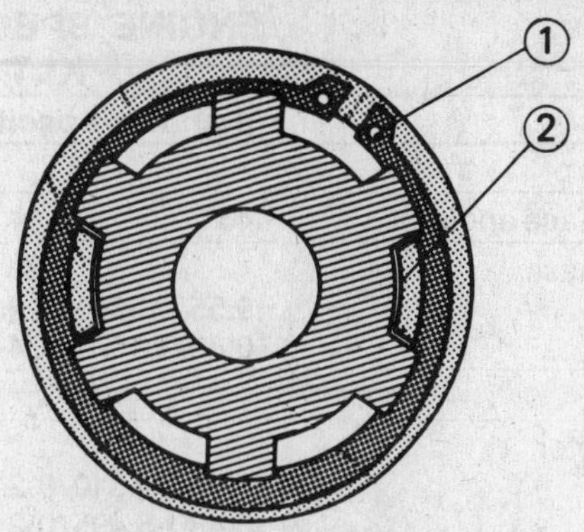

Install circlips (1) and toothed washers (2) on the transmission shafts as shown

ENGINE TORQUE SPECIFICATIONS KLT110

Component	Torque (ft lbs.)
Cylinder head bolts	
8 mm	16
6 mm	7.3
Manifold bolts	7.3
Valve adjuster locknuts	6.5
Oil pipe banjo bolts	13
Cam sprocket bolts	8.7*
Clutch housing nut	46
Secondary gear nut	53
Oil drain plug	22
Engine mounting bolts	
Front and rear	22
Cylinder head	13
Engine bracket bolts	13
Magneto rotor nut	31
Spark plug	10

*Use a non-permanent thread-locking compound

ENGINE TORQUE SPECIFICATIONS KLT 160

Component	Torque (ft lbs.)
Cylinder head bolts	
8 mm	18 (oiled)
6 mm	7.3 (oiled)
Oil pipe banjo bolts	11
Cam sprocket bolt	22 (oiled)
Valve adjuster locknuts	8.7
Recoil starter pulley bolt	43
Recoil starter shaft nut	8.7
Secondary clutch hub nut	14.5 (oiled)
Secondary clutch spring bolts	11
Primary clutch nut	14.5 (oiled)
Oil drain plug	58
Oil filter screen plug	58
Engine mounting bolts	
Front and rear	22
Cylinder head	15
Engine bracket bolts	15
Final gear bearing retainer	6.5*
Oil pipe banjo bolts	11
Shift/clutch release pins	33*
Spark plug	14.5

*Use a non-permanent thread-locking compound

ENGINE SPECIFICATIONS
KLT 110

Component	Standard Specification (mm/in.)	Service limit (mm/in.)
Cylinder head warp	—	0.05/0.0020
Valve seating surface angle	45°	—
Valve head thickness		
Intake	0.55-0.85/0.022-0.034	0.4/0.016
Exhaust	0.85-1.15/0.034-0.045	0.5/0.020
Valve bend	—	0.05/0.002
Valve stem diameter		
Intake	5.495-5.510/0.2163-0.2169	5.48/0.2157
Exhaust	5.480-5.495/0.2157-0.2163	5.47/0.2153
Valve guide ID	5.520-5.532/0.2173-0.2178	5.60/0.2210
Valve seat width		
Intake	0.80-1.15/0.031-0.0453	—
Exhaust	0.85-1.15/0.034-0.0453	—
Valve seating surface dia.		
Intake	25.1-25.3/0.988-0.996	—
Exhaust	22.2/0.874	—
Valve spring free length		
Inner (plain)	33.5/1.32	32.01.26
Inner (progressively wound)	34.8/1.37	33.2/1.31
Outer (plain)	36.8/1.45	35.5/1.40
Outer (progressively wound)	37.5/1.48	36.0/1.42
Rocker arm ID	10.000-10.015/0.3937-0.3943	10.05/0.3957
Rocker arm shaft OD	9.980-9.995/0.3929-0.3935	9.95/0.3917
Cam lobe height (IN & EX)	28.750-28.858/1.1319-1.1361	28.65/1.1280
Cam chain length (21 pins)	127.00-127.48/5.00-5.02	128.9/5.07
Cylinder ID	51.000-51.012/2.0078-2.0083	51.10/2.012
Max. allowable variation	0.001/0.0004	0.005/0.002
Piston diameter	50.965-50.980/2.0065-2.0070	50.83/2.001
Piston/cylinder clearance	0.020-0.047/0.0008-0.0019	—
Piston ring/groove clearance		
Top	0.01-0.05/0.0004-0.0020	0.15/0.006
Second	0.01-0.045/0.0004-0.0018	0.15/0.006
Piston ring groove width		
Top, second	1.20-1.22/0.047-0.048	1.30/0.051
Oil	2.50-2.52/0.098-0.099	2.60/0.102
Piston ring thickness		
Top	1.170-1.190/0.0461-0.0469	1.10/0.0433
Second	1.175-1.190/0.0463-0.0469	1.10/0.0433
Piston ring end-gap		
Top	0.10-0.30/0.004-0.012	0.6/0.024
Second	0.15-0.30/0.006-0.012	0.6/0.024
Engine sprocket dia.	41.10-41.30/1.62-1.63	40.4/1.59
Clutch friction plate thickness	2.95-3.05/0.116-0.120	2.6/0.102
Plate warpage	—	0.3/0.118
Primary gear ID	22.020-22.041/0.8669-0.8678	22.05/0.8681
Primary gear collar dia.	21.972-21.993/0.8650-0.8659	21.95/0.8642
Connecting rod bend	—	0.2 @ 100mm/0.008 @ 3.9 in.
Connecting rod twist	—	0.2 @ 100mm/0.008 @ 3.9 in.
Big end radial clearance	0.008-0.022/0.00032-0.00087	0.7/0.0028
Big end side clearance	0.3-0.5/0.012-0.020	0.7/0.028
Crankshaft run-out	—	0.1/0.0039 TIR
Shift fork finger thickness	4.9-5.0/0.193-0.197	4.8/0.189
Shift fork groove width	5.05-5.15/0.199-0.203	5.3/0.209
Shift fork guide pin dia.	4.9-5.0/0.193-0.197	4.8/0.189
Shift drum groove width	5.05-5.20/0.199-0.205	5.3/0.209

ENGINE SPECIFICATIONS
KLT160

Component	Standard Specification (mm/in.)	Service limit (mm/in.)
Cylinder head warp	—	0.05/0.0020
Valve seating surface angle	45°	—
Valve head thickness		
Intake	0.55-0.85/0.022-0.034	0.4/0.016
Exhaust	0.85-1.15/0.034-0.045	0.5/0.020
Valve bend	—	0.05/0.002
Valve stem diameter		
Intake	5.495-5.510/0.2163-0.2169	5.48/0.2157
Exhaust	5.480-5.495/0.2157-0.2163	5.47/0.2153
Valve guide ID	5.520-5.532/0.2173-0.2178	5.60/0.2210
Valve seat width (IN & EX)	0.5-1.0/0.020-0.040	—
Valve seating surface dia.		
Intake	28.9-29.1/1.14-1.15	—
Exhaust	24.9-25.1/0.98-0.99	—
Valve spring free length		
Inner	37.8/1.49	36.2/1.43
Outer	40.35/1.59	38.7/1.52
Rocker arm ID	13.000-13.018/0.5118-0.5125	13.05/0.5138
Rocker arm shaft OD	12.976-12.994/0.5109-0.5116	12.96/0.5102
Cam lobe height (IN & EX)	40.071-40.179/1.5776-1.5818	39.97/1.5736
Cam chain length (21 pins)	127.00-127.36/5.00-5.02	129.9/5.11
Cylinder ID	60.990-61.002/2.4012-2.4016	61.10/2.406
Max. allowable variation	0.01/0.0004	0.05/0.002
Piston diameter	60.950-60.965/2.3996-2.4002	60.81/2.394
Piston/cylinder clearance	0.025-0.52/0.00098-0.0020	—
Piston ring/groove clearance		
Top	0.015-0.065/0.0006-0.0026	0.17/0.007
Second	0.03-0.0.07/0.0012-0.008	0.17/0.007
Piston ring groove width		
Top	0.81-0.83/0.0319-0.0327	0.91/0.0358
Second	1.02-1.04/0.0402-0.0409	1.12/0.0440
Oil	2.51-2.53/0.0988-0.0996	2.61/0.103
Piston ring thickness		
Top	0.765-0.795/0.0301-0.0313	0.70/0.028
Second	0.97-0.99/0.0381-0.0.0390	0.90/0.035
Piston ring end-gap		
Top	0.15-0.30/0.006-0.012	0.6/0.024
Second	0.15-0.35/0.006-0.014	0.6/0.024
Primary clutch housing ID	116.0-116.2/4.567-4.575	116.5/4.587
Primary clutch shoe groove depth	1.0-1.3/0.04-0.05	0.5/0.02
Secondary clutch friction plate thickness	2.8-2.9/0.110-0.004	2.4/0.095
Secondary clutch plate warpage	0.15/0.006 (max)	0.3/0.012
Secondary clutch spring free length	24.0-25.0/0.96-1.0	23.5/0.94
Primary drive gear backlash	0.02-0.11/0.0008-0.0043	0.14/0.006
Crank diameter	23.959-23.980/0.9433-0.9441	23.94/0.943
Secondary gear ID	25.000-25.021/0.9843-0.9851	25.03/0.9854
Secondary gear collar dia.	24.970-24.985/0.9831-0.9837	24.95/0.9823
Connecting rod bend	—	0.2 @ 100 mm/0.008 @ 3.9 in.
Connecting rod twist	—	0.2 @ 100 mm/0.008 @ 3.9 in.
Big end radial clearance	0.008-0.019/0.00032-0.00075	0.07/0.0028
Big end side clearance	0.2-0.3/0.008-0.012	0.5/0.020
Crankshaft run-out	—	0.1/0.0039 TIR
Shift fork finger thickness	4.9-5.0/0.193-0.197	4.8/0.189
Shift fork groove width	5.05-5.15/0.199-0.203	5.3/0.209
Shift fork guide pin dia.	5.9-6.0/0.232-0.236	5.8/0.228
Shift drum groove width	6.05-6.20/0.238-0.244	6.3/0.248

Fuel Systems

GAS TANK

Removal

1. Remove the seat.
2. Be sure the fuel petcock is "OFF."
3. Disconnect the fuel line at the petcock.
4. Remove the bolt at the rear of the gas tank.
5. Tilt the tank up and remove it from the frame.

Inspection

1. Pour the gasoline out into a suitable container and check it for water, foreign matter, etc.
2. Remove the petcock (see below) and clean it thoroughly.

Installation

1. Be sure the rubber cushions on the frame tubes are in place.
2. Slip the tank into position. Install the bolt.
3. When fitting the fuel line, be sure it is pushed onto the fitting as far as possible and secured with the safety clip.
4. Turn on the petcock and check for leaks before operating the machine.

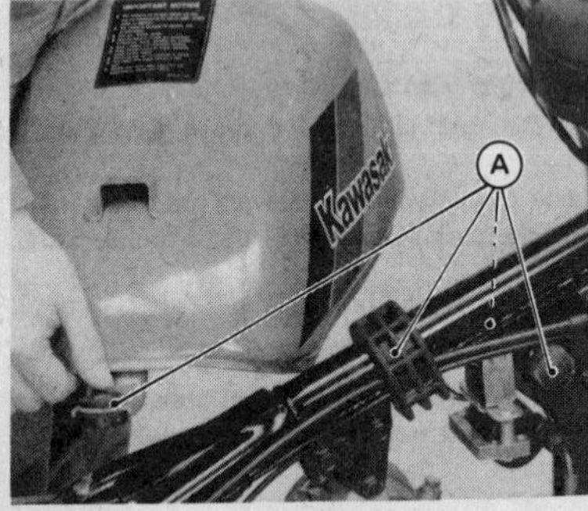

Be sure the rubber cushions on the frame (A) are in place when installing the tank

Float bowl components: float pivot pin (A), main jet (B), bleed pipe (C) and pilot jet (D)

CARBURETOR (KLT 110)

Removal

1. Be certain that the fuel petcock is "OFF."
2. Disconnect the fuel line from the petcock.

Keihin carburetor (110)

3. Disconnect the overflow line from the carburetor float bowl. Disconnect the bleed line from the side of the carburetor.
4. Loosen the carburetor cap.
5. Loosen the carburetor's manifold clamp screw.
6. Move the air cleaner hose spring away from the carburetor.
7. Pull the air cleaner hose off of the carburetor intake.
8. Pull the carburetor out of the manifold.
9. Unscrew the carb cap and pull out the throttle slide assembly.
10. Drain the gasoline remaining in the float bowl into a safe container and dispose of it properly.
11. If the throttle slide assembly is not to be serviced, wrap it in a clean cloth and arrange it out of the way to avoid damaging it.

Disassembly

1. To disassemble the throttle slide, compress the spring and disengage the cable from the slide.
2. Separate the spring and slide.
3. Remove the needle keeper spring clip. Shake the needle out of the slide.

CAUTION: *Do not remove the needle clip from the needle. Position is critical.*

4. Remove the float bowl screws.
5. Remove the float bowl carefully, taking care not to damage the float assembly. If the float bowl resists, hold it tightly and strike it with the screwdriver handle until it breaks free.
6. Pull out the float pivot pin.
7. Lift out the float assembly and needle.
8. Unscrew and remove the main jet.
9. Unscrew and remove the pilot jet.
10. Unscrew and remove the bleed pipe.
11. Push the needle jet out from the top of the carburetor with your finger or a wooden dowel.
12. Remove the throttle stop screw and pilot jet from the side of the carb. Do not loose the springs.

Inspection

1. Refer to the "General Information" section of this manual for detailed carburetor inspection procedures.
2. Clean all metal parts in a safe, mild solvent.

CAUTION: *The carburetor has non-removable plastic parts which may be damaged by a strong solvent.*

3. Clean air and fuel passages by blowing with compressed air. Do not insert wire or the like into passages as this may alter their calibrated dimensions.

Assembly

Assembly is the reverse of disassembly. Note the following points:

1. Use new O-rings, gaskets, etc.
2. The needle jet is inserted from the bottom of the carburetor, small diameter first. It will be pushed into its final position when the bleed pipe is tightened.
3. Do not overtighten jets.
4. Check that the needle clip is positioned in the fourth groove from the top.
5. When installing the pilot screw, turn it in gently until it is lightly seated, then back it out 1-3/8 turns.
6. When inserting the throttle slide assembly into the carburetor body, align the slot in the slide with the tab in the body. Do not force the slide in. Be sure the needle enters the jet correctly.
7. Be sure the floats are correctly installed. The needle tang must be lower than the pivot.
8. Check float level (see "Maintenance").

Installation

Installation is the reverse of removal. Note the following points:

1. Be sure the carburetor is firmly seated in the manifold and positioned vertically. Tighten the clamp screw securely.
2. Be sure all lines are firmly connected and are secured with safety clips.
3. Turn on the fuel and check for leaks before operating the machine.
4. Check throttle operation before attempting to start the machine.
5. Be certain the air cleaner hose is seated all around the carb intake and not folded or crimped.

CARBURETOR (KLT 160)

Removal

1. Be certain that the fuel petcock is "OFF."
2. Disconnect the fuel line from the petcock.
3. Disconnect the overflow line from the carburetor float bowl.

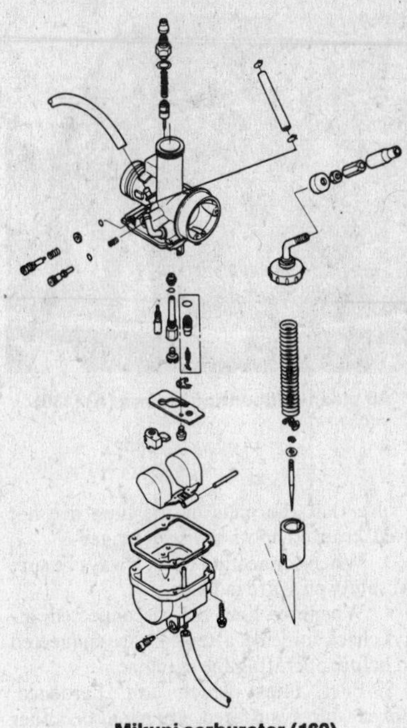

Mikuni carburetor (160)

4. Disconnect the bleed line from the side of the carburetor.
5. Unscrew the starter plunger assembly from the carburetor body.
6. Loosen the carburetor cap.
7. Loosen the carburetor's manifold clamp screw.
8. Move the air cleaner hose spring away from the carburetor.
9. Pull the air cleaner hose off of the carburetor intake.
10. Pull the carburetor out of the manifold.
11. Unscrew the carb cap and pull out the throttle slide assembly.
12. Drain the gasoline remaining in the float bowl into a safe container and dispose of it properly.
13. If the throttle slide assembly is not to be serviced, wrap it in a clean cloth and arrange it out of the way to avoid damaging it.

Disassembly

1. To disassemble the throttle slide, compress the spring and disengage the cable from the slide.
2. Separate the spring and slide.
3. Remove the needle keeper spring clip. Shake the needle out of the slide.

CAUTION: *Do not remove the needle clip from the needle. Position is critical.*

Float bowl components: float pivot pin (A), main jet (B), bleed pipe (C) and pilot jet (D)

4. Remove the float bowl screws.
5. Remove the float bowl carefully, taking care not to damage the float assembly. If the float bowl is stuck, hold it tightly and strike it with the screwdriver handle until it breaks free.
6. Remove the plastic main jet cup from the float bowl.
7. Pull out the float pivot pin.
8. Lift out the float assembly and needle.
9. Remove the plate mounting screw.
10. Remove the needle seat holder.
11. Remove the needle seat and O- ring.
12. Unscrew and remove the main jet.
13. Unscrew and remove the pilot jet.
14. Unscrew and remove the bleed pipe. There is an O-ring above the bleed pipe. Shake it out now or with the needle jet.
15. Push the needle jet out from the top of the carburetor with your finger or with a wooden dowel. Note the O-ring located below the jet, if it has not already been removed.
16. Remove the throttle stop and pilot screws along with their springs and O-rings.

Inspection

1. Refer to the "General Information" section of this manual for detailed carburetor inspection procedures.
2. Clean all metal parts in a safe, mild solvent.

CAUTION: *The carburetor has non-removable plastic parts which may be damaged by a strong solvent.*

3. Check the condition of the starter plunger O-ring and replace it if it is knicked or damaged.
4. Clean air and fuel passages by blowing with compressed air. Do not insert wire or the like into passages as this may alter their calibrated bores.

Assembly

Assembly is the reverse of disassembly. Note the following points:

1. Use new O-rings and gaskets.
2. The needle jet is inserted into the bottom of the carburetor, long end first. It will be pushed into its final position when the bleed pipe is tightened.

The long end on the needle jet (A) is inserted first

3. Do not forget the O-ring installed above the bleed pipe.
4. Do not forget the throttle stop and pilot screw O-rings.
5. Check that the needle clip is positioned in the fourth groove from the top.
6. When installing the pilot screw, turn it in gently until it is lightly seated, then back it out 1- 1/4 turns.
7. When installing the throttle slide in the carburetor, be sure it is positioned correctly. Do not force the slide in. Be sure the needle enters the jet correctly.
8. Check float level (see "Maintenance").

Installation

Installation is the reverse of removal. Note the following points:

1. Be sure the carburetor is firmly seated in the manifold and positioned vertically. Tighten the clamp screw securely.
2. Be sure all lines are firmly connected and are secured with safety clips.
3. Turn on the fuel and check for leaks before operating the machine.
4. Check throttle operation before attempting to start the machine.
5. Be certain the air cleaner hose is seated all around the carburetor intake and not folded or crimped.

FUEL PETCOCK

The fuel petcock is fitted with filter screens on the pipes inside the fuel tank.

Removal

1. Remove the fuel tank.
2. Drain off the gasoline.
3. Remove the petcock securing bolts with washers and remove the petcock.

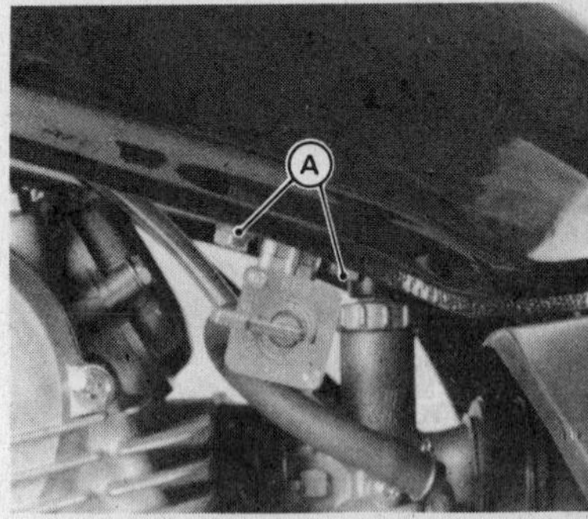

Petcock mounting screws (A)

Petcock filter screens

Inspection

1. Clean the filter screens in a solvent to remove all dirt and other foreign matter.
2. Check filter screen condition. If punctured, or if they cannot be properly cleaned, replace them.
3. Check the condition of the petcock O-ring and replace it if deformed, knicked or otherwise defective.

4. Check the condition of the nylon washers and replace as necessary.
5. Clean the petcock mating surface on the tank to ensure a good seal.

Installation

1. Fit the petcock, nylon washers and bolts. Tighten them evenly.
2. Connect the fuel line and ensure it is secured with the safety clip.
3. Check for leaks before operating the machine.

AIR CLEANER

NOTE: *See "Maintenance" for filter element service.*

Removal

1. Remove the seat.
2. Remove the rear fender.
3. Remove the filter element.
4. Remove the air cleaner mounting bolts.
5. Disconnect the hose to the mouth of the carburetor.
6. Lift the air cleaner out of the frame.

Air cleaner mounting screws (A) (110)

Air cleaner mounting screws (A) (160)

Installation

Installation is the reverse of removal.

FUEL LINES

1. Fuel lines should be checked periodically for condition.
2. Whenever fuel lines are disconnected, be sure that the ends of the lines are not rotted, cracked or otherwise damaged.
3. When connecting lines, always be sure that safety clips are in place.
4. Whenever lines are disconnected, always check for leaks after they are connected and before operating the machine.
5. Fuel lines which are hardened, cracked, have suffered abrasion or other damage must be replaced.

CARBURETOR SPECIFICATIONS

	KLT 110	KLT 160
Make	Keihin	Mikuni
Type	PC 18	VM22SS
Main jet	102	110
Main air jet	130	—
Pilot jet	35	22.5
Starter jet	—	35
Throttle slide cutaway	3.0	3.5
Jet needle	N17A	5J14
Needle clip position	4th from top	4th from top
Needle jet	—	0-2
Pilot screw (turns out)	1 3/8	1 1/4
Service fuel level (mm/in.)	2.5 ± 1/0.10 + 0.04	5.0 ± 1/0.20 ± 0.04
Float Height (mm/in.)	20/0.8	33.3/1.3

Electrical System

IGNITION SYSTEM

CAUTION: *Do not run the engine with any wiring leads disconnected. This may cause damage to sensitive electronic components.*

1. In the event of no spark or a weak spark, first check spark plug condition.
2. If a new plug does not remedy the problem, remove the spark plug cap from the high tension lead and check cap resistance with an ohmmeter. If the cap is electrically open, replace it.
3. Before beginning extensive system troubleshooting procedures, first check wiring and connectors. Be sure that all connectors are clean and dry. Check wiring for defective insulation, breaks and other obvious signs of damage.
4. If the problem cannot be isolated in this manner, check ignition system components as follows.

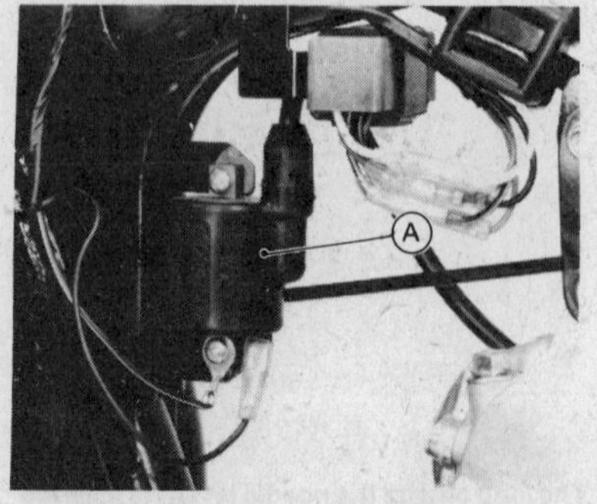

Ignition coil (A) (110)

Ignition Coil

1. The ignition coil is located beneath the fuel tank and can be checked in place.
2. An ohmmeter is used to check primary and secondary coil resistance.
3. Remove the seat. See "Chassis."
4. Remove the gas tank. See "Fuel Systems."
5. Disconnect the low tension lead from the ignition coil. The lead is black on the 110 and green/white on the 160.
6. Measure the resistance between the low tension terminal on the coil and the coil core. It should be:
   KLT 110: 0.34-0.52 ohms
   KLT 160: 0.18-0.28 ohms
7. If the primary winding resistance is too high, it indicates a broken circuit. If too low, it shows defective insulation. In either case, the ignition coil must be replaced.
8. Check secondary coil resistance by first disconnecting the lead from the spark plug. Remove the spark plug cap from the lead.
9. Check the resistance between the high tension lead and the coil core. It should be 3.2-4.8 K ohms for both models. Resistance which is too low indicates a short in the coil; resistance which is too high indicates broken wiring. In either case, the coil must be replaced.

Ignition coil (A) (160)

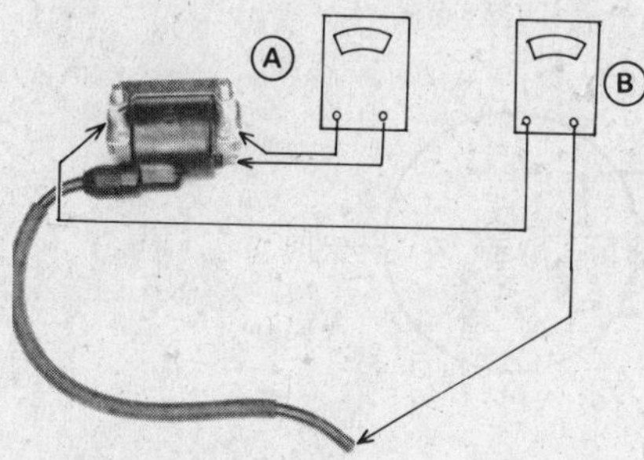

Checking primary winding (A) and secondary winding (B) resistance

NOTE: *When replacing the coil, ensure that the contact surfaces are clean and all connections clean and tight.*

Exciter Coil

KLT 110

1. To check the exciter coil, disconnect the red lead from the harness on the frame behind the engine.
2. Check resistance between the red lead and ground on the engine.
3. The reading should be 180-280 ohms. If exciter coil resistance is not within this range, replace the magneto stator.

KLT 160

1. To check the exciter coil, disconnect the red and black/red leads at the plastic connector on the frame behind the engine.
2. Check resistance across the red and black/red leads.
3. The reading should be 100-190 ohms. If the exciter coil resistance is not within this range, replace the magneto stator.

Pickup Coil

KLT 110

1. To check pickup coil resistance, disconnect the magneto wires at the plastic connector behind the engine.
2. Measure the resistance between the brown and the white leads.
3. It should be 90-140 ohms. If the reading is not within this range, replace the pickup coil.

Pickup coil (A) air gap (B) should be 0.7 mm (0.03 in.)

KLT 160

1. To check pickup coil resistance, disconnect the pickup coil leads (black and black/yellow) at the plastic connector.
2. Check resistance between the black and black/yellow wires. It should be 90-160 ohms.
3. If the reading is not within this range, replace the pickup coil.
4. Remove the left side engine cover.
5. Check the air gap between the pickup coil and the projection on the magneto rotor.

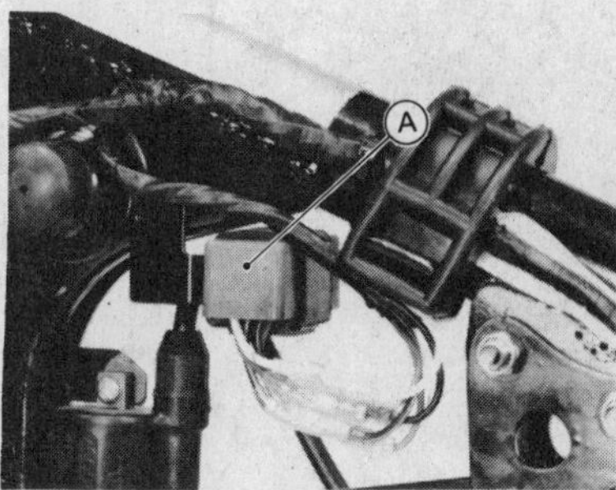

CDI unit (110)

CDI unit (160)

Meter Negative (−) Lead Connection	Meter Positive (+) Lead Connection					
Lead (Lead Color)	Pickup Coil (White)	Pickup Coil (Chocolate)	Ground (Black/Yellow)	Ignition Coil (Black)	Exciter Coil (Red)
Pickup Coil (White)		40 – 160 kΩ	40 – 160 kΩ	∞	60 – 500 kΩ
Pickup Coil (Chocolate)	30 – 150 kΩ		0 Ω	∞	1 – 6 kΩ
Ground (Black/Yellow)	30 – 150 kΩ	0 Ω		∞	1 – 6 kΩ
Ignition Coil (Black)	60 – 240 kΩ	1 – 6 kΩ	1 – 6 kΩ		5 – 20 kΩ
Exciter Coil (Red)	250 – 1,000 kΩ	60 – 240 kΩ	60 – 240 kΩ	∞	

CDI unit specifications (110)

Unit: kΩ

Meter Negative (−) Lead Connection	Meter Positive (+) Lead Connection						
Lead Color	R	BK/R	BK	BL	G/W	BK/W	BK/Y
R		∞	∞	∞	∞	∞	∞
BK/R	25 – 180		10 – 50	10 – 50	∞	35 – 180	10 – 50
BK	2 – 10	2 – 10		0.1 – 0.4	∞	2 – 10	0.1 – 0.4
BL	2 – 9	2 – 10	0.1 – 0.4		∞	2 – 10	0
G/W	∞	∞	∞	∞		∞	∞
BK/W	0	∞	∞	∞	∞		∞
BK/Y	2 – 10	2 – 10	0.1 – 0.4	0	∞	2 – 10	

CDI unit specifications (160)

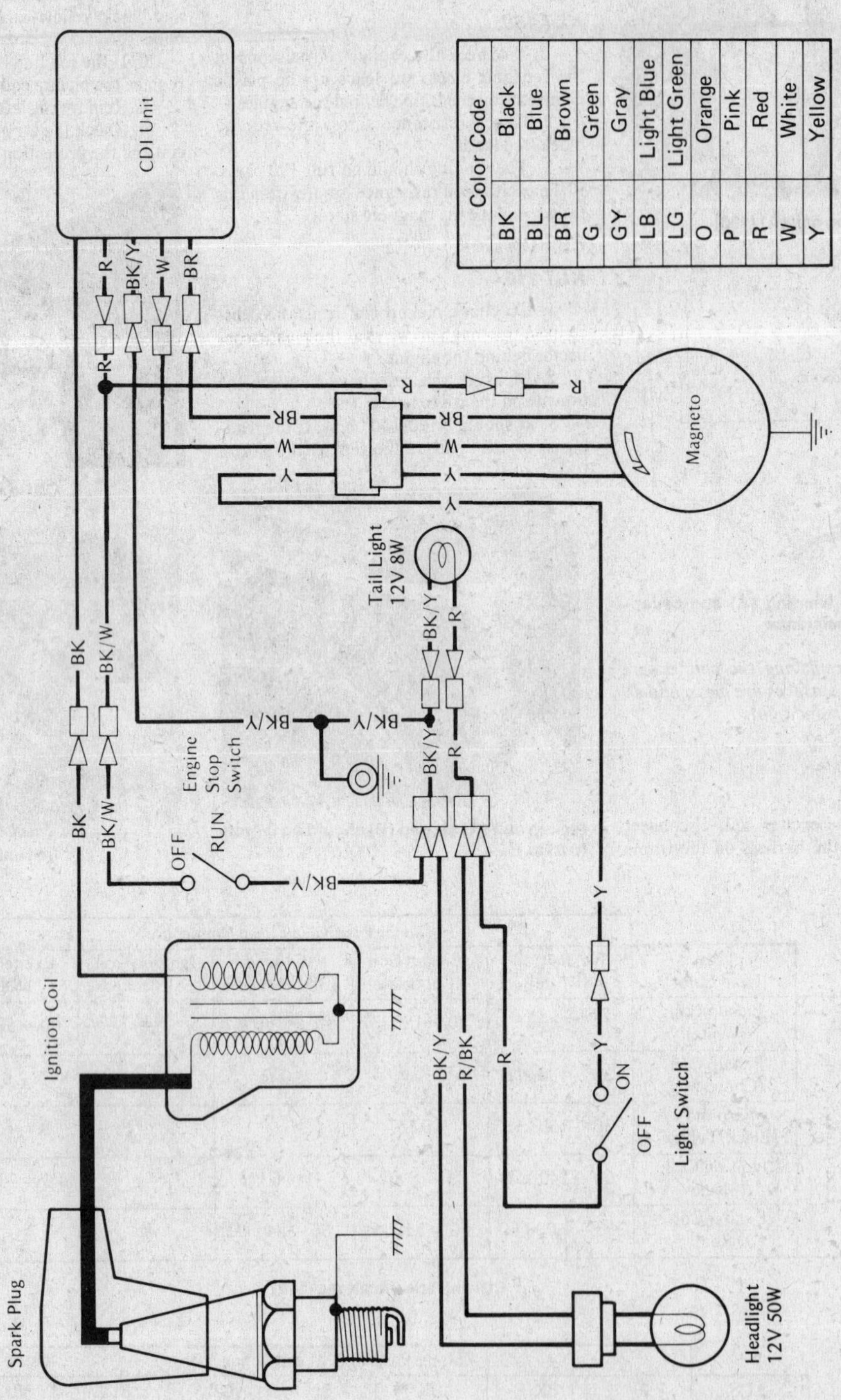

Color Code	
BK	Black
BL	Blue
BR	Brown
G	Green
GY	Gray
LB	Light Blue
LG	Light Green
O	Orange
P	Pink
R	Red
W	White
Y	Yellow

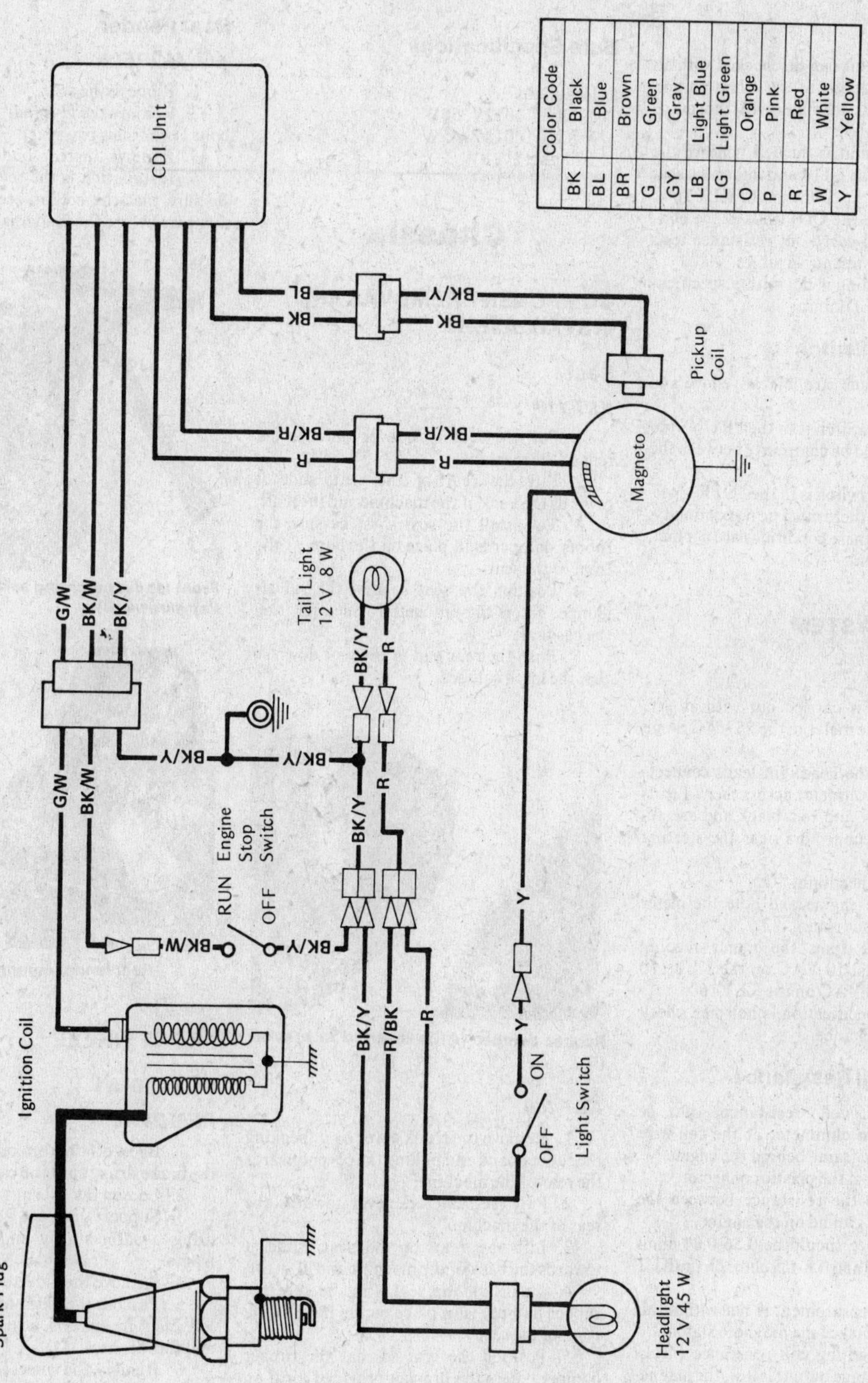

Color Code	
BK	Black
BL	Blue
BR	Brown
G	Green
GY	Gray
LB	Light Blue
LG	Light Green
O	Orange
P	Pink
R	Red
W	White
Y	Yellow

KLT 160

6. The air gap should be 0.7mm (0.03 in.). If it is not correct, loosen the two mounting screws and reposition the coil to give the correct gap.

CDI Unit

1. The CDI unit can be checked with an ohmmeter if inspection of the other ignition system components does not reveal the source of the problem.
2. The CDI unit is located beneath the fuel tank on the KLT 110 and under the seat on the left side of the frame on the KLT 160.
3. Disconnect the CDI leads at the plastic connector and carry out resistance tests according to accompanying tables.
4. If any reading is not within specification, replace the CDI unit.

Engine Stop Switch

1. Switch leads are black/yellow and black/white.
2. When the switch is in the "RUN" position, there should be continuity between the two leads.
3. When the switch is in the "OFF" position (either one), there must be no continuity.
4. If both of these conditions are not met, replace the switch.

LIGHTING SYSTEM

AC Output

1. This test is carried out with an AC voltmeter. Set the meter to the 25 VAC range or equivalent.
2. Leaving the headlight leads connected, connect the voltmeter across them. Leads are black/yellow and red/black and are accessible at the connectors near the steering head lug.
3. Turn the headlight "ON."
4. Start the engine and note the meter readings at various rpm.
5. At 3,000 rpm, the meter reading should be at least 10 VAC on the KLT 110 and at least 11.5 VAC on the KLT 160.
6. If this specification is not met, check lighting coil resistance.

Lighting Coil Resistance

1. Lighting coil resistance can be checked with an ohmmeter at the coil wire connector on the frame behind the engine.
2. Disconnect the plastic connector.
3. Measure the resistance between the yellow lead and ground on the engine.
4. Resistance should be 0.56-0.84 ohms on the KLT 110 and 0.8-1.5 ohms on the KLT 160.
5. If the measurement is not within this specification, replace the magneto stator.
6. If the lighting coil resistance checks out, but AC voltage output is low, the magneto rotor magnets may be defective. Replacing the rotor is the solution.

Light Switch

1. Check the light switch by disconnecting the yellow and red switch leads at the connectors near the steering head lug.
2. When an ohmmeter is placed across the leads, it should show no resistance when the switch is in the "ON" position and infinite resistance when the switch is in the "OFF" position.
3. If both of these conditions are not met, replace the light switch.

Bulb Specifications

Headlight
KLT 110 12V, 50W
KLT 160 12V, 45W
Tailight 12V, 8W

Chassis

COMPONENT REMOVAL AND INSTALLATION

Seat

KLT 110

1. Pull the seat lock lever towards the rear of the machine.
2. Lift the rear of the seat, slide it towards the back of the machine and lift it off.
3. To install the seat, first be sure the rubber damper is in place on the hook at the front of the seat.
4. Position the seat so that the rubber damper enters the bracket provided for it on the gas tank.
5. Push the rear end of the seat down so that the latch catches.

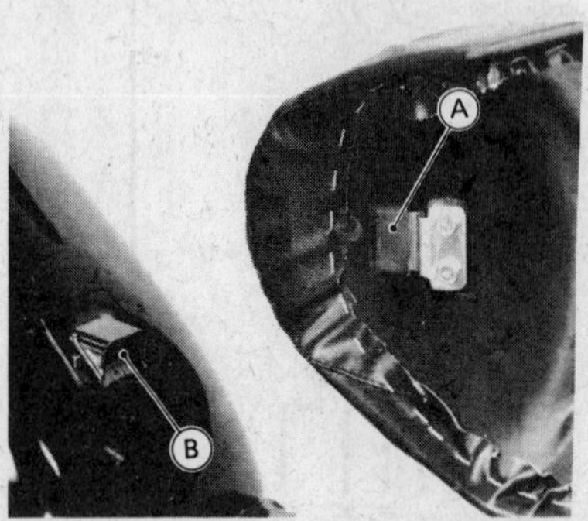

Rubber damper (A) is inserted in bracket (B)

KLT 160

1. Remove the trunk cover by unhooking the rubber band and pulling the cover towards the rear of the machine.
2. Pull the seat lock lever towards the rear of the machine.
3. Lift the rear of the seat, slide it towards the back of the machine and lift it off.
4. To install the seat, first be sure the rubber damper is in place on the hook at the front of the seat.
5. Position the seat so that the rubber damper enters the bracket provided for it on the gas tank.
6. Push the rear end of the seat down so that the latch catches.
7. Slip the hooks on the front of the trunk cover into the slots on the seat bracket. Connect the rubber band.

Front Fender

ALL MODELS

1. Remove the front wheel.
2. Remove the four fender mounting bolts and lockwasher and flat washer on each.
3. Remove the fender.
4. Installation is the reverse of removal.

Rear Fender

ALL MODELS

1. Remove the seat.
2. Remove the four rear fender mounting bolts (two front, two rear).
3. Remove the rear fender.
4. Installation is the reverse of removal. Be sure that the collars are in place in the dampers before the fender is mounted.

Front fender mounting screws (A) and mudflap screws (B)

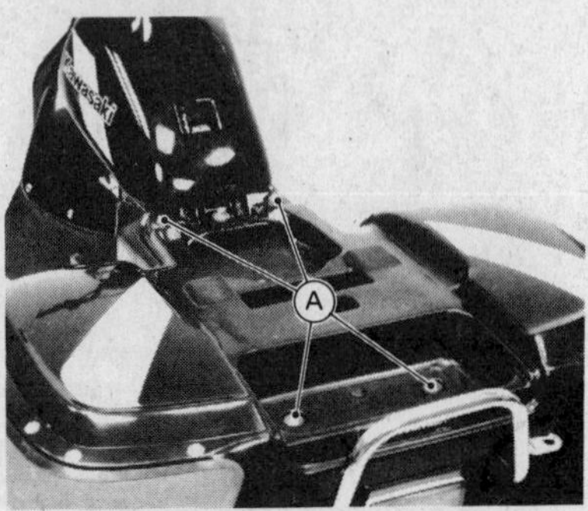

Rear fender mounting bolts (A)

FRONT WHEEL

KLT 110-A1

REMOVAL

1. Back off the brake cable adjuster at the brake drum until the cable is slack.
2. Loosen the axle nut.
3. Support the front wheel off the ground using a safe, sturdy support beneath the frame.
4. Remove the axle nut.
5. Pull out the axle noting location of the left and right spacers, bearing cap (right side) and flat washers.
6. Remove the wheel from the forks.
7. Remove the brake plate from the drum.
8. Remove the lug nuts and separate the hub from the wheel.

NOTE: *If the wheel bearings are going to be removed, leave the hub on the wheel.*

INSTALLATION

1. Mount the hub on the wheel, positioning it so that the valve stem is on the opposite side of the wheel from the drum.

2. Install the lug nuts and tighten them in a cross pattern until the correct torque of 30 ft. lbs. is reached.
3. Place the brake plate in the drum.
4. Lightly grease the axle with a medium- weight chassis grease.
5. Install the left-side flat washer and left-side spacer on the axle.
6. Position the wheel/brake assembly in the forks, ensuring that the fork lug engages the slot on the brake plate.
7. Slide the wheel in place and slide the axle through enough to hold it.
8. Position the bearing cap and the right-side spacer between the wheel and the fork and push the axle through.
9. Place the flat washer on the axle.
10. Install the axle nut.
11. Adjust the brake and apply it several times to center the brake plate.
12. Tighten the axle nut to 54 ft. lbs.
13. Make final brake adjustment as outlined in "Maintenance."

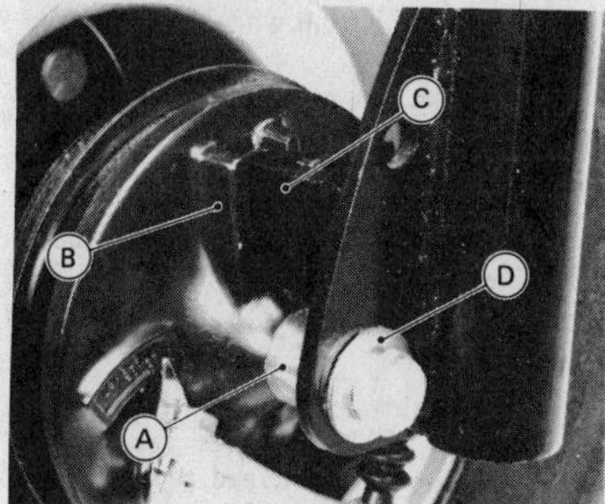

Be sure spacer (A) and flat washer (D) are in place; engage fork lug (C) with slot (B)

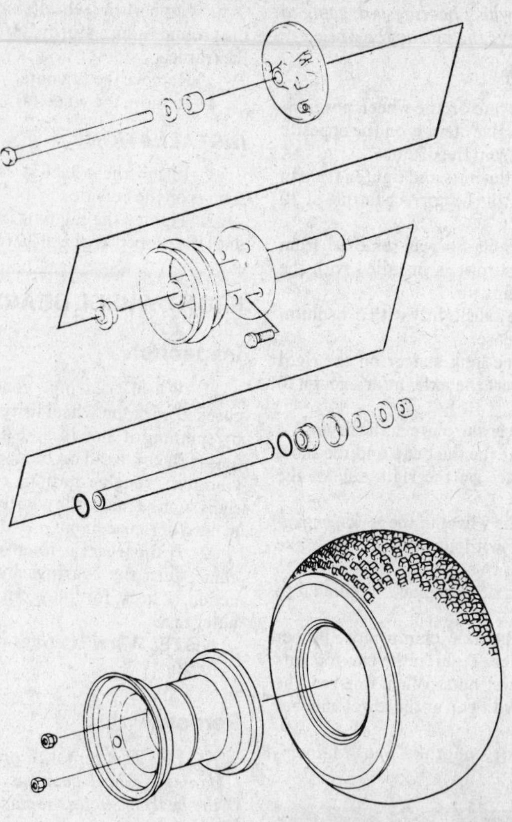

Front wheel assembly (110-A1)

KLT 110-A2, KLT 160

REMOVAL

1. Run the cable adjuster at the brake drum down until the cable is slack.
2. Loosen the four axle clamp nuts on the right side of the axle.
3. Support the front wheel a couple of inches off the ground by placing a sturdy, safe support beneath the frame.
4. Unscrew and remove the axle, sliding it out to the right side.
5. Note the locations of the spacers and bearing cap.
6. Remove the wheel from the forks.
7. Remove the brake plate from the drum.
8. Remove the four lug nuts and separate the hub from the wheel.

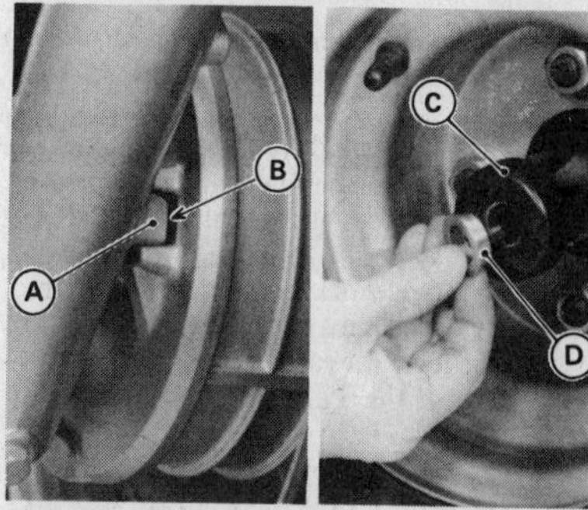

Engage fork lug (A) with slot (B); be sure dust seal (C) and spacer (D) are in place

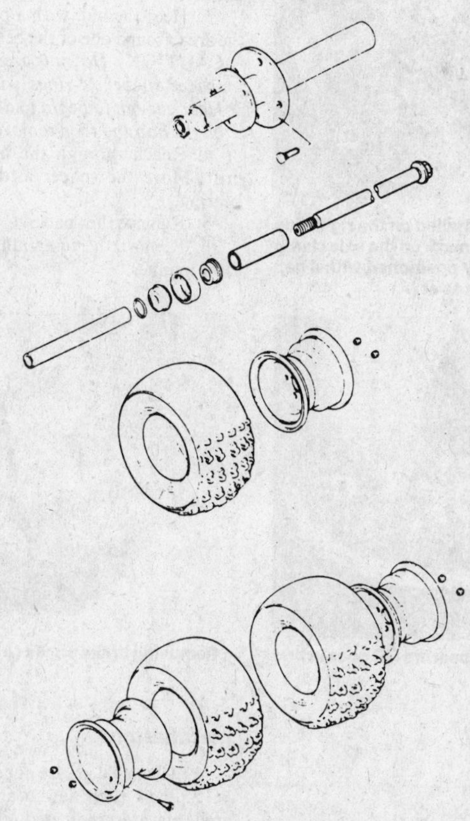

Front wheel assembly (110-A2, 160)

NOTE: *If the wheel bearings are going to be removed, leave the hub on the wheel.*

INSTALLATION

1. Mount the hub on the wheel, positioning it so that the valve stem is on the opposite side of the wheel from the drum.
2. Install the lug nuts and tighten them in a cross pattern until the correct torque of 30 ft. lbs. is reached.
3. If the axle clamp was removed from the fork leg, be sure it is installed with the "UP" mark pointing up.
4. Grease the axle lightly with a medium-weight chassis grease.
5. Position the long spacer on the right fork tube and insert the axle in far enough to hold it.
6. Install the brake plate in the drum.
7. Check that the dust cap and the short spacer are in place on the right side of the wheel.
8. Position the wheel in the forks, engaging the fork lug with the slot in the brake plate.
9. Slide the axle into place. Tighten it to 51 ft. lbs.
10. Tighten the axle clamp nuts. Proper torque is 7.3 ft. lbs. Tighten the two top nuts first, then the lower nuts. When finished, the clamp should have a gap at the lower end, but not the upper.
11. Adjust the front brake. See "Maintenance."

Long spacer (D) is installed on the right side of the axle. The "UP" mark on the axle clamp (C) must be correctly positioned with a gap at (B) and flush surfaces at (A)

The long side of the bearing (A) goes in first

REAR WHEELS

All Models

REMOVAL

1. Loosen the four lug nuts on the wheel(s) you wish to remove.
2. Support the wheel(s) an inch or so off the ground using a sturdy, safe stand beneath the frame.
3. Remove the lug nuts.
4. Remove the wheel(s).

INSTALLATION

1. Install the wheel(s) so that the valve stem is on the outside.
2. Tighten the lug nuts in a cross pattern until the proper torque of 30 ft. lbs. is reached.

FRONT WHEEL BEARINGS

Inspection

1. Wheel bearing condition can be checked with the wheel installed in the forks by spinning it slowly and listening for any noise. Place a hand on the fork tube to detect vibration, rough rotation, etc. If there are signs such as these, the wheel bearings may be in need of replacement.
2. If the wheel is removed from the machine, turn the bearings by hand to check action. Check for play between inner and outer races.

NOTE: *Wheel bearings must be replaced in pairs.*

Removal

NOTE: *The removal procedure usually damages wheel bearings. Do not remove the bearings unless replacement is intended.*

1. Remove the front wheel from the machine.
2. Remove the brake plate from the drum.
3. Heat the hub with a propane torch in the area around one of the bearings.

CAUTION: *Do not overheat. Bearings spacer rubber O-rings will be damaged. Heat enough to begin to discolor the paint on the hub and then remove heat source.*

4. Reach through the hub with a long drift. Move the spacer aside. Tap out the bearing.
5. Remove the spacer.
6. Remove the remaining bearing in the same manner.

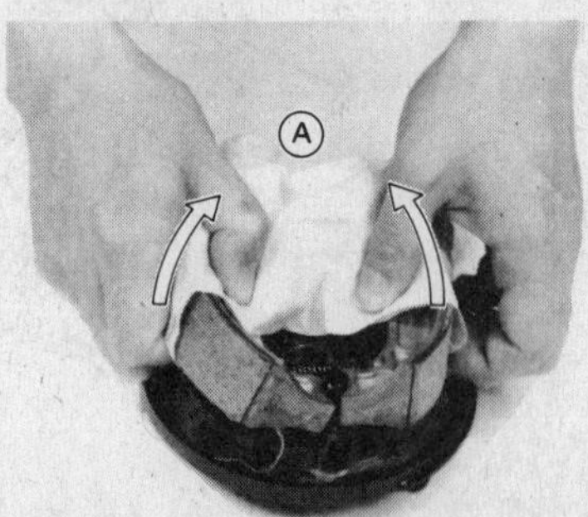

Removing brake shoes (A) from the drum

Installation

1. Clean old grease out of the hub.
2. Pack each new bearing with a good grade of waterproof, medium-weight bearing grease. Place a quantity of the grease in the hub.
3. Clean and deburr the bearing seats in the hub.
4. Install one bearing. The long side of the bearing (relative to the circlip) goes in first (sealed side out). Use a suitably-sized bearing driver to drive the bearing straight into its seat. Be sure it is not cocked or tilted.
5. Before the spacer is installed, check O-ring condition. Replace the O-rings if they show signs of damage.
6. Position an O-ring about 6mm from each end of the spacer.
7. Install the spacer.
8. Install the remaining bearing (long side in, sealed side out).

FRONT BRAKE

Removal And Disassembly

1. Run down the front brake cable adjusters as far as possible.
2. Disconnect the cable from the brake lever on the drum.
3. Remove the front wheel from the machine.
4. Remove the brake plate from the drum.
5. Remove the drum, if required, by taking off the three nuts and bolts.
6. Brake components can be inspected in place. See below.

Inspection

1. Check the general condition of the brake linings. If the linings are scored, grooved or otherwise damaged, replace them.
2. Check the linings for an oil-soaked condition. If there are signs of lubricant penetration, they must be replaced.
3. Measure lining thickness. If either of them measures less than 1.5mm (0.6 in.) at the thinnest point, replace them.
4. Check the condition of the brake drum. If the inner surface is scored or grooved, the drum may have to be replaced. It may be possible to have the drum turned down on a lathe to remove minor scoring, but the final drum inside diameter must not exceed the wear limit specification (see below).
5. Measure the inside diameter of the brake drum. If it exceeds 110.75mm (4.36 in.), replace it.
6. Check that the drum is not cracked.
7. Remove rust, dirt and corrosion from the brake drum with emery cloth.
8. Break the glaze on brake linings with emery cloth.

CAUTION: *Do not blow out brake components with compressed air or breathe brake dust. It represents a health hazard.*

9. To replace the linings, grasp both of the shoes and fold them towards the center of the brake plate.
10. Check the condition of the brake return springs. Replace the pair if they are broken, deformed, badly rusted or seem weak.
11. To remove the brake cam from the plate, first scribe a mark on lever and cam to position the lever for easy installation.
12. Remove the brake lever pinch bolt and carefully pull the lever off the cam.
13. Tap the cam out of the brake plate from the outside. Note O-ring location.
14. Clean the cam in solvent and use emery cloth to remove any rust or corrosion.

15. Check the diameter of the cam bushing area and replace it if the measurement is less than 11.8mm (0.47 in.).

16. Check the diameter of the brake plate hole and replace the plate if the measurement exceeds 12.7mm (0.51 in.).

17. Check that the cam is not bent and that the lever splines are not torn or broken.

18. Check the brake plate for cracks.

Assembly And Installation

1. Clean all metal parts thoroughly in a solvent.

2. Lubricate the brake cam bushing area and brake shoe seat with a waterproof, medium-weight chassis grease.

3. Install the cam in the brake plate. The mark on the brake shoe seat must point towards the center of the plate.

4. Fit the brake cam O-ring.

5. Fit the brake lever on the cam, aligning the position marks made prior to removal.

6. Install and tighten the lever pinch bolt.

7. Lightly grease the brake shoe pivot on the brake plate. Lubricate the brake shoe holes to which the return springs attach.

CAUTION: *Keep lubricant well clear of the linings. Do not use too much as it may work its way onto the linings.*

8. Assemble the shoes and return springs.

9. Install the shoes and springs onto the brake plate. Ensure that they are firmly seated.

10. Install the brake drum on the hub if it was removed. Tighten the bolts and nuts to 22 ft. lbs.

11. The remainder of the procedure is the reverse of removal.

FRONT FORKS (KLT 110- A1)

Removal

1. Remove the front wheel.

2. Remove the front fender (four bolts, washers).

3. Remove the gas tank. See "Fuel Systems."

4. Disconnect the brake cables from both hand levers. The front brake cable is already free. The rear brake adjusters must be run down to provide enough slack to effect removal.

5. Remove the throttle lever housing mounting bolts.

6. Remove the screws which secure the switch housing to the left side of the handlebars.

7. Remove the screws which securę the rubber cover to the upper triple clamp. Remove the cover.

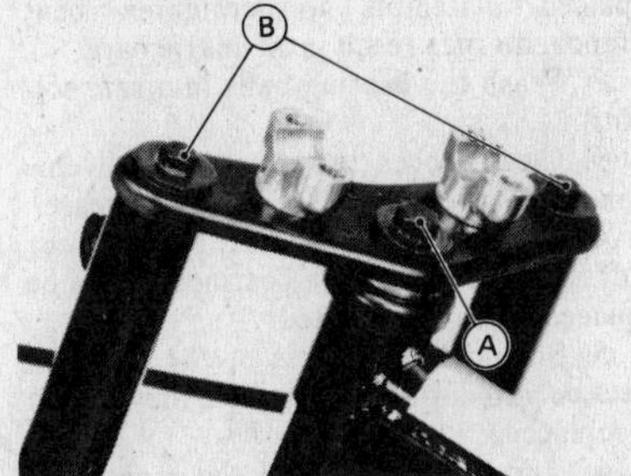

Steering stem bolt (A); upper triple clamp bolts (B)

8. Remove the handlebar clamp bolts.

9. Remove the handlebars.

10. Remove the headlight.

11. Remove the steering stem bolt and washer.

12. Remove the upper triple clamp bolts above the fork tubes. Remove the washers.

13. Remove the upper triple clamp.

14. Support the fork assembly with one hand and unscrew the steering stem bearing adjuster nut.

CAUTION: *Steering stem bearing balls may come out as the nut is loosened.*

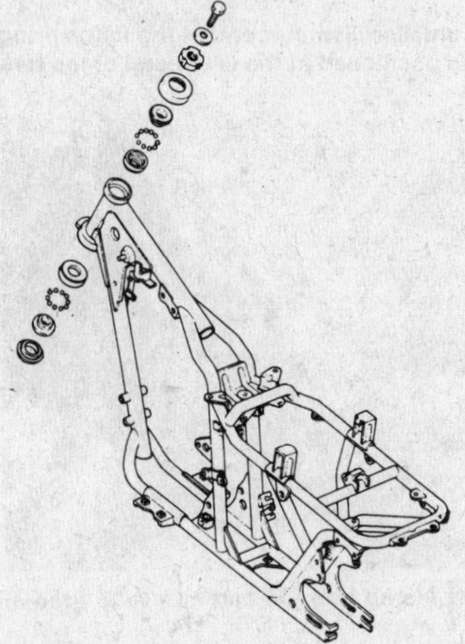

Steering stem bearing assembly (all models)

15. Remove the dust cover from the steering stem.

16. Remove the upper race from the steering stem.

17. Lower the forks until they are clear of the frame.

18. Remove the bearing balls from the lower race to avoid loss.

Inspection

1. If the fork tubes or the steering stem are bent, the assembly must be replaced.

2. Wash the bearing balls in a safe solvent.

3. Clean the bearing races with a solvent-soaked rag to remove all traces of old grease.

4. Check the balls for rust, pitting, wear and/or flat spots. All of the bearings should be replaced if damage is noted.

5. Should the surfaces of the bearing races be pitted, rusted or rippled, they should be replaced.

6. Run a finger around the races. The surfaces must be smooth and without indentations, ripples or other imperfections.

7. To replace the races in the frame lug, drive them out with a hammer and drift. The race on the steering stem is removed with a hammer and chisel.

Installation

1. New steering stem races are fitted to the head lug by driving them in with a suitable driver. Be sure that they are driven straight in and are fully seated.

2. Smear the races with a good grade of waterproof, medium-weight bearing grease and imbed the bearing balls in the frame race and the steering stem race.

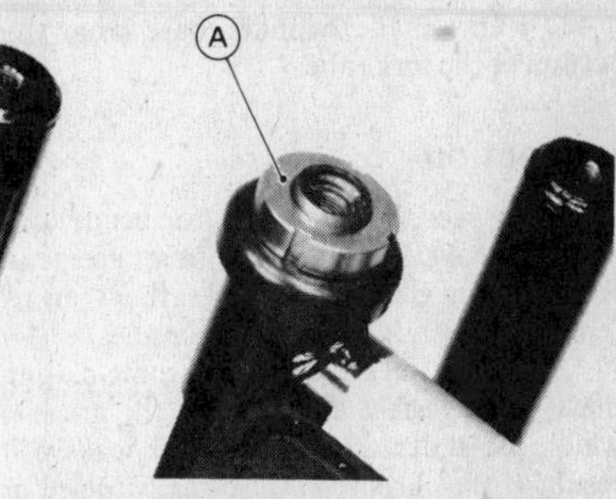

Steering stem bearing adjuster nut (A)

3. Bearing ball specifications are:

Upper: 6mm, 23 ea.
Lower: 8mm, 19 ea.

4. Slip the forks into the frame head lug ensuring that none of the balls in the lower race are lost.

5. Hold the forks in place while installing the upper race, dust cover and adjuster nut.

6. Adjust the bearings as outlined in "Maintenance."

7. The remainder of the procedure is the reverse of removal. Note the following torque ratings:

Upper triple clamp bolts: 22 ft. lbs.
Steering stem bolt: 40 ft. lbs.
Handlebar clamp bolts: 13 ft. lbs.

HYDRAULIC FRONT FORKS

Removal

1. Remove the front wheel.

2. Loosen the two clamp bolts securing each fork tube to the steering stem assembly.

3. Hold the fork tube. Remove the upper clamp bolt.

4. Remove the fork tube.

Disassembly

1. Loosen the clamp screw and pull off the rubber boot.

2. Press down on the plug at the top of the fork tube and remove the retaining ring.

3. Holding the plug against the fork spring tension, release pressure slowly until spring tension is released.

4. Remove the top plug with the O-ring.

5. Remove the short spring.

6. Remove the spring seat.

7. Remove the long spring.

8. Pour off the old fork oil.

9. Remove the allen bolt and gasket from the bottom of the fork slider. Separate the fork components.

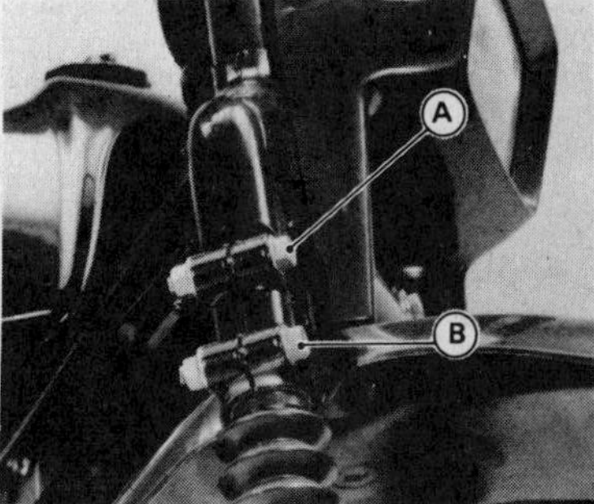

Upper (A) and lower (B) fork the tube clamp bolts

10. Remove the piston assembly from the top of the fork tube.

11. Remove the cylinder base from the bottom of the fork tube.

Inspection

1. Inspect the fork tubes for bends such as might have been incurred in an accident. Replacement is recommended rather than attempting to straighten bent fork tubes.

2. On the fork tubes the chrome plating must be in perfect condition in the area on which the slider oil seal rides, or leaks will result. If the chrome in this area is peeled or damaged, the tube should be replaced.

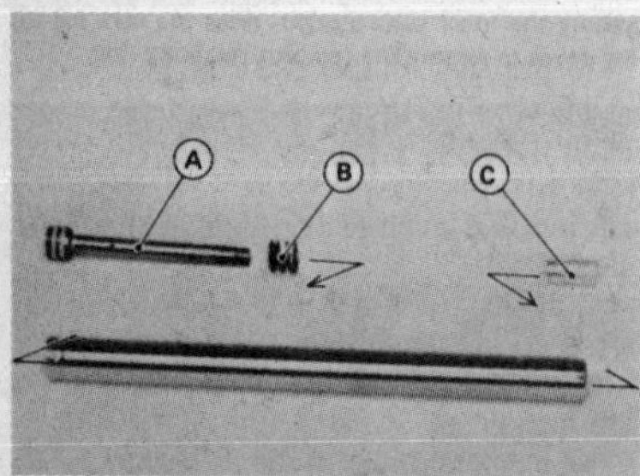

Hydraulic fork components: piston and cylinder assembly (A), spring (B) and cylinder base (C)

3. Minor rust and corrosion on the fork tubes should be removed by a low-abrasive method.

4. Check the condition of the fork springs. Compare the heights of the springs from each fork leg. Spring heights should be equal.

5. Clean all damper components in a safe solvent. Be sure they are clean before installation.

6. Clean all metal parts in a safe solvent. Lubricate them lightly with fork oil before installation.

7. New fork slider seals should be used once the forks have been disassembled.

8. Remove the dust cover from the top of each slider.

9. Remove the slider oil seal circlip.

10. Pry out the old seal with a small screwdriver or the like, taking care to protect the top edge of the slider which you are using as a fulcrum.

11. Drive the new seal straight in. Be sure it is not cocked or otherwise damaged as it is driven in. The seal must be far enough in the slider so that the circlip can be installed.

12. Oil the seal lips before installation.

Assembly

Assembly is the reverse of disassembly. Note the following points.

1. Use a non-permanent thread- locking compound on the threads of the slider allen bolt. Tighten the bolt to 14.5 ft. lbs.

2. Add fork oil as outlined below.

Changing Fork Oil

1. SAE 5W-20 oil is recommended for the forks.

2. Fork oil should be changed every 90 days of machine use.

3. Fork capacity is 88cc (3 oz.) after a rebuild and 75cc (2.6 oz.) for a routine change. This is the capacity of each fork leg.

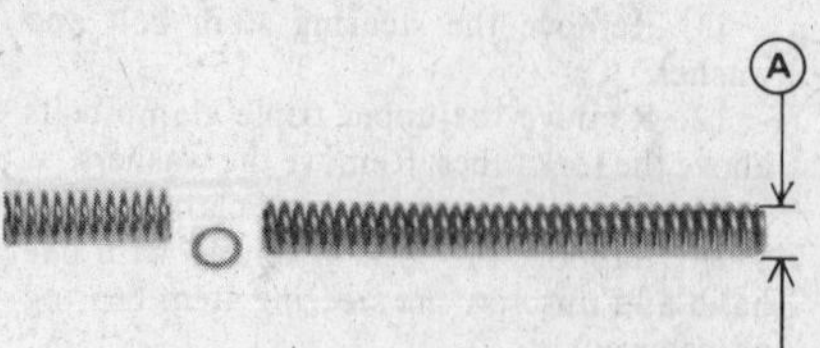

The smaller diameter end of the long spring (A) is positioned at the lower end of the fork tube

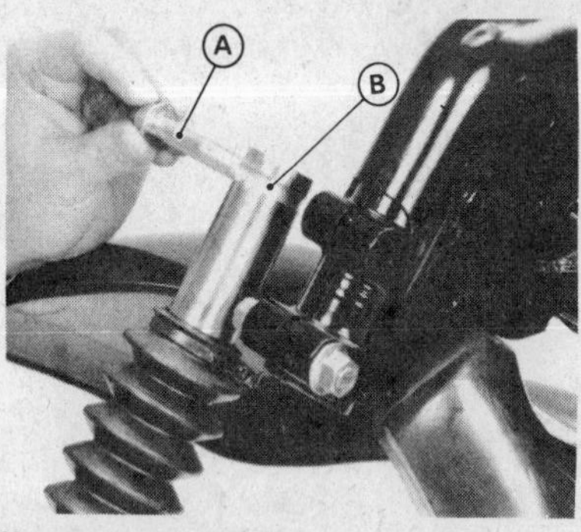

Upper clamp bolt (A) and fork tube groove (B)

4. Remove the fork leg from the steering head assembly as outlined above.

5. Remove the top plug retaining ring and the plug as noted in the "Disassembly" section, above. Remove the springs.

6. Pour off the old oil.

7. Add the proper grade and quantity of oil to the fork leg.

8. With the fork fully compressed and held vertically, measure the distance from the top of the fork tube to the oil. It should be 140mm (5.5 in.). If necessary, add or drain off oil until this specification is obtained.

Installation

1. When installing the fork springs, install the long spring so that the smaller diameter end is facing down.

2. When installing the fork legs on the steering stem, be sure the leg with the axle clamp is on the right side.

3. Insert the fork leg into the holder and slip the top clamp bolt into place. Note that the fork leg must be properly positioned so that the groove at the top aligns with the bolt hole.

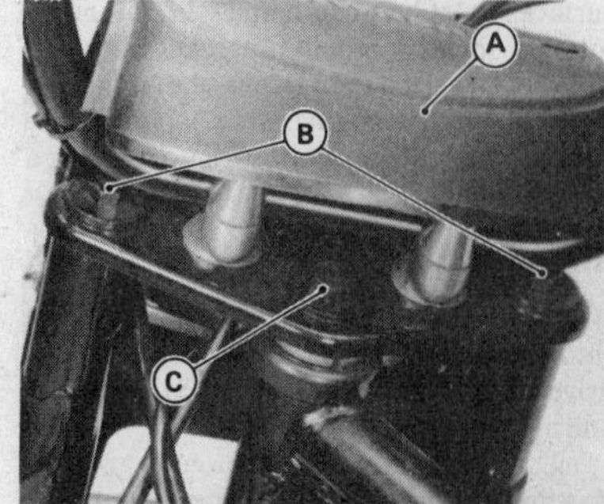

Rubber cover (A), upper triple clamp bolts (B) and steering stem bolt (C)

4. Tighten the upper clamp bolt to 22 ft. lbs.

5. Tighten the lower clamp bolt to 22 ft. lbs.

STEERING STEM

KLT 110-A1

The steering stem and front forks constitute one assembly. Refer to the "Front Forks" section.

KLT 110-A2, KLT 160

REMOVAL

1. Remove the front wheel.
2. Remove the front fender.
3. Remove the fork tubes from the steering stem assembly.
4. Remove the gas tank. See "Fuel Systems."
5. Disconnect the brake cables from the hand levers. The front brake cable should already be free. The rear brake adjusters must be run down to provide enough slack to effect removal.
6. Remove the throttle lever housing mounting bolts.
7. Remove the screws which secure the switch housing to the left side of the handlebars.
8. Remove the screws which secure the rubber cover to the upper triple clamp. Remove the cover.
9. Remove the handlebar clamp bolts.
10. Remove the handlebars.
11. Remove the headlight.
12. Remove the steering stem bolt and washer.
13. Remove the upper triple clamp bolts above the fork leg holders. Remove the washers.
14. Remove the upper triple clamp.
15. Support the steering stem assembly with one hand and unscrew the steering stem bearing adjuster nut.

CAUTION: *Steering stem bearing balls may come out as the nut is loosened.*

16. Remove the dust cover from the steering stem.
17. Remove the upper race from the steering stem.
18. Lower the steering stem until it is clear of the frame.
19. Remove the bearing balls from the lower race to avoid loss.

INSPECTION

1. Check that the steering stem assembly is not bent or deformed. If it is, it should be replaced. Attempts to straighten bent components may result in an unsafe part.
2. Wash the bearing balls in a safe solvent.
3. Clean the bearing races with a solvent-soaked rag to remove all traces of old grease.
4. Check the balls for rust, pitting, wear and/or flat spots. All the bearings should be replaced if damage is noted.
5. Should the surfaces of the bearings races be pitted, rusted or rippled, they should be replaced.
6. Run a finger around the races. The surfaces must be smooth and without indentations, ripples or other imperfections.

7. To replace the races in the frame lug, drive them out with a hammer and drift. The race on the steering stem is removed with a hammer and chisel.

ASSEMBLY

1. New steering stem races are installed in the head lug by driving them in with a suitable driver. Be sure that they are driven straight in and are fully seated.
2. Smear the races with a good grade of waterproof, medium-weight bearing grease and imbed the bearing balls in the frame race and the steering stem race.
3. Bearing ball specifications are:
 Upper: 6mm, 23 ea.
 Lower: 8mm, 19 ea.
4. Slip the steering stem into the frame head lug ensuring that none of the balls in the lower race are lost.
5. Hold the assembly in place while installing the upper race, dust cover and adjuster nut.
6. Adjust the bearings as outlined in "Maintenance."
7. The remainder of the procedure is the reverse of removal. Note the following torque ratings:
 Upper triple clamp bolts: 22 ft. lbs.
 Steering stem bolt: 40 ft. lbs.
 Handlebar clamp bolts: 13 ft. lbs.

REAR AXLE

KLT 110

REMOVAL

1. Support the rear wheels off the ground by placing a safe, sturdy support beneath the frame. Don't obstruct access to the skid plate. It must be removed to take off the axle.
2. Remove the lug nuts and take off the wheels.
3. Remove the axle nut cotter pin on each side.

Brake drum (A) and axle shaft nuts (B)

4. Remove each axle nut and washer.
5. Pull off the hubs.
6. Remove the air cleaner case. See "Fuel Systems."
7. Remove the engine sprocket cover.
8. Remove the chain case screws and pull the upper half of the case back and clear of the machine.
9. Remove the skid plate.
10. Remove the lower half of the chain case.
11. Remove the engine sprocket by removing the circlip from the shaft.
12. Remove the drive chain.
13. To disassemble the brake, remove the brake drum cover bolts. Remove the cover.

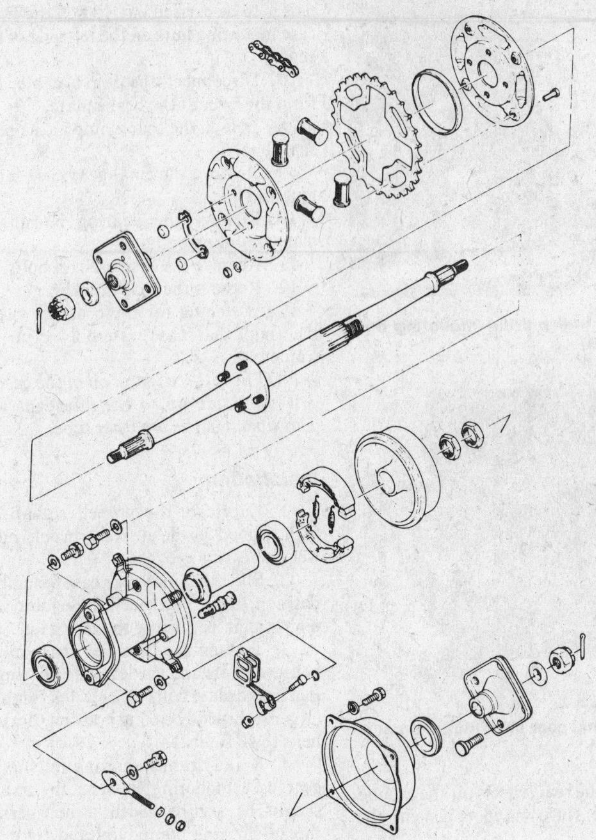

Rear axle assembly (110)

14. Apply the rear brake to secure the axle. Remove the axle shaft nuts (two).
15. Pull off the brake drum.
16. Bend down the sprocket nut locking tabs.
17. Remove the sprocket nuts.
18. Remove the sprocket assembly.
19. Disconnect the brake cables from the brake plate.
20. Remove the axle mounting bolts.
21. Remove the axle.

INSTALLATION

1. Installation is the reverse of removal. Note the following points.
2. Tighten the axle mounting bolts to 43 ft. lbs.
3. Tighten axle shaft nuts to 58 ft. lbs. Tighten the inner nut first; then tighten the outer nut while holding the inner in place.

Hand lever adjuster (A)

Foot pedal adjuster (A)

4. When connecting the rear brake cables, the pedal cable is attached to the lower slot on the brake drum lever and the hand lever cable is attached to the upper slot.
5. Tighten sprocket nuts to 22 ft. lbs. The nuts should be tightened evenly in a cross pattern. After the proper torque is reached, bend up the locking tabs.
6. Grease the splines on each end of the axle before fitting the hubs.
7. Tighten axle nuts to 65 ft. lbs.
8. Use new cotter pins on the axle nuts.

KLT 160

REMOVAL

1. Remove the axle nut cotter pin on each side.
2. Loosen the axle nuts.

Removing the brake drum mounting nuts (A) with tools (B)

Removing the final gear case mounting nuts (A) with tools (B)

3. Support the rear wheels off the ground by placing a safe, sturdy support beneath the frame.

4. Remove the axle nuts and pull off the wheels with hubs.

5. If the brake components are to be serviced, remove the brake drum cover bolts and remove the cover. Remove the two brake drum mounting nuts on the axle shaft. The axle can be secured while this is done by applying the rear brake. Remove the brake drum.

Final gear case mounting bolts (A), bracket (B) and boot clamp screw (C)

Bearing housing/brake plate mounting bolts (A)

6. If service to the final gear case internals is to be carried out, loosen the final gear case mounting nuts on the left side of the axle shaft.

7. Disconnect the brake cable and rod from the lever at the brake plate.

8. Loosen the rear clamp at the propeller shaft boot.

9. Remove the final gear case mounting nuts and bolts.

10. Remove the bearing housing/brake plate mounting bolts.

11. Remove the case bracket bolts.

12. Remove the case bracket.

13. Watching for the breather tube, pull the final gear case assembly clear of the frame.

NOTE: *If there is still oil in the case, place it right side up so the lubricant will not drain out of the breather tube.*

Installation

1. Lubricate the propeller shaft splines with a good grade of waterproof, medium-weight bearing grease.

2. Slide the final gear case assembly into position, engaging the sliding joint and the pinion joint by turning the rear axle.

3. Tighten the final gear case mounting bolts and nuts and the left-side bearing housing/brake plate bolts to 22 ft. lbs. Tighten the larger right-side bearing housing/brake plate bolts to 40 ft. lbs.

4. Brake drum mounting nuts and final gear case mounting nuts on the axle shaft should be secured with a non-permanent thread- locking compound and tightened to 61 ft. lbs.

5. If the brake drum cover was removed, check that the lip side of the dust seal faces out. Lubricate the lip with a bit of grease.

6. Be sure to install the cover so that the drain hole points down.

joint by turning the rear axle.

3. Tighten the final gear case mounting bolts and nuts and the left-side bearing housing/brake plate bolts to 22 ft. lbs. Tighten the larger right-side bearing housing/brake plate bolts to 40 ft. lbs.

4. Brake drum mounting nuts and final gear case mounting nuts on the axle shaft should be secured with a non-permanent thread- locking compound and tightened to 61 ft. lbs.

5. If the brake drum cover was removed, check that the lip side of the dust seal faces out. Lubricate the lip with a bit of grease.

6. Be sure to install the cover so that the drain hole points down.

7. Route the breather hose along the left side of the frame and insert it into the rear end of the frame top tube.

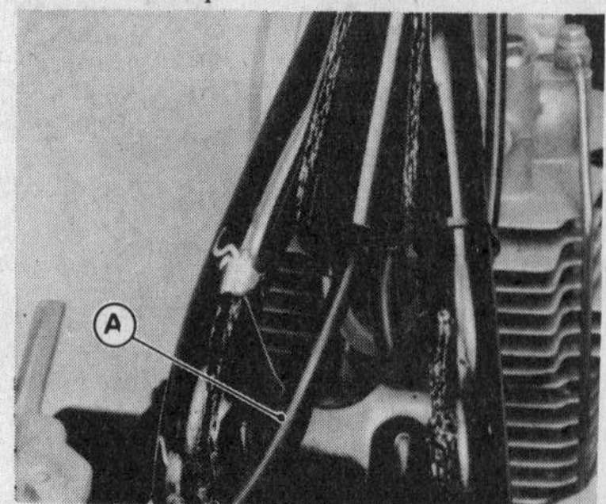

Insert the breather hose (A) into the rear end of the frame top tube

8. Connect the brake rod and cable. The rod is connected to the lower slot on the brake plate lever.

9. Grease the splines on the ends of the axle shaft with a good grade of waterproof, medium-weight bearing grease.

10. Install the wheels with hubs.

11. Tighten the axle nuts to 110 ft. lbs.

12. Use new cotter pins on the axle nuts.

13. Check final gear case oil level before operating the machine.

REAR BRAKE

Removal and Disassembly

1. Remove the cotter pin from the axle nut on the right hand rear wheel.

2. Loosen the axle nut.

3. Support the rear wheels off the ground by placing a safe, sturdy support beneath the frame.

4. Remove the axle nut.

5. Remove the right hand rear wheel and hub.

6. Remove the brake drum cover.

7. Remove the two axle shaft (brake drum mounting) nuts.

8. Remove the brake drum.

9. Brake components can be inspected in place. See below.

Inspection

1. Check the general condition of the brake linings. If they are scored, grooved or otherwise damaged, replace them.

2. Check the linings for an oil-soaked condition. If there are indications of this, the linings must be replaced.

3. Measure lining thickness. If either of them measures less than 2mm (0.8 in.) at the thinnest point, replace them.

4. Check the condition of the brake drum. If the inner surface is scored or grooved, the drum may have to be replaced. It may be possible to have it turned down on a lathe to remove minor scoring, but the final drum inside diameter must not exceed the wear limit specification (see below).

5. Measure the inside diameter of the brake drum. If it exceeds 130.75 mm (5.15 in.), replace it.

6. Check that the brake drum is not cracked.

7. Remove rust, dirt and corrosion from the brake drum with emery cloth.

8. Break the glaze on brake linings with emery cloth.

CAUTION: *Do not blow out brake components with compressed air or breathe brake dust. It represents a health hazard.*

9. To replace the linings, grasp both of the shoes and fold them towards the center of the brake plate.

10. Check the condition of the brake return springs. Replace the pair if they are broken, deformed, badly rusted or seem weak.

11. To remove the brake cam from the plate, first scribe a mark on lever and cam to indicate their relative positions for reassembly.

12. Disconnect the brake rod and/or brake cable(s) from the brake plate lever.

13. Remove the brake lever pinch bolt and carefully pull it off the cam.

14. Tap the cam out of the bearing housing from the left side. Note O-ring location.

15. Clean the cam in solvent and use emery cloth to remove any rust or corrosion.

16. Check the diameter of the cam bushing area and replace it if the measurement is less than 11.8mm (0.47 in.).

17. Check the diameter of the bearing housing cam hole and replace the housing if the measurement exceeds 12.7mm (0.51 in.).

NOTE: *Replacement of the bearing housing requires removal of the axle assembly.*

18. Check that the cam is not bent and that the lever splines are not torn or broken.

19. Check for stress cracks around the cam hole in the bearing housing.

Assembly And Installation

1. Clean all metal parts thoroughly in a solvent.

2. Lubricate the brake cam bushing area and brake shoe seat with a waterproof, medium-weight chassis grease.

3. Install the brake cam in the bearing housing. The mark on the brake shoe seat must point towards the center of the bearing housing.

4. Fit the brake cam O-ring.

5. Install the brake lever on the cam, aligning the position marks made prior to removal.

6. Install and tighten the lever pinch bolt.

7. Lightly grease the brake shoe pivot on the bearing housing. Lubricate the brake shoe holes to which the return springs attach.

CAUTION: *Keep lubricant well clear of the linings. Do not use too much of it as it may work its way onto the linings.*

8. Assemble the shoes and return springs.

9. Install the shoes and springs onto the bearing housing. Ensure that they are firmly seated.

10. Install the brake drum on the axle shaft.

11. Install and tighten the two large axle shaft (brake drum mounting) nuts. These nuts should be secured with a non-permanent thread-locking compound on the KLT 160. Proper torques are:

KLT 110: 58 ft. lbs.
KLT 160: 61 ft. lbs.

Tighten the innermost nut first, then torque the outer nut while holding the inner in place.

12. Grease the lips of the dust seal in the brake drum cover.

13. Install the cover. Be sure the water drain hole points down.

14. The remainder of the procedure is the reverse of disassembly. Grease the axle splines before installing the hubs. Be certain that the axle nuts are correctly torqued and that new cotter pins are used on them:

Removing a rear axle bearing

KLT 110: 65 ft. lbs.
KLT 160: 110 ft. lbs.

REAR AXLE BEARINGS

KLT 110

1. Remove the rear axle.

2. Remove the sprocket and the brake components. Refer to "Rear Axle, Removal" for procedures.

3. Inspect and replace the bearings in the same manner as the front wheel bearings. See "Front Wheel Bearings," above for procedures.

KLT 160

Replacement of the axle bearings requires disassembly of the final gear case. This requires special tools and critical assembly skills and should be left to a qualified expert.

GENERAL TORQUE SPECIFICATIONS ①

Thread dia. (mm)	Torque (ft lbs.)
5	2.5-3.6
6	4.3-5.6
8	10-14
10	19-25
12	33-45
14	54-72
16	83-115
18	125-165
20	165-240

① Unless otherwise noted.

CHASSIS TORQUE SPECIFICATIONS KLT 110

Component	Torque (ft lbs.)
Engine bracket bolts	13
Front wheel lug nuts	30
Front axle nut (A1)	54
Rear sprocket nuts	22
Rear axle nuts	65
Axle shaft locknuts	58
Axle mounting bolts	43
Steering stem bolt	40
Steering stem adjusting nut	14.5
Upper triple clamp bolts	22
Handlebar clamp bolts	13
Front axle (A2)	51
Fork slider allen bolts (A2)	14.5*
Front axle clamp nuts (A2)	7.3
Fork tube clamp bolts (A2)	22
Front brake drum mounting bolts (A2)	22

* Use a non-permanent thread-locking compound

CHASSIS TORQUE SPECIFICATIONS KLT 160

Component	Torque (ft lbs.)
Engine bracket bolts	14.5
Front wheel lug nuts	30
Front axle	51
Axle shaft (brake drum mounting) locknuts	61
Rear axle nuts	110
Final gear case mounting bolts	22
Axle bearing housing mounting bolts	40
Front brake drum mounting bolts	22
Steering stem bolt	40
Steering stem adjusting nut	14.5
Upper triple clamp bolts	22
Fork tube clamp bolts	22
Fork slider allen bolts	14.5*
Front axle clamp nuts	7.3
Handlebar clamp bolts	13

* Use a non-permanent thread-locking compound

Kawasaki Triples

MODEL COVERAGE

S1 (250)	KH400
KH250	H1 (500)
S2 (350)	KH500
S3 (400)	H2 (750)

INDEX

General Specifications

Model	*S1-B/C*	*S1-B*	*KH250*	*S2*	*S3*	*KH400*	*H1-A/D*	*H1-E/F*	*KH500*	*H2*	*H2-B/C*
DIMENSIONS											
Dry weight (lbs)	326.3	339.0	348.0	329.6	353.0	357.0	383.7①	407.0	423	423.4	448.0
Overall length (in.)	79.1	79.5	79.7	79.1	79.7	79.7	82.5	82.1	82.1	82.5	83.1
Overall width (in.)	31.5	32.3	32.3	31.5	32.3	32.3	33.1	32.9	32.9	33.5	33.9
Overall height (in.)	43.1	41.0	43.1	43.1	44.5	44.5	42.5	44.9	44.9	45.1	46.5
Wheelbase (in.)	52.4	53.7	54.1	52.4	53.7	53.7	55.1	55.5	55.5	55.5	56.5
Ground clearance (in.)	5.9	6.0	6.1	6.3	6.0	5.9	5.3	5.7	5.7	6.9	6.3
Tire size:											
Front	3.00 x 18	3.00 x 18	3.25 x 18	3.00 x 18	3.25 x 18	3.25 x 18	3.25 x 19	3.25 x 19	3.25 x 19	3.25 x 19	3.25 x 19
Rear	3.25 x 18	3.25 x 18	3.50 x 18	3.50 x 18	3.50 x 18	3.50 x 18	4.00 x 18	4.00 x 18	4.00 x 18	4.00 x 18	4.00 x 18
ENGINE											
Displacement (cc)	249	249	249	346.2	400.4	400.4	498.0	498.0	498.0	748.0	748.0
Bore x Stroke (mm)	45 x 52.3	45 x 52.3	45 x 52.3	53 x 52.3	57 x 52.3	57 x 52.3	60 x 58.8	60 x 58.8	60 x 58.8	71 x 63	71 x 63
Compression ratio (: 1)	7.5	7.5	7.5	7.3	6.5	6.5	6.8	6.8	6.8	7.0	7.0
Induction	piston-port	piston-port	piston-port	piston-port	piston-port	piston-port	piston-port	piston-port	piston-port	piston-port	piston-port
Lubrication	Superlube	Superlube	Superlube	Superlube	Superlube	Superlube	Injectolube	Injectolube	Injectolube	Injectolube	Injectolube
Carburetion (Mikuni)	VM22SC	VM22SC	VM22SC	VM24SC	VM26SC	VM26SC	VM28SC	VM28SC	VM28SC	VM30SC	VM30SC
TRANSMISSION											
Primary reduction	2.22	2.22	2.22	2.22	2.22	2.22	2.41	2.41	2.41	1.88	1.88
Final reduction	3.29	3.43	3.43	3.07	2.96	2.73	3.00	3.00	3.00	3.13	3.13
Overall reduction (5th)	7.03	7.31	7.31	6.56	6.25	5.85	5.84	5.84	5.84	4.76	4.76
Gearbox ratios											
1st	2.86	2.86	2.86	2.86	2.86	2.86	2.20	2.20	2.20	2.17	2.17
2nd	1.79	1.79	1.79	1.79	1.79	1.79	1.40	1.40	1.40	1.47	1.47

3rd	1.35	1.35	1.35	1.35	1.35	1.09	1.09	1.09	1.11	1.11
4th	1.12	1.12	1.12	1.12	1.12	0.92	0.92	0.92	0.92	0.92
5th	0.96	0.96	0.96	0.96	0.96	0.81	0.81	0.81	0.81	0.81
ELECTRICAL SYSTEM										
Ignition	battery/coil	battery/coil	battery/coil	battery/coil	magneto CDI	battery/coil or CDI	magneto CDI	magneto CDI	magneto CDI	magneto CDI
Generator	Alternator	Alternator	Alternator	Alternator	Alternator	Alternator	Alternator	Alternator	Alternator	Alternator
System voltage	12	12	12	12	12	12			12	12
CHASSIS										
Frame type						Tubular, double-cradle				
Steering angle (deg)	42	42	42	40	40	42②	39	39	39	NA
Caster (deg)	62	62	62	62	62	61	63	63	62	63.5
Trail (in.)	4.3	4.3	4.3	4.4	4.4	4.3	4.3	4.3	4.3	4.1

① Disc brake models—401.3
② Disc brake models—40
NA Not available

MAINTENANCE

NOTE: *Common maintenance procedures are explained in detail in "General Information."*

LUBRICATION

Engine

The crankshaft bearings, cylinders, and pistons are lubricated by the Kawasaki Superlube (250–400cc) or Injectolube (500 and 750cc) oil injection system.

The system does not require maintenance except for a periodic check on the oil pump cable adjustment provided that the oil tank is kept full of oil. Any good quality injected two-stroke oil recommended for air-cooled engines may be used in the oil tank.

NOTE: *If the tank ever runs out of oil, or if the feed line is disconnected for any reason, it will be necessary to bleed the system before operating the motorcycle. Refer to the "Lubrication System" for procedures.*

Transmission

The transmission and clutch are lubricated by an oil bath. The correct amount and grade of oil recommended for your model is listed in the "Maintenance Data" chart.

CAUTION: *SAE 10W30 or SAE 10W40 oil or ATF is recommended. However, this does not mean that the two can be mixed. Either one or the other should be used exclusively. If it is desired to change from one to the other the transmission must be flushed clean first.*

CHECKING OIL

1. The machine should be on the center stand, preferably on a level surface when checking the transmission oil level.
2. The oil level should be checked with the engine warm.
3. A dipstick is provided in the rear of the right crankcase cover. To check the oil level unscrew it and wipe it off. Reinsert, screwing the dipstick cap in. The oil level should be between the maximum and minimum marks on the dipstick. If the level is too low, add oil until the level is correct. Do not overfill. Let the oil distribute itself for a minute or so, then recheck the level.

CHANGING OIL

The transmission oil should be changed at least every 2,000 miles after break-in.

1. Oil should be changed when the engine is at or close to operating temperature.
2. The machine should be on the center stand and parked on a level surface.
3. Remove the dipstick.
4. Remove the drain plug and allow the oil to drain off for several moments.
5. Check the condition of the drain

Transmission drain plug location

plug gasket. Replace with a new one if damaged or cracked. Refit the drain plug and tighten firmly. Torque it to 36–52 ft lbs.

6. Fill the transmission with the correct type and quantity of oil. Capacities are given in the "Maintenance Data" chart. After filling, allow a moment or two for the oil to distribute itself, then check the level with the dipstick.

NOTE: *The use of oil additives is not recommended, since these may cause clutch slippage.*

Front Forks

1. SAE 10W oil is recommended for the front forks. If slightly stiffer damping characteristics are desired use SAE 20W. If softer damping is needed use SAE 5W.

2. Fork oil should be changed every 4,000 miles.

3. To drain the fork oil, remove the drain plug at the lower portion of one of the fork sliders. Allow the oil to drain into a suitable container; pump the slider up and down several times. After most of the oil is expelled, turn the forks all the way to the right to completely drain the right fork leg, or to the left for the left fork leg. Check the condition of the drain plug gasket. Replace it if necessary. Refit and tighten the drain plug.

Fork drain screw (H2 shown)

4. Repeat the procedure with the other fork leg.

5. Remove the fork filler caps from the top of each fork leg. The handlebar holders may have to be removed and the bars pulled back to allow access to the filler caps. Loosening the triple clamp pinch-bolts may make removal easier.

Removing the fork filler caps

6. Add the correct quantity and viscosity of oil to each fork leg. Capacities for each model are giving in the "Maintenance Data" chart.

Chassis Lubrication

1. Wheel and steering head bearings are lubricated with bearing grease. This should be accomplished every 4,000 miles. Refer to the "Chassis" section for procedures.

SERVICE CHECKS AND ADJUSTMENTS

Drive Chain

1. The chain should have about ¾ in. (20 mm) of total up-and-down free-play measured in the middle of the lower chain run.

2. *Before* checking or adjusting the chain slack, the following conditions should be met:

a. The machine should be off the center stand, and with a rider sitting on the seat;

b. The chain should be clean and well lubricated;

c. The chain should have been checked for any tight spots by slowly rotating the wheel and checking for variances in the chain tension at different points.

If a tight spot exists, the chain should be adjusted to the prescribed free-play at the tight spot.

3. To adjust the chain, first back off the rear brake adjuster nut if a rod-operated brake is fitted.

4. Remove the axle nut cotter pin and loosen the axle nut several turns. Loosen the sprocket hub securing nut (if fitted). Loosen the locknut on each adjuster bolt.

5. Turn each of the adjuster bolts in by equal amount until chain tension is approximately correct.

Loosening the axle nut

6. Check wheel alignment by means of the adjusting marks inscribed on both sides of the swing arm. Be sure that both adjusters are lined up with the same mark on each side. If not, turn one of the adjuster bolts in or out so that alignment is achieved.

7. Tighten the sprocket nut and the axle nut and check the chain tension. Correct it if necessary. After adjustment is correct, torque the axle nut to 42–50 ft lbs. Fit a new cotter pin. Tighten the adjuster locknuts. Readjust the rear brake.

Clutch

Two adjustments are made to the clutch: cable adjustment and the pushrod adjustment. Usually, the pushrod need not be adjusted unless the clutch malfunctions. Cable adjustment must always be maintained at the proper specification.

To adjust the clutch:

1. Loosen the clutch cable adjuster nut at the handlebar and screw in the adjuster to give a gap of 5–6 mm (0.20–0.24 in.) between the end of the adjuster and the locknut.

2. Loosen the locknut on the adjusting screw at the clutch release mechanism, and back the adjusting screw out 3 or 4 turns.

3. Turn the cable adjuster at the middle of the cable or on the engine cover in or

Adjusting the clutch: A, adjusting screw; B, locknut

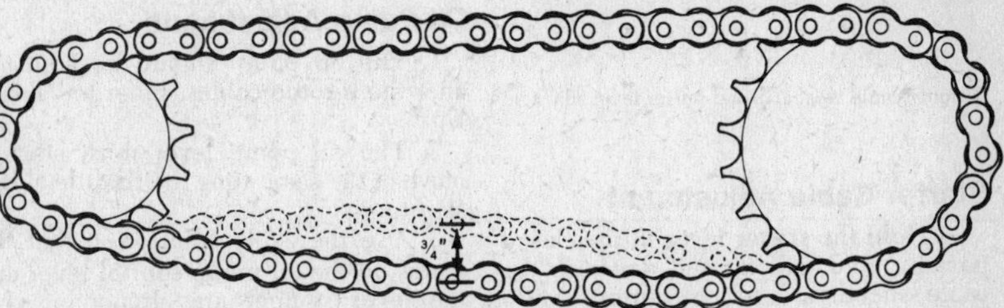

Measuring chain free-play

out until the centerline of the release lever is at a 100° angle from vertical.

4. Screw the adjusting screw in until a resistance is felt, then tighten the locknut.

5. Using the cable adjuster on the handlebar, adjust the free-play of the cable until the hand lever can be moved 1/16–1/8 (2–3 mm) before the clutch starts to disengage.

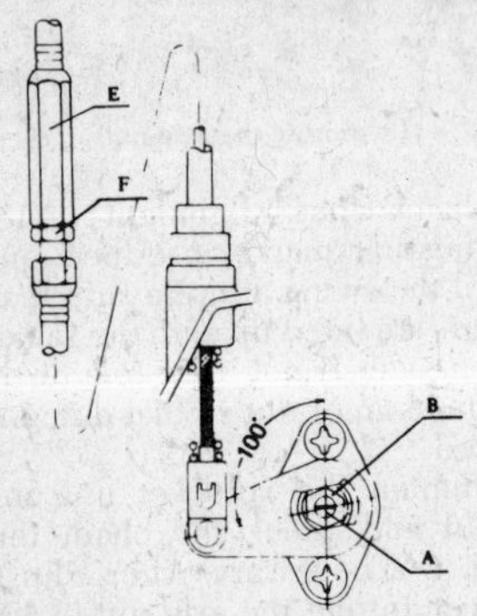

Use the cable adjuster (E) to position clutch release lever as shown

6. The adjuster at the hand lever is used for minor adjustments and to maintain the cable free-play at the proper amount while riding.

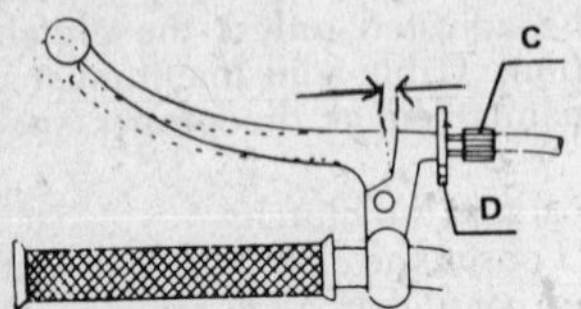

Clutch lever free-play is measured between the hand lever and the lever holder

Throttle Cables

1. Using the adjuster at the twist-grip adjust the cable so that the twist-grip can be rotated 5°–10° before the throttle slides start to open.

2. For other adjustments to the cables, refer to "Tune-Up."

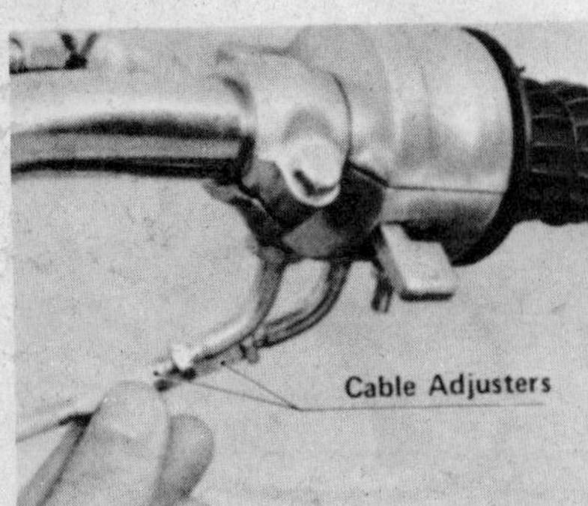

Throttle cable twist grip and starter lever adjusters

Starter Cable Adjustment

1. Hold the starter lever in the closed position, and pull up and down on the cable sheath at each carburetor while turning the adjuster in or out until you can move the sheath 1–2 mm (0.04–0.08 in.) then tighten the locknut.

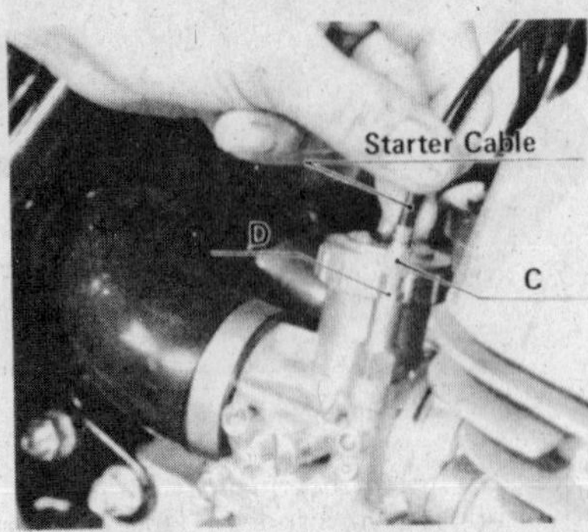

Adjusting the starter lever cable: adjuster, C; locknut, D

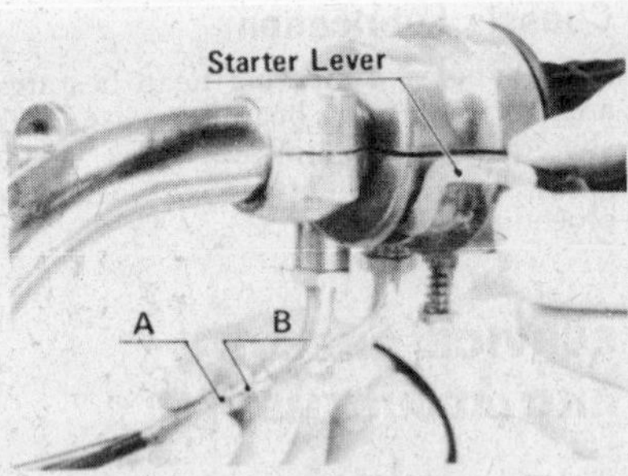

Starter lever handlebar adjuster

2. Using the adjuster at the twist-grip, set the starter cable free-play for 3–4 mm (0.12–0.16 in.)

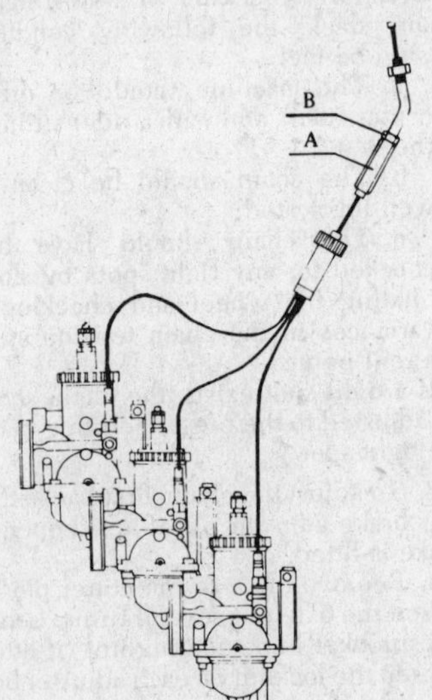

Starter lever cables and handlebar adjuster (A and B)

Oil Pump Adjustment

1. The oil pump should be adjusted after the throttle cables. Refer to "Tune-Up."

2. The oil pump lever must start to move at the same time the throttle slides start to open.

3. Use the cable adjuster so that the marks on the oil pump control lever and the lever stopper are aligned at zero throttle opening.

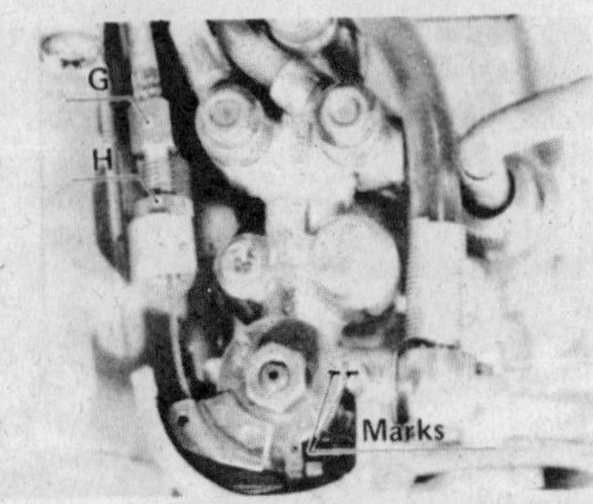

Adjust the oil pump cable so that the marks align (H1 shown)

Brakes

FRONT DISC

1. The brake lever is fitted with an adjusting screw on some models. The lever should have 5 mm (3/16 in.) of free-play, measured at the tip of the lever. To adjust, loosen the locknut and turn the adjusting screw in or out. Then tighten the locknut.

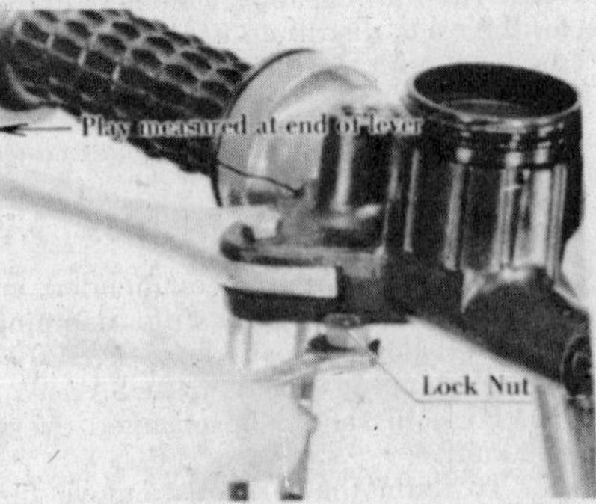

Adjusting disc brake lever free-play

2. Maintain the brake fluid level in the master cylinder at the level line inscribed on the inside of the master cylinder. Although the fluid level may drop slightly as the pads wear, this drop should not be significant.

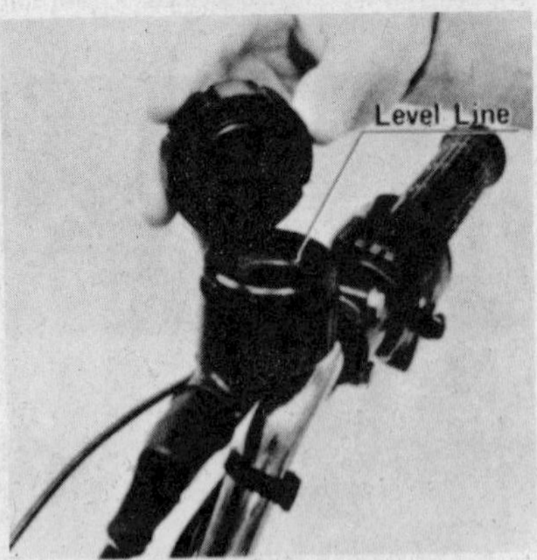

Maintain brake fluid level at the marked line

3. Pads should be checked periodically for wear. Replace them when worn to or near the red limit line. Refer to "Chassis" for pad replacement procedures.

4. The brake hoses should be checked for seepage or abrasion damage often,

and should be replaced if they show wear or leakage of any kind. Make sure that the lines touch the frame or forks at the mounting points only.

5. Every 8,000 miles or 1 year, the brake system should be flushed and refilled with fresh fluid. Refer to "Chassis" for procedures.

FRONT DRUM

1. Use the cable adjuster on the cable end to allow about ¼ in. (6 mm) of brake handlebar lever free-play before the shoes contact the drum. This free-play is to be measured between the lever and the lever holder.

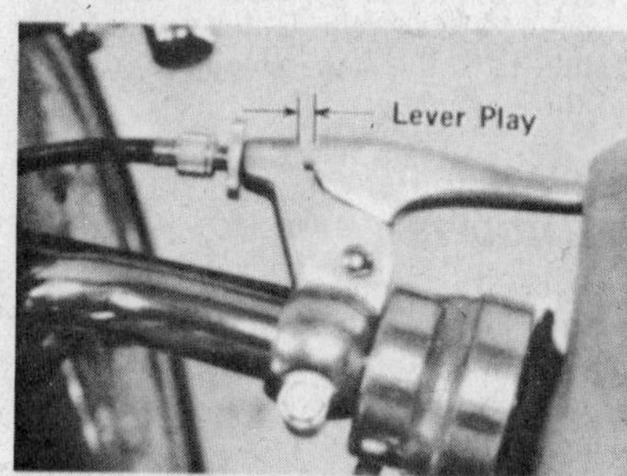

Adjust the brake cable so that the correct amount of play is available before the linings contact the drum

2. This free-play can be maintained as the shoes wear by using the adjuster at the handlebar lever.

3. The linkage of twin-leading shoe front brakes ordinarily does not need adjustment. If the backing plate has been disassembled, or adjustment is felt to be necessary because of weak brakes, proceed as follows:

a. Raise the front wheel off the ground so that the wheel can spin freely;

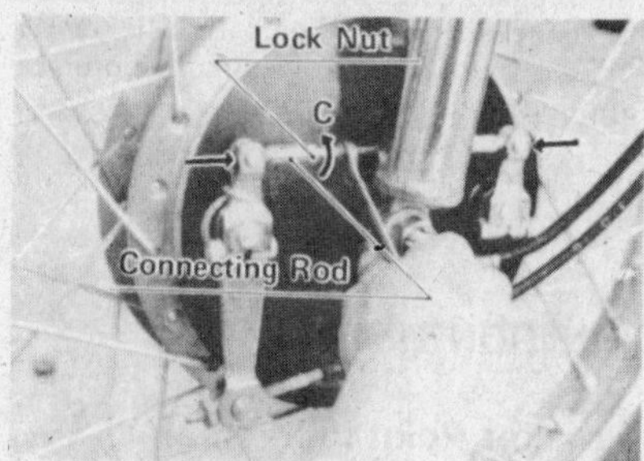

Adjusting the brake cam connecting rod

b. Loosen the locknut on the connecting rod and turn the connecting rod down one turn so that the rear brake lever is moved to the rear, increasing the distance between the levers. This allows the front shoe to be adjusted without interference from the rear one;

c. Turn the cable adjuster in until the front shoe just begins to contact the drum;

d. Turn the connecting rod up, decreasing the distance between the levers, until the rear shoe just begins to contact the drum; the connecting rod will no longer turn easily. At this point both shoes should begin to contact the drum at the same time. Tighten the locknut;

e. Adjust the brake cable free-play as previously described.

REAR BRAKE

Use the adjusting nut on the end of the cable or rod so that the brake pedal has 1 in. of free-play before the linings contact the drum.

NOTE: *If the angle between the brake cable or rod and the lever on the brake plate exceeds 90° when the brake is applied with all adjustment taken up, the lining thickness should be checked.*

BRAKE LIGHT SWITCH

The switch should be checked for operation after the brake is adjusted. The rear brake light switch is mounted in a slotted bracket and secured by locknuts. Moving the light switch up on the bracket allows the brake light to turn on sooner. Moving it down allows it to come on later. Generally, the brake light should come on just as the linings contact the drum.

Steering Stem Bearings

The steering stem bearings should be checked periodically and adjusted if necessary. Refer to the "Chassis."

FUEL SYSTEM

1. Fuel system maintenance involves cleaning the petcock and filter, cleaning or replacing the air cleaner, and cleaning the carburetors.

2. The carburetors should be removed, disassembled, and cleaned every 4,000 miles. The procedures are outlined in "Fuel Systems."

3. The petcock should be serviced every 2,000 miles. On H-series and newer 250–400cc, shut the fuel off, then unscrew and remove the petcock sediment bowl. Take out the fuel filter screen. On older S-series, disconnect the fuel lines at the carburetor and turn the petcock to "R" to drain the fuel tank. Unscrew the nut to remove the petcock. Clean the parts in solvent and install. Check for leaks.

Removing the petcock (standard type)

4. The air cleaner should be serviced or replaced every 2–3,000 miles, depending on conditions. If the air cleaner is the paper type, it should be kept free of water, solvents, etc.

5. To remove the air cleaner element:

250–400cc: remove the left sidecover and loosen the thumb screw on the air cleaner housing. Pull out the air cleaner housing along with the element. Remove the two screws which secure the element to the housing.

500cc: loosen the clamp screws securing the air cleaner hose to each carburetor

Removing the air cleaner (S-series)

Maintenance Data

Model	Fuel Tank Capacity (gal)	Oil Tank Capacity (qt)	Transmission Oil Capacity (qt)	Fork Oil① Capacity (cc/oz)	Tire Pressure (psi) Front/Rear
250	3.7	1.6	1.16	210/7.1	24/31
350	3.7	1.6	1.16	210/7.1	24/31
S3	3.7	1.6	1.16	155/5.3	24/31
KH400	3.7	1.6	1.16	141–149/4.8–5.0	25/28
H1/A-D	4.0	2.5	②	③	26/31
H1-E/F, KH500	4.2	2.5	1.3	170/5.6	26/31
H2	4.5	2.1	1.5	160/5.5	26/31
H2-B/C	4.5	2.1	1.5	175/5.9	26/31

① Each leg
② Front drum: 1.7
Front disc: 1.3
③ Front drum: 230/7.8
Front disc: 160/5.5

and the clamp screw at the air cleaner housing, and remove the hose assembly. Remove the left-side carburetor after loosening the clamp screw. Remove the air cleaner mounting screw and remove the housing and element together through the left-side of the frame.

750: remove the left sidecover. Remove the rubber silencer beneath the seat. Loosen the air hose clamp screw on the air cleaner housing. Remove the housing mounting screw. Remove the front mounting bracket for the left sidecover. Push the air hose out of the way and remove the air cleaner and housing complete from the left-side of the frame.

6. Inspect the condition of the air cleaner element and replace it if torn or otherwise damaged. The sponge gasket must also be in good condition. If damaged, the element must be replaced.

Wash the element in pure gasoline and blow it dry. The elements used on these motorcycles are the dry-type, and should therefore be kept free of oil, oily solvents, etc.

On the 750, clean the felt part of the air cleaner in solvent, and apply a small amount of oil to the felt portion only. Keep the oil away from the element. Glue the felt portion on securely if it is loose.

Periodic Maintenance①

Daily (before each ride)
- Check lighting equipment and horn operation
- Check operation and adjustment of the brakes
- Tire condition
- Chain tension
- Cable adjustments
- Oil injection tank level

Weekly
- Transmission oil level
- Tire pressure (cold)
- Spoke tension
- Battery electrolyte level
- Chain condition
- Critical nuts and bolts

Monthly
- Trickle charge stored battery

Every 200 miles
- Lubricate chain

Every 2000 miles
- Change transmission oil
- Remove, clean and lubricate chain
- Lubricate control and instrument cables
- Check oil pump adjustment
- Clean fuel petcock
- Check brake fluid level (disc brake)
- Clean and gap spark plugs
- Clean points and check timing
- Clean or replace air filter
- Adjust brakes
- Decarbonize engine and exhaust system

Every 4000 miles
- Change fork oil
- Pack wheel and steering head bearings
- Check brake linings
- Check sprocket condition
- Grease speedometer drive mechanism
- Clean carburetors
- Replace spark plugs

Every 8000 miles
- Flush hydraulic disc brake system

① Based on normal usage after break-in is complete

Recommended Lubricants

Oil Tank
- Any high quality two-stroke motorcycle oil for air-cooled engines

Transmission
- SAE 10W30, "SE"
- SAE 10W40, "SE"
- ATF
- SAE 30 (summer)
- SAE 20 (winter)

Forks
- SAE 10
- SAE 20
- SAE 5W

Drive Chain
- Any high quality chain lube specifically developed for motorcycle drive chains

Wheel and Steering Head Bearings
- Lithium or moly-based bearing grease

Cables
- Light motor oil
- Graphite-based lubricant
- Molybdenum disulphide-based lubricant

Grease Fittings
- Chassis grease

TUNE-UP

NOTE: *Common tune-up procedures are explained in detail in "General Information."*

CONTACT BREAKER POINTS

Location

Breaker points are mounted on a plate beneath the cover on the left-side of the engine. The cover is secured by two screws.

Gapping

ALL BREAKER POINT MODELS

Points should be filed (if necessary) and cleaned before gapping.

Loosen screw A and use a screwdriver at the pry point to adjust the gap

1. The breaker point set is secured to its plate by a single screw which is used to adjust the gap. This is not to be confused with the breaker point mounting screws which are used to adjust the ignition timing. A small pry slot for a thin screwdriver blade is also provided.

2. Turn the engine over slowly until one of the three sets of points is fully open. Check the gap for that set of points with the proper feeler gauge. Correct point gap for all models is 0.3–0.4 mm (0.12–0.16 in.).

3. If adjustment is needed, loosen the securing screw ("A" in the accompanying illustration), just enough to allow the gap to be varied, and increase or decrease the point gap with the aid of a small screwdriver applied to the pry slot.

4. Tighten the screw and recheck the gap. Note that the gap may change slightly when the screw is tightened.

5. Repeat the procedure with the two remaining point sets. Try to get the gaps of all three sets as close to one another as possible. That is, the feeler gauge blade should have the same amount of drag in all three point sets.

Replacement

ALL MODELS

1. Breaker points must always be replaced in sets. The contact surfaces of new points should be cleaned with a non-oily solvent to remove any preservative which may be present.

2. Loosen the breaker point terminal nut, disconnect the primary wire, remove the point securing screw, and remove the old point set.

3. Install the new set of points; connect the primary wire, and install the securing screw.

4. Repeat the procedure with the other two point sets. Set the gap on all three point sets and check the ignition timing.

Lubrication

1. A small dab of grease (high melting point is preferred) should be applied to each lubricating felt pad (there are three pads) so that the pad can distribute it onto the breaker cam. Be sure that each pad is adjusted so that it bears lightly on the breaker cam. A drop of light oil should be applied to the points pivot.

2. In any case it is imperative that care be taken to keep the lubricant away from the point contact surfaces.

IGNITION TIMING

Breaker Point Ignition

250, 350, 400

1. Remove the spark plugs and the breaker point cover. Clean and gap all three point sets.

Loosen screws B and move the points with a screwdriver to adjust ignition timing (S-series and KH250)

2. An inspection window is provided on the breaker point mounting plate through which can be seen the timing marks engraved on the alternator rotor. The marks are labeled "L," "R," "C," for the three cylinders. There is a corresponding mark on the breaker plate. In addition, each set of points is labeled for its cylinder.

3. Hook up the ohmmeter or light to any set of points. Turn the engine over slowly in the normal direction of rotation (counterclockwise), until the rotor timing mark for that set of points comes into view.

4. The light or meter should react indicating that the points have opened as soon as the rotor mark aligns with the mark on the breaker plate. If this happens, the ignition timing for that cylinder is correct. If the meter or light reacts before the marks align, the timing for that cylinder is too advanced; if the meter or light reacts after the rotor mark passes the breaker plate mark, the timing is too retarded.

5. To adjust the timing, loosen the two point set mounting screws ("B" in the accompanying illustration), and use a small screwdriver at the pry points indicated to move the points to the left or right as necessary so that the points will begin to open as soon as the timing marks align. Secure the mounting screws and recheck the timing.

6. Repeat the procedure with the two remaining sets of points.

It can be seen that in order to correct advanced timing, the points should be moved in the direction of crankshaft rotation. To correct retarded timing, move the points opposite the direction of crank rotation. All three cylinders must be timed correctly before the procedure can be considered complete.

NOTE: *If any of the points cannot be moved far enough to correct the timing, excessive wear of the heel is probably the cause, and all three of the point sets should be replaced.*

H1

The ignition timing for the left cylinder *must* be set first. The points for the left cylinder are positioned at the top of the breaker mounting plate. It can be seen that these points are mounted directly on the breaker plate and rotating the entire plate is the only means of adjusting the timing for the left cylinder. This in turn will change the timing for the center and right cylinders.

Timing marks are provided on the rotor which can be used to set the timing under most circumstances. If the breaker plate has been removed from the engine or the timing pointer moved, timing must be reset with a dial indicator.

1. Remove the spark plugs and the breaker points cover. Clean and gap the three sets of points.

2. Attach the ohmmeter or test light to ground and to the terminal of the points for the left cylinder.

3. Slowly rotate the engine in the normal (counterclockwise) direction of rotation. At the instant that the "L" mark on the rotor aligns with the leading (left) edge of the timing pointer ("E" in the illustration), the meter or light should react indicating that the points have begun to open. If this is the case, the timing for the left cylinder is correctly adjusted. The other cylinders must still be checked, however.

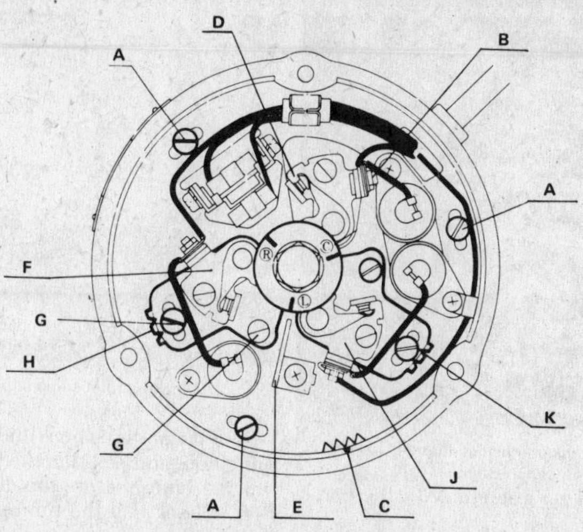

Breaker point assembly (H1)

4. If the left cylinder timing was not correct, do not move the rotor; leave the marks aligned; loosen the three screws which secure the breaker plate to the engine. (These are lettered "A" in the illustration.) Using a small screwdriver at the pry point provided, rotate the breaker plate as necessary to correct the timing. Then tighten the screws.

CAUTION: *Do not move the rotor while the breaker plate screws are loose or timing may be lost.*

5. After tightening the breaker plate screws, move the pointer ("E") so that its leading edge is aligned with the "L" mark on the rotor. The position of the pointer will have changed when the breaker plate is moved.

6. Hook up the meter or test light to ground and to the terminal of the points for the right cylinder. Turn the crankshaft counterclockwise as before until the "R" mark on the rotor aligns with the leading edge of the timing pointer. The tester should indicate that the points have just begun to open when the marks align. If the points do not do so, loosen the two mounting screws for the right cylinder's points (lettered "G" in the illustration), and use a screwdriver and the pry point provided "H") to move the points in the direction necessary so that they will just begin to open when the timing marks are aligned. Tighten the mounting screws and recheck the timing.

7. Repeat the procedure (Step 6) for the remaining set of points (center cylinder).

If timing has been lost for any reason, or if a more accurate method of setting the timing is required, a dial indicator should be used.

1. After removing the spark plugs, cleaning and gapping the points, etc., fit the dial indicator into the left cylinder spark plug hole. Turn the engine over slowly until the gauge needle reaches a point and begins to reverse. This is piston top dead center. Turn the crankshaft a few degrees in either direction to confirm the finding, then place the piston at TDC and zero the gauge.

2. Turn the engine opposite to the normal direction of rotation (clockwise) until the dial gauge indicates about 4 mm (0.16 in.) before TDC. The breaker points for the left cylinder will be closed at this point.

3. Hook up the ohmmeter or test light to the points for the left cylinder. Check that they are closed. Slowly rotate the engine in the normal (counterclockwise) direction of rotation. When the dial gauge indicates that the piston is at the proper number of millimeters or inches before TDC, the points should begin to open as indicated by the reaction of the tester.

Proper timing specifications are as follows:

H1 (drum front brake)	0.136 in. (3.45 mm) (25°) BTDC
H1 (disc front brake)	0.088 in. (2.23 mm) (20°) BTDC

4. If timing is not correct, loosen the three screws which secure the breaker plate to the engine, and use a screwdriver at the pry point provided to rotate the plate so that the points for the left cylinder start to open when the piston is properly positioned at the correct distance before TDC.

5. When correct timing of the left cylinder has been accomplished, and maintaining the left cylinder's piston at the timing specification given in Step 3, check the alignment of the rotor timing mark and the timing pointer. If the rotor mark is not aligned with the leading (left) edge of the pointer, move the *pointer* so that alignment is achieved. Do not move the rotor.

6. Timing of the right and center cylinders must still be accomplished. This can be done either with the dial gauge, or simply by aligning the rotor and pointer as outlined in the previous section.

CDI Ignition

KH400

1. Remove the left engine cover.

2. The mark on the magneto stator

Stator and crankcase marks aligned (KH400)

plate should be aligned with the crankcase mark.

3. If the marks are not aligned, remove the magneto flywheel, loosen the three stator plate screws, and rotate the plate so that the marks are in alignement.

4. Tighten the screws securely and install the flywheel.

5. Timing is checked with a strobe light.

6. Connect the strobe light to the left cylinder.

7. Start and run the engine at 4,000 rpm. The timing mark on the flywheel should align with the crankcase mark at this engine speed.

8. If the marks do not align, rotate the stator plate as in Steps 3–4 above until alignment is achieved.

H1

A dial gauge should be used to set the timing.

1. Remove the spark plugs, the rotor cover and the distributor cover.

2. Place the right cylinder at top dead center, and check that the timing mark on the distributor plate is aligned with "T" mark on the engine case.

Line up the timing mark on the distributor plate with the "T" mark on the engine case (H1 battery-CDI)

3. Slowly rotate the crankshaft so that one of the magnetic projections of the signal generator rotor is aligned with the pickup coil. Check the gap between the projection and the coil with a feeler gauge. Proper gap is 0.4–0.6 mm (0.016–0.024 in.). If adjustment is necessary, loosen the two coil mounting screws (1 and 2 in the illustration) and move the coil so that the gap is correct.

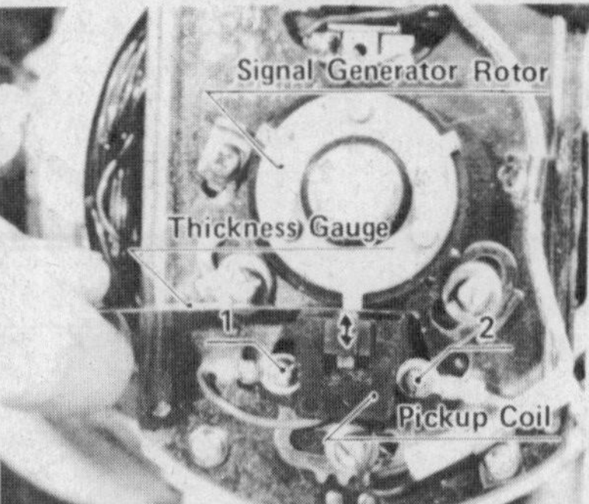

Checking rotor-to-pickup coil gap

4. Fit the dial gauge into the left spark plug hole and position the piston at 0.136 in. (3.45 mm) before top dead center.

5. Check that the timing marks on the rotor and the top of the pickup coil are aligned as shown in the illustration. If they are not, loosen the three pickup coil adjusting screws (3, 4, and 5 in the illustration), and move the coil so that the marks align. Secure the screws.

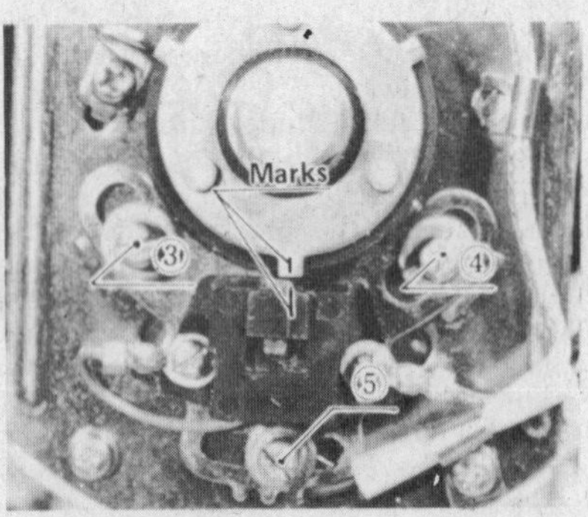

With the piston properly positioned, line up the timing marks after loosening screws 3, 4, and 5

6. Check that the timing pointer (No. 6 in the illustration) aligns with the mark on the rotor as shown. If it does not, loosen the pointer screw, and move it so that alignment is achieved. Note that the piston must remain at the correct distance BTDC during this operation.

Timing pointer "6" can be used to check ignition timing after it is aligned with the rotor mark

NOTE: *Once this pointer is correctly aligned, it can be used to check the timing, or reset the timing whenever the pickup coil is removed.*

H1-E/F, KH500

The ignition system on the H1-E and following 500 models is somewhat different than the battery/CDI system found on early models.

1. Timing is checked with a strobe light. With the engine running at 4,000 rpm, and the strobe light connected to the left spark plug, the timing mark on the rotor ("A" in the illustration) should align with the stationary pointer.

The mark "A" should align with the pointer at 4000 rpm (H1-E, KH500)

2. If adjustment is necessary, proceed as follows:

3. Remove the left cylinder's spark plug and install a dial gauge.

4. Turn the engine over using a 13 mm wrench on the Signal Generator rotor bolt until the left cylinder is at TDC. Zero the gauge.

5. Turn the engine *clockwise* until the gauge indicates that the left piston is 2.4 mm (0.1157 in.) or 23° before TDC.

6. With the piston in this position, the mark on the rotor ("A" in the illustration) should align with the stationary timing pointer. If it does not, loosen the pointer securing screw, and move the *pointer* (not the rotor) so that they align.

7. Tighten the pointer screw. Turn the crankshaft slowly in the normal direction of rotation (counterclockwise) until the next timing mark appears ("B" in the illustration). Align this mark with the pointer. With these marks aligned, the trailing edge of one of the rotor projections must align with the edge of the pickup coil projection.

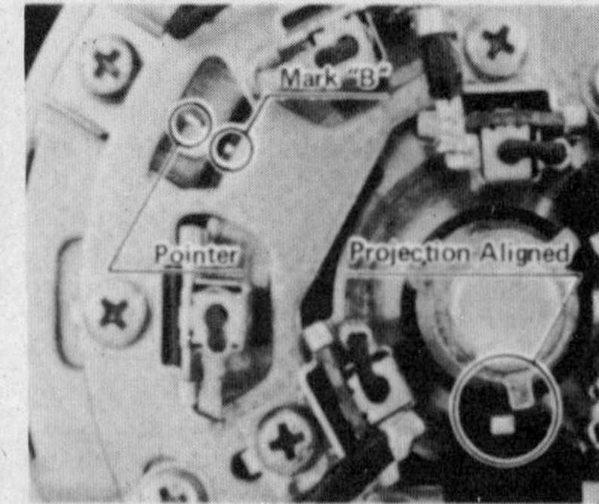

Mark "B" aligned with the pointer as trailing edge of rotor projection aligns with edge of the pickup coil projection (H1-E, KH500)

8. If it does not, loosen the three stator mounting plate screws, and rotate the plate so that alignment is obtained. Tighten the screws securely.

9. Turn the rotor clockwise a few degrees until the rotor projection and the pickup coil projection are directly in line.

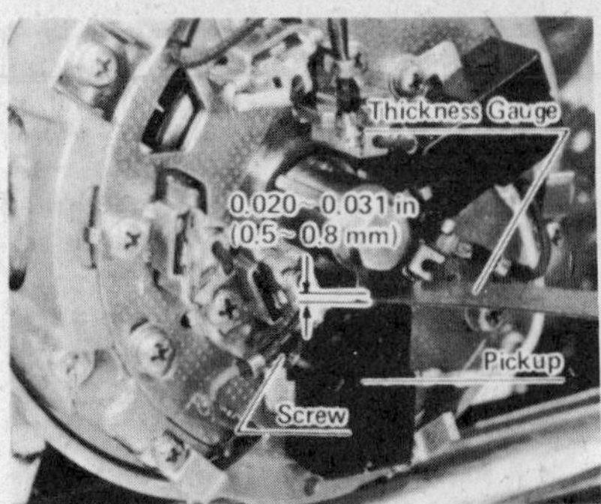

Pickup coil/rotor projection gap H1-E/F, KH500

Measure the gap between them with a feeler gauge. It should be 0.5–0.8 mm (0.020–0.031 in.). If not within specification, loosen the two pickup coil screws and move the coil up or down until the gap is correct. Tighten the screws securely.

10. To check the timing, use a strobe light as outlined in Step 1. Mark "A" should align with the pointer at 4,000 rpm.

H2

1. Timing can be checked with a standard automotive stroboscopic timing light if one is available. Connect the light to the left cylinder plug lead. Start the engine. At 4,000 rpm, the rotor "L" mark should line up with the timing pointer. If it does not, timing must be adjusted.

2. Timing for each cylinder is adjusted independently; therefore, use the strobe light to check the right and center cylinder timing as well.

3. Turn the engine over so that the magnetic projection of the rotor is aligned with any one of the pickup coils. Check the gap between the two. Correct gap should be 0.5–0.8 mm (0.020–0.031 in.). If adjustment is necessary, loosen the two coil mounting screws and move the coil so that the gap is correct. Then secure the screws. Repeat the procedure with the other two pickup coils.

Rotor/pickup coil gap (H2)

CAUTION: *The coils must be moved by hand only. Do not pry the coil toward or away from the rotor, as this risks breaking the coil housing.*

4. Insert a dial gauge into the left cylinder. Set the piston to 3.13 mm (0.123 in.) before top dead center.

5. Check that the timing pointer is aligned with the "L" mark on the rotor. If it is not, bend the pointer so that alignment is achieved.

Aligning the timing pointer (H2)

6. Turn the rotor slightly so that the "S" mark for the left cylinder aligns with the timing pointer. When this is done, note that the trailing edge of the rotor's magnetic projection should be aligned with the mark on the pickup coil for the left cylinder. If these marks are not aligned, loosen the two pickup coil mounting plate screws, and move the coil in the direction necessary to align the marks. When the rotor "S" mark is aligned with the timing pointer and the trailing edge of the magnetic projection is aligned with the mark on the pickup coil, the timing is correct for the left cylinder.

With the "S" mark aligned, the trailing edge of the rotor projection must align with the pickup coil mark. If adjustment is necessary, loosen the mounting screws and move the coil (H2)

7. Timing for the remaining two cylinders must be checked as well. Since the timing pointer was set correctly in Step 5, it is only necessary to align the "S" mark for the right and center cylinders with the timing pointer and check the alignment of the trailing edge of the rotor projection and the timing mark atop each pickup coil. If adjustment is necessary, loosen the pickup coil mounting plate screws and move the coil as necessary to effect timing.

8. After checking timing on all three cylinders, check dynamic timing with a strobe light.

CARBURETORS

Adjusting Float Level

EARLY MODELS

1. Remove the carburetors.

2. Turn the carburetor upside down, and remove the four float bowl screws carefully lifting off the float bowl.

3. Remove the float bowl gasket.

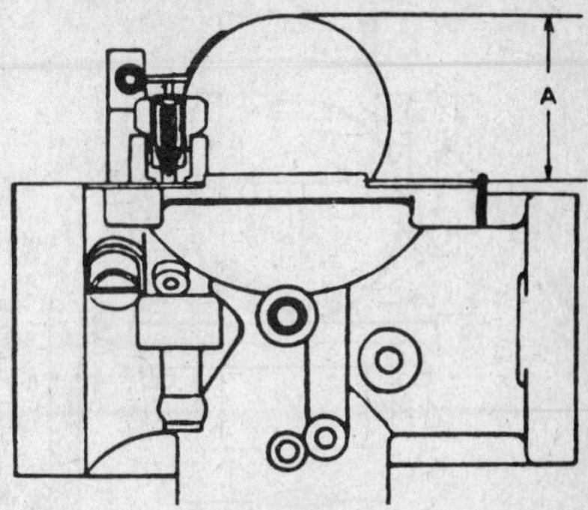

Float level "A" is the distance from the float bowl gasket surface (gasket removed) to the top of the float

4. Float level can be measured with a steel rule or a vernier caliper. Float level is defined as the distance from the float bowl gasket surface (gasket removed) to the top of the float, when the tang of the float arm is just touching the float needle.

NOTE: *Lower the float down until the tang just contacts the float needle. Hold the float in this position, then measure the float level.*

5. Compare the value obtained with the correct specification for your machine. If the float level is too high or low, pull out the pin which holds the float in place, and bend the tang very slightly to correct the adjustment.

NOTE: *If float level is too high, bend the tang away from the carburetor body. If too low, bend it toward the carburetor body.*

6. Refit the float and recheck the adjustment.

CAUTION: *Bend only the float tang to make an adjustment. Do not bend the float arms. The floats must be level. If the floats show different heights, the float assembly should be replaced. This indicates that the float assembly has been mishandled. It is very important that all three carburetors have the same float level.*

7. Float level will not be correct if the needle is worn or if there is foreign matter on the needle seat.

LATE MODELS

The following procedure may be used on later model machines provided that the special gauge is available. If it is not, check level as outlined for early models.

1. Remove the carburetor from the manifold with the feed line connected, but the fuel off.

2. Remove the float bowl and fit the special gauge (see illustration) in its place.

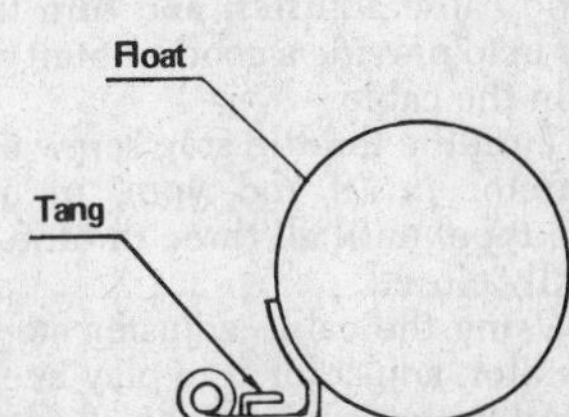

To adjust float/fuel level, bend the tang only

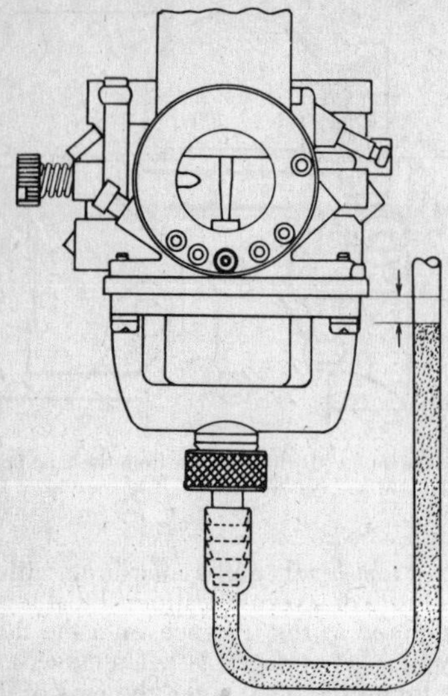
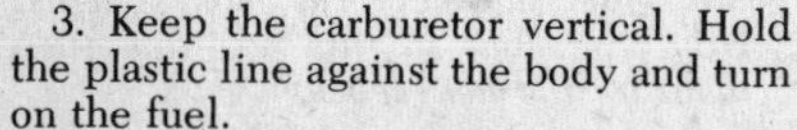

Fuel level is measured from the bottom of the carburetor body if the bowl fitting is available

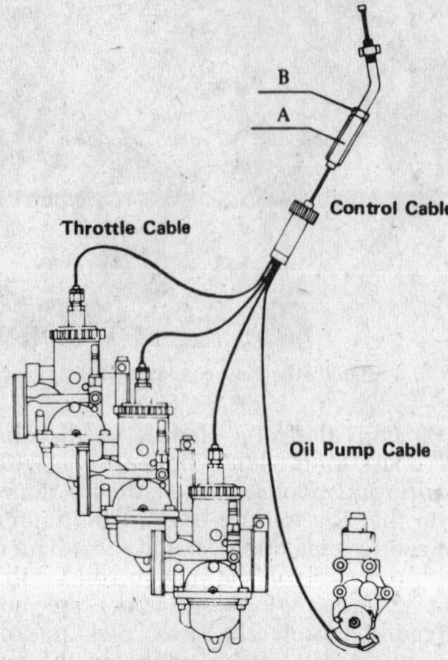

Throttle cable linkage

3. Keep the carburetor vertical. Hold the plastic line against the body and turn on the fuel.

4. The gas in the line should come up to a point 2–4 mm (0.08–0.16 in.) below the float bowl mating surface on 500 and 750s. Proper level for 250 to 400 machines is 4–6 mm (0.16–0.24 in.).

Carburetor Synchronization

Carburetor synchronization includes adjustments to the throttle cables, the idle speed, and the idle mixture. Cable adjustments are necessary to ensure that all three throttle slides move together.

Before attempting adjustment, the following conditions should be met:

a. The tank should have a good supply of gasoline;

b. The carburetors must be vertically aligned, not tilted to one side or the other;

c. Carburetor clamp screws should be tight;

d. The engine should be at normal operating temperature.

A cable adjuster is fitted to the top of each carburetor and another at the twist-grip. One throttle cable runs from the twist-grip to a junction box. There, it is connected to the oil pump cable and three throttle cables which run to the carburetors. Therefore, each cable must be adjusted.

When reading the following, note that some carburetors have the throttle stop rod (idle adjustment) screw located on the carburetor cap, while on others it is a wheel on the side of the body.

1. Loosen the locknut on the twist-grip throttle cable adjuster, and turn the adjuster in to provide a good amount of freeplay in the cable.

2. Turn the throttle stop screw of each carburetor *in* (if rod-type), or *out* (if wheel-type) until all three throttle slides are fully closed.

3. Using the cable adjuster atop each carburetor, adjust for zero play in each of the carburetor cables. This is done by loosening the adjuster locknut, lifting the cable out of the adjuster as far as possible without lifting the slide, and turning the adjuster out until it meets the cable sheath. Check that it is not possible to lift the cable out of the adjuster without lifting the slide as well. But take care that the cable adjuster is not turned out so far as to partially lift the slide. The slide must remain in the fully closed position. Be sure to tighten the adjuster locknut.

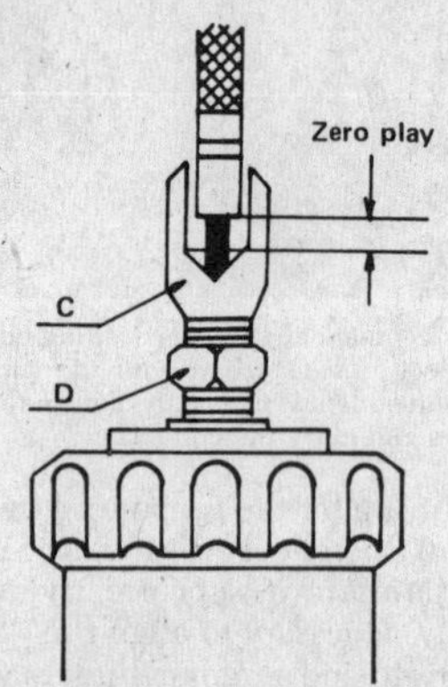

Use the adjuster "C" to effect zero play between the adjuster and the cable sheath

4. Turn the pilot air screw on each carburetor in until lightly seated, then back each one out the prescribed number of turns as indicated for your model in the "Tune-Up Specifications" chart.

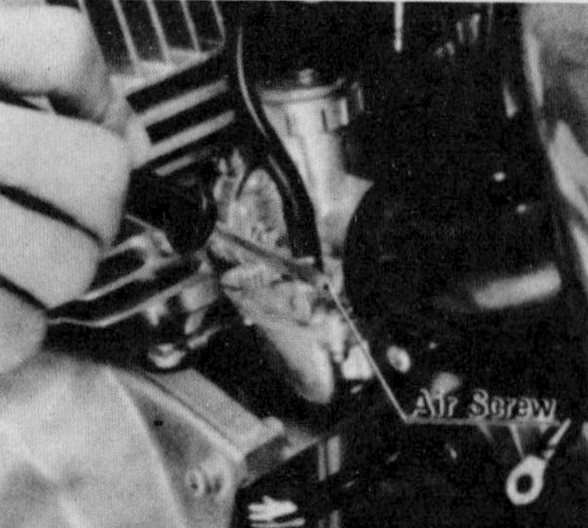

Adjusting the pilot air screw (KH400 shown)

5. Start the engine, running it for a minute or so. Then turn the throttle stop screw on each carburetor in or out in small, equal increments until the lowest smooth idle speed is obtained. It is critical that the throttle stop screws be turned the same amount for each of the three carburetors.

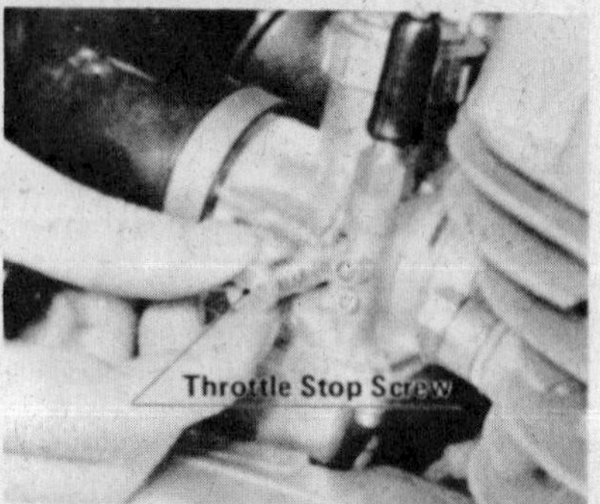

Throttle stop screw (S2 shown)

Throttle stop screw (S1 shown)

6. Place your hands over the ends of each muffler and check for equal pressure. If the pressure here is not equal for all three cylinders, either one cylinder is leading the others (idle speed too high), or is dragging (idle speed too low). Make fine adjustments to that cylinder by adjusting the pilot air screw or the throttle stop screw. It should not be necessary to turn either adjustment screw more than a small amount to equalize the backpressure. If it is, there has either been a mistake in settings, or there is a mechanical defect in the fuel system or engine, or ignition system.

7. After synchronization is complete, turn each of the throttle stop screws in or out in small, equal increments, until the recommended idle speed is reached.

8. Turn the throttle twist-grip adjuster so that the twist-grip has 5–10° of free rotational movement before the throttle slides begin to lift.

9. Check the oil pump cable adjustment. Refer to "Maintenance."

A further check of slide synchronization can be accomplished after removing the air cleaner hoses from the carburetors. Turn the twist-grip slowly while observing the movement of the throttle slides. All three should begin to move at the same time. Turn the twist-grip until the cutouts in the slides just clear the upper portion of the carburetor bore. Slide a finger in along the upper surface of the bore to ensure that each cutout is just even with the top surface of the bore. All three slides must be in the

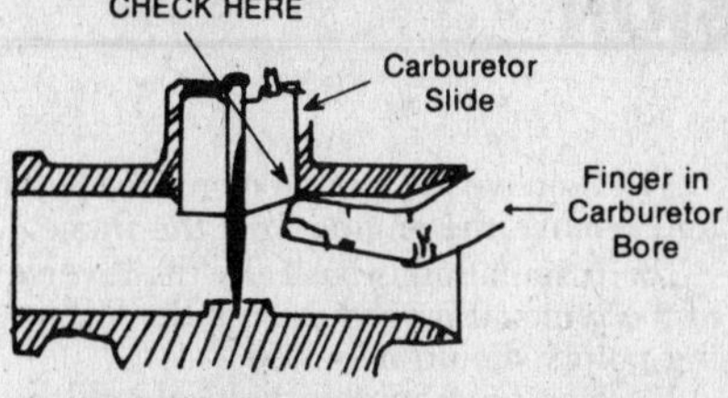

Checking throttle slide synchronization

Slide heights must be even as shown in the lower drawing

same position. If any one is too high or too low, use the cable adjusters atop each carburetor to effect adjustment. Allow the slides to close, and recheck cable adjustment.

NOTE: *After setting cable adjustments, turn the front forks slowly lock-to-lock with the engine idling. Any variation in idle speed as this is done would indicate that the throttle cable(s) are too tightly adjusted or are binding somewhere along the routing.*

Tune-Up Specifications

	S1	*S1-B/C, KH250*	*S2, S3*	*KH400*	*H1 (Breaker Point Ignition)*	*H1 (CDI)*	*H1-E/F, KH500*	*H2*
Standard spark plug (NGK)	B-9HCS	B-9HCS	B-9HCS	B-8HS	B-9HCS	BUHX	B-9HS-10	B-9HS-10
Spark plug installation torque (ft lbs)	18–22	18–22	18–22	18–22	18–22	18–22	18–22	18–22
Spark plug gap (in./mm)	0.024–0.028/0.6–0.7	0.024–0.028/0.6–0.7	0.024–0.028/0.6–0.7	0.035–0.039/0.9–1.0	0.016–0.020/0.4–0.5	—	0.035–0.039/0.9–1.0	0.035–0.039/0.9–1.0
Ignition timing (in./mm BTDC)	0.102/2.60 (23°)	0.102/2.60 (23°)	0.102/2.60 (23°)	0.102/2.60 (23°)	②	0.136/3.45 (25°)	0.116/2.94 (23°)	0.123/3.13 (23°)
Point gap (in./mm)	0.012–0.016/0.3–0.4	0.012–0.016/0.3–0.4	0.012–0.016/0.3–0.4	—	0.012–0.016/0.3–0.4	—	—	—
Carburetor pilot air screw (turns out)	1½	1¼	1½	1¼	1½	③	1¼	④
Idle speed (rpm)	1300–1500	1300–1500	1300–1500	1200–1300	1150–1250	1150–1250	1150–1250	1150–1250
Float level (in./mm)	0.99/25.0	1.00/25.5	1.00/25.5	①	0.94/24.0⑤	0.94/24.0⑤	0.94/24.0⑤	0.94/24.0⑤
Compression (psi)⑥	142	142	150	150	142	142	142	142

① 4–6 mm (0.16–0.24 in.) below edge of carburetor body
② Drum front brake: 0.136/3.45 (25°)
Disc front brake: 0.088/2.23 (20°)
③ Early CDI: 1¼
H1-B: 1½
H1-C, H1-D: 1¼
④ H2, H2-A: 1½
H2-B/C 1¾
⑤ 2–4 mm (0.08–0.16 in.) below edge of carburetor body
⑥ If variance is 45 psi or more overall or more than 15 psi between cylinders, a top end overhaul is needed.

ENGINE AND TRANSMISSION

NOTE: *For engine component inspection techniques and procedures, refer to "Engine Rebuilding" under the General Information section.*

Engine Removal and Installation

Clean the engine thoroughly before removal to take away as much grease and road grime as possible. Be especially attentive to the cylinder base and the crankcase mating areas.

1. Warm the engine and drain off the transmission oil. Replace the drain plug hand-tight.
2. Remove the spark plugs.
3. Turn the fuel petcock to the "S" position (standard type petcock), disconnect the fuel lines from the carburetors and unbolt and remove the fuel tank.
4. Remove the complete exhaust system from the motorcycle.
5. Remove the three phillips head mounting screws from the oil pump cover and lift the cover up (500, 750) or remove it (250–400).
6. Unscrew the tachometer cable fitting and disconnect the cable from the engine.

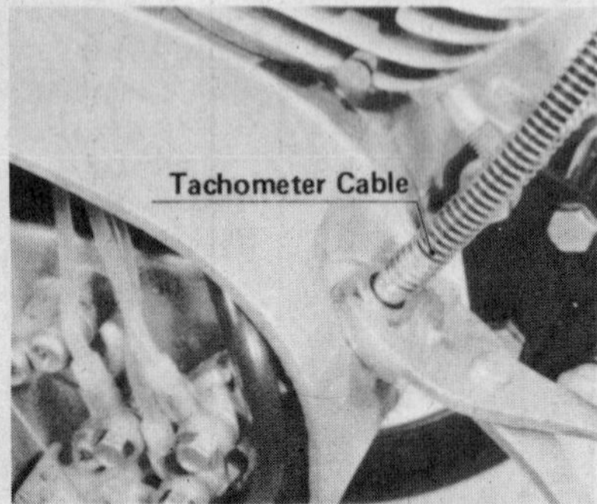

Disconnecting the tach cable (S-series)

7. Remove the distributor cap (early H1 battery-CDI only).

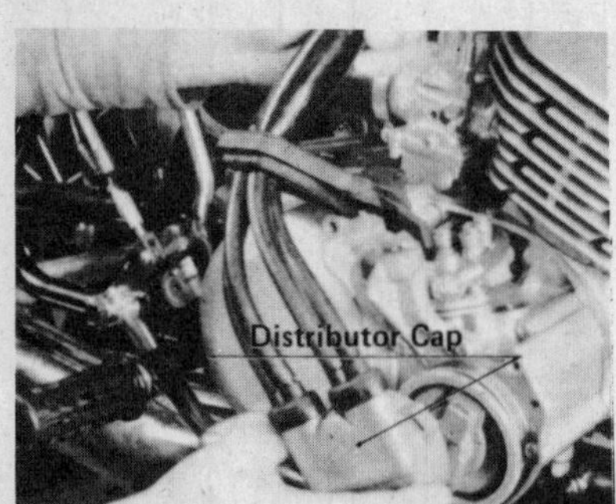

Removing the distributor cap (H1 battery-CDI)

8. Remove the air cleaner connecting tubes.
9. Remove the carburetors after loosening the clamps which secure them to the intake manifold. Tie them out of the way with the cables attached.
10. Remove the shift lever pinch-bolt and remove the shift lever and the shift lever pivot bolt.

Disconnecting the oil pump cable

11. Disconnect the oil pump control cable from the oil pump control lever and cable holder.
12. Disconnect the oil tank delivery line at the pump. Plug the end of the line to prevent the oil tank from draining.

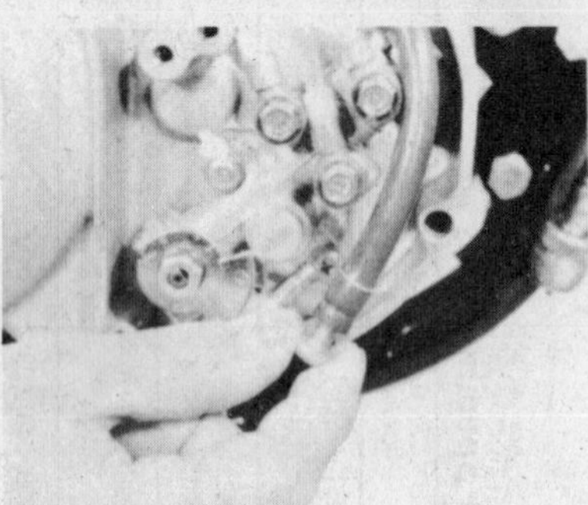

Plugging the oil delivery line

13. Remove the four phillips head screws from the countershaft sprocket cover and remove the cover.
14. Remove the masterlink (if fitted) from the drive chain. If no masterlink is fitted then loosen the rear axle nut and sprocket nut, loosen the chain adjusters and move the wheel forward and slip the chain off the countershaft sprocket.

    NOTE: *If the sprocket is to be removed later, loosen the sprocket nut before disengaging the chain.*
15. Slacken the clutch cable; disconnect the cable from the clutch release mechanism after straightening the lever tongue, then disconnect the cable from the engine cover.
16. Disconnect the alternator leads from the main harness at the connectors under the seat.

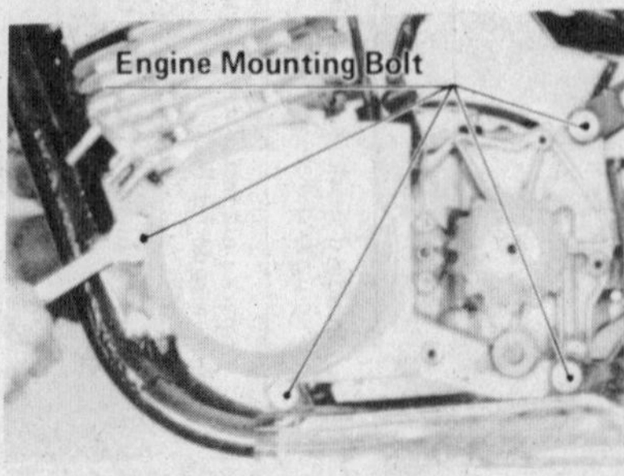

Engine mounting bolts

17. Remove the engine mounting bolts and remove the engine from the frame.
18. Installation is basically the reverse of the removal procedure, but the following points should be noted:
19. Engine mounting bolts should be properly torqued. Refer to the "General Torque Specifications" chart.
20. Coat the threads of the engine case screws with anti-seize compound or a general purpose lubricant to prevent them from seizing in the engine cases. Install them with an impact driver.
21. Replace any worn or damaged exhaust pipe gaskets.
22. Make sure that all fuel and oil lines are properly seated and secured with circlips.
23. After refilling the transmission and bleeding the oil pump, check all points of adjustment: cables, chain, rear brake, ignition timing, carburetor synchronization, oil pump cable adjustment, etc.
24. Install the drive chain masterlink spring clip (if fitted) with the closed end facing the direction of rotation.
25. After starting the engine, check around the carburetor and air cleaner for air leaks.

TOP END

The components in the top end are the cylinder heads, cylinders, pistons, piston rings, wrist pins, and the connecting rod small end bearings. All of these can be removed for inspection and service with the engine in the frame. No special tools are needed to remove these components.

Cylinder Head, Cylinder and Piston

REMOVAL

Clean the engine thoroughly before beginning.

1. Remove the fuel tank and exhaust header pipes.
2. Loosen the carburetor connecting bands, and remove the carburetors from the intake manifolds.
3. Disconnect the spark plug leads and remove the spark plugs. Disconnect the oil lines at the cylinder on models so equipped.
4. Loosen the four cylinder head nuts from each cylinder ¼ turn at a time in an "X" pattern. When all of the nuts are

Removing the cylinder head

loose, remove them and their washers from the studs. Carefully lift off the cylinder head, and remove the head gasket beneath it as well.

NOTE: *If the cylinder head will not come off the cylinder, tap it at the bottom with a soft-faced mallet until it is free. Take care not to break the cooling fins.*

To remove the cylinder, place one of the outside pistons at top dead center.

5. Lift that cylinder up and off the studs. When the cylinder spigot clears the crankcases, insert a clean, lint-free rag between the cylinder and crankcases. This will catch any piece of broken ring which may drop out when the piston comes out of the cylinder bore. Continue lifting up the cylinder until the piston clears the bore, then place it in a safe place with the lower end up to await service.

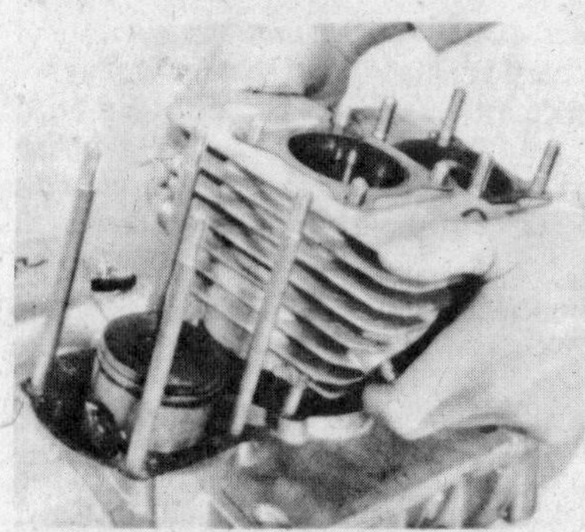

Removing a cylinder

NOTE: *Pistons must be reinstalled into their proper cylinder; therefore, mark the position of each piston before removal.*

6. Remove the wrist pin circlips with needlenose pliers. The rag should remain in place while doing this to prevent one of the circlips from falling into the crankcase.

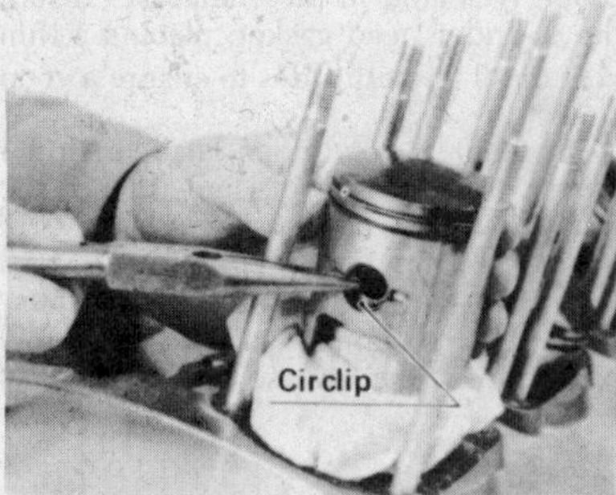

Removing a wrist pin circlip

IMPORTANT: *New circlips must be used on reassembly.*

Grasp the piston with one hand, and push out the wrist pin with a suitable drift. If the pin will not come out, the piston crown may be heated, evenly and gently, with a propane torch. If the pin still resists, it is advisable to use a special tool to remove it. This consists of a steel band or bands which fits around the piston while an attached screw device is used to push out the pin.

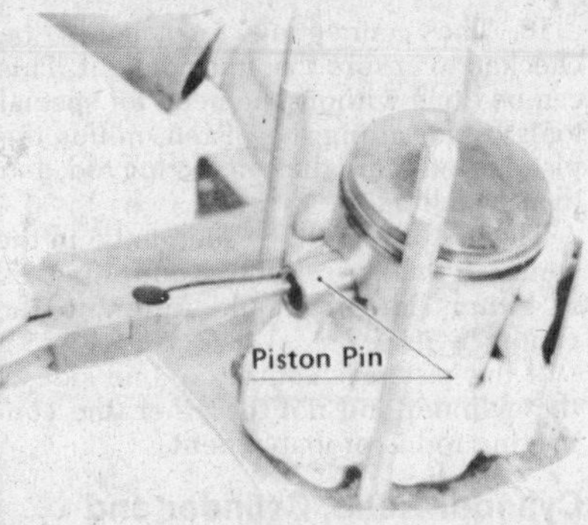

Removing the wrist pin

7. When the wrist pin is about ¾ in. out of the piston, grasp the exposed end with needlenose pliers, and pull it out until it is clear of the connecting rod. Remove the piston and small end needle bearing from the connecting rod.

CAUTION: *Never strike the wrist pin or attempt to use force to drive it out. The connecting rod may be bent in the attempt.*

Cylinder and Piston

INSPECTION

1. Inspect the surface of the cylinder walls for scoring or other damage. It is recommended that the cylinder be lightly honed.

2. After honing, inspect the cylinder walls again. If scores or scratches deeper than 0.001–0.002 in. (0.025–0.050 mm) remain in the walls, the cylinder should be rebored and the next oversize piston fitted.

3. Make a visual inspection of the piston. It should be free of scoring or signs of extreme wear. If any damage has occurred, it may be possible to save the piston by polishing the damaged area with an oilstone, or with #400 grit sandpaper or crocus cloth. However, if score marks are deeper than 0.002–0.003 in. (0.050–0.075 mm), or if the scored area is wider than 0.5 in., it is recommended that the piston be replaced.

If the piston is sanded, do so to yield a cross-hatch pattern.

4. Check that the piston ring locating pins are not excessively worn. If they are, the piston should be replaced. Check the fit of the wrist pin in the piston; if the wrist pin is a very loose fit, the piston and wrist pin should be replaced.

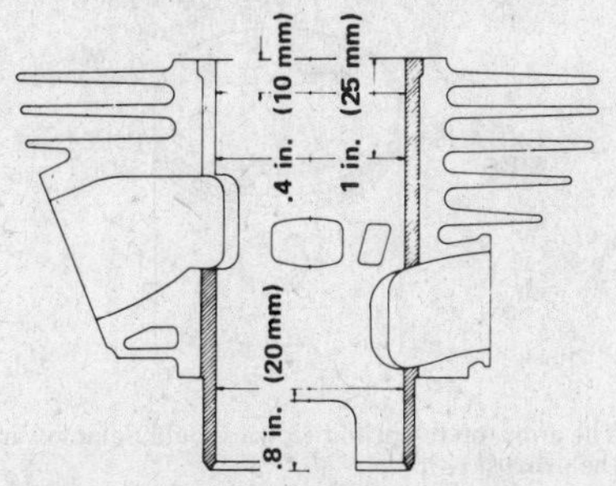

Cylinder bore measurement points

5. Measure the cylinder bore diameter in three locations, as shown, in directions both parallel and perpendicular to the crankshaft (six measurements). If any of the measurements are greater than the service limit given at the end of this section or if any two measurements vary by more than 0.05 mm (0.002 in.), the cylinder should either be bored to an oversize or replaced. This checks cylinder wear, taper, and out-of-round. Oversized pistons are available in two sizes: 0.5 mm and 1.0 mm.

6. Measure the piston diameter at a point 5 mm (0.2 in.) from the bottom of the skirt and perpendicular to the wrist pin. Then measure the cylinder diameter at a point 5 mm (0.2 in.) up from the bottom of the cylinder also perpendicular to the wrist pin. The difference between the two measurements is the piston-to-cylinder clearance. If the clearance is greater than the service limit given at the end of the section, a new piston should be fitted. If this does not bring the clearance into specification, the cylinder will have to be bored and an oversize piston fitted.

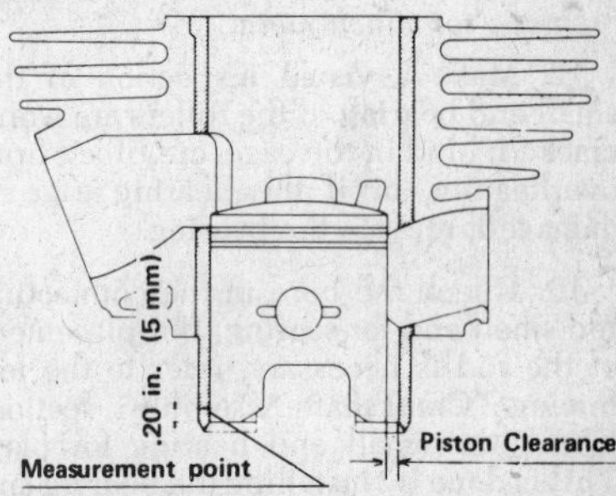

Piston-to-cylinder clearance

7. After boring the cylinder, or whenever the rings are replaced, the cylinder should be honed so that a cross-hatched finish is produced. Also, it is important that the edges of the ports be bevelled slightly. This can be done with some emery cloth.

8. Be sure that the piston rings are free in the grooves, and that the grooves have not been closed up by having metal pushed into them as might occur if the piston has seized. The ring grooves should be cleaned of any carbon build-up after the rings have been removed.

9. With the rings installed in their grooves, measure the piston ring groove side clearance with a feeler gauge. If the clearance is greater than the service limit given at the end of this section, replace the rings as a set. If fitting new rings does not bring the side clearance into the proper tolerance, replace the piston as well.

If the side clearance is not sufficient, it is probable that the piston has suffered seizure damage (metal being pushed into the ring grooves). In this case, the piston must be replaced.

10. Remove the rings from the piston by carefully spreading the end-gap with your thumbs and moving the part of the ring opposite the end-gap off the piston. Place each ring on a flat surface such as a piece of plate glass to check for warpage. If either ring is warped or twisted, replace the rings as a set.

11. Assuming that the cylinder bore is

not excessively worn, measure the end-gap for both piston rings. Insert each ring into the bore about 5 mm (0.2 in.) from the bottom of the cylinder. Push the ring into the bore using the piston; this will ensure that the ring is perpendicular to the cylinder wall.

Check that the ring is contacting the cylinder wall at all points. Place the cylinder with the ring in it on a white paper under strong light. If you can see the paper between the ring and the cylinder wall, replace the rings, or check the cylinder bore diameter.

Measure the end-gap with a feeler gauge. If the end-gap of any ring is greater than the service limit given at the end of this section, replace all rings.

New rings should also be checked in this manner before installation. If the end-gap of a new ring is too small, use a fine file to remove as much material from the ring ends as necessary.

NOTE: *Be sure to check the gap often during this operation as it is easy to remove too much metal.*

12. Make a visual inspection of the small end bearing. If the rollers are worn, cracked, bind in the cage, are blued from overheating, or if the bearing cage is damaged, replace the bearing.

13. Check the bore in the connecting rod small end for scoring. If replacement of the rod is necessary, refer to the following "Crankshaft Assembly" section. Check the small end bearing for play. This is done by installing the bearing and wrist pin in the connecting rod and feeling for up-and-down play between the wrist pin and connecting rod. If play is noticeable, replace the bearing.

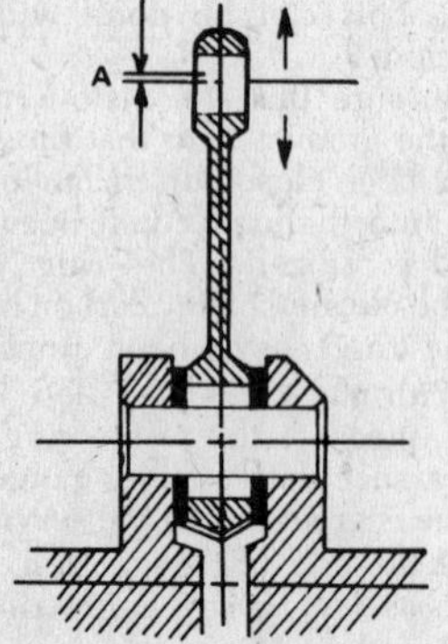

Check the con rod for vertical play which would indicate a worn big end bearing

14. If the wrist pin shows any blueing, which is indicative of overheating or lack of lubricant, it and the needle bearing should be replaced.

15. Check the connecting rod for radial (up-and-down) play on the crankpin. There must be absolutely none. If any play is evident, this indicates a badly worn big end bearing. Procedures for measuring the con rod radial and axial clearance and crankshaft service steps are given under "Crankshaft Assembly," which follows.

16. The connecting rod should be checked to ensure that it is not bent. This can be done without the need for special tools by installing the piston, minus the piston rings, onto the connecting rod, and then installing the cylinder.

The piston should be seen to be in the center of the bore. If the piston is moved to either side, it should return to the center by itself.

If the piston is contacting one side of the cylinder and not the other, the connecting rod is probably bent.

Cylinder Head, Cylinder and Piston

INSTALLATION

1. Refit the piston rings to the piston; note that the top ring has a chrome outside edge and is also chamfered while the bottom ring is un-chamfered. If the bottom ring has a expander behind it, install this into the ring groove first. Install the rings, beginning with the bottom ring, by spreading them slightly and sliding them down over the piston and into their respective grooves. The rings must be installed with the number and letter facing up and the end-gap over the locating pins in the grooves.

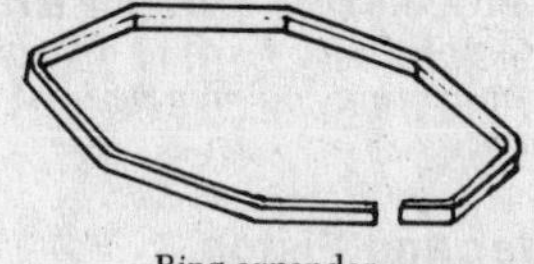

Ring expander

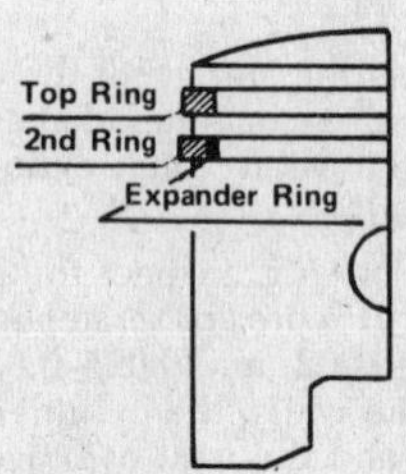

Piston ring location

2. Fit one of the *new* wrist pin circlips into the far side of the piston; the gap in the circlip should face either up or down. Install the wrist pin into the near side of the piston so that about ⅛ in. of the wrist pin is visible protruding from the inside of the piston. The wrist pin should be a push-fit, but gentle heat may be applied to facilitate installation as on removal.

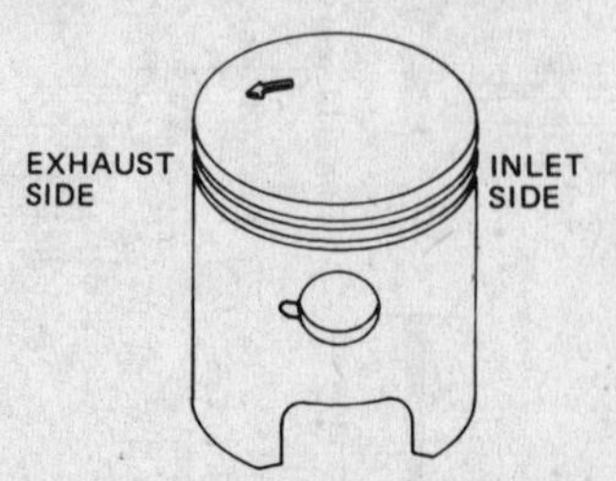

The arrow on the piston crown should point toward the exhaust port

3. Install the small end bearing into the connecting rod. Lubricate it with two-stroke oil.

4. Place the piston over the connecting rod with the arrow stamped on the top of the piston pointing to the exhaust side of the engine.

5. Carefully line up the wrist pin with the connecting rod small end bearing, and push the wrist pin through until it is centered between the circlip grooves.

6. Install a new circlip into the groove in the near side of the piston. Be sure that both circlips are firmly seated in their grooves with the gap in the circlip facing either up or down.

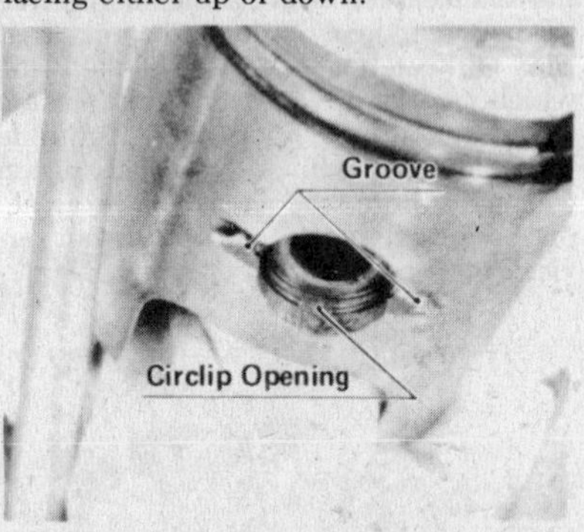

Make sure that the gap in the circlip is positioned downward and that the clip is firmly seated in its groove

7. Lightly lubricate the piston rings and the piston skirt with two-stroke oil.

8. Install a new cylinder base gasket, making sure that it is installed correctly.

9. Place the piston at top dead center. Align the piston rings so that the ring ends are directly over the locating pins.

10. Take up the cylinder, make sure that the cylinder walls are lightly coated with oil and fit the cylinder on the crankcase studs.

11. Lower the cylinder over the piston while compressing the piston rings with your fingers until the piston has fully entered the bore.

12. Make sure that the cylinder is properly seated in the crankcase. Install the cylinder head gasket; placing a thin coat of oil on both sides to ensure a good seal.

13. Refit the cylinder head, cylinder head washers and nuts and tighten the nuts in an "X" pattern in increments of about 5 ft lbs to the proper torque of 16 ft lbs for 250–500 models, 30 ft lbs for 750s.

14. The remainder of the assembly procedure is the reverse of disassembly.

CRANKCASE COVER COMPONENTS

The alternator, or magneto countershaft sprocket, and clutch release mechanism are found beneath the left crankcase covers; while beneath the right crankcase cover are the oil pump, tachometer drive, primary drive gears, and the clutch.

To remove the alternator or magneto assembly, a special puller is necessary, while a holder of some sort will be necessary to remove the clutch, primary gear, and the countershaft sprocket.

In all cases, these parts can be serviced with the engine in the frame.

Alternator

S-SERIES, KH250

Removal

1. Remove the two phillips head mounting screws from the points cover and remove the cover.

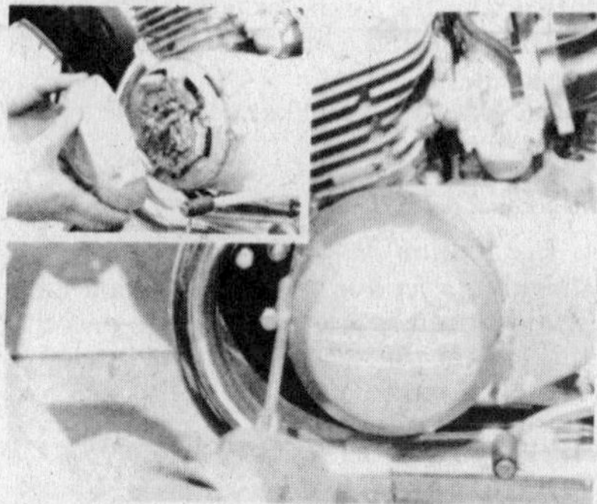

Removing the points cover (S-series, KH250)

2. Remove the neutral switch wire from the neutral switch.

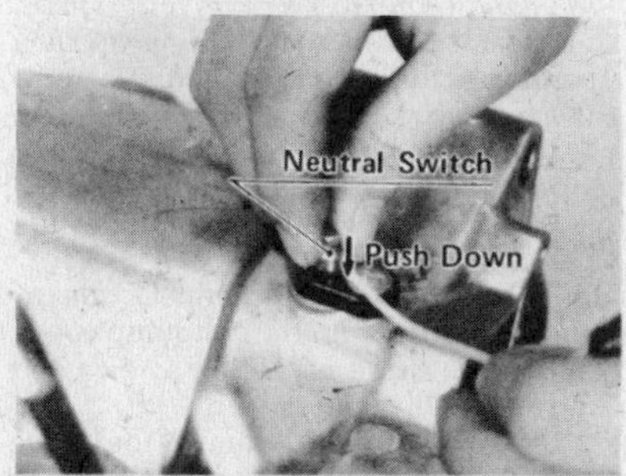

Disconnecting the neutral switch

3. Disconnect the point and alternator wiring from the wire harness at the connectors.
4. Remove the breaker cam bolt.

Removing the breaker cam bolt

Removing the stator assembly

NOTE: *When removing the breaker cam bolt or using the rotor puller it will be necessary to keep the crankshaft from turning. Engage the transmission and apply the rear brake.*

5. Remove the four phillips head screws from the left crankcase cover and remove the cover, breaker plate, and stator as an assembly.

Removing the rotor

6. Remove the rotor with a rotor puller. Screw the puller into the center of the rotor to remove it from the tapered end of the crankshaft. Remove the woodruff key from the crankshaft.

Removing the woodruff key

Inspection

For inspection of the alternator components refer to the "Electrical System" section.

Installation

Assembly is the reverse of disassembly, however, note the following points.

1. Install the woodruff key in the slot in the end of the crankshaft.
2. Lubricate the tapered portion of the crankshaft with a thin coat of grease to make removal easier the next time.
3. Make sure that no metal objects have become attached to the rotor.
4. Draw the rotor down on the crankshaft with the mounting bolt. Do not attempt to drive the rotor onto the crankshaft by force as striking the rotor can affect its magnets.
5. Be sure that the rotor does not rub on the stator.
6. Check the ignition timing.

KH400

Removal

1. Remove the gearshift lever. Remove the front and rear sections of the left crankcase cover. Remove the front section's gasket.
2. Engage the transmission, apply the rear brake, and remove the magneto rotor bolt.
3. Using the special puller, remove the rotor.
4. Disconnect the magneto/alternator wiring. Remove the three stator plate screws and take off the stator plate.

Installation

1. Installation is the reversal of removal. When installing the stator plate, be sure that the timing marks on the plate and the crankcase are aligned.

H1-H1-D, H2

Removal

1. Remove the shift lever and the sprocket cover.

Removing the left engine cover (H1-A/D H2)

2. Remove the three mounting screws (on H1 models) or two mounting screws (H2) and remove the left engine cover.
3. Remove the neutral switch wire from the neutral switch.
4. Disconnect the ignition and alternator wiring from the wire harness at the connectors.

Disconnecting the wiring (H2)

5. CDI models: Remove the signal generator rotor bolt and pull off the signal generator rotor.

NOTE: *When removing the signal generator bolt or using a rotor puller, it will be necessary to hold the crankshaft from turning. Engage the transmission and apply the rear brake.*

6. H1 without CDI: Mark the breaker plate so that it can be installed in the same position as it is removed from. Remove the breaker cam bolt, the three

Removing the rotor

Removing the breaker plate (H1, breaker point ignition)

mounting screws, and remove the breaker plate.

7. H2 models: Remove the three stator mounting screws and remove the stator.

8. Remove the alternator rotor with a rotor puller. Screw the puller into the center of the rotor to remove it from the tapered end of the crankshaft. Remove the woodruff key from the crankshaft.

Inspection

For inspection of the alternator components, refer to the "Electrical System."

Installation

Assembly is the reverse of disassembly. However, note the following points:

1. After installing the alternator woodruff key, push the alternator rotor onto the shaft. Do not strike the rotor while installing it as this may affect its magnetic properties.

A bit of lubricant applied to the crankshaft taper will make future removal of the rotor easier.

Align the slot in the rotor with the pin on the alternator rotor (H1, battery-CDI)

2. Align the slot in the signal generator rotor with the pin on the alternator rotor. On the H1 with breaker point ignition, align the slot in the breaker cam with the pin on the rotor.

Line up the slot in the cam with the pin on the alternator rotor (H1, breaker point ignition)

H1-E/F, KH500

Removal

1. Proceed as for H1-H1D, H2 outlined above, Steps 1–4.

2. Remove the stator plate screws, and take off the plate complete with pick-up coils and carbon brushes. Remove the plate slowly as the brushes are spring-loaded.

3. Remove the screws which secure the stator windings.

4. Remove the signal generator rotor bolt, the signal generator rotor, and use the special puller to remove the alternator rotor.

Inspection

For inspection of the components, refer to "Electrical Systems."

Installation

Install components in the reverse of disassembly. Reset the ignition timing as outlined in "Tune-Up."

Countershaft Sprocket

REMOVAL

1. Remove the shift lever and the sprocket cover.

2. Remove the sprocket nut from the end of the countershaft after bending back the locktab.

NOTE: *When removing the sprocket nut it will be necessary to hold the countershaft from turning. If the engine is in the frame this can be done by placing the transmission in High gear and applying the rear brake while removing the nut. If the engine has been removed from the frame, wrap a piece of old drive chain around the sprocket and lock the other end in a vise.*

Bending down the locking tab on the countershaft sprocket nut

3. Loosen the rear axle nut and move the rear wheel forward in the swing arm until the chain can be lifted off the countershaft sprocket.

4. Slide the sprocket off of the countershaft.

INSTALLATION

Installation is the reverse of the removal procedure. Ensure that the sprocket nut is firmly tightened and that the tab on the washer is bent up across one of the nut flats.

Right Crankcase Cover Components

RIGHT CRANKCASE COVER

Removal

NOTE: *On all models, the oil pump, tach and pump drive gears will remain in the cover when it is removed. They can be left undisturbed unless service is necessary.*

It will be necessary to bleed the pump before operating the machine, since the lines must be disconnected to remove the crankcase cover.

1. 250–400 only: Disconnect the tachometer cable from the oil pump cover. Remove the three mounting screws and remove the oil pump cover.

2. 500, 750 only: Remove the three mounting screws from the oil pump cover and slide the cover up the tachometer cable. Disconnect the tachometer cable and remove the oil pump cover.

3. Remove the three oil line banjo bolts and disconnect the oil lines from the pump and slip them out of the right crankcase cover. Be sure to keep track of the banjo bolt gaskets. Disconnect the oil pump cable from the control lever and remove it from the crankcase cover.

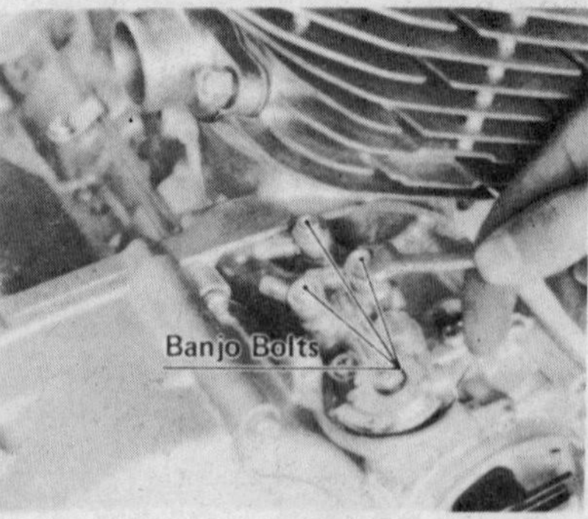

Removing the oil line banjo bolts (H1 shown)

4. H1 battery-CDI only: Unclip the distributor cap and remove it.

5. Remove the oil tank line from the oil pump by unscrewing the banjo fitting. Remove the banjo fitting from the oil line and plug the end of the line with a small screw.

6. Remove the kick-starter lever

pinch-bolt and pull the lever off the kick-starter shaft.

7. Drain the transmission oil. Place a drip pan beneath the crankcase cover.

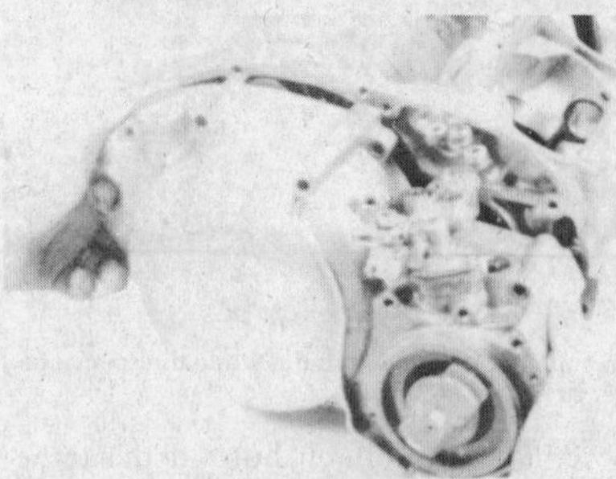

Removing the right crankcase cover (H1, battery-CDI)

8. Remove the mounting screws and remove the crankcase cover; tap it carefully with a plastic mallet to break the seal if stuck.

9. Remove the cover gasket.

Installation

Installation is in the reverse order of disassembly, however note the following points:

1. A new cover gasket should always be used upon assembly.

2. H1 battery-CDI only: The ignition timing will have to be set when the cover is installed:

a. Use a dial gauge to set the right cylinder at TDC;

Line up the mark on the timing plate with the "T" mark on the engine case (H1, battery-CDI)

b. Turn the rotor until the mark on the rotor is pointing to the "T" mark on the crankcase cover;

c. Holding the rotor in this position mount the cover on the engine as described below. Be sure that the right cylinder is still at TDC.

3. Hold the cover in place and make sure that the oil pump gear and the distributor gear (H1 battery-CDI) are meshed with their drive gears. Install the mounting screws and tighten them in an "X" pattern a little at a time until they are all tight. Secure with an impact tool.

4. Refill the transmission with the correct amount of oil.

5. Bleed the oil pump and adjust the control cable.

OIL PUMP

The pump is removed along with the right-side cover. For service to the oil pump refer to "Lubrication System."

TACHOMETER AND OIL PUMP DRIVES

1. Remove the right crankcase cover as previously described.

2. Pull the tachometer gear assembly out of the cover from the outside with pliers. On 500 and 750s, the nylon tach gear and thrust washer can be removed from the inside of the cover at this time.

Removing the tach gear shaft (500, 750)

3. S-series: Remove the two phillips screws from the tachometer gear holder in the inside of the case. Remove the holder, gear shaft and nylon oil pump gear, noting the location of any thrust washers.

Removing the tach gear assembly (250–400)

4. Inspect the condition of all of the gears, replace any with badly worn, chipped, broken, or missing teeth.

5. Inspect the condition of the oil seal in the tachometer bushing. If the lips of the oil seal appear to be damaged, replace the seal with a new one.

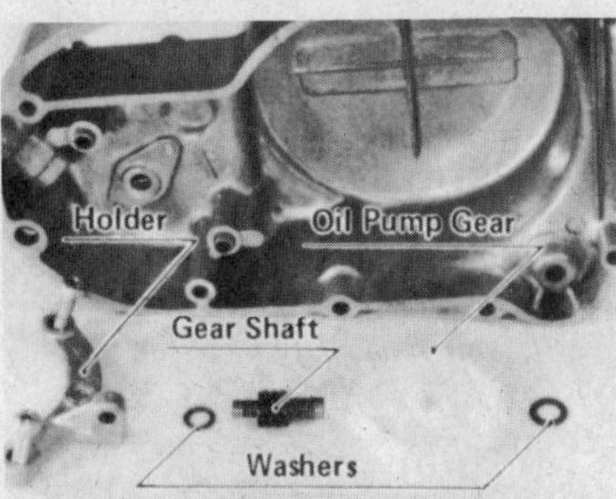

Left crankcase cover tach and pump gears (250–400)

6. Check the O-ring for condition, if it is torn or cracked it should be replaced.

7. To install the tachometer gear assembly, replace the gear shaft, oil pump gear, and gear holder (250–400). Be sure that the slot in the gear shaft is fitted to the tab on the oil pump drive. On 500–750, hold the driveshaft gear and thrust washer in place.

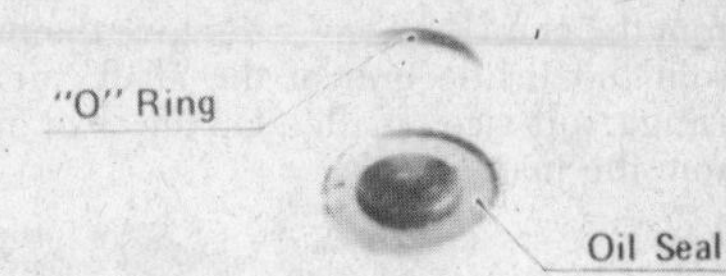

Check the tach oil seal and O-ring

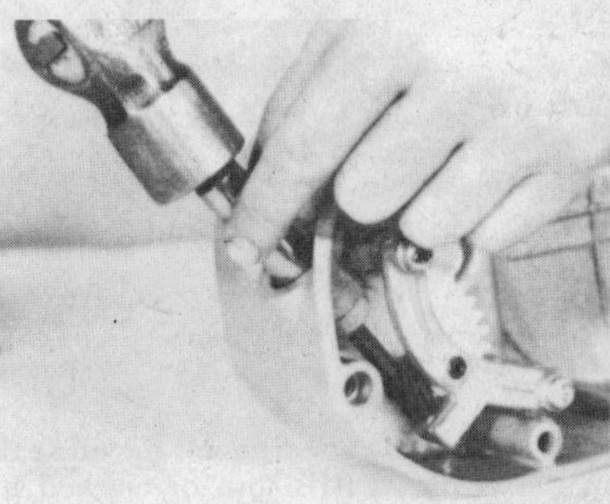

Installing the tach gear assembly (250–400)

8. Slip the tachometer driveshaft through the bushing, and press the assembly into the case. Take care not to damage the O-ring or the oil seal. Check that the gears line up when pressing in the shaft. Note that a pin on the shaft must engage the slot in the tach gear (500–750).

9. Install the right crankcase cover.

DISTRIBUTOR (H1 BATTERY-CDI)

1. Remove the right crankcase cover as previously described.

2. While holding the rotor remove the pinion gear nut from the end of the distributor shaft. Remove the pinion gear from the shaft.

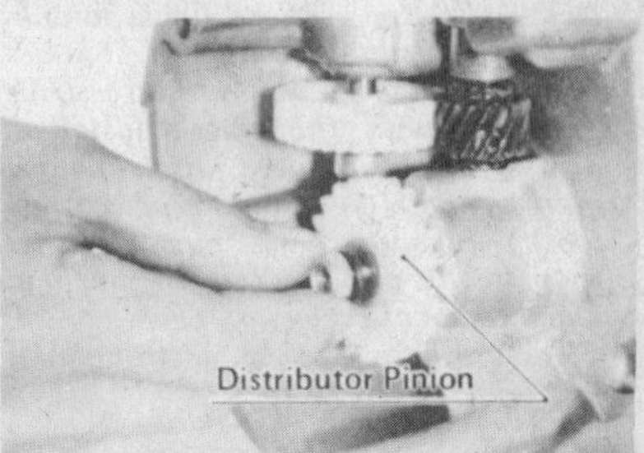

Removing the distributor pinion gear nut (H1, battery-CDI)

3. Pull the rotor off the shaft, and remove the insulator from the crankcase cover.

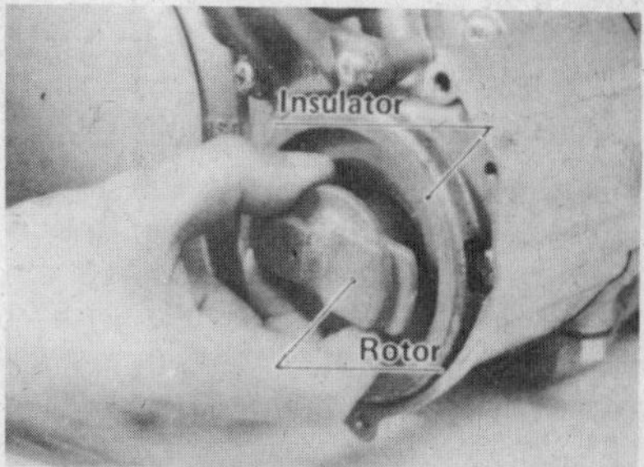

Removing the rotor (H1, battery-CDI)

4. To remove the distributor shaft from the crankcase cover, remove the pin from the inside end of the shaft, then, using a soft-faced mallet, tap the shaft out from the inside.

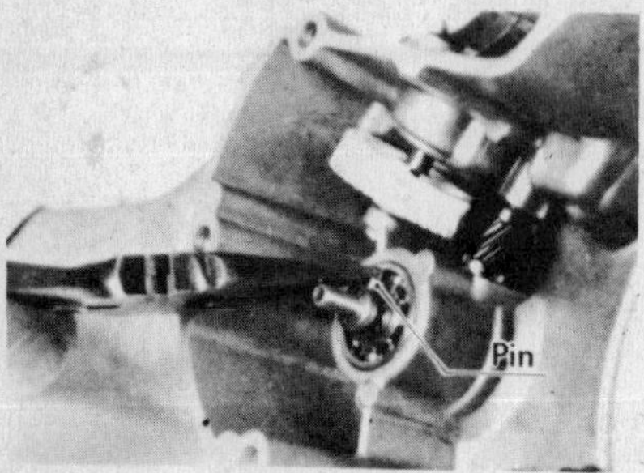

Remove the pin to remove the distributor driveshaft (H1, battery-CDI)

5. Check the condition of the oil seal in the cover, if it is torn or cracked it should be replaced.
6. Replace the rotor if it is cracked or chipped.
7. Inspect the pinion gear and replace it if any of the teeth are chipped or missing.
8. Inspect the shaft for bends and replace if bent. Check the bearing condition. Rotation must be smooth and effortless.
9. Inspect the condition of the threads on the end of the shaft. Replace the shaft if they are chipped or stripped.
10. Installation is the reverse of removal.

CLUTCH

Removal

1. Drain the transmission oil.
2. Remove the right crankcase cover as previously described.

NOTE: *If the primary drive (crankshaft) gear must be removed, it is advisable to loosen the primary drive gear nut with the clutch installed. Stuff a rag between the clutch and primary gears to lock them in place, then loosen the nut. Using impact (rather than steady pressure) on this nut will make removal easier.*

3. Loosen the five clutch spring plate bolts gradually and evenly, then remove them.
4. Remove the pressure plate with the clutch springs, and spring guides. On H2 models, remove the retaining ring from the clutch housing.
5. Remove the spring plate pusher from the center of the hub.

Clutch springs and retaining ring

6. Remove the clutch steel and friction plates. Note the steel bands fitted between each pair of friction and steel plates. Handle them carefully. Note the order of the plates and bands as they are removed. All components must be installed in the same order.

Removing the spring plate pusher

7. Remove the clutch hub nut. To remove the hub nut, either hold the hub stationary with the special tool, as shown, or engage the transmission and lock the countershaft sprocket in place.

Removing the clutch hub nut while the special tool keeps clutch from turning

8. Pull the clutch hub off the transmission mainshaft, and then remove the thrust washer behind the hub.

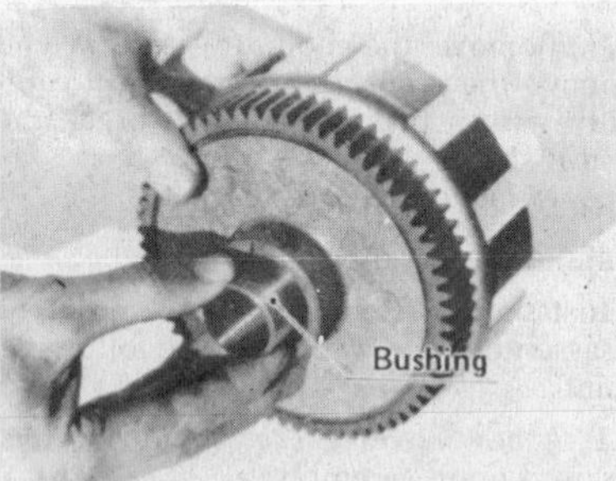

Checking the clutch housing bushing for play

9. Remove the clutch housing. The housing needle bearing will remain in the housing in most cases. Remove the bushing and thrust washer from the mainshaft.
10. To remove the clutch release mechanism and the pushrods: remove the countershaft sprocket cover, disconnect the clutch cable from the clutch release assembly, and unscrew the two mounting bolts. Remove the release mechanism and the pushrods.

Removing the clutch release assembly

Removing the pushrod

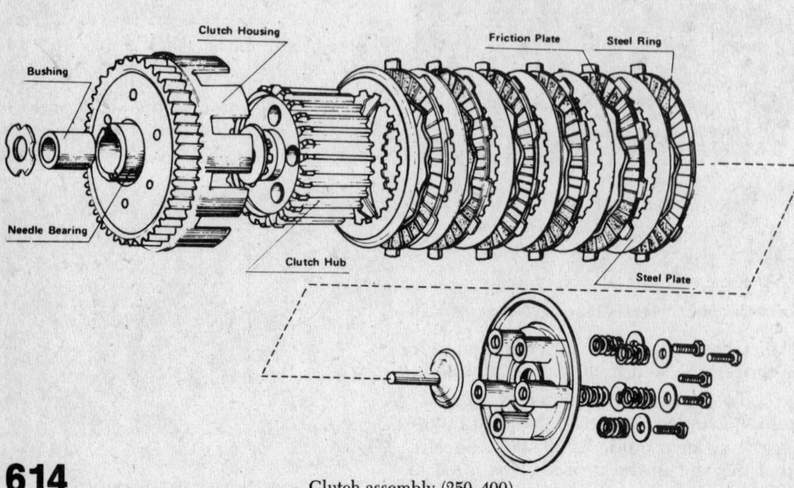

Clutch assembly (250–400)

Inspection

1. Refer to the "Specifications" charts at the end of this section for individual models.

2. Check clutch spring free length, friction plate thickness, and steel plate warpage. If plate warpage exceeds 0.2 mm (0.008 in.), replace the plates as a set.

3. Check the clearance between the tabs on the friction plates and the slots in the clutch housing. If the clearance exceeds the service limit given in the "Specifications" chart, replace the housing. If replacing the housing does not bring the clearance into specification, the friction plates will also have to be replaced.

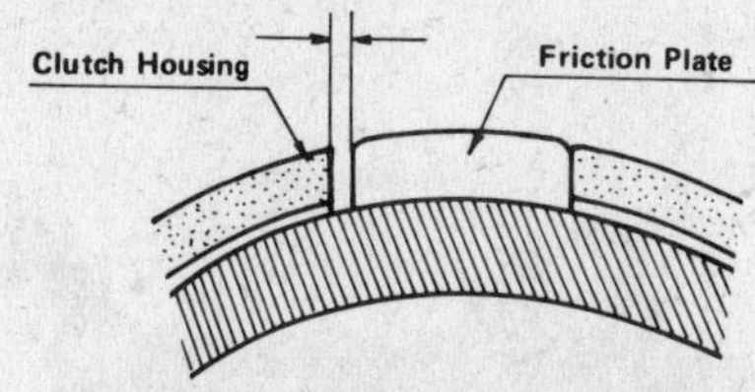

Check the clearance between the clutch housing and the friction plate tabs

4. Check the condition of housing gear. The gear teeth should be free of wear. If any of the gear teeth are broken or extremely worn, replace the clutch housing and check the condition of the gear with which the worn gear meshes (the primary drive gear). Minor imperfections of the teeth may be remedied with an oilstone. Any gear which is worn enough to necessitate replacement should have its mating gear replaced as well, since it, too, is undoubtedly worn.

5. Place the bushing on the mainshaft and check for play. If play is noticeable, replace the bushing. Be sure that the bushing is free of score marks.

Check the bushing for excessive play in the clutch housing. If any is evident, check the condition of the housing needle bearing as well and replace both bushing and bearing if necessary.

6. Inspect the condition of the needle bearing; if the rollers are scored or discolored or the roller cage is damaged, the bearing should be replaced.

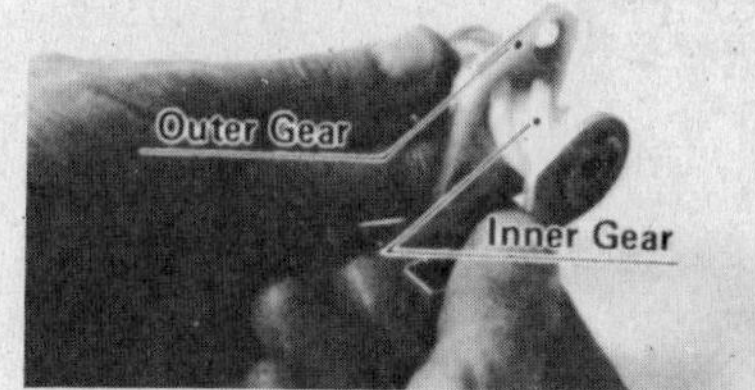

The inner and outer release gears should mesh smoothly

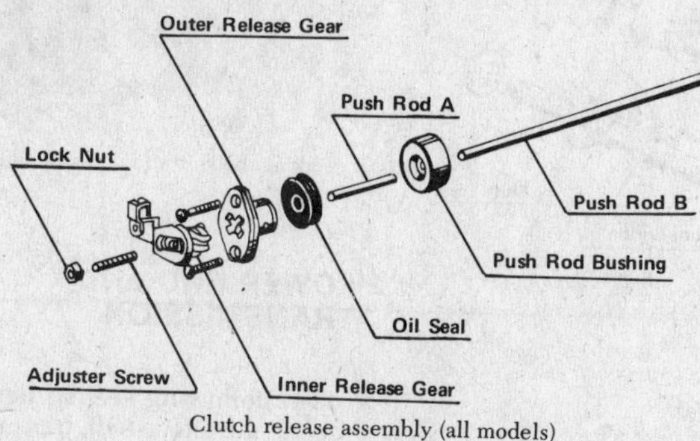

Clutch release assembly (all models)

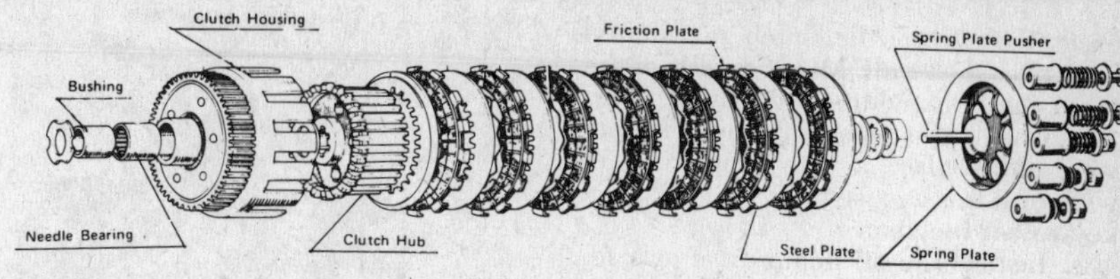

Clutch assembly (H1)

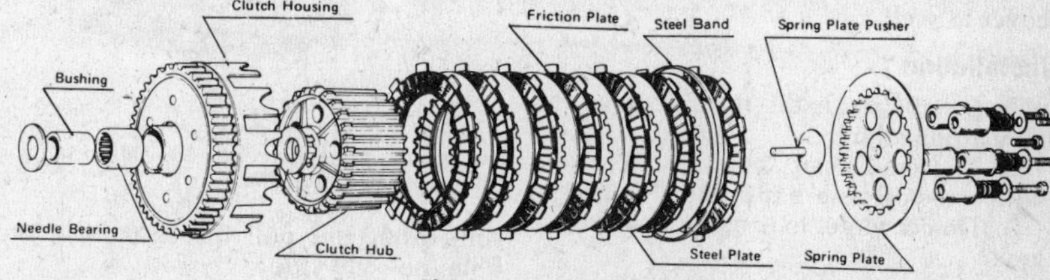

Clutch assembly (H2)

7. Check the general condition of the clutch release assembly pieces. The inner and outer release gears should mesh smoothly together. If they do not, check for damage and replace them.

Installation

1. Clean all metal parts in a solvent. Lubricate them with transmission oil before assembly.

2. Install the clutch components in the reverse of the removal procedure, referring to the accompanying illustrations if necessary. Be sure that all thrust washers are correctly installed.

3. Be sure that the steel bands are in place between the friction and steel plates.

4. Tighten the clutch hub nut securely.

5. Spring plate bolts should be tightened gradually and evenly.

PRIMARY GEAR

Removal

1. As noted, the primary drive gear nut should be loosened with the clutch installed.

2. Stuff a rolled up rag between the primary and the clutch housing gears to lock them in place, then remove the oil pump drive gear bolt from the end of the crankshaft. Remove the oil pump drive gear and lockwasher.

3. Bend down the locktab on the primary gear nut washer and unscrew the nut.

Removing the pump drive gear assembly

4. Remove the distributor drive gear (H1 battery-CDI), lockwasher, and the primary drive gear. Remove the key from the crankshaft.

Bending back the primary gear nut washer locktab

Distributor gear (H1, battery-CDI)

Inspection

1. Check the gear teeth for wear. Replace if necessary. If the primary gear is

excessively worn, the clutch gear should be replaced as well. Minor defects of the teeth can be remedied with an oilstone.

2. Check the woodruff key for step-wear and replace it if it shows signs of wear or if it is a loose fit in the crankshaft keyway or the gear.

3. Inspect the oil pump drive gear for worn teeth and replace it if necessary. Inspect the pump driven gear in the case cover as well.

Installation

1. Installation is the reverse of the removal procedure.

2. The crankshaft should be smeared with some oil before installing the gears.

3. Do not forget to install the woodruff key.

The primary gear nut washer projection must be fitted into the hole in the primary gear

4. When installing the primary gear nut lockwasher be sure that the projection on the washer is fitted into the hole in the primary gear. Tighten the primary gear nut securely, and bend up the side of the washer against the flat on the nut.

SHIFTER MECHANISM

Removal

On all models the shift arm and shaft can be removed and inspected with the engine in the frame.

1. Remove the right crankcase cover and clutch assembly.

2. Remove the gearshift pedal and the countershaft sprocket cover.

3. Disengage the shifter arm from the

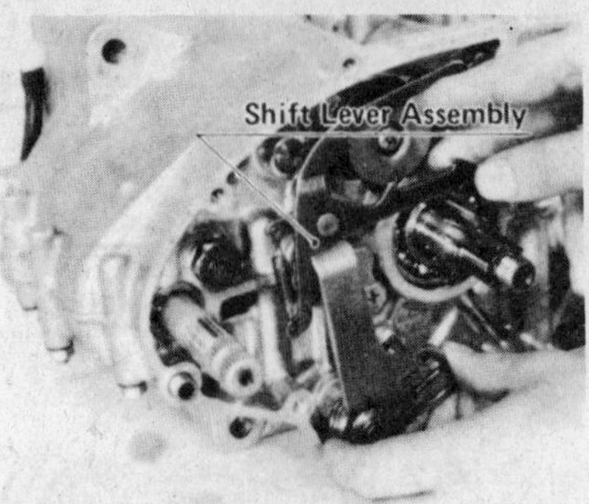

Disengaging the fingers from the shift drum and pulling out the shifter shaft

shift drum and pull the shift lever out from the right-side.

4. Remove the mounting screws, and remove the set lever and its spring and the positioning plate.

Removing the set lever

Inspection

1. Check the splines on the gearshift shaft for wear or splintering, and replace the shaft if they are too badly damaged to properly secure the gearshift pedal.

2. Check the shaft for a bent condition and replace it if bent.

3. Check the shift arm for straightness. Check the shift fingers for straightness, and especially for wear at the tips.

4. Inspect the shifter return spring and replace it if broken, or if the ends of the spring show signs of twisting or fatigue.

Removing the shift drum positioning plate

Check the shifter return spring for damage

5. Check the other springs in the shift linkage and replace any that are deformed, damaged, or weakened.

6. Inspect the set lever and replace it if worn.

Installation

1. Installation is the reverse of the removal procedures.

2. When installing the return spring, be sure that both ends of the spring bear tightly against the pin. The spring ends should be parallel to one another. This will provide the tension needed to keep the (foot) shift lever in position after each shift.

3. Be sure that the spring is secure in the crankcase.

4. When installing the positioning plate, stake the head of the mounting screws with a punch.

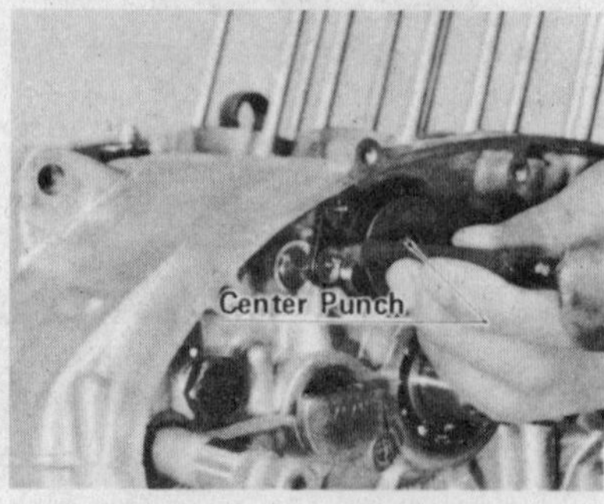

Staking the shift drum positioning plate screw

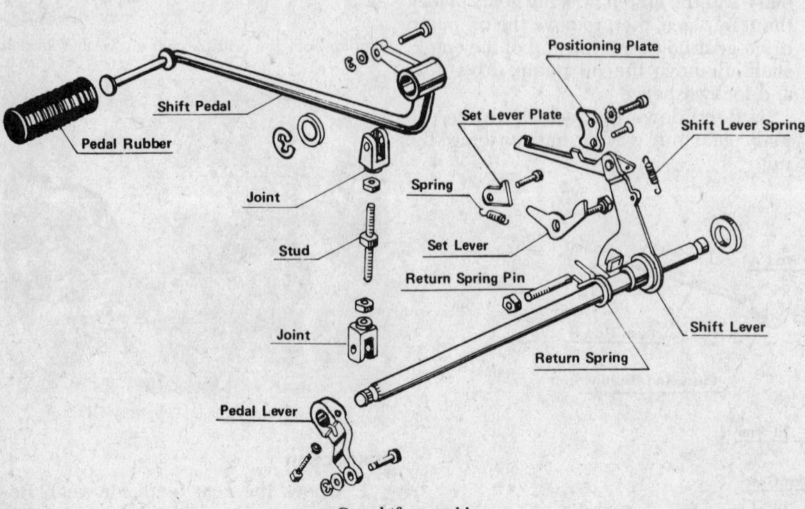

Gearshift assembly

LOWER END AND TRANSMISSION

The following section deals with service to the crankshaft, transmission, kick-starter mechanism, shifter (drum) assembly, crankcase bearings, and seals. Removing the engine and splitting the crankcases is necessary to service these components.

Splitting the Crankcases

1. Remove the engine from the frame. Remove the top end assembly. Remove the side cover components: alternator, countershaft sprocket, clutch, primary drive gear, shifter mechanism, clutch release mechanism.
2. Remove the oil receiver on the right-side of the engine.

Removing the oil receiver plate

3. Remove the kick stopper bolt.

Loosen the kick stopper bolt

4. Turn the engine upside down and remove the mounting nuts. Turn each nut ¼ turn at a time until they are all loose and then remove them.
5. Tap all around the crankcase mating surface with a soft-face or a plastic mallet. When the lower case comes free, remove it. The crankshaft and gear clusters will remain in the upper crankcase half.

Lower crankcase nuts

Engine Specifications

250

Item	*Standard (mm/in.)*	*Service Limit (mm/in.)*
Bore (standard)	45.016/1.772	45.15/1.778
Piston clearance	0.025/0.001	0.1/0.004
Piston skirt diameter (standard)	44.991/1.771	—
Top ring groove width	1.5/0.06	—
Top ring groove depth	2.5/0.1	—
Second ring groove width	1.5/0.06	—
Second ring groove depth	2.5/0.1	—
Top ring end-gap	0.2–0.3/0.008–0.012	0.8/0.031
Second ring end-gap	0.2–0.3/0.008–0.012	0.8/0.031
Top ring side clearance	0.09–0.13/0.003–0.005	0.17/0.007
Second ring side clearance	0.05–0.09/0.002–0.003	0.12/0.005
Clutch spring free-length	34.5/1.358	32.5/1.280
Friction plate thickness	3.0/0.118	2.7/0.106
Friction plate-to-clutch housing clearance	0.05–0.45/0.002–0.0217	—
Small end bearing radial clearance	0.003–0.022/0.00012–0.00088	0.1/0.004
Big end bearing radial clearance	0.025–0.035/0.00098–0.00138	0.1/0.0039
Con rod side clearance	0.4–0.5/0.0157–0.0197	0.7/0.0276
Crankshaft run-out	0.040–0.050/0.0016–0.0020	0.1/0.0039

350

Item	*Standard (mm/in.)*	*Service Limit (mm/in.)*
Bore (standard)	53.000–53.019/2.0866–2.0873	53.15/2.0925
Piston clearance	0.031/0.0012	0.1/0.004
Piston skirt diameter (standard)	52.975/2.0856	—
Top ring groove width	1.5/0.59	—
Top ring groove depth	2.5/0.0984	—
Second ring groove width	1.5/0.59	—
Second ring groove depth	2.5/0.0984	—
Top ring end-gap	0.2–0.3/0.008–0.012	0.8/0.031
Second ring end-gap	0.2–0.3/0.008–0.012	0.8/0.031
Top ring side clearance	0.09–0.13/0.0035–0.0051	0.17/0.0067
Second ring side clearance	0.05–0.09/0.0020–0.0035	0.12/0.0047
Clutch spring free-length	28.7/1.130	26.7/1.051
Friction plate thickness	3.0/0.118	2.7/0.106

6. To remove the crankshaft from the crankcase, tap upward on one end of the shaft with a plastic mallet. Lift out the crankshaft carefully.

7. Inspection of the transmission gears can be carried out with the gear clusters in place. Do not remove the gear clusters unless it is necessary to do so.

Removing the gear clusters

8. Lift out the mainshaft, complete with gears, by tapping upward on the clutch end of the shaft with a plastic mallet to free it if necessary.

9. Remove the countershaft and gears in the same manner.

10. Before removing the shift drum and forks, mark the location of each fork so that they may be installed in their proper locations.

11. Remove the set lever and the positioning plate to remove the shift drum.

12. 500, 750 models: bend back the locktab on the drum guide pins and remove the pins. Slip the shift drum out from the right-side and remove the selector forks.

Remove the guide pins to remove the shift drum from the forks (H-series)

13. 250–400 models only: Remove the circlip from the selector fork rod and slip the rod out of the crankcase, remove the two selector forks. Remove the cotter pin from the selector fork on the shift drum and remove the guide pin. Slip the drum out of the crankcase and remove the remaining selector fork.

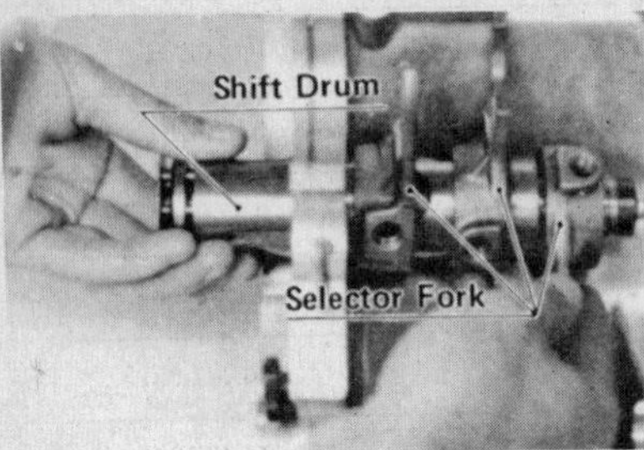

Removing the shift drum

Engine Specifications (cont.)

350

Item	Standard (mm/in.)	Service Limit (mm/in.)
Friction plate-to-clutch housing clearance	0.05–0.45/0.002–0.022	—
Small end bearing radial clearance	0.003–0.022/0.0001–0.0008	0.1/0.004
Big end bearing radial clearance	0.025–0.035/0.0001–0.0014	0.1/0.004
Con rod side clearance	0.4–0.5/0.016–0.019	0.7/0.027
Crankshaft run-out	0.04–0.05/0.0016–0.0020	0.1/0.004

400

Item	Standard (mm/in.)	Service Limit (mm/in.)
Bore (standard)	57.0/2.24	57.1/2.244
Piston clearance	0.031/0.0012	0.1/0.004
Piston skirt diameter (standard)	56.12/2.209	—
Top ring groove width	1.5/0.59	—
Top ring groove depth	2.5/0.098	—
Second ring groove width	1.5/0.59	—
Second ring groove depth	2.5/0.098	—
Top ring end-gap	0.2–0.3/0.008–0.012	0.8/0.031
Second ring end-gap	0.2–0.3/0.008–0.012	0.8/0.031
Top ring side clearance	0.09–0.13/0.0035–0.0051	0.17/0.0067
Second ring side clearance	0.05–0.09/0.0020–0.0035	0.12/0.0047
Clutch spring free-length	28.7/1.130	26.7/1.051
Friction plate thickness	3.0/0.118	2.7/0.106
Friction plate-to-clutch housing clearance	0.05–0.45/0.002–0.022	—
Small end bearing radial clearance	0.003–0.022/0.0001–0.0008	0.1/0.004
Big end bearing radial clearance	0.025–0.035/0.0001–0.0014	0.1/0.004
Con rod side clearance	0.4–0.5/0.016–0.019	0.7/0.027
Crankshaft run-out	0.04–0.05/0.0016–0.0020	0.1/0.004

500

Item	Standard (mm/in.)	Service Limit (mm/in.)
Bore (standard)	60.015–60.040/2.3628–2.3638	60.15/2.3681
Piston clearance	①	0.1/0.004
Piston skirt diameter (standard)	59.975/2.3612	—
Top ring groove width	1.5/0.06	—
Top ring groove depth	2.7/0.1063	—
Second ring groove width	1.5/0.06	—

14. Lift the kick-starter assembly out of the crankcase.

15. Remove the spring guide and return spring.

16. Remove the two circlips and the holder plate.

17. Remove the snap-ring from the shaft and remove the gear holder and gear from the shaft.

Removing the shift rod shaft circlip (250–400)

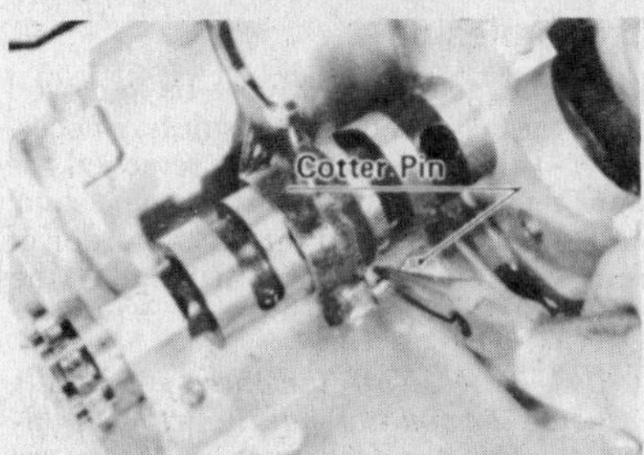

Remove the cotter pin and the shift fork guide pin to remove the shift drum

Removing the shift drum

Removing the kick-starter return spring

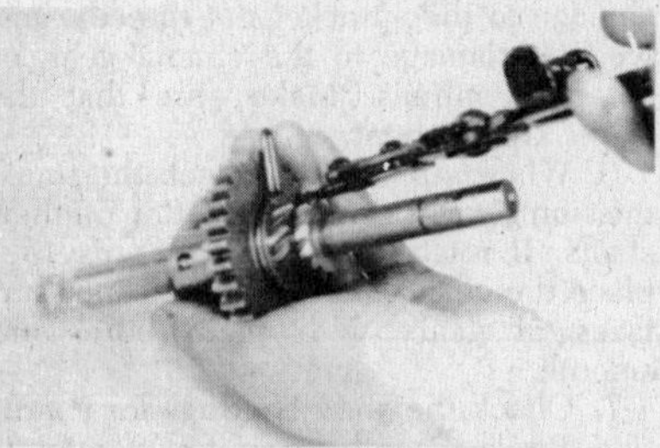
Removing the kick-starter shaft snap-ring

Engine Specifications (cont.)

500

Item	Standard (mm/in.)	Service Limit (mm/in.)
Second ring groove depth	2.7/0.1063	—
Top ring end-gap	0.2–0.3/0.008–0.012	0.8/0.031
Second ring end-gap	0.2–0.3/0.008–0.012	0.8/0.031
Free end-gap Top Second	 7.0/0.276 9.5/0.374	 — —
Top ring side clearance	0.09–0.13/0.0035–0.0051	0.17/0.0067
Second ring side clearance	0.05–0.09/0.002–0.0035	0.12/0.0047
Clutch spring free-length	36.0/1.417	34.0/1.339
Friction plate thickness	2.7–2.9/0.106–0.114	2.5/0.098
Friction plate-to-clutch housing clearance	0.1–0.4/0.0039–0.0157	—
Small end bearing radial clearance	0.003–0.022/0.00012–0.00088	0.01/0.00039
Big end bearing radial clearance	0.025–0.035/0.001–0.0013	0.1/0.0039
Con rod side clearance	0.4–0.5/0.015–0.019	0.7/0.028
Crankshaft run-out	0.04/0.0016	0.1/0.0039

①73 and earlier: 0.062–0.070/0.0024–0.0028
74 and later: 0.057–0.065/0.0022–0.0026

750

Item	Standard (mm/in.)	Service Limit (mm/in.)
Bore (standard)	71.000–71.019/2.795–2.796	71.15/2.8012
Piston clearance	0.074/0.0029	0.1/0.004
Piston skirt diameter (standard)	70.946/2.793	—
Top ring groove width	1.5/0.06	—
Top ring groove depth	3.23/0.1272	—
Second ring groove width	1.5/0.06	—
Second ring groove depth	3.23/0.1272	—
Top ring end-gap	0.2–0.4/0.008–0.016	0.8/0.031
Second ring end-gap	0.2–0.4/0.008–0.016	0.8/0.031
Free end-gap	8.0/0.315	—
Top ring side clearance	0.09–0.13/0.0035–0.0051	0.17/0.0067
Second ring side clearance	0.05–0.09/0.002–0.0035	0.12/0.0047
Clutch-spring free-length	32.0/1.26	30.0/1.18
Friction plate thickness	2.7–2.9/0.106–0.114	2.5/0.098
Friction plate-to-clutch housing clearance	0.09–0.4/0.0035–0.0157	—
Small end bearing radial clearance	0.003–0.022/0.00012–0.00088	0.01/0.00039

Engine Specifications (cont.)

750

Item	Standard (mm/in.)	Service Limit (mm/in.)
Big end bearing radial clearance	0.023–0.041/0.001–0.0013	0.1/0.0039
Con rod side clearance	0.4–0.5/0.015–0.019	0.7/0.028
Crankshaft run-out	0.04/0.0016	0.1/0.0039

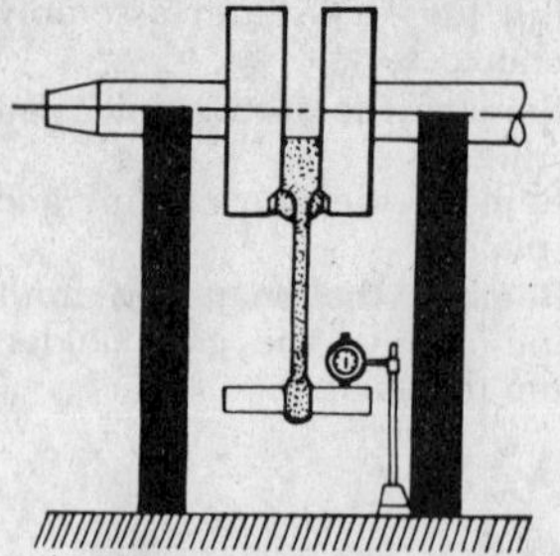
Checking for a bent connecting rod

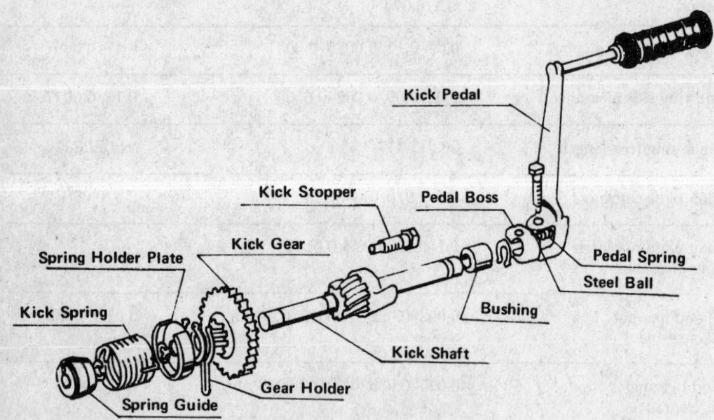

Kick-starter components

Crankshaft

The crankshaft is a pressed together unit. Therefore, in the event of damaged crank, crank bearings, or connecting rods the crankshaft should be replaced as a unit.

1. Lubricate the big end bearings with two-stroke oil. Rotate the rod slowly around the crankpin. The movement should be smooth and noiseless.
2. With the crankshaft mounted in a jig, and a dial indicator mounted to bear against the small end of the connecting rod, check the vertical movement of the rod. It should not exceed the service limit given for big end bearing radial play in the "Specifications" chart at the end of this section. If the movement exceeds this figure, the con rod big end bearing is worn, and the crankshaft should be replaced.

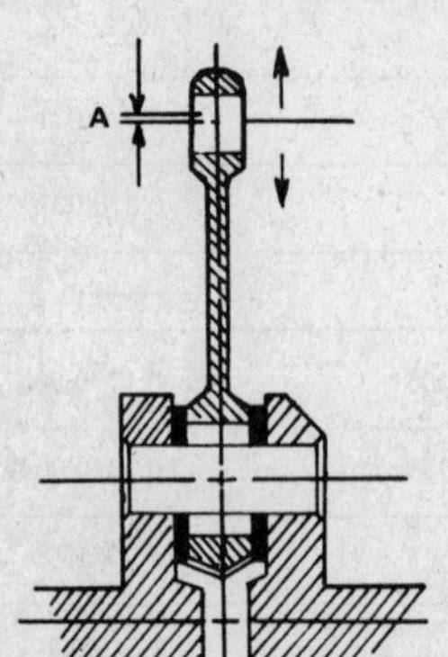

Check for big end bearing radial play

3. Check the connecting rod side clearance with a feeler gauge placed between the rod big end and one of the flywheels. Side clearance should be 0.4–0.5 mm (0.0157–0.0197 in.), if the side clearance is more than 0.7 mm (0.0276 in.), the crankshaft should be replaced.

Checking connecting rod big end bearing-to-flywheel clearance

4. Mount the crankshaft in a set of V-blocks, and mount a dial guage to the main bearings. Rotate the crankshaft slowly and note the indicator readings. The maximum allowable run-out is 0.10 mm (0.0039 in.). If run-out exceeds this figure, replace the crankshaft.
5. With the crankshaft mounted in a jig, as shown, insert a shaft of the same diameter as the wrist pin into the small end bearing. Measure the distance between the base of the jig and the shaft on both sides of the rod, any difference in the two measurements indicates the con rod is bent. Also check that the shaft is parallel to the crankshaft; if not the con rod is twisted.
6. Clean and lubricate the main bearings. Check that each bearing rotates smoothly. If, in any bearing, play can be felt or rotation is other than smooth, the bearing is beyond its service life.
7. The crankshaft oil seals must be in good condition to maintain fuel transfer compression in the individual crankcase compartments. If the seal lips are damaged or worn, or if there is evidence of leaking (discoloration), the seals should be replaced. Scratches on the surface of the outer seals, caused by pinching when the crankcases are assembled, are not harmful.

Transmission

1. The gears should not be removed from their shafts unless absolutely necessary. If the gears are being removed, be sure that each gear, thrust washer, shim, and snap-ring is laid out in the order of removal so that it can be installed in the proper location.

CAUTION: *Note the three steel balls inside the countershaft Fourth gear (S-series). If the transmission shafts are disassembled, refer to the exploded views of the transmissions as a guide to assembly. Note, however, that the number and location of the thrust washers fitted to individual transmissions may vary from the illustrations. These are used to adjust gear clearances (see below), and may differ from machine to machine.*

2. Check each of the gears for chipped, broken, or worn teeth. If any gear shows evidence of such damage, it should be replaced. In addition, the gear with which it meshes should be replaced as well, since it has undoubtedly been overstressed. Minor imperfections can be removed with an oilstone.
3. Check the inner splines on those gears so equipped, and replace the gear if the splines are worn or broken. Inspect the corresponding splines on the shafts. The shafts should be replaced if damaged.
4. Inspect the engaging dogs on gears which have them. The dogs must not be worn, chipped, or broken. Replace the gear if they are.
5. Inspect the transmission shafts for damage to the sprocket nut threads, and wear or damage to the clutch, gear, or sprocket splines. Make sure that the shafts are not bent.
6. Where applicable, check the transmission gears for smooth rotation on their shafts. If rotation is rough or noisy, replace the gear. Check that the inner surfaces of gears with plain bores are smooth.
7. Check the shaft bearings for condition. Replace any bearing if movement is balky or noisy, or if there is damage or

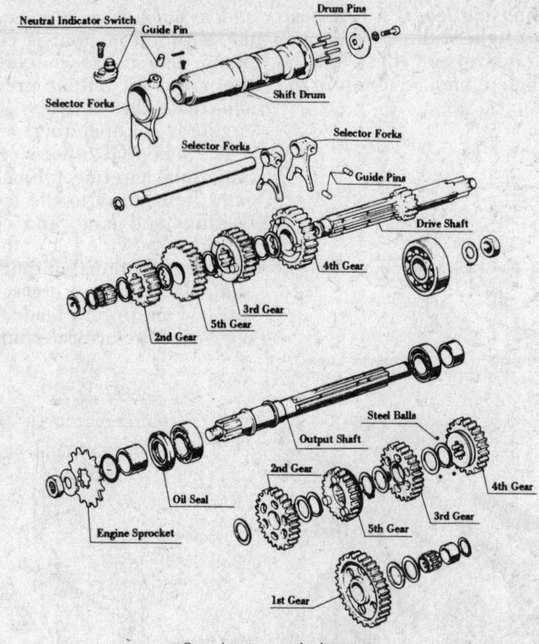

S-series transmission

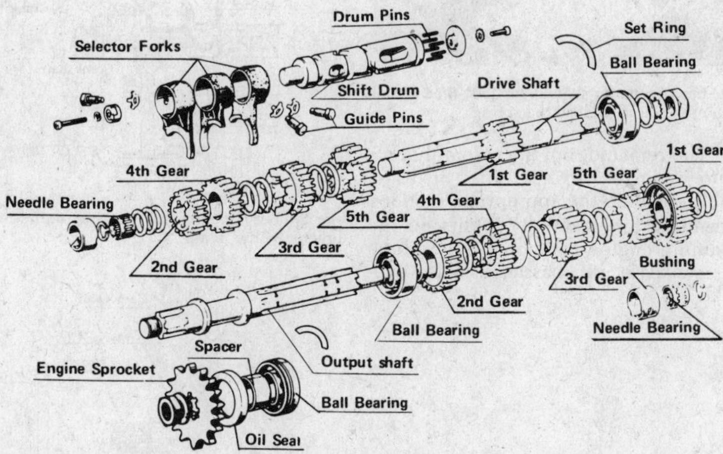

H-series transmission

discoloration to the bearings or races.

8. With the gear clusters assembled in the cases, check the gear side clearances with a feeler gauge as follows:

a. Clearance between the mainshaft Second gear and the bearing;

b. Clearance between the countershaft First gear and the bearing;

c. Clearance between the countershaft Second gear and Fourth gear (500, 750) or Fifth gear (250–400) snapring.

In each case, clearance should be 0.020 in. (0.5 mm) or less. To bring the clearance to within the proper specification, add a transmission shaft thrust washer where shown in the exploded views of the transmissions.

CAUTION: *If the addition of the washer makes the shaft difficult to turn, delete it.*

Shift Drum

1. The shift drum itself should be inspected for wear in the selector fork guide pin grooves, damaged guide pin lockwashers, and scoring or wear of the bearing surfaces.

2. The selector fork shaft (250–400) should be inspected for wear in those areas on which the selector forks ride. Roll the shaft along a flat surface to check it for a bent condition. Replace the shaft if bent.

3. Check the selector forks themselves. Note any wear to the fork bore. Check the fingers for bends, or for chipping or wear. Replace any fork on which such defects are noted.

Checking selector fork-to-gear clearance

4. Check the guide pins for wear, and replace them if damaged.

5. Check the shift drum pins. Replace any broken, worn or missing pins.

6. With a feeler gauge measure the clearance between the selector fork fingers and the groove in the gears. The standard clearance is 0.05–0.25 mm (0.002–0.01 in.); if the clearance exceeds 0.6 mm (0.024 in.), the gear and/or the selector fork should be replaced.

Kick-Starter

1. Rotate the gear on its shaft splines; operation should be smooth. Check for damage to the gear teeth (inner and outer) and to the shaft.

2. Check the condition of the splines on the end of the kick-starter shaft and replace the shaft if the splines cannot maintain a good grip on the kick lever.

Checking the movement of the kick-starter gear on its shaft

3. Inspect the return spring and replace it if the ends are broken or deformed.

4. The gear holder should be a snug fit on the gear.

Assembly of Crankcases

1. Check that the oil passages and the transmission breather hole are clear. Blow them out with compressed air if possible.

Be sure that the bearing set rings are properly installed

2. Clean the crankcase mating surfaces thoroughly.

3. Make sure that the crankshaft main bearings set rings are properly installed in the upper crankcase and install the crankshaft. Seat the main bearings by tapping them lightly with a plastic mallet.

4. Fit the transmission shafts into the upper crankcase. Position the selector forks so that the center fork faces the front

of the engine and the outer fork faces the rear. Fit the countershaft first and then the mainshaft. Be sure that the selector forks are correctly fitted to the grooves in the proper gears. The center fork is fitted to the mainshaft 3rd gear and the left and right forks are fitted to the countershaft 5th and 4th gears, respectively.

Seating crankshaft bearings

Position the selector forks as shown before installing the gears (250–400 shown)

5. Assemble the kick-starter. Be sure that the circlips and snap-ring are properly seated in the shaft. Install the kick-starter assembly in the case, noting that the end of the gear holder should be fitted into the boss in the crankcases. After the cases are assembled the return spring must be preloaded and the kick stopper installed.

The kick-starter gear holder should be seated in the crankcase boss

6. Apply a thin coat of gasket sealer to the crankcase surfaces. Install the lower crankcase. Tighten the crankcase nuts in an X pattern in 3 ft lb increments starting from the center of the case. Torque the 8 mm nuts to 18 ft lbs and the 6 mm nuts to 11 ft lbs.

7. Install the kick-starter lever on the shaft and rotate it counterclockwise about 150° and holding the lever in this position install and tighten the kick stopper bolt. Release the lever and check that the spring has sufficient preload to return the lever to the stop.

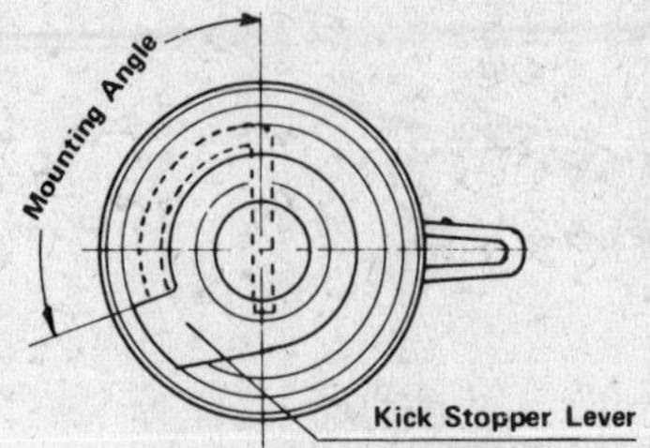

Rotate the kick-starter shaft about 150°, then install the stopper bolt to preload the spring

8. The remainder of the assembly procedure is in the reverse order of disassembly. Refer to the appropriate sections preceeding for assembly details on the remaining engine components. Pre-lube the crankcase oil passages with two-stroke oil.

LUBRICATION SYSTEM

Both Superlube and Injectolube systems include an oil reservoir, oil feed line, oil pump, and oil delivery lines. The pumps are of the plunger type and are driven by the end of the crankshaft through reduction gears. The amount of oil fed to the induction passage delivery line and crankcase drillway (Injectolube) is determined by two variables: the speed of plunger operation and the length of plunger stroke. These variables are set by the engine rpm and the degree of throttle opening, respectively. The pump effectively meters the amount of oil according to engine speed and load and, as a result, no more and no less than the required amount is consumed. The pump also houses a check valve that keeps the oil output pressure constant and seals the delivery line when the engine is not operating.

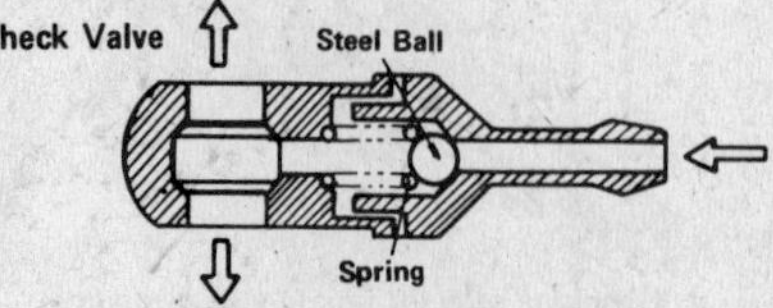

The essential difference between the Superlube and Injectolube systems is the extra lubrication to the crankshaft main bearings and large end connecting rod bearings provided by the Injectolube type. An additional output port in the oil pump leads to a drillway in the crankcase, which in turn leads to smaller passages to these critical points.

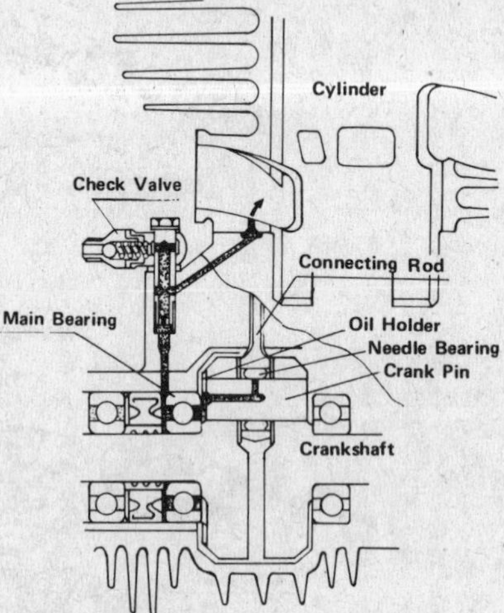

Injectolube: the crankshaft bearings are lubricated directly by the pump

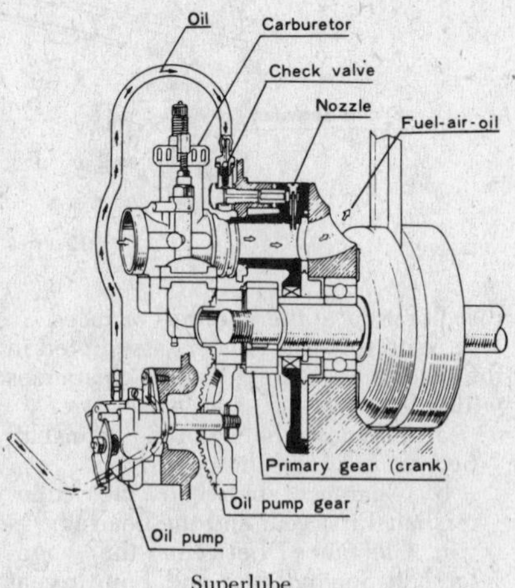

Superlube

OIL PUMP

Removal and Installation

1. 250–400 only: Disconnect the tachometer cable from the oil pump cover. Remove the three mounting screws and remove the cover.

2. 500 and 750 only: Remove the three mounting screws from the oil pump cover and slide the cover up on the tachometer cable. Disconnect the tachometer cable and remove the oil pump cover.

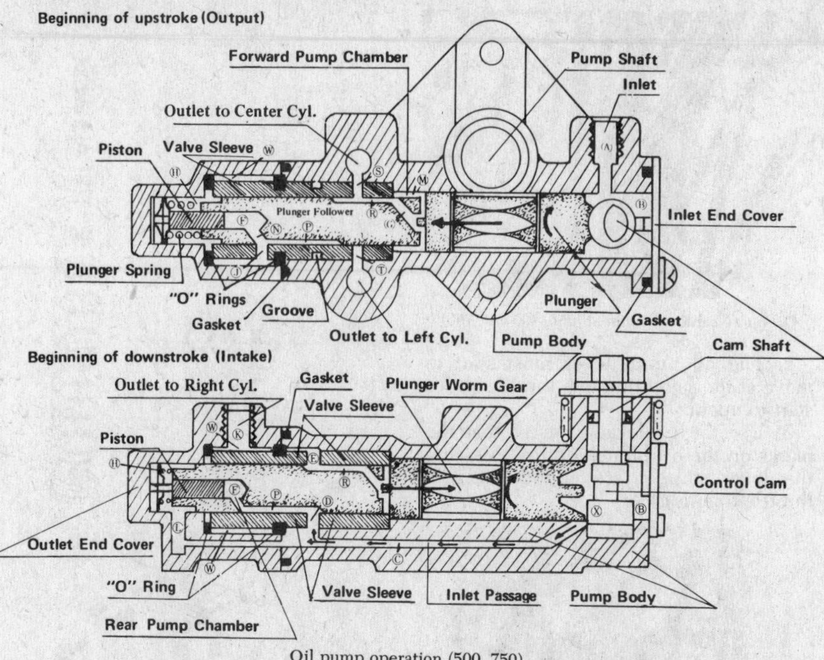

Oil pump operation (500, 750)

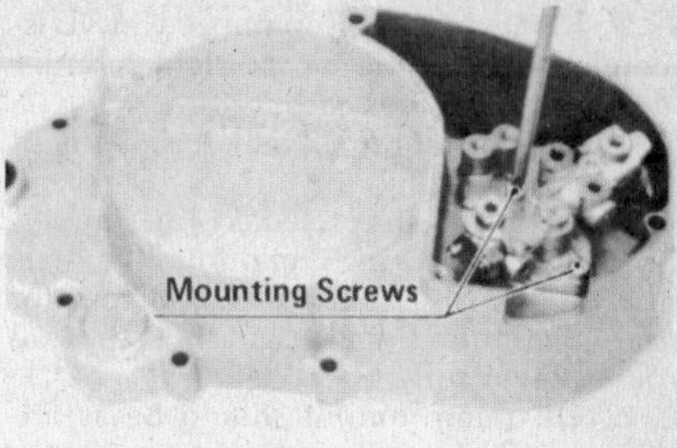

Oil pump mounting screws (250–400 and 750)

Oil pump mounting screws (500)

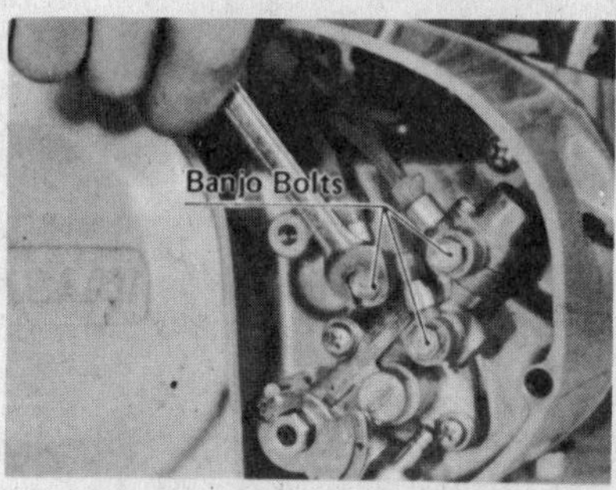

Disconnecting the banjo bolts (250–400)

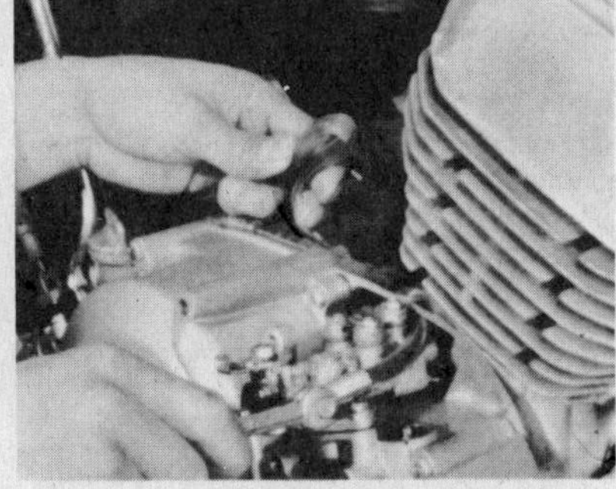
Disconnecting the oil tank line (H1 shown)

3. Remove the three oil line banjo bolts and disconnect the oil lines from the pump. Cover the ends of the oil lines with a plastic bag secured with a rubber band to prevent dirt from entering the system.

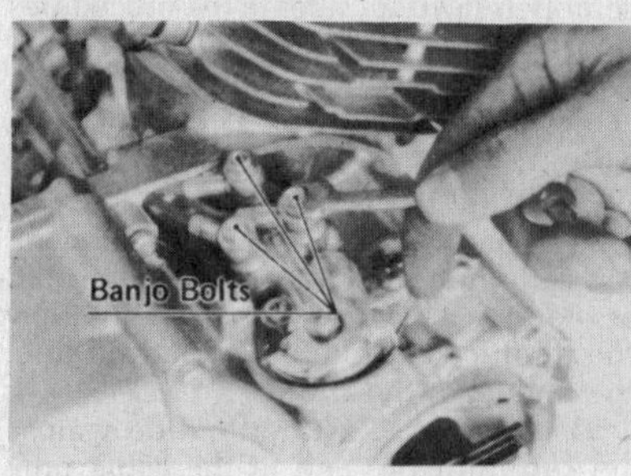

Disconnecting the banjo bolts (500)

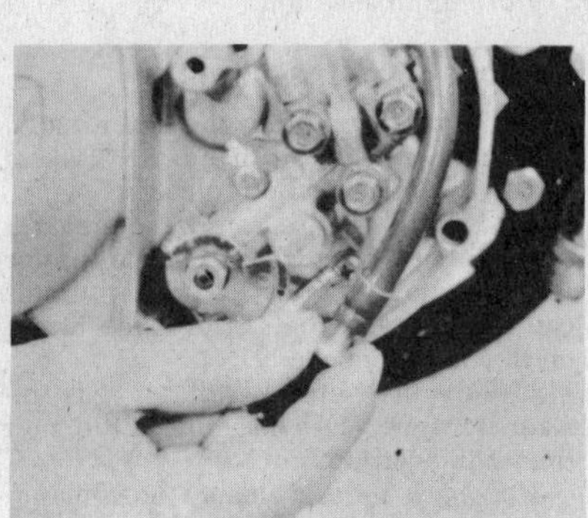
Plugging the delivery line

4. Disconnect the oil pump cable from the pump control lever.

5. Remove the oil tank line from the oil pump by unscrewing the banjo fitting. Remove the banjo fitting from the oil line and plug the end of the line with a small screw.

6. Remove the two phillips head mounting screws and pull the pump off the right crankcase cover.

7. To install, mount the pump to the right crankcase cover with the two mounting screws. Be sure that the tab on the oil pump drive is fitted into the slot in the oil pump driveshaft.

8. Install the oil lines. Make certain that they are securely fastened, and that all gaskets are in place.

9. Connect the pump control cable and adjust it as described below.

10. Bleed the oil lines as described below.

Pump Repair

The factory advises against attempting to disassemble and repair the oil pump. The internal parts are machined to very exacting tolerances and it is highly unlikely that the pump can be reassembled to factory specifications. In addition to this, oil pump failure is *very* seldom due to internal malfunction.

The condition of pump o-rings is critical. Replace the o-rings if in doubtful condition.

Pump Output

H2-B/C

1. Drain the gas tank and refill it with a gas/two-stroke oil mixture in a ratio of 20:1.

2. Remove the oil pump cover. Detach the banjo bolt and oil line from the right-side carburetor and fit a 6 mm screw to the carburetor.

3. Loosen the banjo bolt at the oil pump and take out the check valve. Tighten the banjo bolt.

4. Check that the oil tank has plenty of oil. Run the free end of the disconnected oil line into a measuring cup or something similar.

5. Start the engine. While running it at 2,000 rpm, hold the oil pump open for three minutes.

6. Measure the amount of oil collected. Proper output is 0.17–0.20 oz. (4.9–5.9 cc).

7. If output is not within this amount, check oil pump o-ring condition. Replace them if damaged. If the problem is not rectified, replace the pump.

8. Flush out the gas tank; bleed the oil pump.

OTHER MODELS

1. Drain the gas tank and refill it with a gas/two-stroke oil ratio of 20:1.

2. Remove the oil pump cover. Disconnect the oil line for the right cylinder at the crankcase or carburetor.

3. Check that the oil tank has plenty of oil.

4. With the disconnected line emptying into a measuring cup or the like, start the engine and run it at 2,000 rpm for three minutes while holding the oil pump lever fully open.

5. Oil pump output should be as follows:

500: 0.17–0.20 oz. (5.1–5.8 cc)
H2: 0.23–0.26 ox. (6.8–7.5 cc)
250: 0.11–0.13 oz. (3.2–3.9 cc)
350, 400: 0.13–0.15 oz. (3.8–4.4 cc)
"S1," "S2-2" (pump marks): 0.11–0.13 oz. (3.8–4.4 cc)

6. If output is unsatisfactory, check oil pump o-rings and replace if in bad or doubtful condition. If this does not rectify the problem, replace the pump.

7. Flush the gas tank and bleed the pump.
after the throttle cables.

PUMP BLEEDING

The oil pump must be bled of air between the pump and check valve, and between the reservoir and pump whenever the pump is removed, the delivery lines are disconnected, or the reservoir has run dry.

1. Remove the oil pump access cover.

2. Start and run the engine at 2,000 rpm while holding the pump control lever in the fully open position.

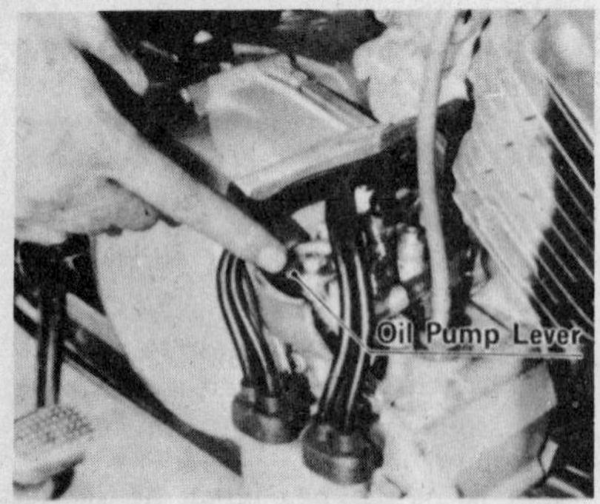

Hold the lever fully open while bleeding the pump (H1 shown)

3. Observe the output delivery line. Any air bubbles in the system should disappear quickly. If they do not, check the tightness of the input and output line banjo bolts.

4. If there are air bubbles in the reservoir oil delivery line, disconnect it at the pump and allow oil to flow through it until the bubbles are gone, then reconnect it and repeat Steps 2 and 3. The reservoir delivery line must not be disconnected while the engine is running.

OIL PUMP CABLE ADJUSTMENT

1. The oil pump should be adjusted after the throttle cables. Refer to "Tune-Up."

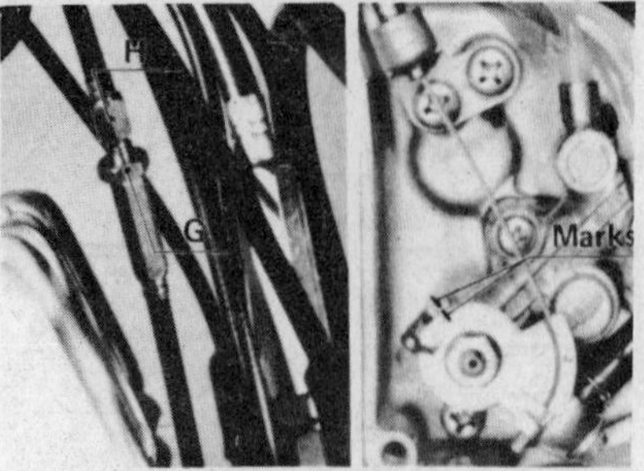

Oil pump cable adjustment (250–400 and 750)

2. The oil pump lever must start to move at the same time the throttle slides start to open.

3. Use the cable adjuster so that the marks on the oil pump control lever and the lever stopper are aligned at zero throttle opening.

Oil pump cable adjustment (500)

FUEL SYSTEM

NOTE: *For carburetor theory, component inspection, and troubleshooting, refer to "Carburetors" in the "General Information" section.*

Removal and Installation

Before disassembling the carburetors, have overhaul kits on hand. All gaskets and O-rings should be replaced.

1. Carburetors are removed one at a time. Before removing each carburetor from the manifold, loosen the carburetor cap ring nut and the starter cable fitting on the carburetor body.

2. Turn the petcock "off" if it is the standard type, and disconnect the fuel line at the carburetor.

3. Loosen the air cleaner hose clamp screw on either outside carburetor, and remove the air cleaner hose.

4. Loosen the carburetor clamp screw at the manifold and pull off the carburetor. Disconnect any breather or overflow lines.

5. Lift up the rubber cap cover, unscrew the cap ring nut, and pull out the throttle slide assembly. Unscrew the starter plunger unit. Drain the fuel from the float bowl.

6. Repeat the procedure for the two remaining carburetors.

7. Installation is the reverse of the above. Be certain that the carburetors are vertical on their manifolds. Secure the manifold and air cleaner hose screws. On machines with "diaphragm" petcocks, turn the petcock to the "prime" position to fill the float bowls with fuel.

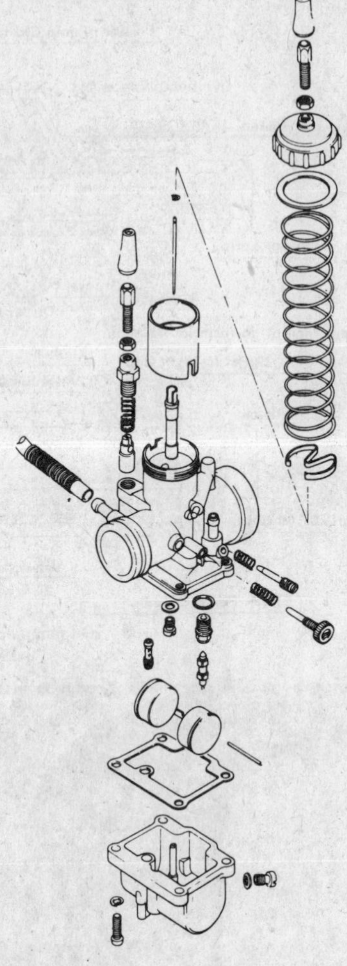

Mikuni carburetor SC-series

Disassembly

If disassembly of the throttle slide assembly is desired, refer to the procedures below. If a throttle-stop rod is used to adjust the idle speed, as on some models, see Step 1 and following. On models with a body-mounted screw for idle adjustment, begin with Step 2.

1. The idle speed adjusting screw on the carburetor cap has a small cotter pin at the top. Removing this pin will allow the throttle stop rod to be removed from the bottom of the slide.

2. Compress the throttle slide against the cap until the end of the cable protrudes from the bottom of the slide. Slip the cable end free of the slide, then remove the spring and slide.

3. Remove the spring seat from the inside of the slide, then turn it upside down to remove the needle and clip.

NOTE: *Do not remove the clip from the needle unless making a tuning change.*

4. Turn the carburetor upside down, and remove the four float bowl screws. Remove the float bowl.

NOTE: *If the carburetor is old and has*

never been disassembled, the float bowl may be stuck to the gasket. Use a soft-faced (plastic) mallet to tap around the bowl until it is free. Restraint should be exercised while doing this.

5. Push out the float pivot pin by hand or with a small punch, and remove the float assembly.

CAUTION: *Carefully note or mark the top side of the float assembly, since damage could occur if the attempt were made to install the float incorrectly.*

6. Remove the float needle.
7. With a suitable socket, unscrew and remove the float needle seat.
8. Unscrew and remove the main jet.

CAUTION: *All fuel jets are very malleable and must be removed and installed with care to avoid damage.*

9. Unscrew and remove the pilot jet.
10. The needle jet is located above the main jet and is a press-fit in the carburetor body. Removal is not usually necessary unless the jet is to be replaced. To remove the needle jet, remove the washer press-fitted into the carburetor just beneath the needle jet. Use a small wooden dowel to tap the bottom of the needle jet and force it into the carburetor bore.

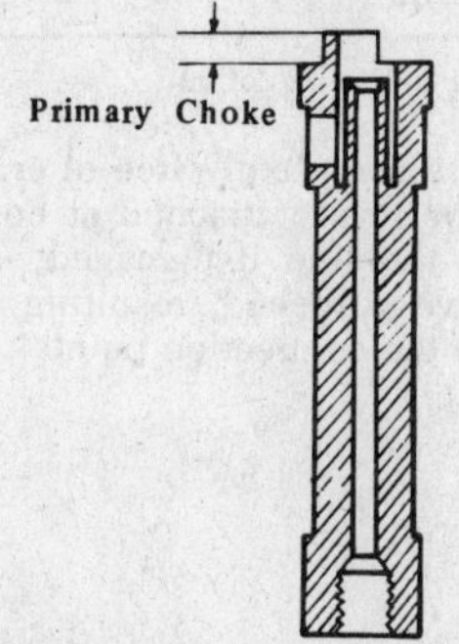

Install the primary choke of the needle jet facing the air cleaner side of the carburetor; the cutout faces the engine side

CAUTION: *When installing the needle jet note that it must be installed with the cutout at the top of the jet facing the ENGINE side of the carburetor.*

Assembly

1. All gaskets should be replaced when overhauling a carburetor.
2. On models with a rod-operated throttle slide, assemble by first fitting the carburetor cap onto the throttle cable. Install the stop rod through the bottom of the slide and secure it with the cotter pin to the top of the idle adjusting screw on the carburetor cap.
3. Install the needle, making sure that the needle clip is properly positioned, and that the clip position is the same for all three carburetors.
4. Install the spring seat, return spring, and engage the throttle cable on the slide in the reverse of the disassembly procedure.
5. Install the pilot jet, being careful when screwing the jet in that it is properly seated.
6. Install the needle jet, as on removal, with a wooden dowel drift, tapping it into its seat from the carburetor bore. Install the washer.

Be sure that the jet is installed with the cutout at the top facing the engine side of the carburetor.

7. Install the main jet.
8. Install the fiber gasket onto the float needle seat and screw the needle seat into the carburetor.
9. Insert the float needle into the seat, and position the float assembly over the needle, ensuring that the correct side faces up. Slip the float pivot pin into the holder.
10. Check the float level as outlined in "Tune-Up."
11. Fit a new float bowl gasket. Refit the float bowl, insert the four phillips head screws and tighten them gradually, and in an "X" pattern.
12. Refit the pilot air screw. Screw it in gently until seated, then back it out the prescribed number of turns given in the "Carburetor Specifications" chart at the end of this section. This is an approximate setting and may have to be readjusted after the engine is started.
13. Install the throttle stop screw (if fitted) to the carburetor body.
14. Install the carburetor on the manifold, slip in the throttle slide and needle and secure the cap ring nut. Fit the plunger assembly to the carburetor body. Secure the manifold clamp screw.
15. Refer to the "Maintenance" and "Tune-Up" sections if necessary to adjust the pilot air and throttle adjustment stop screws, cables, and slide synchronization.

FUEL PETCOCK

Two types of petcocks are in use: the standard three-position type, and a diaphragm type. The diaphragm petcock is left in the "on" position at all times except when switching to "reserve." Use the "prime" position to fill the carburetor float bowls if they have been emptied. No fuel should flow out of the petcock in the "on" and "reserve" positions unless the engine is running.

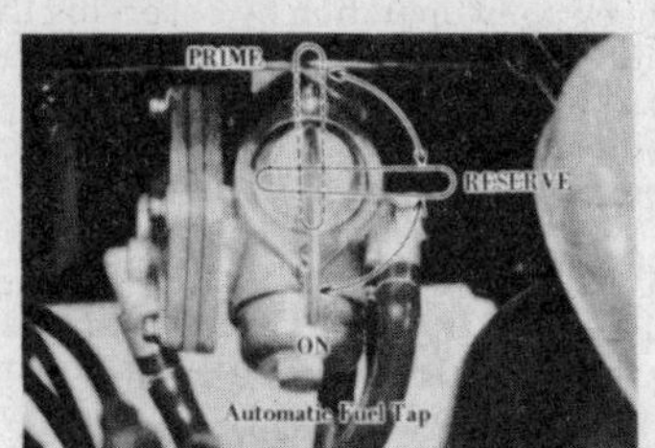

Diaphragm-type petcock (pre-1975)

1. The petcocks contain a wire mesh filter which should be removed and cleaned every few months, or at 2,000 mile intervals.
2. If a sediment bowl is fitted, turn the petcock lever so that fuel will not flow, and unscrew and remove the sediment bowl, O-ring, and filter screen. On petcocks without sediment bowls, the filter screens are fitted to the petcock intake pipes inside the tank. Remove and drain the gas tank, unscrew the petcock nut, and remove the petcock from the tank.

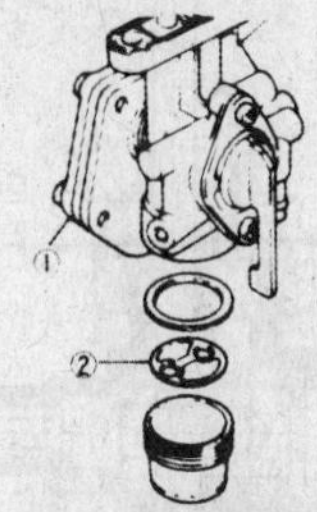

Petcock body (1), and filter screen (2)

3. Clean all metal parts in solvent. Be sure that the filter screens are clean.
4. Make sure that the petcock fully shuts off the gas (standard type), or does not leak gas in the "on" position (diaphragm type). If leakage is noted, the petcock should be replaced.
5. Check the condition of the sediment bowl O-ring, or petcock gasket, and replace it if damaged.
6. Replace the filter and sediment bowl. Do not overtighten the bowl. After installation, check for leaks.
7. If water has accumulated in the gas tank, some or most of it can be removed if the standard-type petcock is fitted by disconnecting the fuel lines at the petcock, placing a suitable container beneath it to catch the gasoline, and turning the petcock lever to the "Reserve" position. Letting the fuel flow for several seconds in this manner should remove any water present around the petcock pipe in the gas tank.
8. After extended periods of time, removal and thorough cleaning of the petcock is recommended. Remove the gas tank and drain off all the fuel. Unscrew and remove the petcock body from the gas tank. Unscrew and remove the sediment bowl and filter.
9. On diaphragm-type petcocks, remove the diaphragm plate securing screws, and remove the plate and diaphragm.

Removing the petcock (diaphragm-type)

10. Clean the fuel pipe filters and the petcock body thoroughly in gasoline. Be sure that all passages are clear.
11. Assembly is the reverse of disassembly. On diaphragm-type petcocks,

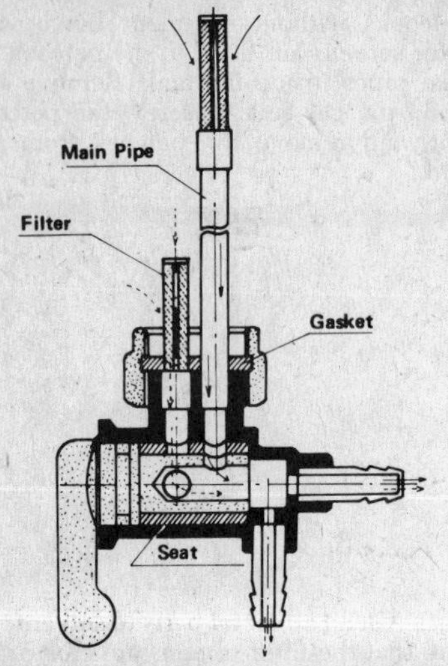

Standard-type petcock showing fuel filter screens

align the air vents in the petcock body, diaphragm, and plate as illustrated.

12. Check the condition of the sediment bowl O-ring and replace it if damaged. Check the mounting nut gasket and replace it if cracked or crushed.

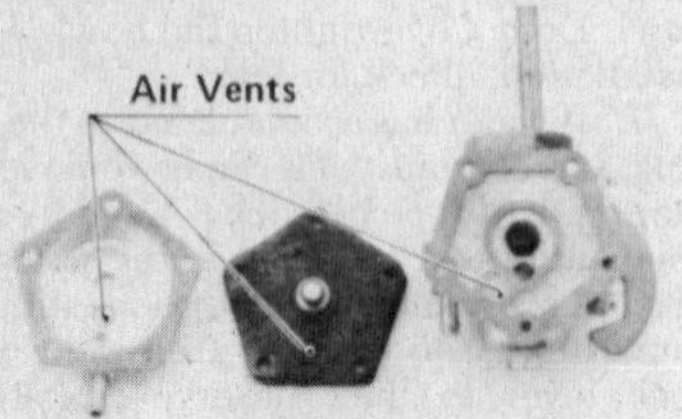

On diaphragm-type petcocks, be sure that the air vents are aligned when assembling

Carburetor Specifications①

Model	*Carburetor*	*Main Jet*	*Needle Jet*	*Needle*	*Pilot Jet*	*Slide Cut-away*	*Air Screw (turns out)*
S1, KH250	VM22SC	75	O—0	4EJ8—3 or 4EJ7—3	20.0	2.0	1½
S2	VM24SC	85	O—2	4EJ4—3	25.0	2.0	1½
S3	VM26SC	85	O—2	4EJ9—3	17.5	2.5	1¼
KH400	VM26SC	77.5	O—6/4	4EJ4—3	20	2.5	1¼
Early H1 (with CDI)	VM28SC	100	O—2	5GL3—3	30.0	3.0	1¼
Early H1 (without CDI)	VM28SC	90	O—2	5EH7—3	30.0	2.5	1½
H1-B	VM28SC	95	O—4/8	5DJ19—4	30.0	2.0	1½
H1-C	VM28SC	100	O—2	5GL3—3	30	3.0	1¼
H1-D, H1-E/F	VM28SC	92.5	O—4/8	5DJ19—4	30	2.5	1¼
KH500	VM28SC	90	O—4/8	5DJ19—4	30	2.5	1¼
H2, H2-A	VM30SC	97.5	O—6/8	5EJ15—3	35	2.5	1½
H2-B/C	VM30SC	102.5	O—6/8	5EJ15—4	40	2.5	1¾

① Specifications may differ according to model year, manufacturing lot, etc.

13. After assembly, check for leaks.

14. On diaphragm petcocks, be sure that the vacuum line is airtight, or fuel flow will be cut off. The vacuum line should be completely free of cracks and should be firmly attached at both ends. Replace the line if damaged, or if the ends have stretched, resulting in loose fitting at the connection points.

ELECTRICAL SYSTEM

IGNITION SYSTEM

Breaker Point Ignition

BREAKER POINTS

1. The general condition of the breaker points should be checked as outlined in "General Information" and the points replaced if pitted or worn beyond repair.

CONDENSERS

1. Condensers are best checked with a capacitance tester. Capacitance should be 0.18 mf for 250–400 machines, and 0.22 mf for the H1. If less, replace the condenser.

2. If no special test equipment is available, the condenser(s) may be checked for a short circuit with a low voltage DC test light. Disconnect the condenser wire from the point terminal. Check for continuity between the condenser lead and the condenser body. There should be none. If continuity exists, the condenser must be replaced. Even if there is no continuity, however, this does not guarantee that the condenser is in working order, as there are other things which might be wrong with it, such as partial insulation breakdown.

3. Points which pit, burn, or rapidly wear out would indicate a bad condenser. Check point operation by observing them with the engine running. Noticeable sparking or arcing between the breaker point contact surfaces indicate a bad condenser.

IGNITION COILS

1. A defective ignition coil is most easily found by comparing the performance of the three coils.

2. Remove the spark plug leads from the plugs. Insert a metal pin or nail into each of the plug leads in turn and hold the nail about an eighth of an inch from the cylinder head while kicking over the engine. In each case a fat, blue spark should be produced. If one of the coils produces a spark noticeably weaker than the others, it must be replaced.

3. An ohmmeter or continuity light can be used to check the primary winding of the ignition coil. Disconnect the coil low tension terminals and connect the tester across them. There must be continuity. An ohmmeter should show a relatively low resistance, not more than a few ohms at most. If any one coil has a primary winding resistance higher or lower than the other two, it should be replaced.

4. An ohmmeter can be used to check the resistance of the ignition coil secondary winding. Resistance should be about 10K Ω. If any one coil shows a resistance different from the other two, it should be replaced. Secondary winding resistance is checked by connecting the meter leads to the high-tension lead and to a low-tension terminal. All coil leads should be disconnected while testing.

CDI (H1/A–D)

The following points should be noted on H1 models with battery/CDI:

a. If the battery is installed incorrectly (i.e., connections reversed), the CDI components will be burned out as soon as the ignition is switched on. Exercise extreme care when connecting the battery;

b. Do not connect or disconnect the battery at any time that the ignition switch is on or the engine is running. This will damage the rectifier. A burned-out diode will completely drain the battery if the machine is run;

c. Battery connections must be kept clean and tight at all times;

d. The wiring between CDI units "A" and "B" (refer to wiring diagram) must be properly connected, free of damaged insulation, loose connections, etc. If trouble is traced to the wiring between the units, the units must be checked since they may have been damaged;

e. The black ground wires from the CDI units must be well grounded, or a no-spark condition will arise;

f. The CDI units are sealed, and no repairs can be effected; if damaged, the units must be replaced;

g. The rubber mounts for the CDI units must be in good condition. The units are very susceptible to damage from vibration.

TESTING

1. Before attempting to troubleshoot a CDI system, first check the above points for possible causes.
2. If spark is absent from only one plug, the trouble is either a defective plug or plug lead.
3. Check the ignition timing and the signal generator rotor-to-pickup coil gap as directed in "Tune-Up."
4. Check the condition of the plug leads. Replace them if damaged, cracked, etc.
5. Check the condition of the distributor cap. If the cap is cracked or chipped in any way, it must be replaced.
6. Disconnect the pickup coil leads at the connector and use an ohmmeter to measure the resistance between the leads. Resistance should be 300–400 Ω. If the correct resistance is not obtained, check the condition of the pickup coil wires, or replace the unit if necessary.

Checking the resistance of the pickup coil

7. To test the CDI "A" unit, an ohmmeter can be used. Disconnect the unit leads. Connect the positive ohmmeter lead to the "A" unit black lead, and the negative meter lead to the unit's gray (or slate) lead. The ohmmeter must show infinite resistance (no continuity).

Connect the positive lead of the meter to the gray unit lead, and the negative meter lead to black unit lead. Resistance must be infinite.

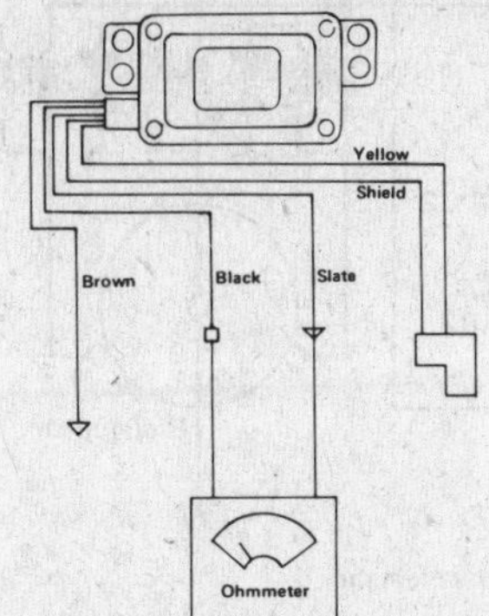

Testing unit "A" with an ohmmeter

These tests are checks for proper operation of the thyristor. If readings are not infinite in both cases, the "A" unit must be replaced.

8. To check CDI unit "B," a voltmeter (at least 500v DC), a DC ammeter and a 12v battery are needed.

Make connections as shown in the illustration: one lead of the ammeter to the positive battery terminal and the other ammeter lead to the brown "B" unit lead. Black unit lead to the battery negative terminal, negative battery terminal to the negative voltmeter lead, and positive voltmeter lead to the slate colored "B" unit lead.

All of the following conditions must be met: the "B" unit must emit a high-pitched hum; the voltmeter must read 370–500v; the ammeter must read 1.8 ± 0.5A with no fluctuation of the ammeter needle.

If any one of these conditions is not met, the "B" unit must be replaced.

9. Check the units "A" and "B" together as shown in the illustration. All of the following conditions must be met:

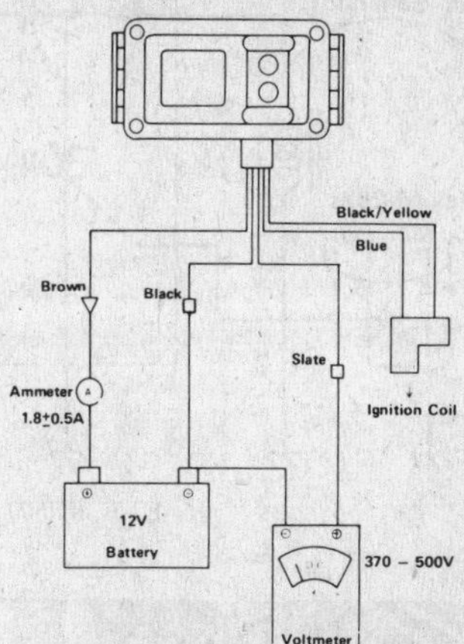

Testing unit "B" with an ohmmeter

unit "B" must emit a high-pitched hum; the voltmeter must read 370–500v; the ammeter must read 2.0 ± 0.5A with no fluctuation of the meter needle.

CDI (H1-E/F, KH500)

The CDI system used on these models is fundamentally different from the battery-CDI used on earlier 500s.

IGNITION WINDING

1. Unplug the brown and orange leads at the connector and check the resistance between them on the alternator side.
2. Resistance should be 115 ohms. If this reading is not obtained, replace the stator.

PICKUP COILS

1. The two pickup coils are connected in parallel. Disconnect the white wires' connector and check resistance between the white wire (alternator side) and ground on the frame.

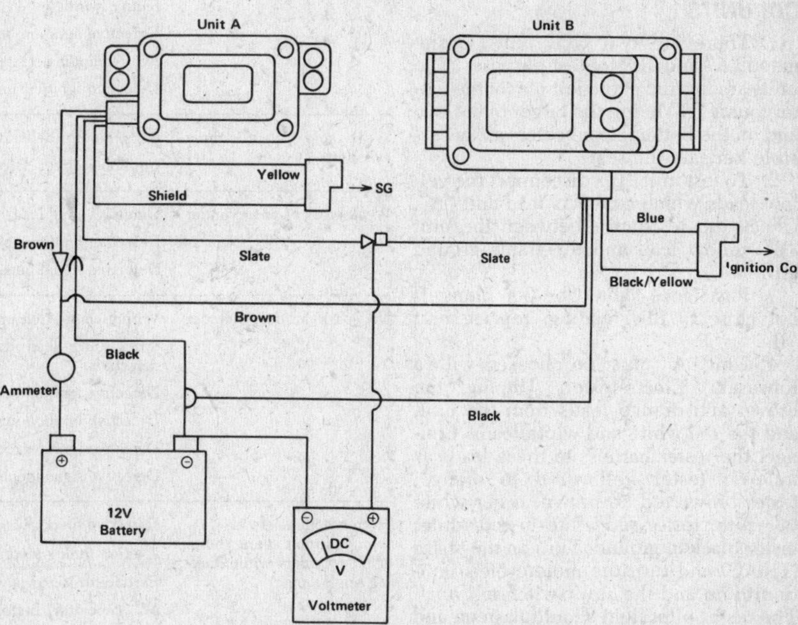

Checking the CDI units A and B together

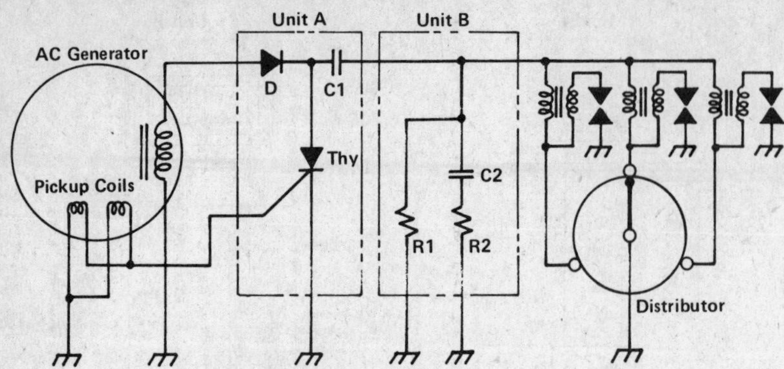

H1-E, KH500 electronic-CDI schematic

3. A faulty ignition unit for any one cylinder may cause a no-spark condition at all three. To check the ignition units, disconnect the three light green wires going from the ignition rectifier unit to the ignition units. Connect one wire at a time to its proper ignition unit and check for spark at that cylinder. If spark is evident at two cylinders only, the ignition unit for the dead cylinder is defective.

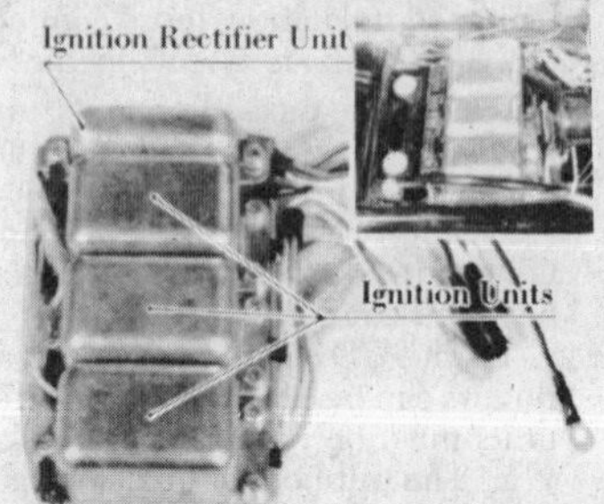

Ignition and ignition rectifier units (H2)

Testing the pickup coils

2. Resistance should be 130 ohms.

3. If this reading is not obtained, measure the resistance of each pickup coil separately. Unscrew the pick-up coil ground terminal and check resistance between the white wire and the ground wire of each coil. Resistance in each case should be 260 ohms. Replace any coil if resistance is not very close to this value.

DISTRIBUTOR

Refer to "Charging System," following for distributor rotor tests.

CDI UNITS

1. There are two CDI units, designated "A" and "B" for test purposes. The units are located at the left rear of the battery, unit "A" being the larger of the two and on the bottom. Connectors are accessible beneath the seat.

2. To test unit "B," disconnect the yellow leads which connects it to unit "A". Check the resistance between the unit "B" yellow lead and the frame ground terminal.

3. Resistance should be 300 ohms. If not close to this reading, replace unit "B".

4. Unit "A" must be checked with a Kawasaki Electrotester. Unplug the brown and orange leads from the unit, and the red/white and white leads. Connect the tester harness to these leads as follows: tester yellow/red to orange; tester brown/red, to brown; tester white to white; tester red/white to red/white; tester black to ground. Turn on the tester (110AC) and turn the motorcycle's ignition to on and the stop switch to "run." The tester pilot light should flash on and off. If it does not, replace the unit.

CDI (H2)

Before attempting to troubleshoot this system, the cause of the problem must be narrowed down as much as possible. Refer to the "Magneto CDI Troubleshooting" chart. Component test procedures are given below.

NOTE: *Do not run the motorcycle with the battery disconnected, as this may cause the ignition units to break down.*

1. Check for spark at each plug. A strong blue-white spark should be produced in each case. If there is no spark or weak spark at one plug, check that plug, its lead, and its ignition coil.

2. If there is strong spark at all three plugs, yet the engine will not start, check that the plug leads are connected to the correct plugs. If they are, the problem is not in the electrical system, unless the ignition timing is quite far off the mark.

4. If spark is absent from only one cylinder, and the plug and lead is in good condition, follow the procedure below to isolate the problem. The source of the problem must be one of the following: the ignition coil, the ignition unit, the ignition rectifier, or the signal generator:

a. Disconnect two of the green wires coming from the ignition rectifier and going to the ignition units, one for the bad cylinder, and one from either of the good cylinders. Reverse the connections. If the bad cylinder shows spark and the good cylinder is now without spark, the problem is a defective ignition rectifier;

Magneto CDI Troubleshooting

Problem	*Possible Causes*	*Inspection/Remedy*
No spark at any cylinder	Wiring connections broken; defective wiring	Check wiring connections and insulation.
	Defective ignition rectifier	Replace.
	AC generator defective	Replace.
	Defective ignition unit	Replace.
Weak spark at all three cylinders	AC generator defective	Replace.
	Ignition rectifier defective	Replace.
Weak spark at one cylinder	Defective plug lead	Replace.
	Defective ignition coil	Replace.
	Defective signal generator	Replace.
No spark at one cylinder	Wiring connection broken	Check wiring connections and insulation.
	Spark plug lead damaged or defective	Replace.
	Defective ignition coil	Replace.
	Defective ignition unit	Replace.
	Defective ignition rectifier	Replace.
	Defective signal generator	Replace.
High-speed misfire although strong spark shows at all cylinders while kicking engine over	Defective spark plug(s)	Replace.
	Ignition timing incorrect	Adjust.
	Carburetor settings wrong	Adjust.
	AC generator high-speed coil defective	Replace.

b. If there is no spark at the bad cylinder, reverse the plug wires of the bad cylinder and either of the good cylinders. Disconnect the red wire from the ignition unit to the ignition coil for the bad cylinder and for the good cylinder whose plug lead you reversed, and reverse the connections. Check for spark. If spark shows at the bad cylinder, the problem is the ignition coil. If there is no spark, proceed to the next test;

c. Connect the plug leads in the normal way, but leave the coil wires reversed. Take the white wire coming from the bad cylinder's ignition unit and switch it with the white wire coming from the good cylinder's ignition unit. If the bad cylinder shows spark, its ignition unit is defective. If it does not, the signal generator coil is defective.

Be sure to connect all wiring in the proper manner after testing has been completed. Check ignition timing as described in Chapter 3 if a signal generator coil has been replaced.

OHMMETER TESTS

All CDI system components can be checked with an ohmmeter.

Ignition Unit

1. Using the R x 10 range of the ohmmeter, check the resistance between the black and the light green ignition unit leads. With the positive meter lead connected to the black lead, resistance should be infinite (no reading). With the positive meter lead connected to the light green lead, resistance should be infinite. If the readings are not correct, the ignition unit is defective and must be replaced.

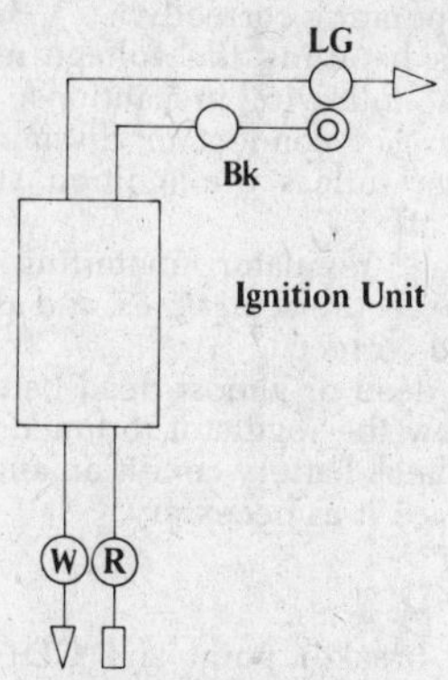

Ignition unit leads (H2)

2. Using the R x 100 range of the ohmmeter, check the resistance between the light green and the red ignition unit leads. Connecting the positive meter lead to the light green unit lead and the negative meter lead to the red lead, the ohmmeter needle should jump and then indicate infinite resistance. Reversing the connections should show the same reaction. If the meter does not react properly, the ignition unit is defective.

Ignition Rectifier

1. Using the R x 10 meter range, test the ignition rectifier by checking resistance between the black/white lead and the blue, white, and green leads in turn. If the positive meter lead is connected to the black/white wire and the negative lead is connected to the others one at a time, a resistance of about 35 Ω should be obtained between the black/white, the blue, and the green leads, and a resistance of about 90 Ω between the black/white and the white leads.

If the negative ohmmeter lead is connected to the black/white wire, and the test repeated, an infinite resistance should be obtained in all three cases. If the readings are not correct, the ignition rectifier is defective.

2. Using the R x 10 range, measure the resistance between the black/white lead and each of the light green leads one at a time. With the positive meter lead connected to the black/white lead and the negative to the light green leads, an infinite resistance should be indicated in all three cases. If the negative meter lead is connected to the black/white wire, and the positive to the light green wires, a resistance of about 35 Ω should be obtained in all three cases. If the readings are not correct, the ignition rectifier unit is defective.

Regulator/Rectifier

This unit accomplishes the dual purposes of voltage rectification (AC to DC) and voltage regulation. It functions in both ignition and charging circuits. The following tests may therefore determine the cause of a fault in either circuit.

1. To test this unit, use the R x 10 meter scale and measure the resistance across the black and the red leads. If the positive ohmmeter lead is connected to the black regulator lead, a resistance of about 70 Ω should be obtained. If the connections are reversed, a resistance of about 1K Ω should be indicated.

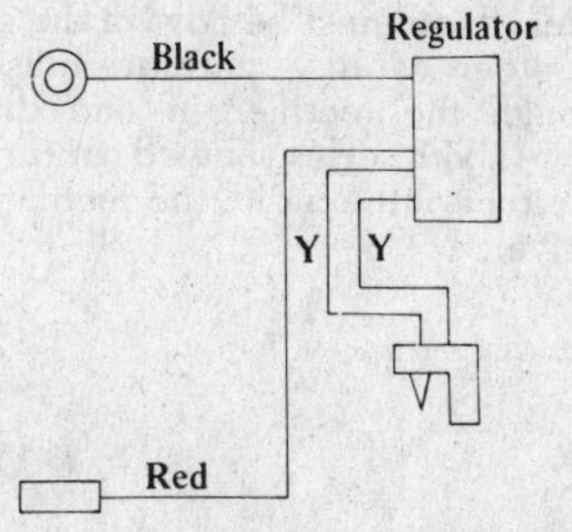

Regulator unit leads

2. Check the resistance between the black lead and each yellow lead, one at a time. If the positive meter lead is connected to the black regulator lead, a resistance of about 25 Ω should be obtained in each case. If the negative meter lead is connected to the black regulator lead, the resistance in each of the two cases should be about 1K Ω.

3. Check the resistance between the red lead and each of the yellow leads in turn (R x 10 range). Connecting the positive meter lead to the red wire should yield a resistance of 1K Ω at one yellow lead, and about 4K Ω at the other yellow lead.

Connecting the negative meter lead to the red wire should yield a resistance of about 25 Ω across each yellow lead.

4. Connect a 16v DC power source across the regulator black and red leads (positive battery terminal to the red lead).

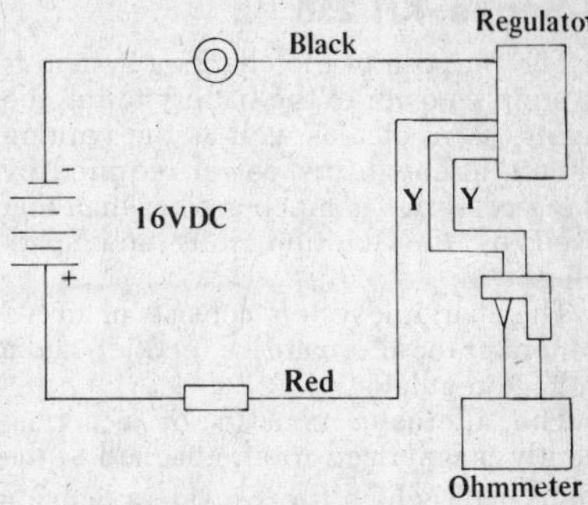

Checking the regulator

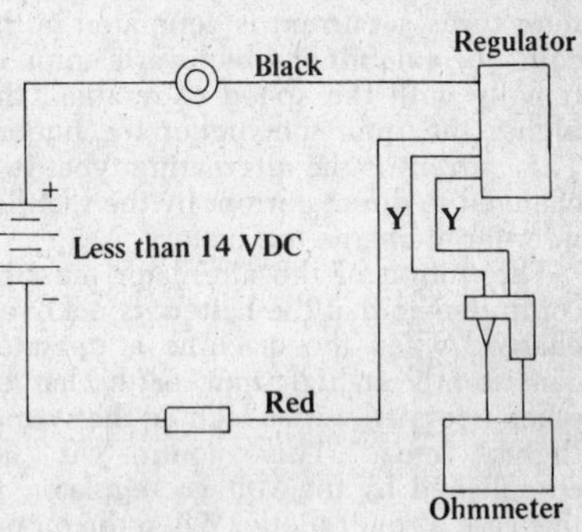

Regulator test

Check the resistance across the yellow leads. Resistance should be infinite one way, and about 500 Ω when the ohmmeter leads are reversed.

5. Connect a DC source less than 14v across the black and the red regulator leads (positive battery terminal to the black lead), and connect the ohmmeter across the yellow regulator leads. Resistance should be infinite, and if the meter connections are reversed, an infinite resistance should also be obtained.

If the regulator fails any of the above tests, it is defective.

AC Generator

The generator should be tested at normal operating temperature, but not when it is hot from operation.

1. Check the resistance between the two yellow leads. It should be 0.4 Ω.

2. Check the resistance between each yellow lead and ground. Resistance should be infinite.

3. Resistance between the blue and the green alternator leads should be about 5.0 Ω.

4. Resistance between the black generator wire and each of the white leads, in turn, should be 200 Ω. This tests the signal generator.

If readings are not correct, the alternator is defective.

Ignition Coil

1. Resistance between the white coil lead and the coil core should be about 0.8 Ω.

CHARGING SYSTEM

S-Series, KH 250

The purpose of the charging system is to supply power to the battery to run the lights, horn, etc., as well as the ignition circuit, although the power required by the accessories is much greater than that used by the ignition coils and spark plugs.

The charging system consists of an AC generator (or alternator), a rectifier, and a voltage regulator.

The alternator consists of a permanently magnetized rotor, attached to the crankshaft, which turns inside a housing (or stator) to which three coils are attached, 120° apart. The coils are wired as shown in the illustration. As the magnetic rotor turns, a current is generated in the coils, the amount of which varies proportionally with the speed of rotation: the higher the rpm, the higher the output. This current is the alternating type. It is changed to direct current by the rectifier in order to charge the battery.

The output of the alternator must be controlled so that the battery is not overcharged when the machine is operated consistently at high rpm, or discharged when operated with a load on the system (lights, etc.). This control is accomplished by the voltage regulator, in this case a zener diode. When the output of the alternator exceeds the voltage required by the battery, the zener diode allows the excess to flow to ground.

1. In the event of charging system failure, the battery itself should be checked first. If the battery will not hold a charge or overcharges, test each cell with a hydrometer.
2. If the battery is in good condition, check that all electrical connections in the circuit are clean and tight.
3. If the battery overcharges, suspect the voltage regulator.
4. If the battery discharges, suspect the alternator, the rectifier, or the regulator.

ALTERNATOR

Alternator tests can be carried out with an ohmmeter.

1. Disconnect the alternator connectors at the voltage regulator and the rectifier. Check for continuity between the yellow, the pink, and the white leads testing two leads at a time. There should be continuity between all three because the coils are all connected. If there is no continuity between any two wires, the assembly must be replaced.

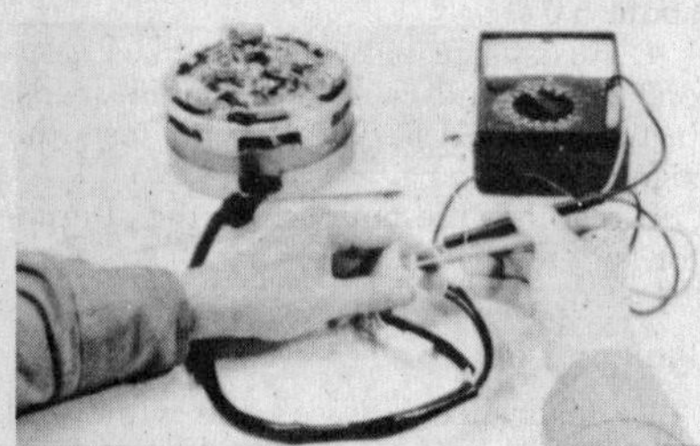

Checking for continuity between the stator leads

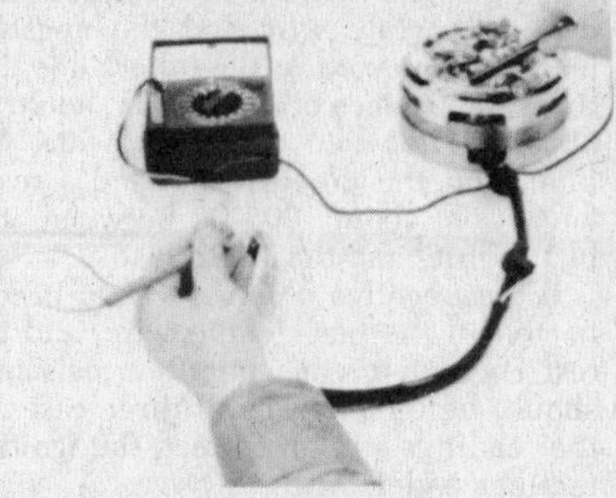

Checking for continuity between the stator leads and the housing

2. Check for continuity between each lead and the housing. There must be no continuity. If there is in any case, the assembly must be replaced.

RECTIFIER

The rectifier can be checked with an ohmmeter or continuity light.

1. Disconnect the rectifier wiring at all points.
2. Hook up the negative tester lead to the black rectifier wire, and the positive lead to each yellow lead, one lead at a time. Note whether or not there is continuity. Current must either flow or not flow in all three cases. Now switch the tester leads so that the negative lead is connected to the yellow and the positive to the rectifier black lead and repeat the tests. In each case there must be continuity or no continuity all three times.

Now compare the two sets of tests. If there was current flow in the first series, there must be none in the second. If there was no current flow in the first series, there must be flow in the second. In other words, current must flow through the rectifier in one direction only. If both series showed continuity, or if neither of them did, the rectifier is defective.

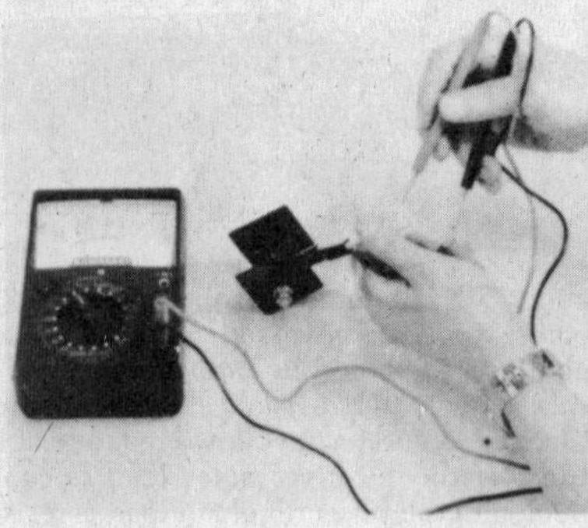

Testing the rectifier

REGULATOR

The voltage regulator can be checked with an ohmmeter.

1. Disconnect the regulator wires and remove it from the motorcycle.
2. Check the resistance between the brown and the black lead. It should be more than 1K Ω.
3. Check for current flow in both directions between each of the regulator leads (white, yellow, pink) and the black lead.

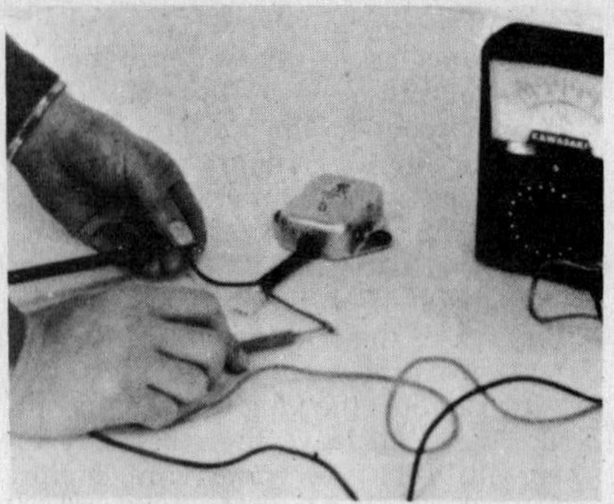

Testing the voltage regulator

There should be no continuity shown in either direction.

4. Connect a 12v battery positive battery terminal to the brown lead, and negative battery lead to the black lead. Check that there is no current flow from the black to the brown lead.
5. Wire another battery in series with the first so that the total input is over 16v. Check for current flow from the brown to the black lead. If there is flow, the regulator is operating correctly.

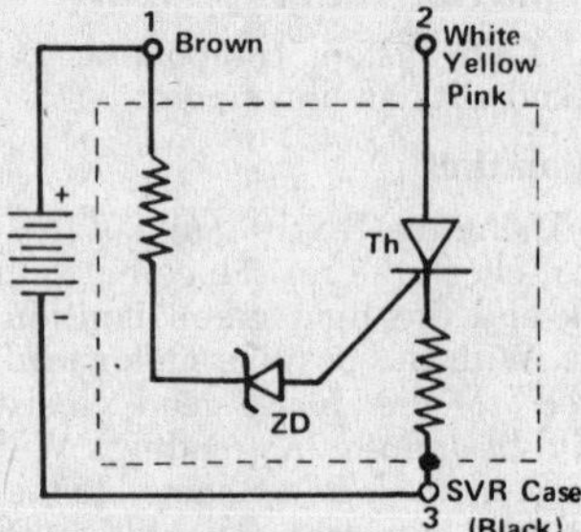

Regulator test set-up

When handling the voltage regulator, obey the following precautions:

1. Do not connect or disconnect the regulator unless the ignition switch is turned off.
2. The regulator mounting screws must be secure at all times, and all wiring must be correct.
3. A dead or almost dead battery will not allow the regulator to function properly. Check battery condition and charge or replace it as necessary.

H1/A–D

Both breaker point and CDI models are fitted with an alternator to charge the battery. The alternator consists of an electromagnetic rotor which turns inside a housing to which three sets of coils are attached. The movement of the magnetic field of the rotor through the coils generates an alternating current in them. The current is changed to direct current by the rectifier and used to charge the battery.

The amount of electrical power generated by the alternator is determined by the voltage regulator. This device maintains a voltage of 14.5 volts across the battery at high speed. The regulator varies the strength of the rotor's magnetic field. When field strength is high, alternator output is high, and vice versa, at a given rpm.

ALTERNATOR

The alternator can be tested with an ohmmeter.

1. Remove the alternator stator and rotor from the machine.

Checking for resistance between the alternator slip rings (H1)

2. Check the resistance between the rotor slip rings. Resistance should be 3.5–5.5 Ω. If resistance is lower than this amount, the rotor field coils are shorted. If infinite, there is an open circuit. In either event, the rotor must be replaced.

3. Check the condition of the rotor slip ring carbon brushes. The length of new brushes is 14 mm. If the length of the brushes is less than 9.5 mm, they should be replaced.

4. Check for continuity between each of the three yellow leads, two leads at a time. (If the leads were numbered, 1, 2, 3, check for continuity between 1–2, 1–3, and 2–3.) There must be continuity in all cases. If any test shows an open circuit, replace the stator assembly.

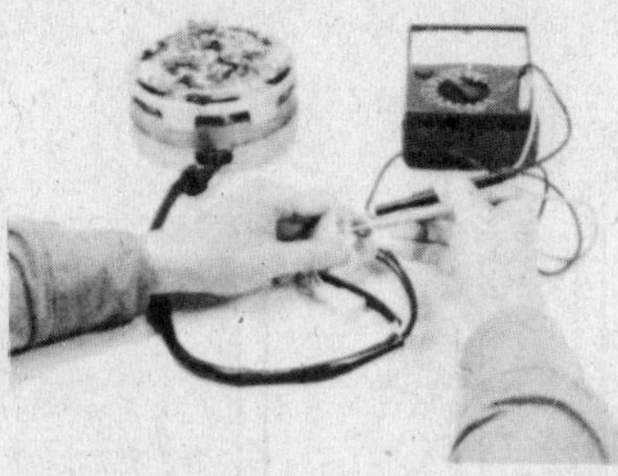

Checking for continuity between the stator leads

5. Check for continuity between the stator housing and each of the yellow leads. Resistance should be infinite. If there is current flow in any case, replace the stator assembly.

RECTIFIER

The rectifier can be checked with an ohmmeter or continuity light.

1. Check for continuity between each of the rectifier leads after removing it from the machine.
   Yellow (3) to Black
   Blue to Black
   Red to Black
   Blue to Yellow (3)
   Red to Yellow (3)

In each case, there should be current flow when the tester leads are hooked up to each set of leads indicated above, but no current flow when the tester leads are reversed. Continuity in both directions or no continuity in either direction for the pairs of leads indicates a defective rectifier.

NOTE: *Be sure to test all three yellow leads and the other lead where shown.*

REGULATOR

An ohmmeter or a DC voltmeter can be used to check the regulator.

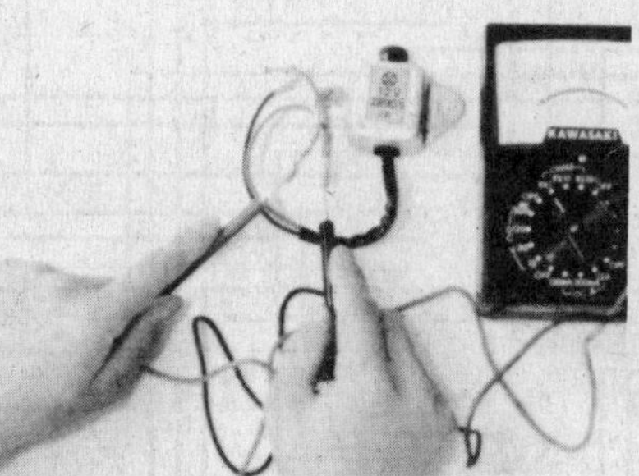

Checking the voltage regulator

1. After removing the regulator from the machine, measure the resistance between the brown and the black leads. Resistance should be 53–55 Ω. If the resistance is not within 10% of this value, replace the regulator.

2. Install the regulator on the motorcycle, secure it, and be sure that all connections are correct. Start the engine and rev to 5,000 rpm. At this point a voltmeter connected to the positive battery terminal and ground should indicate 14–15 volts. If voltage is incorrect, replace the regulator.

NOTE: *This test assumes that the battery and the alternator are in good condition. Check them first before replacing the regulator.*

H1-E/F, KH500

CHARGE WINDINGS

1. Disconnect the two yellow wires at the two-lead plug, and check resistance (on the alternator side of the circuit) between the two yellow wires. It should be about 0.25 ohms.

2. If this reading is not obtained, the stator must be replaced.

DISTRIBUTOR

1. Remove the alternator cover and the plate for the brushes and pick-up coils.
2. Clean the slip rings thoroughly.
3. Check the resistance between the outer ring and the separated section of the inner ring. Resistance should be infinite. If not, replace the rotor.
4. Check resistance between the inner ring and the rotor shaft. Again, resistance must be infinite or replacement of the rotor is necessary.

BRUSHES

1. A wear-limit line is marked on each brush and they should be replaced when worn to this mark.

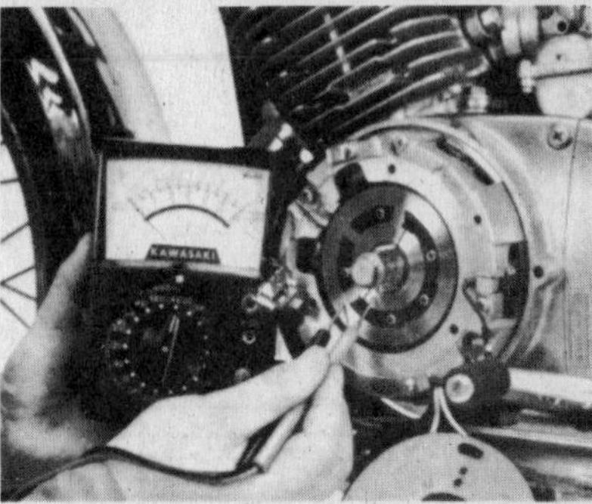

Checking resistance between the inner and outer slip-rings

Checking resistance between the inner ring and the rotor shaft

REGULATOR

1. The regulator may be checked in place on the motorcycle. For the test to be valid, the battery must have a charge of at least 13v.

2. The regulator is mounted inside of the left side cover. Disconnect the red lead from the regulator and connect the positive lead of an ammeter (12a range) to the red lead coming from the regulator and the negative tester lead to the red lead from the battery.

3. Connect a 30v DC voltmeter, positive lead to the battery positive terminal, negative lead to the battery negative terminal.

4. At idle, current should be less than 2a, and voltage 14.5–15.5v.

5. At 3,000 rpm, readings should be the same.

6. With the headlight on low-beam, and at idle, current should be less than 5a, voltage 12–13v. At 3,000 rom, current should be unchanged, and voltage 14.5–15.5v.

7. Assuming that the alternator, battery, etc., are in good condition, the regulator is defective if these readings are not obtained.

H2

Tests for the H2 charging system components are included in the preceding "CDI (H2)" section, due to the construction of this motorcycle's electrical system. The "magneto" or alternator which powers the ignition circuit also charges the battery after its output is changed to direct current by the rectifier. The rectifier also accomplishes voltage regulation. This is not to be confused with the "ignition rectifiet" which functions only in the ignition circuit.

WIRING DIAGRAMS

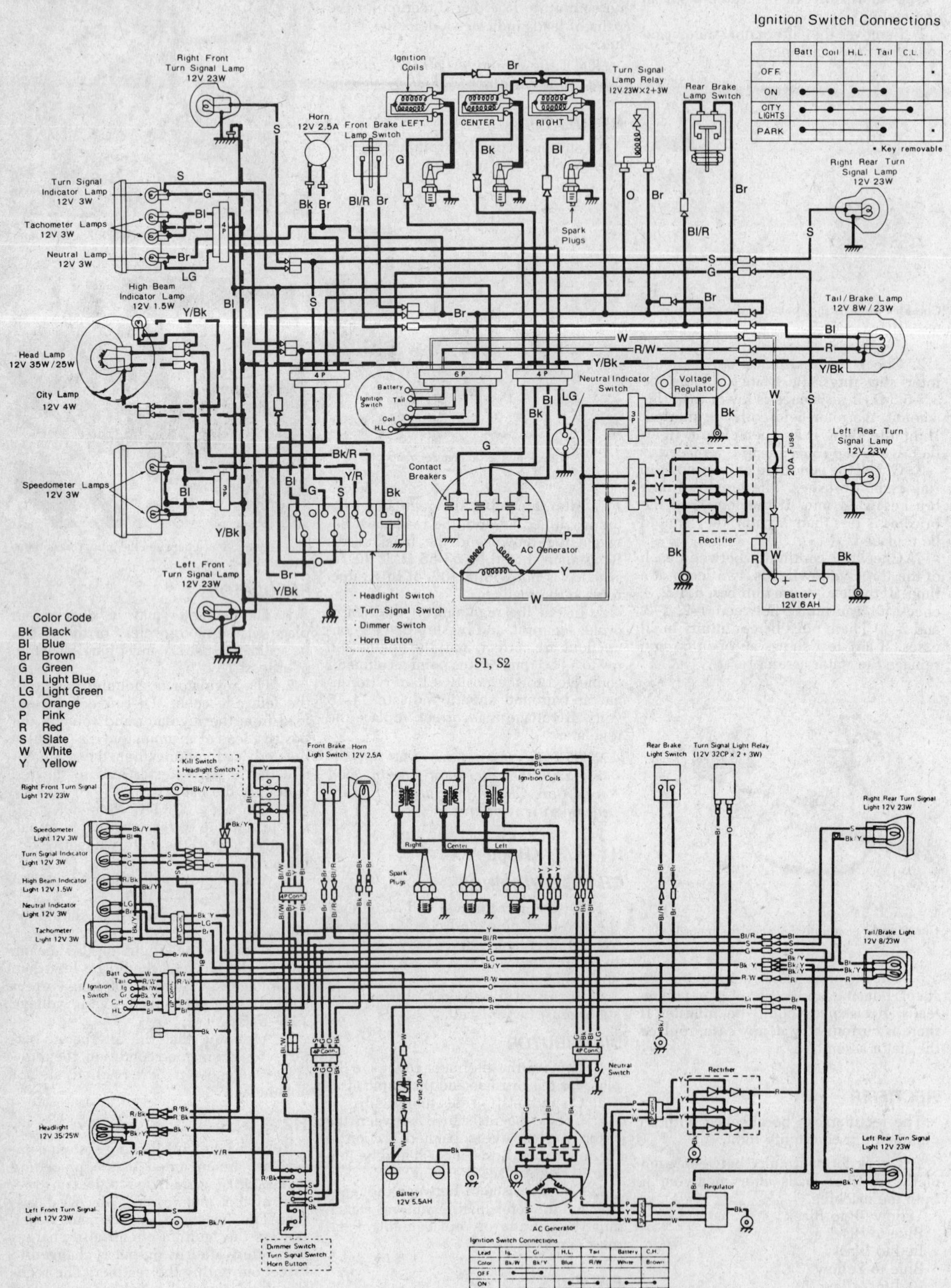

S1, S2

S1-B/C, KH250, S3

WIRING DIAGRAMS

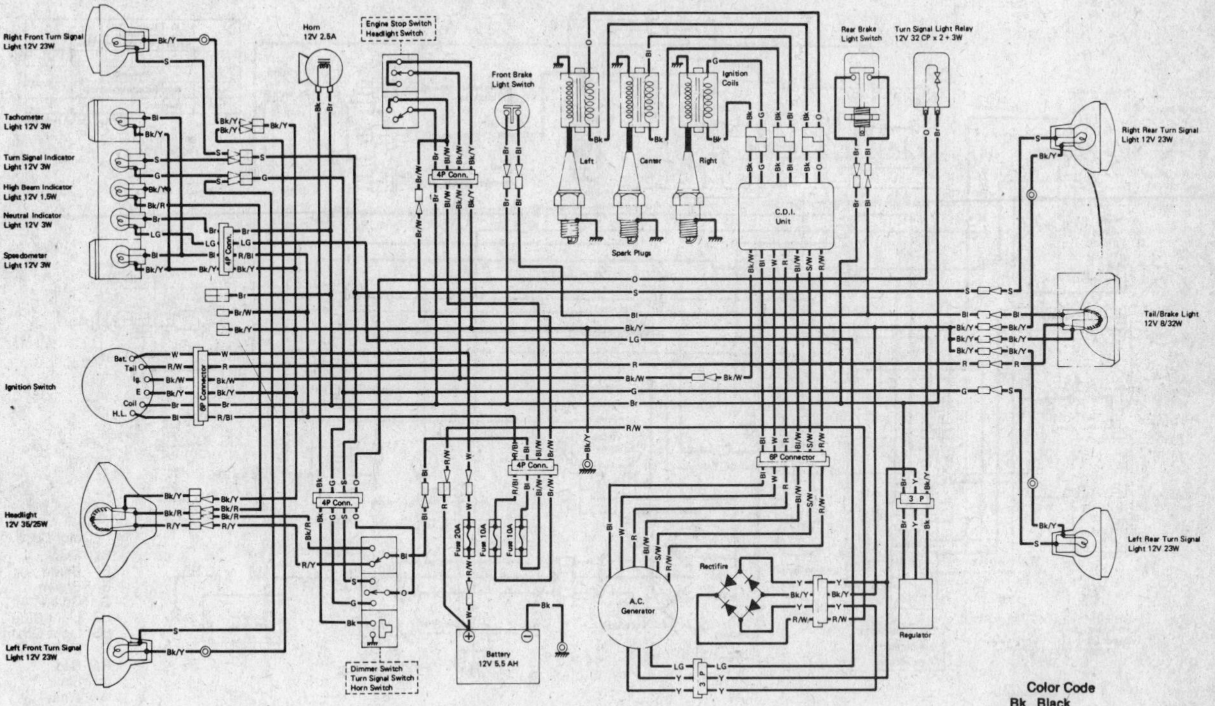

Lead	Ignition	E	H.L.	Tail	Battery	Coil
Color	Bk/W	Bk/Y	Blue	Red	White	Brown
OFF	●	●				
ON			●	●	●	●
PARK	●	●		●	●	

(194-0)

Color Code

- Bk Black
- Bl Blue
- Br Brown
- G Green
- LB Light Blue
- LG Light Green
- O Orange
- R Red
- S Slate
- W White
- Y Yellow

KH400

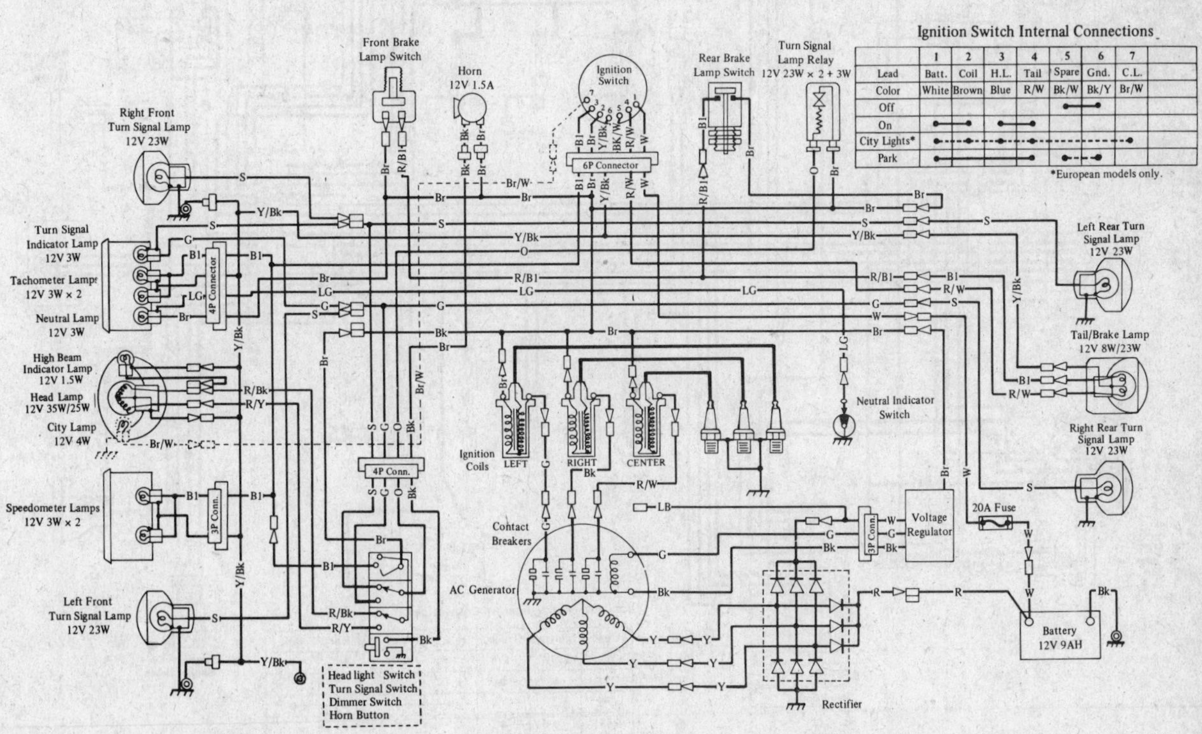

Ignition Switch Internal Connections

	1	2	3	4	5	6	7	
Lead	Batt.	Coil	H.L.	Tail	Spare	Gnd.	C.L.	
Color	White	Brown	Blue	R/W	Bk/W	Bk/Y	Br/W	
Off					●	●		
On	●	●	●	●				
City Lights*	●	●	●	●			●	
Park	●			●	●	●		

*European models only.

H1, Breaker point ignition

WIRING DIAGRAMS

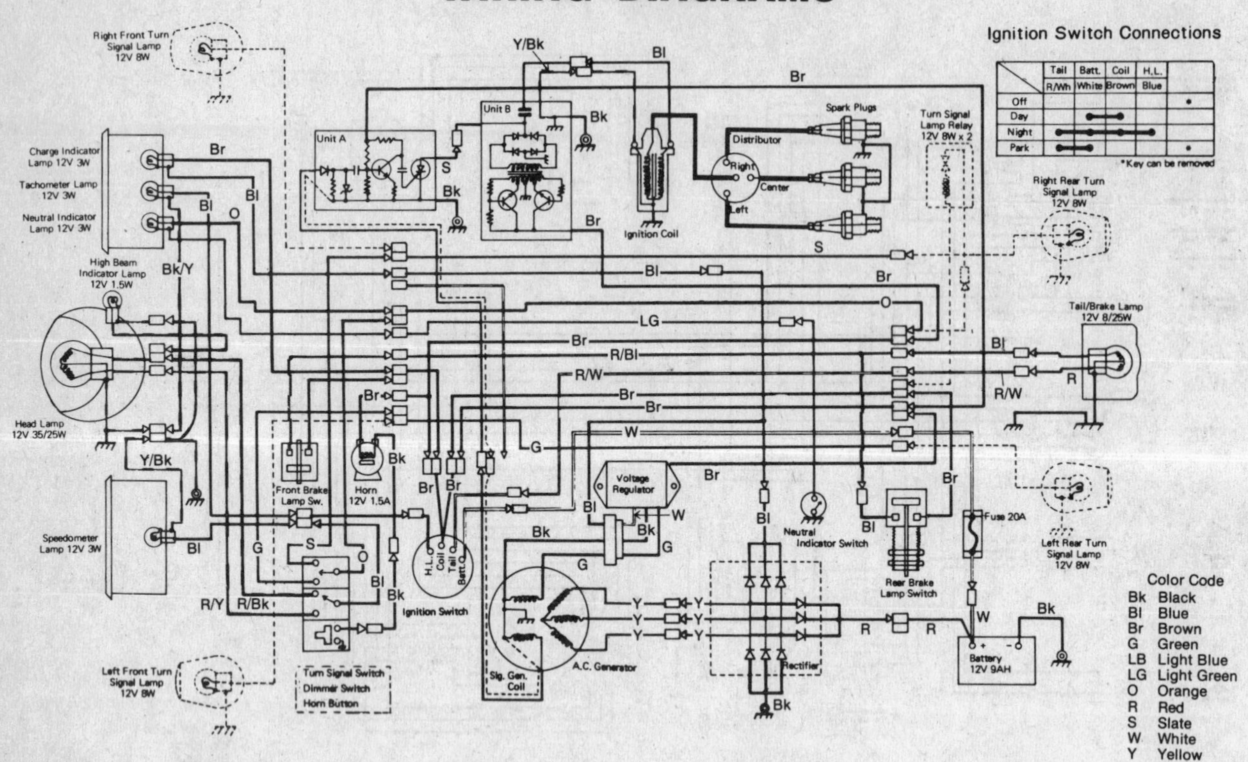

Ignition Switch Connections

	Tail	Batt.	Coil	H.L.	
	R/Wh	White	Brown	Blue	
Off					•
Day		●—	—●		
Night	●—	—●—	—●—	—●	
Park	●—	—●			•

*Key can be removed

H1, Battery CDI

Right Front Turn Signal Light 12V 23W
Speedometer Light 12V 3W
Turn Signal Indicator Light 12V 3W
High Beam Indicator Light 12V 1.5W
Neutral Indicator Light 12V 3W
Tachometer Light 12V 3W
Brake Light Failure Indicator Light 12V 3W
Ignition Switch
Headlight 12V 35/25W
Left Front Turn Signal Light 12V 23W
Engine Stop Switch
Headlight Switch
Dimmer Switch
Turn Signal Switch
Horn Button
Front Brake Light Switch
Ignition Coils
Spark Plugs
A.C. Generator
Neutral Switch
Regulator
SSM UNIT
Turn Signal Light Relay (12V 23W x 2 + 3W)
Horn 12V 2.5A
Fuse 20A
Rear Brake Light Switch
Battery 12V 9AH
Right Rear Turn Signal Light 12V 23W
Tail/Brake Light 12V 5/21W
Left Rear Turn Signal Light 12V 23W
Outage Indicator Switch

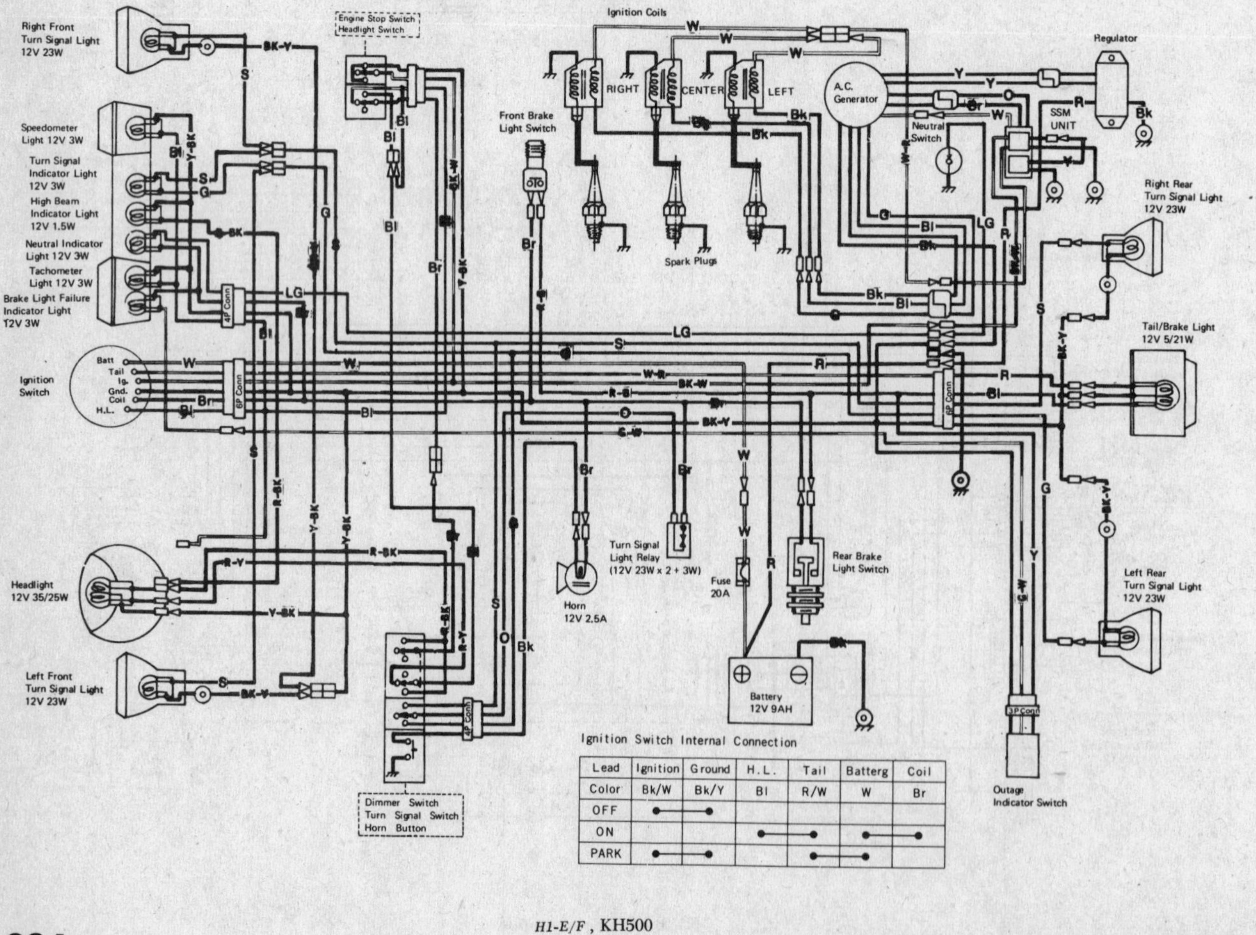

Ignition Switch Internal Connection

Lead	Ignition	Ground	H.L.	Tail	Batterg	Coil
Color	Bk/W	Bk/Y	Bl	R/W	W	Br
OFF	●—	—●				
ON			●—	—●	●—	—●
PARK	●—	—●		●—	—●	

H1-E/F, KH500

WIRING DIAGRAMS

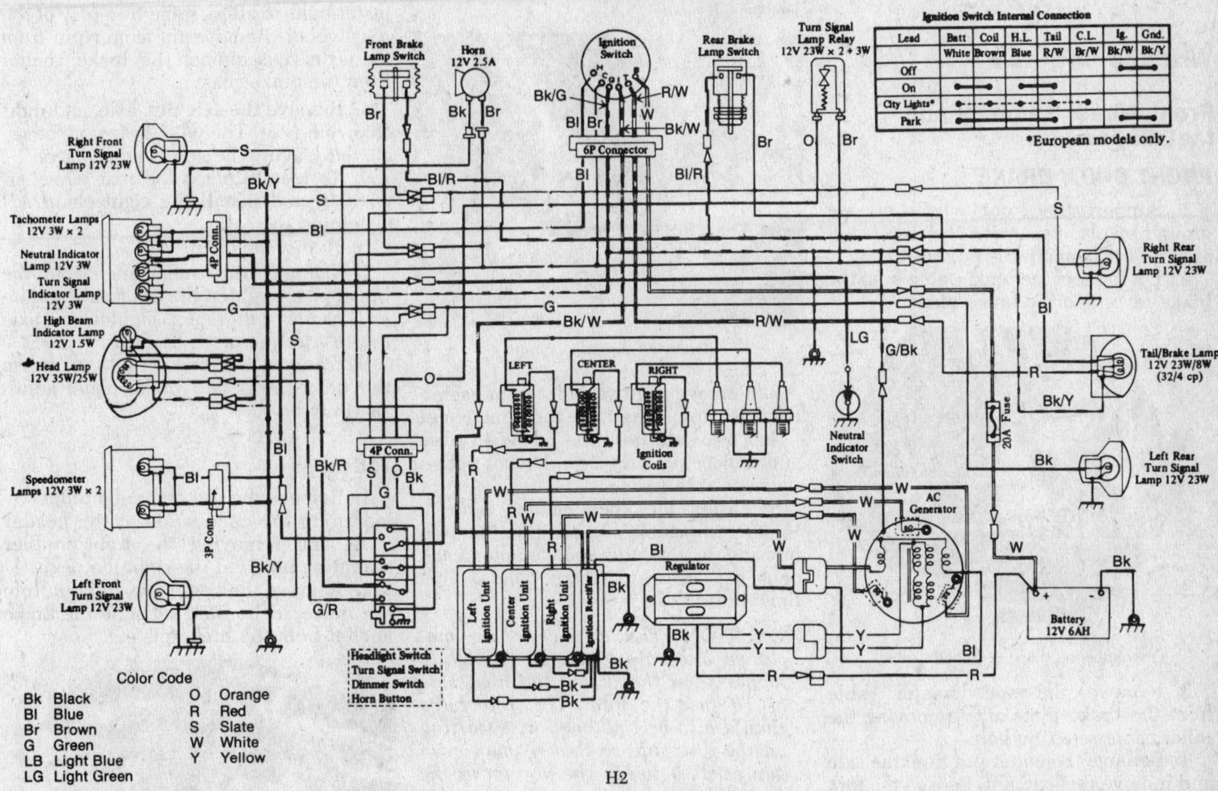

Ignition Switch Internal Connection

Lead	Batt	Coil	H.L.	Tail	C.L.	Ig.	Gnd.
	White	Brown	Blue	R/W	Br/W	Bk/W	Bk/Y
Off						●	●
On	●	●	●	●			
City Lights*	● (dashed)	● (dashed)	● (dashed)	● (dashed)	● (dashed)		
Park	●			●		●	●

*European models only.

H2

Right Front Turn Signal Light 12V 23W

Engine Stop Switch
Headlight Switch

Speedometer Light 12V 3W

Turn Signal Indicator Light 12V 3W

High Beam Indicator Light 12V 1.5W

Neutral Indicator Light 12V 3W

Tachometer Light 12V 3W

Brake Light Failure Indicator Light 12V 3W

Ignition Switch (Batt, Tail, Ig., Gnd., Coil, H.L.)

Headlight 12V 35/25W

Left Front Turn Signal Light 12V 23W

Ignition Coils

RIGHT CENTER LEFT

Front Brake Light Switch

Spark Plugs

Turn Signal Light Relay (12V 23Wx2+3W)

Horn 12V 2.5A

Fuse 20A

Rear Brake Light Switch

Battery 12V5.5AH

A.C. Generator

Neutral Switch

SSM Unit

Regulator

Right Rear Turn Signal Light 12V 23W

Tail/Brake Light 12V8/23W

Left Rear Turn Signal Light 12V 23W

Outage Indicator Switch

Dimmer Switch
Turn Signal Switch
Horn Button

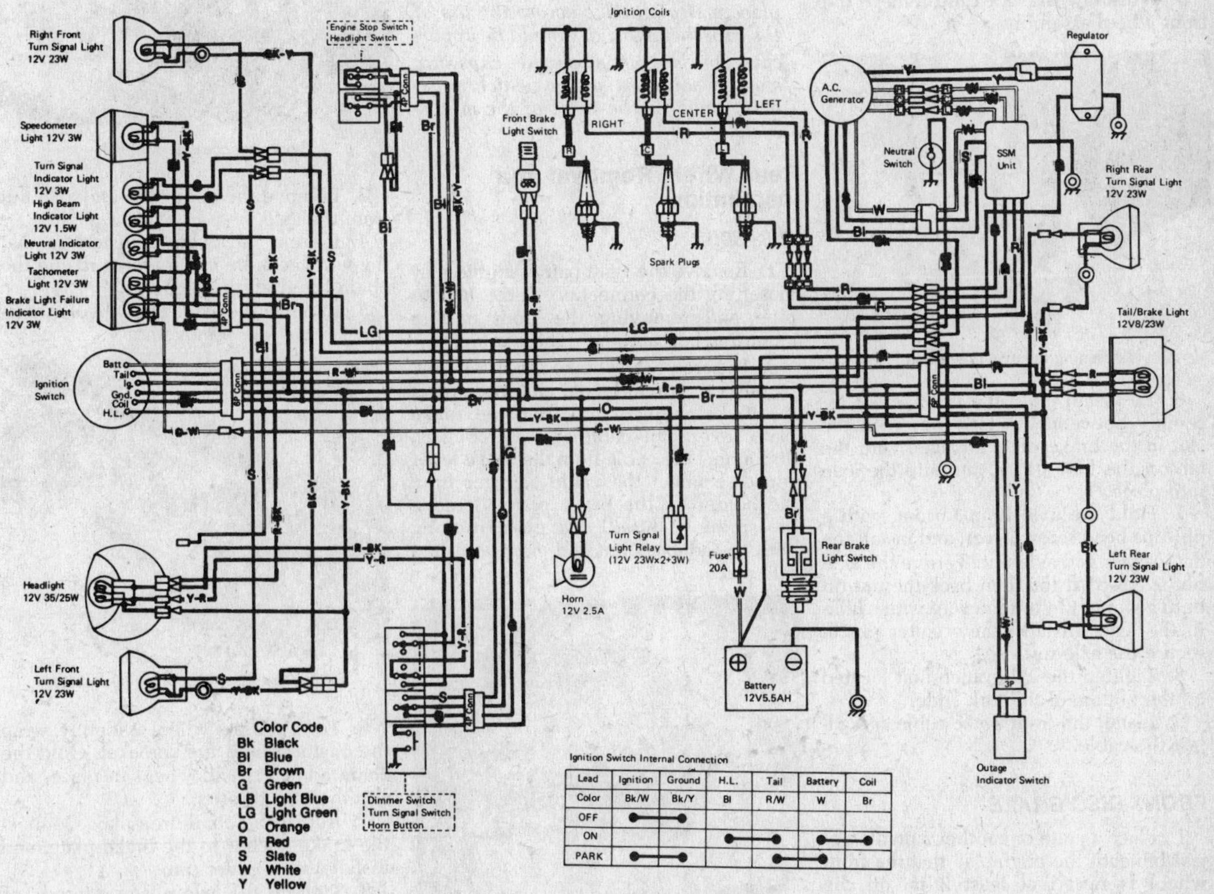

Color Code

- Bk Black
- Bl Blue
- Br Brown
- G Green
- LB Light Blue
- LG Light Green
- O Orange
- R Red
- S Slate
- W White
- Y Yellow

Ignition Switch Internal Connection

Lead	Ignition	Ground	H.L.	Tail	Battery	Coil
Color	Bk/W	Bk/Y	Bl	R/W	W	Br
OFF	●	●				
ON			●	●	●	●
PARK	●	●		●	●	

H2-B/C

CHASSIS

WHEELS, BRAKES

Front Wheel Removal and Installation

FRONT DRUM BRAKE

1. Support the front wheel off the ground by placing a crate or another suitable object beneath the engine.
2. Disconnect the brake cable from the brake lever and the brake plate.

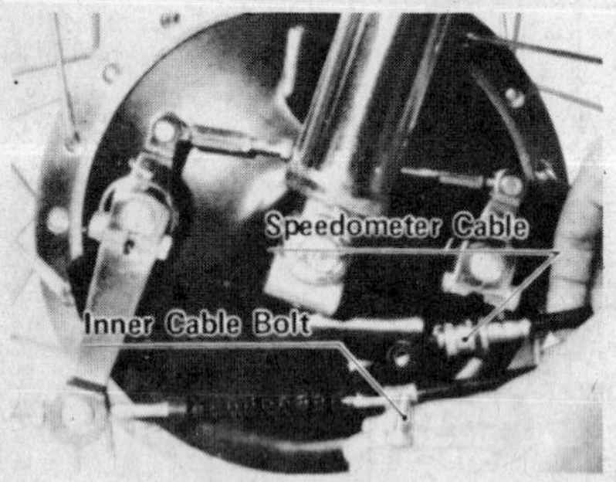

Disconnecting the speedometer cable

3. Remove the speedometer cable from the brake plate after removing the inner cable securing bolt.
4. Remove the cotter pin from the axle and remove the axle nut. Loosen the fork slider pinch-bolt.
5. Withdraw the axle, and remove the front wheel assembly.

Loosening the axle pinch bolt

6. To install, hold the front wheel assembly between the fork legs with the slot in the brake plate engaged with the tab on the fork slider, and slip the axle into place.
7. Hold the axle from turning with a phillips head screwdriver, and install the flat washer and axle nut. Torque the axle nut to 48–61 ft lbs then back the nut off until a slot in the nut lines up with a hole in the axle. Install a new cotter pin to secure the axle nut.
8. Tighten the axle pinch-bolt located on the bottom of the fork slider.
9. Install the front brake cable and adjust the cable.

FRONT DISC BRAKE

1. Place a crate or another suitable object beneath the engine so that the front wheel is raised at least 2 in. off the ground.
2. Unscrew the speedometer cable from the drive housing on the brake plate.

Removing the axle capnuts

3. Remove the two bolts from each of the axle caps and remove the front wheel.
4. To install, hold the wheel in place and replace the axle caps. Do not tighten the caps at this time.
5. Fasten the speedometer cable to the drive housing, and position the drive housing so that the speedometer cable does not have any sharp bends. Then tighten the axle caps.

CAUTION: *The axle caps are machined unevenly (one side is slightly higher than the other) the high side MUST face the front. The front bolts should also be tightened first starting on the disc side so that a small even gap exists between the bottom of the fork slider and the rear of the axle cap. If in doubt which side is the high side, place a straightedge across the top of the cap; the high side should be apparent. On late models, the caps are marked with an arrow which must point towards the front of the motorcycle.*

Rear Wheel Removal and Installation

250–500

1. Remove the right pair of mufflers by loosening the connection at the header pipe and removing the front muffler mounting bolt and the right rear footpeg.
2. Unscrew the brake adjuster nut. Depress the brake pedal and disconnect the brake cable or rod from the brake plate lever. On cable-operated brakes, disconnect the cable from the brake lever and disconnect the cable adjuster from the holder on the brake plate. Remove the spring (if fitted) and place it along with the adjuster nut and clevis pin in a safe place.

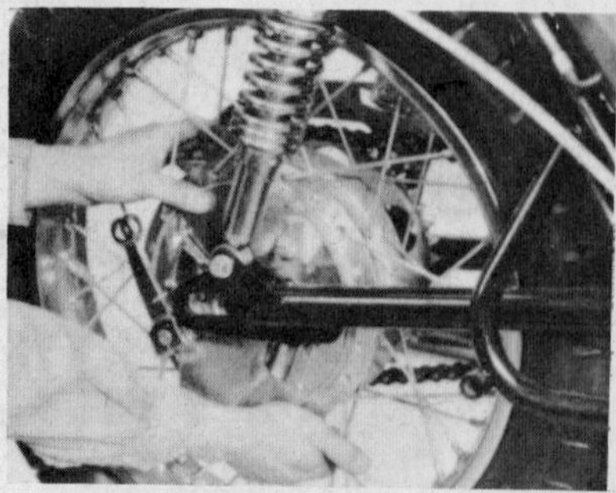

Removing the rear wheel

3. Loosen the chain adjuster locknut on each adjuster. Then back off the adjuster bolts to allow some free-play of the rear wheel. Remove the cotter pin from the axle. Disconnect the brake anchor from the brake plate.
4. Remove the axle nut, axle, and right chain adjuster. The wheel can now be removed leaving the sprocket in place.
5. To install, place the rear wheel in position and install the right chain adjuster and the axle.
6. Adjust the chain.
7. Connect the brake anchor to the brake plate, tighten the nut firmly and install a new cotter pin. Tighten the axle nut to a torque of 48–61 ft lbs.
8. Connect the brake cable or rod to the brake lever and brake plate, adjust the brake.

750

1. Remove the right pair of mufflers by loosening the connection at the header pipe, and removing the front muffler mounting bolt and the right footpeg.
2. Remove the cotter pin and nut from the brake anchor and separate the brake anchor from the brake plate.

Removing the axle nut (H2)

3. Remove the cotter pin and axle nut from the axle.
4. Loosen the chain adjusters so that the wheel can be moved forward and the chain lifted off the sprocket.
5. Remove the axle. The wheel assembly can now be removed.

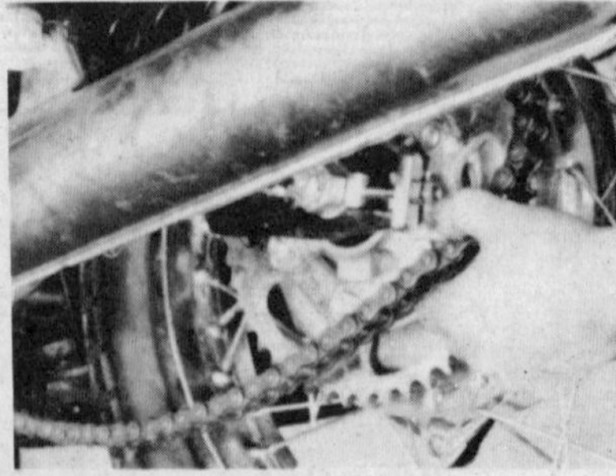

Lifting the chain off the sprocket (H2)

6. To install the wheel assembly, wrap the chain around the sprocket. Hold the chain adjusters and wheel in place, and slip the axle through.
7. Adjust the chain free-play. Connect the brake anchor to the brake plate, and install a new cotter pin.
8. Tighten the axle nut to a torque of 83.2–90.4 ft lbs, then back it off until a

slot in the axle nut is in line with a hole in the axle. Install a new cotter pin.

9. Connect the brake rod to the brake lever, and adjust the brake pedal free-play.

Sprocket Assembly

The rear sprocket assembly consists of the sprocket, sprocket hub, sprocket hub bearing, and the rubber dampers which will remain in the wheel when it is removed.

REMOVAL AND DISASSEMBLY

1. Disconnect the drive chain. Unscrew the large sprocket hub nut and remove the assembly from the swing arm.
2. Bend down the tabs on the sprocket nut locking plates. Unscrew the nut and remove the sprocket from the hub.

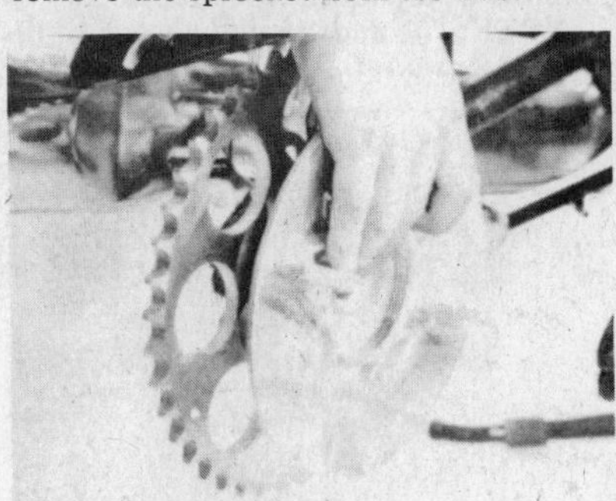

Removing the sprocket hub

3. To remove the hub bearing, first remove the sprocket shaft by tapping it out from the sprocket side of the hub. Use a plastic mallet or block of wood so that the sprocket shaft threads will not be damaged when struck.
4. Take off the sprocket shaft collar.
5. Use an elbow-shaped tool to pry out the oil seal. If the oil seal is damaged on removal, as is likely, a new one must be fitted.
6. Drive the bearing out toward the sprocket side of the hub with a suitable drift or bearing driver. Tap the bearing evenly around its circumference to avoid distorting the hub.

INSPECTION

1. For bearing inspection and lubrication, refer to "Wheel Bearings," below.
2. Check the condition of the sprocket. If the sprocket is warped, or if the sprocket teeth are worn or hooked, the sprocket should be replaced along with the chain and the countershaft sprocket.
3. Check the condition of the sprocket nuts, bolts, and locking plates. Replace any nuts or bolts with rounded flats, stripped threads, or those which are bent or cracked. Bolts must be tightened securely upon installation. It is also recommended that they be secured with a thread locking compound. The locking plates must not have fatigued or cracked edges, since these are used to lock the nuts in place. Replace the plates if damaged in any way.
4. Check the condition of the oil seal and replace it if the lips are damaged.
5. Inspect the sprocket shaft for broken or stripped threads.
6. Check the condition of the rubber dampers in the wheel hub. These take up any driveline shocks when the clutch is released and have an important effect on chain and sprocket life. Replace any damper which is hardened, crushed, or damaged.

In instances where the damper is a tight fit in the hub, some engine oil or dishwashing liquid can be used to facilitate removal and installation.

ASSEMBLY

1. Assembly is the reverse order of disassembly procedure.
2. Lubricate the bearing as described in "Wheel Bearings," below. The bearing should be driven into place with a bearing driver or a suitable substitute.
3. Grease the lips of the oil seal before installation. The seal should be pressed into the hub with care.
4. Tap the sprocket shaft into the hub from the wheel side.
5. When connecting the chain masterlink, install the spring clip closed end facing the direction of chain rotation. Tighten the sprocket hub nut securely.

Drum Brake Service

All models use a single-leading shoe rear brake, while, a twin-leading shoe is used on the front brake. Kawasakis use brakes in which the lining is bonded to the brake shoe, therefore, are purchased and replaced as a single unit.

1. Brakes can be inspected in place on the brake plate.

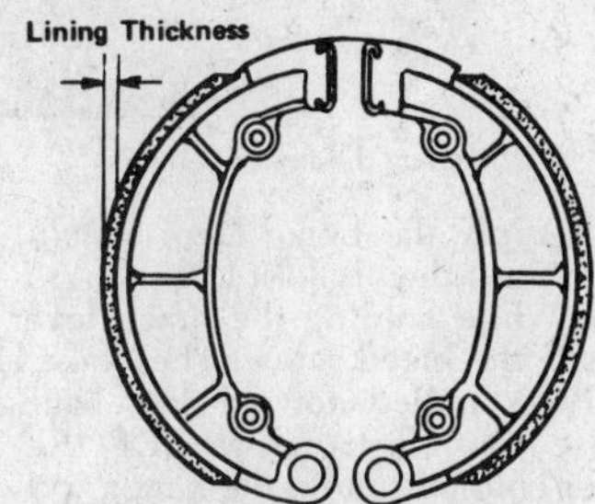

Check lining thickness

2. Inspect the shoes for wear. There should be at least 0.12 in. (3 mm) of lining material left (measured at the lining's thinnest point) or the shoes must be replaced.
3. Use a large vernier caliper to measure the inside diameter of the brake drum. If the diameter is found to be less than the service limit given in the "Chassis Specifications" chart, the hub should be replaced.
4. Inspect the linings for scoring or grooves. These may be caused by particles of dirt which have entered the drum. If badly scored, the shoes should be replaced. If scoring of the shoes is evident, it would be wise to inspect the brake drum for the same type of damage.

Be sure that there is no oil or grease present on the brake linings. Oil-impregnated linings must be replaced. If the linings do show this condition, determine the source of the lubricant: defective wheel bearing oil seals, excessive chain lube, etc.

5. If the linings are usable, rough up the surface with a piece of coarse sandpaper. Then clean the linings thoroughly with alcohol or laquer thinner. Clean the brake drum with the same solvent.
6. To disassemble the brake plate, simply grasp each shoe and fold them toward the center of the brake plate. They may be installed in the same manner.

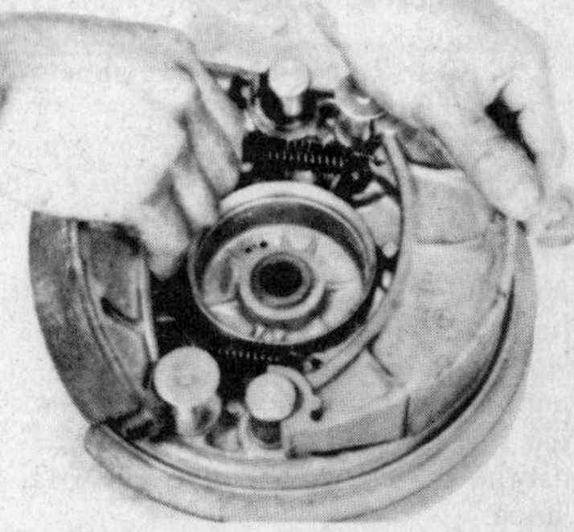

Removing the brake shoes from the brake plate

7. Remove the brake lever pinch-bolt(s) and pull the lever(s) off the splined brake camshaft(s).

NOTE: *The plurals refer to the twin-leading shoe brakes.*

8. Push the brake cam(s) out of the brake plate from the outside using hand-pressure or by tapping with a plastic mallet. Remove the dust seals (if fitted) from the brake plate.
9. Check that the brake lever pinch-bolts are not bent. This can easily happen if they are overtightened. Replace any bolts which are in this condition. Inspect the brake lever splines and replace the lever(s) if these are worn or torn.
10. Inspect the splines on the brake cam(s). These should be in good condition. Check that the brake cams are not bent and that they can rotate freely in the brake plate passage. If it will not, use a fine grade of sandpaper on the camshaft and the surface of the brake plate passage.
11. Clean the cam(s) thoroughly in a solvent to remove any old grease, rust or corrosion. Use sandpaper or emery cloth to polish the cams. Clean off any residue; before reassembly, smear the cams with chassis grease.
12. Inspect the brake plate for cracks or fractures, and replace it if necessary.
13. On twin-leading shoe brakes, the brake plate linkage should be checked. The connecting rod is secured to each brake lever by a clevis pin and cotter pin. These pins can be removed after the cotter pin is taken off. They should be checked for wear, especially on high mileage machines, and replaced if necessary.
14. Check the condition of the brake springs, noting any twisted or fatigued hooks. Replace any broken, rusted, or old springs with new ones. Be sure that the lever springs are in good condition. Check the length of the brake springs against the specification given in the "Chassis Specifications" chart.

15. Clean all parts thoroughly with a suitable solvent, making a special effort to remove the dust and built-up dirt from the brake plate.

16. When reassembling the hub, note the following points:

a. Ensure that the brake cams are lubricated with chassis grease and that any shims which were on the cams are in place;

b. The use of new dust seals is recommended;

c. Lubricate the brake shoe pivot points with a little grease;

d. Install the shoes as on removal. Hook them together with the springs, and fold them down over the brake cam(s) and pivot(s).

On twin-leading shoe brakes, position the front brake lever so that it forms a 90° angle with the brake cable when the shoe begins to contact the drum. Position the rear lever parallel to the front lever. Adjust the linkage as described in "Maintenance."

Brake Drums

1. Upon disassembly of the hub, inspect the brake drum surface for condition. The drums must be clean and free from score marks or rust.

2. Rust can be removed from the drum surface with sandpaper. Polish the surface until it is shiny, then clean it thoroughly.

3. Alcohol or lacquer thinner can be used to remove dirt or deposits from the drum.

4. The drum should be checked for concentricity. An out-of-round condition is usually noticeable as an on-off-on feeling when the brake is applied while riding. With the wheel assembly mounted on the machine, spin the wheel while applying the brake very lightly. The rubbing noise of the brakes against the drum should be heard for the entire revolution of the wheel.

5. An out-of-round condition and most scoring can be removed by having the drum turned on a lathe. If the rim needs to be trued, have this done before any work on the drum is performed, as the action of the spokes while truing the rim may further aggravate the drum warpage.

Disc Brake Service

When handling disc brake fluid, observe the following cautions:

a. Brake fluid absorbs moisture very quickly, and then becomes useless. Therefore, never use fluid from an old or unsealed container;

b. Brake fluid will quickly damage paint. Place a protective cover on the gas tank;

c. Use only DOT #3 or DOT #4 brake fluid.

FLUSHING

The brake system should be flushed out every 8,000 miles, or once a year.

1. Attach a length of vinyl tube to the bleed screw on the brake caliper, and put the other end into a small container.

2. Remove the master cylinder cap, and the diaphragm. Loosen the bleed screw. Pull the brake lever slowly to the handgrip. Repeat until the master cylinder is almost empty.

3. Add new brake fluid to the master cylinder and continue squeezing and releasing the brake lever until the new fluid begins to come out of the vinyl tube. Bleed the system as outlined below.

BLEEDING

1. Needed for this operation are a torque wrench, a small cup, and a vinyl tube.

2. Be sure that the reservoir is topped up. After checking the reservoir level, replace the diaphragm.

3. Connect the vinyl tube to the bleed screw on the caliper, making sure that it is a tight fit; then insert the other end of the tube into a small container with several inches of brake fluid in it. Be sure that the end of the tube is below the level of the fluid in the container.

Bleeding the front disc brake

4. Apply the brake lever *slowly* several times, then hold it ON.

5. While holding the brake lever on, loosen the bleed screw. The brake lever will be pulled toward the handgrip. Close the bleed screw BEFORE the lever bottoms out on the handgrip.

6. Repeat the procedure until the fluid issuing from the lower end of the tube is completely free of air bubbles.

NOTE: *During the operation, keep a check on the reservoir fluid level, maintaining it near its normal position.*

7. Tighten the bleed screw to 4.5–6.7 ft lbs.

8. Top up the reservoir to the level line.

PAD REPLACEMENT

Two-Piece Caliper

1. Remove the front wheel.

2. Remove the phillips head screw from the back of the inside caliper half, and remove the inside pad (pad B).

3. Squeeze the brake lever carefully until the outside pad (pad A) can be removed. Do not force the piston out more than is necessary.

4. Inspect the pads for wear. If either pad is worn past the red line, replace both pads as a set.

5. Inspect the pads for score marks.

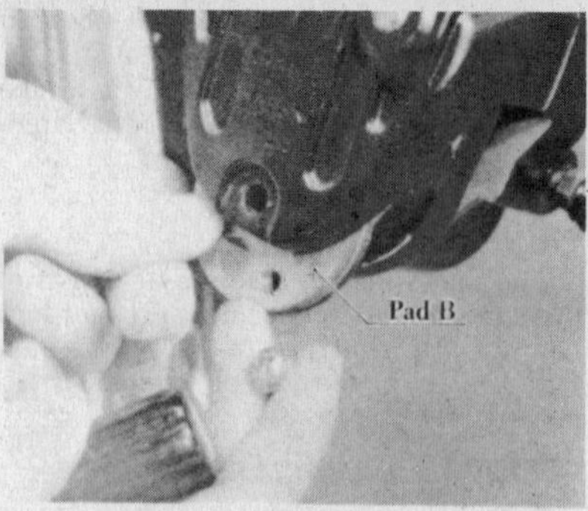

Removing the inner brake pad

Minor scoring can be removed with sandpaper. Be sure that there is no oil or grease present on the pads. Fluid-impregnated pads must be replaced.

NOTE: *The pads should always be replaced as a set.*

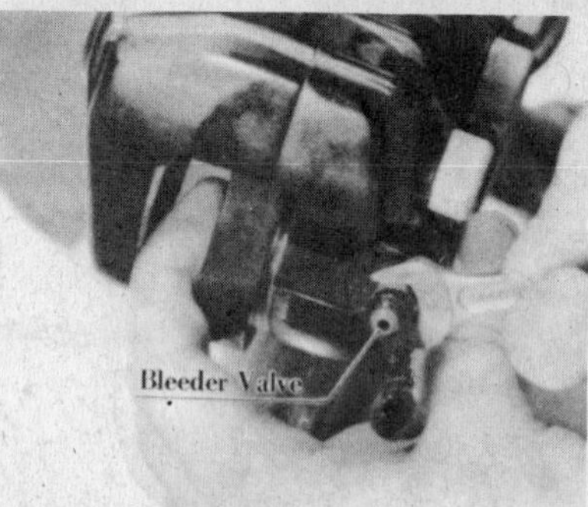

Open the bleeder valve and push in the outer pad "A"

6. To install, open the bleeder valve slightly to relieve pressure, then push the piston in all the way and close the valve. Be prepared for brake fluid to exit the bleeder valve when the piston is forced in.

7. Install the outside pad (pad A), making certain that the groove in the pad is aligned with the positioning pin.

8. Install the inside pad (pad B), apply thread locking compound to the securing screw and install the screw.

9. Install the front wheel. Check the fluid level in the master cylinder. Note that fitting new pads in the place of a pair which were considerably worn will result in a rise in the reservoir fluid level. If it gets too high, drain off any excess fluid via the caliper bleed screw. If the brake lever feels soft or spongy, the brake should be bled.

10. Avoid hard application of the brake for about 50 miles until the new pads are seated.

One-Piece Caliper

1. Remove the front wheel.

2. Remove the mounting screw for the inner pad (pad B) and take off the metal plate. Remove the pad.

3. Push the caliper body to the right side of the motorcycle and take out the outer pad (pad A). If removal is difficult, gently apply the brake lever until the pad is forced out.

4. Check the pads for wear and replace them, as a set, if either is worn to the red wear limit line.

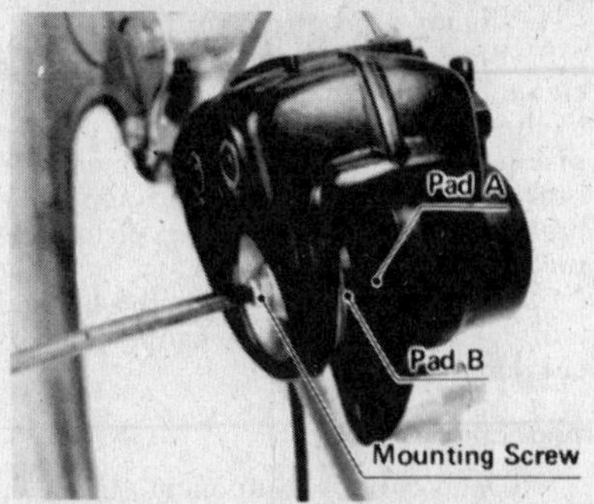

On one-piece calipers, remove the mounting screw to take out pad B

5. Check for score marks. Minor scoring can be removed with sandpaper. Be sure there is no oil or grease present on the pads. Fluid-impregnated pads must be replaced.

6. To install the pads, loosen the bleeder valve slightly and push in the piston as far as possible. Tighten the valve. Install pad A. Install pad B, aligning the pad tongue with the groove in the caliper. Fit the plate. Secure the screw with a thread locking compound (non-permanent).

7. Check fluid level and bleed front brake.

8. If new pads are fitted, avoid hard application of the brake for about 50 miles.

TWO-PIECE CALIPER

Removal and Disassembly

1. Disconnect the brake line pipe from the caliper half, place the rubber cap from the bleeder valve over the end of the brake line to prevent dirt from entering the system.

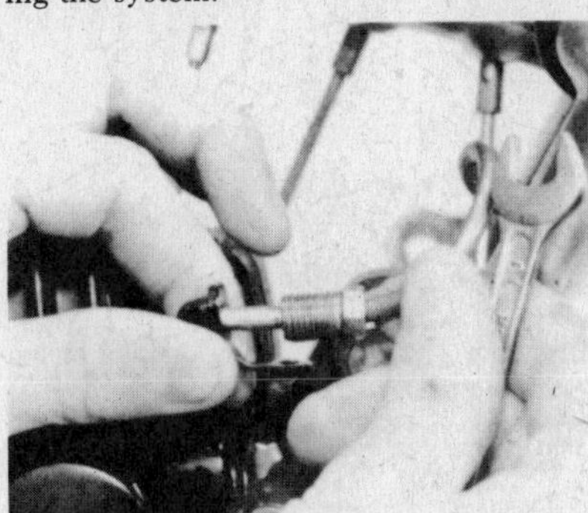
Plug the end of the brake line with the bleeder valve cap to prevent fluid loss

2. Loosen the two allen head shafts a few turns. Remove the two mounting bolts holding the caliper to the fork slider, and remove the caliper.

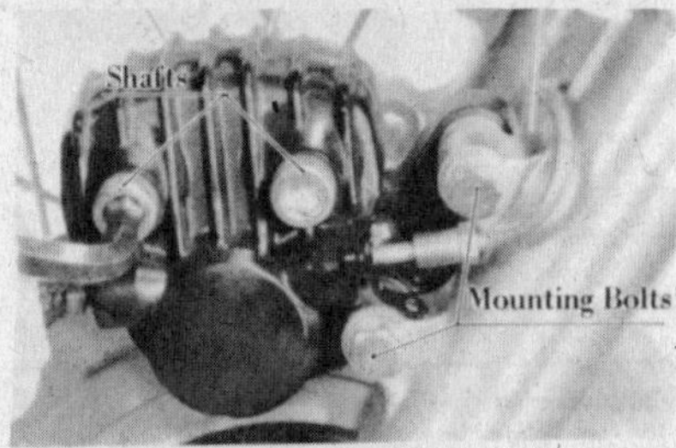

Loosen the allen bolt shafts before removing the caliper mounting bolts

3. Remove the pads from the caliper. Unscrew the two allen head shafts evenly, and then remove the inside caliper half and the caliper mounting bracket, pulling them straight off. Pull the allen head shafts from the outside caliper, being careful not to damage the shafts or the O-rings.

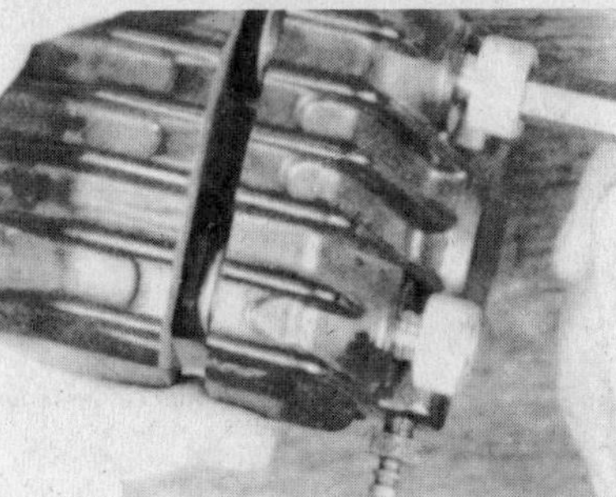
Unscrew the shafts evenly.

4. Remove the band and the dust seal from the piston in the outside caliper half.

5. The piston can be removed from the outside caliper half by blowing compressed air into the brake line inlet. If compressed air is not available, reconnect the brake line and pump the brake lever to force the piston out.

NOTE: *These are the only recommended methods for removing the piston.*

6. Remove the piston ring from the cylinder.

Inspection

NOTE: *Caliper components should be kept free of any solvent. Parts should be cleaned only in brake fluid.*

1. Inspect the piston for scoring along the sides or for other signs of wear. Replace as necessary.

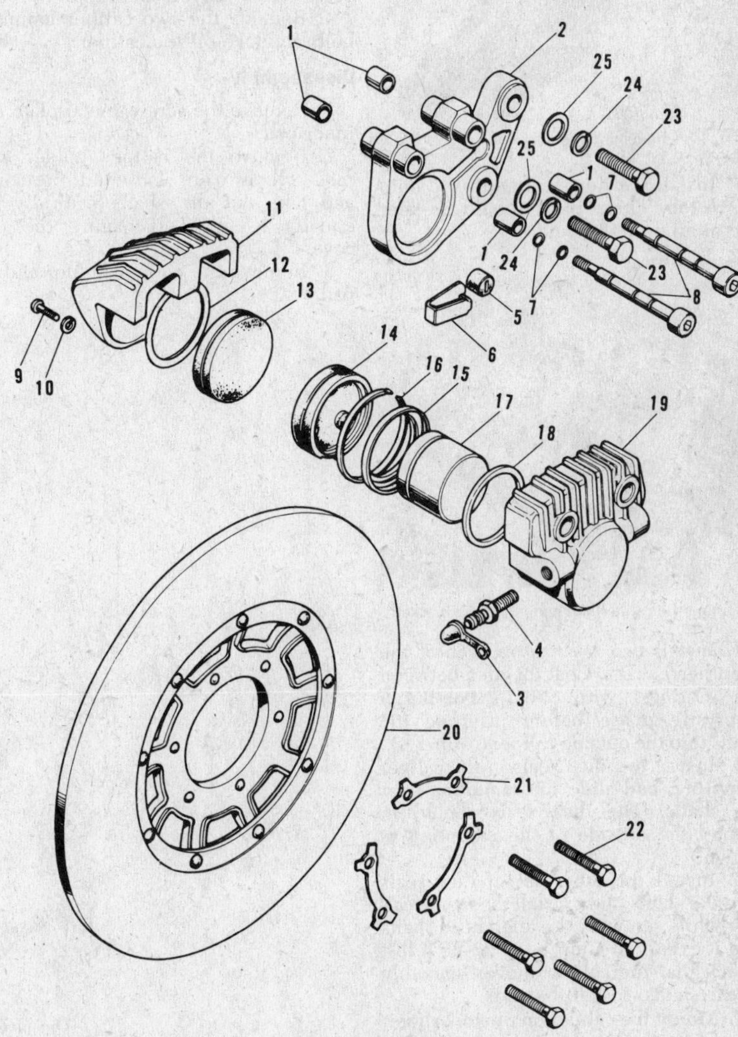

Two-piece caliper assembly

1. Dust seal
2. Caliper mounting
3. Bleeder valve cap
4. Bleeder valve
5. Bushing
6. Stopper
7. O-ring
8. Shaft
9. Screw
10. Lockwasher
11. Caliper B (inner)
12. Ring
13. Pad B (inner)
14. Pad A (outer)
15. Dust seal
16. Band
17. Piston
18. Ring
19. Caliper A (outer)
20. Disc
21. Lockwasher
22. Bolt
23. Bolt
24. Lockwasher
25. Washer

2. Replace any damaged seals in the unit. All seals should be replaced every two years regardless of appearance.

3. Refer to the chart at the end of this section for specifications.

Assembly and Installation

1. Clean the components in brake fluid, be sure to clean the ring groove inside the cylinder.

2. Lubricate the piston ring and piston with fresh brake fluid, and insert them into the cylinder in that order. Push the piston in as far as possible.

Removing the dust seal

3. Install the dust seal and band onto the piston. These parts should be kept free of oil or brake fluid.

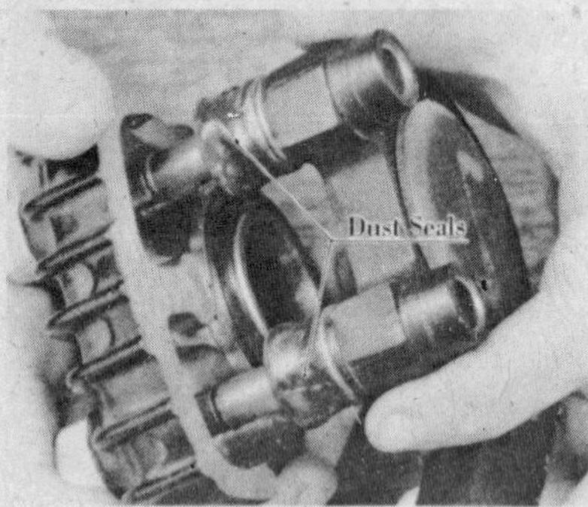

Joining the caliper half and mounting bracket

4. Install two O-rings on each of the allen head shafts. Coat the area between the O-rings with PBC (PolyButyl-Cuprysil) grease before inserting the shafts into the outside caliper (caliper A).

5. Install two dust seals in the caliper mounting, and slide the mounting over the shafts. The dust seals should fit around the outside of the mounting as shown.

6. Install the other set of dust seals onto the shafts, then install the inside caliper while screwing the allen head shafts into it evenly to a torque of 22–26 ft lbs. Check that the caliper moves smoothly on the shafts. Install the pads.

7. Mount the caliper on the fork slider, torque the mounting bolts to 18–24 ft lbs, then connect the brake line. Bleed the brake system as previously described.

ONE-PIECE CALIPER

Removal

1. Remove the front wheel.

2. If the caliper is to be disassembled, remove the two caliper holder shaft nuts on the wheel side of the caliper.

Loosen the caliper holder shaft nuts before removing the caliper mounting bolts

3. Disconnect the brake line from the caliper and cap the end with the bleeder valve cap to prevent fluid loss.

4. Remove the two caliper mounting bolts and take off the caliper.

Disassembly

1. Remove the screw, metal plate, and inner pad.

2. Remove the caliper holder shaft nuts which were loosened previously and take out the shafts carefully and equally to avoid damaging the dust covers.

3. Remove the caliper holder and the pad.

4. Remove the piston dust seal.

5. Block the caliper opening with a clean, heavy cloth. Apply compressed air to the brake line fitting to push out the piston. If not available, reconnect the brake line to the caliper and apply the brake lever to push out the piston. Be prepared for spilled fluid.

6. Remove the fluid seal with a hooked tool, taking care that the caliper bore is not damaged.

Inspection

1. Clean caliper components in clean brake fluid only. Do not use solvents.

2. Check the piston for scuffing or imperfections and replace it if damaged.

3. Replace the piston seal as a matter of preventive maintenance, and dust covers and o-rings if damaged.

4. Refer to the chart at the end of this section for caliper specifications.

Assembly

1. Fit the fluid seal into the caliper.

2. Lubricate the outsides of the piston with clean brake fluid and push it carefully into the caliper by hand as far as possible.

3. Fit the dust seal into its groove.

4. Apply a light coat of high-temperature waterproof grease (PBC) to the holder holes and caliper holder shafts. With the dust covers and o-rings and caliper holder in place, carefully insert the shafts, turning them as they are inserted.

5. Fit the spacers to the shafts, pro-

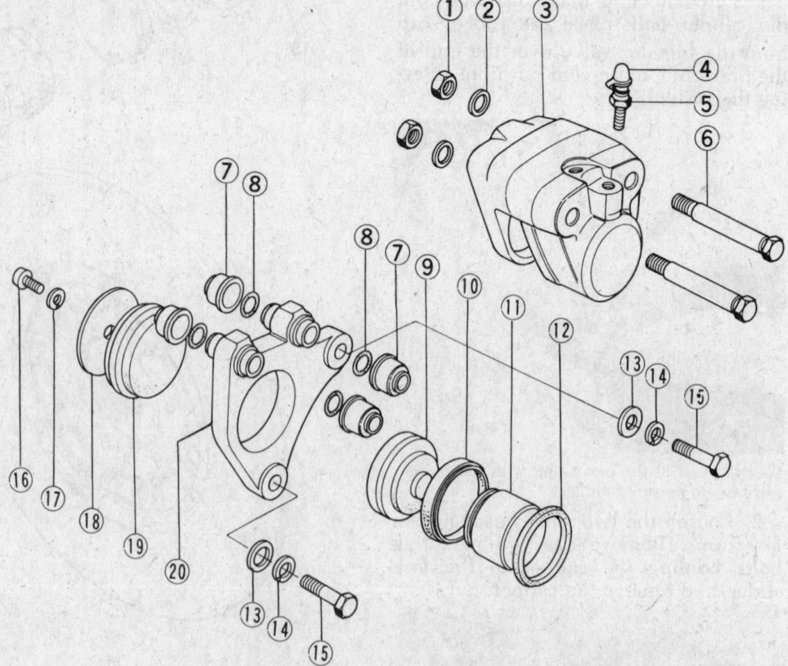

One-piece caliper assembly

1. Nut
2. Spacer
3. Caliper
4. Bleeder valve cap
5. Bleeder valve
6. Caliper holder shaft
7. Dust cover
8. O-ring
9. Pad A
10. Dust seal
11. Piston
12. Piston seal
13. Washer
14. Lockwasher
15. Caliper mounting bolt
16. Mounting screw
17. Lockwasher
18. Metal plate
19. Pad B
20. Caliper holder

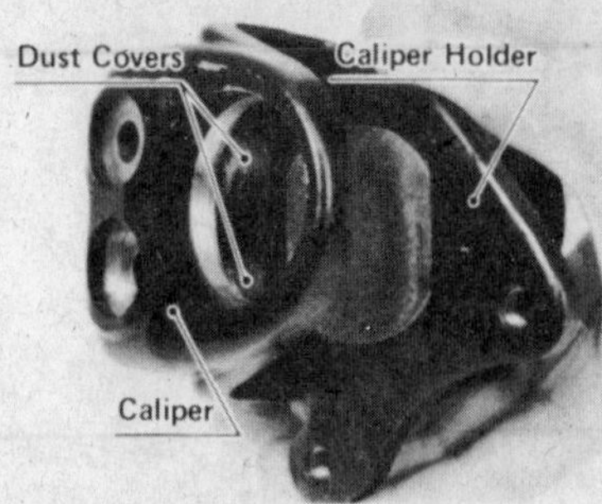

Assembling the caliper components

truding side facing the caliper. Screw on the nuts, tightening them to the proper torque after installing the caliper on the fork slider.

6. Install the pads as outlined in "Pad Replacement" preceeding.

Installation

1. Tighten the caliper mounting bolts to 25–33 ft lbs.
2. Tighten the caliper holder shaft nuts to 17.5–20 ft lbs.
3. Connect the brake line to the caliper and tighten the fitting to 12–13 ft lbs.
4. Check fluid level in the master cylinder and bleed the brake.

BRAKE DISC (EARLY)

1. Check the disc for run-out by securing a dial gauge to the fork slider. If run-out is 0.012 in. (0.3 mm) or more, remove the disc and check for warpage. If the disc is not warped, suspect the wheel bearings.

2. Measure the disc thickness. Replace the disc if less than 0.217 in. (5.5 mm).

3. To remove the disc, remove the front wheel, bend down the locking tabs on the disc securing bolts, and remove the bolts.

4. When installing the disc, care should be taken to tighten the bolts evenly and gradually until the proper torque of 12–16 ft lbs is reached. Ensure that the locking tabs are bent up against the flats on the disc bolts.

BRAKE DISC (*LATER*)

The "later" disc is used with the one-piece caliper.

1. Inspect the disc as outlined for the "Early" type above. Maximum allowable run-out is 0.012 in. (0.3 mm). Minimum thickness is 0.24 in. (6.0 mm).

2. When installing the disc, tighten the bolts to 25–33 ft lbs.

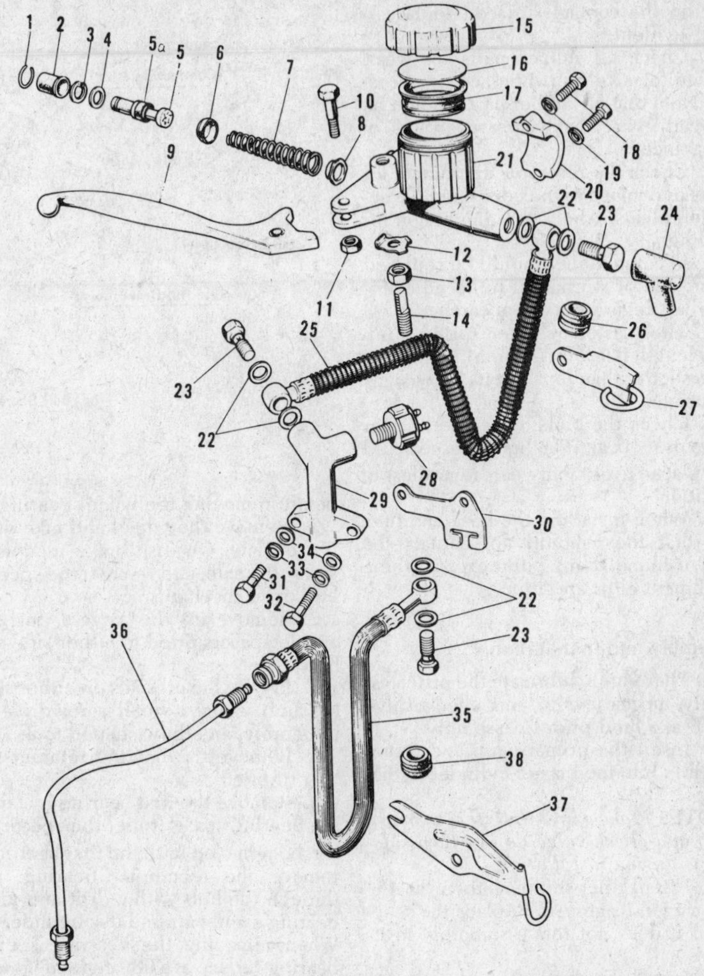

Disc brake master cylinder assembly

1. Dust seal stopper
2. Dust seal
3. Circlip
4. Piston stopper
5. Piston assembly
5a. Secondary cup
6. Primary cup
7. Spring assembly
8. Check valve assembly
9. Brake lever
10. Bolt
11. Nut
12. Lockwasher
13. Nut
14. Bolt
15. Cap
16. Plate
17. Cap seal diaphragm
18. Bolt
19. Washer
20. Master cylinder mounting
21. Master cylinder body
22. Washer
23. Banjo bolt
24. Dust cover
25. Hose
26. Grommet
27. Bracket
28. Pressure switch
29. 3-way fitting
30. Guide
31. Bolt
32. Bolt
33. Lockwasher
34. Washer
35. Hose
36. Pipe
37. Bracket
38. Grommet

MASTER CYLINDER

Removal and Disassembly

1. Disconnect the brake fluid line from the master cylinder.
2. Remove the two mounting bolts and the master cylinder assembly.
3. Remove the reservoir cap, seal, and plate. Drain the brake fluid.
4. Unscrew the mounting bolt and nut, then remove the brake lever.
5. Using a piece of heavy wire bent into a hook at the end, remove the securing ring and the dust seal. Be careful not to damage the seal.
6. Remove the securing snap-ring, then remove the stopper plate, piston assembly, primary cup, spring assembly, and check valve. Leave the secondary cup on the piston unless replacement is necessary. Do not remove the spring seat from the spring.

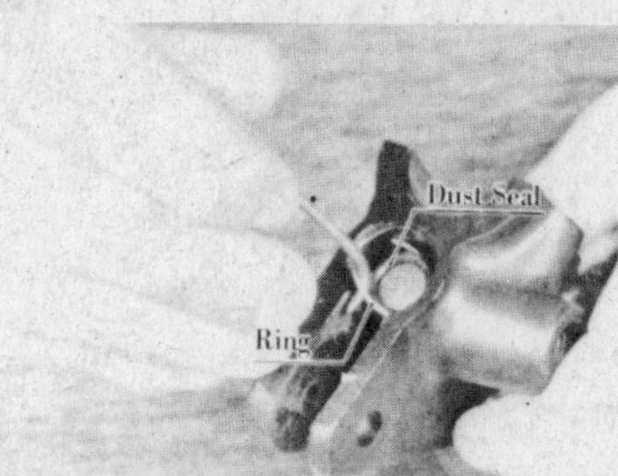

Removing the dust seal and ring from the master cylinder

NOTE: *Do not clamp the master cylinder tightly in a vise, as distortion may result.*

Inspection

1. Wash all parts in new brake fluid only.
2. Check the master cylinder port for clogging due to foreign matter.
3. Be sure that the reservoir is clean.
4. Check the walls of the master cylinder for grooves or score marks.
5. Check the outlet end for dents or other damage.

In the event of any permanent damage, replace the master cylinder body.

6. Check the piston for wear or rust and replace as necessary.
7. Check the condition of the cylinder cup noting any evidence of grooved

wear on the contact surface. Replace if any is evident.

8. Check all rubber parts for wear, damage, or swelling. Replace as necessary. Note that all rubber parts should be replaced every two years regardless of appearance.

9. Check the reservoir diaphragm for cracks or damage to the edges and the accordion pleats. Check the diaphragm for swelling.

These components should be replaced if damaged or worn, and replaced every two years regardless of appearance.

10. The master cylinder spring minimum length is 1.9 in. (48 mm). Replace it if it is shorter than this or if it shows signs of damage.

11. Check the brake hose and line for cracks or seepage. The brake hose should be replaced every four years regardless of condition.

12. When installing the hose and line, note that they should not contact the forks or frame at any point except where attachment clips are fitted.

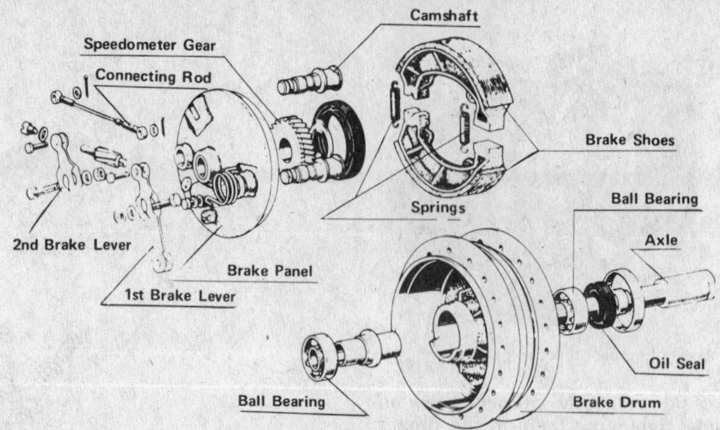

Front drum brake assembly

Assembly and Installation

1. Thoroughly lubricate the piston assembly, primary cup, and check valve with brake fluid prior to assembly.

2. Insert the primary cup and piston assembly into the master cylinder in that order.

NOTE: *Make sure that the primary cup and check valve do not turn sideways during installation.*

3. Install the stopper, then fit the snap-ring in its groove. Replace the snap-ring if it does not rotate smoothly in its groove.

4. Install the dust seal and seal stopper. Make absolutely certain that the seal seats properly in the piston groove.

5. Install the brake lever.

6. Hold the cylinder and squeeze the lever to make certain that it operates smoothly. Put a finger over the hose connection: you should be able to detect suction when the lever is released.

7. Fill the reservoir with brake fluid and install the cap.

8. Squeeze and release the lever several times until the fluid is pumped out the hose connection. Do not squeeze the lever to the limit of its travel or damage to the secondary cup may result.

9. Squeeze the lever, cover the hose connection with a finger, then release the lever: it should return to its original position quickly and smoothly.

10. Mount the assembly on the handlebar, and tighten the top mounting bolts first.

11. Adjust the brake lever to have less than 3/16 in. free-play.

12. Connect the brake hose, fill the reservoir, and bleed the system as previously described.

Wheel Bearings

REMOVAL

Removal of the wheel bearings necessitates removing the hub oil seals. These must be replaced with new ones upon reassembly. Clean the outside of the hub before removing the wheel bearings.

1. Remove the wheel and take out the brake plate. On disc brake models, unscrew the axle, and remove the speedometer drive mechanism.

2. Remove any dust covers, dust seals, or axle spacers fitted to either side of the hub.

3. Pry out the oil seals on either side of the hub using a small screwdriver, or, preferably, an elbow-shaped tool.

4. Remove the bearing retainer snap-ring (if fitted).

5. Remove the first bearing by tapping the bearing spacer tube; the spacer tube can be removed with the first bearing. To remove the remaining bearing, reach through the hub with a drift and tap the bearing evenly around its circumference. When removing the bearing, keep the bearing surface at a 90° angle to its seat in the hub.

NOTE: *On some models, especially high mileage machines, the hub should be heated gently with a propane torch in the vicinity of the bearing bosses to facilitate removal.*

INSPECTION

NOTE: *The following bearing inspection checks refer to the sprocket hub bearing as well as the wheel bearings.*

1. Clean the bearings and spacer tube in a suitable solvent, removing all of the old grease. At this point, it would be wise to clean out the hub as well.

2. Check the bearing bosses in the hub for scuffs, cracks, or distortion. If they are in any way damaged, the hub must be replaced.

3. Check the condition of the spacer tube and replace if damaged.

4. Apply a few drops of light oil to the bearing, and spin it. The bearing must rotate smoothly and freely. Any roughness or binding in rotation will necessitate a new bearing.

5. Place the bearing on a flat surface. Place your fingers on the outer bearing race to hold it steady. Try to move the inner race back and forth. In a good bearing, it will not be possible to move the inner race. If it is, the bearing must be replaced.

6. Note that bearings must be replaced in pairs.

ASSEMBLY

1. Obtain a good grade of wheel bearing grease to lubricate the wheel bearings.

2. Pack the grease in the bearing. A common method of doing this is to place a goodly amount of the grease in the palm of one hand. Taking the clean, dry, bear-

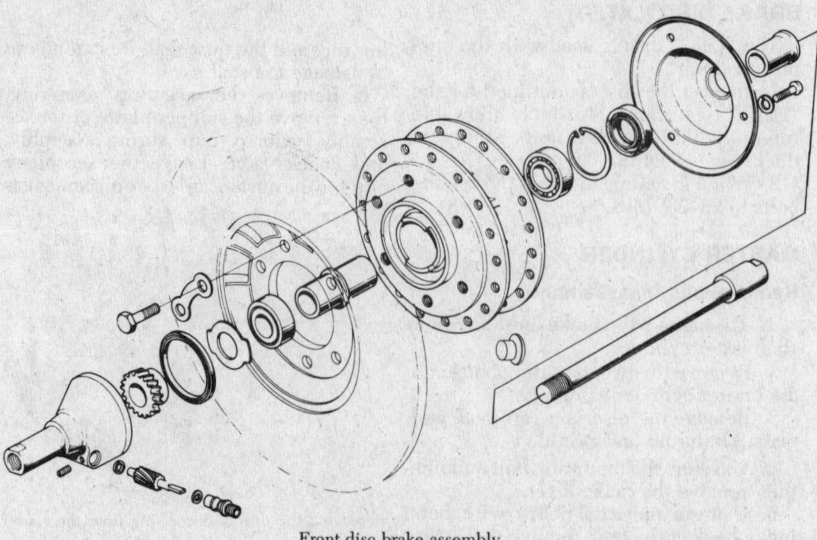

Front disc brake assembly

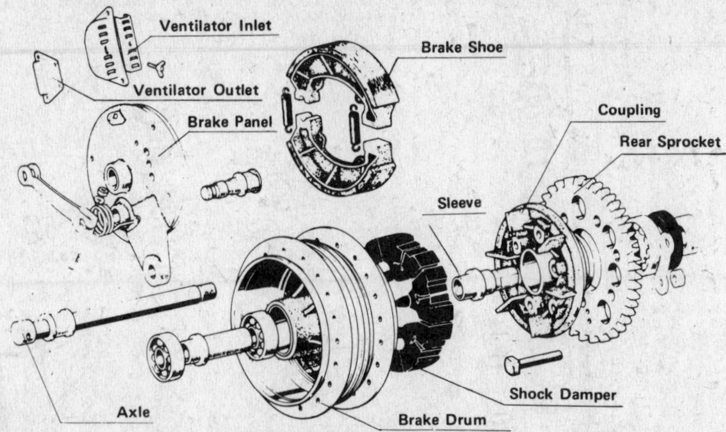

Rear brake assembly (H1)

ing, press one section of it into the grease. Turn the bearing until the grease has been deposited around the entire circumference. The packing process is complete when the grease begins to come out of the upper side of the bearing. Place an amount of grease in the hub as well.

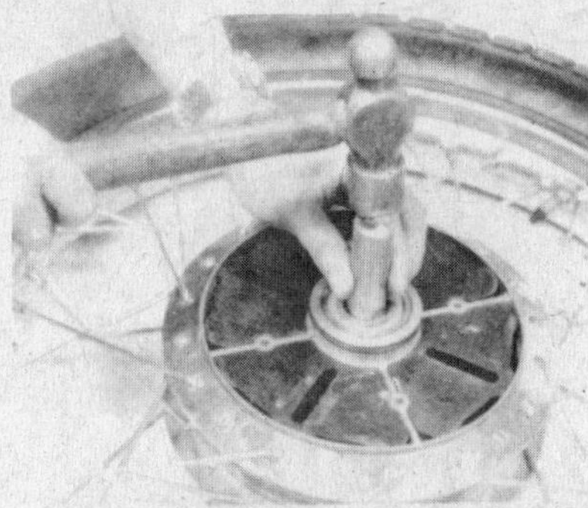
Installing a wheel bearing

3. Heat either side of the wheel hub with a propane torch as on removal of the bearings. Place one of the bearings in the hub, and make sure that it is seated.

Any bearing to which a retainer is fitted should be installed first. On most machines the axle can be used as a drift to install the first bearing. Insert the axle into the bearing until the larger diameter end rests on the bearing. Center the bearing in the bearing boss, then strike the axle sharply until the bearing is seated.

4. Fit the spacer, and install the other wheel bearing.

5. Press in new oil seals on both sides of the hub.

6. Tighten the axle to 51–80 ft lbs. on disc brake wheels.

FRONT FORKS

Early Type

REMOVAL AND DISASSEMBLY

1. Remove the front wheel and fender.
2. If a disc brake is fitted, remove the caliper from the left fork leg.
3. Remove the fork filler caps.
4. Loosen the upper (if fitted) and lower triple clamp pinch-bolts.

Removing the fork filler caps

5. Withdraw the fork legs one at a time from the steering stem.
6. Remove the spring from the top of the fork tube and invert the fork leg over a suitable container to pour out the oil.

Loosening the lower triple clamp pinch bolts

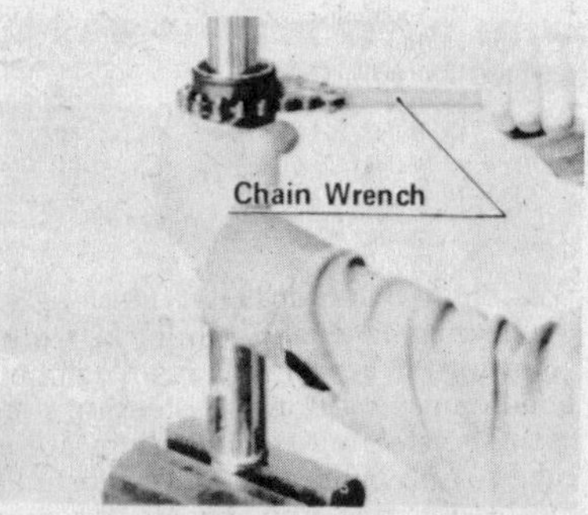

Removing the slider nut

7. Clamp the bottom of the fork slider in a wood jaw vise, lift up the slider dust seal, and unscrew the slider nut with a chain wrench or pipe wrench.

NOTE: *If neither of these tools are available, wrap the slider nut with a piece of old inner tube and tighten a heater hose clamp around the inner tube. With the clamp tightened securely, grasp the screw fitting with a pair of vise-grips and unscrew the nut.*

8. Grasp the fork tube with one hand and the slider with the other and pull them apart.
9. Remove the oil seal from the slider nut.

INSPECTION

1. Measure the free-length of the fork spring. Replace both if either is found to be less than the service limit given in the "Chassis Specifications" chart at the end of this section.
2. Install the fork tube and sliding bushing into the slider. Check that the tube slides smoothly, with a minimum of play.
3. Check the inside bore of the sliding bushing for score marks. Replace if scored.
4. Install the sliding bushing on the fork tube and check for play, if play is excessive replace the bushing.
5. Install the sliding bushing into the slider, it should be a light press fit. If it is a loose fit in the slider replace the bushing.
6. Check the fork tube for any dents, score marks or bends, replace if defective. The plating must be in good condition.
7. Inspect the slider and the slider nut for broken or stripped threads, and replace as necessary.
8. Inspect the filler cap O-ring and replace it if it is torn, cracked, or nicked.

ASSEMBLY AND INSTALLATION

1. Install a new oil seal into the slider nut and lubricate it before installing it on the fork tube.
2. Install the fork tube and sliding bushing into the slider and screw the slider nut onto the slider securely.
3. Slip the dust seal down over the slider nut.
4. Fill the forks with the correct amount and grade of oil and install the spring holder and the spring.
5. To install the fork legs, slip them up and through the steering stem. Replace the filler caps, and tighten the lower triple clamp pinch-bolts making sure that the top of the fork legs are even with the top of the upper triple clamp.
6. Check that the filler caps are tight and tighten the upper triple clamp pinch-bolts (if fitted). On models with a disc brake, refit the caliper to the left fork leg.
7. Install the front fender and wheel, and check the forks for smooth and proper operation.

Later Type

The late-type forks are used on late model 400–750 machines.

REMOVAL AND DISASSEMBLY

1. Refer to Steps 1–5 under "Early Type" forks for removal procedures.
2. Remove the fork spring and pour out the oil.

3. Remove the dust cover from the top of the fork slider.

4. Remove the allen bolt from the bottom of the fork slider. The damper cylinder into which the allen bolt is threaded may turn with the bolt making removal impossible. If this happens, it may be possible to free the bolt using an impact driver. Alternately, a special tool is used which is threaded to the top of the cylinder, holding it in place while the allen bolt is removed.

5. After removing the allen bolt, separate the fork slider from the fork tube.

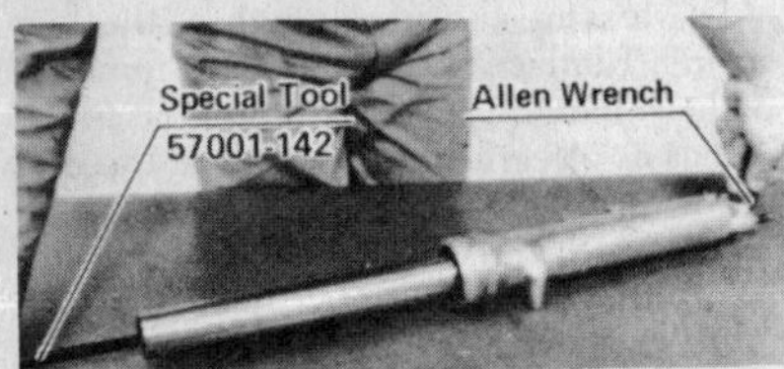

Using the special tool to remove the slider allen bolt

6. Remove the circlip from the bottom of the fork tube to remove the damper components.

7. Remove the slider oil seal circlip and pry out the slider. New seals must be used on assembly.

INSPECTION

1. Measure the free length of the fork springs and compare to the serviceable limit given in the "Chassis Specifications" chart.

2. Clean the damper components in a solvent and check for wear, especially of the cylinder ring. Lubricate all components before assembly.

ASSEMBLY AND INSTALLATION

1. Assembly is the reverse of disassembly. A special tool is used to install the cylinder components into the fork leg.

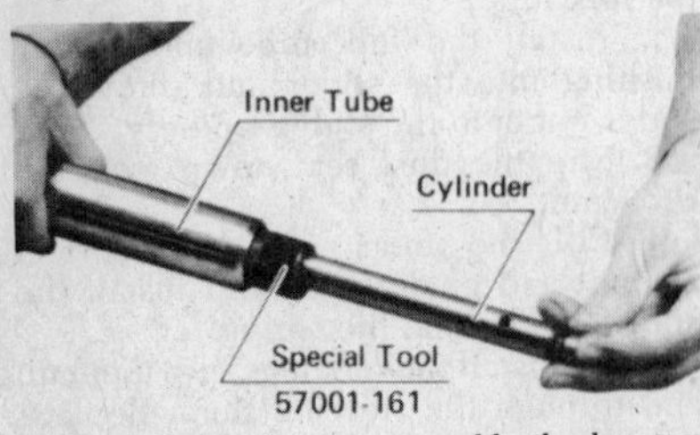

Using the special tool to assemble the late type front fork

2. Press new oil seals into the sliders insuring that they are not tilted and are fully seated. Install the washer and circlip, being sure that it is seated in its groove. Lubricate the seal lips with fork oil before installing the slider on the tube.

3. Refer to Steps 3–7 under "Early Type" forks for remaining operations.

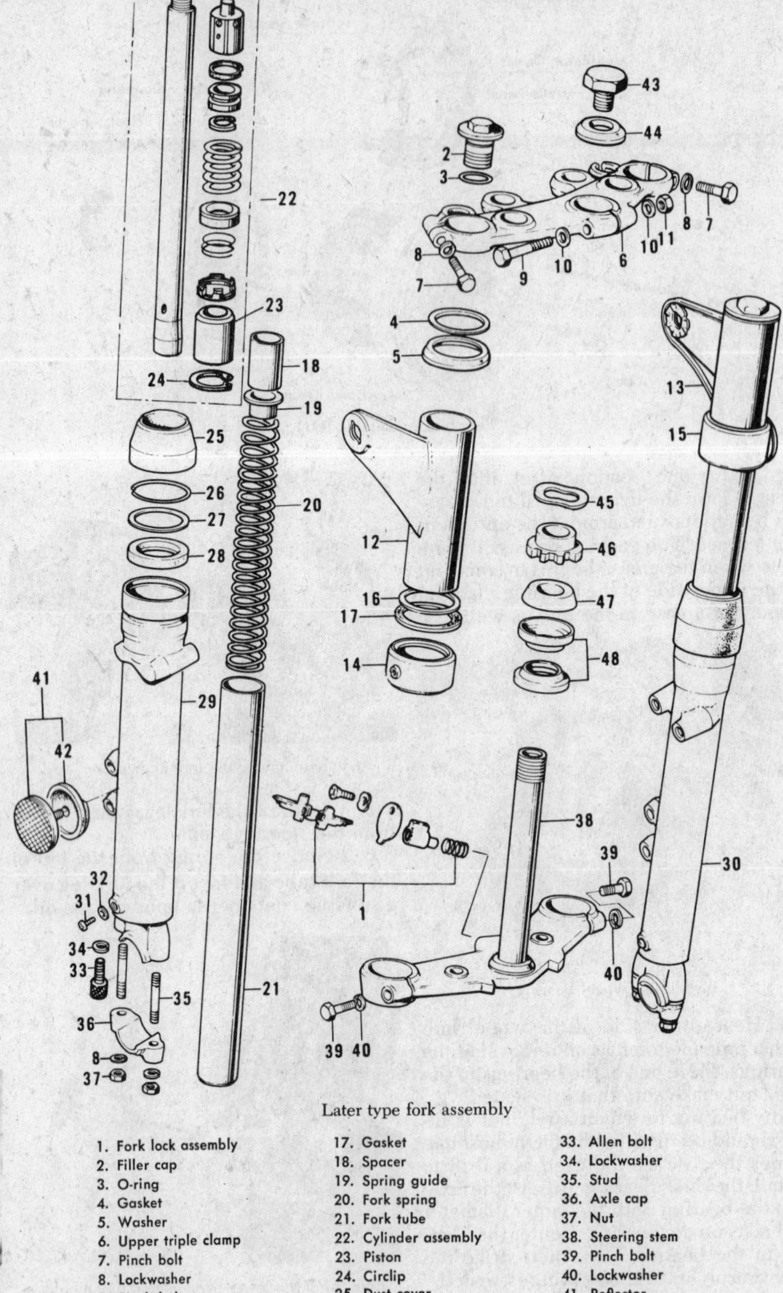

Later type fork assembly

1. Fork lock assembly
2. Filler cap
3. O-ring
4. Gasket
5. Washer
6. Upper triple clamp
7. Pinch bolt
8. Lockwasher
9. Pinch bolt
10. Lockwasher
11. Nut
12. Headlight bracket, left
13. Headlight bracket, right
14. Guide
15. Guide
16. Washer
17. Gasket
18. Spacer
19. Spring guide
20. Fork spring
21. Fork tube
22. Cylinder assembly
23. Piston
24. Circlip
25. Dust cover
26. Circlip
27. Washer
28. Oil seal
29. Fork slider, left
30. Fork slider, right
31. Drain plug
32. Gasket
33. Allen bolt
34. Lockwasher
35. Stud
36. Axle cap
37. Nut
38. Steering stem
39. Pinch bolt
40. Lockwasher
41. Reflector
42. Damper rubber
43. Steering stem bolt
44. Washer
45. Washer
46. Stem locknut
47. Cap
48. Bearing race

STEERING STEM ASSEMBLY

Bearing Adjustment

On models equipped with a friction steering damper, the damper should be loosened (counterclockwise) as much as possible so that it does not interfere with the bearing movement while checking or adjusting the bearings. If an oil damper is fitted, remove it from the steering stem.

1. The steering stem bearings are uncaged ¼ in. balls. They are adjusted by means of a ring nut beneath the upper triple clamp.

2. To check bearing adjustment, support the front wheel off the ground. Grasp the tip of the front fender, place your other hand beneath the lower triple clamp at the frame lug.

3. Attempt to move the fork by pulling up on the tip of the fender. If play or movement can be felt, at the lower triple clamp, the bearings are adjusted too loosely or worn.

4. Turn the forks slowly from lock-to-lock. Movement should be smooth, silent, and effortless. If any binding or uneven movement is felt, the balls and races are either too tightly adjusted or they are worn. If the steering feels uniformly stiff, the bearings are too tightly adjusted. If any noise is noted, the bear-

ings are damaged, or some are missing.

5. With the front wheel off the ground, release the front forks from a few degrees off the centered position. The forks should fall freely to either side of their own weight. If they will not, the bearings are too tightly adjusted, the steering stem is bent, the races are extremely worn, or some of the bearings are missing.

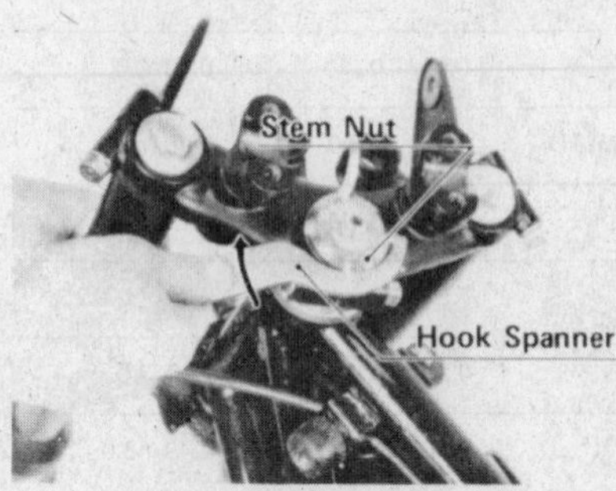

Adjusting the steering head bearings

6. To adjust the bearings, remove the front wheel, front forks, handlebars, and the upper triple clamp. The bearings are adjusted by means of the stem adjuster nut under the upper triple clamp.

7. Tighten or loosen the adjuster nut a little at a time until the steering stem adjustment conforms to that outlined above. Temporarily install the forks, upper triple clamp, and the steering stem nut to check the adjustment.

8. If proper adjustment is not possible, the bearings and races will probably need to be replaced.

Disassembly

1. Remove the front wheel, front forks, and handlebars. If a friction steering damper is fitted remove it by removing the cotter pin from under the lower triple clamp, and unscrewing the damper rod and removing the friction plates. If an oil shock is fitted unbolt it from the lower triple clamp.

2. Disconnect the wiring inside the headlight shell, and remove the headlight shell.

3. Unscrew the steering stem nut and disconnect the speedometer and tachometer cables from their instruments. Remove the upper triple clamp.

4. Loosen the steering stem adjuster nut with a pin wrench, then hold the steering stem up while unscrewing the adjuster nut the rest of the way off. Remove the steering stem top cone race and ball bearings from the top race.

5. Carefully pull the steering stem out from the bottom. Some of the ball bearings from the lower race will probably fall out at this time so be prepared for this.

6. Remove the bottom cone race, dust seal, and dust seal washer from the steering stem if they are to be replaced. These will have to be pried off with a chisel, therefore only remove them if necessary.

CAUTION: *Take care not to damage the steering stem when removing the lower cone race.*

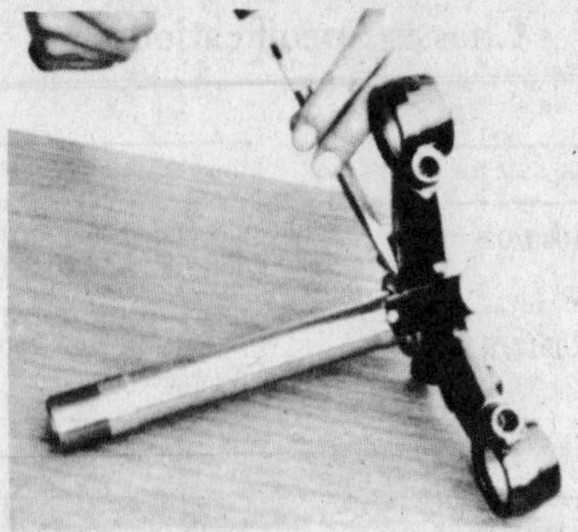
Removing the lower cone race from the steering stem

7. The bearing races in the frame lug are a press-fit and should not be removed unless replacement is necessary. If replacement is necessary the old races can be removed by reaching through the frame lug with a suitable punch and tapping the race evenly around its circumference to remove it from the inside of the frame lug. Be sure that the race does not become cocked in its seat upon removal.

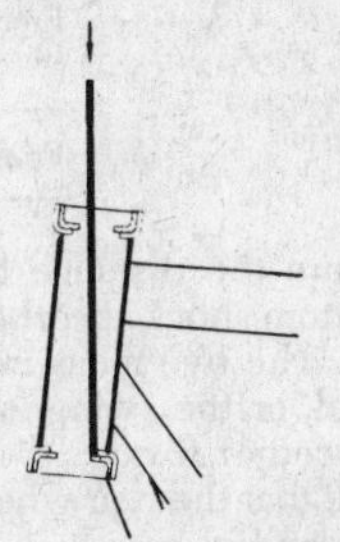
Removing the frame races

New races are installed with a suitable sized bearing driver: i.e., one which will drive the race square into this seat. Be certain that the race goes straight in.

These races can also be installed using a block of hard wood of sufficient size to cover the race in place of a bearing driver.

Inspection

1. Wash the ball bearings in a suitable solvent.

2. Clean all of the old grease from the bearing race surfaces, steering stem, and frame lug.

3. Inspect the bearing race surfaces. They must be clean and smooth. That is free from any cracks, scoring, rust, or indentations. Run your finger around each of the bearing races. Note any roughness or ripples on the race surface. If any imperfections are noted, both the sets of races and all of the balls must be replaced.

4. Check the balls themselves for rust, pitting, scoring, or flat spots. If the balls are found to be defective in any way, the balls and both sets of races must be replaced.

NOTE: *Balls and races must always be replaced in a set as worn races will destroy new balls and worn balls will destroy new races.*

5. Check the dust seal for condition and replace if torn or cracked.

6. Check the steering stem for cracks or a bent condition; this is especially important if the bike has been involved in a spill.

Installation

1. Install the dust seal washer, dust seal, and lower cone race on the steering stem. Use a good grade of bearing grease to coat the bottom cone race and the upper race in the frame lug.

2. Embed 19 balls into the grease in both the bottom cone race and the top race.

3. When the balls are in place, slip the steering stem through the frame lug and hold it in place while refitting the top cone race and threading on the adjuster nut.

4. Tighten the adjuster nut all of the way by hand, rotating the steering stem to work the grease into the balls.

Disc Brake Specifications

Measurement	Standard (in./mm)	Service Limit (in./mm)
Disc thickness (two-piece caliper) (one-piece caliper)	0.276/7.0 0.27–0.28/6.9–7.1	0.217/5.5 0.24/6.0
Disc run-out	Less than 0.004/Less than 0.1	0.012/0.3
Caliper cylinder ID (two-piece caliper)	1.5031–1.5039/38.18–38.20	1.5045/38.215
Caliper cylinder ID (one-piece caliper)	1.687–1.689/42.850–42.900	1.69/42.92
Caliper piston OD (two-piece caliper)	1.5006–1.5019/38.115–38.148	1.5002–38.105
Caliper piston OD (one-piece caliper)	1.685–1.686/42.788–42.820	1.68/42.75
Master cylinder, cylinder ID	0.5512–0.5529/14.00–14.04	0.5543/14.08
Master cylinder piston OD	0.5495–0.5506/13.95–13.98	0.5496/13.960
Master cylinder primary, secondary cup diameter	0.577–0.596/14.65–15.15	0.571/14.50
Master cylinder spring free-length	2.01/51.0	1.89/48.0

Chassis Specifications

250–400

Measurement	Standard (in./mm)	Service Limit (in./mm)
Swing arm pivot shaft run-out	0.004/0.1	0.020/0.5
Swing arm sleeve/bushing clearance	0.0059/0.15	0.0217/0.55
Rim run-out	0.04/1.0	0.12/3.0
Front (drum brake) drum ID	7.087/180.0	7.116/180.75
Rear drum ID	7.087/180.0	7.116/180.75
Brake lining thickness	0.20/5.0	0.12/3.0
Front drum brake spring free-length	1.85/47.0	1.97/50
Rear brake spring free-length	2.20/56.0	2.32/59.0
Front fork spring free-length	14.21/361.0	13.78/350.0

500–750

Measurement	Standard (in./mm)	Service Limit (in./mm)
Swing arm pivot shaft run-out	0.004/0.1	0.020/0.5
Swing arm sleeve/bushing clearance	0.0059/0.15	0.0217/0.55
Rim run-out	0.04/1.0	0.12/3.0
Front (drum brake) drum ID	7.874/200.0	7.904/200.75
Rear drum ID (H1)	7.087/180.0	7.116/180.75
Rear drum ID (H2)	7.874/200	7.904/200.75
Brake lining thickness	0.20/5.0	0.12/3.0
Rear brake spring free-length (H1)	2.36/60.0	2.48/63.0
Rear brake spring free-length (H2)	2.62/66.5	2.74/69.5
Front drum brake spring free-length	2.62/66.5	2.74/69.5
Front fork spring free-length	13.58/345.0	13.19/335.0

General Torque Specifications

Coarse Threads

Diameter (mm)	Torque (ft lbs)
5	2.5–3.5
6	4.6–6.4
8	11.6–15.9
10	22.4–30.4
12	39.1–54.2
14	60.0–83.2
16	94.0–130
18	130–181
20	188–253

Fine Threads

Diameter (mm)	Torque (ft lbs)
5	2.5–3.5
6	4.0–5.6
8	9.8–13.4
10	18.4–25.3
12	32.5–44.8
14	53.5–73.8
16	83.2–116
18	123–166
20	166–239

5. Tighten the adjuster nut until the steering stem turns freely, but has no play.

6. Install the fork tubes, headlight assembly, and upper triple clamp, flat washer, and steering stem nut. Check that the stem moves freely of its own weight when released from 5°–10° off center.

7. Install the front fender, front wheel, and handlebars.

SWING ARM

All Models

INSPECTION

1. Disconnect the chain. Remove the rear wheel and sprocket assembly.

2. Remove the shock absorbers and chain guard.

3. Measure the distance between the top and bottom shock absorber mounts on both sides. The two measurements must be identical, or the swing arm will have to be replaced or fixed.

4. Check that the rear wheel mounting plates are parallel.

5. Grasp the legs of the swing arm and attempt to move it from side-to-side. Any noticeable side-play will indicate that the swing arm bushings in the frame need replacement.

The swing arm is most likely to be damaged if the machine is operated for any length of time with a broken or otherwise defective shock absorber.

REMOVAL

1. Proceed as above. Then remove the swing arm pivot shaft nut, and pull out the pivot shaft.

2. Remove the swing arm. Note the dust caps and O-rings on either side of the swing arm.

3. The swing arm should be inspected for cracks or fractures, especially around the welds.

After removal of the swing arm, the short sleeves and steel bushings can be replaced. This should be done every 10,000 miles, or more often depending on how the machine is used, or if the bushings are worn (see "Inspection," above).

INSTALLATION

Installation is the reverse of the removal procedure. Be sure that all nuts and bolts are secure before operation.

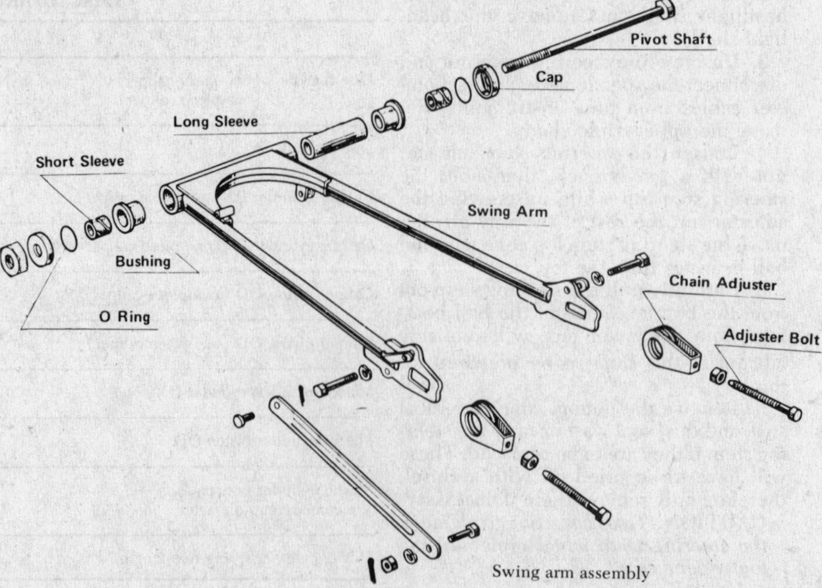

Swing arm assembly

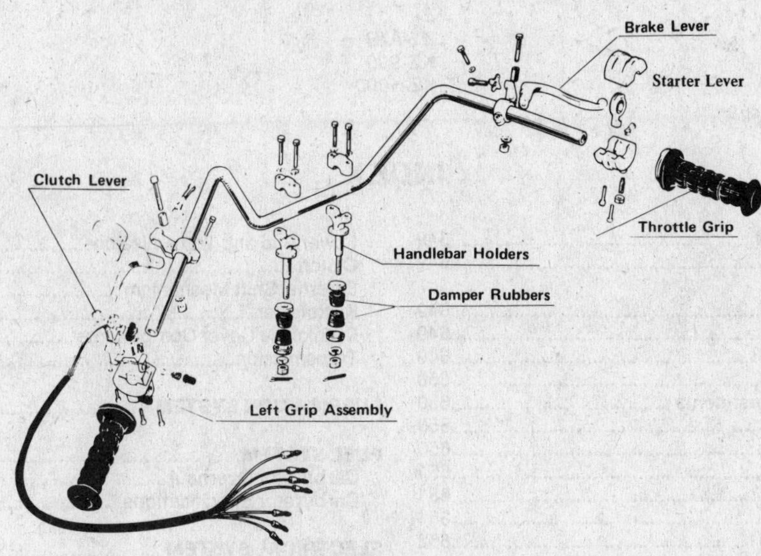

H1- Handlebar Assembly

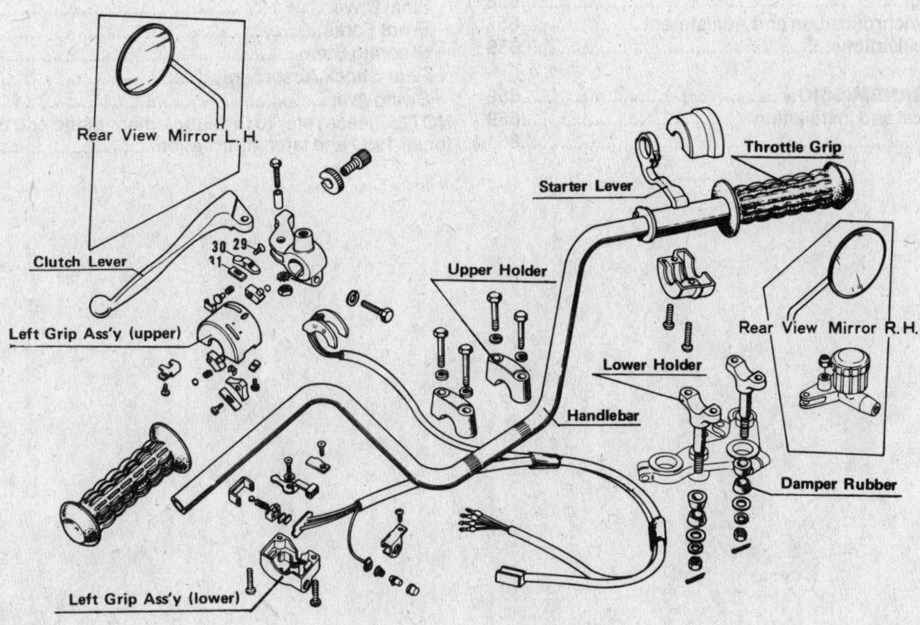

H2- Handlebar Assembly

Kawasaki 900/1000

MODEL COVERAGE

Z1
Z1-A/B
KZ-900
KZ-1000

INDEX

GENERAL INFORMATION

SERIAL NUMBER LOCATION

In order to prevent possible confusion when purchasing parts, always refer to the engine and frame serial numbers. The frame number is stamped on the left side of the steering lug, while the engine number is behind the cylinders on the top right side of the crankcase.

Frame number location

Engine number location

MAINTENANCE

NOTE: *Common maintenance procedures are explained in detail in the "General Information" section.*

LUBRICATION

Motor Oil

For use in all temperatures, Kawasaki recommends SAE 20W-50 or SAE 10W-40 motor oil, service rating "SE" or "SF."

Checking Oil Level

1. Check the oil level when the engine is warm.
2. A sight glass is provided at the lower part of the clutch case. The oil level should be between the upper and lower level marks.

Changing Oil

1. Change oil at 2,000 mile intervals or 60 days (summer)/30 days (winter); whichever comes first.

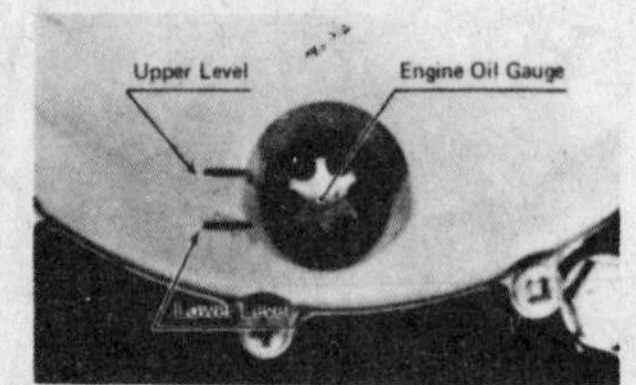

Oil level view window

2. Use 20W-50 or 10W-40 oil, service rated "SE" or "SF."
3. For the 900, engine oil capacity is 3.5 qts, minus filter. If oil *and* filter are being changed, capacity is 4.2 qts. For the 1000, capacities are approximately 3.2 qts minus the filter, and 3.9 qts if both oil and filter are changed.
4. Run the engine until normal operating temperature is reached, and place the motorcycle on its center stand.
5. Remove the engine and oil filter drain plugs, and allow the oil to drain into a suitable receptacle.
6. Remove the oil filter, if it is to be replaced, at this time by removing the filter mounting bolt, and dropping out the filter.
7. Rotate the engine several times, with the key off, to assure complete drainage.
8. Wipe off any metal filings which may be stuck to the magnetic drain plug, and install the plug. Intall the filter assembly, or filter drain plug only, as the case may be.
9. Torque the drain plug to 29 ft lbs (4.0 kg/m), the filter mounting bolt to 18 ft lbs (7.5 kg/m), and the filter drain plug to 16 ft lbs (2.2 kg/m).
10. Fill the engine with oil. The oil level should be between the two lines at the level window located on the right side crankcase clutch cover.
11. Check level after the engine has been running several minutes.

Oil Filter (Disposable)

1. A disposable cartridge oil filter is fitted, and should be changed every 4,000 miles or every other oil change.
2. When installing a new filter, make sure that the spring and both O-rings are in good condition, and replace them as necessary. The filter mounting assembly should be cleaned with clean gasoline, and blown dry, before the new filter is installed.
3. After securing the bolt to 18 ft lbs (2.5 kg/m, replenish the oil supply, and run the engine to check for any possible oil leaks.
4. Note that engine oil capacity is 4.2 qts for the 900 and 3.9 qts for the 1000 when changing this filter.

Oil Filter (Strainer)

The oil strainer is located at the oil pump pickup, and may be removed for cleaning after the oil pan is unbolted and lowered as described in the "Lubrication System" section. The strainer is secured to the pump body by 3 screws.

Clean the strainer in solvent, or replace it with a new one if it is damaged, then install the strainer and oil pan using a new pan gasket. After refilling the engine with oil, start the engine and check for oil leaks.

Oil Pressure

The engine oil pressure should be checked once a year, or whenever an oil pressure problem is suspected. Either the factory gauge (Part No. 57001-125), or a suitable substitute, can be connected at the oil gallery access hole at the right side of the engine after the plug has been removed. The gauge should read 2.8 lbs/in.^{2} (0.2 kg/cm^2) with the engine running at 3,000 rpm, and the engine oil temperature approximately 140° F (60° C), or operating temperature. If the reading proves unsatisfactory, determine and correct the fault (restricted oil passage, clogged filter, pressure relief valve failure, etc.). Consult the "Lubrication System" section for additional information.

NOTE: *Apply Loctite® to the plug threads before installing it in the gallery access hole.*

Engine and oil filter drain plug and filter mounting bolt locations

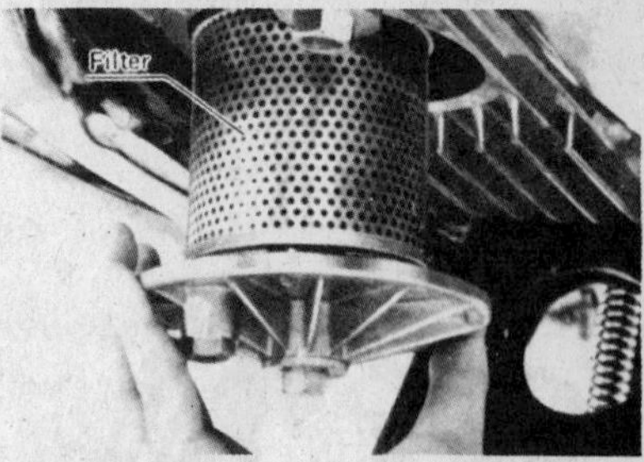

Removing the oil filter assembly

Oil pump oil filter location

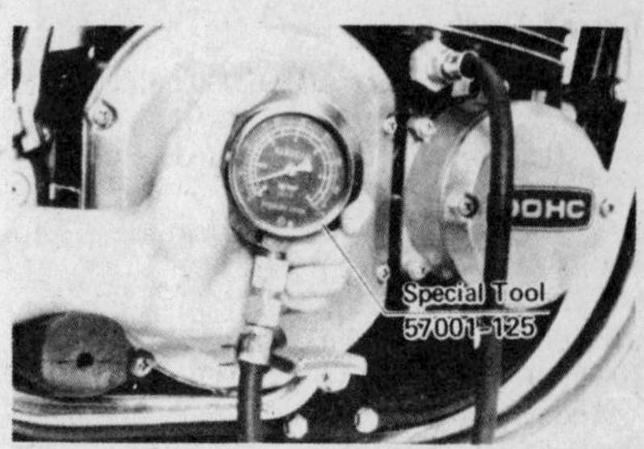

Checking oil pressure

Chain Oiler (73–74 Models)

The 73 and 74 models are equipped with a drive chain oiler, which, in conjunction with hand lubrication using a chain lubricant, is intended to keep chain wear to a minimum. The tank for the oiler is located under the seat, and has a dipstick and a filler cap. The tank should be kept filled with 30W or 40W oil.

The pump can be adjusted for oil flow. "0"

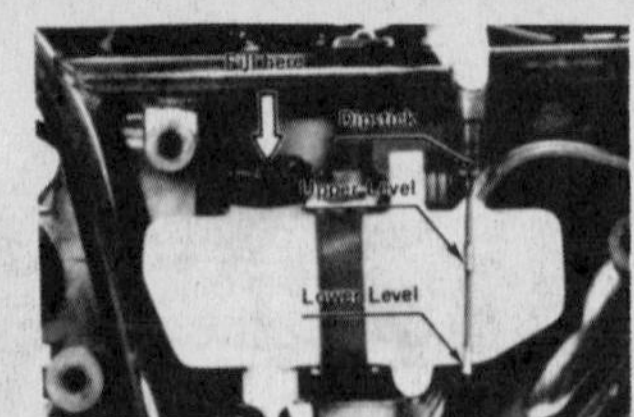

Keep the tank filled with 30 or 40W

Pump cover location

Pump output adjuster

or "1" supplies the least oil, and "5" is for maximum output. The chain should be kept wet, but not dripping.

Do not rely on the oiler to provide all the necessary chain lubrication these machines require. Every 200 miles, or more often if used in wet or dusty conditions, the chain should be hand lubricated.

Front Forks

1. The change interval is 6,000 miles or one year.
2. Recommended oil is SAE 10W or 10W20, non-detergent.
3. Fork capacities (per fork leg) are as follows:

900 (1973–75)	5.7 oz./170 cc
900 (1976)	6.5 oz./192 cc
1000 (1977–81)	5.7–6.0 oz./170–178 cc

Add an additional 0.6 oz. (15 cc) per leg if the forks have been disassembled.

4. To change the oil, remove the drain screw from the bottom of each slider and pump the slider up and down to expel the oil. Install the drain screws. Support the front wheel off the ground.
5. Loosen the upper triple clamp pinch bolts and remove the fork top bolts. Add the correct amount of oil to each fork leg.

SERVICE CHECKS AND ADJUSTMENTS

Drive Chain

1. The chain should have about 30–35 mm (1.2–1.4 in.) of total up-and-down free-play measured in the middle of the lower chain run.
2. Before checking or adjusting the chain slack, the following conditions should be met:
   a. The motorcycle should be placed on the center stand so that the rear wheel is off the ground;
   b. The transmission should be placed in neutral;
   c. The chain should be clean and well-lubricated;
   d. The chain should have been checked for any tight spots by slowly rotating the wheel and checking for variances in the chain tension at different points. If a tight spot exists, the chain tension should be adjusted to the prescribed free-play at the tight spot. Note, however, that such a condition is indicative of a worn chain and probably worn sprockets, which should be replaced as soon as possible.
3. To adjust the chain, first back off the rear brake adjuster nut on drum rear brakes. Loosen the brake anchor nut on disc brake models, loosen the nut on the caliper anchor.
4. Remove the axle nut cotter pin and loosen the axle nut several turns. Loosen the locknut on each chain adjuster bolt.

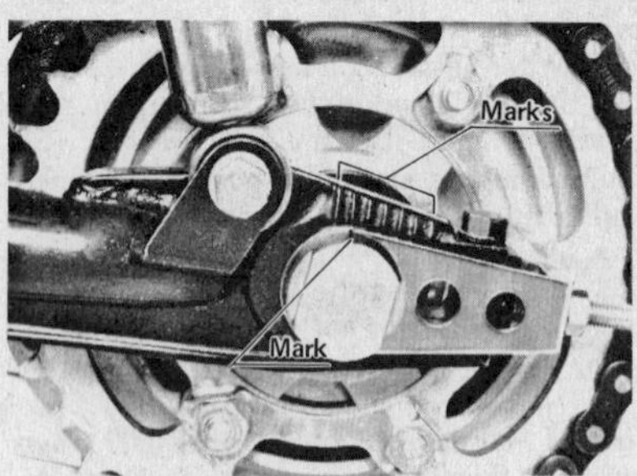

Rear wheel alignment marks

5. Turn each of the adjuster bolts in or out by equal amounts until the chain tension is approximately correct.
6. Check wheel alignment by means of the aligning marks inscribed on both sides of the swing arm. Be sure that both adjusters are lined up with the same mark on each side. If not, turn one of the adjuster bolts in or out so that alignment is achieved.
7. Tighten the axle nut and adjuster bolt nuts and check the chain tension. The chain tension should also be checked with the weight of a rider sitting on the motorcycle when it is off the center stand; the chain should still have at least ½ in. of free-play. Correct if necessary. After adjustment is correct, torque the axle nut to 72–100 ft lbs.

Fit a new cotter pin. Tighten the brake anchor nut. Readjust the rear brake on drum brake models.

NOTE: *If the engine sprocket is removed, be sure to reinstall it so that the stamped numbers face the engine. Otherwise, chain alignment will be incorrect.*

Clutch

1. Loosen the knurled locknut at the hand lever, turn the thumbscrew into its seat to provide maximum cable play, then secure the locknut.
2. Loosen the locknut at the center of the cable, and screw in the adjuster to provide maximum cable play.
3. Remove the cover to gain access to the pushrod adjusting screw.
4. Loosen the locknut, and back out the adjusting screw until it turns loosely.

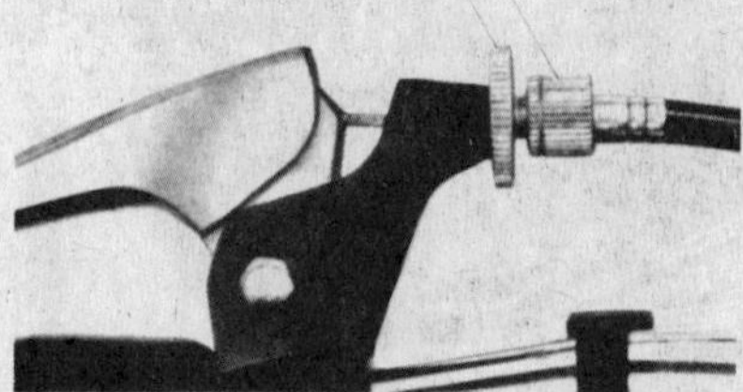

Cable adjusting points

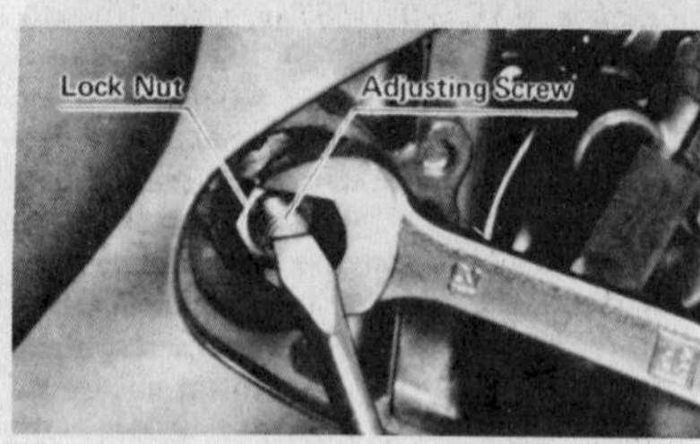

Drain plug location

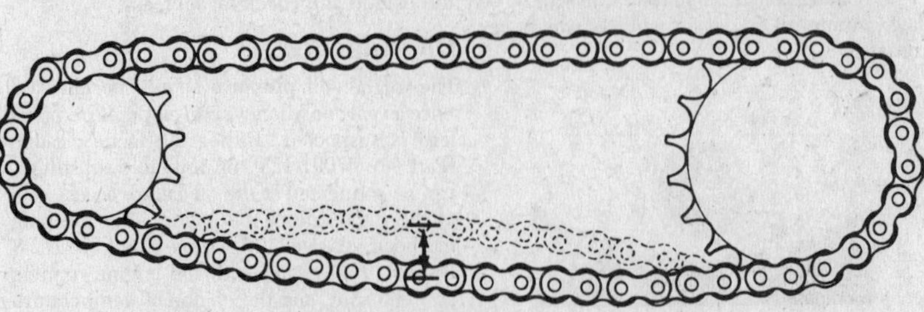

Chain slack should be measured at the middle of the lower run

5. Gently turn in the adjusting screw to the point where it suddenly becomes hard to turn, then back it out ½ turn from that point, and secure the locknut while holding the screw steady with a screwdriver.

6. Making sure that the cable sleeve ends do not catch on the edge of the cable seat, take up the cable play at the cable center until there is from $^1/_{16}$–$^1/_8$ in. (2–3 mm) play at the hand lever, then secure the cable center adjuster locknut.

7. Make fine adjustments at the hand lever, if necessary, until the cable play is within its specified limits, then secure the thumbscrew locknut, and replace the oil pump cover.

Throttle Cables

900

Adjust the cables by loosening the locknut on the opening cable, and adjusting out any slack before securing the locknut again. Loosen the locknut on the closing cable, and adjust it so there is about $^1/_{16}$ in. (2 mm) of play in the throttle grip, then secure the locknut. The adjustment may be varied according to personal preference and riding style, however, too tight an adjustment may cause the cables to stretch prematurely.

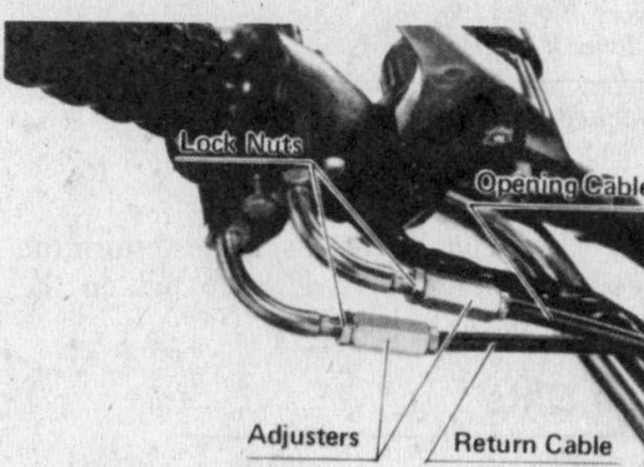

Always adjust the opening cable first

1000

1. There should be about 2–3 mm of throttle grip play.

2. With the throttle grip pushed completely closed, check that there is no clearance between the cable bracket and the pulley stopper.

3. If adjustment is necessary, loosen the locknuts and screw both cable adjusters in fully to give maximum throttle play.

4. Turn out the adjuster on the closing cable until there is no clearance between the cable bracket and pulley stopper when the throttle grip is pushed completely closed.

5. Turn the adjuster on the opening cable out to give 2–3 mm of throttle grip play. Tighten the locknuts.

6. If the cables cannot be properly adjusted with the upper adjusters, use those on the lower ends of the cables.

Brakes

FRONT DISC BRAKE

1. The front disc brake is automatically adjusted when in use, and therefore the condition of the brake pads should be checked periodically for wear. When either pad is worn down to the red or green limit line, the pads should be replaced.

2. The brake lever is adjustable; however, the need for adjustment, other than to reduce vibration of the lever, indicates excessive wear of some of the brake components.

3. Adjust the lever by loosening the locknut, and turning the adjusting bolt a fraction of a turn so that the lever has less than $^3/_{16}$ in. (5 mm) of play. Hold the adjusting bolt steady while securing the locknut, and make sure that there is still play in the lever after the locknut is tightened.

4. The brake fluid should be drained and refilled, along with a careful check of each component in the system once each year, or every 6,000 miles.

REAR DISC BRAKE

1. Check the pads periodically for wear and replace the set when they are worn to the stepped portion.

2. The brake pedal should have 8–10 mm (0.32–0.40 in.) of freeplay before the pushrod contacts the master cylinder piston. Adjust, if necessary, by loosening the pushrod locknut and turning the pushrod. Tighten the locknut and check brake operation. Readjust the brake light switch, if necessary.

3. Brake pedal position should be 20–30 mm (0.8–1.2 in.) below the top of the footpeg. If it is too high, loosen the pushrod locknut and turn the pushrod to give plenty of freeplay. Use the adjusting bolt to adjust pedal height. Tighten the pushrod locknut and check pedal freeplay.

Rear brake pedal freeplay

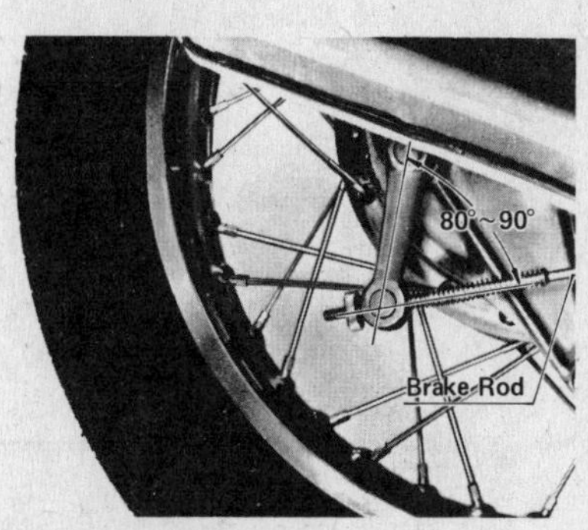

Correct brake rod to lever angle when the brakes are applied

REAR DRUM BRAKE

1. Check the position of the brake pedal in relation to the right front foot rest. It should be about $^1/_{16}$ in. (2 mm) lower than the foot rest, and can be adjusted by loosening the adjusting bolt locknut, and rotating the bolt until the desired adjustment is attained. Be sure to secure the locknut, once a suitable adjustment is arrived at.

2. Apply the brake and note the angle formed between the actuating lever and the brake rod. If the angle is not within 80–90°, remove the lever and reposition it to correct the angle.

CAUTION: *The brake linings must be checked for wear before the lever is repositioned to avoid damage to the drum caused by worn linings. Wear indicators are fitted to late models.*

3. Make the fine adjustment by screwing in the brake rod adjusting nut until the brake pedal travel is within ¾–1¼ in. (20–30 mm) from the rest position to the fully applied position.

4. With the machine on the center stand, spin the rear wheel to check for dragging, and either readjust the brakes, or disassemble and repair the assembly to adjust for this.

NOTE: *An adjustment made with the machine on its center stand may not be the same once the machine is resting on both wheels.*

BRAKE LAMP SWITCH

The front brake lamp switch is hydraulically operated, and therefore needs no adjustment. The rear brake lamp switch is mechanical, and requires periodic adjustment to compensate for stretching of its spring, damage to the brake pedal, or to suit your preference for when the lamp comes on.

Adjust the switch by loosening the two mounting nuts, and moving the switch up or down so that the brake lamp will light after ½–¾ in. (15–20 mm) of pedal movement. Secure the locknuts when a suitable adjustment has been attained.

CAUTION: *Do not rotate the switch body itself while performing the adjustment, as this may damage the wiring.*

Rear brake light switch

Air Filter

The element should be cleaned every 3,000 miles.

To remove the filter element, open the seat, take the screen off the air cleaner, and pull the element out.

Clean the element with gasoline or some other volatile solvent, then blow it dry from the inside out with compressed air. Do not use any cleaner which will not evaporate completely.

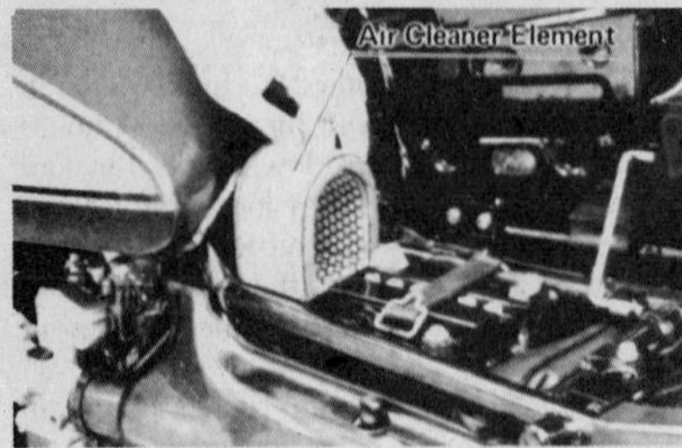

Removing the filter element

Inspect the element and sponge gaskets for signs of wear or damage, and replace the element if either are damaged. The gaskets can be glued on if they've come loose and are still in good condition. Be careful, when installing the element, not to crimp the gaskets.

Replace the element every 6,000 miles or after 5 cleanings.

Fuel System

The fuel filter, located in the fuel tap, and the fuel lines, should be removed and cleaned at the prescribed intervals, or whenever fuel delivery problems are suspected. Simply turn the fuel tap to the stop ("S") position, and unscrew the cup to gain access to the filter. Fuel flow at both the on and reserve positions can be checked at this time.

If there is any indication of water in the gas, turn the tap to the reserve position, and allow the fuel to flow out into a suitable container until only pure gas comes out. Remove the drain plugs from the bottom of each carburetor, and drain the float bowls also.

CAUTION: *Do not start the engine until any spilled gasoline has completely evaporated, or has been wiped up. If the tap allows any gas to pass while in the stop position, the tap should be replaced, or gas may leak into the crankcase and dilute the oil.*

The sediment cup must be removed to gain access to the filter

Clean the filter screen and cup, and reinstall them on the tap using a new O-ring, if necessary. Inspect the fuel lines for cracks or damage, and replace them as necessary. Straighten out any kinks or sharp bends in the lines, and make sure that the filler cap vent is not plugged, as this can interfere with normal fuel delivery.

Steering Stem Bearings

Check for proper adjustment by supporting the front wheel off the ground, grasping the fork sliders and pushing and pulling them in line with the motorcycle. No free-play should be felt. If it is, the bearings are too loosely adjusted.

Turn the forks slowly from lock-to-lock. Movement should be free, smooth, and noiseless. When released from a position a few degrees off center, the forks should fall freely to the side. If they do not, the bearings are too

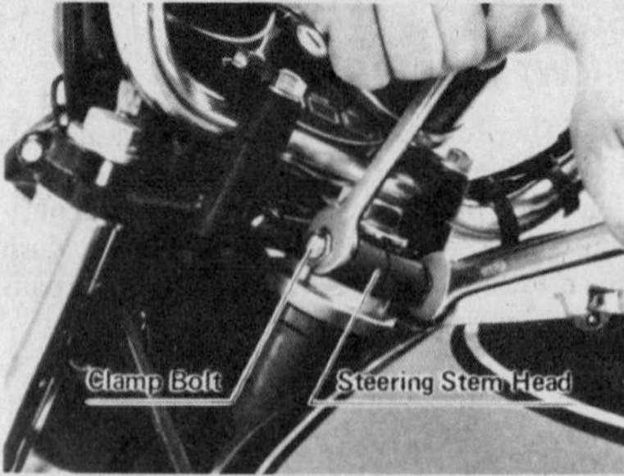

Loosening the steering stem rear clamp bolt

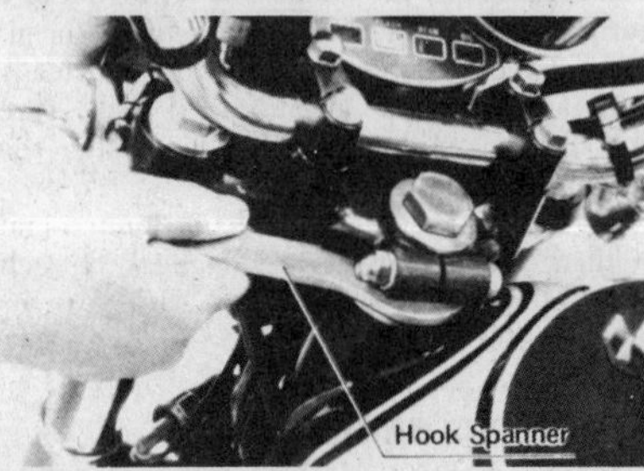

Make the adjustment slightly snug if the bearings and races have just been replaced

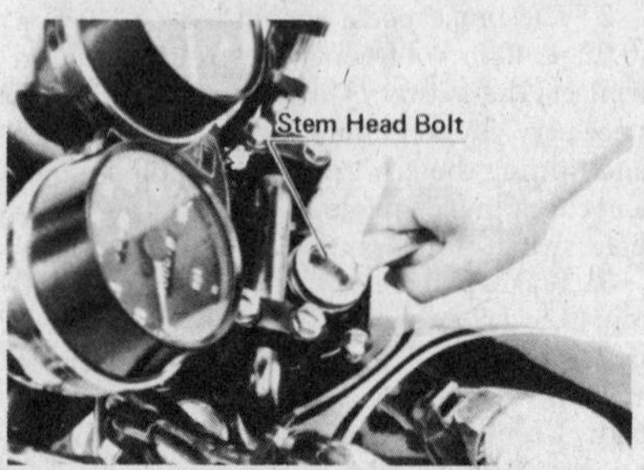

tightly adjusted. If the bearing movement is rough or noisy, the bearings and races are probably worn.

Adjust the bearings in the following manner:

1. Loosen the steering stem head bolt, and the clamp bolt shown in the accompanying illustration.

Tightening the lower triple clamp bolt

Periodic Maintenance Intervals ①

Daily
- Brake adjustment
- Engine oil level
- Cable adjustments
- Chain slack
- Lights and safety devices

Weekly
- Battery electrolyte level
- Spokes for tightness
- Tire pressure (cold)

Every 2000 Miles
- Change engine oil
- Clean and gap plugs
- Adjust points and check timing
- Check chain wear
- Clean fuel system

Every 3000 Miles
- Clean air filter
- General lubrication

Every 4000 Miles
- Replace oil filter
- Check valve clearance

Every 6000 Miles
- Renew brake fluid
- Change fork oil
- Replace air cleaner element

Every 12000 Miles
- Repack wheel bearings

① Based on normal usage after break-in is completed

2. Use a suitable hook spanner to turn the steering stem locknut down to tighten the steering, or up to loosen it.

Maintenance Data

	900	*1000*
Engine Capacity (qt/l)		
Oil change only	3.5/3.3	3.2/3.0
Oil and filter	4.2/4.0	3.9/3.7
Chain Oiler (qt/l)	0.95/0.9	—
Front Forks (oz/cc) (each leg)		
Normal change	①	5.7–6.0/170–178
After disassembly	②	6.3–6.6/185–193
Tire Pressures (psi)		
Front	26	28
Rear	31	32
Rear (high-speed or two-up)	36	36
Tire Wear Limits (mm/in.)		
Front	1.0/0.04	1.0/0.04
Rear	2.0/0.08	2.0/0.08
Battery		
Type	Yuasa 12N-14-3A	Yuasa 12N-14-3A
Capacity (amp hours)	14	14
Voltage	12	12
Charging rate (amps)	1.4	1.4

① 1973–75: 5.7/170
1976: 6.5/192
② 1973–75: 6.3/185
1976: 7.1/207

Recommended Lubricants

Engine
SAE 20W-50, "SE" or "SF"
SAE 10W-40, "SE" or "SF"

Chain oiler
SAE 30W
SAE 40W

Front Forks
SAE 10W, non-detergent

Control Cables
Motor oil
Graphite-based lubricant
Molybdenum disulphide-base lubricant

Tach, Speedometer Cables
Light-duty, lithium-base grease

Wheel Bearings, Steering Stem Bearings
Waterproof, medium weight bearing grease

Grease Fittings
Waterproof, medium-weight chassis grease

Chain
SAE 90W

3. Secure the head bolt and clamp, then loosen the two lower clamp bolts to let them reseat themselves, and retighten the bolts evenly. The upper clamp bolts should be torqued to 12–13 ft lbs (1.6–1.8 kg/m), and the two lower clamp bolts should be torqued to 40–43 ft lbs (5.4–6.0 kg/m).

TUNE-UP

NOTE: *Common tune-up procedures are explained in detail in the "General Information" section.*

VALVE CLEARANCE

Before you start read the following:

An oil film can form between the adjusting shim and the top of the valve which can cause misleading measurements. You may find that the clearance isn't what you expected it to be after the correct shim is installed, and this film is the reason. To avoid this, do the following:

1. Measure the clearance as directed in the "Adjustment" Section.
2. Remove and measure the shim to determine what you need (i.e., if the clearance is 0.006 in., a 0.002 in. shim will result in a clearance of 0.004 in.).
3. Kick the engine through a couple dozen times with the spark plugs out and the ignition switch "Off" to remove the film, then measure the clearance again.

CAUTION: *Never rotate the engine with any of the adjusting shims removed as this may damage the cam and tappet.*

NOTE: *The type of valve tappets used in all models up to engine number Z1E-08979 have caused shim fracturing problems on some machines. If your machine is equipped with this type of tappet, consult the "Engine Disassembly; Camshafts" Section for additional information.*

Adjustment

1973 MODELS

1. Open the seat all the way and remove the fuel tank, then remove the valve cover and cover gasket. Remove the spark plugs.
2. Rotate the engine so that the cam lobe (the highest portion of the cam) for the valve to be checked is pointing directly away from the valve lifter.

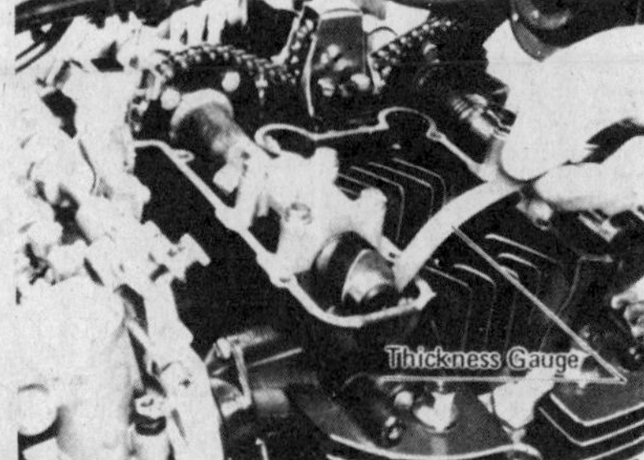

Be sure that the gauge is between the shim and the cam lobe

Using the special tool to remove the shim

3. Measure the clearance between the cam and the valve shim using a thickness gauge. The clearance should be within 0.002–0.004 in. (0.05–0.10 mm) for both the intake and exhaust valves. If the feeler gauge of the proper clearance will not fit between the cam and the shim, or if it slides through with little or no resistance, the clearance should be adjusted. It should be noted that some of the valves may not require adjustment. Clearance is correct if the next size thinner gauge fits easily and if the next size thicker will not fit, or fits with great resistance.
4. If the clearance is in need of adjustment, rotate the engine so that the cam lobe presses the lifter down, install the special tool (Part No. 57001-109) as illustrated, then rotate the engine so that the cam lobe points directly away from the tappet, and remove the shim.

NOTE: *The tappet is notched so that the shim can be grasped.*

5. If the valve clearance was less than 0.002 in., use a thinner shim; if the clearance was greater than 0.004 in., use a thicker shim. Shims are available in 0.05 mm increments from 2.00 mm to 3.20 mm. Consult the accompanying Valve Adjustment Chart.
6. If the valve seat is worn to the point where the smallest shim will not provide the correct clearance, check for excessive wear or burning of the valve and seat. Bring the clearance within the specified limits by removing the valve and grinding down the top of the stem slightly while holding the valve in a V-block to keep it at right angles to the side of the grinder. There must be at least 0.16 in. (4.1 mm) of stem above the valve spring collar groove.

1974–78 MODELS

Marks are inscribed on the camshaft sprocket to facilitate the valve adjustment procedure.

1. Check valves when the engine is cold.
2. Remove the gas tank and valve cover. Remove the spark plugs.

Sprocket alignment marks

3. Check that the cam cap bolts are torqued to 8.8 ft lbs.
4. Working with one of the camshafts, turn the engine over until the marks on the cam sprocket align with the cylinder head mating surface.
5. Check the clearance at the two closed valves.
6. Turn the sprocket 180° until the marks align again, and check clearance at the other two valves.
7. Repeat the procedure with the other camshaft.
8. Clearance is adjusted in the same manner as outlined for 1973 models (see above), Steps 2–6.

1979 AND LATER MODELS

Check clearance as outlined above for earlier models.

Correct clearance is 0.002–0.006 in. (0.05–0.15 mm) for both intake and exhaust valves.

Be sure that the correct cam sprocket marks are used (see illustration).

When fitting new shims, be sure that the correct chart is referred to.

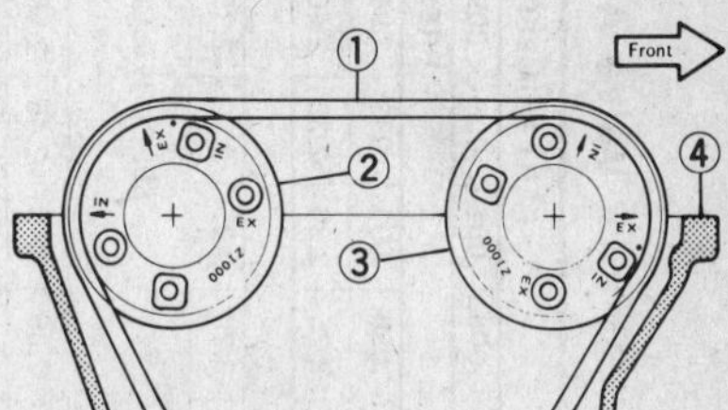

Late model cam sprockets: Cam chain (1), intake sprocket (2), exhaust sprocket (3), head mating surface (4)

CAMSHAFT CHAIN

1978 and Earlier

Wear to the chain and chain guide roller causes excessive slack in the chain which must be adjusted out periodically. Adjust the chain every 1,000 miles, or when performing a tune-up, or whenever it becomes noisy enough to warrant an adjustment. Chain noise can be heard as a rattle at an idle speed, or a high-pitched whine while running.

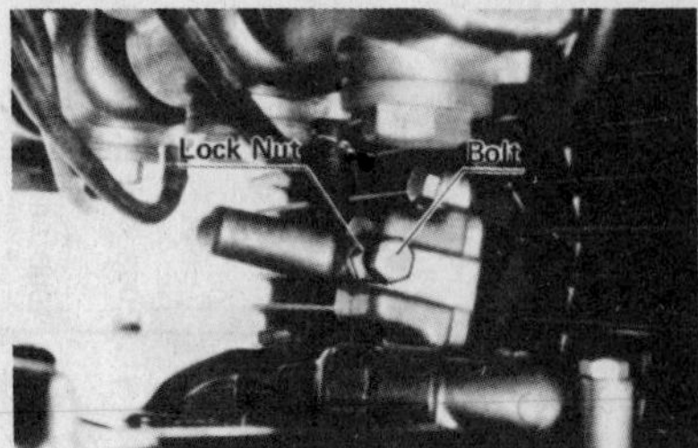

Cam chain adjuster

Valve Adjustment Chart (900)

		PART NUMBER PREFIX 12037-																								
	P/N SUFFIX	-001	-002	-003	-004	-005	-006	-007	-008	-009	-010	-011	-012	-013	-014	-015	-016	-017	-018	-019	-020	-021	-022	-023	-024	-025
	PRESENT SHIM SIZE																									
	INCHES	.079	.081	.083	.085	.087	.089	.091	.093	.094	.096	.098	.100	.102	.104	.106	.108	.110	.112	.114	.116	.118	.120	.122	.124	.126
	MILLIMETERS	2.00	2.05	2.10	2.15	2.20	2.25	2.30	2.35	2.40	2.45	2.50	2.55	2.60	2.65	2.70	2.75	2.80	2.85	2.90	2.95	3.00	3.05	3.10	3.15	3.20
VALVE CLEARANCE INCHES	MILLIMETERS																									
.000-.001	0.00-0.04		2.00	2.05	2.10	2.15	2.20	2.25	2.30	2.35	2.40	2.45	2.50	2.55	2.60	2.65	2.70	2.75	2.80	2.85	2.90	2.95	3.00	3.05	3.10	3.15
.002-.004	0.05-0.10	SPECIFIED CLEARANCE/ NO CHANGE REQUIRED																								
.005-.007	0.11-0.19	2.10	2.15	2.20	2.25	2.30	2.35	2.40	2.45	2.50	2.55	2.60	2.65	2.70	2.75	2.80	2.85	2.90	2.95	3.00	3.05	3.10	3.15	3.20		
.008-.009	0.20-0.24	2.15	2.20	2.25	2.30	2.35	2.40	2.45	2.50	2.55	2.60	2.65	2.70	2.75	2.80	2.85	2.90	2.95	3.00	3.05	3.10	3.15	3.20			
.010-.011	0.25-0.29	2.20	2.25	2.30	2.35	2.40	2.45	2.50	2.55	2.60	2.65	2.70	2.75	2.80	2.85	2.90	2.95	3.00	3.05	3.10	3.15	3.20				
.012-.013	0.30-0.34	2.25	2.30	2.35	2.40	2.45	2.50	2.55	2.60	2.65	2.70	2.75	2.80	2.85	2.90	2.95	3.00	3.05	3.10	3.15	3.20					
.014-.015	0.35-0.39	2.30	2.35	2.40	2.45	2.50	2.55	2.60	2.65	2.70	2.75	2.80	2.85	2.90	2.95	3.00	3.05	3.10	3.15	3.20						
.016-.017	0.40-0.44	2.35	2.40	2.45	2.50	2.55	2.60	2.65	2.70	2.75	2.80	2.85	2.90	2.95	3.00	3.05	3.10	3.15	3.20							
.018-.019	0.45-0.49	2.40	2.45	2.50	2.55	2.60	2.65	2.70	2.75	2.80	2.85	2.90	2.95	3.00	3.05	3.10	3.15	3.20								
.020-.021	0.50-0.54	2.45	2.50	2.55	2.60	2.65	2.70	**2.75**	2.80	2.85	2.90	2.95	3.00	3.05	3.10	3.15	3.20									
.022-.023	0.55-0.59	2.50	2.55	2.60	2.65	2.70	2.75	2.80	2.85	2.90	2.95	3.00	3.05	3.10	3.15	3.20										
.024-.025	0.60-0.64	2.55	2.60	2.65	2.70	2.75	2.80	2.85	2.90	2.95	3.00	3.05	3.10	3.15	3.20											
.026-.027	0.65-0.69	2.60	2.65	2.70	2.75	2.80	2.85	2.90	2.95	3.00	3.05	3.10	3.15	3.20												
.028-.029	0.70-0.74	2.65	2.70	2.75	2.80	2.85	2.90	2.95	3.00	3.05	3.10	3.15	3.20													
.030-.031	0.75-0.79	2.70	2.75	2.80	2.85	2.90	2.95	3.00	3.05	3.10	3.15	3.20														
.032-.033	0.80-0.84	2.75	2.80	2.85	2.90	2.95	3.00	3.05	3.10	3.15	3.20															
.034-.035	0.85-0.89	2.80	2.85	2.90	2.95	3.00	3.05	3.10	3.15	3.20																
.036-.037	0.90-0.94	2.85	2.90	2.95	3.00	3.05	3.10	3.15	3.20																	
.038-.039	0.95-0.99	2.90	2.95	3.00	3.05	3.10	3.15	3.20																		
.040-.041	1.00-1.04	2.95	3.00	3.05	3.10	3.15	3.20																			
.042-.043	1.05-1.09	3.00	3.05	3.10	3.15	3.20																				
.044-.045	1.10-1.14	3.05	3.10	3.15	3.20																					
.046-.047	1.15-1.19	3.10	3.15	3.20																						
.048-.049	1.20-1.24	3.15	3.20																							
.050-.051	1.25-1.29	3.20																								

INSTALL THIS SHIM

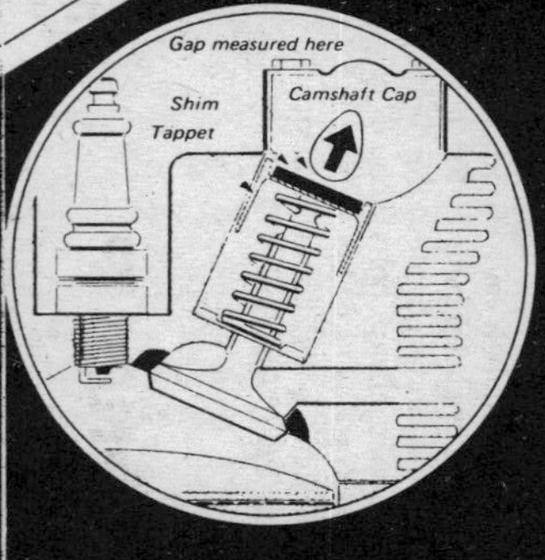

Gap measured here

Shim

Tappet

Camshaft Cap

1. To use the chart, locate the measured gap on the vertical column on the left. Find the thickness of the old shim in the top horizontal column and look down that column to find the required new shim.
2. If the valve clearance is greater than 0.10mm (.004"), use a thicker shim to correct to the specified clearance.
3. If the valve clearance is less than 0.05mm (.002"), select a thinner shim. NOTE: If there is no clearance between the shim and the cam, select a shim which is several sizes smaller and then remeasure the gap.
4. Do not put shim stock under the shim. This may cause the shim to pop out at high rpm.
5. NOTE: Check the valve clearance with the cam lobe pointing directly away from the valve, as pictured. Checking the clearance at any other cam position may result in improper valve clearance.

Valve Adjustment Chart (KZ1000, 1978 and Earlier)

PART NUMBER 12037-	001	002	003	004	005	006	007	008	009	010	011	012	013	014	015	016	017	018	019	020	021	022	023	024	025
	PRESENT SHIM SIZE																								
MILLIMETERS	2.00	2.05	2.10	2.15	2.20	2.25	2.30	2.35	2.40	2.45	2.50	2.55	2.60	2.65	2.70	2.75	2.80	2.85	2.90	2.95	3.00	3.05	3.10	3.15	3.20
MILLIMETERS																									
0.00 ~ 0.05 mm		2.00	2.05	2.10	2.15	2.20	2.25	2.30	2.35	2.40	2.45	2.50	2.55	2.60	2.65	2.70	2.75	2.80	2.85	2.90	2.95	3.00	3.05	3.10	3.15
0.05 ~ 0.10	SPECIFIED CLEARANCE/NO CHANGE REQUIRED																								
0.10 ~ 0.14	2.05	2.10	2.15	2.20	2.25	2.30	2.35	2.40	2.45	2.50	2.55	2.60	2.65	2.70	2.75	2.80	2.85	2.90	2.95	3.00	3.05	3.10	3.15	3.20	
0.15 ~ 0.19	2.10	2.15	2.20	2.25	2.30	2.35	2.40	2.45	2.50	2.55	2.60	2.65	2.70	2.75	2.80	2.85	2.90	2.95	3.00	3.05	3.10	3.15	3.20		
0.20 ~ 0.24	2.15	2.20	2.25	2.30	2.35	2.40	2.45	2.50	2.55	2.60	2.65	2.70	2.75	2.80	2.85	2.90	2.95	3.00	3.05	3.10	3.15	3.20			
0.25 ~ 0.29	2.20	2.25	2.30	2.35	2.40	2.45	2.50	2.55	2.60	2.65	2.70	2.75	2.80	2.85	2.90	2.95	3.00	3.05	3.10	3.15	3.20				
0.30 ~ 0.34	2.25	2.30	2.35	2.40	2.45	2.50	2.55	2.60	2.65	2.70	2.75	2.80	2.85	2.90	2.95	3.00	3.05	3.10	3.15	3.20					
0.35 ~ 0.39	2.30	2.35	2.40	2.45	2.50	2.55	2.60	2.65	2.70	2.75	2.80	2.85	2.90	2.95	3.00	3.05	3.10	3.15	3.20						
0.40 ~ 0.44	2.35	2.40	2.45	2.50	2.55	2.60	2.65	2.70	2.75	2.80	2.85	2.90	2.95	3.00	3.05	3.10	3.15	3.20							
0.45 ~ 0.49	2.40	2.45	2.50	2.55	2.60	2.65	2.70	2.75	2.80	2.85	2.90	2.95	3.00	3.05	3.10	3.15	3.20								
0.50 ~ 0.54	2.45	2.50	2.55	2.60	2.65	2.70	2.75	2.80	2.85	2.90	2.95	3.00	3.05	3.10	3.15	3.20									
0.55 ~ 0.59	2.50	2.55	2.60	2.65	2.70	2.75	2.80	2.85	2.90	2.95	3.00	3.05	3.10	3.15	3.20										
0.60 ~ 0.64	2.55	2.60	2.65	2.70	2.75	2.80	2.85	2.90	2.95	3.00	3.05	3.10	3.15	3.20											
0.65 ~ 0.69	2.60	2.65	2.70	2.75	2.80	2.85	2.90	2.95	3.00	3.05	3.10	3.15	3.20												
0.70 ~ 0.74	2.65	2.70	2.75	2.80	2.85	2.90	2.95	3.00	3.05	3.10	3.15	3.20													
0.75 ~ 0.79	2.70	2.75	2.80	2.85	2.90	2.95	3.00	3.05	3.10	3.15	3.20														
0.80 ~ 0.84	2.75	2.80	2.85	2.90	2.95	3.00	3.05	3.10	3.15	3.20															
0.85 ~ 0.89	2.80	2.85	2.90	2.95	3.00	3.05	3.10	3.15	3.20																
0.90 ~ 0.94	2.85	2.90	2.95	3.00	3.05	3.10	3.15	3.20																	
0.95 ~ 0.99	2.90	2.95	3.00	3.05	3.10	3.15	3.20																		
1.00 ~ 1.04	2.95	3.00	3.05	3.10	3.15	3.20																			
1.05 ~ 1.09	3.00	3.05	3.10	3.15	3.20																				
1.10 ~ 1.14	3.05	3.10	3.15	3.20																					
1.15 ~ 1.19	3.10	3.15	3.20																						
1.20 ~ 1.24	3.15	3.20																							
1.25 ~ 1.30	3.20																								

INSTALL THIS SHIM

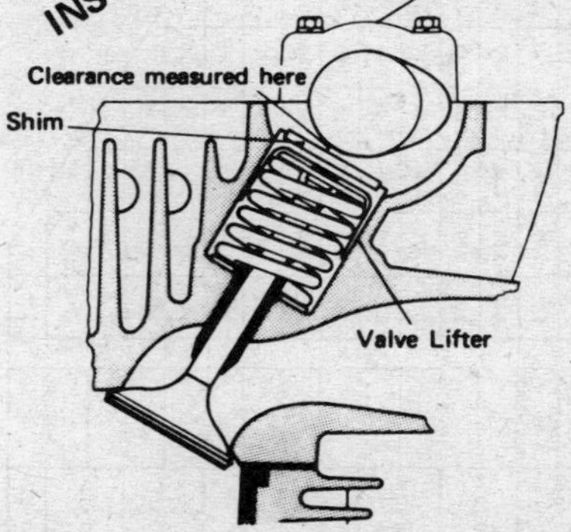

1. Measure valve clearance (cold).
2. Check present shim size.
3. Match clearance in vertical column with present shim size in horizontal column.
4. The shim specified where the lines intersect is the one that will give you the proper clearance.

NOTES: 1. Check the valve clearance with the proper method in text (Pgs. 15 ~ 16). Checking the clearance at any other cam position may result in improper valve clearance.

2. If there is no clearance between the shim and the cam, select a shim which is several sizes smaller and then remeasure the gap.

CAUTION 1. Do not put shim stock under the shim. This may cause the shim to pop out at high rpm.

2. Do not grind the shim. This may cause it to fracture.

Valve Adjustment Chart (KZ1000, 1979 and Later)

	PRESENT SHIM SIZE																								
PART NUMBER 12037	001	002	003	004	005	006	007	008	009	010	011	012	013	014	015	016	017	018	019	020	021	022	023	024	025
MILIMETERS	2.00	2.05	2.10	2.15	2.20	2.25	2.30	2.35	2.40	2.45	2.50	2.55	2.60	2.65	2.70	2.75	2.80	2.85	2.90	2.95	3.00	3.05	3.10	3.15	3.20
VALVE CLEARANCE																									
0.00 ~ 0.05			2.00	2.05	2.10	2.15	2.20	2.25	2.30	2.35	2.40	2.45	2.50	2.55	2.60	2.65	2.70	2.75	2.80	2.85	2.90	2.95	3.00	3.05	3.10
		2.00	2.05	2.10	2.15	2.20	2.25	2.30	2.35	2.40	2.45	2.50	2.55	2.60	2.65	2.70	2.75	2.80	2.85	2.90	2.95	3.00	3.05	3.10	3.15
0.05 ~ 0.15 mm	SPECIFIED CLEARANCE/NO CHANGE REQUIRED																								
0.15 ~ 0.19	2.05	2.10	2.15	2.20	2.25	2.30	2.35	2.40	2.45	2.50	2.55	2.60	2.65	2.70	2.75	2.80	2.85	2.90	2.95	3.00	3.05	3.10	3.15	3.20	
0.20 ~ 0.24	2.10	2.15	2.20	2.25	2.30	2.35	2.40	2.45	2.50	2.55	2.60	2.65	2.70	2.75	2.80	2.85	2.90	2.95	3.00	3.05	3.10	3.15	3.20		
0.25 ~ 0.29	2.15	2.20	2.25	2.30	2.35	2.40	2.45	2.50	2.55	2.60	2.65	2.70	2.75	2.80	2.85	2.90	2.95	3.00	3.05	3.10	3.15	3.20			
0.30 ~ 0.34	2.20	2.25	2.30	2.35	2.40	2.45	2.50	2.55	2.60	2.65	2.70	2.75	2.80	2.85	2.90	2.95	3.00	3.05	3.10	3.15	3.20				
0.35 ~ 0.39	2.25	2.30	2.35	2.40	2.45	2.50	2.55	2.60	2.65	2.70	2.75	2.80	2.85	2.90	2.95	3.00	3.05	3.10	3.15	3.20					
0.40 ~ 0.44	2.30	2.35	2.40	2.45	2.50	2.55	2.60	2.65	2.70	2.75	2.80	2.85	2.90	2.95	3.00	3.05	3.10	3.15	3.20						
0.45 ~ 0.49	2.35	2.40	2.45	2.50	2.55	2.60	2.65	2.70	2.75	2.80	2.85	2.90	2.95	3.00	3.05	3.10	3.15	3.20							
0.50 ~ 0.54	2.40	2.45	2.50	2.55	2.60	2.65	2.70	2.75	2.80	2.85	2.90	2.95	3.00	3.05	3.10	3.15	3.20								
0.55 ~ 0.59	2.45	2.50	2.55	2.60	2.65	2.70	2.75	2.80	2.85	2.90	2.95	3.00	3.05	3.10	3.15	3.20									
0.60 ~ 0.64	2.50	2.55	2.60	2.65	2.70	2.75	2.80	2.85	2.90	2.95	3.00	3.05	3.10	3.15	3.20										
0.65 ~ 0.69	2.55	2.60	2.65	2.70	2.75	2.80	2.85	2.90	2.95	3.00	3.05	3.10	3.15	3.20											
0.70 ~ 0.74	2.60	2.65	2.70	2.75	2.80	2.85	2.90	2.95	3.00	3.05	3.10	3.15	3.20												
0.75 ~ 0.79	2.65	2.70	2.75	2.80	2.85	2.90	2.95	3.00	3.05	3.10	3.15	3.20													
0.80 ~ 0.84	2.70	2.75	2.80	2.85	2.90	2.95	3.00	3.05	3.10	3.15	3.20														
0.85 ~ 0.89	2.75	2.80	2.85	2.90	2.95	3.00	3.05	3.10	3.15	3.20															
0.90 ~ 0.94	2.80	2.85	2.90	2.95	3.00	3.05	3.10	3.15	3.20																
0.95 ~ 0.99	2.85	2.90	2.95	3.00	3.05	3.10	3.15	3.20																	
1.00 ~ 1.04	2.90	2.95	3.00	3.05	3.10	3.15	3.20																		
1.05 ~ 1.09	2.95	3.00	3.05	3.10	3.15	3.20																			
1.10 ~ 1.14	3.00	3.05	3.10	3.15	3.20																				
1.15 ~ 1.19	3.05	3.10	3.15	3.20																					
1.20 ~ 1.24	3.10	3.15	3.20																						
1.25 ~ 1.29	3.15	3.20																							
1.30 ~ 1.34	3.20																								

INSTALL THIS SHIM

Camshaft Cap

Clearance measured here

Shim

Valve Lifter

1. Align the sprocket mark with the cylinder head surface, and measure the clearance (cold).
2. Check present shim size.
3. Match clearance in vertical column with present shim size in horizontal column.
4. Select one of the shims specified where the lines intersect. Either shim will give you the proper clearance.

NOTE: If there is no clearance between the shim and the cam, select a shim which is several sizes smaller and then remeasure the clearance.

CAUTION

1. Do not put shim stock under the shim. This may cause the shim to pop out at high rpm, causing extensive engine damage.
2. Do not grind the shim. This may cause it to fracture, causing extensive engine damage.
3. Check the valve clearance with the proper mathod in the text. Checking the clearance at any other cam position may result in improper valve clearance.

Allowing the chain to go unadjusted will increase the rate of wear, cause unnecessary noise, and may lead to chain failure. When adjusting the chain no longer keeps it from making noise, either the chain is stretched out, or the guide rollers are worn out, and either or both must be replaced.

ADJUSTMENT

1. Remove the points cover. Turn the engine over a couple of times in the normal direction of rotation, then align the "T" mark for either set of pistons with the stationary timing mark.
2. Loosen the cam chain adjuster locknut and back out the adjusting bolt. Then retighten the bolt and secure the locknut.

NOTE: *When rotating the engine, turn it only in the normal direction of rotation. Do not turn it backwards if you pass the timing mark.*

1979 and Later

ADJUSTMENT

Cam chain tension is set automatically on these models. No manual adjustment is required.

CONTACT BREAKER POINTS

Breaker Point Gap Adjustment

FEELER GAUGE METHOD

1. Rotate the crankshaft until the points set to be adjusted is at its widest opening (the highest point of the cam lobe). Check the gap using a suitable thickness gauge. If the gap is not within the specified limits of 0.012–0.016 in. (0.3–0.4 mm), loosen the screws and use a screwdriver at the pry point to increase or decrease the gap as necessary. The optimal setting is 0.014 in. (0.35 mm), and the thickness gauge should move between the points with some slight resistance; the next larger and smaller sizes should be obviously too thin and too thick respectively. Recheck the adjustment after securing the screws, and run a business card through the points to remove any dirt from the thickness gauge.
2. Rotate the engine until the other points set is at its widest position, and adjust them in the same manner.

DWELL METER METHOD

1. Although setting breaker point gaps with a feeler gauge as outlined above should produce fairly accurate results, the use of a dwell meter is even more accurate.
2. Connect the dwell meter: one lead to ground on the engine, the other lead to the points' wire terminal or spring.
3. Select the 8-cylinder or 4-cylinder scale.
4. Start and idle the engine at 800–1,000 rpm. Dwell should be 23° when read on an 8-cylinder scale, or 46° on a 4-cylinder scale.
5. If dwell is not correct, adjust the point gaps as outlined above so that the meter gives the correct reading.

Ignition Timing

The breaker points on the left fire cylinders 1 and 4. Those on the right fire cylinders 2 and 3. Timing is set for each pair of cylinders.

Timing marks "1.4" and "2.3" on the advancer are for the left and the right side points respectively.

STATIC TIMING

1. Clean and adjust the points as described in the "Contact Breaker Points" Section.
2. Rotate the engine until the "F" mark on the timing advancer for the set of points to be adjusted is slightly to the left of the timing mark located just above the advancer.
3. Connect a timing light or ohmmeter to the appropriate set of points with one lead on either the leaf spring or the points wire mounting bolt, and the other on a ground

Aligning the timing mark

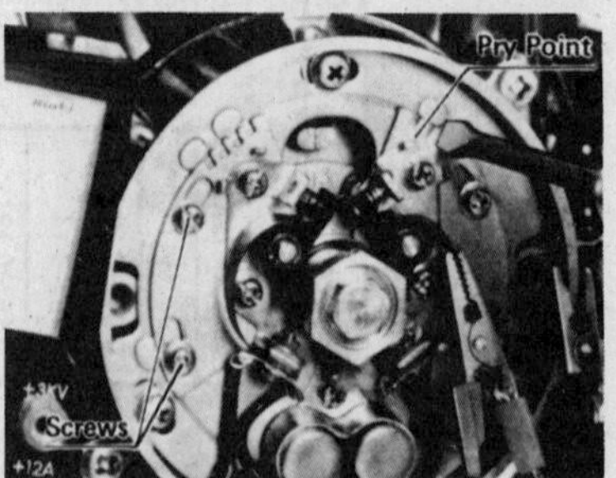

Adjusting the points adjusting plate

Mounting plate mounting screws

(i.e., an engine cooling fin, the frame, etc.). Turn on the ignition switch, if a timing light without a power source is used.

NOTE: *Leaving the key on will cause the points to burn and pit, so leave it on only when necessary.*

4. Rotate the engine until the "F" mark is aligned with the timing mark. The light should react as the two come together. If it does, the timing is correct and you should now do the other set of points; if not, go on to the next step.

5. Loosen the adjusting plate mounting screws, and use a screwdriver at the pry point to position the points so that they just begin to open as the timing marks come into alignment. Always rotate the engine back past the point of alignment by a few degrees before trying again. If the adjusting plate will not travel far enough to arrive at a suitable adjustment, loosen the 3 mounting plate screws and rotate the plate to provide more room for adjustment. Secure the screws and recheck the timing before going on to the other set of points.

DYNAMIC TIMING

1. Clean and adjust the points as described in the "Contact Breaker Points" Section.

2. Run the engine until its normal operating temperature is reached, and adjust the idle, if necessary, to within 800–1,000 rpm as described in the "Carburetor Synchronization and Adjustment" Section.

3. Connect the strobe light according to the manufacturer's instructions, so that the impulses from cylinders 1 and 4 are monitored. Aim the light at the timing marks. The "F" 1.4 mark should be aligned with the timing index mark. If it isn't, loosen the mounting screws, and use a screwdriver at the pry point until the marks do line up.

4. Repeat the above steps on the "F" 2.3 mark.

5. Advance the engine speed to about 2,900–3,100 rpm and check both sets of points. If the timing is off, the advance mechanism is probably at fault.

NOTE: *The idle speed can be regulated by either the throttle stop screw or the throttle grip tensioner.*

6. If the timing is unsteady, remove the contact breaker plate assembly and examine the advance unit. Look for weak or broken springs, or a bent advancer shaft. If either spring is defective, replace both of them. If the advancer shaft is bent (noticeable as the engine is turned over), remove the advancer unit and bend the shaft until total run-out is less than 0.004 in. (0.1 mm), or replace the assembly. When reinstalling the advance unit, make sure that the pin is located in the hole.

ELECTRONIC IGNITION

The ignition timing is pre-set. Due to the nature of the system, no routine maintenance is required.

CARBURETOR SYNCHRONIZATION AND ADJUSTMENT

Preliminary Adjustment

1973 MODELS

Perform the following operations as a prelude to the actual adjustment anytime the carbs are rebuilt or replaced, of if the engine idles especially rough.

1. Remove the carburetors.

2. Turn the throttle stop screw in or out until there is about ⅜ in. (10 mm) between the bracket and the underside of the screw head.

3. Loosen the closed-throttle stopper locknut, and rotate the eccentric stopper screw until there is about 1/16 in. (1.5–2.0 mm) clearance between the stopper and the top of the pulley.

4. Locate the notch cut into the throttle valve, then loosen the locknut and rotate the adjusting screw until there is about 0.024–0.028 in. (0.6–0.7 mm) clearance between the notch and the bottom of the carburetor bore, and secure the locknut.

NOTE: *This is a very delicate operation which must be performed on each of the carbs, so that the adjustment is as close as possible for all 4.*

Throttle stop screw adjustment

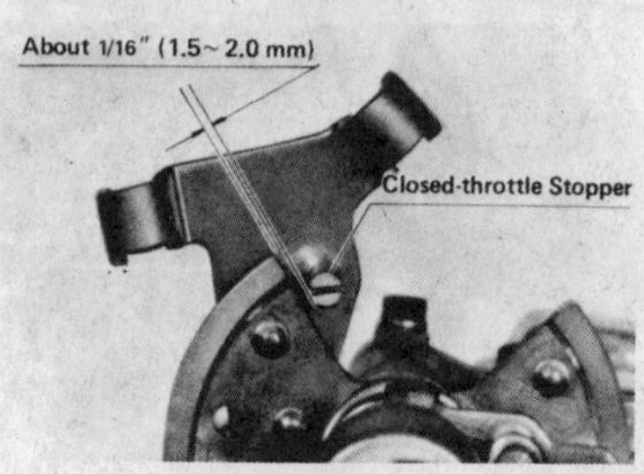

Closed-throttle stopper adjuster

Throttle valve adjusting screw and locknut

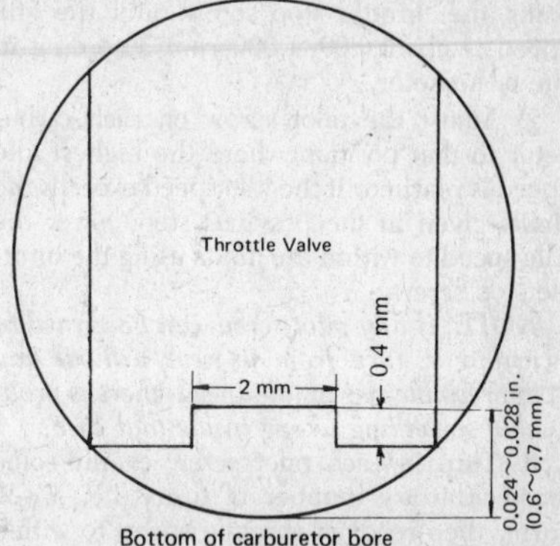

Throttle valve clearance

Adjusting the opened-throttle stopper

Adjusting the pilot mixture

5. Open the throttle by rotating the pulley until the bottom edge of the lowest of the 4 throttle valves is even with the top of the carburetor bore, then rotate the open-throttle stopper screw so that the pulley is stopped at that point.

6. Gently turn each of the carburetor pilot screws into their seats, then back them all out 1½ turns.

1974–76

1. The procedure is to be carried out anytime the carburetors have been rebuilt or replaced, or if the engine runs very roughly.

2. The procedure for 1974 and later models is essentially the same as for 1973 models as outlined above except for the following points:

a. The clearance between the closed throttle stopper and the top of the pulley (Step 3) should be 2–3 mm (about ⅛ in.).

b. The pilot screws (Step 6) should be turned 1¼ turns off their seats.

Adjustment

1973–76

1. Turn the pilot screws in until they bottom lightly, then turn each of them out 1½ turns on 1973 models or 1¼ turns on 1974 and later machines. Run the engine for at least 5 minutes until normal operating temperature is reached, then adjust the engine idle speed

using the throttle stop screw until the idle speed is about 800–1,000 rpm according to the tachometer.

2. Adjust the pilot screw on each carburetor to that position where the highest idle speed is reached. If the idle speed exceeds the limits given in the previous step, lower the idle speed to within the limits using the throttle stop screw.

NOTE: *If any pilot screw can be turned to within ½ turn from its seat without any appreciable rise in idle speed, there is probably something wrong inside that carb.*

3. Turn in each pilot screw evenly some small arbitrary number of turns (i.e., ¼–½ turn), then readjust the idle speed to within the specified limits.

4. Adjust the manifold vacuum of each carburetor using one of the following methods, depending on the equipment available. The machine should be standing in a good airflow to keep the engine operating temperature down.

Without Vacuum Gauges

This procedure is very imprecise by its very nature and should not be attempted except in "emergency" situations. Vacuum gauges are virtually essential.

1. Pay careful attention to the exhaust noise, and place your hands behind the mufflers to feel the exhaust pressure.

2. Compensate for any variations in exhaust noise or pressure by making adjustments to the throttle valve adjusting screws for the carburetor(s) in question. Use either the special tool (Part No. 57001-120), or suitable substitutes to loosen the locknut and rotate the adjusting screws. Backing the screw(s) out will increase pressure, and turning it in will decrease it. Try to keep the idle speed as low as possible while maintaining a balanced pressure for all 4 carbs. Be sure to secure each locknut while holding the adjusting screw steady with a screwdriver.

CAUTION: *If the special tool is not available, you can use a screwdriver and a box-end wrench, but be careful not to bend or place excessive pressure on any of the adjusting screws while loosening or securing the locknuts as this may cause damage to the carburetor.*

NOTE: *Adjusting the vacuum on one carb will cause changes in the pressure on all of the others, so be prepared to compensate for this.*

3. Readjust the pilot screws on any carburetors which have been readjusted, then readjust the idle speed to within 800–1,000 rpm by adjusting the throttle stop screw.

With Vacuum Gauges

1. Remove the rubber caps from the vacuum fittings on the cylinder head (Engine Nos. up to Z1E-01000) or carb holders (Engine No.s from Z1E-02174), and attach the vacuum gauges.

2. With the engine running at idle speed, close down the vacuum gauge intake valve until the gauge needle flutters less than 2 cm Hg (0.8 in. Hg).

3. The normal manifold vacuum gauge reading is 20–23 cm Hg (8–9 in. Hg) for each cylinder. If any gauge reads less than 15 cm Hg (6 in. Hg), recheck the pilot screw adjustment, and make sure that the carb holder hose clamps and spark plugs are secure.

4. Balance the carbs by readjusting the throttle valve adjusting screws as described in Step 2 of the "Without Vacuum Gauges" Section. All of the carbs should be adjusted to within 2 cm Hg (0.8 in. Hg) of each other. Read the Caution after Step 2.

5. Open the throttle and allow it to snap shut several times while watching to see if the vacuum gauge readings remain the same. Readjust any carburetor whose reading has changed.

6. Remove the vacuum gauges, replace the rubber covers, readjust the pilot air screws on any carbs which have been adjusted, and adjust the idle speed to about 800–1,000 rpm.

NOTE: *Inability to obtain synchronization or proper idling may be due to incorrect carburetor float levels, obstruction of air or fuel passages, etc. Refer to "Fuel Systems."*

Preliminary Adjustment
1977–80

1. The preliminary adjustment should be carried out anytime the carburetors have been rebuilt or replaced or if the engine runs very roughly.

2. Turn the idle adjusting screw to give 1.6–2.0 mm (about ¹/₁₆ in.) between the throttle cable bracket end and the stopper on the pulley.

3. Push the throttle completely closed. Clearance between the bracket end and the stopper should be zero, and should return to 1.6–2.0 mm when the throttle is released. If it will not do this, replace the cable bracket.

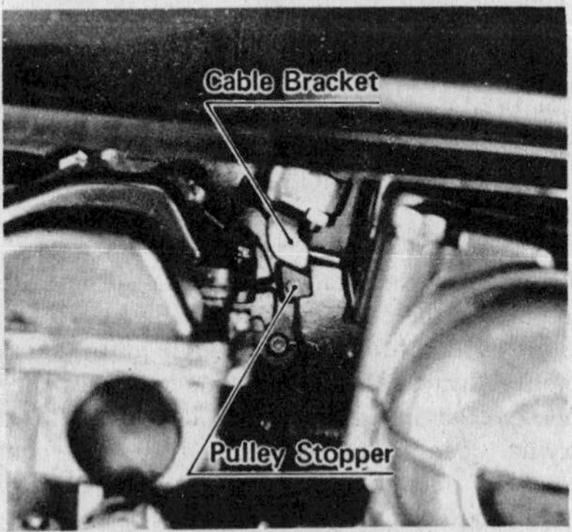

4. Remove the carburetors from the motorcycle.

5. Remove the carburetor caps.

6. On each carburetor, loosen the adjusting screw locknut and turn the screw so that there is 0.7 mm (0.028 in.) between the throttle valve and the bottom of the carburetor bore. Tighten the locknuts and install the carburetor caps.

7. Open the throttle pulley until the bottom edges of the carburetor valves are even with the top of the carburetor bores. Adjust the pulley stop screw so that the pulley travel will be stopped at that point.

8. Remove the carburetor float bowls.

9. Turn each pilot screw in until it bottoms lightly, then back each one out 1¼ turns. Install the float bowls.

10. Refit the carburetors and adjust the cables.

Adjustment
1977–80

1. Start the engine and allow it to reach operating temperature.

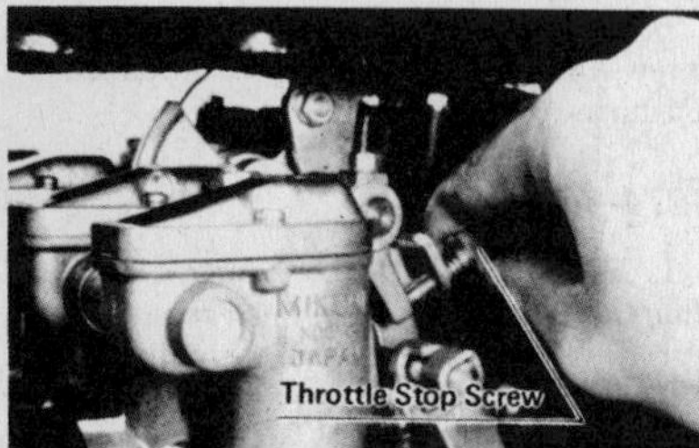

Adjusting the throttle stop screw

Vacuum gauge fitting (shown is a later model; earlier models were pressed into the head)

Adjusting the throttle valves using the special tool

Vacuum gauge installation

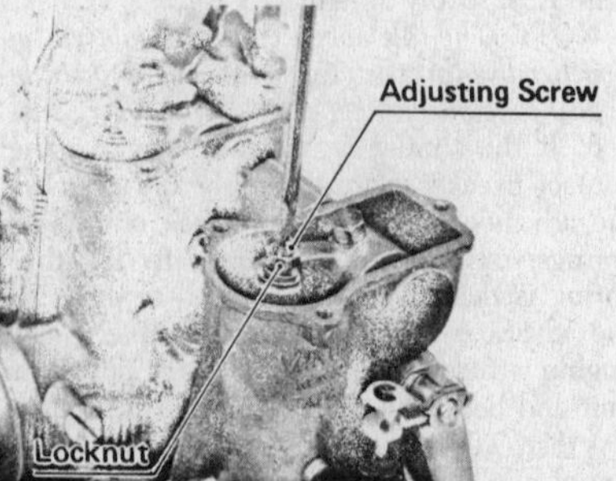

Adjusting the throttle valves

2. Use the idling screw to set the idle speed to 950–1050 rpm. Snap the throttle open a few times to ensure that the idle speed does not change.

3. Remove the gas tank and install an auxilliary tank to supply fuel to the carburetors during the synchronization procedure. Install the vacuum gauge set.

4. With the engine idling and at operating temperature, not the vacuum gauge readings. Normal vacuum should be 24–28 cm Hg (8–9 in. Hg), with the difference between cylinders being less than 2 cm Hg (0.8 in. Hg).

5. If the vacuum difference between cylinders is more than 2 cm Hg, remove the carburetor caps, loosen the adjusting screw locknuts, and turn the adjusting screw(s) so that idle vacuum for all four cylinders is as close as possible.

6. Tighten the adjusting screw locknuts. Readjust the idle speed, if necessary. Open and close the throttle a few times to ensure that the adjustments remain the same.

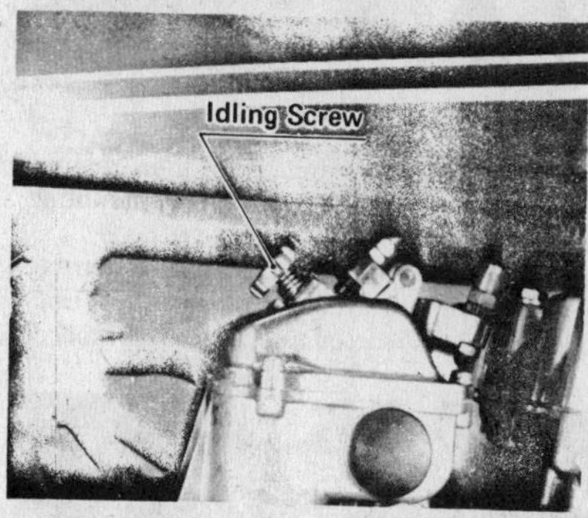

1981

These models are fitted with CV-type carburetors.

Adjustment procedure is basically the same as described for 1977–80 models, above. Note the following points:

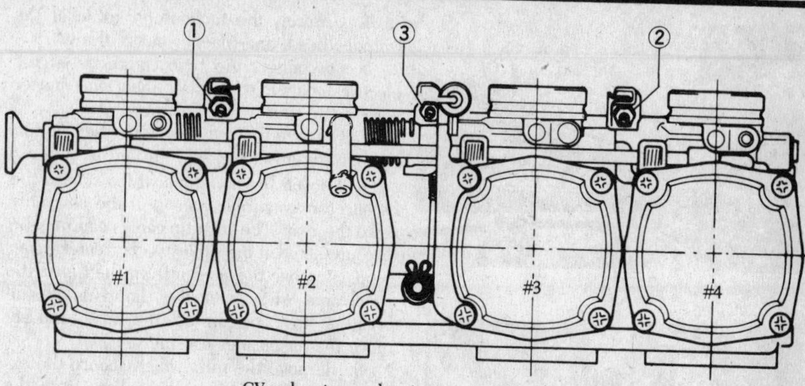

CV carburetor synchronization screws (1.2.3)

a. disconnect the fuel tap and two vacuum switch hoses. Put the petcock on the "prime" position.

b. the adjustment screws are accessible without removing carburetor caps. There are three of them. Use the adjustment screw on the left to lower cylinder No. 1 vacuum. Use the screw on the right to lower cylinder No. 4 vacuum. The center screw will lower cylinders Nos. 1 and 2 simultaneously.

ENGINE AND TRANSMISSION

NOTE: *For engine rebuilding techniques and component inspection methods, refer to the "Engine Rebuilding" section under "General Information."*

ENGINE REMOVAL AND INSTALLATION

Removal

1. Remove the engine and oil filter drain plugs, and allow the engine to drain thoroughly.

NOTE: *If the engine will not run and therefore cannot be warmed as an aid in draining the oil, kick it through several times to assure as complete a drainage as possible.*

2. Remove the plastic side covers, open and unhook the seat, turn the fuel tap to the "S" poition, disconnect the fuel lines, disengage the gas tank tang from the rubber retaining band, and pull the tank off from the back.

3. Disconnect the black and green ignition coil leads at the coils, then disconnect the spark plug leads at the plugs.

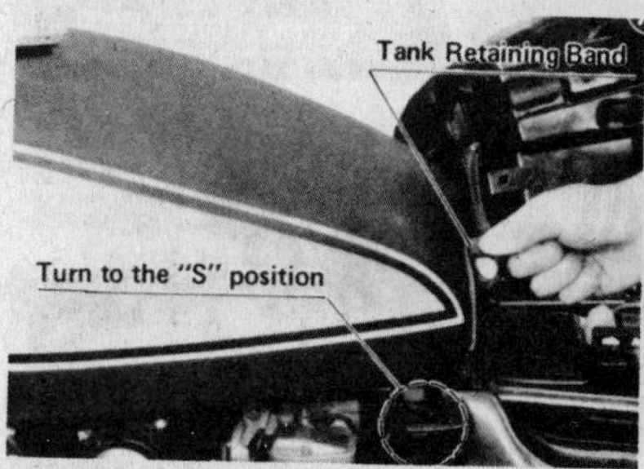

Tune-Up Specifications

	900 (1973)	900 (1974 and Later)	1000 (1977–78)	1000 (1979–81)
Valve clearance (cold)				
Intake (mm/in.)	0.05–0.10/0.002–0.004	0.05–0.10/0.002–0.004	0.05–0.10/0.002–0.004	0.05–0.15/0.002–0.006
Exhaust (mm/in.)	0.05–0.10/0.002–0.004	0.05–0.10/0.002–0.004	0.05–0.10/0.002–0.004	0.05–0.15/0.002–0.006
Compression (psi)				
Standard	121	121	128–156	128–156
Serviceable limit	85	85	100	100
Max allowable variation between cylinders	14	14	14	14
Spark Plugs (NGK)				
Standard	B-8ES	B-8ES	B-8ES	B-8ES
Hot	B-7ES	B-7ES	B-7ES	B-7ES
Cold	B-9ES	B-9ES	B-9ES	B-9ES
Gap (mm/in.)	0.7–0.8/0.028–0.032	0.7–0.8/0.028–0.032	0.7–0.8/0.028–0.032	0.7–0.8/0.028–0.032
Breaker point gap (mm/in.)	0.3–0.4/0.012–0.016	0.3–0.4/0.012–0.016	0.3–0.4/0.0012–0.0016	—
Ignition timing				
deg BTDC @ 1500 rpm	5	20	20	—
deg BTDC @ 3000 rpm	40	—	—	—
deg BTDC @ 2350 rpm	—	40	40	—
Carburetors				
Idle speed (rpm)	800–1000	800–1000	950–1050	950–1050
Pilot screws (turns out)	1½	①	1¼	Pre-set
Synchronization				
range (cm/in. HG)	20–23/8–9	20–23/8–9	20–24/8–9	20–24/8–9
max variation (cm/in. HG)	2/0.8	2/0.8	2/0.8	2/0.8

① 1974: 1½
1975: 1¼
1976: 1⅜

Disconnecting the coil leads

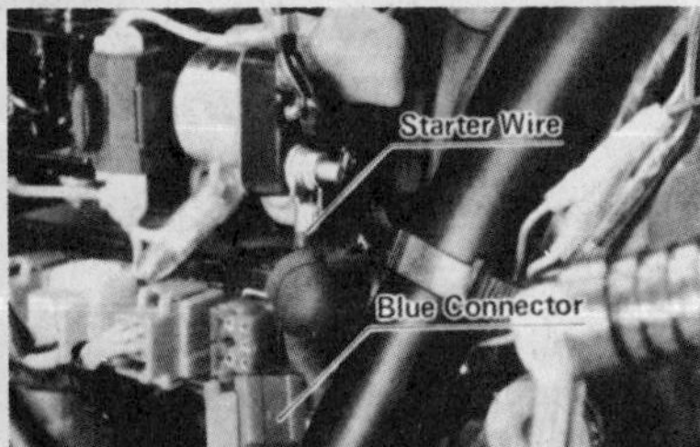

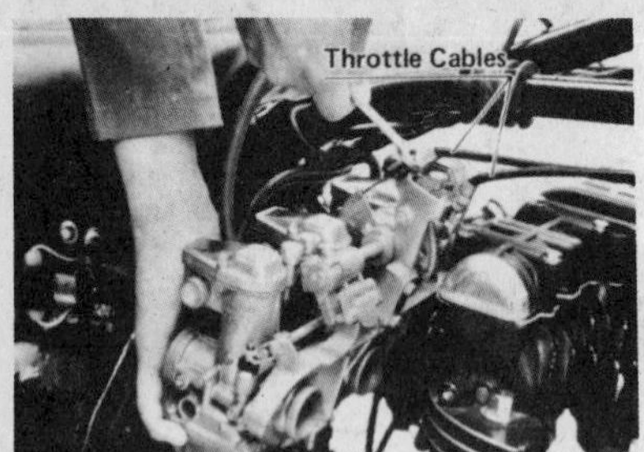

Removing the carburetor assembly

Removing the air cleaner assembly

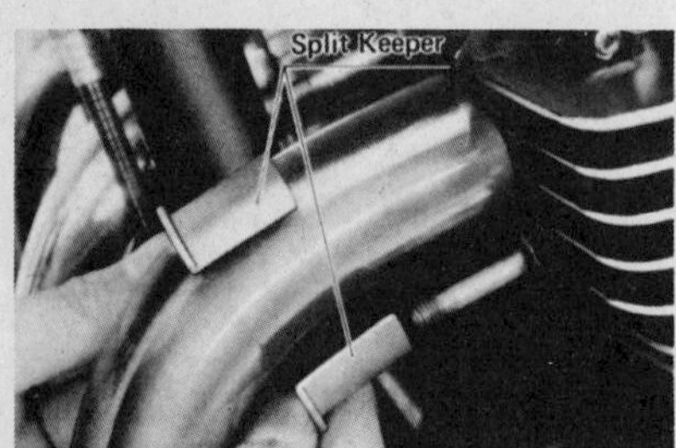

Removing the keepers

4. Unscrew the tachometer cable at the cylinder head, and place it out of the way.

5. Disconnect the blue connector at the electrical panel, then disconnect the starter wire at the starter relay terminal.

6. Remove the right footrest, then unbolt the battery ground wire (−) from the engine.

7. Loosen the 8 clamps which secure the carburetor assembly, then pull the assembly off to the rear. The throttle cables can now be discounnected at the pulley with greater ease.

8. Remove the screen from the top of the air cleaner, slide back the clamp on the oil breather hose, disconnect the hose, and remove the air cleaner assembly.

9. Remove the nuts which secure the exhaust pipe collars, free the collars from the cylinder head studs, and remove the split keepers.

10. Remove the exhaust system rear mounting bolts, then push the two mufflers on either side forward to remove them. If you wish to contend with each pipe individually, disconnect the muffler connecting hose clamp from each pair.

11. Remove the left front footrest, shift lever, and starter cover and gasket.

12. Remove the chain oiler pump cover, if fitted, disconnect the inlet hose from the pump, and plug it with a screw as shown in the illustration.

13. Remove the chain cover, pull the cotter pin out of the clutch release lever, disengage the clutch cable, remove the engine sprocket guard, and remove the clutch pushrod from the driveshaft.

14. Bend back the lockwasher locking tab, secure the sprocket with either the special tool (Part No. 57001-118), or a suitable substitute, and remove the sprocket nut and sprocket.

15. On rear disc brake models, remove the rear brake master cylinder bolts and side cover bracket. Remove the brake lamp switch and spring, back off the brake rod adjusting nut until maximum pedal play is reached, then loosen the brake pedal position adjusting bolt locknut, and back out the bolt so that the pedal is held down, out of the way.

16. Jack or lever the engine up to take the weight off the mounting bolts, then remove the nuts from the 3 long engine mounting bolts.

17. Remove the short engine mounting bolt from the lower center mounting on each side, the right rear engine mounting bracket

Securing the intake hose

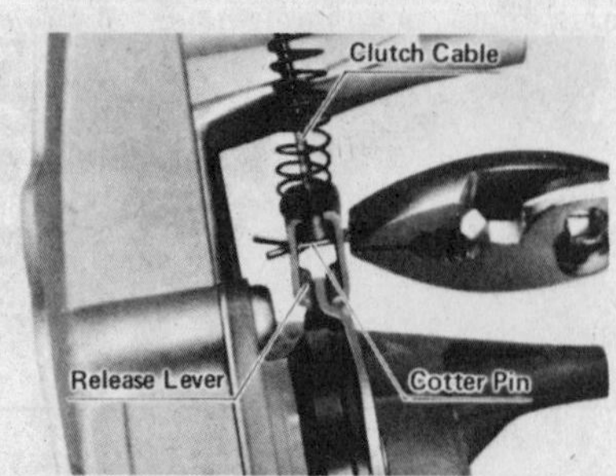

Disconnecting the clutch cable

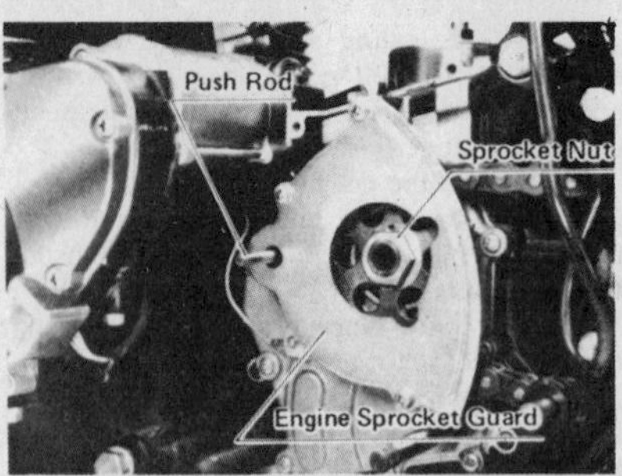

Removing the sprocket nut

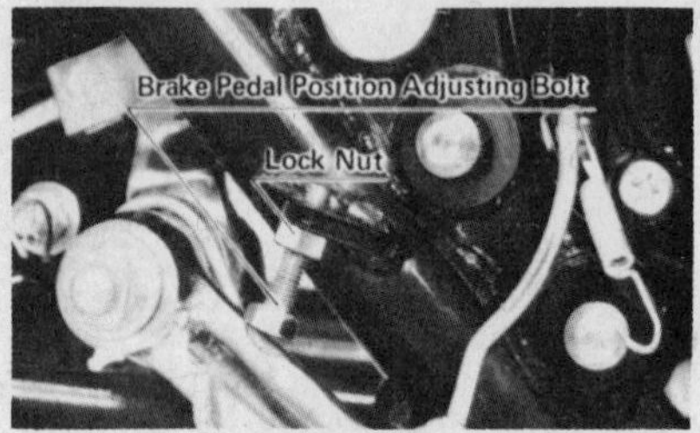

Keeping the pedal out of the way

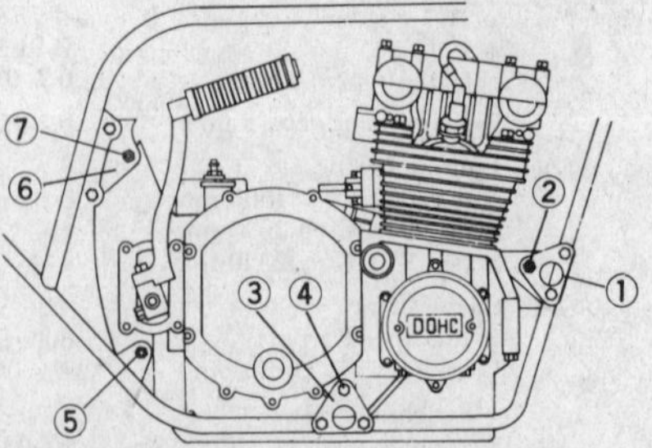

Engine mounting bolt locations

1. Front bracket
2. Front bolt
3. Lower center bracket
4. Lower center bolt
5. Rear lower bolt
6. Rear upper bracket
7. Rear upper bolt

The brackets must be clear before the engine can come free

bolts, the center and right side front mounting brackets, and the 3 long bolts.

18. With the engine held level, slowly lift it up about 1 in., then move it to the right slightly until the rear of the engine slips over the lower right rear mounting.

19. Raise the front of the engine a little so that it will clear the frame, then drop down the left side, and pull the engine out diagonally and upwards to the right.

Installation

1. Mount, but do not secure, the 3 engine mounting brackets before inserting the engine bolts. Insert the engine bolts, secure the bracket mounting bolts, and then tighten the engine mounting bolts. The 3 long bolts are inserted from the left side of the machine. Two spacers go on the rear upper bolt; a long one on the left side of the engine, and a short one on the right side. Secure the bracket bolts to 14.5–16.5 ft lbs (2.0–2.3 kg/m), the 3 long (12 mm) bolts to 47–50 ft lbs (6.5–7.0 kg/m, and the two shorter bolts (10 mm) to 26–29 ft lbs (3.5–4.0 kg/m).

2. Install the engine sprocket with the chain already on it, and secure the sprocket nut to 87–108 ft lbs (12–15 kg/m). A new lockwasher should be used, and the chain adjustment can be loosened if the sprocket and chain will not go on the shaft. Note that the sprocket must be installed with the stamped numbers facing the engine. Otherwise chain alignment will be incorrect.

3. An oil seal guide (Part No. 57001-130), or a suitable substitute, should be used when installing the chain cover in order to avoid damaging the rubber seal. The pin in the output shaft must be aligned with the groove in the chain oil pump shaft before the cover will go on, on models with a rear chain oiler.

4. Install the carburetor assembly, taking care that the clamps are secured well enough to prevent any air leaks.

5. Install the inside mufflers first, and then the outside ones. The collar can be used to hold the split keeper while installing the pipe. Secure the muffler connecting hose clamp to prevent any exhaust leaks, then secure the

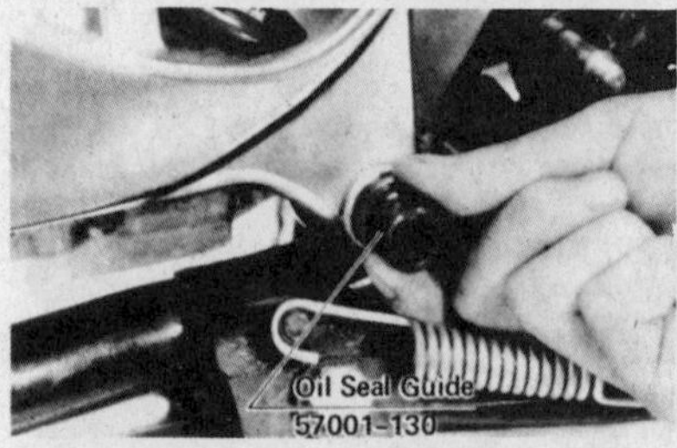

Using the guide to protect the cover oil seal

rear mounting bolts and the bolts at the cylinder head, in that order.

6. Connect the spark plug wires to the plugs. The wires are numbered in accordance with their respective cylinders counting from left to right.

7. Replenish the oil supply with high quality (SE) oil, and kick the engine through several times to circulate the oil before firing it up. Refer to the "Maintenance" Chapter for capacities.

8. Give the machine a thorough going over, and make all the necessary adjustments.

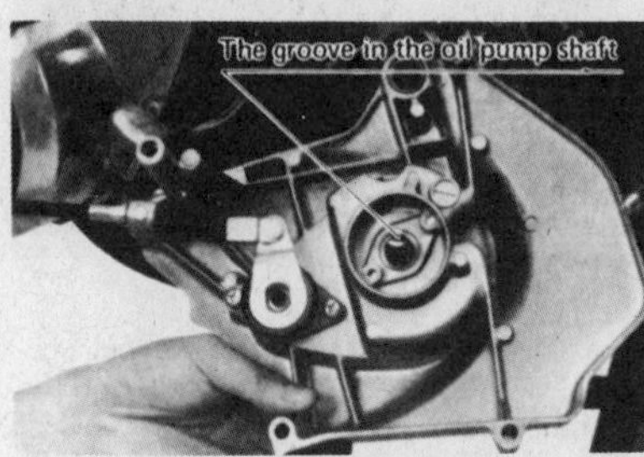

Lining up the pin and groove

Installing the split keepers and collar

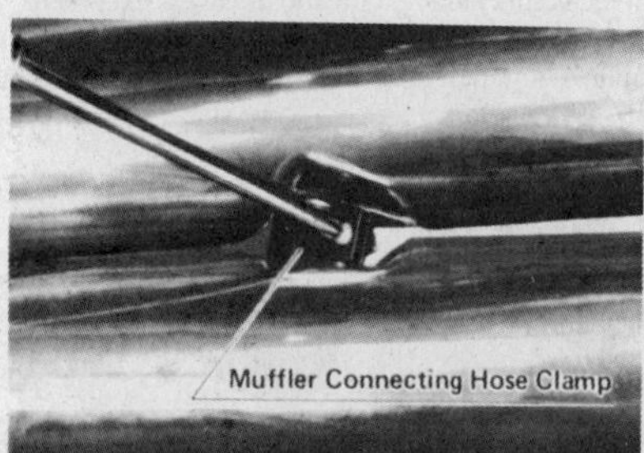

Securing the hose clamp

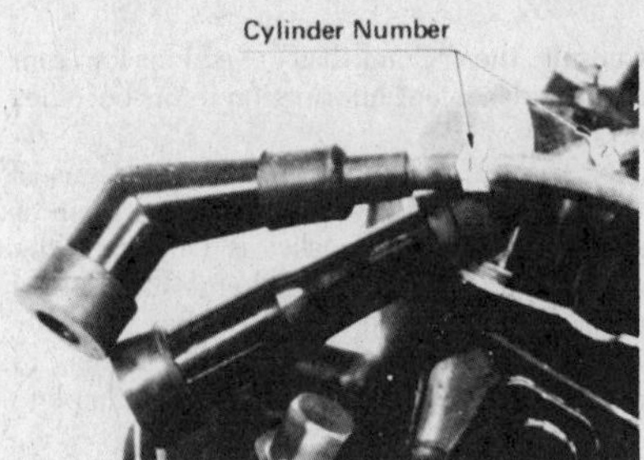

Put the right leads on the right plugs

TOP END

Camshafts

REMOVAL

1. Remove the gas tank.

2. Remove the tool tray. Remove the air cleaner silencer.

3. Disconnect the spark plug leads. Remove the contact breaker cover and gasket.

4. Turn the engine over until the "T" mark for cylinders 1 and 4 lines up with the timing mark.

5. Remove the valve cover and gasket.

6. Remove the chain guide sprocket, then unbolt the camshafts caps and separate the split bushing halves for installation in their original positions unless they are to be replaced. Remove the camshafts.

7. Unscrew the tachometer cable, and remove the tach pinion to avoid any possible damage to the camshaft worm during the installation procedure.

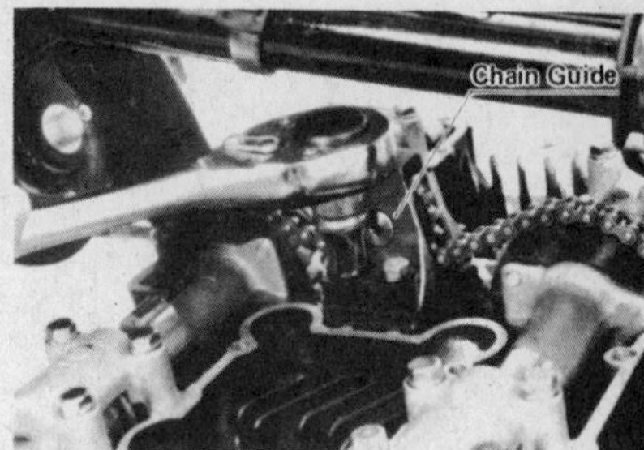

Removing the cam chain guide

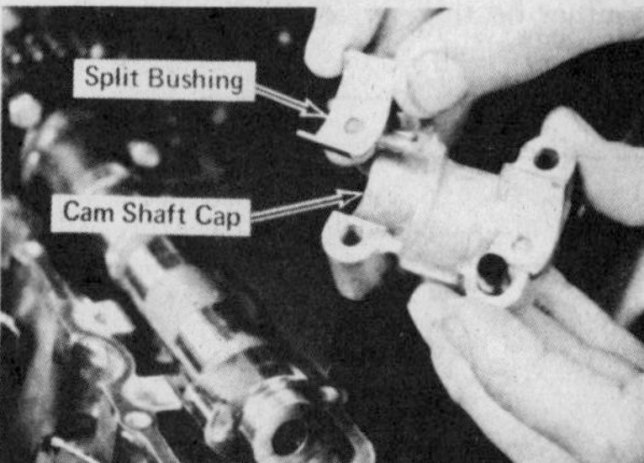

Removing the bushings and caps

Removing the exhaust camshaft

INSPECTION

1. Clean all parts in a suitable solvent, then blow them dry.

2. Inspect the camshafts for signs of wear, scored lobes, or damage, and replace them as necessary based on the following information.

   a. Measure the height of each cam lobe with a micrometer, and replace the cam as necessary if the lobes are worn past their serviceable limits as given below:

900

	Standard	*Service Limit*
Intake	1.4276 ~ 1.4307 in. (36.26 ~ 36.34 mm)	1.4236 in. (36.16 mm)
Exhaust	1.4079 ~ 1.4110 in. (35.76 ~ 35.84 mm)	1.4039 in. (35.66 mm)

1000

	Standard	*Service Limit*
Intake	1.4256 ~ 1.4327 in. (36.21 ~ 36.39 mm)	1.4220 in. (36.12 mm)
Exhaust	1.4059 ~ 1.4200 in. (35.71 ~ 35.89 mm)	1.4024 in. (35.62 mm)

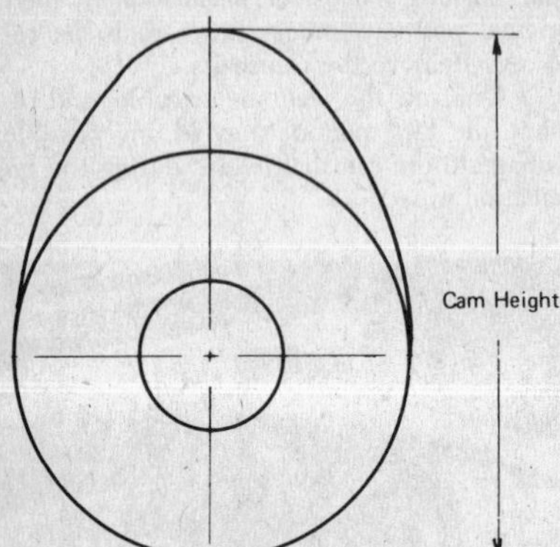

Make the measurement along here

b. Measure the diameter of each of the camshaft bearing surfaces with a micrometer, and replace the camshaft as necessary if either bearing surface is worn past its serviceable limit:

Standard	*Service Limit*
0.9633 ~ 0.9638 in. (24.467 ~ 24.480 mm)	0.9614 in. (24.420 mm)

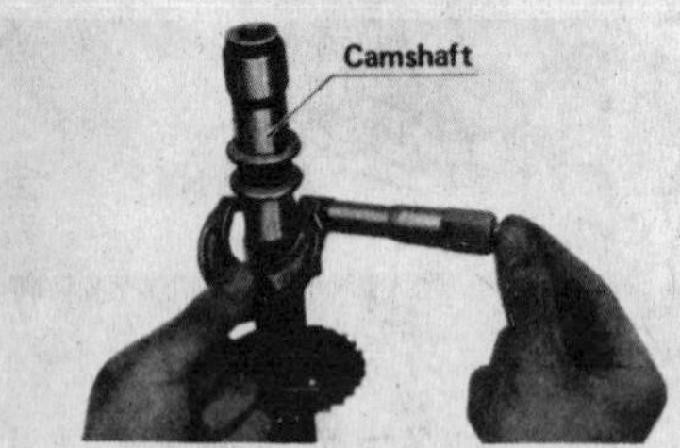

Measuring the bearing surfaces

3. Remove the cam chain sprocket from the camshafts, keeping them separate for replacement in their original locations, and place the shafts on V-blocks so that they ride on the bushing surfaces, or in a lathe. Rotate the shafts and use a dial indicator to check run-out along the sprocket mounting surface. Replace any cam whose run-out exceeds the service limit given below:

Standard	*Service Limit*
under 0.0008 in. (under 0.02 mm)	0.004 in. (0.10 mm)

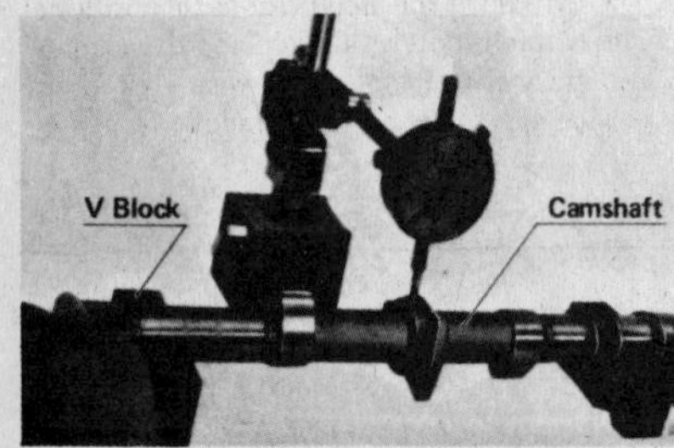

Checking camshaft run-out

4. Inspect the camshaft bushings for signs of wear, scoring, or damage, and replace them as a set per camshaft if worn past their serviceable limit of 0.0063 in. (0.16 mm). The standard clearance between the bushings and the camshafts is 0.008–0.0025 in. (0.020–0.064 mm). Measure the clearance in the following manner:

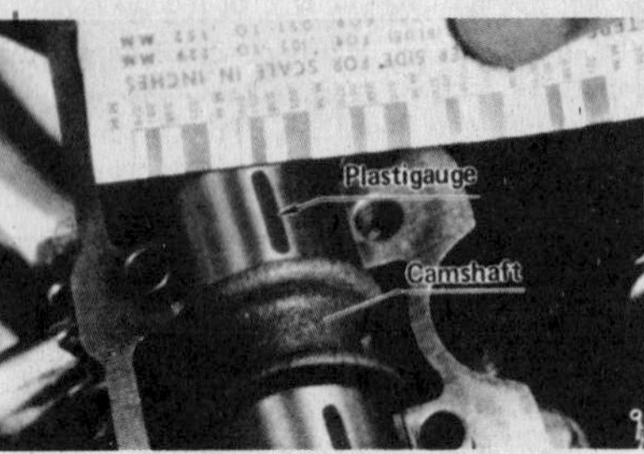

Checking bearing wear with plastigage

a. Remove the camshafts and cut sections of Plastigage® to the width of the bushing, and place a strip on the lower half of each bushing, parallel to the camshaft, and so that the plastigage will be between the bushing and the shaft.

b. Fit the cam chain over the sprocket so that the cam is held stationary, and fit and secure the caps and bolts as directed in the "Camshaft Installation" Section.

c. Remove the camshaft and use a micrometer to measure the plastigage in order to determine the camshaft/bushing clearance. Excessive clearance in any of the 4 bushings for each of the camshafts will necessitate replacing all 4 bushings for that cam.

5. The cam chain is of the endless variety, and should not be removed unless replacement is necessary. In most cases excessive chain noise can be traced to wear of the guide rollers, in which case they should be replaced.

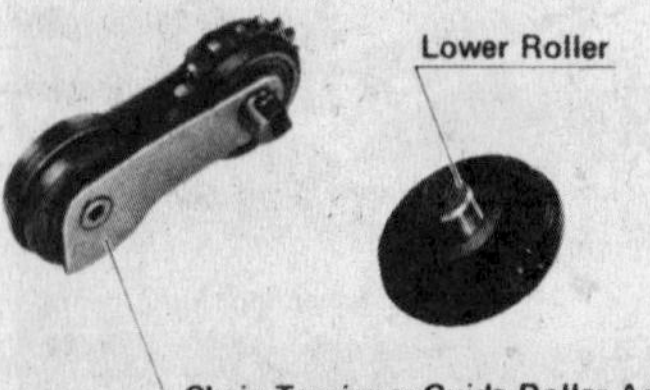

Check these for wear

Consult the "Crankshaft" Section for cam chain replacement information if this becomes necessary.

6. Inspect the cam sprockets for signs of wear or damaged teeth, and replace them as necessary. If one sprocket is damaged, the chances are good that the other is also in need of replacement, and the chain has probably also been affected. It's best, for that reason, to replace the sprockets and chain as a complete system.

NOTE: *On models with engine numbers before Z1E-04654, there have been instances of severe engine damage caused by the sprocket mounting bolts loosening and backing out. A new shouldered bolt (Part No. 92003-41) is available, and should be used to replace the original bolts. Use Liquid Lock-Super (Part No. K41012-014) or a suitable thread locking compound, and torque the bolts to 7 ft lbs (1.0 kg/m).*

A sprocket secured with a new type bolt

INSTALLATION AND CAMSHAFT TIMING

1. Installation is basically in the reverse order of removal. Use new gaskets whenever possible.

2. Remove the breaker point cover, then rotate the crankshaft, using a wrench on the large crankshaft nut while holding the cam chain up so that it doesn't get caught and so that the slack between the crankshaft and the exhaust cam sprocket is taken up, until the "T" alignment mark for cylinders 1 and 4 is aligned with the timing mark. This brings the number 1 and 4 pistons into the TDC (top dead center) position.

3. Slip the exhaust camshaft through the cam chain, and position it so that the mark on the sprocket is aligned with the cylinder head surface and facing toward the front of the engine, then pull the chain taut and fit it onto the exhaust camshaft sprocket. The camshafts have "L" and "R" marked on them for installation purposes.

CAUTION: *The chain must be properly seated on the crankshaft and chain guide or the timing will not be accurate.*

Rotate the engine forward

Lining up the sprocket mark

4. Starting with the next chain link pin above the one which coincides with the exhaust sprocket mark, count to the 28th, then slip the intake camshaft through the chain so the 28th pin and the "28" mark on the intake camshaft sprocket are aligned as illustrated.

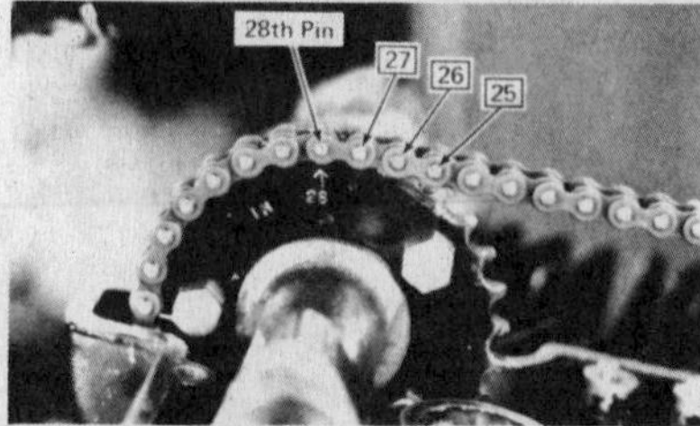

Lining up the 28th pin and mark

Start counting here

NOTE: *Do not begin counting at the exhaust sprocket mark; start at the next pin above that point.*

5. Position all the split bushing halves in their original locations unless they've been replaced.

6. Position the camshaft caps so that the arrow points toward the exhaust side, and so that the number on the cap matches the number on the head.

7. Seat the camshaft by partially tightening the left-side cap bolts, then fully torque all of the bolts to 105 in. lbs (1.2 kg/m) in the order shown in the accompanying illustration.

CAUTION: *If you are bench assembling the head without the cam chain installed, great care must be taken not to bend any valves*

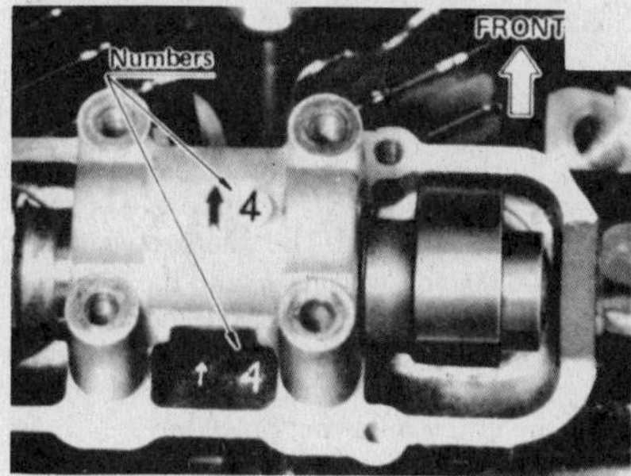

Match the stamped numbers when installing the bearing caps

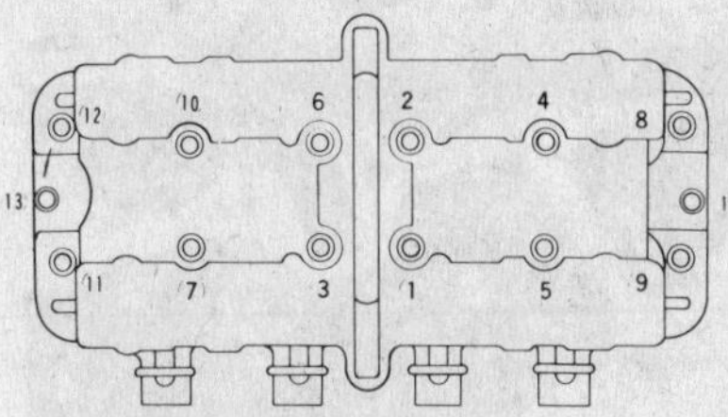

Cylinder head bolt tightening pattern

Both lobes pointing down . . .

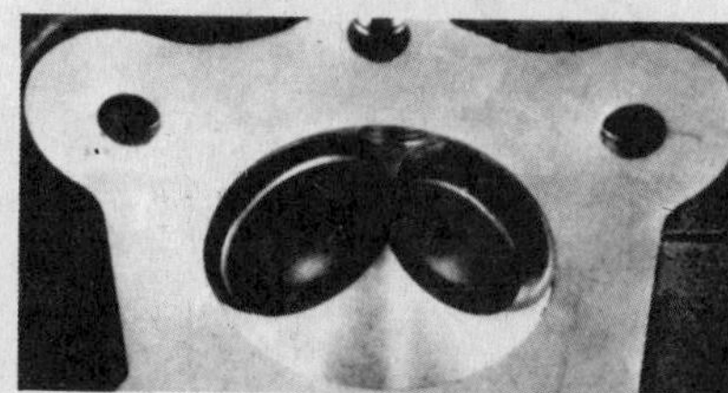
. . . will cause the valves to hit . . .

. . . and this is the result

by securing the bearing caps with the cams improperly positioned. Be sure that the cam lobes do not depress both valves of any one cylinder at the same time, and place styrofoam, under the head to prevent bending the valves on the bench surface. Do not tighten both camshafts into place at the same time, and do not secure the caps until the valve timing is set (Step nos. 2–4) with the cam chain in position.

8. Liberally oil the cam assembly, then install the chain guide sprocket assembly, and adjust the cam chain tension as described in the "Tune-Up" Chapter.

9. Rotate the crankshaft 2 or 3 complete revolutions until number 1 and 4 pistons are at TDC ("T" mark aligned with timing mark), then check that the marks on the exhaust and intake camshaft sprockets are properly aligned, as illustrated, indicating that the cam timing is correct.

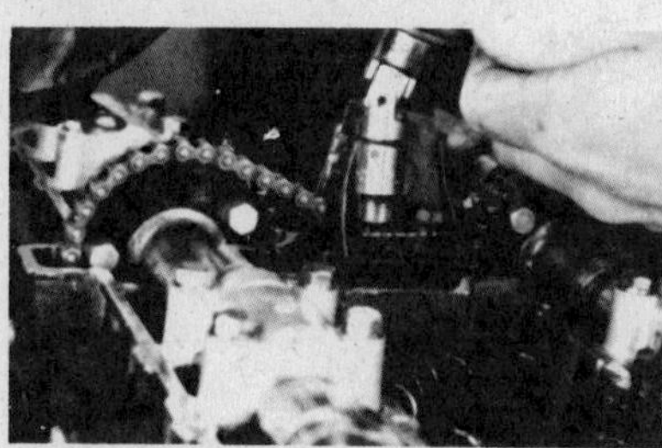
Securing the chain guide

CAUTION: *Do not attempt to rotate the engine by using a wrench on the camshaft sprocket mounting bolts; use the large nut on the crankshaft instead. If any unusual resistance is felt when rotating the engine, stop immediately and make sure that the timing is correct or valve damage may occur.*

10. Install the tachometer pinion and cable, then mount and secure the valve cover and cover gasket to 70 in. lbs (0.8 kg/m) torque.

11. Adjust the valve clearances as described in the "Tune-Up" Chapter.

Cylinder Head

The cylinder head is made of aluminum alloy into which the valve guides are pressed, and the valve seats are cast. The valve seats must be cut to their specified angles to assure efficient sealing, and to prevent the valve from overheating by promoting heat dissipation.

Normal wear to the valve lifter and cam surfaces can be adjusted for up to 0.04 in. (1.0 mm). Once this limit has been exceeded through seat wear or grinding, the valve stem end can be ground down to increase clearance. The head will have to be replaced if the adjustment limit is exceeded again.

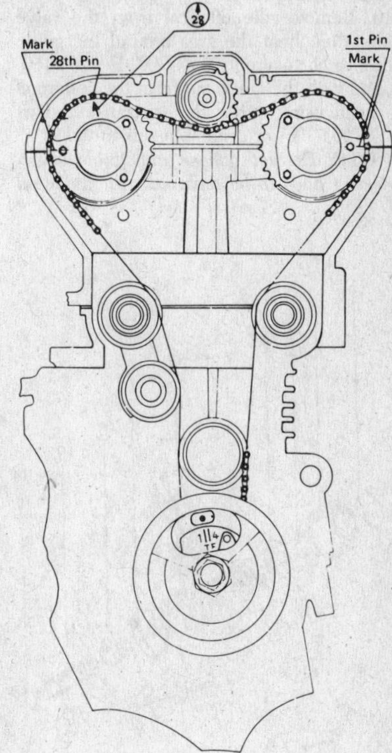

Timing mark alignment

Installing the tachometer pinion

REMOVAL AND DISASSEMBLY

1. Fully open the seat, and remove the tank.

2. Remove the exhaust system as described in Steps 9 and 10 of the "Engine Removal" Section.

3. Remove the carburetor assembly after loosening the 8 hose clamps which secure it.

4. Remove the camshafts as described in the "Camshafts Removal" Section.

5. Disconnect the spark plug wires from the plugs, and remove the plugs.

6. Remove the bolt from either end of the heat, and the 12 cylinder head nuts using either the special tool (Part No. 57001-111) or any suitable socket wrench.

7. Remove all of the valve tappets and shims, keeping them separate for installation in their original locations.

8. Remove the cylinder head and head gasket. Tap the head with a soft mallet to break it free from its seat if necessary.

9. Compress the valve springs, using either the special tool (Part No. 57001-107) or a suitable substitute, until the split keepers can be removed, then remove the valve, springs, and spring retainer, keeping them separate for installation in their original locations.

NOTE: *All of the valves do not necessarily have to be removed, however this is the recommended practice.*

10. Remove the oil seal from the valve guide, then heat the area around the guide with a torch to about 250°– 300° F (120°–150° C), and drift the guide out from the bottom of the head using either the special drift (Part No. 57001-108) or a suitable substitute.

NOTE: *Do not remove any guide which doesn't have to be replaced. Any guide oil seal which is damaged or removed should be replaced. Consult Step 4 of the following section for additional information.*

Removing the head bolts

Oil Seal

Removing the oil seal

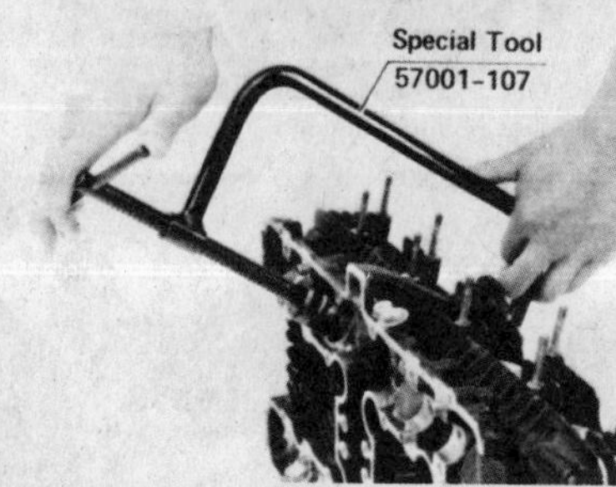
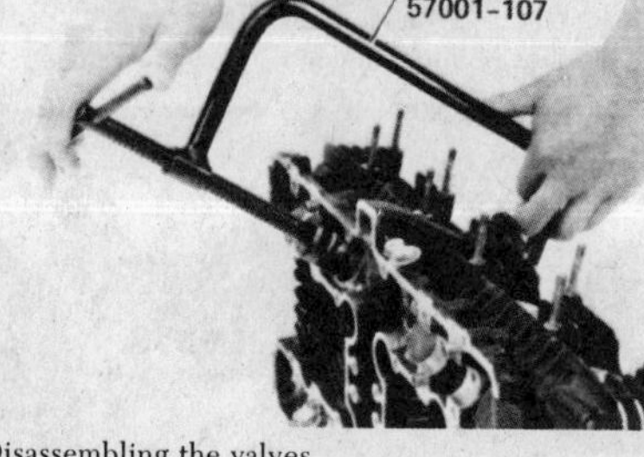

Disassembling the valves

Drifting out a valve guide

One complete valve and tappet assembly

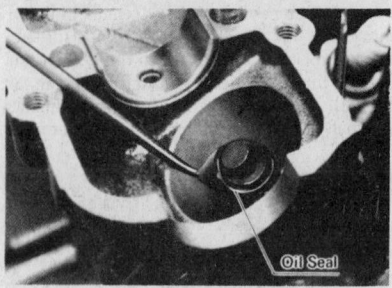

INSPECTION

1. Clean all parts other than seals and gaskets in a suitable solvent, then blow them dry. Carbon deposits on the piston and head assemblies can be softened with a decarbonizing solvent, and scraped off with a blunt instrument such as a butterknife. Do not use a caustic soda solution to clean aluminum parts such as the head and pistons, however, it may be used on the valves. Avoid gouging the piston crown or removing any metal. It is not necessary to restore the components to a like-new condition. Periodically, as you work, wipe the surface clean with a clean rag soaked in clean gasoline. If this is done with the cylinder still in place, you can catch the carbon flakes by pressing a line of grease around the piston on top of the rings. Rotating the piston will leave the grease ring with the carbon trapped in it on the cylinder, and it can then be wiped out. The cylinder-head assembly should be disassembled before being decarbonized.

2. Inspect the cylinder head for warpage on the gasket surface by laying a straightedge across the head and measuring the distance between the straightedge and the gasket surface with feeler gauges. The standard warpage is under 0.002 in. (0.05 mm), and the serviceable limit is 0.10 in. (0.25 mm). If the warpage exceeds this limit, the head must be replaced. It is possible to straighten a warped head using one of the following procedures:

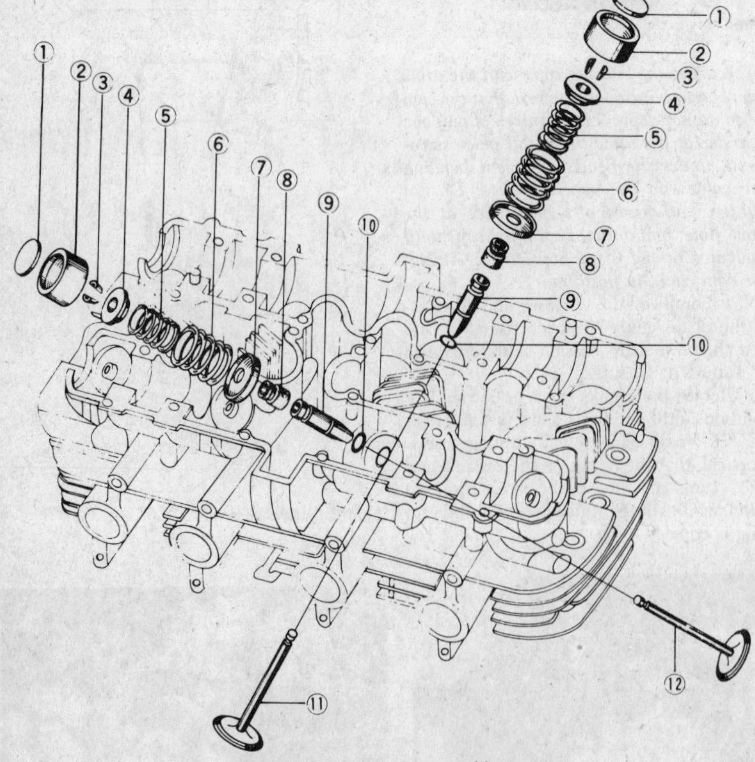

Cylinder head and valve assemblies

1. Shim
2. Valve lifter
3. Split keeper
4. Valve spring retainer
5. Inner valve spring
6. Outer valve spring
7. Valve spring seat
8. Oil seal
9. Valve guide
10. Circlip
11. Exhaust valve
12. Inlet valve

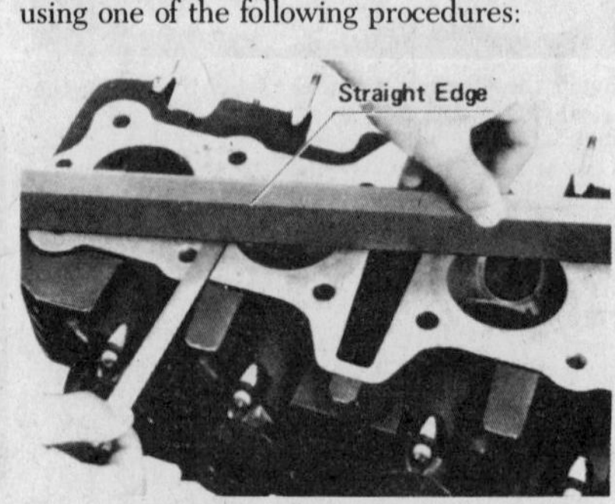

Checking the head for warpage

a. Place a sheet of fine grit emery paper on a flat surface and move the head around in a figure-eight motion while applying mild pressure. It is better to work slowly with mild pressure than quickly with heavy pressure. Don't remove any more metal than is necessary.

b. An alternative method is to use a piece of glass and a fine valve grinding compound instead of the emery paper.

c. Check the results with Prussian blue dye or red lead. To do this, lay out some very fine sandpaper on a flat surface. Coat the gasket surface on the head with the dye and allow it to dry. Move the head very gently over the sandpaper just long enough to remove the dye, then look at the gasket surface. If the head is flat, all of the dye will have been removed. If there is still dye on the heat, repeat the entire process, replace the head, or consult your local dealer.

3. Inspect the valves for a worn, bent, burned, or damaged condition, and replace them as necessary. Perform the following operations on each valve:

a. Measure the valve head thickness using vernier calipers, and replace the valve if the head is thinner than the service limit given below:

Standard	Service Limit
0.034 ~ 0.045 in. (0.85 ~ 1.15 mm)	0.020 in. (0.5 mm)

b. Carefully inspect the seating surface of the valve and the condition of the stem, and repair the valve if possible using a valve refacer. The valve seating surface angle is 45°.

c. Place the valve in a pair of V-blocks,

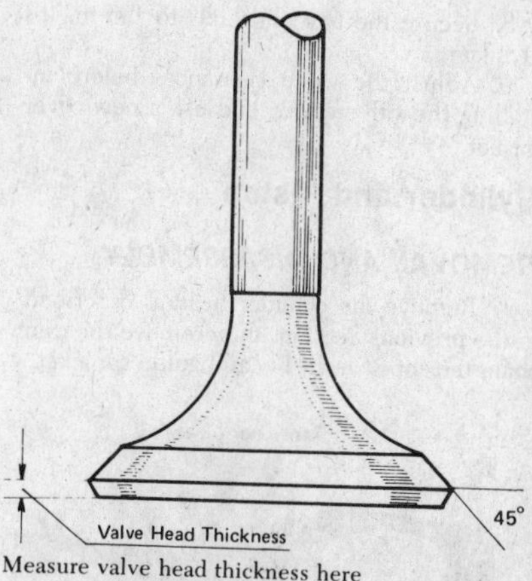

Measure valve head thickness here

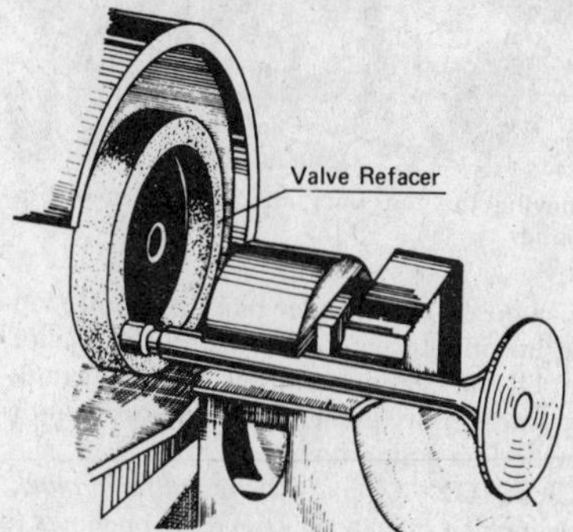

Refacing the valve stem

and check its run-out with a dial indicator. The valve must be replaced if its run-out exceeds the service limit of 0.002 in. (0.05 mm).

d. Measure the valve stem in at least 4 places using a micrometer held at right angles to the stem, and replace the valve if it is worn past the service limits given below at any point:

	Standard	Service Limit
Intake	0.2742 ~ 0.2748 in. (6.965 ~ 6.980 mm)	0.272 in. (6.90 mm)
Exhaust	0.2738 ~ 0.2744 in. (6.955 ~ 6.970 mm)	0.272 in. (6.90 mm)

4. Measure the bore of each valve guide in at least 4 places, using a small bore gauge and a micrometer, and replace the guide if any of the measurements exceed the service limits given below:

Standard	Service Limit
0.2756 ~ 0.2762 in. (7.000 ~ 7.015 mm)	0.279 in. (7.08 mm)

If a bore gauge and micrometer are not available, insert a new valve into the guide, set a dial indicator against the stem, and move the stem back and forth to measure valve/valve guide clearance, then do it again while moving the stem in a direction at right angles to the first measurement. The guide will have to be replaced if the valve/valve guide clearance exceeds the service limits given below:

	Standard	Service Limit
Intake	0.002 ~ 0.005 in. (0.050 ~ 0.124 mm)	0.010 in. (0.25 mm)
Exhaust	0.003 ~ 0.006 in. (0.071 ~ 0.142 mm)	0.009 in. (0.24 mm)

5. Inspect the valve seat for signs of wear, scoring, burning, or damage, then measure the width of the seat. The seat must be smooth

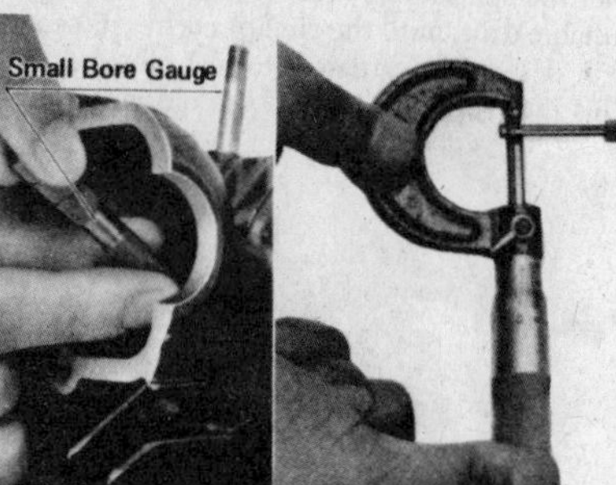

Measuring valve guide inside diameter

Measuring valve/valve guide clearance

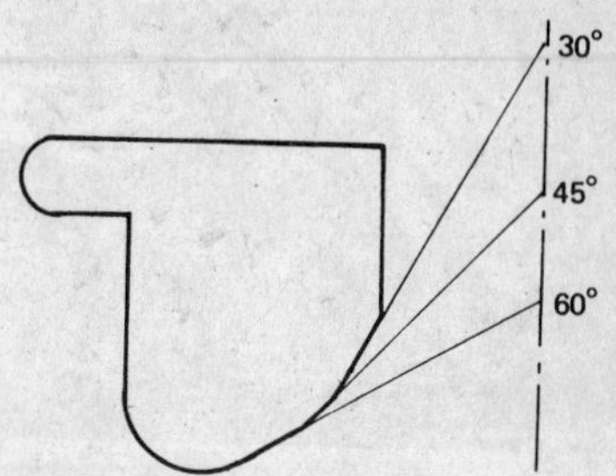

Valve seat dimensions

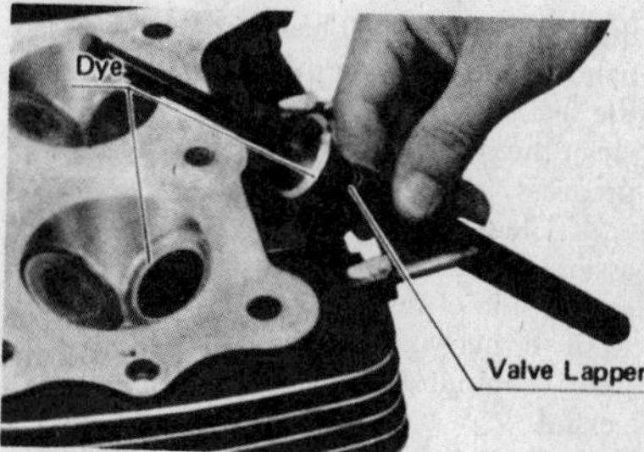

Checking valve/valve seat contact

and undamaged, and must measure 0.04–0.06 in. (1.0–1.5 mm). 30°, 45°, and two 60° cutters are available for valve seat repairs. Proceed in the following manner:

NOTE: *The following procedure will be of value only if the valve and seat are in good condition.*

a. Remove the valve and apply machinist's dye to the valve seat, then use a lapper to tap the valve lighty into place. The dye pattern on the valve will give an indication of the condition of the seat. Compare it with the illustration.

b. Carefully cut the seating surface with the 45° cutter, taking care to remove only as much metal as is necessary to provide a good surface.

c. Carefully cut the area inside the seting surface with the 30° cutter, and cut the area outside the seating surface with the 60° cutter. If done properly, the seating surface should be within the specified limits all the way around.

6. If the seat has just been cut, or if the seat looks alright and you just wish to ensure a good seal between the seat and valve, lap the valves in at this time in the following manner:

a. Lightly oil the valve stem and insert it into the guide.

b. Apply a light coat of lapping compound to the seat. It is best to apply a few evenly spaced daubs rather than a random application, and it's a good idea to start off with coarse compound and finish with fine compound.

c. Slip a gas line, or a valve lapper, over

Cutting a valve seat

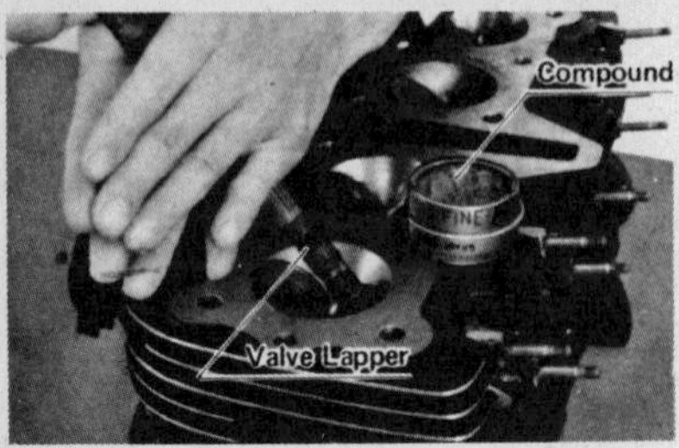

Lapping in a valve

the stem and rotate it back and forth in your hands while applying mild pressure against the seat by pulling on the gas line. Stop and clean the seat periodically to check on your progress.

d. Clean the seat area when smooth, and assemble the valve. Pour some gas into the spring side of the head and allow the head to sit. If there is no leakage through the seat after 15 minutes, the lapping has been successful.

7. Inspect the valve springs for a pitted, collapsed, or damaged condition, and replace them as necessary. Perform the following checks also:

a. Measure the valve spring free lengths using vernier calipers, and replace the springs as a complete set if any are shorter than the serviceable limits given below:

	Standard	*Service Limit*
Inner	1.42 in. (36.0 mm)	1.38 in. (35.0 mm)
Outer	1.55 in. (39.3 mm)	1.50 in. (38.0 mm)

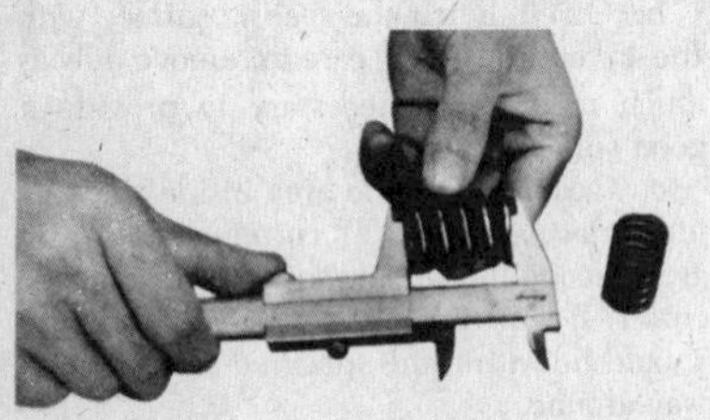
Checking valve spring free length

b. Stand each spring up on a flat surface, and set a perpendicular reference point next to it. If any spring is tilted more than 0.075 in. (1.9 mm) on 900 models or 0.059 in. (1.5 mm) on 1000 models, replace it.

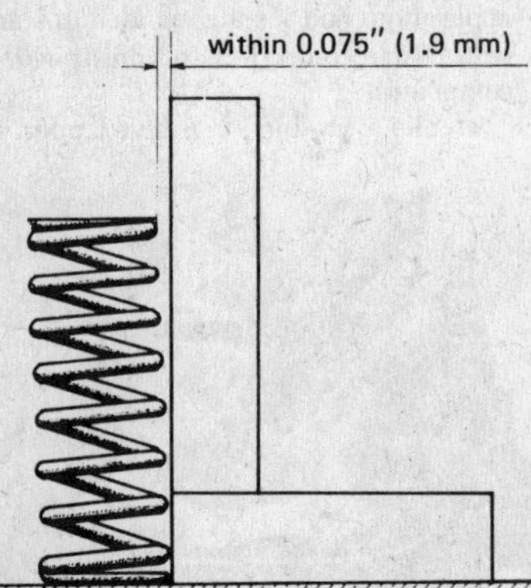

Measuring valve spring tilt

NOTE: *Valve springs should always be replaced as a complete set to assure efficient operation.*

8. Inspect the valve tappets and adjusting shims for signs of wear or damage and replace them as necessary.

NOTE: *The type of valve tappets used in all models up to engine number Z1E-08979 have caused shim fracturing problems on some machines. A new redesigned tappet (Part No. 12032-005) is available as a replacement for the old type (Part No. 12032-004). It is recommended that all old style tappets be replaced. The new type of tappet, recognizable by the lack of a navel in the tappet/shim mating area, can be used in conjunction with the shim already in use, however this is not recommended as the old shim may have begun to fracture.*

The old style tappets should be replaced

ASSEMBLY AND INSTALLATION

1. Assembly is basically in the reverse order of disassembly, and installation is in the reverse order of removal. Use new gaskets, valve guide seals, O-rings, and valve split keepers.

2. Install the circlip in its groove in the valve guide, and liberally oil the guide. Heat the area around the guide hole with a torch to about 250°–300° F (120°–150° C), and drive the guide in from the top of the head using either the special tool (Part No. 57001-108) or a suitable drift, until the circlip reaches its seat.

3. Use a 7 mm reamer to ream the guides. This must be done even if the old guides are used. Always rotate the reamer to the right, and keep rotating it as it's withdrawn.

Drifting in a valve guide

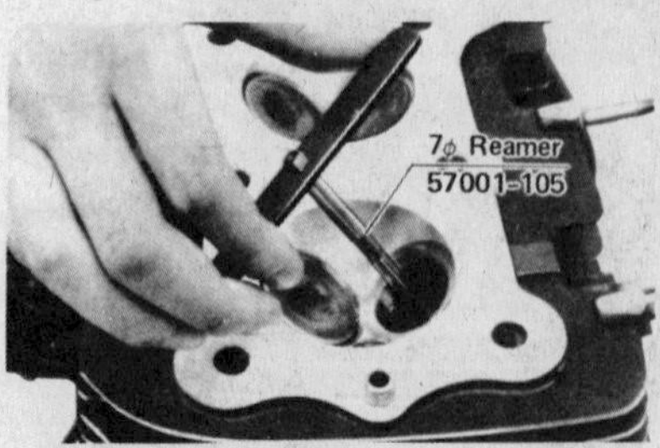

Reaming out a valve guide

4. Lap the valve into its seat as directed in the preceeding "Inspection and Repair" Section.

5. Install the tappets and shims to their original locations.

6. Use a new head gasket to prevent compression leakage, and install the gasket so the side with the wider folded-over metal edges is facing up.

Installing a new head gasket

7. Tighten the cylinder head nuts gradually and evenly to 25 ft lbs (3.5 kg/m) on 900 models or 27–31 ft lbs (3.7–4.3 kg/m) on the 1000 in the order shown in the accompanying illustration.

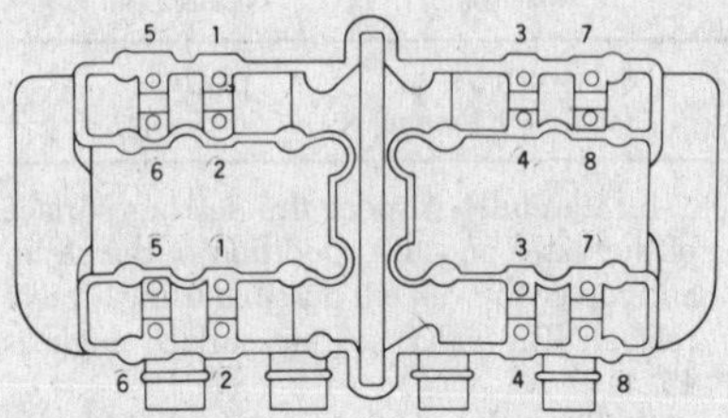

Bolt tightening pattern

8. Secure the two end bolts to 105 in. lbs (1.2 kg/m).

9. Adjust the valve clearances before installing the valve cover, and use a new cover gasket.

Cylinder and Piston

REMOVAL AND DISASSEMBLY

1. Remove the cylinder head as described in the previous Section, then remove the cam chain tensioner assembly and guide sprocket.

Removing the tensioner and guide sprocket assemblies

2. Loosen the cylinder block by gently tapping up on alternate ends with a soft mallet, then lift the cylinder and gasket off the crankcase studs. A pry point at the crankcase joint is provided on some models.

CAUTION: *As you lift the cylinder block, stuff clean rags in the crankcase openings to prevent foreign matter, such as broken rings, from falling into the crankcase, and to prevent possible piston damage caused by pistons striking the crankcase studs.*

3. Remove the piston pin circlips with a pair of needle-nosed pliers, then remove the piston pin with the special tool (Part No. 57001-114 for the 900, 57001-910/914 for the 1000) or a suitable substitute. The pins can be removed also by heating the piston crown with a torch, and driving the pin out while carefully supporting the connecting rod to prevent damage to it or the big end bearings. Keep the pins with their pistons, and mark the pistons for replcement in their original positions.

Removing the piston pin circlip

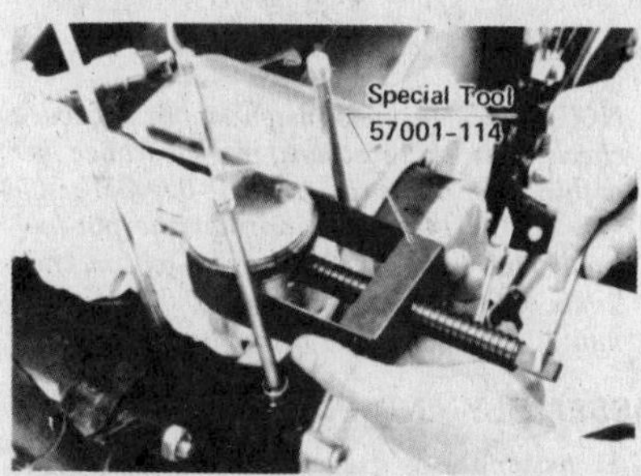

Removing the piston pin

4. Remove the piston rings using either the special tool (Part No. 57001-115), a suitable substitute, or by hand, taking care not to damage the piston. When removing rings by hand, spread the ring ends with your thumbs, and push up on the opposite side of the ring to remove it.

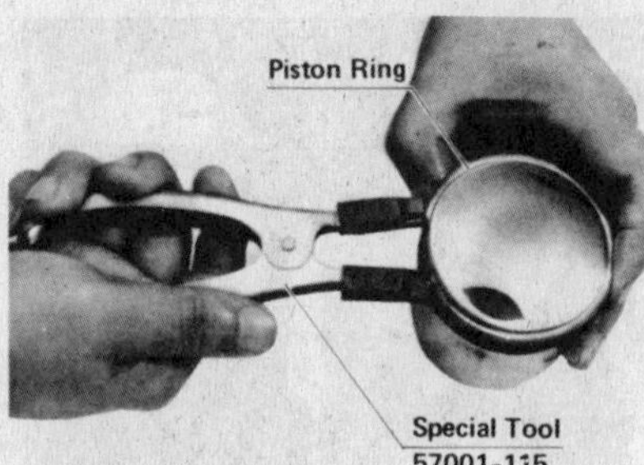

Removing the rings with the special tool

NOTE: *Do not remove the rings unless you are planning to replace them, as rings shouldn't be reused once they've been removed.*

INSPECTION

1. Clean all parts other than gaskets, O-rings, and seals, in a suitable solvent, then blow them dry taking care to blow clear all oil passages. Decarbonize all components as described in the preceding "Inspection" Section. Piston ring grooves can be cleaned with a broken piece of piston ring.

2. Inspect the cylinder block for damage to the cooling fins or either of the gasket mating surfaces, or for badly scored cylinder walls, and replace the assembly as necessary. Use a cylinder gauge to check the cylinder wall dimensions of each cylinder in the three areas shown, and take two measurements at 90° from one another, at each location. If any of the measurements exceeds the service limits given below, or if there is a difference of more than 0.002 in. (0.05 mm) between any two measurements, all the cylinders will have to be bored and honed.

900

Standard	*Service Limit*
2.5984 ~ 2.5992 in. (66.000 ~ 66.019 mm)	2.602 in. (66.10 mm)

1000

Standard	*Service Limit*
2.7559 ~ 2.7567 in. (70.000 ~ 70.019 mm)	2.7598 in. (70.10 mm)

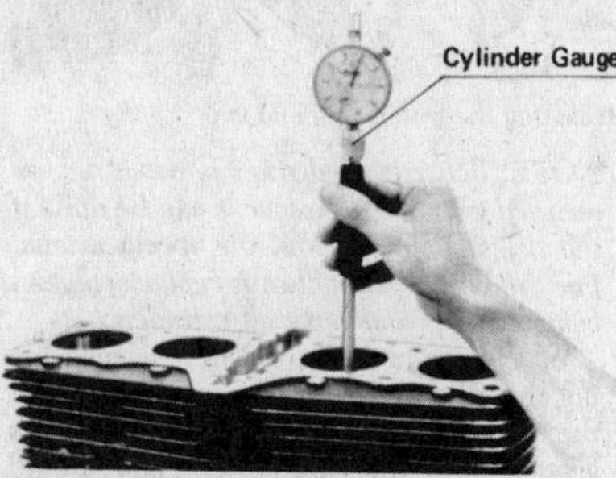

Measuring the cylinder bore

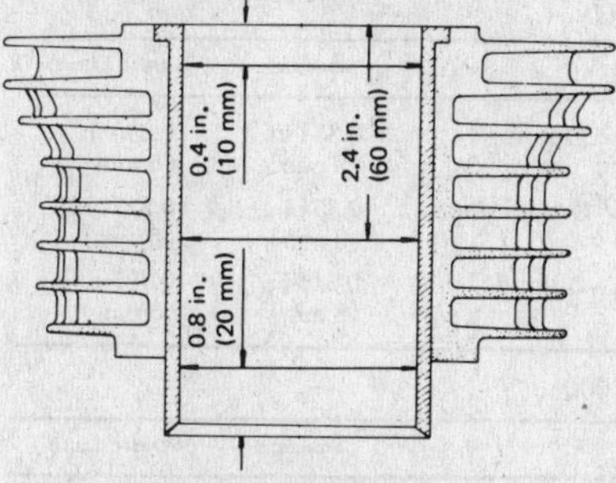

Cylinder bore measurement points

3. Measure the piston diameter at a point about 0.2 in. (5 mm) up from the bottom of the piston skirt and at right angles from the piston pin holes. Replace the piston if the diameter is under the service limits:

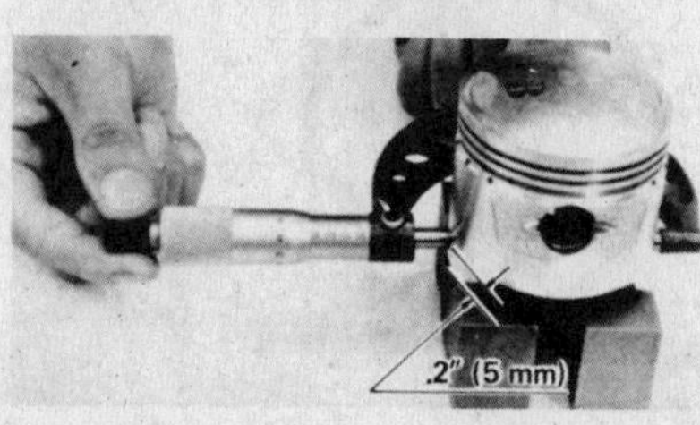

Measuring the piston

900

Standard	*Service Limit*
2.5956 ~ 2.5965 in. (65.93 ~ 65.95 mm)	2.590 in. (65.80 mm)

1000

Standard	*Service Limit*
2.7535 ~ 2.7543 in. (69.94 ~ 69.96 mm)	2.7480 in. (69.8 mm)

4. Subtract the piston diameter from the cylinder measurement to arrive at the piston/cylinder clearance. The clearance must be returned to standard whenever the cylinder is replaced or bored, however, if only the piston is replaced, clearance may exceed the limit, but must not be less than the minimum clearance of 0.0025–0.003 in. (0.060–0.079 mm) (900) or 0.0020–0.0028 in. (0.050–0.069 mm) (1000).

5. When boring and honing the cylinders, adhere to the following rules:

a. The inside diameter of any cylinder must not vary by more than 0.0004 in. (0.01 mm) at any point along its bore.

b. Replacement pistons are available in 0.020 in. (0.5 mm) and 0.040 in. (1.0 mm) oversizes. If boring in excess of 1 mm over standard is every necessary, the cylinder block must be replaced since replacement sleeves are not made available by the factory.

c. To avoid cylinder distortion due to unbalanced metal temperatures, bore the cylinders in either the 2-4-1-3 or 3-1-4-2 order.

d. Allow the metal to cool completely after boring before taking any measurements, as the diameter may change due to the temperature incease.

e. After the boring is completed, the piston/cylinder clearance should be returned to standard.

6. In the event of piston seizure in the bore, the cylinder should be honed, or at least smoothed out with #400 emery cloth, and the piston should be treated likewise. Make sure that the rings are till free if they aren't to be replaced. If the damage is heavy, the cylinder will have to be bored and the piston replaced. Try and determine why the piston seized before running the engine again. Look for air leaks, improper mixture adjustments, improper timing, or insufficient piston/cylnder clearance.

7. Inspect the piston rings and ring grooves for signs of wear or damage. The rings should be replaced if their condition is even slightly questionable, and the piston must be replaced if the ring grooves are unevenly worn or damaged. Make the following measurements:

Measuring the piston ring grooves

a. Measure the width of the ring grooves using a thickness gauge, and replace the piston if the grooves exceed the service limits given below:

900

	Standard	*Service Limit*
Top Groove	0.059 ~ 0.060 in. (1.50 ~ 1.52 mm)	0.063 in. (1.60 mm)
Second groove	0.059 ~ 0.060 in. (1.50 ~ 1.52 mm)	0.063 in. (1.60 mm)
Bottom groove	0.098 ~ 0.099 in. (2.50 ~ 2.52 mm)	0.102 in. (2.60 mm)

1000

	Standard	*Service Limit*
Top groove	0.048 ~ 0.049 in. (1.23 ~ 1.25 mm)	0.052 in. (1.33 mm)
Second groove	0.048 ~ 0.049 in. (1.22 ~ 1.24 mm)	0.052 in. (1.32 mm)
Bottom groove	0.099 ~ 0.100 in. (2.51 ~ 2.53 mm)	0.102 in. (2.60 mm)

b. Measure the thickness of the piston rings using a micrometer, and replace the rings if worn thinner than the service limits given below:

900

	Standard	*Service Limit*
Top ring	0.0567 ~ 0.0573 in. (1.440 ~ 1.455 mm)	0.0535 in. (1.36 mm)
Second ring	0.0579 ~ 0.0587 in. (1.470 ~ 1.490 mm)	0.055 in. (1.40 mm)
Oil ring	0.0973 ~ 0.0980 in. (2.470 ~ 2.490 mm)	0.0945 in. (2.40 mm)

1000

	Standard	*Service Limit*
Top and Second rings	0.0461 ~ 0.0469 in. (1.170 ~ 1.190 mm)	0.0433 in. (1.10 mm)

c. Measure the clearance between the ring grooves and rings using a thickness gauge at various pints around the piston, and replace the necessary components if the clearance exceeds the service limits given below:

900

	Standard	*Service Limit*
Top ring	0.0018 ~ 0.0031 in. (0.045 ~ 0.080 mm)	0.007 in. (0.18 mm)
Second ring	0.0004 ~ 0.0020 in.	0.006 in.
Oil ring	(0.010 ~ 0.050 mm)	(0.15 mm)

1000

	Standard	*Service Limit*
Top ring	0.0016 ~ 0.0032 in. (0.040 ~ 0.080 mm)	0.0059 in. (0.15 mm)
Second ring	0.0012 ~ 0.0028 in. (0.030 ~ 0.070 mm)	0.0059 in. (0.15 mm)

d. Measure ring end gap by placing the ring in a new cylinder, and using a thickness gauge to determine wear. If a new cylinder is not available, make the measurement at the bottom of the least worn cylinder where wear is minimal. If the gap is less than the limits given below, the ring ends can be filed as long as care is taken to file them flat, and if all burrs are removed. If the gap is worn greater than the service limits, the ring must be replaced.

900

Standard	*Service Limit*
0.008 ~ 0.016 in. (0.2 ~ 0.4 mm)	0.028 in. (0.7 mm)

1000

Standard	*Service Limit*
0.012 ~ 0.020 in. (0.30 ~ 0.50 mm)	0.032 in. (0.8 mm)

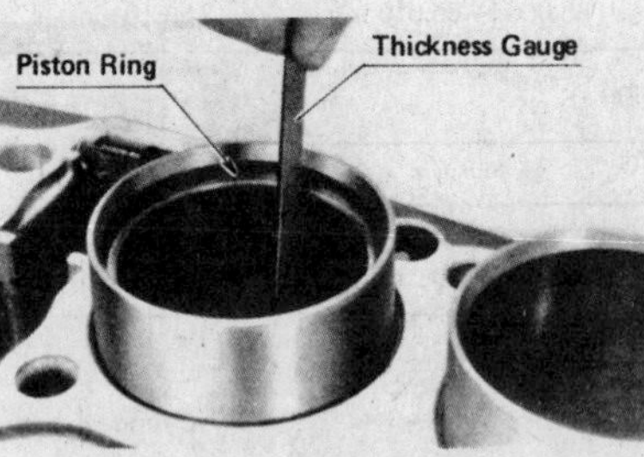

Measuring the piston ring end gap

NOTE: *Reusing used rings is not a recommended practice, however it can be done if the rings conform to all the specifications. For the best results, always replace rings in complete sets and hone all cylinders.*

e. Determine ring tension by measuring the ring gap while the ring is free. If the gap is less than the service limits given below, the ring is weak and should be replaced.

900

	Standard	*Service Limit*
Top ring	0.354 in. (9 mm)	0.236 in. (6 mm)
Second ring	0.354 in. (9 mm)	0.236 in. (6 mm)
Oil ring	0.315 in. (8 mm)	0.197 in. (5 mm)

1000

	Standard	*Service Limit*
Top ring	0.28 in. (7.0 mm)	0.16 in. (4.0 mm)
Second ring	0.32 in. (8.0 mm)	0.20 in. (5.0 mm)

Determining ring tension

8. Measure the diameter of the piston pin using a micrometer, then measure the inside diameter of the piston pin hole in the piston, and the diameter of the connecting rod small end bearing. Replace the necessary components if the pin diameter is too small, or if the pin hole or bearing diameter is too large as indicated by the service limits given below:

	Standard	*Service Limit*
Piston pin	0.6691 ~ 0.6693 in. (16.994 ~ 17.000 mm)	0.6677 in. (16.96 mm)
Piston pin hole	0.6694 ~ 0.6701 in. (17.0035 ~ 17.0115 mm)	0.6724 in. (17.08 mm)
Small end O.D.	0.6694 ~ 0.6698 in. (17.003 ~ 17.014 mm)	0.6713 in. (17.05 mm)

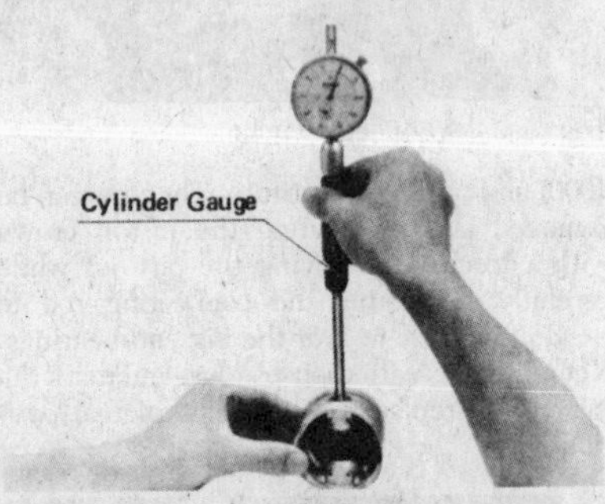

Measuring the piston pin hole

NOTE: *When a new piston or pin is used, check that the piston-to-pin clearance is within the limits of 0.0026–0.00057 in. (0.0066–0.0145 mm), and that the pin-to-small end bearing clearance is within the limits of 0.00012–0.00079 in. (0.003–0.020 mm), and replace any necessary parts.*

ASSEMBLY AND INSTALLATION

1. Assembly is basically in the reverse order of disassembly, and installation is in the reverse order of removal. Use new gaskets, seals, O-rings, and piston pin circlips.
2. Liberally lubricate the piston pins before installing them, and install the pistons so that the arrow marked on the piston crown points forward.

Be sure that the pistons are installed correctly

On 1000 models, if parts such as pistons or piston pins are being replaced, note the following:

a. Some piston pins are marked on the edge, and these should be used with pistons marked "A." Unmarked pins should be used with "B" pistons.

b. Install pistons marked "2" in cylinder bores with the same number, and unnumbered pistons in unnumbered bores.

CAUTION: *Do not attempt to drive in a pin without firmly supporting the connecting rod to prevent possible damage to the rod and big end bearing. Heat the piston crown with a torch or heated rags as an aid in installation.*

3. Always use new piston pin circlips, taking care to position the clip so that its open end is not aligned with either groove in the piston.

4. Install the piston rings with their lettered "N") side up. Be careful not to mix the first and second rings. The outer edge of the top ring is chamfered, and the lower outer edge of the second ring is notched as illustrated.

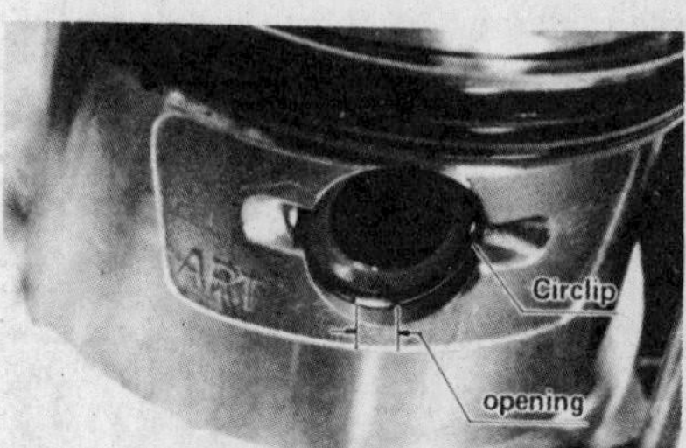

This will prevent the clip from coming free

Install the rings with the "N" up

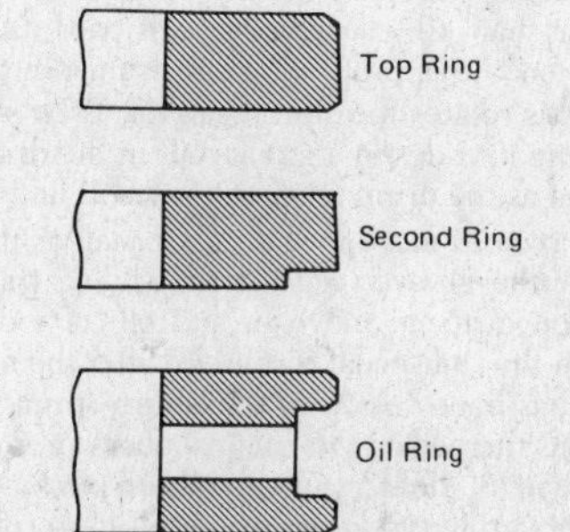

The rings must go on the correct lands

NOTE: *The green coating on the top and bottom rings is to prevent scuffing, and is not intended to be permanent.*

5. Place the two alignment pins into the forward tension stud hole on either side of the crankcase. **Do not put the pins into the rear holes.** Apply a small amount of liquid gasket to the four innermost rear studs. Install the cylinder base gasket.

6. Rotate the top and bottom rings so that their end gaps are facing forward, and the center ring so that its gap faces the rear. On models with three-piece oil rings, stagger the rails about 30° on either side of the expander gap. Thoroughly lubricate the pistons and rings with fresh engine oil.

7. Lift up the cam chain so that it doesn't get caught, then rotate the crankshaft until all of the pistons are at about the same hight, and install the positioning rods (Part No. 57001-112 for the 900, 57001-532 for the 1000) to

Alignment pin installation

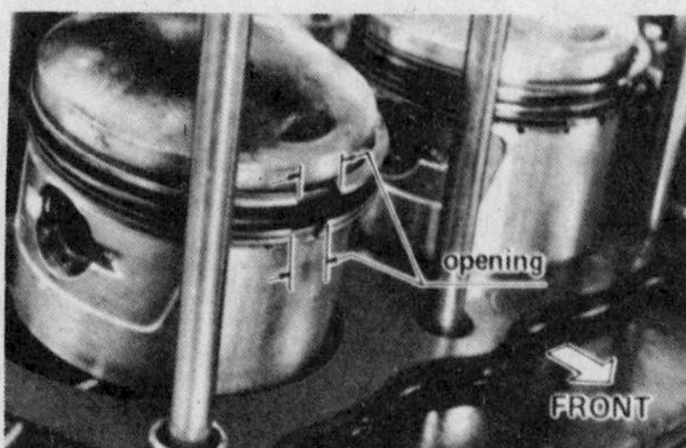

Aligning the ring gaps for maximum compression

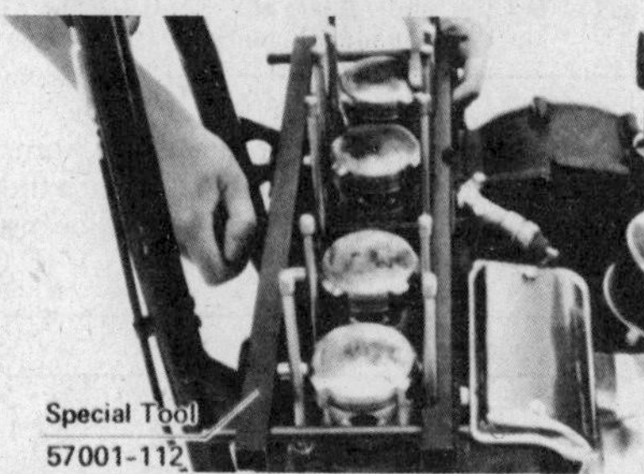

Lining up the pistons with the special tool

hold them level. Wooden slats can be used effectively in place of the special tool.

8. Compress the piston rings using either the special positioning rod or ring compressors lubricate the cylinder walls thoroughly with fresh engine oil, and start the cylinder block down on the pistons. The ring compressors will have to be lowered and then removed as the rings enter the cylinder. Remove the positioning rod after the rings are in the bore.

NOTE: *It's a good idea to enlist the aid of a second set of hands during this operation so that one person can work with the cylinder block, and the other can keep track of the ring situation.*

9. After the engine is fully assembled, tuned, and lubricated, crank it through several times before actually starting it to ensure adequate lubrication of the top end components.

CRANKCASE COVER COMPONENTS

Clutch

DISASSEMBLY

1. Drain the engine oil as described in the "Maintenance" section. The oil in the oil filter, and the filter assembly, can be left as is.

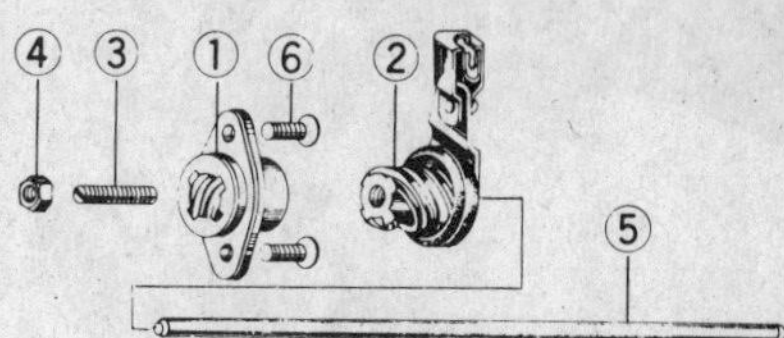

Clutch release mechanism assembly

1. Outer release gear
2. Inner release gear
3. Adjusting screw
4. Locknut
5. Pushrod
6. Screw

2. Remove the clutch cover and cover gasket, then remove the pressure plate bolts, clutch springs, and the pressure plate.

Removing the pressure plate bolts

3. Remove the clutch pushrod, and tilt the motorcycle so the steel ball (release bearing) will fall out.

NOTE: *The clutch assembly need not be further disassembled unless the clutch hub or housing is damaged.*

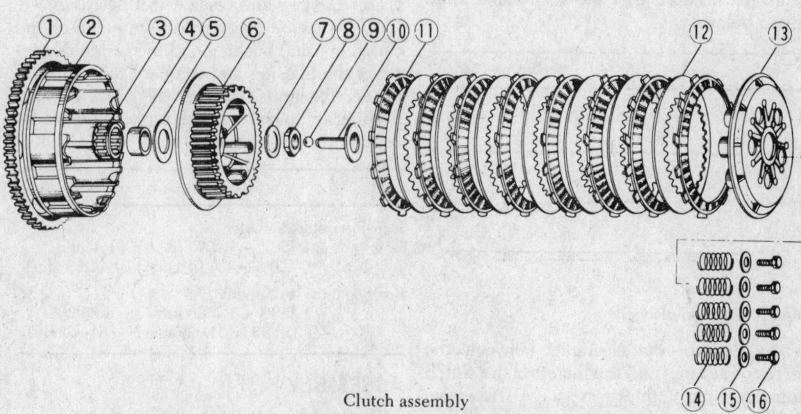

Clutch assembly

1. Reduction drive gear
2. Clutch housing
3. Needle bearing
4. Bushing
5. Washer
6. Clutch hub
7. Washer
8. Nut
9. Steel ball
10. Pusher
11. Friction plate
12. Steel plate
13. Pressure plate
14. Clutch spring
15. Washer
16. Bolt

4. Remove the clutch plates by either tilting the bike or by lifting them out with a hooked piece of wire, then keep the clutch hub from turning by using either the special tool (Part No. 57001-119) or a suitable substitute, and remove the hub mounting nut.

5. Remove the outer washer, the hub, and the inner washer. Clutch housing removal will necessitate complete engine disassembly with the engine removed from the frame as described in the "Splitting the Crankcases" Section.

Removing the release bearing

Removing the hub mounting nut

6. Remove the chain cover as described in the "Final Drive" Section of the "Chassis" section, then remove the clutch release inner gear by twisting it out, and the outer gear.

INSPECTION

1. Clean all parts other than the cover gasket and the friction plates in a suitable solvent, then blow them dry.

2. Inspect the clutch plates and discs for a worn, damaged, scored, or burned condition, and replace them as necessary. Friction discs should be replaced as a complete set if any are damaged or worn past the serviceable limits given below:

Standard	*Service Limit*
0.146 ~ 0.154 in. (3.7 ~3.9 mm)	0.134 in. (3.4 mm)

Measure friction plates here

3. Measure the clearance between the friction disc tangs and the fingers of the clutch housing using a thickness gauge. Excessive clearance will result in noisy operation. If you replace the discs check the clearance again, and if it still exceeds the service limit given below, replace the housing.

Standard	*Service Limit*
0.002 ~ 0.012 in. (0.04 ~ 0.30 mm)	0.020 in. (0.5 mm)

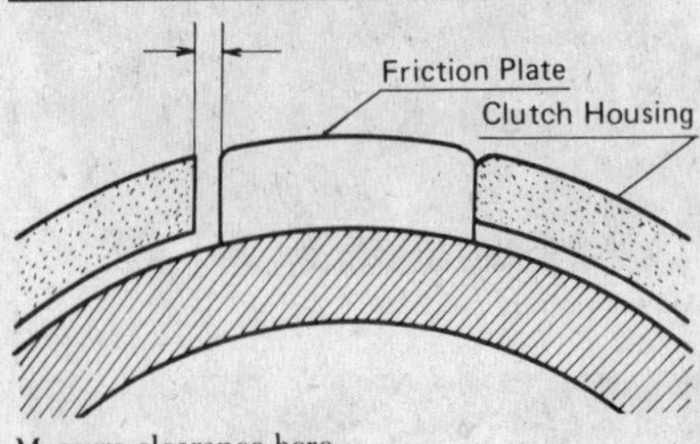

Measure clearance here

4. Place the clutch plates on a flat surface, and use a thickness gauge to measure warpage. Replace any plate if it is warped more than the limits given below:

	Standard	*Service Limit*
Friction plate	under 0.006 in. (under 0.15 mm)	0.012 in. (0.30 mm)
Steel plate	under 0.008 in. (under 0.20 mm)	0.016 in. (0.40 mm)

5. Inspect the clutch springs for a worn, pitted, or collapsed condition, and replace the entire set if any are worn past the following free length limits:

Standard	*Service Limit*
1.33 in. (33.8 mm)	1.27 in. (32.3 mm)

6. Inspect the clutch hub and housing for signs of wear or damage, and replace them as necessary. Light damage to any gear teeth can be repaired with an oilstone, but severely damage teeth, fingers, or hub splines will necessitate replacing the housing and/or hub.

7. Inspect the clutch pushrod, release bearing, and worm teeth of the release gears for signs of wear, pitting, or damage, and replace them as necessary. The release gears must be replaced as a set.

8. Inspect the pressure plate for signs of wear, fatigue, cracks, or severe warpage, and replace it as necessary.

9. Inspect the clutch housing needle bearing for signs of discoloration, wear, or other visible damage and replace it if necessary.

10. Measure the outside diameter of the clutch housing bushing and the inside diameter of the housing and compare the values to the service limits. If either the housing or the bushing are to be replaced, replace the needle bearing as well.

	Standard	*Service Limit*
Housing inside diameter	1.4567 ~ 1.4573 in. (37.000 ~ 37.016 mm)	1.458 in. (37.03 mm)
Bushing outside diameter	1.2590 ~ 1.2596 in. (31.980 ~ 31.995 mm)	1.258 in. (31.96 mm)

ASSEMBLY

1. Assembly is basically in the reverse order of disassembly. Use a new cover gasket.

2. Keep the clutch hub from rotating as in the disassembly procedure, and secure the hub nut to 87–108 ft lbs (12–15 kg/m). Remember that the correct order is washer-hub-washer-hub nut.

NOTE: *The washer between the clutch hub and the hub nut has "outside" marked on it and must be properly installed.*

3. Install the friction and steel plates, starting with a friction disc and then alternating them.

4. Install the release bearing and pushrod in the driveshaft, then install the pressure plate, springs, washers, and mounting bolts, securing them in a cross pattern. Tighten the bolts to 78–98 in. lbs (0.9–1.1 kg/m).

5. Liberally lubricate the two release gears with cup grease before installing them. The release lever should be positioned as illustrated.

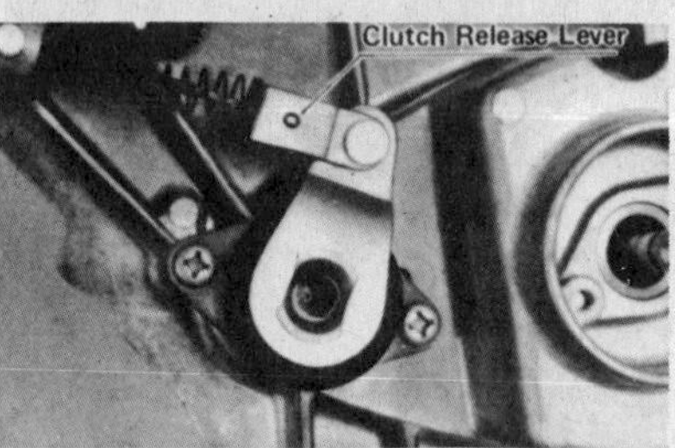

The release lever should be positioned like this

6. Secure the outer gear mounting after applying Loctite® or a suitable thread sealer, to the threads.

7. Refill the engine with oil.

External Shift Mechanism

Operating the shift pedal (1) rotates the shifter shaft (2), causing the shift pawl (3) to catch on the appropriate shift drum pin (4), and this rotates the shift drum (5). Each shift fork pin (6) rides in a groove cut in the drum, so that as the drum turns the forks (21 and 22) are forced to move to the right or left as they follow the groove, causing the sliding transmission gears to move in and out of mesh. When the shift pedal is released after the next gear has been selected, the return spring (7) returns the pedal to its original position. A detent arm (8), held against the drum pin by the detent spring (9), keeps the drum from rotating which would cause the transmission to pop out of gear. A Neutral detent pin (11), fitted inside the shift drum positioning pin (10), and acted on by a spring (12), drops into the drum positioning groove when the drum is rotated into the Neutral position.

Worn or broken parts could allow the shift drum to turn randomly, resulting in damage to the transmission and engine (through over-revving). A transmission which will not shift can often be traced to a damaged return spring, shift pawl, or pawl spring, and a tired or broken detent arm spring can cause a transmission to stick in gear or pop out of gear under power.

REMOVAL

1. Remove the chain cover and drive-sprocket as described in the "Final Drive" Section of the "Chassis" section.

2. Disconnect the Neutral switch lead.

3. Remove the transmission cover, cover gasket, sprocket distance collar, and O-ring. A

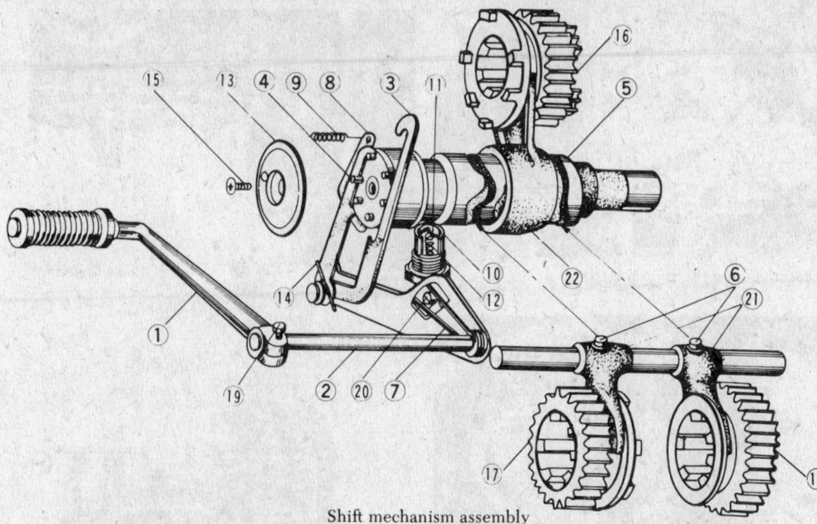

Shift mechanism assembly

1. Shift pedal
2. Shaft
3. Shift pawl
4. Shift drum pin
5. Shift drum
6. Shift fork pin
7. Return spring
8. Detent arm
9. Detent arm spring
10. Shift drum positioning pin
11. Neutral detent pin
12. Spring
13. Shift drum pin holder
14. Pawl spring
15. Screw
16. Drive 3rd gear
17. Output 5th gear
18. Output 4th gear
19. Bolt
20. Return spring pin
21. Shift fork
22. Shift fork

Neutral Switch

Disconnecting the neutral switch lead

"O" Ring

Sprocket Collar

bearing puller may be used if the collar proves difficult to remove.

4. Remove the shift lever assembly and detent lever mounting bolt, then unhook the spring and remove the lever.

INSPECTION

1. Clean all parts other than gaskets and O-rings in a suitable solvent, then blow them dry.
2. Inspect the shift lever spring, shift pawls, pawl spring, and detent arm spring for signs of wear or damage, and replace them as necessary.
3. Measure the free length of the detent arm spring using vernier calipers, and replace it if it is longer than the service limits given below:

Standard	*Service Limit*
0.917 in. (23.3 mm)	0.984 in. (25.0 mm)

INSTALLATION

1. Check the return spring pin for a tight fit, and remove it and coat the threads with Loctite before installing it if it was loose.

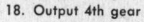

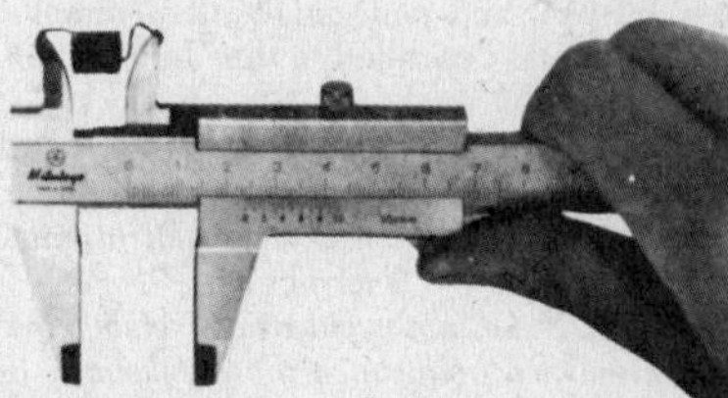

Measuring the return spring free length

Make sure that the return spring pin is secure

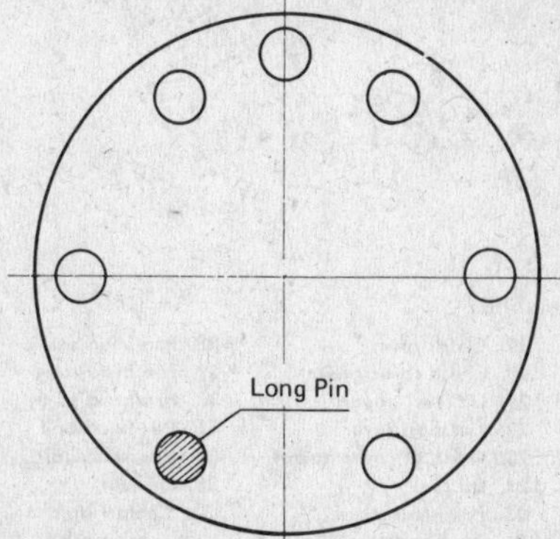

Correct positioning of the long pin is essential

Long pin installed

2. Make sure that the longest shift drum pin is in the position illustrated, if the pins were removed. Failure to properly position the long pin will keep the Neutral light from operating correctly.
3. Install the detent lever taking care to position it so that it rides on the shoulder of its mounting bolt, and so that it doesn't get caught between the bolt and crankcase.

The detent lever must be able to move freely

4. Install a new O-ring behind the sprocket to prevent oil leakage.
5. Use an oil seal guide (Part No. 57001-130) or a suitable substitute while installing the transmission cover so that the shift shaft seal isn't damaged.
6. Install the sprocket collar after the transmission cover is installed to avoid damaging the output shaft oil seal.
7. Grease the pushrod before installing it.

Always use a new O-ring to be sure

Protecting the seal will pay off

LOWER END AND TRANSMISSION

Splitting the Crankcases

DISASSEMBLY

1. Remove the engine from the frame as described in the "Engine Removal and Installation" Section.

2. Remove the kickstarter pedal, spring cover, and cover gasket, then pull out the spring guide and unhook and remove the spring.

Removing the kick starter spring

3. Remove the clutch hub as described in the "Clutch" Section only if the clutch housing or ball bearing is to be removed from the driveshaft..

4. Remove the contact breaker cover, breaker plate assembly, and advance mechanism as described in the "Electrical System" section, then remove the right-side engine cover.

5. Disconnect the leads from the Neutral light switch and the oil pressure switch.

6. Remove the dynamo wires from the clamps, then remove the dynamo cover and cover gasket.

7. Remove the transmission cover and cover gasket, then remove the sprocket distance dollar and O-ring. A bearing puller may be used to remove the collar if necessary.

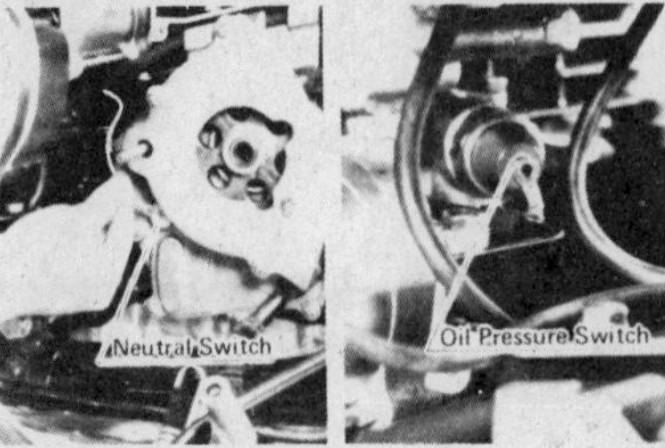

Disconnecting the switch leads

8. Remove the shift lever assembly.

9. Remove the starter assembly.

10. Remove the 5 crankcase bolts from the top side of the crankcase. The two cable clamps will also come free, and these should be replaced in their original positions.

11. Invert the engine and remove the oil filter, oil pan, and pan gasket, then remove the oil pump as described in the "Lubrication System" section.

12. Remove the 17 6 mm crankcase bolts (two of which have cable clamps under them and both should be replaced in their original positions), and the 8 8 mm bolts.

CAUTION: *Do not accidentally remove the 4 bolts which hold down the crankshaft.*

Cable clamp locations

Remove the crankcase bolts evenly

13. Screw 3 8 mm bolts into the jack bolt positions provided in the lower crankcase, and turn them in evenly to separate the crankcase halves. The cases can be gently tapped with a soft mallet to help loosen them.

CAUTION: *Do not attempt to pry the cases apart.*

Jack bolt positions

14. Remove the driveshaft, clutch housing, output shaft, and kickstarter shaft.

INSPECTION

1. Clean all metal components in a suitable solvent, then blow them dry taking care to clear all oil passages.

2. Inspect the crankcases, studs, clutch housing, and component systems for signs of wear or damage, and either repair or replace

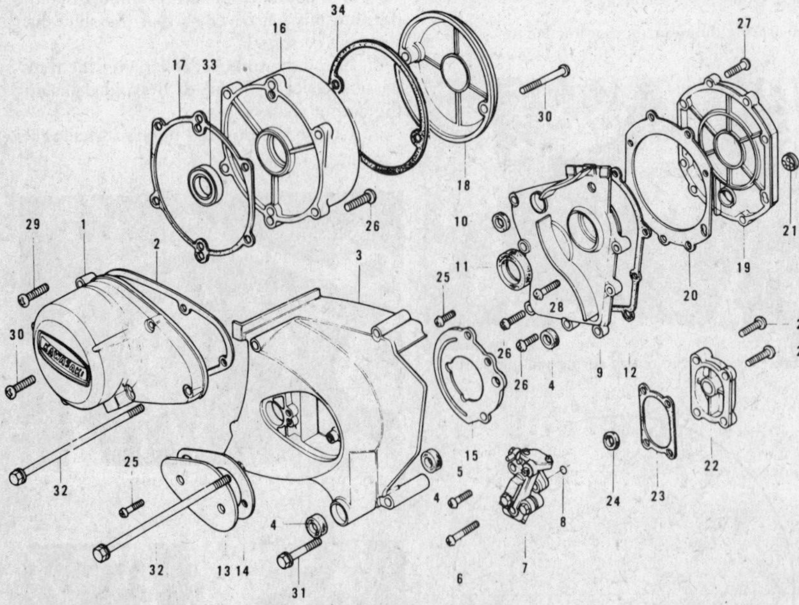
Engine cover assemblies

1. L.H. engine cover
2. L.H. engine cover gasket
3. Front chain cover
4. Oil seal
5. Pan head screw
6. Pan head screw
7. Oil pump assy
8. Oil pump O-ring
9. Transmission cover
10. Oil seal
11. Oil seal
12. Transmission cover gasket
13. Oil pump cover
14. Oil pump cover gasket
15. Engine sprocket cover
16. R.H. engine cover
17. R.H. engine cover gasket
18. Contact breaker cap
19. Clutch cover
20. Clutch cover gasket
21. Oil level gauge
22. Kickshaft cover
23. Kickshaft cover gasket
24. Oil seal
25. Pan head screw
26. Pan head screw
27. Pan head screw
28. Pan head screw
29. Pan head screw
30. Pan head screw
31. Hex head bolt
32. Hex head bolt
33. Oil seal
34. Contact breaker cap gasket

The assemblies ready for removal

them as necessary. For further disassembly procedures for the kick starter, driveshaft, output shaft, shift drum, crankshaft, and cam chain, follow the following "Assembly" Section.

ASSEMBLY

1. Assembly is basically in the reverse order of disassembly. Use all new gaskets, seals, and O-rings wherever applicable.

2. Install the O-ring for the main engine oil passage as illustrated.

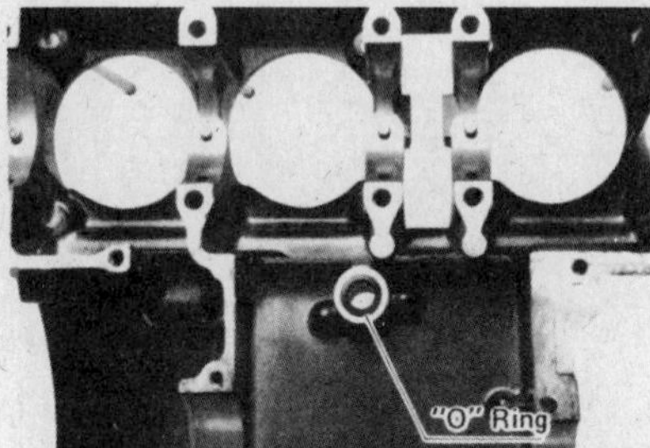

Main oil passage O-ring location

Be sure to install all the pins

3. When installing the output, drive, and kick starter shafts, the crankcase set pins must go into the holes in the respective bushings on the shafts, and the set ring for each ball bearing must be fit into its groove.

4. Thoroughly clean the crankcase mating surfaces, and apply a liquid gasket compound to the surface of the lower case half. Be careful not to use so much compound that it runs down into the crankcase after the halves are joined.

5. Secure the 8 8 mm bolts to 18 ft lbs (2.5 kg/m) torque, evenly following the order numbers on the lower case half. The threads of bolts 6 and 8 should be *coated with Loctite, and* #1 sealer (the hardening type) should be applied to the underside of the bolt heads.

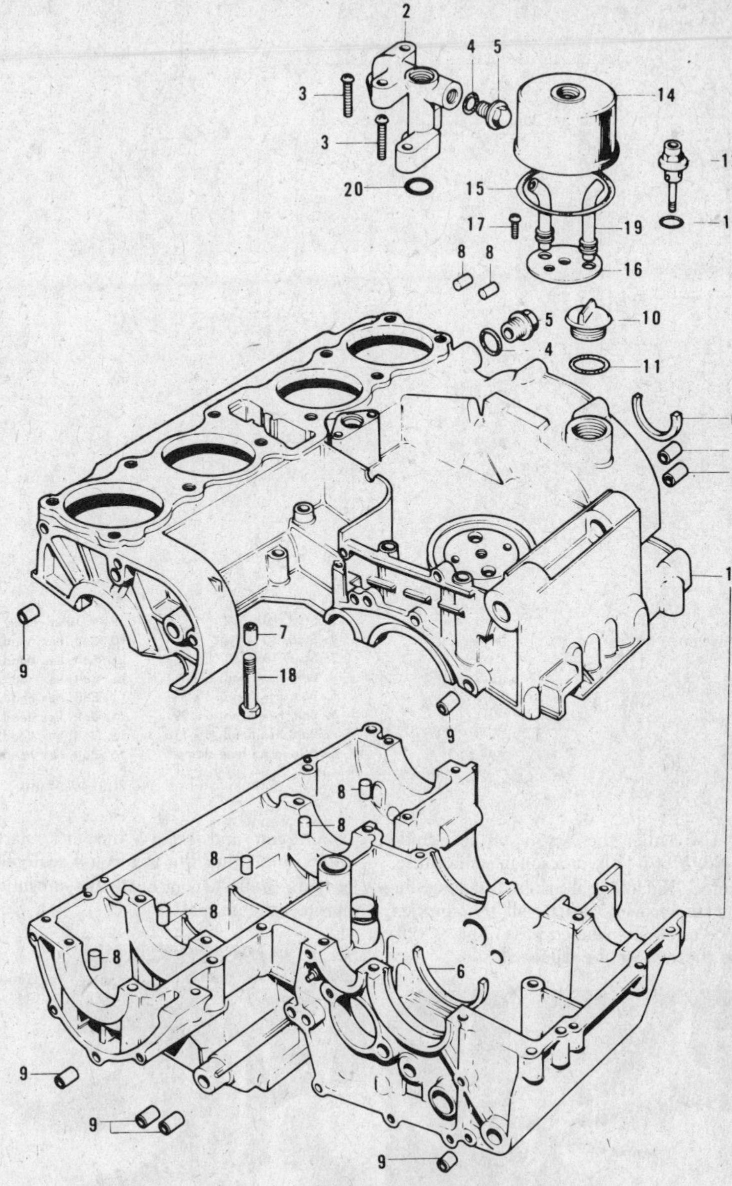

Crankcase assembly

1. Crank case set
2. Pipe
3. Pan head screw
4. O-ring
5. Plug
6. Ring, bearing set
7. Dowel pin
8. Dowel pin
9. Dowel pin
10. Oil filler plug
11. O-ring
12. Breather bolt
13. O-ring
14. Breather body
15. Breather body O-ring
16. Breather plate
17. Pan head screw
18. Hex head bolt
19. Tube
20. O-ring

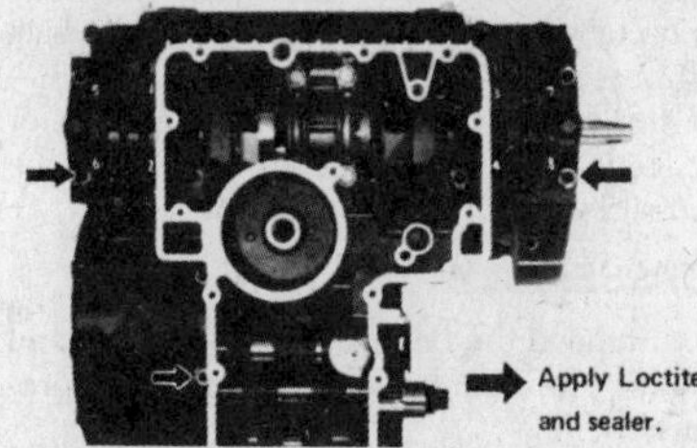

Bolts which must be sealed

6. Secure the 22 6 mm bolts to 70 in. lbs (0.8 kg/m). Coat the threads of the remaining bolt depicted in the accompanying illustration with Loctite, and apply #1 sealer (the hardening type) to the underside of the bolt head.

7. Install the O-ring depicted in the accompanying illustration, and check that the oil pump gear meshes correctly with the crankshaft gear when installing the pump. Apply Loctite to the pump mounting bolts, and secure them to 70 in. lbs (0.8 kg/m) torque.

8. To aid in installing the starter, lightly oil the O-ring.

9. Install the O-ring on the output shaft before installing the transmission cover to prevent oil leaks.

Installing the oil pump

Output shaft O-ring

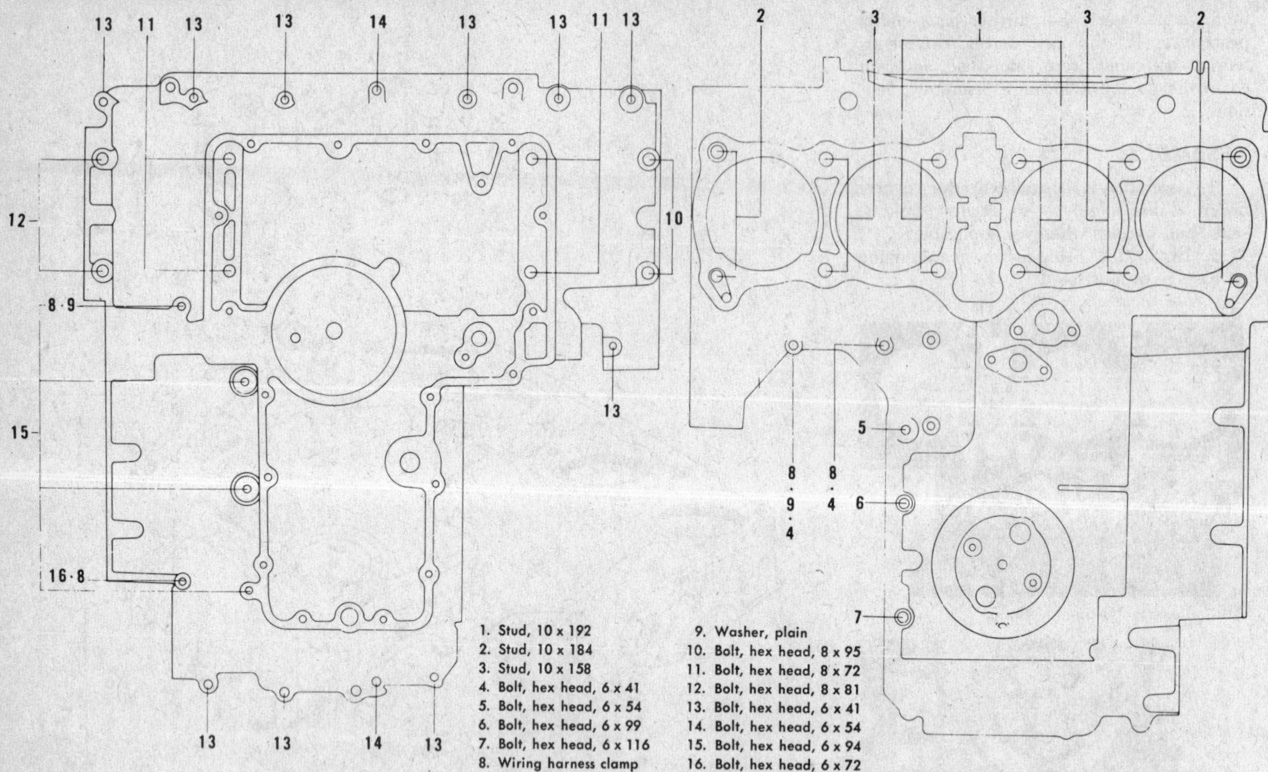

Crankcase bolt and stud locations

10. Use either the factory oil seal guide (Part No. 57001-130), or a suitable substitute, to protect the oil seal while installing the transmission cover, and install the sprocket distance collar after the cover is in place, otherwise the seal will be damaged.

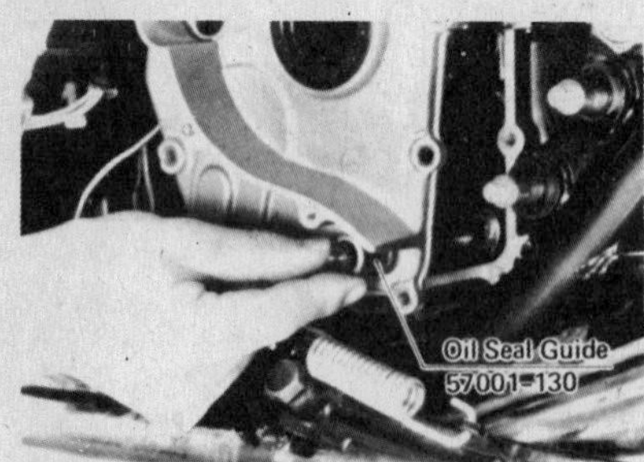

Installing the transmission cover

11. Apply Loctite to the 3 upper right engine cover mounting screws.
12. Align the pin and groove when installing the advance mechanism.
13. Rotate the kickstarter shaft all the way to the right before hooking the spring into the hole in the shaft.

The kickstarter must be preloaded before the spring is installed

14. Mount and secure the kick starter cover, using either the factory oil seal guide (Part No. 57001-131) or a suitable substitute, to protect the oil seal.

Installing the kick starter cover

Kick Starter

The kick gear ⑧ which is constructed with a ratchet on one side, is always meshed with 1st gear of the output shaft, and turns freely any time the output shaft is turning. The kick shaft ① is splined, and a ratchet gear ③ mounted on this shaft is pushed toward the kick gear by a spring ④. When no kicking is being done, however, the lever on the ratchet gear hits a stopper ⑥, and the ratchet gear is prevented from meshing with the kick gear ratchet.

When the pedal ② is kicked, the lever moves out from behind the stopper and the ratchet gear meshes with the kick gear ratchet. The kick gear then turns, turning the output shaft 1st gear which turns the crankshaft over via the driveshaft 1st gear and the clutch gear, and starts the engine.

When the kick pedal ② is released, the kick spring ⑤ returns the pedal to its original position. As the pedal returns, the ratchet gear lever (and the ratchet gear) is guided away from the kick gear by the stopper, and the ratchet gear returns to its rest position.

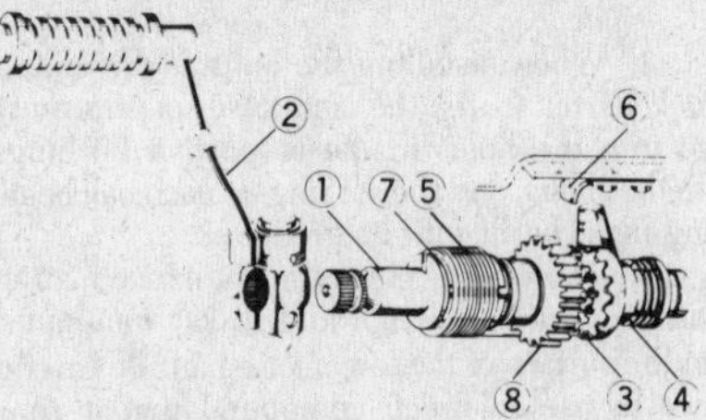
Kick starter assembly

1. Kick shaft
2. Kick pedal
3. Ratchet gear
4. Spring
5. Kick spring
6. Stopper
7. Spring guide
8. Kick gear

If the kick pedal return spring weakens or breaks, the kick pedal will not return completely or at all, and the ratchets will stay partially meshed and make noise while the engine is running. Kick mechanism noise may also occur when the kick gear bushing or kick shaft becomes worn.

If the teeth of either ratchet are worn or damaged, the ratchet will slip and it will be impossible to kickstart the engine.

DISASSEMBLY

1. Remove the engine from the frame, and separate the crankcases as described previously.
2. Remove the circlip (1), cap (2), coil spring (3), ratchet (4), circlips (1), washer (5), kick gear (6), washer (7), and bushing (8) from the kick shaft (10).

INSPECTION

1. Clean all parts in a suitable solvent, then blow them dry.

2. If the kick starter made a ratcheting noise while the engine was running, check the pedal return spring and the kick gear bushing and shaft for wear. Wear on these parts, and damage to the kick gear teeth are the most common kick starter problems. If any of these parts appear worn, pitted, collapsed (in the case of the spring), or damaged, they should be replaced. The ratcheting gears should be replaced as a set if either is damaged, as indicated by slipping of the kick starter pedal.

3. Measure the inside diameter of the kick gear, and replace it if it is worn past its service limit given below:

Standard	Service Limit
0.8653 ~ 0.8661 in. (21.979 ~ 22.000 mm)	0.8681 in. (22.05 mm)

4. Measure the outside diameter of the kick start shaft, and replace it if it is worn past its service limit given below:

Standard	Service Limit
0.8637 ~ 0.8646 in. (21.939 ~ 21.960 mm)	0.8626 in. (21.91 mm)

ASSEMBLY

1. Assembly is basically in the reverse order of disassembly. The oil seal (13) should be replaced.

2. When the ratchet is assembled to the kick shaft, align the mark on the ratchet with the mark on the shaft.

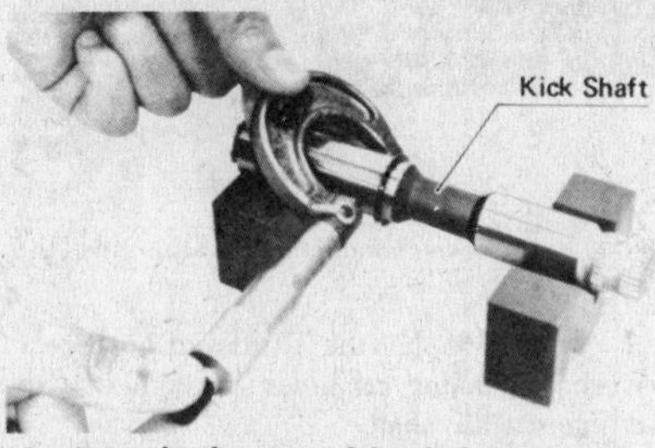

Measuring the diameter of the shaft

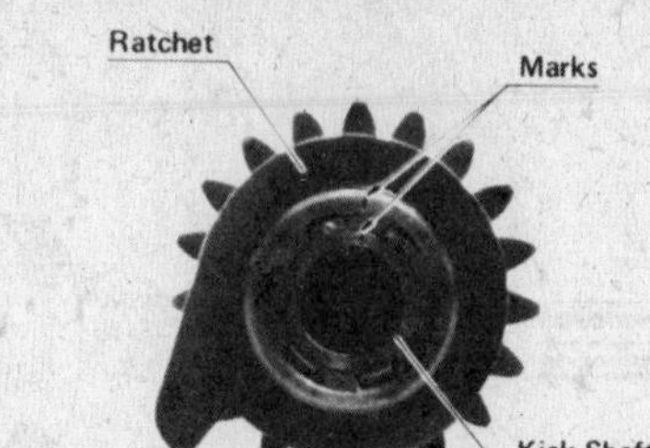

These marks must be alignment

Transmission

A 5-speed, constant mesh, return-shift type transmission, housed in the crankcases, is used on these models to put the power on the ground. The driveshaft runs off the clutch, and drives the output shaft which drives the chain which drives the rear wheel.

The 3 shift forks ride on gears D3 ("D" means Driveshaft, "O" means Output shaft, and the number indicates which gear), O4, and O5, and can move them along the shaft, although each gear must rotate with its shaft. Gears D1 and D2 are fixed to the driveshaft; gears D4, D5, O1, O2, and O3 are free to rotate on the shaft, but cannot move along the shaft.

Inside gear O4, 3 steel balls are located 120° apart, and serve to facilitate Neutral location when shifting from 1st gear. When the motorcycle is stopped and the output shaft is not turning, one or two of these balls falls down into its respective groove in the output shaft. When the shift pedal is operated to shift from First toward Second, gear O4 starts moving, but halfway toward its Second gear position, the steel ball(s) hits the end of the groove(s) in the output shaft, stopping gear O4 from moving, stopping the shift drum from turning, and leaving the transmission gears in the Neutral position.

Trouble in shifting could be caused by wear of the shift forks, the shift fork grooves in the gears, shift fork guide pins, or the grooves in the shift drum. It could also be the result of bent shift forks, or of damage to the tongues on the side of the gears or the holes that they go into. If there is trouble in the external shift mechanism or with the clutch release, this could also cause difficulty in shifting.

Transmission noise will result from gear teeth damage, or damage or wear of the gear bushings, shaft, bearings, etc.

DISASSEMBLY

1. Remove the engine from the frame, and separate the crankcases as described previously. Before removing the gear clusters from the crankcase, the gears should be checked for backlash. Consult the "Inspection" Section for additional information.

2. Remove the bushing (1), circlip (2), shim (3), needle bearing (4), washers (5 and 6), Second gear (7), Fifth gear (8), Fifth gear bushing (9), and the toothed washer (10).

3. Remove the retaining ring (11), Third gear (12), the next retaining ring (11), the toothed washer (10), and Fourth gear (13), then pull the bearing (14) with a suitable bearing puller.

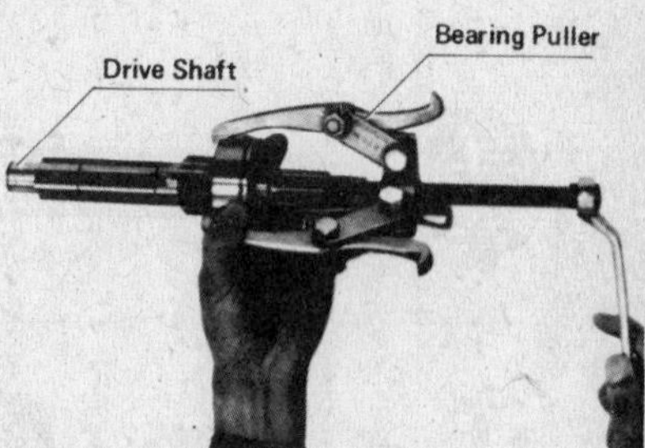

Drive shaft bearing removal

4. Remove the bushing (15), retaining ring (2), shim (3), needle bearing (4), washers (5 and 6), First gear (16), and shim (17).

5. Rotate the shaft while removing the Fourth gear (29) so that the 3 balls (30) will move, then pull the bearing (18) from the shaft using a suitable bearing puller, and remove the washer (19), Second gear (20), the Second gear bushing (21), and the toothed washer (22) from the shaft.

6. Remove the circlip (23), Fifth gear (24), the next circlip (23), the toothed washer (22), Third gear (25), and the washer (26).

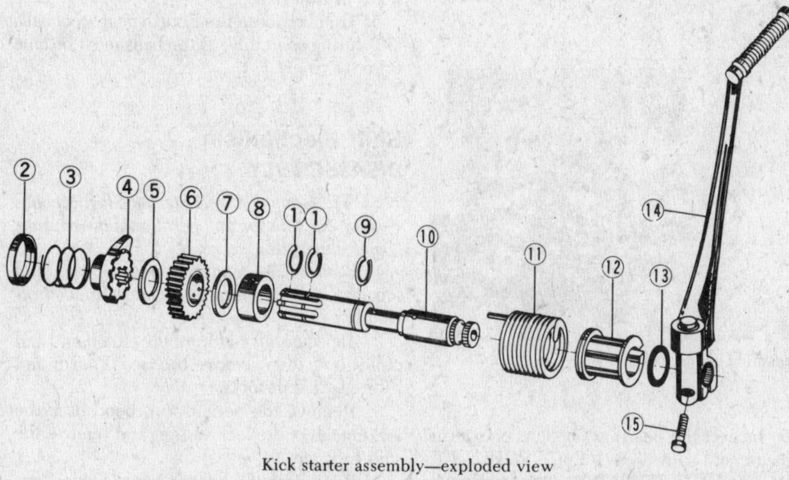

Kick starter assembly—exploded view

1. Retaining ring
2. Cap
3. Coil spring
4. Ratchet
5. Washer
6. Kick gear
7. Washer
8. Bushing
9. Retaining ring
10. Kick shaft
11. Kick spring
12. Spring guide
13. Oil seal
14. Kick pedal
15. Clamp bolt

INSPECTION

1. Clean all parts in a suitable solvent, then blow them dry. The oil seal (35) which has already been removed during the initial disassembly procedure, should be replaced. Bearings should be washed with clean gasoline, blown dry, and lubricated with clean oil. DO NOT SPIN UNLUBRICATED BEARINGS.

2. Inspect all parts for signs of wear, damage, pitting, or chipped gear teeth, and replace them as necessary. Gears with chipped or damaged teeth, dogs, or dog holes should be replaced as gear systems rather than as individuals since they act upon one another.

3. Check for excessive gear backlash in all 5 gears by holding one gear steady while rotating the gear it meshes with back and forth. A dial indicator set against the gear which is moved will provide the necessary information. The difference between the highest and lowest reading is the backlash. In cases where the backlash exceeds the limits given below, replace both gears:

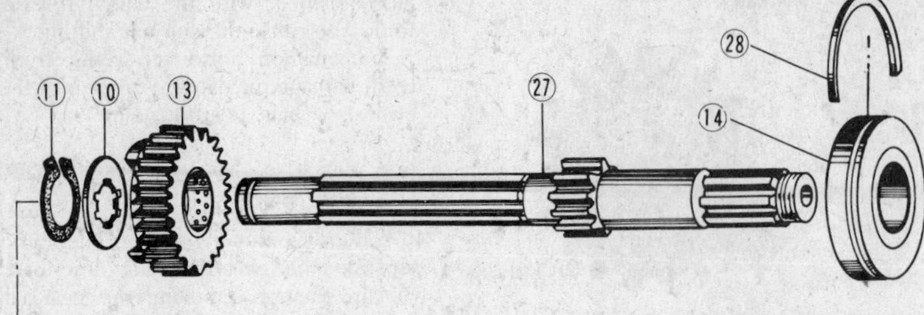

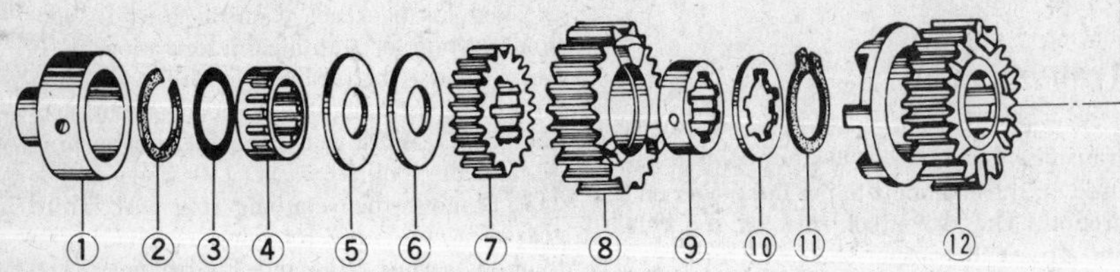

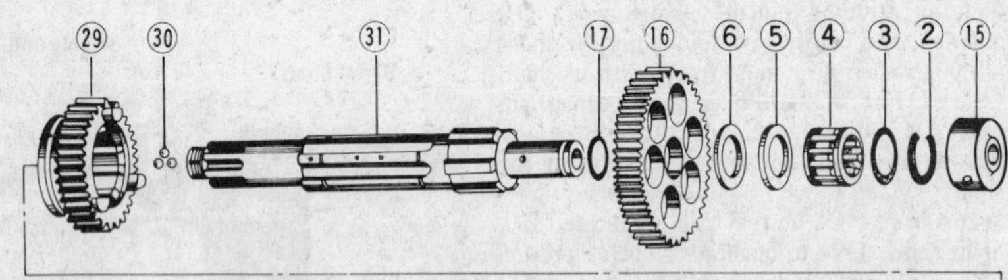

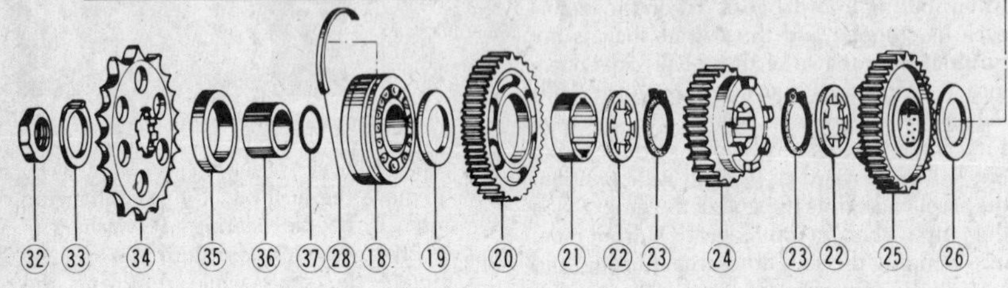

Transmission assembly—exploded view

1. Bushing
2. Retaining ring
3. Shim
4. Needle bearing
5. Washer
6. Washer
7. 2nd gear (D)
8. 5th gear (D)
9. 5th gear Bushing
10. Toothed washer
11. Retaining ring
12. 3rd gear (D)
13. 4th gear (D)
14. Bearing
15. Bushing
16. 1st gear (O)
17. Shim
18. Bearing
19. Washer
20. 2nd gear (O)
21. 2nd gear bushing
22. Toothed washer
23. Retaining ring
24. 5th gear (O)
25. 3rd gear (O)
26. Washer
27. Driveshaft
28. Set ring
29. 4th gear (O)
30. Steel balls
31. Output shaft
32. Nut
33. Lockwasher
34. Engine sprocket
35. Oil seal
36. Engine sprocket collar
37. O-ring

900

	Standard	*Service Limit*
1st gear	0.0008 ~ 0.0075 in. (0.02 ~ 0.19 mm)	0.0098 in. (0.25 mm)
2nd–5th gears	0.0024 ~ 0.0091 in. (0.06 ~ 0.23 mm)	0.0118 in. (0.30 mm)

1000

	Standard	*Service Limit*
All gears	0.0024 ~ 0.0091 in. (0.06 ~ 0.23 mm)	0.0118 in. (0.30 mm)

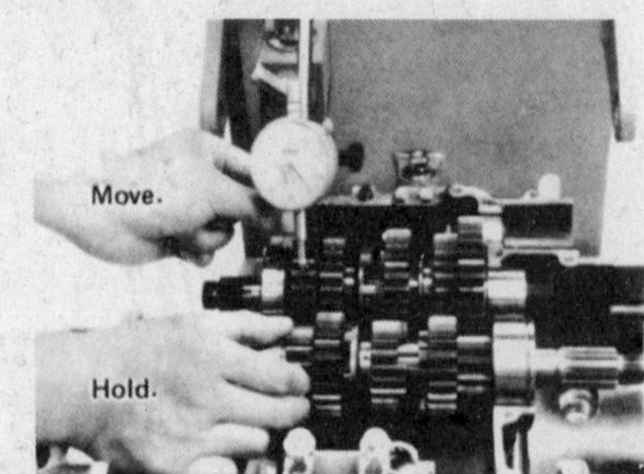

Measuring gear backlash

4. Measure the inside diameter of each gear, then measure the outside diameter of the shafts, subtract the two, and replace any gear which exceeds the service limits given below:

900

Gear	*Standard*	*Service Limit*
Drive 4th, output 3rd	0.0008 ~ 0.0024 in. (0.020 ~ 0.062 mm)	0.0064 in. (0.162 mm)
Drive 5th	0.0063 ~ 0.0096 in. (0.160 ~ 0.245 mm)	0.0136 in. (0.345 mm)
Output 1st	0.0011 ~ 0.0024 in. (0.027 ~ 0.061 mm)	0.0063 in. (0.161 mm)
Output 2nd	0.0118 ~ 0.0182 in. (0.300 ~ 0.463 mm)	0.0222 in. (0.563 mm)

1000

	Standard	*Service Limit*
Output 1st	0.0011 ~ 0.0024 in. (0.027 ~ 0.061 mm)	0.0063 in. (0.16 mm)
Output 2nd, Drive 5th	0.0010 ~ 0.0030 in. (0.025 ~ 0.075 mm)	0.0067 in. (0.17 mm)
Output 3rd, Drive 4th	0.0008 ~ 0.0024 in. (0.020 ~ 0.062 mm)	0.0063 in. (0.16 mm)

5. Inspect the bearings for signs of external damage, and spin them (ONLY WHEN LUBRICATED) to check for rough motion or noisy operation, and replace them as necessary.

6. Inspect all the assorted hardware, and replace any circlips which are twisted, or any washers which are worn or scored.

ASSEMBLY

1. Assembly is basically in the reverse order of disassembly. Use plenty of fresh motor oil as an assembly lubricant.
2. Press on the ball bearings so that the set ring groove is toward the end of the shaft.

The set ring groove should be toward the end of the shaft

3. Make sure that the Third and Fifth gear driveshaft bushing oil holes ae aligned with the holes in the shaft.
4. Make sure that the Second and Fifth gear (output shaft) oil holes ae aligned with the holes in the shaft.
5. Do not grease the Fourth gear steel balls (30) during assembly, as the balls must be able to move freely.

Shift Mechanism

DISASSEMBLY

NOTE: *Consult the "External Shift Mechanism" Section for an operational description and illustration.*

1. Remove the engine from the frame, and separate the crankcases as described previously.
2. Tap the shift rod from the clutch end and pull it out, then remove the two (Fourth and Fifth gear) shift forks.
3. Remove the detent arm, bend back the locking tab of the lockwasher, and remove the shift fork pin.
4. Bend back the locking tab of the lockwasher, then unscrew and remove the drum positioning bolt. The cap bolt need not be removed from the top of the positioning bolt.

Removing the shift rod and forks

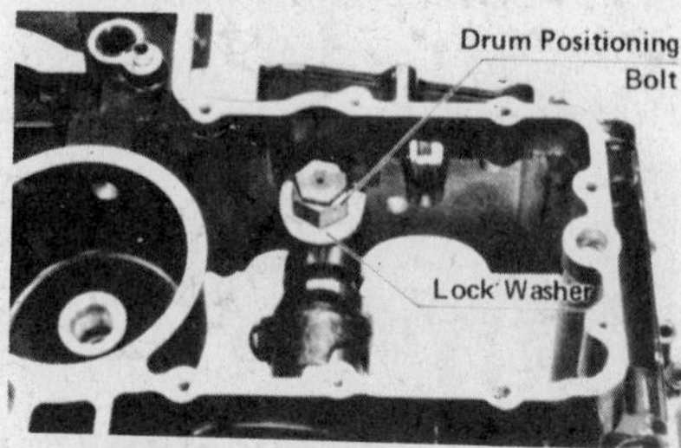

Remove the positioning bolt, but do not loosen the cap bolt

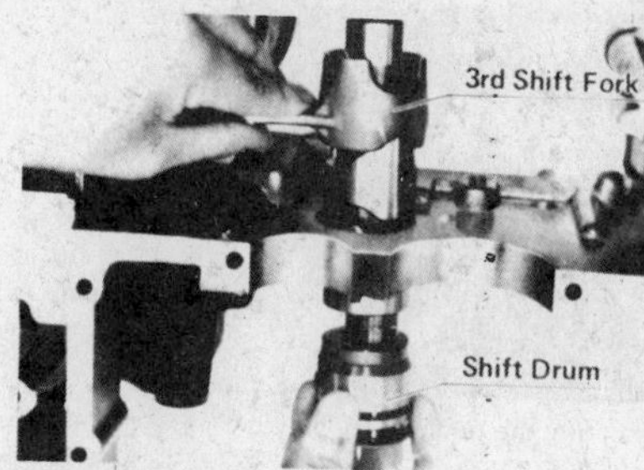

Removing the shift drum

5. Pull the shift drum out of the crankcase along with the third gear shift fork.

INSPECTION

1. Clean all parts in a suitable solvent, then blow them dry.

2. Inspect the shift forks for a worn, pitted, bent, or damaged condition, and replace them as necessary. A bent fork will allow the transmission to pop out of gear under power. If the thickness of the shift fork prongs is less than the service limit listed below, the fork will have to be replaced.

Standard	Service Limit
0.228 ~ 0.236 in. (5.80 ~ 6.00 mm)	0.224 in. (5.70 mm)

Measuring the shifter forks

3. Inspect the shift drum for signs of wear or damage, and replace it as necessary. Compare it to a new one if possible. Measure the width of the shift fork grooves, and replace the drum if worn past the service limits given below:

Standard	Service Limit
0.238 ~ 0.242 in. (6.05 ~ 6.15 mm)	0.246 in. (6.25 mm)

ASSEMBLY

1. Assembly is basically in the reverse order of disassembly.

2. Rotate the shift drum to the Neutral position when installing the drum positioning bolt. The bolt should be coated with Loctite and torqued to 44–57 ft lbs (6.0–8.0 kg/m).

3. The Third gear shift fork is different from the other two, and should be installed so that the short end goes on the drum first, and so that it faces the Neutral switch.

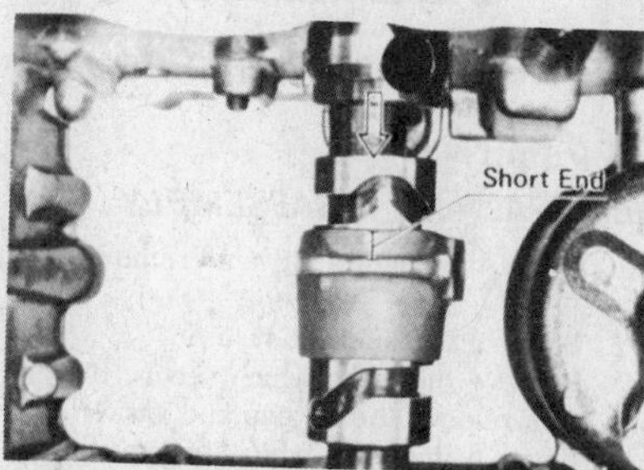

Install the third gear shift fork with the short end as shown

Crankshaft and Cam Chain

REMOVAL

1. Remove the engine from the frame, and separate the crankcases as described previously.

The crankshaft assembly ready to go

2. Remove the crankshaft bearing cap, lift the crankshaft out of the upper case half, and slip the cam chain from it.

3. The crankshaft end bearings may now be removed by using a suitable puller.

INSPECTION

1. Clean the assembly in a suitable solvent, then blow it dry, taking care to clear any oil passages. Lubricate the assembly with fresh motor oil before attempting to spin the bearings.

2. Remove the bearing from each end of the crank, and place it in a V-block. Place a suitable arbor into the connecting rod small end, and measure the difference in height over a 100 mm (4 in.) length, using a dial indicator, to determine the amount which a connecting rod is bent. The standard for this is under 0.002 in./100 mm (under 0.05 mm/100 mm), and the crankshaft assembly should be replaced if the measurement is over the service limit of 0.008 in. (0.20 mm).

3. Use the method described above to determine whether or not a rod is twisted by

Checking the rods for a bent condition

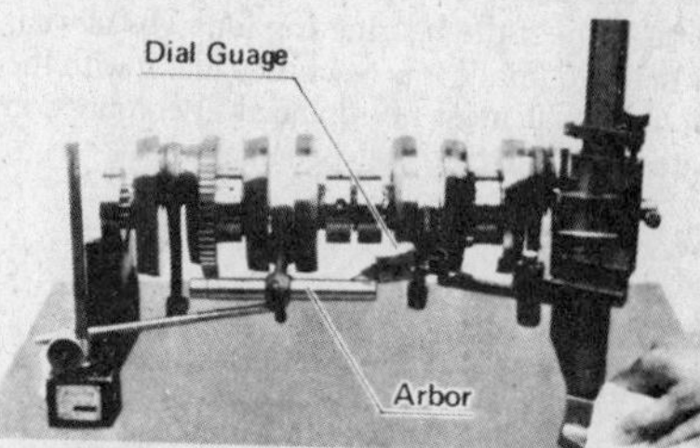

Checking the rods for a twisted condition

checking the amount in which the arbor varies from parallel over a 100 mm length of arbor. The standard for this is the same as that given in the previous step.

4. Check for big end radial clearance by setting the crank, with the end bearings removed, in V-blocks with a dial indicator set against the connecting rod to be checked. Push the rod against the gauge, and then pull it away. The difference between the two readings is the radial clearance. If the clearance for any of the rods exceeds the service limit listed below, the crankshaft will have to be replaced.

Standard	Service Limit
0.0006 ~ 0.0012 in. (0.016 ~ 0.030 mm)	0.0031 in. (0.08 mm)

Measuring bearing radial clearance

5. Measure the connecting rod side clearance using a thickness gauge as shown in the illustration. If the clearance on any of the connecting rods exceeds the service limits given below, the crankshaft will have to be replaced.

Standard	Service Limit
0.012 ~ 0.016 in. (0.3 ~ 0.4 mm)	0.024 in. (0.6 mm)

6. With the end bearings removed and the crankshaft in that old V-block set up once again, rotate the crank slowly with a dial indicator set against each of the bearings in order. The difference between the highest and lowest reading is the runout. The crankshaft must be replaced if the run-out exceeds the service limit given below:

Standard	*Service Limit*
under 0.0012 in. (under 0.03 mm)	0.004 in. (0.10 mm)

7. Clean the bearings with clean gasoline, blow them dry, then lubricate them with fresh motor oil. DO NOT SPIN UNLUBRICATED BEARINGS. Spin the bearings by hand and check for smooth motion and quiet operation. If the bearings are noisy or rough they must be replaced. Only the end bearings can be replaced without a major crankshaft rebuild.

8. Inspect the bearing cap for signs of wear or damage. Since it is machined along with the crankcase, it must be replaced in conjunction with the crankcase if it is damaged.

INSTALLATION

1. Installation is in the reverse order of removal.
2. Align each pin in the upper crankcase with the pin hole in each bearing before slipping the crankshaft into place.
3. The crankshaft bearing cap is bored along with the crankcase, so that it must be installed with the arrow pointing toward the front of the engine. Secure the bolts with 18 ft lbs (2.5 kg/m) torque in the numbered sequence.

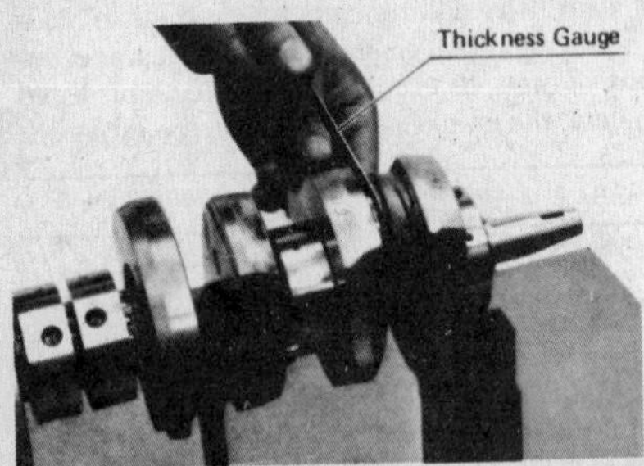

Measuring bearing side clearance

Measuring crankshaft run-out

Set pins installed

Bearing cap installed

LUBRICATION SYSTEMS

ENGINE LUBRICATION

Oil Pump

REMOVAL AND DISASSEMBLY

1. Drain the engine oil and remove the filter.
2. Remove the exhaust system.
3. Remove the bolts which secure the oil pan, then remove the oil pan and gasket.
4. Remove the bolts which secure the oil pump, then remove the oil pump.
5. Secure the pump in a wood-jawed vise, or take precautions to avoid deforming the pump body, then remove the circlip, main gear, alignment pin, and shim.
6. Remove the screws which secure the pump housing halves together, then gently tap the two shafts alternately until the halves can be separated without damaging the shafts.

Engine with oil pan removed

Removing the circlip and main gear

Separating the pump body halves

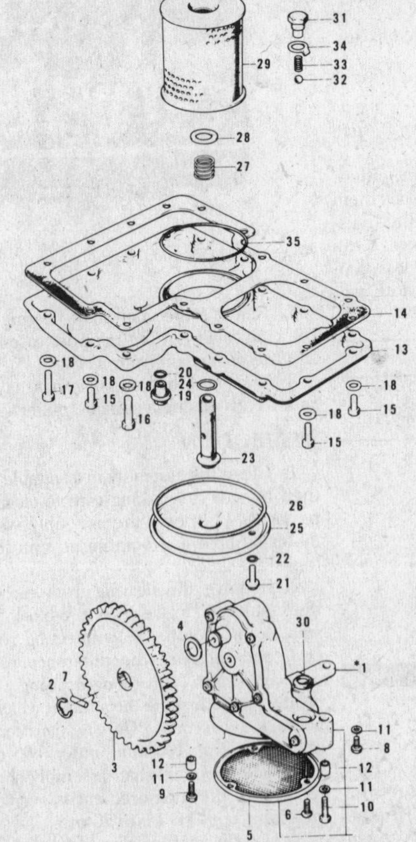

1. Oil pump assy
2. Circlip
3. Oil pump gear
4. Oil pump washer
5. Oil pump strainer
6. Screw, pan head
7. Dowel pin
8. Hex head bolt
9. Hex head bolt
10. Hex head bolt
11. Plain washer
12. Dowel pin
13. Oil pan
14. Oil pan gasket
15. Hex head bolt
16. Hex head bolt
17. Hex head bolt
18. Plain washer
19. Oil drain plug
20. O-ring
21. Oil drum plug
22. O-ring
23. Oil filter bolt
24. O-ring
25. Oil filter cover
26. O-ring
27. Oil filter spring
28. Plain washer
29. Oil filter element
30. O-ring
31. Check valve bolt
32. Ball
33. Check valve spring
34. Lock washer
35. O-ring

Lubrication system assembly

INSPECTION

1. Clean the pump components thoroughly in a suitable solvent, then blow them dry.
2. Inspect all parts for a worn or damaged condition, and replace them as necessary. All gaskets and O-rings should be replaced as a matter of course.
3. Assemble the two internal gears in one side of the pump body, and check the clearance between each gear and the pump body with feeler gauges. The standard clearance on 900 models is 0.0001–0.0014 in. (0.003–0.036 mm), and the pump must be replaced if it is worn past its serviceable limit of 0.004 in. (0.10 mm). On the 1000, standard clearance is 0.0004–0.0033 in. (0.011–0.083 mm), the service limit being 0.006 in. (0.14 mm).

Checking gear/pump body clearance

4. Inspect the strainer screen for a damaged, worn, or permanently clogged condition, and replace it as necessary.

ASSEMBLY AND INSTALLATION

1. Assembly is in the reverse order of disassembly, and installation is in the reverse order of removal.
2. Make sure that the gasket surface of both pump body halves is in perfect condition, and is absolutely clean, and always use a new gasket during assembly.
3. Use Loctite®, or a suitable thread sealing compound, on all of the assembling screws and mounting bolts, and torque the mounting bolts to 70 in. lbs (0.8 kg/m).
4. Make sure that the pump and crankshaft gears mesh properly.
5. Make sure that the sump pan gasket surfaces are perfectly clean, use a new pan gasket, and tighten the pan securing bolts in a crossed sequence to avoid deforming the gasket.

Oil Pressure Switch

For information on oil pressure switch repair and troubleshooting, consult the "Electrical System" Chapter.

Drive Chain Oil Pump

OPERATIONAL DESCRIPTION

An output (countershaft) shaft-drive, plunger-type oil pump is fitted on the Z1 (1973–74 models) to provide lubrication for the drive chain. Oil flow is regulated by both the pump cam setting (which can be manually adjusted for rate of flow) and by engine rpm, since the output shaft drives both the pump and the rear wheel simultaneously. When the pump lever is adjusted for minimum (0 on a scale from 0–5) flow, the length of plunger travel is also at a minimum, and vice versa.

Oil for the pump is contained in a separate

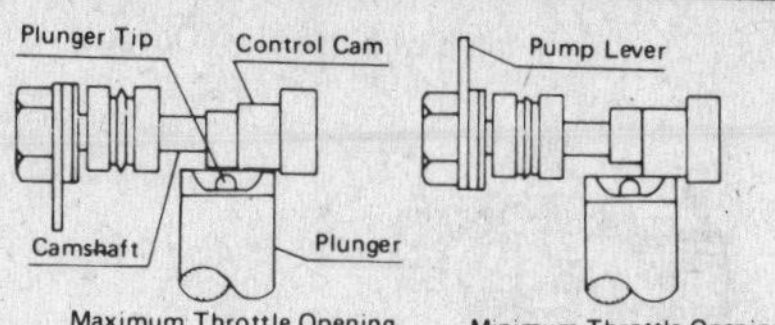

Pump adjustment

chain oiler tank located under the seat, and is gravity fed to the pump through a hose. A non-return check valve is mounted on the output side of the pump, and the oil flows through the hollow pump shaft to the output shaft where it exits through drillings near the drive sprocket. As the output shaft rotates, the oil is flung onto the chain. The accompanying illustration shows the details of the pump's operation. Oil flows into the pump at point A, and along passage B into chamber C. When the plunger moves toward the camshaft on its intake stroke, some space (F) is left between the plunger follower and the cylinder wall. At this time the follower is so positioned that passage D in the follower is aligned with a hole in the valve sleeve, and the oil flows from chamber C through passage D through space E into the empty area F. As the plunger returns on its pumping stroke it rotates back to its original position, causing passage G to be aligned with the outlet hole in the sleeve instead of D being aligned with the inlet hole, and the plunger's motion decreases area F causing the oil to flow into the check valve inlet H. The pressure exerted by the oil presses the ball back, compressing the check valve spring, and allowing the oil to flow through the valve and eventually to the chain.

PUMP REMOVAL AND DISASSEMBLY

1. Remove the oil pump cover, slide back the hose clamp, and disconnect the hose.

NOTE: *Insert the cover screw into the hose, as illustrated, to prevent oil leakage.*

2. Remove the two pump mounting screws, and remove the pump.
3. Wrap cloth around the pump shaft (1) to protect it, then pull it out with pliers. A spacer (2) should come out with the shaft.
4. Remove the shaft bushing (5), then remove the O-ring (3) and oil seal (4).

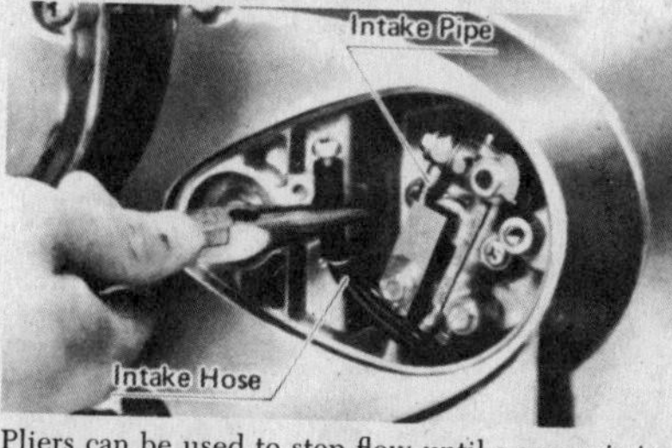

Pliers can be used to stop flow until a screw is inserted

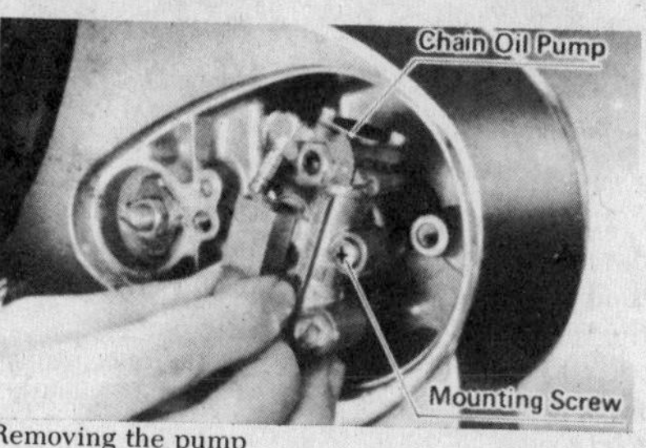

Removing the pump

5. Remove the cap screws and top cap (6), then remove the plunger spring (7), plunger guide stopper (8), and O-ring (9).
6. Remove the cap screws and bottom cap (10), then remove the O-ring (11).
7. Gently press on the bottom of the plunger (14) with a thin rod to remove the top plunger (13), guide (12), and bottom plunger (14) from the pump body (17).
8. Remove the control cam (15) and V-ring (16).
9. Remove the banjo bolt (18) and banjo assembly, and the check valve securing bolt (29) and check valve housing (30).

INSPECTION

1. Clean all but the rubber parts in a suitable solvent, then blow all but the check valve assembly dry.

CAUTION: *The pressure exerted by compressed air may damage the check valve.*

2. Inspect all parts for a worn or damaged condition. The O-rings and the check valve are the only parts which are expected to wear, and consequently are the only available replacement components available. If other parts are worn or damaged, the entire pump assembly should be replaced.
3. Check that the check valve will pass oil in only one direction, and that it isn't clogged. The valve can be easily cleaned with gasoline or solvent in a syringe.
4. Whenever the pump is disassembled, or if the pump oil tank runs dry while the pump is in operation, air will enter the pump, which must then be bled. Do this by removing the bleeder bolt (28) until oil starts to run from the hole, then secure the bolt.

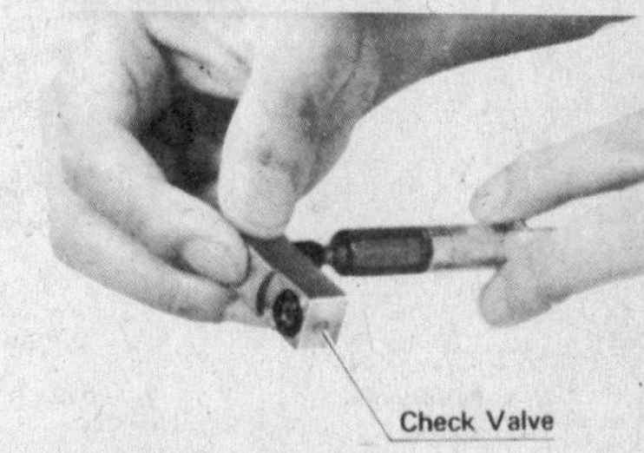

Testing the check valve

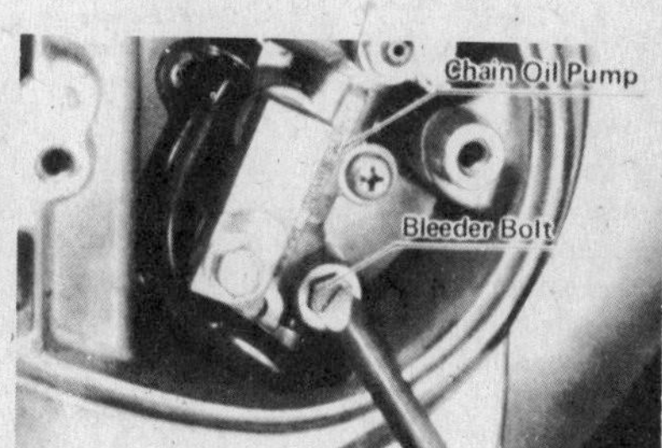

Bleeding the pump

ASSEMBLY AND INSTALLATION

1. Assembly and installation are in the reverse order of removal and disassembly.
2. Lubricate the oil seal with clean oil before pressing it into position.
3. Lubricate the O- and V-rings, plungers, and plunger guide before assembly.
4. Rotate the rear wheel until the pin in the output shaft is brought into alignment with the groove in the oil pump shaft. This is essen-

Beginning of Downstroke (Intake)

Beginning of Upstroke (Output)

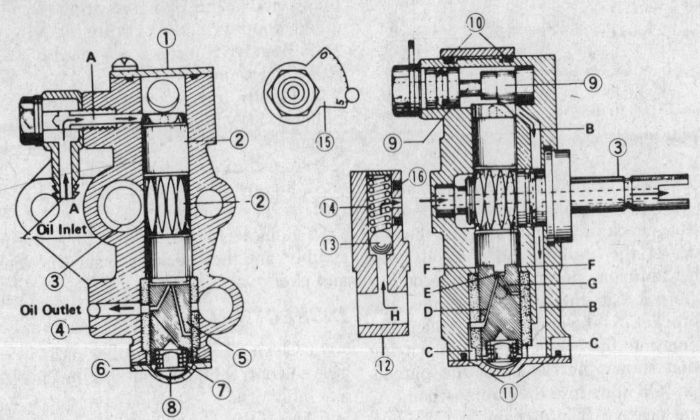

Pump operation

1. End cover
2. Plunger
3. Pump shaft
4. Pump body
5. Plunger follower
6. End cover
7. Plunger spring
8. Spring seat
9. Control cam
10. O-ring
11. O-ring
12. Check valve
13. Steel ball
14. Spring
15. Pump lever
16. O-ring

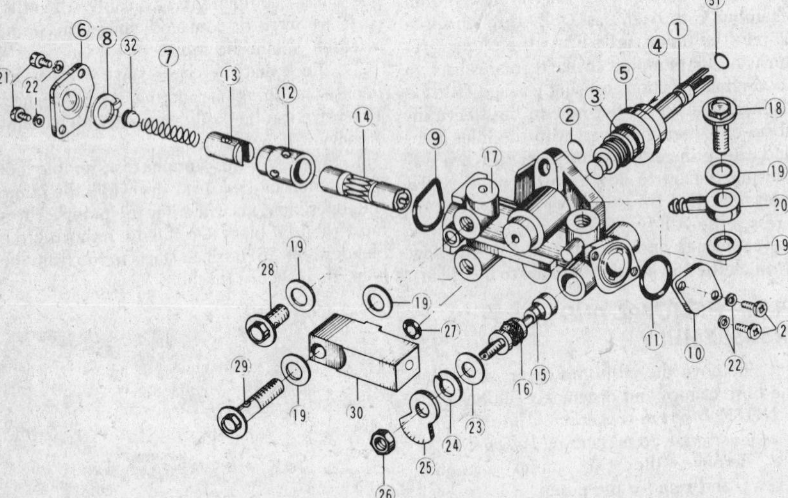

Pump assembly

1. Pump shaft
2. Spacer
3. O-ring
4. Oil seal
5. Bushing
6. Cap
7. Plunger spring
8. Plunger guide stopper
9. O-ring
10. Cap
11. O-ring
12. Plunger guide
13. Plunger
14. Plunger
15. Control cam
16. V-ring
17. Oil pump body
18. Banjo bolt
19. Washer
20. Banjo
21. Bolt
22. Lockwasher
23. Washer
24. Lockwasher
25. Control lever
26. Nut
27. O-ring
28. Bleeder bolt
29. Bolt
30. Check valve
31. O-ring
32. Spring seat

tial for correct installation as otherwise the pump will not seat correctly.

5. Apply Loctite®, or some other suitable thread sealer, to the pump mounting screws before installing them.

6. Bleed the pump as directed in Step 4 of the preceding Section before securing the pump cover.

7. Check the oil level in the chain oiler pump tank.

FUEL SYSTEMS

CARBURETOR OVERHAUL (1973–75)

Carburetor Bank

REMOVAL AND INSTALLATION

1. Disconnect the fuel lines at the gas tank, then remove the tank.

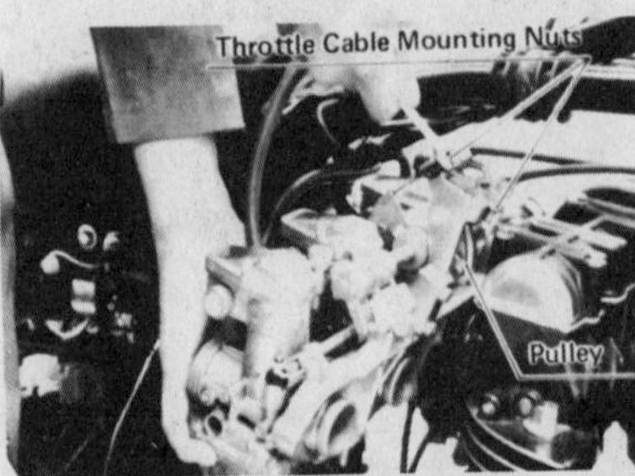

Removing the carburetor bank assembly

2. Loosen the 4 intake manifold clamps at the front, and the 4 air cleaner hose clamps at the back, then pull the carburetor bank off to the rear.

3. Loosen the throttle cable mounting nuts, and disconnect the cables from the pulley.

4. Installation is in the reverse order of removal. Note the following:

a. All clamps must be secure enough to prevent air leaks, especially at the intake manifold.

b. Adjust the throttle cables as described in the "Tune-Up" section.

Individual Carburetor

REMOVAL AND INSTALLATION

1. Remove the carburetor bank as described in the previous Section.

2. Remove the throttle stop screw locknut (1) from both the carburetor to be removed and its companion, then remove the double washer link (2).

3. Remove the throttle stop screw (53), stop screw spring (54), and the spring seat (4).

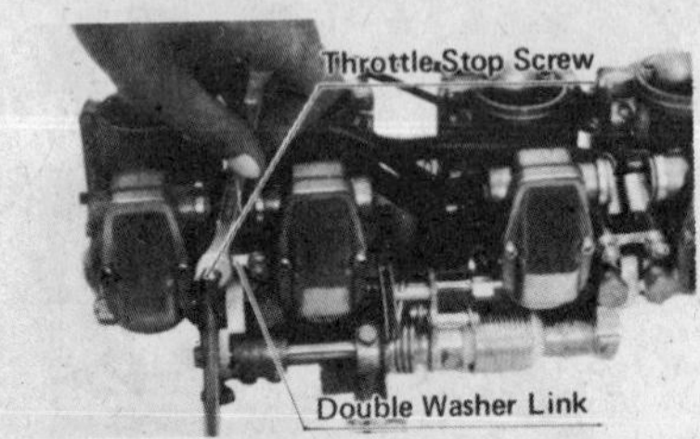

Removing the stop screw locknut

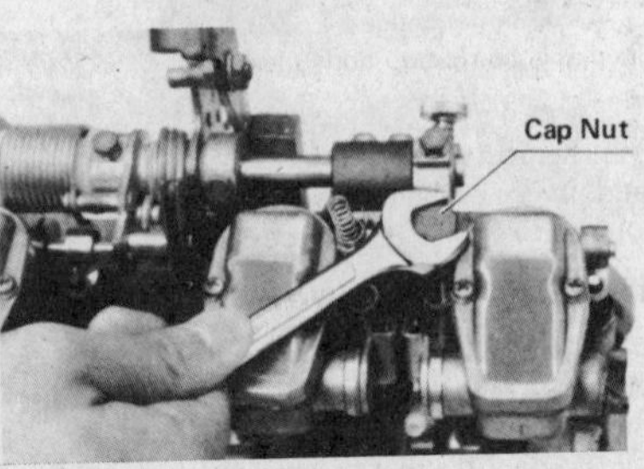

Removing the cap nut

4. Remove the cap nut (52) from the linkage of the carburetor which is to be removed, then remove the spring (3) and seat (4).

CAUTION: *Upon removal of the cap nut the spring may pop out. Be prepared to catch it.*

5. Remove the 4 mounting screws and swing the pair of carburetors you are working with away from the plate. The object of your attentions may now be pulled off to the side.

Removing a pair of carbs

6. Installation is in the reverse order of removal. Use Loctite, or some other suitable sealer, on the mounting screws.

Linkage

DISASSEMBLY AND ASSEMBLY

1. Remove all of the carburetors from the mounting plate as described in the previous Section.

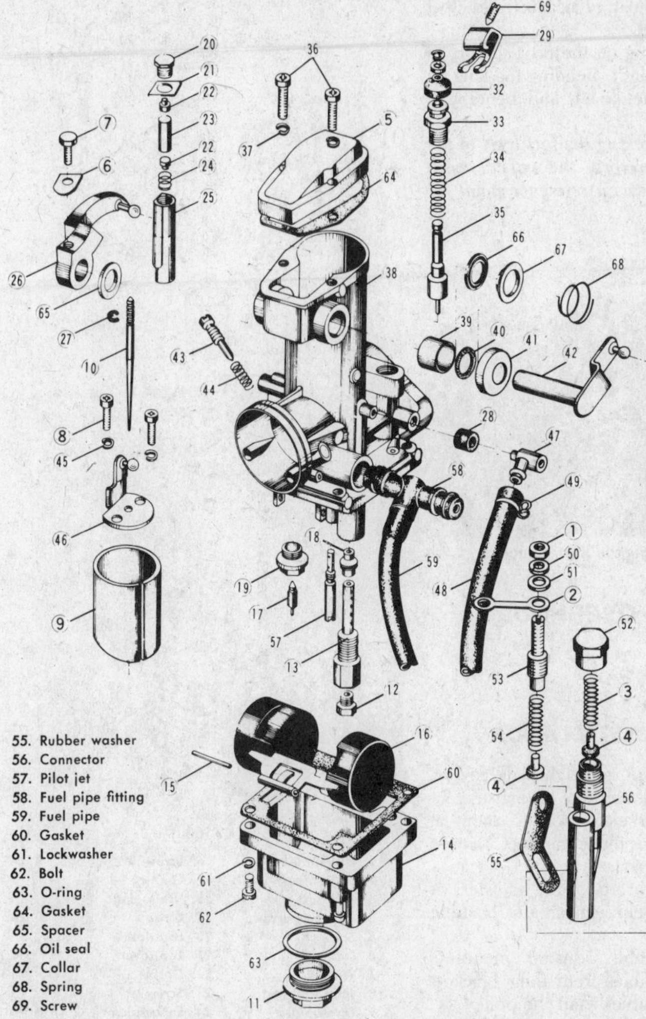

1. Throttle stop screw lock-nut
2. Double washer link
3. Spring
4. Spring seat
5. Top cover
6. Lockwasher
7. Bolt
8. Screw
9. Throttle valve
10. Jet needle
11. Drain plug
12. Main jet
13. Air bleed pipe
14. Float bowl
15. Pin
16. Float
17. Float valve needle
18. Needle jet
19. Valve seat
20. Guide screw
21. Lockwasher
22. Spring seat
23. Pin
24. Spring
25. Connector
26. Level assembly
27. Circlip
28. Hose
29. Level
30. Circlip
31. Ring
32. Cap
33. Guide screw
34. Spring
35. Plunger assembly
36. Bolt
37. Lockwasher
38. Mixing chamber
39. Hose
40. Washer
41. Cup
42. Lever assembly
43. Air screw
44. Spring
45. Lockwasher
46. Bracket assembly
47. Air vent pipe fitting
48. Air vent pipe
49. Clamp
50. Lockwasher
51. Washer
52. Cap nut
53. Throttle stop screw
54. Spring
55. Rubber washer
56. Connector
57. Pilot jet
58. Fuel pipe fitting
59. Fuel pipe
60. Gasket
61. Lockwasher
62. Bolt
63. O-ring
64. Gasket
65. Spacer
66. Oil seal
67. Collar
68. Spring
69. Screw

Carburetor assembly

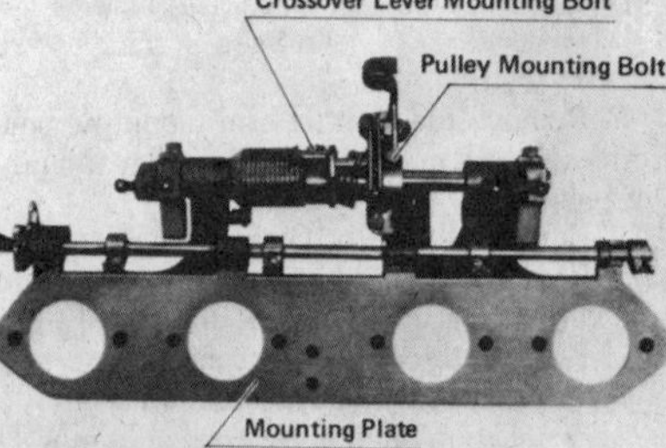

Mounting plate assembled

Removing the springs

2. Remove the crossover lever and pulley mounting bolts, then unhook the crossover spring from the pulley pin, and the throttle return spring from the crossover lever pin.

3. Remove the bolt which secures the linkage arm to the shaft from either of the arms,

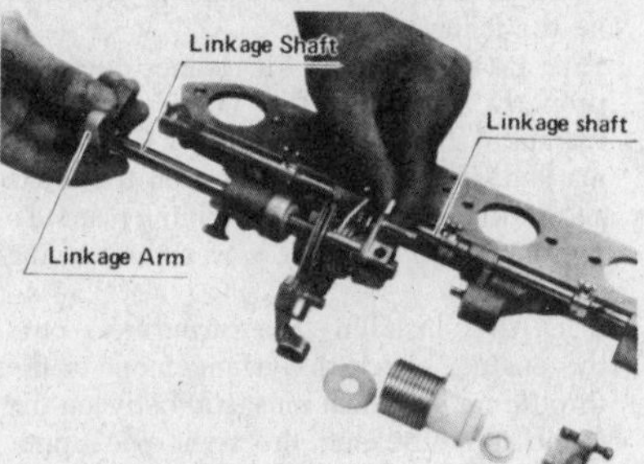

Removing the linkage shaft

then pull the shaft out from the opposite end. The other arm need not be removed.

NOTE: *The starter (choke) linkage need not be removed unless it is defective.*

4. Assembly is in the reverse order of disassembly. Lubricate the shafts at this time.

Carburetor

DISASSEMBLY

1. Remove the carburetor to be disassembled as described in the "Individual Carburetor Removal and Installation" Section. The fuel may be drained from the float bowl by removing the drain plug (11) and washer (63).

NOTE: *Consult the "Individual Carburetor Removal and Installation" Section for a labeled exploded view illustration.*

2. Remove the top cover mounting screws (36) and washers (37), then remove the cover (5) and cover gasket (64).

3. Bend flat the lockwasher tab (6), then remove the bolt (7). The lever assembly (42) can now be removed along with its associated components. The connector assembly (56) can now be further disassembled if so desired.

Removing the lever assembly mounting bolt

4. Remove the two screws (8) which secure the bracket assembly (46) to the throttle valve (9), and lift the bracket, complete with the lever assembly (26) and connector assembly (25), out of the bore. The connector assembly may be further broken down by removing the guide screw (20) and components (21–24).

5. Remove the throttle valve (9) and needle (10) from the bore, taking care not to damage the needle.

6. Remove the plunger assembly (35) after removing the lever (29), cap (32), and the guide screw (33).

7. Remove the float bowl securing screws (62), the float bowl (14), the bowl gasket (60), the float (16), float pivot (15), and the float valve needle (17).

8. Remove the main jet (12) and air bleed pipe (13), then invert the carburetor and gently press out the needle jet (18) with a

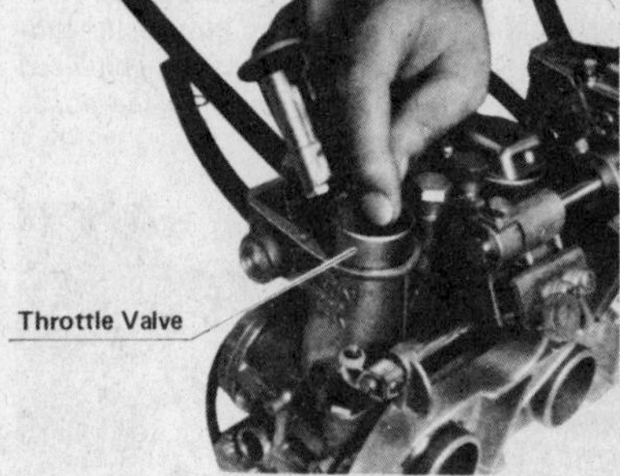

Removing the throttle valve

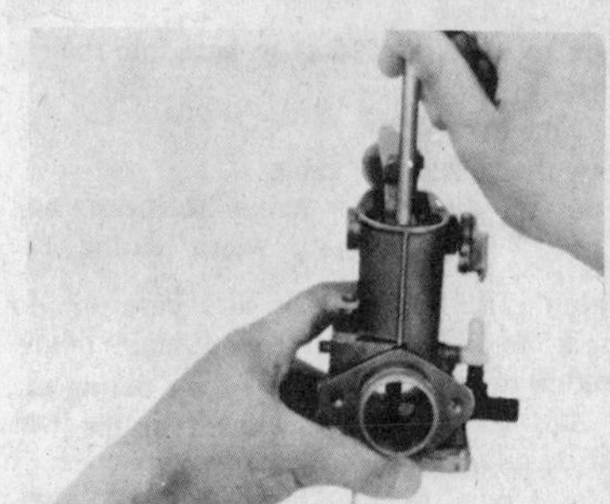

Removing the needle jet

wooden rod or some other suitable instrument.

9. Remove the valve seat (19), the pilot jet (57), the pilot air screw (43) and spring (44), and any other remaining items such as the fuel lines and their hardware.

ASSEMBLY

1. Assembly is in the reverse order of disassembly. Use all new gaskets and O-rings.

2. Do not overtighten the jets when installing them in the carburetor body.

3. Make certain that the jet needle is installed in the same position as when it was re-

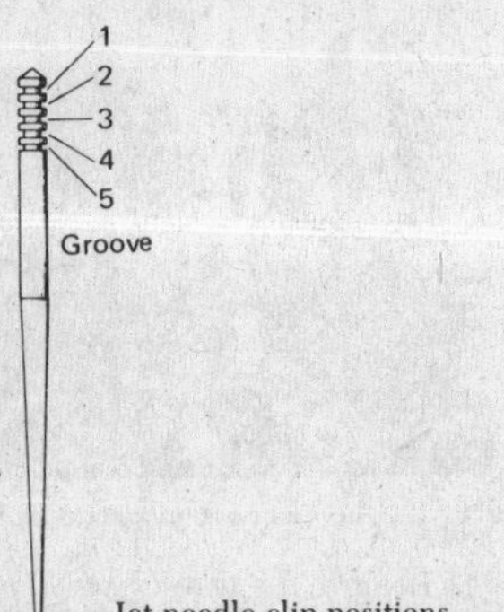

Jet needle clip positions

moved. The clip should be in the third groove from the top on all models except the 1975 (2nd groove from top).

4. Adjust the height of the float as described in the following Section if necessary, and adjust the carburetor as described in the "Tune-Up" section.

Float Height Adjustment

1. Turn the fuel tap to the "Off" position, remove the overflow vent tube (which will interfere with the knurled knob), and remove the float bowl drain plug. Be prepared to catch the fuel which will run out.

2. Install the fuel level measuring device (Part No. 57001-122 for the Z1, 57001-208 for the KZ900) in place of the drain plug.

NOTE: *The original fuel level gauge hose (Part No. 99990-020) was incorrectly calibrated, and has been subsequently replaced with the part number given in the above Step.*

Special tool installed

3. Hold the plastic tube against the carburetor body and turn the fuel tap to the "On" position. The gas level in the hose should come up to 0.10–0.18 in. (2.5–4.5 mm) below the edge of the carburetor body.

4. If the fuel level is incorrect, the float must be adjusted in the following manner:

a. Drain the fuel from the float bowl, then remove the bowl. Be prepared to catch the float, float pivot pin, and float needle.

b. Bend the tang on the float slightly to adjust the float height. Bending the tang up will lower the fuel level, and bending it down will raise it.

NOTE: *When checking the fuel level of the inside two carburetors, the outside carb base may be used as a reference point for the gauge.*

Bending the tang adjusts the float height

CARBURETOR OVERHAUL (1976–80)

Carburetor Bank

REMOVAL AND INSTALLATION

1. Remove the left and right side covers. Remove the gas tank and tool kit and tray.

2. Loosen the air cleaner duct clamp at each carburetor and remove the duct. Loosen the carburetor clamps.

3. Screw in the throttle cable adjusters as far as possible to yield a maximum of cable play.

4. Loosen the cable adjuster mounting nuts, remove the cables from their brackets and disengage the cables from the pulley.

5. Remove the carburetor air vent tubes from the air cleaner cap and pull them out towards the engine. Pull the carburetor overflow tubes out of their guide.

6. Remove the carburetor assembly.

7. Installation is the reverse of removal. Note the following points:

a. Be sure that the air cleaner ducts are properly installed. The outer ducts are marked "R" and "L" and "UP" is also marked. Check that the lines on the ducts align with the lines on the holding plate. To position the ducts, first loosen the holding plate screws.

b. After installing the carburetors onto the engine, check the arrangement of the throttle cables which must run between the frame top tube and the right-side upper cradle tube and must be free of kinks or sharp bends.

Individual Carburetor

REMOVAL AND INSTALLATION

All carburetor parts with the exception of the starter plungers and the fuel line 3-way joint can be removed without removing the carbs from their mounts. If individual removal is required, proceed as follows:

1. Remove the carburetors from the engine as outlined above. Remove the idle screw and spring.

2. Remove the carburetor top covers.

3. Detach the throttle return spring.

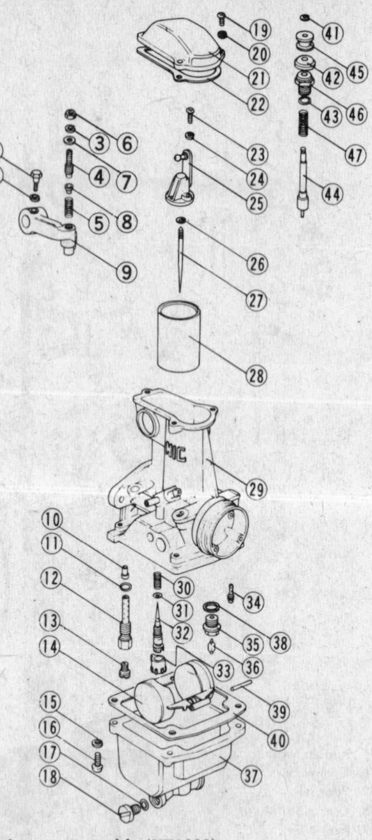

Carburetor assembly (KZ1000)

1. Mounting bolt
2. Lockwasher
3. Lockwasher
4. Adjusting screw
5. Spring
6. Locknut
7. Washer
8. Joint ball seat
9. Throttle arm
10. Needle jet
11. O-ring
12. Air bleed pipe
13. Main jet
14. Float
15. Lockwasher
16. Screw
17. O-ring
18. Drain plug
19. Screw
20. Lockwasher
21. Top cover
22. Gasket
23. Screw
24. Lockwasher
25. Throttle valve bracket
26. Circlip
27. Jet needle
28. Throttle valve
29. Carburetor body
30. Spring

4. Remove the throttle arm mounting bolt from each carb and remove the pulley mounting bolt.

5. Remove the throttle shaft set plate.

6. Remove the rubber cap from each outside carburetor. Push out the throttle shaft.

7. Remove the carburetor mounting screws (2 ea) and take off the individual units.

8. Installation is the reverse of removal. Note the following points:

a. Use a non-permanent thread-locking compound on the mounting screws.

b. Grease the throttle shaft before installation.

c. Perform the initial synchronization sequence as outlined in the "Tune-Up" section.

Carburetor

DISASSEMBLY

1. To remove the throttle valve assembly, first remove the throttle shaft as outlined above under "Individual Carburetor Removal and installation," Steps 1–6.

2. Lift up the linkage and pull out the throttle valve and jet needle.

3. To remove the needle, remove the two

screws which secure the throttle valve bracket.

4. Remove the four screws and take off the float bowl and gasket.

5. Unscrew and remove the pilot screw, O-ring, and spring.

6. Remove the main jet, air bleed pipe, and pilot jet.

7. Push out the float pivot pin. Remove the float and float needle. Unscrew and remove the float valve seat and gasket.

8. To remove the needle jet, push it out from the top of the carburetor with a wooden dowel.

ASSEMBLY

1. Assembly is in the reverse order of disassembly. Use all new gaskets and O-rings.

2. Do not overtighten the jets when installing them in the carburetor body.

3. Make certain that the jet needle is installed in the same position as when it was removed. The clip should be in the third groove from the top.

4. Adjust the height of the float as described in the following Section if necessary, and adjust the carburetor as described in the "Tune-Up" section.

Float Height Adjustment

1. Turn the fuel tap to the "Off" position, remove the overflow vent tube (which will interfere with the knurled knob), and remove the float bowl drain plug. Be prepared to catch the fuel which will run out.

2. Install the fuel level measuring device (Part No. 57001-208) in place of the dain plug.

3. Hold the plastic tube against the carburetor body and turn the fuel tap to the "On" position. The gas level in the hose should come up to 0.10–0.18 (2.5–4.5 mm) below the edge of the carburetor body.

4. If the fuel level is incorrect, the float must be adjusted in the following manner:

a. Drain the fuel from the float bowl, then remove the bowl. Be prepared to catch the float, float pivot pin, and float needle.

b. Bend the tang on the float slightly to adjust the float height. Bending the tang up will lower the fuel level, and bending it down will raise it.

NOTE: *When checking the fuel level of the inside two carburetors, the outside carb base may be used as a reference point for the gauge.*

CARBURETOR OVERHAUL (1981)

Carburetor Bank

REMOVAL AND INSTALLATION

1. Remove the gas tank.

2. Loosen the carburetor clamps on the manifold side.

3. Move the spring bands back from the carb mouths.

4. Disconnect the throttle cable, vacuum lines and feed lines.

5. Pull the carburetors back until free of the manifolds and out to the right side.

6. Installation is the reverse of removal. Note the following points:

a. Route the throttle cable between the right fork leg and the head pipe, and the right side of the frame top tube.

b. Connect the two hoses of the vacuum switch to carbs Nos. 1 and 4. Connect the fuel feed line to carb No. 2.

Carburetor

DISASSEMBLY AND ASSEMBLY

1. Carburetor disassembly is straightforward. Observe the following precautions when working on the carburetors.

2. Take care when removing the throttle slide that the diaphragm is not ripped.

3. The pilot screw is covered with a plug which must be pried off. It is recommended that this item remain in place unless absolutely necessary.

4. The coasting enricher diaphragm cover on the side of the unit has a painted screw in the middle. Do not turn or disturb this screw.

5. When assembling, the pilot screw plug must be held in place with a bonding agent. A new plug should be used.

FUEL TAP

1. Turn the tap to the "Off" position, then disconnect the fuel lines.

2. Remove the tank, or raise and support the back of it.

3. Unscrew the sediment cup on early models and remove the O-ring and strainer.

4. Remove the screw which secures the valve and lever, and remove those parts.

5. The tap may be removed from the tank by loosening the nut or screws which secures it to the tank.

NOTE: *Removing the fuel tap body from the gas tank is not recommended unless replacement is necessary.*

Carburetor Specifications

Type	*Main Jet*	*Air Jet*	*Needle Jet*	*Jet Needle*	*Pilot Jet*	*Throttle Valve Cutaway*	*Pilot Screw*	*Fuel Level*
VM28SC (Z1, 1973–74)	112.5	1.0	P-8	5J9-3	20	2.5	1½ turns out	32 ± 1 mm (1.26 ± 0.04 in.)
VM28SS (Z1, 1975)	112.5	1.0	O-8	5J9-2	17.5	1.5	1¼ turns out	32 ± 1 mm (1.26 ± 0.04 in.)
VM26SS (KZ900)	115	1.6	O-6	5DL31-3	17.5	1.5	1⅜ turns out	32 ± 1 mm (1.26 ± 0.04 in.)
VM26SS (KZ1000)	107.5	na	O-8	5CN8-3	17.5	1.5	1¼ turns out	32 ± 1 mm (1.26 ± 0.04 in.)
VM28SS (1979–80)	102.5	na	O-4	5CN17-3	15	2.0	pre-set	33 ± 1 mm (1.30 ± 0.04 in.)
BS34 (J-models)	127.5	na	Y-6	5FL749	37.5	na	1¼ turns out	18.6 mm (0.73 in.)
BS34 (K, M-models)	122.5	na	Y-1	5FL51	37.5	na	1¼ turns out	18.6 mm (0.73 in.)

ELECTRICAL SYSTEMS

CHARGING SYSTEM

Alternator

OUTPUT TEST

Before checking the alternator, make sure that the battery, rectifier, and regulator are all good, and be sure that the battery is fully charged. Dynamo failure can be traced to either a short, an open circuit (burned-out wire), or a loss of rotor magnetism.

Test the dynamo in the following manner:

1. Remove the right-side plastic cover, and disconnect the green regulator lead from the connector panel. Be sure that all accessories are turned off.

2. Rotate the hand tester switch to the 30 VDC (from 0–30 volts of DC) scale, and connect it across the battery so that the negative (−) tester lead goes to the negative battery terminal, and the positive (+) tester lead goes to the battery positive terminal.

3. Start the engine and run it at 4000 rpm, taking note of the meter reading. A reading of 15–20 VDC is normal, and a lower reading indicates a defective dynamo.

NOTE: *For convenience sake, the throttle grip adjusting screw can be used to keep the engine turning at 4000 rpm. Hold the throttle open until the tach reads correctly, then turn in the adjusting screw.*

4. Turn off the engine and disconnect the tester leads from the battery, then set the tester to the 12 amp DC range, and switch the tester leads to the appropriate meter sockets.

5. Disconnect the wire which runs from the fuse to the starter relay, and connect the positive (+) tester lead to the white wire on the fuse side, and the negative (−) tester lead to the white wire on the relay side. This puts the tester in series with the rectifier and battery so that battery charging current can be measured.

CAUTION: *Do not use the electric starter if the tester is connected in series directly at the battery terminal instead of as directed in*

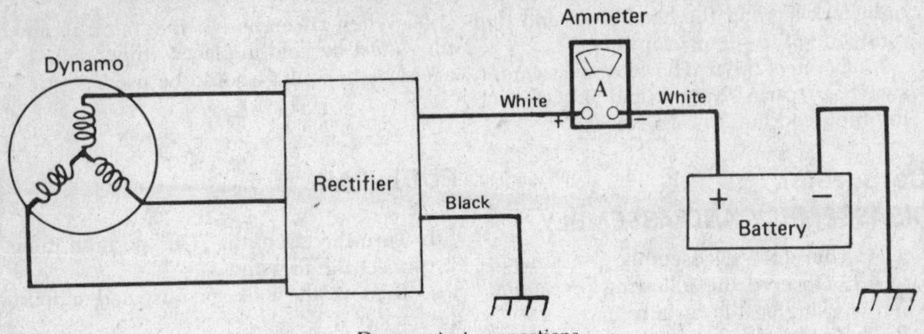

Dynamo test connections

the preceding Step, or the reverse starting current will damage the meter.

6. Start the engine and run it at 4000 rpm, taking note of the meter reading. A reading of 9.5 amps or more is normal, and a lower reading indicates a defective dynamo.

7. Determine whether the problem is in the windings or the rotor in the following manner:

a. Disconnect the blue plug from the connector panel, and use the R x 1 scale on the tester to determine the resistance between each pair of wires going to the plug: blue/pink, blue/yellow, and pink/yellow.

b. The resistance between any two of the wires should be 0.45–0.6 ohms; less indicates shorted coils, and a higher resistance or none at all indicates open coils. If the coils are defective, the stator must be replaced.

c. Measure the resistance between each dynamo wire and ground (the chassis,

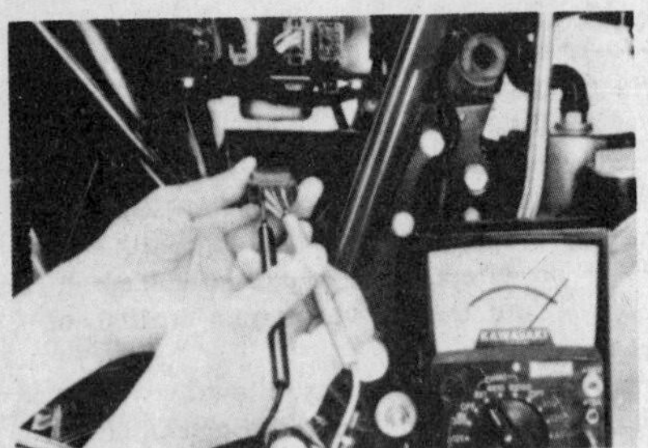
Testing the connector panel plug

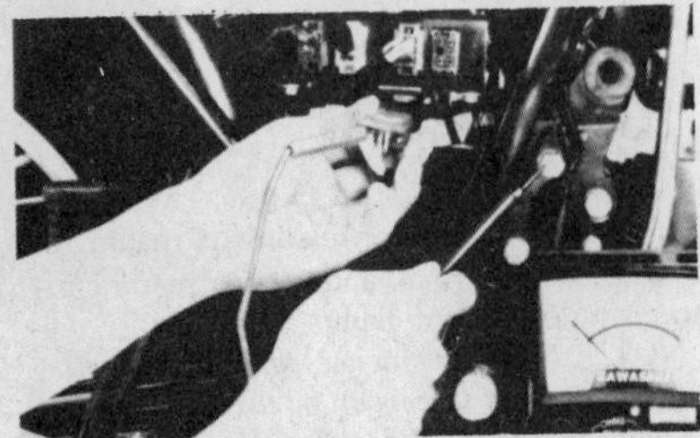
Measuring resistance between the leads and ground

engine, etc.) using the highest resistance scale on the tester.

d. No reading (∞) is normal, and any reading indicates a short which means the stator must be replaced.

e. If the coils have normal resistance, but voltage and current checks indicate that the dynamo is defective, the rotor magnets are probably bad, and the rotor will have to be replaced.

REMOVAL AND INSTALLATION

1. Remove the chain cover as described in the "Engine Removal and Installation" Section.

2. Remove the right-side plastic cover, and disconnect the blue dynamo wire, and the wires from the oil pressure and Neutral indicator switches, then release the wires from the cable clamps.

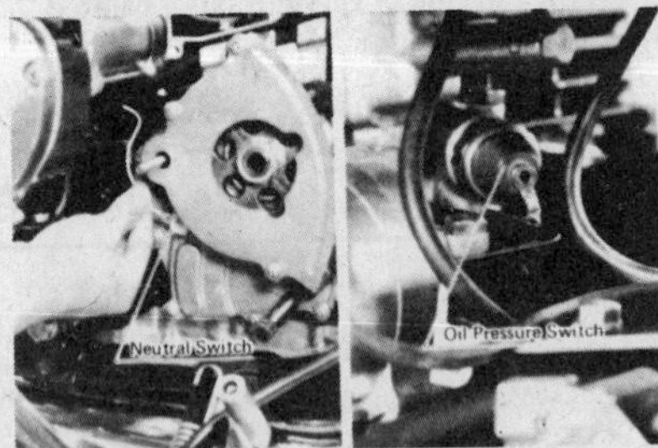

Disconnecting the switches

3. Remove the left-side engine cover, and remove the allen bolts which secure the stator to the cover.

NOTE: *If only the rotor is to be removed, it is not necessary to disconnect the wiring or remove the stator.*

4. Remove the starter idle gear.

5. Keep the rotor from turning by holding it with either the special tool (Part No. 57001-117) or a suitable substitute, and remove the rotor mounting bolt.

6. Hold the rotor still as described above, and use either the special tool (Part No. 57001-116) or a suitable substitute to remove the rotor-starter clutch assembly.

CAUTION: *Hammering on the rotor will demagnetize the magnets, leaving the rotor useless.*

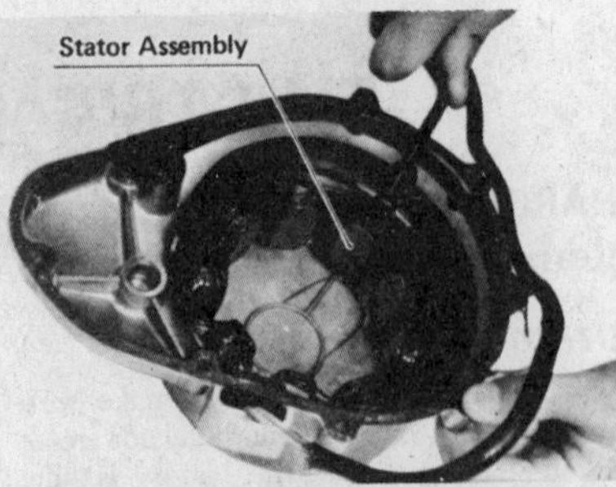

Removing the stator

Removing the idle gear assembly

Removing the rotor mounting bolt

Removing the rotor and starter clutch assembly

7. Remove the woodruff key, thin shim, starter clutch gear, needle bearing, gear damper, and thick shim, in that order, from the crankshaft, then remove the rollers, springs, and spring caps from the starter clutch.

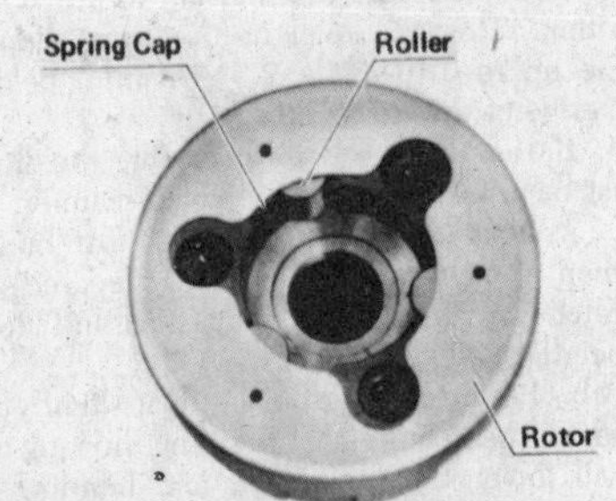

Starter clutch assembly

Disassembling the starter clutch

8. Secure the rotor in a wood-jawed vise, or wrap it to protect it if a metal vise is to be used, and remove the allen bolts to separate the rotor and starter clutch.

9. Installation is in the reverse order of removal. Use a new cover gasket, apply Loctite or some other suitable sealer to the allen bolts, and be sure to use an oil seal guide when installing the chain cover.

10. Place the thick shim onto the crankshaft

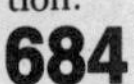

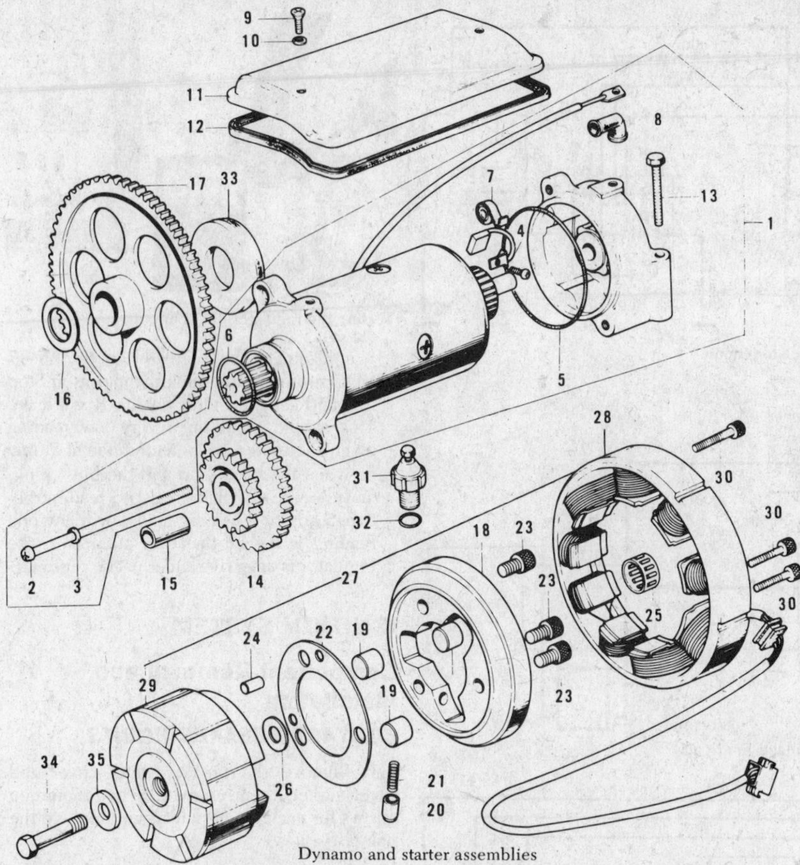

Dynamo and starter assemblies

1. Starting motor assy
2. Pan head screw
3. Spring washer
4. Carbon brush
5. O-ring
6. O-ring
7. Carbon brush spring
8. Starting motor terminal cap
9. Hex head bolt
10. Plain washer
11. Starting motor cover
12. Starting motor cover gasket
13. Hex head bolt
14. Starting motor gear
15. Piston pin
16. Thrust washer
17. Starting clutch gear
18. Starting clutch
19. Roller
20. Plug
21. Spring
22. Clutch starting plate
23. Bolt
24. Dowel pin
25. Needle bearing
26. Plain washer
27. Dynamo assy
28. Stator assy
29. Rotor
30. Allen bolt
31. Oil pressure switch assy
32. Oil pressure switch O-ring
33. Damper rubber
34. Hex head bolt
35. Plain washer

with its chamfered side facing in before installing the starter clutch.

11. Spin the clutch gear so that the rollers

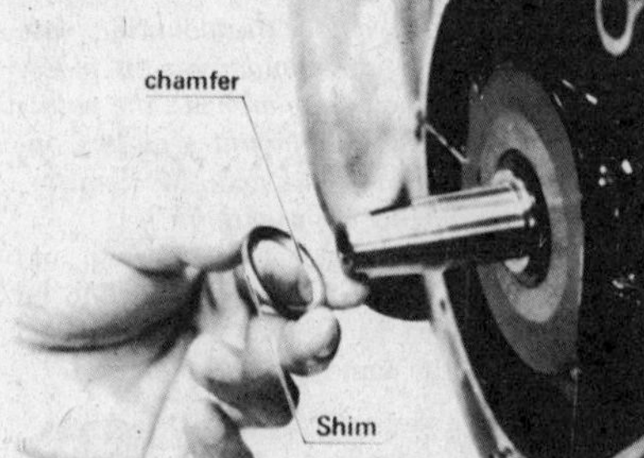

Install the shim with the chamfered side in

will move enough to allow it to go on when installing the starter clutch.

12. Apply Loctite, or another suitable sealer, to the rotor mounting bolt threads before installing it, and torque the bolt to 18 ft lbs (2.5 kg/m).

Rectifier

A six-diode (two for each of the alternator's 3 output phases) rectifier is used to convert the AC current produced by the dynamo into the DC current needed to run the battery charging, ignition, lighting, and horn circuits.

Diodes can only conduct current from negative to positive, and therefore they convert AC to DC. If the rectifier, or any of the diodes, goes bad it will conduct in both directions, or not at all, leading to a discharged battery.

RESISTANCE TEST

1. Disconnect the white rectifier plug from the connector panel, and the white lead going to the battery.

2. With the tester set on the R x 10, or the R x 100 range, check the resistance between the white rectifier lead and each of the yellow leads, the yellow leads and the white lead, the black lead and each yellow lead, and each yellow and black lead. This means a total of 12 measurements.

3. The resistance should be low in one direction, and about ten times as great in the other. If the readings are high or low in either direction for any pair of wires, the rectifier is defective and must be replaced.

NOTE: *The lower reading should be within ⅓ scale of zero ohms regardless of the type of tester used.*

CAUTION: *When removing or installing a rectifier, do not loosen or tighten the nut*

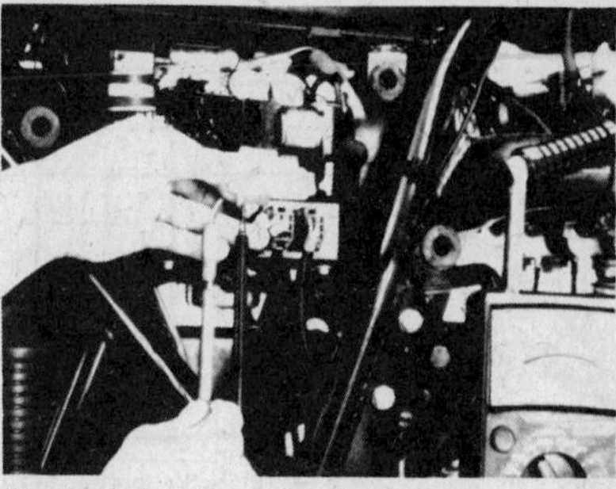

Testing the rectifier

which holds the rectifier assembly together as this will damage the unit.

Regulator

The regulator is a sealed solid state unit which must be replaced if defective. It functions to limit voltage to a maximum of about 15–16 volts, and is so constructed to act over each of the 3 phases of dynamo output.

Two symptoms which would indicate the possibility of a faulty regulator are repeated battery discharging or overcharging. Overcharging is indicated by the need to top up the electrolyte level more frequently than normal, and by light failures when running at high rpms. Discharging is indicated by a battery which checks out okay, but goes dead quickly after being charged.

OPERATIONAL TEST

In Circuit

NOTE: *Make sure that the battery is in good condition, and is well charged before beginning the test.*

1. Set the tester to the 30 VDC range, and connect it across the battery (tester negative lead to battery negative terminal, and tester positive lead to battery positive terminal).

2. Run the engine, with all lights and accessories turned off, at 4000 rpm while checking the meter. If the meter reads between 15–16 volts, the regulator is functioning normally; if it reads over 16 volts the regulator is either improperly connected or defective; and if the reading is less than 15 volts either the dynamo, rectifier, or regulator needs to be replaced. Go on to the next Step if the reading was low.

3. Turn off the engine, but leave the tester connected as is. Disconnect the green regulator plug from the connection panel under the right-side plastic cover. Run the engine at 4000 rpm and check the meter reading. If the reading is within 15–20 volts the regulator is defective; if the reading is less, then either the dynamo or rectifier is defective.

4. Before replacing the regulator, make sure that all the connections are clean and snug, as poor connections could cause misleading test results.

Out of Circuit

CAUTION: *When removing the regulator do not loosen or remove the screws in the regulator body. The screws aid in heat dissipation, and the unit will overheat if they are not properly installed.*

1. Set the meter on the R x 10 or R x 100 scale. There should be 1,000–1,100, ohms resistance between the black and brown leads, and no reading (∞) between any other two

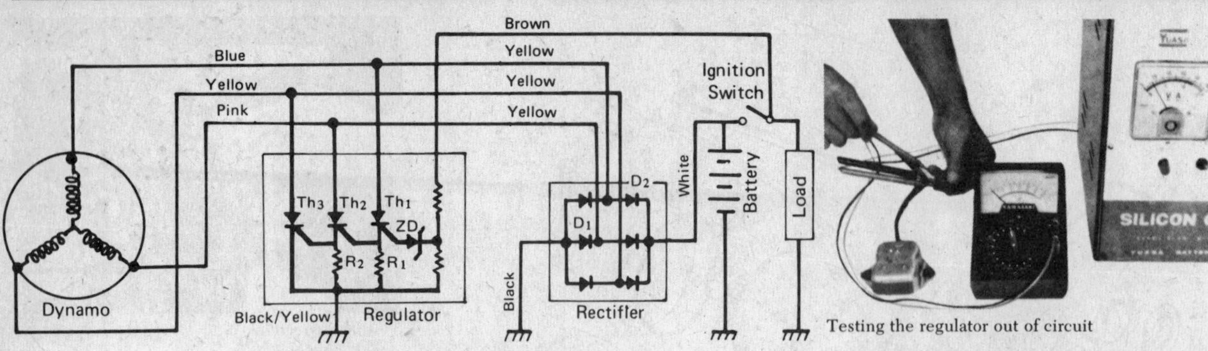

Rectifier and regulator circuit

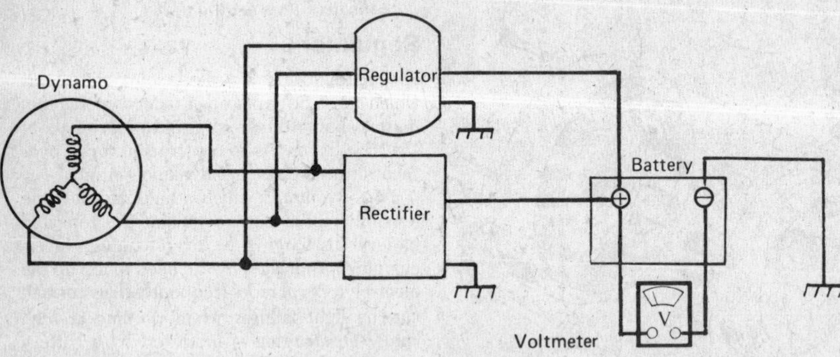

Testing with the regulator in circuit

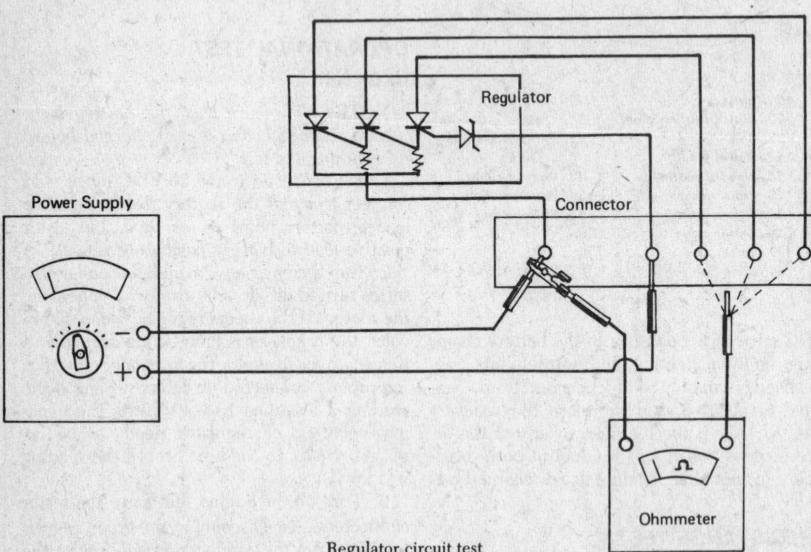

Regulator circuit test

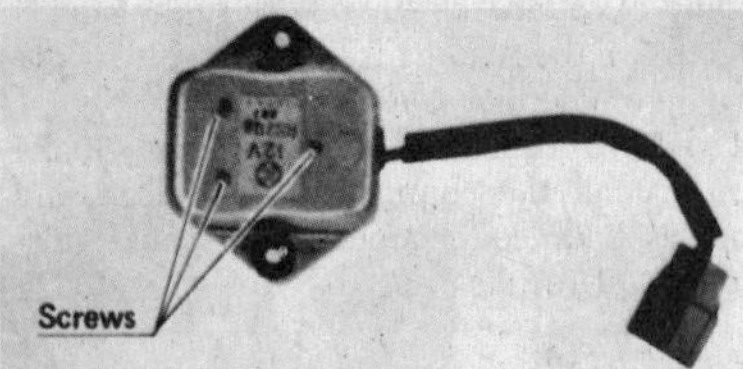

Do not remove these screws

leads, or between the black or brown and any other lead. Any other results indicate that the regulator is defective.

2. For this test a 14 VDC and a 16–17 VDC power source must be available. If the sources used cannot provide sufficient power, the tests will be inaccurate, and if more than 18 volts are passed through the regulator it may be damaged. Proceed as follows:

CAUTION: *If the voltage source and regulator are connected backwards for even a moment, the regulator will be damaged.*

a. Connect the regulator to the 14 VDC source as shown in the accompanying illustration.

b. Set the meter to either the R x 10 or the R x 100 range, and check that there is no reading (∞) between the black lead and the pink, yellow, or blue lead. If the meter gives any reading for any wire, the regulator is defective.

CAUTION: *When performing the next test, be sure that the black and brown leads never touch the meter leads at the same time or the meter will be damaged.*

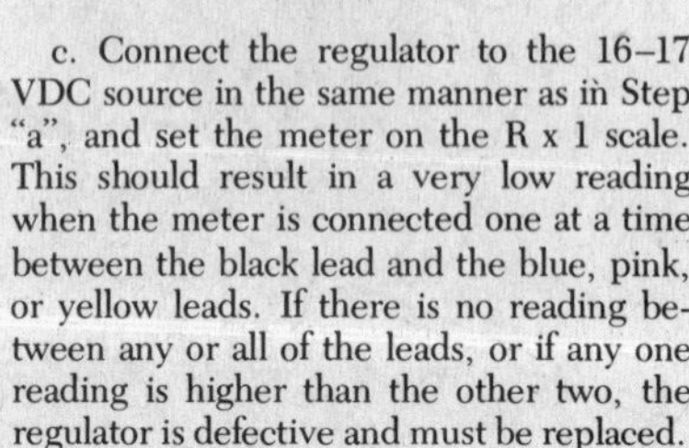
Testing the regulator out of circuit

c. Connect the regulator to the 16–17 VDC source in the same manner as in Step "a", and set the meter on the R x 1 scale. This should result in a very low reading when the meter is connected one at a time between the black lead and the blue, pink, or yellow leads. If there is no reading between any or all of the leads, or if any one reading is higher than the other two, the regulator is defective and must be replaced.

IGNITION SYSTEM

Component Removal and Installation

CONTACT BREAKER POINTS

1. Remove the breaker point cover and cover gasket, then remove the two mounting screws for each set of points, and remove the points.

Removing the point mounting screws

NOTE: *You may remove the mounting plate with the points and condensers in place, and then install a new plate with the points and condenser already mounted on it. Consult the "Automatic Advance Mechanism" Section for further information.*

2. Loosen the nut at the leaf spring, and disconnect the condensers if they are to be reused. It is best to replace the points and condensers at the same time.

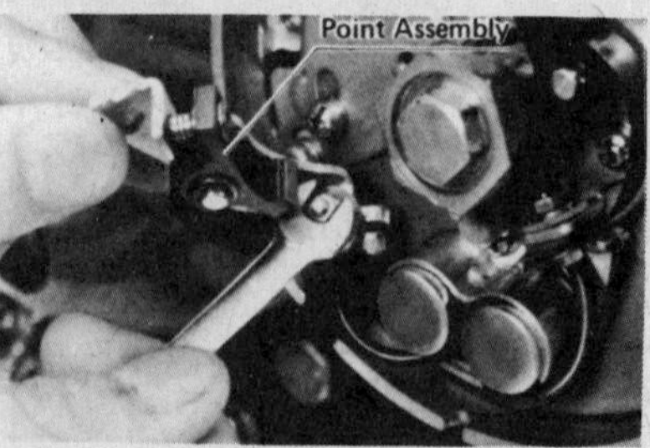

Disconnecting the condensers from the points

3. When installing the points make sure that the wire connectors are positioned on the

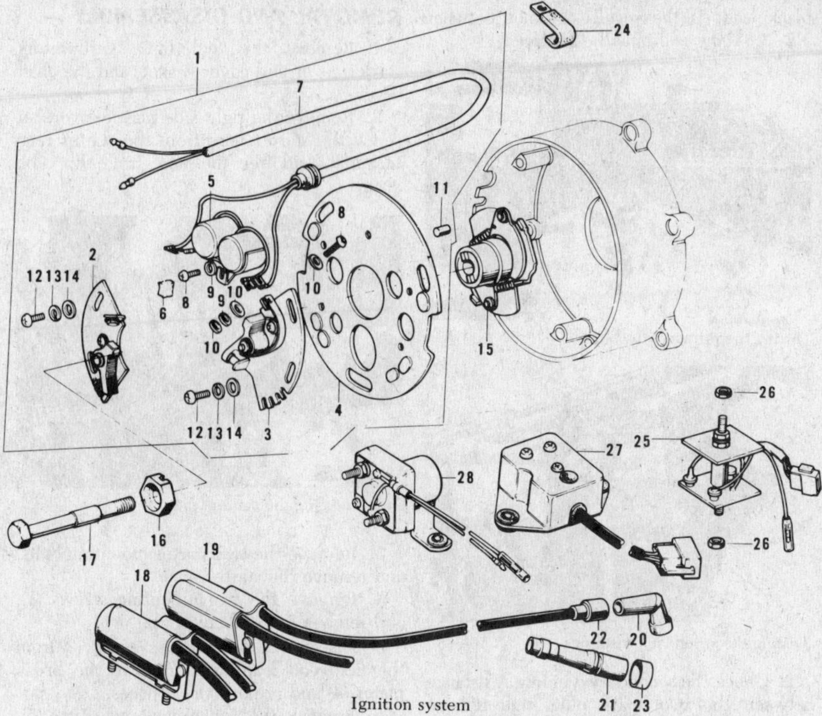

Ignition system

1. Contact breaker assy
2. Contact breaker
3. Contact breaker
4. Contact breaker plate
5. Condenser
6. Oil felt
7. Contact breaker wiring harness
8. Pan head screw
9. Spring washer
10. Plain washer
11. Dowel pin
12. Pan head screw
13. Spring washer
14. Plain washer
15. Spark advancer assy
16. Spark advancer washer
17. Spark advancer bolt
18. Ignition coil
19. Ignition coil
20. Spark plug cap
21. Spark plug cap
22. High tension cord grommet
23. Spark plug cap grommet
24. High tension cord clamp
25. Rectifier
26. Nut
27. Voltage regulator
28. Magnetic switch assy

outer part of the insulating washer. Do not overtighten the nuts as this may damage the washers causing electrical leakage.

CONDENSERS

1. The condensers are secured to the mounting plate by a single mounting screw. If they are being removed in conjunction with the points, follow Step 1 in the previous section, then remove the condensers mounting screw and disconnect the lead wires.

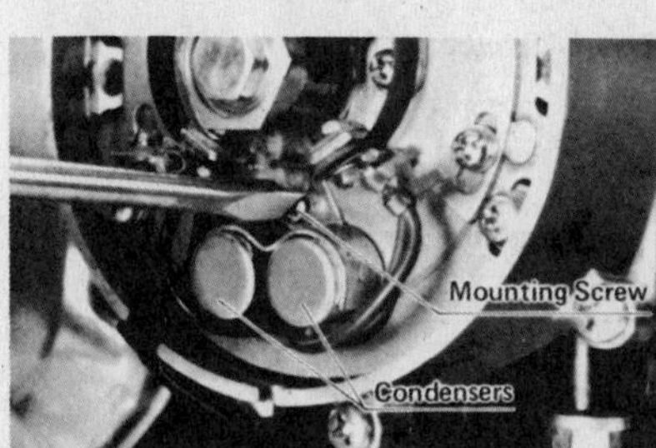

Removing the condensers

2. If the condensers alone are to be removed, remove the mounting screw and loosen the nuts at the lead spring to free the wires. Consult Step 3 in the previous Section.

Testing Condensers

Condensers are generally not tested for poor operation since they are so inexpensive to replace. Arcing across the points when they are open, badly pitted or burned points, or damaged leads indicate the need for condenser replacement.

The condensers can be tested by replacing them and checking for improved performance, or by testing them with a capacitor tester as illustrated. The condenser specifications are 0.25± 0.03 mfd., 1000 VDC.

AUTOMATIC ADVANCE MECHANISM

1. Remove the points cover and cover gasket.

2. Hold the crankshaft rotation nut steady with one wrench, then remove the bolt from the end of the shaft with another.

Removing the shaft nut

Removing the plate mounting screws

3. Remove the 3 mounting plate mounting screws to remove the plate, and remove the advance mechanism.

4. Disassemble the unit, replace any damaged parts (or the whole unit), assemble it so

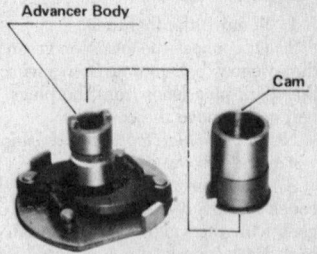

The cam slips right off the advancer body

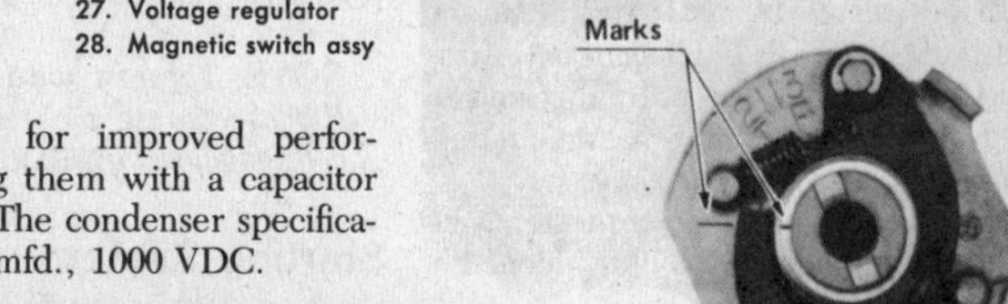

Line up these marks when assembling the unit

Greasing the shaft

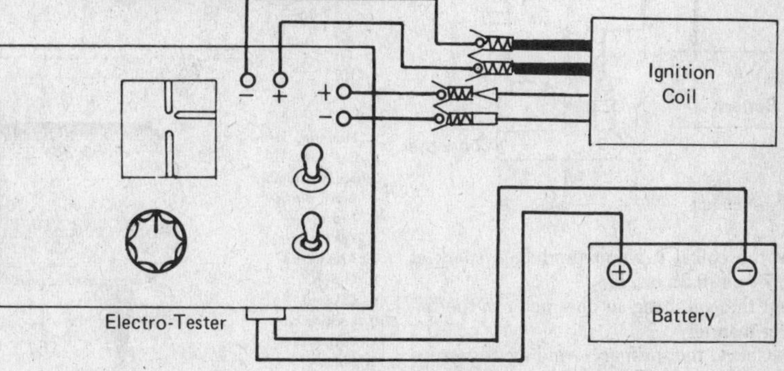

Condenser test circuit

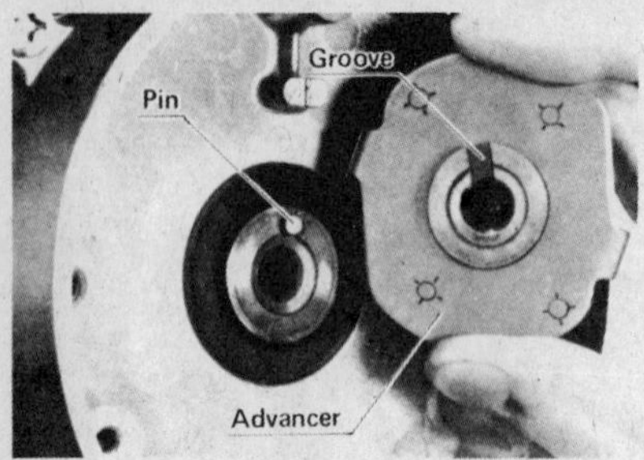

Lining up the groove and pin

that the marks line up, and grease the shaft before installing the breaker cam.

5. When installing the mechanism be sure that the pin on the crankshaft fits into the groove in the back of the advancer, and that the crankshaft rotation nut is properly seated.

IGNITION COILS

1. Remove the fuel tank.
2. Disconnect the black or green wire (as the case may be), and the brown wire, remove the spark plug leads from the plugs, and unbolt and remove the coil(s).

   NOTE: *The high tension leads cannot be removed from the coil.*
3. When installing coils match the color coded black and green wires. The brown wire goes with the yellow-red lead from the battery. Each plug lead is numbered for the appropriate cylinder.

Testing Coils

Coils can be stested by replacing them and seeing if performance is enhanced, by testing them with an electro-tester, or by checking for a shorted or open condition using an ohmmeter.

Hook up the coil to the electro-tester as indicated in the accompanying illustration. Replace the coil if it won't produce a spark at least 7 mm (0.28 in.) long.

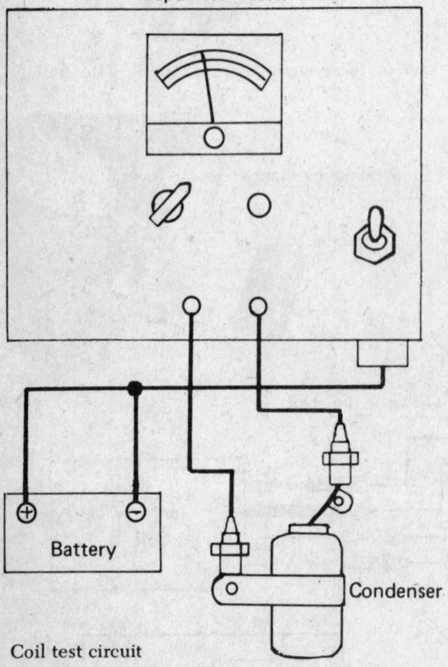

Coil test circuit

Test the coil using an ohmmeter in the following manner:

1. Check the primary winding resistance between the red/yellow lead and the green or black lead. If the results are not between 3.2–3.8 Ω the coil must be replaced.

Testing the primary windings

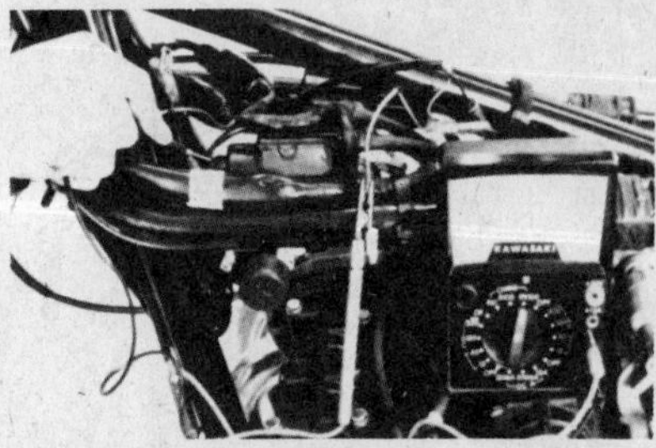
Testing the secondary windings

2. Check the secondary winding resistance between the two spark plug high tension wires. If the result is not about 30K Ω the coil must be replaced.
3. Set the ohmmeter on its highest scale and check the resistance between the brown wire and the plug wires or the coil core. If the reading is not infinity (∞), the coil must be replaced.

   NOTE: *The test with an ohmmeter is not 100% accurate as it doesn't test for high voltage shorts (insulation breakdown).*

Starting System

CAUTION: *Do not keep the starter button depressed if the starter motor doesn't respond as this may burn out the starter windings. Do not continue to operate the starter for more than 30 seconds if the engine doesn't start, and let it cool off for about 2 minutes if you do operate it for long.*

REMOVAL AND DISASSEMBLY

1. Remove the fuel tank, carburetors, starter cover and cover gasket, and the chain cover.
2. Remove the right-side plastic cover, unscrew the starter wire from the starter relay terminal, and free the wire from the cable clamp.

Disconnecting the starter leads

3. Remove the two starter mounting bolts, and remove the starter.
4. Remove the two mounting screws (1), and remove the end cover (2).
5. Disconnect the brush assembly (3) from the field coil lead, then remove the brush plates (4) and remove the brushes.
6. Remove the remaining end cover (5), and remove the yoke assembly (6) and armature (7).
7. Remove the starter clutch as described in the "Dynamo Removal and Installation" Section.

INSPECTION

1. Inspect the carbon brushes for excessive wear or damage, and replace them if worn past the standard of ½ in. (13–13 mm) by ¼ in. (7 mm) or more. Always replace the brushes as a pair.
2. Inspect the brush springs for a worn, damaged, or collapsed condition and replace them as necessary. The spring tension should be 20–24 oz (560–680 g) as measured with a spring gauge, but the spring may be considered serviceable if it will snap the brush firmly into place.

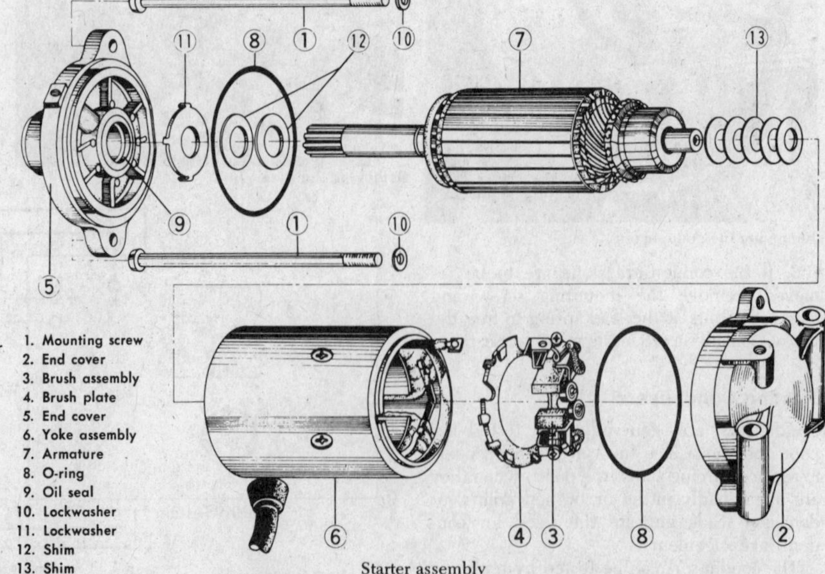

Starter assembly

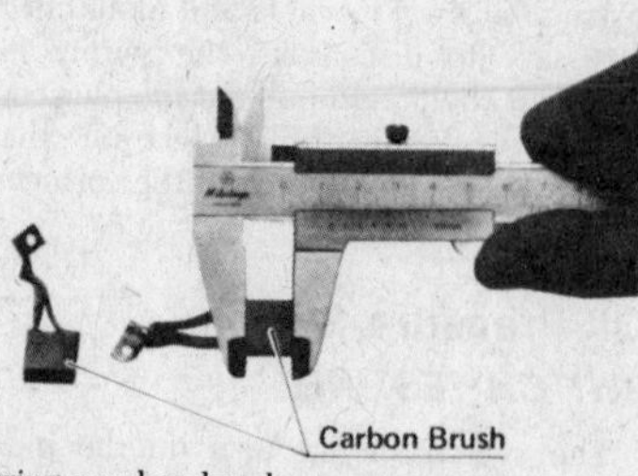

Measuring a carbon brush

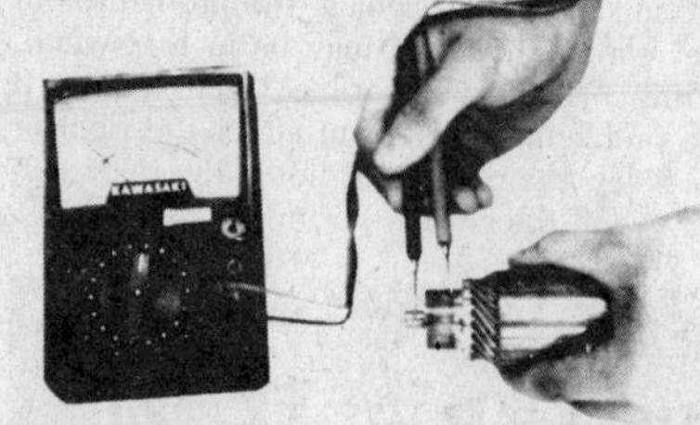
Testing resistance between the commutator and shaft

3. Inspect the commutator for a worn, scored, or otherwise damaged condition, and turn it down or clean it up with fine emery paper if necessary. If brush dust is caught in the commutator grooves it must be cleaned out thoroughly, and the mica should be cut square as illustrated.

4. Test the commutator in the following manner:

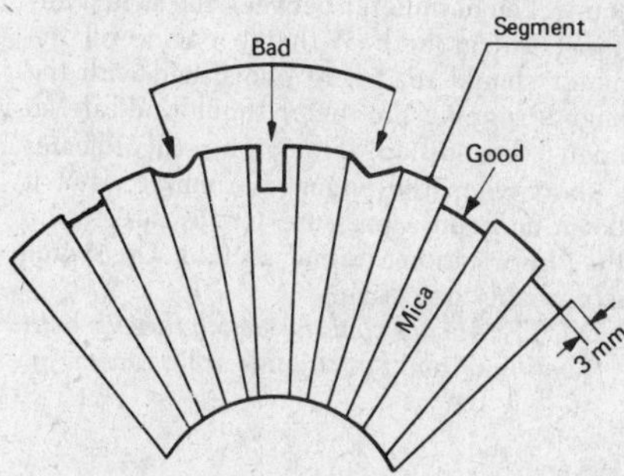

The commutator grooves should look like the "good" one

a. Turn the meter switch to the R x 1 scale, and measure the resistance between each two segments of the commutator. High resistance or no reading at all between any two, indicates that wire is open and the armature must be replaced.

b. Turn the meter switch to the highest scale, and measure the resistance between the commutator and the shaft. Any reading at all indicates that the armature is grounded.

c. If the above checks do not reveal a problem, and after checking the other starter circuit components no fault is discovered, the nature of the problem may be such that it cannot be isolated with a meter. Therefore if after thoroughly checking the system the starter still fails to turn over, or only operates feebly, replace the armature.

5. Test the field coils in the following manner:

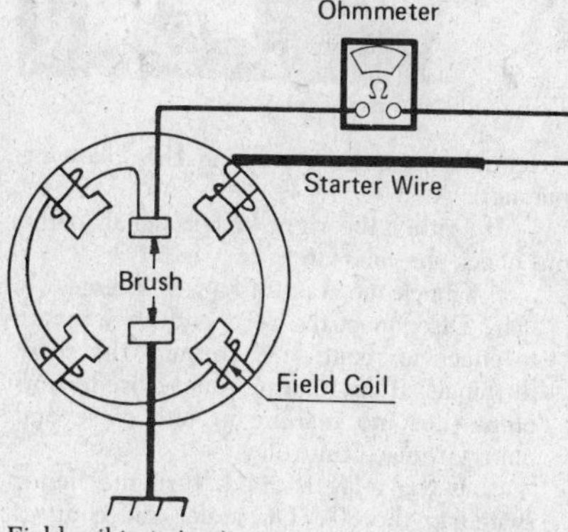

Field coil test circuit

a. Turn the meter switch to the R x 1 scale, and measure the resistance between the carbon brush on the positive side, and the starter lead. If the reading is not close to zero ohms, or if there is no reading, the field coils are open and the yoke assembly must be replaced.

Testing the resistance between the positive brush and the yoke

b. Turn the meter switch to the highest scale, and measure the resistance between the positive side brush and the yoke (housing). Any reading indicates that the coils are shorted to ground, and the yoke must be replaced.

6. Test the starter relay in the following manner:

a. Disconnect the starter wires from the relay, and connect a meter set on the R x 1 scale, across the relay terminals.

b. Press the starter button and see if the meter reads zero ohms. If the relay clicks once and the meter reads zero, the relay is good. If it clicks, but the meter does not read zero, the relay is defective and must be replaced. If the relay doesn't click at all, disconnect the black and yellow/black wires and measure the resistance across them. If the reading is not close to zero, the relay is defective.

c. If the reading is zero, the relay may be good, but there may be no current getting to it. Turn the tester switch to the 30 VDC scale and connect the negative (−) meter lead to the yellow/black relay lead, and the positive (+) tester lead to the black wire. When the starter button is pushed, the meter should read battery voltage. If it doesn't the problem is in the wiring. If the meter reads battery voltage, but the relay doesn't click, the relay is defective.

7. If the starter works, but doesn't disengage after the engine starts, the starter clutch rollers or gear may be damaged or worn. Such damage could also prevent the starter from engaging properly, or could cause noisy operation while the engine is running.

The clutch should not be able to rotate in the direction of the arrow

Test the clutch by rotating the clutch gear by hand. It should not be able to turn in the direction of the arrow, but should turn freely in the opposite direction. If the clutch does not operate correctly, or if it operates noisily, disassemble and inspect all components for wear or damage, and replace those whose condition is even marginal.

NOTE: *Damage to either the starter clutch gear, the idle gear, or the starter gear may cause damage to the other gears. Inspect them all carefully if any are damaged or excessively worn.*

ASSEMBLY AND INSTALLATION

1. Assembly is in the reverse order of disassembly, and installation is in the reverse order of removal.

Testing resistance between segments

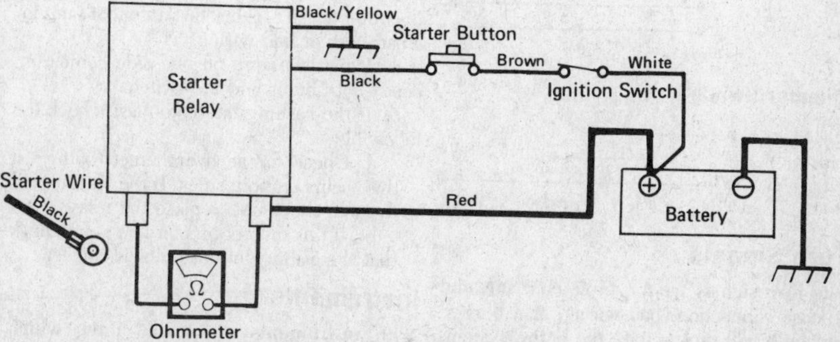

Starter relay contact test circuit

2. Carefully clean off any dust from the shaft as this may result in premature wear, and dampen the shaft felts with fresh oil.

3. Take care not to damage the O-rings and oil seals when installing the end covers, and align the marks on the covers and housing.

Make sure that the marks are aligned on both ends

4. Lubricate the O-ring with a small amount of fresh oil before slipping the starter into place.

5. Apply Loctite, or another suitable sealer, to the starter mounting bolts before installing them.

ELECTRICAL EQUIPMENT

Switches

The switches are not repairable, and must be replaced if defective. The switches can be disassembled and cleaned, but no replacement parts are available.

Use a meter to determine whether the connections given in the following charts are good. The meter should read zero ohms for any of these connections.

Intermittent loss of spark to either pair of cylinders may be caused by a shorted kill switch. The best way to test for this is to remove the switch from the circuit, and see whether or not you continue to drop cylinders.

Ignition Switch

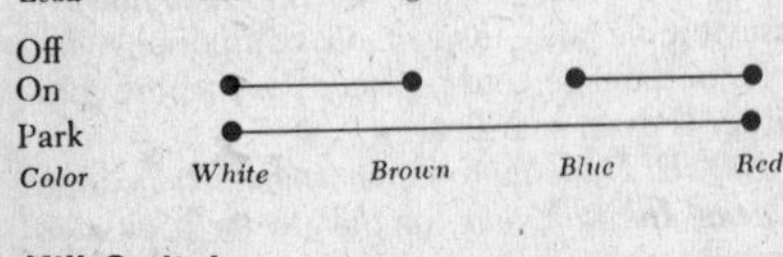

Kill Switch

On	●	●
Off		
Color	Brown	R/Y

Headlight Switch

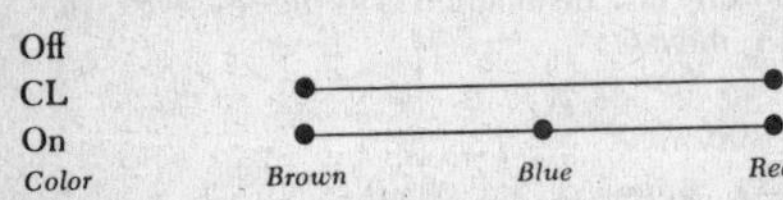

Dimmer Switch

Turn Signals

The turn signals are a complete circuit, and a loose connection, bad wiring, or a burned out bulb will incapacitate the entire system. Usually, if the trouble is common to both the left and right turn signals, the problem is in the relay, although it may be in the switch, wiring, or due to a poorly charged battery. If the problem is isolated in either the right or left sides, the problem is not in the relay, but may be in the switch, wiring, or bulbs.

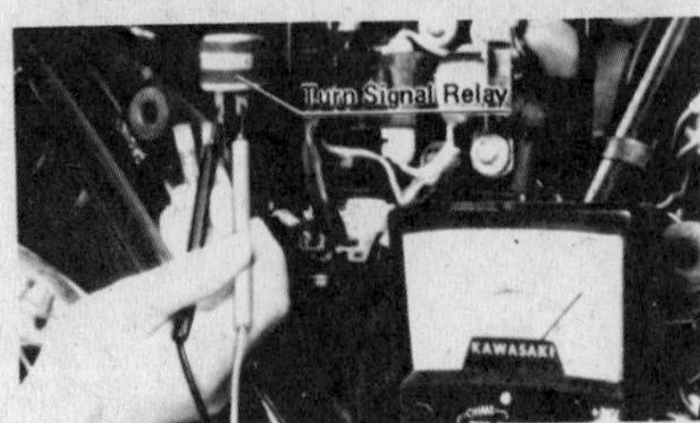

Testing the turn signal relay

Troubleshoot the system in the following manner:

1. If neither the right or left signals come on, check the following:
   a. Check the state of battery charge.
   b. Disconnect the relay and use a meter to check for continuity through the relay terminals. If the reading is not close to zero ohms (i.e., no reading or one of several ohms), replace the relay.
   c. If the relay is good, turn the meter switch to the 30 VDC scale, and connect the positive (+) meter lead to the brown wire which goes to the relay, and the negative (−) tester lead to the orange wire. Turn on the ignition, and flip the turn signal switch from right to left. If the meter registers battery voltage but the lamps don't work, recheck the wiring and bulbs. If the meter doesn't register battery voltage, either the switch or wiring is bad.
2. If both the right or left signals come on and stay on, or blink too slowly, check the following:
   a. Check the state of battery charge.
   b. Check all of the wiring connections.
   c. Check that the bulbs, both the flasher and the indicator, are of the correct wattage.
   d. Replace the relay if the above Steps check out.

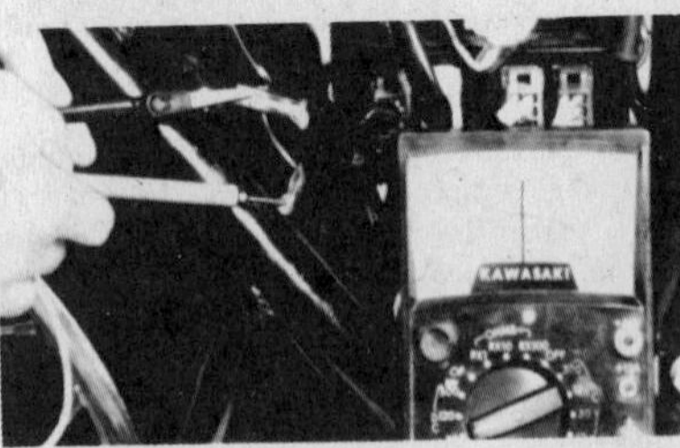

Testing the relay leads

3. If one lamp on one side comes on, but the other doesn't, check the lamp that's out for a bad bulb or bad wiring.
4. If neither lamp on one side comes on, check both bulbs and the switch.
5. If the flashing rate is too fast, check the following:
   a. Check for an overcharged battery if this occurs on both sides. If the battery and dynamo check out, replace the relay.
   b. If this only occurs on one side, check that the wattage of the bulbs is correct.

Instruments

Both instruments are sealed units which cannot be repaired except for bulb replacement. Replace the bulbs by disconnecting the instrument from its cable and mount (it is not necessary to disconnect the wiring in the headlight shell), and pull out the plug connector for the offending bulb. Make sure that you replace the bulb with one of the correct wattage.

Oil Pressure Switch

SWITCH TESTING

The switch should turn on the indicator light when the key is on but the engine is not running. If the light doesn't come on, disconnect the lead from the switch and use an ohmmeter to check for continuity between the switch body and the switch terminal. A dead short indicates that the problem is either in the wiring or bulb. If the reading is not zero ohms, the switch is defective and must be replaced.

If the lamp stays on and you've already followed the instructions in the preceding Section, disconnect the lead from the switch, and connect an ohmmeter between the switch terminal and ground. With the engine off the meter should read zero ohms, and with the engine running the meter should indicate an open (∞) condition. If the meter still indicates a short when the engine is running, shut it down and run a pressure test as directed in the "Lubrication System" section. The switch is probably defective.

NOTE: *Always coat the switch threads with Loctite, or another suitable sealer, when installing it.*

Horn

Most horn troubles, unless caused by maladjustment, can be traced to the contacts. The contacts wear and must be periodically adjusted. If adjusting the contacts doesn't correct the problem, the contacts are probably dirty or pitted.

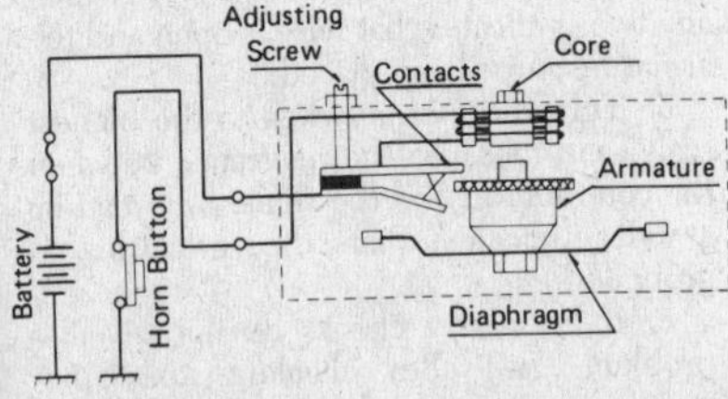

Horn diagram

ADJUSTMENT

1. Remove the fuel tank, then disconnect the black horn wire, and connect a meter into the circuit so that the positive (+) tester lead goes to the black wire on the horn side, and the negative (−) tester lead goes to the remaining black wire.

2. Turn on the ignition, and depress the horn button while turning in the adjusting nut until the horn sounds its best. Keep the horn current between 1.8 and 2.5 amps.

CAUTION: *Do not turn the adjusting nut in too far as this may damage the spring inside the horn, and increase the horn current to a point where the horn coil may be burned out.*

3. If the horn doesn't sound right, first make sure that no cables or other components are touching it, and if this doesn't help, clean the contacts as described in the following Section.

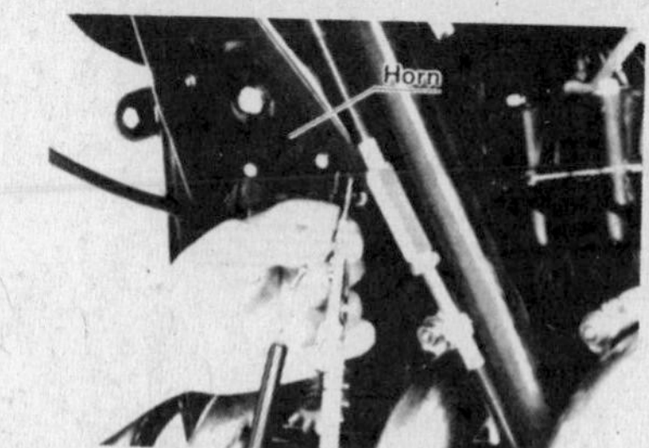

Testing the horn

Horn adjusting nut location

5. Inspect the horn assembly for signs of water damage, and replace the gasket with a homemade one if it appears to be water damaged.

ELECTRICAL TROUBLESHOOTING

If you've got an electrical problem that you can't trace, especially if it is an intermittent one, chances are that it's due to poor contact of the male and female connectors in the electrical panel. This may be due to the failure of one of the connectors to seat properly in the plastic plug jack, so when the panel is plugged together one of the pins or receptors backs out causing a poor contact. Vibration can also figure in this, causing a poor connection while the machine is running, but checking out okay when sitting dormant.

Alleviate this sort of problem by tugging at each wire until a loose one is discovered, then push it back in until you feel the small locking tang reach its seat. Pull on the offending wire a few times again to make sure that it's now properly seated.

The following table will help you locate a connector-based problem more easily:

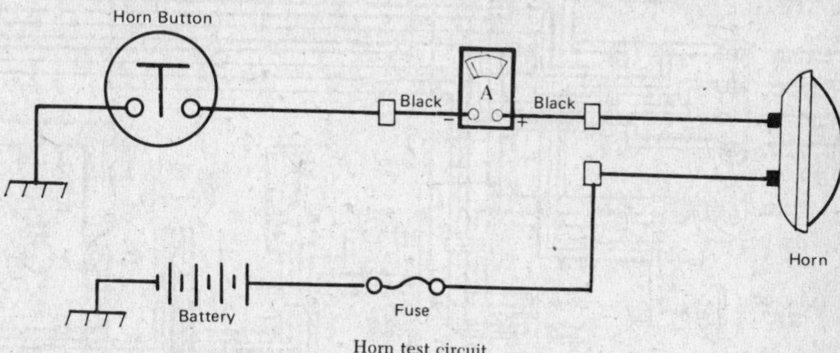

Horn test circuit

REPAIR

CAUTION: *Do not loosen the core or armature mounting as this will necessitate fine adjustments not given here.*

1. Check horn continuity with a meter connected to the black and brown leads. If the reading is close to zero ohms, the horn should be adjusted.

2. If the reading is several ohms, if there is no reading, or if adjustment will not correct the problem, remove the screws around the perimeter of the horn to disassemble it.

3. Clean the contacts with fine sandpaper or emery cloth until you get a reading of zero ohms resistance across the contacts.

4. If there is still high resistance, or if there is still no reading, the coil is burned out and the horn must be replaced.

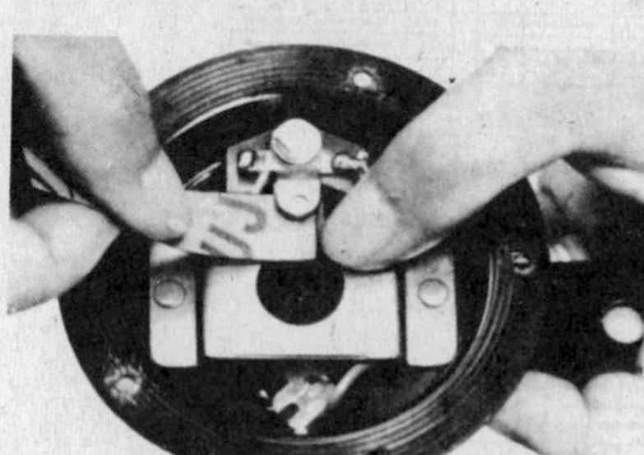
Cleaning the contacts

Blue Plug:	The blue plug contains 3 leads from the dynamo, one lead from the Neutral light, and one from the oil pressure warning light. A poor connection here could mean the battery would not charge, leading to a dead battery, or failure of one of the warning lights to illuminate.
Green Plug:	The green plug goes to the voltage regulator. A poor connection here could overcharge the battery, possibly causing it to boil over. Usually, the first indication of a problem is burning out of the headlamp or other lamps.
White Plug:	The white plug leads to the rectifier. A bad connection here could fail to charge the battery, leading to a dead battery.
Brown Plug:	The brown plug supplies the main electrical harness, including the starter, the lights, the horn, and the ignition. Poor connection could mean no lights, no horn, no electric start, or no ignition.

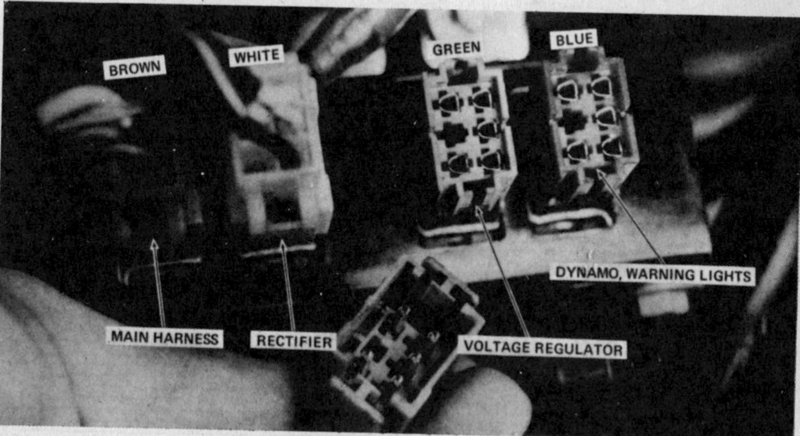

Electrical panel location

WIRING DIAGRAMS

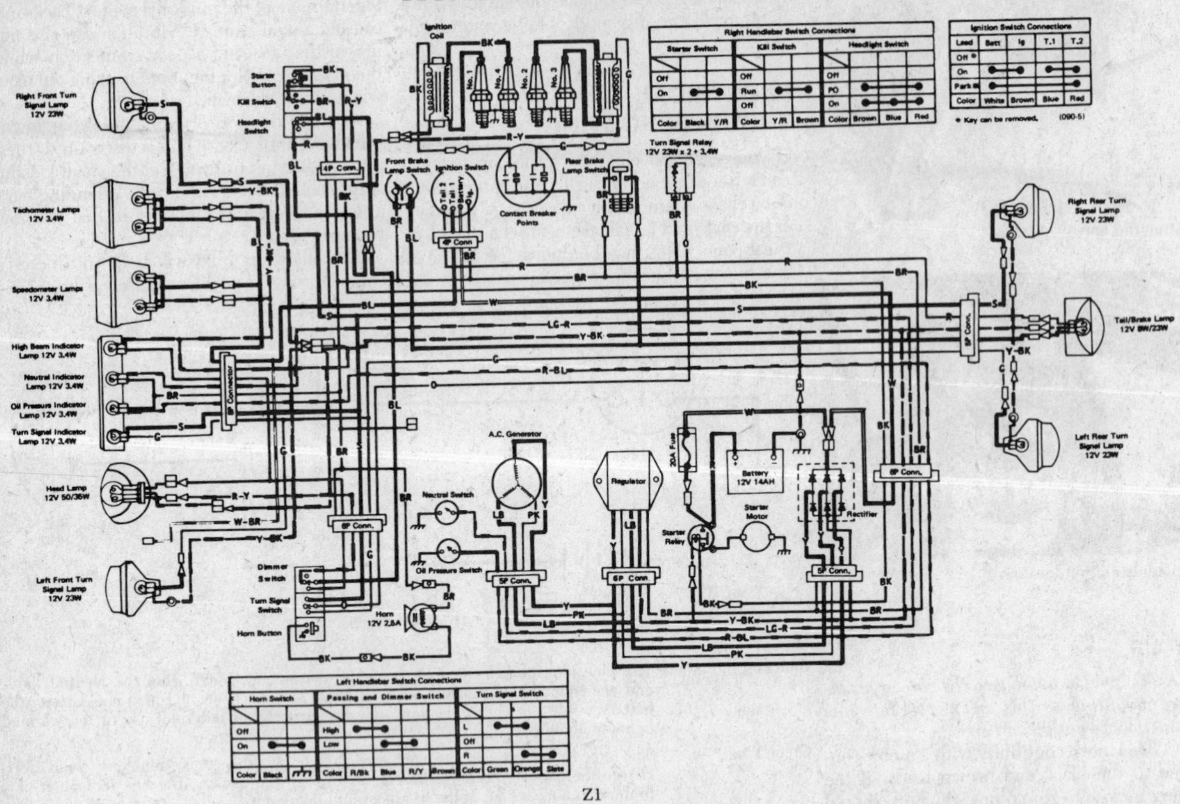

Z1

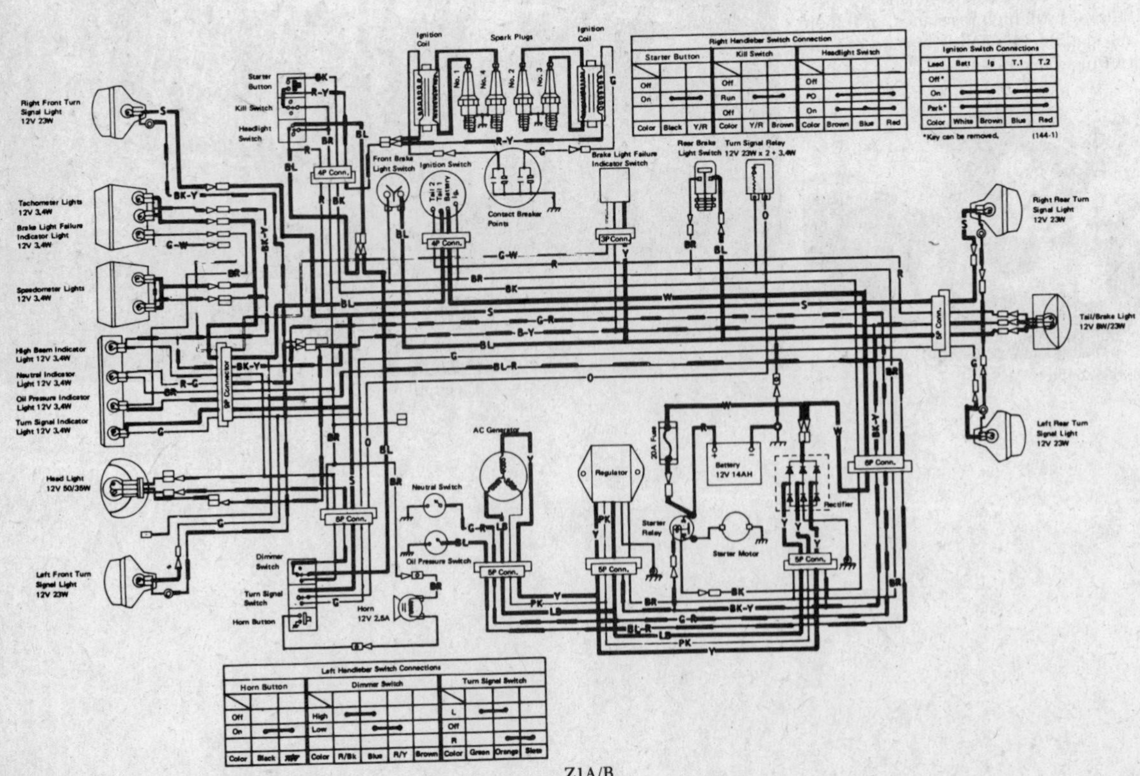

Z1A/B

WIRING DIAGRAMS

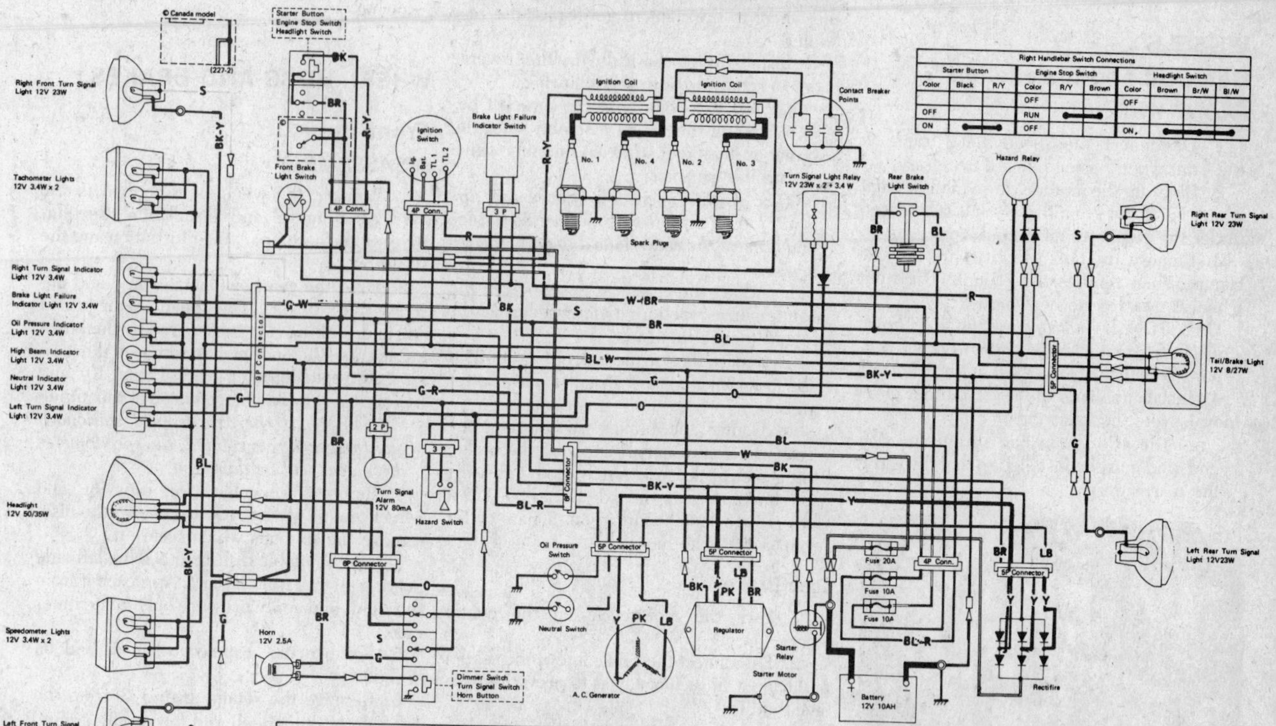

Right Handlebar Switch Connections									
Starter Button			Engine Stop Switch			Headlight Switch			
Color	Black	R/Y	Color	R/Y	Brown	Color	Brown	Br/W	Bl/W
			OFF			OFF			
OFF			RUN	●	●				
ON	●	●	OFF			ON	●	●	●

Left Handlebar Switch Connections											
Horn Button			Dimmer Switch					Turn Signal Switch			
Color	Black	⏚	Color	Bk/R	Blue	R/Y	Brown	Color	Green	Orange	Slate
OFF			HI	●	●			Left	●	●	
ON	●	●	LO		●	●					
								Right		●	●

Hazard Switch			
Color	Green	Slate	Orange
OFF			
ON	●	●	●

(214-3)

Ignition Switch Connection				
Lead	Ignition	Battery	Tail 1	Tail 2
Color	Brown	White	Blue	Red
OFF				
ON	●	●	●	●
PARK		●		●

KZ900

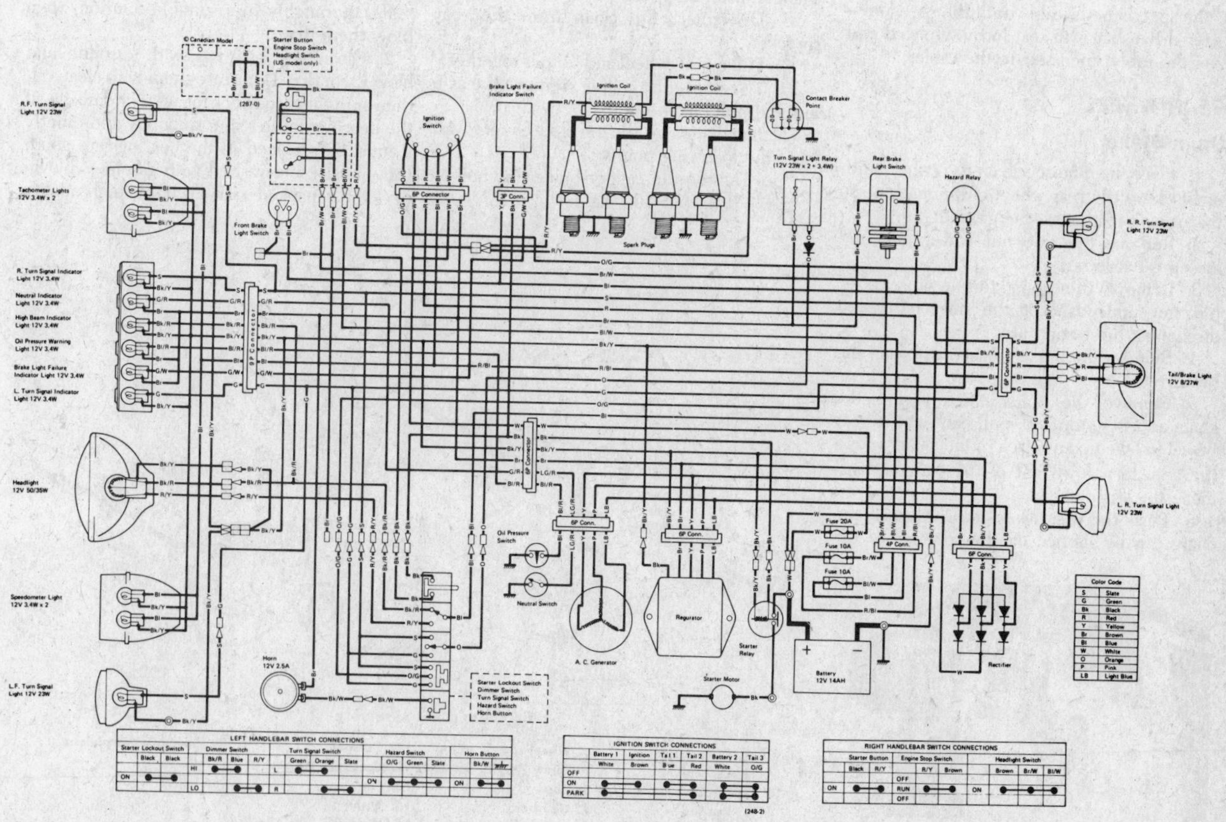

Color Code	
S	Slate
G	Green
Bk	Black
R	Red
Y	Yellow
Br	Brown
Bl	Blue
W	White
O	Orange
P	Pink
LB	Light Blue

LEFT HANDLEBAR SWITCH CONNECTIONS																	
Starter Lockout Switch			Dimmer Switch				Turn Signal Switch				Hazard Switch				Horn Button		
	Black	Black		Bk/R	Blue	R/Y		Green	Orange	Slate		O/G	Green	Slate		Bk/W	⏚
			HI	●	●		L	●	●								
ON	●	●									ON	●	●	●	ON	●	●
			LO		●	●	R		●	●							

IGNITION SWITCH CONNECTIONS						
	Battery 1	Ignition	Tail 1	Tail 2	Battery 2	Tail 3
	White	Brown	Blue	Red	White	O/G
OFF						
ON	●	●	●	●	●	●
PARK	●			●	●	●

(248-2)

RIGHT HANDLEBAR SWITCH CONNECTIONS									
Starter Button			Engine Stop Switch			Headlight Switch			
	Black	R/Y		R/Y	Brown		Brown	Br/W	Bl/W
			OFF						
ON	●	●	RUN	●	●	ON	●	●	●
			OFF						

KZ1000

CHASSIS

WHEELS

Removal and Installation

FRONT WHEEL

1. Disconnect the speedometer cable at the front wheel, using pliers if necessary.
2. Block up the motorcycle so that the front wheel is off the ground, or use a jack placed under the engine to raise the bike.
3. Remove the nuts which secure the axle clamps, then remove the clamps. The front wheel is now free to be removed.

CAUTION: *Do not operate the front brake while the front wheel is removed or the caliper piston will be forced out of the cylinder.*

4. Installation is in the reverse order of removal. Note the following:

a. The axle clamp has a front and rear end, and must be installed so that the gap at the rear is even.

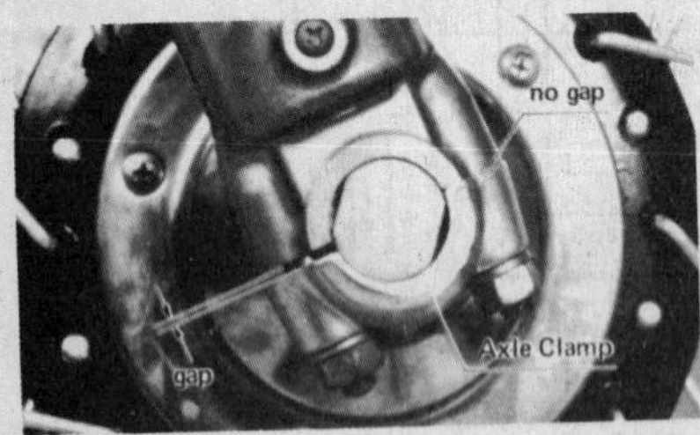

Axle clamp correctly installed

b. Secure the front clamp nut first, and then the rear, to a specified torque of 13–14.5 ft lbs (1.8–2.0 kg/m). Check for an even gap at the rear.

c. Rotate the front wheel while installing the speedometer cable until the speedometer drive shaft will seat in the grooved end of the cable, then secure the cable.

REAR WHEEL

Drum Brake

1. Place the motorcycle on its center stand, or block up the rear wheel of the machine so that it isn't resting on the ground.
2. Remove the axle nut cotter pin, and loosen the axle nut.
3. Remove the brake torque link cotter pin, nut, and washer at the brake hub, then disconnect the torque link.
4. Remove the brake adjuster nut from the brake rod.
5. Remove the bolts which secure the chain adjuster stoppers, pull back on the rear wheel to take up any slack in the chain, rotate the adjusters down out of the way, and remove the stoppers.
6. Push the rear wheel forward until the chain can be slipped off the sprocket to the left, then pull the wheel back and off the frame. It may be necessary to shift the top of the wheel to the right to get it past the rear fender.

Chain adjuster stopper location

7. Installation is basically in the reverse order of removal. Note the following:

a. Start the chain onto the sprocket before slipping the wheel assembly onto the frame or it will get stuck on the nuts which secure the sprocket.

NOTE: *If this operation proves too difficult, loosen the left-side muffler mounting, and remove the chain guard to gain greater access.*

b. Adjust the chain, as described in the "Maintenance" section, before securing the axle and torque link nuts.

c. Secure the torque link nut to 22–25 ft lbs (3–3.5 kg/m) and install a new cotter pin.

d. Center the brakes by spinning the rear wheel and sharply applying the brake, then secure the axle nut without releasing the brake. Secure the axle nut to 95–115 ft lbs (13–16 kg/m), and install a new cotter pin. Adjust the brakes.

Disc Brake

1. Park the motorcycle on the center stand.
2. Disconnect the brake line at the caliper and hang it in such a way as to prevent excessive fluid loss.
3. Unbolt the torque link at the caliper.
4. Remove the chain guard.
5. Loosen the axle nut. Disengage the caliper from the torque link.
6. Back off both chain adjuster bolts and bend the adjusters down and out of the way. Push the wheel forward as much as possible.
7. Remove the bolts and take out the chain adjuster stoppers.
8. Disconnect the chain from the rear sprocket.
9. Pull off the wheel and caliper together.
10. To remove the caliper, remove the axle nut and pull out the axle.
11. Installation is the reverse of removal. Note the following points:

a. Tighten the caliper brake line bolt to 21–22 ft lbs (2.9–3.1 kg/m).

b. After installing the wheel, bleed the brake as outlined in the brake section following.

WHEEL HUBS AND BRAKES

Front Hub

DISASSEMBLY

1. Remove the wheel as described in the "Wheels Removal and Installation" Section. Refer to the accompanying illustration and the "Caution."
2. Hold the gearbox (9) stationary, and unscrew the axle (17). The speedometer pinion (16) and bushing (14) are secured by the bushing set pin (13), and may be removed if necessary. The speedometer gears (12 and 10), and the oil seal (11) may be removed at this time.

CAUTION: *If the axle is held stationary and the gearbox is rotated, the speedometer drive gear will be damaged.*

3. Remove the collar (18), caps (8), and wheel cap (6). If you wish to remove the disc, remove the six bolts which secure it.
4. Use a suitable drift to knock the left-side bearing (4) free from its seat. Approach it from the right, and apply pressure only to the inner race.
5. Remove the distance collar (5) and oil seal (2).
6. Remove the retaining ring (3) from the left-side of the wheel, and tap evenly around the inner race of the right-side bearing until it comes out.
7. Consult the "Front Disc Brake" Section for additional information on the front disc brake master cylinder and caliper assemblies.

INSPECTION

1. Clean all parts, except the bearings and seals, thoroughly in a suitable solution, then blow them dry.
2. Clean the bearings with gasoline and blow them dry. Lubricate them with clean oil, then spin them to check for wear or damage. If the bearing doesn't spin smoothly and quietly it must be replaced. If the bearings are good, they must be rewashed with gasoline, blown dry, and repacked with a suitable high quality

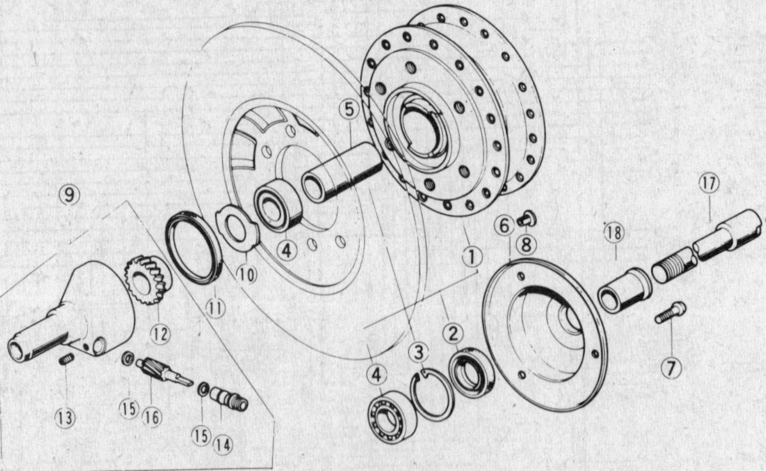

Front hub assembly

1. Drum assembly
2. Oil seal
3. Circlip
4. Bearing
5. Distance collar
6. Wheel cap
7. Screw
8. Cap
9. Gearbox
10. Speedometer gear
11. Oil seal
12. Speedometer gear
13. Pin
14. Bushing
15. Washer
16. Speedometer pinion
17. Axle
18. Collar

bearing grease. Spin the bearing a few times to circulate the grease evenly.

CAUTION: *Never spin dry bearings under any circumstances.*

3. Check all parts for a worn or damaged condition, and replace them as necessary. Oil seals must be replaced if even only slightly damaged or cracked, and should be replaced as a matter of course.

4. Consult the "Front Disc Brake—Disc" Section for additional information concerning the disc.

ASSEMBLY

1. Assembly is basically in the reverse order of disassembly.

2. Replace the oil seals with new ones, and install the bearings using either the special bearing driver holder and bearing driver (Part No. 57001-139 and 57001-140) or a suitable substitute.

3. Align the speedometer drive, as illustrated, during installation.

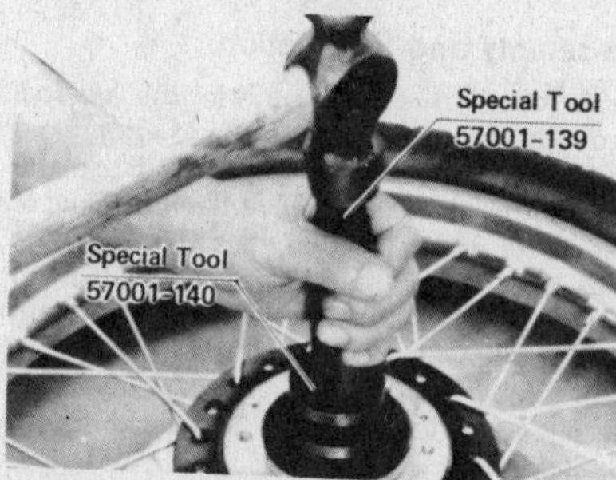

Installing a wheel bearing

Installing the speedometer drive

4. Remember to hold the gearbox stationary and screw in the axle to avoid damaging the speedometer gear drive.

Front Disc Brake

CAUTION: *Read and observe the following before beginning any work on the disc brake assemblies:*

1. Never re-use old brake fluid.

2. Do not use fluid from a container that has been left unsealed, or that has been open a long time.

3. Do not mix two types of fluid for use in the brakes. This lowers the brake fluid boiling point and could cause the brake to be ineffective. It may also cause the rubber brake parts to deteriorate. Recommended fluids are shown below.

NOTE: *The type of fluid originally used in the disc brake is not available in most areas, but it should be necessary to add very little fluid before the first brake fluid change. After changing the fluid, use only that one type thereafter.*

Atlas Extra Heavy Duty
Shell Super Heavy Duty
Texaco Super Heavy Duty
Wagner Lockheed Heavy Duty
Girling Amber

The correct fluid will come in a can labeled SAE J-1703 or D.O.T.3. Do not use fluid that does not have one of these markings.

4. Don't leave the reservoir cap off for any length of time as moisture may be absorbed into the fluid.

5. Don't change the fluid in the rain, or when a strong wind is blowing.

6. Use only disc brake fluid, isopropyl alcohol or ethyl alcohol for cleaning brake parts, but do not allow rubber parts to remain in contact with the alcohol for more than 30 seconds.

7. Brake fluid will damage painted surfaces; any spilled fluid should be wiped off immediately.

8. Do not use gasoline, motor oil, or any other mineral oils near disc brake parts; these oils cause deterioration of rubber brake parts. If oil spills on any brake parts it is very difficult to wash off and will eventually reach and break down the rubber.

9. If any of the brake line fittings or the bleeder valve is loosened at any time the air must be bled from the brake.

10. Prescribed torque values for tightening disc brake parts mountings are as above.

Brake lever	45 ~ 60 in. lbs	0.5 ~ 0.7 kg/m
Brake lever adjuster	70 ~ 100 in. lbs	0.9 ~ 1.2 kg/m
Master cylinder clamp	55 ~ 75 in. lbs	0.63 ~ 0.88 kg/m
Fitting (banjo) bolts	19 ~ 23 ft lbs	2.5 ~ 3.3 kg/m
Brake pipe nipple	150 ~ 155 in. lbs	1.7 ~ 1.8 kg/m
3-way fitting mounting	45 ~ 50 in. lbs	0.5 ~ 0.6 kg/m
Pressure switch	135 ~ 170 in. lbs	1.5 ~ 2.0 kg/m
Caliper shafts	22 ~ 26 ft lbs	3.0 ~ 3.6 kg/m
Caliper mounting	19 ~ 23 ft lbs	2.5 ~ 3.3 kg/m
Bleeder valve	70 ~ 85 in. lbs	0.8 ~ 1.0 kg/m
Disc mounting bolts	140 ~ 190 in. lbs	1.6 ~ 2.2 kg/m

BRAKE PADS

Replacement

1. Read the cautionary notes at the beginning of the "Front Disc Brake" Section.

2. Remove the front wheel as described in the "Wheels Removal and Installation" Section.

3. Remove the mounting screw which secures pad B (see the illustration), and remove the pad.

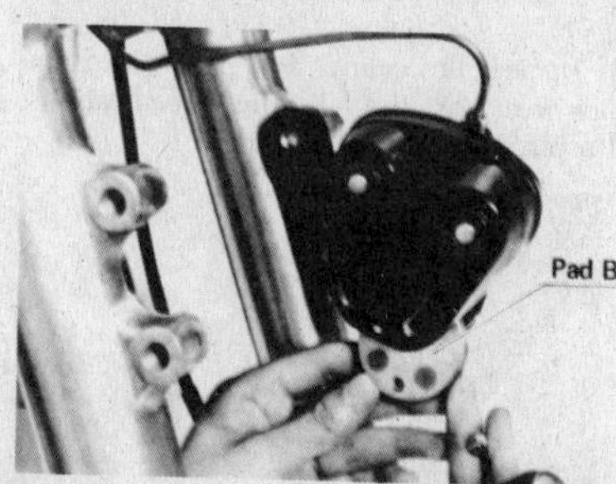

Removing pad B

4. Pump the brake lever several times until the piston forces pad A out, and remove the pad.

5. Loosen the bleeder valve slightly, press the piston in by hand as far as it will go, then close the valve.

CAUTION: *Some brake fluid will leak out of the bleeder during this operation. Be prepared to catch it with a rag.*

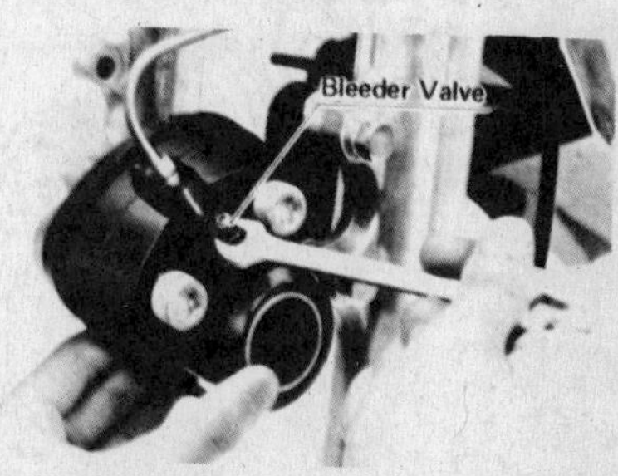

Opening the bleeder valve reduces the pressure in the caliper slightly

6. On 1975 and earlier models, align the groove in pad A with the ridge in the caliper, then insert the pad. On 1976 models, simply install the pad.

7. Install pad B in the caliper aligning the tongue on the pad with the groove in the caliper on 1976 models, and use either Loctite or some other suitable thread sealer on the mounting screw.

CALIPER (1975 AND EARLIER)

Removal and Disassembly

1. Remove the front wheel.

2. Unscrew the brake pipe nipple and disconnect the pipe.

Loosening the brake pipe nipple

3. If the caliper is to be disassembled, loosen the allen head shafts at this time.

4. Remove the mounting bolts, then remove the caliper.

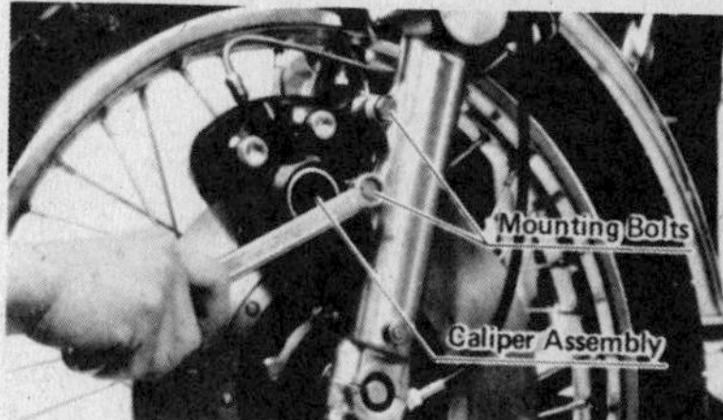

Removing the caliper

5. Unscrew the allen head shafts (1) evenly, alternating between the two a little at a time, then remove caliper B (2). Pad B (3) may be removed at this time by removing its securing screw (12).

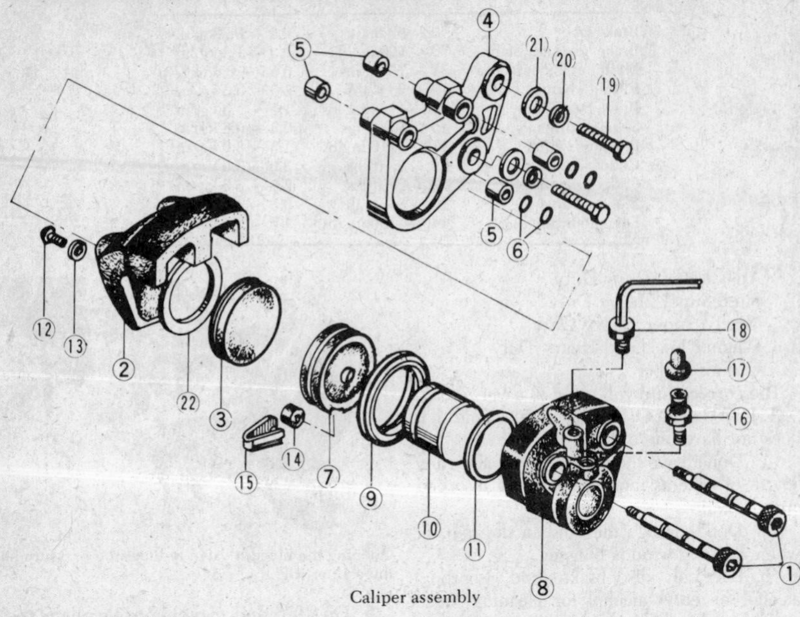

Caliper assembly

1. Allen head shaft
2. Caliper B
3. Pad B
4. Caliper holder
5. Boots
6. O-ring
7. Pad A
8. Caliper A
9. Piston dust seal
10. Piston
11. Seal
12. Screw
13. Lockwasher
14. Bushing
15. Stopper
16. Bleeder valve
17. Bleeder valve cap
18. Nipple
19. Mounting bolt
20. Lockwasher
21. Washer
22. Ring

6. Remove the bolts which secure the caliper holder (4), taking care not to damage the boots (5) or O-rings (6), then remove pad A (7).

7. Remove the two shafts (1) from caliper A (8), then remove the piston dust seal (9) and pull the piston (10) straight out without twisting it. The piston may also be blown out with compressed air through the brake line outlet, if it is reluctant to leave its seat.

8. Remove the seal (11), taking care not to damage the cylinder wall. A special tool (Part No. 56019-111) is available for this job, however a suitable substitute may be used.

Blowing out the piston

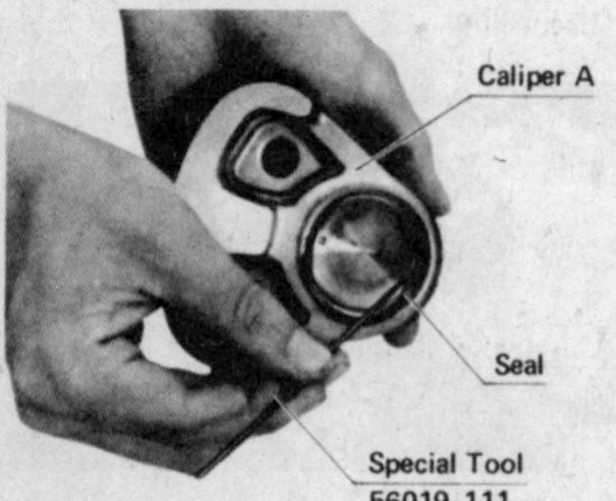

Removing the seal

Inspection

1. Inspect the brake pads for damage or excessive wear and replace them as necessary. If the surface of either pad is worn to the red or green warning line, the pads should be replaced, preferably as a pair. Grease or oil on the pads can be removed with triclorethylene or gasoline. If the pads are oil impregnated, they should be replaced.

2. Inspect the oil seals for a worn, damaged, or cracked condition and replace them as necessary. If the seal around the piston, which serves to maintain the proper pad/disc clearance, is bad, one pad will wear more rapidly than the other, and the constant friction caused by the dragging pad will cause a sharp increase in brake and brake fluid temperature which might result in damage to the various assemblies. Replace the seal if any of the following conditions exist:

a. Oil leakage around pad A.

b. The brake overheats under normal conditions.

c. Pad A and B wear unevenly.

d. The seal is stuck to the piston.

e. If the seal has been reused once already.

3. Inspect the caliper and piston for damage or wear past the following specifications, and replace them as necessary:

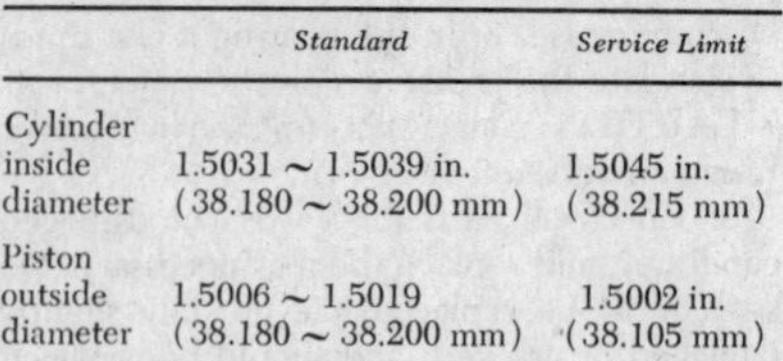

	Standard	Service Limit
Cylinder inside diameter	1.5031 ~ 1.5039 in. (38.180 ~ 38.200 mm)	1.5045 in. (38.215 mm)
Piston outside diameter	1.5006 ~ 1.5019 (38.180 ~ 38.200 mm)	1.5002 in. (38.105 mm)

4. If there is a mushy feeling at the hand lever when the brake is applied, it may be due to excessive clearance between the caliper halves. This is not a problem concerning braking efficiency, and has only to do with the feeling at the hand lever. Check on this in the following manner:

a. Assemble the caliper as described in the "Assembly and Installation" Section. Be sure that the caliper shafts are torqued to 22–26 ft lbs.

b. Check the clearance between the caliper halves using a 0.012 in (0.30 mm) feeler gauge. If the clearance is greater than this, the caliper must be replaced.

Assembly and Installation

1. Assembly is basically in the reverse order of disassembly. Use new O-rings and fluid seals whenever possible, and use the torque specifications given at the beginning of the "Disc Brake" Section.

2. Clean all of the caliper components with either brake fluid or alcohol, then coat them all liberally with fresh brake fluid.

3. Bleed the system thoroughly, after it is installed, as described in the "Bleeding the Brake System" Section.

DISC (1975 AND EARLIER)

Removal and Installation

1. Remove the front wheel.

2. Bend down the lockwasher locking tabs, and remove the disc mounting bolts to free the disc for removal.

3. When installing the disc, use new lockwashers whenever possible. Torque the mounting bolts to 104–190 in. lbs (1.6–2.2 kg/m), then bend the locking tab against the flat of the bolt.

Inspection

1. Clean any oil off the surface of the disc using either trichlorethylene or gasoline.

2. Inspect the disc for deep score marks or wear, and measure the disc with a micrometer at its most worn part. The disc can be cut safely up to 0.050 in. to remove score marks.

Checking clearance between the caliper halves

Checking the disc for wear

but if the scoring, or wear, runs deeper than the disc's serviceable thickness of 0.217 in. (5.5 mm), the disc must be replaced. Standard thickness for the disc is 0.276 in. (7.0 mm).

3. Check the disc for a warped condition. If the disc is warped, less than 0.004 in. (0.1 mm) it needn't be replaced, but if it is warped in excess of 0.012 in. (0.3 mm), it must be replaced.

CALIPER (1976 AND LATER)

Removal

1. Remove the front wheel.
2. If the caliper is to be disassembled, loosen the caliper shaft nuts.

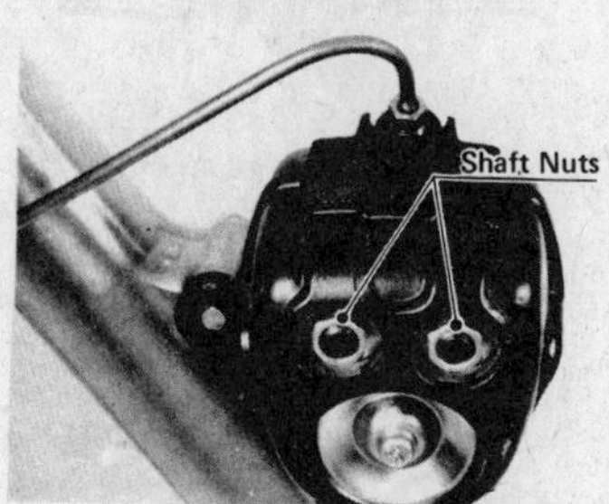

Caliper shaft nuts (1976 and later)

3. Disconnect the brake line at the caliper and plug the end with the bleeder valve cap.
4. Remove the caliper-to-fork slider mounting bolts. Remove the caliper.

Disassembly

1. Remove the mounting screw for Pad B and remove the pad.
2. Remove the caliper shaft nuts. Carefully pull out the caliper shafts (unscrewing each a little at a time) and spacers. Note the dust covers.
3. Remove the caliper holder. Remove Pad A.
4. Remove the piston dust seal. To remove the piston, apply compressed air at the brake line fitting. If not available, reconnect the brake line to the caliper and apply the brake to force out the piston.
5. Remove the fluid seal from the caliper, taking care not to scratch the walls.

Inspection

1. Check piston and caliper bore diameters against the following:

Bore ID	
Standard	42.850–42.900 mm/ 1.687–1.689 in.
Serviceable limit	42.92 mm/1.69in.
Piston OD	
Standard	42.788–42.820 mm/ 1.685–1.686 in.
Serviceable limit	42.75 mm/1.68 in.

2. Clean all parts in clean brake fluid. The use of new seals is recommended.

Assembly

1. Lubricate all parts with new brake fluid during the assembly process.
2. Lubricate the caliper shafts with PBC (high-temperature, water-resistant) grease.
3. Assembly is the reverse of disassembly. Install the spacers with the protruding side facing in. Tighten caliper shaft nuts after mounting the caliper on the slider.

Installation

1. Tighten the mounting bolts to 25–33 ft lbs.
2. Tighten the caliper shaft nuts to 17.5–20.0 ft lbs.
3. Tighten the brake line fitting to 12–13 ft lbs.
4. Bleed the system after installation of pads and wheel.

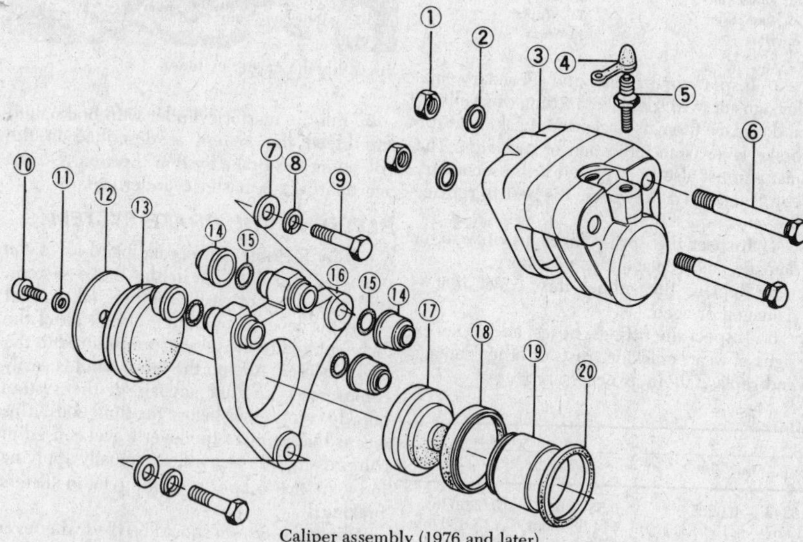

Caliper assembly (1976 and later)

1. Nut
2. Spacer
3. Caliper
4. Bleeder valve cap
5. Bleeder valve
6. Caliper holder shaft
7. Flat washer
8. Lock washer
9. Caliper mounting bolt
10. Mounting screw
11. Lock washer
12. Metal plate
13. Pad B
14. Dust cover
15. O-ring
16. Caliper holder
17. Pad A
18. Dust seal
19. Piston
20. Fluid seal

DISC (1976 AND LATER)

Removal and Installation

1. To remove the disc, bend down the lockwashers and remove the mounting bolts.
2. To install, tighten the bolts to 25–33 ft lbs.

Inspection

1. Standard disc thickness is 6.9–7.1 mm (0.27–0.28 in.). Serviceable limit is 6 mm (0.24 in.).
2. Max. allowable run-out is 0.3 mm (0.012 in.).

MASTER CYLINDER

Removal and Disassembly

1. Read the cautionary notes at the beginning of the "Front Disc Brake" Section.
2. Remove the right-side rear view mirror.
3. Open the bleeder valve on the caliper, and pump all of the brake fluid out of the system.
4. Remove the banjo bolt which secures the brake line to the master cylinder, then remove the rest of the brake line as desired.
5. Remove the clamp bolts which secure the master cylinder, and remove the cylinder.
6. Remove the reservoir cap (1), diaphragm plate (2), and diaphragm (3), then empty out any residual brake fluid.
7. Remove the brake lever (4), then use either the special tool (Part No. 56019-111) or a suitable substitute to remove the dust cover stopper (5). Remove the dust cover (6).

Removing the dust cover stopper

8. Remove the retaining ring (7) using retaining ring pliers, then remove the stopper (8), piston (9), primary cup (10), spring (11), and check valve (12) from the master cylinder body (22).

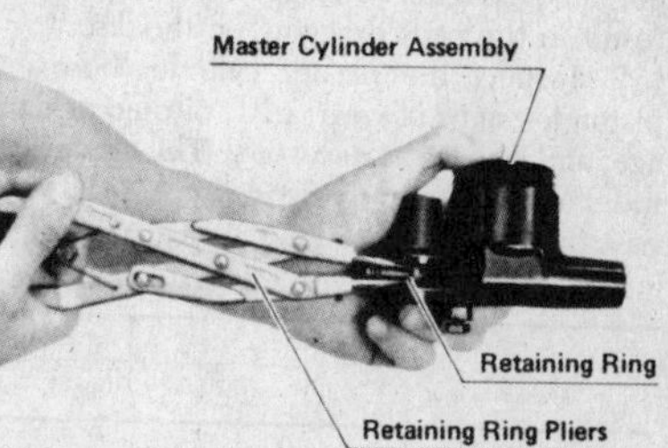

Removing the retaining ring

CAUTION: *Do not attempt to remove the secondary cup (13) from the piston as this will damage the cup.*

9. Any remaining components such as the pressure switch (29), the 3-way fitting (30), the

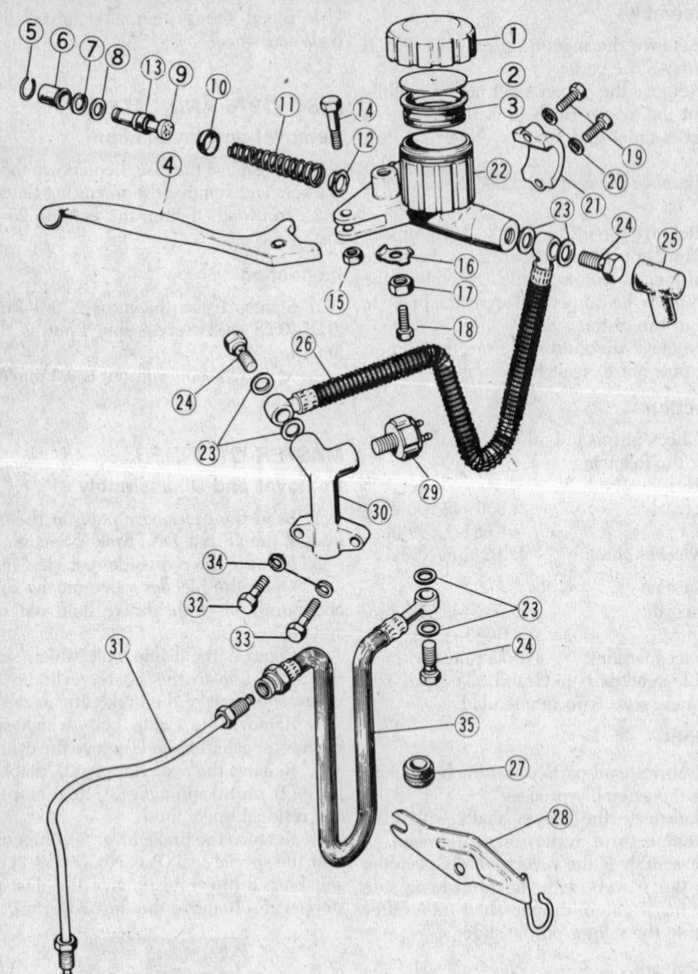

Master cylinder assembly

1. Cap	10. Primary cup	19. Bolt	27. Grommet
2. Plate	11. Spring assembly	20. Washer	28. Bracket
3. Cap seal	12. Check valve assembly	21. Master cylinder mounting	29. Pressure switch
4. Brake lever	13. Secondary cup	22. Master cylinder body	30. 3-way fitting
5. Dust seal stopper	14. Bolt	23. Washer	31. Pipe
6. Dust seal	15. Nut	24. Banjo bolt	32. Bolt
7. Circlip	16. Lockwasher	25. Dust cover	33. Bolt
8. Piston stopper	17. Nut	26. Hose	34. Washer
9. Piston assembly	18. Bolt		35. Hose

brake lines (35) and pipe (31) may be removed at this time.

Inspection

1. Clean all parts in clean brake fluid, then blow them dry. Use compressed air to blow out all passages. A clogged relief port will result in the pads dragging on the disc.
2. Inspect the master cylinder bore and piston for signs of wear, rust, pitting, or damage, and replace as necessary. The master cylinder and piston must also be replaced if worn past their serviceable limit.
3. Inspect the primary and secondary cups for signs of wear, damage, rotting, or swelling, and replace them as necessary. Leaking at the brake lever is an indication of bad cups. The piston must also be replaced if the secondary cup is damaged, however, it's best to replace the cups as a set.
4. Inspect the spring for signs of wear or damage, and replace it as necessary.
5. Replace the rubber dust cover if it is damaged or aged.
6. Inspect the fittings, hoses, and pipes for signs of wear, cracking, rust, or other damage and replace them as necessary.

Measurement	*Standard*		*Service Limit*	
	Single Disc	*Dual Disc*	*Single*	*Dual*
Cylinder inside diameter	0.5512 ~ 0.5529 in. (14.000 ~ 14.043 mm)	0.6248 ~ 0.6265 in. (15.870 ~ 15.913 mm)	0.5543 in. (14.080 mm)	0.6280 in. (15.950 mm)
Piston outside diameter	0.5495 ~ 0.5506 in. (13.957 ~ 13.984 mm)	0.6231 ~ 0.6242 in. (15.827 ~ 15.854 mm)	0.5472 in. (13.900 mm)	0.6209 in. (15.770 mm)
Primary, second cup diameter	0.5768 ~ 0.5965 in. (14.650 ~ 15.150 mm)	0.6476 ~ 0.6673 in. (16.450 ~ 16.950 mm)	0.5709 in. (14.500 mm)	0.6417 in. (16.300 mm)
Spring length (free)	2.008 in. (51.0 mm)	1.709 in. (43.4 mm)	1.890 in. (48.0 mm)	1.594 in. (40.5 mm)

7. The necessary specifications for determining the serviceability of the master cylinder components are as above.

Assembly and Installation

1. Assembly is basically in the reverse order of disassembly. Make sure that all internal parts are perfectly clean, and liberally coat them all with clean brake fluid before installing.
2. Make sure that the primary cup and the check valve are not installed backwards, and make sure that they aren't distorted or turned sideways after insertion.
3. Use either the factory tool (Part No. 56019-110) or a suitable substitute to install a new retaining ring in its groove in the cylinder wall. The same tool can be used to install the boot and boot stopper.
4. Install the master cylinder so that the small projection is toward the throttle grip. Secure the lower camp bolts first, then secure the upper bolts. The bolts should be torqued to 55–75 in. lbs (0.63–0.88 kg/m).

Installing the retaining ring

Installing the master cylinder

5. Fill the master cylinder with brake fluid and bleed the system as described in the "Bleeding the Brake System" Section. Do not overtighten the master cylinder cap.

BLEEDING THE BRAKE SYSTEM

A mushy feeling at the brake hand lever can often be traced to air in the brake system. Brake fluid is not easily compressed, so that when the lever is operated, almost all of the force applied to the lever is transmitted to the brake caliper. Air, on the other hand is easily compressed, so that any air in the system quickly compresses before the fluid does. This means that some of the lever travel is used in compressing the air without actually applying force to the caliper, resulting in inefficient braking.

The brake system should be bled whenever the action at the hand lever feels soft or spongy, whenever brake fluid is changed, or whenever a brake line fitting has been loosened or disconnected. Bleed the brake system in the following manner:

NOTE: *Read the cautionary notes at the beginning of the "Front Disc Brake" Section.*

1. Remove the reservoir cap and check that there is plenty of fluid in the reservoir. The fluid level must be checked several times during the bleeding operation, and replenished as necessary. If the fluid in the reservoir runs completely out at any time during the bleeding operation, air will enter the system, and the procedure will have to be begun again.
2. Slowly pump the brake lever until no air bubbles can be seen rising up through the fluid from the holes at the bottom of the reservoir. When no more bubbles appear, the master cylinder end of the brake system has been purged of all air.

Fill the reservoir to the level line

3. Replace the reservoir cap, and run a clear plastic hose from the caliper bleeder valve into a container. Pump the brake lever until it becomes hard, then, while holding the lever squeezed, quickly open (turn counterclockwise) and close the bleeder valve. Repeat the operation until no more air can be seen coming out into the plastic hose. During this process repeatedly check the fluid level in the reservoir, and replenish it as necessary.
4. If a double disc has been fitted, repeat the above Step on the other side.
5. When the system has been bled, replace the rubber cap on the bleeder valve(s), and check the fluid level in the reservoir once more. The handlebars must be turned so that the reservoir is level, and the fluid must come up to the level line scribed inside the reservoir.

NOTE: *If twin brakes are used and it becomes difficult to get a firm feeling at the lever, bleed the brake closest to the master cylinder first. Stretching the brake hoses while pumping up the system will help eliminate air bubbles trapped in the system.*

Rear Disc Brakes

Read the preliminary procedures under "Front Disc Brake" before beginning any work.

BRAKE PADS

Replacement

1. Remove the pad cover on the caliper.
2. Remove the two clips from the pins.
3. Hold down the anti-rattle springs and pull out the pins. Remove the pads and shims.
4. To install new pads, remove the bleed valve cap and attach a plastic hose to the nipple, running the other end of the hose into a suitable container.
5. Open the bleed valve slightly and push both pistons in as far as possible using one of the old pads. Close the bleed valve.
6. Insert the pads and shims. Note that each shim is installed so that the triangular hole points towards the front of the motorcycle.

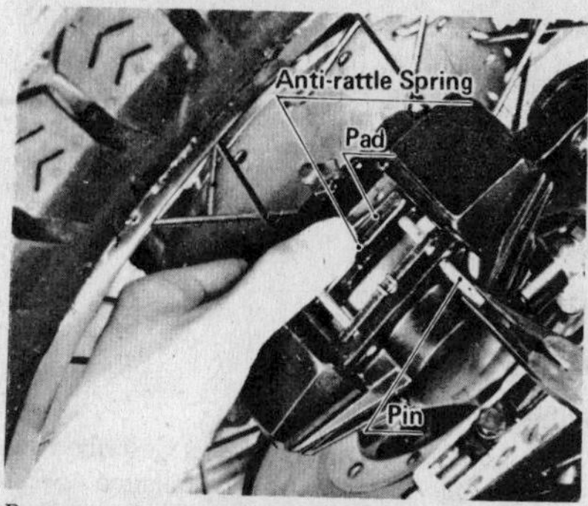

Removing the pad pins

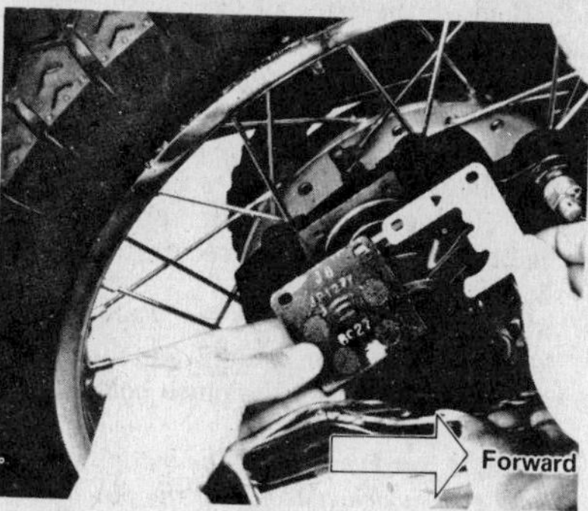

Correct shim installation

7. Check the master cylinder fluid level. Pump up the brake system with the rear brake pedal until operation is normal before operating the motorcycle.

CALIPER

Removal and Disassembly

1. The caliper is removed along with the rear wheel. Refer to the "Rear Wheel (Disc Brake)" removal and installation Section.
2. Remove the brake pads as outlined above.
3. Remove the two caliper allen bolts and separate the caliper halves.
4. Remove the piston dust seals and the caliper O-rings.
5. Apply compressed air to the caliper fluid passages in order to remove the pistons from the caliper halves.
6. Carefully pry out the piston fluid seals with a hooked tool.

Inspection

1. Check piston and caliper bore diameters against the following:

Bore ID

Standard	42.850–42.900 mm/ 1687–1.689 in.
Serviceable limit	42.92 mm/1.69 in.

Piston OD

Standard	42.788–42.820 mm/ 1.685–1.686 in.
Serviceable limit	42.75 mm/1.68 in.

2. Clean all parts in clean brake fluid. The use of new seals is recommended.

Assembly and Installation

1. Assembly is the reverse of disassembly.
2. Tighten the caliper allen bolts to 20–23 ft lbs (2.8–3.2 kg/m).
3. Install the caliper as outlined in the "Rear Wheel (Disc Bake)" removal and installation Section.

DISC

Removal and Installation

1. To remove the disc, bend down the lockwashers and remove the mounting bolts.
2. To install, tighten the bolts to 25–33 ft lbs (3.4–4.6 kg/m).

Inspection

1. Standard disc thickness is 6.9–7.1 mm (0.27–0.28 in.). Serviceable limit is 6 mm (0.24 in.).

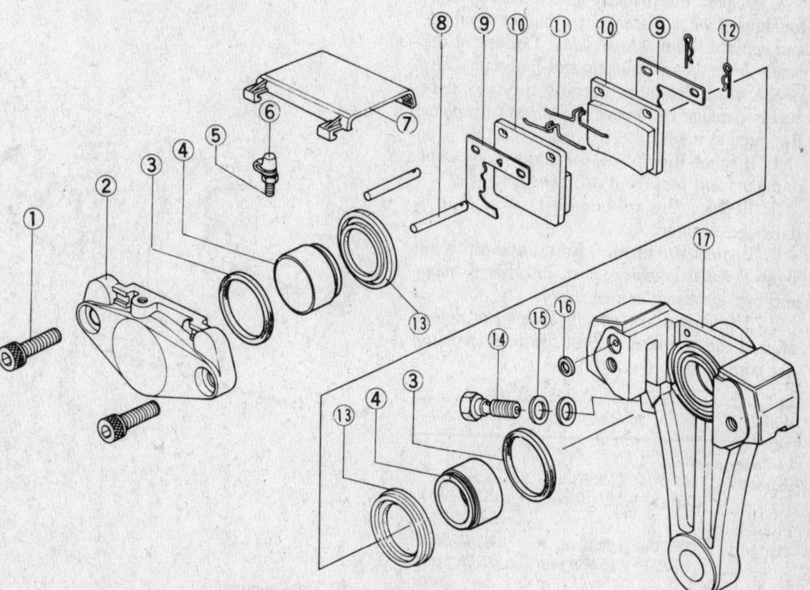

Rear caliper assembly

2. Max. allowable run-out is 0.3 mm (0.012 in.).

MASTER CYLINDER

Removal and Disassembly

1. Remove the right side cover.
2. Disconnect the brake line at the master cylinder, taking adequate precautions to wipe up the brake fluid that spills.
3. Remove the two mounting bolts and remove the master cylinder from the motorcycle.
4. Remove the pushrod dust cover.
5. Remove the master cylinder cap and pour off the brake fluid.
6. Use a thin screwdriver to remove the retainer and take out the piston stopper and piston. Do not remove the secondary cup from the piston as it will be damaged.

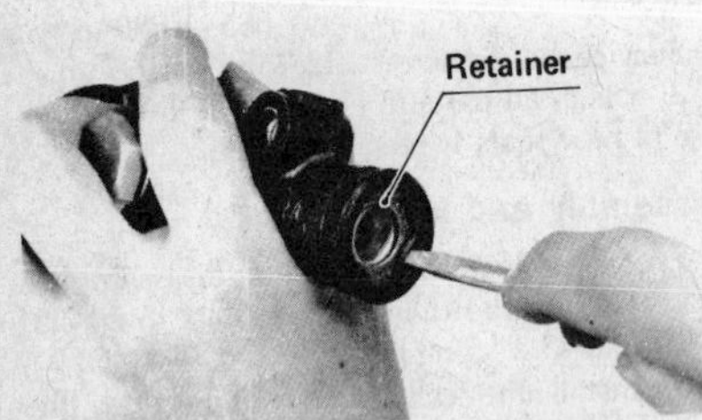

Removing the retainer

7. Remove the return spring and primary cup by applying compressed air to the brake fluid outlet hole.

Inspection

1. Clean all parts in clean brake fluid, then blow them dry. Use compressed air to blow out all passages. A clogged relief port will result in the pads dragging on the disc.
2. Inspect the master cylinder bore and piston for signs of wear, rust, pitting, or damage, and replace as necessary. The master cylinder and piston must also be replaced if worn past their serviceable limit.
3. Inspect the primary and secondary cups for signs of wear, damage, rotting, or swelling, and replace them as necessary. Leaking at the brake lever is an indication of bad cups. The piston must also be replaced if the secondary cup is damaged, however, it's best to replace the cups as a set.
4. Inspect the spring for signs of wear or damage, and replace it as necessary.
5. Replace the rubber dust cover if it is damaged or aged.
6. Inspect the fittings, hoses, and pipes for signs of wear, cracking, rust, or other damage and replace them as necessary.
7. The necessary specifications for determining the serviceability of the master cylinder components are as follows:

	Standard	*Service Limit*
Cylinder inside diameter	0.6248 ~ $.6265 in. (15.870 ~ 15.913 mm)	0.628 in. (15.95 mm)
Piston outside diameter	0.6231 ~ 0.6242 in. (15.827 ~ 15.854 mm)	0.620 in. (15.75 mm)
Cup diameters	0.648 ~ 0.667 in. (16.45 ~ 16.95 mm)	0.642 in. (16.30 mm)
Spring free length	1.62 in. (41.2 mm)	1.54 in. (39.0 mm)

Assembly and Installation

1. Assembly is the reverse of disassembly. Be sure the spring is installed with the spring seat side facing out.
2. Be sure that the primary cup is properly inserted and not turned or installed backwards.

Rear Hub

DRUM BRAKE

Disassembly

1. Remove the rear wheel as described in the "Wheels Removal and Installation" Section. Refer to the accompanying illustration.
2. Remove the axle nut (25), washer (27), and distance collar (24), then remove the axle (23) by withdrawing it through the left side.
3. Remove the panel assembly (1) from the hub (10) then disassemble the panel assembly in the following manner:
   a. Remove the two cotter pins (9) and double washer (8) which secure the brake shoes.
   b. Use a punch to mark the original position of the brake cam lever (2) and the brake cam (5), then remove the pinch bolt (3) and lever.
   NOTE: *Lever removal can be made easy by using a screwdriver to pry at the pinch bolt slot while pulling the lever off the cam.*
   c. Remove the dust seal (4), then remove the brake shoes (6) and cam (5) by prying the shoes up evenly and removing them along with the cam.
   d. Remove the brake return springs (7) from the shoes.
4. Separate the coupling assembly (15) from the hub (10), then disassemble it in the following manner:
   a. Remove the shock damper rubbers (12), distance collar (16), axle sleeve collar (20), and oil seal (19).
   b. Tap evenly around the bearing (18) inner race from the inside of the coupling assembly (15) with a suitable drift until the bearing comes out.
5. Tap evenly around the inner race of the panel side bearing (14) from the sprocket side until it comes out, remove the distance collar (13), then tap evenly around the inner race of the coupling assembly side bearing (11) from the panel side until it comes out.
6. The rear sprocket (28) can be removed by bending up the lockwasher locking tabs, and removing the mounting nuts and bolts.
   NOTE: *If just the sprocket is to be removed it is not necessary to disassemble the hub. Remove the left-side mufflers, the sprocket mounting bolts, the rear wheel, and then the sprocket.*

Inspection

1. Clean all parts, other than the brake shoes, seals, and rubber dampers in a suitable solvent, then blow them dry.
2. Inspect the brake drum for a warped, scored, or damaged condition, and replace it as necessary. Measurements should be taken in no less than two different places. If the drum is scored or worn out of round it can be turned down as long as turning it doesn't exceed the specified limits which are as follows:

Measuring the rear hub

Standard	*Service Limit*
7.874 ~ 7.881 in. (200.00 ~ 200.185 mm)	7.904 in. (200.75 mm)

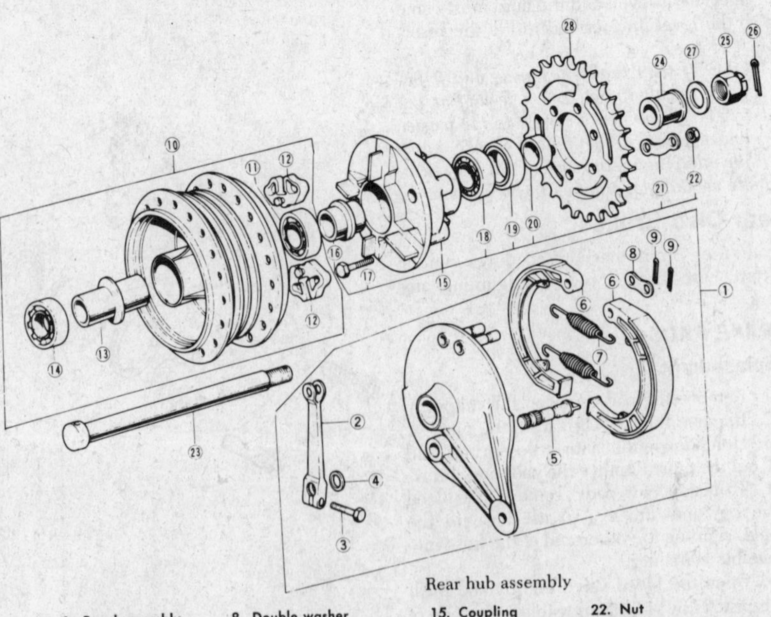

Rear hub assembly

1. Panel assembly
2. Brake cam lever
3. Bolt
4. Dust seal
5. Brake cam
6. Brake shoe
7. Spring
8. Double washer
9. Cotter pin
10. Drum assembly
11. Bearing
12. Shock damper rubber
13. Spacer
14. Bearing
15. Coupling
16. Distance collar
17. Bolt
18. Bearing
19. Oil seal
20. Sleeve collar
21. Washer
22. Nut
23. Axle
24. Distance collar
25. Nut
26. Cotter pin
27. Washer
28. Rear sprocket

3. Inspect the brake shoes for excessive or uneven wear, or for oil or grease impregnation, and replace them as necessary. Surface glazing or high spots can be removed by sanding. The shoes should be measured in several spots, and they must be replaced if worn anywhere past their serviceable limits which are as follows:

Standard	Service Limit
0.1909 ~ 0.2146 in. (4.85 ~ 5.45 mm)	0.118 in. (3.00 mm)

4. Inspect the brake return springs for a worn, pitted, collapsed, or otherwise damaged condition, and replace them as necessary. The brake spring free length specifications are as follows:

Standard	Service Limit
2.62 in. (66.5 mm)	2.72 in. (69.0 mm)

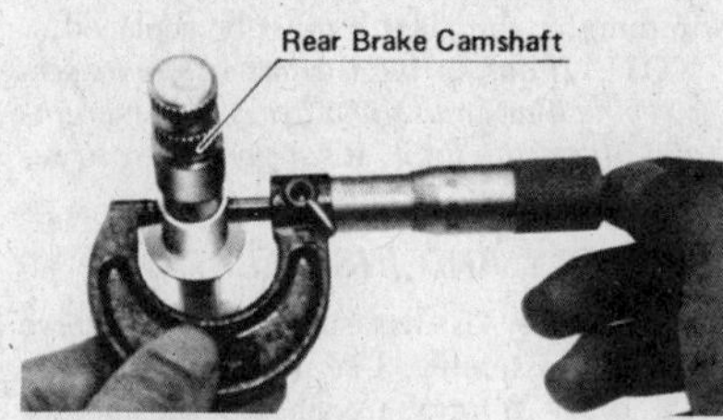

Measuring the brake camshaft

5. Inspect the brake camshaft and backing plate for signs of wear or damage, and replace them individually or as a pair as necessary. These measurements are critical if efficient braking is to be maintained, and therefore should be done with micrometers as illustrated. The service limits for these items are as follows:

	Standard	Service Limit
Camshaft	0.6676 ~ 0.6687 in. (16.957 ~ 16.984 mm)	0.6626 in. (16.83 mm)
Shaft hole	0.6693 ~ 0.6704 in. (17.000 ~ 17.027 mm)	0.6764 in. (17.18 mm)

Measuring the inside diameter of the camshaft hole

Measuring rear axle run-out

6. Measure the rear axle run-out in the manner indicated, and replace it if run-out exceeds 0.008 in. (0.2 mm).

7. Inspect the rubber dampers for signs of cracking, damage, or rotting, and replace them as necessary.

Assembly

1. Assembly is in the reverse order of disassembly. Use new oil seals, locking tabs, and cotter pins whenever possible.

NOTE: *The small cotter pins which secure the brake shoes to the backing plate are sometimes difficult to locate. In a case like this, mechanic's wire will work as a substitute. Loop it through the holes in the pivots at least twice.*

2. Use either the special factory tools (Part Nos. 57001-139 and 57001-140), or a suitable substitue, when installing the bearings and oil seals.

3. When installing the rear sprocket, torque the mounting nuts to 23–30 ft lbs (3.1–4.2 kg/m), and bend the locking tab up against a flat of the nut.

4. Lubricate the brake pivots, brake shoe anchor pins, brake return spring ends, and the brake camshaft surface and groove with grease. Be sure that the camshaft groove is filled, but take care not to overlubricate, as this may result in grease on the brake shoes and drum.

DISC BRAKE

Disassembly

1. Remove the rear wheel from the motorcycle. Remove the axle and brake caliper.

2. Remove the sprocket nuts and washers. Remove the sprocket from the coupling.

3. Separate the sprocket coupling from the wheel hub.

4. Remove the coupling collar from the left and the coupling sleeve from the right of the coupling.

5. Pry out the bearing grease seal. Remove the circlip and tap out the bearing from the wheel side of the coupling.

6. Remove the rubber dampers from the hub. Remove the disc-side collar.

7. Unbolt and remove the brake disc.

8. Pry out the grease seal on the disc side, remove the circlip, and reach through the hub from the disc side to tap out the left-side bearing. Remove the wheel bearing spacer. Remove the other bearing in the same manner.

Inspection

1. Check the rubber dampers for damage and replace them if necessary.

2. Clean the wheel bearings in a solvent, oil them lightly, and check operation. Bearing rotation should be smooth, noiseless, and effortless. Replace the bearings as a set if any one is damaged.

Assembly

1. Assembly is the reverse of disassembly.

2. Pack the bearing with a good grade of bearing grease. Use new grease seals.

3. Tighten the sprocket nuts to 25–33 ft lbs (3.4–kg/m).

FINAL DRIVE

Removal

NOTE: *The drive chain may be cut or broken with a chain breaker if it is going to be discarded and replaced. Otherwise, the chain must never be cut.*

1. Remove the chain cover in the following manner:

a. Remove the chain oil pump cover screws and cover on models so equipped.

b. Slide back the hose clamp and disconnect the inlet hose from the pump. One of the cover screws can be used to plug the hose to prevent oil leakage.

c. Remove the left footrest and shift pedal. The clamp bolt must be completely removed before the shifter can be removed.

d. Remove the starter cover and cover gasket.

e. Remove the chain cover mounting bolts, then remove the cover.

f. Remove the cotter pin from the clutch release lever, and disconnect the clutch cable.

2. Loosen the cylinder exhaust flange bolts and the muffler mounting bolts for the two left-hand mufflers, and either remove or swing the pipes up out of the way.

3. Remove the lower mounting bolt from the left-side rear shock absorber.

4. Loosen the chain adjusters and back off the adjusting nuts so that the chain is as loose as possible.

5. Remove the rear axle cotter pin, loosen the axle nut, and push the rear wheel forward in the swing arm.

6. Remove the engine sprocket in the following manner:

a. Remove the clutch pushrod and sprocket guard.

b. Bend back the lockwasher locking tab.

c. Secure the sprocket so that it won't turn by using the special tool (Part No. 57001-118), a suitable substitute, or by engaging the transmission in Low gear, then remove the sprocket and disengage the chain.

7. Disconnect the rear brake torque link at the rear hub, remove the brake rod adjusting nut and disconnect the rod from the lever by rotating the brake backing plate, and remove the two pinch bolts and stoppers at the swing arm chain adjusters.

NOTE: *Remove the spring and link pin from the brake lever and put them back on the rod to avoid losing them.*

8. Push the left shock absorber out of the swing arm, loop the chain over the swing arm, and slide the rear wheel out of the swing arm.

9. Remove the nut from the swing arm pivot shaft, and withdraw the shaft. Tilt the swing arm until the pivot section clears the frame, then drop the chain through the gap.

Inspection

1. Check the drive chain for signs of wear, cracks on the rollers, bushings, or roller links, or for kinking or binding, and replace it if any of these conditions exist. Thoroughly lubricating the chain may help free kinked or bound links.

2. Replace the chain if it is worn more than 2% of its original length. This can be determined by measuring the chain in either of the following manner:

a. Stretch the chain taut by using the chain adjusters, or by hanging a 20 lb (10 kg) weight on the bottom run of the chain.

b. Remove the chain guard and measure the length of 20 links along a straight line from the center of the first pin to the center of the twenty-first pin.

c. If the length of the chain exceeds the standard length of 15.0 in. (381 mm) by more than 5/16 in. (8 mm), the chain must be replaced.

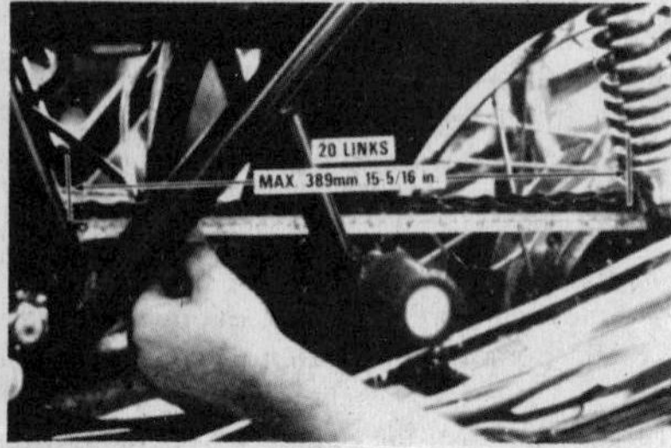

Measuring the chain

3. Inspect both the drive (engine) and driven sprockets for signs of wear, damage, or a warped condition, and replace them as necessary if worn past the service limits given below:

a. Engine sprocket diameter:

900

Standard	Service Limit
3.376 ~ 3.384 in. (85.76 ~85.96 mm)	3.346 in. (85.0 mm)

1000

Standard	Service Limit
3.11 ~ 3.12 in. (79.01 ~ 79.21 mm)	3.08 in. (78.3 mm)

b. Rear sprocket diameter and run-out:

900

Diameter		Runout	
Standard	Limit	Standard	Limit
8.560 in. (217.4 mm)	8.484 in. (215.5 mm)	under 0.012 in. (under 0.3 mm)	0.020in. (0.5 mm)

1000

Diameter		Runout	
Standard	Limit	Standard	Limit
7.39 ~ 7.41 in. (187.77 ~ 188.27 mm)	7.38 in. (187.4 mm)	under 0.012 in. (under 0.3 mm)	0.020in. (0.5 mm)

Measuring rear sprocket diameter

Installation

1. Installation is basically in the reverse order of removal.
2. Make sure that the chain adjustment is loose enough to allow the engine sprocket and chain to fit properly, then readjust it afterwards.
3. Make sure that the lockwasher tab seats in the hole in the sprocket, and bend up one side of the washer after securing the sprocket nut.
4. Secure the sprocket nut to 87–108 ft lbs (12–15 kg/m).
5. Use an oil seal guide (Part No. 57001-130) to prevent damage to the seal while installing the chain cover.
6. Rotate the rear wheel until the pin inside the output shaft and the groove in the chain oil pump shaft are in alignment before installing the cover.

FRONT FORKS

Fork Tubes

REMOVAL AND DISASSEMBLY

1. Remove the front wheel as described in the "Wheels Removal and Installation" Section.
2. Remove the front fender mounting bolts and fender.
3. Remove the brake caliper and place it out of the way.

NOTE: *The caliper need not be disconnected from the brake line pipe, however the assembly should be tied to or rested on something to avoid bending the pipe.*

4. Remove the bolt (2) from the top of the tube if the fork is to be disassembled once it's removed. If only the slider is to be removed, it may be done now by removing the allen bolt (30) from the bottom.

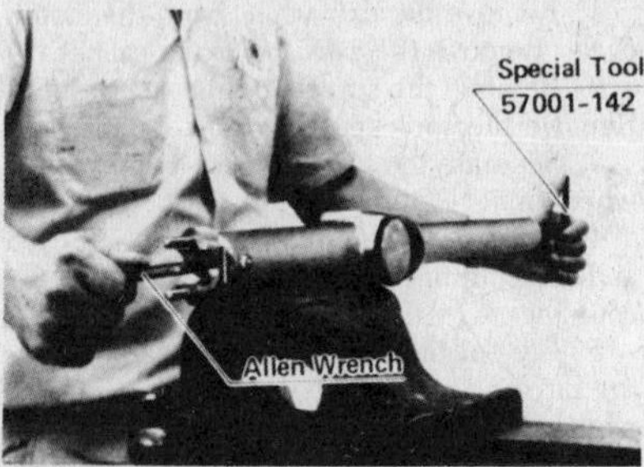

Disassembling the fork tube and slider

Clamp bolt locations

NOTE: *If you've removed or loosened the top bolt (2), the cylinder assembly (19) will rotate and you won't be able to remove the allen bolt without the assistance of the special factory tool (Part No. 57001-142).*

5. If you wish to remove the entire fork leg, remove the top bolt (2) and the clamp bolts (6 and 16), and pull the assembly down and out. If you use screwdrivers to spread the clamps on the stem head (4) and stem (15) assemblies the legs will come out more easily.
6. Invert the assembly and dump out the spring (18) and fork oil. If the allen bolt (30) has been removed, the inner tube assembly (19) will also come out.
7. Remove the circlip (36) from the inner tube using snap-ring pliers, and remove the cylinder assembly (20) from the tube.
8. Remove the dust seal (21) from the outer tube (25), then remove the circlip (22) and oil seal (24) using a sharp hook.

NOTE: *Once the oil seal has been disturbed it must be replaced.*

INSPECTION

1. Clean all of the components in a suitable solvent, then blow them dry.
2. Inspect all parts for signs of wear, scoring, stripped threads, warpage, or other damage and replace them as necessary.
3. Inspect the inner tube for a bent condition by rolling it across a flat surface, and have it straightened out if it isn't too severely bent.
4. Inspect the spring for a collapsed or damaged condition, and measure it to check its free length. If the spring is shorter than 19.09 in. (485 mm) for the 900 or 17.91 in. (455 mm) for the 1000 it must be replaced.

NOTE: *If one spring is shorter than its serviceable limit, and the other is only marginally above the limit, it's a good idea to replace them both at this time.*

ASSEMBLY AND INSTALLATION

1. Assembly is basically in the reverse order of disassembly. Use new seals.

On 1974–76 forks, use the special tool for inserting the cylinder assembly into the inner tube.

2. When installing new oil seals, use the special tool (Part No. 57001-141) to install the seal. Lubricating the seal will make installation easier.

If progressively-wound fork springs are fitted, install them with the close coils toward the top of the forks.

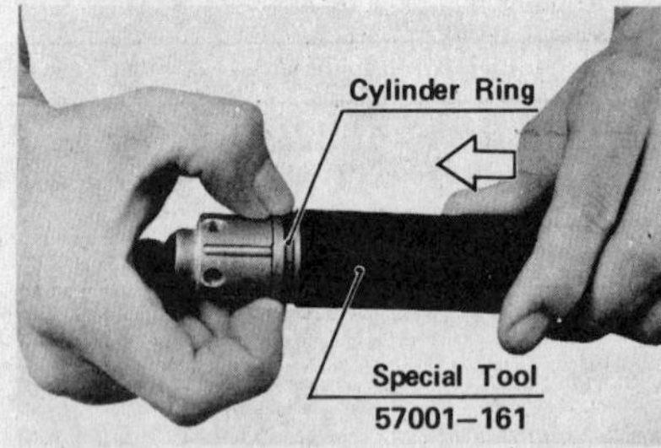

Assembling the damper components with the special tool (1974–76)

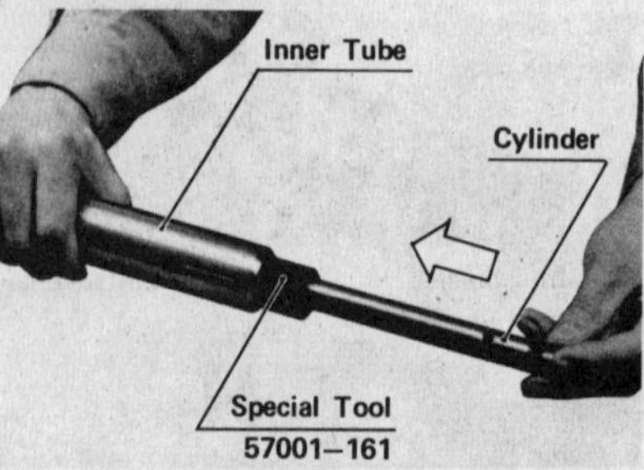

Assembling the fork tube (1974–76)

3. Before tightening the top clamp, make sure that the flange surface of the bolt in the top of the tube is level with the top of the steering stem.
4. Secure the upper clamp bolt to 140–155

in. lbs (1.6–1.8 kg/m), and the lower clamp bolt to 40–43 ft lbs (5.4–6.0 kg/m).

STEERING STEM

Removal

1. Remove the front wheel as described in the "Wheels Removal and Installation" Section.
2. Remove the fender mounting bolts and fender.
3. Remove the bolt from the bottom of the headlight shell and the two screws from the sides, which serve to secure the beam assembly, and remove and unplug the beam assembly.
4. Unplug the turn signal wires, and disconnect the main wiring harness connectors.
5. Remove the turn signals and headlight shell after removing the mounting hardware.
6. Disconnect the tachometer cable at the cylinder head.
7. Remove the mounting bolts which secure the instrument and ignition switch cluster, and remove the assembly. Remove the gas tank.
8. Remove the mirrors (if applicable), then disconnect the front brake pressure switch wires.
9. Remove the mounting bolts for the master cylinder, the 3-way fitting, and the caliper, then remove the entire brake system while taking care not to damage the brake line pipe.
10. Unbolt the handlebars and allow them to rest on the tubes as illustrated, then loosen

Front fork assembly—exploded view

1. Lock assy
2. Top bolt
3. O-ring
4. Stem head
5. Clamp bolt
6. Clamp bolt
7. Lockwasher
8. Nut
9. Washer
10. Headlight stay
11. Headlight stay
12. Stay guide
13. Washer
14. Gasket
15. Steering stem
16. Bolt
17. Lockwasher
18. Spring
19. Inner tube
20. Cylinder
21. Dust seal
22. Circlip
23. Washer
24. Oil seal
25. Outer tube
26. Outer tube
27. Gasket
28. Drain plug
29. Gasket
30. Allen bolt
31. Stud
32. Axle
33. Nut
34. Reflector
35. Rubber washer
36. Circlip

Removing the instrument cluster mounting bolts

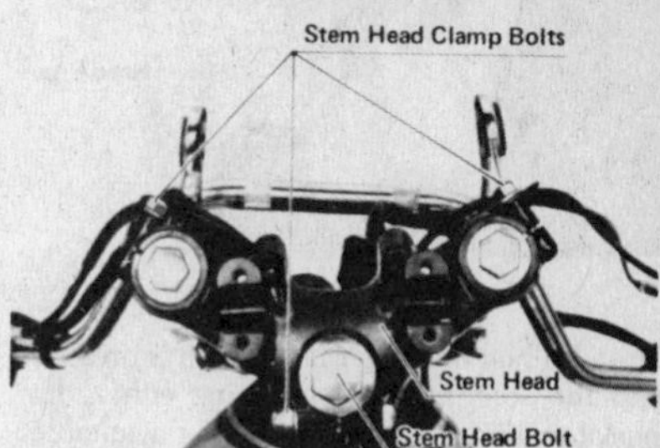

Clamp bolt locations

Installing the oil seal

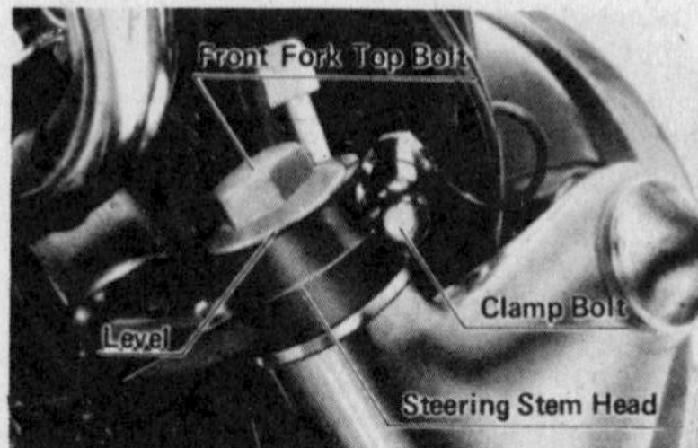

Lining up the tube in the triple clamp

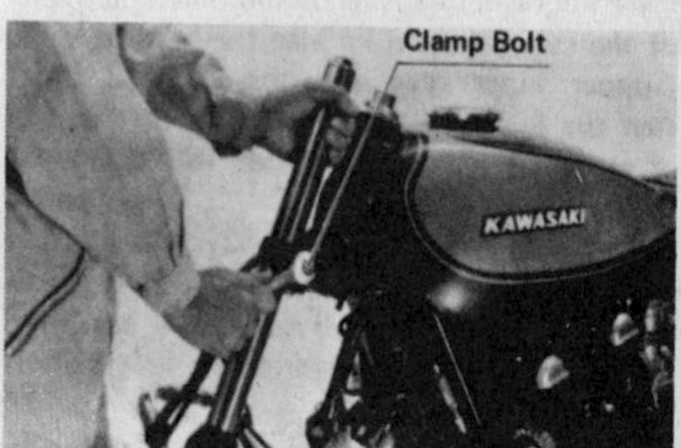

Removing the lower clamp bolts

the 3 stem head clamp bolts, remove the stem head bolt, and remove the stem head.

11. Rest the handlebars on the frame, remove the two lower clamp bolts, the fork ears (headlight stay), and the fork tubes.

12. Remove the steering stem locknut using a suitable hook spanner, and drop the stem out from the bottom. Remove the stem cap, upper inner race, and the bearings.

CAUTION: *When withdrawing the stem, be prepared to catch the lower race bearings in a suitable receptacle. Always keep the two bearing groups separate for installation in their original locations.*

13. Remove the bearing races; only if they must be replaced, by drifting them out with a suitable soft face drift. Drove the lower race out from the top, and the upper race out from the bottom. Tap evenly around the circumference of the race while removing the races.

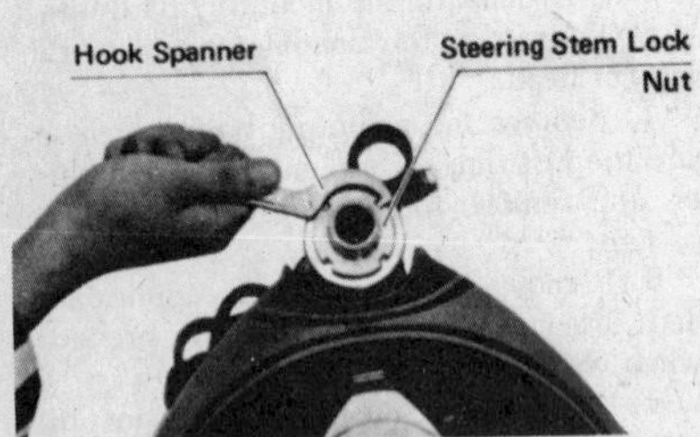

Removing the stem locknut

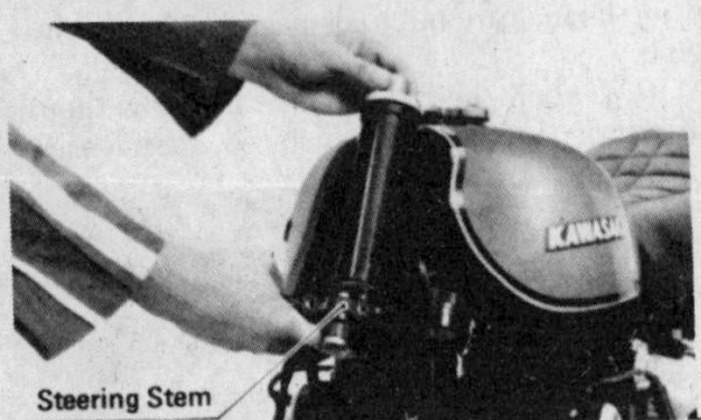

Removing the steering stem

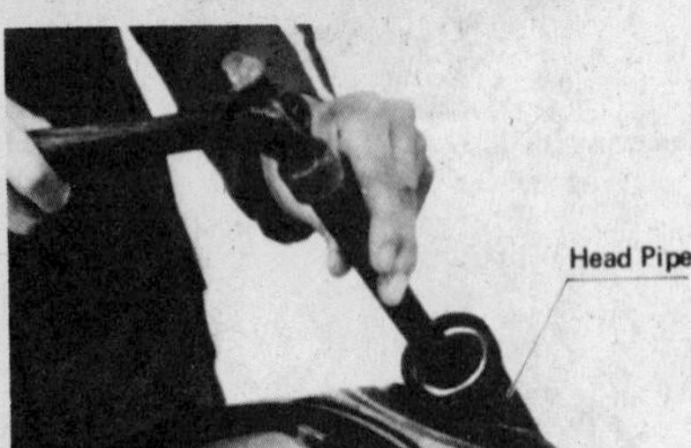

Drifting out the lower race

14. Pull off the lower race which is pressed onto the steering stem by using either the special tool (Part No. 57001-135) or a suitable substitute. Try not to damage the grease seal under the race, or stretch it and pull it off over the race.

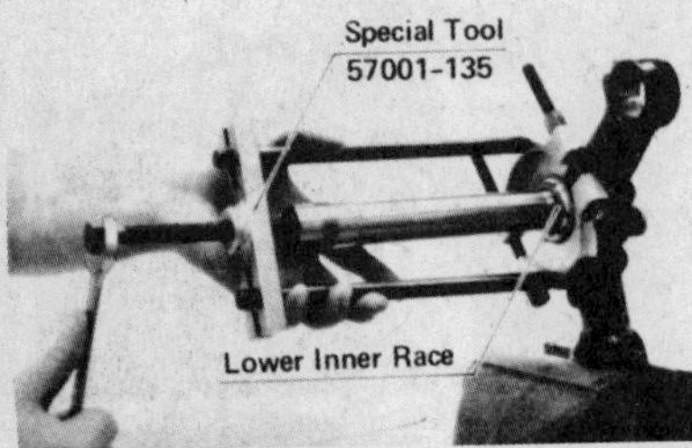

Pulling off the stem lower race

Inspection

1. Clean all parts, other than gaskets and seals, in a suitable solvent, and blow them dry.

2. Inspect all parts for signs of wear, stripped threads, or damage, and replace them as necessary.

e. Visually inspect the stem for a tilted condition and replace it if not perpendicular to the clamp.

4. Inspect the bearings and races for signs of wear, scoring, or damage, and replace them as complete sets as necessary. Bright spots on the inner portion of the race indicate advanced wear, and may cause jerky steering.

Installation

1. Installation is basically in the reverse order of removal.

2. Liberally oil the outer races and drive them into the head pipe using either the special tools (Part Nos. 57001-139 and 57001-138) or a suitable substitute such as a soft-faced drift. Be sure that they seat evenly in the pipe.

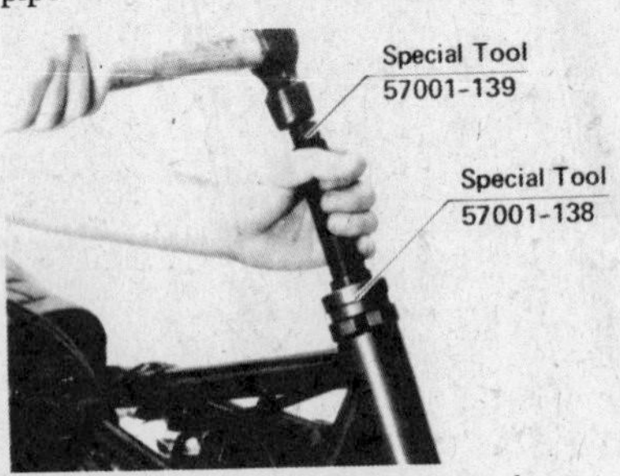

Installing the races using the special tools

3. Oil the lower inner race and drive it into the stem using either the special tool (Part No. 57001-137) or a suitable substitute. The race can be driven on using the clamping edges of a vise if necessary, but this is hard on the bottom of the clamp.

Driving on the lower inner race

NOTE: *If the special tools are being used, install a new seal before driving on the race. If you are going to drive it on using the edges of a vise, it's best to drive on the race and then stretch the seal on over the race.*

4. Liberally grease the bearing races, and stick the bearings in the grease. The upper race takes 19 bearings, and the lower race takes 20.

5. Insert the stem into the frame head, then install the upper inner race, cap, and locknut.

6. Use a suitable hook spanner to tighten the locknut until the stem moves smoothly and freely to either side, but no play exists in the bearings.

7. Position the fork ears and guides between the two halves of the stem assembly, then slide the fork tubes up through them so that they protrude about 1¼ in. (30 mm) at the top. Snugging up the lower clamp bolt will hold the tubes in position.

Fork tubes properly positioned

8. Position the handlebar assembly as illustrated, making sure that all the wires and cables are correctly routed.

9. Install the stem head, and secure the stem head bolt and the rear clamp bolt.

10. Loosen the lower clamp bolt, position the fork tube so that the flange surface of the fork top bolt is flush with the upper surface of the steering stem head, then secure the upper and lower clamp bolts. The 3 upper clamp bolts should be secured to 140–155 in. lbs (1.6–1.8 kg/m), and the two lower clamp bolts should be torqued to 40–43 ft lbs (5.4–6.0 kg/m).

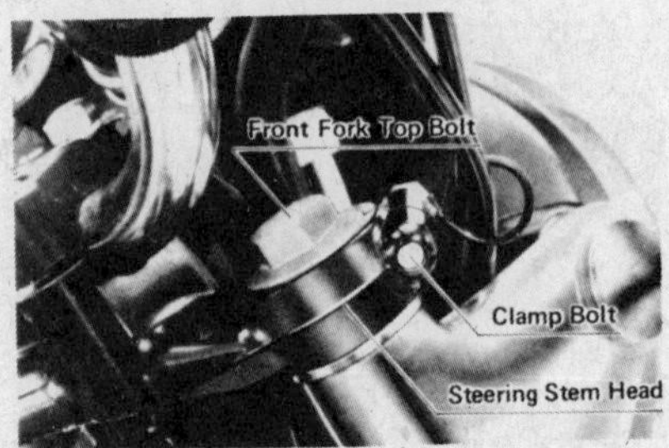

Fork tubes ready to be secured

NOTE: *Secure the lower clamp bolts first, then the upper bolts.*

11. Mount and bleed the disc brake assembly as described in the "Front Disc Brake" Section.

12. Mount and secure the ignition switch and instrument cluster, then mount, but do not secure, the headlight shell and turn signals.

13. Start, but do not tighten, the bolt which goes in the bottom of the headlight. Adjust the vertical height of the shell, then secure the shell, the bottom bolt, and the turn signals.

14. Connect the wiring harness connectors, then connect and install the headlight lamp unit.

NOTE: *The left turn signal lead goes to the green wire, and the right lead goes to the gray wire.*

15. Mount and secure the front fender, the brake hose clamp, and the front wheel.

REAR SHOCK ABSORBERS

Removal, Disassembly and Installation

1. Remove the mounting nut from the upper end, and the bolt from the lower end of each shock. If there is not sufficient clearance for the removal of the bottom mounting bolt,

it will be necessary to loosen or remove the mufflers on the side in question.

2. Remove the mounting bolts for the chrome bar, and remove the bar, then pull the shock free of the mounting stud.

3. Disassemble the shock by compressing it until the upper keepers are free to be removed, then remove the keepers, cover, and spring. The upper mounting eye can now be unscrewed and removed if it or the rubber stopper is to be replaced.

NOTE: *The shock can be compressed in a vise or by pressing it against the floor while someone else removes the keepers.*

4. Assembly and installation are in the reverse order of removal and disassembly. If you want to look racy, it's not necessary to replace the cover.

Inspection

1. Once the shock is disassembled, check its dampening action by pushing in the piston rod, and then pulling it back out. The rod should slip smoothly in until seated, and should take more effort to pull it back out than to push it in. Both shocks should react to this test in the same manner.

2. Replace the shocks, preferably as a set, if one or both fails the above test, if the seals leak, or if the rod is bent.

SWING ARM

900

REMOVAL AND DISASSEMBLY

1. Remove the rear wheel as described in the "Wheels Removal and Installation" Section.

2. Remove the rear shock absorber lower mounting bolts, then unscrew the swing arm pivot shaft nut, withdraw the shaft, and remove the swing arm.

3. Pull the sleeve (5) out of each end of the swing arm.

4. Position the distance collar (9) so that it seats against either bushing (6), or at least so it's off center, then, using a suitable bar as a drift, gently drift out the opposite side bushing. Invert the swing arm and remove the remaining bushing.

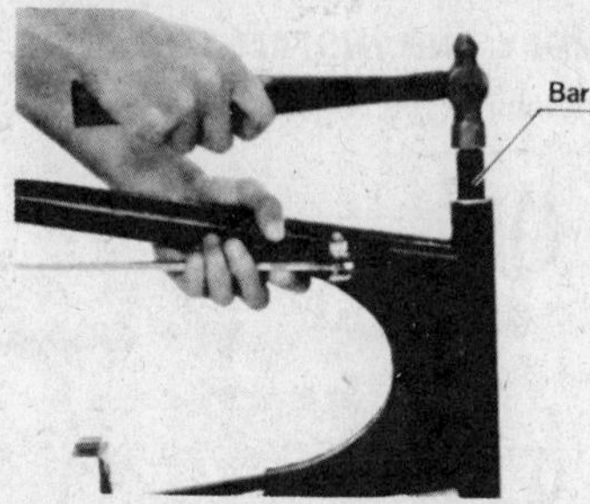

Drifting out a bushing

INSPECTION

1. Clean all parts in a suitable solvent, then blow them dry.

2. Inspect the swing arm for stress signs, cracks, bends, or other damage, and have it repaired or replace it as necessary.

NOTE: *Any necessary welding should be done by a professional to assure rigidity and correct alignment.*

3. Inspect the sleeves for signs of wear or damage, and replace them as a set if either is in need of replacement. The standard outside diameter of a sleeve is 0.8653–0.8661 in. (21.979–22.171 mm), and the sleeve must be replaced if worn past its serviceable limit of 0.864 in. (21.95 mm).

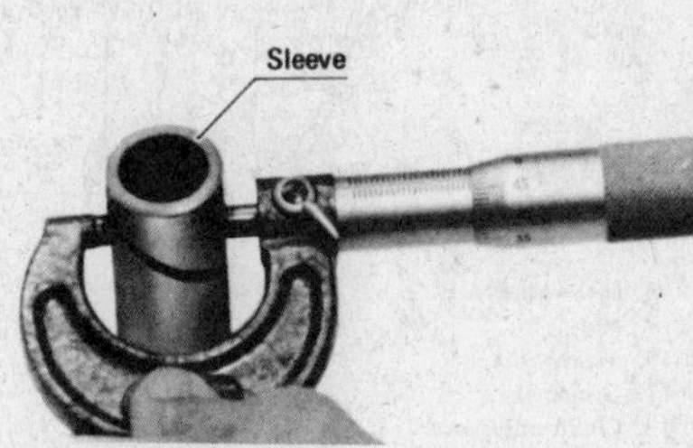

Measuring a sleeve for wear

4. Inspect the bushings for signs of wear or damage, and replace them as a set if either is in need of replacement. The standard inside diameter of a bushing is 0.8712–0.8729 in. (22.128–22.171 mm), and the bushing must be replaced if worn past its serviceable limit of 0.881 in. (22.37 mm).

5. Inspect the pivot shaft for signs of wear, scoring, excessive run-out, or other damage, and replace it as necessary. Check the run-out with a dial indicator and a pair of V-blocks as illustrated. If the run-out exceeds the standard allowance of under 0.004 in. (under 0.1 mm), the shaft must be straightened or replaced.

Measuring a bushing

Checking the pivot shaft run-out

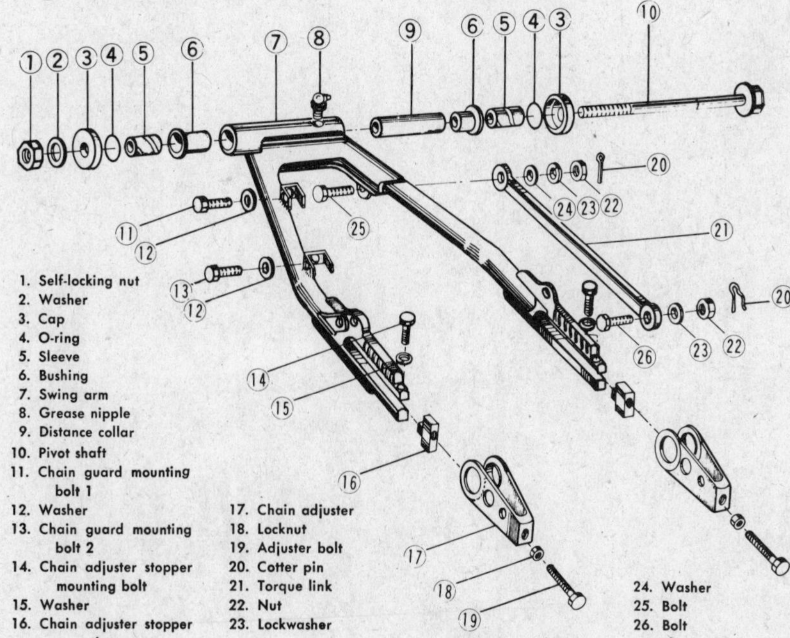

Swing arm—exploded view

ASSEMBLY AND INSTALLATION

1. Assembly is in the reverse order of disassembly, and installation is in the reverse order of removal. New O-rings and bushings should be used whenever possible, and the bushings should be oiled before being installed.

2. Thoroughly grease the swing arm by applying grease through the grease nipple until it runs out either end of the swing arm, then wipe off the excess.

3. Secure the pivot shaft to 87–108 ft lbs (12–15 kg/m).

1000

REMOVAL AND DISASSEMBLY

1. Remove the mufflers. Remove the rear wheel.

2. Detach the brake hose from the swing arm clips.

3. Remove the lower mounting bolt of each shock absorber.

4. Remove the swing arm pivot shaft nut and pull out the pivot shaft. Remove the swing arm. Note the dust cap on either end of the swing arm.

5. The swing arm needle bearings will be damaged on removal. Be sure to have new ones on hand prior to disassembly. Pull out the swing arm sleeve. Reach through the swing arm with a suitable drift and drive out one of the needle bearings. Repeat the procedure with the other.

INSPECTION

1. Measure the outside diameter of the swing arm sleeve at both ends. Standard diameter is 0.8656–0.8661 in. (21.987–22.000 mm). Service limit is 0.8646 in. (21.96 mm). Replace the sleeve and both bearings if it is worn beyond this limit.

2. Check the pivot shaft for a bent condition and replace it if it is bent more than 0.008 in. (0.2 mm).

ASSEMBLY AND INSTALLATION

1. Assembly is the reverse of disassembly. Lubricate the needle bearings with oil before installation, then apply chassis grease to the grease nipple until some shows at both ends of the swing arm.

2. Tighten the pivot shaft nut to 58–87 ft lbs (8.0–12.0 kg/m).

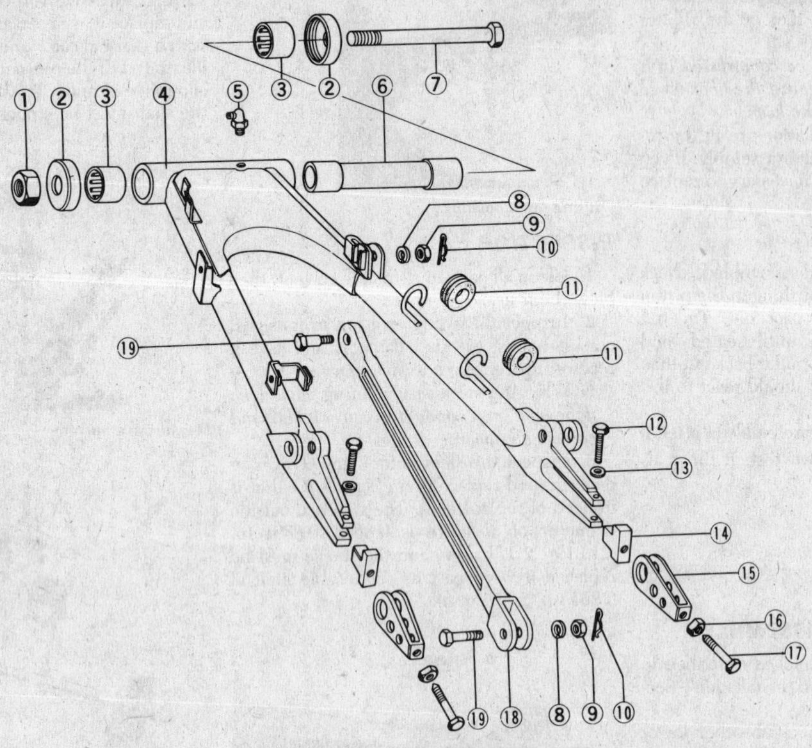

Swing arm assembly (KZ1000)

1. Pivot shaft nut
2. Cap
3. Needle bearing
4. Swing arm
5. Grease fitting
6. Swing arm sleeve
7. Pivot shaft
8. Lockwasher
9. Nut
10. Safety clip
11. Grommet
12. Chain adjuster stopper mounting bolt
13. Washer
14. Chain adjuster stopper mounting
15. Chain adjuster
16. Locknut
17. Adjusting bolt
18. Torque link
19. Bolt

Supplement

This supplemental information applies to models manufactured after 1980 or the year(s) indicated. All other relevant data on these machines can be found in the body of the preceding section.
The information below is organized in the same manner as the main section.

Maintenance

LUBRICATION

Front Forks

1. Release air pressure from forks before draining oil.

2. Use SAE 10W20 oil. Capacities per leg for a routine change are as follows:

J-models (81)	300cc (10.1 oz.)
K, M-models (81)	320cc (10.8 oz.)
R, J-models (82 and later)	290cc (9.8 oz.)
K, M-models (82 and later)	295cc (1.1 oz.)

3. Add about 20-30cc (0.68-1.0 oz.) per leg when refilling forks after rebuilding.

4. Pressure forks. Standard pressures are:

J-Models	3.6-5.0 psi
K,M,R-Models	5.7-8.5 psi

SERVICE CHECKS AND ADJUSTMENTS

Clutch

1. Loosen the knurled locknut at the hand lever and turn the adjuster in to maximum cable free-play.

2. Use the adjuster mid-way along the cable to maximize cable free-play.

3. Remove the clutch adjusting screw cover on the left side of the engine.

4. Loosen the locknut. Turn the adjusting screw CCW until it becomes hard to turn, then turn it 1/4 turn clockwise.

5. Hold the adjusting screw in this position and tighten the locknut.

6. Use the cable adjuster mid-way along the cable to give ^{16}-1/8 in. (2-3mm) of play at the hand lever. This distance is measured between the hand lever and the lever holder.

7. Use the adjuster at the hand to lever to make fine adjustments.

Engine And Transmission

TOP END

On models with a hy-vo cam chain instead of the single-row unit used on earlier machines, there are several differences in top end components and service procedures. Note the following points.

Camshafts

1. J/R, K and M-models use different camshafts. They are identified by grooves adjacent to the sprocket on the right-hand side of the cam. Cam marks are as follows:
J/R-models: the intake camshaft has one groove, the exhaust cam, none.
K-models: the intake camshaft has two grooves, and so does the exhaust cam.
M-models: the intake camshaft has two grooves, the exhaust camshaft has gear teeth for the tachometer drive.

2. Cam lobe service limits are as follows:
J/R-models: Intake: 36.80mm (1.449 in.)
Exhaust: 36.40mm (1.443 in.)
K/M-models: In & Ex: 35.91mm (1.414 in.)

Cam Sprockets

1. Cam sprockets are identical for both intake and exhaust cams, but different mounting holes are used depending on which camshaft they are mounted to.

2. When mounting a sprocket on the Intake cam, use the holes with square recesses (marked "IN").

3. When mounting a sprocket on the Exhaust cam, use the holes with round recesses (marked "EX").

4. Tighten sprocket bolts to 11 ft. lbs. after applying non-permanent thread-locking compound.

Valve Timing

1. Be sure that camshafts are installed so that the "R" and "L" marks are on the correct sides of the engine.

2. Refer to the illustration of timing marks. The alignment is made when the "T" 1.4 mark on the timing advance mechanism is lined up with the timing mark at the crankshaft.

Fuel System

CARBURETORS

Refer to the exploded view of the BS 34 constant-velocity carburetor as a guide for disassembly. See chart for specifications. Service procedures are as outlined in "General Information."

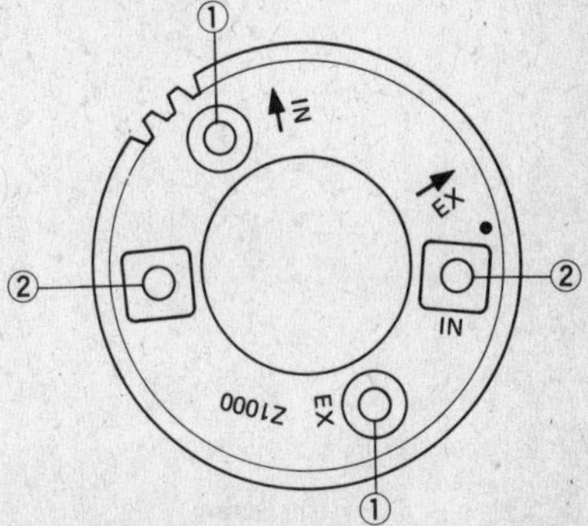

Exhaust cams are mounted to the square-recessed holes (1); intake cams mount to the round recessed holes (1)

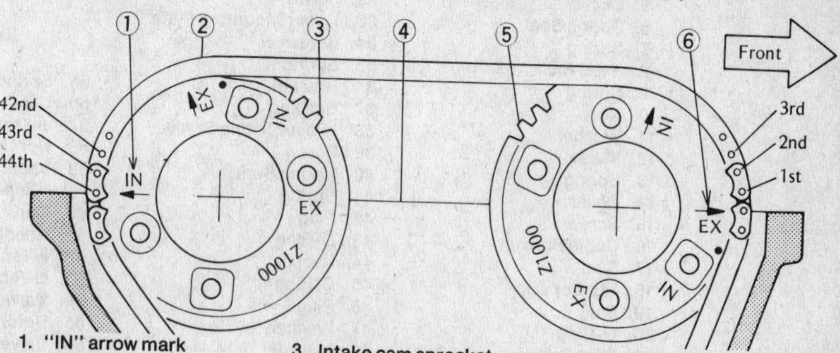

1. "IN" arrow mark
2. Cam chain
3. Intake cam sprocket
4. Cover mating surface
5. Exhaust cam sprocket
6. "EX" arrow mark

Timing marks aligned when centrifugal timing advance mark "T" 1.4 is aligned with the timing mark at the crankshaft

CARBURETOR SPECIFICATIONS

Type	J-Models BS 34	R-Models BS 34
Main jet	117.5R	127.5%
Needle jet	Y-2	Y-4
Jet needle	5CF59	5C50-1
Pilot jet	37.5	37.5
Starter jet	1:45; 2:0.8	45
Main air jet	85	85
Pilot air jet	350	350
Pilot screw	pre-set	pre-set
Service fuel level (mm/in.)	3/0.12	3/0.12
Float height	18.6/0.73	18.6/0.73

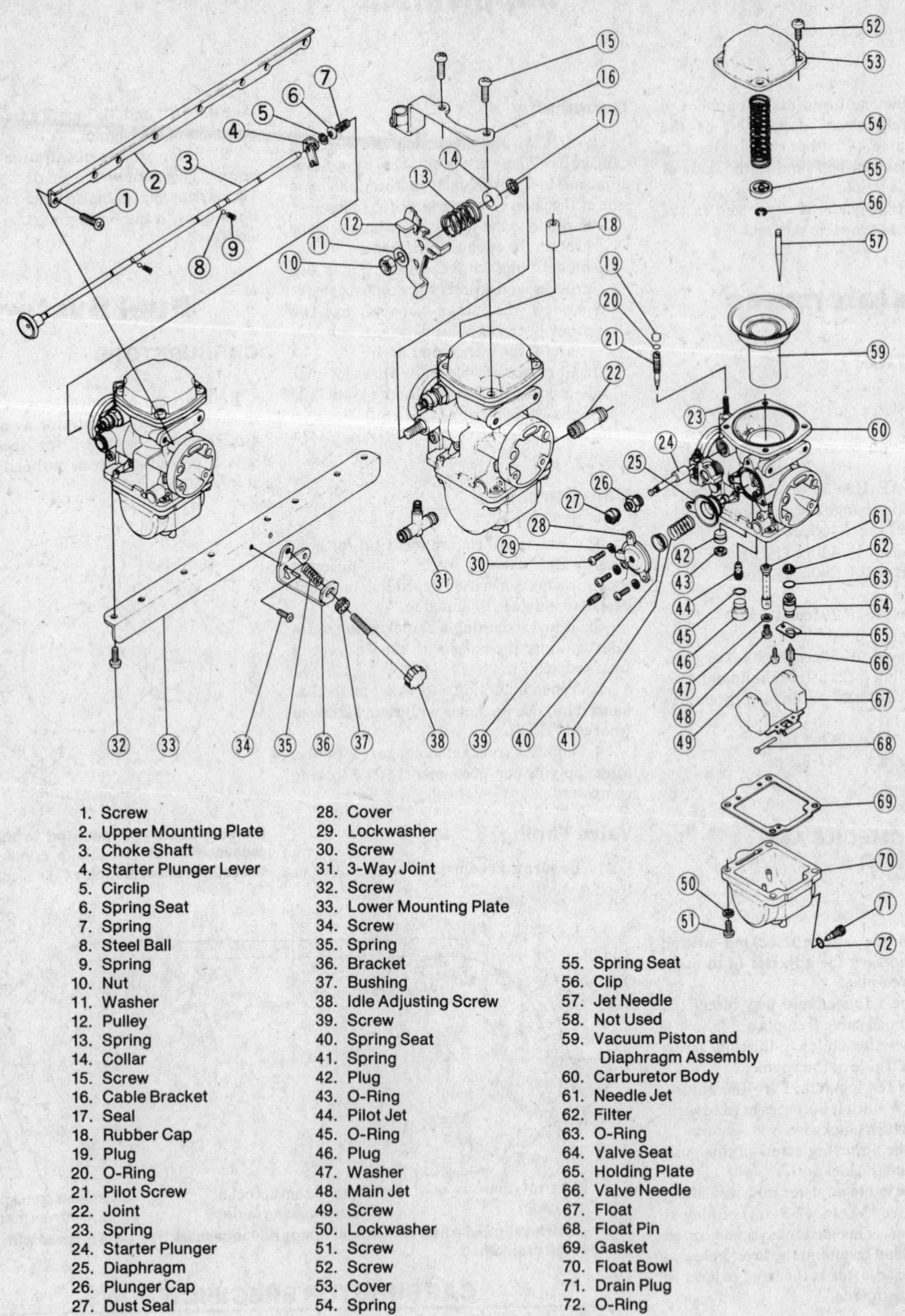

1. Screw
2. Upper Mounting Plate
3. Choke Shaft
4. Starter Plunger Lever
5. Circlip
6. Spring Seat
7. Spring
8. Steel Ball
9. Spring
10. Nut
11. Washer
12. Pulley
13. Spring
14. Collar
15. Screw
16. Cable Bracket
17. Seal
18. Rubber Cap
19. Plug
20. O-Ring
21. Pilot Screw
22. Joint
23. Spring
24. Starter Plunger
25. Diaphragm
26. Plunger Cap
27. Dust Seal
28. Cover
29. Lockwasher
30. Screw
31. 3-Way Joint
32. Screw
33. Lower Mounting Plate
34. Screw
35. Spring
36. Bracket
37. Bushing
38. Idle Adjusting Screw
39. Screw
40. Spring Seat
41. Spring
42. Plug
43. O-Ring
44. Pilot Jet
45. O-Ring
46. Plug
47. Washer
48. Main Jet
49. Screw
50. Lockwasher
51. Screw
52. Screw
53. Cover
54. Spring
55. Spring Seat
56. Clip
57. Jet Needle
58. Not Used
59. Vacuum Piston and Diaphragm Assembly
60. Carburetor Body
61. Needle Jet
62. Filter
63. O-Ring
64. Valve Seat
65. Holding Plate
66. Valve Needle
67. Float
68. Float Pin
69. Gasket
70. Float Bowl
71. Drain Plug
72. O-Ring

BS model carburetor assembly

Kawasaki KZ 650/750

MODEL COVERAGE

KZ 650-B
KZ 650-C
KZ 650-D
KZ 750-E/H/L
KZ 650-D/F/H

INDEX

MAINTENANCE

NOTE: *Common maintenance procedures are explained in detail in the "General Information" section.*

LUBRICATION

Motor Oil

For use in all temperatures, Kawasaki recommends SAE 10W-40 motor oil, service rating "SE." SAE 10W-50 or 20W-50 can also be used.

Checking Oil Level

1. The KZ650/750 has a wet-sump lubrication system, all of the oil being contained in the crankcases.
2. A sight glass is provided just below the clutch housing on the right side of the engine to allow oil level to be checked.

3. Be sure that the motorcycle is parked on the center stand and on a level surface.
4. If the engine has just been shut off, allow it to sit for a few minutes before checking the level.
5. With the above conditions met, the oil level should be between the upper and lower level marks inscribed by the inspection glass. If the level is too low, add enough oil to bring the level up even with the top level mark. If the oil level is too high, siphon some of the excess off. Do not overfill the crankcase.
6. If the oil and filter have just been changed, the engine should be allowed to idle for several minutes before checking the level to give the filter case a chance to fill up.

Changing Oil

1. The recommended oil change interval is 1800 miles or three months, whichever comes first.
2. Oil should be changed when the engine is warm. This ensures more complete draining, and makes it more likely that the oil will carry off any particulate matter with it.

Removing the drain plug

3. With the motorcycle parked on the center stand, and a suitable container (at least 3½ qt. capacity) placed beneath the engine, remove the crankcase drain plug and allow the oil to drain off. After draining seems to be complete, kick the engine over a few times with the kickstarter to drain off the oil in the filter. This is not necessary if the filter is being changed at the same time.
4. Install the drain plug and tighten it to 10–12 ft lbs.
5. If the filter is being changed, refer to "Oil Filter," below.
6. Add about 3.2 qts. (3.0 l) of SAE 10W-40, 10W-50 or 20W-50 oil to the crankcase. Start the engine and allow it to idle for a couple of minutes. Shut it off, let it sit a few minutes more, then check the oil level. Add oil, if necessary, to bring the level up to the upper level mark.

If the filter is being changed at the same time, it will be necessary to add more oil (3.7 qts./3.4.1). See the following section.

Oil Filter

1. The oil filter should be changed at every other oil change (3600 miles/6 months).
2. Proceed as outlined above ("Changing Oil," Steps 2–4). Place the container beneath the oil filter.
3. Remove the oil filter mounting bolt and take out the filter.
4. Hold the filter element steady and twist out the filter bolt.
5. Check the condition of the filter bolt and filter cover O-rings. If they are knicked, flattened, hardened, discolored, or otherwise damaged, the O-rings should be replaced.
6. Before fitting the new filter element, lightly oil the grommets on both sides. When installing the element onto the filter bolt, be sure that the grommets do not slip out of place.

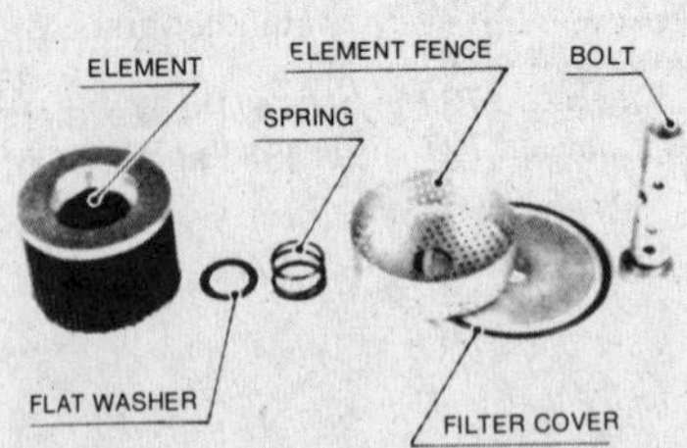

Oil filter components

7. Wipe off the large o-ring's mating surface on the crankcase. Lightly oil the large o-ring and the filter bolt o-ring.
8. Install the filter assembly and tighten the bolt to 13–16 ft lbs.
9. Add 3.7 qts. (3.5 l) of the proper grade of oil to the crankcase and check the oil level as previously described.

NOTE: *If the filter components have been completely disassembled, the correct reassembly order is: filter bolt, filter cover, element fence, spring, flat washer, and filter element.*

Front Forks (Standard)

1. SAE 10W oil is recommended for KZ650-B front forks, SAE 15W for other models.
2. Fork oil should be changed every 6000 miles or 12 months, whichever comes first.
3. Place a container beneath one of the fork sliders and remove the drain plug. Pump the slider up and down by applying the front brake and pushing on the forks until all of the old oil is expelled. Examine the plug gasket, replacing it if it is damaged, then refit the plug.

Removing the fork drain screw

Repeat the procedure with the other fork slider.

4. Examine the drained oil. If it contains water, or is exceptionally dirty, it may be that the dust covers on top of the fork sliders are damaged and allowing foreign matter to get past. Check that the dust covers are properly secured and replace them if they are cracked or otherwise damaged.
5. Support the front wheel off the ground. Remove the filler bolt from the top of the fork leg. On late models, the rubber cap must be removed first.
6. Add the correct quantity of oil to each fork leg. This amounts to 165 cc (5.6 oz.) for KZ650-B models, and 160 cc (5.4 oz.) for later models. These amounts apply to routine oil changes. If the forks are being refilled after rebuilding, add an additional 20–30 cc (0.68–1.0 oz.) per fork leg.
7. Inspect the filler bolt o-rings for damage and replace them if necessary. Install the bolts and tighten them securely. Install the cap, if fitted.
8. After several miles of operation, check the area around the fork slider seals for leaks or seepage. Even a minimal amount will require replacement of the seals. A coating of grime building up in this area over a period of time is also indicative of ineffective seals.

Front Forks (Air-Type)

CAUTION: *Air fork adjustments must be co-ordinated with rear shock settings according to factory specifications. Refer to the "Chassis" section for proper settings.*

1. SAE 10W oil is recommended for air forks.
2. Place the motorcycle on the center stand.
3. Depressurize each fork leg by means of the air valve at the top of the fork legs.
4. Remove the handlebars.
5. Remove the fork drain screw at the lower end of the slider. Pump out the fork oil by pumping the forks up and down.
6. Refit the drain screw, securing it with a non-permanent thread-locking compound.
7. Remove the filler cap and pull out the fork spring.
8. Add the proper amount of oil to each fork leg.

9. Fork capacities are as follows:

KZ 650D/F	225 cc
KZ 650H	270 cc
KZ 750E	230 cc
KZ 750H	260 cc

NOTE: *If the fork is being rebuilt, add about 20 cc more per leg.*

10. After refitting the filler caps, adjust front fork air pressure. See "Chassis."

Chasis Lubrication

1. The swing arm pivot is fitted with a single grease fitting in the middle of the pivot. A good grade of chassis grease should be applied about every 6,000 miles, or once a year—whichever comes first.

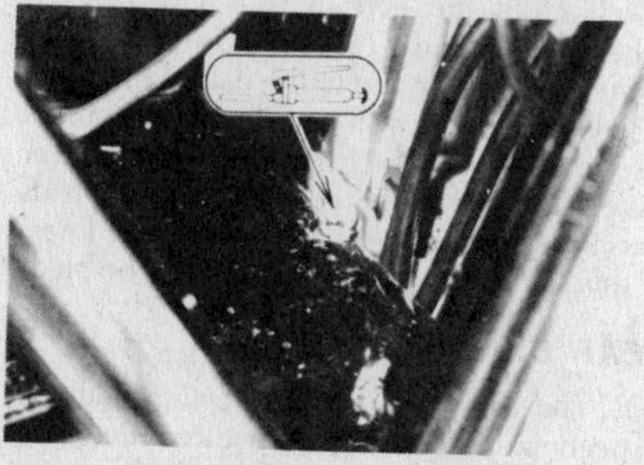

Swing arm grease fitting

Apply the grease until some of it appears at both ends of the swing arm to ensure thorough lubrication. Wipe off the excess.

2. Every 2 years or 12,000 miles—whichever comes first—the wheel bearings and steering stem bearings should be repacked. Refer to the "Chassis" section for procedures.

3. At 3,000 mile intervals, or more often if the machine is used in wet or inclement weather, various control and chassis pivot points should be lubricated with multi-purpose grease or motor oil. These include the hand lever pivots, side and center stand pivots, and carburetor choke pivots.

SERVICE CHECKS AND ADJUSTMENTS

Drive Chain

1. The chain should have about 20–30 mm (0.75–1.2 in.) of total up-and-down free-play measured in the middle of the lower chain run.

2. Before checking or adjusting the chain slack, the following conditions should be met:

a. The motorcycle should be placed on the center stand so that the rear wheel is off the ground;

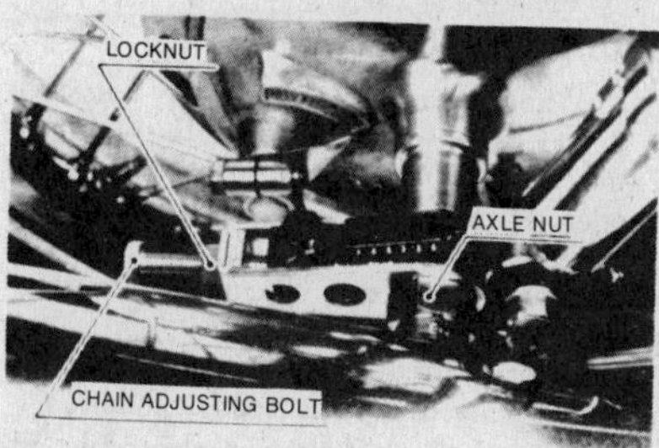

b. The transmission should be placed in neutral;

c. The chain should be clean and well-lubricated;

d. The chain should have been checked for any tight spots by slowly rotating the wheel and checking for variances in the chain tension at different points. If a tight spot exists, the chain tension should be adjusted to the prescribed free-play at the tight spot. Note, however, that such a condition is indicative of a worn chain and probably worn sprockets, which should be replaced as soon as possible.

REAR DRUM BRAKE MODELS

1. Back off the rear brake adjusting nut several turns. Remove the securing clip and loosen the brake anchor nut on the brake plate.
2. Loosen the chain adjuster bolt locknuts.
3. Remove the cotter pin and loosen the axle nut several turns.
4. Turn both chain adjuster bolts in by equal amounts until chain tension is approximately correct. Make sure that the notch on each chain adjuster is aligned with the same corresponding swing arm mark on each side.
5. Tighten the chain adjuster bolt locknuts.
6. Spin the rear wheel and then apply the rear brake hard, and hold it on. While holding the brake on, tighten the axle nut. The axle nut should be tightened to 72–101 ft lbs.
7. Recheck chain slack. Readjust if necessary.
8. Tighten the brake anchor nut and fit the securing clip. Readjust the rear brake.

REAR DISC BRAKE MODELS

1. Remove the cotter pin and loosen the torque link nut. Remove the axle nut cotter pin and loosen the axle nut.
2. Loosen the chain adjuster bolt locknuts.
3. Turn both chain adjuster bolts in by equal amounts until chain tension is approximately correct. Make sure that the notch on each chain adjuster is aligned with the same corresponding swing arm mark on each side.
4. Tighten the chain adjuster bolt locknuts. Tighten the axle nut to 72–101 ft lbs. Recheck the chain tension.
5. Tighten the torque link nut to 19–25 ft lbs. Fit the cotter pins to the axle and torque link nuts.

Checking Chain Wear

1. Chain wear is checked by measuring a length of chain and comparing it to the standard specification.

2. With the machine on the center stand, hang a weight of 10 kg (about 15 lbs) from the middle of the lower chain run. Measure the length of twenty chain links. This will be twenty-one pins. The standard length of a new chain is 317.5 mm (12.5 in.). The serviceable limit is 323 mm (12.7 in.). If the measured length between 21 pins exceeds this limit, the chain must be replaced.

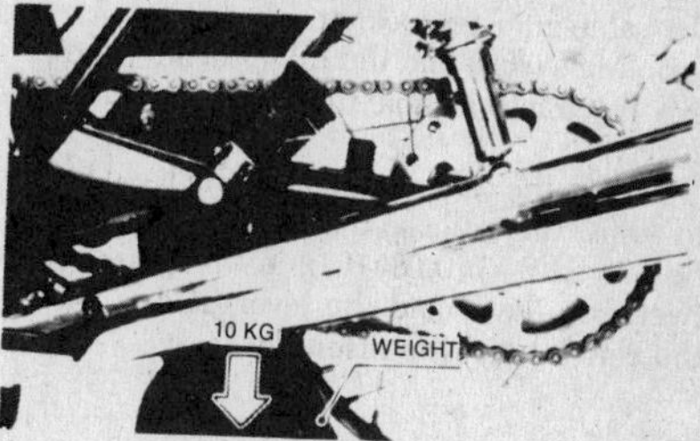

Checking chain wear

Clutch

1. Clutch cable adjustment must always be maintained at the proper specification. If the cable has insufficient free-play, the clutch will slip and rapidly burn out. If it has too much play, the clutch will not disengage completely, resulting in hard shifting and creeping at stops.

2. Use the cable adjuster at the handlebar or on the cable to maintain the correct amount of cable slack. The clutch hand lever should be able to be moved 2–3 mm (0.08–0.12 in.) measured between the lever and the lever holder before the clutch begins to disengage.

Drive chain slack is measured in the middle of the lower chain run

The clutch lever should have 2–3 mm of play before the clutch begins to disengage

If clutch operation is not satisfactory after making this adjustment, proceed as follows:

3. Loosen the locknut on the adjuster mid-way down the cable and screw the adjuster in as far as possible, providing the cable with plenty of slack.

4. Loosen the locknut on the cable adjuster at the hand lever and turn the adjuster so that there is a gap of 5–6 mm (0.20–0.24 in.) between the adjuster and the locknut.

5. Remove the clutch adjuster cover. Loosen the adjuster locknut and back the adjusting screw off two or three turns.

6. Turn the adjusting screw in until it becomes hard to turn. From this point, back the screw off ½ turn. Hold the screw in this position and tighten the locknut.

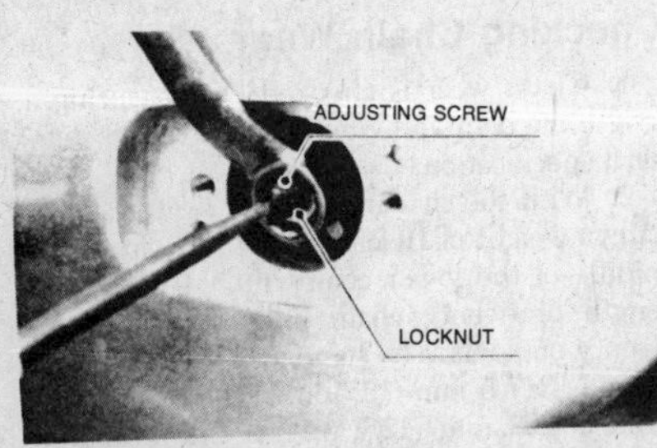

Adjusting the clutch

7. Take up all of the cable slack with the cable adjuster mid-way on the cable. Tighten the cable adjuster locknut.

8. Make sure that the cable sheath is properly fitted into its hole in the engine sprocket cover.

9. Use the cable adjuster at the hand lever to adjust the cable so that the hand lever can be moved 2–3 (0.08–0.12 in.) measured between the lever and the lever holder before the clutch begins to disengage.

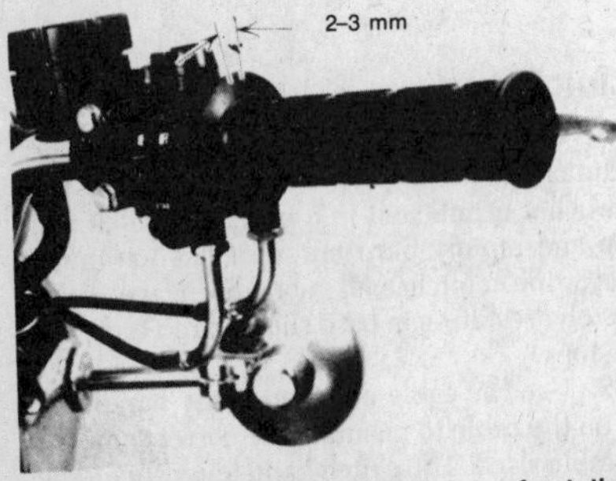

The twist-grip should have 2–3 mm of rotation before the slides begin to open

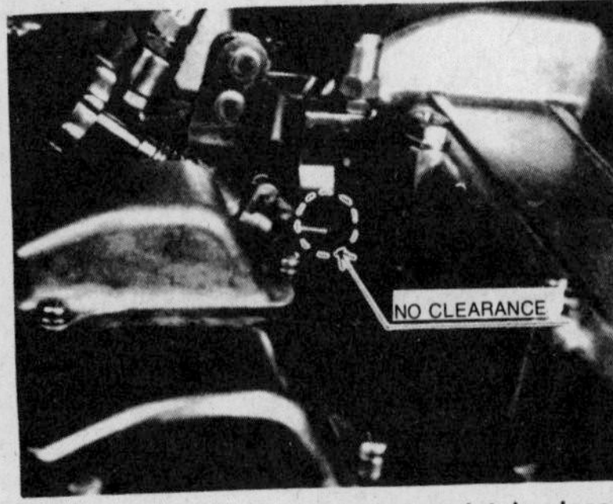

When the throttle is pushed completely closed, there should be no clearance between the cable bracket and the stopper

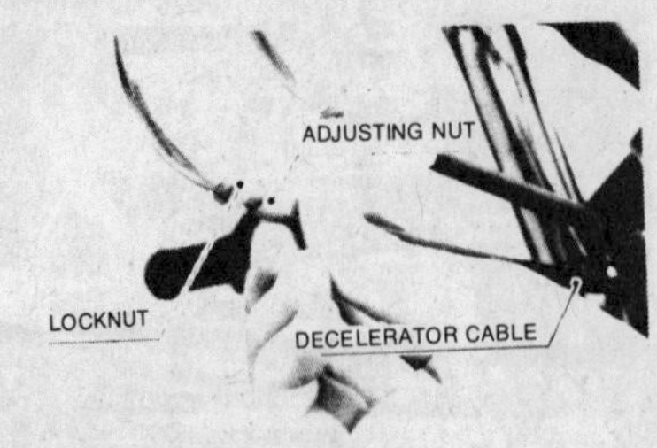

Adjusting the throttle cables

Throttle Cables

1. When the cables are properly adjusted, it should be possible to rotate the twist-grip 2–3 mm (0.08–0.12 in.) before the slides begin to open. Further, when the throttle is pushed completely closed, there should ge no clearance between the cable bracket and the stopper.

If either of these checks indicates that adjustment is necessary, proceed as follows:

2. Loosen the locknuts on the cable adjusters at the twist-grip and screw the adjusters in as far as possible, giving the cables plenty of slack.

3. Turn the decelerator cable adjuster out until there is no clearance between the cable bracket and the stopper when the twist-grip is pushed to the completely closed position. Tighten the locknut.

4. Turn the accelerator cable adjuster out until the twist-grip can be rotated 2–3 (0.08–0.12 in.) before the slides begin to lift. Tighten the locknut.

NOTE: *If the cables cannot be properly adjusted with the adjusters at the twist-grip, use those at the carburetors.*

5. To check that the cables have sufficient slack, start the engine and allow it to idle while turning the handlebars slowly from lock-to-lock. Idle speed must not be affected. If it is, it is probable that the cables are too tightly adjusted, are incorrectly routed, or are binding somewhere along their route.

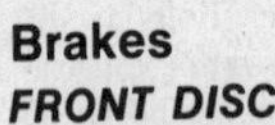

Brakes

FRONT DISC

Disc brakes need no attention other than a periodic check of fluid level and pad wear.

1. After removing the reservoir cap and rubber diaphragm, check to see if the fluid is up to the level mark on the inside of the master cylinder. If the level is below the level mark, add enough DOT 3 brake fluid to bring the level up to the mark. Reinstall the diaphragm and the cap, and tighten securely.

NOTE: *The fluid level will drop slightly as the pads wear.*

2. Check the brake pad wear, and replace the pads in a set if either one is worn to the red limit line.

Refer to "Chassis," for brake system service procedures.

3. If the brake lever feels spongy, bleed the system. This procedure can also be found in "Chassis."

4. There should be 3–5 mm (0.12–0.20 in.) of front brake lever travel. An adjusting bolt is fitted to the underside of the master cylinder for this purpose. If adjustment is necessary, bend up the tab on the adjusting bolt locknut, loosen the locknut, and turn the adjusting bolt very slightly in one direction or the other so that the hand lever has the correct amount of travel. Hold the bolt in this position, and tighten the locknut to 13–16.5 ft lbs. Bend down the tab over one of the flats of the nut.

This adjustment will usually not have to be reset once lever travel is correct. If the lever travel becomes excessive and the brake pads are satisfactory, suspect air in the brake lines. In this event, the system will have to be bled.

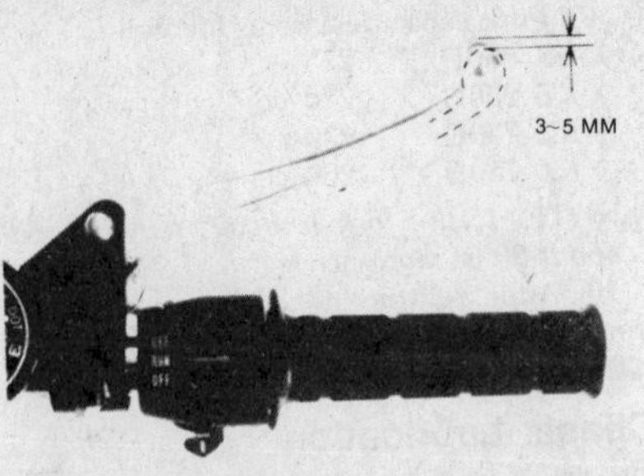

The brake lever should have 3–5 mm of movement

REAR DISC

1. The transparent master cylinder allows inspection of the fluid level without removing the master cylinder cap. If the fluid level is below the level mark, remove the cap and diaphragm and add enough DOT 3 brake fluid to bring the level up to the mark. Reinstall the diaphragm and cap and tighten it securely.

2. Check the brake pads for wear and replace them as a set if they are worn to the red limit line.

3. The rear brake pedal should have 8–10 mm (0.32–0.40 in.) of freeplay. If adjustment is necessary, loosen the brake pushrod locknuts and turn the pushrod until freeplay is corrected. Tighten the locknuts.

NOTE: *Before tightening the locknuts, he sure the sleeve is properly seated on the brake rod joint, as illustrated.*

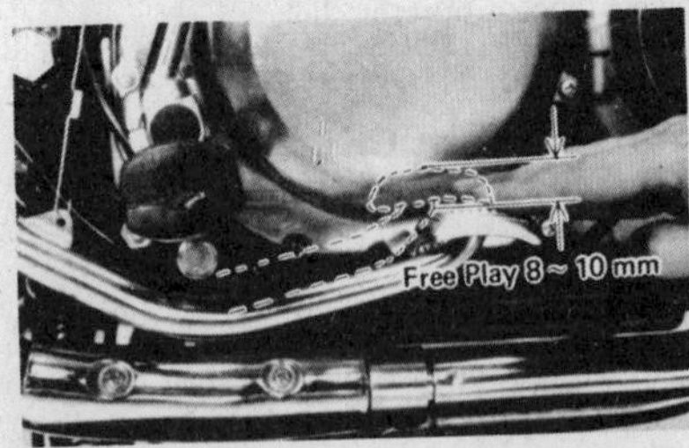

The rear disc brake pedal should have 8–10 mm of free play

4. Brake pedal height should be 20–30 mm (0.8–1.2 in.) below the upper surface of the footpeg. If pedal height is too high, loosen the brake pushrod locknuts, slide down the dust cover, and shorten the pushrod, providing plenty of play in the pedal. Then adjust pedal position with the adjusting bolt.

If pedal height is too low, loosen the adjusting bolt locknut and turn the bolt to yield the proper height. Tighten the locknut. Check brake pedal travel, and adjust if necessary.

REAR DRUM

1. The rear brake pedal should have 20–30 mm (0.8–1.2 in.) of freeplay before the shoes contact the drum. Use the adjusting nut on

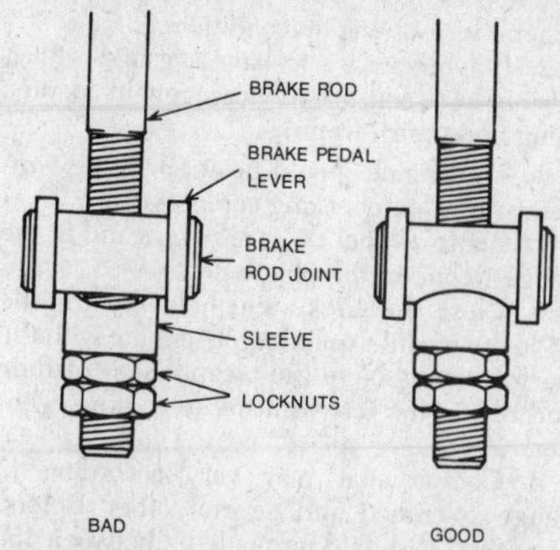

Be sure that the sleeve is properly seated on the brake rod joint

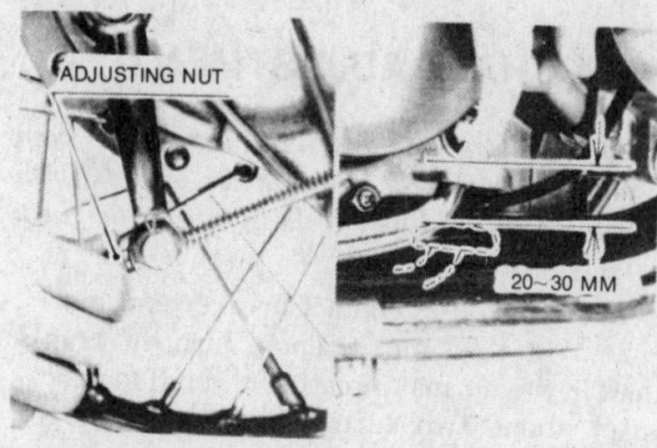

Adjust the rear drum brake to give 20–30 mm of pedal play before the linings contact the drum

the back of the brake rod to make this adjustment.

The adjustment should be made with the machine on its wheels and the weight of a rider on the seat. The pedal should be depressed lightly by hand to find the freeplay.

2. After making this adjustment, check that the brakes do not drag after application. Check the operation of the rear brake light and adjust if necessary.

3. At rest, the brake pedal should be positioned 20–30 mm (0.8–1.2 in.) below the upper surface of the footpeg. If adjustment is necessary, back off the brake adjusting nut and use the pedal stopper bolt to change the pedal height. Readjust the brake after this correction is made.

4. A pointer is provided indicating brake shoe condition by means of a "usable range" when the brake is fully applied. When the pointer leaves this range, the brake shoes must be replaced.

5. When the brakes are fully applied, the angle formed by the brake rod and the brake lever should be approximately 90°. If the angle exceeds this amount, brake effectiveness will be greatly reduced. If necessary, remove the brake lever and move it one or more splines on the brake cam to restore the angle. Do not disturb the brake wear indicator when this is done.

The angle between the brake lever and rod should be 80–90° when the brake is fully applied

Brake Light Switches

The switches should be checked for operation after the brakes are adjusted. The rear brake light switch and adjuster nut are mounted on a slotted bracket. The rear switch is adjusted by holding the switch and turning the adjuster nut to effect adjustment. Moving the switch upon the bracket allows the brake light to turn on sooner. Moving it down allows the light to turn on later. Do not turn the switch to effect adjustment as the wires will become twisted and may break. Generally, the brake light should come on after the pedal has moved 15 mm (0.6 in.).

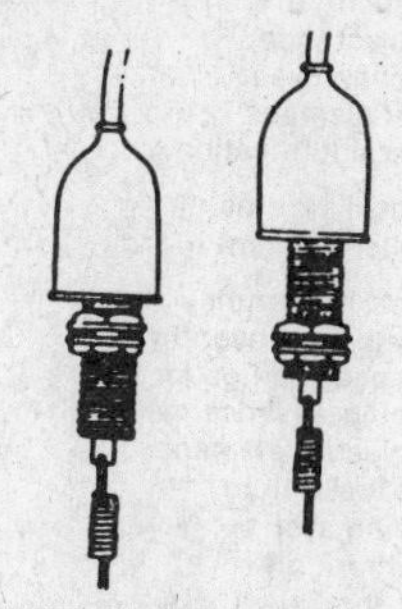

Brake light switch adjustments

The front switch is activated by the pressure of the brake fluid in the brake line. This switch is not adjustable; if defective, it must be replaced.

Headlight Adjustment

1. Set the machine about 25 feet away from the perpendicular to a wall, preferably of a color which reflects light well.

The machine should be off the stand, and with a rider putting his weight on the machine as in operation.

2. Switch on the high beam. The headlight high beam should be parallel to the ground and should hit the wall directly in front of the machine.

3. Vertical adjustment is made by loosening the two headlight shell mounting bolts slightly and pivoting the shell up or down.

4. Lateral adjustment is accomplished by means of the screw on the right side of the headlight. Turning the screw clockwise will move the beam to the left; turning it counterclockwise will move it to the right.

Headlight lateral adjustment screw

FUEL SYSTEM

Fuel system maintenance involves cleaning or replacing the air filter, cleaning the fuel petcock sediment cup and filter screens, and cleaning the carburetor float bowls.

The normal service interval is 3,000 miles. The air filter element should be replaced every 6,000 miles.

Air Filter

1. Open the seat. Unscrew and remove the air cleaner cap. It will be necessary to lift the end of the tank to clear the cap. Remove the air filter element.

Air cleaner cap location

2. Clean the element with a high flash-point solvent. Do not use a solvent such as kerosene or anything else which will leave an oily residue on the element. After cleaning, dry the element by applying compressed air to the inside area.

3. After about five such cleanings, or every 6,000 miles, the filter element should be replaced with a new one.

4. Check that the sponge gaskets are properly secured to the element. If they are not, stick them on with an adhesive. If the gaskets or the element itself is damaged or holed, it should be replaced.

5. Installation is the reverse of removal. When installing the air cleaner cap, screw it on until a click is heard.

Petcock

1. The petcock has a sediment cup and a filter screen just above it, and also has filter screens on the intake pipes inside the gas tank.

2. Shut the fuel off. Unscrew and remove the sediment cup. Take out the filter screen. Clean any dirt or debris from the cup. Brush the surface of the filter screen to remove any trapped foreign matter. Check the condition of the gasket and replace it if it is crushed or knicked.

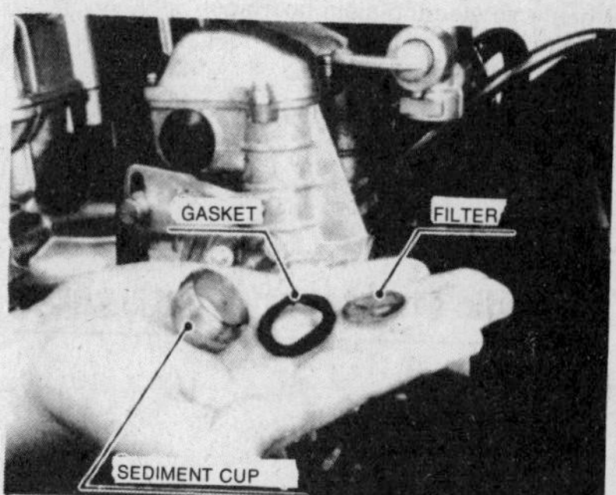

Petcock sediment cup components

3. If water was present in the cup, place a container beneath the petcock and turn on the gas in the "reserve" position. Drain off the gasoline until there is no water left in the fuel.

4. Refit the filter screen, the gasket, and the cup. Turn on the gas and check for leaks before operating the motorcycle.

5. At longer intervals, the filter screens inside the tank should be attended to. Disconnect the fuel line from the petcock. Remove the gas tank and drain off the gasoline. Remove the two screws which secure the petcock to the tank. Carefully clean the intake pipe filters. Check the petcock sealing o-ring for damage and replace it if necessary.

Carburetors

1. Although thorough cleaning of the carburetors necessitates their removal from the motorcycles, water and foreign matter can be removed from the float bowls simply by removing the drain plug and allowing the contents to drain into a suitable container. Be sure the petcock is off before removing any of the drain plugs.

2. It is also possible to clean the jets by removing the float bowls. Refer to the "Fuel System" section for procedures.

Removing the float bowl drain plug

Recommended Lubricants

Engine
- SAE 10W-40, service rating "SE"
- SAE 10W-50, service rating "SE"
- SAE 20W-50, service rating "SE"

Front forks
- KZ650-B: SAE 10W
- KZ650-C/D: SAE 15W
- Other models: SAE 10W

Disc brakes
- DOT 3 standard hydraulic disc brake fluid

Control cables
- Light motor oil
- Graphite-based lubricant
- Molybdenum-disulphide-based lubricant

Tach, speedometer cables; throttle twist-grip
- Light duty grease

Wheel and steering stem bearings
- Waterproof, medium-weight bearing grease

Grease fitting
- Waterproof, medium-weight chassis grease

Drive chain
- Lubricant developed specifically for motorcycle drive chains

Periodic Maintenance Intervals①

Before each ride
- Safety items
- Operation of lights
- Chain adjustment
- Control cable adjustment
- Brake operation

Weekly
- Engine oil level
- Tire pressure (check when cold)
- Battery electrolyte level

Every 200 miles
- Lubricate chain

Every 500 miles
- Check drive chain slack
- Check tightness of critical fasteners

Every 1800 miles/3 months
- Change engine oil

Every 3000 miles/6 months
- Check brakes and brake fluid level
- Check clutch
- Adjust carburetors
- Check cable free-play
- Check spokes and rim run-out
- Clean fuel system
- Clean and gap spark plugs
- Check point gap and ignition timing
- Adjust cam chain
- Check valve clearance
- Check drive chain wear
- Clean air filter element
- Perform general lubrication

Every 3600 miles/6 months
- Change oil filter element

Every 6000 miles/12 months
- Check steering stem bearing play
- Check brake pads/linings for wear
- Lubricate timing advance mechanism
- Replace air cleaner element
- Change disc brake fluid
- Lubricate swing arm
- Change front fork oil

Every 12000 miles/24 months
- Repack wheel bearings and steering stem bearings
- Repack speedometer gear housing
- Grease drum brake cam

① Based on normal usage after initial service and break-in are completed

Maintenance Data

Fuel capacity	16.8 1/4.4 gal.
Oil capacity	
When changing oil only	3.0 1/3.2 qts.
When changing oil and filter	3.5 1/3.7 qts.
Front forks (each leg)	
KZ650-B	165 cc/5.6 oz.①
KZ650-C/D	160 cc/5.4 oz.①
KZ650-D/F	225 cc/7.6 oz.①
KZ650-H	270 cc/9.1 oz.①
KZ750-E	230 cc/7.8 oz.①
KZ750-H	260 cc/8.8 oz.①
Tire pressure	
Front	28 psi
Rear (solo)	32 psi
Rear (two-up or high-speed)	36 psi
Battery	
Make/Model	Yusa/YB10L
Voltage/Output	12v/10 ah
Continuous charging rate	1.0 amp

① When refilling forks after rebuilding, add an additional 20-30 cc (0.68–1.0 oz.) per leg to the given quantities

TUNE-UP

Common tune-up procedures are explained in detail in the "General Information" section.

COMPRESSION TEST

1. A compression check should be made before each tune-up since this will provide a general idea of engine condition.

2. It is necessary to have a gauge with a flexible hose and the proper screw-in adapter (plug holes are 14 mm).

3. The engine should be at operating temperature when checking compression.

4. Remove all of the spark plugs and fit the gauge to one of the plug holes.

5. Close the choke and hold the throttle wide open while spinning the engine with the starter motor. Note the compression reading and repeat the test with the remaining cylinders.

6. Compression may vary according to gauge tolerance and several other factors. However, it should normally be between 156 and 185 psi. All cylinders must be within 15 psi of this range and of each other.

CAM CHAIN ADJUSTMENT

NOTE: *Late models have automatic cam chain adjustment. For earlier models with a manually adjusted chain, the procedure is as follows.*

1. Remove the contact breaker cover.

2. With a 17 mm wrench, turn the crankshaft in the normal direction of rotation (clockwise) about two turns. Then position the corner of the timing advance mechanism near the Nos. 2 and 3 timing marks so that it aligns with the stationary timing mark.

NOTE: *Do not turn the crankshaft backwards to achieve this alignment. If you go past the point of aligment, continue turning the crankshaft in the normal direction of rotation.*

3. Loosen the cam chain tensioner locknut and back the bolt off a couple of turns. Cam chain tension will be set automatically.

4. Tighten the tensioner bolt to 61–78 in. lbs. Tighten the locknut.

5. Refit the contact breaker cover.

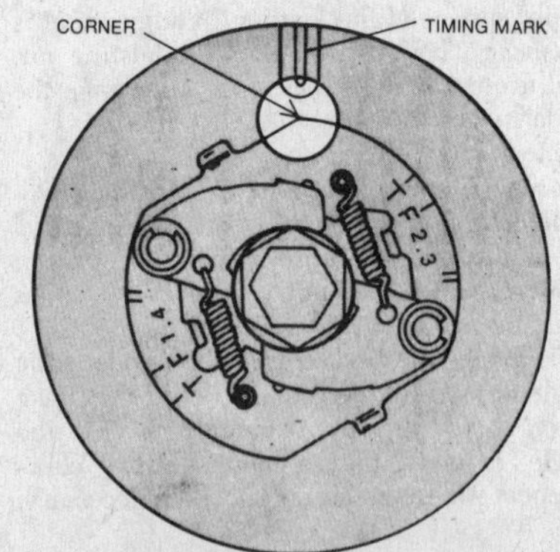

Crankshaft position for cam chain adjustment

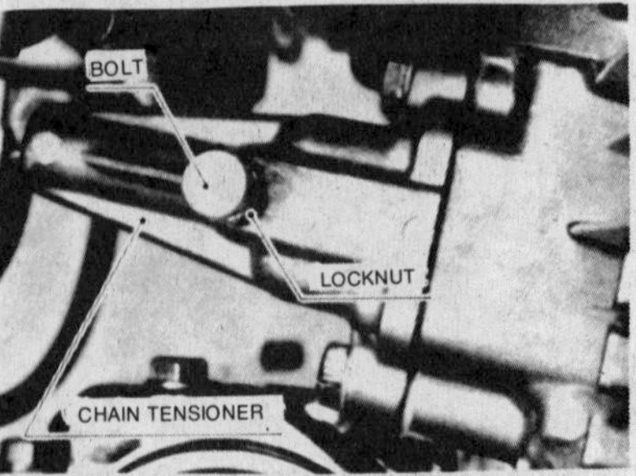

Cam chain tensioner

6. If adjustment does not remedy excessive cam chain noise, it is probable that the cam chain or the chain guides are worn to the point of replacement.

VALVE ADJUSTMENT

Checking Clearance

NOTE: *Valve clearance must be checked when the engine is COLD.*

1. Remove the gas tank. Remove the ignition coils.
2. Remove the cylinder head cover bolts and take off the cover.
3. Remove the contact breaker cover.
4. Using a 17 mm wrench, turn the crankshaft over until the line marked "Ex" on the exhaust cam sprocket is pointing forward and is aligned with the cylinder head surface. With the engine in this position, clearance can be checked at the exhaust valves of cylinders Nos. 1 and 3.
5. With a feeler gauge of the proper thickness, measure the clearance at the exhaust valves of cylinders Nos. 1 and 3. (Cylinders are numbered consecutively from left to right.)

The correct clearance is 0.08–0.18 mm (0.003–0.007 in.). A feeler gauge of the proper thickness should be a light slip fit between the cam and the valve lifter. If the measured clearance is not within this range, the clearance must be adjusted by substituting shims of the proper thickness. Refer to "Adjusting Clearance," below.

Cam sprocket position to check the valve clearance at the exhaust valves for cylinders Nos. 1 and 3

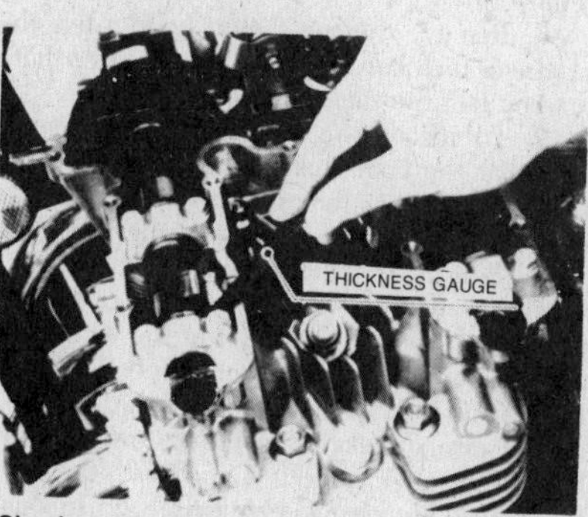

Check valve clearance between the cam lobe and the tappet

6. Turn the engine over until the line marked "Ex" for the exhaust cam sprocket is pointing towards the rear of the engine and is aligned with the cylinder head surface. In this position, the exhaust valves for the remaining two cylinders (Nos. 2 and 4) can be checked.
7. To check the clearance of the intake valves, turn the engine over until the arrow marked "T" on the intake cam sprocket is pointing towards the rear of the engine and is aligned with the cylinder head surface. Check the clearance of the intake valves for cylinders Nos. 1 and 3.

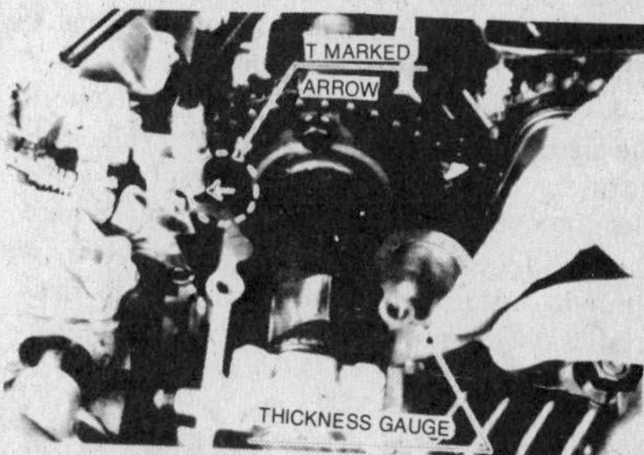

Cam sprocket position for checking valve clearance at the intake valves for cylinders Nos. 1 and 3

As for the exhaust valves, proper clearance is 0.08–0.18 mm (0.003–0.007 in.).

8. Turn the engine over again until the arrow marked "T" is pointing towards the front of the engine and aligned with the cylinder head surface. Check the clearance at the intake valves for cylinders Nos. 2 and 4.

Valve Adjustment Chart

	PRESENT SHIM SIZE																								
PART NUMBER (92025-	1090	1091	1092	1093	1094	1095	1096	1097	1098	1099	1100	1101	1102	1103	1104	1105	1106	1107	1108	1109	1110	1111	1112	1113	1114
THICKNESS (mm)	2.00	2.05	2.10	2.15	2.20	2.25	2.30	2.35	2.40	2.45	2.50	2.55	2.60	2.65	2.70	2.75	2.80	2.85	2.90	2.95	3.00	3.05	3.10	3.15	3.20
VALVE CLEARANCE (mm)																									
0.00~0.03			2.00	2.00	2.05	2.10	2.15	2.20	2.25	2.30	2.35	2.40	2.45	2.50	2.55	2.60	2.65	2.70	2.75	2.80	2.85	2.90	2.95	3.00	3.05
0.04~0.07		2.00	2.00	2.05	2.10	2.15	2.20	2.25	2.30	2.35	2.40	2.45	2.50	2.55	2.60	2.65	2.70	2.75	2.80	2.85	2.90	2.95	3.00	3.05	3.10
0.08~0.18	SPECIFIED CLEARANCE / NO CHANGE REQUIRED																								
0.19~0.22	2.05	2.10	2.15	2.20	2.25	2.30	2.35	2.40	2.45	2.50	2.55	2.60	2.65	2.70	2.75	2.80	2.85	2.90	2.95	3.00	3.05	3.10	3.15	3.20	
0.23~0.27	2.10	2.15	2.20	2.25	2.30	2.35	2.40	2.45	2.50	2.55	2.60	2.65	2.70	2.75	2.80	2.85	2.90	2.95	3.00	3.05	3.10	3.15	3.20		
0.28~0.32	2.15	2.20	2.25	2.30	2.35	2.40	2.45	2.50	2.55	2.60	2.65	2.70	2.75	2.80	2.85	2.90	2.95	3.00	3.05	3.10	3.15	3.20			
0.33~0.37	2.20	2.25	2.30	2.35	2.40	2.45	2.50	2.55	2.60	2.65	2.70	2.75	2.80	2.85	2.90	2.95	3.00	3.05	3.10	3.15	3.20				
0.38~0.42	2.25	2.30	2.35	2.40	2.45	2.50	2.55	2.60	2.65	2.70	2.75	2.80	2.85	2.90	2.95	3.00	3.05	3.10	3.15	3.20					
0.43~0.47	2.30	2.35	2.40	2.45	2.50	2.55	2.60	2.65	2.70	2.75	2.80	2.85	2.90	2.95	3.00	3.05	3.10	3.15	3.20						
0.48~0.52	2.35	2.40	2.45	2.50	2.55	2.60	2.65	2.70	2.75	2.80	2.85	2.90	2.95	3.00	3.05	3.10	3.15	3.20							
0.53~0.57	2.40	2.45	2.50	2.55	2.60	2.65	2.70	2.75	2.80	2.85	2.90	2.95	3.00	3.05	3.10	3.15	3.20								
0.58~0.62	2.45	2.50	2.55	2.60	2.65	2.70	2.75	2.80	2.85	2.90	2.95	3.00	3.05	3.10	3.15	3.20									
0.63~0.67	2.50	2.55	2.60	2.65	2.70	2.75	2.80	2.85	2.90	2.95	3.00	3.05	3.10	3.15	3.20										
0.68~0.72	2.55	2.60	2.65	2.70	2.75	2.80	2.85	2.90	2.95	3.00	3.05	3.10	3.15	3.20											
0.73~0.77	2.60	2.65	2.70	2.75	2.80	2.85	2.90	2.95	3.00	3.05	3.10	3.15	3.20												
0.78~0.82	2.65	2.70	2.75	2.80	2.85	2.90	2.95	3.00	3.05	3.10	3.15	3.20													
0.83~0.87	2.70	2.75	2.80	2.85	2.90	2.95	3.00	3.05	3.10	3.15	3.20														
0.88~0.92	2.75	2.80	2.85	2.90	2.95	3.00	3.05	3.10	3.15	3.20															
0.93~0.97	2.80	2.85	2.90	2.95	3.00	3.05	3.10	3.15	3.20																
0.98~1.02	2.85	2.90	2.95	3.00	3.05	3.10	3.15	3.20																	
1.03~1.07	2.90	2.95	3.00	3.05	3.10	3.15	3.20																		
1.08~1.12	2.95	3.00	3.05	3.10	3.15	3.20																			
1.13~1.17	3.00	3.05	3.10	3.15	3.20																				
1.18~1.22	3.05	3.10	3.15	3.20																					
1.23~1.27	3.10	3.15	3.20																						
1.28~1.32	3.15	3.20																							
1.33~1.38	3.20																								

INSTALL THE SHIM OF THIS THICKNESS (mm)

Cam
Valve Lifter
Shim
Clearance measured here

1. Measure the clearance (when cold).
2. Check present shim size.
3. Match clearance in vertical column with present shim size in horizontal column.
4. The shim specified where the lines intersect is the one that will give you the proper clearance.

NOTE: If there is no clearance, select a shim which is several sizes smaller and then measure the clearance.

CAUTION

1. Do not put shim stock under the shim. This may cause the shim to pop out at high rpm causing extensive engine damage.
2. Do not grind the shim. This may cause it to fracture, causing extensive engine damage.
3. Check the valve clearance with the proper method in the text. Checking the clearance at any other cam position may result in improper valve clearance.

If the measured clearance is not within the proper range, the valves must be adjusted as outlined under "Adjusting Clearance," below.

Adjusting Clearance

1. Valve clearance is adjusted by removing the fitted shim from beneath the valve lifter and fitting another thicker or thinner one.
2. First it is necessary to find the true valve clearance. If the clearance is not within the specified range, use feeler gauges between the cam and valve lifter until the true clearance is determined. The feeler gauge blade should be a light slip fit.
3. Remove the camshaft. Remove the valve lifter. This procedure is outlined below.
4. Remove the installed shim and check the size marked on it. Refer to the "Valve Adjustment Chart," find the measured valve clearance and the present shim size. Where the two lines intersect, find the correct new shim to install. Shims are available in sizes from 2.0–3.2 mm in increments of 0.05 mm.

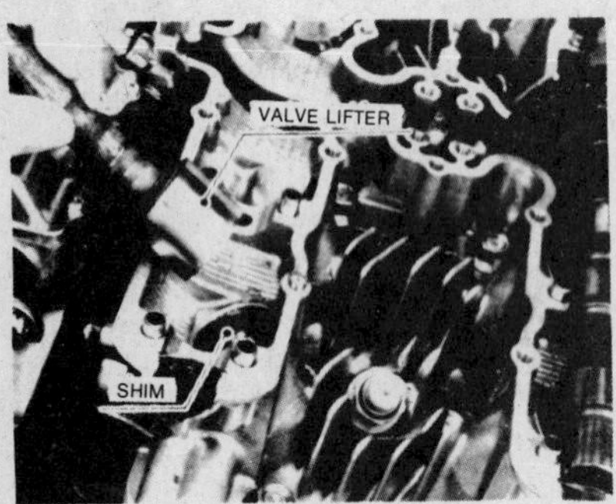

Valve lifter (tappet) and adjusting shim

5. Before adjusting the valve clearance, note the following points:
   a. never put shim stock beneath the shim; it may pop out.
   b. never grind a shim; this may cause it to fracture.
   c. if the smallest available shim will not yield the proper clearance, the valve seat is probably worn. In this case, inspect the valve seat and stem installed height. Refer to the "Engine and Transmission" section.
6. After fitting a shim of the correct size as derived from the "Valve Adjustment Chart," refit the camshaft and recheck the clearance in the normal manner.

CAMSHAFT REMOVAL AND INSTALLATION

CAUTION: *On late models, the cam chain and the valve timing marks of the cam sprockets was changed. The chain on early models was a single-row type; late models have a hy-vo chain. Early cam sprockets are marked with arrows and "T" letters; later models have "IN" and "Z6EX" marks on 650s and "Z7EX" on 750s for valve timing.*

To remove the camshaft(s) for valve adjustment, proceed as follows:

1. Turn the crankshaft over until the "T" mark for cylinders Nos. 1 and 4 is aligned with the stationary timing mark. This puts those cylinders at top dead center.
2. Remove the screw and remove the tachometer pinion holder stopper. Pull the

Remove the tachometer pinion holder stopper

tachometer pinion holder and pinion with the tach cable off the cylinder head.
3. Remove the cam chain tensioner.
4. Remove the cam chain upper chain guide sprocket (4 allen bolts).
5. Remove the camshaft cap bolts and remove the caps.
6. Remove the camshafts. Loop a length of wire or the like around the cam chain so that it won't fall into the crankcases.
7. To install the camshafts, first make sure that the crankshaft is still positioned so that the "T" mark for cylinders Nos. 1 and 4 is aligned with the stationary timing mark.
8. Pull the camshaft chain taut to remove any kinks in it. Install the exhaust camshaft noting that the notched end of the camshaft goes to the right side of the engine. Position the exhaust cam so that the arrow marked "T" on the cam sprocket is pointing towards the front of the engine and is aligned with the cylinder head surface. Keeping the cam in this position, pull the cam chain taut and loop it over the cam sprocket. On late models the exhaust cam is installed so that the "Z6EX" or "Z7EX" mark is aligned with the cylinder head surface.
9. Install the intake camshaft, positioning it so that the arrow marked "T" on the cam sprocket is pointing towards the rear of the engine and is aligned with the cylinder head surface. On late models, the mark on the in-

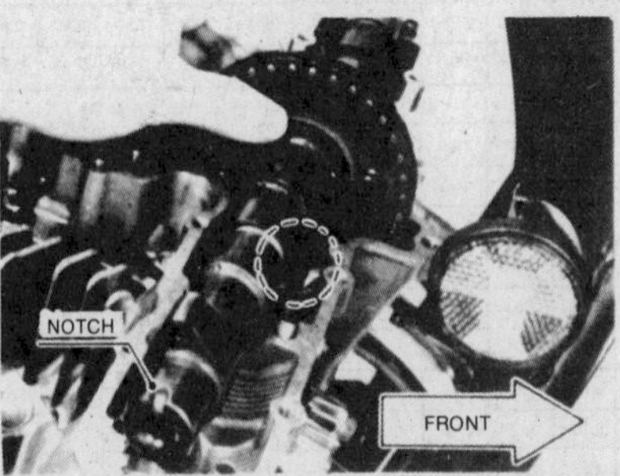

The notch on the end of the cam must be positioned on the right side

Align the arrow marked "T" with the cylinder head surface. On late models the mark "Z6EX" is to be aligned

Correct positioning of the intake cam sprocket (early models)

take cam sprocket which should be aligned with the cylinder head surface is indicated by the letters "IN."
10. Find the cam chain pin pointed at by the exhaust cam "T" arrow or "Z6EX"/"Z7EX" index mark. With this pin as "zero," count off thirty-six (36) pins on early models with the single-row chain, or forty-five (45) pins on late models with the hy-vo chain. Be sure that the index mark on the intake cam sprocket points towards this 36th pin or between pins 45 and 46 on hy-vo chain engines. If it does not, the camshafts are not properly aligned, and engine damage will be the result if the engine is rotated.

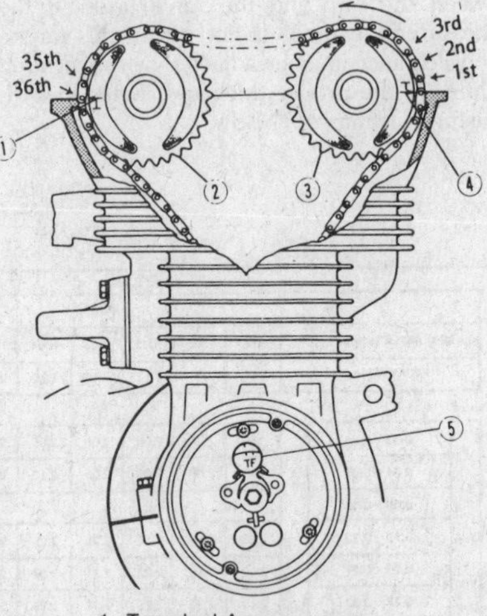

Correct valve timing (early models)

When installing the cam caps, match the number on the caps with the number on the head. Install the caps so that the arrows point towards the exhaust side of the engine

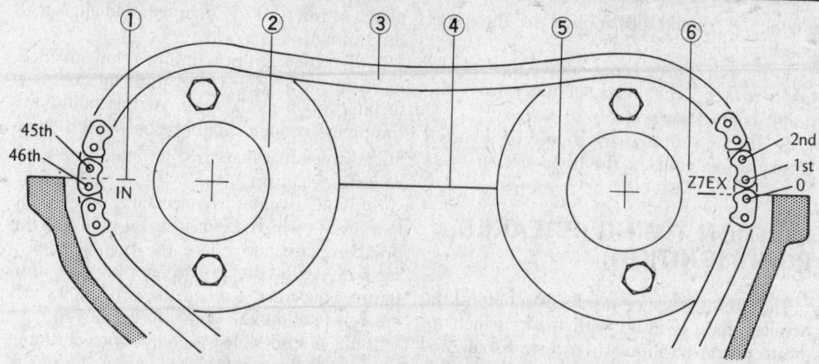

1. "IN" mark
2. Intake cam sprocket
3. Cam chain
4. Cylinder head mating surface
5. Exhaust cam sprocket
6. "Z6EX" or "Z7EX" mark

Correct valve timing for late models

11. Before installing the camshaft caps, note that the caps are identified by a number. Match the number on the cap with that on the cylinder head. Install the caps so that the arrows on the caps point towards the exhaust side of the engine.

12. Partially tighten the left-inside cam caps first to seat the camshaft. Then tighten the cap bolts in the order shown in the illustration until the proper torque of 7.9–10.8 ft lbs is reached.

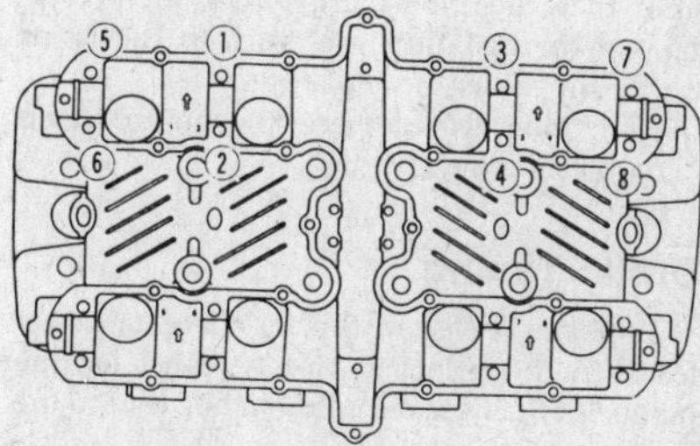

Cam cap bolt tightening sequence

13. Install the upper chain guide sprocket assembly and tighten the allen bolts to 6.5–7.9 ft lbs. The bolts should be secured with a non-permanent thread-locking compound.

14. Install the cam chain tensioner assembly. Note that the red side of the assembly gasket must face the cylinder. Apply liquid gasket to both sides of the assembly bolt washers. Tighten the bolts evenly to 5.1–6.5 ft lbs.

15. Recheck the valve timing before rotating the engine. Turn the engine over slowly at first. If any resistance is felt, stop at once and determine the cause. Improper valve timing may cause the valves to hit the pistons or each other. Turn the engine through several complete revolutions and realign the "T" mark for cylinders Nos. 1 and 4. Check that the cam sprocket marks are still aligned as before.

16. Apply a small amount of high temperature grease to the tachometer pinion shaft, and insert the pinion and pinion holder into the cylinder head. Secure the pinion holder with the holder stopper and screw.

17. Lubricate all of the top end components before refitting the cylinder head cover.

CONTACT BREAKER POINTS

Location

The points and condensers are located on the right end of the crankshaft beneath the points cover. The timing advance mechanism is fitted onto the crankshaft behind the breaker point base plate.

Replacement

1. Points sets are available complete with condensers already mounted on the breaker plate. Disconnect the primary wires at the connectors. Carefully pull the wires through, noting the proper routing. Remove the three screws which secure the breaker plate. When the new plate is fitted, position it so that the securing screws are approximately centered in their slots, and adjust the point gaps and the ignition timing.

2. If the points are purchased separately, disconnect the primary wire at each point set, remove the securing screws, and remove the old points. When installing new points, note that the proper installation of the insulating washers at the primary terminal is critical. If improperly installed, no spark will occur. There is a small insulating washer which fits around the terminal bolt and two insulating washers, one immediately on either side of the terminal bracket. All connectors (condenser, primary wire, points spring) are made on the outer sides of these washers (i.e., no connector must touch the bracket, which is a ground).

3. New points may have a protective coating on the contact surfaces to prevent oxidation. Clean off these surfaces with a non-oily solvent before attempting to start the machine.

Removing the contact breakers

4. If the motorcycle will not start immediately after installation of new points, check that the primary wire connections are tight, that the insulating washers at the primary terminal are properly installed, and that the contact surfaces are thoroughly cleaned.

5. Condensers are easily replaced after disconnecting the lead at the primary terminal, and removing the securing screw.

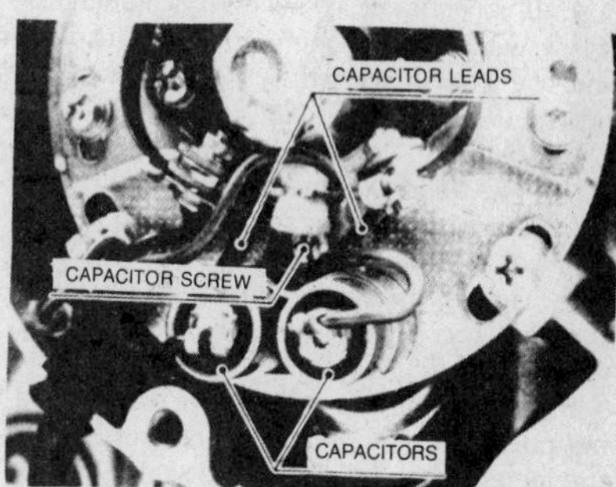

Capacitor securing screw

Gapping

FEELER GAUGE METHOD

Periodic gapping is necessary to compensate for erosion of the contact surfaces due to electrical arcing and for wear of the fiber heel. As the heel wears, the points will open later relative to the rotation of the crankshaft, thus retarding the time slightly.

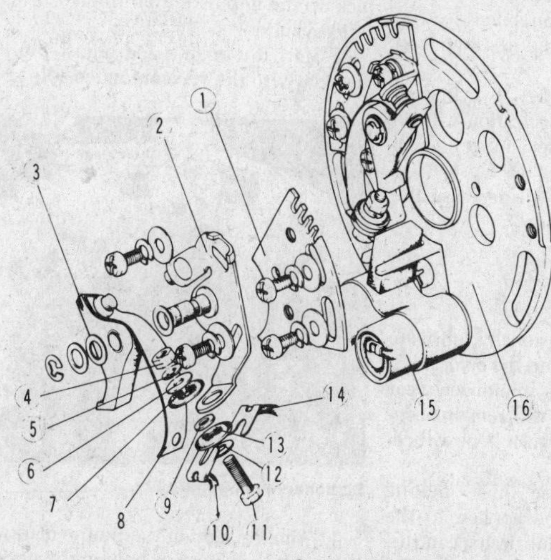

1. Contact breaker adjusting plate
2. Contact breaker base plate
3. Contact breaker
4. Nut
5. Lockwasher
6. Flat washer
7. Large insulator
8. Spring
9. Small insulator
10. Contact breaker lead
11. Bolt
12. Flat washer
13. Large insulator
14. Capacitor lead
15. Capacitor
16. Contact breaker plate

Contact breaker assembly

Points should be filed (if necessary) and cleaned before gapping.

1. Remove the points cover.
2. Turn the engine over until one of the two sets of points is fully open.
3. With the proper feeler gauge blade, check the gap. The proper specification is 0.3–0.4 mm (0.012–0.016 in.), and the blade should be a slip fit between the points if the gap is correct.

Checking the point gap. Loosen the screws indicated by arrows to adjust the gap

4. If adjustment is necessary, loosen the screws which secure the point set to its plate, and use a small screwdriver at the pry point provided to adjust the gap.

   CAUTION: *Loosen the screws just enough to allow the points to be moved. If loosened too much, the points will snap shut instead of holding the gap.*

5. Tighten the screws and recheck the gap. It may change slightly when the screw is tightened.
6. Repeal the procedure with the remaining points set. Try to adjust both sets so that the feeler gauge blade has the same "feel" in both sets. This will help to ensure accurate timing.
7. If it is not possible to gap the points correctly, the fiber heel is evidently worn; the points should then be replaced.

DWELL METER METHOD

Point gap can also be adjusted with the aid of a dwell meter if one is available. "Dwell" is the amount of time the points are closed relative to crankshaft revolution and is expressed in degrees.

The adjustment is made with the engine idling, the positive meter connections lead to the primary wire terminal, and negative lead to the engine (ground).

With the meter set to the "8 cylinder" range, the proper dwell specification will be 23.75°; if set to the "4 cylinder" range, it will be 47.5°.

Increasing the point gap will decrease the dwell reading, and vice-versa.

Lubrication

1. It is necessary to occasionally lubricate the cam follower fiber heel and the pivot point of the contact breaker. This minimizes wear and ensures that the timing will remain accurate for a longer period. A worn heel will retard the timing.
2. A small dab of grease (high melting point, if possible) should be applied to the lubricator wick so that the lubricator can distribute it onto the breaker cam. A drop of engine oil should be applied to the pivot point.
3. In both cases it is imperative that care be taken to keep the lubricant away from the points contact surface.
4. The lubricating wick should be adjusted so that it just contacts the breaker cam.

IGNITION TIMING (BREAKER POINT IGNITION)

The timing advance mechanism behind the breaker plate is fitted with marks which indicate piston position when they are aligned with the stationary timing mark (visible through the inspection hole in the breaker plate). There are two sets of marks, identified 1.4 and 2.3 to indicate which cylinders they represent.

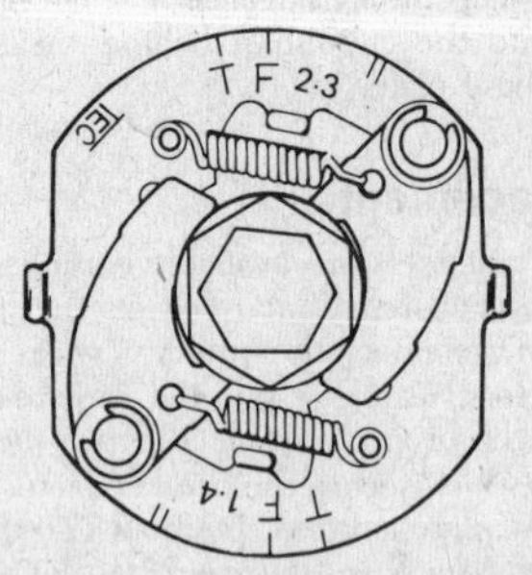

Timing advance mechanism ignition timing marks

The timing marks on the advance mechanism are interpreted as follows: "T" indicates top dead center, "F" is the fixed advanced firing point, which is when the plug fires before the automatic timing advancer comes into play and is about 10° BTDC. An additional pair of

Observing the breaker plate, note that the points set on the left are marked "1.4." They control the timing for those two cylinders. The righthand points, marked "2.3," control the timing for the remaining cylinders.

Dynamic Timing

1. Clean and gap both sets of points as described previously.
2. Hook up the strobe light according to the directions of the light's manufacturer to pick up the impulses from the No. 1 (left outside) cylinder.
3. Start the engine and adjust the idle, if necessary, to the recommended idle speed.

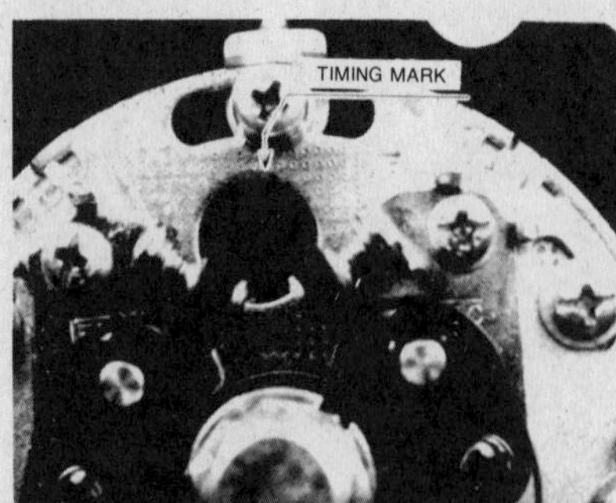

Stationary timing mark

4. Aim the light at the timing marks visible through the inspection hole in the points base plate. At idle, the "F" mark should align with the timing index mark.
5. To check ignition timing at full advance, increase the engine speed until the motor is turning 3,000–3,400 rpm. At this point, the timing index mark should be between the two full advance marks scribed into the timing advance mechanism.
6. If adjustment is necessary, loosen the two screws which secure the 1.4 points to the breaker plate and rotate the points using a screwdriver at the pry point provided until timing is correct. Loosen the two screws just enough to allow the points to be moved.

   If it is not possible to achieve correct timing by moving the points alone, center the securing screws at the median adjustment position. Then loosen the three screws which secure the breaker plate itself. Rotate the plate until the timing is corrected.

7. Repeat the procedure, this time having the strobe light pick up cylinder No. 2. If adjustment is necessary, loosen the two screws which secure points set 2.3 to its plate, and use a small screwdriver at the pry point provided to move the set so that proper mark alignment is achieved. Tighten the screws.
8. If it is not possible to achieve full advance alignment without moving the breaker base plate or points set 2.3 all the way to the end of their range of allowable travel, it is possible that the points are either incorrectly gapped, or that they are worn to the point where they must be replaced.
9. If other troubles are encountered, see "Troubleshooting" below.

Static Timing

1. Connect one of the test light or tester leads to the primary wire terminal for the points set "1.4." Ground the other lead to the engine.
2. If the test device is not self-powered, turn the ignition switch *on* and be sure the kill switch is in the "on" position as well.
3. Turn the engine over in the normal direction of rotation until the "F" mark for cylinders 1 and 4 align with the timing index mark. The test instrument should react at the instant these marks align, indicating that the points have opened. If they do not, loosen the two screws and rotate the points so that the points are just opening when the marks align. If it is not possible to do so and the points have been moved to the end of their possible adjustment range, set them at the median position and tighten the screws. Loosen the three breaker base plate screws and rotate the plate so that correct timing is achieved.
4. Repeat the procedure with points set

Adjusting the timing

2.3, first rotating the engine so that the timing marks for those cylinders are brought into alignment with the stationary timing mark. If adjustment is necessary, loosen the two screws which secure these points and rotate them so that correct timing is achieved. Tighten the screws and recheck the timing.

Troubleshooting

1. If the static method is used, the reaction of the test light or meter should be positive when the points open. If the instrument seems to hesitate before indicating that the points are open, it may be because of defective condensers or dirty or pitted points surfaces.

2. If it is necessary to move the base plate or the points plate to the extreme end of the adjustment range to effect proper timing, the points or points heel is probably worn to the limit, and the set should be replaced.

3. If the dynamic method is used, the various timing marks should hold their positions steadily at given rpms. If they seem to move erratically, check the condition of the timing advance mechanism behind the base plate. Check for weak or broken springs or stiff movement of the advancer weights. When the breaker cam is turned so that the weights move outwards, and then is released, it should return to the original position. If it does not, the springs are too weak and must be replaced. Try penetrating oil to ease movement of the mechanism if it is stiff. If this fails, replace the mechanism.

IGNITION TIMING (ELECTRONIC IGNITION)

The ignition timing is preset. No routine adjustment is required.

CARBURETORS (650)

Carburetor adjustments to be made during a tune-up include checking the float level, idle speed and mixture, and carburetor synchronization.

Adjusting Float Level

1. Float level is a measure of the amount of gasoline which will be in float bowls during operation. While it is a critical specification, it will not normally need readjustment once properly set. Float level, therefore, need not be checked at every tune-up, but should be attended to from time to time.

2. Float level is checked with the carburetors in place on the motorcycle. To do this, a special gauge (Part no. 57001-208) is needed.

3. Shut off the fuel petcock. Remove the drain plug of one of the carburetors and fit the fuel level gauge. Turn the petcock on. Fuel should flow into the float bowl until it is 2.5–4.5 mm (0.098–0.177 in.) below the edge of the carburetor body as shown in the illustration.

4. If the fuel level is not correct, remove the carburetors and take off the float bowl(s). Bend the float tang a small amount. Bending the tang up lowers the fuel level, while bending it down raises the fuel level.

5. All carburetors must have the same fuel level. Measure all before changing any. Note that the measured float level will be inaccurate if the float needle tip is worn, or if there is foreign matter on the needle seat.

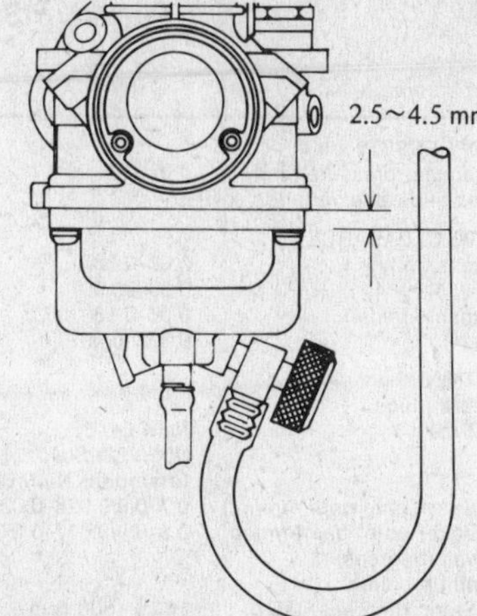

Fuel level measurement

Idle Speed, Mixture, Synchronization

NOTE: *The following adjustments must be made when the engine is at operating temperature. Other tune-up operations (valve adjustment, ignition timing, etc.) should be performed first.*

1. Later models have pilot *air* screws on the sides of the carburetor bodies. To adjust the pilot air screws, screw each one in until it is lightly seated, then back it out two turns.

2. Early models have pilot *fuel* screws fitted under the float bowls. They are covered with plastic extenders and need not be adjusted unless they have been disturbed. In this case, remove the extenders, and turn each pilot fuel screw in until it is lightly seated, then back it out 1⅛ turn. Fit the extenders so that the small ridge points towards the front.

3. After the engine has run for about five minutes to attain operating temperature, adjust the idle speed to 950–1,050 rpm by means of the idle adjusting screw.

4. Remove the gas tank and supply gas to the carburetors by means of longer fuel lines. Removal of the tank is necessary to gain access to the carburetor throttle slide adjusting screws.

5. Remove the carburetor caps.

6. Fit the vacuum gauges to the fittings provided on the manifolds.

Adjusting the air screw

7. Start the engine and allow it to reach operating temperature.

8. With the engine running at idle, close the vacuum gauge dampers (if fitted) until needle fluctuation is less than 3 cm Hg.

9. Normal vacuum at idle should be 19–24 cm Hg. The maximum allowable difference between any two cylinders is 2 cm Hg. If adjustment is necessary, loosen the throttle slide adjusting screw locknut(s) and turn the adjusting screw(s) so that all four carburetors show the same vacuum reading. Backing the screws out decreases vacuum, while screwing them in increases it.

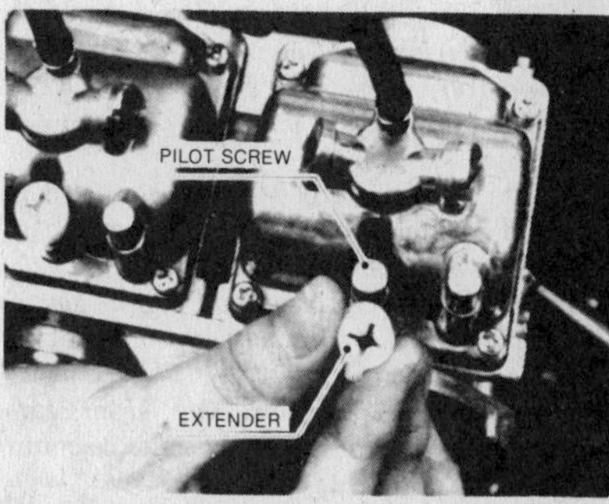

Pilot screw and extender

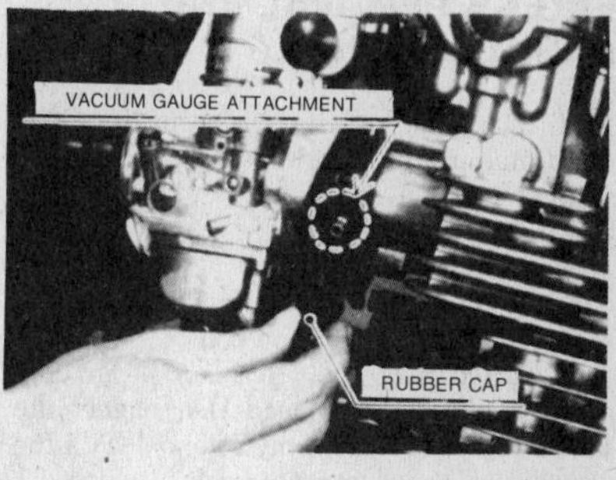

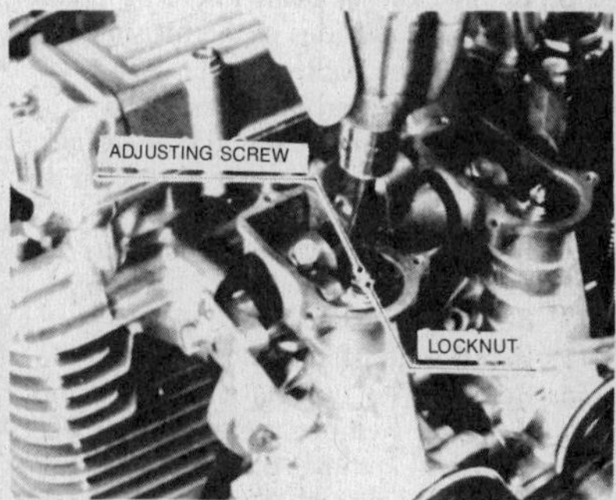

Adjusting the throttle slides

CARBURETORS (750)

The 750 models are equipped with four CV-type carburetors.

Adjusting Float Level

Float level is checked with special gauge Part No. 57001-1017. Correct float level is 3.0–5.0 mm (0.12–0.20 in.) below the bottom edge of the carburetor body.

Refer to the "650" section for details, if necessary. The procedure is the same, only the specification differs.

Idle Speed, Mixture, Synchronization

NOTE: *The following adjustments must be made when the engine is at operating temperature.*

1. The idle mixture is preset. Adjustment is not necessary.
2. Idle speed is 1,000–1,100 rpm and is adjusted by means of the knob between carburetors #2 and #3.
3. Remove the gas tank and supply gas to the carburetors by means of longer fuel lines.
4. Remove the rubber cap from carburetor No. 3 and disconnect the vacuum hoses from Nos. 1, 2, and 4.
5. Attach the vacuum gauges.
6. Turn the fuel petcock lever to the "PRI" position.
7. With the engine idling, close the vacuum damper valves until flutter is less than 3 cm Hg.
8. Engine vacuum at idle should be about 22 cm Hg. The difference between cylinders should be less than 2 cm Hg.
9. If the difference between any two cylinders is greater than this, use the synchronization screw between the carburetors to effect adjustment.

Tune-Up Specifications

	650 (1976–79)	650 (1981)	750
COMPRESSION			
Cranking pressure (psi)	156–185	156–185	156–185
Max allowable variation (psi)	15	15	15
VALVE CLEARANCE			
Intake (mm/in.)	0.08–0.18/ 0.003–0.007	0.08–0.18/0.003–0.007	0.08–0.18/0.003–0.007
Exhaust (mm/in.)	0.08–0.18/ 0.003–0.007	0.08–0.18/0.003–0.007	0.08–0.18/0.003–0.007
IGNITION			
Spark plugs			
Type	NGK B-7ES ND W22ES-U Champion N-4MC	NGK B-7ES ND W22ES-U	NGK B-8ES ND W24ES-U
Spark plug gap (mm/in.)	0.7–0.8/0.028–0.032	0.7–0.810.028–0.032	0.7–0.8/0.028–0.032
Breaker point gap (mm/in.)	0.3–0.4/0.012–0.016	na	na
Dwell (degrees)	①	na	na
Ignition timing			
Static (degrees BTDC)	10 @ 1500 rpm	10 @ 1500 rpm	10 @ 1500 rpm
Fully advanced (degrees BTDC)	35 @ 3200 rpm	35 @ 3200 rpm	35 @ 3200 rpm
CARBURETION			
Idle speed (rpm)	950–1050	950–1050	1000–1100
Pilot screw setting (turns out)			
Pilot air screw	2	—	—
Pilot fuel screw	1 1/8	preset	preset
Vacuum range (cm Hg.)	19–24	19–24	22
Uniformity (cm Hg.)	2	2	2

① If read on a dwell meter "4 cyl" scale: 47.5°. On an "8 cyl" scale: 23.75°.

ENGINE AND TRANSMISSION

NOTE: *Engine rebuilding techniques and procedures are explained in detail in the "General Information" section.*

ENGINE REMOVAL AND INSTALLATION

1. Drain the oil and the oil in the filter. After draining is completed, tighten the oil drain plug to 9.5–12.0 ft lbs., and the oil filter bolt to 13–16 ft lbs.
2. Remove the gas tank.
3. Remove the side covers.
4. Remove the ignition coils.
5. Disconnect the alternator 4-pin connector and the green lead. Disconnect the starter motor lead from the solenoid. Pull the solenoid off the electrical panel.
6. Remove the air cleaner housing mounting bolts from both sides of the housing.
7. Remove the baffle plate.
8. Remove the carburetor assembly.
9. Remove the ducts from the air cleaner.
10. Disconnect the breather hose from the breather cover.
11. Remove the air cleaner housing.
12. Remove the left footpeg.
13. Remove the shift lever.
14. Remove the starter motor cover.
15. Remove the two clutch cable clamps from the frame. Remove the engine sprocket cover bolts and remove the cover. Remove the cover knock pins if they remain in the crankcase.

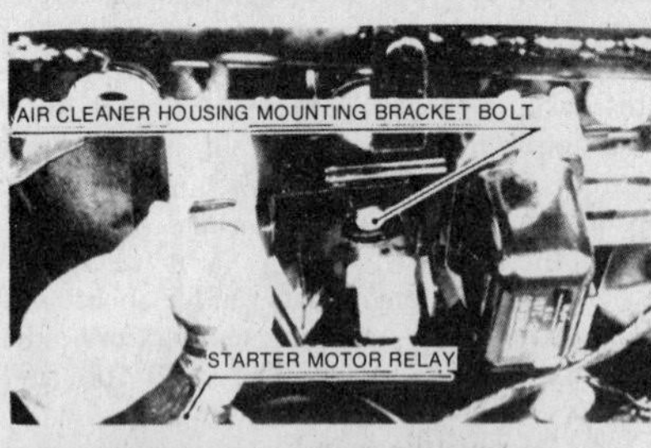

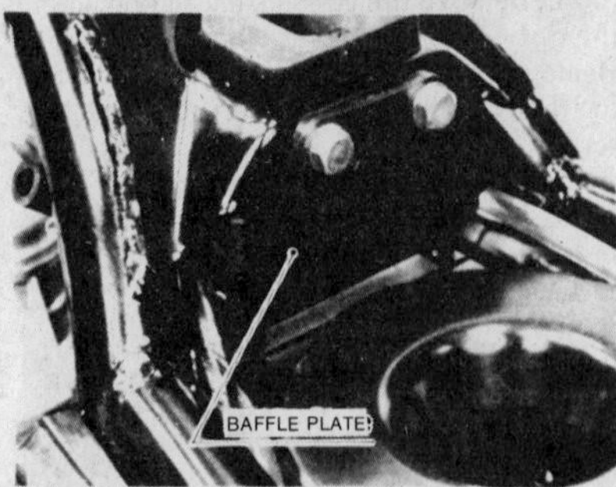

Remove the baffle plate

16. Remove the clutch pushrod. Disconnect the neutral switch lead from the switch.
17. Disconnect the clutch cable from the hand lever. Remove the cable from the motorcycle along with the engine sprocket cover.
18. Remove both mufflers.
19. Disconnect the rear brake light spring.
20. Disconnect the battery negative lead from the engine. Disconnect the blue and brown rear brake light switch leads.
21. Disconnect the black, green, and blue/red contact breaker point leads.
22. On rear drum brake models, back off the brake adjusting nut to give the pedal plenty of play. On rear disc brake models, remove the rear brake master cylinder. Run down the brake pedal adjusting bolt to depress the pedal as much as possible.
23. Remove the right footpeg.
24. Disconnect the tach cable from the cylinder head.
25. Loosen the rear brake torque link nut, the axle nut, and back off the chain adjuster bolts. Move the wheel forward as far as possible.
26. Remove the engine sprocket nut.
27. Jack the engine up slightly to facilitate mounting bolt removal.
28. Remove the engine mounting bolts. The rear upper bolt has a spacer.

Engine mounting bolts (right side)

Engine mounting bolts (left side)

29. Lift the engine straight up and move it slightly to the right so that the rear and front slips over the lower right rear and the lower right front engine mounts.

30. Lift up the right side to clear the oil pan, and remove the engine from the frame.

31. Installation is the reverse of removal. Note the following points:

a. Tighten the bracket bolts to 14.5–20.0 ft lbs. Tighten the four engine mounting bolts to 25–33 ft lbs.

b. Tighten the engine sprocket nut to 54–61 ft lbs. Be sure to bend down the side of the toothed washer over one of the nut flats.

TOP END

Cylinder Head Removal

The cylinder head can be removed with the engine still in the frame.

1. Remove the gask tank. Remove the ignition coils.

2. Remove the contact breaker cover. Turn the engine over using a 17 mm wrench on the special bolt and align the "T" mark for cylinders Nos. 1 and 4 with the stationary timing mark.

3. Remove the screw and remove the tach pinion holder stopper. Pull off the tach pinion holder and pinion along with the cable, freeing it from the cylinder head.

NOTE: *Attempting to install the cams with the tach pinion in the cylinder head may damage the gear.*

4. Remove the cylinder head cover bolts and remover the cover. Remove the cover gasket.

5. Remove the cam chain tensioner from the cylinders.

6. Remove the four allen bolts and take off the upper chain guide sprocket.

7. Remove the 16 camshaft cap bolts and the caps.

8. Remove the camshafts. Wire up the cam chain to prevent its falling into the crankcase.

9. Remove the two cylinder head bolts and the 12 nuts. Remove the cylinder head. Remove the cylinder head gasket and o-rings.

Cylinder and Piston Removal

1. Remove the cylinder head, head gasket, and o-rings.

2. Remove the front chain guide sprocket and tensioner guide sprocket.

3. With a large screwdriver, pry the cylinder loose on each side. Pry slots are provided. Lift off the cylinder block.

4. Wrap a clean cloth around the piston bases to prevent the wrist pin snap-rings or foreign matter from entering the crankcases.

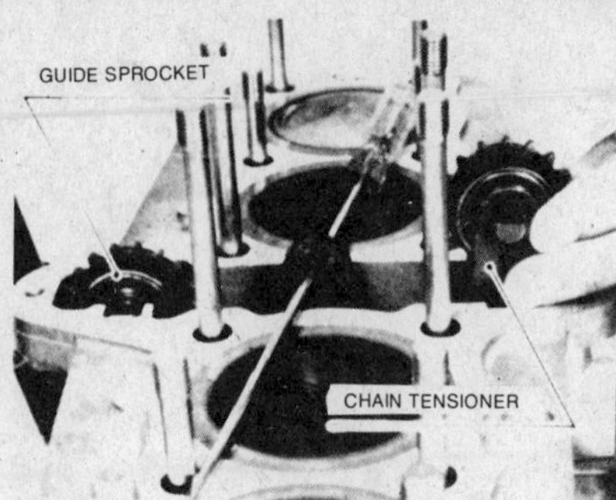

Removing the cam chain tensioner

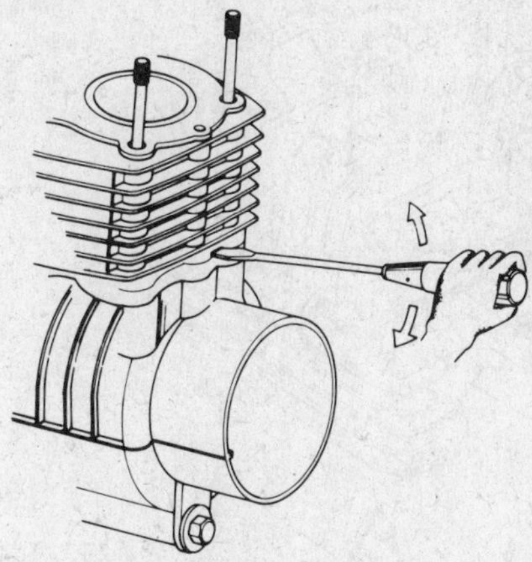
Prying loose the cylinders

5. Remove the snap-rings from each piston.

6. Push out the wrist pin and remove each piston. If the pin resists removal, gently heat the piston crown to facilitate removal.

NOTE: *Mark the location of each piston to ease assembly. Pistons must be reinstalled in their original cylinders.*

Inspection

CAMSHAFTS

1. Examine the camshaft lobes for scoring and wear. If the lobes are visibly imperfect, the camshafts should be replaced.

2. Measure the height of each cam lobe with a micrometer. Standard cam height is 35.73–35.87 mm (1.407–1.412 in.). Replace the cam if the height of any lobe is less than 35.65 mm (1.404 in.).

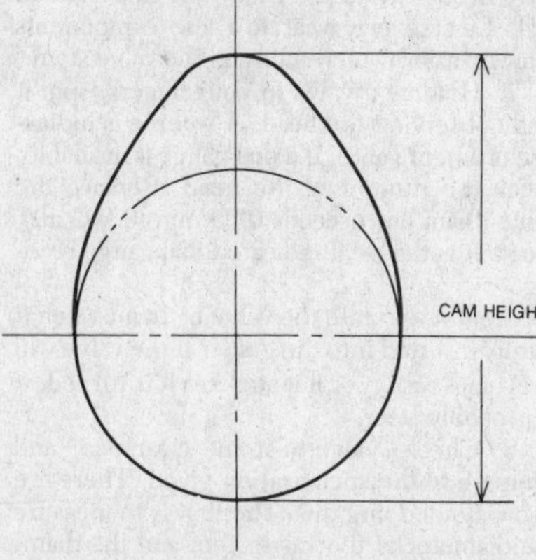

Measure cam height with a micrometer

3. Use Plastigauge® to measure cam bearing journal wear. After applying the Plastigauge®, 7.9–9.4 ft lbs. Be sure to install each cap in its original location and with the arrows on the caps pointing towards the exhaust side of the engine.

Standard clearance is 0.090–0.132 mm (0.0035–0.0052 in.). The serviceable limit is 0.19 mm (0.0075 in.). If the bearing clearance exceeds this limit, measure the cam journals and the camshaft bearing inside diameters to determine which is at fault.

4. Measure the cam journal diameter with a micrometer. Standard diameter is 21.949–21.970 mm (0.8641–0.8650 in.). Replace the cam if the measured diameter is less than 21.936 mm (0.8636 in.).

5. Install the bearing caps onto their correct positions with the arrows pointing towards the exhaust side of the engine. Tighten the cap bolts to 7.9–9.4 ft lbs. Measure the inside diameter of each cam bearing. Standard ID is 22.060–22.081 mm (0.8685–8693 in.). The serviceable limit is 22.12 mm (0.8709 in.). If greater than this limit, the caps must be replaced along with the cylinder head.

6. Check the bearing caps and the corresponding surfaces in the head for scoring or signs of obvious wear. The caps and cylinder head must be replaced if the damage is evident.

7. Check the run-out of each camshaft by mounting the cams in a set of v-blocks and measuring run-out with a dial gauge set at the center of the cam. Standard run-out is less than 0.01 mm (0.0004 in.). The cam must be replaced if run-out exceeds 0.1 mm (0.004 in.).

CHAIN GUIDES

Inspect the chain guides for wear and replace them if they show signs of damage.

CYLINDER HEAD

1. Clean any traces of head gasket material from the cylinder head mating surface. Place a straight edge across the mating surface and check for warpage by attempting to slip feeler gauge blades between the head and straight edge. Maximum allowable head warpage is 0.05 mm (0.002 in.). At this point, the head should be milled to restore a flat mating surface.

2. Use a wire brush fitting on a power drill to decarbonize the combustion chambers. The valves should be left in place as this is done, as it minimizes the chance of causing damage to the valve seats.

VALVE ASSEMBLY

1. To remove the valves, and install them properly, a suitable C-clamp is necessary. Remove the valve lifters and shims. Compress the valve springs and remove the split collars, retainers, springs, oil seal clips, and seals. Remove the spring seats. Inspect the valves, guides, springs, and valve seats in the following manner. Keep each assembly separate so that every piece can be installed in its original location. New valve seals must always be used on assembly.

2. If considerable mileage has been covered, the valve springs should be replaced as a matter of course. Always replace valve springs as a set.

3. Each valve must be free to move up and down in its guide with little resistance.

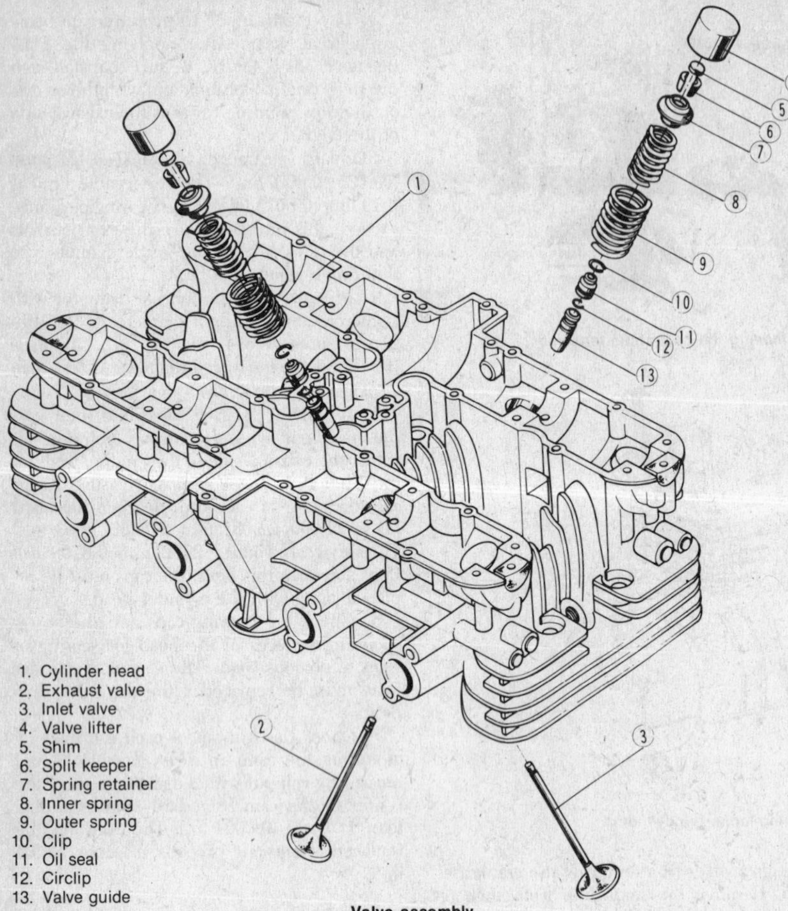

Valve assembly

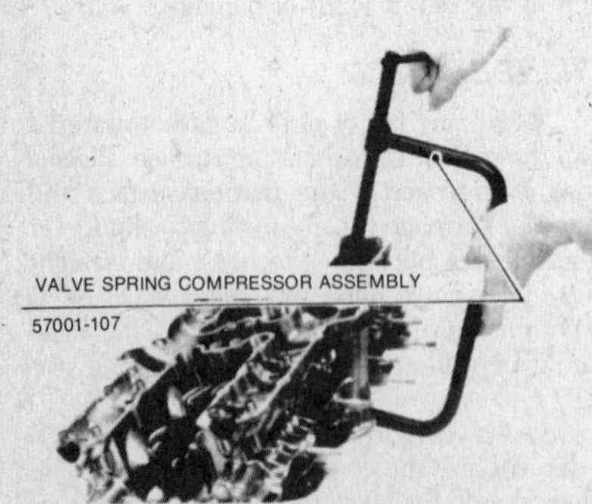

Removing the valves

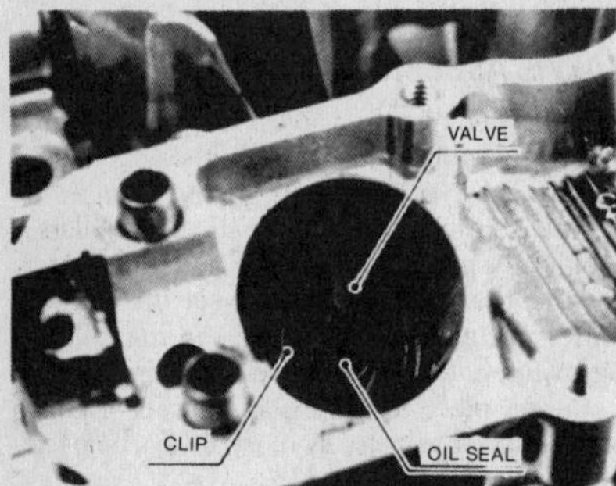

Valve stem, oil seal, and retaining clip

Any sticking or binding as the valve is moved in the guide will indicate that the valve stem or guide is in poor condition.

4. Inspect the valve, paying close attention to the edges of the valve head for pitting, burnt or broken edges, excessive carbon build-up, etc. A certain amount of carbon and lead deposits on the valve face and the top of the exhaust valve are inevitable. Heavy deposits should be carefully scraped off with a dull knife, or a wire wheel, and the valve finished up with very fine emery cloth.

Do not touch the valve seating area during these operations.

If the valve has burnt or broken edges, it must be replaced.

5. Carbon deposits should not extend too far up along the valve stem. This would indicate a worn or cracked valve guide.

6. Wet, oily deposits on the back of the valve head is indicative of a worn guide or bad seal. Less severe wear to these components show up as brown oil stains on the valve stem.

7. Holding a valve in your fingers, spin it while observing the head. A wobble is indicative of a bent valve. If a dial gauge is available, check the run-out of the head. Replace the valve if run-out exceeds 0.05 mm (0.002 in.). Run-out is the total indicated dial gauge reading.

Attempt to rotate the valve by hand when it is fully inserted into the guide. If the valve will not rotate easily, or if it sticks as it is turned, it is probably bent.

8. Check valve-to-stem clearance and compare to the specification given. There are two ways of doing this. The first is to measure the diameter of the valve stem and the diameter of the inside of the guide and subtract

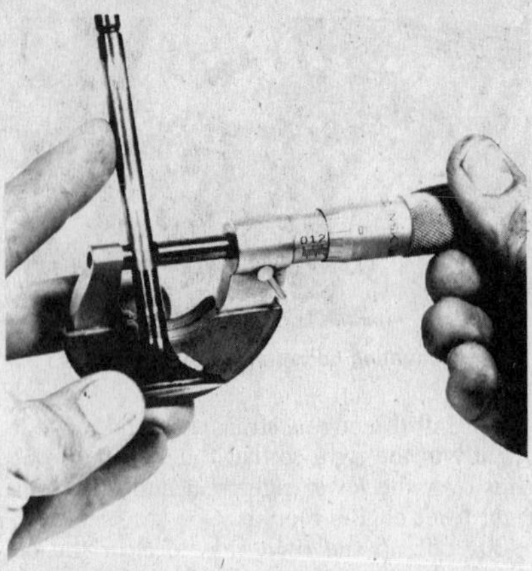

Measuring valve stem diameter

the difference. Another way, somewhat easier, is to insert the valve into the guide, holding it about ½ in. off the seat, and check the total amount of allowable movement in two directions using a dial gauge.

For the direct-measurement method, specifications are as follows:

The standard valve inside guide diameter, for both intake and exhaust valve guides is 7.000–7.015 mm (0.2756–0.2762 in.). Guides should be replaced with new ones if inside diameter exceeds 7.08 mm (0.2787 in.).

Intake valve stem diameter, which should be measured at four places along the valve stem is 6.965–6.980 mm (0.2742–0.2748 in.). The valve should be replaced if any of the measurements is less than 6.90 mm (0.2717 in.).

Exhaust valve stem diameter, which should be measured at four places along the length of the valve stem, is 6.950–6.970 mm (0.2736–0.2744 in.). Replace the valve if any of the measurements is less than 6.89 mm (0.2713 in.)

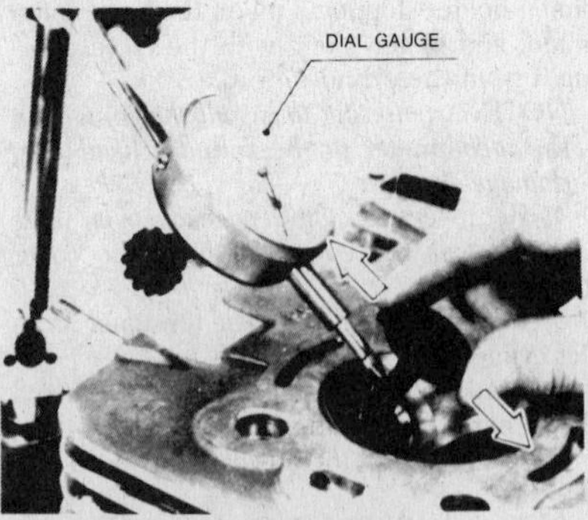

Checking valve-to-stem clearance

If the valve-to-guide clearance is checked by inserting the valve into its guide and checking for movement, the specifications are as follows:

For the intake valves, standard clearance is 0.049–0.085 mm (0.0019–0.0033 in.). Replace the valve or guide (whichever shows signs of wear) if the measurement is more than 0.24 mm (0.0094 in.).

For the exhaust valves, standard clearance is 0.057–0.124 mm (0.0022–0.0049 in.), and the maximum acceptable measurement is 0.19 mm (0.0075 in.).

9. To remove valve guides, use a suitable drift, or tool No. 57001-163. Heating the head in an oven will facilitate removal and installa-

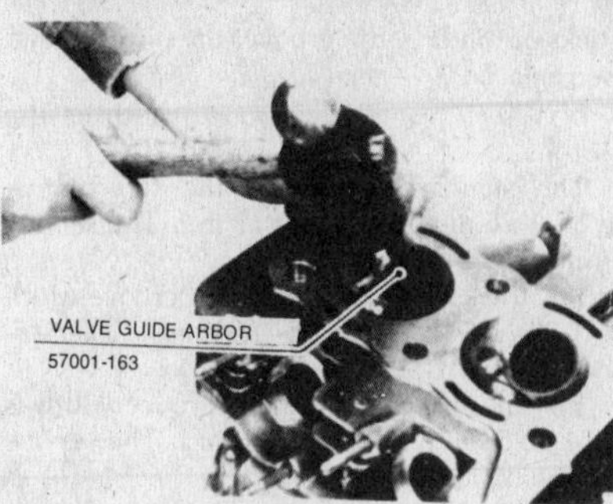

Removing a valve guide

tion. Heat the head to 248–302° F. Be sure the set rings are in place on the guides before installation. Be sure the guides are fully seated.

After installing a guide, it must be reamed to the proper size. Use tool No. 57001-162.

10. After installing new guides, the valve seat should be recut and the valves lapped in.

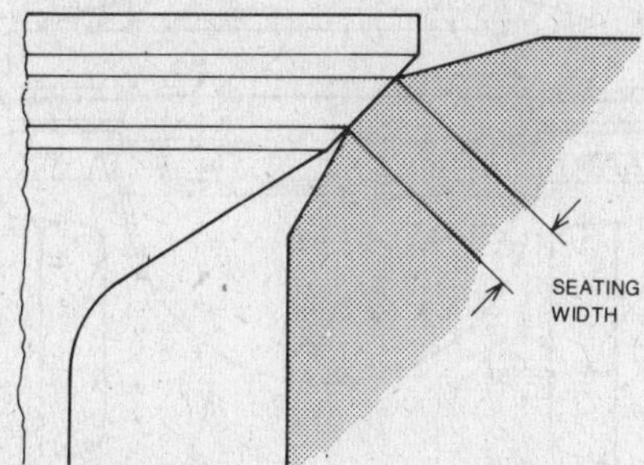

Valve seat width measurement point

Cutting

1. To determine whether the valve seat needs to be cut, carry out the following test using machinist's dye.

NOTE: *The valve and guide must be in serviceable condition for the test to be conclusive.*

2. Apply the dye to the valve seat and lap the valve into place. Note where the dye adheres to the valve seating surface.

3. The valve seating surface must be in the middle of the valve face. Check that the seat in the head is the proper thickness (0.5–1.0 mm/0.02–0.04 in.).

4. If the valve seat requires cutting, use a 45° cutter first. Do not cut any more material than is absolutely necessary, or it may be impossible to adjust the valves after you are done.

5. Use a 30° cutter on the *intake* valve seats to cut the surface inside the seating area. Use a 60° cutter on the surface outside the seating area. On exhaust valve seats, the 60° cutter only is required.

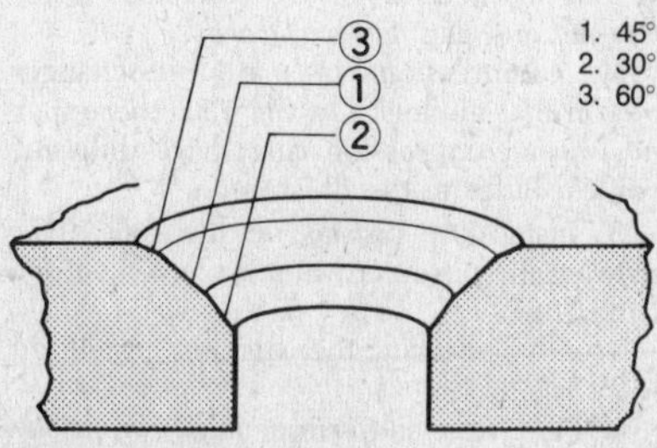

Valve seat profile

6. After the seats have been recut, lap the valves into place.

7. Install the valves and measure the distance from the spring seating area in the head to the end of the valve stem. Since cutting removes material from the valve seat, a thinner valve adjustment shim will probably have to be fitted. Refer to the accompanying chart after measuring the valve height.

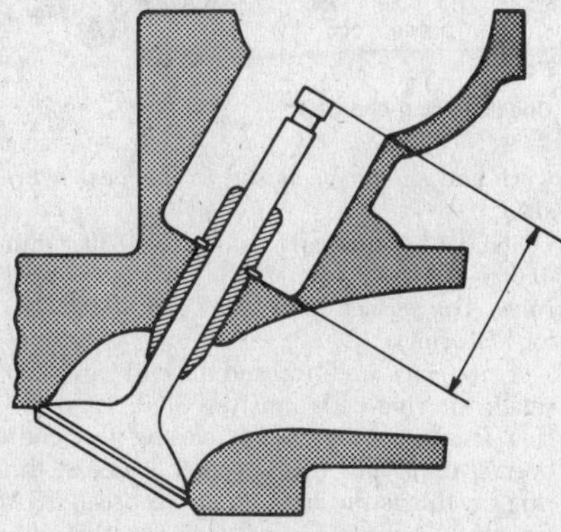

Measure valve height after cutting

NOTE: *If valve height exceeds 37.54 mm no shim is available to give the correct valve clearance. In this case, replace the valve and remeasure. If a new valve does not measure less than this amount, the cylinder head must be replaced.*

Service

Valve Height Measurement (mm)	*Assembly with this shim:*	*After checking valve clearance, final shim may be in this range:*
36.60–36.64	2.85 mm	2.85–3.20 mm
36.65–36.69	2.80	2.80–3.20
36.70–36.74	2.75	2.75–3.15
36.75–36.79	2.70	2.70–3.10
36.80–36.84	2.65	2.65–3.05
36.85–36.89	2.60	2.60–3.00
36.90–36.94	2.55	2.55–2.95
36.95–36.99	2.50	2.50–2.90
37.00–37.04	2.45	2.45–2.85
37.05–37.09	2.40	2.40–2.80
37.10–37.14	2.35	2.35–2.75
37.15–37.19	2.30	2.30–2.70
37.20–37.24	2.25	2.25–2.65
37.25–37.29	2.20	2.20–2.60
37.30–37.34	2.15	2.15–2.55
37.35–37.39	2.10	2.10–2.50
37.40–37.44	2.05	2.05–2.45
37.45–37.49	2.00	2.00–2.40
37.50–37.54	2.00	2.00–2.35

CYLINDERS AND PISTONS

1. Make a visual inspection of the cylinder bore, noting any imperfections. The cylinder walls should be uniformly smooth.

2. With an inside micrometer, measure the diameter of each cylinder bore at three places along its length. The measurement points should be about 10 mm (0.4 in.) below the top of the cylinder, 60 mm (2.4 in.) below the top, and 20 mm (0.8 in.) from the bottom of the cylinder. Make measurements in two directions, 90° apart, both parallel to and perpendicular to the piston wrist pins.

If the largest measurement exceeds 62.10 mm (2.445 in.) for 650cc machines, or 66.10 mm (2.602 in.) for 750s, or if the difference between any two measurements exceeds

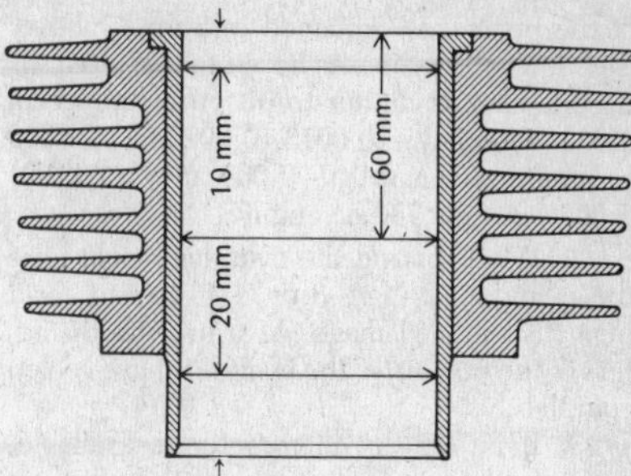

Cylinder bore measurement points

0.05 mm (0.0020 in.), the cylinders must be bored out to the first oversize.

NOTE: *Maximum allowable bore size is 63.0 mm (2.4803 in.) on the 650 and 67.0 mm (2.638 in.) on the 750. If it is necessary to bore the cylinders out in excess of this figure, the cylinder block must be replaced.*

3. Make a visual inspection of the pistons. Scoring, scuffing, or seizure marks on the piston skirts may be removed with a fine grade of emery or crocus cloth if they are not too severe. Sanding should be done in a cross-hatch pattern. If the damage is severe (more than about ½ in. wide), the pistons should be replaced.

4. The rings must be free to move in the piston grooves. If they cannot, either they are carbon clogged (which necessitates replacing the rings and cleaning out the grooves), or metal has been pushed into the grooves by a piston seizure. In this event, pistons and rings must be replaced. Carbon-clogged rings are almost always broken when an attempt is made to remove or free them, so be prepared to buy a new set.

5. Measure the diameter of the pistons at a point about 5 mm (0.2 in.) from the bottom edge of the skirt and perpendicular to the wrist pin. 650 pistons should be replaced if the measured diameter is less than 61.8 mm (2.433 in.). 750 piston replacement limit is 65.8 mm (2.591 in.).

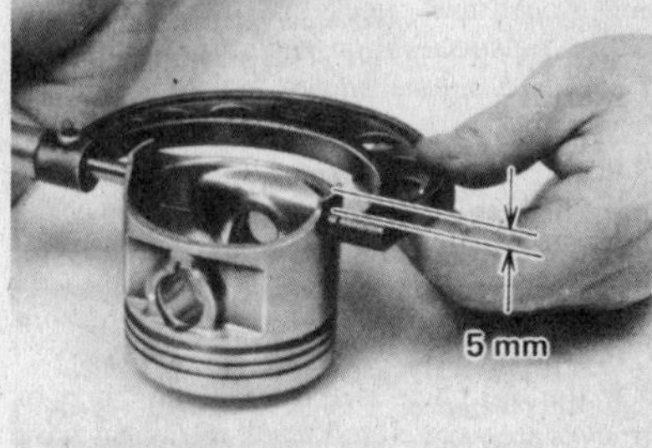

Measure piston diameter 5 mm (0.2 in.) from the bottom edge of the skirt and perpendicular to the wrist pin

6. In the event that the cylinder bore and pistons are already oversize, the serviceable limit for the bores is 0.1 mm (0.004 in.) over the size to which the cylinder was bored. The serviceable limit for oversized pistons is 0.15 mm (0.006 in.) less than the oversize. If the cylinder bore is unknown, a rough approximation can be obtained by measuring the bore diameter at the very bottom of the bore.

7. If the cylinders need boring, obtain the new pistons first. Pistons are available in 0.5 and 1.0 mm oversizes. Measure the diameter

of the pistons as explained in Step 5, above, then have the cylinders bored to that size plus the standard cylinder-to-piston clearance of 0.032–0.055 mm (0.0013–0.0022 in.) for 650 cc engines, or 0.040–0.067 mm (0.0015–0.0026 in.) for 750 cc engines.

8. When boring the cylinder block, bore the cylinders 2-4-1-3 or 3-1-4-2 to avoid heat distortion damage. Measure the diameters of the bore *after* the cylinders have cooled completely.

9. If an inside micrometer is available, measure the inside diameter of the wrist pin holes. The wrist pins should be a light push fit into the holes. If too loose, the pistons should be replaced.

Maximum allowable wrist pin hole diameter is 15.07 mm (0.5933 in.).

10. Check the condition of the wrist pins. Measure the diameter of the pins at three places along their length and compare the diameter to the service specification; the minimum allowable pin diameter is 14.96 mm (0.589 in.). Replace them if under this limit, or if they are discolored from overheating.

11. The wrist pins ride directly on the connecting rod small ends. Measure the inside diameters of the small ends and compare to the serviceable limit of 15.05 mm (0.5925 in.). If worn beyond this point, the rod must be replaced.

12. Be sure that all oil passages in the cylinder are clear.

13. Replace the cylinder base O-rings. Check that any o-rings and the important knock pins fitted to the cylinders are in their proper locations before installation.

PISTON RINGS

Checks to be made on the piston compression rings include side clearance and end-gap. These checks should be made on both new and used rings.

1. Piston ring side clearance for compression rings and one-piece oil rings is checked with the rings installed on the piston. Insert a feeler gauge blade between the ring and the ring groove and check that the clearance is within the specification given:

Standard side-clearance for the top compression ring is 0.04–0.08 mm (0.0016–0.0032 in.).

Standard side clearance for the lower compression ring is 0.03–0.07 mm (0.0012–0.0028 in.).

Serviceable limit for both rings is 0.15 mm (0.0060 in.).

If the clearance is too large, the rings or grooves are worn. If too small, metal may have been pushed into the grooves due to a piston seizure. Check that the grooves are not just carboned up. If new rings do not bring the clearance to the proper value, the pistons must be replaced.

2. To remove the rings from the piston, use a ring spreader. They are available at most auto stores. Decarbonize the ring grooves.

3. To check the ring end-gap, ensure first that the cylinder bore is not excessively worn. Place each ring, in turn, into the bottom of its cylinder and push it in an inch or less using the piston skirt to align the ring in the bore. Measure the end-gap with a feeler gauge. If the end-gap is larger than the service limit, the rings must be replaced. If the measured end-gap of new rings is too large, the cylinder is

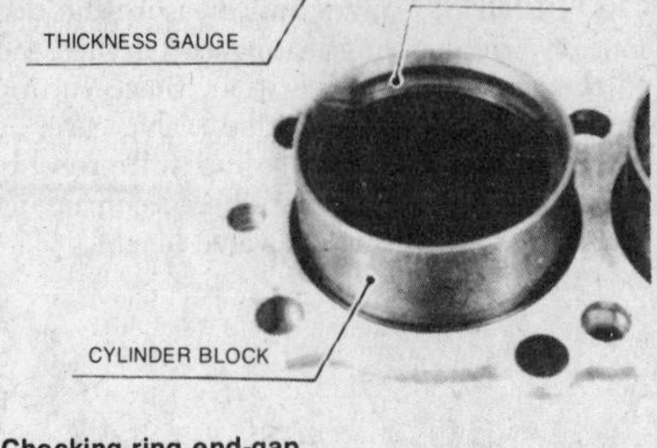

Checking ring end-gap

worn and should be bored to the next oversize.

Standard end-gap is 0.15–0.30 mm (0.006–0.012 in.) for both top and second rings. The service limit is 0.7 mm (0.028 in.) for both rings.

If new rings are fitted and the end-gap is too small, the ring ends must be filed. Hold the ring steady as illustrated, closing the ends over a thin, fine file. Do not squeeze the ring, as this is the easiest way to break it. A few strokes of the file will increase the end-gap.

CAUTION: *Do not make more than a few strokes before checking the end-gap again. It is easy to remove too much metal.*

Do not allow the file to slip out of the ring, as this risks breaking it.

4. Check the free end gap of both compression rings. Standard is 8 mm (0.32 in.). Replace the rings if the measured free end-gap is less than 5 mm (0.20 in.).

Filing ring ends

Measuring ring free end-gap

5. Roll each ring around its own groove and ensure that this can be done easily. If a ring

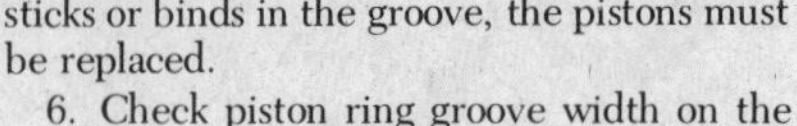

sticks or binds in the groove, the pistons must be replaced.

6. Check piston ring groove width on the pistons.

The standard width for the top ring is 1.23–1.25 mm (0.048–0.049 in.). The service limit is 1.33 mm (0.052 in.).

For the second ring, standard groove width is 1.22–1.24 mm (0.048–0.049 in.). The service limit is 1.32 mm (0.052 in.).

For the oil ring, standard groove width is 2.51–2.53 mm (0.099–0.100 in.). The service limit is 2.60 mm (0.102 in.).

Piston and Cylinder Installation

1. Install the oil ring expander, then the two steel oil rails. The rails are interchangeable. Be sure that the expander ends butt together.

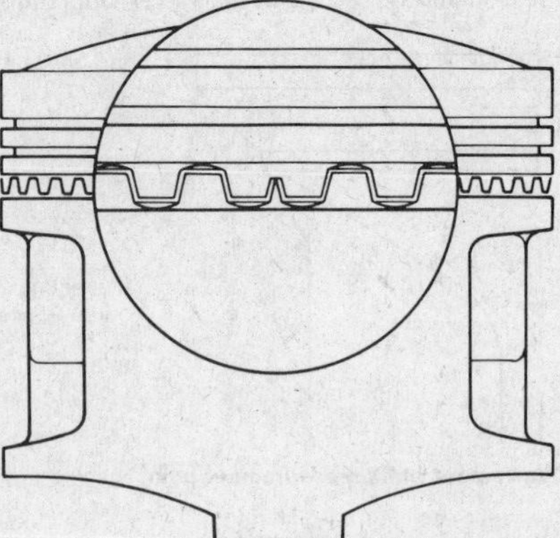

Be sure that the expander ends butt together

Always install rings so that the letter near the end-gap faces up

2. Install the compression rings so that the side marked "R" or "N" (the small letter near the end-gap) faces *upwards*.

The compression rings are interchangeable on 650 models. On the 750, the upper and lower compression rings have different profiles. Refer to the illustration.

3. Install the pistons on the rods. The arrow on the piston crown must face the front of the engine.

4. After installing the wrist pin, install the snap-rings.

NOTE: *New snap-rings must be used. Never reuse old snap-rings.*

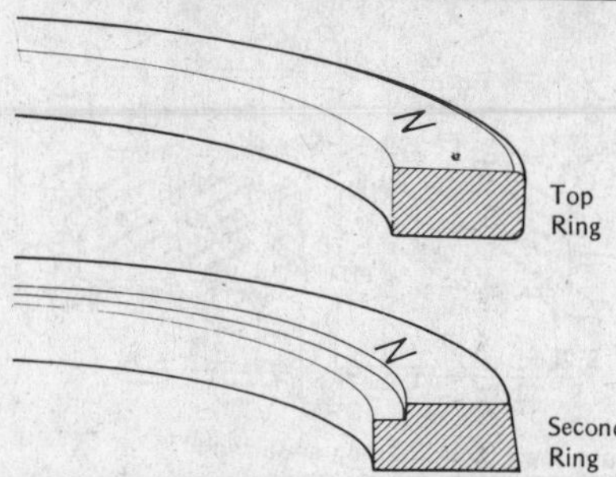

Upper and lower compression rings (750)

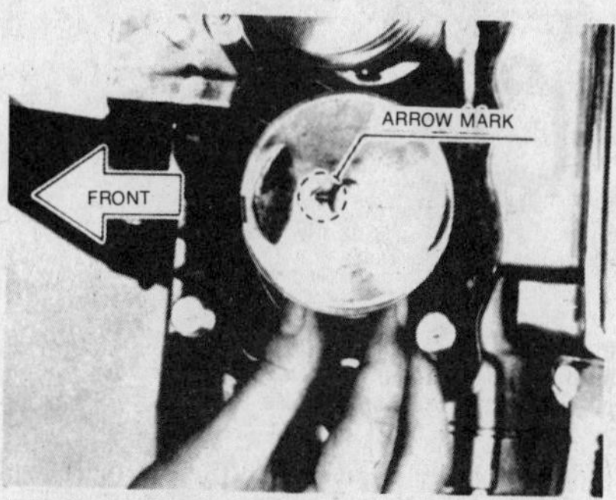

Install the pistons so that the arrows on the crowns point towards the front of the engine

Be sure that the snap-rings are firmly seated. When installing the snap-rings, do not compress them any more than is necessary to effect installation.

5. Arrange the piston ring end-gaps on the pistons so that the end-gap of the top ring and the oil ring expander face the front of the engine and the end-gap of the second compression ring faces the rear of the engine. The end-gaps of the two oil rails should be positioned about 30° on either side of the expander end-gap.

Stagger the ring end-gaps

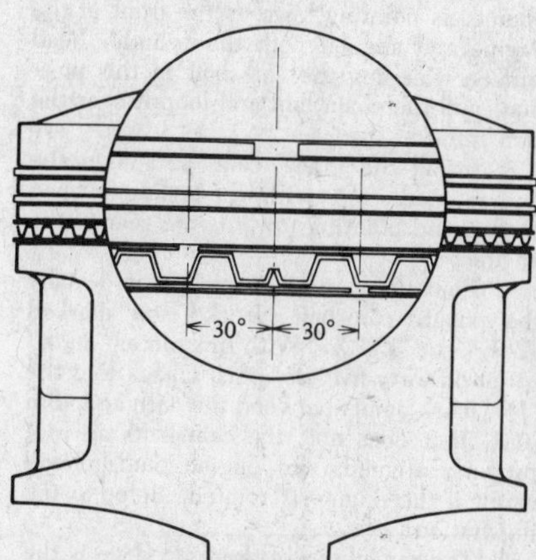

Oil rails should be arranged about 30° on either side of the expander end-gap

6. Lubricate the rings and piston skirts with fresh motor oil.

7. If the cam chain guide roller has been removed, install it. From engine No. KZ650BE019151, install the rubber dampers on the roller shaft ends using an adhesive with the side marked "Up" facing upwards.

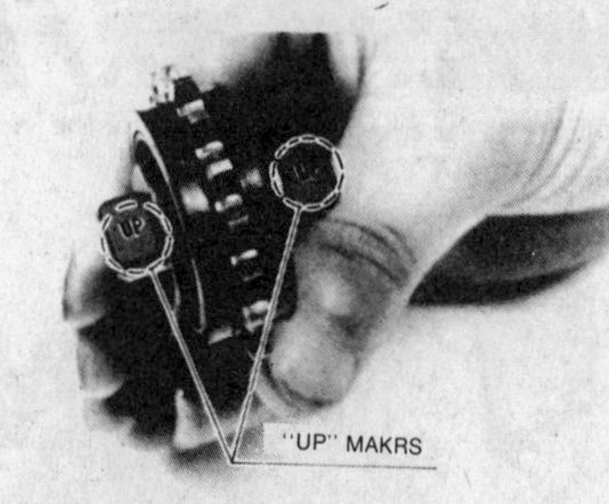

Install the cam chain guide roller so that the marks face "Up"

8. Install the chain guide and tensioner sprockets in the cylinder block. From engine No. KZ650BE019151, fix the rubber dampers onto the sprocket shaft ends with an adhesive, the side marked "UP" facing upwards.

9. Blow out the oil passages and orifices in the cylinder block. Check that the two oil passage orifices are in place and that the small hole in each orifice faces up. Install the orifice o-rings.

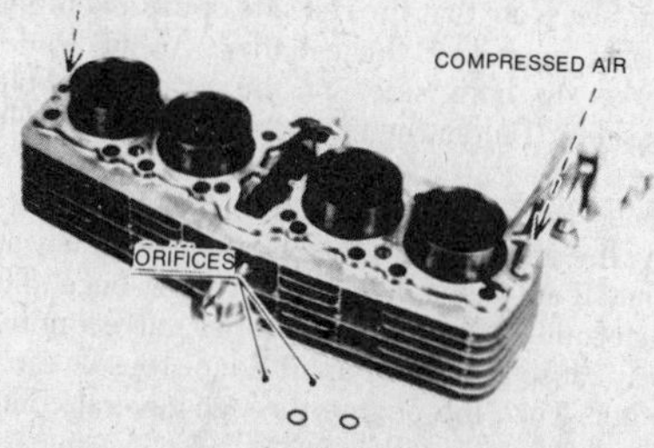

Blow out the cylinder block oil passages with compressed air. Be sure that the orifices and o-rings are fitted before installation

10. Use new cylinder base o-rings.

11. Install a new cylinder base gasket. Fit the gasket so that the "L" mark is on the left side of the cam chain cutout. Apply a liquid gasket compound to both sides of the cylinder base gasket around the rearmost section of the cam chain cutout.

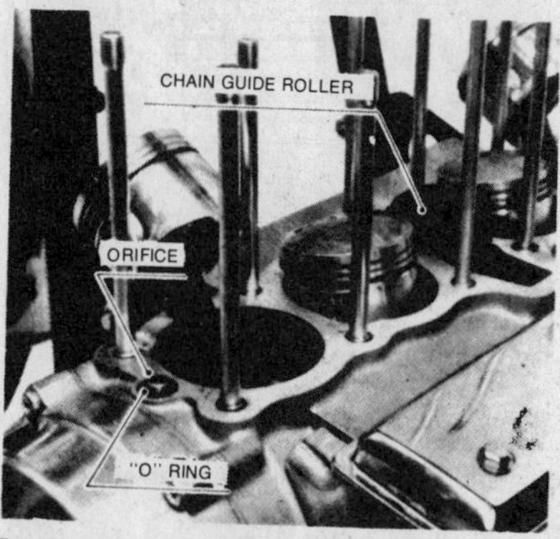

Be sure that the orifices, o-rings, and the chain guide roller are in place

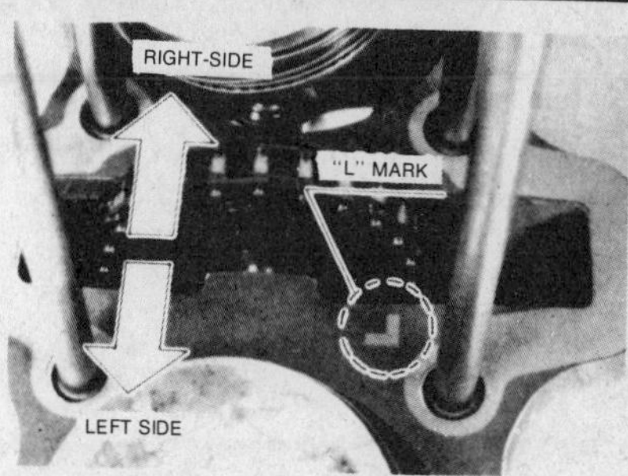

The cylinder base gasket must be installed so that the "L" mark is on the left side of the cam chain cut-out

12. Pull the cam chain taut, making sure that it is properly engaged with the crankshaft sprocket and not kinked or off the sprocket teeth.

13. Turn the crank so that all of the pistons are at about the same height.

14. Install the special piston bases to hold the pistons in position. Be sure that the piston rings are properly positioned. Install the cylinder block. Piston ring compressors will facilitate the job.

Cylinder Head Installation

1. Blow out all of the oil passages in the cylinder head with compressed air.

2. Use a new head gasket and o-rings. "Top" is marked on some head gaskets, and should be correctly positioned.

3. Install the gasket and the two o-rings. Fit the cylinder head, pulling the cam chain up through the cut-out as the head is lowered into position.

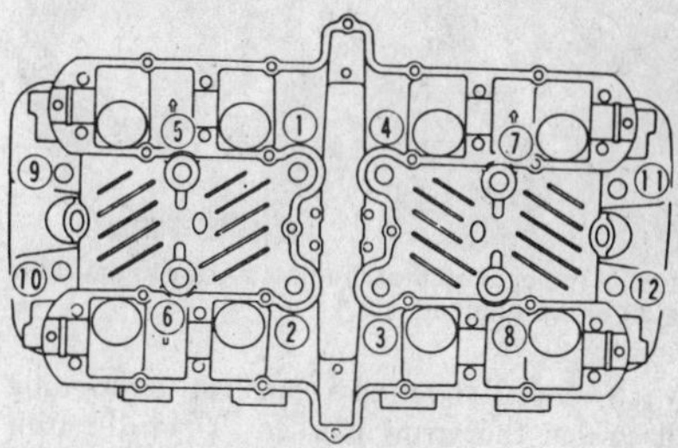

Cylinder nut tightening sequence

4. Tighten the cylinder head nuts gradually and in the order shown in the accompanying illustration. Tighten all of the nuts to about 18 ft lbs. first, then, in the pattern shown, give them a final tightening to 27–31 ft lbs.

5. Tighten the cylinder head bolts to 16–20 ft lbs. Install the valve shims and lifters in their original locations.

6. Install the camshafts as outlined below. NOTE: *If any valve service was performed, it will be necessary to adjust the valve clearance.*

Valve Timing

The cam sprocket timing marks are different depending on whether the engine has the older single-row cam chain, or the later hy-vo chain. The hy-vo chain is used on 750 engines and later 650s.

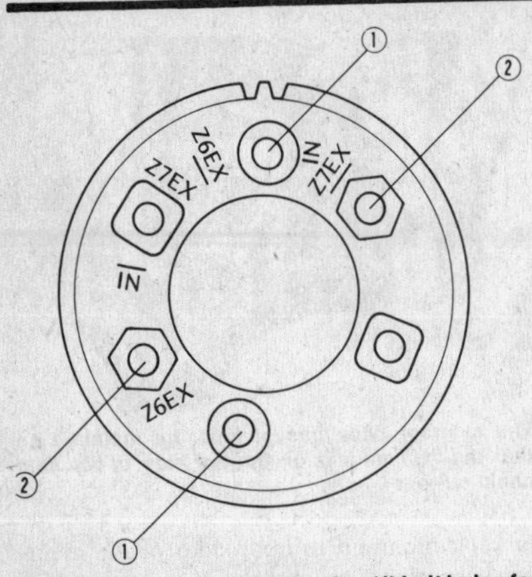

Hy-vo chain cam sprocket marks: (1) bolt holes for intake cam; (2) bolt holes for exhaust cam

Align the arrow marked "T" with the cylinder head surface

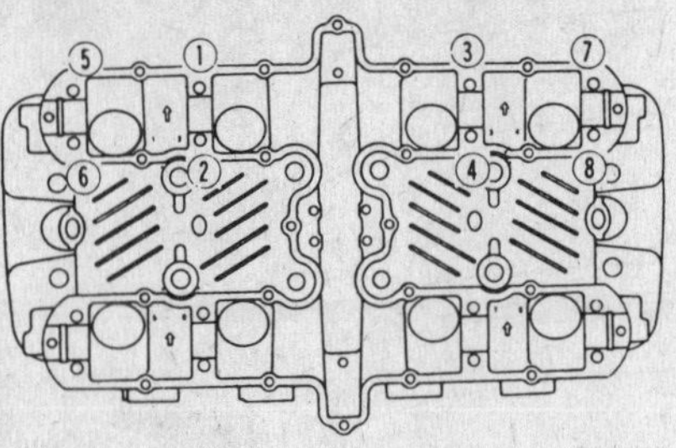

Cam cap bolt tightening sequence

SINGLE-ROW CAM CHAIN

1. To install the camshafts, first make sure that the crankshaft is positioned so that the "T" mark for cylinders Nos. 1 and 4 is aligned with the stationary timing mark.

2. Pull the camshaft chain taut to remove any kinks in it. Install the exhaust camshaft noting that the notched end of the camshaft goes to the right side of the engine. Position the exhaust cam so that the arrow marked "T" on the cam sprocket is pointing towards the front of the engine and is aligned with the cylinder head surface. Keeping the cam in this position, pull the cam chain taut and loop it over the cam sprocket.

Install the cam so that the notch goes to the right side of the engine

3. Install the intake camshaft, positioning it so that the arrow marked "T" on the cam sprocket is pointing towards the rear of the engine and is aligned with the cylinder head surface.

4. Find the cam chain pin pointed at by the exhaust cam "T" arrow. With this pin as "zero" count off thirty-six (36) pins. Check that the "T" arrow of the intake cam sprocket points towards this 36th pin. If it does not, the camshafts are not properly aligned, and engine damage will be the result if the engine is rotated.

5. Before installing the camshaft caps, note that the caps are identified by a number. Match the number on the cap with that on the cylinder head. Install the caps so that the arrows on the caps point towards the exhaust side of the engine.

6. Partially tighten the left-inside cam caps first to seat the camshaft. Then tighten the cap bolts in the order shown in the illustration until the proper torque of 7.9–10.8 ft lbs. is reached.

The arrow marked "T" of the intake cam sprocket must be aligned with the cylinder head surface and indicate the 36th cam chain pin

7. Install the upper chain guide sprocket assembly and tighten the allen bolts to 6.5–7.9 ft lbs. The bolts should be secured with a nonpermanent thread-locking compound.

8. Install the cam chain tensioner assembly. Note that the red side of the assembly gasket must face the cylinder. Apply liquid gasket to both sides of the assembly bolt washers. Tighen the bolts evenly to 5.1–6.5 ft lbs.

9. Recheck the valve timing before rotating the engine. Turn the engine over slowly at first. If any resistance is felt, stop at once and determine the cause. Improper valve timing may cause the valves to hit the pistons or each other. Turn the engine through several complete revolutions and realign the "T" mark for cylinders Nos. 1 and 4. Check that the cam sprocket marked are still aligned as before.

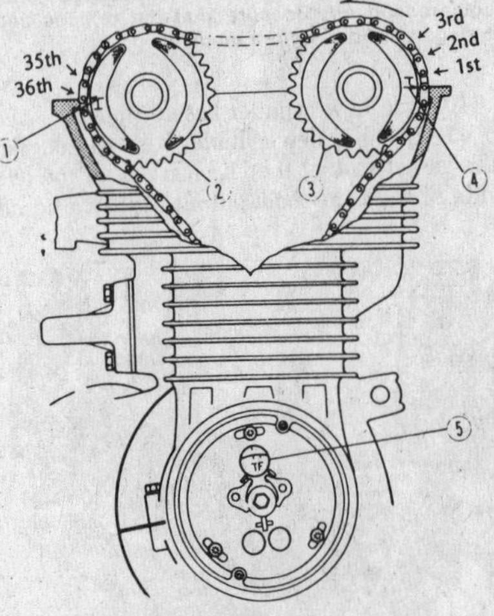

1. T-marked Arrow
2. Inlet Camshaft Sprocket
3. Exhaust Camshaft Sprocket
4. T-marked Arrow
5. #1, 4 TDC Mark

Valve timing alignments

Install the chain tensioner gasket so that the red side faces the cylinder. Use liquid gasket compound on the tensioner bolts

10. Apply a small amount of high temperature grease to the tachometer pinion shaft, and insert the pinion and pinion holder into the cylinder head. Secure the pinion holder with the holder stopper and screw.

11. Lubricate all of the top end components before refitting the cylinder head cover.

12. Recheck the valve clearance.

13. After the engine has been completely reassembled, start it and allow it to reach operating temperature. Then let it cool completely and retorque the head nuts and bolts.

HY-VO CAM CHAIN

This procedure applies to 750 cc engines, and later 650s.

1. First make sure that the crankshaft is positioned so that the "T" mark for cylinders Nos. 1 and 4 is aligned with the stationary timing mark.

2. Pull the cam chain taut to remove any kinks in it. Install the exhaust camshaft noting that the notched end of the camshaft goes on the right side of the engine. Position the exhaust cam so that the line marked "Z6EX" on 650 engines or "Z7EX" on 750 engines is pointing towards the front of the engine and aligned with the cylinder head surface. Keeping the camshaft in this position, pull the chain taut and loop it over the cam sprocket.

3. Install the intake cam, and align the line marked "IN" with the cylinder head surface and pointing towards the rear of the engine.

4. Find the cam chain pin pointed at by the exhaust camshaft sprocket line marked "Z6EX" or "Z7EX." With this pin as "zero," count off forty-five (45) pins. Check that the "IN" mark points between the 45th and 46th pins. If it does not, the camshafts are not properly aligned, and engine damage will result if the engine is rotated. Refer to the illustration.

5. The remainder of the procedure is the same as described for single-row cam chain models, above Steps 5–13.

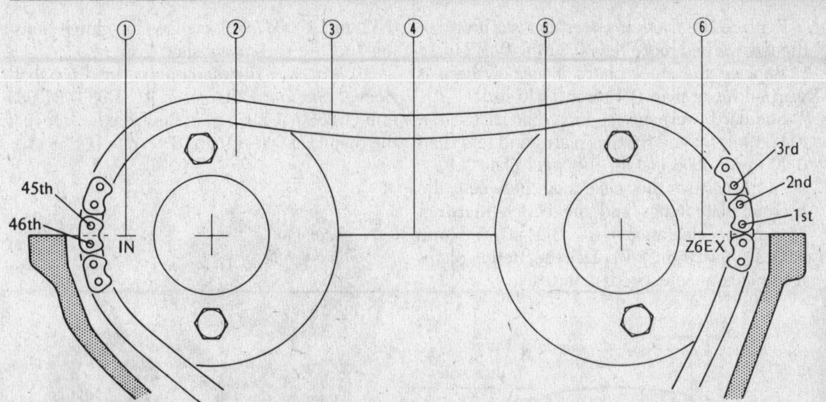

Correct valve timing for hy-vo chain models: (1) IN mark; (2) intake cam sprocket; (3) cam chain; (4) cylinder head surface; (5) exhaust cam sprocket; (6) Z6EX mark for 650s; 750s are marked Z7EX

CRANKCASE COVER COMPONENTS

The following section deals with the removal, inspection, and installation of those components found beneath the left and right crankcase covers. These include the clutch, breaker points, alternator, clutch release mechanism, engine sprocket, external shift assembly, and kickstarter spring. These components can all be serviced with the engine in the frame.

Clutch

REMOVAL

1. Drain the oil. Refit the drain plug and tighten it to 9.5–12.0 ft lbs.
2. Disconnect the rear brake light switch spring.
3. On drum rear brake models, back off the brake adjusting nut to give the pedal plenty of play. On disc rear brake models, remove the master cylinder. Loosen the pedal height adjusting bolt locknut and turn the bolt to hold the pedal down and out of the way.
4. Remove the right side footpeg.
5. Mark the position of the kickstarter relative to its shaft, then remove it. It may be necessary to spread the kickstarter clamp slightly after removing the pinch bolt so that it can easily be removed from the kickstarter shaft splines.
6. Detach the contact breaker leads from the clamps below the clutch cover.
7. Remove the ten clutch cover screws, and take off the clutch cover and its gasket.
8. Remove the clutch spring bolts, washers, and springs.
9. Remove the spring plate, take out the plate pusher, and tilt the motorcycle to the right so that the steel ball will come out.
10. Remove the clutch plates.
11. Stop the clutch hub from turning using the special tool, or a suitable substitute, and remove the clutch hub nut and its lockwasher.
12. Remove the clutch hub, housing, needle bearing, drive shaft sleeve, and spacer.

Removing the spring plate pusher and steel ball

Removing the clutch hub nut

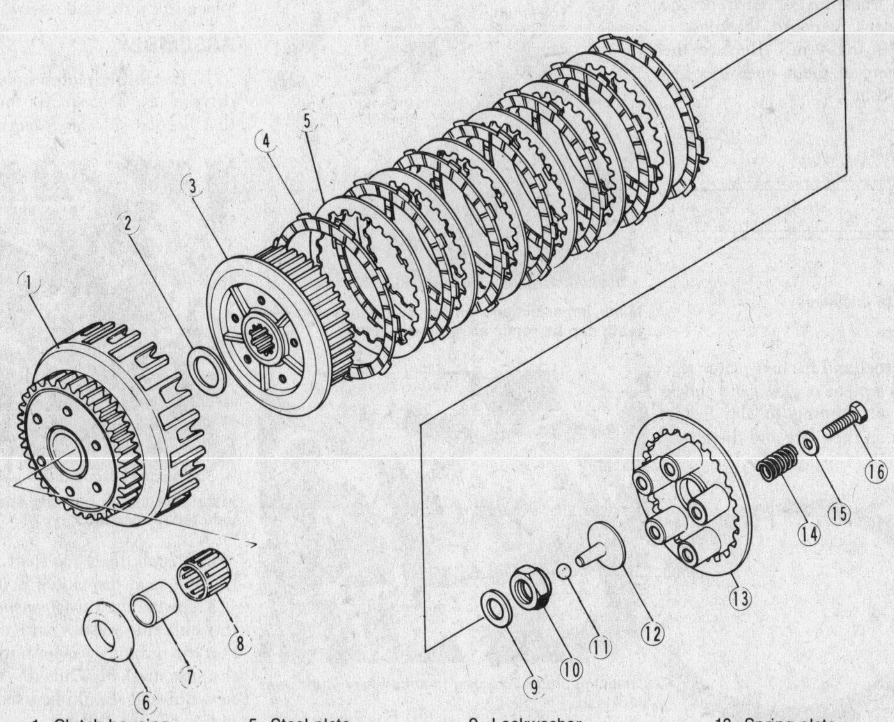

1. Clutch housing
2. Thrust washer
3. Clutch hub
4. Friction plate
5. Steel plate
6. Spacer
7. Sleeve
8. Needle bearing
9. Lockwasher
10. Nut
11. Steel ball
12. Spring plate pusher
13. Spring plate
14. Clutch spring
15. Washer
16. Bolt

Clutch assembly

Note the thrust washer between the hub and housing.

INSPECTION

The following checklist may help to diagnose clutch trouble.

If the clutch does not disengage properly, this may be caused by:

a. Excessive lever play/cable adjustment;
b. Warped or rough clutch plates;
c. Uneven clutch spring tension;
d. Deteriorated engine oil;
e. Too much oil in the engine, or oil of too high a viscosity;
f. Clutch housing frozen on the drive shaft;
g. Defective clutch release mechanism;
h. Unevenly worn clutch hub or clutch housing;

If the clutch slips, some possible causes are:

a. Insufficient cable play;
b. Worn friction plates;
c. Weak clutch springs;
d. Sticking clutch cable;
e. Defective clutch release mechanism;
f. Unevenly worn clutch hub or clutch housing.

Too much noise in the clutch can be caused by:

a. Excessive shaft/clutch gear backlash;
b. Damaged gear teeth;
c. Excessive friction plate/housing clearance;
d. Worn or damaged housing needle bearing;
e. Weak or damaged damper rubbers;
f. Metal particles in the housing gear teeth.

1. Check the lengths of each of the clutch springs. If one or more of the springs is shorter than the others, replace the set.

2. Check the thickness of each of the clutch friction plates. Standard thickness is 3.7–3.9 mm (0.146–0.154 in.). Replace the plates as a set if any of them measures less than 3.5 mm (0.138 in.).

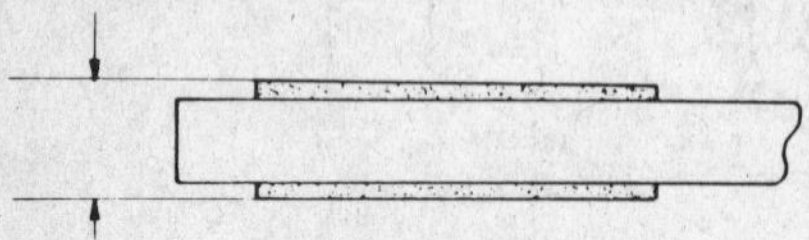

Measure friction plate thickness

3. Place each steel and friction plate on a flat surface, such as a piece of glass, and check plate warpage by attempting to slip feeler gauge blades between the plate and the glass.

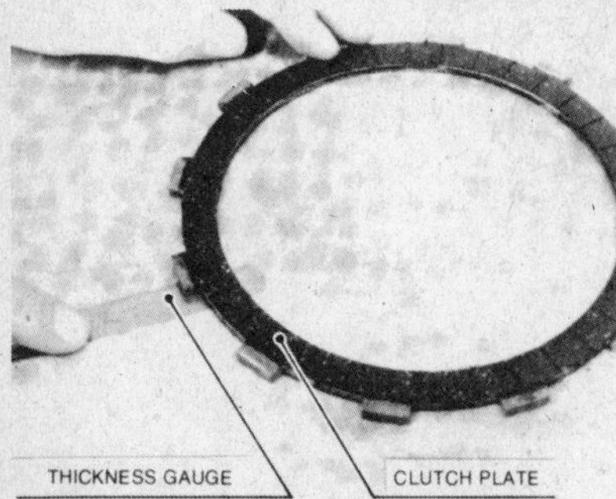

Checking a friction plate for warpage

Replace the friction plates as a set if any of them is warped more than 0.3 mm (0.012 in.).

Replace the steel plates if any of them is warped more than 0.4 mm (0.016 in.).

Standard warpage is less than 0.15 mm (0.006 in.) for the friction plates and less than 0.20 mm (0.008 in.) for the steel plates.

4. Measure the clearance between the friction plate tangs and the clutch housing. Standard clearance is 0.34–0.75 mm (0.0133–0.0295 in.). Replace the friction plates if the clearance exceeds 1.0 (0.4 in.).

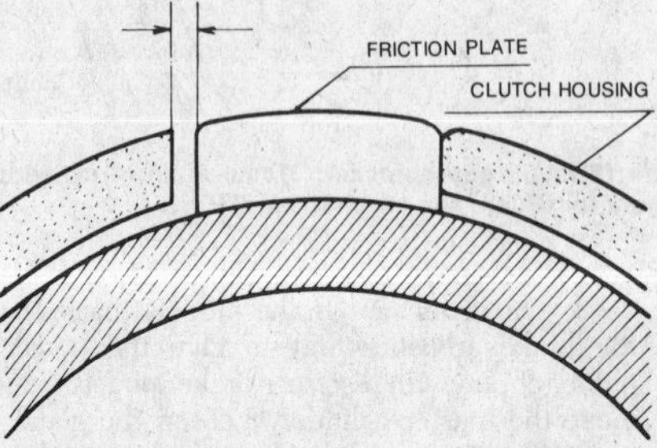

Measure the clearance between the friction plate tabs and the clutch housing

5. Check the clutch housing for wear caused by the tangs of the friction plates. Minor indented wear can be removed with an oilstone. If the indentations are too deep, however, the housing should be replaced.

6. Check the condition of the clutch housing gear teeth. Minor damage to the teeth can be removed with an oilstone. If this is not possible, the housing must be replaced. If the housing gear teeth shows signs of wear, inspect the secondary shaft gear as well. The gears should be replaced as a set.

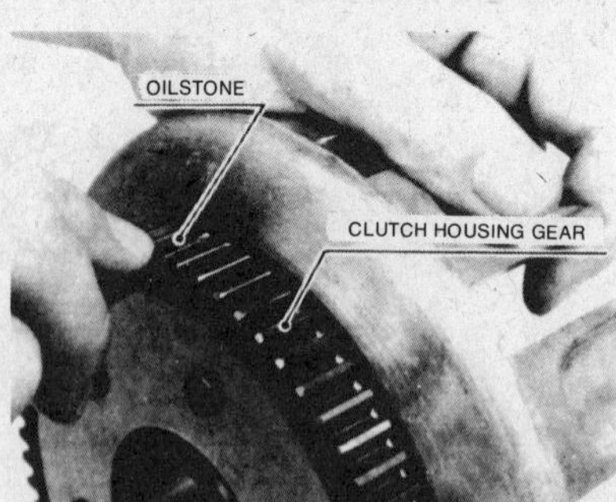

Minor imperfections on the clutch housing gear teeth can be removed with an oilstone

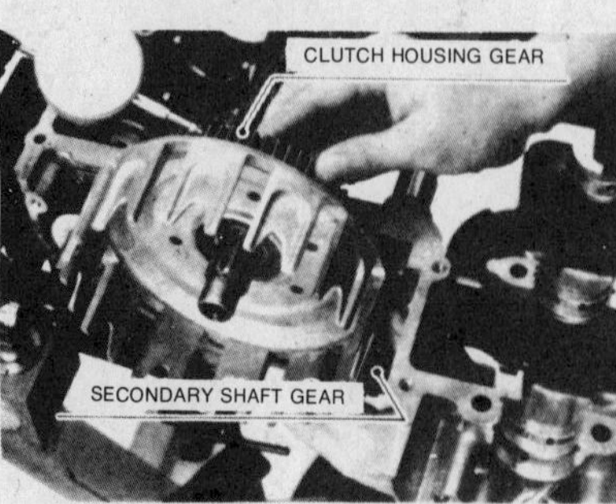

Checking clutch housing-to-secondary shaft gear backlash

7. With a dial gauge, measure clutch housing gear/secondary shaft gear backlash. Standard gear backlash is under 0.08 mm (0.0031 in.). If the measured backlash exceeds 0.12 mm (0.0047 in.), replace the clutch housing and the secondary shaft gear.

8. Measure the diameter of the drive shaft sleeve. Standard diameter is 31.980–31.995 mm (1.2590–1.2956 in.). Replace the sleeve if the diameter is less than 31.96 mm (1.258 in.).

Measuring drive shaft sleeve and clutch housing inside diameter

9. Measure the inside diameter of the clutch housing. Standard diameter is 37.000–37.016 mm (1.4567–1.4573 in.). Replace the housing if the measured diameter is greater than 37.03 mm (1.458 in.).

10. Check the condition of the housing needle bearing and replace it if it is blued or discolored, or if rotation is faulty, or there are flat spots on the needles.

11. If the clutch housing or the drive shaft sleeve are ever replaced, the needle bearing should be replaced as a matter of course.

12. Check the splines of the clutch hub where the steel plates ride. Minor wear can be repaired with an oilstone. If damage is excessive, the hub should be replaced.

13. Check the fit of the hub on its shaft. It should be fairly tight. If the hub is very loose, check the inner splines for damage, and replace the hub if necessary.

ASSEMBLY

1. Install the clutch housing spacer on the drive shaft. The spacer must be installed so that the flat side faces *outwards*.

Install the clutch housing spacer so that the flat side faces outwards

2. Install the drive shaft sleeve, the needle bearing, and the clutch housing.

3. Install the thrust washer, the clutch hub, the hub nut washer and the hub nut. Note that the hub nut washer must be installed with the side marked "Outside" facing outwards. A new hub nut should be used. Tighten the hub nut to 87–118 ft lbs.

4. Install one of the friction plates, then alternate steel and friction plates until all are fitted. New plates should be generously coated with fresh engine oil before installation.

Fit the hub nut washer with the "Outside" mark facing out

5. Fit the steel ball and pusher. They should be lubricated with a high melting-point grease.

6. Install the spring plate, washers, and the bolts. Tighten the bolts in a cross pattern to 6.5–7.9 ft lbs.

7. Make sure that the two thrust washers are in place on the kickstarter shaft. Check that the two clutch cover knock pins are in place. Fit a new cover gasket, and install the cover. Lubricate the lips of the kickstarter shaft oil seal before installation to avoid damaging the seal. An oil seal guide (57001-265) can also be used.

8. The remainder of the procedure is the reverse of removal.

Kickstarter Spring

REMOVAL

1. Remove the clutch cover. Remove the clutch assembly.

2. Pull off the thrust washers and the spring guide.

3. Remove the kickstarter return spring.

Removing the thrust washers and spring guide

INSPECTION

1. Replace the spring if it is broken, or so weakened that it cannot hold the kickstarter lever firmly in place.

Installing the kickstarter return spring

INSTALLATION

1. Turn the kickstarter shaft as far as possible clockwise, insert one end of the return spring into the shaft, insert the spring guide, and install the other end of the spring into the crankcase hole using a pair of needle-nosed pliers.

2. Install the two thrust washers. The thinner washer is installed on the shaft first.

3. The remainder of the procedure is the reverse of removal.

Timing Advance Mechanism

REMOVAL

1. Remove the contact breaker point cover.

2. Remove the three contact breaker mounting plate screws and take off the plate.

3. Disconnect the oil pressure indicator switch lead.

4. Use a 17 mm wrench on the crankshaft rotation to keep the engine from turning over and remove the timing advancer mounting bolt. Take off the rotation nut and the timing advance mechanism.

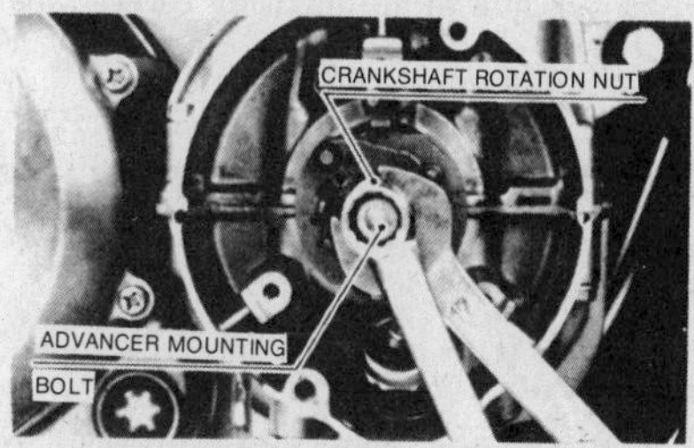

Removing the timing advancer mounting bolt

INSPECTION

1. Refer to "Tune-Up," for breaker point inspection.

2. The timing advance mechanism springs should have enough tension to return the breaker cam to its original position when it is turned as far as possible and then released. If they cannot, replace the springs if lubricating the assembly will not ease the movement.

3. If disassembly of the unit is desired, take off the breaker cam. Remove the two C-rings, washers, and weights. Remove the thrust washers from the shafts.

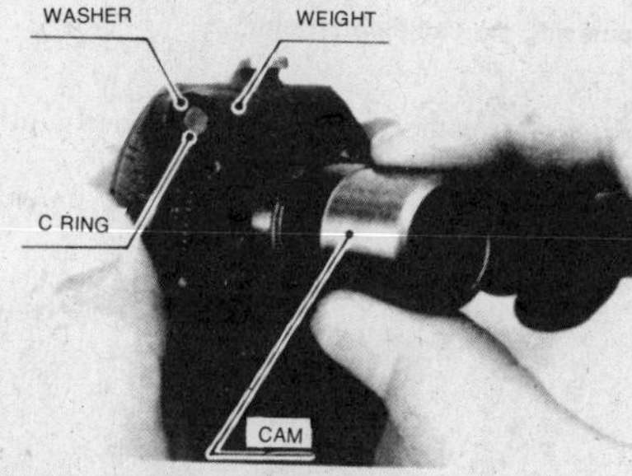

Timing advance unit components

INSTALLATION

1. Clean the advance mechanism thoroughly, and fill the groove in the advancer body with grease.

2. When installing the breaker cam, align the mark on the cam with the small hole in the timing advance mechanism body.

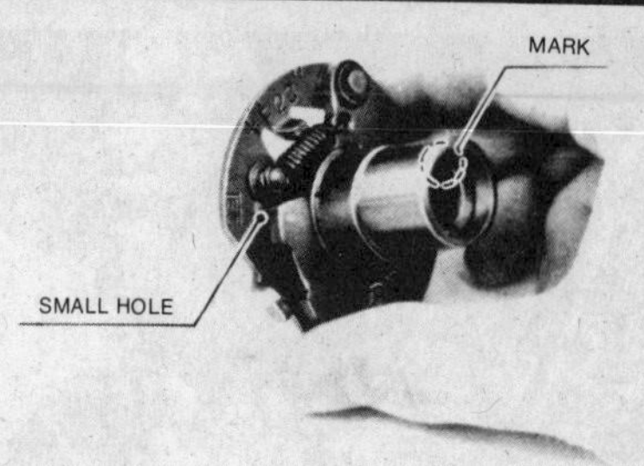

When fitting the breaker cam, align the mark on the cam with the small hole on the body

3. When installing the timing advance mechanism on the crankshaft, match the notch in the mechanism with the pin on the end of the crank.

4. Install the crankshaft rotation nut and the advancer mounting bolt. The notches in the nut fit the projections of the timing advance mechanism.

5. Tighten the bolt to 16.5–19.5 ft lbs.

6. Connect the oil pressure indicator switch lead. The lead must point towards the rear.

7. Install the contact breaker mounting plate. Adjust the ignition timing.

Oil Pressure Indicator Switch

REMOVAL

1. Remove the timing advance mechanism.

2. Remove the bolt and lockwasher and remove the lead from the switch.

3. Unscrew and remove the switch.

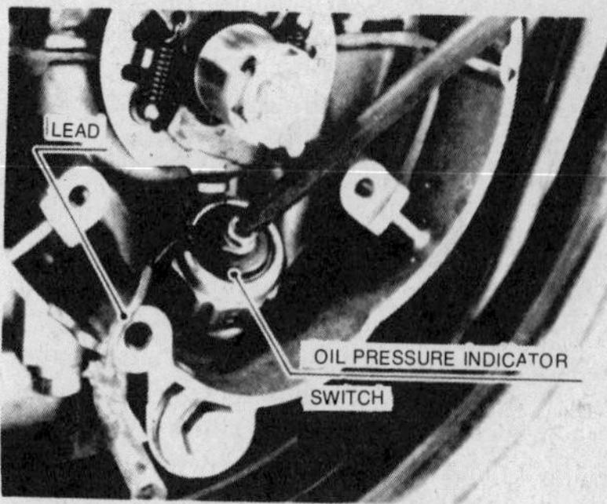

Disconnecting the oil pressure indicator switch lead

INSTALLATION

1. Tighten the switch to 9.5–12.0 ft lbs.

2. The switch lead must point towards the rear.

Alternator

REMOVAL

1. Remove the left side-cover and disconnect the alternator 4-pin connector and the green lead.

2. Remove the engine sprocket cover. Disconnect the neutral indicator switch lead. Pull the alternator wiring harness out to the left.

3. Remove the alternator cover screws and remove the cover and gasket.

4. If desired, remove the three allen bolts which secure the armature windings to the cover and remove the armature. Remove the three field coil allen bolts and take out the field coil.

5. Hold the rotor steady with the special

Disconnecting the green lead

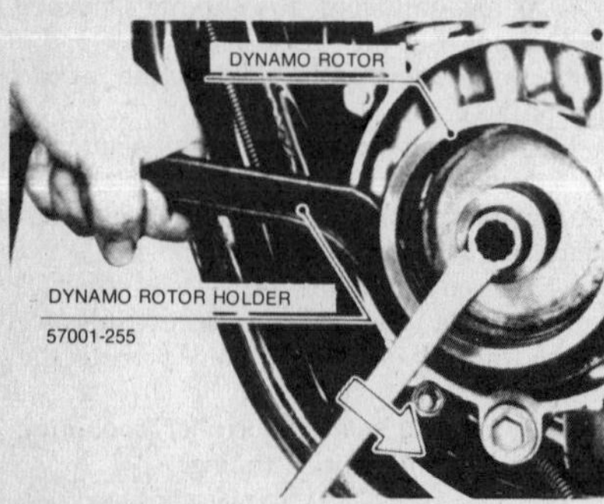

Removing the alternator rotor bolt

tool, or by placing the engine in gear and applying the rear brake, and remove the rotor bolt.

6. Holding the rotor steady as before, remove the rotor with the special tool (No. 57001-254).

INSTALLATION

1. Installation is basically the reverse of removal. Note the following points:

a. Be sure that the crankshaft taper is perfectly clean and free of oil or foreign matter.

b. Tighten the rotor bolt to 42–46 ft lbs.

c. Apply a non-permanent thread-locking compound to the armature and field coil allen bolts if these components were removed. Use a liquid gasket compound around the wiring grommets.

d. Check that the two knock pins are in place before installing the cover.

e. Route the alternator wiring harness between the external shift mechanism cover and the crankcase.

Engine Sprocket

REMOVAL

1. Remove the left footpeg.
2. Remove the shift lever pinch bolt and pull off the shift lever.
3. Remove the starter motor cover.
4. Remove the engine sprocket cover.
5. Remove the axle nut cotter pin and loosen the axle nut.
6. Remove the cotter pin or safety clip and loosen the rear torque link nut.
7. Loosen the chain adjuster bolt locknuts and back off the chain adjuster bolts as far as possible. Push the wheel forward.
8. Bend down the locking tab on the engine sprocket nut. Hold the engine sprocket in place using either the special tool (57001-306) or by putting the machine in gear and applying the rear brake. Remove the sprocket nut. Pull the sprocket off its shaft with the chain attached.

INSTALLATION

1. Install the sprocket onto the shaft with the chain looped around it.
2. Fit the lockwasher, engaging it with the hole in the sprocket. Install the sprocket nut and tighten it to 54–61 ft lbs. Bend down a tab of the washer over one of the flats of the nut.
3. Check that the knock pin is in place and install the sprocket cover. Use the shift shaft oil seal guide (57001-266) if possible.
4. Fit the shift lever, aligning it so that the pedal is even with the alternator cover lower right bolt.
5. Fit the footpeg. Adjust the clutch.

Clutch Release Mechanism

The clutch release mechanism is inside the engine sprocket cover.

REMOVAL

1. Remove the engine sprocket cover.
2. Remove the cotter pin from the release lever and disengage the cable from the fitting.

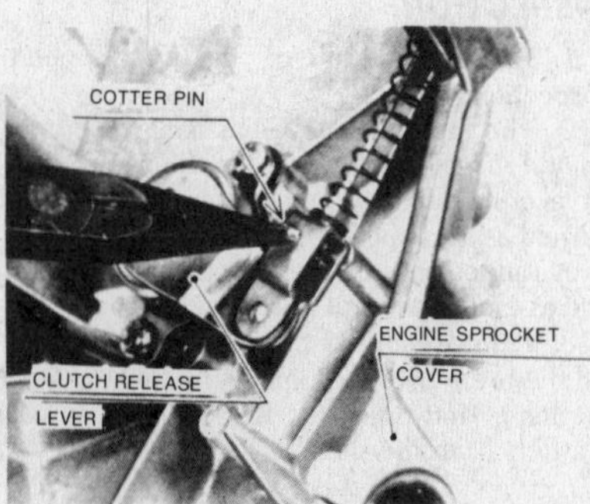

Removing the cable cotter pin

3. Remove the two mounting screws and take out the release mechanism.
4. Remove the circlip. Separate the inner and outer release gears.

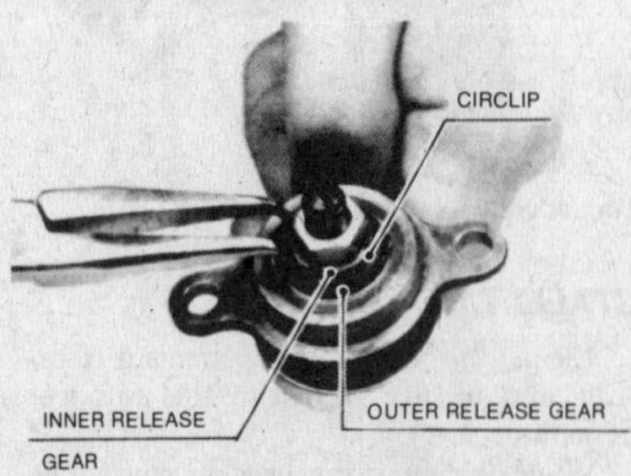

Removing the clutch release mechanism circlip

INSTALLATION

1. Clean the release balls in a solvent and lubricate them with chassis grease. There are eleven balls.
2. Fit the inner gear onto the outer gear. When fully meshed, the release lever and the outer gear must be positioned as shown in the illustration. The machined side of the outer gear must face upwards. Install the circlip.

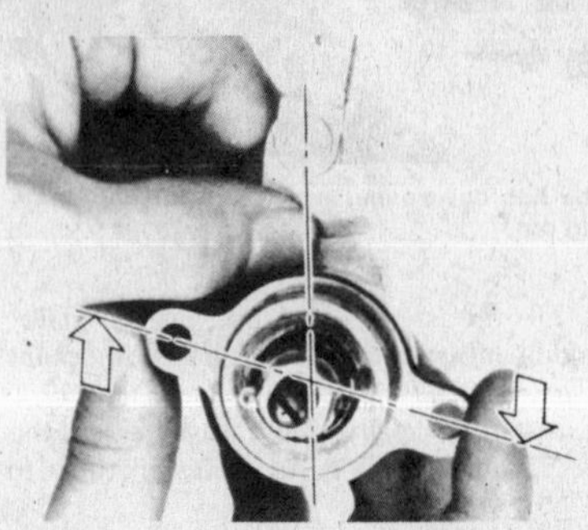
Align the release lever and the outer gear as shown

3. Use a non-permanent thread-locking compound on the release mechanism mounting screws.
4. The remainder of the procedure is the reverse of removal. Adjust the clutch after installation is completed.

External Shift Mechanism

REMOVAL

1. Remove the engine sprocket cover. Remove the engine sprocket cover. Remove the engine sprocket.
2. Disconnect the neutral indicator switch lead. Remove the clutch pushrod.

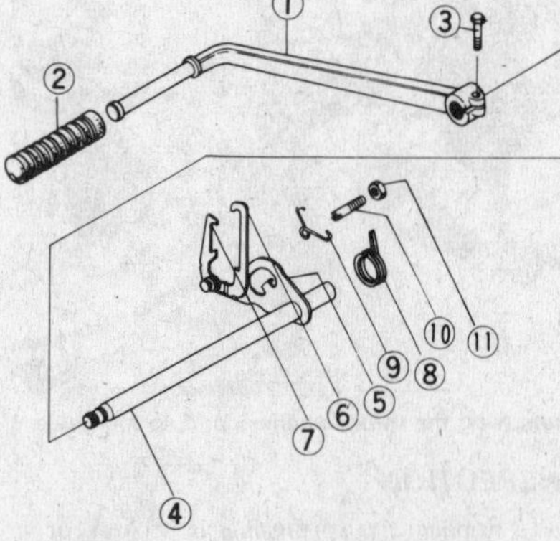

1. Shift pedal
2. Pedal rubber
3. Bolt
4. Shift shaft
5. Shift lever
6. Overshift limiter
7. Shift mechanism arm
8. Return spring
9. Pawl spring
10. Return spring pin
11. Locknut

External shift mechanism assembly

3. Remove the engine sprocket chain guard.
4. Place a suitable container beneath the cover to catch the oil which will drain off. Remove the seven shift mechanism cover screws and pull off the cover. Install one of the screws in its hole to stop the oil flow.
5. Remove the output shaft collar. If the collar is difficult to remove, use a bearing puller. Remove the o-ring.

6. Disengage the shift mechanism arm and the overshift limiter arm from the shift drum and pull out the external shift mechanism.

CAUTION: *Do not pull the shift rod out of the crankcases more than 40 mm (1.6 in.) or the shift forks will fall into the oil pan, requiring splitting the crankcases.*

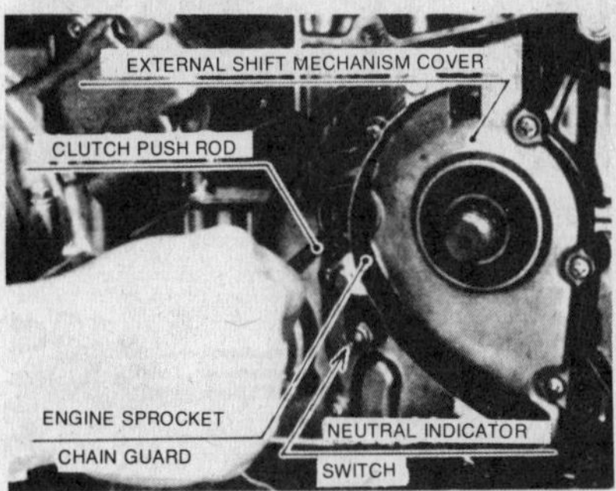

Removing the clutch push rod

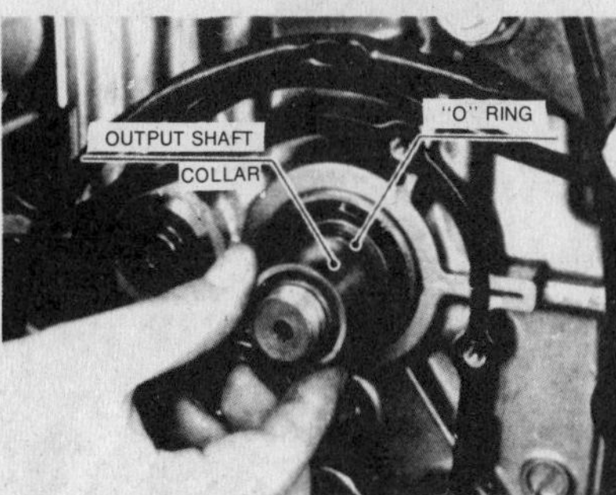

Removing the output shaft collar

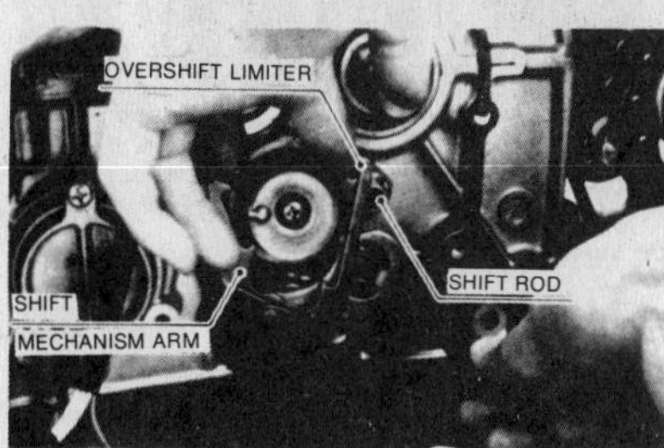

Removing the external shift mechanism

INSPECTION

1. Check the shift mechanism and overshift limiter arms for wear.
2. Check the return spring for damage, and replace it if it is broken.
3. Check that the shift drum pins are not broken or worn.
4. Check that the output shaft o-ring is in good condition.
5. Check that the return spring pin is secure in the cases. If not, remove it and reinstall with a non-permanent thread-locking compound on the threads. The pin should protrude about 20 mm (0.8 in.) from the crankcases.

INSTALLATION

1. Check that the return spring is properly fitted to the shaft.
2. If the shift drum pins have been removed, check that the long pin is installed in the position shown.

The return spring pin should protrude 20 mm (0.8 in.) from the case

Correct position of the long shift drum pin

3. Install the external shift mechanism shaft, engaging the arms with the shift drum pins.

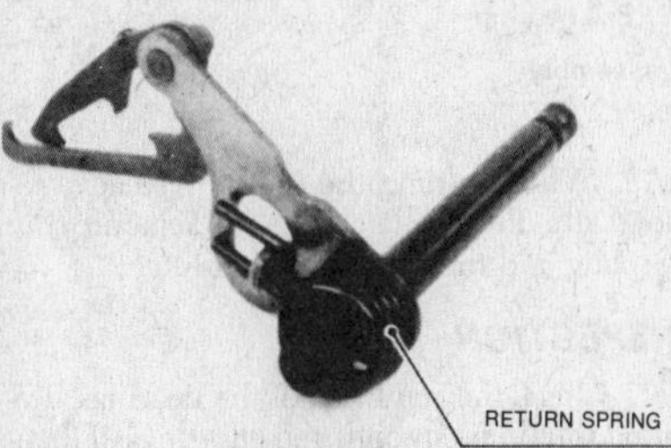

Return spring installation

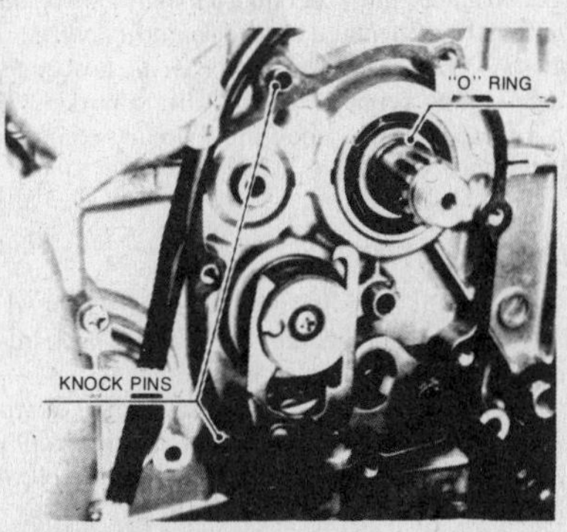

Knock pins and o-ring in position

4. Check that the two knock pins are in place in the crankcase.
5. Install the shaft o-ring.
6. Apply high-temperature grease to the lips of the clutch pushrod oil seal and the output shaft collar oil seal.
7. Use the shift shaft oil seal guide (57001-266), and install the cover. The aluminum washer for the lower left screw must be replaced with a new one.
8. Install the output shaft collar.
9. Install the chain guard, using a non-permanent thread-locking compound on the threads.
10. The remainder of the procedure is the reverse of removal.

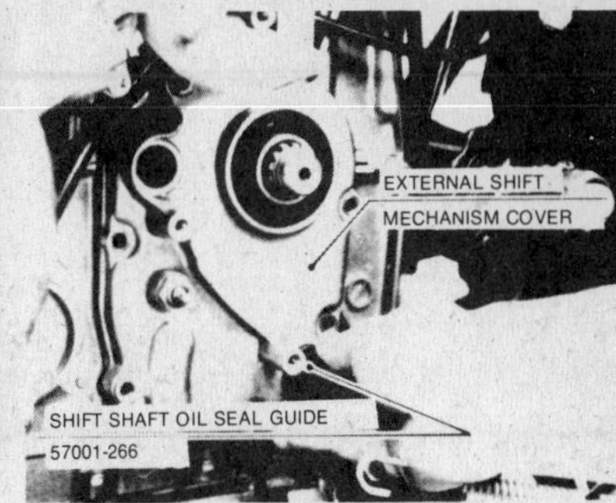

Installing the external shift mechanism cover

Secondary Shaft/ Starter Motor Clutch

REMOVAL

1. Remove the mufflers.
2. Remove the engine sprocket cover, clutch, and oil pump.
3. Remove the secondary shaft bearing stopper screws and pull off the secondary shaft.

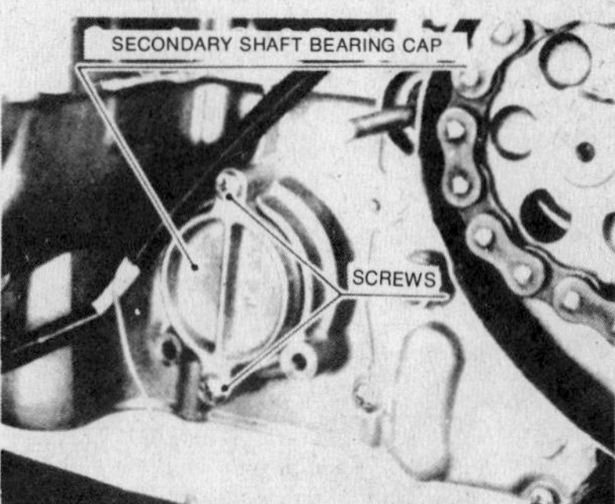

Remove the secondary shaft bearing cap

Tap the left side of the secondary shaft inwards to remove the right-side bearing

4. Remove the two screws and remove the secondary shaft bearing cap.
5. Tap the left side of the secondary shaft inwards until the right-side bearing comes out.
6. Hold the secondary sprocket and starter clutch assembly together and remove the shaft.
7. Disengage the secondary sprocket and starter clutch assembly from the primary chain and remove them from the bottom of the engine.
8. Remove the secondary shaft gear circlip. Use a bearing puller to remove the gear from the shaft.
9. If removal of the starter motor idler gear is desired, remove the circlip, pull off the shaft, and remove the idler gear.

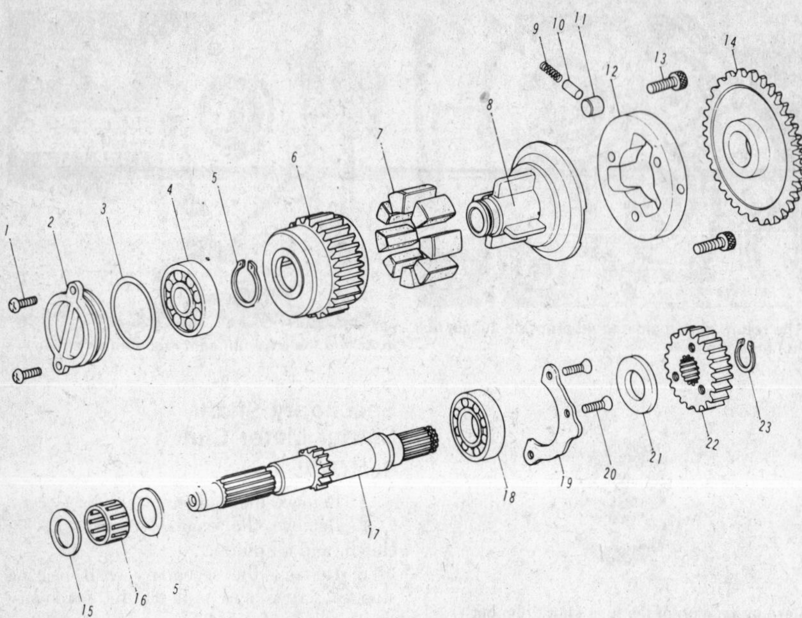

1. Screw
2. Bearing cap
3. O-ring
4. Ball bearing
5. Circlip
6. Secondary sprocket
7. Rubber damper
8. Inner coupling
9. Spring
10. Spring cap
11. Roller
12. Starter motor clutch
13. Allen bolt
14. Starter clutch gear
15. Washer
16. Needle bearing
17. Secondary shaft
18. Ball bearing
19. Bearing stopper
20. Screw
21. Thrust washer
22. Secondary shaft gear
23. Circlip

Secondary shaft assembly

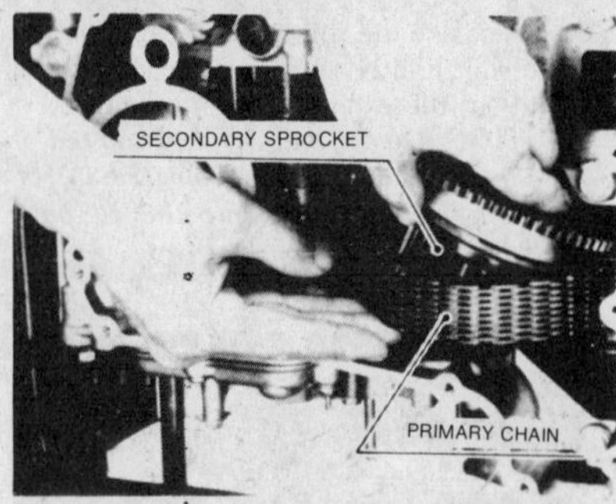

Engaging the primary chain with the secondary sprocket

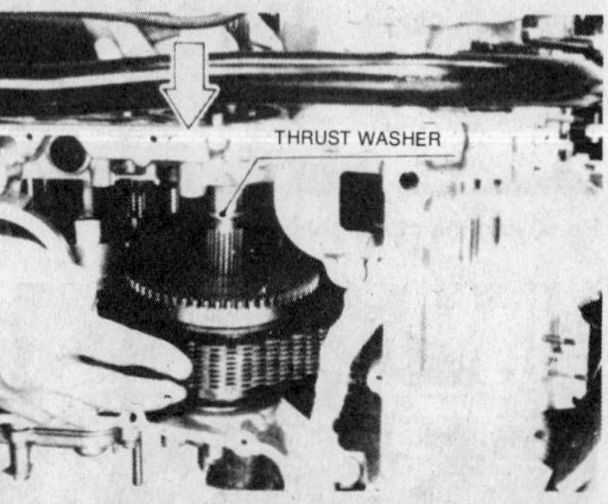

Installing the secondary shaft

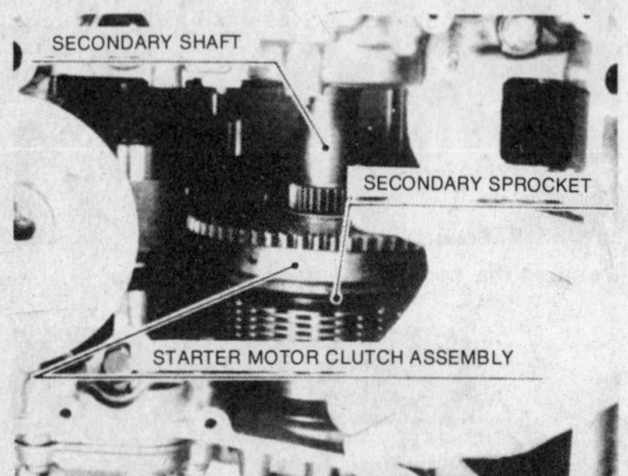

Removing the secondary sprocket and starter motor clutch assembly

10. To disassemble the shaft, remove the starter clutch gear, needle bearing, and washer.
11. Remove the rollers, spring, and the three spring caps from the starter motor clutch.
12. Remove the circlip and pull off the secondary sprocket. Note the rubber dampers.

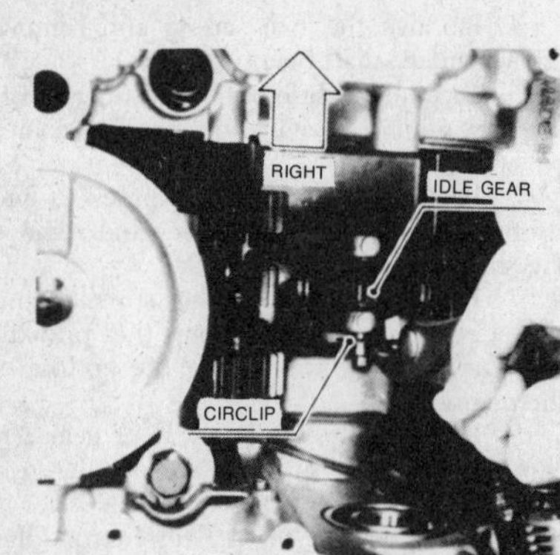

Removing the starter motor idler gear

13. While holding the coupling steady, remove the three allen bolts to separate the coupling and the starter motor clutch.

INSPECTION

1. Check the condition of the bearings. Rotation should be smooth and effortless. If damage is noted, or if there is play between the inner and outer races, replace the bearings.
2. Check the secondary shaft sprocket teeth. Minor damage can be remedied with an oilstone. Extensive damage or wear, however, necessitates replacement of the sprocket. If this is necessary, check the primary chain as well, since it, too, is probably worn.

INSTALLATION

1. Install the idler gear if it was removed. The gear must be installed so that the protruding side points to the right.
2. Reassemble the secondary shaft components, referring to the diagram for proper assembly order if necessary. Apply some oil to the rubber dampers before fitting.
3. Use a non-permanent thread-locking compound on the allen bolt threads and tighten the bolts to 24–27 ft lbs.
4. Install the thrust washer, starter motor clutch, and needle bearing assembly into the seconday sprocket and starter motor clutch assembly.
5. Engage the primary chain around the sprocket.
6. Install the thrust washer onto the secondary shaft and put the secondary shaft into the sprocket assembly.
7. Install the shaft bearing on the right side of the engine using a bearing driver or suitable substitute. Press the bearing in until it is fully seated.
8. Be sure that the oil pump knock pins are in place.

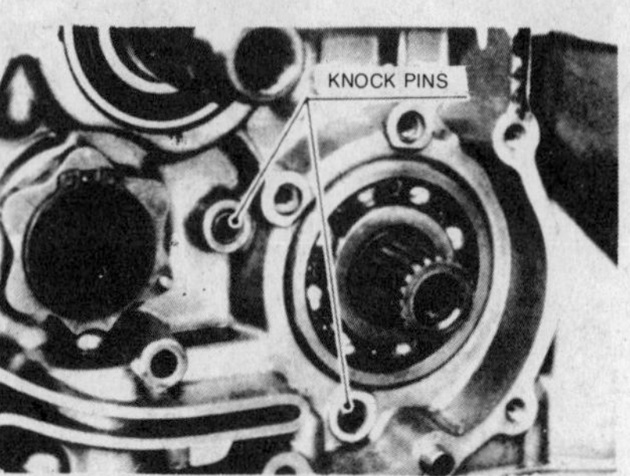

Be sure that the oil pump knock pins are in place

9. Install the secondary shaft bearing stopper with the two short screws and tighten the screws lightly. Install the oil pump, making sure that the gears mesh correctly.
10. Apply a non-permanent thread-locking compound to the oil pump bolt and tighten the bolt and the two screws. Then tighten the secondary shaft bearing stopper screws. Peen each screw to prevent loosening.
11. Fit the secondary shaft bearing cap.
12. Install the large flat washer onto the secondary shaft. Oil the shaft and press on the gear. A special gear installation tool (57001-535) is available. Install the circlip.
13. The remainder of the procedure is the reverse of removal.

LOWER END AND TRANSMISSION

Splitting the Crankcases

If the transmission alone is to be serviced, it is not necessary to remove the top end components. If the crankshaft must be taken out, however, the top end (cylinder head, cylinders, pistons) must be removed.

1. Remove the engine from the frame.

2. Remove the starter motor. Disconnect the neutral indicator switch.
3. Remove the alternator cover. Remove the alternator rotor if the crankshaft is going to be serviced.
4. Remove the engine sprocket chain guard. Remove the external shift mechanism cover.
5. Remove the output shaft collar, using a bearing puller if it is difficult to remove.
6. Remove the external shift mechanism.
7. Remove the secondary shaft bearing cap.
8. Remove the contact breaker assembly. Disconnect the oil pressure switch lead. Remove the timing advance mechanism.
9. Remove the clutch assembly.
10. Remove the secondary shaft bearing stopper screws.
11. Remove the twelve upper crankcase bolts.

Upper crankcase half bolts

12. Remove the oil filter. Remove the oil pan, gasket, and oil passage o-rings. There are three of them.
13. Remove the oil pump.
14. Remove the secondary shaft and starter motor clutch assembly. Refer to the section above for removal details.
15. Remove the eight 6 mm lower crankcase bolts and the two 8 mm bolts. Split the crankcases. Pry at the two indicated pry points if necessary.
16. Upper and lower crankcase halves are machined together. Therefore, they must be replaced in a set.
17. The 8 mm lower crankcase bolts should be replaced after five removals.
18. To install the cases, first set the shift drum in the neutral position.
19. Check that the following pieces are in place in the upper crankcase half: two knock pins, drive shaft and output shaft set rings and set pins, oil passage plug, and starter motor idler gear.
20. Check that the following components are in place in the lower crankcase half: kickstarter shaft assembly, two oil passage nozzles, five crankshaft main bearing inserts.

Shift drum in the neutral position

Be sure that the indicated components are in place

Bearing inserts, oil passage nozzles, and kickstarter assembly

21. Blow oil passages in the cases clear with compressed air.
22. Be sure that the crankcase mating surfaces are clean and dry, and free of old gasket material.
23. Install the transmission shafts in the upper crankcase half. Be sure that the crankcase set pins engage the holes in the needle bearing outer races and the set rings into the grooves in the ball bearings. The cases will not mate if the shafts are not properly seated.
24. Lubricate the transmission assembly with motor oil. Apply oil to the crankshaft main bearing inserts as well.
25. Check that the output shaft first gear will turn freely. If it does not, replace the steel washer with a thinner one (0.5 mm). Check that the clearance between the drive shaft second gear and the copper washer is 0.1–0.3 mm (0.004–0.012 in.). If it is not within specification, change or add steel washers until the clearance is correct. The steel washers are available in 1.0, 0.7, and 0.5 mm thicknesses.
26. Apply a liquid gasket material to the lower crankcase mating surface as shown in the illustration.

CAUTION: *Do not allow the gasket material to enter bearing or shaft areas or oil passages.*

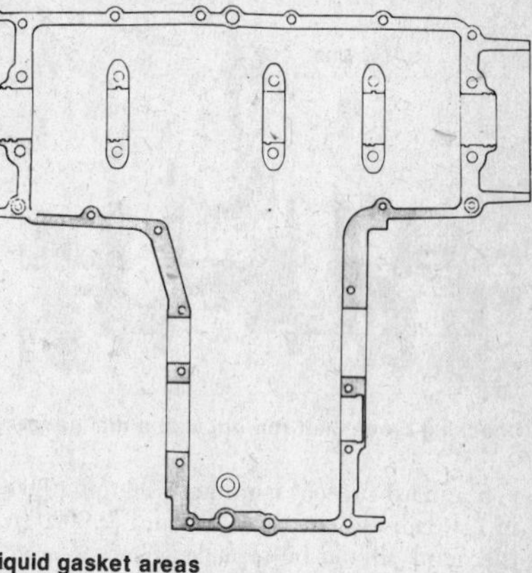
Liquid gasket areas

27. Install the lower crankcase half onto the upper half, engaging each gearshift fork with its gear groove.

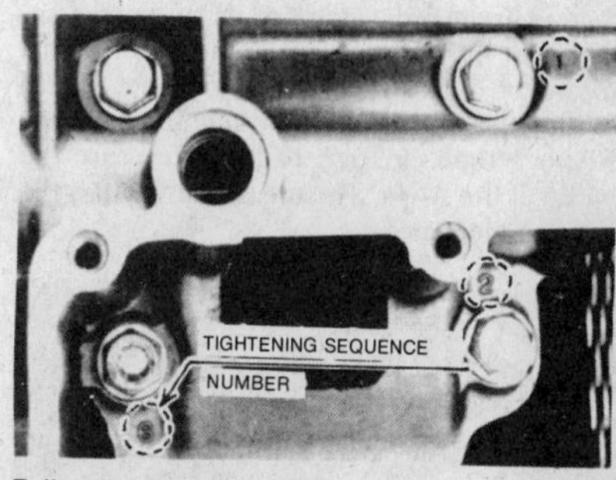

Follow the tightening sequence number when assembling the cases

Lower crankcase half bolts

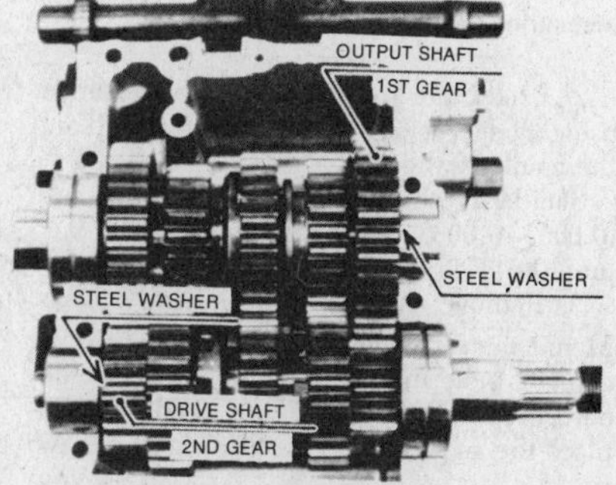

Transmission shaft shim locations

28. Install the lower crankcase bolts. The tightening sequence numbers are embossed on the lower crankcase half. Tighten the 8 mm bolts to about 11 ft lbs all around, then go back for a final tightening of 16.5–19.5 ft lbs.
29. Tighten the 6 mm bolts to 5.2–7.9 ft lbs.
30. Check that the transmission shafts turn freely and that shifting is smooth.
31. Install the secondary shaft assembly. Refer to the section above for assembly details.
32. The remainder of the procedure is the reverse of disassembly. Refer to the "Crankcase Cover Components" sections for assembly details.

Crankshaft Assembly

REMOVAL

1. Remove the engine from the frame.
2. Remove the top end components: cams, cylinder head, cylinders, pistons.
3. Remove the transmission.
4. Lift out the crankshaft and primary chain and camshaft chain. Remove the two chains from the crankshaft.

INSPECTION

Crankshaft

1. Blow out the crankshaft oil passages with compressed air.
2. Mount the crankshaft on a set of v-blocks and check the run-out at the center main bearing with a dial gauge. Run-out will be the true indicated reading.

Checking crankshaft run-out with a dial gauge

Standard run-out is under 0.02 mm (0.0008 in.). If run-out exceeds 0.05 mm (0.0020 in.), the crank should be replaced.

3. Measure the main bearing clearance with Plastigauge®. Cut strips of the material to the width of the bearings and place them on the crank journals parallel with the crank. Install the lower crankcase. Tighten the lower crankcase 8 mm bolts to about 11 ft lbs all around in the order stamped on the crankcase, then go back and tighten them to a final torque of 16.5–19.5 ft lbs. Be sure not to turn or disturb the crankshaft during the operation. Remove the crankcase half and measure the width of the strips. The measured width is the bearing clearance.

Measuring bearing clearance with plastigauge

Standard bearing clearance is 0.034–0.076 mm (0.0013–0.0030 in.). If the clearance exceeds 0.11 mm (0.0043 in.), the bearing inserts should be replaced, and the crankshaft journals checked for wear.

4. Measure each of the crankshaft journals. Standard diameter is 35.984–36.000 mm (1.4167–1.4173 in.). If the diameter is less than 35.964 mm (1.4159 in.), or if the journals are scored, the crankshaft should be replaced.

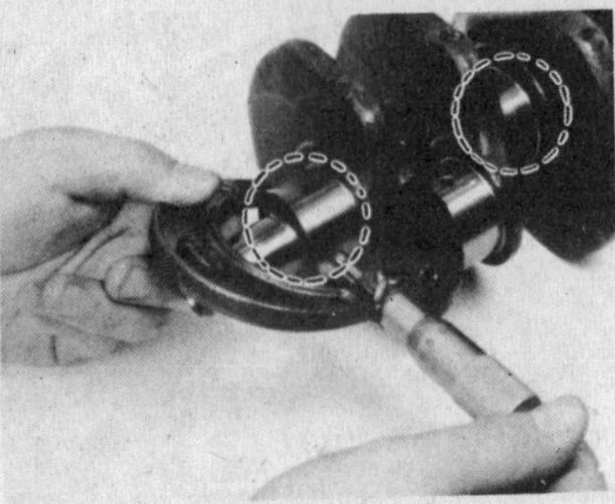

Measuring the crankshaft journal diameter

Checking crankshaft side clearance

5. Install the crank in the crankcase half. Levering it to one side, as illustrated, measure the side clearance with a feeler gauge. Standard side clearance is 0.05–0.15 mm (0.0020–0.0059 in.). If clearance exceeds 0.40 mm (0.0157 in.), the crankcases must be replaced.

NOTE: *The cases are machined in pairs and must be replaced as a set.*

Connecting Rods

1. To remove the connecting rods, remove the big end cap nuts and pull off the rods. Be sure to mark them for location. Do not mix the rods and caps. Caps can only be installed on their own rod.

Measuring connecting rod side clearance

2. Check the rod big end side clearance, using a feeler gauge between the big end and the crank flywheels.

Standard clearance is 0.15–0.25 mm (0.0059–0.0098 in.) If clearance exeeds 0.45 mm (0.0177 in.), replace the rod.

3. Remove the con rod bearing inserts. Mount the rod as illustrated and measure the con rod bend over a 100 mm distance. Standard bend is under 0.05 mm (0.002 in.) Replace the rod if bend exceeds 0.2 mm (0.008 in.).
4. Turn the rod 90° and measure twist.

Checking the rod for a bent condition

Standard twist is under 0.05 mm (0.002 in.). Replace the rod if twist exceeds 0.2 mm (0.008 in.) over a 100 mm distance.

NOTE: *If any or all of the rods are to be replaced, be sure that each pair of rods (1 and 2 or 3 and 4) have the same weight mark. The weight mark is a capital letter stamped on the big end.*

5. Check con rod bearing clearance with Plastigauge®. Standard clearance is 0.041–0.067 mm (0.0016–0.0026 in.) If clearance exceeds 0.1 mm (0.0040 in.), replace the bearing inserts.

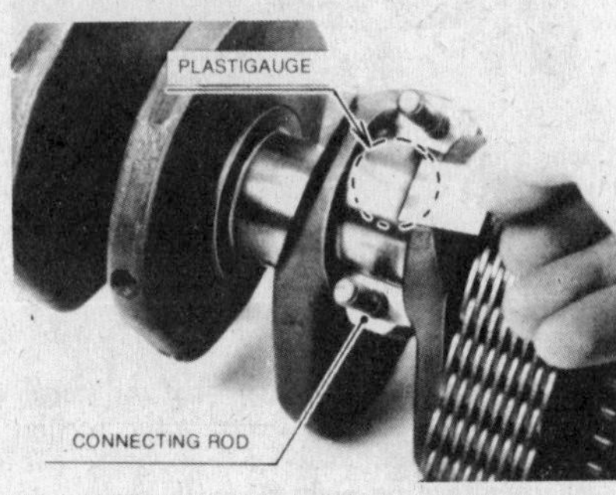

Measuring rod bearing clearance with plastigauge

6. If the con rod bearings are in need of replacement, the correct size insert must be chosen. To do this, first measure each of the rod journals with a micrometer.

If the measured journal diameter is less the 34.97 mm (1.3768 in.), replace the crankshaft.

Standard journal diameter is 34.984–34.994 mm (1.3773–1.3777 in.). If the measured diameter is less than this amount, but not under the serviceable limit, use new bearing inserts marked with *blue* paint.

If the measured diameter of the journal is 34.984–34.994 mm (1.3773–1.3777 in.), do not mark it.

If the diameter is 34.995–35.000 mm (1.3778–1.3780 in.) mark the journal with a "zero."

NOTE: *Ignore any marking already on the crankshaft.*

Bolt the rod and cap together with the bearing inserts removed. Tighten the rod bolts to 16–19 ft lbs, the standard torque. Measure the inside diameter of the rod big end.

If the inside diameter is 38.009–38.016 mm (1.4964–1.4967 in.), mark the rod with a "zero."

If the inside diameter is 38.000–38.008 mm (1.4961–1.4964 in.), do not mark the rod.

Refer to the following chart and cross-reference the rod and crank markings to determine which bearing inserts to use.

Bearing Insert Chart

Crank- shaft Marking / Con-Rod Marking	0	No mark
0	Black (PN 13034-051)	Brown (PN 13034-052)
No mark	Blue (PN 13034-050)	Black (PN 13034-051)

Bearing insert thicknesses are as follows:

Blue 1.485–1.490 mm/0.0585–0.0587 in.
Black 1.480–1.485 mm/0.0583–0.0585 in.
Brown 1.475–1.480 mm/0.0581–0.0583 in.

Primary Chain

1. With the crankshaft and the secondary shaft in place, check the primary chain slack. Replace the primary chain if slack exceeds 27 mm (1.08 in.).
2. The replacement chain is a Tsubakimoto Hy-Vo 3/8P-1W 76-link chain.

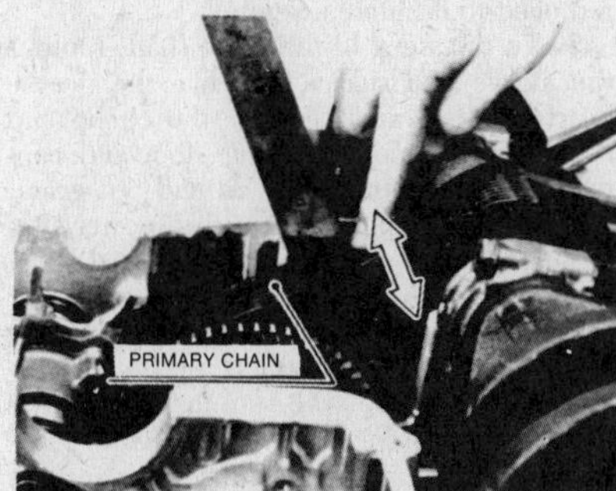

Checking primary chain free-play

Camshaft Chain

Stretch the chain by applying a force of about 5 kg. (10.4 lbs.), and measure the length of a 20-link section of the chain.

The standard length is 160.0 mm (6.30 in.) The chain should be replaced if the 20-link section measures more than 162.4 mm (6.39 in.).

INSTALLATION

1. Lubricate the bearing inserts thoroughly and install each rod on its own journal. Be sure that the rod caps are correctly installed. Fit the caps onto the rods so that the weight marks align. Install and tighten the rod nuts to 16–19 ft lbs.

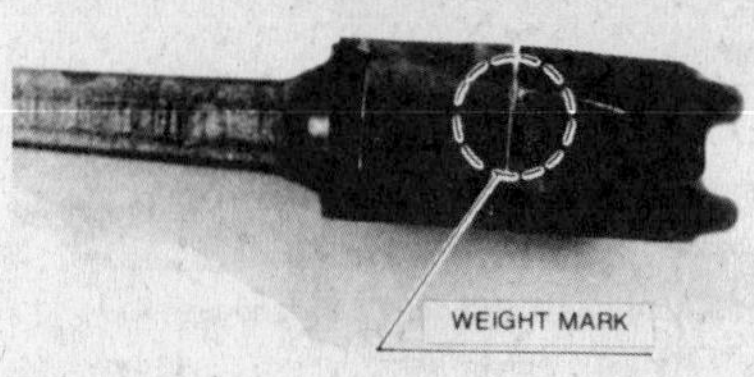

Install the caps on the rods so that the weight marks align

2. Lubricate the crankshaft bearings. Be sure that the primary and cam chain are fitted and properly engaged on their sprockets. Install the crankshaft in the upper crankcase half.
3. Apply high-temperature grease to the lips of the oil seals and fit the seals to either side of the crankshaft. The arrows on the faces of the seals must face *outwards*. The arrows should indicate the direction of crankshaft rotation (clockwise from the right side of the engine).
4. Fit the crankcase halves together as outlined in the "Splitting the Crankcases" section.

Oil seal installation

Transmission

REMOVAL

1. Split the crankcases.
2. Remove the transmission gear shafts from the upper case half.

NOTE: *Do not disassemble the shafts unless it is necessary. Components can be inspected in place (see below). Shaft circlips are not reusable and must be replaced with new ones on assembly.*

3. Pull out the shift rod and remove the two shift forks from the lower case half.

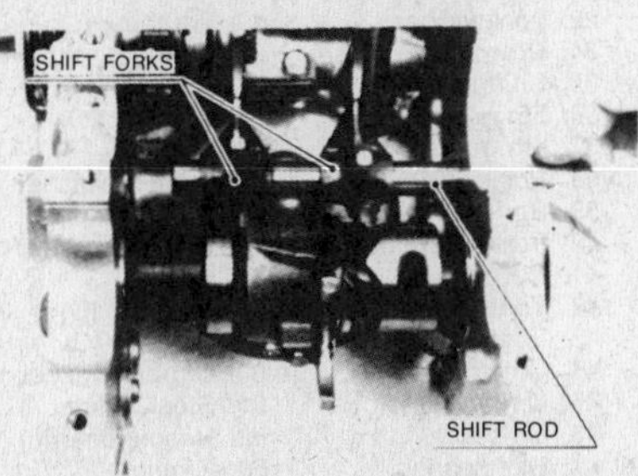

Removing the shift rod

4. Remove the shift drum positioning bolt, spring, and pin.
5. Bend down the washer tab and remove the shift drum guide bolt.

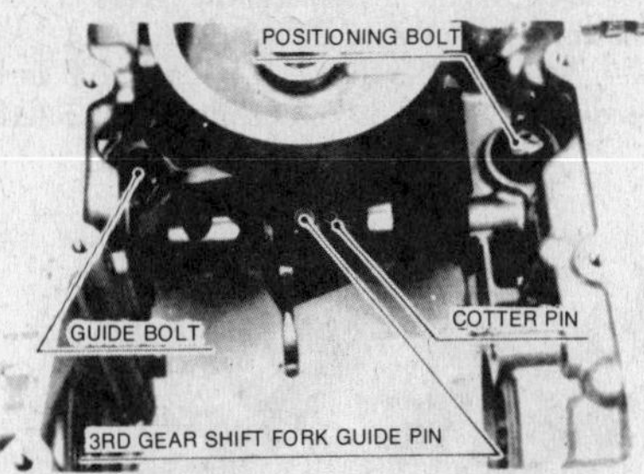

6. Remove the cotter pin and remove the 3rd gear shift fork guide pin.
7. Remove the operating plate circlip and the plate.
8. Pull the shift drum out a small way and remove the 3rd gear shift fork. Remove the shift drum from the crankcase.

INSPECTION

1. Lubricate the transmission shaft bearings and check their rotation. It should be smooth, effortless, and noiseless. If the rotation is rough or halting, or if play is noticeable in the outer race, the bearings should be replaced.

Replace bearings as a set.

2. Check the needle bearings for flattened or discolored needles. Replace them if damage is noted.

Measure the diameter of the transmission shafts where the needle bearings ride, and also the outer races of the needle bearings.

Standard shaft diameter is 19.980–19.993 mm (0.7866–0.7871 in.). Replace the shaft and the needle bearing if the measured diameter is less than 19.96 mm (0.7858 in.).

Checking needle bearing wear

Measure the inside diameter of the outer needle bearing races. Standard diameter is 26.014–26.024 mm (1.0242–1.0245 in.). Replace the outer race and the needle bearing if the measured inside diameter is 26.04 mm (1.025 in.).

3. Make a visual inspection of the gears. Look for pitting of the gear teeth. This will be most noticeable at the very base of the teeth. Gears with pitted teeth should be replaced, as should the gear with which they mesh.

Check the gear dogs for chipping or wear. Check the gear dog holes and recesses for wear and damage.

Some of the gears are splined to the shafts, others rotate freely. Check that the freely rotating gears can do so without binding or rough rotation. The bush inside diameters of these gears should be measured if the shafts are disassembled. Refer to "Disassembly," below.

4. Install the transmission shafts in the crankcase and check the backlash of each of the pairs of gears with a dial gauge. Set the gauge against one of the gears and attempt to rotate it while holding the meshing gear steady. Standard backlash is 0.17 mm (0.007 in.). Replace any pair of gears where backlash exceeds 0.25 mm (0.010 in.).

Checking gear backlash

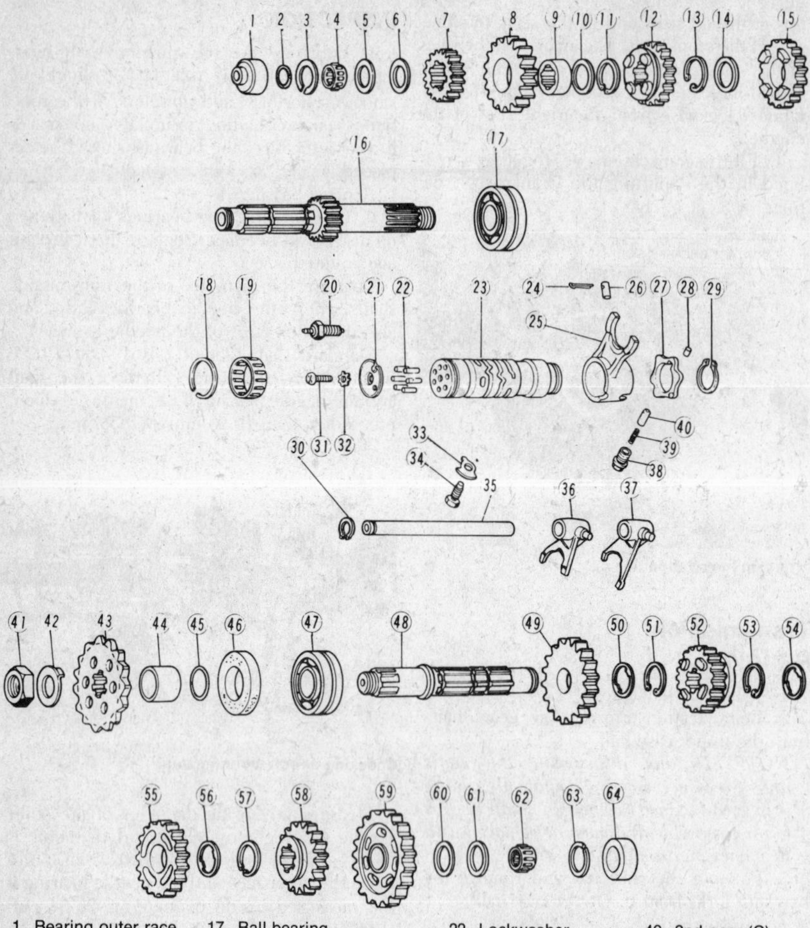

1. Bearing outer race
2. O-ring
3. Circlip
4. Needle bearing
5. Steel washer
6. Copper washer
7. 2nd gear (D)
8. 5th gear (D)
9. Copper bushing
10. Washer
11. Circlip
12. 3rd gear (D)
13. Circlip
14. Washer
15. 4th gear (D)
16. Drive shaft
17. Ball bearing
18. Circlip
19. Needle bearing
20. Neutral indicator switch
21. Shift drum pin plate
22. Shift drum pin
23. Shift drum
24. Cotter pin
25. 3rd gear shift fork
26. Guide pin
27. Operating plate
28. Pin
29. Circlip
30. Circlip
31. Screw
32. Lockwasher
22. Lockwasher
34. Drum guide bolt
35. Shift rod
36. 5th gear shift fork
37. 4th gear shift fork
38. Positioning bolt
39. Spring
40. Positioning pin
41. Nut
42. Toothed washer
43. Engine sprocket
44. Collar
45. O-ring
46. Oil seal
47. Ball bearing
48. Output shaft
49. 2nd gear (O)
50. Splined washer
51. Circlip
52. 5th gear (O)
53. Circlip
54. Splined washer
55. 3rd gear (O)
56. Splined washer
57. Circlip
58. 4th gear (O)
59. 1st gear (O)
60. Copper washer
61. Steel washer
62. Needle bearing
63. Circlip
64. Bearing outer race

Transmission and shift drum assembly

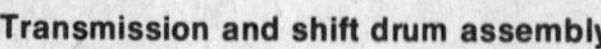

5. Visually inspect the shift forks for chipping or wear to the fingers. Measure the thickness of each of the shift fork fingers. Standard thickness is 4.9–5.0 mm (0.19–0.20 in.;. Replace any fork on which the fingers measure less than 4.7 mm (0.18 in.).

6. Measure the gear shift fork groove width on the gears. Standard width is 5.05–5.15 mm (0.199–0.203 in.). Replace the gears if the width is wider than 5.25 mm (0.207 in.).

7. Measure the diameter of each shift fork guide pin. For the 3rd gear shift fork, standard diameter is 7.985–8.000 mm (0.3144–0.3150 in.) and the fork should be replaced if the measured diameter is less than 7.93 mm (0.312 in.). For the 4th and 5th gear shift forks, standard diameter is 7.9–8.0 mm (0.311–0.315 in.), and the forks should be replaced if the pin measures less than 7.85 mm (0.309 in.).

8. Measure the diameter of each shift drum groove. Standard groove width is 8.05–8.20 mm (0.317–0.323 in.). Replace the shift drum if the groove width is greater than 8.25 mm (0.325 in.).

9. Measure the length of the shift drum positioning spring. Standard spring free-length is 32.3 mm (1.27 in.). The spring should be replaced if it measures less than 30.7 mm (1.21 in.).

SHAFT DISASSEMBLY AND ASSEMBLY

1. Have new circlips on hand before disassembling the shafts. Once removed, circlips cannot be reused. Lay out each piece as it is removed to facilitate assembly.

2. To disassemble the drive shaft: remove the sleeve and spacer. Remove the needle bearing outer race. Remove the circlip and remove the needle bearing, steel and copper washers. Remove the 2d and 5th gears. Remove the copper bushing and washer. Remove the circlip and remove the 3rd gear. Remove the circlip and remove the washer and the 4th gear. Remove the ball bearing from the shaft using a puller.

3. To disassemble the output shaft: remove the needle bearing outer race. Remove the circlip and pull off the needle bearing and the steel and copper washers. Remove the 1st and 4th gears. Remove the circlip and remove the splined washer, 3rd gear, and splined washer. Remove the circlip and the 5th gear. Remove the circlip, splined washer and 2d gear. Remove the ball bearing using a bearing puller.

4. Check gear-to-shaft clearance by measuring the inside diameter of each of the bushed gears and the corresponding area of the shaft on which they ride.

Standard clearance for 2d, 3rd, 4th, and 5th gears (both output and and drive shafts) is 0.020–0.062 mm (0.0008–0.0024 in.). Replace the gear(s) if clearance exceeds 0.16 mm (0.0063 in.).

Measuring shaft and gear clearance

Standard clearance for the 1st output shaft gear is 0.014–0.048 mm (0.0006–0.0019 in.). Replace the gear if clearance exceeds 0.15 mm (0.006 in.)

5. Assemble the shafts in the reverse of the disassembly order. Use *new* circlips.

6. For the drive shaft, install the circlips so that the opening of the circlips aligns with one of the grooves in the shaft. Be sure to install the 5th gear copper bushing so that the oil

Checking gear shift fork finger wear

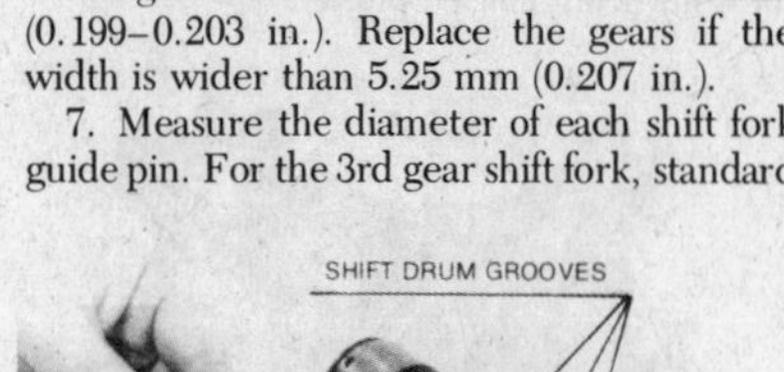

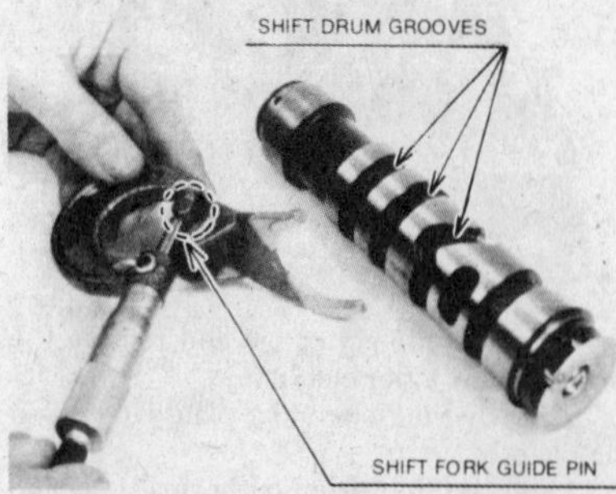

Checking the gear shift fork pins and drum grooves for wear

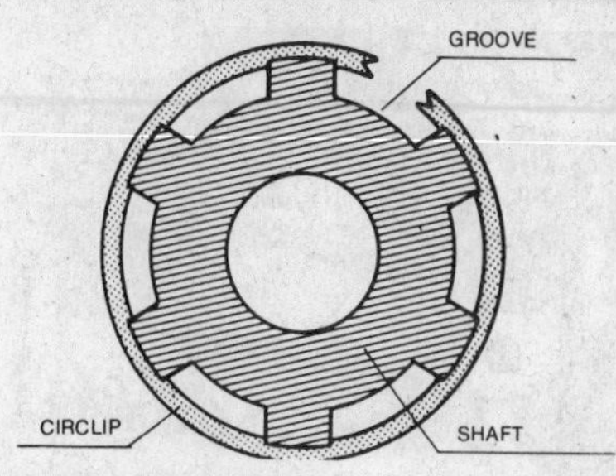

Correct circlip installation

When fitting the 5th gear copper bushing, align the oil holes

hole in the bushing aligns with the oil hole in the shaft.

The proper assembly order for the drive shaft is: 1st gear (part of the shaft) 4th gear, washer, circlip, 3rd gear, circlip, washer, copper bushing, 5th gear, 2d gear, copper washer, steel washer, needle bearing, circlip, bearing race.

7. To assemble the output shaft, install the circlips so that the opening of the circlip aligns with one of the shaft grooves. Install the splined washers so that their teeth do not coincide with the circlip opening.

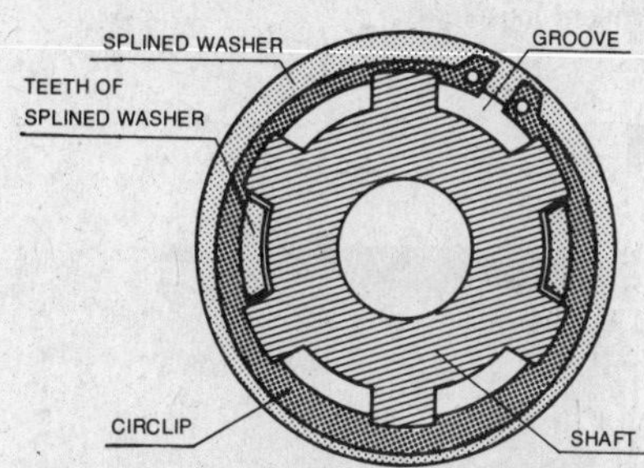

Correct splined washer and circlip installation

The proper assembly order is: (starting from the engine sprocket side (2d gear, splined washer, circlip, 5th gear, circlip, splined washer, 3rd gear, splined washer, circlip, 4th gear, 1st gear, copper washer, steel washer, needle bearing, circlip, bearing race.

INSTALLATION

1. If the shift drum pins have been removed, make sure that the long pin is installed in the proper hole. Refer to the illustration. Use a new pin plate screw lockwasher and be sure that the pin plate screw is firmly tightened.
2. Install the needle bearing, pressing it on so that the end of the bearing is even with the left end of the hole.
3. Place the 3rd gear shift fork into position in the crankcase half positioned so that the short side faces the neutral indicator switch.

Be sure that the long shift drum pin is positioned as shown

Install the 3rd gear shift fork as illustrated

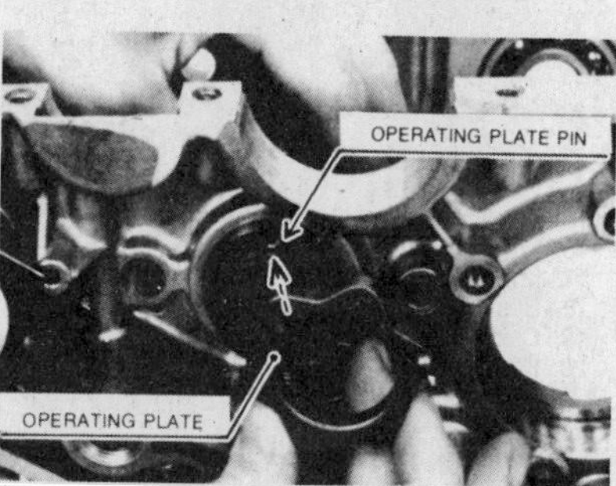

Fitting the operating plate

Install the shift drum sliding it through the shift fork.

4. Install the operating plate onto the shift drum and fit its circlip.
5. Seat the shift drum guide bolt washer in the crankcase and install and tighten the bolt. Bend the tab over the flat of the bolt.
6. Install the 3rd gear shift fork guide pin and use a new cotter pin. The shift fork pin should be inserted into the middle of the three shift fork grooves. The cotter pin should be inserted from the long side of the shift fork.
7. Install the shift drum positioning pin, spring, and bolt.

Insert the cotter pin from the right side. Do not forget the positioning bolt

8. Set the shift drum into the neutral position.
9. Lubricate the shift rod and shift fork fingers. Insert the rod, running it through the two shift forks while fitting the shift fork pins into the shift drum grooves.

NOTE: *The shift forks are not interchangeable.*

The 4th gear shift fork has fingers of about equal length. Note their proper positions on the shift rod by referring to the accompanying illustration.

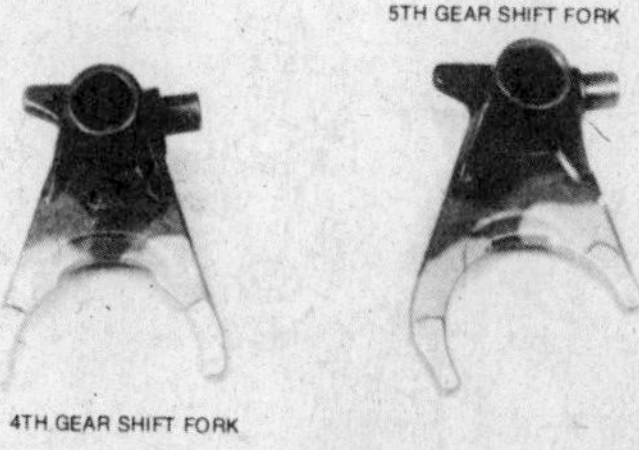

Differentiate the 4th and the 5th gear shift forks

Proper shift fork installation

Kickstarter

REMOVAL

1. Split the crankcases. The transmission can remain in place.
2. Remove the spring guide. Remove the kickstarter return spring.
3. Remove the circlip from the shaft bushing. Remove the shaft stopper screws and stopper and pull off the bushing.
4. Remove the shaft assembly.
5. Straighten the lockwasher ends and remove the stopper.
6. Remove the circlip on the end of the shaft and remove the spring seat, spring, and ratchet gear.
7. Remove the circlip, and take off the washer and kick gear.

INSPECTION

1. Make a visual inspection of the kick gear, and replace it if there is any damage to the gear teeth or to the ratchet mechanism.
2. Measure the inside diameter of the kick gear. Standard diameter is 20.000–20.021 mm (0.7874–0.7882 in.). Replace the gear if the inside diameter exceeds 20.07 mm (0.790 in.).
3. Measure the diameter of the kickstarter shaft in the area on which the kick gear rides. Standard shaft diameter is 19.959–19.980 mm (0.7858–0.7866 in.). Replace the shaft if the diameter is less than 19.94 mm (0.7850 in.).

INSTALLATION

Installation is the reverse of removal. Note the following points:

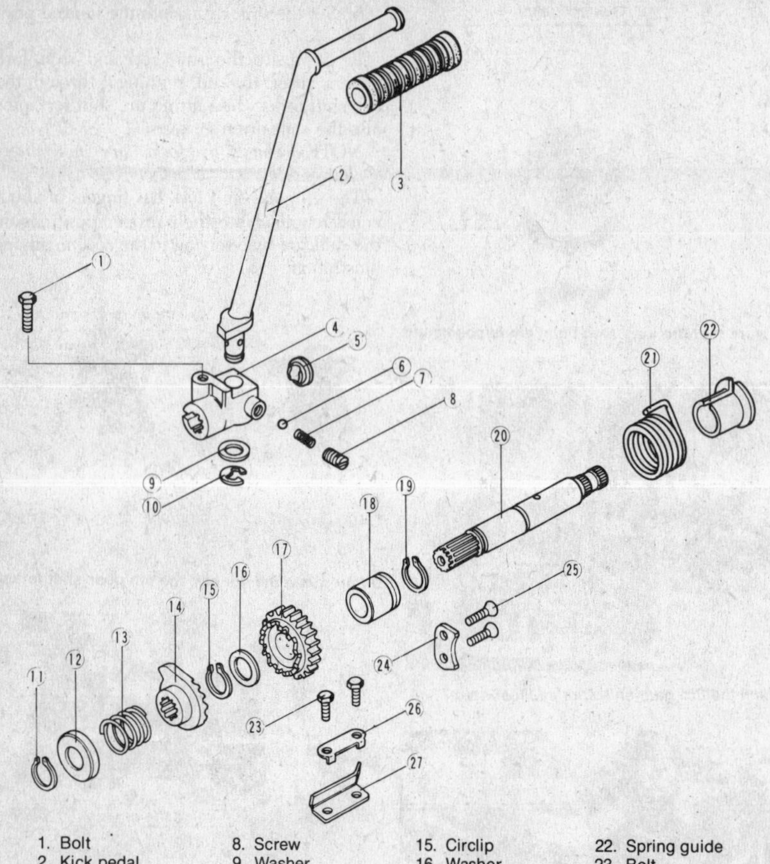

Kickstarter shaft assembly

Install the ratchet gear arm stopper as shown

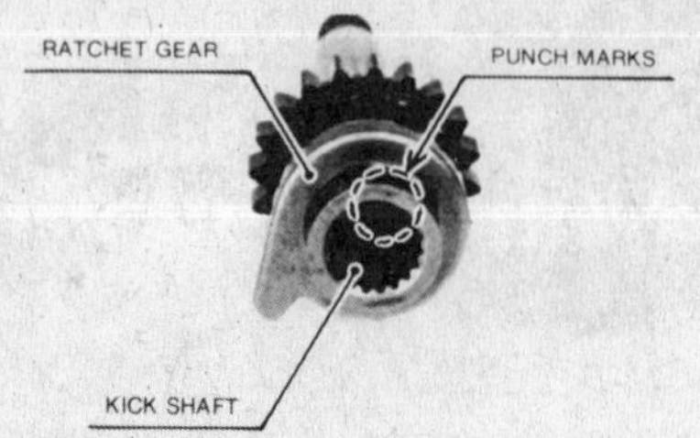

Align the shaft and ratchet gear punch marks when installing

1. Install the ratchet gear arm stopper as shown in the illustration. Use a new lockwasher. Tighten the two stopper bolts to 5.1–6.5 ft lbs. Be sure to bend the ends of the lockwasher over the stopper bolts.
2. Lubricate the gears with engine oil and the bushing with some high temperature grease before installation.
3. When installing the ratchet gear, align the punch mark on the gear with the punch mark on the shaft.
4. After tightening the kickstarter shaft stopper screws, peen both screw heads to prevent loosening.

LUBRICATION SYSTEM

OIL PRESSURE

1. To check the oil pressure, a special gauge (No. 57001-164) and adapter (No. 57001-403) are needed.
2. Oil pressure should be checked when the engine is at normal operating temperature.

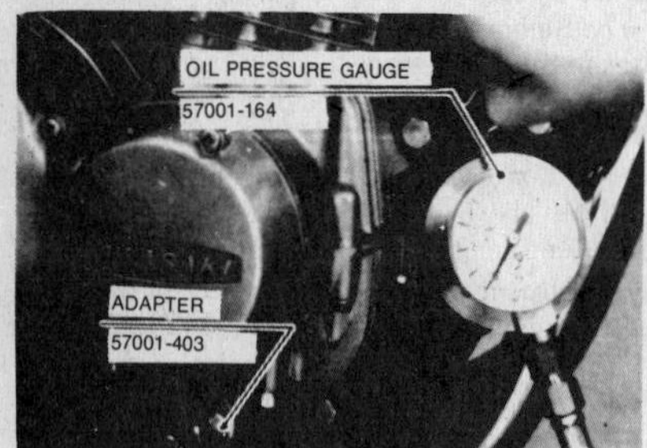

Checking oil pressure

3. With the engine *off*, remove the oil passage plug below the breaker points case. Be cautious of the hot oil. Fit the adapter and gauge.
4. Start and run the engine to 4,000 rpm. Oil pressure should be 28–36 psi.
5. If oil pressure is significantly below this figure, remove and inspect the oil pump and oil pressure relief valve.
6. The oil pressure gauge is also used to check oil pressure relief valve operation. This item is checked with the engine *cold*.
7. When checking with the oil cold, measured pressure should not fall too much below 63 psi nor exceed 85 psi regardless of rpm. If the oil pressure is too low, the relief valve may be stuck open. If it is too high, the relief valve may be stuck in the closed position. Refer to the appropriate section below for relief valve inspection.

OIL PUMP

Removal

1. With the motorcycle placed on the center stand, remove the drain plug and drain off the oil. Remove the oil filter as well.
2. After the oil has been drained, install the drain plug and tighten it to 9.5–12.0 ft lbs.
3. Remove the mufflers.
4. Remove the clutch. Refer to the "Engine and Transmission" chapter.
5. Remove the 15 oil pan bolts and remove the pan. Remove the gasket and the three oil passage o-rings.

Oil pan bolts

6. Remove the oil pump mounting bolt and the two mounting screws and take off the pump. Note that there are two knock pins on the crankcase.

Inspection

1. Measure the clearance between the inner rotor and the outer rotor. Standard clearance is 0.05–0.23 mm (0.0020–0.0091

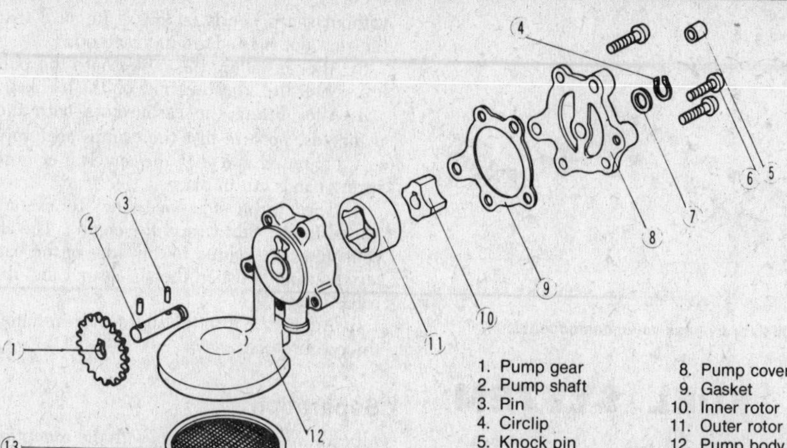

Oil pump components

in.). The rotors should be replaced if clearance exceeds 0.30 mm (0.012 in.).

2. Measure the clearance between the outer rotor and the pump body. Standard clearance is 0.15–0.21 mm (0.0059–0.0083 in.). Replace the rotors or the oil pump body if the clearance exceeds 0.30 mm (0.012 in.).

Oil pump mounting screws and bolt

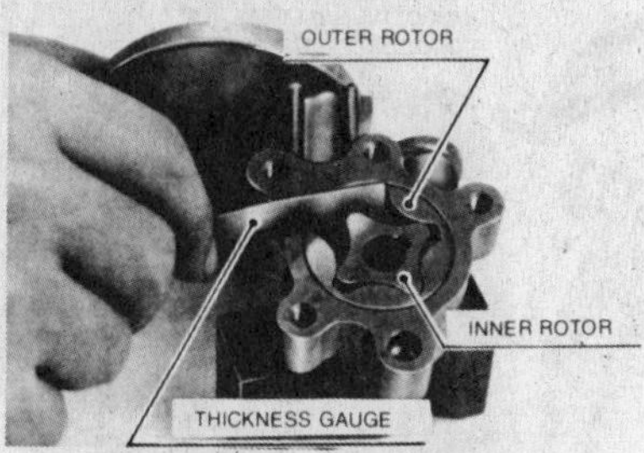

Checking inner-to-outer rotor clearance

3. Place a straightedge across the pump body and then probe beneath it with a suitably sized feeler gauge blade to determine rotor side clearance. Standard clearance is 0.02–0.07 mm (0.0008–0.0028 in.). Replace the rotors or the pump assembly if clearance exceeds 0.12 mm (0.0047 in.).

Disassembly

1. Remove the circlip and washer on the pump shaft end.
2. Remove the oil pump cover screws and remove the pump cover and gasket.
3. Remove the rotors.
4. Remove the pin and pull off the oil pump gear and shaft.
5. Slide off the pump gear and take the pin from the shaft.

Assembly

1. Assembly is the reverse of disassembly. Use a new gasket. Be sure that all of the internals are well oiled and the pump turns smoothly after assembly.

Installation

1. Before installing the oil pump, fill it with clean motor oil.
2. Check that the two knock pins are in place.
3. Be sure that the oil pump gear and the pump drive gear are properly meshed.
4. Use a non-permanent thread-locking compound on the oil pump mounting bolt. Peen the two mounting screws to lock them in place.
5. Replace the three oil passage o-rings with new ones.
6. Tighten the oil pan bolts to 5.1–6.5 ft lbs.

OIL PRESSURE RELIEF VALVE

1. The oil pressure relief valve is fitted to the oil pan. To remove the pan, refer to "Oil Pump: Removal," Steps 1–5.

2. Unscrew the relief valve and remove it from the oil pan.

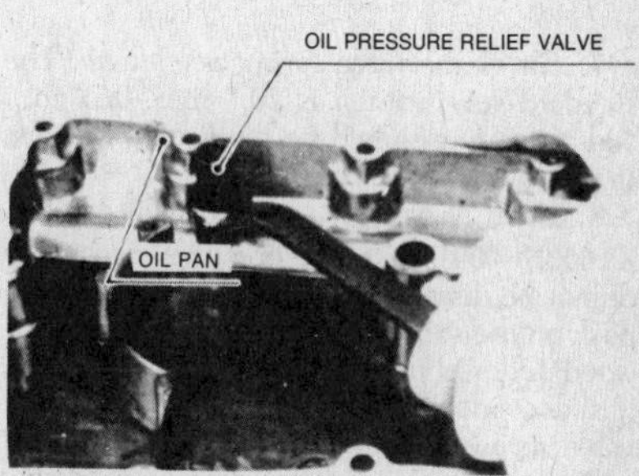

Removing the oil pressure relief valve

3. For models with engine numbers prior to KZ65OBE000144, the relief valve can be disassembled and inspected. This cannot be done for later models.

4. To disassemble the relief valve on engines prior to KZ650BE000144, press down on the washer with a screwdriver and take out the circlip. Remove the washer, spring, and piston.

5. Check the piston and the inside of the valve body for scoring or other signs of wear.

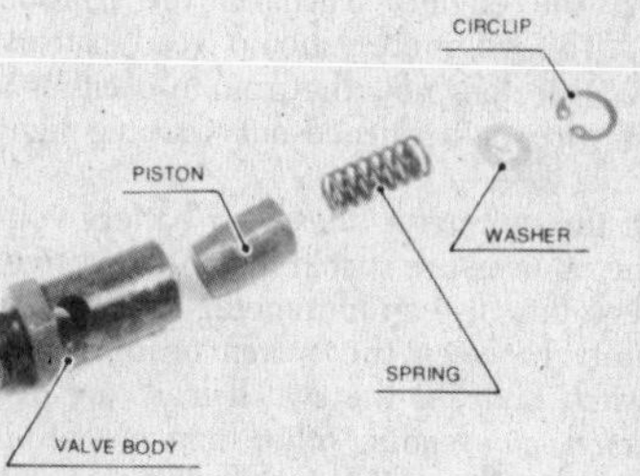

Relief valve components (early)

6. Measure the diameter of the piston and the inside diameter of the valve body to determine piston-to-body clearance. The standard specification is 0.020–0.103 mm (0.0008–0.0041 in.). Replace the piston if clearance exceeds 0.13 mm (0.0051 in.).

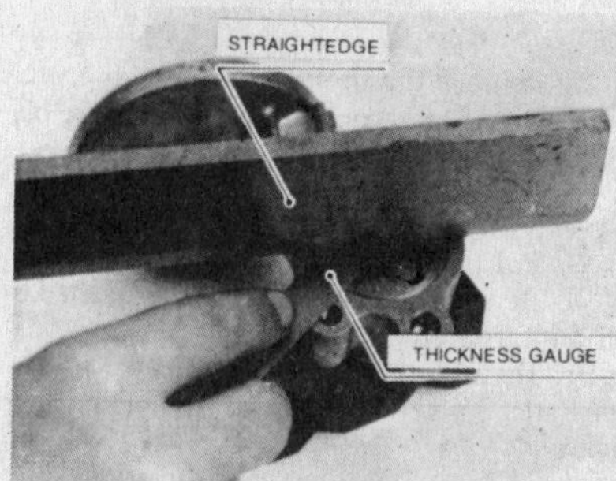

Checking rotor side clearance

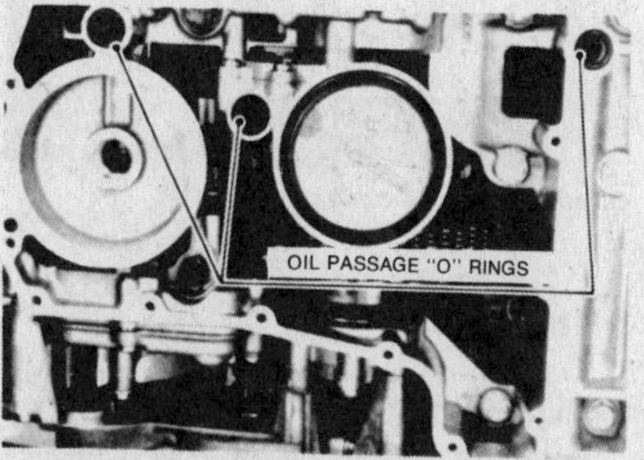

Replace the three oil passage o-rings with new ones

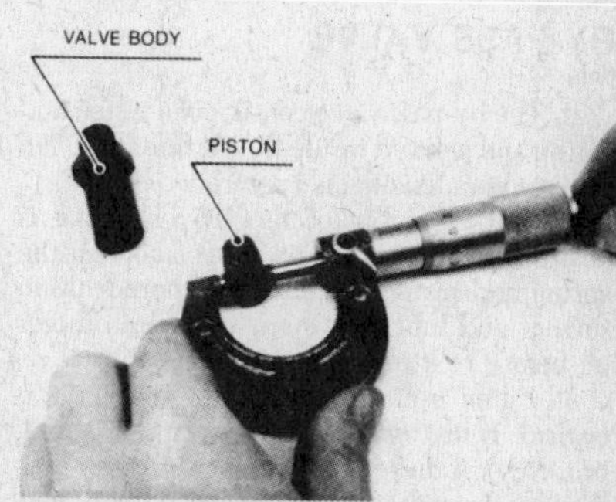

Measuring relief valve piston diameter (early)

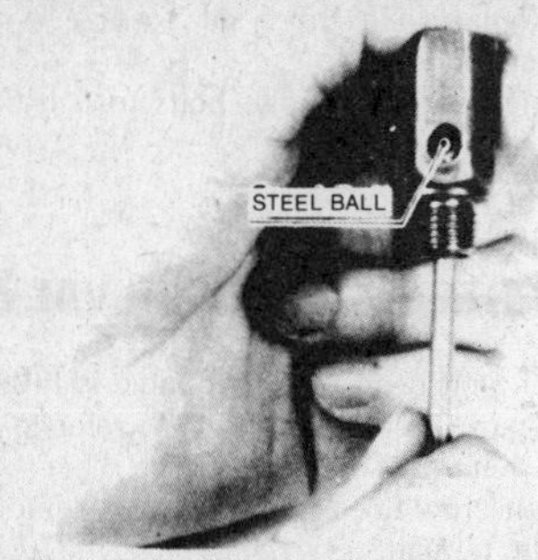

Checking relief valve operation (late)

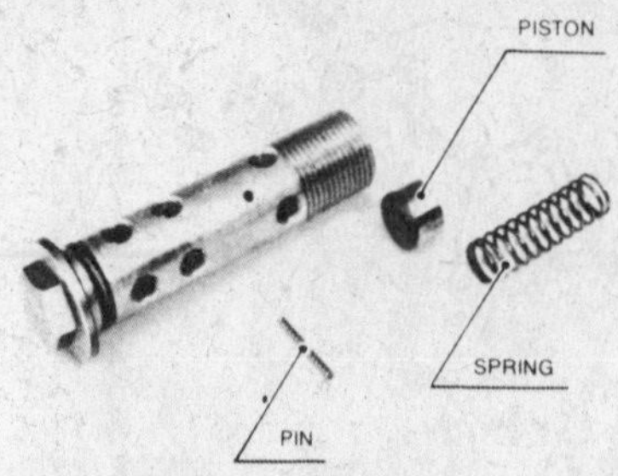

Oil filter by-pass valve components

7. Check the valve spring free length. The standard specification is 20.1 mm (0.79 in.), and the spring should be replaced if it is less than 19.1 mm (0.75 in.) long.

8. For models after Engine No. KZ650BE000144, the oil pressure relief valve cannot be disassembled. The only check is to push on the steel ball in the valve body with a wooden dowel or the like and make sure that it slides smoothly and is fully seated by the valve spring pressure. Any rough movement which cannot be cured by cleaning the valve assembly thoroughly in a solvent will necessitate replacing the valve assembly.

CAUTION: *Do not attempt to disassemble the valve.*

OIL PRESSURE INDICATOR SWITCH

1. The switch should go on when the ignition is turned on. If it does not, check it by first disconnecting the switch lead. Then, connect the positive lead of a 30V DC voltmeter to the lead, and ground the negative meter lead on the engine. Turn on the ignition switch. The voltmeter should read battery voltage. If it does not, the trouble is either a broken wire or a burned-out warning light bulb.

2. If the voltmeter does read battery voltage, the oil pressure switch may be defective. To check this, use an ohmmeter to check for continuity between the switch terminal and the switch body. If the switch leads are disconnected, any reading other than zero ohms indicates that the switch is defective.

3. If the switch does not turn the warning light out at any engine speed above idle, check the oil pressure with a pressure gauge as outlined at the beginning of this chapter. If oil pressure is satisfactory, the switch is defective and should be replaced.

BY-PASS VALVE

1. The by-pass valve consists of a piston and spring and is fitted inside the oil filter bolt. No routine maintenance is required.

2. If disassembly of the by-pass valve is desired, remove the pin and take out the spring and piston. Clean them thoroughly in solvent and lubricate them with clean motor oil before refitting.

3. Filter bolt rubber o-ring condition is critical. If the o-rings are chipped, hardened, or torn, or if there is any doubt as to their condition, they should be replaced with new ones.

FUEL SYSTEM

CARBURETOR OVERHAUL (650)

Removal

1. Remove the gas tank. Drain the carburetor float bowls.

2. Screw in the throttle cable adjusters near the twist-grip to give the cables plenty of play.

3. Loosen the manifold clamp for each carburetor.

4. Move the spring bands which secure the air cleaner hoses to the carburetors.

Removing the carburetors

5. Pull the carburetors off the manifolds as an assembly.

6. Loosen the throttle cable adjuster nuts and disconnect the cables from the pulley. Remove the carburetors from the motorcycle.

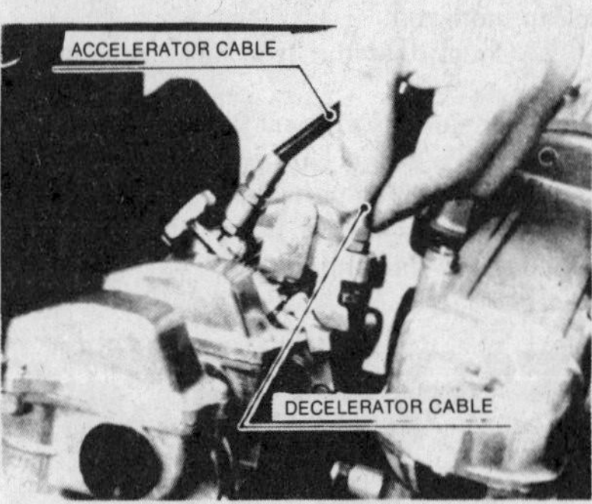

Disconnecting the cables

Installation

1. Installation is basically the reverse of removal. Note the following points:

2. Be sure that the throttle cables are correctly routed. They should run between the top frame tube and the right side cradle tube without sharp bends or kinks. Be sure that they are not twisted around each other.

3. After installing the cables onto the pulley, center the adjusting nuts on the bracket.

4. After fitting the carburetors onto the manifolds, be sure that the clamps are properly tightened and that the air cleaner hose spring bands are in place.

5. The carburetor overflow tubes are routed to the right rear of the engine. The air vent tubes are routed to the sides of the battery housing between the air cleaner and the baffle plate.

6. Adjust the throttle cables after installing the carburetors.

Separation

All carburetor components with the exception of the linkage mechanism and starter plungers can be removed and inspected without separating the carburetors from their mounting plate. If this separation is required, proceed as follows:

1. Remove the carburetors from the motorcycle.

2. Remove the idle adjusting screw and spring.

3. Remove the carburetor covers.

4. Unscrew and remove the throttle arm mounting bolts and the pulley mounting bolt. Note the lockwashers on each bolt.

Remove the throttle arm mounting bolts and the pulley mounting bolt

Remove the throttle shaft set plate and rubber cap

5. Remove the throttle return spring.

6. Remove the phillips screw and take off the throttle shaft set plate.

7. Remove the rubber shaft caps from the end carburetors.

8. Pull the throttle shaft out to the left side.

9. Remove the mounting screws and take off the carburetors.

10. To refit the carburetors, reverse the separation procedure. Note the following points:

a. Use a non-permanent thread-locking compound on the mounting screws.

b. Apply a thin coat of grease to the throttle shaft before inserting it through the carburetors.

c. Perform a mechanical synchronization of the carburetors (see below).

Disassembly

As noted, all carburetor components with the exception of the linkage mechanism and the starter plungers can be removed without separating the carburetors from their mounting plate. To disassemble the carburetors in this manner, proceed as follows:

1. Refer to Steps 1–8 under "Separation" above.
2. Lift out the linkage and throttle valve assemblies.

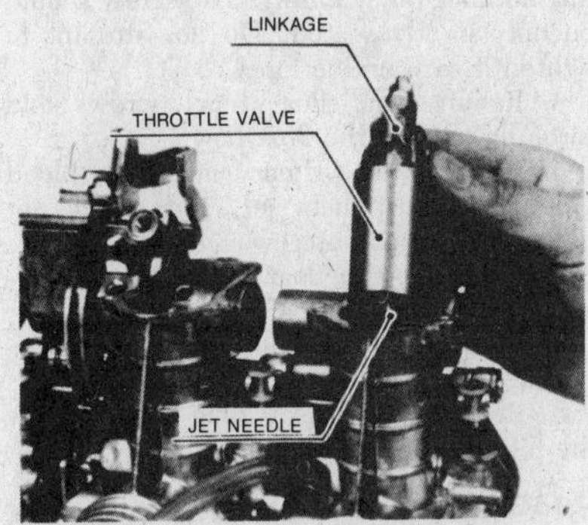

Removing the throttle slide assembly

3. If desired, remove the two screws inside the throttle valve(s) and take out the jet needle. Note the position of the needle clip. Do not change the position of the clip unless tuning adjustments are being made.
4. On early model carburetors, remove the pilot fuel screw extenders and unscrew and remove the pilot screw, o-ring and spring. On later model carburetors, unscrew and remove the pilot air screw, spring, and o-ring from the carburetor body.
5. Unscrew and remove the float bowl screws and carefully remove the float bowl and float bowl gasket.

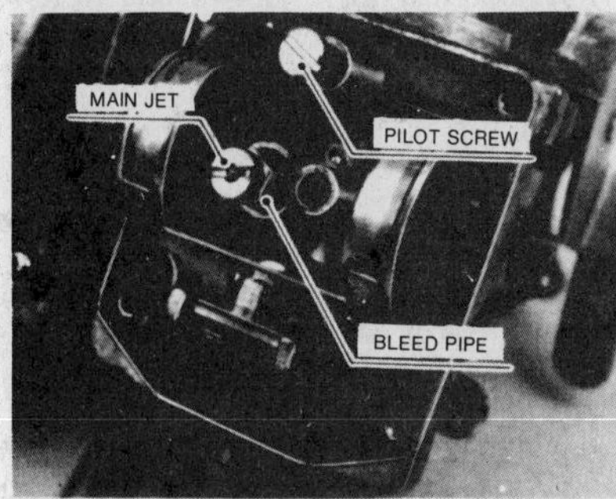

Float bowl components

6. Unscrew and remove the main jet, air bleed pipe, and pilot jet.
7. Push out the float pin and remove the float assembly.
8. Remove the float needle. Unscrew and remove the float needle seat and gasket.
9. If the carburetors have been removed from their mounting plate, unscrew and remove the starter plunger after first removing the plunger cap.
10. From the top of the carburetor, push out the needle jet using a soft wooden dowel or the like.

Assembly

1. Assembly is basically the reverse of disassembly. Note the following points:
2. Check the condition of all gaskets and o-rings and replace them if they are damaged.
3. Be sure that the jet needle clip is in the 4th groove from the top, unless tuning changes were made.
4. Do not overtighten the fuel jets when installing them in the carburetor body.
5. When installing the pilot fuel screws on early model carburetors, screw them in until they are lightly seated, then back each one out 1⅛ turn. Fit the plastic extender with the projection facing the front. When installing pilot air screws to the carburetor bodies on later model carburetors, screw them in until they are lightly seated, then back each one out two full turns.

The pilot screws may have to be readjusted after the carburetors are installed.

6. Perform a mechanical synchronization of the carburetors (see below).
7. After installing the carburetors, make sure that all fuel lines are secure. Turn on the gas and allow the units to sit for a few minutes before operating the motorcycle to check for leaks.

Mechanical Synchronization

Any time the carburetors have been disassembled, it is wise to perform a preliminary mechanical synchronization prior to installation. After installation, the carburetors should

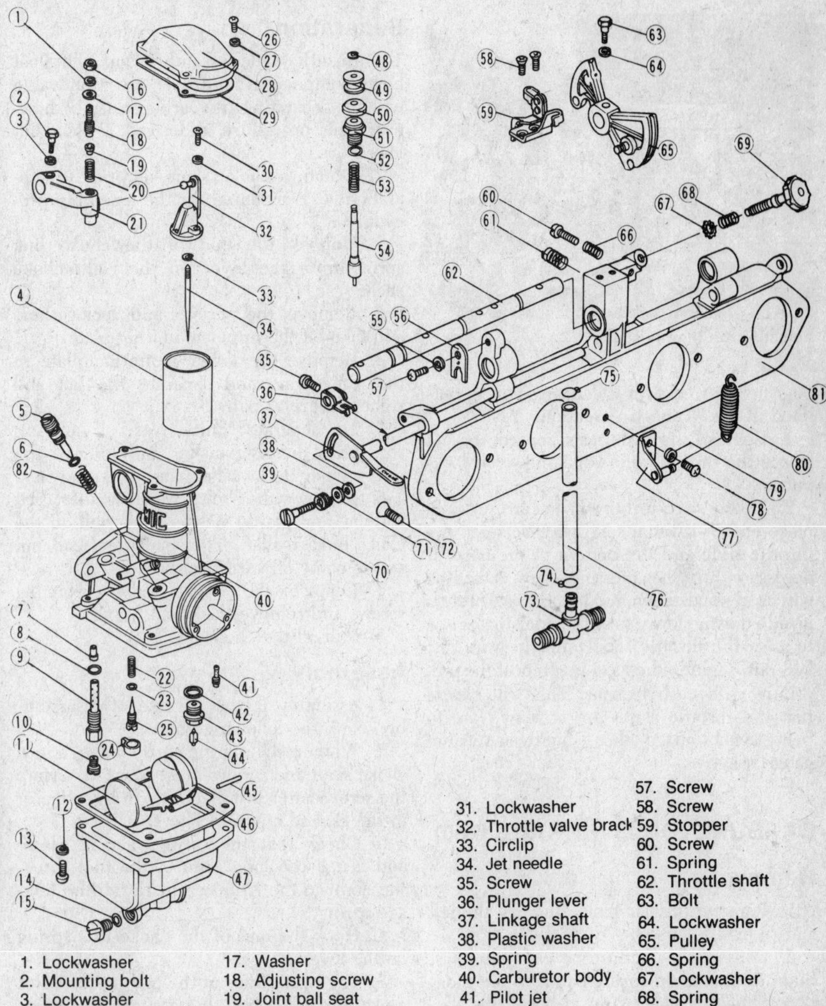

1. Lockwasher
2. Mounting bolt
3. Lockwasher
4. Throttle valve
5. Air screw (only on air-screw type)
6. O-ring (only on air-screw type)
7. Needle jet
8. O-ring
9. Air bleed pipe
10. Main jet
11. Float
12. Lockwasher
13. Screw
14. O-ring
15. Drain plug
16. Locknut
17. Washer
18. Adjusting screw
19. Joint ball seat
20. Spring
21. Throttle arm
22. Spring (only on pilot-screw type)
23. O-ring (only on pilot-screw type)
24. Extender (only on pilot-screw type)
25. Pilot screw (only on pilot-screw type)
26. Screw
27. Lockwasher
28. Top cover
29. Gasket
30. Screw
31. Lockwasher
32. Throttle valve brack
33. Circlip
34. Jet needle
35. Screw
36. Plunger lever
37. Linkage shaft
38. Plastic washer
39. Spring
40. Carburetor body
41. Pilot jet
42. Gasket
43. Valve seat
44. Valve needle
45. Float pin
46. Gasket
47. Float bowl
48. Clip
49. Bush
50. Dust seal
51. Plunger cap
52. O-ring
53. Spring
54. Starter plunger
55. Lockwasher
56. Set plate
57. Screw
58. Screw
59. Stopper
60. Screw
61. Spring
62. Throttle shaft
63. Bolt
64. Lockwasher
65. Pulley
66. Spring
67. Lockwasher
68. Spring
69. Idle adjusting screw
70. Screw
71. Flat washer
72. Screw
73. 3-way joint
74. Clamp
75. Clamp
76. Fuel hose
77. Bracket
78. Screw
79. Lockwasher
80. Spring
81. Mounting plate
82. Spring (only on air-screw type)

Carburetor assembly

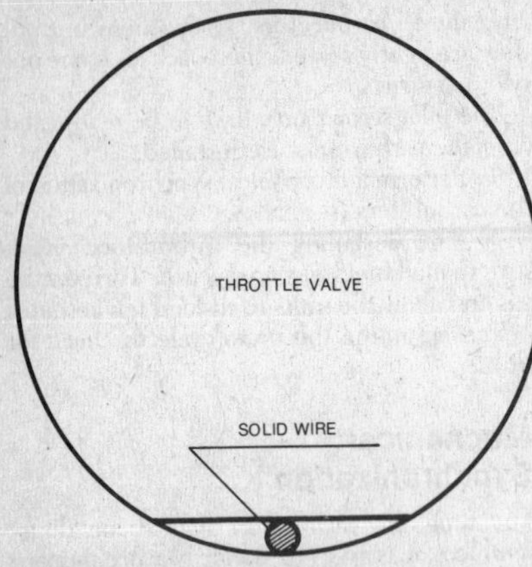

Throttle slide mechanical synchronization

Adjusting the throttle slides

Carburetor Specifications

	KZ650 (1976)	KZ650 (1977–1980)	KZ650 (1981)	KZ750
Type	VM24SS	VM24SS	VM24SS	CV34
Main jet	102.5	102.5	92.5	62/125
Needle jet	0–8	0–8	0–5	NA
Needle	5DL31-4	5DL31-4	5CL30-4	NO1A
Needle clip position	4	4	4	NA
Pilot jet	15	15	15	35
Pilot screw (turns out)	1⅛	2	preset	preset
Throttle slide	1.5	1.5	1.75	NA
Fuel level (mm/in.)	30/1.2	30/1.2	23/0.91	36.5/1.44

be synchronized with vacuum gauges as outlined in the "Tune-Up" section.

1. Remove the carburetor top covers and loosen the throttle slide adjusting screw locknuts.
2. Taking each carburetor in turn, insert a piece of 0.5–1.0 mm solid wire between the throttle slide and the bottom of the bore. If necessary, turn the adjusting screw so that the wire is trapped. Then, holding the carburetors upside down, slowly turn the adjusting screw to raise the throttle slide until the wire just falls out. Tighten the locknut. Repeat the procedure with each locknut. This will ensure that the throttle slides are at least close to being synchronized, thus simpifying vacuum gauge usage.

CARBURETOR OVERHAUL (750)

Removal

1. Remove the gas tank. Remove the left and right side covers.
2. Loosen the carburetor clamp screws. Slide the manifold spring bands to one side.
3. Slide the clamps up and pull the vacuum lines off the carburetors.
4. Loosen the locknuts of the throttle cable adjuster, and free the adjuster from the bracket.
5. Disconnect the overflow tubes from the air cleaner box.
6. Pull the carburetors out and to the right, disconnecting the cable end from the pulley as soon as it becomes accessible.

Installation

Installation is basically the reverse of removal. Note the following points:

1. Install the carb clamps so that the one for carb No. 2 has the opening pointing upwards, and that the others point downwards.
2. Run the throttle cable between the right fork leg and the head pipe, and the right side of the frame top tube.
3. Adjust the throttle cable.

Separation

The throttle slide assembly and the float bowl components and jets are removable without separating the carburetors. If, however, this procedure is desired, it is as follows:

1. Obtain a choke shaft kit prior to separation. It is essential for the assembly procedure.
2. Unhook the end of the choke link spring from the lever on the right choke shaft.
3. Remove the screws and lockwashers and take off the upper mounting plate.
4. Remove the lower mounting plate in the same way, and separate the left and right carburetor pairs.
5. To separate units Nos. 1 and 2, straighten the flat washer and remove the nut, washer, lockwasher, and choke lever.
6. Remove the bolt, wave washer, flat washer, and plastic washer, and pull off the choke linkage shaft. The small steel ball and spring come off with the shaft.
7. Remove the choke valve retaining screws and remove the choke valves.
8. Pull off the choke shaft.

Assembly

1. Assembly is the reverse of disassembly. Note the following points:
2. When installing the choke valve, a new choke shaft and screws must be used. Crimp the screws after installation with the adapter in the kit and a pair of pliers.
3. Check that the o-rings are in place, and install the long pipe of the fuel three-way joint to the No. 3 carb. Install the linkage spring.
4. Hook the end of the choke link spring on the lever.
5. The centerlines of the carburetor bores must be parallel both horizontally and vertically. If not, loosen the mounting screws and align the carburetors. Then retighten the screws.

Disassembly

The major components of each carburetor can be serviced without separating the assembly.

1. Remove the throttle slide cover screws and take off the cover and spring. Carefully pull out the throttle slide assembly.
2. If removal of the needle is desired, unscrew the holder.
3. To remove the pilot screw, punch and pry off the plug. Turn the pilot screw in carefully until it is fully seated, counting the number of turns. The screw must be reset to this number on assembly. The screw should be only lightly seated. Do not attempt to tighten it with undue force.
4. Remove the float bowl screws and carefully take off the float bowl.
5. Remove the primary main jet, bleed pipe, secondary main jet, and needle jet holder. All items unscrew.
6. Push out the float pivot pin and remove the floats and float needle.
7. Push out the needle jet from the carburetor mouth.
8. Remove the plastic plug and unscrew the pilot jet beneath it.

Assembly

Assembly is straightforward. Note the following points:

1. Be sure that the slide diaphragm is correctly installed. The diaphragm is located with a tab. The lip must be seated in its groove all the way around. The slide must move up and down with light finger pressure.
2. Fit the pilot screw by screwing it in until lightly seated as on disassembly, then backing it off the same number of turns you counted in the disassembly procedure.
3. Use a new pilot screw plug and bond it in place.

Fast Idle Adjustment

1. Check that there is 4–6 mm (0.16–0.24 in.) clearance between the pin on the idling link and the fast idle cam when the choke lever is fully pushed down.

ELECTRICAL SYSTEM

NOTE: *The charging system may be one of two types. The early type used separate regulator and rectifier, the regulator being the mechanical type. The later system has an integral regulator/rectifier unit.*

Determine the system in use before beginning tests, then refer to the appropriate section.

CHARGING SYSTEM (EARLY)

Alternator Output Test

1. Before attempting this test, check the condition of the battery. If the battery charge

is less than 12 v, charge the battery. If a full charge cannot be obtained, the battery should be replaced.

2. Carry out the test with the engine at operating temperature.

3. Remove the left side cover.

4. Be sure that the ignition switch is turned off.

5. Disconnect the regulator green and brown leads from the regulator. Connect these two leads together.

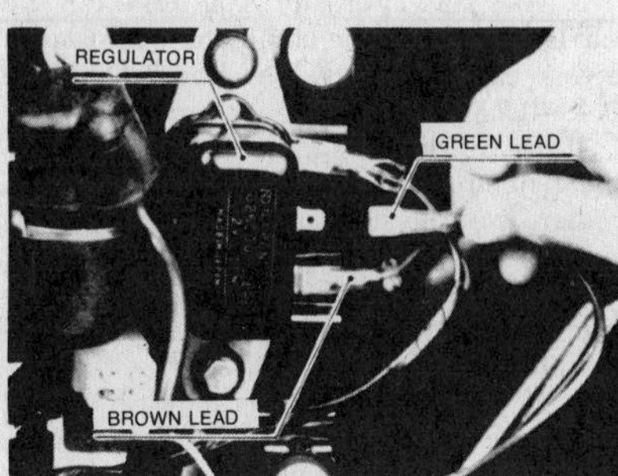

Disconnecting the regulator leads

NOTE: *When connecting the two leads be sure that the connection is not grounded. Do not leave the two leads connected any longer than is necessary. Be sure that they are disconnected immediately after the test is carried out.*

6. Open the seat and disconnect the battery negative lead from the battery terminal.

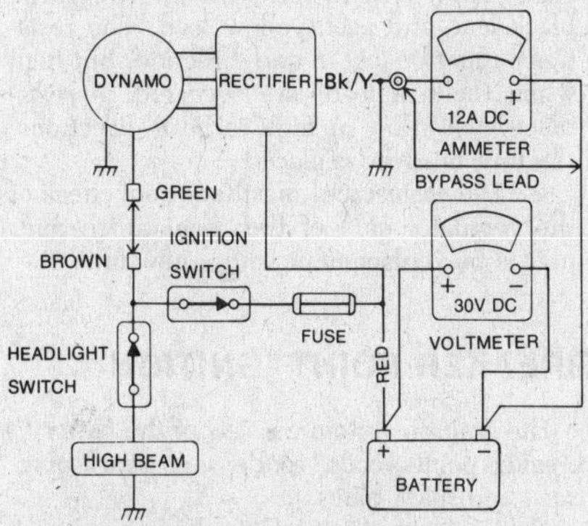

Circuit diagram for alternator output test

7. Connect an ammeter in series with the battery, connecting the meter negative lead to the battery negative lead and the meter positive lead to the battery negative terminal.

8. To avoid damage to the meter during the test, connect a by-pass wire to the battery negative terminal and the meter negative lead.

9. Connect a DC voltmeter (at least 30v DC) across the battery.

10. Start the engine with the kickstarter.

CAUTION: *Do not use the electric starter to start the engine as this may cause damage to the ammeter. Make sure that all connections are tight. A loose connection may damage electrical components.*

11. Turn on the headlight and set it to high beam.

12. Disconnect one end of the by-pass lead.

13. Run the engine at 4,000 rpm, and note the meter readings. They should be as follows:

a. The voltmeter should read 15 v

b. The ammeter should read about 3 amps

14. If either reading is somewhat lower than these figures, check the field coil and armature resistance as outlined below.

Alternator Test

1. In the event that the measured output of the alternator is not with specification, the armature windings and field coil windings should be checked for shorts or open circuits. This can be done with an ohmmeter.

2. Disconnect the 4-pin electrical connector on the electrical panel.

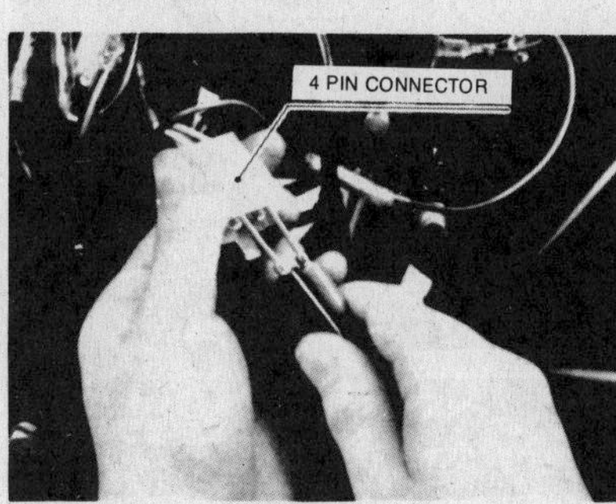

Checking armature windings for continuity

3. With the ohmmeter set on the R x 1 range, check the resistance between each of the three yellow leads in turn. In each case, resistance should be 0.4–0.6 ohms. If resistance is greater than this, there is probably an open circuit and the armature must be replaced. If resistance is zero, there is probably a short in the system, and, again, the armature must be replaced.

4. Using the highest range on the ohmmeter, measure the resistance between each of the three yellow leads in turn and a ground on the chassis. Resistance should be infinite. If there is any reading short of this, the armature must be replaced.

5. Disconnect the green field coil wire and measure the resistance between the wire and ground on the chassis. Field coil resistance should be 2.7–3.4 ohms. If the resistance reading is not within this specification, the field coil must be replaced.

Removal

1. To remove the alternator, remove the left side cover and disconnect the alternator 4-pin connector and the green lead.

2. Remove the engine sprocket cover.

3. Disconnect the neutral indicator switch lead and pull out the wiring towards the left side.

4. Remove the four alternator cover screws and remove the cover and gasket.

5. Remove the armature allen bolts to remove the armature from the cover; remove the three field coil allen bolts to remove the field coil.

Installation

1. Apply a liquid gasket compound around each of the armature grommets before fitting.

2. Use a non-permanent thread-locking compound on the allen bolts.

3. When installing the alternator cover, be sure that the two knock pins are in place. Use a new gasket.

4. Arrange the wiring between the crankcase and the external shift mechanism cover.

5. The remainder of the procedure is the reverse of removal.

Rectifier

1. With the ingition switch off, remove the left side cover. Disconnect the white lead from the battery positive terminal, and disconnect the rectifier black lead. Disconnect the 4-pin connector on the electrical panel.

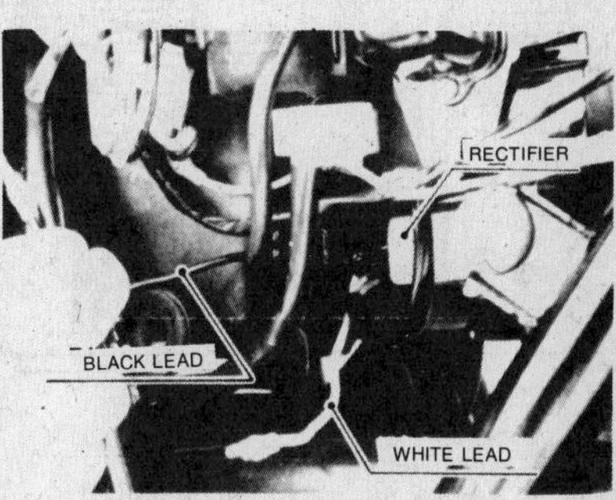

Checking the rectifier

2. Using the R x 10 or the R x 100 range on the ohmmeter, check the resistance in both directions between the white lead and each yellow lead, and then between the black lead and each yellow lead. In each case, resistance should be low in one direction, and approximately ten times as high in the opposite direction.

3. If any check indicates that resistance is high in both directions, or low in both directions, the rectifier is defective and must be replaced.

Regulator

1. The regulator should be checked if the battery overcharges or discharges. If this happens, check the battery first, before attempting any regulator tests. These tests will not be accurate if the battery is defective or is not fully charged.

2. Other symptoms of a defective regulator include bulbs burning out at high rpm, or the need to constantly add water to all of the battery cells.

3. Remove the headlight and disconnect the 9-pin connector therein. Turn the ignition switch *on*, and be sure that all lights are turned *off*.

4. Connect a DC voltmeter (at least 30v scale) across the battery. Start the engine and run it at 1,600 rpm. The voltage reading should be 14–15 v.

5. Gradually increase engine speed and recheck the meter reading with the engine running at 4,000 rpm. The reading should still be 14–15 v.

NOTE: *Engine speed must increase directly from 1,600 rpm to 4,000, and must not decrease at any point during this time. If engine speed is allowed to drop, the readings may be incorrect. If this happens, start the test over from the beginning.*

6. If the voltage reading is 14–15 v in both cases, the regulator is satisfactory. If it was not, test the regulator as outlined below.

NOTE: *If the motorcycle is still under warranty, replace the regulator at this point rather than carrying out the following tests.*

7. Remove the left side cover and disconnect the black, green, and brown leads from the regulator.

8. With an ohmmeter, check the resistance across the middle and upper terminals with the points P_0 in position 1. There should be zero resistance. If there is any resistance indicated, the points are probably dirty and should be cleaned with emery cloth and/or a non-oily solvent.

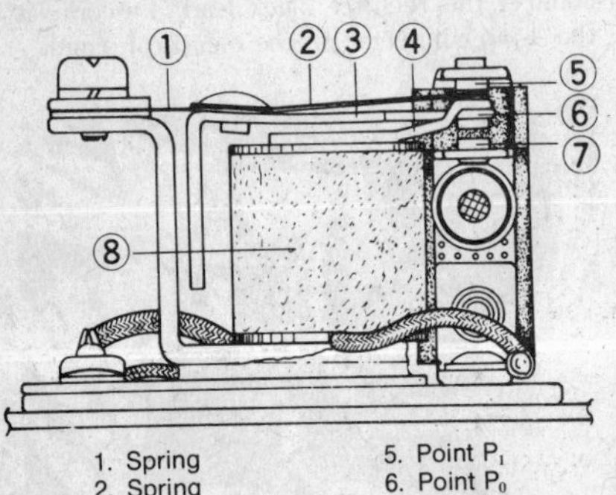

1. Spring
2. Spring
3. Armature
4. Adjuster Arm
5. Point P_1
6. Point P_0
7. Point P_2
8. Relay Coil

Voltage regulator components

9. With the points in position 2, resistance should be 9 ohms. If resistance is not correct, the regulator must be replaced.

10. Connect the ohmmeter across the middle and lower terminals. In position 1, the resistance reading should be about 100 ohms. If the reading is not correct, the regulator must be replaced. In position 2, resistance should be zero. If it is greater than this, the points are probably dirty and should be cleaned with emery cloth and a non-oily solvent.

11. If cleaning the points does not get resistance down to zero ohms, replace the regulator.

12. Press down on the armature and check the armature gap with a feeler gauge. It should be 0.3 mm (0.012 in.) or more. If the gap is not correct, bend the holder for point P_2, until it is.

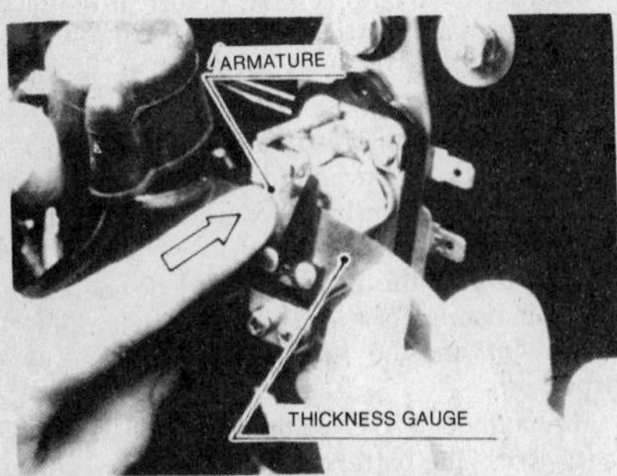

Checking armature gap

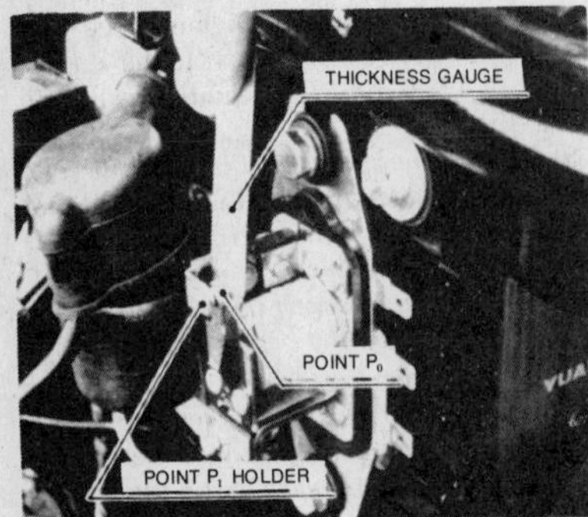

Checking the gap between points P_2 and P_0

13. Check the gap between points P_2 and P_0 with a feeler gauge. The gap should be 0.30–0.45 mm (0.012–0.018 in.). If the gap is incorrect, bend the holder for point P_1 to correct it.

14. Connect a DC voltmeter across the battery terminals and start the engine, noting the voltage at various engine speeds. If the voltage was not between 14–15 volts, adjust the output by bending the adjuster arm. Bending the arm up increases the voltage output, and bending it down decreases it.

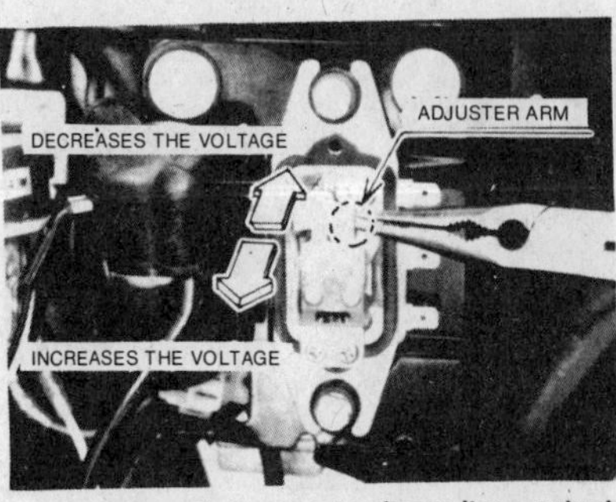

Bending the adjuster arm to alter voltage output

15. Start the engine and read the voltage with the engine running below 1,600 rpm. It should be 14–15 v. If the voltage is too low, bend the adjuster arm up. If it was too high, bend the arm down. Be sure the ignition is *off* when making these adjustments.

16. Check the voltage with the engine running at 4,000 rpm. If it is less than the specified 14–15 v, bend the holder for point P_2 down. If it is greater, bend the P_2 holder up.

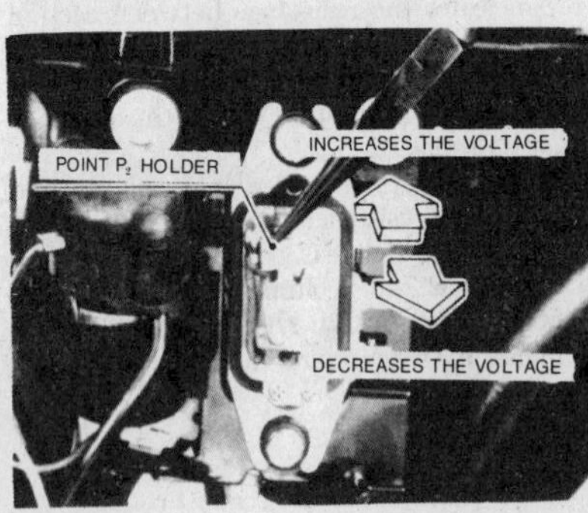

Bending the P_2 holder to alter voltage output

17. Fit the regulator cover and recheck voltage output.

CHARGING SYSTEM (LATE)

System Check

1. Always check battery condition and state-of-charge before beginning system tests or suspecting failure of the other components.

2. The battery must be in good condition and fully charged before carrying any other tests or the results may be incorrect.

3. Connect a DC voltmeter across the battery terminals. With the engine running at 4,000 rpm, the reading should be about 14.5 v.

If the reading is higher than this value, the rectifier/regulator is defective. If lower, check the alternator and the regulator/rectifier.

Alternator Test

1. Remove the engine sprocket cover and disconnect the three yellow leads.

2. With an AC voltmeter set on the 250 v range, check the voltage across pairs of the yellow leads with the engine running at about 4,000 rpm. This no-load test should give about 50 v across each pair of leads.

3. A static alternator coil test can be carried out with an ohmmeter. Resistance across each pair of yellow leads should be 0.48–0.72 ohms.

If the resistance is infinite, the wiring has an open circuit. If lower, there is a short. In either case, the stator must be replaced.

4. With the ohmmeter set on the highest scale, check resistance between each yellow lead and the stator core. Resistance must be infinite in each case.

5. If the ohmmeter tests indicate normal resistance, but the no-load test (Step 2) indicates low voltage output, the rotor magnets may be weakened. Replacement of the rotor is the solution.

Regulator/Rectifier

1. Remove the electrical panel beneath the left side cover.

2. Disconnect the white/red lead and 6-pin connector.

3. With an ohmmeter set to the 10 or 100 ohm range, check the resistance in both directions between the white/red lead and each yellow lead in turn, then between the black lead and each yellow lead. The resistance must be low in one direction, but high when the test leads are reversed. If resistance shows low or high in both directions, the unit must be replaced.

4. The easiest and most foolproof check of the regulator side of the regulator/rectifier unit is by replacement with a new unit.

BREAKER POINT IGNITION

The ignition system consists of the battery, breaker points, coils, condensers, spark plug caps, and spark plugs.

There are two sets of breaker points and two ignition coils. Each coil fires two cylinders. They are paired No. 1 and 4, and No. 2 and 3.

1. In the event of failure of the ignition system, first check the fuses; if all are in working order, check that the snap connectors for the coils and breaker points are all clean and tight.

2. At this point refer to chapters 2 and 3 for inspection procedures for the breaker points, plugs, and battery. If these items are all in working order, the problem may be isolated to the coils, condensers, or plug caps.

3. If only one cylinder fails to fire, and the problem is not a loose connection or defective spark plug, suspect the plug cap. The caps are fitted with a resistor to prevent radio interference while in operation, and heat and vibration may cause the value of this resistor to increase considerably, even to becoming an open circuit.

The easiest way to see if a misfire is due to a defective cap is to switch the plug lead of the non-firing cylinder with its corresponding cylinder (1–4, 2–3). If the dead cylinder begins to fire and the other cylinder ceases, the problem is the plug cap. The caps should be replaced as a set.

Functional caps will have a resistance of 5,000–7,500 ohms. Usually, when resistance reaches about 9,000 ohms, the plug for that cap will no longer fire.

Caps are easily removable by unscrewing them from their cables.

4. Defective condensers are seldom a problem, since these are now usually replaced along with the breaker points. Defective condensers will cause considerable arcing or sparking between the breaker point contacts while the machine is running, and this should be cause for replacement before they fail completely. Badly burned or pitted point contact surfaces can also be caused by defective condensers, as well as by improper adjustment. If the points are in bad condition, replace them and the condensers as well.

5. Condenser capacity can be checked with electrical test equipment (if available) in place on the machine, provided the condenser is first disconnected from the primary terminal. Capacitance should be 0.24 MFD. The resistance of the condensers should be in excess of 10 MΩ. A variation of 10% in either reading is allowable.

6. Coils should really be checked on a Kawasaki Electrotester, where a good coil should be able to produce a 6 mm (0.24 in.) spark. If this is not available, however, some clue to coil condition (although not necessarily as conclusive) can be gained by measuring the resistance of the primary and secondary windings with an ohmmeter.

7. With the ohmmeter set to the R x 1 range, check the resistance between the coil yellow/red lead and the green or black lead. Resistance of the primary winding should be about 4 ohms. If less, the winding is shorted; if greater, there is an open circuit. In either case the coil must be replaced.

8. To check secondary winding resistance, check the resistance between the two spark plug leads using the R x 100 scale. Resistance should be about 23K ohms. If resistance is somewhat less than this amount, it is probable that the coil winding has started to break down; if resistance is greater, there is an open circuit. In either case the coil should be replaced.

9. Using the highest available ohmmeter range, check for resistance between the yellow/red lead and the coil core and between one of the spark plug leads and the core. Resistance in each case should be infinite. If there is any reading, replace the coil.

10. Check the condition of the spark plug leads and replace the coil if the leads are in any way damaged.

ELECTRONIC IGNITION

Ignition Coils

1. The most reliable check of ignition coil condition is carried out on a Kawasaki Electrotester if available. The coils should be able to produce a 7 mm arc.

If an Electrotester is not available, check the coils with an ohmmeter as follows.

2. Remove the spark plug caps. Connect the ohmmeter across each pair of spark plug leads. This checks the secondary winding resistance which should be 12–18 K ohms.

3. Disconnect the low tension leads from the coil and check resistance across the coil's low tension terminals. It should be 1.8–2.7 ohms.

If both resistance checks are not within specification, the coil must be replaced.

Pick-Up Coils

1. Check the resistance between the black lead and the blue lead and between the yellow lead and red lead. In both cases, resistance should be 360–540 ohms.

2. Check resistance between each lead and ground on the engine using the meter's highest scale. Resistance must be infinite.

3. If any resistance readings are not within these specifications, the pick-up coil(s) are defective.

IC Igniter

Check the IC Igniter circuitry with an ohmmeter according to the accompanying chart. Replace the unit if all meter readings are not in accordance with the chart.

Resistance readings are measured on the Kawasaki Hand Tester and may vary if another instrument is used. However, they should be consistent in any case.

STARTING SYSTEM

The starting system consists of the starter motor and clutch, the solenoid, the handlebar-mounted starter button, and clutch-operated lockout switch, which prevents starter operation unless the clutch is disengaged.

When the clutch lever is pulled in, and the starter button is pushed, battery current activates the starter solenoid, sending current directly from the battery to the starter motor and turning the engine over.

The starting system is quite reliable and it is unlikely that major problems will arise.

Testing

1. If the starter motor spins, but the engine does not, suspect the starter motor clutch.

2. If the engine turns over very slowly, the problem may be a low battery, too thick oil usually caused by extremely low temperatures, or a defective starter motor.

3. If the engine does not turn over at all, turn on the headlight, pull in the clutch, and hit the starter button. If the headlight retains its brightness, the starter motor is not drawing current, and the trouble may be confined to the starter button, lockout switch, wiring and wiring connections, or a defective starter motor solenoid. If the headlight dims, this indicates that the motor is drawing current, and the trouble may be a low battery or a defective starter motor. Check the battery as outlined in Chapter 2, "Maintenance."

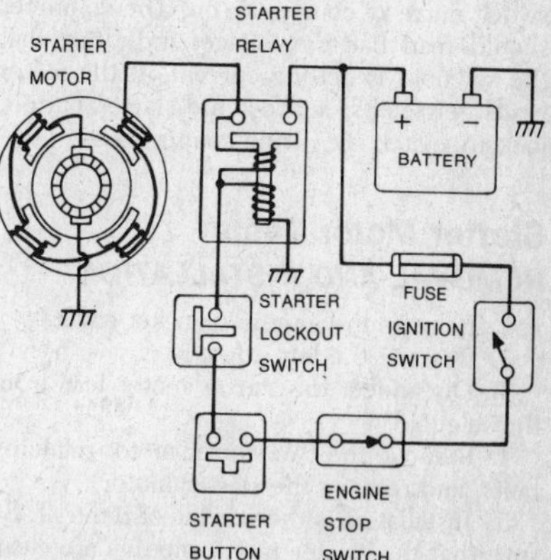

Starter motor circuit

Solenoid Test

1. Disconnect the two high-tension leads from the starter solenoid and connect an ohmmeter set to the R x l scale across the terminals.

2. With the ignition switch on, pull in the clutch and hit the starter button. The ohmmeter should read zero ohms. The solenoid should make a clicking sound as well. If a click is heard, but resistance does not read zero, the solenoid is defective and must be replaced.

3. Disconnect the two low-tension solenoid leads (black and yellow/red) and measure the resistance across them. It should be close to zero ohms. If it is not, the solenoid is defective and must be replaced.

4. If the solenoid checks out according to the above tests, but still will not work, check that it is getting current by connecting a 30v DC voltmeter across the black and yellow/red leads from the wiring harness. Pull the clutch

Checking secondary winding resistance

Meter Range	Connections	Location	Reading*
x 1 kΩ	Meter (+) → Black/Yellow Meter (–) → Black, Green	At the 4-pin connector for the ignition coils	∞
x 100 Ω	Meter (+) → Black, Green Meter (–) → Black/Yellow	"	200 ~ 500 Ω
	Meter (+) → Yellow/Red Meter (–) → Black/Yellow	"	200 ~ 600 Ω
	Meter (+) → Black/Yellow Meter (–) → Yellow/Red	"	300 ~ 700 Ω
x 1 kΩ	Meter (+) → Blue (Red) Meter (–) → Black (Yellow)	At the 4-pin connector for the pick-up coils	25 ~ 45 kΩ
	Meter (+) → Black (Yellow) Meter (–) → Blue (Red)	"	20 ~ 40 kΩ

IC Igniter test chart

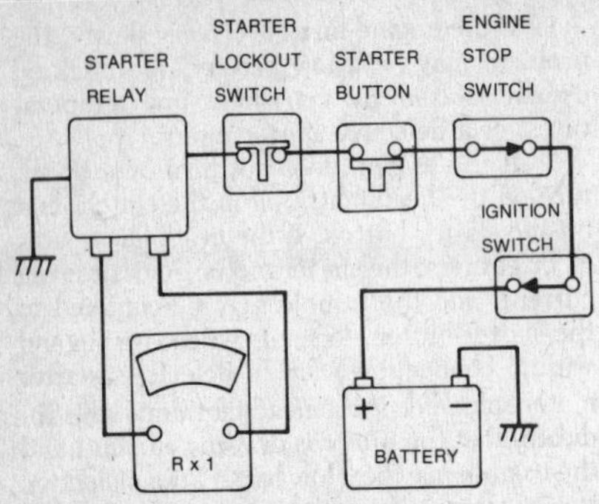

Checking the relay (solenoid)

lever and hit the starter button. The ignition switch must, of course, be on. The voltmeter should read battery voltage, indicating that the solenoid is getting current. If the meter reads zero volts, suspect the starter button, lockout switch, or wiring connections.

Starter Motor Tests

REMOVAL AND INSTALLATION

1. Remove the engine sprocket cover.
2. Remove the left side cover.
3. Disconnect the starter motor lead from the solenoid.
4. Remove the two starter motor retaining bolts, and remove the starter motor.
5. Installation is the reverse of removal. Be sure that the starter motor mounts are clean (this is an electrical ground) and that the starter motor o-ring is in good condition.

INSPECTION

1. The starter motor can be disassembled after removing the two long screws and separating the components.
2. Check carbon brush length. Standard brush length is 12–13 mm (0.47–0.51 in.). The brushes must be replaced if their measured length is less than 6 mm (0.24 in.).
3. Brush springs should be checked. Spring tension should be 560–680 gr, but they may be considered serviceable if they will hold the brushes firmly in place.
4. Clean the commutator surface thoroughly and polish it with fine emery cloth. Check mica undercut depth. Standard depth is 0.5–0.8 mm (0.020–0.032 in.). The armature should be replaced if the depth is less than 0.2 mm (0.008 in.).
5. Measure the resistance between each of the commutator segments using the lowest ohmmeter scale. Resistance should be zero. If any of the tests shows resistance, the windings may be open and the armature must be replaced.

Checking for continuity between the commutator segments

6. Using the highest ohmmeter range, measure the resistance between the commutator and the armature shaft. Resistance must be infinite. Any reading indicates a short and necessitates replacing the armature.
7. To check the field coils, measure the resistance between the starter motor terminal and the positive side carbon brush. Resistance must be close to zero. If it is not, there may be an open circuit in the field coils and the yoke assembly must be replaced.

Checking for field coil continuity

8. Using the highest meter scale, measure the resistance between the positive side brush and the starter motor body. Resistance must be infinite. If there is continuity, this indicates a short in the field coils, and the yoke assembly must be replaced.
9. To check the starter clutch, turn the idler gear by hand. When viewed from the left side of the engine, the idler gear should turn counterclockwise freely, but should not turn clockwise. If operation is not correct, disassemble the starter clutch and check for worn or damaged parts.
10. When assembling the starter motor, align the notch on the end plate with the tongue on the housing, and align the mark on the end covers with the lines on the housing.

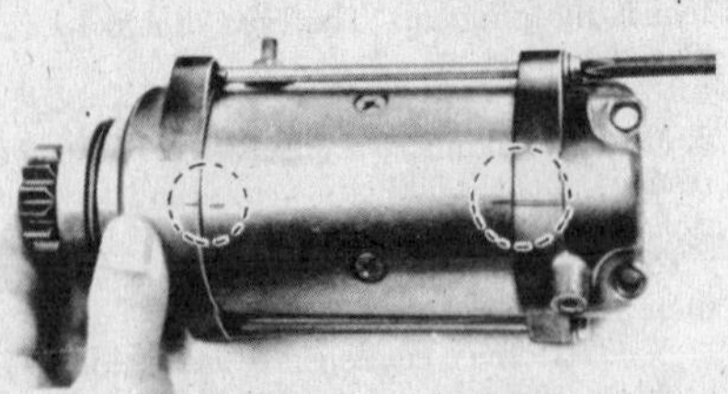

When assembling the starter motor, align the marks

Starter Lockout Switch

1. Remove the gas tank. Disconnect the two lockout switch black leads.
2. Connect an ohmmeter set to the R x 1 scale across the switch leads and pull in the clutch lever. The meter should read zero ohms. If it does not, the switch is defective and must be replaced.

HEADLIGHT

Removal

1. Remove the two retaining screws and pull the headlight out of the shell.
2. Disconnect the socket from the headlight.
3. Remove the pivot screws and nuts. Remove the rubber dampers.
4. Remove the beam horizontal adjusting screw. A nut, spring seat, and spring will come off as well.
5. Separate the outer and inner rims.
6. Remove the two screws to separate the beam unit from the inner rim and mounting rim.

Installation

1. Install the sealed beam unit in the mounting rim fitting the raised portion into

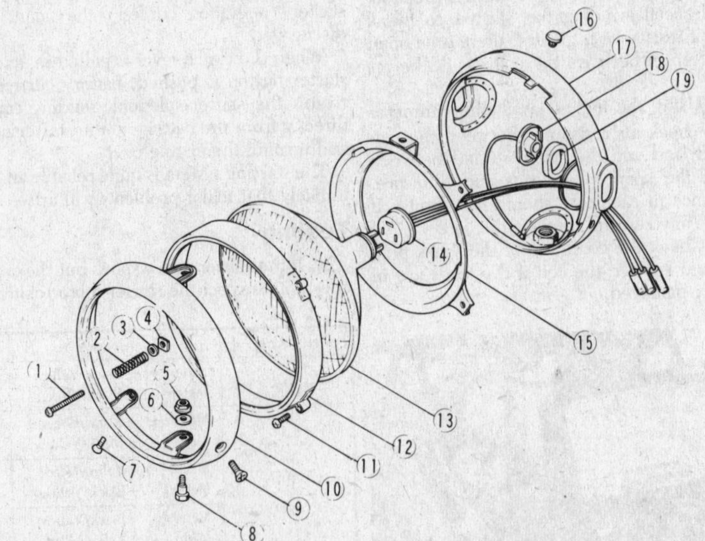

1. Adjusting screw
2. Spring
3. Spring seat
4. Nut
5. Nut
6. Rubber damper
7. Screw
8. Pivot screw
9. Retaining screw
10. Outer rim
11. Screw
12. Inner rim
13. Sealed beam unit
14. Socket
15. Mounting rim
16. Plug
17. Housing
18. Collar
19. Damper

Headlight components

the holders. The "top" of the beam (which is so marked) must be in that position.

2. Note that the spring seat on the horizontal adjusting screw goes between the spring and the bracket.

3. Adjust the horizontal beam after installation.

ELECTRICAL SWITCHES

Switches can be checked with an ohmmeter or a continuity light. In all cases, check the appropriate bulbs first.

Ignition Switch

KZ650-B

1. Disconnect the 4-pin connector inside the headlight shell.

2. With the ignition switch in the "off" position, there should not be continuity between any of the wires.

3. With the ignition switch in the "on" position, there should be continuity between the white and brown wires, and between the blue and the red wires.

4. In the "park" position, there should be continuity between the white and the red wires.

5. If the swtich fails any of the above tests, replace it.

KZ650-C/D AND LATER, KZ750

1. Disconnect the 6-pin connector inside the headlight shell.

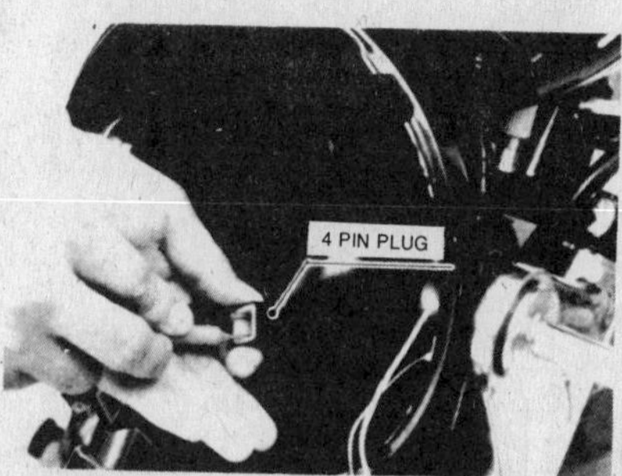

Checking the ignition switch

2. With the switch in the "off" position, there should not be continuity between any of the wires.

3. With the switch in the "on" position, there should be continuity between the white and brown wires (or between the white, brown, and yellow on later models), between the blue and red wires, and between the white and orange/green wires.

4. With the switch in the "park" position, there should be continuity between the white and red wires and between the white and orange/green wires.

5. If the switch fails any of the above tests, replace it.

Headlight Switch

KZ650-B

1. Remove the gas tank. Disconnect the brown, blue/white, and brown/white leads going to the switch.

2. With the switch "off," there should be no continuity.

3. With the switch "on," there should be continuity between all three leads.

4. If the switch fails the test, disassemble it and clean the contacts. If this fails to restore normal operation, the switch should be replaced.

KZ650-C/D

1. Remove the gas tank. Disconnect the brown, brown/white, and blue/white leads going to the switch.

2. With the switch in the "off" position, there should be continuity between the brown/white and the blue/white leads.

3. With the switch in the "on" position, there should be continuity between all three leads.

4. If the switch fails the test, disassemble it and clean the contacts. If this fails to restore normal operation, the switch should be replaced.

Dimmer Switch

1. Remove the gas tank. Disconnect the red/black, blue, and red/yellow leads from the switch.

2. With the switch in the "hi" position, there should be continuity between the red/black and the blue leads.

3. With the switch in the "low" position, there should be continuity between the blue and the red/yellow leads.

4. If the switch fails to operate normally, disassemble it and clean the contacts. If this does not restore proper operation, replace the switch.

Front Brake Light Switch

1. Disconnect the wires and check for continuity across the switch terminals when the brake lever is pulled. If there is no continuity, replace the switch.

CAUTION: *When removing the switch, be careful of spilled brake fluid. Use a non-permanent thread-locking compound on the switch threads, but keep it away from the lower fourth of the threads to avoid contaminating the brake fluid. Bleed the system after installing the new switch.*

Rear Brake Light Switch

1. Disconnect the two leads from the switch.

2. Check for continuity between the two switch leads when the pedal is depressed. If there is no continuity, replace the switch.

Brake Light Failure Indicator Switch

1. Turn on the ignition. Apply and release either brake. The indicator light should go on when the brake light does, and go off when the brake light does.

2. Remove the brake light bulb. The indicator bulb should go on when the brake is applied, and it should flash when the brake is released.

3. If the brake light failure indicator switch does not behave in the prescribed manner, check all wiring connections. If they are sound, replace switch.

Turn Signals

KZ650-B

1. If both left and right turn signals fail to come on at all, first check the battery. If the battery is satisfactory, proceed to check the relay.

2. Disconnect the relay leads and check for continuity across the terminals. Resistance should be zero. If resistance is more than this, replace the relay.

3. If the relay is satisfactory, use a 30 v DC voltmeter, connecting the positive meter lead to the brown relay lead and the negative meter lead to the orange relay lead. With the ignition switch "on," turn the turn signal switch to the "R" and "L" positions. The voltmeter should read battery voltage in either position. If it does not, check the wiring connections, fuse, or ignition switch. If battery voltage is read, but the turn signals still do not work, check all writing connection.

4. If the left and right turn signals do come on, but will not flash or flash very slowly, first check that the battery is not low. Check that all wiring connections are clean and tight. Check that all of the turn signal bulbs are the correct wattage. If all of these are correct, replace the relay.

5. If one light on one side comes on and will not blink, either the other light on that side is burned out or is not the correct wattage, or the wiring is broken or improperly connected.

6. If neither light on one side comes on, both bulbs on that side are burned out, or the turn signal switch is defective.

7. If the turn signal bulbs flash too quickly, and this occurs on one side only, the bulbs on that side are of too high a wattage. If both sides flash too quickly, it may indicate that the battery is being overcharged (check the voltage regulator), or that the turn signal relay is defective.

KZ650-C/D AND LATER

1. If neither the left nor the right turn signals come on at all, check that battery voltage is normal.

2. Remove the left side cover. Disconnect the brown lead and the relay diode from the turn signal relay and check for continuity between the relay terminals. Resistance should be zero ohms. If there is any resistance noted, replace the relay.

3. If the relay is satisfactory, disconnect the relay diode from the orange lead. Set the ohmmeter to the R x 10 or R x 100 range. Check for resistance in both directions across the diode. Resistance should be relatively low in one direction. If resistance is low or high in both directions, replace the diode.

4. If both relay and diode are satisfactory, use a 20v DC voltmeter and connect the positive meter lead to the brown relay lead, and the negative meter lead to the orange lead. With the ignition switch on and the hazard switch off, turn the turn signal indicator switch to the "R" and "L" positions. In each case, the meter should indicate battery voltage. If it does not, check the fuse, the ignition switch, and the wiring. If battery voltage is obtained, but the turn signals will still not work, check all wiring connections.

5. If both left and right turn signals come and stay on or flash slowly, check that battery voltage is normal. Check all wiring connections. Check that the turn signal and indicator

bulbs are of the correct wattage. If all of the above points are correct, replace the relay.

6. If one light on one side comes on and will not blink, either the other light on that side is burned out or is not the correct wattage, or the wiring is broken or improperly connected.

7. If neither light on one side comes on, both bulbs on that side are burned out, or the turn signal switch is defective.

8. If the turn signal bulbs flash too quickly, and this occurs on one side only, the bulbs on that side are of too high a wattage. If both sides flash too quickly, it may indicate that the battery is being overcharged (check the voltage regulator), or that the turn signal relay is defective.

Hazard Circuit

1. If failure occurs, first check the ignition switch and turn signal circuits as outlined above.

2. Remove the gas tank. Disconnect the grey and green hazard switch leads.

3. Set a DC voltmeter to the 20v range, and connect the positive meter lead to the grey lead from the left switch housing, and the negative meter lead to the other grey lead. With the hazard switch on, and the turn signal switch off, turn the ignition switch to the "on" and then to the "park" positions. The meter should read battery voltage.

4. Connect the voltmeter to the green lead and repeat the test. The same result should be obtained.

5. If battery voltage is not obtained, the fuse, hazard switch or wiring connections are at fault.

6. To check the switch itself, disconnect the orange/green, green, and grey hazard switch leads under the gas tank. When the switch is "off" there should be no continuity between the leads. When the switch is "on," there should be continuity between all three of the leads. If this is not the case, replace the switch.

7. Remove the right side cover and disconnect the hazard relay leads. Check the resistance across the relay terminals. It should be 60 ohms. If the measure resistance is not in this range, replace the relay.

Horn

1. If the horn fails to sound, check that the battery is not too low.

2. With an ohmmeter set on the R x 1 range, disconnect the horn wires and check for continuity across the horn terminals. Resistance should be zero. If any resistance is noted, replace the horn.

3. If horn resistance is satisfactory, connect a voltmeter across the horn wires, and with the ignition on, push the horn button. When this is done, the meter should read battery voltage. If it does, replace the horn. If not, check the fuse, ignition switch, and wiring connections.

Bulb Chart①

Headlight	50/35W
Tail/Brake light	8/27W
Speedometer lights	3.4W
Tachometer lights	3.4W
Neutral indicator light	3.4W
High beam indicator	3.4W
Turn signals	
KZ650-B, front and rear	23W
Other models, front	8/23W
rear	23W
Turn signal indicators	3.4W
Oil pressure indicator	3.4W
Brake light failure indicator	3.4W

① All 12v

WIRING DIAGRAMS

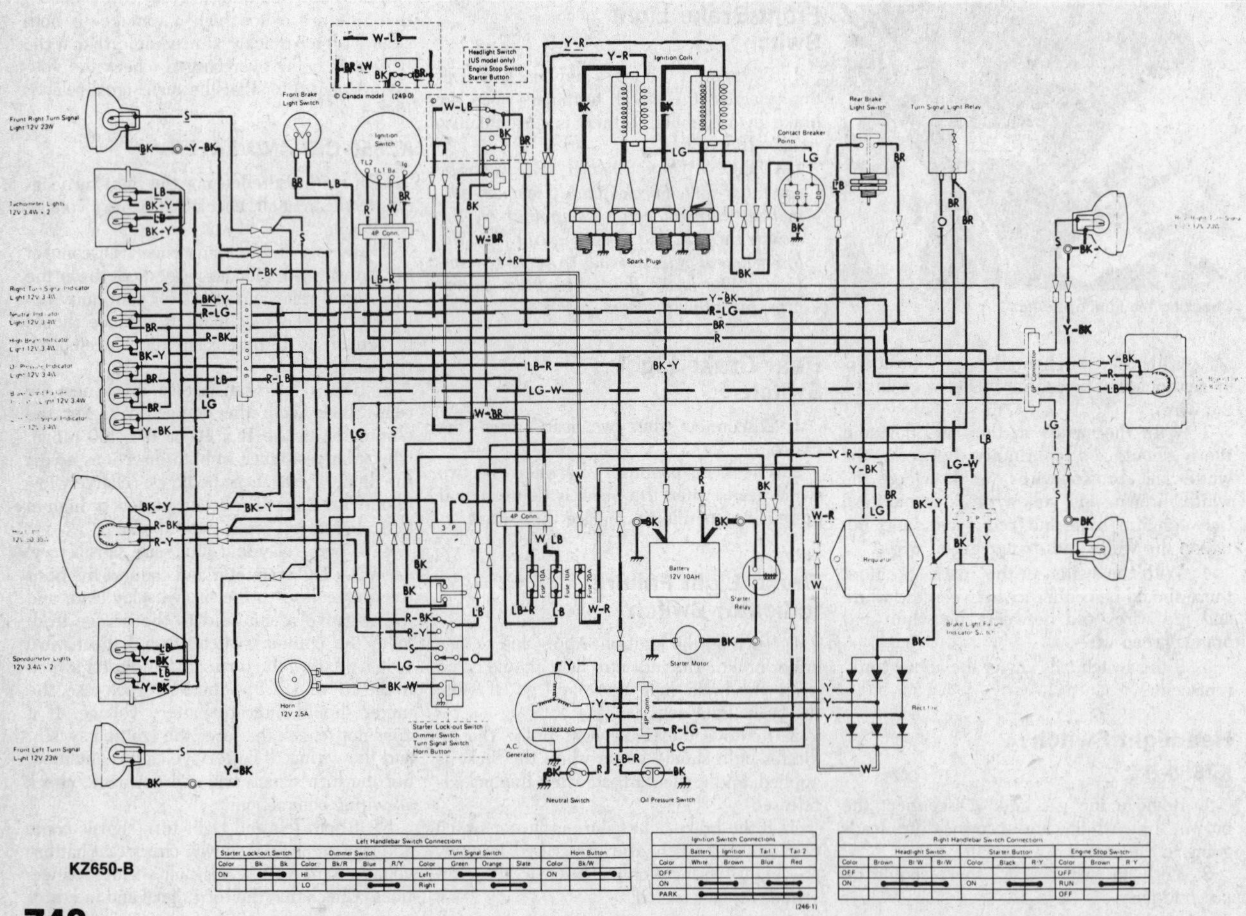

KZ650-B

WIRING DIAGRAMS

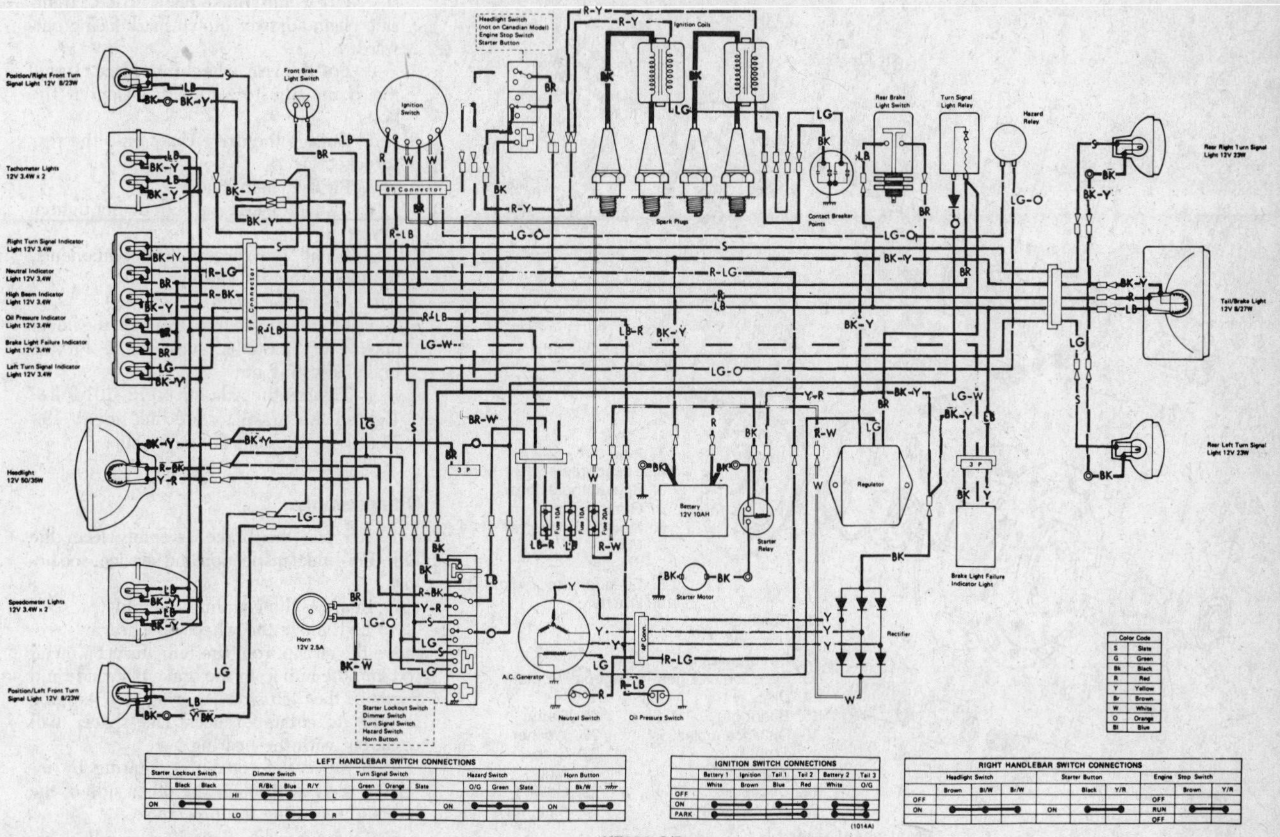

Color Code	
S	Slate
G	Green
Bk	Black
R	Red
Y	Yellow
Br	Brown
W	White
O	Orange
Bl	Blue

LEFT HANDLEBAR SWITCH CONNECTIONS

Starter Lockout Switch		
	Black	Black
ON	●	●

Dimmer Switch			
	R/Bk	Blue	R/Y
HI	●	●	
LO		●	●

Turn Signal Switch			
	Green	Orange	Slate
L	●	●	
R		●	●

Hazard Switch			
	O/G	Green	Slate
ON	●	●	●

Horn Button		
	Bk/W	Ground
ON	●	●

IGNITION SWITCH CONNECTIONS

	Battery 1	Ignition	Tail 1	Tail 2	Battery 2	Tail 3
	White	Brown	Blue	Red	White	O/G
OFF						
ON	●	●	●	●	●	●
PARK	●			●	●	●

(1014A)

RIGHT HANDLEBAR SWITCH CONNECTIONS

Headlight Switch			
	Brown	Bl/W	Br/W
OFF			
ON	●	●	●

Starter Button		
	Black	Y/R
ON	●	●

Engine Stop Switch		
	Brown	Y/R
OFF		
RUN	●	●
OFF		

KZ650-C/D

CHASSIS

WHEELS

Front Wheel Assembly

SINGLE DISC BRAKE

Removal and Installation

1. Support the front wheel off the ground by placing a jack or other suitable means of support beneath the engine.
2. Disconnect the speedometer cable from the wheel.
3. Loosen, but do not remove, the four axle clamp nuts. Loosen the axle nuts.
4. Remove the axle clamp nuts, lockwashers, and clamps. Drop the front wheel down and remove it from the motorcycle.
5. Insert a suitably sized wedge of wood between the disc brake pads to prevent their being moved out of position in the event that the brake lever is operated.

NOTE: *Do not allow the brake disc to touch the ground.*

6. Installation is the reverse or removal. Note the following points:

a. Place the wheel in position and gradually lower the motorcycle until the forks engage the axle.

b. Fit the axle caps noting that they *must* be fitted so that the arrow on the caps points towards the *front* of the motorcycle. Install the axle cap nuts loosely.

Correct axle cap installation

c. Turn the speedometer gear housing so that it points towards the two o'clock position. Be sure that the small projection on the housing does not catch on the fork tube.

d. Tighten the axle nuts to 51–65 ft lbs. Turn the speedometer gear housing clockwise until it stops.

e. Tighten the front axle cap nuts *first*, tightening them to 11.5–16.0 ft lbs. Then tighten the rear axle cap nuts. Note that there will be a gap between the cap and the slider at the rear of the slider.

f. Connect the speedometer cable, turning the wheel slowly to fully engage the cable end.

CAUTION: *Do not operate the motorcycle until front brake operation has been checked. Pump the brake several times and then check operation before riding.*

Disassembly

1. Remove the disc-side axle nut and remove the speedometer gear housing.
2. Straighten the tabs on the brake disc washers. Remove the disc bolts, washers, speedometer gear drive holding plate, gear drive, and the brake disc.
3. Pull out the axle. Remove the collar.
4. Remove the screws and washers and the hub cap.
5. Use a small screwdriver or a hooked tool and pry out the grease seal. Remove the circlip.
6. Insert a rod into the hub from the speedometer gear side and tap evenly around the circumference of the right-side bearing to remove it from the hub. The bearing spacer will come out as well.
7. Insert the rod into the other side of the hub and tap out the remaining bearing in the same manner.

Assembly

1. Pack the bearings with a good grade of bearing grease. Put a small handful in the hub as well.
2. Use wheel bearing driver or similar tool to drive home one of the bearings. Drive the

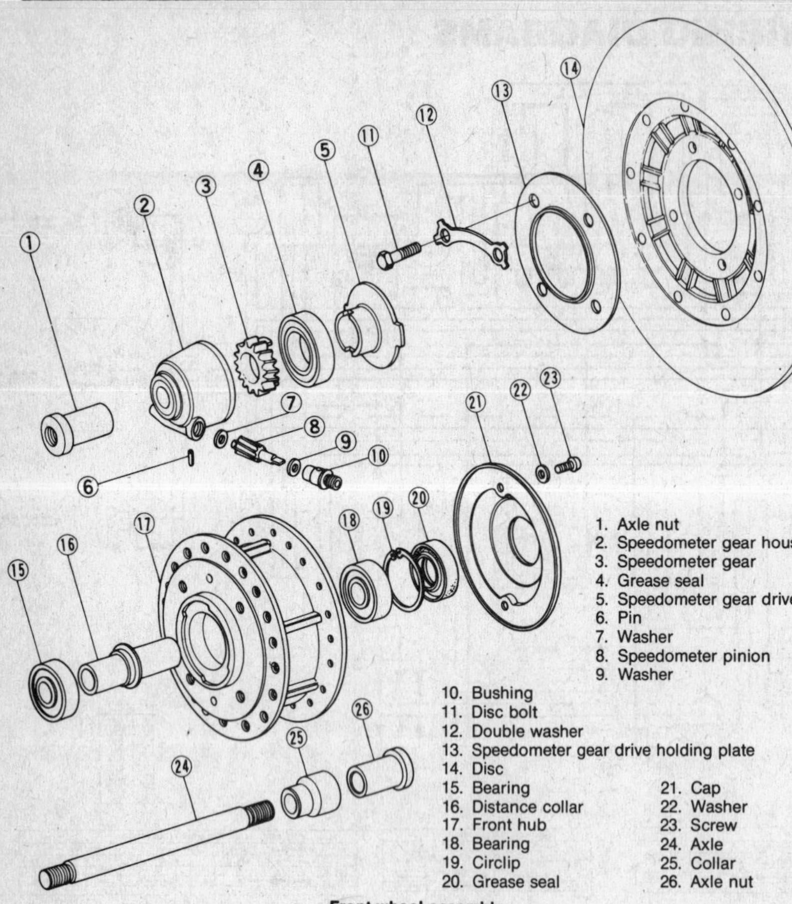

1. Axle nut
2. Speedometer gear housing
3. Speedometer gear
4. Grease seal
5. Speedometer gear drive
6. Pin
7. Washer
8. Speedometer pinion
9. Washer
10. Bushing
11. Disc bolt
12. Double washer
13. Speedometer gear drive holding plate
14. Disc
15. Bearing
16. Distance collar
17. Front hub
18. Bearing
19. Circlip
20. Grease seal
21. Cap
22. Washer
23. Screw
24. Axle
25. Collar
26. Axle nut

Front wheel assembly

bearing in until it is fully seated. Install the spacer and the remaining bearing.

3. Use new grease seals. Seals should be pressed in until the face of the seal is flush with the surface of the hub.

4. Fit the speedometer gear drive into the hub notches. The gear drive holding plate must be installed with the plain side facing the hub.

5. Tighten the disc mounting bolts to 25–33 ft lbs. Bend up the washer tabs against the bolt flats.

6. Clean off any grease or foreign matter which may have gotten on the disc with a non-oily solvent.

DUAL DISC BRAKE

Removal and Installation

Removal and installation of the front wheel is accomplished in the same manner as for the single disc outlined above except that the calipers must be removed from the fork sliders first. After reinstalling the wheel, tighten the caliper mounting bolts to 25–33 ft lbs.

Disassembly

Hub disassembly for the cast-wheel models is the same as for the single disc described above. The only difference is that two brake discs must be removed.

Assembly

Assembly of the hub is the same as outlined for the single disc, above. If wheel bearings of the sealed type are used, install them with the seals facing inwards to keep out dirt and foreign matter.

Rear Wheel Assembly

DRUM BRAKE

Removal and Installation

1. Park the motorcycle on the center-stand.

2. Disconnect the rear brake light switch spring from the brake pedal.

3. Unscrew and remove the adjusting nut from the brake rod. Press down on the brake pedal and disengage the rod from the brake hub lever. Remove the rod spring.

4. Remove the safety clip from the rear torque link bolt on the hub. Remove the nut, lockwasher, and bolt.

5. Remove the cotter pin and loosen the axle nut.

6. Remove the chain guard.

7. Loosen the chain adjuster bolt locknuts on each side and back out the adjusting bolts. Push the wheel forward as far as possible.

8. Remove the bolts and take out the chain adjuster stoppers.

9. Disengage the chain from the rear sprocket. Pull off the wheel.

10. Installation is basically the reverse of removal. Note the following points:

a. If the wheel has been disassembled, check that the coupling collar, coupling sleeve, rubber damper, and brake plate are in place.

b. Insert the rear axle through the left-side chain adjuster (notch mark facing outwards), coupling collar, coupling, coupling sleeve, rear hub, brake plate, spacer, right-side chain adjuster (notch mark facing outwards).

c. Put the rear wheel into place. Install the chain adjuster stoppers. Tighten the bolts.

d. Engage the drive chain onto the rear sprocket.

e. Fit the chain guard.

f. Install the axle nut, but do not tighten it yet.

g. Install the torque link components, tightening the nut loosely.

h. Adjust the chain.

i. Fit the brake rod through the lever (having first installed the spring). Fit the brake adjusting nut.

j. Tighten the axle nut to 72–101 ft lbs. Tighten the brake torque link nut to 19–25 ft lbs and install the safety clip.

Disassembly

1. Remove the brake assembly from the hub. For brake inspection and service, see below.

2. Remove the coupling assembly.

3. To remove the wheel hub bearings, remove the circlip from the hub. Insert a metal rod into the hub from the brake plate side and remove the left-side bearing by tapping around its circumference. The spacer will come out with the bearing.

4. Remove the remaining bearing by inserting the rod through the other side of the hub and repeating the procedure.

5. To disassemble the wheel coupling, remove the coupling collar from the right side and the coupling sleeve from the opposite side.

6. Temporarily fit the rubber dampers to the wheel hub and install the coupling to facilitate sprocket removal.

7. Bend down the washers on the sprocket nuts, and remove the nuts. Remove the sprocket. Remove the sprocket bolts.

8. Remove the coupling from the hub. Using a small screwdriver or a hooked tool, pry out the coupling grease seal. A new seal must be used on assembly.

9. Tap out the coupling bearing using a suitable drift, tapping around the circumference of the bearing from the wheel side of the coupling.

Assembly

1. Pack the coupler bearing with a good grade of bearing grease and install it in the coupler using a bearing driver. Drift the bearing straight in until it is fully seated.

2. Use a new coupler grease seal and press the seal into place until the face of the seal is flush with the coupler surface.

3. Fit the sprocket bolts, the sprocket, and the washers and sprocket nuts.

CAUTION: *Be sure to install the sprocket so that the tooth number stamped on the sprocket faces away from the wheel. If this is not done properly, the chain may jump off the sprocket during operation.*

4. Fit the coupler onto the hub to facilitate tightening of the sprocket nuts. Tighten the nuts gradually and in a cross pattern until they are torqued to 26–32 ft lbs. Bend up the tabs on the washers to secure the nuts.

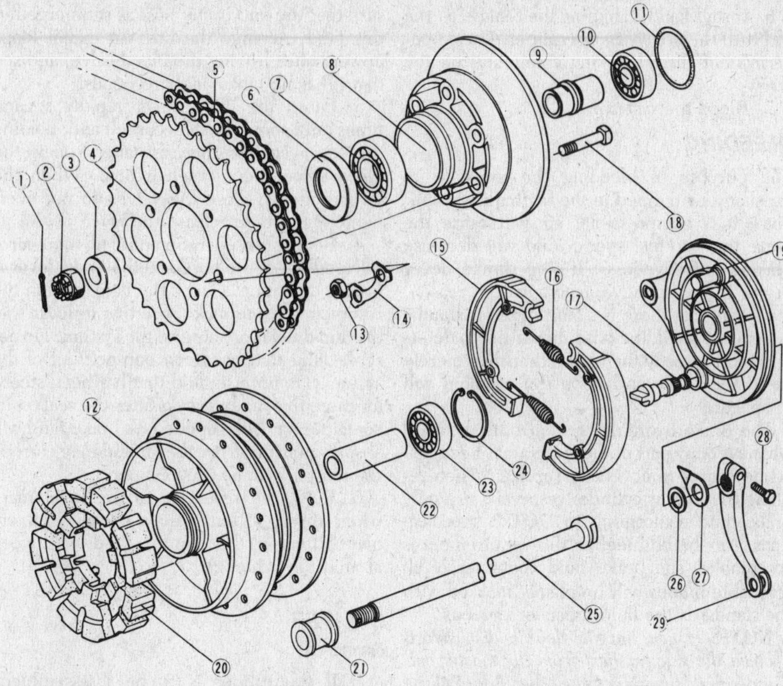

1. Cotter pin
2. Axle nut
3. Coupling collar
4. Rear sprocket
5. Drive chain
6. Grease seal
7. Ball bearing
8. Coupling
9. Coupling sleeve
10. Ball bearing
11. O-ring
12. Drum assembly
13. Nut
14. Double washer
15. Brake shoe
16. Spring
17. Brake camshaft
18. Bolt
19. Brake panel
20. Rubber damper
21. Spacer
22. Distance collar
23. Ball bearing
24. Circlip
25. Axle
26. Dust seal
27. Wear indicator
28. Bolt
29. Brake cam lever

Rear wheel assembly

5. Remove the coupler from the hub and fit the coupling sleeve to the right (wheel) side and the coupling collar to the left side.

6. Pack the wheel bearings with a good grade of bearing grease and place a small handful in the hub as well. Drive them into place with a bearing driver or suitable drift. Do not forget to install the bearing spacer. Drive the bearings into the hub until they are fully seated.

7. Check the hub o-ring for condition and replace it if necessary.

DISC BRAKE

Removal and Installation

1. Park the motorcycle on the center stand.

2. Remove the cotter pin and loosen the torque link nut.

3. Remove the chain guard.

4. Loosen the locknuts on the chain adjuster bolts on both sides and back off the adjuster bolts as far as possible.

5. Remove the axle nut cotter pin and loosen the axle nut.

6. Push the wheel forward as far as possible.

7. Remove the bolts and lockwashers and remove the chain adjuster stoppers.

8. Disengage the chain from the rear sprocket.

9. Pull out the rear wheel and caliper.

10. Remove the axle nut and the left-side chain adjuster. Remove the axle and the right-side adjuster.

11. Remove the coupling assembly and rubber damper from the hub and take out the wheel. Reposition the axle in the swing arm to support the caliper assembly.

12. Place a suitable block of wood between the brake pads to prevent their being knocked out of position if the brake pedal was accidentally operated.

NOTE: *Do not allow the brake disc to touch the ground. Always position the wheel with the disc up.*

13. Installation is the reverse of removal. Note the following points:

a. Clean off the old grease and relubricate the o-ring on the rear hub.

b. Remove the wedge from the brake pads and remove the axle if it has been refitted.

c. Slip the wheel into place, installing the rubber damper and coupler assembly. Note that the coupling sleeve must be in place.

d. Fit the caliper into place over the disc and install the axle. The right-side chain adjuster must be installed so that the washer-welded side is towards the left. The hub components should be arranged in the following order: caliper holder, collar, rear hub, coupling sleeve, coupling, coupling collar, left-side chain adjuster (with the alignment mark facing outwards). Fit the axle nut.

e. Install the wheel onto the swing arm.

f. Install the chain adjuster stoppers. Tighten the bolts.

g. Engage the drive chain onto the sprocket.

h. Install the chain guard. Be sure that the front inside part of the chain guard is inserted between the two holding plates.

i. The remainder of the procedure is the reverse of removal.

CAUTION: *Check brake operation before operating the motorcycle. Pump the brake pedal several times and check efficiency before riding. The brake may not work upon first operating the pedal.*

Disassembly

1. To disassemble the coupling, temporarily install the coupling onto the hub. Bend down the washer tabs and remove the sprocket nuts and remove the sprocket.

2. Remove the coupling from the wheel. Remove the coupling collar from the left and the coupling sleeve from the right side.

3. Using a small screwdriver or a hooked tool, pry out the coupling grease seal. A new seal must be used on assembly.

4. Tap out the bearing from the wheel side.

5. Remove the collar from the disc side of the wheel.

6. Bend down the washer tabs and remove the brake disc bolts to remove the disc.

7. Pry out the grease seal using a small screwdriver or a hooked tool. A new seal must be used on assembly.

8. Remove the circlip.

9. Tap or press on the distance collar to remove one of the wheel bearings. Remove the collar and the remaining bearing by tapping it out.

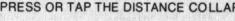

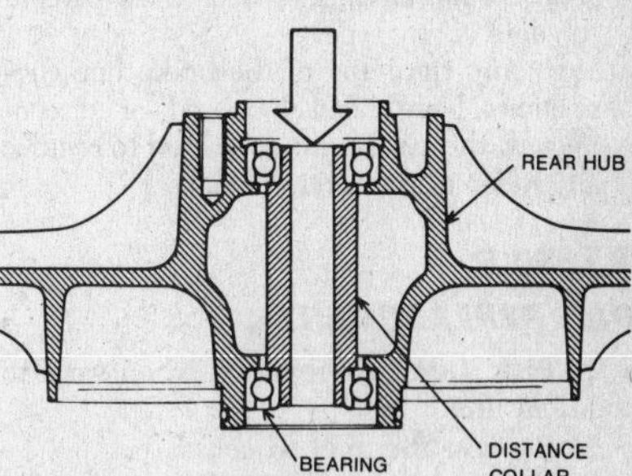

Removing the wheel bearings

should be smooth, noiseless, and free of binding or unevenness. If any of the above conditions exist, both bearings should be replaced.

4. Place each bearing on a flat surface and hold the inner race firmly in place. Attempt to move the outer race up and down. If any play is evident, the bearings should be replaced.

Assembly

1. Pack the coupling bearing with a good grade of bearing grease and install it using a bearing driver or a suitable substitute.

2. Press in a new coupling grease seal until the face of the seal is level with the coupling surface. Grease the seal lip.

3. Install the rear sprocket with the numbered side facing outwards. Tighten the sprocket nuts to 26-32 ft lbs. Bend up the tabs on the washers.

CAUTION: *Be sure that the sprocket is installed with the numbered side facing outwards.*

4. Install the bearings in the hub by driving them in with a bearing driver or suitable substitute. Drive the bearings in until they are fully seated. Do not forget the distance collar. If the bearings are the sealed type, install them with the sealed side facing inward.

5. Install the circlip.
6. Install the grease seal, pressing it in as far as possible.

FRONT DISC BRAKE

Before attempting work on the hydraulic disc brake system, note the following points:

a. Never use brake fluid from an old or an unsealed container. Brake fluid is hydroscopic—it absorbs moisture—and therefore quickly becomes useless unless kept in a sealed environment.

b. Never reuse brake fluid which has been flushed from the system.

c. The system uses DOT 3 brake fluid. This standard is marked on the can. Do not use any other type. Do not mix types or brands of brake fluid, as they may not be compatible.

d. When handling brake fluid, cover all painted parts (such as the gas tank) which may be accidentally damaged by spillage. Brake fluid will remove paint in short order.

e. Keep brake fluid away from the pads and disc surfaces. If there is contact, clean them off immediately with a non-oily solvent. If pads cannot be cleaned, replace them.

f. With the exception of the pads and disc, all internal caliper and master cylinder parts should be cleaned in new brake fluid *only*. Do not attempt to clean these parts in solvents of any type.

g. Any time any of the brake line connections have been loosened or disconnected, the system must be bled to remove air. Refer to the section below.

KZ650-B

PAD REPLACEMENT

1. Pads should be replaced when worn to the limit line.
2. Remove the front wheel.
3. Remove the mounting screw for the inner pad (Pad B) and remove the pad, lockwasher, and metal plate.
4. Move the caliper body as far as possible to the right and remove Pad A. If removal is not possible, apply the brake lever several times until the pad comes out.
5. Install Pad A first. Attach a hose to the bleed valve and run one end into a container. Loosen the bleed valve, and push the piston in by hand as far as possible. Then close the valve. Install the pad. Wipe up any spilled brake fluid immediately.

NOTE: *If a shim is fitted to the pad, install the pad so that the shim is towards the front of the bike.*

6. Install Pad B, aligning the tongue on the pad with the groove in the caliper. Use a non-permanent thread-locking compound on the screw.
7. Bleed the system.

BLEEDING

The purpose of bleeding the brake is to expel any air trapped in the hydraulic system. Since it is compressible, air will cause the brake lever to feel spongy and will decrease braking effectiveness. If the brake lever begins to feel spongy for no apparent reason, it is likely that there is a fault in the hydraulic system. (It would be wise, however, to determine and remedy the fault rather than merely bleed the brake and hope the problem will disappear).

The brake hydraulic system must be bled whenever any part of the system has been disconnected or removed for service. When refilling the master cylinder reservoir, use only brake fluid conforming to DOT 3 specifications. Any brand meeting this requirement is acceptable. The brake fluid container of all reputable brands will be plainly marked with the standards the fluid meets or exceeds.

NOTE: *If you have a double disc setup, bleed the side furthest from the master cylinder first, then bleed the other side. Pulling and tapping on the lines will help expel any air bubbles trapped in the system. If you find that you can't get the system bled properly and the master cylinder has been dry for awhile, the seals inside the cylinder may have become dried and cracked. In this case rebuild the master cylinder.*

1. Top up the reservoir with brake fluid and replace the cap to keep dirt and moisture out and the fluid in. Cover the gas tank with a thick cloth to avoid damage due to spilled brake fluid.
2. Attach one end of a small diameter rubber hose to the bleed valve on the caliper, and place the other end in a jar which contains several inches of clean, new brake fluid. Be sure that the end of the hose is submerged in this fluid. Arrange the hose so that it loops upward after leaving the bleed valve, and see that it has no kinks or sharp bends.
3. Pump the brake lever rapidly several times until some resistance is felt and, holding the lever against the resistance, open the bleed valve about one-half turn. When the lever bottoms, close the valve (do not overtighten) and then release the lever.
4. Repeat this operation until no more air is released out of the hose and the brake lever is firm in operation. Check the fluid level in the reservoir often to make sure that it doesn't go dry and draw more air into the system. Do not reuse fluid that has been pumped out of the system. Do not use fluid that has been stored for more than a few weeks after the seal on its container has been opened, as brake fluid will absorb moisture from the air and may corrode the master cylinder and caliper.
5. Refill the reservoir to the level mark when through (but do not overfill). Avoid overtightening the cap or fluid will weep around the cap edge.

CALIPER

Removal

1. If the caliper is to be disassembled, loosen the caliper holder shaft nuts at this time.
2. Disconnect the brake pipe from the caliper. Plug the end with the bleed valve cap to prevent fluid leakage.
3. Remove the caliper mounting bolts and take off the caliper.

Disassembly

1. Remove the screw for Pad B and remove the pad. Remove the lockwasher and metal plate.
2. Remove the caliper holder shaft nuts and remove the caliper shafts and spacers. This should be done carefully to avoid damage to the dust covers and o-rings.

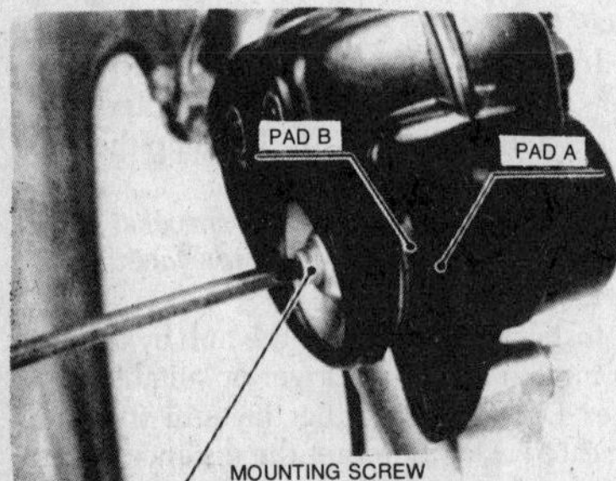

Removing the mounting screw

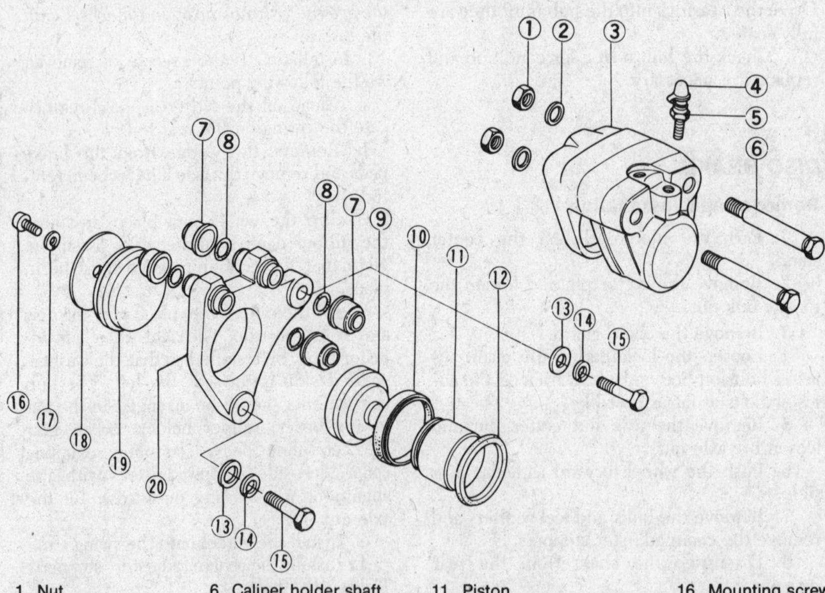

Caliper assembly

3. Remove the caliper holder and take out Pad A.
4. Remove the piston dust seal.
5. Cover the caliper opening with a clean, heavy cloth. Apply compressed air to the brake line fitting to force out the caliper piston. If a compressed air source is not available, the piston can be removed by reconnecting the brake line to the caliper and applying the brake.
6. Using a small, hooked tool, remove the fluid seal, taking care not to damage the bore surface.

Inspection

1. Check piston and caliper bore diameters agaimnst the following:

Bore ID	
Standard	42.850–42.900 mm/ 1.687–1.689 in.
Serviceable limit	42.92 mm/1.69 in.
Piston OD	
Standard	42.788–42.820 mm/ 1.685–1.686 in.
Serviceable limit	42.75 mm/1.68 in.

2. Clean all parts in clean brake fluid. The use of new seals is recommended.
3. The fluid seal should be replaced every other time that the pads are replaced, or if there is fluid leakage around the pad, a problem with brake overheating, there is a difference in the wear of the two pads, or if the seal is stuck to the piston. If the fluid seal is replaced, replace the dust seal as well.
4. Inspect the dust covers and o-rings and replace them if they are cracked or otherwise damaged.

Assembly

1. Lubricate all parts with new brake fluid during the assembly process.
2. Lubricate the cliper shafts with PBC (high-temperature, water-resistant) grease.
3. Assembly is the reverse of disassembly. Install the spacers with the protruding side facing in. Tighten caliper holder shaft nuts after mounting the caliper on the slider.

Installation

1. Tighten the mounting bolts to 25–33 ft lbs.
2. Tighten the caliper shaft nuts to 17.5–20.0 ft lbs.
3. Tighten the brake line fitting to 12–13 ft lbs.
4. Bleed the system after installation of pads and wheel.

MASTER CYLINDER

Removal

1. Read the cautionary notes at the beginning of the "Front Disc Brake" Section.
2. Remove the right-side rear view mirror.
3. Open the bleeder valve on the caliper, and pump all of the brake fluid out of the system.
4. Remove the banjo bolt which secures the brake line to the master cylinder, then remove the rest of the brake line as desired.
5. Remove the clamp bolts which secure the master cylinder, and remove the cylinder.

Disassembly

1. Remove the reservoir cap, diaphragm plate, and diaphragm, then empty out any residual brake fluid.
2. Remove the brake lever, then use either the special tool (Part No. 56019-111) or a suitable substitute to remove the dust cover stopper. Remove the dust cover.
3. Remove the retaining ring using retaining ring pliers, then remove the stopper, piston, primary cup, spring, and check valve from the master cylinder body.

CAUTION: *Do not attempt to remove the secondary cup from the piston as this will damage the cup.*

4. Any remaining components such as the pressure switch, the 3-way fitting, the brake lines and pipe may be removed at this time.

Inspection

1. Clean all parts in clean brake fluid, then blow them dry. Use compressed air to blow out all passages. A clogged relief port will result in the pads dragging on the disc.
2. Inspect the master cylinder bore and piston for signs of wear, rust, pitting, or damage, and replace as necessary. The master cylinder and piston must also be replaced if worn past their serviceable limit.
3. Inspect the primary and secondary cups for signs of wear, damage, rotting, or swelling, and replace them as necessary. Leaking at the brake lever is an indication of bad cups. The piston must also be replaced if the secondary cup is damaged, however, it's best to replace the cups as a set.
4. Inspect the spring for signs of wear or damage, and replace it as necessary.
5. Replace the rubber dust cover if it is damaged or aged.
6. Inspect the fittings, hoses, and pipes for signs of wear, cracking, rust, or other damage and replace them as necessary.
7. The necessary specifications for determining the serviceability of the master cylinder components are as follows:

Cylinder inside diameter	
Standard	14.000–14.043 mm/ 0.5512–0.5529 in.
Serviceable limit	14.080 mm/0.5543 in.
Piston outside diameter	
Standard	13.957–13.984 mm/ 0.5495–0.5506 in.
Serviceable limit	13.900 mm/0.5472 in.
Primary, secondary cup diameter	
Standard	14.650–15.150 mm/ 0.5768–0.5965 in.
Serviceable limit	14.500 mm/0.5709 in.
Spring free-length	
Standard	51.0 mm/2.008 in.
Serviceable limit	48.0 mm/1.890 in.

Assembly and Installation

1. Assembly is basically in the reverse order of disassembly. Make sure that all internal parts are perfectly clean, and liberally coat them all with clean brake fluid before installing.
2. Make sure that the primary cup and the check valve are not installed backwards, and make sure that they aren't distorted or turned sideways after insertion.
3. Use either the factory tool (Part No. 56019-110) or a suitable substitute to install a new retaining ring in its groove in the cylinder wall. The same tool can be used to install the boot and boot stopper.
4. Install the master cylinder so that the small projection is toward the throttle grip. Secure the lower camp bolts first, then secure the upper bolts. The bolts should be torqued to 55–75 in. lbs (0.63–0.88 kg/m).
5. Fill the master cylinder with brake fluid and bleed the system as described in the "Bleeding" section. Do not overtighten the master cylinder cap.

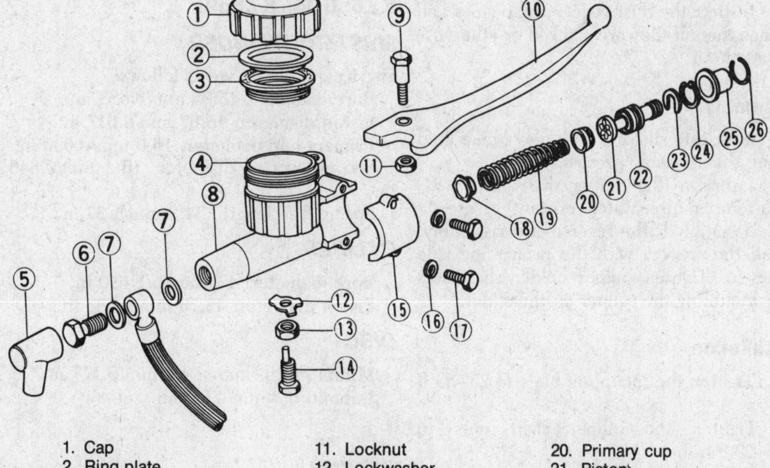

1. Cap
2. Ring plate
3. Diaphragm
4. Reservoir
5. Dust cover
6. Banjo bolt
7. Flat washer
8. Master cylinder body
9. Pivot bolt
10. Brake lever
11. Locknut
12. Lockwasher
13. Locknut
14. Adjusting bolt
15. Clamp
16. Flat washer
17. Clamp bolt
18. Check valve (only on KZ650-C/D)
19. Spring
20. Primary cup
21. Piston
22. Secondary cup
23. Stopper
24. Retaining ring
25. Dust seal
26. Dust seal stopper

Master cylinder assembly

DISC

Removal and Installation

1. To remove the disc, bend down the lockwashers and remove the mounting bolts.
2. To install, tighten the bolts to 25–33 ft lbs.

Inspection

1. Standard disc thickness is 6.9–7.1 mm (0.27–0.28 in.). Serviceable limit is 6 mm (0.24 in.).
2. Max. allowable run-out is 0.3 mm (0.012 in.).

KZ650-C/D

PAD REPLACEMENT

1. Pads should be replaced when they are worn to the limit lines.
2. Remove the caliper mounting bolts and take the caliper(s) off the fork sliders.
3. Remove the mounting screw for the inner pad (Pad B) and remove the pad along with the lockwasher and metal plate.
4. Slide the caliper holder to the piston side and remove Pad A.
5. Remove the cap from the caliper bleed valve and fit one end of a plastic line to it, running the other end into a suitable container.
6. Loosen the bleed valve and push the piston in by hand as far as possible. Close the valve.
7. Install Pad A. Fit the pad so that the shim is towards the front of the motorcycle.
8. Install Pad B, aligning the tongue on the pad with the groove in the caliper. Use a non-permanent thread-locking compound on the pad mounting screw.

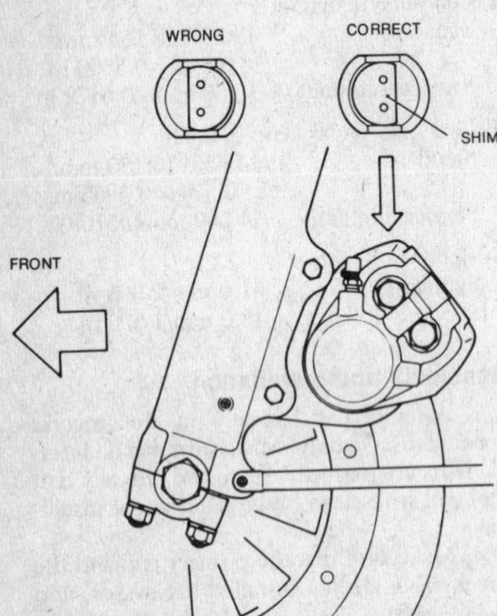

Install the pad so that the shim is towards the front of the motorcycle

9. Install the calipers onto the fork sliders, tightening the mounting bolts to 25–33 ft lbs.
10. Check the fluid level in the master cylinder, and bleed the system.

CAUTION: *Operate the brake lever several times to position the brake pads. Check brake operation before attempting to ride the motorcycle.*

BLEEDING

Refer to the "Bleeding" section for the KZ650-B, above. The procedure is the same.

CALIPER

Removal

1. If the calipers are to be disassembled, first loosen the caliper holder shaft nuts.
2. Disconnect the brake line at the caliper and arrange the line upwards to avoid fluid loss.
3. Remove the caliper mounting bolts and take off the calipers.

Disassembly

1. Remove the screw for Pad B and remove the pad. Remove the lockwasher and metal plate.
2. Remove the caliper holder shaft nuts and remove the caliper shafts and spacers. This should be done carefully to avoid damage to the dust covers and o-rings.
3. Remove the caliper holder and take out Pad A.
4. Remove the piston dust seal.
5. Cover the caliper opening with a clean, heavy cloth. Apply compressed air to the brake line fitting to force out the caliper piston. If a compressed air source is not available, the piston can be removed by reconnecting the brake line to the caliper and applying the brake.
6. Using a small, hooked tool, remove the fluid seal, taking care not to damage the bore surface.

Inspection

1. Check piston and caliper bore diameters against the following:

Bore ID	
Standard	38.180–38.230 mm/ 1.503–1.505 in.
Serviceable limit	38.25 mm/1.506 in.
Piston OD	
Standard	38.116–38.148 mm/ 1.501–1.502 in.
Serviceable limit	38.08 mm/1.499 in.

2. Clean all parts in new brake fluid. The use of new seals is recommended.
3. The fluid seal should be replaced every other time that the pads are replaced, or if there is fluid leakage around the pad, a problem with brake overheating, there is a difference in the wear of the two pads, or if the seal is stuck to the piston. If the fluid seal is replaced, replace the dust seal as well.
4. Inspect the dust covers and o-rings and replace them if they are cracked or otherwise damaged.

Assembly

1. Lubricate all parts with new brake fluid during the assembly process.
2. Lubricate the caliper shafts with PBC (high-temperature, water-resistant) grease.
3. Assembly is the reverse of disassembly. Install the spacers with the protruding side facing in. Tighten caliper holder shaft nuts after mounting the caliper on the slider.

Installation

1. Tighten the mounting bolts to 25–33 ft lbs.
2. Tighten the caliper shaft nuts to 17.5–20.0 ft lbs.
3. Tighten the brake line fitting to 12–13 ft lbs.
4. Bleed the system after installation of pads and wheel.

MASTER CYLINDER

Service procedures for the master cylinder on the KZ650-C/D are the same as for that outlined for the KZ650-B. Refer to that section, above.

Note that master cylinder specifications are different, however. They are as follows:

Bore inside diameter	
Standard	15.870–15.913 mm/ 0.6248–0.6265 in.
Serviceable limit	15.95 mm/0.6280 in.
Piston outside diameter	
Standard	15.827–15.854 mm/ 0.6231–0.6242 in.
Serviceable limit	15.77 mm/0.6209 in.
Primary, secondary cup diameter	
Standard	16.45–16.95 mm/ 0.6476–0.6673 in.
Serviceable limit	16.30 mm/0.6417 in.
Spring free-length	
Standard	39.2–43.2 mm/ 1.54–1.70 in.
Serviceable limit	37.2 mm/1.46 in.

DISC

Removal and Installation

1. To remove the disc(s), remove the wheel, bend down the washer locktabs and remove the mounting bolts.
2. To install, tighten the disc bolts to 25–33 ft lbs. Bend up the locktabs across the bolt flats.

Inspection

The disc can be inspected without removing it from the machine.

1. Check disc run-out with a dial gauge. Standard run-out is less than 0.15 mm (0.006 in.). Maximum allowable run-out is 0.3 mm (0.012 in.). If run-out exceeds this figure, replace the disc.
2. Standard disc thickness, measured with a micrometer, is 4.9–5.1 mm (0.19–0.20 in.). Replace the disc if the measured thickness is less than 4 mm (0.16 in.).

KZ650D4, KZ650F

MASTER CYLINDER

Serviceable limits are as follows:

Bore diameter: 15.95 mm/0.628 in.
Piston diameter: 15.67 mm/0.617 in.
Primary cup diameter: 16.0 mm/0.630 in.
Secondary cup diameter: 16.4 mm/0.646 in.
Spring free length: 34.8 mm/1.37 in.

CALIPER

Bore diameter: 42.92 mm/1.690 in.
Piston diameter: 42.75 mm/1.683 in.

DISC

Minimum thickness: 4.5 mm/0.177 in.
Runout: 0.3 mm/0.012 in.

KZ650H

MASTER CYLINDER

Bore diameter: 12.78 mm/0.503 in.
Piston diameter: 12.50 mm/0.492 in.
Primary cup diameter: 12.8 mm/0.503 in.
Secondary cup diameter: 13.1 mm/0.516 in.
Spring free length: 47.2 mm/1.858 in.

CALIPER

Bore diameter: 42.92 mm/1.690 in.
Piston diameter: 42.75 mm/1.683 in.

DISC

Minimum thickness: 4.5 mm/0.177 in.
Runout: 0.3 mm/0.012 in.

KZ750

MASTER CYLINDER

Bore diameter: 15.95 mm/0.628 in.
Piston diameter: 15.80 mm/0.622 in.
Primary cup diameter: 16.0 mm/0.630 in.
Secondary cup diameter: 16.4 mm/0.646 in.
Spring free length: 34.7 mm/1.37 in.

CALIPER

Bore diameter: 42.92 mm/1.690 in.
Piston diameter: 42.75 mm/1.683 in.

DISC

Minimum thickness: 4.5 mm/0.177 in.
Runout: 0.3 mm/0.012 in.

REAR BRAKES

Rear Drum

REMOVAL

1. Remove the rear wheel. Take out the brake panel.
2. Using rags to avoid getting grease or oil on the brake linings, remove the linings by folding them in towards the center of the brake panel. Disengage the springs and remove the linings.
3. Mark the position of the cam lever relative to the cam so that it can be reinstalled in the same position. Unbolt and remove the lever. Remove the lining wear indicator, dust seal, and the cam.

INSPECTION

1. Measure the inside diameter of the brake drum. Standard diameter is 180.0–180.2 mm (7087–7.094 in.). Replace the drum if the measured diameter is greater than 180.75 mm (7.116 in.).
2. Measure the thickness of the brake linings at their thinnest point. Thickness of new linings is 4.86–5.80 mm (0.191–0.228 in.). Linings should be replaced as a set if either measures less than 2.5 mm (0.098 in.) at the thinest point.
3. Check the linings for uneven wear and sand down any high spots. Clean the linings thoroughly afterwards.
4. Remove any foreign matter imbedded in the linings with a wire brush.
5. Clean the linings with a non-oily solvent to remove any oil or grease. If the linings cannot be cleaned in this manner, replace them.
6. Check the free-length of each of the brake return springs. Standard free-length is 66.0–67.0 mm (2.60–2.64 in.). Replace the springs as a set if either measures more than 69.0 mm (2.72 in.).
7. Measure the diameter of the brake cam where it rides on the brake panel, and measure the inside diameter of the cam hole as well. Replace the cam if the diameter is less than 16.83 mm (0.663 in.). Replace the brake panel if the hole diameter is more than 17.22 mm (0.678 in.).
8. Wipe the old grease from the brake cam and lubricate it thoroughly with a good grade of chassis grease. Fill the cam groove with grease. Grease the brake shoe anchor pin as well. Be sure not to get any grease on the linings.

INSTALLATION

1. Install the camshaft.
2. Fit the return springs onto the shoes and bend the linings over the anchor and cam in the reverse of the removal process.
3. Fit the dust seal and install the wear indicator onto the cam so that it points to the extreme right of the letters "USABLE RANGE."
4. Install the cam lever in the position marked on removal, and tighten the bolt.

Rear Disc (1976–1979)

NOTE: *Before attempting any work on the rear disc brake, read the cautions provided in the beginning of the section "Front Disc Brake," above.*

PAD REPLACEMENT

1. Remove the rear wheel.
2. Unbolt and remove the caliper.
3. Remove the mounting screw for the inner pad (Pad B) and remove the pad along with the lockwasher and metal plate.
4. Slide the caliper holder to the piston side and remove Pad A.

If pad A is difficult to remove, apply the brake pedal to force it out.

5. To install the pads, remove the cap on the bleed valve, and fit a plastic hose, running the other end of the hose into a suitable container.
6. Open the bleed valve slightly and push in the piston as far as it will go by hand. Close the valve.
7. Install Pad A in the caliper holder, aligning the groove of the pad with the ridge in the caliper holder.
8. Install Pad B, aligning the tongue on the pad with the groove in the caliper. Use a non-permanent thread-locking compound on the pad mounting screw.
9. Bleed the system.

Align the tongue on the pad with the groove on the caliper

CAUTION: *Apply the brake several times and check brake efficiency before operating the motorcycle. The pedal may not function the first time it is operated.*

CALIPER

Removal

1. Remove the rear wheel.
2. If the caliper is to be disassembled, loosen the caliper holder shaft nuts at this point.
3. Disconnect the brake line at the caliper and arrange the line at a high spot to prevent fluid loss.

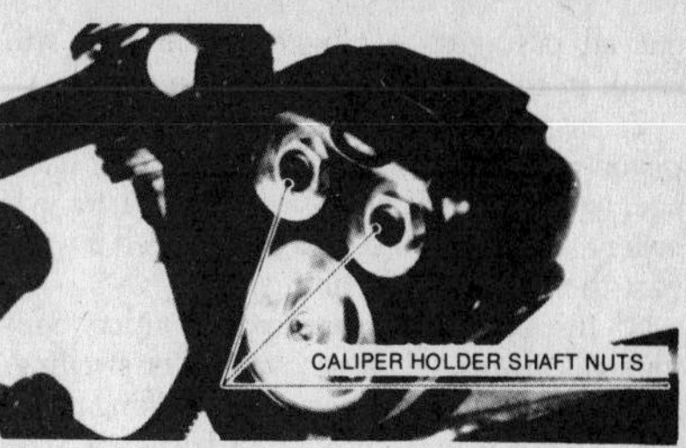

4. Remove the torque link nut at the caliper and remove the caliper from the motorcycle.

Disassembly

Disassemble the caliper in the same manner as described for the KZ650-C front brake calipers, above.

Inspection

1. Measure the piston diameter. Standard diameter is 42.788–42.820 mm (1.6846–1.6858 in.). Replace the piston if the measured diameter is less than 42.75 mm (1.683 in.).
2. Measure the caliper bore diameter. Standard bore diameter is 42.850–42.900 mm (1.6870–1.6890 in.). Replace the caliper body if the bore exceeds 42.92 mm (1.690 in.).

Assembly

1. Lubricate all parts with new brake fluid during the assembly process.
2. Lubricate the caliper shafts with PBC (high-temperature, water-resistant) grease.
3. Assembly is the reverse of disassembly. Install the spacers with the protruding side facing in. Tighten caliper holder shaft nuts after mounting the caliper on the slider.

Installation

1. Tighten the mounting bolts to 21–22 ft lbs.
2. Tighten the caliper shaft nuts to 17.5–20.0 ft lbs.
3. Tighten the brake line fitting to 12–13 ft lbs.
4. Bleed the system after installation of pads and wheel.

MASTER CYLINDER

Removal

1. Remove the right side cover.
2. Disconnect the brake line fitting on the master cylinder. Watch for split brake fluid. Wipe up any spills immediately.
3. Remove the master cylinder mounting bolts and take off the master cylinder.

Disassembly

1. Remove the pushrod dust cover.
2. Remove the master cylinder cap and pour off the brake fluid.
3. Use a thin screwdriver to remove the retainer and take out the piston stopper and piston. Do not remove the secondary cup from the piston as it will be damaged.
4. Remove the return spring and primary cup by applying compressed air to the brake fluid outlet hole.

Inspection

1. Clean all parts in clean brake fluid, then blow them dry. Use compressed air to blow

out all passages. A clogged relief port will result in the pads dragging on the disc.

2. Inspect the master cylinder bore and piston for signs of wear, rust, pitting, or damage, and replace as necessary. The master cylinder and piston must also be replaced if worn past their serviceable limit.

3. Inspect the primary and secondary cups for signs of wear, damage, rotting, or swelling, and replace them as necessary. Leaking at the brake lever is an indication of bad cups. The piston must also be replaced if the secondary cup is damaged, however, it's best to replace the cups as a set.

4. Inspect the spring for signs of wear or damage, and replace it as necessary.

5. Replace the rubber dust cover if it is damaged or aged.

6. Inspect the fittings, hoses, and pipes for signs of wear, cracking, rust, or other damage and replace them as necessary.

7. The necessary specifications for determining the serviceability of the master cylinder components are as follows:

Cylinder bore diameter	
Standard	14.000–14.043 mm/ 0.5512–0.5529 in.
Serviceable limit	14.08 mm/0.5543 in.
Piston outside diameter	
Standard	13.957–13.984 mm/ 0.5495–0.5506 in.
Serviceable limit	13.90 mm/0.5472 in.
Primary, secondary cup diameter	
Standard	14.65–15.15 mm/ 0.577–0.596 in.
Serviceable limit	14.50 mm/0.571 in.
Spring free-length	
Standard	49.1–53.2 mm/ 1.93–2.09 in.
Serviceable limit	46.5 mm/1.83 in.

Assembly

1. Coat all parts with clean, new brake fluid before assembly.

2. Install the return spring. The spring seat side must face outwards.

3. Install the primary cup. Be sure that it is not installed backwards or turned sideways after installation.

4. Install the piston and stopper. Install the retainer in as far as it will go.

5. Install the diaphragm and master cylinder cap. Fit the pushrod dust cover.

6. If the master cylinder plug has been removed, use a new gasket and tighten the plug to 29–36 ft lbs.

Installation

1. Tighten the brake line banjo bolt to 21–22 ft lbs. Be sure that the metal pipe comes to the right side of the stopper on the master cylinder.

2. Bleed the system.

Rear Disc (KZ650D4)

MASTER CYLINDER

Bore diameter: 14.08 mm/0.554 in.
Piston diameter: 13.80 mm/0.543 in.
Primary cup diameter: 14.0 mm/0.551 in.
Secondary cup diameter: 14.6 mm/0.575 in.
Spring free length: 32.4 mm/1.28 in.

CALIPER

Bore diameter: 42.92 mm/1.690 in.
Piston diameter: 42.75 mm/1.683 in.

DISC

Minimum thickness: 6.0 mm/0.236 in.
Runout: 0.3 mm/0.012 in.

Rear Disc (KZ750)

MASTER CYLINDER

Bore diameter: 14.08 mm/0.554 in.
Piston diameter: 13.77 mm/0.542 in.
Primary cup diameter: 14.1 mm/0.555 in.
Secondary cup diameter: 14.5 mm/0.571 in.
Spring free length: 37.2 mm/1.465 in.

CALIPER

Bore diameter: 42.92 mm/1.690 in.
Piston diameter: 42.75 mm/1.683 in.

DISC

Minimum thickness: 6.0 mm/0.236 in.
Runout: 0.3 mm/0.012 in.

FRONT FORKS (STANDARD)

KZ650-B

REMOVAL

1. Support the front wheel of the motorcycle well off the ground by placing a jack or other sturdy support beneath the engine.

2. Remove the front wheel.

3. Remove the fender.

4. Remove the caliper from the fork slider by removing the two mounting bolts. Support the caliper so that it does not stretch the brake line or bend the pipe.

5. If the fork leg is to be disassembled after removal, loosen the top bolt at this point.

6. Loosen the upper and lower triple clamp bolts.

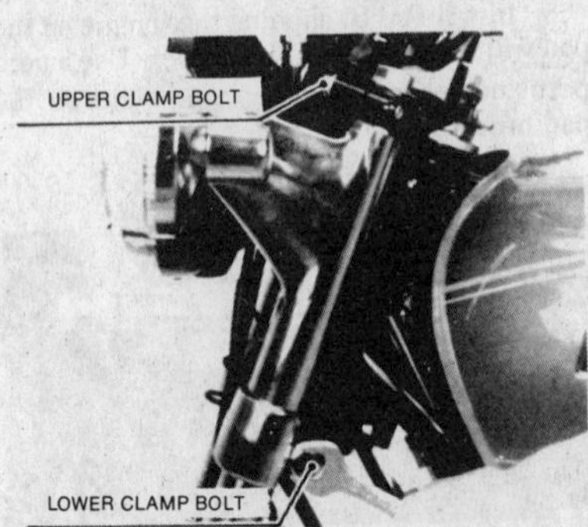

7. Pull the fork leg down and with a twisting motion to free it from the triple clamps. Repeat the procedure with the other fork leg.

DISASSEMBLY

1. Remove the top bolt. Remove the spring seat and spring. Pour off the oil. It may be necessary to pump the slider to expel all of the oil.

2. Remove the dust seal.

3. Use the special tool to stop the cylinder from turning and remove the allen bolt from the bottom of the fork slider.

If the special tool is not available, it may be possible to remove the allen bolt by temporarily installing the spring and top bolt and then loosening the allen bolt.

4. Remove the fork slider from the fork leg.

5. Remove the cylinder base.

6. Remove the retaining ring on the cylinder and slide the cylinder and piston unit and its spring out of the top of the fork tube.

7. Remove the circlip inside the end of the fork tube and pull out the collar, valve, spring, and valve seat.

8. Remove the spring and circlip and pull the piston off the cylinder.

9. Remove the fork slider oil seal retainer using a small screwdriver or a hooked tool. Remove the washer. Pry out the oil seal with a small screwdriver or hooked tool. It will probably be necessary to heat the slider around the area of the seal before removal is possible. New seals must always be used on assembly.

INSPECTION

1. Check the free length of each fork spring. Standard length is 487.5–493.5 mm (19.19–19.43 in.). Replace the springs as a set if either of them measures less than 477.5 mm (18.80 in.).

2. Check the fork tube for damage such as bends or other accident damage. Be sure that the chrome plating is in good condition on the tube, especially in the area on which the oil seals ride. If it is chipped or cracked, replace the tube.

CAUTION: *Do not attempt to straighten crash-damaged or bend fork tubes. Replace them with new ones.*

ASSEMBLY

1. With the piston ring guide (Part No. 57001-161) fit the cylinder and piston assembly into the bottom of the fork tube.

2. Install the collar. Install the circlip in the fork tube, noting that the rounded side of the circlip faces the collar.

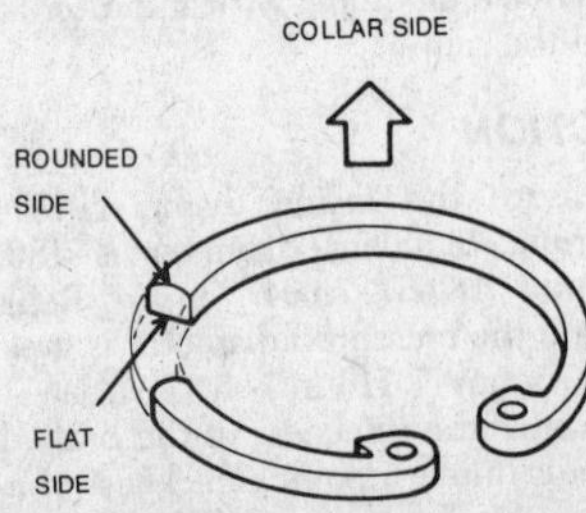

Install the circlip with the rounded side towards the collar

3. Use a liquid gasket material on both sides of the allen bolt gasket. Use a non-permanent thread-locking compound on the allen bolt itself. Tighten the allen bolt to 14.5–19.0 ft lbs.

4. Use new fork slider oil seals, driving the seals straight in until they are seated properly. Oil the lips of the seal before fitting the slider to the fork tube.

5. Refer to the "Maintenance Data" chart at the end of the "Maintenance section for fork oil capacity.

6. When fitting the fork springs, be sure that they are installed with the close coils towards the top.

7. Tighten the top bolts to 18–22 ft lbs.

INSTALLATION

1. Push the fork leg up into the triple clamps until the upper surface of the top bolt flange is flush with the upper surface of the triple clamp.

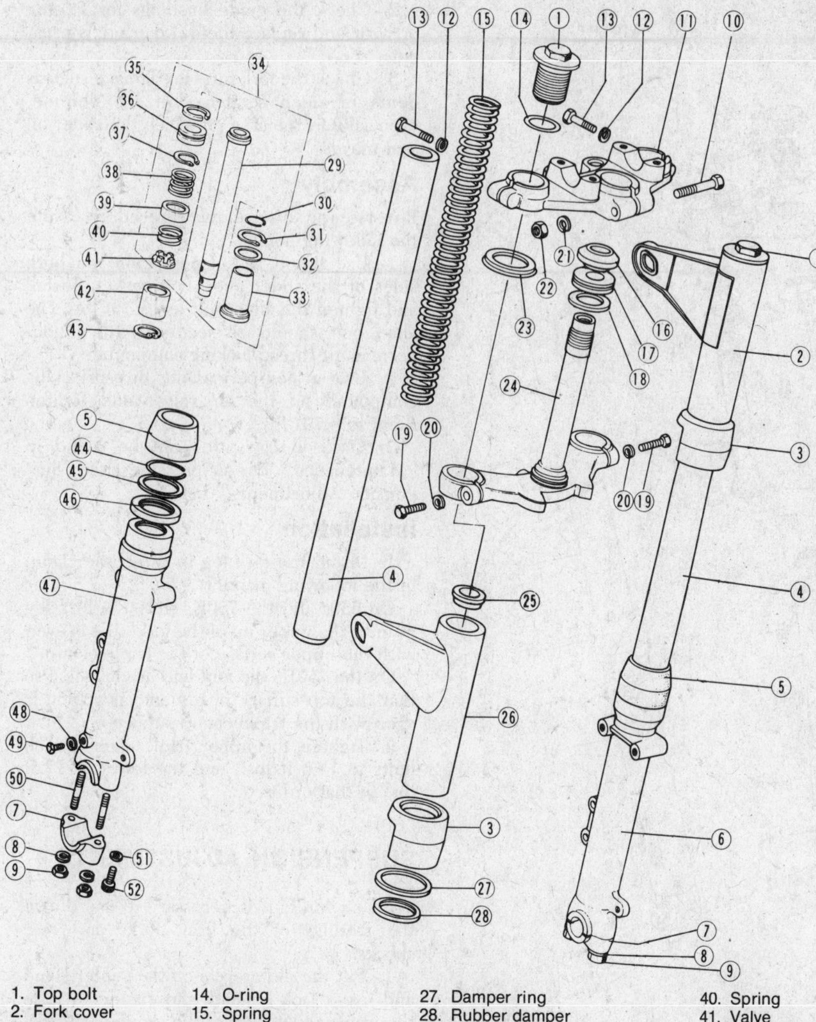

1. Top bolt
2. Fork cover
3. Base cover
4. Inner tube
5. Dust seal
6. Outer tube
7. Axle clamp
8. Lockwasher
9. Clamp nut
10. Clamp bolt
11. Stem head
12. Lockwasher
13. Clamp bolt
14. O-ring
15. Spring
16. Lower inner race
17. Grease seal
18. Washer
19. Clamp bolt
20. Lockwasher
21. Lockwasher
22. Nut
23. Ring cap
24. Steering stem
25. Spring seat
26. Fork cover
27. Damper ring
28. Rubber damper
29. Cylinder
30. Retaining ring
31. Circlip
32. Valve
33. Cylinder base
34. Cylinder and piston unit
35. Piston ring
36. Piston
37. Circlip
38. Spring
39. Valve seat
40. Spring
41. Valve
42. Collar
43. Circlip
44. Retainer
45. Washer
46. Oil seal
47. Outer tube
48. Gasket
49. Drain screw
50. Stud
51. Gasket
52. Allen bolt

Front fork assembly (KZ650-B)

2. Tighten the upper triple clamp bolts to 11.5–16.0 ft lbs. Tighten the lower triple clamp bolts to 25–33 ft lbs.
3. Tighten the top bolt to 18–22 ft lbs., if this has not been done already.
4. Install and tighten the caliper mounting bolts to 25–33 ft lbs.
5. Install the fender and the front wheel.

KZ650-C/D

REMOVAL

1. If the fork leg is to be disassembled after removal, remove the rubber cap from the top of the fork leg and loosen the top bolt.
2. Support the front wheel firmly well off the ground by placing a jack or other suitable support beneath the engine.
3. Remove the front wheel.
4. Remove the fender.
5. Loosen the upper and lower triple clamp bolts. Pull the fork leg down with a twisting motion and remove it from the machine; repeat the procedure with the other fork leg.

DISASSEMBLY

1. Remove the top bolt and take out the spring and spring seat.
2. Pour out and discard the oil. It may be necessary to pump the slider several times to expel all of the oil.
3. Remove the dust seal from the top of the slider.
4. Use the special tool to stop the cylinder from turning and remove the allen bolt from the bottom of the fork slider.

If the special tool is not available, it may be possible to remove the allen bolt by temporarily refitting the spring and top bolt and attempting to loosen the allen bolt.

5. Separate the fork slider from the fork tube.
6. Remove the cylinder base and valve.
7. Slide the piston and cylinder and the spring out of the top of the fork tube.
8. Remove the oil seal retained from the top of the fork slider with a hooked tool. Remove the washer. With a small screwdriver or a hooked tool, remove the slider oil seal. It may be necessary to gently heat the slider in the area around the seal before removing it. New seals must always be used on assembly.

INSPECTION

1. Check the free length of the fork springs. Standard free length is 494.5 mm (19.47 in.). The spring should be replaced if the measured length is less than 485 mm (19.09 in.). Springs should be replaced in sets to ensure equal damping characteristics.
2. Check the fork tubes for bends or other accident damage. Replace the tubes if they are bent.

CAUTION: *Do not attempt to straighten bent tubes.*

3. Check the condition of the chrome plating on the tubes, especially in the area on which the oil seals ride. Scratched or nicked plating may cause oil leaks. If this is the case, replace the tube.

ASSEMBLY

1. Assembly is basically the reverse of disassembly. Note the following points:
   a. Using the special piston ring guide (Part No. 570010161), and turning the fork tube upside down, install the cylinder and piston assembly into the tube from the top end.
   b. Apply a liquid gasket compound to both sides of the allen bolt gasket. Use a non-permanent thread-locking compound on the allen bolt threads, tightening it to 14.5–19.0 ft lbs.
   c. Use new fork slider oil seals. Oil the lips of the seal before inserting the fork tube into the slider.
   d. Refer to the "Maintenance Data" chart at the end of chapter 2 for the correct quantity and grade of oil.
   e. After installing the fork leg into the triple clamp, tighten the top bolt to 18–22 ft lbs.

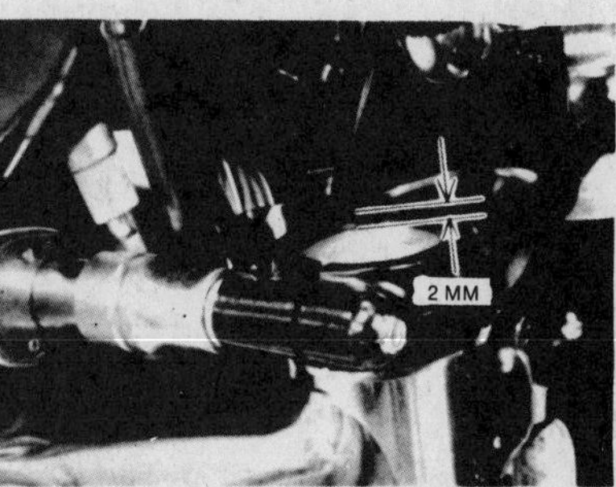

Install the fork tube so that it is about 2 mm below the top surface of the upper triple clamp

INSTALLATION

1. Install the fork leg into the triple clamps until the top edge of the tube is 2 mm below the upper surface of the upper triple clamp.
2. Tighten the upper triple clamp pinch bolts to 11.5–16.0 ft lbs.
3. Tighten the lower triple clamp pinch bolts to 25–33 ft lbs.

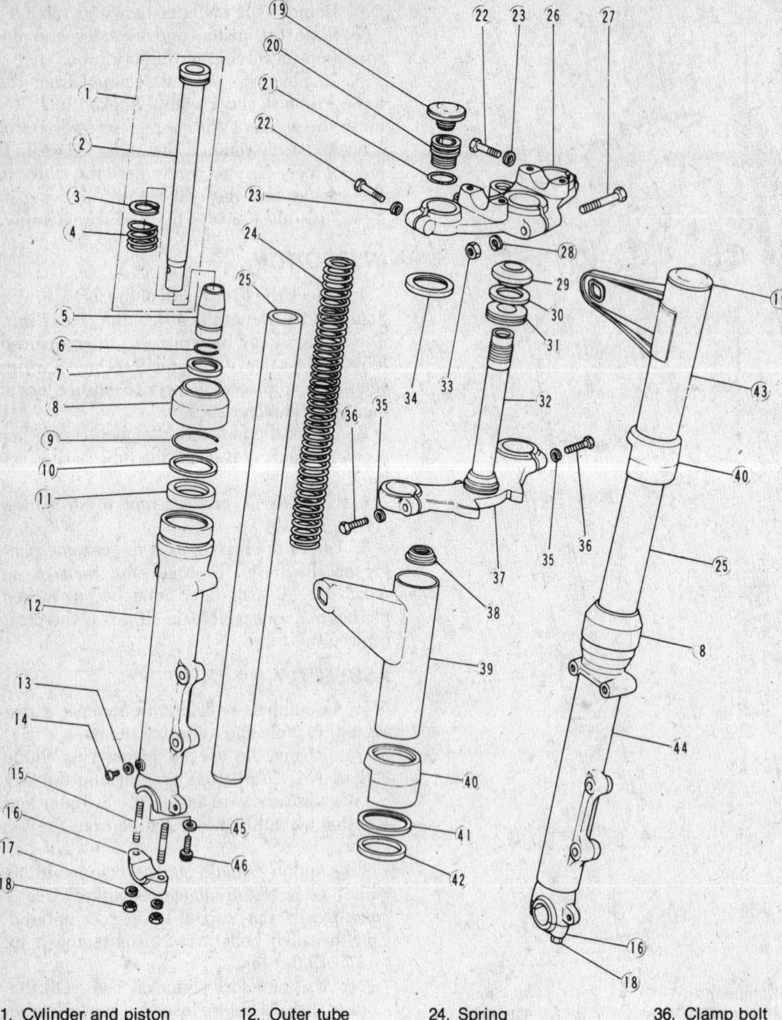

1. Cylinder and piston unit
2. Cylinder
3. Piston ring
4. Spring
5. Cylinder base
6. Retainer
7. Valve
8. Dust seal
9. Retainer
10. Washer
11. Oil seal
12. Outer tube
13. Gasket
14. Drain screw
15. Stud
16. Axle clamp
17. Lockwasher
18. Nut
19. Rubber cap
20. Top bolt
21. O-ring
22. Clamp bolt
23. Lockwasher
24. Spring
25. Inner tube
26. Stem head
27. Clamp bolt
28. Lockwasher
29. Lower inner race
30. Washer
31. Grease seal
32. Steering stem
33. Nut
34. Ring cap
35. Lockwasher
36. Clamp bolt
37. Stem base
38. Spring seat
39. Fork cover
40. Base cover
41. Damper ring
42. Rubber damper
43. Fork cover
44. Outer tube
45. Gasket
46. Allen bolt

Front fork assembly (KZ650-C/D)

4. Tighten the top bolt to 18–22 ft lbs if this has not already been done.
5. Install the fender and the front wheel.

FRONT FORKS (AIR TYPE)

Removal

1. Remove the caliper(s) from the fork leg(s).
2. Remove the front wheel.
3. Remove the fender.
4. Loosen the top plug.
5. Loosen the upper and lower triple clamp bolts. Pull the fork leg down and free of the triple clamps.

Disassembly

1. Remove the air valve and o-ring.
2. Remove the top plug, o-ring, and spring. Pump out the oil.
3. Remove the allen bolt from the bottom of the slider and separate the slider from the fork tube.
4. Remove the cylinder and spring from the top of the fork tube.
5. Remove the seal retainer from the fork slider and pry out the seal. It may be necessary to heat the top of the slider gently to get the seal out. New seals must be used when assembling.

Inspection

1. Measure the free-length of the fork springs and replace both of them if either measures less than the service limit:

KZ650D/F 491 mm/19.3 in.
KZ650H, KZ750E 497 mm/196.6 in.
KZ750H 483 mm/19.0 in.

2. Check the guide bushings for scoring or wear and replace them if damage is present.
3. Check the fork tube for damage such as dents or deep scratches in the chrome, especially in the area on which the slider oil seal moves.

Assembly

Reverse the disassembly procedure. Note the following points:

1. Use liquid gasket compound on both sides of the slider allen bolt gasket. Install and tighten the allen bolt to 16.5 ft lbs. The allen bolt should be secured with a non-permanent thread-locking compound.
2. Use a non-permanent thread-locking compound on the air valves and tighten them to 8.7 ft lbs.
3. Fork oil capacities can be found in "Maintenance." For air pressures, see "Suspension Adjustments," below.

Installation

1. Install the fork leg in the triple clamp in the following manner:

On 650s and the 750E, slide the fork leg in until the upper lip of the fork tube is even with the upper surface of the triple clamp.

On the 750H, the fork legs are installed so that the top surface of the air valve plug is even with the triple clamp surface.

2. Tighten the upper triple clamp pinch bolts to 14.5 ft lbs., and the lower to 27 ft lbs. in that order.

SUSPENSION ADJUSTMENTS

With air forks, it is necessary to coordinate the settings of the front forks and rear shocks.

1. Put the motorcycle on the center stand and use a jack beneath the engine to raise the front wheel clear of the ground.
2. Front forks must be cold when checking air pressure.
3. Pressure must be checked with the special gauge. Tire pressure gauges will give misleading readings.
4. Fork air pressure should be as follows:

H-models	7.1–14.0 psi
Other models	8.5–13.0 psi

5. Fork leg pressures must be within 1.4 psi.
6. Inject air with a pump, but do it slowly. CAUTION: *Pressures exceeding 36 psi may damage the oil seals.*
7. Use only air or nitrogen gas.
8. Rear shocks are adjusted for Spring Force at the bottom and for Damping Force at the top. The settings must conform to the following limits:

Spring Force Setting	Damping Force Setting
1 or 2	1 or 2
2 or 3	2 or 3
3 or 4	3 or 4
4 or 5	3 or 4

STEERING STEM ASSEMBLY

Bearing Adjustment

1. To check bearing adjustment, support the front wheel off the ground. Grasp the bot-

toms of the fork sliders and attempt to move the forks back and forth in line with the motorcycle. Push and pull on the fork sliders. There should be no detectable movement. If there is, the bearings must be adjusted.

Checking for steering stem bearing play

2. Turn the forks slowly from lock-to-lock, again with the front wheel off the ground. Movement should be smooth, silent, and effortless. If any binding or uneven movement is felt, the balls and races are either too tightly adjusted or they are worn. If the steering feels uniformly stiff, the bearings are too tightly adjusted. If any noise is noted, the bearings are damaged or some are missing.

3. With the front wheel off the ground, release the front forks from a few degrees off the centered position. The forks should fall to either side of their own accord. If they will not, the bearings are too tightly adjusted, the steering stem is bent, the races are extremely worn, or some of the bearings are missing.

4. To adjust the bearings, first remove the gas tank. Be sure that the front wheel is firmly supported off the ground.

5. Loosen the lower triple clamp pinch bolts.

6. Loosen the upper triple clamp head pinch bolt, and loosen the steering stem head bolt.

7. Back out the steering stem locknut one or two turns until it turns without resistance using the special wrench.

NOTE: *Do not loosen the locknut more than two turns. To do so risks loosing some of the ball bearings.*

8. Tighten the steering stem locknut to 19.5–24.0 ft lbs. If a torque wrench is not available, turn the locknut until resistance is felt (the locknut becomes hard to turn), then turn it another $^{1}/_{16}$ turn (about 20°).

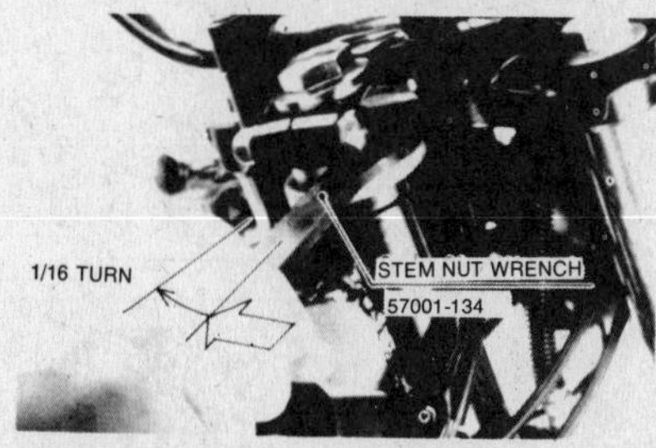

Adjusting the steering stem bearings ($^{1}/_{16}$ turn after the locknut becomes hard to turn)

9. Check that bearing adjustment conforms to the checks outlined above.

10. Tighten the steering stem head bolt to 29–36 ft lbs. Tighten the pinch bolt to 11.5–16.0 ft lbs.

11. Tighten the lower triple clamp pinch bolts to 25–33 ft lbs.

12. Check bearing adjustment. If the bearings still do not function properly, remove the steering stem and check the parts for wear.

Disassembly

1. Remove the gas tank.
2. Remove the front wheel.
3. Remove the handlebars.
4. Remove the headlight. Disconnect the turn signal leads. Remove the turn signals.
5. Remove the headlight shell. Remove the starter locknut switch.
6. Disconnect the tachometer cable at the instrument. Remove the nuts which secure the instruments and remove them.
7. Remove the front fender.
8. Disconnect the front brake light switch leads.
9. Remove the disc brake line joint from the lower triple clamp.
10. Remove the caliper(s) from the fork slider(s).
11. Loosen the upper triple clamp pinch bolts.
12. Loosen the steering stem head clamp bolt and remove the stem head bolt.
13. Tap lightly on the underside of the upper triple clamp with a plastic mallet and remove it.
14. Remove the fork covers.
15. Loosen the lower triple clamp pinch bolts. Pull out the fork legs.
16. Hold up the lower triple clamp and unscrew the steering stem locknut. When the locknut is completely off the stem, carefully lower the stem assembly out of the head lug. Note that some of the balls in the lower race will drop out as the stem is lowered.
17. Remove the steering stem cap and upper inner race and remove the balls from the upper race.

Removing the upper inner race

18. Inspect the bearings and races as outlined below. If replacement of the frame races is required, remove them by driving them out of the frame lug with a drift and hammer.

19. A special tool is required to remove the lower inner race from the steering stem if replacement is required. The race is pressed on. If the race is removed, replace the grease seal beneath it.

Inspection

1. Wash the ball bearings in a suitable solvent. Ball bearing size is ¼ in.

2. Clean all of the old grease from the bearing race surfaces, steering stem, and frame lug.

3. Inspect the bearing race surfaces. They must be clean and smooth and free of any cracks, scoring, rust, or indentations. Run your finger around each of the bearing races. Note any roughness or ripples on the race surface. If any imperfections are noted, both sets of races and all of the balls must be replaced.

4. Check the balls themselves for rust, pitting, scoring, or flat spots. If the balls are found to be defective in any way, the balls and both sets of races must be replaced.

NOTE: *Balls and races must always be replaced in a set because worn races will destroy new balls and worn balls will destroy new races.*

5. Check the grease seal for condition and replace if torn or cracked.

6. Check the steering stem for cracks or a bent condition; this is especially important if the bike has been involved in a spill.

Assembly

1. The frame lug races have been removed, lubricate the new races and drive them into place.

2. Replace the steering stem grease seal with a new one and drive the lower inner race onto the stem.

3. Lubricate the top frame lug race and the lower inner race with a thick coating of a good grade of bearing grease. Install the balls, imbedding them into the grease.

There are 19 balls in the upper race and 20 in the lower race.

4. Install the steering stem into the frame lug, fit the upper inner race and cap.

5. Install and tighten the steering stem locknut to 19.5–24 ft lbs. Check bearing play. Refer to the "Bearing Adjustment" section, above.

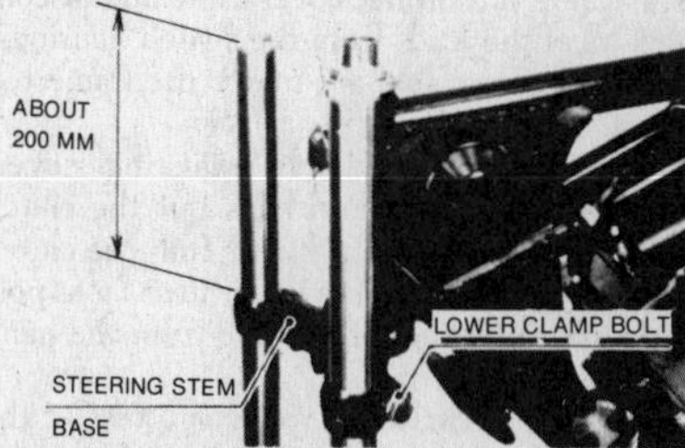

Position the legs so that the tops are about 200 mm (7.9 in.) above the lower triple clamp

6. Install the fork legs. The legs should be positioned so that their tops are about 200 mm (7.9 in.) above the lower triple clamp. Tighten the triple clamp pinch bolts temporarily to hold the fork legs in place.

7. Install the rubber damper, damper ring, base cover, fork cover, and ring cap (in that order).

8. Install the upper triple clamp, the lockwasher, and flat washer (flat side facing down). Screw on the stem head bolt loosely. Be sure that the wiring harness and the cables go in from of the stem head.

9. On KZ650-B models, loosen the lower triple clamp bolts, and align the upper surface of the top bolt flange flush with the upper surface of the upper triple clamp. Tighten the upper clamp bolts to 11.5–16.0 ft lbs.

10. For the KZ650-C/D, slide each fork leg up until the end of the tube is about 2 mm (0.08 in.) below the top surface of the upper triple clamp.

11. Tighten the stem head bolt to 29–36 ft lbs. Tighten the rear clamp bolt to 11.5–16.0 ft lbs.

12. Tighten the lower triple clamp pinch bolts to 25–33 ft lbs.
13. Install the handlebars.
14. Install the master cylinder and calipers.
15. Install the brake line joint. Be sure that the cable guide is included with each bolt. Tighten the bolts to 5.1–6.5 ft lbs.
16. Install the instruments. Be sure that the left switch wiring harness and the right switch wiring harness run between the upper triple clamp and the instruments. Note the rubber dampers fitted both above and below the triple clamp.
17. Afix the instrument cables.
18. Connect the front brake light switch. The wires may be connected to either terminal.
19. Run the plugs and wiring into the headlight shell. Install the turn signals. Connect the turn signal leads. The left turn signal takes the green lead. The right takes the grey lead. Both black/yellow leads are connected to the black/yellow plug.
20. The remainder of the procedure is the reverse of removal.

HANDLEBARS

Removal

1. Remove the mirrors.
2. Remove the gas tank.
3. Disconnect and remove the throttle cables. This is done by running the cable adjusters in as far as possible, splitting the twistgrip, and disconnecting the throttle cables from the drum.
4. Slide the rubber cover aside and disconnect all of the leads from the switch housings. The lead connectors are under the frame top tubes.
5. Remove the clutch adjusting cover. Loosen the locknut and back out the clutch adjusting screw several turns. Run the clutch cable adjuster at the handlebar in as far as possible and disconnect the cable from the hand lever.
6. Using a small screwdriver, press in the starter lockout switch tab which catches in the hole on the underside of the clutch lever holder. Remove the switch.
7. Remove the master cylinder.
8. Remove the handlebar clamp bolts and remove the handlebars.

Installation

1. Run the wiring leads between the upper triple clamp and the instrument holder. Fit the handlebars.
2. Tighten the clamp bolts to 11.5–16.0 ft lbs. The bars should be angled slightly away from the center line of the front forks.
3. Tighten the master cylinder bolts to 4.3–6.5 ft lbs. Note that the clamp is installed with the small projection towards the throttle twist-grip.
4. Connect the wiring. Note that one of the starter locknut black leads is connected to a black lead of the main wiring harness, while the other black lead is connected to the black lead from the right switch housing on the handlebar.
5. The remainder of the procedure is the reverse of removal. Adjust the clutch, clutch cable, throttle cables, etc.

REAR SHOCK ABSORBERS

Removal

1. Park the motorcycle on the centerstand.
2. Remove the mufflers.
3. Remove the grab bar mounting bolt.
4. Remove the cap nut from the top of the shock absorber. Remove the grab bar.
5. Lifting up the rear wheel as necessary, remove the lower shock bolt. Remove the shock.

Inspection

1. The shock absorbers are sealed units, and cannot be disassembled for repair. If defective they must be replaced. Always replace shock absorbers in pairs, even if only one is damaged, to ensure even operation. Riding the motorcycle with unequally operating shocks may cause instability.
2. If the shocks leak oil, or if they were damaged in an accident, replace them. Check for dents in the damper unit, or a bent damper rod.
3. Compress each shock as far as possible and release it. The shock should return smoothly to its full length. If the shock snaps back suddenly, the damper unit is defective and the unit should be replaced.
4. If one shock feels weaker than the other when compressing it, replace both.
5. Check the rubber bushings at either end of the unit and replace them if they are cracked or hardened.

Installation

Installation is the reverse of removal. Tighten the lower shock bolt to 19–25 ft lbs. Tighten the upper cap nut to 19–25 ft lbs.

SWING ARM

Inspection

1. Place the motorcycle on the centerstand.
2. Remove the mufflers.
3. Remove the rear wheel. For disc rear brake models, disengage the brake hose from the swing arm guides and hang or support the caliper so that it does not pull on the brake line.
4. Unbolt the shock absorbers from the swing arm.
5. Check the swing arm by moving it slowly up and down. There should not be abnormal friction.
6. Grasp both swing arm tubes and attempt to move the swing arm from side-to-side. There should be no lateral play.
7. If there is lateral play, or abnormal resistance to vertical swing arm movement, the swing arm bushings should be replaced.

Removal

1. Proceed as outlined above, Steps 1–4.
2. Remove the pivot shaft nut and pull out the pivot shaft.
3. Remove the swing arm from the machine. The dust cover on each side of the swing arm will come off.

Disassembly

1. Swing arm bushes, once removed, must be replaced with new ones. Have the new ones on hand prior to disassembly. If the condition of the bushes is questionable, measure their inside diameter in place on the swing arm.
2. Remove the safety clip from the torque link bolt. Remove the nut and bolt and separate the torque link from the swing arm.

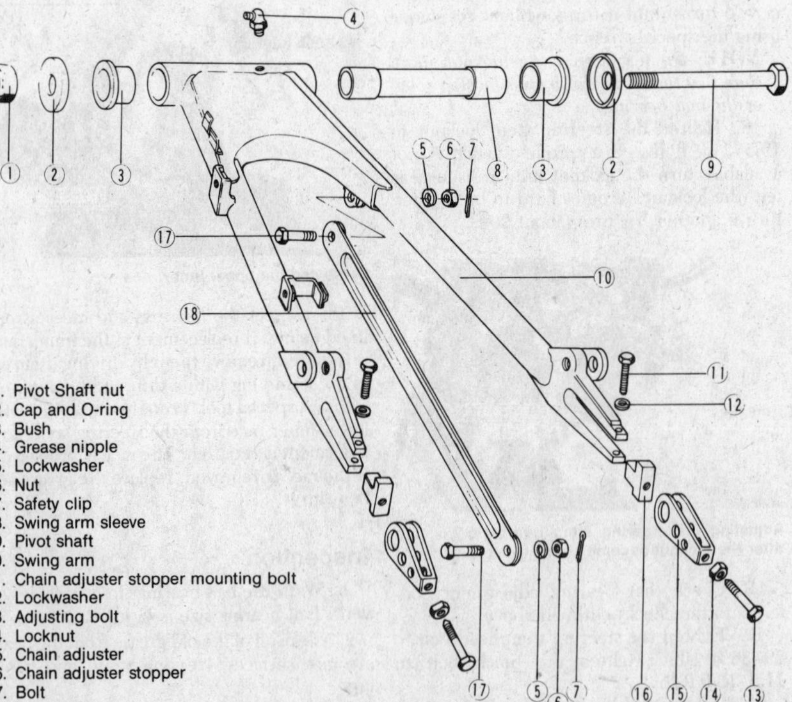

Swing arm components

3. Remove the swing arm sleeve.

4. Insert a suitable bar or rod through the swing arm and knock out the bush on the other side. Remove the remaining bush in the same manner.

Inspection

1. Measure the outside diameter of each end of the swing arm sleeve. Standard diameter is 21.979–22.00 mm (0.8653–0.8661 in.). The sleeve should be replaced if the measured diameter is less than 21.95 mm (0.864 in.).

2. Unless the bushes have been removed, in which case they must be replaced in any event, measure the inside diameter with a cylinder gauge. Standard ID is 22.055–22.088 mm (0.8683–0.8686 in.). Replace the bushes if the measured diameter is greater than 22.29 mm (0.878 in.).

3. To measure the swing arm pivot shaft run-out, mount the shaft in a set of v-blocks and measure run-out with a dial gauge set in the middle of the shaft.

In this case, run-out is the total amount of gauge movement. Standard run-out is under 0.1 mm (0.004 in.). The shaft should be replaced or straightened if run-out exceeds 0.14 mm (0.006 in.). If run-out exceeds 0.7 mm (0.028 in.), or if the shaft cannot be straightened, it must be replaced with a new one.

Assembly

1. Assembly is basically the reverse of disassembly. Note the following points:

a. Oil the new bushes before driving them into place with a press. Be sure that the bushes are properly seated.

b. Clean off all the old grease from the swing arm sleeve and lubricate it with fresh chassis grease. Be sure to grease the grooves especially.

c. Tighten the torque link nut to 19–25 ft lbs., and install the safety clip.

Installation

1. Be sure that the dust caps are in place on either end of the swing arm before installation.

2. Put the left side of the swing arm through the drive chain.

3. Insert the pivot shaft from the right side. Tighten the pivot shaft nut to 58–87 ft lbs.

Supplement

This supplemental information applies to models manufactured after 1980 or the year(s) noted. All other relevant data on these machines can be found in the body of the preceding section. The information below is organized in the same manner as the main section.

Maintenance

LUBRICATION

Changing Oil

Drain plug torque is 27 ft. lbs.

Final Drive Gearbox (750 Shaft)

1. With the machine parked on a level surface, gearbox oil level should be even with the lower portion of the inspection plug hole.

2. Recommended oil is API GL-5 or GL-6. Use SAE 90 for ambient temperatures above 42°F, SAE 80 for temperatures below 42°F.

CAUTION: *Do not mix brands of oil.*

3. Oil level should be checked every 6200 miles.

4. Gearbox oil change interval is 18,600 miles.

5. To change the gearbox oil:

a. Gearbox should be at operating temperature.

b. Park the machine on a level surface.

c. Remove the inspection plug. Remove the drain plug.

d. After draining is completed, refit drain plug and torque to 14 ft. lbs.

e. Add oil until level is even with lowest threads of inspection hole. Capacity is 0.19L (6.4 oz).

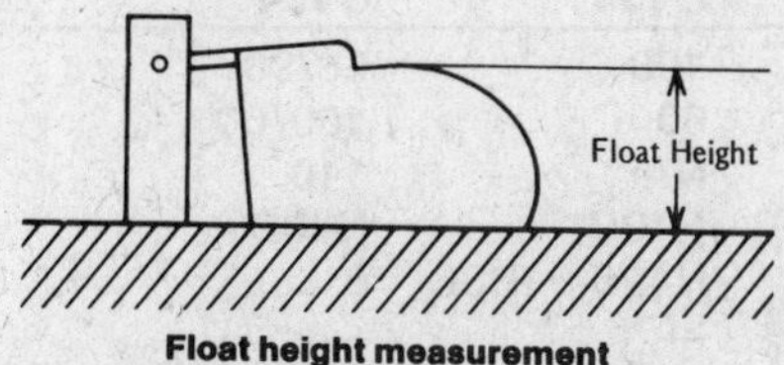

Float height measurement

Front Forks (750)

See main section for procedures. Recommended oil is SAE 5W20. Quantities per leg at routine change are as follows:

KZ 750F/N	250cc (8.5 oz.)
KZ 750P (82)	260cc (8.8 oz.)
KZ 750P (83)	300cc (10.2 oz.)

NOTE: *When rebuilding forks, add about 20-30cc (0.68-1.0 oz.) per leg to these quantities.*

SERVICE CHECKS AND ADJUSTMENTS

Clutch

750 SHAFT

Use the cable adjusters at the hand lever or in middle of cable to maintain free-play of 2-3mm (0.08-0.12 in.) between the hand lever and the lever holder (see illustration in main section).

750 CHAIN DRIVE

Adjustment is as described in main section.

650 (1981 AND LATER)

1. Adjust cable as outlined in main section to give 2-3mm (0.08-0.12 in.) of free-play between hand lever and lever holder.

2. Loosen the adjusting screw locknut. Turn the adjusting screw CCW until resistance is felt. Turn it 1/4 turn clockwise. Hold it in this position and tighten the locknut.

3. Check hand lever free-play and correct with the cable adjusters, if necessary, to give the correct amount.

Brakes

FRONT DISC

Some models have an inspection glass for fluid level check so removal of the reservoir cap is not required.

Tune-Up

CARBURETORS (650)

1. BS32 constant velocity carburetors are used on 1982 and later models in place of the VM24SS.

2. Float level is 3 ± 1mm below the edge of the carburetor body. The level gauge can be fitted to the drain pipe on the float bowl or in place of the drain screw itself if the factory fitting is available.

3. Float height is adjusted by bending the float tang. It should be 18.6mm (0.73 in.) when measured as shown in the illustration.

4. Pilot screws are protected by caps and are not an adjustment item.

5. Idle speed should be 1000 ± 50 rpm and can be adjusted with the idle speed knob. Adjust when engine is at operating temperature.

6. Vacuum variation between carburetor must be less than 2 cm HG when synchronizing. Procedure is as outlined in the main section.

CARBURETORS (750)

1. Either CV34 or BS34 carburetors may be found on these models. Procedures may be found in the main section. Note the following:

2. The pilot screws on most models are covered by a plug and are not adjustable. On other models (those with an accessible pilot screw) the correct setting is two turns out from the seated position.

3. Service fuel levels are:

KZ 750 N	4 ± 1mm
Z 750 P	3 ± 1mm
A/F Models	0.5mm

4. Other specifications and procedures are as described in the main section.

Fuel System

CARBURETOR OVERHAUL

Late model KZ 650s as well as 750 "P" models are equipped with "BS" model constant-velocity carburetors. Refer to the exploded view as a guide to disassembly. Other 750 machines have the "CV 34" units described in the main section.

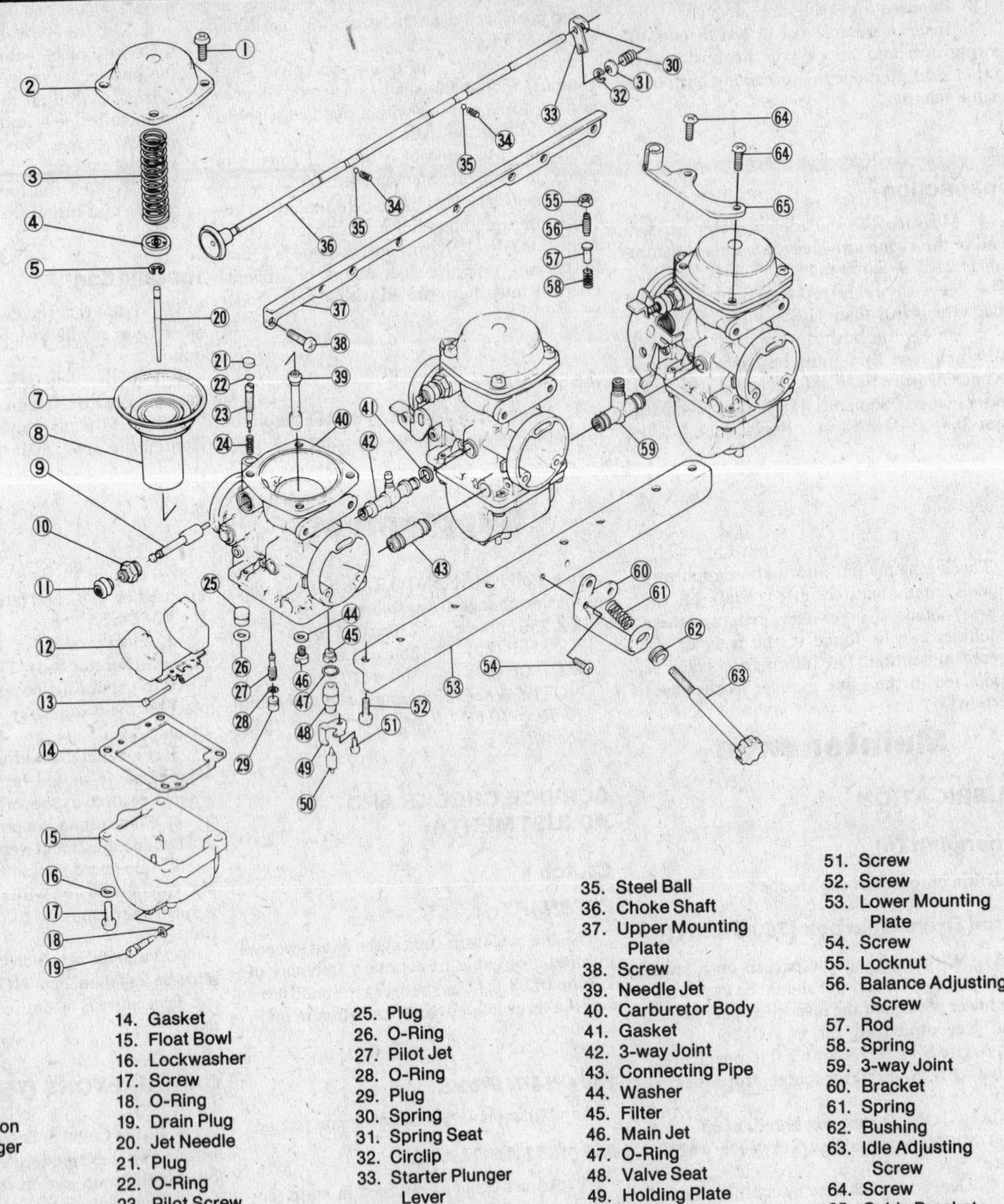

1. Screw
2. Cover
3. Spring
4. Spring Seat
5. Circlip
7. Diaphragm
8. Vacuum Piston
9. Starter Plunger
10. Plunger Cap
11. Dust Seal
12. Float
13. Float Pin
14. Gasket
15. Float Bowl
16. Lockwasher
17. Screw
18. O-Ring
19. Drain Plug
20. Jet Needle
21. Plug
22. O-Ring
23. Pilot Screw
24. Spring
25. Plug
26. O-Ring
27. Pilot Jet
28. O-Ring
29. Plug
30. Spring
31. Spring Seat
32. Circlip
33. Starter Plunger Lever
34. Spring
35. Steel Ball
36. Choke Shaft
37. Upper Mounting Plate
38. Screw
39. Needle Jet
40. Carburetor Body
41. Gasket
42. 3-way Joint
43. Connecting Pipe
44. Washer
45. Filter
46. Main Jet
47. O-Ring
48. Valve Seat
49. Holding Plate
50. Valve Needle
51. Screw
52. Screw
53. Lower Mounting Plate
54. Screw
55. Locknut
56. Balance Adjusting Screw
57. Rod
58. Spring
59. 3-way Joint
60. Bracket
61. Spring
62. Bushing
63. Idle Adjusting Screw
64. Screw
65. Cable Bracket

BS 34 carburetor assembly

CARBURETOR SPECIFICATIONS

Type	KZ 650 (1982-On) BS32	KZ 750N CV34	KZ 750P BS34	KZ 750F CV34	ZN 750A CV34
Main jet	107.5R	65/90	110R	100	68/90
Main air jet	250	100/60	250	60	100/60
Pilor air jet	37.5	110	300	NA	110
Jet needle	4D30	N10A	4BE3	N10C	N10D
Needle jet	Y-7	N426-01B36	Z-2	N426-01B36	6
Starter jet	55	—	—	—	—
Fuel level (mm/in.)	3/0.12	4/0.16	3/0.12	0.5/0.02	0.5/0.02
Float height (mm/in.)	18.6/0.73	21/0.84	18.6/0.73	14./0.56	14/0.56

Kawasaki KZ400/440

MODEL COVERAGE

KZ400 D,S,A,B,C
KZ440 A,B,C,D

INDEX

MAINTENANCE

NOTE: *Common maintenance procedures are explained in detail in "General Information."*

LUBRICATION

Checking Oil Level

1. To get an accurate oil level reading, the engine must be warm and the machine must be parked on the centerstand on a level surface.
2. Early moels have a dipstick fitted to the oil filter cap on top of the crankcase. The cap must be fully screwed in to get the reading. Maintain the oil level between the upper and lower level marks.
3. Other models have a sight glass on the side of the crankcase. Oil level should be maintained between the upper and lower level marks inscribed on the crankcase beside the glass.

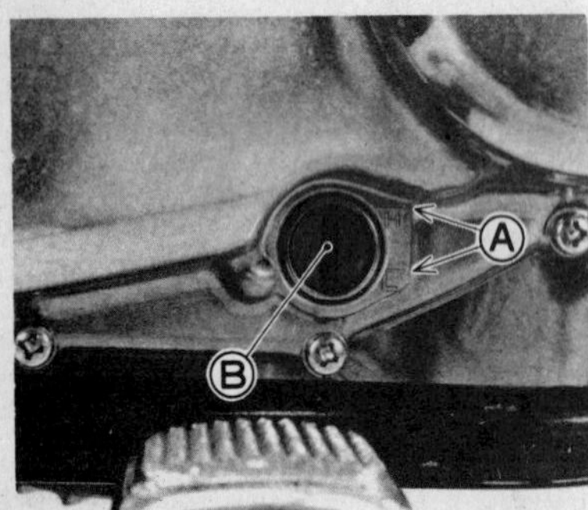

Oil level sight glass (B) and level lines (A)

Changing Oil

1. The oil change interval is 1,800 miles. SAE 10W-40, 10W-50, or 20W-50 service rating "SD" or "SE" is recommended.
2. Change oil when the engine is at operating temperature. The machine should be parked on the center stand and on a level surface to ensure full drainage of the oil.
3. Remove the filler cap. Remove the drain plug from the bottom of the crankcase and allow the oil to drain.

4. Clean off the plug (it is magnetic to trap metal particles). Check the condition of the O-ring. Refit, tightening the plug to 14.5-18 ft lbs. on 1974-77 models and 22 ft lbs. on newer machines.
5. If the filter is to be changed, refer to the following section.
6. Add the correct grade and quantity of oil. If the filter has been changed, add 3.0 1/3.2 qt. If the filter has not been changed, add 2.6 1/2.8 qt.

General Specifications

<table>
<tr><th></th><th>KZ400D</th><th>KZ400S</th></tr>
<tr><td>ENGINE</td><td></td><td></td></tr>
<tr><td>Displacement (cc)</td><td colspan="2">389</td></tr>
<tr><td>Bore x Stroke (mm)</td><td colspan="2">64 x 62</td></tr>
<tr><td>Compression ratio</td><td colspan="2">9.0 : 1</td></tr>
<tr><td>Lubrication</td><td colspan="2">trochoid oil pump; wet sump system</td></tr>
<tr><td>Carburetion</td><td colspan="2">Twin Keihin constant velocity CVB 36</td></tr>
<tr><td>Ignition</td><td colspan="2">Battery and coil</td></tr>
<tr><td>Starting</td><td>electric and kick</td><td>kick</td></tr>
<tr><td>TRANSMISSION</td><td></td><td></td></tr>
<tr><td>Type</td><td colspan="2">constant mesh</td></tr>
<tr><td>No. speeds</td><td colspan="2">5</td></tr>
<tr><td>Clutch</td><td colspan="2">wet, multi-disc</td></tr>
<tr><td>Gear ratios (: 1)</td><td></td><td></td></tr>
<tr><td>1st</td><td colspan="2">2.751</td></tr>
<tr><td>2nd</td><td colspan="2">1.684</td></tr>
<tr><td>3rd</td><td colspan="2">1.273</td></tr>
<tr><td>4th</td><td colspan="2">1.040</td></tr>
<tr><td>5th</td><td colspan="2">0.889</td></tr>
<tr><td>Primary reduction (: 1)</td><td colspan="2">2.435</td></tr>
<tr><td>Final reduction (: 1)</td><td colspan="2">3.000</td></tr>
<tr><td>Overall drive ratio (: 1)</td><td colspan="2">6.493 (high gear)</td></tr>
<tr><td>CHASSIS</td><td></td><td></td></tr>
<tr><td>Dry weight (lbs)</td><td>375</td><td>366</td></tr>
<tr><td>Wheelbase (in.)</td><td colspan="2">53.5</td></tr>
<tr><td>Overall length (in.)</td><td colspan="2">81.6</td></tr>
<tr><td>Overall width (in.)</td><td>31.8</td><td>31.1</td></tr>
<tr><td>Ground clearance (in.)</td><td colspan="2">4.93</td></tr>
<tr><td>Brakes</td><td></td><td></td></tr>
<tr><td>Front</td><td>Disc</td><td>Drum, twin-leading shoe</td></tr>
<tr><td>Rear</td><td colspan="2">Drum, single-leading shoe</td></tr>
<tr><td>Tires</td><td></td><td></td></tr>
<tr><td>Front</td><td colspan="2">3.25 x 18</td></tr>
<tr><td>Rear</td><td colspan="2">3.50 x 18</td></tr>
</table>

7. Allow the engine to idle for a few minutes, then check the oil level and top up if necessary.

Oil Filter

1. A cartridge-type oil filter is fitted to the bottom of the crankcases. The filter should be changed at every other oil change or at intervals of about 3,600 miles.
2. Drain the oil as described above. Unscrew and remove the oil filter.
3. Install the new filter element ensuring that the O-rings are in good condition and properly fitted. Tighten the filter to 11-14.5 ft lbs.

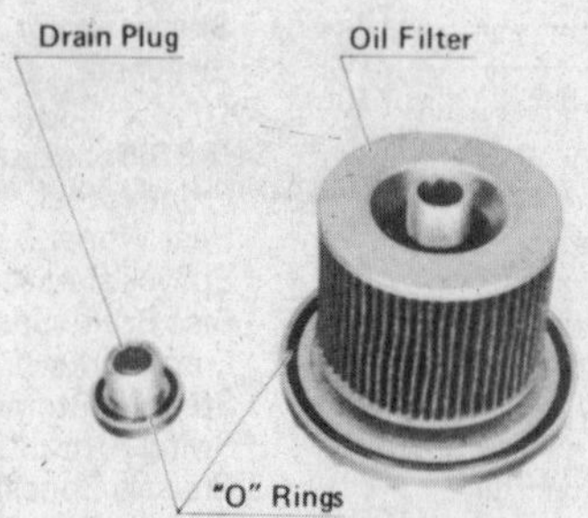

Oil filter and drain plug O-rings

4. Add 3.0 1/3.2 qts of oil to the engine, then check oil level as described above.

FRONT FORKS

Checking Oil

1. Front fork oil level should be checked about every 3,600 miles.
2. Support the front wheel off the ground.
3. Remove the filler cap from the top of each fork leg.

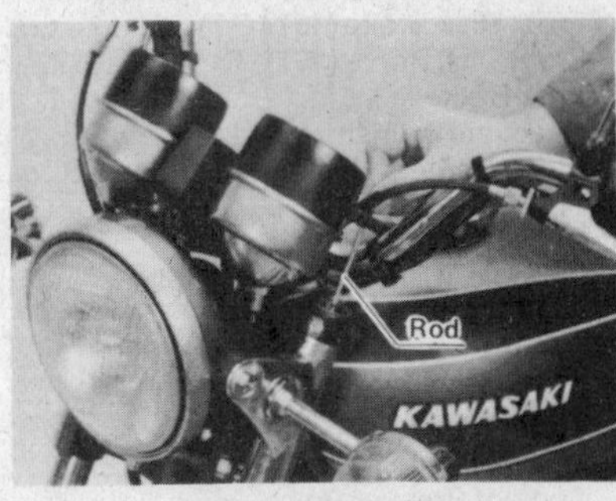

Checking fork oil level

4. On 1978 and later models, remove the fork springs from each leg.
5. Insert a suitable rod into the fork leg to check level which is measured from the top of the fork tube. Add oil, if necessary, to bring the level up to specification. Oil levels are:

1974-76 .... 350mm/13.8 in.
1977 B, C .... 417mm/16.4 in.
1978, 1982-On .... 435mm/17.1 in.
1979-81 B, C .... 435mm/17.1 in.
1979-On A, D .... 475mm/18.7 in.

Changing Oil

1. Fork oil should be changed about every 6,200 miles.
2. SAE 5W-20 oil is recommended.
3. Remove the drain bolt from the bottom of one slider. Apply the front brake and push forward on the handlebars with the machine off its stand to pump out the oil. Repeat with the other fork leg.
4. After fitting the drain bolts, and with the machine on the center stand and the front wheel supported off the ground, remove the filler caps from the top of each fork leg and add the correct grade and quantity of oil.
5. Check the condition of the filler cap O-rings, then refit and tighten them to 18-22 ft lbs.

6. When changing fork oil, add about 130cc (4.5 oz.) to each fork leg.

CHASSIS LUBRICATION

1. The swing arm is fitted with a grease nipple and should be lubricated with a high-quality chassis grease about every 1,800 miles. Apply grease until some appears at either end of the swing arm.

2. At the same intervals, lightly oil brake lever fittings and carburetor linkage. Lubricate controls and cables.

3. Lubrication on the wheel bearings, brake cams, speedometer gear housing, and steering stem bearings is required every 2 years or about 12,000 miles. Use a high-quality bearing grease for these operations.

Swing arm grease fitting

Refer to "Chassis" for procedures.

SERVICE CHECKS AND ADJUSTMENTS

Drive Chain

1. The chain should have 20-25mm (3/4-1 in.) of total up and down movement. This is measured in the middle of the lower chain run and at the tightest point of the chain, if such a tight spot exists.

2. When checking chain slack, the machine should be parked on the center stand, and the chain must be clean and well-lubricated.

Loosening the coupling sleeve nut

3. If adjustment is necessary, remove the safety clip and loosen the brake anchor nut on the brake plate. Loosen the axle nut after removing the cotter pin.

4. Loosen the coupling sleeve nut.

5. Loosen the adjuster bolt or adjuster nut locknuts. Turn the adjuster bolts or nuts in or out until the proper chain slack is attained. Be sure that the index notch on the adjusters align with the same swing arm reference mark on both sides.

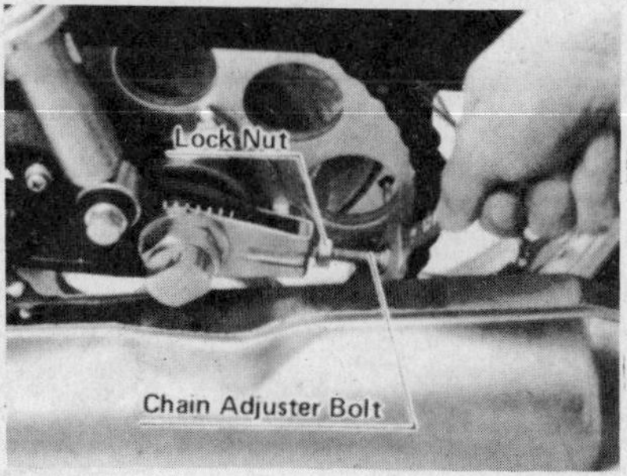

Adjusting the chain

6. Tighten the locknuts, the coupling sleeve nut, and the axle nut. Recheck chain slack. If correct, fully tighten the axle nut to 95-116 ft lbs. Tighten the brake anchor nut to 20-22 ft lbs. The use of the new cotter pin is recommended.

7. Check rear brake and brake light switch adjustments.

8. Periodically (1,800 miles) the chain should be checked for wear. Refer to "Chassis."

Drive Belt

With the motorcycle on the centerstand, the drive belt should give a deflection of 0.5 in. (13 mm) when a 10 lb. weight is applied to the middle of the bottom belt run.

2. Adjustment is done in the same way as with chain drives, by moving the rear wheel.

3. Before the axle nut is tightened following a belt adjustment, spin the wheel and apply the rear brake hard to center the drum. Then tighten the axle nut.

CAUTION: *Drive belts must be replaced when the nylon on the belt teeth is worn through at any point or if proper adjustment cannot be obtained.*

Clutch

1. Using the adjuster at the handlebar, maintain clutch cable free-play so that when the clutch lever is pulled, there is a gap of 2-3 mm (0.08-0.12 in.) between the lever and the lever bracket before the cluch begins to disengage.

If clutch operation is not satisfactory in spite of the above adjustment, or if new plates have been fitted, proceed as follows:

2. Slide back the dust cover from the cable adjuster located about halfway along the cable. Screw the adjuster in to put as much slack in the cable as possible.

3. Loosen the locknut at the handlebar cable adjuster and turn the adjuster so that there is a gap of 5-6mm (0.02-0.24 in.) between the adjuster and the locknut.

4. Remove the clutch adjusting cover. Loosen the locknut and back the adjusting screw out 3-4 turns.

5. Turn the screw in until resistance is felt.

On 1974-77 models, turn the screw *out* 1/2 turn and tighten the locknut.

On newer models, turn the screw *in* 1/4 turn and tighten the locknut.

6. Take up all of the cable slack with the main cable adjuster. Refit the adjuster dust cover.

7. Use the handlebar adjuster to give the correct amount of clutch cable free-play as in Step 1.

Adjusting the clutch

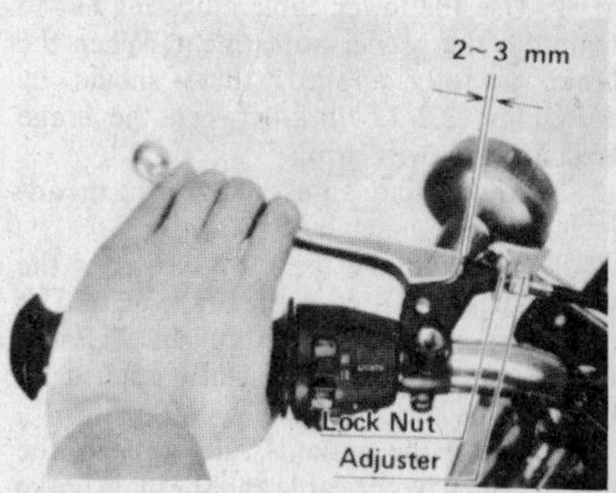

Proper clutch cable free-play

Throttle Cables (Dual)

1. Loosen the locknuts for the throttle cable adjusting nuts at the twist-grip, and screw both adjusting nuts in to yield as much cable free-play as possible.

2. Turn the adjusting nut for the decelerator cable out three turns. If this takes up all the play at the twist-grip, loosen the decelerator adjuster locknut (at the carburetors), and turn the adjuster to yield a small amount of free-play, then tighten the locknut.

3. Turn the accelerator cable adjusting nut at the twist-grip out until twist-grip play is almost gone, then tighten the locknut.

4. Turn the decelerator adjusting nut in

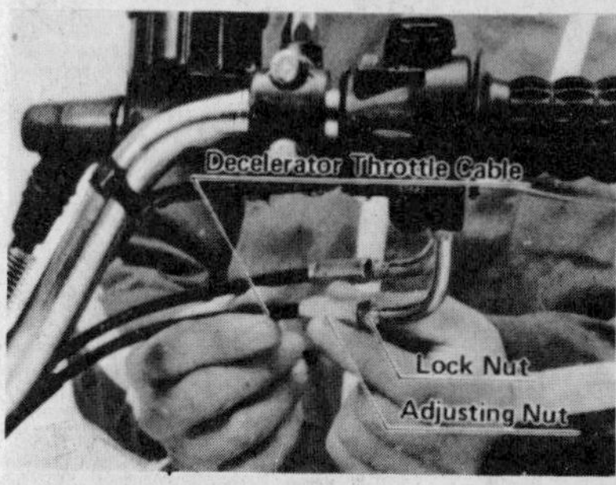

Turning the decelerator adjusting nut out

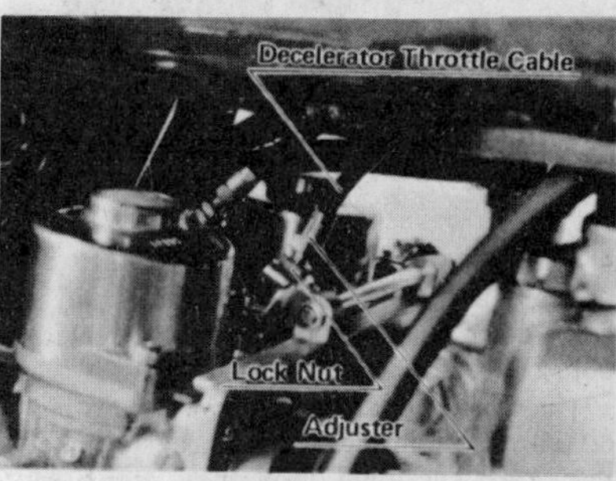

Decelerator cable adjuster at the carburetor

until the desired amount of twist-grip free-play is obtained, which should generally be about 10-15° of grip rotation.

5. Check the tightness of all locknuts. Check throttle operation before riding the motorcycle.

Throttle Cable (Single)

Later models have a single throttle cable in place of the "pull-pull" twin cable system. Adjust the cable to give 10-15° of grip rotation before the butterfly valves start to open.

Front Drum Brake

1. Use the lower cable adjusting nut to maintain the proper adjustment. When the brake is fully applied, there should be 55-65mm (2.2-2.6 in.) between the brake lever and the twist-grip.

2. Make minor adjustments using the adjuster at the handlebar.

3. Check brake wear by means of the wear indicators fitted to the brake plate. The indicators must stay within the "Usable Range" when the brake is fully applied, or linings must be replaced.

4. When the brake is fully applied, the angle formed by the cable and the main brake lever at the brake plate must be within 80-90°. If the angle exceeds this amount, brake effectiveness will be reduced. Further, the main and secondary brake levers should be parallel. This adjustment can be made with the threaded connecting rod, but is usually not necessary unless the brake plate has been disassembled, or new shoes have been fitted. Refer to "Chassis" for this procedure.

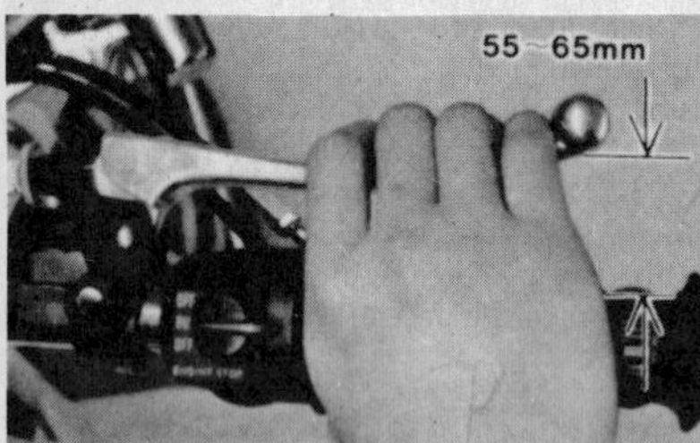

Proper front drum brake lever free-play

An angle in excess of 80–90° will result in reduced brake effectiveness

Front Disc Brake (1974-77)

1. Check pad wear. When either pad is worn down to the stepped portion, replace both as a set.

2. Check fluid level. A level line is inscribed on the inside of the master cylinder reservoir. The fluid level may drop very slightly as the pads wear. Before adding fluid, refer to the "Chassis" section which provides proper procedures for disc brake work.

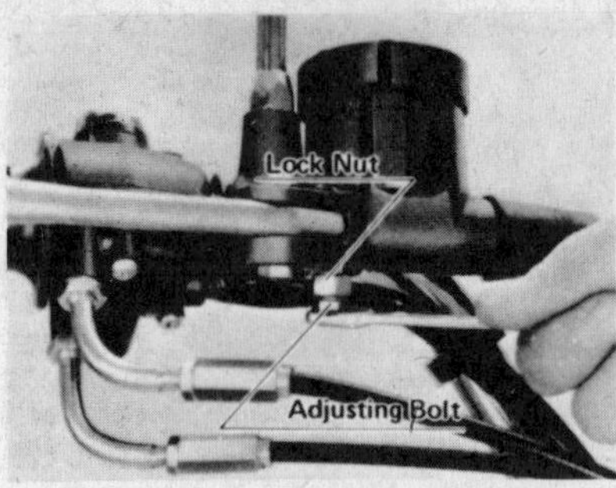

Disc brake lever adjuster

The brake fluid should be changed each year or every 6,200 miles, whichever comes first. Refer to "Chassis" for procedures.

3. Check brake lever play. The tip of the lever should not move more than 5 mm (0.10 in.) before the brake is applied. If adjustment is necessary, an adjusting bolt is fitted to the underside of the lever bracket. Bend down the tab on the lockwasher, loosen the locknut while holding the adjusting bolt steady, then turn the bolt very slightly so that lever travel is corrected.

4. Tighten the locknut to 13-16.5 ft lbs. Bend down the lockwasher tab.

Front Disc Brake (1978 Later)

1. Check pad wear. When either pad is worn down to the stepped portion or to the notch, replace both as a set.

2. Check fluid level. A level sight glass is provided on the master cylinder reservoir. Maintain level at the scribed line. Fluid level may drop slightly as pads wear. Before adding fluid, refer to the "Chassis" section which provides proper procedures for disc brake work.

The brake fluid should be changed every year or every 6,200 miles, whichever comes first. Refer to "Chassis" for procedures.

Rear Brake

1. The brake pedal is adjustable for position. It should be set so that the knurled surface of the pedal is 20-30mm (0.8-1.2 in.) below the top of the footpeg rubber.

2. If adjustment is necessary, back off the brake adjusting nut. Loosen the locknut on the pedal height adjustment bolt, and turn the bolt so that pedal height is correct. Tighten the locknut. Adjust the rear brake.

3. The brake is correctly adjusted if the pedal is free to move 20-30mm (0.8-1.2 in.) before the linings contact the drum. Adjustment is made with an adjusting nut on the end of the brake rod.

Brake pedal free-play

4. When the brake is fully applied, the wear indicator must be within the "Usable Range" or the lining will have to be replaced. Further, the angle formed by the brake lever and rod when the brake is applied should be about 80-90°. If the angle exceeds this amount, braking effectiveness will be reduced. It is possible to remove the lever from the brake cam and reposition it so that the proper angle is not exceeded when the brake is applied.

5. After adjusting the brake, check the operation of the brake and the adjustment of the brake light switch.

Brake Light Switch

1. The front brake light switch for disc brakes is not adjustable. The front drum brake light switch does not need routine adjustment.

2. The rear brake light switch is fitted to a slotted bracket and secured by a locknut. The brake light should go on after about 15mm (0.6 in.) of pedal travel, or shortly before the linings contact the drum. Make the adjustment by loosening the locknut and moving the switch up or down as necessary. Moving the switch up will allow the light to go on sooner and vice versa.

CAUTION: *Do not turn the switch body itself during adjustment or the electrical connections may be damaged.*

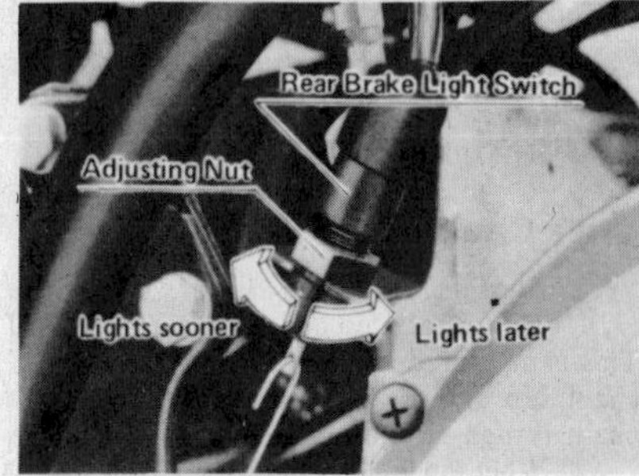

Headlight Adjustment

1. Set the machine about 25 feet away from and perpendicular to a wall, preferably of a color which reflects light well.

The machine should be off the stand, and with a rider putting his weight on the machine as in operation.

2. Switch on the high beam. The headlight high beam should be parallel to the ground and should hit the wall directly in front of the machine.

3. Vertical adjustment is made by loosening the two headlight shell mounting bolts slightly and pivoting the shell up or down.

4. Lateral adjustment is accomplished by means of the screw on the right-side of the headlight.

Steering Stem Bearings

1. The bearing adjustment should be checked about every 3,600 miles. Refer to "Chassis" for inspection and adjustment procedures.

FUEL SYSTEM

1. Fuel system maintenance involves

cleaning the petcock filter, cleaning or replacing the air cleaner, and cleaning the carburetors.

This should be done about every 1,800 miles.

2. Shut off the fuel, and place a funnel or a channel-shaped piece of cardboard or heavy paper beneath one of the carbs. Remove the float bowl drain plug and allow the fuel to drain into a suitable container. Repeat with the other carb. Refit the drain plugs. Check for leaks before operating the machine.

At more frequent intervals, the carburetors should be removed, disassembled, and cleaned. Refer to "Fuel System" for procedures.

3. Be sure that the fuel petcock is "Off." Unscrew and remove the sediment cup. Reach into the petcock body and pull out the O-ring and filter screen strainer. Clean in solvent. If the screen is punctured, replace it.

4. Place a container beneath the petcock and turn it to the "Reserve" position which will serve to remove any water which may have accumulated in the bottom of the gas tank.

5. Check the condition of the O-ring, and replace it if damaged. Install the strainer, O-ring, and sediment cup, and tighten it securely. Check for leaks before operation.

Air Cleaner Service

REMOVAL

1. On 1974-76 models, the element is reached by removing the left side cover, removing the housing sidecover screw and taking out the element.

2. On later models, open the seat, remove the tool kit and tray and take out the (dry type) element, or open the seat, remove the air cleaner housing mounting bolts and take out the housing (wet type).

SERVICE

1. Two types of air cleaner element can be found on these motorcycles. Service procedures will vary for each.

2. Clean dry type elements by washing in a non-oily solvent. Dry by applying compressed air from the inside.

CAUTION: *Do not use solvents with a dangerously low flashpoint, or those which may leave and oily residue, like kerosene.*

1. Clean wet type elements by first removing it from the frame. Clean it by soaking in a safe, high flashpoint solvent. Squeeze dry. Soak the element in SAE 30 oil and squeeze out as much of the oil as possible.

CAUTION: *Handle the sponge element carefully. Do not wring it out, as the material may tear.*

4. Check the condition of the element and replace it if torn or punctured.

5. The maximum service life of the element is about 6,000 miles or 5 cleanings, whichever comes first. After this, a new element should be fitted.

INSTALLATION

1. Installation is the reverse of removal. Install the element so that the element holes match the air cleaner ducts.

Periodic Maintenance Intervals ①

Daily
- Brake adjustment
- Engine oil level
- Cable adjustments
- Chain slack
- Lights and safety equipment

Weekly
- Battery electrolyte level
- Spokes for tightness
- Tire pressure (cold)

Every 150 Miles
- Lubricate drive chain

Every 1800 Miles
- Change engine oil
- Grease swing arm
- Lubricate controls and cables
- Check chain wear
- Adjust carburetors
- Clean fuel system
- Clean and gap spark plugs
- Adjust cam chain
- Check points and ignition timing
- Clean air filter

Every 3600 Miles
- Replace oil filter
- Checking steering head bearings
- Adjust valves
- Check brake wear
- Check fork oil level

Every 6200 Miles
- Replace air cleaner element
- Change fork oil
- Flush and renew brake fluid

Every 12,000 Miles or 2 Years
- Repack wheel bearings
- Repack steering stem bearings
- Lubricate brake cams
- Lubricate speedometer gear housing

① Based upon normal usage after break-in is complete

RECOMMENDED LUBRICANTS

Engine
- SAE 10W-40, service rating "SD" or "SE"
- SAE 10W-50, service rating "SD" or "SE"
- SAE 20W-50, service rating "SD" or "SE"

Forks
- SAE 5W-20

Control Cables
- Motor oil
- Graphite-base lubricant
- Molybdenum disulphide-base lubricant

Tach, Speedometer Cables
- Light-duty grease

Wheel Bearings, Steering Stem Bearings
- Waterproof, medium-weight bearing grease

Grease Fitting
- Waterproof, medium-weight chassis grease

Tune-Up

NOTE: *Common tune-up procedures are explained in detail in "General Information."*

IMPORTANT: *In all relevant procedures, not that the normal direction of rotation of this engine's crankshaft is counterclockwise when viewed from the right-side.*

CAM CHAIN ADJUSTMENT

1. The cam chain adjuster is located between the cylinders at the front of the engine.

2. Remove the breaker point cover from the right-side of the engine. Remove the cam chain tensioner cap and O-ring.

3. Remove the spark plugs.

4. Turn the engine over using a 17 mm wrench on the crankshaft *nut* at the points compartment. Turn the crankshaft counterclockwise while observing the tensioner pushrod which is in the center of the pushrod guide.

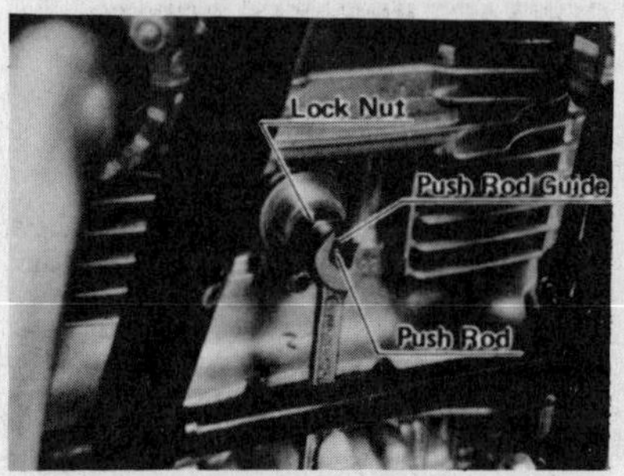

Adjusting the cam chain

5. Continue turning the engine over until the pushrod reaches the innermost point, then stop.

NOTE: *Hold the crankshaft in place. Do not turn the engine backward.*

6. The end of the pushrod should be flush with the pushrod guide if adjustment is correct. If adjustment is necessary, loosen the large locknut on the tensioner, and turn the guide until the guide and pushrod are flush.

CAUTION: *If the pushrod protrudes even a small bit from the guide, the adjustment is too tight and damage may result.*

7. Tighten the locknut. Refit the tensioner O-ring and cap. Replace the point cover and spark plugs.

VALVE ADJUSTMENT (1974-76)

NOTE: *Valves must be adjusted when the engine is cold.*

1. Remove the contact breaker point cover from the right-side of the engine.

2. Remove the spark plugs.

3. Remove the cylinder head cover caps from each side of the head. Remove the four valve clearance adjuster plugs.

4. Clearance for both intake and exhaust valves is 0.004-0.006 in./0.10-0.15mm.

5. Using a 17mm wrench on the crank-

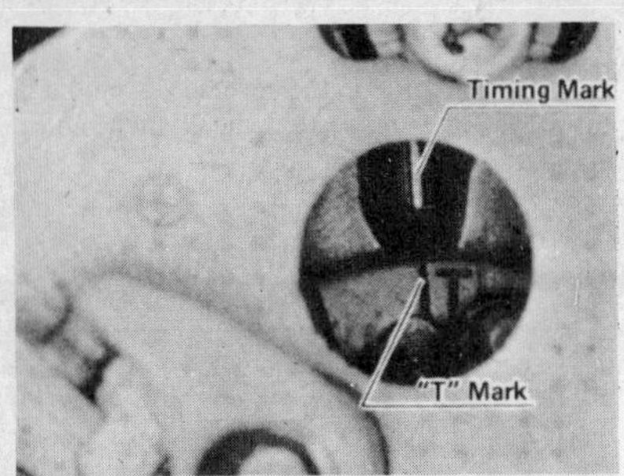

Align the "T" mark for valve adjustment

Checking valve adjustment

shaft nut at the points compartment, turn the engine over counterclockwise until the intake valve for the right cylinder opens and begins to close.

6. Continue turning the engine over in the same direction while observing the timing marks through the hole in the breaker plate. About 1/4 of a turn after the intake valve closes, the "T" mark will appear. Align the "T" mark with the stationary timing mark, as illustrated.

7. The right-side piston has now been positioned at top dead center (TDC) on its compression stroke. Both valves for the right cylinder should be closed.

8. Check the valve clearance by inserting the proper-sized feeler gauge between the valve stem and the rocker arm.

Turn the rocker arm shafts as shown to increase or decrease clearance

9. If adjustment is necessary, loosen the rocker arm shaft locknut, and turn the shaft carefully in either direction to increase or decrease the clearance as necessary. Refer to the illustration. Do not turn the shaft more than 180°. The punch mark on the shaft must continue to face inward toward the "+" and "−" marks.

To increase valve clearance, turn the shaft toward the "+" mark; to decrease it, turn it toward the "−" mark.

10. Hold the shaft in position, while tightening the locknut to 18-22 ft lbs. After tightening, recheck clearance.

11. Repeat the procedure for the other right cylinder valve.

12. Turn the crankshaft CCW 360° (one full turn) until the "T" mark again aligns. The left piston is now at TDC on its compression stroke and the left cylinder valves can now be adjusted.

VALVE ADJUSTMENT (1977 AND LATER)

NOTE: *Valves must be adjusted when the engine is cold.*

1. Remove the contact breaker point or pickup coil cover from the right side of the engine.
2. Remove the spark plugs.
3. Remove the four valve adjuster caps.
4. Clearance for the intake and the exhaust valves is the same. Clearances are:

1977 .... 0.005-0.006 in./0.13-0.15mm
1978-On 0.007-0.009 in./0.17-0.22mm

5. Using a 17mm wrench on the crankshaft nut, turn the engine over counterclockwise until the intake valve for the right cylinder opens and begins to close.
6. Continue turning the engine over in the same direction while observing the timing marks through the hole in the breaker plate. About 1/4 turn after the intake valve closes, the "T" mark will appear. Align the "T" mark with the stationary timing mark.
7. The right-side piston has now been positioned at TDC on the compression stroke. Both valves for the right piston should now be adjusted.
8. Check the valve clearance by inserting a feeler gauge blade of the right size between the valve and adjuster. It should be a slip fit. If adjustment is required, loosen the locknut on the adjuster and turn the adjuster until there is a slight drag on the blade as it is pulled through. Tighten the locknut (11 ft. lbs.) while holding the adjuster in place.
9. Repeat the procedure for the other valve of the right side cylinder.
10. Turn the engine 360° CCW until the "T" mark again aligns with the timing mark and check the left-side valves.

CONTACT BREAKER POINTS

Location

1. The points are located beneath a cover on the right-side of the engine.
2. A single set of points is used and they are opened by a breaker cam fitted to the crankshaft.

Replacement

1. Replacement of the points is easily accomplished by loosening the wire terminal nut, and disconnecting the primary wire and condenser wire from the points terminal. Remove the points base screw and lift them off. Remove the condenser securing screw.
2. Clean the contact surfaces of new points with a non-oily solvent prior to fitting.
3. When connecting the primary wire and condenser lead, be sure that the insulating washers for the points terminal are all present and correctly installed. If there is continuity between the primary wire and the

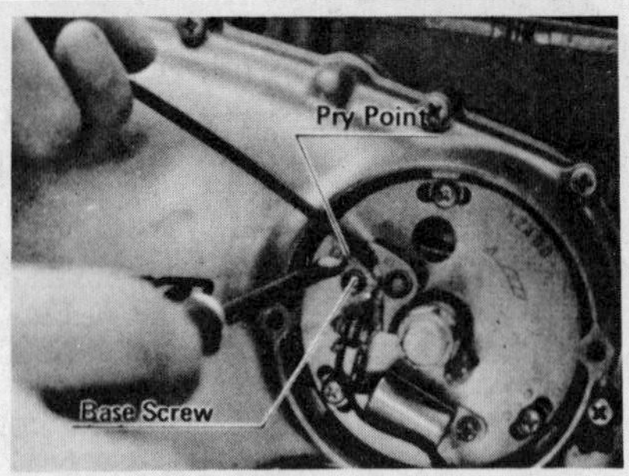

Loosen the base screw and move points with a screwdriver at the pry point to adjust gap

engine (ground) when the points are open, the engine will not run.

Gapping

1. Clean the points if necessary before gapping.
2. Remove the spark plugs. Using a 17 mm wrench on the crankshaft nut, turn the engine counterclockwise until the points are open to their maximum gap. Check with a feeler gauge. Proper point gap is 0.3-0.4mm (0.012-0.016 in.).
3. If adjustment is necessary, loosen the point base screw just enough to allow the points to be moved. Use a small slothead screwdriver at the pry point provided to adjust the gap. Tighten the screw and recheck.
4. Clean off the points to remove any foreign matter which may have been deposited by the feeler gauge.

Lubrication

1. A felt pad is positioned to bear against the breaker cam and distribute lubricant.
2. Periodically, apply a bit of high temperature grease to the left-side of the pad. Do not overlubricate as this risks fouling the points.

IGNITION TIMING (1974-80)

Dynamic Timing

1. Clean and gap the breaker points.
2. Hook up the strobe light according to the manufacturer's instructions. The timing marks are visible through the inspection hole in the breaker plate.

Full advance timing marks

3. Start the engine. At idle, the "F" mark on the timing advance mechanism must align with the stationary timing mark. At 3,000 rpm and above, the twin full-advance marks must align with the stationary timing mark.
4. If adjustment is necessary, loosen the

three breaker point base plate screws, and rotate the plate in either direction, as necessary, so that the marks align.

5. Once timing has been set for the full advance marks or for the "F" mark, the other should align as well. If only one of them can be brought into alignment, suspect trouble with the automatic timing advance mechanism.

6. When alignment is achieved, tighten the base plate screws and recheck.

Static Timing

1. Clean and gap the points before checking the timing.

2. Hook up the test light or ohmmeter-one lead to ground, the other to the points wire terminal. Be sure that the ignition is off and the engine kill button is turned to an "Off" position.

3. Using a 17mm wrench on the crankshaft nut, turn the engine over in the normal (counterclockwise) direction, until the "F" mark on the timing advance mechanism (visible through the inspection hole in the breaker base plate) comes into view.

4. Continue turning the engine over. As the "F" mark aligns with the stationary timing mark, the test light or meter should react, indicating that the points have begun to open.

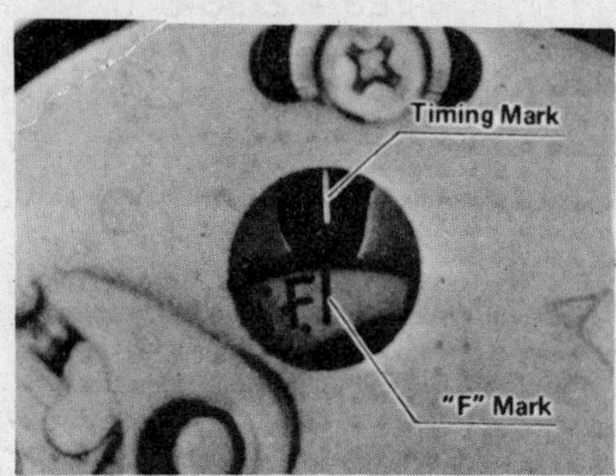

Stationary advance timing mark "F"

5. If the points do not begin to open as these marks align, loosen the three breaker base plate screws after aligning the "F" mark and rotate the base plate in the direction necessary so that the points just begin to open when the marks align.

IGNITION TIMING (1981-AND LATER)

Transistorized ignitions used on late models do not require adjustment.

CARBURETORS (1974-76)
Adjusting Float Level

Generally, float level need not be adjusted unless fuel delivery problems have been noted, or if the machine has covered considerable mileage.

1. Drain the float bowls by removing the drain plugs.

2. Fit float level gauge No. 57001-208 to the float bowl. Turn on the fuel petcock.

3. The fuel level should be 2-4mm (0.08-0.16 in.) below the carburetor body-to-float bowl mating surface.

4. If adjustment is necessary, remove the carburetors, take off the float bowls, and remove the float assemblies.

5. Bend the float tang to correct the level.

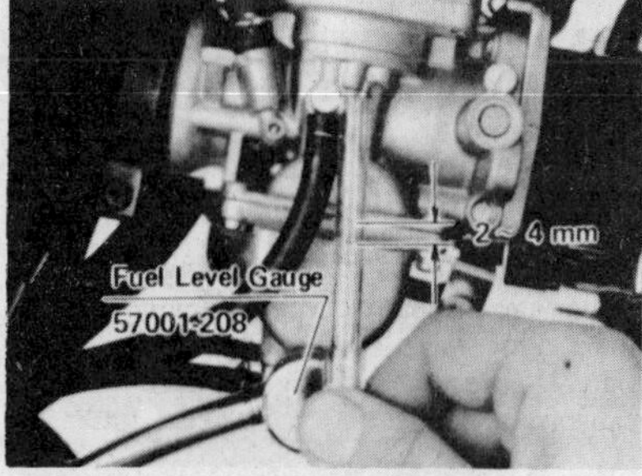

Checking carburetor fuel level

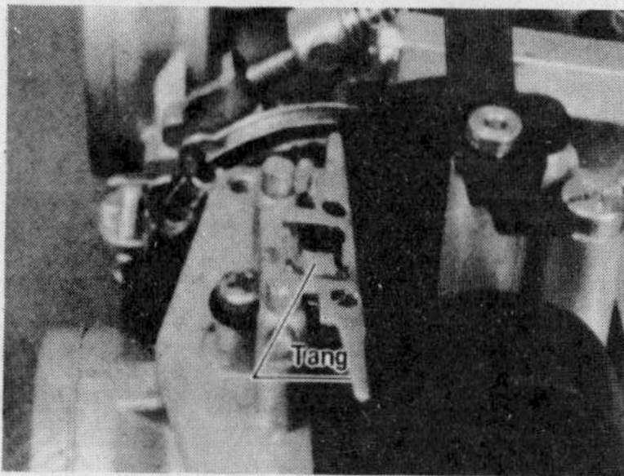

Bend the tang to adjust fuel level

Bending the tang toward the carburetor body will lower the float level. Bending it down, or away from the carburetor body, will raise the float level.

Idle Speed and Mixture

NOTE: *These adjustments must be made when the engine is at operating temperature.*

1. If engine idling is very poor, the following procedure may be necessary: remove the carburetors from the manifolds. Turn the pulley as far as possible and check that both butterfly valves are parallel to the carburetor bores. If they are not, loosen the pulley stop screw locknut and turn the stop screw so that this is achieved. Tighten the locknut. Install the carburetors and check cable free-play. This procedure will not ordinarily be necessary, and most routine tune-ups can start with Step 2.

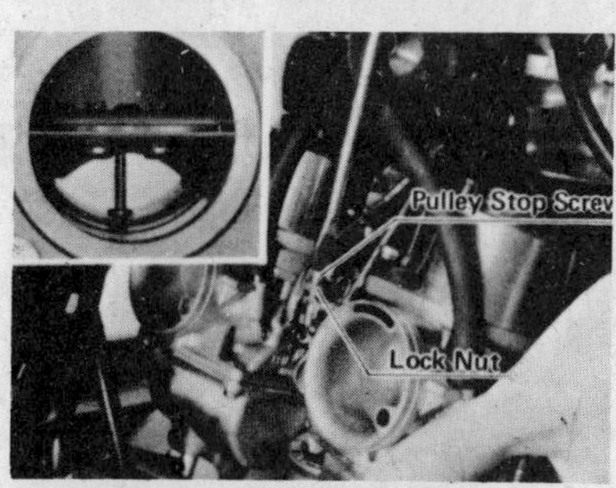

Use the pulley stop screw if butterfly valves are not parallel to the bores when opened fully

Adjusting the pilot screw

2. With the engine at operating temperature, back out the throttle stop screw until the engine idles at the lowest rpm at which it can run smoothly.

3. Turn each pilot screw in or out until the highest idle speed is reached.

4. Adjust the idle with the throttle stop screw to 1,100-1,300 rpm.

5. Turn each pilot screw in and out after noting their positions. If the idle speed rises when this is done, repeat Steps 2-4.

6. After the correct setting for each pilot screw has been determined, turn each one *in* 1/16 turn.

7. Rev the engine a few times and ensure that idle speed does not change. Check for proper cable free-play and operation.

Throttle Synchronization

1. Throttle synchronization is made easy with vacuum gauges 57001-127 and adapters 57001-401. Balance adjuster 57001-167 is also used. If the gauges are not available, refer to Steps 7 and following, below.

2. Fit the vacuum gauges to the carburetors.

3. With the engine at operating temperature and idling at 1,100-1,300 rpm, adjust the gauges so that needle flutter is less than 3 cm Hg. Standard vacuum should be 22-27 cm Hg. If the difference between the two gauges' readings is more than 1 cm Hg, stop the engine and remove the fuel tank.

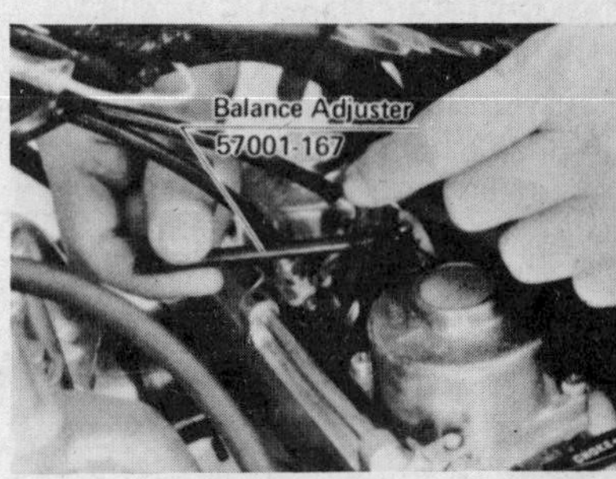

Using the balance adjuster

4. Use the balance adjuster on the balance adjuster screw so that vacuum is equalized. The motorcycle will run at this point on the gas left in the carburetors.

5. After equalizing vacuum, reinstall the tank, adjust both pilot screws by equal amounts so that vacuum is 22-27 cm Hg, then turn each in 1/16 turn.

6. Remove the gauges and adpaters and use the throttle stop screw to adjust idle speed to 1,100-1,300 rpm.

7. If vacuum gauges are not available, check synchronization by placing a hand over the end of each muffler. Check that there is no difference in pressure or noise between the cylinders.

8. If there is, remove the gas tank, and adjust the balance adjuster screw to equalize the pressure. The engine will run on the fuel left in the carburetors. After equalizing pressure, install the tank and adjust the idle speed to 1,100-1,300 rpm.

CARBURETORS (1977 AND LATER)

Adjusting Float Level

The procedure is the same as described for 1974-76 carburetors, above, with the following changes:

1. Float level gauge part number is 57001-1017.
2. Fuel level is 3-5mm (0.12-0.20 in.) below the carburetor body-to-float bowl mating surface.

Idle Speed and Mixture

1. Adjust idle speed when the engine is at operating temperature.
2. Idle speed should be 1,100-1,300 rpm and is adjusted with the knob between the carburetors.
3. The pilot screws are not adjustable. To tamper with them may violate clean air ordinances.
4. After idle speed is adjusted, rev the engine a few times to check the engine returns to set value. Turn the handlebars from side to side. If idle speed changes, check throttle cable free-play.

Throttle Synchronization

Butterfly valves are synchronized by means of the balance adjusting screw between the two carburetors. The procedures is the same as described for 1974-76 carburetors above.

Fast Idle Adjustment

1. Adjust idle speed with the knob until it is 1,100-1,300 rpm.
2. Check that there is 4-6mm (0.16-0.24 in.) clearance between the pin on the idling link cam and the fast idle cam when the choke lever is fully pushed down.
3. Open or close the gap on the idle link to meet the specification.

TUNE-UP SPECIFICATIONS

	1974-76	1977	1978-On
VALVE CLEARANCE			
Intake (mm/in.)	0.10-0.15/0.004-0.006	0.13-0.15/0.005-0.006	0.17-0.22/0.007-0.009
Exhaust (mm/in.)	0.10-0.15/0.004-0.006	0.13-0.15/0.005-0.006	0.17-0.22/0.007-0.009
IGNITION SYSTEM			
Point gap (mm/in.)	0.3-0.4/0.012-0.016	0.3-0.4/0.012-0.016	0.3-0.4/0.012-0.016 ①
Spark plugs (NGK/ND)			
Standard	B-8ES/W24ES	B-8ES/W24ES	B-7ES/W22ES-U
Hot	B-7ES/W22ES	B-7ES/W22ES	B-6ES/W20EP
Cold	B-9ES/W27E	B-9ES/W27E	B-8ES/W24ES
Spark plug gap (mm/in.)	0.7-0.8/0.028-0.032	0.7-0.8/0.028-0.032	0.7-0.8/0.028-0.032
CARBURETORS			
Idle speed (rpm)	1,100-1,300	1,100-1,300	1,100-1,300
Max. vacuum variation (cm Hg)	1.0	1.0	1.0
Vacuum at idle (cm Hg)	22-27	22-27	22-27
Pilot screw setting	1/16 turn from max rpm	—	—
COMPRESSION (psi)			
Standard	142-156	142-156	142-156
Service limit	107	107	107
Max. variation between cylinders	14	14	14

① Except transistorized ignition

ENGINE AND TRANSMISSION

NOTE: *For engine component inspection techniques and procedures, refer to "Engine Rebuilding" under the "General Information" section.*

ENGINE REMOVAL AND INSTALLATION

NOTE: *Some models may have shims at the engine/frame mounting points. Note their locations when removing and be sure they are properly repositioned when the engine is installed.*

1. Drain the oil and filter.
2. Remove the gas tank. Disconnect the plug leads and loosen the spark plugs.
3. Disconnect the blue primary (breaker points) wire from the connector. Disconnect the tach cable.
4. Remove the left and right-side covers and disconnect the two electrical connectors. Disconnect the electric starter cable (if fitted) from the starter solenoid.

5. Remove the carburetors (refer to "Fuel System" if necessary for procedures).
6. Remove the exhaust system and passenger footpegs. Remove the left rider's footpeg and side stand spring. Remove the gearshift lever.
7. Remove the countershaft sprocket (left rear crankcase) cover. Remove the masterlink and disengage the chain from the countershaft sprocket.

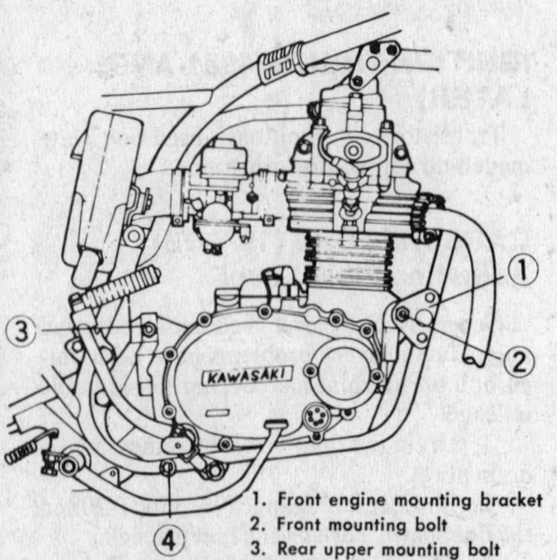

1. Front engine mounting bracket
2. Front mounting bolt
3. Rear upper mounting bolt
4. Rear lower mounting bolt

Engine mounting bolts

8. Disconnect the rear brake light. Unscrew the switch adjusting nut until the portion beneath the mounting bracket can be squeezed, then push the switch out of the bracket.

9. Disconnect the tube from the breather. Remove the bracket bolts from the frame and breather cover (top engine mounting bolts). Unbolt and remove the breather cover.

10. Remove the engine mounting bolts. Raise the engine slightly as the bolts are removed to avoid thread damage. Note that the rear bolts are fitted with spacers and/or shims. Remove the left front engine mounting bracket. Move the clutch cable and sprocket cover out of the way.

11. Lift up the engine and remove it from the left-side of the frame, bringing the top out first.

12. Installation is the reverse of removal. Note the following points:

After installing the engine, fit the left front engine mounting bracket. Tighten the upper bolt and then the lower to 16-19 ft lbs.

13. Lift the engine slightly to install the mounting bolts. Note the rear bolts have spacers fitted between the frame and the left-side of the engine. The lower spacer may have shims added. After tightening the bolt to the proper torque (25-31 ft lbs), check to see if the spacer is tight. If not, add more shims to take up the clearance.

14. Install mounting bolt nuts with the spring side out, and tighten to 25-31 ft lbs.

15. Use a gasket sealer to hold the breather cover O-ring in place if necessary. Tighten cover bolts to 13-16.5 ft lbs.

16. When installing the sprocket cover, the oil guide seal guide should be used to avoid damage to the seal. Route wires in front of the upper mounting bolt spacer.

17. Use new exhaust pipe cylinder head gaskets. Install the shift lever so that it is aligned with the alternator cover lower right-hand screw.

18. When installing the carburetors, note that the cable should run along the right-hand side of the frame tube.

19. Adjust chain, brake light switch, etc.

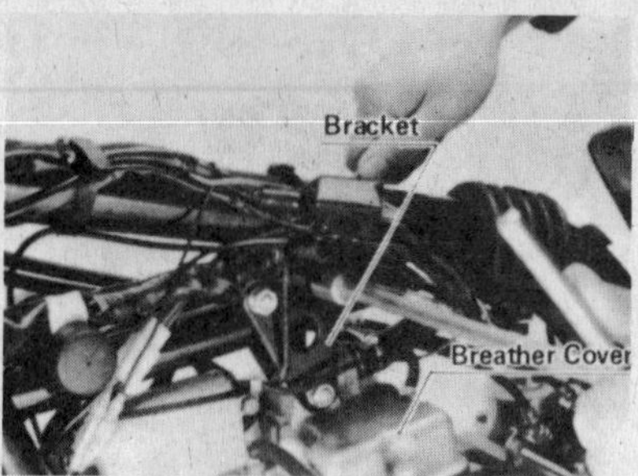

Removing the breather cover bracket

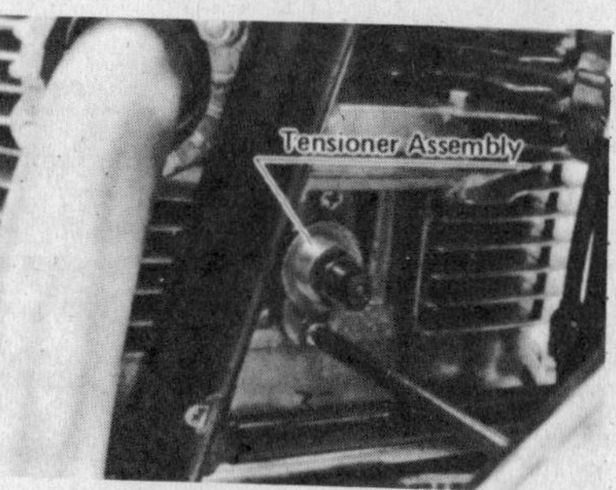

Removing the cam chain tensioner

Removing the cam sprocket bolts

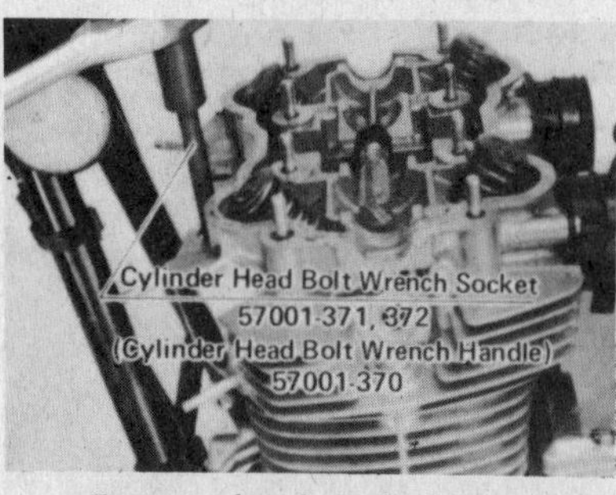

Removing the cylinder head bolts

CYLINDER HEAD

The cylinder head can be removed with the engine in the frame. On 1974-76 models, several special tools are needed for removal and installation.

The head assembly consists of the breather cover, cylinder head cover, head, camshaft, and valve train.

REMOVAL

1. Remove the gas tank. Remove the ignition coil and bracket. Remove the breather cover bracket (three bolts). Disconnect the breather tube. Unbolt and remove the breather cover. Tap with a plastic mallet to free it if necessary.

2. Disconnect the tach cable. Remove the head cover nuts or bolts, and remove the cylinder head cover. Note the O-rings.

3. Remove the cam chain tensioner as follows:

KZ400: Remove the cam chain tensioner cap and O-ring; remove the tensioner screws and pull out the tensioner assembly, complete.

KZ440: Loosen the tensioner lock bolt. Remove the tensioner mounting bolts and take off the tensioner body and O-ring.

CAUTION: *Once the mounting bolts on the KZ440 are loosened, they must be removed completely. Special installation procedures are required. Refer to the "Installation" section following. Failure to follow the procedures may result in engine damage.*

4. Remove the breaker point (or pickup coil) cover. Using a 17mm wrench on the crankshaft *nut,* turn the engine over, and unbolt the camshaft sprocket as the bolts become accessible. Disengage the cam chain from the sprocket. On 1977 and later models, remove the camshaft bearing caps.

5. Loop a length of wire or something similar through the cam chain and secure it to a fixed point to prevent the chain from falling into the cylinder when the camshaft is removed. Remove the cam sprocket and cam.

6. Remove the exhaust system. Remove the left and right-side covers, and remove the carburetors. Refer to "Fuel System" for procedures if necessary.

7. Remove the spark plugs.

8. Remove the external oil line on models so equipped.

9. Remove the cylinder head bolts, loosening bolts gradually and in a cross pattern. Remove the cylinder head. Remove the head gasket.

Disassembly

1. To remove the rocker arms and shafts on 1974-76 models, remove the cap from each side of the cylinder head cover. Remove the nut from each rocker arm shaft, and remove the plate.

2. Pull out the rocker arm shafts with a pliers, protecting the shafts with a rag. Mark the shafts and rocker arms so that they will be installed in their original locations.

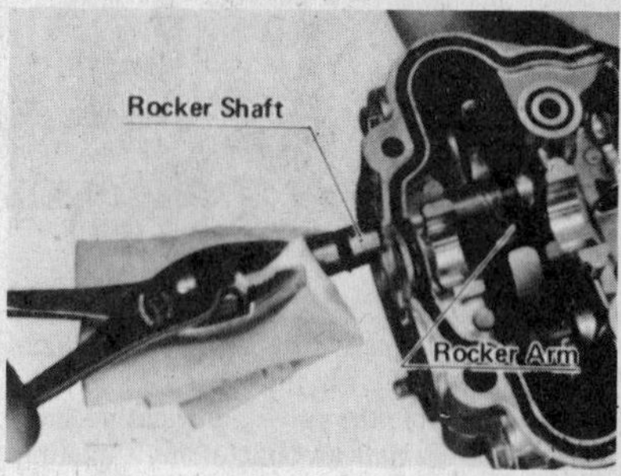

Extricating a rocker arm shaft

3. On 1977 and later models, the rocker arm shafts can be removed by simply unscrewing them from the head cover. Mark them for position to ensure correct installation.

4. Remove the valves by compressing the springs and taking out the keepers. Remove the oil seals from the guides after removing the retaining clip.

Inspection

1. Refer to the specification charts at the end of this section for standard and service limits.

2. If removal of the valve guides is required, heat the head to 250-300° F (120-150° C), and drive out the guide. To install, make sure that an O-ring is fitted to the head side of the guide, and drive it in, heating the head as before.

3. Ream the guide after installation.

Assembly

The use of new O-rings and gaskets is recommended.

1. Lightly lubricate each rocker arm shaft O-ring and push the shafts into place, securing their rocker arms in the process. On 1974-76 models, note that the larger contact pad of the rocker arms ride on the camshaft. Turn each shaft so that the punch mark faces the center of the head cover. Install, but do not tighten, the shaft nuts.

2. Check that all O-rings are in place in the head cover. Secure them with gasket sealer if necessary. Note that the large mat-

Be sure that the shafts are fitted with the punch marks facing the center of the head cover

Cylinder head gasket and O-rings

The unmarked arrow aligns with the head surface when the timing advancer edge is aligned with the timing mark

Cover O-ring and gasket location

Holding plates installed

The "T" mark on the sprocket aligns with the head surface when the timing advance "T" mark aligns with the timing mark

ing surface O-ring is fitted with a tab which must fit into a notch in the cover.

3. Assemble the valves, lubricating each valve with a small amount of high melting point grease before inserting it into its guide.

4. When installing the valve springs, note that both inner and outer springs are progressively wound and are installed with the close coils toward the cylinder head.

The cam is installed with the notch on the right-side of the engine and the sprocket arrows face to the right as well

Installation

1. Fit a new head gasket. Be sure that the O-rings on either side are in place.

2. Install the head, bringing the cam chain up through the passage in the head as it is lowered on the studs.

3. Install the cylinder head holding plates (57001-165), and tighten the stud nuts.

4. Place the cam sprocket on the camshaft. The notched end of the camshaft is located on the *right-side* of the engine, and the side of the cam sprocket with arrows also faces the right-side of the engine.

5. Lubricate the cam bearings and lobes, and slip the cam through the cam chain and fit the chain onto the sprocket.

6. Turn the engine over so that the "T" mark aligns with the timing mark. Turn the engine *counterclockwise* exactly 90° past this point until the timing advance mechanism aligns with the timing mark as illustrated.

7. Disengage the cam chain from the sprocket, and turn the camshaft until the notch on the right end faces directly upward.

8. On early models the cam sprocket has two arrows. One is marked with a "T," the other is unmarked. Turn the sprocket so that the unmarked arrow points toward the front of the engine and is parallel with the head cover mating surface. Fit the cam chain onto the sprocket. On later models, the cam sprocket has only one mark and this must be positioned towards the front of the engine with the cam notch 180° away.

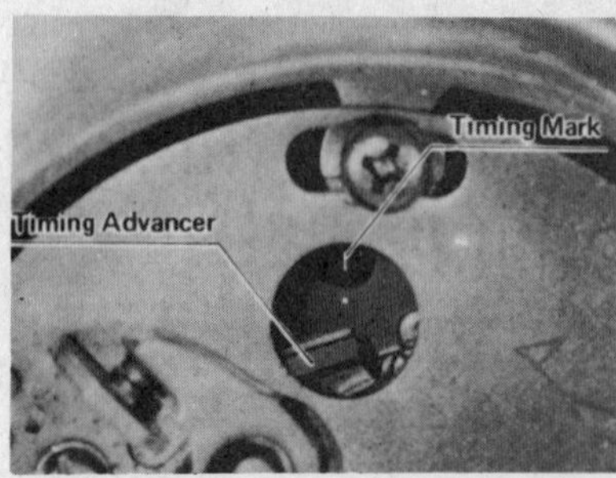

Align the timing advancer as shown to effect valve timing

9. Position the sprocket up against the cam bolt holes. The bolt holes will not be aligned.

10. Hold the cam steady, and slowly turn the crankshaft until the bolt holes align. Fit the cam sprocket bolts which should be coated with a thread locking compound and tightened to 10.0-11.5 ft lbs.

11. Check that valve timing is correct. Turn the crankshaft so that the "T" mark on the timing advance mechanism is aligned with the stationary timing mark. At this position, the cam sprocket arrow marked "T" must be pointing toward the front of the engine and be parallel to the head cover mating surface. If it is not, valve timing is not correct, and must be done again.

12. Remove the cylinder head holding plates. Lubricate the components. Install the cam bearing caps, if fitted, with the arrows facing the front of the engine. Tighten the bolts in a cross pattern to 9 ft lbs.

13. Turn the crankshaft so that the "T" mark on the timing advance mechanism is aligned with the timing mark.

14. Install the cylinder head cover, which has been prepared for installation in Steps 1-2. Fit the eight cover nuts, tightening them in the order shown gradually until the proper torque of 18-22 ft lbs. is reached.

15. Install the four remaining head bolts and tighten them gradually and in the order shown to the proper torque; 8 mm bolts—18-22 ft lbs; 6 mm bolts—8-9.5 ft lbs.

16. Lubricate the tachometer gear with high melting-point grease, insert it, and connect the tach cable.

17. KZ400: refit the tensioner assembly. Assembly order is: pushrod, spring, gasket, holder, pushrod guide, and nut. KZ440: Tension installation is critical. Proceed as follows:

a. Back out the lock bolt a few turns.

b. Put the flat washer and long spring on the pushrod end with the flats.

c. Compress the spring and insert the pushrod into the tensioner body until the flattened end engages the recess at the bottom of the tensioner body.

d. Holding the pushrod in this position, turn in the lock bolt through the body into the rod to keep the rod in place.

CAUTION: *Do not use any bolt longer than 14mm, as it may cause damage. Never loosen the lock bolt before installing the tensioner.*

e. Put the balls and retainer and small spring on the pushrod. Fit the O-ring.

f. Place the assembled tensioner on the engine. Fit and secure the bolts.

g. Loosen the lock bolt several turns until it releases the pushrod. Tighten the lock bolt to 7 ft lbs.

18. Install the breather cover, holding the O-ring in place with gasket sealer if necessary. Tighten the breather bolts gradually and in a cross pattern until a torque of 13-16.5 ft lbs is reached.

19. The remainder of the procedure is the reverse of removal. Adjust the valves and cam chain after assembly is complete.

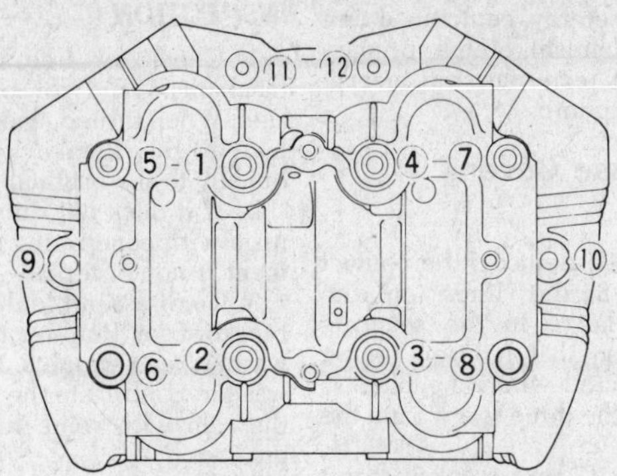

Cylinder head and head cover bolt tightening sequence

CYLINDER AND PISTON

Removal

1. Remove the cylinder head components and cam chain tensioner as outlined in the preceding section.
2. Pull up the cylinders, taking care that the pistons do not hit the crankcases when they come out of the bores.
3. Remove the cylinder base gasket, noting the positions of the oil passage O-rings.
4. Wrap a clean wrag around the base of the piston, and use a needlenose pliers to take out the wrist pin circlips.
5. Push out the wrist pin. If the pin resists removal, the piston crown may be heated slightly. Alternately, use special factory tools 57001-910 and 57001-913.

Mark each piston for position so that it can be reinstalled in its own bore.

Inspection

1. Refer to the specifications chart at the end of this section for service limits. Note the following points;

a. Pistons are available in two oversizes: 0.5mm and 1.0mm. Measure piston diameter 5mm (0.2 in.) from skirt bottom. Measure bore 10mm (0.4 in.) and 60mm (2.4 in.) from top; 25mm (1 in.) from bottom;

b. If boring is necessary, standard piston-cylinder clearance is 0.034-0.054 mm/0.001-0.002 in.;

c. In addition to fitted end-gap and side clearance, used rings should be checked for free end-gap to check for loss of tension;

d. When fitting new parts, try to fit a marked piston pin to a piston with an "A" mark on the crown, and an unmarked pin with an unmarked piston.

Use pistons marked with "2" on the crown in cylinders marked in the same way, and fit unnumbered pistons into the unnumbered cylinders.

Installation

1. Top and bottom compression rings are not interchangeable and must be installed as illustrated, and with the manufacturer's mark near the end-gap facing *upward.*

Piston and pin marks

Piston and cylinder marks

2. The arrow on the piston crown must face the exhaust port.
3. Use new wrist pin snap-rings in all cases.
4. On models with a one-piece oil ring, arrange the end gaps so that the top compression and the oil ring gaps face the exhaust side and the second compression ring faces the intake side of the engine.

On models with a three-piece oil ring, arrangement should be the same except that the oil ring rails must be positioned about 30° on either side of the oil expander, whose gap should face the exhaust side of the engine.

5. Fit a new cylinder base gasket, ensuring that the O-rings are in place. Fit new O-rings to the cylinders, if necessary.
6. Lightly lubricate the rings and piston skirts with motor oil. Use piston base 57001-340 to hold the pistons in place, and ring compressor 57001-921 and adapter A/57001-924 to squeeze the rings so that the cylinders may be installed.
7. Pull the cam chain through the cylinders as they are lowered down on the studs. Secure the chain so that it will not fall into the engine.
8. The rest of the procedure is the reverse of removal.

Install rings with the mark facing upward

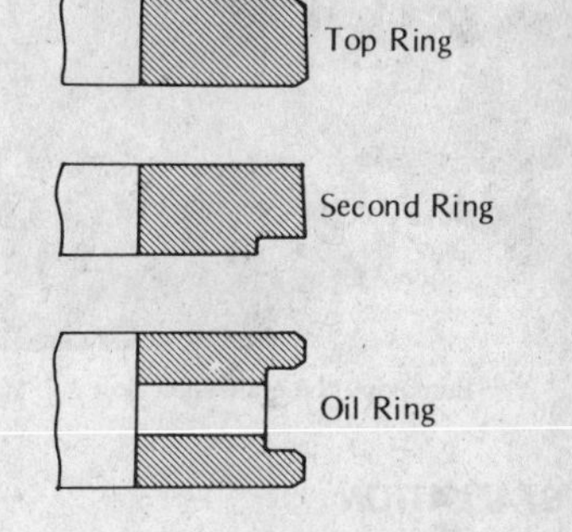

Note that the two compression rings are not interchangeable

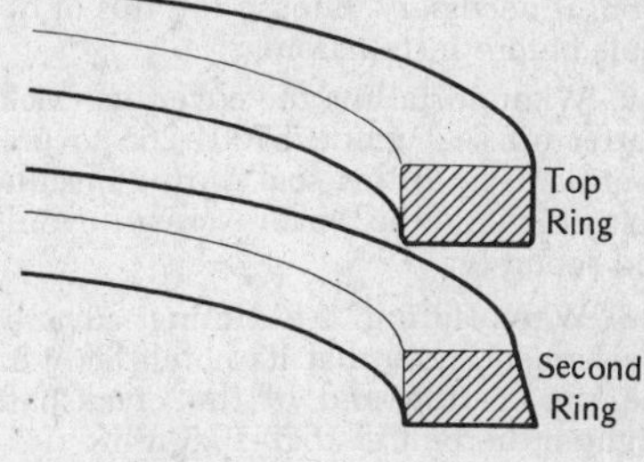

Compression ring profiles (1977-On)

CRANKCASE COVER COMPONENTS

Right Crankcase Cover Components

The right crankcase cover houses the

breaker points assembly, centrifugal timing advance mechanism, clutch, primary drive components, external shift mechanism, and the oil pump.

Right Crankcase Cover

REMOVAL

1. Drain the oil. Remove the contact breaker cover. Scribe lines on the breaker plate relative to the securing screw positions so that ignition timing can be approximated when the plate is refitted. Remove the three screws and the plate.
2. Holding the 17 mm crankshaft nut with a wrench, break loose the crankshaft bolt. Remove it, and the timing advance mechanism.
3. Remove the right footpeg. Scribe a mark across the kick-starter lever and its shaft to mark its position, then remove the bolt and pull off the kick-starter lever.
4. Placing a pan beneath the cover to catch any oil residue, remove the 12 cover screws and pull off the cover, using a plastic mallet to break it loose if necessary.

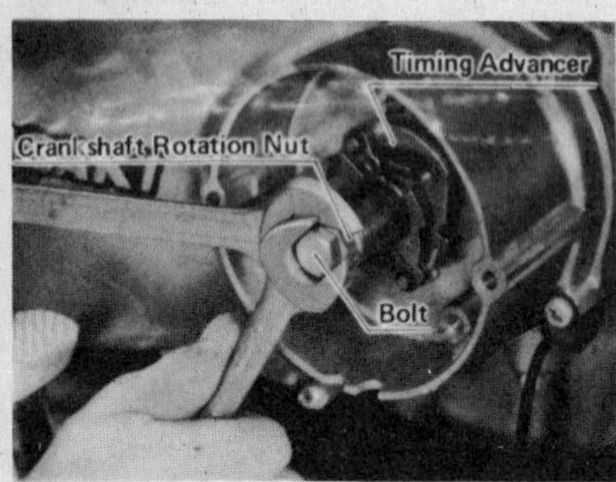

Removing the crankshaft bolt

INSTALLATION

1. Use a new cover gasket. Check the condition of the kick-starter and crankshaft oil seals in the cover, and replace them if necessary. Grease the lips of the seals before installation.
2. When installing the cover, use kick-starter oil seal guide 57001-265 to prevent damage to this seal during installation. Tighten the cover screws evenly and securely.
3. When fitting the timing advance mechanism, note that its notch fits with the pin on the end of the crankshaft. Tighten the bolt to 16.5–19.5 ft lbs.
4. The remainder of the procedure is the reverse of removal. Reset the ignition timing.

Timing Advance Mechanism

REMOVAL

1. Remove the contact breaker cover. Scribe lines on the breaker plate relative to the securing screw positions, so that ignition timing can be approximated when the plate is refitted. Remove the three screws and the plate.
2. Holding the 17 mm crankshaft nut with a wrench, break loose the crankshaft bolt. Remove it, and the timing advance mechanism.

INSPECTION

1. Check for free movement of the mechanism and for proper spring tension. When turned against its stop and released, the breaker cam must return quickly to the original position.
2. If it does not, lubricate the mechanism with penetrating oil. If no improvement is noted, replace the springs.
3. To disassemble the unit, pull off the breaker cam. Remove the two "C" rings, washers, and weights. Remove the thrust washers. Lubricate the shaft and inside of the cam with some high melting point grease.
4. When assembling, align the mark on the breaker cam with the cut-out notch on the mechanism body.

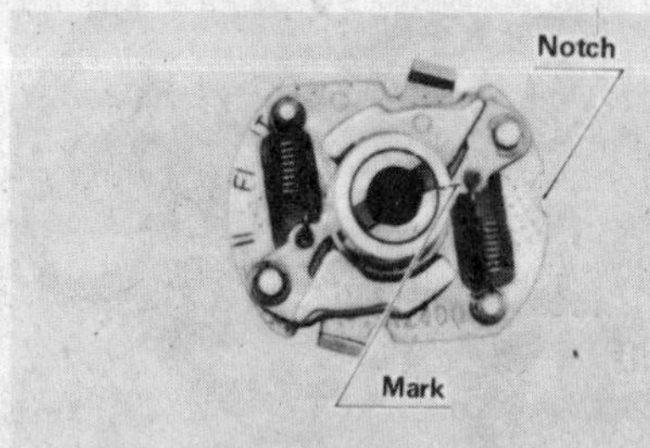

When assembling the timing advance mechanism, align the mark with the notch

INSTALLATION

1. Installation is the reverse of removal. Align the notch in the mechanism with the pin on the crankshaft.
2. Tighten the crankshaft bolt to 16.5–19.5 ft lbs.

Clutch and Primary Drive

REMOVAL

Before removing the components, check primary chain wear.

The primary chain is allowed a maximum of 20 mm (0.8 in.) of total up and down movement which is measured in the middle of the upper chain run. If movement exceeds this amount, replace the chain.

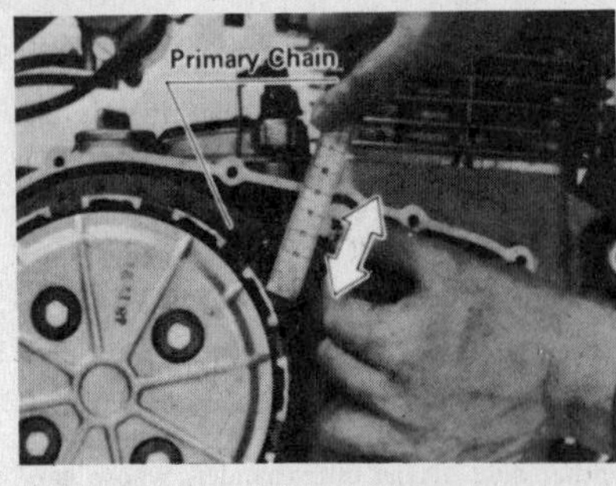

Checking primary chain wear

If replacement is necessary, use "Tsubakimoto Hy-Vo" No. 3/8P-5/8W 74-link chain only.

1. Remove the right crankcase cover as outlined in the preceding procedure.
2. Remove the clutch spring bolts, washers, and springs. Remove the pressure plate. Remove the pusher. Tilt the motorcycle to the right so that the steel ball comes out of the clutch shaft.

Removing the oil pump drive gear

3. Remove the clutch hub circlip and the shims behind it. Remove the clutch plates and the clutch hub. Note the thrust washer behind the hub.
4. Remove the circlip from the crankshaft (primary) gear. Pull off the clutch housing, chain, and crankshaft gear together.
5. Remove the oil pump drive gear from the back of the clutch housing, if desired, by removing the circlip. Note the locating pin.

INSPECTION

1. Check the clutch and gears as outlined in "Engine Rebuilding" and by referring to the specifications at the end of this section.
2. Check chain guide thickness. Standard is 7.5 mm (0.3 in.). Serviceable limit is 3.5 mm (0.14 in.).

INSTALLATION

1. Fit the oil pump drive gear onto the clutch housing, noting that the protruding side of the gear faces the housing.
2. Assemble the crankshaft gear, chain, and clutch housing. Note that the protruding side of the crankshaft gear faces *out.* Fit the assembly, rotating the oil pump gear by hand if necessary so that it meshes with the drive gear. Install the crankshaft gear circlip.

Install the crankshaft primary gear with the protruding side outward

3. Fit the thick thrust washer to the clutch assembly, followed by the hub. Install the shims and the clutch hub circlip. There should be no axial play of the clutch hub on its shaft. If there is, remove the circlip, and add more shims until the play is taken up.
4. Install the clutch plates in the following order: friction plate, steel ring, steel plate, and alternating in this manner, fitting a steel ring last.
5. Install the steel ball and the pusher.
6. Install the pressure plate, aligning the marks on the plate and the clutch hub. Install the springs, washers, and

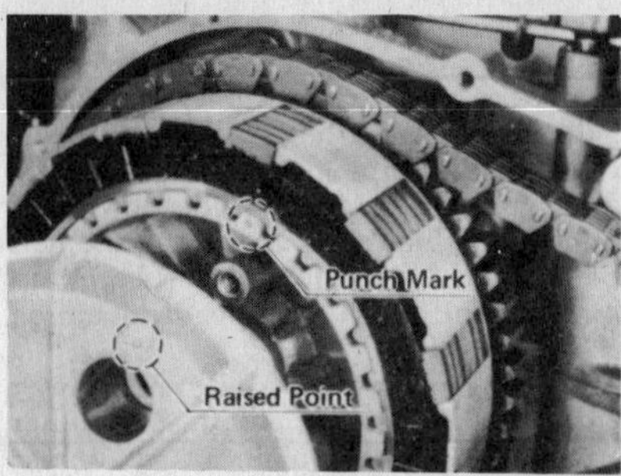

Align the marks on the pressure plate and clutch hub

spring bolts, tightening them evenly and in a cross pattern.

7. The remainder of the procedure is the reverse of removal.

Oil Pump

REMOVAL

1. Remove the right crankcase cover and the clutch and primary drive assembly. Refer to the preceding procedures.

2. Remove the four oil pump screws and pull off the pump. Note the O-rings in the crankcase.

INSPECTION

Refer to "Lubrication System."

INSTALLATION

1. Installation is the reverse of removal.

2. Lubricate the pump with motor oil before installation.

Shift Mechanism

The shift mechanism in the right crankcase cover consists of the shift shaft, return spring, and shift arm or pawl.

REMOVAL

1. Remove the right crankcase and the clutch and primary drive assembly. Refer to the preceding procedures.

2. Remove the left rider footpeg. Remove the side stand and spring. Remove the gearshift lever.

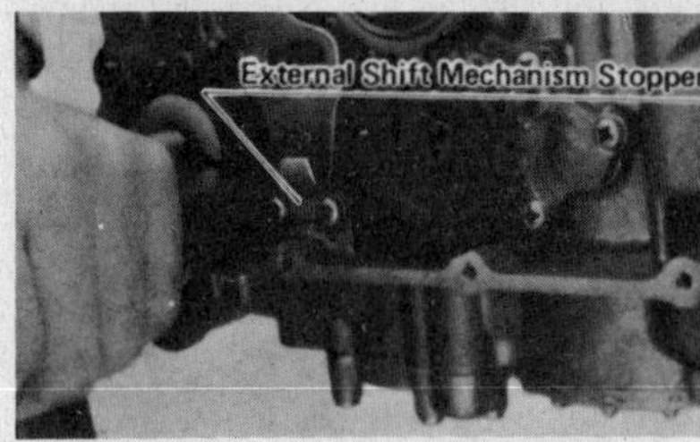

Removing the shift mechanism stopper

3. Remove the left rear crankcase (engine sprocket) cover.

4. Remove the shift mechanism stopper. Disengage the fingers of the shifter pawl from the shift drum and pull out the shaft.

INSTALLATION

1. Be sure that the shifter return spring is properly installed with the spring arms on either side of the return spring pin.

2. Use oil seal guide 57001-264 to protect the shift shaft oil seals in the crankcase and the engine sprocket cover when installing the shift shaft. Engage the pawl with the shift drum pins.

3. Use thread locking compound on the shift mechanism stopper screws.

Left Crankcase Cover Components

The left crankcase covers house the engine (countershaft) sprocket, the clutch release mechanism, the alternator, and the electric starter sprocket and chain (on "D" models).

Left Crankcase Covers

REMOVAL AND INSTALLATION

1. Remove the left rider's peg. Remove the sidestand and spring. Remove the shift lever.

2. Remove the four screws and take off the sprocket cover.

3. To remove the alternator cover, first remove the sprocket cover (Steps 1 and 2).

4. Remove the right-side frame cover and disconnect the alternator field coil leads from the connector.

5. Remove the wiring guide just above the countershaft sprocket.

6. Remove the starter motor cover and gasket. Remove the eight alternator cover screws and take off the cover. Disconnect the oil pressure and neutral indicator leads.

7. Installation is the reverse of removal. Use shift shaft oil seal guide 57001-264 when installing the countershaft sprocket cover. Be sure that the electrical wiring is correctly routed.

Clutch Release Mechanism

REMOVAL AND INSTALLATION

1. The clutch release mechanism is incorporated in the countershaft sprocket cover.

2. Remove the sprocket cover. Remove the cotter pin from the clutch cable fitting, and disengage the cable from the fitting, and from the cover.

Disconnecting the clutch cable from the fitting

3. Remove the chain guide screws.

4. Remove the two clutch release outer gear screws and separate the two gears.

5. Clean the release mechanism in solvent, dry, and lubricate thoroughly with grease.

6. Assemble the release mechanism, fitting the worm gears together so that, as they begin to mesh, the raised point on the outer gear aligns with the punch mark on the inner gear.

The raised point and punch mark should align as the gears begin to mesh

Clutch release mechanism installation

7. Use thread locking compound on the outer gear screws. Install the mechanism as shown.

8. The remainder of installation is the reverse of removal.

Countershaft Sprocket

REMOVAL AND INSTALLATION

1. Remove the countershaft sprocket cover.

2. If special engine sprocket holder 56019-040 is available, disconnect the chain, bend down the tab on the sprocket nut lockwasher, and remove the nut.

3. If it is not available, place the transmission in gear, bend down the tab on the sprocket washer, and remove the sprocket nut, applying the rear brake if necessary to hold the sprocket.

4. To install, tighten the sprocket nut to 87–105 ft lbs and bend down the washer tab. If the chain was disconnected, be sure to install the masterlink spring clip with the closed end facing the direction of chain rotation.

Alternator and Starter Assembly

REMOVAL

1. Remove both left-side covers as outlined in the preceding procedures.

Removing the starter motor bolts

2. To remove the starter motor, first remove the cover and disconnect the lead at the motor.

3. Remove the two 10 mm bolts on the right-side of the starter motor body.

4. Tap lightly on the starter motor body with a plastic mallet to move it to the right and disengage the shaft from the gear.

CAUTION: *Do not tap the motor shaft itself.*

Tapping out the starter motor

5. To remove the alternator rotor, hold the rotor steady with the special tool (alternately, engage the transmission and apply the rear brake to lock the crankshaft, and remove the rotor bolt by turning it in a *clockwise* direction).

CAUTION: *The rotor bolt is a LEFT-HAND thread.*

6. Remove the rotor and starter clutch assembly using special puller 57001-254 while holding the rotor in place. Note the thrust washer behind the rotor.

7. Pull off the starter chain and sprocket.

8. The field coil and alternator armature windings are in the cover. To remove them (not necessary for testing), remove the starter motor chain guide and sprocket guide. Remove the three armature allen bolts and remove the armature. Remove the three field coil allen bolts on the outer side of the cover and remove the field coil.

INSPECTION

1. For alternator and starter motor tests, refer to "Electrical System."

2. Disassembly of the starter clutch is not necessary unless it has been malfunctioning. To check operation of the starter clutch, fit the sprocket and rotor assembly to the crankshaft. When the rotor is turned, by hand, in a counterclockwise direction, the sprocket should turn as well. If the rotor is turned in the clockwise direction, the sprocket should not turn.

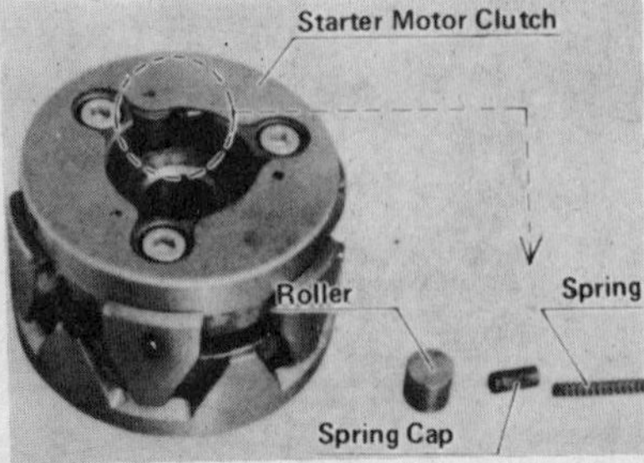

Starter clutch components

To disassemble the starter clutch, remove the three allen screws, and take out the springs, spring caps, and rotors. Check for wear of the rollers.

3. Check the starter motor chain by measuring its length. Extend the chain by stretching it with a force of about 10 lbs. A twenty-link length of chain (standard) measures 155.5 mm (6.1 in.); service limit is 157.8 mm (6.2 in.)

INSTALLATION

1. Fit the starter clutch to the rotor, using thread locking compound on the bolts and tightening to 24–27 ft lbs.

2. Install the field coil, use thread locking compound on the bolts and tighten to 5.1–5.8 ft lbs. Use the same procedure and torque on the armature bolts. Fit all wiring into their grommets and properly fit the grommets in the case.

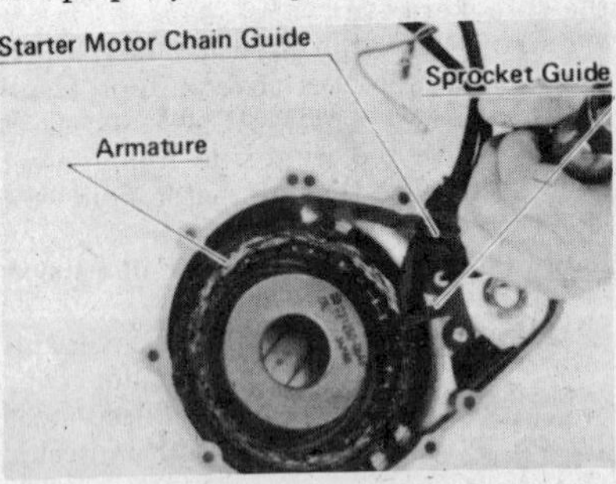

Installing the sprocket guide

3. Use thread locking compound when installing the sprocket guide and starter motor chain guide. The sprocket guide bends outward.

4. Put a little oil on the starter motor O-ring, and install the starter motor. Install the sprockets and chain.

5. Put some high melting point grease on the rotor thrust washer and put it behind the rotor, installing the rotor assembly on the crankshaft. Install the rotor bolt (left-hand thread), and tighten it to 47–51 ft lbs while holding the rotor in place.

6. The remainder of the procedure is the reverse of removal.

Lower End and Transmission

Engine removal is required for these components: crankshaft, transmission, shift drum assembly, balancer assembly, and kick-starter.

Removal of the top end components is required for crankshaft service, but the top end may be left in place for service and inspection of the kick-starter, transmission, or balancer.

Splitting the Crankcase

1. Drain the oil and remove the filter. Remove the engine from the frame. If crankshaft service is required, remove the top end components. Refer to the preceding procedures.

2. Remove the crankcase covers and all of the components therein: clutch and primary drive, external shift mechanism, countershaft sprocket, starter motor, and alternator assembly.

3. Remove the six upper crankcase half bolts and the carburetor overflow/breather tube guide.

4. Turn the engine upside down and remove the fourteen lower crankcase half bolts. Remove the lower case half, tapping carefully with a plastic mallet to free it if necessary.

The lower case half will come away with the kick-starter shaft. The other components will remain in the upper case half.

Transmission

1. Check the gears in place. Check gear backlash. Standard is 0.06–0.23 mm (0.0024–0.0092 in.), while the serviceable limit is 0.3 mm (0.012 in.).

2. To remove the transmission, lift the shafts and gears together out of the case.

3. Disassembly of the transmission shafts must be done carefully. Lay out each component as it is removed for ease of assembly.

4. For the mainshaft, take out the clutch pushrod and oil seal. Remove the shaft needle bearing outer race. Remove the circlip and take off the needle bearing and any shims fitted.

5. Remove the 2d and 5th gears, the copper bushing and splined washer. Remove the circlip followed by 3rd gear.

6. Remove the circlip, splined washers, and 4th gear.

7. Remove the bushing and shaft ball bearing together using the special puller.

8. To disassemble the countershaft, remove the needle bearing outer race, circlip, needle bearing, and shim(s).

9. Remove the 1st and 4th gears, splined washer, 3rd gear, splined washer, circlip, and 5th gear.

10. Remove the circlip, splined washer, and 2d gear. Remove the oil seal, collar, and O-ring. Remove the shaft ball bearing with the special tool.

11. Check gear-shaft clearances.

12. Assembly is the reverse of disassembly. Refer to the exploded view for part locations. New circlips should be used, and special tool 57001-380 should be used to install circlips without damage.

13. After assembly of the shafts, check side play. If evident, use shims as necessary on the engine side of the needle bearings to eliminate play. Shaft ball bearings must be pressed into place.

Shift Drum

1. Remove the transmission shafts.

2. Remove the shift drum stopper.

3. Remove the shift drum positioning bolt, O-ring, spring, and plunger on top of the upper crankcase half.

4. Remove the cotter pin and guide pin from the shift fork (3rd gear), which rides on the shift drum. Pull out the shift drum, and remove the operating plate circlip, operating plate, and shift fork.

5. Pull out the shift rod and the two remaining shift forks. They are not interchangeable. Note positions.

6. Check all parts for wear.

7. Insert the shift rod into the crankcase and through the two shift forks. The

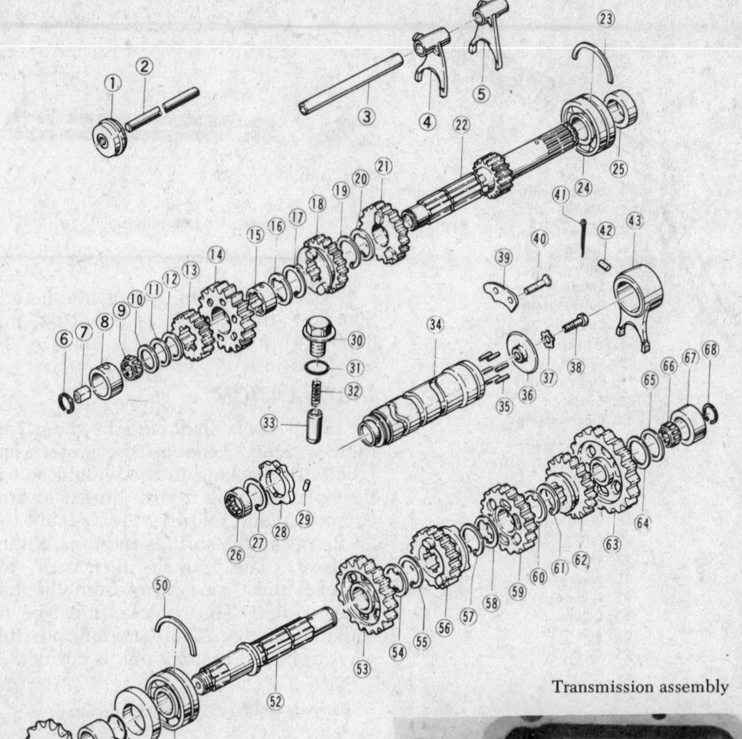

1. Oil seal
2. Clutch pushrod
3. Shift rod
4. 5th gearshift fork
5. 4th gearshift fork
6. Circlip
7. Bushing
8. Needle bearing outer race
9. Needle bearing
10. Shim
11. Bronze shim
12. Shim
13. 2nd gear
14. 5th gear
15. Copper bushing
16. Splined washer
17. Circlip
18. 3rd gear
19. Circlip
20. Splined washer
21. 4th gear
22. Mainshaft
23. Set ring
24. Bearing
25. Bushing
26. Shift drum needle bearing
27. Circlip
28. Operating plate
29. Operating plate pin
30. Shift drum positioning bolt
31. O-ring
32. Spring
33. Pin
34. Shift drum
35. Pins
36. Drum pin plate
37. Lockwasher
38. Screw
39. Shift drum stopper
40. Screw
41. Cotter pin
42. Guide pin
43. 3rd gearshift fork
44. Countershaft sprocket nut
45. Toothed washer
46. Countershaft sprocket
47. Countershaft collar
48. O-ring
49. Oil seal
50. Set ring
51. Bearing
52. Countershaft
53. 2d gear
54. Splined washer
55. Circlip
56. 5th gear
57. Circlip
58. Splined washer
59. 3rd gear
60. Splined washer
61. Circlip
62. 4th gear
63. 1st gear
64. Shim
65. Shim
66. Needle bearing
67. Needle bearing outer race
68. Circlip

Transmission assembly

Removing the shift drum stopper

Removing the shift drum positioning bolt assembly

Removing the shift drum

Shift fork positions

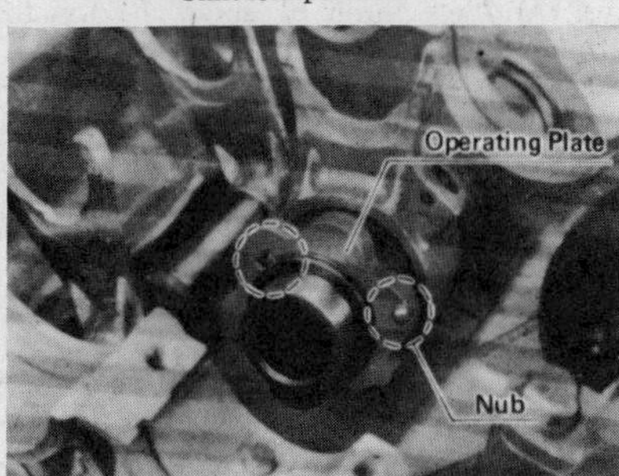

Shift drum operating plate installation. The nub faces out.

shift forks are not interchangeable. Note that the fork on which the guide pin is located in the center of the fork is located on the clutch side of the engine.

8. Insert the shift drum into the crankcase fitting the shift fork as this is done. The pin housing on the shift fork faces the crankshaft.

9. Install the operating plate pin, if it was removed, and fit the operating plate, nub facing out. Install the circlip.

10. Insert the shift fork guide pin, cotter pin, and secure the cotter pin.

11. Fully install the shift drum and engage the guide pins for the other two shift forks with the drum grooves.

12. Install the shift drum stopper screws, which should be peened for security. Install the shift drum positioning bolt components after turning the drum, if necessary, so that the plunger is properly in place.

Kick-Starter

1. Bend up the tabs on the lockplate of the ratchet gear arm stopper bolts, and remove the bolts and stopper.

2. Remove the spring guide circlip.

3. Remove the spring guide. Remove the return spring.

4. Remove the kick-starter shaft collar circlip. Remove the shaft stopper and collar.

5. Remove the kick-starter shaft.

6. Remove the gear and thrust washer. Remove the spring side circlip, and take off the spring cap and spring.

7. Remove the ratchet gear and the other circlip.

8. Check all parts for wear.

9. Assembly is the reverse of disassembly. When fitting the ratchet gear, align the punch mark on the gear with the notch on the shaft.

10. When fitting the return spring, turn the shaft as far as possible clockwise, insert one end of the return spring into the crankcase and the other end into the kick-

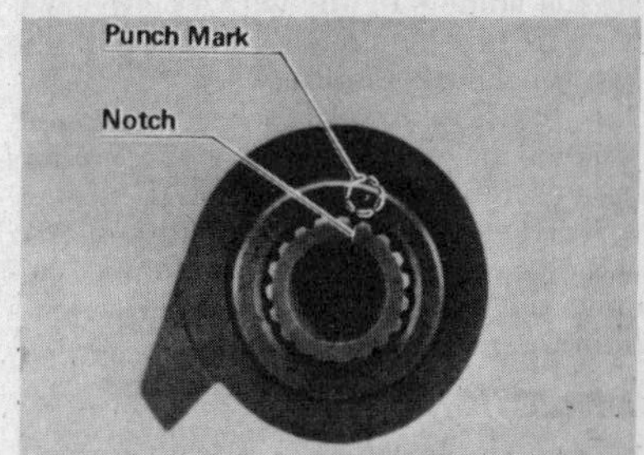

Align the notch and punch mark when assembling the ratchet gear onto the shaft

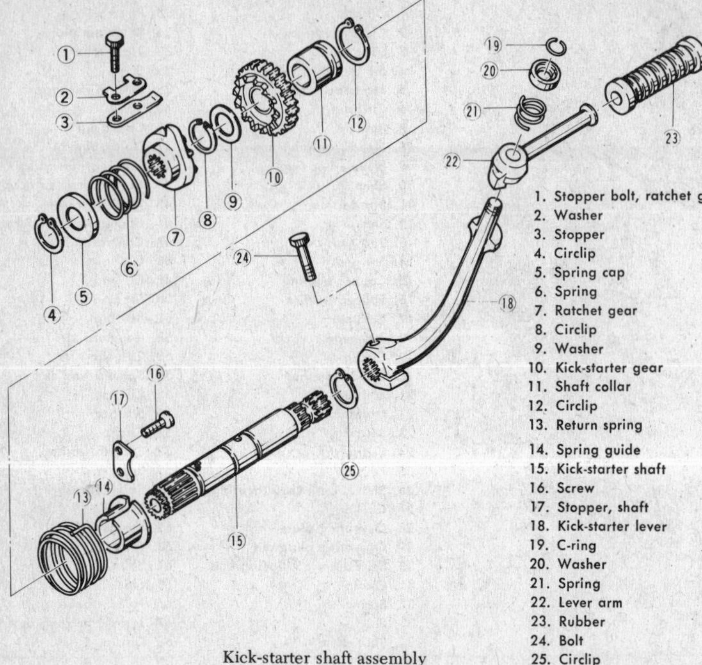

1. Stopper bolt, ratchet gear arm
2. Washer
3. Stopper
4. Circlip
5. Spring cap
6. Spring
7. Ratchet gear
8. Circlip
9. Washer
10. Kick-starter gear
11. Shaft collar
12. Circlip
13. Return spring
14. Spring guide
15. Kick-starter shaft
16. Screw
17. Stopper, shaft
18. Kick-starter lever
19. C-ring
20. Washer
21. Spring
22. Lever arm
23. Rubber
24. Bolt
25. Circlip

Kick-starter shaft assembly

Measure a 20-link length.

Checking the balancer chain for wear

starter shaft. Hold the spring in this position, and fit the spring guide.

11. Use a bit of high melting point grease on the inside of the collar. Peen the shaft stopper screws for security. Bend down the tabs on the ratchet gear arm stopper bolt lockplate.

Balancer

REMOVAL

1. Remove the four bolts and two screws from the crankshaft bushing cap. Note that the cap has an arrow pointing toward the front of the engine, and it must be refitted in the same way.
2. Remove the balancer chain guide.

Removing the crankshaft bushing cap

3. Remove the balancer holder bolts, tap the holders lightly with a plastic mallet to free them, if necessary; then lift the entire balancer assembly away.
4. If disassembly of the unit is desired, remove the chain. Remove the holders from each balance weight and the shims.
5. Tap off the sprockets with a plastic mallet. Remove the springs and pins. Remove the bolts, and separate the weights from their shafts.

INSPECTION

1. Measure the diameters of the balancer shafts and the inside diameters of the holders. Compare to the serviceable limits.

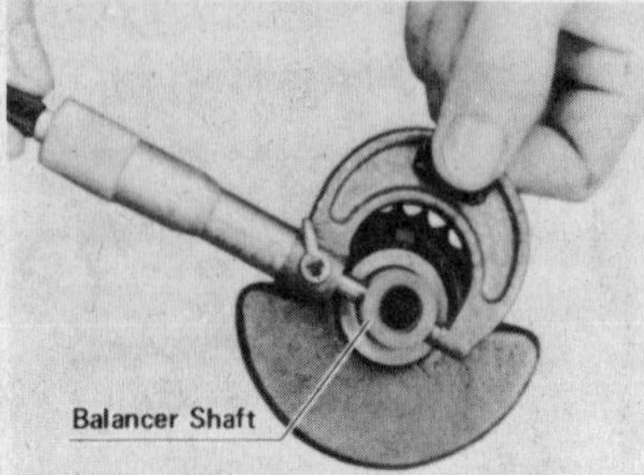

Measuring balancer shaft diameter

2. Apply a force of about 10 lbs to stretch the balancer chain and measure a 20-link length. Standard length is 160 mm (6.30 in.). Serviceable limit is 162.4 mm (6.38 in.).
3. Check chain guide thickness. Each must be at least 1.0 mm (0.04 in.) or better.
4. Check balancer spring free-length. Standard free-length is 9.8–10.4 mm (0.39–0.41 in.). Serviceable limit is 9.0 mm (0.35 in.).

INSTALLATION

1. Oil each shaft and fit them into their weights. Line up the larger shaft hole with the hole in the weight and fit the bolt, securing it with thread locking compound and torquing to 7.9–9.5 ft lbs.
2. Install the springs and pins. Fit the sprocket. The punch mark on the sprocket must face away from the balancer weight. The sprocket must be installed as shown. There are four possible ways to install it. Only one is correct.

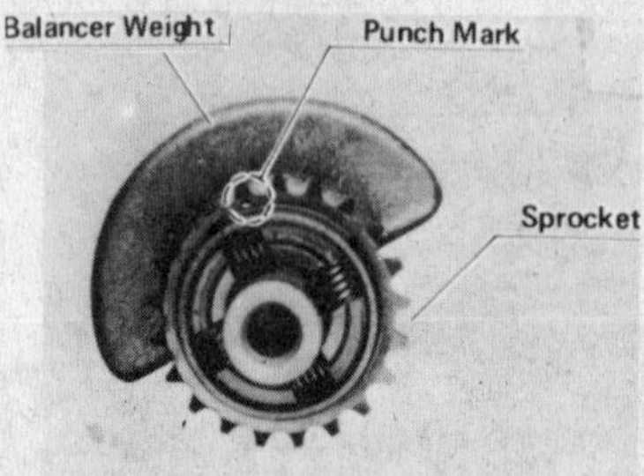

Sprocket installed correctly

3. Install the sprocket side shims. The smaller diameter shim is installed first. Fit the holders onto the shaft. Note that the machined side of each holder faces the weight.

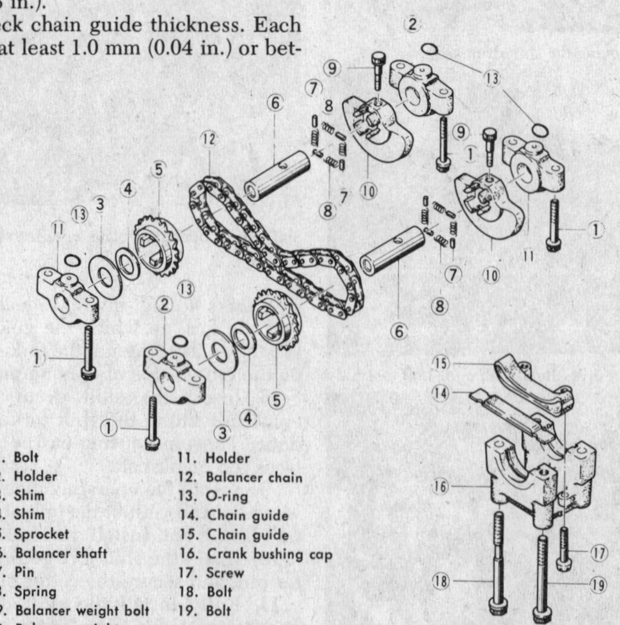

1. Bolt
2. Holder
3. Shim
4. Shim
5. Sprocket
6. Balancer shaft
7. Pin
8. Spring
9. Balancer weight bolt
10. Balancer weight
11. Holder
12. Balancer chain
13. O-ring
14. Chain guide
15. Chain guide
16. Crank bushing cap
17. Screw
18. Bolt
19. Bolt

Balancer assembly

Install holders with the machined side facing the weight

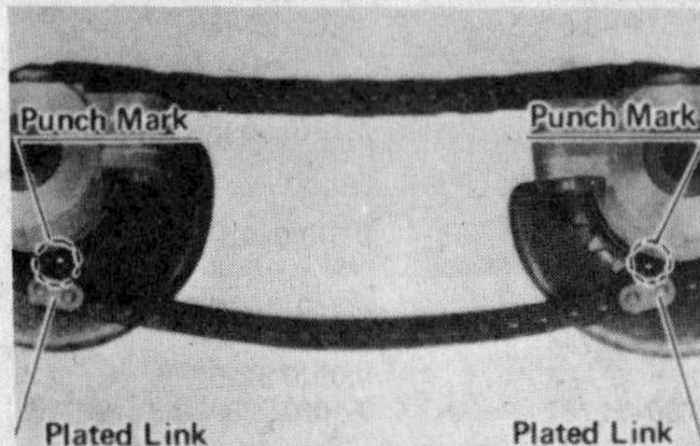

The chromed links must align with the sprocket punch marks

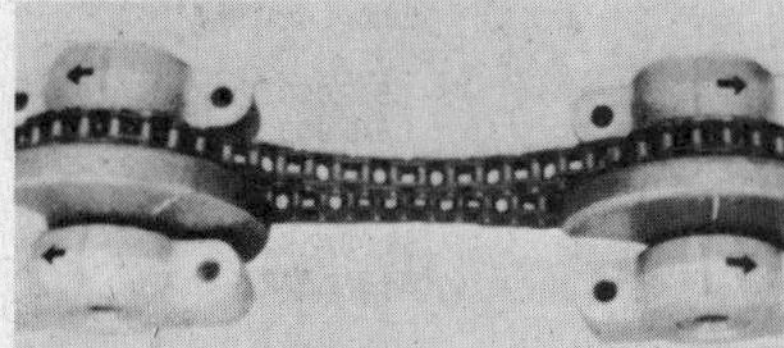
Install the assembly with the holder arrows pointing outward

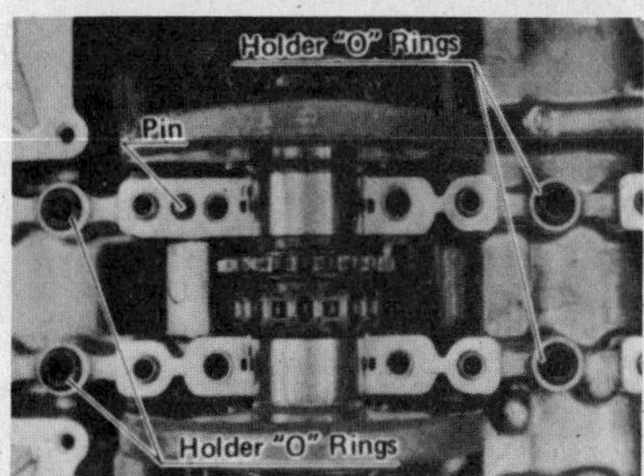

The pin and O-rings must be in place

Turn the crankshaft so that the oil holes align with the crankcase mating surface

4. Install the chain on the balancer sprockets. The two chromed links on the chain must align with the punch marks on the sprocket tooth of each sprocket. Turn the holders so that the arrow on each holder points away from the crankshaft.

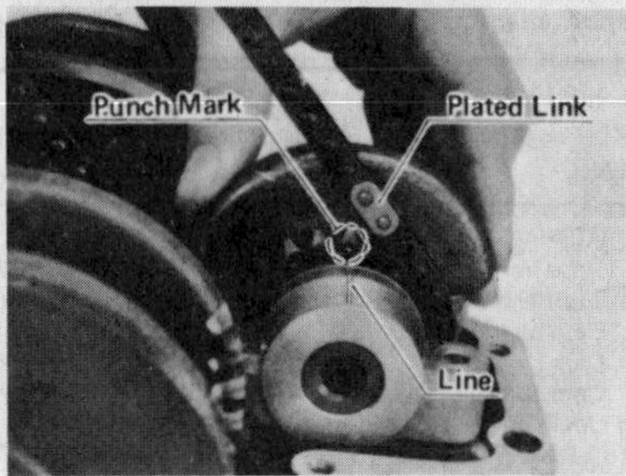

Align the chrome-plated link, sprocket punch mark, and holder line

Balancer assembly correctly installed. The weights must be directly upright.

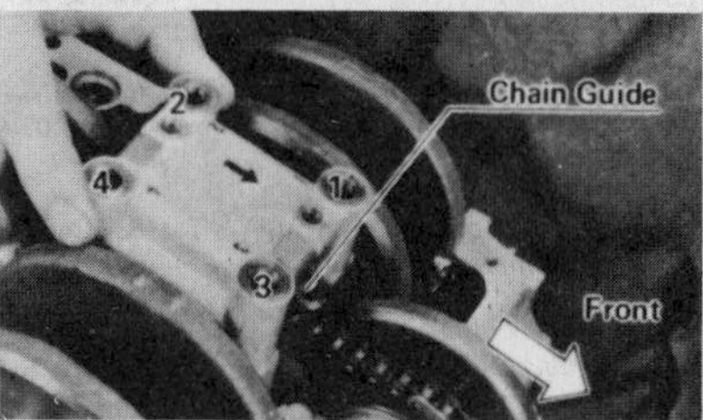

The crankshaft bushing cap is installed with the arrow facing the front of the engine

5. Check that the holder O-rings and the pin are in place in the crankcase.

6. Turn the crankshaft so that the oil holes are even with the upper crankcase mating surface, as shown, and facing the front of the engine.

7. Holding the balancer assembly taut after alignment (Step 4), place one unit in position in the crankcase. Turn the sprocket punch mark so that it aligns with the mark on the holders. Engage the balancer chain with the crankshaft sprocket, and install the remaining unit, aligning the marks as before.

8. With the balancer in place, check that each chrome chain link is aligned with the holder marks. The balance weights must be directly upright, not cocked to either side.

9. Make sure that each holder is well-seated in its locating pin. Install the holder bolts and tighten to 10–11.5 ft lbs.

10. Install the balancer chain guides: one under the upper chain run, one in the crankshaft bushing cap.

11. Oil the crankshaft bushing cap lightly, and install it with the arrow facing the front of the engine. Install the screws, securing them with thread locking compound. Tighten the bushing cap bolts in a cross pattern to 18–22 ft lbs.

Cranksahft

REMOVAL

1. Remove the top end components, including the pistons. Remove the crankcase cover components and split the crankcases. Remove the transmission and the balancer assembly. Refer to the preceding sections for procedures.

2. Remove any balancer holder O-rings which are loose to prevent loss. Remove the pin in the crankcase which secures the camshaft chain guide locating pin.

3. Remove the crankshaft and cam chain. Remove the chain guide, if desired, by pulling out the locating pin.

4. Remove the connecting rods, noting the alignment of the cap and rod marks. The caps must be installed correctly.

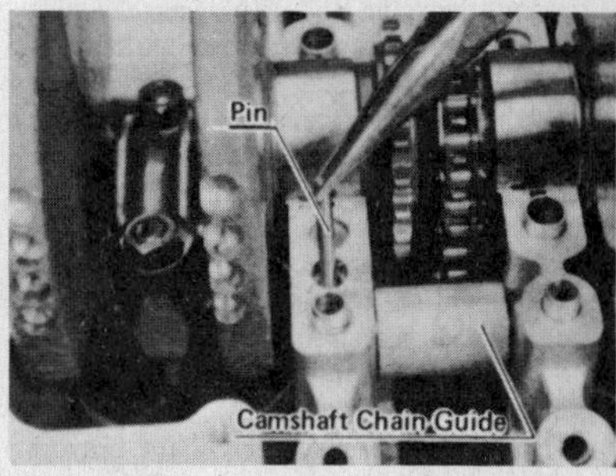

Removing the chain guide pin

INSPECTION

1. Check that the rods are not bent or twisted.

2. Check the condition of the rod bearings. Use Plastigage® to measure rod-crankshaft journal clearance which is set at 0.041–0.071 mm (0.0016–0.0027 in.). Serviceable limit is 0.1 mm (0.0039 in.).

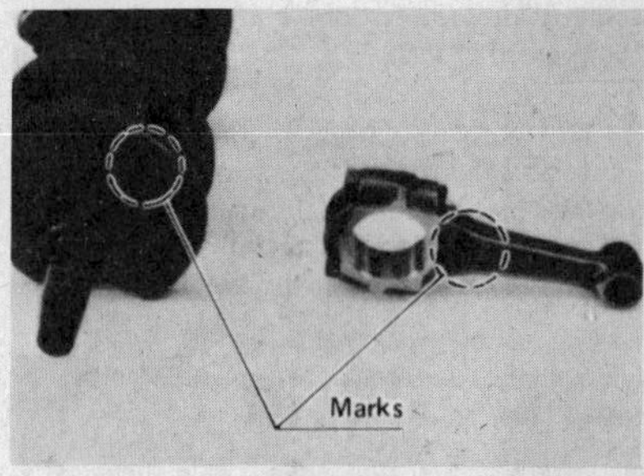

Con rod and crankshaft marks

3. Rods and crankshaft journals are "sized." A mark, or a lack of a mark, on the rods is significant. Crankshaft journals will also have a mark or no mark—but this is not significant, since they refer to factory dimensions. Since the journals wear, they must be measured, and marked accordingly. Proceed as follows:

a. Measure the diameter of the rod journals. If diameter is 35.994–36.000 mm (1.4171–1.4173 in.), mark the journal ("1").

If diameter is 35.984–35.994 mm (1.4167–1.4171 in.), leave the journal unmarked.

NOTE: *Ignore any marks already present on the crankshaft.*

b. Note the mark or lack of mark on the rods. An unmarked rod has a big end diameter of 39.000–39.010 mm (1.5354–1.5358 in.). A marked rod has a diameter of 39.010–39.016 mm (1.5358–1.5361 in.).

This diameter is measured with the rod cap in place and properly torqued. It does not include the bearing inserts;

c. Bearing inserts are color coded, and are available in three thicknesses:

Blue 1.485-10490mm (0.05846-0.05866 in.)

Black 1.480-1.485mm (0.05827-0.05846 in.)

Brown 1.475-1.480mm (0.5856-0.05827 in.)

d. After measuring and marking the crankshaft and noting the con rod marks, select the proper bearing insert according to the following:

If the crank journal is marked, and the rod is not, use the BROWN inserts.

If both journal and rod are marked, use the BLACK inserts.

If the crank is unmarked, but the rod is, use the BLUE inserts.

If neither is marked, use the BLACK inserts.

4. After fitting new bearing inserts, check connecting rod side clerance.

5. Check crankshaft run-out.

6. Measure crankshaft main bearing diameter. Check main bearing clearance with Plastigage® and replace the main bearing inserts if excessive.

7. Install the bushing cap and tighten the bolts to the proper torque (18-22 ft lbs). Measure crankshaft thrust clearance as shown. Mesure between the bushing cap and center portion of the flywheel. Standard is 0.10-0.20 mm (0.0039-0.0078 in.). If greater than 0.45 mm (0.0177 in.), the crankcases and the bushing cap must be replaced together.

NOTE: *Cap and cases are line-bored when assembled at the factory, and must therefore be replaced in sets.*

ASSEMBLY

1. Lubricate the rod bearings, and install the rods on the crankshaft, ensuring that the rod and cap marks align as shown. Oil the rod bolts and tighten the nuts to 24-27 ft lbs.

The rod caps must be fitted so that the marks align

Crankcase Assembly

1. Clean the case mating surfaces thoroughly. Blow out oil passages.

2. Install the main bearings inserts. Be sure that these and all other components are oiled during assembly.

3. Check that the transmission shaft locating pins and bearings set rings are in place.

4. If the camshaft chain guide was removed, install it. The grooved end of the guide pin goes toward the alternator side of the engine.

ENGINE AND TRANSMISSION SPECIFICATIONS

	Standard (mm/in.)	Serviceable Limit (mm/in.)
CAMSHAFT		
Lobe height	38.39-38.47/1.511-1.515	38.3/1.508
Journal diameter	27.94-27.96/1.010-1.101	27.90/1.098
Cam bearing clearance	0.043-0.101/0.0017-0.0040	0.19/0.0075
Cam run-out	less than 0.02/0.0008	0.1/0.0039
Cam chain (20 links)	160.0/6.30	162.4/6.39
Chain guide thickness		
front	3.3/0.13	1.5/0.059
rear	4.5/0.15	2.0/0.079
ROCKER ARMS		
Shaft diameter	12.966-12.984/0.5105-0.5112	12.940/0.5095
Rocker arm ID	13.000-13.018/0.5118-0.5125	13.05/0.5138
CYLINDER HEAD		
Max. allowable warpage	—	0.25/0.0098
VALVES		
Head thickness	0.75-1.25/0.030-0.050	0.5/0.020
Stem diameter		
Intake	6.965-6.980/0.2742-0.2748	6.860/0.2701
Exhaust	6.955-6.970/0.2738-0.2744	6.850/0.2700
Run-out	—	0.05/0.0020
Valve guide ID	7.000-7.015/0.2756-0.2762	7.10/0.280
Valve-to-guide clearance		
Intake	0.02-0.05/0.0008-0.0020	0.1/0.0394
Exhaust	0.03-0.06/0.0012-0.0024	0.1/0.0394
Valve spring free-length		
Inner	32.4/1.28	31.0/1.22
Outer	37.3/1.47	36.0/1.42
Valve spring tilt		
Inner	0.85/0.034	1.5/0.060
Outer	0.98/0.039	1.5/0.060
PISTONS AND CYLINDERS (400)		
Cylinder diameter (standard)	63.984-64.004/2.5191-2.5198	64.08/2.521
Piston diameter (standard)	63.94-63.96/2.517-2.518	63.8/2.512
Piston-cylinder clearance	0.034-0.054/0.0013-0.0021	—
Piston pin diameter	14.994-15.000/0.5903-0.5906	14.96/0.589
Piston pin hole ID	15.004-15.011/0.5907-0.5910	15.08/0.594
Con rod small end ID	15.003-15.014/0.5907-0.5911	15.05/0.593
PISTONS AND CYLINDERS (440)		
Cylinder diameter	—	67.60/2.661
Piston diameter	—	67.30/2.650
Piston-cylinder clearance	—	0.035-0.062/0.0014-0.0024
Piston pin diameter	14.994-15.000/14.96/0.589	0.5903-0.5906
Piston pin hole ID	15.004-15.011/0.5907-0.5910	15.08/0.594
Con rod small end ID	15.003-15.014/0.5907-0.5911	15.05/0.593
PISTON RINGS		
Ring thickness		
top	1.460-1.475/0.0575-0.0581	1.38/0.0543
second	1.475-1.490/0.0581-0.0587	1.40/0.0551
oil	2.475-2.490/0.0974-0.0980	2.40/0.0945
Groove width		
top, second	1.50-1.52/0.059-0.060	1.60/0.063
oil	2.50-2.52/0.098-0.099	2.60/0.102
Ring side clearance		
top	0.025-0.060/0.0010-0.0024	0.160-0.0063
second, oil	0.010-0.045/0.0004-0.0018	0.145-0.0057
Fittend end-gap		
all	0.2-0.4/0.008-0.016	0.7/0.028
Free end-gap		
top	8.0/0.31	5.0/0.20
second	10.5/0.41	7.5/0.30
oil	9.0/0.35	6.0/0.24
LOWER END		
Rod misalignment	less than 0.05/0.002 per 100 mm	0.2/0.008
Rod bearing-to-journal clearance	0.041-0.071/0.0016-0.0030	0.1/0.0039
Rod big end side clearance	0.15-0.25/0.006-0.0010	0.45/0.177
Crankshaft run-out	less than 0.02/0.0008	0.05/0.0020
Main bearing clearance	0.036-0.078/0.0014-0.0031	0.11/0.0043
Main bearing journal diameter	35.984-36.000/1.4167-1.4173	35.94/1.415
Crankshaft thrust clearance	0.10-0.20/0.004-0.008	0.45/0.018
BALANCER		
Shaft diameter	19.967-19.980/0.7861-0.7866	19.93/0.7846
Holder ID	20.007-20.028/0.7877-0.7885	20.08/0.7905
Chain length (20 links)	160.0/6.30	162.4/6.39
Chain guide thickness		
upper	2.0/0.079	1.0/0.039
lower	2.5/0.098	1.0/0.039
Spring free-length	9.8-10.4/0.39-0.41	9.0/0.35

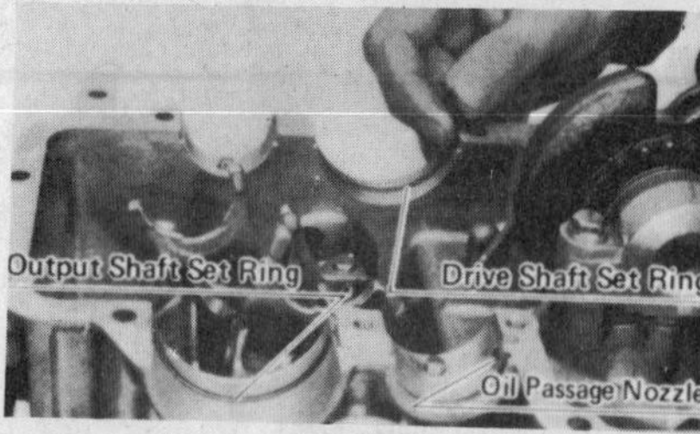

Check that the set rings and locating pins are in place

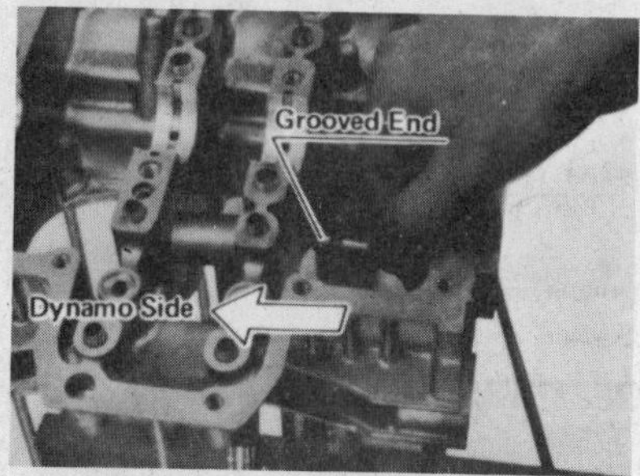

The grooved end of the chain guide locating pin must be on the dynamo (alternator) side

Lower crankcase half components

Upper crankcase half components

The alternator side oil seal is installed with the spring side facing the crankshaft. The ridge on the seal fits into the groove.

5. Install the crank and cam chain. Note that the alternator side of the crankshaft is fitted with an oil seal which must be installed with the spring side facing toward the crank. The ridge on the seal must fit into the groove in the crankcase.

6. Install the cam chain guide pin.

7. Check that the oil passage O-ring and the balancer assembly holder O-rings are in place. Install the balancer assembly.

8. Install the crankshaft bushing cap with chain guide, arrow pointing toward the front of the engine. Install the capscrew, securing them with thread locking compound. Install the capbolts, tightening to 18–22 ft lbs in a cross pattern.

9. Install the shift drum and forks. Install the transmission shafts and gears. Check that the pushrod oil seal is in place. Be sure that the output (countershaft), oil cup is in place on the right-side of the shaft (lower crankcase half). Install the kick-starter assembly.

10. Apply a liquid gasket compound to the upper case half. Install the lower case half. Tighten the lower case 8 mm bolts in the order shown. Proper torque is 18–22 ft lbs. Tighten the bolts gradually and evenly until the proper torque is reached. Tighten the 6 mm bolts gradually and in the order shown to 5.8–7.3 ft lbs.

11. Tighten the upper crankcase bolts to 5.8–7.3 ft lbs.

12. The remainder of the procedure is the reverse of disassembly. Refer to the preceding sections.

ENGINE AND TRANSMISSION SPECIFICATIONS

	Standard (mm/in.)	Serviceable Limit (mm/in.)
CLUTCH AND TRANSMISSION		
Clutch spring free-length	33.8/1.33	32.3/1.27
Friction plate thickness	2.9-3.1/0.11-0.12	2.5/0.10
Max allowable warpage		
steel plate	under 0.15/0.006	0.30/0.012
friction plate	under 0.20/0.008	0.40/0.016
Friction plate-to-clutch housing clearance	0.15-0.40/0.006-0.016	0.60/0.024
Clutch-to-shaft clearance	0.020-0.062/0.0008-0.0024	0.162/0.006
Primary chain max. play	—	20/0.8
Chain guide thickness	7.5/0.30	3.5/0.14
Shifter pawl spring free-length	29.4/1.16	31.0/1.22
Gear backlash	0.06-0.23/0.002-0.009	0.3/0.012
Shifter fork finger thickness	4.9-5.0/0.19-0.20	4.7/0.185
Gear fork groove width	5.05-5.15/0.200-0.203	5.25/0.207

General Torque Specifications①

Thread Diameter (mm)	*Torque (ft lbs)*
Coarse	
5	2.5–3.5
6	4.5–6.5
8	11.5–16.0
10	22–30
12	39–54
14	60–83
16	94–130
18	130–181
20	188–253
Fine	
5	2.5–3.5
6	4.5–5.5
8	10–13.5
10	19–25
12	33–45
14	54–74
16	83–116
18	123–166
20	166–239

① Unless otherwise noted

Engine Torque Specifications

Part	*Torque (ft lbs)*
Engine mounting bolts	25–31
Engine mounting bracket bolts	
front	16–19
rear	11.5–14.5
Breather cover bolts	13–14.5
Cylinder head cover nuts	18–22
Cylinder head bolts, 8 mm	18–22
Cylinder head bolts, 6 mm	7.9–9.4
Cam sprocket bolts	10–11.5
Rocker arm shaft nuts	18–22
Alternator rotor bolt	47–51
Starter clutch bolts	24–27
Field coil bolts	5.1–5.8
Armature bolts	5.1–5.8
Countershaft sprocket nut	87–108
Crankcase bolts, 8 mm	18–22
Crankcase bolts, 6 mm	5.8–7.3
Balancer holder bolts	10–11.5
Balancer weight bolts	7.9–9.4
Crankshaft bushing capbolts	18–22
Connecting rod bolts	24–27
Timing advance mechanism bolt	16.5–19.5
Neutral indicator	11–14.5
Oil pressure indicator	10–11.5
Oil filter bolt	11–14.5
Drain plug	14.5–18

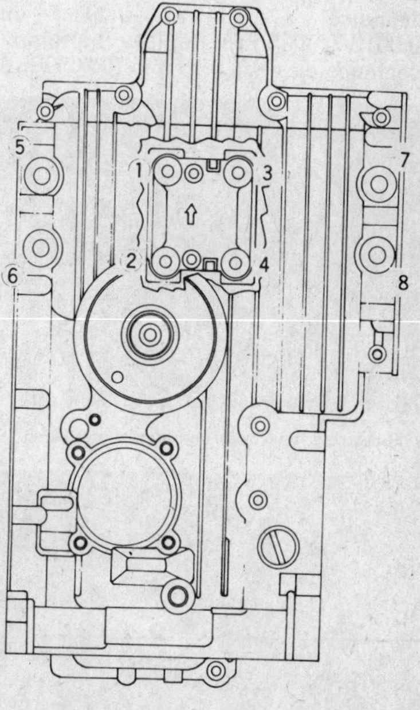

Crankcase bolt tightening order

LUBRICATION SYSTEM

OIL PRESSURE

1. Remove the oil pressure indicator switch, and connect the oil pressure gauge adapter (57001-400).
2. At engine operating temperature, pressure should be 57 psi at 4,000 rpm.
3. If pressure is low, check the oil pump.

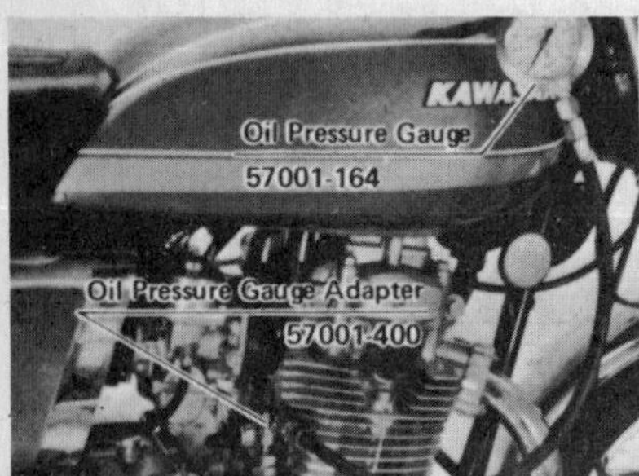

Checking oil pressure

OIL PUMP

Removal

1. The pump is located on the right-side of the lower crankcase half. Access to the pump is obtained by removing the clutch. Refer to "Engine and Transmission" for procedures, if necessary.

Inspection

1. Measure inner-to-outer rotor clearance. Standard is 0.025–0.115 mm (0.0010–0.0045 in.). Replace the rotors if clearance exceeds 0.21 mm (0.0083 in.).
2. Check wear to the sides of the rotors by laying a straightedge across the pump and checking clearance between the straightedge and the rotors. Standard clearance is 0.03–0.09 mm (0.0012–0.0035 in.). Replace the rotors if clearance exceeds 0.15 mm (0.0059 in.).

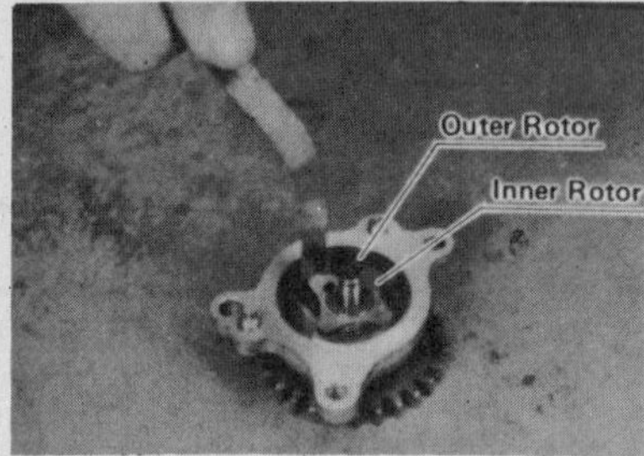

Measuring inner rotor-to-outer rotor clearance

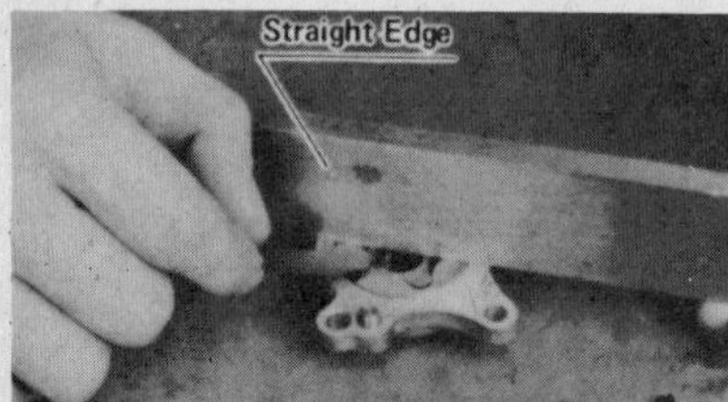

Checking rotor side wear

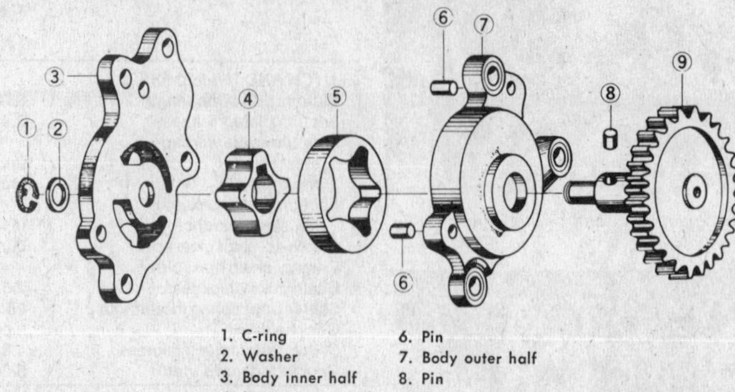

Oil pump components

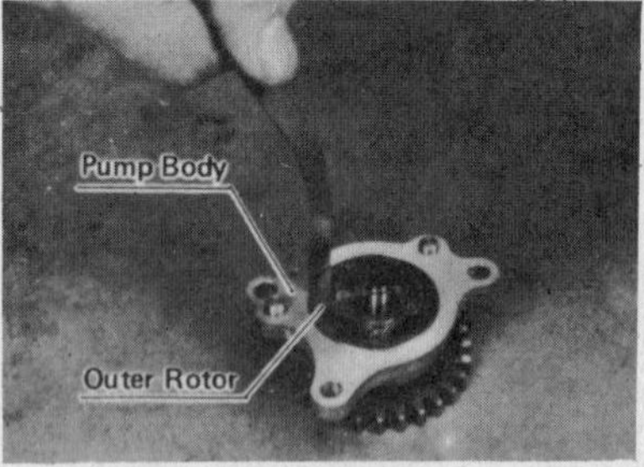

Checking outer rotor-to-pump body clearance

3. Check the clearance between the outer rotor and the pump body. Standard clearance is 0.10–0.15 mm (0.004–0.006 in.). Replace either the outer rotor or the pump body (depending on which is worn), if clearance exceeds 0.25 mm (0.0098 in.).

Disassembly

1. Remove the C-ring and washer from the gear shaft.
2. Separate the body halves and remove the rotors.
3. Remove the shaft pin to remove the gear from the body half.

Assembly

1. Assembly is the reverse of disassembly. Note that the sides of the rotors with the punch marks face away from the gear when installed.

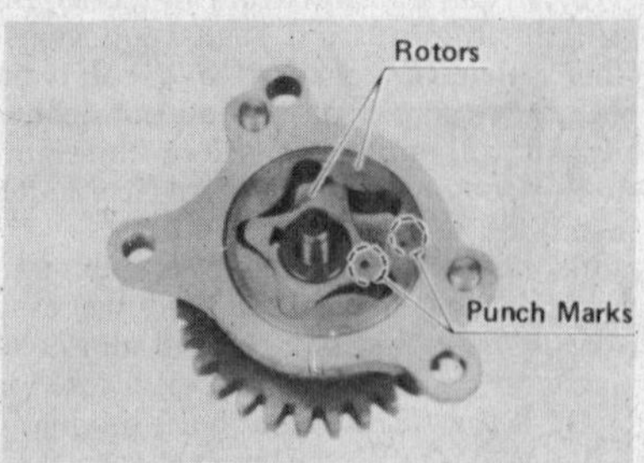

Install rotors with the punch marks facing outward

Installation

1. Oil the pump internals thoroughly before installation. Use new O-rings if necessary. Be sure that the O-rings are in place.

OIL PRESSURE RELIEF VALVE

1. The oil pressure relief valve is located in the lower crankcase half.
2. To remove the valve, separate the case halves as outlined in "Engine and Transmission." Unscrew the valve from the case.
3. To disassemble the valve, remove the circlip, and take out the washer, spring, and valve piston.

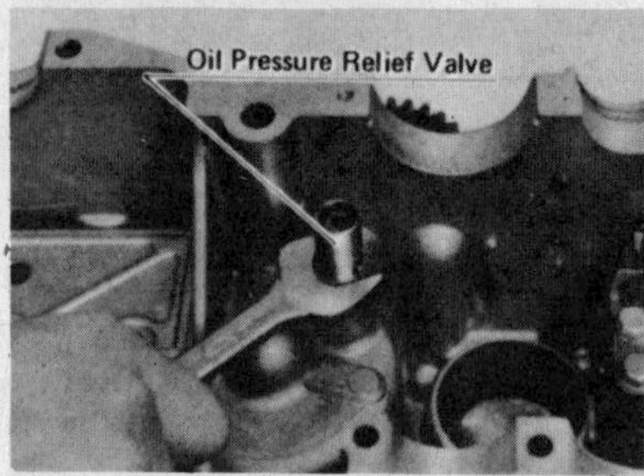

Removing the oil pressure relief valve

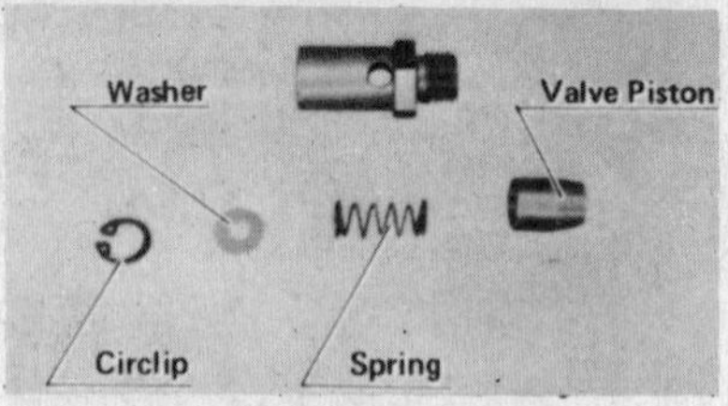

Pressure relief valve components

4. Measure the diameter of the piston. Measure the inside diameter of the valve body. Standard clearance is 0.020–0.103 mm (0.0008–0.0041 in.). Replace either the piston or the body (depending on which is worn), if clearance exceeds 0.13 mm (0.0051 in.).
5. Measure the free-length of the spring. Standard value is 20.6 mm (0.811 in.). Serviceable limit is 19.0 mm (0.748 in.).
6. Assembly is the reverse of disassembly. Use thread locking compound when installing the valve in the crankcase.

OIL PRESSURE INDICATOR SWITCH

1. If the bulb fails to light when the ignition switch is turned on, disconnect the wire from the pressure switch.
2. Check for continuity between the switch terminal and the switch body.If resistance is noted, or if there is no continuity, the switch is defective. If there is continuity (no resistance), check the bulb and wiring.
3. The warning buld should go off when the engine passes 1,500 rpm. If it does not, stop the engine and disconnect the switch lead. Connect an ohmmeter or continuity light between the switch lead and the engine (ground). There should be no resistance when the engine is off, and infinite resistance (no continuity) when rpm is above 1,500.

Checking the oil pressure indicator switch

4. If continuity is noted with the engine turning over 1,500 rpm, check oil pressure. If oil pressure is satisfactory, replace the indicator switch. Use thread locking compound when installing the switch. Tighten it to 10.0-11.5 ft lbs.

FUEL SYSTEM

Refer to "Carburetors" in the "General Information" section for carburetor theory, inspection, and troubleshooting.

GAS TANK

Removal

1. Turn off the fuel petcock. Slide the fuel line clamps off the petcock fitting, and disconnect the two fuel lines from the petcock.
2. Open the seat. Unhook the rubber tank strap, and pull the tank backward and off the machine.

Installation

1. Installation is the reverse of removal.
2. Secure all fuel line connections. Check for leaks before operation.

CARBURETORS (1974-76)

Removal

The carburetors are removed together.

1. Remove the gas tank.
2. Remove the left and right sidecovers.
3. Loosen the rubber intake manifold clamp screws and the air cleaner duct clamp screws and move the duct clamps away from the carburetors.
4. Pull the carburetors out of the intake manifolds and move them as far as possible to the right-side of the motorcycle.
5. Adjust the cable adjusters at the twistgrip to yield the maximum amount of throttle cable free-play. Unscew each of the cable adjusters at the carburetors from its bracket

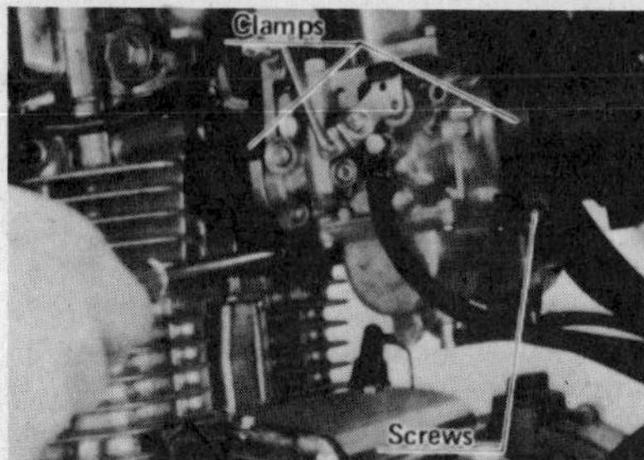

Loosening the carburetor clamp screws

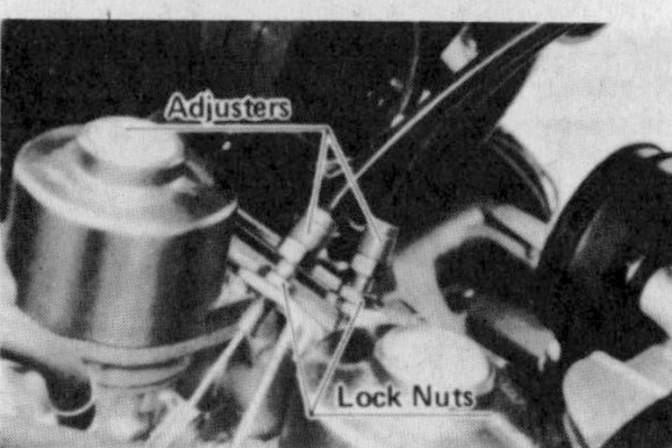

Cable adjusters are detached from their brackets to remove carburetors

and disengage each throttle cable from the pulley.

6. Remove the carburetors from the machine, taking care to pull the overflow and breather tubes out of their guide.

Disassembly

1. Drain the fuel from each float bowl. Although not necessary for disassembly, the carbs may be removed from their mounting plate by removing the two screws which secure each one, and disconnecting the choke linkage and balance screw connection.

Removing the main jet and keeper spring

2. Remove the carburetor caps. Pull out the throttle slide and remove the slide gasket. To remove the needle, remove the retaining screw.
3. Remove the screw securing the cover plate made accessible by removal of the slide. Unscrew and remove the main and slow air jets.
4. Remove the float bowl screws, and take off the float bowl.
5. Lift out the jet keeper spring. Push out the float pivot pin. Remove the float and float needle.
6. Unscrew the float needle seat retainer, and pull out the seat.
7. Pull out the main jet. Turn the carb right side up and allow the needle jet to drop out.
8. Unscrew and remove the starter jet. Remove the pilot passage plug, and unscrew the pilot jet and slow jet.

Assembly

1. Reverse the disassembly procedure. Use new gaskets and O-rings.

Installation

1. Check that the butterfly valves are parallel to the carburetor bores when the pulley is rotated fully. If not, loosen the pulley stop screw locknut and turn the screw to make the adjustment. Tighten the locknut.
2. Engage the accelerator throttle cable with the pulley, and screw the cable adjuster all the way into its bracket. Install the decelerator cable in the same manner. Screw both cable adjusters out about halfway of their length.

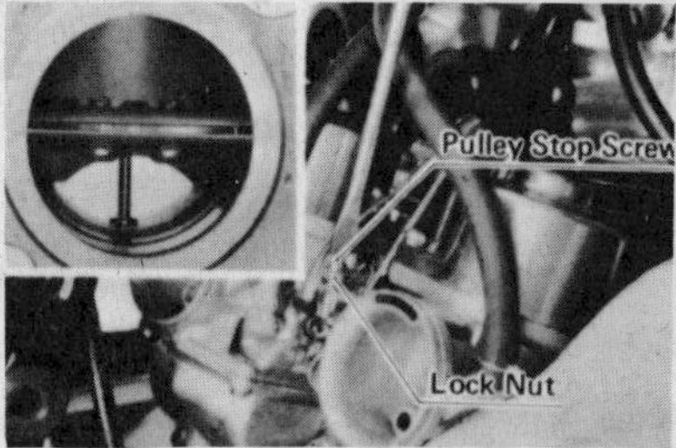

Use the pulley stop screw, if necessary, so that the butterfly valves are parallel to their bores when the pulley is opened as far as possible

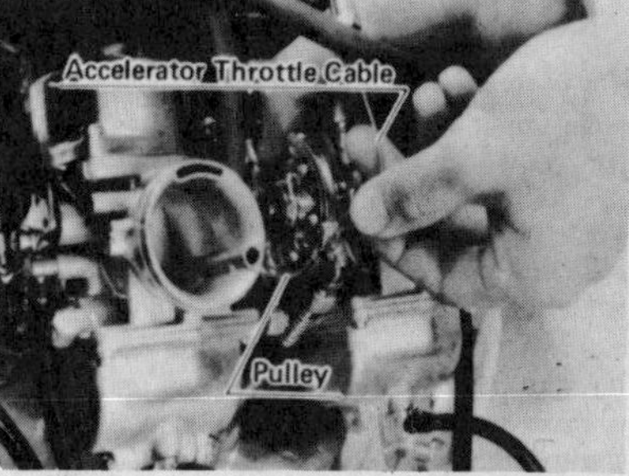

Attaching the accelerator cable to the pulley

3. The remainder of the procedure is the reverse of removal. Be sure that all lines are correctly routed and properly secured. Adjust the throttle cables.

Check for proper operation before riding the machine.

CARBURETORS (1977 AND LATER)

Removal

1. Remove the gas tank. Remove the left and right side covers.
2. Disconnect the lead from the oil pressure switch to avoid damage during removal.
3. Loosen the carburetor clamp screws. Some models have springs on the air cleaner side. Roll the springs away from the carburetors.
4. Disconnect throttle cables and hoses at the carburetors.
5. Pull the carburetors out of the intake manifold hoses and then the air cleaner hoses and take them out to the right side.

Disassembly

Refer to the exploded view of the carburetor assembly for disassembly and assembly

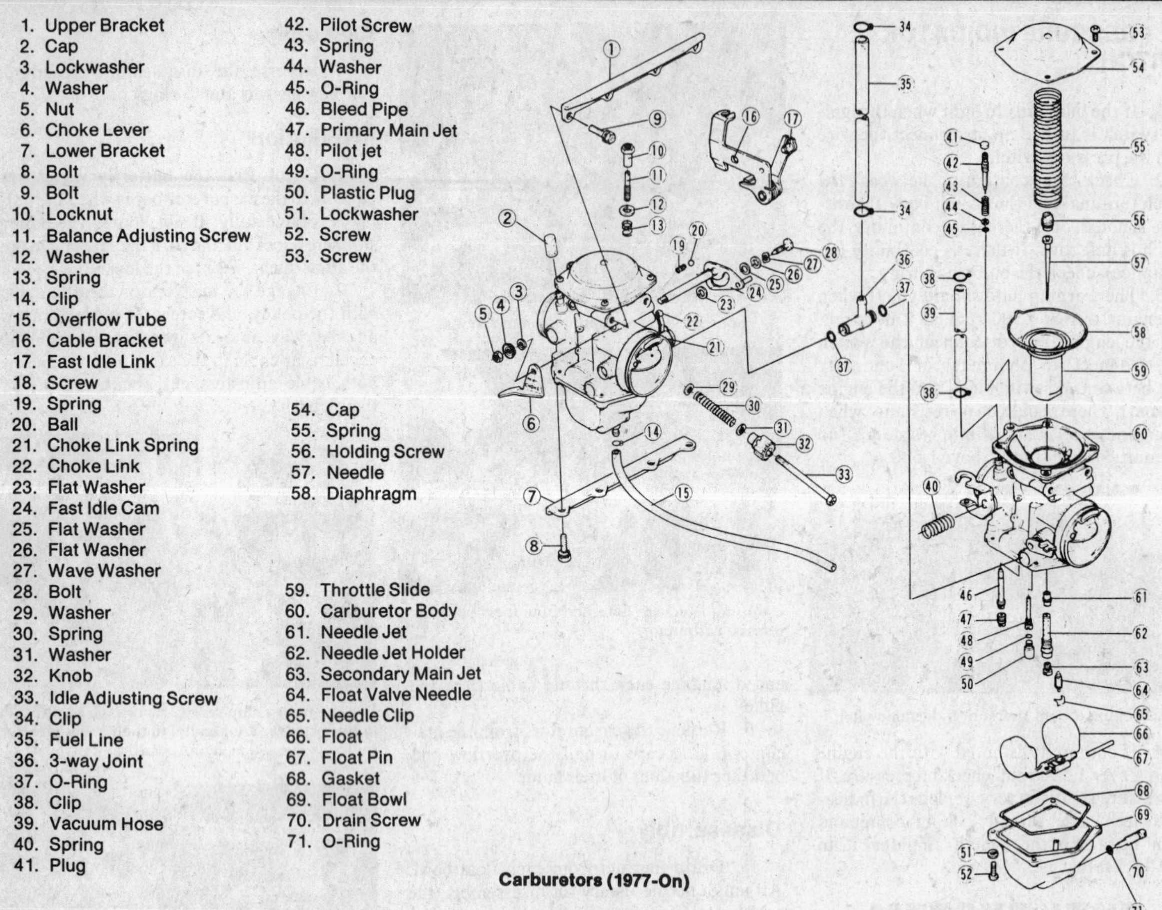

Carburetors (1977-On)

information. Carburetors may have minor variations depending on model and year.

1. Drain the gasoline from each float bowl and dispose of it safely.
2. Remove the carburetor caps. Remove the spring. Carefully pull out the diaphragm and throttle slide assembly taking care not to puncture or otherwise damage the rubber diaphragm.
3. Remove the float bowl screws. Carefully take off the bowl. If it is stuck, tap around the sides with the screwdriver handle until it is free. Do not pry or use excessive force.
4. Push out the float pin. Take out the float and needle assembly.
5. Unscrew the secondary main jet, needle jet holder, primary main jet and bleed pipe.
6. Remove the plastic plug and O-ring and unscrew the pilot jet.
7. Turn the carburetors right side up and push out the needle jet with a wooden dowel.

NOTE: *Pilot jet removal may violate emissions regulations.*

Assembly

1. Clean all metal parts in a safe solvent. Use low pressure compressed air to blow out passages in jets and carburetor bodies.
2. The use of new gaskets and O-rings is recommended.
3. Assembly is the reverse of disassembly. Do not overtighten jets.
4. When fitting the throttle slides, engage the diaphragm tab with the cutout provided.

Installation

1. Check that both butterfly valves open and close smoothly with no binding.
2. Check the clearance of each valve relative to the carburetor bore. If they differ, loosen the locknut and turn the balance adjusting screw until clearance is the same for both.
3. The remainder of the installation procedure is the reverse of removal. Adjust throttle cable(s) after installation. Be sure that all lines and connections are secure.
4. Check for gas leaks before riding the motorcycle.

CARBURETOR SPECIFICATIONS

	KZ400 (1974-76)	KZ400 (1977-On)	KZ440A, D	KZ440B, C
Type	CVB36	CV32	CV36	CV36
Primary Main Jet	125	70	62 (1980) 65 (1981-On)	68
Secondary Main Jet	—	90R	88	90
Jet Needle	—	003001	N02A	N03A
Main Air Jet	60	120	130	130
Secondary Air Jet	90	50	50	50
Pilot Air Jet	—	130	125	125
Pilot Fuel Jet	35	35	35	35
Pilot Screw (turns out)	1½	pre-set	pre-set	pre-set
Fuel Level (mm/in.)	33.5/1.32	3-5/0.12-0.20	3-5/0.12-0.20	3-5/0.12-0.20
Butterfly Angle	10°30′	—	—	—

ELECTRICAL SYSTEMS

IGNITION SYSTEM (1974-80)

1. The ignition system consists of a single set of points, a condenser, and the ignition coil. The coil has two leads—one for each plug—and the cylinders therefore fire at the same time. However, since only one cylinder is on the compression stroke at any time, there is a waste spark at the other cylinder.

2. Since the two plug leads are interdependent (one connected to each end of the secondary coil), disconnecting one lead will result in a lack of spark at both cylinders. Therefore, if one plug is dirty, fouled, or defective, neither cylinder will have spark.

3. If there is no spark, and common items such as fuse, plugs, points, and wiring connections have been checked, remove the plug caps and check for spark by grounding the leads against the cylinder head. If there is spark, one or both of the caps is defective. Replace both.

4. Check the condenser. If the proper test equipment is available, the condenser should rate 0.22 mfd. Alternately, check the condition of the points. Pitting, a burned-looking condition, or mounds and matching depressions are signs of arcing which is caused by a defective condenser. Replace both points and condenser if these conditions are noted.

5. Check the condition of the ignition coil primary winding by disconnecting the two primary winding leads and checking resistance across them (blue and red/yellow). Resistance should be 3.8-4.2 ohms.

6. If the primary winding is within these limits, check the secondary winding by measuring resistance across the two spark plug leads. It should be approximately 13K ohms.

7. If either of these tests indicates a resistance not within the given specifications, replace the coil.

IGNITION SYSTEM (1981 AND LATER)

These models use a transistorized ignition system replacing the breaker points of earlier years.

1. If ignition problems arise, first be sure that all wiring is in good order, connections tight and clean, etc.

2. Ignition timing is not adjusted, but the mechanical timing advance mechanism behind the pickup coil is the same as on earlier models. Be sure that the mechanism is clean and free to move the balance weights. Check that the springs are in good condition.

3. To check the pickup coil, remove the gas tank and disconnect the leads. Check that there is infinite resistance between either lead and the chassis. Check the resistance between the leads is 360-540 ohms.

4. The ignition coil can be checked as outlined for 1974-80 models, above.

CHARGING SYSTEM

The charging system consists of the alternator, rectifier, and regulator.

Alternator

1. Before carrying out the following alternator output test, be sure that the battery is fully charged. A low or defective battery will cause misleading readings. If the battery will not hold a full charge, replace it.

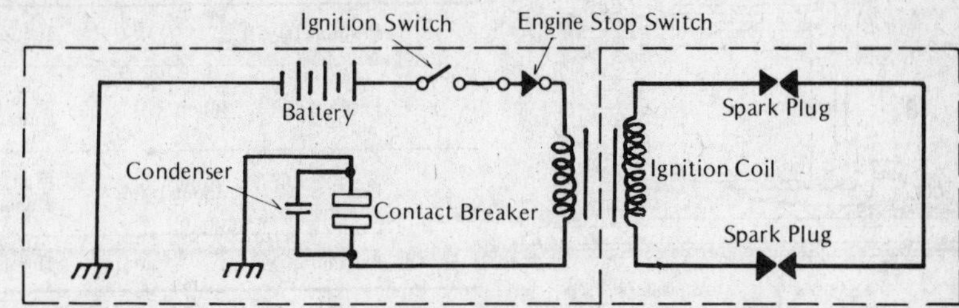

Ignition circuit wiring

2. Remove the left sidecover and the headlight. Disconnect the 6-wire connector beneath the sidecover and the 9-wire connector in the headlight shell. Disconnect the white rectifier lead from the battery positive lead.

3. Set a DC voltmeter to the 30v range. Connect the positive meter lead to the rectifier white lead and the negative meter lead to ground on the frame.

4. Remove the right sidecover. Disconnect the green and the brown regulator leads from terminals "F" and "I." Connect these two leads together.

NOTE: *Carry out the test as quickly as possible and disconnect the green and brown leads from each other as soon as the test is finished. Be sure that the leads are insulated from the frame.*

5. Start the engine and allow it to idle at 1,100-1,300 rpm. The voltmeter should read 14v DC or more. If less than this amount, either the alternator or the rectifier is defective.

CAUTION: *Do not let the engine turn above idle speed or the electrical components may be damaged.*

6. If the proper voltage reading was not obtained, check the rectifier as outlined in the following procedure. If the rectifier is satisfactory, check the alternator current output as follows.

7. Connect a 1 ohm-200W variable resistor, one lead to the rectifier white lead and the other to ground on the frame. Set the resistor at its maximum resistance and start the engine. Adjust the resistor to maintain a voltmeter reading of 14.5v, while gradually raising rpm to 5,000.

8. Stop the engine. Disconnect the voltmeter and the resistor lead to the rectifier white wire.

9. Connect an ammeter, set to the 30a DC range, to the variable resistor and to the rectifier white wire. This will put the meter, resistor, and rectifier in series. Be sure that all connections are tight. Start and run the engine at 5,000 rpm. The meter should read 13a DC. If the current reading is lower, the alternator is defective.

To determine which alternator component is faulty, proceed as follows:

10. Remove the right sidecover and disconnect the plug just below the regulator. With an ohmmeter, check the resistance between each of the three leads. Resistance should be 0.4-0.6 ohms. If any measurement shows infinite resistance, the armature has an open circuit and must be replaced.

11. With the highest meter range set to operate, measure resistance between each of the three leads and the frame (ground). Resistance should be infinite in each case. If a reading less than this is noted, the armature must be replaced as there is a short circuit.

12. Using the low range on the ohmmeter, check resistance between the field coil leads: green and black. It must be 4.8 ohms. An infinite reading indicates a break in the field coil, while a lower one indicates a short. In either case, replace the coil.

Rectifier

1. A full-wave rectifier with six diodes is used. An ohmmeter is used to check the rectifier.

2. Remove the left sidecover, disconnect the white rectifier lead from the battery and disconnect the rectifier black lead. The engine must be off.

3. Remove the right sidecover and disconnect the plug below the regulator.

4. Using the 10 or 100 ohm meter range, check resistance between the white lead and each yellow lead in turn, and then between the black lead and each yellow lead. Resistance measurements must be taken in both directions: that is, reverse the meter probes after each reading and take another.

Note the readings. If there is low resistance in one direction, there must be 10 times the amount when the leads are reversed. If any set of readings are either low or high in both directions, the rectifier must be replaced.

Regulator (Mechanical)

1. Remove the left sidecover and disconnect the 6-wire connector. Remove the headlight and disconnect the 9-wire connector in the shell.

2. Set a voltmeter to the 30v DC range and connect it across the battery. Start the engine and run it at 1,600 rpm. The meter should read 14-15v.

NOTE: *As in the alternator test, the battery must be fully charged.*

3. Increase engine speed. At 4,000 rpm, the meter reading should gain be 14-15v.

NOTE: *Proceed to 4,000 rpm from a starting point of 1,600. If rpm returns to idle speed, increase it gradually to 1,600 and then to 4,000.*

4. If voltage was not correct in both cases, proceed with the following checks:

NOTE: *If the machine is still under warranty, the regulator should be replaced at this point.*

5. Remove the right sidecover; disconnect the black, green, and brown regulator

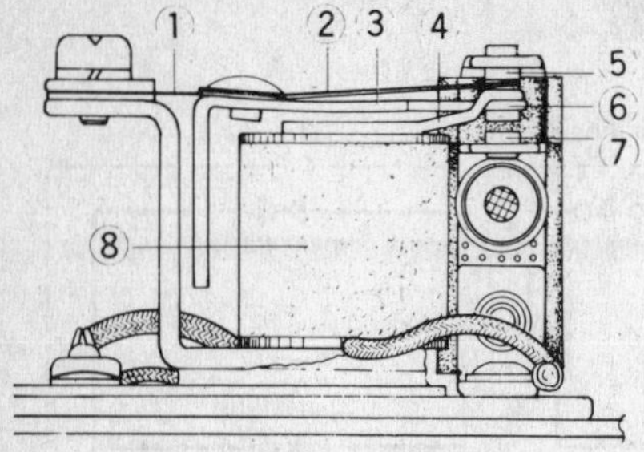

1. Spring
2. Spring
3. Armature
4. Adjuster arm
5. Point P_1
6. Point P_0
7. Point P_2
8. Relay coil

Voltage regulator components

Regulator Resistance

Terminal	Point P_0	Resistance	Results
F—I	Position 1①	0 Ω	If more than 0 Ω, points P_0 and P_1 are dirty or fouled.
	Position 2②	about 9 Ω	If no reading, resistor Rf is open. If no resistance, there is a short. Replace regulator.
F—E	Position 1①	about 100 Ω	If no reading, the relay coil is open. If no resistance, there is a short. Replace regulator.
	Position 2②	0 Ω	If more than 0 Ω, points P_0 and P_1 are dirty or fouled.

① Points P_0 and P_1 are in contact by spring force.
② Points P_0 and P_1 are in contract by pressing on the armature with a finger.

leads from terminals "E," "F," and "I." Remove the regulator cover.

6. With the ohmmeter set to the low range, check the resistance according to the chart:

7. Clean points with solvent if necessary. If badly pitted, use emergy cloth. If the points cannot be cleaned to achieve zero ohms resistance, replace the regulator.

8. Press down on the armature and check

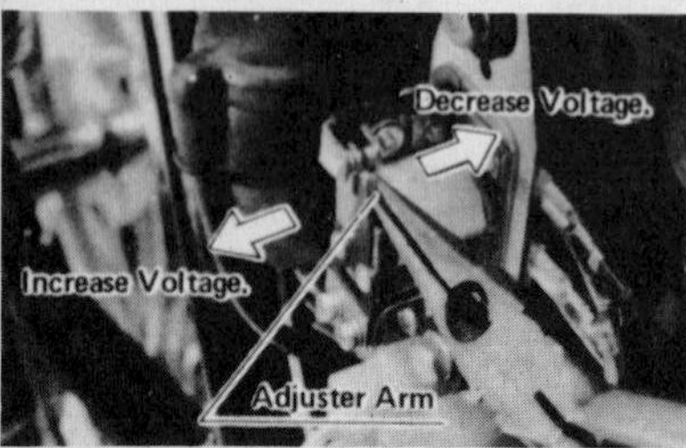

Bending the adjuster arm to correct regulator output

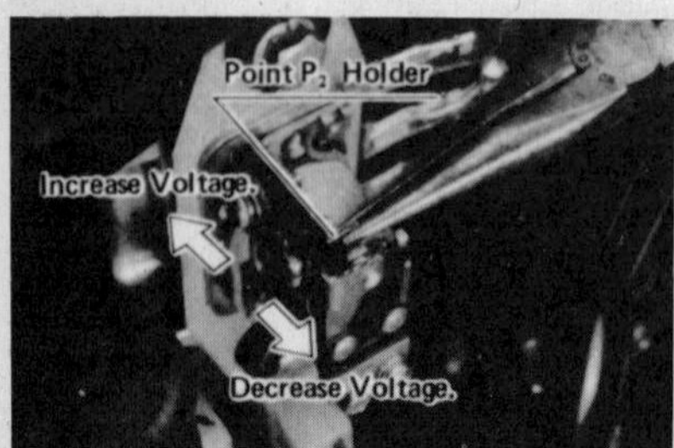

Bending the P_2 holder to correct regulator output

the gap. It should be 0.3 mm (0.012 in.). If not correct, bend the P_2 holder.

9. Check the gap between P and P_0. It should be 0.30-0.45 mm (0.012-0.018 in.). If adjustment is needed, bend the holder for P_1.

10. Assemble the regulator and make all connections. Recheck regulator output as described previously. If voltage was too high, or too low, adjust by bending the adjusting arm. Bending the arm out away from the machine will increase the output voltage and vice versa.

11. Recheck output. At 2,000 rpm, output should be 14-15v. Adjust again, if necessary as in Step 10.

12. Check output at 4,000 rpm. If voltage was too high or too low, bend the P_2 holder. Bend it toward the machine to increase voltage, and vice versa.

13. Recheck at 2,000 and 4,000 rpm.

Regulator/Rectifier

This solid-state component is not adjustable. When the engine is running above idle, the regulator should develop about 14.5v across the battery terminals. The battery must be in a good state of charge for an accurate reading. If voltage is not within this range, the unit must be replaced.

The rectifier section of this unit can be checked for resistance as described for earlier types, above.

STARTER MOTOR

1. Refer to "Engine and Transmission" for removal and installation procedures. See "Left Crankcase Cover Components, Alternator, and Starter Assembly."

2. Disassemble the starter motor by removing the body screws.

3. Carbon brush length is 11.0-12.5 mm (0.4-0.5 in.) new. Serviceable limit is 6.0 mm (0.24 in.).

4. Clean the commutator surface with a solvent, polishing with fine emery cloth if necessary.

5. Clean out the commutator grooves and check their condition. Standard groove depth is 0.5-0.8 mm (0.02-0.03 in.), while the serviceable limit is 0.2 mm (0.008 in.).

6. There must be little or no resistance between each of the commutator segments. Use low meter range when checking. Resis-

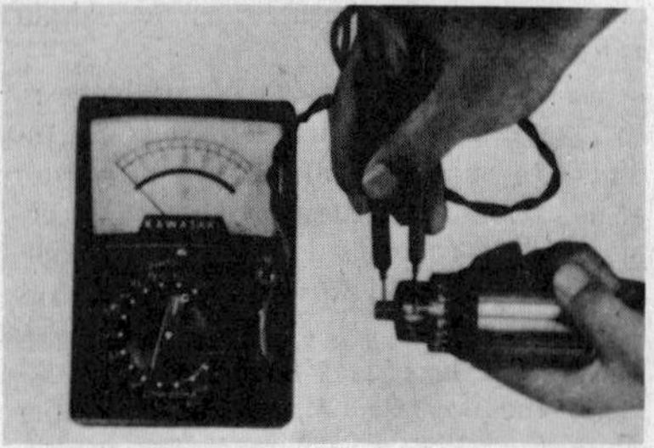

Checking the starter motor armature for continuity between segments

tance between the segments and the armature shaft must be infinite. Use high range when checking.

7. Check resistance between the positive carbon brush and the starter motor lead. There must be no or very little resistance. If considerable resistance is noted, the field coils must be replaced. Use the lowest meter range when making this check.

8. Check resistance between the positive carbon brush and the starter motor body. It must be infinite, or there is a short necessitating replacement of the field coils. Use the highest meter range when making this check.

Solenoid

1. After disconnecting the motor lead from the solenoid, connect an ohmmeter, set on the low scale, across the solenoid terminals. Push the starter button. Resistance when the button is pushed must be zero. If higher, replace the solenoid.

2. If the solenoid does not click when the starter button is pushed, disconnect the black and yellow/red solenoid leads and check resistance across the terminals. It must be close to zero ohms. If higher, replace the solenoid.

3. Check that voltage is getting to the solenoid from the battery. If so, replace the solenoid if it failed any of the above tests.

SWITCHES

Ignition Switch

1. In the "Off" position, all four switch leads must be insulated (no continuity) from each other.

2. In the "On" position, there must be continuity between the white and brown leads and between the blue and red leads.

3. In the "Park" position, there must be continuity betwen the white and red leads; none between the others.

Headlight Dimmer Switch

1. In the "high beam" position, there must be continuity between the blue and red/black leads.

2. In the "low beam" position there must be continuity between the red/yellow and blue leads.

Brake Light Switches

DISC BRAKE

1. Disconnect the leads from the switch which is just above the lower triple clamp. Continuity should exist when the brake lever is pulled. If not, replace the switch.

2. Protect plated or painted surfaces from possible brake fluid spillage when removing the switch.

3. Apply thread locking compound to the threads of the new switch, but not on the lower quarter of the threads to avoid contamination of the brake fluid.

4. Bleed the brake lines.

DRUM BRAKE

1. Front drum brake light leads are in the headlight shell (blue and brown).

2. Rear brake light switch leads are accessible at the rear of the gask tank.

3. Continuity between the leads must be present when the brake lever or pedal is applied, or the switch must be replaced.

CHASSIS

FRONT WHEEL

Removal and Installation

DISC BRAKE

1. Support the front wheel off the ground.
2. Remove the axle nut cotter pin. Remove the nut and washer.
3. Remove the axle clamp nuts from the slider. Remove the clamp.
4. Support the wheel and pull out the axle to remove the wheel.

To install the wheel:

5. Be sure that the speedometer cable is located on the inside of the fender bracket. Fit the speedometer gear housing to the wheel.
6. Install the wheel, slipping the axle through from the disc side.
7. Install the axle clamp. Note that the arrow on the bottom of the clamp must point toward the front of the motorcycle. The clamp is machined unevenly so that there will be a gap between the clamp and the slider at the rear of the slider. Install the washers and nuts, but do not tighten them.

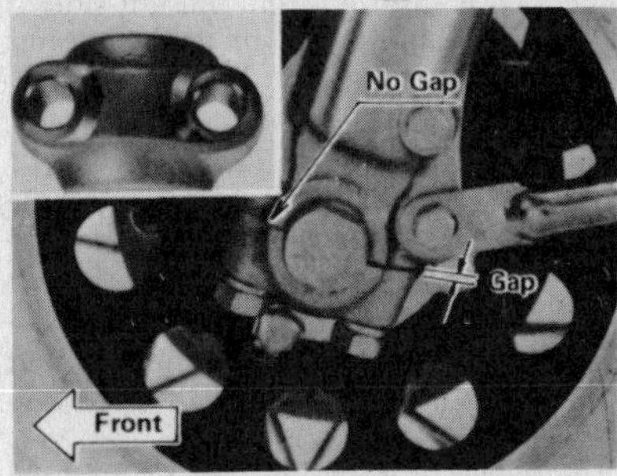

Install the axle clamp as shown

8. Install and tighten the axle nut to 72–94 ft lbs. Check that the speedometer gear housing does not move when this is done. Use a new cotter pin.
9. Tighten the front axle clamp nut to 13.0–14.5 ft lbs, then tighten the rear nut to the same torque.

DRUM BRAKE

1. Support the front wheel off the ground.
2. Remove the brake cable cotter pin and unscrew the adjusting nut to disconnect the cable from the brake plate. Take out the brake lever fitting.
3. Disconnect the speedometer cable from the brake plate after removing the securing bolt.
4. Unbolt the brake anchor from the slider and the brake plate.
5. Remove the axle nut. Remove the axle clamp nuts and the clamp.
6. Lift the wheel slightly, and pull out the axle, then remove the wheel from the machine.

To install the wheel:

7. Put the wheel into position between the sliders. Insert the axle from the brake plate side. Install the axle clamp.

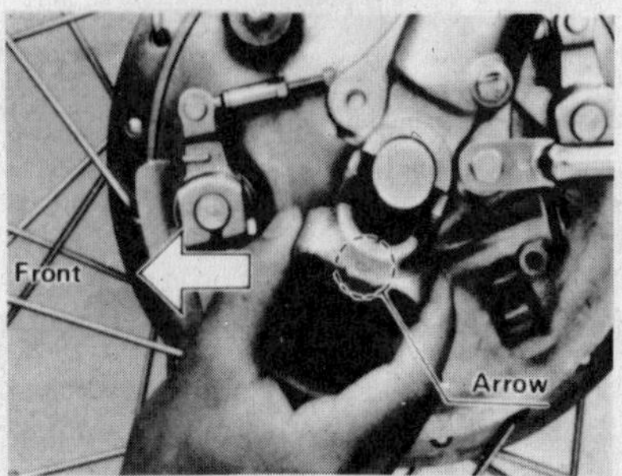

The axle clamp arrow points toward the front of the motorcycle

Install, but do not tighten, the clamp nuts. Note that the arrow stamped on the clamp points toward the front of the motorcycle. The clamp is machined unevenly. When installed, there will be a gap between the clamp and the slider at the rear of the slider.

8. Fit, but do not tighten, the axle washer and nut.
9. Install the brake anchor, tightening the nuts to 19.5–22.0 ft lbs.
10. Tighten the axle nut to 72–94 ft lbs. Tighten the forewardmost clamp nut to 13.0–14.5 ft lbs, and then tighten the rear one to the same torque.
11. The remainder of the procedure is the reverse of removal.

Disassembly

DISC BRAKE

1. To disassemble the speedometer gear housing, disconnect the cable. Pull out the gear drive with snap-ring pliers. Remove the bush and pinion after drilling out the locating pin. Pack the assembly with grease prior to assembly.
2. Unbolt and remove the disc. Remove the disc-side hub cap.
3. Pry out the disc side grease seal. Remove the bearing retainer circlip.
4. Using a drift, tap around the outer race of the speedometer gear side wheel bearing until the disc side bearing is driven out.
5. Remove the remaining grease seal and speedometer drive. Remove the remaining wheel bearing by tapping out from the inside.

DRUM BRAKE

1. Remove the brake linings from the brake plate by pulling them apart until free of their cams.
2. To remove the brake levers and linkage from the brake cams, first mark the positions of the levers relative to the cams. Remove the pinch-bolts. Remove the levers, return spring, wear indicator, etc. Push the cams out of the brake plate noting the dust seals.
3. Remove the speedometer pinion gear by unscrewing the bushing.
4. Remove the hub cap (axle nut side).
5. Pry out the grease seal. With a suitable drift, tap around the race of the right-side wheel bearing until the left-side bearing is free. Remove the remaining bearing in the same manner.
6. Remove the speedometer gear using a gear puller. Remove the remaining grease seal.

Inspection

1. Axle run-out (max. standard) is 0.1 mm (0.004 in.). Serviceable limit is 0.2 mm (0.008 in.). Although it may be possible to straighten slightly bent axles, those with a run-out which exceeds 0.7 mm (0.028 in.) must be replaced.

Measured run-out is the total gauge variation.

2. Check wheel bearings for rough rotation, binding, looseness, etc., after removing old grease and oiling lightly.
3. Grease seals which have been removed must be replaced with new ones.

If the seals are still in place, check for obvious damage, hardening, etc.

4. For brake disc inspection, refer to the "Disc Brake" section, following.
5. Check brake lining thickness. Standard is 4.75–5.20 mm (0.19–0.20 in.). Serviceable limit is 2.5 mm (0.10 in.).

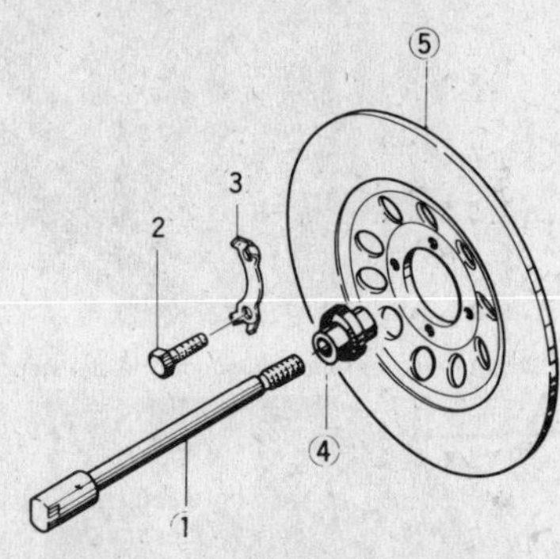

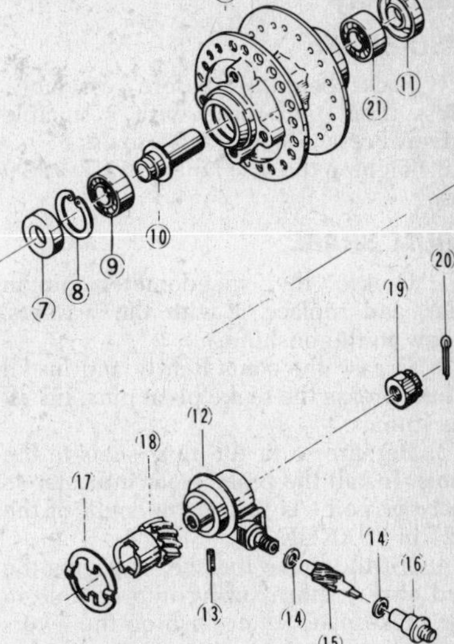

1. Axle
2. Bolt
3. Lockplate
4. Cap
5. Brake disc
6. Wheel hub
7. Grease seal
8. Circlip
9. Wheel bearing
10. Spacer
11. Grease seal
12. Speedometer gear housing
13. Pin
14. Washer
15. Speedometer pinion
16. Bush
17. Gear drive
18. Speedometer gear
19. Axle nut
20. Cotter pin
21. Wheel bearing

Front disc brake wheel assembly

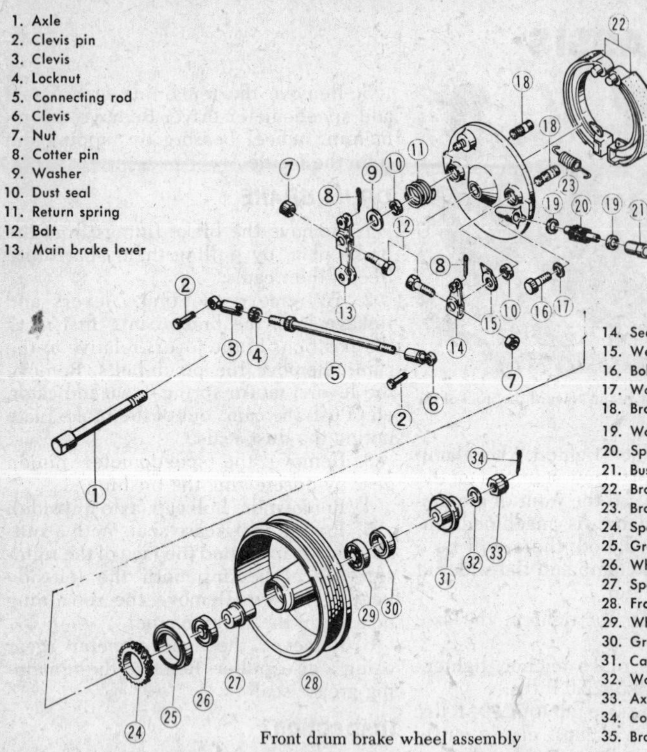

1. Axle
2. Clevis pin
3. Clevis
4. Locknut
5. Connecting rod
6. Clevis
7. Nut
8. Cotter pin
9. Washer
10. Dust seal
11. Return spring
12. Bolt
13. Main brake lever
14. Secondary brake lever
15. Wear indicator
16. Bolt
17. Washer
18. Brake cam
19. Washer
20. Speedometer pinion gear
21. Bush
22. Brake shoes
23. Brake springs
24. Speedometer gear
25. Grease seal
26. Wheel bearing
27. Spacer
28. Front hub
29. Wheel bearing
30. Grease seal
31. Cap
32. Washer
33. Axle nut
34. Cotter pin
35. Brake plate

Front drum brake wheel assembly

6. Check brake drum inside diameter. Standard is 180.0–180.2 mm (7.086–7.094 in.). Serviceable limit is 180.75 mm (7.116 in.).

7. Check brake spring free-length. Standard is 46.7–47.3 mm (1.84–1.86 in.). Serviceable limit is 48.5 mm (1.91 in.).

8. Brake cam diameter (standard) is 14.957–14.984 mm (0.5889–0.5899 in.). Serviceable limit is 14.83 mm (0.584 in.). Cam hole diameter is 15.000–15.027 mm (0.5906–0.5916 in.). Serviceable limit is 15.18 mm (0.598 in.).

9. Wheel bearing numbers are as follows:
Disc brake: #6302
Drum brake:
left #6302Z
right #6302

Assembly

DISC BRAKE

1. Pack bearings before assembly. Press them into place with a suitable driver. Press in new grease seals.

2. Tighten the disc bolts to 11.5–16.0 ft lbs.

DRUM BRAKE

1. Grease the speedometer pinion gear, and replace it with the washers. Screw in the bushing.

2. Grease the cams lightly and install them. Grease the brake pivot pins. Install the linings.

3. Be sure to fit the dust seals to the cams. Install the brake wear indicator so that the point is just to the right of the "E" in "RANGE."

4. Fit the brake linkage, engaging the end of the return spring into its hole in the brake plate, then push on the levers aligning the reference marks made before removal.

5. Assemble the hub, packing the bearings with grease and pressing them in with a suitable drift. If the speedometer gear was removed, peen it in four places for security after pressing it on.

6. The remainder of the procedure is the reverse of disassembly.

LINKAGE ADJUSTMENT

1. Fit the wheel to the motorcycle and secure it at all points.

2. Support the front wheel off the ground.

3. Loosen the connecting rod locknut and turn the rod one turn in the direction shown.

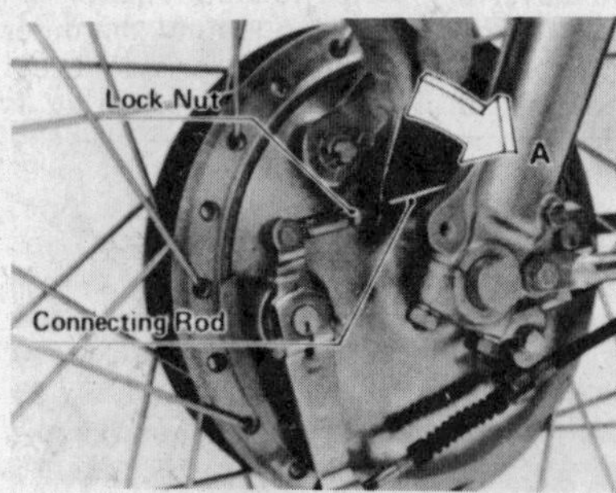

Drum brake linkage adjustment, initial step

Drum brake linkage adjustment, second step

4. Spin the wheel slowly and turn in the cable adjusting nut until the shoe controlled by the main brake lever just touches the drum.

5. Continue turning the wheel, and turn the connecting rod in the direction "B" shown until the secondary shoe just touches the drum.

6. The brakes are now synchronized. Tighten the connecting rod locknut. Adjust the cable as outlined in "Maintenance."

REAR WHEEL

Removal and Installation

1. Disconnect the brake anchor from the brake plate.

2. Disconnect the brake light switch spring from the brake pedal. Remove the brake adjusting nut from the brake rod. Disconnect the rod from the brake lever.

3. Remove the axle nut. Take out the axle.

4. Remove the axle spacer from the right-side of the wheel. Move the wheel as far as possible to the right to detach it from the coupling and remove it from the motorcycle.

To install the wheel:

5. Reverse the removal procedure. The axle is inserted from the left-side of the wheel. Tighten the brake anchor nut to 19.5–22 ft lbs. Then tighten the axle nut to 94–116 ft lbs.

Disassembly

1. Mark the position of the lever relative to the brake cam. Remove the pinchbolt, wear indicator, and dust seal.

2. Remove the brake lever. Pull the brake shoes, complete with the cam, out of the brake plate. Spread the shoes to disassemble.

3. Reach through the hub with a long punch and tap out the right-side wheel bearing. Remove the spacer and tap out the left-side bearing from the inside of the hub.

Inspection

1. Axle run-out (max. standard) is 0.05 mm (0.002 in.). Serviceable limit is 0.2 mm (0.008 in.). Although it may be possible to straighten slightly bent axles, those with a run-out which exceeds 0.7 mm (0.028 in.) must be replaced.

Measured run-out is the total gauge variation.

2. Check wheel bearings for rough rotation, binding, looseness, etc., after removing old grease and oiling lightly.

3. Check brake lining thickness. Standard is 5.35–6.05 mm (0.21–0.24 in.). Serviceable limit is 2.5 mm (0.10 in.).

4. Check brake drum inside diameter. Standard is 180.0–180.2 mm (7.086–7.094 in.). Serviceable limit is 180.75 mm (7.116 in.).

5. Check brake spring free-length. Standard is 56.0 mm (2.20 in.), while serviceable limit is 58.0 mm (2.28 in.).

6. Brake cam diameter (standard) is 16.957–16.984 mm (0.6676–0.6687 in.). Serviceable limit is 16.83 mm (0.663 in.). Cam hole diameter is 17.000–17.027 mm (0.6693–0.6704 in.). Serviceable limit is

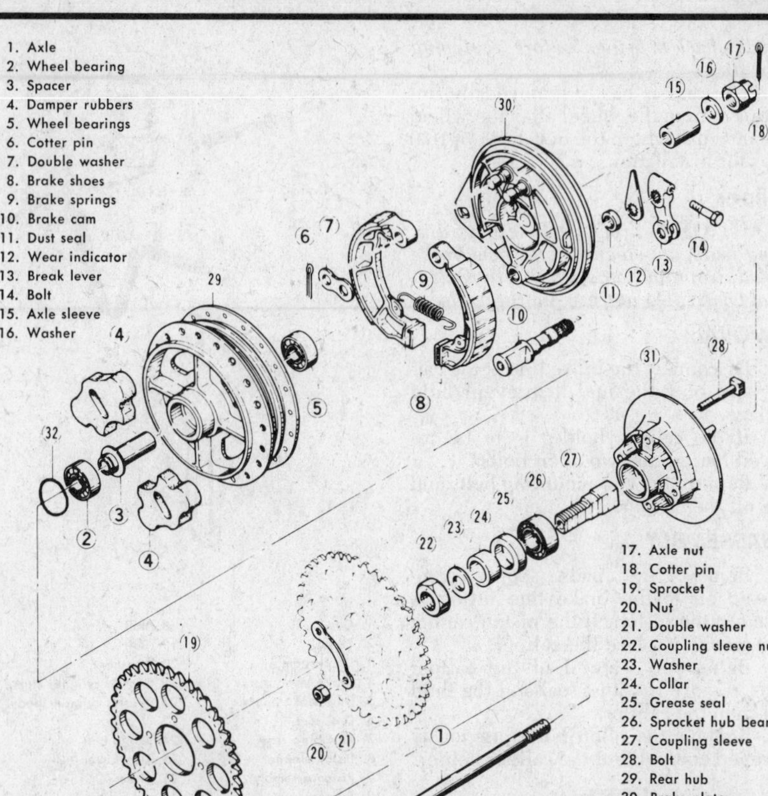

Rear wheel and sprocket assembly

17.18 mm (0.676 in.).

7. Wheel bearing numbers are as follows:

Left: #6303
Right: #6303Z

Assembly

1. Grease the cam lightly before installation. Grease the brake plate pins as well.

2. Assembly is the reverse of disassembly. When fitting the brake wear indicator, have it point just to the right of the "E" in "RANGE."

SPROCKET ASSEMBLY

Removal

1. Disconnect the drive chain. Follow the rear wheel removal procedure as previously outlined, and in addition, remove the coupling sleeve nut and washer. The wheel and sprocket assembly can then be removed from the motorcycle together.

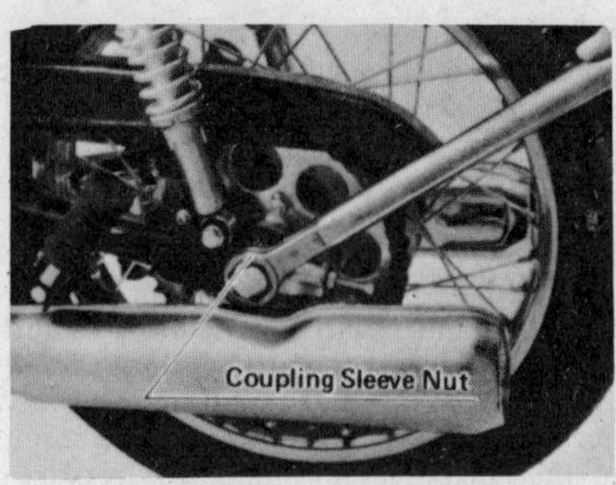

Loosening the coupling sleeve nut

Disassembly

1. Bend down the locking tabs on the sprocket nuts. Remove the nuts and the sprocket. Detach the coupling from the rear wheel.

2. Pull out the sleeve and collar.

3. Remove the grease seal by prying it out.

4. Use a suitable drift to tap out the coupling bearing. The bearing is driven out of the sprocket side of the coupling.

Inspection

1. Check condition of the coupling rubber dampers in the wheel hub. Replace any which are damaged.

2. Check the condition of the coupling bearing in the same manner as wheel bearings. Repack with new grease before installation.

3. Check the sprocket teeth for condition. Check diameter. Standard is 217.4 mm (8.56 in.). Serviceable limit is 215.5 mm (8.48 in.).

4. Sprocket run-out is less than 0.3 mm (0.012 in.); replace the sprocket if it is warped more than 0.5 mm (0.020 in.).

5. Chain condition can be checked by stretching the chain with about 25 lbs pressure and measuring the length of a 20-pin section of chain. Standard length is 317.5 mm (12.50 in.); replace the chain if the measurement is over 323 mm (12.7 in.).

Assembly

1. Reverse the disassembly procedure. Repack the bearing with grease. Tighten sprocket nuts to 25–31 ft lbs.

Installation

Refer to "Rear Wheel Removal and Installation" for procedures. Be sure that the chain masterlink spring clip is installed with the closed end facing the direction of chain rotation.

DISC BRAKE SERVICE

When servicing the hydraulic disc brake system, observe the following precautions:

a. Brake fluid absorbs moisture. Therefore, never add fluid from an old or an unsealed container;

b. Do not add fluid which has been pumped out of the system. Add new fluid only;

c. Protect all plated and painted surfaces from possible contact with spilled brake fluid;

d. Do not mix types of brake fluid. Use DOT 3 brake fluid only. The following types are recommended:

Atlas Extra Heavy-Duty
Shell Super Heavy-Duty
Texaco Super Heavy-Duty
Wagner Lockheed Heavy-Duty
Girling Amber

Flushing

1. Attach a clear plastic hose which will fit snugly to the caliper bleed nipple and put the other end in a quantity of brake fluid in a suitable container.

2. Open the bleed nipple and apply the brake lever in slow, even strokes until all of the old fluid is pumped out.

3. Close the bleed nipple. Refill the reservoir with fresh fluid. Open the nipple, apply the lever, and, holding it against the handgrip, close the nipple and quickly release the lever.

4. Repeat this procedure until the new fluid begins to come out of the hose.

5. Bleed the air from the system.

Bleeding

This should be done after flushing, or if any brake line junction has been disconnected, or if the brake lever feels spongy or the brake is inefficient.

1. Top up the fluid reservoir if necessary.

2. With the reservoir cap off, slowly pump the lever several times until no air bubbles can be seen rising from the passages at the bottom.

3. Replace the cap. Fit a length of plastic hose which will fit snugly to the caliper bleed nipple, immersing the other end of the hose in a quantity of brake fluid in a suitable container.

4. Apply the brake lever several times until it becomes hard. Hold it tightly and loosen the bleed nipple, then close it quickly.

5. Release the lever. Repeat this procedure until brake fluid only comes out of the hose, and no air bubbles.

Pad Replacement

1. When either pad is worn down to the stepped portion, replace both as a set.

2. Remove the front wheel. Remove the screw from the inner caliper half, tak-

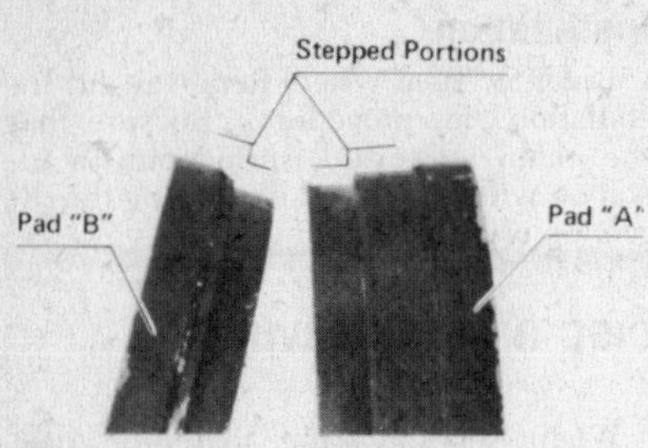

Replace pads when either is worn to the stepped portion

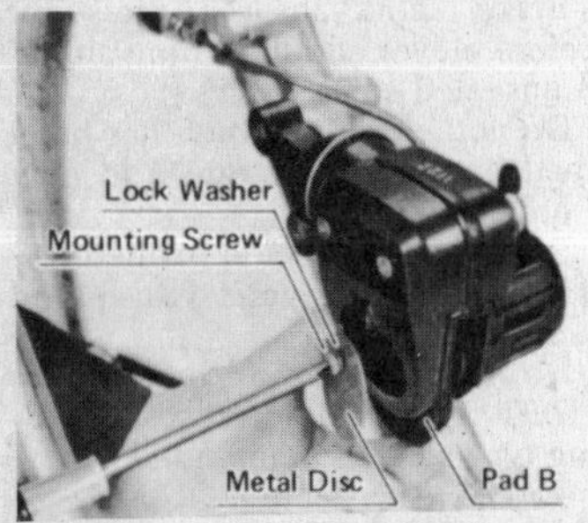

Removing pad B

ing off its washer and the metal plate. Remove the inner pad ("B").

3. Apply the brake lever until the outer pad ("A") is pushed out.

4. Loosen the bleed nipple slightly, push the piston in as far as possible, then tighten the nipple.

5. Place the shim on the rear of the outer pad, shim projection over pad projection, align the pad projection with the slot in the bottom of the caliper, and insert the pad.

6. Install the "B," metal disc, and screw. Use thread locking compound on the screw.

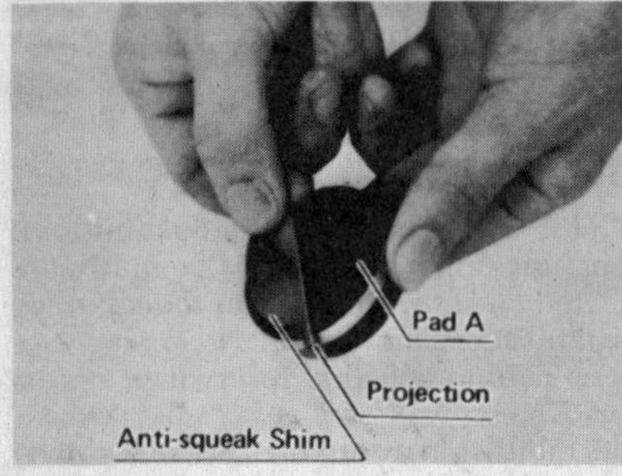

Fit the shim projection over the pad projection

7. Check reservoir fluid level.

NOTE: *After fitting new pads, avoid hard application of the brake for at least 50 miles. Replace the dust seal and piston fluid seal every other time the pads are replaced. Refer to "Caliper" for procedures.*

Disc

1. The disc may be checked in place.

2. Measure thickness. Standard is 6.95–7.05 mm (0.27–0.28 in.). Serviceable limit is 5.5 mm (0.22 in.).

3. Check run-out. Standard is 0.1 mm (0.004 in.) or less. Serviceable limit is 0.3 mm (0.012 in.).

NOTE: *If run-out is excessive, check that the reading is not being caused by bad wheel bearings before replacing the disc.*

4. The disc is easily removed by unbolting it from the wheel after the wheel is removed. Tighten the nuts to 11.5–16.0 ft lbs for installation.

Caliper

CAUTION: *Caliper parts (except disc and pads) are cleaned with new brake fluid, isopropyl alcohol, or ethyl alcohol ONLY. Do not use anything else.*

REMOVAL

1. Disconnect the brake line at the caliper and plug the end to prevent fluid spillage.

2. If the caliper holder is to be removed loosen the two allen bolts.

3. Remove the two mounting bolts and take off the caliper.

DISASSEMBLY

1. Remove the pads. Apply compressed air to the brake line fitting to force out the piston. If the piston cannot be removed, replace the caliper.

2. Being very careful of the caliper walls, remove the dust seal and the fluid seal from the caliper.

3. Remove the allen bolts previously loosened and pull out the caliper holder.

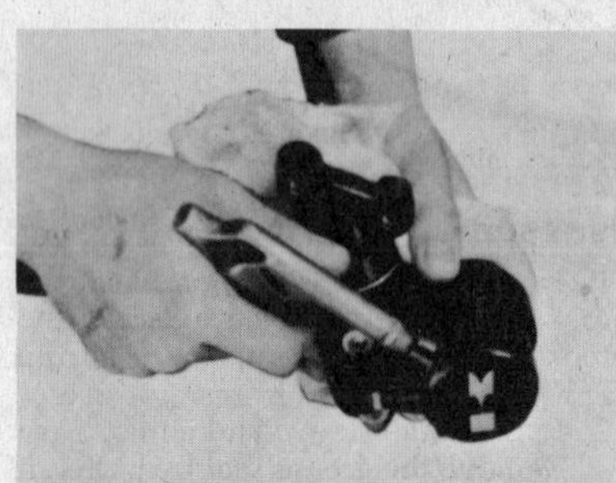

Removing the piston from the caliper with compressed air

INSPECTION

1. Check the dimensions of all parts against the specifications given in the "Chassis Specifications" chart at the end of this section.

2. Replace the fluid seal if leakage around the pad is noted, if there is a large difference in wear between the pads, or if the seal is stuck to the piston.

ASSEMBLY

1. Clean caliper internals (except pads) with new brake fluid, isopropyl alcohol, or ethyl alcohol.

2. Assembly is the reverse of disassembly. Be sure that the caliper holder dust cover is properly secured. Coat the sides of the piston with brake fluid before inserting it into the caliper.

INSTALLATION

1. Installation is the reverse of removal. Tighten allen bolts to 22–26 ft lbs, and mounting bolts to 18–24 ft lbs. Tighten banjo bolts to 18–24 ft lbs.

2. Bleed the system.

Master Cylinder

REMOVAL

1. Remove the right-side mirror.

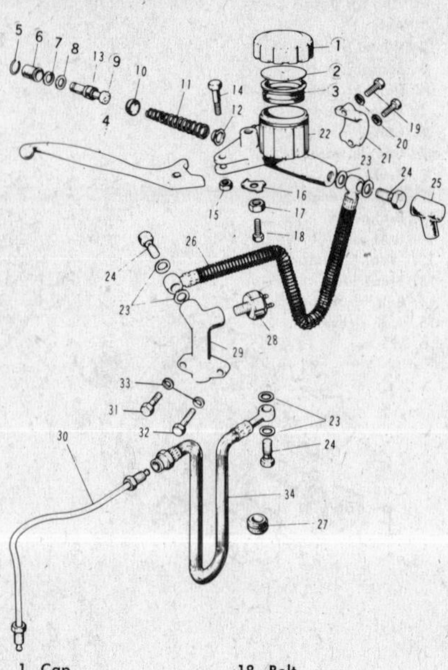

1. Cap
2. Plate
3. Diaphragm
4. Brake lever
5. Dust seal stopper
6. Dust seal
7. Retaining ring
8. Piston stopper
9. Piston assembly
10. Primary cup
11. Spring assembly
12. Check valve assembly
13. Secondary cup
14. Bolt
15. Nut
16. Lockwasher
17. Nut
18. Bolt
19. Bolt
20. Washer
21. Master cylinder clamp
22. Master cylinder body
23. Washer
24. Banjo bolt
25. Dust cover
26. Hose
27. Grommet
28. Brake light switch
29. 3-way joint
30. Pipe
31. Bolt
32. Bolt
33. Washer
34. Hose

Master cylinder assembly

2. Slip off the banjo fitting dust cover and disconnect the brake line from the master cylinder; note the washer on either side of the banjo.

3. Remove the two clamp bolts, taking care that fluid is not spilt, and remove the master cylinder.

Disassembly

1. Remove the reservoir cap and diaphragm and pour out the brake fluid.

2. Remove the brake lever. Use the special master cylinder stopper remover to remove the dust seal stopper and then take out the dust seal.

3. Remove the retaining ring and remove the stopper, piston, primary cup, spring, and check valve out of the master cylinder. Do not remove the secondary cup from the piston.

Inspection

1. Check the master cylinder components against the standard specifications given in the "Chassis Specifications" chart at the end of this section.

2. Check for obvious defects to the master cylinder bore and the piston body.

3. Inspect the rubber parts for damage or rotting and swelling. The cups should be slightly larger than the cylinder bore. If leakage at the master cylinder has occurred, replace both cups. Replacement of the secondary cup requires replacement of the piston as well.

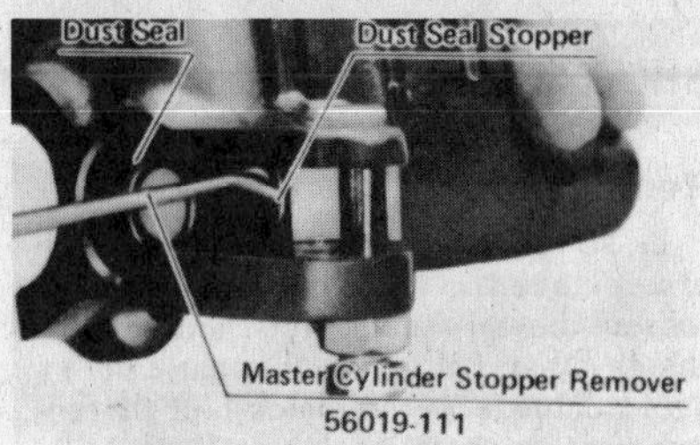

Removing the dust seal stopper

ASSEMBLY

1. Clean all parts in new brake fluid or isopropyl or ethyl alcohol.

CAUTION: *Do not use anything else to clean brake parts.*

2. Smear the parts and the inner walls of the master cylinder with brake fluid.
3. Check that the primary cup and check valve are installed facing the right direction, and are not misaligned during installation.

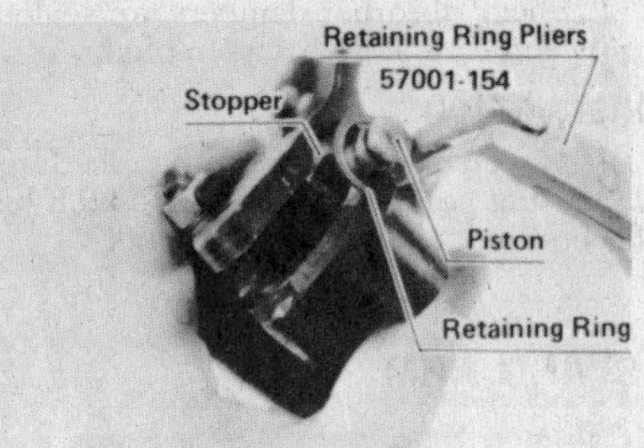

Installing the retaining ring

4. Install the check valve, spring, primary cup, and piston. Fit the piston stopper.
5. Install a new retaining ring, ensuring that it is properly seated in its groove. Install the dust seal and stopper.
6. The remainder of the procedure is the reverse of disassembly.

INSTALLATION

1. When installing the master cylinder, note that the small projection on the clamp goes on the twist-grip side.
2. Tighten the upper bolt first to 4.3–6.5 ft lbs, then the lower bolt to the same torque. Tighten the banjo bolt to 18–24 ft lbs and bleed the system.

FRONT FORKS

Removal

1. Remove the front wheel. Remove the fender.
2. On disc brake models, unbolt the caliper, supporting it out of the way to avoid bending the pipe.
3. If disassembly of the fork leg is required, loosen the filler cap(s) at this point.
4. Loosen the upper and lower triple clamp pinch-bolts.
5. Pull out the fork leg twisting it as necessary until it is free of the triple clamps.
6. Remove the remaining fork leg in the same manner.

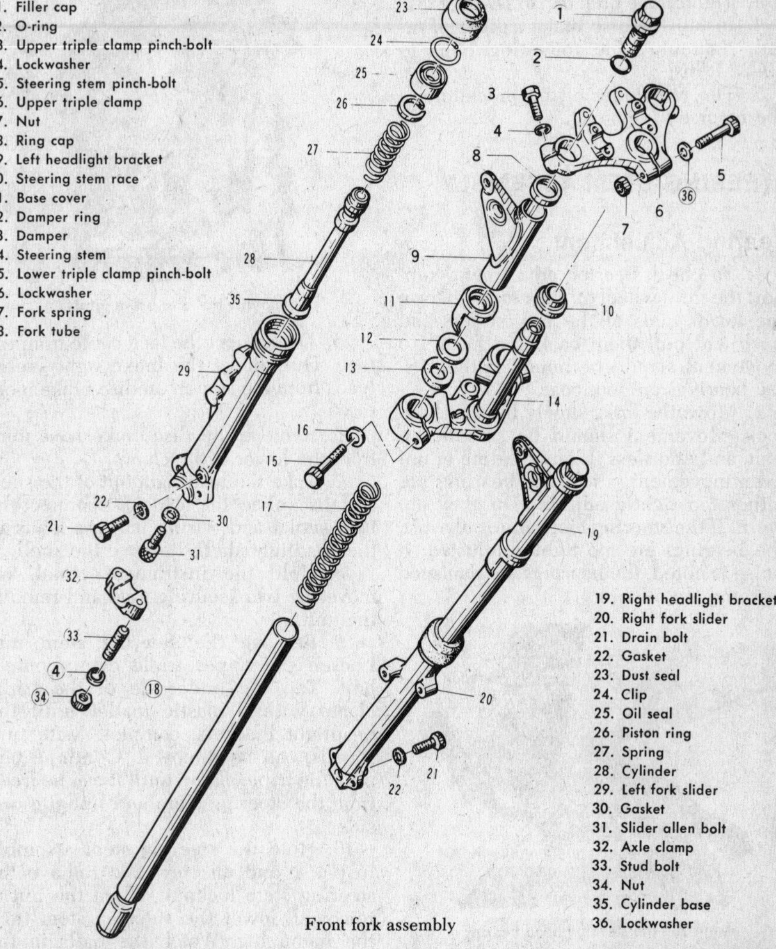

Front fork assembly

Disassembly

1. Remove the filler cap and take out the fork spring. Pour the fork oil out, pumping the slider to remove it all.
2. Pry up the dust seal from the top of the slider.
3. Insert the special piston holder to secure the cylinder and remove the allen bolt from the bottom of the slider. It may be possible to remove the allen bolt without the tool, but if the cylinder assembly begins to turn as the bolt is loosened, the tool will be necessary.
4. Pull the fork slider from the fork tube. Remove the cylinder components from the top of the fork tube.
5. Remove the slider oil seal clip and pull out the oil seal. Remove the cylinder base from the slider.

Inspection

1. Check spring free-length. Standard is 475 mm (18.7 in.). If either spring is compressed below 465 mm (18.3 in.), both springs should be replaced to ensure equal damping characteristics.
2. Check damper components for wear. Replace as necessary.

Assembly

1. Use new fork slider oil seals.
2. Install the cylinder base in the slider.
3. Press a new oil seal into the slider after lubricating the seal's outer side to facilitate assembly. Install the clip.

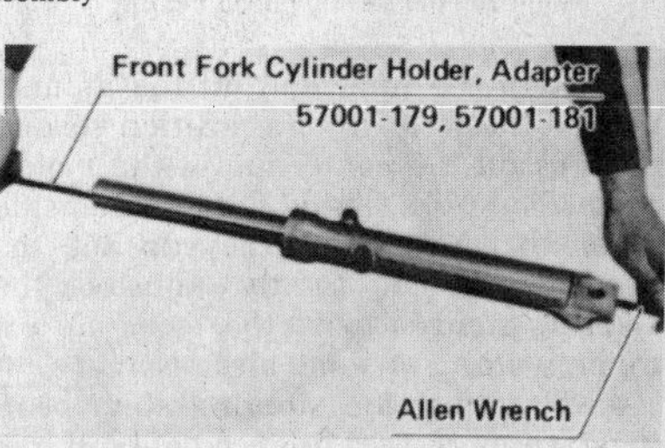

Removing the slider allen bolt with the special tool

4. Install the cylinder assembly in the fork tube inserting it so that the end protrudes from the bottom of the fork tube.
5. Oil the inner lips of the slider seal, fit the bottom of the cylinder into the cylinder base, sliding the slider all the way onto the fork tube.
6. Use thread locking compound on the allen bolt and tighten it.
7. Install the slider dust seal. Refill the forks with the correct grade and quantity of oil (refer to "Maintenance"). Fit the spring (close coils toward the top of the fork) and the filler cap.

Installation

1. Install the fork leg into the triple clamps until the edge of the top of the tube is flush with the upper triple clamp surface.
2. Tighten the upper triple clamp pinch-bolt to 11.5–13.0 ft lbs, and then the lower triple clamp pinch-bolt to 14.5–22.0 ft lbs.

3. Tighten the filler cap to 18–22 ft lbs.
4. Install the disc brake caliper, if fitted, tightening the mounting bolts to 19–23 ft lbs.
5. The remainder of the procedure is the reverse of removal.

STEERING STEM ASSEMBLY

Bearing Adjustment

1. To check bearing adjustment, support the front wheel off the ground. Grasp the lower ends of the fork sliders and push and pull them back and forth. No movement should be noted. If there is, the bearings are too loose.
2. Move the forks slowly from lock-to-lock. Movement should be smooth, silent, and effortless. If any binding or uneven movement is felt, the bearings are either too tightly adjusted, or they are worn. If the steering feels uniformly stiff, the bearings are too tightly adjusted. If noise is noted, the bearings are damaged or some are missing.

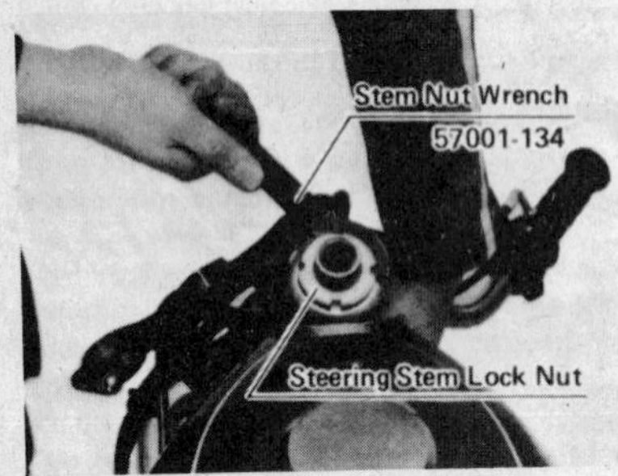

Adjusting the steering head bearings

3. With the front end off the ground, release the forks from a position several degrees off the centerline of the motorcycle. The forks should fall to either side when this is done. If they do not, the bearings are too tightly adjusted, the steering stem is bent, the races are extremely worn, or some are missing.
4. To adjust the steering stem bearings, support the front wheel off the ground, loosen the steering stem bolt and the pinch-bolt. Use the special wrench to tighten or loosen the steering stem locknut (just under the upper triple clamp), until bearing action conforms to those standards in Steps 1–3.
5. Tighten the steering stem nut to 40 ft lbs. Tighten the pinch-bolt to 11.5–13.0 ft lbs. Momentarily loosen the lower triple clamp pinch-bolts, and then tighten them to 14.5–22.0 ft lbs. Recheck bearing adjustment. If proper adjustment is not possible, the bearings and races may be worn and in need of replacement.

Removal

1. Drain the disc brake fluid, if applicable.
2. Remove the front wheel. Unbolt the master cylinder from the handlebar, disconnecting the brake line from the joint on the lower triple clamp.
3. Remove the caliper and the lower brake hose.
4. Remove the front fender. Remove the forks.

Removing the disc brake joint

5. Disconnect the tach cable from the tach. Disconnect the brake light switch leads from the switch on disc brake models.
6. Remove the disc brake hose joint from the lower triple clamp.
7. Take the headlight out of the shell and disconnect the leads. Disconnect the turn signal and wiring harness leads in the headlight shell. Remove the shell.
8. Hold the instrument panel, remove the two securing nuts and remove the unit.
9. Remove the steering stem nut. Loosen the upper triple clamp pinch-bolt. Tap the underside of the triple clamp with a plastic mallet until the headlight brackets, complete with turn signals, can be removed. Continue tapping the triple clamp until it can be freed from the steering stem and hung to one side.
10. Hold the steering stem assembly in place; and unscrew and remove the steering stem locknut. When the nut is removed, lower the steering stem from the frame lug. Watch the balls in the lower race as they will fall out as the stem is lowered. The upper balls are accessible after removing the cap.

Inspection

1. The bearing balls are standard ¼ in. in size, and 19 are used in each race.
2. Clean balls in solvent. Wipe old grease off races. Check the balls for rust, dents, pitting, and other damage. Check that the race surfaces are perfectly smooth and without dents, cracks, or ripples.
3. If any parts are damaged, replace bearings and races as a set.
4. Remove races from the frame by punching them out. Drive new races straight in.
5. Remove the steering stem race, if necessary, with a hammer and punch. The race is pressed onto the stem.

Installation

1. Lubricate the races with bearing grease and press 19 balls into the frame race and the steering stem race. Raise the stem carefully into position and screw on the stem locknut.
2. The remainder of installation is the reverse of removal. When fitting the headlight brackets, note that the ring cap goes on the top and the damper, damper ring, and stem base cover are at the bottom.

SHOCK ABSORBERS

Removal

1. To remove one of the shock absorbers, remove the grab bar mounting nuts, loosen the top shock nuts, and remove the grab bar. Lifting up the rear wheel to avoid damage to the shock bolt threads, remove the lower shock bolt. Remove the capnut and washers and remove the shock absorber.
2. To remove the other shock, repeat the procedure.

Inspection

1. Check for damping by compressing the shock absorber as much as possible, then releasing. If the shock springs quickly back to full length, the damping unit is defective.

Replace shocks in pairs even if only one is bad.

2. Shock absorber dampers are sealed units and cannot be disassembled.

Installation

1. Reverse the removal procedure. Mounting point torque is 19.5–24.0 ft lbs for both upper and lower mounts.

SWING ARM

Inspection

1. Remove the rear wheel, sprocket assembly, and shock absorbers.
2. Measure the distance between the top and bottom shock absorber mounts on both sides. The two measurements must be identical, or the swing arm will have to be replaced.
3. Check that the rear wheel mounting plates are parallel.
4. Grasp the swing arm and attempt to move it from side to side. Any noticeable side play indicates worn bushings which will need replacement.

Removal

1. Proceed as above (Step 1).
2. Remove the swing arm pivot shaft nut and pull out the shaft. Remove the swing arm noting the dust cap on each end which will come off.
3. Remove the chain guard and brake anchor from the swing arm.

Disassembly

1. Pull out the sleeve from each side of the swing arm. Remove the distance collar.
2. Measure bush inside diameter. Tap out the bush from each side, if worn. If bushes are removed, they must be replaced with new ones.

Inspection

1. Measure the outside diameter of the sleeves. Standard is 21.979–22.000 mm (0.8653–0.8661 in.). Serviceable limit is 21.95 mm (0.864 in.). Replace sleeves as a set of either is worn.
2. Check the inside diameter of each bush. Standard is 22.030–22.063 mm (0.8673–0.8686 in.). Serviceable limit is

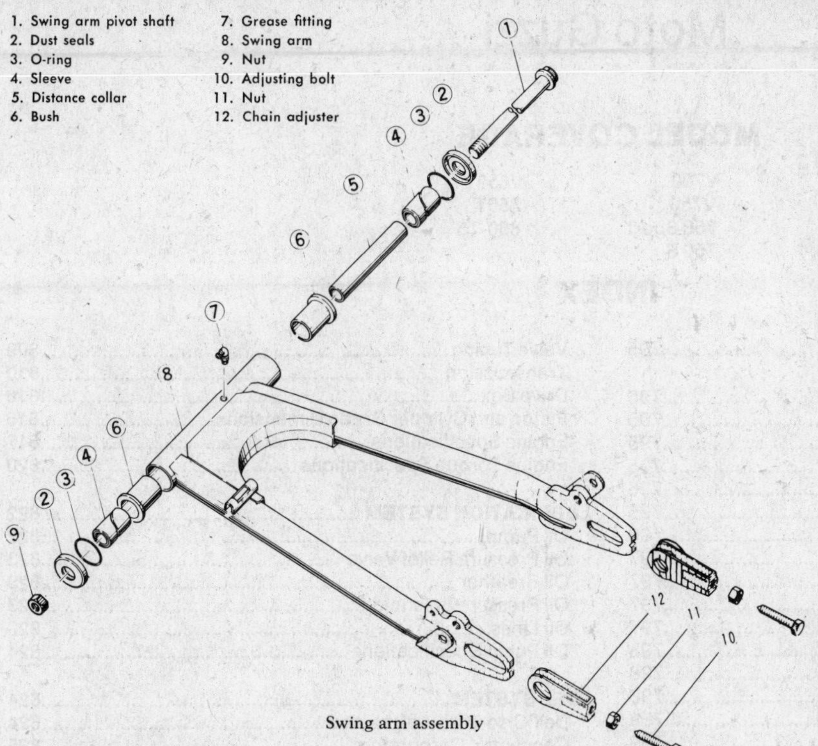

Swing arm assembly

22.26 mm (0.876 in.). Replace the bushes as a set if either is worn.

3. Check pivot shaft run-out. Standard is 0.1 mm (0.004 in.) or less. Replace the shaft if run-out exceeds 0.2 mm (0.008 in.).

Assembly

1. Oil new bushes and press them into place.
2. Lubricate the sleeves with chassis grease before installation.

Installation

1. Installation is the reverse of removal. Insert the pivot shaft into the frame from the right. Ensure that the dust caps are in place. Tighten the shaft nut to 72–94 ft lbs. Check that the swing arm pivots freely.

General Torque Specifications①

Thread Diameter (mm)	Torque (ft lbs)
Coarse	
5	2.5–3.5
6	4.5–6.5
8	11.5–16.0
10	22–30
12	39–54
14	60–83
16	94–130
18	130–181
20	188–253
Fine	
5	2.5–3.5
6	4.5–5.5
8	10–13.5
10	19–25
12	33–45
14	54–74
16	83–116
18	123–166
20	166–239

① Unless otherwise noted

Chassis Torque Specifications

Part	Torque (ft lbs)
Axle nuts	
front	72–94
rear	94–116
Front axle clamp nuts	13.0–14.5
Fork filler caps	18–22
Upper triple clamp pinch-bolts	12–13
Lower triple clamp pinch-bolts	14.5–22.0
Steering stem nut	40
Steering stem nut clamp bolt	11.5–13.0
Handlebar clamp bolts	14.5–18.0
Drum brake anchors	19.5–22.0
Sprocket nuts	25–31
Shock absorber mounts	19.5–24.0
Swing arm pivot shaft nut	72–94
Spokes	1.8–2.2

Disc Brake Torque Specifications

Part	Torque (ft lbs)
Disc mounts	11.5–16.0
Caliper shafts	22–26
Caliper mounts	18–24
Bleed nipple	5.7–7.2
Brake pipe nipple	12–13
Banjo bolts	18–24
Hose joint	3.6–4.3
Master cylinder clamp	4.3–6.5
Brake lever	3.6–5.0
Lever adjuster locknut	13.0–16.5

Chassis Specifications

Part	Standard (mm/in.)	Serviceable Limit (mm/in.)
Axle run-out		
front	0.1/0.004	0.2/0.008
rear	0.05/0.002	0.2/0.008
Drum brake lining thickness		
front	4.75–5.20/0.19–0.20	2.5/0.10
rear	5.35–6.05/0.21–0.24	2.5/0.10
Drum brake inside diameter		
front and rear	180.0–180.2/7.086–7.094	180.75/7.116
Brake spring free-length		
front	46.7–47.3/1.84–1.86	48.5/1.91
rear	56.0/2.20	58.0/2.28
Brake cam diameter		
front	14.957–14.984/0.5889–0.5899	14.83/0.584
rear	16.957–16.984/0.6676–0.6687	16.83/0.663
Cam hole diameter		
front	15.000–15.027/0.5906–0.5916	15.18/0.598
rear	17.000–17.027/0.6693–0.6704	17.18/0.676
Rear wheel sprocket		
diameter	217.4/8.56	215.5/8.48
run-out	0.3/0.012	0.5/0.020
Drive chain		
20-pin length	317.5/12.50	323/12.7
Disc brake disc		
thickness	6.95–7.05/0.270.28	5.5/0.22
run-out	0.1/0.004	0.3/0.012
Disc brake caliper		
cylinder ID	38.10–38.15/1.500–1.502	38.17/1.503
piston OD	37.97–38.02/1.495–1.497	37.90/1.492
Disc brake master cylinder		
cylinder inside diameter	14.000–14.043/0.5512–0.5529	14.08/0.5543
piston outside diameter	13.957–13.984/0.5495–0.5506	13.90/0.5472
cup diameters	14.65–15.15/0.577–0.596	14.50/0.571
spring free-length	51.0/2.01	48.0/1.89
Front fork spring free-length	475/18.7	465/18.3
Swing arm		
sleeve OD	21.979–22.000/0.8653–0.8661	21.95/0.864
bush ID	22.030–22.063/0.8673–0.8686	22.26/0.876

Moto Guzzi

MODEL COVERAGE

V700
V750
750 Sport
750 S
V850
850T
850-T3

INDEX

General Specifications

	V700	V750	750 Sport/S	V850	850T	850-T3
DIMENSIONS						
Wheelbase (in.)	56.9	57.8	57.8	58.8	57.8	57.8
Length (in.)	87.5	88.3	85.2	88.3	86.6	86.6
Width (in.)	31.2	32.6	27.5	31.3	30.7	30.7
Height (in.)	41.2	42.1	40.7	32.5	41.7	41.7
Minimum ground clearance (in.)	5.9	5.9	5.9	5.9	5.9	5.9
Curb weight (lbs)	536	502	495	548	520	526
ENGINE						
Type	four-stroke; pushrod operated overhead valves					
Number of cylinders	2	2	2	2	2	2
Configuration	90°	90°	90°	90°	90°	90°
Bore x Stroke (mm)	80 x 70	83 x 70	82.5 x 70	83 x 78	83 x 78	83 x 78
Displacement (cc)	703.7	757.5	748.4	844.0	844.0	844.0
Compression ratio (: 1)	9	9	9.8	9.2	9.5	9.5
Maximum rpm	6000	6500	7200	6500	6000	7000
Carburetion (Dell'Orto)						
right	S.S.I	VHB 29 CD	VHB 30 CD	VHB 29 CD	VHB 30 CD	VHB 30 CD
left	S.S.I.	VHB 29 CS	VHB 30 CS	VHB 29 CS	VHB 30 CS	VHB 30 CS
Lubrication	pressure; pump gear or chain driven from crankshaft					
TRANSMISSION						
Clutch type	flywheel mounted; dry, twin driven plates					
Gearbox type	constant mesh gears					
Engine/gearbox ratio (1 :)	1.375	1.375	1.235	1.235	1.235	1.235
Internal gear ratios (1 :)						
first	2.230	2.230	2.000	2.000	2.000	2.000
second	1.333	1.333	1.388	1.388	1.388	1.388
third	0.954	0.954	1.047	1.047	1.047	1.047
fourth	0.750	0.750	0.869	0.869	0.869	0.869
fifth	—	—	0.750	0.750	0.750	0.750
Secondary drive type	constant speed double joint cardan shaft					
Overall gear ratios (1 :)						
first	14.180	13.413	10.806	11.424	11.424	11.643
second	8.473	8.015	7.499	7.929	7.929	8.080
third	6.063	5.735	5.657	5.980	5.980	6.095
fourth	4.768	4.510	4.695	4.964	4.964	5.059
fifth	—	—	4.052	4.284	4.284	4.366
PERFORMANCE						
Maximum speed in gears (mph)						
first	41.0	38.5	47.5	42.2	41.0	44.5
second	59.6	64.6	68.7	61.2	58.9	63.1
third	74.5	89.2	91.2	81.9	78.0	85.4
fourth	106.0	115.0	111.8	102.1	94.0	102.9
fifth	—	—	130.0	120.1	120.1	121.1

Maintenance

NOTE: *Common maintenance procedures are explained in detail in "General Information."*

Lubrication

ENGINE

Checking

A dipstick is incorporated into the crankcase filler plug and has maximum and minimum marks on it. When checking the oil level, the engine should be warm. The filler plug must be screwed one turn into its threads to make the level reading on all models except the 850T/T3, where it should be fully threaded in. Maintain the oil level at the top dipstick mark.

Changing

1. The oil should be changed every 1800 miles under normal conditions.
2. Use SAE 10W–50 or 20W–50 oil, service rating "SE".
3. The oil should be changed when the engine is at operating temperature. Remove the drain plug at the rear of the oil pan to drain off the oil. After draining is complete, add the correct amount of oil for your machine (refer to the "Maintenance Data" chart). Run the engine for a minute, then recheck the level. Top up if necessary.

OIL FILTER

All Models Except 850T/T3

A wire mesh oil filter screen is fitted around the oil pump intake. The screen should be removed for cleaning about every 15000 miles.

1. Drain the oil.

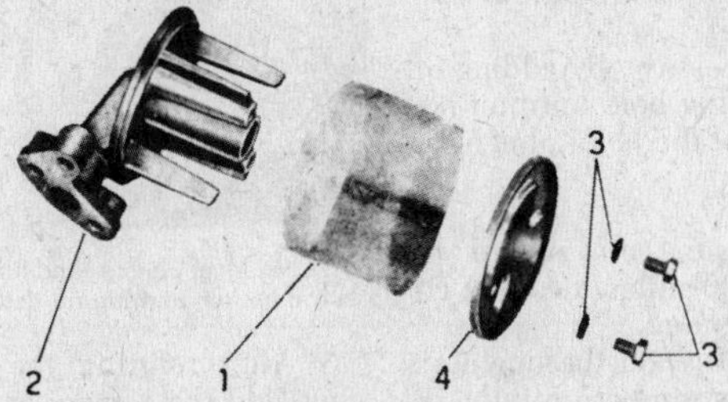

Oil filter screen assembly: 1, screen; 2, housing; 3, bolts and washers; 4, cover

2. Remove the oil pan bolts. If the pan will not come free, tap around the sides with a plastic mallet. Do not attempt to pry the pan off.

3. Remove the two filter cover bolts, and take away the filter screen. Clean it in a solvent and dry thoroughly.

4. Installation is the reverse of removal. Use a new pan gasket.

Tighten the pan bolts gradually and evenly.

850T/T3

Most 850T and all T3 models have an oil filter screen and a replaceable cartridge oil filter, both of which are fitted to the oil pan. Cleaning of the filter screen and replacement of the cartridge filter are necessary about every 15,000 miles.

1. Drain the oil.
2. Remove the oil pan bolts. If the pan resists removal, tap around the sides with a plastic mallet. Do not attempt to pry the pan off.
3. Remove the filter screen, clean it in a solvent and dry thoroughly before installation.
4. Unscrew and remove the filter cartridge and replace it with a new unit.
5. Installation is the reverse of removal. Use a new pan gasket. Tighten the pan bolts gradually and evenly.

TRANSMISSION

Checking

1. A level plug is fitted to the right side of the transmission housing to enable the level to be checked periodically. This should be done every 1800 miles.

Transmission oil level plug (A), filler (B), and drain plug (C)

2. Check when the engine is at operating temperature. When the plug is removed, the oil should just begin to seep out of the plug hole.

3. Top up, if necessary, by adding oil through the filler plug hole until oil just begins to seep out of the level plug hole.

Changing

1. The transmission oil should be changed every 6,000 miles. SAE 90 EP gear oil is recommended.

2. Change the oil when the engine is at operating temperature. Carefully remove the drain plug at the very bottom of the transmission and allow the old oil to drain for several minutes. When fitting the drain plug, be very careful not to overtighten it. It is easy to strip the threads.

3. Add 1¾ pints (0.75 l) of SAE 90 oil through the filler plug. After allowing the oil to settle for a moment, check the level. Top up if necessary.

DRIVE BOX

Checking

1. A level plug is provided to check the drive box oil, which should be done every 1,800 miles. When the plug is removed, the oil should just begin to seep out.

The oil should be checked when the engine is warm.

When removing or installing the level plug, it is important to do this carefully. It is very easy to strip the threads in the drive box.

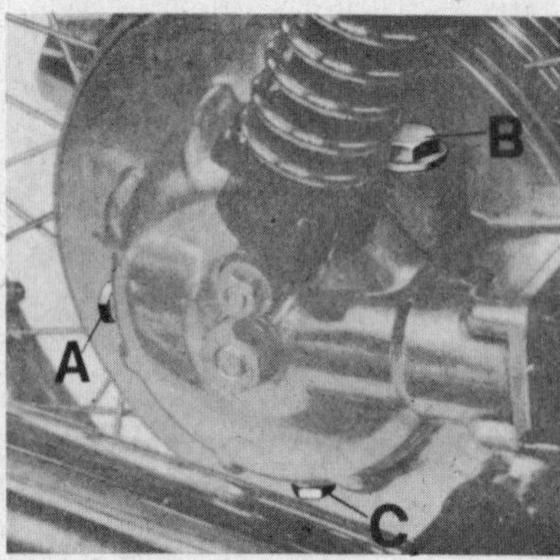

Drive box level plug (A), filler (B) and drain plug (C) (early)

Changing

1. Drive box oil should be changed every 6,000 miles. Change the oil when the unit is at operating temperature.

2. On early models, a drain plug is provided. Sport and 850s have a cover plate secured by allen screws. After removing the screws, tap the sides of the cover to break it free.

Drive box level plug (A) and filler (B). Remove cover plate at bottom to drain oil (later models)

3. After refitting the cover or drain plug, add the correct amount of SAE 90 EP oil through the filler plug. Refer to the "Maintenance Data" chart.

4. After allowing the oil to settle for a moment, check the level and top up if necessary.

FRONT FORKS

1. The front fork oil should be changed every 12,000 miles, or every year, whichever comes first.

2. V7, V750, and V850 models use standard hydraulically damped forks, while Sport and 850T/T3 models utilize forks in which the dampers are sealed units (much like rear shocks). The oil added to this type of fork is used only to lubricate the internal components, and does not affect damping characteristics.

3. ATF can be used in all forks, although any quality oil designed for motorcycle forks is also acceptable.

4. Drain one fork leg at a time. Remove the drain plug at the bottom of the fork slider. Pump the forks up and down several times to expell all of the old oil. Refit the drain plugs.

5. On Sport and 850T/T3 models, place a support beneath the crankcase to prevent the forks from collapsing when the filler caps are removed. Remove the bolts which secure the instrument bracket to the forks.

Fork drain plug (A) and filler cap (B) (Sport shown)

6. Remove the filler cap from each fork leg. Add the correct quantity of fork oil for your model as given in the "Maintenance Data" chart.

NOTE: *Slight leakage at the fork seals on Sport and 850T/T3 models may be due to an excess of oil in the fork, and is no cause for concern. Since the fork dampers are sealed, the leakage of lubricating oil will not affect fork operation.*

CHASSIS LUBRICATION

1. The steering head and wheel bearings should be lubricated with a good grade of bearing grease every 12,000 miles.

2. The swing arm pivot bearings should be packed with bearing grease whenever the swing arm is removed.

Service Checks and Adjustments

CLUTCH

1. Maintain clutch cable adjustment so that the clutch handlebar lever can be moved ⅛ in. (4 mm) before the clutch begins to disengage. This distance is measured between the clutch lever and lever bracket as illustrated, and can be made either with the cable adjuster on the handlebar, or with that on the transmission.

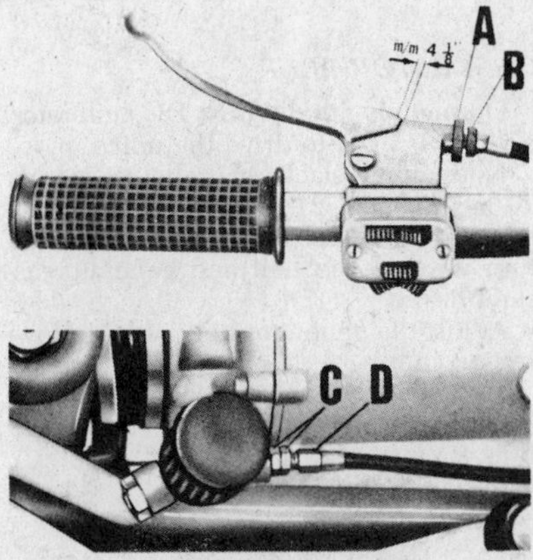

Clutch adjustment can be made with either the handlebar adjuster (A,B) or the lower cable adjuster (C,D)

2. If adjustment of the cable to the proper specification does not result in good clutch operation, check the adjustment of the clutch pushrod adjuster on the rear of the transmission, which is fitted to 850 and 750 Sport models.

The pushrod is adjusted by means of a screw and locknut on the clutch operating lever.

3. To check this adjustment, run the clutch cable adjusters in until there is maximum freeplay. Measure the distance between the center of the cable fitting in the lever and the transmission rear cover. This distance should be 67–69 mm for Eldorado models; and for Sport and 850T/T3 models: 65 mm for machines with disc or rod-operated rear brakes; 75 mm for machines with cable-operated rear brakes. To make the adjustment, loosen the locknut and turn the screw until the distance is correct. Next, adjust the clutch cable as described in Step 1.

SHIFTER MECHANISM

If noisy and difficult gear shifts are encountered, and the clutch has been adjusted properly, they may be remedied by adjusting the shift mechanism. This is located at the rear of the transmission.

To adjust, loosen the locknut and turn the adjusting screw (V700, V750) or eccentric nut (850s and 750 Sport) in or out until a position is arrived at where the gears will shift smoothly both up and down and where neutral can readily be found. Then hold the screw or eccentric nut in position and tighten the locknut.

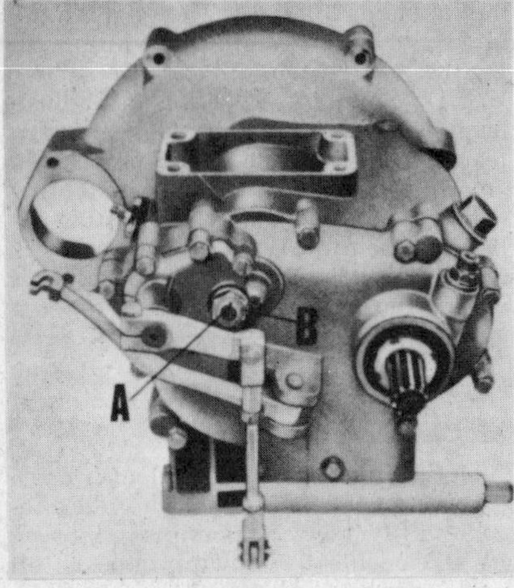

Shifter adjuster: adjusting screw (A), locknut (B) (V700, V750)

BRAKES

Disc Brake

1. A periodic check of the master cylinder fluid level and pad wear is the only routine maintenance required. The fluid level should not be allowed to drop more than 8 mm (0.3 in.) below the maximum mark inscribed inside the master cylinder. The level will drop somewhat as the pads wear, but when this point is reached, fresh fluid should be added.

Never use brake fluid from an unsealed container.

Take precautions to ensure that the fluid does not contact painted surfaces.

Use DOT 3 hydraulic brake fluid.

2. The brake system should be flushed and refilled with fresh fluid at least once a year. Refer to "Chassis" for procedures.

3. If brake operation is not satisfactory, or if the lever feels mushy, the system should be bled. Refer to "Chassis" for procedures.

4. A clearance of 0.05–0.15 mm (0.002–0.006 in.) must be maintained between the lever end and the piston. The adjustment can be effected with the screw on the lever bracket. This adjustment is usually not necessary unless the master cylinder has been disassembled.

5. About every 3,000 miles, the pads should be checked for wear. To remove the pads: remove the dust cover, remove the tapered pin and spring, remove the retainer pins, and take out the pads. Both pads must be at least 6 mm (0.2 in.) thick. If either is less than this amount, replace them as a set.

New pad thickness is 9 mm (0.35 in.).

Installation is the reverse of removal. Note that fitting new pads may result in a rise of the master cylinder fluid level. Drain off any excess fluid by means of the bleed screw on the caliper if the level is above the maximum mark. Hold the brake on, loosen the bleed screw (fluid will flow out and the lever will be pulled to the handgrip). Tighten the screw before releasing the lever.

NOTE: *Avoid hard application of the brake for at least fifty miles after fitting new pads.*

6. It will not be necessary to bleed the brake lines after fitting new pads. Operate the brake lever several times to position the pads before riding.

Front Drum Brake

Twin-Leading Shoe

1. A twin-leading shoe type brake is fitted to all models with a front drum brake with the exception of the V7 Sport.

2. The brake adjustment is correct if the brake lever on the handlebar can be moved 20–25 mm (¾–1 in.) before the shoes contact the drum. This distance is measured at the tip of the lever.

3. If adjustment is necessary, use the cable adjuster at the brake plate so that the proper amount of lever movement is obtained. For fine adjustments, use the adjuster at the handlebar.

Four-Leading Shoe

1. The V7 Sport front drum brake is a four-leading shoe type. Two independent cables are used, along with a common adjuster at the handlebar which allows both cables to be adjusted simultaneously.

2. The brake lever at the handlebar should have 20–25 mm (¾–1 in.) of free movement before the shoes contact the drum. This is measured at the tip of the lever. For minor adjustments, use the handlebar adjuster to obtain the proper freeplay.

3. If the handlebar adjustment has been used up, or if brake operation is not satisfactory, proceed as follows:

4. Run the handlebar adjuster all the way in. Disconnect the right side brake cable from the lever at the brake plate. Use the cable adjuster on the brake plate for the left side brake cable to give 20–25 mm (¾–1 in.) of movement at the handle-

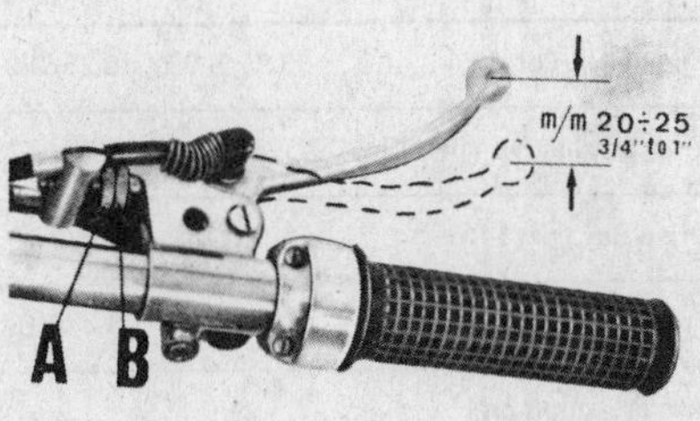

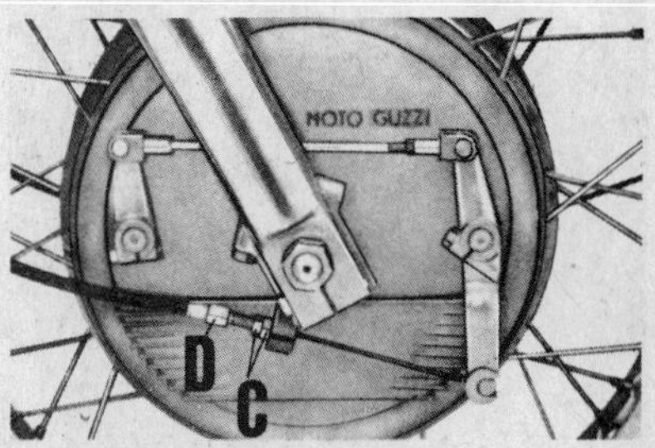

Front drum brake adjustment. Make minor adjustments with the handlebar adjuster (A,B); major adjustments with that on the brake plate (C,D). On Sport models be sure to adjust both brake plates when using the lower brake plate adjuster

bar lever before the left side shoes contact the drum.

5. Reconnect the right side brake cable. Apply the handlebar lever, ensuring that it is still adjusted to the proper amount of movement. Check that the right side brakes are contacting the drum by pushing on the brake plate lever with your thumb. If this lever can be moved with the brake applied, it indicates that there is too much slack in the right cable. Use the adjuster at the brake plate to take up slack until the right side shoes are in contact with the drum.

6. Apply the brakes, and check for movement of the brake plate levers on both sides by pushing on them. If both sides are in contact with the drum, no movement will be possible.

7. Make final adjustments of handlebar lever movement with the adjuster at the handlebar.

Rear Drum Brake

1. The rear brake may be either cable or rod-operated. A twin-leading shoe unit is used on late models.

The brake should be adjusted so that the brake pedal can be moved 20–25 mm (¾–1 in.) before the shoes contact the drum. On rod-operated brakes, this adjustment should be checked with the machine off the stand, and a rider in place on it.

2. Rod-operated brakes are adjusted by means of the thumb screw at the end of the rod.

Cable-operated brakes are adjusted by means of locknuts on the cable adjuster.

STEERING HEAD

1. A periodic check should be made of the steering head bearings. With the front wheel supported off the ground, the forks should swing easily from lock to lock. If the forks are tight or if movement is noisy, the bearings should be adjusted. Also check for excessive play by grasping the fork sliders and pushing and pulling on them. No play should be noticeable.

2. On V700, V750, and V850 models, two locknuts beneath the upper triple clamp are used to adjust the bearings. Loosen the uppermost nut, and turn the lower so that bearing action conforms to the standards in Step 1. Then tighten the upper nut against the lower while holding the lower in place.

3. On Sport and 850T models, adjustment is accomplished by loosening the rearmost upper triple clamp pinch bolt, loosening the nut beneath the steering damper knob, and using the adjusting nut beneath the triple clamp to make the fork movement conform to those standards outlined in Step 1.

Steering head bearing adjusting nuts (A,B) (early models shown)

FUEL SYSTEM

Air Cleaner

Models fitted with an air cleaner use a paper element type. When the filter becomes dirty it may be possible to prolong its service life by blowing deposits off with compressed air. It is preferable, however, to simply replace the element.

The element should be checked about every 6,000 miles under normal conditions.

To remove the air filter on the T3:

1. Lift the seat, supporting it by its rod.
2. Remove the tool box.
3. Remove the gas tank.
4. Disconnect the wiring from the battery (negative first) and unbolt the brackets.
5. Unhook the springs and remove the rubber oil breather manifold.
6. Remove the nut securing the oil breather to the housing, disconnect the lines and take out the oil breather.
7. Remove the air filter.
8. Installation is the reverse of the removal procedure.

Fuel Filters

1. Mesh filter screens are fitted to the fuel petcocks and each carburetor. These filters should be serviced every 6,000 miles.

2. The petcock filters are reached by removing and draining the gas tank. Unscrew and remove the petcocks. Clean the filters in a solvent and blow dry. Replace them if punctured or damaged.

3. The carburetor fuel filters are located beneath the feed banjos on the carburetor bodies. After removing the banjo securing screw, lift off the banjo and remove the filter screen. Clean in solvent. Replace them if punctured or damaged.

Removing the carburetor fuel filter screen

GENERATOR BELT

On models fitted with a DC generator, a v-belt is used to drive the unit.

Normal belt slack (A) is about 1 cm per 10 kgs (0.39 in./21 lbs). Avoid overtightening the belt as this may cause premature wear to the belt and generator assemblies.

Adjust the generator belt in the following manner:

1. Remove the three bolts (B) which secure the outer half-pulley to the pulley hub, then remove the half-pulley.

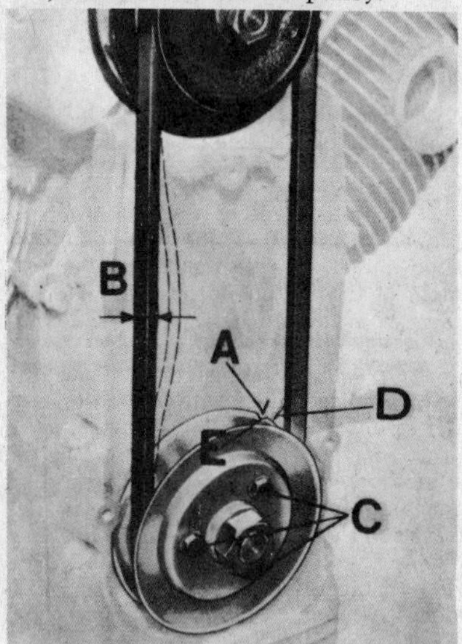

Generator belt tension (A)

Maintenance Data

	V700	V750	V7 Sport/S	V850	850T	850-T3
Engine Oil (qt/l)	3.25/3.0	3.25/3.0	3.7/3.5	3.25/3.0	3.7/3.5	3.2/3.0
Transmission Oil (pts/l)	1.75/0.75	1.75/0.75	1.75/0.75	1.75/0.75	1.75/0.75	1.75/0.75
Drive Box (oz/l)	6.1/0.18	6.1/0.18	12.0/0.36	12.0/0.36	12.0/0.36	8.5/0.25
Front Forks @ leg (oz/l)	5.4/0.16	5.4/0.16	1.8/0.05	5.4/0.16	1.8/0.05	2.0/0.06
Tire Pressure (psi) front	21	21	28	21	25	25
rear (solo)	25	25	33	25	31	31
rear (two-up)	28	28	36	28	36	36

2. Add or remove spacing collars as necessary. Removing spacers will increase belt tension and installing spacers will decrease it. Spacers should be removed or installed one at a time and, if more than one spacer is removed, the extras should be placed at the front and rear of the pulley so as not to throw the pulleys out of alignment.

3. Replace the outer half-pulley and secure the three mounting bolts. Recheck the adjustment and repeat the operation until a satisfactory adjustment is attained.

GENERATOR

Every 6,000 miles the generator commutator should be cleaned with a clean cloth slightly moistened with gasoline.

If carbon or copper dust has settled in the mica insulators, it should be blown clean with compressed air.

At this time inspect the brushes and replace them if chipped or excessively worn. Be sure the brushes make perfect contact with the commutator.

Periodic Maintenance Intervals①

Weekly
- Check battery electrolyte level
- Check tire pressure

Every 300 miles
- Check crankcase oil level

Every 600 miles
- Lubricate controls and cables

Every 1800 miles
- Change engine oil
- Check valve adjustment
- Clean and gap spark plugs
- Check transmission oil level
- Check drive box oil level
- Lubricate contact breaker cam felt

Every 6000 miles
- Change transmission oil
- Change drive box oil
- Clean petcocks and fuel filters
- Check and clean battery terminals
- Clean generator commutator
- Change air filter

Every 12000 miles
- Repack wheel and steering head bearings
- Change fork oil
- Change disc brake fluid
- Clean starter motor commutator

Every 15000 miles
- Clean oil filter screen
- Change replaceable filter (if fitted)

① Based on normal usage after break-in is complete

Recommended Lubricants

Engine
- SAE 10W—50, service rating "SE"
- SAE 20W—50, service rating "SE"

Transmission and Drive Box
- SAE 90EP

Front Forks
- ATF
- SAE 30W
- SAE 20W

Control Cables
- Light motor oil
- Graphite-based lubricant
- Molybdenum disulphide-based lubricant

Tach, Speedometer Cables
- Light-duty grease

Wheel, Steering Head Bearings
- Waterproof wheel bearing grease

Tune-Up

NOTE: *Common tune-up procedures are explained in detail in "General Information."*

Valve Adjustment

NOTE: *Valves must be adjusted when the engine is cold.*

V700, V750, V850

1. Remove the valve covers. Remove the spark plugs.

2. Place the transmission in gear, and rotate the rear wheel to turn the engine over in the following manner.

3. Beginning with either cylinder, turn the rear wheel in the normal direction until the intake valve for that cylinder opens and just begins to close.

4. Using a flexible swizzle stick or similar non-rigid object, insert it carefully into the spark plug hole until it touches the piston crown.

5. Continue turning the rear wheel slowly. The piston should rise. When the piston reaches the highest point of its travel, stop. The piston should now be at TDC (top dead center) and on the compression stroke. Turn the wheel a few degrees in either direction to verify that the piston is at the top of its stroke. Check that there is clearance at both valves. If there is not, the piston is at the top of the *exhaust* stroke, and the engine must be turned 360° to obtain the compression stroke.

6. When the piston is at TDC on the compression stroke, the valves can be adjusted. Correct clearance is 0.15 mm (0.0059 in.) for the intake valve, and 0.25 mm (0.0098 in.) for the exhaust valve.

The measurement is made between the valve stem and the rocker arm.

7. If adjustment is necessary, loosen the locknut and turn the adjusting screw in or out until the feeler gauge is a drag fit. Tighten the locknut while holding the adjusting screw in place. Recheck the adjustment after tightening the locknut.

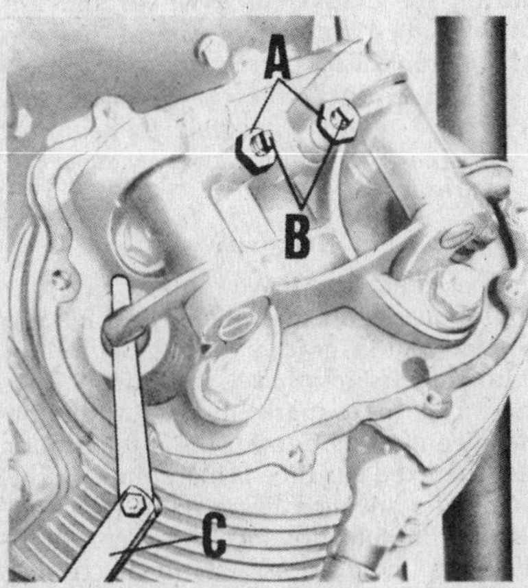

Valve adjustment is made with the screws (B) after loosening locknuts (A)

8. Repeat the procedure for the remaining cylinder, turning the engine over to position that piston at TDC on the compression stroke.

9. Before installing the valve cover screws, coat the threads with oil or an anti-seize compound to facilitate future removal. Tighten the screws gradually and in a cross pattern.

750 SPORT/S, 850T/T3

These models have timing marks on the flywheel, making it easy to position the piston at top dead center for valve adjustment.

1. Remove the spark plugs. Remove the valve covers. Remove the rubber cap from the inspection hole on the right side of the crankcase.

2. The flywheel has several marks among which are "S" and "D". "S" indicates that the left cylinder is at TDC and "D" that the right cylinder is at TDC when the letters are aligned with the slash mark on the side of the inspection hole.

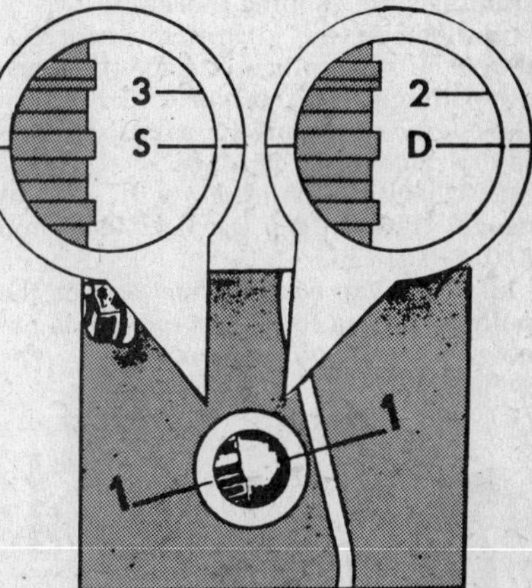

TDC for the left cylinder occurs when flywheel mark "S" aligns with timing mark "1." "D" is TDC for the right cylinder. Nos. "2" and "3" are fixed advance firing points.

3. Engage the transmission. Using the rear wheel, turn the engine over until either of these marks appears through the inspection hole, then line up the letter with the mark on the hole. Check for clearance at both valves for that cylinder (i.e. if the "S" mark is aligned, check the left cylinder).

If there is clearance at both valves, the piston is at TDC on the compression stroke and the valves for that cylinder can be adjusted. If there is not clearance at both valves, the piston is at TDC on the exhaust stroke, and the engine must be turned 360° to get it on the compression stroke.

4. Correct clearance for both intake and exhaust valves is 0.22 mm (0.0089 in.). The measurement is made between the valve stem and the rocker arm.

5. If adjustment is necessary, loosen the locknut and turn the adjusting screw until the clearance is correct. Hold the adjusting screw in place while tightening the nut. Recheck the adjustment afterwards.

6. Turn the engine over so that the remaining cylinder is at TDC on the compression stroke and repeat the procedure.

7. Before installing the valve cover screws, coat the threads with oil or an anti-seize compound to facilitate future removal. Tighten the screws gradually and in a cross pattern.

Contact Breaker Points

LOCATION

1. The points are located beneath a cap just inside the right cylinder.
2. 750 Sport and 850T/T3 models use dual points, while other models have a single point set with a rotor and distributor cap.

GAPPING

Points should be filed (if necessary) and cleaned before gapping.

V700, V750, V850

A single set of points is used, which simplifies the gapping procedure.

1. Remove the distributor cap. Remove the spark plugs. Engage the transmission, and use the rear wheel to turn the engine over until the points are open to their maximum gap.
2. Check the point gap with a feeler gauge. Proper gap is 0.42–0.48 mm (0.016–0.018 in.).
3. If the gap is not correct, loosen the points securing screw just enough to enable the fixed point to be moved.

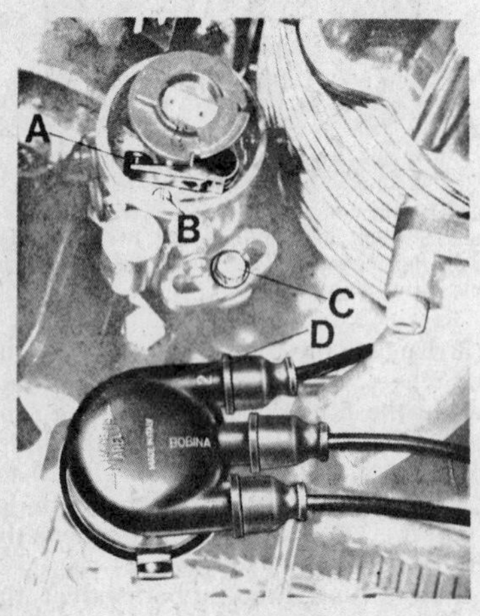

Point gap adjustment (A) is made after loosening screw (B). Bolt (C) is for ignition timing adjustment. Plug lead #2 from distributor cap (D) is for the left cylinder.

Adjust the gap with a thin screwdriver applied at the pry point. Tighten the screw and recheck the gap.

750 Sport, 850T/T3

These models utilize two sets of breaker points. Each set is gapped separately.

1. Remove the points cap. Remove the spark plugs. Engage the transmission, and use the rear wheel to turn the engine over until one of the sets of points is open to the maximum gap.
2. Check the gap with a feeler gauge. Proper clearance is 0.37–0.43 mm (0.014–0.017 in.) for the Sport and T3, and 0.42–0.48 mm (0.016–0.018 in.) for the 850T.
3. If the gap is not correct, loosen the two screws which secure the points (see illustration) just enough to enable the fixed point to be moved. Adjust the gap with a thin screwdriver applied at the notch provided. Tighten the screws and recheck the point gap.

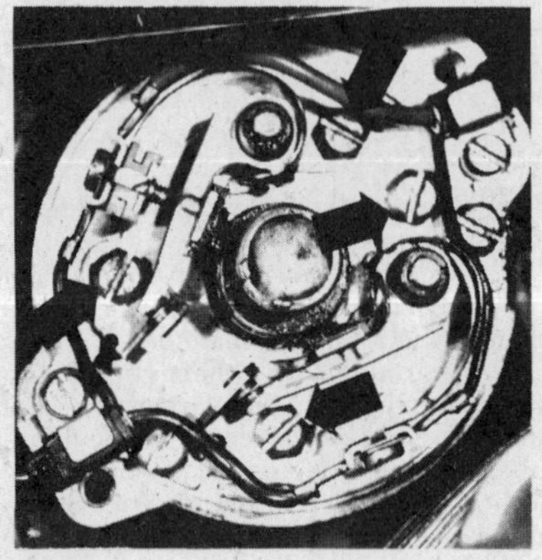

To adjust point gap, loosen the screws (arrows) for each point set. Loosening the wrong screws for the lower point set will necessitate resetting the ignition timing

4. Turn the engine over until the other points set is open, and repeat the procedure.

LUBRICATION

When the points are gapped, a few drops of clean motor oil should be applied to the lubricating felt.

Care should be taken not to overlubricate the felt, since this may cause fouling of the points.

Ignition Timing

On DC generator models, the generator drive pulley on the crankshaft is fitted with several marks which indicate piston position when aligned with a stationary mark on the crankcase.

On alternator models, the timing marks are on the crankshaft flywheel and are visible when the rubber cap on the side of the crankcase is removed.

NOTE: *Points must be cleaned and gapped before checking the timing. Dirty points will cause inaccurate readings.*

GENERATOR MODELS

The generator drive pulley has four timing marks on the inner lip which are used to set the ignition timing. Beginning with the first of these, and proceeding *clockwise* these marks represent: the top dead center position for the left cylinder (B), the fixed advance firing point (C), the automatic advance firing point (D), and, finally, the total advance firing point (E). There is, in addition, a stationary timing mark on the crankcase.

NOTE: *The crankshaft rotates clockwise when viewed from the front.*

Generator models timing marks

Spark plug leads are numbered "1" and "2" for the right and left cylinders respectively.

Dynamic Timing

1. Remove the generator belt cover. Hook the strobe light up to the left cylinder, and, illuminating the timing marks, run the engine. At the following rpm, the pulley marks should align with the stationary mark in this manner:
   a. Mark "C" at 1200 ± 100 rpm
   b. Mark "D" at 2200 ± 100 rpm
   c. Mark "E" at 3600 ± 100 rpm
2. If the marks do not line up with the stationary mark at the proper engine speed, loosen the distributor shaft lock bolt, and rotate the distributor a few degrees in the direction necessary so that alignment is achieved. In most cases it will not be necessary to turn the distributor more than a few degrees. Tighten the lock bolt and recheck the timing.
3. If it is not possible to get the "E" (full advance mark) aligned, either the automatic advance unit is not working correctly, or the breaker points are worn to the point of replacement.

Static Timing

1. Remove the generator belt cover. Remove the distributor cap. Hook up the continuity light or test light so that one lead is connected to ground, and the other to the primary wire terminal or moveable point.
2. Turn the engine over slowly until the contact on the distributor rotor approaches the vicinity of the distributor cap contact for the left cylinder (which is marked "2" on the distributor cap). The engine should be turned in the normal running direction—the generator drive pulley will rotate clockwise when viewed from the front of the engine.
3. Continue to rotate the engine slowly. The test light should react at the moment the mark "C" on the pulley aligns with the stationary timing mark.
4. If the test light does not indicate that the points have opened when the "C" mark and the stationary mark are aligned, loosen the distributor shaft lock bolt and rotate the distributor a few degrees in the direction required so that

alignment is achieved. Tighten the lock bolt and recheck the timing.

ALTERNATOR MODELS

Timing marks are provided on the flywheel to set the ignition timing. Because of the dual-point ignition, timing must be checked for both cylinders.

NOTE: *Crankshaft rotation is clockwise when viewed from the front.*

The breaker points which are connected to the *red* primary wire are the points for the *right* cylinder; the points with the *green* primary wire are for the *left* cylinder.

Each cylinder also has three timing marks on the flywheel and these are as follows (refer to the illustration):

"S" and "D": "S" is the top dead center position for the left cylinder; "D" is TDC for the right cylinder.

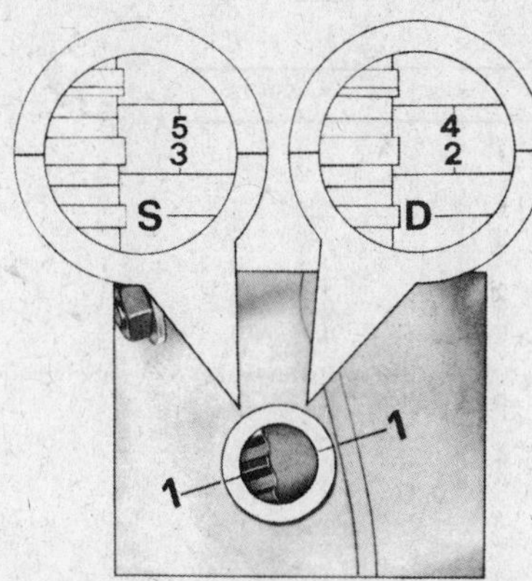

Alternator models flywheel timing marks

"2" and "3": these marks indicate the fixed advance firing points for the right and left cylinders respectively. They indicate piston positions of 13° before TDC for the Sport, or 8° before TDC (850T) or 2° before TDC (T3): that is, the firing point before the automatic advance mechanism comes into effect.

"4" and "5": these are the full advance firing points for the right and left cylinders respectively. They indicate piston positions of 39° BTDC (Sport), 34° BTDC (850T) or 33° BTDC (T3): that is, the full advance firing point.

Dynamic Timing

The right cylinder *must* be timed first.

1. Remove the inspection cap from the crankcase so that the timing marks on the flywheel are visible. Remove the points cap. Clean and gap the points.
2. Hook up the strobe light according the manufacturer's instructions to time the right cylinder.

All of the following rpm values are plus or minus 200 rpm.

3. Start the engine, aiming the strobe light at the flywheel marks. The mark indicated as "2" in the illustration must align with the mark on the side of the inspection hole at rpm up to 1000 (T3) or 1500 (other models). At 6,000 rpm (T3) or 4,400 rpm (other models) and above, the mark indicated as "4" must align with the mark on the side of the inspection hole.
4. If the marks do not align at the given rpm, loosen the two round head screws which secure the points plate to the housing, and rotate the entire plate a few degrees in the direction necessary to bring the marks into alignment. Tighten the screws and recheck the timing.
5. Having timed the right cylinder, the remaining cylinder must be checked as well. Proceeding as before, the mark "3" must align with the inspection hole mark at 1,500 rpm, (T3:1,000 rpm) while the mark "5" must align at 4,400 rpm (T3: 6,000 rpm).
6. If adjustment is necessary, loosen the two hex-head screws which secure the left cylinder's breaker points to the points plate and move the points with a thin screwdriver at the pry point provided so that the marks can be brought into alignment.

It will be noted that adjusting the timing for the right cylinder will affect both cylinders, while the left cylinder is adjusted independently.

Static Timing

The right cylinder *must* be timed first.

1. Remove the inspection cap from the crankcase so that the timing marks on the flywheel are visible. Remove the spark plugs. Remove the right cylinder valve cover. Remove the points cap. Clean and gap the points.
2. Hook up the test light to the points for the right cylinder (red lead).
3. Engage the transmission and use the rear wheel to turn the engine over in the normal running direction until the right cylinder's intake valve open and begins to close. Continue turning the engine over, slowly, until the "D" mark on the flywheel aligns with the mark on the inspection hole. The right cylinder is now at TDC on the compression stroke.

Right cylinder TDC mark (D)

4. Turn the engine backwards until the fixed advance timing mark ("2" in the illustration) comes into view and passes the inspection hole timing mark.
5. Turn the engine in the normal direction of rotation once more. As the "2" mark aligns with the inspection hole mark, the points should open as indicated by the reaction of the test light.
6. If this is not the case, loosen the two round head screws which secure the points plate and rotate the entire plate in the necessary direction so that the points begin to open as these marks align. Tighten the screws and recheck the timing.
7. The left cylinder must now be set. Turn the engine over in the normal direction of rotation until the "S" mark (left cylinder at TDC) is aligned with the inspection hole mark. Now repeat the timing procedure outlined above to see if the points open when the mark "3" aligns with the inspection hole mark. If they do not, loosen the two screws which secure the left cylinder's points to the plate, and position them so that they open when the marks align. Tighten the screws and recheck the timing.

It will be noted that adjusting the timing for the right cylinder will affect timing for both cylinders, while the left cylinder is adjusted independent of the other.

Carburetors

Three adjustments to be made to the carburetors are the idle mixture, idle speed, and synchronization.

Carburetor adjustments must be made when the engine is at operating temperature, preferably after all of the other tune-up operations outlined have been carried out.

1. Ensure that the throttle cables have enough freeplay so that the throttle slides are closing fully.
2. Turn the pilot screws in very carefully until they bottom lightly, then back them out the proper number of turns for your model (refer to the "Tune-Up Specifications" chart).
3. Start the engine (which should already be at operating temperature). With the engine idling at 1000–1200 rpm (T3:900–1000 rpm), disconnect one of the spark plug leads, and turn the pilot screw for the running cylinder in or out so that the cylinder is running at the highest

Pilot screw (A) and throttle stop screw (B)

speed. It should not be necessary to alter the adjustment more than ½ turn from the given setting. If it *is* necessary, suspect a dirty idle passage or damage to the pilot screw's tapered tip.

4. Connect the spark plug lead, rev the engine a few times to clean it out, then disconnect the other lead, and repeat the procedure with the other cylinder.

5. When both pilot screws have been adjusted in this manner, connect both leads, rev the engine a few times, and set the idle speed in this manner:

6. When either spark plug lead is disconnected, the other cylinder should fire 4–5 times before stalling.

Adjust the throttle stop screws so that this condition is met.

7. When both plug leads are connected, idle speed should be 1000–1200 rpm (T3:900–1000 rpm). If this is not the case, turn both throttle stop screws by equal amounts until the desired idle speed is obtained.

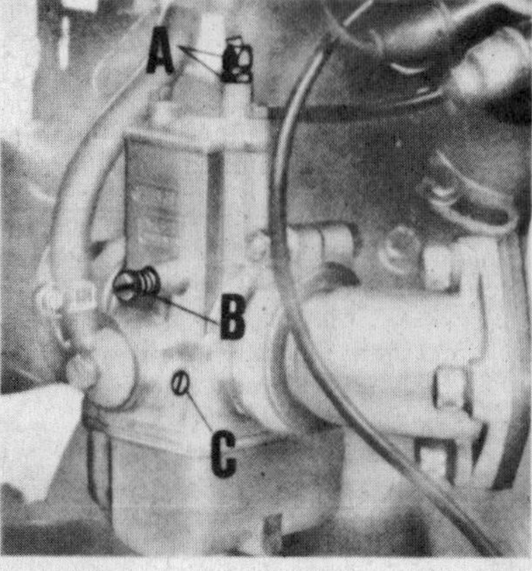

Cable adjuster (A), throttle stop screw (B), pilot screw (C)

8. To synchronize the throttle slides, first remove the air cleaner assembly (if fitted), the rubber sleeves, and the velocity stacks (if fitted), so that the carburetor intakes are readily accessible.

9. Place a finger in each carburetor bore and check that both slides begin to rise at exactly the same time when the twist grip is turned.

An alternative method is to turn the twist grip until one of the slides just clears the carburetor bore and check that the other is in the very same position.

10. If an adjustment is necessary, turn the throttle cable adjusters on the carburetor caps in or out until the slides are sychronized.

Tune-Up Specifications

	V700	V750	750 Sport/S	V850	850T	850-T3
Ignition						
Spark plug heat range①						
normal	225	225	240	225	240	225
cold	240	240	275	240	275	240
Spark plug gap (in./mm)						
normal	0.024/0.6	0.024/0.6	0.024/0.6	0.024/0.6	0.024/0.6	0.024/0.6
cold	0.019/0.5	0.019/0.5	0.019/0.5	0.019/0.5	0.019/0.5	0.019/0.5
Breaker point gap (in./mm)	0.016–0.018/ 0.42–0.48	0.016–0.018/ 0.42–0.48	0.014–0.017/ 0.37–0.43	0.016–0.018/ 0.42–0.48	0.016–0.018/ 0.42–0.48	0.014–0.017/ 0.37–0.43
Valve Clearance						
Intake (in./mm)	0.0059/0.15	0.0059/0.15	0.0089/0.22	0.0059/0.15	0.0089/0.22	0.0089/0.22
Exhaust (in./mm)	0.0098/0.25	0.0098/0.25	0.0089/0.22	0.0098/0.25	0.0089/0.22	0.0089/0.22
Carburetors						
Pilot screw (turns out)						
left	1½	1½	2–2½	1½	2–2½	1½
right	1½	1¾–2	2¼–2¾	1¾–2	2¼–2¾	1½
Idle Speed (rpm)	1000–1200	1000–1200	1000–1200	1000–1200	1000–1200	900–1000

① Refers to Marelli and Bosch heat range numbers. Refer to the Spark Plug Comparison chart for equivalent plugs by other manufacturers

Engine and Transmission

NOTE: *For engine component inspection procedures, refer to "Engine Rebuilding" under General Information.*

Engine Removal and Installation

Due to the weight of the engine-transmission assembly, engine removal should not be undertaken by less than two people. Cleaning the unit thoroughly before removal is recommended.

V700, V750, V850

1. Run the engine until its normal operating temperature is reached, then drain the oil. Drain the transmission oil.

2. Remove the battery covers from both sides, then disconnect the battery cables.

3. Disconnect the speedometer cable from the transmission housing.

4. Remove the tank, seat, and battery, then remove the battery support plate.

5. Disconnect the throttle and choke cables at the carburetors, or remove the carburetors and position them out of the way.

6. Disconnect the clutch, starter, and neutral indicator cables from their mounting positions on the engine.

7. Disconnect and remove the ignition coil, distributor cap, spark plug leads, and the distributor rotor.

8. Remove the generator covers, generator belt guard, and the generator unit. It is not entirely necessary to remove the generator; it may be repositioned to gain sufficient clearance.

9. Remove the exhaust system.

10. Block the engine to keep it from falling out of the frame, then remove the bolts which secure the engine-transmission assembly to the frame. Remove the engine by slipping it forward, tilting it to the right, and lifting it out of the frame.

11. Installing the engine is a reversal of the removal process.

SPORT AND 850T/T3

1. Drain the engine and transmission oil.

2. Remove the gas tank. Disconnect and remove the battery. Remove the air cleaner, if fitted.

3. Unbolt and carburetors and manifolds from the cylinder heads, and remove them along with the twist grip and cables.

4. Remove the mufflers.

5. Disconnect all wiring and control cables at the engine: tach and speedometer, clutch cable, electric starter lead, solenoid wires, ignition coil high and low tension leads, etc. Remove the alternator cover. Code the wires to the terminals before disconnecting them.

6. Place a sturdy crate or a scissors jack beneath the oil pan so that it supports the engine at about the same height as the center stand.

7. Remove the rear wheel. Unbolt the rear shocks from the swing arm. Remove the disc brake caliper, if applicable. Loosen each of the chrome swing arm bushing locknuts. The bushings should be removed carefully with a screwdriver so that the locknut does not change its position on the threads.

8. Loosen the clamp on the engine

side of the drive shaft rubber boot. Pull the swing arm off the machine.

NOTE: *The drive shaft coupling splines are a very tight fit and some effort may be needed to separate them.*

9. Remove the exhaust pipe mounting clamps from the frame. Remove the gearshift linkage.

10. Unbolt the battery box from the engine. Unbolt the lower frame rails from the main frame assembly.

11. Very carefully lift up the main frame assembly complete with the front end to separate it from the engine and frame rails. The engine/transmission unit will remain in place supported by the centerstand and crate or jack.

12. Installation is the reverse of the above. Be sure all wiring connections are correct. Be sure that the frame rail bolts are very tight, and the swing arm is properly aligned when refitted.

Top End

CYLINDER HEAD

Removal

1. Remove the gas tank. Remove the exhaust pipe. Disconnect the spark plug lead. Remove the plug.
2. Unbolt the carburetor mainfold from the head. Disconnect the oil feed line at the head.
3. Remove the valve cover and gasket.
4. Remove the rocker arm shaft lock bolts, and push out the rocker arm shafts.

Removing the rocker arm shafts

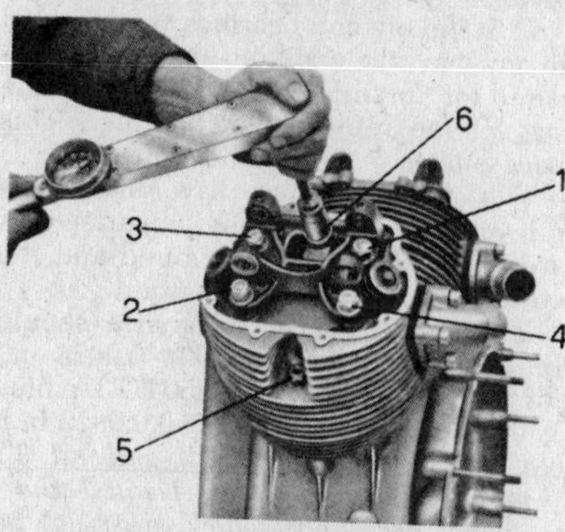

Cylinder head bolt tightening and loosening

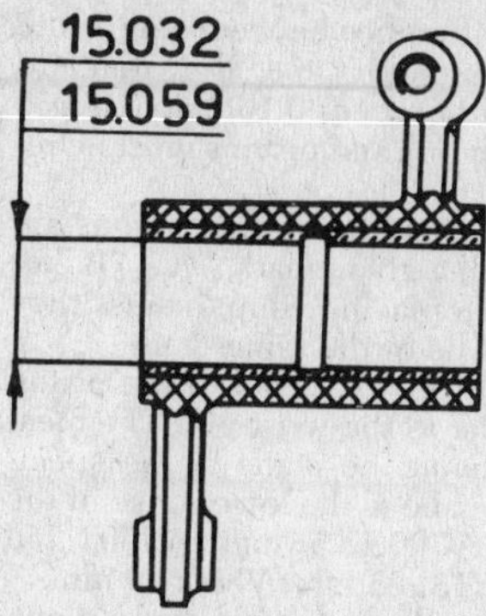

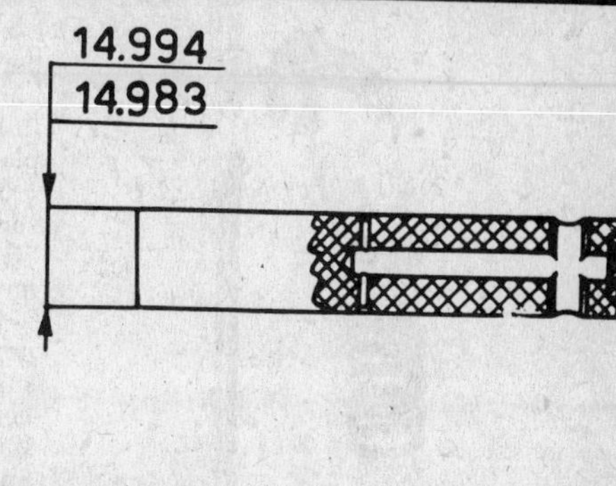

Rocker arm and shaft dimensions

When the shaft is removed, lift out the rocker arms complete with the spring and thrust washer. Remove the pushrods.

5. Loosen each cylinder head nut about ¼ turn, then remove them. Remove the rocker arm support.

6. Remove the head and the head gasket. If the head is stuck, tap carefully at the sides with a plastic mallet.

7. Remove the valves by compressing the spring(s) and taking out the keepers.

Inspection

1. Maximum allowable head warpage is 0.05mm (0.002 in.).
2. Rocker arm shaft-to-bore clearance must be within 0.038–0.076mm (0.0015–0.0029 in.).
3. Valve guide-to-stem clearance should be within 0.013–0.015mm (0.0005–0.0019 in.) for the intake valves, and 0.020–0.057mm (0.0008–0.0022 in.) for the exhaust valves.

If the clearance exceeds these specifications, replace the valves or guides.

4. To replace the valve guides, heat the head to about 200° C., and drive the guides out with a suitable drift. Drive new guides in fully. New guides must be reamed to the proper size after installation. Oil the ream lightly when it encounters interference. Remove metal chips as soon as they occur, and always continue to rotate the ream when removing or installing it.
5. The valve seats and seating areas should be no less than 0.8 mm (0.032 in.) wide at the narrowest point, nor wider than 1.5 mm (0.060 in.)

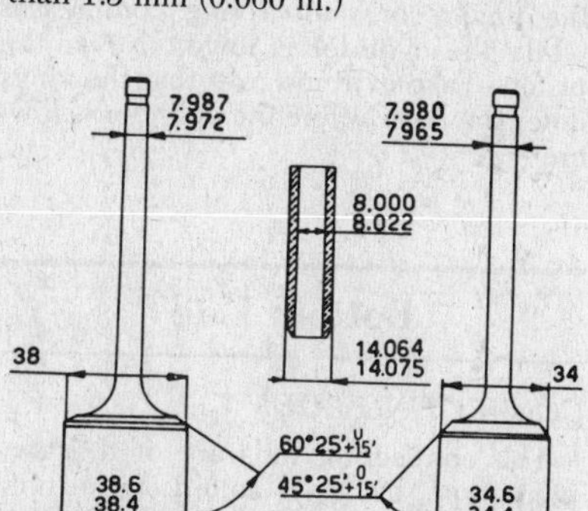

Valve and valve seat dimensions: intake (left), exhaust (right) (V700)

Seat dimensions are shown in the accompanying illustrations.

6. For other component specifications, refer to the illustrations.

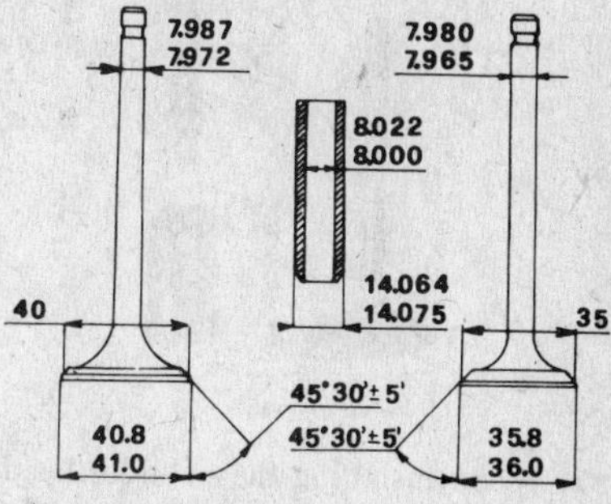

Valve and valve seat dimensions: intake (left), exhaust (right) (All except V700)

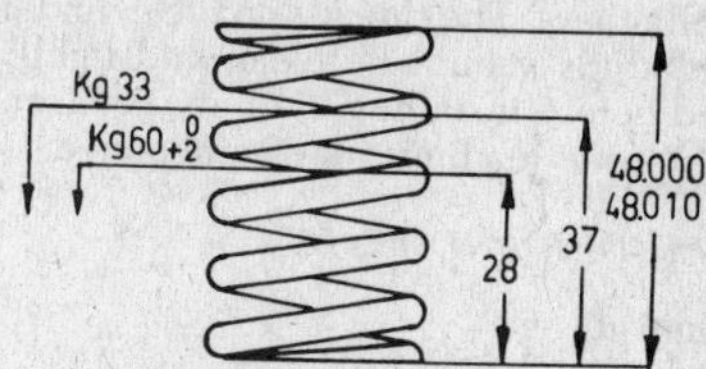

Valve spring dimensions in mm (V700)

Installation

1. Installation is the reverse of the removal procedure.
2. Use new valve keepers and a new head gasket.

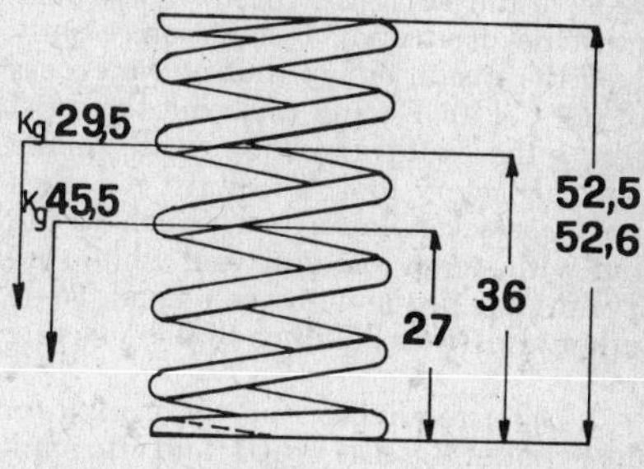

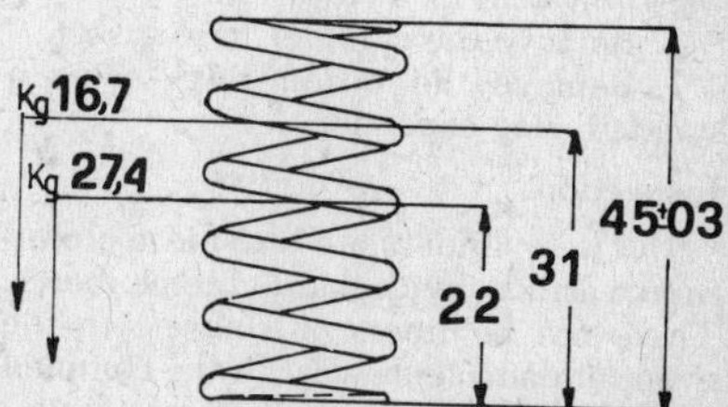

Valve spring dimensions in mm (All except V700)

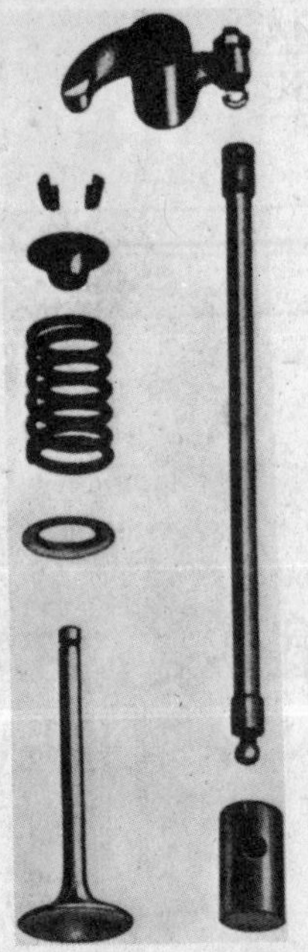

Valve assembly

3. When installing the cylinder head, nuts must be torqued in a cross pattern a few ft lbs at a time until the specified torque is reached. This is 29–32 ft lbs on Sport and 850T/T3 models, and 27 ft lbs on all others. The threads on the cylinder head studs should be clean and lightly oiled before installing the nuts, or incorrect torque readings may be obtained.

CYLINDER AND PISTON

Removal

1. Remove the cylinder head.
2. Rotate the piston to TDC, and lift off the cylinder until the spigot clears the crankcase. Stuff a clean lint-free rag beneath the cylinder to catch any foreign matter.
3. Continue lifting off the cylinder until it is clear of the piston.
4. To remove the piston from the rod, remove the wrist pin circlips. New ones must be used upon installation. Gently heat the piston crown (but not in excess of 60° C/140° F), and push out the wrist pin, either with a suitable drift, or the special factory tool. The wrist pin must not be struck a blow. Always push the pin out with steady pressure and while supporting the piston with a free hand. To do otherwise risks bending the connecting rod.
5. After removing a piston, mark it for its cylinder (i.e. LH or RH) and also mark the exhaust side so that the piston can be installed the correct way. Keep each wrist pin with its own piston.
6. Remove the cylinder base gasket.
7. Remove the piston rings using a standard ring expander.

Inspection

1. The cylinders are one-piece aluminum castings with hard-chrome bores. There are no liners or sleeves. In the event of damage or wear to the chromed surface of the bore, the entire cylinder and piston must be replaced.
2. If the difference between any of the bore measurements and the standard bore diameter exceeds 0.10 mm (0.00039 in.), the cylinders and pistons must be replaced.
3. Note that cylinders and pistons are stamped with a grade mark, "A," "B," or "C". When replacing components, they must always be of the same grade.
4. Measure the diameter of the piston perpendicular to the wrist pin. The measurement should be made at the specified distance above the lower edge of the skirt, viz.: V700:18.5 mm; V750, 750 Sport, 850T/T3: 35 mm; V850: 20 mm.
5. Compare the measured piston diameter with the standard diameter for pistons of that class. If the difference exceeds 0.055–0.065 mm (0.0021–0.0025 in.), replace the pistons with new ones of the same grade class.
6. If new pistons are fitted, compare their weights if a balance is available. Pistons should be within 1.5 grams of one another. If the weight difference exceeds this, it is possible to file some material from the bottom of the skirt of the heavier piston. If this is done, ensure that there are no burrs remaining by sanding with a fine emery cloth.

PISTON RINGS

1. Side clearance (installed on the piston) is 0.030–0.062 mm (0.0011–0.0024 in.) for all rings.
2. Ring end-gap must be within 0.30–0.45 mm (0.011–0.018 in.) for compression rings, and 0.25–0.40 mm (0.010–0.016 in.) for oil rings.

Installation

1. Fit a new cylinder base gasket.
2. Assemble the rings on the piston. When installing the piston on the rod, ensure that it is installed correctly. Heat the piston as on removal. Use new wrist pin circlips.
3. Stagger the ring end-gaps 90° apart so that no two adjacent rings have the end-gaps aligned. In addition, the end gaps should not be directly in line with the wrist pin holes.
4. Coat the piston rings and piston skirt with clean motor oil before installing the cylinder. Oil the cylinder bore lightly. Compress the piston rings with the fingers or with a ring compressor while the cylinder is lowered over the piston. Take extreme care that the rings enter the bore before the cylinder is lowered.

Bottom End

CONNECTING RODS

The connecting rods are of the two-piece type, having a bolted cap to hold the big end bearing. The small end has a pressed-in bush. The rods ride side-by-side on the crankshaft.

It is possible to remove the rods with the engine in the frame. If, however, the big end bearings show more than normal wear, the crankshaft must be removed for inspection and service.

The following procedure is for the removal of the rods. If replacement of the big end bearings only is desired, they are accessible after removing the oil pan and oil pipe. Top end removal is not necessary.

Removal

1. Drain the engine oil. Remove the oil pan.
2. Remove the cylinder heads, cylinders, and pistons. Remove the oil pump filter screen assembly and the oil pipe.
3. Some models have locking tabs on the rod nuts. If these are fitted, bend them back. Remove the rod nuts. Pull off the rod cap and remove the rod. Remove the other rod in the same manner.

NOTE: *Keep the individual rod assemblies separate. Rods and caps are not interchangeable.*

Con rod assembly

Inspection

1. If replacement of the bushing is necessary, drive the old one out of the rod with a punch. Press in the new bushing, drill the oil hole, and ream it to the correct size of 22.020–22.041 mm (0.8669–0.8678 in.)
2. If the big end bearings are damaged in any way, the crankpin should be measured for possible wear to determine the size of the replacement bearings. This necessitates removing the crankshaft.

The crankpin must have an almost mirror-like finish. If any imperfections are noticed, it must be ground and the correct oversized bearings fitted.

3. Big end bearing clearance should be 0.011–0.061 mm (0.0004–0.0024 in.) for all models except the 850T/T3, which is 0.030–0.054 mm (0.0012–0.0.0022 in.).

CAUTION: *Some 850T and all T3 models have specially treated (hardened) crankpins which must not be ground down for the fitting of oversized bearings. Be sure to check with a*

Crankpin Diameters (750 Sport):

Original Diameter	Undersize 0.254 mm (0.010 in.)	0.508 mm (0.020 in.)	0.762 mm (0.030 in.)
43.893–43.994 mm (1.730–1.732 in.)	43.729–43.740 mm (1.720–1.722 in.)	43.475–43.486 mm (1.710–1.712 in.)	43.221–43.232 mm (1.700–1.702 in.)

Crankpin Diameters (850/T3):

Original Diameter	Undersize 0.254 mm (0.010 in.)	0.508 mm (0.020 in.)	0.762 mm (0.030 in.)
Blue mark on shoulder of flywheel side: 44.008–44.014 mm (1.7339–1.7341 in.) White mark on shoulder of flywheel side: 44.014–44.020 mm (1.7341–1.7348 in.)	43.754–43.766 mm (1.7240–1.7244 in.)	43.500–43.512 mm (1.7139–1.7144 in.)	43.246–43.258 mm (1.7039–1.7044 in.)

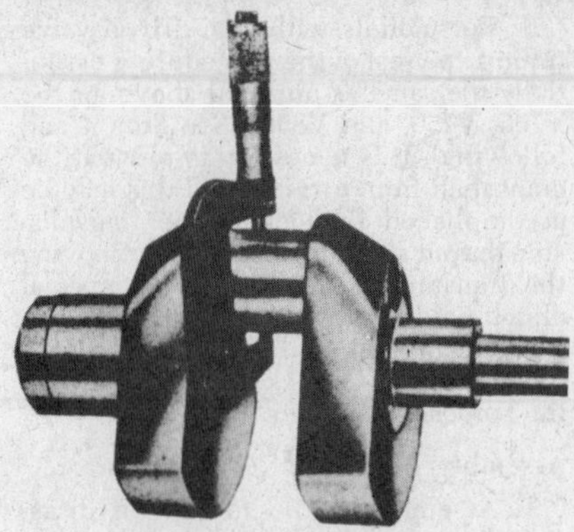

Measuring crankpin diameter

Moto Guzzi dealer, who is provided with a list of 850T machines fitted with these cranks.

4. If the crankpin is reground, the shoulder relief radius must be restored. This should be 1.5 mm (0.059 in.) for the V700, V750, and V850; 2.0–2.5 mm (0.078–0.090 in.) for the 750 Sport and 850T models without hardened crankpins.

5. With the rods assembled on the crankshaft, check the lateral movement. If the bearings are in good condition, this should be 0.011–0.061 mm (0.0004–0.0024 in.)

6. Check the con rod side clearance. This should be 0.3–0.5 mm (0.012–0.020 in.).

7. Check that the rod is not bent. The big and small ends must be within 0.03 mm (0.0012 in.) of true, or the rod must be replaced.

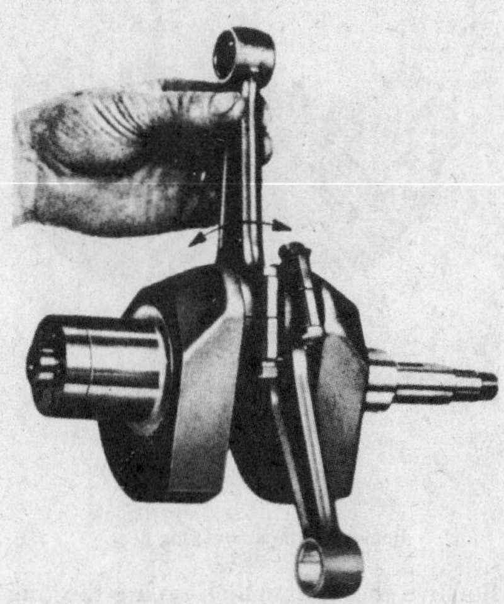

Checking rod lateral movement

Measuring rod side clearance

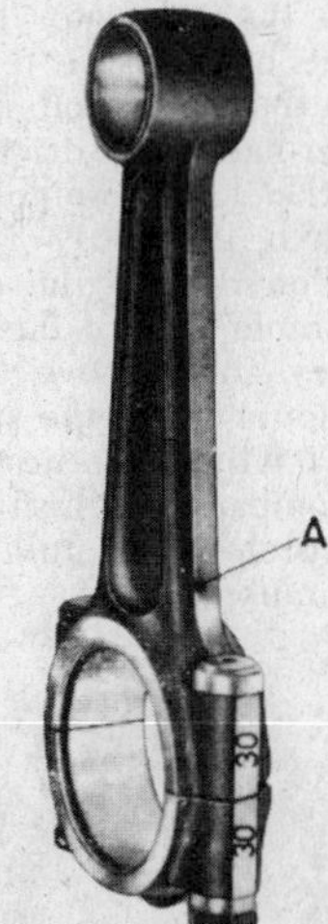

Connecting rod and cap correctly assembled: note milled edge of rod and cap

8. If new rods are fitted, they should be weighed complete with bearings, bolts, and nuts. Rod assemblies must be within 3 g of each other. If a difference greater than this is noted, select another rod for use, until the weights are matched.

Installation

1. Be sure the big end bearing is well lubricated before fitting. New rod nuts should always be used.

2. When installing the rods, ensure that the oil hole on the side faces *upwards* for the left-hand cylinder's rod,

Big End Bearings:

Original Thickness	Oversize 0.254 mm (0.010 in.)	0.508 mm (0.020 in.)	0.762 mm (0.030 in.)	1.016 mm (0.040 in.)
1.534–1.543 mm (0.06039–0.06074 in.)	1.661–1.670 mm (0.06539–0.065748 in.)	1.788–1.797 mm (0.07–0.07074 in.)	1.915–1.924 mm (0.07539–0.07574 in.)	2.042–2.051 mm (0.08039–0.08074 in.)

Crankpin Diameters (V700, V750, V850):

Original Diameter	Undersize 0.254 mm (0.010 in.)	0.508 mm (0.020 in.)	0.762 mm (0.030 in.)	1.016 mm (0.040 in.)
44.013–44.033 mm (1.7328–1.7336 in.)	43.759–43.779 mm (1.7228–1.7236 in.)	43.505–43.525 mm (1.7128–1.7136 in.)	43.251–43.271 mm (1.7028–1.7036 in.)	42.997–43.017 mm (1.6928–1.6936 in.)

and *downwards* for the right-hand cylinder's rod.

3. When fitting the rod caps, ensure that the milled side of the cap is adjacent to the milled side of the rod. On some models numbers are printed on one side of the cap and the rod, and these must align.

4. Torque the rod nuts to 33–35 ft lbs for 750 Sport and 850T/T3 models, 25 ft lbs on other models.

Timing Chest

V700, V750, V850

Disassembly

Although it is possible to remove the timing gears without removing the engine from the frame, a special tool will be needed to set the valve timing if this is done. Refer to the "Valve Timing" section if such a tool is available. If it is not, removal of the engine is necessary.

1. Remove the engine from the frame.
2. Remove the generator belt cover and belt. The belt can be removed by withdrawing the three bolts which secure the outer half of the driving pulley.
3. Secure the clutch assembly with the special tool (No. 12911801) or a suitable substitute, then remove the nut which secures the inner half of the generator driving pulley and remove the pulley half. Then mount either the special tool (No. 12905300 which is indicated by No. 24 in the accompanying illustration), or a suitable substitute, to the pulley hub and remove the crankshaft nut.

Removing the pulley hub

4. Remove the screws which secure the timing cover to the crankcase, then remove the cover. Tap the cover gently with a wood block and hammer to break its seal, if necessary. Remove the seal ring from the cover if necessary.
5. Remove the cam wheel securing nut, then remove the cam wheel. The clutch should still be secured as directed in Step No. 3 by the special tool (16).
6. Remove the oil pump gear from its tapered shaft with the pump gear puller (No. 32906302 which is indicated by No. 15 in the accompanying illustration) or a suitable substitute. The clutch must be secured by the special tool (16).
7. Remove the crankshaft timing gear from the end of the crankshaft. The gear is a keyed on press fit and must be pulled with a suitable puller.

Removing the cam wheel nut

Removing the oil pump gear

Assembly

1. Assembly is in the reverse order of disassembly.
2. Consult the "Valve Timing" section for instructions on installing the three timing chest gears.
3. When installing the timing cover, some provision must be made to protect the seal ring. This is easily done by using the special tool (No. 12908300).
4. Install and adjust the generator belt as described in "Maintenance."

750 SPORT, 850T/T3

Early models of this series are fitted with the same type of gear drive assembly as the V700, V750, and V850. Later models have a chain-driven assembly.

Disassembly

Remove the engine from the frame.

2. Remove the alternator cover. Detach the alternator brush spring from the brush. Remove the screws which secure the stator and remove it. Remove the rotor allen bolt. Use the special puller (No. 14906600) to remove the alternator rotor.

3. For models with gear-driven valve timing, the rest of the procedure is essentially the same as outlined above for the V700, V750, and V850. (See Step 4 and following). It is necessary to prevent the crankshaft from turning, and this may be accomplished by locking the transmission output shaft in place, or by removing the transmission and using the special clutch holding device (No. 12911801).

4. On models with chain-driven timing, remove the sprocket nuts and pull off the sprockets together.

Assembly

1. Assembly is the reverse of disassembly.
2. Refer to the "Valve Timing" section, following, to install the gears or sprockets correctly.
3. When installing the timing cover, a guide is available to prevent damage to the oil seal.

Clutch

ALL MODELS

Removal

1. Remove the engine from the frame. Unbolt the transmission unit.
2. Secure the starter ring gear using either the factory tool (No. 12911801 which is indicated by No. 16 in the accompanying illustration) or a suitable substitute.

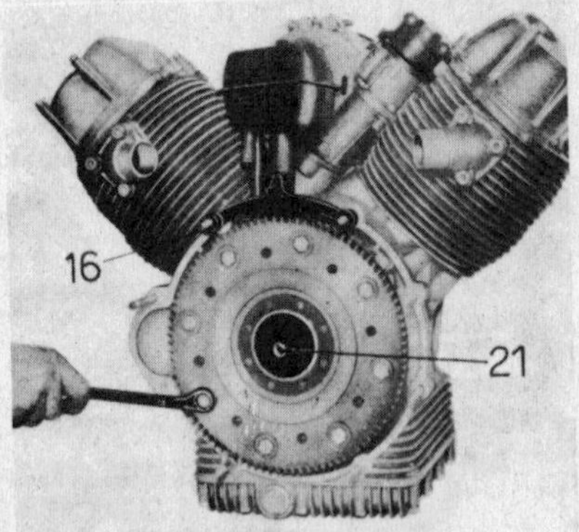

Removing the starter ring gear

Remove the bolts which secure the ring gear to the flywheel, then remove the clutch assembly.

NOTE: *The bolts must be removed evenly in a crossed pattern to avoid deforming the pressure plate.*

3. Remove the bolts which secure the flywheel, which serves as a clutch hub to the crankshaft, and remove the flywheel.

The springs should be pressure tested to check their efficiency. The following are the specificiations:

V700

With the spring compressed to 20 mm (0.7874 in.), the load should be 16 ± 10% kg (35.27 ± 10% lbs).

With the spring compressed to 17 mm (0.6692 in.), the load should be 24 ± 10% kg (52.9 ± 10% lbs).

Clutch assembly

OTHER MODELS:

With the spring compressed to 20 mm (0.7874 in.), the load should be 21 ± 25% kg (46.3 ± 25% lbs).

With the spring compressed to 17 mm (0.6692 in.), the load should be within 28.7–29.7 kg (64.6–66.8 lbs).

5. Each friction plate should be 8 mm (0.3149 in.) thick as measured at a point on which there is friction material and the plates must be replaced if worn down to 7.5 mm (0.2953 in.).

Installation

1. Assembly is basically in the reverse order of disassembly.
2. Secure the flywheel to the crankshaft by means of bolts and lockwashers, then torque the bolts down to 30 ft lbs.
3. Insert the clutch springs into their housings in the flywheel, then mount the pressure plate so that the punch-marked tooth on the pressure plate is in alignment with the arrow marked on the flywheel.

NOTE: *There is an arrow on the flywheel which indicates TDC and which serves as a reference mark for assembling the clutch pressure plate.*

4. Mount the clutch dismantling and assembling tool (No. 12906500 which is indicated by No. 21 in the accompanying illustration) on the crankshaft, screwing it down enough so the clutch plates and ring gear can be so positioned that the securing bolts can be screwed down into the flywheel. The flywheel's motion must be blocked by using either the factory tool (No. 12911801) or a suitable substitute. Tighten ring gear bolts to 22 ft lbs. Remove the dismantling and assembling tool.

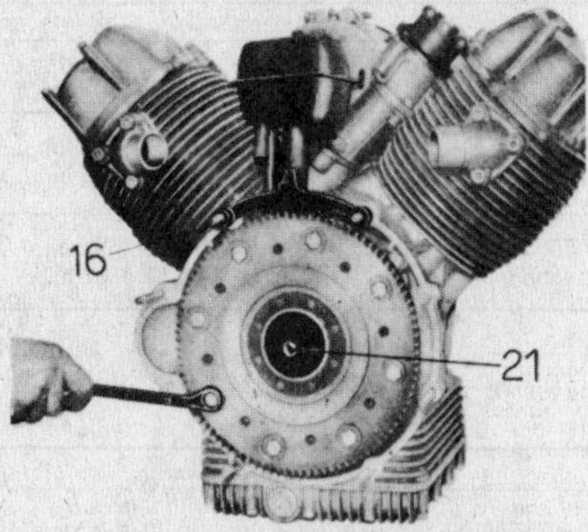

Installing the starter ring gear

NOTE: *The purpose of the dismantling and assembling tool is to properly align the teeth of the plates in the hub so the bolts will be able to be turned down into the flywheel.*

5. Complete the assembly in the reverse order of disassembly, then adjust the clutch.

CRANKSHAFT AND CAMSHAFT

Removal

1. Remove the engine from the frame. Remove the transmission.
2. Remove the cylinder heads, cylinders, and pistons. Remove the timing chest and the gears or sprockets therein. Refer to the appropriate preceeding sections.
3. Remove the clutch assembly and the flywheel. Remove the distributor shaft (generator models) or the points assembly and housing with shaft (alternator models).
4. Remove the cam tappets from the crankcase.

NOTE: *Mark the tappets so that they can be installed in their original locations.*

5. Remove the oil pan. Unbolt and remove the oil pipe and the oil pump filter screen assembly. Remove the oil pump.
6. Unbolt and remove the connecting rods.
7. Remove the camshaft flange (timing side) and take out the cam.
8. Remove the flywheel side crankshaft flange bolts, and use the special tool (No. 12913600) to remove the flange from the housing. Remove the crankshaft.
9. Remove the timing side flange from the crankcase.

Removing the main bearing flange

Inspection

1. Measure the diameter of the timing and flywheel side main bearing journals, and then the inside diameters of the main bearings. Two measurements should be made of each journal, 90° apart, to check for ovalization.

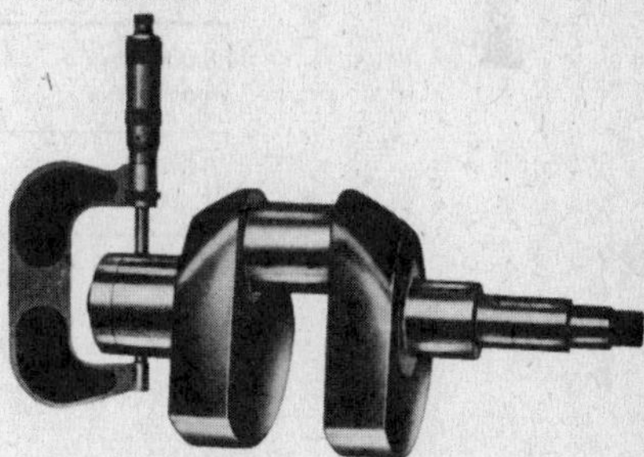
Measuring main bearing diameter

Bearing clearances must be within the following limits:

Crankshaft-to-timing side main bearing: 0.025–0.057 mm (0.00098–0.00224 in.).

Crankshaft-to-flywheel side main bearing: 0.030–0.068 mm (0.00118–0.00270 in.).

2. If the bearing clearances are not within the proper limits, new bearings should be fitted. If the journals are scored or are not within the standard values given, they should be ground down, and undersized bearings fitted. This must be done according to the following specifications:

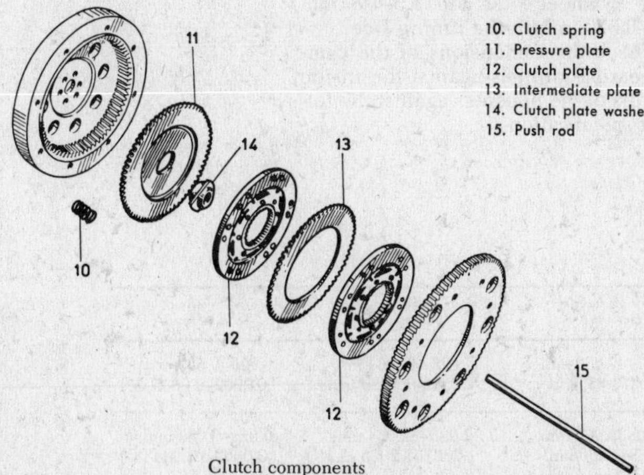

Clutch components

a. Diameter of flywheel side main bearing journal:

Original Diameter	Undersize 0.2 mm (0.00787 in.)	0.4 mm (0.0157 in.)	0.6 mm (0.02362 in.)	0.8 mm (0.03149 in.)
53.970 mm (2.1248 in.)	53.770 mm (2.1169 in.)	53.570 mm (2.1090 in.)	53.370 mm (2.1013 in.)	53.170 mm (2.0930 in.)
53.951 mm (2.1240 in.)	53.751 mm (2.1162 in.)	53.551 mm (2.1033 in.)	53.351 mm (2.1004 in.)	53.151 mm (2.0926 in.)

b. Diameter of the timing side bearing journal:

Original Diameter	Undersize 0.2 mm (0.00787 in.)	0.4 mm (0.01574 in.)	0.6 mm (0.02362 in.)	0.8 mm (0.03149 in.)
37.975 mm (1.4951 in.)	37.775 mm (1.4872 in.)	37.575 mm (1.4793 in.)	37.375 mm (1.4715 in.)	37.175 mm (1.4636 in.)
37.959 mm (1.4944 in.)	37.759 mm (1.4866 in.)	37.559 mm (1.4787 in.)	37.359 mm (1.4707 in.)	37.159 mm (1.4629 in.)

c. Inside diameter of flywheel side main bearing:

Original Diameter	Undersize 0.2 mm (0.00787 in.)	0.4 mm (0.01574 in.)	0.6 mm (0.02362 in.)	0.8 mm (0.03149 in.)
54.000 mm (2.1260 in.)	53.800 mm (2.1171 in.)	53.600 mm (2.1102 in.)	53.400 mm (2.1024 in.)	53.200 mm (2.0945 in.)
54.019 mm (2.1267 in.)	53.819 mm (2.1188 in.)	53.619 mm (2.1109 in.)	53.419 mm (2.1031 in.)	53.219 mm (2.0952 in.)

d. Inside diameter of timing side main bearing:

Original Diameter	Undersize 0.2 mm (0.00787 in.)	0.4 mm (0.01574 in.)	0.6 mm (0.02362 in.)	0.8 mm (0.03149 in.)
38.000 mm (1.4961 in.)	37.800 mm (1.4883 in.)	37.600 mm (1.4803 in.)	37.400 mm (1.4725 in.)	37.200 mm (1.5646 in.)
38.016 mm (1.4967 in.)	37.816 mm (1.4889 in.)	37.616 mm (1.4809 in.)	37.416 mm (1.4731 in.)	37.216 mm (1.5652 in.)

NOTE: *Replacement main bearings come already mounted in their flanges.*

3. If the crankshaft journals are ground to an undersize, the relief radius must be restored. This should be 3 mm (0.118 in.) for the flywheel side and 1.5–1.8 mm (0.058–0.070 in.) for the timing side.

4. Check the dimensions of the camshaft bearing journals against the inside diameters of the housings against the following specifications.

V700, V750, V850:

	Camshaft Journals Diameter	Housing in Crankcase Diameter	Fitting Clearance
Timing side	46.975–47.000 mm (1.8494–1.8504 in.)	47.025–47.064 mm (1.8511–1.8529 in.)	0.025–0.089 mm (0.0009–0.0035 in.)
Flywheel side	31.975–32.000 mm (1.2588–1.2598 in.)	32.025–32.064 mm (1.2607–1.2623 in.)	0.025–0.089 mm (0.0009–0.0035 in.)

750 Sport, 850T/T3:

	Camshaft Journals Diameter	Housing in Crankcase Diameter	Fitting Clearance
Timing side	46.984–47.000 mm (1.814–1.8504 in.)	47.025–47.050 mm (1.8511–1.8524 in.)	0.025–0.066 mm (0.0009–0.0026 in.)
Flywheel side	31.894–32.000 mm (1.259–1.260 in.)	32.025–32.050 mm (1.2607–1.2618 in.)	0.025–0.066 mm (0.0009–0.0026 in.)

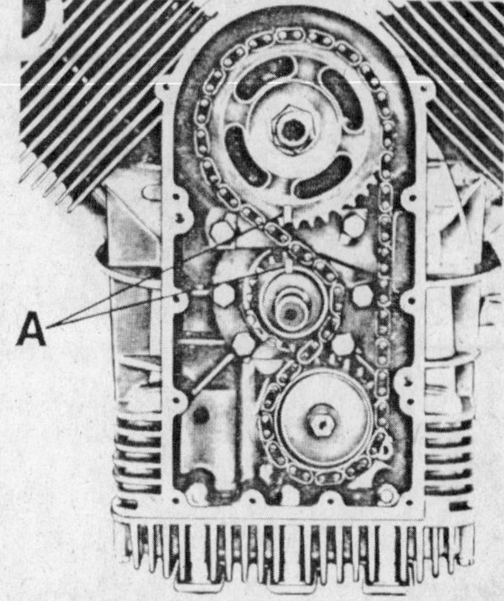

Timing marks aligned (Chain-driven timing)

5. Inspect the tappets for signs of wear, scoring, or other damage, and replace them if necessary. Slight score marks can be removed with fine emery paper. The tappet-camshaft contact area must be perfectly smooth or both components will wear out quickly. The tappets must move smoothly in their guides with no hesitation or binding, and the guides must not be scored or worn. Oversized tappets are available, and the guides must be reamed to the proper size if these are going to be used. Compare tappet and guide sizes against the following specifications:

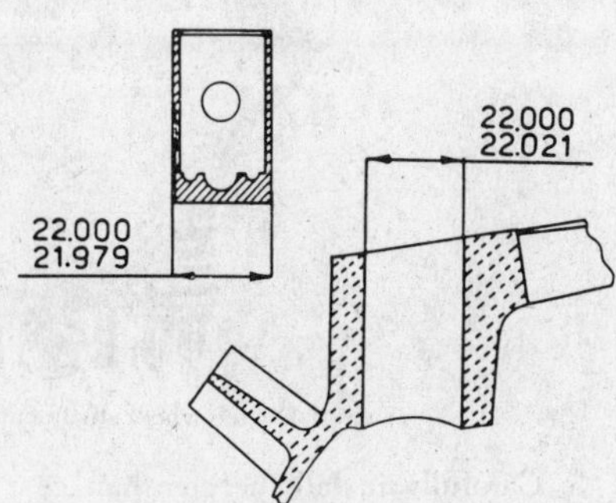

Tappet and guide dimensions

		I/D of Guides	O D of Tappets	Fitting Clearance
Original		22.021–22.000 mm (0.8669–0.8661 in.)	22.000–21.979 mm (0.8661–0.9046 in.)	0–0.042 mm (0–0.0016 in.)
Oversize	0.05 mm (0.0019 in.)	22.071–22.050 mm (0.8688–0.8680 in.)	22.050–22.029 mm (0.8680–0.8672 in.)	0–0.042 mm (0–0.0016 in.)
	0.10 mm (0.0039 in.)	22.121–22.100 mm (0.8708–0.8700 in.)	22.100–22.079 mm (0.8700–0.8692 in.)	0–0.042 mm (0–0.0016 in.)

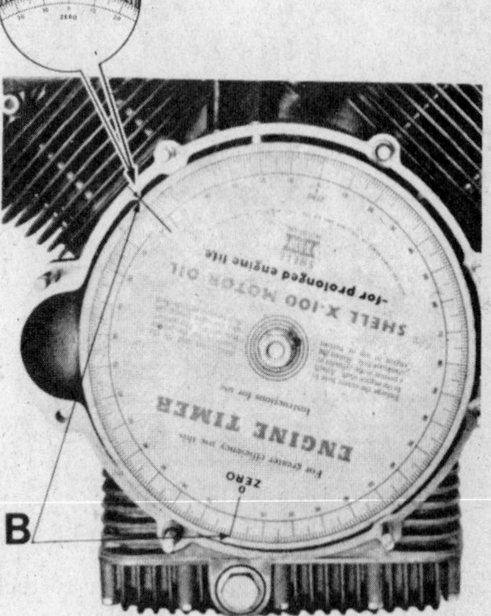

Degree wheel aligned for valve timing (All except Sport)

Assembly

1. The use of new oil seals is recommended, regardless of the apparent condition of the original seals. New woodruff keys should also be used.
2. All components should be coated with plenty of clean engine oil during the assembly procedure. This is especially critical of bearing surfaces.
3. Mount and secure the timing side main bearing and flange assembly.
4. Install the crankshaft, then the flywheel side main bearing and flange. The lubrication passages in the flange must be aligned with the passages in the crankcase, and the seal in the flange should be protected during installation with a guide (Tool No. 12912000).

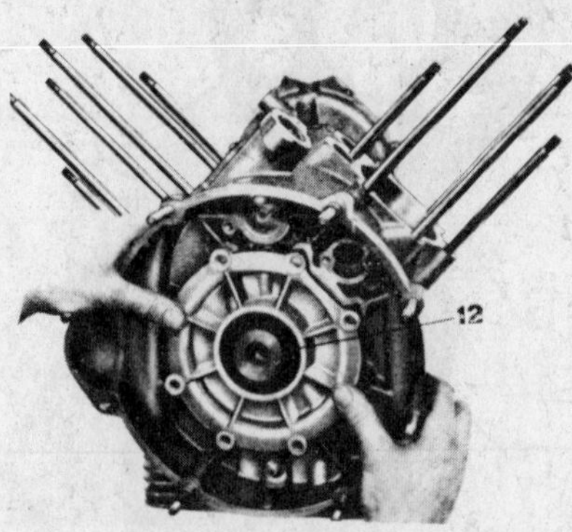

Mounting the flywheel side main bearing flange

5. The remainder of the assembly procedure is the reverse of disassembly.

Refer to the "Valve Timing" section following to properly install the timing gears or sprockets.

Valve Timing

CHAIN DRIVEN TIMING

1. Correct valve timing is easily obtained by aligning the marks on the crankshaft and camshaft sprockets when the sprocket and chain assembly is installed.

GEAR DRIVEN TIMING

V700, V750, V850

The intake valve opens at 24° BTDC and closes 58° ABDC; the exhaust valve opens at 58° BBDC, and closes 22° ATDC.

1. Adjust the tappets to 0.5 mm (0.0195 in.). Rotate the flywheel until its timing mark is in alignment with the timing mark on the crankcase.
2. Mount a degree wheel on the flywheel in such a manner that the zero on the degree wheel, the arrow on the flywheel, and the line of the crankcase are all aligned. (See (A) on the accompanying illustration.)
3. Rotate the flywheel 122° (the distance indicated by (B) in the illustration) in the direction of normal engine operation until the exhaust valve of the left-hand cylinder begins to open.
4. At this point, the only timing gear which should be installed is the oil pump gear. Mount the crankshaft timing gear on the crankshaft, then, using a screwdriver, rotate the camshaft counterclockwise until the rocker arm on the exhaust valve of the left hand cylinder begins to touch the valve.
5. Mount the cam wheel on the camshaft in such a manner that the dowel slots in the camshaft and cam wheel will align without necessitating moving the crank or camshaft, and insert the pin.

NOTE: *It is a good idea, when installing new gears, to mark the teeth which are engaged in the cam wheel and the crankshaft timing gear, and the point on the wheel where it is keyed to the shaft with a daub of paint for future reference.*

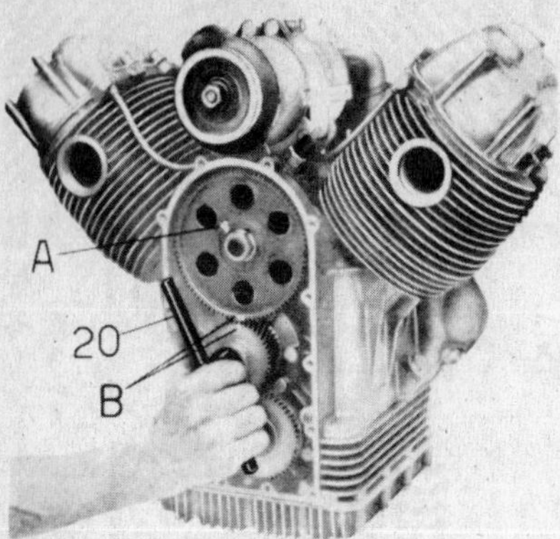

Aligning timing marks

Marking the gears for future reference

6. Adjust the tappets to their correct specifications.

750 Sport

The following procedure applies to Sport models with gear-driven timing.

The camshaft specifications are as follows: intake valve opens 40° BTDC, closes 70° ABDC; exhaust valve opens 63° BBDC, closes 29° ATDC.

1. Set all valves to a clearance of 0.5 mm (0.019 in.). Rotate the flywheel until the arrow on it aligns with the projection on the crankcase (clutch side). This positions the right-hand cylinder at TDC, with both valves closed.
2. Fit a degree wheel to the flywheel, aligning the TDC mark of the degree wheel with the flywheel arrow and the crankcase projection.
3. Turn the flywheel 117° in a counterclockwise direction. At this point, the exhaust valve for the right-hand cylinder will begin to open once the timing is correctly set.
4. Install the oil pump gear; then fit the crankshaft timing gear and secure it. Use a screwdriver to turn the camshaft in a counterclockwise direction until the right cylinder's rocker arm just touches the exhaust valve.

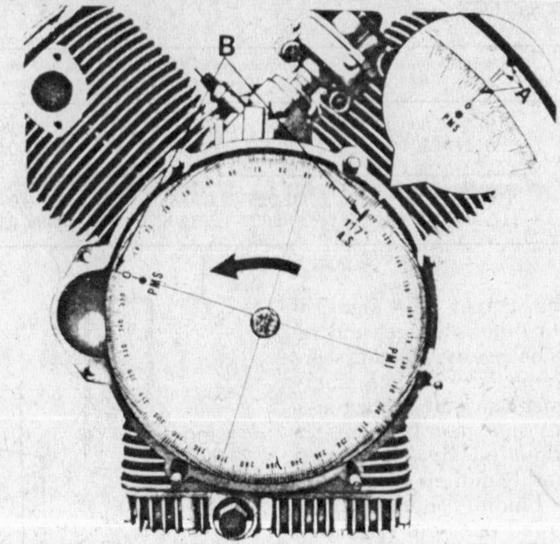

Degree wheel alignment for valve timing (V7 Sport)

5. Carefully install the camshaft gear so that the dowel pin can be inserted into the camshaft without moving either the crankshaft or the camshaft.
6. Mark the teeth of the gears that engage, and the position of the dowel pin on the camshaft gear with daubs of paint to facilitate any future retiming. Secure the camshaft gear.
7. Set the valve clearance to 0.22 mm (0.0086 in.). Check the opening and closing of the valves against the cam specifications.

Alternate Method

A special tool is designed for this job to transfer the timing marks on the fitted camshaft gear to a new replacement.

1. Remove the timing gears.
2. Insert the pin of the special tool (no. 12913800, 25 in the illustration) into the camshaft gear slot. Loosen the tool's bolt, and turn the arm so that it indicates the two marked teeth on the cam gear. Tighten the bolt, and remove the tool from the old gear.
3. Fit the tool to the new replacement camshaft gear, inserting the pin into each of the five slot until the notch on the tool's arm will bracket two gear teeth perfectly.
4. Mark these two teeth with paint. Also mark the slot into which the tool's pin was inserted.
5. If the crankshaft gear is being replaced as well (it should be if the cam gear was worn or damaged), copy the index mark onto the replacement gear by counting the number of teeth between the gear's keyway and the marked tooth.
6. Install the crankshaft gear, then the cam gear, inserting the pin into the marked slot, and ensuring the marked teeth of the two gears engage when the engine is rotated.

NOTE: *It is important that the camshaft not be disturbed while the gears are removed if this procedure is used.*

Transmission

The V700 and V750 use a four-speed transmission, while a five-speed is found on the 750 Sport and 850 models.

REMOVAL AND DISASSEMBLY

Four-Speed Models

1. Drain the transmission oil.

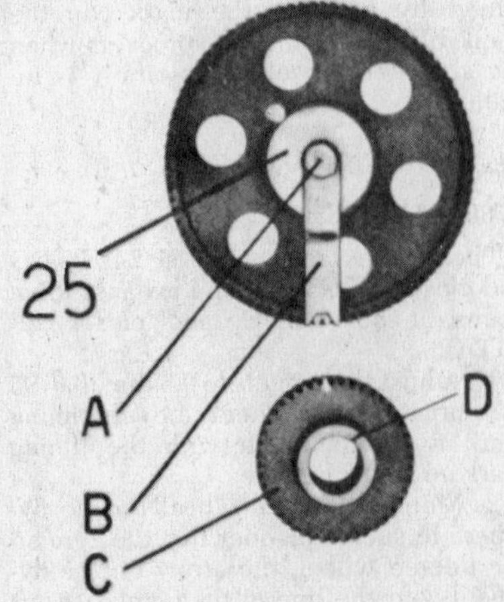

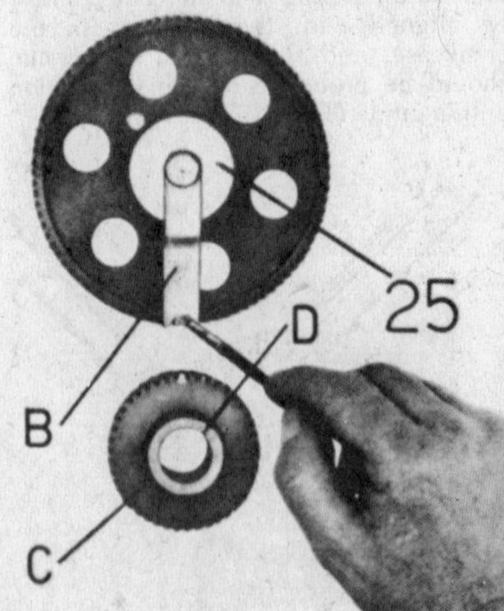

Using the special tool to transfer timing marks

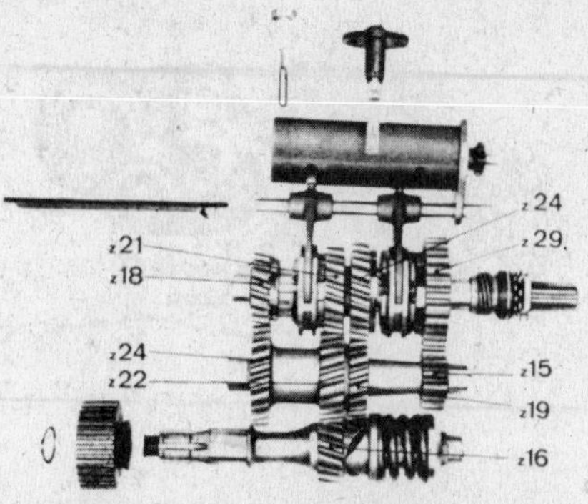

Four-speed transmission assembled

Removing the layshaft lockring

Shifter inner body assembly

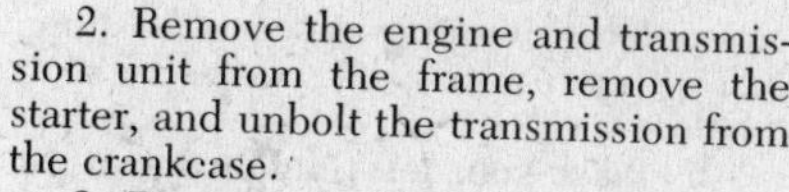

2. Remove the engine and transmission unit from the frame, remove the starter, and unbolt the transmission from the crankcase.

3. Remove the clutch release lever and shifter.

4. Disengage the tab washer on the layshaft nut (if fitted), then use special factory tools Nos. 12907100 and 12905400 to hold the layshaft in place and remove the nut.

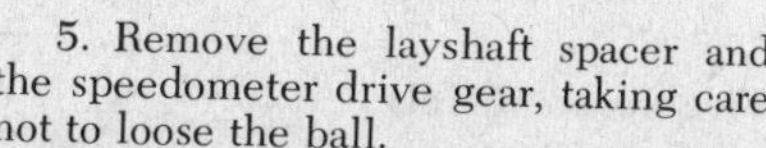

5. Remove the layshaft spacer and the speedometer drive gear, taking care not to loose the ball.

6. Remove the shifter cover screws, then remove the cover assembly which includes the shaft, sector, return spring and offset adjusting screw.

7. Remove the gearbox cover mounting screws and cover, then remove the clutch outer body, clutch cage, and clutch push-rod. Tap the cover with a wood block and hammer, if necessary, to loosen it.

8. Remove the clutch inner body circlip, the oil pick-up plate, the drain plug, and the pawl and spring which are housed in the drain plug.

9. Remove the gear control cam plate and the shifter inner body assembly which includes the plungers, pawls, and pawl springs.

10. Remove the shifter drum rod, disengage the shifter forks from the drum grooves, then remove the drum.

11. Remove the shifter fork shaft, then disengage and remove the forks from the layshaft sliding gears.

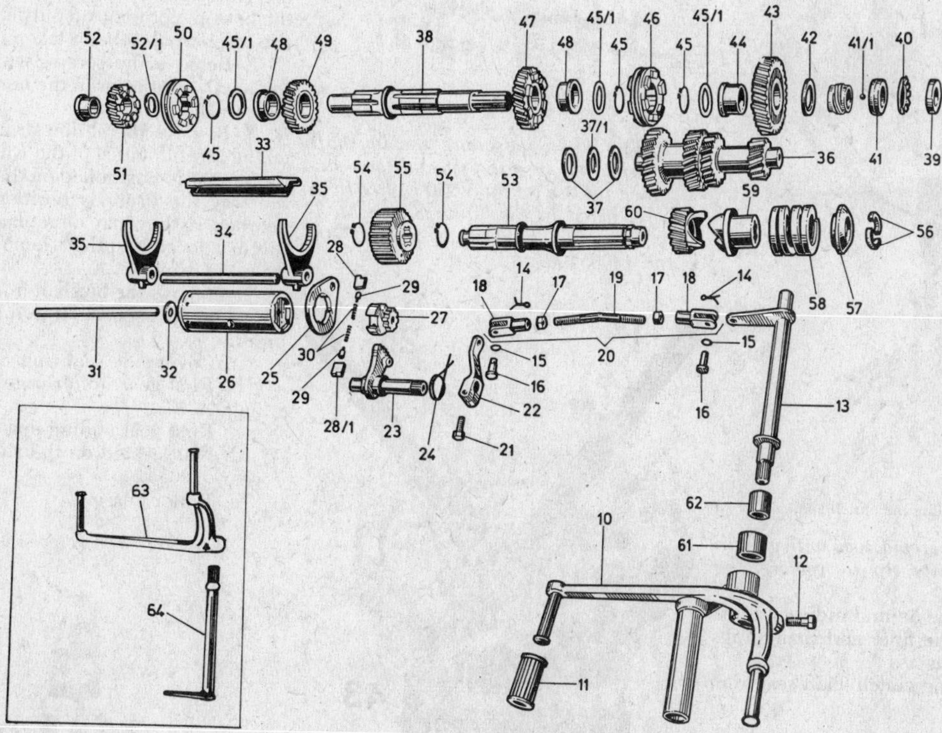

10. Gearshift, rocker type, l/h pedal
11. Gearshift pedal rubber
12. Gearshift pedal screw
13. L/h operation shaft, c/w lever
14. Gearshift operating rod cotter pin
15. Gearshift rod pins washer
16. Gearshift control rod pin
17. Adjusting on rod nut
18. Gearshift rod fork
19. Gearshift rod
20. Rod c/w forks
21. Lever-to-crankcase screw
22. Gearshift operating lever
23. Shifter guard nut
24. Starter pin return spring
25. Camplate
26. Gear selection drum
27. Inner, selector body
28. R/h selector plunger
    L/h selector plunger
29. Selector plunger pawl
30. Plunger spring
31. Selector drum rod
32. Shim 0.6 mm (0.023 in.)
    Shim 0.8 mm (0.031 in.)
    Shim 1 mm (0.039 in.)
    Shim 1.2 mm (0.047 in.)
33. Oil pick up cup
34. Fork operating shaft
35. Gear selector fork
36. Gear box main shaft
37. Main shaft high gear end thrust washer
37/1. Main shaft seal, intermediate
38. Layshaft
39. Layshaft lock-ring
40. Safety lock-ring washer
41. Spacer
41/1. Tachometer gear retaining ball
42. Adjusting washer
43. 1st gear c/w bushing
44. 1st gear bushing
45. Layshaft circlip
45/1. Thrust circlip-to-bush washer
46. Sliding 1st and 2nd gear sleeve
47. 2nd gear c/w bushing
48. 2nd and 3rd gear bushing
49. 3rd gear c/w bushing
50. Sliding 3rd and high gear sleeve
51. Top gear
52. Floating high gear bush
52/1. Bush-to-shaft thrust washer
53. Clutch shaft
54. Clutch inner body circlip
55. Inner clutch body
56. Cush drive plate semi-collar
57. Cush drive plate
58. Cush drive spring
59. Sliding muff
60. Clutch shaft counter gear
61. Guiding operating shaft bush
62. Inner operating shaft bush
63. Gearshift r/h lever
64. R/h lever shaft

Four-speed transmission components

12. Remove the layshaft assembly and disassemble it in the following order:
   a. Adjusting washer
   b. First gear
   c. Circlip
   d. Second gear
   e. Fourth gear floating bushing
   f. Fourth gear
   g. Thrust washer
   h. Third gear

13. Remove the mainshaft assembly including the thrust washers and spacers.

14. Remove the clutch shaft complete with the cush drive assembly; then remove the two cush drive plate keepers, the cush drive plate, the cush drive spring, the sliding sleeve, and the clutch shaft-to-mainshaft driving gear. The easiest way to disassemble this assembly is by clamping the shaft on a press or in a wood-jawed vise and using either the special tool (No. 12905900 which is indicated by No. 23 in the accompanying illustration), or a suitable substitute to compress the spring.

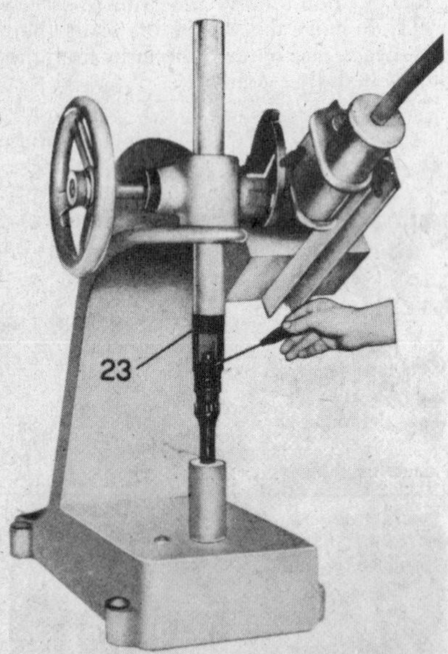

Disassembling the clutch shaft

NOTE: *Use a screwdriver with a daub of grease on its tip to remove the keepers.*

15. Remove the neutral indicator unit.

16. Remove the filler and drain plugs from the housing.

17. Remove the clutch shaft seal from the gearbox and the layshaft seal from the gearbox cover.

18. Remove, only if replacement is deemed necessary, the following bearings in the manner indicated:
   a. Remove the layshaft bearing.
   b. Remove the mainshaft bearing.
   c. Drift out the clutch shaft bearing with an appropriate drift.
   d. Remove the gearbox cover mainshaft and clutch shaft bearings.
   e. Drift out the layshaft bearing with an appropriate drift.

NOTE: *Heating the cases to about 150–160° C (300–350° F) will make removing the bearings considerably easier.*

Neutral indicator (A)

Five Speed Models

1. Follow steps 1–7 in the "Four Speed Models" section. The transmission should be in its Neutral position.

Five-speed transmission assembled

NOTE: *When loosening the layshaft securing nut, use the special tools designed for use on the V850 rather than those listed in the "Four-Speed Models" section. These are Nos. 12907100 and 14905400.*

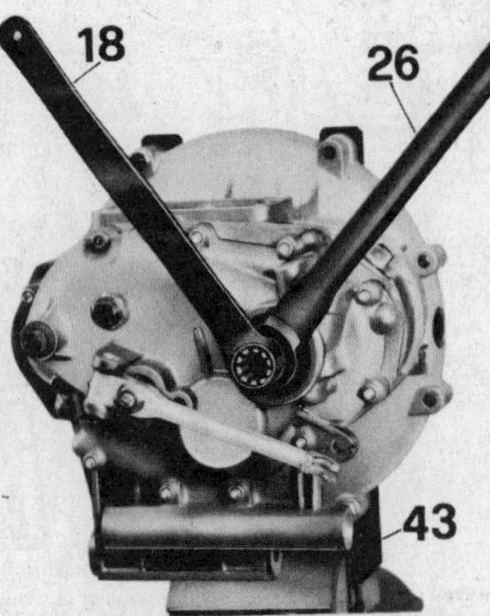

Loosening the layshaft nut

2. Remove the layshaft from its bearing in the cover, taking care not to lose the tachometer gear shim.

3. Remove the shifter fork rod, then remove the high gear shifter fork.

4. Remove the high gear sliding dog gear from the layshaft, then remove the layshaft high gear.

5. Remove the mainshaft high gear along with its roller cage and bushing in the following manner:
   a. Depress the stop pin down into its housing using a suitable pointed instrument, then turn the bushing in either direction and withdraw the gear, complete with roller cage and bushing, to within reaching distance of the shaft hole.
   b. Place your left thumb against the spring loaded stop pin, to prevent it from springing off into the cosmos, and at the same time withdraw the gear assembly with your right hand.
   c. Remove the stop pin and spring assembly.

Shift drum (arrow)

6. Remove the breather plug from the top of the transmission housing and remove the spring. The pawl will remain in the housing for removal only after the entire assembly has been taken down.

7. Remove the screws which secure the neutral indicator in the housing, then remove the indicator.

8. Remove the shifter drum and rod, taking careful notice of the way in which the shims are positioned on the drum and the way the drum is positioned in the gearbox, so they may be replaced in their original locations; then remove the rod from the drum.

9. Remove the layshaft from the gearbox, then disassemble it in the following order:
   a. Cover side seal ring.
   b. First gear, roller cage, and bushing
   c. First gear sliding dog gear
   d. Nut located on the side of fourth gear
   e. Roller bearing.

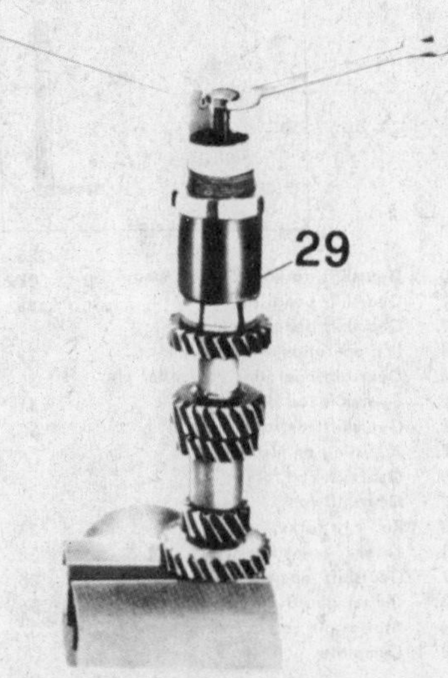

Removing the mainshaft inner bearing race

f. Adjusting washers
g. Fourth gear, roller cage, and bushing
h. Fourth gear sliding dog gear
i. Fixed sleeve on shaft
j. Shim
k. Third gear, roller cage, and bushing

10. Remove the mainshaft assembly from the gearbox, taking care to note the positions of the shims for reassembly in their original positions. The mainshaft inner bearing race may be removed with either the special puller (No. 14928500 which is indicated by No. 29 in the accompanying illustration) or a suitable substitute.

11. Bend back the locking tabs, then remove the clutch body retaining ring from the clutch side of the clutch shaft using either the special tools (Nos. 14912800 and 14912600 which are indicated by Nos. 27 and 28 in the accompanying illustration) or suitable substitutes.

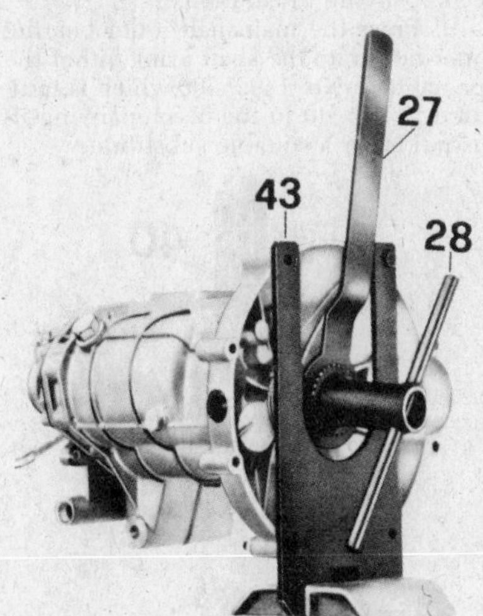

Removing the retaining ring

12. Remove the clutch fixed body, taking care to note the position of the seals between the body and the bearing and the seals in the shaft groove.

13. Remove the clutch shaft from the bearing taking care not to lose the oil scoop between the shaft and bearing.

NOTE: *Tap the end of the shaft gently with a soft mallet if it is reluctant to leave its seat.*

14. Remove the inner roller bearing race and the spacer nut from the clutch shaft using either the special puller (No. 14928500 which is indicated by No. 29 in the accompanying illustration) or a suitable substitute.

15. Install the clutch shaft in a wood-jawed vise, then use either the special tool (No. 12905900), or a suitable substitute, to compress the spring enough so the keepers can be removed; then remove the tool and slip off the cush plate, spring, sliding sleeve, and the intermediate gear.

NOTE: *Use a screwdriver with a daub of grease on its tip to remove the keepers.*

16. Remove the bearings from the

Removing the clutch shaft inner bearing race

gearbox in the following manner, especially if they have been secured with Loctite®:

a. Place the gearbox in an oven and heat it up to 150–160° C (300–350° F).
b. Remove the mainshaft roller bearing.
c. Remove the mainshaft roller bearing outer race.
d. Remove the clutch shaft seal, the lockplate securing bolts, and the lockplate, then drift out the clutch shaft bearing.

17. Remove the shifter merchanism from the transmission cover by carefully tapping the assembly free with a soft mallet, then remove the shifter return spring, the spring guide pin, the operating pawls, the pawl return springs, and the shifter adjusting screw and locknut.

If the pawls must be removed, do so by removing the pins with the aid of a 3–4 mm (0.11–0.15 in.) tool; the pawl springs will come out with the pins. A 10 mm (0.39) reamer may be used to ream out the pawl housings.

18. Remove the bearings from the gearbox cover in the following manner, especially if they have been secured with Loctite®:

a. Place the cover in an oven and heat it up to 150–160° C (300–350° F).
b. Remove the mainshaft bearing.
c. Remove the clutch shaft bearing.
d. Remove the layshaft seal and the lockplate securing screw, then remove the lockplate.
e. Remove the layshaft bearing.

INSPECTION

1. Inspect the fifth gear bushing retainer and spring for signs of wear, damage, or, in the case of the spring, a collapsed condition and replace them as necessary. The spring should show a load of 1.40 kgs (3.08 lbs) when compressed to a length of 8 mm (0.031 in.).

2. Check the clearances between the layshaft gear bushings and the shaft (V700 and V750 models). The clearances should be as follows:

a. The inside diameter of the first, second, and third gear bushings must be within 27.040–27.061 mm (1.0646–1.0655 in.).
b. The outside diameter of the layshaft bushing support for first, second, and third gears must be within 26.987–27.000 mm (1.0624–1.0630 in.).
c. The bushing-to-layshaft fitting clearance must be within 0.040–0.074 mm (0.0016–0.0028 in.).
d. The inside diameter of the fourth gear floating bushing must be within 20.007–20.028 mm (0.7877–0.7885 in.).
e. The outside diameter of the layshaft floating bushing support for fourth gear must be within 19.987–20.000 mm (0.7868–0.7874 in.).
f. The bushing-to-layshaft fitting clearance must be within 0.007–0.041 mm (0.0003–0.0016 in.).

3. Check the clearances between the layshaft bushings and gears (V700 and V750 models). The clearances should be as follows:

a. The outside diameter of the first, second, and third gear bushings must be within 31.060–31.099 mm (1.2228–1.2243 in.).
b. The inside diameter of the first, second, and third gears must be within 31.000–31.025 mm (1.2205–1.2214 in.).
c. The negative clearance for the gear bushings must be within 0.035–0.099 mm (0.0014–0.0039 in.).
d. The outside diameter of the fourth gear floating bushing must be within 22.960–22.939 mm (0.9309–0.9031 in.).
e. The inside diameter of the fourth gear must be within 23.021–23.000 mm (0.9063–0.9055 in.).
f. The clearance between the fourth gear and its floating bushing must be within 0.040–0.082 mm (0.0016–0.0032 in.).

4. Inspect the clutch shaft assembly for signs of wear or damage and replace the necessary components. The sliding sleeve must be able to slide smoothly and freely and the engaging teeth must be devoid of chips, score marks, or other damage.

5. Inspect the cush plate assembly, making sure that the retainer is not cracked or damaged, the plate grooves are not rough or damaged, and that the drive spring is not collapsed or damaged, and replace any parts as necessary.

ASSEMBLY

Four Speed Models

1. Assembly is basically in the reverse order of disassembly. Lubricate all parts, other than those surfaces on which a sealant is used, with clean oil as you put them together and make certain that all parts are perfectly clean.

2. Press all bearings into the cover and case using light applications of GREEN Loctite® at your own discretion. Make absolutely certain that no Loctite® gets into the bearings. When installing the layshaft bearing in the case, make sure you use a bottom plate to protect the fourth gear floating bushing.

CAUTION: *The Loctite® must be allowed to set for at least 12 hours before you continue with the assembly.*

3. Install the clutch shaft seal ring on the gearbox.

4. Install the mainshaft with the two thrust washers and the intermediate washer between the roller bearing and the fourth gear side of the shaft.

5. Place the fourth gear, its floating bush, and the thrust washer on the bearing; then insert the assembled layshaft (except for the first gear) through the thrust washer and gear and into the bearing.

6. Install the assembled clutch shaft assembly in the gearbox, using either the special tool (No. 12910700 which is indicated by No. 14 in the accompanying illustration) or a suitable substitute, to protect the seal ring.

NOTE: *Failure to install the shaft correctly will result in damage to the seal ring and eventual oil leakage on the clutch.*

Protect the seal before installing the clutch shaft

7. Install the shifter forks to the two sliding dog gears, install the shifter drum, then insert the fork ends in the drum grooves.

8. Slip the fork shaft through the forks, then mount the camplate on the shaft.

9. Rotate the shifter drum until the shifter pawl enters the fourth gear position hole and the sliding dog gear engages the second gear.

10. Install the assembled shifter inner body which includes the springs, plungers, and pawls.

11. Slip the first gear and an adjusting washer on the layshaft.

12. Install the oil pick-up plate and the neutral indicator unit in the gearbox; then mount the gearbox cover and a new cover gasket, making sure the indicator doesn't interfere with the mating of the box and cover. A light coating of a gasket sealer may be used at your discretion.

NOTE: *When securing the cover screws, do so evenly in a cross pattern to avoid deforming the cover gasket.*

13. Mount the speedometer driving gear, spacer, and lockwasher on the layshaft; then install the lock ring using either the special tools (Nos. 12907100 and 12905400) or suitable substitutes. Secure the ring by bending the locking tab in the lock ring slot.

14. Assemble the sector quadrant and shifter shaft assembly, the shifter return spring and the offset adjusting screw, along with its washer and locknut, to the shifter cover; then mount the cover assembly using a new gasket and making sure that the quadrant is engaging the shifter inner body. A light coat of a gasket sealer may be used at your discretion.

NOTE: *When securing the cover, tighten the short and long screws evenly in a cross pattern to avoid deforming the cover gasket.*

15. Mount the gear shifter operating lever on the shifter shaft, securing it by means of the two circlips which fit in the clutch shaft grooves.

16. Install the clutch rubber tube, pressure rod, inner body, cage and outer body, and seal ring; then mount the clutch operating lever to the gearbox by means of its pin and cotterpin.

17. Check the shift mechanism. If shifting is not satisfactory, adjust by loosening the locknut and turning the adjusting screw. This adjuster is located on the rear cover, above the clutch lever.

Five Speed Models

1. Assembly is basically in the reverse order of disassembly. Lubricate all parts, other than those surfaces on which a sealant is used, with clean oil as you put them together and make sure that all parts are perfectly clean.

2. When installing the bearings, it is recommended that a light coat of GREEN Loctite® be used on the outer races and bearing housings. Be very careful to avoid getting any Loctite® in the bearings and allow them to set for about 12 hours before continuing with the assembly. Install the bearings as follows:

a. Install the clutch shaft bearing into its gearbox housing.

b. Press the outer layshaft bearing race into its gearbox housing.

c. Install the mainshaft bearing in its gearbox housing.

d. Press the layshaft bearing in its housing in the gearbox cover.

e. Install the mainshaft bearing in its cover housing.

f. Install the clutch shaft bearing.

3. Install the layshaft bearing retainers in the gearbox cover, making sure that they seat absolutely flush with the outer bearing races. Mill away any projections which may prevent a perfect seal and use a light coat of green Loctite®, taking care not to allow any of it to penetrate the bearing.

NOTE: *Use only the modified type retainers (part No. 14213802) for the best results.*

4. Install the clutchshaft seal in the gearbox.

5. Install the layshaft seal in the gearbox cover.

6. Install the selector shaft seal in its housing in the gearbox cover.

7. Assemble the shifter body by inserting the pawls and springs and securing them to the shifter body with flexible pins; then install the shifter quadrant shaft, gear, and return spring to the shifter body and mount the assembled body to the gearbox cover.

8. Shim up the mainshaft so the distance between the cover bearing and the gearbox bearing is within 167.1–167.2 mm (6.578–6.582 in.). Shims are available in the following sizes: 0.2, 2.1, 2.2, and 2.4 mm (0.0788, 0.8274, 0.8668, 0.9456 in.) and may be fitted on the gearbox end of the shaft with bronze spacers between them. The part numbers are given in the accompanying illustration.

9. Press the mainshaft roller bearing inner race onto the shaft using either the special tool (No. 14928600 which is indicated by No. 40 in the accompanying illustration) or a suitable substitute.

Installing the mainshaft inner bearing race

10. Assemble the following components on the layshaft gearbox end:

a. Slip the second gear bushing on the shaft so the bushing head faces the transmission cover.

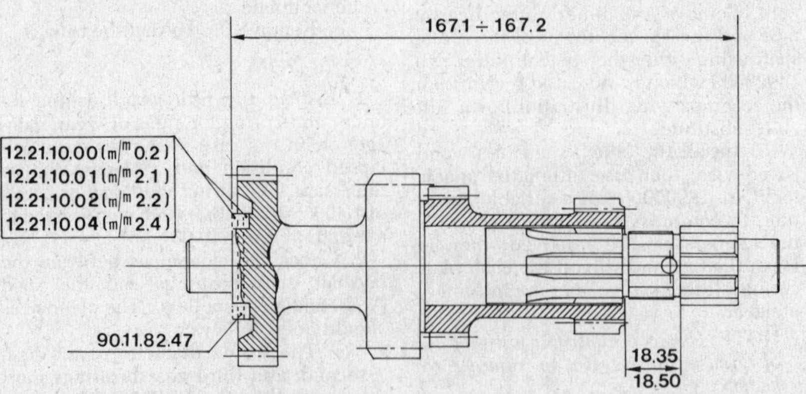

Shimming the mainshaft

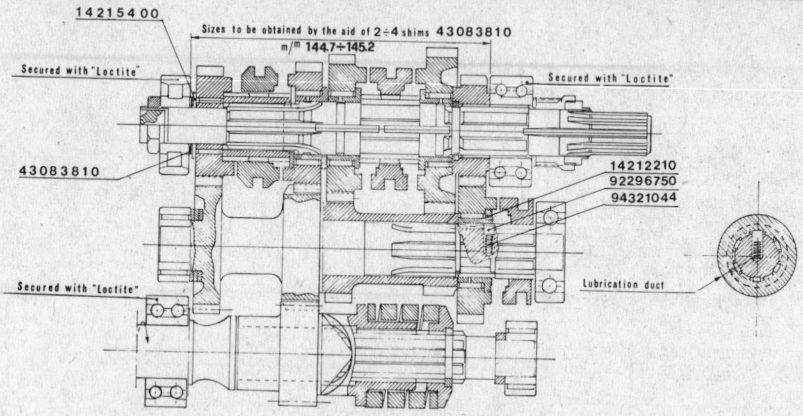

Shimming the layshaft

b. Fit the second gear roller cage on the second gear bushing, then mount the second gear on the cage so its engaging dogs are facing the gearbox cover.

c. Slip the third gear bushing on the shaft so its head faces the second gear, assemble the third gear roller cage on the bushing, then install the third gear on the roller cage so its engaging dogs are facing the gearbox.

d. Place a shim on the shaft, install the fixed sleeve on the shaft with its stepped down end facing the third gear, then slip the third and fourth gear sliding sleeve onto the shaft with its stepped down end facing the third gear.

e. Slip the fourth gear bushing on the shaft, install the roller cage on the bushing, then position the fourth gear on the shaft so its engaging dogs face the sliding sleeve.

11. Assemble the following components on the layshaft gearbox cover end:

a. Slip the first and second gear engaging sleeves on the shaft.

b. Position the first gear bushing on the shaft so its head faces second gear, fit the first gear roller cage on the bushing, then install the first gear on the roller cage.

c. Position the seal in its groove in the shaft, then slip the fourth gear on the shaft so its stepped down end is fitted on the seal ring.

12. Shim the layshaft on the fourth gear side until the distance between the shims and the fourth gear is within 144.7–145.2 mm (5.692–5.715 in.). This can generally be accomplished with between two and four shims.

13. Mount the roller bearing on the fourth gear end of the layshaft, secure the nut on the fourth gear end of the shaft by hammering the nut tang with a chisel along the line of the shaft groove, then mount the assembled layshaft in the transmission housing.

14. Assemble the first, second, third, and fourth gear shifting forks on the layshaft dog gears.

15. Install the splined shifter drum, along with its shaft and a spacer, in the gearbox. Then look through the hole in the ratchet pawl to see if the pawl hole is aligned with one of the six holes in the drum. If the holes are misaligned, replace the spacer with larger or smaller ones until both holes are in perfect accord.

16. Position the nubs of the shifter forks in the drum grooves using either the special tool (No. 14929300 which is indicated by No. 41 in the accompanying illustration) or a suitable substitute.

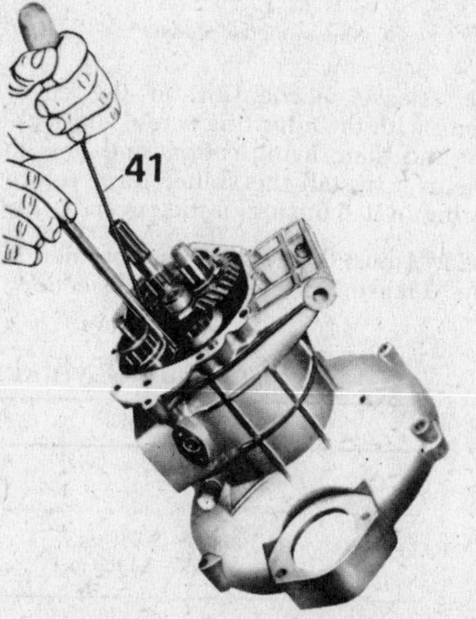

Fitting the shifter forks to the drum

17. Temporarily secure the peg, spring, and cap in their gearbox housing.

18. Slip the shifter fork retaining rod through the fork eyes.

19. Mount and secure the neutral indicator to the gearbox, making sure that the blade contacts the button on the drum.

20. Assemble the clutch shaft assembly in the following manner:

a. Install the idle gear so its engaging dogs face the gearbox cover, then position the coupling sleeve so its engaging dogs face the idle gear.

b. Slip the cush spring and spring plate on the shaft, then use either the special tool (No. 12905900), or a suitable substitute, to compress the spring enough so two new keepers can be installed.

c. Secure the spacer nut, then install the clutch shaft roller bearing inner race in the cover using either the special tool (No. 14928600 which is indicated by No. 40 in the accompanying illustration) or a suitable substitute.

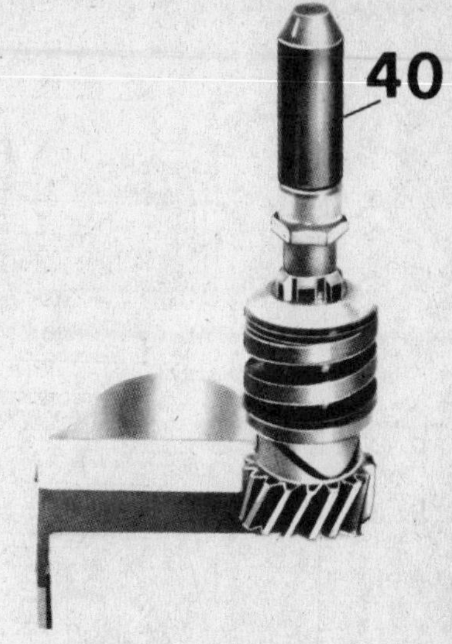

Installing the clutch shaft bearing inner race

d. Install, on the gearbox end of the shaft, the oil seal in its groove, and the oil scoop between the shaft and gearbox bearing; then mount the shaft assembly in the gearbox bearing and retaining ring.

21. Assemble the mainshaft assembly in the following manner:

a. Mount the fifth gear roller cage and gear on the bushing, then slip the gear, cage, and bushing assembly on the splined portion of the shaft.

b. Mount the spring in its drilling in the shaft, then position the stop pin on top of the spring.

c. Depress the spring with the thumb of your left hand while slipping the fifth gear assembly over it, then rotate the bushing to either the right or left until the stop peg seats into one of the bushing's six splines.

d. Slip the fifth gear engaging sleeve and shifter fork onto the shaft, so the fork eye slips over the fork rod, then engage the fork nub in the drum groove.

22. Assemble the gearbox cover in the following manner:

a. Install the retaining washer on the shifter drum along with one or more shims.

b. Shift the drum into the neutral position, place a new cover gasket on the mating surface, mount the cover while tapping it lightly with a soft mallet to properly seat all of the shafts and mating surfaces, then lightly screw in the four cover screws.

NOTE: *A sparing application of a suitable gasket sealer may be used at your own discretion, but make sure none of it gets inside the gearbox.*

c. Slip the shim, speedometer drive gear, and the drive gear stop ball onto the layshaft, then temporarily secure the layshaft securing nut.

d. Mount either the special tool or any suitable substitute which you can use to shift the transmission, onto the shifter shaft.

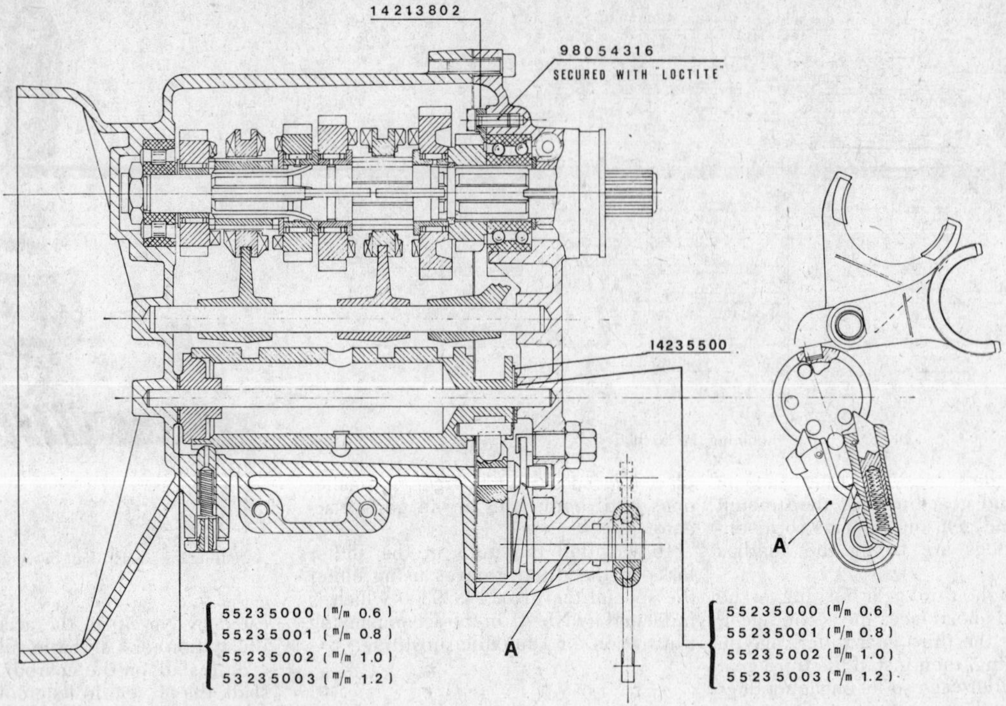

Shimming the gearbox

e. Loosen the locknut and rotate the adjusting nut on the rear cover until a suitable adjustment is achieved in which all gears, including Neutral, can be easily engaged. If ease of shifting cannot be attained, remove the gearbox cover and add or remove spacer shims from between the gearbox and the shift drum to alleviate shifting problems related to First and Third gears, or between the gearbox cover and the drum to alleviate shifting problems related to Second and Fourth gears. 0.6, 0.8, 1.0, and 1.2 mm (0.023, 0.031, 0.039, and 0.047 in.) shims are available

f. Remount the cover and recheck the gearbox operation. If all of the gears engage smoothly, including Neutral, secure the layshaft nut using either the special tools (Nos. 14905400 and 12907100) or suitable substitutes, then hammer the nut with a chisel at the shaft groove to lock it into place.

g. Secure the cover mounting screws, remove the tool from the shifter shaft, and mount and secure the shift lever on the shifter shaft.

h. Secure the oil breather plug which serves to secure the gearbox spring and stop peg.

23. Mount the bearing inner body seal, inner body, safety washer, and the inner body locking nut on the clutch shaft using either the special tools (Nos. 14912800 and 14912600) or suitable substitutes, then bend one of the locking tabs into one of the locknut grooves.

24. When installing the clutch unit on the mainshaft and gearbox cover, position the small rubber tube in the shaft, mount the inner body, mount the throwout bearing on the inner body, and mount the inner body and seal on the gearbox cover. Then slip the clutch pushrod into the operating shaft at the gearbox end, mount the release mechanism on the cover along with the adjusting screw and locknut and then, using cotters and pins to secure it, install the shifter lever return spring in its housing in the cover.

25. Adjust the gearbox as described in the "Transmission Adjustment" section.

Drive Box

Disassembly

1. Remove the drive box drain plug or cover and filler plug and allow the oil to drain.

Piston and Cylinder Grade Dimensions

	Class A	*Class B*	*Class C*
V700			
Piston	79.952–79.958 mm (3.1477–3.1480 in.)	79.958–79.964 mm (3.1480–3.1482 in.)	79.964–79.964 mm (3.1482–3.1485 in.)
Cylinder	80.000–80.006 mm (3.1496–3.1499 in.)	80.006–80.012 mm (3.1499–3.1501 in.)	80.012–80.018 mm (3.1501–3.1503 in.)
V750			
Piston	82.958–82.964 mm (3.2260–3.2262 in.)	82.964–82.970 mm (3.2262–3.2264 in.)	82.970–82.976 mm (3.2264–3.2266 in.)
Cylinder	83.000–83.006 mm (3.2677 3.2679 in.)	83.006–83.012 mm (3.2679–3.2681 in.)	83.012–83.018 mm (3.2681–3.2683 in.)
750 Sport			
Piston	82.458–82.464 mm (3.2463–3.2465 in.)	82.464–82.470 mm (3.2465–3.2467 in.)	82.470–82.476 mm (3.2467–3.2469 in.)
Cylinder	82.500–82.506 mm (3.2480–3.2482 in.)	82.506–82.512 mm (3.2482–3.2484 in.)	82.512–82.516 mm (3.2484–3.2486 in.)
V850, 850T/T3			
Piston	82.968–82.974 mm (3.2664–3.2666 in.)	82.974–82.980 mm (3.2666–3.2668 in.)	82.980–82.986 mm (3.2668–3.2671 in.)
Cylinder	83.000–83.006 mm (3.2677–3.2679 in.)	83.006–83.012 mm (3.2679–3.2681 in.)	83.012–83.018 mm (3.2681–3.2683 in.)

Engine Specifications

V700	
Cylinder diameter:	80.000–80.018 mm (3.1496–2.1503 in.)
Piston diameters:	
—at piston top	79.600–79.650 mm (3.1338–3.1358 in.)
—below top ring	79.700–79.750 mm (3.1378–3.1397 in.)
—below 2nd ring	79.000–79.100 mm (3.1102–3.1141 in.)
—at recess below oil scrapers	79.100–79.150 mm (3.1149–3.1161 in.)
—5 mm (0.196 in.) below top oil scraper recess	79.922–79.940 mm (3.1465–3.1472 in.)
—selection diameter at 18.5 mm (0.728 in.) over piston bottom edge	79.952–79.970 mm (3.1477–3.1484 in.)
—at piston bottom	79.922–79.940 mm (3.1465–3.1472 in.)
—piston pin housing diameter	22.000–22.006 mm (0.8661–0.8663 in.)
Piston pin diameter	22.001–22.006 mm (0.86614–0.86634 in.)
Mainshaft diameter, flywheel side	53.970–53.951 mm (2.1248–2.1240 in.)
Mainshaft diameter, timing side	37.975–37.959 mm (1.4951–1.4944 in.)
I/D of main bearings c/w flange:	
—flywheel side	54.000–54.019 mm (2.1260–2.1268 in.)
—timing side	38.000–38.016 mm (1.4961–1.4967 in.)
Undersize range of main bearings available as spare parts:	0.2 mm (0.00787 in.) 0.4 mm (0.01574 in.) 0.6 mm (0.02362 in.) 0.8 mm (0.03149 in.)
Crankpin diameter	44.013–44.033 mm (1.7328–1.7336 in.)
Diameter of con-rod big end bearing housing	47.130–47.142 mm (1.8559–1.8574 in.)
Original thickness of con-rod bearings	1.534–1.543 mm (0.06039–0.06070 in.)
Oversize range of big end bearings	0.254 mm (0.010 in.) 0.508 mm (0.020 in.) 0.762 mm (0.030 in.) 1.016 mm (0.040 in.)
I/D of small end bushing (after pressing in):	22.020–22.041 mm (0.8669–0.8677 in.)
I/D of camshaft housings in crankcase	
—timing side	47.025–47.064 mm (1.8511–1.8529 in.)
—flywheel side	32.025–32.064 mm (1.2607–1.2623 in.)
Diameter of camshaft journals	
—timing side	46.975–47.000 mm (1.8494–1.8504 in.)
—flywheel side	31.975–32.000 mm (1.2588–1.2598 in.)
Diameter of tappet guides	22.021–22.000 mm (0.8669–0.8661 in.)
O/D of original tappet	22.000–21.979 mm (0.8661–0.9046 in.)
Tappet oversize range	0.05 and 0.10 mm (0.0019 and 0.0039 in.)
I/D of rocketr arms	15.032–15.059 mm (0.5918–0.5929 in.)
Diameter of rocker arms spindles	14.983–14.994 mm (0.5899–0.5903 in.)
I/D of inlet and exhaust valve guide housings	14.000–14.018 mm (0.5512–0.5519 in.)
O/D of inlet and exhaust valve guides (original)	14.064–14.075 mm (0.5537–0.5541 in.)
(spares)	14.107–14.118 mm (0.55541–0.55545 in.)
I/D of inlet and exhaust valve guides (after pressing-in)	8.000–8.022 mm (0.3149–0.3158 in.)
Diameter of inlet valve stem	7.972–7.987 mm (0.3138–0.3144 in.)
Diameter of exhaust valve stem	7.965–7.980 mm (0.3136–0.3142 in.)
Diameter of inlet valve head	38.4–38.6 mm (1.5118–1.5197 in.)
Diameter of exhaust valve head	34.4–34.6 mm (1.3543–1.3622 in.)

2. Remove the rear wheel.

3. Remove the four nuts or bolts which secure the drive box and remove the box along with the shaft and sleeve.

4. Remove the drive shaft from the sleeve, the two circlips from the shaft, and the sleeve from the bevel pinion.

5. Remove the drive box gasket and oil seal.

6. Bend back the locking tab then, using either the special tool (No. 12907100 which is indicated by No. 18 in

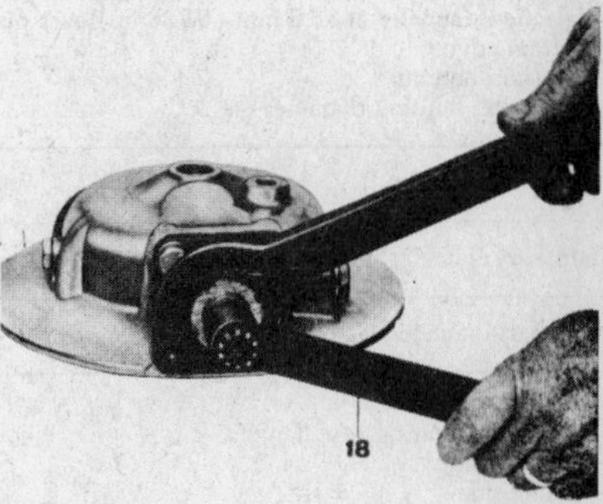

Removing the bevel pinion lockring

the accompanying illustration) or a suitable substitute, remove the lock-ring which secures the bevel pinion.

7. Remove the bearing housing, then further disassemble it by removing the bevel pinion, both bearings, the shims, and the spacer.

8. Remove the housing-to-drive box gasket and seal ring.

Removing the roller bearing outer race

9. Bend back the locking tabs, remove the eight bolts which secure the flange to the drive box, then remove the flange. Remove the seal ring and bearing from the flange.

10. Remove the gaskets from between the flange and shim, and from between the shim and drive box.

11. Remove the internally toothed sleeve and bevel crown from the rear wheel coupling, then remove the bevel crown gear from the sleeve by removing the lockwashers and bolts.

12. Remove the roller bearing stop screw, plate, bearing cage, and the inner race, then remove the outer race by using either the special puller or a suitable substitute.

Engine Specifications (cont.)

V750 and V850

Cylinder diameter:	83.000–83.018 mm (3.2677–3.2683 in.)
Piston diameters:	
—at piston top	82.600–82.650 mm (3.2520–3.2538 in.)
—below top ring	82.700–82.750 mm (3.2558–3.2578 in.)
—below 2nd ring	82.000–82.100 mm (3.2283–3.2322 in.)
—at recess below oil scrapers	82.100–82.150 mm (3.2322–3.2342 in.)
—5 mm (0.196 in.) below top oil scraper recess	82.928–82.946 mm (3.2648–3.2655 in.)
—selection diameter at 18.5 mm (0.728 in.) over piston bottom edge	82.958–82.976 mm (3.2660–3.2667 in.)
—at piston bottom	82.928–82.946 mm (3.2648–3.2665 in.)
—piston pin housing diameter	22.000–22.006 mm (0.8661–0.8663 in.)
Piston pin diameter	22.001–22.006 mm (0.86614–0.86634 in.)
Mainshaft diameter, flywheel side	53.970–53.951 mm (2.1248–2.1240 in.)
Mainshaft diameter, timing side	37.975–37.959 mm (1.4951–1.4944 in.)
I/D of main bearing c/w flange:	
—flywheel side	54.000–54.019 mm (2.1260–2.1268 in.)
—timing side	38.000–38.016 mm (1.4961–1.4967 in.)
Undersize range of main bearings available as spare parts:	0.2 mm (0.00787 in.)
	0.4 mm (0.01574 in.)
	0.6 mm (0.02362 in.)
	0.8 mm (0.03149 in.)
Crankpin diameter	44.013–44.033 mm (1.7328–1.7336 in.)
Diameter of con-rod big end bearing housing	47.130–47.142 mm (1.8559–1.8574 in.)
Original thickness of con-rod bearings	1.534–1.543 mm (0.06039–0.06070 in.)
Oversize range of big end bearings	0.254 mm (0.010 in.)
	0.508 mm (0.020 in.)
	0.762 mm (0.030 in.)
	1.016 mm (0.040 in.)
I/D of small end bushing (after pressing in):	22.020–22.041 mm (0.8669–0.8677 in.)
I/D of camshaft housings in crankcase	
—timing side	47.025–47.064 mm (1.8511–1.8529 in.)
—flywheel side	32.025–32.064 mm (1.2607–1.2623 in.)
Diameter of camshaft journals	
—timing side	46.975–47.000 mm (1.8494–1.8504 in.)
—flywheel side	31.975–32.000 mm (1.2588–1.2598 in.)
Diameter of tappet guides	22.021–22.000 mm (0.8669–0.8661 in.)
O/D of original tappet	22.000–21.979 mm (0.8661–0.9046 in.)
Tappet oversize range	0.05 and 0.10 mm (0.0019 and 0.0039 in.)
I/D of rocker arms	15.032–15.059 mm (0.5918–0.5929 in.)
Diameter of rocker arms spindles	14.983–14.994 mm (0.5899–0.5903 in.)
I/D of inlet and exhaust valve guide housings	14.000–14.018 mm (0.5512–0.5519 in.)
O/D of inlet and exhaust valve guides (original)	14.064–14.075 mm (0.5537–0.5541 in.)
(spares)	14.107–14.118 mm (0.55541–0.55545 in.)
I/D of inlet and exhaust valve guides (after pressing-in)	8.000–8.022 mm (0.3149–0.3158 in.)
Diameter of inlet valve stem	7.972–7.987 mm (0.3138–0.3144 in.)
Diameter of exhaust valve stem	7.965–7.980 mm (0.3136–0.3142 in.)
Diameter of inlet valve head	40.8–41.0 mm (1.605–1.615 in.)
Diameter of exhaust valve head	35.8–36.0 mm (1.409–1.417 in.)

13. Remove the roller bearing cage retaining ring, drive box oil seal, wheel-to-drive box spacer, and the level plug and gasket.

14. If you wish to remove the universal double joint, gaiters, and bands, you'll have to either remove the engine and transmission assemblies from the frame or remove the swing arm assembly.

Assembly

1. Assembly is in the reverse order of disassembly. Use new gaskets, seals, and lockwashers.

Refer to the "Engine Torque Specifications Chart."

2. Replace the oil drain plug, position the rear wheel-to-drive box spacer and press the drive box oil seal into place.

3. Install the bearing cage retaining ring, roller bearing outer race, bearing cage, and inner race, then secure the bearing stop screw and plate.

4. Assemble the bevel crown to the internally toothed sleeve by means of the securing bolts and locking tabs.

5. Press the bearing and seal ring into the drive box flange, position new gaskets on the drive box and box flange, then mount the flange to the box.

NOTE: *Do not secure the locking tabs until after the bevel gear adjustment is performed as directed in the "Bevel Gear Adjustment" section.*

6. Install the front bearing, bearing spacer, distance adjusting shims, and the rear bearing into the bearing housing.

7. Mount the spacer shim and adjusting shims onto the bevel pinion and slip the pinion shank into the bearing housing, then secure it with a lock-ring and lock-ring safety washer using either the special tool (No. 12907100) or a suitable substitute.

NOTE: *After the bevel gear adjustment is carried out, secure the lock-ring by bending the lockwasher locking tab. Consult the "Bevel Gear Adjustment" section for additional information.*

8. Secure the bearing housing and bevel pinion to the drive box by means of the securing nuts and washers.

NOTE: *This must not be done until the bevel gear adjustment is carried out as directed in the "Bevel Gear Adjustment" section.*

9. Install the ball bearing to the swing arm and secure it with a circlip.

10. Install the double joint in the swing arm bearing and fit the gaiters and bands over the joint. The bands should be used to secure the gaiters on the swing arm side only.

NOTE: *If the engine and transmission have been removed from the frame, the front side of the gaiters must be secured when installed in the engine and transmission assembly.*

11. Position the circlips in their grooves in the drive shaft, then install the shaft into the double joint and bevel drive sleeve.

12. Insert the splined portion of the bevel pinion into the sleeve and secure it without locking the four bolts and lockwashers which secure the drive box to the swing arm. Then insert the rear

Engine Specifications (cont.)

750 Sport	
Cylinder diameter:	82.500–82.516 mm (3.2480–3.2486 in.)
Piston diameter	82.458–82.476 mm (3.2463–3.2469 in.)
Piston pin diameter	22.000–22.004 mm (0.8661–0.8663 in.)
Piston pin hole diameter	22.000–22.006 mm (0.8661–0.8663 in.)
Mainshaft diameter, flywheel side	53.951–53.970 mm (2.1240–2.1248 in.)
Mainshaft diameter, timing side	37.959–37.975 mm (1.4944–1.4951 in.)
I/D of main bearings c/w flange —flywheel side —timing side	 54.000–54.019 mm (2.1260–2.1268 in.) 38.000–38.016 mm (1.4961–1.4967 in.)
Undersize main bearings available	0.2 mm (0.00787 in.) 0.4 mm (0.01574 in.) 0.6 mm (0.02362 in.) 0.8 mm (0.03149 in.)
Crankpin diameter	43.893–43.994 mm (1.730–1.732 in.)
Original thickness of con-rod bearings	1.537–1.543 mm (0.0604–0.0607 in.)
Diameter of con-rod big end bearing housing	47.130–47.142 mm (1.8559–1.8574 in.)
Oversize range of big end bearings	0.254 mm (0.010 in.) 0.508 mm (0.020 in.) 0.762 mm (0.030 in.)
I/D of small end bushing (after pressing in)	22.025–22.045 mm (0.8670–0.8678 in.)
I/D of camshaft housings in crankcase —timing side —flywheel side	 47.025–47.050 mm (1.8511–1.8529 in.) 32.025–32.050 mm (1.2607–1.2623 in.)
Diameter of camshaft journals —timing side —flywheel side	 46.984–47.000 mm (1.814–1.850 in.) 31.894–32.000 mm (1.259–1.260 in.)
Diameter of tappet guides	22.021–22.000 mm (0.8669–0.8661 in.)
O/D of original tappet	22.000–21.979 mm (0.8661–0.9046 in.)
Tappet oversize range	0.05 and 0.10 mm (0.0019 and 0.0039 in.)
I/D of rocker arms	15.032–15.059 mm (0.5918–0.5929 in.)
Diameter of rocker arms spindles	14.983–14.994 mm (0.5899–0.5903 in.)
I/D of inlet and exhaust valve guide housings	14.000–14.018 mm (0.5512–0.5519 in.)
O/D of inlet and exhaust valve guides (original) (spares)	14.064–14.075 mm (0.5537–0.5541 in.) 14.107–14.118 mm (0.55541–0.55545 in.)
I/D of inlet and exhaust valve guides (after pressing-in)	8.000–8.022 mm (0.3149–0.3158 in.)
Diameter of inlet valve stem Diameter of exhaust valve stem	7.972–7.987 mm (0.3138–0.3144 in.) 7.965–7.980 mm (0.3136–0.3142 in.)
Diameter of inlet valve head Diameter of exhaust valve head	40.8–41.0 mm (1.605–1.615 in.) 35.8–36.0 mm (1.409–1.417 in.)
850T/T3	
Cylinder diameter:	83.000–83.018 mm (3.2677–3.2683 in.)
Piston diameter	82.968–82.986 mm (3.2664–3.2671 in.)
Piston pin diameter	22.000–22.004 mm (0.8661–0.8663 in.)

Correct gear engagement

Pinion too deep in crown

Crown too far from pinion

wheel spindle through the left-hand side of the swing arm and into the drive box, then secure the four bolts and remove the spindle.

13. Replenish the drive box oil supply.

BEVEL GEAR ADJUSTMENT

1. Adjust the pinion-to-crown clearance of the bevel gear set to 0.010–0.015 mm (0.0039–0.0059 in.). Make sure the meshing surfaces of the gears are in proper contact.
2. Check for correct teeth contact in the following manner:
   a. Coat the crown teeth with lead oxide, then rotate the pinion while

Engine Specifications (cont.)

Piston pin hole diameter	22.000–22.006 mm (0.8661–0.8663 in.)
Mainshaft diameter, flywheel side	53.951–53.970 mm (2.1240–2.1248 in.)
Mainshaft diameter, timing side	37.959–37.975 mm (1.4944–1.4951 in.)
I/D of main bearings c/w flange —flywheel side —timing side	 54.000–54.019 mm (2.1260–2.1268 in.) 38.000–38.016 mm (1.4961–1.4967 in.)
Undersize main bearings available	0.2 mm (0.00787 in.) 0.4 mm (0.01574 in.) 0.6 mm (0.02362 in.) 0.8 mm (0.03149 in.)
Crankpin diameter —Blue mark —White mark	 44.008–44.014 mm (1.7339–1.7341 in.) 44.014–44.020 mm (1.7341–1.7344 in.)
Original thickness of con-rod bearings	1.537–1.543 mm (0.0604–0.0607 in.)
Diameter of con-rod big end bearing housing	47.130–47.142 mm (1.8559–1.8574 in.)
Oversize range of big end bearings	0.254 mm (0.010 in.) 0.508 mm (0.020 in.) 0.762 mm (0.030 in.)
I/D of small end bushing (after pressing-in)	22.025–22.045 mm (0.8670–0.8678 in.)
I/D of camshaft housings in crankcase —timing side —flywheel side	 47.025–47.050 mm (1.8511–1.8529 in.) 32.025–32.050 mm (1.2607–1.2623 in.)
Diameter of camshaft journals —timing side —flywheel side	 46.984–47.000 mm (1.814–1.850 in.) 31.894–32.000 mm (1.259–1.260 in.)
Diameter of tappet guides	22.021–22.000 mm (0.8669–0.8661 in.)
O/D of original tappet	22.000–21.979 mm (0.8661–0.9046 in.)
Tappet oversize range	0.05 and 0.10 mm (0.0019 and 0.0039 in.)
I/D of rocker arms	15.032–15.059 mm (0.5918–0.5929 in.)
Diameter of rocker arms spindles	14.983–14.994 mm (0.5899–0.5903 in.)
I/D of inlet and exhaust valve guide housings	14.000–14.018 mm (0.5512–0.5519 in.)
O/D of inlet and exhaust valve guides (original) (spares)	14.064–14.075 mm (0.5537–0.5541 in.) 14.107–14.118 mm (0.55541–0.55545 in.)
I/D of inlet and exhaust valve guides (after pressing-in)	8.000–8.022 mm (0.3149–0.3158 in.)
Diameter of inlet valve stem Diameter of exhaust valve stem	7.972–7.987 mm (0.3138–0.3144 in.) 7.965–7.980 mm (0.3136–0.3142 in.)
Diameter of inlet valve head Diameter of exhaust valve head	40.8–41.0 mm (1.605–1.615 in.) 35.8–36.0 mm (1.409–1.417 in.)

Crown too close to pinion

Pinion too far from crown

Engine Torque Specifications

Part		Torque (ft lbs)
Cylinder head	750 Sport, 850T/T3:	29–32
	V700, V750, V850:	27
Rocker arm shaft bolts		4.2–5.7
Connecting rod nuts	750 Sport, 850T/T3:	33–35
	V700, V750, V850:	25
Flywheel bolts		30
Crankshaft bearing flanges		22
Ring gear bolts		22
Camshaft flange bolts		22
Camshaft gear/sprocket nut		108
Oil pump screws		22
Filter screen cover plate		7
Filter screen housing		22
Oil pipe bolts		22
Hollow oil delivery bolts		11–16
Gearbox bearing retainer bolt		7
Layshaft securing nut		115–129
Filler cap, gearbox		22
Level and Drain plugs, gearbox		14
Gearbox nut, 24 mm hex		50–57
Filler cap, drive box		22
Level and drain plugs, drive box		18
Drain plate allen bolts, drive box		7
Bevel gear bearing retainer nut, 36 mm hex, drive box		129–144
Crown wheel bolt, 13 mm hex		31
Flange bolts		18
Drive box securing nuts, 13 mm hex		25

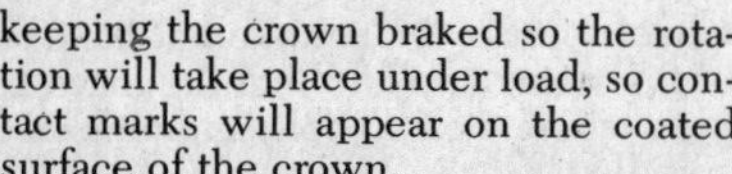

keeping the crown braked so the rotation will take place under load, so contact marks will appear on the coated surface of the crown.

b. Make sure that the contact is correct by comparing it with the accompanying illustration. If the contact marks are incorrect, go onto the next step.

3. If the contact pattern is not correct, consult the following steps and illustrations to arrive at a solution:

NOTE: *After adding or removing shims, readjust the pinion-to-crown clearance before rechecking the contact pattern.*

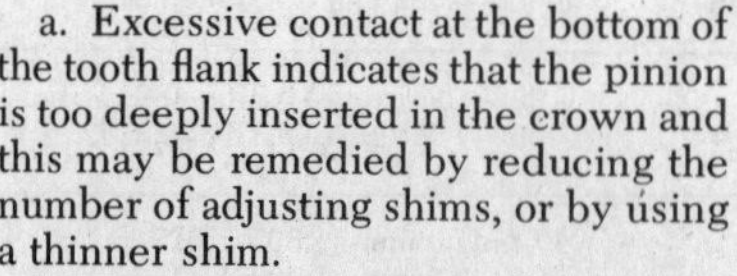

a. Excessive contact at the bottom of the tooth flank indicates that the pinion is too deeply inserted in the crown and this may be remedied by reducing the number of adjusting shims, or by using a thinner shim.

b. Excessive contact at the heel of the tooth indicates that the crown is too far from the pinion and this may be remedied by increasing the number of shims, or by using a thicker shim.

c. Excessive contact at the crest of the tooth indicates that the pinion is too far from the crown and this may be remedied by increasing the number of shims, or by using a thicker shim.

d. Excessive contact at the top land of the tooth indicates that the crown is too close to the pinion and this may be remedied by reducing the number of shims, or by using thinner shims.

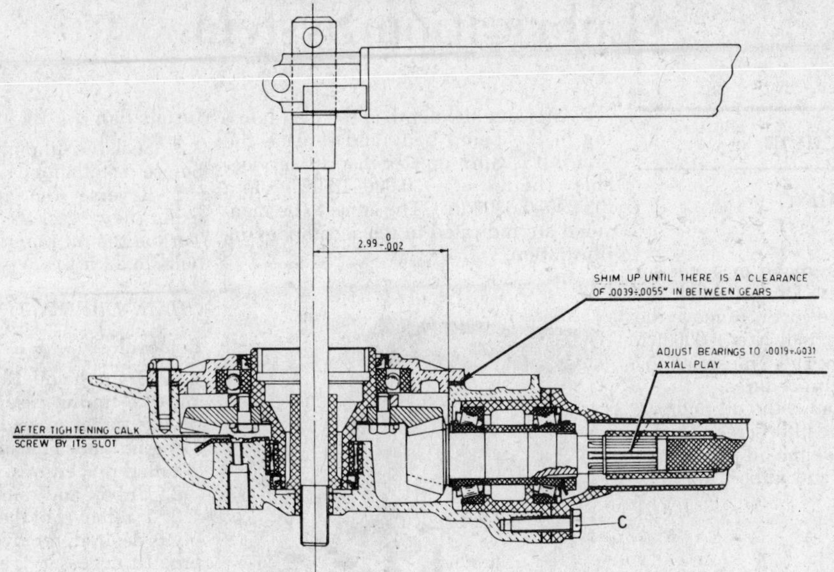
2.99 - 0 / .002
SHIM UP UNTIL THERE IS A CLEARANCE OF .0039÷.0055" IN BETWEEN GEARS
ADJUST BEARINGS TO .0019÷.0031 AXIAL PLAY
AFTER TIGHTENING CALK SCREW BY ITS SLOT
C
Assembling the drive box

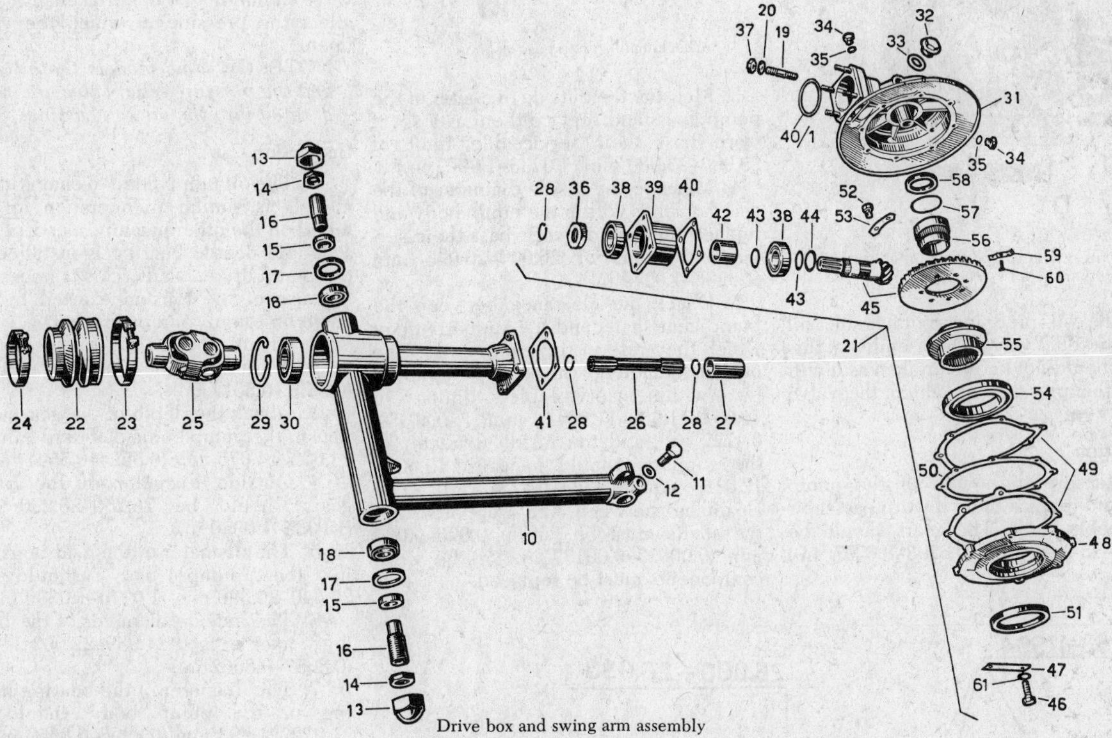
Drive box and swing arm assembly

10. Swing arm
11. Rear clamp screw
12. Clamp screw washer
13. Cap nut
14. Spindle nut
15. Spacer
16. Support spindle
17. Spindle seal
18. Taper roller bearing
19. Drive box-to-swing arm bolt
20. Drive box bolts washer
21. Wheel drive complete, rear
22. Rubber gaiter
23. Large gaiter-to-drive box band
24. Small gaiter-to-drive box band
25. Layshaft to drive shaft double joint
26. Drive shaft
27. Drive shaft and bevel drive sleeve
28. Drive shaft and bevel gears seal
29. Circlip
30. Ball bearing
31. Rear drive box
32. Drive box oil filler plug
33. Oil filler plug gasket
34. Oil level and drain plug
35. Oil level and drain plug washer
36. Bevel gear retaining nut
37. Drive box bolts nut
38. Taper roller in housing bearing
39. Housing bearing
40. Drive box-to-bearing housing gasket
40/1. Rear drive box seal
41. Bearing housing gasket
42. Bearings distance piece
43. Spacer-to-bearing shim
    Bevel gears spacer shim
44. Bevel set spacer
    Bevel set spacer
    Bevel set spacer
45. Bevel gear set
46. Flange
47. Flange fixing bolt lock plate
48. Drive box flange
49. Flange-to-spacer and spacer-to-drive box gasket
50. Shim 0.8 mm (0.031 in.)
    Shim 0.9 mm (0.035 in.)
    Shim 0.1 mm (0.039 in.)
    Shim 1.1 mm (0.043 in.)
    Shim 1.2 mm (0.047 in.)
    Shim 1.3 mm (0.051 in.)
51. Seal
52. Bevel gear-to-journal bolt
53. Bevel gear bolts-to-journal bearing lock plate
54. Ball bearing
55. Journal bearing
56. Roller bearing
57. Cage retaining ring
58. Seal
59. Bearing stop plate
60. Roller bearing stop plate screw
61. Flange securing screw washer

Lubrication System

Oil Pump

GEAR DRIVEN TIMING

Removal

1. Remove the alternator or generator drive belt and pulley. Drain the oil. Remove the timing case cover. Remove the oil pump gear using tool No. 32906302. Refer to the "Engine and Transmission" section for detailed procedures.
2. Unbolt and remove the oil pump.
3. If removal of the filter screen assembly is desired, remove the oil pan, the oil pipe (if necessary), and unbolt the filter assembly.

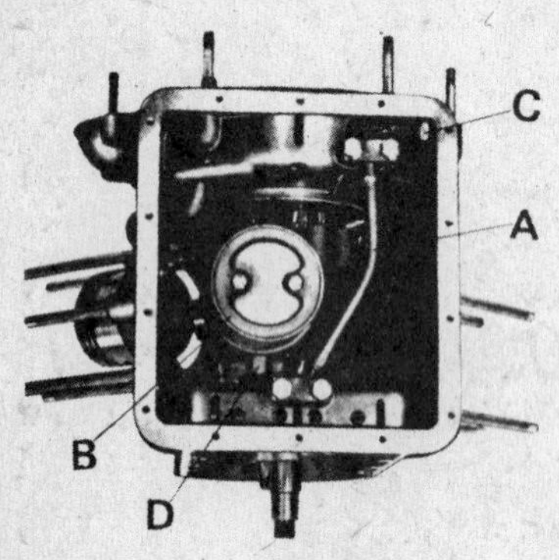

Lubrication system components: A, oil pipe; B, filter; C, pressure relief valve; D, oil pump

4. The oil pipe incorporates the oil pressure relief valve. Disassembly of this valve should not be undertaken as it will affect the pressure at which the valve opens.

Inspection

1. Measure the width of the pump gears and replace them if worn past their serviceable limit. The gears should be 15.983–15.994 mm (0.6293–0.6297 in.) wide.
2. Measure the depth of the gear housing in the pump body and replace the unit if it is worn greater than its serviceable limit of 16.000–16.027 mm (0.6299–0.6309 in.). The areas to be measured are indicated in the accompanying illustration.

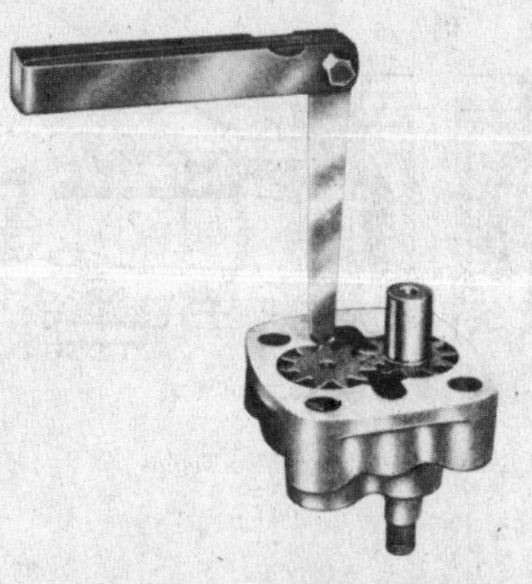

Checking oil pump gear clearance

3. Measure the outside diameter of the pump gears and replace them as a set if worn past their serviceable limit of 25.993–25.980 mm (1.0233–1.0227 in.).
4. Measure the inside diameter of the gear housings within the pump body and replace the unit if worn past their serviceable limits of 26.000–26.033 mm (1.0236–1.0249 in.).
5. Check the clearance between the pump gear shafts and the supports upon which they ride in the pump body. The outside diameter of the gear shafts should be within serviceable limits of 11.994–11.983–11.994 mm (0.4717–0.4722 in.), and the inside diameter of the supports should measure 12.000–12.018 mm (0.4724–0.4731 in.). The clearance between the supports and the shafts must be within 0.006–0.035 mm (0.00023–0.00137 in.) or the worn components must be replaced.

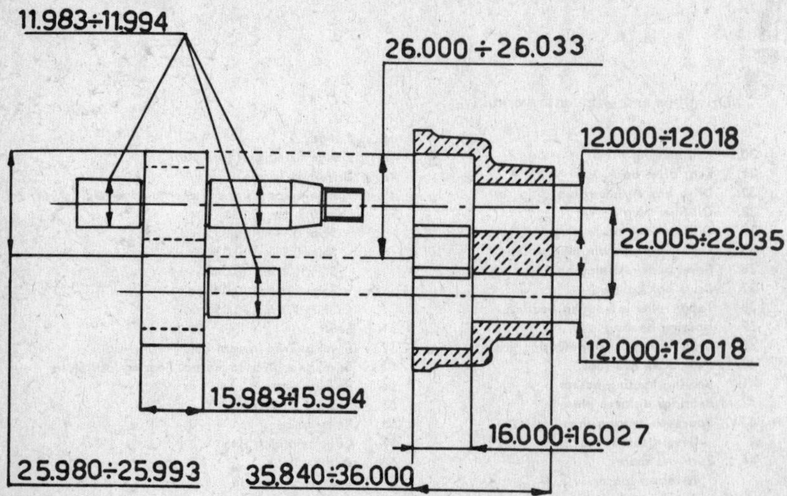

Oil pump dimensions (gear-driven timing)

Installation

1. Soak the oil pump in clean motor oil before installation.
2. Reverse the removal procedure, using new gaskets where applicable. Torque the oil pump and filter assembly bolts to 22 ft lbs.

CHAIN DRIVEN TIMING

Removal

1. Drain the oil. Remove the alternator and the timing case cover. Remove the timing sprockets and chain. Refer to the "Engine and Transmission" section for detailed procedures.
2. Unbolt and remove the oil pump.
3. If removal of the filter screen assembly is desired, remove the oil pan, the oil pipe (if necessary), and unbolt the filter assembly.
4. The oil pipe incorporates the oil pressure relief valve. Disassembly of this valve should not be undertaken, as it will affect the pressure at which the valve opens.

NOTE: *On some models the oil pipe and the pressure relief valve are incorporated into the oil pan casting.*

Inspection

1. The oil pump fitted to chain timing models is similar in operation to that found on the other machines, except that a double needle bearing is installed on the pump driven shaft. This is necessary because of the tension exerted by the chain on the oil pump sprocket.
2. Check the width of the pump gears. They should be 13.973–14.000 mm (0.5501–0.5511 in.).
3. Check the depth of the gear housings in the pump body. Standard value is 14.032–14.075 mm (0.5524–0.5541 in.).
4. Outside diameter of the pump gears should be 26.250–26.290 mm (1.0335–1.0350 in.).
5. The diameter of the gear housings in the pump body should be 26.340–26.390 mm (1.0370–1.0390 in.).
6. The outside diameter of the bearing race is 21.989–22.002 mm (0.8657–0.8662 in.).
7. The diameter of the bearing housing in the pump body should be 21.072–21.993 mm (0.8296–0.8659 in.).
8. The inside diameter of the bearing race should be 9.990–10.002 mm (0.3933–0.3938 in.).
9. Check the diameters of the pump shafts, 9.985–10.000 mm (0.3931–0.3937 in.).
10. Replace any parts which are not within the limits given.

Installation

1. Soak the oil pump in clean motor oil before installation.
2. Reverse the removal procedure, using new gaskets where applicable. When installing the timing sprocket assembly, refer to the "Valve Timing" section of "Engine and Transmission" to ensure that this is set correctly.

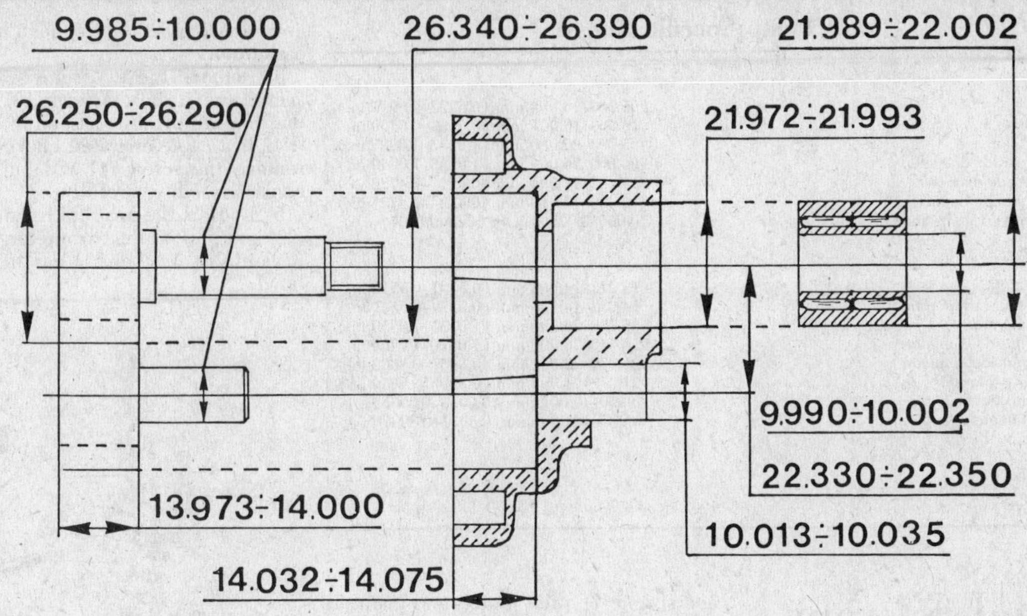

Oil pump dimensions (chain-driven timing)

Oil pump components (gear-driven timing)

Oil pressure solenoid (A)

3. Torque the oil pump and filter assembly bolts to 22 ft lbs.

Oil Pressure Relief Valve

The relief valve is mounted on the oil pipe inside the crankcase on most models, or in the oil pan casting on models with a cartridge type oil filter.

This is a maintenance-free item, which must be replaced if it fails to function properly.

The relief valve opens whenever oil pressure exceeds the prescribed rating. When the valve opens, the pressure drops and the valve will stay open until pressure returns to normal.

The standard maximum pressure is 35.6–42.7 psi (2.5–3.0 kg/sq cm) for the 700cc engine, and 54.0–60.0 psi (3.9–4.2 kg/sq cm) for all 750 and 850cc models.

Disassembly of the relief valve must not be undertaken as it will affect the operation of the valve.

Oil Breather

Situated on the top of the crankcase between the cylinders, the oil breather box contains a diaphragm held closed by a spring. When the oil pressure relief valve opens, the excess pressure is discharged into the breather box. The oil mist is separated out: the oil returning to the crankcase, and air released into the atmosphere.

If the machine has not been used for some time, it is possible for deposits to form on and eventually clog the breather diaphragm. This will result in oil leakages due to the lack of venting. If this is noted, remove the fuel tank, disconnect all of the lines running to the breather, remove the securing bolt, and remove the breather.

By means of a stiff, thin, rod inserted into the main breather box tube, check that the diaphragm is free to move. If it is not, soak the box in a suitable solvent until the diaphragm can be freed.

Oil Pressure Solenoid

A crankcase-mounted solenoid is fitted which is connected to a warning light to indicate whether proper oil pressure is being maintained.

The warning light should go out as soon as the engine is started. If it does not, or if it comes on while running, stop the engine immediately, and determine the cause of oil pressure failure.

Oil Lines

External oil lines which feed the cylinder heads should be checked for cracks or abrasion damage periodically, and replaced if even minor damage is noted.

Breather lines are rubber and should be inspected for dry-rotting or cracking, and replaced as necessary.

Oil Pump Specifications

Gear-Driven	
Gear width	15.983–15.994 mm (0.6293–0.6297 in.)
Depth of housing in pump body	16.000–16.027 mm (0.6299–0.6309 in.)
Gear outside diameter	25.993–25.980 mm (1.0233–1.0227 in.)
Gear housing inside diameter	26.000–26.003 mm (1.0236–1.0249 in.)
Gear shaft outside diameter	11.983–11.994 mm (0.4717–0.4722 in.)
Shaft support inside diameter	12.000–12.018 mm (0.4724–0.4731 in.)
Clearance between shafts and supports	0.006–0.035 mm (0.0023–0.0137 in.)
Chain-Driven	
Gear width	13.973–14.000 mm (0.5501–0.5511 in.)
Depth of housing in pump body	14.032–14.075 mm (0.5524–0.5541 in.)
Gear outside diameter	26.250–26.290 mm (1.0335–1.0350 in.)
Gear housing inside diameter	26.340–26.390 mm (1.0370–1.0390 in.)
Bearing race outside diameter	21.989–22.002 mm (0.8657–0.8662 in.)
Bearing housing diameter	21.072–21.993 mm (0.8296–0.8659 in.)
Bearing race inside diameter	9.990–10.002 mm (0.3933–0.3938 in.)
Pump shaft diameter	9.985–10.000 mm (0.3931–0.3937 in.)
Oil Pressure	
V700	35.6–42.7 psi (2.5–3.0 kgs/sq cm)
All other models	54.0–60.0 psi (3.8–4.2 kgs/sq cm)

Fuel System

The V700 uses a carburetor with a separate float bowl. All other models are equipped with Dell'Orto concentric float bowl carburetors featuring an accelerator pump, except for a very few 1973 or 1974 machines which were fitted with Amal Concentric carburetors.

Dell'Orto Carburetors

NOTE: *Numbers in the text refer to parts labelled in the exploded views of the carburetors.*

V700

Removal

1. After ensuring that the fuel petcocks are "off," remove the float bowl drain plug (22) to drain off the gas, catching it in a suitable container.
2. Remove the spring clip (2) from the carburetor cap ring nut (1), then unscrew the nut and remove the cap (3), and the spring, slide, and needle (4, 5, 6) as an assembly.
3. Disconnect the fuel feed line from the float bowl. Alternately, remove the banjo bolt (18), banjo (19), and filter screen (20) from the float bowl.
4. Unscrew the choke assembly (16).
5. Loosen the manifold clamp screw and remove the carburetor.

Disassembly

1. If disassembly of the throttle slide assembly is desired, compress the slide spring to disengage the throttle stop rod from the slide. The components can then be separated.
2. Remove the float bowl banjo if this has not yet been done, removing the filter screen, then the float bowl cap (17), float and needle (23, 24).
3. Remove the float bowl securing bolt (10), venturi block (6/1), pilot air screw and spring (7), pilot jet (8), and main jet (13), and jet holder and needle jet (14).

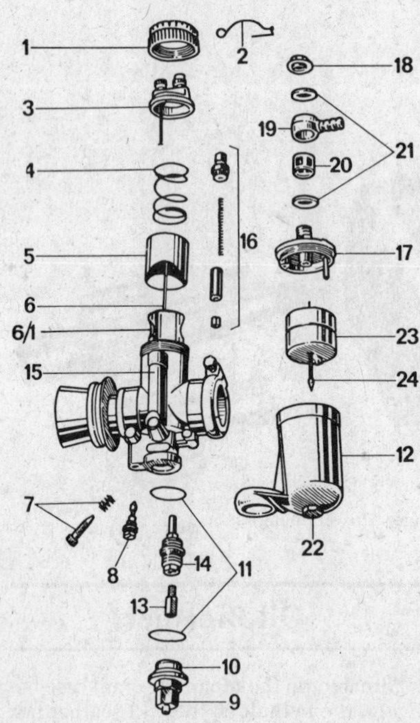

Carburetor components (V700). See text for references

Assembly and Installation

1. Use new gaskets and o-rings.
2. When installing the pilot air screw, turn it in until it bottoms lightly, then back it out 1–1½ turns.
3. When fitting the carburetor, be sure it is positioned vertically. Check throttle action and check for fuel leaks before starting the machine.

750 AND 850 MODELS

Removal

1. Removal of the gask tank is recommended to facilitate carburetor removal. Remove the air cleaner, if fitted.
2. Ensuring that the fuel petcocks are "off," disconnect the fuel feed line at the carburetor.
3. Remove the two screws (8) which secure the carburetor cap (13) and pull out the throttle slide assembly.
4. If a cable-operated choke is fitted, remove the screw (1) and pull out the choke assembly carefully.
5. Loosen the manifold clamp screw (22) and pull off the carburetor, handling it carefully, as there is gas in the float bowl.

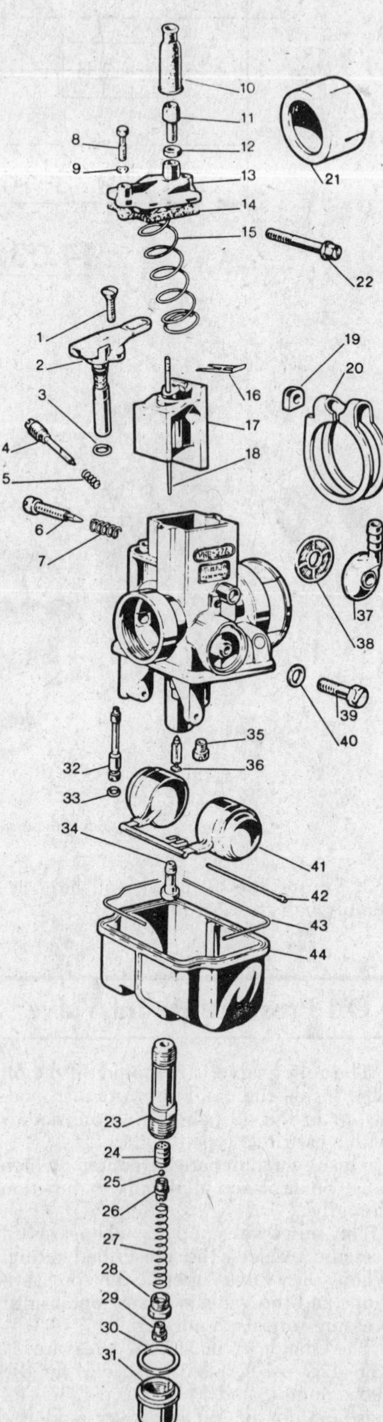

Carburetor components (All except V700). See text for references

Disassembly

1. Disassembly of the throttle slide components is easily accomplished by removing the return spring from its seat on the slide and disengaging the cable. To remove the needle, push the clip out with a screwdriver. Note needle clip position before this is done.
2. On models with a lever-operated choke, remove the securing screw (1) and carefully pull out the choke assembly (2, 3).
3. Remove the fuel feed banjo screw (39), the banjo (37), and filter screen (38).
4. Remove the float bowl nut (31).
5. Unscrew and remove the main jet and accelerator pump assembly (23–29). It is not necessary to disassemble these components for routine cleaning. If replacement of the main jet is desired, it may be unscrewed from the accelerator pump assembly without disturbing the other components.
6. Remove the float bowl (44).
7. Pull out the float pivot pin (42), and lift off the float (41) and float needle (36).
8. Remove the needle jet (34). Unscrew the pilot jet (35) and the starter jet (32).
9. Remove the pilot screw (4) and the throttle stop screw (6) and their springs.

Removing the float assembly

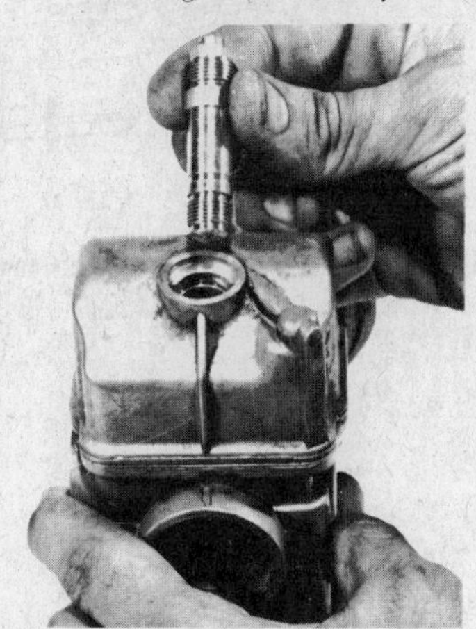

Removing the main jet and accelerator pump assembly

Assembly and Installation

1. The use of new gaskets and o-rings is recommended, although they may be reused if undamaged.
2. When installing the pilot screw, turn it in until it bottoms lightly, then back it out the number of turns indicated in the "Carburetor Specifications" chart.
3. When installing the carburetor, be sure it is positioned vertically.
4. The throttle slide consists of two parallel plates. This must be installed so that the smaller of the plates faces *away from* the engine.
5. Check throttle action and check for fuel leaks before starting the machine.

Concentric Carburetors

A few late model machines may be fitted with Amal Concentric carburetors. Disassembly of the unit will be clarified by referring to the exploded view provided.

Petcocks and Fuel Lines

1. The electrovalve needs no maintenance. If it is operating correctly, there will be a distinct "click" when the ignition key is turned.
2. The manual petcock should be operated from time to time to check operation. If the "reserve" position has not been used for extended periods of time, it is possible that quantities of water may accumulate in the bottom of the gas tank. Disconnect the fuel line at the manual petcock to check operation in all three positions. When in the "Off" position, the petcock must stop fuel flow completely, or replacement is in order.
3. Both petcocks are equipped with a fuel filter screen. At extended intervals, they should be removed from the gas tank, and the filters washed in solvent to remove any trapped matter.

Carburetor Specifications

	V700	*V750*	*750 Sport*	*V850*	*850T*	*850-T3*
Carburetor type	S.S.I.	VHB29CD/CS	VHB30CD/CS	VHB29CD/CS	VHB30CD/CS	VHB30CD/CS
Venturi diameter (mm)	29	29	30	29	30	30
Throttle slide	80	60	40	60	40	40
Atomizer	265	265	265	265	265	265
Main jet	120	145	142	145	142	120
Pilot jet	55	45	50	45	50	50
Needle	M14	SV5	V9	SV9	V9	V9
Float	14 g	NA	10 g	NA	10 g	10 g
Starter jet	——	80	80	80	80	80
Needle clip setting (notches from top)	3	2	2	2	2	2
Pilot screw (turns out) left	1–1½	1½–2	2–2¼	1¾–2	2–2¼	1½
right	1–1½	2–2½	2¼–2¾	1–1½	2¼–2¾	1½

NA Not available
—— Not applicable

4. Check fuel lines periodically for cracks, dry-rotting, or abrasion damage. Replace them if any is noted.

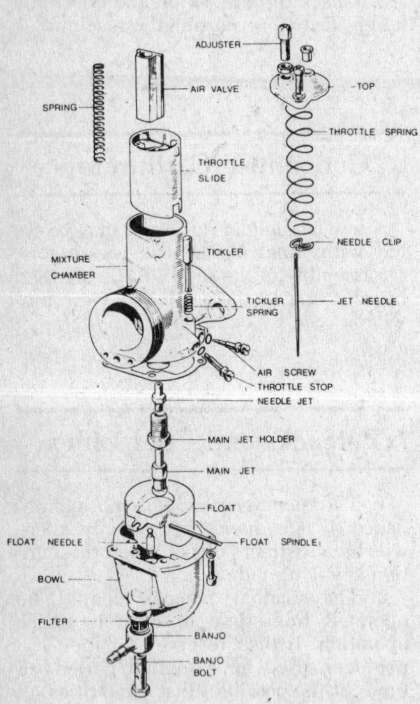

Amal Concentric carburetor components

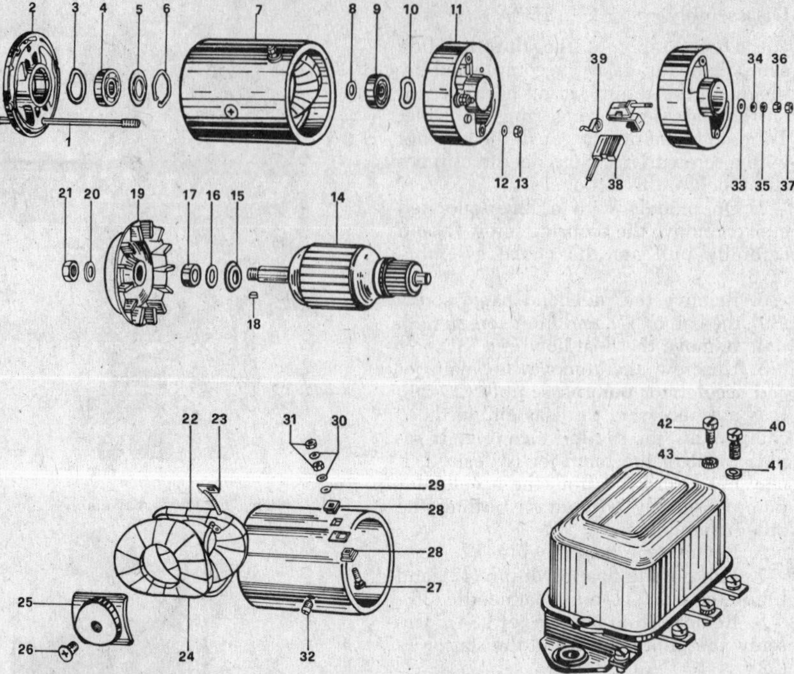

Generator components

1. Generator DN 62 M, complete
2. Stud
3. End cover
4. Spring washer
5. Grease retainer
6. Retaining ring bearing
7. Body complete with coils generator
8. Flat washer
9. Ball bearing
10. Washer spring
11. Holder assembly brush
12. Washer spring
13. Fixing nut cover
14. Armature
15. Grease retainer
16. Shim 0.1 mm
    Shim 0.2 mm
17. Spacer
18. Woodruff key
19. Pulley with fan
20. Washer spring
21. Securing nut pulley
22. Oil with square terminal feed
23. Cable connector grounding
24. Coil with small terminal field
25. Shoe pole
26. Pole shoe screw
27. Terminal screw DF
28. Insulating block
29. Flat washer
30. Washer spring
31. Terminal nut
32. Dowel locating
33. Washer insulating
34. Flat washer
35. Washer spring
36. Terminal securing nut
37. Terminal end nut
38. Brush
39. Spring brush
    IR 50 BA complete regulator
40. Screw for terminals D/61 DF, OF, D/31
41. Washer spring
42. Screw for DF terminal
43. Toothed washer

Electrical System

V700, V750, and V850 utilize a DC generator in conjunction with a mechanical voltage regulator for charging. The ignition system has a single contact point set with rotor and distributor cap.

750 Sport and 850T/T3 models are fitted with an alternator, rectifier, and regulator. The ignition system has two sets of points, and twin coils.

DC Charging System

GENERATOR

The models with DC generators come equipped with a Marelli DN 62 Type N generator which, at 2400 rpm, produces 300 watts at 12 volts. The unit is of the open construction type, has two poles, and operates in conjunction with a separate regulator unit. The rotor spins on two permanently lubricated ball bearings which are intended to be maintenance free items. The cover assembly is attached by means of two studs which pass through the unit. There are two terminals D+/51 (A) and DF (B), located on the commutator end of the housing which are used to connect the regulator wiring to the generator. The D+ terminal is connected to the positive brush and the DF terminal is connected to one end of the rotor assembly. When the generator is attached to the regulator, the D+ and DF terminals of both units must be connected.

Generator Data

Generator specifications applicable at room temperature (20° C, 68° F).

NOTE: *When carrying out tests, disconnect possible grounds.*

Field winding resistance: $4.6 \pm 0.2\ \Omega$

Connection speed (no load) tension 13V:1500 rpm

Load rating (tension 13V, current 23A):2300 rpm

Check dialectric rigidity by feeding 50V, 50 Hz AC for three seconds. Check insulation resistance by feeding 500V DC. Resistance must be over 2M Ω.

Dimensions

Brush spring load: 1000–1100 gms (2.2–2.4 lbs.)

ID of pole shoes: 65.7–66.0 mm (2.59–2.60 in.)

OD of rotor: 64.9–65.0 mm (2.55–2.56 in.)

Generator with Regulator

Connection voltage: 11.5–13.0V

Recovery current: 2–8A

No-load adjusting voltage: 13.8–14.4V

Current limiter on: 28.5–30.5A

Load at rated voltage: 300W

Troubleshooting the Generating System

The following is the most direct approach to take in locating generating system difficulties:

1. The following items are indicators of a faulty generating system:

a. Failure of the generator light to go off.

b. Repeated or sudden battery discharging.

c. Excessive battery water evaporation indicating an overcharged state.

2. In testing the generating system do not commit the following mistakes which will result in damage to the system:

a. Do not reverse the generator polarity.

b. Do not short or ground any wires unless specifically instructed to do so.

c. Do not operate the engine while the generator output terminal is disconnected.

d. Always connect positive to positive and the negative to negative when connecting a charger or booster to the battery.

e. Keep the generator and regulator units connected.

3. Check for a faulty generator light in the following manner:

a. If the ignition is on and the light remains on, disconnect the generator leads at their terminals. If the light stays on, check for a short between these two leads.

b. If the generator light doesn't go on when the ignition switch is turned on, check the bulb; if satisfactory, check for a short between the two leads. If the light still doesn't come on, reverse the two leads. If the light still doesn't come on, check for an open circuit in the following manner:

(A) Connect the two leads of a voltmeter to ground and the DF generator terminal and check for a reading. Go on to the next step if a reading is obtained. No reading indicates an open circuit between the DF terminal and the battery. Correct this, then see if the light goes on when the ignition is turned on.

(B) Either connect or disconnect both generator leads, turn the ignition switch on, and momentarily ground the D+ terminal lead only. If the light does not come on, check for a burned out bulb, blown fuse, faulty bulb socket, or an open condition between the D+ terminal and the ignition switch. Remove the ground from the D+ terminal if the light comes on and, with both terminals connected, ground the generator.

(C) If the light still hasn't come on, check for open circuits between the wiring harness and the No. 1 terminal, generator brushes, slip rings, and field windings.

(D) If the light came on in the first step and there was a voltmeter reading, replace the regulator.

(E) Consult the next section if the light stays on when the motor is running.

4. Locate the reason for an undercharged battery in the following manner:

a. Make sure the reason the battery keeps going down is not because the accessories have been left on without the engine running.

b. Check the drive belt for proper tension.

c. Check the battery for shorting with a voltmeter or hydrometer indicated by one or more dead cells.

d. Inspect all writing for loose or poor connections.

e. Connect the leads of a voltmeter from ground to the generator "BAT" terminal, then the no. 1 terminal, then the no. 2 terminal. No reading indicates an open condition between the battery and the voltmeter connection.

DC Generator Troubleshooting

Possible Causes	*Remedy*
Generator does not charge battery	
Blown fuse on generator or battery (+) terminal	Check and, if necessary, replace fuse. Fuse contact could also be defective or fuse could be improperly housed in its seat
Break in charge circuit	Locate break and repair it. Breaks are generally due to loose or oxidated terminals
Slack generator belt	Adjust belt to correct tension
Faulty battery	Check battery
Generator does not charge battery	
Defective contact of brushes with commutator; dirty commutator; brushes not freely sliding in holders or worn out	Clean commutator, clean brush holders, or replace brushes
Grounded brush holder	Reset brush holder insulation and replace it if necessary
Grounded or broken rotor winding	Replace rotor
Short-circuited rotor	Clean carefully between rotor blades. Make sure that there are no welding drops on front face and especially on back side of commutator ring. If so, remove them. Failing to attain a good result, replace rotor.
Rotor unwelded from commutator	Renew welding if rotor does not show any other fault
Broken, short-circuited, or grounded field windings	Replace field coils unless grounding is spotted and eliminated
Generator lacks residual magnetism	Re-excite generator by connecting, for an instant, the (+) and (−) field winding terminals to (+) and (−) battery terminals
Faulty regulator	Replace
Generator is slow to start battery charge	
Faulty regulator unit	Replace
Partially short-circuited rotor	Replace rotor
Partially short-circuited field windings	Replace field windings
Grounded field windings	Replace windings if grounding cannot be eliminated
Battery gets only partially charged	
Oxidation of regulator unit contacts	Clean regulator unit contacts
Loose or defective connections inside regulator unit	Check and make connections positive
Faulty battery	Check battery
Generator overcharges battery	
Faulty generator grounding	Re-establish connection
Excitation circuit and generator (+) in direct short circuit	Overhaul system and eliminate fault
Faulty regulator windings	Replace
Battery discharges over generator	
Faulty regulator unit	Replace
Generator tension is not constant and exceeds prescribed value	
Faulty regulator unit	Replace
Tension oscillates and is not constant	
Oxidation of regulator unit contacts	Clean regulator unit contacts
Regulator unit with altered air gaps, loose screws, etc.	Replace
Overheating of generator	
Short circuited rotor	Replace rotor
Regulator unit damaged or out of setting	Replace
Brushes wear out too quickly	
Offset commutator	Turn commutator and remove excess mica
Excessive pressure of brush holder springs	Take spring pressure down to correct load
Brushes of poor quality	Replace brushes and fit with original parts
Excessive sparking at commutator	
Break in rotor winding	Replace rotor
Rotor unwelded from commutator	Renew weldings if there is no other fault
Offset commutator	Turn commutator and remove excess mica
Loose brush holder springs	Replace springs or restore correct spring load
Worn out brushes	Replace brushes
Mica protruding from commutator bars	Remove excess mica

DC Generator Troubleshooting (cont.)

	Noisy generator operation
Rotor rubs against pole shoes	Make sure pole shoes are correctly secured to casing. Replace bearings

5. Check the generator in the following manner if the problem hasn't yet been discovered:

a. Disconnect the battery ground wire, connect an ammeter so the current will pass through it from the generator D+ terminal to the lead which was connected to the D+ terminal, and reconnect the battery ground wire.

b. Turn on all of the accessories and attach a carbon pile across the battery terminals. Operate the engine until the maximum current output is obtained.

c. If the generator is good, amperage output will be within 10 percent of its rated output. Go back and recheck the previous steps.

d. Ground the generator by inserting a screwdriver through the generator test hole if amperage isn't within 10 percent of its normal rating.

e. Recheck with a carbon pile as described above. If the reading is still not within 10 percent, the regulator must be replaced.

f. Recheck with a carbon pile and overhaul the generator if the reading still isn't within 10 percent of its rated amperage.

6. Locate the reason for an overcharged battery in the following manner:

a. Check the state of battery charge with a voltmeter or hydrometer.

b. Connect the leads of a voltmeter to ground and to the generator DF terminal to check for an open reading (zero). The voltage, in any case, should not exceed 12 volts at 0° F. Discrepancies in measurements taken in cold and hot conditions are to be expected.

7. If the above test proves that the circuit is good and excessive water evaporation still indicates an overcharged battery, separate the generator end frames and check the field windings for a shorted condition in the following manner:

a. Connect the leads of an ohmmeter from the brush lead clip to the end frame and then reverse the connections. The ohmmeter must be set on its lowest range scale.

b. If both readings are zero, check for a grounded brush lead. This is probably caused by a missing or damaged insulating washer or insulating screw sleeve.

c. If, after replacing the insulating elements, both readings are still zero, the regulator is defective and must be replaced.

REGULATOR

These models use the Marelli IR 50 BA type regulator which is a three coil unit and is mounted to the frame. The unit is not repairable or adjustable and must be replaced if defective.

AC Charging System

The following applies to 750 Sport and 850T/T3 models which are fitted with an alternator.

ALTERNATOR

NOTE: *Disconnect all wires at the alternator before carrying out the following tests.*

1. The commutator slip-rings should be cleaned with a solvent to remove any carbon build-up. Minimum commutator diameter is 28.6 mm (1.13 in.).
2. Check the carbon brushes for wear. Both must make good contact with the commutator. Replace the brushes if wear seems excessive.
3. Check for continuity between the commutator slip-rings. If an ohmmeter is available, resistance should be 6.3 ohms. If there is no continuity, replace the rotor.
4. Check for continuity between the stator terminals. Resistance should be 0.5 ohms. If there is no continuity, or if resistance is infinite, replace the stator.

REGULATOR

The regulator is located beneath the gas tank. The following specifications apply at 4500 rpm:

Test load: 13 A
Adjusting voltage: 13.9–14.8 V
Set load at nominal voltage: 330–360 W

RECTIFIER

The easiest and surest rectifier test is done by replacing the suspect unit with one known to be in working order.

Ignition System

1. Noise suppressor spark plug caps are fitted which have a resistance of 5,000 ohms. In the event of a misfire or lack of spark not attributable to other components, check the resistance of the cap(s). Replace them as a set if resistance is not close to the specification. Broken or cracked insulation inside the caps may also cause ignition problems, especially in wet weather.
2. Ignition coil resistance across the low tension terminals should be about 3 ohms. Resistance between the high tension (spark plug) lead and one of the low tension terminals should be about 6,200 ohms.

If readings are not close to these specifications, replace the coil.

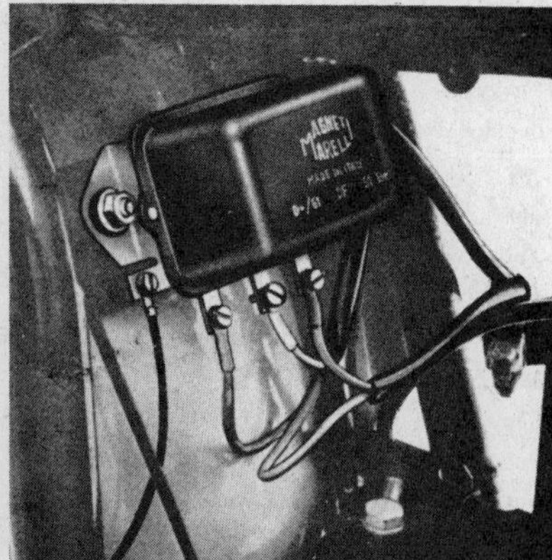

Voltage regulator

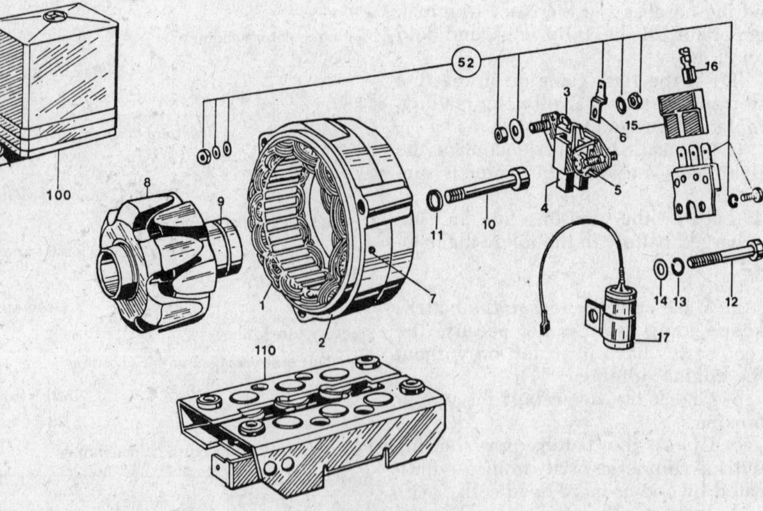

Alternator components

1. Stator
2. Stator housing
3. Brush holder
4. Brushes
5. Springs
6. Clamp
7. Band
8. Rotor
9. Slip ring
10. Rotor bolt
11. Washer
12. Bolt
13. Lockwasher
14. Washer
15. Casing
16. Connector
17. Condensor
52. Clamp parts set
100. Voltage regulator
110. Rectifier

Electric Starter

V700, V750, V850, 850T/T3

These models use a starter motor with an integral solenoid. When the starter button is pushed, the current passes through the solenoid, which is an electromagnetic switch and the switch makes contact with the two high tension terminals visible on the rear of the solenoid. This allows current to flow from the battery to the starter motor which then begins to turn. At the same time, the movement of the solenoid switch referred to moves a lever which is attached to the starter motor gear, forcing the gear into engagement with the crankshaft ring gear.

750 SPORT

The operation of this starter motor is similar to that described above, except that the solenoid is not involved in engaging the starter motor gear. Instead, it merely allows current flow through the starter motor windings. When the starter turns, centrifugal force and a threaded armature shaft cause the starter motor gear to move along the armature shaft to engage the crankshaft ring gear.

TROUBLESHOOTING

The most common starter fault is due to wear of the armature bushings. This will cause the armature to contact the field coils, creating a short circuit.

This fault is especially common in models which use the 0.4 hp Bosch starter (750 Sport).

In this case, the starter will turn the engine over slowly or not at all and will show signs of overheating if repeated attempts at starting are made. When the starter button is pushed, the warning lights will dim indicating that the starter is drawing current.

This trouble can easily be checked by removing the starter. Check for play of the armature shaft. There should be none. If play is noticeable, the drive side bushing is worn.

On the starter found on models except the Sport, bushing replacement is simple since it is outboard of the starter gear.

On the Sport starter, it is necessary to remove the starter gear. This is accomplished by pushing down the sleeve on the drive end of the armature shaft, which will reveal a lock ring in a groove. Pry out the ring, and remove the sleeve, spring, and starter gear assembly. Remove the two through-studs and take off the drive side end plate complete with bushing.

At this point the starter should be handled carefully, since if the brush side armature shaft cap has been removed, it is possible for the armature to fall out of the starter body.

If the bushing is damaged, it can be purchased already installed in a new end plate. This is recommended. If the starter has been subjected to some stress, it is possible that the end plate itself is cracked.

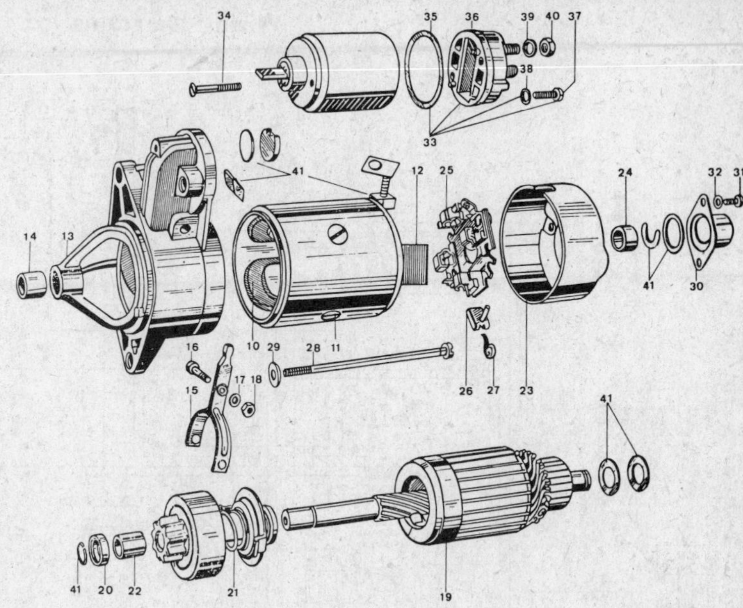

Electric starter components (All except Sport)

10. Field coil assembly
11. Field coil screws
12. Insulator
13. Ratchet cover, with bush
14. Bush, drive side
15. Engagement lever
16. Screw
17. Washer
18. Nut
19. Armature
20. Stop ring
21. Starter ratchet assembly
22. Starter ratchet bush
23. End cover, brush side, with bush
24. Bush, end cover
25. Brush holder
26. Brush set
27. Brush spring
28. Through bolt
29. Washer
30. Cap
31. Screw
32. Washer
33. Solenoid
34. Screw
35. Shim
36. Cap
37. Screw
38. Washer
39. Washer
40. Nut
41. Rebuild kit

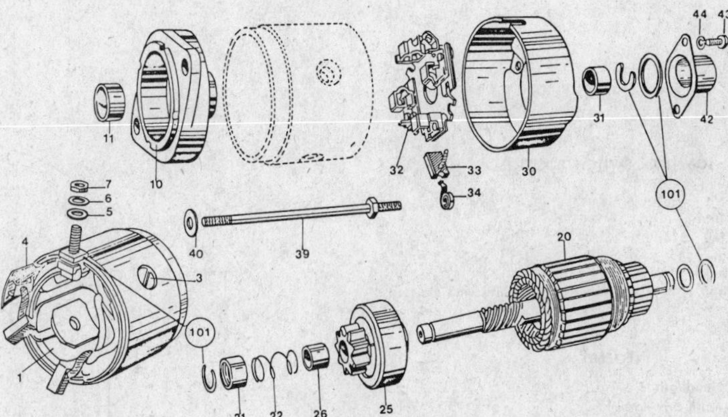

Electric starter components (V7 Sport)

1. Field coil assembly
3. Screw
4. Insulator
5. Washer
6. Washer
7. Nut
10. Drive side end cover
11. Drive side bushing
20. Armature
21. Sleeve
22. Spring
25. Starter gear assembly
26. Bushing
30. Brush side end cover
31. Brush side bushing
32. Brush holder
33. Brushes
34. Brush spring
39. Through bolt
40. Washer
42. End cap
43. Screw
44. Washer
101. Rebuild kit

Starter engagement mechanism

1. Control lever
2. Release spring
3. Release spring housing ring
4. Sleeve
5. Coupling spring
6. Coupling hub
7. Flywheel ring gear
8. Pinion gear
9. Roller freewheel

Wiring Diagrams

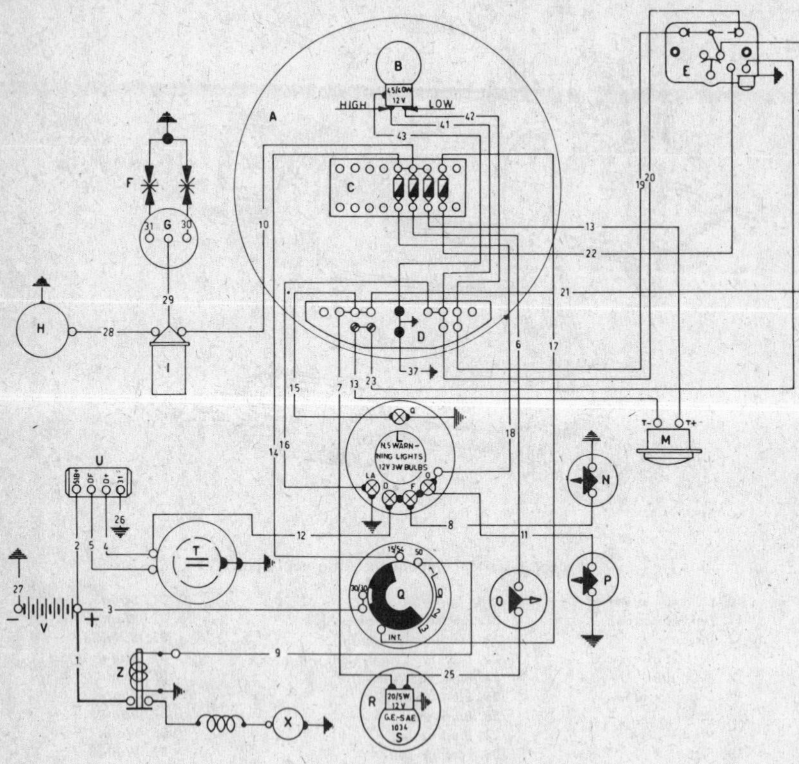
V700

IGNITION SWITCH POSITION

0—
1—30/30 Int.
2—30/20 Int. 15/54
3—30/30 Int. 15/54 50

LEGEND

A Headlight
B Main light bulb
C Terminal block with fuses
D Distributing block
E Light switch and horn button
F Spark plug
G Distributor
H Contact breaker
I H.T. coil
L Speedometer and warning light bulbs
M Horn
N Neutral indicator cut-out
O Stop light cut-out
P Oil pressure cut-out
Q Ignition switch
R Number plate and tail light
Plate illumination and stop light
T Generator
U Regulator
V Battery
Z Starter motor relay
X Starter motor

IGNITION SWITCH POSITION

0—
1—30/30 Int.
2—30/30 Int. 15/54
3—30/30 Int. 15/54 50

Note: Position 3 does not serve on machines with starter button.

LEGEND

A Headlight
B Main driving lights
C Terminal block with fuses
D Distributing block
E Light switch and horn button
F Spark plugs
G Distributor
H Contact breaker
I H.T. coil
L Starter button
M Horn
N Neutral indicator cut-out
O Stop light cut-out
P Oil pressure cut-out
Q Ignition switch
R Number plate and tail light
S Plate illumination and stop light
T Generator
U Regulator
V Battery
Z Starter motor solenoid
X Starter motor
AA Speedometer (with illumination bulb)
BB Rev-counter (with illumination bulb)
CC Lights indicator (red)
DD Neutral indicator (orange)
EE Generator charge indicator (red)
FF Oil pressure indicator (red)
K Relay for starter selenoid

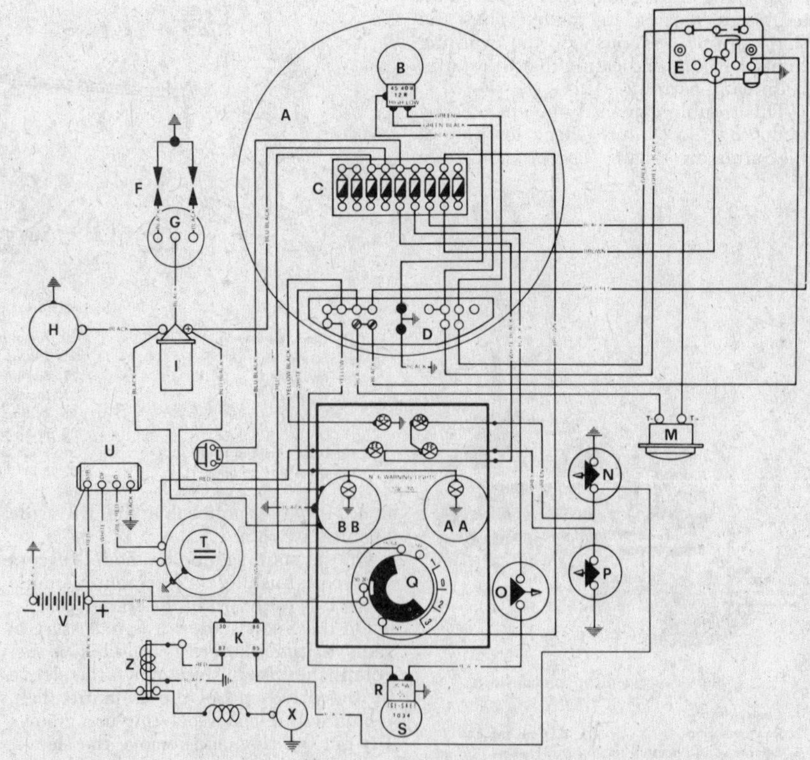
V750

Wiring Diagrams

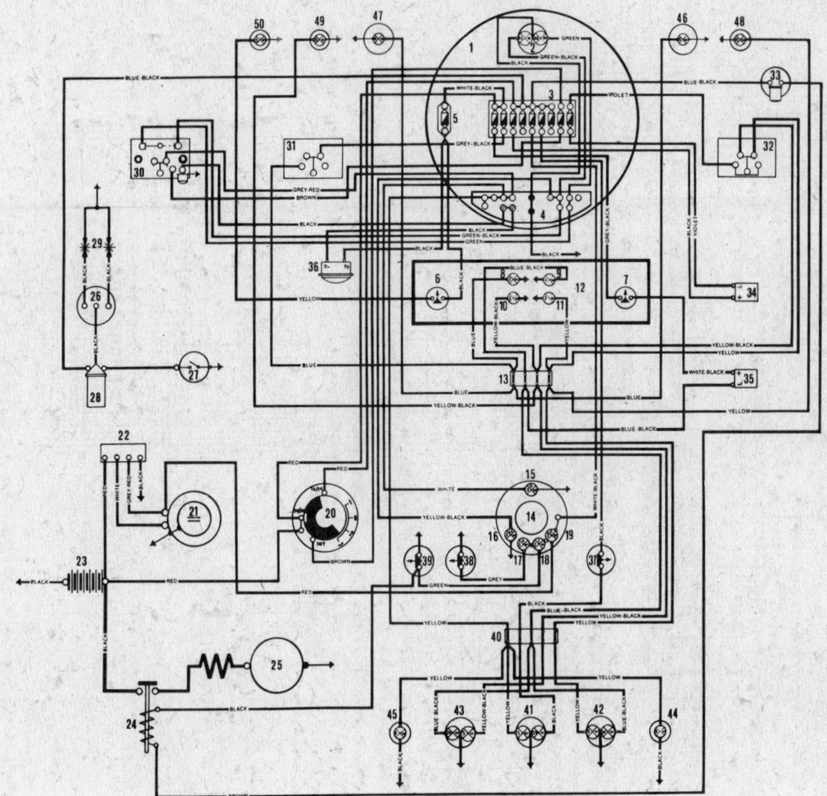

V750 (Police)

LEGEND

1. Headlight
2. High and low beam lamp (45/40W—12V)
3. Terminal block with fuses
4. Distribution block in headlight
5. Fuse for horn and additional light
6. Cut-out for additional light
7. Cut-out for rear amber flashers
8. Red warning lamp for front red lights (bulb 3W—12V)
9. Blue warning light for amber rear lamps (bulb 3W—12V)
10. Green warning lamp for L/H flasher (bulb 3W—12V)
11. Green warning lamp for R/H flasher (bulb 3W—12V)
12. Instrument panel
13. Front distributing block
14. Mile speedometer
15. Speedometer illumination lamp (3W—12V)
16. Red warning light for high beam (bulb 3W—12V)
17. Red oil pressure indicator (bulb 3W—12V)
18. Amber neutral indicator lamp (bulb 3W—12V)
19. Red indicator light for insufficient battery charge
20. Ignition switch
21. Generator
22. Regulator
23. Battery
24. Starter motor relay
25. Starter motor
26. Distributor
27. Contact breaker
28. H.T. coil
29. Spark plug
30. Light switch and horn button
31. Front side red lights switch
32. Turn signal flashing lamps switch
33. Start button
34. Turn flashers cut-out (28W—12V)
35. Amber rear lights cut-out (40W—12V)
36. Horn
37. Stop light cut-out, rear brake
38. Oil pressure solenoid
39. Neutral indicator cut-out
40. Rear distributing block
41. Number plate and stop light (5/20W—12V)
42. R/H rear light amber flasher (bulb 5/20W—12V)
43. L/H rear light amber flasher (bulb 5/20W—12V)
44. R/H rear light, blue (bulb 5W—12V)
45. L/H rear light, blue (bulb 5W—12V)
46. R/H red front light (bulb 15W—12V)
47. L/H red front light (bulb 15W—12V)
48. R/H amber turn indicator (bulb 15W—12V)
49. L/H amber turn indicator (bulb 15W—12V)
50. Additional light for police duties
51. Stop light cut-out, front brake

IGNITION SWITCH POSITION

0—
1—30/30 Int.
2—30/30 Int. 15/54
3—Not applicable for systems incorporating starter button

Wiring Diagrams

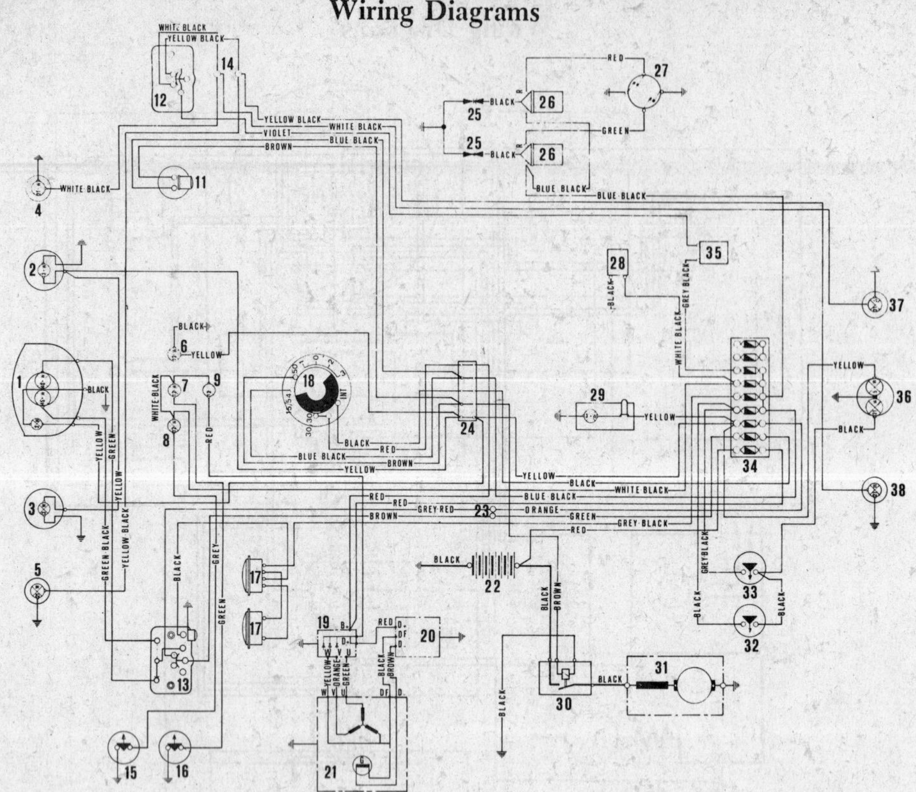

V7 Sport

1. Headlight (lamp—40/45W—12V and 4W—12V)
2. Speedometer (3W—12V)
3. Tachometer (3W—12V)
4. R/H front turn light indicator (21W—12V bulb)
5. L/H front turn light indicator (21W—12V bulb)
6. Green warning light (12W—12V bulb)
7. Orange warning light neutral indicator (12W—12V bulb)
8. Red warning light oil pressure (12W—12V)
9. Red warning light generator charge (12W—12V bulb)
11. Start button
12. Turn lights switch
13. Light switch and horn button
14. 3-way faston
15. Oil pressure indicator cut-out
16. Neutral indicator cut-out
17. Horn
18. Ignition switch
19. Rectifier
20. Voltage regulator
21. Alternator
22. Batteries
23. Connectors
24. Distributing Block
25. Spark plug
26. H.T. coil
27. Double contact breaker
28. Electrovalve (fuel)
29. Courtesy lamp (3W—12V bulb)
30. Starter motor relay
31. Starter motor
32. Front stop light cut-out
33. Rear stop light cut-out
34. Terminal block with fuses
35. Flasher unit
36. Number plate and stop light (21/5W—12V bulb)
37. R/H rear turn light indicator (21W—12V bulb)
38. L/H rear turn light indicator (21W—12V bulb)

IGNITION SWITCH POSITION

0—
1—30/30 Int.
2—30/30 Int. 15/54
3—30/30 Int. 15/54 50

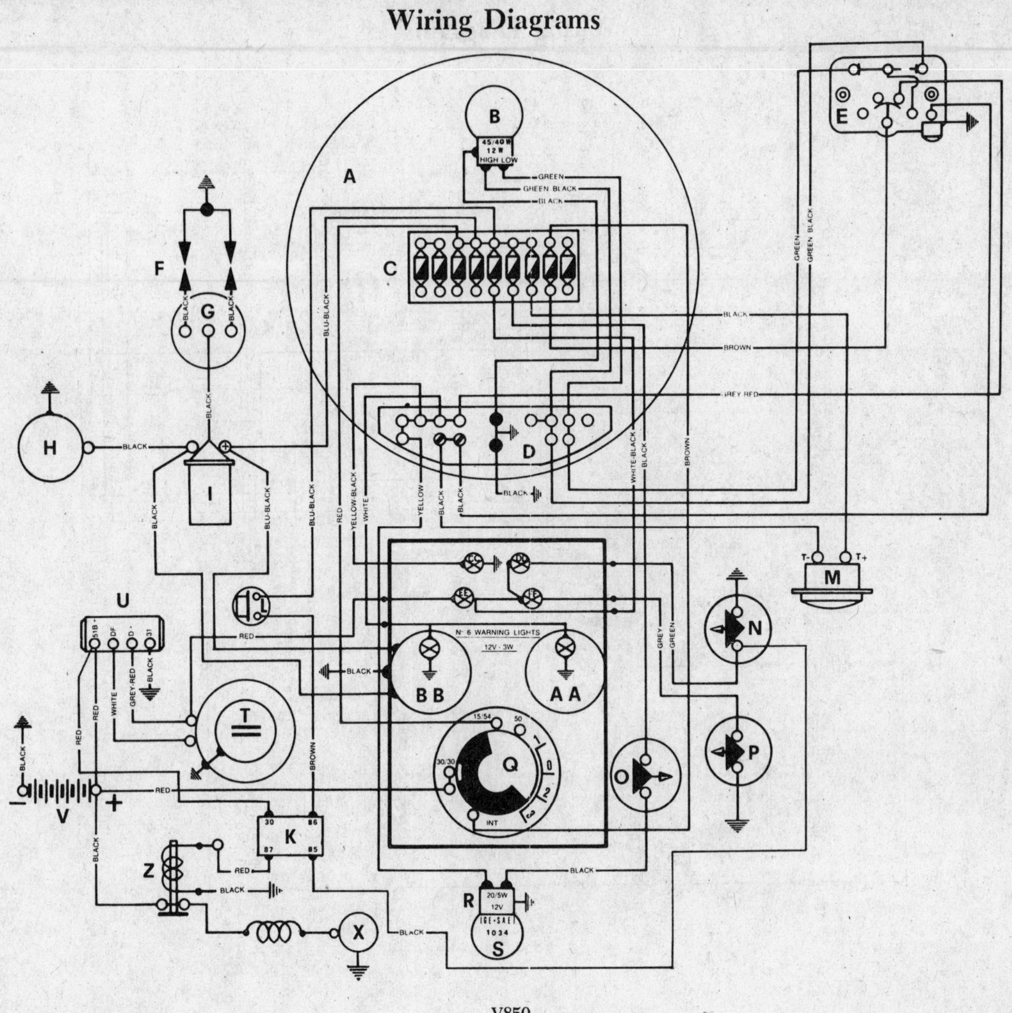

V850

LEGEND

A Headlight
B Main driving lights
C Terminal block with fuses
D Distributing block
E Light switch and horn button
F Spark plugs
G Distributor
H Contact breaker
I H.T. coil
L Starter button
M Horn
N Neutral indicator cut-out
O Stop light cut-out
P Oil pressure cut-out
Q Ignition switch
R Number plate and tail light
S Plate illumination and stop light
T Generator
U Regulator
V Battery
Z Starter motor solenoid
X Starter motor
AA Speedometer (with illumination bulb)
BB Rev-counter (with illumination bulb)
CC Lights on indicator (red)
DD Neutral indicator (orange)
EE Generator charge (red)
FF Oil pressure indicator (red)
K Relay for starter solenoid

IGNITION SWITCH POSITION

0—
1—30/30 Int.
2—30/30 Int. 15/54
3—30/30 Int. 15/54 50

Note: Position 3 does not serve on machines with starter button.

Wiring Diagrams

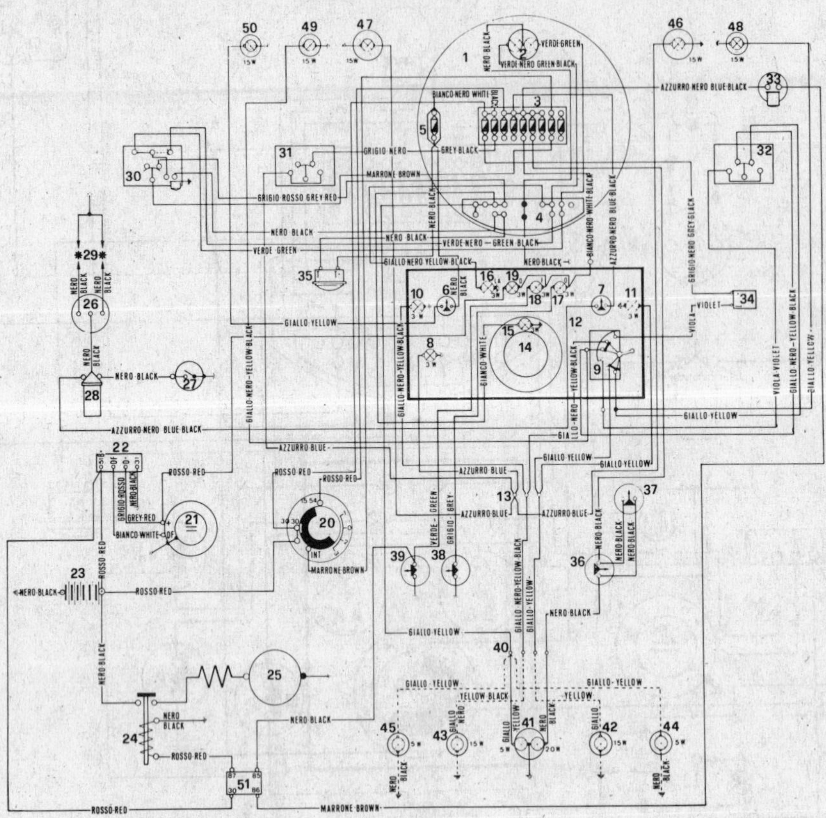

V850 (Police)

LEGEND

1. Headlight
2. High and low beam bulb (45/40W—12V)
3. Terminal block with fuses
4. Distributing block in headlight
5. Horn fuse
6. Courtesy light cut-out
7. Coil disconnection cut-out
8. Red warning light, front red lights on
9. Turn lights and rear flashing lights switch
10. Green warning light, L/H turn light on (3W—12V bulb)
11. Green warning light, R/H turn light on (3W—12V bulb)
12. Instrument panel
13. Shunting connection, front
14. Mile speedometer
15. Bulb, speed, illumination (3W—12V)
16. Red warning light, high light on (3W—12V bulb)
17. Red warning light, oil pressure (3W—12V bulb)
18. Orange warning light, neutral indicator (3W—12V bulb)
19. Red warning light, generator charge (3W—12V)
20. Ignition switch
21. Generator
22. Voltage regulator
23. Battery
24. Starter motor relay
25. Starter motor
26. Distributor
27. Contact breaker
28. Coil
29. Spark plug
30. Light switch and horn button
31. Ground switch for relay
32. Turn lights, front red lights, and radio control switch
33. Starter button
34. Flasher unit for turn lights, and rear lights
35. Horn
36. Rear brake stop cut-out
37. Front brake stop cut-out
38. Oil pressure hydraulic cut-out
39. Neutral indicator cut-out
40. Rear shunting connections
41. Plate and stop light (5/21W—12V bulb)
42. Rear orange flashing light (21W—12V bulb), R/H
43. Rear orange flashing light, L/H (21W—12V bulb)
44. Rear R/H blue light (5W—12V bulb)
45. Rear L/H blue light (5W—12V bulb)
46. Front R/H red light (21W—12V bulb)
47. Front L/H red light (21W—12V bulb)
48. Front R/H turn light indicator (orange) (15W—12V bulb)
49. Front L/H orange turn light indicator (15W—12V bulb)
50. Supplementary light
51. Starter motor solenoid relay

Wiring Diagrams

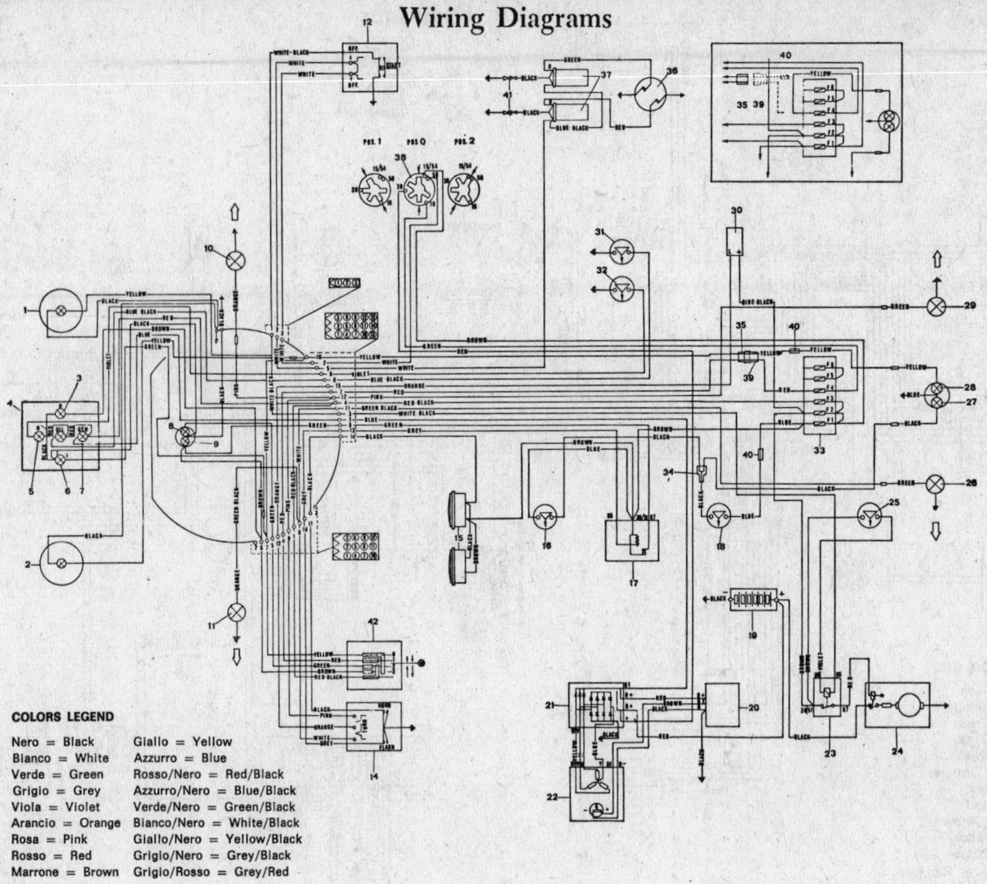

COLORS LEGEND
Nero = Black
Bianco = White
Verde = Green
Grigio = Grey
Viola = Violet
Arancio = Orange
Rosa = Pink
Rosso = Red
Marrone = Brown
Giallo = Yellow
Azzurro = Blue
Rosso/Nero = Red/Black
Azzurro/Nero = Blue/Black
Verde/Nero = Green/Black
Bianco/Nero = White/Black
Giallo/Nero = Yellow/Black
Grigio/Nero = Grey/Black
Grigio/Rosso = Grey/Red

850-T3

1. Speedometer (bulb 3W)
2. Tachometer (bulb 3W)
3. High beam indicator light (1, 2W)
4. Oil pressure indicator light (1, 2W)
5. Neutral indicator light (1, 2W)
6. Low beam indicator light (1, 2W)
7. Generator charge indicator light (1, 2W)
8. Low beam (40W)
9. High beam (45W)
10. Right front turn signal light (21W)
11. Left front turn signal light (21W)
12. Engine starting and stopping switch
13. Lighting switch
14. Switch; turn signal, horns, flashing light
15. Horns Power 7A
16. Front brake stop light cut-out
17. Flashing light relay
18. Rear brake stop light cut-out
19. Battery
20. Regulator
21. Rectifier
22. Alternator
23. Starter motor relay
24. Starter motor
25. Clutch cable cut-out
26. Left rear turn signal (21W)
27. Rear brake stop light (21W)
28. Number plate and parking light (5W)
29. Right rear turn signal (21W)
30. Flasher unit
31. Oil pressure cut-out
32. Neutral position cut-out
33. Terminal block with fuses (16A)
34. 3-way connector
35. 4-way connector
36. Contact breaker
37. Coils
38. Ignition switch (3 positions)
39. 4-way connector
40. 2-way connector
41. Spark plugs
42. Light switch, with stop device from position High-Low Beam to position Parking light

Wiring Diagrams

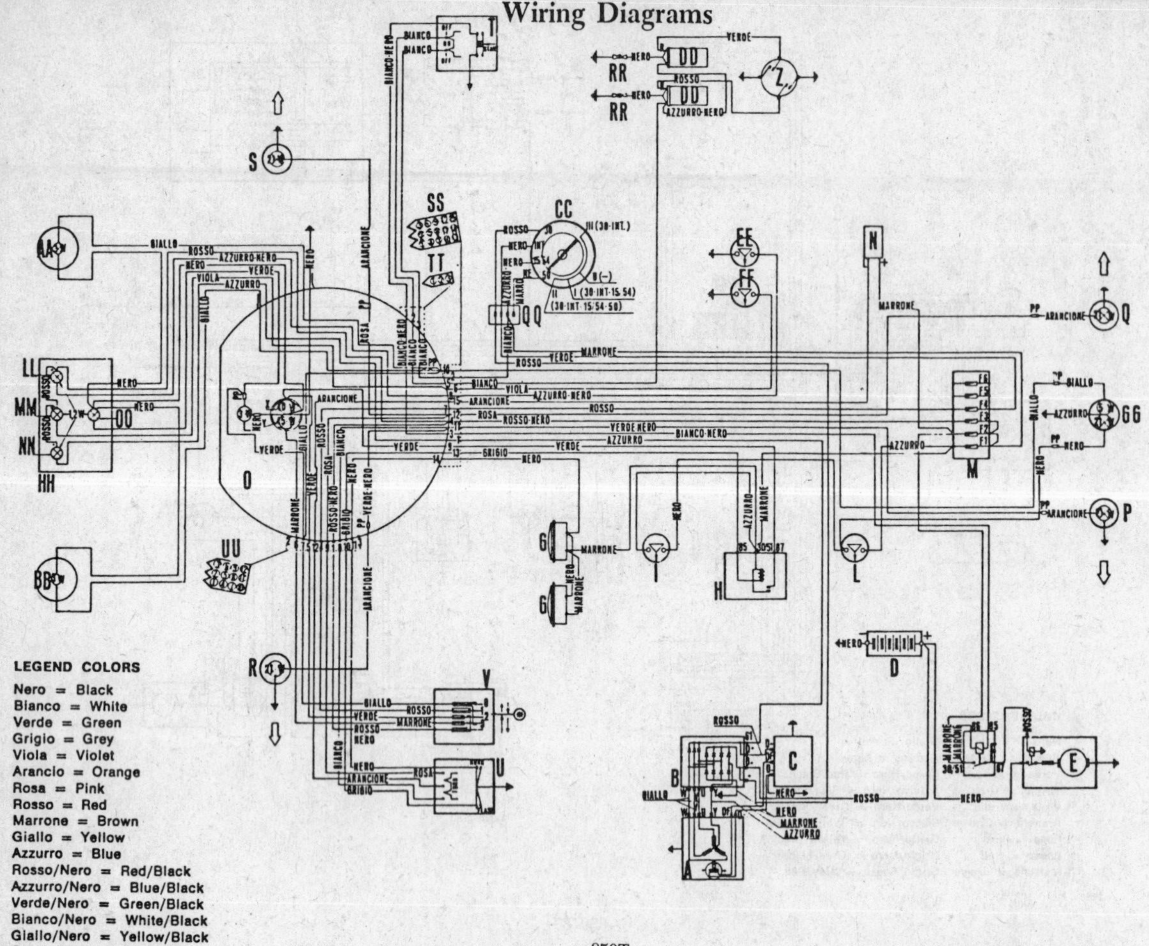

850T

A Alternator
B Rectifier
C Voltage regulator
D Battery
E Starter motor
F Relay for starter motor
G Horn
H Relay flashing light
I Hydrostop
L Rear stop light cut-out
M Terminal fuse holder
N Flasher unit (turning lights)
O Asymmetric headlight
P Rear turning light, left
Q Rear turning light, right
R Front turning light, left
S Front turning light, right
T Engine starting and stopping switch
U Horn, flashing light, turning lights, control switch
V Lights switch, with travel cut-out from dimmer to town driving and parking light
AA Speedometer
BB Tachometer
CC Ignition switch
DD H.T. coil
EE Oil pressure indicator cut-out
FF Neutral indicator cut-out
GG Number plate and stop light
HH Instrument panel
LL Oil pressure indicator light (red)
MM Neutral indicator light (orange)
NN Battery charge indicator light (red)
OO Parking indicator light (red) (USA version)
PP Faston connectors
QQ 4-way connector AMP
RR Spark plugs
SS 15-way connector MOLEX
TT 3-way connector MOLEX
UU 12-way connector MOLEX
X Low beam light
Y High beam light
Z Contact breaker

FUSES

F1-15A. Horn, stop lights—Turning lights relay
F2-15A. Starter motor relay—Flasher unit
F3-15A. Headlights—Indicator lights LL MM NN
F4-15A. Parking lights—Indicator light OO
F5-15A. Spare fuse

Chassis

Wheel Removal

FRONT DRUM BRAKE

1. Support the front wheel several inches off the ground.
2. Disconnect the brake cable(s) from the lever(s) on the brake plate(s).
3. Remove the axle nut. Loosen the pinch bolts. Pull out the axle.
4. Installation is the reverse of removal. Be sure to engage the anchor studs on the brake plate with the slot(s) in the slider(s).

REAR DRUM BRAKE

1. Flip up the rear fender section if hinged fender is fitted.
2. Disconnect the brake cable or rod from the lever on the rear brake plate.
3. Remove the axle nut. Loosen the swing arm axle pinch bolt. Remove the brake anchor nut and disengage the anchor from the brake plate.
4. Remove the axle. Move the wheel as far as possible to the left to disengage it from the drive box and remove the wheel, tilting the machine to the side if necessary.
5. Installation is the reverse of removal.

FRONT DISC BRAKE

1. Support the front wheel off the ground.
2. On machines with a single disc, remove the axle nut, loosen the axle pinch bolts, and pull out the axle to remove the wheel.
3. On machines with a dual-disc, unbolt the right-side caliper from the fork slider. Remove the axle nut. Loosen the axle pinch bolts. Pull out the axle, noting

the position of any spacers, and remove the wheel.

4. Installation is the reverse of removal

REAR DISC BRAKE

1. Remove the left exhaust pipe.
2. Remove the axle nut. Loosen the swing arm axle pinch bolt. Pull out the axle.
3. Disengage the caliper from the disc.
4. Remove the caliper from the pin on the swing arm and hang it from the motorcycle lifting handgrip.
5. Lean the machine to the right and remove the wheel.
6. Installation is the reverse of removal.

Wheels

DRUM BRAKES

1. To remove brake shoes, remove the pinch bolts which secure the brake lever(s) to the cam(s). Mark the position of the lever(s) on the cam(s) to facilitate assembly.
2. Remove the lever linkage. Tap the brake cam(s) out of the brake plate, collecting any dust seals which may be fitted. Pull the brake shoes apart to release the cam(s).
3. It is recommended that brake return springs over three years old be replaced as a matter of preventive maintenance.
4. Assembly is the reverse of the above. Grease the cam(s) before installation.

BRAKE LINKAGE

1. Twin-leading shoe brake plates are fitted with an adjustable rod which connects the two brake levers on the brake plate. The rod is adjusted at the factory, and further adjustment is not usually necessary. It is neither necessary nor recommended to disturb the rod adjustment when removing the brake levers from the plate. If the position of the main lever is marked on its cam before removal, the linkage can be reinstalled in the proper position with no trouble, since the secondary lever will only go on its cam one way.
2. If it is felt that the linkage is improperly adjusted, proceed as follows. On the Sport four-leading shoe brake, disconnect one of the brake cables while adjusting the opposite brake.
3. With the wheel mounted on the machine and properly secured, remove the clevis pin which joins the linkage rod to the main brake lever. Loosen the rod locknut.
4. Have an assistant apply the brake until the shoes just contact the drum. With your hand, push against the secondary lever until the shoe contacts the drum. The eye of the rod and the hole in the main lever should align at this point. If they do not, lengthen or shorten the rod by screwing it in or out until these holes line up.
5. Fit the pin. Tighten the rod locknut.

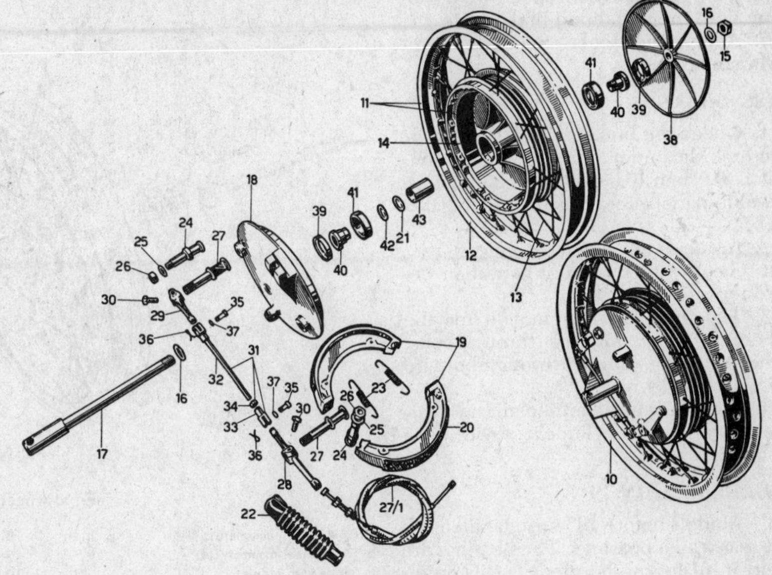

Front wheel assembly (twin-leading shoe brake)

10. Front wheel, complete
11. Front wheel, w/bearings
12. Rim
13. Spokes
14. Hub
15. Axle nut
16. Washer
17. Axle
18. Brake plate
19. Brake shoes
20. Linings
21. Shim
22. Rubber cover
23. Return springs
24. Brake pin
25. Washer
26. Nut
27. Brake cam
27/1. Cable
28. Main lever
29. Secondary lever
30. Pinch bolt
31. Brake linkage
32. Adjusting rod
33. Clevis
34. Locknut
35. Clevis pin
36. Cotter pin
37. Washer
38. Cover
39. Grease seal
40. Bushing, flanged
41. Roller bearings
42. Shim
43. Spacer

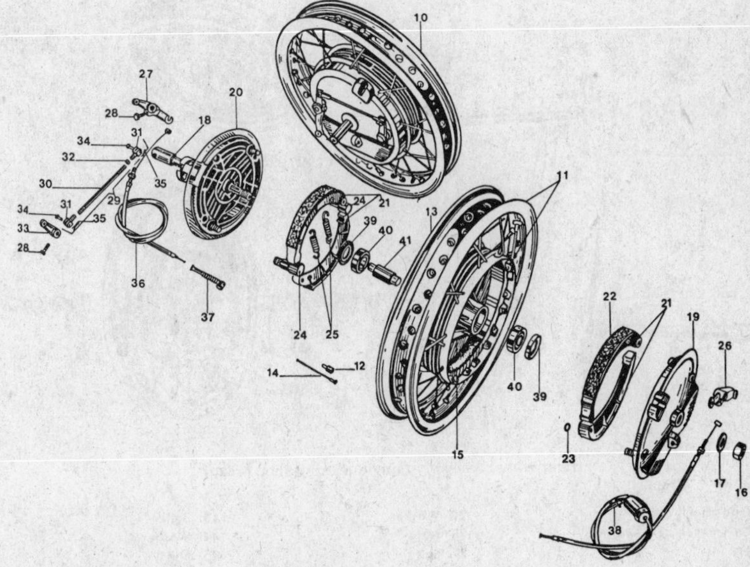

Front wheel assembly (V7 Sport, drum brake)

10. Front wheel, complete
11. Rim and hub
12. Spoke nipple
13. Rim
14. Spokes
15. Hub
16. Axle nut
17. Washer
18. Axle
19. Brake plate, right
20. Brake plate, left
21. Brake shoes
22. Brake linings
23. Dust seal
24. Brake cams
25. Return springs
26. Main brake lever, right
27. Main brake lever, left
28. Pinch bolt
29. Brake linkage
30. Adjusting rod
31. Clevis
32. Locknut
33. Secondary lever
34. Clevis pin
35. Cotter pin
36. Brake cable
37. Rubber cover
38. Brake cable w/switch
39. Grease seal
40. Wheel bearings
41. Spacer

6. On Sport models, repeat the procedure with the remaining brake plate.

7. Adjust the brake as outlined in "Maintenance."

DISC BRAKES

1. Check the brake disc for scoring or run-out. Maximum allowable lateral run-out is 0.2 mm (0.008 in.). Maximum allowable radial run-out is 0.06 mm (0.002 in.).

2. In the event of excessive disc run-out, check wheel bearing condition before replacing the disc.

3. The disc(s) can be removed from the wheel by removing the through-bolts. When refitting, torque through-bolts to 15.8–17.3 ft lbs.

4. For disc brake maintenance and caliper and master cylinder service, see below.

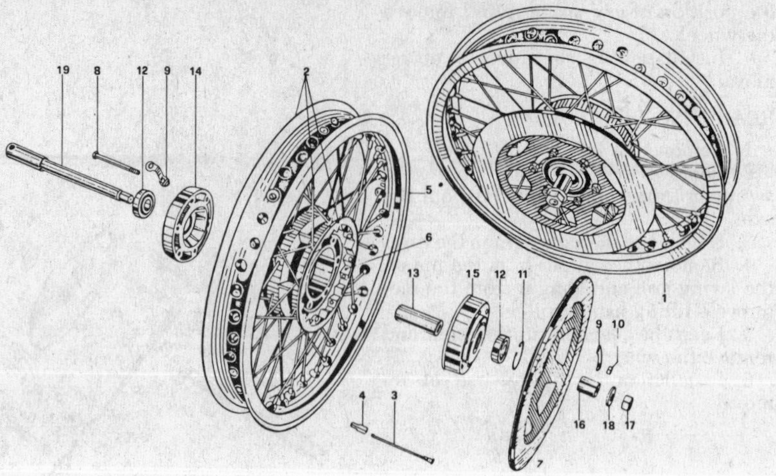

Front wheel assembly (850T)

1. Front wheel, complete
2. Front wheel assembly
3. Spoke with nipple
4. Balance weight
5. Rim
6. Hub
7. Brake disc
8. Disc bolt
9. Lock plate
10. Nut
11. Circlip
12. Wheel bearing
13. Spacer
14. Flange, left
15. Flange, right
16. Spacer
17. Axle nut
18. Washer
19. Axle

WHEEL BEARINGS

1. Models before 1974 use tapered roller rear wheel bearings. The bearings are held in place by the grease seals on either side of the hub, and can usually be removed by reaching through the hub with a punch to pop out the bearing. The outer bearing race will remain in the hub. New grease seals will probably be necessary.

There may be spacer shims in the rear wheel assembly, since the bearings are adjustable. To adjust the tapered roller bearings, proceed as follows:

a. Clean the bearings in solvent to remove the old grease, then oil lightly.

b. Install the bearing assembly using whatever shims are necessary placed between the left bearing and the spacer so that when the wheel is installed on the swing arm, and the rear axle nut is tightened to the proper torque of 100 ft lbs, wheel rotation becomes stiff. This is the zero bearing play position.

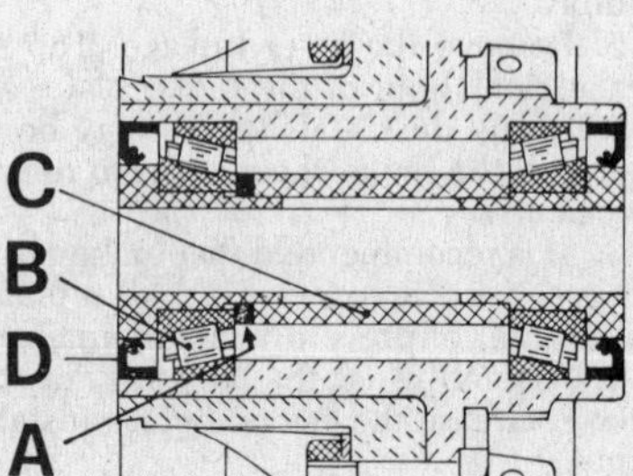

Tapered roller bearing adjustment: A, spacer; B, bearing roller; C, spacer tube; D, grease seal

c. Disassemble the hub again and add a shim of 0.10 mm (0.0039 in.) thickness. Bearing adjustment is now correct. The wheel should have an axial play of 0.05 mm (0.002 in.) with ungreased bearings.

d. Disassemble and pack the bearings.

2. Front wheels and late model rear wheels are fitted with common ball bearings. On disc brake wheels the bearings will come away with the flanges after unbolting the brake disc(s). It is therefore not necessary to remove the bearings for inspection or repacking.

3. For other wheel assemblies, refer to the illustrations.

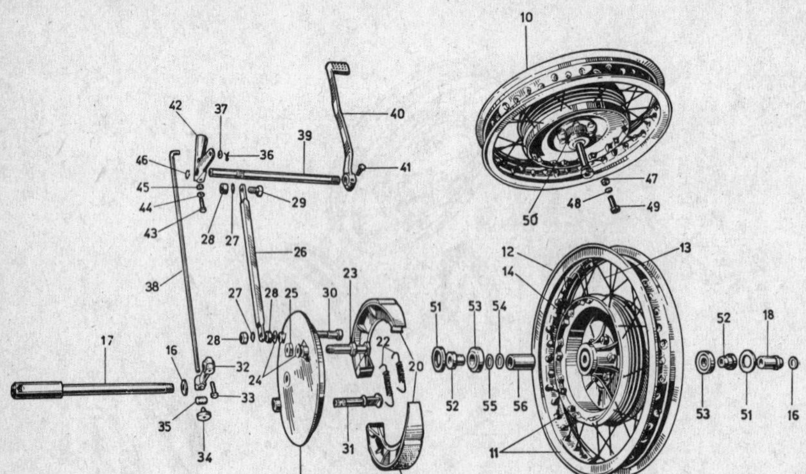

Rear wheel assembly (single-leading shoe brake)

10. Rear wheel, complete
11. Rear wheel, c/w bearings
12. Rim
13. Spoke
14. Hub
15. Axle nut
16. Washer
17. Axle
18. Spacer
19. Brake plate
20. Brake shoes
21. Linings
22. Return springs
23. Pin
24. Washer
25. Nut
26. Brake anchor
27. Washer
28. Nut
29. Bolt
30. Screw
31. Brake cam
32. Brake lever
33. Pinch bolt
34. Adjusting screw
35. Fitting
36. Cotter pin
37. Washer
38. Brake rod, RH
39. Brake shaft
40. Brake pedal, RH
41. Pinch bolt
42. Lever
43. Bolt
44. Washer
45. Nut
46. Circlip
47. Nut
48. Washer
49. Bolt
50. Drive flange
51. Grease seal
52. Flanged bushing
53. Wheel bearings, tapered roller
54. Adjustment shim
55. Washer
56. Bearing spacer
57. Brake pedal, LH
58. Lever, LH
59. Brake rod, LH

Disc Brake System

FLUSHING

1. The brake system should be flushed every year and refilled with new fluid. Use DOT 3 fluid or equivalent.

2. Remove the rubber cap from the bleed nipple on the caliper and attach of suitably sized length of plastic hose, immersing the other end of the hose in new

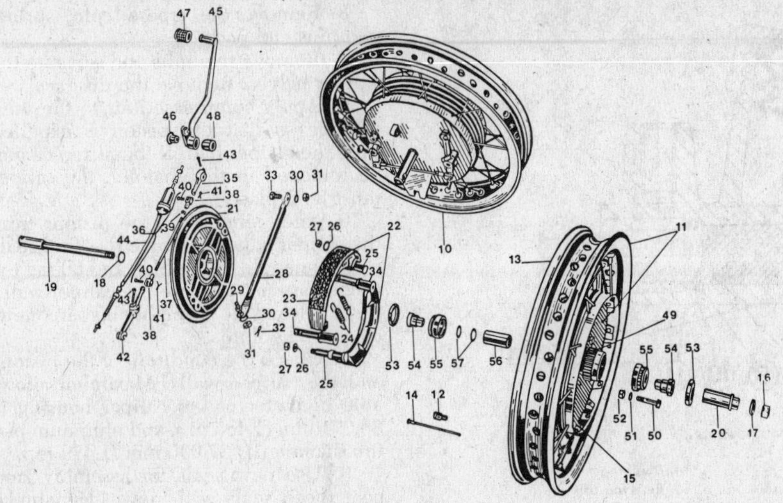

Rear wheel assembly (V7 Sport)

10. Rear wheel, complete
11. Rim and hub
12. Balance weight
13. Rim
14. Spoke and nipple
15. Hub
16. Axle nut
17. Washer
18. Washer
19. Axle
20. Axle spacer
21. Brake plate
22. Brake shoes
23. Brake linings
24. Return springs
25. Brake pin
26. Washer
27. Nut
28. Brake anchor
29. Screw
30. Washer
31. Nut
32. Cotter pin
33. Bolt
34. Brake cams
35. Secondary brake lever
36. Brake linkage
37. Adjusting rod
38. Clevis
39. Locknut
40. Clevis pin
41. Cotter pin
42. Main brake lever
43. Pinch bolt
44. Brake cable w/switch
45. Brake pedal
46. Bush
47. Pedal rubber
48. Cap
49. Drive flange
50. Flange bolt
51. Washer
52. Nut
53. Grease seal
54. Flanged bushing
55. Tapered roller bearing
56. Bearing spacer
57. Shim

fluid which has been placed in a container. Remove the master cylinder cap and diaphragm.

3. Apply the brake, then loosen the bleed nipple. Apply the brake lever several times as the old fluid is expelled. Do not allow the master cylinder to empty. Add the new fluid as needed to maintain fluid level. Continue pumping the brake lever until new fluid begins to be expelled from the hose.

4. Tighten the bleed nipple, top up the master cylinder, and bleed the brake system in the usual manner.

BLEEDING

1. Bleeding should be accomplished after flushing, or if the brake lever feels spongy with an accompanying loss of braking power.

2. On integral brake systems, where two calipers are fed by one master cylinder, the caliper farthest from the master cylinder should be bled first.

3. Remove the rubber cap from the bleed nipple on the caliper and attach a suitably sized length of transparent plastic hose. Put a couple of inches of new brake fluid in a container and immerse the free end of the hose in it.

4. Apply the brake. Loosen the bleed nipple and the brake lever will be pulled to the end of its stroke. Observe the fluid discharged when this is done. Allow the lever to return *slowly* to its normal position. Wait several seconds before reapplying the brake. Continue the operation until the fluid being discharged from the plastic hose is free of air bubbles. Apply the brake lever, then tighten the bleed nipple and check brake operation before riding.

5. The fluid level in the master cylinder must be kept up during the bleeding operation. After the operation is complete, top up the reservoir to the marked line.

NOTE: *The front wheel should point straight ahead while bleeding front calipers.*

MASTER CYLINDER

1. The master cylinder should not be disassembled unless defective operation has been traced to it. Fluid leaking from the lever side of the master cylinder necessitates replacement of the piston seals.

2. Drain the fluid from the reservoir. Disconnect the fluid line at the master cylinder, cleaning off any dirt before disconnecting. Cover the open end of the feed line with a small plastic bag or the like to prevent the entry of foreign matter.

3. Remove the brake lever. Remove the master cylinder from the handlebar.

4. Special tool No. 14926400 is inserted into the feed line side of the master cylinder and used to push out the piston assembly. This must be done carefully to avoid scoring the cylinder walls. Remove the spring and guide bush from the cylinder.

5. To disassemble the piston, remove the lock ring, seal, and washer.

6. Carefully clean the piston components and master cylinder body in clean brake fluid.

CAUTION: *Do not use solvents or anything else to clean these components.*

7. Maximum allowable master cylinder passage diameter is 15.92 mm (0.621 in.). Minimum allowable piston diameter is 15.83 mm (0.617 in.).

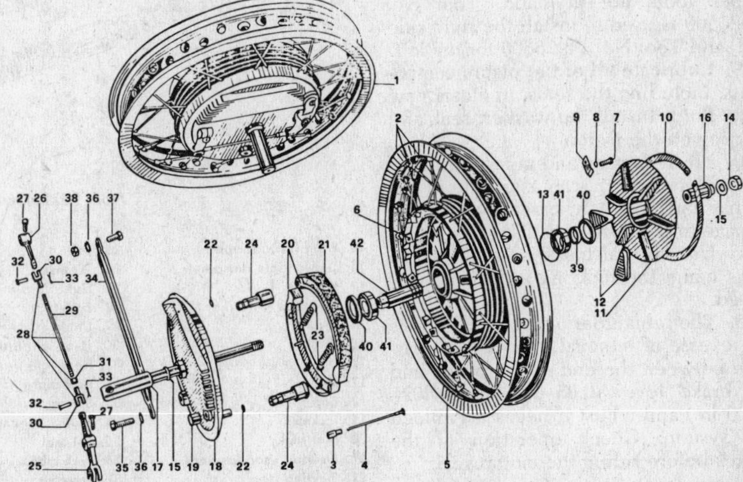

Rear wheel assembly (850T)

1. Rear wheel, complete
2. Rear wheel
3. Balance weight
4. Spoke with nipple
5. Rim
6. Hub
7. Bolt
8. Washer
9. Lockplate
10. Circlip
11. Drive coupling
12. Plastic bushes
13. O-ring
14. Axle nut
15. Washer
16. Spacer
17. Axle
18. Brake plate
19. Bush
20. Brake shoe
21. Brake lining
22. Dust seal
23. Return spring
24. Brake cams
25. Main brake lever
26. Secondary brake lever
27. Pinch bolt
28. Brake linkage
29. Adjusting rod
30. Clevis
31. Locknut
32. Clevis pin
33. Cotter pin
34. Brake anchor
35. Bolt
36. Washer
37. Bolt
38. Nut

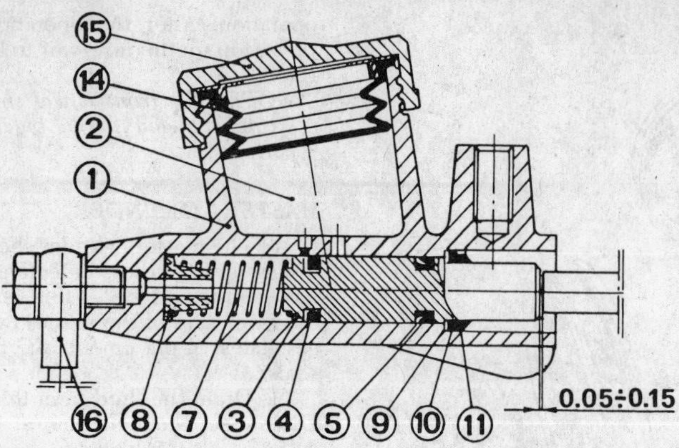

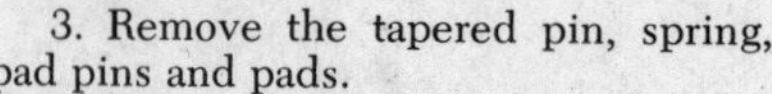

Master cylinder components

1. Master cylinder
2. Reservoir
3. Piston assembly
4. Piston seal
5. Piston seal
7. Spring
8. Guide bush
9. Washer
10. Seal
11. Lockring
14. Diaphragm
15. Reservoir cap
16. Banjo fitting

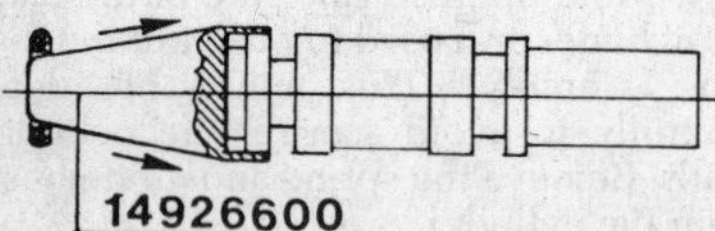

Installing the piston seal with the special tool for the left-side seal

8. The seals on either end of the piston are fitted into grooves and require special tools to act as bushes so that they can be installed without damage. If the master cylinder leaks on the lever side, these seals must be replaced, but if they appear to be in good condition, and the cylinder does not leak, they should not be disturbed unless new seals and the proper tools are at hand. Tool No. 14926500 is used to install the right side seal, and Tool No. 14926600 for the left.

9. Lubricate all of the piston components, including the seals, in clean, new brake fluid. Install the washer, seal, and lockring on the piston.

10. Fit the spring and guide bush.

11. Install the piston assembly in the caliper pushing it in carefully to avoid damage to the bore or seals.

12. Use special tool No. 14926700 to press home the lockring until it is fully seated.

13. The remainder of the procedure is the reverse of removal. Check the clearance between the end of the piston and the brake lever (0.05–0.15 mm/0.002–0.006 in.) and adjust if necessary. Bleed the system. Check operation of the brakes before riding the motorcycle.

CALIPER

1. Disconnect and plug the brake line at the caliper.

2. Remove the caliper from its mounting.

3. Remove the tapered pin, spring, pad pins and pads.

4. Remove the bolts and separate the caliper halves. Remove the dust seals.

5. Apply compressed air to the fluid passage so that the piston is expelled from the caliper half. If the piston cannot be removed in this manner, the caliper must be replaced.

6. After removal of the pistons from the caliper halves, remove the fluid seals using a needle or the like, and taking extreme care not to score the caliper wall.

7. Clean all components in new, clean brake fluid.

8. Check the condition of the pistons and the caliper walls. Maximum allowable diameter of the caliper housing is 38.071 mm (1.485 in.), and minimum piston diameter is 37.930 mm (1.479 in.).

9. Use new seals for assembly, and coat these seals with new, clean brake fluid. Install the piston seal carefully into its groove. Lightly lubricate the pistons with brake fluid and press them into their calipers using hand pressure only.

10. Install the dust seals into their re-

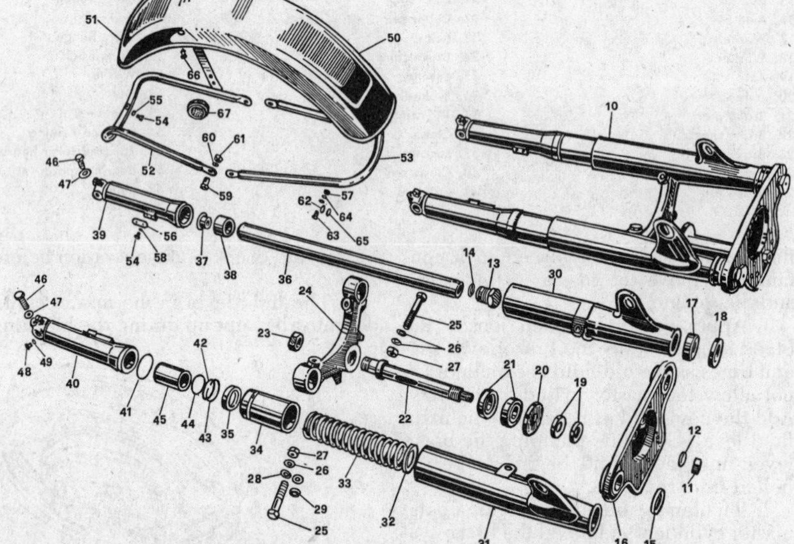

Front forks assembly (V700, V750, V750)

10. Front forks, complete
11. Upper triple clamp nut
12. Washer
13. Filler cap
14. O-ring
15. Washer
16. Upper triple clamp
17. Bush
18. Cap
19. Locknuts
20. Dust seal
21. Steering head bearings
22. Steering stem
23. Nut
24. Lower triple clamp
25. Bolt
26. Washers
27. Nut
28. Eyelet
29. Cable guide ring
30. Headlight bracket, right
31. Headlight bracket, left
32. Dust seal
33. Spring
34. Spring housing
35. Oil seal
36. Fork tube
37. Lockring
38. Bushing
39. Fork slider, right
40. Fork slider, left
41. O-ring
42. Adjusting washer
43. Circlip
44. Adjusting shim
45. Bushing
46. Bolt
47. Washer
48. Drain plug
49. Washer
50. Front fender
51. Decal
52. Bracket, front
53. Bracket, rear
54. Screw
55. Washer
56. Plate
57. Nut
58. Washer
59. Bolt
60. Washer
61. Nut
62. Eyelet
63. Screw
64. Washer
65. Ring
66. Plug
67. Reflector

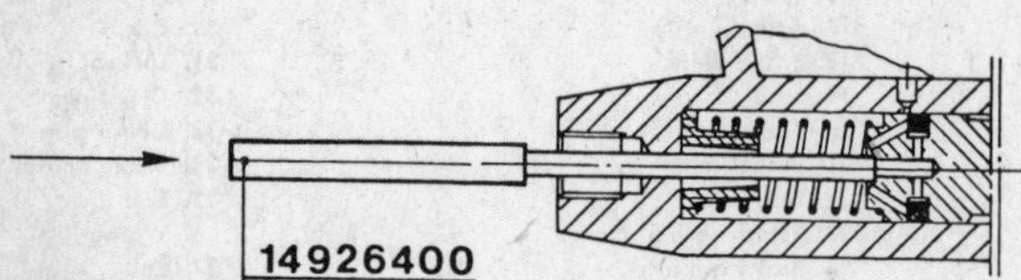

Removing the piston assembly with the special tool

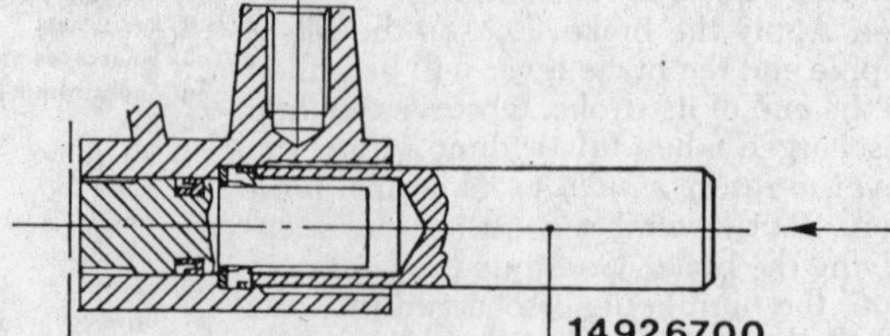

Pushing home the lockring with the special tool

spective caliper halves, making sure they are properly seated.

11. After insuring that the caliper half mating surfaces are perfectly clean, join the two halves, tightening the caliper bolts to 28–32 ft lbs.

12. Install the caliper on its mount, tightening the mounting bolts to 28–32 ft lbs.

13. Install the pads. Connect the brake lines, bleed the system. Check brake operation before riding the motorcycle.

Front Forks and Steering

V700, V750, V850

Removal and Disassembly

1. Disconnect the clutch and brake cables at the handlebars, remove the clamp screws and caps, and remove the handlebars.

2. Remove the instrument panel mounting screws, disconnect the electrical cables and the speedometer drive, then remove the instrument panel.

Removing the upper triple clamp

Steering stem locknuts

3. Remove the speedometer from the instrument panel.

4. Remove the nut and fork filler caps from the top triple clamp then pull the clamp using an appropriate wrench and tool No. 60910500 or a suitable substitute puller.

5. Remove the steering stem lock-ring (B) and lock-cap (A) from the top of the steering stem.

6. Remove the pinch bolts which secure the bottom triple clamp to the fork tubes.

7. Either drain the forks now by removing the drain plugs or pull out the tube and slider assemblies and then invert and drain the oil.

8. Remove the spring housings and springs as an assembly, then remove the headlight bracket bottom plate.

9. Remove the spring housings, then remove the seal ring and rubber ring from the housings.

10. Remove the circlip and adjusting washer, then remove the fork bottom cover and bushing.

11. Remove the bottom slider bushing lock-ring, then extract the bushing.

12. Remove the nut which secures the steering stem, from the bottom of the lower triple clamp, then remove the stem.

Inspection

1. Using a micrometer or calipers, check the diameter of the tubes at the chromed portion, which must extend 120 mm (4.722 in.), and replace them if worn past their serviceable limit of 34.720–34.695 mm (1.3669–1.3659 in.). Using feeler gauges, check the clearance between the tubes and bushings and replace them if worn past their serviceable limit of 0.040–0.015 mm (0.0015–0.0041 in.) at the top bushing, and 0.020–0.044 mm (0.0007–0.0017 in.) at the bottom bushing.

2. Inspect the top bushings for signs of wear, damage, or scoring which would interfere with the proper operation of the forks, or which could damage the fork tubes, and replace them as necessary. Using inside and outside micrometers, measure the bushings and replace them if worn past their serviceable limits of 34.760–34.800 mm (1.3685–1.370 in.) for the inside diameter, and 40.010–39.971 mm (1.5751–1.5735 in.) for the outside diameter.

3. Inspect the bottom bushings. Their values are 34.700–34.739 mm (1.3661–1.3676 in.) for the inside diameter, and 39.950–39.911 mm (1.5728–1.5712 in.) for the outside diameter.

4. Inspect the fork bottom covers for damage or scoring of their inner surfaces and replace them as necessary. Using an inside micrometer, measure the inside diameter of the cover, then use feeler gauges to measure the clearances between the cover and the top and bottom bushings, and replace the components if worn past their serviceable limits. The inside diameter of the cover should be 40.010–40.050 mm (1.5751–1.5767 in.). The clearance between the cover and the top bushing should be 0–0.079 mm (0–0.10031 in.), and the clearance between the cover and the bottom bushing should be 0.099–0.100 mm (0.0038–0.0039 in.).

5. Inspect the fork springs for signs of wear, fatigue, excessive tilt, or damage and replace them as necessary. A new spring should be 230 ± 15 mm (9.0551 in.), and should be replaced if collapsed more than 3%. With a load of 110 ± 4 lbs the spring should be 170 mm (6.6929 in.), and with a load of 231 ± 8 lbs, the spring should be 104 mm (4.0945 in.).

Assembly and Installations

1. Install the top and bottom fork cover bushings, then secure them with bushing lock-rings. Use new lock-rings if the old ones are distorted.

2. Install the fork tubes complete with the sliders, then position the adjusting washer in the top portion of the cover and install the circlip in the cover groove.

3. Place the fork cover gasket, cover, and spring housing in position.

4. Carefully press the seal ring into position, then secure the spring housing using Tool No. 12912600 (labeled "11" in the accompanying illustration) or a suitable substitute.

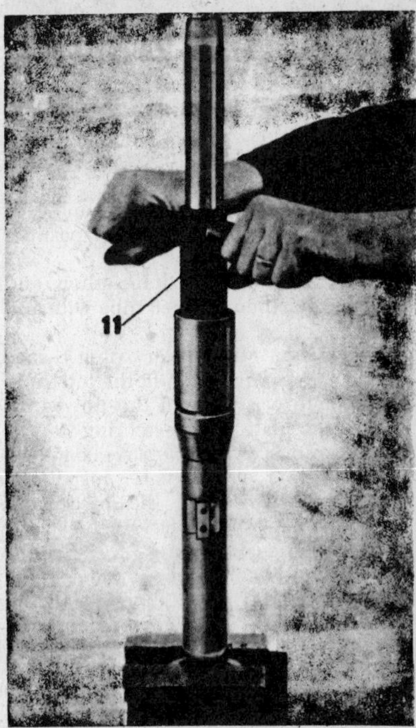

Installing a slider oil seal with the special tool

5. Slip the fork springs over the fork tubes and position them in the spring housing; then insert the fork tubes in the bottom triple clamp and headlight bracket using Tool No. 12909500 (labeled "4" in the accompanying illustration), or a suitable substitute, to position them.

6. Install the pinch bolts and secure the headlight bracket, then secure the steering stem to the bottom triple clamp with its nut.

7. Pack the steering head bearings with fresh grease and install them in the frame neck, then slip the steering stem and fork assembly into position so the stem seats fully inside the neck, and install the steering stem cap.

8. Position the steering stem lock-ring and adjust the steering play. The forks should pivot freely in the fork neck

Lining up the fork components with the special tool

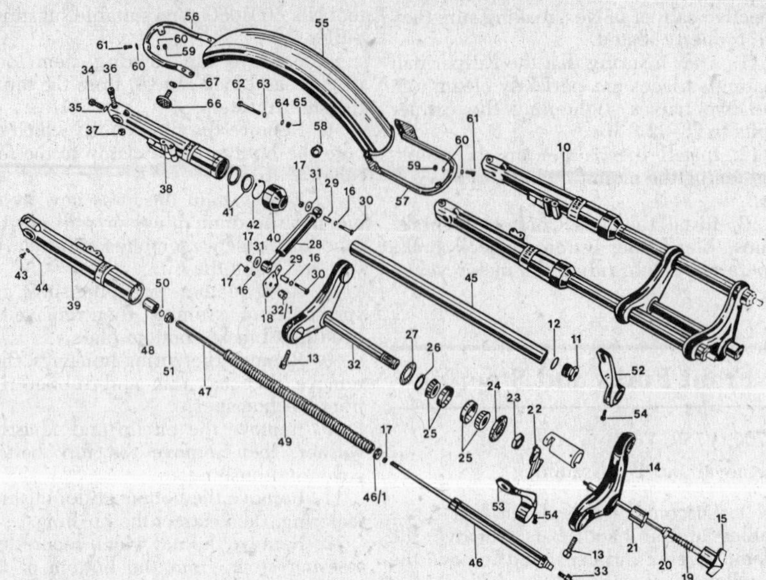

Front fork components (Sport, 850T/T3)

10.	Front fork, complete	30.	Screw	48.	Cap
11.	Filler cap	31.	Shim	49.	Spring
12.	O-ring	32.	Lower triple clamp	50.	Circlip
13.	Pinch bolt	32/1.	Bushing	51.	Bottom cup
14.	Upper triple clamp	33.	Screw	52.	Headlight bracket, right
15.	Steering damper knob	34.	Screw	53.	Headlight bracket, left
16.	Washer	35.	Washer	54.	Screw
17.	Nut	36.	Screw	55.	Fender
18.	Plate	37.	Nut	56.	Fender bracket, front
19.	Spring	38.	Right fork slider	57.	Fender bracket, rear
20.	Bushing	39.	Left fork slider	58.	Grommet
21.	Top nut	40.	Dust cover	59.	Nue
22.	Steering lock plate	41.	Oil seals	60.	Washer
23.	Bearing adjustment nut	42.	Circlip	61.	Screw
24.	Cup	43.	Drain plug	62.	Screw
25.	Tapered roller steering head bearings	44.	Washer	63.	Washer
26.	Shim	45.	Fork tube	64.	Washer
27.	Dust seal	46.	Damper	65.	Nut
28.	Steering damper	46/1.	Rubber damper ring	66.	Reflector
29.	Spacer	47.	Damper rod	67.	Rubber washer

without binding. When the steering is to your satisfaction, fit and secure the lock cap using Tool No. 60910500 or a suitable substitute.

9. Position the rubber rings and caps in the headlight brackets, then position the top triple clamp plate.

10. Install the fork drain plugs and their gaskets, then fill each tube with fork oil.

11. Position the filler plug seals, washers, and plugs, then fit the top triple clamp plate washer, and the nut which secures the plate, to the steering stem.

12. Mount the handlebar clamps on the top triple clamp plate, install the speedometer drive on the instrument panel, connect the electric cables, and secure the speedometer.

13. Mount the instrument panel on the top triple clamp plate, then install the handlebars and their clamp caps and screws.

750 SPORT, 850T/T3

Removal and Disassembly

1. Drain the fork oil. Support the front wheel off the ground. Remove the front wheel. Remove the brake caliper(s) from the forks, if disc brake. Remove the front fender.

2. Detach the electrical switches.

3. Remove the hydraulic steering damper unit, and engagement knob assembly.

4. Unbolt the headlight, disconnect the wiring, and remove the headlight unit. Remove the turn signal indicators.

5. Disconnect the tach and speedometer cables. Remove the instruments and warning light wiring and panel screws. Remove the panel.

6. Loosen the upper triple clamp pinch bolts. Remove the steering stem nut, the fork filler caps, and the upper triple clamp. Remove the headlight bracket. Disconnect wiring or control cables from the handlebars and remove the bars from the forks.

7. If removal of the forks only is desired, loosen the lower triple clamp pinch bolts, and pull down on the fork leg to remove it.

8. If removal of the steering stem and fork assembly is desired, remove the steering stem nut and take away the fork and steering assembly.

9. To disassemble the fork leg, secure the fork slider in a soft-face vise and remove the bolt at the very bottom of the slider. Pull the fork tube out of the slider, and remove the spring and damper assembly from the tube.

10. Remove the rod circlip. Remove the bottom cap and spring. Unscrew the rod from the damper.

11. Remove the dust seal from the top of the slider, followed by the circlip. Pry out the slider seals.

Inspection

1. Check that the chrome plating of the fork tubes is in good condition. Diameter of the fork tubes should be 34.72–34.74 mm (1.366–1.367 in.).

2. Tube-to-slider clearance is 0.010–0.085 mm (0.0004–0.0033 in.).

3. Inside diameter of the fork slider should be 34.75–34.79 mm (1.368–1.370 in.).

4. Fork spring free length is 418.5–423.5 mm (16.48–16.67 in.).

5. Fork dampers are sealed units and cannot be disassembled. Check that the units have equal damping rates. If one leaks or shows damage, replace both to ensure equal damping characteristics.

6. Check the damping characteristics of the steering damper. If it leaks or has lost its damping ability, replace it. The unit cannot be disassembled.

7. Check the condition of the steering stem bearings. Replace them if signs of wear or damage are evident. Rollers should be bright and smooth over their whole surface.

8. Check the condition of the outer races in the steering head. Races must be perfectly smooth and free of wear or ripples. If damaged the races must be replaced, and this is accomplished by removing them from the frame with a punch, and pressing the replacements straight in.

Assembly and Installation

1. The use of new seals and rubber parts is recommended.

2. Assemble the fork slider by carefully pressing in the new seals until they are seated then fitting the circlip. Lubri-

cate seal lips with ATF. Install the dust seals on the sliders.

3. Install the rubber ring on the damper rod. Install the locknut, screw the damper rod into the damper tube and secure it with the locknut.

4. Fit the fork spring, bottom cap and circlip assembly.

5. Fit the damper assembly into the fork tube and the tube into the slider.

6. To assemble the steering stem, fit the dust cap, shim and bearing race onto the lower triple clamp steering stem in that order. Install the steering assembly on the frame, then the top bearing and dust cover. Install the steering stem nut and tighten it so that the steering stem will turn freely but without any play.

7. The remainder of the procedure is the reverse of removal. Add the proper amount of ATF to each fork leg.

Swing Arm

Removal and Disassembly

1. Remove the rear wheel. Remove the disc brake caliper, if necessary. Unbolt the shocks from the swing arm.

2. The swing arm can be removed complete with the drive box. If removal of the box is desired, drain the oil and unbolt it from the swing arm.

3. Loosen one of the clamps on the drive shaft rubber boot.

4. Remove the cap nuts from the pivot pins, if fitted (early models).

5. Loosen the swing arm pivot pin locknuts. Do not unscrew the locknuts. Just loosen them enough so the pins can be unscrewed. Try to keep the locknuts at the same place on the pins to preserve alignment upon assembly.

6. Unscrew the pivot pins. Pull off the swing arm assembly.

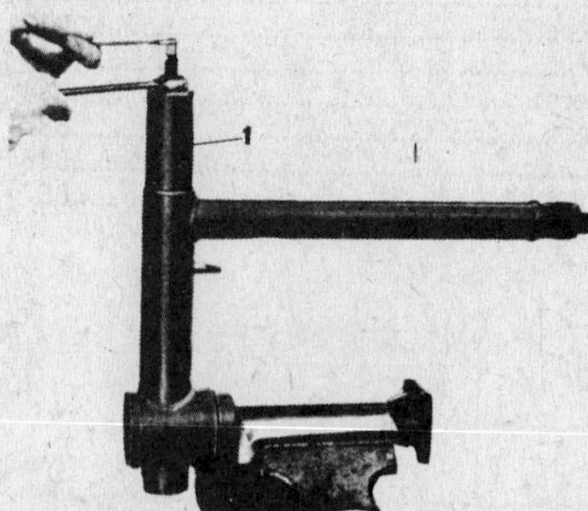

Removing the swing arm bearing race

7. Remove any grease seals or dust seals or spacers from either end of the swing arm. To remove the bearings, use special tool No. 12904700.

Assembly and Installation

1. Lubricate the bearings with bearing grease and install them. Press in the seals and spacers.

2. Install the swing, engaging the universal coupling with the shaft.

3. Fit the pivot pins, screwing them in equally until the swing arm can pivot freely but shows no signs of lateral play. Secure the locknuts.

4. The remainder of the procedure is the reverse of removal.

Rear Shock Absorbers

ALL MODELS EXCEPT SPORT

1. The shocks absorbers are sealed units. If leakage or other damage occurs, they must be replaced.

SPORT

1. Sport models are fitted with adjustable Koni® rear shock absorbers.

2. The standard factory setting is approximately 1½ turns from the minimum damping position. The maximum damping position is 2¼ turns.

3. If a change in damping rate is desired, remove the shocks from the motorcycle. Compress the spring, remove the collar, and remove the spring.

4. The rubber stopper should be moved down the damper shaft. Use a screwdriver or the like to pry it down off the top eyelet, if necessary, but take care not to damage or knick the damper shaft's chrome surface. Moving the rubber stopper down will expose a locknut against the top eyelet.

5. Use the right size wrench to hold the locknut, then insert a rod into the eyelet and break it loose, then remove it. Remove the locknut. If the locknut resists removal, secure the damper shaft in a soft-faced vise by the threaded portion, then loosen the locknut as far as possible. Remove the damper shaft from the vise, and remove the locknut.

CAUTION: *Do not attempt to secure any part of the damper shaft which must enter the damper during adjustment or operation. The shaft is very easily knicked and the damper oil seal will be ruined.*

6. Remove the rubber stopper from the damper shaft. Refit the eyelet, and locknut, but do not tighten them excessively.

7. The adjuster mechanism is at the very bottom of the damper unit. Push the damper shaft in as far as possible without using excess pressure, then turn it a few degrees in either direction while maintaining a light pressure. The bottom of the shaft will engage the adjustment mechanism which can be felt when it happens.

8. Turn the damper shaft to the left until it stops. This is the minimum damping position. Turn the damper shaft to the right until the desired damping position is reached. Adjustments are made in increments on ¼ turn. Maximum damping position is 2¼ turns.

9. After adjustment, pull the damper shaft out an inch or so to disengage it from the adjustment mechanism. Refit the rubber stopper. Secure the eyelet and locknut.

10. Both shocks must have the same adjustment to provide satisfactory operation.

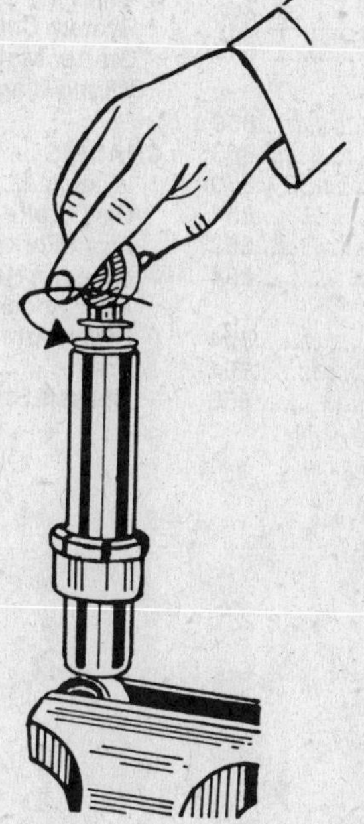

Adjusting the damping rate on Koni® shocks (Sport only)

Chassis Torque Specifications

Part	Torque (ft lbs)
Lower frame rail allen bolts (Sport, 850T/T3)	58
Center stand	25
Battery bracket bolts	18
Footpegs	14
Swing arm pivot pin locknuts	58
Brake anchor, rear drum brake	32
Rear Shock absorbers	
top	22
bottom	32
Rear axle pinch bolt	32
Axle nuts, front and rear	101–107
Triple clamp pinch bolts	32
Fork filler caps	86–108
Fork slider allen bolts	32
Fork damper securing bolt	22
Fork slider axle pinch bolts	32
Top steering stem nut (Sport, 850T/T3)	122–129
Disc brake caliper mounts	28–32
Disc brake caliper bolts	28–32

NORTON

MODEL COVERAGE

Atlas
G15CS
N15CS
P-11
Commando 750
Commando 850

INDEX

General Specifications

	Commando 850	Commando 750 (Standard)	Commando 750 (Combat)	Atlas	G15CS N15CS	P-11
DIMENSIONS						
Net Weight (lbs)	422–436	390	390	410	N.A.	N.A.
Ground Clearance (in.)	6	6	6	6	N.A.	N.A.
Wheelbase (in.)	57	56¾	56¾	N.A.	N.A.	N.A.
Overall Length (in.)	88	87½	87½	N.A.	N.A.	N.A.
Overall Width (in.)	26	26	26	26	26	26
Seat Height (in.)	31	31	31	N.A.	N.A.	N.A.
ENGINE						
Displacement (cc)	828	745	745	745	745	745
Bore x Stroke (mm)	77 x 89	73 x 89	73 x 89	73 x 89	73 x 89	73 x 89
Compression Ratio	8.5 : 1	8.9 : 1	10 : 1	7.5 : 1	7.5 : 1	7.5 : 1
Carburetor (Amal)	932	930	932	389 Monobloc or 930	389 Monobloc	930
Ignition	Battery and coil	Battery and coil	Battery and coil	Magneto	Magneto	Battery and coil
TRANSMISSION						
Clutch Type	Diaphragm, multi-plate	Diaphragm, multi-plate	Diaphragm, multi-plate	Dry-type, multi-plate	Dry-type, multi-plate	Dry-type, multi-plate
Gear Ratios (: 1)						
First	11.20	12.40	12.4	11.6•	12.65	12.65
Second	7.45	8.25	8.25	7.70	8.40	8.40
Third	5.30	5.90	5.90	5.52	6.03	6.03
Fourth	4.38	4.84	4.84	4.53	4.96	4.96
CHAINS						
Rear (in.)	5/8 x 3/8 (99 pitches)	5/8 x 3/8 (98 pitches)	5/8 x 3/8 (98 pitches)	5/8 x 1/4 (97 pitches)	5/8 x 0.380 (97 pitches)	5/8 x 0.380 (97 pitches)
Primary (in.)	3/8 (triple row) (92 pitches)	3/8 (triple row) (92 pitches)	3/8 (triple row) (92 pitches)	1/2 x 0.305 (76 pitches)	1/2 x 0.305 (76 pitches)	1/2 x 0.305 (76 pitches)
Camshaft (in.)	3/8 x 0.225 (38 pitches)	3/8 x 0.225 (38 pitches)	3/8 x 0.225 (38 pitches)	3/8 x 0.225 (38 pitches)	3/8 x 0.225 (38 pitches)	3/8 x 0.225 (38 pitches)
Magneto (in.)	—	—	—	3/8 x 5/32 (42 pitches)	3/8 x 5/32 (42 pitches)	—
CHASSIS						
Front Suspension	Rod damper hydraulic forks on all					
Rear Suspension	Swing arm and hydraulic damped shock absorbers on all					
Tire Size						
Front	4.10 x 19	4.10 x 19	4.10 x 19	3.25 x 19	3.25 x 19	3.25 x 19
Rear	4.10 x 19	4.10 x 19	4.10 x 19	4.00 x 18	4.00 x 18	4.00 x 18
ELECTRICAL						
System Voltage	12	12	12	12	12	12
Generator	Alternator on all					

N.A. Not available

Maintenance

NOTE: *Common maintenance procedures are explained in detail in "General Information."*

Lubrication

ENGINE

Oil should be changed every 2500 miles under normal operating conditions. Change oil when engine is warm.

Use SAE 20/50 or SAE 30 "SE" if the average temperature is above 32° F., and SAE 10/30 or SAE 20 "SE" oil if below this.

Checking Oil Level

1. Remove the seat, if necessary (as on Commandos) to gain access to the oil tank cap. Remove the cap.
2. Start the engine and let it run for a few moments until the sump has been scavenged and the oil in the tank is at its normal level as in operation. You can tell when the sump has been emptied, as the oil flow coming from the return line inside the oil tank will become intermittent and splutter somewhat.
3. Check the oil level. On Commando models, a dipstick is provided. The oil level should not exceed the "H" mark, or fall below the "L" mark.

Early Commando machines have an oil level tube adjacent to the oil tank. The oil level should be about half-way up the tube under operating conditions.

On all other models, gauge the oil level against the decal level lines on the side of the tank. Both maximum and minimum levels are marked.

Putting too much oil in will cause it to spill out of the overflow tube while in operation, while too little will cause an excess of heat to be built up in the remaining oil.

Changing Oil

1. Let the engine run until it is warm, then remove the seat (if necessary as on Commando models) and the right side cover (if fitted) to gain access to the tank filler cap and drain plug respectively.
2. Drain the warm oil out into a suitable receptacle. On the 1970 Roadster, the filter junction bolt must be removed to drain the oil tank.

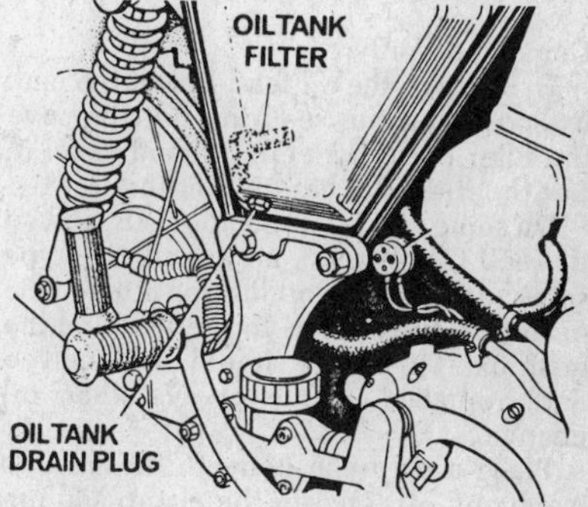

3. Remove the crankcase sump drain plug and allow the sump to drain completely. There should only be a pint or so of oil in the sump.

On early 1973 Commando 750 models, only a small drain plug is fitted to the sump. On the 850 Commando, a large plug with filter is fitted along with a smaller magnetic plug. This small plug should be removed and cleaned when the oil is changed.

4. Clean the sump filter by removing the spring clip, taking out the washer, and pulling out the filter mesh.
5. Wash the filter thoroughly in a suitable solvent to remove all impurities

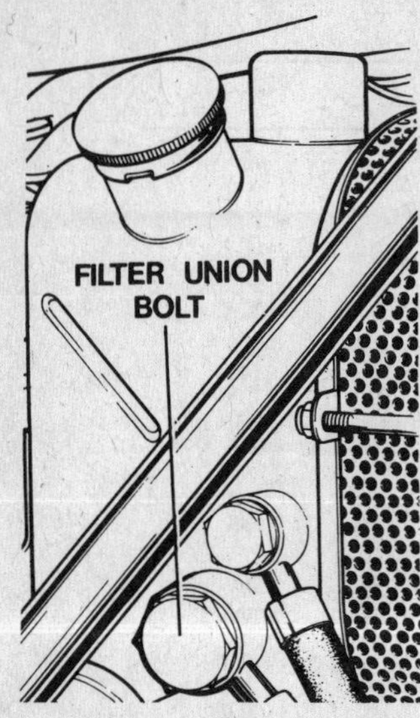

Roadster "S" tank filter bolt (1970)

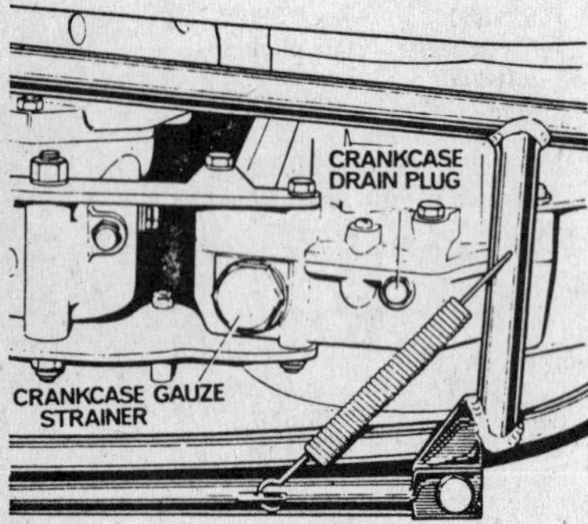

Drain plugs (850 shown)

trapped in it. Also wash out the plug itself checking closely for metal particles.

6. Reassemble the filter in the plug and replace. Tighten the plug firmly.

Commando only:

7. Remove the oil feed line at the tank by loosening the securing nut. Remove the filter (held by a circlip) and clean it. Let the filter dry before refitting it.

On some 1973 Commando 750s, and on the 850 Commando, an automotive-type screw-on cartridge oil filter is fitted to the oil return line, and is located behind the gearbox. This filter should be removed and replaced about every other oil change.

Place a drip pan beneath the filter to catch any oil. Loosen the clamp and unscrew the filter, using a filter strap wrench if necessary.

To install, place a thin coat of oil around the O-ring of the new filter and screw it on hand-tight only. Tighten the clamp. Do not overtighten the clamp as this risks crushing the filter.

Pre-Commando:

For the other models, the factory did not recommend removing the filter on the oil feed pipe as just described for the Commando for fear of causing a leak at this spot by breaking the seal. Instead, the recommended procedure was to remove the oil tank completely and wash it out with kerosene or another suitable solvent.

a. Take off the metal oil pipe junction at the engine by removing the single fastening bolt.

b. Remove all other hose connections to the oil tank such as the crankcase breather, tank breather, etc.

c. Remove the three or four bolts which hold the oil tank to the frame (depending on the model) and remove the tank.

d. Flush the tank with the solvent several times to assure a complete cleansing job. Let the tank drain and dry thoroughly before refitting.

It is not necessary or recommended to perform this operation at every oil change. It should be done occasionally, though, and for certain if the engine has just been rebuilt.

Commando:

Although this should not be necessary for the Commando under normal conditions, the procedure is as follows:

a. Remove the seat and sidecovers from both sides of the machine.

b. Drain the oil as described above.

c. Take off the chain oiler pipe at the point where it enters the felt cartridge by compressing the spring clip and pulling the pipe away. Also remove the oil tank breather and crankcase breather pipes.

d. Unscrew the front and rear oil tank rubber mountings and remove the tank by lifting it to clear the bottom grommet and taking the bottom of the tank out of the frame first.

e. Reassembly is the reverse of the above procedure.

8. Occasionally check the filter in the oil pressure relief valve. To remove the valve, it may be necessary to take out the rocker oil feed banjo bolt immediately below it.

9. Refill the oil tank with the correct amount and grade of oil. Start the engine and let it run for three minutes. Then shut it off and let it sit for another two minutes. Recheck the oil level and fill it up as necessary.

GEARBOX

The change interval is 5000 miles. Oil should be warm when changing. Use SAE 90EP when average temperature is above 32° F and SAE 30 when it is below this.

Checking Oil

To check the level of oil in the gearbox, simply remove the oil level plug at the rear of the outer gearbox cover. The oil should begin to flow gently out.

Changing Oil

NOTE: *The oil should be warm when changing.*

1. Remove the clutch lever inspection cap on the outer cover.
2. Remove the drain plug at the bottom rear of the gearbox and allow the oil to drain out. Replace the drain plug and tighten it firmly, but avoid damaging the fiber washer.
3. Using a small funnel or other suitable device, add oil through the inspection cap. Add the oil slowly, as it is quite thick and must drain through a drilling in the inner cover to get to the gear compartment. When you have added the correct amount of oil (Commando: 1.2 pints; other models: 1 pint), let the oil sit for a minute to ensure that the level is equal in both the inner and outer compartments, then remove the level plug and check as before.
4. Replace the level plug and the inspection cap.

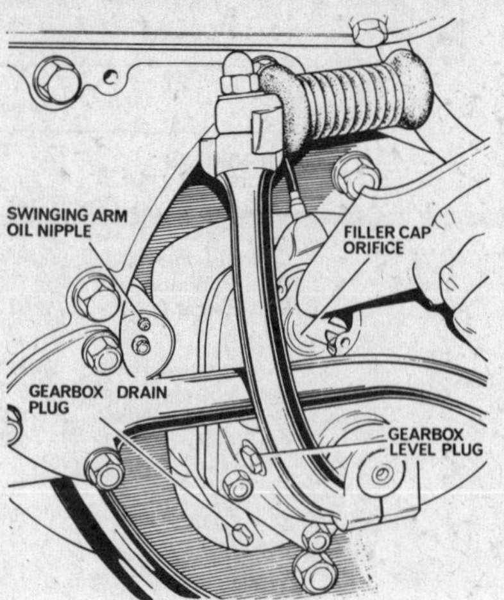

Gearbox plugs (all models)

PRIMARY CHAINCASE

The change interval is every 2500 miles. Change when engine is warm. Use the same type of oil being used in the engine.

Checking Oil Level

To check the primary chaincase oil level, remove the oil level plug at the middle, lower portion of the chaincase. The oil should seep gently out the level is correct.

Changing Chaincase Oil

1. Remove the left-side footpeg.
2. Place a long metal tray or suitable substitute beneath the chaincase, unscrew the central fixing bolt, or the screws around the chaincase cover as on some models, and pull off the chaincase cover just enough to break the joint and let the oil escape.
3. Let the cover sit for a moment until as much of the oil as possible has drained out, then remove the cover.
4. Wash out the cover with kerosene or another suitable solvent.
5. Replace the cover, remove the chain inspection cap, and add the correct amount and grade of oil with the aid of a small funnel. Check the oil level as before.

The primary chaincase for the Commando should be filled with 7 oz. of oil, while on the other models, the correct amount is 4.5 oz.

Never use any type of oil additive or a thicker grade of oil in the primary chaincase in an effort to slow or stop a leak, or for any other rason, as these may affect the operation of the clutch.

CAUTION: *Do not overfill the primary chaincase.*

FRONT FORKS

The oil should be changed every 5,000 miles (Commando), or 10,000 miles (pre-Commando) and refilled with the recommended grade in the correct amount.

1. Remove the small drain screw at the bottom of one fork leg, having a suitable receptacle ready to catch the oil. Push the bike off the center stand and work the forks up and down to completely drain all of the oil in the fork.

2. Allow the oil to drain for several minutes, then replace the drain screw, paying attention to the fiber washer to avoid damaging it. Drain the other fork leg in the same manner.

3. The large filler plug at the top of each fork leg must now be removed. If necessary for your bike, remove the handlebars for increased accessibility to the plugs.

With the bike off the center stand, remove *one* of the filler plugs.

CAUTION: *Do not remove both plugs with the bike off the center stand, or the forks will collapse.*

4. Push down on the front end so that the spring and damper rod rise out of the fork leg.

5. Using two wrenches, remove the filler plug from the damper rod.

6. Put the machine on the center stand so that the spring and damper rod retract into the fork leg, which they will do when the forks extend.

7. Pour the correct amount of oil into the fork leg. Atlas and Commando: 5 oz in each leg; Scramblers: 6.5 oz in each leg.

Oil must be added slowly. It takes time for the oil to seep past the spring and into the slider.

An alternate method to hasten filling is to cover the plug hole with the palm of one hand and then pump the forks up and down slightly.

8. After the oil has been added, push the machine off the stand again to expose the damper rod. Screw the filler plug onto the rod as far as possible, then lock the damper rod nut against it. A little thread locking compound can be used on the filler plug threads, as this will ensure that the damper rod does not come loose in operation.

9. Put the bike back on the center stand and screw the filler plug into the fork leg and tighten firmly. repeat the procedure with the remaining fork leg.

DRIVE CHAIN

The rear chain receives some lubrication from the oil tank by way of the tank breather tube. On Commandos, a felt regulator is incorporated into the tube. A lubricant developed specifically for motorcycle drive chains, however, should be used at regular intervals.

GREASE NIPPLES

On all drum brake models, grease nipples are fitted to the front and rear brake cam pivots. These should be lubricated every 5,000 miles with no more than one stroke of the grease gun to avoid getting grease inside the drum.

Most models also need lubrication of the rear brake pedal pivot and a fitting is provided for this purpose. Grease the pivot every 2,500 miles.

At the same interval, give a few shots of grease to the speedometer drive on the rear wheel.

On Commando models only, there is a nipple on the right side of the swing arm bush housing. This should be attended to every 5,000 miles. Fill it with SAE 140 oil.

To check the swing arm oil level, remove the spindle locating bolt at the top, center, of the swing arm pivot. Fill with oil until it begins to come out of the bolt hole.

CAUTION: *Be sure to use oil only; do not use grease.*

CONTACT BREAKER POINTS

Battery and Coil Ignition

Every 5,000 miles, when checking or replacing the contact breaker points, apply some grease to the breaker cam and to the pivot posts.

At the same time, apply a small amount of light oil to the centrifugal advance mechanism bob weights at their pivots. The advance mechanism is behind the breaker point plate.

In both cases, use the grease and oil very sparingly so you won't foul the points in the process.

Magneto Ignition

The cam ring in the Lucas K2F magneto has two holes drilled into it in which are fitted very small fiber wicks which hold and distribute oil. They are fed by much larger pieces of fiber beneath the cam ring. Every 3,000 miles, add oil sparingly to the cam ring face. Less often, the cam ring may be removed after first removing the center bolt, prying out the points and breaker plate, and very gently pulling out the cam plate. It must be pulled straight out by hand. Removing the cam ring will allow you to oil the fiber elements directly. Do it sparingly.

If the wicks in the ring are missing, as may happen after many miles, the ring can be lightly greased for the same purpose.

Also apply a drop of oil to the breaker point pivot post.

SPEEDOMETER AND TACHOMETER CABLES

The speedometer and tachometer cables should be removed, cleaned, inspected, and lubricated with grease periodically.

1. Disconnect the cables at the instruments or the drive box.

2. Withdraw the cables, leaving the outer housings in place.

3. Clean the cables thoroughly in kerosene, then inspect them for fraying.

4. Completely coat the cables with light-duty grease except for the 6 in. nearest the instruments.

5. Reinstall the cables as removed.

STEERING HEAD BEARINGS

Late Model Commando

If the machine does not have a large chrome hexagon nut at the top of the steering stem, it is the latest design. The fork bearings are therefore ball journal type, but pre-packed with grease at the factory which lasts for the life of the motorcycle. These bearings need neither lubrication nor adjustment of any kind.

All Other Models

Steering head bearing lubrication is necessary at intervals of about 20,000 miles. It is necessary to remove the fork legs and steering stem. Refer to "Chassis" for procedures.

REAR SHOCK ABSORBERS

The Girling rear shock absorbers are maintenance-free sealed units and cannot be disassembled. If a shock absorber weeps oil, it must be replaced.

On some early machines, the upper part of the spring might be greased if it grates against the metal dust cover.

WHEEL BEARINGS

The maintenance interval for both front and rear wheel bearings is 10,000 miles, at which time they should be removed, cleaned, inspected, packed with the approved brand of grease, and replaced. Removal procedure is given in "Chassis."

Service Checks and Adjustments

CLUTCH

The procedure is essentially the same for all models.

1. Remove the clutch activating lever inspection cap on the gearbox and the clutch adjusting screw cap on the primary chaincase.

2. Run the clutch cable adjuster all the way down until there is slack in the cable.

3. Check the free-play of the clutch activating lever in the gearbox outer cover. There should be about ⅛ in. of free movement before the lever touches the clutch pushrod.

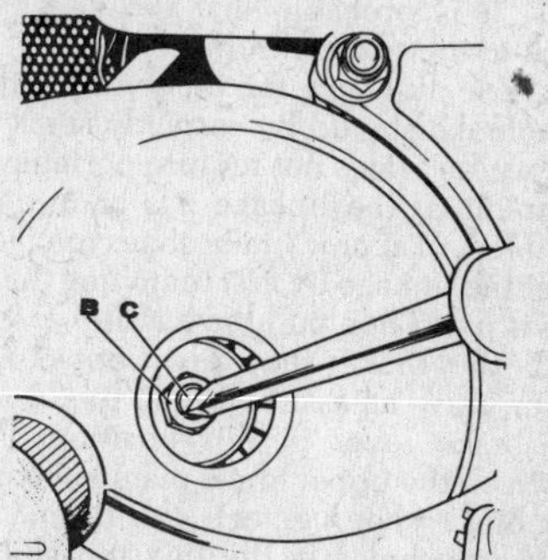

Clutch adjuster locknut (B) and adjuster (C)

4. Adjust, if necessary, by loosening the locknut on the adjusting screw in the center of the clutch hub.

5. Loosen the adjusting screw a few turns until you note the free-play in the gearbox lever.

6. Screw in the adjusting screw until it just touches the clutch pushrod.

7. On Commando models, back the adjusting screw off one full turn, then

tighten the locknut. On all other models, back the screw off ½ to ⅔ of a turn, then tighten the locknut.

8. Make sure that the activating lever has the required free-play. Take up the extra cable slack with the cable adjusters at the gearbox or the handlebar. There should be about ⅛ in. of free movement in the handlebar lever before it engages the clutch for pre-Commando models. This is measured between the hand lever and the lever holder. On the Commando, there should be between 3/16 in. and ¼ in. free movement between the cable outer casing and the adjuster.

BRAKE ADJUSTMENT

Commandos are fitted with either an hydraulic disc or a twin leading shoe drum-type brake at the front, and a single leading shoe at the rear on pre-1975 models. 1975 and later models have a disc at the rear wheel as well. Drum brakes are cable-operated on both wheels.

Other models usually had single leading shoe brakes front and rear, and the rear brake was rod-operated.

On all drum brakes, if the axle nut has been loosened, the brakes must be centralized in the drum before attempting adjustment. This is done by applying the brake hard with the axle nut loose, and then tightening the axle nut while keeping the brake applied. Then adjust the brake as outlined in the following sections.

Commando

FRONT, DRUM TYPE

1. Two adjusters are provided on the front brake cable: at the handlebar and at the drum itself. Usually, the adjuster at the drum is used to compensate for wear of the brake shoes.

Adjust the brakes so that the shoes contact the drum after the handlebar brake lever has moved about 1 in. (measured at the tip of the lever).

2. The angle formed by the cable and the brake plate lever should not exceed 90° when the brake is fully applied. If it does, it is probable that the shoes are worn to the point of replacement.

3. The link rod for the twin leading shoe brake should be correctly set at the factory, and does not require periodic adjustment. If the linkage has been disassembled, or if new brake shoes are fitted, reset the linkage by first removing the top clevis pin. Then pull the handlebar lever until the brake shoe just contacts the drum. Have an assistant hold the handlebar brake lever in this position. Push down on the upper brake plate lever until the brake shoe contacts the drum. The clevis pin holes in the link rod and the lever should line up, if the brakes are correctly adjusted. If not, loosen the link rod locknut, and screw the rod in or out so that the holes line up. Tighten the locknut. Insert the clevis pin and fit the clip. Adjust the brake with the brake plate adjuster.

NOTE: *The pins should be checked periodically and replaced if they show signs of wear, or braking effectiveness will be reduced.*

4. The front brake is equipped with an

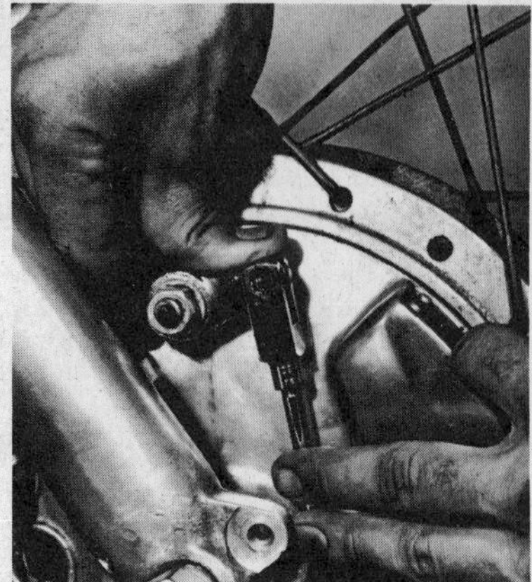

Adjusting tls brake rod

air scoop and an outlet, both of which are blocked off. The plates can be removed if desired, but the wire mesh screens must remain in place.

FRONT, DISC TYPE

1. The only required check besides pad wear is for fluid level. The fluid level should be ½ in. from the top of the reservoir. Add DOT 3 brake fluid only if topping up is necessary. Refit the diaphragm closed end down.

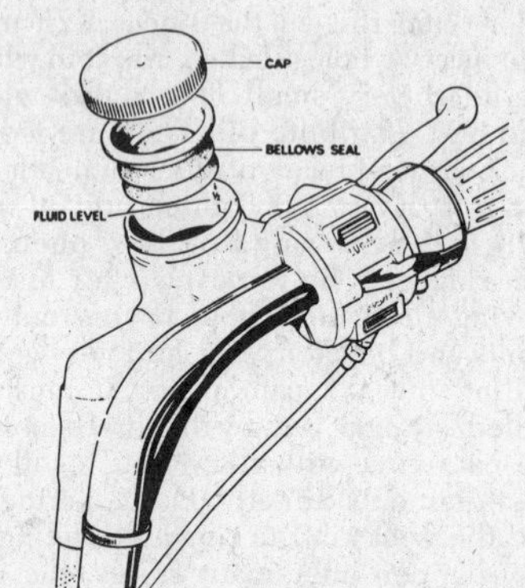

Disc brake fluid level should be ½ in. below the lip of the reservoir

Note that the fluid level may drop slightly as the pads wear. In this case it is not necessary to add additional fluid, since the level will rise when new pads are fitted.

2. Bleeding and flushing procedures for the hydraulic system are provided in "Chassis."

REAR, DRUM TYPE

1. A stop bolt is fitted so that the brake pedal can be positioned to suit rider preference. Adjust this before adjusting the brake. If the stop bolt is moved, check operation of the brake light switch.

2. When the rear brake is fully applied, the lever should not be past the 6 o'clock position. If it is, new linings are necessary. The brake is adjusted with the adjuster on the end of the cable. Allow about 1 in. of pedal travel before the linings contact the drum.

3. Adjust the brake light switch after adjusting the brake. Loosen the securing screws and move the switch up or down as necessary so that the brake light goes on as soon as the pedal is depressed.

4. Be sure that the brake pedal returns to rest against the stopper bolt, and not against the brake light switch, or the switch will be ruined. The switch plunger must *not* be fully compressed when the pedal is resting against its stop.

REAR, DISC TYPE

Check fluid level as outlined for "Front, Disc Type."

Pre-Commando

FRONT AND REAR

1. Adjust the front brake cable to allow about 1 in. of hand lever movement, measured at the tip of the lever, before the linings contact the drum.

The angle formed by the brake arm and the cable should not exceed 90° when the brake is fully applied, or the linings are probably worn to the point of replacement.

2. If the machine is equipped with a pedal stop for the rear brake pedal, this should be adjusted to the desired position first.

3. The rear brake, if rod-operated, must be adjusted with the motorcycle on its wheels and the weight of a rider on it. Allow about 1 in. of pedal movement before the linings contact the drum.

4. In all cases the wheels should be free to turn with no dragging from the brake linings.

PRIMARY DRIVE CHAIN

1974 and Earlier

On pre-Commando models, this adjustment should be made when the engine is at operating temperature.

1. Remove the primary chaincase inspection cap.

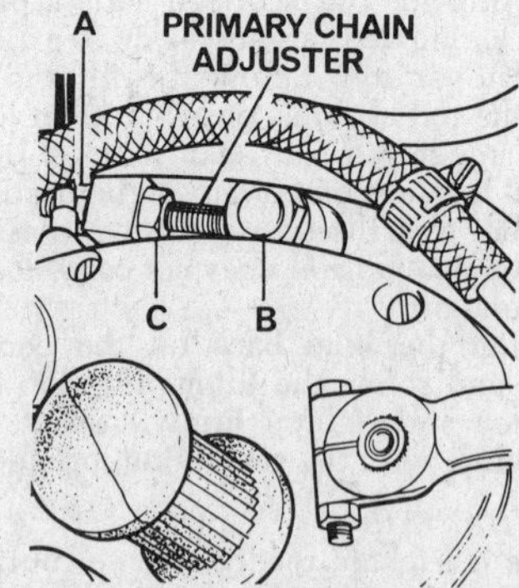

Primary chain adjuster locknuts (A&C) and locking bolt (B)

2. Loosen the large nut on the adjustment assembly on top of the gearbox. Also, loosen the nuts on the lower gearbox mounting stud.

3. On Scrambler models: screw down the adjuster bolt several turns. Pull down hard on the drive chain to take up the slack in the primary chain, then turn the adjuster bolt out until primary chain tension is correct. Tighten the lockbolt.

4. On other models: Back off the adjuster nut on the right several turns. Then tighten the nut on the left. The gearbox will pivot to the left to tighten the pri-

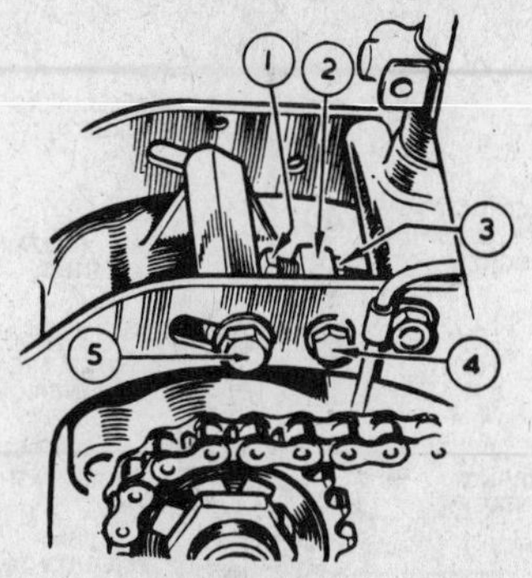

G15CS primary chain adjuster bolt (1), locknut (3), and gearbox lock bolt (5)

mary chain. Tighten the nut until the slack is completely gone, then back it off several turns and tighten the right nut until the correct chain slack is obtained. For Commandos this is ⅜ in. total up and down movement. For models with single-row chains, ½–¾ in.

5. Slowly rotate the chain and check the slack at several points. If the chain has a tight spot, the slack must be set to the correct specification at this point.

6. Tighten the large adjuster nut and the mounting stud nuts.

7. The final drive chain adjustment has been altered and must be checked.

1975 and Later

An automatic chain tensioner is fitted to the primary chain, so no adjustment is necessary.

FINAL DRIVE CHAIN

Before attempting adjustment, the chain must be clean and well lubricated. Check for tight spots and set slack at the tight spot, if any.

1. Loosen the rear axle nuts. Loosen the adjuster locknuts. Back off the rear brake adjuster (drum brake).
2. Pull down on the bottom chain run to ensure the wheel is aligned.
3. Turn each adjuster an equal amount until the chain is a bit looser than desired.
4. Check slack with the motorcycle on its wheels and a rider on it. Readjust, if necessary, until there is ¾ to 1 in. of slack (total up and down movement) measured in the middle of the bottom chain run.
5. Apply the rear drum brake, tighten the axle nuts and recheck chain slack. Tighten the adjuster locknuts.
6. Check that the brake is not dragging. On models with a rod-operated brake, the adjustment will have changed if the wheel was moved. Readjust the brake as necessary.

CAM CHAIN

1. Cam chain tension should be checked periodically. 1975 and later models are fitted with a plug on the timing case cover to allow the tension to be checked. On other models, the cover must be removed to check the tension.
2. Correct cam chain tension is ⅛–3/16 in. of total up-and-down movement measured in the middle of the upper chain run. Adjustment is by means of an adjustable slipper secured by two nuts.

Air Cleaner

1974 and Earlier

This is a paper element on most models, although it differs for each type of machine. Replace the filter paper every 5,000 miles or more often under dusty conditions.

On motorcycles like the Commando with its larger filter box, foam air cleaner elements can be fitted as a replacement. These are superior to paper filters and can be reused by washing them in solvent and oiling as per instructions. Follow the filter manufacturer's recommendations if this is done.

1975 and Later

A foam-type air cleaner is used on these machines. Under normal conditions the filter should be serviced every 3,000 miles by removing it from the machine, washing it in clean gasoline, and squeezing dry. Then soak the filter in motor oil, squeeze off the excess, and install.

Periodic Maintenance Intervals

Weekly
- Check tire pressure

Every two weeks
- Check battery electrolyte level

Every 250 miles
- Check engine oil tank level

Every 1,000 miles
- Check primary chaincase oil level
- Lubricate and adjust rear chain
- Lubricate all control cables
- Adjust both brakes
- Check gearbox oil level

Every 2,500 miles
- Check timing and adjust contact breaker points
- Clean spark plugs and set gaps
- Change primary chaincase oil and check adjustment
- Check clutch adjustment
- Change engine oil
- Clean crankcase oil filter
- Clean, lubricate, and adjust rear chain
- Grease rear brake pedal pivot
- Grease speedometer drive
- Lubricate control cables

Every 3,000 miles
- Lubricate magneto cam ring
- Clean air filter (foam-type)

Every 5,000 miles
- Change gearbox oil
- Change oil in forks (Commando)
- Check steering head bearing adjustment
- Clean contact breaker points
- Lubricate contact breaker cam and auto advance unit
- Grease brake spindles (one stroke of grease gun)
- Check and adjust valve rocker clearances
- Check and adjust cam chain
- Replace air filter element (paper-type)
- Disassemble and clean both carburetors
- Lubricate swing arm bushes (Commando)
- Replace cartridge oil filter

Every 10,000 miles
- Change oil in front forks (pre-Commando)
- Re-pack wheel bearings with grease
- Check front and rear rubber engine mountings for side play (Commando)

Maintenance Data

			Commando			
	Atlas	*G15CS, N15CS, P-11*	*Fastback*	*Roadster*	*SS Hi-Rider*	*Interstate*
Fuel Tank (gal)	3.5	2.5	3.9	2.7, 3.0	2.3	②
Oil Tank (pts)	4.5	4.5	6.0	6.0	6.0	6.0
Gearbox (pts)	1.0	1.0	1.2	1.2	1.2	1.2
Primary Chaincase (oz)	4.5	4.5	7.0	7.0	7.0	7.0
Front Forks @ Leg (oz)	5.0	6.5	5.0	5.0	5.0	5.0
Tire Pressure (psi) ①						
Front	24	24	22	22	22	22
Rear	24	24	24	24	24	24
Chain Slack (in.)						
Primary Drive	½–¾	½–¾	⅜	⅜	⅜	⅜
Rear Drive	¾–1	¾–1	¾–1	¾–1	¾–1	¾–1

① For two-up or extended high-speed operation, add 2 psi, front and 4 psi, rear to given pressures.
② 750—6.0; 850—7.3

Recommended Lubricants

Engine and Primary Chain		
Above 32° F	SAE 20/50	or SAE 30W
Below 32° F	SAE 10/30	or SAE 20W
Gearbox		
Above 32° F	SAE 90EP	
Below 32° F	SAE 30	
Front Forks	SAE 10-30	or SAE 20W
Swing Arm (Commando)	SAE 140	
Grease Fittings	Waterproof, medium-weight chassis grease	
Control Cables	10/30 motor oil Graphite-base lubricant Molybdenum disulphide-base lubricant	
Tach, Speedometer Cables	Light-duty grease	
Wheel and Steering Head Bearings	Waterproof, medium-weight bearing grease	

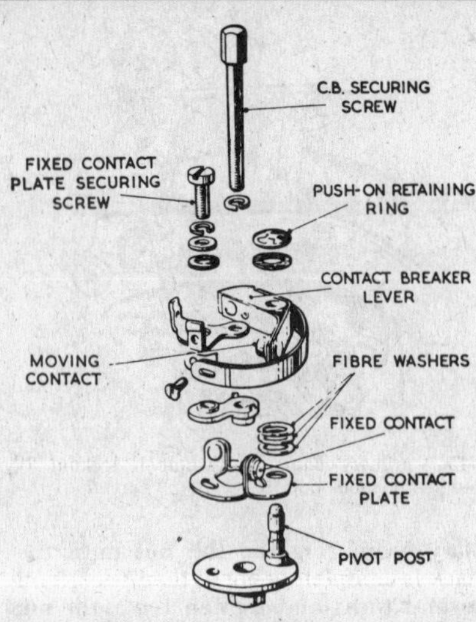

Magneto breaker points assembly

Tune-Up

NOTE: *Common tune-up procedures are explained in detail in "General Information."*

Valve Adjustment

NOTE: *Valves must be adjusted when the engine is cold.*

1. Remove the gas tank after shutting off the fuel taps and disconnecting them at the tank. On some models, the seat must be removed first.
2. Remove the spark plugs, the two exhaust rocker covers, and the intake rocker cover.
3. Turn the engine over with the kickstarter until the left-side intake valve is fully open (the rocker arm will be depressed). The right intake valve will be closed at this point. Check the clearance at the right intake valve with a feeler gauge. It should be 0.006 in. for all models except Combat-equipped Commandos which are set at 0.008 in.

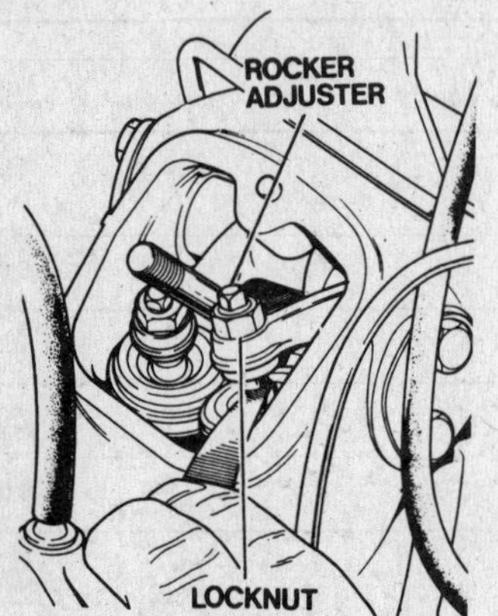

Adjusting the valves

The feeler gauge blade will be a slight drag fit in a correctly adjusted valve.

4. Adjust, if necessary, by loosening the locknut and turning down the adjuster until the feeler gauge blade can be pulled through with a slight drag on it.
5. Hold the adjuster in position and tighten the locknut. Recheck the gap after tightening.
6. Turn the engine over until the right intake valve is depressed, then adjust the left intake valve.
7. Repeat the procedure with the exhaust valves. Proper exhaust valve clearance for all standard engines is 0.008 in. Combat engines are set at 0.010 in.

Contact Breaker Points

MAGNETO IGNITION

The contact breaker points are located beneath the magneto cover on the left-side of the machine.

Removal

1. Loosen the kill-button wire knurled nut at the magneto. This is attached to the post in the center of the magneto cover.
2. Unscrew the cover and place it aside.
3. Loosen the central hex-head securing screw until it is clear of its threads but is still in the center of the contact breaker. It can be used to "break" the points off their tapered shaft by gently levering sideways with the fingers.
4. When the points have been taken off the shaft, remove them completely.

Installation

Installation is the reverse of the removal procedure. Clean the new points with a non-oily solvent to remove the preservative coating. Do not forget to replace the fiber washers on the pivot post. Refer to the illustration for correct position of various parts. Also, apply a drop of oil to the post for lubrication. Note that the points assembly has a key which must fit in its slot. Set the gap upon installation. The ignition timing need not be readjusted.

Gap Adjustment

1. Turn the engine over slowly until the points are fully open. This should be done with care. The points will be open at two positions on the cam ring. These points can be determined by looking at the cam ring itself. There are two "thick" areas. The points will be open when the contact breaker heel passes over these points which are about 6 o'clock and 12 o'clock.
2. Loosen the fixed contact plate securing screw, then use a screwdriver to move the fixed contact plate to the correct gap. Check the gap with the appropriate feeler gauge. It should be 0.012–0.015 in.
3. Tighten the fixed contact plate securing screw and recheck the gap.
4. Check that the gap is the same at both open positions on the cam ring. If it is not, set the gap so that it is within the given specification at both open positions.

CAPACITOR IGNITION

Capacitor ignition systems (or battery and coil ignition) are found on 1967 models as well as on Commandos. The earliest machines equipped with this system had the ignition points located in a canister behind the cylinder barrels and attached to the timing case. The first machines utilized dual points with the condensers mounted on the breaker plate. This set-up was soon replaced with yet another system: Lucas 6CA dual points, individually mounted on the breaker plate, the condensers being remotely positioned. The points on this later system allow each cylinder to be timed separately. This system was used on Commando models also up to engine No. 131257, when the points were relocated to the timing case. Aside from the new location, the points assembly is the same.

Commando 750s (1973) and Commando 850s use another type of breaker point assembly, the Lucas 10CA.

Early 1967 Models

Removal

1. Remove the ignition point cover.
2. If desired, the points assembly may be removed as a unit to reveal the automatic timing advance mechanism. Disconnect the two wires from the snap connectors; remove the two screws which secure the breaker plate and remove the plate.
3. If replacement of the points only is desired, remove the two wires from the snap connectors, release the nut which holds the spring of each breaker point to

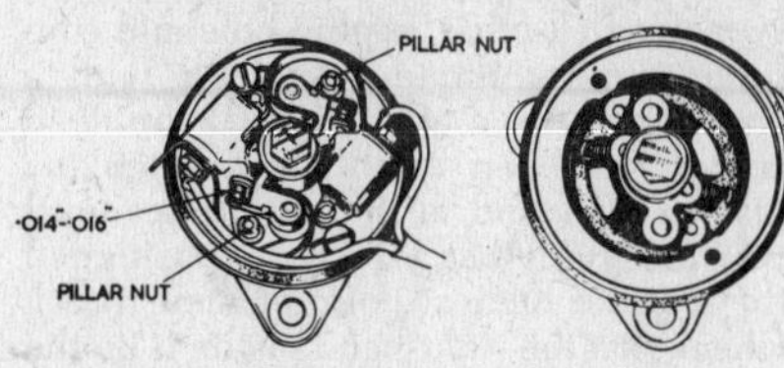

Early battery-and-coil breaker points and advance mechanism

its condensor, being careful of the insulating washers and their positions.

4. Remove the pillar nut which holds each breaker point onto the plate and take away the points.

Installation

Installation is the reverse of the removal procedure. Clean the new points with a solvent to remove the preservative coating. Be sure that all insulating washers are in their proper positions. Apply a drop of oil to the pivot posts.

NOTE: *When refitting the contact breakers, assure that the wires are connected correctly. The yellow-black wire attached to the top contact breaker goes to the coil mounted on the left rear frame down tube. Also, the high tension lead from this coil goes to the drive side cylinder.*

When refitting the contact breaker cover, be sure that the two insulated strips for each condenser are in position.

Gap Adjustment

1. Turn the engine over until one of the breaker points is fully open.
2. Loosen the pillar nut which secures the breaker point fixed plate.
3. Use a screwdriver to adjust the gap by prying between the fixed plate and the contact breaker housing.
4. Using a feeler gauge, set the gap for each breaker point at 0.014–0.016 in.
5. Tighten the pillar nut and recheck the gap.

Late 1967 Models and Commando 750 to Engine No. 131257

These models utilize the Lucas 6CA points assembly, located behind the cylinders.

Removal

1. Remove the points cover.
2. If desired, the breaker points assembly may be removed as a unit to reveal the automatic timing advance mechanism by removing the two large screws which secure the breaker assembly plate.
3. To remove the points themselves, remove the hexagon nut which secures the wire and the contact breaker spring. Be especially careful of the plastic insulator sleeve and the fiber washer.
4. Remove the locking screw (D) and take off the breaker.

Installation

Installation is the reverse of the removal procedure. Ensure that the insulating washers and insulator sleeve are correctly positioned. Smear the pivot post with a bit of grease before refitting. Clean new points with a solvent to remove the preservative coating. When fitting the point cover, be sure it is seated on the rubber washer.

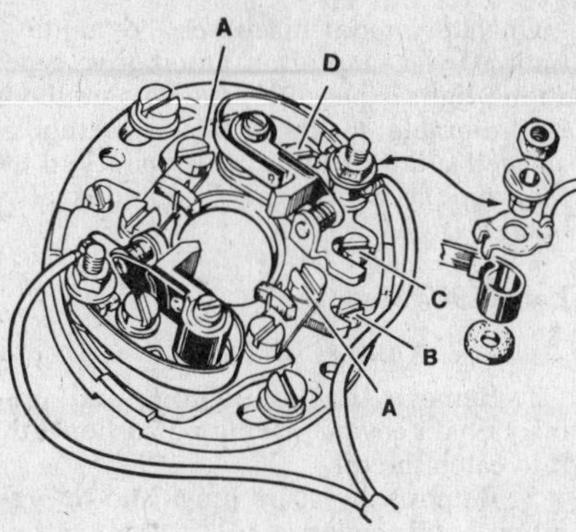

6CA points assembly

Gap Adjustment

1. Turn the engine over until the slash mark on the point cam aligns with the nylon heel of one of the breaker points.
2. Check the gap with the appropriate feeler gauge. It should be 0.014–0.016 in.
3. If adjustment is necessary, loosen the locking screw (D) and turn the eccentric screw (C) until the proper gap is attained.
4. Tighten the locking screw and recheck the gap.
5. Repeat the procedure for the remaining point set.

Commando 750 From Engine No. 131258 to 1972 Models

The points are located beneath the cover on the timing case. This is also a 6CA breaker set and the procedure for removal, replacement, and adjustment is exactly the same as described in the preceding section.

Commando 750 (1973) and Commando 850

These models use Lucas 10CA points assemblies driven off the camshaft.

Removal

1. Remove the points cover.
2. To remove the points assembly complete, remove the two large screws which secure the breaker assembly plate. The ignition timing must be set upon installation if the breaker assembly plate is disturbed.
3. To remove individual points, disconnect the wire, being careful of the plastic and fiber insulators at the terminal.
4. Remove the two screws which secure each set of points to the plate (C and D in the illustration).

Installation

Installation is the reverse of the removal procedure. Assure that the insulating washers and insulator sleeve are correctly positioned. Smear the pivot post with a bit of grease before refitting. Clean new points with a solvent to remove the preservative coating.

Gap Adjustment

1. Turn the engine over until the slash mark on the point cam aligns with the heel of one of the breaker points.
2. Check the point gap. It should be 0.014–0.016 in.
3. If adjustment is necessary, loosen the points securing screws (C and D), and move the point with a small screwdriver until the gap is correct.
4. Tighten the two screws and recheck the gap. Repeat the procedure with the other points set.

Ignition Timing

It is essential that the ignition points be in good condition and correctly gapped before the timing procedure is undertaken.

MAGNETO IGNITION

Adjusting Timing

1. Remove the left and right footpegs and the tachometer drive.
2. Remove the magneto points cover after loosening the kill button wire nut.
3. Place a pan beneath the primary chaincase cover and remove the cover.
4. Take out all of the screws which secure the timing cover. Place a receptacle for oil beneath the timing cover and pull it off, being careful that the conical oil seal fitted to the oil pump nipple is not misplaced.

Oil will dribble out of the drilling in the crankcase. It can be blocked off by inserting one of the cover screws.

5. Remove the spark plugs.
6. Remove the alternator rotor nut and affix the timing disc to the crankshaft.

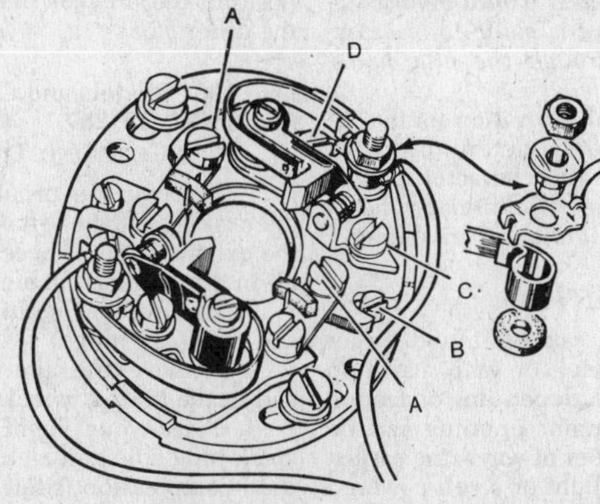

10CA points assembly

7. The pistons must be set to top dead center. Place your thumbs over the spark plug holes and kick the engine over slowly with the kickstarter until compression is felt in one of the cylinders. Now place a short drinking straw or a swizzle stick into that spark plug hole and turn the engine over using a wrench on the rotor nut until the piston's highest point has been ascertained. Work the pistons up and down several times until you are sure that you have it right.

NOTE: *There will be about 4° of "loose" movement of the crankshaft which will indicate TDC.*

8. Attach a stiff wire anywhere that is convenient so that it points to "zero" on the timing disc.

9. Loosen the self-extracting bolt on the timing advance mechanism until the points can be turned freely.

10. Using a small block of wood, or suitable substitute, lock the bob weights of the timing advance mechanism in the "full advance" position.

11. Turn the rotor nut clockwise until the pointer indicates 32° on the timing wheel.

12. Place a very thin piece of paper (cigarette paper is good) between the points and, tugging gently at the paper, assure that the points are closed, trapping the paper. Rotate the points with a wrench on the center nut, maintaining gentle pressure on the paper.

13. The very instant the points begin to separate, the plug will fire. With the small wrench, hold the points at the place that the paper slips out of the points.

14. Turn the self-extracting bolt on the timing advance mechanism with your hand until it is finger tight, then tap the bolt head lightly with a hammer so that the advance mechanism will lock onto the tapered shaft.

CAUTION: *A light tap is all that is needed. Do not smack the bolt with any great force.*

Tighten the bolt.

15. Turn the engine over once or twice, then recheck the timing.

16. Before reassembling the components, be sure to remove the block from the timing advance mechanism. Check the mechanism for free play.

NOTE: *The correct amount of timing advance is 32° of crankshaft rotation which is equivalent to 0.343 in. (8.69 mm) of piston travel. It is possible to use this measurement if the head has been removed, but it would be inaccurate if an attempt is made to measure piston travel through the plug holes due to their angle.*

Also, the point of separation for the ignition points cannot be determined with a test light due to the characteristics of the magneto. A special ohmmeter, however, can be used if one is available.

CAPACITOR IGNITION

Piston position can be found either with a degree wheel, or with marks on the alternator rotor, depending on model. The moment of point opening can be checked in a number of ways, the easiest being with a test light or a self-powered continuity light.

On later model machines, "dynamic" timing by means of an automotive-type strobe light is possible, and this method is preferable to the "static" methods, since it allows timing to be checked at the rpm at which the engine usually operates.

Early 1967 Models

CHECKING TIMING

1. Remove the left footpeg and primary chain cover, placing a pan beneath it to catch the oil.

2. Remove the spark plugs and the ignition points cover.

3. Fit the timing disc onto the crankshaft and place the pistons at top dead center. The left cylinder should be on the firing stroke, as indicated by compression in that cylinder as the piston approaches top dead center and clearance at both valves at TDC.

4. The timing, when fully advanced, is 32°. The advance mechanism is behind the points and it is therefore easier to check the timing in the unadvanced position. This is fine on machines which have not covered a large number of miles. In this case, rotate the crankshaft clockwise a few degrees past 8° as indicated on the timing wheel, then turn it counterclockwise. When the pointer indicates 8°, the points for the left cylinder should just be beginning to open. Verify this by using a test or continuity light.

For machines with this system which have covered a large number of miles, the timing should be checked in the full advance position since the advance unit stops may be worn. To lock the advance unit into full advance position, remove the bolt of the breaker cam and use a screwdriver to turn the cam clockwise until it stops. Using this method, the points should start to open at 32° before top dead center.

ADJUSTING TIMING

To set the timing, proceed as outlined above. Loosen the two securing screws which hold the contact breaker plate and move the plate in the needed direction until the points for the left cylinder begin to open at the correct time. The plate is moved clockwise to retard the timing, counterclockwise to advance it.

Be sure to check the timing on the other cylinder as well. If there is a difference greater than 1° between the two, position the breaker plate so as to split the difference.

Late 1967 Models and Commando to Engine No. 131257

CHECKING TIMING

1. Remove the primary chain cover after taking off the left side footpeg and the exhaust pipe, if necessary. Catch the oil in a suitable container.

2. Remove the ignition points cover and the spark plugs.

3. Remove the alternator rotor bolt and fit the timing wheel.

4. Place your finger over the right spark plug hole and kick the engine over until compression is felt in the cylinder.

5. Insert a short drinking straw or a swizzle stick into the plug hole and continue turning the engine over with a wrench on the rotor bolt until top dead center has been established. Rock the pistons back and forth a few times until you are sure that you have positioned them at the highest point of their travel. Check that the right-hand piston is on the compression stroke by noting clearance at both valves.

NOTE: *There will be about 4° of "loose" movement in the crankshaft which will indicate TDC.*

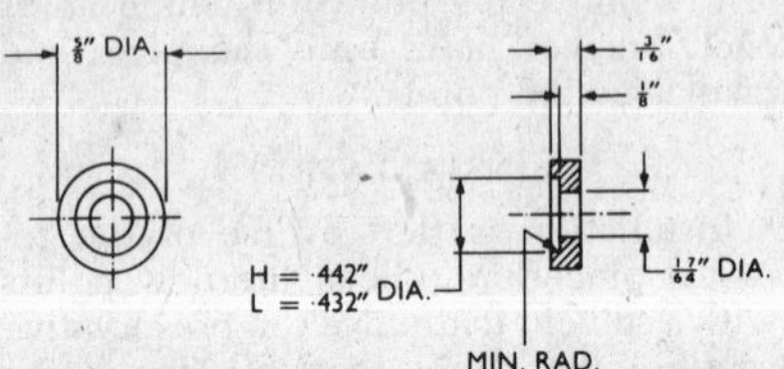

Washer for locking timing advance unit

6. Remove the center bolt of the contact breaker cam and find a washer with a hole large enough to fit over the cam post and bear on the cam itself. Replace the bolt and this washer, turn the cam clockwise to the full advance position, and tighten the bolt. This should lock the cam in the advanced position.

7. Using a piece of wire as a pointer, position it anywhere that is convenient so that it indicates "zero" on the timing disc.

If you have placed the right cylinder piston at TDC on the compression stroke, you will be working with the points with the black/white primary wire. Hook up the test or continuity light.

8. Rotate the crankshaft backward by turning the rotor nut clockwise several degrees past the normal timing advance as indicated by the degree wheel. This will be either 32° or 28° depending on the model. Turn the crank to about 40° before TDC to assure that the points are closed.

9. Slowly turn the nut counterclockwise until the timing wheel indicates the correct reading. At this very point the test light bulb should react, for they will commence to open if the timing is correct.

10. Repeat this procedure for the left cylinder.

ADJUSTING TIMING

If the points do not begin to open at the correct time, refer to the illustration of the 6CA points assembly.

6CA points assembly

1. Loosen the two securing screws (A) and turn the brass eccentric screw (B) until the points open at the correct time.

2. If the correct timing cannot be attained in this manner, set the contact breaker at about the middle of its adjustment range using screw (B), then tighten the securing screws.

3. Loosen the large screws which hold the contact breaker plate to the housing and rotate the entire plate until the points begin to open.

4. Secure the two screws. Turn the engine over 360° and adjust the other points set as previously described. It should not be necessary to move the entire breaker plate again, only the individual point set.

Commando Models After Engine No. 131257

These machines have the points assembly mounted in the timing case on the right side of the camshaft and are fitted with a timing mark on the rotor and an indicator plate beneath a cap at the front of the primary chain cover. The system may be checked for proper timing either with the engine running or at a standstill.

CHECKING TIMING

1. Remove the points cover and the inspection plug from the primary chaincase.

2. Hook up a strobe light in accordance with the manufacturer's recommendations.

3. Start the engine and run it at 2,000 rpm so that the timing is fully advanced. The mark on the rotor should register with the 28° mark on the indicator plate. (Each line indicates two degrees.)

4. If no strobe light is available, the engine can be checked at rest. Remove the points cover and the inspection cap on the primary chaincase.

5. Remove the spark plugs. Remove the intake valve rocker cover. Rotate the engine until the drive side (left) intake rocker opens and closes. This will place the drive side cylinder on the firing stroke.

6. Remove the center bolt of the contact breaker cam. With a washer which has a hole large enough to clear the cam post and bear on the cam itself, replace the bolt, turn the breaker cam until it is in the full advance position, and then tighten the bolt.

7. Connect a test light to ground and to the terminal of the LEFT contact breaker (black/yellow primary wire) and rotate the engine until the indicator plate on the primary chaincase reads 28°. The test light bulb should react at this point as the points separate.

8. Repeat the procedure to check the timing for the right cylinder.

ADJUSTING TIMING

1. Proceed as above. If the points do not open at the correct time, refer to the illustration of the Lucas 6CA or 10CA points.

2. Loosen the securing screws (A) and turn the brass eccentric adjusting screw (B) until the points open at the proper time. Tighten the screws.

3. Rotate the engine 360° and repeat the procedure for the other cylinder.

4. Be sure to remove the breaker cam bolt and the oversized washer, replace the standard washer, and tighten the bolt. Make sure that the advance mechanism works freely.

IGNITION TIMING—WHEN TIMING HAS BEEN LOST

1. If, for any reason, the breaker cam assembly has been removed from its shaft (and this applies to all models equipped with the 6CA or 10CA points system), it is necessary to align it in approximately the correct position before timing can be accomplished.

2. Referring to timing information previously given, locate the drive side (left) cylinder on its compression stroke, and place the piston at 28° before TDC.

3. Place the breaker cam assembly onto its shaft so that the bobweight pivots of the automatic timing advance mechanism line up with the point assembly cover screw holes (see illustration). The slot on the cam face (not the timing slash mark, but the slot) will be at approximately nine o'clock.

4. Set the ignition timing as previously described.

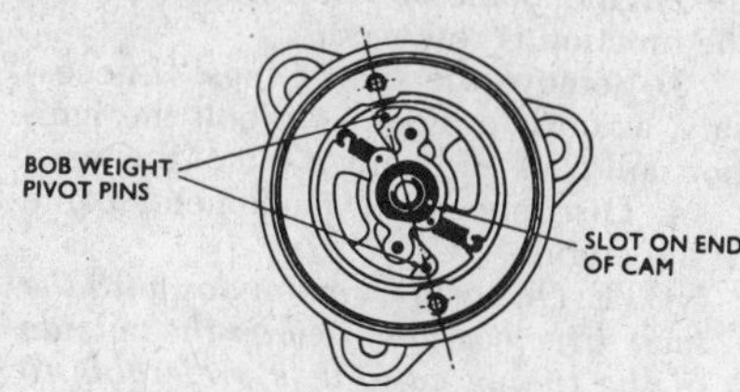

Correct location of timing advance unit

Carburetor Adjustments

These should be made after the other items in this section have been checked, and when the engine is at its normal operating temperature.

IDLE SPEED AND MIXTURE

1. Turn the pilot air screws in until lightly seated, then back them out about 1½ turns.

2. Turn in the throttle stop screws until idle speed is slightly higher than normal.

3. Remove one of the spark plug leads. Keep the engine running on one cylinder by turning in the throttle stop screw for that cylinder until the engine runs, but as slowly as possible.

4. Turn the pilot air screw in or out until the exhaust pulse from the running cylinder is smooth and even.

5. Connect the spark plug lead, rev the engine a few times to clear it out, then disconnect the lead to the cylinder which has been adjusted.

6. Repeat the previous procedure so that the running cylinder fires as slowly and evenly as possible.

7. Connect the lead. Both cylinders will be running and idle speed will be very high. Back out each throttle stop screw by equal amounts until the desired idle speed is reached.

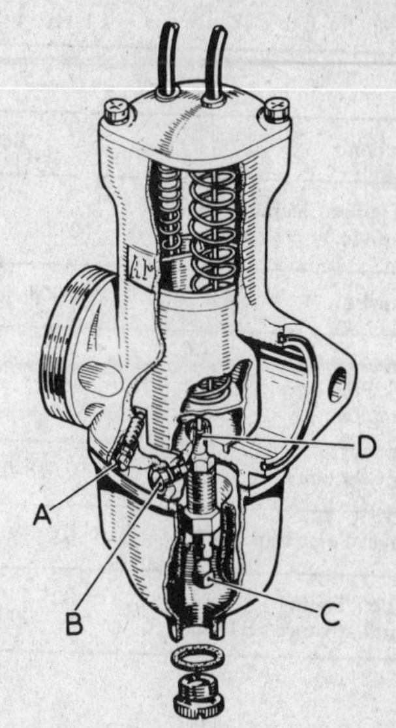

Concentric carburetor throttle stop screw (A), pilot air screw (B), main jet (C) and needle jet (D)

8. Check that both cylinders are firing evenly.

CARBURETOR SYNCHRONIZATION

1. Remove the air cleaner assembly.

2. Twist the throttle fully open to lift up the slides.

3. Position a mirror behind the carburetors or reach into the carburetor bores with the thumb and index finger of one hand.

4. Slowly close the throttle and watch, or feel, the slides as they are being lowered; they should enter their respective bores simultaneously.

5. If the slide positions are unequal, raise or lower one to match the other by turning the adjuster at the top of the carburetor.

6. Another check is to place a finger on each carburetor slide when the throttle is fully closed, then move the twist grip very slightly. Both slides should begin to lift at the same time. Adjust as described above if necessary.

THROTTLE CABLE ADJUSTMENT

On most models, the cable runs from the twist-grip to a junction block, where two shorter cables run to the carburetor tops. One end of each cable is equipped with an adjuster. These are located at the twist-grip and the carburetor tops.

Adjust the long cable so that there is about 2 mm of free-play before actuation.

Adjust the short cables so that there is as close to zero free-play as possible. Check carburetor synchronization as previously described.

After setting the free-play at each cable, start and warm up the engine. Turn the handlebars from side to side and notice any variation in rpm. If a variation occurs, one of the cables is either incorrectly adjusted (not enough free-play) or is binding somewhere along its routing.

Tune-Up Specifications

	Magneto Ignition	Capacitor Ignition (pre-Commando)	Commando (Standard)	Commando (Combat)
Carburetion	Refer to "Fuel System" for standard carburetor settings			
Valve Tappet Clearance (cold) Intake (in.)	0.006	0.006	0.006	0.008
Exhaust (in.)	0.008	0.008	0.008	0.010
Ignition Spark Plug (standard) Champion	N5	N5	N6Y-N7Y	N7Y
Plug Gap (in.)	0.018–0.022	0.023–0.028	0.023–0.028	0.023–0.028
Breaker Point Gap (in.)	0.012–0.015	0.014–0.016	0.014–0.016	0.014–0.016
Ignition Timing (full advance) BTDC	32°	32°	28°	28°

Engine and Transmission

It is important to realize that although the procedures for working on the Norton engine are applicable, with minor variations, to all models, the engine components are usually not interchangeable between Commando and pre-Commando units, even though they may be similar in appearance. Be sure that the correct replacement parts are obtained when necessary.

NOTE: *For engine component inspection procedures, refer to "Engine Rebuilding" under the General Information section.*

ENGINE SERVICE NOTES

1. On all models, the cylinder head and cylinder can be removed without removing the engine from the frame.
2. The clutch and primary drive and timing case components are also accessible for service with the engine in the frame.
3. All transmission components with the exception of the left-side countershaft (or layshaft) bearing can be serviced without removing the transmission.

If necessary, the transmission itself can be removed without disturbing the engine.

4. Most engine work requires only standard tools and a torque wrench. A variety of pullers are needed.

To remove the Commando diaphragm clutch, a special tool *must* be used for safety reasons.

Engine Removal and Installation

COMMANDO

The engine unit may be removed without disturbing the transmission, and this is the easiest method, since removal of the complete assembly requires removal of the rear wheel and swing arm.

1. Remove the seat and fuel tank.
2. Drain the oil from the tank and disconnect the oil pipe junction (one bolt) at the engine. Some oil will come out when the junction is removed.
3. Remove the spark plugs. If necessary, as on late models, unbolt the ignition coil pack and hang it out of the way.
4. Disconnect the tachometer cable at the engine.

NOTE: *On early Commandos with the tach drive box mounted on the outside of the timing case, it is preferable to remove the box itself rather than just the cable, since it is vulnerable to damage if the engine is dropped.*

5. Remove the carburetors complete with manifolds and hang them out of the way by the throttle cable.
6. Remove the exhaust system.
7. Remove the small, engine head steady plates. On models with rubber mounts here, loosen the rubber mount nuts first. Remove the head steady plate from the cylinder head.
8. Remove the gearshift lever.
9. Remove the battery cover. Disconnect the positive terminal of the battery to eliminate the possibility of a short.
10. Disconnect the alternator leads at the snap connectors.
11. Remove the left-side footpeg and the rear brake lever. Remove the primary chaincase cover and remove the alternator, clutch, sprocket, and chain. Refer to "Clutch and Primary Drive."
12. Disconnect the crankcase breather from the engine.
13. Disconnect the ground wire attached to the bottom crankcase stud on the left-side, if fitted.
14. Before removing the mounting plate bolts, provide some means of support for the engine or it will drop several inches before hitting the lower frame rails. A block of wood placed beneath the crankcase is a good idea.
15. Take off the self-locking nut from the bolt which passes through the front engine mount. Withdraw the bolt from the right-side of the frame. Remove the front engine mounting assembly.
16. Remove the rear crankcase mounting nuts and studs, lifting the unit to remove the bottom most stud. Remove the unit from the right-side of the frame.

Installation of the engine and transmission is basically a reversal of the removal procedure.

17. Place the engine in the frame from the right-side of the motorcycle.
18. Fit the three studs and nuts which pass through the rear engine mounting and the crankcase.
19. Supporting the engine, place the front engine mounting assembly in position.
20. Insert the front engine mounting bolt and tighten the self-locking nut to the correct torque setting. Tighten the nuts on the three rear engine mounting studs.
21. Continue reassembly in the reverse of the sequence described for removal.
22. The washers for the finned exhaust pipe nuts should be replaced.
23. Be sure that the exhaust pipe finned nuts are tightened securely. These nuts are best looked after by safety wire fastened by drilling one lobe of the nut and the top cylinder head fin.
24. Check all nuts and bolts for tightness before and after a short ride.

ATLAS

To remove the Atlas engine and transmission as a unit, follow this procedure:

1. Remove the gas tank, disconnecting the fuel lines at the carburetors and taking off the mounting nuts.
2. Remove the head steady bracket.
3. Remove the air cleaner and the carburetors.
4. Drain the oil tank and the engine sump. If work is to be performed on the transmission, drain it also.
5. Unbolt the oil pipe junction at the crankcase. Kicking the engine over a few times after draining the oil tank and before removing the junction will minimize the amount of oil which will dribble out.
6. Remove the exhaust pipes and mufflers.
7. Disconnect the tachometer drive (two screws) at the engine. It is advisable to remove the drive rather than just the cable to avoid hitting it on something as the engine is removed from the frame.
8. Disconnect the battery leads and remove the battery.
9. Remove the rectifier, being very careful of the rectifier bolt.
10. Remove the battery box.
11. Disconnect the crankcase and tank breather hoses to the oil tank and remove the tank (4 bolts).
12. Remove the oil tank platform.
13. Remove the clutch activating lever inspection cap at the top left-hand side of the transmission, pry up the lever with a suitable screwdriver (taking care not to damage the edges of the inspection hole), and remove the clutch cable. Screwing the cable adjuster all the way in makes the job easier. Next, remove the adjuster from the case.
14. Remove both footpegs. Place a pan beneath the primary chaincase cover to

catch the oil when it is removed. Remove the large hexagon nut on the footpeg stud and carefully take off the chrome cover and the rubber washer. Pull off the chaincase cover.

15. Disconnect the alternator leads at the snap connector.

16. Remove the clutch pressure plate by unscrewing the three spring adjustment nuts. These are cylindrical and have two small tabs on the face that bears against the clutch spring to prevent loosening during operation. Removing the nuts will invariably sheer off the tab, making replacement of the nuts advisable. If you must reuse the nuts on the clutch, a knife blade or suitable substitute can be placed between the nut and the spring while removing.

17. Remove the clutch springs and cups.

18. Remove the main clutch nut on the transmission mainshaft and the lock washer. Prevent the hub from turning either with the special tool or by applying the rear brake with the transmission in gear.

19. Remove the three nuts and washers which secure the alternator stator to the stator housing. Pull off the stator.

20. Remove the nut which secures the rotor to the crankshaft and remove the rotor and its woodruff key. A small gear puller is sometimes needed to take the rotor off of the shaft.

21. Disconnect the primary chain. The clutch hub may require a special puller to remove it from the transmission mainshaft, especially if it has not been removed before. In addition, the engine sprocket is fitted onto a tapered portion of the crankshaft and will definitely require a puller. A smaller gear puller can be used in place of the factory sprocket extractor. Be sure to remove the engine sprocket woodruff key.

22. Remove the three screws which fix the stator housing to the mounting plate and the three screws fixing the plate to the crankcase.

23. Remove the nut which is found about halfway between the engine sprocket and the clutch which secures the inner chaincase half.

24. The inner chaincase half is also secured by means of a tab by the nut on the bottom transmission stud. Remove this nut and take away the chaincase half. Disconnect the final drive chain.

25. Proceeding to the four bolts which fasten the upper and lower arms of the engine mounting plates (just before the swing arm), remove the lower bolts and loosen the upper two.

26. Remove the two studs, two bolts, and their respective nuts at the front engine plates.

27. Remove the two bolts which pass through the center stand mounts and the engine mounting plates. Lift the engine and remove the front mounting plates.

28. Remove the engine assembly from the frame.

29. Installation is the reverse of removal.

SCRAMBLERS

For engine service on Scrambler models, note the following points:

1. The engine and transmission are best removed as a unit.

2. The primary chaincase can be left intact during removal.

Refer to removal procedure for Atlas models for initial steps if additional information is needed.

1. Prepare the engine and transmission for removal in the manner outlined for the Atlas, removing the gas tank, exhaust pipes and mufflers, air cleaners, carburetors, oil from tank, and sump.

2. Remove the tachometer drive from the engine, clutch cable at the transmission, oil junction, oil tank and crankcase breather pipes, and alternator connections.

3. Disconnect the rear drive chain.

4. Remove the metal cover over the transmission.

5. Remove the upper front engine mounting bolts. Loosen, but do not remove, the lower front mounts.

6. Remove the right side footpeg and remove the rod from the left side. There are two spacers involved.

7. Unhook the center stand spring.

8. Remove the left side rear engine mounting bolts.

9. Raise the engine slightly to take the pressure off of the lower front bolts which are still in place and remove the nuts. Take away the engine plates, watching for the spacer.

10. Lever the engine forward and lift it up and out of the right side of the frame.

11. Installation is somewhat simplified by first removing the skid plate.

Before replacing the engine in the frame, be certain that the left side footpeg is in its proper position since it cannot be replaced after the engine is in the frame.

12. Begin by placing the engine in the frame from the right side of the bike, rear end first.

13. Insert a length of steel rod or a suitable screwdriver through the rear engine plates and the frame to align the bolt holes.

14. Lever the front of the engine up to replace the lower small mounting bolt and tighten the nuts firmly.

15. Lower the engine and refit the front and rear engine plate bolts.

16. The remainder of the installation procedure is the reverse of the removal procedure.

Top End

REMOVAL

The following procedure gives instructions for removing the head with the engine in the frame.

1. Remove the seat and gas tank. Disconnect the spark plug leads, remove or loosen the plugs; remove the exhaust system.

2. Remove the coil pack, if fitted.

3. On Commando models, remove the head steady side plates, unscrewing the rubber mounting nuts first. Remove the head steady plate from the head.

4. On pre-Commando models, unbolt the head steady from the head and the frame, and remove it.

5. Disconnect the rocker oil feed pipe on each side of the head.

CAUTION: *Each junction has two copper washers. A rag placed over the spark plug hole is a good idea when removing the banjo bolts.*

The rocker oil feed pipe must be placed out of the way so that the head can be removed. On models with neoprene lines, this is not a problem. Earlier machines, however, are equipped with a copper pipe to feed the rockers. This pipe is only flexible to a certain degree. It can be bent out of the way, but take care to avoid crimping it anywhere along its length. The alternate method is to also disconnect the pipe banjo at the crankcase and turn the pipe aside.

6. Remove the exhaust rocker covers and the intake rocker cover.

7. Remove the air cleaner, the carburetors, and the manifolds.

8. On magneto models, removing the front spark plug lead is a good idea.

NOTE: *On Scrambler models, additional steps must be taken at this point.*

a. Remove all of the cylinder head nuts and the bolt on the center of the head. This will leave only the four bolts flanking the spark plug holes;

b. Remove both exhaust rocker spindle retaining plates and remove the spindles. This requires a special tool. Refer to a following section. Be extremely careful of the washer and spring which are found on the spindle;

c. Remove the four remaining cylinder head bolts.

The remainder of the procedure is the same as that for other models.

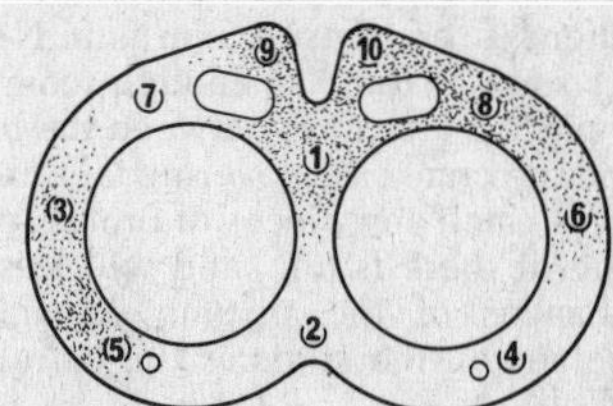

Cylinder head tightening sequence; reverse the order when removing the head

9. The cylinder head can now be taken off. It is secured to the cylinders by five bolts and nuts. First position the pistons at TDC. Loosen the bolts and nuts gradually and in the reverse of the tightening order shown. There are two long nuts concealed in the fins which require an expecially thin wrench to reach them.

As the last of the fasteners is loosened, the head should begin to rise off its seat slightly, due to the pressure of the valve springs. If the head is not free after the last of the fasteners has been removed, it is probably due to carbon build-up as on engines with many miles on them or those with an oil burning problem. In this event, place a block of wood against the cylinder fins at the exhaust port (the fins are strongest here) and rap sharply with a hammer.

10. The head must be removed very carefully. Remember that there are two

studs at the front of the cylinder barrels and three shorter ones in the head itself which must clear. The most important consideration at this point, however, is the pushrods.

11. Straddle the bike. Lift the head several inches off its seat. Slipping your fingers between the head and barrels, push the four pushrods up into the head as far as they will go. They should only protrude about two inches from the head.

12. Pull the head straight up as far as possible and tilt it backward and to one side until two of the pushrods clear their tunnel. Then tilt it to the opposite side so that the other two are clear. After both sets are out of the tunnels, the head can be taken out to one side.

NOTE: *The pushrods are of two lengths. The longer ones activate the intake rockers. These are placed closest to the center of the barrels. Be certain they are correctly located upon reassembly.*

13. The barrels can now be removed. Loosen all nuts securing the barrels to the crankcase. There are nine of them, except on the 850 Commando which has four allen bolts. These should be removed first.

Remove the nuts at the front of the barrels. The others must be loosened as much as possible until they hit the cooling fins. Lift the barrels as much as you can, then loosen the nuts again. Continue until the nuts can be taken off of the studs.

As soon as you have removed the nuts, remove and account for all washers. Be sure that none are left on the barrels, or one can easily fall into the crankcase later.

14. Lift the barrels clear of the crankcase. Ordinarily, the pistons will ride up with them if the transmission is in Neutral. As soon as there is enough room to do so, place a clean rag between the barrels and the crankcase covering the studs. This will catch any pieces of broken piston ring, if there is one, and will lessen the chances of the pistons damaging themselves on the studs as the barrel is pulled off.

CYLINDER HEAD

Maximum allowable warpage across the mating surface is 0.002 in.

ROCKER ARMS

Removal

1. For each rocker arm, remove the rocker spindle retaining plate assembly. This consists of an outer plate, a gasket, an inner plate with two tabs to engage the slots of the rocker spindle and assure it maintains its position, and another gasket. Each element in this assembly is different. Note each position carefully.

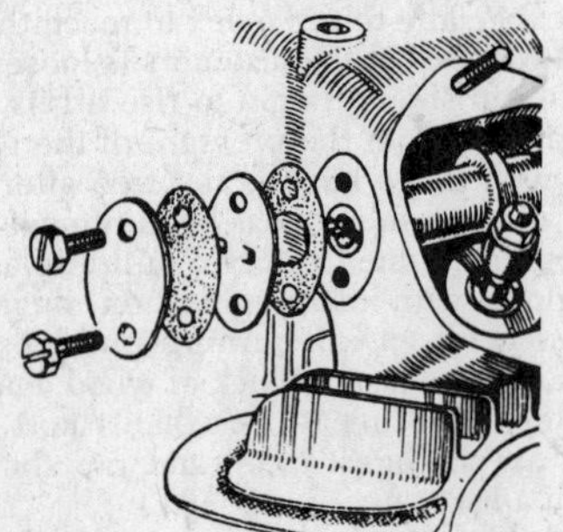

Rocker spindle retaining plate assembly

In most cases the parts will remain together when removed, and need not be taken apart.

2. The rocker spindle is press-fit on the cylinder head. First note the position of the slots in the spindle end. Removal is made much easier, and there is less chance of scoring the spindle or the head, if the head is heated first. Ideally, the head should be placed in an oven and heated to not more than 100° C (212° F). In the case of the Scrambler models, where the factory recommends removing the exhaust rocker spindles prior to removing the head (engine in the frame), a propane torch can be used, with caution, to heat the area around the spindle very gently.

The spindles must be removed with a puller. They are threaded internally to accept special tool no. 064298 for late models. Earlier units could accept the pre-Commando cylinder head bolts ($^5/_{16}$ in W). To remove the spindles, a bolt, a locknut, and a short steel sleeve (or pre-Commando clutch spring cup), can be used as a puller. Thread the locknut most of the way up the bolt, then insert it into the sleeve or spring cup. Screw the bolt as far as possible into the spindle. Tightening the locknut will draw the spindle out of the head.

The oil hole in the spindle must face AWAY FROM the center of the head

4. The rocker arm is flanked by a spring washer, fitted on the side closest to the center of the head, and a plain thrust washer on the opposite side. Be positive that both are accounted for. The thickness of the plain thrust washer should be 0.015 in.

NOTE: *The exhaust rockers can be taken directly out of the head after pulling out the spindle. The intake rockers must be turned upside down and then removed on older models.*

6. The ball end is press-fit in the rocker arm. To remove it, support the rocker arm on an appropriate surface to prevent damage to it, then drive the ball shaft out with a drift. The rocker arm has a drilled oil passage from the spindle to the ball end to lubricate the ball and pushrod cup. Make sure that this passage is clear. Also, note that the ball shaft's oil hole must line up with the oil drilling in the rocker. To reassemble, press the ball shaft into position as far as possible. A standard bench vise faced with wood will do the job.

Installation

The rocker arm assembly must be installed correctly or damage to the components will result.

1. The rocker spindle must be located so that the slots on the outer end are HORIZONTAL; the oil hole on the spindle *must* face away from the center of the head.

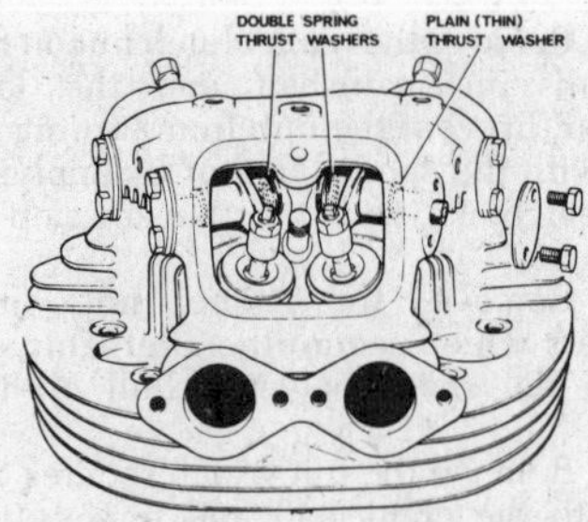

Rocker arm spindle spring and thrust washer installation

2. Fit the spring washer, the rocker arm, and the thrust washer in their proper locations. Remember that the spring washer is closest to the center of the cylinder head.

3. Heat the head, as was done on removal, and press in the spindle. Make sure that the spindle slots are horizontal to engage with the tabs on the spindle locating plate. Also, check to make certain that the spindle is just below flush with the gasket face on the cylinder head.

4. Fit the spindle locating plate. The correct order, from the head out, is:

a. Paper gasket with large center hole
b. Plate with locating tabs
c. Paper gasket
d. Plain oval plate
e. Two fixing bolts

If oil leaks from the locating plate assembly, it may be due to the spindle protruding even slightly from the head, or the plates themselves may be warped. A late modification has been the fitting of copper washers beneath the plate bolts (Part No. 063129). These may be fitted to all previous models.

VALVES AND VALVE SPRINGS

Removal

1. Take out the stud for the intake rocker cover if you are going to remove the intake valves.

2. Using the valve spring compressor, compress the springs far enough to remove the two tapered valve keepers (collets) and release the spring.

3. The valve collar, inner and outer springs, spring seat, and heat insulating washer can be removed. Keep each assembly separate so that the components

can be reassembled together and in their original location.

4. Remove the oil seals from the guide, if fitted. Remove the valve.

5. Intake valves are larger than the exhaust valves, so telling them apart is no problem. The Commando valves, however, are about 0.07 in. longer than those found on previous models, with a corresponding decrease in the length of the pushrods. The shorter valves can be fitted to the Commando, if necessary, provided that a winkel cap of the proper thickness is installed.

Commando valves cannot be fitted to a pre-Commando engine. The pushrods for Commando and pre-Commando models are in no way interchangeable.

6. Check the valve spring free length, for both inner and outer springs, against the figures given in the technical data. If the measured length is less than 0.187 in. from the standard value, the spring must be replaced. Note that valve springs should be replaced as a set.

Installation

NOTE: *The valve springs are progressively wound, and are installed with the close coils towards the cylinder head.*

1. Put some clean oil on the valve stem and place the valve in the guide.

2. Refit the valve seal, if so equipped. New seals must always be used.

3. Replace the heat insulating washer in its seat, then, the valve spring seat, the springs (close coils against the head), and the spring collar.

4. Compress the spring and slip the two keepers into place.

VALVE GUIDES

Removal

Nortons are equipped with cast iron guides, the newer models being fitted with guides grooved to accept an oil seal on the intake side.

All 750 models have a flange around the guide which rests against the surface of the head when the guide is installed. The 850, however, has a spring clip around the guide which accomplishes the same purpose.

Valve guide to valve stem clearance is 0.002–0.004 in

1. To remove the guides, strip the head of valves, springs, rocker arms, etc.

2. Heat the head on a hot plate or in an oven. This is essential as the guides are force fit in the head and any attempt to drive them out without heating is sure to result in either a broken guide or a scuffed or enlarged guide bore. Do not heat the head in excess of 200° C.

3. Use a drift to drive out the guides.

If the guides are broken, or have a great amount of carbon build-up as in the case of the exhaust guides, some difficulty will be encountered in removing them. If this is the case, use a chisel to break off the lower portion of the guide which protrudes into the port.

This operation should be an emergency recourse undertaken only after the standard procedure has been attempted.

Installation

1. To replace the guides, again heat the head to 200° C. The guide must be accurately inserted in the bore so that the valve can seat properly. To accomplish this, take the valve, which will be used in the port on which you are working, and place it in its normal seated position. The valve stem will be used to locate the valve guide in the head as it is driven in. Use the drift again, this time from the other end, and press home the guide until the flange or clip, abuts against the head. Guide bore size on all models is 0.3135–0.3145 in. Use the appropriate ream after installation.

NOTE: *The newer Commando 750s have been fitted with oil seals on the intake guides to eliminate the oil burning which was a problem on some motorcycles. The guides are grooved to accept these seals which must* not *be fitted on the exhaust side. These guides are identical in other respects to the previous units, so changing over to a seal-type is possible, if so desired, by simply replacing the old guides with the new units.*

The 850 is also fitted with oil seals on the intake valve guides, although this guide differs from the earlier one (being fitted with a circlip instead of a flange). In both cases, the oil seals go on the intake side only.

Oversized outside diameter guides are available, if needed, in the following sizes over standard: 0.002 in., 0.005 in., 0.010 in., and 0.015 in.

TAPPETS

Removal and Installation

1. The tappets, which are located at the front of the cylinder block, can be checked in place, or removed by cutting the safety wire and taking out the two screws.

The tappets will come out along with the keeper. Note its position for installation.

2. Since tappets are machined in pairs, it is imperative that they be kept together. If either is damaged, they must be replaced in pairs.

3. Grinding or finishing of the stellite pad which contacts the camshaft is not recommended. Replace the tappets if damage occured.

4. When installing, note that the beveled edges of the tappets (running from top to bottom) must face the front of the engine. Use safety wire after tightening the screws.

CYLINDER

1. Measure the bore at the top (½ in. below the lip), middle, and bottom in two directions 90° apart.

2. Rebore the cylinders if the difference between the largest and smallest of the measurements is 0.005 in. (0.13 mm) or greater, or if any of them is 0.008 in. (0.20 mm) greater than the standard bore diameter specification.

3. Pistons for 750s are available in four oversizes in increments of 0.010 in. and 0.010 and 0.020 in. for the 850.

4. When boring, set piston-to-cylinder clearance at 0.0045 in.

PISTONS AND RINGS

Removal

NOTE: *Mark the pistons "L" or "R" and the front or rear to facilitate installation.*

1. Remove the piston pin circlips.

2. Heat the piston crown gently and evenly. Heat only the crown, not the skirt. Push out the piston pin.

Inspection

1. Ring side clearance should be 0.0015–0.0035 in.

2. Ring end-gap should be 0.012–0.013 in. Replace the rings if the compression ring gap exceeds 0.014 in.

On multi-piece oil rings, the rails may have an end-gap of 0.010–0.040 in.

Installation

1. The design of the piston rings has been changed several times over the years. The top compression ring is chromed on most models, or red-coated.

NOTE: *Do not remove the red coating if present.*

2. On late models the lower compression ring is tapered, while on others it may be stepped. Be sure the rings are installed with the "Top" mark facing upwards. Stepped rings are installed as illustrated.

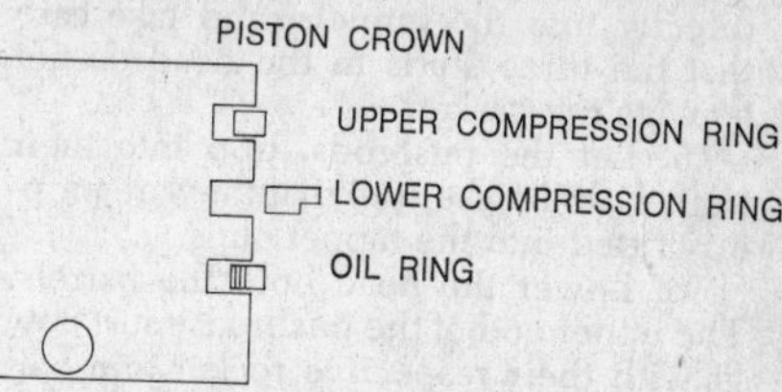

Correct installation of stepped compression ring

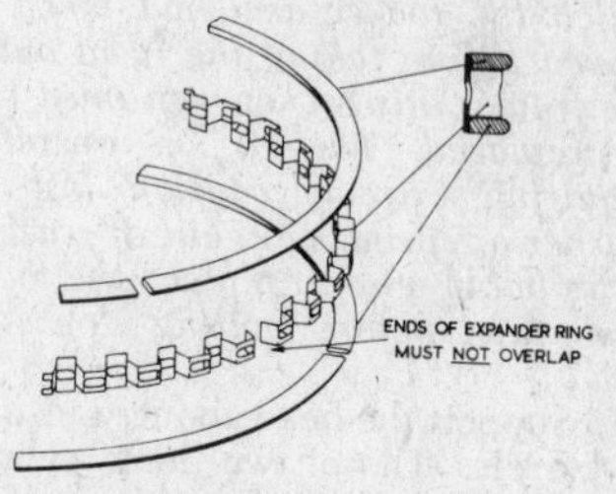

Three-piece oil ring installation

3. Stagger the ring end-gaps around the piston.

4. Fit the pistons to the rods, using new circlips. The rounded ege of the circlip, where applicable, must face the piston.

Be sure the pistons are correctly fitted. 850 models have the crown stamped "RH" or "LH" and the "EX" mark must face the front of the engine.

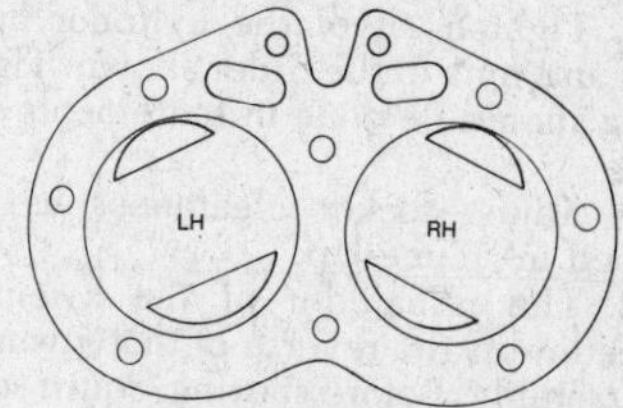

Piston installation (750)

750 Models have valve cut-outs. The exhaust valve cut-out is closer to the edge of the piston and must be positioned towards the front of the engine.

ASSEMBLY

1. Install the cylinders. Tighten the bolts or nuts in a cross pattern until the correct torque is reached.

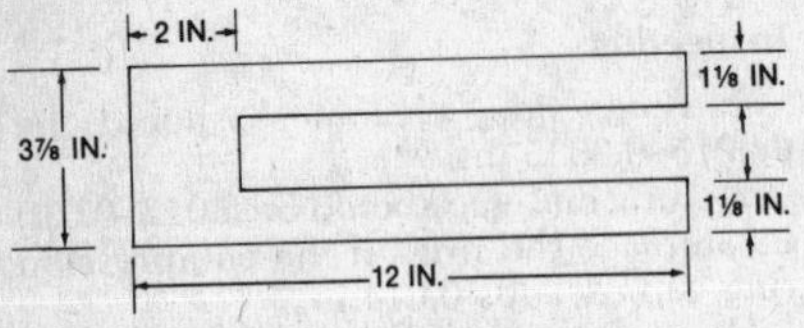

Piston stand dimensions

On 750 models, 20 ft lbs for the two small nuts and 25 ft lbs for the others.

On 850 models, 30 ft lbs for allen bolts, 25 ft lbs for the front nut, and 20 ft lbs for the others.

2. Place the pistons at top dead center.

3. Place the four pushrods up into the head as far as they will go, as described in "Removal." The longer pushrods are to be positioned closest to the center of the head.

4. Carefully position the head over the barrels, so that the pushrods will drop directly into the tunnels, and take care that the three studs in the head do not damage the gasket.

5. Let the pushrods drop into their tunnels and make sure that they are properly fitted into the tappet cups.

6. Lower the head onto the barrels. The upper end of the pushrods must now fit with their respective rocker arm ball ends.

CAUTION: *On Scrambler models for which the rocker arm had to be removed before taking the head out of the frame, this rocker arm must now be replaced. This is an operation requiring extreme caution lest the washer or spring drop out of reach. It is probably wise to replace the rocker arm now, before bolting down the head.*

7. Support the head about ¼ in. off of the barrels. Those two long cylinder sleeve nuts, which are found beneath the exhaust ports, can be used to support the head in this position.

8. Looking through the exhaust and intake rocker boxes, fit each pushrod with the proper ball end. A short piece of wire with a hook at one end can be used to move the pushrods to accomplish this.

9. When you think you have engaged all of the pushrods, remove the nuts which support the head. Check again. Be absolutely certain all of the pushrods are engaged before proceeding further.

10. Tighten all of the cylinder head bolts and nuts in the order shown. Tightening should be done in increments of 5 ft lbs.

11. Adjust rocker clearances as described in "Tune-Up."

12. The remainder of the assembly procedure is the reverse of that given for disassembly. Before starting, squirt some clean engine oil into the pushrod tunnels, the rocker spindles, and the valve stems.

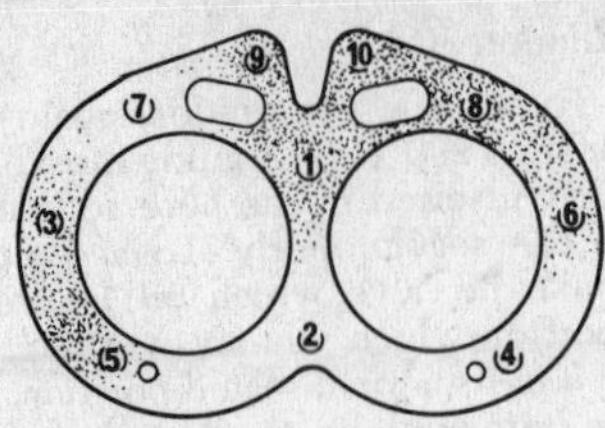

Cylinder head tightening sequence

13. After the engine has been warmed up, allow it to cool and retorque the head bolts and nuts. After the engine is cold, readjust the valves.

Clutch and Primary Drive

COMMANDO 1974 AND EARLIER

Disassembly

1. Remove the left-side footpeg and place a pan beneath the primary chaincase to catch the oil; take off the chaincase fixing bolt and pull off the cover.

2. Disconnect the alternator wires at the snap connectors. Unbolt the stator and pull the wires (carefully) through the inner chaincase half.

3. Remove the sleeve nut and the lockwasher which secures the alternator rotor to the crankshaft. Remove the rotor, using a gear puller if needed, and take out the woodruff key. Use a pair of pliers if it is tight.

4. The triplex chain is endless variety and, therefore, the engine and clutch sprockets and the chain must be removed simultaneously.

CAUTION: *The clutch can only be removed with the aid of a special tool and it is dangerous to attempt to do so without it.*

5. Loosen the clutch adjuster nut and remove the adjuster screw.

6. With the special clutch compressor tool (Part No. 06-0999), screw the center bolt of the tool into the diaphragm spring center. Tighten the nut on the tool's center bolt until the diaphragm spring is free to turn in the clutch sprocket. Stop at this point.

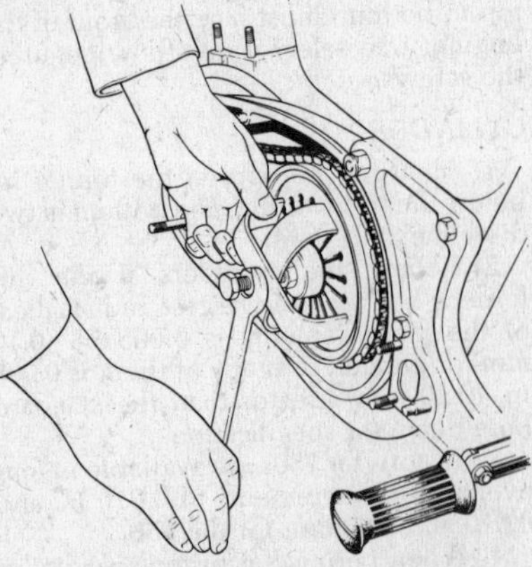

Using special tool to compress diaphragm spring

7. Remove the large circlip which retains the diaphragm spring (there is a groove provided to make removal easier) and take away the spring and the tool together.

8. Remove the nut and washer which secures the clutch hub to the transmission mainshaft; it is necessary to stop the clutch from turning so that this nut can be broken loose. Use the clutch hub tool (Part No. 06-1015) or a suitable substitute. Alternately, put the transmission in gear and apply the rear brake to remove the clutch nut.

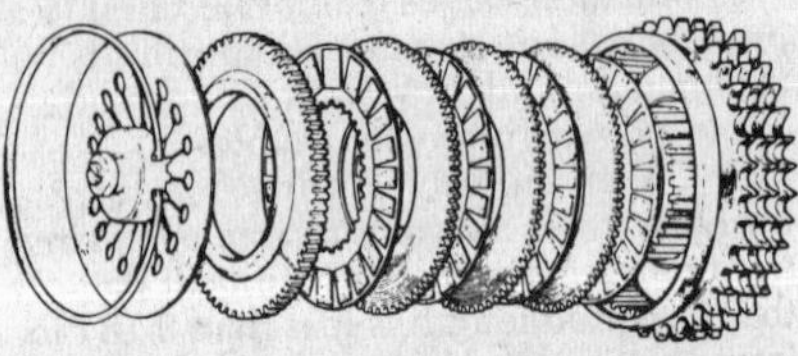

Commando clutch assembly

9. Remove the engine sprocket from its tapered shaft. It is press-fit here and must be removed from the taper with a special tool. The procedure here is to attach the extractor to the sprocket and, after tightening the center bolt, rap it once with a hammer. This should break the sprocket off the shaft. If necessary, a small gear puller can be used instead.

10. The engine sprocket, chain, and clutch hub sprocket can now be taken away. There may be shims behind the clutch hub sprocket. These are used to adjust the true running of the primary chain and should be reassembled in their proper place.

If necessary, a special tool is available which screws into the center of the clutch to aid in removing it from its shaft. It might not be necessary if the clutch has been removed before.

After the assembly has been taken out of the chaincase, remove the engine sprocket woodruff key.

Inspection

1. Maximum allowable plate warpage is 0.012 in. (0.3 mm).

2. Although it operates in the primary chaincase which contains oil to lubricate the chain, this clutch is the "dry" type. The 750's friction plates must have dispersal grooves to get rid of any excess oil which accumulates on them. It may be necessary to cut these grooves if the plate does not have them. Four dispersal grooves spaced 90° apart should be sufficient. On the other side of the friction plate, cut four more grooves offset 45° in relation to the first set and also spaced at 90°.

The plates may have a single groove on each side which is elliptical in reference to the center of the plate.

3. The clutch hub runs on a bearing fitted into the clutch sprocket and located with circlips. To remove the clutch bearing:

a. Take out the small circlip which holds the clutch hub with sleeve extension;

b. Press out the clutch hub;

c. Take out the circlip bearing (the large one);

Commando clutch bearing assembly

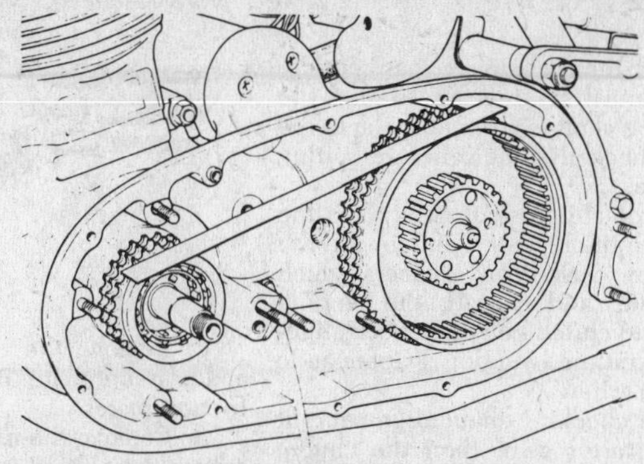

Checking alignment of sprocket and clutch

d. Press out the bearing from the inside of the clutch sprocket.

Check the bearing for smooth, effortless rotation. If the bearing is halting or rough, or if there is any play between the outer and inner races, replace it.

Assembly

1. Assembly is the reverse of disassembly.
2. First install the clutch and engine sprockets without the primary chain. Place a straightedge across the sprockets to check that the chain line is true. If adjustment is necessary, add or remove shims behind the clutch sprocket.
3. When installing the assembly, tighten the clutch nut to 70 ft lbs, and the engine (rotor) nut to 80 ft lbs.
4. After installing the alternator stator, check that the gap between the stator and the rotor is even all the way around. The gap should be about 0.010 in. If the rotor and stator touch at any point, or if the gap is obviously not equal at all points, loosen the stator mounts and try to move it to even out the gap. If this is not possible, check for bent mounting studs.

COMMANDO 1975 AND LATER

Disassembly

1. Disconnect the electric starter terminal. Engage First gear. Remove the two bolts from the left footpeg mounting flange.
2. Remove the primary chaincase drain bolt to drain off the oil.
3. Place a large pan beneath the chaincase to catch any residual oil when the cover is removed. Remove the primary chaincase screws and the electric starter locating screw, and remove the cover. Tap the cover with a plastic mallet or the like to free it if stuck.
4. Remove the gearshift cross-shaft.
5. Apply the rear brake and remove the alternator rotor nut and the fan disc washer behind it.
6. Remove the alternator stator after disconnecting the leads, and remove the three stator securing nuts.
7. Remove the alternator rotor. The rotor is keyed to the crankshaft. If it resists, use a small gear puller or pry it off with two screwdrivers. Remove the woodruff key and any shims fitted.
8. Remove the alternator stator mounting plate.
9. Remove the reduction gear assembly, sleeve, and washer.
10. Remove the starter intermediate gear shaft with the overload device.
11. Remove the small primary chain tensioner nut; then the two remaining nuts, and remove the tensioner. The tensioner plungers must remain in their original bores so mark them before removal.
12. Loosen the clutch adjuster nut and remove the adjuster.
13. With the special clutch compressor tool (Part No. 06-0999), screw the center bolt of the tool into the diaphragm spring center. Tighten the nut on the tool's center bolt until the diaphragm spring is free to turn in the clutch.
14. Remove the large circlip which retains the spring, and take away the spring and tool together.
15. Remove the nut and washer which secures the clutch hub to the transmission mainshaft. It is necessary to stop the clutch from turning so that this nut can be broken loose. Use the clutch hub tool (Part No. 06-1015). Alternately, apply the rear brake after putting the transmission in gear to remove the clutch nut.
16. Break the engine sprocket off its shaft. The shaft is tapered, and the sprocket must be removed with the special extractor. A small gear puller can also be used.
17. The sprocket, chain, and clutch assembly can now be removed. There may be shims behind the clutch. These are used to adjust the true running of the primary chain and must be reinstalled. If any new components are fitted, the chain line should be checked and shims added or subtracted as necessary.

Inspection

Refer to "Commando 1974 and Earlier" for inspection procedures.

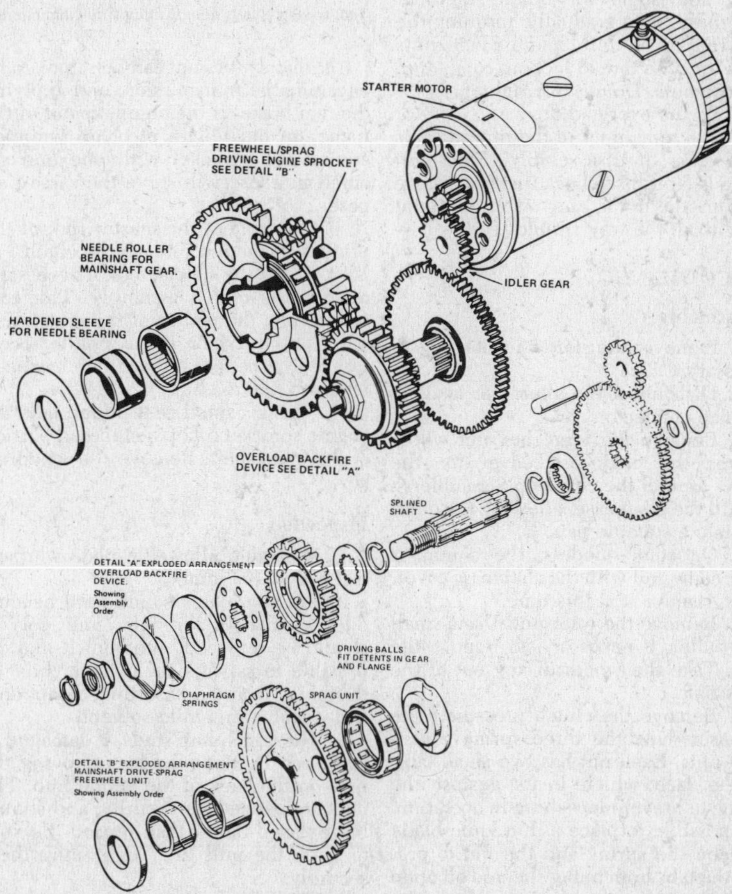

Electric starter drive and reduction assembly

Assembly

1. If the inner chaincase has been removed it must be refitted so that the transmission shaft is perpendicular to the oil seal. Check alignment before bolting up the case.
2. Fit the clutch shaft circlip and the spacer, with the recessed end toward the transmission. Install any spacers which were fitted, and install the engine sprocket and clutch hub and check alignment as outlined under "Commando 1974 and Earlier."
3. After checking chain alignment, fit the large starter gear, then the clutch, sprocket, andprimary chain together. Be sure the engine sprocket is pushed onto its shaft as far as possible.
4. Tighten the clutch nut to 70 ft lbs.
5. Install the clutch plates, first fitting a friction plate, then a steel plate, and alternating until fitting the last (iron) plate. Fit the diaphragm spring with the tool attached, and the large circlip. Remove the clutch tool.
6. Fit the clutch adjuster and locknut.
7. Install the thrust collar into the engine sprocket recess with the small end facing outward.
8. Install the sleeve onto the crankshaft. Fit the starter assembly into the sprocket.
9. Install the large starter gear and bearing over the hardened sleeve and insert it into the assembly.
10. Install the chain tensioner. If the plungers have been removed from their bores, add some oil before refitting. Tighten the nuts gradually, torquing the 5/16 in. nuts to 12 ft lbs, and the 1/4 in. nuts to 5 ft lbs. Use thread locking compound on these nuts. Do *not* overtighten.
11. Fit the overload device.
12. The remainder of the procedure is the reverse of disassembly. Rotor nut torque is 80 ft lbs. Check that the air gap between the rotor and stator is about 0.010 in. all the way around.

PRE-COMMANDO

Disassembly

1. Remove the left-side footpeg if necessary.
2. Disconnect the alternator leads at the snap-connector.
3. Remove the large hex nut which secures the chaincase cover (or the screws around the cover on Scramblers). Pull off the chaincase, allowing the oil to drip into a suitable pan.
4. On some models, the alternator stator comes off with the chaincase cover. If not, remove it at this time.
5. Remove the rotor nut. Use a small gear puller, if necessary, to remove the rotor. Take the woodruff key out of the crankshaft.
6. Remove the clutch pressure plate by unscrewing the three spring adjustment nuts. Each nut has two small tabs, on the face which bears against the spring, to prevent loosening in operation. It is possible to place a thin knife blade between the spring and the nut to prevent the tabs from being sheared off upon removal. Otherwise, the nuts should be replaced upon reassembly.

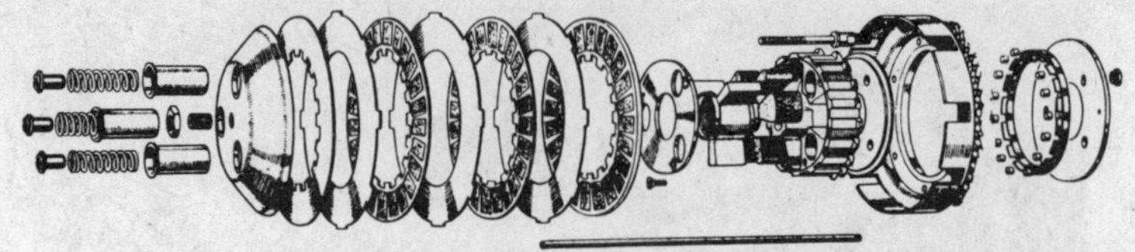

Pre-Commando clutch assembly

7. Remove the clutch springs, cups, and pressure plate. Remove the steel and friction plates.
8. Remove the nut and washer which secure the clutch assembly to the transmission mainshaft.

NOTE: *It is necessary to stop the clutch from turning so that this nut can be removed. You can make a simple, though effective, tool to do this. This consists of a standard clutch plain metal plate and a standard friction plate. Bolting the two together takes the place of spring pressure and will make removal of the center nut much easier.*

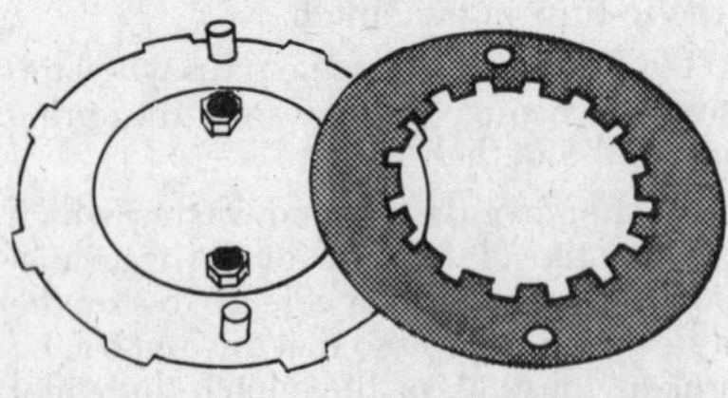

Tool to stop clutch from turning (pre-Commando)

Alternately, the nut can be removed by engaging the transmission, and applying the rear brake. If the engine is out of the frame, an old length of chain wrapped around the sprocket with one end secured in a vise will serve the same purpose.

9. Disconnect the master link of the primary chain and remove the chain.
10. Using the special tool, if necessary, remove the clutch assembly. This tool screws into the center of the clutch and pulls it off the shaft. It may not be necessary to use the tool if the clutch has been removed before.
11. Using a small gear puller, take the engine sprocket off of the tapered portion of the crankshaft. Remove the woodruff key.

Inspection

1. Maximum allowable plate warpage is 0.012 in. (0.3 mm).
2. Friction plates which have become oil-impregnated through long service should be replaced, although it may be possible to salvage them for awhile by dusting with an oil-absorbing compound, and washing in a mild solvent.
3. The clutch hub studs, if damaged or bent, can be removed by removing the nuts on the back of the clutch hub. The nuts are peened for security, and should be replaced rather than reused. Be sure to peen the nuts after tightening them securely.
4. The clutch has rubber shock absorbers in the hub to prevent "snatching" and the damage it might cause. To inspect them, remove the three countersunk retaining screws from the front of the clutch hub and pry off the steel plate. The rubber blocks will come out of the hub easily if they are worn.

Assembly

Assembly is basically the reverse of the disassembly procedure. Note the following points:

1. Be sure to install the chain masterlink spring clip so that the closed end faces the direction of chain rotation.
2. When assembling the clutch, first fit the housing and hub. Install the engine sprocket onto the crankshaft with the boss outward. Fit the primary chain.
3. Install the clutch plates, noting that the single-sided friction plate is installed last with the steel side outward.
4. Replace the spring cups and springs; the cups have a tab to fit a slot on the pressure plate.
5. Screw down the adjusting nut with a fork-like tool. These should be flush with the spring cups after assembly.
6. Replace the rotor and tighten the rotor nut very firmly. It is advisable to secure this nut with thread locking compound.
7. Bolt on the alternator, run the leads through the inner chaincase half, and reconnect them.
8. Kick the engine over several times while watching the rotor, to be sure that it does not contact the alternator stator at any point. An even gap all around the rotor is preferred and washers may be placed behind the stator to accomplish this.

A spacer, about 0.010 in. thick, can be placed around the rotor and used as a guide while tightening the stator nuts.

9. Work the handlebar clutch lever several times and notice the operation of the clutch. The pressure plate must remain parallel to the other plates when it disengages. If it does not (you will notice it coming off the assembly at an angle), adjust the clutch springs.
10. Adjust the clutch as outlined in "Maintenance."

Timing Case

All of the valve and ignition timing gear on the Norton 750 and 850 is contained in the case on the right-side of the crankcase. The oil pump as well as several important oil seals and junctions for the lubrication system are found here also.

The timing is accomplished by means of a small pinion which is fitted to the end of the crankshaft and drives an intermediate gear and sprocket. This sprocket drives the camshaft by means of a short, single-row chain. The oil pump drive gear is also located on the crankshaft.

Commando engines after No. 131257 have the ignition points operating at the right end of the camshaft. Prior to this model, Commandos had the points located in a canister behind the cylinder barrels. The points were timed by another chain from the intermediate sprocket to the distributor sprocket which was secured to its shaft by a pin.

Most other Nortons, including the Atlas and G15CS, were equipped with the Lucas K2F magneto. This unit, too, was located behind the barrels and it was also driven by chain from the intermediate sprocket. The automatic spark advance mechanism for the magneto was integrated with the magneto sprocket and they were secured to the magneto's tapered shaft with a self-locking bolt.

TIMING COVER

Removal

To remove the timing cover, follow the procedure outlined below, with attention to variations for particular models.

1. Disconnect the tachometer drive if it is mounted on the outside of the timing cover.
2. Remove the ignition points cover (after engine No. 131257).
3. Remove the rocker oil feed pipe banjo at the rear of the timing cover. If the engine has been recently run, a little oil may dribble out.

AFTER ENGINE NO. 131257:

4. Remove the ignition point base plate which is secured by two screws, also the wires. It may be helpful to mark the location of the base plate before removal, so that it can be reinstalled without the necessity of resetting the timing.
5. Remove the automatic timing advance center bolt.
6. Screw a withdrawal bolt (Part No. 06-0934) into the center of the advance mechanism to pull it off of the camshaft. Slide hammer 06-4298 can also be used.

ALL MODELS:

7. Place a can beneath the cover to catch the oil. Take out the timing cover screws. There are twelve of them and they are of three different lengths, so note their positions.
8. Pull off the timing cover. If difficulty is encountered, tap around the cover very lightly with a rubber mallet until the cover can be separated. Often a commercial brand of penetrating fluid can be used to break the seal.

Note the oil seal plunger and spring fitted to late 850 models.

9. Oil will dribble out of the drilling in the crankcase at the left (as you look at it) of the timing case. Use one of the cover screws to block off the flow of oil.

TIMING ASSEMBLY

Removal

If the sprockets and chain are to be removed, mark both with paint before removal.

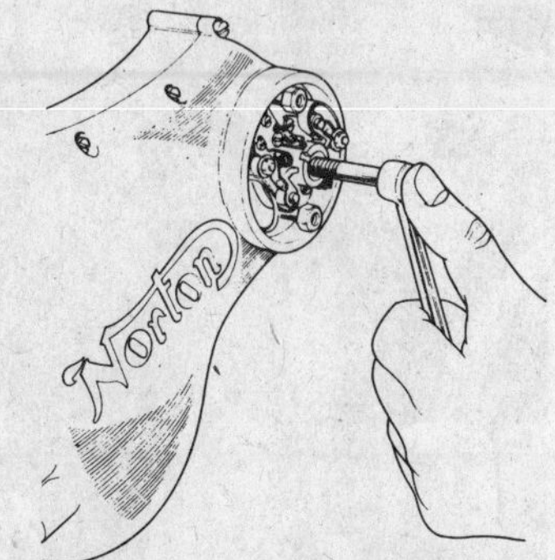

Removing the advance mechanism

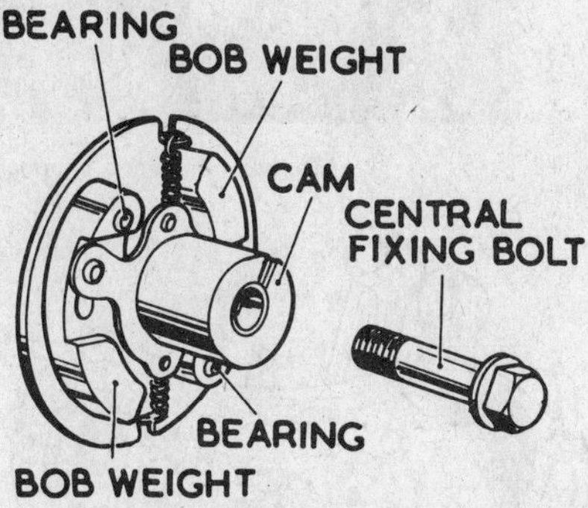

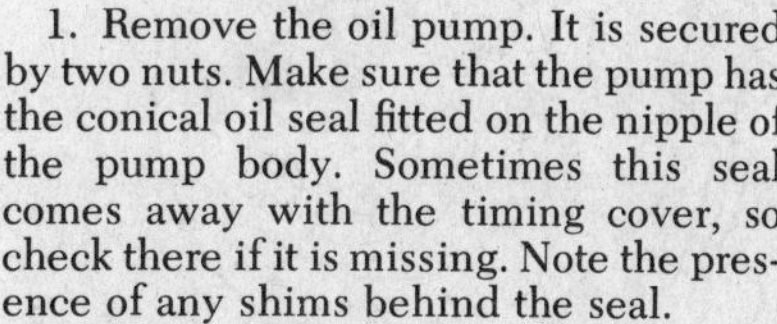

Timing advance mechanism

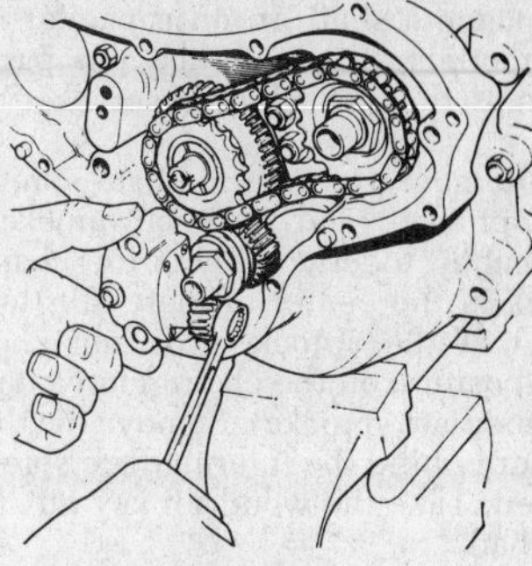

Removing the oil pump

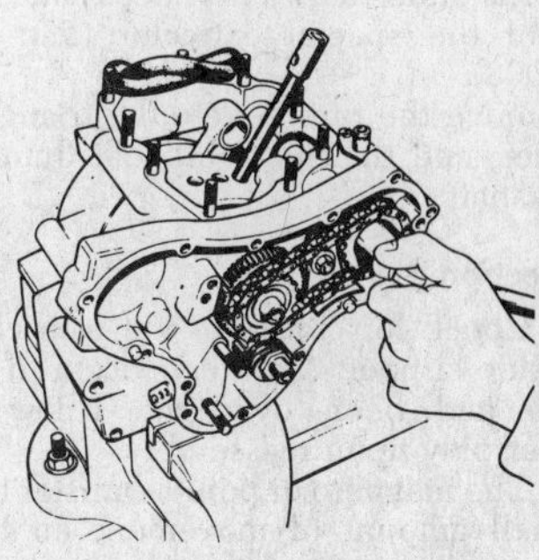

Removing the camshaft sprocket nut

1. Remove the oil pump. It is secured by two nuts. Make sure that the pump has the conical oil seal fitted on the nipple of the pump body. Sometimes this seal comes away with the timing cover, so check there if it is missing. Note the presence of any shims behind the seal.
2. Remove the oil pump drive gear. This has a LEFT-HAND thread onto the crankshaft.
3. Remove the camshaft chain adjuster. This assembly consists of two plain metal plates of varying thickness and a metal slipper which bears on the cam chain and it is fastened by two nuts. The thin metal plate goes on the engine side of the slipper.
4. Remove the nut which secures the camshaft sprocket. The sprocket can be taken off with a gear puller or with the extractor tool (Part No. EST12). The cam sprocket cannot be removed at this point on models with a separate ignition timing chain. For these models:
5. Loosen the magneto sprocket bolt and make sure that the automatic advance mechanism can be removed from

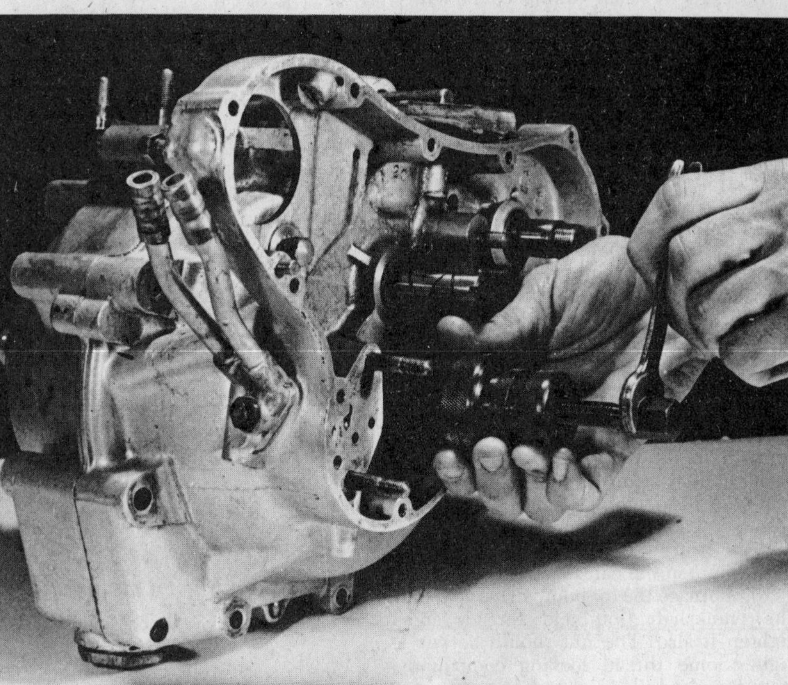

Removing the timing pinion

the magneto shaft or, on capacitor ignition models, drive out the pin passing through the distributor sprocket and shaft.

6. Remove the intermediate sprocket, cam sprocket, and ignition sprocket (if applicable) together. Pinch the chain or chains in the center of their runs to ensure that the sprockets do not change their position on the chain relative to the intermediate sprocket. Remove the thrust washer behind the intermediate sprocket if fitted. Take the woodruff key off of the camshaft.

7. Remove the small timing pinion from the crankshaft. This necessitates the use of the special extractor (Part No. ET2003).

Remove the pinion key, the triangular washer, and the metal oil seal from the crankshaft.

Timing pinion and intermediate sprocket marks aligned

Inspection

1. Check for cracks in the cam chain adjuster slipper. This can occur if the chain had been overtight. Allow for proper play upon reassembly.

2. The magneto or points canister have a small amount of movement on their mountings to adjust the chain tension. Once this movement has been used up, the chain must be replaced.

Installation

1. Replace the metal oil seal, the triangular washer, and the pinion key on the crankshaft.

2. Replace the pinion. Be sure the bevelled edge faces outward. there is a timing "dot" on the outer side of the pinion also.

3. Replace the thrust washer on the intermediate shaft if fitted.

4. Rotate the crankshaft until the small timing dot on the timing pinion is at 12 o'clock.

5. Take the cam timing chain with the intermediate sprocket and cam sprocket, and the ignition timing chain and sprocket if applicable, and position the intermediate gear so that its timing dot aligns with that on the timing pinion.

6. Also fit the cam sprocket on the cam. It is keyed.

7. If the timing has been preserved—fine, but if you are not entirely sure, there is an easy check. There are timing dots on both the intermediate sprocket and the cam sprocket. When the intermediate sprocket is in the correct position, there should be SIX outer plates of the drive chain between the two dots.

8. Replace the distributor or magneto sprocket. If a magneto is fitted, do not tighten the fixing bolt all the way, as the timing must be reset.

9. Stop the engine from turning by placing the transmission in gear or, if the engine is disassembled, place a steel bar through the connecting rod small ends and the bearing on the top of the crankcase. Tighten the camshaft sprocket nut.

10. Replace the oil pump drive gear on the crankshaft (left-hand thread) and tighten it also. The nut should be very tight. Some thread locking compound here is a good idea.

11. Apply a thin coat of gasket compound on the face of the oil pump unless a gasket is fitted, and replace the pump on its studs. Tighten the two nuts evenly and torque both to 15 ft lbs.

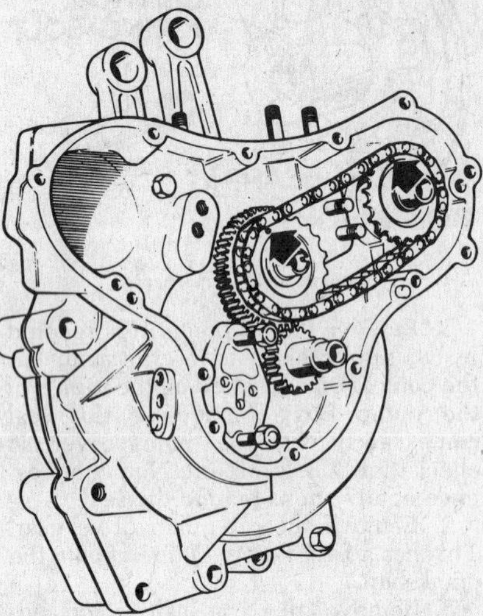

Cam chain correctly timed (six chain plates between the dots on the sprockets)

12. Replace the thin metal plate on the cam chain tensioner with the longest portion from the bolt hole downward.

13. Replace the tensioner slipper itself and, finally, the thick plate. Replace, but do not tighten, the two nuts on the tensioner.

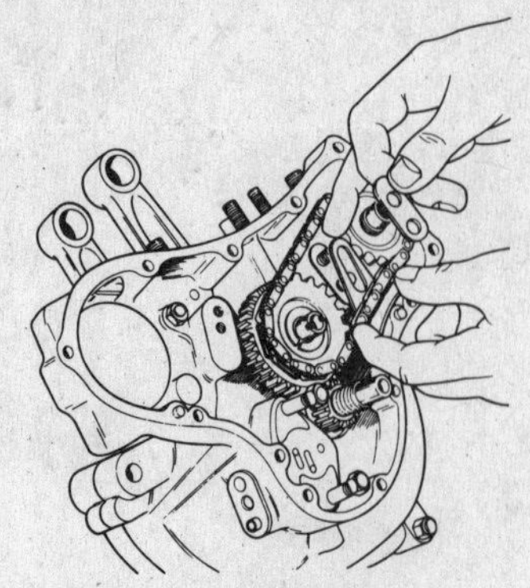

Installing the cam chain tensioner

14. The cam chain tension must now be adjusted. A cut-away timing cover is handy to have for the adjustment of the chain, since it supports the intermediate sprocket spindle and allows a more accurate setting of the chain slack to be made.

1975 and later models have an inspection hole in the timing cover for this purpose.

The tensioner should be adjusted to bear against the lower chain run until there is 3/16 in. play measured in the middle of the upper chain run.

15. If an ignition chain is fitted, this can be adjusted (also to 3/16 in. play in the middle of the upper run) by loosening the two nuts and one bolt which secure the distributor or magneto, and pivoting the unit until the desired tension is reached. A screwdriver can be used to pry behind the unit, as there is a shoulder provided on the case for this.

CAUTION: *Overtightening of the magneto chain can cause binding of the automatic spark advance mechanism. Therefore, ensure that the chain slack is correct and that the advance mechanism moves freely after the timing is adjusted.*

TIMING COVER OIL SEALS

1. To remove the large seal, take out the circlip which secures it and pry the seal out.

2. When replacing the seal, gently heat the cover with a propane torch or suitable replacement and fit the seal with the metal face outward (toward you as you install it).

3. The smaller seal is present on machines after engine No. 131257 and is intended to prevent oil from getting into the points compartment. It fits directly over the camshaft. Pry out the seal with a sharp pointed tool.

4. Warm the cover as before and press the seal into position, metal backing facing you as you install it.

5. The timing cover also has the oil pressure relief valve which is located just above the rocker oil feed pipe junction. The relief valve is spring-loaded to operate at a predetermined pressure and, therefore, needs no attention. The valve does have a wire filter screen fitted which

might be checked and cleaned if necessary.

TIMING COVER

Installation

1. Remove all traces of old gasket and gasket compound from the mating surfaces. The timing cover can be worked on an appropriate surface (such as a sheet of emery cloth placed on a piece of glass) to remove any surface irregularities, scratches, etc.

NOTE: *Early model Nortons had a rather thin paper gasket for the timing cover which was effective only if the mating surfaces were in very good condition. The Commando has a thicker gasket which may be used to advantage on earlier models also. The only difference between this and the earlier gasket (aside from the thickeness and composition of the material) is an extra hole for the points wires. This is not needed for early models and can be removed.*

2. Models fitted with the ignition points at the camshaft must use a guide bush (Part No. 06-1359) over the cam to prevent damage to the oil seal in the timing cover. The threaded portion of the bush is screwed on to the camshaft by hand, as far as possible. Add a little oil to the outside of the bush to make assembly easier.

3. Check the condition and efficiency of the conical seal on the oil pump. If it is deformed, replace it. It should be able to push the timing cover away from the case about 0.010 in. when fitted. If it does not, replace it, or use shim washers behind the seal.

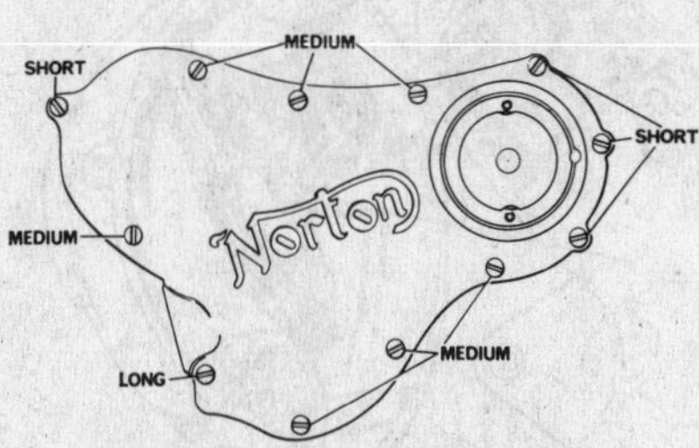

Timing cover screw locations

If the thicker gasket has been fitted to early models, shim washers may be necessary.

4. Refit the timing cover, screw in the 12 cover screws, and tighten them evenly and in a diagonal pattern.

5. Reconnect the rocker oil feedpipe banjo.

6. Reconnect the tachometer drive cable if applicable.

For Commando models after engine No. 131257:

7. Remove the inspection cap on the primary chaincase to expose the indicator plate.

8. Position the engine so that the timing mark on the rotor registers 28° on the indicator plate (each mark equals two degrees).

9. Insert the timing advance mechanism and position it so that the rivets for the bob weights are in line with the two

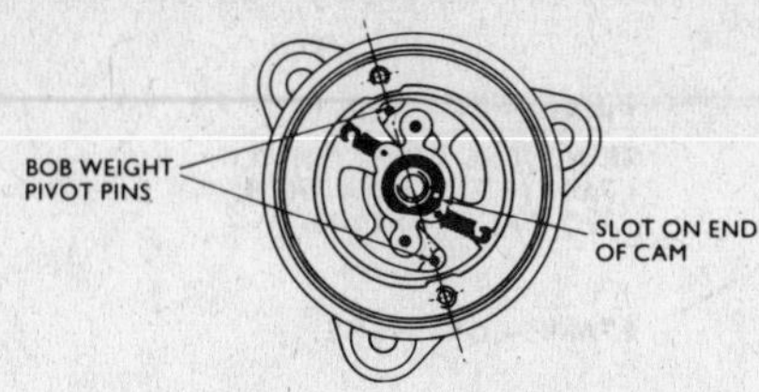

Timing advance mechanism positioned for installation

screw holes for the point cover. The slot (not the slash mark) in the breaker cam should now be about 9 o'cock.

10. Replace the ignition point base assembly. The yellow and black lead is for the drive side cylinder (left point set).

11. Adjust the timing.

Bottom End

Disassembly

1. Remove the engine from the frame. Remove the primary drive and clutch, cylinder head and cylinders, timing cover and timing gear, etc.

2. Unbolt the crankcase studs and remove the screw(s) at the bottom of the cases.

3. Tap against the inside of the left-side crankcase half with a plastic mallet or wooden block to separate the cases. If difficulty is encountered, gently heat the drive side bearing boss. This should only be necessary on relatively new engines.

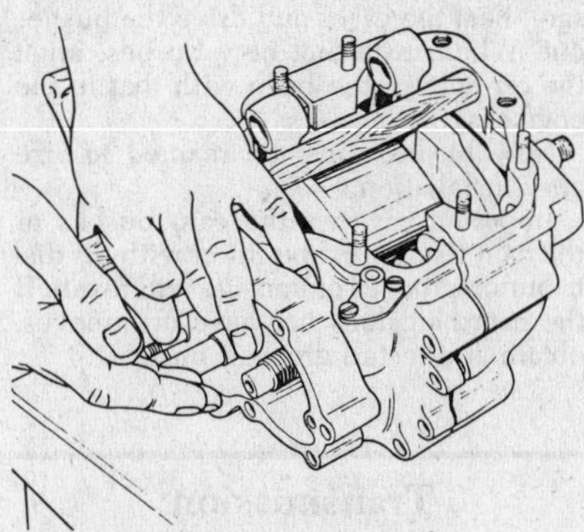

Separating the crankcase halves

4. Take out the camshaft, and the crankcase breather plate and spring, if fitted.

5. Heat the timing side bearing boss, holding the right-side crankcase half, and tap on the timing end of the crankshaft with a plastic mallet to free it.

NOTE: *It is a good idea to use a sleeve over the crankshaft end to avoid damage to it or to the oil pump worm gear threads.*

6. Bearings can be removed from the crank by prying them off.

7. To remove bearing races from the crankcases, heat the case in an oven (not to exceed 200° C), then drop the case onto a wooden block from about a 6 in. height. If removal is difficult, the bearing race can be cooled, after the case is heated, either with a damp rag, or by running an ice cube around the race.

8. The drive side oil seal can be punched out after removing the bearing race. Late models are equipped with a circlip which must be removed before the oil seal.

Assembly

1. Assembly is the reverse of disassembly.

2. On models with a cam-timed crankcase breather, refusal of the case halves to mate is sometimes due to the engaging dogs on the breather plate not properly engaging the camshaft.

3. On models with a roller bearing on the timing side, insure proper lubrication by pouring clean engine oil into the intake rocker box after engine assembly is completed. This oil will drain into the timing case, and then to the bearings.

4. Be sure that all bearings and bushings are well lubricated before reassembling the rest of the engine.

CONNECTING RODS AND JOURNALS

Removal and Installation

1. To remove the rods, remove the rod bolt nuts and pull the rod off the journal with a sharp jerk.

2. Be sure to keep each rod with its own cap. Rods and caps are machined together, and it is essential that the rod-and-cap assemblies be kept separate. In addition, note that there is a slash mark on each which indicates the correct cap position.

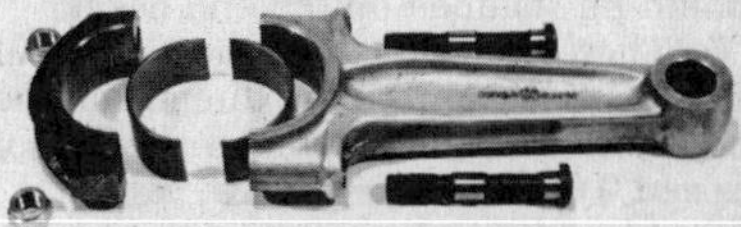

Connecting rod assembly

3. Rod journals must be within 0.001 in. of perfectly round. Minor scoring can be removed with fine emery tape, but if the journal is oval, or heavily scored, it must be reground.

If the crankshaft is reground, be sure that a 0.090 in. radius is restored on the journal shoulder.

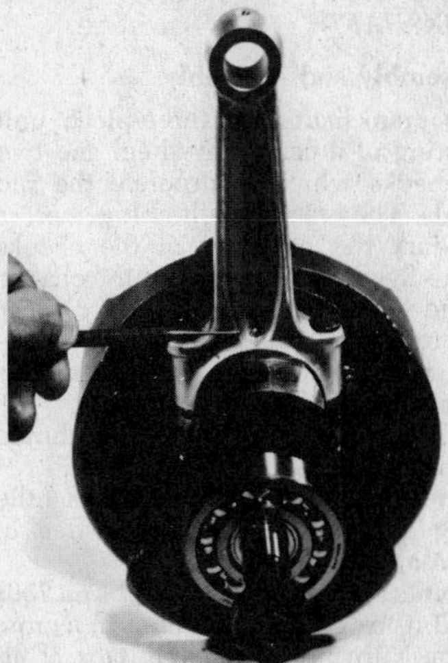

The oil hole at the base of the rods must face outwards

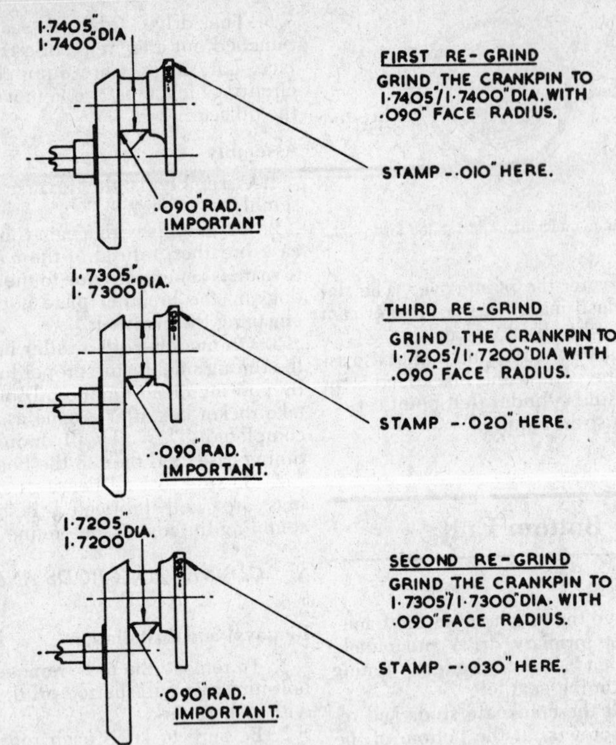

Crank regrinding dimensions

4. Undersized big end bearings are available in four sizes: 0.010 in., 0.020 in., 0.030 in., and 0.040 in.

The size of the replacement bearing should be stamped on the end cheek.

5. There is no bush at the rod small end, the piston pin riding directly on the rod itself. Small end diameter should not exceed 0.6868 in.

6. Assembly is the reverse of removal. Be sure that the mark on each cap aligns with that of its own connecting rod. Install the rods with the oil hole at the lower end pointing AWAY FROM the center of the crankshaft.

7. New rod bolt nuts must be used, and the use of new bolts is recommended as well. Tighten thse nuts to 25 ft lbs.

8. Be sure the big end bearings are well lubricated before assembly.

CRANKSHAFT

Disassembly and Assembly

The crankshaft is a three-piece unit consisting of a center flywheel and two end cheeks which incorporate the rod journals. The crank is bolted together.

1. Mark the positions of the cheeks and the flywheel to eliminate the chance of accidental interchange.

2. Straighten thelock tabs, if applicable, then remove the crankshaft nuts and separate the pieces.

3. Clean out the sludge trap machined into the flywheel.

4. Before assembly, be certain that the mating surfaces are absolutely free of foreign matter.

5. Nuts are torqued to 35 ft lbs on 750s and 30 ft lbs on 850s. Tighten in a cross pattern. Turn up the locking tabs, if fitted. If not, peen the nuts with a punch to lock them in position.

CAMSHAFT

1. After splitting the cases, make the usual inspections of the cam and cam bushes. The bushes must be free of wear or score marks. If replacement is necessary, heat the cases and drive the bushes out. When installing new bushes, align the oil hole in the bush with that in the crankcase.

New bushes must be reamed to size after installation.

Important: Either the cam bushes or the cam itself must be fitted with oil distribution grooves or damage will result. If the camshaft does not have oil grooves, obtain and install grooved bushes.

Transmission

The transmission is basically the same on all models covered here, the major change being the introduction of the left-hand shift for 1975 and later models.

GEARBOX REMOVAL AND INSTALLATION

1. Removal and replacement of all gearbox internal parts with the exception of the layshaft left-side bearing is possible without removing the gearbox shell from the frame. If removal of the entire unit is desired, the engine must be removed on 1969 and earlier models.

2. On 1970 and later units, remove the clutch and primary drive assembly. Remove the rear wheel. Disconnect the chain.

3. Remove the three rear crankcase-to-engine plate bolts or studs.

4. Support the motorcycle on a large block of wood or a crate, remove the rear wheel and the center stand.

5. Remove the top and bottom mounting bolt and stud. Turn the gearbox counterclockwise as far as possible. Push the rear engine mounting towards the rear of the motorcycle, until the cutaway at the bottom right is clear of the crankcase, and continue rotating the gearbox until it can be removed.

In some cases it may be necessary to remove the front main mounting bolt for extra clearance.

6. Installation is the reverse of the above.

OUTER COVER

Disassembly

1. Take off the clutch lever inspection cap on the outer cover and disconnect the clutch cable by prying up the lever and slipping out the nipple. Unscrew the cable adjuster from the case. Drain the transmission oil.

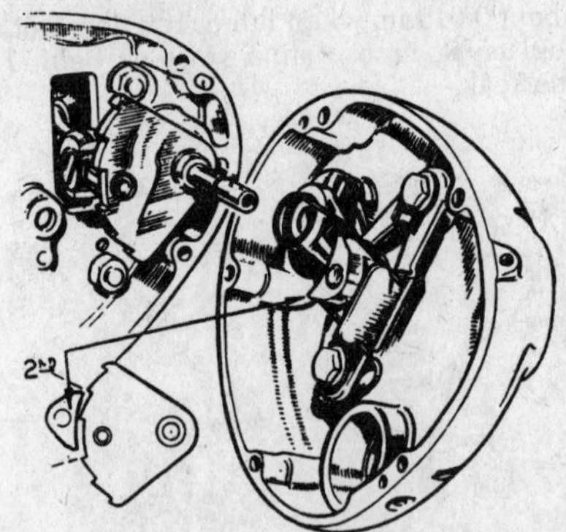
Gearbox outer cover assembly

2. Remove the kick-starter crank bolt and remove the crank. It might be necessary to use a claw-type puller to get the crank off the splined shaft.

3. Remove the right footpeg.

4. Remove the bolt for the gearshift lever, but leave the lever in place.

5. Remove the five screws which secure the outer cover.

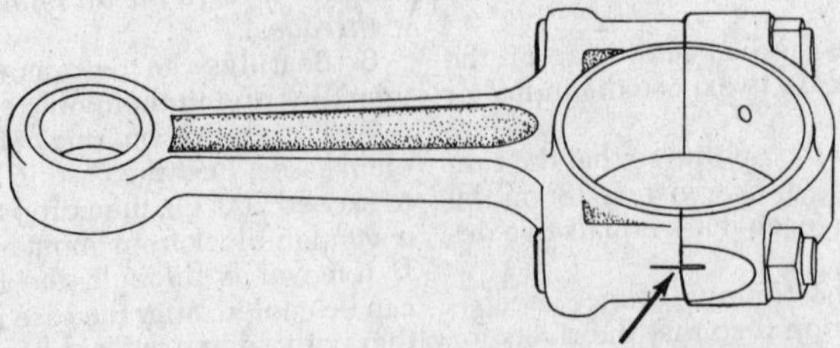
Caps must be installed so that the slash mark on rod and cap align

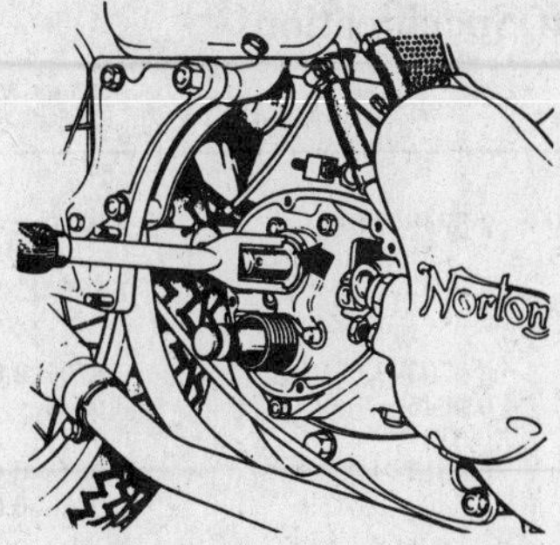

Removing the clutch operating lever

6. Carefully pull off the cover, using the gearshift lever to assist you.
7. Remove the pawl spring.
8. Disengage the shifter return spring legs from the pawl pin, and withdraw the pawl carrier, tapping it if necessary.
9. Remove the shifter stop plate (two bolts), and remove the return spring.

Inspection

1. Check the shifter pawl for unusual wear.
2. The outer cover has two rubber O-rings which act as oil seals. The larger of the two is found on the kick-starter shaft behind a steel bush. The bush may be removed by heating the case and driving it out from the outside after first prying out the O-ring.
3. The smaller O-ring is for the gear shifter shaft. To remove the bush here, heat the cover, gently screw a coarse threaded tap into the bush, and pull it out.
4. Remove any traces of old gasket material from the outer cover mating surface and check the condition of the surface. All abrasions, scratches, etc. should be removed with an oil stone.

Assembly

1. Assembly is the reverse of the previous procedure.
2. When refitting the pawl spring, notice that the cranked leg of the spring will be in the lowest position, the straight leg in the higher.
3. Assure that the pawl concave side is facing the gearshift spindle so that it can remesh with the ratchet plate.
4. Put some clean oil on the kick-starter shaft to avoid bruising the O-ring on reassembly.

INNER COVER

Disassembly

1. Remove the ratchet plate with spindle.
2. Unbolt the clutch operating lever and remove it and its roller from the shaft.
3. Mark the position of the slot in the clutch operating lever shaft on the inner cover so that the shaft can be reassembled in the correct position to give the clutch cable a straight pull. On recent models, the assembly is already marked.
4. Unscrew the lockring on the clutch lever shaft and remove the lockring, the shaft, and the ball.
5. Remove the mainshaft nut which will be exposed after removing the shaft.

Inner cover ready for removal

6. Remove the seven nuts which secure the inner cover to the gearbox shell and pull off the inner cover, tapping lightly at the front end if necessary.
7. Take the kick-starter return spring out of the hole in the kick-starter shaft.
8. Pull the kick-starter shaft out of its bush from the inside of the cover.

Inspection

1. Check the mating surfaces of the inner cover for scratches, abrasions, or knicks. If present, these may be removed with emery cloth. In addition, place the cover on a flat surface, such as a piece of glass, and make sure that it is flat.
2. Check the mainshaft bearing for excessive play, roughness or binding in rotation, or obvious marks of wear. Replace the bearing if necessary by heating the case gently and driving out the bearing.
3. If the kick-starter bush is worn, it can also be removed after heating the case. After the new bush is driven in, it should be reamed to 0.6875–0.6865 in.
4. Check the condition of the kick-starter pawl very carefully. Be sure that the pawl shows no signs of wear or chipping along the edge. The pawl is easily replaced by removing the pin. If this is done, watch for the plunger or spring.
5. Examine the kick-starter stop-piece and the pawl cam which are riveted to the inner cover. Check for looseness on the rivets and re-rivet the stop-piece if necessary.

Assembly

1. Assemble the inner cover in the reverse of the disassembly procedure. Be certain that the clutch operating lever shaft is correctly aligned to give the cable a straight pull.
2. Be sure that the mating surfaces are clean and in good condition. Refit a new gasket.
3. Tighten the inner cover nuts evenly and in a cross pattern to 12 ft lbs. Fit and tighten the mainshaft nut.

GEAR CLUSTER

Disassembly

1. Proceed with the disassembly procedures outlined above. Removing the inner cover will expose the gear assemblies on the two shafts. The upper shaft is the mainshaft and the lower is the countershaft (or layshaft).

Gear cluster and shifter assembled

2. Remove the low gear pinion on the mainshaft. Note that the boss on this gear faces outward.
3. Unscrew the shifter fork spindle and remove it.
4. Remove the shifter forks.
5. Remove the clutch pushrod from the mainshaft.
6. If the clutch has been removed, remove the mainshaft and the gears on it. The sleeve gear will remain in place.
7. Take out the layshaft and the layshaft gears.
8. If disassembly is required past this point, it is necessary to remove the primary chaincase, etc., to gain access to the transmission sprocket.
9. Remove the screw which secures the lock plate on the transmission sprocket.
10. Remove the transmission sprocket nut, which has a LEFT-HAND thread, and remove the sprocket from the shaft.
11. Remove the sleeve gear from the bearing.

Removing the shift fork spindle

12. Remove the dome nut at the bottom of the transmission case and take out the plunger and spring. Remove the neutral switch, if fitted.

13. Remove the bolt fixing the quadrant and the bolt which secures the camplate and remove these components.

14. To remove the layshaft bearing, it is necessary to remove the case. Heat it in an oven (do not exceed 200° C), then tap the case with a plastic mallet to knock out the bearing.

15. The mainshaft bearing can be removed after prying out the oil seal and again heating the case, driving out the bearing with a suitable drift.

Inspection

1. Check the condition of the mainshaft and layshaft bearings. All bearings should rotate with little friction and should be smooth throughout.

2. The bushes for the camplate and quadrant mounting bolts should be checked. Wear would make shifting difficult. The bushes may be removed by heating the case and tapping them out.

3. There are O-ring oil seals on both the camplate and the quadrant. If oil leakage is noticed at the bolts for these components, the seals should be replaced.

4. Examine the gear bushes. They should be free from any score marks and have a smooth finish.

Except for the layshaft first gear and the sleeve gear, the bushes are a slip fit in the gears. Replacement bushes are easily fitted.

Layshaft first gear and sleeve gear bushes are pressed in; on late models the sleeve gear bushes are secured by snaprings. These bushes must be checked in place since removal will destroy them. New bushes are pressed into the gear after chilling the bushes in a freezer for several hours (heating the gear will not work), and must be reamed to the proper size after installation. Do not attempt to replace the bushes unless the correct size reamer is available.

Assembly

1. Fit the mainshaft and layshaft bearings in the case by driving them in. The case should be heated slightly to aid installation. Note that the mainshaft bearing is installed with the sealed side outward. Do not forget the spacer which fits in the mainshaft oil seal.

2. Fit the shifter quadrant, securing it with its bolt and washer. Raise the quadrant so that the very top arm is in line with the top right-hand stud on the transmission case.

3. Insert the cam plate, positioning it so that only the first two teeth on the quadrant are visible through the camplate slot. When the camplate plunger is fitted, the plunger will rest in the High gear notch of the camplate. Secure the camplate with its bolt and washer. Fit the camplate plunger, spring, and domed nut.

4. Replace the sleeve gear, making sure that the spacer which bears on the oil seal is in position.

5. Fit the transmission sprocket and secure it with its nut. The nut has a left-hand thread. Tighten it firmly. Hold the sleeve gear in position to tighten the nut by wrapping a length of drive chain around the sprocket and securing one end. Fit the locking plate and screw.

6. Fit the third gear onto the layshaft noting that the boss on this gear faces the fourth layshaft gear. Tap the fourth layshaft gear onto its shaft. Note that this gear has a small boss on one side which must face the layshaft bearing.

Engine and Transmission Specifications

	Commando 850	*Commando 750*	*Atlas, G15CS, N15CS, P-11*
CYLINDER			
Bore size (in.)	A:3.0315–3.0320 B:3.0320–3.0325	2.8746–2.8754	2.8750–2.8758
Tappet bore size (in.)	1.865–1.875	1.865–1.875	1.865–1.875
PISTONS			
Piston diameter (in.)	3.0271–3.028	2.8703–2.8713	2.8703–2.8713
Piston clearance (in.)	0.0045	0.0045	0.0045
Piston ring end-gap (in.)	0.012	0.013	0.013
Piston ring side clearance (in.)	0.0015–0.0035	0.0015–0.0035	0.0015–0.0035
Wrist pin diameter (in.)	0.6867–0.6869	0.6867–0.6869	0.6866–0.6868
VALVE TRAIN			
Intake Valve			
Head diameter (in.)	1.490	1.490	1.500
Stem diameter (in.)	0.3105–0.3115	0.3105–0.3115	0.309–0.310
Exhaust Valve			
Head diameter (in.)	1.302	1.302	1.312
Stem diameter (in.)	0.312	0.312	0.311
Valve Guides			
Bore (in.)	0.3135–0.3145	0.3135–0.3145	0.3135–0.3145
Valve Springs			
Free-length (inner) (in.)	1.482	1.531	1.531
Free-length (outer) (in.)	1.618	1.700	1.700
Pushrods			
Length (intake) (in.)	8.130–8.166	8.130–8.166	8.194
Length (exhaust) (in.)	7.285–7.321	7.285–7.321	7.351
Rocker Arms			
Spindle bore (in.)	0.4998–0.5003	0.4998–0.5003	0.4998–0.5003
Spindle diameter (in.)	0.4985–0.4998	0.4985–0.4998	0.4985–0.4998
CONNECTING ROD			
Small end bore (in.)	0.6873–0.6878	0.6873–0.6878	0.6873–0.6878
Side clearance (in.)	0.013–0.016	0.013–0.016	0.013–0.016
Big end bearing clearance (max) (in.)	0.001	0.001	0.001
CRANKSHAFT			
Con rod journal diameter (in.)	1.7504–1.7509	1.7504–1.7509	1.7500–1.7505
Bearing journal (drive) (in.)	1.1812–1.1815	1.1812–1.1815	1.1812–1.1815
Bearing journal (timing) (in.)	1.1812–1.1815	1.1807–1.1812 (ball) 1.1812–1.1815 (roller)	1.1807–1.1812
Main bearing (drive) (mm)	30 x 72 x 19	30 x 72 x 19	30 x 72 x 19
Main bearing (timing) (ball) (mm)	——	30 x 72 x 19	30 x 72 x 19
Main bearing (timing) (roller) (mm)	30 x 72 x 19	30 x 72 x 19	——
CAMSHAFT			
Bearing diameter (in.)	0.8735	0.8735	0.8735
Bush bore (in.)	0.8750	0.8750	0.8750
PRESSURE RELIEF VALVE SPRING			
Free-length (in.)	1.171	1.171	1.171
OD (in.)	0.430–0.435	0.430–0.435	0.430–0.435
INTERMEDIATE PINION			
Shaft diameter (in.)	0.5610–0.5615	0.5610–0.5615	0.5610–0.5615
Bush bore (in.)	0.5620–0.5627	0.5620–0.5627	0.5620–0.5627

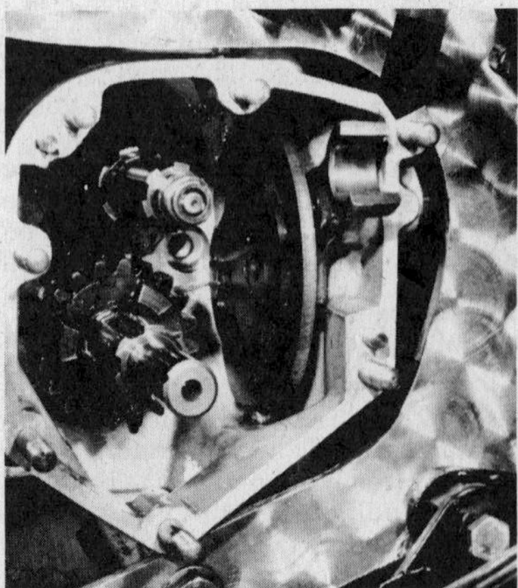

Quadrant upper radius aligned with stud and camplate installed

7. Install the mainshaft with the third gear in place on the shaft. Install the layshaft with third and fourth gears in place.

NOTE: *The layshaft should be pressed into its bearing by hand and should be reasonably tight once in place. If the shaft cannot be inserted by hand, use a fine emery cloth to work the end of the shaft until this is possible. Otherwise removal of the shaft will be very difficult.*

8. Install the mainshaft second gear complete with its shift fork, engaging the shift fork stud into the camplate slot. Note that the camplate may be rotated to the Neutral position (shallow notch), to facilitate installation.

9. Install the layshaft second gear complete with its shift fork and engage the fork stud into the camplate stud. Line up the bores of the shift forks and install and tighten the shift fork spindle.

10. Fit the first gears, noting that the boss on the mainshaft first gear faces outward.

11. Install the roller into the shifter quadrant holding it in place with some grease if necessary.

NOTE: *The roller cannot be installed once the inner cover is fitted.*

12. Fit a new gasket. Install the inner cover. Using a wrench on the camplate bolt, check that the gears can be shifted. Check that the shifter quadrant clears the cut-out in the inner cover when in the First gear position and Fourth gear position. If it does not, the quadrant and camplate are improperly indexed, and the transmission will not have all gears when completed.

13. Refit the inner cover as previously described.

TRANSMISSION	
Mainshaft diameter (clutch side) (in.)	0.8095–0.8105
Mainshaft diameter (kickstarter side (in.)	0.6244–0.6248
Mainshaft bearing (kickstarter side) (in.)	$\frac{5}{8}$ x $1\frac{9}{16}$ x $\frac{7}{16}$
Mainshaft bearing (clutch side) (in.)	$1\frac{1}{4}$ x $2\frac{1}{2}$ x $\frac{5}{8}$
Layshaft bearing (clutch side) (mm)	17 x 40 x 12
Layshaft diameter (clutch side) (in.)	0.6687–0.6692
Layshaft diameter (kickstarter side) (in.)	0.6845–0.6855
Sleeve gear bearing (OD) (in.)	1.2495–1.2500
Sleeve gear bush (OD) (in.)	0.9055–0.9060
Sleeve gear bush (reamed in place) (in.)	0.812–0.813
Layshaft first gear bush (reamed in place) (in.)	0.6865–0.6875
Clutch bearing (Commando) (mm)	35 x 62 x 14

Torque Specifications

Part	Torque (ft lbs)
Cylinder head $\frac{3}{8}$ in. nuts and bolts	30
Cylinder head $\frac{5}{16}$ in. bolt	20
Cylinder base nuts	
large front	30
small front	20
others	25
Cylinder allen bolts (850)	30
Connecting rod bolts	25
Rocker shaft cover plate bolts	8.3
Cam chain tensioner nuts	15
Crankshaft nuts	
750	35
850	30
Alternator stator	10
Alternator rotor nut	80
Engine mounting nuts	25
Oil pump nuts	15
Oil feed banjo bolts	15
Oil pressure relief valve	25
Gearbox inner cover nuts	12
Clutch nut	70
Mainshaft nut	50

Lubrication System

Oil Pump

REMOVAL AND INSPECTION

When rebuilding a severely damaged engine, the pump should always be inspected.

1. Remove the timing cover, after taking off the tach drive (if necessary), and disconnect the rocker oil feed pipe at the cover.

2. Remove the two nuts which secure the pump body and pull off the pump. Remove the oil pump gasket, if fitted.

3. Slowly turn the driveshaft and note any roughness or binding in the movement. The driveshaft should turn smoothly.

4. Grasp the driveshaft gear firmly and push and pull on it. There should be no end-play whatsoever if the pump has oil in it.

5. Check the face of the pump body which mates with the crankcase. Place a straightedge across the stud holes to ensure that the body is not warped. It must, of course, be perfectly flat, or air will be introduced into the oil flow. The mating surface may be lapped flat if necessary after dismantling the pump.

6. Check the conical oil seal on the steel nipple. It must be in very good condition and not deformed. If the seal has been subject to too much pressure, the tapered end will be forced into, and perhaps obstruct, the major oil passage in the timing cover.

Disassembly

1. It is not necessary to remove the pump drive gear to get at the internals, but it may be taken off the driveshaft if desired by taking off the nut which secures it to the shaft and pulling off the gear. Take out the woodruff key also.

2. Remove the four screws in the pump body and take off the brass end plate.

3. Remove the iron plate from the pump body.

4. Using a brass drift, if necessary, tap out the driveshaft. The return side (wide) gear is a close fit on the shaft so the drift will probably be needed.

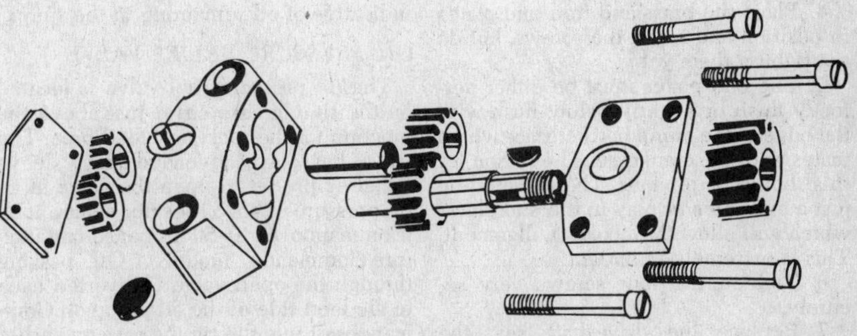

Oil pump disassembled

5. Tap out the shaft for the idler gears. Remove it from the feed side of the pump.

6. Remove both sets of gears.

Inspection

1. Foreign matter in the gear teeth or chipped or worn teeth will be obvious. Under normal operating conditions, however, and assuming that the engine has received routine attention, there should be nothing wrong.

2. If the engine oil in the tank runs down to the crankcase sump after the bike has been sitting for a short time, the problem may be due to loose pump body screws. Another reason may be excessive wear of the shaft bores in the pump body. There is no remedy for this latter cause, other than replacement of the pump body.

3. Check the sides of the oil pump gears and the pump body for wear caused by contact of the gear sides with the body. If there is evidence of wear, assemble the pump dry, and check that there is a slight resistance to turning the driveshaft. If the shaft turns very freely, excessive clearance between the gears and the body may be the cause. Disassemble the pump, and lap the feed side (narrow gears), on a piece of emery cloth placed on a very flat surface. Assemble the pump, tightening the body screws securely. When turning the driveshaft, a slight stiffness should be noted.

Be careful that lapping is done very gradually.

Repeat the procedure on the return gear side. When the pump is reassembled for checking, do not install the feed gears. The driveshaft should be slightly stiff as before.

Finally, assemble the pump completely, and check that the driveshaft is still stiff. Lubricate the pump with motor oil, and continue turning the shaft. Stiffness should disappear as the shaft is turned.

CAUTION: *Be certain that the pump body is cleaned out thoroughly after each lapping operation.*

Reassembly

1. Clean all of the components thoroughly by washing them in a solvent such as kerosene.

2. Reassemble the gears in their proper positions. The small radius on the return (wider) gears must face the inside of the pump body.

3. Replace the idler shaft and the driveshaft.

4. Place the brass and iron end plates in position and insert the screws, but do not tighten them yet.

5. The end plates must be either perfectly flush or slightly below flush with the edge of the pump body surface which mates with the crankcase. The reason for this should be obvious. There should be just a minimum of play in the end plates which will allow their correct alignment. This is extremely important.

6. Tighten the four screws very securely.

7. Replace the driveshaft key, the drive gear, and the fixing nut.

Installation

1. Oil the pump internals well before installing the pump.

2. Apply some gasket compound to the face of the pump, using it sparingly and being very careful not to get it anywhere near the oil passages. Remember that it will spread along the mating surface when compressed. No gasket compound should be used if a gasket is used between the pump body and the engine as on the 850. A new gasket, however, should also be used.

3. Replace the pump on the studs and gradually tighten the two nuts to 15 ft lbs.

System Components

CRANKCASE BREATHER

Latest Commandos have the crankcase breather fitted to the rear of the crankcase (750) or at the timing case (850), and no attention is needed for this type. All others, however, have the breather fitted to, and timed by, the camshaft. The breather mechanism consists of a slotted plate with driving tabs to engage the end of the camshaft, and a spring.

The rotating plate opens and closes openings in a stationary plate and this accomplishes the timing of the breather.

Crankcase breather (early models)

The rotating breather plate must be flat on the mating side and it may be worked on a stone to make it so if necessary. The driving tabs should also be in good condition.

The crankcase breather is connected to the oil tank via a rubber hose. If the engine has been standing a while, oil will usually seep into the crankcase and, when the bike is started, it will come out of the breather for a few moments until the oil pump has completely scavenged the sump. While the motorcycle is in operation, especially at high speeds, the breather will pass oil mist or even pure oil. This is normal; the amounts, however, should not be excessive, as this is indicative of oil remaining in the sump.

OIL PRESSURE RELIEF VALVE

The oil pressure rlief valve is located on the timing case cover just above the junction for the rocker oil feed pipe. The valve has a spring-loaded steel sleeve which is pre-set to open the valve at an oil pressure of 45–55 lbs per square inch (Commando) or 40–50 lbs per square inch (pre-Commando models). Oil passing through the open valve is diverted back to the feed side of the oil pump on Commandos or into the timing case on earlier machines. Although the valve itself does

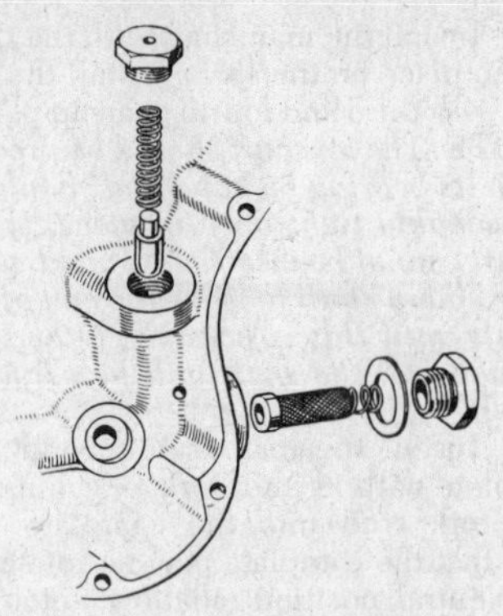

Oil pressure relief valve (Atlas)

not require attention, it does have a wire mesh filter fitted over one end which is easily cleaned after unscrewing the valve.

OIL LINES

1. All external oil lines should be checked periodically for potential cracks or splits, especially at the joints. If the hoses are secured by screw-type hose clamps, these should not be overtightened or they will crack the rubber.

2. The rocker oil feed pipe is especially important. This unit has been known to crack from vibration. It should therefore be inspected closely, especially if engine work has been done, and the pipe moved about. Arrange the pipe so that it does not touch the barrels or head except at the banjo junctions. Alternately, it can be replaced with a flexible hose as used on the latest Commandos.

The sealing ability of the copper washers used at the banjo junctions can be improved by heating them until they are red hot and then allowing them to cool. Be careful when handling after this operation, however, as the washers will be very soft.

Checking the Lubrication System

OIL PRESSURE

Oil pressure can be readily checked on Commando models with the use of the proper gauge. This is fitted at the rocker oil feed pipe junction and a reading is taken when the engine is at operating temperature. The reading should be 45–55 lbs per square in. at 3,000 rpm.

This method cannot be used for the other models because the rocker arms are fed from the oil return line. The alternative method is to acquire another timing cover. This is then drilled centered with the large oil seal and the gauge inserted. There should be 40–50 lbs per square in. pressure when checked as above, or a minimum of 5 lbs at idle, with the pressure rising with the rpm.

OPERATIONAL CHECKS

If you do not have the proper gauge, the lubrication system can be checked over in some manner by doing the following:

1. Run engine for several minutes until the oil is warm, then check the oil level at the tank and top up if necessary.

2. Take a short ride to thoroughly circulate the oil. Stop and remove the crankcase sump drain plug. No more than one or two pints of oil should come out as this is done. Be sure to replace the correct amount of oil.

3. Loosen one of the banjo fittings at the cylinder head and, with the ignition OFF, kick the engine over briskly several times. Oil should seep from the loosened banjo as you do this, proving that it is being fed to the cylinder head rocker assembly.

4. Let the machine sit overnight. Upon starting, observe the flow of oil at the return line inside the oil tank. There may be a steady stream for a few moments and then a sputtering return of oil as the sump is scavenged.

5. Check the condition of the oil seals contained in the timing cover. Removal and installation of these seals is described in Engine and Transmission.

CAUTION: *Because of a difference in the oil passages, the timing covers found on the Commando are NOT INTERCHANGEABLE with those on earlier machines although they are similar at first sight. Therefore, always be sure that you get the proper timing cover in the event that it must be replaced.*

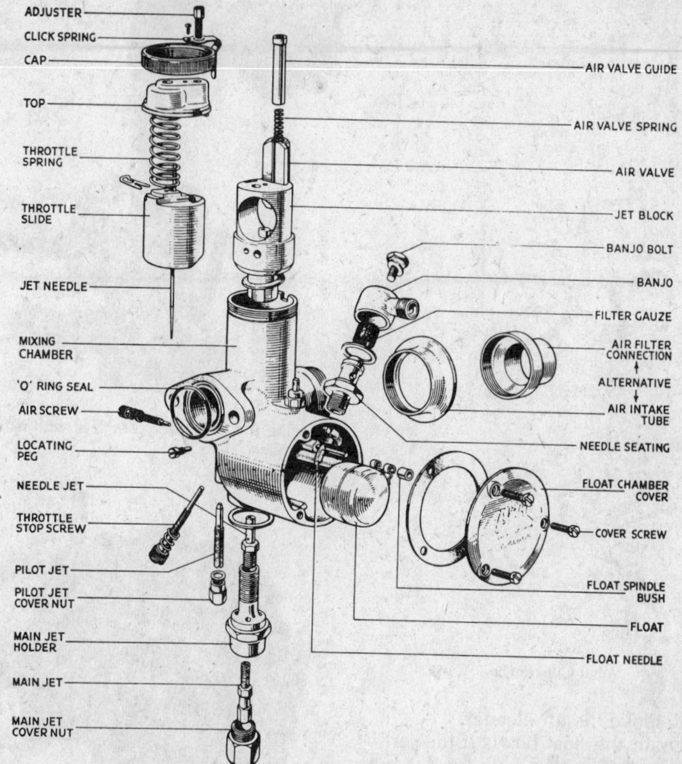

Amal Monbloc

Oil Pump Specifications

Oil Pump Body Material	Cast Iron
Type	Double Gear
Ratio, Feed: Return	1 : 2
Pump Stud Nuts Torque	15 ft lbs
Pressure Relief Valve Spring Free-Length	1.171 in.
Spring Outside Diameter	0.430–0.435 in.
Pressure Relief Valve Torque	25 ft lbs

Fuel Systems

1967 and later models use two Amal Concentric carburetors, while earlier ones are fitted with the Monobloc carburetor. The left-side Monobloc has the float bowl assembly which is used by both carburetors.

Monobloc

Removal and Disassembly

1. Remove the gas tank.
2. Remove the air cleaner.
3. Unscrew the carburetor cap and pull out the slide assemblies.
4. To disassemble the slides, remove the needle clip, and disengage the cable from the slide.
5. Gradually loosen the two carburetor flange nuts, and remove the carburetor.
6. Remove the banjo bolt, and take off the banjo and filter screen.
7. Unscrew and remove the float needle seat. Take out the needle.
8. Remove the main jet cover nut. Unscrew and remove the main jet holder complete with main and needle jets.
9. Remove the pilot jet cover nut. Unscrew and remove the pilot jet.
10. If applicable, remove the float bowl cover (3 screws). Remove the float spindle, float, and spindle bush.

Removing the jet holder and jets

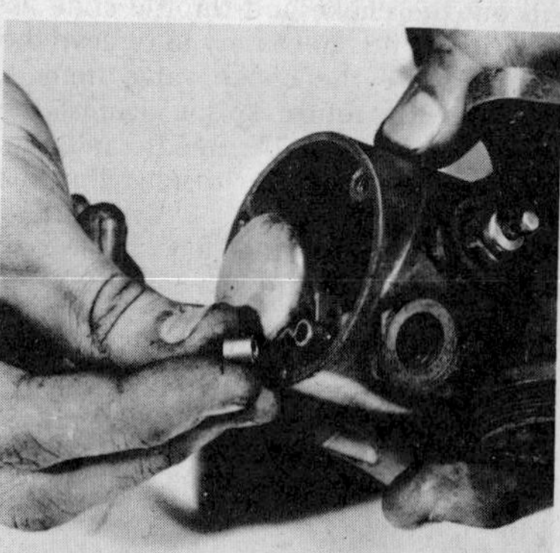
Removing the float spindle bush

11. Remove the pilot air and throttle stop screws.
12. Remove the locating peg, and shake out the jet block.

Assembly and Installation

1. Assembly is the reverse of disassembly. Use new gaskets, O-rings, and fiber washers.
2. Install the throttle slides in the carburetor bodies before tightening the flange nuts. Tighten slowly and evenly, checking for free slide movement as the nuts are tightened. If the slide begins to stick, the nuts are overtightened, warping the carburetor body.

Concentric

Removal and Disassembly

1. Remove the gas tank.

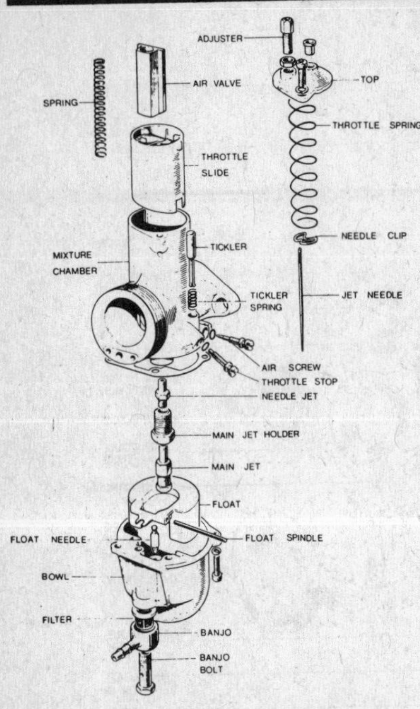

Amal Concentric

2. Remove the air cleaner.

3. Drain the float bowls if the carburetors are fitted with a plug for this purpose.

4. Unscrew the carburetor caps and pull out the choke and throttle slide assemblies. If it is necessary to remove the slide, remove the choke valve from it, compress the return spring against the carb cap, taking out the needle and clip. Remove the slide after disengaging the cable from it.

5. Unscrew the fuel feed banjo bolt on the float bowl and remove the banjo and filter.

6. Remove the float bowl screws. Hold the carburetor upright and remove the bowl complete with float assembly.

7. Lift out the float, needle, and spindle. The spindle may be a light press fit in the bowl.

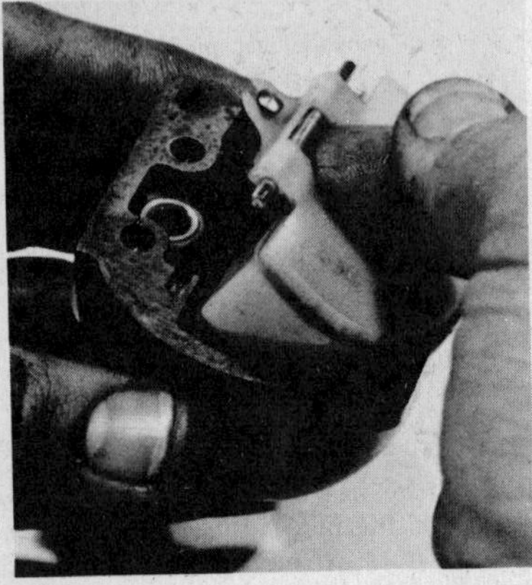

Removing the float, spindle, and float needle

8. Unscrew the main jet holder, complete with main and needle jets.

9. Unscrew the pilot jet, if so equipped. Most late models have a bush for pilot metering, which is in the carburetor body and not removeable.

Removing the jet holder complete with main and needle jets

Removing the pilot jet

10. Remove the throttle stop and pilot air screws.

Assembly and Installation

1. Assembly is the reverse of disassembly. Use new gaskets, O-rings, and fiber washers.

2. Be certain that the mounting flange O-ring is firmly in place before the carburetor is bolted to the manifold. Install the throttle slides in the bodies before tightening the flange nuts. Tighten them slowly and evenly, while checking for free slide movement. If the slide suddenly sticks, the body is being warped by overtightening the flange nuts.

3. Do not overtighten the banjo bolt. If too tight, the banjo may be deformed and leak gas.

Modifications

1. Several modifications have been made to the Amal Concentrics since their introduction. Early models had a small mesh-type fuel filter fitted over the main jet. This sometimes hindered the free movement of the float. Since at most places in the U.S., impurities in gasoline are uncommon, and the fuel system is already equipped with filters in the tank and at the carb banjo, the filter on the main jet is really unnecessary and can be removed.

2. A newer type float bowl has been fitted. This has fuel passages for the pilot jet which take the gas near the bottom of the bowl rather than half-way down as before. This was done to assure a positive fuel flow to the pilot jet regardless of variations in fuel level in the float.

3. The jet holder has been changed to thrust the main jet deeper into the float bowl. Once again, the aim was to assure positive fuel flow.

4. The needle jet and needle have both been changed. the newer type needle jet can be readily identified by the small bleed hole at the base of the jet. Looking closer, it can be seen that the jet's metering orifice has been moved from the very top of the jet to the bottom. This has, of course, necessitated the use of a longer needle. This longer needle can be distinguished from the other by the fact that it has two small rings at the very top of the needle (above the clip grooves). The other needle has three rings.

The short needles will not work with the new needle jets or vice versa. Before buying any replacement parts, be sure that they are identical to the parts you have. Of course, it is preferable, if you have an older Concentric, to switch over to the new system completely.

5. A more precise metering of the fuel flow is now obtained with the use of a brass float needle to replace the standard nylon unit. This brass needle has a rubber tip which should form a better seal with the needle seat.

Carburetor Specifications

	Commando 850	*Commando 750 (1971–on)*	*Commando 750 (1970)*	*Commando 750 (1968–69)*
Amal Type	932	930	930	930
Venturi Size	32 mm	30 mm	30 mm	30 mm
Main Jet	260	220③	220④	220
Needle Jet	0.106	0.106	0.107	0.107
Needle Clip Position	Top	Middle②	Middle	Middle
Needle	928/104	—	—	—
Throttle Slide	3	3	3	3
Pilot Jet	—	25	25	25

Carburetor Specifications

	Commando 750 (Combat)	*Atlas (after 1966), P-11*	*Atlas, G15CS, N15CS*
Amal Type	932	930	389/88RH⑤ 389/87LH
Venturi Size	32 mm	30 mm	1⅛ in.
Main Jet	230①	250	320
Needle Jet	0.106	0.107	0.106
Needle Clip Position	Middle②	Middle	Lowest notch
Needle	——	——	D
Throttle Slide	3	3	3
Pilot Jet	25	25	25

① 220 with mute
② Top with mute
③ 210 with mute
④ 180 with restricted meg; 210 with modified meg
⑤ Without float bowl

NOTE: *Some models, especially in 1966, were equipped by the factory with main jets ranging up to 420 in size. This is far too rich for most applications, especially if the air cleaner and muffler are left stock. The settings were later revised to those shown above.*

Electrical System

Ignition System

LUCAS K2F MAGNETO

A magneto ignition is used on machines prior to 1967.

The magneto consists of an armature (with a condenser incorporated) rotating in a magnetic field. The armature is driven by chain from the intermediate sprocket. The centrifugal timing advance mechanism is incorporated in the magneto sprocket and is located in the timing case. The contact breaker points are found on the opposite side of the armature, beneath the magneto cover, and are opened and closed as they rotate inside a cam ring.

The high tension leads contact the magneto slip ring via carbon brushes and these brushes are also used for the "kill button" and the magneto ground, the latter being found beneath the screw on the right-side (top) of the magneto.

Service

1. Every 2,000 miles, clean the breaker points and adjust the gap. Refer to "Tune-Up." Check the gap opening at both firing points on the cam ring. If one is greater than the other, it is best to compromise the value.

2. Apply a small drop of oil to the breaker point pivot. Also, use some high temperature grease to lubricate the cam ring. Be very careful when using any type of lubricant near the breaker points.

3. Every 5,000 miles, remove the high tension pick-ups, and clean off the carbon brushes. The brushes are mounted on springs and should slide freely in the pick-ups. There must be at least ⅛ in. of the brush protruding from the pick-up for the magneto to work.

Also clean the ground brush after removing its mounting screw.

4. Stuff a clean rag into one of the pick-up holes and kick the engine over a few times to clean off the slip ring. A good deal of oil on the slip ring will indicate a defective oil seal which must be replaced.

5. Remove the timing cover and check the play (up and down) of the magneto sprocket nut. If there is more than 0.005 in. of play, the magneto should be disassembled and the bearings replaced or adjusted.

The following procedure is given for either mechanical (i.e., bearing) or electrical faults:

Removal and Disassembly

1. Remove the timing cover.
2. Remove the magneto points cover.
3. Remove the pick-ups.
4. Unscrew the magneto sprocket bolt and remove the advance mechanism. Remove the two nuts (on studs) and the nut and bolt which secure the magneto to the timing case.
5. Hold the rocker oil feed pipe aside and pull off the magneto.
6. Remove the two safety screws located just by the pick-up holes.

CAUTION: *These screws must be removed before the armature is taken out.*

7. Remove the points; then remove the cam ring, which is a slip fit in the magneto case and must be pulled straight out (with the fingers only). Be careful of the lubricating wicks.

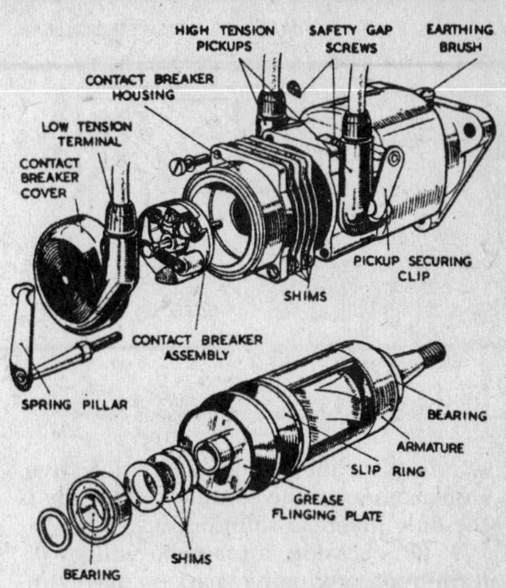

Lucas magneto

8. Remove the two end cover screws and take off the cover. Be careful of the thin metal shims which may be fitted behind the cover.
9. Remove the ground brush and pull out the armature.
10. The magneto sprocket-side bearing race is a press-fit in the housing and a fiber washer is fitted around it. An oil seal is beneath the race. If replacement of the race or oil seal is necessary, heat the housing slightly and tap the race out.

Inspection

1. A simple but relatively effective armature test can be made with a two-volt battery. Screw in the hexagon screw which secures the points into the armature, then connect one of the battery leads to this screw, the other to an ammeter. Then connect the other lead of the ammeter to the ground of the armature itself. The ammeter reading should be about four amps. This is a test of the primary winding.

2. To test the secondary winding (this is the high tension side of the circuit) set up as above. Obtain a length of high tension wire and clamp one end to ground at the armature, supporting the other end from ⅛ to $^3/_{16}$ in. from the slip ring contact. Make and break the connection at the hexagon screw several times quickly, and observe the spark produced. The high tension spark must be able to jump at least a ⅛ in. gap.

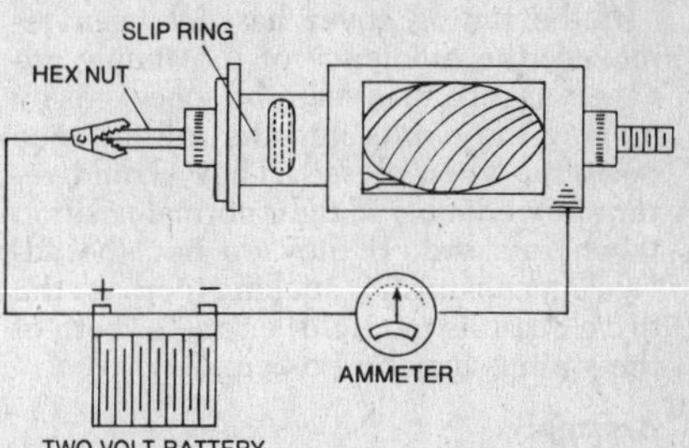

Magneto armature low-tension test

If no spark is produced, the armature

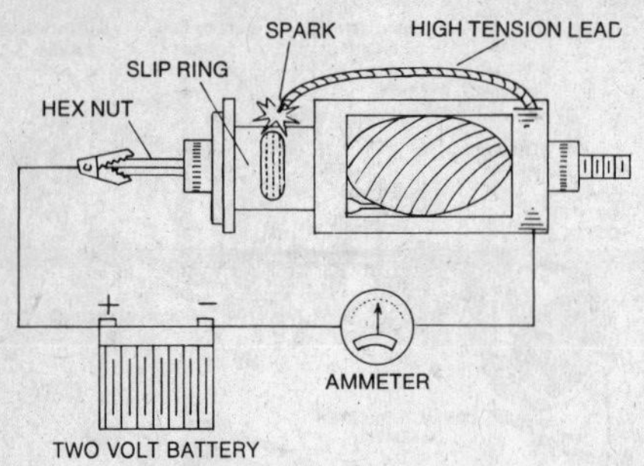

Magneto armature high-tension test

windings or the condenser is defective. Replacement of the complete assembly is the only practical solution.

3. On occasion, a magneto will go intermittent, producing spark on one cylinder, or severe misfiring while running. This is sometimes due to a broken wire within the windings. This cannot be rectified and the armature should be replaced.

4. Magneto bearings are adjustable by removing the thin metal shims from behind the end cover until the end play of the shaft is within acceptable limits.

When the last of these shims have been removed, there is still some possibility of adjustment by adding shims behind the inner races on the armature shaft. However, it requires a special tool to remove or replace the inner races.

Excessive bearing play is most often the result of the drive side outer bearing race, which rides on a rather flimsy fiber insulator, becoming loose.

The ball bearings themselves are held on the inner races by a standard cage. They can be easily removed by simply pulling off by hand as the cage is somewhat flexible.

5. The timing advance mechanism should be inspected. Check for worn sprocket teeth. The two springs which control bob-weight movement should have from 12–14 oz of tension at 1/16 in. extension.

If the machine has been idle for some time, bathe the advance mechanism in light penetrating oil to assure free movement of the weights.

If the timing cover has not been removed, the efficiency of the timing advance mechanism can be checked by moving the points into the full advance position, when closed. They should return immediately to their normal position when released. If they do not, the advance mechanism is sticking (perhaps the drive chain is too tight) or one or both of the springs may be broken.

Assembly

1. If the sprocket-side bearing race has been removed, fit a new oil seal. Bend the tabs of the insulating washer so that the washer fits the bearing race. Install the washer and press in the race.

2. Lubricate the bearings with a good grade of high temperature grease before installation.

3. Refit the armature, the ground brush, safety screws, and end cover.

4. Replacethe point's cam ring.

NOTE: *As on removal, the cam ring must slide directly in. It must be done by hand. Do not force the ring into place. Note that the ring is notched to align with a small stud in the end cover.*

5. Replace the points assembly. The backing plate is "keyed" and must align with its slot. Replace the hexagon screw.

6. Replace the complete magneto and place the timing advance mechanism on the armature shaft.

7. Adjust the magneto drive chain and set the ignition timing.

CAPACITOR IGNITION

The capacitor ignition system utilizes a dual-point and dual-coil set-up. A capacitor is wired in parallel with the battery and should provide spark even if the battery condition is low.

To check each of the components in the event of a lack of spark, follow these procedures:

Ignition Coils

1. The ignition coil for each cylinder can be checked by inserting a nail or other suitable conductive object into the spark plug cap and holding this about ⅛ in. away from the cylinder fins while kicking the engine over briskly. A spark should be able to jump the gap.

2. Pre-1970 and some 1972 models use the Lucas 17M12 coil. The primary winding can be checked by connecting an ohmmeter across the low tension terminals (white and black-white leads or white and black-yellow leads). The reading for the 17M12 coil should be 3.3–3.8 ohms.

Late models are equipped with 17M6 coils. These are 6 volt coils, although the rest of the electrical system remains 12 volt. The 17M6 coils have a ballast resistor wired in series. Resistance for the primary winding is 1.7–1.9 ohms.

The ballast resistor can be tested and should yield a value of 1.8–2.0 ohms.

Condensers

To test the condensers, turn on the ignition and take voltage readings across each set of contact points when open. If no reading is obtained, the condensers have broken down and must be replaced.

If a voltage reading is obtained but there is noticeable arcing and pitting of the ignition points, the condensers should be replaced.

On 1970 models, the condensers are fastened to the coil clips and are reached from beneath.

On 1971 and later models, the coil assembly must be removed and then the condenser pack (2 screws and nuts). Remove the rubber cover which will reveal the condensers mounted individually to the base plate.

2MC Capacitor

The large Lucas 2MC capacitor is mounted in a coil spring secured to the frame.

1. The capacitor should be checked periodically; this can be done by simply disconnecting the battery (tape up the leads to avoid the possibility of a short circuit). The machine should be able to start and run normally. The lights should still work, although they may be dim at low revs, getting brighter as engine speed increases.

2. The capacitor should be mounted with the terminals downward. The single terminal (marked with a red dot) is positive and the double terminal is negative. The terminals are also different sizes, making reversal of the connections almost impossible.

NOTE: *If, by some accident, the connections are reversed, the capacitor will be ruined.*

3. The capacitor can also be checked by removing it from the machine and connecting a fully charged 12 volt battery across it, leaving it this way for about five minutes. Then, disconnect the battery and let the capacitor sit for another five minutes. At the end of this time, a DC voltmeter connected across the capacitor terminals should give a reading of at least 8 volts.

The capacitor has a limited storage life of approximately 18 months at 68° F. or 9 to 12 months at 86° F. Therefore, it would be wise to check the condition of the capacitor regularly.

Charging System

IMPORTANT: *All models are equipped with a 12 volt POSITIVE GROUND system.*

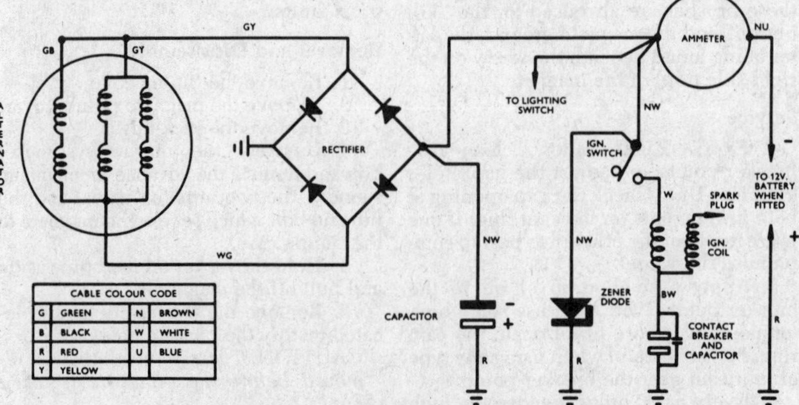

Simplified diagram of Commando wiring system

The charging system consists of the alternator, rectifier, zener diode, and the battery itself. 1975 and later models have two diodes.

The alternator produces alternating current by means of a permanent magnet rotor mounted on the left-side of the crankshaft, which rotates within a stationary six-pole laminated iron stator assembly. Three stators have been used and they are easily distinguishable: the RM15 has three leads while the later types RM21 and RM23 have two leads.

The current produced by the alternator is "rectified" (changed to direct current) by the three-plate rectifier.

The amount of charge which the battery receives is determined by the zener diode. This is essentially a variable resistance ("semi-conductor" is the proper term) which automatically raises or lowers the amount of current flowing into the battery according to its condition and needs.

Although the two types of alternator are similar, charging system troubleshooting procedures are provided for each alternator model.

RM15 SYSTEM

There are several types of this model alternator fitted. Nos. 540, 210, and 18 are found on magneto equipped machines, and 047 and 534 on coil ignition machines.

IMPORTANT: *For the results of the following tests to be valid, the battery must be in good condition and more than half charged.*

Test the system as a whole first by assuring that the battery is receiving the proper charge:

1. Be certain that all electrical connections are clean and tight.
2. Disconnect the 2MC capacitor if fitted.
3. Disconnect the battery negative cable and connect a DC ammeter between the cable and the negative terminal of the battery.
4. Start the engine and run it at 3,000 rpm.
5. Observe the ammeter readings at each of the lighting switch positions.

Switch Position	*Alternator RM15 Type*	
	540, 210, 18	*047, 534*
Off	2.75 amps	2.75 amps
Park. Light	2.0	1.5
Headlight	2.0	1.5

6. If the readings are higher than those given, the battery may be overcharged. This would most probably be caused by a defective zener diode.
7. If the readings are lower than those given, any one of the other components may be at fault. Perform the test again, but disconnect the diode cable. If the readings become higher, the fault is in the diode, which must be replaced.

If the diode cannot be faulted, the alternator should be checked for voltage output. This requires an AC voltmeter (20 volt range) and a 1 ohm resitor capable of carrying 20 amps without overheating.

1. Disconnect the three alternator leads at the snap connector.
2. Connect the resistor in parallel with the AC voltmeter and check the voltage output between the alternator leads. The following values are the minimum acceptable for an alternator in good condition, with the engine turning 3,000 rpm.

Voltmeter and Resistor connected between leads	*Alternator RM15 Type*	
	540, 210, 18	*047, 534*
White-Green and Green-Black	4.0v.	4.0v.
White-Green and Green-Yellow	6.5	6.5
White-Green and Green-Black*	8.5	9.0
Each lead and ground	0.0	0.0

* With Green-Yellow connected to Green-Black

The following conclusions can be drawn from the test results:

A. If all readings are low, the rotor has become demagnetized.

B. If any individual readings are low, a single coil or coils are short circuited.

C. Zero reading indicates that individual coil or coils are open circuits.

D. Any voltage reading obtained with the voltmeter and resistor connected to any lead and ground indicates coil or coils internally grounded.

If the alternator tests out okay, the trouble is probably the rectifier. This component is best checked by replacing it with a known workable rectifier. A bench test is given later however.

RM21 SYSTEM

IMPORTANT: *Before the following tests are carried out, the battery must be in good condition and close to a full state of charge.*

1. Leave the cable connections to the rectifier in place; connect the negative lead of a DC voltmeter (20 volt range) to the center terminal of the rectifier, and the other lead to a ground on the frame or engine. The voltmeter should read battery voltage at this point, if the proper connections are in order.
2. Start the engine and run it at about 3,000 rpm. The voltmeter should register 14.4–16.4 volts.
3. If the voltmeter reading is the proper value, all components are working properly and any trouble with battery charging must be due to the battery itself or to the battery connections.
4. If the voltage reading is higher than the given value, the zener diode is faulty and must be replaced.
5. If the voltage reading is lower than normal, the alternator, rectifier, diode, or 2MC capacitor can be at fault.
6. If the voltage reading is lower than the given value, perform the test again, but disconnect the diode. The voltage reading should read higher than the regulated value of 14.4–16.4 volts. If it does, the diode is faulty. If it does not, the alternator, rectifier, or capacitor may be at fault.
7. Disconnect the 2MC capacitor and repeat the test. If the voltage reading reaches the normal value, the capacitor is faulty and must be replaced. If it does not, the trouble must be in either the alternator or the rectifier.
8. Test the voltage output of the alternator. Disconnect the two leads at the snap connector and connect an AC voltmeter (20 volt range), with a 1 ohm resistor wired in parallel with it, to the two alternator leads.
9. Start the engine and run it up to about 3,000 rpm. The voltmeter should give a reading of 9 volts if the alternator is satisfactory. If it does, the rectifier is at fault and must be replaced. If it does not, further checks can be carried out to determine the cause of the alternator failure.

The alternator may fail due either to a short or an open circuit in the stator windings or a demagnetized rotor.

1. Connect a 110 volt AC 15 watt test light circuit between the alternator leads (one at a time), and the stator laminations. If the light goes on, there is a short circuit in the windings.

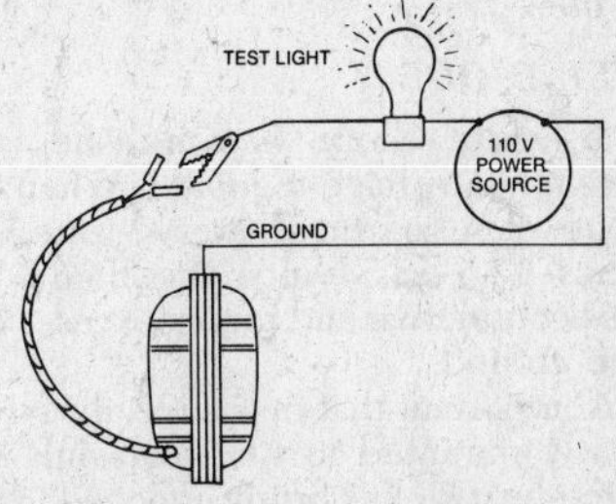

Testing the stator for short circuits

2. It is extremely difficult to carry out a test for an open circuit, so at this point the best thing to do is to fit a replacement rotor and see if this cures the problem. If it does not, the stator is at fault. Since it is plastic-encapsulated, no service is possible and the stator must be replaced.

RM23 SYSTEM

1. Needed for an alternator test are an AC voltmeter and a one-ohm resistor.
2. Disconnect the two alternator leads at the snap connectors and hook up the AC voltmeter across them. Connect the resistor in parallel to the alternator leads.

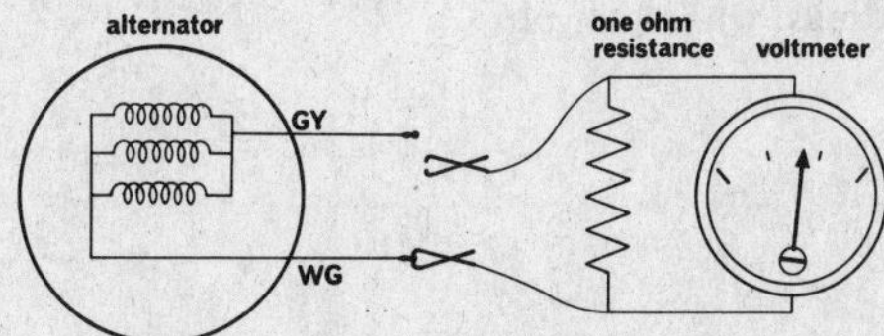

Testing RM21 alternator voltage output

3. Start the engine and run it at 3,000 rpm. The voltmeter reading should be nine volts.

4. If the output is low, the rotor may be becoming demagnetized. The best check is by substitution. If the reading is zero, the stator probably has a broken wire and must be replaced.

System Components

RECTIFIER

A 12-volt test light is needed to carry out the rectifier test.

1. Disconnect the leads and remove the rectifier from the machine. Take care not to disturb the bolt and nut which hold the rectifier plates together as they are set at the factory and disturbing them will affect rectifier output.

2. Assume that the three rectifier plate terminals are numbered 1, 2, 3, and the mounting stud is No. 4.

3. With the test light, check for continuity across the terminals using the following pairs of connections: 1-2, 1-4, 3-4, and 2-3.

4. In each case, reverse the test light leads and again check for continuity.

5. Reading should be as follows: For each connection, there must be continuity in one direction only. If there is no continuity in either direction, or if there is continuity in both directions for one or more of the connections, the rectifier is defective and must be replaced with a new one.

ZENER DIODE

The zener diode accomplishes the function of a voltage regulator. When the voltage across the battery terminals reaches 13.5–15.5 volts, the diode becomes conductive and routes excess voltage to ground.

It is important that the diode always be securely mounted to the heat sink and that the heat sink is firmly attached to the frame. Also, the heat sink should be placed in the cooling airstream.

To test the zener diode, a DC ammeter and voltmeter are needed.

NOTE: *When carrying out this test, the battery must be in good condition and have a full charge. Otherwise the test results will not be valid.*

1. Disconnect the zener diode lead and connect the positive wire of the DC ammeter to the diode and the negative ammeter wire to the lead.

2. Connect the voltmeter across the diode terminal and ground (positive to ground).

3. Be sure that all lights and accessories are OFF.

4. Start and run the engine; note the following meter readings: when the voltmeter reads 12.8 volts or less, the ammeter should show zero current flow. When the ammeter shows 2.0 amps flowing, the voltmeter should read 13.5–15.5 volts.

5. If readings do not conform to the above specifications, replace the zener diode.

ALTERNATOR

The alternator requires no maintenance as such, but the following points should be noted:

1. Clean off the rotor and the stator poles from time to time removing any foreign matter, metal particles, etc.

2. Make sure that the rotor is not worn or scored from contact with the stator poles.

3. There must be no contact between the rotor and the stator poles. Ideally, there should be an even gap between the two all around the rotor. This can be checked with a feeler gauge. Clearance should be about 0.010 in. The position of the stator can be altered by using shim washers behind it placed on the housing studs.

4. Before tightening the stator mounting nuts, place an appropriate spacer around the rotor, then place the stator on its studs. Tighten the nuts with the spacer in place. This will help centralize the stator.

Starter Motor

1975 and later models are equipped with a Prestolite starter motor.

Removal

1. Disconnect the starter high-tension lead.

2. Remove the three screws from the primary chain cover flange and remove the starter noting the O-ring.

Disassembly

1. Mount the starter in a suitable vise.

2. Before disassembly, note that the end covers are marked in relation to the body itself and must be properly lined up when assembling.

3. Remove the two through-bolts.

4. Tap the end of the armature with a platic mallet or the like until the opposite side end cover begins to come off. Stop when the cover has moved about ⅛ in. At this point, hold the armature while attempting to pull off the end cover.

5. After this end cover is removed, tap the brush side of the armature to remove the drive-side end cover.

6. Remove the armature from the starter body, noting that the brushes will spring out as the armature is withdrawn.

Inspection

1. Check the armature bushings for cracks or signs of wear. The drive side bushing can be tapped out with a drift, if replacement is needed, after prying out the oil seal.

The brush-side bushing is removed with a tap.

In both cases, removal and installation can be facilitated by heating the end covers gently.

2. Clean the armature commutator in a solvent to remove any residue or carbon dust.

3. With a continuity tester, check for continuity between each of the commutator segments. All segments must show continuity, or the starter armature must be replaced.

4. Check for continuity between the armature core and the commutator. There must be no continuity here. If there is, replace the starter armature.

Assembly

1. Assembly is the reverse of the disassembly procedure.

2. Before assembly, apply a light coat of molybdenum disulphide grease to each armature bush.

3. After fitting the armature into the body, install the spring shim and thrust washer. Note that the spring shim is closest to the armature.

4. When assembling the end caps, be sure to line up the marks. Use thread locking compound on the through-bolts and torque them to 8 ft lbs. Check that the armature turns easily. Some resistance will be imparted by the brushes which bear against the commutator.

Installation

Be sure that the O-ring is in place when installing the starter.

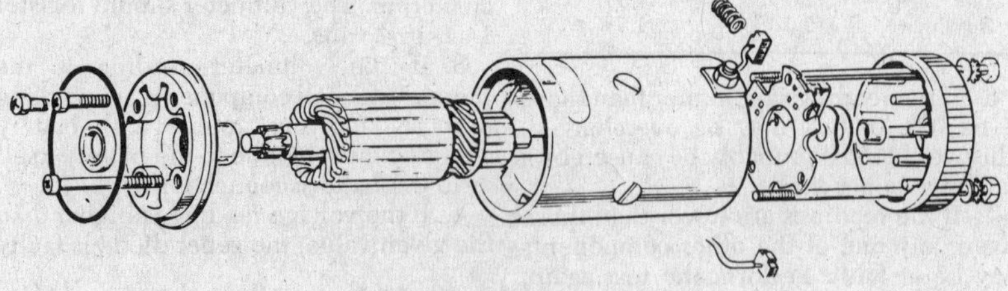

Electric starter assembly

Wiring Diagrams

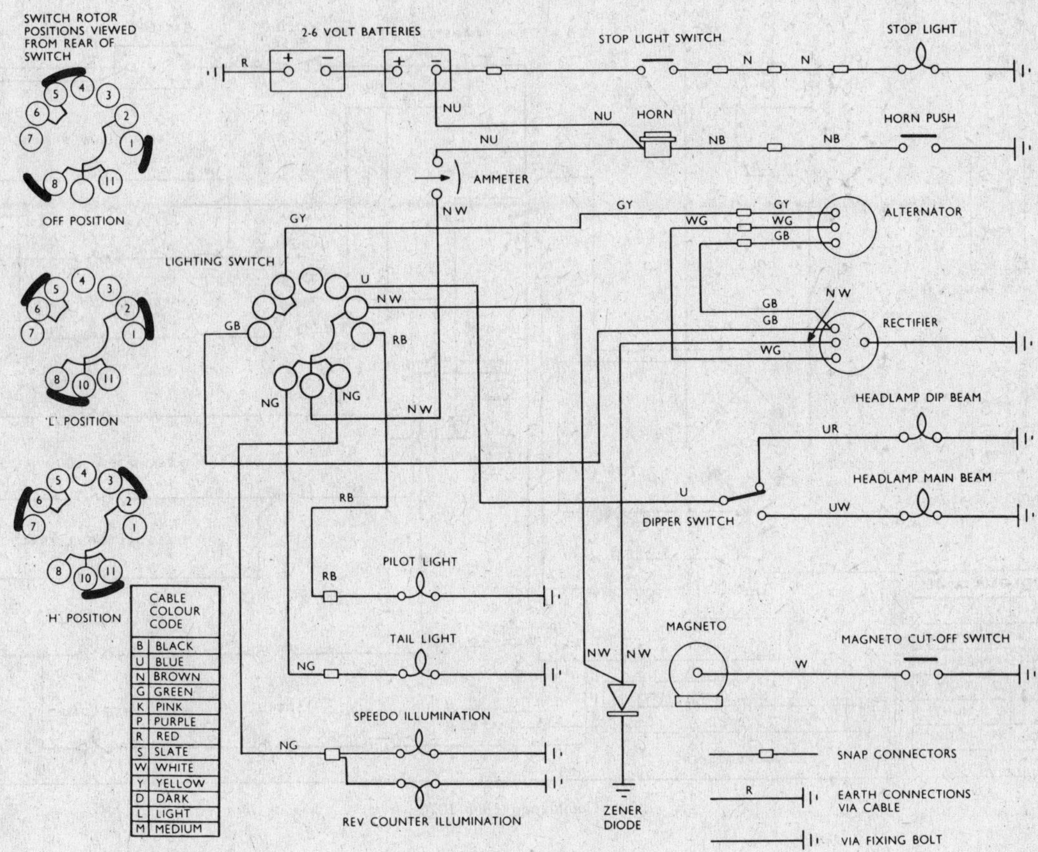

Magneto ignition models

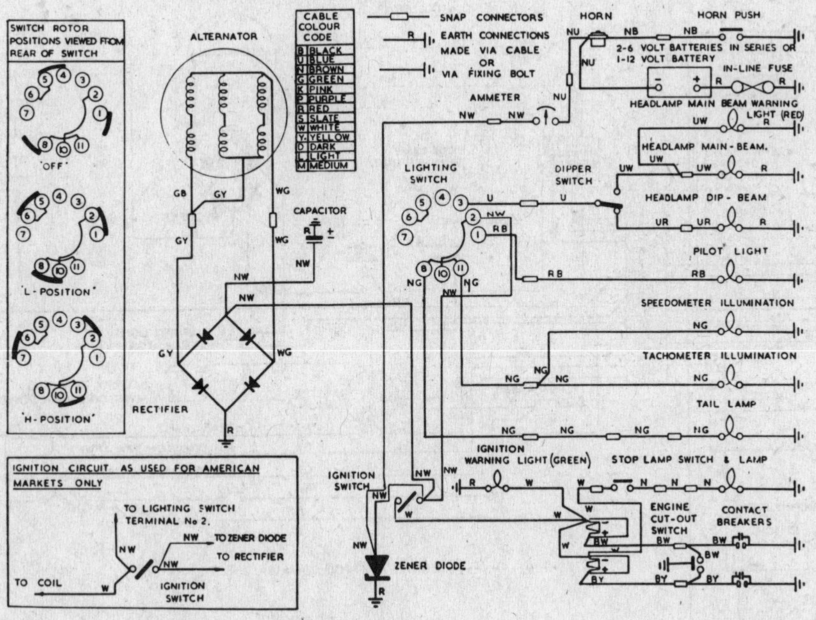

Capacitor ignition 1967 models

Wiring Diagrams

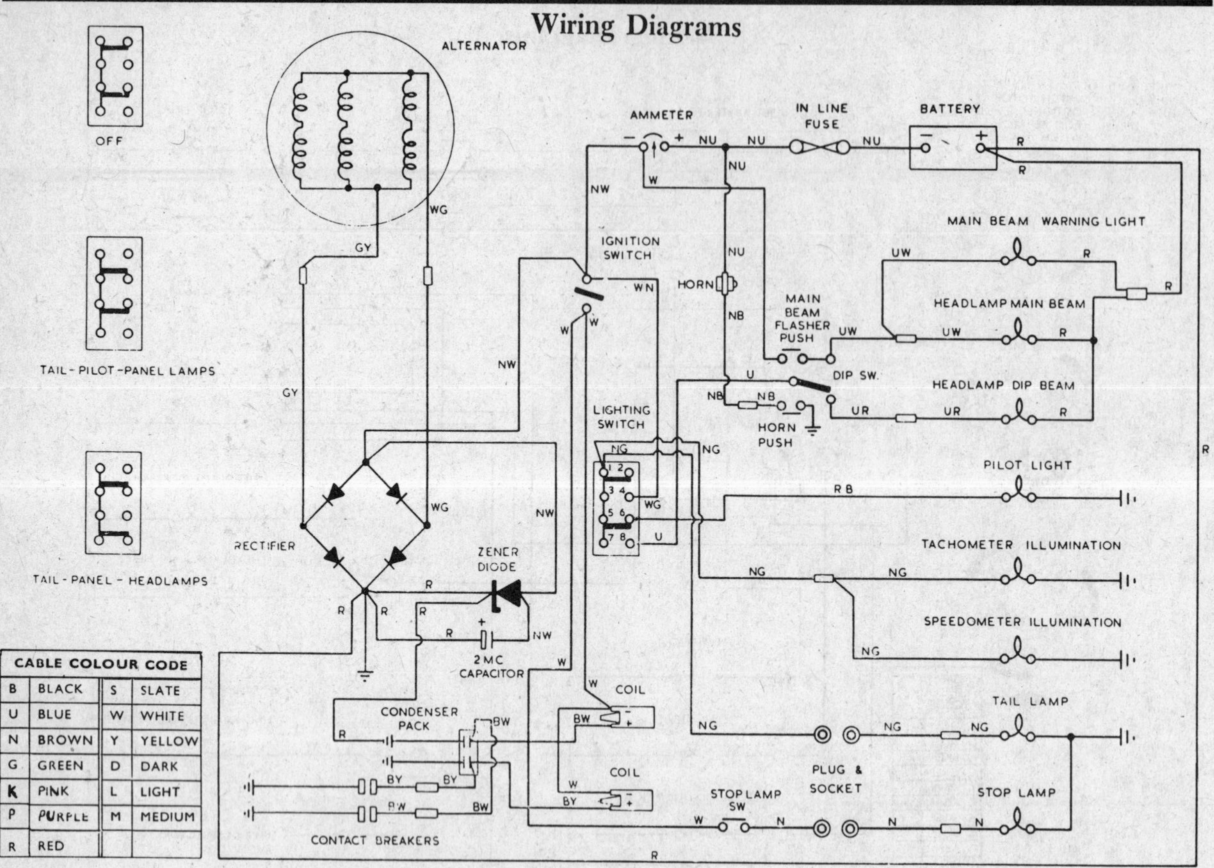

Commando (1968–1970)

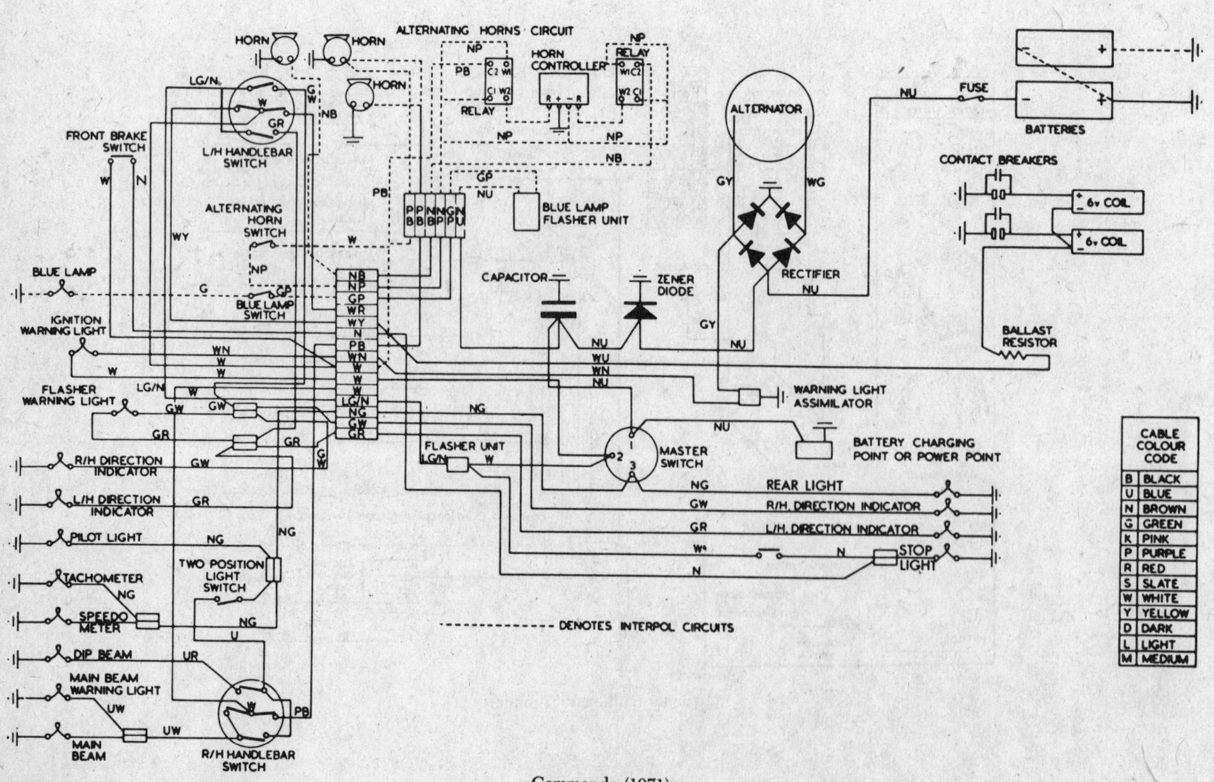

Commando (1971)

Wiring Diagrams

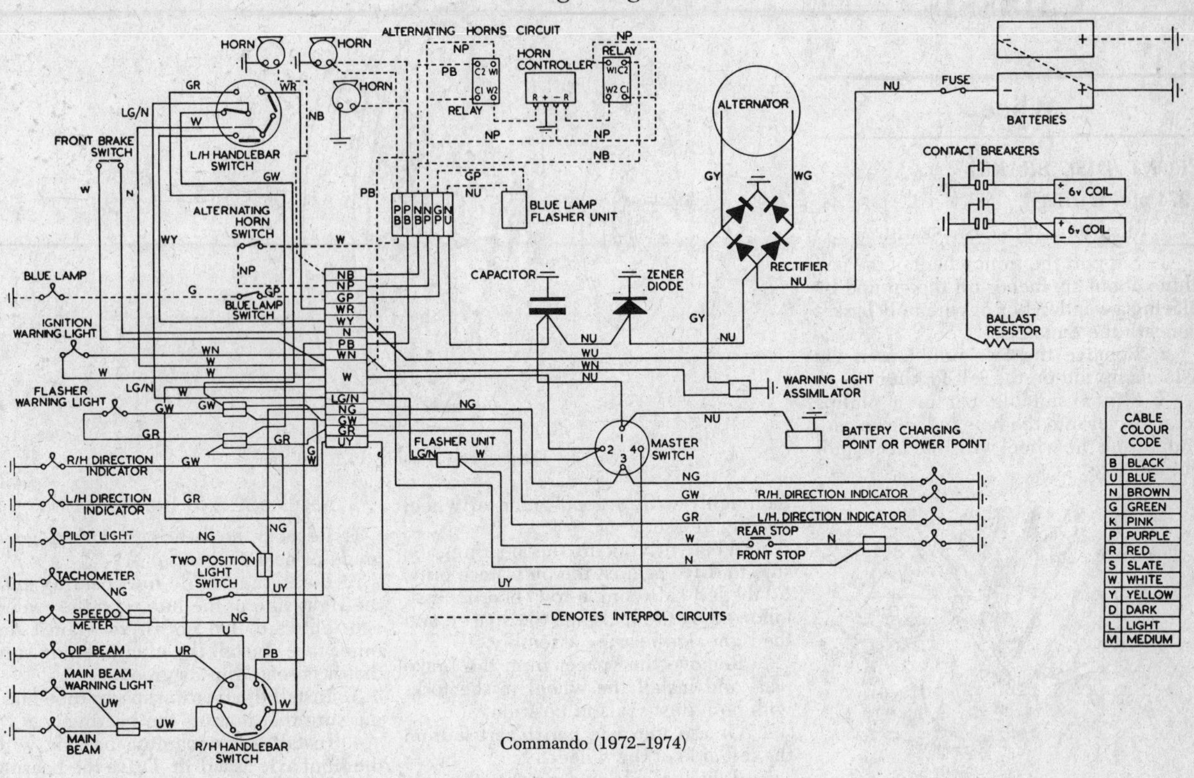

Commando (1972–1974)

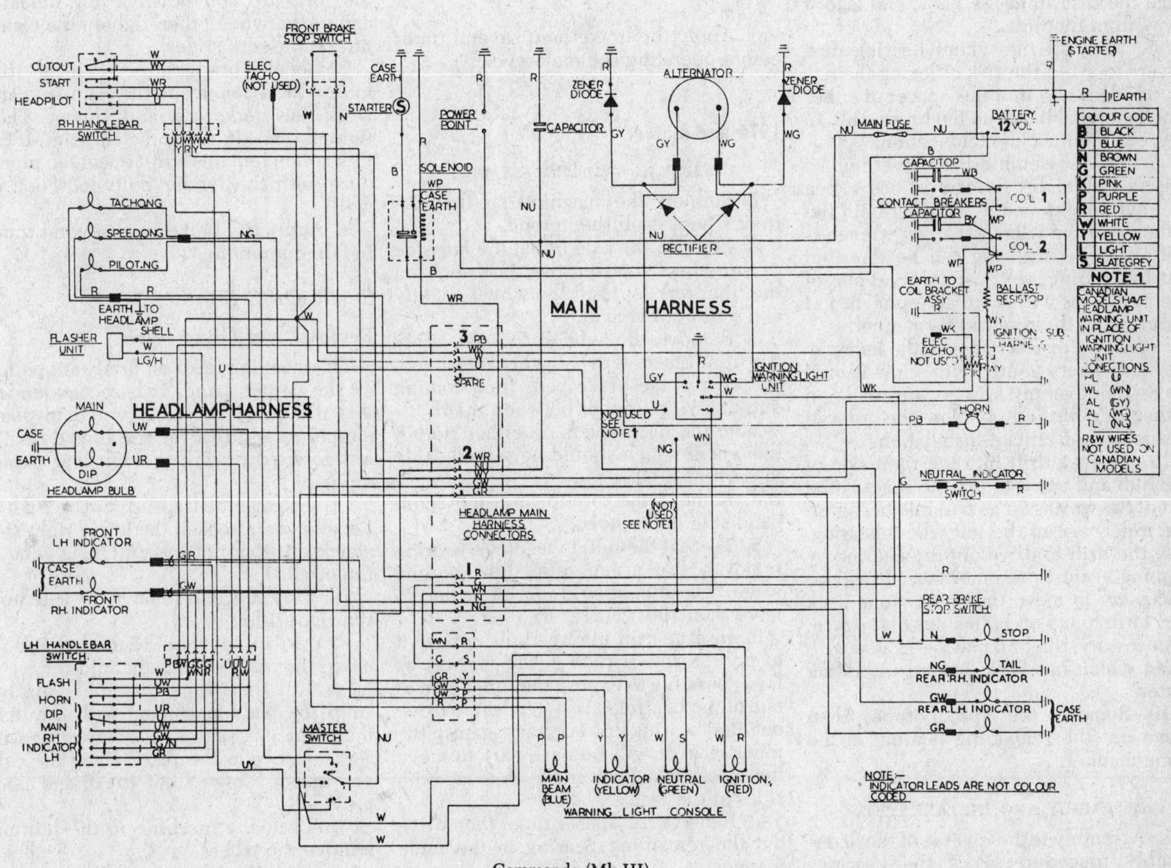

Commando (Mk III)

Chassis

Wheels

FRONT (DISC BRAKE)

1974 and Earlier

REMOVAL AND DISASSEMBLY

1. Support the front wheel of the machine about six inches off the ground by placing a wooden box or wire milk basket beneath the engine.
2. Remove the axle nut; loosen the axle clamp nut on the left fork tube.
3. Slip a suitable bar or a philips screwdriver into the hole in the axle and, supporting the wheel with one hand, pull out the axle.

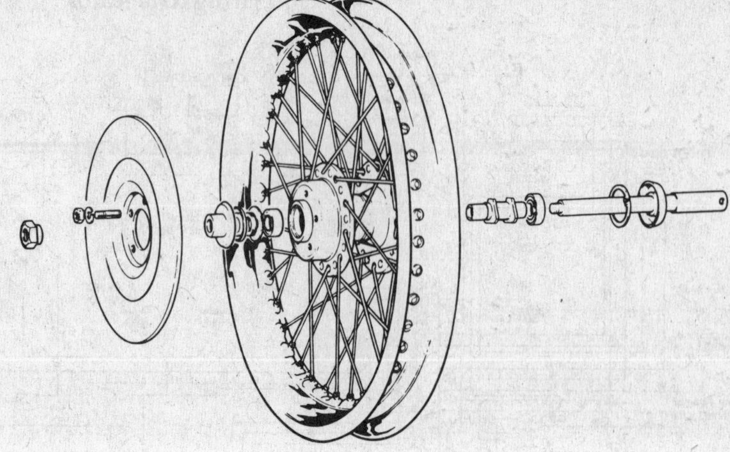

Front wheel assembly (1975 and later)

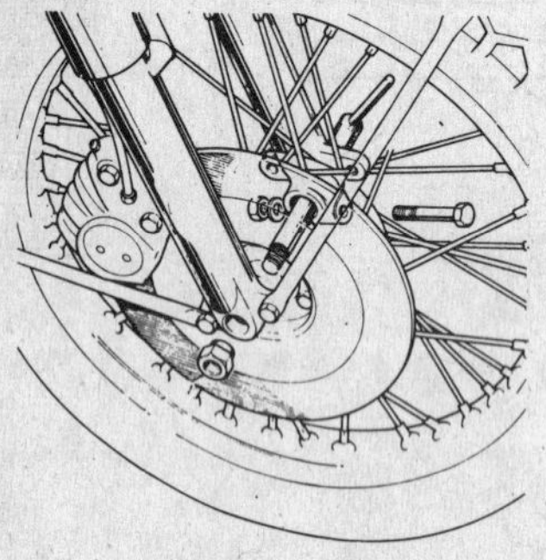

Removing the front wheel (disc brake)

4. Pull the wheel forward, to disengage the disc from the pads, and take it away from the forks.
5. Take off the wheel bearing dust covers to avoid the risk of losing them.
6. Place a ¼ in. thick spacer of either wood or metal between the brake pads, to prevent their accidental ejection.
7. To disassemble the wheel hub, if this is felt to be necessary, use a peg wrench to remove the lockring from the left-side of the wheel. If a peg wrench is not available, the ring can be threaded out by tapping, very carefully, at one of the peg holes with a suitable punch, and unscrewing the ring in this manner.

If the ring resists removal, the hub may be heated very gently with a low flame.

8. Remove any spacers and seals on either side of the hub. Note the order of assembly to facilitate installation.
9. Insert a drift into the right-side of the hub and use it to pry the spacer tube out of the way as far as possible to expose the inner race of the left wheel bearing. Use the drift to drive out the bearing by tapping against the inner race. It will be necessary to move the spacer tube back and forth to tap on both sides of the race. If necessary, the hub may be heated with a rag which has been soaked in boiling water.
10. Remove the spacer tube; then drive out the remaining bearing in the same manner.

ASSEMBLY AND INSTALLATION

1. Assembly is the reverse of the disassembly procedure. Pack the bearings thoroughly with a good grade of wheel bearing grease.
2. When driving in the bearings, be sure to drive against the outer race only. Fit the left-side (single-row) bearing first, followed by the lockring, the spacer, and the right-side bearing assembly.
3. Remove the spacer from the brake pads and install the wheel in the forks with both dust seals in position.
4. Grease the axle and insert it from the left-side of the wheel.
5. Refit the axle and tighten the axle nut firmly. Take the support out from under the bike and work the forks up and down several times. Then tighten the axle clamp nut.

CAUTION: *Do not overtighten the clamp nut.*

6. Apply the brake hard several times before operating the motorcycle.

1975 and Later

REMOVAL AND DISASSEMBLY

1. Support the machine so that the front wheel is off the ground.
2. Remove the axle nut at the left-side of the wheel. Loosen the pinch-bolt on the right fork leg. Lift the wheel slightly and pull out the axle.
3. Remove the wheel. Do not apply the front brake with the wheel removed. To prevent the brake pads from coming out, fit a ¼ in. spacer between them.

Note the dust covers on either side of the wheel which should be placed aside to prevent loss.

4. Remove the circlip from the right-hand side of the hub.
5. To heat the hub to facilitate bearing removal, use a rag dipped in boiling water. The hub should not be heated to more than 100° C (212° F).
6. Insert a drift into the hub and use it to pry the spacer tube out of the way as far as possible to expose the inner race of one of the bearings. Use the drift to drive out the bearing by tapping against the inner race. It will be necessary to move the spacer tube back and forth to tap both sides of the race.
7. Remove the spacer tube; then drive out the remaining bearing in the same manner.

ASSEMBLY AND INSTALLATION

1. Repack the bearings with a good grade of bearing grease.
2. Press the single-row bearing into the right-side of the hub with the sealed side outward. Do not drive against the inner race. Install the circlip, being sure that it is seated in its groove.
3. Install the bearing spacer tube making sure that it abuts the bearing.
4. Install the remaining bearing with the front axle as a drift. Drive the bearing in until it is completely seated. Install the flet seal, spacer, and dust cover on the right-side of the hub.
5. Install the wheel on the motorcycle.
6. After tightening the axle nut, work the forks up and down a few times to center the wheel, then tighten the clamp nut on the fork slider.
7. Check fork action. If it is stiff, loosen the axle nut and the clamp nut and work the forks up and down. Then tighten the axle nut and clamp nut. If the fork action remains stiff, repeat the procedure with the fender bolts loosened as well.
8. Apply the brake hard several times before operation.

REAR (DISC BRAKE)

Removal and Disassembly

The machine must be firmly supported on the center stand. It is recommended that the stand be safety wired in place temporarily so that the machine does not roll forward during the removal procedure.

1. Engage the transmission in First or Second gear. Loosen the lower right-side shock absorber nut and pull it out as far as the circlip.
2. Unscrew and remove the axle from the right-side.
3. Move the wheel to the left and remove the right-side chain adjuster.
4. Lift the caliper assembly up, but keep the pads in contact with the disc, then squeeze the chain adjuster and insert it between the pads. Hang the caliper upside down from the frame hook provided.
5. Lean the machine to the left and remove the wheel.
6. If desired, the sprocket assembly

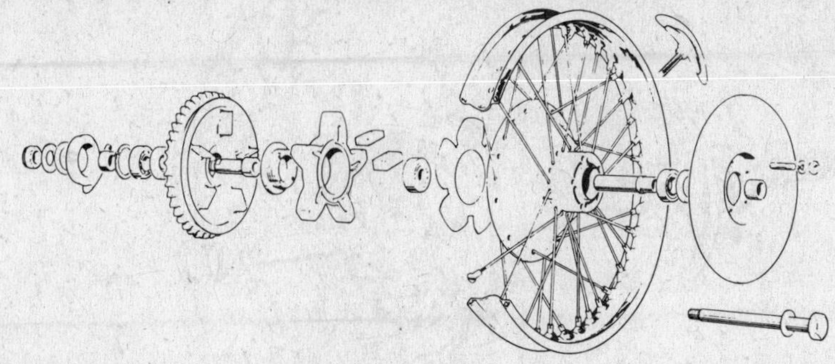

Rear wheel disc brake assembly

may be removed by disconnecting the chain, detaching the speedometer cable, removing the left-side axle nut, and taking off the assembly.

7. To disassemble the rear wheel assembly, first remove the brake disc.

8. Remove the lockring on the left-side of the wheel.

NOTE: *The lockring is a LEFT-HAND thread.*

9. Remove the small spacer from the right-side of the wheel. The end of the bearing spacer tube will be exposed. Use a soft metal or plastic mallet against the protruding end of the tube to drive out the left-side wheel bearing.

If necessary, the hub may be heated, but to no more than 100° C (212° F), with a rag which has been dipped in boiling water.

10. Use a suitable drift on the left end of the spacer tube and use it to drive out the right-side wheel bearing and oil seal.

11. To disassemble the sprocket hub, remove the bearing circlip and drive out the bearing from the oil seal side.

Assembly and Installation

1. Pack the bearings with grease.

2. Install the disc-side wheel bearing first, driving it straight into the hub with pressure applied to the outer race only. The bearing should be pressed in until it is about $^5/_{16}$ in. below the lip of the hub. Install the oil seal so that the outer face is flush with the hub lip.

3. Install the spacer tube. Install the left-side bearing. Install and tighten the lockring.

4. Install the spacer into the right-side oil seal.

5. To assemble the sprocket hub, drive in the bearing first. Fit the bearing locating circlip, sharp side outward, making sure that it is seated in its groove. Install the oil seal, metal side out.

6. The remainder of the assembly procedure is the reverse of disassembly.

7. Before riding the machine, apply the rear brake hard several times to line up the brake pads.

FRONT (DRUM BRAKE)

Late models are equipped with a twin leading shoe front brake, while earlier ones feature a single leading shoe unit. In either case, the procedures are similar.

Removal and Disassembly

1. Place the machine on the center stand.

2. Disconnect the front brake cable from the hub.

3. Remove the axle nut, then loosen the axle clamp nut on the left fork leg.

4. Support the wheel to take the weight off the axle, then insert a bar or a philips screwdriver into the hole on the left-side of the axle and pull it out.

5. Watching that the brake anchor clears the slot in the right fork leg, take the wheel out of the forks.

On the P-11, loosen the axle nut, disconnect the brake anchor, remove the axle caps, and remove the wheel.

6. Remove the dust cover on the left-side of the wheel. Remove the brake backing plate assembly from the drum.

7. To disassemble the wheel hub, if this is felt to be necessary, use a peg wrench to remove the lockring from the left-side of the wheel. If a peg wrench is not available, the ring can be threaded out by tapping, very carefully, at one of the peg holes with a suitable punch, and unscrewing the ring in this manner.

8. Remove the felt washer. Remove the spacer, noting that the flat side bears against the wheel bearing.

9. Insert the axle through the right-side of the wheel. A few blows with a soft-faced mallet will drive the right-side wheel bearing against the tube spacer, and this in turn will force out the left wheel bearing.

CAUTION: *The wheel bearing will not usually "pop" out. In fact, it will be difficult in many cases to notice that it has moved at all. Therefore, after hitting the end of the axle once or twice, try taking out the bearing with your fingers. Under no circumstances should you use undue force on the axle.*

10. Take out the axle and insert it into the left-side of the hub. Use the same method to drive out the right-side bearing.

11. Remove the brake shoes from the backing plate by taking out the bolts which secure the fixed end of the shoes (single leading shoe brake), or removing the circlips (twin leading shoe brake).

Assembly and Installation

1. Pack the bearings with a good grade of bearing grease.

2. Press the left-side (single-row) bearing into place after heating the hub gently to facilitate installation. Tap on the outer bearing race only.

3. Replace the spacer, flat side against the bearing, fit the felt seal, and install the lockring.

4. Insert the spacer tube, small end first, into the hub, until it abuts the bearing already fitted.

5. Fit the right-side (double-row) bearing. Be sure that it is fitted squarely into the hub, then drive it home by tapping around the outer bearing race.

6. Fit the thin steel washer (the smaller of the two), the felt washer, and the large steel washer.

7. Secure the large washer by peening it with a punch across the hub. Replace the dust covers.

8. Replace the wheel, slide in the axle, and replace the axle nut, screwing it down only hand-tight.

9. Apply the handlebar brake lever firmly, and, while maintaining pressure here, secure the axle nut with a wrench. This will serve to centralize the brakes in the drum.

10. Take the bike off the center stand and work the forks up and down several times. Then tighten the axle clamp nut.

REAR (DRUM BRAKE)

Removal and Disassembly

1. It is possible to remove the rear wheel without disturbing the rear brake, drive chain, etc. The wheel is secured to the brake drum by three sleeve nuts beneath the rubber caps on the rear hub or, as on more recent models, by three tongues on the brake hub. If your machine has the rubber caps, remove them and remove the sleeve nuts with a suitable socket wrench. On P-11 models, disconnect the brake anchor.

2. Loosen the axle on the right-side of the wheel and pull it out.

3. Remove the spacer on the right-side of the wheel and remove the speedometer drive. It is not necessary to disconnect the cable, simply place the drive mechanism out of the way.

4. Pull the wheel as far as possible to the right-side of the machine, until it is clear of the studs or tongues, then tilt it as necessary to clear the rear fender and pull it out of the machine.

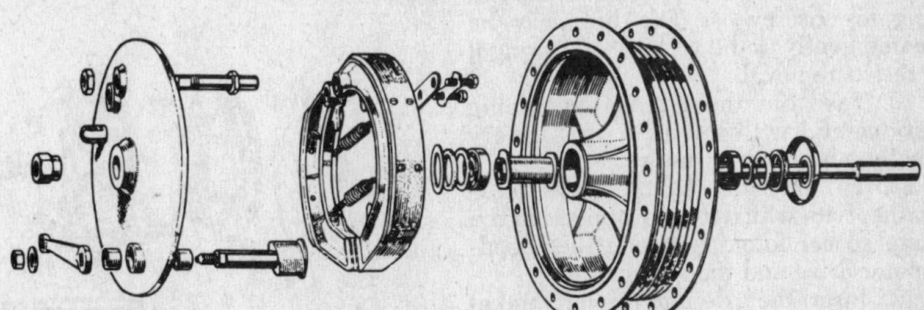

Front hub assembly (pre-Commando)

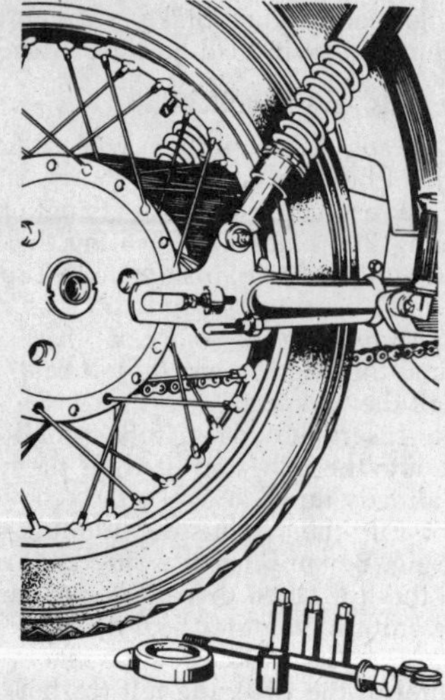
Removing the rear wheel (pre-1971 models)

Removing the rear wheel (1971 and later drum brake models)

5. If so desired, the rear brake drum can be removed by removing the chain guard (not necessary on late Commando models with the "chopped" chain guard) and disconnecting the drive chain.

6. Remove the axle nut.

7. Remove the rear brake adjuster nut if the brake is rod-operated, or disconnect the brake cable if it is cable-operated.

8. Take out the brake drum and backing plate, taking care not to loose the large spacer. Remove the brake shoes, if desired, referring to "Front Wheel, Drum Brake," above.

9. If it is desired to remove or lubricate the bearing, remove the lockring on the right-side of the rear hub. This ring has a LEFT-HAND thread. Use a peg wrench or a suitable punch and tap the ring to unscrew it. The hub may be heated gently in the vicinity of the ring if it resists removal.

10. Take out the felt washer, being very careful with this item as it is very fragile; also remove the spacer.

11. To the axle, fit the large lockwasher with which it is equipped and the large spacer found between the speedometer drive and the swing arm.

12. Insert the axle into the left (brake) side of the wheel and use a soft-faced mallet to strike the axle smartly once or twice. You will feel the brake side bearing give until it bears against a shoulder in the hub. It will have pushed the right side bearing out by an equivalent amount. stop at this point and withdraw the axle.

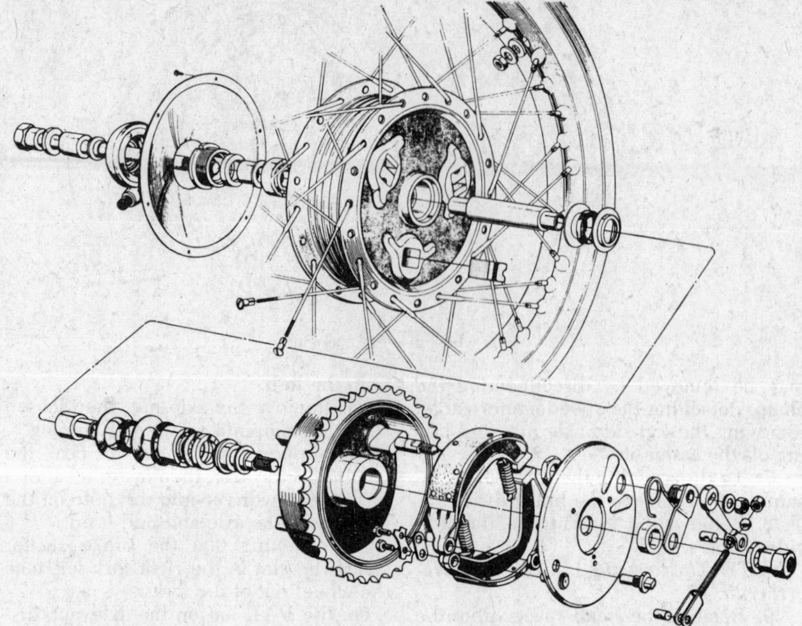
Rear wheel assembly (1971 and later drum brake)

13. Obtain a short piece of steel tubing with a diameter just slightly smaller than the inside diameter of the bearing. The front wheel axle is suitable for this purpose. Insert the tubing, or the threaded end of the axle, into the brake side bearing, center it, and tap lightly until the right side bearing is driven out. The axle will bear against the spacer inside the hub, which in turn will serve to drive out the right-side bearing.

14. Take out the spacer, if it is still in place, and remove the drift you used. Insert the rear axle (and spacer), into the right-side of the wheel. Carefully center it on the brake side bearing and drive this bearing out with a couple of blows on the end of the axle with a soft-faced mallet. The steel cup washer, felt washer, and thin steel washer will come out with the bearing.

Inspection

1. In 1971, an additional bearing was introduced in the rear brake drum. This bearing should be inspected and lubricated at the same time as the wheel bearings.

2. The three tongues on the brake assembly which drive the wheel must be inspected for security. The tongues are brazed into the brake drum. Note that the brazing material must have run all around the tongue bosses when viewed from inside the drum.

Assembly and Installation

1. Fit the right-side (single-row) bearing into the threaded side of the hub.

2. Fit the tube spacer from the left-side with the long end inserted into the single-row bearing.

3. Refit the spacer, the felt washer, and the lockring on the right-hand side of the hub and tighten the lockring. Remember, it has a left-hand thread.

4. Replace the brake side bearing and drive it home using the rear axle and spacer as on removal.

5. Fit the thin steel washer, the felt washer, and the cup washer in that order. Peen the cup washer against the hub with a suitable punch.

6. The rest of the assembly is a reverse of the disassembly procedure. Be sure that the speedometer drive is correctly engaged in the slots of the lockring before tightening the axle.

Also, apply the rear brake pedal hard, then tighten the axle nut (left-side), while holding the brake pedal on to centralize the brakes in the drum.

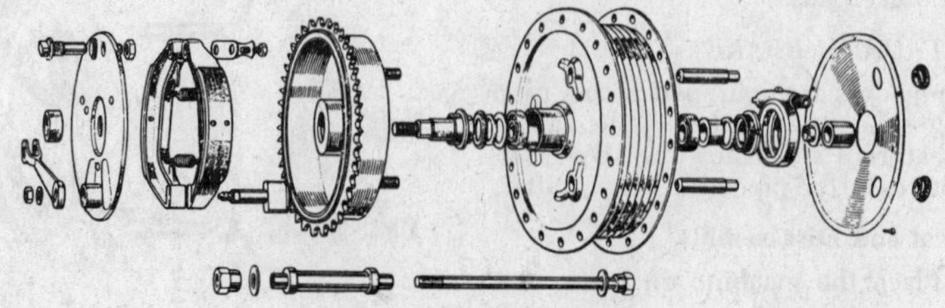
Rear hub assembly (Atlas)

Disc Brake Service

The following precautions should be observed when working on the disc brake system:

a. Use only DOT 3 brake fluid;

b. Never reuse brake fluid drained or flushed from the system. Never use brake fluid from an old or unsealed container. Brake fluid is "hydroscopic" (water-absorbing), and is easily contaminated;

c. Do not allow brake fluid to contact painted surfaces as it can remove the finish.

FRONT DISC BRAKE

Every 18 months or 24,000 miles (whichever comes first), the hydraulic system should be drained and refilled with fresh brake fluid.

1. Attach a length of plastic tubing to the bleeder screw of the hydraulic unit (as illustrated), placing the other end in a suitable container, assuring that the end of the tube is immersed in a small amount of new brake fluid.
2. Turn the bleeder screw one-half turn.
3. Apply the brake slowly, allowing it to return unassisted. Allow a slight pause between each brake application. Be sure that the master cylinder is kept full by adding the new fluid as needed.
4. When clean fluid, which is completely free of bubbles, emerges from the plastic tube, the flushing operation is complete.
5. Apply the brake lever hard, hold it on, and tighten the bleeder screw.

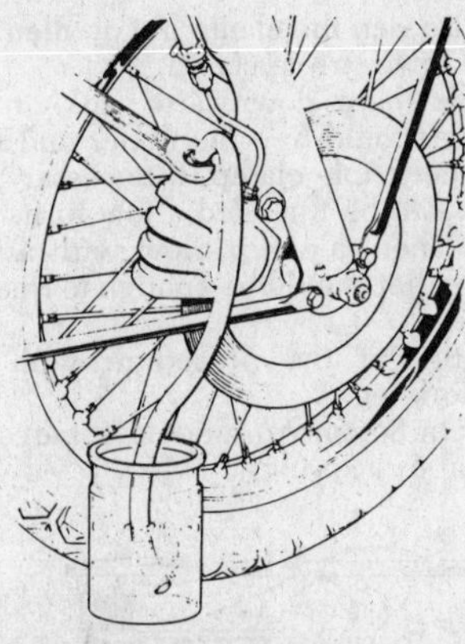

Bleeding the front disc brake

6. Refill the master cylinder to the correct fluid level (one half inch below the top of the cylinder).

In the event of excessive lever travel or a spongy feel in the front brake, the system must be bled, after first determining the cause of the malfunction.

The bleeding procedure is identical to that for flushing the system as described above, except that it is only necessary to continue the process until the bubbles cease to come out of the plastic tube.

Friction Pad Replacement

1. Remove the front wheel.
2. Rotate the friction pads slightly and remove them from the caliper.
3. The pads should be inspected for uneven or excessive wear or scoring. Minimum acceptable thickness is 1/16 in. (1.5 mm).
4. Clean the pad with the aid of a soft brush. Do not use any solvent or wire brush for removing deposits from the pads.
5. Smear the piston faces and brake pad recesses lightly with disc brake lubricant.
6. Remove the master cylinder cap and bellows seal.
7. Press the pistons back into the caliper, observing the brake fluid level in the master cylinder.
8. Smear the edges of the pad backing plate with disc brake lubricant and press the pads against the pistons.

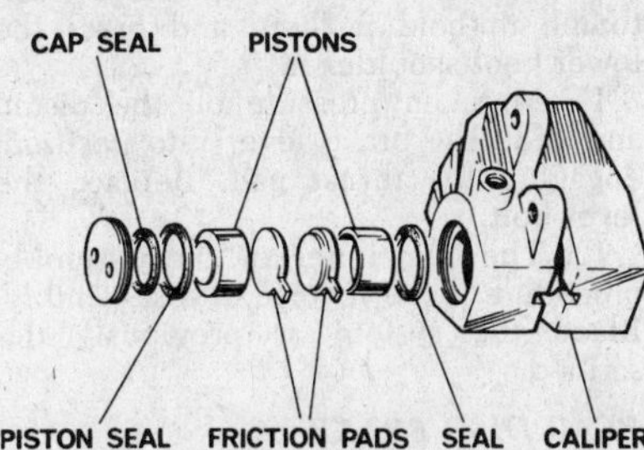

Disc brake caliper assembly

9. Replace the front wheel and spin the wheel while applying the brake lever several times.
10. Check the master cylinder fluid level.

NOTE: *If new pads are fitted, they must always be fitted in pairs. Also, the correct pad must be obtained depending on whether the machine is equipped with cast iron, or stainless steel, discs. The latter is identifiable by the part number (063464) stamped on the outer rim. When new pads are fitted, they must be "broken in" for at least 50 miles by avoiding hard application of the brake.*

Caliper

If the pistons will not move freely in the caliper, this unit should be disassembled and inspected.

DISASSEMBLY

1. Loosen, but do not remove, the caliper end plug.
2. Remove the two caliper bolts and washers and swing the caliper clear of the fork leg, watching for the brake hose.
3. Remove the two friction pads from the caliper.
4. Clean the outer ends of the pistons and the caliper body with alcohol.
5. Place a can below the caliper to catch the brake fluid. Apply the brake lever, and the inner piston will come out into the pad cavity and the fluid will be released.

IMPORTANT: *If the piston is seized, the entire caliper assembly must be replaced.*

6. Loosen the lower brake pipe junction nut and separate the pipe from the caliper.
7. Remove the caliper end plug which was previously loosened and drain out the remaining fluid.
8. Remove the piston from the caliper.
9. Remove the pressure seal from the outer bore.

CAUTION: *Take extreme care not to damage the seal grooves.*

10. Remove the inner piston through the outer cylinder bore. Then remove the pressure seal from the outer bore.
11. Mark the friction pads for position ("inner" and "outer").

INSPECTION

1. Clean the pistons, caliper bores, and seal grooves with ethyl alcohol or clean brake fluid.
2. Examine the pistons for corrosion, wear, scoring, or unevenness of the thrust faces. If there are any irregularities present, the piston must be replaced.
3. Check the caliper bores for corrosion, scratches, abrasion, or damage to the seal grooves.

ASSEMBLY

1. Coat new pressure seals with disc brake fluid and insert the first seal into the inner bore with your fingers, making sure that it is correctly fitted.
2. Coat the inner piston with the brake fluid and insert it into the inner cylinder bore (closed end first) after passing it through the outer bore. Let the piston protrude about 5/16 in. from the inner bore.
3. Fit the other pressure seal to the outer bore groove.
4. Insert the other piston into the other bore (open end first) until about 5/16 in. protrudes from the inner mouth of the bore.
5. Replace the end plug. A new O-ring must be fitted.
6. Fit the friction pads and replace the caliper assembly on the fork leg.
7. Torque down the end plug to 26 ft lbs.
8. Examine the fitting of the metal brake fluid pipe for distortion, cracks, or other damage. Fit the pipe into the caliper. Screw down the junction screw until the metal pipe is just lightly seated.

CAUTION: *Tighten the junction nut with a wrench no more than 60°. This is VERY important.*

9. Loosen the bleed nipple one full turn and connect a bleed tube to it as described earlier in this section. Fill the master cylinder with the recommended brake fluid.
10. Work the brake lever until the fluid begins to flow through the bleed tube. Be sure to keep the master cylinder topped up or air will be drawn into the lines. Hold the brake lever on while adding fluid.
11. When fluid, without bubbles, begins to flow through the bleeder tube, hold the brake lever on and tighten the bleed nipple.
12. Check the brake for sponginess and examine the system for leaks. Recheck the master cylinder fluid level, and fill it up as necessary.

Master Cylinder

REMOVAL AND DISASSEMBLY

1. Disconnect the brake light switch and lift off the rubber switch cover which exposes the hose junction.
2. Disconnect the hose.
3. Remove the four screws and take off the master cylinder assembly.
4. Remove the reservoir cap and bellows seal. Also remove the brake light switch.
5. Remove the brake lever bolt and the brake lever.
6. Carefully pry out the boot circlip, then remove the boot complete with piston and secondary cup.
7. Remove the primary cup washer, primary cup, spreader, spring, and valve assembly. These parts may be removed by GENTLY tapping the edge of the master cylinder assembly on a wooden block.

INSPECTION

1. Clean the master cylinder and piston in brake fluid or methyl alcohol. Inspect the cylinder body for wear of the piston bore.
2. Make sure that the two ports in the reservoir chamber are clear.
3. Inspect the hose junction for cleanliness.
4. Check the body of the master cylinder assembly for any cracks or fractures, especially in the area of the lever bolt.
5. Check for wear of the piston thrust face.

ASSEMBLY

1. Clean all parts and lay them out for reassembly, referring to the exploded diagram.
2. New primary and secondary cups MUST be fitted. Saok the new cups in hydraulic brake fluid for fifteen minutes, kneading them occasionally.
3. Take the secondary cup and place its non-lipped side against the ground "crown" diameter of the piston. Work the cup over the crown by hand, down the piston body, over the shoulder, and into its groove.
4. Fit the boot over the piston (open end toward the piston crown) and ensure that the boot upper end is fitted into the piston groove. Oil the piston assembly lightly with brake fluid.
5. Assemble the valve to the spring. Make sure that the inner plastic bobbin is seated in the valve base and that the plastic spreader is pressed securely into the spring.
6. Fit this assembly into the master cylinder, valve end first, holding the master cylinder bore vertical.
7. Place the primary cup into the bore (open end inward), the washer (convex side upward toward the open end of the cylinder bore). Lightly oil the mouth of the cylinder bore.
8. Take the master cylinder assembly in your left hand and insert the piston assembly into the bore.
9. Apply a gentle rotary action to the piston assembly with your right hand, at the same time maintining pressure downward against the valve spring assembly.
10. Be sure that the lip of the secondary cup enters the bore freely. When the piston has entered the bore, use your left thumb to hold it there and press the lower boot shoulder in.
11. Maintain pressure on the piston and slide the brake lever into position, engaging the thrust pad. Replace the lever bolt.
12. The remainder of the assembly procedure is the reverse of disassembly. Bleed the system as previously described.

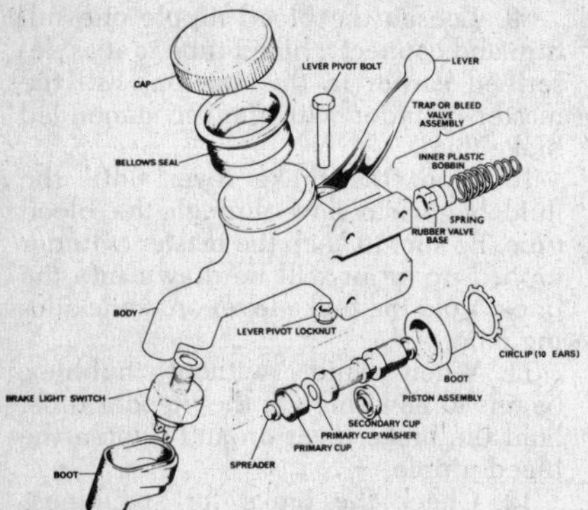

Front disc brake master cylinder assembly

REAR DISC BRAKE

1975 and later models are fitted with an hydraulic disc rear brake. Service procedures for the brake system components are the same as described for the front disc brake.

Adjustment

To adjust the rear brake pedal, loosen the locknut which bears against the brake rod clevis and turn the rod to adjust the pedal.

CAUTION: *Do not loosen the two locknuts at the opposite end of the rod since this will alter the master cylinder piston stroke. This adjustment is made at the factory.*

Front Forks

The fork legs can be removed individually, leaving the steering column in place, or the entire assembly can be taken off at once. The first procedure is given below.

REMOVAL AND DISASSEMBLY

1. Support the front wheel well off the ground. Remove the front wheel, as previously described, and also remove the front fender.
2. Remove the drain plugs at the bottom of the sliders to drain the oil.

On 1974 and earlier disc brake models, remove the hydraulic system completely after placing a ¼ in. spacer between the brake pads.

On 1975 and later models, the brake system cannot be removed completely. Drain the system completely by means of a tube attached to the bleeder screw. Disconnect the brake line at the junctions. Remove the caliper from the slider. Remove the master cylinder.

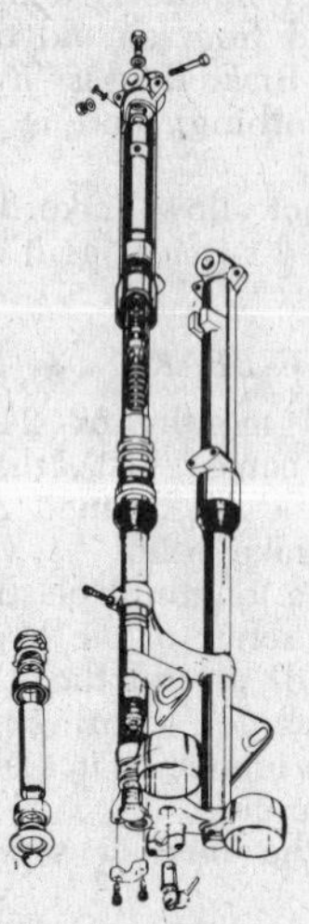

"Slim-line" type forks (Commando)

3. Loosen the filler cap nut at the top of the fork leg until it is clear of the threads in the triple clamp. Then use a thin wrench to loosen the locknut on the damper rod so that the capnut can be removed from the rod. It may be necessary to push up on the fork leg to raise the damper rod enough to gain access to the locknut.
4. Loosen the clamp nut or allen bolt on the lower triple clamp.
5. A sharp downward yank on the fork leg should free the upper end from the upper triple clamp. If necessary, the capnut can be threaded a few turns into place. Then, a sharp blow with a soft-faced mallet should be enough to free the fork leg.
6. Repeat the procedure with the other fork leg.
7. On Scrambler models, remove the external fork springs.

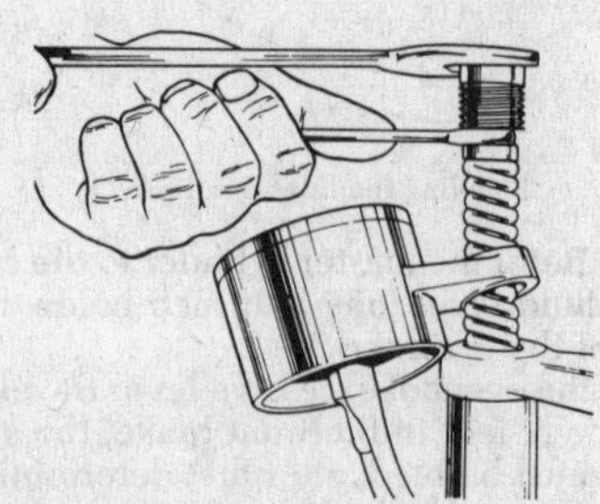

Removing the fork cap nut from the damper rod

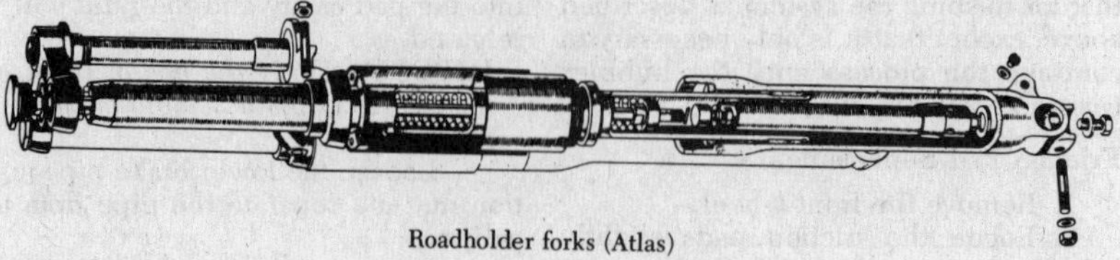

Roadholder forks (Atlas)

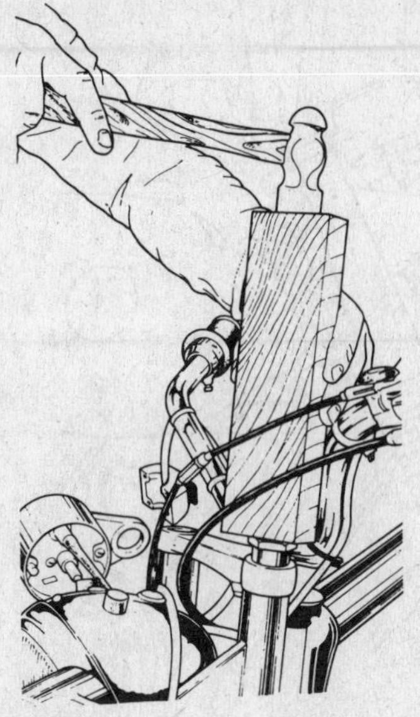

Freeing the fork tube from the upper triple clamp

8. Remove the rubber fork gaiter, if fitted, or the rubber dust cover.

9. Remove the bolt and washer at the very bottom of the fork slider (a thin-walled socket is needed to reach this bolt) and take out the spring and damper assembly from the top of the fork tube.

A fiber washer is placed at the bottom of the damper tube and may remain in the fork slider.

10. The alloy fork slider has an extension screwed into it, the length and type of the extension depending on the model of the machine. To remove the slider, the extension must be taken off first. Most models have holes for the appropriate peg wrench on the extension and, if this tool is available, removal is a simple matter. If the peg wrench is not to be had, however, an alternative method is to fasten a heater hose clamp to the extension (at the bottom portion of the long chrome plated extensions, if that is what you have); vise-grip pliers can then be locked on to the screw assembly of the clamp and used to turn the extension.

Unscrew the extension all the way, then take off the slider from the bottom of the fork tube.

11. Remove the extension from the top of the fork tube and also remove the oil seal, paper washer, and flanged bush (bronze), in that order, from the top of the tube as well.

12. The bottom bush (steel) is held in place by a circlip and can be removed after the circlip is taken off.

13. The damper tube can be disassembled on Atlas and Commando models, if desired, by taking off the nut at the top of the rod, the spacer, and the long spring.

14. Insert a suitable rod through the holes in the damper tube to keep it from turning, and unscrew the damper tube cap nut. Removing the nut at the bottom of the rod will allow the slotted washer, cup, and crosspin to be removed.

15. On Scramblers, the damper tube is diassembled by taking off the bottom nut, the brass seat for the damper valve, the damper valve itself, and the crosspin. Remove the circlip and take off the plunger sleeve.

NOTE: *The oil groove is closest to the bottom of the rod when installed.*

INSPECTION

1. Remove any rust from the exterior of the fork tube with emery cloth. This is most likely to form beneath the headlight supports.

2. Make sure that the inside of the fork tube is clean and smooth.

3. The flanged (bronze) bush should be a close but free sliding fit on the fork tube. It must be replaced if excessive clearance is noticed.

4. The oil seal and paper washer should be replaced with new items if possible. The rubber lip of the seal must be free of cracks, signs of age, dirt, or corrosion.

5. Check the damper tube and assure that it is free of corrosion, foreign matter, and has a smooth interior surface.

6. Make sure that the damper rod is not bent as might happen if it has come loose from the fork capnut during operation.

7. Check the springs for damage.

ASSEMBLY AND INSTALLATION

1. Thoroughly clean all components before assembly. Give all pieces a coat of light oil.

2. Reassemble the damper tube components if this has been taken apart: crosspin cup, slotted washer. Secure the nut at the bottom of the rod, then fit the assembly into the damper tube and secure the damper cap nut.

For Scramblers, the plunger sleeve (oil groove closest to the bottom of the rod), circlip, crosspin, damper valve, valve seat, and rod nut are fitted in that order.

3. Replace the fiber washer on the lower end of the damper tube and insert the tube into the fork slider; secure it there with the bolt and washer at the very bottom of the slider.

4. Fit the bottom (steel) bush and secure it with the circlip. Be sure the circlip is not deformed. Fit a new one if in doubt.

5. From the top of the fork tube, slide on the flanged bush, the paper washer, and the oil seal. Be very careful when sliding the oil seal along the fork tube. It is advisable to apply some oil to the seal lip before refitting. Also, note that the seal is installed with the spring side (open side) facing the flanged bush.

6. Take up the damper rod and fork slider, which have been assembled as directed above, and slip the internal fork spring over the damper rod. Also, fit the spacer and the nut. Be sure that the bevelled side of the nut faces the spring. Screw the nut all the way down to the end of the threads of the damper rod.

7. Take up the slider and damper assembly and insert the spring into the bottom of the fork tube. Carefully bring the fork slider up over the lower and upper bushes.

8. Place the extension into position from the upper end of the fork tube and use it to centralize and press the oil seal into the fork slider. Hand-tighten the extension. Final tightening is best left until the axle has been replaced, as this will keep the slider from turning as the extension is turned.

9. Replace the external spring (if fitted) and the fork gaiter or dust cover.

10. Lightly grease the upper portion of the fork tube and position it in the triple clamps. The clamp nut on the lower triple clamp may be gently tightened to hold the fork leg in place, if necessary.

11. Refill the fork leg with the correct grade and quantity of oil.

12. Push up the fork leg to expose the damper rod and replace the capnut and washer. Tighten the capnut against the locknut on the damper rod, then (loosen the clamp nut on the lower triple clamp if this has been tightened) tighten the fork capnut all the way to pull the fork tube up into its proper position. Retighten the lower triple clamp nut. Replace the brake lines (hydraulic). Torque the caliper bolts to 30 ft lbs.

13. Refit the fender and wheel. Tighten the fork slider extension securely.

Steering Head

The steering head assembly should be removed to lubricate the bearings at the appropriate maintenance interval, or to inspect the condition of the bearings if

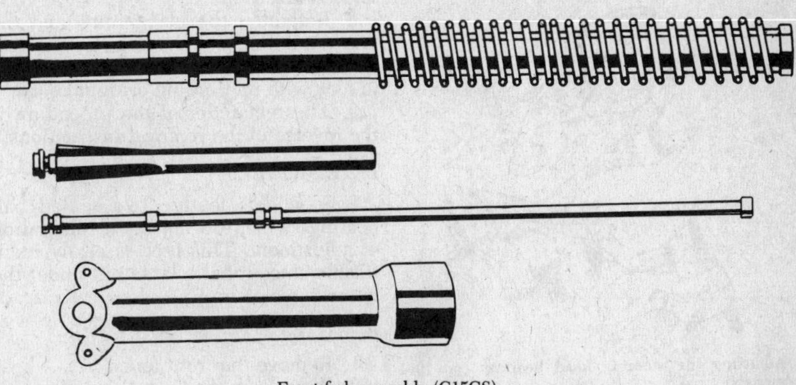

Front fork assembly (G15CS)

normal adjustment procedures do not take play out of the front forks.

NOTE: *Latest Commando models have sealed steering head bearings installed and, therefore, the steering head is not adjustable and should not be removed except if damage is suspected as after a collison.*

EARLY MODELS

The following procedure applies to early models with adjustable steering stem bearings.

Removal

1. Remove the handlebars, the instrument drive cables, and the light wires.
2. Unbolt the headlight and let it hang from the wiring harness.
3. Remove the fork capnuts and remove the tach and speedometer.
4. Remove the front wheel and fender as previously described.
5. Remove the steering damper, if fitted.
6. Remove the fork crown nut (this is the large nut at the rear center of the upper triple clamp). Give the upper triple clamp a blow from beneath with a soft-faced mallet and remove it.
7. Support the forks and unscrew the bearing race adjuster nut; this is a sleeve nut. Watch for the 18 ball bearings in the upper race.
8. Lower the forks and remove the assembly from the frame.
9. The bearing cups in the frame are press-fit. They can be drifted out, if necessary, using a short piece of steel tubing. The cups must come out parallel to the housing, so move the tubing around the circumference of the cup while driving it out.
10. The cone on the steering column can be removed with a suitable chisel or a screwdriver.

Inspection

1. There are 36 bearings in the steering head assembly (18 in each ball race). Be sure that all are present.
2. Inspect the bearing race surfaces for ripples, cracks, rust, pitting, or signs of wear. The bearing surfaces should be smooth.
3. Make sure that the steering column is parallel with the top ends of the fork tubes.
4. Ball bearings are ¼ in. in size. They must be in good condition and free from any deformation.

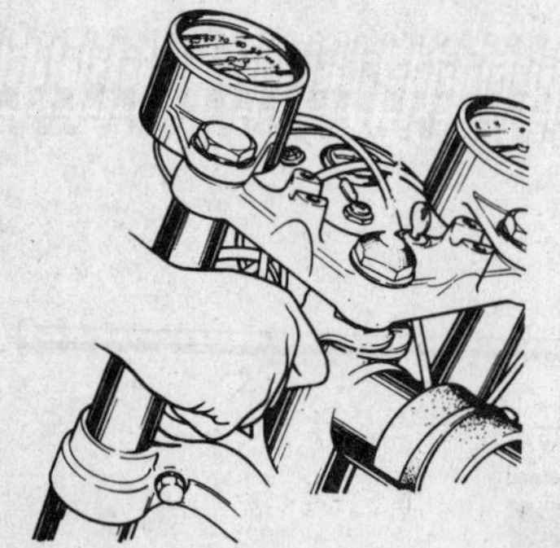

Adjusting the steering head bearings (pre-1971 models)

Checking steering head bearings for excessive play

Installation and Adjustment

1. Replace the cone on the steering column and the bearing races in the frame. A draw bolt should be used to press home the races. All traces of paint or foreign matter must be removed to enable the bearings to be repositioned correctly.
2. Place 18 balls in the cone and in the top cup on the frame, holding them in place by embedding them in stiff grease.
3. Replace the dust cover, then thread on the bearing race adjuster nut (sleeve nut). This must be adjusted later. Make it reasonably tight for now.
4. Replace the upper triple clamp and seat it properly. Replace the fork crown nut, but do not tighten it.
5. Replace the front fender and wheel assembly.
6. Check the play in the front forks by grasping the tip of the front fender, pulling forward, and feeling for play with the other hand placed at the junction of the upper triple clamp and the frame.
7. To adjust the bearings, loosen the clamp nuts on the lower triple clamp (be sure that the fork crown nut is also loose), and tighten the sleeve nut with the appropriate wrench until all play in the forks is taken up.
8. Retighten the clamp nuts and the crown nut. Recheck the forks for play and also see that they can be rotated from lock to lock with no binding or tight spots.
9. The remainder of the procedure is the reverse of the removal instructions.

LATE MODELS

Late models feature two sealed ball bearings which do not need lubrication or adjustment. This type is easily identifiable since it has a large nut under the lower triple clamp.

Removal

1. Remove the front forks.
2. Bend back the locktab and remove the large nut under the lower triple clamp. Remove the triple clamp, tapping down with a plastic mallet while supporting the headlight brackets.
3. Tap the steering stem upward through the bearings to remove the stem and upper triple clamp.
4. The bearings are a press fit in the frame and are separated by a spacer tube. To remove them, move the tube to one side and drift out one of the bearings. Remove the tube and repeat the procedure for the remaining bearing.

Installation

1. Installation is the reverse of the removal procedure.
2. When the triple clamps are installed, do not fully tighten the stem nut. Install the forks, then tighten the fork top bolts, stem nut, and lower triple clamp bolts in that order. Stem nut torque is 15 ft lbs.

Rear Shock Absorbers

The rear shock absorbers are sealed units and the hydraulic damper cannot be serviced. They are adjustable for load and this change is made with the appropriate "C" wrench. The adjuster preloads the spring and turning the adjuster in a clockwise direction provides a stiffer ride when needed (as when carrying two people). Of course, both units must have the same adjustment.

The springs can be removed by:

1. Removing the shocks (one at a time) from the frame.
2. Compressing the spring sufficiently to take out the two keepers at the top.
3. Removing the dust cover (if fitted), and taking off the spring.

NOTE: *Grating noises while in operation are usually eliminated by greasing the inside of the dust cover before installation.*

The rear shocks must have some play on their mountings. It should be possible to twist the shocks slightly to either side and have them return to the center position when released. If the shocks are unable to move in this manner, remove them and check the steel mounting sleeves in the eyelets. The sleeves must protrude from the eyelet slightly. If they do not, fit new sleeves.

When fitting shocks, tighten securing bolts to 28 ft lbs.

On Mk III models, check that the bottom of the right shock clears the caliper mounting plate. Clearance can be increased by fitting a spacer behind the shock mount.

Swing Arm

ATLAS

Removal

1. Remove the chainguard. Disconnect the final drive chain.
2. Remove the rear wheel and the brake assembly.
3. Remove the bolts which attach the bottom of the shock absorbers to the frame.
4. Remove the nut and washer from one end of the swing arm spindle and take out the spindle from the other side of the frame.
5. Push the swing arm forward, turn it to one side, and take it out of the frame.

Disassembly

There are two bushes, separated by a spacer. The bushes must be removed and installed with a press.

Assembly and Installation

1. Press in the new bushes.
2. Replace the swing arm in the frame.
3. Replace and tighten the shock absorber bottom bolts before tightening the swing arm spindle nut.
4. Tighten the swing arm spindle nut and proceed with assembly in the reverse of the removal sequence.

G15CS, N15CS

These scrambler models incorporate two oilite bearings in a steel sleeve.

Removal

1. Remove the chainguard, disconnect the chain, and unbolt the rear shocks from the swing arm.
2. Remove the rear wheel and the brake assembly.
3. Take out the cotter pin on the swing arm spindle and press out the steel sleeve. Remove the swing arm. Watch for the two felt washers as the swing arm is removed.

Disassembly

Each bush must be pressed out in turn with a press. Note that they are flanged.

Assembly and Installation

1. The spindle diameter is 0.990–0.995 in. The bushes are reamed, after installation, to 1.001 in.
2. The steel sleeve is oil filled and this is accomplished by removing the filler screw in the cover plate and injecting a heavy grade of oil until the cavity is filled.
3. The remainder of the procedure is the reverse of removal.

COMMANDO (1974 AND EARLIER)

The swing arm pivots on two flanged bushes which are supported by the swing arm spindle which passes through the rear engine mounting plate.

Removal

1. Remove the threaded rod which secures the end plates for the swing arm bushes.
2. Remove the lockbolt, in the middle of the rear engine mounting, which secures the swing arm spindle.
3. The spindle is threaded on the right-side. It must be removed with a ½ in. bolt. Thread in the bolt and pull out the spindle.
4. Remove the chainguard. Disconnect the drive chain.
5. Remove the rear wheel and the brake assembly.
6. Remove the bottom bolts on the rear shock absorbers.
7. The swing arm can now be removed from the frame.

Disassembly

1. Remove the large O-rings and dust covers from the swing arm.
2. Take out the small O-rings in the recesses of the bushing housings, then support the ends of the swing arm properly and press out the bushes with an arbor press.

Commando swing arm bushings (to 1974)

Inspection

In the event of a damaged or worn swing arm pivot spindle, oversized units are available. These are 0.005 in. larger in diameter than the stock unit. The spindle bore clearance should be 0.0005–0.0020 in.

To fit the oversized spindle, the bearings should be bored, in place, to 0.8807–0.8817 in.

Assembly and Installation

1. Place the dust cover over the bush. The recess in the dust cover for the large O-ring should face inward.
2. Press in the bushes. Again, an arbor press is used.
3. Refit the large O-rings in the dust covers and the small O-rings in the recess in the bush housing.
4. The rest of the procedure is the reverse of that for removal.

COMMANDO (1975 AND LATER)

Removal

NOTE: *New swing arm welch plugs and felt pieces are required if the swing arm is removed.*

1. Loosen the right-side shock absorber and pull out as far as the circlips allow.
2. Hang the brake caliper from the hook provided. Remove the rear wheel.
3. Remove the right rear support plate complete with brake, pedal, and footpeg.
4. Pry out the right-side swing arm pivot welch plug. Remove the felt washers.

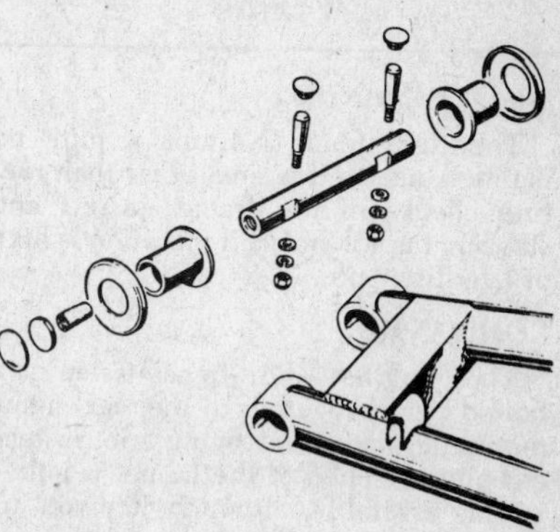

Commando swing arm bushings (1975 and later)

5. Remove the lower rear fender brackets. Remove the oil filter and lines. Remove the horn.
6. Remove the swing arm pivot pins by removing the nuts and driving up from the bottom. Note the rubber plugs.
7. Remove the shock absorber bottom bolts.
8. Remove the swing arm spindle. To do this, screw a bolt with a locknut into the spindle (the main front mounting bolt will work), and pull out the spindle. Disconnect the speedometer cable. Remove the swing arm.

Inspection

1. Check the spindle for wear or scoring. Inspect the bushes for signs of wear.
2. Insert the spindle into place and check for play. There should be none. If play exists, the spindle and the bushes should be replaced.

Disassembly and Assembly

1. Remove the left welch plug.
2. Press out the old bushings.
3. To install new bushes, place the sealing washer over the bush and press it in fully. The bushes do not need to be reamed after installation.
4. Place the felt disc into the recess of the left-side boss after soaking it in SAE 140 oil. Install the welch plug.

Installation

1. Soak the swing arm spindle lubricating wicks in SAE 140 oil and then install one into the left end of the spindle.
2. Place the swing arm into position with the bushes installed and the left-side felt washer and welch plug in place.

3. Carefully push in the spindle, noting the two cutouts which align with the cotter pins. When the spindle is inserted about half-way, install the left-side cotter pin. Then continue pushing in the spindle until the cotter pin mates with the cutout in the spindle.

4. Install the right-hand cotter pin.

5. Remove the bolt used to install the spindle. Install the oil-soaked felt wick into the right-side of the spindle, then the oil-soaked felt washer, and install the welch plug.

6. The remainder of the procedure is the reverse of disassembly.

Checking clearance in the front engine mounting (1974 and earlier)

5. To remove the rear engine mounting, the engine, transmission, oil tank, and the swing arm spindle must be removed.

6. The main mounting bush and the rubber spacers are removed with an arbor press. This is also true for the front assembly, although this unit may be taken out of the frame by itself.

NOTE: *If proper side-play cannot be obtained, the engine mounting tube may be partially collapsed and must be replaced.*

For other engine mounting problems, refer to the following chart:

Vibration Range	*Probable Cause*	*Solution*
0–3000 rpm	Front Mounting OK, Rear Tight	Remove 0.005 in. shim
3000–5000 rpm	Rear Mounting OK, Front Tight	Remove 0.005 in. shim
0–5000 rpm	Front and Rear Mountings Tight	Remove 0.005 in. shim

Frame

PRE-COMMANDO

The rigid frame Nortons require no maintenance in this area other than routine checks of the frame gussets and steering lug for cracks if vibration is high or handling poor.

COMMANDO

The engine and transmission are bolted rigidly together by the rear engine mounting plate. The swing arm, instead of being attached to the frame, is bolted to this assembly, although it pivots independently in the normal manner. Now, the entire engine-transmission-swing arm unit is mounted in the frame at three places by means of polymer filled absorption units. These are located at the very top of the cylinder head, at the front of the crankcase, and above and to the rear of the transmission.

The absorption units must be assembled properly if the system is to work as the designers intended.

The front and rear engine mounting units must be checked for side-play if vibration occurs.

NOTE: *When checking the mountings, 1970 and earlier models may be supported on the center stand. 1971 and later models, however, must be supported with a crate or box on which the lower frame rails can rest. These models cannot be checked while on the stand, since this will put tension on the mountings.*

1974 and Earlier

FRONT MOUNTING

1. For the front engine mounting, be sure that the engine mounting bolt is torqued to the correct value of 25 ft lbs.

2. The total side-play of the front engine mounting should be 0.020–0.025 in. If the side play is reduced, the mounting bush will not function. Side-play is adjusted by means of shim washers of varying thickness. These are available in four sizes: 0.005, 0.010, 0.020, and 0.030 in.

3. If the engine plate is moved and then released, the assembly should react through the elasticity of the mounting bush. If it does not, the shim washers are too thick.

4. To fit new shims, remove the nut on the left side of the assembly, drive out the bolt far enough so that the spacer and the cap can be removed for access to the shim washer, and replace this with one which will give the correct side-play.

5. Reassemble the mounting, torque down the nut to 25 ft lbs, and recheck the side-play.

REAR MOUNTING

1. Checking the side-play for the rear mount is the same as for the front. The value is 0.010–0.015 in. It should be checked on the right-side of the machine.

2. New shims can be fitted by taking off the nut on the right-side and driving out the bolt far enough so that the spacer and cap can be removed.

3. Replace the shim washer with the one selected and refit the cap and spacer.

4. Torque down the nut (25 ft lbs) and recheck side-play.

1975 and Later

The Isolastic mounts on the Mk III are similar to those found on earlier models, although they incorporate an adjusting device.

FRONT MOUNTING

1. Slide the right-side gaiter back to give access to the adjuster and plastic washer.

2. Push the engine as far as possible to the right to take up all the slack in the mounting. Hold the engine in this position and check the clearance between the plastic washer and the plated adjuster collar. If the clearance exceeds 0.010 in. (0.25 mm), adjustment will be necessary.

3. Loosen the mounting main bolt and slide the spring clip clear of the holes in the adjuster. Use a thin screwdriver or a suitable substitute and turn the adjuster until there is no clearance. Then back off the adjuster 1½ holes.

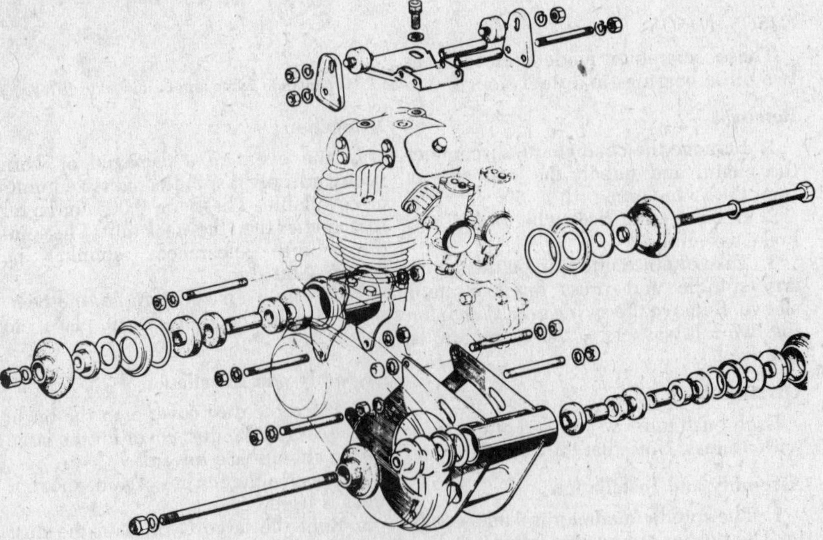

Isolastic mountings (1974 and earlier)

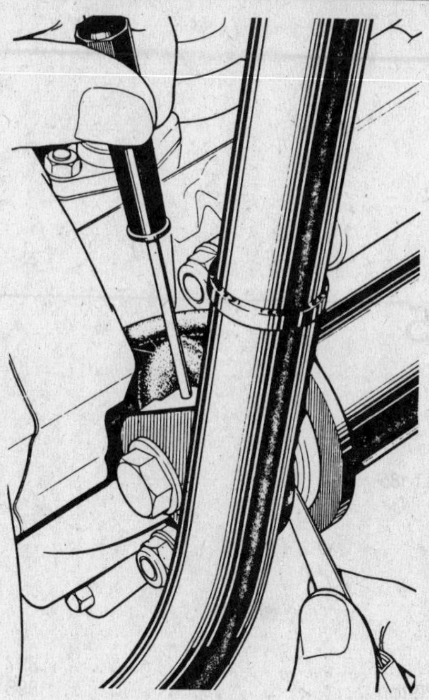
Adjusting clearance (1975 and later)

4. Tighten the main bolt to 30 ft lbs. Clearance should be about 0.006 in. (0.152 mm).

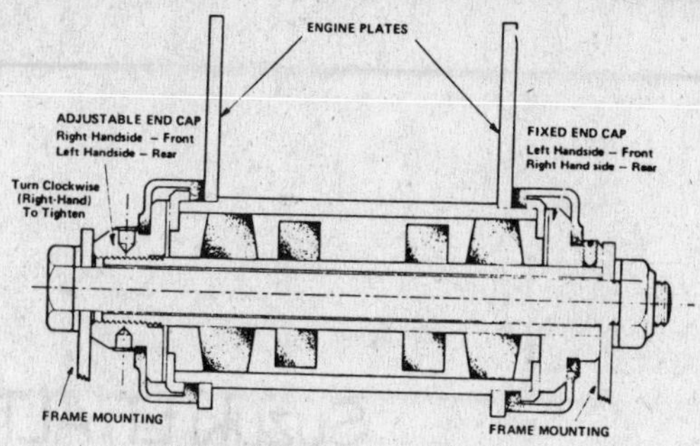

Mounting unit (1975 and later)

Rear Mounting

1. Slide the left-side gaiter back to expose the face ring and plastic washer.

2. Push the rear wheel as far as possible to the left and check the clearance between the plastic washer and the plated adjusting collar. If clearance exceeds 0.010 in. (0.25 mm), the mounting should be adjusted.

3. Loosen the mounting main bolt. Insert a small screwdriver or something similar into the adjuster and turn it until there is no clearance. Then back it off 1½ holes. Tighten the bolt to 30 ft lbs. Clearance should be about 0.006 in. (0.152 mm).

Chassis Specifications

Wheel Bearings (mm)	
Front, left side	17 x 40 x 12
Front, right side	17 x 40 x 16
Rear, left side	17 x 40 x 12
Rear, right side	17 x 40 x 16
Torque Wrench Settings (ft lbs)	
Engine Mounting Bolts (All)	25
Disc Brake Caliper Bolts	25
Disc Brake	
Pad type: Steel backed, molded and bonded friction material	
Pad friction area diam. (in.)	1.65
Pad thickness (in.)	0.37–0.38
Disc diameter (in.)	10.70
Disc width (in.)	0.250–0.260

Suzuki LT/ALT 125/185

MODEL COVERAGE

LT 125 D/E/F
LT 185 E/F
ALT 125 D/E/F
ALT 185

INDEX

SERIAL NUMBER LOCATIONS

In order to prevent possible confusion, always supply the chassis and engine serial numbers when ordering parts.

On LT models, the chassis serial number is stamped on the front downtube on the left side of the frame.

On ALT models, the chassis serial number is stemped on the right side of the steering lug.

On all models, the engine serial number is on the front of the crankcase, visible from the left side of the machine.

MAINTENANCE

NOTE: *Common maintenance procedures are explained in detail in the "General Information" section.*

LUBRICATION

Engine Oil

SAE 10W-40 oil, service rated "SE" or "SF" is recommended.

Engine oil (and filter) should be changed every 600 miles after initial break-in, assuming that the machine operates under normal conditions.

Engine oil capacity is about 1150ml (1.2 qts.) when changing oil and filter.

Checking Oil Level

1. A sight glass is fitted on the right side of the crankcase allowing an easy check of oil level.
2. Oil should be checked after the engine has been running, then shut off and left to sit for a minute.

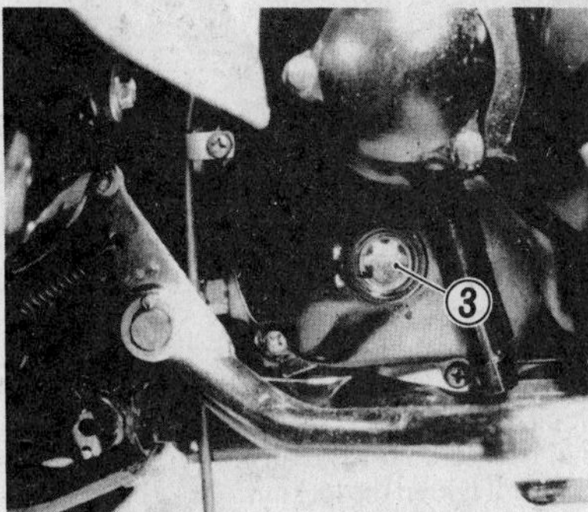

Crankcase oil sight glass (3)

3. The machine must be parked on a level surface for an accurate reading.
4. Oil level should be at, but not above, the "F" mark on the crankcase.
5. If the level is below the mark, remove the filler cap and add the correct grade and type of oil until level is correct.

CAUTION: *Do not overfill the crankcase.*

Changing Oil and Filter

1. Oil should be changed when the engine is warm. This ensures more complete draining and makes it more likely that the oil will carry off any particulates with it.
2. Place a suitable container (about 2 qt. capacity) beneath the crankcase.
3. Remove the filler cap.

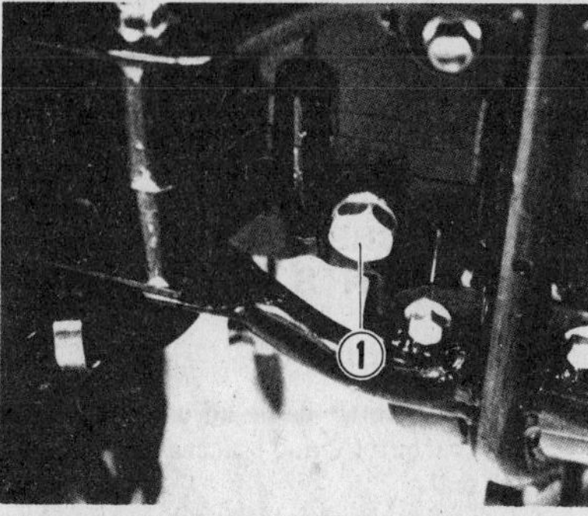

Oil drain plug (1)(125)

4. Remove the drain plug beneath the crankcase.
5. Allow the oil to drain for several minutes.
6. Clean the drain plug. Install it and tighten to 15-18 ft. lbs.
7. Place the container beneath the oil filter cap on the right side of the engine.

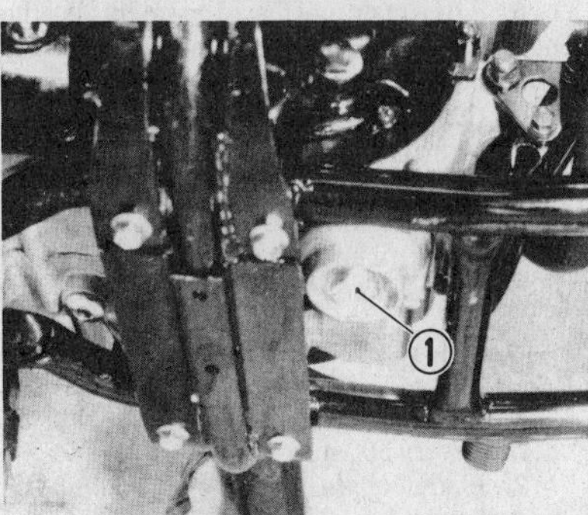

Oil drain plug (1)(185)

Oil filter cap bolts

8. Remove the three screws or bolts and carefully pull the cap off. Note the spring on the inside.
9. Pull out the oil filter and discard it.
10. Clean out the oil filter housing with a rag. Clean the filter cap.
11. Inspect cap O-ring condition. Replace it if it is knicked or damaged in any way.
12. Clean the filter cap mating surface.
13. Check that the O-ring in the filter housing is in position.
14. Install the new filter, closed end out.
15. Check that the filter cap spring is in place.
16. Carefully fit the cap and tighten the three fasteners gradually and evenly.
17. Add about 1150ml (1.2 qts.) of the recommended type and grade oil to the crankcase.
18. Fit the filler cap.

Oil filter installation

19. Let the engine run for a few minutes, then shut it off and check level at the sight glass. Top up if necessary.
20. Check for leaks at the drain plug and filter cap before operating the machine.

Filter Screen

The crankcase has a filter screen in the sump which should be inspected and cleaned at every other oil change (1200 miles).

1. Drain the oil.
2. Remove the three screws at the very bottom of the crankcase which hold the screen cover.

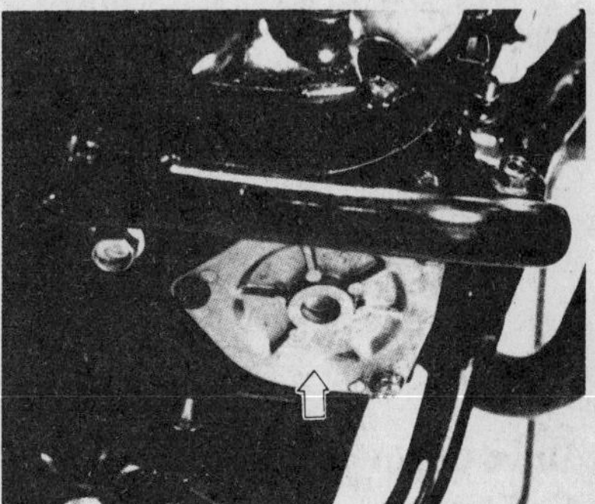

Filter screen cover (125)

Oil filter screen (125)

3. Remove the two screws which hold the filter screen and take it out.
4. Clean the screen thoroughly in a solvent to remove all traces of foreign matter.
5. Check screen condition. If it is punctured, badly clogged or deformed, replace it.
6. Check the matter removed from the screen for metal particulates which would indicate on-going engine wear.
7. Install the screen and tighten the two screws.

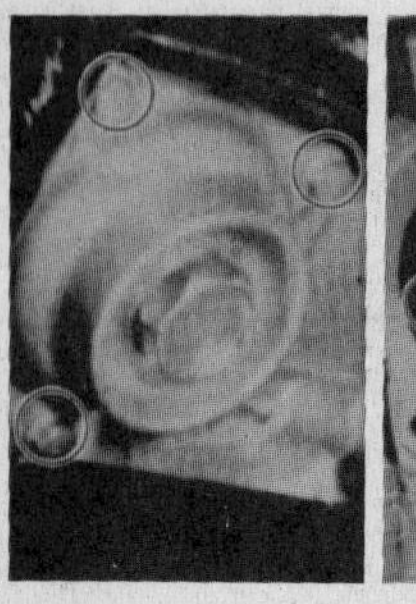

Oil filter screen cover and fasteners (185)

8. Clean the cover mating surface thoroughly.

9. Ensure that the cover O-ring is in good condition. Replace it if knicked or otherwise damaged.

10. Install the cover and refill the crankcase with oil.

Engine Oil Pressure

Oil pressure can be checked if the proper gauge and fitting are available and a method is found of measuring engine rpm.

1. Warm engine oil to 140°F.

2. Remove the oil gallery plug on the right side of the engine in front of the clutch housing and install the pressure gauge.

3. Oil pressure should be 4.3-10.0 psi at 3000 rpm.

4. Oil pressure which is too high may be caused by oil which is too heavy for conditions, or merely too heavy. Other causes include a clogged passage or filter, improperly installed filter, or a combination of these factors.

5. Low oil pressure can be caused by leakage from the gallery, a damaged oil seal, worn engine components or a defective oil pump.

Drive Chain

The chain should be cleaned and lubricated every 600 miles.

The chain is fitted with rubber O-rings between the plates. Use only kerosene to clean it. Do not use gasoline or similar petroleum-based solvents. They may damage the O-rings.

Chain case nuts and clamps

The chain should be lubricated with motor oil only. Do not use commercial chain lubes. They may contain materials which will damage the chain O-rings.

The chain is accessed by removing the seat, rear fender and chain case. The case is secured by two nuts and four clamps.

Rear Axle Housing

The rear axle housing is fitted with a grease nipple for bearing lubrication. Apply grease every 600 miles.

SERVICE CHECKS AND ADJUSTMENTS

Throttle Cable

1. The throttle cable adjuster is located near the carburetor and is accessed by removing the seat.

2. The cable should be adjusted so that free play is about 0.5-1.0mm (0.02-0.04 in.). This distance is measured between the sheath of the cable coming from the carb and the end of the adjuster.

3. Remove the seat.

4. Loosen the adjuster locknut and turn the adjuster in or out until the proper free play is obtained. Tighten the locknut.

5. Replace the seat.

6. After making this adjustment, let the engine idle and turn the handlebars slowly from lock to lock. Any variation in idle speed means that the throttle cable has insufficient free play or is binding somewhere along its route.

7. After making any adjustment to the throttle cable, check throttle operation before riding the machine.

Drive Chain

1. Drive chain free-play should be checked every 600 miles.

2. If the chain is dirty, it should be cleaned and lubricated before checking.

3. The machine must be parked on a level surface with a rider sitting on the seat.

4. An inspection cap is fitted to the chain case for easy free-play checking. Remove the cap.

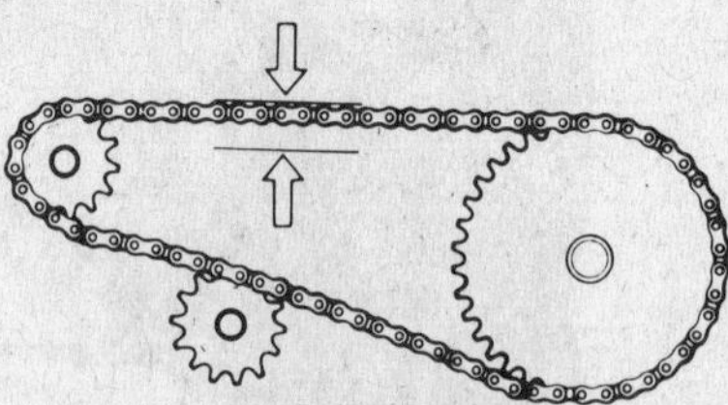

Chain free-play

5. The chain free-play should be:
ALT 185: 10-20mm/0.39-0.79 in.
Other models: 5- 15mm/0.2-0.6 in.
This is the total up-and-down play. If adjustment is necessary, proceed as follows:

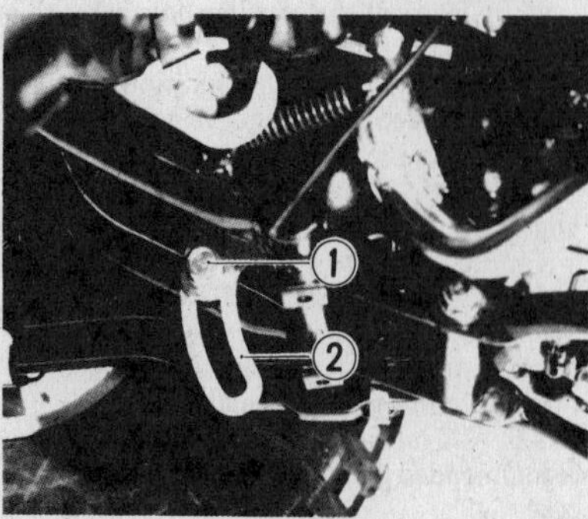

Chain adjuster (2) and lockbolt (1)

6. Remove the skid plate.

7. Loosen the chain adjuster lockbolt.

8. Move the slotted adjuster until chain free-play is correct. Moving the adjuster up reduces free-play.

9. Hold the adjuster in place and tighten the locking bolt. Torque to 51- 73 ft. lbs.

10. Recheck chain free-play at the inspection hole.

11. Periodically, the chain should be checked for wear. Proceed as follows:

a. Remove the seat and rear fender.

b. Remove the skid plate.

c. Remove the two nuts and four clamps that secure the chain case and remove it.

d. Loosen the chain adjuster locking bolt.

e. Push up on the adjuster until all free-play is removed from the chain.

f. Measure the distance between 21 pins on the upper chain run. Maximum allowable distances are:
125 models: 256mm/10.07 in.
185 models: 324mm/12.8 in.

g. If the measured distance exceeds this specification, replace the chain.

h. Adjust the chain to the proper free-play as outlined above.

Clutch

1. The clutch should be adjusted every 1200 miles after break-in is complete.

2. Remove the four screws and take off the clutch cover.

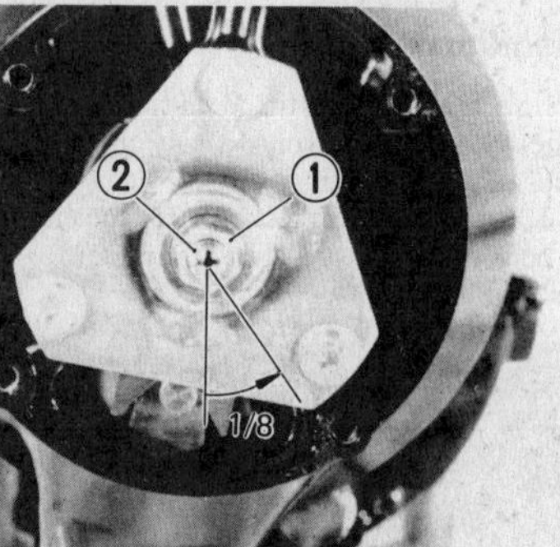

Clutch adjuster screw (2), locknut (1) and adjustment (1/8 turn)

3. Loosen the adjuster screw locknut.

4. Back off the adjuster screw, then turn it clockwise until resistance is felt. Back the adjuster screw off 1/8 turn.

5. Tighten the locknut.

Brake

1. The rear brakes are controlled jointly by the foot pedal and the hand lever on the left side. Both must be adjusted when servicing the brakes. The foot pedal must be adjusted *first*.

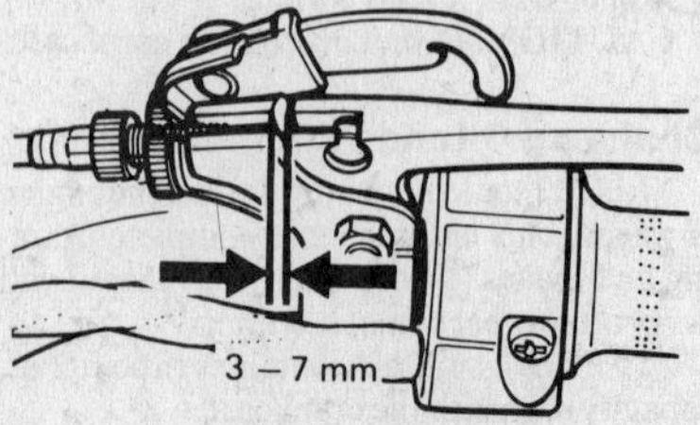

Brake lever free-play

2. The foot pedal is connected to the *lower* of the two cables at the brake plate lever.

3. Use the adjusting nut on the end of the cable so that the foot pedal can move 20-30mm (0.8-1.0 in.) before the linings contact the drum.

4. Check brake hand lever free-play. The lever should have 3-7mm (0.1-0.3 in.) of free play before the linings contact the drum. This specification is measured between the lever and the lever holder.

5. If adjustment is necessary, first run the adjuster at the handlebar all the way in.

6. Use the adjusting nut on the end of the brake cable to give the hand lever the required amount of free-play.

7. Make fine adjustments with the adjuster at the handlebar.

8. After the brakes are adjusted, apply foot pedal or hand lever fully and check that the index mark on the brake camshaft is still within the wear limit range embossed on the axle housing. If it is not, the linings must be replaced.

Tires

1. Tire pressure should be checked before each ride.

2. Always check pressure when tires are cold.

3. Proper tire pressure is 2.2 psi for solo riding.

4. Tire pressures should be checked with an accurate, low-pressure gauge.

5. Never exceed the recommended pressures.

6. When inflating tires, a hand pump is highly recommended. High pressure lines such as found in gas stations should never be used.

WARNING: *Tire condition and tire pressures constitute critical safety factors. Be certain that manufacturer's guidelines are adhered to in all cases.*

7. Tires must be replaced when tread depth is 4.0mm (0.16 in.) or less.

Steering

ALT MODELS

1. Front fork bearing play should be checked every 600 miles.

2. Support the front wheel off the ground.

3. Grasp the forks and attempt to move them back and forth in line with the machine. There should be no play. If there is, bearings are either too loose, or are worn. Refer to "Chassis" for service procedures.

4. Move the handlebars slowly from lock-to-lock. Note any binding, roughness or noise. Movement must be smooth. If it isn't, suspect bearing damage. See "Chassis" for service procedures.

LT MODELS

Toe-in of the front wheels should be checked every 600 miles. This procedure, and subsequent adjustments, are given in the "Chassis" section.

FUEL SYSTEM

Fuel system maintenance involves cleaning the fuel line filter screens, cleaning the air filter and cleaning the carburetor.

Air Filter

1. The filter element should be cleaned and reoiled every 600 miles under normal operating conditions.

2. Remove the seat.

3. Remove the air cleaner case cover after removing the securing screws.

4. Pull out the element snap pin and take out the element.

Air cleaner case cover screws (1)

5. Remove the element from the frame.

6. Clean the element in a safe, non-flammable solvent. Be sure to squeeze the element: do not wring it out as this will damage the pores.

7. When the element is clean, squeeze off the excess solvent.

8. Soak the element in motor oil. Squeeze off the excess, leaving the element slightly wet with the oil.

9. Fit the element onto the frame. Install the assembled components in the case.

NOTE: *If the element is damaged or cannot be cleaned properly, replace it. Check for rips or torn areas, especially along the seam.*

Fuel Filters, Carburetor

Fuel filters are located on the lines inside the gas tank. Service to these items, and carburetor disassembly, is covered in the "Fuel System" section.

TOP END FASTENERS

1. The factory recommends that cylinder head nuts, cylinder base nuts and exhaust pipe and muffler fasteners be tightened every 600 miles.

NOTE: *This procedure must be done when the engine is cold.*

2. Remove the seat.

3. Remove the front fender (LT models) or frame cover (ALT models).

4. Remove the cylinder head cover.

5. Loosen the four 8mm nuts under the cover and the two 6mm nuts on the left side of the engine.

6. Gradually, and in a cross pattern, tighten the 6mm nuts to 5.0-8.0 ft. lbs. and the 8mm nuts to 11.0-14.5 ft. lbs.

7. Loosen the two 6mm cylinder base nuts on the left side of the engine, then re-tighten to 5.0-8.0 ft. lbs.

8. Tighten the exhaust pipe nuts at the cylinder head to 6.5- 8.5 ft. lbs. Tighten the muffler bolts to 13.0- 20.0 ft. lbs.

9. When refitting the cylinder head cover, use liquid gasket material on the mating surface.

MAINTENANCE DATA

Fuel tank (w/reserve)	
LT/ALT 125D	5.0L/1.3 gal.
LT/ALT 125E-F	8.0L/2.3 gal.
LT/ALT 185	8.0L/2.3 gal.
Engine oil	
Routine change	1100 ml/1.16 qts.
Oil & filter change	1150 ml/1.2 qts.
After rebuilding	1200 ml/1.3 qts.
Tire pressure (cold)	
Front and rear	2.2 psi
Oil pressure	4.3-10.0 psi @ 3000 rpm, 140°F

Suzuki LT/ALT 125/185

GENERAL SPECIFICATIONS

	LT 125	ALT 125	LT 185	ALT 185
DIMENSIONS				
Overall length (mm/in.)	1680/66.1	1655/65.2	1680/66.1	1655/65.2
Overall width (mm/in.)	950/37.4	950/37.4	950/37.4	950/37.4
Overall height (mm/in.)	980/38.6	965/38.0	980/38.6	965/38.0
Wheelbase (mm/in.)	1045/41.4	1045/41.4	1045/41.4	1045/41.4
Front track (mm/in.)	650/25.6	—	650/25.6	—
Rear track (mm/in.)	700/27.6	700/27.6	700/27.6	700/27.6
Ground clearance (mm/in.)	110/4.3	110/4.3	110/4.3	110/4.3
Dry weight (kg/lbs.)	129/284	118/260	138/304	125/276
ENGINE				
Type	four-stroke, single cylinder, air-cooled OHC			
Bore (mm/in.)	57.0/2.244	57.0/2.244	63.0/2.480	63.0/2.480
Stroke (mm/in.)	48.8/1.921	48.8/1.921	57.0/2.244	57.0/2.244
Displacement (cc/cu.in.)	124/7.5	124.7.5	178/10.9	178/10.9
Compression ratio (:1)	8.5	8.5	9.0	9.0
Carburetor	VM20SS	VM20SS	VM22SS	VM22SS
Lubrication system	wet sump	wet sump	wet sump	wet sump
Starting system	recoil	recoil	recoil	recoil
TRANSMISSION				
Clutch type	wet multi-plate automatic centrifugal			
Transmission type	5-speeds forward constant mesh; 1-speed reverse			
Primary reduction	3.736 (71/19)	3.736 (71/19)	3.736 (71/19)	3.736 (71/19)
Final reduction	3.769 (49/13)	3.769 (49/13)	3.166 (38/12)	3.166 (38/12)
Gear ratios				
Low	3.545 (39/11)	3.545 (39/11)	3.454 (38/11)	3.454 (38/11)
1st	2.333 (35/15)	2.333 (35/15)	2.500 (35/14)	2.500 (35/14)
2nd	1.500 (30/20)	1.500 (30/20)	1.722 (31.18)	1.722 (31/18)
3rd	1.173 (27/23)	1.173 (27/23)	1.227 (27/22)	1.227 (27/22)
Top	0.913 (21/23)	0.913 (21/23)	0.960 (24/25)	0.960 (24/25)
Reverse	3.090 (34/11)	3.090 (34/11)	2.727 (33/11 × 30/33)	2.727 (33/11 × 30/33)
ELECTRICAL SYSTEM				
Ignition	PEI	PEI	PEI	PEI
Timing (full advance)	10°BTDC below 2000 rpm; 30°BTDC above 3500 rpm			
CHASSIS				
Steering angle	42°30′	38°	38°l/24°0	38°
Caster	2°30′	68°30′	3°30′	68°30′
Trail (mm/in.)	10/0.4	57/2.24	14/0.6	57/2.24
Toe-In (mm/in.)	5-11/0.2-0.4	—	12-18/0.5-0.7	—
Camber	1°	—	2°	—
Turning radius (m/ft.)	2.2/7.2	2.2/7.2	2.2/7.2	2.2/7.2
Front tire size	20 × 7.00-8	22 × 11.00-8	20 × 7.00-8	22 × 11.00-8
Rear tire size	22 × 11.00-8	22 × 11.00-8	22 × 11.00-8	22 × 11.00-8
CAPACITIES				
Fuel tank (1/gal)	5.0/1.3①	5.0/1.3①	8.0/2.1	8.0/2.1

① E/F models: 8.0/2.1

RECOMMENDED LUBRICANTS

Engine
SAE 10W-40 oil, service rated "SE" or "SF"

Drive chain
Motor oil

Air filter
Medium-weight motor oil

Control cables, odometer cable
Light motor oil
Graphite-based lubricant
Molybdenum-disulphide-based lubricant

Throttle lever
Light-duty grease

Rear axle housing
Waterproof, medium-weight bearing grease

Wheels and steering shaft
Waterproof, medium-weight bearing grease

General chassis lubrication
Waterproof, medium-weight chassis grease

PERIODIC MAINTENANCE INTERVALS①

Before each ride
- Check operation of lights
- Check engine oil level
- Check tire pressure and condition
- Check tightness of critical fasteners
- Check throttle and brake operation

Every 600 miles
- Change engine oil
- Change oil filter
- Clean air filter element
- Check battery
- Check brake adjustment and wear
- Check steering operation
- Tighten cylinder, cylinder head and exhaust pipe fasteners
- Tighten all hardware
- General chassis lubrication
- Clean and lubricate drive chain
- Check drive chain free-play
- Lubricate rear axle housing

Every 1200 miles
- Clean oil filter screen
- Adjust clutch
- Lubricate throttle lever, odometer cable, wheel and steering bearings

Every 4 years
- Replace fuel lines

① Based on normal use of the machine after break-in is complete

TUNE-UP

NOTE: *Common tune-up procedures are explained in detail in the "General Information" section.*

COMPRESSION TEST

1. A compression check should be made before each tune-up since this will provide a general idea of engine condition.

2. If a screw-in type gauge is used, note that the spark plug hole is 12mm.

3. Before making this test, check that the cylinder head nuts and bolts are properly torqued (see "Maintenance") and that the valves are properly adjusted (see below). Be sure the compression release cable is disengaged if one is fitted.

4. The engine must be at operating temperature.

5. Remove the spark plug.

6. Fit the compression gauge. If a hold-in type gauge is used, oil the rubber tip to give a better seal.

7. Hold the throttle wide open and crank the engine with the recoil starter.

8. The highest attainable reading is the compression. The standard specifications are:
125 models: 142-199 psi
185 models: 185-241 psi.
The lowest acceptable readings are 114 psi for the 125 and 156 psi for the 185.

9. If compression is too low, squirt a bit of motor oil into the cylinder and repeat the test. If compression increases, suspect worn piston rings or cylinder walls. If it does not, the cause may be a defective head gasket, burnt, poorly seated or incorrectly adjusted valves.

NOTE: *Some models are equipped with a compression release cable. Be sure the cable is properly adjusted before checking the compression.*

CAM CHAIN TENSIONER

1. The cam chain tensioner should be adjusted every 600 miles.

2. The tensioner is a spring-loaded unit which will take up excess slack in the chain when the tensioner rod is released from its normally locked position. For accurate settings, the adjustment must be made when the piston is at TDC on the comparession stroke.

3. Remove the seat.

4. Remove the front fender (LT models) or front frame cover (ALT models).

Magneto rotor "T" mark (1) and stationary timing mark (2)

5. Remove the spark plug.

6. Remove the valve adjuster caps.

7. Remove the gearshift lever.

8. Remove the recoil starter assembly.

9. Rotate the engine until the "T" mark on the magneto rotor aligns with the mark on the crankcase cover. The piston is now positioned at TDC.

10. Check for clearance at both valves. If both valves are closed, the piston is at TDC on the compression stroke and the adjustment sequence may proceed. If there is not clearance at both valves, the piston is at TDC on the exhaust stroke. In this case, rotate the rotor 360° until the "T" mark alignment is reestablished. Now check for clearance at both valves.

11. When the piston is properly located, loosen the locknut on the cam chain tensioner behind the cylinder.

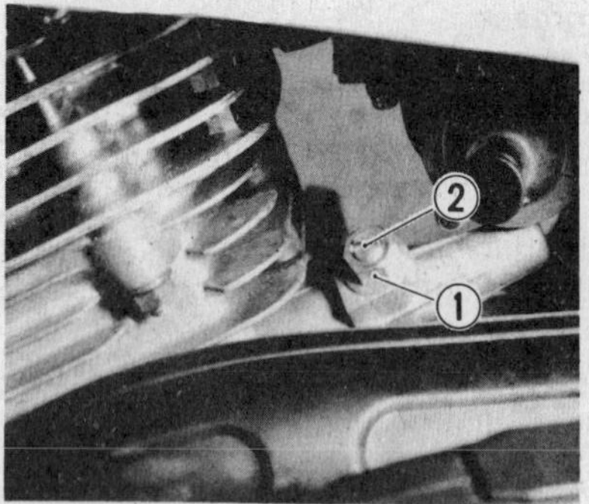

Cam chain tensioner locknut (1) and adjuster screw (2)

12. Turn the adjuster screw one full turn counterclockwise. The spring-loaded tensioner rod will be free to take up chain slack.

13. Tighten the adjuster screw to lock the rod in place.

14. Tighten the locknut.

15. After adjustment, check that chain operation is quiet. If the procedure was done correctly, but the chain is still noisy, it is probable that the rod is sticking due to dirt or the like. The assembly should be removed and thoroughly cleaned. Refer to "Engine and Transmission" for procedures.

VALVE ADJUSTMENT

NOTE: *Valve adjustment must be done when the engine is cold.*

1. Valve clearance must be checked every 600 miles.

2. Remove the seat.

3. Remove the front fender (LT models) or the front frame cover (ALT models).

4. Remove the spark plug.

5. Remove the valve adjuster caps.

6. Remove the gearshift lever.

7. Remove the recoil starter assembly.

8. Rotate the magneto rotor until the "T" mark on the magneto rotor aligns with the mark on the crankcase cover. This will position the piston at TDC.

9. Check for clearance at both valves by attempting to move the adjusters. If there is clearance at both valves, the piston is on the compression stroke and the adjustment sequence can continue. If clearance cannot be detected at both valves, the piston is probably at TDC on the exhaust strike. Rotate the magneto rotor one full turn until the "T" mark alignment is reestablished. Then check for clearance at the valves once more.

Adjusting the valves

10. With the piston at TDC on the compression stroke, check valve clearance.

11. Proper valve clearance is 0.08-0.13mm (0.003-0.005 in.) for both the intake and the exhaust valve.

12. Select a feeler gauge blade near the middle of these specifications and attempt to slip the blade between the valve stem and the adjuster.

13. If clearance is correct, a blade of the proper thickness will be a light slip fit between stem and adjuster.

14. If adjustment is necessary, loosen the adjuster locknut, insert a blade of the proper thickness, and turn the adjuster until the blade is a slip fit—not too loose.

15. When clearance is correct, hold the adjuster in place and tighten the locknut.

16. Recheck clearance after the locknut is secured.

17. Install adjuster caps, recoil starter, spark plug, etc.

18. On machine equipped with a compression release cable, adjust the cable after the valves have been adjusted.

19. After the procedures are complete, check engine compression.

Compression Release Cable

1. Some models are equipped with a compression release cable. The cable should be adjusted after the valves are set.

2. Pull the compression release lever on the handlebar.

3. With the handlebar lever fully pulled in, check clearance between the indicator on the engine lever and the upper surface of the cylinder head cover.

4. Clearance should be nil (zero).

5. Use the cable adjuster at the bracket to make this adjustment. Loosen the two locknuts and move the adjuster on the bracket as required. Tighten the locknuts.

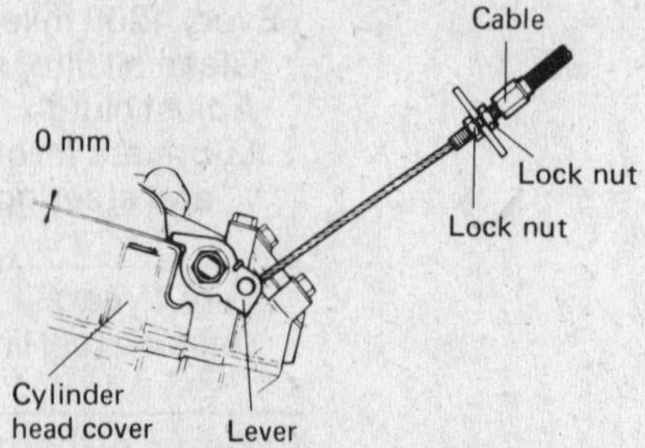

Compression release cable adjustment

IGNITION TIMING

The machine is equipped with a solid-state ignition system which requires no adjustment or routine maintenance.

CARBURETOR

Carburetor adjustments to be made during a complete tune-up include checking the float level, adjusting the idle mixture and adjusting the idle speed.

An aftermarket tachometer is required if idle speed is to be set exactly to specification.

NOTE: *Fuel system adjustments may be ineffective or impossible if the carburetor or air filter are dirty or if there are mechanical faults (such as air leaks) in the system.*

Float Level

1. Float level is a measure of the amount of gasoline which will be present in the float bowl during operation. While it is a critical specification, it will not normally need periodic readjustment once it is properly set. Float level, therefore, need not be checked at every tune-up, but should be attended to from time to time.
2. Remove the carburetor from the machine. Refer to the "Fuel System" section for procedures.
3. Remove the float bowl.
4. Remove the float bowl gasket.
5. Turn the carburetor upside down and lower the float until the tang just touches the tip of the needle.
6. Float level is the distance from the float bowl mating surface (gasket removed) to the top of the float.

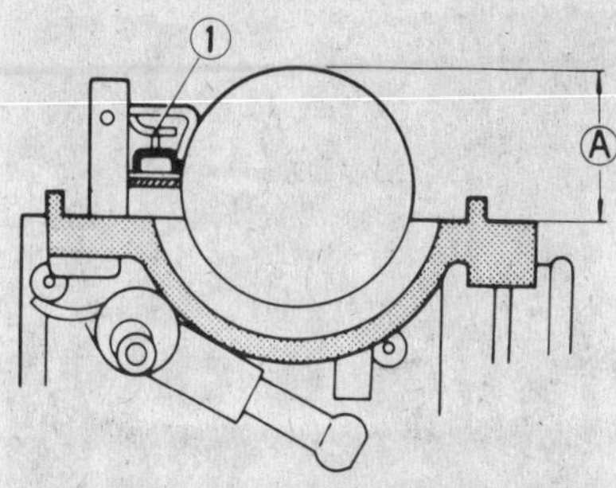

Float level ("A") is adjusted by bending tang (1)

7. Float level is 25.8mm (1.02 in.) with a tolerance of ± 1.0mm (0.04 in.).
8. If the measured float level is not within this range, remove the float by pushing out the pivot pin.
9. Bend the float tang in the required direction to raise or lower the float level. Bending the tang away from the carburetor body raises the float level; bending it towards the carb lower the amount of fuel in the bowl.

Idle Mixture and Idle Speed

1. These adjustments should be made every 600 miles.

NOTE: *Idle speed and mixture adjustments must be made when the engine is at operating temperature.*

2. Carefully turn the pilot screw in until it bottoms, then back it out the following number of turns:

LT/ALT 125D1 3/4
LT/ALT 125E-F1
LT/ALT 1852 1/8

Pilot screw (1) and throttle stop screw (2)

CAUTION: *Turn the screw in carefully. Do not overtighten it or the calibrated tip will be damaged.*

3. Connect a tachometer to the engine.
4. Use the throttle stop screw to adjust idle speed to the proper specification:

LT/ALT 1251500-1600 rpm
LT/ALT 1851350-1450 rpm

5. After idle speed is set, turn the pilot screw 1/2 turn in either direction from the standard setting looking for the highest idle speed. Do not exceed 1/2 turn from the original setting.
6. Readjust idle speed to the standard specification with the throttle stop screw.
7. If these adjustments prove difficult or impossible, suspect dirt or some mechanical defect in the fuel system. Possible causes include air leaks at manifold joints, clogged air or fuel passages in the carburetor, etc. tightly adjusted valves or engine damage of this sort can also make smooth, consistant idling impossible.

TUNE-UP SPECIFICATIONS

	LT/ALT 125	LT/ALT 185
COMPRESSION		
Cranking pressure (psi)	142-199	185-241
Minimum allowable reading (psi)	114	156
VALVE CLEARANCE		
Intake & Exhaust (mm/in.)	0.08-0.13/0.003-0.005	0.08-0.13/0.003-0.005
SPARK PLUG		
OEM	NGK/ND/Champion	NGK/ND/Champion
Standard	D-7EA/X22ES-U/A8YC	D-7EA/X22ES-U/A8YC
Cold	D#8EA/X24ES-U/A6YC	D-8ES/X24ES-U/A6YC
Standard resistor type	DR-7ES/X22ESR#U/RA8YC	DR-7ES/X22ESR-U/RA8YC
Cold resistor type	DR-8ES-L/X24ESR-U/RA6YC	DR-8ES-L/X24ESR-U/RA6YC
IGNITION TIMING	preset	preset
CARBURETION		
Idle speed (rpm)	1500-1600	1350-1450
Pilot screw setting (turns out)	①	2¿
Float level (mm/in.)	25.8/1.02 ± 1.0/0.04	25.8/1.02 ± 1.0/0.04

① D models: 1ı
E-F models: 1

ENGINE AND TRANSMISSION

NOTE: *For engine component inspection techniques and procedures, refer to "Engine Rebuilding" in the General Information section.*

ENGINE REMOVAL AND INSTALLATION

NOTE: *Before removing the engine from the frame, clean both thoroughly.*

1. Engine removal procedures are very similar for all models covered in this section. The following instructions note differences between various machines.

Fuel tank vent hose (1) and mounting bolts (2)

2. Drain the engine oil.
3. Remove the seat.
4. Remove the fuel tank cap.
5. Unhook the fuel tank cap band (if fitted) and disconnect the vent hose from the tank.
6. Remove the four bolts and take off the rear fender.
7. Replace the tank cap.
8. On ALT models, remove the front frame cover bolts and screws. Raise the cover, disconnect the odometer cable and remove the frame cover.

Front frame cover screws (ALT)

9. On LT models, remove the four screws which secure the instrument cluster. Raise the cluster, disconnect the odometer cable and remove the cluster from the machine.
10. On LT models, remove the front fender mounting bolts: there are two at the front and two on each side. Remove the front fender.

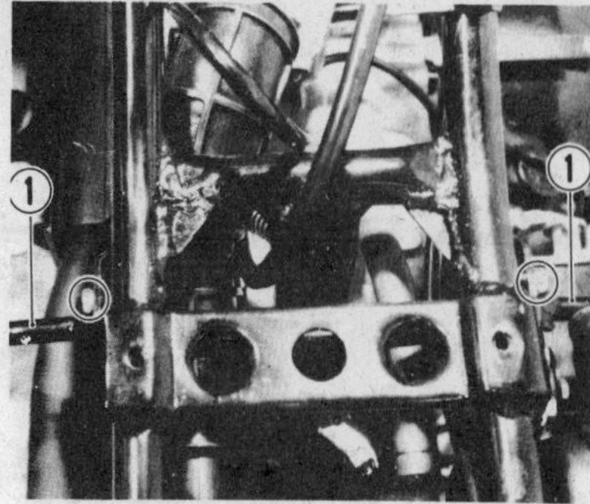

Remove the mounting bracket (1)

11. Remove the fender or cover mounting bracket across the top frame tubes.
12. Remove the exhaust system by removing the two nuts at the cylinder head and the muffler bracket bolt.
13. Remove the skid plate (four bolts).
14. Loosen the drive chain tensioner adjuster bolt.
15. Remove the chain case: there are two nuts and four clamps.

Engine sprocket guide plate (1), fasteners (2,3), locking tab (4) and sprocket nut (5)

16. Remove the engine sprocket guide plate (one bolt, one screw).
17. Remove the engine sprocket nut after bending down the locking tab on the washer.
18. Pull the sprocket off the transmission shaft.

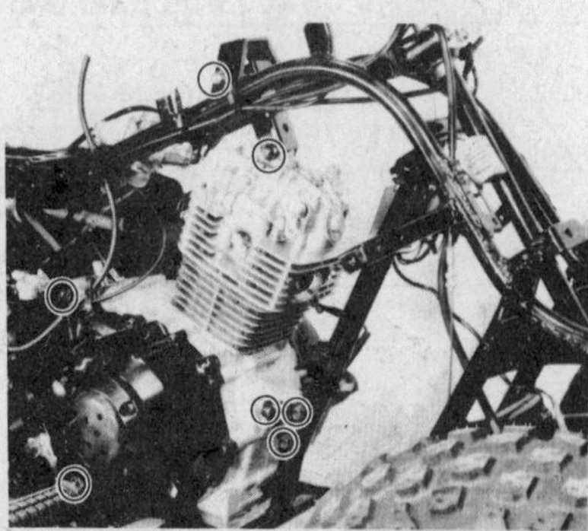

Engine mounting hardware (LT)

19. Be sure the fuel petcock is "OFF." Disconnect the fuel line at the carburetor. Disconnect the vacuum line at the manifold and the overflow line at the float bowl.
20. Loosen the two carburetor clamp screws and pull the carb out of the manifold and air cleaner hoses. Arrange it so that it is not damaged by subsequent removal steps.
21. Disconnect the odometer cable from the engine.
22. Disconnect the breather hose from the back of the crankcase.
23. Locate the wiring connectors near the front of the frame and disconnect wires coming from the engine: lighting, pick-up and power source coils.
24. Disconnect the spark plug cap from the plug.
25. Disconnect the compression release cable from the cylinder head lever on models equipped with one.
26. Remove the gearshift lever.
27. Remove the engine mounting bolts and brackets at the cylinder head, front and rear crankcase and beneath the engine.
28. Take the engine out of the right side of the frame.
29. Engine installation is the reverse of removal. Note the following points:

Engine mounting hardware (ALT)

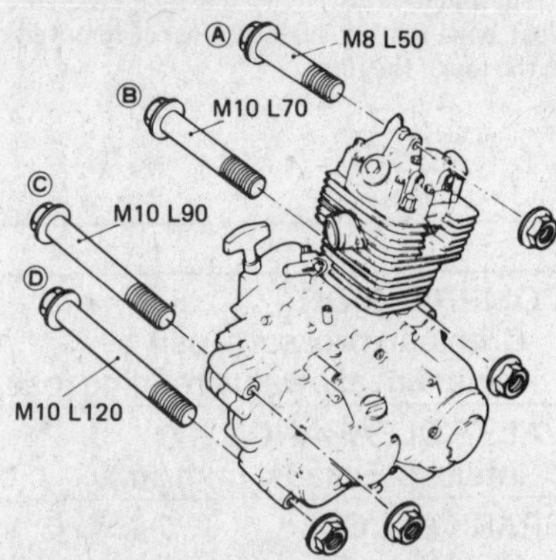

Torque head bolt ("A") to 20-25 ft lbs., others ("B"-"D") to 58-69 ft lbs.

a. Engine mounting bolts use self-locking nuts which cannot be reused. Use new nuts when installing the engine.

b. Tighten the mounting bolt which runs through the cylinder head to 20-25 ft. lbs.

c. Tighten all other mounting bolts to 58-69 ft. lbs.

d. Engine sprocket nut torque is 58-73 ft. lbs. for 125 models, 73-94 ft. lbs. for 185 models.

e. Tighten exhaust pipe cylinder nuts to 7-9 ft. lbs. and the muffler bracket bolt to 13-20 ft. lbs.

f. Be certain that all hoses and lines, electrical connections, control cables, etc., are properly connected and adjusted before starting the engine.

g. Do not forget to add oil before attempting to start the engine.

TOP END

NOTE: *Refer to the General Information section of this manual for common engine rebuilding techniques and inspection procedures.*

Cylinder Head

REMOVAL

1. It is possible to remove the cylinder head with the engine still in the frame. Remove the seat, front fender (LT) or front frame cover (ALT), rear fender, carburetor and exhaust system. Remove the frame bracket on the head. Refer to "Engine Removal and Installation," above for procedures.
2. Remove the spark plug.

Cam chain tensioner mounting bolts

3. Remove the valve adjuster caps.
4. Remove the cam chain tensioner from the left side of the cylinder.
5. Remove the four fasteners that secure the recoil starter assembly (engine left side).
6. Disconnect the compression release cable from the cylinder head cover if equipped with one.
7. Turn the magneto rotor until the "T" mark aligns with the timing mark on the crankcase. Check for clearance at both valves. This indicates that the piston is at TDC on the compression stroke. If one of the valves is tight, rotate the engine 360° and try again. The piston must be at TDC on the compression stroke when removing the head.
8. Refer to the accompanying illustration of the head. Loosen the cylinder head cover bolts gradually and evenly in the order shown.

Cylinder head cover bolt loosening order. Do not remove bolts ("A") which secure the rocker arm shafts

CAUTION: *Do not disturb the two bolts (for rocker arm shafts) with conical recesses marked "A" in the illustration.*

9. When all cover bolts are loose, remove them.
10. Remove the cylinder head cover.
11. Remove the camshaft end cap.
12. Bend down the locking tabs and remove the cam sprocket bolts.
13. Pull the sprocket off the camshaft. Disengage the sprocket from the chain and remove it.
14. Run a rod through the chain so that it will not drop into the crankcase.
15. Remove the camshaft being careful not to loose the timing pin on the end.
16. The head is secured by four nuts on top and two smaller nuts on the left side of the cylinder. Loosen the fasteners gradually and in a cross pattern. Remove the nuts and washers. Note the locations of the copper washers.

Cylinder head nuts

17. Remove the cylinder head. If it is stuck, rap it with a plastic mallet, but do not strike the cooling fins, as they may break.
18. Remove the head gasket.
19. Pull out the compression release shaft from the cylinder head cover, if one is fitted.
20. Remove the rocker arm shaft set bolts (conically recessed heads) from the head cover.
21. Pull the rocker arm shafts out of the cover with pliers.

Rocker arm shaft set bolts (1)

NOTE: *Rocker arms and shims will come out at this time. Keep each shaft with its own rocker arm so all parts can be installed in their original locations.*

22. If valves fail the leakage test, they can be removed for service by compressing the springs and removing the keepers.
23. Worn valve guides can be driven out of the head with a drift in the usual manner.

INSPECTION

Refer to the Engine Rebuilding section of "General Information" for component wear checks and measurement points. Compare the measurements against the standard specifications given in the "Engine Specifications" chart, below.

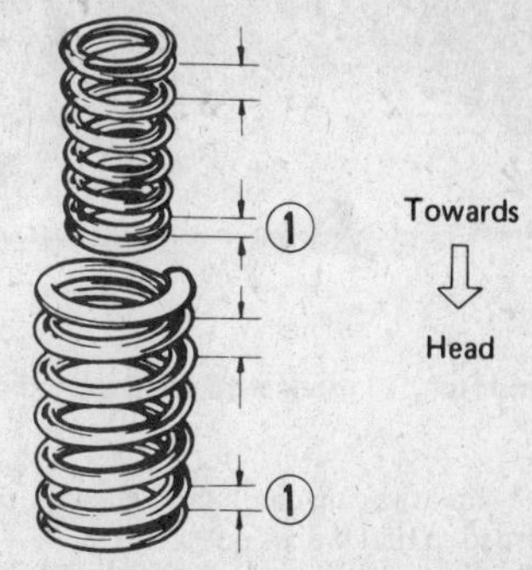

Install valve springs with the close coils (1) towards the head

Cylinder head mating surface dowel pins (1)

INSTALLATION

1. Use new gaskets, O-rings and seals.
2. Install the valve springs with the close coils against the head.
3. Be sure that the two dowel pins are in place on the cylinder mating surface.
4. Install the cylinder head and pull the cam chain through.—
5. Note that the copper washers for the head fasteners are fitted to the same studs that have the dowel pins on the cylinder mating surface.
6. Tighten the nuts gradually and in a cross pattern until the proper torque is reached:

   8mm11-15 ft. lbs.
   6mm5-8 ft. lbs.
7. Install and tighten the cylinder nuts on the left side to 5-8 ft. lbs.
8. Turn the magneto rotor until the "T" mark aligns with the timing mark on the crankcase.

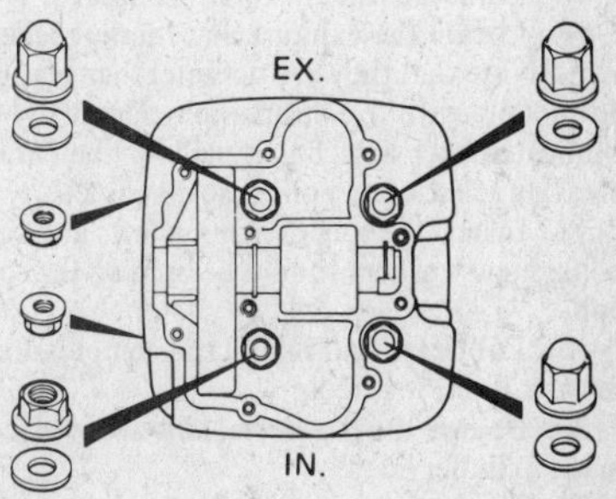

Be sure copper (1) and steel (2) washers are properly located

Align rotor "T" mark with crankcase timing mark

9. Pull the cam chain taut when the rotor is turned so that it does not jam.

10. Grease the camshaft timing pin and fit it to the camshaft.

11. Lubricate the camshaft and install it on the head.

12. Engage the cam sprocket and cam chain.

Position timing pin (1) as shown and align slash marks (2) with cover mating surface

13. Position the camshaft so that the timing pin is at the highest position and that the slash marks on the end of the cam are parallel to the head cover mating surface.

14. With the magneto rotor "T" mark still aligned, and the cam positioned as directed, install the sprocket on the cam without moving either cam or rotor. If this cannot be done, disengage the sprocket from the chain and change its position so that alignment is possible. When assembly is completed, the rotor "T" mark must be aligned with the crankcase timing mark and the camshaft slash marks must be parallel to the cover mating surface. Otherwise valve timing will be incorrect.

15. Use a non-permanent thread locking ompound on the sprocket bolts and tighten them to 7.0-9.5 ft. lbs. Bend up the locking tabs.

16. Lubricate the rocker arm shafts.

17. Locate the exhaust and intake rocker arms. Note that they are not interchangeable on models with a compression release. The exhaust rocker arm has a pad for the compression release lever on these machines.

18. Install the rocker arms, shafts and set bolts. New washers should be used on the set bolts.

19. Lubricate and install the compression release, if one is fitted.

20. Be sure the two dowel pins are in place in the cylinder head.

21. Use gasket compound to seal the head cover mating surface and install the head cover.

Be sure dowel pins (1) are in place

Be sure gaskets are installed on cover bolts

Cover bolt tightening sequence

CAUTION: *Do not apply the compound to the camshaft end cap.*

22. Be sure the gaskets are in place on the two cover bolts.

23. Install the cover fasteners. Tighten the fasteners gradually and in the order shown in the illustration until the correct torque (6.5-8.0 ft. lbs.) is attained.

24. To install the cam chain tensioner, loosen the locking nut, loosen the screw one full turn and compress the pushrod. Tighten the screw. Bolt the tensioner on the cylinder. The piston must be positioned at TDC on the compression stroke. Loosen the screw to free the pushrod, then tighten it and tighten the locking nut.

25. Adjust valves. After the engine has a few miles on it, retorque the fasteners and readjust the valves.

Cylinder And Piston

REMOVAL

1. Remove the cylinder head as outlined above.
2. Remove the cam chain guide.
3. Remove the cylinder base nuts.
4. Pull off the cylinder.
5. Stuff a clean rag into the crankcase to prevent the entry of foreign matter.
6. Remove the wrist pin circlips.
7. Push out the piston wrist pin and remove the piston. Do not strike or try to drive the wrist pin out. Heat the piston crown gently to make removal easier.
8. Remove the cylinder base gasket.

Cylinder nuts

INSPECTION

1. Refer to the Engine Rebuilding section of "General Information" for piston and cylinder inspection procedures.
2. Compare specifications obtained from the engine against the standard specs in the chart below.
3. Piston diameter is measured 15mm above the edge of the skirt.
4. Piston rings are available in two oversizes: 0.5mm and 1.0mm. The compression rings are marked "50" and "100". The 0.5 O.S. oil ring spacer is painted red. The 1.0 O.S. oil ring spacer is yellow.

INSTALLATION

1. The two compression rings are not interchangeable. On 125 models, the top compression ring is chrome-plated, while the second ring is not. On 185 models, the top ring has a rounded profile, while the second ring is wedge-shaped. Be sure the rings are installed in the correct grooves.

Install rings with manufacturer's mark up

Compression ring profiles (185)

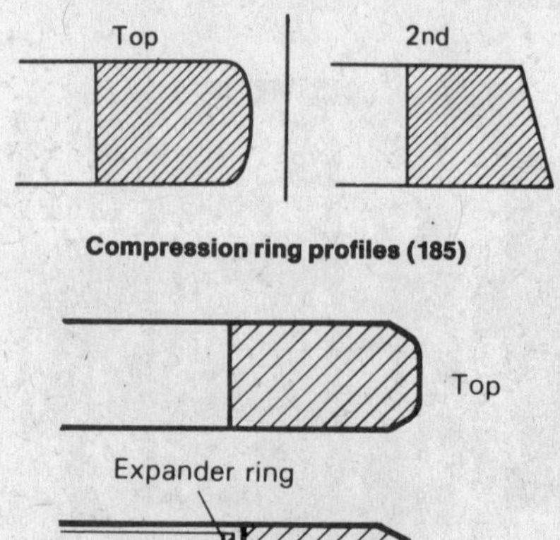

Compression ring profiles (125)

2. Compression rings must be installed with the "R" or "N" mark or oversize mark near the end gap facing up.

3. Position the ring end gaps around the piston as shown in the illustration.

4. When installing the piston, be sure that the arrow on the crown points towards the exhaust port.

5. Be sure that the dowel pins are in place on the cylinder studs on the left side of the engine.

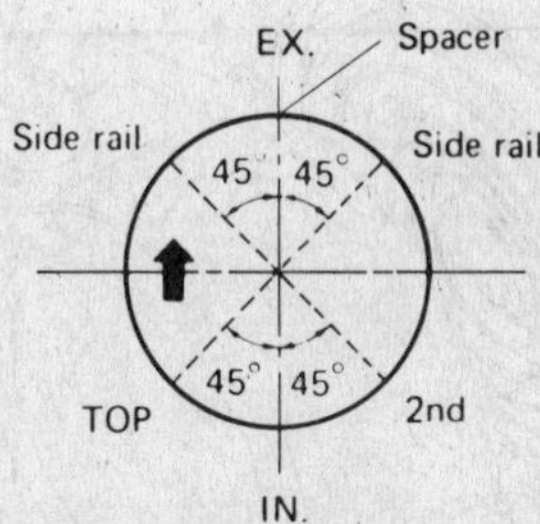

Piston ring end-gaps must be positioned as shown

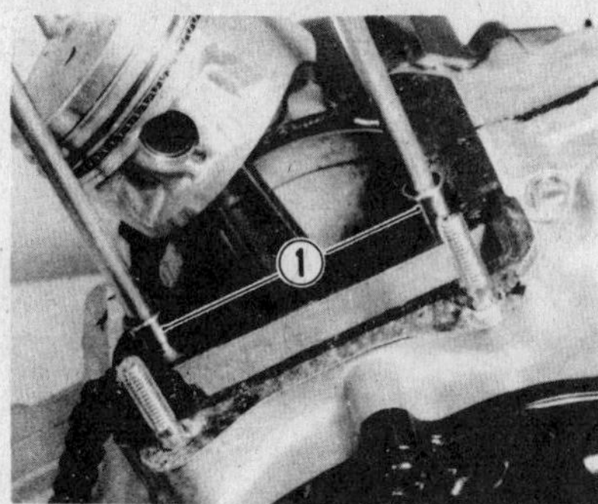

Be sure dowel pins (1) are in place on crankcase

6. Use a new cylinder base gasket.

7. Compress the rings and fit the cylinder while pulling the cam chain through. Keep the chain taut or it may jam on the crank sprocket.

8. Install the cam chain guide. Be sure it is properly seated in its holder in the crankcase.

9. Tighten the cylinder base nuts to 5-8 ft. lbs.

CRANKCASE COVER COMPONENTS

Left Side

REMOVAL

1. Remove the four fasteners that secure the recoil starter assembly and remove the recoil starter.

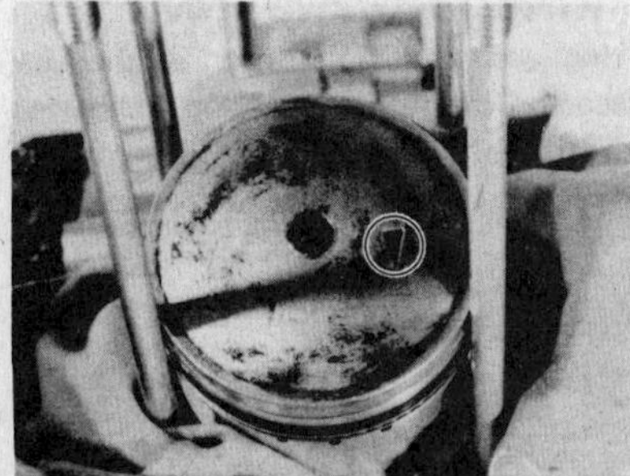

Install piston so that the arrow points towards the exhaust port

Recoil starter fasteners

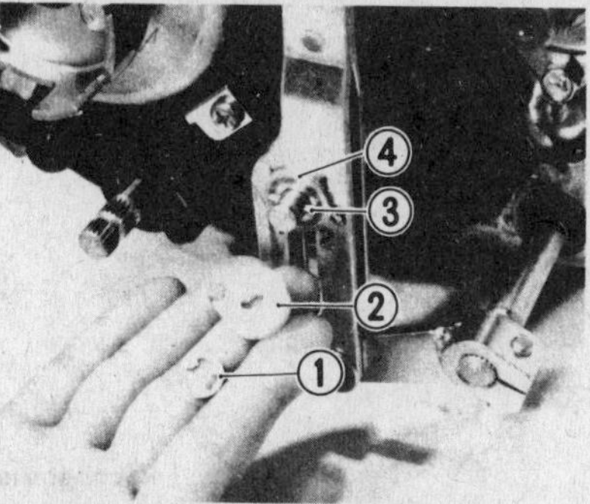

Reverse lever E-ring (1), gear position indicator (2), pin (3) and washer (4)

Removing the rotor nut

Magneto stator screws

2. Remove the reverse lever E-ring. Remove the gear position indicator, pin and washer.

3. Remove the reverse lever arm pinch bolt. Pull the lever off the shaft. Remove the spring, spacer and washer.

4. Remove the magneto nut.

5. Pull the magneto off the crankshaft.

6. Remove the six magneto stator screws and take off the stator assembly.

7. To proceed past this point, the engine oil must be drained.

8. Remove the crankcase cover screws and take off the left side crankcase cover.

9. Remove the gear position indicator gear by removing the E-ring. Remove the pin.

10. If the top end has been removed, the cam chain can be removed.

11. Remove the screw which secures the odometer drive box on the top of the crankcase and pull out the assembly.

INSPECTION

1. Clean all metal parts in a safe solvent.

2. Check gears for damage or wear and replace as required.

3. Use new gaskets and O- rings when assembling.

ASSEMBLY

1. When fitting the gear position indicator gears, align the punch marks as shown.

2. Be sure the two dowel pins are installed in the crankcase before installing the crankcase cover.

3. Use a new crankcase cover gasket.

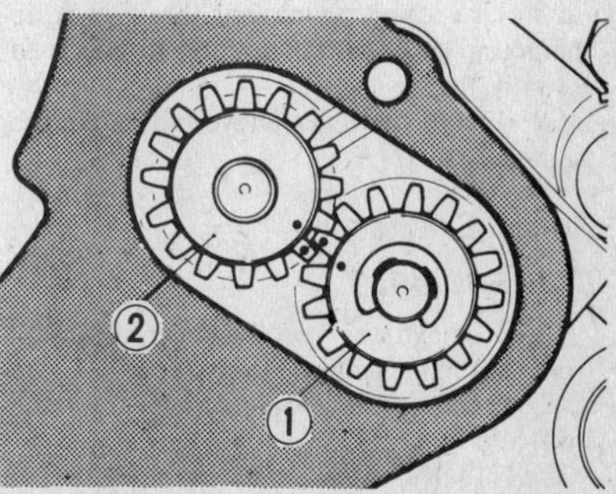

Align punch marks on teeth of gear position indicator gears (1,2)

Be sure crankcase cover dowel pins ("A") are in place

Forwardmost screw may have one or more gaskets

4. Install the cover.

5. On some models, the forwardmost cover screw is fitted with one or more gaskets. Be sure they are replaced if originally equipped.

6. Use a non-permanent thread-locking compound on the magneto stator screws.

7. Clean the rotor and the tapered portion of the crankshaft before the rotor is installed.

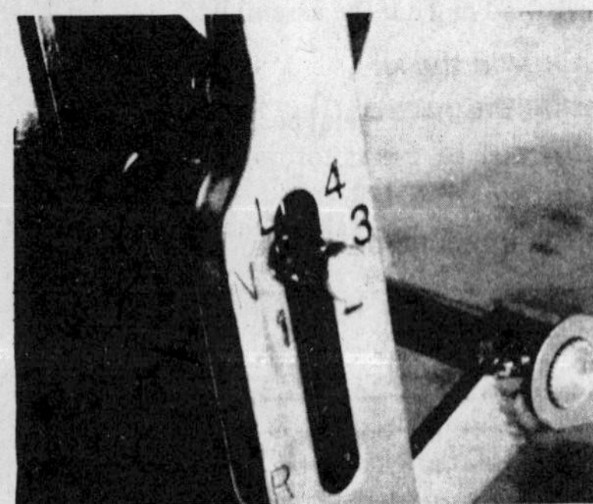

Align pin hole with reverse lever "N"

8. Use a non-permanent thread-locking compound on the rotor nut and tighten it to 36-44 ft. lbs.

9. Install the reverse lever and align the pin hole with "N."

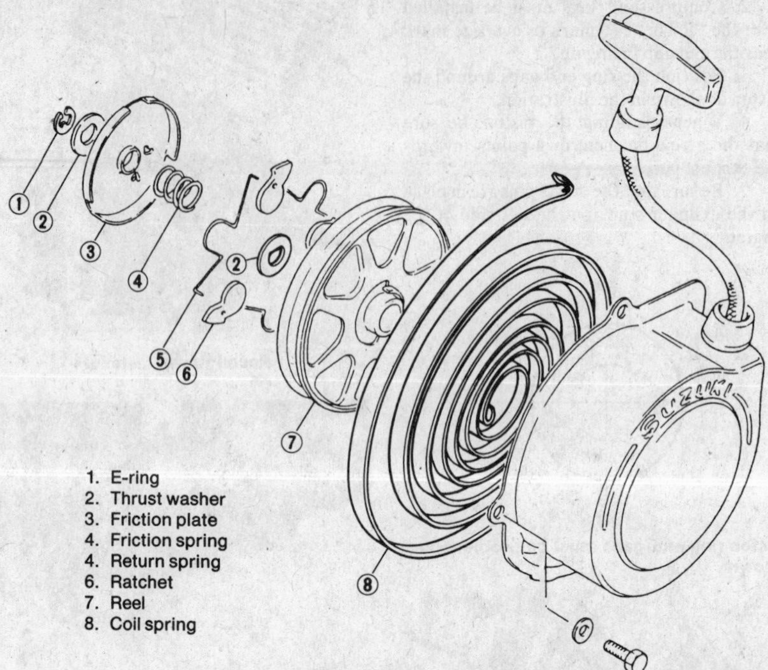

Recoil starter assembly (early)

Recoil Starter

DISASSEMBLY

1. Remove the recoil starter assembly from the engine (four bolts or screws).

2. Remove the E-ring or nut from the shaft and separate the components.

CAUTION: *Watch the expanding spring when the parts are disassembled.*

INSPECTION

1. Clean all parts thoroughly.

2. Check all parts for damage and replace as required.

ASSEMBLY

1. When installing the coil spring, hook the end of the spring onto the rib provided on the case.

2. Grease the spring thoroughly.

3. Wind the starter rope onto the reel. Engage the reel tab with the spring cut-out.

4. Grease the shaft and ratchet before installation.

5. To adjust tension, hook the rope onto the reel and turn it clockwise 3 or 4 times.

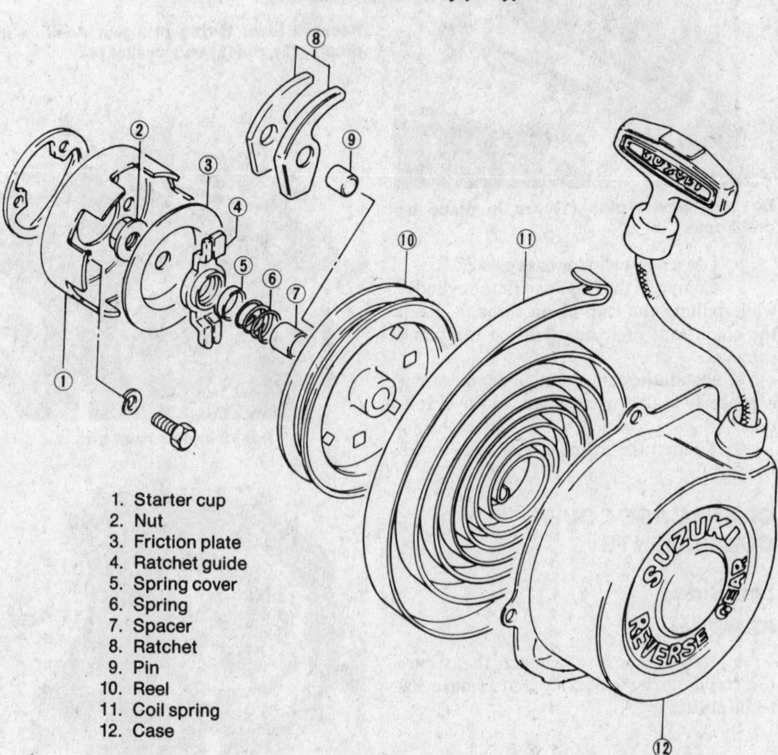

Recoil starter assembly (late)

Right Side

DISASSEMBLY

1. Drain the oil.

2. Remove the oil filter cap.

3. Remove the oil filter element.

4. Remove the clutch adjuster cap.

5. Remove the three outer ball guide screws. Remove the outer ball guide, release ball assembly, inner ball guide and spring.

6. Remove the clutch push plate.

7. Place a drip pan beneath the engine to catch the oil residue.

8. Remove the clutch cover screws.

9. Remove the clutch cover. If the cover is stuck, free it with a plastic mallet.

10. Remove the clutch release lever bolt.

11. Remove the clutch sleeve hub nut.

12. Remove the clutch assembly and primary drive gear.

13. Remove the primary driven gear circlip.

14. Remove the primary driven gear.

15. Slide the oil pump drive gear off its shaft.

16. Remove the oil pump driven gear after removing the circlip.

17. Remove the three oil pump mounting screws and remove the oil pump.

18. Remove the gearshift lever (left side of engine).

19. Pull out the gearshift shaft from the right side.

20. Remove the four screws and take out the cam driven gear. Watch for the pawls, pins and springs which are part of this assembly.

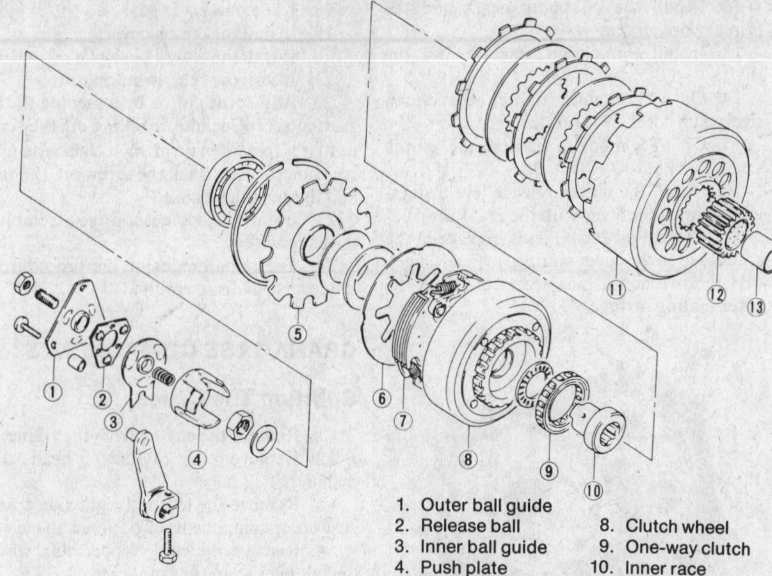

Clutch assembly

Primary driven gear circlip

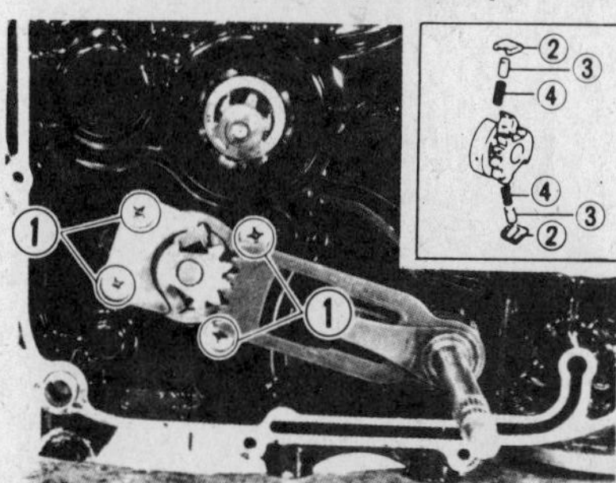

Oil pump drive (1) and driven (2) gears and circlip; oil pump mounting screws

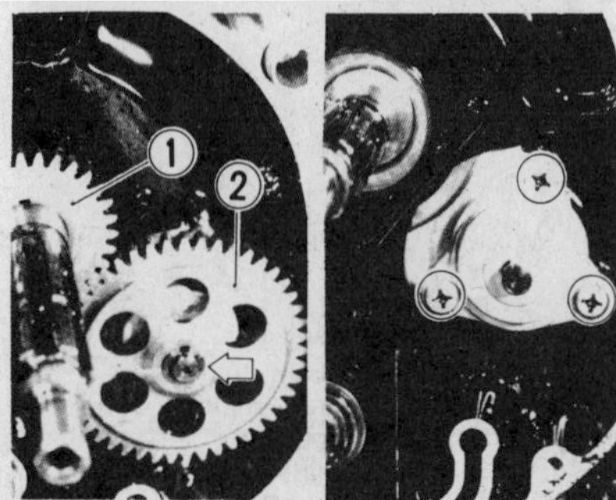

Cam driven gear screws (1); pawls (2), pins (3), springs (4)

INSPECTION

1. To disassemble the clutch, compress the pressure plate, remove the retaining ring and separate the components.

2. Clean all metal parts in a safe solvent and check for obvious signs of wear.

3. Measure the thickness of each clutch drive (friction) plate. Replace the plates as a set if any measures less than 2.6mm (0.10 in.).

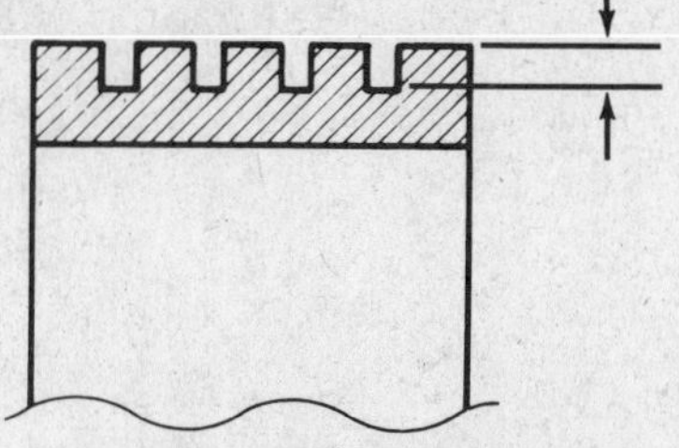

Check clutch shoe grooves

4. Measure drive plate tab width. Replace plates if the tabs are worn or if they average less than 11.0mm (0.43 in.).

5. Check driven (steel) plate warpage. Maximum allowable warp is 0.1mm (0.004 in.).

6. Measure clutch spring free length and replace them as a set if any measures less than 30.2mm (1.19 in.).

7. Inspect the clutch shoes for chipping, cracking, uneven wear or a burnt condition. If the grooves are worn away, or if other signs of damage are evident, replace shoes as a set.

8. Check the clutch wheel for scoring, cracks, etc., and replace if damaged.

9. Check the clutch bearings for damage.

Check the clutch release balls for pitting, wear, etc. If any damage is evident, replace the assembly.

11. Insert the inner race into the one-way clutch and rotate it. Action must be smooth and noiseless. If rotation is rough or binding, replace the clutch bearings.

12. Check the condition of the bearing in the clutch cover. Replace it if it is damaged or if rotation is noisy or binding.

13. Check the oil pump for smooth shaft rotation. The pump cannot be disassembled. Replace the oil pump if the shaft rotation is not smooth and noiseless.

14. Check gearshift shaft components for condition. Check the shaft for a bent condition. Check for chipped gear teeth. Replace defective parts.

15. Replace the gearshift shaft pawl spring if broken or if seems weakened.

16. Inspect the teeth of the primary drive and primary driven gears. Check for broken, chipped or pitted teeth. Check the fit of the driven gear on its shaft. Check for wear or scoring of the gear bushing and shaft. Replace damaged parts.

ASSEMBLY

1. Use new gaskets and O-rings.

2. Be certain all parts are well lubricated during assembly.

3. The oil pump should be soaked with clean motor oil before installation.

4. Oil pump mounting screws should be secured with a non-permanent thread locking compound and tightened to 5-7 ft. lbs.

5. Assemble the clutch by referring to the exploded view. Note the following points:

Lip of the one-way clutch must face away from the cluch wheel

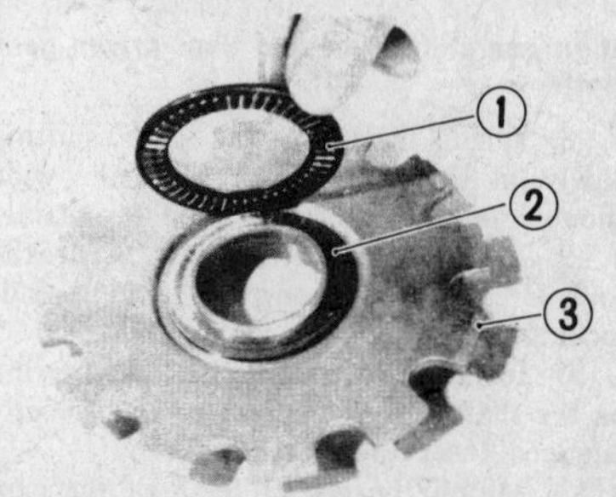

Thrust bearing (1), thrust washer (2), pressure plate (3)

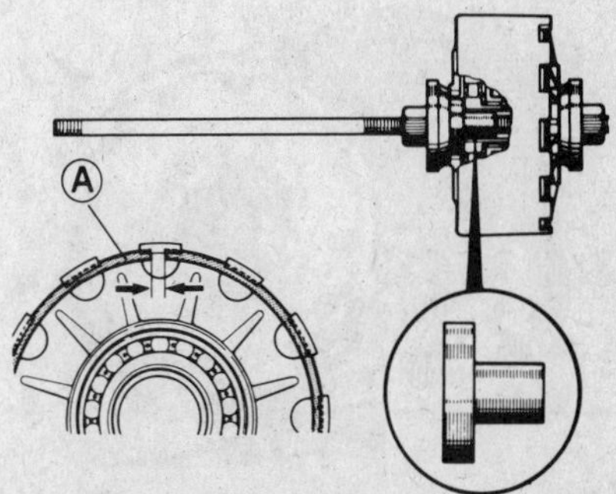

Retaining ring end-gap ("A") must bear against clutch housing finger

a. The lip on the one-way clutch must face away from the clutch wheel when the one-way clutch is fitted.

b. When fitting the shoe assembly to the clutch wheel, engage the wheel tabs with the shoe slots.

c. Be sure to install the thrust washer and thrust bearing on the inner side of the pressure plate.

Shifting pawl wide shoulders ("A") must be on the outside when pawls are fitted

6. Compress the clutch assembly and install the retaining ring.

NOTE: *Both ends of the retaining ring should bear against one of the clutch housing fingers.*

7. Oil the primary drive gear spacer before installation.

Align gearshift shaft and cam driven gear teeth

8. When installing the gear shifting pawls on the cam driven gear, the wide shoulder on the pawls must be on the outside.

9. Install the cam driven gear. Secure the four screws with a non-permanent threadlocking compound.

10. Install the gearshift shaft pawl spring on the shaft with the spring pawls correctly engaged. Insert the gearshift shaft.

11. Match the center teeth of the cam driven gear and the gearshift shaft gear teeth. Check shifting action.

Align clutch release lever with crankshaft

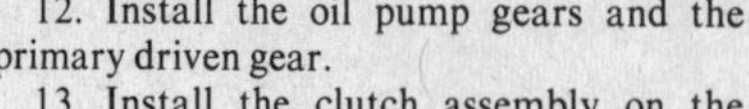

12. Install the oil pump gears and the primary driven gear.

13. Install the clutch assembly on the shaft.

14. On 125 models, tighten the clutch sleeve hub not to 29-44 ft. lbs.

15. On 185 models, tighten the clutch sleeve hub nut to 44-58 ft. lbs.

16. Install the clutch release lever, aligning the tip of the lever with the crankshaft.

17. Check that the oil jet is in place in the crankcase on the cover mating surface. Check that the two dowel pins are in place on the cover mating surface.

Be sure dowel pins ("A") and the oil jet are in place on the crankcase mating surface

18. Use a new cover gasket.

19. Install the clutch cover.

20. Install the clutch push plate.

21. Install the release mechanism.

22. Adjust the clutch by loosening the adjusting screw locknut, backing off the screw until it is free, then turnizng it clockwise until resistance is felt. Back the screw off 1/8 turn and tighten the locknut.

23. Install the odometer drive assembly if it was removed.

24. The remainder of the procedure is the reverse of disassembly.

CRANKCASE COMPONENTS

Splitting The Cases

1. Remove the engine from the frame.
2. Remove the cylinder head and cylinder.
3. Remove the left and right side crankcase cover components as outlined above.
4. Remove the cam stopper bolt, spring and plunger from the crankcase.
5. Remove the crankcase bolts.
6. Separate the case halves. The crank and gear clusters remain in the left crankcase half.
7. Disconnect the shift cam stopper spring.

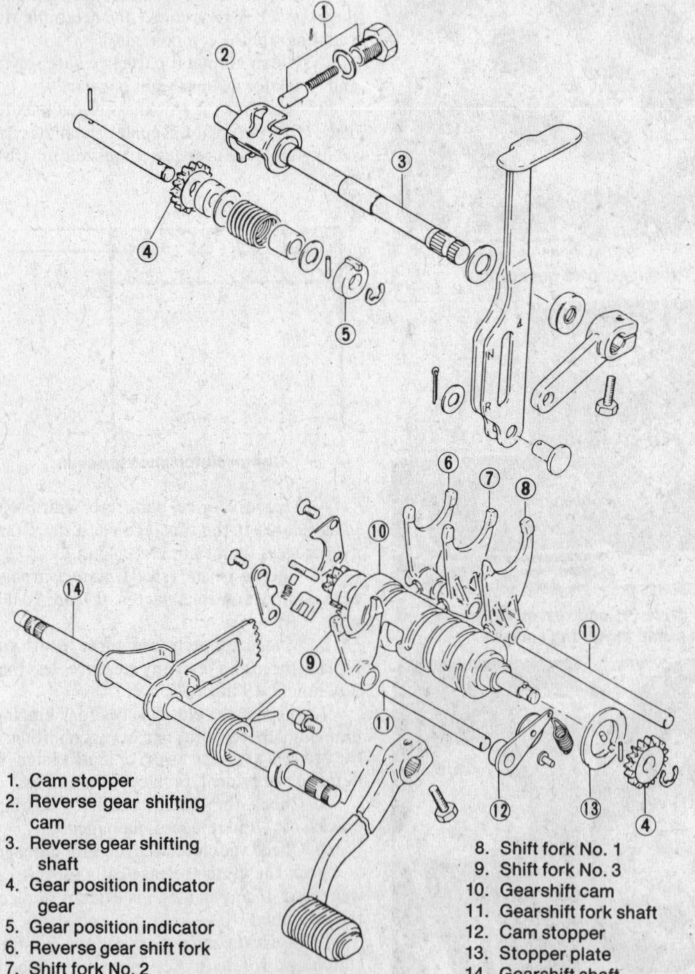

1. Cam stopper
2. Reverse gear shifting cam
3. Reverse gear shifting shaft
4. Gear position indicator gear
5. Gear position indicator
6. Reverse gear shift fork
7. Shift fork No. 2
8. Shift fork No. 1
9. Shift fork No. 3
10. Gearshift cam
11. Gearshift fork shaft
12. Cam stopper
13. Stopper plate
14. Gearshift shaft

Gearshifting assembly

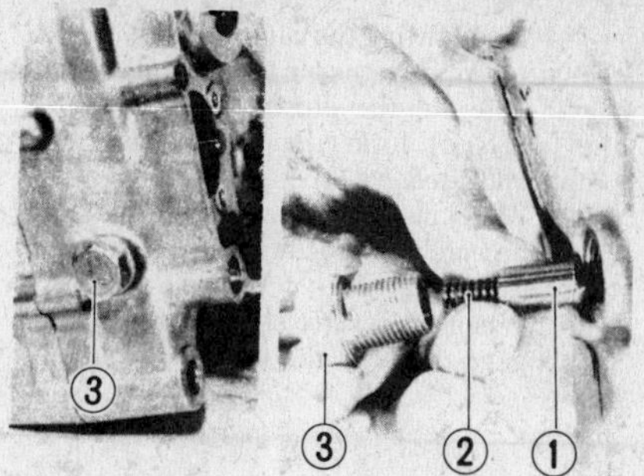

Cam stopper plunger (1), spring (2) and bolt (3)

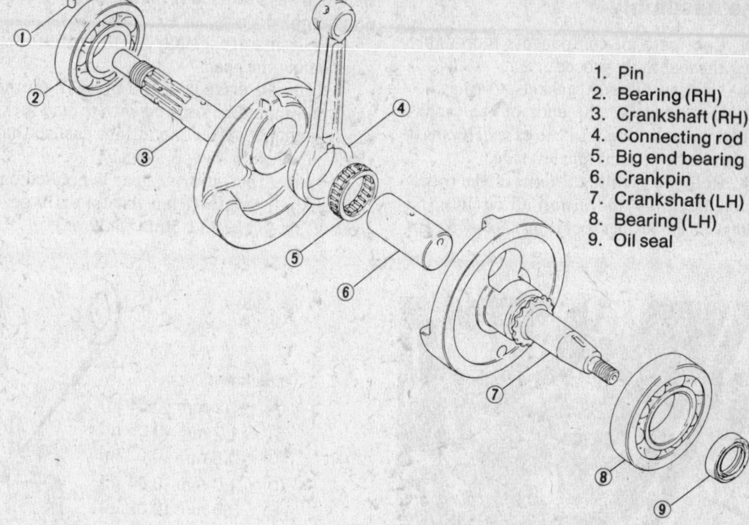

Crankshaft components

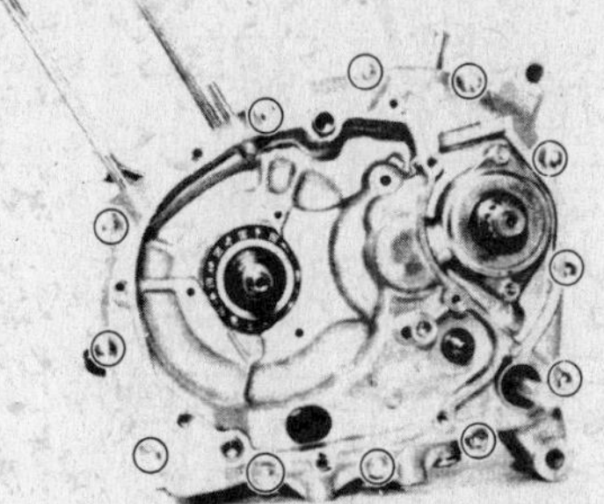
Crankcase screws

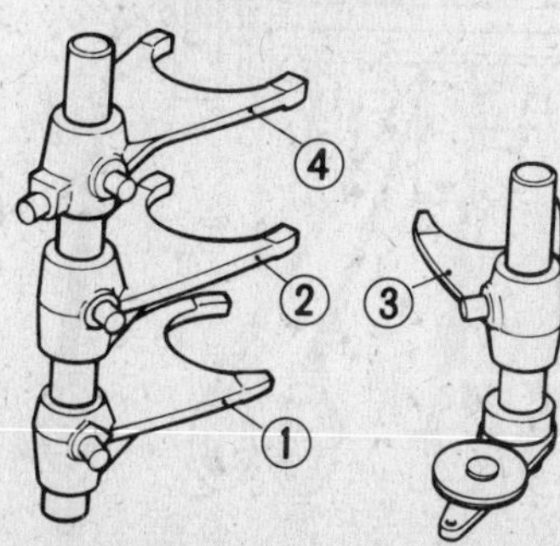

Shift fork installation: 1, top driven gear; 2, 3rd driven gear; 3, 2nd drive gear; 4, reverse driven gear

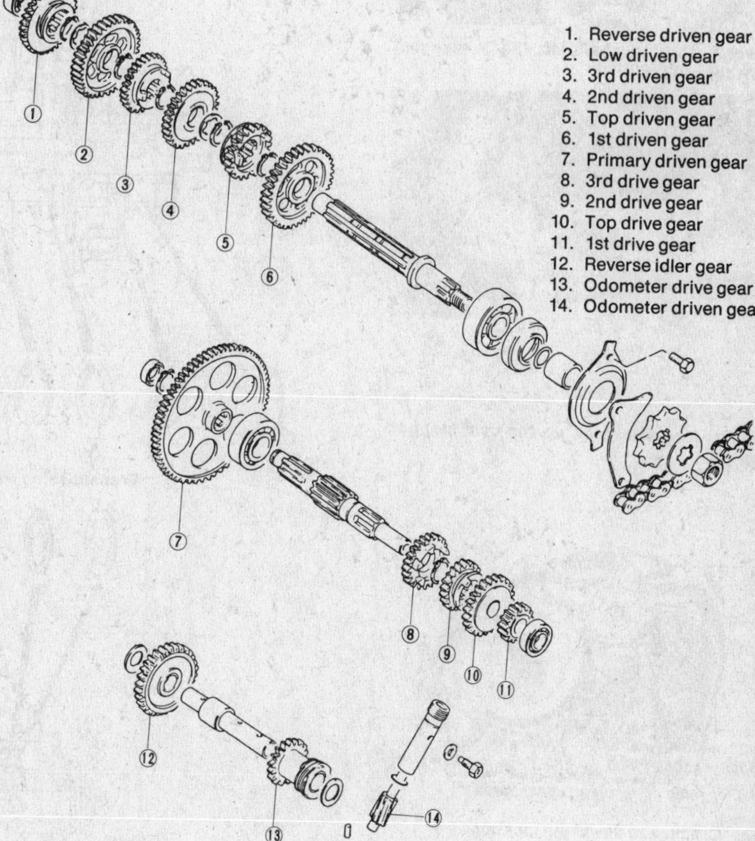

Transmission assembly (125D)

Reverse shaft pin ("B") fits into groove ("A")

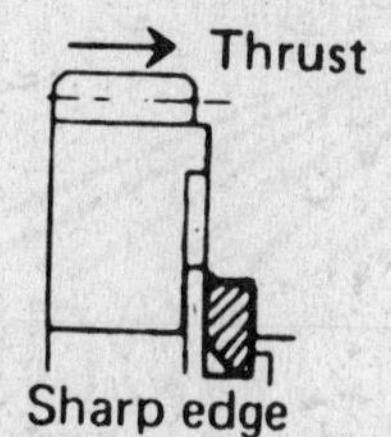

Circlip rounded side must face gear

8. Remove the gearshift fork shafts.
9. Remove the reverse gear shift shaft.
10. Remove the gears, shift forks and shift cam.
11. Remove the odometer driven gear stopper bolt. Remove the odometer gear.
12. Press the crankshaft out of the case.
13. Remove the oil sump filter cap and filter.

Inspection

1. Clean all metal parts in a safe solvent.
2. Check all components for obvious signs of wear as directed in Engine Rebuilding section of "General Information." Compare readings taken at the various measurement points against the standard specifications given in the chart below.

Case Assembly

1. Lubricate all components thoroughly during the assembly procedure.

2. Use new oil seals, gaskets, O-rings.

3. Do not strike the ends of the crankshaft when installing it in the case. The shaft must be drawn in from the left side.

4. Refer to the illustrations of the transmission assembly and install all circlips and washers in the proper locations. New circlips should always be used if the shafts have been disassembled.

5. Circlips are installed with the rounded sides facing the gear.

6. The 1st drive gear is a press fit on the shaft and should be secured with thread locking compound. After mounting, ensure that the adjacent gear can spin freely.

7. After the 1st drive gear is pressed on, countershaft length (from the 1st drive gear to Low) should be 111.5mm (4.39 in.).

8. When fitting the cam stopper plate on the shift cam, align the pin groove and the pin.

9. Refer to the illustration identifying the four shift forks. Be certain they are properly located.

10. When installing the reverse shaft, fit the pin on the shaft into the groove provided in the crankcase.

11. When the reverse shifting shaft is fitted, engage the shaft tab with the cam cut-out.

Reverse shifting shaft tab ("A") engages cam cut-out ("B")

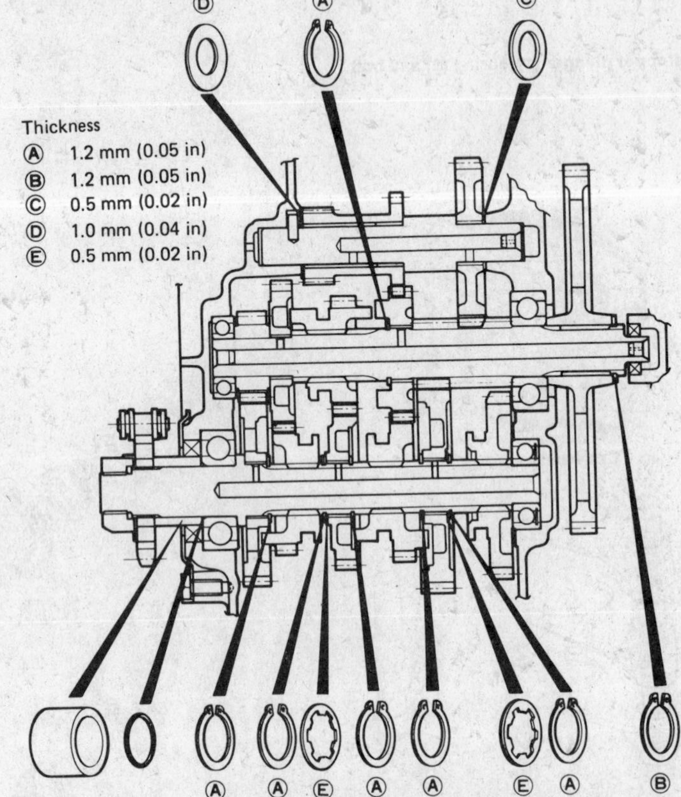

Transmission washers and circlips (125D)

Do not forget to hook up the cam stopper spring

Crankcase dowel pin locations ("A")

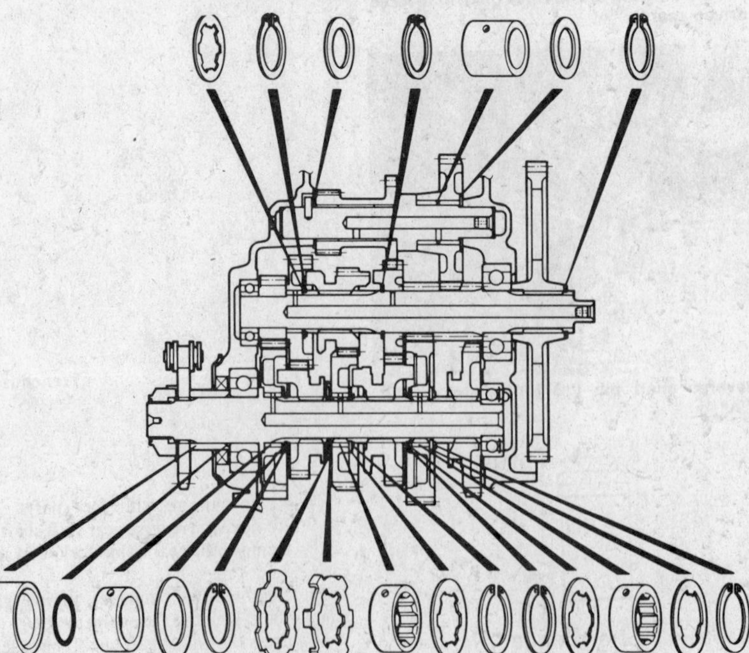

Transmission washers and circlips (125E-F, 185)

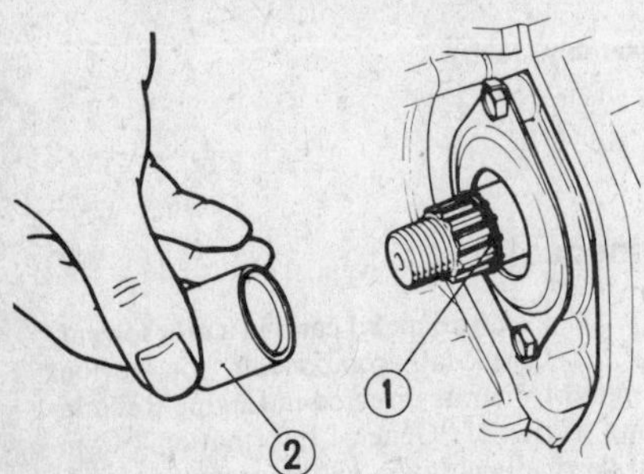

Transmission drive shaft o-ring (1); install spacer (2) with chamfered side in

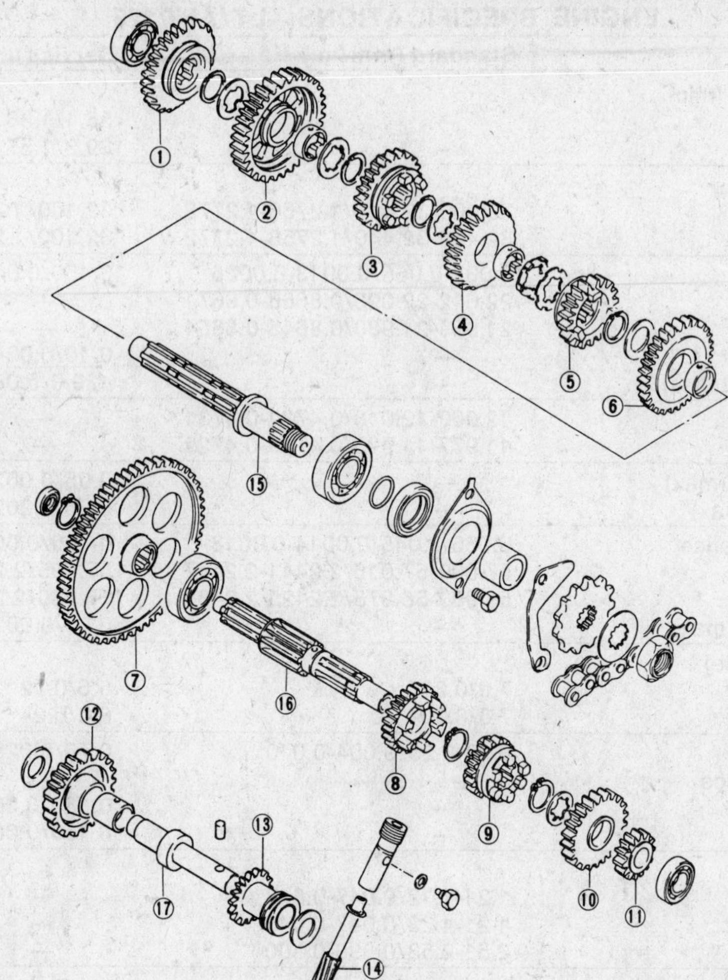

Transmission assembly (125E-F, 185)

12. Do not forget to connect the cam stopper spring.

13. Crankcase mating surfaces should be coated with liquid gasket compound.

NOTE: *Be certain the dowel pins and O-ring are in place on the left crankcase half before mating.*

14. Tighten the crankcase bolts gradually and evenly. Check that the crank and gear shafts can rotate freely as the bolts are tightened.

15. A new O-ring should be used on the transmission drive shaft. Install the O-ring. Fit the spacer with the chamfered side facing in.

16. Tighten the cam stopper bolt to 13-20 ft. lbs.

17. Note that the wide shoulder of the gear shift pawls must face the outside of the engine when the assembly is installed. Use a non-permanent thread locking compound on the screws.

18. When installing the gear shift shaft, be sure the pawl spring is properly engaged. Slip the shaft into place and mesh the center teeth with the center teeth of the shaft cam. Check shifting.

ENGINE SPECIFICATIONS—LT/ALT 125

Part	Standard (mm/in.)	Service limit (mm/in.)
Valve guide-to-stem clearance		
Intake	0.010-0.037/0.0004-0.0015	0.35/0.014
Exhaust	0.030-0.057/0.0012-0.0022	0.35/0.014
Valve guide ID	5.500-5.512/0.2165-0.2170	—
Valve stem OD		
Intake	5.475-5.490/0.2155-0.2161	—
Exhaust	5.455-5.470/0.2148-0.2153	—
Valve run-out (max)	—	0.05/0.002
Valve head thickness (min)	—	0.5/0.02
Valve stem end length	—	2.8/0.11
Valve seat width	0.9-1.1/0.035-0.043	—
Valve head radial run-out	—	0.03/0.001

ENGINE SPECIFICATIONS—LT/ALT 125

Part	Standard (mm/in.)	Service limit (mm/in.)
Valve spring free length (min)		
Inner	—	35.1/1.38
Outer	—	39.9/1.57
Cam lobe height		
Intake	32.400-32.440/1.2756-1.2772	32.100/1.2638
Exhaust	32.400-32.440/1.2756-1.2772	32.100/1.2638
Cam journal clearance	0.032-0.066/0.0013-0.0026	0.150/0.0059
Cam journal ID	22.012-22.025/0.8666-0.8671	—
Cam journal OD	21.959-21.980/0.8645-0.8654	—
Cam run-out (max)	—	0.10/0.004
Cam chain length (20 pitches)	—	129.0/5.08
Rocker arm ID	12.000-12.018/0.4724-0.4731	—
Rocker arm shaft OD	11.977-11.995/0.4715-0.4722	—
Cylinder head warpage (max)	—	0.05/0.002
Head cover warpage (max)	—	0.05/0.002
Piston to cylinder clearance	0.035-0.045/0.0014-0.0018	0.120/0.0047
Cylinder bore	57.000-57.015/2.2441-2.2447	57.095/2.2478
Piston diameter	56.960-56.975/2.2425-2.2431	56.880/2.2394
Cylinder dia. deviation (max)	—	0.05/0.002
Piston ring end-gap (free)		
Top	7.0/0.28	5.6/0.22
Second	7.5/0.30	6.0/0.24
Piston ring end gap	0.10-0.25/0.004-0.010	0.70/0.028
Piston ring side clearance		
Top	—	0.180/0.0071
Second	—	0.150/0.0059
Piston groove width		
Top	1.21-1.12/0.047-0.048	—
Second	1.21-1.23/0.047-0.048	—
Oil	2.51-2.53/0.099-0.100	—
Ring thickness		
Top	0.97-0.99/0.038-0.039	—
Second	1.17-1.19/0.046-0.047	—
Wrist pin bore ID	14.002-14.008/0.5513-0.5515	14.030/0.5524
Wrist pin OD	13.996-14.000/0.5510-0.5512	13.980/0.5504
Con rod small end ID	14.004-14.012/0.5513-0.5517	14.040/0.5528
Con rod lateral play (max)	—	3.0/0.12
Big end side clearance	0.10-0.45/0.0039-0.0177	1.00/0.039
Big end width	15.95-16.00/0.628-0.630	—
Crank web-to-web width	53.0 ± 0.1/2.086 ± 0.004	—
Crankshaft run-out (max)	—	0.05/0.002
Clutch specifications		
Drive plate thickness	2.9-3.1/0.11-0.12	2.6/0.10
Drive plate claw width	11.8-12.0/0.46-0.47	11.0/0.43
Driven plate warpage (max)	—	0.10/0.004
Spring free length (min)	—	27.4/1.08
Transmission specifications		
Shift fork groove clearance	0.10-0.30/0.004-0.012	0.50/0.020
Shift fork groove width		
1st, 2nd, 3rd	5.50-5.60/0.217-0.220	—
Reverse	4.50-4.60/0.177-0.181	—
Shift fork thickness		
1st, 2nd, 3rd	5.30-5.40/0.209-0.213	—
Reverse	4.30-4.40/0.169-0.173	—

ENGINE SPECIFICATIONS, LT/ALT 185

Part	Standard (mm/in.)	Service limit (mm/in.)
Valve guide-to-stem clearance		
Intake	0.010-0.037/0.0004-0.0015	0.35/0.014
Exhaust	0.030-0.057/0.0012-0.0022	0.35/0.014
Valve guide ID	5.500-5.512/0.2165-0.2170	—
Valve stem OD		
Intake	5.475-5.490/0.2155-0.2161	—
Exhaust	5.455-5.470/0.2148-0.2153	—
Valve run-out (max)	—	0.05/0.002
Valve head thickness (min)	—	0.5/0.02
Valve stem end length	—	2.6/0.10
Valve seat width	0.9-1.1/0.035-0.043	—
Valve head radial run-out	—	0.03/0.001
Valve spring free length (min)		
Inner	—	35.1/1.38
Outer	—	39.9/1.57
Cam lobe height		
Intake	33.780-33.820/1.3299-1.3315	33.480/1.3181
Exhaust	32.990-33.030/1.2988-1.3004	32.690/1.2870
Cam journal clearance	0.032-0.066/0.0013-0.0026	0.150/0.0059
Cam journal ID	22.012-22.025/0.8666-0.8671	—
Cam journal OD	21.959-21.980/0.8645-0.8654	—
Cam run-out (max)	—	0.10/0.004
Cam chain length (20 pitches)	—	129.0/5.08
Rocker arm ID	12.000-12.018/0.4724-0.4731	—
Rocker arm shaft OD	11.977-11.995/0.4715-0.4722	—
Cylinder head warpage (max)	—	0.05/0.002
Head cover warpage (max)	—	0.05/0.002
Piston to cylinder clearance	0.030-0.040/0.0012-0.0016	0.120/0.0047
Cylinder bore	63.000-63.015/2.4803-2.4809	63.100/2.4842
Piston diameter	62.965-62.980/2.4789-2.4795	62.880/2.4756
Cylinder dia. deviation (max)	—	0.05/0.002
Piston ring end-gap (free)		
Top		
N Mark	7.5/0.30	6.0/0.24
R mark	7.3/0.29	5.8/0.23
Second		
N mark	8.5/0.33	6.8/0.27
R mark	8.7/0.34	7.0/0.28
Piston ring end-gap	0.10-.25/0.004-0.010	0.70/0.028
Piston ring side clearance		
Top	—	0.180/0.0071
Second	—	0.150/0.0059
Piston groove width		
Top	1.21-1.23/0.047-0.048	—
Second	1.21-1.23/0.47-0.048	—
Oil	2.51-2.53/0.099-0.100	—
Ring thickness		
Top & second	1.170-1.190/0.0461-0.0469	
Wrist pin bore ID	14.001-14.008/0.5513-0.5515	14.030/0.5524
Wrist pin OD	13.994-14.002/0.5509-0.5517	13.980/0.5504
Con rod small end ID	14.004-14.012/0.5513-0.5517	14.040/0.5528
Con rod lateral play (max)	—	3.0/0.12
Big end slide clearance	0.10-0.45/0.004-0.018	1.00/0.039
Big end width	15.95-16.00/0.628-0.630	—
Crank web-to-web width	53.0 ± 0.1/2.087 ± 0.004	—
Crankshaft run-out (max)	—	0.05/0.002

ENGINE SPECIFICATIONS—LT/ALT 125

Part	Standard (mm/in.)	Service limit (mm/in.)
Clutch specifications		
Drive plate thickness	2.9-3.1/0.11-0.12	2.6/0.10
Drive plate claw width	11.8-12.0/0.46-0.47	11.0/0.43
Driven plate warpage (max)	—	0.10/0.004
Clutch spring free-length (min)	—	30.2/1.19
Transmission specifications		
Shift fork groove clearance	0.10-0.30/0.004-0.012	0.50/0.020
Shift fork groove width		
1st, 3rd	5.00-5.10/0.197-0.201	—
2nd	5.50-5.60/0.217-0.220	—
Reverse	4.50-4.60/0.177-0.181	—
Shift fork thickness		
1st, 3rd	4.80-4.90/0.189-0.193	—
2nd	5.30-5.40/0.209-0.213	—
Reverse	4.30-4.40/0.169-0.173	—
Countershaft length (low to 1st)	111.5/4.390	—

ENGINE TORQUE SPECIFICATIONS

Part	Torque (ft lbs.)
LT/ALT 125	
Cylinder head cover bolts	6.5-8.0
Cam sprocket bolts	7.0-9.5
Cylinder head nuts	
8 mm	11-15
6 mm	5-8
Cylinder base nuts	5-8
Magneto rotor nut	36-44
Clutch sleeve hub nut	29-44
Engine oil drain plug	13-15
Engine sprocket nut	58-73
Engine mounting bolt	
8 mm	20-25
10 mm	58-69
Exhaust pipe nuts at cylinder head	6.5-8.5
Muffler bracket bolt	13-20
Gearshift arm stopper bolt	11-17
Gearshift lever pinch bolt	6.0-8.5
LT/ALT 185	
Cylinder head cover bolts	6.5-8.0
Cam sprocket bolts	7.0-9.5
Cylinder head nuts	
8 mm	11-15
6 mm	5-8
Cam chain tensioner adjuster bolt	4.5-6.0
Cylinder base nuts	5-8
Magneto rotor nut	36-44
Clutch sleeve hub nut	44-58
Engine oil drain plug	13-15
Engine sprocket nut	73-94
Engine mounting bolts	
8 mm	20-25
10 mm	58-69
Exhaust pipe nuts at cylinder head	6.5-8.5
Muffler bracket bolt	13-20
Gearshift arm stopper bolt	11-17
Gearshift lever pinch bolt	6.0-8.5

FUEL SYSTEM

CARBURETOR

NOTE: *Refer to the "General Information" section for carburetor theory and trouble-shooting procedures.*

Removal

1. Remove the seat.
2. Unhook the fuel tank cap band, if fitted, and disconnect the tank vent hose from the tank.
3. Remove the four rear fender mounting bolts.
4. Remove the gas cap, if required, and remove the rear fender. Replace the gas cap.
5. Unscrew the starter plunger and pull it out of the carburetor.
6. Unscrew the carburetor cap and carefully pull the slide assembly out of the carburetor.
7. If the slide assembly is not going to be serviced, wrap it in a clean rag and place it out of the way to avoid accidental damage.
8. Disconnect the fuel line, breather hose and overflow hose from the carburetor.
9. Loosen the carburetor clamp screws.
10. Pull the carburetor body free of the intake manifold and air cleaner hoses.

WARNING: *The float bowl contains gasoline. Drain it inot a suitable container and dispose of it properly.*

Disassembly

1. Remove the three screws and take the priming pump from the float bowl.
2. Unscrew the four float bowl screws.
3. Remove the float bowl. If it will not come right off, hold bowl and carburetor body with one hand and rap the bowl with the handle of the screwdriver. When it breaks free, carefully lift the bowl off the carburetor.
4. Remove the float bowl gasket. A new gasket should be used when assembling.
5. Push out the float pivot pin. Carefully lift off the float assembly and the float needle.
6. Unscrew and remove the main jet.
7. Unscrew and remove the main nozzle. An O-ring may come out when the nozzle is taken out.
8. Unscrew and remove the pilot jet.
9. Use a wooden dowel and push the needle jet out from the top of the carburetor. If the O-ring did not come out with the nozzle, it will now.
10. Unscrew and remove the throttle stop (idle speed) screw, O-ring and spring.
11. Unscrew and remove the pilot screw, spring and O-rings.
12. Remove the screw which secures the float needle seat keeper. Remove the keeper, plate, needle seat and O-ring.
13. Remove the drain screw from the float bowl.
14. To disassemble the throttle slide, compress the spring against the carburetor cap, remove the stopper plate inside the slide, and disengage the throttle cable from the slide. Separate all components.
15. The starter plunger assembly may be separated by disconnecting the cable from the plunger.

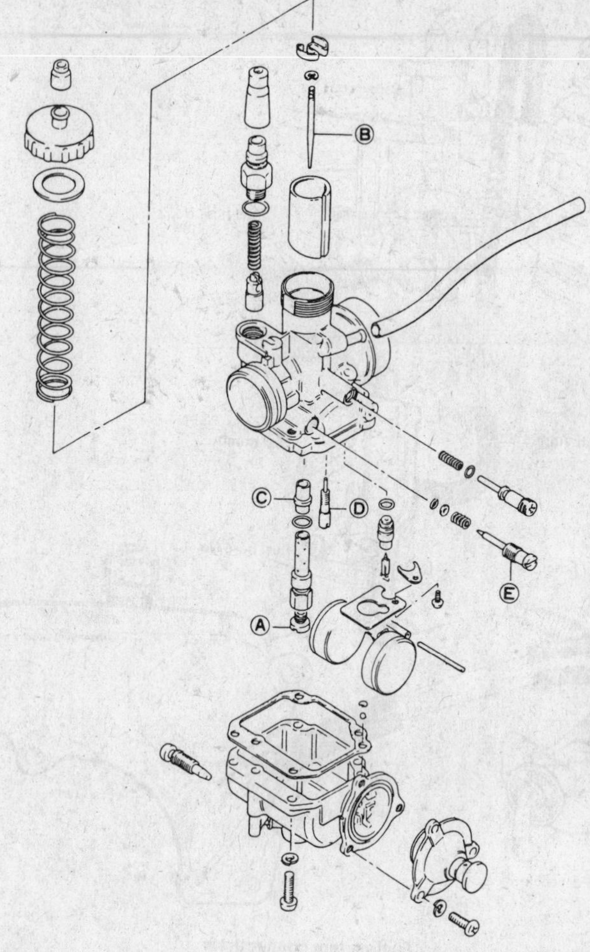

Carburetor: A, main jet; B, needle; C, needle jet; D, pilot jet; E, pilot screw

Inspection

NOTE: *Refer to "General Information" for carburetor service and inspection procedures.*

1. Clean all metal parts in a safe solvent.
2. All gaskets and O-rings should be replaced when assembling the carburetor.

Assembly

Carburetor assembly is basically the reverse of the disassembly procedures. Note the following points:

1. If the needle clip was removed, ensure that it is positioned in the correct needle groove from the top:
   LT/ALT 125: 2nd groove from top
   LT/ALT 185: 3rd groove from top
2. Use a little bit of oil to lubricate O-rings when installing. This will reduce the risk of knicking or tearing them.
3. Do not overtighten jets. They are brass and may be damaged.
4. When fitting the priming pump to the float bowl, position it so that the vent hole faces down.

Installation

1. Lubricate the lips of the manifold and air cleaner hoses to make it easier to install the carburetor.
2. Make sure that the hoses are not folded over or otherwise deformed when the carb is slipped into place.
3. Tighten the clamps after positioning the carburetor vertically.
4. Install the starter plunger.
5. When inserting the throttle slide, ensure that it slips right into the bore. Do not force it. The needle must enter the needle jet directly. Check throttle operation before attempting to start the engine.
6. Be sure that all carburetor lines are properly connected. Be sure safety clips are in place.
7. After installation, turn on the petcock and use the priming pump to prime the carburetor. Check for leaks.
8. Run the engine for several minutes and check again for leaks. Do not operate the machine until certain that all connections are properly made.

PETCOCK

The petcock is located on the front of the fuel tank and is accessible after removing the seat and rear fender.

To remove the petcock, remove the two screws, pull it out, and disconnect the fuel lines.

WARNING: *Watch for fuel leaks.*

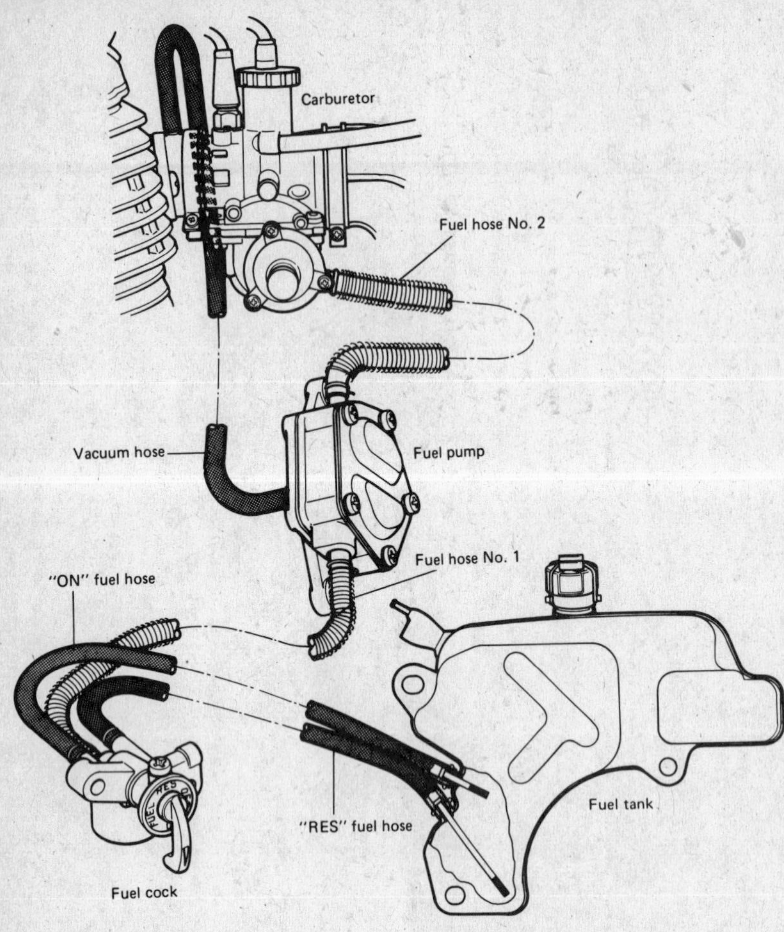

Fuel system connections

FUEL STRAINERS

Each line from the petcock to the gas tank is fitted with a fuel strainer at the tank end.

These lines should not be disconnected unless the tank is almost empty, or gasoline will be spilled.

If the tank is empty, remove the petcock, as outlined above, and disconnect the two lines from the tank.

Clean the strainers in clean solvent and blow them dry. If foreign matter cannot be removed, the strainer(s) must be replaced.

Be sure to connect the lines to the proper fitting. The longer strainer ("RES") is connected to the lower fitting.

WARNING: *Be sure that connections are properly made and tight. Check for leaks before operating the machine.*

FUEL PUMP

1. The fuel pump is mounted on the front of the fuel tank and is accessed by removing the seat and rear fender.

Fuel tank mounting bolts (1)

2. The pump needs no routine maintenance. However, if it fails, or shows signs of leaking, it must be replaced.
3. To remove the pump, remove the two mounting bracket bolts and disconnect the lines.
4. When fitting the pump, note that the line from the petcock goes to the inlet pipe on the pump which is marked "IN."

CAUTION: *When making pump connections, be sure that they are tight. Check for leaks before riding the machine.*

FUEL LINES

Fuel lines should be replaced every four years or whenever any of them shows signs of cracking, hardening or abrasion damage.

Refer to the illustration of the fuel system lines.

FUEL TANK

Removal and Disassembly

1. Remove the seat.
2. Unhook the fuel cap band, if equipped. Disconnect the fuel tank vent hose.
3. Remove the four securing bolts and take off the rear fender.
4. Remove the right side rear wheel. See "Chassis" for procedures.
5. Disconnect the vacuum hose from the fuel pump.
6. Disconnect the fuel line at the carburetor.
7. Remove the three mounting bolts and take out the fuel tank.

CAUTION: *Handle the tank and its contents carefully.*

8. Empty the contents of the tank into a suitable container—one which is safe for the storage of flammable gasoline.
9. Remove the petcock mounting screws.
10. Pull the petcock out and disconnect the lines.
11. Remove the two bracket bolts which secure the fuel pump.
12. Disconnect the lines and remove the fuel pump.

Assembly and Installation

1. Reverse the removal procedure.
2. Be sure that all connections are properly made. Refer to the fuel oine diagram.
3. Be certain that all fuel and vacuum line connections are tight and that all safety clips and clamps are in place.
4. Be sure that tank and component mounting bolts are properly tightened.
5. Fill the tank with fuel and check for leaks before operating the machine.

CARBURETOR SPECIFICATIONS

	LT/ALT 125D	LT/ALT 125E-F	LT/ALT 185
Type	VM20SS	VM20SS	VM22SS
ID No.	18900	18911/12	24400/01
Fuel level (mm/in.)	4.5 ± 0.5/0.18 ± 0.02	4.5 ± 0.5/0.18 ± 0.02	4.5 ± 0.5/0.18 ± 0.02
Float weight (mm/in.)	25.8 ± 1.0/1.02 ± 0.04	25.8 ± 1.0/1.02 ± 0.04	25.8 ± 1.0/1.02 ± 0.04

CARBURETOR SPECIFICATIONS

	LT/ALT 125D	LT/ALT 125E-F	LT/ALT 185
Type	VM20SS	VM20SS	VM22SS
ID No.	18900	18911/12	24400/01
Main jet	100	100	115
Main air jet	1.4	1.4	1.4
Needle	4JR39-2	4JU42-2	5L15-3
Needle jet	0-4	0-2	0-2
Throttle slide cutaway	3.0	2.5	2.0
Pilot jet	20	20	20
Starter jet	30	25	30
Pilot screw (turns out)	1ı	1	2¿
Pilot air jet	1.4	1.4	1.7
Pilot outlet	0.7	0.7	0.7

ELECTRICAL SYSTEM

IGNITION SYSTEM

The major components of the ignition system are the CDI unit, the magneto coil, the ignition coil and the spark plug.

Ignition Coil

The ignition coil is mounted on the frame above the cylinder head.

1. Remove the seat.
2. On LT models, remove the front fender. On ALT models, remove the front frame cover.
3. Disconnect the black ignition coil low tension lead.

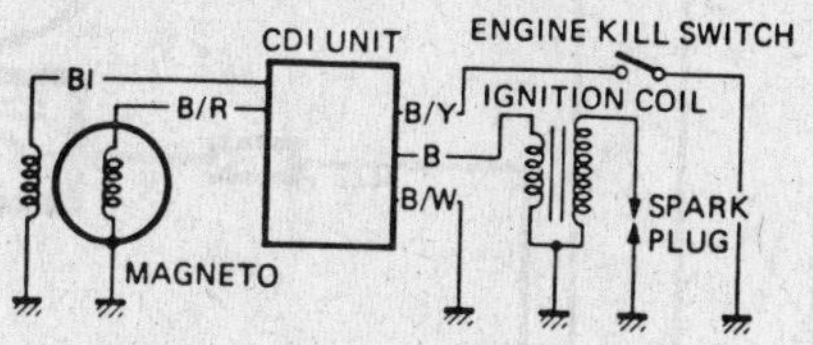

Ignition schematic

4. Measure the resistance between the black lead and a good ground on the chassis. It should be 0.5-1.5 ohms. This is the primary coil resistance. If the reading indicates and open or short circuit, replace the ignition coil.
5. Disconnect the spark plug high tension lead.
6. Measure the resistance between the spark plug cap and a good ground on the chassis. It should be 15-25,000 ohms. This is the secondary coil resistance. If the reading obtained is not within this range, remove the spark plug cap and repeat the test. A good reading at this time indicates a defective cap. If the reading is still not correct, replace the ignition coil.

Magneto Coils

Magneto windings can be checked after disconnecting the wiring on the harness near the cylinder head.

1. Remove the seat.
2. On LT models, remove the front fender. On ALT models, remove the front frame cover.
3. Disconnect the blue and the black/red wires at the connectors near the CDI unit.
4. Check pick-up coil resistance by measuring resistance across the blue wire and ground. It should be about 130-200 ohms.
5. Check magneto power source coil resistance by measuring resistance across the black/red wire and ground. It should be 350-450 ohms.
6. If readings are not within specification, replace the respective components.

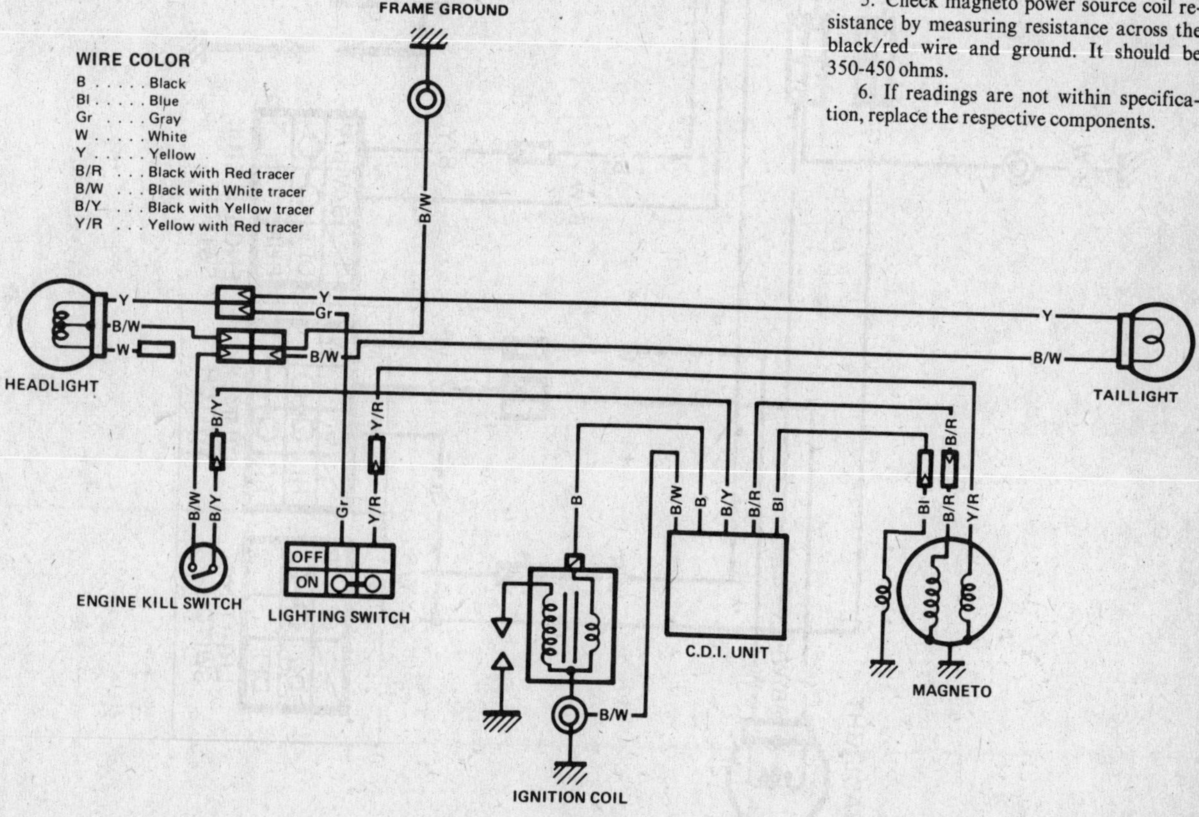

125 Models

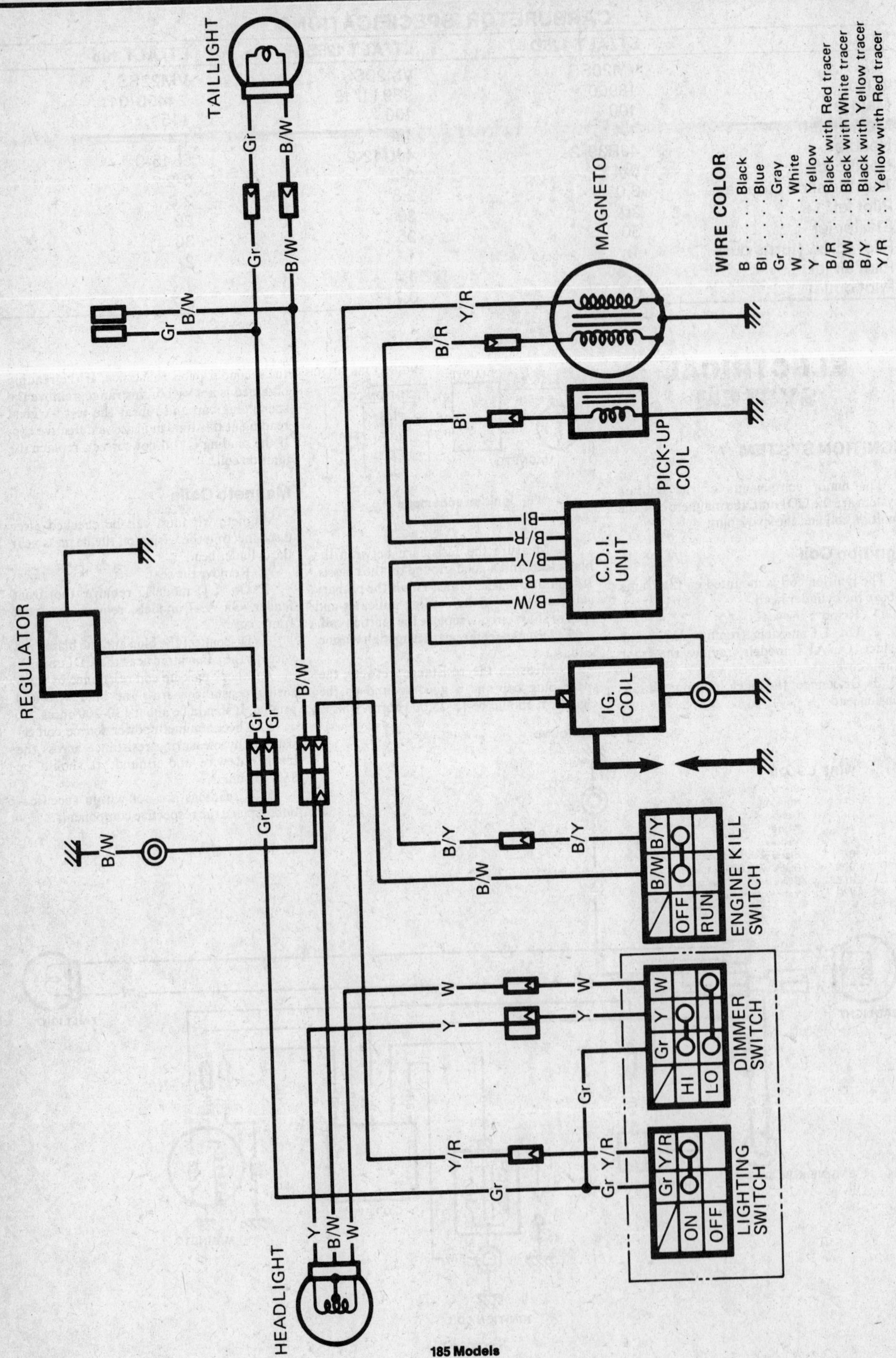

TAILLIGHT
MAGNETO
WIRE COLOR
B . . . . . . Black
Bl . . . . . Blue
Gr . . . . . Gray
W . . . . . . White
Y . . . . . . Yellow
B/R . . Black with Red tracer
B/W . . Black with White tracer
B/Y . . Black with Yellow tracer
Y/R . . Yellow with Red tracer
PICK-UP COIL
C.D.I. UNIT
IG. COIL
REGULATOR
ENGINE KILL SWITCH
OFF
RUN
DIMMER SWITCH
HI
LO
LIGHTING SWITCH
ON
OFF
HEADLIGHT

185 Models

CDI Unit

If the ignition coil, pick-up coil and power source coil all check out, but there is still no spark, suspect the CDI unit. The easiest test method is to replace the unit with a new one.

LIGHTING SYSTEM

The lighting system consists of a coil in the magneto, a regulator (on the 185) and the bulbs themselves.

1. A tachometer and an AC voltmeter are required for this test.
2. Remove the headlight.
3. Set the AC voltmeter to a suitable range for the expected maximum reading. Connect the positive probe to the high or low beam lead (yellow) and the negative probe to a good ground.
4. Start the engine, turn the lighting switch on, and note the readings at the relevant rpm. They are:
LT/ALT 125
Over 5.5 VAC @3000 rpm
Below 8.0 VAC @8000 rpm
LT/ALT 185
Over 9.0 VAC @2000 rpm
Below 14.0 VAC @8000 rpm
5. If the readings are too high on the 185, suspect the voltage regulator.
6. If the readings are too low, check the resistance across the lighting coil lead (yellow/red) and a good ground on the chassis or engine. If the resistance check shows an open or short circuit, the coil is defective.

ELECTRICAL SWITCHES

Switches can be checked with an ohmmeter or a battery-powered test light.

Engine Kill Button

1. The switch can be checked after disconnecting the black/yellow and black/white wires inside the headlight housing.
2. When the switch is set to either "OFF" position, there should be continuity between the black/yellow and black/white wires.
3. When the switch is in the "RUN" position, there should be no continuity.
4. If both these conditions are not met, the switch is defective and must be replaced.

Light Switch

1. The switch can be checked after disconnecting the green and the ywllow/red leads inside the headlight housing.
2. When the switch is in the "ON" position, there should be continuity between the green and the yellow/red leads.
3. When the switch is in the "OFF" position, there must be no continuity.
4. Replace the switch if operation is faulty.

Dimmer Switch

1. The switch can be checked at the plastic connector inside the headlight housing.
2. When the dimmer switch is in the "HI" position, there should be continuity between the green and the yellow leads.
3. When the dimmer switch is in the "LO" position, there should be continuity between the green and the white leads.
4. If both of these conditions are not met, the switch must be replaced.

BULB SPECIFICATIONS

LT/ALT 125
Headlight: 25/25W, 6V
Taillight: 5W, 6V

LT/ALT 185
Headlight: 35/35W, 12V
Taillight: 5W, 12V

CHASSIS

FRONT WHEEL

Removal (ALT)

1. Park the machine on a level surface. Block the rear wheels so the machine won't roll.
2. If the front wheel hub is going to be disassembled, loosen the wheel nuts slightly to facilitate disassembly.
3. Remove both axle nut cotter pins.
4. Loosen both axle nuts.
5. Raise the front of the machine using a safe support beneath the engine. The front wheel will drop out of the forks.

Removal (LT)

1. Park the machine on a level surface. Block the rear wheels so the machine won't roll.
2. Loosen the front wheel nuts slightly.
3. Support the wheels off the ground using a safe support beneath the frame.
4. Remove the wheel nuts.
5. Remove the wheel.

Installation (ALT)

1. Reverse the removal procedure.
2. Tighten the wheels nuts to 15-23 ft. lbs.
3. Slip the wheel into the forks.
4. Lower the frame so that the forks are resting on the axle.
5. Tighten both axle nuts equally until the proper torque of 26-38 ft. lbs. is reached.
6. Install new axle nut cotter pins on both nuts.

Installation (LT)

1. Reverse the removal procedure. Install wheels valve stem out.
2. On 125 models, tighten the wheel nuts to 15-23 ft. lbs.
3. On 185 models, tighten the wheel nuts to 33-47 ft. lbs.

FRONT WHEEL HUB

Removal (ALT)

Loosen the wheel nuts before removing the wheel from the machine.

2. Remove the wheel as outlined above.
3. Remove the axle nuts from the axle.
4. Remove the axle nut spacers.
5. Pull out the axle.
6. Remove the long spacers.
7. Remove the wheel nuts and separate the hub from the wheel.

Removal (LT)

1. Remove the wheel as outlined above.
2. Remove the axle cap, if fitted.

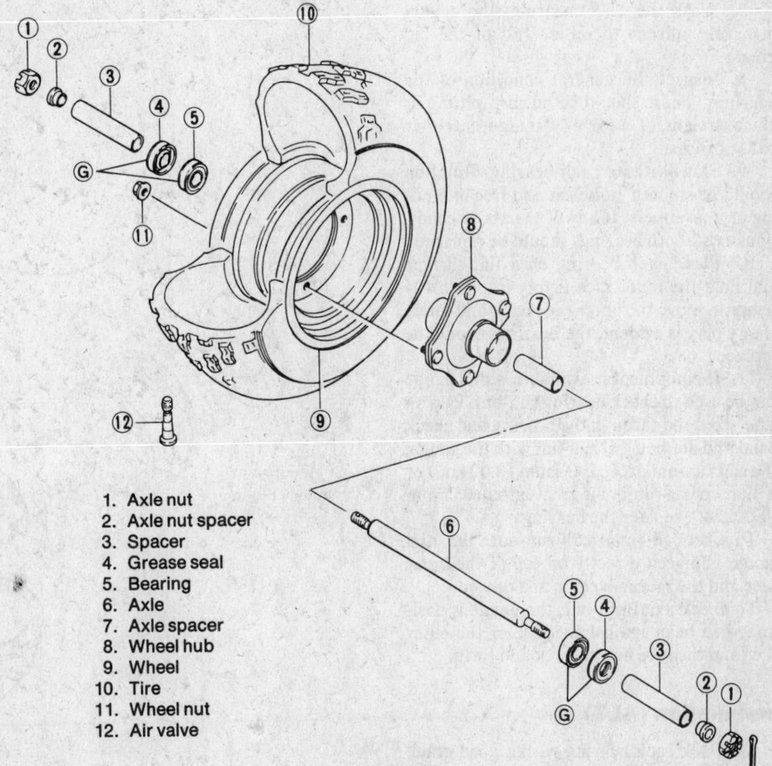

Front wheel (ALT)

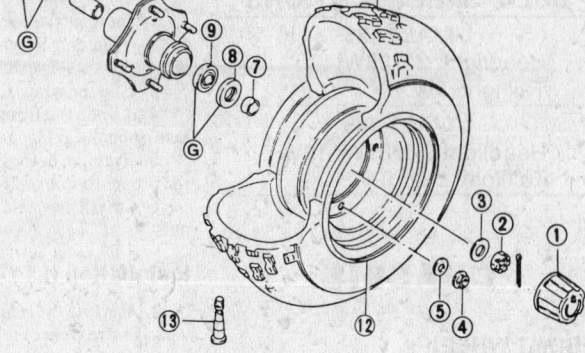

1. Axle cap
2. Axle nut
3. Washer
4. Wheel nut
5. Washer
6. Tire
7. Spacer
8. Grease seal
9. Bearing
10. Wheel hub
11. Spacer
12. Wheel
13. Air valve

Front wheel (LT)

3. Remove the axle nut cotter pin.
4. Remove the axle nut. Remove the washer.
5. Pull the hub off the axle.
6. Remove the spacer from the hub to avoid loosing it.

Inspection (All Models)

1. The wheel bearings are pressed into the hub. Attempted removal may damage bearings.
2. Remove any spacers on the hub.
3. Pry out the grease seals. New seals should be used when assembling.
4. Reach into the hub with a drift and drive out one bearing.
5. Remove the spacer.
6. Remove the remaining bearing in the same manner as the first.
7. Wash the wheel bearings thoroughly in a safe solvent to remove all of the old grease.
8. Inspect the general condition of the bearings. There should be no rust, pitting or obvious signs of wear or damage on either balls or races.
9. Slowly rotate each bearing. Rotation should be smooth, noiseless and free of binding or unevenness. If any of the above conditions exist, both bearings should be replaced.
10. Place each bearing on a flat surface and hold the inner race firmly in place. Attempt to move the outer race back and forth. If any play is evident, the bearings should be replaced.
11. If equipment is available, a dial gauge can be used to check bearing run-out. Pass an axle-sized rod through the bearing and check axial and diametrical run-out with the gauge. If axial run-out exceeds 0.1mm (0.004 in.) or if diametrical run-out is greater than 0.05mm (0.002 in.), replace the bearings.

To check diametrical run-out, the dial gauge is placed directly on top of the outer race and the race moved up and down.

To check axial run-out, the gauge is positioned to bear against the side of the outer race and the race moved back and forth.

Installation (ALT)

1. Pack each bearing with a good grade of waterproof, medium-weight bearing grease.
2. Clean old grease out of the hub and put in a small quantity of fresh grease.
3. Install the right side bearing first. Be sure to press it straight into the hub. Be certain the bearing is properly seated.

NOTE: *Wheel bearings which have a metal seal on one side must be installed with the sealed side out.*

4. Install the spacer.
5. Install the left side bearing.
6. Lubricate the lips of the grease seals and press them into the hub. Using new grease seals is recommended.
7. The remainder of the installation procedure is the reverse of removal. Do not forget the axle spacers. Tighten the wheel nuts to 15-23 ft. lbs. Tighten the axle nuts to 26-38 ft. lbs.

Installation (LT)

1. Pack each bearing with a good grade of waterproof, medium-weight bearing grease.
2. Clean old grease out of the hub and put in a small quantity of fresh grease.
3. Install the inside hub bearing first.

NOTE: *Bearings with a metal shield on one side must be installed with the sealed side out.*

4. Press the inside bearing into place ensuring that it is not cocked or tilted as it is installed. Be sure the bearing is properly seated.
5. Install the spacer.
6. Install the outside bearing.
7. Lubricate the lips of the grease seals and press them into the hub. Using new seals is recommended. Be sure they go straight in and are not cocked or tilted.
8. Install the axle spacer.
9. Install the hub on the axle.
10. Install the washer and axle nut.
11. Tighten the axle nut to 36-58 ft. lbs.
12. Use a new axle nut cotter pin.

REAR WHEELS (ALL MODELS)

Removal

1. Park the machine on a level surface. Block the front wheel(s) so the machine will not roll.

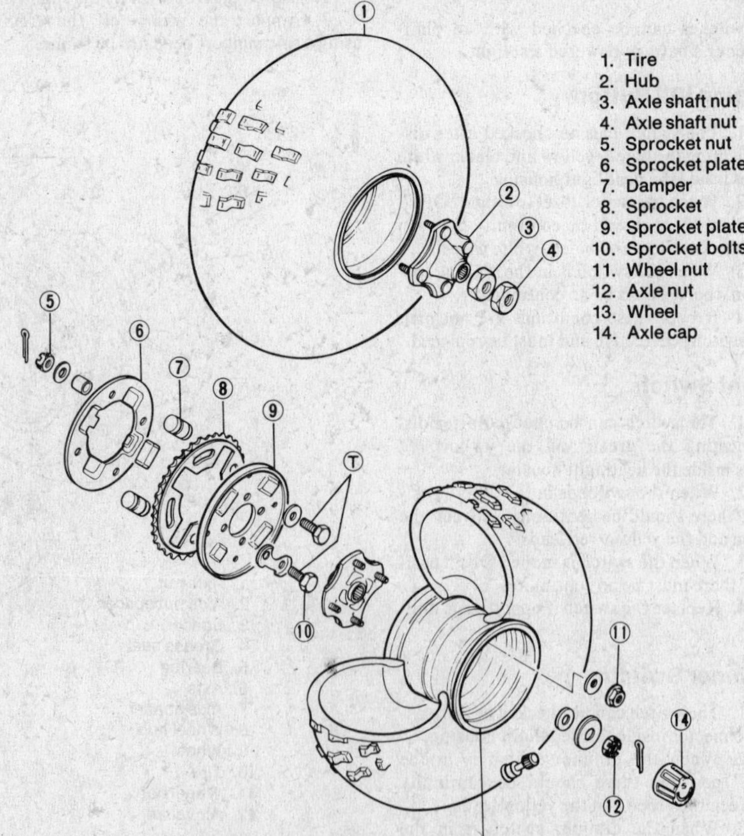

Rear wheel assembly

2. Loosen the wheel nuts.
3. Support the rear wheels an inch or so off the ground by placing a safe, sturdy jack or similar support beneath the frame.
4. Remove the wheel nuts and washers (if fitted).
5. Remove the wheel.

Installation

1. Install the wheel (valve stem out).
2. Install the wheel nut washers, if fitted.
3. Tighten the wheel nuts gradually and in a cross pattern until the proper torque is reached:
125 models: 15-23 ft. lbs.
185 models: 33-47 ft. lbs.

REAR WHEEL HUB (ALL MODELS)

Removal

1. Remove the axle cap, if fitted.
2. Remove the axle nut cotter pin.
3. Loosen the axle nut.
4. Remove the rear wheel as outlined above.
5. Remove the axle nut.
6. Remove the washers.
7. Pull the hub off the axle.

Inspection

1. Check the splines on both the hub and the axle for damage. Replace as required.
2. Clean the hub and axle splines and lubricate with a bit of grease before installation.

Installation

1. Reverse the removal procedure.
2. Tighten the axle nut to 62-83 ft. lbs.
3. Use a nex axle nut cotter pin.
4. Install the axle cap.

REAR SPROCKET

Removal

1. Remove the seat.
2. Remove the rear fender.
3. Remove the four bolts that mount the skid plate and remove the plate.
4. Remove the axle nut cap, if fitted.
5. Remove the axle nut cotter pin.
6. Loosen the axle nut.
7. Support both rear wheels an inch or so off the ground by placing a safe, sturdy support beneath the frame.
8. Remove the rear wheel nuts and take off the rear wheels. If only the sprocket is to be serviced, only the left wheel need be removed.
9. Remove the axle nut.
10. Remove the rear wheel hubs. See above for procedures.
11. Loosen the chain adjuster lock bolt.
12. Remove the chain case by removing the two nuts and releasing the four clamps.
13. Remove the chain tensioners sprocket pinch nut and bolt from the sprocket lever.
14. Remove the sprocket lever snap-ring.
15. Carefully pull the lever off the splined shaft.
16. Remove the engine sprocket guide plate bolt and screw. Remove the guide plate.
17. Flatten the engine sprocket nut locking tab. Remove the sprocket nut. Pull the sprocket off the shaft.
18. Bend down the locking tabs on the rear sprocket bolts.
19. Remove the four sprocket bolts.
20. Remove the sprocket from the axle.

Inspection

1. Check sprocket teeth for wear or damage.
2. To disassemble the sprocket, remove the cotter pins and the four nuts and separate the components.
3. Check the rubber dampers for damage. Replace as required.

Installation

1. Use a non-permanent thread-locking compound on the four sprocket assembly nuts. Tighten the nuts gradually and in a cross pattern until the proper torque of 6.0-8.5 ft. lbs. is reached. Use new cotter pins on the nuts.
2. The remainder of the installation procedure is basically the reverse of removal. Note the following points:
a. New locking tabs and new cotter pin should be used throughout when assembling.
b. Tighten the four sprocket bolts to 29-44 ft. lbs. Bend up the locking tabs.
c. Tighten the engine sprocket nut to 58-73 ft. lbs. on 125 models; 73-94 ft. lbs. on 185 models.
d. When installing the chain tensioner sprocket lever, be sure to align the slot in the lever with the punch mark on the shaft. Tighten the pinch bolt to 15-23 ft. lbs.
e. Do not forget the lever snap-ring.
f. Adjust chain free-play as outlined in "Maintenance".

REAR BRAKES

Disassembly

1. Remove the rear wheels. If only the brakes are to be serviced, remove the right side wheel only.
2. Remove the hub.
3. Remove the two axle shaft nuts.
4. Remove the six brake drum cover bolts.
5. Pull off the brake drum.
6. Pull off the two brake shoes and their springs together.
7. Back off the brake pedal and hand lever cable adjuster nuts at the brake cam lever.
8. Disconnect the cables from the brake cam lever.
9. Remove the pinch bolt holding the cam lever to the cam. Carefully pull off the lever.
10. Tap out the brake cam from the plate.

Inspection

1. Clean all parts thoroughly and check for unusual wear.
2. Minimum allowable brake lining thickness is 1.5mm (0.06 in.). Linings must be replaced as a set if either is thinner than this at any point.
3. Check the brake return springs for rusted, weakened or deformed condition.
4. Measure the brake drum diameter. Maximum allowable diameter is stamped on the drum (150.7mm/5.93 in.). The drum must be replaced as it exceeds this specification.
5. Clean the brake cam. Check the condition of the lever splines. Check that the cam is not cracked or bent.

Assembly

1. Use new brake cam O-rings.
2. Lightly grease the cam before installation.
3. When fitting the brake lever to the cam, align the punch mark on the lever with the slash mark on the cam. Tighten the pinch bolt to 6.0-8.5 ft. lbs.

Rear sprocket bolts

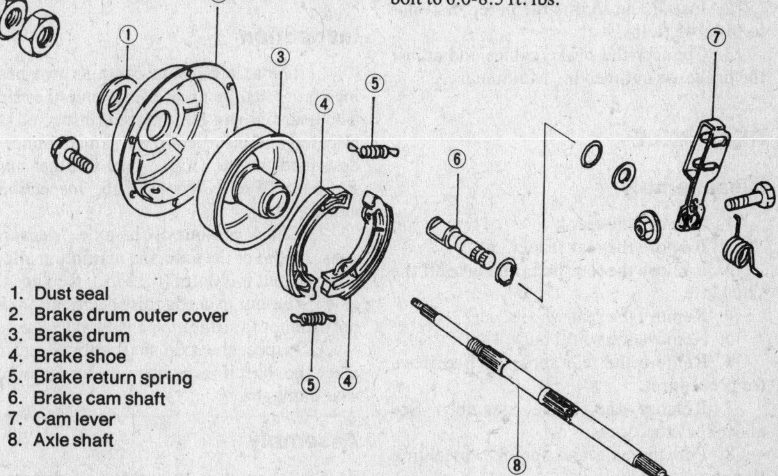

Rear brake assembly

4. Hook the brake lever return spring to the lever.

5. Lightly grease the brake cam and the pivot pin on which the brake shoes ride.

6. Assemble the shoes and their return springs and fold them onto the brake plate.

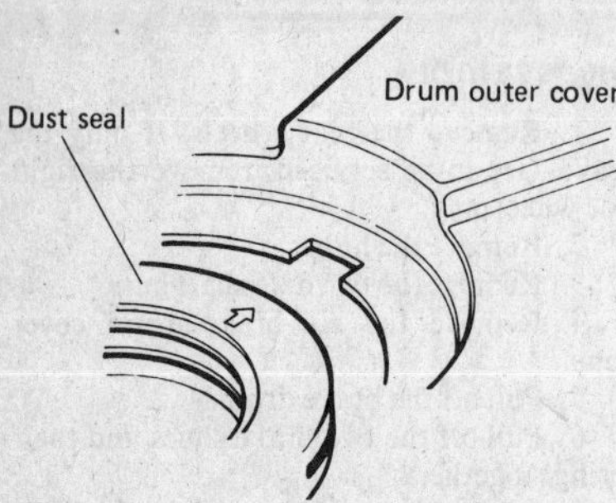

Align dust seal arrow with drum cover notch

7. If a new brake drum cover dust seal is installed, align the arrow on the seal with the notch in the cover. Hold the seal in place with thread-locking compound.

8. Grease the axle splines and apply some to the brake drum dust seal.

CAUTION: *Do not allow grease to contact the axle shaft threads.*

9. Install the drum cover. Tighten the cover bolts to 3-5 ft. lbs.

10. The axle shaft nuts must be secured with a non-permanent thread-locking compound.

Axle shaft nuts (2) must be secured with non-permanent thread-locking compound and properly torqued

11. Install and torque the inner shaft nut to 36-58 ft. lbs.

12. Install and torque the outer shaft nut to 116-145 ft. lbs.

13. Connect the brake cables and adjust the brakes as outlined in "Maintenance."

REAR AXLE

Disassembly

1. Remove the seat.
2. Remove the rear fender.
3. Remove the four bolts and take off the skid plate.
4. Remove the rear wheels.
5. Remove the wheel hubs.
6. Remove the rear sprocket. See above for procedures.
7. Remove the brake assembly. See above for procedures.
8. Pull the axle and sprocket mounting flange out to the left.
9. Move the sprocket mounting flange aside. Remove the ring. Remove the flange from the axle shaft.
10. Remove the brake drum inner cover which is mounted by three nuts with cotter pins.
11. Remove the three bolts mounting the axle housing to the inner chain case. Remove the housing.

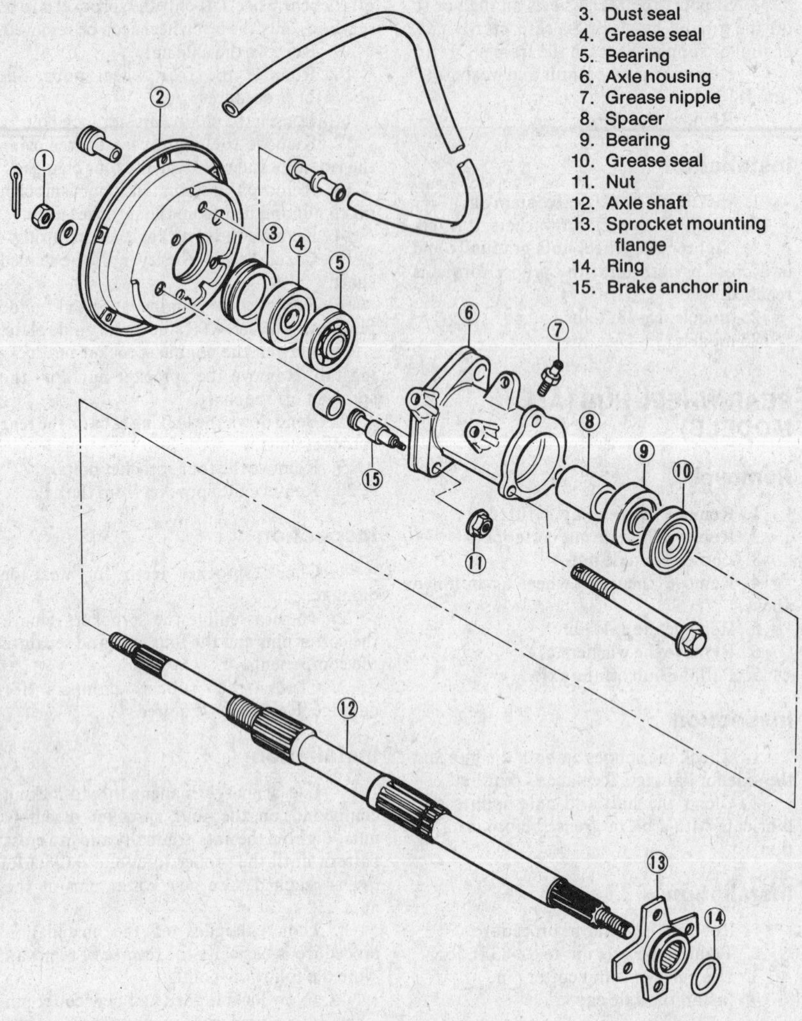

1. Axle housing nut
2. Brake drum inner cover
3. Dust seal
4. Grease seal
5. Bearing
6. Axle housing
7. Grease nipple
8. Spacer
9. Bearing
10. Grease seal
11. Nut
12. Axle shaft
13. Sprocket mounting flange
14. Ring
15. Brake anchor pin

Rear axle assembly

Inspection

1. The axle housing contains two bearings protected by grease seals on either side. The bearings can be removed, inspected, lubricated and installed in the same manner as described for the front wheel hub bearings. Refer to "Front Wheel Hub, Inspection," above.

2. Check run-out of the axle. Measured near the end of the axle, the maximum allowable run-out is 3.0mm (0.12 in.). Replace the axle if run-out exceeds this specification. Do not attempt to straighten a bent axle.

3. Inspect the axle shaft splines and replace the shaft if the splines are torn or otherwise damaged.

Assembly

1. Assembly is the reverse of disassembly.

2. Torque the axle housing mounting nuts to 13-20 ft. lbs. and secure them with new cotter pins. Bend the cotter pins so that they will not contact the brake shoes.

FRONT FORKS (ALT)

Removal

1. Remove the front wheel.
2. Remove the front fender (four screws).
3. Remove the extension from the forks (four bolts).
4. Remove the headlight (two screws).
5. Disconnect the leads and pull the wiring out of the headlight housing.
6. Remove the housing bolts and remove the headlight housing.
7. Run down the brake cable adjuster and disconnect the cable from the hand lever.
8. Remove the throttle lever cover. Disconnect the throttle cable from the lever.
9. Remove the handlebar clamp bolts. Remove the clamps and handlebars.
10. Remove the handlebar holder nuts under the upper triple clamp. Remove the holders.
11. Remove the upper triple clamp by

removing the two bolts above the fork tubes and the crown nut on the steering stem.

12. Hold the forks. Loosen the steering stem nut and lower the forks out of the frame lug.

CAUTION: *Lower race bearing balls may fall out as the forks are lowered free of the frame lug.*

Inspection

1. Wash the ball bearings in a suitable solvent.
2. Clean all the old grease from the bearing race surfaces, steering stem, and frame lug.
3. Inspect the bearing race surfaces. They must be clean and smooth and free of any cracks, scoring, rust, or indentations. Run your finger around each of the bearing races. Note any roughness or ripples on the race surface. If any imperfections are noted both sets of races and all of the balls must be replaced.
4. Check the balls themselves for rust, pitting, scoring, or flat spots. If the balls are found to be defective in any way, the balls and both sets of races must be replaced.

NOTE: *Balls and races must always be replaced in a set because worn races will destroy new balls and worn balls will destroy new races.*

5. Check the steering stem for cracks or a bent condition; this is especially important if the machine has been involved in a spill.
6. The bearing races in the frame lug are press fit and should not be removed unless replacement is necessary. If required, they can be removed by reaching through the frame lug with a suitable punch and tapping the race evenly around its circumference until it comes out. Be sure that the race does not become cocked while attempting removal.
7. The bottom cone race on the steering stem will usually have to be pried or chiseled off. Inspect it in place.

Installation

1. New races are installed with a suitably sized bearing driver, i.e., one which will cover the race and drive it squarely into the seat. Be certain the race goes straight in.
2. Install the lower cone race on the steering stem. Use a good grade of bearing grease to coat the lower cone race and the upper race in the frame lug.
3. Embed 18 bearing balls in the stem lower race and 22 bearing balls in the upper race in the frame lug.
4. When the balls are all in place, slip the steering stem through the frame lug and hold it in place while refitting the upper cone race, dust seal cover and steering stem nut.
5. Tighten the steering stem nut to 29-36 ft. lbs. Work the forks back and forth several times to seat races and balls. Back the stem nut off 1/4-1/2 turn.
6. Check bearing adjustment by noting movement of the fork. It should be smooth and free—but with no play. Turn the steering stem nut as required until fork operation is satisfactory. Grasp the lower ends of the fork tubes after the upper triple clamp is installed and attempt to move them back and forth in line with the machine. If there is play, tighten the steering stem nut. Check that free side-to-side movement of the forks is not inhibited.

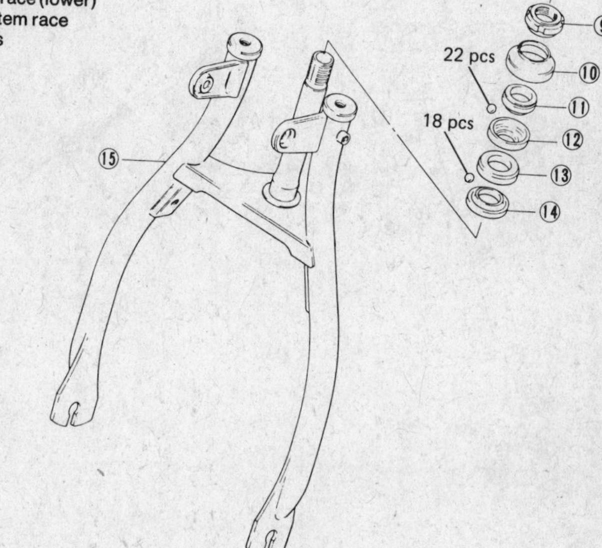

Front fork assembly (ALT)

7. Install the upper triple clamp. Tighten the crown nut to 26-40 ft. lbs. Tighten the bolts above the fork tubes to 26-40 ft. lbs.
8. When installing the handlebar assembly, tighten the holder nuts to 15-26 ft. lbs. Align the handlebars so that the punch mark on the bar matches the mating surface of the holders. Tighten the clamp bolts to 9-15 ft. lbs. Tighten these bolts evenly so the gap between clamp and holder is the same front and rear.
9. The remainder of the procedure is the reverse of removal.
10. Check fork bearing adjustment after assembly.

STEERING (LT 125)

Removal and Disassembly

1. Remove the front wheels.
2. Remove the wheel hubs.
3. Remove the cotter pins and take off the knuckle arm nuts and bolts.
4. Remove the cotter pins and nuts securing the rod-ends to the knuckle arms.
5. Disconnect the rod-ends from the knuckle arms.
6. Remove the knuckle arms from the frame.
7. Remove the seat.
8. Remove the odometer.
9. Remove the front fender.
10. Remove the left and right front grip support tube tightening bolts.
11. Remove the front grip with support tube from the frame (four bolts).
12. Remove the two screws and remove the headlight.
13. Disconnect the wires in the headlight housing and carefully pull them out.
14. Remove the steering shaft wiring clamp.
15. Remove the throttle lever housing screws and remove the cover. Disconnect the throttle cable.
16. Run down the brake adjuster and disconnect the brake cable from the hand lever.
17. Remove the four clamp bolts and take off the handlebars.
18. Remove the steering shaft bottom nut cotter pin, nut and washers.
19. Remove the steering shaft holder nut cotter pins. Remove the nuts and bolts. Remove the holders.
20. Remove the steering shaft from the frame.
21. Remove the tie rods from the steering shaft.

Front grip support tube tightening bolts

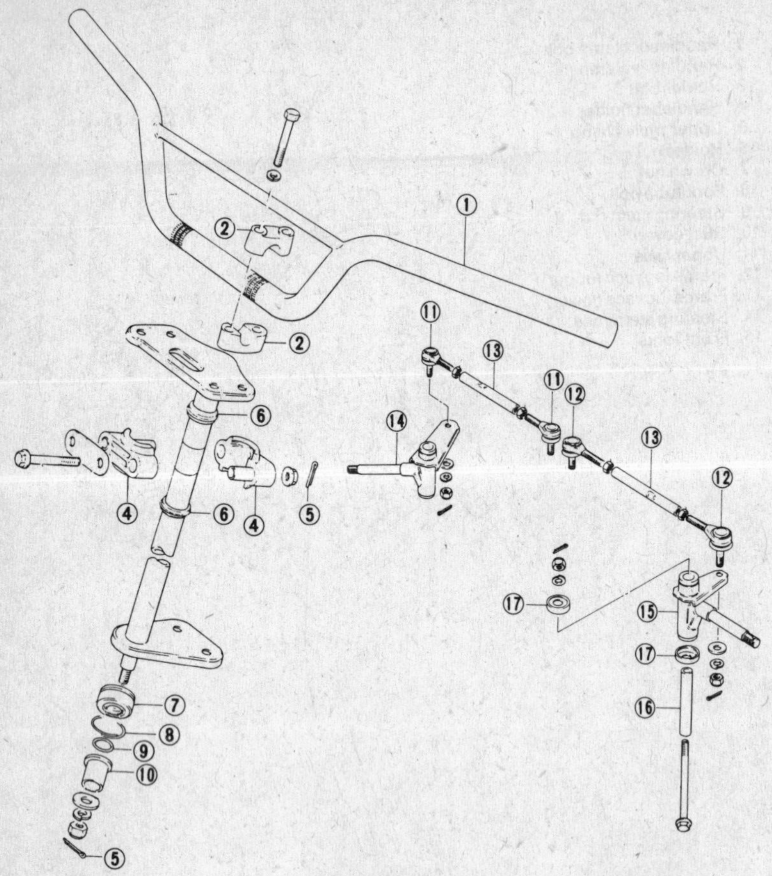

Steering assembly (LT 125)

Inspection

1. Clean metal parts thoroughly in a safe solvent.
2. Check all metal parts for signs of distortion, for cracks, deformation and other obvious indications of damage.
3. Remove the dust caps from the top and bottom of the knuckle arms and take out the spacer. Check for damage.
4. Check the dust seals for cracks or wear and replace if necessary.

Steering shaft dust seal and circlip

5. Check the steering shaft for a bent condition. If it is bent, replace it. Do not attempt to straighten a bent shaft.
6. Check the condition of the steering shaft bushing in the frame and the portion of the lower shaft which rides on it. There should be no play of the shaft in the bushing. If there is, the bushing can be driven out of the frame with a drift and replaced with a new unit.
7. Inspect the dust seal at the lower end of the steering shaft. The seal is secured by a clip.
8. Check holder condition.
9. Be sure both tie-rods are straight. Replace any bent or damaged units.
10. Check all grease and dust seals for condition. Replace as required.

Assembly

NOTE: *All cotter pins in the steering assembly should be replaced with new ones when assembling.*

Grease the dust seal at the bottom of the steering shaft before installing it. Fit the dust seal circlip.

2. Install the tie rods on the steering shaft. Tighten the nuts to 29-44 ft. lbs.

NOTE: *The tie rods must be installed so that the flats are closer to the steering shaft than to the wheels.*

3. Use a good quality bearing grease and lubricate the steering shaft bushing in the frame and the shaft holders.

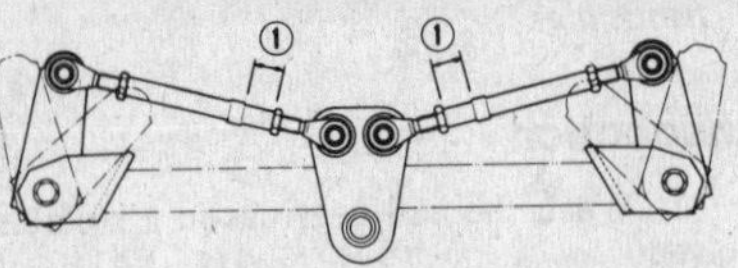

Tie rods are installed with flats (1) closer to steering shaft

4. Install the steering shaft.
5. Install the holders. Dust seals on the holders should be installed so that the gaps face forward.
6. Use a new O-ring on the steering shaft bottom nut.
7. Grease the bottom nut O-ring and install it. Install the washers. Tighten the nut to 16-26 ft. lbs. Use a new cotter pin.
8. Tighten the holder nuts to 13-20 ft. lbs.
9. Grease the knuckle arm spacers and install them. Grease and install the dust caps.
10. Grease the knuckle arm bolts.
11. Install the knuckle arms and tighten the nuts to 29-44 ft. lbs.
12. Connect the tie-rod ends to the steering knuckles. Tighten the nuts to 29-44 ft. lbs.
13. When fitting the handlebars, note that the punch mark should align with the holder mating surface.
14. Tighten the handlebar clamp bolts evenly so that the gap between clamp and holder is equal front and rear. Torque is 7-12 ft. lbs.
15. The remainder of the procedure is the reverse of disassembly. Check the "Chassis Torque Specifications" chart for correct torque settings.
16. Adjust toe-in as described below.

Toe-In Adjustment

NOTE: *Outer locknuts on tie-rods (yellow finish) have left-hand threads.*

1. Park the vehicle on a level surface.
2. Be sure the tires are inflated to the proper specification (2.2 psi).
3. Position the handlebars straight ahead.

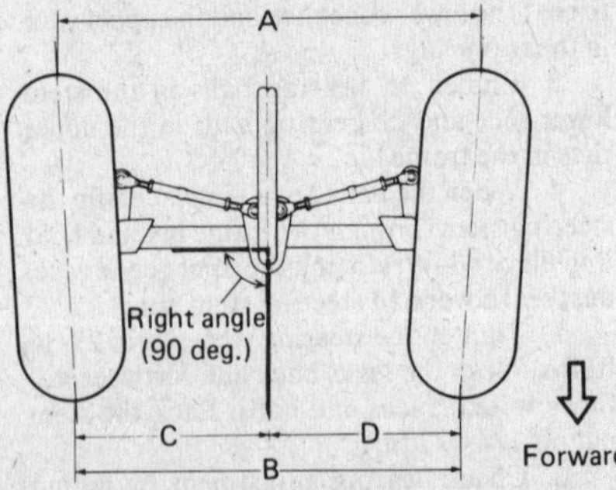

Subtract "B" from "A" for toe-in dimension; "C" and "D" must be equal

4. Measure the distance from centerline to centerline of the two front tires. Measure this distance at the very front of the tires. Make another measurement 180° from the first.

5. Subtract the first measurement from the second. The final figure is toe-in. It should be 5-11mm (0.2-0.4 in.).

6. If this is not the value obtained, adjust as follows.

7. Loosen the two locknuts on each tie-rod.

8. Turn each rod with a wrench on the flats provided as necessary to bring toe-in into specification.

CAUTION: *It is critical that both rods be turned by equal amounts, assuming that other components have not been disturbed or damaged. The distance from the centerline of the steering shaft to the centerline of each tire must be equal.*

9. When toe-in is correct and the distance from the centerline of the steering shaft to the centerline of both tires is equal, tighten the tie-rod locknuts to 16-26 ft. lbs.

FRONT SUSPENSION (LT 185)

Removal And Disassembly

1. Remove the front wheels.
2. Remove the hubs.
3. Disconnect the tie-rods from the knuckle arms by removing the cotter pins and nuts.
4. Remove the knuckle arms by removing the knuckle arm nut cotter pins, nuts and bolts.
5. Remove the upper and lower shock absorber mounting bolts and take off the shock absorbers.
6. Remove the knuckle arm holders from the wishbone arms (two bolts).
7. Remove the wishbone arms.
8. Disconnect the tie-rods from the steering shaft by pulling out the cotter pins on the nuts, removing the nuts and taking off the tie-rods.
9. Remove the seat.
10. Remove the odometer.
11. Remove the front fender.
12. Remove the cotter pin on the steering shaft bottom nut. Remove the bottom nut.
13. Run down the brake adjusters and disconnect the brake cable from the hand lever.
14. Remove the two screws and take off the throttle lever housing cover.
15. Disconnect the throttle cable from the lever.
16. Remove the cable clamp from the steering shaft.
17. Remove the steering shaft holder nut cotter pin. Remove the nuts and bolts. Remove the holders and dust seals.
18. Remove the handlebar clamp bolts and take off the handlebars.
19. Remove the headlight.
20. Disconnect the wiring inside the headlight housing and carefully pull the wires out.
21. Remove the headlight housing.
22. Remove the steering shaft from the frame.

Inspection

1. Clean metal parts thoroughly.
2. Check all metal parts for signs of distortion, for cracks, deformation and other obvious indications of damage.
3. Check the shock absorbers for signs of leakage. Repair is not possible. Replace any leaking units. Shocks should be replaced as a set for uniform performance.
4. Check the shock absorber springs for condition.
5. Check the steering shaft for a bent condition. If it is bent, replace it. Do not attempt to straighten the shaft.
6. Check the steering shaft holders for wear. Replace as necessary.
7. Be sure both tie-rods are straight. Replace any bent or damaged units.
8. Check all dust and grease seals for condition. Replace as required.
9. Inspect wishbone arm bushings for play. There should not be any. If there is, the bushings must be replaced.
10. Check for play of the lower steering shaft bushing. Replace if play is noted.
11. If replacement is required, the steering shaft bushing can be driven out of the frame with a suitable drift.
12. Remove the dust caps from the top and bottom of the knuckle arms and take out the spacer. Check for damage.
13. Inspect the dust seal at the lower end of the steering shaft. The seal is secured by a clip.

Assembly

NOTE: *All cotter pins in the front suspension must be replaced with new ones when assembling.*

1. Grease the dust seal at the bottom of the steering shaft before installing it. Fit the dust seal circlip.
2. Grease the steering shaft bushing in the frame, the portion of the shaft that rides on it, the holders and the portion of the shaft that contacts the holders. Use a good grade of bearing grease.
3. Install the steering shaft.
4. Install the holders. The dust seals on the holders should be installed so that the gaps face forward. Tighten the holder nuts to 13-20 ft. lbs.
5. Use a new O-ring on the steering shaft bottom nut.
6. Grease the bottom nut O-ring and install it. Install the washers. Tighten the bottom nut to 15-26 ft. lbs. Use a new cotter pin.

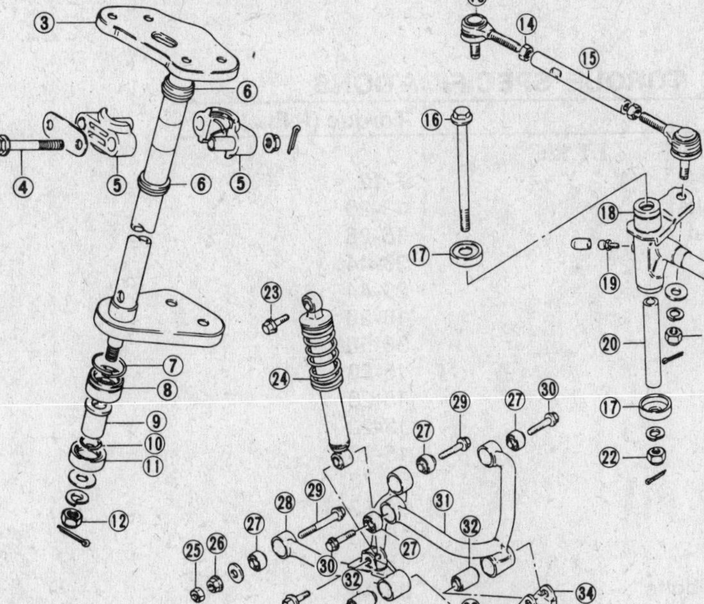

1. Handlebar clamp bolt
2. Clamp
3. Steering shaft
4. Holder bolt
5. Steering shaft holder
6. Dust seal
7. Circlip
8. Dust seal
9. Lower bushing
10. O-ring
11. Dust seal
12. Steering shaft bottom nut
13. Rod-end
14. Locknut
15. Tie rod
16. Knuckle arm bolt
17. Dust seal
18. Knuckle arm
19. Grease nipple
20. Spacer
21. Rod-end nut
22. Knuckle arm nut
23. Shock absorber bolt
24. Shock absorber
25. Wishbone arm front locknut
26. Wishbone arm front nut
27. Bushing
28. Wishbone lower arm
29. Wishbone arm inner bolt (lower)
30. Wishbone arm inner bolt (upper)
31. Upper wishbone arm
32. Bushing
33. Wishbone arm outer bolt
34. Knuckle arm holder

Front suspension (LT 185)

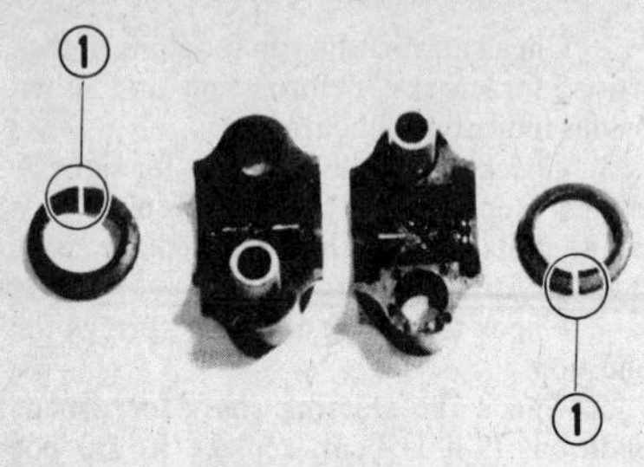

Install dust seals with gaps (1) facing forward

7. Attach tie-rod ends to the steering shaft. Tighten the nuts to 29-44 ft. lbs. Use new cotter pins.

NOTE: *Install the tie-rods so that the flats are closer to the steering shaft than to the wheels.*

8. When fitting the handlebars, note that the punch mark should be aligned with the holder mating surface.

9. Tighten the handlebar clamp bolts evenly so that the gap between clamp and holder is equal front and rear. Bolt torque is 7-12 ft. lbs.

10. The remainder of the procedure is basically the reverse of disassembly. Be certain that all fasteners are correctly torqued. The upper and lower wishbone arm bolts on the frame are tightened to 36-51 ft. lbs.

11. The knuckle arm holder bolts are tightened to 51-73 ft. lbs.

12. Grease the knuckle arm spacers with a good grade of bearing grease and install them. Grease and install the knuckle arm dust caps.

13. Grease the knuckle arm bolts.

14. Install the knuckle arms and tighten the nuts to 30-44 ft. lbs.

15. Connect the tie-rod ends to the knuckle arms. Tighten the nuts to 29-44 ft. lbs.

16. Adjust toe-in as outlined below.

Toe-In Adjustment

NOTE: *Outer locknuts on tie-rods (yellow finish) have left-hand threads.*

1. Park the vehicle on a level surface.
2. Be sure the tires are inflated to the proper specifications.
3. Position the handlebars straight ahead.
4. Measure the distance from centerline to centerline of the two front tires. Measure this distance at the very front of the tires. Make another measurement 180° form the first.
5. Subtract the first measurement from the second. The final figure is the toe-in. It should be 12-18mm (0.5-0.7 in.).
6. If this is not the value obtained, adjust as follows.
7. Loosen the two locknuts on each tie rod.
8. Turn each rod with a wrench on the flats provided as necessary to bring toe-in into specificiation.

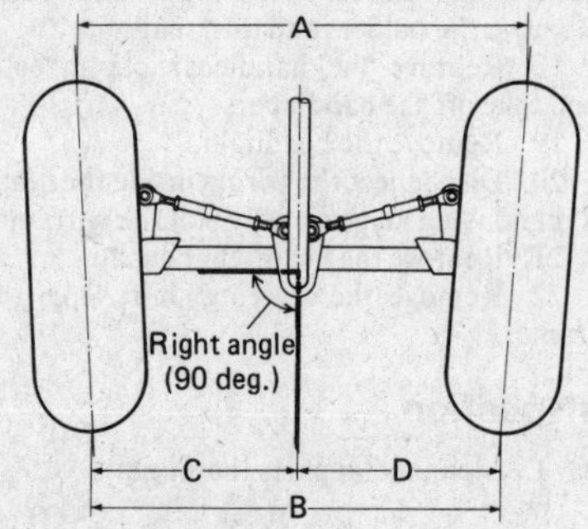

Subtract "B" from "A" for toe-in dimension; "C" and "D" must be equal

CAUTION: *It is critical that both rods be turned by equal amounts, assuming that other components have not been disturbed or damaged. The distance from the centerline of the steering shaft to the centerline of each tire must be equal.*

9. When the toe-in is correct and the distance from the centerline of the steering shaft to the centerline of both tires is equal, tighten the tie-rod locknuts to 16-26 ft. lbs.

GENERAL TORQUE SPECIFICATIONS ①

Bolt thread diameter (mm)	Torque (ft lbs)
Unmarked or marked "4"	
4	0.7-1.5
5	1.5-3.0
6	3-5
8	7-12
10	16-26
12	26-40
14	36-58
16	58-94
18	94-138
Marked "7"	
4	1-2
5	2-5
6	6-9
8	13-20
10	29-44
12	51-73
14	80-116
16	123-181
18	145-203

① Unless otherwise noted

CHASSIS TORQUE SPECIFICATIONS

Part	Torque (ft lbs.)
LT 125	
Handlebar clamp bolts	7-12
Steering shaft holder bolts	13-20
Steering shaft bottom nut	16-26
Knuckle arm bolt	29-44
Tie-rod end nuts	29-44
Tie-rod locknuts	16-26
Front wheel axle nuts	36-58
Front wheel nuts	15-23
Front wheel rim nuts	15-23
Footrest bolts	13-20
Chain tensioner nut	15-23
Chain adjuster bolt	51-73
Rear wheel axle nut	62-83
Rear wheel nuts	15-23
Rear wheel rim nuts	15-23
Rear sprocket mounting bolts	29-44
Rear sprocket nuts	6.0-8.5
Rear axle housing nuts	13-20
Brake cam lever pinch bolt	6.0-8.5
Brake drum outer cover bolts	3-5
Axle shaft nut, inner	36-58*
Axle shaft nut, outer	116-145*

CHASSIS TORQUE SPECIFICATIONS

Part	Torque (ft lbs.)
ALT 125	
Handlebar clamp bolts	9-15
Handlebar holder nuts	15-26
Upper triple clamp bolts and crown nut	26-40
Front axle nuts	36-58
Front wheel nuts	15-23
Front wheel rim nuts	15-23
Footrest bolts	15-23
Chain tensioner nut	15-23
Chain adjuster bolt	51-73
Rear wheel axle nut	62-83
Rear wheel nuts	15-23
Rear wheel rim nuts	15-23
Rear sprocket nuts	6.0-8.5
Rear sprocket mounting bolts	29-44
Rear axle housing nuts	13-20
Brake cam lever pinch bolt	6.0-8.5
Brake drum outer cover bolts	3-5
Axle shaft nut, inner	36-58*
Axle shaft nut, outer	116-145*
LT 185	
Handlebar clamp bolts	7-12
Steering shaft holder nuts	13-20
Steering shaft bottom nut	15-26
Knuckle arm bolt	29-44
Tie-rod end nuts	29-44
Tie-rod locknuts	16-26
Shock absorber mounting bolts	29-44
Front wheel axle nut	36-58
Front wheel nuts	33-47
Footrest bolts	13-20
Chain tensioner nut	15-22
Chain tensioner bolt	51-73
Wishbone arm bolts (frame)	51-73
Knuckle arm holder bolts	29-44
Rear wheel axle nut	62-83
Rear wheel nuts	33-47
Brake cam lever pinch bolt	6.0-8.5
Rear sprocket mounting bolts	29-44
Rear sprocket nuts	6.0-8.5
Rear axle housing nuts	13-20
Wishbone arm front locknut	15-26
Axle shaft nut, inner	36-58*
Axle shaft nut, outer	116-145*
ALT 185	
Handlebar clamp bolts	9-15
Handlebar holder nuts	15-26
Steering stem nut	26-40
Upper triple clamp bolts and crown nut	26-40
Front wheel axle nuts	26-38
Front wheel nuts	15-23
Chain tensioner nut	15-23
Chain adjuster bolt	51-73
Rear wheel axle nut	62-83
Rear wheel nuts	33-47
Rear axle housing nuts	13-20
Rear sprocket mounting bolts	29-44
Rear sprocket nuts	6.0-8.5
Axle shaft nut, inner	36-58*
Axle shaft nut, outer	116-145*

*Use thread locking compound

Suzuki LT 230GE

MODEL COVERAGE

LT 230GE

INDEX

GENERAL SPECIFICATIONS

DIMENSIONS	
Overall length	1690 mm/66.5 in.
Overall width	980 mm/38.6 in.
Overall height	1040 mm/40.9 in.
Wheelbase	1045 mm/41.1 in.
Front track	650 mm/25.6 in.
Rear track	720 mm/28.3 in.
Ground clearance	130 mm/5.1 in.
Seat height	710 mm/28.0 in.
Dry weight	154 kg/340 lbs.
ENGINE SPECIFICATIONS	
Type	OHC 4-stroke
Bore	66.0 mm/2.598 in.
Stroke	67.0 mm/2.638 in.
Displacement	229 cc/14.0 cu. in.
Compression ratio	9.0:1
Carburetor	VM24SS
Starter	Electric/recoil
Lubrication system	Wet sump
Clutch	Wet, multi-plate centrifugal
TRANSMISSION SPECIFICATIONS	
Type	5-speed forward/1-speed reverse
Primary reduction	3.136 (69/22)
Secondary reduction	1.062 (17/16)
Final reduction	3.600 (36/10)
Gear ratios	
1st	3.083 (37/12)
2nd	1.933 (29/15)
3rd	1.444 (26/18)
4th	1.095 (23/21)
5th	0.913 (21/23)
Reverse	2.833 (29/12 × 34/29)
ELECTRICAL SYSTEM	
Ignition	PEI
Timing	31.5° BTDC @ 3800 rpm
CHASSIS	
Caster	3°30′
Trail	25 mm/1.0 in.
Camber	1°30′
Turning radius	2.5 m/8.2 ft.
Front tire size	21 × 8.00-9
Rear tire size	22 × 11.00-8
CAPACITIES	
Fuel tank	10.0 l/2.6 gal w/reserve
Reserve supply	1.0 l/1.1 gal
Engine oil	1900 ml/2.0 qts. (total)

RECOMMENDED LUBRICANTS

Engine
- SAE 10W-40 oil, service rated "SE" or "SF"

Final gearbox
- SAE 90 hypoid gear oil

Front brakes
- DOT 3 or DOT 4 glycol-based brake fluid

Air filter
- Medium-weight motor oil

Control cables, odometer cable
- Light motor oil
- Graphite-based lubricant
- Molybdenum-disulphide-based lubricant

Throttle lever
- Light duty grease

SERIAL NUMBER LOCATIONS

In order to prevent possible confusion, always supply the chassis and engine serial numbers when ordering parts.

The chassis serial number is stamped on the front downtube on the left side of the frame.

The engine serial number is on the front of the crankcase, visible from the left side of the machine.

MAINTENANCE

NOTE: *Common maintenance procedures are explained in detail in the "General Information" section.*

RECOMMENDED LUBRICANTS

Wheel and steering shaft
 Waterproof, medium-weight bearing grease

General chassis lubrication
 Waterproof, medium-weight chassis grease

PERIODIC MAINTENANCE INTERVALS①

Before each ride
- Check operation of lights
- Check engine oil level
- Check tire condition and pressure
- Check tightness of critical fasteners
- Check throttle and brake operation

Every 600 miles
- Change engine oil
- Change oil filter
- Clean air filter element
- Check battery
- Check brake fluid
- Check brake adjustment and wear
- Check steering operation
- Tighten all hardware

Every 1200 miles
- Change final gear box oil
- Tighten cylinder head, exhaust pipe nuts

Every two years
- Replace final gearbox oil

Every four years
- Replace brake lines
- Replace fuel lines

① Based on normal use of the machine after break-in is complete.

LUBRICATION

Engine Oil

SAE 10W-40 oil, service rated "SE" or "SF" is recommended.

Engine oil (and filter) should be changed every 600 miles after initial break-in, assuming that the machine operates under normal conditions.

Engine oil capacity is about 1700ml (1.8 qts.) when changing oil and filter.

CHECKING OIL LEVEL

1. A sight glass is fitted on the right side of the crankcase allowing an easy check of oil level.
2. Oil should be checked after the engine has been running, then shut off and left to sit for a minute.
3. The machine must be parked on a level surface for an accurate reading.
4. Oil level should be at, but not above, the "F" mark on the crankcase.
5. If the level is below the mark, remove the filler cap and add the correct grade and type of oil until level is correct.

CAUTION: *Do not overfill the crankcase.*

CHANGING OIL AND FILTER

1. Oil should be changed when the engine is warm. This ensures more complete draining and makes it more likely that the oil will carry off any particulates with it.

Engine oil sight glass (8) and filler cap (7)

Crankcase drain plug (6)

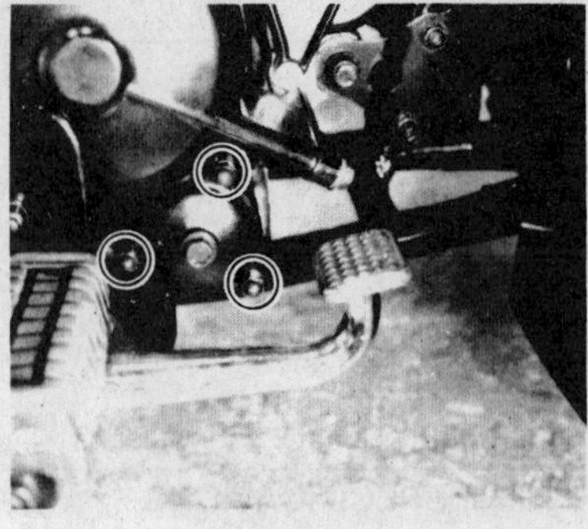
Oil filter cap bolts

Oil filter installation

2. Place a suitable container (about 2 qt. capacity) beneath the crankcase.
3. Remove the filler cap.
4. Remove the drain plug beneath the crankcase.
5. Allow the oil to drain for several minutes.
6. Clean the drain plug. Install it and tighten to 15-18 ft. lbs.
7. Place the container beneath the oil filter cap on the right side of the engine.
8. Remove the three cap nuts and carefully pull the cap off. Note the spring on the inside.
9. Pull out the oil filter and discard it.
10. Clean out the oil filter housing with a rag. Clean the filter cap.
11. Inspect cap O-ring condition. Replace it if it is knicked or damaged in any way.
12. Clean the filter cap mating surface.
13. Check that the O-ring in the filter housing is in position.
14. Install the new filter, closed end out.
15. Check that the filter cap spring is in place.
16. Carefully fit the cap and tighten the three nuts gradually and evenly.
17. Add about 1700ml (1.8 qts.) of the recommended type and grade oil to the crankcase.
18. Fit the filler cap.
19. Let the engine run for a few minutes, then shut it off and check level at the sight glass. Top up if necessary.
20. Check for leaks at the drain plug and filter cap before operating the machine.

Engine Oil Pressure

Oil pressure can be checked if the proper gauge and fitting are available and a method is found of measuring engine rpm.

1. Warm engine oil to 140°F.
2. Remove the gallery plug in the center

Checking oil pressure with gauge (3) at gallery plug (4)

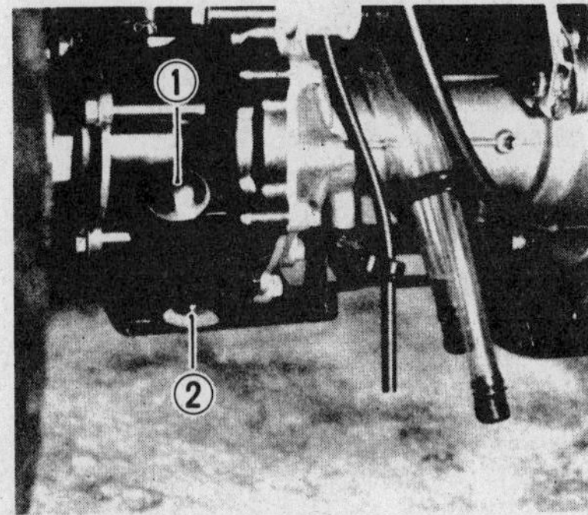

Final gearbox level (filler) plug (1) and drain plug (2)

of the filter cap beneath the clutch housing and fit the pressure gauge.

3. Oil pressure should be 4.3-10.0 psi at 3000 rpm.

4. Oil pressure which is too high may be caused by oil which is too heavy for conditions, or merely too heavy. Other causes include a clogged passage or filter, improperly installed filter, or a combination of these factors.

5. Low oil pressure can be caused by leakage from the gallery, a damaged oil seal, worn engine components or a defective oil pump.

Final Gearbox

SAE 90 hypoid gear oil is recommended for the final gearbox.

Oil should be changed every 1200 miles under normal operating conditions.

Gearbox capacity is 165-175ml (5.9 oz.) when changing.

1. Oil should be changed when the gearbox is at operating temperature to ensure complete draining.
2. Park the machine on a level surface.
3. Place a suitable container beneath the gearbox drain plug.
4. Remove the filler plug.
5. Remove the drain plug. Allow the oil to drain for several minutes.
6. Clean the drain plug and check gasket condition.
7. Install the drain plug and tighten it securely.
8. Add about 165-175ml (5.9 oz.) of SAE 90 hypoid gear oil through the filler hole. The final level should be just even with the lip of the filler hole.
9. Check the filler plug gasket. Install the plug and tighten it securely.

Chassis lubrication points

General Lubrication

Refer to the illustration showing the machine in profile and the lubrication points. "G" is for grease; "O", for oil.

Service intervals will depend on operating conditions.

SERVICE CHECKS AND ADJUSTMENTS

Throttle Cable

1. The throttle cable adjuster is located near the carburetor and is accessed by removing the air cleaner case.
2. The cable should be adjusted so that free-play is about 0.5-1.0mm (0.02-0.04 in.). This distance is measured between the sheath of the cable coming from the carb and the end of the adjuster.
3. Remove the seat.
4. Remove the front fender.
5. Remove the two air cleaner inlet case bolts and remove the inlet case.
6. Loosen the adjuster locknut and turn the adjuster in or out until the proper free play is obtained. Tighten the locknut.

MAINTENANCE DATA

Fuel tank (w/reserve)	10.0 1/2.6 gal.
Fuel reserve	1.0 1/1.1 qt.
Engine oil	
Routine change	1500 ml/1.6 qts.
Oil & filter change	1700 ml/1.8 qts.
After rebuilding	1900 ml/2.0 qts.
Final gearbox	165-175 ml/5.6-5.9 oz.
Tire pressure (f&r) (cold)	
Up to 230 lbs.	2.6 psi
230-375 lbs.	3.6 psi
Oil pressure	4.3-10.0 psi @3000 rpm, 140°F
Battery	
Voltage/output	12v/11 ah
Continuous charging rate	1.1 amps

7. Replace air cleaner case, fender, seat.

8. After making this adjustment, let the engine idle and turn the handlebars slowly from lock to lock. Any variation in idle speed means that the throttle cable has insufficient free play or is binding somewhere along its route.

9. After making any adjustment to the throttle cable, check throttle operation before riding the machine.

Clutch

1. The clutch should be adjusted every 1200 miles after break-in is complete.
2. Drain the engine oil.
3. Remove the right side foot rest.
4. Place a drip pan beneath the right side of the engine.
5. Remove the three bolts which secure the clutch adjuster cap. Remove the cap.
6. Loosen the adjuster screw locknut.
7. Turn the adjuster screw 1/2 turn clockwise, then turn it counterclockwise until resistance is felt.
8. Turn the adjusting screw clockwise 1/8 turn or less. Hold it in place and tighten the locknut.
9. Check adjuster cap gasket condition before refitting. Replace if necessary.
10. Tighten the cap screws evenly.
11. Refill the crankcase with the proper grade and amount of oil.

Clutch adjusting screw and locknut (1 and 2)

Front Brakes

FLUID LEVEL

1. Check fluid level at the sight glass provided on the reservoir.
2. The machine should be parked on a level surface and the front wheel pointed straight ahead for an accurate reading.
3. If the fluid level is below the limit mark provided, clean the reservoir with a clean rag to remove any dirt, then remove the cap and add enough fluid to bring the level up to specification. Do not overfill.
4. Use DOT 3 or DOT 4 brake fluid only.

NOTE: *The machine is equipped at the factory with glycol-based brake fluid. Do not use other types such as silicone or petroleum- based fluids to top up the reservoir or the brake system may be damaged. Brake fluid is hydroscopic. It absorbs moisture. Therefore, do not use fluid from an old or unsealed container. Exercise extreme care in handling the brake fluid. It will remove paint on contact. Be sure the reservoir cap is firmly secured when refitting.*

BRAKE ADJUSTMENT

1. Park the machine on a level surface.
2. Apply the parking brake.
3. Support the front wheels off the ground by placing a secure, safe support beneath the frame. Observe all standard safety precautions.
4. Remove the rubber plug from each wheel.
5. Turn the wheel until the star wheel adjuster on one side of the brake cylinder is accessible. There are adjusters on both sides of the cylinders. It does not matter which is adjusted first.
6. Insert a small slothead screwdriver into the adjuster hole. Work the screwdriver so that the star wheel is made to turn as shown in the illustration.
7. Rotate the wheel gently while the star wheel adjuster is turned. When the wheel is locked, back the adjuster off one notch at a time until it turns without dragging.
8. Repeat the procedure with the adjuster on the other side of the cylinder.
9. Repeat the adjustment sequence with the wheel on the other side.
10. After both wheels are adjusted, apply the brake several times. Spin the wheels to check that the brakes do not drag.
11. Install the rubber plugs.

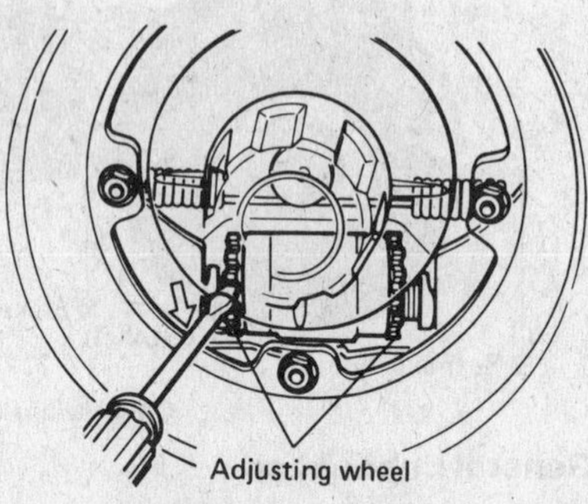

Front brake adjustment

Rear Brakes

1. The rear brakes are controlled jointly by the foot pedal and the hand lever on the left side. Both must be adjusted when servicing the brakes. The foot pedal must be adjusted *first*.
2. The foot pedal is connected to the *lower* of the two cables at the brake plate lever.
3. Use the adjusting nut on the end of the cable so that the foot pedal can move 20-30mm (0.8-1.0 in.) before the linings contact the drum.
4. Check brake hand lever free play. The lever should have 3-7mm (0.1-0.3 in.) of free play before the linings contact the drum. This specification is measured between the lever and the lever holder.
5. If adjustment is necessary, first run the adjuster at the handlebar all the way in.
6. Use the adjusting nut on the end of the brake cable to give the hand lever the required amount of free play.
7. Make fine adjustments with the adjuster at the handlebar.
8. After the brakes are adjusted, apply foot pedal or hand lever fully and check that the index mark on the brake camshaft is still within the wear limit range embossed on the axle housing. If it is not, the linings must be replaced.

Tires

1. Tire pressure should be checked before each ride. Always check pressure when tires are cold.
2. Proper tire pressure is 2.6 psi for loads up to 230 lbs., and 3.6 psi for loads from 230 to 375 lbs.
3. Tire pressures should be checked with an accurate, low-pressure gauge.
4. Never exceed the recommended pressures.
5. When inflating tires, a hand pump is highly recommended. High pressure lines such as found in gas stations should never be used.

CAUTION: *Tire condition and tire pressures constitute critical safety factors. Be certain that manufacturer's guidelines are adhered to in all cases.*

6. Tires must be replaced when tread depth is 4.0mm (0.16 in.) or less.

Steering

Toe-in of the front wheels should be checked every 600 miles. This procedure, and subsequent adjustments, are given in the "Chassis" section.

FUEL SYSTEM

Fuel system maintenance involves cleaning the fuel line filter screens, cleaning the air filter and cleaning the carburetor.

Air Filter

1. The filter element should be cleaned and reoiled every 600 miles under normal operating conditions.
2. Remove the seat.
3. Remove the air cleaner case cover after removing the securing screw.
4. Remove the element securing screw and take out the element.

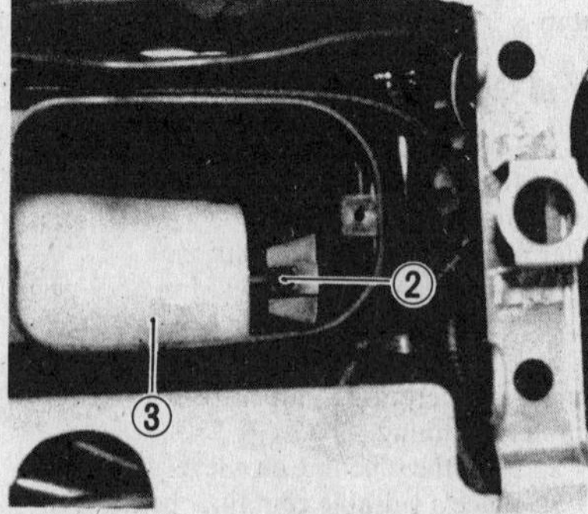

Air filter element (3) and securing screw (2)

5. Remove the element from the frame.
6. Clean the element in a safe, non-flammable solvent. Be sure to squeeze the element: do not wring it out as this will damage the pores.
7. When the element is clean, squeeze off the excess solvent.
8. Soak the element in motor oil. Squeeze off the excess, leaving the element slightly wet with the oil.
9. Fit the element onto the frame. Install the assembled components in the case.

NOTE: *If the element is damaged or cannot be cleaned properly, replace it. Check for rips or torn areas, especially along the seam.*

Fuel Filters and Carburetor

Fuel filters are located on the lines inside the gas tank. Service to these items, and carburetor disassembly, is covered in the Fuel System section.

TOP END FASTENERS

1. The factory recommends that cylinder head nuts, cylinder base nuts and exhaust pipe and muffler fasteners be tightened every 1200 miles.

NOTE: *This procedure must be done when the engine is cold.*

2. Remove the seat.
3. Remove the front fender.
4. Remove the cylinder head cover.
5. Loosen the four 8mm nuts under the cover and the two 6mm nuts on the left side of the engine.
6. Gradually, and in a cross pattern, tighten the 6mm nuts to 5.0-8.0 ft. lbs. and the 8mm nuts to 15.0-18.0 ft. lbs.
7. Loosen the two 6mm cylinder base nuts on the left side of the engine, then retighten to 5.-8.0 ft. lbs.
8. Tighten the exhaust pipe nuts at the cylinder head to 6.5-8.5 ft. lbs. Tighten the muffler bolts to 13.0-20.0 ft. lbs.
9. When refitting the cylinder head cover, use liquid gasket material on the mating surface.

Tune-Up

NOTE: *Common tune-up procedures are explained in detail in the "General Information" section.*

TUNE-UP SPECIFICATIONS

COMPRESSION	
Cranking pressure	171-228 psi
Minimum allowable reading	142 psi
VALVE CLEARANCE	
Intake	0.03-0.08 mm/0.001-0.003 in.
Exhaust	0.08-0.13 mm/0.003-0.005 in.
SPARK PLUG	
OEM	NGK/ND/Champion
Standard	D-7EA/X22ES-U/A8YC
Cold	D-8EA/X24ES-U/A6YC
Standard Resistor type	DR-7ES/X22ESR-U/RA8YC
Cold Resistor type	DR-8ES-L/X24ESR-U/RA6YC
Spark plug gap	0.6-0.7 mm/0.024-0.028 in.
IGNITION TIMING	Preset
CARBURETION	
Idle speed	1350-1450 rpm
Pilot screw setting	2¡ turns out
Float level	24.5 mm/0.96 in. ± 1.0 mm/0.04 in.

COMPRESSION TEST

1. A compression check should be made before each tune-up since this will provide a general idea of engine condition.
2. If a screw-in type gauge is used, note that the spark plug hole is 12mm.
3. Before making this test, check that the cylinder head nuts and bolts are properly torqued (see "Maintenance") and that the valves are properly adjusted (see below).
4. The engine must be at operating temperature.
5. Remove the seat.
6. Remove the front fender.
7. Remove the spark plug.
8. Fit the compression gauge. If a hold-in type gauge is used, oil the rubber tip to give a better seal.
9. Hold the throttle wide open and crank the engine with the starter motor.
10. The highest attainable reading is the compression. The standard specification for this engine is 171-228 psi. The lowest acceptable reading is 142 psi.
11. If compression is too low, squirt a bit of motor oil into the cylinder and repeat the test. If compression increases, suspect worn piston rings or cylinder walls. If it does not, the cause may be a defective head gasket, burnt, poorly seated or incorrectly adjusted valves.

Cam chain tensioner and locknut (1 and 2)

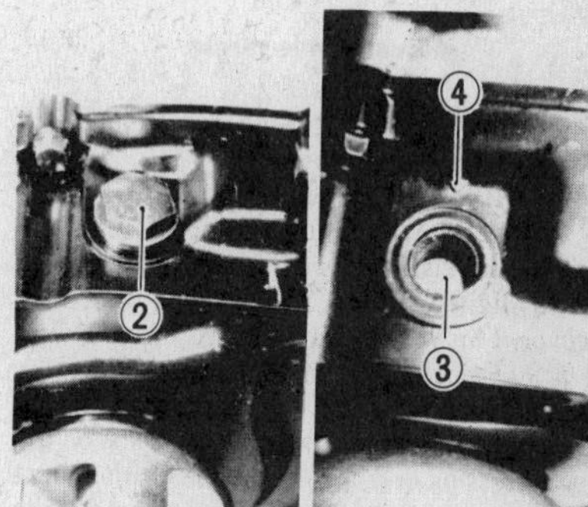

Timing inspection plug (2), "T" mark (3) and crankcase mark (4)

CAM CHAIN TENSIONER

1. The cam chain tensioner should be adjusted every 1200 miles.
2. The tensioner is a spring-loaded unit which will take up excess slack in the chain when the tensioner rod is released from its normally locked position. For accurate settings, the adjustment must be made when the piston is at TDC on the compression stroke.
3. Remove the seat.
4. Remove the front fender.
5. Remove the spark plug.
6. Remove the timing inspection plug from the crankcase cover.
7. Remove the valve adjuster caps.
8. Remove the recoil starter.
9. Rotate the engine until the "T" mark on the rotor aligns with the mark on the crankcase cover. The piston is now positioned at TDC.
10. Check for clearance at both valves. If both valves are closed, the piston is at TDC on the compression stroke and the adjustment sequence may proceed. If there is not clearance at both valves, the piston is at TDC on the exhaust stroke. In this case, rotate the rotor 360° until the "T" mark alignment is reestablished. Now check for clearance at both valves.
11. When the piston is properly located, loosen the locknut on the cam chain tensioner behind the cylinder.
12. Turn the adjuster screw one full turn counterclockwise. The spring-loaded tensioner rod will be free to take up chain slack.
13. Tighten the adjuster screw to lock the rod in place.
14. Tighten the locknut.
15. After adjustment, check that chain operation is quiet. If the procedure was done correctly, but the chain is still noisy, it is probable that the rod is sticking due to dirt or the like. The assembly should be removed and thoroughly cleaned. Refer to "Engine and Transmission" for procedures.

VALVE ADJUSTMENT

NOTE: *Valve adjustment must be done when the enge is cold.*

1. Valve clearance must be checked every 1200 miles.
2. Remove the seat.
3. Remove the front fender.
4. Remove the spark plug.
5. Remove the valve adjuster caps.

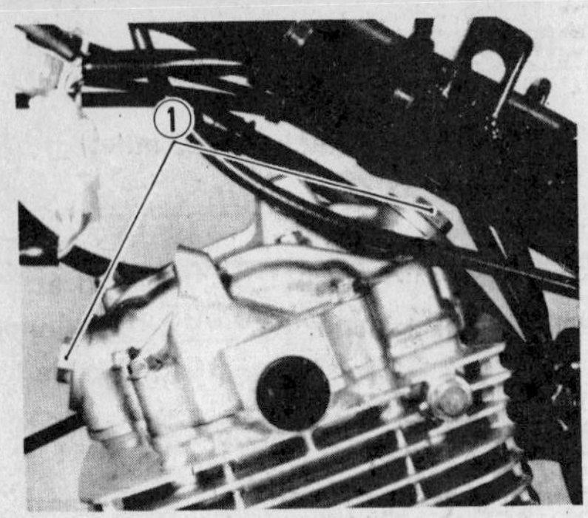

Valve adjuster caps (1)

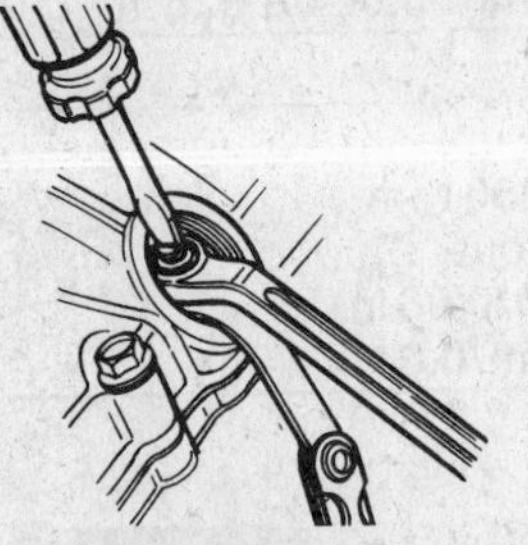
Adjusting the valves

6. Remove the timing inspection plug from the crankcase cover.

7. Remove the recoil starter.

8. Rotate the magneto rotor until the "T" mark visible through the inspection plug hole aligns with the mark on the crankcase cover. This will position the piston at TDC.

9. Check for clearance at both valves by attempting to move the adjusters. If there is clearance at both valves, the piston is on the compression stroke and the adjustment sequence can continue. If clearance cannot be detected at both valves, the piston is probably at TDC on the exhaust stroke. Rotate the magneto rotor one full turn until the "T" mark alignment is reestablished. Then check for clearance at the valves once more.

10. With the piston at TDC on the compression stroke, check valve clearance.

11. Proper valve clearance is 0.03-0.08mm (0.001-0.003 in.) for the intake valve and 0.08-0.13mm (0.003-0.005 in.) for the exhaust valve.

12. Select a feeler gauge blade near the middle of these specifications and attempt to slip the blade between the valve stem and the adjuster.

13. If clearance is correct, a blade of the proper thickness will be a light slip fit between stem and adjuster.

14. If adjustment is necessary, loosen the adjuster locknut, insert a blade of the proper thickness, and turn the adjuster until the blade is a slip fit—not too loose.

15. When clearance is correct, hold the adjuster in place and tighten the locknut.

16. Recheck clearance after the locknut is secured.

17. Install adjuster caps, timing inspection cap, recoil starter, spark plug, etc.

18. After assembly is completed, check compression.

IGNITION TIMING

The machine is equipped with a solid-state ignition system which requires no adjustment or routine maintenance.

CARBURETOR

Carburetor adjustments to be made during a complete tune-up include checking the float level, adjusting theidle mixture and adjusting the idle speed.

An aftermarket tachometer is required if idle speed is to be set exactly to specification.

NOTE: *Fuel system adjustments may be ineffective or impossible if the carburetor or air filter are dirty or if there are mechanical faults (such as air leaks) in the system.*

Float Level

1. Float level is a measure of the amount of gasoline which will be present in the float bowl during operation. While it is a critical specification, it will not normally need periodic readjustment once it is properly set. Float level, therefore, need not be checked at every tune-up, but should be attended to from time to time.

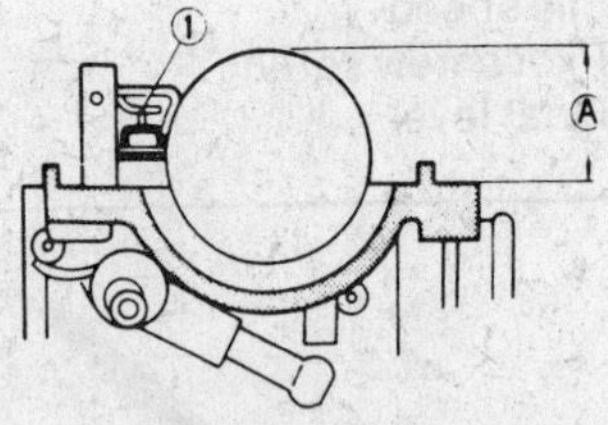

Float level (A) and float tang (1)

2. Remove the carburetor from the machine. Refer to the "Fuel System" section for procedures.

3. Remove the float bowl.

4. Remove the float bowl gasket.

5. Turn the carburetor upside down and lower the float until the tang just touches the tip of the needle.

6. Float level is the distance from the float bowl mating surface (gasket removed) to the top of the float.

7. Float level is 24.5mm (0.96 in.) with a tolerance of ± 1.0mm (0.04 in.).

8. If the measured float level is not within this range, remove the float by pushing out the pivot pin.

9. Bend the float tang in the required direction to raise or lower the float level. Bending the tang away from the carburetor body raises the float level; bending it towards the carb lower the amount of fuel in the bowl.

Idle Mixture And Idle Speed

1. These adjustments should be made every 1200 miles.

NOTE: *Idle speed and mixture adjustments must be made when the engine is at operating temperature.*

2. Carefully turn the pilot screw in until it bottoms, then back it out 2 3/8 turns.

CAUTION: *Turn the screw in carefully. Do not overtighten it or the calibrated tip will be damaged.*

3. Connect a tachometer to the engine.

4. Use the throttle stop screw to adjust idle speed to 1350-1450 rpm.

5. After idle speed is set, turn the pilot screw 1/2 turn in either direction from the standard setting looking for the highest idle speed. Do not exceed 1/2 turn from the original setting.

6. Readjust idle speed to the standard specification of 1350-1450 rpm.

7. If these adjustments prove difficult or impossible, suspect dirt or some mechanical defect in the fuel system. Possible causes include air leaks at manifold joints, clogged air or fuel passages in the carburetor, etc. Tightly adjusted valves or engine damage of this sort can also make smooth, consistant idling impossible.

Engine And Transmission

NOTE: *For engine component inspection techniques and procedures, refer to "Engine Rebuilding" in the General Information section.*

ENGINE REMOVAL AND INSTALLATION

NOTE: *Before removing the engine from the frame, clean both thoroughly.*

1. Drain the engine oil.

2. Remove the seat.

3. Remove the tool tray mounting bolt. Remove the tool tray.

4. Disconnect the negative battery terminal, then the positive terminal. Remove the battery.

5. Remove the Choke knob and the Reverse knob after taking out the securing screws.

6. Remove the four odometer panel mounting bolts.

7. Remove the two front fender mounting bolts near the air cleaner inlet case.

8. Remove the two front fender mounting bolts at the front of the fender.

9. Remove the bracket bolts which secure the front fender to the frame.

10. Pull the fender forward and take it off the machine.

11. Remove the rear fender (four bolts).

12. Remove the exhaust pipe nuts at the cylinder head. Remove the two muffler mounting bolts. Remove the exhaust system.

13. Loosen the air cleaner inlet case clamp screw.

14. Remove the two air cleaner inlet case mounting bolts. Remove the air cleaner inlet case.

15. Disconnect the ground wire on the left side of the frame behind the engine.

16. Locate the electrical connectors near the cylinder head. Disconnect the magneto wires, reverse switch and neutral indicator switch leads.

17. Disconnect the carburetor lines: fuel feed, overflow, vent and vacuum (the vacuum line is fitted to the manifold).

18. Unhook relevant hose clamps.

19. Loosen the carburetor air cleaner and manifold side clamp screws.

20. Remove the carburetor. Place it out of the way to avoid the risk of damage.

21. Unbolt the footrest bracket from the frame (four bolts).

22. Remove the rear reinforcement.

ENGINE SPECIFICATIONS

Part	Standard (mm/in.)	Service limit (mm/in.)
Valve guide-to-stem clearance		
Intake	0.010-0.037/0.0004-0.0015	0.35/0.014
Exhaust	0.030-0.057/0.0012-0.0022	0.35/0.014
Valve guide ID	5.500-5.512/0.2165-0.2170	—
Valve stem OD		
Intake	5.475-5.490/0.2155-0.2161	—
Exhaust	5.455-5.470/0.2148-0.2153	—
Valve run-out (max)	—	0.05/0.002
Valve head thickness (min)	—	0.5/0.02
Valve stem end length	—	2.8/0.11
Valve seat width	0.9-1.1/0.035-0.043	
Valve head radial run-out	—	0.03/0.001
Valve spring free length (min)		
Inner	—	35.1/1.38
Outer	—	39.9/1.57
Cam lobe height		
Intake	33.780-33.820/1.3299-1.3315	33.480/1.3181
Exhaust	32.990-33.030/1.2988-1.3004	32.690/1.2870
Cam journal clearance	0.032-0.066/0.0013-0.0026	0.150/0.0059
Cam journal ID	22.012-22.025/0.8666-0.8671	—
Cam journal OD	21.959-21.980/0.8645-0.8654	—
Cam run-out (max)	—	0.10/0.004
Cam chain length (20 pitches)	—	129.0/5.08
Rocker arm ID	12.000-12.018/0.4724-0.4731	—
Rocker arm shaft OD	11.977-11.995/0.4715-0.4722	—
Cylinder head warpage (max)	—	0.05/0.002
Head cover warpage (max)	—	0.05/0.002
Piston to cylinder clearance	0.04-0.05/0.0016-0.0020	0.120/0.0047
Cylinder bore	66.000-66.015/2.5984-2.5990	66.090/2.6020
Piston diameter	65.955-65.970/2.5966-2.5972	65.880/2.5937
Cylinder dia. deviation (max)	—	0.05/0.002
Piston ring end-gap (free)		
Top	7.5/0.30	6.0/0.24
Second	9.4/0.37	7.6/0.30
Piston ring end gap	0.10-0.25/0.004-0.010	0.70/0.028
Piston ring side clearance		
Top	—	0.180/0.0071
Second	—	0.150/0.0059
Piston groove width		
Top	1.01-1.03/0.0398-0.0406	—
Second	1.22-1.24/0.0480-0.0488	—
Oil	2.01-2.03/0.0791-0.0799	—
Ring thickness		
Top	0.97-0.99/0.038-0.039	—
Second	1.17-1.19/0.046-0.047	—
Wrist pin bore ID	16.002-16.008/0.6300-0.6302	16.030/0.6311
Wrist pin OD	15.996-16.000/0.6298-0.6299	15.980/0.6291
Con rod small end ID	16.006-16.014/0.6302-0.6305	16.040/0.6315
Con rod lateral play (max)	—	3.0/0.12
Big end side clearance	0.10-0.45/0.0039-0.0177	1.00/0.039
Bid end width	17.95-18.00/0.707-0.709	—
Crank web-to-web width	53.0 ± 0.1/2.087 ± 0.004	—
Crankshaft run-out (max)	—	0.05/0.002
Clutch specifications		
Drive plate thickness	2.7-2.9/0.106-0.114	2.4/0.094
Drive plate claw width	11.8-12.0/0.46-0.47	11.0/0.43
Driven plate warpage (max)	—	0.10/0.004
Spring free length (min)	—	27.4/1.08

ENGINE SPECIFICATIONS

Part	Standard (mm/in.)	Service limit (mm/in.)
Transmission specifications		
Shift fork groove clearance	0.10-0.30/0.004-0.012	0.50/0.020
Shift fork groove width		
1st, 2nd, 3rd	4.50-4.60/0.177-0.181	—
Reverse	4.00-4.10/0.157-0.161	—
Shift fork thickness		
1st, 2nd, 3rd	4.30-4.40/0.169-0.173	—
Reverse	3.80-3.90/0.150-0.154	—
Drive shaft specifications		
Secondary bevel gear backlash	0.05-0.32/0.002-0.013	—
Final bevel gear backlash, drive side	0.03-0.64/0.001-0.025	—

ENGINE TORQUE SPECIFICATIONS

Part	Torque (ft lbs)
Cylinder head cover bolts	6.5-8.0
Cylinder head nuts	15-18
Rocker arm shaft bolts	6-7
Cylinder base nuts	5-8
Camshaft sprocket bolts	7.0-8.5
Tensioner adjuster bolt	4.5-6.0
Magneto rotor nut	109-123
Clutch sleeve hub nut	44-58
Clutch shoe nut	65-80
Starter clutch allen bolts	17-20
Clutch release outer nut	7.0-8.5
TDC plug	15-18
Oil pressure check bolt	6.0-8.5
Oil pump bolts	5-7
Crankcase oil drain plug	15-18
Engine mounting bolts	44-52
Exhaust pipe nuts at cylinder head	7-9
Muffler mounting bolts	13-20
Gearshift arm stopper bolt	11-17
Gearshift lever pinch bolt	6-9
Reverse shift cam stopper bolt	13-20
Reverse switch	15-18
Secondary drive gear bevel nut	65-80
Final bearing case bolts (right & left)	15-19
Final drive bevel gear nut	65-80
Final drive bearing stopper	44-47

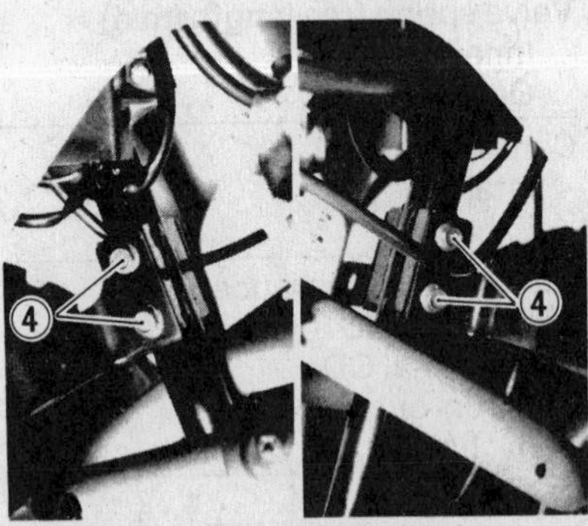

Front fender bracket bolts (4)

Engine mounting bolts

23. Disconnect the odometer cable from the engine.

24. Loosen the reverse lever and the gearshift lever pinch bolts and carefully pull these levers off their splined shafts.

25. Loosen the drive shaft boot clamp screws and slide the boot to the rear.

26. Remove the secondary gear housing outer case bolts. There are eight. Remove the outer case.

27. Remove the secondary driven bevel gear assembly by pulling it out.

28. Disconnect the high tension lead from the starter motor.

29. Remove the starter motor (two bolts).

30. Remove the front engine mounting bolts and brackets.

31. Remove the engine mounting bolts at the back and beneath the crankcase.

32. Take the engine out to the left side.

33. Engine installation is the reverse of removal. Note the following points:

a. Engine mounting bolts use self-locking nuts which cannot be reused. Use new nuts on the mounting bolts. Torque engine mounting nuts to 44-52 ft. lbs.

b. The spline of the secondary driven bevel gear assembly should be lubricated with Lithium-based Molybdenum grease (NLGI No. 2) before installation.

c. Be sure the secondary gear housing outer case dowel pins are in place before fitting the outer case.

d. Coat the outer case mating surface with liquid gasket compound.

e. Tighten the exhaust pipe nuts at the cylinder head to 7-9 ft. lbs. and the muffler mounting bolts to 13-20 ft. lbs.

f. Do not forget to add oil before attempting to start the engine.

g. Be certain that all hose, electrical connections, control cables, etc., are

GENERAL TORQUE SPECIFICATIONS①

Bolt thread diameter (mm)	Torque (ft lbs)
Unmarked or marked "4"	
4	0.7-1.5
5	1.5-3.0
6	3-5
8	7-12
10	16-26
12	26-40
14	36-58
16	58-94
18	94-138

GENERAL TORQUE SPECIFICATIONS①

Bolt thread diameter (mm)	Torque (ft lbs)
Marked "7"	
4	1-2
5	2-5
6	6-9
8	13-20
10	29-44
12	51-73
14	80-116
16	123-181
18	145-203

① Unless otherwise noted

properly connected and adjusted before starting the engine.

TOP END

NOTE: *Refer to the General Information section of this manual for common engine rebuilding techniques and inspection procedures.*

Cylinder Head

REMOVAL

1. It is possible to remove the cylinder head with the engine still in the frame. Remove the seat, front fender, carburetor and exhaust system. Refer to "Engine Removal and Installation", above, for procedures.
2. Remove the cam chain tensioner from the left side of the cylinder.
3. Remove the four screws that secure the recoil starter assembly (engine left side). Remove the recoil starter.
4. Remove the inspection plug on the left crankcase cover.
5. Remove the valve adjuster caps.
6. Turn the rotor until the "T" mark visible through the inspection hole aligns with the timing mark. Check for clearance at both valves. This indicates that the piston is at TDC on the compression stroke. If one of the valves is tight, rotate the engine 360° and try again. The piston must be at TDC on the compression stroke when removing the head.
7. Disconnect the spark plug lead. Remove the spark plug.
8. Refer to the accompanying illustration of the head. Loosen the cylinder head cover bolts gradually and evenly in the order shown.

CAUTION: *Do not disturb the two bolts with conical recesses marked "A" in the illustration.*

9. When all cover bolts are loose, remove them.
10. Remove the cylinder head cover.
11. Remove the camshaft end cap.
12. Bend down the locking tabs and remove the cam sprocket bolts.
13. Pull the sprocket off the camshaft. Disengage the sprocket from the chain and remove it.
14. Run a rod through the chain so that it will not drop into the crankcase.
15. Remove the camshaft being careful not to loose the timing pin on the end.
16. The head is secured by four nuts on top and two smaller nuts on the left side of the cylinder. Loosen the fasteners gradually and in a cross pattern. Remove the nuts and washers. Note the locations of the copper washers.
17. Remove the cylinder head. If it is stuck, rap it with a plastic mallet but do not strike the cooling fins, as they may break.
18. Remove the head gasket.

Recoil starter mounting screws

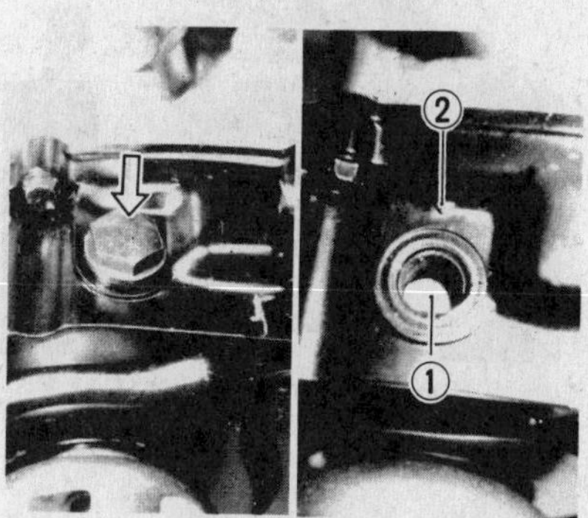

Timing inspection plug (arrow); "T" rotor mark (1) and crankcase timing mark (2)

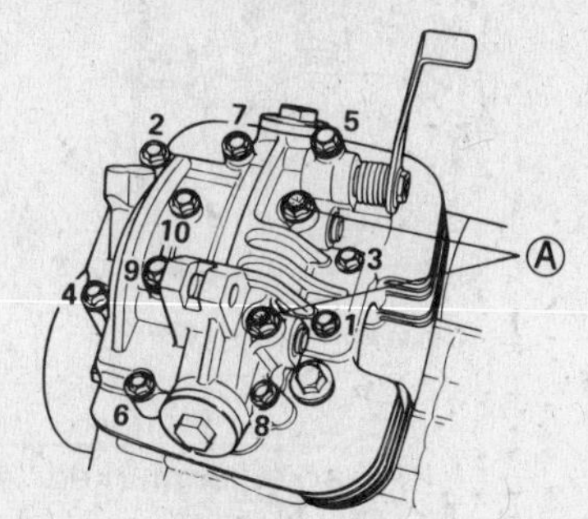

Head cover bolt loosening order. Do not disturb bolts "A"

Upper cylinder head nuts

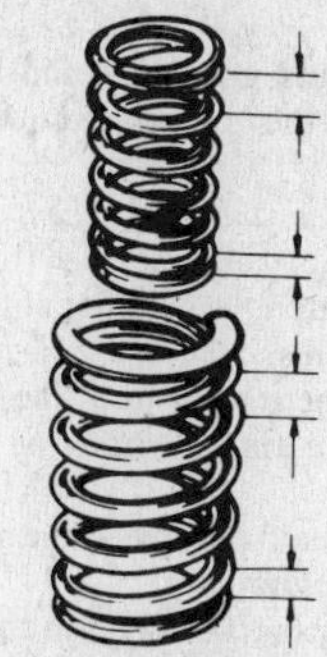

Install valve springs with the close coils towards the head

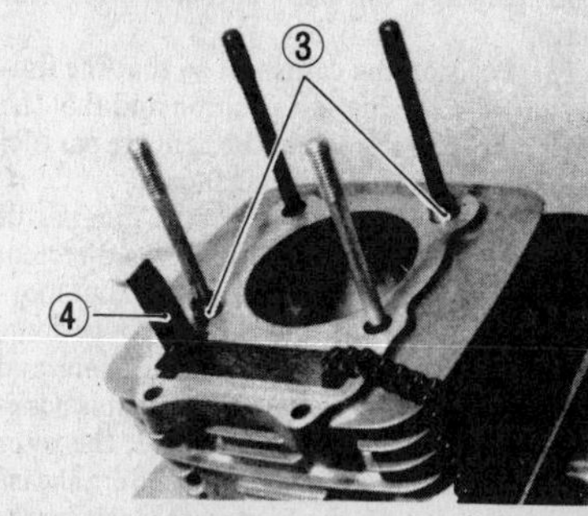

Dowel pins on cylinder mating surface (3) and cam chain guide (4)

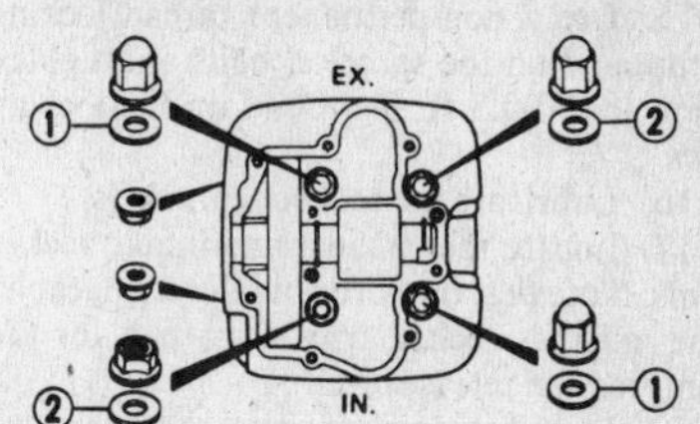

Copper washer (1) and steel washer (2) installation

19. Pull out the compression release shaft from the cylinder head cover.
20. Remove the rocker arm shaft set bolts from the head cover.
21. Pull the rocker arm shafts out of the cover with pliers.

NOTE: *Rocker arms and shims will come out at this time. Keep each shaft with its own rocker arm so all parts can be installed in their original locations.*

INSPECTION

Refer to the Engine Rebuilding section of

"General Information" for component wear checks and measurement points. Compare the measurements against the standard specifications given in the "Engine Specifications" chart, below.

INSTALLATION

1. Use new gaskets, O-rings and seals.
2. Install the valve springs with the close coils against the head.
3. Be sure that the two dowel pins are in place on the cylinder mating surface.
4. Install the cylinder head and pull the cam chain through.
5. Note that the copper washers for the head fasteners are fitted to the same studs that have the dowel pins on the cylinder mating surface.
6. Tighten the nuts gradually and in a cross pattern until the proper torque is reached:

   8mm .... 11-15 ft. lbs.
   6mm .... 5-8 ft. lbs.
7. Install and tighten the cylinder nuts on the left side to 5- 8 ft. lbs.
8. Turn the magneto rotor until the "T" mark aligns with the timing mark on the crankcase.
9. Pull the cam chain taut when the rotor is turned so that it does not jam.
10. Grease the camshaft timing pin and fit it to the camshaft.
11. Lubricate the camshaft and install it on the head.
12. Engage the cam sprocket and cam chain.
13. Position the camshaft so that the timing pin is at the highest position and that the slash marks on the end of the cam are parallel to the head cover mating surface.
14. With the magneto rotor "T" mark still aligned, and the cam positioned as directed, install the sprocket on the cam without moving either cam or rotor. If this cannot be done, disengage the sprocket from the chain and change its position so that alignment is possible. When assembly is completed, the rotor "T" mark must be aligned with the crankcase timing mark and the camshaft slash marks must be parallel to the cover mating surface. Otherwise valve timing will be incorrect.
15. Use a non-permanent thread locking compound on the sprocket bolts and tighten them to 7.0-9.5 ft. lbs. Bend up the locking tabs.
16. Lubricate the rocker arm shafts.
17. Locate the exhaust and intake rocker arms. Note that they are not interchangeable. The exhaust rocker arm has a pad for the compression release level.
18. Install the rocker arms, shafts and set bolts.
19. Lubricate and install the compression release.
20. Be sure the two dowel pins are in place in the cylinder head.
21. Use gasket compound to seal the head cover mating surface and install the head cover.

   CAUTION: *Do not apply the compound to the camshaft end-cap.*
22. Be sure the gaskets are in place on the two cover bolts.
23. Install the cover fasteners. Tighten the fasteners gradually and in the order shown in the illustration until the correct torque (6.5-8.0 ft. lbs.) is attained.
24. To install the cam chain tensioner, loosen the locking nut, loosen the screw one full turn and compress the pushrod. Tighten the screw. Bolt the tensioner on the cylinder. The piston must be positioned at TDC on the compression stroke. Loosen the screw to free the pushrod, then tighten it and tighten the locking nut.
25. Adjust valves. After the engine has a few miles on it, retorque the fasteners and readjust the valves.

Valve timing: align rotor "T" mark (1) with crankcase timing mark (2)

Valve timing: position cam with timing pin (3) upwards and slash marks parallel to cover surface

Cylinder head dowel pins (1)

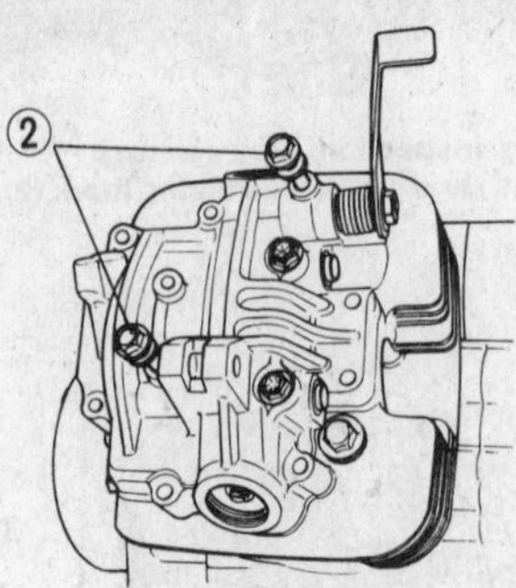

Cover bolt gaskets (2)

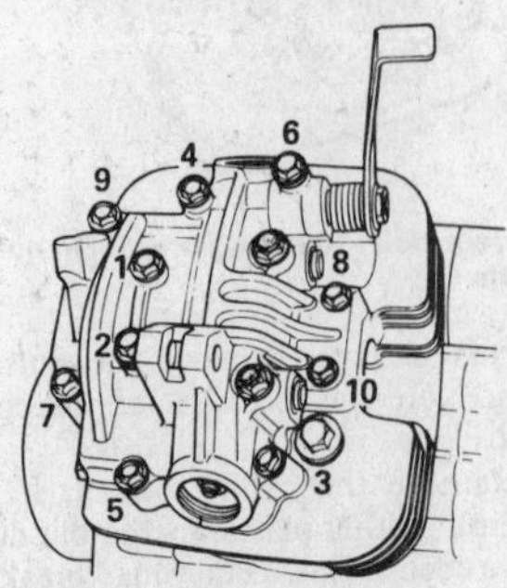

Cover bolt tightening order

Cylinder And Piston

REMOVAL

1. Remove the cylinder head as outlined above.
2. Remove the cam chain guide.
3. Remove the cylinder base nuts.
4. Pull off the cylinder.
5. Stuff a clean rag into the crankcase to prevent the entry of foreign matter.
6. Remove the wrist pin circlips.
7. Push out the piston wrist pin and remove the piston. Do not strike or try to drive the wrist pin out. Heat the piston crown gently to make removal easier.
8. Remove the cylinder base gasket.

INSPECTION

1. Refer to the Engine Rebuilding section of "General Information" for piston and cylinder inspection procedures.
2. Compare specifications obtained from the engine against the standard specs in the chart below.
3. Piston diameter is measured 18mm above the edge of the skirt.
4. Piston rings are available in two oversizes: 0.5mm and 1.0mm. The compression rings are marked "50" and "100". The 0.5 O.S. oil ring spacer is painted red. The 1.0 O.S. oil ring spacer is yellow.

INSTALLATION

1. The second (lower) compression ring has a wedge-shaped profile. The upper compression ng has a rounded profile. Be sure rings are installed in the correct groove.
2. Compression rings must be installed with the "R" mark or oversize mark near the end gap facing up.
3. Position the ring end-gaps around the piston as shown in the illustration.
4. When installing the piston, be sure that the arrow on the crown points towards the exhaust port.

Top

2nd

Compression ring profiles

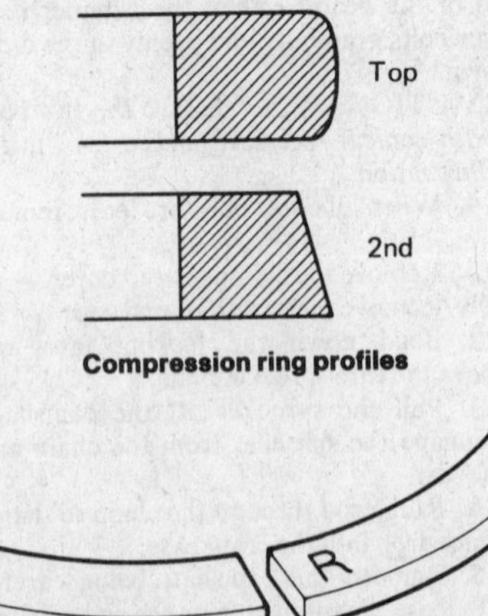

Manufacturer's marks must face up when rings are installed

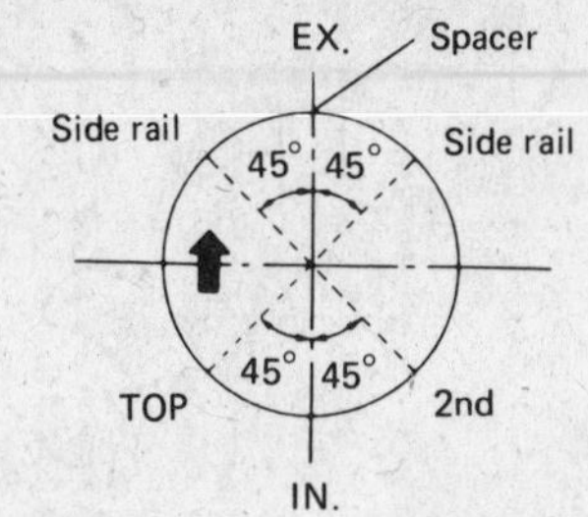

Arrange ring end gaps around piston as shown

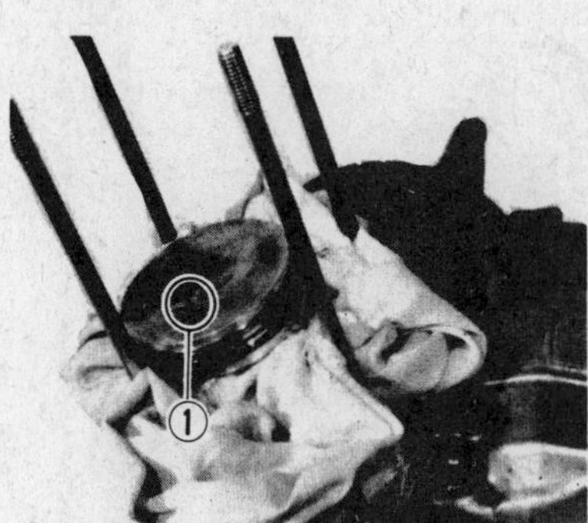

Piston crown arrow (1) must point towards the exhaust port

5. Be sure that the dowel pins are in place on the cylinder studs on the left side of the engine.

6. Use a new cylinder base gasket.

7. Compress the rings and fit the cylinder while pulling the cam chain through. Keep the chain taut or it may jam on the crank sprocket.

8. Install the cam chain guide. Be sure it is properly seated in its holder in the crankcase.

9. Tighten the cylinder base nuts to 5-8 ft. lbs.

CRANKCASE COVER COMPONENTS

Left Side

REMOVAL

1. Remove the recoil starter assembly. Remove the starter motor.
2. Remove the starter cup nut.
3. Remove the starter cup.
4. Remove the lead wire clamp bolt.
5. Remove the magneto cover with neutral indicator switch.
6. Remove the O-ring and neutral indicator switch contact and spring.
7. Remove the starter motor idle gear shaft.
8. Remove the idle gear.
9. Remove the crankshaft spacer.
10. Remove the magneto nut.
11. Remove the starter clutch assembly.
12. Remove the starter clutch gear, bearing and woodruff key.
13. Remove the secondary drive gear nut. Place transmission in "Low" to do this.
14. Remove the gear.
15. Remove the secondary gear housing inner case.
16. Remove the reverse switch.

Cylinder dowel pin locations (1)

Removing the starter cup nut

INSPECTION

1. Clean all parts thoroughly in a safe solvent.
2. Check gears for damage and wear and replace as required.
3. Use new gaskets and O-rings when assembling.

ASSEMBLY

1. Assembly is the reverse of disassembly.
2. Clean the rotor and the tapered portion of the crankshaft before installing it.

Magneto cover screws

3. Use a non-permanent thread-locking compound on the rotor nut.

4. Rotor nut torque is 109-123 ft. lbs.

Recoil Starter

DISASSEMBLY

1. Remove the recoil starter assembly from the engine (four bolts).
2. Remove the nut and separate the components.

CAUTION: *Watch the expanding spring when the parts are disassembled.*

INSPECTION

1. Clean all parts thoroughly.
2. Check all parts for damage and replace as required.

ASSEMBLY

1. When installing the coil spring, hook the end of the spring onto the rib provided on the case.
2. Grease the spring thoroughly.
3. Wind the starter rope onto the reel. Engage the reel tab with the spring cut-out.
4. Grease the shaft and ratchet before installation.
5. To adjust tension, hook the rope onto the reel and turn it clockwise 3 or 4 times.

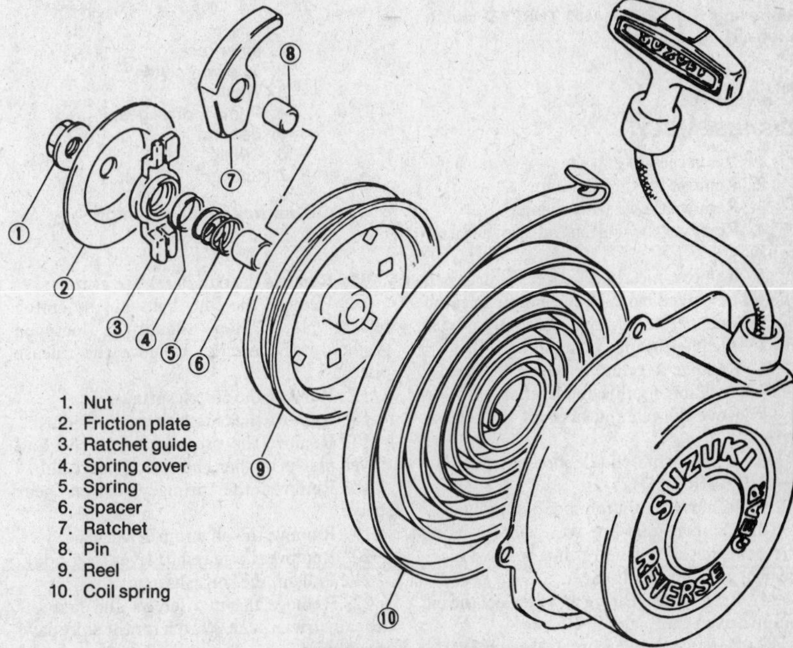

Recoil starter assembly

Clutch cover screws

Clutch release outer guide assembly

Removing the LEFT-HAND THREAD clutch shoe nut

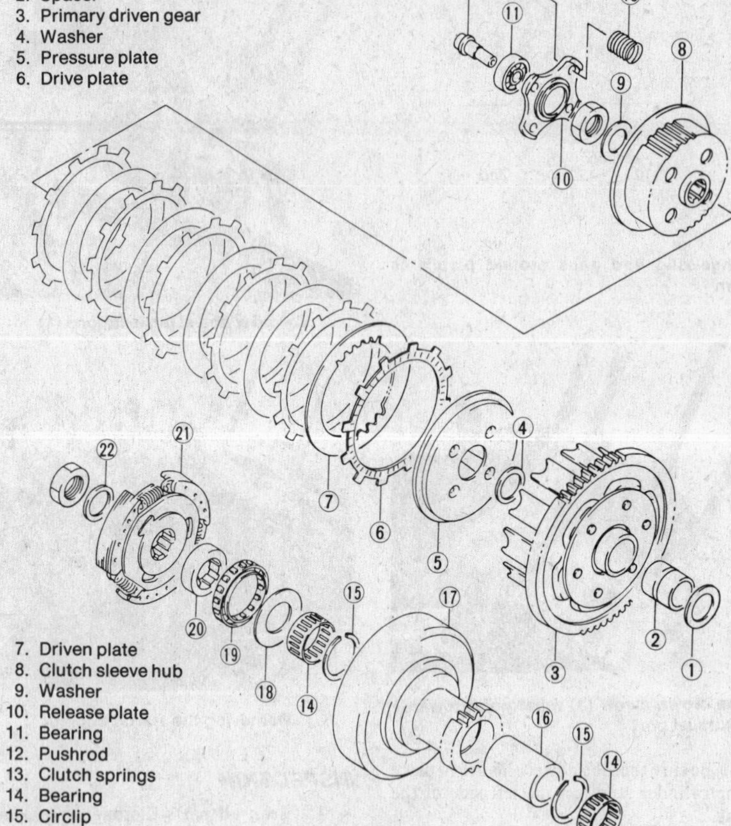

1. Washer
2. Spacer
3. Primary driven gear
4. Washer
5. Pressure plate
6. Drive plate
7. Driven plate
8. Clutch sleeve hub
9. Washer
10. Release plate
11. Bearing
12. Pushrod
13. Clutch springs
14. Bearing
15. Circlip
16. Spacer
17. Primary drive gear
18. Washer
19. One-way clutch
20. Spacer
21. Shoe
22. Lockwasher

Clutch assembly

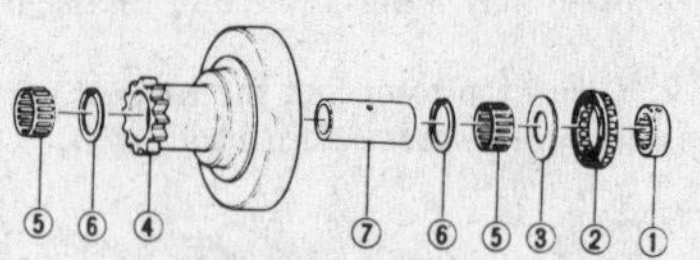

1. Inner race
2. One-way clutch
3. Washer
4. Primary drive gear
5. Bearing
6. Circlip
7. Spacer

One-way clutch assembly

Right Side

DISASSEMBLY

1. Drain the oil.
2. Remove the oil filter cap.
3. Remove the oil filter element.
4. Remove the clutch release adjuster cap.
5. Remove the clutch cover. A drip pan should be placed beneath the engine to catch oil residue before removal. If the cover is stuck, free it with a plastic mallet.
6. Remove the clutch release outerguide, release ball, inner guide and washer.
7. Rove the pin and take off the release arm.
8. Remove the clutch shoe nut (LEFT-HAND THREAD).
9. Remove the clutch shoe assembly.
10. Remove the one-way clutch inner race, the clutch, washer, primary drive gear, bearings, circlips and spacer.
11. Remove the E-ring and take off the oil pump driven gear.
12. Remove the oil pump (three screws).
13. Remove the clutch release arm.
14. Remove the four bolts on the clutch release plate. They should be loosened gradually and evenly. Remove the release plate.
15. Remove the clutch springs.
16. Remove the clutch sleeve hub nut.
17. Remove the pressure disc, drive and driven plates, washer and clutch sleeve hub.
18. Remove the primary driven gear spacer.
19. Remove the oil pump drive gear.
20. Remove the gearshift lever (left side).
21. Pull out the shift shaft.
22. Remove the two screws and take off the cam driven gear. Watch for the shift pawl assembly.

INSPECTION

1. Clean all metal parts in solvent and check for obvious signs of wear.
2. Measure the thickness of each clutch drive (friction) plate. Replace the plates as a set if any measures less than 2.4mm (0.094 in.).
3. Measure drive plate tab width. Replace plates if the tabs are worn or if they average less than 11.0mm (0.43 in.).
4. Check driven (steel) plate warpage. Maximum allowable warp is 0.1mm (0.004 in.).
5. Measure clutch spring free length and replace them as a set if any measures less than 27.4mm (1.08 in.).
6. Inspect the clutch shoes for chipping, cracking, uneven wear or a burnt condition. If the grooves are worn away, or if other signs of damage are evident, replace shoes as a set.
7. Check the clutch wheel for scoring, cracks, etc., and replace if damaged.
8. Check the one-way clutch bearing for damage.
9. Check the clutch release balls for pitting, wear, etc. If any damage is evident, replace the assembly.
10. Check the starter clutch rollers for damage. Check springs for tension.
11. Check the oil pump for smooth shaft rotation. The pump cannot be disassembled. Replace it if shaft rotation is not smooth and noiseless.

12. Check gear shift components for chipped teeth, a bent condition, etc.

ASSEMBLY

1. Use new gaskets and O-rings.
2. Be certain all parts are well lubricated during assembly.
3. The oil pump should be soaked with clean motor oil before installation.
4. Oil pump mounting screws should be secured with a non-permanent thread locking compound and tightened to 5-7 ft. lbs.
5. Assembly is basically the reverse of disassembly. The following points should be especially noted:
   a. Clutch sleeve hub nut torque is 44-58 ft. lbs.
   b. Clutch spring bolts should be tightened gradually and in a cross pattern.
   c. When fitting the clutch shoe spacer, align the oil hole with the crankshaft oil hole.

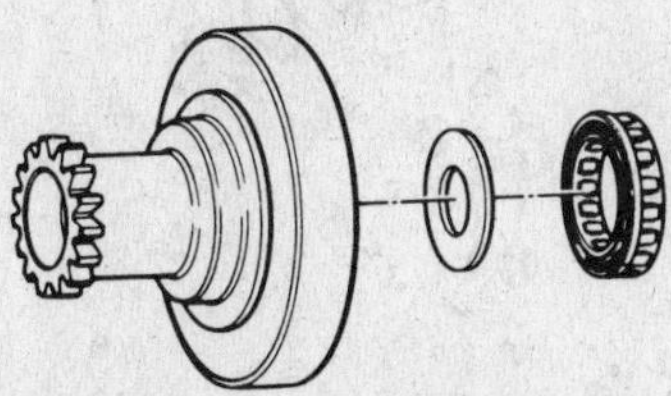

One-way clutch installation

Clutch shoe spacer hole (1) must align with crankshaft oil hole

Clutch cover dowel pins (2) and oil jet (3) locations

   d. Shoe nut torqueis 65-80 ft. lbs. This is a LEFT-HAND THREAD.
   e. Clutch release nut torque is 7.0-8.5 ft. lbs.
   f. Be sure oil jets and dowel pins are in place before fitting the clutch cover.

Align release arm pin (4) with pin guide (5)

Crankcase bolts

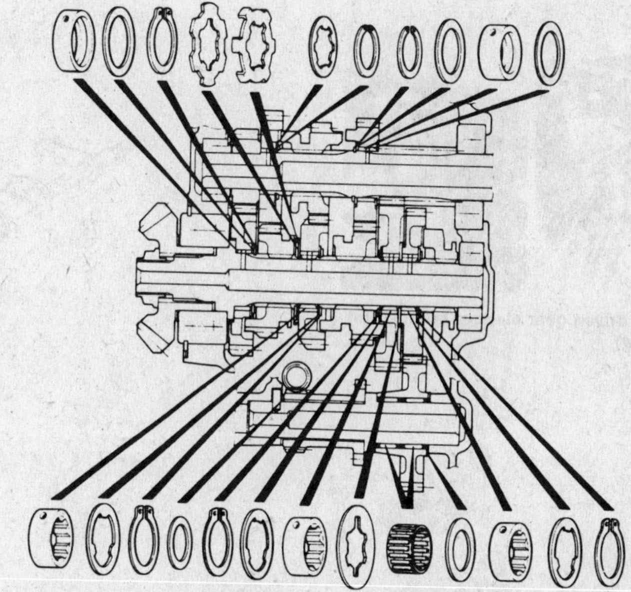

Transmission component installation

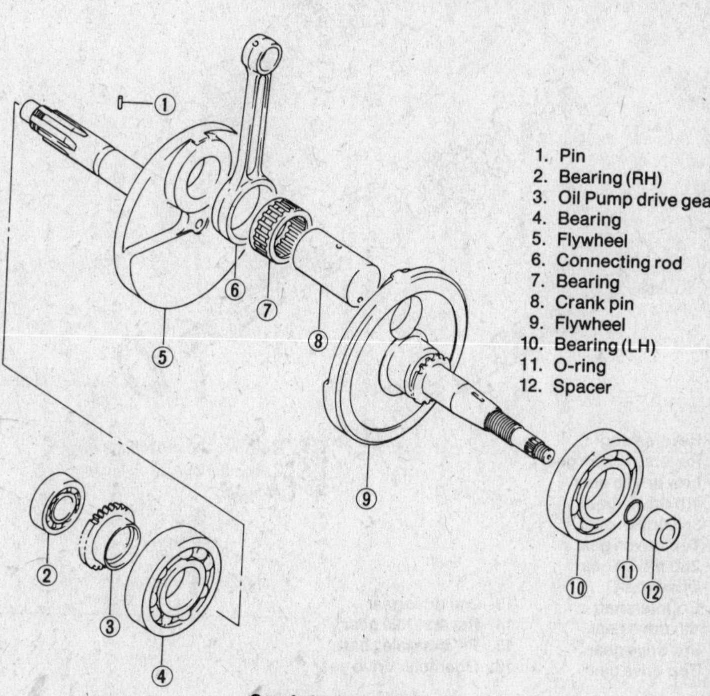

Crankshaft assembly

Shift fork shafts

1. Gearshift lever
2. Reverse gear shifting cam
3. Reverse cam stopper
4. Reverse gear switch
5. Cam driven gear
6. Reverse dog shift fork
7. Gear shift fork No. 1
8. Gear shift fork No. 2
9. Shift fork shaft No. 1
10. Shift cam stopper plate
11. Shift cam
12. Neutral indicator switch
13. Gear shift fork No. 3
14. Shift fork shaft No. 2
15. Shift cam stopper
16. Gearshift shaft

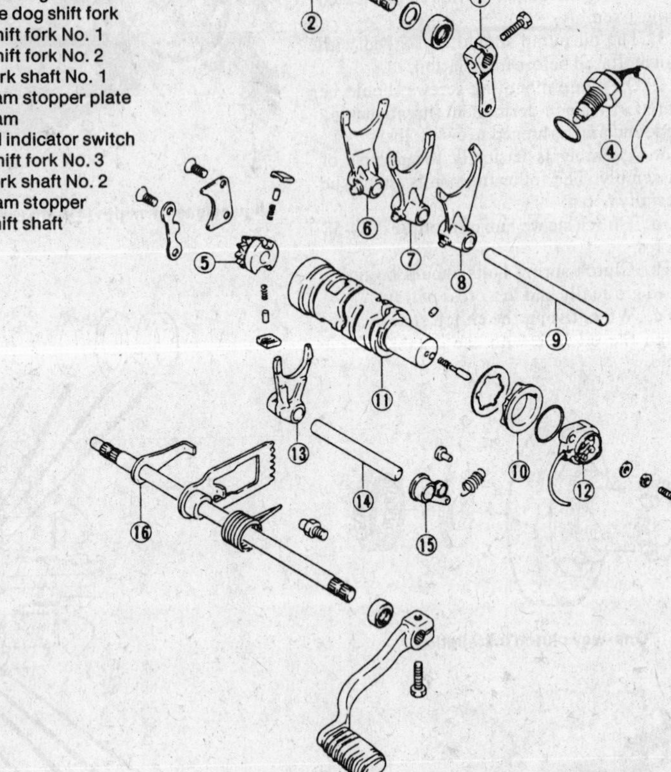

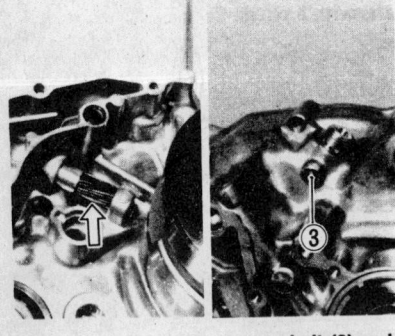

Odometer driven gear stopper bolt (3) and gear (arrow)

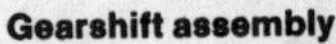

Gearshift assembly

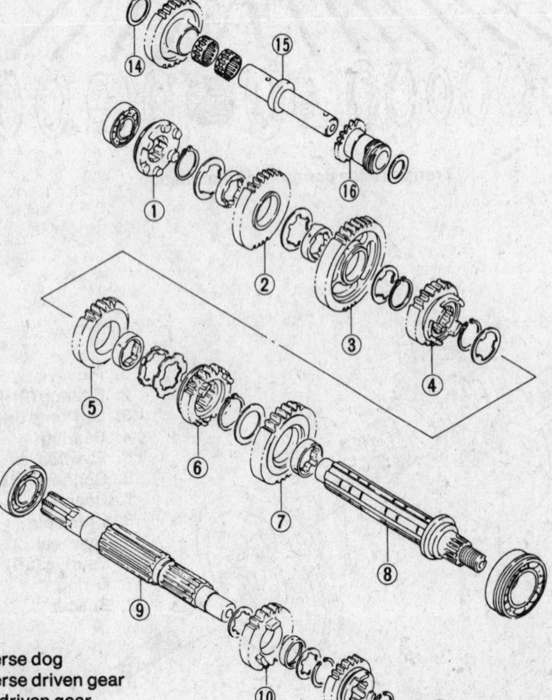

1. Reverse dog
2. Reverse driven gear
3. Low driven gear
4. 4th driven gear
5. 3rd driven gear
6. Top driven gear
7. 2nd driven gear
8. Drive shaft
9. Countershaft
10. 4th drive gear
11. 3rd drive gear
12. Top drive gear
13. 2nd drive gear
14. Reverse idle gear
15. Reverse idle shaft
16. Odometer drive gear

Transmission assembly

Proper thrust washer installation

g. When fitting the cover, align the clutch release arm pin with the pin guide.

CRANKCASE COMPONENTS

Splitting The Cases

1. Remove the engine from the frame.
2. Remove the cylinder head and cylinder.
3. Remove the left and right side crankcase cover components as outlined above.
4. Remove the cam stopper bolt, spring and plunger from the crankcase.
5. Remove the crankcase bolts.
6. Separate the case halves. The crank and gear clusters remain in the left crankcase half.
7. Remove the gearshift fork shafts.
8. Remove the reverse gear shift shaft.
9. Remove the gears, shit forks and shift cam.
10. Remove the odometer driven gear stopper bolt. Remove the odometer gear.
11. Press the crankshaft out of the case.

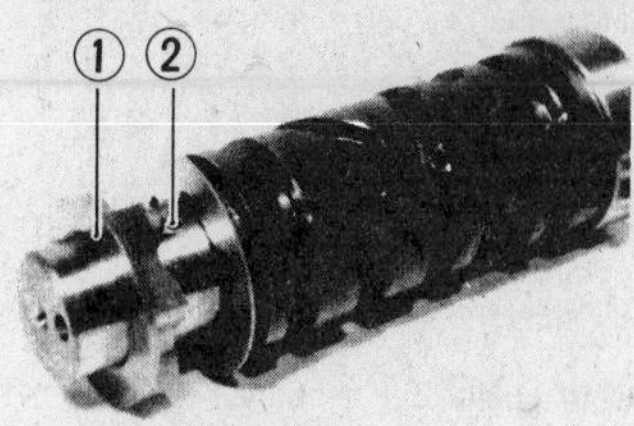

Align pin groove (1) with pin (2)

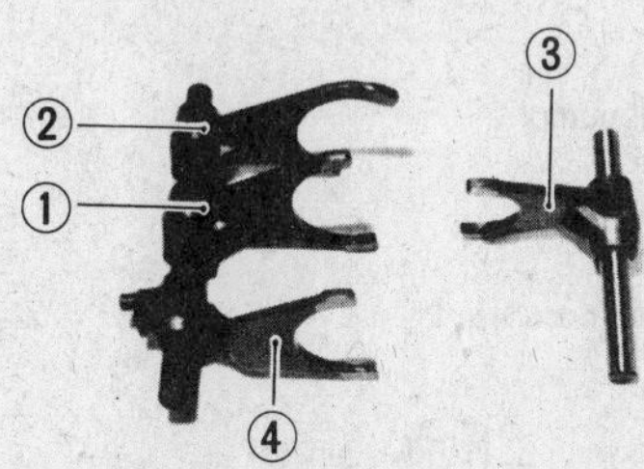

Shift forks: (1), 4th driven gear; (2), top driven gear; (3), 3rd driven gear; (4), Reverse

Crankcase half dowel pins (1) and o-ring (2)

12. Remove the oil sump filter cap and filter.

Inspection

1. Clean all metal parts in a safe solvent.
2. Check all components for obvious signs of wear as directed in Engine Rebuilding section of "General Information." Compare readings taken at the various measurement points against the standard specifications given in the chart below.

Case Assembly

1. Lubricate all components thoroughly during the assembly procedure.
2. Use new oil seals, gaskets, O-rings.
3. Do not strike the ends of the crankshaft when installing it in the case. The shaft must be drawn in from the left side.
4. Refer to the illustrations of the transmission assembly and install all circlips and washers in the proper locations. New circlips should always be used if the shafts have been disassembled.
5. Circlips are installed with the rounded sides facing the gear.
6. The 2nd drive gear is a press fit on the shaft and should be secured with thread locking compound. After mounting, ensure that the adjacent gear can spin freely.

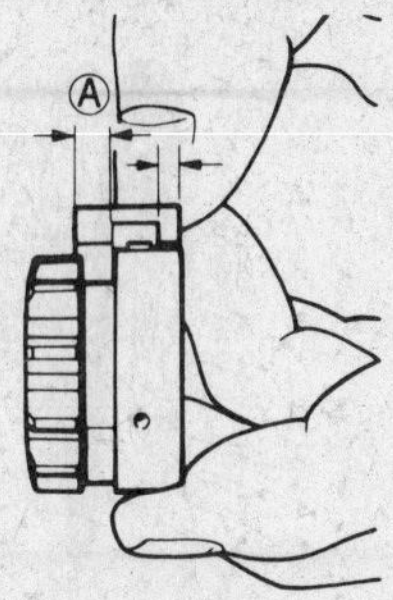

Wide shoulder of the pawl (A) must face away from the engine

7. When fitting the cam stopper plate on the shift cam, align the pin groove and the pin.
8. Refer to the illustration identifying the four shift forks. Be certain they are properly located.
9. When installing the reverse shaft assembly, align the pin groove and the pin.
10. Crankcase mating surfaces should be coated with liquid gasket compound.

NOTE: *Be certain the dowel pins and O-ring are in place on the left crankcase half before mating.*

11. Tighten the crankcase bolts gradually and evenly. Check that the crank and gear shafts can rotate freely as the bolts are tightened.
12. Tighten the cam stopper bolt to 13-20 ft. lbs.
13. Tighten the reverse switch to 15-18 ft. lbs.
14. Note that the wide shoulder of the gear shift pawls must face the outside of the engine when the assembly is installed. Use a non-permanent thread locking compound on the screws.
15. When installing the gear shift shaft, be sure the pawl spring is properly engaged. Slip the shaft into place and mesh the center teeth with the center teeth of the shaft cam. Check shifting before proceding.

FUEL SYSTEM

CARBURETOR

NOTE: *Refer to the "General Information" section for carburetor theory and troubleshooting procedures.*

Removal

1. Remove the seat.
2. Remove the Choke knob.
3. Remove the Reverse knob.

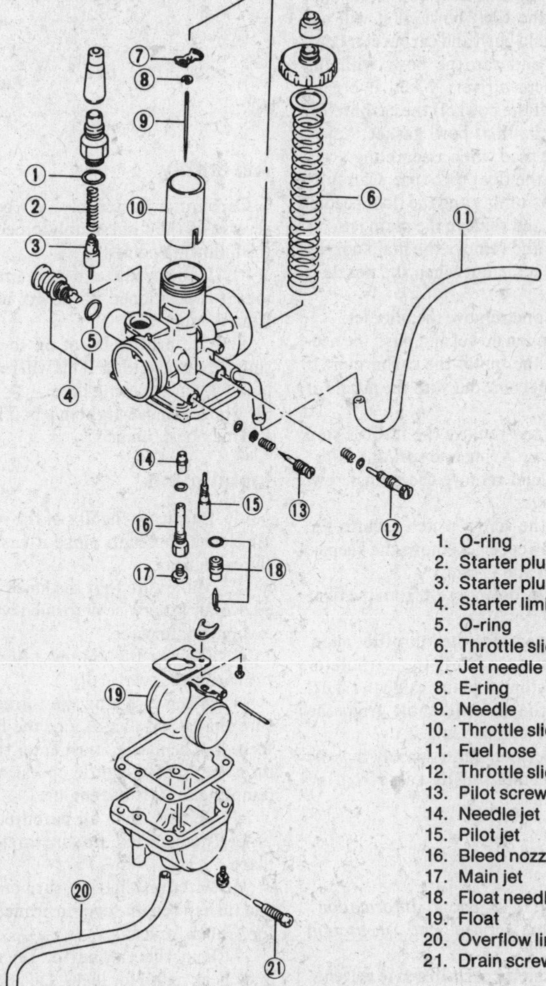

1. O-ring
2. Starter plunger spring
3. Starter plunger
4. Starter limiter
5. O-ring
6. Throttle slide spring
7. Jet needle stopper plate
8. E-ring
9. Needle
10. Throttle slide
11. Fuel hose
12. Throttle slide stop screw
13. Pilot screw
14. Needle jet
15. Pilot jet
16. Bleed nozzle
17. Main jet
18. Float needle and seat
19. Float
20. Overflow line
21. Drain screw

Carburetor

4. Remove the four odometer panel mounting screws.
5. Remove the panel.
6. Remove the two front fender mounting bolts near the odometer panel.
7. Remove the two front fender mounting bolts from the front of the machine.
8. Remove the four bolts that secure the fender brackets to the frame.
9. Pull the fender forward and free of the frame.
10. Remove the two bolts securing the air cleaner inlet case. Remove the case.
11. Unscrew the starter plunger assembly from the carburetor body. Arrange the plunger cable so that it will not be accidentally damaged.
12. Unscrew the carburetor cap and carefully pull the slide assembly out of the carburetor.
13. If the slide assembly is not going to be serviced, wrap it in a clean rag and place it out of the way to avoid accidental damage.
14. Loosen the carburetor clamp screws.
15. Pull the carburetor body free of the intake manifold and air cleaner hoses.

CAUTION: *The float bowl contains gasoline. Drain it into a suitable container and dispose of it properly.*

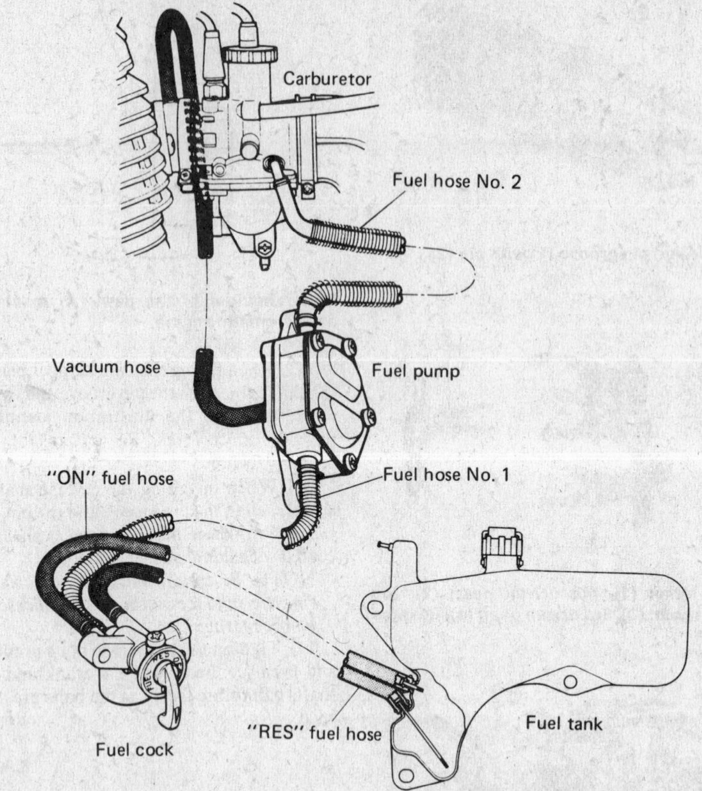

Fuel system hoses and components

Disassembly

1. Unscrew the four float bowl screws.
2. Remove the float bowl. If it will not come right off, hold bowl and carburetor body with one hand and rap the bowl with the handle of the screwdriver. When it breaks free, carefully lift the bowl off the carburetor.
3. Remove the float bowl gasket. A new gasket should be used when assembling.
4. Push out the float pivot pin. Carefully lift off the float assembly and the float needle.
5. Unscrew and remove the main jet.
6. Unscrew and remove the main nozzle. An O-ring may come out when the nozzle is taken out.
7. Unscrew and remove the pilot jet.
8. Use a wooden dowel and push the needle jet out from the top of the carburetor. If the O-ring did not come out with the nozzle, it will now.
9. Unscrew and remove the throttle stop (idle speed) screw, O-ring and spring.
10. Unscrew and remove the pilot screw, spring and O-rings.
11. Remove the screw which secures the float needle seat keeper. Remove the keeper, plate, needle seat and O-ring.
12. Remove the drain screw from the float bowl.
13. To disassemble the throttle slide, compress the spring against the carburetor cap, remove the stopper plate inside the slide, and disengage the throttle cable from the slide. Separate all components.
14. The starter plunger assembly may be separated by disconnecting the cable from the plunger.

Inspection

NOTE: *Refer to "General Information" for carburetor service and inspection procedures.*

1. Clean all metal parts in a safe solvent.
2. All gaskets and O-rings should be replaced when assembling the carburetor.

Assembly

Carburetor assembly is basically the reverse of the disassembly procedures. Note the following points:

1. If the needle clip was removed, ensure that it is positioned in the 4th needle groove from the top.
2. Use a little bit of oil to lubricate O-rings when installing. This will reduce the risk of knicking or tearing them.
3. Do not overtighten jets. They are brass and may be damaged.

Installation

1. Lubricate the lips of the manifold and air cleaner hoses to make it easier to install the carburetor.
2. Make sure that the hoses are not folded over or otherwise deformed when the carb is slipped into place.
3. Tighten the clamps after positioning the carburetor vertically.
4. When inserting the throttle slide, ensure that it slips right into the bore. Do not force it. The needle must enter the needle jet directly. Check throttle operation before attempting to start the engine.
5. Be sure that all carburetor lines are properly connected. Be sure safety clips are in place.
6. After installation, turn on the petcock and turn the engine over to prime the carburetor. Check for leaks.
7. Run the engine for several minutes and check again for leaks. Do not operate the machine until certain that all connections are properly made.

PETCOCK

The petcock is located on the front of the fuel tank and is accessible after removing the seat and rear fender.

To remove the petcock, remove the two screws, pull it out, and disconnect the fuel lines.

CAUTION: *Watch for fuel leaks.*

FUEL STRAINERS

Each line from the petcock to the gas tank is fitted with a fuel strainer at the tank end.

These lines should not be disconnected unless the tank is almost empty, or gasoline will be spilled.

If the tank is empty, remove the petcock, as outlined above, and disconnect the two lines from the tank.

Clean the strainers in clean solvent and blow them dry. If foreign matter cannot be removed, the strainer(s) must be replaced.

Be sure to connect the lines to the proper fitting. The longer strainer ("RES") is connected to the lower fitting.

CAUTION: *Be sure that connections are properly made and tight. Check for leaks before operating the machine.*

Fuel Pump

1. The fuel pump is mounted on the front of the fuel tank and is accessed by removing the seat and rear fender.
2. The pump needs no routine mainten-

Petcock mounting bolts (4) and fuel pump mounting bolts (5)

CARBURETOR SPECIFICATIONS

Type	VM24SS
Venturi size	24 mm/0.94 in.
ID No.	18A00/18A01
Main jet	115
Needle	4JR40-4/4JR45-4
Needle jet	0-2
Throttle slide cutaway	1.5
Pilot jet	17.5
Starter jet	30
Pilot screw (turns out)	2¡
Float height	2.45 ± 1.0 mm/0.96 ± 0.04 in.
Idle speed	1400 ± 50 rpm

ance. However, if it fails, or shows signs of leaking, it must be replaced.

3. To remove the pump, remove the two mounting bracket bolts and disconnect the lines.

4. When fitting the pump, note that the line from the petcock goes to the inlet pipe on the pump which is marked "IN."

CAUTION: *When making pump connections, be sure that they are tight. Check for leaks before riding the machine.*

FUEL LINES

Fuel lines should be replaced every four years or whenever any of them shows signs of cracking, hardening or abrasion damage.

Refer to the illustration of the fuel system lines.

FUEL TANK

Removal and Disassembly

1. Disconnect the fuel tank vent hose.
2. Remove the seat.
3. Remove the four securing bolts and take off the rear fender.

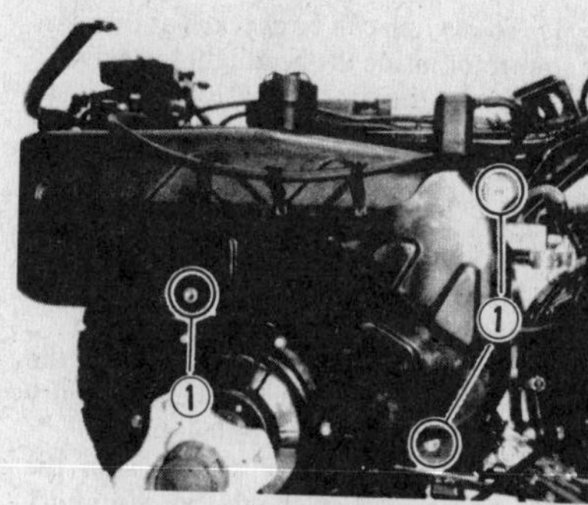

Fuel tank mounting bolts

4. Remove the right side rear wheel. See "Chassis" for procedures.
5. Disconnect the vacuum hose from the fuel pump.
6. Disconnect the fuel line at the carburetor.
7. Remove the three mounting bolts and take out the fuel tank.

CAUTION: *Handle the tank and its contents carefully.*

8. Empty the contents of the tank into a suitable container—one which is safe for the storage of flammable gasoline.
9. Remove the petcock mounting screws.
10. Pull the petcock out and disconnect the lines.
11. Remove the two bracket bolts which secure the fuel pump.
12. Disconnect the lines and remove the fuel pump.

Assembly and Installation

1. Reverse the removal procedure.
2. Be sure that all connections are properly made. Refer to the fuel line diagram.
3. Be certain that all fuel and vacuum line connections are tight and that all safety clips and clamps are in place.
4. Be sure that tank and component mounting bolts are properly tightened.
5. Fill the tank with fuel and check for leaks before operating the machine.

Electrical System

IGNITION SYSTEM

The major components of the ignition system are the CDI unit, the magneto coil, the ignition coil and the spark plug.

Ignition Coil

1. Remove the seat.
2. Remove the front fender.
3. Disconnect the ignition coil low tension leads: black/white and white/blue.
4. Resistance between these two leads should be about 2 ohms. This is the primary coil resistance. If open (infinite resistance) or shorted (zero resistance), replace the ignition coil.
5. Disconnect the spark plug high tension lead.
6. Measure the resistance between the spark plug cap and the white/blue lead. It should be 10-25,000 ohms. This is the secondary coil resistance. If not within this range, replace the ignition coil.

Magneto Coil

1. Remove the seat.
2. Remove the front fender.
3. Disconnect the pick-up and power source coil lead connectors.
4. Measure pick-up coil resistance (blue and green leads). It should be 70-160 ohms.
5. Measure power source coil resistance (brown and pink wires). It should be 150-250 ohms.
6. Replace the pick-up coil or the alternator if the reading(s) are not within these ranges.

CDI Unit

If the ignition coil, pick-up coil and power source coil all check out, but there is still no spark, suspect the CDI unit. The easiest test method is to replace the unit with a new one.

CHARGING SYSTEM

NOTE: *The battery must be in good condition and fully charged or results of the alternator output check will not be valid.*

1. Remove the seat.
2. Remove the tool tray.
3. Set the ignition switch to the LIGHT position.
4. Start the engine and run it at 5000 rpm. Check the voltage across the battery terminals. It should be 14-15 VDC.
5. If voltage is too high, suspect the regulator/rectifier unit. If it is too low, the problem may be the regulator/rectifier or the alternator.
6. Disconnect the three yellow alternator leads at the plastic connector.
7. With the engine running at 5000 rpm, check for voltage across all three yellow leads, two at a time. The meter must be set to an AC range. In each case, the reading should be at least 55 VAC.
8. If the AC voltage readings are not within this range, further tests are required.
9. If all three measurements are low, and about equal, suspect a faulty rotor.
10. If one or more of the readings is low, suspect the alternator windings.
11. Shut off the engine and check the resistance across each pair of yellow alternator leads with an ohmmeter. If all three readings are similar, suspect a defective rotor. If one or two of the readings are very low or high, suspect the alternator windings.
12. Check resistance between each lead and the stator core. The readings must be infinite. If it is not, the coils are grounded and the alternator stator must be replaced.
13. If the alternator passes all its tests, but charging voltage is not within specification, replace the regulator/rectifier.

STARTING SYSTEM

The starting system consists of the starter motor and clutch, the starter relay, neutral relay, reverse switch, neutral switch, starter button, engine stop switch, ignition switch and battery.

Testing

1. If the starter motor spins when the starter button is pressed, but the engine does not, the problem is likely a defective starter clutch. Refer to the "Engine and Transmission" section for removal procedures.

2. If the engine turns over very slowly, possible causes include cold weather, oil which is of too high a viscosity for conditions, a low battery or a defective starter motor.

3. If the engine fails to turn over, but the starter motor is drawing current, the problem may be due to a low battery or a defective starter motor.

4. If nothing at all happens when the starter button is pushed, check that all switches are properly set and then that all are properly functioning. If they are, suspect the starter relay.

5. A clattering sound when the starter button is pushed may be caused by a defective starter motor or defective relay.

Starter Relay

1. If the battery is known to be in good condition, and nothing at all happens when the starter button is pushed, check the starter relay.

2. Disconnect the high tension cable at the starter motor. When the starter button is pushed, there should be an audible "click" which indicates that the relay is operating.

3. For access to the relay, remove the seat. Remove the relay cover.

4. Disconnect the high tension cable from the positive terminal of the battery. Reconnect the low tension (system) lead to the battery.

5. Check for continuity across the high tension relay terminals. There should be continuity when the starter button is pushed. If there is not, replace the relay.

6. Disconnect the black/white and yellow/black starter relay wires. Check resistance across the wires. It should be about 3-7 ohms. Replace the relay if resistance is not within this range.

Neutral Relay

1. This relay can be checked with an ohmmeter once it is removed from the machine.

2. Refer to the illustration of the relay connector.

3. Apply a 12 VDC source across the terminals "1" and "2" with the positive lead of the source connected to "1".

4. Check for continuity across terminals "3" and "4". If there is none, replace the relay.

Starter Motor

REMOVAL AND DISASSEMBLY

1. Disconnect the high tension lead at the starter motor.

2. Remove the two mounting bolts.

3. Take off the starter.

4. Remove the two through bolts and separate the end caps.

5. Take the armature out of the casing.

INSPECTION

1. Check for electrical continuity between the commutator and the armature core using an ohmmeter or test light and battery. If continuity exists, the armature coil is grounded and the starter motor must be replaced.

2. Check for continuity between all of the commutator segments. Continuity must exist in each case.

3. Examine carbon brushes for damage to the contact surfaces. Measure the length of each brush. Replace the set if either measures less than 6mm (0.24 in.).

4. The mica undercut of the commutator should be at least 0.2mm (0.008 in.). Any carbon deposits should be cleaned out of the commutator grooves and a piece of hacksaw blade or the like used to increase undercut depth, if necessary.

5. Polish the commutator with fine emery cloth and clean it thoroughly before installation.

6. Check the condition of the bearing in the end cap. Replace it if damage or wear is evident. Check condition of the bushing in the brush end cap.

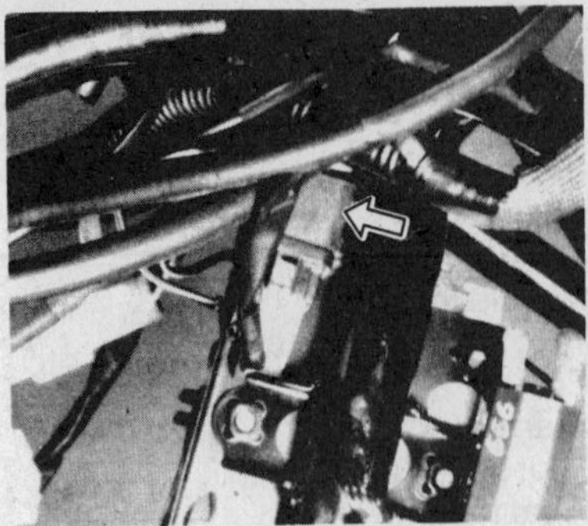

Neutral relay location

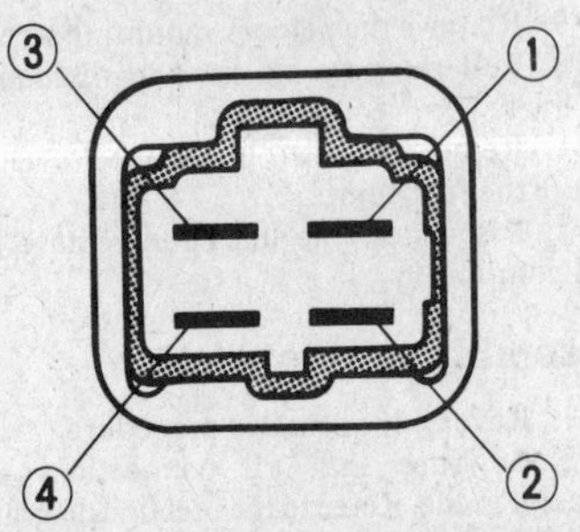

Neutral relay connectors (see text)

Starter motor components

Starter motor alignment marks

ASSEMBLY AND INSTALLATION

1. The use of new O-rings and a new oil seal is recommended.

2. Apply a small amount of moly grease to the brush side of the armature.

3. When installing the brush end cap, align the protrusion of the brush holder with the groove on the cap.

4. Grease the bearing and the lips of the oil seal before installing the cap.

5. When the end caps are fitted, align their marks with the marks on the case.

6. Through bolts should be secured with a non-permanent thread-locking compound.

7. Oil the O-ring before fitting the starter to the engine.

ELECTRICAL SWITCHES

Switches can be checked with an ohmmeter or battery-powered test light.

Emergency Stop Switch

1. The switch can be checked at the plastic connector inside the headlight housing.

2. Disconnect the plastic connector holding the Stop Switch wires.

3. When the switch is set to the "OFF" position, there should be continuity between the black/white and black/yellow wires.

4. When the switch is in the "RUN" position, there should be continuity between the orange and orange/white wires.

5. If both of these conditions are not met, the switch is defective and must be replaced.

Starter Button

1. The switch can be checked at the plastic connector inside the headlight housing.

2. When the starter button is pushed, there must be continuity between the orange/white and yellow/green wires.

Dimmer Switch

1. The switch can be checked at the plastic connector inside the headlight housing.

2. When the dimmer switch is in the "HI" position, there should be continuity between the green and the yellow wires.

3. When the dimmer switch is in the "LO" position, there should be continuity between the green and the white wires.

Ignition/Lighting Switch

1. The switch can be checked at the plastic connector inside the headlight housing.

2. When the switch is "OFF" there should be continuity between the black/yellow and black/white wires.

3. When the switch is "ON" there should be continuity between the red and orange wires.

4. When set to the "LIGHT" position, there should be continuity between the red, orange and green wires.

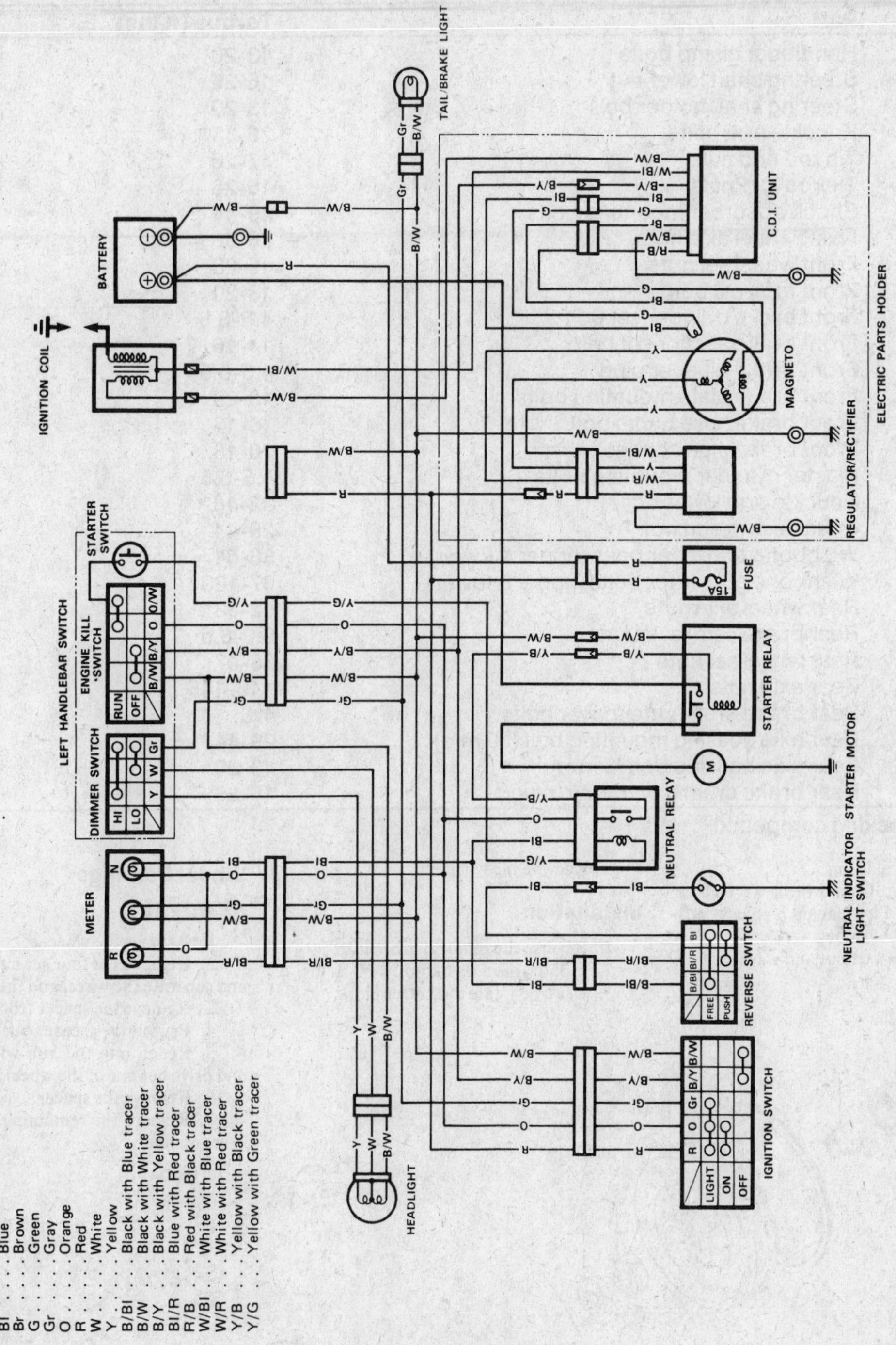

Wiring diagram

5. If the switch does not pass all of these tests, replace it.

Neutral Switch

1. The lead is accessible on the wiring harness near the carburetor.
2. When "ON" there should be continuity between the blue wire and ground.
3. When "OFF" there should be no continuity to ground.

Reverse Switch

1. The switch leads are accessible on the wiring harness near the carburetor.
2. When the transmission is in NEUTRAL, there should be continuity between the blue and the blue/black wires.
3. When the transmission is in REVERSE, there should be continuity between the blue/red and the blue wires.

Bulb Specifications
Headlight 45/45W
Tailight 5W
Odometer light 3.4W
Reverse indicator 3.4W
Neutral indicator 3.4W

CHASSIS

FRONT WHEELS

Removal

1. Park the machine on a level surface.
2. Apply the parking brake.
3. Remove the plastic axle nut cap.
4. Remove the cotter pin from the axle nut.

CHASSIS TORQUE SPECIFICATIONS

Part	Torque (ft lbs)
Handlebar clamp bolts	13-20
Steering shaft lower nut	16-26
Steering shaft holder bols	13-20
Knuckle arm bolts	26-33*
Tie rod end nuts	17-26
Tie rod locknuts	16-26
Shock absorber mounting bolts	29-44
Front wheel axle nuts	36-58
Front wheel set nuts	15-23
Front footrest bolts	13-20
Front brake cylinder set bolt	4.5-6.5
Front brake anchor set bolt	11-16
Front brake bleeder plug	4.5-6.5
Front brake plate mounting bolts	13-20
Front brake hose banjo bolt	15-18
Front brake pipe connecting nut	10-13
Master cylinder mounting bolts	4.5-6.5
Knuckle arm lower bolt	32-48*
Knuckle arm end nut	29-44
Wishbone arm inner bolts (upper & lower)	36-51
Wishbone arm outer bolts (upper & lower)	87-123*
Rear wheel axle nuts	62-83
Rear brake cam lever nut	6.0-8.5
Rear wheel set nuts	33-47
Rear axle nuts	116-145
Rear brake drum outer cover bolts	4-6
Rear axle housing mounting bolt (10 mm)	29-44
Rear axle housing bolt (8 mm)	13-20
Rear brake drum cover drain plug	16-26

*Use thread locking compound

5. Loosen the axle nut.
6. Support the front wheels an inch or two off the ground by placing a sturdy, safe support beneath the frame.
7. Remove the axle nut and washer.
8. Remove the wheel.

Installation

1. Reverse the removal procedure.
2. Tighten the axle nut to 36-58 ft. lbs.
3. Use a new axle nut cotter pin.

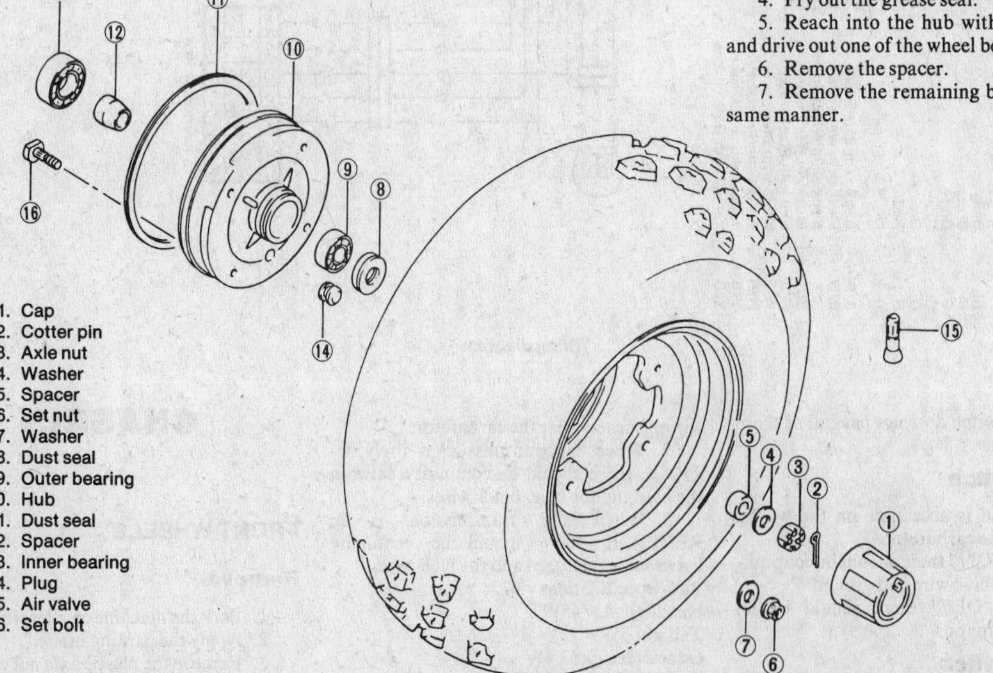

Front wheel assembly

Wheel Bearings

REMOVAL

1. Remove the wheel.
2. Remove the four set nuts and washers and separate the wheel and the hub.
3. Remove the spacer from the hub.
4. Pry out the grease seal.
5. Reach into the hub with a long drift and drive out one of the wheel bearings.
6. Remove the spacer.
7. Remove the remaining bearing in the same manner.

INSPECTION

1. Wash the wheel bearings thoroughly in a safe solvent to remove all of the old grease.

2. Inspect the general condition of the bearings. There should be no rust, pitting or obvious signs of wear or damage on either balls or races.

3. Slowly rotate each bearing. Rotation should be smooth, noiseless and free of binding or unevenness. If any of the above conditions exist, both bearings should be replaced.

4. Place each bearing on a flat surface and hold the inner race firmly in place. Attempt to move the outer race back and forth. If any play is evident, the bearings should be replaced.

5. If equipment is available, a dial gauge can be used to check bearing run-out. Pass an axle-sized rod through the bearing and check axial and diametrical run-out with the gauge. If axial run-out exceeds 0.1mm (0.004 in.) or if diametrical run-out is greater than 0.05mm (0.002 in.), replace the bearings.

To check diametrical run-out, the dial gauge is placed directly on top of the outer race and the race moved up and down.

To check axial run-out, the gauge is positioned to bear against the side of the outer race and the race moved back and forth.

INSTALLATION

1. Pack each bearing with a good grade of bearing grease.

2. Clean old grease out of the hub. Place a small quantity of fresh grease in the hub.

3. Install the inner bearing first. Be sure the bearing is pressed straight into the hub, not cocked or tilted.

NOTE: *Be sure bearing is installed with the sealed side facing out.*

4. Install the spacer.

5. Press in the outside wheel bearing. Be sure it is pressed straight in and not cocked or tilted.

6. Use a new grease seal. Lightly lubricate the seal lips and press it straight into the hub. Be sure it is flush with the hub boss.

7. Assemble the wheel and hub. Tighten the four set nuts gradually and in a cross pattern until the specified torque of 15-23 ft. lbs. is reached.

REAR WHEELS

Removal

1. Park the machine on a level surface.

2. Block the front wheels so the machine will not roll.

3. Remove the plastic axle nut cap.

4. Remove the cotter pin from the axle nut.

5. Loosen the axle nut.

6. Support the rear wheels an inch or so off the ground by placing a sturdy, safe support beneath the frame.

7. Remove the axle nut and washers.

8. Remove the wheel.

9. Remove the four set nuts and washers to separate the wheel from the hub.

Inspection

1. Check the condition of the hub splines and the mating splines on the rear axle.

2. Grease the splines lightly before fitting the wheel.

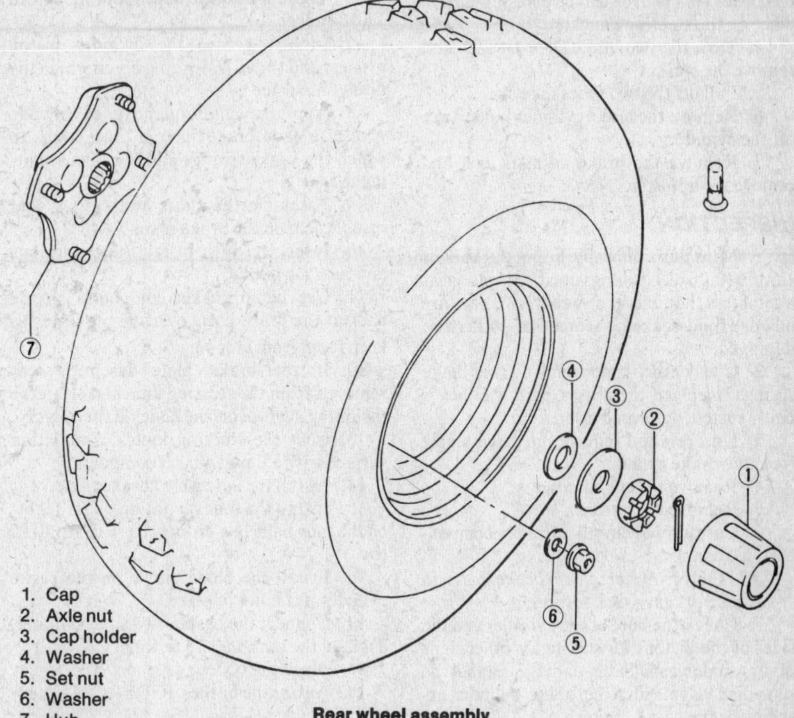

1. Cap
2. Axle nut
3. Cap holder
4. Washer
5. Set nut
6. Washer
7. Hub

Rear wheel assembly

Installation

1. Assemble the wheel and hub.

2. Tighten the four set nuts gradually and in a cross pattern until the specified torque of 33-47 ft. lbs. is reached.

3. Slip the wheel onto the axle carefully making sure that the splines mate.

4. Install the axle nut washers. Fit the axle nut. Torque it to 62-83 ft. lbs.

5. Install a new cotter pin.

FRONT BRAKE

Inspection

1. The front brake shoes can be checked after removing the front wheel and hub.

2. Minimum allowable brake lining thickness is 1.5mm (0.06 in.). If either lining of a pair measures less than this at any point, both shoes must be replaced.

3. Check linings for fluid or grease-soaked condition. Replace them if there is evidence of this sort of damage.

4. Check the linings for scoring or signs of unusual wear. If any is noted, determine the cause. Then replace the brake shoes.

5. Check the surface of the brake hub. It should be smooth and featureless. If any scoring or other wear is noted, it can be removed by having the hub turned down on a lathe. The maximum allowable hub diameter, which is embossed on the inner side, cannot be exceeded.

6. Measure the inside diameter of the brake drum. If it exceeds 142.7mm (5.62 in.), it must be replaced.

7. Check the brake plate assembly for any signs of fluid leakage. If any is noted, determine the cause and fix it before operating the machine.

8. Use compressed air to blow brake dust out of the brake assembly.

CAUTION: *Wear a protective mask to avoid inhaling potentially dangerous particulate matter.*

Bleeding

1. Brakes should be bled if the hand lever develops excessive travel and/or a spongy feel. The procedure is also required if fluid is changed, any part of the fluid system is disconnected or fluid is allowed to drop to a very low level.

2. The hydraulic drum brake system used on these machines can be bled in the same manner as is described for hydraulic disk brakes in the "General Information" section of this manual.

Brake Plate

DISASSEMBLY

1. Remove the front wheel and hub.

2. Disconnect the brake line at the brake plate. Plug the end of the line to prevent leakage.

3. To remove the entire brake plate, remove the four bolts which secure it to the steering knuckle. The brake can be disassem-

Brake plate mounting bolts

bled after removal, or can be disassembled in place on the steering knuckle.

4. Turn the two brake shoe pins 90° and remove the springs.

5. Pull off the two shoes together.

6. Remove the brake cylinder bolts. Take off the cylinder.

7. Remove the brake adjuster bolt and remove the adjuster.

INSPECTION

1. Minimum allowable lining thickness is 1.5mm (0.06 in.). Linings must be replaced as a set if less than this at any spot, or if they are oil or fluid-soaked, scored or otherwise damaged.

2. Check the condition of the brake springs. Replace them as a pair if either is badly rusted, deformed or broken.

3. Unscrew and remove the bleed nipple from the brake cylinder.

4. Remove the cylinder boots.

5. Remove the pistons.

6. Carefully clean all cylinder components in clean, fresh brake fluid.

CAUTION: *Never clean brake parts in gasoline or other such solvents.*

7. Check the bore of the cylinder and the sides of the pistons for scoring or other signs of unusual wear. Such damage cannot be remedied. Replacing the brake cylinder assembly is the only solution.

8. Check the condition of the boots. The cylinder must be replaced if damage is detected or if it leaks.

9. Check that the star wheel adjusters on the adjuster assembly can move freely. Do not move them very much or brake adjustment will be way off when the brake plate is assembled.

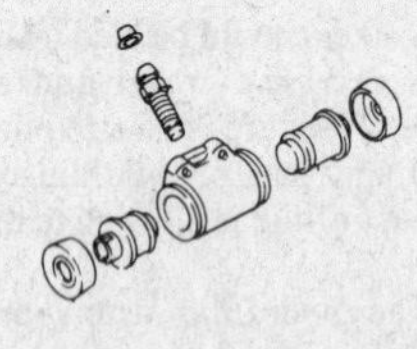

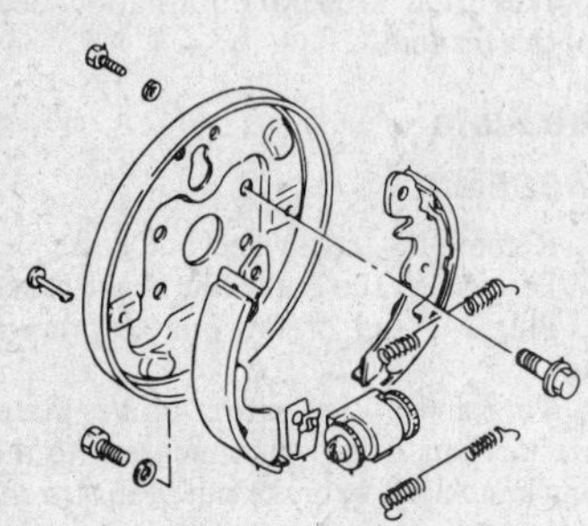

Front brake components

Assembly

1. Clean the brake plate thoroughly, removing all dirt and other foreign matter.

2. Lubricate brake cylinder and pistons with clean brake fluid when assembling.

3. When fitting the cylinder boots, be certain that they are properly seated.

4. Apply a liquid gasket compound to the brake plate surfaces on which the brake cylinder and the adjuster are mounted.

5. Tighten the cylinder bolts to 4.5-6.5 ft. lbs.

6. Tighten the adjuster mounting bolt to 11-16 ft. lbs.

7. Lightly grease the cylinder piston grooves and the adjuster grooves on which the brake shoes ride.

8. Apply a small quantity of silicone grease to each brake shoe in those areas to which the brake springs and the pins are attached.

9. Assemble the shoes and springs and install them on the brake plate.

10. Insert the pins. Install the pin springs and turn the pins 90°.

11. Use liquid gasket compound on the back of the brake plate over the pin heads to keep them from moving.

12. If the brake plate assembly was removed from the steering knuckle, clean the mounting surface on the knuckle thoroughly.

13. Coat the steering knuckle mounting surface with a liquid gasket compound.

14. Install the assembled brake plate.

15. Install the four mounting bolts. Tighten the four bolts in a cross pattern to 13-20 ft. lbs.

16. Install the bleed nipple on the brake cylinder if it is not in place.

17. Connect the brake line to the cylinder. Tighten the nut to 10-13 ft. lbs.

18. Bleed the system.

19. Adjust the brakes. Refer to "Maintenance."

Master Cylinder

DISASSEMBLY

1. Place heavy cloth beneath the master cylinder to prevent damage to paint caused by leaking fluid.

2. Unscrew the brake line banjo bolt at the master cylinder.

3. Remove the two bolts mounting the master cylinder to the handlebar.

4. Remove the master cylinder assembly.

5. Remove the brake lever.

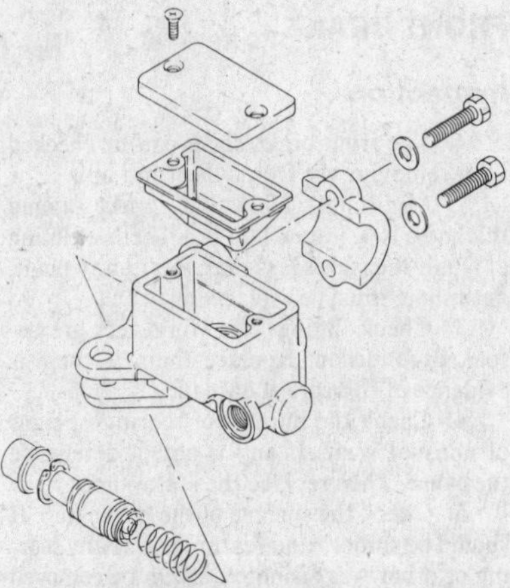

Master cylinder components

6. Remove the reservoir cap.

7. Remove the diaphragm.

8. Pour off and discard any brake fluid in the reservoir.

9. Pull out the rubber boot.

10. Remove the circlip from the cylinder bore.

11. Remove the piston, primary cup and spring.

INSPECTION

1. Clean all parts in fresh, clean brake fluid.

2. Check the cylinder bore for any signs of scoring or wear.

3. Check the piston for scoring. Replacement is the only remedy for damage.

4. Check that rubber parts are not hardened, cracked or deformed by swelling. Replace any parts which are not in obviously perfect condition.

ASSEMBLY

1. Assembly is the reverse of disassembly.

2. Lubricate the piston and primary cup with clean brake fluid before fitting.

3. Be sure that the circlip is properly seated.

4. When installing the reservoir on the handlebars, tighten the upper bolt first. Then tighten the lower bolt. There is a gap between the clamp and the reservoir on the lower side. Correct torque for these bolts is 4.5-6.5 ft. lbs.

5. After connecting the brake line banjo bolt, fill the reservoir with fresh fluid. Bleed the system as outlined in the "General Information" section.

REAR BRAKE

Disassembly

1. Remove the rear wheels.

2. Remove the four bolts that secure the skid plate to the frame. Remove the skid plate.

3. Remove the brake drum outer cover (six bolts).

4. Remove the two axle nuts.

5. Pull off the brake drum with axle.

6. Pull off the two brake shoes and their springs together.

7. Back off the brake pedal and hand lever cable adjuster nuts at the brake cam lever.

8. Disconnect the cables from the brake cam lever.

9. Remove the pinch bolt holding the cam lever to the cam. Carefully pull off the lever.

10. Tap out the brake cam from the plate.

Inspection

1. Clean all parts thoroughly and check for unusual wear.

2. Minimum allowable brake lining thickness is 1.5mm (0.06 in.). Linings must be replaced as a set if either is thinner than this at any point.

3. Check the brake return springs for rusted, weakened or deformed condition.

4. Measure the brake drum diameter. Maximum allowable diameter is stamped on the drum (150.7mm/5.93 in.). The drum must be replaced if it exceeds this specification.

5. Clean the brake cam. Check the condition of the lever splines. Check that the cam is not cracked or bent.

Assembly

1. Use a new brake cam O-ring.

2. Lightly grease the cam before installation.

3. When fitting the brake lever to the

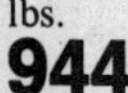

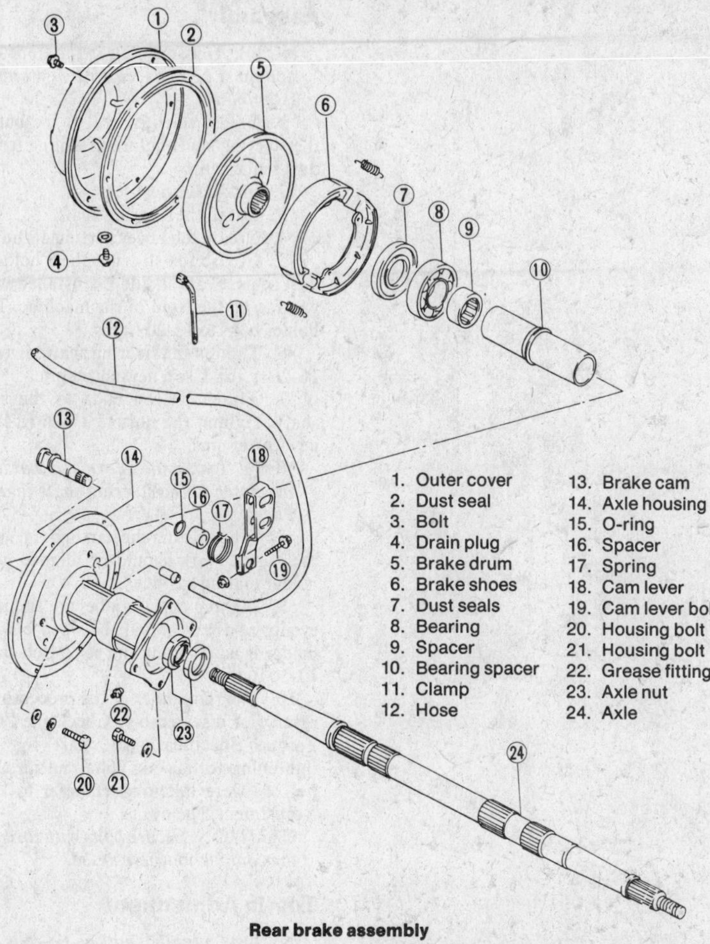

Rear brake assembly

cam, align the punch mark on the lever with the slash mark on the cam. Tighten the pinch bolt to 6.0-8.5 ft. lbs.

4. Lightly grease the brake cam and the pivot pin on which the brake shoes ride.
5. Assemble the shoes and their return springs and fold them onto the brake plate.
6. Grease the axle splines and apply some to the brake drum dust seal.

CAUTION: *Do not allow grease to contact the axle shaft threads.*

7. Apply liquid gasket compound to the axle flange.
8. Install the axle.
9. Apply liquid gasket compound to the circumference of the final driven gear.
10. The axle nuts require thread locking compound. Tighten the inner axle nut to 116-145 ft. lbs. Then install and tighten the outer axle nut to the same torque.
11. Use liquid gasket compound on the brake drum cover dust seal and gasketing.
12. Install the brake drum cover and tighten the six bolts to 4-6 ft. lbs.
13. Connect the brake cables and adjust the brakes as outlined in "Maintenance."
14. Install the skid plate.

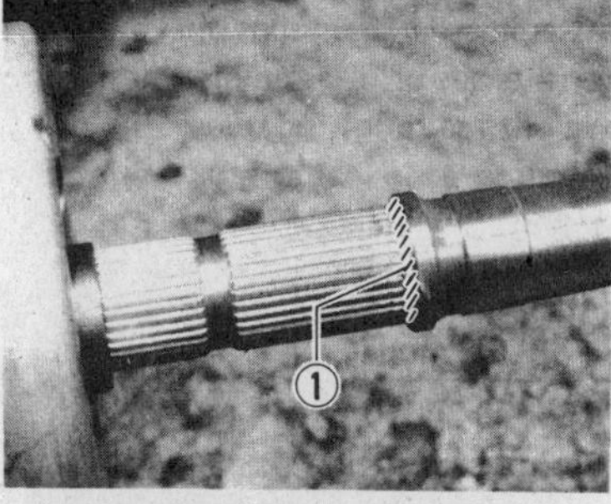

Liquid gasket application point (1)

Liquid gasket application point (2)

FRONT SUSPENSION

Disassembly

1. Remove the front wheels.
2. Remove the front brake plate assemblies.
3. Disconnect the left and right brake hoses from the holders.
4. Remove the cotter pins and nuts and disconnect the tie rods from the steering knuckles.
5. Remove the shock absorber upper mounting bolt.
6. Remove the upper and lower wishbone arm mounting bolts.
7. Remove the upper and lower wishbone arms, the shock and the steering knuckle from the machine as an assembly.
8. Remove the lower shock mounting bolt and take off the shock absorber.
9. Remove the lower wishbone arm from the steering knuckle.
10. Remove the cotter pin and nut of the wishbone arm end from the steering knuckle.
11. Remove the knuckle arm and brake hose guide.
12. Separate the upper wishbone arm and steering knuckle by pressing out the arm end.
13. Remove the four bolts and take the front plate from the chassis.
14. Loosen the nuts and remove the brake hose stopper rings.
15. Disconnect the brake hose from the brake pipe.
16. Remove the brake hose joint bolt. Take off the brake hose and pipe.
17. Disconnect the throttle cable from the housing on the handlebar.
18. Run down the rear brake cable adjusters and disconnect the brake cable from the hand lever.
19. Remove the headlight (two screws).
20. Disconnect the wiring at the plastic connectors inside the housing.
21. Remove the handlebar bolts and take off the handlebars.
22. Remove the four bolts and take off the headlight bracket with headlight housing.
23. Remove the cotter pins and nuts and disconnect the tie-rods from the steering shaft.
24. Remove the two steering shaft holder bolts.
25. Remove the steering shaft holders and dust seals.
26. Remove the steering shaft lower nut.
27. Pull the steering shaft out of the frame.
28. Remove the clip and dust seal from the bottom of the steering shaft.
29. Remove the dust seal and O-ring from the frame.

Inspection

1. Clean metal parts thoroughly.
2. Check all metal parts for signs of distortion, for cracks, deformation and other obvious indications of damage.
3. Check the shock absorbers for signs of leakage. Repair is not possible. Replace any leaking units. Shocks should be replaced as a set for uniform performance.
4. Check the shock absorber springs for condition.
5. Check the steering shaft for a bent condition. If it is bent, replace it. Do not attempt to straighten the shaft.
6. Check the steering shaft holders for wear. Replace as necessary.
7. Be sure both tie-rods are straight. Replace any bent or damaged units.
8. Check all dust and grease seals for condition. Replace as required.
9. Inspect wishbone arm bushings for play. There should not be any. If there is, the bushings must be replaced.
10. Check for play of the lower steering shaft bushing. Replace if play is noted.

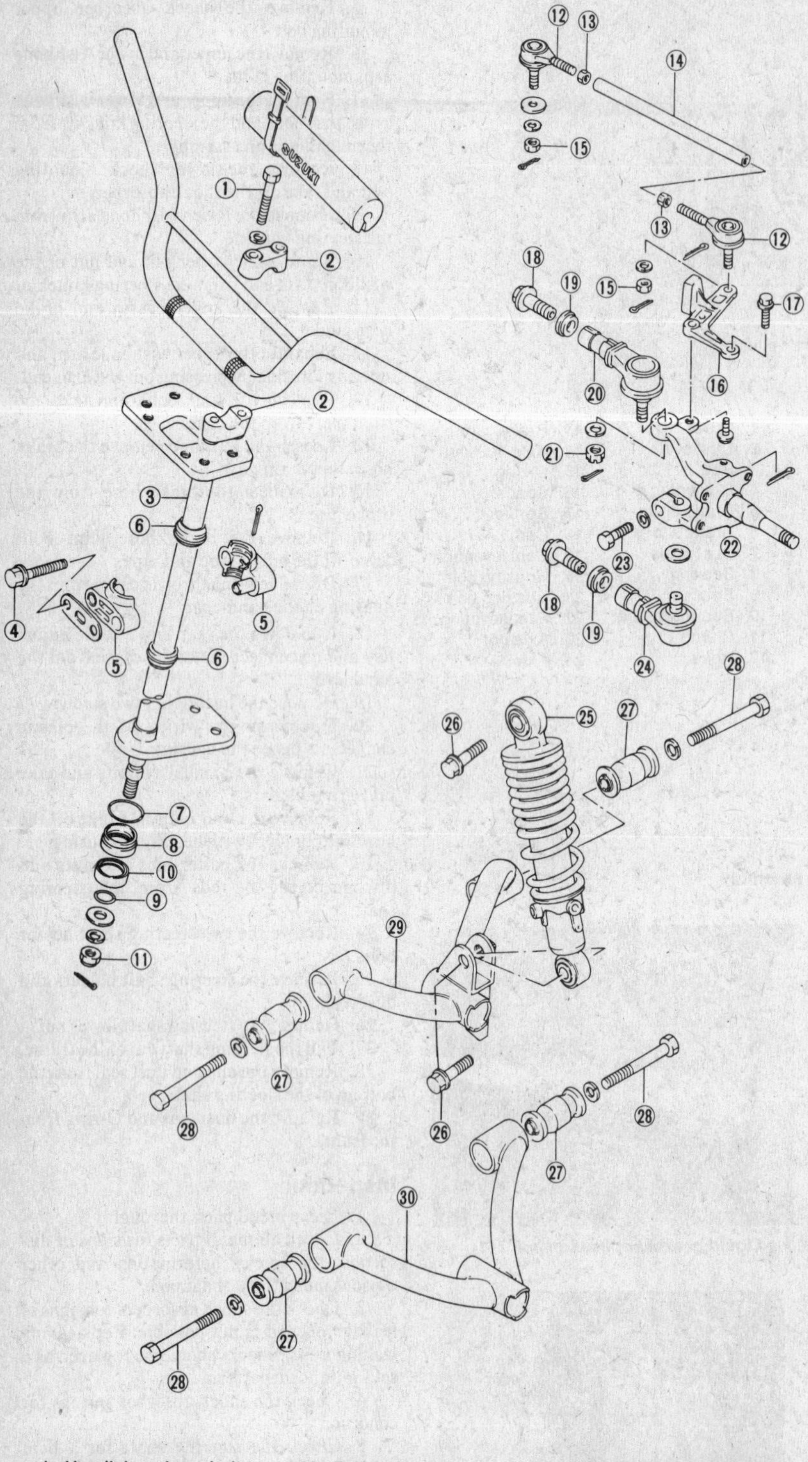

Assembly

NOTE: *All cotter pins in the front suspension must be replaced with new ones when assembling.*

1. Grease the dust seal at the bottom of the steering shaft before installing it. Fit the dust seal circlip.
2. Install the dust seal.
3. Install the steering shaft.
4. Grease the lower portion of the shaft.
5. Grease the steering shaft holders and dust seals. Seals should be installed with the gap facing the front of the machine. Tighten holder bolts to 13-20 ft. lbs.
6. Tighten the steering shaft lower nut to 16-26 ft. lbs. Use a new cotter pin.
7. Attach tie-rod ends to the steering shaft. Tighten the nuts to 17-26 ft. lbs. Use new cotter pins.

NOTE: *Install the tie-rods so that the flats are closer to the steering shaft than to the wheels.*

8. When fitting the handlebars, note that the punch mark should be aligned with the holder mating surface.
9. Tighten the handlebar clamp bolts evenly so that the gap between clamp and holder is equal front and rear. Bolt torque is 13-20 ft. lbs.
10. The remainder of the procedure is the reverse of disassembly. Check the "Chassis Torque Specifications" chart for correct tightening torque for bolts and nuts. If the tie-rods were taken apart, refer to "Toe-In Adjustment," below.

CAUTION: *Secure bolts with thread locking compound where noted.*

Toe-In Adjustment

NOTE: *Outer locknuts on tie-rods (yellow finish) have left-hand threads.*

1. Park the vehicle on a level surface.
2. Be sure the tires are inflated to the proper specifications.

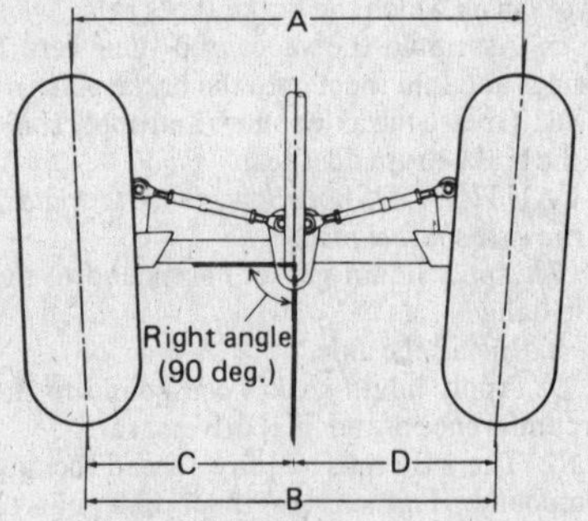

Toe-in adjustment: B minus A must equal 15-21 mm (0.6-0.8 in.), while C and D must be equal

3. Position the handlebars straight ahead.
4. Measure the distance from centerline to centerline of the two front tires. Measure this distance at the very front of the tires. Make another measurement 180° from the first.
5. Subtract the first measurement from the second. The final figure is the toe-in. It should be 15-21mm (0.6-0.8 in.).
6. If this is not the value obtained, adjust as follows.
7. Loosen the two locknuts on each tie rod.

1. Handlebar clamp bolt
2. Handlebar clamp
3. Steering shaft
4. Holder bolt
5. Steering shaft holder
6. Dust seal
7. Dust seal clip
8. Dust seal
9. O-ring
10. Dust seal
11. Steering shaft lower nut
12. Rod end
13. Tie rod locknut
14. Tie rod
15. Rod end nut
16. Steering knuckle arm
17. Knuckle arm bolt
18. Steering knuckle end bolt
19. Knuckle end stopper
20. Wishbone arm end
21. Steering knuckle end nut
22. Steering knuckle
23. Steering knuckle arm bolt
24. Wishbone arm end
25. Shock absorber
26. Shock absorber bolt
27. Bushing
28. Suspension arm pivot bolt
29. Wishbone upper arm
30. Wishbone lower arm

Front suspension

8. Turn each rod with a wrench on the flats provided as necessary to bring toe-in into specification.

CAUTION: *It is critical that both rods be turned by equal amounts, assuming that other components have not been disturbed or damaged. The distance from the centerline of the steering shaft to the centerline of each tire must be equal.*

9. When the toe-in is correct and the distance from the centerline of the steering shaft to the centerline of both tires is equal, tighten the tie-rod locknuts to 16-26 ft. lbs.

REAR AXLE HOUSING

Removal

1. Remove the rear fender.
2. Remove the rear wheels.
3. Remove the rear brake assembly.

Rear axle housing mounting bolts

4. Disconnect the brake breather hose from the drum.
5. Remove the three housing bolts on brake side of housing.
6. Loosen the drive shaft boot clamp screw.
7. Remove the three final case mounting bolts.
8. Remove the final gear case with the axle housing.
9. Remove the four bolts to separate the rear axle housing from the final gear case.

Inspection

1. Maximum allowable axle run-out is 3.0mm (0.12 in.).
2. Remove/inspect/install wheel bearings as described for Front Wheel bearings, above.

Installation

Installation is the reverse of removal. Refer to the "Chassis Torque Specifications" chart for torque values.

Suzuki Triples

MODEL COVERAGE

GT380
GT550
GT750

INDEX

MAINTENANCE

NOTE: *Common maintenance procedures are explained in detail in "General Information."*

LUBRICATION

Engine

Suzuki recommends SAE 30W CCI oil for engine lubrication. If Suzuki CCI oil is not available, one of the types listed below will suffice.

American	Permalube SAE 30W
Atlantic	Atlantic Aviation SAE 30W
Castrol	Heavy Duty SAE 30W
Gulf	Gulfpride SAE 30W
Humble	ESSO, ENCO, Humble SAE 30W
Kendall	Dual Action, Super Duty SAE 30W
Mobil	Mobil A SAE 30W
Phillips	Sixty-Six SAE 30W
Pure	Super Duty Purelube SAE 30W
Richfield	Richlube Premium SAE 30W
Shell	Shell X—100 SAE 30W
Texaco	Havoline SAE 30W

Gearbox

The gearbox (transmission) and clutch are lubricated by an oil bath. SAE 20W/40 is recommended for all models.

Gearbox oil level screw (1)

CHECKING OIL

A phillips head level screw is threaded into the right crankcase cover just behind the clutch housing. Check the oil level in the gearbox by removing the screw when the machine is parked on the centerstand on a level surface.

Oil should just begin to seep out of the level hole if the level is correct.

Check oil on warm engine.

CHANGING OIL

NOTE: *Oil should be changed when the engine is warm.*

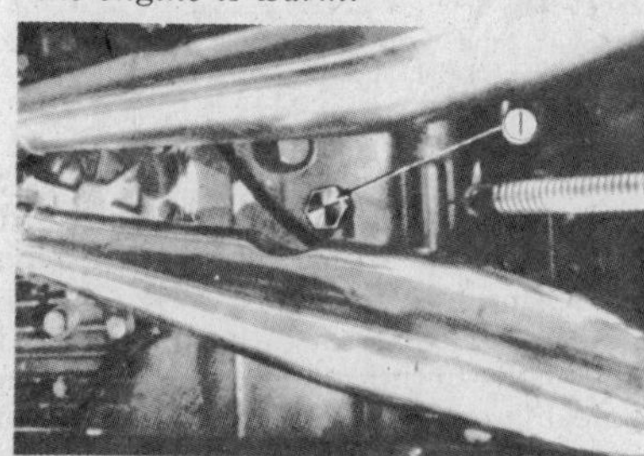

Gearbox oil drain plug (1)

General Specifications

	GT380	*GT550*	*GT750*
ENGINE			
Type	two-stroke	two-stroke	two-stroke
No. cylinders	3	3	3
Displacement (cc)	371	543	738
Bore x stroke (mm)	54 x 54	61 x 62	70 x 64
Compression ratio	7.2 : 1	6.7 : 1	6.7 : 1
Induction timing	piston port	piston port	piston port
Cooling system	Ram Air System	Ram Air System	water-cooled
TRANSMISSION			
Clutch type	wet, multi-disc	wet, multi-disc	wet, multi-disc
No. gears	6	5	5
Primary reduction ratio	2.833 : 1	2.242 : 1	1.673 : 1
Final reduction ratio	2.67 : 1	2.500 : 1	3.133 : 1
TRANSMISSION			
Gear ratios : 1			
First	2.333	2.846	2.846
Second	1.500	1.736	1.736
Third	1.157	1.363	1.363
Fourth	0.904	1.125	1.125
Fifth	0.782	0.923	0.923
Sixth	0.708	—	—
LUBRICATION			
Engine	CCI	CCI	CCI
Transmission	oil bath	oil bath	oil bath
IGNITION			
System type	battery and coil	battery and coil	battery and coil
ELECTRICAL SYSTEM			
System voltage	12v	12v	12v
Generator	alternator	alternator	alternator
CHASSIS			
Suspension			
Front	Telescopic forks, oil-dampened		
Rear	Swing arm with hydraulically-dampened springs		
Steering angle (r & l)	42°	42°	40°
Caster	61°	61°	63°
Trail (in.)	4.6	4.6	3.74
Wheelbase (in.)	54.3	57.7	57.8
Ground clearance (in.)	5.7	5.7	5.5
OVERALL DIMENSIONS			
Weight (dry) (lbs)	377	441	507
Length (in.)	82.3	86.4	87.2
Width (in.)	32.1	32.1	34.0
Height (in.)	44.3	45.7	44.3
TIRES			
Front	3.00-19	3.25-19	3.25-19
Rear	3.50-18	4.00-18	4.00-18

1. Every 2,000 miles (after break-in), remove the crankcase filler cap; remove the drain plug at the bottom of the crankcase, and drain the gearbox oil into a container.

2. Replace the drain plug, fitting it with a new washer as necessary, and add the correct amount and grade of oil through the filler cap.

3. Gearbox capacities are:
GT380J-K—3.0 pt (1420 cc)
GT380L-A—3.2 pt (1500 cc)
GT550—3.2 pt (1500 cc)
GT750—4.7 pt (2200 cc)

NOTE *If the engine has been rebuilt, more oil will have to be added before operation. This is because the normal oil change procedure leaves a certain amount of the lubricant in the transmission. If the engine has just been reassembled add:*
GT380—3.2 pt (1500 cc)
GT550—3.4 pt (1600 cc)
GT750—5.3 pt (2500 cc)
Use the level plug to determine final level.

Front Forks

1. SAE 5W/20, 10W/20 or Automatic Transmission Fluid is recommended for the front forks.

2. To drain the fork oil, do one fork tube at a time. Place a container beneath the phillips head drain plug which is located at the lower portion of the fork slider. To drain the right fork tube, turn the forks all the way to the right; turn to the left to drain the left fork tube.

Fork drain plug (2)

3. After the oil has been allowed to drain for a couple of minutes, pump the forks up and down several times to expel all of it. Check the drain plug washer for condition, replacing it if need be, then refit the drain plug, and remove the cap at the top of each fork.

4. Support the front wheel off the ground. Remove the filler cap at the top of each fork leg. Refill each fork tube with the correct amount and grade of oil. (Refer to the "Maintenance Data" chart at the end of this section.

Cooling System (GT750)

The cooling system capacity is 9.5 pt. (4.5 ltr). The system is filled at the factory with a solution of 50% antifreeze-and-summer coolant and 50% distilled water. This is the standard water-to-coolant ratio and it should be maintained unless the machine is operated in extremely cold weather. In this case, see the "Coolant Solution" chart for appropriate mixing ratios.

MAINTENANCE

1. Check the coolant level daily.
2. The correct solution level is 0.2–0.6 in. (5–15 mm) from the bottom of the reservoir tank. Refer to the illustration. Maintain the level at this point. Note that a white level plate is located in the radiator filler pipe for visual checks.
3. When adding coolant to maintain the solution level, use *distilled water only.*

CAUTION: *Tap water must never be used because of the uncertain properties in various geographic locales (i.e., mineral content, etc.).*

4. Every two years or 20,000 miles, the cooling solution should be drained and refilled with a fresh amount. See below.

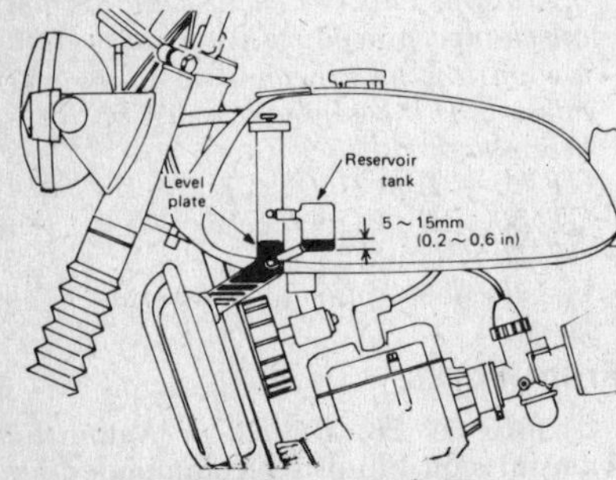

GT750 radiator water level

Coolant Solution

Operation in Air Temperature Below (°F)	Mixing Ratio of Antifreeze (%)	Amt. of Antifreeze/Distilled Water for 4.5 ltr (9.5 pt)	
		(ltr)	(pt)
14	30	1.35/3.15	2.90/6.60
5	35	1.60/2.90	3.40/6.10
–4	40	1.80/2.70	3.80/5.70
–13	45	2.00/2.50	4.20/5.30
–24	50	2.25/2.25	4.75/4.75

FLUSHING AND CHANGING THE COOLANT

1. Remove the radiator cap. Remove the cooling system drain plug at the front, lower portion of the crankcase, and drain the solution.
2. Flush the system by running a garden hose or the like through the system for several minutes.
3. Replace the drain plug, and fill the system with water.
4. Start and run the engine for about ten minutes.

GT750 water drain plug

5. Drain the system completely, and refill it with the proper mixture of distilled water and antifreeze.

NOTE: *The drained water should be colorless; if not, refill and drain after running the engine as described above until the water is colorless.*

6. Add ½ oz. (14 gr.) of Suzuki "Bars Leaks" or another reputable radiator antileak formula. If in a liquid form, the proper amount is 70 cc (0.15 pt).
7. Run the engine for ten minutes, until the thermostat is open, then check the coolant level. Top it up with the correct mixture of distilled water and antifreeze. After running the engine until hot, once again check the coolant level.

CAUTION: *Do not mix different brands of antifreeze. Also, keep antifreeze off painted surfaces, since they will be easily damaged by contact.*

Carburetor Linkage

The carburetor linkage for 380 and 550 L-A models is fitted with a pair of grease fittings at the tops of the throttle slide shaft holders. Chassis grease should be applied to the fittings until excess appears at the shaft.

Drum Brake Camshafts

The brake opening cams should be attended to every 2,000 miles, and should receive a shot of chassis grease.

Swing Arm Pivot Shaft

Lubricate the swing arm pivot shaft with chassis grease every 4,000 miles.

SERVICE CHECKS AND ADJUSTMENTS

Air Cleaner

1. The air cleaner may be either the paper element or the polyurethane (foam) type.
2. If a paper element type is fitted, remove it from the machine (every 2,000 miles or more often depending on conditions) by lifting up the rear of the gas tank slightly, removing the two air cleaner fitting bolts beneath the back of the tank, loosening the carburetor clamps, and taking out the filter. Clean by brushing off dirt, and blow off any remainder with compressed air applied to the inside of the filter. After 3 such cleanings, the element should be replaced.
3. If a "foam" type filter is fitted, remove it every 2,000 miles by removing the fitting bolts beneath the rear of the tank, loosening the carburetor clamps, and taking out the air cleaner from the right-side of the machine. Divide the cleaner case in two by removing the six nuts. Then take out the filter element by removing the two phillips head screws. Wash the filter in gasoline. Squeeze it dry. Then give the filter a light coat of CCI or SAE 30W oil, squeeze out the excess and reinstall.

Fuel Petcock

The petcock is fitted with a filter screen and this should be cleaned periodically in gasoline. Remove any sediment from the bowl as well.

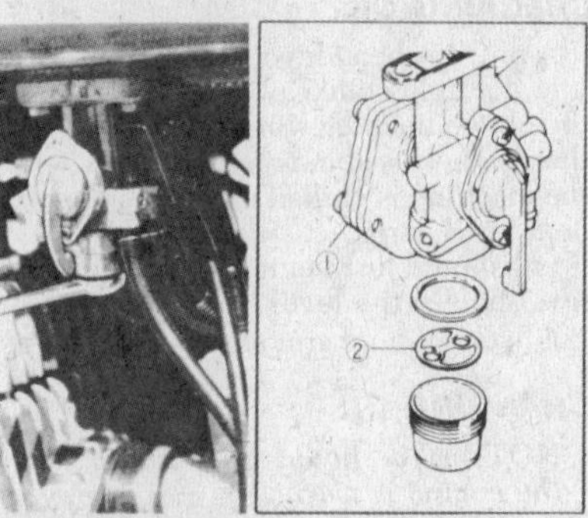

Removing the petcock sediment bowl (left). Diaphragm case (1) and filter screen (2)

Throttle Cables

Throttle cable adjustment will depend on the type of linkage used. Generally, on SC-series carburetors, 1972–73, the cables should be set to have about 2–3 mm (0.08–0.1 in.) of free-play between the cable end and the adjuster on top of the carburetor for the GT550 and GT750; set the adjusters on the GT380 to give 3–5 mm (0.1–0.2 in.).

1974 and later models use a dual-cable linkage. Use the cable adjusters at the carburetors so that when average thumb pressure (0.22–0.44 lbs./100–200 g) is applied to either cable mid-way between the cable adjuster and the pulley, the cable will be deflected 3–5mm (0.12–0.20 in.).

Be sure that both cables have the same free-play.

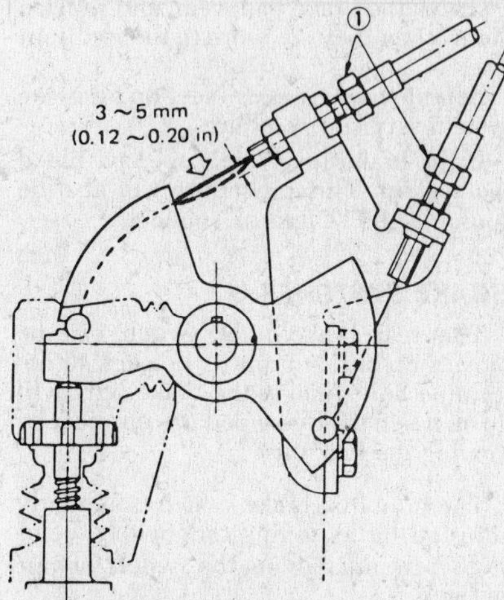

Each cable should have the same amount of free-play as illustrated (L-A models)

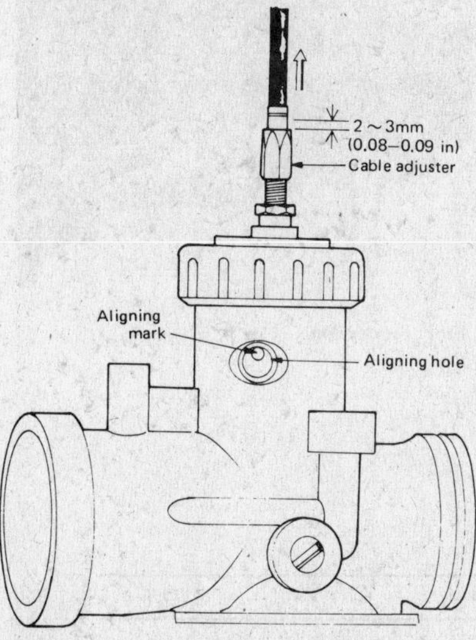

Throttle cable adjustment at the carburetor (GT550, GT750)

The cable adjuster(s) at the twist-grip should be set to allow 0.5–1.0 mm (0.02–0.04 in.) on the GT750, and 1.0–2.0 mm (0.04–0.08 in.) on the GT380 and GT550.

After setting this adjustment, idle the engine and turn the handlebars lock-to-lock noting any increase or variation in idle speed. If the revs go up, the cables are probably adjusted too tightly. Also check to make sure that the cables are not binding anywhere along the route from the twist-grip to the carburetors.

On "J" and "K" models, the throttle slides should be synchronized after setting the cable adjuster on the carburetor top and before setting the twist-grip adjustment.

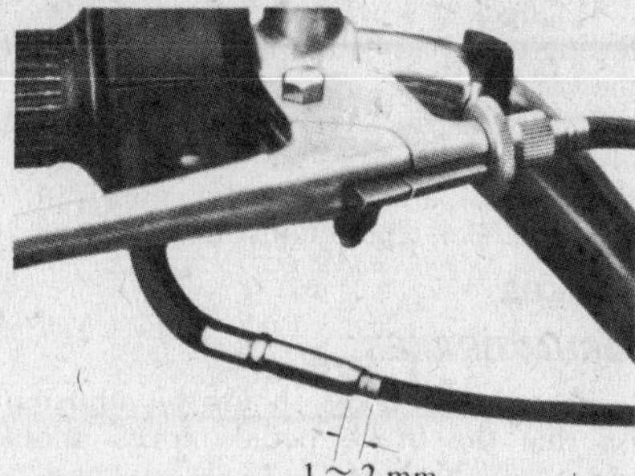

Throttle cable twist-grip adjustment (GT380, GT550)

Check the oil pump cable adjustment afterward.

Oil Pump

NOTE: *Carburetor adjustments and throttle cable free-play must be set before the oil pump.*

GT750L-A

The oil pump rod adjustment can be checked after removing the oil pump cover. The lines on the pump lever and pump body should align.

If the throttle is opened all the way, the punch marks should align.

Oil pump alignment marks (GT7501-A)

OTHER MODELS

1. Remove the oil pump cover.
2. Remove the carburetor slide alignment plug(s).
3. Adjust the throttle cable(s) as described above.
4. Turn the throttle so that the punch marks on the slides are at the top of the alignment plug holes.
5. At this point, the alignment mark on the oil pump lever should be lined up with the line on the pump body. If it is not, turn the pump cable adjuster in or out (after loosening the locknut) so that the marks align.

Proper oil pump cable adjustment. Note the position of the pump lever and the carburetor slide

Clutch

Two adjustments must be made: the clutch adjustment itself, and the clutch cable adjustment.

GT750

1. Remove the clutch cover.
2. Run down the cable adjusters either on the crankcase or at the handlebar so that the clutch lever (in the case) has a bit of free-play before clutch disengagement begins.
3. The lever should have about 0.018 in. (0.5 mm) of play. As necessary, loosen the clutch shaft locknut and adjust the inner nut until the proper amount of play is evident in the shaft. Tighten the locknut.
4. Adjust the clutch cable using the adjusters on the crankcase or the handlebar so that the clutch handlebar lever has 0.12–0.16 in. (3–4 mm) of play before clutch disengagement begins.

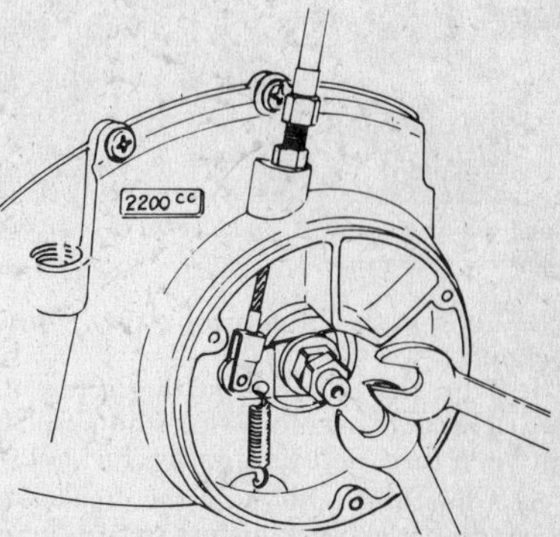

Loosening the clutch adjuster locknuts (GT750)

Clutch adjuster (3) and locknuts (2) (GT750)

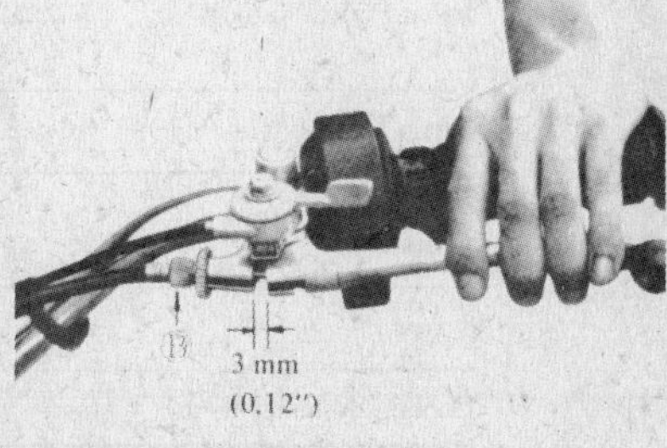

Setting clutch lever free-play with the handlebar cable adjuster (B)

GT380, GT550

1. Remove the clutch cover.
2. Run the clutch cable adjusters at the handlebar or the crankcase down so that the clutch cable has plenty of free-play.

Clutch adjuster screw (B) and locknut (A) (GT380, GT550)

3. Loosen the clutch adjusting screw locknut.
4. Turn the clutch adjusting screw in until a bit of resistance is felt, then back it out ¼–½ turn, and tighten the locknut.
5. Adjust the cable with the crankcase or handlebar cable adjusters so that there is about 0.16 in. (4 mm) of handlebar lever movement before clutch disengagement begins.

Drive Chain

The chain should have 0.6–0.8 in. (15–20 mm) of total up-and-down movement measured in the middle of the bottom chain run. The chain must be clean and well-lubricated before adjustment.

To adjust the chain:

1. Remove the rear axle nut cotter pin and loosen the nut.
2. Loosen both adjuster locknuts.
3. Back off the rear brake adjustment a few turns.
4. Turn the adjusting bolts IN to tighten the chain, OUT to loosen it.
5. Turn both adjusters equal amounts.
6. Check rear wheel alignment by referring to the adjusting marks scribed on the swing arm.
7. When the wheel is properly aligned, tighten the adjuster locknuts, the axle nut, and replace the cotter pin.
8. Recheck chain adjustment.

Brakes

DRUM BRAKES

Rear drum brakes should be adjusted so that the brake pedal moves about 0.8–1.2 in. (20–30 mm) before the brakes fully contact the drum.

Use the brake pedal adjuster, where fitted, to adjust pedal position for ease of operation. Then adjust the brake by turning the adjustment nut on the brake rod.

Note that the brake should be adjusted or at least checked each time the chain is adjusted.

Front drum brakes are four-leading shoe units on the GT550 and GT750. Both cables must be adjusted so that the brakes fully contact the drum when the handlebar lever is pulled about 0.8–1.2 in. (20–30 mm).

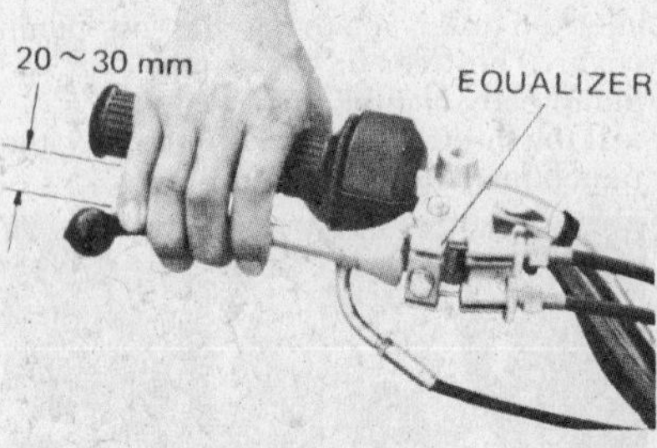

Front brake lever play before brakes contact the drum

DISC BRAKES

Disc brakes need no attention other than an occasional check of fluid level and pad wear.

After removing the reservoir cap, note that the brake fluid level should be approximately at the level mark. 1974 and later models have a see-through reservoir, so cap removal is not necessary.

NOTE: *The fluid should be set at this mark when new pads are fitted or when the hydraulic system is overhauled or any component removed. The level will drop slightly as the pads wear.*

Check the brake pad wear, and replace them when they are worn to the red limit line.

Refer to the "Chassis" section for brake system service procedures.

If the brake lever feels spongy, bleed the system. This procedure can also be found in the "Chassis" section.

BRAKE SWITCHES

The rear brake light switch can be moved up or down on its bracket, to determine how quickly the brake light will go on when the brake pedal is applied, by moving the locknuts.

The front disc brake switch is similarly adjusted by loosening the switch securing screw and moving the switch forward or back.

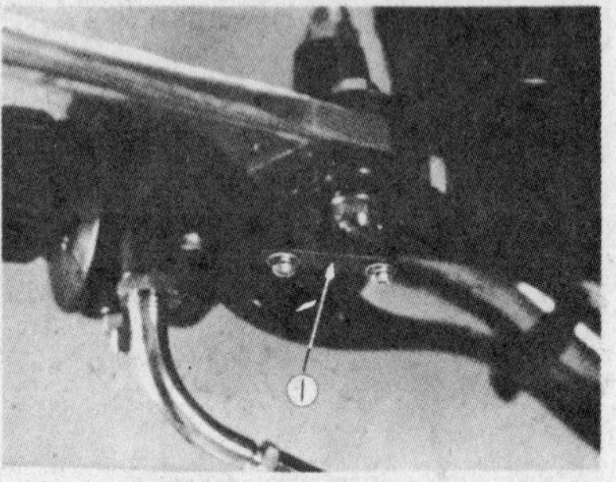

Front brake light switch (disc brake)

Maintenance Data

	GT380J-K	*GT380L-A*	*GT550J-L*	*GT550M-A*	*GT750J-K*	*GT750L-A*
Gas Tank (gal)	4.0	4.0	4.0	4.0	4.5	4.5
Oil Tank (pt/cc)	2.7/1280	2.5/1190	2.5/1190	2.5/1190	3.8/1800	3.8/1800
Transmission (pt/cc)	3.0/1420	3.2/1500	3.2/1500	3.2/1500	4.7/2200	4.7/2200
Front Forks (oz/cc) @ leg	7.1/210	4.9/145	7.9/235	5.4/160	7.9/235	5.4/160
Chain freeplay (in./mm)	0.6–0.8/15–20	0.6–0.8/15–20	0.6–0.8/15–20	0.6–0.8/15–20	0.6–0.8/15–20	0.6–0.8/15–20
Tire pressure (psi) front	26	26	23①	23①	26②	26②
rear	28①	28①	26②	26②	28③	28③
Cooling System (pt/cc)	—	—	—	—	9.5/4500	9.5/4500

① Add 3 psi for two-up or high-speed
② Add 2 psi for two-up or high-speed
③ Add 4 psi for two-up or high-speed

Periodic Maintenance[1]

Every 2000 Miles
- Clean and gap spark plugs
- Check oil pump adjustment
- Change transmission oil
- Adjust carburetors
- Check cylinder and cylinder head fasteners
- Clean air filter
- Clean and gap points
- Chassis lubrication
- Brake and clutch checks and adjustments

Every 4000 Miles
- Replace spark plugs
- Decarbonize top end
- Clean fuel petcock
- Check steering stem bearings
- Clean oil tank outlet union filter

Every 8000 Miles
- Change fork oil
- Overhaul carburetors
- Flush disc brake system

[1] Based on normal usage after break-in is completed

Recommended Lubricants

Engine
- Suzuki CCI

Transmission
- SAE 20W/40

Front Forks
- SAE 5W/20
- SAE 10W/20
- ATF

Disc Brake System
- DOT 3
- DOT 4

Control Cables
- 10W-30 motor oil
- Graphite-based lubricant
- Molybdenum disulphite-base lubricant

Instrument Cables
- Light-duty grease

Wheel and Steering Stem Bearings
- Waterproof, medium-weight bearing grease

Grease Fittings, brake cams, pivots
- Waterproof, medium-weight chassis grease

Drive Chain
- Good quality lubricant developed specifically for motorcycle drive chains

TUNE-UP

NOTE: *Common tune-up procedures are explained in detail in "General Information."*

CONTACT BREAKER POINTS

Replacement

NOTE: *New points are coated with a preservative to prevent the contact surfaces from rusting. Be sure to remove the coating with a solvent before installing the points.*

1. To replace a set of points, remove the small nut and bolt which secure the wiring to the breaker point set; remove the adjustment screw, and take off the old set of points.

2. When installing the new points, be sure that the fiber insulating washers are correctly located.

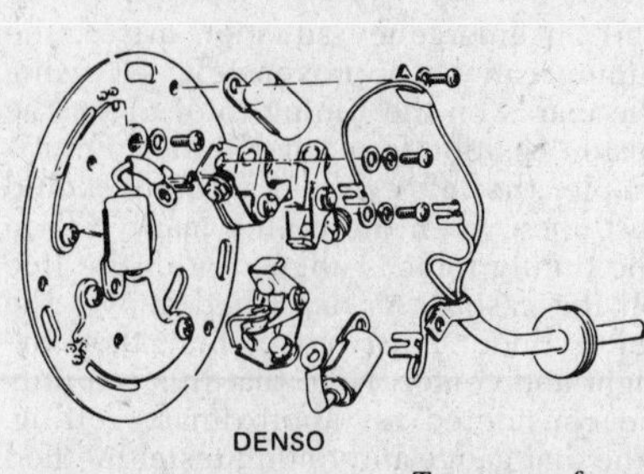

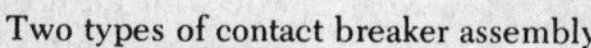

Two types of contact breaker assembly

Contact breaker assembly components

1. Contact point base
2. Contact point set plate
3. Timing plate
4. Aligning mark
5. Movable plate

Both "Denso" and "Kokusan" contact breaker assemblies are used, and it is important to find which manufacturer supplied the assembly for your machine when ordering parts. Refer to the illustration comparing the two types of breaker assemblies.

Adjustment

NOTE: *Always clean the points before gapping.*

1. Turn the engine over until any one of the points is fully open. Check the gap with the appropriate feeler gauge. The acceptable point gap for all models is 0.30–0.40 mm (0.012–0.016 in.).

2. To adjust the gap, simply loosen the screw which secures the breaker point to its mounting plate; use a small screwdriver to move the breaker point by means of the small slot cut out of the assembly, until the correct gap is obtained.

NOTE: *The right and center breaker points (indicated by letters "R" and "L" stamped on the base plate) are mounted on movable mounting plates which are fastened to the base plate by two screws. These two screws are loosened to adjust ignition timing only, and it is not necessary to disturb them to set the point gap.*

Also note that the points for the left cylinder are mounted directly on the base plate; but it is still necessary to loosen only a single screw to set the gap.

4. Tighten the adjusting screw, and recheck the gap with the feeler gauge.

5. Repeat this procedure for the other two cylinders.

IGNITION TIMING

A dial gauge (to determine piston position) is necessary for ignition timing. Since all three machines use battery-and-coil ignitions, a test or continuity light or an ohmmeter/point checker can be used to find when the points separate.

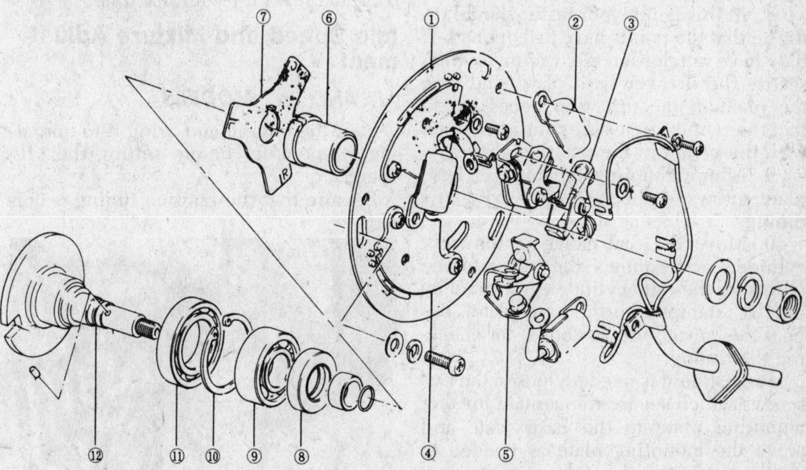

Contact breaker assembly (GT750)

1. Contact point base
2. Condenser
3. Contact point assembly
4. Contact point set plate
5. Contact point shifting plate
6. Point breaker cam
7. Timing plate
8. Oil seal
9. Camshaft inner bearing
10. Circlip
11. Camshaft outer bearing
12. Camshaft

Adjusting the point gap

1. Remove the points cover and the spark plugs.

2. Clean and gap each of the points as described above.

NOTE: *For each model, the timing of the LEFT cylinder must be set first. Note that the left cylinder's contact breaker is mounted directly on the points assembly base plate. The entire base plate is moved to adjust the timing of this cylinder, and this, quite naturally, will affect the timing of the other two cylinders.*

3. Fit the dial gauge into the left cylinder's spark plug hole, then turn the engine over until the dial gauge needle peaks and begins to reverse direction.

4. Turn the engine back and forth until the dial gauge indicates that the piston has reached its highest point of travel. Let the piston stay in this position (TDC), then zero the gauge.

5. Hook up your timing tester. Attach one lead to ground on the engine case, and the other to the movable point terminal for the left cylinder. Note that "L" is stamped adjacent to the left cylinder's breaker points for identification.

6. Refer to the "Tune-Up Specifications" chart at the end of this section for the correct timing settings for your model.

7. Turn the engine backward until the dial gauge indicates that the piston has moved the correct distance below TDC.

8. At this point, your tester should indicate that the points have just opened. If they have not, loosen the 3 screws which secure the breaker base plate, and turn the plate in the direction necessary so that the points are just beginning to open with the piston in the position above.

9. After tightening the breaker base plate screws, recheck the left cylinder's timing.

10. Move the dial gauge to the right cylinder, and connect the tester to the points for the right cylinder (indicated by the "R" stamped on the base plate). Repeat the procedure, as above, for checking the timing.

If adjustment is needed, loosen the two screws which secure the contact breaker mounting plate to the base plate and move the mounting plate as needed to get the points to open at the correct point.

11. Repeat the procedure for the center ("C") points.

CAUTION: *Note that the piston position specifications for the center cylinder of certain models is NOT the same as for the left and right cylinders.*

If an emergency situation arises, the timing can be approximately set using the marks on the timing rotor to set the piston position for each cylinder. For example, the left cylinder's points should just open when the timing mark "L" on the timing rotor is aligned with the line on the casing. As described above, the left cylinder must be set first, then the right and center. Note that this can only be considered an approximate setting. The dial gauge and timing tester method is the recommended procedure.

CARBURETOR ADJUSTMENTS

Float Level

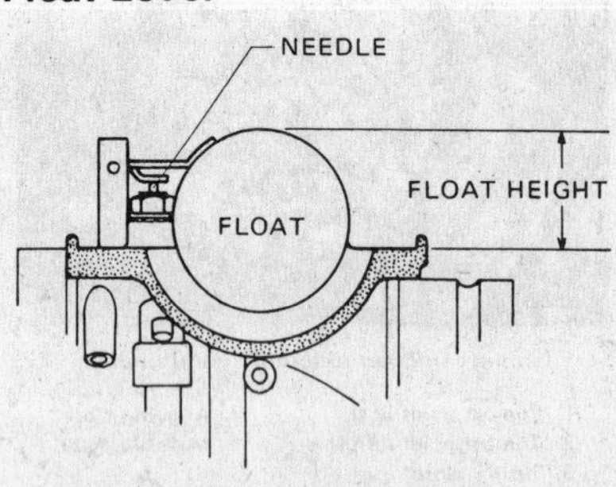

Carburetor float height measurement

To adjust the float level on these carbs, first remove the carburetor float bowl and float. Make sure that there's no gas inside the float due to a pinhole leak, then refit the float and, holding the carburetor upside down, lower the float gradually until the float tongue just touches the upper end of the needle. Now, measure the distance between the float bowl gasket fitting surface and the bottom of the float (gasket removed).

If the distance is less than specified, the fuel level is too high; if more than specified, too low. To adjust, bend the float tang only, never the mounting pivot.

Refer to the "Tune-Up Specifications" chart at the end of this section for the correct float level for your machine.

Idle Speed and Mixture Adjustment

"J" AND "K" MODELS

Start the engine and bring it to operating temperature before setting the idle speed.

Be sure that the ignition timing is correct.

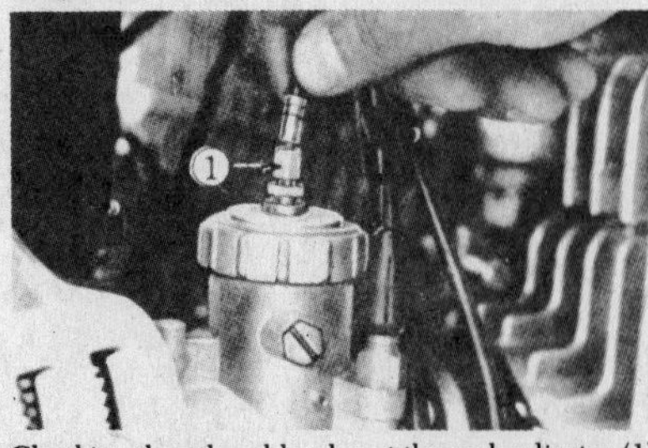

Checking throttle cable play at the carb adjuster (1)

If possible, replace the standard spark plugs with ones of a slightly hotter heat range while setting the idle speed.

1. After setting the cable free-play with the carburetor cap adjusters (see "Maintenance") screw each of the pilot air adjustment screws in until it is *lightly* seated, then back it out the specified number of turns:

GT380, GT550 1¼ turns out
GT750 1½ turns out

2. Screw in each of the throttle stop screws until lightly seated, then back each of them out an equal amount (about 3½ turns).

3. Refer to the accompanying illustration to clarify the procedure. Basically, it

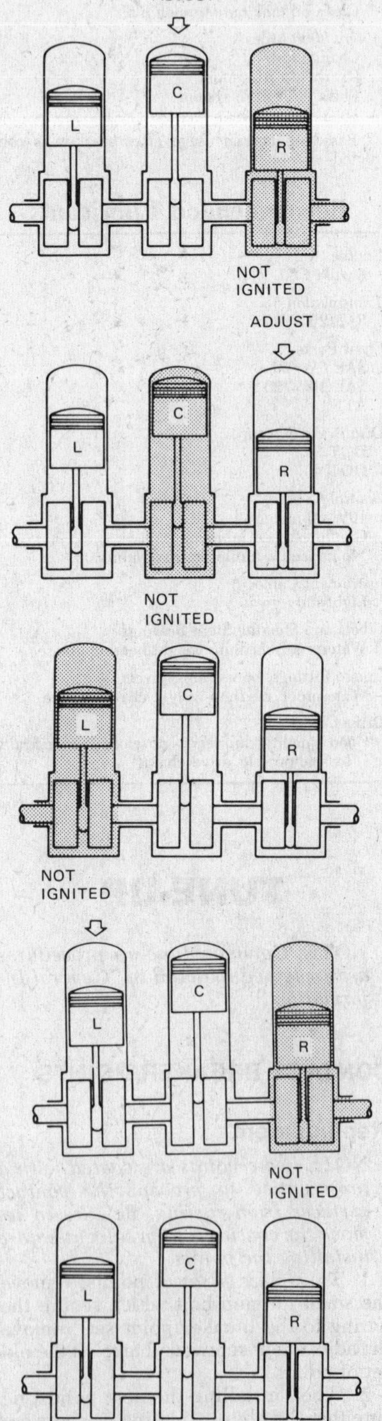

Five steps for adjusting the idle speed and mixture

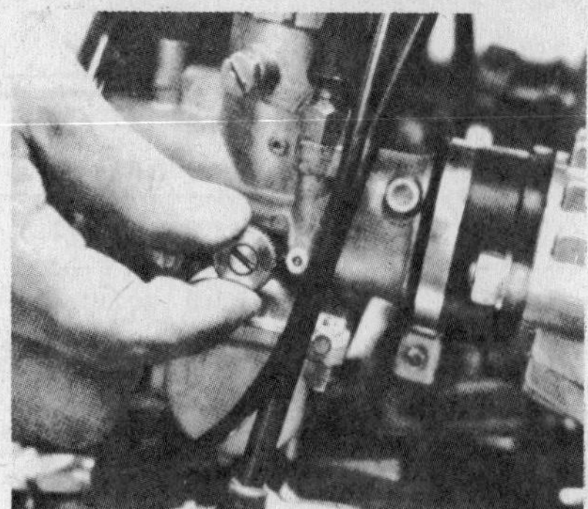

Adjusting the idle speed

involves disconnecting one cylinder, then setting the idle speed on one of the two remaining running cylinders.

a. With the engine running, disconnect the spark plug lead of the right cylinder, and set the idle speed of the two running cylinders to 1100 rpm by turning the throttle stop screw of the *center* cylinder carburetor only.

b. Reconnect the right cylinder plug lead; disconnect the center cylinder lead. Then set the idle speed to the same rpm as above, using the throttle stop screw for the right cylinder carburetor *only*.

c. Reconnect the center cylinder spark plug lead; disconnect the left cylinder lead. Note the rpm reading on the tachometer. Call this value "X" rpm.

d. Connect the left cylinder lead; disconnect the right cylinder lead. Use the throttle stop screw of the left cylinder carburetor to adjust the tachometer reading to "X" rpm.

e. Now connect the right cylinder lead so that the machine is firing on three cylinders. Turn each of the throttle stop screws out an equal amount to bring the idle speed to 1000 rpm (GT750) or 1100 rpm (GT380, GT550).

4. Proceed to throttle slide synchronization.

GT380, GT550 "L-A" MODELS

1. Make the adjustments when the engine is at operating temperature. Be sure that all items in the ignition systems (plugs, points, etc.) have been correctly set.

2. Adjust throttle cable free-play (see "Maintenance").

3. Turn each pilot air screw in until it is seated, then back each out the number of turns shown in the "Tune-Up Specifications" chart.

4. Using the idle speed wheel, set idle at 1500 rpm.

5. Refer to the illustration "Five steps for adjusting the idle speed and mixture." The procedure for L-A models is essentially the same as for J-K models outlined above.

a. Disconnect the right cylinder's spark plug cap, and adjust the throttle slide adjustment nut on the center cylinder so the engine will run at 1000 rpm.

b. Reconnect the right cylinder; disconnect the center cylinder's plug lead and use the right cylinder's slide adjustment nut to set idle at 1000 rpm as before.

c. Connect the center cylinder. Disconnect the left cylinder's plug lead and note engine rpm.

d. Connect the left cylinder's lead. Disconnect the right cylinder's lead. Note engine rpm. Use the throttle slide adjustment nut of the left cylinder to adjust idle speed to the same value obtained in Step "c."

e. With all cylinders connected, rev the engine a few times to clean the plugs, and set idle speed to 1100 rpm with the idle speed wheel.

GT750 "L-A" MODELS

1. Make adjustments when the engine is at operating temperature. Adjust points, plugs, ignition timing and throttle cables before this procedure.
2. Turn each pilot screw in until lightly seated, then back each out ¼ turn for GT750L or ¾ turns for FT750M-A.
3. Turn the idle speed screw to achieve an idle speed of 3000 rpm.
4. Disconnect the left and center spark plug caps. Adjust the idle speed screw so that the engine idles at 1000 rpm.
5. Connect the lead for the center cylinder; disconnect the lead for the right cylinder. Adjust the center cylinder's throttle stop screw to obtain an idle of 1000 rpm.
6. Connect the lead for the left cylinder. Disconnect the lead for the center cylinder. Adjust the left cylinder's throttle stop screw to obtain an idle speed of 1000 rpm.
7. Connect all three leads, rev the engine a few times to clean off the plugs; set idle speed to 1000 rpm using the idle speed screw.

Throttle Slide Synchronization

"J" AND "K" MODELS

1. Accomplish the setting of the cable adjusters and the idle speed and mixture as described above.

SC-series carburetor pilot air screw (1) and throttle stop screw (2)

2. Remove the carburetor alignment hole plugs.
3. Turn the twist-grip about half-open, so that the punch marks on the carburetor slides are aligned with the upper surface of the alignment hole.
4. Use the cable adjusters on each carburetor cap to bring the slides into alignment. Refer to the illustration of the correct slide alignment.

Correct throttle slide alignment

Incorrect throttle slide adjustment

5. Replace the alignment hole plugs.
6. Set the throttle cable adjuster near the twist-grip to give the following cable free-play:

GT380, GT550	1–2 mm (0.04–0.08 in.)
GT750	0.5–1.0 mm (0.02–0.04 in.)

7. After all adjustments have been made, start the engine, and turn the handlebars lock-to-lock and note any variation in engine speed. This would indicate that the cable was adjusted too tightly, or that the throttle cable is binding or being pinched somewhere along its route.

NOTE: *After throttle cable adjustments, always check the oil pump cable adjustment. Refer to "Maintenance."*

"L-A" MODELS

Because of the pulley and linkage used, slide synchronization is not usually necessary unless the linkage has been disassembled. In any event, removal of the carburetors and linkage is necessary. Refer to "Fuel System" for procedures.

Tune-Up Specifications

	Spark Plugs (NGK/ND)	Spark Plug Gap (in./mm) NGK	ND	Breaker Point Gap (in./mm)	Ignition Timing (mm) R	C	L	Pilot Screw (turns out)	Idle Speed (rpm)	Float Level (in./mm)
GT380J, K	B-7ES/W22ES	0.028–0.032/0.7–0.8	0.024–0.028/0.6–0.7	0.012–0.016/0.3–0.4	2.99	2.93	2.99	1¼	1100	0.96/24.3
GT380L	B-8ES/W24ES	0.028–0.032/0.7–0.8	0.024–0.028/0.6–0.7	0.012–0.016/0.3–0.4	2.40	2.40	2.40	1¼	1100	1.01/25.8
GT380M	B-8ES/W24ES	0.028–0.032/0.7–0.8	0.024–0.028/0.6–0.7	0.012–0.016/0.3–0.4	2.30	2.25	2.30	1¼	1100	1.01/25.8
GT380A	B-8ES/W24ES	0.028–0.032/0.7–0.8	0.024–0.028/0.6–0.7	0.012–0.016/0.3–0.4	2.09	2.05	2.09	1¼	1100	1.01/25.8
GT550J, K	B-7ES/W22ES	0.028–0.032/0.7–0.8	0.024–0.028/0.6–0.7	0.012–0.016/0.3–0.4	3.37	3.37	3.37	1¼	1100	0.96/24.3
GT550L	B-7ES/W22ES	0.028–0.032/0.7–0.8	0.024–0.028/0.6–0.7	0.012–0.016/0.3–0.4	3.37	3.37	3.37	1½	1100	1.01/25.8
GT550M, A	B-8ES/W24ES	0.028–0.032/0.7–0.8	0.024–0.028/0.6–0.7	0.012–0.016/0.3–0.4	3.37	3.37	3.37	1½	1100	1.01/25.8
GT750J, K	B-7ES/W22ES	0.028–0.032/0.7–0.8	0.024–0.028/0.6–0.7	0.012–0.016/0.3–0.4	3.64	3.42	3.64	1½	1000	1.07/27.3
GT750L	B-6ES/W20ES	0.028–0.032/0.7–0.8	0.024–0.028/0.6–0.7	0.012–0.016/0.3–0.4	3.64	3.42	3.64	¼	1000	1.08/27.6
GT750M	B-8ES/W24ES	0.028–0.032/0.7–0.8	0.024–0.028/0.6–0.7	0.012–0.016/0.3–0.4	3.62	3.42	3.62	¾	1000	1.08/27.6
GT750A	B-8ES/W24ES	0.028–0.032/0.7–0.8	0.024–0.028/0.6–0.7	0.012–0.016/0.3–0.4	3.63	3.42	3.63	¾	1000	1.08/27.6

ENGINE AND TRANSMISSION

NOTE: *For engine component inspection techniques and procedures, refer to "Engine Rebuilding" under the General Information section.*

ENGINE SERVICE

Removal

GT380

1. Clean the engine thoroughly before removal.
2. Shut off the fuel petcock, and disconnect the fuel lines at the petcock.
3. Free the gas tank from its mounts, lifting it up at the rear and removing it from the machine.
4. Disconnect the 3 spark plug wires from the spark plugs.
5. Disconnect the alternator wires at the plastic couplers beneath the left side cover.
6. Disconnect the contact breaker point wires at the coupler.
7. Disconnect the oil line at the bottom of the oil tank, catching the oil in a container, or plugging the hole. Remove the drain plug for the transmission oil at the bottom of the crankcase, and allow the oil to drain for several moments.
8. Loosen the clamps which secure the left-side carburetor to the manifold and to the air cleaner, and pull the carburetor free, placing it carefully out of the way. The carburetors are located by a pin on the manifold. Do not twist or tilt the unit while removing.
9. Loosen the clamps which secure the center and right-side carbs to the air cleaner, then remove the air cleaner from the machine.
10. Loosen the clamps securing the center and right carburetors to the manifold, and pull off the carbs.

On 1974 and later models, disconnect the throttle cables and remove the carbs together after loosening the clamp screws and removing the air cleaner.

11. Remove the oil pump cover just beneath the right carb; disconnect the oil pump cable.
12. Disconnect the tachometer cable at the engine. Remove the rear brake light switch from its bracket.

Removing the oil pump cover

13. Remove the right-side rider's footpeg; pull off the rear brake pedal.
14. Remove the nuts which secure the exhaust pipe clamps to the cylinders, then remove the passenger footpegs. Remove the right and left exhaust pipes and mufflers. Loosen the clamps securing the center mufflers to the exhaust pipe, and pull the mufflers back until they are free of the pipe. Then remove the pipe.
15. Remove the left rider's footpeg, then loosen the pinch-bolt and pull the gearshift lever off the splined shaft.
16. Remove the clutch adjuster cover (left-side).
17. Remove the countershaft sprocket cover. Remove the 3 bolts, and remove the countershaft sprocket from the shaft. Move the chain out of the way so that it will not interfere with the engine removal.
18. Remove the Ram Air cover.
19. Remove all of the engine mounting nuts and bolts, take out the rear engine mounting plates, and take the engine out of the frame.

Removing the rear engine mounting plate

Engine mounting bolt locations

GT550

1. Clean the engine thoroughly prior to removal.

2. Shut the fuel petcock off, and disconnect the fuel line at the petcock. Remove the rubber strap securing the back of the gas tank, and lift up the back of the tank and remove it from the machine.

3. Disconnect the negative lead of the battery at the battery terminal.

4. Remove the 3 spark plug caps from the plugs. Disconnect the contact breaker wires at the plastic coupler beneath the right side cover.

5. Remove the rear brake light switch from its bracket. Then remove the brake pedal after removing the right footpeg and loosening the rear brake cable.

6. Disconnect the tachometer cable at the engine.

7. Disconnect the starter motor lead at the solenoid located beneath the left side cover.

8. Disconnect the alternator wires at the plastic couplers beneath the left side cover. Note that the alternator coupler and the rectifier coupler are similar in appearance, but have different markings. Be certain that they are properly connected upon reassembly.

Rectifier (top) and alternator coupler designations

9. Remove the oil pump cover, then disconnect the cable from the pump lever and from the engine.

10. Remove the oil line at the tank. Either catch the oil in a container, or plug the hole in the tank with a rubber plug (an inner tube valve cap should work).

11. Drain off the transmission oil.

12. Loosen the clamps which secure the air cleaner to the carburetors and remove the air cleaner ("J" and "K" models).

13. Loosen the clamps securing the carbs to the manifold, and remove them. Pull the carburetors straight off the manifold. Do not attempt to twist or turn them as they are located by a pin on the manifold.

NOTE: *On 1974–76 models which use a pulley and linkage assembly to open and close the carburetor slides, the throttle cables must be disconnected, and the carburetors taken out together.*

14. Remove the left-side rider's footpeg. Loosen the pinch-bolt and remove the gearshift lever from the splined shaft.

15. Remove the clutch mechanism cover, and then the countershaft sprocket cover.

16. Remove the 3 bolts which secure the countershaft sprocket to the shaft, then turn the locking plate half a pitch of the splines until it can be removed from the shaft. Remove the sprocket by pulling it off. Arrange the chain so that it will not interfere with the engine removal.

17. Remove the Ram Air cover.

18. Remove the nuts which secure the exhaust pipe clamps to the cylinder. Remove the passenger footpegs. Take off the right and left mufflers and exhaust pipes.

19. Loosen the clamps which secure the center mufflers to the center exhaust pipe, and pull the mufflers back and free from the pipe. Remove the exhaust pipe from the machine.

Engine mounting bolt locations

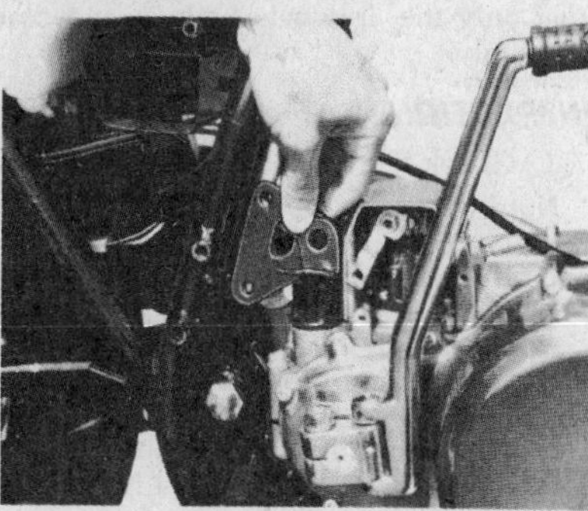

Removing the rear engine mounting plate

20. Remove all of the engine mounting nuts and bolts, the rear engine mounting plates, and remove the engine from the right-side of the frame.

GT750

1. Drain the cooling system by loosening the water drain plug at the front, center, of the engine. Drain the transmission oil.

Water drain plug location

Disconnect the oil feed line at the oil tank and either drain the oil or plug the tank.

2. Disconnect the starter motor lead from the battery terminal.

3. Shut off the fuel petcock, disconnect the fuel lines at the petcock, and remove the gas tank by detaching the rubber strap from the rear of the tank and sliding the tank back and up from the frame mounts.

4. Disconnect the radiator inlet hose, and remove the fan assembly and bracket.

5. Remove the passenger footpegs, loosen the muffler clamp screws, and remove the exhaust pipe bolts on the cylinder head. Remove the exhaust system.

6. Remove the left side cover, which will expose the electrical connections. Refer to the accompanying illustration. Disconnect the alternator (1), contact breaker (2), and starter motor (3) leads, and then disconnect the ground wire from the frame.

Alternator (1), contact breaker (2), and starter motor (3) leads

7. Remove the air cleaner by removing the set bolts on top and the 3 carburetor clamp screws.

8. Remove the left-side footpeg, the shift lever, and the countershaft sprocket cover. Bend down the locktab on the countershaft sprocket nut, remove the nut, and pull off the sprocket. It is not necessary to disconnect the chain. Arrange the chain out of the way so that it does not interfere with the engine removal.

9. Disconnect the clutch, oil pump, and tachometer cables at the engine. Disconnect the carburetor cables and remove the carburetors.

10. Remove the right-side footpeg and the rear brake pedal.

11. Remove the engine mounting nuts and bolts, the mounting plates, and take the engine out of the frame.

Installation

ALL MODELS

To install the engine, reverse the removal procedure. It is important that all important nuts and bolts be properly tightened. Torque specifications are given at the end of this section. The joints of the exhaust pipe coupler tubes should be coated with a temperature-resistant sealant before reassembly.

New exhaust pipe gaskets (at the cylinders) should be used. Leave a gap of 1 mm (0.04 in.) between the cylinder and the exhaust pipe clamp when installing the exhaust system.

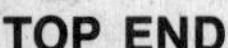

Cylinder head nut loosening order (GT380, GT550)

Removing a piston wrist pin circlip

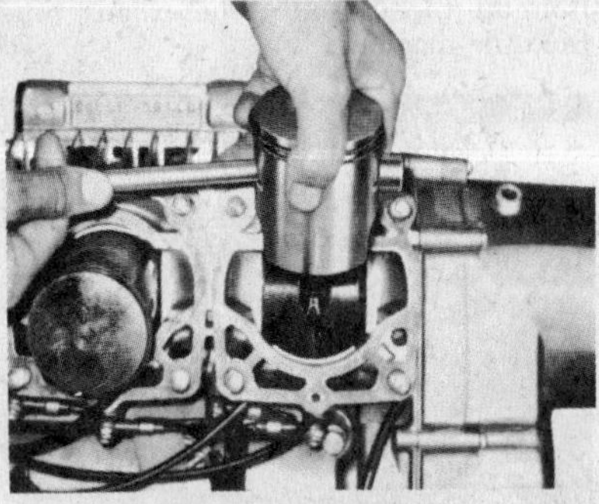

Removing a wrist pin

TOP END

GT380, GT550

It is possible to remove the head and barrels with the engine still in the frame. To do this, remove the gas tank, disconnect the spark plug leads; remove the Ram Air scoop, the carburetors, and exhaust system.

REMOVAL

1. The cylinder head is a one-piece casting and is secured to the cylinders by 12 thru-studs which are anchored in the barrels.

2. Refer to the illustration for cylinder head nut loosening order. Loosen each nut about ¼ turn at a time until they are free of tension, then remove them completely.

3. Lift the head clear of the studs and remove it. Remove the head gaskets. If the head resists removal, tap lightly all around the head-barrels joint with a soft-faced mallet to free it.

4. The 3 cylinders are separate, and each is secured to the crankcase by 4 nuts on studs which are anchored in the case. Each cylinder is removed separately.

5. Pull out the SRIS hoses on the intake side of the cylinders. Loosen the nuts for either outside cylinder gradually in a cross pattern, then remove the nuts and the washers beneath them. Pull off the cylinder, tapping gently on the underside of the fins to free it from the case as necessary.

6. Remove the cylinder base gaskets.

7. Pistons must be reinstalled into their proper cylinder; therefore, mark the position of each piston before removal. Stuff a clean, lint-free rag into the crankcase under the pistons. To remove the pistons, pry out the wrist pin circlips with a small screwdriver or needlenose pliers.

The wrist pin can then be pushed out with a suitable sized drift. Discard the circlips. New ones must be used upon assembly.

8. If, for some reason, the wrist pin will not yield to the normal method of removal, low heat may be applied to the piston crown to aid removal. Take care that only the crown is heated, and that sparingly.

INSPECTION

1. Check the head for warpage.

Note that *each cylinder's* mating surface must be checked as well as the overall head warpage. Observe the following tolerances:

a. No individual mating surface may be warped more than 0.03 mm (0.0012 in.).

b. No individual mating surface may be more than 0.1 mm (0.004 in.) below the line of the others.

c. Total warpage of the head must not exceed 0.15 mm (0.006 in.).

2. On the GT380, the top piston ring is wedge shaped, the upper surface of the ring being inclined 7° above the horizontal.

The lower ring on the GT380 is flat.

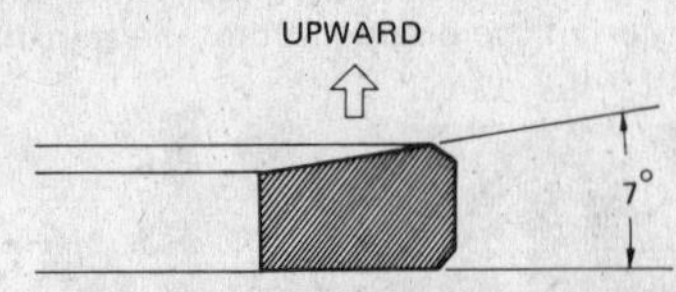

Correct installation of the wedge-shaped piston ring

On the GT550, both rings are wedge shaped. Needless to say, the rings on the GT380 are not interchangeable, and the wedged ring must always be installed in the top ring groove.

On all rings, a letter stamped on the top indicates the side which must face UPWARD.

3. Standard ring end-gap is 0.15–0.35 mm (0.006–0.014 in.). Rings must be replaced if end-gap exceeds:

GT380—1.0 mm (0.04 in.)
GT550—0.7 mm (0.028 in.)

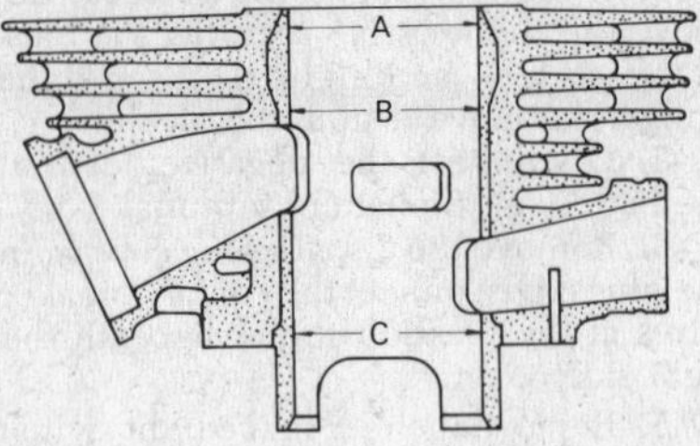

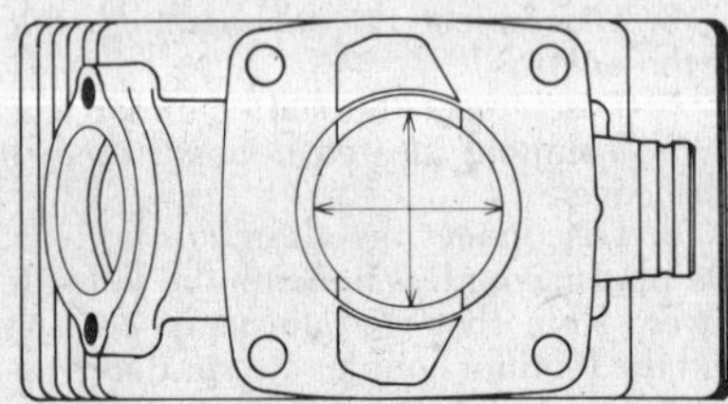

Cylinder bore measurement points (A, B, and C)

4. The cylinder bores should be checked for both taper and ellipticity. Measure the diameter of the bore at the top, middle, and bottom keeping the micrometer in the same plane; the readings should be taken at 6 mm (0.24 in.) below the top of the cylinder; 5 mm (0.20 in.) above the exhaust port; and 5 mm (0.20 in.) below the intake port.

Then take another set of readings at the same positions on the cylinder, but 90° from the first set.

If the difference between the largest and smallest of the six readings exceeds 0.1 mm (0.004 in.), the cylinders must be rebored to the next oversize, and then honed.

Oversized pistons are available in diameters 0.5 mm and 1.0 mm greater than standard.

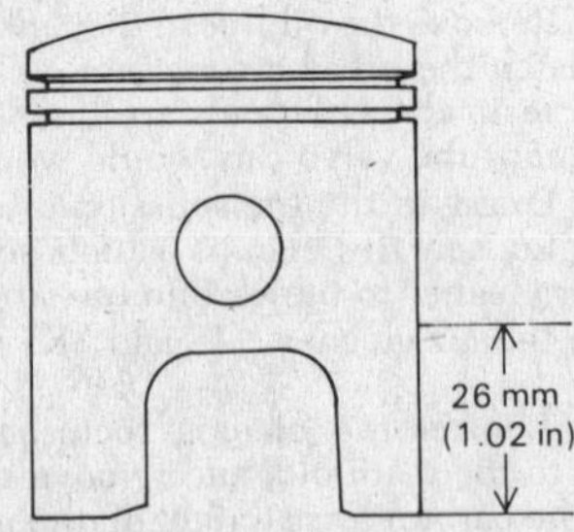

Piston diameter measurement point

5. Piston-to-cylinder clearance (standard) is 0.045 mm (0.0018 in.). Determine the clearance by measuring the diameter of the cylinder bore at a point 20 mm (0.79 in.) below the top of the cylinder, measuring from back to front of the cylinder.

Measure the diameter of the piston at a point 26 mm (1.02 in.) above the bottom ton wrist pin. Maximum acceptable piston-to-cylinder clearance (used) is 0.1 mm (0.004 in.). After this, the cylinders must be bored to fit oversized pistons.

NOTE: *After boring the cylinder, the edges of the ports must be chamfered according to the dimensions shown in the illustration.*

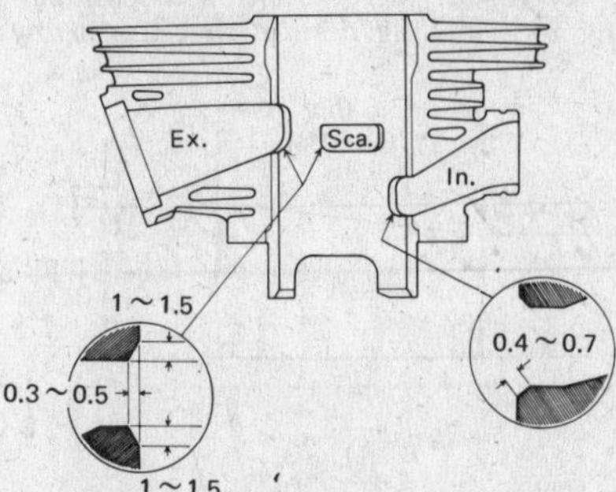

Port chamfer dimensions

NOTE: *Even if the cylinder has not been bored, check that the edges of the ports are not sharp. If they are, chamfer them with emery cloth or a small file.*

ASSEMBLY

1. Be sure that the rings are correctly installed on the pistons, with the lettered side of the ring facing up. Note that the wedge shaped ring of the GT380 is installed in the uppermost ring groove.
2. Install each piston on its own connecting rod, making certain that the arrow stamped on the piston crown points toward the EXHAUST port. Use new wrist pin circlips when refitting the pistons. Install the wrist pins using firm, steady pressure as on removal.
3. Use new cylinder base and cylinder head gaskets.

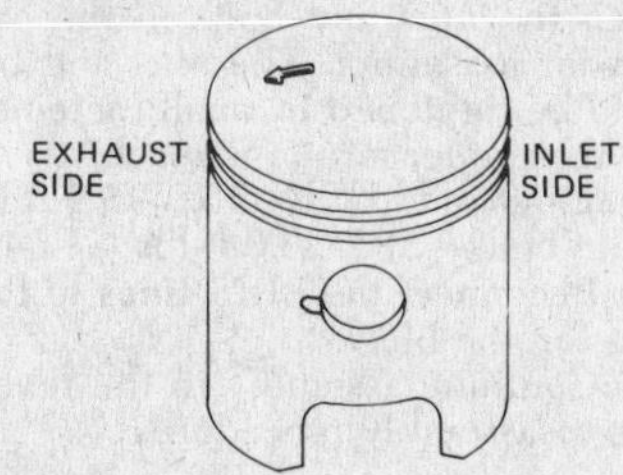

The arrow on the piston crown must point toward the exhaust port when the piston is installed

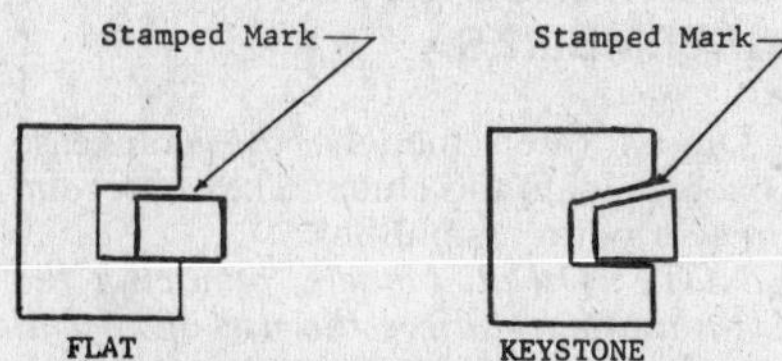

The stamped side of the piston ring is installed facing up

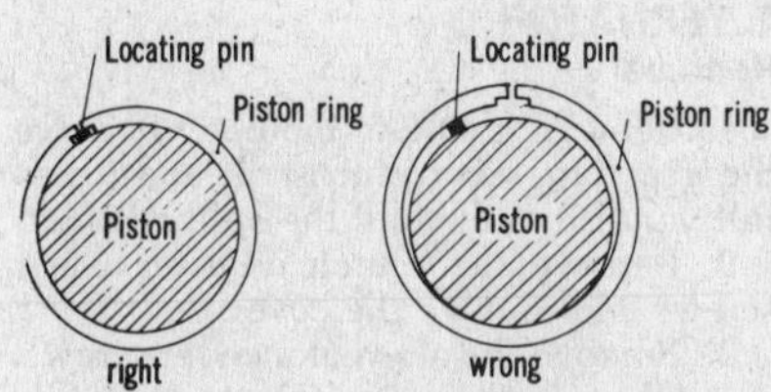

Correct and incorrect installation of the rings

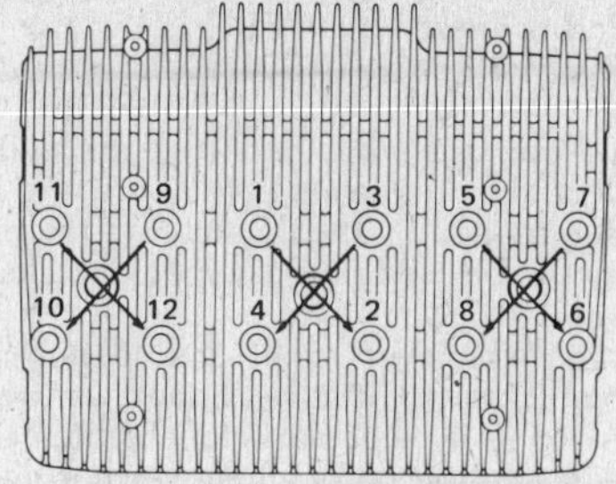

Cylinder head nut tightening order

4. Arrange the rings so that the ring ends are aligned with the locating pin in each ring groove. This is most important.
5. Lubricate the connecting rod small end, the rings, and the cylinder walls before installing the cylinders. Use CCI oil.
6. Slide each cylinder down over the piston while compressing the piston rings with your fingers. When the cylinder is seated on the crankcase, tighten the cylinder nuts gradually and in an "x" pattern.
7. Refit the cylinder heads and tighten the nuts gradually and in the pattern shown until the proper torque (18–29 ft lbs) is reached.
8. Refer to the accompanying illustration when installing the rubber intake manifold. Note that the notch "C" on the manifold must engage the rib on the cylinder "D" which will allow proper installation of the carburetors.

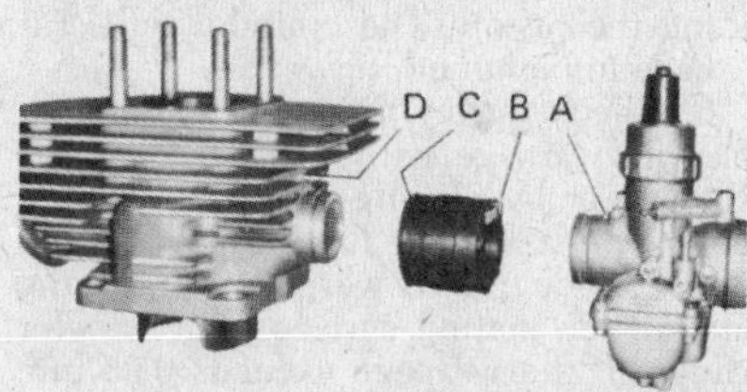

Locating pins and slots insure correct carburetor alignment

Exhaust pipe clamp clearance upon installation

9. When installing the exhaust pipes, allow 1–2 mm (0.04–0.08 in.) clearance between the cylinder and the exhaust pipe clamp.

GT750

REMOVAL

1. It is possible to remove the cylinder head and block without removing the engine from the frame. Loosen the water drain plug at the front, center, of the engine to drain the cooling system. Remove the gas tank, disconnect the radiator inlet hose and remove it; loosen the water by-pass hose clamp; disconnect the spark plug caps; remove the exhaust pipes; remove the carburetors.
2. Loosen the cylinder head nuts and bolts gradually (about ¼ turn at a time) in the order shown. When there is no longer any tension on the nuts and bolts, remove them all and take off the cylinder head. Remove the head gasket.

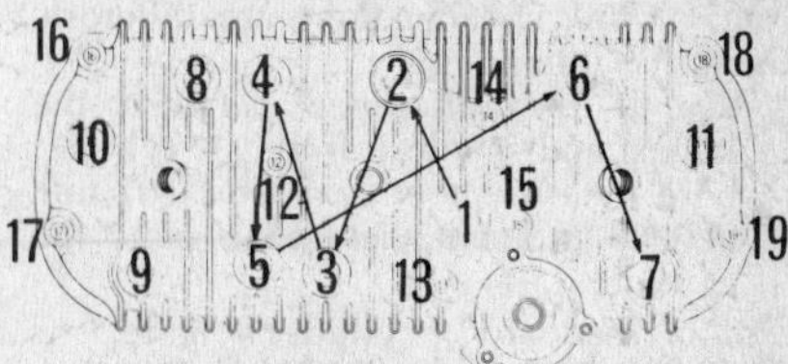

Cylinder head nut and bolt loosening order

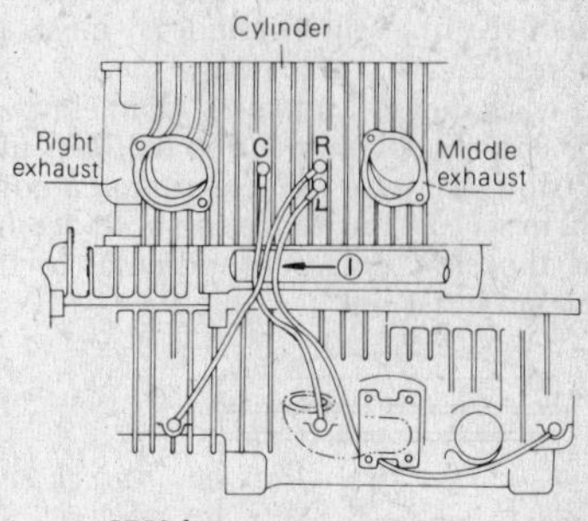

SRIS hose arrangements

3. Remove the SRIS lines from the cylinder. Remove the cylinder set nut behind the right cylinder. Lift the cylinder up and free of the pistons.

CAUTION: *Do not allow the pistons to strike the cylinder studs when they drop free of the cylinder.*

4. Remove the cylinder base gasket.
5. Pistons must be reinstalled into their proper cylinder; therefore, mark the position of each piston before removal. Stuff a clean, lint-free rag into the crankcase under the pistons. To remove the pistons, pry out the wrist pin circlips with a small screwdriver or needlenose pliers.

The wrist pin can then be pushed out. Discard the circlips; new ones must be used upon assembly.

6. If, for some reason, the wrist pin will not yield to the normal method of removal, low heat may be applied to the piston crown to aid removal. Take care that only the crown is heated, and that sparingly.

Be sure that each wrist pin is installed with its own piston upon reassembly.

INSPECTION

1. Check the head for warpage. Warpage exceeding 0.04 mm (0.001 in.) must be remedied.
2. Wrist pin play in the rod small end should not exceed 0.05 mm (0.002 in.).
3. Note that both rings on the GT750 pistons are wedge-shaped.

Maximum allowable ring end-gap is 0.7 mm (0.027 in.). Replace the rings if the end-gap exceeds this figure.

Standard ring end-gap is 0.15–0.35 mm (0.006–0.014 in.).

4. Piston ring side-clearance should be 0.030–0.095 mm (0.001–0.004 in.). If side-clearance is excessive, replace the rings.

5. Refer to GT380, GT550 "Inspection" for bore measurement points.

Although the procedures are similar for the GT750, specifications are different. Note the following:

a. If the difference between the largest and smallest of the six cylinder bore measurements exceeds 0.07 mm (0.0028 in.), bore and then hone the cylinders.

b. Standard cylinder bore is 70.000–70.015 mm (2.7559–2.7565 in.). If any of the readings exceed this measurement by more than 0.07 mm (0.0018 in.), the cylinders must be bored.

c. Standard piston diameter is 69.950–69.965 mm (2.7539–2.7545 in.). Piston diameter is measured at a point 32 mm (1.26 in.) above the bottom edge of the skirt and perpendicular to the piston wrist pin.

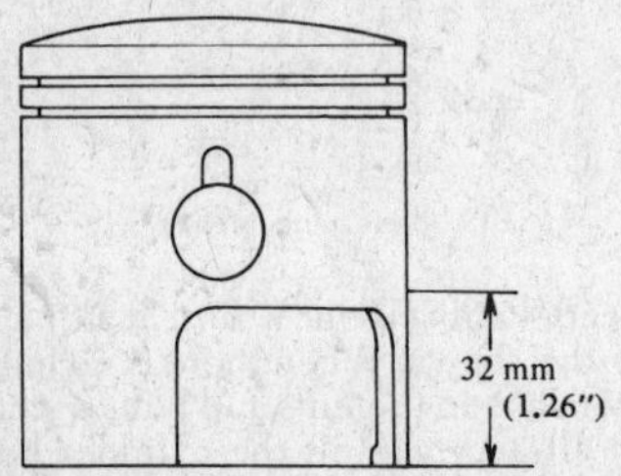

Piston diameter measurement point

d. Standard piston-to-cylinder clearance is 0.045–0.055 mm (0.0018–0.0022 in.) and may be determined by subtracting the diameter of the piston from the largest of the cylinder bore measurements obtained. Maximum allowable clearance is 0.07 mm (0.0028 in.).

e. Another method of checking the clearance is to insert a feeler gauge of the proper thickness into the bore, and then insert the piston. Using a spring scale, pull out the feeler gauge. Between 2.2–4.4 lbs (1–2 kg) should be sufficient to pull out the feeler gauge.

Checking piston-to-cylinder clearance with a feeler gauge and spring scale

f. Oversized pistons are available in two sizes: 0.5 and 1.0 mm. These pistons have the following diameters:

1st oversize
(0.5 mm): 70.450–70.465 mm (2.7736–2.7742 in.)

2nd oversize
(1.0 mm): 70.950–70.965 mm (2.7933–2.7939 in.)

Note that when reboring the cylinders, the dimension of the bore will be determined by the diameter of the pistons to be used plus the specified clearance.

g. Whenever the cylinders are bored, they must be honed as well. Also, it is necessary to chamfer the edges of the ports whenever boring is accomplished. The ports should be chamfered to the dimensions shown in the accompanying illustration.

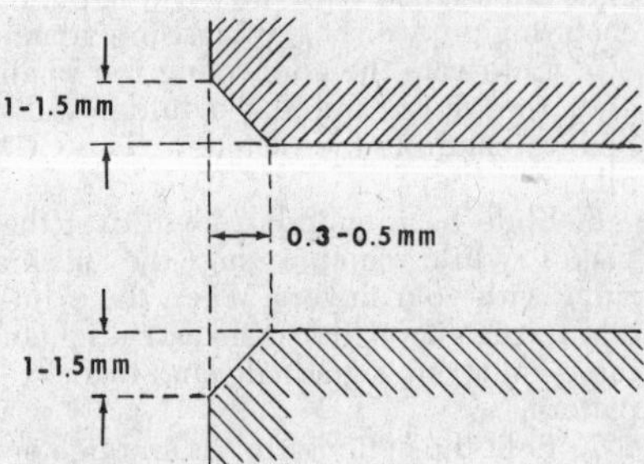

Port chamfer dimensions

h. If piston-to-cylinder clearance exceeds 0.07 mm (0.0028 in.) and the bore does not show excessive taper or wear, it may be possible to bring the clearance within tolerance by replacing the piston. The cylinder will still have to be honed, however.

6. Check the cylinder block top surface for warpage with a straightedge (as shown), or by placing the block, upside down, on a known flat surface. Determine the degree of warpage by probing around the mating surface with a feeler gauge. If the warpage exceeds 0.05 mm (0.002 in.), the mating surface must be lapped, or the block replaced.

Checking the cylinders for warpage

7. If the proper equipment is available, the block should be checked with air pressure for tightness. No leakage should be detected at a pressure of 3 kg/cm² (42.6 psi).

ASSEMBLY

NOTE: *Pistons must be installed in their original locations. If new pistons are fitted, note that the crown is stamped with either an "R" or "L." "R" pistons are always installed in the right cylinder, while "L" pistons are installed in the left and the center cylinders.*

1. Be sure that the piston rings are correctly installed, lettered side UP. If old rings are used, be sure that they are installed in their former location on the piston they came from.

2. Install each piston on its connecting rod, making certain that the arrow

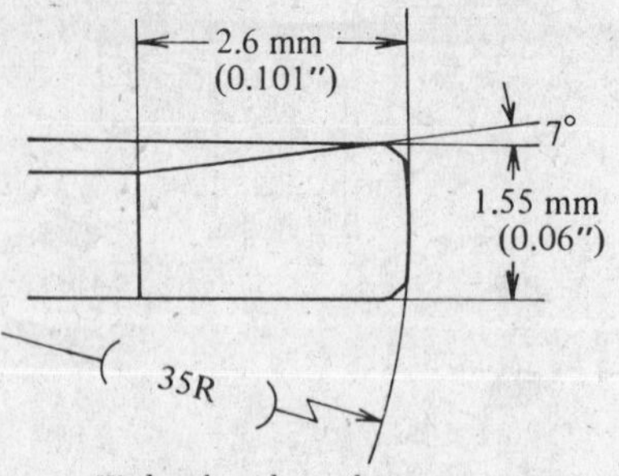

Wedge-shaped ring dimensions

stamped on the piston crown points toward the EXHAUST port. Use new wrist pin circlips when refitting the pistons.

3. Replace the 3 water passage O-rings at the front (top) of the crankcase with new ones. Fit a new cylinder base gasket.

4. Arrange the piston rings so that the ring ends are aligned with the locating pin in each ring groove. This is very important.

5. Lubricate the connecting rod small end, the rings, and the cylinder walls before installing the cylinder block. Use CCI oil.

6. Piston ring compressors should be used to hold the rings in while the block is fitted over the studs and slipped down over the pistons.

7. Replace and tighten the cylinder set nut.

8. Refit the cylinder head, and tighten the nuts and bolts in the order given for loosening. The nuts and bolts should be tightened in small increments until the proper torque is reached:

8 mm nuts and bolts—13.0–15.9 ft lbs.
10 mm bolts—21.7–29.0 ft lbs.

9. Reconnect the SRIS lines to their fittings on the block.

10. Continue assembly in the reverse of the disassembly procedure.

CRANKCASE COVER ASSEMBLIES

On all three models, the crankcase covers contain the clutch, alternator, and breaker point assemblies.

NOTE: *On all models, removing the alternator requires the use of special tools.*

GT380

LEFT CRANKCASE COVER AND ALTERNATOR

Removal

1. Remove the left footpeg. Remove the gearshift lever pinch-bolt and (carefully) pull the lever off the splined shaft.

2. Remove the clutch adjuster cover screws and remove the cover.

3. Remove the alternator cover screws, and take off the cover. Note that this cover is fitted with a gasket.

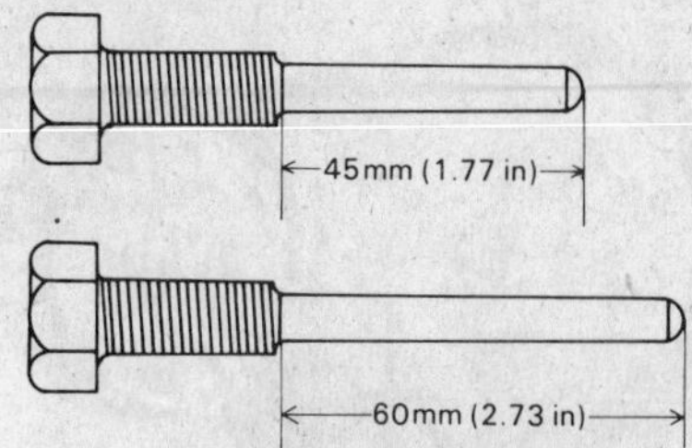

Two types of rotor puller: 45 mm length (top) for the Kokusan and 60 mm for the Denso rotors

4. Disconnect the Neutral switch wire from the switch.

5. Remove the 3 stator screws, then take off the stator.

NOTE: *If a Nippon Denso alternator is fitted, lift the carbon brush off the slip-ring by hand while removing the stator.*

6. Two types of alternator are fitted, therefore a different rotor puller is needed depending on which type you are working with.

The Nippon Denso alternator requires a puller with a 60 mm (2.36 in.) unthreaded portion.

The Kokusan Denki alternator requires a puller with a 45 mm (1.77 in.) unthreaded portion.

7. If the engine has been removed from the frame, or the cylinders removed, lock the crankshaft in place with the special tool (No. 09910–20113) placed under the piston.

If the engine is still in the frame, and the cylinders have not been removed, place the transmission in First gear, and have an assistant apply the rear brake while removing the rotor.

8. Remove the rotor bolt, then use the special tool and remove the rotor itself. To remove the rotor, tighten the puller to 6.6–10 ft lbs.

9. To gain access to the countershaft sprocket, remove the sprocket cover after disengaging the clutch cable from the clutch release mechanism, and unscrewing the cable adjuster from the sprocket cover. The sprocket cover is secured by 4 screws.

Inspection

1. All electrical tests are given in the "Electrical Systems" section.

2. Check that the rotor does not have scoring or wear marks on it, as it might if it has contacted the stator.

Assembly

1. Reverse the removal procedure.

2. When refitting the stator, take care that the carbon brush (if fitted) is held out of the way while the stator is positioned.

3. Make sure that the stator and rotor are separated by an even air gap all the way around. Move the stator on its mounting screws as necessary to achieve this.

4. If the rotor and stator touch at any point, one of them is not mounted correctly.

5. Tighten the rotor bolt to 6.6–10 ft lbs.

RIGHT CRANKCASE COVER COMPONENTS

The right crankcase cover contains the breaker point assembly, and removing the cover will reveal the clutch assembly and the crank and kickstarter drive gears.

A special tool is sometimes necessary to remove the clutch hub. It must be held stationary while the hub nut is removed.

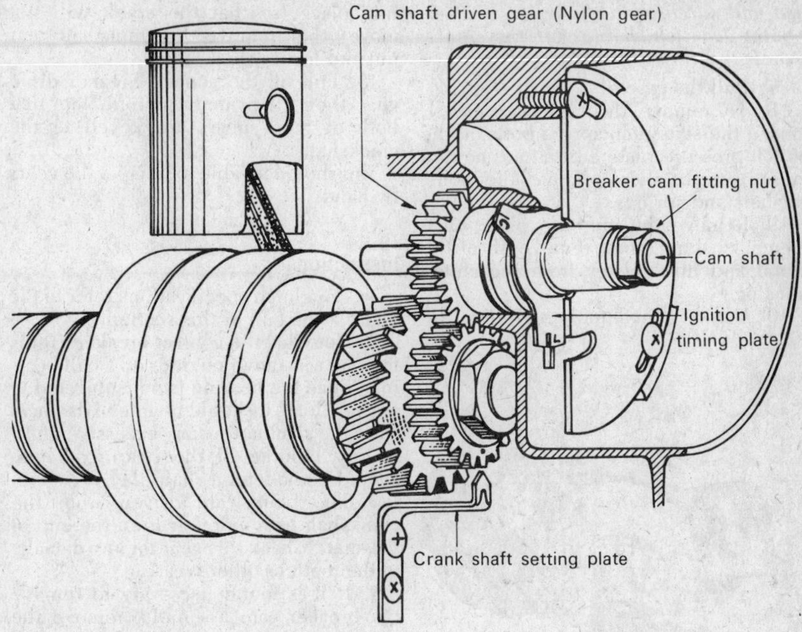

Breaker cam drive (GT380)

Removal and Disassembly

1. Drain the transmission oil.
2. Remove the right-side footpeg.
3. Remove the breaker points inspection cap.
4. Disconnect the points wires, remove the 3 base plate screws, and remove the contact breaker assembly.
5. Remove the kickstarter pinch-bolt, and pull the kickstarter off the splined shaft.

Right crankcase cover screws (GT380)

6. Remove the right crankcase cover securing screws. There are 9 of them; note that two are found inside the points compartment.

CAUTION: *It is not necessary to remove the breaker cam nut to remove the right case cover. To attempt to do*

Clutch assembly (GT380)

1. Clutch housing
2. Clutch hub thrust washer
3. Clutch hub
4. Clutch hub nut
5. Clutch hub nut lockwasher
6. Friction plate
7. Steel plate
8. Clutch pressure plate
9. Clutch spring
10. Clutch spring bolt
11. Washer
12. Pushrod
13. Pushrod
14. Pushrod oil seal
15. Push crown
16. Push crown oil seal
17. Clutch release assembly screw device
18. Clutch adjuster screw
19. Washer
20. Locknut
21. Cover
22. Dust seal
23. Screw
24. Spring

so will surely ruin the nylon breaker point gear which runs off the crankshaft.

7. Pull the case off.
8. To remove the clutch assembly, loosen the six clutch spring bolts on the clutch pressure plate a bit at a time in a cross pattern, then remove the bolts, washers and springs.
9. Remove the pressure plate, push crown, pushrod, then remove all of the metal and fiber plates from the clutch housing.
10. Use a punch to bend down the

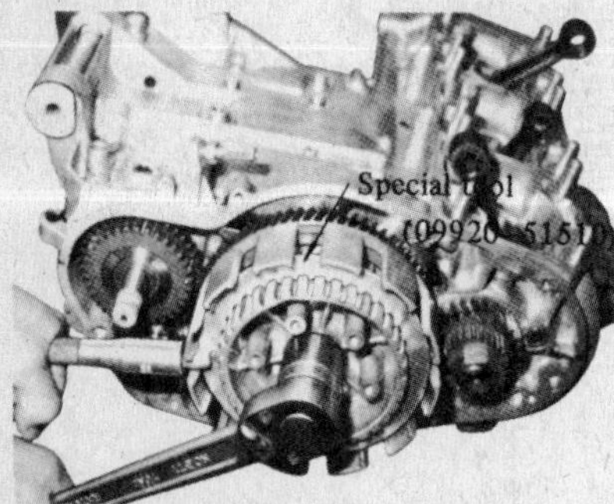

Removing the clutch hub nut

clutch hub nut lockwasher. Then remove the nut.

11. Take off the clutch hub, thrust washer, and housing.
12. Take off the kickstarter gear, the ratchet wheel, and the spring.
13. To remove the crankshaft gears, first remove the crankshaft setting plate. Bend down the tab on the lockwasher.
14. Use the shop tool or a suitable substitute to lock the right connecting rod

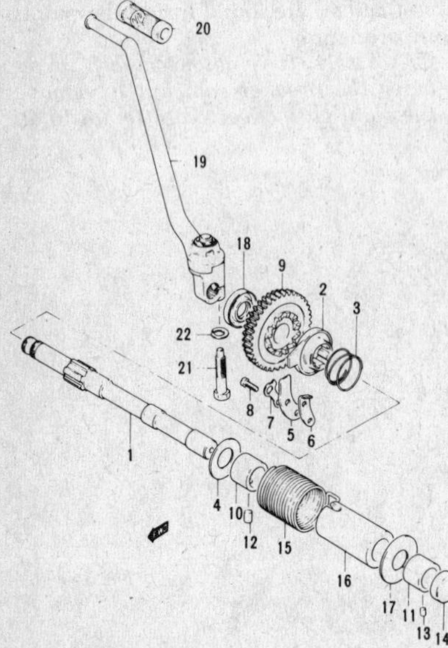

Kickstarter assembly (GT380)

1. Kickstarter shaft
2. Ratchet wheel
3. Spring
4. Thrust washer
5. Kickstarter guide
6. Stopper plate
7. Stopper washer
8. Stopper bolt
9. Kickstarter drive gear
10. Shaft bushing
11. Shaft bushing
12. Dowel pin
13. Dowel pin
14. Shaft plug
15. Return spring
16. Return spring guide
17. Washer
18. Shaft oil seal
19. Kickstarter lever
20. Rubber
21. Pinch-bolt
22. Lockwasher

into place (so that the crank will not move), then remove the crankshaft gear nut and lockwasher.

15. Pull off the contact breaker drive gear, then the primary pinion. Note that both of these gears are keyed to the crankshaft.

You should be able to remove the gears by hand.

Inspection

1. For clutch specifications refer to the chart at the end of this section.
2. Note that the contact breaker cam is fitted to a shaft which rides on a ball bearing. Since the bearing is not subjected to any real load, it should be free of damage. Turn the shaft noting any excessive noise or any binding of the bearing. There should be no lateral shaft play.
3. The points are driven from the crankshaft by a nylon gear on the end of the shaft. Check this gear for any damage to the teeth or other wear.
4. If it is found necessary to remove the breaker cam assembly, remove the shaft nuts, nylon gear, timing plate, and pull out the shaft. An oil seal is fitted over the bearing. After removing the seal, take off the bearing retaining circlip, and tap out the bearing from the inside of the case.

A new oil seal must be used upon reassembly.

Assembly and Installation

1. Reverse the removal procedure. Note the following points.
2. Install the primary pinion woodruff key, then the pinion. Install the contact breaker drive gear key, then the gear.

Tighten the crankshaft nut to 36 ft lbs. Install the crankshaft setting plate. Secure the plate screws with a thread locking compound.

3. Install the kickstarter mechanism lining up the punch mark on the ratchet wheel with the punch mark on the shaft.
4. Install the clutch assembly. Note the thrust washer between the hub and housing. When installing the plates, fit a steel plate *first*, then alternate friction and steel plates. When tightening the clutch hub nut, hold the housing as on removal. Tighten the nut to 36–43 ft lbs. Bend up the lockwasher tab.
5. Tighten the clutch spring bolts gradually and in a cross pattern to 2.9–5.1 ft lbs.
6. Engine timing marks *must* be properly aligned to accomplish ignition timing. Proceed as follows:
   a. Turn the crankshaft so that the punch mark on the contact breaker drive gear is lined up with the mark on the crankshaft setting plate.
   b. Line up the scribed line marked "L" on the 3-pronged timing rotor with the mark on the crankcase cover.
   c. Match the locating pin on the crankcase with the hole in the right crankcase cover, and replace the cover. NOTE: *A new gasket should always be installed. Also be sure to grease the lips of the kickstarter oil seal before installing the cover.*

Timing rotor correctly positioned for case cover installation

7. Refit and tighten the cover screws. Install the breaker plate. Be sure that the wires are correctly positioned so that they are not pinched between the plate and the inside of the cover.
8. Adjust the clutch after assembly is complete.

GT550

LEFT CRANKCASE COVER AND ALTERNATOR

The procedures for removing and installing the right crankcase cover components on the 550 are essentially the same as described for the 380, above. Refer to that Section.

RIGHT CRANKCASE COVER COMPONENTS

Removal

1. Drain the transmission oil if this has not already been done. Remove the right-side footpeg.
2. Remove the kickstarter lever pinch-bolt and carefully pull the lever off the splined shaft.
3. Remove the right crankcase cover securing screws, and pull off the cover.

   NOTE: *It is not necessary to remove the breaker points.*
4. Loosen the clutch spring screws gradually and evenly. Then remove the screws, caps, and springs. Take off the pressure plate, the push crown, and the clutch plates.
5. Bend down the tab on the clutch hub nut lockwasher. While holding the clutch with the special tool, loosen and remove the clutch hub nut.
6. Grasping the clutch housing AND the starter clutch gear with your hands, as illustrated, pull the assembly off the clutch shaft.

   NOTE: *It is important that the starter clutch gear be taken off along with the clutch housing, or the other starter clutch components may drop off the housing when it is removed.*

Removing the clutch hub nut

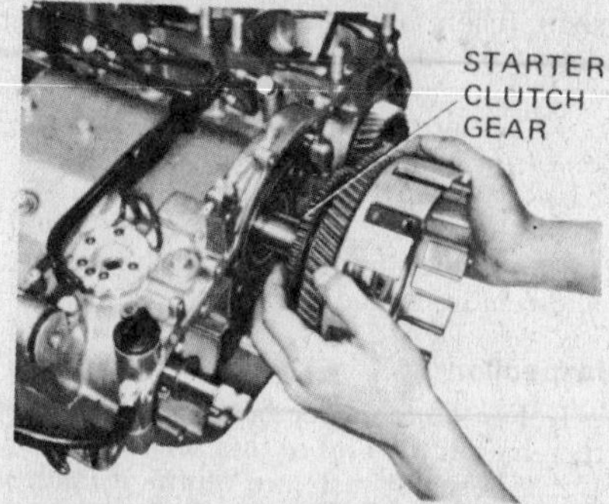

Pulling off the clutch housing and starter clutch gear assembly

7. Pull out the gear shifter shaft.

8. Remove the oil guide plate. The securing screws will have to be removed with an impact driver. Remove the kickstarter shaft thrust washer. Take off the circlip, washer, spring, and ratchet wheel.

Removing the gearshifter shaft

9. Remove the starter motor cover.

10. Remove the securing screws and take out the starter motor.

Removing the oil guide plate

Inspection

1. For clutch specifications refer to the chart at the end of this section.

2. The contact breaker assembly is mounted in the right side-cover, and is accessible after removing the small cover plate. The breaker cam is mounted on a shaft which is driven by the crankshaft primary gear. The shaft rides on two bearings. Since the bearings are not subject to any real load, they should be free of damage. Turn the shaft noting any excessive noise or binding; check the shaft for lateral play. There should be none.

3. The breaker points compartment is kept free of oil by a seal installed beneath the 3-pronged timing plate rotor. If this seal is removed, it must be replaced. The seal should be replaced, as necessary, at the first sign of oil in the points case.

4. The breaker point shaft bearings are retained by a circlip accessile after removing the oil seal.

5. Check the condition of all gear teeth, noting any chipped or worn teeth.

6. If the crankshaft primary gear is damaged, remove it by bending down the lockwasher, removing the nut, and pulling the gear off the crankshaft. Note that the gear is located by a woodruff key.

7. Disassembly of the starter clutch is not recommended unless the unit is defective.

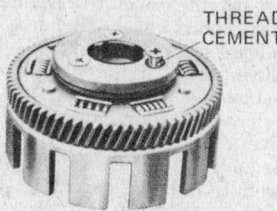

Starter clutch securing screws

With an impact driver, remove the 3 phillips head screws which secure the starter clutch assembly to the back of the clutch housing. Take off the cover plate. The starter clutch can be inspected in place.

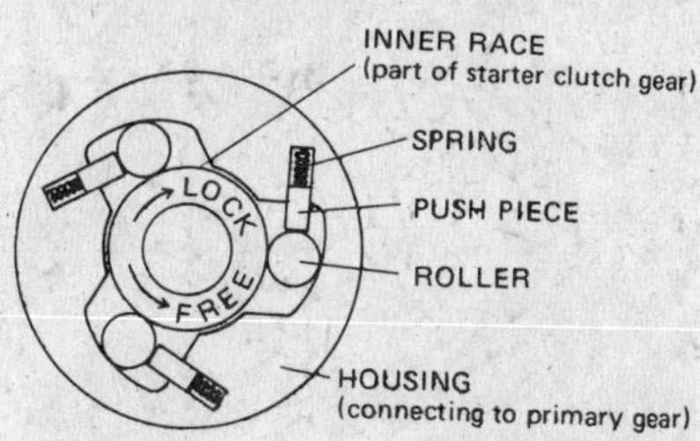

Starter clutch components

Check the rollers and the housing cutouts for wear or damage. Replace as necessary.

NOTE: *When refitting, be certain that the starter clutch housing screws are secured with thread locking compound and are installed with an impact driver.*

Assembly and Installation

Reverse the disassembly procedure. Note the following:

1. The ratchet wheel punch mark must be aligned with the mark on the kickstarter shaft. Turn the wheel so that the boss rests against the stopper plate.

2. The oil guide plate screws should be secured with an impact driver.

3. Torque the clutch hub nut to 36–43 ft lbs. Bend up the lockwasher tab.

4. Torque the clutch spring screws to 2.9–5.1 ft lbs. They should be tightened gradually and in a cross pattern.

5. When installing the cover, note that the contact breaker cam shaft pin must be properly engaged with the primary gear.

6. Adjust the clutch after assembly is complete.

GT750

LEFT CRANKCASE COVER COMPONENTS

The breaker points are located beneath a cover at the forward, left-side of the engine. Behind the points are the starter clutch assembly, water pump drive gear, electric starter gears, and the tachometer drive gear. The countershaft sprocket is beneath the rear left side-cover.

Removal

1. Drain the transmission oil. Disconnect the tachometer cable at the engine.

2. Remove the contact breaker cover plate. Marking the position of the stator will speed reassembly. Remove the 3 stator securing screws, and take off the stator.

3. Remove the starter clutch cover. The contact breaker cam shaft assembly will come off with it.

4. Remove the circlip which retains the nylon water pump drive gear, and take off the gear.

5. Remove the electric starter idler gear.

6. Remove the starter clutch assembly bolt, then remove the assembly. Note that two special tools are needed to accomplish this.

7. Loosen the set bolt and take out the tachometer driven gear and sleeve.

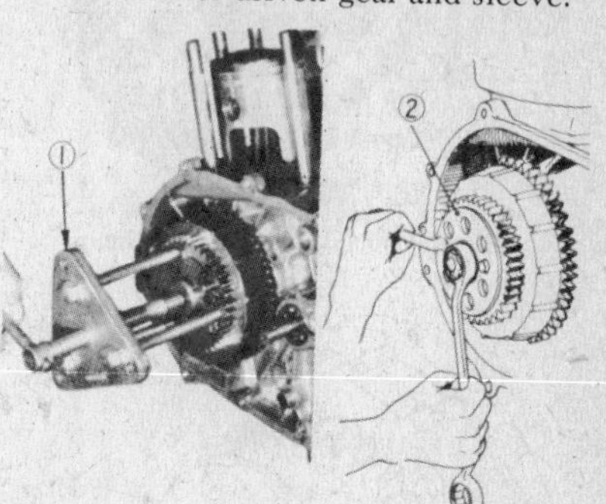

Special tools (1, 2) in use removing the starter clutch components

Water pump drive gear (1); electric starter gear (2); tachometer drive gear sleeve (3) and set bolt

8. Remove the countershaft sprocket cover after removing the left footpeg, and removing the gearshift lever.

9. Bend down the tab on the sprocket lockwasher. Remove the nut. Remove the lockwasher from the shaft, then pull off the sprocket.

10. Remove the oil seal retainer.

11. Remove the gearshift switch.

NOTE: *Steps 10 and 11 are not neces-*

sary unless either of the components are defective, or the crankcases are to be split.

Inspection

1. Check the gear teeth for chipping or wear. Replace any damaged gear.
2. Check the starter clutch rollers and the housing for wear.
3. The contact breaker camshaft rides on two bearings which are mounted in the starter clutch cover. Check the rotation of the shaft. It should be smooth and effortless. Make sure that rotation is not rough or binding. Check the shaft for lateral play.

An oil seal keeps the points compartment free of oil. If seepage is noted, replace the seal. If the seal is taken off the shaft, a new seal should always be fitted.

To remove the smaller of the bearings from the starter clutch cover, first remove the snap-ring, then drive out the bearing.

The punch mark and pin must align

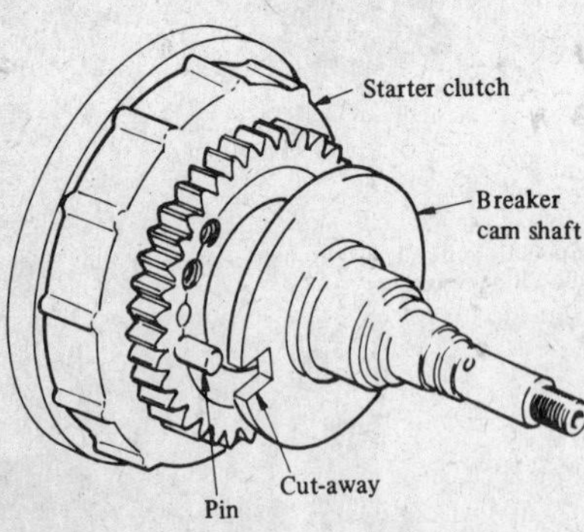

Installing the breaker cam

Assembly

1. Reverse the disassembly procedure. Note that the punch mark on the starter clutch housing must align with the pin on the water pump drive gear. Secure the gear-to-housing bolts with thread locking compound.
2. Tighten the starter clutch mounting bolt to 33–40 ft lbs. The starter clutch must be held with the special tool.
3. When refitting the cover, note that the slot cut into the plate of the contact breaker camshaft must engage the pin on the water pump gear.

RIGHT CRANKCASE COVER COMPONENTS

The right crankcase covers contain the alternator and clutch assemblies, and the kickstarter return spring assembly.

Removal

Note that the removal of the alternator rotor requires a special puller.

1. If the clutch is to be removed, drain the transmission oil. Remove the alternator cover.
2. Unscrew the brush holder screws, holding the holder very securely while doing it. A spring bears on the brushes and will attempt to push them out of the holder as the holder is removed. Take the holder off very slowly, so that the brushes do not spring out too quickly.
3. Remove the alternator stator.
4. Remove the alternator rotor bolt. Then use the special puller to remove the rotor.
5. Remove the clutch release mechanism inspection cover. Remove the clutch release shaft nuts, and take off the clutch lever. Detach the clutch cable from the clutch cover.
6. Remove the right footpeg and rear brake lever.
7. Remove the kickstarter pinch-bolt, then carefully pull the kickstarter lever off the splined shaft.
8. Remove all of the securing screws, and pull off the clutch cover.
9. To disassemble the clutch, loosen the six clutch bolts gradually and evenly

Clutch pressure plate (1) and shaft (2)

and when they are all loose, remove them, the springs, and finally the clutch pressure plate and shaft.

10. Take out the clutch plates.
11. Remove the clutch hub nut after bending down the tab on the lockwasher. The clutch housing must be held in place while removing the nut.
12. Remove the hub, then screw two draw bolts into the clutch hub bushing spacer and take it and the bushing off the shaft. Then take off the clutch housing, noting the location of the thrust washers on the assembly.

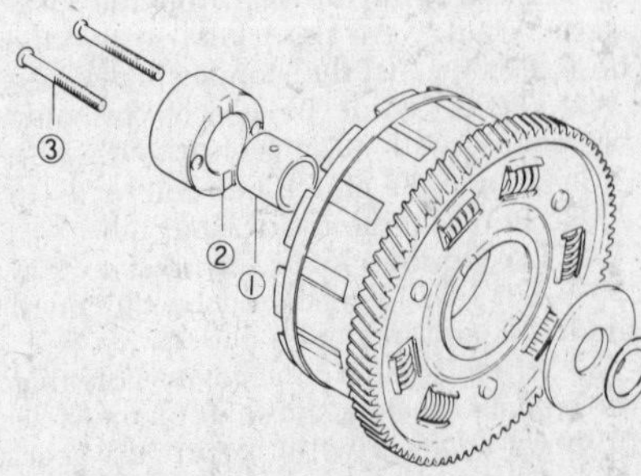

Clutch hub bushing (1), spacer (2), and draw bolts (3)

13. Remove the transmission oil reservoir plate fitted on the crankcase if the cases are going to be split.
14. Remove the kickstarter shaft spring guide, then disengage the spring, and remove it and its holder.

Inspection

1. For clutch specifications, refer to the chart at the end of this section.
2. Alternator tests are outlined in the "Electrical Systems" section.
3. Check the mating surfaces of the right side-covers for nicks or scratches. Remove with emery cloth. Remove any traces of old gasket or gasket compound from the mating surfaces.
4. Check the kickstarter shaft oil seal. Replace if defective.

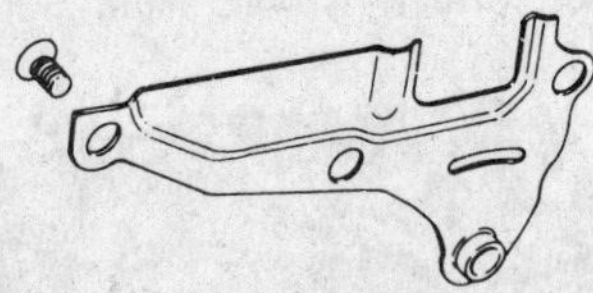

Transmission oil reservoir plate

Assembly

1. Reverse the disassembly procedure. Note the following:
2. Use thread locking compound on the transmission oil reservoir plate securing screws and tighten them with an impact driver.
3. Oil the clutch housing bushing and spacer thoroughly with transmission oil. Be sure that the thrust washers are correctly located, and install the assembly.
4. Replace the hub, and tighten the hub nut to 29–40 ft lbs.
5. Squirt some oil into the hole in the clutch sleeve shaft. Install the plates and pressure plate.
6. Adjust the clutch as outlined in the "Maintenance" section.
7. Grease the lips of the kickstarter shaft oil seal before refitting the cover. Be sure to use a new cover gasket.
8. When refitting the kickstarter lever, align the mark on the lever with that on the shaft.

LOWER END AND TRANSMISSION

Splitting the Crankcases

ALL MODELS

1. Remove the engine from the frame. Remove the cylinder head, barrels and pistons.
2. Remove the left and right crankcase covers and the components therein.
3. Remove the oil pump.
4. Remove the electric starter if so equipped.
5. Remove the oil reservoir guide plates where fitted, and the oil seal housing on the transmission shaft if so equipped.

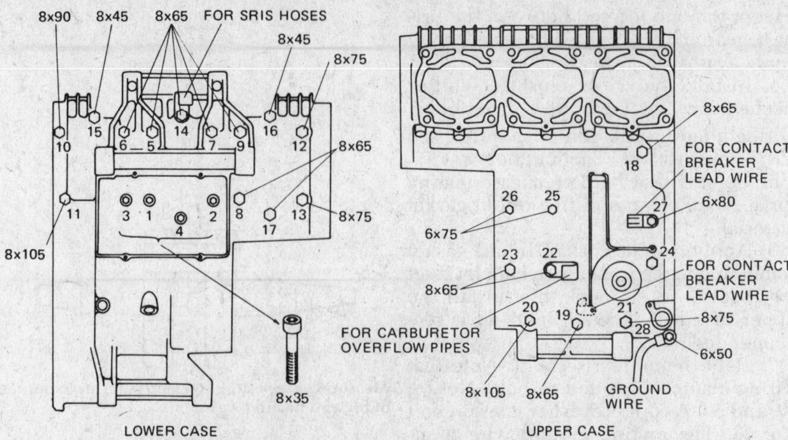

Crankcase bolt loosening and tightening order (GT550)

Crankcase bolt loosening and tightening order (GT380)

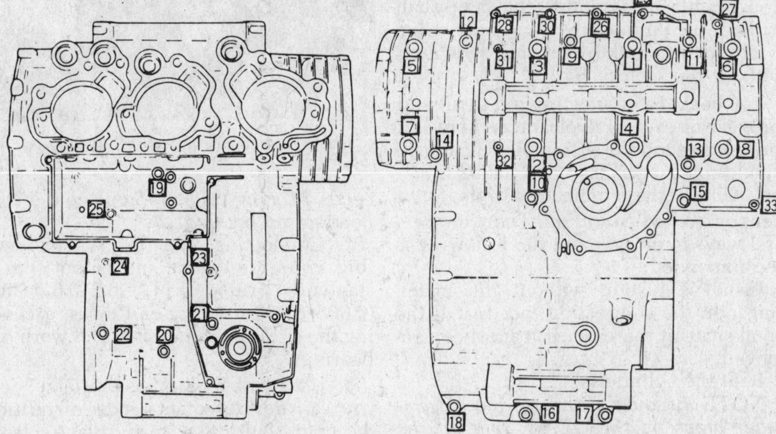
Crankcase bolt loosening and tightening order (GT750)

6. Loosen all of the crankcase bolts on the top and bottom crankcase halves in the reverse of the order shown (the numbers are stamped on the cases).

7. Turn the engine so that the correct side faces up, then tap around the crankcase halves' mating surface with a soft-faced mallet. Lift off the upper crankcase half. The crankshaft and gear clusters will stay in the lower case half.

Assembling the Cases

For crankshaft and transmission inspection procedures, see below.

GT380, GT550

1. Generously bathe the crankshaft assembly, especially the bearings, in Suzuki CCI oil.

2. Position each crankshaft oil seal close to the bearing side.

3. Position the pins of each crankshaft bearing so that it sits in its slot in the lower crankcase.

4. When installing the gear clusters, make sure that the bearings are matched with their dowel pins.

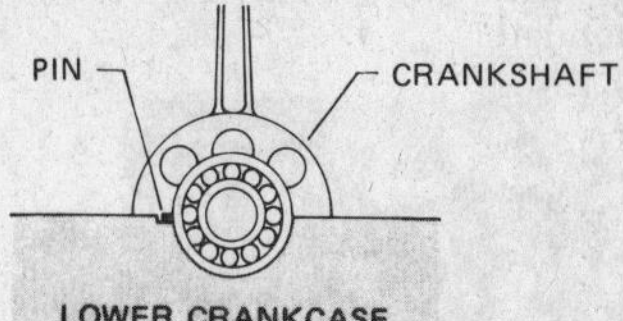

Crank bearing locating pin engaged in lower case

5. Check for smooth operation of all the gears and the shift mechanism.

6. GT550: Fit the boss of the countershaft oil reservoir in the groove in the lower crankcase to properly position the oil passage.

7. Make sure that the transmission shafts can be rotated smoothly by hand.

8. Align the kickstarter shaft and ratchet wheel punch marks. Position the starter return spring so that its end is properly seated. Preload the spring by

Fit the countershaft boss into its groove

Aligning the kickstarter ratchet wheel and shaft punch marks

turning the shaft ¾ turn counterclockwise until the boss of the ratchet wheel is resting on the stopper plate.

9. Be sure that both crankcase halves have clean mating surfaces. Remove any traces of old gasket compound.

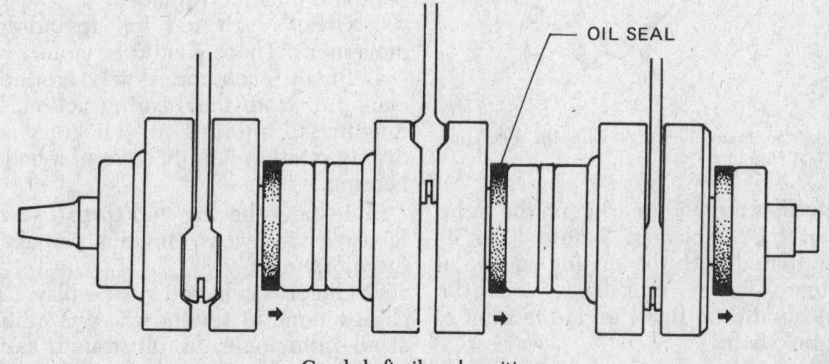

Crankshaft oil seal positions

10. Apply a light coat of a liquid gasket material to the upper case half. Let it set for about five minutes, then install the upper case half. Suzuki Bond #4 is recommended.

Kickstarter return spring fitted into the case cutout

11. Install the crankcase bolts and the hose and wiring clamps where applicable. Tighten the bolts in the order indicated by the numbers stamped on the crankcases.

Proper torque settings are:

GT380:
6 mm bolts—9.4 ft lbs.
8 mm bolts—14.5 ft lbs.
GT550:
6 mm—4.4–7.3 ft lbs.
8 mm—9.5–17 ft lbs.

12. Complete the assembly of the right and left crankcase cover components as described in those Sections. Refill the transmission with the correct quantity and grade of oil.

GT750

NOTE: *If the crankcase halves have been replaced, be sure to install the transmission gears supplied with the new parts. Cases and gears are color-coded. Refer to the "Transmission" Section, below.*

1. Lubricate the crankshaft assembly thoroughly with Suzuki CCI before installation.
2. Insert the crankshaft assembly into the lower case, and position the crank bearings so that the punch marks on the bearing races align with the crankcase mating surface.

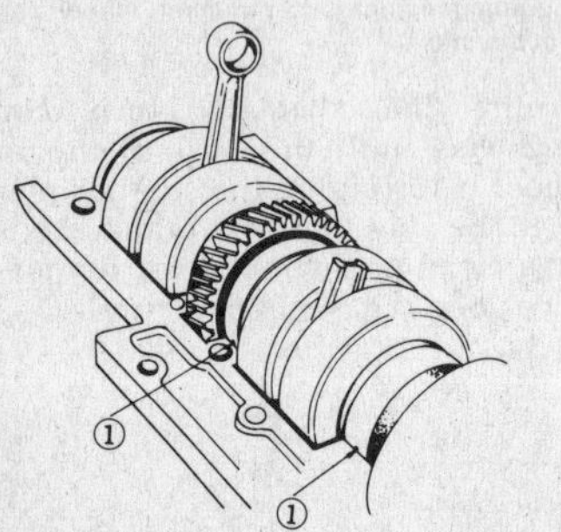

Aligning the crank bearings with the crankcase marks (GT750)

Note that the end bearing on the right-side of the crankshaft should have its mark aligned with the mating surface at the rear of the crankshaft, while the others should be lined up at the front of the crankshaft.

3. Push all of the crankshaft oil seals (except the one located between the primary gear and the right-side crankthrow) firmly against their bearings.
4. Install the gear clusters, shifter mechanism, and kickstarter assemblies. For detailed installation procedures, see the "Transmission" Section, below.
5. Be sure that both crankcase mating surfaces are clean and free of old gasket material.
6. Apply a light coat of liquid gasket compound to the upper case half, let it set for about 5–10 minutes, then install the upper case half. Suzuki Bond #4 is recommended.
7. Refit the crankcase bolts. Note that wiring clamps are fitted to bolts Nos. 8, 10, and 14. A copper washer goes on bolt No. 13. The engine ground wire is attached to bolt No. 22.

Attach the remaining clamps for the wiring to bolt No. 6.

8. Tighten the bolts in the order indicated by the numbers on the crankcase. Note the following torque specifications:

6 mm bolts—4.3–7.2 ft lbs.
8 mm bolts—9.4–16.7 ft lbs.
10 mm bolts—18.1–28.9 ft lbs.

9. Fill the transmission with the correct amount (2500 cc) of oil.

Crankshaft

ALL MODELS

The crankshafts on all three machines are pressed together. It is impossible to disassemble or assemble the crankshaft without the proper press, and impossible to align the crankthrows and flywheels without the factory jigs.

1. Check the connecting rod small end for wear or excessive clearance between the bearing and the piston pin. Clearance should not exceed 0.05 mm (0.002 in.).
2. Check the connecting rods for a bent or twisted condition. There are several ways to do this, but the following is recommended:

Install a piston, without the piston rings, on the connecting rod. Install the crankshaft in the case, if it has been removed.

Refit the cylinder(s).

NOTE: *Because of the one-piece cylinder block on the GT750, refit all the pistons and check all of the rods at the same time.*

Push the piston crown left and right with the piston at top dead center. The piston should return to the center of the cylinder bore when released from the right or left. If it does not, and stays off to one side of the cylinder bore, the rod is bent and must be replaced.

3. Check each rod for up-and-down movement. There should be none.
4. Rotate each rod slowly around its crankpin. Note the bearing action. Any roughness, binding, or clicking noise during rotation is indicative of a bad rod bearing.
5. Inspect the big end thrust washers for excessive wear, obvious damage, or discoloration.
6. Check each rod's side-play. This can be done in several ways. A suitable sized right-angle, as illustrated, can be placed on the crankshaft, and used to

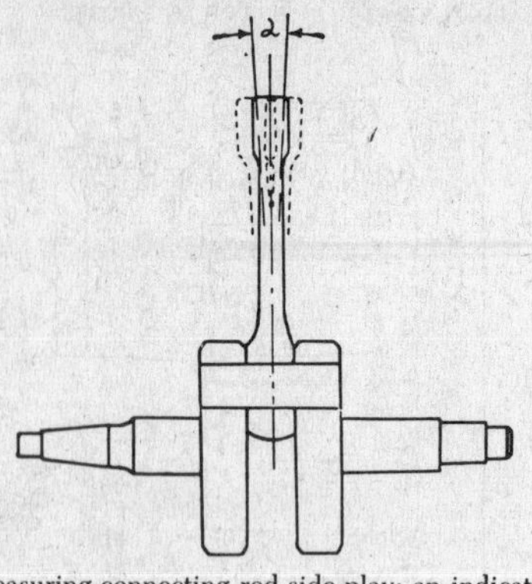

Measuring connecting rod side-play: an indication of big end bearing wear

measure play at the rod small end. Or a dial gauge can be attached to measure small end side-play.

Standard small end side-play is 0.5–0.8 mm (0.02–0.03 in.). If play equals or ex-

Checking a connecting rod for straightness

ceeds 3.0 mm (0.12 in.), replace the connecting rod bearing.

7. Connecting rod thrust clearance (big end side-to-side movement) has a standard value of 0.2–0.6 mm (0.008–0.023 in.). Big end thrust exceeding these values is indicative of worn rod bearings.
8. If a set of V-blocks is available, or if you can devise some means of turning the crankshaft on a steady plane, check the crankshaft for run-out. If the run-out is measured at a crank flywheel or bearing, divide the result by two, and this will give the amount of bend in the crankshaft.

If more than 0.08 mm (0.003 in.) of bend is indicated, the assembly will have to be straightened.

If the run-out is not excessive, it may be remedied by striking the flywheel with a soft metal mallet where the greatest amount of run-out is measured. Recheck the crank alignment, and repeat as necessary.

9. Check the rotation of the main bearings, noting any rough movement or noises during rotation. Inspect the oil seals, especially around the lips, for a condition which might cause leakage.

Note that if any bearing is damaged or worn, all of the crank bearings must be replaced. The same is true of the crank oil seals.

Transmission

GT380, GT550

1. The gear clusters can be lifted out of the lower crankcase. Before doing so, however, note the location of each gear. Note also that the transmission shaft bearings are located by "C" rings.

2. Before removing the shift fork spindles, mark each fork for location to facilitate assembly.

3. After the shift forks are removed, the shift drum can be taken out if the drum stopper, stopper pawls and gear indicator switch are removed.

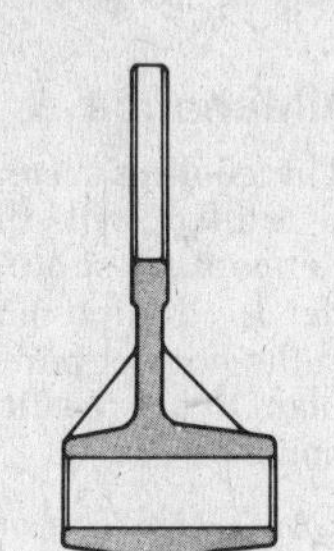

GT550 shift fork differences

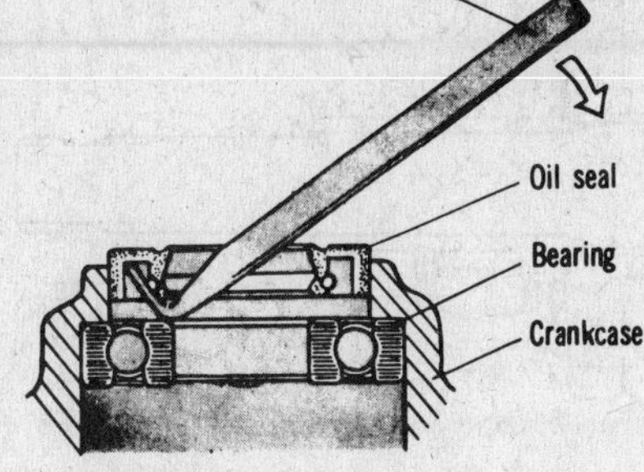

Removing an oil seal

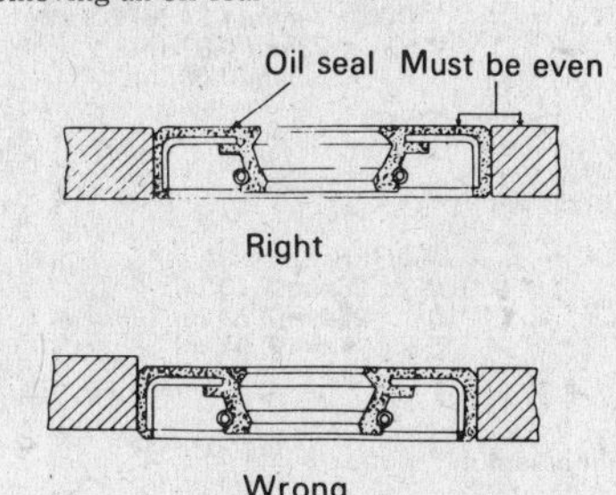

Correct and incorrect oil seal installation

4. Be certain that the transmission and kickstarter shafts are correctly located with the pins in the lower crankcase and that the "C" rings are installed and fitted properly into the bearings.

5. Make sure that the transmission shafts turn smoothly after installation.

6. When assembling the kickstarter shaft, insure that the punch mark on the shaft aligns with that on the ratchet wheel. Be sure that the return spring is correctly fitted with the spring end in place in the case. Make sure that the kickstarter shaft is assembled as shown in the illustration.

GT750

1. The countershaft Second gear must be removed from its shaft with an arbor press if in need of replacement. After this has been done twice, the entire assembly must be replaced.

Measuring gear backlash

2. Gears are color-coded to the crankcases. The color code and chart are shown below.

3. Check all gears for wear by checking the gear backlash. Lock one gear into position and move the other against it while measuring total rotational movement with a dial gauge. The average backlash for the first, second, third, and kickstart gears is 0–0.05 mm (0–0.002 in.), and for all other gears it is 0.05–0.1 mm (0.002–0.004 in.).

Crankcase Color Code

Crankcase Color	*1st, 2nd Driven Gears*	*Kickstart Drive Gear*
Brown Black Red Yellow	Yellow	Brown
Blue Green White	White	Yellow

4. Average clearance between the shift forks and spindles is 0.05–0.1 mm (0.002–0.004 in.).

5. Thickness of the shift fork fingers is (standard) 4.95–5.05 mm (0.195–0.198 in.). Replace any fork whose fingers measure less than 4.90 mm (0.19 in.).

6. Inspect the shift drum for damage. Note any irregular wear of the grooves. Standard diameter of the shift drum is 44.90–44.98 mm (1.76–1.77 in.).

7. If gears are being replaced, when you purchase gear replacements for the first and/or second gear, you will get two gears in a package. One is marked with a dab of white paint, the other with yellow paint. The crankcase is color-coded, so

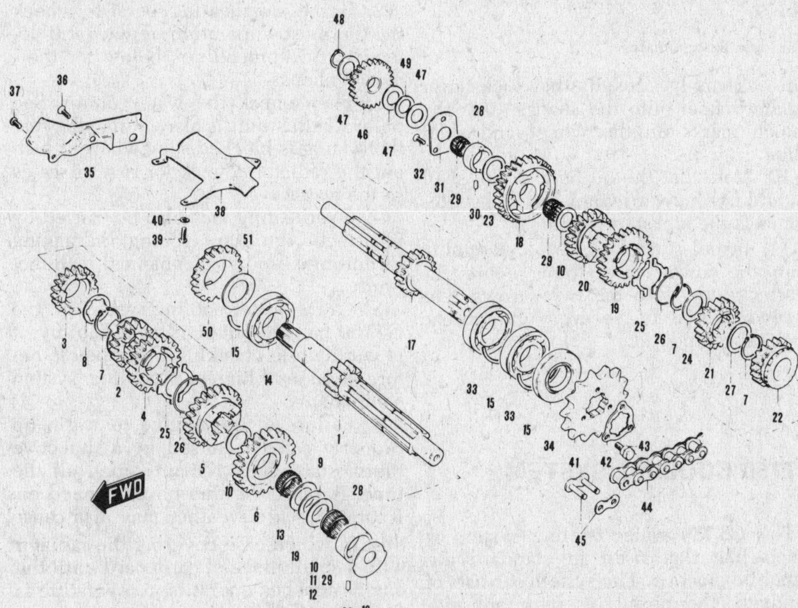

GT380 gear clusters

1. Countershaft (12T)
2. 2nd drive gear (16T)
3. 3rd drive gear (19T)
4. 4th drive gear (21T)
5. 5th drive gear (23T)
6. 6th drive gear (24T)
7. 3rd drive gear circlip
8. 3rd drive gear lockwasher
9. 6th drive gear thrust washer
10. 6th drive gear thrust washer
11. 6th drive gear thrust washer
12. 6th drive gear thrust washer
13. 6th drive gear bearing
14. Countershaft bearing
15. Countershaft C-ring
16. Countershaft retainer
17. Mainshaft (28T)
18. 1st driven gear (24T)
19. 2nd driven gear (27T)
20. 3rd driven gear (22T)
21. 4th driven gear (19T)
22. 5th driven gear (18T)
23. 1st driven gear thrust washer
24. 4th driven gear washer (right-hand)
25. 2nd driven gear ring
26. 2nd driven gear circlip
27. 4th driven gear thrust washer
28. Transmission shaft bushing
29. Transmission shaft bearing
30. Transmission shaft bushing pin
31. Driveshaft retainer
32. Retainer screw
33. Bearing
34. Driveshaft oil seal
35. Oil reservoir cup
36. Screw
37. Screw
38. Oil guide plate
39. Oil guide plate screw
40. Lockwasher
41-1. Engine sprocket (14T Std)
41-2. Engine sprocket (16T Opt)
42. Engine sprocket plate
43. Plate bolt
44. Drive chain assembly
45. Chain joint
46. Kickstarter idle gear
47. Kickstarter idle gear thrust washer
48. Idle gear circlip
49. Idle gear washer
50. Kickstarter driven gear
51. Kickstarter driven washer

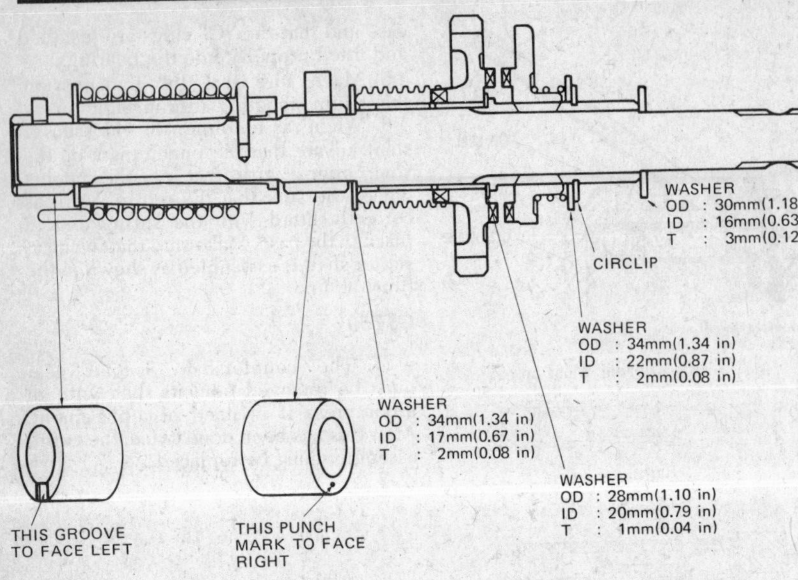

GT550 kickstarter shaft assembly

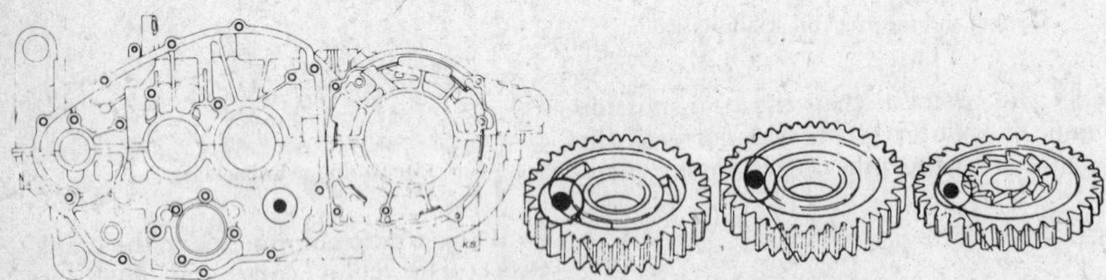

GT750 gear and crankcase color identification marks

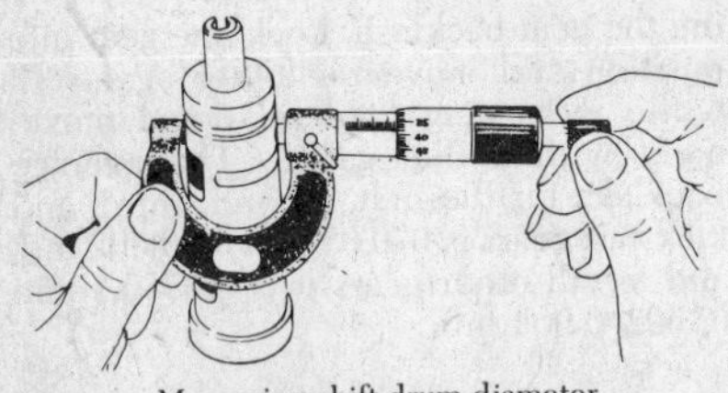

Measuring shift drum diameter

check the chart for the appropriate gear to use.

If, for example, the cases are coded brown, the yellow gear will be used. If they are coded green, the white marked gear must be installed.

8. When replacing the kickstarter gear, the same procedure applies, except that the gears are coded yellow and brown.

9. Oil all components thoroughly before assembly. Insert the kickstarter ratchet wheel onto the shaft so that the punch marks on the wheel and shaft align.

10. Note that the oil hole in the shaft should face upward when the kickstarter contacts the kickstarter guide.

11. Install the kickstarter assembly into the lower case, then secure the starter guide with the two screws. The screws should be secured with thread locking compound.

Kickstarter shaft and lever marks aligned properly

GT750 COOLING SYSTEM

The GT750 water cooling system is much like that used in standard automobile practice. The system consists of a radiator, thermostat, reservoir tank, cylinder block and head water jacket, fan, and water pump.

The water pump is located in the lower crankcase. A centrifugal-type unit, it is driven off the crankshaft through the starter clutch gear.

The pump takes water from the radiator and circulates it through the cylinder block and head water jacket, the thermostat, the radiator, and then back to the pump.

When the engine is cold, the thermostat routes the water directly back to the pump via the by-pass hose, rather than having it pass through the radiator.

A thermostat-activated switch controls the electric fan.

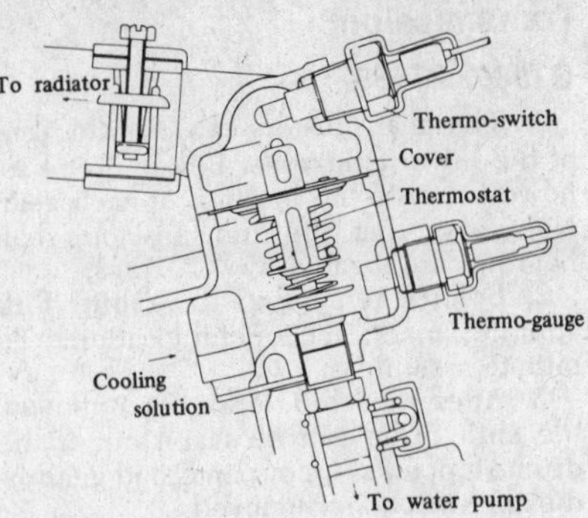

Thermostat and temperature control components

Maintenance

The cooling system should be drained and refilled with the proper amount of water/coolant solution every two years. Refer to "Maintenance", for procedures and the correct percentages of water and coolant to use to suit various climatic conditions.

CAUTION: *Use only distilled water in the cooling system.*

Troubleshooting

1. In case of engine overheating, first check the coolant level, and top up as necessary. Check the system for leaks as well.

2. If the overheating persists, check the thermostat operation; replace it if defective. See procedures below for thermostat checks.

3. Then check the water pump. See below. If this unit is okay, it may be that the system is blocked somewhere. Flush out the radiator. Check for rust or scales in the water.

4. Overheating may also be caused by incorrect ignition timing, dragging (drum) brakes, or a mechanical malfunction.

Since the water cooling system on the GT750 has a reputation for reliability, it is worthwhile checking these points before disassembling any cooling system components.

5. Failure of the engine to warm up properly can be caused by a defective thermostat which remains open all the time. Replace the thermostat if need be. Extremely cold weather may also cause this, in which case covering the radiator with a small piece of cardboard until the engine reaches operating temperature is recommended.

6. Excessive noise in the engine not caused by the crankshaft, clutch or gears may be due to either a defective water pump bearing or a loose or bent impeller. Replace the pump or impeller as needed.

Radiator

REMOVAL

1. Drain out the coolant solution.

2. Remove the gas tank, the radiator inlet and outlet hoses, the coolant inlet line, the reservoir tank and its hose, and the cooling fan and shroud.

3. Remove the radiator crash bars and the radiator assembly.

NOTE: *When the radiator assembly is removed, keep each set of shims and washers separate and mark their locations. The radiator must be correctly installed.*

INSPECTION

1. Inspect the radiator for damage, signs of leakage, mud-encrusted or dirty cooling fins. Check that the fins are not bent or otherwise damaged. Slight leakage can be remedied with a radiator additive designed for that purpose.

2. Internal damage to the radiator, such as that which might have been caused by the freezing of the coolant solution, cannot be repaired, and the unit must be replaced.

3. If more than 20% of the total radiator cooling surface area is incapacitated by fin damage or irremovable deposits, replace the radiator.

4. Inspect the radiator cap for condition. The cap is designed to maintain a system pressure of about 27 psi (1.9 kg/cm²).

The radiator cap is fitted with a safety valve, "A" (see the accompanying illustration).

It is installed for releasing steam from the system.

It is pressed down prior to removing the radiator cap on a hot engine and will open "B" allowing any builtup steam to

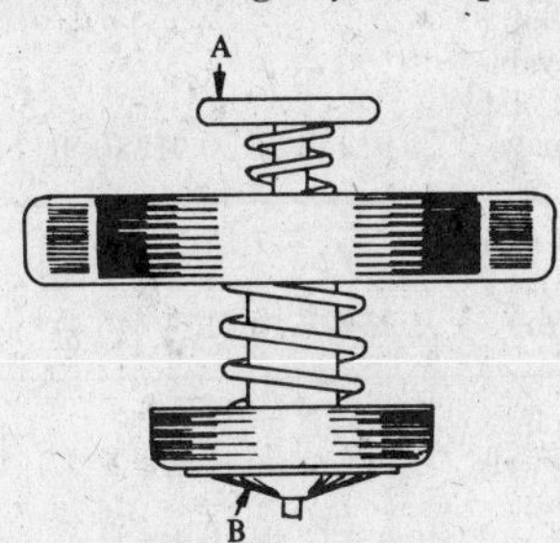

Radiator cap with safety valve ("A" and "B")

escape safely so that the cap can be removed.

5. The radiator cap may be checked by placing a weight of 15.4 lbs (7 kg) on it as shown to observe whether or not the cap opens.

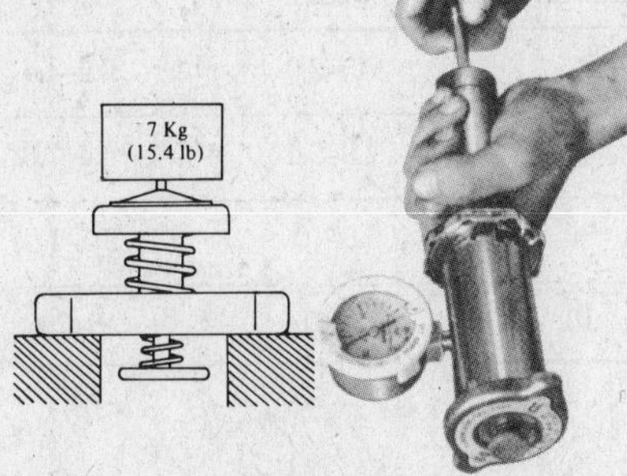

Two radiator cap tests

6. If a pressure gauge is available, the cap should begin to open at about 27 psi (1.9 kg/cm²).

Replace the cap if it fails the pressure test.

7. Check the condition of all hoses and replace any which show even minor cracking or rotting.

INSTALLATION

1. To install the radiator, reverse the removal procedure. Note the following points.

2. There are 3 different sizes of washers used to mount the radiator and these are color-coded. The radiator must be mounted correctly to prevent vibration and stress damage.

The following information concerns the proper placement of washers:

a. Washer "A" is 2.0 mm (0.079 in.) thick.

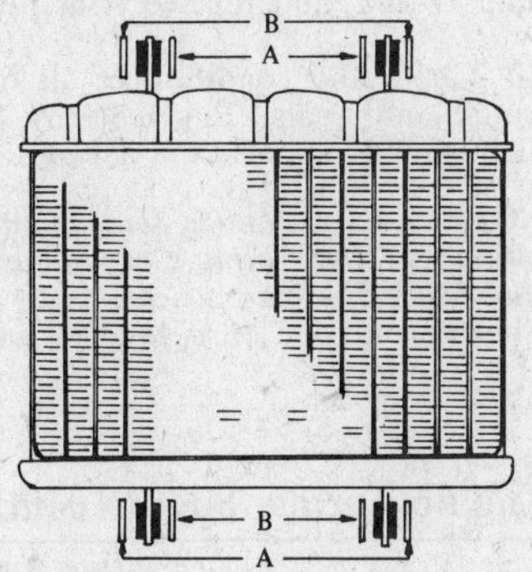

Radiator mounting shims (refer to the text procedures)

Washer "B" is 1.6 mm (0.063 in.) thick.
Washer "C" is 0.8 mm (0.031 in.) thick.

b. When the radiator is marked with white circles on the mounting plates, install the washers as illustrated.

c. When the radiator is not marked, mount it only with "B" washers.

d. In instances where there is a white circle at the top only, fit "A" and "B" washers to the top mount as illustrated, and fit only "B" washers to the bottom.

e. In instances where only the bottom mount is marked, fit "B" washers only to the top mount, and "A" and "B" washers, as illustrated, to the bottom.

f. If, after installing the washers in their prescribed positions, there is still a gap, use "C" washers as shims until a flush mounting is obtained.

Thermostat

The thermostat is used to direct the flow of the coolant solution. When the coolant reaches 180°F, the thermostat opens and circulates the water through the radiator.

The thermostat is the wax-pellet type and the valve is designed to open and close with the expansion and contraction of the pellet.

1. Make sure that the pellet is not cracked or damaged in any way.

2. To check operation, immerse the thermostat in water and heat the water noting the operation of the thermostat as the temperature climbs.

3. At 180°F, the valve should begin to open; at 203°F, it should be completely open. The operating stroke of the thermostat in this position should be 8.0 mm (0.3 in.).

If the thermostat operation does not coincide with this standard operation, replace the thermostat.

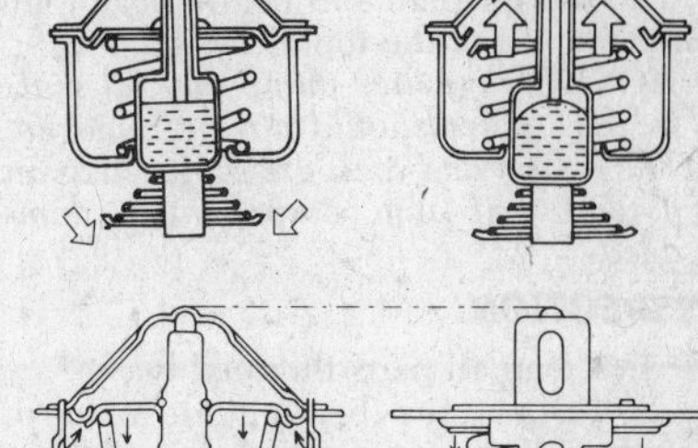

Thermostat operation

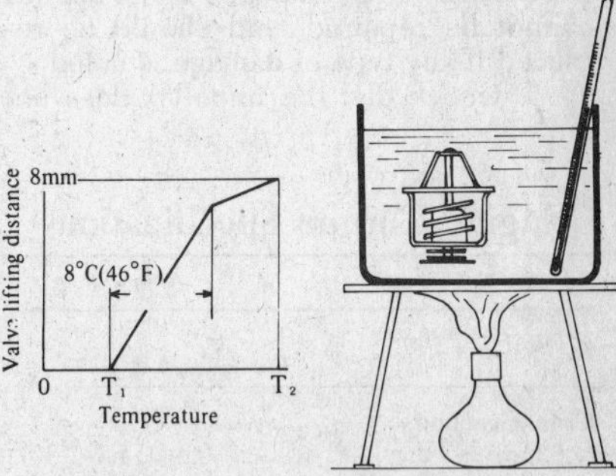

Thermostat operation as a function of water temperature

Water Pump

REMOVAL

1. Drain the coolant.
2. Remove the center muffler.
3. Carefully remove the water pump cover, taking care not to damage the mating surface.
4. Remove the impeller circlip with a pair of snap-ring pliers, then remove the impeller.

Removing the impeller circlip

5. Remove the water pump holder circlip with the snap-ring pliers.

6. Then pull out the pump holder with a pair of pliers.

CAUTION: *Protect the mechanism by covering the pump driven shaft with a rag or piece of rubber while withdrawing the holder. Do not allow the pliers to contact the driven shaft directly.*

DISASSEMBLY

The water pump driven shaft and bearing can be removed from the holder by heating the holder assembly to 165–185° F.

The driven shaft and bearing can then be taken out of the top of the holder.

NOTE: *The water pump and oil seals in the holder should not be removed. The holder and seals are replaced as an assembly if any component is damaged.*

INSPECTION

1. Clean all parts thoroughly.
2. Inspect the bearing for wear or damage. If bearing action is rough or noisy, replace the bearing.
3. Inspect the pump driven shaft for wear or damage. If the shaft is rusted or has corrosion built up on it, remove such deposits with emery cloth.
4. Inspect the impeller blades for deflection or other damage. The impeller cannot be repaired, and should be replaced if any type of damage is noted.
5. Check that the impeller does not contact the crankcase or pump case. If it does, check the shaft and bearing.
6. Nominal clearance between the impeller and the crankcase is 0.5–1.5 mm (0.02–0.59 in.).
7. Check the water pump drive gears and bearings for any wear or damage.
8. Inspect the pump sealing seat and corresponding area of the pump holder for wear or scoring. Replace both the sealing seat and the holder if any unusual marks are noted.
9. Check the condition of the pump holder O-ring, and replace it as necessary.
10. Check the condition of all other O-rings and seals. Replace any part which is even suspected of damage.

NOTE: *The coolant is sealed with a pump seal, the sealing seat, and an O-ring inside the sealing seat.*

The transmission oil is held by an oil seal.

There are, in addition, two more O-rings outside of the pump holder.

ASSEMBLY

1. Assembly is the reverse of the disassembly and removal procedure.
2. Lubricate the holder with fresh oil during installation. Align the holder port with the crankcase port. The notch on the holder top will align with the crankcase bolt.
3. Insert the impeller onto the pump driven shaft and secure it with the circlip. Check the gap between the impeller and crankcase with a feeler gauge. It should be 1.5 mm (0.59 in.). If the gap is not correct, remove the pump driven shaft from the holder, and realign it in the holder.
4. Apply a liquid gasket material to both sides of the water pump case gasket before mounting the pump case.
5. Refill the system with the correct amount and mixture of water/coolant solution.

Engine Torque Specifications

Part	Torque (ft lbs)
GT380, GT550	
Crankcase bolts	
6 mm	9.4①, 4.4–7.3②
8 mm	14.5①, 9.5–17②
Cylinder head nuts	18–29
Cylinder base nuts	18–29
Crankshaft primary gear nut	36
Rotor bolt	6.6–10
Oil pump	1.5–2.9
Oil pump cover	1.5–2.9
Clutch spring nuts	2.9–5.1
Clutch hub nut	36–43
Starter motor	2.9–5.1
Starter motor cover	1.5–2.9
Oil line banjo bolts	1.8
Breaker cam nut	36
Engine mounting nuts and bolts	23–29

Engine Torque Specs (cont.)

Part	Torque (ft lbs)
Engine mounting plate bolts	10–17
GT 750	
Crankcase bolts	
6 mm	4.3–7.2
8 mm	9.2–16.7
10 mm	18.1–28.9
Cylinder head	
8 mm	13.0–15.9
10 mm	21.7–29.0
Clutch hub nut	29–40
Starter clutch bolt	33–40
Engine mounting nuts and bolts	23–29
Engine mounting plate bolts	10–17

① Model GT380
② Model GT550

Clutch Specifications

	GT380, GT550 in. (mm)	GT750 in. (mm)
Friction disc standard thickness	0.138 (3.5)	0.11–0.12 (2.9–3.1)

Clutch Specifications (cont.)

	GT380, GT550 in. (mm)	GT750 in. (mm)
Friction disc wear limit	0.126 (3.2)	0.107 (2.7)
Maximum allowable steel plate warpage	0.012 (0.3)	0.012 (0.3)
Clutch spring standard length	1.15 (38.4)	1.59 (40.4)
Maximum allowable spring collapse	0.055 (1.4)	0.055 (1.4)

General Nuts and Bolts

Bolt Diameter	Torque (ft lbs) Unmarked Bolt	Torque (ft lbs) "S" Marked Bolt
5	1.5–2.9	2.2–4.4
6	2.9–5.1	4.4–7.3
8	6.6–10	9.5–17
10	13–20	18–29

LUBRICATION SYSTEM

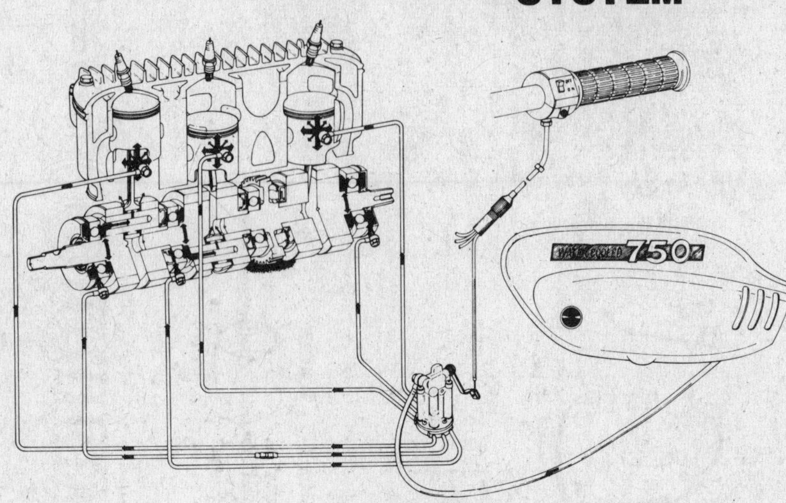

GT750 CCI system

OIL PUMP

NOTE: *Due to the exacting tolerance to which it is made, the oil pump should never be disassembled. If trouble is traced to the pump, the unit must be replaced rather than repaired.*

Troubleshooting

Before beginning any repair of the lubrication system, refer to the following, as it may help.

In the event of piston seizure not caused by any engine component failure, check the oil pump cable adjustment; then check for air in the oil lines (see "Bleeding," below), clogged lines, defective SRIS check valves (see "SRIS", below), low quality oil, or a blocked oil tank filler cap breather hole.

In case of excessive smoking at the exhaust pipe, check the oil pump cable adjustment; check for clogged or pinched SRIS lines, faulty SRIS check valves, or low quality oil (see "SRIS", below).

In case of excessive oil consumption, check the oil pump cable adjustment, and then check for oil leakage at the pump or lines.

If abnormal oil consumption is noted, and assuming that the cable is properly adjusted, the oil pump should be replaced, and a known workable oil pump substituted. If this does not cure the problem, the check valves may be defective.

Adjustment

This procedure is covered in "Maintenance".

Bleeding

The oil pump is fitted with a bleed screw. Refer to the illustration.

1. In the event of air bubbles in the line from the oil tank to the pump loosen the bleed screw, and observe the oil flow. When the oil seems to be free of air bubbles, retighten the screw.

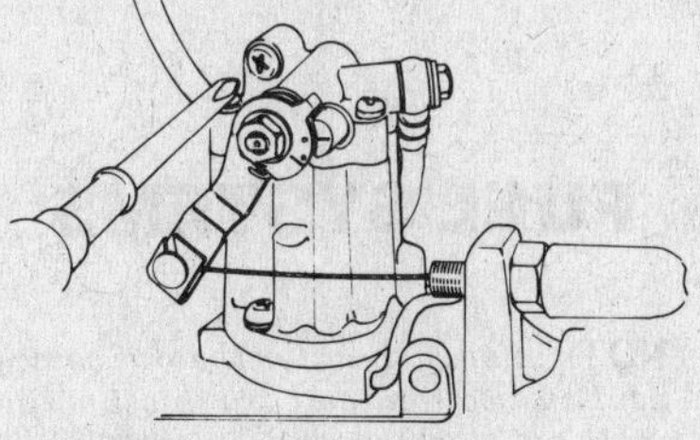

Oil pump air bleed screw

2. Check the lines from the oil pump to the engine for air bubbles. If present, they may be removed in either of the following ways, depending on the amount of air present in the lines:

a. If only a small amount of air bubbles are present, start the engine, and, with your hand, hold the oil pump lever full on until you feel all of the air is expelled from the lines.

b. If a larger quantity is present, remove the oil pump (see "Removal", below), and force clean CCI oil into each of the oil feed lines as shown. After this is done, refit the pump, and carry out procedure "a" above.

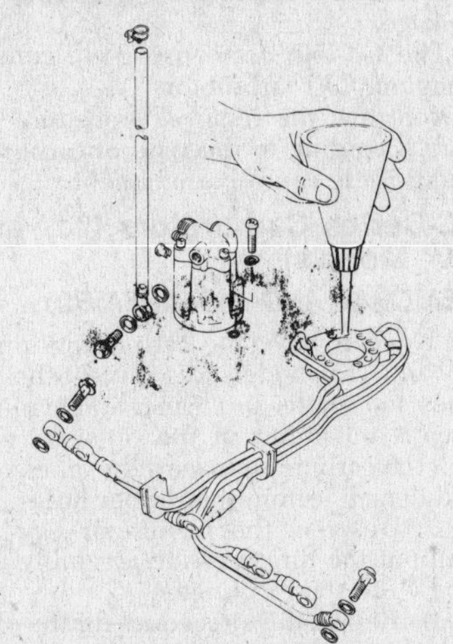

Priming the CCI lines

Pump Removal and Installation

1. Remove the oil pump cover.
2. Disconnect the pump cable from the pump lever. Disconnect and plug the feed line from the oil tank.
3. Remove the securing screws, and remove the oil pump.
4. If the pump-to-engine feed lines are removed, blow them clear; check the external condition of the lines and gaskets. Replace any worn components.
5. Before installing the lines, force Suzuki CCI oil into the crankcase oil passages.
6. Be sure that the lines are properly connected. Tighten the banjo bolts to 1.8 ft lbs.
7. After the lines are installed, fill them with CCI oil. Then install the pump, and connect the oil tank feed line. Bleeding the system, as described above, is recommended.

SRIS

NOTE: *The arrangement of the SRIS pipes is important, so note their location before removing them.*

REMOVAL

1. Remove the oil line guide plate from the lower crankcase, where fitted.
2. Disconnect the SRIS lines at the crankcase lower side by removing the securing clips with a screwdriver.
3. The SRIS check valves will be either press-fit into position (as on early models), or threaded in.

INSPECTION

1. Check the lines for cracks, leaks, or other damage.
2. Check the operation of the check valves with a syringe as shown. The valves should be able to form an effective seal against oil traveling in this direction.
3. The newer type valves are fitted with a nylon mesh filter, and this should be cleaned if the lines are disconnected.

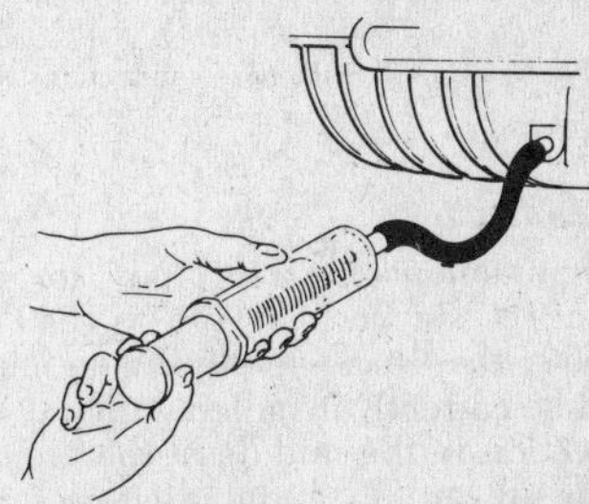

Checking SRIS check valve operation

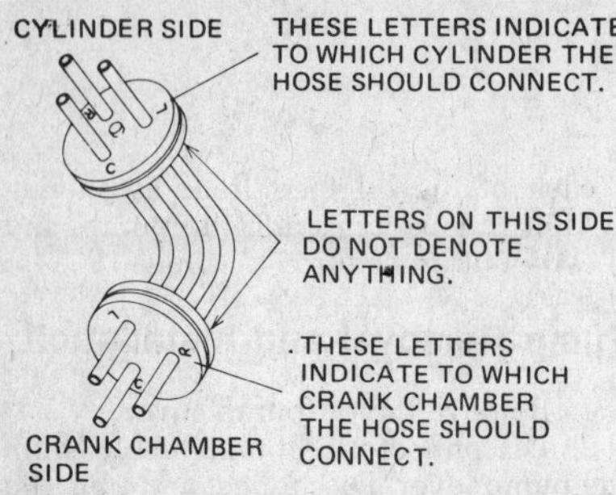

GT380 and GT550 SRIS hose grommets and hose positions

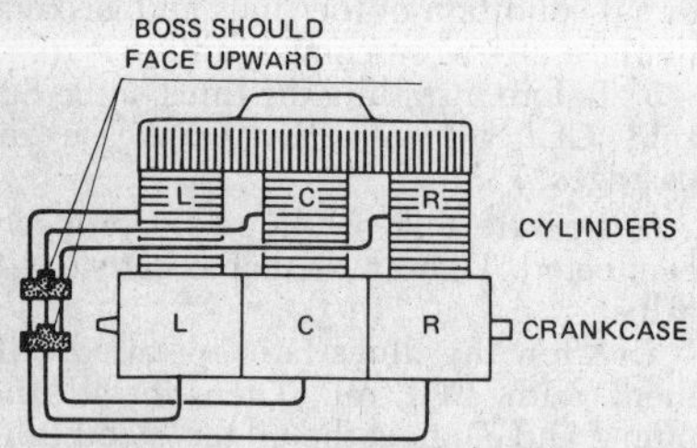

SRIS lines (GT380, GT550)

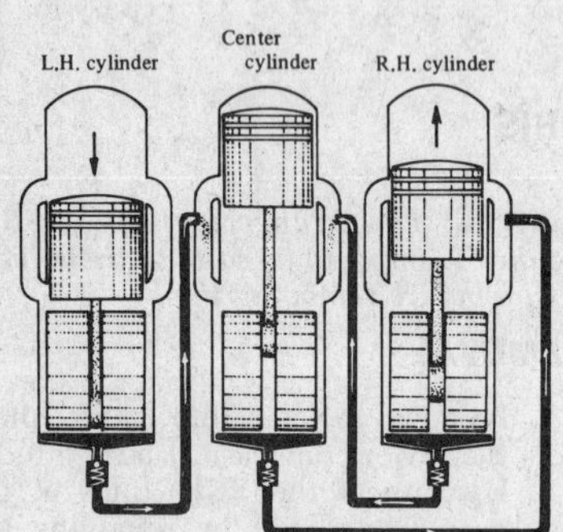

GT750 early SRIS setup

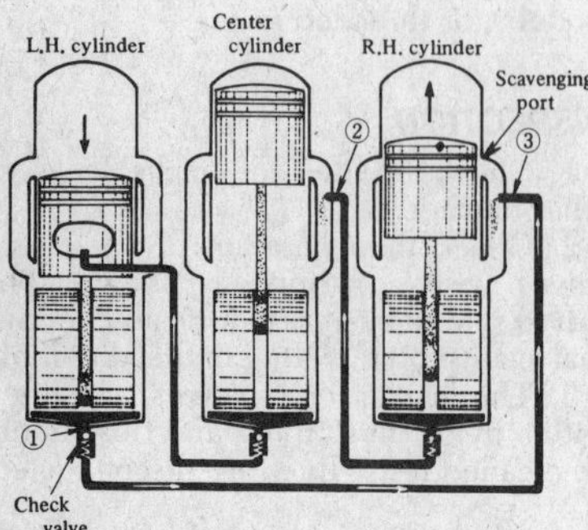

Later GT750 SRIS hose connections

ASSEMBLY

Arrangement of the pipes for each model is shown. On the GT380 and GT550, the lines' mounting grommets must be correctly installed with the small projection in the middle of the grommet facing upward. Be certain that each SRIS line is connected to its proper cylinder.

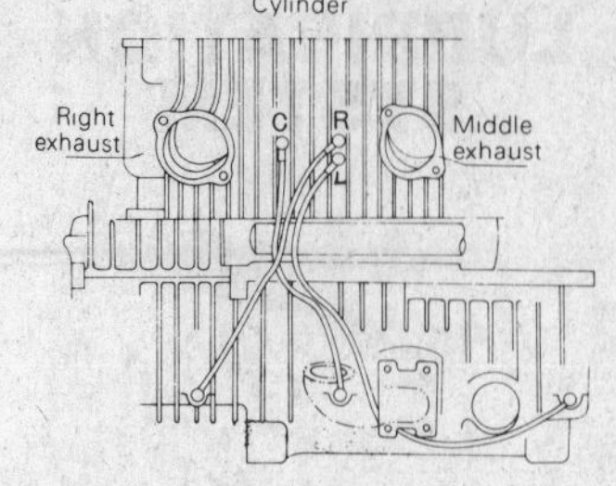

SRIS line connections

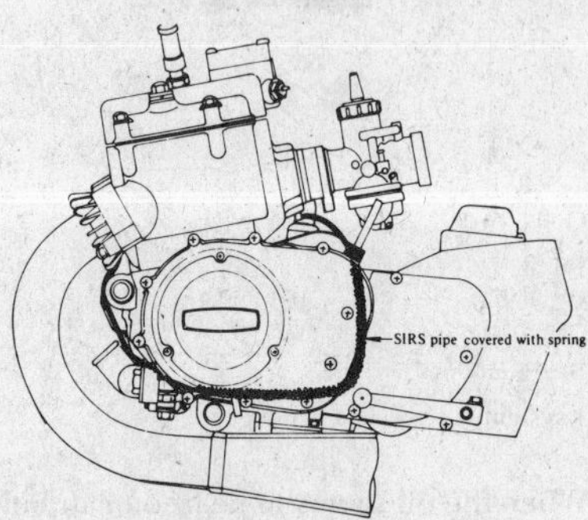

Later type SRIS lines (GT750)

FUEL SYSTEMS

NOTE: *For carburetor theory, component inspection, and troubleshooting, refer to "Carburetors" in the General Information section.*

CARBURETORS

The GT380, GT550, and GT750 all use different types of Mikuni carburetors.

All "J" and "K" models (1972–73) use cable-operated "SC" series carbs. The GT380 and GT550 "L-A" (1974–76) also use these carburetors, but throttle slide movement is controlled by a pulley and linkage.

The GT750 "L-A" use BS40 constant vacuum (CV) carburetors.

Note that the removal procedure will vary according to the type of carburetor and throttle control arrangment.

SC-Series Carburetors ("J" and "K" Models)

REMOVAL AND DISASSEMBLY

1. To remove the carburetors on all "J" and "K" models, disconnect the fuel lines, loosen the air cleaner and manifold clamps on either of the outside carbs, pull the carburetor toward the air cleaner and detach it from the rubber hoses.
2. Unscrew the carburetor cap and pull out the throttle slide assembly. Unscrew the starter plunger.
3. Repeat this procedure for the other two carburetors.

CAUTION: *The carburetors are aligned on the manifold hoses by a slot and rib arrangement; therefore, never attempt to twist the carburetor while it is still attached to the manifold hose.*

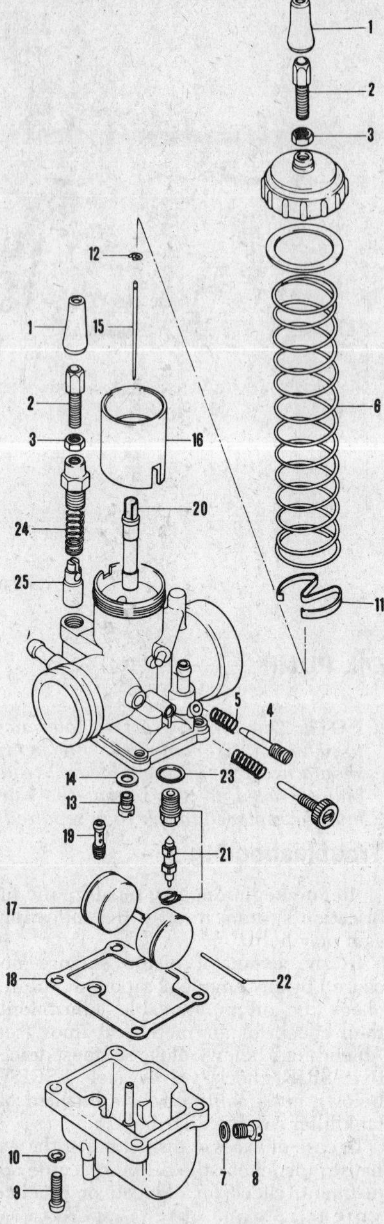

Mikuni SC-series carburetor

1. Dust cover
2. Cable adjuster
3. Locknut
4. Pilot air screw
5. Spring
6. Throttle slide return spring
7. Washer
8. Drain plug
9. Float bowl screw
10. Lockwasher
11. Needle retainer
12. Needle clip
13. Main jet
14. Washer
15. Needle
16. Throttle slide
17. Float assembly
18. Float bowl gasket
19. Pilot jet
20. Needle jet
21. Float needle and seat
22. Float pin
23. Washer
24. Spring
25. Starter plunger

4. Detach the throttle cable from the throttle slide, and free the slide and needle.

5. Remove the clip which holds the needle in the slide, and remove the needle from the top of the slide.

NOTE: *The small circlip on the needle determines midrange mixture; note which groove the clip is positioned in if it is to be removed for any reason.*

6. Turn the carburetor body upside down. Remove the float bowl screws.

7. Carefully remove the float bowl and gasket. Push out the float pin, and remove the float.

8. Remove the float needle; unscrew and remove the float needle seat.

9. Unscrew the pilot jet. Unscrew and remove the main jet from the carburetor body.

10. Unscrew and remove the pilot air screw and the throttle stop screw from the carburetor body.

11. Remove the needle jet, if desired, by very gently drifting it out through the throttle slide passage in the body, tapping from the main jet side.

ASSEMBLY AND INSTALLATION

1. To assemble, reverse the disassembly procedure. Use all new gaskets, O-rings and washers.

NOTE: *If the needle jet was removed, install it so that the cut-out at the top of the jet faces the ENGINE side of the carburetor.*

2. Set the float level as described in "Tune-Up".

3. After installation, set the cable slides, and tune the carburetors as described in "Tune-Up".

SC-Series Carburetors ("L-A" Models)

REMOVAL AND DISASSEMBLY

1. Disconnect the fuel line and vacuum hose. Remove the gas tank. Remove the air cleaner assembly.

2. Run the throttle cable adjusters down and disconnect the throttle cables from the pulley.

3. Loosen the carburetor manifold clamp screws and take out the carburetors.

4. Remove the choke lever screw. Exercise caution when removing the screw as the lever is spring-loaded.

5. Loosen the starter rod screws and pull out the starter rod.

6. Remove the two carburetor cap screws from each carburetor, and pull out the throttle slide assemblies.

7. Disassembly of the throttle slide assemblies is neither necessary nor recommended for routine cleaning, since the slides must be synchronized during assembly. If replacement of any parts is necessary, the slide components must of course be disassembled. This is done by lifting up the rubber boot on one of the slide assemblies. Remove the upper and lower throttle slide adjustment nuts, disengaging the throttle rod from the throttle slide arm. Separate the components.

8. If the removal of the needle is required, remove the needle set plate screws and take out the needle.

9. Repeat the procedure with the remaining throttle slides, if necessary. Do not mix slides and needles. Keep them separate for installation in their own carburetors.

10. To disassemble the linkage, remove the throttle slide arm pinch screws and pull off the arms, removing their woodruff keys from the shaft. Remove the shaft stopper screw and separate the components.

Linkage components, L-A Models: (1) Throttle slide arm; (2) Throttle slide shaft; (3) shaft stopper; (4) pulley

11. To disassemble the carburetors themselves, remove the float bowl screws, and take off the float bowl and gasket.

Main jet (1) and pilot jet (2)

12. Push out the float pin and remove the float assembly and float needle.

13. Unscrew and remove the main jet, pilot jet, and float needle seat and their washers, if fitted.

14. The needle jet may be removed after the washer is removed with a wooden drift by tapping it gently out of the carburetor from the main jet side (driving it into the bore).

15. Unscrew and remove the starter plunger assembly, and pilot air and throttle stop screws.

ASSEMBLY AND INSTALLATION

1. Use new o-rings, gaskets, and washers. Assembly of the carburetor body is the reverse of disassembly. Note that the needle jet is positioned by means of a pin at the lower portion of the needle jet holder. Carefully insert the needle jet so that the slot in the jet aligns with this

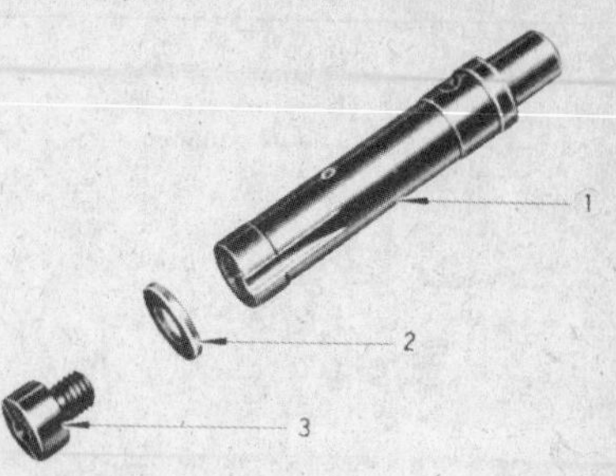

Needle jet with locating slot (1); washer (2) and main jet (3)

pin, and press home. Do not force the jet until alignment is ensured.

2. If the pulley and linkage was disassembled, be sure the carburetor cap screws are in place in the cap casting before refitting the linkage. Install the linkage in the reverse of disassembly. Note that the pulley and throttle slide arms are located by keys.

Throttle slide shaft installation: woodruff key (1) to locate arms. Install the stopper (3) so the lug (2) enters its hole in the holder column

When installing the slide shaft stopper, align the lug of the stopper with the hole in the shaft holder column.

3. Lubricate the shaft grease fitting with chassis grease until some shows at the shaft.

4. Position the pulley so that the thick side bears against the throttle slide stop screw, and secure the pulley pinch screw.

5. Lubricate the bearing surfaces of the throttle slide arms and insert the arm shafts.

6. When installing the slides, be sure the cut-away faces the front of the carburetor. If the slide has a punch mark, it must be installed on the side of the carburetor with an inspection plug.

7. Thread the upper throttle slide adjustment nut on so that a few threads from the throttle rod protrudes.

Throttle slide arm (1), adjusting nut (2), and throttle rod (3)

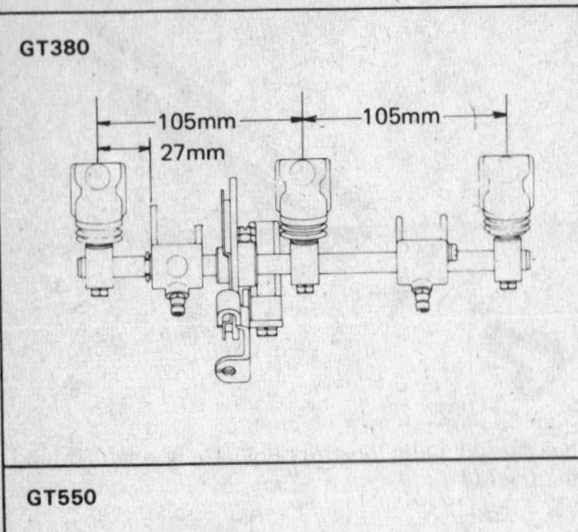

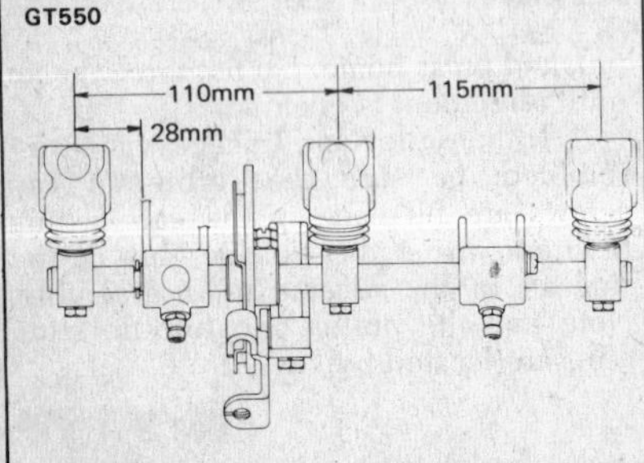

Throttle slide arm installation positions

8. Secure the throttle slide arms at the proper distances apart. Refer to the illustrations.

9. Synchronize the slides after completing assembly.

THROTTLE SLIDE SYNCHRONIZATION

1. Turn the throttle slide stop screw in as far as possible, then back it out 1½ turns.

2. Use the throttle slide adjustment nut atop each carburetor so that there is a gap of 0.8–1.0 mm (0.031–0.039 in.) between the bottom edge of the slide and the carburetor bore. The measurement is made on the engine side of the carburetors.

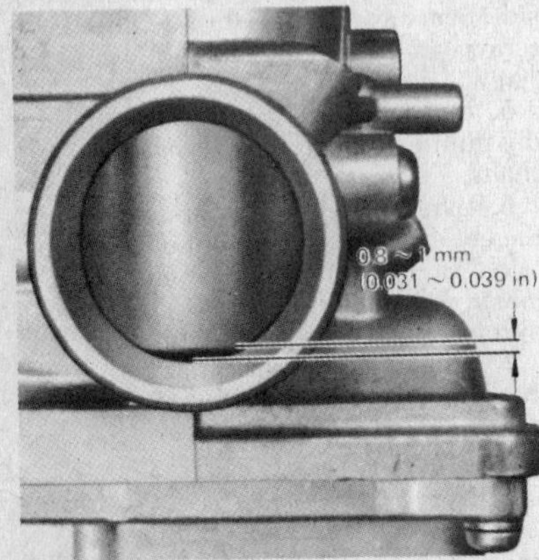

Slide synchronization, initial step using the slide adjustment nut

3. Turn the pulley to the full-open position and check that the distance between the top of the carburetor bore and the bottom edge of the throttle slide is 0.5–1.0 mm (0.02–0.039 in.). If it is not, adjust the full-open stop screw until the proper clearance is obtained.

4. Hold the pulley so that any of the

Slide synchronization, second step using the full-open stop screw

throttle slides is perfectly aligned with the top of the carburetor bore. As in the above instances, check at the engine side of the carburetor, aligning the bottom edge of the slide with the top of the bore.

5. All three slides must be in the same position for synchronization. After aligning the one slide as in Step 4, hold the pulley in place, and use the throttle slide adjustment nut to bring the other two slides into alignment. Tighten the nuts securely.

6. Adjust the pilot air screws, cables, and make final adjustments as outlined in "Tune-Up."

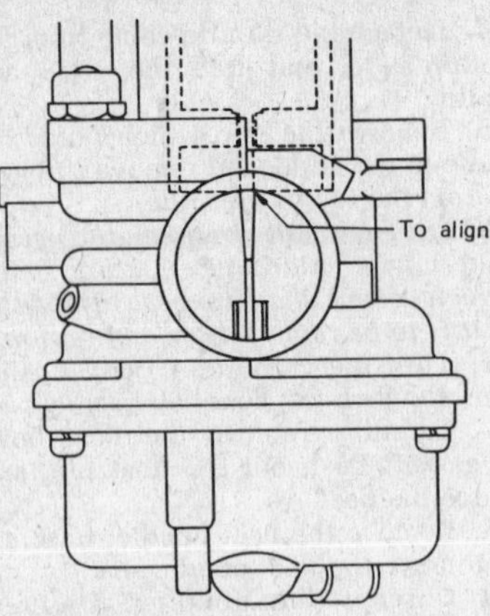

Slide synchronization, final step: all three slides must align as shown

CV-Carburetor

The GT750L-A models use three BS40 constant velocity carburetors.

REMOVAL

1. Disconnect the fuel and vacuum lines. Remove the gas tank and air cleaner.

2. Run the throttle cable adjusters down all the way and disengage the cables from the pulley.

3. Loosen the oil pump control rod adjusting nut and disconnect the rod from the lever.

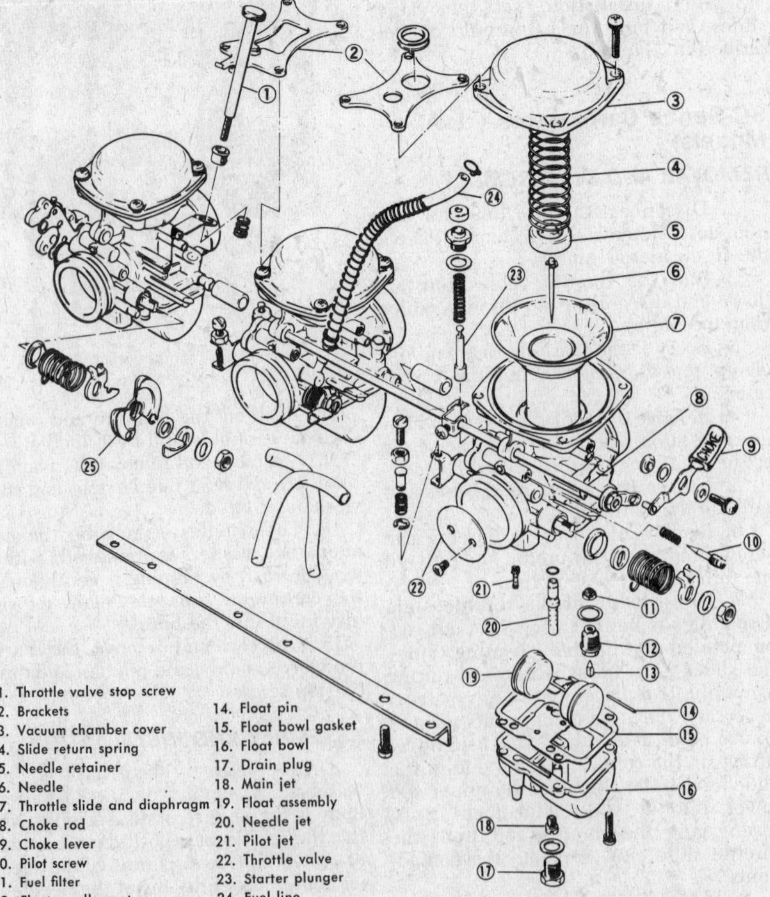

BS40 CV carburetor assembly

Oil pump adjusting nut (1) and control rod (2)

4. Loosen the carburetor manifold clamp screws. Remove the carburetors as a unit.

DISASSEMBLY

All major carburetor components are accessible for cleaning or service without separating the three units. Disassembly of the linkage is not recommended unless absolutely necessary (see Step 1).

1. Loosen the three choke rod screws and pull out the rod after disengaging it from the choke lever and turning it to clear the lever. Turn the throttle adjusting screws out so that there is clearance between the end of the screw and the throttle lever.

Choke rod (1), choke rod screw (2) and choke lever (3)

Throttle adjusting screw (1) and throttle lever (2)

Remove the bracket screws holding the carburetors together.

2. Remove the four vacuum chamber cover screws and remove the cover, return spring, and throttle slide.

NOTE: *Do not mix the throttle slides. Each must be reinstalled in its own carburetor.*

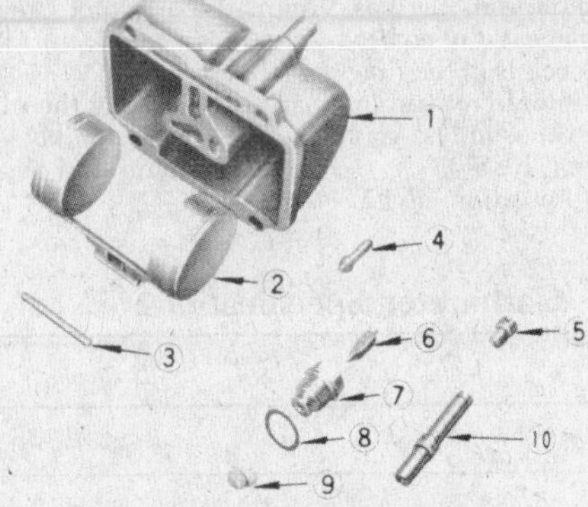

Float bowl components

1. Float bowl
2. Float assembly
3. Float pin
4. Pilot jet
5. Main jet
6. Float needle
7. Needle seat
8. Seat gasket
9. Fuel filter
10. Needle jet

3. Remove the drain plug from the float bowl.

4. Unscrew and remove the main jet.

5. Remove the float bowl screws and take off the bowl and gasket.

6. Push out the float pin and remove the float assembly.

7. Remove the float needle. Unscrew and remove the float needle seat. Remove the fuel filter.

8. Unscrew and remove the pilot jet from the float bowl.

9. Remove the needle jet from the carburetor.

ASSEMBLY AND INSTALLATION

1. Assembly is the reverse of disassembly. Note that the diaphragm is notched for proper installation.

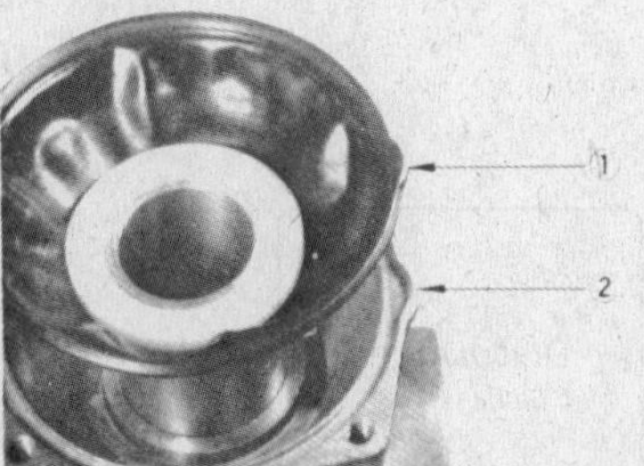

Install the diaphragm so the tab engages the carburetor notch (1 and 2)

Use a thread-locking agent on the choke rod screws (1)

2. Use a non-permanent thread-locking compound on the choke rod screws.

3. Synchronize the throttle valves by aligning the edge of the valves with the edge of the No. 1 by-pass outlet. Use the throttle adjusting screws to make this adjustment.

4. Adjust the pilot screws, the cables (after installation) and make final adjustments as outlined in "Tune-Up."

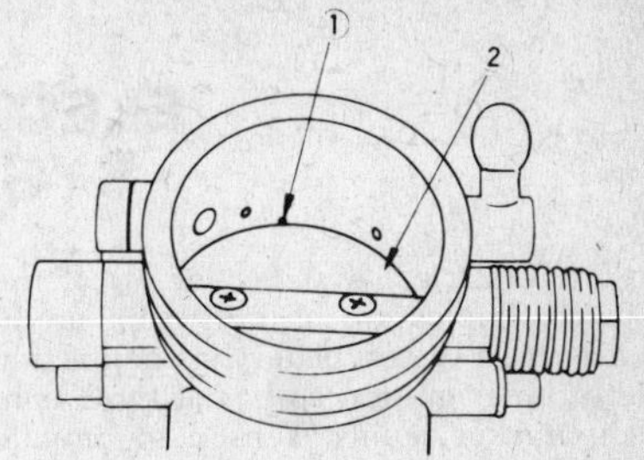

Synchronize the throttle valves by aligning each with the edge of the by-pass outlet (1) with the throttle adjusting screws

Throttle adjusting screws

Fuel Petcock

Occasionally check the fuel petcock. The sediment bowl should be removed and cleaned. The filter should be washed in gasoline and blown dry.

Before refitting the sediment bowl, check the condition of the gasket. Replace it if it is damaged or worn looking.

The petcock can be removed from the gas tank by removing the two securing nuts. In this event, closely check the condition of the O-ring which seals the gas tank at that joint and replace it if need be.

Note that the fuel petcock is of the diaphragm type. The lever should remain in the "ON" position at all times unless you are switching to reserve. ("RES").

Use the prime ("PRI") position ONLY if the carburetor float bowls have been drained for some reason. When the engine is started, turn back to "ON" immediately.

After removing the plate at the back of the fuel petcock, check the condition of the diaphragm and replace it as necessary.

Carburetor Specifications①

Model	Type	Main Jet	Needle Jet	Needle②	Throttle Slide	Pilot Jet
GT380J, K	VM24SC	80	O-4	4DH7-2	3.0	22.5
GT380L, M, A	VM24SC	80	O-2	4DH7-2	3.0	25
GT550J, K	VM28SC	R&L : 95 C : 92.5	O-5	5DH21-3	2.5	27.5
GT550L, M, A	VM28SC	R&L : 97.5 C : 95	P-0	5DH21-4	2.5	25
GT750J, K	VM32SC	R&L : 102.5 C : 100	R&L : P-4 C : P-3	5F16-3	2.5	30
GT750L	BS40	R&L : 110 C : 107.5	Z-0	4DN18-3	120	47.5
GT750M, A	BS40	R&L : 110 C : 107.5	Z-0	4DN18-4	110	45

① For float level and pilot screw settings, refer to "Tune-Up"
② The last number refers to needle clip position, counting from the top groove

ELECTRICAL SYSTEMS

The electrical systems for all of the Suzuki Triples are basically similar. In each case a 12-volt battery in conjunction with three ignition coils and three contact breaker points is used to provide spark.

The GT550 and GT750 are fitted with electric starters. The GT550 starter drives the engine through the clutch; while the GT750 starter drives the crankshaft through an intermediate gear.

CHARGING CIRCUIT

In the event of electrical troubles such as the battery overcharging, or failing to hold a charge, perform the following tests:

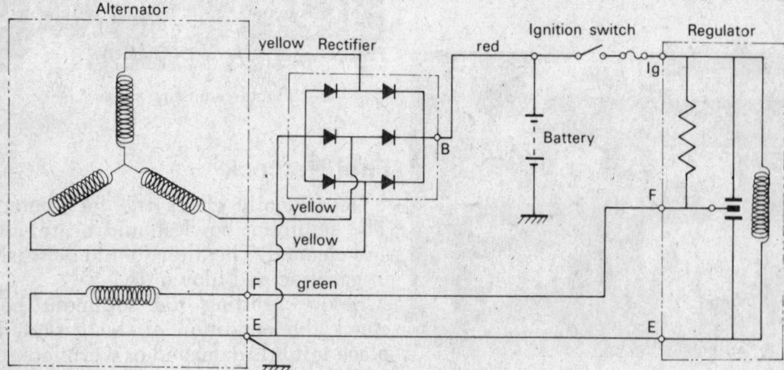

Charging circuit

a. If the battery is overcharging, the problem is probably the voltage regulator.

b. If the battery is going dead, the problem may be the regulator, rectifier, or alternator.

Perform the tests outlined below.

Component Tests (GT380, GT550)

CAUTION: *For all of the following "in circuit" tests, the battery must be fully charged, or erroneous results will be obtained.*

VOLTAGE REGULATOR

1. Start the engine and run it at 2500 rpm. Measure the voltage across the positive battery terminal and ground. A reading of 13.5–14.5 volts should be obtained. If the reading is too high, replace the regulator, or carry out further tests on it as described below. If the voltage reading is lower than the amount specified, test the regulator and then the other components.

2. With the engine OFF, disconnect the voltage regulator. With the ohmmeter, measure the resistance between the green and the orange leads. Resistance should be zero. If the meter reads resistance, replace the voltage regulator.

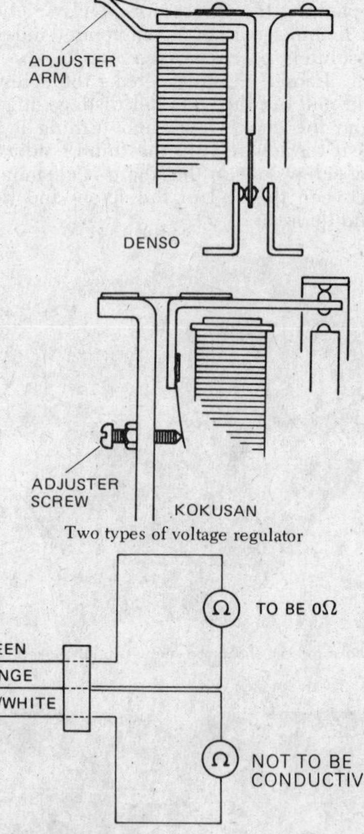

Two types of voltage regulator

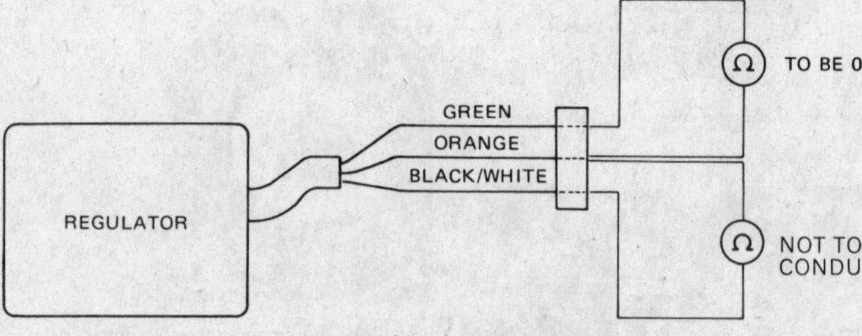

Voltage regulator resistance tests

3. Measure the resistance between the orange and the black/white leads. Resistance should be infinite. If resistance is less than this value, replace the alternator.

4. Remove the regulator cover. Press down on the regulator arm, so that the moving contact point is not in contact with either of the stationary points. Measure the resistance between the green and the orange leads. Resistance should read about 10 ohms. If the resistance is not near this value, adjustment is not possible, and the regulator must be replaced.

5. Refer to the accompanying illustra-

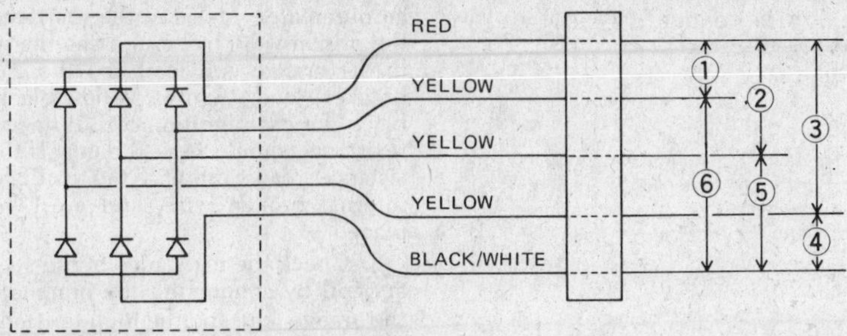

Rectifier test points

tions. Note that two types of regulators are used.

On the "Denso" regulator, bend the adjusting arm to attain the proper voltage. Bend the adjuster arm *up* to raise voltage output, and *down* to decrease output.

On the "Kokusan" regulator, turn the adjusting screw *in* to increase the voltage output, and *out* to decrease output.

RECTIFIER

If the regulator seems to be okay, check the operation of the rectifier. This is done with an ohmmeter. The rectifier must be disconnected.

Refer to the illustration which shows the wiring of the rectifier. Note that each of the six diodes will pass current in one direction only.

Connect the negative lead of the ohmmeter to the red rectifier wire. Then connect the positive meter lead to each of the yellow rectifier leads in turn. The meter must show less than a few ohms resistance in all three cases.

Now reverse the connections so that the positive meter lead is connected to the red rectifier lead, and the negative meter lead is connected to each of the yellow rectifier wires in turn. The meter must read a higher resistance in each case.

If the rectifier has been satisfactory to

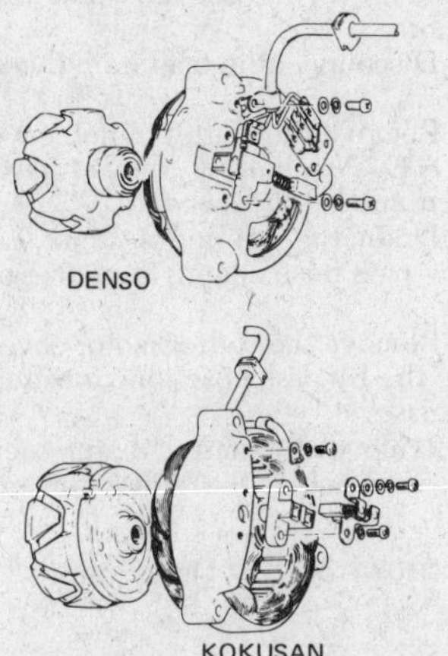

The two types of alternator in use

this point, connect the positive meter lead to the black/white rectifier lead and the negative meter lead to each of the yellow rectifier wires in turn. Resistance in each case must be close to zero.

Now reverse the meter leads and perform the tests again between the black/white lead and each of the yellow leads. Resistance should be much higher.

If the resistance in any of the above cases differs from the normal reading, the rectifier *must* be replaced.

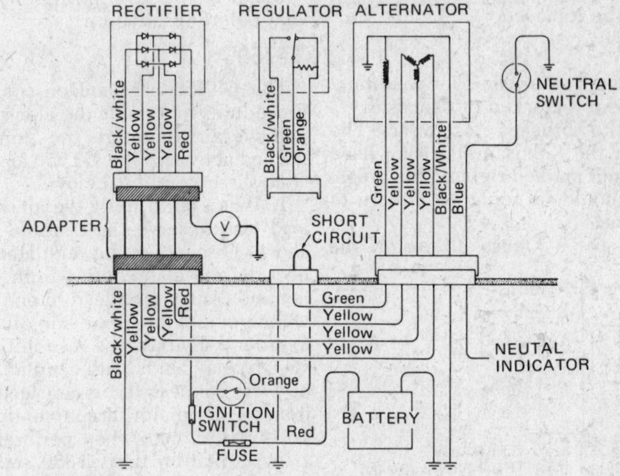

Alternator no-load test (GT380, GT550)

ALTERNATOR

No-Load Test

CAUTION: *The alternator no-load test must be performed quickly to avoid burning out the alternator coils.*

1. The battery must be fully charged.
2. The alternator should be cold.
3. Disconnect the voltage regulator coupler. Then use a small piece of wire to connect the green wire from the alternator to the orange battery wire. Refer to the "short circuit" in the illustration.
4. Disconnect the red lead coming from the rectifier at the rectifier wiring coupler, and connect it to one side of a voltmeter; connect the other side of the voltmeter to ground, as shown.
5. Start the engine and take voltage readings at 1500 and 2500 rpm. Take the readings quickly to avoid damaging the alternator. Compare the readings to the proper specifications for your make of alternator below:

	Output	
Alternator	*1500 rpm*	*2500 rpm*
Denso	18v	31v
Kokusan	22v	40v

Stator Coil Test

1. Remove the alternator stator.
2. Check the resistance between each of the yellow leads and the stator body. This is a test for a grounded coil. In each case, the resistance should be infinite. If, in any case, it is not, the stator assembly must be replaced.
3. Check the continuity between each of the 3 yellow leads. If the 3 leads were assigned the letters "A," "B," and C," you would check the continuity between A–B, A–C, and B–C.

In each case, the ohmmeter should read less than 1 ohm resistance. The exact specifications are 0.26–0.1 ohms for the Denso alternator, and 0.43–0.1 ohms for the Kokusan coil.

If the resistance in any of the 3 tests is higher than this value, an open circuit exists, and the stator assembly must be replaced.

ROTOR TEST

1. Check the resistance between each of the rotor slip-rings and the rotor core. In each case, resistance should be infinite.

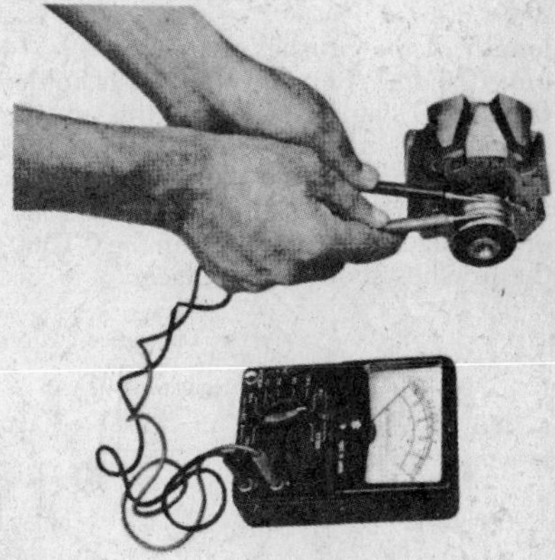
Checking for continuity between the rotor slip-rings

If it is not, the slip-ring(s) are grounded, and the rotor must be replaced.

2. Check the resistance between the slip-rings themselves. It should be 10.5–11.5 ohms for the Denso rotor, and 4–5 ohms for the Kokusan unit. If the

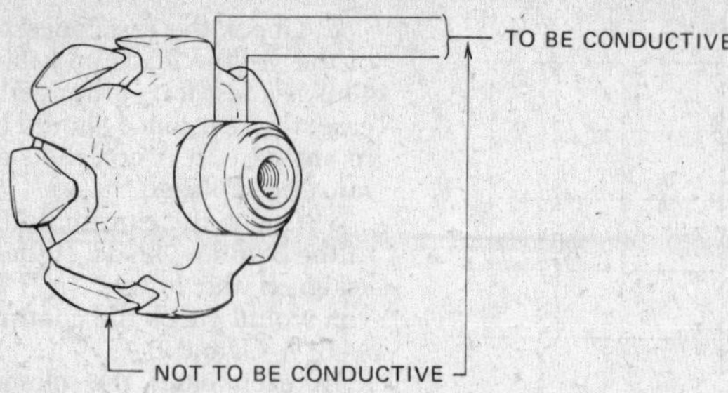

Rotor resistance test points

resistance is not close to this value, the rotor must be replaced.

BRUSHES

Check the rotor brushes for condition. Replace them if cracked or damaged.

Check the brushes for wear. The brushes for the Kokusan alternator have the wear limit marked right on the brush, and they should be replaced if worn to near the line.

If you have a Denso alternator, the

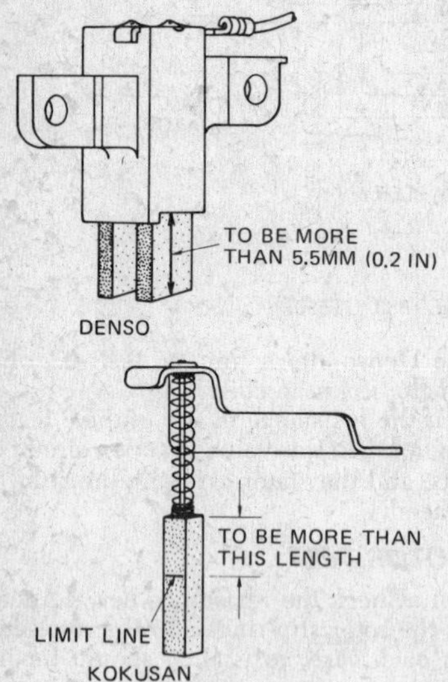

Carbon brush wear limits

length of the brushes, when new, is 14 mm (0.6 in.). Remove the brush holder from the stator assembly, lift up the spring, and measure the length of the brush protruding from the holder. If it is less than 5.5 mm (0.22 in.) on the GT550, or less than 7 mm (0.28 in.) on the GT380, the brushes should be replaced.

Clean the rotor slip-rings with a solvent before installation.

GT750

The GT750 uses a Denso alternator. Procedures for testing the electrical components are therefore the same as described above for the GT550 and GT380. Note the exceptions below:

1. When performing the alternator no-load test, observe the cautions outlined above. Disconnect the regulator; disconnect the red lead coming from the rectifier and connect the lead to one side of a voltmeter and the other side of the meter to ground. By-pass the fuse in the starter switch relay lead. With a suitable length of wire, connect the green lead coming from the alternator directly to the battery positive terminal. Then perform the test as described for the GT380 and GT550. Specifications are as follows:

1500 rpm	above 16v
2500 rpm	above 27v

2. After removing the brush holder, lift up the spring so that the brush is free, and measure the length of the brush protruding from the holder. Brush length, when new, is 12.5 mm (0.49 in.); replace if measured length is less than 5.5 mm (0.22 in.).

IGNITION CIRCUIT

Coil

1. If an electrotester is available, check each coil with it. A good coil should be able to produce a constant spark over a 6 mm (0.24 in.) gap for a period of about 5 minutes.

2. The coils can also be checked with an ohmmeter. Measure the resistance of the primary coil by connecting the meter to the orange coil lead and the contact breaker lead (white, yellow/black, or black) for each ignition coil. Primary coil resistance should be 4–6 ohms. If the resistance reads infinity, the coil has an internal broken wire, and must be replaced.

3. Check the resistance of the secondary coil by connecting the ohmmeter to the orange lead and the high-tension lead (not including the spark plug cap). Resistance should be 15–25,000 ohms. If much lower than this figure, the coil has a short circuit; if much higher, there is an open circuit in the coil. In either case, replacement is the only alternative.

Condensers

Check the capacitance of each condenser with an electrotester if one is available. It should be 0.16–0.20 mfd for each one. Replace the condensers if the reading falls short of this value.

STARTER MOTOR

GT550, GT750

REMOVAL

GT550

1. Remove the exhaust system. Drain the transmission oil.

2. Remove the right-side crankcase cover and the clutch assembly. Refer to "Engine and Transmission".

3. Unbolt and remove the starter motor cover from the bottom of the crankcase. Disconnect the motor lead. Pull off the gears, and take the starter motor out of the housing.

GT750

1. Remove the gas tank and the carburetors.

2. Disconnect the lead from the starter relay.

3. Remove the starter clutch cover.

NOTE: *The contact breaker assembly need not be disturbed.*

4. Drain the cooling system. Loosen the by-pass hose clamp, then take off the hose.

5. Remove the starter motor cover. Remove the by-pass hose junction from the crankcase.

6. Remove the starter motor securing bolts, then move the motor toward the

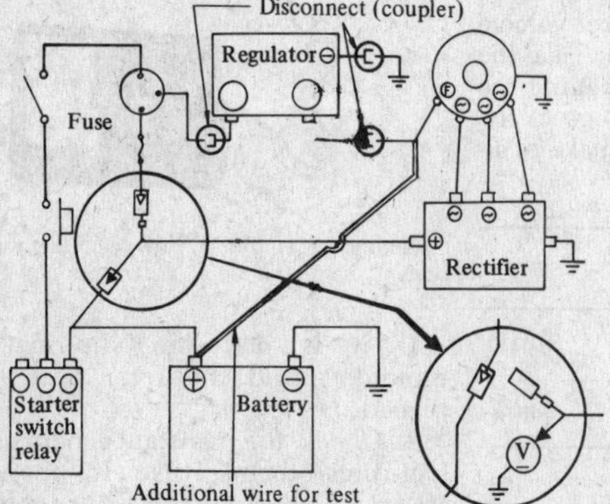

Alternator no-load test (GT750)

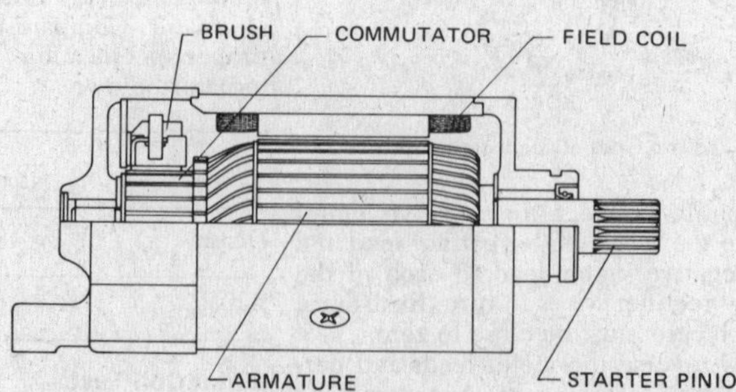

Starter motor cutaway view

clutch side of the engine, and remove it from the crankcase housing.

INSPECTION

1. Before disassembling the motor, check for lateral play of the armature shaft. Play should be very slight (0.2 mm; 0.008 in.).

2. If play of the shaft is evident, it is indicative of a worn bush or bushes.

3. Disassemble the starter motor by removing the through-bolts. Take off the commutator end plate and the drive side end plate. Note the location of all thrust washers behind the plates.

4. The bushes are located in the end plates. Check their condition. Note any cracks or heavy scoring on the bushes. If the armature has grounded out against the field coils, this will be very evident by score marks on the armature and coils; this condition is almost always due to worn bushes, so replace them. The bushes can be driven out with a suitable drift, and new units pressed in. Lubricate the bushes with a bit of grease after installation.

5. Clean off the commutator surface with some solvent.

6. Check the depth of the mica undercut on the commutator. Minimum acceptable depth is 0.2 mm (0.008 in.) on the GT750, and 0.3 mm (0.012 in.) on the GT550.

If the undercut is less than these amounts, use a small, thin file or a piece of hacksaw blade to increase the undercut. The standard depth is 0.05–0.8 mm (0.02–0.03 in.). Clean the commutator very thoroughly after cutting.

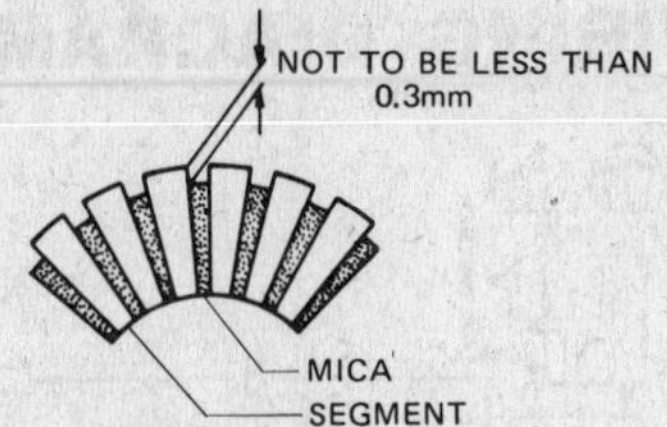

Starter motor commutator mica undercut

7. With an ohmmeter or continuity light, check for continuity between the commutator and the armature shaft. If there is continuity, the commutator is grounded, and the armature must be replaced.

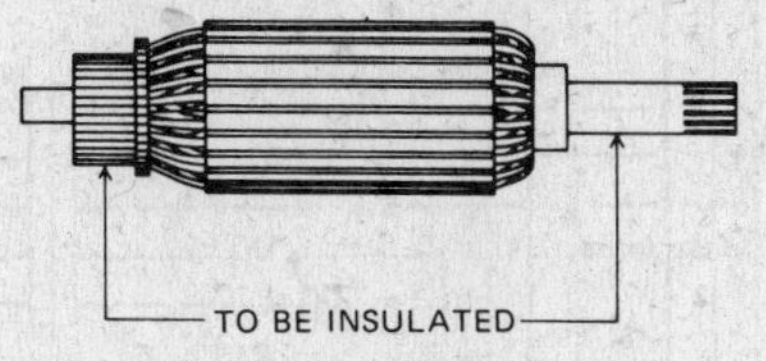

Commutator ground test

8. Check for continuity between the starter motor terminal and the positive brush as illustrated; then check for continuity between the terminal and the field coils. In both cases, the test should show continuity.

9. Check the brushes for wear or cracks. Compare the brush length with the replacement limits given in the illustration.

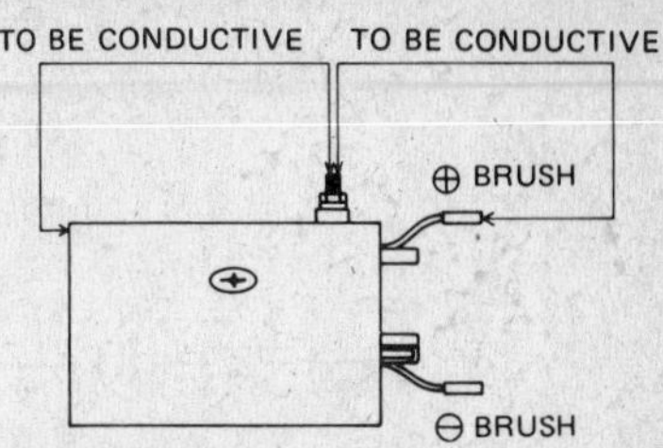

Field coil and brush tests

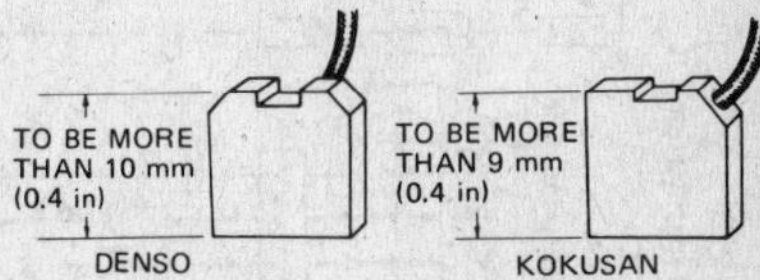

Carbon brush wear limits

ASSEMBLY AND INSTALLATION

Assembly and installation are accomplished by reversing the above procedures.

Starter Relay

When the starter button is pushed, the relay should be heard to click. If the relay is doubtful, by-pass it to see if the starter works.

The relay can be fixed sometimes by removing the cover. Check the condition of the points. If burnt, clean them off with emery cloth or sandpaper.

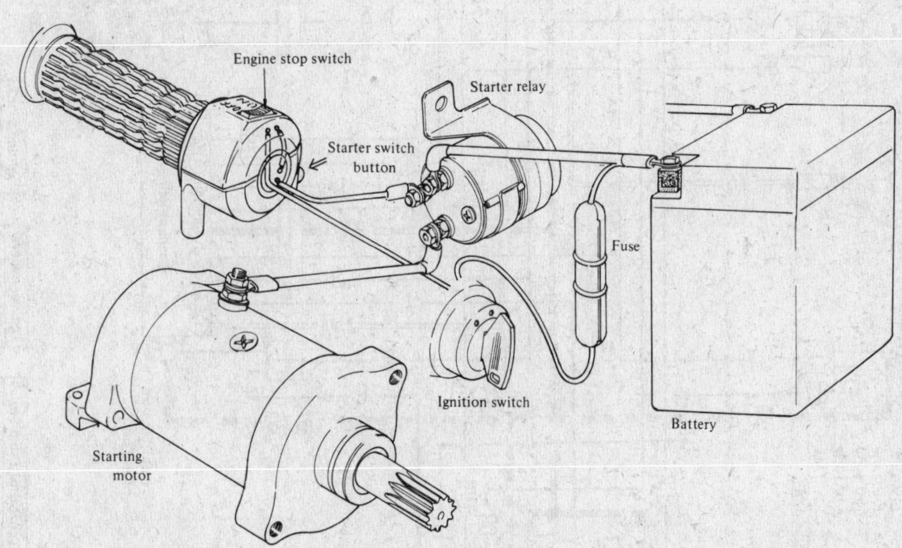

WIRING DIAGRAMS

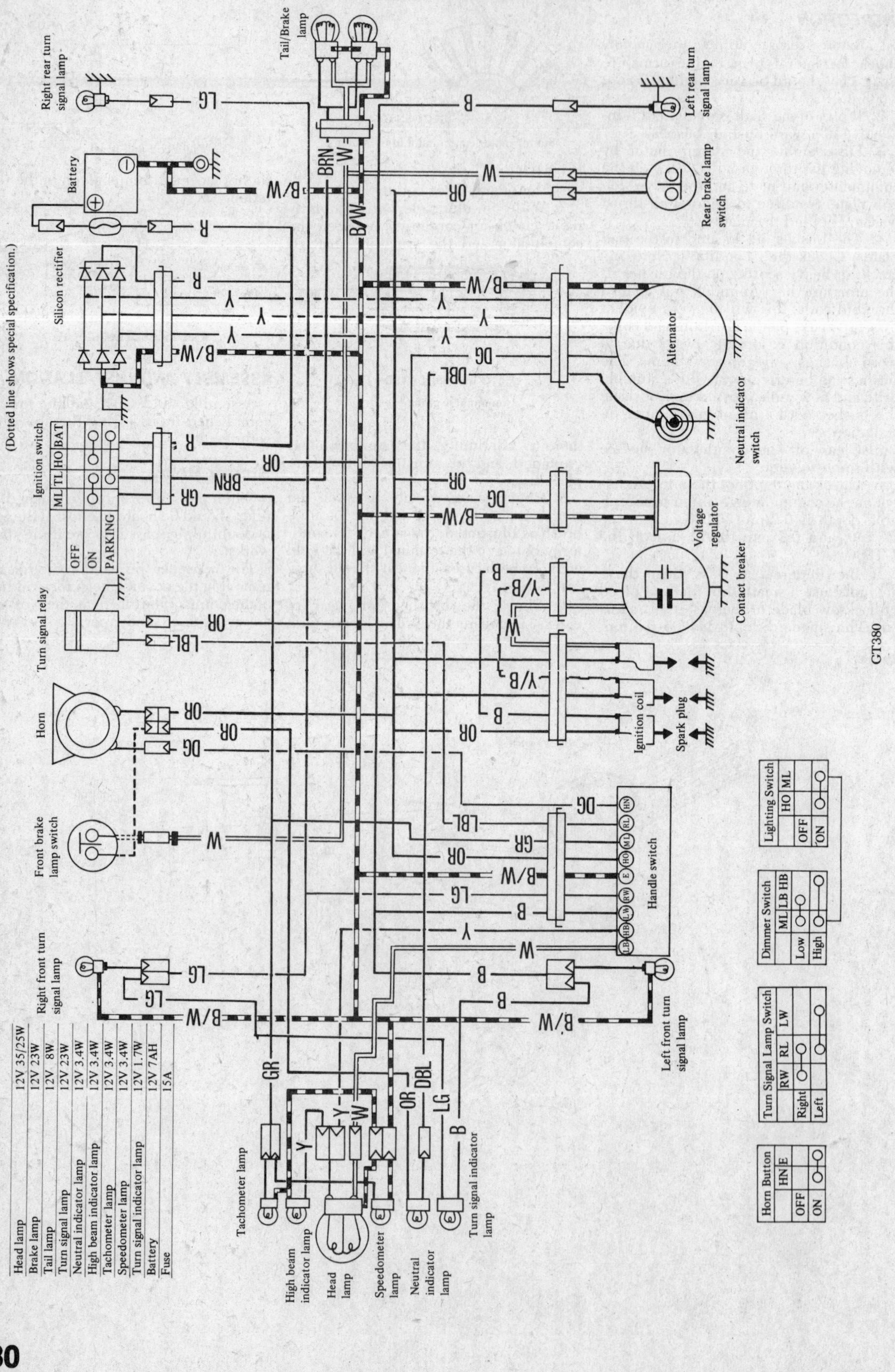

GT380

(Dotted line shows special specification.)

Head lamp	12V 35/25W
Brake lamp	12V 23W
Tail lamp	12V 8W
Turn signal lamp	12V 23W
Neutral indicator lamp	12V 3.4W
High beam indicator lamp	12V 3.4W
Tachometer lamp	12V 3.4W
Speedometer lamp	12V 3.4W
Turn signal indicator lamp	12V 1.7W
Battery	12V 7AH
Fuse	15A

Ignition switch

	ML	TL	HO	BAT
OFF				
ON				
PARKING				

Lighting Switch

	HO	ML
OFF		
ON		

Dimmer Switch

	ML	LB	HB
Low			
High			

Turn Signal Lamp Switch

	RW	RL	LW
Right			
Left			

Horn Button

	HN	E
OFF		
ON		

Right rear turn signal lamp
Tail/Brake lamp
Left rear turn signal lamp
Battery
Rear brake lamp switch
Silicon rectifier
Alternator
Neutral indicator switch
Voltage regulator
Contact breaker
Turn signal relay
Ignition coil
Spark plug
Horn
Front brake lamp switch
Handle switch
Right front turn signal lamp
Left front turn signal lamp
Tachometer lamp
High beam indicator lamp
Head lamp
Speedometer lamp
Neutral indicator lamp
Turn signal indicator lamp

WIRING DIAGRAMS

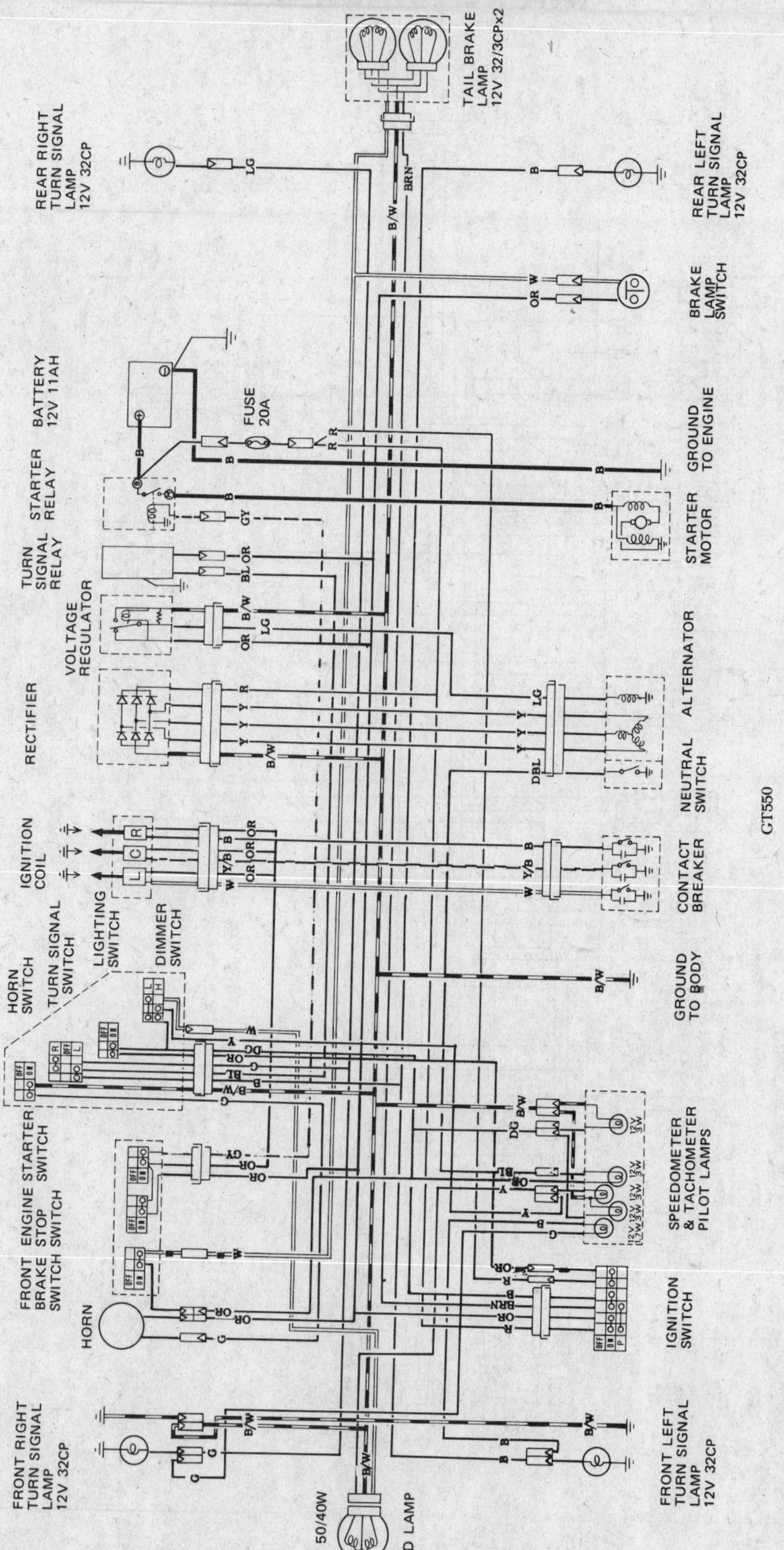

FRONT RIGHT TURN SIGNAL LAMP 12V 32CP

12V 50/40W HEAD LAMP

HORN

FRONT BRAKE SWITCH

ENGINE STOP SWITCH

STARTER SWITCH

HORN SWITCH

TURN SIGNAL SWITCH

LIGHTING SWITCH

DIMMER SWITCH

IGNITION COIL

RECTIFIER

VOLTAGE REGULATOR

TURN SIGNAL RELAY

STARTER RELAY

BATTERY 12V 11AH

FUSE 20A

REAR RIGHT TURN SIGNAL LAMP 12V 32CP

TAIL BRAKE LAMP 12V 32/3CP×2

REAR LEFT TURN SIGNAL LAMP 12V 32CP

BRAKE LAMP SWITCH

GROUND TO ENGINE

STARTER MOTOR

ALTERNATOR

NEUTRAL SWITCH

CONTACT BREAKER

GROUND TO BODY

SPEEDOMETER & TACHOMETER PILOT LAMPS

IGNITION SWITCH

FRONT LEFT TURN SIGNAL LAMP 12V 32CP

GT550

WIRING DIAGRAMS

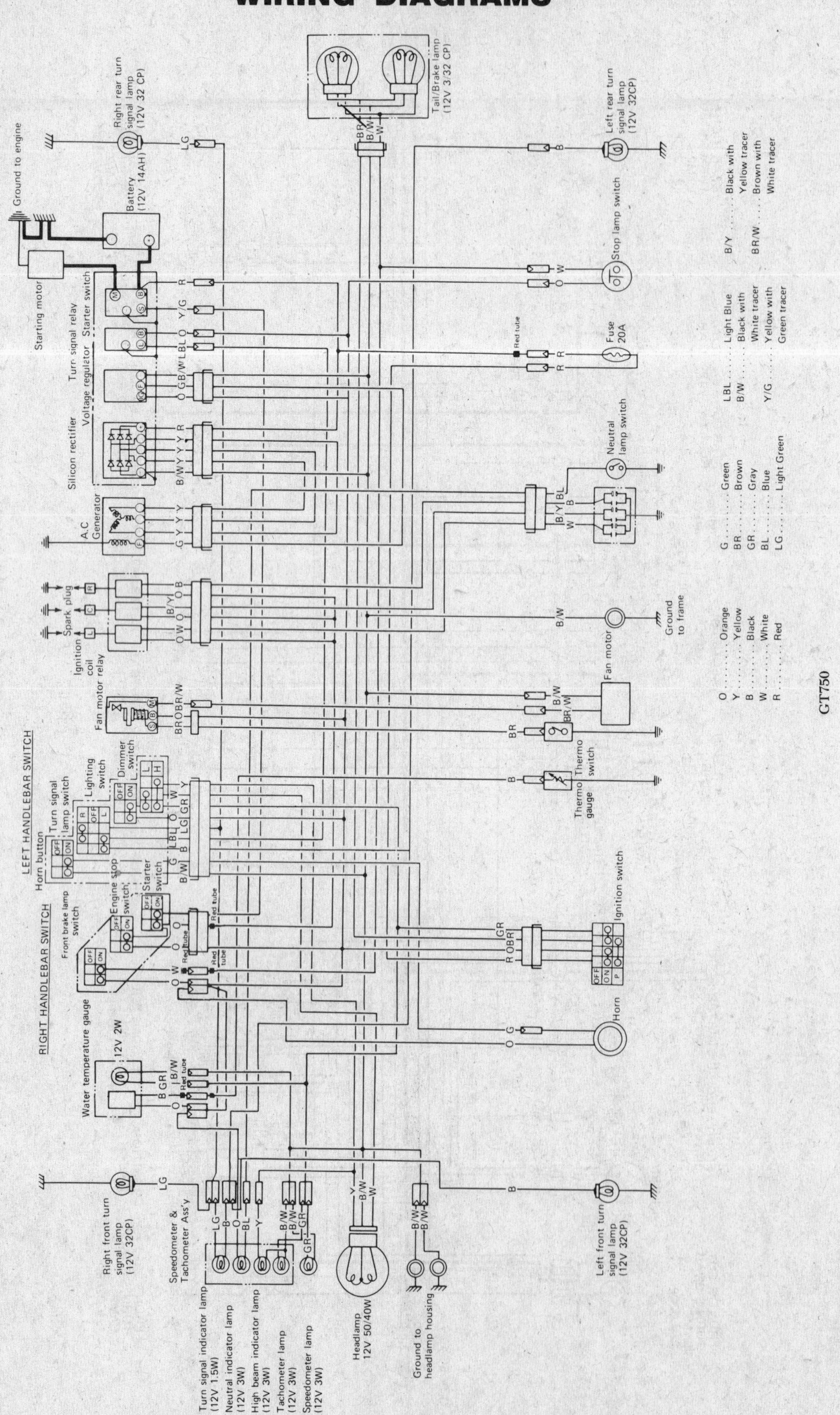

CHASSIS

WHEELS, HUBS, AND BRAKES

Removal and Installation

FRONT

Drum Brake

The front drum brake is a four-leading shoe unit on the GT550 and GT750, and a twin-leading shoe brake on the GT380.

1. Support the front end of the machine well off the ground.
2. Disconnect the brake cable(s) at the hub.
3. Remove the brake anchor bolt(s) which secure the brake anchor(s) to the sliders.
4. Disconnect the speedometer cable at the hub. Loosen the axle nut.
5. Remove the axle holder capnuts, take off the caps, and remove the front wheel from the forks.
6. Installation is the reverse of the removal procedure. Refer to the "Torque Specifications" chart at the end of this section for the proper tightening torque for the nuts and bolts.

Disc Brake

1. Support the front end off the ground.
2. Disconnect the speedometer cable at the hub.
3. Remove the axle holder capnuts, remove the caps, and remove the front wheel from the forks.
4. Installation is the reverse of the removal procedure. Refer to the "Torque Specifications" chart at the end of this section. for the correct torque values.

REAR

1. Remove the chain guard.
2. Disconnect the rear brake cable at the hub.
3. Disconnect the brake anchor on the brake hub.
4. Remove the axle nut cotter pin, and loosen the axle nut.
5. Loosen each of the chain adjuster bolts as far as possible.
6. Remove the rear axle clamp bolts.
7. Move the wheel forward as far as possible, then disengage the drive chain from the sprocket.
8. Pull the wheel back and remove it from the frame.

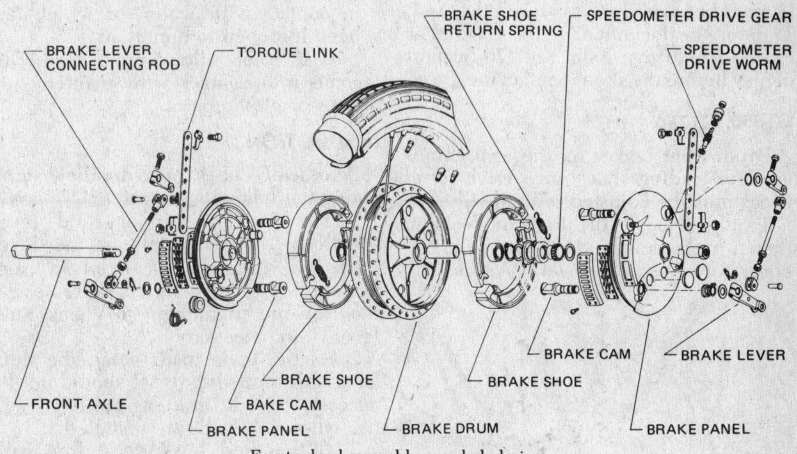

Front wheel assembly—exploded view

Drum Brakes

INSPECTION

1. Check the condition of the brake linings. If the linings are scored or oil-impregnated, they should be replaced.
2. Clean the linings with sandpaper, and wash them off with a solvent. Use the sandpaper to break the glaze on the linings.
3. Check the condition of the brake drum, noting any scoring. Clean off the drum surface with sandpaper as used on the linings, and clean it thoroughly with a solvent afterward.
4. If the drums are scored or if they are warped (as indicated by an on-off-on feeling when the brake is applied), they can be turned down on a lathe.
5. Measure the diameter of the brake linings installed on the backing plate. Check the diameter obtained against the replacement limit shown below.

NOTE: *When measuring the diameter of the linings installed on the backing plate, be sure that the brake cams lie flat.*

6. Measure the diameter of the brake drums. Check the reading obtained against the wear limits given below.

Brake Replacement Limits

Diameter	*GT380 mm (in.)*	*GT550, GT750 mm (in.)*
Brake shoe		
Front	176 (6.93)	194 (7.64)
Rear	176 (6.93)	176 (6.93)
Brake drum		
Front	180.7 (7.11)	200.7 (7.90)
Rear	180.7 (7.11)	180.7 (7.11)

7. Check the condition of the brake return springs, and replace them if they are badly rusted or corroded, or if the ends of the springs are twisted or damaged.
8. The brake cams may be lubricated after removing the brake shoes, removing the brake lever pinch-bolts, and carefully pulling the levers off the splined cams; the cams are then tapped out of the brake backing plate using a soft-faced mallet.
9. Clean off the brake cams with a solvent; remove any rust with emery cloth or sandpaper. Lubricate the cams with chassis grease, and install.

ADJUSTMENT

Adjustment of the brake rods will not be necessary unless the brake hub has been completely disassembled.

GT380

The GT380 drum front brake is a twin-leading shoe unit. To adjust the brake rod, loosen the locknut on the rod; turn the rod in the direction "1" shown in the illustration. Pull the handlebar brake lever full on. This will mean that one shoe is contacting the brake drum. Now turn the rod

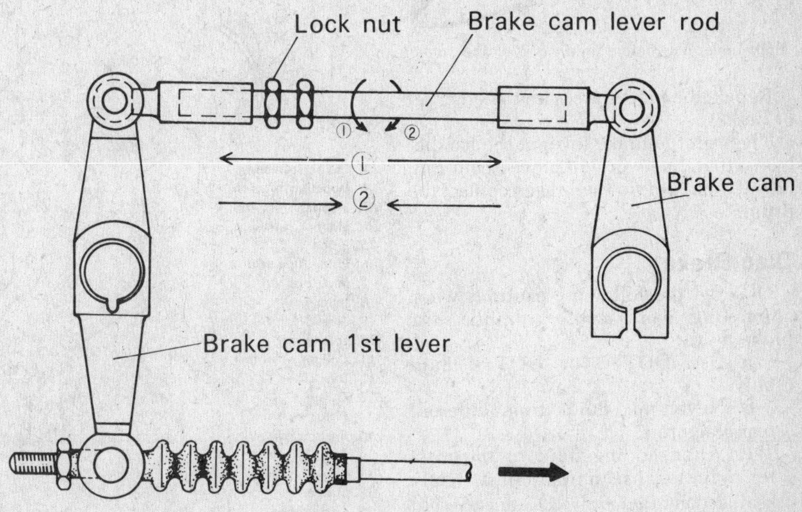

GT380 drum brake adjustment

in the direction "2", opposite the way you turned it first, until the other shoe contacts the drum, at which time it will no longer be possible to turn the rod. Tighten the locknut. Set the handlebar brake lever to give about 1 in. (20–30 mm) of play before the shoes contact the drum.

GT550, GT750

Drum front brakes on these machines are four-leading shoe units. Each set of shoes must be adjusted individually.

To adjust, loosen the brake rod locknut, then turn the brake rod to shorten the distance between brake levers "A" and "B"

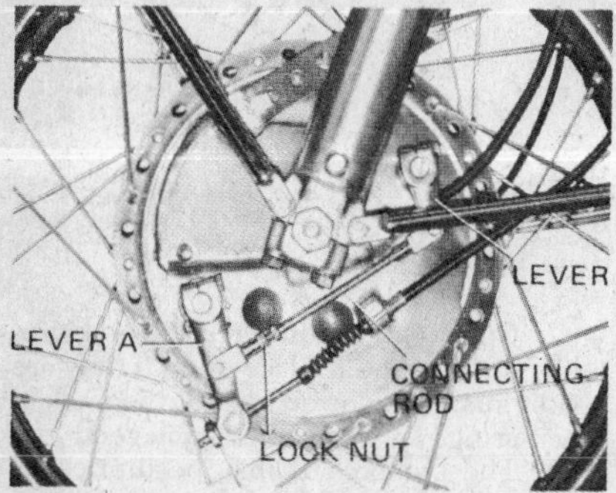

GT550, GT750 drum brake adjustment procedure

in the illustration. The rod should be turned so that it will be threaded into lever "A".

Push lever "A" so that the shoes contact the drum; hold this lever in position with your hand, and with your other hand, unscrew the brake rod from lever "A" until you feel that the shoe controlled by lever "B" has contacted the brake drum. The rod will no longer be able to be turned by hand at this point. Tighten the locknut.

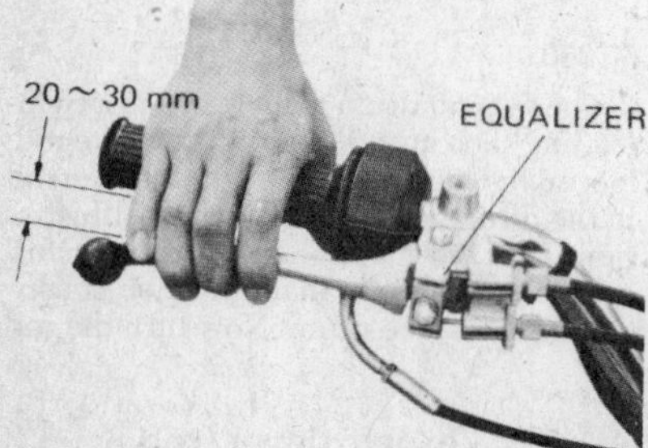

Brake lever play before brakes contact the drum

Repeat the procedure with the other set of brakes.

Then set the brake lever at the handlebar so that the lever will move about 1 in. (20–30 mm) before the brakes contact the drum.

Disc Brakes

Observe the following cautions when attempting work with hydraulic disc brake fluid:

a. Use DOT 3 or DOT 4 fluid only.

b. Never mix fluids from different manufacturers.

c. When adding fluid to the master cylinder, use fluid from a tightly sealed container only. Do not use old fluid, or fluid which has been stored for even a short time in an unsealed container.

d. Do not use fluid which has come in contact with water, or which has been left open to humid air.

e. Do not allow brake fluid to come into contact with painted surfaces or plastic parts.

INSPECTION

Perodically check the hydraulic system, noting the following points:

1. The master cylinder fluid level should be approximately at the level mark. On "L" and later models, a "see-through" reservoir is fitted, so removing the cap and diaphragm to check fluid level is not necessary.
2. As the brake pads wear, the fluid level will drop slightly. It should not be necessary to add fluid, as the level will rise when new pads are installed.
3. If the fluid level does drop well below the level mark, carefully check the system for leaks. Check the hoses for abrasions or cracks, and the caliper(s) for leaky seals.
4. Keep an eye on the pad wear, and replace them when they are worn to near the red limit line. See below.
5. Check that the hoses do not contact the frame or forks at any places except their fastening points.

BLEEDING

This procedure should be necessary only if any of the brake components have been disassembled, or if the brake level travel is excessive or feels spongy.

On the GT750, bleed one caliper at a time.

1. Remove the dust cap from the caliper bleed valve, and fit a suitable piece of plastic or rubber hose to it. A transparent hose is preferred.
2. Arrange the hose so that it loops upward, then immerse the other end in a clean container with a couple of inches of new brake fluid in it.
3. Squeeze the handlebar lever several times, then hold it hard on.
4. Open the bleed valve ½ turn while holding the lever on. The lever will be pulled to the twist-grip as the fluid is expelled. Hold the lever in position against the twist-grip; do not release it.
5. Tighten the bleed valve; release the lever; then repeat the procedure until all air has been expelled from the lines.

NOTE: *Keep track of the fluid in the reservoir during the bleeding operation, and refill it as necessary.*

6. After bleeding is complete, fill the reservoir to the proper level, and refit the diaphragm and secure the cap tightly.

PAD REPLACEMENT

1. Remove the front wheel.
2. Remove the securing screw and take out the inner brake pad.
3. Squeeze the brake lever and remove the main pad. On installation, lightly coat the sides and back of the replacement main pad with the special grease which is supplied with the pads. Do not use common grease for this purpose.
4. Open the bleeder valve slightly to relieve the pressure, then push the piston in all the way and close the valve.
5. Insert the main pad making certain that the groove is properly aligned with the positioning pin.
6. Install the inner pad, apply a small amount of thread locking compound to the securing screw, and tighten it firmly.
7. Install the front wheel.

CALIPER

Removal

1. Remove the front wheel.
2. Disconnect the brake line at the caliper and use the rubber cover of the bleeder valve to plug the end of the brake line to prevent fluid loss.

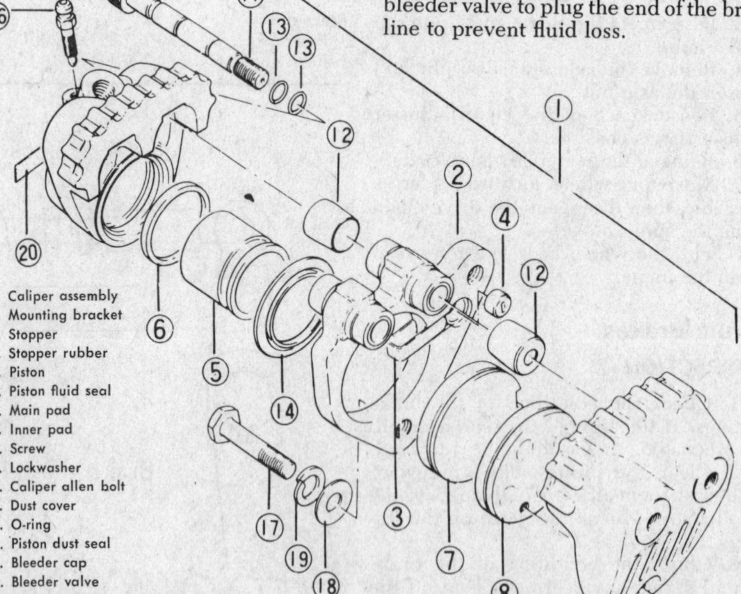

Caliper assembly

3. If the caliper is to be disassembled after removal, loosen the two caliper (allen) bolts now.

4. Remove the mounting bolts and take off the caliper.

Disassembly

1. Remove the allen bolts and separate the caliper halves.
2. Remove the inner pad securing screw and remove the pad.
3. Remove the main pad.
4. Remove the piston dust seal. Use compressed air applied to the brake line connection to force out the piston.
5. Remove the piston seal from the caliper taking care not to scratch the caliper walls.

Inspection

1. Clean all metal parts in new brake fluid only. Do not use solvents.
2. Measure the diameter of the piston and the inside diameter of the caliper bore, and compare the readings to the standard specifications and wear limits.
3. Check the sides of the piston and caliper bore for scuffing and replace the components if damaged.

Assembly

The use of new fluid seals, dust seals, and o-rings is recommended.

1. Coat the piston seal with new brake fluid and insert it into the caliper, ensuring that it is properly seated.
2. Lightly lubricate the caliper walls and sides of the piston with new brake fluid and install the piston in the caliper, being careful that the seal is not damaged when installing the piston.
3. Caliper allen bolts must be lubricated with special Suzuki grease before installation. The remainder of the procedure is the reverse of disassembly. Be sure the allen bolts' dust covers are in place.

Installation

Installation is the reverse of removal. Bleed the system as outlined above.

MASTER CYLINDER

Removal

1. Disconnect the brake switch.
2. Disconnect the brake line at the master cylinder, taking appropriate precautions against fluid spillage.
3. Loosen the master cylinder cap and the brake lever bolt. Remove the mounting bolts and take off the master cylinder. Drain the fluid.

Disassembly

1. Remove the brake lever.
2. Remove the boot stopper, plate, and boot.
3. Remove the snap ring and take out the piston assembly.

Inspection

1. Clean metal parts in new brake fluid only.
2. Clean piston and cylinder bore for wear against specifications given in the Disc Brake chart.
3. The use of new rubber parts such as the primary and secondary cup is recommended.

Assembly and Installation

1. Assembly is the reverse of disassembly. Lubricate all parts with new brake fluid before installing.
2. Bleed the system.

BRAKE DISC

1. Check disc thickness and run-out and compare to the standard specifications.
2. Replace the disc if worn or scored. If run-out is excessive, first check that the wheel bearings are not worn.
3. If the disc is removed, tighten bolts to 11–18 ft lbs. when installing.

Disc Brake Specifications

Part	*Standard (mm/in.)*	*Serviceable Limit (mm/in.)*
Caliper bore	38.18–38.20/1.5031–1.5039	38.22/1.5047
Caliper piston OD	38.15–38.18/1.5020–1.5031	38.10/1.5000
Master cylinder bore		
380, 550	14.00–14.04/0.5512–0.5527	14.05/0.5531
750	15.87–15.91/0.6248–0.6264	15.92/0.6268
Master cylinder piston OD		
380, 550	13.96–13.98/0.5496–0.5504	13.94/0.5488
750	15.83–15.85/0.6232–0.6240	15.81/0.6224

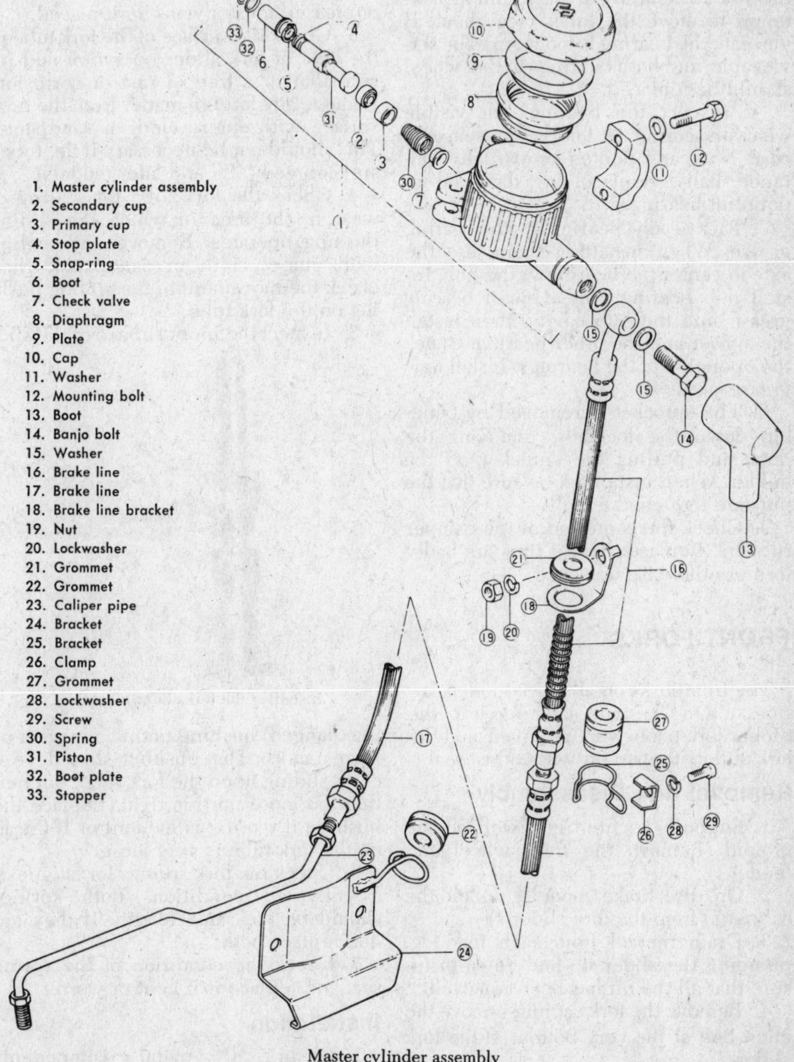

Master cylinder assembly

HUBS

1. After removing the brake drum(s) from the hub on drum brake-equipped wheels, the wheel bearings can be removed for inspection and lubrication.

2. The bearings should be packed every 12,000 miles. Use a good grade of bearing grease.

3. The grease is kept in the hub by seals on either side of the bearing assembly. These seals should be replaced if they are removed.

4. On front wheels, remove the speedometer drive assembly from the hub, and the bearing retainer circlip.

5. On rear wheels, remove the final drive sprocket assembly. This is simply pulled off the hub. It is not necessary to unbolt the sprocket from the sprocket holder.

6. Drive out each bearing from the hub by reaching through the hub and tapping the bearing with a suitable drift.

Note that the sprocket assembly is also fitted with a bearing.

7. Thoroughly clean the bearings in solvent and dry them with compressed air. Check each bearing for excessive looseness of the balls or play of the inner bearing race.

Place the bearing on a flat surface, hold the outer race firmly in place, and then attempt to move the inner race about. If you can, the bearing is too worn to be serviceable, and both bearings in that wheel should be replaced.

8. Inspect the bearings for visible wear or scoring or for the presence of rust. Note any dented or partially flattened balls. Replace any damaged or doubtful bearings.

7. Pack each bearing with bearing grease. When installing them, use the axle to center the bearing in the hub. Install one bearing, put a bit of bearing grease into the hub cavity, then install the spacer and the other bearing. Check the operation of the bearings. Install new grease seals.

8. The sprocket is removed by bending down the locktabs, removing the nuts, and pulling the sprocket off the holder. When installing, be sure that the nuts are tightened evenly.

9. Check the condition of the damper rubbers. Replace them if they are badly torn or otherwise damaged.

FRONT FORKS

The front forks on all three models are similar. On "L" and later models, the rubber fork boots were removed, and the fork sliders topped off with a dust seal.

Removal and Disassembly

1. Support the front end well off the ground. Remove the front wheel and fender.

2. On disc brake models, unbolt the caliper(s) from the fork slider(s).

3. Drain the oil from each fork leg, pumping the slider up and down to insure that all the oil has been removed.

4. Remove the fork capnut; remove the allen bolt at the very bottom of the fork slider.

5. Lift up the fork boot or the dust seal to gain access to the circlip at the top of the slider. Remove the circlip with a pair of snap-ring pliers. Then remove the slider from the fork leg.

6. Loosen the upper and lower triple clamp pinch-bolts, and pull down on the fork leg to remove it from the machine.

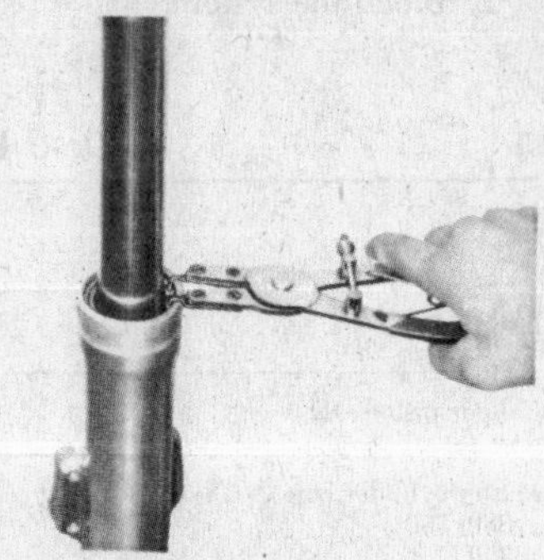

Removing the fork slider circlip

Inspection

1. Check the condition of the fork tubes. Bent tubes must be replaced unless a press is available to straighten them.

2. A fork tube which has been kinked or creased must always be replaced.

3. Check the surface of the fork tube in the area of fork slider operation and insure that it is free of rust or corrosion. Remove any foreign matter from the tube surface with emery cloth or sandpaper. This should not be necessary if the tubes are chromed ("L" and later models).

4. Check the fork tube for scoring or wear in the area in which the sliding bushing operates. Remove any scoring with emery cloth or sandpaper, then check the movement of the sliding bushing on the fork tube.

5. Inspect the inner surface of the sliding (flanged) bushing noting any wear or score marks. The bushing should be a close sliding fit on the fork tube: but neither too loose nor too tight. Replace the bushing if scoring is evident or if the fit on the fork tube is very loose.

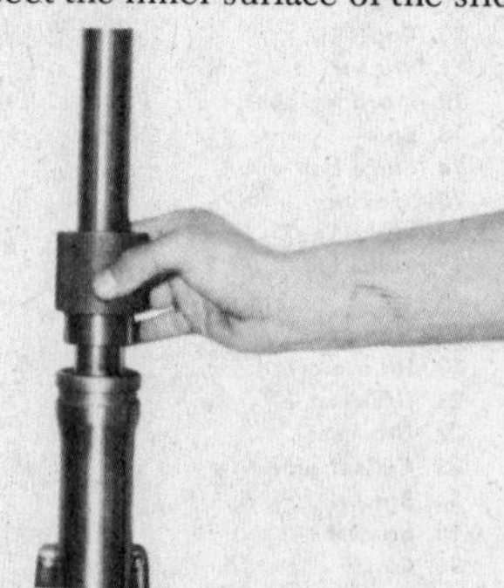

Installing the fork slider oil seal

6. Check the fork springs for fatigue or a collapsed condition. Both springs should be the same length. If they are not, replace both.

7. Check the condition of the spring seat and replace it if bent or worn.

Installation

1. Clean all metal components thoroughly in a solvent, then lubricate them prior to assembly.

2. New fork slider oil seals must be used. Install the seals in the sliders as shown. They should be installed after the slider has been positioned on the tube since this will help center the seal.

3. The O-rings on the fork capnuts should be replaced if they show signs of age or wear.

4. Assembly is the reverse of the disassembly procedure. Note the following:

When installing the fork tubes in the triple clamps, make sure that the top of the tube is flush with the top surface of the upper triple clamp. Lock the tube in place by tightening the upper and lower triple clamp pinch-bolt gradually.

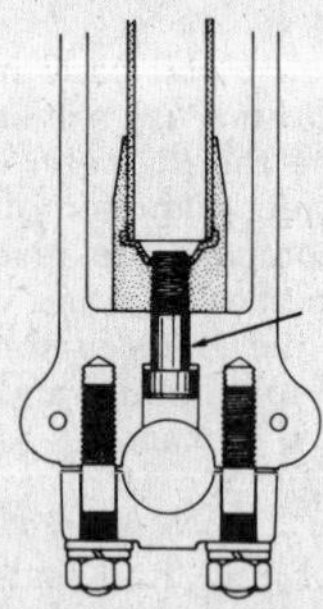

Slider allen bolt in position

When replacing the fork slider allen bolt, push the slider up so that it is "bottomed", then tighten the bolt.

When refitting the fork springs, note that the tapered end of the spring faces *down* (toward the spring seat).

Add the correct quantity of oil to each fork leg, and refit the capnuts.

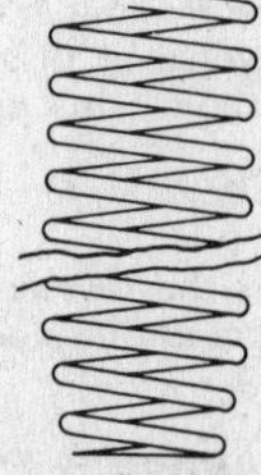

Proper installation of the fork spring

Be sure that all nuts and bolts are firmly tightened.

STEERING STEM

Inspection

1. With the front wheel off the ground, the front forks should swing freely to either side when released.

2. Check the movement of the forks by turning them slowly lock-to-lock. Note any resistance, rough movement, noise, or halting action while moving the forks.

3. Grasp the forks at the bottom of the sliders and attempt to move them back and forth in line with the machine. There should be no play at all. If play exists, the steering stem bearings are in need of adjustment.

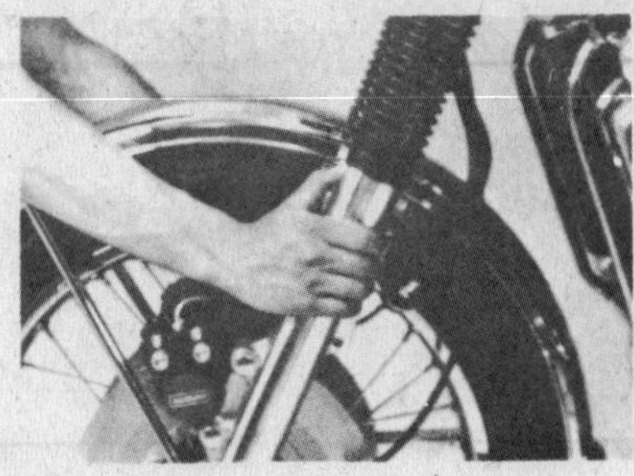
Checking steering stem bearing adjustment

4. Note that a squirrelly feeling in the handling of the machine at low speeds may be due to the steering stem bearings being too tight. It may also be due to low tire pressure, so check that.

5. If the forks have movement in line with the machine, the bearings are too loose, and the adjustment nut should be tightened.

6. Any unusual noise or balky movement of the forks is probably due to worn or damaged balls or races, and the steering stem should be removed and these parts checked.

Adjustment

1. Remove the instruments, handlebars, etc.
2. Loosen the 3 upper triple clamp pinch-bolts. Remove the fork crown nut. Strike the underside of the triple clamp with a soft-faced mallet and remove it.
3. Remove the dust seal from the steering stem.
4. With a suitable wrench, or with a blunt punch and hammer, tighten or loosen the steering stem nut as needed to achieve proper bearing adjustment.
5. As described above, the forks should swing freely from side-to-side, and the movement should be smooth.

Removal

1. Support the front wheel well off the ground, and remove the wheel, fender, brake calipers (disc brake), front forks, instruments and handlebars. Remove the headlight assembly and the fork ears.
2. Loosen the rear pinch-bolt on the upper triple clamp; remove the fork crown nut.
3. Hit the underside of the triple clamp with a soft-faced mallet and remove it.
4. Remove the dust cover. Begin loosening the steering stem nut, and, as it is loosened, grasp the underside of the lower triple clamp, holding it in place until the nut is removed from the steering stem.
5. After the nut is removed, carefully lower the steering stem and remove it from the frame.

Inspection

1. Wash all of the bearing balls in solvent to remove the old grease.
2. Clean off the bearing races.
3. Check the condition of the balls. Note any rust, pitting, dented balls, or scoring.
4. Check the condition of the ball races. The race surface must be smooth. Note any cracks, rust, denting, or a rippled surface.
5. If any damage is evident, balls and races should be replaced as a set.
6. Smear the surface of the lower race with bearing grease, and embed the balls in the grease to hold them in place during installation.

Assembly

Reverse the removal procedure. Hold the steering stem in place on the frame; make sure that all of the balls are in place, then screw on the nut. Adjust the bearings as described above.

REAR SHOCK ABSORBERS

The shock absorbers are sealed units. If they fail to function properly, or leak oil, they must be replaced.

SWING ARM

With the back wheel supported off the ground, check the swing arm for lateral play. There should be none.

If the swing arm bushings are worn (in which case lateral play will be evident), or if the swing arm is cracked or bent, remove the swing arm for service.

1. Remove the rear wheel assembly.
2. Remove the chain guard; unbolt the shock absorbers from the swing arm.
3. Remove the swing arm spindle nut and pull out the spindle; remove the swing arm from the frame.
4. Inspect the bushings for wear and replace as necessary.
5. Installation is the reverse of the removal procedure.

Chassis Torque Specifications

Part	*Torque (ft lbs)*
Axle nuts	
Front	26–38
Rear	36–58
Front axle capnuts	11–18
Upper triple clamp pinch-bolts	
Fork tubes	14–22
Center nut	11–18
Lower triple clamp pinch-bolts	14–22
Steering stem center nut	43–72
Drum brake anchors	
Front	14–22
Rear	14–18
Swing arm spindle nut	36–54
Rear shock absorber nuts	14–18

General Torque Specifications

Bolt Diameter (mm)	*Torque (ft lbs)*	
	Unmarked Bolts	*"S" Marked Bolt*
5	1.5–2.9	2.2–4.4
6	2.9–5.1	4.4–7.3
8	6.6–10	9.5–17
10	13–20	18–29

Suzuki GS 750/850

MODEL COVERAGE

GS 750
GS 750 E
GS 750 L
GS 850 G/GL/GN
GS 850 GT/GLT

INDEX

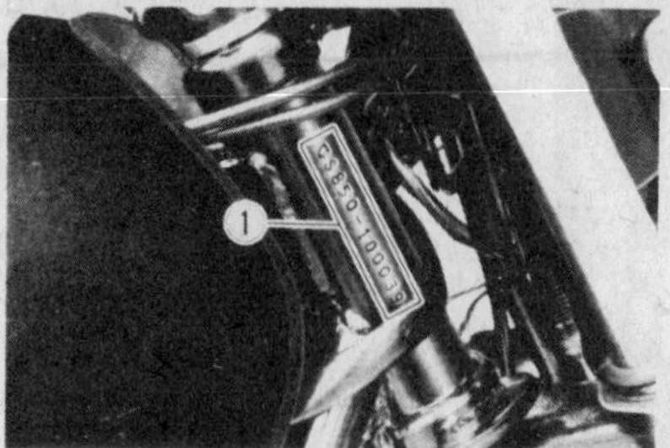

Frame serial number location

Engine serial number location

General Specifications

	GS 750/E	GS 750L	GS 850G/GL/GN	GS 850GT/GLT
Dimensions and Weight				
Overall length	2,225 mm (87.6 in.)	2,230 mm (87.8 in.)	2,230 mm (87.8 in.)	2,230 mm (87.8 in.)
Overall width	870 mm (34.3 in.)	890 mm (35.0 in.)	865 mm (34.1 in.)	865 mm (34.1 in.)
Overall height	1,170 mm (46.1 in.)	1,245 mm (49.0 in.)	1,190 mm (46.9 in.)	1,190 mm (46.9 in.)
Wheelbase	1,490 mm (58.7 in.)	1,510 mm (59.4 in.)	1,490 mm (58.7 in.)	1,500 mm (59.1 in.)
Ground clearance	150 mm (5.9 in.)	160 mm (6.3 in.)	160 mm (6.3 in.)	160 mm (6.3 in.)
Dry weight	223 kg (492 lbs)	233 kg (514 lbs)	253 kg (558 lbs)	253 kg (558 lbs)
Engine				
Type	Four-stroke cycle, air-cooled, DOHC	Four-stroke cycle, air-cooled, DOHC	Four-stroke cycle, air-cooled, DOHC	Four-stroke, air-cooled, DOHC
Number of cylinders	4	4	4	4
Bore	65.0 mm (2.56 in.)	65.0 mm (2.56 in.)	69.0 mm (2.72 in.)	69.0 mm (2.72 in.)
Stroke	56.4 mm (2.22 in.)	56.4 mm (2.22 in.)	56.4 mm (2.22 in.)	56.4 mm (2.22 in.)
Piston displacement	748 cc (45.6 cu in.)	748 cc (45.6 cu in.)	843 cc (51.4 cu in.)	843 cc (51.4 cu in.)
Compression ratio	8.7:1	8.7:1	8.8:1	8.8:1
Carburetors (4)	MIKUNI VM26SS	MIKUNI VM26SS	MIKUNI VM26SS	MIKUNI BS32SS
Air cleaner	Polyurethane foam element	Polyurethane foam element	Polyurethane foam element	Polyurethane foam element
Starter system	Electric and kick	Electric and kick	Electric and kick	Electric
Lubrication system	Wet sump	Wet sump	Wet sump	Wet sump
Transmission				
Clutch	Wet multi-plate type	Wet multi-plate type	Wet multi-plate type	Wet multi-plate type
Transmission	5-speed constant mesh	5-speed constant mesh	5-speed constant mesh	5-speed constant mesh
Primary reduction	2.152 (99/46)	2.152 (99/46)	1.775 (87/49)	1.775 (87/49)
Final reduction	2.733 (41/15)	2.733 (41.15)	3.090 (34/11)	3.090 (34/11)
Gear ratios, Low	2.571 (36/14)	2.571 (36/14)	2.500 (35/14)	2.500 (35/14)
2nd	1.777 (32/18)	1.777 (32/18)	1.777 (32/18)	1.777 (32/18)
3rd	1.380 (29/21)	1.380 (29/21)	1.380 (29/21)	1.380 (29/21)
4th	1.125 (27/24)	1.125 (27/24)	1.125 (27/24)	1.125 (27/24)
Top	0.961 (25/26)	0.961 (25/26)	0.961 (25/26)	0.961 (25/26)
Drive chain	TAKASAGO #630SO, 96 links	TAKASAGO #630SO, 96 links	—	—
Chassis				
Front Suspension	Telescopic, oil dampened	Telescopic, oil dampened	Telescopic, pneumatic	Telescopic pneumatic
Rear suspension	Swing arm, oil dampened, spring 5-way adjustable	Swing arm, oil dampened, spring 5-way adjustable	Swing arm	Swing arm
Steering angle	40° (right & left)	40°	40°	40°
Caster	63°	62°30′	62°	62°
Trail	107 mm (4.21 in.)	100 mm (3.9 in.)	113 mm (4.45 in.)	113 mm (4.45 in.)
Turning radius	2.6 m (8.5 ft)	2.5 m (8.2 ft)	2.6 m (8.5 ft.)	2.6 m (8.5 ft.)
Front brake	Disc	Twin disc	Twin disc	Twin disc
Rear brake	Disc	Disc	Disc	Disc
Front tire size	3.25H 19–4PR	3.25H 19–4PR	3.50H 19–4PR	3.50H 19–4PR
Rear tire size	4.00H 18–4PR	4.50 H17–4PR	4.50H 17–4PR	4.50H 17–4PR

MAINTENANCE

NOTE: *Common maintenance procedures are explained in detail in the "General Information" section.*

LUBRICATION

SAE 10W-40 motor oil, service rating "SE" or "SF" is recommended for all temperatures.

Checking Oil Level

1. The 750/850 has a wet-sump lubrication system, all of the oil being contained in the crankcases.

2. Allow the engine to run for several minutes before checking the oil level.

3. A sight glass or inspection window is provided on the right side of the engine just below the kickstarter. With the machine parked on level ground and on the center stand, and the engine shut off, check the oil level by reference to the marks inscribed on the crankcase. Oil level should be between the "L" and "F" marks.

4. If the oil level is at or near the lower level mark, add enough oil to bring it up to the "F" mark, but do not overfill the crankcase.

Changing Oil

1. The recommended oil change interval is 1,500 miles or 3 months, whichever comes first.

2. Oil should be changed when the engine is warm. This ensures more complete draining and makes it more likely that the oil will carry off any particulate matter with it.

3. Place a suitable container (about 4 qt capacity) beneath the engine and remove the drain plug. Allow the oil to drain for several minutes. Check the condition of the drain plug gasket and replace it if necessary. Refit and tighten the drain plug securely.

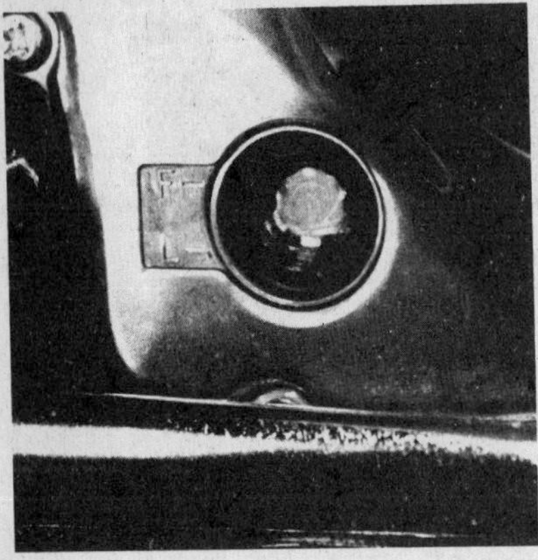
Oil level sight glass

4. If the oil filter is to be replaced, see "Oil Filter," below.

5. If only the oil is being changed, add about 2.8 l (3.0 qt) of oil to the crankcase. If both oil and filter are being changed, add about 3.4 l (3.6 qt).

These amounts are approximations. Make final determination by checking the oil level at the inspection window, and top up to the upper limit line. Start the engine and allow it to idle for about 10 seconds. Shut it off and let it sit for another minute. Check the oil level at the inspection window. Top up the crankcase, if necessary, so that the level is at or near the "F" mark. Do not overfill. Start the engine and allow it to idle for about 10 seconds. Shut it off and let it sit for another minute. Check the oil level at the inspection window. Top up the crankcase, if necessary, so that the level is at or near the "F" mark. Do not overfill.

Oil Filter

1. The oil filter should be changed at every other oil change, or every 3,000 miles.
2. After draining off the crankcase oil, place a drip pan or container beneath the oil filter cover at the front of the engine.
3. Remove the filter cover bolts and take off the cover. Pull the old oil filter.
4. Install the new filter.
5. Before refitting the filter cover, check the condition of the O-ring and replace it if it is knicked or otherwise damaged. Be sure that the mating surface is clean. Lightly oil the cover O-ring before refitting the cover.

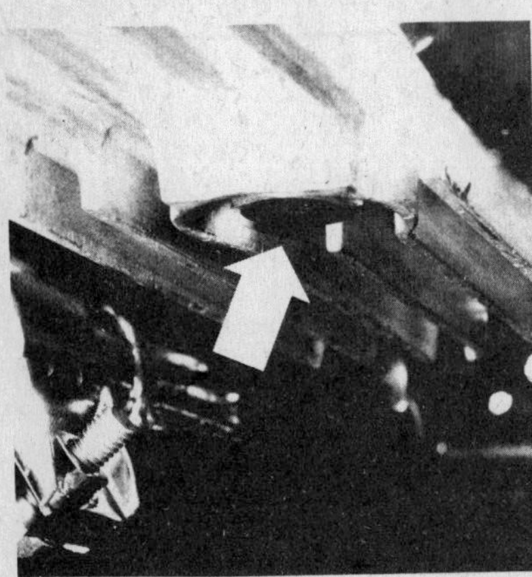
Crankcase drain plug

Oil filter cover bolts

6. Tighten the cover bolts gradually to a torque of 4.3-5.8 ft lbs.

Filter Screen

The oil filter screen should be cleaned every 6,000 miles, or about once a year.

The filter screen is easily reached after removing the exhaust pipes and the oil pan.

Use a new oil pan gasket on assembly. Be sure to tighten the pan bolts evenly to avoid distortion. Tighten the pan bolts to 7.2 ft lbs.

Engine Oil Pressure

1. Be sure that the engine has the proper quantity of oil (between the "F" and "L" marks on the inspection window).
2. Start the engine and run it until oil temperature reaches about 60° C (140° F).
3. Remove the oil gallery plug at the right side of the engine just below the cylinders and install the special oil pressure gauge.
4. Start the engine and run it at about 3,000 rpm while checking the gauge reading. Oil pressure should be about 1.42 psi or more (0.1 kg/cm^2).
5. If the oil pressure is below this limit, remove and inspect the oil pump internals.
6. When fitting the oil gallery plug, be sure to secure it with a non-permanent threadlocking compound. Tighten the plug securely.

Drive Shaft

The secondary drive box and the final drive box both use SAE 90 EP hypoid gear oil.

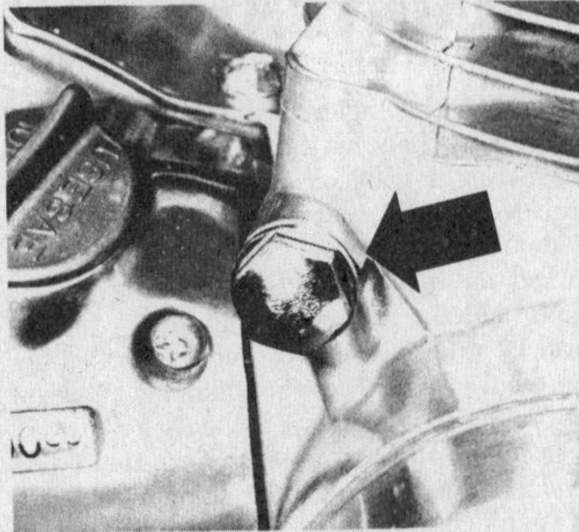
Oil pressure gauge gallery plug

1. To check the oil levels, park the motorcycle on the centerstand on a level surface. Remove the gear shift lever and the secondary drive box cover. Remove the oil level screw. If the level is correct, oil will just begin to come out of the level hole.

To check the final drive box level, remove the level plug/filler cap. Oil should just start to come out if the level is correct.

2. To change oil in the drive boxes, run the motorcycle until operating temperature is reached.
3. Remove the gear shift lever and the secondary drive box cover. Remove the secondary drive box filler plug, drain plug, and level screw.
4. Refit the drain plug. Add SAE 90 gear oil until it begins to come out of the level screw hole. The amount is about 340–400 cc (11.5–13.5 oz).
5. The final drive box oil is changed in the same manner. Capacity is 280–330 cc (9.5–11.2 oz).

Front Forks

GS 750

1. Proper oil for the front forks is a 50/50 mixture of ATF (Automatic Transmission Fluid) and SAE 10W-30 motor oil.
2. Fork capacity is 180 cc (6.1 oz) per fork leg for all except "L" models which is 280 cc (9.5 oz) for each leg.

Front fork drain plug

3. Fork oil should be changed every 6,000 miles, or once a year.
4. Place a container beneath one of the fork sliders and remove the drain plug. Pump the slider up and down until all the oil is expelled. Examine the plug gasket, then refit the plug. Repeat the procedure with the other slider.
5. Examine the drained oil. If it contains water or is exceptionally dirty, it may be that the dust covers are damaged and allowing foreign matter to get past. This will also damage fork seals quickly. Check that the dust covers are properly secured and replace them if cracked, ripped, or otherwise damaged.
6. Support the front wheel off the ground by placing a scissors jack or similar device beneath the engine.

7. Remove the handlebar clamp bolts and move the bars to one side or the other to allow access to the fork filler caps.

8. Remove the fork filler caps. Often loosening the upper triple clamp pinch bolts will make it easier to remove the caps. Since the caps are under spring tension, care should be exercised when removing them.

9. Remove the upper fork springs to facilitate the job of adding the fork oil. Add 180 cc (6.1 oz) to each leg.

10. Inspect the filler cap O-rings for damage and replace them if necessary. Fit the springs and caps, tightening them securely. Tighten the triple clamp pinch bolts if they were loosened. Secure the handlebars, tightening the forwardmost bolts first.

GS 850

Routine oil changes are not necessary on the GS 850. Refer to "Chassis" for service procedures.

Fork air pressure should be checked every 6 mos. in the following manner:

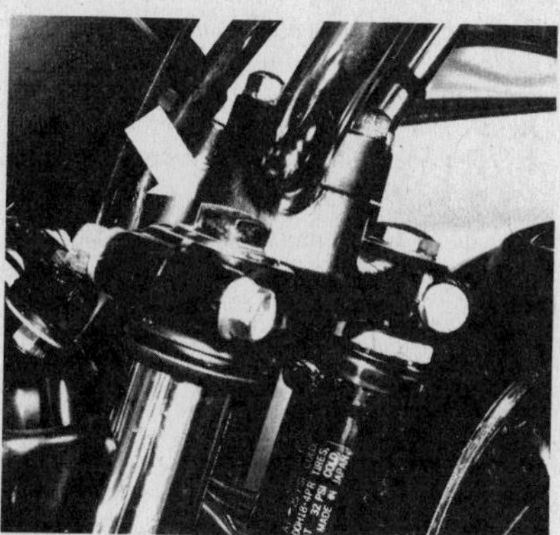

Front fork filler cap

1. Check fork air pressure every 6 mo. Make the check when the forks are "cold" (i.e. before riding).

2. The motorcycle should be on the centerstand with the front wheel off the ground.

3. Pressure is checked with a special gauge. Remove the air valve caps. Turn the valve on the end of the special tool clockwise until it locks. Then turn the other tool valve counterclockwise until it turns freely. Mount the gauge, turning the valve nut clockwise until it stops. Turn the valve on the end of the special tool clockwise until it locks. Pressure should be 8.5–17.0 psi.

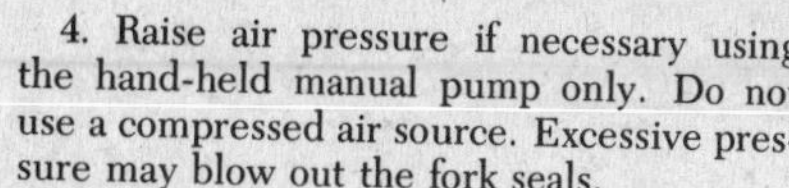

4. Raise air pressure if necessary using the hand-held manual pump only. Do not use a compressed air source. Excessive pressure may blow out the fork seals.

5. Fork legs should be less than 1.4 psi apart.

Drive Chain

1. The drive chain is equipped with rubber O-rings between the plates to seal in the lubricant. At periodic intervals, however, some lubrication of the chain rollers is necessary.

2. About every 600 miles, clean the chain with kerosene.

CAUTION: *Do not use gasoline or any other solvents to clean the chain as the O-rings may be damaged.*

3. After cleaning and drying the chain, lubricate the rollers with 80 or 90W oil. Wipe off any excess.

NOTE: *Do not use commercial chain lubricants on the rollers, as they may cause damage to the O-rings.*

The chain O-rings can be damaged by steam cleaning, high-pressure spray, and certain solvents, keep this in mind when cleaning the motorcycle.

4. If rust is seen to develop on the rollers, lubricate them at more frequent intervals.

Chassis Lubrication

1. The swing arm pivot (750) is fitted with a grease nipple which should be lubricated with a high-quality chassis grease every 12,000 miles or 2 years.

2. Wheel and steering head bearings are lubricated with bearing grease, the service interval being 12,000 miles or 2 years.

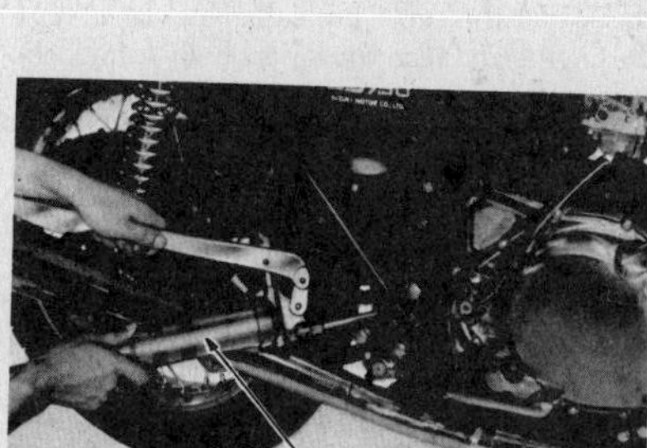

Lubricating the swing arm

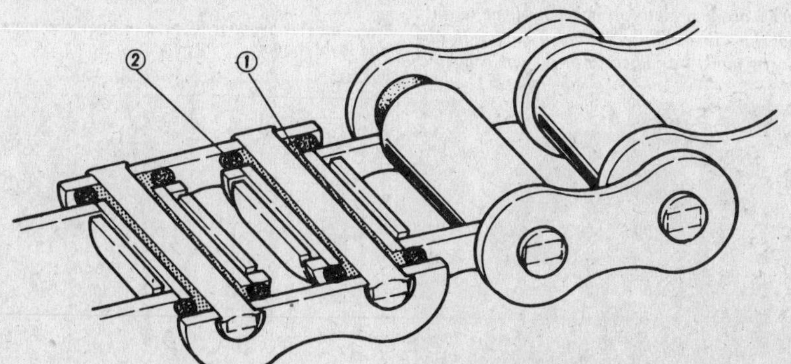

Drive chain lubricant (1) and sealing O-rings (2)

SERVICE CHECKS AND ADJUSTMENTS

Drive Chain

1. The chain should have about 20–30 mm (0.8–1.2 in.) of total up-and-down free-play measured in the middle of the lower chain run.

2. Before checking or adjusting the chain slack, the following conditions should be met:

a. The motorcycle should be placed on the center stand so that the rear wheel is off the ground;

b. The transmission should be placed in neutral;

c. The chain should be clean and well-lubricated;

d. The chain should have been checked for any tight spots by slowly rotating the wheel and checking for variances in the chain tension at different points. If a tight spot exists, the chain tension should be adjusted to the prescribed free-play at the tight spot. Note, however, that such a condition is indicative of a worn chain and probably worn sprockets, which should be replaced as soon as possible.

3. Remove the axle nut cotter pin and loosen the axle nut several turns. Loosen the locknut on each chain adjuster bolt.

4. Turn each of the adjuster bolts in or out by equal amounts until the chain tension is approximately correct.

5. Check wheel alignment by means of the aligning marks inscribed on both sides of the swing arm. Be sure that both adjusters are lined up with the same mark on each side. If not, turn one of the adjuster bolts in or out so that alignment is achieved.

6. Tighten the axle nut and adjuster bolt

Drive chain adjustment alignment marks

nuts and check the chain tension. The chain tension should also be checked with the weight of a rider sitting on the motorcycle when it is off the center stand; the chain should still have at least ½ in. of free-play. Correct if necessary. After adjustment is correct, torque the axle nut to 62–83 ft lbs.

Fit a new cotter pin.

Clutch

1. Cable adjustment must always be maintained at the proper specification. If the cable

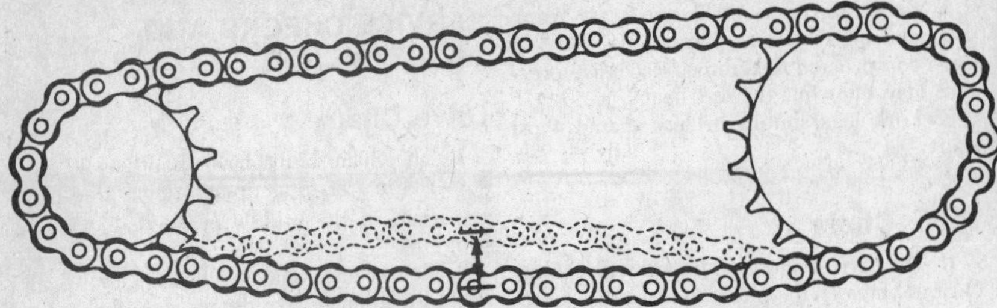

Drive chain free-play is measured at the middle of the lower chain run

has insufficient free-play, the clutch will slip and rapidly burn out. If it has too much play, the clutch will not completely disengage, resulting in hard shifting and creeping at stops.

2. Use the cable adjuster at the handlebar or engine to correct the amount of cable slack. The clutch hand lever should be able to be moved 4 mm (0.16 in.) measured between the lever and the holder before the clutch begins to disengage.

If clutch operation is not satisfactory after making this adjustment, proceed as follows:

3. Screw the cable adjuster at the lever in all the way, increasing cable free-play. Back off the locknut and turn the cable adjuster at the engine in as well.

4. Remove the clutch adjuster cover plate. Loosen the clutch adjusting screw locknut. Back off the adjusting screw 2–3 turns.

5. Turn the adjusting screw clockwise until resistance is felt, then turn it counterclockwise 1/4 turn. Holding the screw in this position, tighten the locknut.

6. Turn the cable adjuster at the engine out until there is about 4 mm (0.16 in.) of free-play in the hand lever. Tighten the locknut on the engine cable adjuster.

7. Make any further fine adjustments with the adjuster at the hand lever.

Clutch cable engine adjuster

Throttle Cables

A dual-cable system is used on all except models with CV carbs. The cables are equipped with adjusters at the twist grip and the linkage.

1. The cable which opens the throttles should have 0.5–1.0 mm (0.02–0.04 in.) of freeplay measured between the end of the cable sheath and the end of the adjuster.

2. The cable which closes the throttles should have zero clearance between the end of the cable and the adjuster.

CV carburetor-equipped models (GS 850GT/GN/GLT) have only a single throttle cable. Adjust it to 0.5–1.0 mm (0.02–0.04 in.) of freeplay.

3. Use the cable adjuster at the handlebar to make and maintain this adjustment. To check that the cable has sufficient slack, start the engine and turn the forks slowly from lock-to-lock. Idle speed must not increase. If it does, it indicates that the cable has insufficient free-play, is incorrectly routed, or is binding at some point.

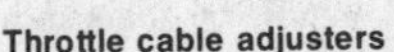

Throttle cable adjusters

Brakes

FRONT

Disc brakes ordinarily need no attention other than a periodic check of the fluid level and pad wear.

1. The fluid level should be between the "Upper" and "Lower" level marks on the see-through master cylinder reservoir. If the level is below the lower level mark, add enough DOT 3 brake fluid to bring it above the mark.

NOTE: *Brake fluid is hydroscopic. It absorbs moisture. Therefore, do not use fluid from an old or unsealed container. Exercise extreme care in handling the brake fluid. It will remove paint on contact. Be sure to tighten the reservoir cap securely.*

NOTE: *The fluid level may drop slightly as the pads wear.*

2. Check brake pad wear and replace the pads as a set if either is worn to the red limit line.

Brake master cylinder reservoir upper and lower fluid level marks

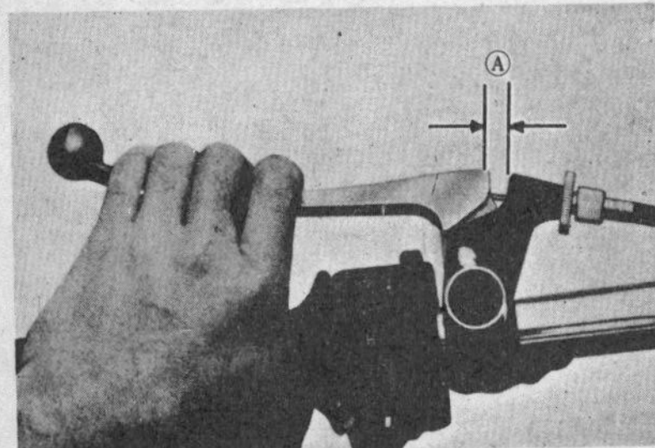

Clutch cable free-play (A) should measure about 4 mm (0.16 in.)

Clutch adjuster locknut (A) and adjusting screw (B)

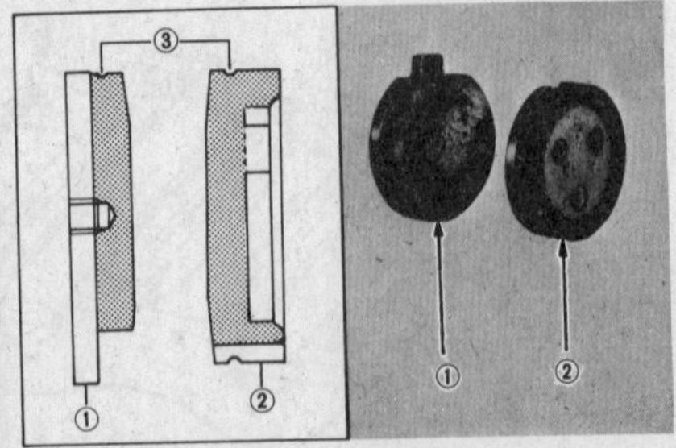

Fixed pad (1) and piston pad (2) should be replaced as a set when worn to the red limit line (3)

3. The front brake lever should have 15–25 mm (0.6–1.0 in.) of travel measured at the tip of the lever. If lever travel is excessive, it is possible that the system needs bleeding.

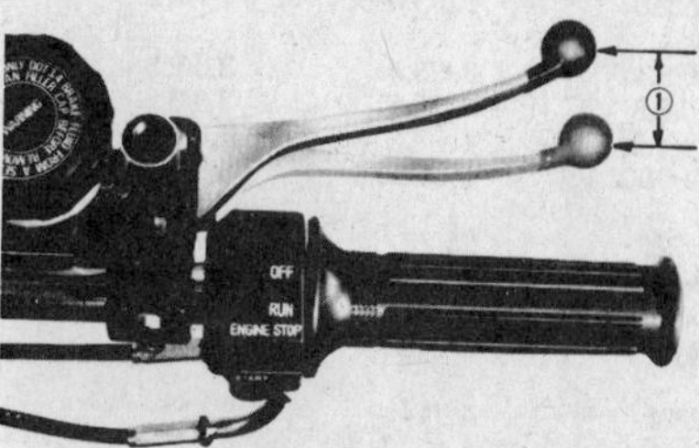

The front brake lever should have 15–25 mm (0.6–1.0 in.) of movement (1)

Rear brake master cylinder fluid level lines

REAR

1. Inspection procedures are virtually the same as for the front brake. Maintain the fluid level between the lines on the master cylinder reservoir.

2. To check pad wear, remove the plastic caliper cover. Pads should be replaced when they are worn to the red-marked stepped portion.

3. To adjust brake pedal height, loosen the locknut on the return stopper bolt on the footpeg bracket. Loosen the brake pushrod locknut. Turn the pushrod until the pedal is about 10 mm (0.4 in.) below the top of the footpeg rubber. Tighten the pushrod locknut. Adjust the clearance between the brake pedal arm and the stopper bolt to 0.5 mm (0.02 in.). Tighten the stopper bolt locknut. Check that the brake pedal has 9–26 mm (0.35–1.0 in.) of free-play.

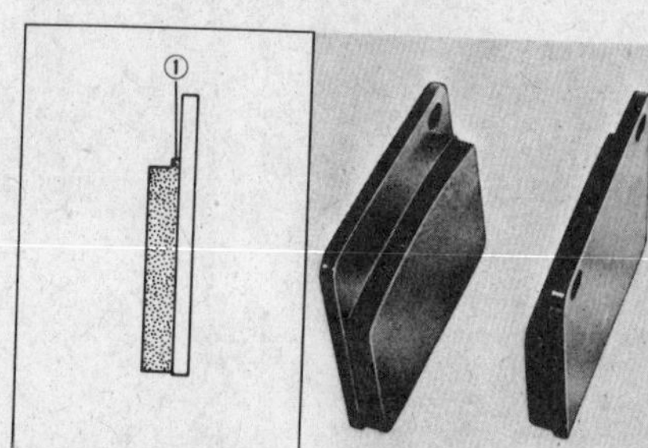

Rear disc brake pads should be replaced when worn to the stepped portion (1)

Brake Light Switches

The switches should be checked for operation after the brakes are adjusted. The rear brake light switch and adjuster nut are mounted on a slotted bracket. The rear switch is adjusted by holding the switch and turning the adjuster nut to effect adjustment. Moving the switch up on the bracket allows the brake light to turn on sooner. Moving it down allows the light to turn on later. Do not turn the switch to effect adjustment as the wires will become twisted and may break.

The front switch is activated by the pressure of the brake fluid in the brake line. This switch is adjusted by loosening the two securing screws and moving the switch body.

Brake pedal free-play should be 9–26 mm (0.35–1.0 in.)

FUEL SYSTEM

Fuel system maintenance involves cleaning the petcock fuel filter screen, cleaning the air filter, and cleaning the carburetors.

The normal service interval is 3,000 miles.

Air Filter

1. Remove the left side cover and the air cleaner box cover.

2. Remove the securing screw and take out the air cleaner element.

3. Remove the two element screws and separate the filter from the element.

4. Wash the filter in gasoline. Squeeze out the excess gas.

NOTE: *Remove the excess gasoline by squeezing the filter. Do not wring it out, as this risks ripping it.*

5. Soak the filter in clean motor oil. Squeeze off the excess.

6. Fit the filter to the element and reinstall.

Carburetors

1. Although major overhaul of the carburetors requires their removal as a unit, the float bowls and jets can be cleaned with the units in place.

2. Drain the fuel from the float bowls.

3. Remove the four securing screws from each float bowl and carefully lower the bowls until they are clear of the floats. It may be helpful to disconnect the overflow tubes before removal.

4. Unscrew the pilot jet. Unscrew and remove the main jet and the main jet holder/emulsion tube. Blow the jets clear, then reinstall. Clean out any residue from the float bowl. When installing, be sure to position the float bowls carefully to avoid damage to the floats. Tighten the screws gradually and evenly. Check for leaks before operating the motorcycle.

Brake pedal return stopper bolt

Brake pushrod locknut

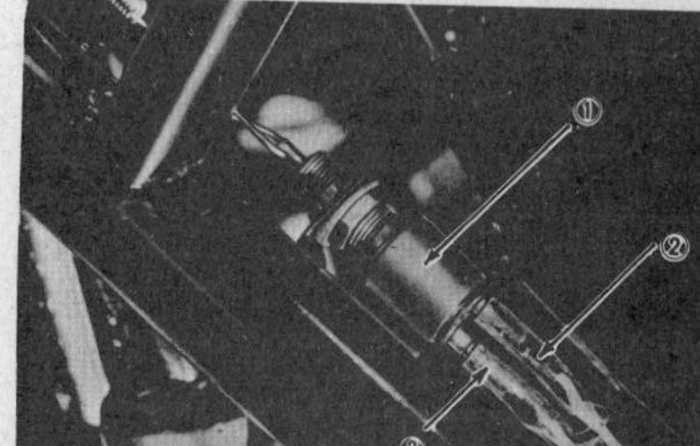

Rear brake light switch (1); white lead (2), amber lead (3)

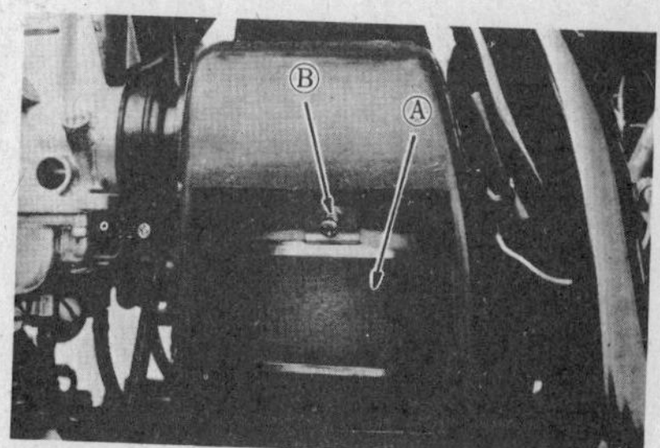

Air cleaner element (A) and securing screw (B)

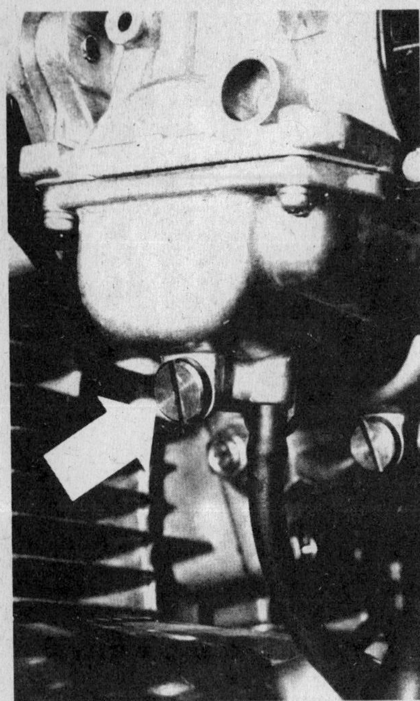

Float bowl drain plug

Maintenance Data

	750/E	750L	850
Fuel capacity (gal/1)	4.8/18	3.4/13	5.8/22
Fuel reserve (gal/1)	0.5/2.0	0.8/3.0	1.1/4.2
Engine oil (qt/1)			
Oil change	3.6/3.4	3.6/3.4	3.0/2.8
Oil and filter change	4.0/3.8	4.0/3.8	3.8/3.6
After rebuilding	4.4/4.2	4.4/4.2	4.0/3.8
Front forks (oz/cc)(each leg)	6.1/180	9.5/280	8.5/250
Tire pressure (psi)			
solo, normal speeds (front/rear)	25/28	25/28	25/28
solo, continuous high speeds (f/r)	28/32	28/32	28/32
two-up, normal speeds (f/r)	25/32	25/32	25/28
two-up, continuous high speeds (f/r)	28/36	28/40	32/40
Battery			
voltage/output (v/ah)	12/14	12/14	12/14
continuous charging rate (amps)	1.4	1.4	1.4
Oil pressure (psi)			
warm engine @ 3000 rpm	1.42	1.42	1.42

Recommended Lubricants

Engine
- General, all temperature: SAE 10W-40, service rating "SE" or "SF"
- Above 14° F (−10° C): SAE 20W-50, service rating "SE" or "SF"
- Above −4° F (−20° C): SAE 10W-50, service rating "SE" or "SF"
- Between −4° F (−10° C) and 86° F (30°C): SAE 10W-30, service rating "SE" or "SF"

Front forks (750)
- ATF/SAE 10W-30 motor oil, 50-50 mixture

Front forks (850)
- SAE 10W-20 oil

Disc brake systems
- DOT 3 or DOT 4 standard disc brake fluid

Control cables
- Light motor oil
- Graphite-based lubricant
- Molybdenum-disulphide-based lubricant

Tach, speedometer cables; throttle twist-grip
- Light duty grease

Wheel and steering head bearings
- Waterproof, medium-weight bearing grease

Grease fittings
- Waterproof, medium-weight chassis grease

Drive chain
- SAE 90W oil
- SAE 80W oil

Gear boxes
- SAE 90 EP gear oil

Periodic Maintenance Intervals①

Before each ride
- Safety items
- Operation of lights
- Chain adjustment
- Control cable adjustment
- Brake operation
- Engine oil level

Weekly
- Tire pressure (check when cold)
- Battery electrolyte level

Every 750 miles
- Lubricate drive chain

Every 1,500 miles/3 months
- Change engine oil

Every 3,000 miles/6 months
- Change oil filter
- Lubricate controls and cables
- Lubricate contact breaker cam felt pad
- Clean air filter
- Adjust carburetors
- Check timing
- Clean and gap spark plugs
- Adjust clutch
- Check compression
- Check oil pressure
- Check tappet clearances
- Check disc brake fluid level
- Check brake pads for wear
- Check tightness of critical nuts and bolts
- Check condition of chain and sprockets
- Check condition of fuel lines
- Check spokes for tightness
- Check swing arm bushings
- Check steering stem bearings

Every 6,000 miles/12 months
- Change front fork oil (750)
- Clean sump oil filter screen
- Grease twist-grip housing

Every 12,000 miles/24 months
- Replace all fuel lines
- Replace brake lines and fluid
- Replace master cylinder internals
- Replace caliper internals
- Repack wheel bearings
- Repack speedometer drive housing
- Grease swing arm
- Grease steering stem bearings

① Based on normal usage after break-in and initial service are completed.

TUNE-UP

NOTE: *Common tune-up procedures are explained in detail in the "General Information" section at the end of the manual.*

COMPRESSION TEST

1. A compression check should be made before each tune-up since this will provide a general idea of engine condition.
2. It is necessary to have a gauge with a flexible hose and the proper screw-in adapter (plug holes are 14 mm).
3. The engine should be at operating temperature when checking compression.
4. Remove all of the spark plugs and fit the gauge to one of the plug holes.
5. Close the choke and hold the throttle wide open while spinning the engine with the starter motor. Note the compression reading and repeat the test with the remaining cylinders.
6. Compression may vary according to gauge tolerance and several other factors. However, it should normally be between 128 and 171 psi. All cylinders must be within 15 psi of this range and of each other.

CAM CHAIN TENSIONER

The cam chain tension is maintained automatically, and no routine adjustments are necessary once the tensioner has been set correctly.

To check tensioner operation, refer to "Cam Chain Tensioner" under the "Top End" section of "Engine and Transmission."

VALVE ADJUSTMENT

Checking Valve Clearance

NOTE: *Valve clearance must be checked when the engine is cold.*

1. Remove the gas tank, the cylinder head cover, and the points cover.
2. Valve clearance is checked by inserting a feeler gauge blade between the cam lobe and the tappet shim. To do this, the cam lobes must be properly positioned or the measured clearance will be inaccurate. Refer to the illustration showing proper cam lobe positions.
3. Correct valve clearance is 0.03–0.08 mm (0.0012–0.0032 in.) for both intake and exhaust valves. The clearance is correct if a feeler gauge blade in this range is a light drag fit between the cam lobe and tappet shim.
4. Use a 17 mm wrench on the special crankshaft nut to turn the engine over (in the normal direction of rotation-clockwise as seen from the right side) until the exhaust cam for the No. 1 (left) cylinder is in the position indicated. Check the valve clearance for the exhaust valves at cylinders Nos. 1 and 2.

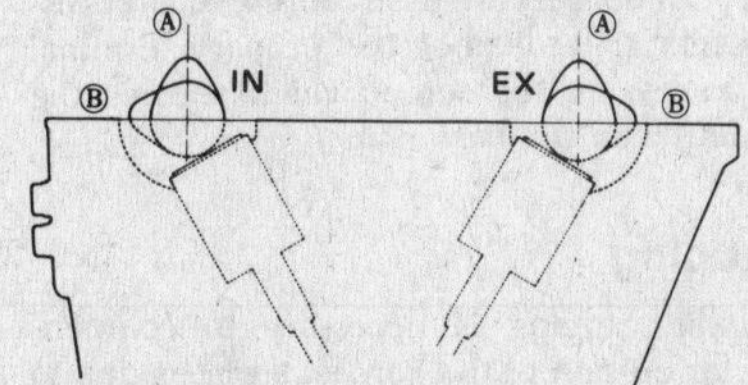

Camshaft lobe locations (A or B) when checking valve clearance

Rotating the engine in the normal direction of rotation

Exhaust lobe cam for No. 1 cylinder in position for checking clearance

Checking valve clearance

Rotate the engine 180°

Intake cam lobe for No. 1 cylinder in position for checking clearance

5. After checking the clearance at the exhaust valves for cylinders Nos. 1 and 2, turn the crankshaft 180° again in the normal direction of rotation until the *intake* cam lobe of the No. 1 cylinder is at the position illustrated.

Exhaust cam lobe for No. 4 cylinder in position for checking clearance

Intake cam lobe for No. 4 cylinder in position for checking clearance

Check the valve clearance of the intake valves for cylinders Nos. 1 and 2.

6. Turn the crankshaft 180° again in the normal direction of rotation until the exhaust cam lobe of cylinder No. 4 is at the position illustrated. Check the clearance of the exhaust valves of cylinders Nos. 3 and 4.
7. Turn the crankshaft an additional 180° until the intake cam lobe of the No. 4 cylinder is positioned as illustrated. Check the valve clearance of cylinders Nos. 3 and 4.

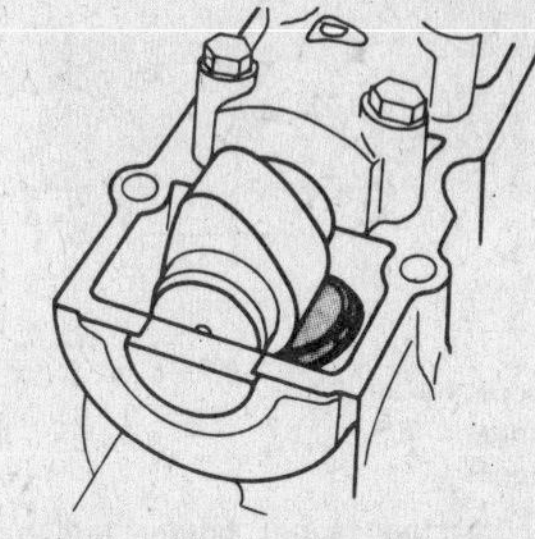

Valve clearance shim and tappet notch

Adjusting Valve Clearance

1. Adjustments to the valve clearances, if necessary, are made by replacing existing tappet shims with new ones of varying thicknesses. A special tool is necessary to hold down the tappet to remove the old shim and install the new one. In addition, a micrometer may be helpful.
2. If the valve clearance is not within the proper range when checking it as outlined above, continue slipping feeler gauges between the cam lobe and shim until the actual clearance is determined. The feeler gauge blade will be a light drag when pulled through. Record the actual clearance.
3. To remove the shims, first rotate the tappet with your fingers until the notch is accessible. Use the special tool to depress the

tappet and remove the shim with a pair of forceps.

NOTE: *Be sure that the special tool is correctly installed. It must have a firm purchase of the tappet. Refer to the illustration.*

Depressing the tappet with the special tool

4. Note the thickness of the removed shim which is marked on it. "265," for example, indicates a thickness of 2.65 mm.

It is possible to use the marked thickness on the shim to calculate valve clearance provided that the shim in question is not worn. It is more accurate, however, to measure the thickness of the removed shim with a micrometer to be sure. Referring back to the actual measured clearance (Step 2, above), calculate the necessary shim thickness which will bring the valve clearance into the proper range.

The proper shim thickness is arrived at by subtracting the specified clearance from the actual measured clearance and adding or subtracting this number to the thickness of the removed shim.

If, for example, the actual measured valve clearance was 0.10 mm, shim thickness must be increased by at least 0.02 mm to bring the clearance back to the maximum allowable figure of 0.08 mm. If the thickness of the removed shim was 2.50 mm, the new shim must be at least 2.50 + 0.02 = 2.52 mm. The closest shim to this size is 2.55 mm, and this shim, when fitted, will bring the valve clearance into the specified range.

NOTE: *Shims are available in increments of 0.05 mm from 2.15 mm to 3.10 mm.*

If the measure clearance is too small, a thinner shim must be fitted. If, or example, the measure clearance is 0.01 mm, shim thickness must be decreased by at least 0.02 mm to bring the clearance to within specification. If the fitted shim in this instance is 2.75 mm thick, the new shim must be 2.75 − 0.02 = 2.73. The closest available shim is 2.70, and this will give a clearance which is within the tolerance range.

5. After calculating the clearance change necessary and finding the correct replacement shim, install the new shim and recheck the clearance.

NOTE: *Lightly lubricate the new shim with motor oil on both sides before fitting it and checking the clearance. Install the new shim with the thickness number facing the tappet.*

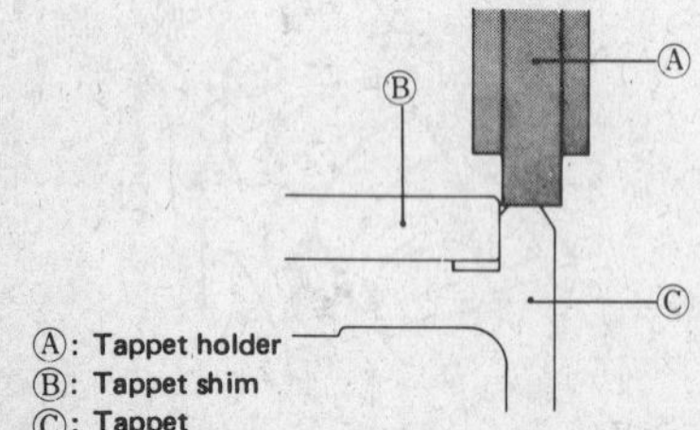

Be sure that the tappet holder tool has firm purchase on the tappet: tappet holder (A), shim (B), tappet (C)

Removing an adjusting shim

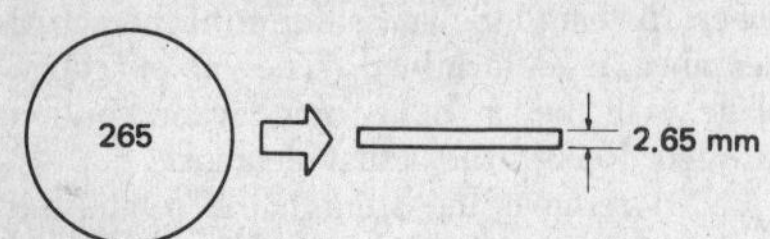

Thickness of the shims is marked on them

Tappet Shim Size Chart

No.	Thickness (mm)	Part No.
1	2.15	12892-45000
2	2.20	12892-45001
3	2.25	12892-45002
4	2.30	12892-45003
5	2.35	12892-45004
6	2.40	12892-45005
7	2.45	12892-45006
8	2.50	12892-45007
9	2.55	12892-45008
10	2.60	12892-45009
11	2.65	12892-45010
12	2.70	12892-45011
13	2.75	12892-45012
14	2.80	12892-45013
15	2.85	12892-45014
16	2.90	12892-45015
17	2.95	12892-45016
18	3.00	12892-45017
19	3.05	12892-45018
20	3.10	12892-45019

To Calculate Shim Size

Clearance Too Tight	
Required clearance	0.03–0.08 mm
Measured clearance	
Difference	
Old shim thickness	
−Difference	
New shim thickness	

Clearance too Loose	
Measured clearance	
Required clearance	0.03–0.08 mm
Difference	
Old shim thickness	
+Difference	
New shim thickness	

CONTACT BREAKER POINTS

Location

The points and condensers are located on the right end of the crankshaft beneath the points cover. The timing advance mechanism is fitted onto the crankshaft behind the breaker point base plate.

Replacement

1. Points sets are available complete with condensers already mounted on the breaker plate. Removal is accomplished by disconnecting the primary wires and removing the three screws which mount the breaker plate to the engine. It is of course necessary to reset the ignition timing after the new breaker plate is installed.

2. If the points are purchased separately, disconnect the primary wire at each point set, remove the securing screw, and remove the old points. When installing new points, note that the proper installation of the insulating washers at the primary terminal is critical. If improperly installed, no spark will occur. There is a small insulating tube which fits around the terminal bolt and two insulating washers, one immediately on either side of the terminal bracket. All connectors (condenser, primary wire, points spring) are made on the outersides of these washers (i.e., no connector must touch the bracket, which is a ground).

3. New points may have a protective coating on the contact surfaces to prevent oxidation. Clean off these surfaces with a non-oily solvent before attempting to start the machine.

4. If the motorcycle will not start immediately after installation of new points, check that the primary wire connections are tight, that the insulating washers at the primary terminal are properly installed, and that the contact surfaces are thoroughly cleaned.

5. Condensers are easily replaced after disconnecting the lead at the primary terminal and removing the screw which secures the condenser to the base plate.

Gapping

Periodic gapping is necessary to compensate for erosion of the contact surfaces due to electrical arcing and for wear of the fiber heel. As the heel wears, the points will open later relative to the rotation of the crankshaft, thus retarding the timing slightly.

Points should be filed (if necessary) and cleaned before gapping.

1. Remove the points cover.
2. Using the special nut, turn the engine over until one of the two sets of points is fully open.
3. With the proper feeler gauge blade, check the gap. The proper specification is 0.35 mm (0.018 in.), and the blade should be a slip fit between the points if the gap is correct.
4. If adjustment is necessary, loosen the screw which secures the point set to its plate,

Point gap (A) is adjusted after loosening the screw (arrow)

and use a small screwdriver at the pry point provided to adjust the gap.

CAUTION: *Loosen the screw just enough to allow the points to be moved. If loosened too much, the points will snap shut instead of holding the gap.*

5. Tighten the screw and recheck the gap. It may change slightly when the screw is tightened.
6. Repeat the procedure with the remaining points set. Try to adjust both sets so that the feeler gauge blade has the same "feel" in both sets. This will help to ensure accurate timing.
7. If it is not possible to gap the points correctly, the fiber heel is evidently worn; the points should then be replaced.

Lubrication

1. It is necessary to occasionally lubricate the cam follower fiber heel and the pivot point of the contact breakers. This minimizes wear and ensures that the timing will remain accurate for a longer period. A worn heel will retard the timing.
2. A small dab of grease (high melting point, if possible) should be applied to the lubricator wick so that the lubricator can distribute it onto the breaker cam. A drop of engine oil should be applied to the pivot points.
3. In both cases it is imperative that care be taken to keep the libricant away from the points contact surface.
4. The lubricating wick should be adjusted so that it just contacts the breaker cam.
5. This lubrication should be carried out every 3,000 miles.

IGNITION TIMING

Transistorized Ignition

GS 850GT/GLT models are equipped with a solid-state ignition system which requires no maintenance or periodic inspection.

Timing marks: A, top dead center; B, fixed advance firing point; C, full advance firing point

Breaker Point Ignition

DYNAMIC TIMING

1. Clean and gap both sets of points as described previously.
2. Hook up the strobe light according to the directions of the light's manufacturer to pick up the impulses from the No. 1 (left outside) cylinder.
3. Start the engine and adjust the idle, if necessary, to the recommended idle speed (1000 rpm).
4. Aim the light at the timing marks visible through the inspection hole in the points base plate. At idle, the "F" mark should align with the timing index mark.
5. To check ignition timing at full advance, increase the engine speed until the motor is turning 2,500–3,000 rpm. At this point, the timing index mark should be aligned with the full advance mark scribed into the timing advance mechanism.
6. If adjustment is necessary, carefully loosen the three base plate screws and rotate the plate so that the proper marks align at the specified rpm. Establishing this alignment at full advance is recommended. Tighten the base plate screws.
7. Repeat the procedure, this time having the strobe light pick up cylinder No. 2. If adjustment is necessary, loosen the two screws which secure points set 2.3 to its plate, and

The "F" mark should align with the timing mark (B) at idle

The full-advance firing mark (C) should align with the timing mark (D) above 2500 rpm

Timing for cylinders 1 & 4 is adjusted by loosening the three screws (E) and rotating the breaker plate

Timing for cylinders 2 & 3 is adjusted by loosening the two screws (A) and moving plate (B)

use a small screwdriver at the pry point provided to move the set so that proper mark alignment is achieved. Tighten the screws.

8. If it is not possible to acieve full advance alignment without moving the base plate or points set 2.3 all the way to the end of their range of allowable travel, it is possible that the points are either incorrectly gapped, or that they are worn to the point where they must be replaced.

STATIC TIMING

1. Connect one of the test light or tester leads to the primary wire terminal for the points set "1.4." Ground the other lead to the engine.
2. If the test device is not self-powered, turn the ignition switch *on* and be sure the kill switch is in the "on" position as well.
3. Turn the engine over in the normal direction of rotation until the "F" mark for cylinders 1 and 4 align with the timing index mark. The test instrument should react at the instant these marks align, indicating that the points have opened. If they do not, loosen the three base plate screws and rotate the base plate so that the points just open when these timing marks are in alignment. Moving the base plate clockwise will retard the timing; counterclockwise will advance it.

Cylinders 1 and 4 are now correctly timed. Tighten the base plate screws and recheck.

4. Repeat the procedure with points set 2.3. If adjustment is necessary, loosen the two screws which secure these points to their mounting plate and use a small screwdriver at the pry point provided. Tighten the screws and recheck the timing.

CARBURETORS

Carburetor adjustments to be made during a tune-up procedures include checking the float level, setting the idle mixture, idle speed, and carburetor synchronization.

All models except the GS 850GT/GLT use Mikuni VM26SS carburetors which are standard throttle-slide types. The GT/GLTs use BS32SS constant velocity (CV) units. Working procedures and specifications are therefore different.

Also, pilot screws on 1978 and later machines are pre-set and need no adjustment. This to meet clean air requirements.

Adjusting Float Level

1. Float level is a measure of the amount of gasoline which will be in the float bowls during operation. While it is a critical specification, it will not normally need readjustment once properly set. Float level, therefore, need not be checked at every tune-up, but should be attended to from time to time.

2. A special gauge is available which allows the float level to be checked with the carburetors still on the motorcycle.

3. Remove the float bowl drain plug and install the gauge. Turn the petcock to the "Prime" position to refill the bowl, then turn it back to "On." Start the engine and allow it to idle at 1000–1100 rpm.

4. Hold the gauge line up against the carburetor body to check the float level. The level should be 2.5–3.5 mm (0.10–0.14 in.) on GS 750/E models, 3.0–4.0 mm (0.12–0.16 in.) on GS 750L and GS 850G/GL/GN, and 4.5–5.5 mm (0.18–0.22 in.) for the GS 850GT/GLT.

This is the distance between the fuel level in the gauge and the float bowl mating surface as shown in the illustration. If float level is not correct, proceed as follows.

5. Remove the carburetors as a unit. Remove the float bowl and the float bowl gasket.

6. With a vernier caliper, measure the distance from the float bowl mating surface to the top of the float. Float heights are as follows:

GS 750/E	25–27 mm (0.98–1.1 in.)
GS 750L, GS 850G/GL/GN	23–25 mm (0.91–0.98 in.)
GS 850GT/GLT	21.4–23.4 mm (0.84–0.92 in.)

Checking float level (A)

Measuring float height (H)

Increase float height by bending the tang towards (B); decrease it by bending towards (A)

If float height is not within this range, push out the float pin to remove the float. Bend the float tang in the desired direction to raise or lower the float level. Bending the tang away from the carburetor body raises the fuel level; bending it towards the carburetor body lowers the fuel level.

Throttle slide locknut (A)

Idle Mixture and Idle Speed

1. These adjustments must be made with the engine at operating temperature.

2. Turn each pilot air screw in until it is lightly seated, then back them out 1¼ turns on 1977 models. On 1978 and later machines the pilot screw is preset and djustment is not necessary.

3. Adjust the idle speed to 1,000 rpm using the throttle stop screw.

Synchronization (VM26SS)

1. A set of vacuum gauges are necessary to synchronize the carburetors.

2. Use longer fuel lines and raise the gas tank sufficiently so that the carburetor caps can be removed.

3. Remove the carburetor caps.

4. Install the vacuum gauges.

5. Start the engine and set it to run at about 1,500 rpm.

6. Note the vacuum gauge readings. Equalize the readings of all four carburetors by loosening the throttle slide locknuts and turning the adjusting screws to raise or lower the slides.

7. Readjust the idle speed to 1,000 rpm and adjust the throttle cables.

Synchronization (BS32SS)

Synchronization of the BS32SS units found on the GS 850GT/GLT is basically the same as outlined above for the VM26SS carbs. The throttle valve adjusters, however, are between the carburetors rather than beneath the carb tops. Delete Step 3.

Pilot air screw (arrow)

Throttle stop screw

Vacuum gauge fitting on manifold

Carburetor synchronizing screws (GT/GLT)

There are three valve adjusting screws (see illustration). Loosen the locknut before attempting adjustment. The screws ("B," "A," and "C" in the illustration) adjust carburetors 1, 2, and 4 respectively.

Tune-Up Specifications

	GS 750/E	GS 750L, GS 850G/GL/GN	GS 850GT/GLT
Compression			
Cranking pressure (psi)	128–171	128–171	128–171
Max allowable variation (psi)	15	15	15
Valve Clearance			
Intake (mm/in.)	0.03–0.08/ 0.0012–0.0032	0.03–0.08/ 0.0012–0.0032	0.03–0.08/ 0.0012–0.0032
Exhaust (mm/in.)	0.03–0.08/ 0.0012–0.0032	0.03–0.08/ 0.0012–0.0032	0.03–0.08/ 0.0012–0.0032
Ignition			
Spark plugs			
OEM	NKG/ND	NGK/ND	NGK/ND
Standard	B-8ES/W24ES-U	B-8ES/W24ES-U	B-8ES/W24ES-U
Cold	B-9ES/W27E	B-9ES/W27E	B-9ES/W27E
Hot	B-7ES/W22ES	B-7ES/W22ES	B-7ES/W22ES
Spark plug gap (mm/in.)	0.6–0.7/ 0.024–0.028	0.6–0.8/ 0.024–0.032	0.6–0.8/ 0.024–0.032
Point gap	0.3–0.4/ 0.012–0.016	0.3–0.4/ 0.012–0.016	0.3–0.4/ 0.012–0.016
Ignition timing			
Static (degrees BTDC)17	17	17	17
Max (degrees BTDC @ 2500 rpm)	37	37	37
Carburetion			
Idle speed (rpm)	1000	1000	1000
Pilot Screw (turns out)	1	preset	preset
Float height (mm/in.)	25–27/ 0.98–1.1	23–25/ 0.91–0.98	21.4–23.4/ 0.84–0.92

① 1977: 1¼
Later models: preset

ENGINE AND TRANSMISSION

NOTE: *For engine component inspection techniques and procedures, refer to "Engine Rebuilding" in the General Information section.*

ENGINE REMOVAL AND INSTALLATION

GS 750

1. Drain the oil.
2. Remove the gas tank.
3. Disconnect the battery negative terminal.
4. Remove the left side cover. Disconnect the alternator leads, the starter solenoid negative terminal, and the points wires.
5. Disconnect the spark plug wires from the plugs.
6. Remove the air cleaner box. Remove the carburetors.
7. Disconnect the tachometer cable from the cylinder head.
8. Remove the exhaust header pipes.

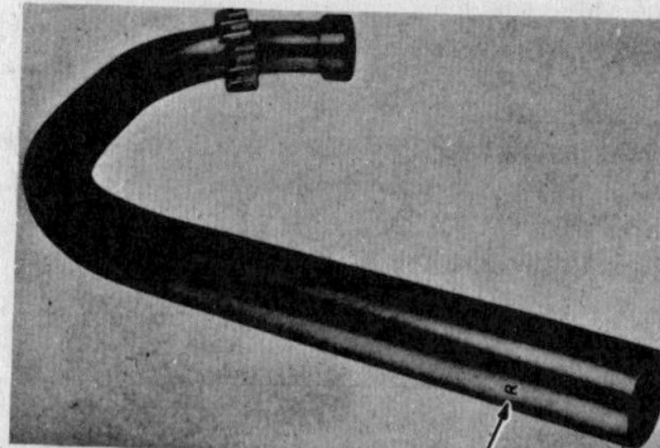

Exhaust header pipes have their locations marked

9. Remove the left-side rider's footpeg.
10. Remove the clutch adjuster cover. Remove the screws which secure the sprocket cover and take off the cover.
11. Remove the engine sprocket.
12. Remove the right-side rider's footpeg. Remove the rear brake lever.
13. Remove the engine mounting bolts. Take the engine out from the right side of the frame.
14. Installation is the reverse of removal. Tighten the long bolts to 29 ft lbs and the short bolts to 14.5 ft lbs.
15. Be sure all hoses and wires are correctly routed and clamped where applicable.

Unbolting the cam chain idler

16. When installing the exhaust header pipes, note that their proper positions are indicated by a stamped letter near the end of each pipe. "L" is for the No. 1 cylinder, "C" for cylinders Nos. 2 and 3, and "R" for No. 4.
17. After installation, check the oil level, drive chain tension, and throttle cable adjustments before starting the engine.

GS 850

1. Drain the oil from the crankcase.
2. Remove the gear shift lever and the secondary drive box cover. Remove the drive box drain plug.
3. With the fuel petcock lever turned to "On" or "Res," disconnect the lines from the petcock. Disconnect the fuel sensor wire at the lower left side of the gas tank. Remove the tank securing bolt and take off the gas tank.
4. Disconnect the intake pipe from the breather cover.
5. Remove the side covers. Disconnect the battery leads. Disconnect the alternator wires, starter relay negative terminal, breaker point or ignition unit wires, neutral switch, gear position, oil pressure gauge wires and spark plug leads.
6. Remove the air cleaner box.
7. Remove the carburetors.
8. Loosen the drive shaft boot clamp and move the boot towards the rear. Remove the four bolts securing the universal joint and the drive shaft.
9. Remove the brake pedal and the right side footpeg.
10. Remove the exhaust system.
11. Remove the horn.
12. Disconnect the clutch and tachometer cables.
13. Remove the engine breather cover.
14. Support the engine with a jack and remove the engine mounting bolts and nuts. Remove the engine from the right side of the frame.
15. Installation is the reverse of removal. Note the following points.
16. Tighten 10 mm mounting bolts to 26 ft. lbs., and 8 mm bolts to 18 ft. lbs.

17. Use thread locking compound on the drive shaft bolts, and tighten them to 18–22 ft. lbs.

18. Secure exhaust pipe bolts to 7–10 ft. lbs., and muffler bolts to 13–20 ft. lbs.

19. Check all levels and cable adjustments before starting the engine.

TOP END

Cylinder Head Removal

1. It is possible to remove the cylinder head with the engine still in the frame provided that the gas tank, exhaust header pipes, air cleaner box, carburetors, and related cables and wires are removed or disconnected.

2. Remove the cylinder head cover.

3. Remove the cam chain adjuster by first loosening the adjuster screw locknut, tightening the adjuster screw, then removing the three cam chain adjuster mounting bolts.

4. Unbolt and remove the cam chain idler between the cam sprockets (four bolts).

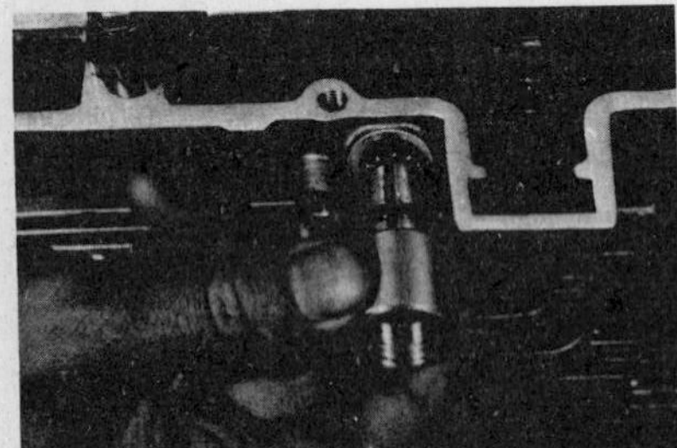

Removing the tach drive stopper

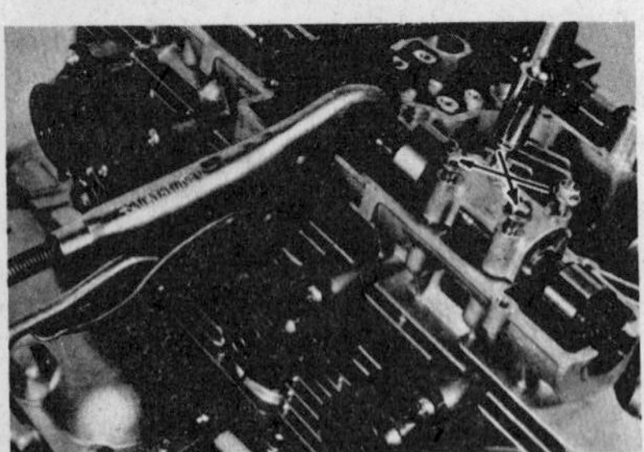

Clamp the cam securely before removing the bearing caps

5. Remove the tachometer drive gear stopper screw, the stopper itself, and pull out the drive gear.

6. Clamp one of the camshafts securely in place using a vise-grip pliers or the like. Be sure to keep the jaws of the pliers clear of the cam lobes.

7. Remove the four bolts which secure each of the two cam bearing caps. These bolts should be loosened gradually and in a cross pattern.

8. Remove the vise-grip pliers. Remove the cam bearing caps. Remove the camshaft. Repeat the procedure with the remaining camshaft. Loop a length of wire around the cam chain and secure it to keep the chain from falling down into the crankcase.

9. To remove the cylinder head, first remove the adjustment shims from each valve. Mark them so that they can be reinstalled in their original locations. Valve adjustment must be checked upon assembly at any rate. Remove the two 6 mm set bolts, one at each side. Then remove the twelve 8 mm nuts. These nuts must be loosened gradually and in a cross-pattern beginning with the centermost nuts. After all the nuts have been removed, lift off the cylinder head, striking it carefully at the sides with a plastic mallet if it is struck.

10. Remove the tappet from each valve. Mark their locations.

Cylinder and Piston Removal

1. Remove the cylinder head as outlined above.

2. Grasp the cylinder block and move it straight up until it is clear of the studs. If the block is stuck, strike it carefully at the sides with a plastic mallet, but watch that no damage is done to the fins.

3. Mark the location of each piston before removal using a felt-tip marker or suitable substitute. Remove the piston wrist pin circlips and disgard them, new ones being required on assembly.

CAUTION: *Do not allow the circlips to fall into the crankcase. To avoid having to split the cases to retrieve a clip, cover the crankcase openings with a cloth.*

4. Press out the wrist pins with the special tool. Alternately, the pins can be removed by gently heating the piston crown and pushing the pin out with a suitable drift. Be sure to support the piston with one hand while doing this. Push the pin out with steady pressure. Never strike the pin in an attempt to remove it. This risks bending the connecting rod.

5. Remove the cylinder base gasket.

Inspection

CAMSHAFTS

1. Check the dam lobes for scoring or other imperfections. The lobes must be perfectly smooth. Replace the cam(s) if any damage is visible.

2. Use a micrometer to measure the height of each cam lobe and compare the readings against the following specifications:

750

Valve	Standard	Serviceable Limit
Intake	36.265–36.295 mm/ 1.4278–1.4289 in.	36.15 mm/ 1.4232 in.
Exhaust	35.735–35.765 mm/ 1.4069–1.4081 in.	35.60 mm/ 1.4016 in.

850

Valve	Standard	Serviceable Limit
Intake	36.320–36.360 mm/ 1.4299–1.4315 in.	36.02 mm/ 1.4181 in.
Exhaust	35.770–35.810 mm/ 1.4083–1.4098 in.	35.47 mm/ 1.3965 in.

3. Inspect the cam journal bearings for scratches or imperfections.

4. Bearing clearance is most easily checked with Plastigage®. Be sure that the cam bearing caps are properly installed (align the arrows on the caps and head) and are torqued to 7.0 ft lbs. Standard bearing clearance is 0.020–0.054 mm (0.0008–0.0021 in.) and the serviceable limit is 0.15 mm (0.0059 in.).

5. Check the run-out of each camshaft by mounting each one in a set of v-blocks and measuring the run-out in the center with a dial indicator. Standard run-out is 0.03 mm (0.0012 in.), while the serviceable limit is 0.1 mm (0.0039 in.).

CAM CHAIN TENSIONER

1. Check that the pushrod is free to move in and out. If it sticks or binds, replace the tensioner.

CYLINDER HEAD

1. Clean any traces of head gasket material from the cylinder head mating surface. Place a straight edge across the mating surface and check for warpage by attempting to slip feeler gauge blades between the head and straight edge. Standard head warpage is about 0.03 mm (0.0012 in.) while the serviceable limit is 0.25 mm (0.0098 in.). If the head is warped beyond this point, flatness should be restored by having the head milled.

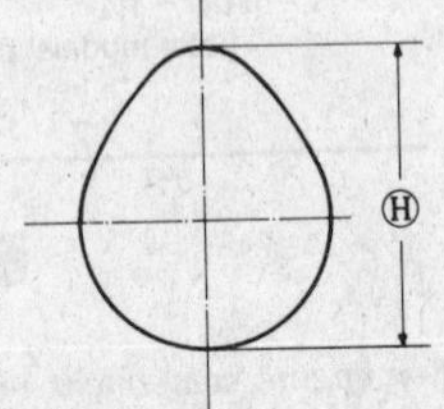

Cam lobe height (H)

Checking the cam chain tensioner pushrod for free movement

2. Use a wire brush fitting on a power drill to decarbonize the combustion chambers. The valves should be left in place as this is done, as it minimizes the chance of causing damage to the valve seats.

VALVE ASSEMBLY

Before removing the valves, check their sealing ability by pouring a small quantity of gasoline into each port and allowing the head to sit for about five minutes. If the valves are properly seating, leakage into the combustion chamber will be minimal.

1. To remove the valves, and install them properly, a suitable C-clamp is necessary. Compress the valve springs and remove the split collars, retainers, springs, seals, and spring seats. Inspect the valves, guides,

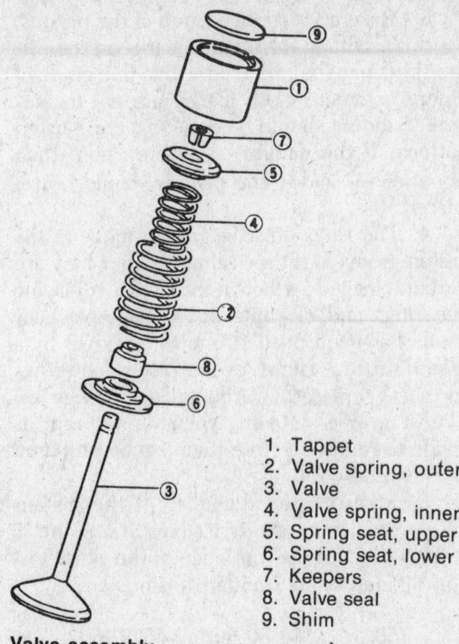

Valve assembly

springs, and valve seats in the following manner. Keep each assembly separate so that every piece can be installed in its original location. New valve seals must always be used on assembly.

2. If considerable mileage has been covered, the valve springs should be replaced as a matter of course. Always replace valve springs as a set.

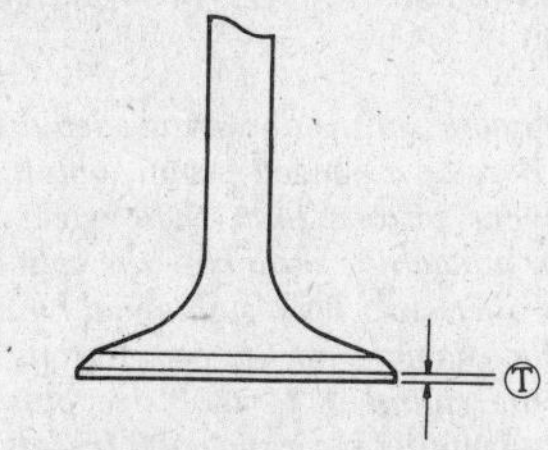

Valve face thickness (T)

Measure the free-length of each valve spring and compare the reading to the following specifications.

Inner springs have a standard free-length of 35.3–37.0 mm (1.39–1.46 in.) and a serviceable limit of 33.8 mm (1.33 in.)

Outer springs have a standard free-length of 43.0–43.3 mm (1.69–1.70 in.) and a serviceable limit of 41.5 mm (1.63 in.).

Replace the springs if any is compressed more than the serviceable limit.

3. Each valve must be free to move up and down in its guide with little resistance. Any sticking or binding as the valve is moved in the guide will indicate that the valve stem or guide is in poor condition.

4. Inspect the valve, paying close attention to the edges of the valve head for pitting, burnt or broken edges, excessive carbon build-up, etc. A certain amount of carbon and lead deposits on the valve face and the top of the exhaust valve are inevitable. Heavy deposits should be carefully scraped off with a dull knife, or a wire wheel, and the valve finished up with very fine emery cloth.

Do not touch the valve seating area during these operations.

If the valve has burnt or broken edges, it must be replaced.

5. Check the thickness of the valve face as shown in the accompanying illustration. Standard thickness is 0.8–1.2 mm (0.0315–0.0472 in.). The valve should be replaced if thickness is less than 0.5 mm (0.0197 in.).

6. Carbon deposits should not extend too far up along the valve stem. This would indicate a worn or cracked valve guide.

7. Wet, oily deposits on the back of the valve head is indicative of a worn guide or bad seal. Less severe wear to these components show up as brown oil stains on the valve stem.

8. Holding a valve in your fingers, spin it while observing the head. A wobble is indicative of a bent valve. If a dial gauge is available, check the run-out of the head. Replace the valve if run-out exceeds 0.05 mm (0.002 in.). Run-out is the total indicated dial gauge reading.

Checking valve-to-guide clearance

Attempt to rotate the valve by hand when it is fully inserted into the guide. If the valve will not rotate easily, or if it sticks as it is turned, it is probably bent.

9. Check the valve-to-guide clearance. To do this, insert each valve into its guide, hold it about ½ in. off its seat, and check allowable movement in two directions with the aid of a dial indicator.

For the intake valves, standard clearance is 0.02–0.05 mm (0.0008–0.0019 in.) and the serviceable limit is 0.09 mm (0.0035 in.).

For the exhaust valves, standard clearance is 0.03–0.06 mm (0.0012–0.0024 in.) and the serviceable limit is 0.10 mm (0.0039 in.).

If the clearance exceeds the serviceable limit, the valve stems should be checked for wear (Step 10). If they are within the serviceable limits. The valve guides must be replaced.

10. Measure the diameter of the valve stem at three places along its length.

For intake valves, the standard diameter is 6.965–6.980 mm (0.2742–0.2748 in.). The valve must be replaced if the measured diameter is less than 6.90 mm (0.2716 in.).

For the exhaust valves, the standard diameter is 6.955–6.970 mm (0.2738–0.2744 in.). The valve must be replaced if the measured diameter is less than 6.805 mm (0.2679 in.).

A quick check of the operational worthiness of a valve and guide can be accomplished by dipping the valve stem in oil and inserting it into its guide. Place a finger over the other end of the guide. Pull the valve a little way out of the guide and release it. The valve should be drawn back into the guide by suction if the components are in serviceable condition.

11. Guides can be removed with a suitable drift. Heating the head in an oven beforehand will facilitate removal. After a guide is removed, the guide hole should be reamed with a 12.2 mm reamer.

12. Valve guides should be installed with the head at room temperature. Oiling the guide hole and guide will facilitate installation. Be certain that the guide is fully seated.

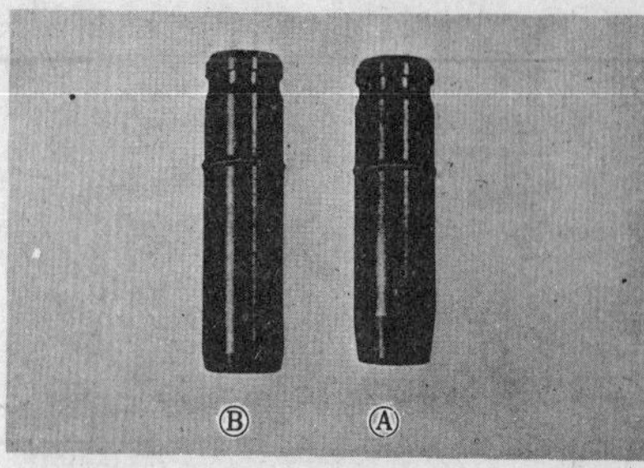

Intake guides (A) and exhaust guides (B) are not interchangeable

Reaming a valve guide

NOTE: *Exhaust and intake guides are different. The intake guides have a more pronounced bevel at the lower end.*

13. After installation, the guide should be reamed with a 7 mm reamer. Clean the inside of the guide thoroughly after this operation.

14. After installing a new guide, the valve seat should be recut and the valve lapped in.

15. Valve seat width should be checked with red lead. Coat the valve seating area on the head with the red lead, than install the valve, rotating it back and forth. Inspect the seating area on the valve. The seating area should be 1.0–1.2 mm (0.04–0.05 in.) all the way around the valve. If the seating area is greater than 1.5 mm (0.06 in.), or is uneven, the valve seat in the head must be recut. Refer to "Valve Seat Service," below.

16. Installation of the valve assembly is the reverse of removal. Note than the upper and

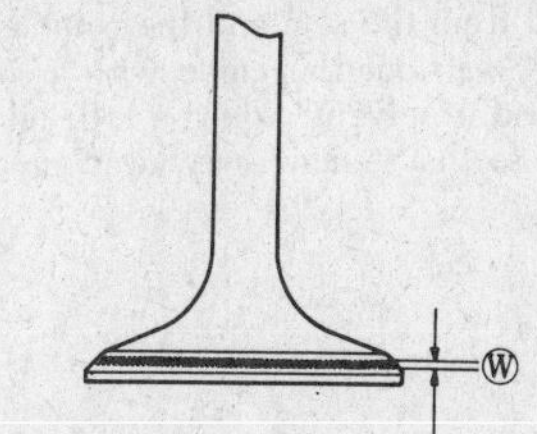

Valve seat width (W)

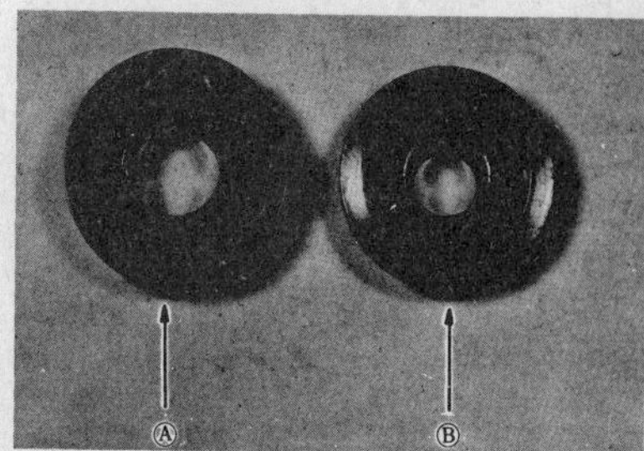

Upper (A) and lower (B) valve spring seats are different

Springs are installed with the close coils (arrows) towards the head

lower spring seats are different, the lower spring seat having a larger hole. Coat the length of each valve stem, and the lips of the valve seals, with molybdenum disulfide lubricant before installation.

17. Note that the valve springs are progressively wound. They must be installed so that the close coils are towards the head.

VALVE SEAT SERVICE

1. Valves should be lapped into their seats if the leakage test shows poor sealing, if the valve edges or seat in the head are pitted, if the motorcycle has covered considerable mileage, or if new valves or guides are fitted.

2. Clean off all carbon build-up on the surface of the combustion chamber. Place three small dabs of valve lapping paste around the circumference of the valve head and place the valve into the guide.

3. If you have a lapping tool, use it as the manufacturer directs. Usually the tool will turn the valve back and forth while rotating it around the seat at the same time. Do not use excessive pressure during the operation.

If you do not have such a tool, a piece of thick fuel line placed over the valve stem works just as well. Turn the valve back and forth and rotate it to a new position every few seconds.

NOTE: *Check the condition of the valve face and seat frequently. When a smooth, even finish is evident, stop lapping. Excessive lapping may lead to a pocketed valve.*

4. Remove the valve and clean it thoroughly. Remove any traces of lapping compound from the seat and the combustion chamber. Swab out the guide with a cotton swab soaked in solvent. Squirt a little oil into the guide so that it may carry away any particles inside.

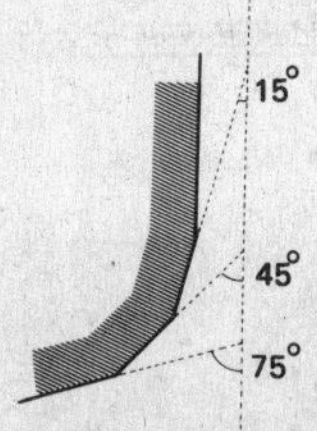

Valve seat dimensions

5. Check the width and condition of the valve seat. The seat should be about 1.0–1.2 mm (0.04–0.05 in.) wide, all the way around. If seat width is too narrow or too large, or if width varies, or if pitting still remains, the seat must be recut and the valve replaced.

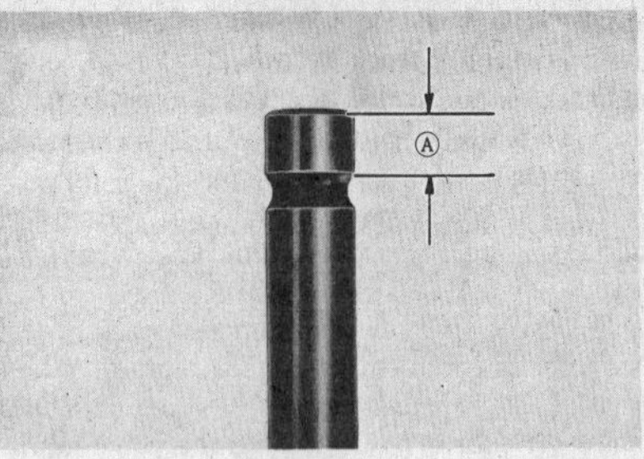

Do not reduce dimension (A) to less than 4.0 mm (0.16 in.)

6. Three cuts are necessary to restore a valve seat to a serviceable condition. First, make cuts at 15° and 75°, removing as little material as possible. Next, use a 45° cutter to produce a valve seat width of 1.0–1.2 mm (0.04–0.05 in.). This cut must be done very carefully; if too much material is removed, the valve may move so close to the camshaft that proper adjustment is made impossible.

7. After recutting the valve seat, lap the valve into place as outlined above.

8. If cutting the valve seat had raised the valve so much that valve adjustment is not possible, it is permissible to grind some material from the end of the valve stem to reduce its length. The distance from the valve keeper groove to the tip of the valve must not be reduced to less than 4.0 mm (0.16 in.), however, or the valve must then be replaced. When installing a valve whose tip has been ground, be sure that the tip still protrudes above the valve keepers.

9. Valves must be adjusted on assembly if lapping or cutting procedures have been carried out

CYLINDERS AND PISTONS

1. Make a visual inspection of the cylinder bore, noting any imperfections. The cylinder walls should be uniformly smooth.

2. With an inside micrometer, measure the diameter of each bore at the top, middle, and bottom. Make measurements in two directions, 90° apart, both parallel and perpendicular to the piston wrist pins.

On 750s with a standard bore, no measurement should exceed 65.100 mm (2.5629 in.).

On 850s with standard bores, no measurement should exceed 69.080 mm (2.7197 in.).

Maximum allowable difference between cylinders is 0.1 mm (0.004 in.).

Standard cylinder inside diameter is as follows:

750 65.000–65.015 mm/2.5591–2.5596 in.
850 69.000–69.015 mm/2.7165–1.7171 in.

If any bore measurement exceeds the service limits above, the cylinders should be bored out to the first oversize. Oversized pistons are 0.5 and 1.0 mm above standard.

NOTE: *When boring cylinders, allow adequate time between cuts for the block to cool. This will eliminate the danger of warpage. Bore cylinders in order 2, 4, 1, 3.*

3. Make a visual inspection of the pistons. Scoring, scuffing, or seizure marks on the piston skirts may be removed with a fine grade of emery or crocus cloth if they are not too severe. Sanding should be done in a cross-hatch pattern. If the damage is severe (more than about ½ in. wide), the pistons should be replaced.

4. The rings must be free to move in the piston grooves. If they cannot, either they are carbon-clogged (which necessitates replacing the rings and cleaning out the grooves), or metal has been pushed into the grooves by a piston seizure. In this event, pistons and rings must be replaced. Carbon-clogged rings are almost always broken when an attempt is made to remove or free them, so be prepared to buy a new set.

5. Measure the diameter of the pistons perpendicular to the wrist pins at a point 15 mm (0.6 in.) above the edge of the skirt. Piston diameters for standard pistons are:

750 64.80 mm (2.5512 in.)
850 68.880 mm (2.7118 in.)

If the pistons measure less than this, they should be replaced. If wear of this kind has occurred, the cylinders are probably worn as well, and the solution is to have them bored out to the next oversize.

Standard piston diameters are 64.945–64.960 mm (2.5569–2.5575 in.) for the 750 and 68.945–68.960 mm (2.7144–2.7150 in.) for the 850.

Note: *If oversized pistons are needed due to a worn bore or damaged piston, obtain the replacement pistons first, then have your dealer or a machine shop bore the cylinders to the proper size. This is obtained by measuring the diameter of the new pistons and boring the cylinders to that size plus the piston-to-cylinder clearance of 0.050–0.060 mm (0.0020–0.0024 in.).*

Oversized pistons are available in 0.5 mm and 1.0 mm sizes.

6. Check the condition of the piston wrist pins and replace them if step-wear or discoloration is evident. The wrist pins should be a snug fit in the piston holes. If they are too

Measure piston diameter 15 mm above the edge of the skirt

loose, the pistons and pins should be replaced.

Check the diameter of the wrist pins at three places along their length. Standard wrist pin diameter is 15.995–16.000 mm (0.6297–0.6299 in.). Replace the pin if any reading is less than 15.96 mm (0.6283 in.).

Check the diameter of the wrist pin bores in the pistons. Standard size is 16.002–16.008 mm (0.6300–0.6302 in.). Replace the pistons if the bore is larger than 16.08 mm (0.6331 in.).

Check the diameter of the small end bores. Standard bore size is 16.006–16.014 mm (0.6302–0.6305 in.). The rod must be replaced if the bore exceeds 16.05 mm (0.6319 in.).

Standard piston-to-wrist pin clearance is 0.002–0.013 mm (0.0001–0.0005 in.). The service limit is 0.12 mm (0.0047 in.).

Standard rod-to-wrist pin clearance is 0.006–0.019 mm (0.0002–0.0007 in.). The service limit 0.080 mm (0.0031 in.).

7. Although not as conclusive as a direct measurement, the condition of the wrist pins and small ends can be checked by inserting the pins and checking for vertical movement. There should be none. If there is noticeable movement in the pins, either the pins or the rods, or both, are in need of replacement. If the rod small ends are discolored or scored, the rods should be replaced.

8. Check the connecting rods for a bent condition. This can be accomplished with two small rectangular blocks of metal of equal thickness. Insert the wrist pins into the rods, and position the pieces of metal beneath them on either side of the rods and resting on the crankcase. Rotate the engine so that the wrist pin rests on the blocks. Both sides of the wrist pin must contact the metal blocks, or the rod is bent and must be replaced.

9. Before installation, decarbonize the piston crowns. Remove any carbon from the ring grooves with a piece of broken ring or a very thin screwdriver. Be careful not to scratch the grooves.

Carefully check the cylinder, cleaning the bores thoroughly. If considerable mileage has been covered, honing the cylinders and fitting new rings is recommended. If the cylinders are honed, make a strenuous effort to clean them thoroughly afterwards, preferably with very hot soapy water and a stiff brush. This is to remove any abrasive particles deposited by the hone in the course of the operation.

Remove any traces of gasket material from the cylinder base and the head mating surface.

10. Be sure that all oil passages in the cylinder are clear.

11. Replace the cylinder base o-rings. Check that any o-rings and the important dowel pins fitted to the cylinders are in their proper locations before installation.

PISTON RINGS

Piston rings should be checked for side clearance, thickness, end-gap (installed) and free end-gap. These checks should be made on both new and used rings.

1. Piston ring side clearance is checked with the rings installed on the piston. Insert a feeler gauge blade between the ring and the ring groove and check that the clearance is within the proper specification. They are as follows:

a. For the top ring, standard clearance is 0.020–0.055 mm (0.0008–0.0022 in.) and the serviceable limit is 0.18 mm (0.007 in.).

b. For the second ring, standard clearance is 0.020–0.060 mm (0.0008–0.0024 in.) and the serviceable limit is 0.15 mm (0.0059 in.).

c. For the oil ring, the serviceable limit is 0.15 mm (0.006 in.).

If the clearance is too large, the rings or grooves are worn. If too small, metal may have been pushed into the grooves due to a piston seizure. Check that the grooves are not just carboned up. If new rings do not bring the clearance to the proper value, the pistons must be replaced.

Measuring piston ring end-gap

2. To remove the rings from the piston, use a ring spreader. They are available at most auto stores. Decarbonize the ring grooves.

3. Measure the thickness of the two compression rings. Standard thickness for the top ring is 1.175–1.190 mm (0.0463–0.0469 in.), and for the second compression ring 1.170–1.190 mm (0.0460–0.0469 in.). Serviceable limit for both compression rings is 1.10 mm (0.043 in.).

4. If possible, check the width of the piston ring grooves. For the compression rings, groove width (standard) is 1.21–1.23 mm (0.0476–0.0484 in.), while the serviceable limit is 1.30 mm (0.051 in.). For the oil ring, standard groove width is 2.51–2.53 mm (0.0988–0.0996 in.), while the serviceable limit is 2.60 mm (0.102 in.).

If the groove width is greater than the serviceable limit, the piston must be replaced.

5. To check the ring end-gap, ensure first that the cylinder bore is not excessively worn. Place each compression ring, in turn, into the bottom of its cylinder and push it in an inch or more using the piston skirt to align the ring in the bore. Measure the end-gap with a feeler gauge. If the end-gap is larger than the service limit, the rings must be replaced. If the measured end-gap of new rings is too large, the cylinder is worn and should be bored to the next oversize.

Standard end-gap for both compression rings is 0.1–0.3 mm (0.004–0.012 in.). Rings must be replaced if end-gap exceeds 0.6 mm (0.024 in.) for the 750s and 0.7 mm (0.028 in.) for the 850s.

If new rings are fitted and the end-gap is too small, the ring ends must be filed. Hold the ring stady as illustrated, closing the ends over a thin, fine file. Do not squeeze the ring, as this is the easiest way to break it. A few strokes of the file will increase the end-gap.

CAUTION: *Do not make more than a few strokes before checking the end-gap again. It is easy to remove too much metal.*

Do not allow the file to slip out of the ring as this risks breaking it.

6. Check the free end-gap of the compression rings with a vernier caliper. On the 750, standard free end-gap is 8 mm (0.31 in.) while the serviceable limit is 6 mm (0.24 in.) for both rings.

On the 850, standard free end-gap for the top ring is 9 mm (0.35 in.) and the serviceable limit is 7.2 mm (0.28 in.). For the lower compression ring the values are 9.5 mm (0.37 in.) and 7.6 mm (0.30 in.).

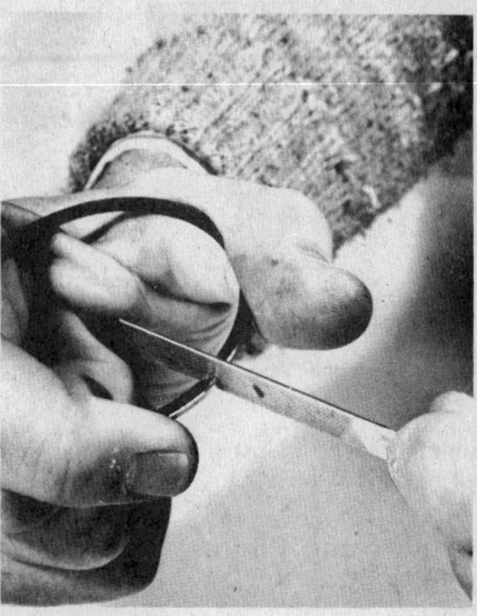
Filing ring ends

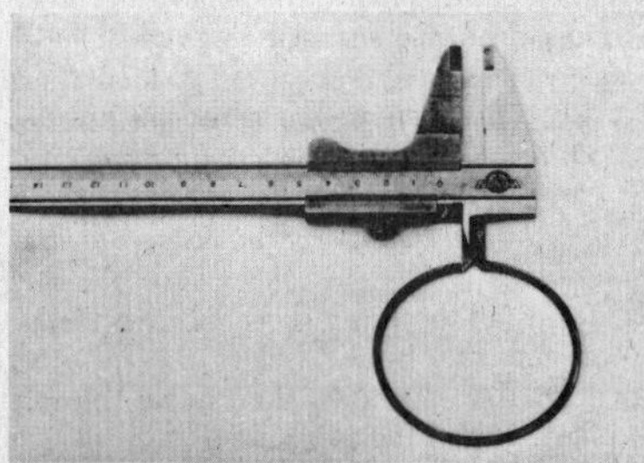
Measuring free end-gap

CAM CHAIN TENSIONER

1. Check that the cam chain tensioner pushrod can move in and out smoothly. If it sticks or binds, remove it by first removing the lock screw. Lubricate the pushrod with molybdenum disulfide lubricant and the pushrod guide with motor oil. If lubrication does not ease the movement, the assembly must be replaced.

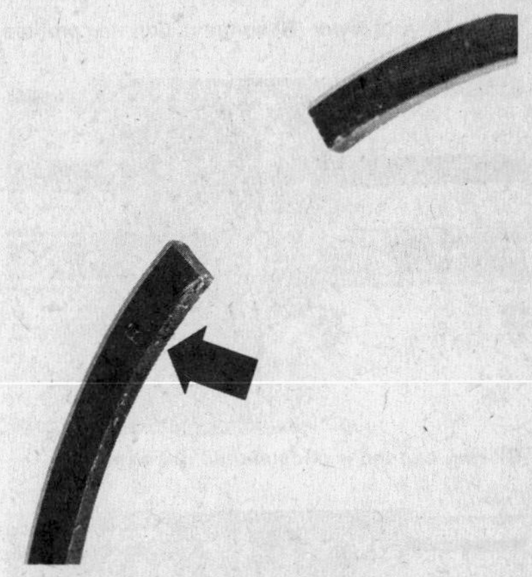
Always install rings so that the letter near the end-gap faces up

2. If the unit has been disassembled, position the lock shaft and holder as illustrated before assembly. Oil the lock shaft first. Tighten the shaft assembly to 22.3–25.3 ft lbs.

3. The handle is fitted to the holder by means of a left-hand thread. Turn the handle

Tensioner lock shaft and holder positioned for installation

counterclockwise to install it. Install the lock shaft nut and tighten it to 5.8–7.2 ft lbs.

Cylinder and Piston Installation

1. When installing the piston rings, note that the compression rings are installed with the manufacturer's mark (the small letter near the end-gap) facing *up*. All rings must have the same mark.

NOTE: *The compression rings are not interchangeable. The upper compression ring is chrome-plated. The lower one has a wedge-shaped cross-section. Refer to the illustration.*

2. To install the three-piece oil ring, install one rail on the piston below the oil ring groove, fit the expander, then move the rail into place. Install the top rail.

If "N"-marked rings are being used, be sure that the oil ring expander ends do not overlap.

Upper (A) and lower (B) compression ring profiles

Oil ring expander ends should not overlap

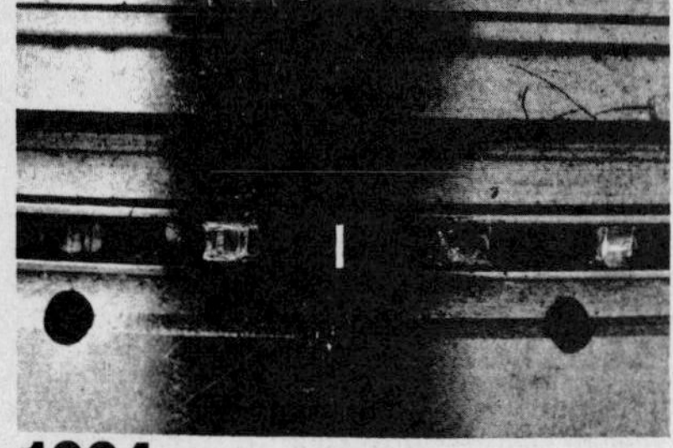

3. Use a ring-expander when installing the compression rings to reduce the chance of breaking them.

4. Ring end-gaps must be staggered around the piston so that they do not overlap. Compression ring end-gaps should be positioned at 45° on either side of the piston centerline on the intake side. The oil ring expander end-gap

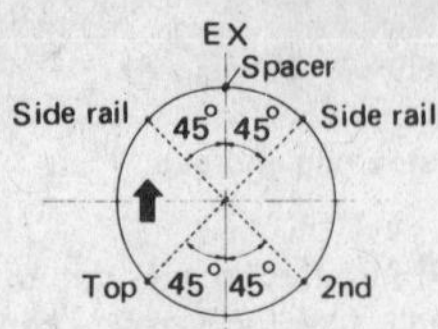

Ring end-gap positions

Fit the pistons with the arrows pointing towards the exhaust ports

should be positioned directly at the front of the piston with the rail end-gaps at 45° on either side of it. Refer to the accompanying illustration.

5. Install the pistons on their connecting rods so that the arrow stamped onto the piston crown points towards the exhaust (front) of the engine.

NOTE: *Be sure to use new wrist pin circlips.*

6. Oil the connecting rod small ends. Slip the wrist pins into place, heating the piston crown as on removal if necessary. Install the wrist pin circlips with a needle-nosed pliers. Be sure that each circlip is firmly seated in its groove and arranged so that the circlip end-gap and the cut-out in the piston do *not* align.

7. Lubricate the rings and piston skirts with clean motor oil.

8. Install the cylinder base gasket.

9. Compress the piston rings and install the cylinders.

Cylinder Head Installation

1. Fit the cylinder head gasket.

2. Install the cylinder head. Run the head nuts down until they are just hand-tight. Note that the four crown nuts and copper washers are installed on the outermost studs.

3. Refer to the illustration for cylinder head nut tightening order. Nuts should be tightened gradually and in a cross-pattern until the proper torque of 25.3–29.0 ft lbs is reached.

4. Install the two 6-mm set bolts and tighten them to 5.1–8.0 ft lbs.

5. Oil and install the valve tappets and shims.

6. If the camshaft sprockets were removed, install each sprocket onto the proper cam, referring to the accompanying illustrations. Tighten the sprocket bolts to 7.2 ft lbs.

Cylinder head bolt tightening order. (A) indicates the positions of the copper washers; (B) are the 6 mm set bolts

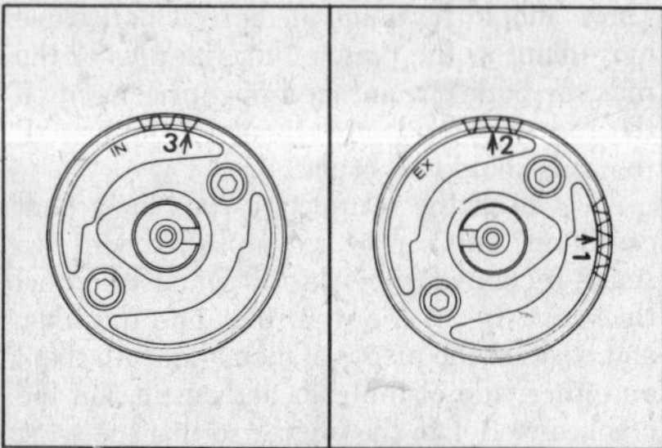

Proper cam sprocket installations

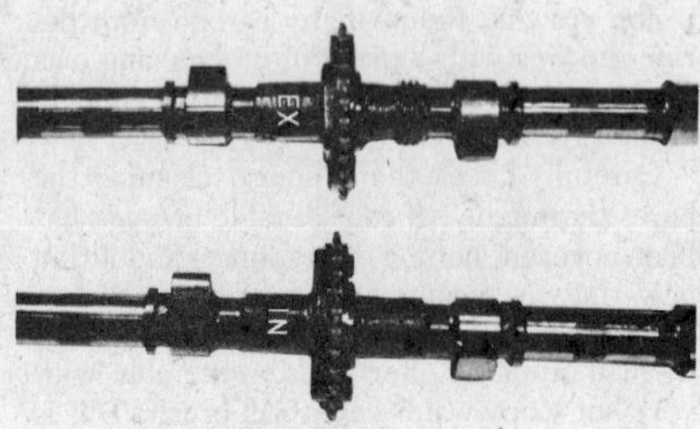

Camshafts are marked for identification

Cams are marked (L) and (R) for proper installation

Engine positioned at TDC for cylinders 1 & 4

Turn the sprocket so that the arrow mark (A) is flush with the cylinder head mating surface

7. Lubricate the cylnder head bearings with clean engine oil. Coat the journal areas of each camshaft with molybdenum disulfide lubricant.

8. Put each camshaft in place, noting that they are marked either "IN" or "EX." In addition, the left and right sides of each cam is marked to aid installation.

9. Engage the cam chain with the cam sprockets.

10. Remove the points cover. Slowly turn the engine over in the normal direction of rotation (clockwise a seen from the right side) until the "T"mark on the timing plate for cylnders 1 and 4 is aligned with the stationary timing mark.

11. Take up the cam chain slack, disengaging the chain from the exhaust cam sprocket. Turn the exhaust cam so that the arrow mark on the sprocket (marked "1") is flush with the cylinder head cover mating surface. At this point, the other arrow (marked "2") will point towards the vertical. Pull up the cam chain and engage the chain with the exhaust cam sprocket in this position.

12. The exhaust cam arrow mark ("2") now points towards a cam chain pin. Starting with this pin, count off 20 pins. Turn the intake camshaft so that the arrow (marked "3") on the intake camshaft sprocket points towards this 20th pin. Refer to the illustration.

Valve timing is now set correctly.

13. Secure both camshafts with vise-grips as on removal, and install the bearing caps.

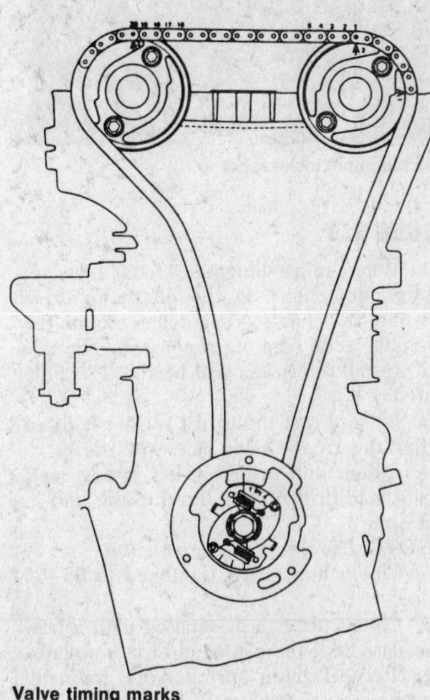

Valve timing marks

Bearing caps are installed so that the arrow on the cap points in the same direction as the arrow on the head

Note that the caps must be installed so that the arrow on the cap points in the same direction as the corresponding arrow embossed in the head.

14. Install the cam bearing cap bolts. Tighten the bolts gradually and evenly in a cross-pattern until the proper torque (2.9–4.3 ft lbs) is reached.

15. Install the tachometer drive gear.

16. Install the timing chain idler, torquing the bolts to 4.3–5.8 ft lbs.

17. To install the cam chain tensioner, turn the lock shaft handle counterclockwise while pushing the pushrod in as far as possible. Continue turning the handle until it refuses to turn further. Tighten the lockscrew to keep the pushrod in place. Bolt the adjuster assembly to the cylinder. Back out the lockscrew ¼ to ½ turn. Hold the lockscrew in place and tighten its locknut.

18. To check the operation on the cam chain tensioner, turn the lock shaft handle counterclockwise while turning the engine over opposite the normal direction of rotation. Release the handle and turn the engine slowly in the normal direction of rotation (clockwise as seen from the right side). The lock shaft handle should rotate by itself. If it does not, or if it rotates in a halting manner, remove and disassemble the tensioner as outlined in the tensioner service section preceeding.

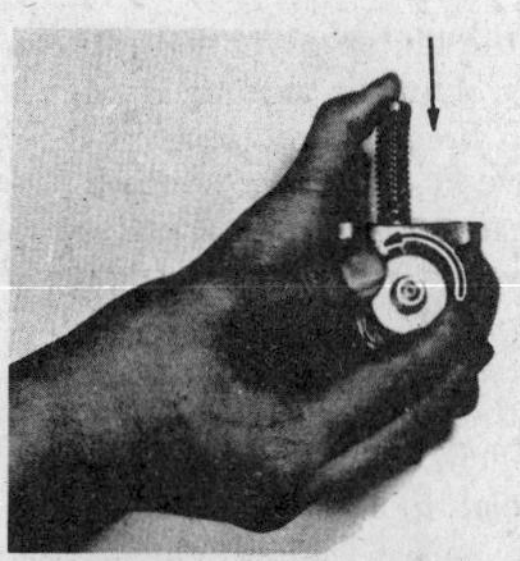

Fitting the cam chain tensioner

Oil separators

19. Adjust the tappets.

Cylinder head cover bolt tightening order

20. The remainder of the assembly procedure is the reverse of disassembly. Install the four oil separators in the cylinder head cover in the positions illustrated. Tighten the 16 cylinder head cover bolts gradually and in the order illustrated until a torque of 5.1–8.0 ft lbs is reached.

CRANKCASE COVER COMPONENTS

The following sections deal with the removal, inspection, and installation of those components found beneath the left and right crankcase covers. These include the clutch, oil pump, breaker points, alternator, starter drive, and shift mechanism. These components can be serviced with the engine in the frame.

Note the following points:

a. Always remove and install crankcase cover screws with an impact driver to prevent damage to the screw heads. Coat the threads of the screws with a bit of lubricant or anti-seize paste before installing to facilitate future removal.

b. New cover gaskets should always be used. Remove any traces of old gasket or gasket sealing compound from the covers and the crankcase mating surfaces.

c. During the disassembly procedure it may be necessary to keep the engine from turning over while a component is removed. There are several ways to do this. If

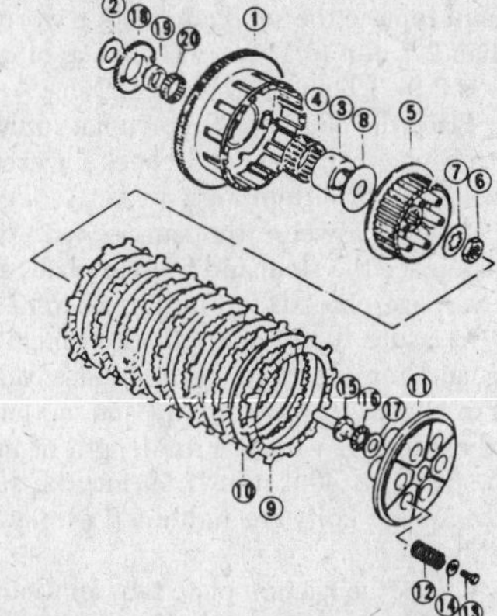

1. Clutch housing
2. Washer
3. Spacer
4. Needle bearing
5. Clutch hub
6. Hub nut
7. Washer
8. Washer
9. Friction plate
10. Steel plate
11. Pressure plate
12. Clutch spring
13. Spring bolt
14. Washer
15. Lifter
16. Needle bearing
17. Washer
18. Oil pump drive gear
19. Spacer
20. Bearing

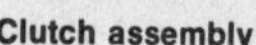

Clutch assembly

the engine is in the frame, place the transmission in gear and apply the rear brake. If the engine has been removed from the frame, loop a length of old drive chain around the countershaft sprocket and secure the end in a vise. Engage the transmission and the engine will not turn over.

Clutch (750)

REMOVAL

1. Drain the oil.
2. Loosen the pinch bolt and carefully pull the kickstarter lever off of its splined shaft.
3. Remove the clutch cover screws. Remove the clutch cover. If the cover is stuck, tap carefully at its sides with a plastic mallet to free it.
4. Remove the clutch cover gasket. A new one should be used on assembly.
5. Gradually, and in a cross pattern, loosen the six clutch spring bolts until they are free. Remove the bolts, washers, springs, and pressure plate. Remove the washer, bearing, and lifter.
6. Remove the clutch friction and steel plates, first making note of their order of installation.
7. Lock the clutch hub in place using either the special tool or by locking the transmission in place. Bend down the lock tab on the clutch hub nut. Loosen and remove the nut. Pull off the clutch hub.
8. Screw two 6-mm bolts into the primary driven gear spacer and pull the spacer out.
9. Remove the clutch housing and primary driven gear.

INSPECTION

1. Check the condition of the kickstarter shaft oil seal. If it leaks, or if the lips show signs of damage, pry out the old seal with a small screwdriver. Press the new seal straight into the cover. Apply some oil or grease to the seal lips before installation.
2. Check the condition of the clutch cover mating surface. Remove any burrs or imperfections with an oilstone.
3. Measure the thickness of each friction plate and replace the set if any plate is worn to less than 2.7 mm (0.11 in.). Thickness of new plates is 2.9–3.1 mm (0.114–0.122 in.).
4. Place the clutch plates on a flat surface, such as a piece of glass, and check for excessive warpage by attempting to slip a feeler gauge blade between the surface and the plate. Replace the steel and friction plates as a set if warpage exceeds 0.3 mm (0.12 in.).
5. Measure the free-length of each clutch spring and replace them as a set if any are found to be less than 39.0 mm (1.54 in.) long, or if their length varies. Free-length of new clutch springs is 40.4 mm (1.59 in.). Be sure that the spring bolts are tightened evenly on assembly.
6. Check the friction plate tabs for wear or damage. Check the clutch housing for indented wear caused by the tabs. Remove any burrs with a file or oilstone.
7. Check the corresponding splines of the clutch hub and steel plates for indented wear.
8. Check the condition of the housing bearing. Rollers must be in good condition, free of any obvious signs of damage, discoloration, etc. Replace the bearing if imperfections are noted.
9. Check the condition of the lifter bearing, looking for obvious signs of damage.
10. Check the pressure plate for cracks.
11. Inspect the primary driven gear teeth for wear or pitting.

ASSEMBLY

1. Assembly is basically the reverse of disassembly.
2. When fitting the clutch housing, note that the tabs on the oil pump drive gear must engage the cut-outs on the back of the housing.
3. Install the spacer, making sure it is fully seated.
4. Install the housing thrust washer, making sure that the washer is installed with the grooved side facing the clutch housing.
5. After fitting the clutch hub, install the hub and tighten it to 29.0–43.4 ft lbs. Bend down the lockwasher tab to secure the nut.
6. After installing the steel and friction plates, the lifter assembly, and the pressure plate, install and tighten the clutch spring bolts. Tighten the bolts gradually, and in a cross pattern until the desired torque of 2.9–4.3 ft lbs is reached.

Clutch (850)

REMOVAL

1. Drain the oil.
2. Remove the kickstarter lever, if fitted.
3. Remove the right side footpeg.
4. Disconnect the clutch cable at the cover.
5. Remove the clutch cover screws. Remove the cover, tapping around it with a plastic mallet to break it free if it is stuck. You should have a drip pan beneath the cover to catch excess oil.
6. Gradually and evenly loosen and remove the six pressure plate spring bolts. Remove the pressure plate and springs.
7. Remove the clutch plates.
8. Lock the clutch hub in place using either the special tool or by locking the transmission in place. Bend down the locktab on the clutch hub nut. Remove the nut. Remove the clutch hub.
9. Screw two 6-mm bolts into the primary driven gear spacer and pull the spacer out. Remove the clutch housing and primary driven gear.
10. Disassemble the clutch hub, if desired, by squeezing the driven plate with a pliers and removing the piano wire clip.

INSPECTION

Refer to "Inspection" for the 750 clutch given above. Procedures are the same. Specifications may differ. For the 850, they are as follows:

1. The thickness of new friction plates is 2.7–2.9 mm (0.11–0.12 in.). They should be replaced as a set if any measures less than 2.4 mm (0.094 in.).
2. Replace the plates as a set if any friction plate is warped more than 0.2 mm (0.008 in.) or any steel plate more than 0.1 mm (0.004 in.).
3. Standard clutch spring free-length is 40.4 mm (1.59 in.), and the serviceable limit is 38.8 mm (1.53 in.).
4. Friction plate tabs should be at least 11.0 mm (0.43 in.) wide.

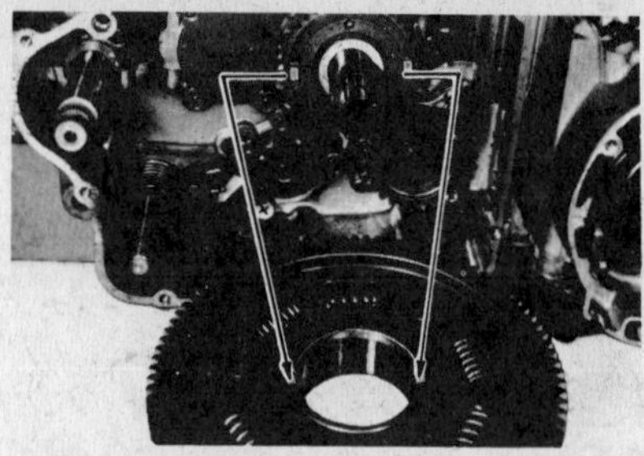
When fitting the clutch housing, the oil pump drive gear tabs must engage the cut-outs on back of the housing

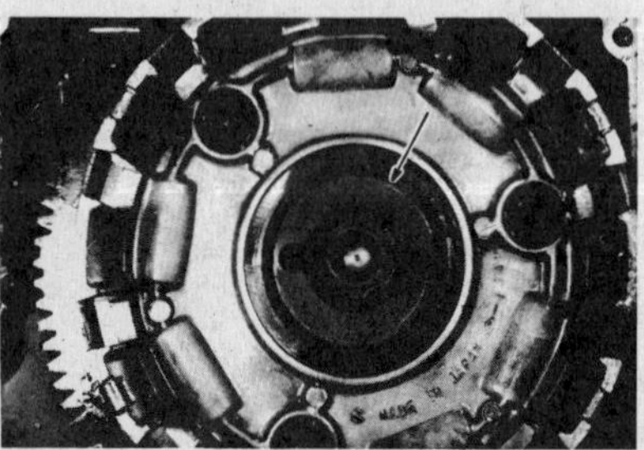
Spacer installed

Thrust washer installed

Clutch hub nut lockwasher

ASSEMBLY

1. When reinstalling the clutch housing, fit the projections on the oil pump drive gear into the clutch gear notches. Rotate the assembly to be sure of proper installation.
2. Install the spacer and be sure it is fully seated.
3. Be sure that the thrust washer is fitted so that the grooved side faces inwards.
4. Clutch hub assembly has spring seat, spring, and driven plate fitted to the hub in that order.

NOTE: *Use a new piano wire clip.*

5. Clutch hub nut is tightened to 36–51 ft. lbs.
6. Clutch plates are installed with a friction plate first, then steel and friction plates alternately. Tighten spring bolts gradually and in a cross-pattern to 8–10 ft. lbs.

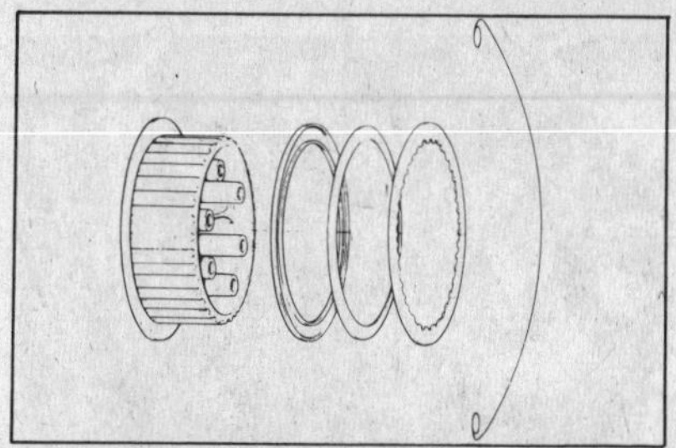

Clutch hub assembly

7. Use a new clutch cover gasket. When fitting the cover, be sure that the clutch lever rack and pinion is properly engaged.

Oil Pump

REMOVAL

1. Drain the oil. Remove the clutch assembly as outlined above.
2. Remove the three screws and pull off the oil pump.

INSPECTION

Refer to "Lubrication System," for inspection procedures.

INSTALLATION

Installation is the reverse of removal. Be sure that the two o-rings are in place behind the oil pump. Use a non-permanent thread locking compound on the pump mounting screws.

Be sure that the o-rings are in place behind the oil pump

Tighten the spring bolts in a cross pattern

Gearshift Mechanism

REMOVAL

1. Drain the oil. Remove the clutch assembly as outlined above.
2. Loosen the pinch bolt and carefully pull the gearshift lever off its splined shaft.
3. Pull out the gear shift shaft.
4. Remove the cam guide and pawl lifter plate screws and take off those parts and the cam gear and pawls.

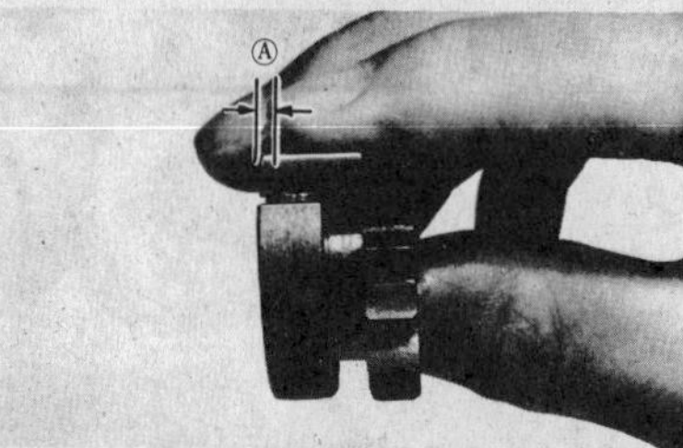

The narrow side of the gearshift pawl (A) is fitted as shown

INSPECTION

1. Check the gearshift return spring for damage.
2. Check the meshing gear teeth for condition.

INSTALLATION

1. Installation is the reverse of removal. Be sure that the gearshift return spring arms are fitted to either side of the arm stopper pin.
2. When fitting the gearshift pawls to the cam gear, note that the narrow side of the pawls are installed closest to the shift drum.
3. Mesh the shift gears as illustrated.
4. Secure the cam guide and pawl lifter screws with a non-permanent thread locking compound.

NOTE: *The four gearshift component screws are somewhat shorter than the other securing screws in the clutch housing. If other components, such as the oil pump or bearing retainers, are removed at the same time, be sure not to confuse the screws.*

Breaker Point Assembly

REMOVAL

1. Remove the breaker points cover. Disconnect the two leads at the top of the air cleaner or at the primary terminals.
2. Scribe a mark on the breaker plate and housing to facilitate ignition timing. Remove the three securing screws and take off the breaker plate.
3. Remove the timing advance mechanism bolt. Slide off the timing advance mechanism.

Correct gearshift ratchet installation

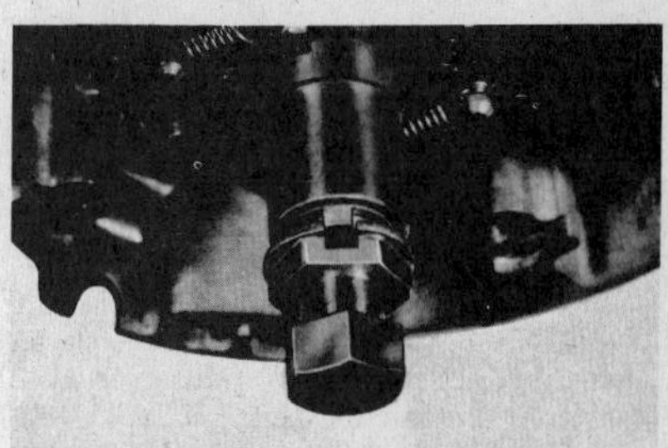

Tighten the advance mechanism bolt to 13.0–20.3 ft lbs.

INSPECTION

1. The timing advance mechanism movement must be free. When the breaker cam is turned so that the weights move out to the fully extended position, releasing the cam should result in its returning to the original location. If it will not, try penetrating oil or the like to ease movement. Check for weak springs. Replace the unit if proper action cannot be obtained.

INSTALLATION

1. Installation is the reverse of removal. When installing the timing advance mechanism note that it is located by a pin.
2. Tighten the timing advance mechanism bolt to 13.0–20.3 ft lbs.
3. When installing the breaker plate, line up the scribed marks made before removal. If no marks were made, it is necessary to retime the ignition. Timing should be checked in any case.

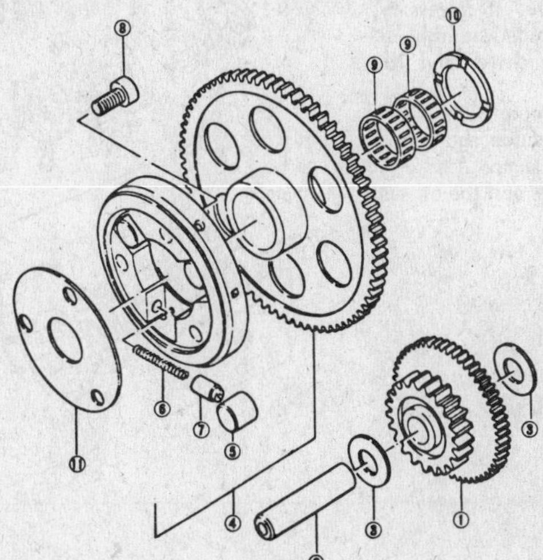

1. Idler gear
2. Shaft
3. Thrust washer
4. Starter clutch
5. Roller
6. Spring
7. Plunger
8. Bolt
9. Bearing
10. Washer
11. Shim

Starter clutch assembly

Alternator/Starter Drive

REMOVAL

1. Remove the alternator cover.
2. Lock the crankshaft and remove the alternator rotor mounting bolt.
3. The rotor is a push-fit onto the tapered crankshaft. It can be removed using either a slide-hammer or a large gear puller.
4. Remove the starter clutch and the starter gear.
5. Remove the idler gear pin complete with the idler gears and washers.

INSPECTION

1. Refer to "Electrical System," for alternator tests.
2. Check the condition of the starter drive gears and replace them if the teeth are worn or broken.
3. The starter clutch should be replaced if defective, a condition indicated if the starter motor, but not the engine, turns over when the starter button is pushed.
4. Check the condition of the starter gear needle bearings. The bearings should be replaced when the rollers show any signs of damage such as flat spots, pitting, or discoloration.

INSTALLATION

1. The thrust washer behind the starter gear must be installed correctly. The washer's hole has a bevel on one side, the other side being plain. The washer must be installed so that the bevelled side faces the crankshaft bearing.
2. Note that a washer is installed on either side of the idler gear.
3. Clean the crankshaft taper thoroughly with a solvent before installing the components. Tighten the rotor bolt to 43.4–50.6 ft lbs. on 750s or 65–73 ft. lbs. on the 850s, non-permanent thread locking compound is recommended.

LOWER END

Disassembly

1. Remove the engine from the frame.
2. Remove the cylinder head and cylinder and piston assembly. Refer to "Top End," above.
3. Refer to the "Crankcase Cover Components" procedures above, if necessary, and remove the ignition timing assembly, alternator rotor and starter drive, and the clutch assembly.
4. Remove the starter motor.
5. Remove the spring guide and return spring from the kickstarter shaft.
6. Remove the two bolts and the oil seal holder.

A thrust washer is installed on either side of the idler gear

Degrease the crankshaft taper thoroughly before fitting the starter clutch

Starter gear thrust washer correctly installed

7. Remove the two screws which secure the gear switch body.
8. On shaft-drive models, remove the secondary drive and driven gear boxes from the crankcase.
9. Remove the oil pump, gear shift mechanism, shifter cam plate and transmission shaft bearing retainers which are found beneath the clutch.
10. Remove the 11 or 12 upper crankcase bolts.
11. Turn the engine over and remove the oil pan and the lower crankcase bolts. The 8-mm bolts should be loosened gradually and in a cross pattern, starting at the center and working out towards the sides of the engine.
12. Separate the crankcase halves. If the cases are stuck, first check that all of the bolts have been removed. Then tap around the edges with a plastic mallet to unstick them.

Remove the securing screws before attempting to split the cases. Screws (A) are shorter than the others

Checking rod small end movement

Checking clearance between the flywheel and the rod big end

13. Lift out the crankshaft and connecting rod assembly.

Inspection

1. The crankshaft is a pressed-together unit. Rod big ends ride in needle bearings. If

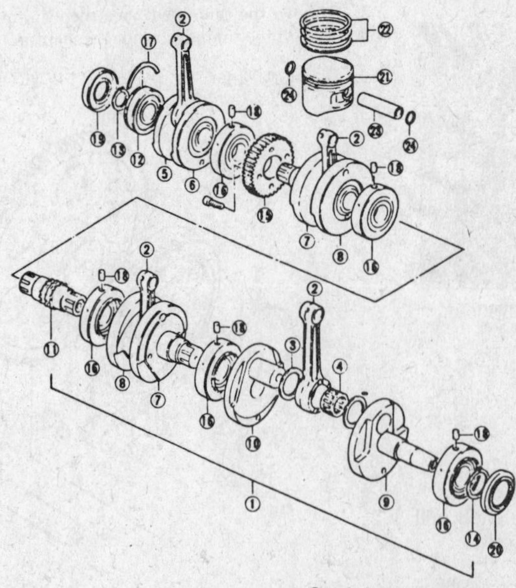

Crankshaft assembly

1. Crankshaft ass'y
2. Connecting rod
3. Washer
4. Bearing
5. RH crankshaft
6. RH crankshaft web
7. Middle crankshaft
8. Middle crankshaft web
9. LH crankshaft
10. LH crankshaft web
11. Timing chain drive shaft
12. RH bearing
13. Circlip
14. Circlip
15. Primary drive gear
16. Bearing
17. RH bearing C ring
18. Pin
19. RH oil seal
20. Starter clutch gear oil seal
21. Piston
22. Piston ring set
23. Piston pin
24. Circlip

replacement of a rod or rod bearing or crankshaft bearing is necessary, the crankshaft will have to be disassembled. This work must be carried out by some one with the right tools and familiarity with the operation.

2. With a dial gauge, check rod side movement at the small end. Total deflection must not exceed 3 mm (0.14 in.). If it does, it indicates that the big end bearing is worn to the point of replacement.

3. With a feeler gauge, check the clearance between the connecting rod big end and the crankshaft flywheel. Standard clearance is 0.10—*0.55 mm (0.004*–0.026 in.). The serviceable limit is 1.0 mm (0.04 in.).

4. Mount the crankshaft in a set of v-blocks. With a dial indicator, measure crank run-out at the main bearings and crank ends. Standard maximum run-out is 0.03 mm (0.0012 in.). If run-out exceeds 0.06 mm (0.002 in.), the assembly must be replaced.

5. Check the condition of each crankshaft bearing by rotating them slowly and checking for unusual behavior. Bearing outer races must not be too loose. Rotation should be smooth, quiet, and effortless.

6. With a dial gauge, check the diametrical clearance of each crank bearing. Standard clearance is 0.015–0.040 mm (0.0006–0.0016 in.). Bearings which exceed 0.08 mm (0.0031 in.) must be replaced.

Assembly

1. Use new crankshaft oil seals. The right-side oil seal must be installed on the crankshaft as illustrated. Lubricate the seal lips before installation.

Check crank run-out at the points indicated

Right-side oil seal installed

Be sure the bearing locating holes (B,C) are fitted to the pins (A,D)

Lower case half O-ring (A)

Crankcase bolt tightening order

2. When installing the crank assembly in the upper case half, be sure that each bearing is properly seated onto its locating pin.

3. Be sure that the o-ring is installed in the lower case half. Refer to the illustration.

4. Apply Suzuki Bond #4 (Part No. 99000-31030) to the lower crankcase half mating surface.

5. After ensuring that the two case halves are correctly mated, install and tighten the 8-mm lower crankcase bolts. The bolts must be tightened gradually and in the order shown in the illustration (a cross pattern starting with the center bolts). Tighten the 8-mm bolts to 14.5 ft lbs.

6. Tighten the 6-mm crankcase bolts to 7.2 ft lbs.

7. Use a non-permenent thread-locking compound on the bearing retainer plate screws.

SECONDARY DRIVE GEAR

Disassembly

1. Knock the end plug out of the housing with a drift.

2. Bend back the shaft nut locktab. Hold the shaft in position, and remove the nut.

NOTE: *Use a new nut when assembling.*

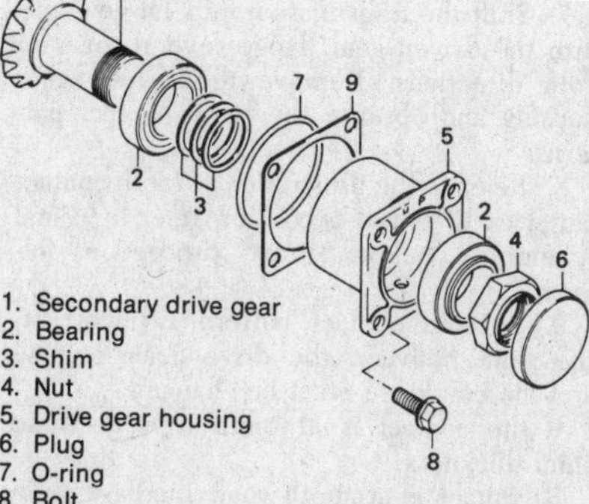

1. Secondary drive gear
2. Bearing
3. Shim
4. Nut
5. Drive gear housing
6. Plug
7. O-ring
8. Bolt
9. Shim

Secondary drive gear

3. Use a plastic mallet or wood block and hammer to tap the drive gear out of the housing.

4. Remove—and save—the drive shaft shims.

5. Remove the inner bearing from the drive gear. A gear puller must be used.

6. Drive the bearing out of the housing.

Inspection

1. Check the bevel gear teeth for pitting, wear, or chips.

2. Closely check the tapered roller bearings for scored, worn, or overheated (bluish) rollers. Check for damage to the cage. Check that the bearing races are smooth and featureless.

NOTE: *If the bevel (drive) gear is damaged, the driven gear with which it meshes must also be replaced.*

Assembly

1. Install the outer bearing in the housing.

2. Install the inner bearing on the shaft of the bevel gear.

3. Install all of the original shims on the shaft.

4. Install the drive shaft into the housing and install the other bearing. Lubricate the bearings with SAE 90 gear oil.

5. Using a new shaft nut, secure the shaft in place and tighten the nut to 87–109 ft. lbs.

Preload Adjustment

After the drive gear assembly has been put together, the tapered roller bearings must be chcked and, if necessary, adjusted.

1. Use a small torque wrench to determine how much torque is required to rotate the gear shaft.

2. The proper specification is 2.60–4.35 in lbs.

Turn the shaft around in both directions several times before making this check in order to seat the bearings.

3. If the torque is below specification (i.e. the shaft turns too freely), decrease shim thickness.

If the torque is greater than the specification, increase shim thickness.

Shims are available in numerous increments from 1.60–2.00 mm.

Be sure to reotate the shaft in both directions before each preload check.

4. After preload is correctly adjusted, remove the drive gear nut, clean and degrease the threads, and refit the nut tightening it to the correct torque (87–109 ft. lbs.).

5. Bend the collar of the nut over into the notch in the drive gear shaft.

6. Press a new plug into the housing so that it is 1.5 mm below the housing shoulder.

7. See "Clearancing Operations," below.

SECONDARY DRIVEN GEAR

Disassembly

1. Bend down the locktab and remove the driven gear nut.

2. Remove the flange. Remove the oil seal.

3. Remove—and save—the shaft shims and spacer.

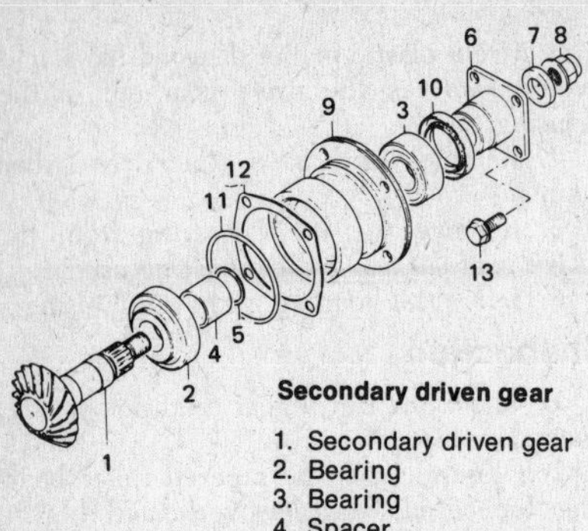

Secondary driven gear

1. Secondary driven gear
2. Bearing
3. Bearing
4. Spacer
5. Shim
6. Universal joint flange
7. Washer
8. Nut
9. Driven gear housing
10. Oil seal
11. O-ring
12. Shim
13. Bolt

4. Use a puller to take off the inner bearing. Drive the other bearing out of the housing.

Inspection

1. Check the gear teeth for pitting, wear, or chips.
2. Closely inspect the tapered roller bearings for scored, worn, or overheated (bluish) rollers. Check for damage to the cage. Check that the bearing races are smooth and featureless.

NOTE: *If the driven gear is damaged, the drive gear with which it meshes must also be replaced.*

3. Use a new oil seal on assembly.

Assembly

1. Assembly is the reverse of disassembly. Install the bearings and the spacer and shims which were removed. Lubricate the bearings with SAE 90 gear oil. Do *not* install the oil seal until bearing preload is adjusted.
2. Use a new shaft nut and tighten it to 65–80 ft. lbs.

Preload Adjustment

1. Turn the shaft several times in either direction to seat the bearings.
2. Use a small torque wrench to determine how much torque is necessary to turn the shaft. It should be 3.45–6.05 in lbs.
3. If the required torque is under the given specification, decrease shim thickness.

If the shaft torque is above the specification, increase the shim thickness.

NOTE: *After changing shims, be sure to turn the shaft in both directions several times before rechecking preload.*

4. Shims are available in several increments from 1.60–2.00 mm.
5. After preload is correct, remove the nut, washer, and propeller shaft flange. Fit a new oil seal making it flush with the housing shoulder.
6. Degrease the shaft threads. Coat them lightly with a non-permanent thread-locking compound. Install the shaft, washer, and nut.

Torque the nut to 65–80 ft. lbs.

7. Bend the collar of the nut into the notch in the driven gear shaft.
8. Refer to "Clearancing Operations," below.

Clearancing Operations

Install the drive gear housing with "UP" in the proper position

1. Fit the housing shims—without o-rings—onto the housings. Install the housings on the crankcase.

NOTE: *Be certain that the housings are installed with the "UP" side correctly located.*

2. Tighten the housing bolts to 15–19 ft. lbs.
3. Fit a dial gauge to the secondary driven gear flange and check backlash.

It should be 0.08–0.13 mm (0.003–0.005 in.).

Install the driven gear housing with "UP" in the proper position

4. If backlash is not correct, the shim between the secondary driven gear housing and the crankcase must be changed.

If backlash is too low, increase shim thickness.

If backlash is too high, decrease shim thickness.

Shims are available in 0.35, 0.40, 0.50, and 0.60 mm thicknesses.

5. After backlash is corrected, tooth contact must be checked.
6. Remove the secondary driven gear housing. Clean and degrease the gear teeth and coat several of the teeth with machinists dye. Reinstall the housing with the correct shim and tighten the bolts to 15–19 ft. lbs. It is not necessary to use the o-ring.
7. Shift the transmission into 1st gear and turn the driven gear flange several turns in both directions. Remove the driven gear housing and observe the tooth contact patterns.
8. Refer to the illustration of tooth contact patterns. If contact is correct, refer to "Final Assembly," below. If not, proceed as follows:
9. If tooth contact pattern is incorrect, the shim between the drive gear housing and the crankcase must be changed.

If the contact is at tooth top, decrease shim thickness.

If contact is at tooth roof, increase shim thickness.

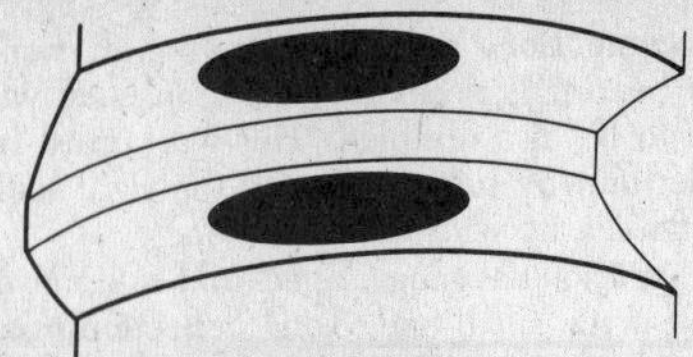

Correct tooth contact pattern

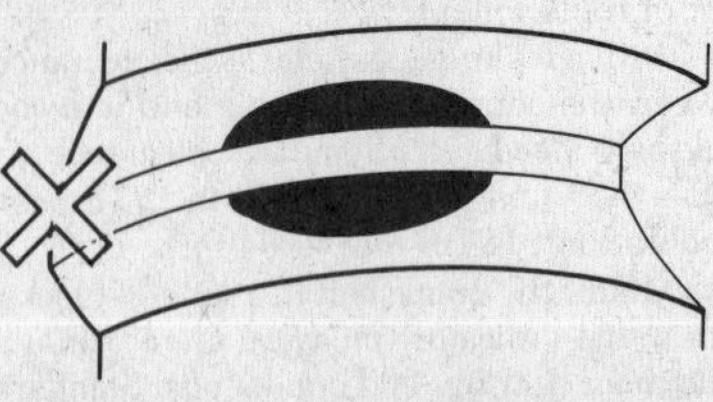

Contact at tooth top (increase shim thickness)

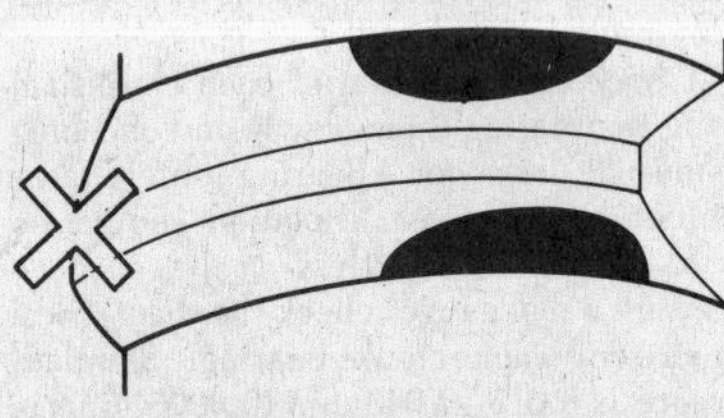

Contact at tooth roof (decrease shim thickness)

Shims are avilable in 0.35, 0.40, 0.45, and 0.50 mm sizes.

NOTE: *After adjusting tooth contact, recheck backlash.*

FINAL ASSEMBLY

1. After tooth contact and gear backlash are both correct, remove the two housings from the crankcase.
2. Clean the gears thoroughly and coat them with gear oil.
3. Use new o-rings on the housings and oil lightly.
4. Fit the housings, noting that the "UP" side is marked. Use a non-permanent thread locking compound on the housing bolts and tighten them to 15–19 ft. lbs.
5. Tighten the drain plug to 15–22 ft. lbs. Do not forget to add oil. Capacity is 11.0–13.5 oz (340–400 cc) of SAE 90 EP hypoid gear oil.

TRANSMISSION (750)

Disassembly

1. Separate the crankcase halves as described above under "Lower End."
2. Pull out the shift fork shafts and remove the shift forks and cam stopper.
3. Remove the shift drum stopper spring holder and take out the pin and spring. Remove the shift drum.

Inspection

NOTE: *Do not disassemble the gear set unless inspection shows that replacement of individual gears is necessary. Gear shaft circlips are not reusable and must be replaced with new ones whenever the gear set is taken apart.*

If the gear set is disassembled, carefully

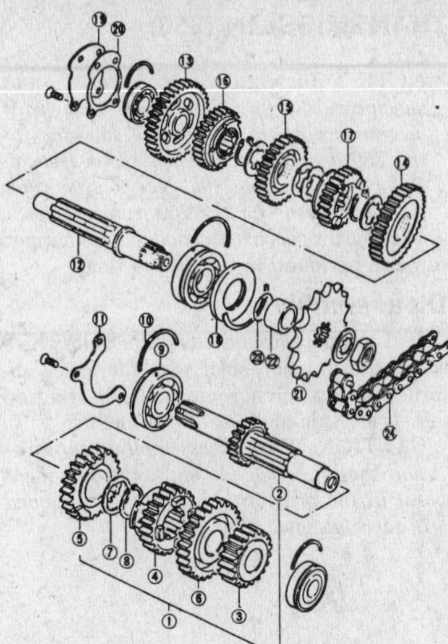

1. Countershaft ass'y
2. Countershaft
3. 2nd drive gear
4. 3rd drive gear
5. 4th drive gear
6. 5th drive gear
7. Washer
8. Circlip
9. RH bearing
10. C ring
11. Bearing holder
12. Driveshaft
13. 1st driven gear
14. 2nd driven gear
15. 3rd driven gear
16. 4th driven gear
17. 5th driven gear
18. Oil seal
19. Plate
20. Gasket
21. Engine sprocket
22. Spacer
23. O ring
24. Drive chain

Transmission assembly

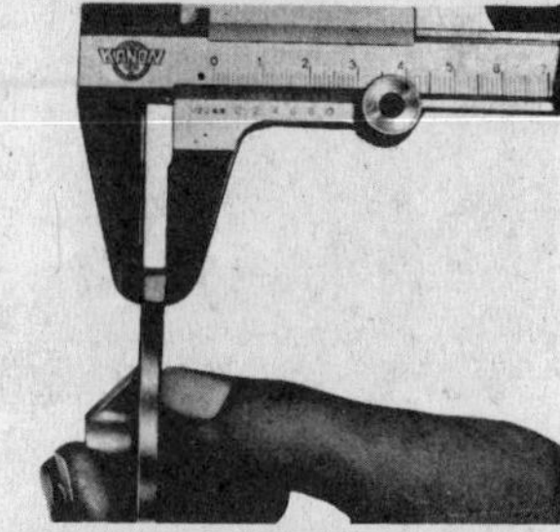

Checking shift fork finger thickness

Align the punch marks on the kick drive gear with that on the shaft

Measuring gear backlash with a dial gauge

lay out each piece in the order it is removed to facilitate reassembly.

1. Flush the transmission shaft bearings with clean motor oil and check operation. Bearing rotation must be smooth, effortless, and quiet. There must be no play between the inner and outer bearing races. If damage is noted, replace the bearings as a set.

2. Install the countershaft and mainshaft assemblies in the crankcase and measure gear backlash with a dial gauge. "Backlash" is the amount of movement noticeable in a gear when the gear with which it meshes is locked in place.

For 1st, 2d, and 3rd gears, standard backlash is 0.04 mm (0.002 in.) or less. The serviceable limit is 0.1 mm (0.004 in.).

For 4th and 5th gears, standard backlash is 0.05–0.1 mm (0.002–0.004 in.). The serviceable limit is 0.15 mm (0.006 in.)

Note that gears are always replaced in pairs.

3. Check the gear teeth for damage, wear, or pitting. Pay close attention to the very base of the teeth. Gears are surface-hardened, and if this hardened layer is damaged, what is left will not last long. Check the engaging dogs and/or dog slots on each gear for chipping or wear. Check that splined gears are a good fit on their shaft (neither too loose nor too tight) and that the splines on the shafts and on the gears are in good condition. Check that gears with plain bores can rotate freely but are not too loose on their shafts. Check all parts for damage due to overheating or lack of lubricant.

4. Check the shift forks for wear or chipping to the fingers or pin. Measure the thickness of the fingers. Standard thickness is 4.95–5.05 mm (0.195–0.199 in.). The serviceable limit is 4.85 mm (0.191 in.).

5. Check the shift fork shafts for a bent condition and replace them if they are not perfectly straight.

6. Check the shift drum for wear or damage to the grooves.

7. Inspect the shift drum bearing for damage and replace it if it is not in good condition.

8. Check the kickstarter return spring for damage and replace it if it is weak or broken.

9. Inspect the splines on the kickstarter shaft and replace the shaft if the splines are

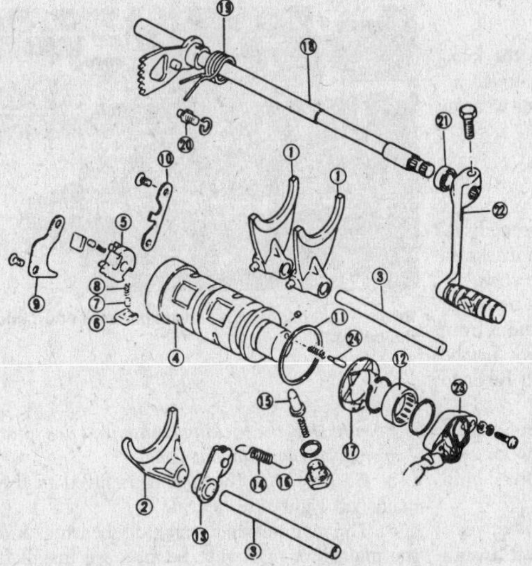

1. 4th & 5th driven gear shift fork
2. 3rd drive gear shift fork
3. Gear shift fork shaft
4. Shift drum
5. Cam driven gear
6. No. 1 pawl
7. Pin
8. Spring
9. Pawl lifter
10. Cam guide
11. Washer
12. Bearing
13. Cam stopper
14. Spring
15. Cam stopper
16. Stopper holder
17. Stopper plate
18. Gear shift shaft
19. Spring
20. Arm stopper
21. Oil seal
22. Gear shift lever assembly
23. Gear shift switch body
24. Gear shift contact switch

Shifter assembly

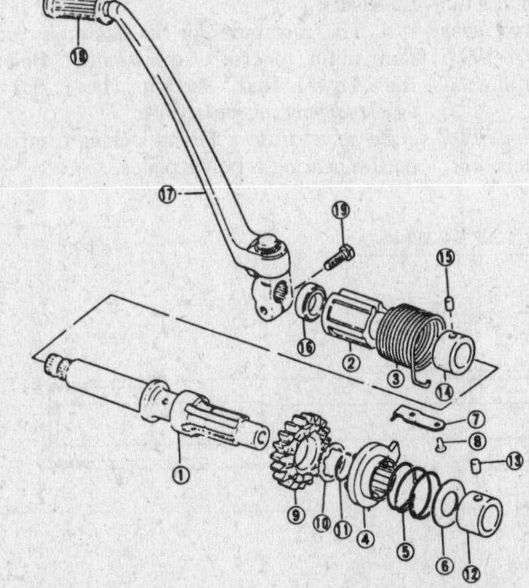

1. Kick starter shaft
2. Spring guide
3. Spring
4. Kick starter
5. Spring
6. Plate
7. Starter guide
8. Screw
9. Kick starter drive gear
10. Washer
11. Circlip
12. LH bushing
13. Dowel pin
14. RH bushing
15. Dowel pin
16. Oil seal
17. Kick starter lever ass'y
18. Cover
19. Bolt

Kickstarter assembly

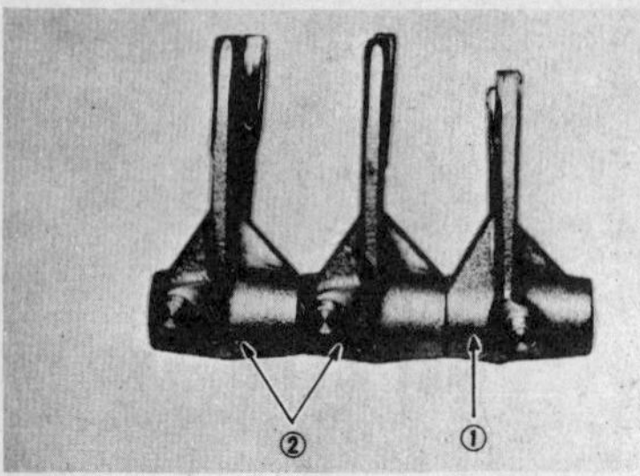

Third gear shift fork (1); fourth and fifth gear shift fork (2)

Be sure that the o-ring is fitted to the mainshaft right-side bearing

Shift fork installation

Install the shaft bearings so that the sealed side faces outwards

distorted or worn to the point that the kickstarter lever cannot be properly secured.

10. Check the kickstarter gears for wear or damage to the teeth.

Assembly

1. If the kickstarter shaft has been disassembled, be sure to align the punch marks on the kick drive gear with that on the shaft.

2. When installing the shift forks, note that the shift fork for the 3rd gear is different from those for 4th and 5th gears. The fork for the 3rd gear is installed on its own shaft. Refer to the illustrations.

3. If the gear clusters have been disassembled, refer to the exploded view for correct component locations. New circlips should always be used.

Note the special washers installed between the 5th and 3rd gears on the mainshaft. Install the washers so that the tabs in the one match the grooves in the other.

4. The countershaft 2d gear must be pressed onto its shaft. Fit this gear so that the distance between the 1st countershaft gear and the 2d countershaft gear is 109.4–109.5 mm (4.307–4.311 in.). Refer to the illustration.

NOTE: *The 2d countershaft gear should be installed with a bearing locking compound.*

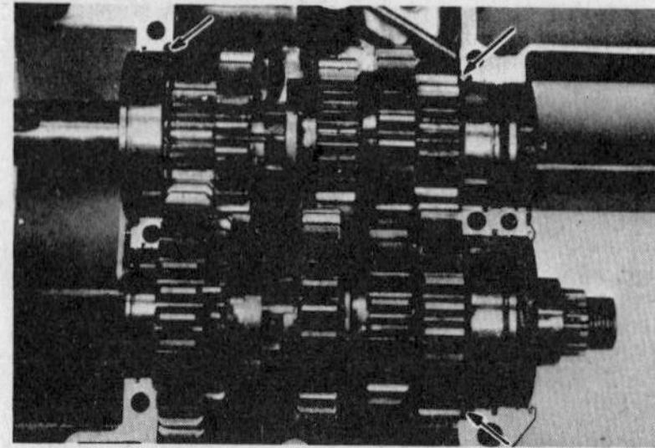
Be sure that the bearing dowel pins are fitted into the cut-outs

Be sure that the locking compound does not spread to the adjacent gear.

5. Be sure that the O-ring is fitted to the mainshaft right-side bearing.

6. The countershaft left-side bearing and the mainshaft right-side bearing are installed with the oil seal sides facing outward.

7. Be sure that the bearing dowel pins are fitted to the cut-outs provided when installing the shafts.

8. The remainder of the assembly procedure is the reverse of disassembly. Refer to the "Lower End" section, above, for the crankcase mating procedure.

Be sure to use a thread locking compound on the bearing retainer plates.

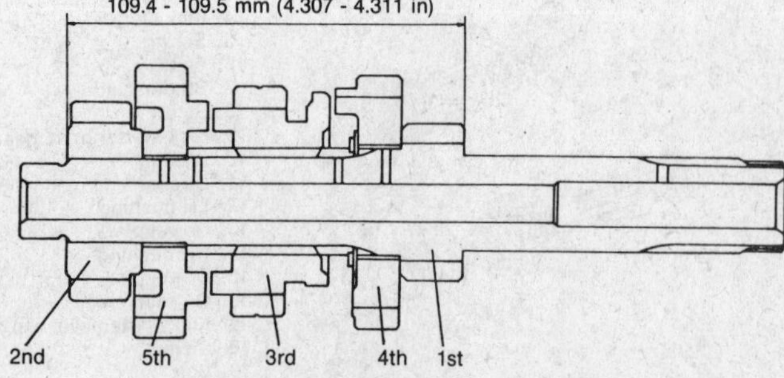

Correct position of 2d countershaft gear

TRANSMISSION (850)

NOTE: *Inspection procedures and specifications for the gears and shift mechanism of the 850 is the same as for the 750 described in the previous section. Before dismantling the gear shafts, refer to "Inspection" for the 750 transmission.*

Kickstarter service for models so equipped can also be found in the 750 section.

Disassembly

1. To disassemble the countershaft (which is the transmission shaft with the shock absorber spring), first remove the bearing on the spring side and also the spacer.

CAUTION: *When disassembling transmission shafts, be sure to lay each component out in the order in which it was removed to facilitate assembly.*

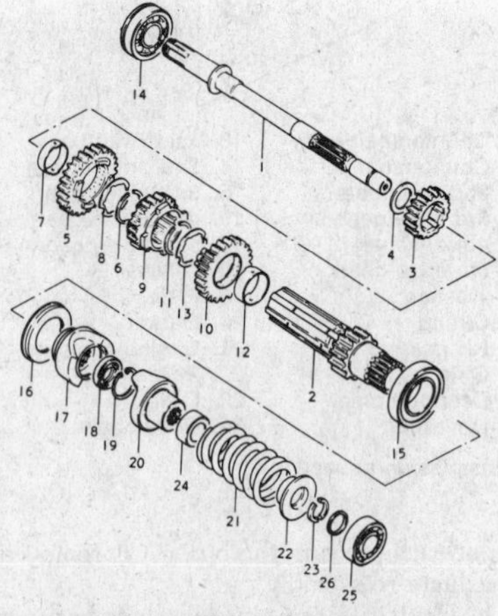

Countershaft assembly (GS 850)

1. Inner countershaft
2. Outer countershaft
3. 2nd drive gear
4. Washer
5. 5th drive gear
6. Circlip
7. Spacer
8. Lock washer
9. 3rd drive gear
10. 4th drive gear
11. Circlip
12. Spacer
13. Lock washer
14. Bearing
15. Bearing
16. Oil seat
17. Output cam dog
18. Oil seal
19. Circlip
20. Input cam dog
21. Spring
22. Sliding stopper
23. Stopper
24. Spring guide
25. Bearing
26. Spacer

2. With the special spring compressor, compress the spring and remove the two stoppers.

3. Carefully remove the other gear components noting location and direction of installation on the shaft.

4. The mainshaft is easily disassembled after removal of the bearings and circlips.

Inspection

See "Inspection" under "Transmission (750)," above.

Assembly

1. Always use circlips where applicable.

2. Note direction of mounting of gears.

3. Clean all metal components in solvent before mounting. Lubricate inner surfaces of gears before installing them on their shafts.

4. Refer to the exploded illustration of the transmission shafts. Note also the following points.

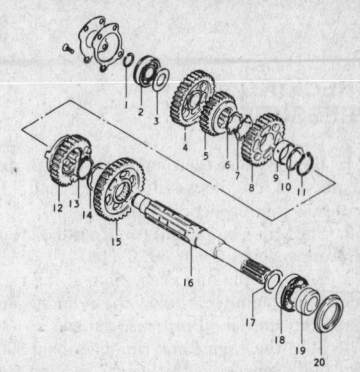

Always align oil holes in shafts, bushings, and gears

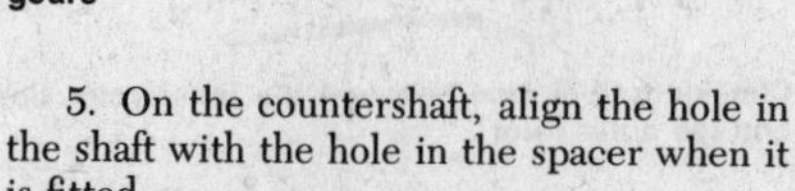

Be sure that the circlip is properly installed

Mainshaft assembly (GS 850)

1. Circlip
2. Bearing
3. Washer
4. 2nd driven gear
5. 5th driven gear
6. Washer
7. Lock washer
8. 3rd driven gear
9. Bushing
10. Washer
11. Circlip
12. 4th driven gear
13. Circlip
14. Washer
15. 1st driven gear
16. Drive shaft
17. Washer
18. Bearing
19. Spacer
20. Oil seal

5. On the countershaft, align the hole in the shaft with the hole in the spacer when it is fitted.

6. Be sure that the locating washer is fitted to the spacer dogs. Install the circlip to the side where the thrust is as shown in the illustration.

7. Be sure that the oil hole in the 3rd gear shift fork groove aligns with the oil hole in the countershaft. The same holds true of the 5th gear spacer. Also be sure that the spacer faces the proper direction.

8. Use moly paste on both sides of the washer fitted after the 2d gear and to the area of the outer countershaft bore 20–30 mm (0.8–1.2 in.) from each end of the shaft. Oil bearing surfaces.

9. Install the inner shaft into the outer. Mount the output cam dog on the outer shaft. Align the cutout on the cam dog with the oil hole in the countershaft.

10. Apply moly paste to the splines of the input cam dog and mount it on the inner countershaft.

11. Mount the spring, guide, and sliding stopper. Compress the spring and fit the stoppers.

12. For the mainshaft, the same precautions hold true. Be sure that the components are installed in the proper order facing the right direction.

13. After installing the 4th driven gear, install the circlip, then the washer. Temporarily position the circlip beyond the groove. Align the hole in the spacer with that in the shaft. Fit the 3rd gear.

14. Install the lockwasher, then the washer and turn the washer to align the lockwasher tongue with the washer cutout.

15. Fit the circlip installed earlier into its groove. Install it as shown in the illustration.

16. Align the oil hole in the 5th gear shift fork groove with the hole in the mainshaft.

LUBRICATION SYSTEM

CHECKING OIL PRESSURE

1. Be sure that the engine has the proper quantity of oil (between the "F" and "L" marks on the inspection window).
2. Start the engine and run it until oil temperature reaches about 60° C (140° F).
3. Remove the oil gallery plug at the right side of the engine just below the cylinders and install the special oil pressure gauge.
4. Start the engine and run it at about 3000 rpm while checking the gauge reading. Oil pressure should be about 1.42 psi or more (0.1 kg/cm²).
5. If the oil pressure is below this limit, remove and inspect the oil pump internals.
6. When fitting the oil gallery plug, be sure to secure it with a non-permanent thread-locking compound. Tighten the plug securely.

OIL PUMP

Removal

1. The oil pump is located just behind the clutch. "Engine and Transmission," for clutch removal procedures.
2. Remove the three securing screws and take off the oil pump.

Disassembly

1. Remove the circlip and pull off the pump gear.
2. Remove the securing screw.
3. Drive out the pins towards the transmission side of the pump.
4. Separate the pump case halves and take out the internals.

Inspection

1. Clean all parts thoroughly in a solvent.
2. Check the clearance between the inner rotor tip and the outer rotor. It must be 0.2 mm (0.008 in.) or less.
3. Check the clearance between the outer rotor and the pump body. It must be 0.25 mm (0.0098 in.) or less.
4. Place a straight edge across the pump body and check the side clearance between the straight edge and the sides of the rotors. Side clearance must be 0.15 mm (0.0059 in.) or less.
5. If any of the above clearances are not within the given specifications, the oil pump must be replaced.

Checking clearance between the inner rotor tip and the outer rotor

Assembly

Assembly is the reverse of disassembly. Lubricate all internal components with clean engine oil before assembly. Apply a non-permanent thread-locking compound to the securing screw.

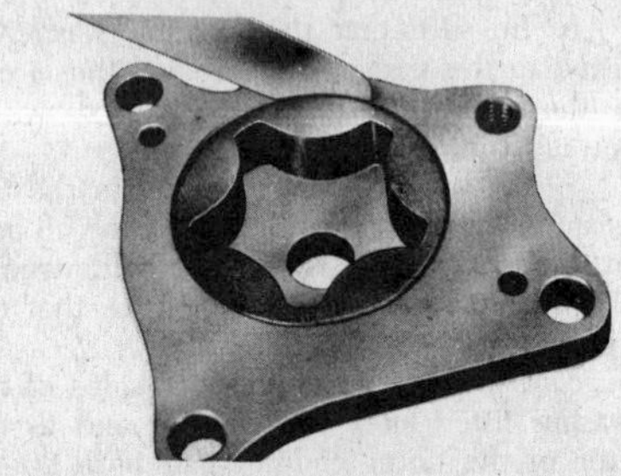

Checking clearance between the outer rotor and the pump body

Installation

1. Be sure that the two o-rings are in place behind the oil pump. The use of new o-rings is recommended.
2. Secure the three oil pump mounting screws with a non-permanent thread-locking compound.

OIL FILTER SCREEN

The oil filter screen should be cleaned every 6,000 miles, or about once a year.

The filter screen is easily reached after removing the exhaust pipes and the oil pan.

Use a new oil pan gasket on assembly. Be sure to tighten the pan bolts evenly to avoid distortion. Tighten the pan bolts to 7.2 ft lbs.

Checking rotor side clearance

FUEL SYSTEM

VM26SS CARBURETOR OVERHAUL

The following procedures apply to the VM26SS standard throttle slide carburetors.

Removal

The carburetors must be removed from the engine as an assembly.

1. Remove the gas tank.
2. Remove the air cleaner and the air cleaner box.
3. Disconnect the overflow lines from the from the linkage. Disconnect the choke cable, if fitted.
4. Loosen the securing clamps and pull the carburetors off the manifolds.
5. Drain the carburetor float bowls.

Installation

1. Installation is the reverse of removal.
2. Adjust the throttle cable free-play after connecting the cables. Be sure that all lines are tightly secured. Check for fuel leaks before starting the engine.

Disassembly

1. It is not necessary to separate the carburetors from their mounting plate to service the float bowl components and jets. This step is only necessary if the throttle slide is to be removed.
2. Remove the four carburetor caps.
3. Remove the five bolts which secure the throttle shaft. Four of the bolts are found beneath the carburetor caps, and the fifth secures the pulley to the throttle shaft.
4. Remove the screw which secures the stopper plate just to the right of the leftmost carburetor, and remove the stopper plate.
5. Pull out the throttle shaft.
6. Remove the four choke shaft screws. Remove the spring-loaded screw in the choke actuating lever slot. Pull out the choke shaft.
7. Remove the screws (2 ea) which secure the carburetor bodies to the mounting plate. Separate the carburetors.
8. Lift out the throttle arm complete with the throttle slide assembly. If replacement or repositioning of the needle is desired, remove the two screws which secure the throttle slide bracket to the slide.
9. Unscrew and remove the pilot air screw, its o-ring and spring.
10. Unscrew and remove the starter plunger assembly.

Remove the screws which secure the carbs to the mounting plate

11. Turn the carburetor upside down and remove the four float bowl retaining screws. Take the float bowl off carefully to avoid damage to the floats. Remove the float bowl gasket.
12. Unscrew and remove the main jet. Unscrew and remove the main jet holder/emulsion nozzle.
13. Unscrew and remove the pilot jet.
14. Push out the float pin and remove the float bulbs. Take out the float needle. Unscrew and remove the float needle seat.
15. Press out the needle jet from the carburetor bore side.

Cleaning

The carburetors have non-removeable plastic parts. Clean the body only in a solvent or carburetor cleaner which is safe for plastic. Blow all air and fuel passages clear with compressed air.

Clean the fuel jets in a solvent and blow them clear. Never insert anything into the jet bores to clear them if they are clogged as this risks ruining their calibration.

Inspection

1. Check the throttle slide surfaces for scoring or signs of wear. The slide should be smooth. The movement of the slide in the carburetor body should be very easy.
2. Examine the jet needle for wear along

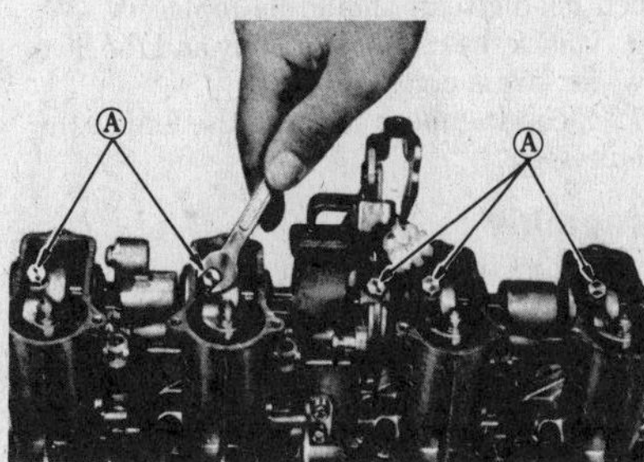

Removing the throttle shaft bolts

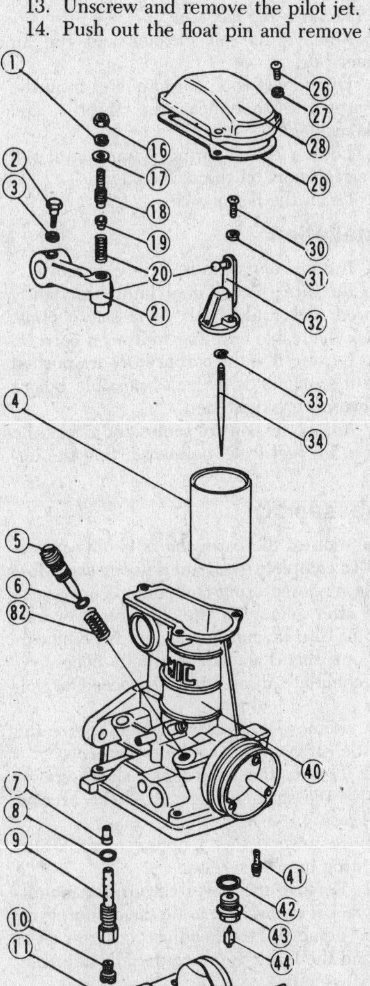

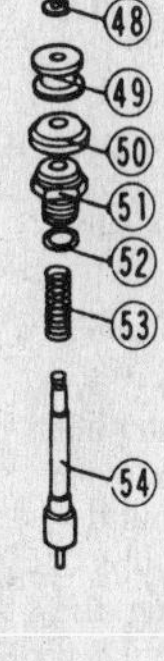

1. Lockwasher
2. Throttle arm shaft bolt
3. Lockwasher
4. Throttle slide
5. Pilot air screw
6. O-ring
7. Needle jet
8. O-ring
9. Nozzle
10. Main jet
11. Floats
12. Lockwasher
13. Screw
14. O-ring
15. Drain plug
16. Locknut
17. Washer
18. Adjusting screw
19. Ball seat
20. Spring
21. Throttle arm
26. Screw
27. Lockwasher
28. Cap
29. Gasket
30. Screw
31. Lockwasher
32. Bracket
33. Clip
34. Jet needle
40. Carburetor body
41. Pilot jet
42. Gasket
43. Needle seat
44. Float needle
45. Pivot pin
46. Gasket
47. Float bowl
48. Clip
49. Bush
50. Dust seal
51. Plunger cap
52. O-ring
53. Spring
54. Starter plunger

Carburetor assembly

the tapered portion as indicated by bright spots or unevenness of the taper. Also check the needle for nicks, and replace it if any damage is noted. Be sure that the needle clip is repositioned in the original groove.

3. After many miles, the needle and needle jet should be replaced, as these parts are subject to wear. Wear of these components may show up as a rich running condition in the mid-throttle range. If the needle seems worn, it would be best to replace the needle jet as well.

4. Check the float needle for wear of the tip or foreign matter and replace if necessary. Check the needle seat for corrosion or foreign matter. Clean off the seat if only dirty. Corroded needle seats should be replaced.

5. Check the carburetor body and the float bowl for stress cracks.

6. Inspect the pilot air screws. The taper of the screws should be very even. Replace if the screw tip is blunted.

Assembly

Assembly is basically the reverse of disassembly. Note the following points:

1. Use new gaskets and o-rings.
2. Do not overtighten the jets when fitting them to the carburetor body.
3. Check the float height.
4. On 1977 models only, screw the pilot screws in until they are lightly seated, then back them off 1¼ turns. Other models have preset pilot screws.
5. Check that the needle clip is positioned in the proper groove.
6. The screws which mount the carb bodies to the mounting plate should be secured with a non-permanent thread-locking compound.
7. Grease the throttle shaft and the lips of the throttle shaft seals before installing the shaft. Tighten the throttle shaft bolts to 2.5 ft lbs.
8. After the carburetors have been mounted on their plate, adjust the full-throttle stopper as follows: back off the idle adjuster screw until there is some clearance between the end of the screw and the pulley. Loosen the throttle slide adjusting screw locknuts and back off the adjusting screws so that the throttle slides are completely closed. This adjustment should be made carefully so that all four carburetors are as close as possible. Open the throttles as far as possible. Adjust the full-throttle stopper so that when this is done, the bottom edge of the slides will be 0.5–1.0 mm (0.02–0.04 in.) above the top of the carburetor bore, as illustrated. After installation has been completed, synchronize the throttle slides as outlined in the "Tune-Up" chapter.

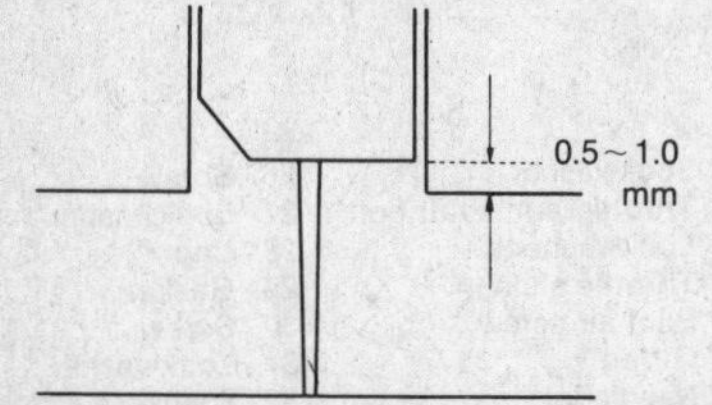

Adjust the full-throttle stopper so that the slides can be lifted 0.5–1.0 mm above the edge of the carburetor bore

Full-throttle stopper (B)

BS32SS CARBURETOR OVERHAUL

Unlike the standard carburetors in which the throttle slides are controlled directly by cable and linkage, the CV carburetor features a throttle plate controlled by the cable and twist-grip. This plate varies engine vacuum which itself determines the movement of the throttle slide.

Removal

1. Remove the gas tank.
2. Remove the air cleaner and the air cleaner box.
3. Disconnect the overflow lines from the carburetors. Disconnect the throttle and choke cables.
4. Loosen the securing clamps and pull the carburetors off the manifolds.
5. Drain the float bowls.

Installation

1. Installation is the reverse of removal.
2. Be sure that all fuel lines are tightly secured and fitted with their safety clips. Check that cable and line routing is correct.
3. Be sure that the carburetors are pushed onto the manifolds as far as possible before the clamps are tightened.
4. Adjust the control cables and check the system for fuel leaks before starting the engine.

Disassembly

Separation of the carburetors is only necessary if a complete overhaul is necessary. Most of the main metering components are accessible after removing the float bowl or carburetor cap. If routing cleaning is being carried out, this is all that is usually necessary. For complete disassembly, proceed as follows.

1. Remove the screws which secure the throttle cable and choke lever brackets.
2. Loosen the four choke shaft screws, remove the shaft, levers and choke bracket and lever.
3. Remove the upper carburetor mounting bracket screws.
4. Remove the lower carburetor mounting bracket screws. Separate the carburetors.
5. Remove the idle adjusting screw lever nut and the lever. Remove the idle adjusting screw assembly.
6. Remove the float bowl screws and carefully take off the float bowl. If it is stuck, tap it lightly with a screwdriver handle or the like while holding it in place.
7. Push out the float pivot pin and remove the float assembly.
8. Remove the float needle. Unscrew and remove the float needle seat.
9. Unscrew and remove the main jet. Note the washer beneath it.

Idle adjusting screw lever nut (6)

10. Remove the plug. Unscrew and remove the pilot jet.
11. Unscrew and remove the carburetor cap screws. Remove the cap, spring, and throttle slide assembly.
12. Push out the needle jet.

Cleaning

Clean the carburetor body in clean solvent designed for this job and which is safe for plastic parts.

Blow all air and fuel passages clear with compressed air.

Do not allow carburetor cleaner or any other solvent to contact the throttle slide diaphragm.

Clean the fuel jets in a solvent and blow them clear. Never insert anything into the jet bores to clear them if they are clogged as this risks ruining their sensitive calibration.

Inspection

1. Check the throttle slide diaphragm for punctures or tears. The slide must be replaced if damage is evident.
2. Check the throttle slide surfaces for scoring or signs of wear. The slide should be smooth. The movement of the slide in the carburetor body must be very easy and without binding.
3. Examine the jet needle for wear along the tapered portion as indicated by bright spots or unevenness of the taper. Also check the needle for handling damage such as nicks and replace it if any damage is noted.
4. After many miles, the needle and needle jet should be replaced, as these parts are subject to wear. Wear of these components may show up as a rich running condition in the mid-throttle range. If the needle seems worn, it would be best to replace the needle jet as well.
5. Check the float needle for wear of the tip or foreign matter and replace if necessary. Check the needle seat for corrosion or foreign matter. Clean off the seat if only dirty. Corroded needle seats should be replaced.
6. Check the carburetor body and the float bowl for stress cracks.
7. Clean the mesh filter on the end of the needle seat.

Assembly

Reverse the disassembly procedure and note the following points:

1. Always use new gaskets and o-rings.
2. Be sure that the throttle slide diaphragm is properly seated in the groove provided and that the locating tab of the diaphragm is fitted into the cutout.

3. Do not overtighten the jets when screwing them into the carb.

4. Check float height (see "Tune-Up").

5. Use a non-permanent thread locking compound on the idle adjusting bracket screws of the No. 3 carb.

6. Use a non-permanent thread locking compound on the upper and lower carburetor mounting bracket screws.

7. Be sure that the throttle shaft lever is installed as illustrated.

8. Non-permanent thread locking compound should be used on the choke shaft screws. These screws also fit tapered ends into countersinks in the shaft. Be sure they are correctly aligned.

9. After assembly is completed, and before the units are installed, perform a rough synchronization of the throttle valves by aligning the edge of each valve with the first bypass hole in the carb throats.

10. After installatcon, check float level and synchronize units. Adjust idle. Refer to "Tune-Up."

Throttle shaft lever correctly fitted

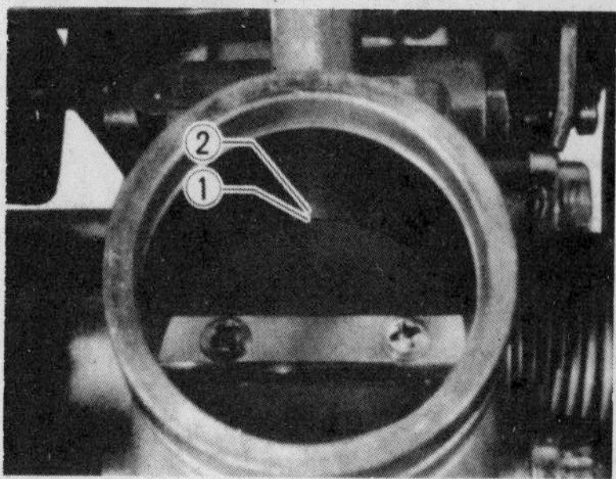

Throttle valve edge (1) aligned with bypass hole (2)

Carburetor Specifications

	GS 750/E	*GS 750L*	*GS 850G/GL/GN*	*GS 850GT/GLT*
Main jet	105	102.5	102.5	115
Pilot jet	22.5	15	15	40
Needle jet	P-1	0–4	0–4	X-5
Jet Needle	5F21-3	5DL36-2	5DL36-2	5D50
Throttle slide	2.5	1.5	1.5	—
Air jet	1.1	1.2	1.2	1.7
Bore (mm/in.)	26/1	26/1	26/1	32/1.26

ELECTRICAL SYSTEM

CHARGING SYSTEM

Alternator Output Test

The following test should be carried out if the battery fails to charge or overcharges. Before attempting the test, note the following:

a. Check the condition of the battery with a hydrometer. Test results will not be valid if the battery is defective. The battery must be *fully* charged. Charge the battery before beginning the test if it is not.

b. Check that all electrical connections are clean and tight. Check that the rectifier and regulator are properly mounted.

1. Remove the headlight switch knob and shut off the headlight or remove the 10A light fuses.
2. Raise the seat to gain access to the wiring connections. Disconnect the yellow wire from the regulator.
3. Disconnect the white/green alternator lead and the white/red rectifier lead and connect the two together.
4. Connect a DC voltmeter across the battery.
5. Making sure that all lights are off, start the engine and run it at a steady 5000 rpm while making note of the voltmeter reading. The voltmeter must read at least 17 volts. If it does, it shows that the alternator and rectifier are in serviceable condition. If the voltage reading is less than 17 volts, either the alternator or the rectifier or both are faulty. Procede to the components tests following.

If the voltage reading is satisfactory, the problem is probably the regulator. Test it as described below.

Starter solenoid (1), rectifier (2), regulator (3)

Regulator/Rectifier

While early models have separate regulator and rectifier units (see illustration), all others have both functions combined in a single sealed unit.

The regulator/rectifier can be tested with a simple continuity tester.

1. Disconnect all of the rectifier/regulator leads.
2. Put the positive probe of the tester on the red lead, and the negative probe on the yellow, white/blue, white/red, and black/white leads in turn.

There must be continuity in each case. Now reverse the probes. There must be no continuity.

3. Put the negative probe of the tester on the black/white lead, and the positive probe on the yellow, white/blue, and white/red leads in turn.

There must be continuity in each case. Now reverse the probes. There must be no continuity.

4. Connect the positive probe to the black/white lead and the negative probe to the yellow lead. The tester should show continuity.
5. Now connect the positive probe to the yellow, white/blue, white/red, and black/white leads in turn while the negative probe is connected to the red lead. There should be no continuity.
6. Connect the positive probe to the black/white lead and the negative probe to the white/blue and white/red leads in turn. There must be no continuity.

If the regulator/rectifier fails to pass any of the continuity tests in Steps 2–6, it must be replaced.

Regulator Test

1. For the test to be valid, the battery must be in good condition and fully charged as for the alternator test just described. Be sure all electrical connections are clean and tight.
2. If the alternator output test outlined above has been carried out, reconnect all wiring to its original condition.
3. Connect a DC voltmeter across the battery terminals.
4. With all lights shut off, start and run the engine at 5000 rpm while noting the voltmeter reading.
5. The voltmeter must read at least 14.0–15.5 volts (or more). If it does not, and the alternator/rectifier test above indicates that those two components are satisfactory, it indicates that the regulator is at fault and must be replaced. No repairs are possible.

NOTE: *Electrical components are supplied by two manufacturers (Denso or Kokusan). When replacing parts, be sure that all are of the same make.*

Alternator Test

The alternator stator can be checked with a continuity tester or an ohmmeter.

1. Disconnect the three alternator leads (white/green, white/blue, yellow).
2. Check for continuity between each lead and the others. There must be continuity in each case. No continuity indicates a broken wire and necessitates replacement of the stator.

If an ohmmeter is being used, there should be about 0.65 ohms resistance between the leads. Too great or too low a resistance reading is indicative of stator damage and requires replacement of the unit.

3. Check for continuity between each of the alternator leads and the stator body. There must be *no* continuity here. If there is, it indicates an internal short which will necessitate replacement of the stator.
3. Check for frayed or stripped wires and repair them if found.

NOTE: *If replacement of the stator is necessary, make sure that it is of the same manufacture (Denso or Kokusan) as the rotor.*

Rectifier Test

The rectifier consists of six diodes arranged to produce full-wave rectification of the alternator's output into direct current.

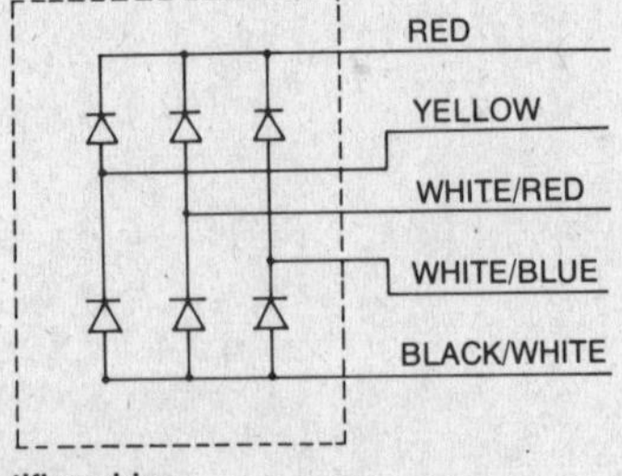

Rectifier wiring

All six diodes must be tested and all six must function properly or the unit will require replacement.

The rectifier can be checked with either a continuity tester or an ohmmeter.

CAUTION: *Do not use a megger.*

1. Disconnect all of the rectifier leads. They are: yellow, white/red and white/blue from the alternator; red from the battery; and black white from ground.

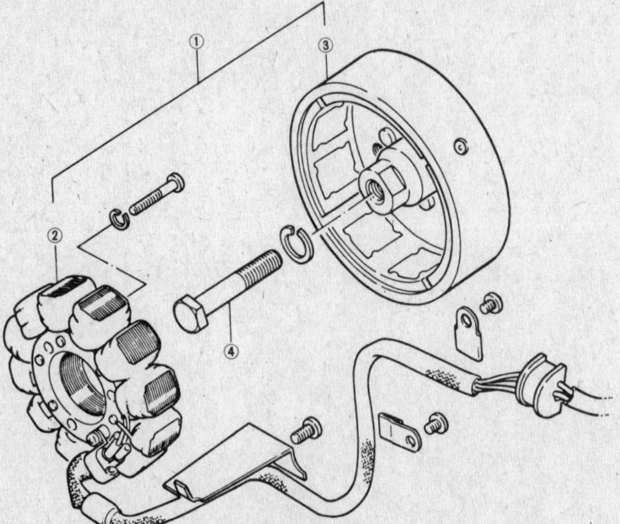

Alternator assembly (1), stator (2), rotor (3), rotor bolt (4)

CAUTION: *Be sure that all of the leads are disconnected, especially the red output wire or the rectifier may be damaged during the test.*

2. Place one lead of the continuity tester or ohmmeter on the red lead's terminal and the other to the yellow, white/red, and white/blue leads in turn. Note whether or not there is continuity or not.

Now reverse the tester leads and make the check with the same wires. Note whether there is continuity or not.

There must be continuity in one direction only. If there is continuity in neither direction, or in both directions for any of the diodes, the rectifier must be replaced.

3. Carry out the same tests between the yellow, white/red, and white/blue leads and the black/white (ground) terminal.

Once again, there must be continuity and in only one direction for each lead tested or the rectifier must be replaced.

BREAKER POINT IGNITION SYSTEM

The ignition system consists of the battery, breaker points, coils, condensers, spark plug caps, and spark plugs.

There are two sets of breaker points and two ignition coils. Each coil fires two cylinders. They are paired No. 1 and 4, and No. 2 and 3.

1. In the event of failure of the ignition system, first check the fuses; if all are in working order, check that the snap connectors for the coils and breaker points are all clean and tight.

2. At this point refer to inspection procedures for the breaker points, plugs, and battery. If these items are all in working order, the problem may be isolated to the coils, condensers, or plug caps.

3. If only one cylinder fails to fire, and the problem is not a loose connection or defective spark plug, suspect the plug cap. The caps are fitted with a resistor to prevent radio interference while in operation, and heat and vibration may cause the value of this resistor to increase considerably, even to becoming an open circuit.

The easiest way to see if a misfire is due to a defective cap is to switch the plug lead of the non-firing cylinder with its corresponding cylinder (1–4, 2–3). If the dead cylinder begins to fire and the other cylinder ceases, the problem is the plug cap. The caps should be replaced as a set.

Functional caps will have a resistance of 5,000–7,500 ohms. Usually, when resistance reaches about 9,000 ohms, the plug for that cap will no longer fire.

Caps are easily removable by unscrewing them from their cables.

4. Defective condensers are seldom a problem, since these are now usually replaced along with the breaker points. Defective condensers will cause considerable arcing or sparking between the breaker point contacts while the machine is running, and this should be cause for replacement before they tail completely. Badly burned or pitted point contact surfaces can also be caused by defective condensers, as well as by improper adjustment. If the points are in bad condition, replace them and the condensers as well.

5. Condenser capacity can be checked with electrical test equipment (if available) provided the condenser is first disconnected from the breaker plate.

Capacitance should be 0.25 MFD for Kokusan condensers and 0.18 MFD for Denso condensers.

6. If the condensers are not suspect, check the ignition coils. Coils can be checked for continuity of the windings. Check for continuity between the two low-tension wires. Resistance should be about 4 ohms. If there is no continuity, the primary winding is broken and the coil must be replaced.

Check for continuity on the high-tension side of each coil. Resistance is c. 15K ohms. Disconnect the two spark plug leads of one of the coils and check the continuity between them. If none exists, replace the coil. Repeat the test with the other coil. Remember you will be checking continuity between plug leads 1 and 4 and leads 2 and 3.

TRANSISTORIZED IGNITION SYSTEM

1. Disconnect the signal generator wires at the plastic coupler. Check resistance between the blue and green leads on the signal generator side. Standard resistance is 250–360 ohms.

2. If the signal generator resistance is satisfactory, remove the Nos. 1 and 2 spark plugs, connect them to their caps, and ground them against the cylinder head.

3. Remove the left side frame cover. Disconnect the signal generator leads at the coupler.

4. Turn the ignition switch "on." Connect the positive probe of an ohmmeter (set to the ohms x 1 range) to the blue lead of the *ignitor* side of the circuit, and the negative probe to the green lead, also on the ignitor side. The moment the probes are connected, the No. 1 plug should fire. The moment the probes are disconnected, the No. 2 plug should fire. If this happens, the ignitor is in workable condition.

5. Other parts of the system, such as plugs, plug caps, and ignition coils, are the same as described for the "Breaker Point Ignition System," above. Refer to that section if the electronic components check out and the problem persists.

STARTING SYSTEM

The starting system consists of the starter motor and clutch, the solenoid, and the handlebar-mounted starter switch. When the button is pressed, the electrical circuit to the solenoid is closed and the solenoid is activated, sending the battery current directly to the starter motor. The starting system is quite reliable and it is unlikely that any major problems will arise.

Testing

1. If, when pressing the starter button, the starter motor spins but the engine does not, the problem is probably the starter clutch. Refer to the "Engine and Transmission" chapter for removal procedures.

2. If the engine turns over very slowly, possible causes include cold weather and/or oil of too high viscosity, a low battery, or a defective starter motor.

3. If the engine fails to turn over and the warning lights dim when the starter button is pushed, causes may be a low battery or a defective starter motor.

4. If nothing at all happens when operating the starter button, check the button's electrical connections. If these are serviceable, suspect the starter solenoid.

5. A clattering sound when the starter button is operated may be caused by a defective solenoid or starter motor.

Starter Motor

REMOVAL AND INSTALLATION

1. Disconnect the cable from the battery positive terminal.

2. Disconnect the starter motor cable from the starter motor.

3. Remove the starter motor cover. Remove the alternator cover.

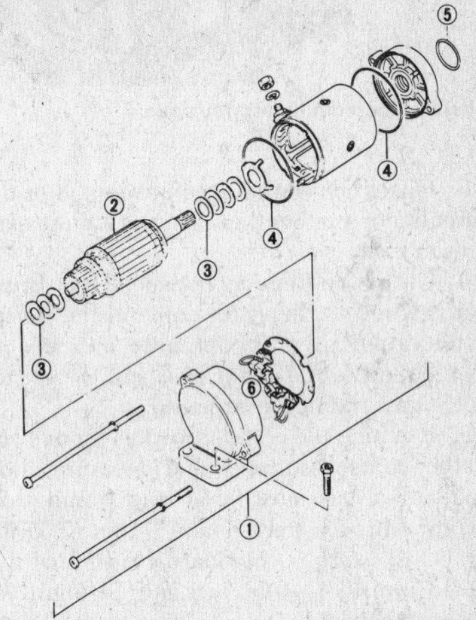

1. Starter motor assembly
2. Armature
3. Shims
4. Oil seal
5. O-ring
6. Brushes

Starter assembly

4. Remove the starter motor gear. Remove the mounting screws and take out the starter motor.

INSPECTION

Two makes of starter motor are used, Denso and Mitsuba. Although the starters are similar in appearance, some specifications differ.

1. Take out the two screws and remove the starter side cover.

2. Check electrical continuity between the commutator and armature core using a multitester or test light and battery. If continuity exists, the armature coil is grounded and the complete starter motor unit must be replaced.

Brush (1), brush spring (2) and commutator (3)

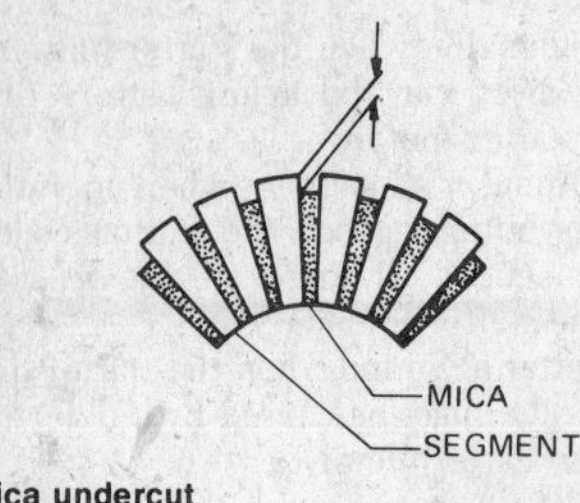

Mica undercut

Polishing the commutator surface

3. Check for continuity between all of the commutator segments. Continuity must exist in each case.

4. Check continuity between the brush that is wired to the stator coil and the starter motor cable. Lack of continuity indicates an open circuit in the stator coil, and the starter motor unit should be replaced.

5. Examine the carbon brushes for damage to the contact surfaces and measure their length. Brushes must be at least 6 mm (0.24 in.) for Mitsuba starters and 9 mm (0.35 in.) for Denso starters. Standard brush length is 12–13 mm (0.47–0.51 in.) and 14 mm (0.55 in.) respectively.

6. The mica undercut of the commutator should be at least 0.2 mm (0.008 in.). The standard specification is 06 mm (0.02 in.). Any carbon deposits should be cleaned out of the commutator grooves, and a piece of hacksaw blade or the like used to increase the undercut depth if necessary. Refer to the illustration.

7. Polish the commutator with fine emery cloth and clean it thoroughly before installation.

STARTER SOLENOID

1. If the battery is in reasonably good condition, and nothing at all happens when the starter button is pushed, check the solenoid.

2. Disconnect the starter cable at the starter motor. When the button is pushed, there should be an audible "click" which indicates that the solenoid is opening.

3. If further testing is necessary, remove the solenoid from the machine.

CAUTION: *Be sure to disconnect the cables at the battery before disconnecting the solenoid terminals.*

Checking resistance of the primary circuit

4. Connect a fully charged 12-volt battery to the solenoid low-tension terminal and the solenoid mounting bracket. Check for continuity across the high-tension leads with an ohmmeter or self-powered test light. If there is no continuity, replace the solenoid.

5. If an ohmmeter is available, check the resistance of the solenoid's primary winding by placing on meter probe on the low-tension terminal and the other on the mounting bracket. Primary winding resistance should be in the neighborhood of 3.5 ohms. If it is not, replace the solenoid.

ELECTRICAL COMPONENTS

Switch and component tests can be carried in most instances with an ohmmeter or test light with a self-contained power source.

NOTE: *After disconnecting the switch, be sure you are testing the switch side of the circuit.*

Ignition Switch

The four-pronged ignition switch plastic connector is inside the headlight shell. After removing the headlight and disconnecting the connector, check for continuity between each of the leads while moving the switch to each position in turn.

When the switch is "off," there should not be continuity between any of the leads.

When the switch is "on," there should be continuity between the red and orange leads and between the gray and brown leads.

When the switch is in the "P" position, there should be continuity between the red and the brown leads.

If the switch does not pass all of the above tests, replace it.

Headlight Switch

The headlight switch coupler is accessible after removing the gas tank.

When the switch is in the "on" position, there should be continuity between the orange and the green wires and between the white/green and the white/red wires.

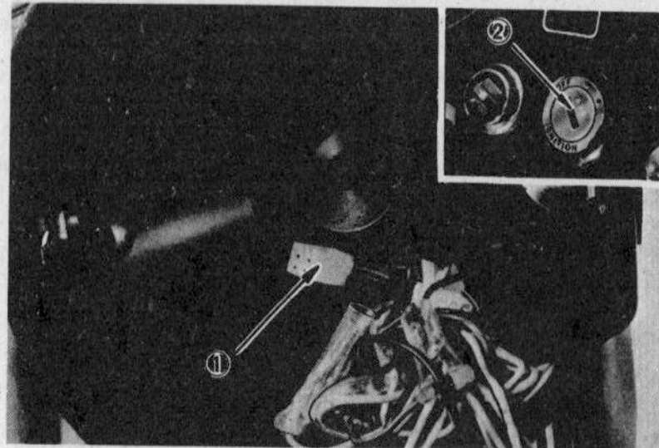
Ignition switch coupler

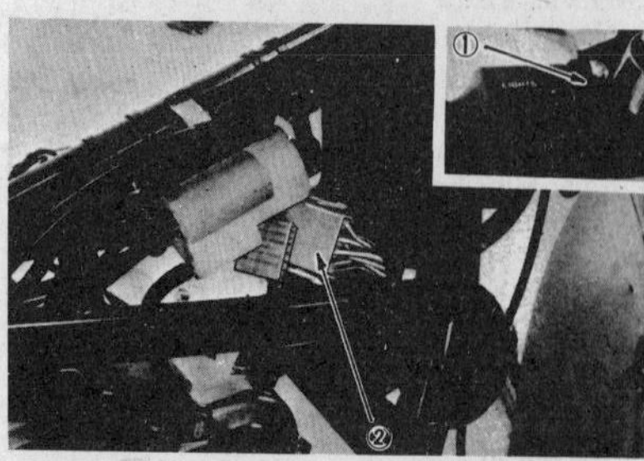
Lighting switch coupler

Dimmer Switch

The dimmer switch wiring is incorporated with the headlight switch coupler.

In the "L" position, there should be continuity between the white and the green leads.

In the "H" position, there should be continuity between the yellow and the green leads.

Front Brake Light Switch

Disconnect the white and orange switch leads inside the headlight shell. These leads should show continuity when the brake hand lever is operated.

Rear Brake Light Switch

Disconnect the white and orange leads from the switch and check for continuity across the switch terminals when the brake pedal is depressed. If there is none, try moving the switch on its bracket as far as possible. If there is still no reaction, replace the switch.

Horn and Horn Switch

If the horn fails to sound, the easiest way to check it is to disconnect the two wires at the horn itself and connect a 12-volt battery across the terminals. If the horn sounds, the switch is probably defective, barring loose connections in the circuit.

To check the horn switch, uncouple the large plastic connector beneath the gas tank and check for continuity between the green and black/white wires when the horn button is operated. There should be continuity. If there is not, there is undoubtedly a loose wire in the circuit.

Turn Signal Switch

Disconnect the leads from the switch and check for continuity between them with the switch in both positions in turn.

For the right turn signal, there should be continuity between the light green and light blue leads.

For the left turn signal there should be continuity between the black and the light blue leads.

Kill Button/Starter Button

The kill button and starter button are combined into one three-pronged coupler inside the headlight shell.

When the kill button is in the "Run" position, there should be continuity between the orange and the orange/white wires.

When the starter switch is pushed, there should be continuity between the yellow/green and the orange/white wires.

Bulb Chart

Light	*Wattage*
Headlight	50/35
Taillight/Brake light	8/23
Turn signals	23
Turn signal indicator	3.4
Instrument illuminators	3.4
High-beam indicator	3.4
Oil pressure warning light	3.4
Neutral indicator light	3.4

WIRING DIAGRAMS

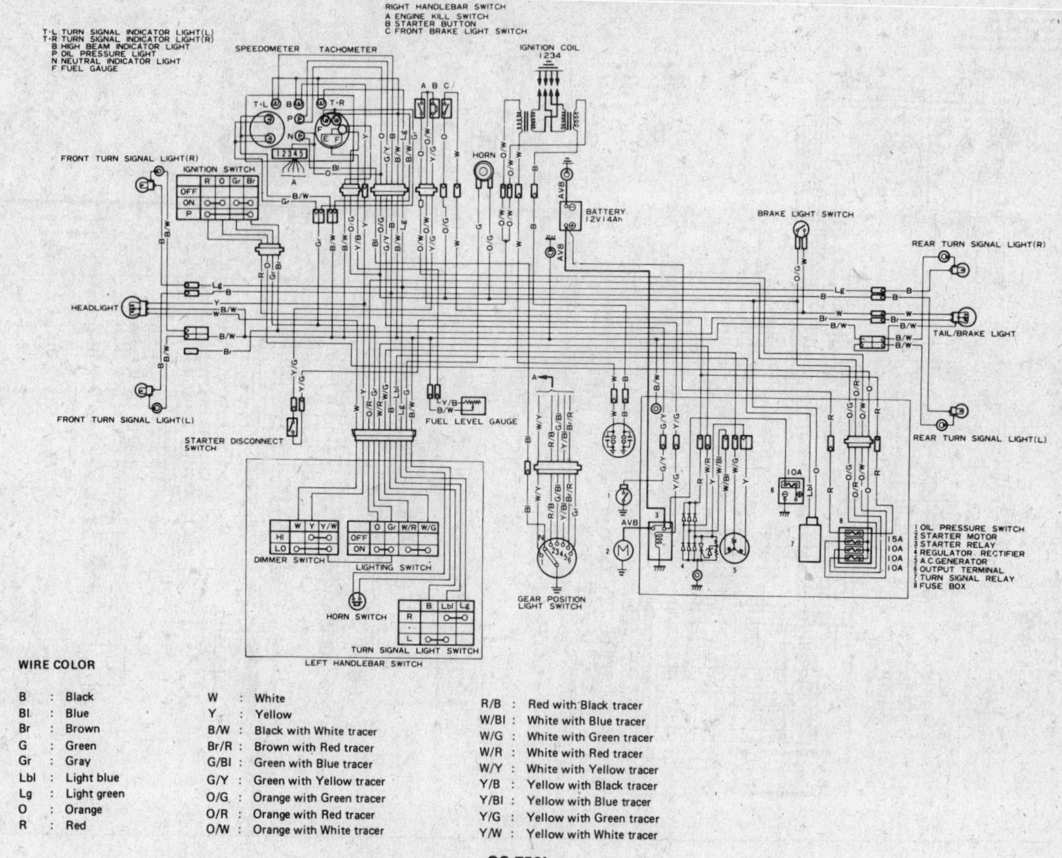

GS 750L

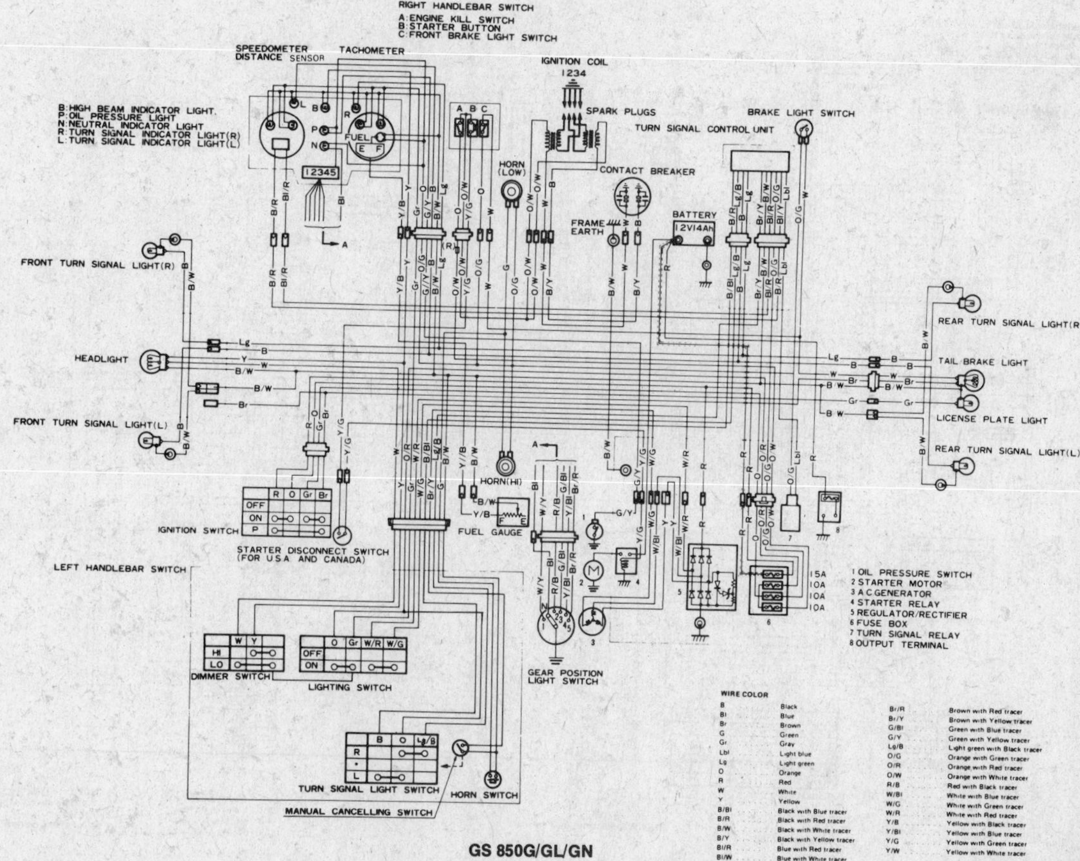

GS 850G/GL/GN

WIRING DIAGRAMS

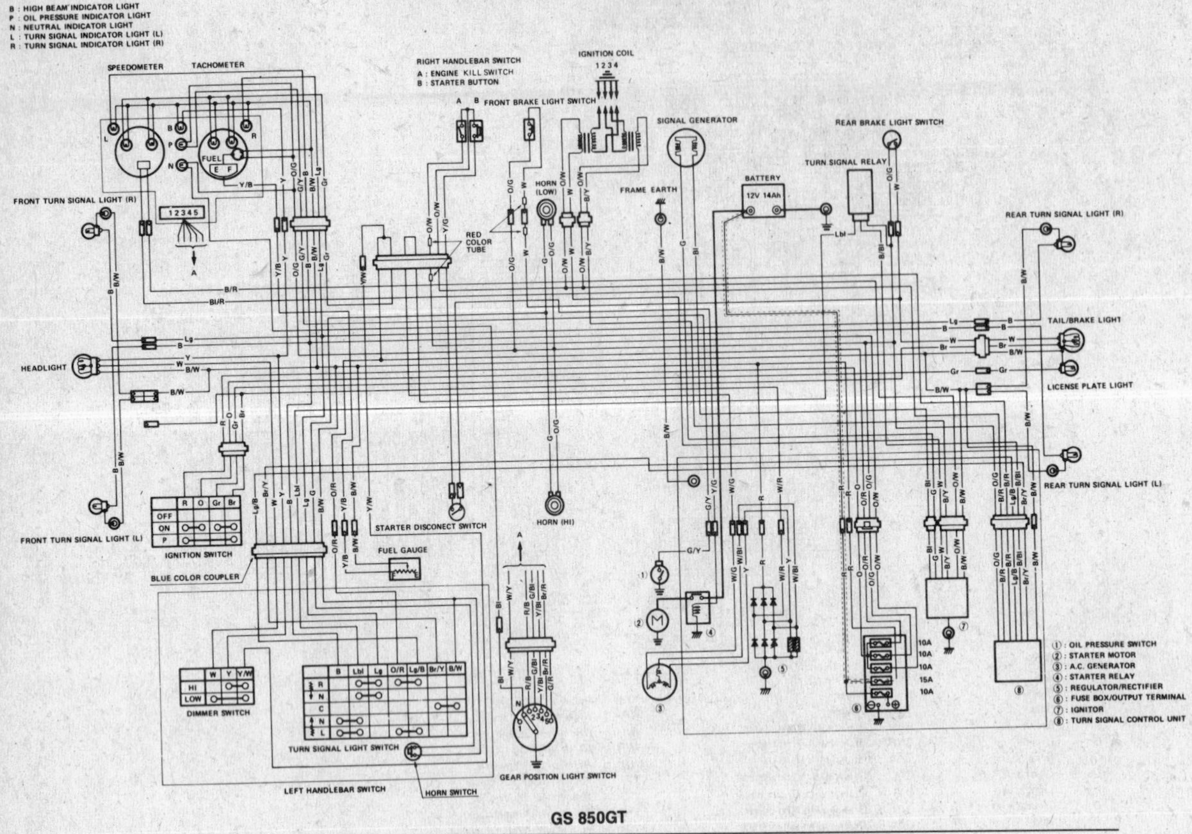

GS 850GT

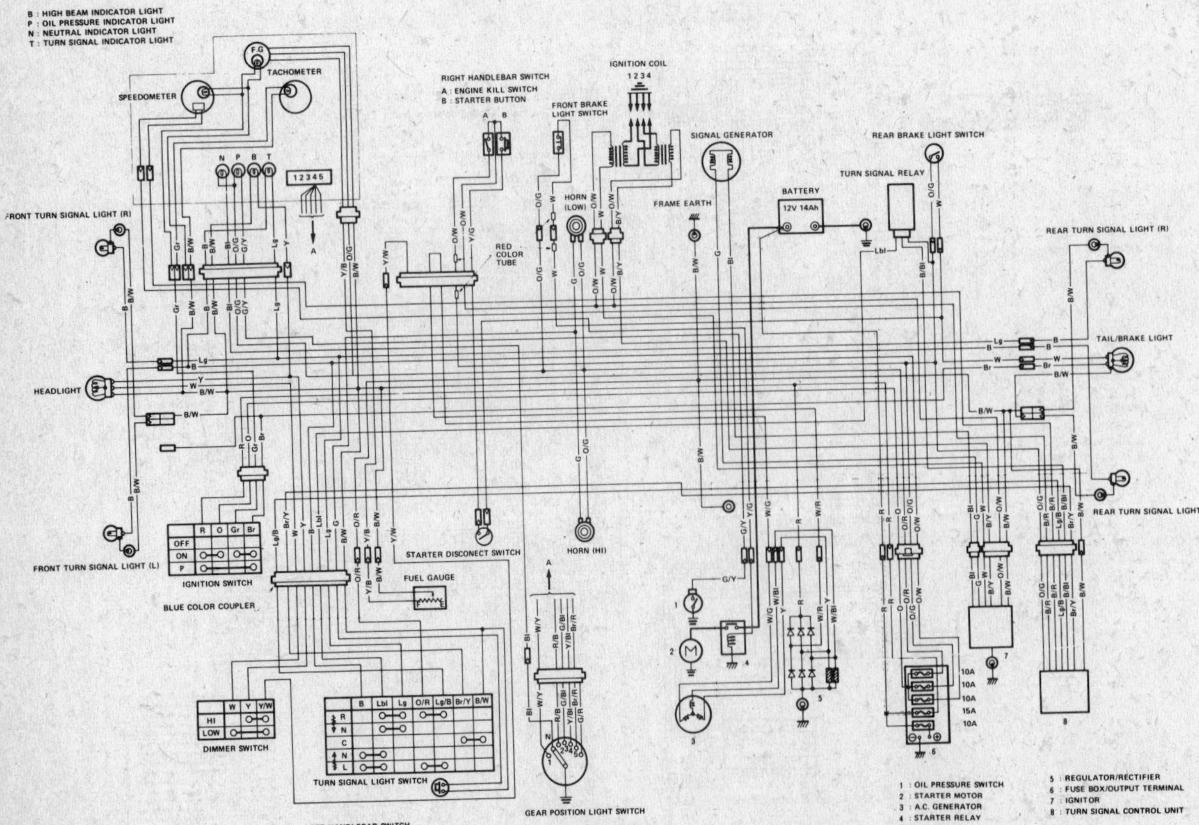

B : HIGH BEAM INDICATOR LIGHT
P : OIL PRESSURE INDICATOR LIGHT
N : NEUTRAL INDICATOR LIGHT
T : TURN SIGNAL INDICATOR LIGHT

SPEEDOMETER · TACHOMETER · F.G · RIGHT HANDLEBAR SWITCH · A : ENGINE KILL SWITCH · B : STARTER BUTTON · IGNITION COIL 1 2 3 4 · FRONT BRAKE LIGHT SWITCH · SIGNAL GENERATOR · REAR BRAKE LIGHT SWITCH · TURN SIGNAL RELAY · BATTERY 12V 14Ah · FRAME EARTH · HORN (LOW) · RED COLOR TUBE · FRONT TURN SIGNAL LIGHT (R) · REAR TURN SIGNAL LIGHT (R) · TAIL/BRAKE LIGHT · HEADLIGHT · REAR TURN SIGNAL LIGHT (L) · FRONT TURN SIGNAL LIGHT (L) · IGNITION SWITCH · BLUE COLOR COUPLER · STARTER DISCONECT SWITCH · HORN (HI) · FUEL GAUGE · DIMMER SWITCH · TURN SIGNAL LIGHT SWITCH · LEFT HANDLEBAR SWITCH · GEAR POSITION LIGHT SWITCH

1 : OIL PRESSURE SWITCH
2 : STARTER MOTOR
3 : A.C. GENERATOR
4 : STARTER RELAY
5 : REGULATOR/RECTIFIER
6 : FUSE BOX/OUTPUT TERMINAL
7 : IGNITOR
8 : TURN SIGNAL CONTROL UNIT

GS 850GLT

WIRING DIAGRAMS

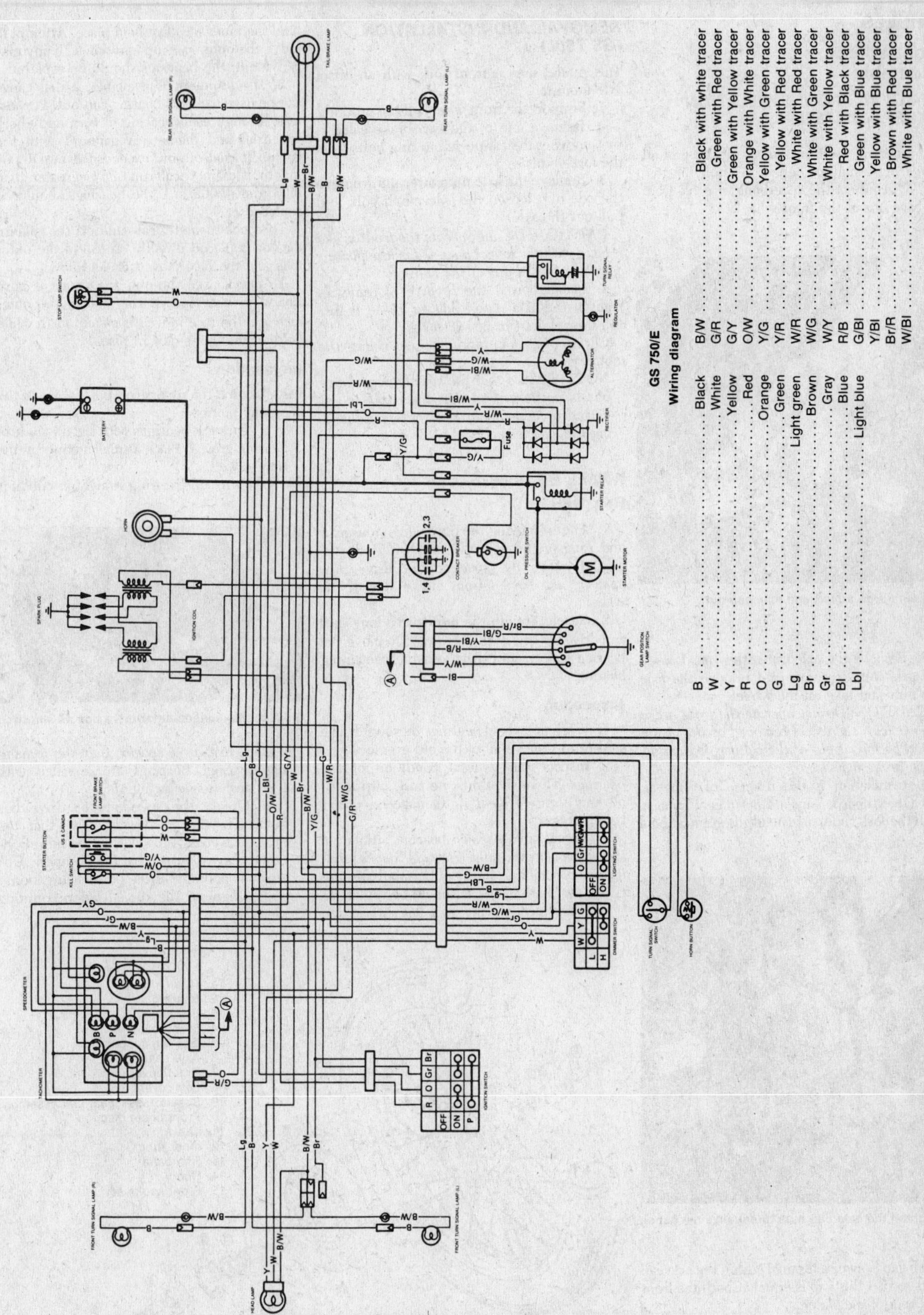
GS 750/E
Wiring diagram
B .... Black
W .... White
Y .... Yellow
R .... Red
O .... Orange
G .... Green
Lg .... Light green
Br .... Brown
Gr .... Gray
Bl .... Blue
Lbl .... Light blue
B/W .... Black with white tracer
G/R .... Green with Red tracer
G/Y .... Green with Yellow tracer
O/W .... Orange with White tracer
Y/G .... Yellow with Green tracer
Y/R .... Yellow with Red tracer
W/R .... White with Red tracer
W/G .... White with Green tracer
W/Y .... White with Yellow tracer
R/B .... Red with Black tracer
G/Bl .... Green with Blue tracer
Y/Bl .... Yellow with Blue tracer
Br/R .... Brown with Red tracer
W/Bl .... White with Blue tracer

CHASSIS

WHEELS

Front Wheel Assembly

REMOVAL AND INSTALLATION (EXCEPT GS 750L)

1. Support the front wheel off the ground by placing a support beneath the engine.
2. Disconnect the speedometer cable from its drive box at the front wheel.

Axle nut (large arrow) and axle cap nuts

3. Remove the axle nut cotter pin. Loosen the axle nut. Unscrew and remove the axle cap nuts and take off the wheel.

CAUTION: *Do not operate the front brake lever with the wheel removed or the piston will be forced out of the caliper, necessitating brake work.*

4. Installation is the reverse of removal. Note that the axle caps are not meant to mate with the fork sliders. Instead, there must be a small gap between them. Tighten the axle cap nuts so that this gap is equal at both the front and rear of the slider.

Tighten the axle cap nuts to equalize the gaps

Tighten the axle cap nuts to 11–18 ft lbs.
Tighten the axle nut to 26–38 ft lbs.
Check front brake operation before riding the motorcycle.

REMOVAL AND INSTALLATION (GS 750L)

This model uses a front fork with an offset axle mount.

1. Support the front wheel off the ground.
2. Remove one of the two brake calipers by removing the caliper mounting bolts from the fork slider.
3. Remove the axle nut cotter pin, remove the axle nut, loosen the axle pinch bolt, and pull out the axle.

CAUTION: *Do not operate the front brake lever with the wheel removed or the pistons will be forced out of the calipers.*

4. Installation is the reverse of removal. Tighten the axle pinch bolt to 11–18 ft lbs. and the axle nut to 26–38 ft lbs.

Check brake operation before riding the motorcycle.

NOTE: *Be sure that the speedometer drive box is positioned so that the cable is not kinked or excessively bent before tightening the axle nut.*

WHEEL BEARINGS

Removal

1. After removing the front wheel, unscrew and remove the axle nut and withdraw the axle. Remove the speedometer drive box, spacers, and covers from either side of the wheel.
2. Reach through the hub with a long drift and drive out one of the bearings. Remove the bearing spacer, and drive out the remaining bearing.

Inspection

1. Wash the wheel bearings thoroughly in a solvent to remove all of the old grease.
2. Inspect the general condition of the bearings. There should be no rust, pitting, or obvious signs of wear or damage on either balls or races.
3. Slowly rotate the bearing. Rotation should be smooth, noiseless, and free of binding or unevenness. If any of the above conditions exist, both bearings should be replaced.
4. Place each bearing on a flat surface and hold the inner race firmly in place. Attempt to move the outer race up and down. If any play is evident, the bearings should be replaced.
5. If equipment is available, a dial gauge can be used to check bearing run-out. Pass the axle through each bearing in turn and check the axial and diametrical run-out with the gauge. If axial run-out exceeds 0.1 mm (0.004 in.) or if diametrical run-out is greater than 0.05 mm (0.002 in.), the bearings should be replaced.

To check diameterical run-out, the dial indicator is placed directly on top of the outer race and the race moved up and down.

To check axial run-out, the gauge is positioned to bear against the side of the outer race and the race moved back and forth while holding the inner race in place.

Installation

Installation is the reverse of removal. Note the following points:

a. Pack the bearings with a good grade of bearing grease. Place a small amount in the hub as well.

b. Drive one bearing straight in until it is seated. Install the spacer, then the remaining bearing. Bearings are installed with their sealed side facing out.

Position the speedometer drive box as shown

c. Grease the speedometer drive box before installation. Install it so that the drive tabs engage the slots in the hub. Position the drive box so that the stamped "Up" arrow is pointing in the correct direction.

d. Degrease the disc(s) before refitting the wheel.

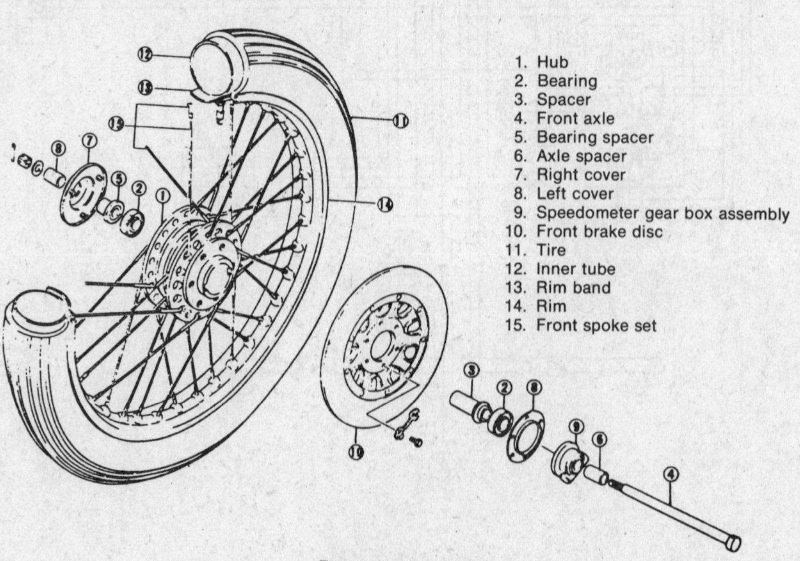

1. Hub
2. Bearing
3. Spacer
4. Front axle
5. Bearing spacer
6. Axle spacer
7. Right cover
8. Left cover
9. Speedometer gear box assembly
10. Front brake disc
11. Tire
12. Inner tube
13. Rim band
14. Rim
15. Front spoke set

Front wheel assembly

Brake anchor and caliper mounting bolts

Chain adjuster support bolt (1), cotter pin (2) and axle nut (3)

Rear Wheel Assembly

REMOVAL AND INSTALLATION (GS 750)

1. Remove the chain guard (2 bolts).
2. Remove the rear axle nut cotter pin. Loosen the axle nut.
3. Remove the two chain adjuster support bolts.
4. Remove the caliper anchor bolt. Remove the two caliper mounting bolts. Lift the caliper from its bracket and hang it out of the way. Be careful that the brake line is not twisted or otherwise subjected to stress.
5. Loosen the chain adjuster bolts and turn both adjusters down and out of the way so that the wheel can be taken off. Remove the chain adjuster supports.
6. Push the wheel forward as far as possible and disengage the chain from the rear sprocket.
7. Pull the wheel back and turn it to the side to remove it from the machine.
8. Installation is the reverse of removal. Note the following points:
   a. Install the wheel and the brake caliper. Tighten the chain adjuster support bolts to the proper torque (11–15 ft lbs), and the other nuts and bolts so that they are just hand-tight or a little more. Adjust the chain tension.
   b. Tighten the axle nut to 62–83 ft lbs.
   c. Spin the wheel while altering caliper position slightly so that there is no or little drag from the brake pads. With the caliper in this position, tighten the mounting bolts to 15–22 ft lbs.
   d. Tighten the caliper anchor nut to 15–22 ft lbs.

REMOVAL AND INSTALLATION (GS 850)

1. Park the bike on the centerstand on a firm, level surface.
2. Insert a phillips screwdriver into the right side of the centerstand.
3. Remove the upper shock absorber nuts and pull the shocks off the mounting lugs.
4. Use a 14 mm wrench or socket and ratchet on the rearmost caliper bolt to raise the swing arm slightly. As this is done, insert a bar through the right muffler support and swing arm hole.
5. Remove both shocks.
6. Disconnect the brake anchor from the caliper.
7. Remove the axle nut cotter pin and the axle nut. Pull out the axle while holding the caliper. Hang the caliper from the upper shock absorber mount.
8. Detach the wheel from the differential and remove it from the machine.
9. To remove the wheel from the fender well, it may be necessary to compress the front forks. Bleed pressure from the forks slowly. Turn the forks to the right and use the fork compressing tool.
10. Installation is the reverse of removal. Be sure that all components are properly torqued:

Axle nut: 62–83 ft lbs. (G/GL/GN)
36–58 ft lbs. (GT/GLT)
Brake anchor bolt: 15–22 ft lbs.
Shock nuts: 15–22 ft lbs.

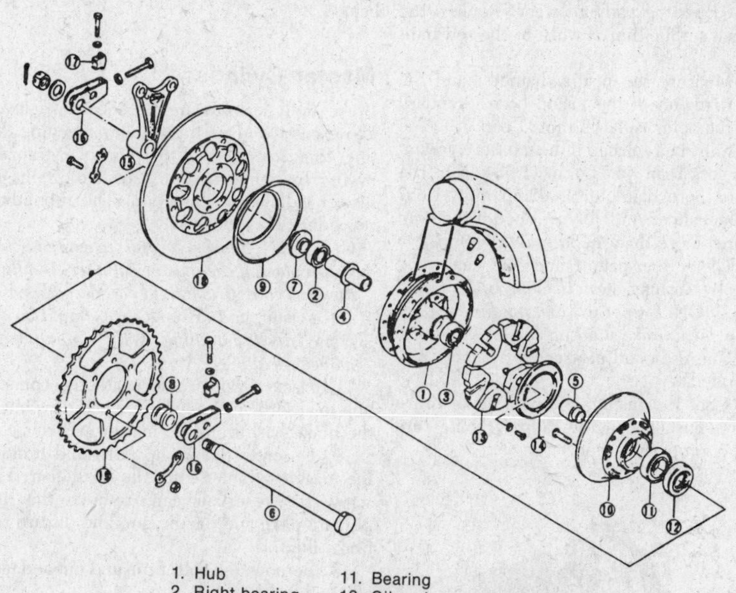

1. Hub
2. Right bearing
3. Left bearing
4. Bearing spacer
5. Bearing holder
6. Rear axle
7. Right spacer
8. Left spacer
9. Hub cover
10. Sprocket nub
11. Bearing
12. Oil seal
13. Damper rubbers
14. Plate
15. Caliper bracket
16. Chain adjuster
17. Chain adjuster supporter
18. Rear brake disc
19. Rear sprocket

Rear wheel assembly

WHEEL BEARINGS

Removal

1. Remove the axle nut and pull out the axle making careful note of the relative locations of the components such as chain adjuster plates, caliper bracket, and spacers which will come off.
2. Separate the sprocket hub from the wheel.
3. Reach through the hub with a long drift and drive out one of the bearings. Remove the spacer and drift out the remaining bearing.

Inspection

Check bearing condition as outlined for the front wheel bearings, above.

Installation

Installation is the reverse of the removal procedure. Note the following points:

a. Thoroughly pack each bearing with a good quality bearing grease. Put a small amount of grease in the hub as well.
b. Drive the bearings straight in until they are seated. Install the bearings so that the sealed sides face outwards.

Sprocket Hub

1. The sprocket hub contains a bearing and an oil seal. The bearing can be removed by prying out the oil seal and driving the bearing out towards the sprocket side of the hub. Inspection is the same as for wheel bearings described above.
2. Installation is accomplished by driving the bearing straight into the hub (from the sprocket side) until it is seated. The bearing should be lubricated with bearing grease.

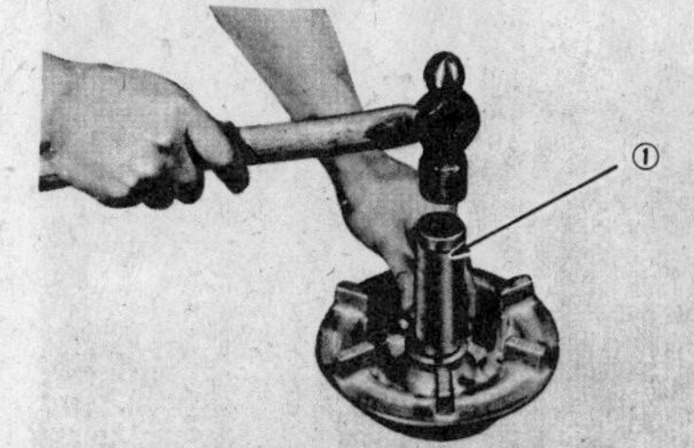

Removing the sprocket hub bearing

3. A new grease seal must always be used. Press it straight into the hub from the sprocket side. Grease the lips of the seal before installing the axle.

4. Check the shock absorber rubbers in the hub for damage and replace them if necessary.

Sprocket

1. Check the sprocket teeth for a hooked condition or other obvious signs of wear or damage. A worn sprocket should be replaced along with the chain and engine sprocket.

2. To remove the sprocket, bend down the securing nut lock tabs and remove the nuts. Installation is the reverse of removal.

FRONT BRAKE SERVICE (EXCEPT GS850GT/GLT)

Pad Replacement

1. Support the front wheel off the ground by placing a support beneath the engine. Remove the wheel.

2. Remove the screw which secures the fixed (inner) pad to the caliper and remove the pad.

3. Move the caliper over as far as possible and take out the remaining pad.

4. Pads which are worn to the red limit line must be replaced.

5. Installation is the reverse of removal. The screw which secures the fixed pad should be secured with a non-permanent thread-locking compound.

6. Before installing the moving (outer) pad, lightly smear its back and sides with the special silicone pad grease. The grease helps to keep pad operation smooth by repelling dirt and water as well as providing lubrication. Do not get any of the grease on the disc side of the pad.

7. Avoid heavy braking for at least fifty miles to allow the pads to seat properly.

Caliper

Leakage of brake fluid from around the caliper piston indicates a bad piston seal or damage to the piston or caliper bore. The cause should be investigated and remedied immediately. To remove, inspect, and rebuild the caliper assembly:

1. Remove the front wheel. Slightly loosen the two caliper shaft bolts.

Caliper mounting bolts

Caliper shaft bolts

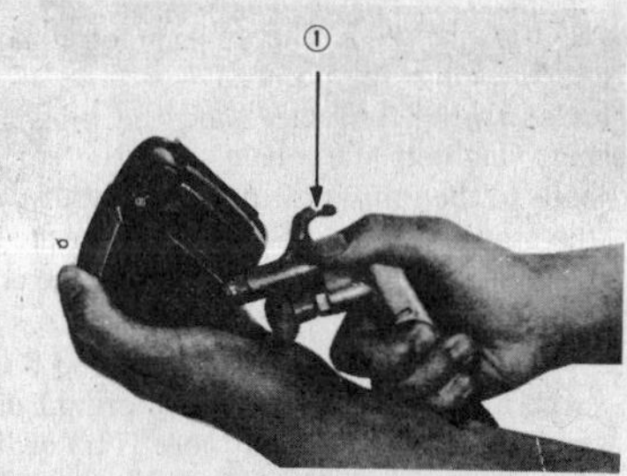

Removing the piston with compressed air

2. Disconnect the brake line fitting at the caliper and catch the brake fluid which will drain off in a suitable container. Discard this brake fluid. Used brake fluid should never be reused. Pump the brake lever to flush out all the fluid.

3. Remove the fixed pad securing screw. Remove the fixed pad, then the moving pad.

4. Remove the two caliper mounting bolts and separate the caliper from the fork slider.

5. Unscrew and remove the two caliper shaft bolts. Remove the caliper holder.

6. Remove the piston boot. Apply compressed air to the brake line drilling on the caliper and force out the piston.

7. Remove the dust seal and piston seal.

8. Check the pads for wear. Replace the pads as a set if either is worn to the red limit line.

9. Measure the piston diameter and the inside diameter of the piston bore. Standard piston diameter is 42.82 mm (1.686 in.). The piston must be replaced if the measured diameter is less than 42.77 mm (1.684 in.). The standard bore diameter is 42.85 mm (1.687 in.). The caliper must be replaced if the bore measures more than 42.89 mm (1.689 in.).

10. Clean the piston and the seals and o-rings by washing them in clean brake fluid.

CAUTION: *Do not use any fluid other than clean, new brake fluid on the brake parts.*

11. The use of all new rubber parts is recommended.

12. Coat the piston seal with fresh brake fluid and install it in the caliper, being sure that it is properly seated.

Caliper holder (1)

Measuring piston diameter

Piston seal in place (1)

13. Put the caliper holder in place. Lightly coat the piston with fresh brake fluid and install it in the caliper.

14. Install the pads, smearing the back and sides of the piston pad with the special silicone pad grease.

15. Smear the caliper shaft bolts with the special shaft grease. Install the shaft bolts and tighten them gradually and evenly until the proper torque (18–25 ft lbs.) is reached.

16. When fitting the caliper to the fork slider, tighten the caliper mounting bolts to 18–29 ft lbs. Tighten the brake line bolt to 11–18 ft lbs.

17. Refill the master cylinder with new brake fluid and bleed the lines as outlined below.

Master Cylinder

Brake fluid leakage around the brake lever and excessive lever travel (after bleeding the lines to make sure that there is no air trapped in the hydraulic system) are indications of master cylinder malfunction. The rebuilding procedure is as follows:

CAUTION: *Be very careful, when removing and replacing the master cylinder, in filling the reservoir. Brake fluid can damage paint and plastic, and extreme care should be exercised in its handling. Wipe up any spills immediately.*

1. Place a cloth underneath the connection to absorb any spilled fluid and disconnect the brake hose from the master cylinder.

2. Unscrew the clamp bolts and remove the master cylinder from the handlebar. Unscrew the reservoir cap, remove the diaphragm plate and diaphragm, and discard the brake fluid.

3. Remove the cotter pin and nut and take off the hand lever.

4. Remove the rubber boot. Using the special tool, remove the circlip from the master cylinder bore.

5. Using a soft wood drift or the like, push the piston assembly out of the bore from the line side. Be sure that this is done carefully to avoid scratching the bore.

6. Remove the two screws which hold the

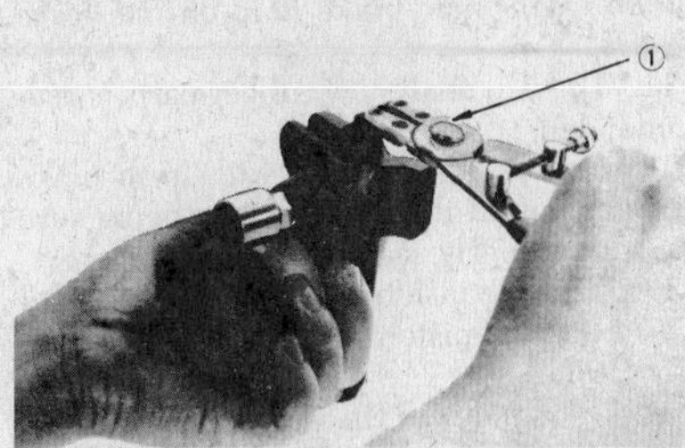

Removing the master cylinder assembly circlip

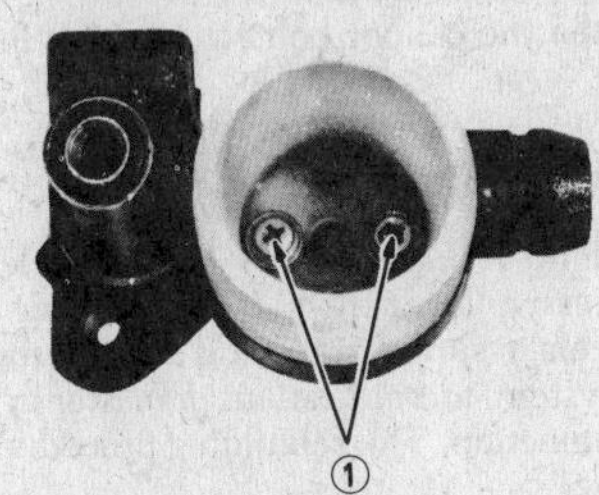

Reservoir securing screws

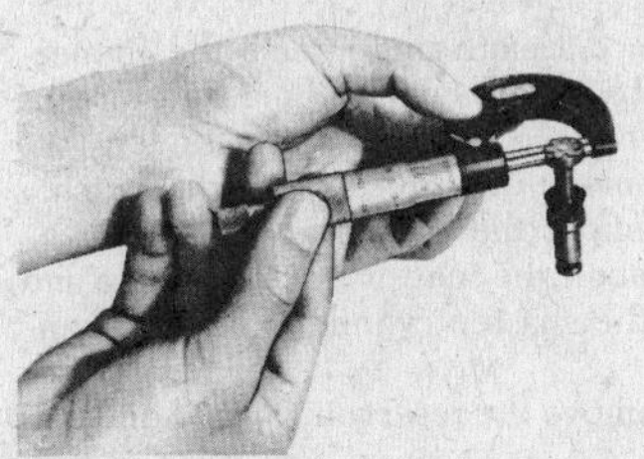
Measuring the piston diameter

master cylinder reservoir and remove it and its o-ring.

7. Measure the diameter of the master cylinder piston and the piston bore. Specifications differ depending on whether the single or double-disc set-up is fitted.

For single-disc models, the standard piston diameter is 13.96 mm (0.550 in.), and the piston should be replaced if the diameter is less than 13.94 mm (0.549 in.). The standard bore diameter is 14.00 mm (0.551 in.), and the master cylinder should be replaced if the measured bore diameter is more than 14.05 mm (0.553 in.).

For double-disc models, the piston diameter is 15.80 mm (0.622 in.) and the bore diameter is 15.87 mm (0.625 in.).

8. If fluid leakage was noted around the bottom of the master cylinder reservoir, the fault probably lies with the reservoir o-ring which should be replaced.

9. Clean the piston assembly in new brake fluid only. The use of new rubber parts (boot, primary and secondary cups) is recommended.

10. Assembly is basically the reverse of disassembly. Lightly lubricate the master cylinder bore and the piston assembly with clean new brake fluid before inserting the piston assembly in the bore. The piston assembly should be inserted as a unit, not one piece at a time. Be sure that the check valve does not become cocked or unseats the spring as it is inserted.

11. The use of a new circlip is recommended. Be sure that the circlip is properly seated in its groove, with the sharp edge away from the spring.

12. When mounting the master cylinder on the handlebar, allow a clearance of about 2 mm (0.08 in.) between the master cylinder clamp and the twist grip.

13. When tightening the brake line bolt, arrange the line so that it is about 15° from vertical. Tighten the bolt to 11–18 ft lbs.

14. Refill the system with fresh brake fluid and bleed the line as outlined below.

Installing the piston assembly

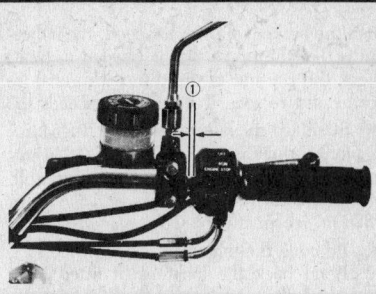

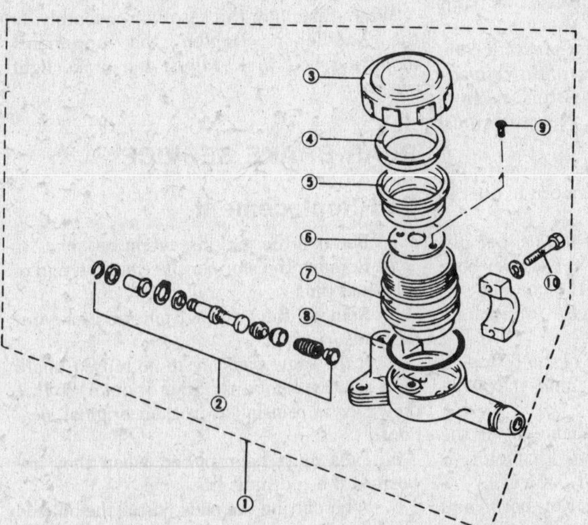

1. Master cylinder assembly
2. Piston cup set
3. Oil reservoir cap
4. Diaphragm plate
5. Diaphragm
6. Reservoir plate
7. Reservoir
8. "O" ring
9. Screw
10. Bolt

Master cylinder assembly

Install the master cylinder assembly about 2 mm (0.08 in.) away from the twist-grip

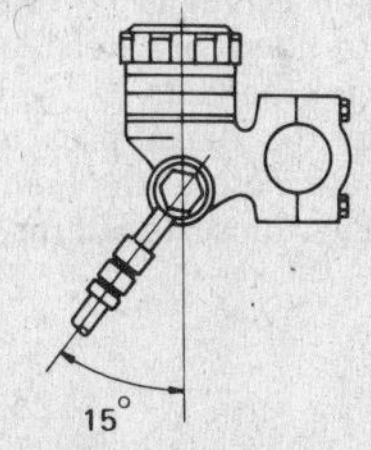

Tighten the banjo bolt so that the fitting is positioned as shown

Measuring brake disc thickness

Checking brake disc run-out

Disc Service

The brake disc normally requires no service of any kind. However, if the disc becomes scored for any reason, it should be replaced and a new set of pads should be installed. A badly scored disc will reduce the effectiveness of the brake and shorten pad life considerably. If the front brake lever oscillates or fluctuates when the brake is applied at speed, the indication is that the brake disc is warped or bent. Check the run-out of the disc with a dial indicator and replace it if run-out exceeds 0.3 disc. Standard thickness is 6.7 mm (0.264 in.) for single front discs and 6.0 mm (0.236 in.) for double front disc, while the serviceable limits are 6.00 mm (0.236 in.) and 5.50 mm (0.220 in.) respectively. To replace the disc:

1. Remove the wheel.
2. Bend back the locktabs (if fitted), unscrew the bolts, and remove the disc from the hub.
3. Mount the new disc on the hub and tighten the bolts evenly to 11–18 ft lbs. using new loktabs (if fitted) or thread-locking compound to secure the bolts.
4. Examine the brake pads and replace them if they are close to the limit of wear or have worn in an unusual pattern.

Bleeding

The brake hydraulic system must be bled whenever any part of the system has been disconnected or removed for service. When refilling the master cylinder reservoir, use only brake fluid conforming to DOT 3 specifications. Any brand meeting this requirement is acceptable. The brake fluid container of all reputable brands will be plainly marked with the standards the fluid meets or exceeds.

NOTE: *If you have a double disc setup, bleed the side furthest from the master cylinder first, then bleed the other side. Pulling and tapping on the lines will help expel any air bubbles trapped in the system. If you find that you can't get the system bled properly and the master cylinder has been dry for awhile, the seals inside the cylinder may have become dried and cracked. In this case rebuild the master cylinder.*

1. Top up the reservoir with brake fluid and replace the cap to keep dirt and moisture out and the fluid in. Cover the gas tank with a thick cloth to avoid damage due to spilled brake fluid.
2. Attach one end of a small diameter rubber hose to the bleed valve on the caliper, and place the other end in a jar which contains several inches of clean, new brake fluid. Be sure that the end of the hose is submerged in this fluid. Arrange the hose so that it loops upward after leaving the bleed valve, and see that it has no kinks or sharp bends.
3. Pump the brake lever rapidly several times until some resistance is felt and, holding the lever against the resistance, open the bleed valve about one-half turn. When the lever bottoms, close the valve (do not overtighten) and then release the lever.
4. Repeat this operation until no more air is released out of the hose and the brake lever is firm in operation. Check the fluid level in the reservoir often to make sure that it doesn't go dry and draw more air into the system. Do not reuse fluid that has been pumped out of the system. Do not use fluid that has been stored for more than a few weeks after the seal on its container has been opened, as brake fluid will absorb moisture from the air and may corrode the master cylinder and caliper.
5. Refill the reservoir to the level mark when through (but do not overfill). Avoid overtightening the cap or fluid will weep around the cap edge.

FRONT BRAKE SERVICE (GS 850GT/GLT)

Pad Replacement

1. Remove the two caliper-to-axle bolts and take the caliper from the holder.
2. Remove the pads and shim.

Caliper axle bolts

3. Install the new pads. They must always be replaced as a set. Do not use pad grease on this brake system.
4. When refitting the caliper, push the piston in all the way to facilitate assembly.
5. Tighten the caliper axle bolts to 11–15 ft lbs.
6. Avoid heavy braking for about fifty miles after installing new pads to allow them to seat properly.

CAUTION: *Do not operate the brake lever while the caliper is removed or the piston will be ejected.*

Caliper

Leakage of brake fluid from around the caliper piston indicates a bad piston seal or damage to the piston or caliper bore. The cause should be investigated and remedied immediately. To remove, inspect, and rebuild the caliper:

1. Disconnect the brake line at the caliper and squeeze the lever repeatedly until all of the fluid is pumped out of the system. Discard this fluid.
2. Remove the two axle bolts which secure the caliper to the holder.
3. Remove the two bolts which secure the caliper holder to the fork slider.
4. Stuff a clean rag into the caliper and apply *low pressure* air to the brake line banjo hole to push out the piston.

CAUTION: *Do not use high pressure compressed air. Keep fingers out of the caliper.*

5. Remove the boot and piston seal from the caliper and discard them. New seals must be used.
6. Check the brake pads for wear. Replace them as a set if either is worn to the red limit line.
7. Check the surfaces of the caliper piston and the inner surfaces of the caliper bore for scoring, pitting, or rust. The components should be replaced unless these surfaces are in perfect condition.
8. Measure the diameter of the piston. It should be 38.098–38.148 mm (1.4999–1.5019 in.).
9. Measure the inside diameter of the caliper bore. Standard bore diameter is 38.180–38.256 mm (1.5031–1.5061 in.).
10. Clean the piston, interior bore, and caliper passages in clean brake fluid.

CAUTION: *Do not use any fluid other than clean, new brake fluid on the brake parts.*

11. The use of all new rubber parts is recommended.
12. Coat the piston seal with fresh brake fluid and install it in the caliper, being sure that it is properly seated.
13. Coat the inside of the caliper bore and the sides of the piston with brake fluid before installation.

The remainder of the procedure is the reverse of disassembly. Note the following points.

Grease the caliper axles and tighten axle bolts to 11–15 ft lbs.

Tighten the caliper bolts to 18–29 ft lbs.

Master Cylinder

Brake fluid leakage around the brake lever and excessive lever travel (after bleeding the lines to make sure that there is no air trapped in the system) are indications of master cylinder malfunction. The rebuilding procedure is as follows:

CAUTION: *Be very careful, when removing and replacing the master cylinder. Brake fluid can damage paint and plastic, and extreme care should be exercised in its handling. Wipe up any spills immediately.*

1. Place a cloth underneath the connection to absorb any spilled fluid and disconnect the hose from the master cylinder.
2. Remove the front brake light switch.
3. Remove the brake lever.
4. Unbolt the master cylinder clamp and remove the master cylinder from the handlebar.
5. Remove the reservoir cap and drain off the fluid.
6. Remove the reservoir and o-ring.
7. Pry out the piston dust seal boot.
8. Use a pair of snap-ring pliers, remove the circlip. Take out the piston assembly.
9. Master cylinder bore diameter is 15.870–15.913 mm (0.6248–0.6265 in.). Piston diameter is 15.827–15.854 mm (0.6231–0.6242 in.).
10. Assembly is the reverse of disassembly. Clean all metal parts in clean brake fluid. All rubber parts should be replaced. Lubricate the bore and piston assembly with brake fluid before assembly.

When installing the reservoir assembly on the handlebar, tighten the uppermost mounting bolt first. Adjust the brake light switch.

REAR BRAKE SERVICE

Pad Replacement

1. Remove the pad inspection cap.
2. Remove the stopper pin from the end of each pad pin.
3. Remove the two pad pins and take out the pads.
4. If the same pads are to be reused, mark their relative locations (inner or outer) so that they can be reinstalled in their original locations.
5. Pads must be replaced when they are worn to the red limit line.
6. When fitting the pads, install the outside pad first. Be sure that the springs are not left out. Install the pad pins and the stopper pins.

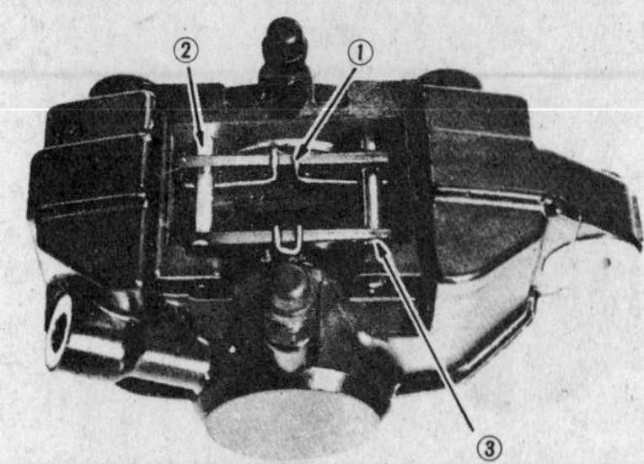

Rear disc brake pad springs (1), pins (2) and pads (3)

NOTE: *Although it is possible to install new pads with the caliper installed, Suzuki warns that the piston boots may be displaced when this is done. If this happens, it will be necessary to remove the caliper and then install the pads.*

Caliper

1. Disconnect the brake line at the caliper.
2. Unbolt the caliper anchor.
3. Remove the two caliper mounting bolts and take off the caliper.
4. Remove the pad inspection cap. Remove the stopper pins, the pad pins, springs, and pads.
5. Unscrew and remove the two caliper allen bolts, and separate the caliper halves.
6. Remove the piston boots. Apply compressed air to the fluid passage of each caliper half to force the pistons out of their bores.

Caliper allen bolts (1)

7. Measure the diameter of each piston and each piston bore and compare the measurements.

Standard piston diameter is 38.15 mm (1.502 in.) and the pistons should be replaced if the diameter is less than 38.18 mm (1.501 in.).

Standard bore diameter is 38.18 mm (1.503 in.) and the caliper should be replaced if either bore measures more than 38.19 mm (1.504 in.).

8. Clean all parts in clean, fresh brake fluid. It is recommended that the piston boots, piston seals, and fluid passage seal be replaced with new parts.
9. When assembling the caliper, be sure that the fluid passage seal is in place. Tighten the allen bolts to 18–25 ft lbs.
10. Tighten the caliper mounting bolts to 18–30 ft lbs., and the brake anchor nut to 15–22 ft lbs.
11. When fitting the fluid line, arrange it so that the line runs parallel to the centerline of the caliper. Tighten the fitting bolt to 11–18 ft lbs.

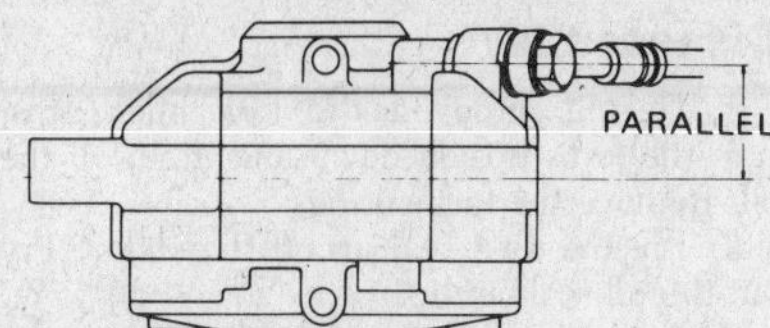

Tighten the banjo bolt so that the brake line is parallel to the caliper body

Master Cylinder

NOTE: *Late models have a modified rear master cylinder in which the reservoir itself is separated from the piston/cylinder housing and is connected by a hose. Other than this, procedures and specifications are the same.*

1. Remove the right-side rider's footpeg.
2. Remove the brake pedal and remove the cotter pin from the brake rod. Push out the clevis pin.
3. Disconnect the brake line at the master cylinder.
4. Remove the two master cylinder mounting bolts and take off the master cylinder.
5. Remove the master cylinder cap, diaphragm plate and diaphragm and pour out the brake fluid.
6. Remove the pushrod boot. Remove the pushrod circlip using the special tool or a suitable substitute. Push the piston assembly out from the opposite side.
7. Remove the two screws securing the master cylinder reservoir and remove it and the o-ring.
8. Measure the diameter of the piston and that of the cylinder bore.

Standard piston diameter is 13.96 mm (0.550 in.), and the piston should be replaced if the measured diameter is less than 13.94 mm (0.549 in.).

Standard bore diameter is 14.00 mm (0.551 in.), and the master cylinder should be replaced if the measured diameter exceeds 14.05 mm (0.553 in.).

9. Clean all parts in clean, fresh brake fluid. The use of new cups and o-ring is recommended.
10. Assembly is the reverse of disassembly. Lightly lubricate the piston assembly with clean, fresh brake fluid. Insert the assembly into the master cylinder as a unit. Be sure that the check valve and spring are properly seated and that the primary cup does not become cocked inside the bore.
11. When fitting the circlip, be sure that it is properly seated.
12. After mounting the master cylinder to the frame (bolt torque: 11–15 ft lbs.) and connecting the fluid line (bolt torque: 11–18 ft lbs.), refill the master cylinder with clean, fresh brake fluid and bleed the system.

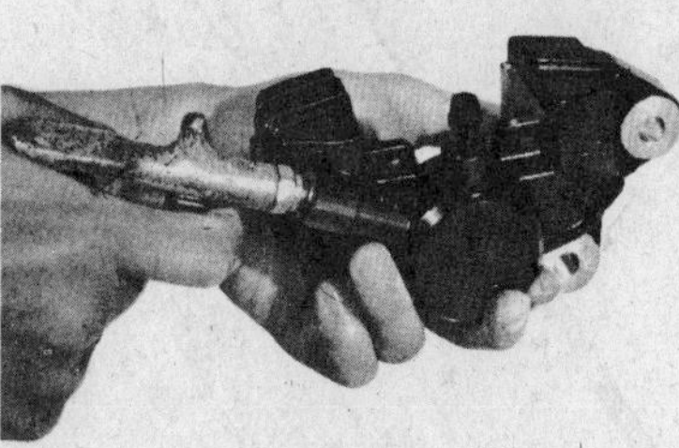

Removing the piston with compressed air

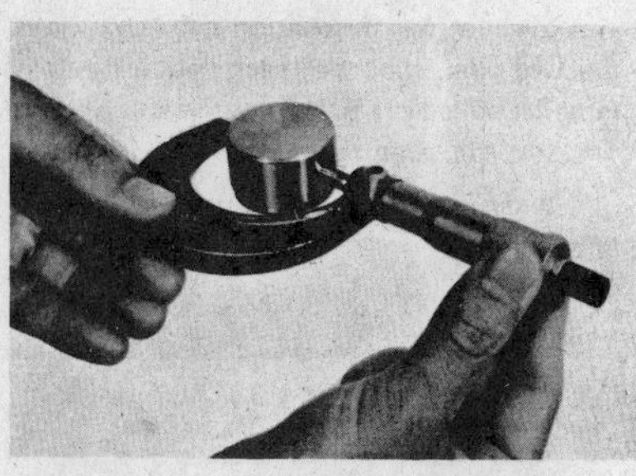

Measuring piston diameter

Bleeding

Bleeding the rear brake system is carried out in the same manner as for the front brake outlined above. The rear caliper has two bleed nipples, unlike the front which has only one. Bleed the wheel side nipple first, then the outer nipple.

FRONT FORKS (GS 750)

Removal

1. Support the front wheel off the ground. Remove the front wheel and fender.
2. Remove the caliper(s) from the fork slider.

CAUTION: *Do not allow the caliper(s) to hang by the brake hose. Tie them out of the way with string or wire.*

3. Remove the fork filler cap at the top of each fork leg. Loosen the upper triple clamp pinch bolts to facilitate filler cap removal.

NOTE: *It may be necessary to remove the handlebars to do so, but the controls may be left connected, and the bars gently laid to one side when the mounting bolts are removed.*

4. Loosen the upper and lower triple clamp pinch bolts.

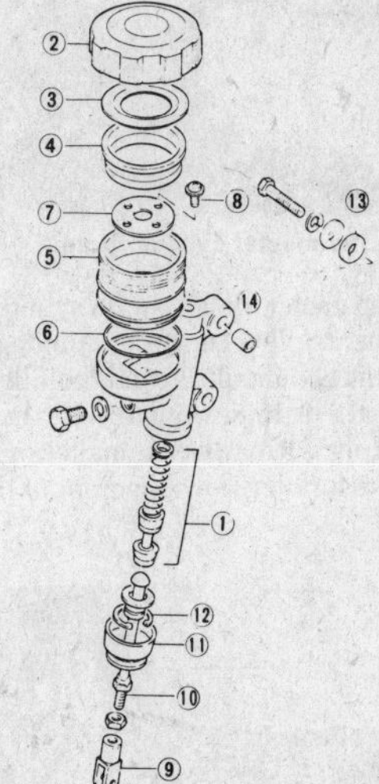

1. Piston & cup set
2. Cap
3. Diaphragm plate
4. Diaphragm
5. Reservoir
6. "O" ring
7. Reservoir plate
8. Screw
9. Clevis
10. Push rod
11. Boot
12. Circlip
13. Mounting rubber washer
14. Spacer

Rear brake master cylinder assembly

Brake rod cotter pin (1), footpeg mount (2), brake pedal (3)

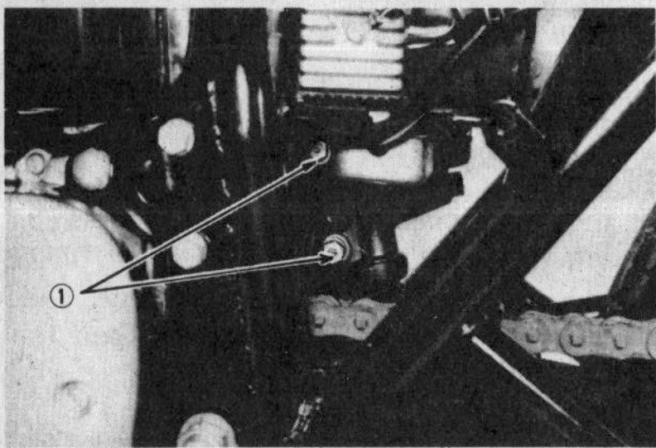

Master cylinder mounting bolts (1)

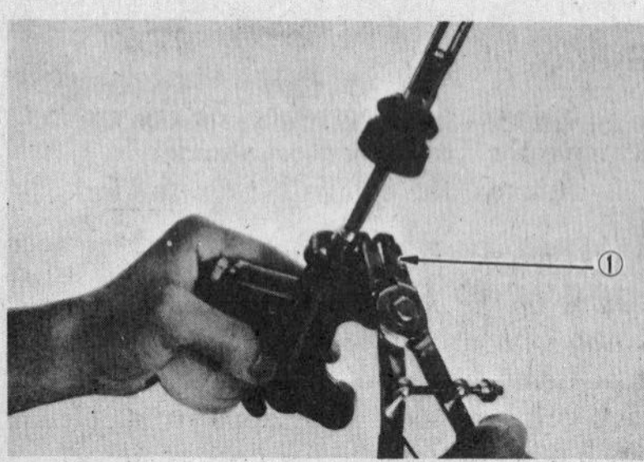

Removing the master cylinder circlip

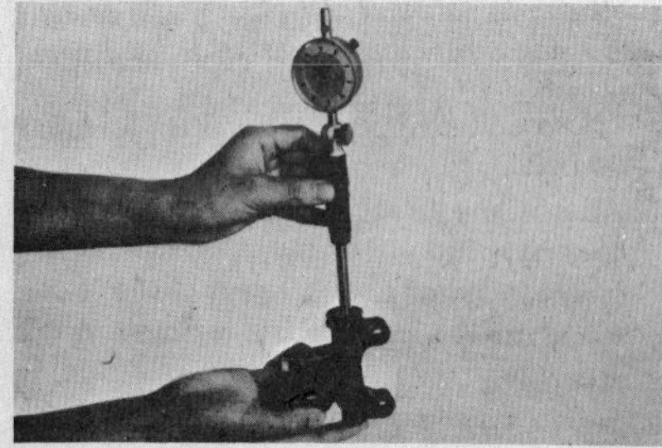
Measuring the master cylinder bore

5. Grasp each fork leg, in turn, and remove it from the triple clamps by pulling downward. If this is difficult, install the filler cap(s), threading them in several turns, then strike them sharply with a plastic mallet or the like to drive the fork leg down and out of the triple clamps.

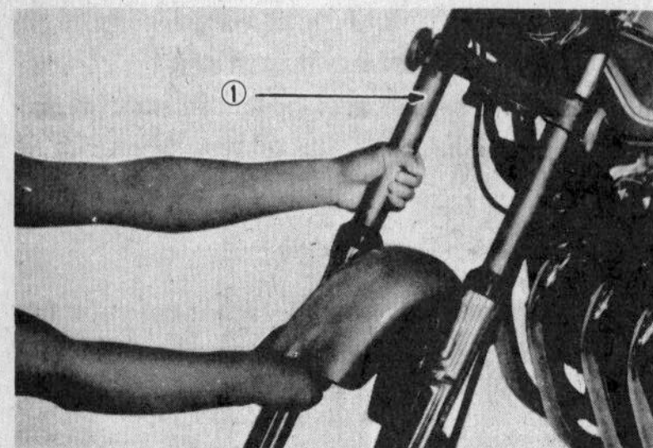

Removing a fork leg

Disassembly

1. Having removed the fork filler caps, turn the forks upside down and drain off the oil. Remove the fork springs.
2. Pry the dust seal up off the slider. Pry out the oil seal circlip.
3. Remove the bolt at the bottom of the fork slider and separate the fork components.

Inspection

1. Inspect the fork tubes for bends such as might have been incurred in an accident. Replacement is recommended rather than attempting to straighten bent fork tubes.
2. Check that the surface of the tube on which the slider components move is smooth and free of rust or scoring. Minor rusting should be removed with fine emery cloth.

On fork tubes, the chrome plating must be in perfect condition. If it is peeled or damaged, the fork tube must be replaced if oil leaks occur.

3. Check the spring condition. Make sure the spring heights are equal.
4. Check that all damper components are clean.
5. Replace the fork filler cap o-rings if they are not in good condition.
6. Clean all metal parts thoroughly in a solvent and lubricate them lightly with fork oil before assembly.
7. New fork slider oil seals should always be used once the forks have been disassembled. Pry out the old seals with a small screwdriver or the like, taking care to protect the top edge of the slider which you are using as a fulcrum. Drive the new seal straight in, being sure it is not cocked or otherwise damaged as it is driven in. The old seal can be used to drive in new seals. Drive the new seal in just far enough to allow the circlip to be installed. Oil the lips of the seal thoroughly before assembly.

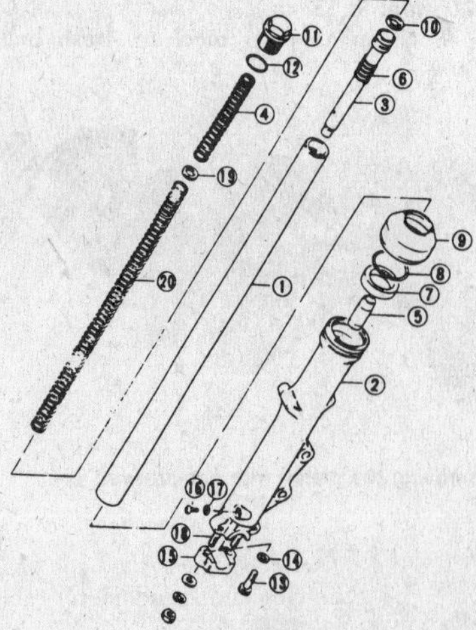

1. Inner tube	11. Cap bolt
2. Outer tube	12. "O" ring
3. Seat pipe	13. Bolt
4. Short spring	14. Gasket
5. Oil lock piece	15. Axle holder
6. Rebound spring	16. Screw
7. Oil seal	17. Gasket
8. Oil seal stopper ring	18. Stud bolt
9. Dust seal	19. Washer
10. Piston ring	20. Long spring

Front fork assembly

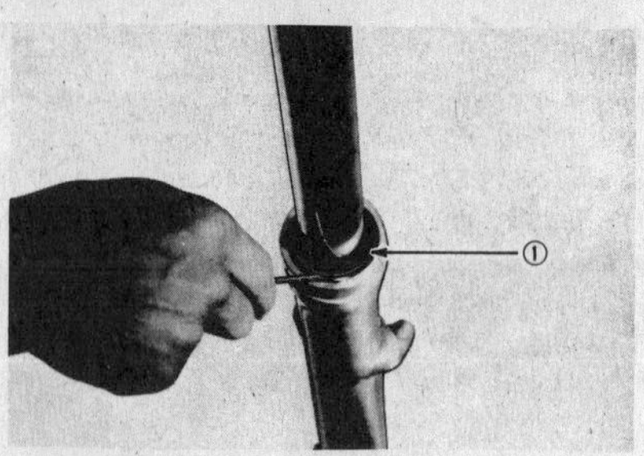

Removing the oil seal circlip

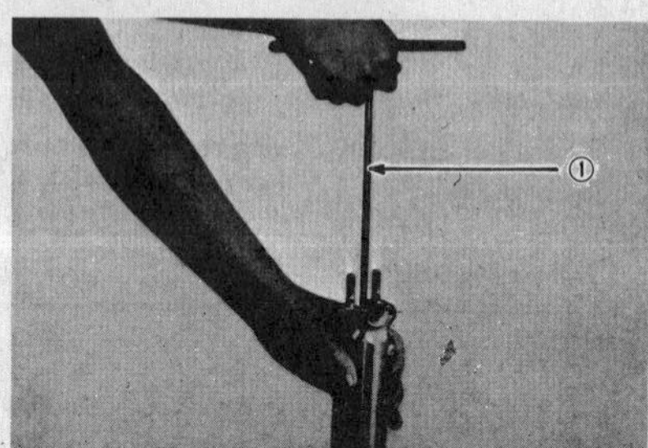

Removing the fork slider bolt

Assembly

Assembly is the reverse of disassembly. Lubricate all components with fork oil before installation.

Fill each fork leg with motor oil.

Installation

1. Install the fork leg in the triple clamps until the top edge of the fork leg is just flush with the top surface of the upper triple clamp.
2. Tighten the upper triple clamp pinch bolts to 15–22 ft lbs., and the lower ones to 11–18 ft lbs. Tighten the fork filler caps securely.
3. The remainder of the installation procedure is the reverse of removal.

FRONT FORKS (GS 850)

Removal

1. Remove the brake caliper(s) from the forks.

CAUTION: *Do not allow the caliper(s) to hang by the brake hose. Tie them out of the way with string or wire.*

2. Support the front wheel well off the ground by placing a jack or the like beneath the engine. Remove the front wheel and front fender.
3. After removing the valve cap at the top of each fork, slowly bleed the forks of air.
4. Loosen the upper triple clamp pinch bolt. Loosen the fork cap bolt. Loosen the lower triple clamp pinch bolts. Grasp each fork leg, in turn, and remove it from the triple clamps by pulling downwards.

Disassembly

1. Remove the fork cap and pull out the spring.
2. Drain off the fork oil, pumping the slider to remove it all.
3. Remove the dust seal.
4. Remove the allen bolt at the bottom of the fork slider. If the damper assembly inside turns with the allen bolt, it may be possible to break it loose by temporarily installing the

spring and fork cap and attempting to loosen the bolt. Otherwise, the special tool will have to be used.

5. Remove the fork slider from the fork tube. Remove the damper assembly.

6. Remove the fork slider oil seal snap-ring, washer, and oil seal.

Inspection

1. Inspect the fork tubes for bends such as might have been incurred in an accident. Replacement is recommended rather than attempting to straighten bent fork tubes.

2. Check that the surface of the tube on which the slider components move is smooth and free of rust or scoring. Minor rusting should be removed with fine emery cloth.

On fork tubes, the chrome plating must be in perfect condition. If it is peeled or damaged, the fork tube must be replaced if leaks occur.

3. Check the spring condition. Make sure that the spring heights are equal.

Springs should be replaced if either is under 416 mm (16.4 in.).

4. Check that all damper components are clean.

5. Replace the fork cap o-rings if they are not in good condition.

6. Clean all metal parts thoroughly in a solvent and lubricate them lightly with fork oil before assembly.

7. New fork slider oil seals should always be used once the forks have been disassembled. Pry out the old seals with a small screwdriver or the like, taking care to protect the top edge of the slider which you are using as a fulcrum. New seals should be installed after the fork tube has been installed in the slider to avoid having it cocked to one side.

Assembly

1. Assembly is the reverse of disassembly. Tighten the slider allen bolt to 15–19 ft lbs.

2. When installing the fork springs, note that they are inserted so that the close spring coils are located at the upper end of the fork tube.

3. Add 251 cc (8.5 oz) of SAE 10W/20 oil to each fork leg.

4. Install the fork legs as outlined below.

Installation

1. Install each fork leg so that the top lip of the tube is flush with the upper surface of the triple clamp.

2. Tighten the upper triple clamp pinch bolt to 15–22 ft lbs.

3. Tighten the lower triple clamp pinch bolts to 11–18 ft lbs.

4. Air pressure of the front forks must be matched with rear suspension settings. See "Suspension Adjustments," below.

STEERING STEM ASSEMBLY (GS 750)

Bearing Adjustment

1. The steering stem bearings are uncaged balls. They are adjusted by means of a ring nut beneath the upper triple clamp.

2. To check bearing adjustment, support the front wheel off the ground. Grasp the tip of the front fender and place your other hand beneath the lower triple clamp at the frame lug.

3. Attempt to move the fork by pulling up on the tip of the fender. If play or movement can be felt at the lower triple clamp, the bearings are adjusted too loosely or are worn. An alternate method is to grasp the fork sliders and attempt to move them back and forth in line with the motorcycle. No play should be noted.

4. Turn the forks slowly from lock-to-lock. Movemement should be smooth, silent, and effortless. If any binding or uneven movement is felt, the balls and races are either too tightly adjusted or they are worn. If the steering feels uniformly stiff, the bearings are too tightly adjusted. If any noise is noted, the bearings are damaged or some are missing.

5. With the front wheel off the ground, release the front forks from a few degrees off the centered position. The fork should fall freely to either side of their own weight. If they will not, the bearings are too tightly adjusted, the steering stem is bent, the races are extremely worn, or some of the bearings are missing.

6. To adjust the bearings, remove the upper triple clamp. The bearings are adjusted by means of the adjuster nut under the upper triple clamp.

7. Tighten or loosen the adjuster nut a little at a time until the steering stem adjustment conforms to that outlined above.

Steering head bearing adjuster nut

8. If proper adjustment is not possible, the bearings and races will probably need to be replaced.

Disassembly

1. Support the front wheel off the ground. Disconnect the clutch cable at the hand lever. Disconnect the tach and speedometer cables at the instruments.

2. Remove the headlight. Disconnect the wiring inside the headlight shell and remove the shell.

3. Remove the master cylinder from the handlebar. Remove the brake line guide which is secured to the upper triple clamp.

4. Remove the bolts securing the brake line joint to the lower triple clamp. Unbolt the caliper(s) from the fork slider(s) and remove the entire brake system.

5. Disconnect the instrument wiring, remove the two mounting bolts and remove the instruments.

6. Remove the handlebar bolts and take off the handlebars.

7. Remove the front wheel.

8. Loosen the upper and lower triple clamp pinch bolts and remove the fork assembly.

9. Loosen the rear pinch bolt on the upper triple clamp. Remove the steering stem bolt. Remove the upper triple clamp.

10. Loosen the steering stem adjuster nut with a pin wrench, then hold the steering stem up while unscrewing the adjuster nut the rest of the way off. Remove the steering stem top cone race.

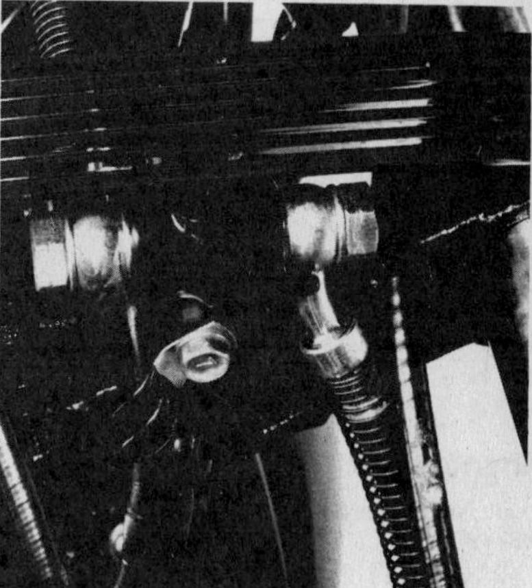

Brake line joint

Upper and lower triple clamp pinch bolts (1 & 2)

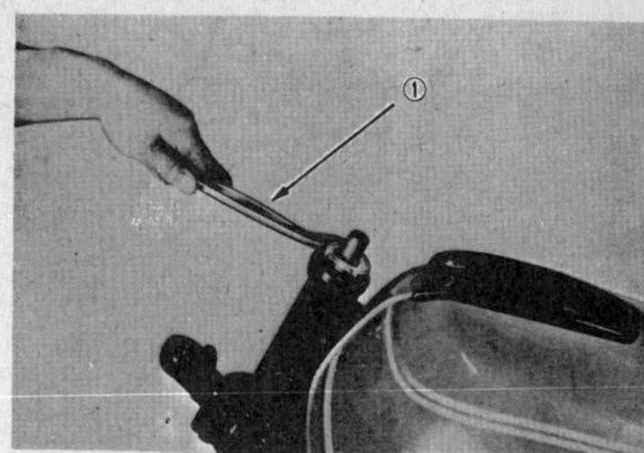

Removing the adjusting nut

11. Carefully lower the steering stem out from the bottom. Some of the ball bearings from the lower race will probably fall out at this time so be prepared for this.

12. Remove the bottom cone race from the steering stem if it is to be replaced. This will have to be pried off with a chisel; therefore only remove it if necessary.

13. The bearing races in the frame lug are a press-fit and should not be removed unless re-

placement is necessary. If replacement is necessary, the old races can be removed by reaching through the frame lug with a suitable

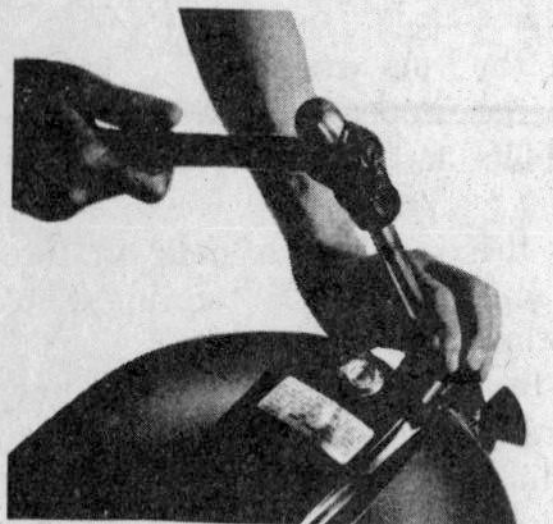
Driving out a steering stem bearing

punch and tapping the race evenly around its circumference to remove it from the inside of the frame lug. Be sure that the race does not become cocked in its seat upon removal.

New races are installed with a suitably sized bearing driver, i.e., one which will drive the race squarely into its seat. Be certain that the race goes straight in.

These races can also be installed using a block of hard wood of sufficient size to cover the race in place of a bearing driver.

Inspection

1. Wash the ball bearings in a suitable solvent.
2. Clean all of the old grease from the bearing race surfaces, steering stem, and frame lug.
3. Inspect the bearing race surfaces. They must be clean and smooth and free of any cracks, scoring, rust, or indentations. Run your finger around each of the bearing races. Note any roughness or ripples on the race surface. If any imperfections are noted, both sets of races and all of the balls must be replaced.
4. Check the balls themselves for rust, pitting, scoring, or flat spots. If the balls are found to be defective in any way, the balls and both sets of races must be replaced.

NOTE: *Balls and races must always be replaced in a set because worn races will destroy new balls and worn balls will destroy new races.*

5. Check the steering stem for cracks or a bent condition; this is especially important if the bike has been involved in a spill.

Installation

1. Install the lower cone race on the steering stem. Use a good grade of bearing grease to coat the bottom cone race and the upper race in the frame lug.
2. Embed 18 balls into the grease of the top frame lug and 18 balls into the grease of the lower cone race.
3. When the balls are in place, slip the steering stem through the frame lug and hold it in place while refitting the top cone race and threading on the adjuster nut.
4. Tighten the adjuster nut all the way by hand, rotating the steering stem to work the grease into the balls.
5. Tighten the adjuster nut until the steering stem turns freely, but has no play.
6. Install the fork tubes, headlight assembly, and upper triple clamp, and steering stem bolt. Check that the stem moves freely to the steering lock of its own weight when released from 5°–10° off center; if not check for:
   a. Steering bearings too tight;
   b. Bent steering stem;
   c. Worn races or balls.
7. Install the front fender, front wheel, and handlebars.
8. When installing the handlebars, adjust them so that the punch mark aligns with the mating face of the handlebar holder. Install the handlebar clamps, and tighten the front bolt first. Tighten the bolts to 9–15 ft lbs.
9. When connecting the headlight's wiring, note that the turn signal lead wires are both black and the wiring harness leads are black for the left-side turn signal and light green for the right-side signal.

STEERING STEM ASSEMBLY (GS 850)

The GS 850 has tapered roller steering stem bearings in place of the uncaged balls used on the 750. The behavior of the front fork/stem assembly relative to bearing adjustment is as outlined under "Bearing Adjustment" for the GS 750, above- Steps 2–5, although the causes for bearing trouble given there are not necessarily applicable. Bearing adjustment is somewhat more complicated, and is given as part of the "Assembly" procedure, below.

Disassembly

1. Remove the gas tank.
2. Remove the headlight bulb and reflector assembly, disconnect the wiring inside, and remove the headlight shell.
3. Disconnect the tach and speedo cables from the instruments.
4. Remove the handlebar cover. Remove the meter assembly.
5. Remove the connection coupler at the end of the lead wire.
6. Loosen the rear pinch bolt of the upper triple clamp and loosen the steering stem lock nut.
7. Remove the front forks. Refer to the section above.
8. Remove the headlight shell brackets. Unbolt the brake line junction beneath the lower triple clamp. Unbolt the master cylinder. Unbolt the handlebars from the upper triple clamp.

Upper triple clamp pinch bolt (1) and locknut (2)

9. Remove the upper triple clamp steering stem lock nut. Remove the upper triple clamp.
10. Loosen the bearing adjusting nut holding the steering stem assembly from below while the nut is taken off. Lower the assembly out of the frame lug.

Inspection

Wipe off any old grease and check the bearings and races for the usual signs of damage.

The lower bearing must be removed from the steering stem with a puller.

The races in the frame lug are to be driven out in the usual manner, and installed by pressing into place.

Assembly

1. Thoroughly grease the bearings and races with a good brand of bearing grease.
2. Insert the steering stem into the frame lug, hold it in place, and install the upper bearing and dust seal.
3. Screw on the adjusting nut. Now adjust the bearings to the proper play in the following manner.
4. Tighten the adjusting nut just enough so that there is no excessive play in the steering stem assembly, but it still turns freely.
5. Tighten the steering stem adjusting nut to 29–36 ft lbs.

Turn the steering stem back and forth several times to seat the bearings.

6. Loosen the adjusting nut, then tighten it just enough so that there is no play in the assembly.
7. Install the upper triple clamp. Tighten the steering stem locknut to 15–22 ft lbs. Tighten the pinch bolt behind it to 11–18 ft lbs.
8. Loosen the adjusting nut slightly. Torque the steering stem nut to 26–38 ft lbs.
9. Check operation of the steering stem. It must turn freely, of course. If too tight, or too loose, first loosen the steering stem nut, then turn the adjusting nut until operation is correct.
10. The remainder of the procedure is the reverse of removal. Tighten the handlebar bolts to 9–15 ft lbs.

REAR SHOCKS

Rear shocks are sealed units which cannot be disassembled or repaired. If a shock is damaged due to accident, leaks oil, or if damping is unsatisfactory, it must be replaced.

Shock absorbers should always be replaced in sets to ensure uniform damping.

Removal and Installation

1. The shock absorbers can be removed after their upper and lower fasteners are taken off.
2. To remove the spring, first set the cam ring on the softest position. Compress the

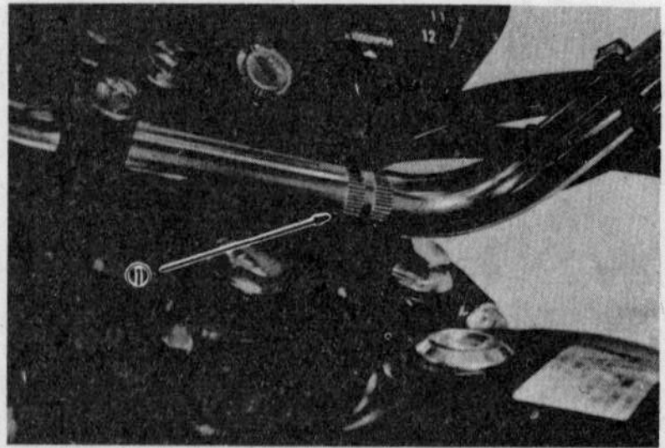
Install the bars so that the punch mark aligns with the clamp surface

spring by hand or with the aid of levers and remove the spring retainers.

3. Check damper operation by pushing the damper rod in as far as possible and then pulling it out. It should be more difficult to pull the damper rod out if the shock damper is functioning properly. Furthermore, both shocks should behave in exactly the same manner.

4. When refitting the shock absorbers, tighten the lower bolt to 15–22 ft lbs, and the top nut to the same torque.

Spring/Damper Settings

Rear shock absorbers on the GS 850 have a four-position damper adjustment as well as the usual five-position spring adjustment.

The spring and damper adjustment must be matched according to the following chart:

Spring setting	Damper setting
1	1 or 2
2	2 or 3
3	3 or 4
4	3 or 4
5	4

CAUTION: *Any spring/damper combinations other than those given may cause unsafe riding conditions. Be sure that both units are set to the same adjustments. Nos. "1." refer to the softest spring and damper setting.*

Be sure to check and, if necessary, adjust the front forks as well. See below.

SUSPENSION ADJUSTMENTS

The unique nature of the GS 850 suspension system requires that rear shock spring/damper settings be matched to front fork air pressure for maximum handling.

CAUTION: *Suspension components must be matched according to the following chart or unsafe riding conditions may arise.*

Rear spring setting	Rear damper setting	Front fork air pressure (psi)
1	1	8.5–17
1	2	11–13
2	2	11–13
2	3	11–13
3	3	14–16
3	4	14–16
4	3	14–16
4	4	14–16
5	4	17

WARNING: *Only the suspension settings indicated by this chart are considered safe. Do not adjust only the front or rear suspension to the neglect of the other.*

SWING ARM (GS 750)

Inspection

Grasp the rear tire and attempt to move it from side to side. There should be no movement allowable. If there is, assuming that the rear wheel bearings are in good condition, it indicates bad swing arm bearings which should be replaced.

Removal and Installation

1. Remove the rear wheel as outlined above.
2. Remove the right-side rider's footpeg. Remove the rear brake lever.
3. Disconnect the brake rod at the clevis. Remove the two master cylinder mounting bolts.
4. Remove the rear shock absorbers.
5. Remove the swing arm pivot shaft nut

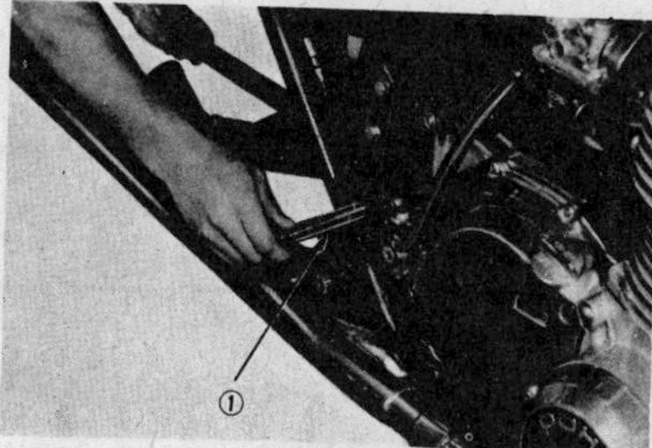

Removing the swing arm pivot

and take out the pivot shaft. Remove the swing arm from the frame.

6. Remove the brake anchor and the caliper and master cylinder from the swing arm.
7. Using special tool no. 00941-44510, remove the needle bearings from the swing arm. Once removed, the bearings must be replaced.
8. Assembly is the reverse of disassembly. Install the bearings with the aid of the special tool. Be sure to lubricate the bearings thoroughly before installation. Grease the spacers and dust caps as well.
9. When installing the pivot shaft, tighten its nut to 36–58 ft lbs.

SWING ARM (GS 850)

Removal

1. Remove the rear wheel.
2. Remove the brake caliper.
3. Remove the rear drive box.
4. Move the rubber boot aside. Disconnect and remove the brake light switch.
5. Remove the cotter pin from the master cylinder pushrod.

Swing arm nut (1) and pivot bolt (2)

6. Remove the swing arm nuts on each side and loosen the pivot shafts. Remove the swing arm.

Be cautious that the bearings do not fall out of either side of the pivot tube.

Inspection

Tapered roller swing arm bearings are fitted and, after washing them in a clean solvent to remove the old grease, the rollers, races, and cages should be inspected in the usual manner. Look for scored, pitted, rusted, or otherwise damaged rollers or races. Damage would be unlikely unless the bearings were not lubricated.

Installation

1. Grease the bearings with a good grade of bearing grease.
2. Tighten the pivot shafts to 2.5–3.0 ft lbs.

CAUTION: *The gaps between the frame and swing arm should be even on both sides.*

3. Tighten the locknuts to 80–94 ft lbs.

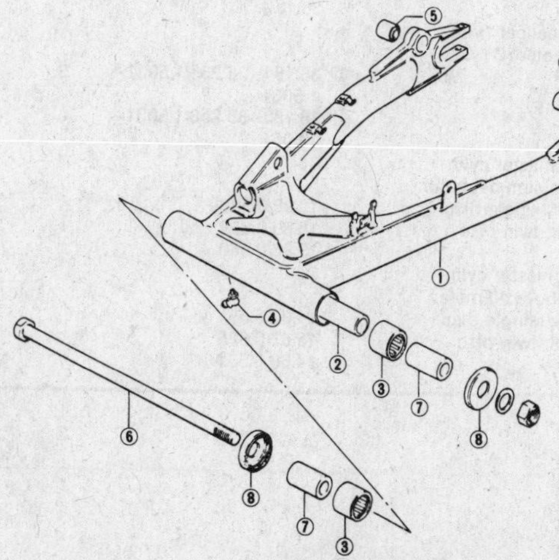

1. Rear swinging arm
2. Spacer
3. Bearing
4. Grease nipple
5. Rear bushing
6. Pivot shaft
7. Spacer
8. Dust seal cover

Swing arm assembly

Chassis Torque Specifications ①

Part	GS 750	GS 850G/GL/GN	GS 850GT/GLT
Brake line bolts	11–18	11–18	11–18
Front master cylinder mounting bolts	4–6	4–6	4–6
Front caliper mounting bolts	18–29	18–29	18–29
Front caliper shaft bolts	18–25	18–25	11–15
Rear master cylinder mounting bolts	11–15	11–15	11–18
Rear caliper mounting bolts	18–29	18–29	15–22
Rear caliper shaft bolts	18–25	18–25	18–26
Rear brake anchor	15–22	15–22	15–22
Bleed nipples	4–7	4–7	4–7
Disc mounting bolts	11–18	11–18	11–18
Front axle nut	26–38	26–38	26–38
Front axle cap nuts	11–18	11–18	11–18
Rear axle nut	36–58	62–83	36–58
Swing arm nuts	36–58	80–94	80–94
Swing arm pivot bolts	—	2.5–3.0	2.5–3.0
Chain adjuster bolts	11–15	—	—
Handlebar mounting bolts	9–15	9–15	9–15
Rear shocks	15–22	15–22	15–22
Footpegs	20–31	20–31	20–31
Upper triple clamp pinch bolts	15–22	15–22	15–22
Lower triple clamp pinch bolts	15–22	11–18	11–18
Steering stem locknut or bolt	26–38	26–36	26–36
Steering stem pinch bolt	11–18	11–18	11–18

① in ft. lbs.

Chassis Specifications

Part	Standard (mm/in.)	Serviceable limit (mm/in.)
Brake disc thickness		
single disc wheels	6.7/0.264	under 6.00/0.236
double disc wheels	6.0/0.240	under 5.5/0.220
Brake disc runout	0.1/0.004	0.3/0.012
Axle runout	0.15/0.006	0.25/0.010
Tire tread depth		
front	—	1.6/0.06
rear		2.0/0.08
Wheel rim runout	—	2.0/0.08
Brake caliper piston diameter (except GT/GLT)		
front	42.82/1.686	under 42.77/1.684
rear	38.15/1.502	under 38.13/1.501
Brake caliper piston diameter (GT/GLT)		
front	38.098–38.148/1.4999–1.5019	—
rear	38.098–38.148/1.4999–1.5019	—
Brake caliper bore diameter (except GT/GLT)		
front	42.85/1.687	over 42.89/1.687
rear	38.18/1.503	over 38.19/1.504
Brake caliper bore diameter (GT/GLT)		
front	38.180–38.256/1.5031–1.5061	—
rear	38.180–38.256/1.5031–1.5061	—
Brake master cylinder piston diameter		
front, single disc	13.96/0.550	under 13.94/0.549
front, twin disc	15.80/0.622	—
rear	13.96/0.550	under 13.94/0.549
Brake master cylinder bore diameter		
front, single disc	14.00/0.551	over 14.05/0.553
front, twin disc	15.87/0.625	—
rear	14.00/0.551	over 14.05/0.553

Triumph

MODEL COVERAGE

250
TR25W

500
T100C, "Trophy Trail"
T100R, "Daytona"

650
TR6R, "Trophy"
TR6C, "Trophy"
T120R, "Bonneville"

750 Twins
TR7V, "Tiger 750"
T140V, "Bonneville 750"

750 Triples
T150, "Trident"
T150V, "Trident"

INDEX

MAINTENANCE

NOTE: *Common maintenance procedures are explained in detail in "General Information."*

LUBRICATION

Engine

NOTE: *Always change oil when the engine is at operating temperature.*

TR25W

1. Remove the right side-panel.
2. Using a suitable container and funnel to catch the oil, remove the oil tank filter located in the lower right corner of the tank. Clean the filter in solvent.
3. Allow the tank to drain for about five minutes, then lean the machine toward the right side to make sure that all the oil has been removed.
4. Remove the four attaching nuts and the oil sump filter located at the bottom of the crankcase. Also, disconnect the supply and scavenge lines at the crankcase union nut.
5. Wash the sump filter in solvent, then allow it to air dry or blow it dry with compressed air.
6. Reinstall the sump filter and gasket, connect the supply and scavenge lines, and reinstall the oil tank filter.
7. Add the recommended oil to the tank until it reaches the correct level mark on the dipstick. Do not overfill it, as excessive venting will result.
8. Let the engine run for several minutes, then recheck the oil level and top up if necessary.

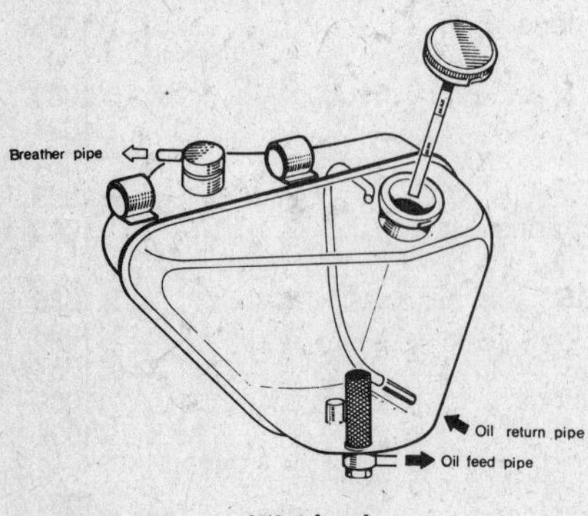

250 oil tank

500 AND 650

1. Remove the sump drain plug and filter.
2. Thoroughly clean the filter in solvent.
3. Allow the oil to drain for approximately five minutes, then reinstall the filter (with gasket) and the sump drain plug.
4. Remove the oil tank filler cap.
5. Position a container under the oil tank, then remove the tank drain plug or disconnect the oil feed line.
6. Remove the oil tank filter and clean it thoroughly in solvent.
7. If possible, clean the oil tank with

General Specifications

	TR25W	*T100C*	*T100R*	*TR6R °*	*TR6C °*
DIMENSIONS					
Net weight (lbs)	320.0	337.0	341.0	365.0	365.0
Overall Height (in.)	43.25	38.0	38.0	38.0	38.0
Overall Width (in.)	28.0	26.5	26.5	27.5	27.5
Overall Length (in.)	83.0	83.25	83.25	84.0	84.0
Wheelbase (in.)	53.0	53.5	53.5	55.0	55.0
Seat Height (in.)	32.0	—	—	—	—
Ground Clearance (in.)	8.5	7.5	7.5	6.0	6.0
ENGINE					
Displacement (cc)	250	490	490	649	649
Bore x Stroke (mm)	67 x 70	69 x 65.5 (2)	69 x 65.5 (2)	71 x 82 (2)	71 x 82 (2)
Compression Ratio	10 : 1	9.0 : 1	9.1 : 1	9.0 : 1	9.0 : 1
Carburetor Type and Model	Amal 928/1	②	③	Amal R930/23	Amal R930/23
TRANSMISSION					
Clutch Type	wet, multi-plate	wet, multi-plate	wet, multi-plate	wet, multi-plate	wet, multi-plate
Internal Gear Ratios					
1st	2.65	2.47	2.47	2.44	2.44
2nd	1.65	1.61	1.61	1.69	1.69
3rd	1.24	1.22	1.22	1.24	1.24
4th	1.00	1.00	1.00	1.00	1.00
5th	—	—	—	—	—
Sprockets (no. of teeth)					
Engine	23	26	26	29	29
Clutch	52	58	58	58	58
Gearbox	15	18	18	18	18
Rear Wheel	①	46	46	46	46
CHASSIS					
Front Suspension	rod damper or shuttle valve-type telescopic			shuttle valve-type telescopic	
Rear Suspension	swing arm with hydraulically dampened shocks				
Tire Size: front	3.25 x 18	3.25 x 19	3.25 x 19	3.25 x 19	3.25 x 19
rear	4.00 x 18	4.00 x 18	4.00 x 18	4.00 x 18	4.00 x 18
ELECTRICAL					
System Voltage	12	12	12	12	12
Generator Type	alternator				

	T120R °	*T150*	*TR7V*	*T140V*	*T150V*
DIMENSIONS					
Net Weight (lbs)	365.0	470.0	402	408	460
Overall Height (in.)	38.0	43.5	38.0	38.0	43.5
Overall Width (in.)	27.5	32.5	33.0	33.0	32.5
Overall Length (in.)	84.0	86.0	87.5	87.5	86.0
Wheelbase (in.)	55.0	56.25	55.0	55.0	56.3
Seat Height (in.)	—	32.0	31.5	31.5	32.0
Ground Clearance (in.)	5.0	6.5	6.0	6.0	6.5
ENGINE					
Displacement (cc)	649	741	747	747	741
Bore x Stroke (mm)	71 x 82 (2)	67 x 70 (3)	76 x 82 (2)	76 x 82 (2)	67 x 70 (3)
Compression Ratio	9.0 : 1	9.0 : 1	8.6 : 1	8.6 : 1	9.5 : 1
Carburetor Type and Model	Amal R930/9 & L930/10	Amal 626	Amal R930/89	Amal L930/92 & R930/89	Amal 626
TRANSMISSION					
Clutch Type	wet, multi-plate	wet, single-plate	wet, multi-plate	wet, multi-plate	wet, single-plate
Internal Gear Ratios					
1st	2.44	2.44	2.59	2.59	2.59
2nd	1.69	1.69	1.84	1.84	1.84
3rd	1.24	1.19	1.40	1.40	1.40
4th	1.00	1.00	1.19	1.19	1.19
5th	—	—	1.00	1.00	1.00
Sprockets (no. of teeth)					
Engine	29	28	29	29	28
Clutch	58	50	58	58	50
Gearbox	18	18	20	20	18
Rear Wheel	46	52	47	47	53
CHASSIS					
Front Suspension	telescopic, hydraulically dampened				
Rear Suspension	swing arm with hydraulically dampened shocks				
Tire Size: front	3.25 x 19	3.50 x 19	3.25 x 19	3.25 x 19	4.10 x 19
rear	4.00 x 18	4.10 x 18	4.00 x 18	4.00 x 18	4.10 x 19
ELECTRICAL					
System Voltage	12	12	12	12	12
Generator Type	alternator				

° Optional 5-speed gearbox available. Ratios: 1st—2.585; 2nd—1.837; 3rd—1.400; 4th—1.192; 5th—1.000.
① 52 tooth standard; 49 tooth optional.
② Amal 376/273 prior to serial no. H.57083; Amal 628/8 after serial no. H.57083.
③ Amal 376/324 and 325 before serial no. H.5708; Amal 626/9 and 10 after serial no. H.5708.

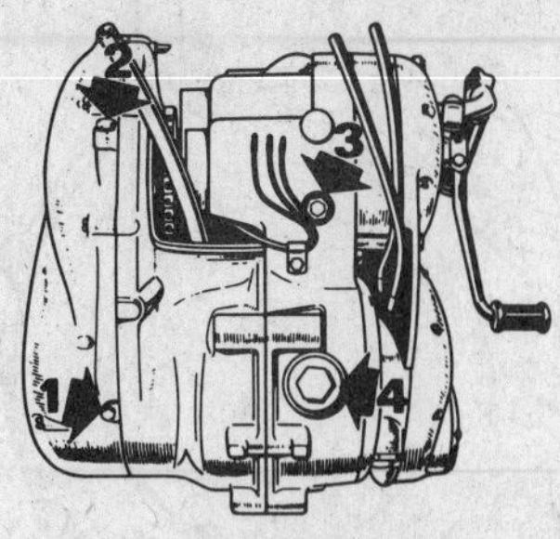

500 models
1. Primary chaincase level plug
2. Primary chaincase drain plug and chain tensioner adjustment
3. Gearbox drain and level plug
4. Sump drain and filter plug

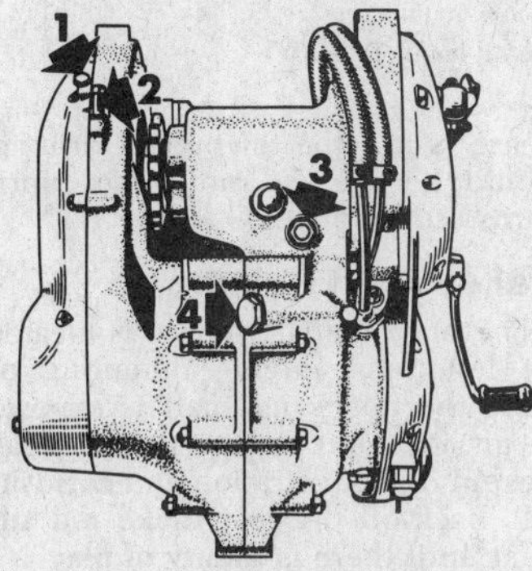

650, 750 Twins
1. Primary chaincase level plug
2. Primary chaincase drain plug and chain tensioner adjustment
3. Gearbox drain and level plug
4. Sump drain and filter plug

flushing oil. If it is not available, use kerosine, but make sure all traces are removed before filling the tank with oil.

8. Fill the tank with the recommended lubricant. The correct level is 1½ in. below the filler cap. Do not exceed this level, as excessive venting will result.

9. Allow the engine to run for several minutes, and recheck the oil level, topping it up if necessary.

TR7V, T140V

Note that the oil for these models is carried in the frame backbone. A filter is also fitted at the bottom of the frame oil reservoir.

1. When the engine is warm, remove the hex-head sump drain plug from beneath the engine. This plug houses the sump filter as well.

2. Allow the oil to drain from the sump for at least ten minutes. Clean the sump plug filter in a suitable solvent, check the condition of the gasket, then replace the filter and the drain plug.

3. Remove the oil reservoir filler cap. Remove the drain plug from the center of the base plate at the very bottom of the frame oil reservoir. Allow to drain for at least ten minutes.

4. Remove the four nuts which secure the cover plate at the bottom of the reservoir, and remove the plate from the studs. Noting the location of the two gaskets (one above the filter base flange, and the other below), clean the filter in a suitable solvent.

5. Flushing the reservoir with kerosene is recommended.

6. The filter gaskets should be replaced. Refit the filter, cover plate, cover plate nuts, and drain plug. Fill the reservoir with the correct amount and recommended grade of oil. Check the oil level after the engine has been run for several miles.

T150, T150V

1. When the engine is warm, remove the six nuts and lockwashers which secure the crankcase sump filter plate to the bottom of the crankcase. Carefully remove the plate. Allow the oil to drain for about ten minutes.

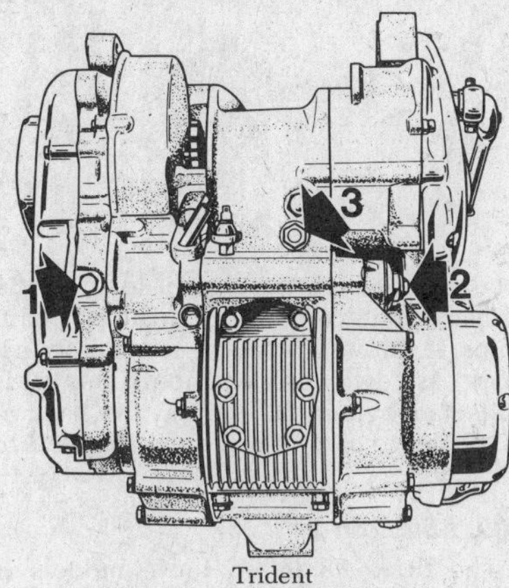

Trident
1. Primary chaincase drain plug
2. Oil filter housing cap
3. Gearbox drain and level plug

2. Clean the sump filter in a solvent. The gaskets on either side of the filter should be replaced upon reassembly. Replace the filter, noting that the pocketed end is towards the rear of the engine. Tighten the nuts gradually and evenly.

3. Remove the oil tank filler cap, and the right side-panel. Drain the oil from the oil tank, then remove the tank oil filter, and wash it in a solvent.

4. Flushing out the oil tank with kerosine is recommended.

5. Remove the cartridge-type main feed oil filter. This is located beneath the large cap nut just below the forward end of the gearbox outer cover. Note that the filter is pulled out with a pair of needle-nosed pliers. There is a spring immediately beneath the cap nut, and an O-ring on the end of the filter. The filter should be replaced every time the oil is changed.

6. When replacing the filter, be sure that the O-ring and the fiber washer are in good condition.

CAUTION: *When the filter is refitted, be sure that the hole in the filter faces inward.*

Refill the oil tank with the correct quantity and recommended grade of oil. Check the level with the dipstick after the engine has run for several miles.

Gearbox

All gearbox components, including the shifter and kick-start mechanisms, are lubricated by oil splash. The oil should be changed at 500 miles in new or reconditioned engines, and at every recommended service interval thereafter.

NOTE: *Drain oil when it is warm.*

TR25W

1. Remove the nylon filler plug and the dipstick from the top of the gearbox.

2. Remove the plug on the bottom of the gearbox and drain the oil.

3. After draining, reinstall the plug, making sure that the sealing O-ring is in good condition.

4. Fill the gearbox with the recommended lubricant to the line marked on the dipstick.

OTHER MODELS

1. Remove the transmission drain plug located at the bottom of the gearbox.

2. After letting the oil drain for about ten minutes, reinstall the drain plug, but without the level plug that normally screws into it.

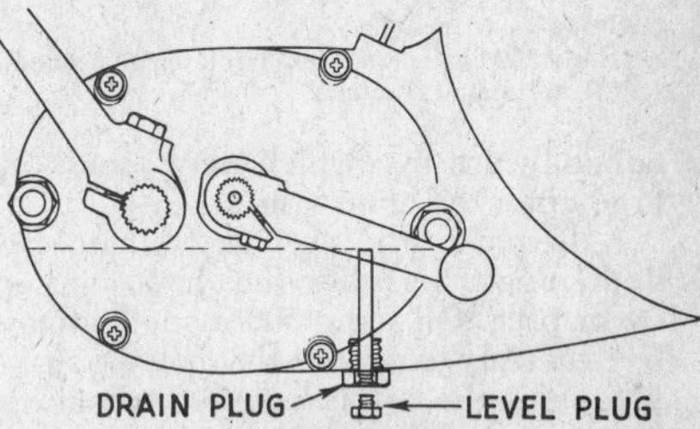

Gearbox drain and level plug

3. Remove the gearbox oil filler plug on the case cover and add fresh oil until it flows out the level plug hole.

4. Reinstall the level plug.

Primary Chaincase

Like the gearbox, the primary chaincase is lubricated by oil bath. On all models, the primary oil supply is contained within the case, where a collection chamber and a feed pipe provide direct lubrication to the primary chain and sprockets.

TR25W

1. On early machines, two of the chaincase securing screws serve as drain and level plugs. On later bikes, a vertical drain plug is provided at the bottom of the case and the forwardmost of the lower chaincase securing screws serves as a level plug.

2. Remove the chain inspection cap on top of the chaincase.

3. Remove the drain plug or screw and level screw.

4. Let the oil drain for about ten minutes, then reinstall the drain plug or screw.

5. Pour the specified amount of the recommended lubricant into the chaincase through the chain inspection cap until it flows out the level screw hole.

6. Reinstall the level screw and chain inspection cap.

NOTE: *Oil containing molybdenum disulphide or graphite, or oil additives, must not be used in the primary chaincase.*

TWINS

On models after about 1971, the primary chaincase oil is automatically supplied by oil forced through the drive side crankshaft bearing. The level is main-

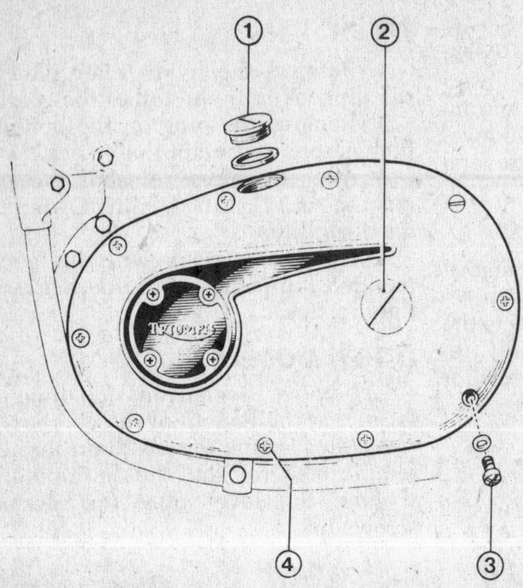

Early 250 chaincase filler (1), clutch adjustment cap (2), level (3) and drain (4) screws

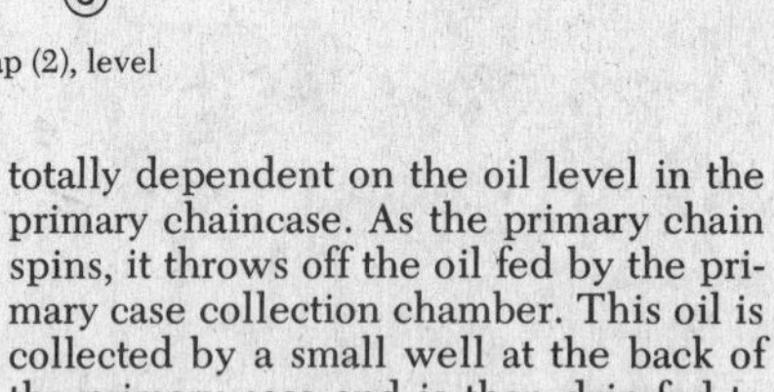

Chaincase oil level (Trident)

tained by drillings which allow excess oil to re-enter the crankcase.

1. Remove the primary chaincase drain plug. This is also the chain adjuster cover plug. On some 500 models it may be necessary to remove the footpeg, striking it after the bolt is loosened to remove it from its taper.

2. Allow the oil to drain for about 10 minutes. Reinstall the drain plug. On older models, remove the level plug.

3. Remove the filler plug at the top of the case. On the older models, add the correct grade oil until it begins to seep from the level plug hole. Refit the level plug and filler plug.

On the more recent machines, add only about ¼ pint of motor oil. The level will come up to the proper amount as the machine is ridden. Check with the level plug.

T150, T150V

1. The primary chaincase is lubricated by oil forced through the crankshaft bearing as outlined for late-model Twins.

2. After removing the drain plug and allowing several minutes for the oil to drain off, refit the drain plug. Add no more than ½ pint of motor oil. The level will rise as the machine is ridden, and will be maintained at the proper level by drillings in the crankcase.

Front Forks

1. Drain each fork leg separately.

2. Remove the drain bolt at the bottom of the fork slider. Hold the front brake and pump the forks several times to expel all the oil.

3. Refit the drain plug. Remove the filler cap at the top of the fork leg.

NOTE: *On machines with resiliently-mounted handlebars, the handlebars may have to be removed to gain access to the filler caps.*

4. Add the correct amount and type of oil, refit the cap; repeat the procedure with the remaining fork leg.

Final Drive Chain

TR25W

Lubrication of the final drive chain is totally dependent on the oil level in the primary chaincase. As the primary chain spins, it throws off the oil fed by the primary case collection chamber. This oil is collected by a small well at the back of the primary case and is then drip-fed to the chain.

500, 650, 750-3

The drive chain on these models is lubricated by means of an overflow tube from the neck of the oil tank. The flow is adjusted by means of a screw with a tapered tip threaded into the oil junction block in the neck of the tank. The screw is accessible after removing the tank filler cap. To increase oil flow to the chain, turn the screw counterclockwise. To decrease flow, turn the screw clockwise.

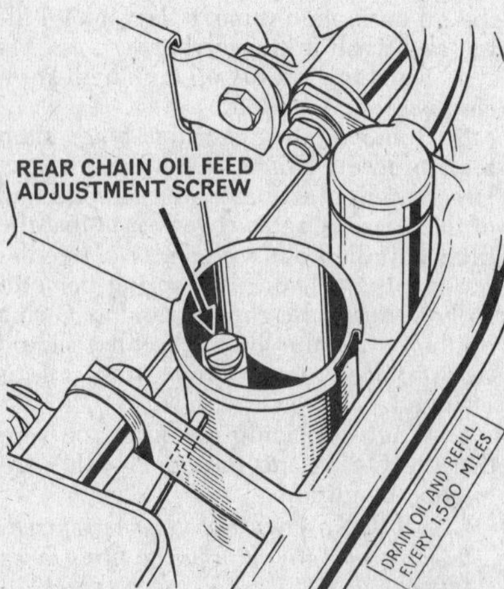

Chain oiler adjustment screw location (500, 650, and Trident)

750 TWINS

The chain should be lubricated by hand at intervals, depending on conditions. No automatic oiler is fitted.

Grease Nipples

Both the front and rear drum brake cams, and the swinging arm pivot are fitted with grease nipples. The brake cams should be given only one stroke of a hand grease gun; the swinging arm pivot should be greased until the lubricant spurts out the pivot O-rings.

Brake Pedal Spindle

The brake pedal spindle is located on the left, rear, engine mounting plate. Since the operating shaft is exposed to the air, it should be coated with grease to prevent dirt penetration and corrosion.

1. Back off the rear brake rod adjustment until there is plenty of play.

2. Remove the pedal retaining nut and pedal.

3. Clean up the operating shaft and bore of the pedal with fine emery cloth.

4. Apply the recommended grease to the shaft and reinstall the pedal. Make sure you don't forget the spring and washer that accompany the retaining nut.

Wheel and Steering Head Bearings

1. These bearings should be packed with a good grade of bearing grease every 12,000 miles.

2. Refer to "Chassis" for removal and installation procedures.

SERVICE CHECKS AND ADJUSTMENTS

Clutch

TR25W, TWINS

1. Run down the clutch cable adjuster(s) until there is plenty of freeplay in the clutch hand lever.

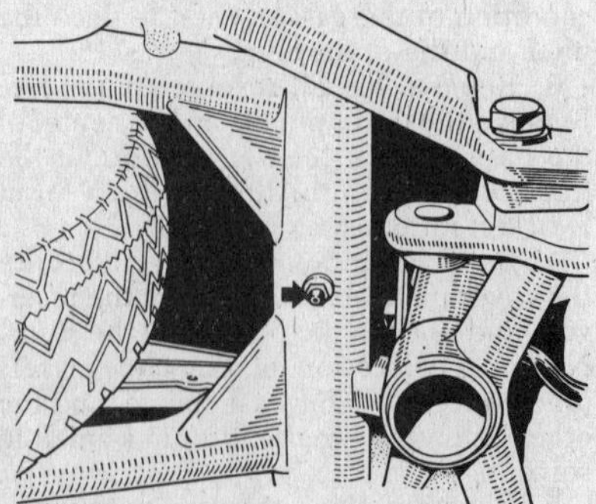

Swing arm grease nipple (650)

2. Remove the clutch adjustment cap on the primary chaincase.

3. Loosen the adjustment nut. Turn the adjusting screw out a few turns, then turn it in until resistance is felt.

4. At this point, back the adjusting screw off the following number of turns:

TR25W: 1
500: ½
650, 750: 1

5. Tighten the adjusting screw locknut while holding the screw in position. Use the cable adjusters to allow ⅛ in. (3 mm) of freeplay between the clutch hand lever and the lever holder before the clutch begins to disengage.

T150, T150V

1. Remove the four screws which secure the clutch inspection plate to the primary chaincase.

2. Run down the clutch cable adjusters both at the handlebar and the chaincase cover so that there is plenty of slack in the clutch cable.

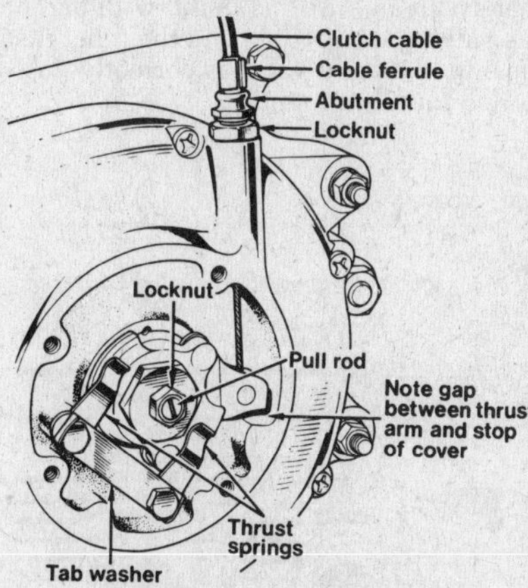

Trident clutch adjustment

3. Loosen the small locknut on the end of the clutch pull-rod. Then turn the large nut until the proper setting is obtained. This will be not less than 0.005 in. measured between the rear face of the large adjuster nut and the ball bearing in the actuating plate. Be sure that the clutch pull-rod does not turn, and retighten the small locknut. Recheck the setting.

4. Adjust the cable so that there is just a very small amount of freeplay at the handlebar lever.

Primary Chain Adjustment

ALL MODELS

An occasional adjustment is necessary to compensate for chain wear. Excess chain slack is taken up by tightening the tensioner bolt.

1. Remove the primary chaincase filler or inspection cap. Place a pan beneath the chaincase and remove the tensioner plug. On most models, the chaincase oil will drain off.

2. Chain slack should be as follows:

TR25W: ¼ in. (6 mm)
Trident: ½ in. (12 mm)
Others models: ⅜ in. (9.5 mm)

This is total up-and-down movement. If adjustment is necessary, use a screwdriver to turn the tensioner bolt until tension is correct.

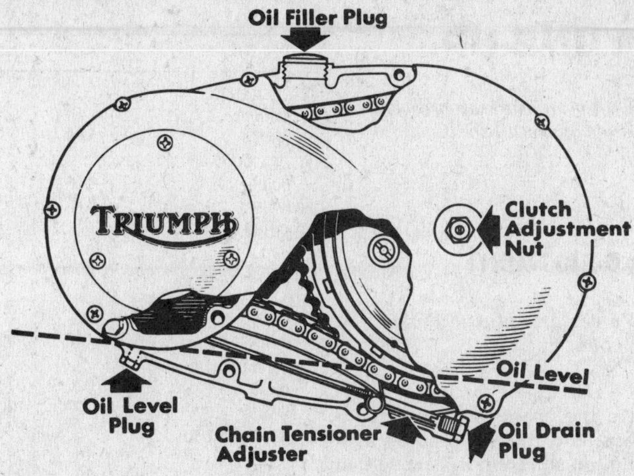

500 and 650 chaincase

3. After refitting the tensioner plug, refer to "Primary Chaincase" lubrication to fill and check oil level.

Final Drive Chain

1. Chain slack should be ¾ in. (19 mm) total up-and-down movement measured in the middle of the chain run with the machine on its wheels. With the bike on the center stand, the slack should be 1¾ in. (43 mm).

Measure at the chain's tightest point.

2. If adjustment is necessary, loosen the axle nut and the brake anchor. Move the wheel by turning the adjustment bolts by equal amounts.

3. Apply the rear brake and tighten the axle nuts.

Brakes

DISC BRAKES

1. The brakes are self-adjusting. Maintain the fluid level at ¼ in. below the top of the master cylinder.

2. Brake pads should be replaced when either of them reaches a lining thickness of 1/16 in. (1.6 mm).

FRONT DRUM

1. On single-leading shoe brakes, use the adjuster at the wheel so that the hand lever can be moved about 1 in. (measured at the tip of the lever) before the shoes contact the drum.

2. On twin-leading shoe brakes, hand lever travel should be the same (1 in., measured at the tip of the lever) and is effected by using the adjuster at the hand lever.

REAR DRUM

1. If a change in pedal position is desired, do this before adjusting the brake.

2. Use the adjuster at the end of the brake rod so there is ½ in. (12 mm) of pedal movement before the shoes contact the drum. The measurement should be made with the weight of a rider on the motorcycle.

Periodic Maintenance Intervals

Every 250 Miles
- Check oil tank level
- Check chain oiler adjustment (where applicable)

Every 1000 Miles
- Lubricate cables
- Grease swing arm pivot and brake fittings
- Remove and clean final drive chain
- Check primary chaincase oil (1970 and later)
- Change primary chaincase oil (1969 and earlier)

Every 1500 Miles
- Change engine oil (650, 750 Twins)

Every 2000 Miles
- Lubricate contact breaker

Every 3000 Miles
- Check gearbox oil level
- Grease brake pedal spindle

Every 4000 Miles
- Change engine and primary chaincase oil (500 T150)
- Change disposable oil filter element (where applicable)

Every 6000 Miles
- Change gearbox oil
- Change front fork oil
- Repack wheel bearings

Every 12000 Miles
- Grease steering head bearings

Recommended Lubricants

Engine and Primary Chaincase
- SAE 20W/50, "SE"
- SAE 10W/40, "SE"

Gearbox
- SAE 90 EP

Front Forks
- 1972 and later: ATF
- 1971 and earlier: SAE 10/40, SAE 20W, SAE 30W

Drive Chain
- Lubricant designed specially for motorcycle drive chains

Grease Fittings
- A high grade chassis grease

Wheel and Steering Head Bearings
- A high grade bearing grease

Controls and Cables
- Tach and speedometer: chassis grease
- Others: light motor oil graphite or molybdenum disulphide lubricant

TUNE-UP

NOTE: *Common tune-up procedures are explained in detail in "General Information."*

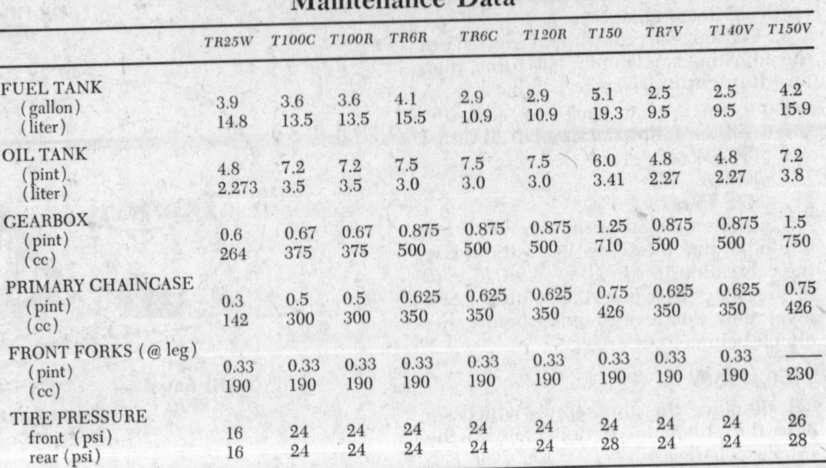

Maintenance Data

	TR25W	T100C	T100R	TR6R	TR6C	T120R	T150	TR7V	T140V	T150V
FUEL TANK										
(gallon)	3.9	3.6	3.6	4.1	2.9	2.9	5.1	2.5	2.5	4.2
(liter)	14.8	13.5	13.5	15.5	10.9	10.9	19.3	9.5	9.5	15.9
OIL TANK										
(pint)	4.8	7.2	7.2	7.5	7.5	7.5	6.0	4.8	4.8	7.2
(liter)	2.273	3.5	3.5	3.0	3.0	3.0	3.41	2.27	2.27	3.8
GEARBOX										
(pint)	0.6	0.67	0.67	0.875	0.875	0.875	1.25	0.875	0.875	1.5
(cc)	264	375	375	500	500	500	710	500	500	750
PRIMARY CHAINCASE										
(pint)	0.3	0.5	0.5	0.625	0.625	0.625	0.75	0.625	0.625	0.75
(cc)	142	300	300	350	350	350	426	350	350	426
FRONT FORKS (@ leg)										
(pint)	0.33	0.33	0.33	0.33	0.33	0.33	0.33	0.33	0.33	—
(cc)	190	190	190	190	190	190	190	190	190	230
TIRE PRESSURE										
front (psi)	16	24	24	24	24	24	24	24	24	26
rear (psi)	16	24	24	24	24	24	28	24	24	28

VALVE ADJUSTMENT

NOTE: *Valves are adjusted when the engine is cold.*

TR25W

1. Remove the spark plug, rocker inspection caps, and rocker spindle plate. Also, put the transmission in gear so that the engine can be easily rotated by turning the rear wheel.
2. Rotate the engine in the normal running direction until the intake valve has just completely closed.

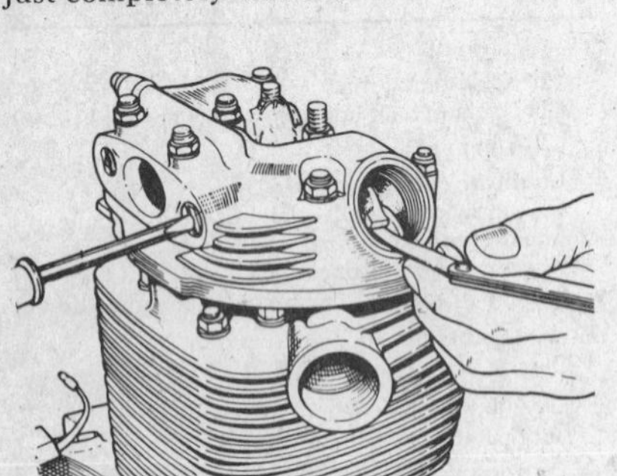

Valve adjustment (250)

NOTE: *This point can be accurately located by feeling the pushrod. When the valve is completely closed, the pushrod will be free to rotate.*

3. The engine is now correctly positioned for checking the exhaust valve clearance. Slide the appropriate feeler gauge between the valve stem and the tappet, and check for a snug slip-fit.
4. If an adjustment is necessary, loosen the rocker spindle locknuts opposite the spindle cover plate. Turn the slotted exhaust valve spindle in a clockwise direction until the rocker arm just touches the valve stem, then turn it back again until the correct clearance is obtained. Tighten up the locknut and recheck the adjustment.
5. Rotate the engine forward again until the exhaust valve is just about to open. This is the correct position for checking the intake valve tappet clearance.
6. Check the clearance with the proper feeler gauge and, if necessary, readjust it to meet specifications. The procedure for adjusting the intake valve clearance is the same as that outlined for the exhaust valve except that the rocker spindle should first be turned counterclockwise, rather than clockwise.

Twins

1. Remove the spark plugs and rocker box inspection caps.

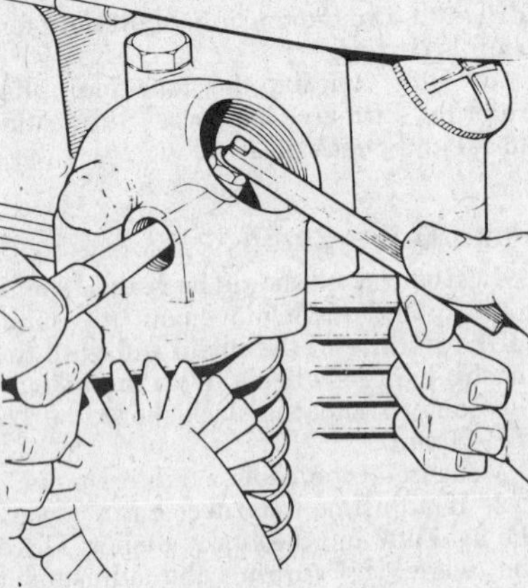

Valve adjustment (500)

2. On 500cc models, remove the large plugs on the side of each rocker box. The feeler gauge is inserted through these holes.
3. Slowly turn the engine over until the left exhaust valve is fully open. Now check the clearance of the right exhaust valve.
4. Insert the proper thickness feeler gauge between the valve stem and rocker arm. The feeler gauge should be a snug slip-fit if the clearance is correct.
5. If adjustment is necessary, loosen the adjuster locknut and turn the adjuster to effect the proper clearance. Hold the adjuster in place and tighten the nut. Recheck the clearance.
6. Turn the engine over so that the right exhaust valve is fully open, then check the adjustment of the left exhaust valve. Repeat this procedure with the intake valves.

NOTE: *If, in an emergency situation, feeler gauges of the proper thickness are not available, clearances can be set approximately by turning the adjuster in until it is finger-tight, then backing it out ¼ turn per 0.010 in. until the given clearance is obtained. Check this setting with a feeler gauge as soon as possible.*

T150, T150V

1. Remove the spark plugs and rocker box inspection caps.
2. Beginning with the intake cam, rotate the engine until two valves are opened by the same amount (approximately 1/16 in.). At this point, with one of the valves just opening and the other just closing, the third valve is correctly positioned for adjustment.

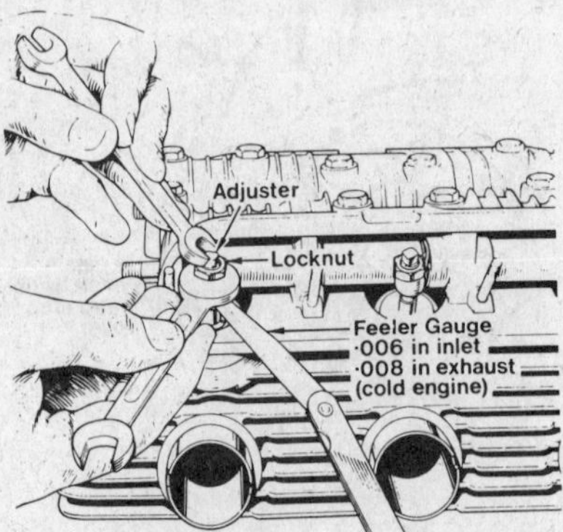

Valve adjustment (Trident)

3. Insert the appropriate feeler gauge and, if necessary, loosen the adjuster locknut and turn the adjuster until a snug slip-fit is obtained. Tighten the locknut and recheck the clearance.
4. Continue rotating the engine until the conditions outlined in step 2 are met for another intake valve. Repeat the procedure on the remaining intake and exhaust valves.
5. Install the spark plugs and rocker box inspection caps.

CONTACT BREAKER POINTS

NOTE: *When installing new points, the contact surfaces should be wiped with a solvent to remove any preservative coating.*

TR25W

The contact breaker point assembly is located behind the circular cover on the right side of the engine.

REMOVAL

1. Remove the breaker point cover.
2. Remove the securing nut, nylon

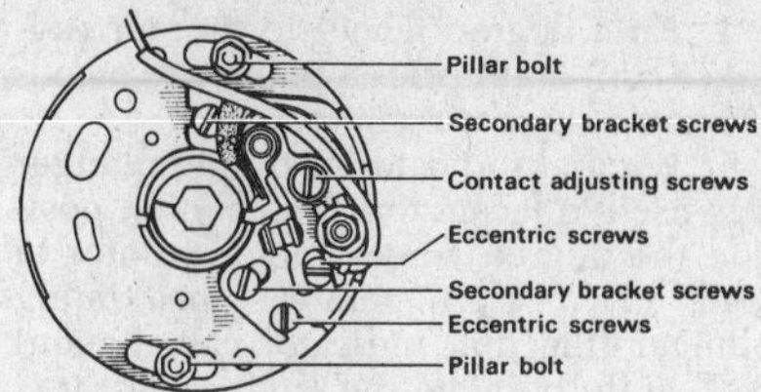

Breaker points (250)

sleeve, and contact breaker lead.

3. Remove the contact adjusting screw, then lift the unit out.

INSTALLATION

Installation is a reversal of the removal procedure. Do not forget to install the fiber washer that fits between the moving point spring and the fixed point backing plate.

GAP ADJUSTMENT

1. Put the transmission in gear and rotate the engine by turning the rear wheel until the nylon heel of the contact breaker is aligned with the scribed mark on the breaker cam.
2. Loosen the contact adjusting screw and turn the eccentric screw until a snug slip-fit is obtained with the appropriate feeler gauge.
3. Tighten the adjusting screw and recheck the gap.

500 (Before H57083)

The point assembly is located behind a circular cover plate on the right side of the engine, and is driven off the right exhaust camshaft.

REMOVAL

1. Remove the points cover and gasket.

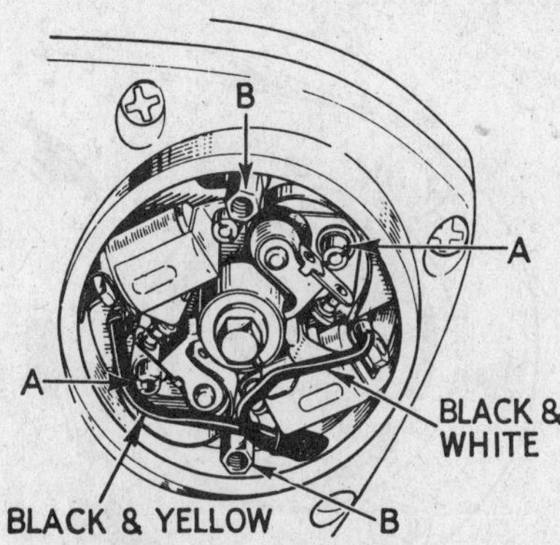

Breaker points (500 before H57083): sleeve nuts (A) and pillar bolts (B)

2. Remove the two sleeve nuts ("A" in the illustration), withdraw the points and condenser, and carefully disconnect the primary wire.

INSTALLATION

Installation is the reverse of removal. Add a drop of motor oil to the point pivots before refitting.

GAP ADJUSTMENT

1. Remove the spark plugs.
2. Rotate the engine until the nylon heel of one set of points aligns with the mark scribed on the breaker cam.
3. Insert the appropriate feeler gauge and, if necessary, loosen sleeve nuts "A" (see illustration) and shift the breaker point plate until a snug slip-fit is achieved.
4. Repeat the above for the other set of points.
5. Check to make sure the breaker plate is correctly positioned. The set of points with the black/yellow lead should be situated toward the rear. Also make certain that the pillar bolts are in the center of their adjustment slots.

500 (H57083 and Later), 650, 750 Twin

The points are beneath a cover plate on the right, front side of the engine.

REMOVAL

1. Remove the cover plate.
2. Remove the primary wire terminal nut, and disconnect the wire, noting any insulators and their positions.
3. Remove the contact locking screw and remove the points.

INSTALLATION

Installation is the reverse of removal. Lubricate the pivot with a drop of oil. Note wire connections.

GAP ADJUSTMENT

1. Turn the engine over until the scribed mark on the breaker cam aligns with the nylon heel of one of the points.
2. Check the gap with the proper feeler gauge. It should be a snug slip-fit if correct. If adjustment is necessary, loosen the contact locking screw, and turn the contact eccentric adjusting screw until the gap is correct. Tighten the locking screw and recheck gap.
3. Repeat the procedure with the other set of points.

T150, T150V

The procedure for removal, installation, and gapping is the same as outlined for 650 and 750 Twins, above, except that three sets of points must be gapped. Note wire color codes by referring to the accompanying illustration.

IGNITION TIMING

NOTE: *Points should be cleaned and gapped before setting ignition timing.*

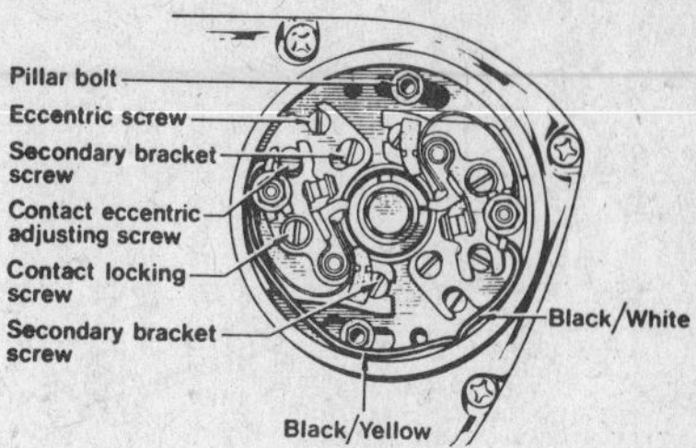

Breaker points (500 after H57082 and other twins)

TR25W

INITIAL PROCEDURE

Before actually setting static timing, the piston must be located at the specified number of degrees before top dead center and the automatic spark advance mechanism must be locked in the fully advanced position.

1. Remove the small inspection cover at the front of the primary chaincase.
2. As can be seen through the aperture, a timing mark is scribed on the face of the alternator rotor and a pointer is mounted at the bottom of inspection hole.
3. Rotate the engine until it is on its compression stroke (i.e., both valves closed), then align the rotor mark and pointer. The piston is now located 37° before top dead center.
4. An alternate method of locating the piston, only possible on later machines, is by using Triumph special plunger and body (no. 61-2915 and 61-D572). Locate the piston on its compression stroke, then rotate the engine gently backward while applying slight pressure to the plunger. The plunger will drop into position, locking the piston at 37° before top dead center.
5. Now that the piston is correctly located, the automatic advance unit must be locked in the fully advanced position. This is necessary because, due to manufacturing tolerances, slight variation in spark timing will occur at one end of the advance curve or the other. In general, it is preferred that this variation does not affect high speed performance; therefore the mechanism should be set at the fully advanced position so that any fluctuations will occur only at idle speeds.
6. Carefully remove the cam central bolt and fit an extra washer on the bolt.

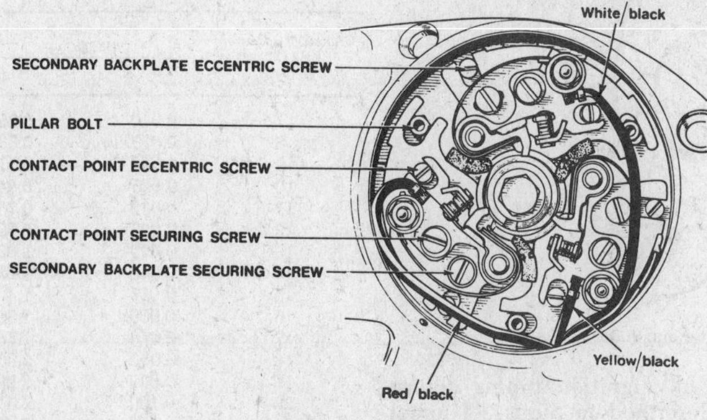

Breaker points (Trident)

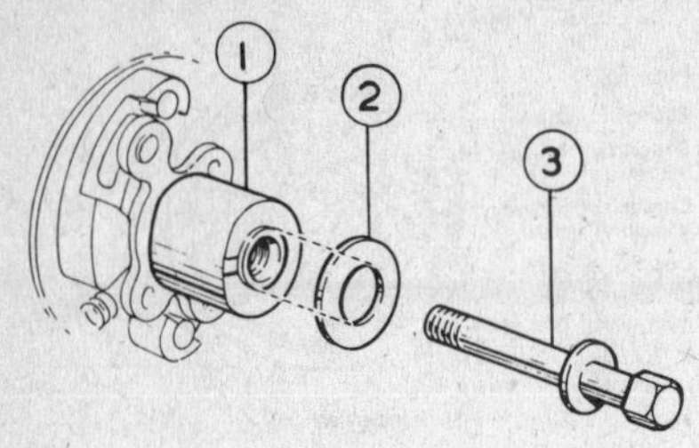

Locking the breaker cam (1) with an oversized washer (2) and central bolt (3)

This washer should have a hole just large enough to clear the cam inner bearing (see illustration).

7. Reinstall the bolt, but before tightening it, rotate the cam counterclockwise until the advance weights are fully extended. Hold the weights in this position and tighten the central bolt.

8. After setting the final ignition timing, don't forget to remove the extra washer on the central bolt.

STATIC TIMING

1. With the piston correctly located and the advance mechanism locked in the full advance position, the ignition timing can now be set.

2. Hook up the test or continuity light: one lead to ground, the other to the primary wire terminal or points spring.

3. Loosen the two secondary bracket screws, and turn the eccentric screw in either direction until the points just open. Tighten the bracket screws.

4. If the points will not open using this method, set the eccentric screw in the middle of its adjustment range. Loosen the two pillar bolts which secure the large points plate, and rotate the entire plate until the points open. Make any necessary fine adjustments with the eccentric screw.

DYNAMIC TIMING

1. Remove the inspection cover at the front of the primary chaincase.

2. Hook up the strobe light. At engines speeds above 3,000 rpm, the mark on the alternator rotor should align with the fitted pointer.

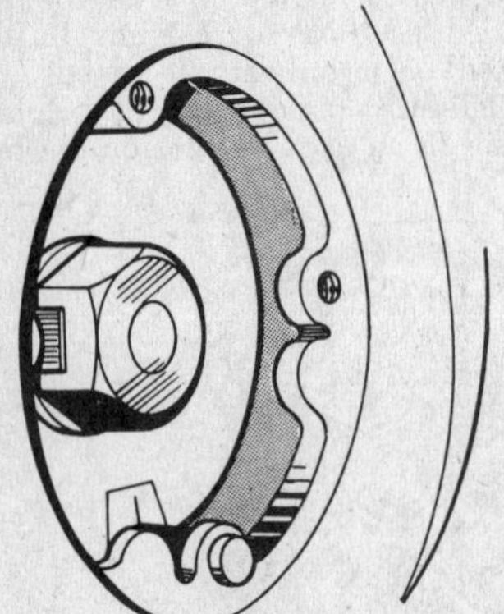
Rotor and stator marks (250)

3. Make any ignition timing adjustments as described in Steps 3-4 under "Static Timing."

500 (Before H57083)

INITIAL PROCEDURE

Before setting ignition timing, the piston must first be positioned at top dead center.

1. Remove the spark plugs and rocker box inspection caps.

2. Put the transmission in gear so that the engine can be rotated by turning the rear wheel.

3. Locate the piston at top dead center, using a dial indicator, Triumph timing plunger and body no. D571/2, or, if necessary, a stick positioned in the spark plug hole. The right cylinder must be on the compression stroke.

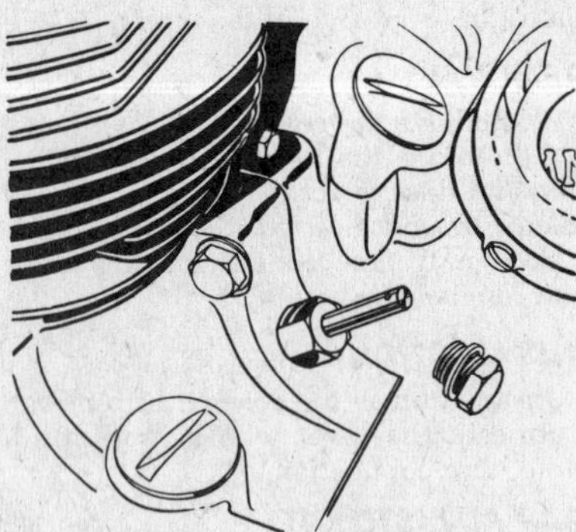
Timing plunger is position (500)

STATIC TIMING

1. Remove the automatic advance unit and check the degree range stamped on the back. Make a note for future reference and reinstall the unit. A special extractor must be used to remove the unit.

2. Double the auto-advance range and subtract it from the fully advanced degree figure (38°). This is the correct static setting for the engine. Example:

AUTO-ADVANCE
DEGREE RANGE = 12°
FULLY ADVANCED
2 × 12° = 24°
38° − 24° = STATIC
TIMING

3. If a stick is used to locate top dead center, convert the degree figure into inches or millimeters by using the chart, then scribe a corresponding mark on the stick.

500 Twin Crankshaft Degree Conversion Chart

Crankshaft position (BTDC) Degrees	Piston position (BTDC) in.	mm
7	0.010	0.25
8	0.015	0.38
9	0.020	0.51
10	0.025	0.64
11	0.030	0.76
12	0.035	0.89
13	0.040	1.02
14	0.048	1.22
15	0.055	1.40
16	0.060	1.52
17	0.070	1.78
18	0.080	2.03
19	0.090	2.29
20	0.100	2.54
21	0.110	2.79

4. Fit a degree wheel to the auto advance unit and fasten a pointer to a convenient case cover screw.

5. If a dial indicator or timing plunger was used to locate top dead center, position the degree wheel and/or pointer to read TDC. Then remove the timing plunger (the dial indicator can remain) and carefully rotate the engine until it is at 38° before top dead center (right cylinder on the compression stroke), as indicated by the degree wheel and pointer.

6. Connect a timing light to the right cylinder points (black/yellow primary wire). Rotate the engine backward to a point below the static timing position. slowly approach the prescribed setting and, if necessary, adjust the breaker plate so that the points are just opening when the setting is reached.

Adjust the timing by rotating the breaker plate after loosening the pillar bolts "B."

7. Rotate the engine forward 360° and repeat the procedure on the second set of points, noting that the main breaker plate must not be disturbed.

NOTE: *To fine-tune the ignition timing, it is permissible to vary the breaker point gap slightly so that both cylinders are timed exactly the same. To advance the spark, open the points approximately 0.001 in. per crankshaft rotation degree.*

DYNAMIC TIMING

After locating top dead center and installing a timing disc as previously described, connect the strobe light on the right cylinder points. If a 6 or 12-volt external power supply is needed, *do not* use the motorcycle battery. AC current pulses in the bike's low tension wiring can trigger the strobe light and lead to incorrect readings.

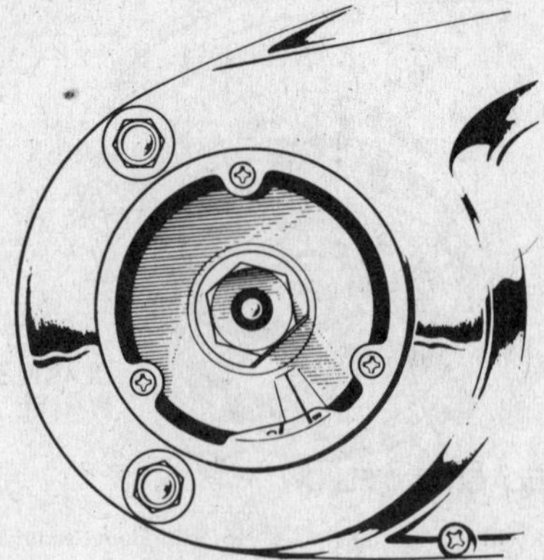
Rotor and stator timing marks with Adaptor D2014 (500)

Aim the strobe light at the timing disc and rev the engine until the auto advance mechanism is actuated (2,000 rpm). The pointer and 38° BTDC on the disc should be exactly in line. If they are not, loosen the contact breaker-plate pillar bolts and make the necessary adjustment. Repeat the procedure for the other cylinder. Remember that the main breaker plate must not be disturbed after setting the right cylinder.

500 (H57083 and Later)

INITIAL PROCEDURE

These models are fitted with alternator rotor marks and timing plunger stops at TDC and 38° BTDC for each cylinder.

First make sure the auto advance unit is correctly positioned on the camshaft locating peg. Lock the auto advance in the full advance position using a suitably sized washer which will bear on the breaker cam when the bolt is tightened (see illustration). Remove the plugs and rocker box covers.

STATIC TIMING

1. Remove the plug behind and between the cylinders. Turn the engine over slowly in the normal direction of rotation until the right cylinder is on the compression stroke, and close to TDC.

2. Install timing plunger and body Nos. D653/D654 and rotate the engine slowly applying slight pressure to the plunger until it drops into the crankshaft hole. The engine should now be at TDC and the right cylinder should be on the compression stroke. Check that there is clearance at both valves. If not, turn the crankshaft 360° to locate the right cylinder on its compression stroke.

3. Lift out the plunger, and rotate the engine backwards. When the plunger drops for the second time, the piston is at the firing point of 38° BTDC.

4. If no timing plunger is available, the piston can be positioned at the firing point by removing the inspection cap from the front of the primary chaincase. After establishing the right piston at TDC on its compression stroke, turn the engine backwards until the rotor and stator marks align. This will be the full advance firing point.

NOTE: *Later machines have the stator pointer built in, but some earlier models require the use of adaptor No. D2014 which has two marks, "B" and "C." Use the line marked "C."*

5. When the piston is positioned as outlined, a timing or test light should indicate that the right cylinder's points have just opened. The points for the right cylinder have the black/yellow primary wire.

6. If adjustment is necessary, loosen the two pillar bolts, and rotate the entire point plate until the points just open. Tighten the bolts.

7. Turn the engine 360°, engage the plunger or line up the rotor and stator marks to position the piston at 38° BTDC, and check that the left cylinder (black/white primary wire) just open. If they do not, loosen the two secondary bracket screws, and turn the eccentric screw until timing is corrected. Tighten the bracket screws.

NOTE: *If timing has been lost completely, as after rebuilding the engine, it is advisable to set the points plate and the eccentric screws at about the middle of their adjustment range before resetting the timing.*

DYNAMIC TIMING

1. A strobe light can be used by means of the rotor and stator timing marks beneath the plate at the forward end of the primary chaincase.

NOTE: *If the strobe light requires a battery power source, do not use the motorcycle battery.*

2. The marks should align above 2,000 rpm. Check the right cylinder (black/yellow primary wire) first, and adjust the timing, if necessary, by moving the point plate as explained in Step 6, above. Repeat the test with the left cylinder, changing the timing by moving the left cylinder points only as explained in Step 7, above.

650, 750 Twin

1. The procedures are the same as for 500 (H57803 and later) since the points are the same type. Note the following:

2. The plunger and body to be used are D2195/D572.

3. If the machine does not have a stator pointer, use D2014. If dynamic timing is being carried out with this pointer, use line "B."

T150, T150V

The Trident is equipped with one set of points for each cylinder. The firing order is one-three-two. The right (no. one) cylinder point lead is white/black; the center (no. two) red/black, and the left (no. three) yellow/black.

STATIC TIMING

NOTE: *Early model Tridents. have three timing marks scribed onto the rotor, 120° apart, each one for a different cylinder. Late models have two sets of timing marks which are distinguished by "A" or "B."*

When timing late engines before Serial No. PG 01603, use the "A" timing marks. For engines after PG 01603, line up the "B" timing marks.

1. Remove the spark plugs and rocker box inspection caps. Put the transmission in gear so that the engine can be rotated by turning the rear wheel.

2. Locate approximate top dead center by rotating the engine until no. 1 piston is at the top of its compression stroke (i.e., both valves closed with clearance at the tappets).

3. Install Triumph timing plunger and body no. D1858, then slowly rotate the engine backward until the plunger locks the crankshaft at 38° BTDC.

4. If the automatic advance unit is not installed, assemble it loosely with an extra washer on the central bolt to lock the cam in the fully advanced position. If it is installed, remove the central bolt and add the extra washer. The washer should have a hole just a little larger than the cam bearing.

5. When the auto-advance unit is fully advanced, the no. 1 cylinder points should just be opening. If this is not the case, loosen the secondary breaker plate screws and shift the plate until the points begin to open.

6. Remove the timing plunger and locate the no. 3 cylinder at TDC on the compression stroke. Rotate the engine backwards until the plunger indicates that the piston is at 38° BTDC. Repeat the procedure outlined above on the no. 3 cylinder points, then again on no. 2 cylinder points.

7. Remove the extra washer on the central bolt.

DYNAMIC TIMING

1. Remove the two top screws of the Triumph patent plate on the primary chaincase. Just loosen the bottom screw, as it will serve as a pointer.

2. Remove the ignition inspection plate located at the front of the primary chaincase.

3. Connect the strobe light to the right cylinder as instructed by the strobe man-

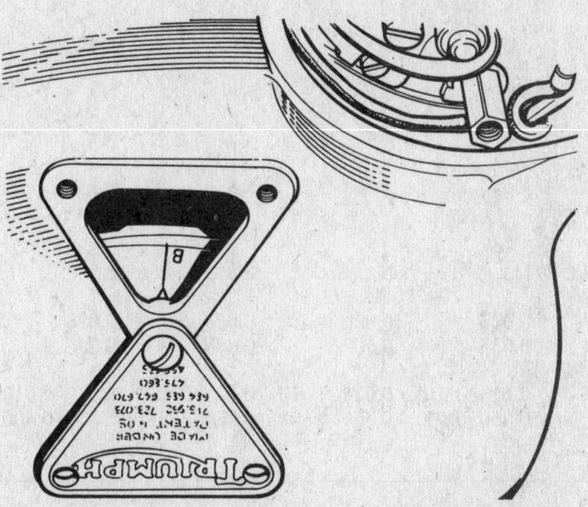

Trident timing marks (from Engine No. PG01603)

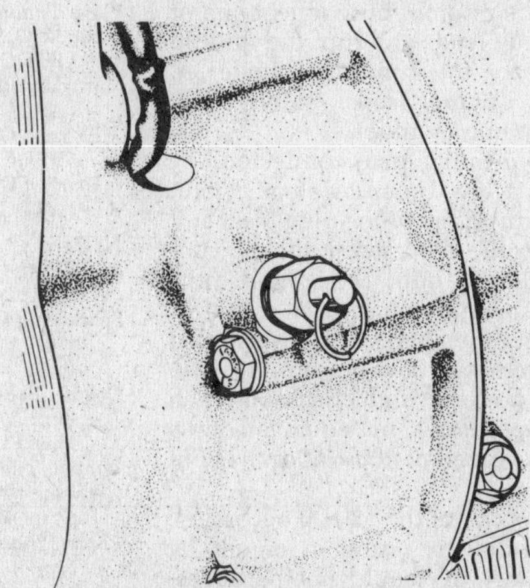
Timing plunger installed (Trident)

ufacturer. If the unit requires an external power source, *do not* use the motorcycle battery. AC pulses in the machine's low tension wiring can trigger the strobe light and lead to incorrect readings.

4. At engine speeds above 2,000 rpm, one of the three marks on the alternator rotor (exposed by the Triumph patent plate) should line up directly with t bottom plate screw. If adjustment is necessary, loosen the no. 1 point set secondary bracket and shift the plate until the marks are aligned. Tighten the plate securing screws.

5. Repeat the above procedure on no. 2 cylinder (center), then no. 3 cylinder (left).

6. Reinstall the patent and inspection plates.

CARBURETOR ADJUSTMENTS

Idle Speed and Mixture

NOTE: *Make these adjustments when the engine is at operating temperature.*

SINGLE-CARBURETOR

1. Make sure there is some freeplay in the throttle cable so the slide will close fully.

2. Turn the pilot air screw in until it is lightly seated, then back it out 2½ turns. Start the engine. Adjust the idle speed (throttle stop) screw so that the engine idles at about 750 rpm.

3. Make any fine adjustments by turning the pilot air screw in either direction so that an even idle is obtained. It should not be necessary to vary this screw more than ½ turn from the standard setting. If it is, there may be something wrong with the carburetor or engine. Check for fuel blockages, air leaks, etc.

4. Use the throttle cable adjuster to take up most of the slack in the cable. The twist grip should have 10–15° or rotation before the slide begins to rise.

TWIN-CARBURETOR

1. Make sure there is some slack in the main throttle cable so that the slides will close fully.

2. Screw each pilot air screw in gently until it is seated, then back them out 2½ turns.

3. Start the engine. Disconnect one of the spark plug leads and turn the throttle stop screw for the running cylinder in until the engine runs slowly but smoothly on one cylinder.

4. With *both* plug leads connected, rev the engine a few times to clean it out. Then disconnect the *other* plug lead, and turn the throttle stop screw for the running cylinder in until the engine runs slowly but smoothly on the one cylinder.

5. Connect the spark plug lead so that both cylinders will now be running. Idle speed will be very high. Back out each throttle stop screws by equal amounts until an idle speed of 500–750 rpm is obtained.

6. To smooth out the idle, if necessary, turn each pilot air screw in or out by equal amounts. It should not be necessary to turn either of them more than ½ turn. If it is, there is probably a defect in the system: air leaks, fuel flow problem, impure gasoline, etc.

7. Synchronize the throttle slides.

8. Use the adjuster on the main throttle cable so that the slide begin to rise after about 10–15° of twist-grip rotation.

Carburetor Synchronization, Twins

On twin-carburetor models, the throttle slides must be synchronized or one cylinder will lead the other while running. This operation should be carried out after setting the idle speed and mixture.

1. Remove the air cleaner(s).

2. Position a mirror behind the carburetors or reach into the bores with the thumb and index finger of one hand.

3. Twist open the throttle slides, and feel, or watch, as the slides enter the bores. They should begin to enter their respective bores simultaneously.

4. An alternate method is to place a finger on each carburetor slide when closed, and then turn the twist-grip slightly. Both slides should begin to lift at the same time.

5. If adjustment is necessary, use the cable adjusters on the top of each carburetor raising or lowering them so the

Tune-Up Specifications

	TR25W	T100C	T100R	TR6R	TR6C
CARBURETION			(See text procedures)		
VALVES					
Valve Tappet Clearance (cold):					
Intake (in.)	0.008	0.002	0.002	0.002	0.002
Intake (mm)	0.203	0.050	0.050	0.050	0.050
Exhaust (in.)	0.010	0.004	0.004	0.004	0.004
Exhaust (mm)	0.254	0.100	0.100	0.100	0.100
Valve Timing:					
Intake Opens (BTDC)	51°	34°	40°	34°	34°
Intake Closes (ABDC)	68°	55°	52°	55°	55°
Exhaust Opens (BBDC)	78°	48°	61°	55°	55°
Exhaust Closes (ATDC)	37°	27°	31°	34°	34°
IGNITION					
Spark Plug (standard) (Champion)	N3	N4	N4	N3	N3
Spark Plug Gap:					
(in.)	0.020–0.025	0.020	0.020	0.025	0.025
(mm)	0.508–0.635	0.508	0.508	0.635	0.635
Contact Breaker Gap:					
(in.)	0.015	0.015	0.015	0.014–0.016	0.014–0.016
(mm)	0.381	0.381	0.381	0.350–0.400	0.350–0.400
Ignition Timing:					
Crankshaft Position (advanced)	37°	38°	38°	38°	38°
Piston Position (BTDC):					
(in.)	0.342	0.330	0.330	0.415	0.415
(mm)	8.687	8.380	8.380	10.4	10.4

	T120R	T150	TR7V	T140V	T150V
CARBURETION			(See text procedures)		
VALVES					
Valve Tappet Clearance (cold):					
Intake (in.)	0.002	0.006	0.008	0.008	0.006
Intake (mm)	0.050	0.152	0.20	0.20	0.15
Exhaust (in.)	0.004	0.008	0.006	0.006	0.008
Exhaust (mm)	0.100	0.203	0.15	0.15	0.20
Valve Timing:					
Intake Opens (BTDC)	34°	50°	NA	NA	50°
Intake Closes (ABDC)	34°	64°	NA	NA	64°
Exhaust Opens (BBDC)	55°	67°	NA	NA	67°
Exhaust Closes (ATDC)	34°	47°	NA	NA	47°
IGNITION					
Spark Plug (standard) (Champion)	N3	N3	N3	N3	N3
Spark Plug Gap:					
(in.)	0.025	0.020	0.025	0.025	0.020
(mm)	0.635	0.500	0.635	0.635	0.50
Contact Breaker Gap:					
(in.)	0.014–0.016	0.014–0.016	0.014–0.016	0.014–0.016	0.014–0.016
(mm)	0.350–0.400	0.350–0.400	0.350–0.400	0.350–0.400	0.350–0.400
Ignition Timing:					
Crankshaft Position (advanced)	38°	38°	38°	38°	38°
Piston Position (BTDC):					
(in.)	0.415	0.357	0.415	0.415	0.357
(mm)	10.4	9.07	10.4	10.4	9.07

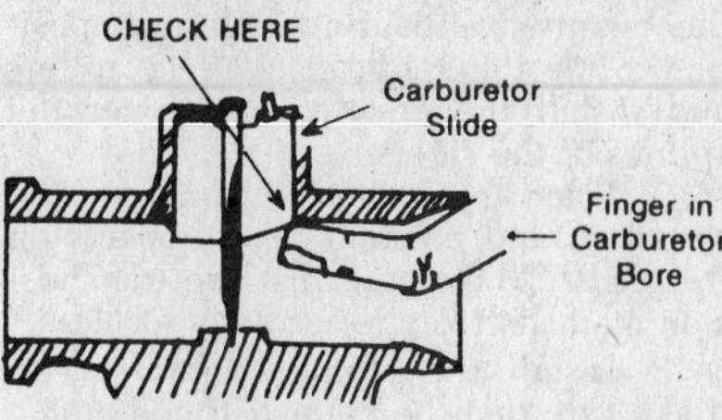

Checking carburetor synchronization

slide movements match. Allow each adjuster some part in making the adjustment. Do not screw either of them out too much, or that slide may not close fully.

6. Check the adjustment of the throttle cable(s), using the adjuster(s) near the twist-grip so that the slides begin to rise after about 10–15° of grip rotation.

Triples

Due to type of linkage used, throttle slides should be synchronized first. There are two possible methods:

1. Remove the carburetor assembly from the motorcycle. Looking through the engine side of the carburetors, turn the idle speed screw so that one of the slides (any one) is being held open about 0.010 in. Loosen the locknut and turn the adjuster at the top of each carburetor so that the other two slides are open the same amount. Check by opening the throttles and ensuring that all three slides clear the bore at the same time. Be sure the locknuts are tightened.
2. Alternately, check synchronization with the carbs in place on the machine using sight or feel according to the procedure outlined under "Carburetor Synchronization, Twins," above.
3. With the engine at operating temperature, turn each pilot air screw in until lightly seated, then back each out 2½ turns. Start the engine, and use the idle speed screw to set idle at 500 rpm.
4. Use the cable adjuster at the carburetor end to give about 10–15° of twist-grip rotation before the slides begin to rise.

ENGINE AND TRANSMISSION

NOTE: *For engine component inspection and service procedures, refer to "Engine Rebuilding" under the "General Information" section. Triumph engine specifications are given at the end of this "Engine and Transmission" section.*

TR25W

Engine Removal and Installation

1. Remove the fuel tank.
2. Remove the exhaust system by disconnecting the exhaust pipe clamp at the head, and removing the two muffler mounting bolts.
3. Remove the right side-cover and unbolt the skid plate from frame tubes. Drain the oil.
4. Disconnect the valve rocker oil line from the metal T-connection and disconnect the flexible scavenge line from the crankcase line at the rear.
5. Disconnect the alternator, oil pressure switch (if applicable), and contact breaker point leads from their snap connectors at the electrical box. Disconnect the spark plug wire.
6. Remove the carburetor flange nuts and tie the carburetor out of the way. Leave the rubber connecting hose attached to the air filter housing.
7. Disconnect the top engine mount (at the rocker cover).
8. Remove the chainguard front extension and remove the master link from the chain.
9. Disconnect the clutch cable using a suitable box wrench as a lever on the operating arm.
10. Loosen the footpeg mounting bolt and swing the footpeg down.
11. Remove the remaining engine mount bolts. Note that spacers are installed between the engine and frame at the right side of the front and bottom bolts.
12. Remove the rear, engine mounting plate and lift the engine unit out of the frame from the right side.

Installation is in reverse order of removal. Be sure to replace the two spacers correctly. Double-check all hardware and electrical connections when completed.

Top End

REMOVAL

On the TR25W, the cylinder head and barrel may be removed with the engine in the frame. The procedure is as follows:

1. Remove the fuel tank.
2. Unbolt the engine mount at the cylinder head and push the bracket up out of the way.
3. Remove the carburetor from the head, leaving it suspended by the throttle cable.
4. Remove the exhaust system by disconnecting the exhaust pipe clamp at the head and removing the two, muffler mounting bolts.
5. Remove the spark plug and disconnect the rocker oil feed line.
6. Rotate the engine until the piston is at top dead center of the compression stroke (both valves closed, clearance at the rocker arms).
7. Remove the six cylinder head nuts; if the head will not move, free it with a rubber mallet.
8. Lift the head, rotate it around the pushrods to clear the frame, and remove it from the engine.

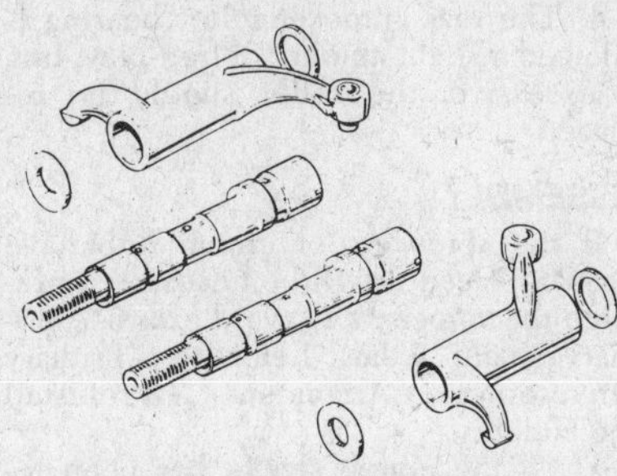

Valve train

9. To remove the barrel, first rotate the engine until the piston is at the bottom of the stroke and then gently lift the barrel off. Steady the piston as the barrel is withdrawn so that it will not be damaged.
10. To remove the piston, it will be necessary to heat it slightly to facilitate removal of the wrist pin. First remove the wrist pin circlips. After the piston is warm, the wrist pin should slide out fairly easily. Mark the front of the piston inside the skirt to facilitate reassembly.

INSPECTION

Refer to "Engine Rebuilding" for service procedures.

Oversized pistons are available in +0.020 and +0.040 sizes.

If the con rod bush must be replaced, refer to the T100C, T100R engine section for removal and installation procedures. Valve guides are removed and installed in the usual manner. The exhaust valve guide is counterbored at the lower end.

INSTALLATION

1. When installing the piston rings, note that the lower compression ring is marked "TOP" and must be installed in the second groove with this mark facing upwards. The top compression ring is probably chromed.
2. Warm the piston and install it, in correct position, on the connecting rod. Insert the piston pin before the piston has a chance to cool. Install *new* circlips and make sure that they are seated properly. Install a new cylinder base gasket and support the piston with two pieces of wood approximately ½ in. square by 6 in. long. Stagger the ring gaps 120 degrees apart, liberally oil the rings, and install a ring compressor. If a ring compressor is unavailable, it is possible to compress the

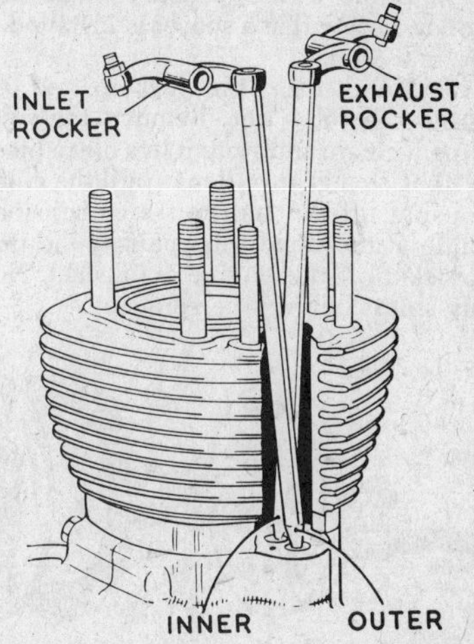

Pushrod installation

rings by hand, one at a time, as the barrel is slipped over the piston. Be careful. Slide the barrel over the piston and remove the compressor and wood blocks.

3. Install the two pushrods, noting that the outer one operates the intake valve. The top of the exhaust valve pushrod is painted red for identification, as it is slightly shorter than the intake pushrod. *The pushrods must be positioned correctly.*

4. Install the rocker box on the cylinder head using a new gasket, then torque the nuts to 7 ft lbs. Install a new head gasket and fit the head onto the barrel. Place the pushrod ends into the rocker arm ends, making absolutely sure that they are positioned correctly, as illustrated. Keep a light, downward pressure on the head and rotate the engine until the piston is at top dead center of the compression stroke. In this position both valves will be fully closed (clearance at both rocker arms). Tighten the cylinder head nuts, gradually to the figures given in specifications at the end of this section.

5. Check and adjust valve clearances, etc.

Clutch and Primary Drive

DISASSEMBLY

1. If the engine is mounted in the frame, remove the left-side footpeg and brake pedal.

2. Drain the oil from the primary chaincase remove the screws, and take off the primary drive cover. It may be necessary to tap the cover with a rubber mallet to break it free.

3. Remove the four, clutch-spring retaining nuts and withdraw the pressure plate, springs, and cups.

4. Withdraw the clutch plates.

5. Keep the clutch from turning by applying the rear brake, and remove the clutch center nut (after the locktab has been bent back).

6. Remove the locktab and spacer, and withdraw the clutch pushrod.

7. To remove the clutch completely, it is necessary to remove the alternator. To remove the stator (enclosing the rotor), take off the three mounting nuts, pull the alternator lead through the grommet, and pull the stator off the studs.

8. Remove the primary chain tensioner, noting that a spacer is installed on the rear stud.

9. Bend back the locktab and unscrew the rotor nut. Remove the rotor, wipe it clean, and store it in a clean place.

10. Use a gear puller to pull the clutch housing off the transmission mainshaft, while at the same time pulling the front sprocket off the engine crankshaft. Note any shims behind the sprocket.

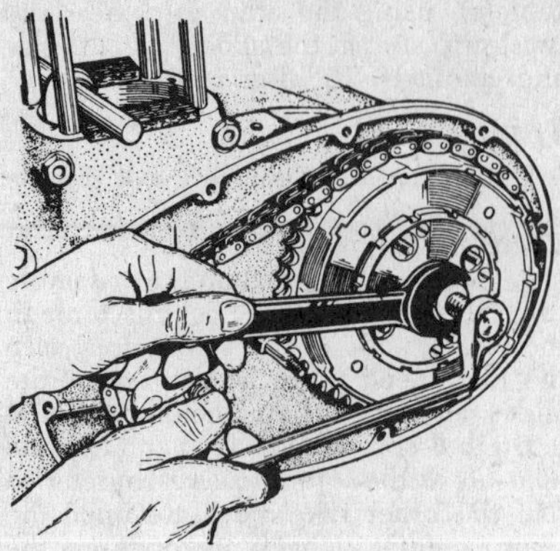

Removing the clutch housing

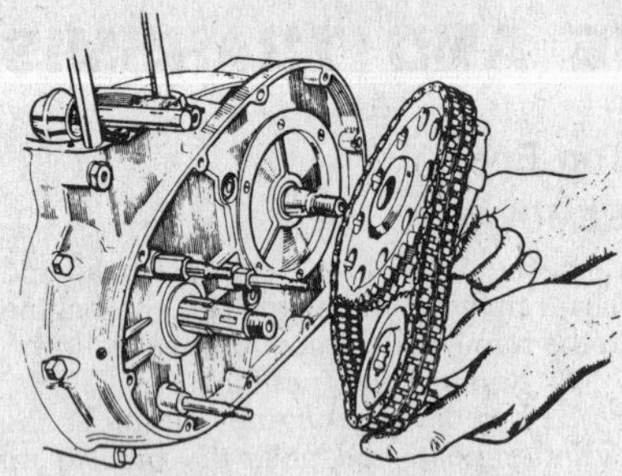

Installing the primary drive

INSPECTION

1. If the thickness of the friction discs measures less than 0.137 in., they should be replaced.

2. To examine the dampers located in the clutch center, remove the four screws adjacent to the clutch spring housings and pry off the retaining plate. The dampers need not be replaced unless they are visibly damaged or worn. It may be necessary to lubricate them when installing; it is recommended that a liquid detergent be used. *Do not use petroleum-based oil or grease.*

3. The clutch center slots should be smooth and undamaged or jerky clutch engagement will result. Check clutch spring free length, and if less than 1.60 in., replace the springs as a set.

4. The rear sprocket roller bearing is allowed a slight amount of free-play, but, if excessive, the roller should be replaced.

ASSEMBLY

If the sprockets or clutch hub have been replaced it will be necessary to realign the sprockets to avoid excessive primary chain wear. Refer to "Primary Drive Sprocket Alignment." To reinstall the clutch:

1. If the clutch sleeve has been removed, smear it with grease and place

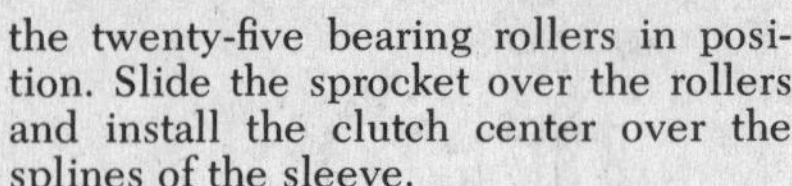

the twenty-five bearing rollers in position. Slide the sprocket over the rollers and install the clutch center over the splines of the sleeve.

2. Place the primary chain over the sprockets and position the sprockets on the shafts. Make sure that the transmission mainshaft key is correctly located.

3. Install the clutch center spacer. Make sure that the mainshaft and clutch retaining nut threads are clean and dry. Install a new locktab and apply a small amount of thread-locking compound to the mainshaft threads before installing the retaining nut. Torque the nut to 60–65 ft lb.

4. Install the alternator rotor on the crankshaft with the marks facing out, making sure that the key is located correctly. Install a new locktab, apply a drop of thread-locking compound to the threads, then tighten the retaining nut to 60 ft lbs.

5. Pass the stator lead through the grommet at the front of the crankcase. Fit the stator over the studs and partially tighten the nuts. Check that there is an equal air gap between the rotor and stator at all points using an 0.008 in. feeler gauge. Variations can be corrected by repositioning the stator.

6. To adjust primary chain tension, loosen the rear stator retaining nut and adjust the tensioner to provide ¼ in. free-play on the top run of the chain midway between the sprockets. Retighten the stator nut.

7. Install the clutch discs and plates, alternately, into the clutch housing, beginning with a disc. Insert the clutch pushrod into the mainshaft.

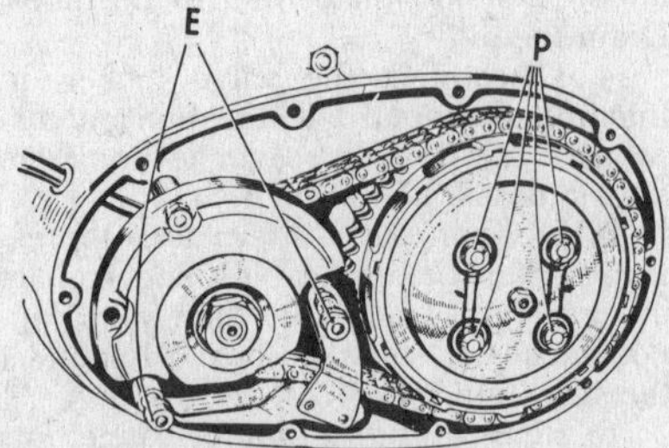

Primary chain (E) and pressure plate (P) adjustment points

8. Install the pressure plate complete with springs and cups. Make sure the spring cup location pips are seated in the slots in the pressure plate.

9. Install and tighten the four spring nuts until the first coil of each spring is just outside of its cup. Improper spring tension will cause excessive pressure at the handlebar lever or clutch slip. Check to see if the springs are tightened evenly by pulling the clutch lever in and kicking the engine over. If any wobble is noticeable at the pressure plate as it turns, tighten or loosen the springs as necessary until it runs true.

10. Adjust the clutch by means of the screw and locknut at the center of the pressure plate so that the clutch operating lever is angled approximately 30° away from the crankcase/side-cover joint.

11. Clean the crankcase and primary cover mating surfaces, apply a thin coat of

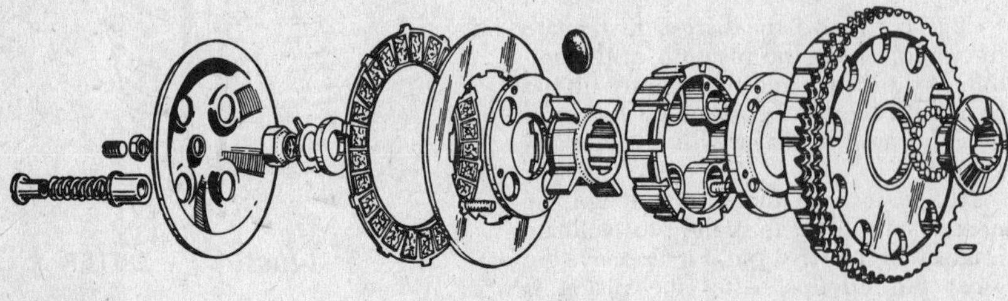

Clutch assembly

gasket cement, and mount the cover using a new gasket. If it is possible to use a torque wrench, tighten the screws to 3.5–4.5 ft lbs.

12. Fill the primary chaincase with oil and adjust the clutch lever free-play if necessary.

Transmission Countershaft Sprocket and Oil Seal

To examine or remove the countershaft final drive sprocket, first remove the six screws that retain the plate surrounding the shaft. Pry the plate loose and remove it with its oil seal, taking note of the felt washer that protects the seal from dirt and grit. Check for oil leakage at the back of the plate and replace the plate oil seal if necessary. Install the seal with the lip facing the countershaft sprocket.

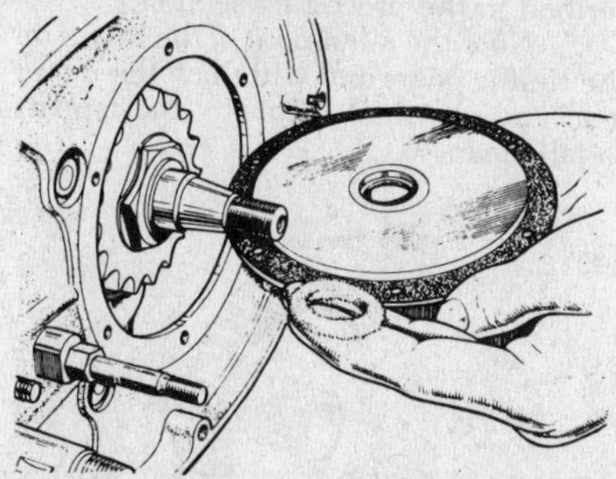

Gearbox sprocket cover and seal

If the sprocket teeth are hooked or if the sprocket is damaged, it should be replaced (along with the drive chain and rear wheel sprocket if it too is worn). To remove the sprocket bend back the locktab, apply the rear brake, then unscrew the retaining nut. Disconnect the drive chain and pull the sprocket off the shaft. Examine the countershaft oil seal at this time. If it shows signs of leakage, remove the circlip, pry out the seal, and replace it with a new one. Coat the new seal with oil to facilitate installation. Examine the sprocket boss for wear, which may have been causing the seal to leak. Lightly oil the boss when installing the sprocket to avoid damaging the seal. Torque the sprocket retaining nut to 100 ft lbs. When installing the round plate, make sure the gasket is in good condition or use a new one. A new felt washer should be used behind the oil seal. Make sure that the small boss cast into the rear of the plate is installed in the four o'clock position, or else it will contact the drive chain.

Primary Drive Sprocket Alignment

Assemble and install the clutch unit—without the primary chain—on the transmission shaft. Install the crankshaft sprocket. (The sprocket spacer must be installed with the chamfered end against the sprocket.). Place a straightedge against the sprockets. If the sprockets are aligned properly, the straightedge will make contact both evenly. Shims of different thicknesses are available for installation behind the crankshaft sprocket to correct misalignment.

Transmission and Shifter Mechanism

DISASSEMBLY

1. If the top end has not been disassembled, position the piston at top dead center of the compression stroke to avoid distorting the inner camshaft bushing (due to valve spring pressure) as the inner crankcase cover is removed. Drain the transmission oil at this time.

2. Disassemble the primary drive and clutch assembly including the countershaft sprocket, described previously. This is necessary to permit the transmission mainshaft to be withdrawn along with the inner crankcase cover at the right (timing) side of the engine.

3. To remove the right-side outer cover, first take off the kick-start and shift levers. Remove the cover retaining screws, noting that the screws are of different lengths and must be replaced in their original positions.

4. Unscrew the kick-start return spring anchor and remove the spring.

5. Remove the ignition advance unit from the inner cover.

6. Take out the remaining inner cover mounting screws and tap the cover with a rubber mallet to break the joint seal. Withdraw the cover complete with transmission gear cluster. As the cover is removed, exert a slight inward pressure on the end of the camshaft to avoid disturbing the valve timing.

7. Depress the two plungers in the shift linkage quadrant and withdraw the quadrant and spring.

8. Remove the camplate pivot cotter pin from the outside of the cover. Screw one of the small inner cover screws into the pivot and pull the pivot out with a pair of pliers.

9. Remove the camplate, shift forks, and fork shaft.

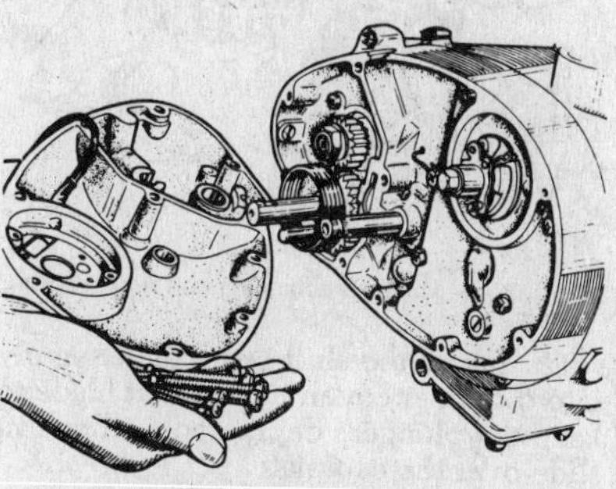

Removing the outer timing cover

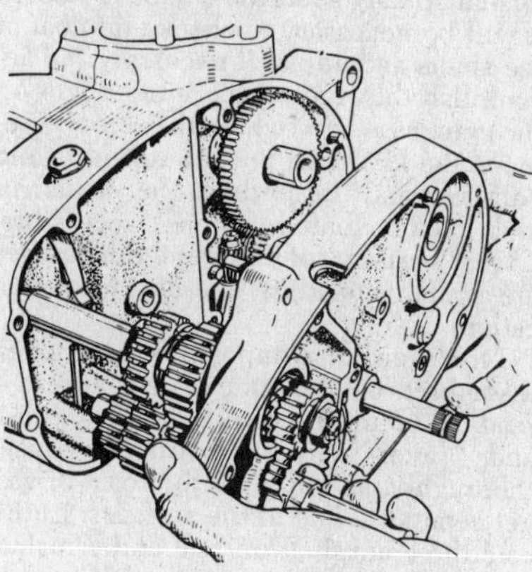

Removing the inner timing cover

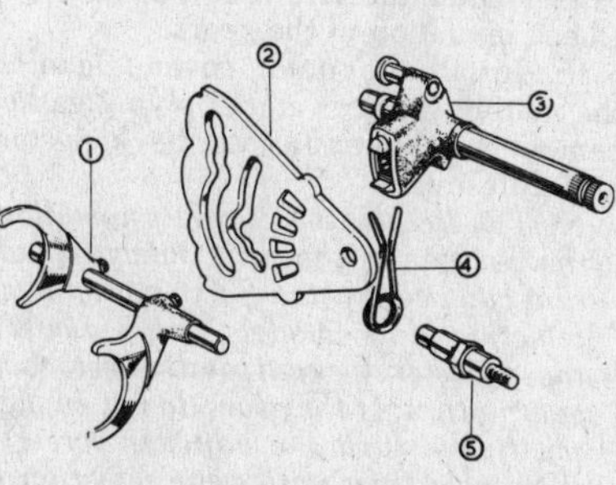

Shifter mechanism

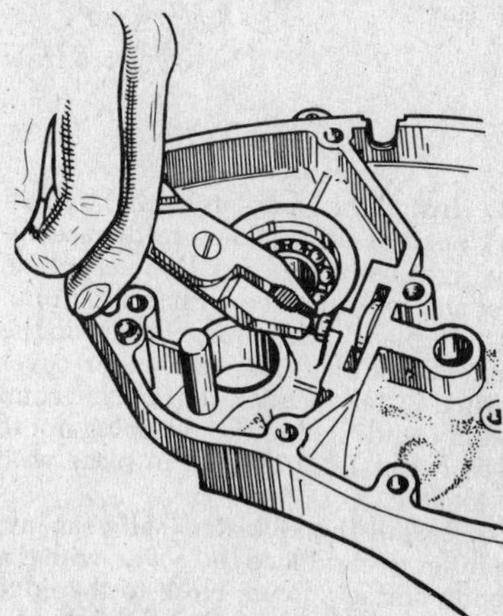

Removing the camplate pivot pin

10. Withdraw the countershaft, complete with gear assembly and mainshaft sliding gear. To remove the mainshaft assembly from the cover, unscrew the kickstart ratchet retaining nut and remove the ratchet components from the shaft.

NOTE: *When removing the countershaft gears, note that second gear is retained by a circlip.*

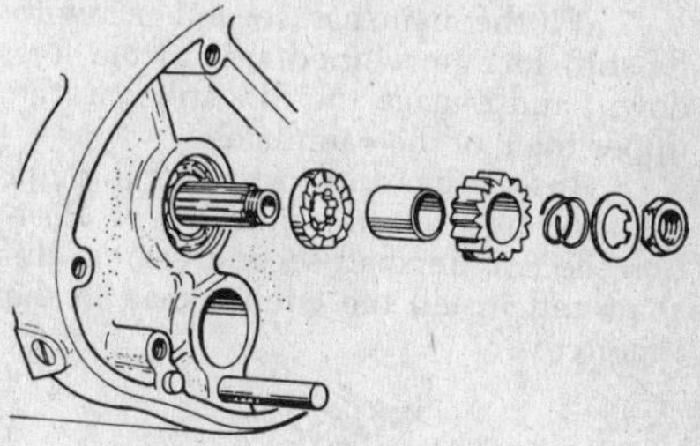

Kickstarter ratchet assembly

11. The two gears remaining on the mainshaft are an interference fit. Remove by clamping the gears in a vise (protected from the jaws with pieces of wood or cloth) and driving the shaft out using a soft metal drift.

12. If it is desired to remove the left-side transmission bearing from the case, drive the pinion out of the bearing and remove the oil seal. The crankcase should be heated with a propane torch before the bearing is driven out to avoid damage to both the bearing and case.

ASSEMBLY

1. To reinstall the left-side bearing (if removed), heat the crankcase very gently

around the area of the bearing housing, moving the torch slowly and evenly to prevent distortion. Install the bearing and fit a new oil seal.

2. If necessary, install a new inner cover bearing, having first heated the cover in an oven. Use new oil seals in the cover.

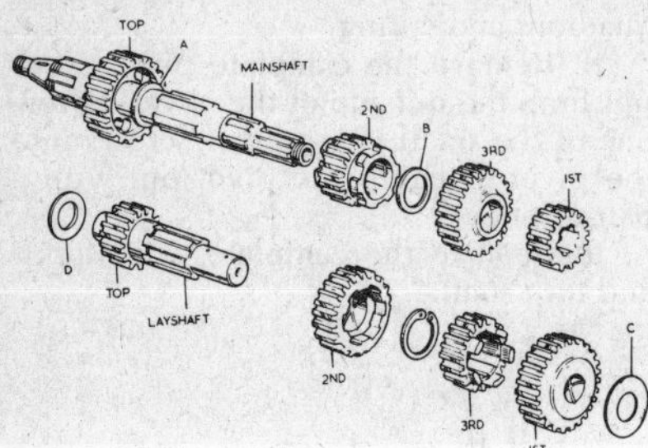

Transmission gears

3. Install the camplate with the small mark positioned as shown in the accompanying illustration. Install the camplate pivot and lock in place with a cotter pin.

4. Replace the mainshaft gears on the shaft, fit the shaft into the inner cover bearing, install the kick-start ratchet components, and tighten the retaining nut to 50–55 ft lbs. Lock the nut in place with the locktab.

5. Install the kick-start half-gear into the inner cover. Place the cover, with the outside surface down, close to the edge on your workbench so that the half-gear shaft is over the edge but the gear is retained in the cover. Place the countershaft first gear shim over the bearing in the half-gear shaft. Use a small amount of grease to hold it in position.

6. Engage the mainshaft and countershaft first gears and fit the shift fork into the countershaft third gear with the machined (flat) side of the fork up. Engage the roller (button) of the fork in the lower camplate track.

7. Fit the mainshaft second gear with its shift fork (machined side of the fork down) and engage the fork roller in the upper track of the camplate.

8. Insert the shift fork shaft through the forks and into the inner cover. Position the countershaft second gear on the shaft and install the countershaft in the inner cover.

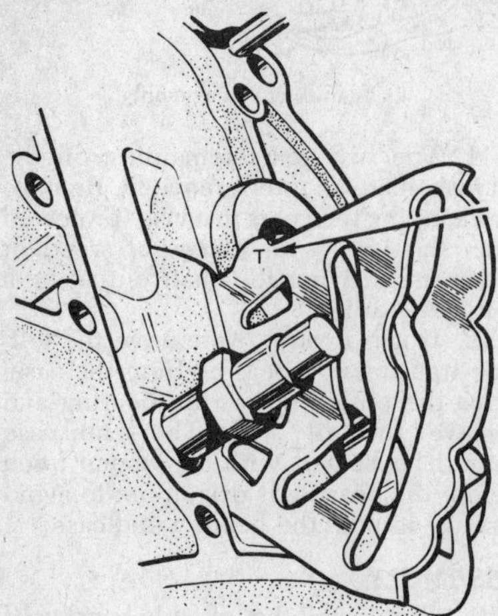

Installing the camplate

9. Place the mainshaft fourth gear thrust washer over the shaft, retaining it with a dab of grease. Install the countershaft thrust washer, making sure that the side with the radius faces the gear.

10. Lubricate all components with motor oil and rotate the shafts to confirm that they are free of binding.

11. If the shift return spring has been removed, it must be reinstalled so that the marked (painted) side of the coil faces the shift quadrant body. If the spring is unmarked, install it in the position in which it appears in the accompanying illustration (in line with the two pins) by trial and error.

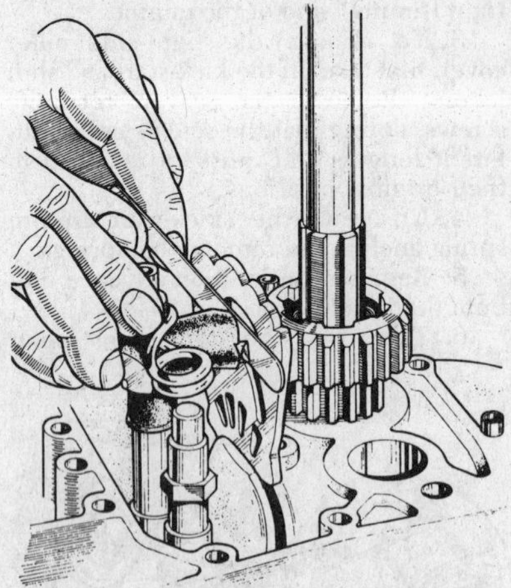

Installing the shifter mechanism and return spring

12. Install the shift quadrant assembly into the inner cover, using a flat blade to keep the plungers depressed so they can slide over the camplate.

13. If the inner case, mainshaft, countershaft, or any gears have been replaced, it will be necessary to check end-float of the shafts and adjust if necessary. To accomplish this, mount the inner cover on the crankcase and tighten the screws. Remove the kick-start ratchet assembly and half-gear and the ends of the mainshaft and countershaft will be accessible. Thrust washers of different thicknesses are available to adjust end-float to specification.

14. When all components have been assembled on the inner cover and it is ready to be installed, clean the crankcase and inner cover mating surfaces thoroughly, and apply a thin coat of gasket cement to one of the surfaces. Lubricate the crankshaft oil seal and camshaft end, and mount the cover on the crankcase. Tighten the screws to 3.5–4.5 ft lbs. Check operation of the gears.

15. Install the outer cover, cleaning the mating surfaces and applying gasket cement as above. Install the kick-start and shift levers.

NOTE: *Before the cover is installed, the position of the shift linkage quadrant can be adjusted for smoother gear selection (late models only). Loosen the adjuster locknut and select each gear in turn. If the gears do not engage positively, turn the adjuster screw a little at a time until gear selection is satisfactory. Do not turn the screw more than ¼ turn from vertical in either direction. Tighten the locknut when adjustment is complete.*

16. Install the primary drive and clutch assembly and refill the transmission and primary case with oil.

Bottom End

DISASSEMBLY

1. Drain the oil from the engine, transmission, and primary case. Remove the engine.

2. Remove the cylinder head, piston, and barrel.

3. Remove the primary drive and clutch assembly.

4. Remove the right-side outer cover and then take off the inner cover, complete with transmission gearset, as described in the preceding section.

5. Note the alignment of the marks on the timing gears and withdraw the upper gear and camshaft, allowing the tappets to fall clear.

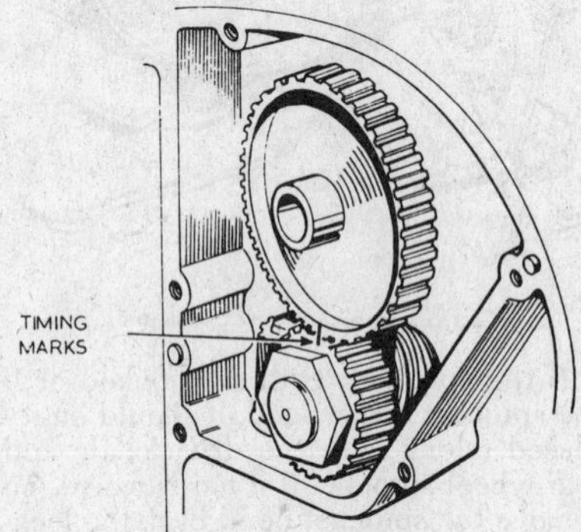

Timing gear marks

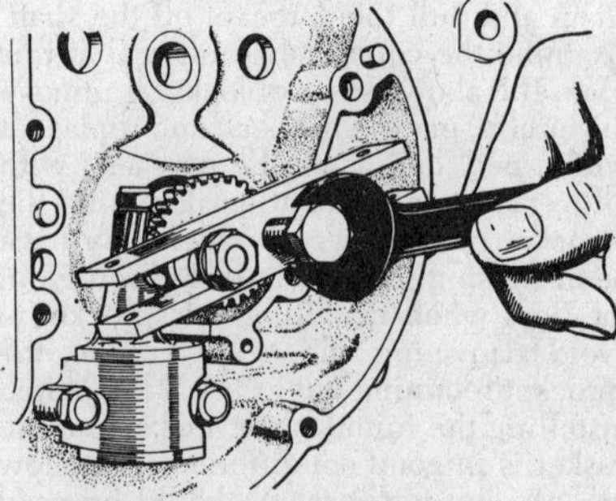

Removing the crankshaft pinion

6. Insert a bar through the connecting rod small-end, place blocks of wood under the bar to protect the crankcase, and unscrew the nut at the end of the crankshaft. The bar will keep the engine from turning over as the nut is broken free.

7. Remove the small timing gear with a suitable gear puller.

8. Take off the nut and remove the oil pump drive-gear.

9. From the left side of the crankcase, remove the three bolts at the lower front of the case, the two stud nuts at the center of the case, and the remaining two stud nuts at the cylinder base.

10. Remove the woodruff keys from the crankshaft ends and separate the crankcase halves by tapping with a rubber mallet.

11. Lift away the right crankcase, and remove the crankshaft assembly. Note the number of shims used, if any, between the right-side flywheel and main bearing.

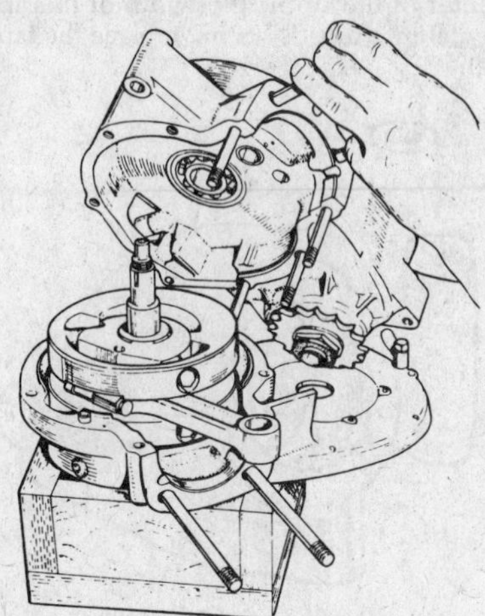

Separating the crankcase halves

MAIN BEARINGS

The inner and outer races of the left-side roller bearing are separated as the crankcase halves are split. The outer race can be driven out after the case has been heated in an oven. The inner race, remaining on the crankshaft, can be pulled off using a suitable gear puller. The right-side (timing side) ball bearing assembly can be driven out after heating the case.

New bearings can be installed in the cases in the same manner, after the cases have been heated.

CONNECTING ROD BEARINGS AND CRANKSHAFT ASSEMBLY

The connecting rod can be removed by simply unbolting the bearing cap. Loosen the nuts alternately, a turn at a time, to prevent distortion. To facilitate reassembly, the connecting rod and cap have been marked with a center punch. Note the direction in which the marks face.

Examine the bearing shells and crankpin carefully for signs of wear, scoring, and other damage. If it is necessary to regrind the crankshaft, bearings are available in 0.010, 0.020, and 0.030 in. undersizes. It is very important that the radius at either end of the crankpin is machined to 0.070–0.080 in. when regrinding. Do not attempt to refinish the bearing shells or file the bearing cap mating surfaces to reduce bearing clearances.

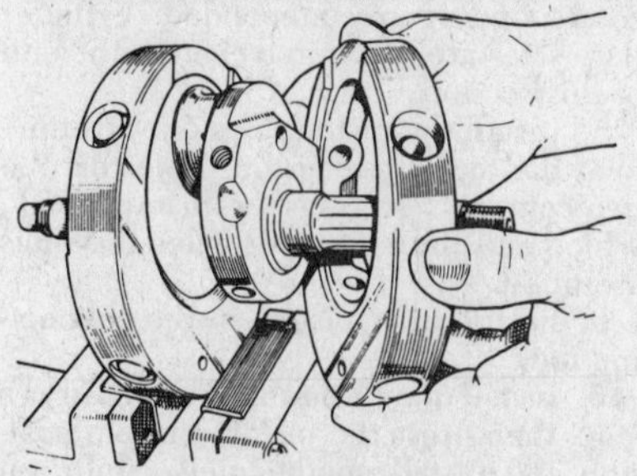

Removing a flywheel

If the crankshaft is to be reground, the flywheels must be removed. Loosen the four, short, flywheel retaining bolts (closest to the crankpin) first to avoid distortion. Remove the remaining four bolts and separate the flywheels. Clean the oil sludge trap, located in the right flywheel. Unscrew the plug and clean the passage with solvent and compressed air.

When reinstalling the flywheels, make sure that the flywheel incorporating the sludge trap is fitted on the *right* side. Apply a drop of thread-locking compound to the threads of each flywheel retaining bolt and tighten evenly to 50 ft lbs.

When installing the connecting rod on the crankshaft, make sure that the rod bearing shells are properly located in the connecting rod and cap. The oil hole should face the drive (left) side flywheel. Lubricate the bearing surfaces with fresh engine oil and install the bearing cap, taking note of the position of the punch marks to ensure that the cap is installed in its original position. It is recommended that new connecting rod bolts and nuts be used as a precaution against breakage. Clean the threads, apply a drop f thread-locking compound, and tighten the nuts to 22 ft lbs. Using a pressure oil can, force oil into the passage at the right end of the crankshaft until it is coming out around the connecting rod bearing. This indicates that the oil passages are not restricted and are full of oil.

ASSEMBLY

1. On the TR25W, the crankshaft end-float must be checked. Proceed with step 2, below, omitting the gasket cement. Check crankshaft end-float, disassemble the cases again and add or remove thrust washers as necessary between the flywheel and right-side main bearing to adjust end-float to within 0.002–0.005 in. Then start with step 2 again and follow the remainder of the assembly procedure.
2. Place the crankshaft assembly into the drive-side crankcase. Clean the crankcase mating surfaces and apply a thin coat of gasket cement to the mating surface of one of the cases. Fit the crankcase halves together and install the three bolts and four nuts. Tighten evenly to 16–18 ft lbs.
3. Rotate the crankshaft to make sure that it turns freely. If it does not, the cause of the trouble must be determined and rectified. Look for incorrect main bearing alignment or insufficient crankshaft endplay.
4. Install the small timing gear on the end of the crankshaft, taking care to locate the woodruff key properly. Tighten the retaining nut to 50–55 ft lbs.
5. Install the oil pump drive-gear on the pump shaft using the special locknut (or a suitable replacement) as originally installed.
6. Place the two tappets into their bores with the thinner end of the tappet foot facing forward. Install the camshaft and timing gear unit, with the timing marks aligned, and fit the thrust washer on the end of the camshaft (late models only).

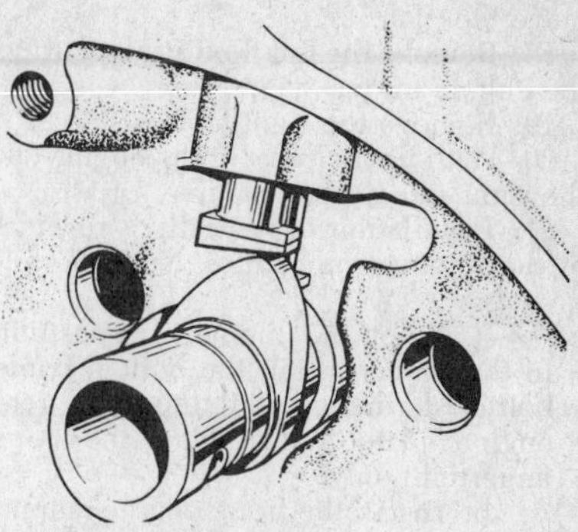

Note position of tappet contact pad

NOTE: *On early engines there are two marks on the camshaft timing gear—a dash and a V. On these engines the dash must be ignored and the marks aligned as illustrated. On later engines that do not have the V mark, simply align the dash marks.*

7. Install the right-side inner cover complete with transmission gearset and install the outer cover.
8. Install the primary drive and clutch assembly.

T100C AND T100R

Engine Removal and Installation

1. Remove the gas tank and disconnect the spark plug leads.
2. Disconnect the battery terminals and the connectors at the two ignition coils.
3. Remove the ignition coils, taking care not to damage the outer casings.
4. Disconnect the snap connectors between the contact breaker assembly and the condensers.
5. Remove the two cylinder-head torque stays.
6. Disconnect the tachometer drive cable.
7. Remove the carburetor(s) complete with air cleaners.
8. Disconnect the rocker oil feed line, taking care not to bend it.
9. Drain the oil tank and disconnect the delivery lines to the engine.
10. Drain the engine sump, primary chaincase, and transmission.
11. Loosen the clutch adjustment at the handlebar, then disconnect and remove the clutch cable.
12. Remove the exhaust header pipes and mufflers.
13. Remove the final, drive-chain master link and withdraw the chain.
14. Disconnect the alternator leads at their snap connectors underneath the engine.
15. Remove the bolts securing the front engines plates and withdraw the plates.
16. Remove the stud securing the bottom of the engine to the frame and the bolt securing the rear engine plates to the transmission case.
17. Have a helper support the engine, then remove the two nuts securing the right rear engine plate to the frame. Re-

move the plate.

18. Remove the left front stud securing the engine torque stay.

19. Remove the right footrest.

20. With the helper, lift the engine out the right side of the machine.

21. Installation is basically a reversal of the removal procedure. Note the following:

a. When the engine is in position in the frame, install the bottom frame bolt first, then install the right rear engine plate and tighten the bolts fingertight only.

b. Install the front, engine mounting plate, then tighten all mounting bolts snugly.

Top End

REMOVAL

The cylinder head and barrel can be removed without taking out the engine.

1. Disconnect the leads from the battery terminals and remove the fuel tank.
2. Disconnect the high tension cables and wiring harness from the ignition coils, then remove the coils. Take care not to damage the coil outer casings.
3. Remove the cylinder head torque stays.
4. Remove the rocker oil feed line.
5. Remove the two nuts from the studs at the bottom of the exhaust rocker box.
6. Remove the two phillips screws from the top of each rocker box, loosen all eight cylinder head bolts and remove the central head bolts.

Rocker box stud nuts and bolt (500)

7. Remove the exhaust rocker box, then remove the intake rocker box in the same manner. Take care not to lose the six plain washers (one under each bottom securing nut).
8. Remove the pushrods and mark them for reassembly position.
9. Remove the exhaust header pipes.
10. Disconnect the fuel lines and plug the ends. Disconnect the throttle linkage at the carburetor(s).
11. Remove the remaining four cylinder head nuts by turning each one a little at a time in an X pattern.
12. Remove the cylinder head complete with intake manifold(s) and carburetor(s). If the cylinder head is being serviced, rather than being removed to gain access to another part of the engine, remove the intake manifolds and carburetor(s).
13. Remove the pushrod tubes, remembering to replace the rubber seals during assembly.
14. Remove the cylinder head gasket.
15. Wedge a piece of rubber between the intake and exhaust tappets to prevent them from falling into the case when the barrel is removed.
16. Rotate the engine until the pistons are both at TDC, then remove the eight cylinder base nuts and washers.
17. Raise the barrel high enough to stuff some clean, no-lint rags into the case openings. It is also a good idea to fit some kind of rubber protectors over the cylinder studs to prevent damage to the connecting rods when the barrel is removed.
18. Lift off the barrel carefully, supporting the pistons when they are free.
19. Remove and mark the tappets for reassembly.

ROCKER BOXES

The rocker spindles can be removed by driving them out with a suitable drift. Once out, the spindles will release the rocker arms and washers. Clean the parts in kerosine or a cleaning solvent, then blow them dry with compressed air. Also blow out the spindle oil drillings with compressed air. Upon reassembly, the spindle oil seals should be replaced.

If the rocker ball pins require replacement, drive them out with a suitable drift and press the new ones in with the drilled flat toward the rocker spindles.

The rocker boxes can be reassembled using a 7/16 in. x 6 in. bar, ground to a taper at one end. This bar serves as an alignment tool for the spindles. Before beginning assembly, note that two of the washers removed from the spindles have a smaller diameter than the other washers. These are thrust washers and they must be assembled last—against the right inner face of the rocker box.

Grease two plain washers and position them on either side of the center bearing boss. Position the left rocker arm, bringing it into line with the alignment bar, and locate the plain washer, spring washer, and thrust washer as shown in the accompanying illustration. Repeat this for the right rocker arm, then oil the spindle and slide it as far into the rocker box as possible. Tap it in the remaining distance with a soft-faced hammer.

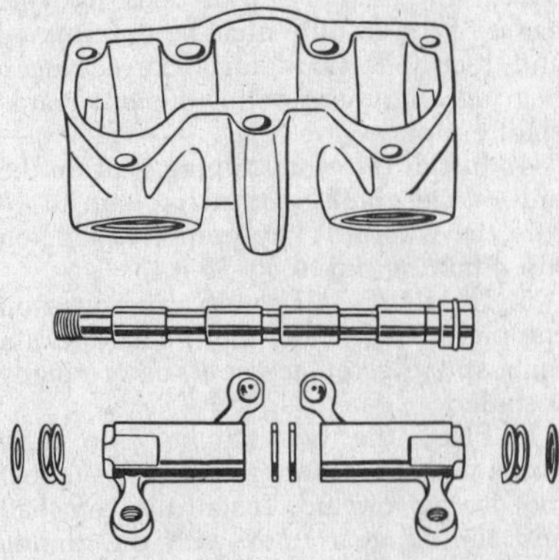

Rocker arms and spindle (500)

TAPPETS AND GUIDE BLOCKS

The only wear likely to be apparent on the tappets is at their tips which are plated with Stellite. Over a long period of time, an indentation will be worn in the center of the tip. If the width of this indentation exceeds 3/32 in., replace the tappet.

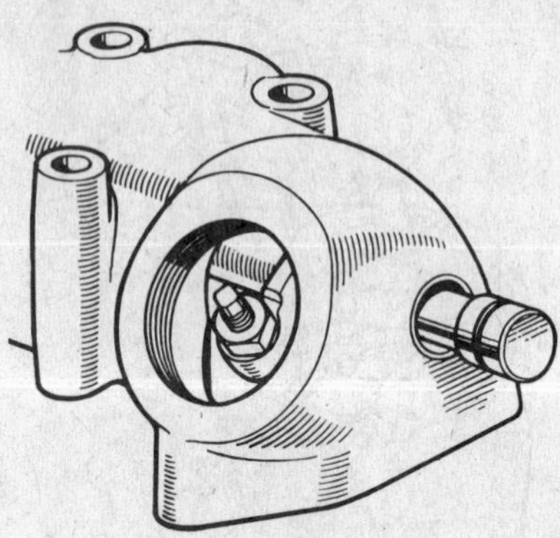

Installing the rocker box spindle

Tappet guide block assembly

It is not necessary to remove the press-fit tappet guide blocks to check their condition. Simply insert the tappet and rock it back and forth in the block. There should be little or no lateral play. See specifications for allowable clearances.

CYLINDERS

The difference between the largest and smallest of the six bore measurements must not exceed 0.13 mm (0.005 in.), or reboring is necessary.

PISTONS

1. Remove the inner and outer piston pin retaining circlips, then attach a piston pin removal tool and press out the pin.
2. Lay out and mark the pistons, piston pins, and retaining circlips for reassembly.
3. Remove the piston rings one at a time by lifting an end of the ring out of its groove and holding a thin piece of metal between it and the piston. Slide the piece of metal around the circumference of the piston while at the same time gently lifting the raised part of the ring upwards.
4. Replacement pistons are available in three oversizes. These sizes and the corresponding recommended cylinder bore sizes are given in a chart at the end of this section.
5. Install the piston rings one at a time over the top of the piston. Note that the two compression rings are marked TOP, which must face upwards when the rings are fitted.
6. Position the piston on the connecting rod.
7. Install one new retaining circlip as a stop, then press the piston pin into position and install another new circlip on the other side.

Install compression rings with the "Top" mark facing upwards

NOTE: *It is advisable to heat the piston to 100° C prior to assembly.*

ASSEMBLY

1. Position new guide block O-ring seals at the base of the cylinder block.
2. If it was removed, lightly grease the outside surface of the exhaust guide block, then carefully align the guide block and cylinder locating holes and drive the block into position with Triumph special tool no. Z23 or a suitable drift.
3. Repeat the above step for the intake guide block, then install the locking bolts.
4. After installing the guide blocks, make sure that the exhaust guide block oil drillways are free from obstruction.
5. Install the tappets in the guide blocks after thoroughly lubricating them with oil. Wedge them in position.
6. Install the cylinder base gasket, making certain that the gasket does not obscure the oil feed drillway in the crankcase.
7. Fit ring compressors over the piston rings, then carefully slide the cylinder down over the pistons. Remove the ring compressors as soon as the rings are positioned within the cylinder. Continue lowering the cylinder block and then remove the rags in the crankcase openings as late as possible.
8. Install the cylinder base attaching nuts.
9. Replace or anneal the cylinder head gasket.
10. Clean the mating cylinder head and cylinder surfaces, then grease the gasket and position it on the cylinder.
11. Coat the tappet guide blocks with grease and position the pushrod cover tubes with new O-rings seals.
12. Position the cylinder head and install the four outer and one central head bolt finger-tight.
13. Place a small amount of grease in the bottom cup of each pushrod, then locate the intake pushrods in their respective bores. This will have to be done by "feel."
14. When the pushrods are properly positioned, remove the spark plugs and turn the engine over until both intake pushrods are level and at the bottom of their travel.
15. Install the intake rocker box.
16. Repeat the above procedure for the exhaust rocker box, noting that the central cylinder head bolts should be tightened to torque specifications before tightening the underside securing nuts.
17. Turn the engine over several times to make sure the valves are operating properly, then reinstall the torque stays and secondary ignition coils.
18. Connect the rocker oil feed line, using either new copper washers or annealed, used ones.
19. The remainder of the assembly procedure is a reversal of the disassembly instructions. Adjust valve tappet clearances.

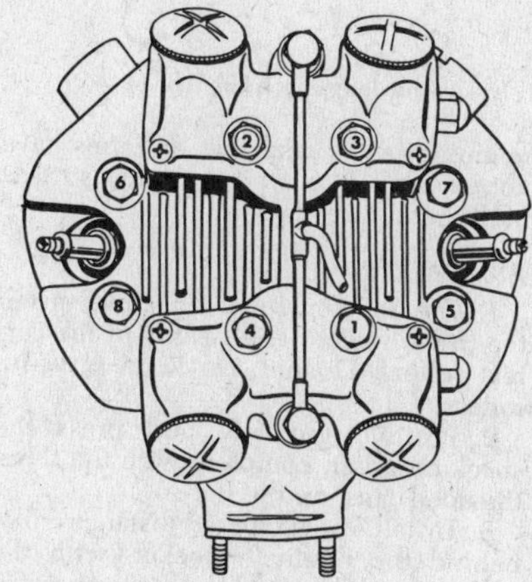

Cylinder head bolt tightening sequence

Clutch

DISASSEMBLY

1. Remove the left exhaust header pipe.
2. Loosen the rear brake adjustment until the pedal drops clear of the primary cover.
3. Remove the left footrest.
4. Drain the oil from the chaincase, then remove the chain tension adjuster.
5. Remove the ten, recessed cover-securing screws and withdraw the cover and paper gasket.
6. Remove the chain tensioner assembly.
7. The clutch pressure plate is held in place by three, slotted adjuster nuts. To remove these nuts, slide a knife or screwdriver blade under the nut and loosen it with Triumph tool no. D364 (supplied with tool kit) or a suitable substitute.

NOTE: *The clutch nuts are fitted with locking tabs which may be sheared off by removal. If so, replace them.*

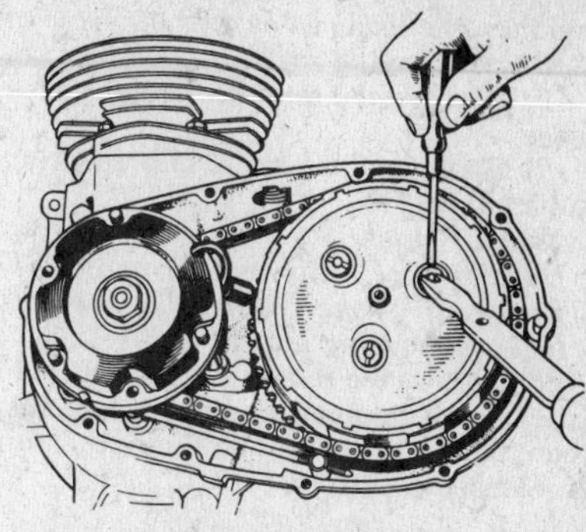

Removing the clutch nuts

8. Remove the clutch springs, cups, and pressure plate assembly.
9. The clutch plates can be removed with the use of two, narrow, hooked tools made of 1/32 in. wire.

INSPECTION

1. If the thickness of the discs is 0.030 in. (0.75 mm), or more, less than specified, they should be replaced.
2. Check the fit of the plate on the shock absorber unit. There should be little radial clearance.
3. Measure the clutch spring length and compare with specifications. If a spring has shortened by 0.10 in. (2.5 mm) or more, replace the set.

ASSEMBLY

1. Install the clutch plates and discs; the innermost position must be occupied by a bonded plate.
2. Install the cups, pressure plate, springs, and slotted adjuster nuts.
3. True the clutch pressure plate by first tightening the pressure-plate, slotted adjuster nuts until they are even with the clutch pins, and then by kicking the engine over and observing the rotation of the plate, and then making any necessary adjustment until the plate turns evenly. If the plate wobbles even slightly, it must be corrected.

Primary Drive and Clutch Hub

DISASSEMBLY

1. Remove the primary cover as previously described.
2. Remove the clutch assembly as previously described.
3. Disconnect the alternator stator leads at their snap connectors under the engine.
4. Remove the three stator securing nuts and withdraw the stator from over its mounting studs. Unscrew the sleeve nut

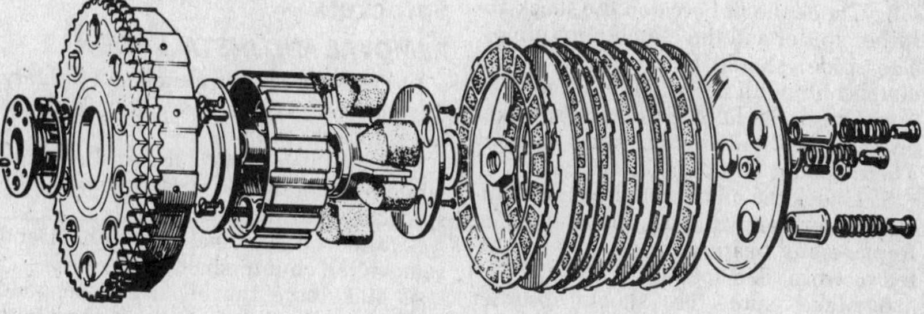

Clutch assembly

and then the lead can easily be removed.

5. Remove the rotor.

6. Remove the rotor key and distance piece.

7. Remove the clutch hub securing nut and cup.

NOTE: *Machines prior to serial no. H49833 have a tab washer and a different cup washer, rather than the self-locking securing nut.*

8. Screw the body of extractor no. Z13 into the clutch hub until it bottoms, then tighten the center bolt until the hub is released.

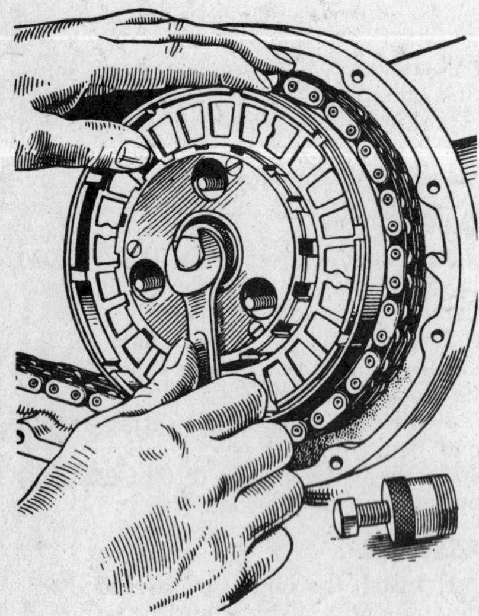

Removing the clutch housing

9. Assemble extractor no. Z151 and D662/3 on the engine sprocket and tighten its center bolt until the engine sprocket is released.

10. Withdraw the engine sprocket, clutch hub, and primary chain together.

11. Remove the transmission mainshaft key and check the oil seal for leakage.

INSPECTION

1. Inspect the clutch shock absorber for worn rubbers or punctures. They can be removed by prying them out, small rubbers first. Replace as necessary. When reassembling, apply thread-locking compound to the cover plate securing screws.

2. First thoroughly clean the primary chain then check it for wear by scribing two marks on a flat surface 12 in. apart, and centering two pivot pins at the scribe marks. Fully compressed, the chain link pivot should line up with the marks; fully stretched, it should not extend more than ¼ in. beyond the marks.

3. Check the fit between the shock absorber spider and the clutch hub splines. The spider should be a push fit on the clutch hub, with no radial movement.

4. Check the fit of the engine sprocket on the crankshaft in the same manner. There should be no radial movement.

5. Check the clutch hub bearing diameter, rollers, and clutch sprocket bearing. Replace any bearing rollers that are pitted or worn. See specifications.

6. Make sure the shock absorber spider is a good fit in the inner and outer

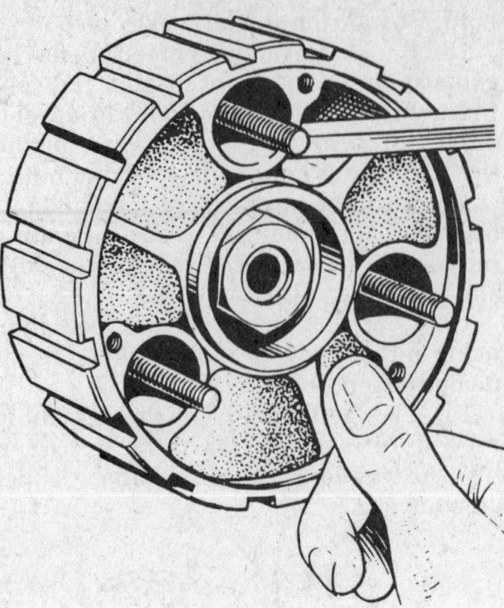

Installing clutch hub rubbers

retaining plates, and that the arms have not excessively scored the inner surface of the retaining plates.

ASSEMBLY

1. Grease the clutch hub and install the thrust washer and twenty of the correct rollers. Do not use ¼ in. x ¼ in. rollers!.

2. Position the hub and press the shock absorber, complete with the three threaded pins, on the hub.

3. Install a new tapered distance collar behind the engine sprocket, with the taper toward the crankshaft main bearing and oil seal.

4. Install the transmission mainshaft key and tap the clutch hub onto its taper.

5. Lubricate the primary chain and lay it over the clutch sprocket.

6. Wrap the chain around the engine sprocket, then position the sprocket on the crankshaft.

7. Place clutch locking tool Z13 in the clutch plate housing, then install the cup washer and self-locking nut. Torque the nut to specifications.

NOTE: *On machines before serial no. H49833, install the tab washer with the long tab in the hole in the shock absorber spider, install the securing nut and bend a tab to lock the nut.*

8. Install the alternator rotor, making sure that the key or locating peg is correctly positioned.

9. Install the alternator stator. Put a 0.008 in. (0.2 mm) feeler gauge between each stator pole and the rotor. Turn over the engine to make sure that the rotor and stator do not touch.

Transmission Countershaft Sprocket

REMOVAL AND INSTALLATION

1. Disassemble the clutch and primary drive as previously described. Remove the sprocket cover.

2. Bend back the tab washer and, while holding the rear brake, remove the sprocket securing nut.

3. Slide off the final drive chain and remove the countershaft sprocket.

4. Make sure the oil seal is in good condition, then lubricate the ground boss of the new sprocket and position it on the transmission mainshaft.

5. Replace the tab washer, screw on the securing nut finger-tight, then, with the chain in place, tighten the nut to torque specifications.

6. Oil the bushing that protrudes from the mainshaft high gear and install the sprocket cover with a new paper gasket.

7. The remainder of installation is a reversal of the removal procedure.

Clutch and Shifter Operating Mechanisms

DISASSEMBLY

1. Remove the right exhaust header pipe and footrest.

2. Drain the gearbox oil.

3. Disconnect the clutch cable from the actuating lever.

4. Remove the two nuts and four recessed screws that secure the gearbox outer cover. Remove the kick-starter.

5. Hold the gearshift lever in one hand, then tap the cover with a soft-faced mallet until it is free to be removed.

6. Unscrew the two nuts inside the gearbox outer cover and remove the shifter return springs complete with the thrust buttons and distance pieces.

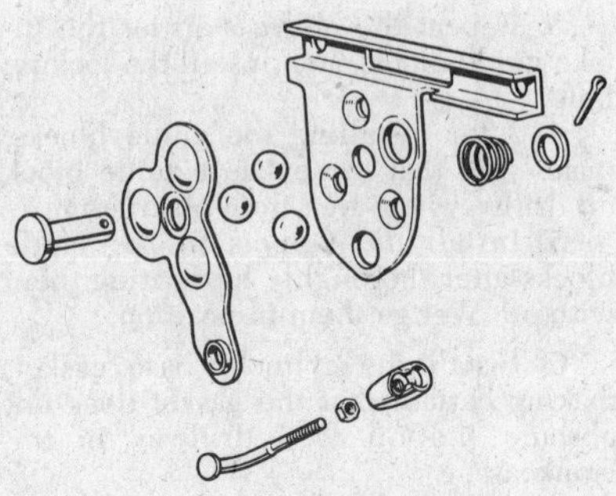

Clutch operating mechanism

7. Unscrew the countersunk screw that secures the clutch operating mechanism and withdraw the assembly.

8. Remove the shifter lever pinch bolt, remove the lever, and then withdraw the shaft from the cover.

9. Remove the cotter pin from the clutch operating shaft. This will release the clutch operating balls.

10. Remove the two cotter pins and disconnect the plungers and springs from the shifter quadrant.

11. If the shifter spindle bushing requires replacement, heat the outer cover to 100° C and drive it out with a suitable, shouldered drift. Drive in the new bushing before the cover has a chance to cool.

Clutch mechanism installed

NOTE: *A drift for removing and installing the shifter spindle bushing can be made from a piece of ¾ in. diameter bar. Machine the bar to a diameter of ⅝ in. and cut a length of ¾ in.*

ASSEMBLY

1. Install the shifter quadrant springs, plungers, and securing cotter pins, then install a new O-ring on the spindle.
2. Lubricate the spindle and O-ring with oil, then insert the spindle in the cover.
3. Assemble the clutch-operating mechanism balls in their recesses and install the shaft and clutch lever in the order shown in the accompanying illustration. Don't forget to install the spring and washer before replacing the cotter pin.

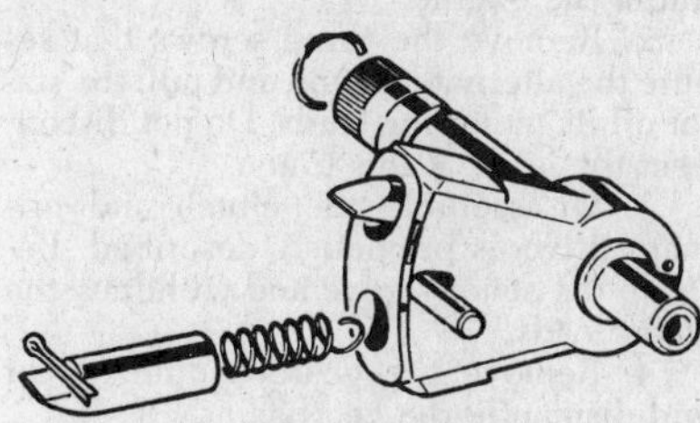

Shifter mechanism

4. Install the distance collar on the end of the shifter quadrant shaft, then install the clutch operating mechanism in the cover and secure it in place with the countersunk screw.
5. Install the distance pieces over the studs, then connect the shifter return springs and thrust buttons. Install the return spring cover plate and tighten the securing nuts.
6. Install the gearbox outer cover with sealant, tighten the securing screws, and install the kick-start lever.
7. Refill the transmission with oil.

Gearbox and Kick-Starter Mechanism

DISASSEMBLY

1. Disassemble the primary drive and clutch as previously described. Remove the transmission mainshaft nut and key.
2. Remove the gearbox outer cover, noting that the gearbox should first be positioned in fourth gear.
3. Remove the two inner gearbox cover retaining screws, then remove the entire gearbox assembly by tapping the clutch end of the mainshaft with a mallet.
4. Remove the camplate cotter pin, then withdraw the camplate spindle.
5. Pry off the kick-starter return spring and remove the distance piece. Withdraw the kick-starter spindle.
6. Remove the camplate index plunger and place it aside.
7. Remove the selector fork spindle and disengage the selector forks from the camplate.
8. Remove the layshaft and kick-starter pawl, plunger, and spring.
9. Drive the mainshaft assembly out of the bearing with a soft-faced mallet.
10. Remove the countershaft sprocket as previously described, then drive the mainshaft high gear into the gearbox with a soft metal drift and hammer.
11. To remove the mainshaft right bearing, heat the cover to 100° C and drive it out with a suitable, shouldered drift. Install the new bearing while the cover is still hot. Replace the securing circlip.
12. To remove the high gear bearing on the left side of the machine, pry out the oil seal and remove the retaining circlip. Heat the case around the bearing to 100° C, then drive it out with a suitable, shouldered drift. Install the new bearing while the case is still hot. Replace the oil seal with the lip and spring toward the bearing, then replace the retaining circlip.
13. If it is necessary to replace the mainshaft high gear bushing, press it out with a drift measuring 5.0 x ⅞ in., having ¾ in. of one end machined to 13/16 in. diameter. Install the new bushing with the same drift, making certain the bushing oil groove is at the gear teeth end. The bushing should then be reamed to the size given in specifications.
14. The layshaft right needle roller bearing can be removed by heating the kick-starter spindle to 100° C and tapping it off with a block of wood.
15. The layshaft left needle roller bearing is of the closed-end type and can be removed through the countershaft sprocket cover plate aperture. Heat the case to 100° C and drive the bearing into the gearbox with a suitable drift. Install the new bearing while the case is still hot. A special drift, for which dimensions are given in the accompanying illustration, must be used to install the new bearing.

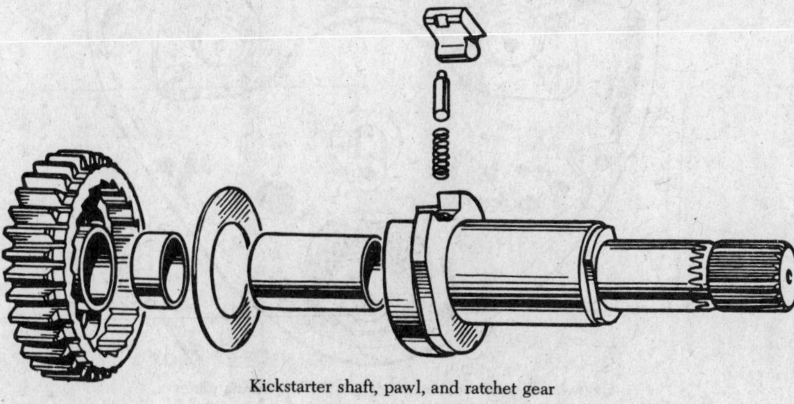

Kickstarter shaft, pawl, and ratchet gear

ASSEMBLY

1. If all replacement bearings have been installed with new seals and circlips, install the layshaft thrust washer over the needle roller cage, and hold it in position with a dab of grease.
2. Lubricate the mainshaft and layshaft captive gears, then assemble the mainshaft in the inner gearbox cover.
3. Install the plunger, spring, and pawl on the kick-starter spindle, then insert the assembly in the inner gearbox cover and slide the layshaft assembly into the kick-starter bearing. Remember to install the mainshaft distance piece between the mainshaft assembly and the main bearing in the inner cover.
4. Position the selector forks on the shafts as shown in the accompanying illustration and insert the selector fork spindle to hold them in position.

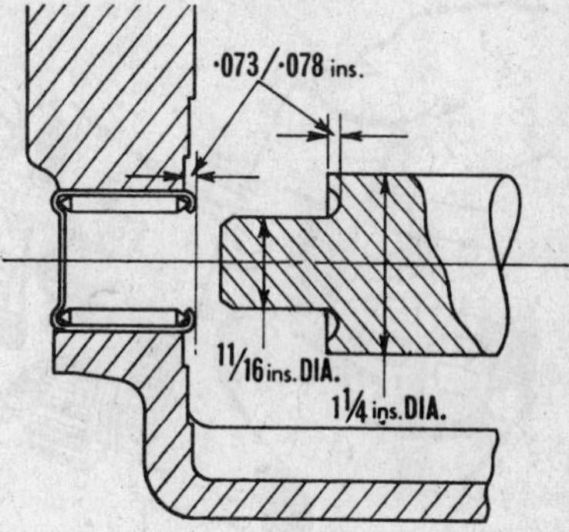

5. Assemble the camplate in the outer cover and locate the selector fork rollers in their camplate tracks.
6. Install the camplate spindle and secure it with a new cotter pin. Install the camplate index plunger and spring.
7. Operate the selector forks manually to make sure that each selector fork is on its appropriate shaft. When the camplate is moved to its full extent, both selector rollers should move to the full extent of the camplate grooves in both directions. If not, the selector forks will have to be disengaged and reversed.
8. Install the distance piece over the kick-starter shaft, then secure the end of the return spring with its retaining screw.

NOTE: *Use a screwdriver to tension the return spring before connecting it and installing the return spring plate.*

9. The remainder of the assembly procedure is a reversal of the disassembly instructions.

Bottom End

CAMSHAFT SERVICE (ENGINE INSTALLED)

It is not necessary to separate the crankcase halves in order to replace the camshafts.

Removal and Installation

1. Remove the rocker boxes.
2. Remove the timing cover.
3. Remove the oil pump (see "Lubrication Systems"), and temporarily block the crankcase holes to prevent oil spillage. Make sure you remember to open these holes before reinstalling the oil pump.

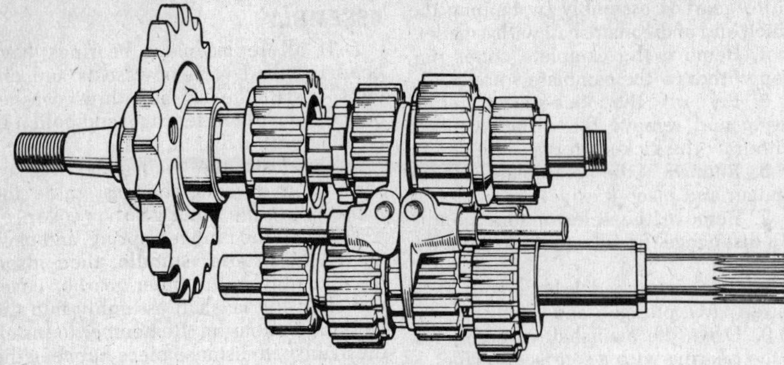

Gear cluster and shift forks

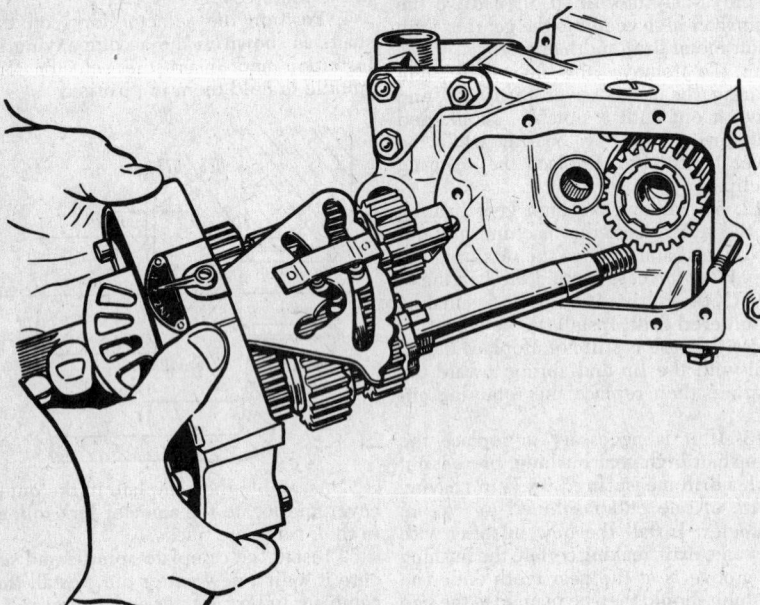

Installing the gearbox components

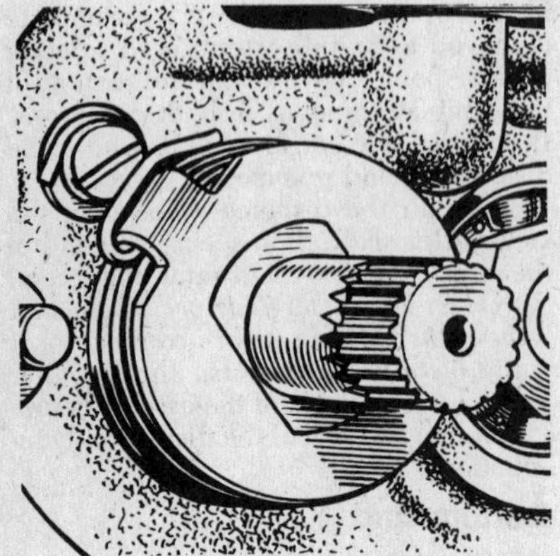

Kickstarter return spring installed

4. Extract the intake and exhaust camwheels. The camshaft retaining plates can now be seen.

5. Carefully pull the camshafts out the right side of the machine. Make sure the breather disc and spring, located behind the intake cam, do not fall into the crankcase. Also, lean the machine to the left when removing the cams so that the cam followers do not fall into the crankcase.

6. Assemble the rotary breather valve and spring to the new intake camshaft, then install both cams, making certain that the slot in the end of the intake cam fully engages the dog on the breather valve.

7. Reinstall the camshaft retainer plates and secure them in place with new screws.

8. The remainder of the assembly procedure is a reversal of the removal instructions.

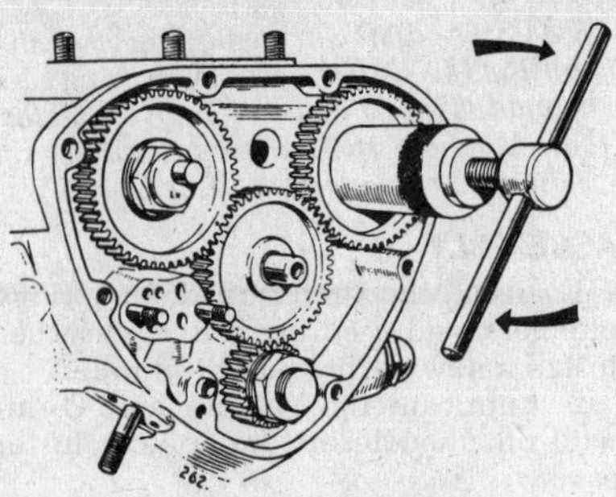

Removing a camshaft gear

CRANKCASE

Disassembly

1. Remove the primary chaincase cover and disconnect the alternator leads under the engine.

2. Remove the three screws that secure the alternator stator, and pull the stator off its mounting studs. Do not disconnect the leads at this time.

3. Disassemble the clutch and primary drive as previously described. Remove the stator sleeve and withdraw the stator leads.

4. Remove the gearbox outer cover and dismantle the gearbox.

5. Remove the rocker boxes, cylinder head, cylinder barrel, and pistons.

6. Disconnect the clutch cable and remove the carburetor(s).

7. Remove the contact breaker cover and the oil pump, then remove the crankshaft pinion. The camshaft pinions can also be removed at this time.

NOTE: *The crankshaft pinion nut has a right-hand thread, but the camshaft nuts are left-hand threads.*

8. Remove what's left of the engine from the frame.

9. Clamp the crankcase firmly in a vise at the bottom mounting lug and remove the bolt and two screws at the cylinder base.

10. Remove the stud at the front of the engine and the two nuts next to the gearbox housing.

11. Attach Triumph extractor no. Z151 and separate the cases.

12. After the cases are apart, remove the crankshaft assembly. Remove the

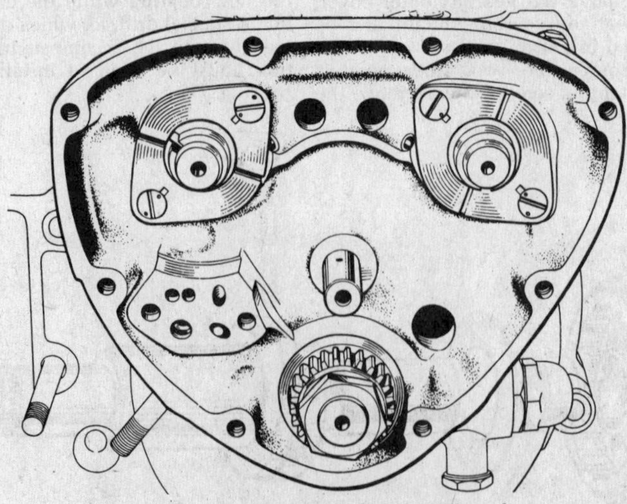

Camwheels removed, revealing camshaft retaining plates

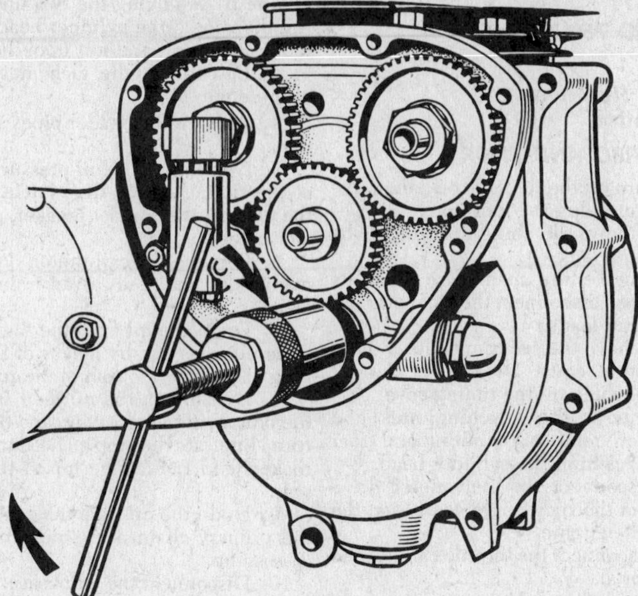

Removing the crankshaft pinion

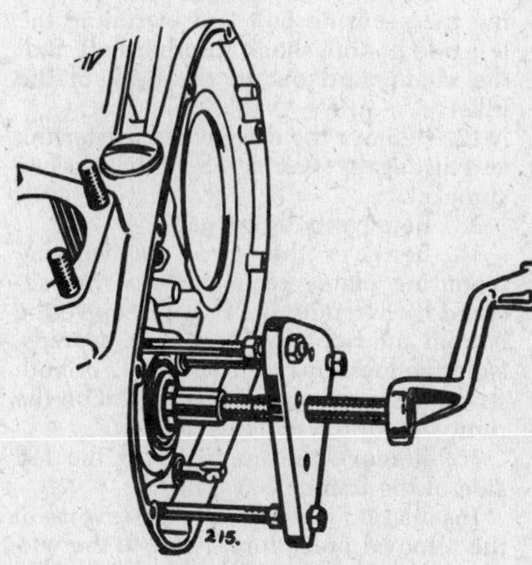

Separating the case halves with tool no. Z151

breather valve from within the intake camshaft bushing in the left case.

Crankshaft and Connecting Rods

DISASSEMBLY

1. Clamp the crankshaft assembly in a soft-jawed vise and place a rag over any sharp edges to protect the connecting rods.

2. Unscrew the cap retainer nuts a little at a time to avoid distortion, then remove the caps and connecting rods.

NOTE: *The connecting rods, caps and nut are center-punched to facilitate reassembly.*

3. Using a large impact driver, unscrew the oil tube retainer plug from the right end of the big-end journal. If necessary, drill a hole ⅛ in. deep and ⅛ in. in diameter to eliminate the locking effect of the plug center punch.

4. Remove the flywheel bolt next to the big-end journal, then pull out the oil tube with a hooked piece of stiff wire through the flywheel bolt location hole.

5. Thoroughly clean all parts in solvent, then blow them dry with compressed air. Make sure the oil drillways are blown clear.

6. To remove the flywheel, unscrew the two remaining bolts and press the crankshaft out of the right side plain bearing with a five ton press.

NOTE: *Before removing the flywheel, make certain it is marked for reassembly.*

INSPECTION

Inspect the big-end journals for any signs of scoring, etc., and measure the journal diameter. Compare with specifications. Light score marks can be removed with fine grade emery cloth, but make sure all metal filings are removed before reassembly. If the scoring is light, new connecting rod shell bearings should be installed; if the scoring is extensive, the journals should be reground to an appropriate undersize.

NOTE: *The replaceable big-end bearing shells are pre-sized to give the correct dimensions. Under no circumstances should they be scraped, or the connecting rod and cap filed to alter the bearing dimensions.*

ASSEMBLY

1. Position the oil tube in the crankshaft, aligning the flywheel bolt holes with those in the crankshaft. Temporarily install one of the flywheel bolts to secure it in position.

2. Apply thread-locking sealant to the oil tube plug and install it in the crankshaft. Center-punch the crankshaft opposite the slot to lock the plug in position.

3. Heat the flywheel to 100° C, then position it over the crankshaft with the center punch mark to the right. Turn the flywheel through 180° to get it over the crankshaft web, then turn it to the correct position relative to the crankshaft and align the bolt holes.

4. Coat the flywheel bolt threads with a thread-locking sealant, then install and torque them to specifications.

5. If a new or reground crankshaft, or a new flywheel was installed, the assembly should be rebalanced.

6. Check to make sure all the oil drillways are free from obstruction, then install the connecting rods and caps. Torque the retaining nuts to 27 ft lbs.

7. Last, force oil through the crankshaft, right main-bearing journal drillway until it is expelled at both big-end bearings. This will provide assurance that the drillway is free from obstruction.

Camshaft Bushings

The intake and exhaust camshafts run in bronze bushings in the left case and are butted directly into the right case. To remove the bushings in the left case, a tap will be necessary. The ideal size is ⅞ in. diameter x 9 whitworth.

When a good thread has been cut in the bushing, heat the case to 100° C and screw in the appropriate bolt. Grip the bolt in a vise and tap the case with a soft-faced mallet until the bushing is free. The replacement bushings are pre-sized but will require a light reaming to meet specifications. After reaming the new bushings, make sure the crankcase is thoroughly cleaned to remove any metal filings.

Main Bearings

To remove the left main bearing heat the case to 100° C and drive it out with tool no. Z14. The right main bearing prior to H65573 is a bronze bushing, and is removed by first removing the lock plate, heating the case to 100° C, then driving it out with a suitable, shouldered drift. It is advisable to replace the left bearing oil seal while the engine is apart, even if it appears to be in good condition. This is installed with the open face outwards.

To install the left bearing, first make sure that its housing is clean, then heat the case to 100° C and drive the bearing into position with a tubular drift the same size as the bearing outer race. A suitable size would be 2¾ in. diameter x 6 in. long.

To install the right bronze bushing, heat the case to 100° C and then press the bushing into position. Let the case cool, then line-ream the bushing to specifications. Tool no. Z134 is available for this purpose. To use it, the case halves must be assembled and the reamer inserted through the right main bearing, with the

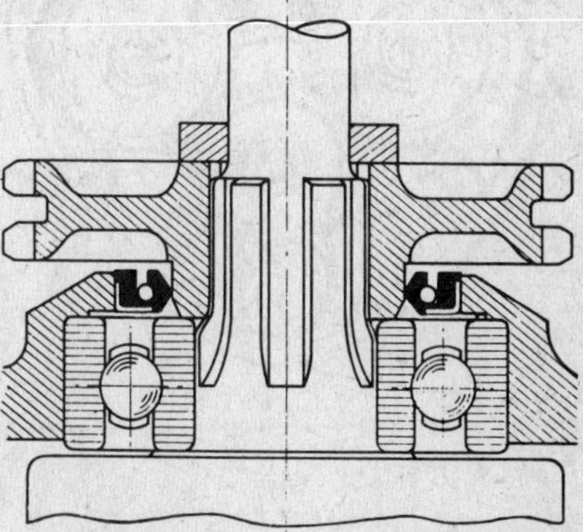

Left main bearing oil seal installation

pilot end located in the left main bearing. Reamer Z134 is also available in 0.010, 0.020, and 0.030 undersizes.

After H65573 the right bearing is the ball-type and is removed and installed in the same manner as the left bearing.

After both bearings have been installed, press the oil seal into the left case, open face outwards.

Assembly

1. Thoroughly clean the mating crankcase halves, giving special attention to the locating dowels.
2. Position the left case on two wooden blocks, lubricate the main bearing and camshaft bushings and then install the breather valve and spring in the intake cam bushing. Assemble both camshafts, making sure the intake cam slot engages the breather valve dog.
3. Carefully install the crankshaft assembly, making sure the fit in the bearing is good.
4. Apply fresh joining compound to the mating surfaces, then position the connecting rods in the center and lower the right case over the crankshaft. When the halves are mated, check to make sure the crankshaft and camshafts are not binding. The crankshaft should rotate freely, while the camshafts should offer only slight resistance.
5. The remainder of the assembly procedure is a reversal of the disassembly instructions. Make sure all timing pinions are correctly located.

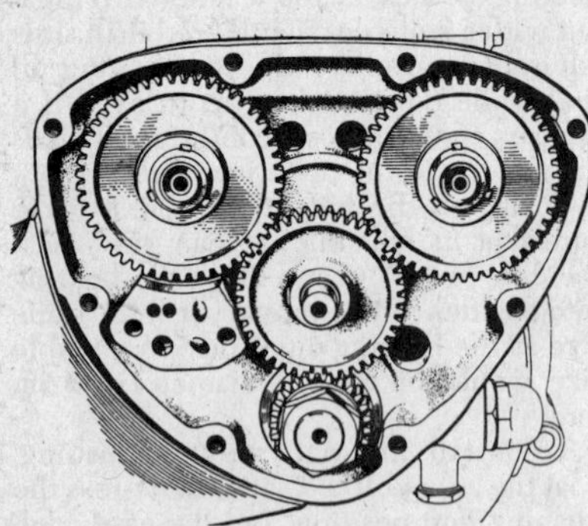

Timing marks (T100C)

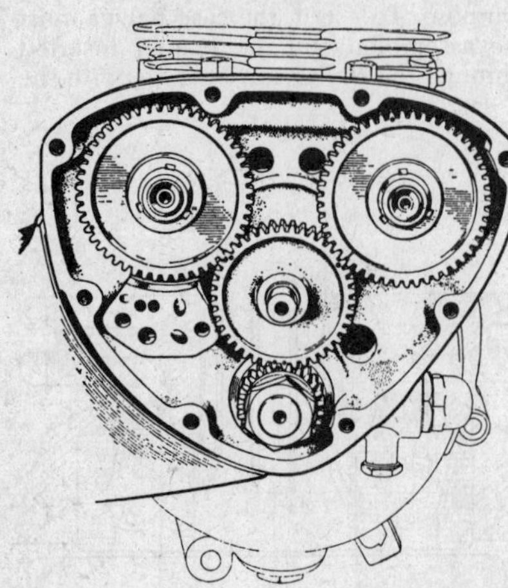

Timing marks (T100R)

650 AND 750 TWINS

Engine Removal and Installation

TR6R, TR6C, AND T120R

1. Turn off the fuel petcock, then disconnect and plug the fuel lines.
2. Remove the three securing bolts and the fuel tank.
3. Remove the main fuse from its holder, then disconnect the right and left ignition coil leads.
4. Remove the securing bolts and the two ignition coils. Disconnect the oil pressure switch on the timing cover.
5. Remove the attaching nuts and bolts, then remove the front and rear torque stays from the cylinder head.
6. Disconnect the tachometer drive cable from the right-angle gearbox at the front of the engine.
7. Disconnect the throttle cable at the carburetor(s).
8. On single carburetor engines, remove the air cleaner.
9. Remove the carburetor(s).
10. Disconnect the rocker oil feed line, taking care not to bend it excessively.
11. Drain the engine sump, oil tank, and transmission.
12. Disconnect all lines from the oil tank.
13. Back off the clutch adjustment at the handlebar until there is plenty of slack, then disconnect the cable at the operating arm on the right side of the engine.
14. Remove the exhaust headers and mufflers.
15. Disconnect the final drive-chain master link and remove the chain.
16. Disconnect the two generator leads at the bottom of the engine.
17. Remove the front chainguard securing bolt and loosen the rear mounting bolt. Pull the chainguard back several inches to get it out of the way.
18. Remove the four bolts and one nut securing the left and right rear engine-mounting plates. Remove the plates.
19. Remove the nuts and washers from one side of the front upper and lower mounting plates.
20. Remove both right-side rocker boxes.
21. Remove the left lower bolts securing the rear frame to the front frame.
22. Pull out the front upper and lower mounting studs, then lift the engine out the left side of the frame. A helper at this point will greatly reduce the possibility of dropping the engine.

Installation is basically a reversal of the removal procedure. To make sure the wiring harness is properly connected, refer to the appropriate wiring diagram.

TR7V, T140V

1. Shut off the fuel taps, and disconnect the fuel lines. Remove the rubber cap from the top, center, of the gas tank, and remove the sleeve nut below. Take the tank off the frame.
2. Detach the torque stay from the engine by removing the two nuts securing the stay to the cylinder head and removing the bolt and nut from the frame.
3. Disconnect the tachometer cable at the engine.
4. Remove the header pipes and mufflers.
5. Disconnect the oil pressure switch at the timing cover, the clutch cable at the engine, the contact breaker, coil, and alternator leads.
6. Remove the carburetor(s) from the manifold(s) and pull away from the air cleaner.
7. Drain the oil from the frame backbone oil reservoir by means of the drain plug at the very bottom of the reservoir.
8. Disconnect the oil feed line from the bottom of the reservoir, and the oil return line at the top. Disconnect the rocker feed line at the top of the reservoir.
9. Drain the oil from the gearbox and the primary chaincase. Drain the crankcase sump.
10. Disconnect the crankcase breather hoses at the left, rear of the crankcase by loosening the hose clamp screws.
11. Remove the chainguard by removing the securing bolt and loosening the left side bottom shock absorber bolt. Pull the chainguard out of the back of the bike.
12. Remove the drive chain masterlink and disengage the chain from the gearbox sprocket.
13. Remove both footpegs.
14. Remove the two rear engine mounting plates each of which are secured by five nuts and bolts. Remove the bottom and front engine mounting studs. Note the location of the spacers. For both studs, the wide spacer is installed on the right side of the motorcycle.
15. Remove the engine from the left side of the frame.

Installation is essentially the reverse of the removal procedure. Refer to the wiring diagrams in the "Electrical Systems" section to insure that all connections are correct. Refer to "Tune-Up and Maintenance" for the proper grades and quantities of oil.

TOP END

Removal

650 TWINS

1. Remove the fuel tank.
2. Disconnect the battery terminal leads.
3. Disconnect and remove the secondary ignition coils, taking care not to damage the alloy cases.
4. Remove the front and rear torque stays.
5. Disconnect the rocker oil feed line, taking care not to bend it excessively.
6. Remove the rocker inspection caps.
7. Remove the three nuts from the securing studs on the underside of the exhaust rocker box.
8. Remove the exhaust rocker box

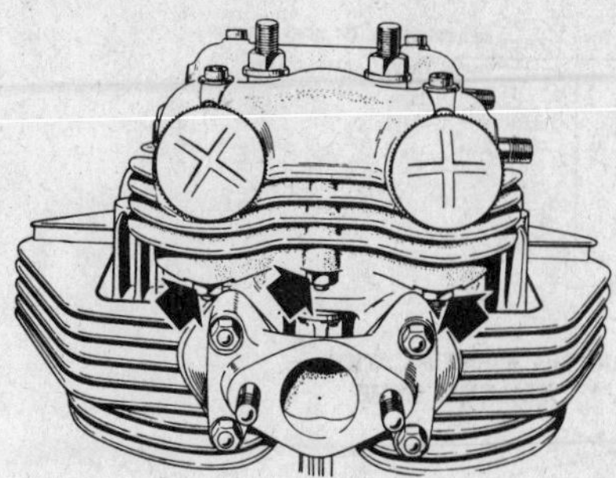

Exhaust rocker box securing nuts (650, 750 Twin)

outer securing bolts and the central cylinder-head bolts.

9. Remove the intake rocker box in the same manner, noting that the outer securing bolts may have to be loosened only a little at a time because of clearance difficulties.

10. Make sure to collect the six plain washers that fit underneath the securing nuts. They often stick to the cylinder-head flanges.

11. Withdraw and lay out the pushrods so that they can be installed in their original position.

12. Remove the carburetor(s) and the intake manifold.

13. Remove the exhaust header pipes.

14. Loosen the cylinder head nuts, a little at a time, in a cross pattern. Lift off the cylinder head.

15. Remove the pushrod cover tubes and rubber O-ring seals.

16. Check the tappet guide blocks for sharp edges that could cut into the pushrod O-ring seals. Smooth out any of these sharp edges or rough areas with a fine grade emery cloth.

17. Remove the copper cylinder-head gasket.

18. Wedge a piece of rubber between the intake and exhaust tappets to prevent them from falling into the crankcase when the cylinder is removed.

19. Rotate the engine until both pistons are at top dead center, then remove the cylinder block attaching nuts at the base of the block.

20. Carefully lift up the cylinder block and, as soon as there is enough room, stuff some clean lint-free rags into the crankcase openings. At this time it is also advisable to fit rubber protectors (or a suitable substitute) over the cylinder base studs.

21. Remove the cylinder base gasket and make sure the two locating dowels are in position on the crankcase.

22. Remove the tappets from the cylinder block and mark them for reassembly.

23. Invert the cylinder head on a bench, remove the locking bolts, then drive out the tappet guide blocks with a suitable drift. Make sure the intake and exhaust guide blocks are marked for reassembly, as the exhaust block has drilled oilways and the intake block does not.

TR7V, T140V

1. Remove the fuel tank after shutting off the petcocks and disconnecting the fuel lines. Remove the carburetor(s) from the head.

2. Disconnect the wires from the battery terminals. Remove the exhaust pipes and mufflers.

3. Disconnect the rocker feed line by removing the domed nut on each rocker spindle.

4. Remove the torque stay by removing the nut at each rocker box. Remove the torque stay bolt and nut on the frame.

5. Remove the rocker box inspection covers. Also remove the three nuts from the studs beneath each rocker box. Account for the washer on each of the studs.

6. Remove the securing bolts on the opposite side of each rocker box, and finally the two larger securing nuts on top. Remove the rocker boxes from the head.

7. Remove the pushrods and place them in a safe place.

8. There are ten cylinder head nuts and bolts. Loosen each one a single turn at a time until they can be turned easily, then remove them. Lift off the cylinder head.

9. New O-rings must be used on the ends of the pushrod cover tubes. New rocker box gaskets should also be used. Be sure that the rocker box mating surfaces are in good condition before refitting.

Rocker Boxes

DISASSEMBLY

1. Carefully drive out the rocker spindle, using a soft metal drift.

2. Remove the rocker arms and washers.

3. Remove the rocker oil seals.

4. If the rocker ball pins require replacement, drive them out with a suitable drift, then press in the new ones with the drilled flat toward the rocker spindle.

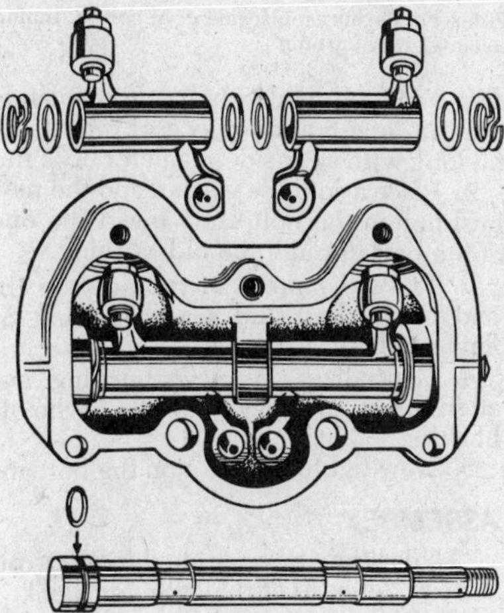

Rocker box assembly (650, 750 Twin)

ASSEMBLY

1. Assemble the rocker boxes using Triumph seal compressor D2221 and a 7/16 x 6 in. bolt with one end ground to a taper.

2. Apply grease to two of the plain washers and position them on either side of the center spindle bearing boss.

3. Position the left rocker arm and insert the alignment bolt, then install the outer plain and spring washers.

4. Position the right rocker arm in the

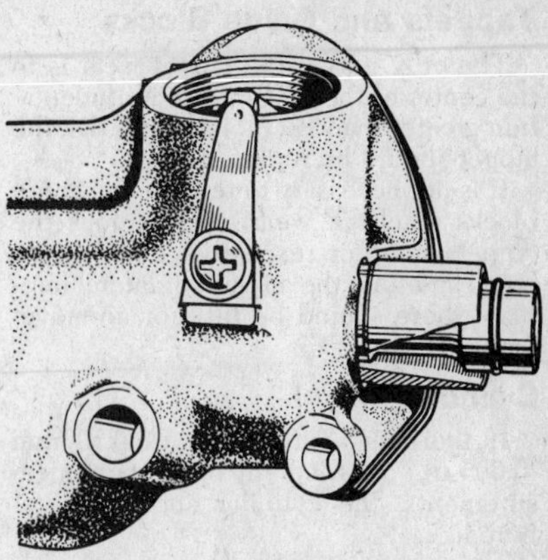

Installing the rocker arm spindle

same manner.

5. Install a new oil seal on the spindle, then coat the whole spindle with oil.

6. Slide the spindle into seal compressor no. D2221 (or a suitable replacement) and through the rocker box, pushing the alignment bolt out the other end. The final positioning of the spindle may require a few taps with a hammer and soft metal drift.

Valves and Valve Springs

REMOVAL

1. Compress the valve springs with the spring compressor and remove the split retainers with a narrow, straight-slot screwdriver.

2. Remove each valve and spring, making certain they are marked and matched for reassembly.

NOTE: *The intake and exhaust valves are marked "IN" and "EX," respectively.*

INSTALLATION

1. Assemble the inner and outer springs with the top and bottom cups over the valve guide.

2. Lubricate the valve stem with a little graphite oil, then slide the valve into position.

3. Compress the spring and install the two retainer halves in the exposed groove of the valve stem.

Valve Guides

Triumph engines are equipped with replaceable bronze valve guides. To remove an old guide, use Triumph special tool 61-6013 or fabricate one to the dimensions given. This is a mild steel bar about 5 in. long and 0.5 in. diameter with a 1 in. section at one end machined to 5/16 in. When installing the new guide, first lightly grease the guide then press or drive it into place, using the special tool. When new valve guides have been installed, it will be necessary to recut the valve seats and grind in the valves.

NOTE: *The intake and exhaust valve guides are almost identical in appearance, except in length. The shorter guides are for the intake valves and the longer guides are for the exhaust valves.*

Tappets and Guide Blocks

The only noticeable tappet wear is in the center of the Stellite tip. An indentation greater than $^3/_{32}$ in. indicates that the tappet should be replaced.

It is not necessary to remove the guide blocks to check wear. Simply rock the tappets in their respective guide block bores and note the amount of lateral freeplay; there should be little or no movement.

Cylinder Barrel

If there is a difference of 0.13 mm (0.005 in.) between any of the bore measurements, the cylinder should be rebored.

Pistons

1. Make sure the crankcase opening edges are covered with lint-free rags to protect the aluminum alloy connecting rod from being damaged.
2. Remove the inner and outer piston pin retaining circlips, then attach a piston pin removal tool and press out the pin.
3. Lay out and mark the pistons, pins, and retaining circlips for reassembly.
4. Remove the piston rings one at a time by lifting an end of the ring out of its groove and holding a thin piece of metal between it and the piston. Slide the piece of metal around the circumference of the piston while at the same time gently lifting the raised part of the ring upwards.
5. Replacement pistons (650) are available in three or four oversizes. These sizes and the corresponding recommended cylinder bore sizes are given in a chart at the end of this section.

TR7V and T140V pistons are available in four oversizes in increments of 0.010 in. Also note that the cylinders and pistons for these models are paired up according to a three-step grading system when the engine is assembled at the factory. There are three sizes "L" (Low), "M" (Medium), and "H" (High).

Refer to the accompanying illustrations for cylinder bore and piston skirt measurement points. Then refer to the "Suitable Re-bore Sizes" chart at the end of this section.

6. Install the piston rings one at a time over the top of the piston. Note that the two compression rings are marked "TOP" to ensure correct assembly position. This mark must face upwards when the rings are fitted.
7. Position the piston on the connecting rod.
8. Install one new retaining circlip as a stop, then press the piston pin into position and install another new circlip on the other side.

NOTE: *If there is no alternative and the piston pin must be driven into its bore, it is advisable to heat the piston to 100°* C prior to assembly.

Piston Pin and Small End Bushing

Inspect the piston pin for center "step wear," scoring, or burring, then slide it into the small-end connecting rod bushing, and make certain that there is no lateral free-play. If there is, replace the bushing in the following manner:

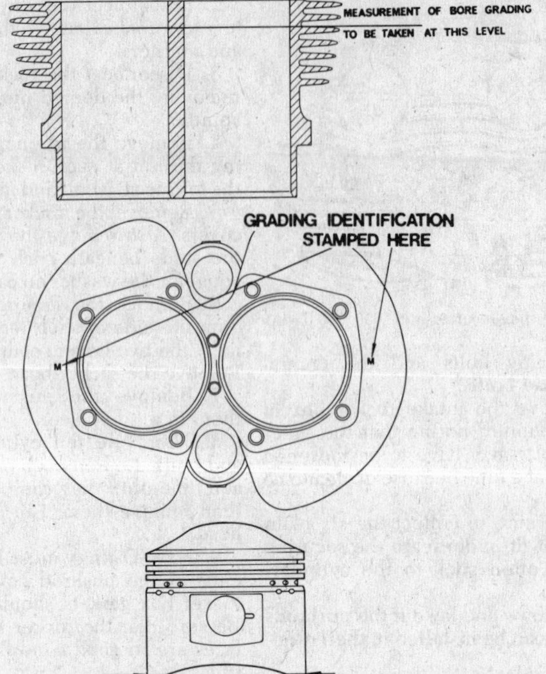

750 Twin piston and cylinder wear measurement points and cylinder grading marks

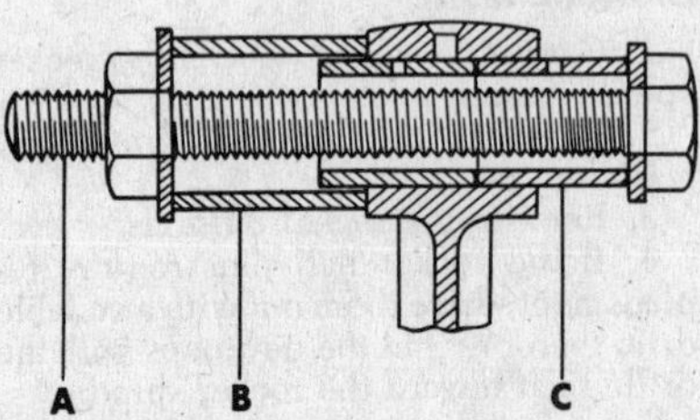

Piston pin bushing replacement: A, bolt; B, tubing collar; C, new bushing

1. Find a threaded bolt approximately 4 in. in length and a piece of tubing $1\frac{1}{4}$ in. long with an inside diameter of ⅞ in.
2. Place a suitable washer and the new bushing on the bolt, then insert the end of the bolt through the old bushing.
3. Place the piece of tubing over the end of the bolt and screw the nut on finger-tight.
4. Centralize the new bushing and align the oil drillway with that in the old bushing.
5. Now tighten the nut on the bolt and

ASSEMBLY

1. Position new guide block O-ring seals at the base of the cylinder block.
2. Lightly grease the outside surface of the exhaust guide block, then carefully align the guide block and cylinder locating holes and drive the block into position with Triumph special tool no. 61-6008 or a suitable drift.
3. Repeat the above step for the intake guide block, then install the locking bolts.
4. After installing the guide blocks, make sure that the exhaust guide block oil drillways are free from obstruction.
5. Install the tappets in the guide blocks as shown in the accompanying illustration, after thoroughly lubricating

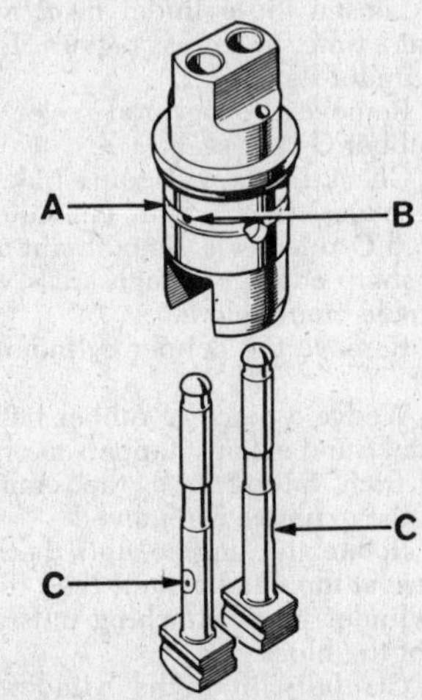

Tappet and guide block (A) oil passage (B, C) alignment

them with oil. Wedge them into position.

6. Install the cylinder base gasket, making certain that the gasket does not obscure the oil feed drillway in the crankcase.
7. Fit ring compressors over the pistons, then carefully slide the cylinder down over the pistons. Remove the ring compressors as soon as the rings are positioned within the cylinder. Continue lowering the cylinder block and then remove the rags in the crankcase openings as late as possible.
8. Install the cylinder base attaching nuts.
9. Replace or anneal the cylinder head gasket.
10. Clean the mating cylinder head and cylinder surfaces, then grease the gasket and position it on the cylinder.
11. Coat the tappet guide blocks with grease and position the pushrod cover

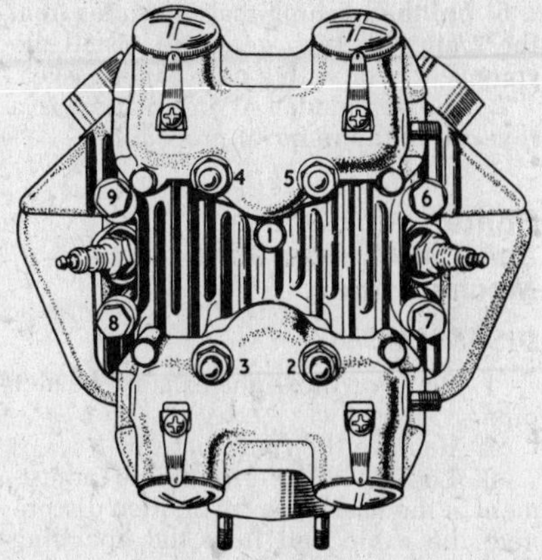

Cylinder head bolt tightening order (650)

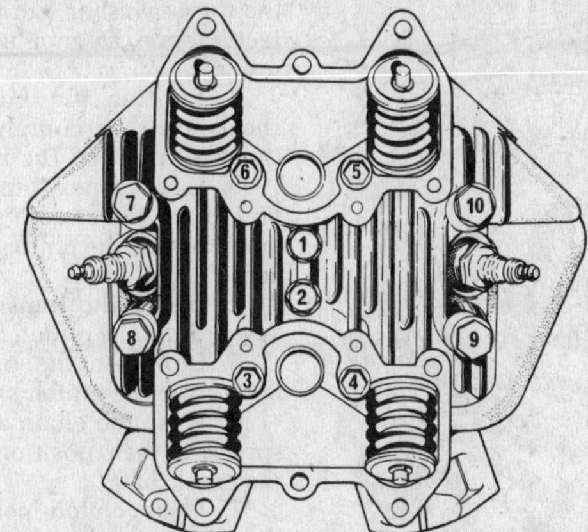

Cylinder head bolt tightening order (750 Twin)

tubes with new O-ring seals.

12. Position the cylinder head and install the head nuts and bolts finger-tight.

13. Place a small amount of grease in the bottom cup of each pushrod, then locate the intake pushrods in their respective bores. This will have to be done by "feel."

14. When the pushrods are properly positioned, turn the engine over until both intake pushrods are level and at the bottom of their travel.

15. Install the intake rocker box.

16. Repeat the above procedure for the exhaust rocker box, noting that the central cylinder-head bolts should be tightened to torque specifications before tightening the underside securing nuts.

17. Turn the engine over several times to make sure the valves are operating properly, then reinstall the torque stays and secondary ignition coils.

18. Connect the rocker oil feed line, using either new copper washers or annealed, used ones.

19. The remainder of the assembly procedure is a reversal of the disassembly instructions. Adjust valve tappet clearances.

Clutch

Service procedures are basically the same for the 650 and 750cc twins, except that the larger models have a triplex primary drive chain in place of the duplex chain found on the 650.

DISASSEMBLY

1. Remove the left exhaust header pipe.

2. Loosen the rear brake adjustment until the pedal drops clear of the primary cover.

3. Remove the left footrest.

4. Drain the oil from the chaincase, then remove the chain tension adjuster.

5. Remove the ten, recessed, cover-securing screws and withdraw the cover and paper gasket.

6. Remove the chain tensioner assembly.

7. The clutch pressure plate is held in place by three, slotted adjuster nuts. To remove these nuts, slide a knife or screwdriver blade under the nut and loosen it with Triumph tool no. D364 (supplied with tool kit) or a suitable substitute.

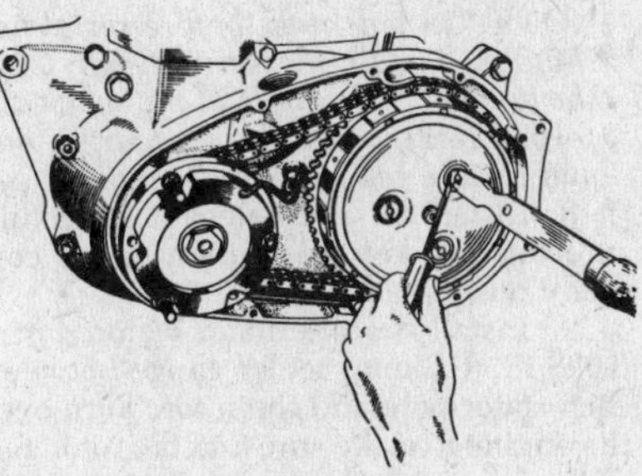
Removing the clutch nuts

NOTE: *The nuts are fitted with locking tabs which may be sheared off by removal. If so, replace them.*

8. Remove the clutch springs, cups, and pressure plate assembly.

9. The clutch plates can be removed with the use of two, narrow, hooked tools made of 1/32 in. wire.

INSPECTION

1. If the thickness of the discs is 0.030 in. (0.76 mm), or more, less than specified, they should be replaced.

2. Check the fit of the plate on the shock absorber unit. There should be little radial clearance.

3. Measure the clutch spring length and compare with specifications. If a spring has shortened by 0.10 in. (2.5 mm) or more, replace the whole set.

ASSEMBLY

1. Install the clutch plates and discs, keeping in mind that the innermost position must be occupied by a bonded plate.

2. Install the cups, pressure plate, springs, and slotted adjuster nuts.

3. True the clutch pressure plate by first tightening the pressure-plate, slotted adjuster nuts until they are even with the clutch pins, and then by kicking with engine over and observing the rotation of the plate, and then making any necessary adjustment until the plate turns evenly. If the plate wobbles even slightly, it must be corrected.

Primary Drive and Clutch Hub

DISASSEMBLY

1. Remove the primary cover as previously described.

2. Remove the clutch assembly as previously described.

3. Disconnect the alternator stator leads at their snap connectors under the engine.

4. Remove the three, stator securing nuts and withdraw the stator from over its mounting studs. Unscrew the sleeve nut and then the lead can easily be removed.

5. To remove the rotor, bend back the tab washer, and remove the locknut.

6. Remove the rotor key and distance piece.

7. Remove the clutch hub securing nut and cup.

NOTE: *Machines prior to serial no. H49833 have a tab washer and a different cup washer, rather than the self-locking securing nut.*

8. Screw the body of extractor no. Z13 into the clutch hub until it bottoms, then tighten the center bolt until the hub is released.

9. Assemble extractor no. Z151 and D662/3 on the engine sprocket and tighten its center bolt until the engine sprocket is released.

10. Withdraw the engine sprocket, clutch hub, and primary chain together.

11. Remove the transmission main-

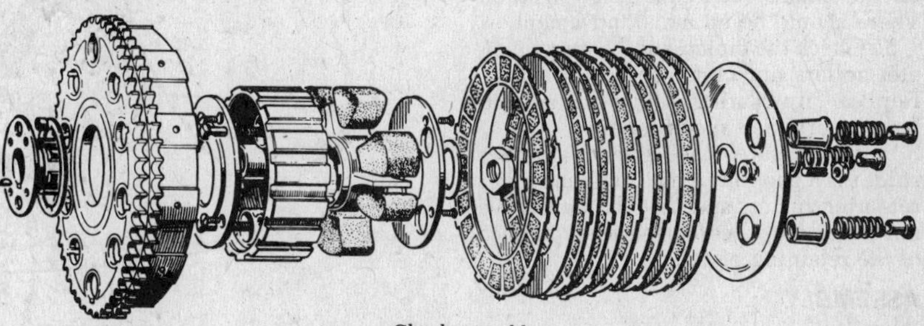
Clutch assembly

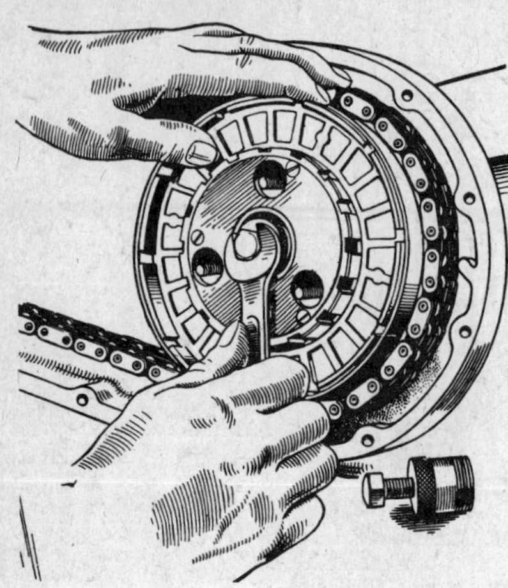

Removing the clutch housing

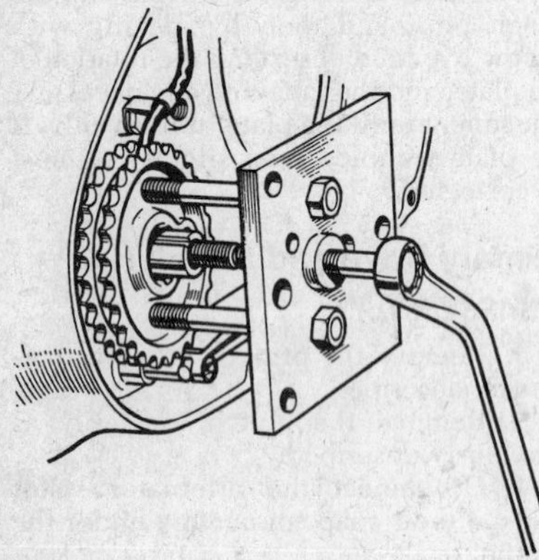

Removing the engine sprocket

shaft key and check the oil seal for leakage.

INSPECTION

1. Inspect the clutch shock absorber for worn rubbers or punctures. They can be removed by prying them out, small rubbers first. Replace as necessary. When reassembling, apply thread-locking compound to the cover-plate securing screws.
2. First thoroughly clean the primary chain then check it for wear by scribing two marks on a flat surface 12 in. apart, and centering two pivot pins at the scribe marks. Fully compressed, the chain link pivot should line up with the marks; fully stretched, it should not extend more than ¼ in. beyond the marks.
3. Check the fit between the shock absorber spider and the clutch hub splines. The spider should be a push fit on the clutch hub, with no radial movement.
4. Check the fit of the engine sprocket on the crankshaft in the same manner. There should be no radial movement.
5. Check the clutch hub bearing diameter, rollers, and clutch sprocket bearing. Replace any bearing rollers that are pitted or worn. See specifications.
6. Make sure the shock absorber spider is a good fit in the inner and outer retaining plates, and that the arms have not excessively scored the inner surface of the retaining plates.

ASSEMBLY

1. Grease the clutch hub and install the thrust washer and twenty of the correct rollers. Do not use ¼ in. x ¼ in. rollers!
2. Position the hub and press the shock absorber, complete with the three threaded pins, on the hub.
3. Install a new tapered distance collar behind the engine sprocket, with the taper toward the crankshaft main bearing and oil seal.
4. Install the transmission mainshaft key and tap the clutch hub onto its taper.
5. Lubricate the primary chain and lay it over the clutch sprocket.
6. Wrap the chain around the engine sprocket, then position the sprocket on the crankshaft.
7. Place clutch-locking tool Z13 in the clutch plate housing, then install the cup washer and self-locking nut. Torque the nut to specifications.

NOTE: *On machines before serial no. H49833, install the tab washer with the long tab in the hole in the shock absorber spider, install the securing nut and bend a tab to lock the nut.*

8. Install the alternator rotor, making sure that the key or locating peg is correctly positioned.
9. Install the alternator stator. Put a 0.008 in. (0.2 mm) feeler gauge between each stator pole and the rotor. Turn over the engine to make sure that the rotor and stator do not touch.
10. The remainder of the assembly procedure is a reversal of the disassembly instructions.

Transmission Countershaft Sprocket

REMOVAL AND INSTALLATION

1. Disassemble the clutch and primary drive as previously described. Remove the sprocket cover.
2. Bend back the tab washer and, while holding the rear brake, remove the sprocket securing nut.
3. Slide off the final drive chain and remove the countershaft sprocket.
4. Make sure the oil seal is in good condition, then lubricate the ground boss of the new sprocket and position it on the transmission mainshaft.
5. Replace the tab washer, screw on the securing nut finger-tight, then, with the chain in place, tighten the nut to torque specifications.
6. Oil the bushing that protrudes from the mainshaft high gear and install the sprocket cover with a new paper gasket.
7. The remainder of installation is a reversal of the removal procedure.

Shifter, Kick-Starter, and Clutch Operating Mechanisms

DISASSEMBLY

1. Remove the right exhaust header pipe.
2. Remove the right footrest.
3. Loosen the clutch cable adjustment at the handlebar lever, then disconnect the cable end from the operating lever in the gearbox outer cover.
4. Drain the gearbox oil into a suitable container.
5. Put the transmission in high gear.
6. Remove the top and bottom nuts and recessed screws that secure the gearbox outer cover. Depress the kick-start lever slightly and tap the cover lightly until it is free.
7. Loosen the kick-starter cotter pin nut a few turns, then drive out the cotter pin.
8. Slide the lever off the shaft and remove the kick-starter quadrant and spring assembly.
9. Apply the rear brake, bend back the tab washer, and remove the kick-starter ratchet pinion securing nut.
10. Remove the pinion, ratchet, spring, and sleeve.
11. If the kick-starter quadrant is to be replaced, drive out the spindle with a suitable drift and hammer. Install the new spindle so that the kick-starter lever location flat is correctly positioned with respect to the quadrant.
12. Remove the shifter foot pedal from the shaft.
13. Remove the guide plate, plunger quadrant, and curved return springs.
14. Remove the two screws that secure the clutch operating mechanism. Remove the securing cotter pin and disassemble the mechanism.

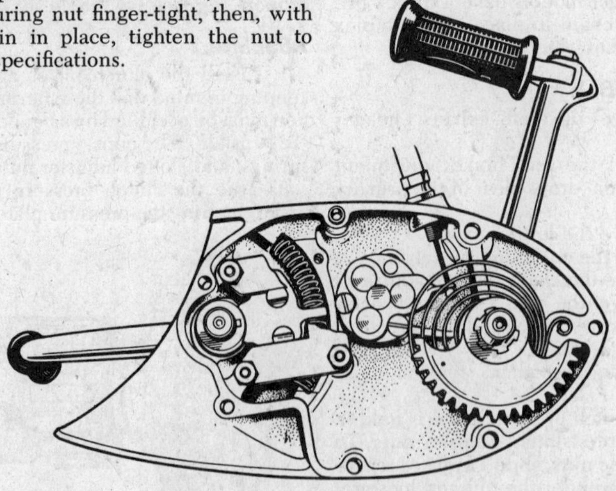

Gearbox outer cover assembled

INSPECTION

Kick-Starter

Inspect the ratchet teeth for burrs, chips, or rounded edges. Make sure the ratchet spring is in good condition and that the thin-walled steel bushing is a clearance fit in the kick-start pinoin. Examine the kick-starter stop peg to make certain it is firmly pressed into the inner cover and is not distorted in any way.

If it is necessary to replace the kick-start spindle bushing, heat the cover to 100° C, then drive out the bushing with a suitable, shouldered drift. Drive in the new bushing while the cover is still hot.

Shifter

If the shifter spindle bushing requires replacement (outer cover), heat the cover surrounding the bushing to 100° C and drive the bushing out with a suitable, shouldered drift. Drive in the new bushing before the cover has a chance to cool.

The inner cover spindle bushing will probably never need replacement, since it suffers an insignificant amount of wear. If it does require replacement, however, it will be necessary to tap the bushing, heat the cover, install an appropriate bolt and then drive it out.

Clutch Operating Mechanism

The clutch operating mechanism is constantly immersed in oil, so wear should be negligible. Inspect the balls for pitting, etc., and make sure they operate smoothly in the plates.

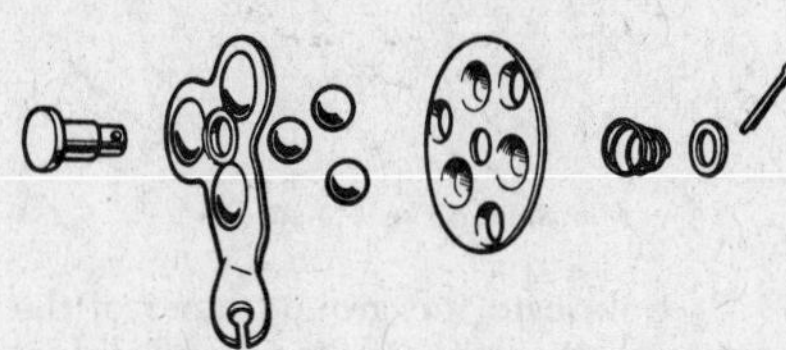

Clutch operating mechanism

ASSEMBLY

1. Assemble and install the clutch operating mechanism, using the accompanying illustration for reference.
2. Install a new rubber O-ring on the shifter spindle and install the spindle in the outer cover bushing, using a few drops of oil to aid installation.
3. Install the two quadrant-return springs, making certain they are correctly located over the step in the cover.

NOTE: *To facilitate connecting of the springs, first install the shifter pedal and clamp it in place, thereby allowing the quadrant to turn and the springs to be compressed.*

4. Install the retainer plate with its four securing nuts and lock washers.
5. Install the plungers and springs, taking care that they don't go springing off somewhere during assembly.
6. Install the kick-starter thin-walled steel sleeve, spring pinion, and ratchet.
7. Install the tab washer and the retaining nut, then torque the nut to specifications and lock it by bending up the washer tab. Do not overtorque the nut as it may cause the thin sleeve to collapse.

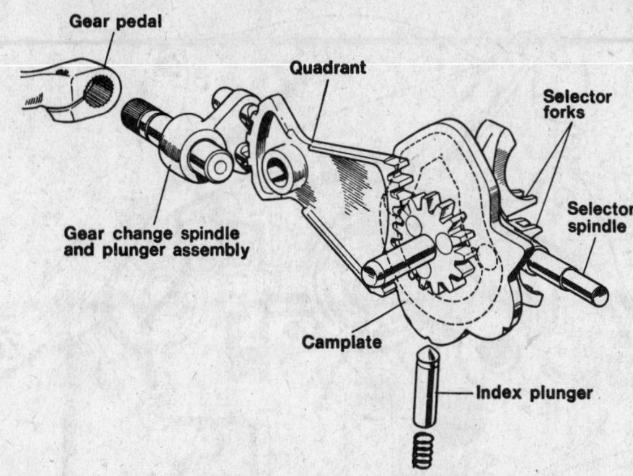

Shifter mechanism (4-speed)

8. Connect the return spring to the kick-starter quadrant as shown in the accompanying illustration.
9. Install the spindle in the kick-starter bushing and connect the return spring to the anchor peg at the rear of the cover.
10. Install the oil seal over the spindle and assemble the kick-starter lever and securing cotter pin.
11. Clean the outer cover joining surface and apply fresh sealing compound. Make sure the two locating dowels are in position.

Kickstarter return spring installed

12. Move the kick-starter lever halfway through its stroke, then fit the outer cover on the gearbox.
13. Before installing the remaining parts, make sure the kick-start lever is fully operational and returns to its upright position.
14. The rest of the assembly is a reverse of the disassembly procedure.

Gearbox Service

DISASSEMBLY

1. Remove the gearbox outer cover as previously described, leaving the gearbox engaged in high gear.
2. Remove the right rear engine plate.
3. Bend back the tabs on the lockwasher, apply the rear brake, and unscrew the kick-starter pinion ratchet retaining nut from the gearbox mainshaft.
4. Remove the clutch and primary drive as previously described. Don't forget to remove the mainshaft key.

Refer to the appropriate procedures, below, for 4-speed or 5-speed service.

4-Speed:

5. Remove the large dome nut from under the gearbox and withdraw the camplate indexing plunger and spring.
6. Remove the allen screw, phillips screw, and bolt that secure the inner gearbox cover. Tap the cover with a mallet until it is free.
7. Remove the selector fork spindle and then withdraw the mainshaft assembly.
8. Remove the layshaft and remaining gears.
9. Remove the camplate and spindle

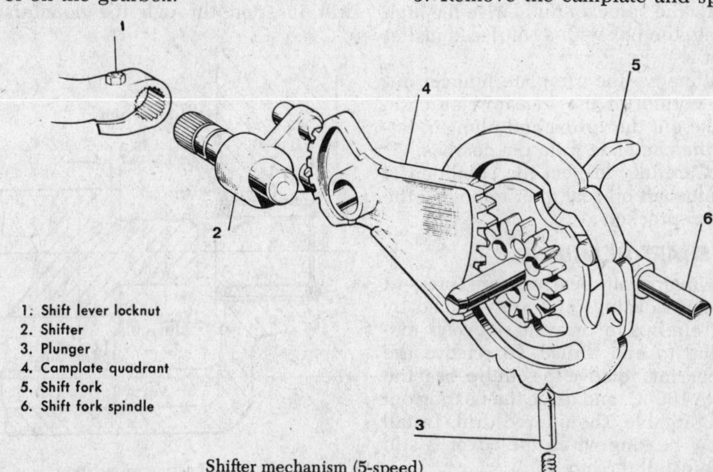

Shifter mechanism (5-speed)

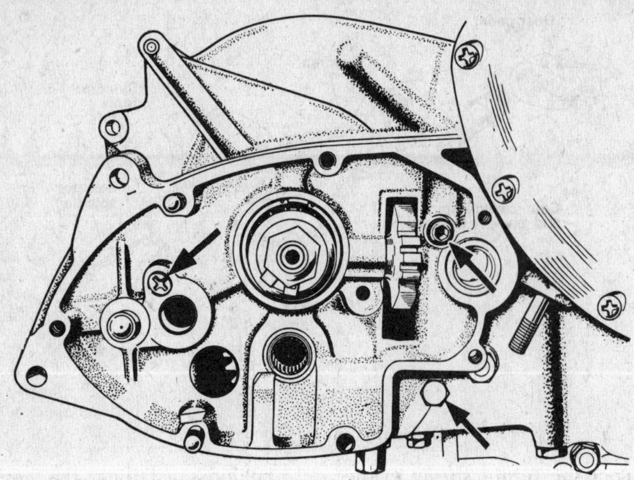

Gearbox inner cover removal

assembly and then remove the two bronze thrust washers located over the needle roller bearings.

10. Remove the circular countershaft sprocket cover from the primary inner cover. Remove the sprocket securing nut.

11. Drive the mainshaft high gear through into the gearbox with a suitable drift. Replace the oil seal.

5-Speed:

5. Remove the allen bolt, phillips screw and bolt and remove the gearbox inner cover, tapping it outward with a softfaced mallet if necessary.

6. Remove the engaging dog pinion from the countershaft. Remove the circlip from the countershaft.

7. Pull out the shift fork rod, then remove the countershaft first gear along with the shift fork.

8. Remove the countershaft second gear, then remove the mainshaft with its first, second, and third gears in position.

9. Take out the mainshaft fourth gear and the countershaft third gear together with the two shift forks.

10. Remove the countershaft fourth and fifth gears.

11. Remove the two thrust washers over the countershaft needle bearings: one on each countershaft bearing.

12. To remove the mainshaft high gear, remove the plate from the inside primary chaincase at the back of the clutch. Bend back the locking plate, and unscrew the sprocket nut. Drive the high gear into the box with a soft-faced mallet or drift.

13. Remove the camplate plunger nut at the bottom of the transmission case, and take out the spring and plunger. Remove the camplate from the gearbox.

14. Carefully inspect the condition of the mainshaft oil seal after removing the gearbox sprocket.

MAINSHAFT BEARINGS

The mainshaft bearings are press-fit into their housings and are retained by spring circlips to prevent sideways motion due to end thrust. To remove the right bearing, remove the circlip, heat the cover to 100° C, and drive the bearing out with a suitable, shouldered drift. Install the new bearing while the cover is still hot. Reinstall the circlip.

To remove the high gear bearing on the left side, pry out the large oil seal, then remove the retaining circlip. Heat the case around the bearing to 100° C, then drive the bearing out with tool no. Z15 or a suitable, shouldered drift. Install the new bearing while the base is still hot. Install the circlip and press in a new seal.

To replace the high gear bushing, (4-speed transmission) press it out with a suitable, shouldered drift. This drift can be fabricated by machining ¾ in. on one end of a ⅞ in. x 5 in. bar to 13/16 in. diameter. The bushing must be pressed out from the tooth side of the gear. Install the new bushing in the same manner, making sure the oil groove in the bushing is on the tooth side of the gear. Ream the bushing to the size given in specifications and make sure any filings are removed from the case before reassembly.

LAYSHAFT BEARINGS

Remove the right bearing by heating the cover to 100° C and pressing or driving it out with a drift similar to the one shown in the accompanying illustration. Press in the new bearing, while the cover is still hot, from the inside of the cover until 0.073-0.078 in. of the bearing protrudes, as shown in the accompanying illustration.

Remove the left bearing by heating the cover housing to 100° C and driving it through into the gearbox with a suitable drift inserted through the countershaft sprocket aperture. Press the new bearing into place while the cover is hot. It must protrude 0.073-0.078 in. inside the gearbox.

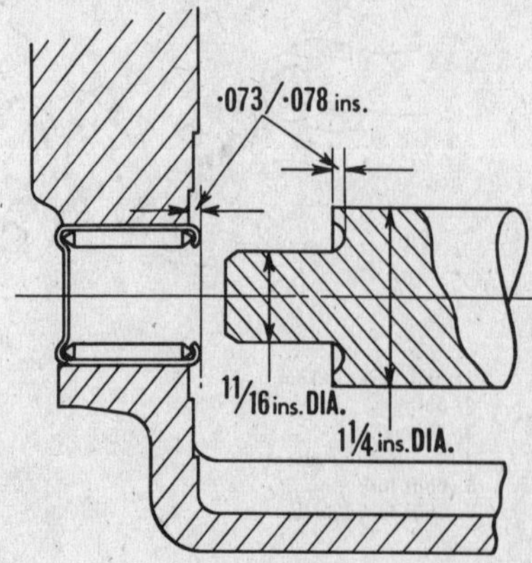

Layshaft bearing installation

MAINSHAFT HIGH GEAR BEARINGS (5 SPEED)

The mainshaft high gear is fitted with two caged needle bearings (one in each end). Press them out and in together with a drift of the dimensions shown in the illustration.

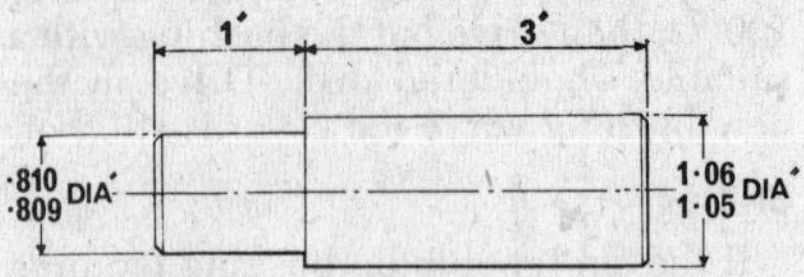

High gear needle bearing drift dimensions

ASSEMBLY

4-Speed

1. Drive a new oil seal up to the main bearing with the lip and spring toward the bearing.

2. Press the high gear into the bearing.

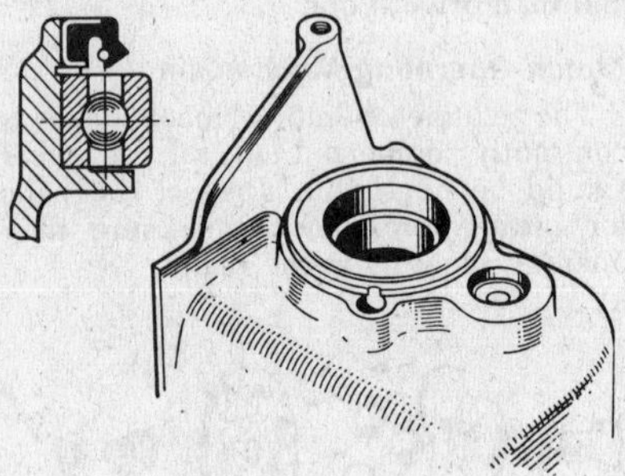

Mainshaft oil seal (4-speed)

3. Lubricate the ground taper of the countershaft sprocket with oil and slide it on to the high gear. Screw on the securing nut finger-tight.

4. Connect the final drive chain over the sprocket, then tighten the securing nut to specifications with tool no. Z63 or a suitable substitute.

5. Lubricate the extended nose of the high gear with oil, then reinstall the sprocket cover with a new paper gasket.

6. Lubricate the camplate spindle and install it in its housing within the gearbox.

7. Assemble the camplate plunger and spring in the domed retaining nut and screw it into position under the gearbox. Don't forget the fiber washer.

8. Locate the camplate plunger in the notch between second and third gear.

9. Position the thrust washer over the inner needle roller bearing. Coat the washer with grease to hold it in place and note that the grooved surface of the washer should be toward the layshaft.

10. Lubricate the captive mainshaft and layshaft gears, then assemble them in a cluster as shown in the accompanying illustration.

11. Grease the camplate rollers, then position them on the selector forks as shown in the accompanying illustration.

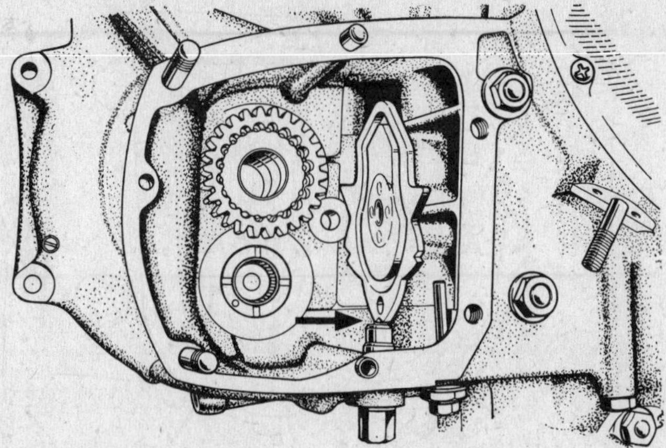
Gearbox assembly with camplate notch between 2d and 3rd gear engaged (4-speed)

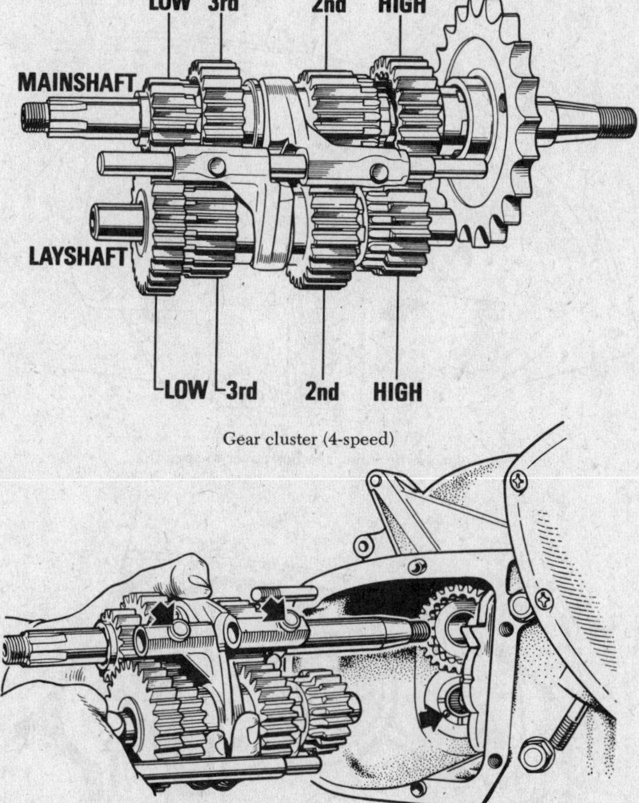

Gear cluster (4-speed)

Installing the gearbox components (4-speed)

NOTE: *The selector fork with the smaller radius is for the mainshaft cluster.*

12. Install the mainshaft and layshaft cluster in the gearbox. As the shafts are being located in their respective bearings, the gears should be slid into position and aligned so that the selector fork rollers engage the camplate and the selector forks are approximately aligned.

13. Lubricate the selector fork spindle with oil, then slide it through the forks, shoulder end first, until it is fully situated in the gearbox housing.

14. Make sure the camplate quadrant is moving freely in the inner cover, then position the layshaft thrust washer over the bearing in the inner cover. Hold it in place by smearing it with grease.

15. Thoroughly lubricate all parts in the gearbox with a pressure oil can, then apply fresh sealer to the joining surface of the gearbox. Make sure the two locating dowels are in position.

16. Begin to install the inner cover assembly, and when the joining surfaces are about ¼ in. apart, position the camplate quadrant in the middle point of its travel, and quickly complete the installation. This will align the camplate middle tooth with the mainshaft centerline.

17. Install the gearbox securing screws and nut, then temporarily install the gearbox outer cover assembly and check out the gearbox operation. If there is a problem, chances are the quadrant teeth are not correctly engaged with the camplate pinion.

18. The remainder of the assembly procedure is a reversal of the disassembly instructions.

5-Speed

1. Replace the camplate after lubricating the camplate spindle with some gearbox oil.

2. Refit the mainshaft oil bearing noting that the lip faces the mainshaft bearing. A new oil seal must always be used.

3. Push the mainshaft high gear into the bearing. Put some transmission oil on the tapered boss of the gearbox sprocket and place it on its shaft, in place, then replace the sprocket nut, tightening it by hand for the time being.

4. Run the drive chain over the gearbox sprocket. Apply the rear brake and tighten the sprocket nut as tight as possible.

5. Lubricate the end of the high gear which protrudes into the primary chaincase, and refit the cover plate. A new paper gasket should be used.

6. Replace the thrust washer over the inner needle bearing. The grooved surface of the thrust washer must face the countershaft. The washer may be held in place by smearing the rear surface with a bit of grease.

7. Refer to the accompanying illustration, and set the camplate in the "neutral" position, and refit the cam plunger, spring, and bolt on the bottom of the gearbox.

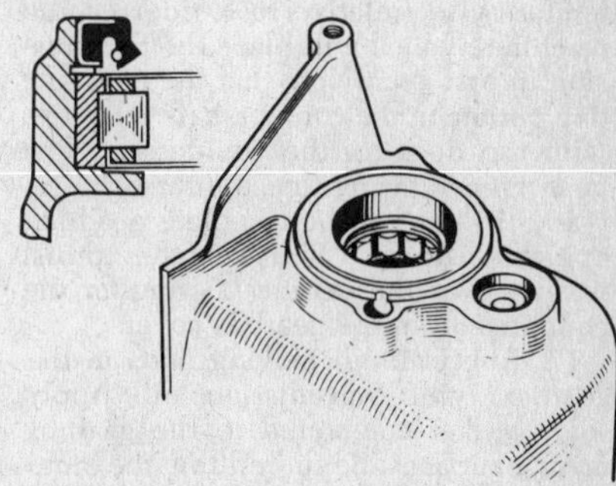
Gear cluster (5-speed)

8. With gearbox oil, lubricate the needle bearing in the high gear and the countershaft bearing. Place the mainshaft high gear onto the mainshaft. Also refit the shift fork to the mainshaft. Note that the three shift forks are all different, and this one has a large engaging pin and no cutaway on the housing.

9. Insert the mainshaft assembly into the high gear, engaging the pin on the shift fork with the camplate groove. Use onto the mainshaft. Also refit the shift fork to the mainshaft. Note that 10. Replace the countershaft with its two highest gears into the gearbox, engaging these gears with their mainshaft counterparts. Note that none of the sliding gear dogs will be engaged if the transmission is set at neutral.

11. Refit the countershaft third gear and its shift fork. This shift fork has a large engaging pin and a cutaway on the housing. Refit the mainshaft third gear

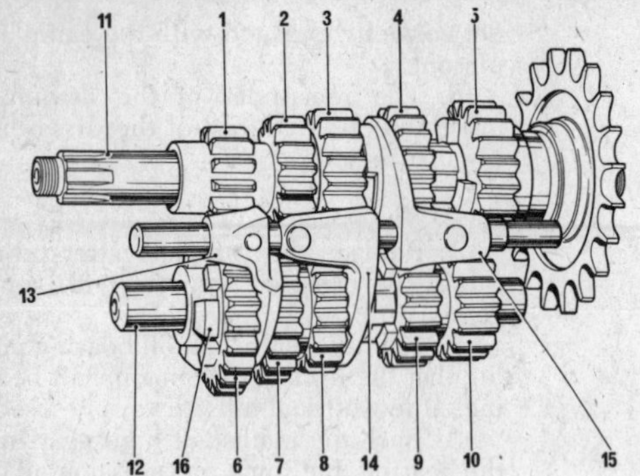

Gearbox mainshaft oil seal and roller bearing (5-speed)

1. 1st gear (Mainshaft)
2. 2nd gear
3. 3rd gear
4. 4th gear
5. 5th gear
6. 1st gear (Countershaft)
7. 2nd gear
8. 3rd gear
9. 4th gear
10. 5th gear
11. Mainshaft
12. Countershaft
13. 1st gear countershaft shift fork
14. 3rd gear countershaft shift fork
15. Mainshaft shift fork
16. Countershaft dog pinion

and engage it with the corresponding countershaft gear.

12. Lubricate the countershaft second gear bushing and replace the gear on the countershaft.

13. Replace the first and second gears onto the mainshaft. Refit the countershaft first gear with its shift fork. Note that this shift fork has the smaller engaging pin.

14. Insert the shift fork rod. Replace the circlip on the end of the countershaft, and replace the engaging dog pinion against the circlip.

15. Turn the camplate counterclockwise (relative to a rider on the machine), which will place the transmission in first gear. Note that the engaging dog pinion on the countershaft will mesh with the dogs on the countershaft first gear, groove facing the countershaft.

16. Insure that the camplate quadrant operates freely. Replace the thrust washer over the needle bearing for the countershaft in the gearbox cover.

17. Lubricate all moving parts in the gearbox with transmission oil. Apply some gasket compound to the gearbox mating surfaces. Begin refitting the inner cover. When the inner cover is about ¼ in. away from the mating surfaces, position the camplate quadrant as shown using the special tool (60-6128). If not available, line up the top edge of the second tooth on the quadrant with an imaginary horizontal line through the center of the gearshift spindle housing. This housing is at the extreme forward part of the inner cover, and is shown occupied by the special tool in the illustration of the inner cover.

18. Refit the inner cover securing bolt and screws tightening them lightly. Assemble the outer cover and gearshift lever and check that the shifter operates properly. If not, it is probable that the quadrant teeth are not properly engaged with the camplate gear.

19. Assuming that the shifting is working properly, tighten the inner cover securing bolt and screws, and refit the kickstarter assembly, the outer cover, and refill the gearbox and primary chaincase with the correct amounts and grades of oil.

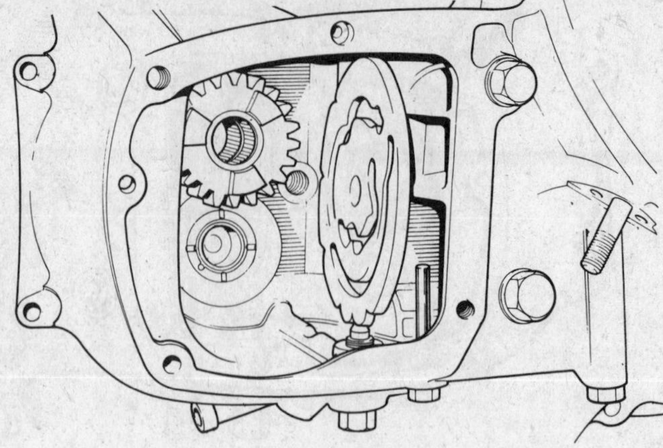

Camplate installed: gearbox in neutral (5-speed)

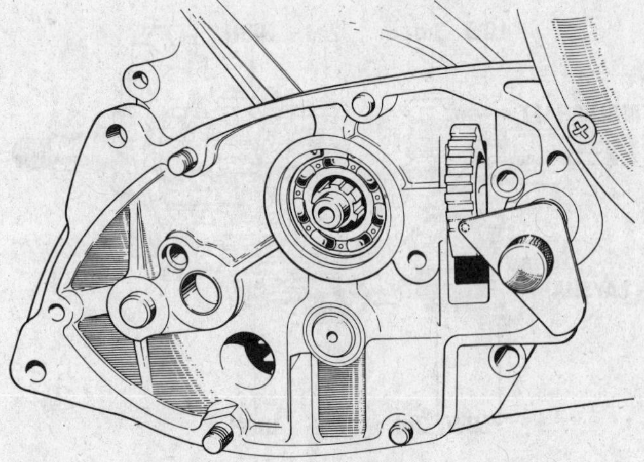

Refitting the inner gearbox cover (5-speed)

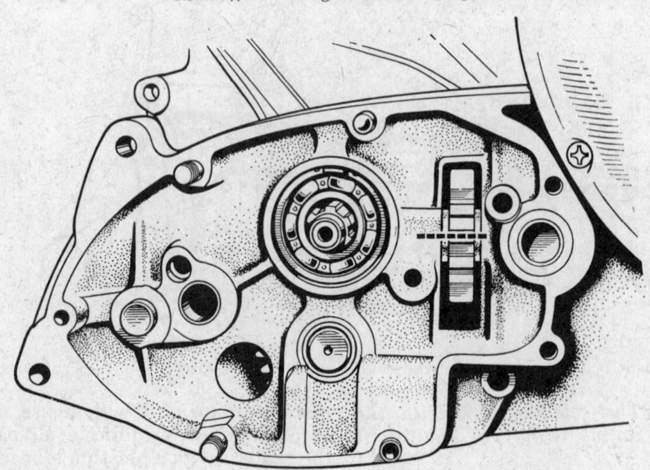

Installing the gearbox inner cover while aligning quadrant

Bottom End

DISASSEMBLY

1. Remove the primary chaincase cover and disconnect the alternator leads under the engine.

2. Remove the three screws that secure the alternator stator, and pull the stator off its mounting studs. Do not disconnect the leads at this time.

3. Disassemble the clutch and primary drive as previously described. Remove the stator sleeve and withdraw the stator leads.

4. Remove the gearbox outer cover and dismantle the gearbox.

5. Remove the rocker boxes, cylinder head, cylinder barrel, and pistons.

6. Disconnect the clutch cable and remove the carburetor(s). Remove the timing cover. Note that the screws are of different lengths.

7. Remove the contact breaker cover and the oil pump, then remove the crank-

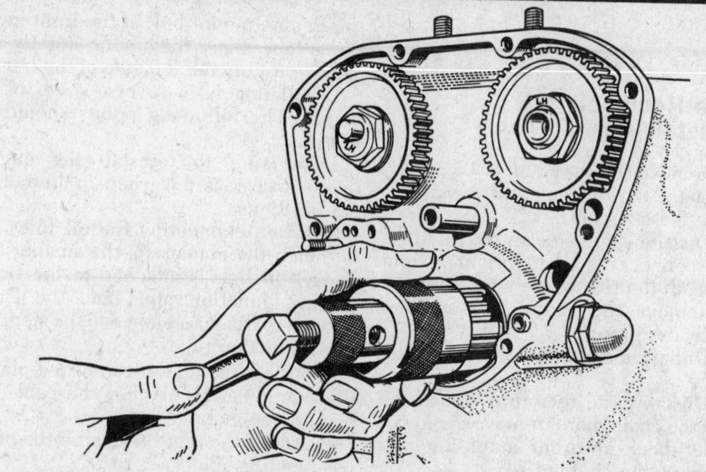

Removing the crankshaft pinion

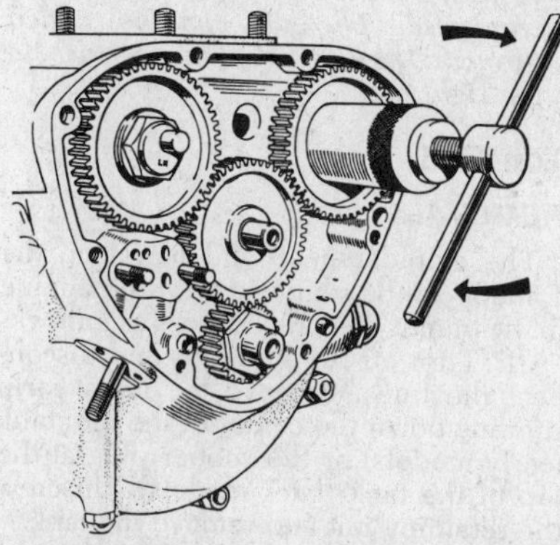

Removing the camplate pinions with tool no. D2213

shaft pinion. The camshaft pinions can also be removed at this time.

NOTE: *The camshaft pinion nuts are left-hand threads. The crankshaft nut has a right-hand thread.*

8. Remove what's left of the engine from the frame.
9. Remove the crankcase filter and oil-way plug.
10. Clamp the crankcase firmly in a vise at the bottom mounting lug and remove the three bolts and two screws near the cylinder base.
11. Remove the four remaining studs and the two nuts next to the gearbox housing.
12. Attach Triumph extractor no. 61-6064 and separate the cases.
13. Remove the breather valve from within the intake camshaft bushing in the left case.

Separating the case halves

CRANKSHAFT AND CONNECTING RODS DISASSEMBLY

1. Clamp the crankshaft assembly in a soft-jawed vise and place a rag over any sharp edges to protect the connecting rods.
2. Unscrew the cap retainer nuts a little at a time to avoid distortion, then remove the caps and connecting rods.

NOTE: *The connecting rods, caps, and nut are center-punched to facilitate reassembly.*

3. Using a large impact driver, unscrew the oil tube retainer plug from the right end of the big-end journal. If necessary, drill a hole ⅛ in. deep and ⅛ in. in diameter to eliminate the locking effect of the plug center punch.
4. Remove the flywheel bolt next to the big-end journal, then pull out the oil tube with a hooked piece of stiff wire through the flywheel bolt location hole.
5. Thoroughly clean all parts in kerosine or a cleaning solvent, then blow them dry with compressed air. Make sure the oil drillways are blown clear.
6. To remove the flywheel, unscrew the two remaining bolts and press the crankshaft out of the right-side bearing with a five ton press.

NOTE: *Before removing the flywheel, make certain it is marked for reassembly.*

INSPECTION

Inspect the big-end journals for any signs of scoring, etc., and measure the journal diameter. Compare with specifications. Light score marks can be removed with fine-grade emery cloth, but make sure all metal filings are removed before reassembly. If the scoring is light, new connecting rod shell bearings should be installed; if the scoring is extensive, the journals should be reground to an appropriate undersize.

NOTE: *The replaceable big-end bearing shells are pre-sized to give the correct dimensions. Under no circumstances should they be scraped, or the connecting rod and cap filed to alter the bearing dimensions.*

ASSEMBLY

1. Position the oil tube in the crankshaft, aligning the flywheel bolt holes with those in the crankshaft. Temporarily install one of the flywheel bolts to secure it in position.
2. Apply thread-locking sealant to the oil tube plug and install it in the crankshaft. Center-punch the crankshaft opposite the slot to lock the plug in position.
3. Heat the flywheel to 100° C, then position it over the crankshaft with the center punch mark to the right. Turn the flywheel through 180° to get it over the crankshaft web, then turn it to the correct position relative to the crankshaft and align the bolt holes.
4. Coat the flywheel bolt threads with a thread-locking sealant, then install and torque them to specifications.
5. If a new or reground crankshaft, or a new flywheel was installed, the assembly should be rebalanced.
6. Check to make sure all the oil drillways are free from obstruction, then install the connecting rods and caps. Torque the retaining nuts to 28 ft lbs.
7. Last, force oil through the crankshaft, right main-bearing journal drillway until it is expelled at both big-end bearings. This will provide assurance that the drillway is free from obstruction.

CAMSHAFT BUSHINGS

The intake and exhaust camshafts run in bronze bushings.

To remove the bushings in the left case, a tap will be necessary. The ideal size is ⅞ in. diameter x 9 whitworth.

When a good thread has been cut in the bushing, heat the case to 100° C and screw in the appropriate bolt. Grip the bolt in a vise and tap the case with a soft-faced mallet until the bushing is free. The replacement bushings are pre-sized but will require a light reaming to meet specifications. After reaming the new bushings, make sure the crankcase is thoroughly cleaned to remove any metal filings.

To remove the bushings in the right case, heat the area around the bushing to 100° C, then drive it out with a suitable, shouldered drift. Install the new bushing while the case is still hot, making sure the oil drillway holes are aligned.

MAIN BEARINGS

To remove the left main bearing, heat the case to 100° C and drive it out with tool no. Z14. Only the right main bearing spool remains in the case, and is removed by first removing the lock plate, heating the case to 100° C, then driving it out with tool no. Z162 or a suitable, shouldered drift. It is advisable to replace the left bearing oil seal while the engine is apart, even if it appears to be in good condition.

To install the left and right bearings, first make sure that their housings are clean, then heat the cases to 100° C and drive the bearings into position with a

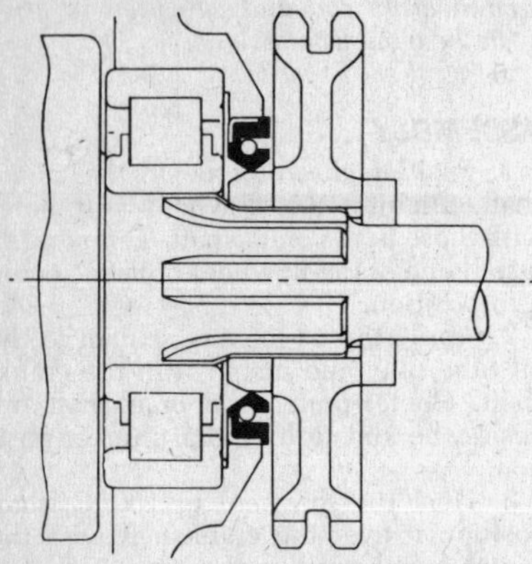

Left main bearing oil seal installation

tubular drift the same size as the bearing outer race. A suitable size would be 2¾ in. diameter x 6 in. long.

After both bearings have been installed, press the oil seal into the left case. This is installed with the spring side facing away from the bearing.

ASSEMBLY

1. Thoroughly clean the mating crankcase halves, giving special attention to the locating dowels. Install the oilway plug.
2. Position the left case on two wooden blocks, lubricate the main bearing and camshaft bushings and then install the breather valve and spring in the intake cam bushing. Assemble both camshafts, making sure the intake cam slot engages the breather valve dog, if fitted.
3. Carefully install the crankshaft assembly, making sure the fit in the bearing is good.
4. Apply fresh joining compound to the mating surfaces, then position the connecting rods in the center and lower the right case over the crankshaft. When the halves are mated, check to make sure the crankshaft and camshafts are not binding. The crankshaft should rotate freely, while the camshafts should offer only slight resistance.
5. The remainder of the assembly procedure is a reversal of the disassembly instructions. Torque all bolts and nuts to specifications.

T150

Engine Removal and Installation

1. Remove the fuel tank.
2. Drain the oil tank and crankcase. Remove the oil cooler.
3. Disconnect the rocker box oil lines, then disconnect the oil supply lines from underneath the rear of the crankcase.
4. Remove the carburetors and exhaust header pipes.
5. Unbolt and remove the right-side footpeg.
6. Unscrew the retaining bolt at the front of the chainguard, remove the lower left-side shock absorber mounting nut, and remove the chainguard.
7. Remove the masterlink and pull the drive chain off the countershaft sprocket.
8. Disconnect the alternator and contact breaker point leads at their connectors. Remove the spark plugs.
9. Turn the cable adjuster at the clutch lever all the way in until the cable is completely slack. Take out the four, clutch, inspection-cover retaining screws and disconnect the clutch cable from the release lever.
10. Disconnect the tachometer cable from the tachometer drive at the front of the crankcase.
11. Pull the engine breather tube off at the rear of the inner primary chaincase.
12. Unscrew the pinch-bolt and pull the brake pedal off its shaft.
13. Unscrew the nut from the kickstart lever shaft and drive out the locating pin by tapping on the end of the threads with a small hammer. Remove the kickstarter lever.
14. Unscrew the five bolts and nuts from the right-side rear engine mount plate. Unscrew the swing arm shaft nut and remove the plate. It is not necessary to remove the left mount plate.
15. Unscrew the nut from the long engine mount bolt underneath the crankcase and drive the bolt out. Note the position of the spacer between the crankcase and frame lug before removing the bolt.
16. Support the engine and remove the engine mount bolt at the front frame down-tube. Raise the engine slightly and remove it from the left side of the frame.

Installation is in reverse order of removal. The following points should be noted:

1. Be sure to reinstall the engine mount spacers and washers in their original positions.
2. When connecting the oil lines underneath the crankcase, the smaller (delivery) oil line is attached to the small, straight, junction pipe, and the larger (scavenge) line is attached to the stepped-down junction pipe.
3. Adjust the clutch cable free-play at the handlebar lever after the cable has been reconnected.
4. Adjust the rear brake after the pedal has been installed.

NOTE: *Before starting the engine, ½ pt of oil should be poured into the crankcase. The oil can be added through the timing plug aperture in the right case.*

Top End

REMOVAL

The cylinder head and barrel on the Trident can be removed with the engine in the frame. The procedure is as follows:

1. Turn off the fuel taps and disconnect the lines. Remove the metal strip running down the center of the fuel tank (early models) or the rubber plug at the top of the tank (later models). Unscrew the retaining nut and remove the tank.
2. Loosen the oil line clamps at the oil cooler and pull the lines off their connector pipes. Mark the lines and pipes to facilitate correct reassembly. *Do not unscrew the large hexagonal connectors from the cooler.* Unbolt the oil cooler bracket from the frame and remove the cooler. Note that the bracket is insulated from the frame with rubber bushings to protect the cooler from vibration.
3. Disconnect the throttle cable from the linkage at the carburetors and disconnect the choke cable at the handlebar lever. Loosen the carburetor-to-intake manifold clamps and remove the carburetors as a unit.
4. Unscrew the exhaust header pipe

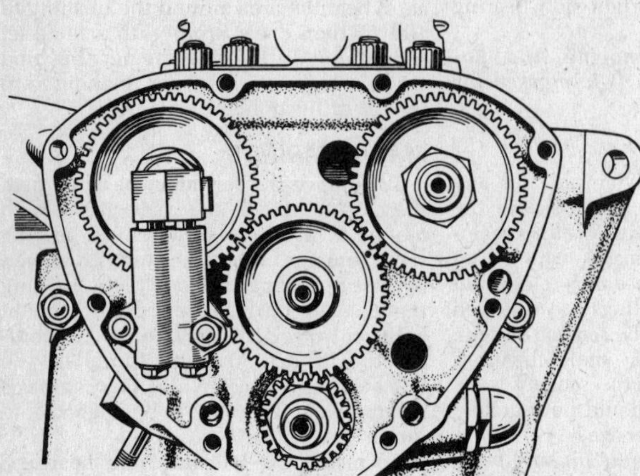

Timing gear mark alignment (650)

Timing gear mark alignment (750 Twin)

nuts at the cylinder head. Disconnect the mufflers from the pipes and remove the header pipe assembly.

5. Unbolt and remove the top engine mount (cylinder head stay).

6. Unscrew the two acorn nuts that secure the rocker oil feed lines to the rocker shafts and tie the pipes out of the way. Remove the access covers and completely loosen the valve adjusters to relieve the head studs of valve spring pressure.

7. Remove the two, small end bolts and three nuts (at the underside of the cylinder head) that secure the rocker boxes to the head. Loosen the head bolts and nuts gradually, in the sequence shown, and then lift off the rocker boxes.

8. Remove the spark plugs, unscrew the remaining cylinder head bolts, and lift the head carefully off the studs. Remove the pushrod tubes and pushrods.

9. To prevent the tappets from falling into the crankcase when removing the barrel, wrap electrical tape around the top of each tappet.

10. Loosen the cylinder-barrel retaining nuts gradually, in the sequence shown, to prevent distortion. Lift the barrel carefully off the crankcase, taking care to support the pistons as they are exposed by the cylinders so that they won't be damaged on the crankcase flange. Mark the tappets so they can be replaced in their original positions. *This is very important.*

11. Remove the piston wrist pin circlips, heat the piston crown, and remove each piston, marking it for location (L,R,C) and mark the front or back for position.

12. To disassemble the rocker mechanism, tap the rocker shafts out from the threaded end. Be sure to install the thrust washers and springs in their correct positions when assemblying.

Cylinders

Maximum allowable wear is 0.005 in.

Pistons

These are available in four oversizes, in increments of 0.010 in.

Tappets

The tappet guide blocks, pressed into the base flange of the cylinder, should not normally need replacement. If it does become necessary to replace them, the dowels must be drilled out and the cylinder must be heated before the guides can be pressed out. New dowels will have to be used along with the new guides.

INSTALLATION

1. Carefully install the rings on the pistons. Note that the compression rings are tapered, and the work "top" must be installed facing up.

2. Be sure to coat each moving part with fresh engine oil or assembly lube during installation.

3. Warm the pistons and install them, in their original positions on the connecting rods. Insert the wrist pins before the pistons have a chance to cool. Install *new* circlips and make sure that they are properly seated.

Engine and Transmission Specifications—TR25W

PISTON	
Material	"Lo-Ex" aluminum
Compression ratio	10 : 1
Clearance (bottom of skirt)	0.0023–0.0028 in. (0.05842–0.07112 mm)
Clearance (top of skirt) (Both measured on major axis)	0.0042–0.0053 in. (0.10668–0.13462 mm)
PISTON RINGS	
Material—compression (top)	Brico BSS 0.5004 cast iron
Material—compression (center)	Brico 8 cast iron
Material—scraper	Brico BSS 0.5004 cast iron
Width—compression (top and center)	0.0625 in. (1.5875 mm) 0.0615–0.0625 in.)
Width—scraper	0.125 in. (3.175 mm) (0.124–0.125 in.)
Depth—compression (top and center)	0.108–0.114 in. (2.7432–2.8956 mm)
Depth—scraper	0.094–0.100 in. (2.3876–2.540 mm)
Clearance in groove	0.001–0.003 in. (0.0254–0.0762 mm)
Fitted gap—(maximum)	0.013 in. (0.3302 mm)
Fitted gap—(minimum)	0.009 in. (0.2283 mm)
Connecting rod (length between centers)	5.312 in. (134.92 mm)
Internal die of small end	0.6892 in. (17.51 mm)
CYLINDER BARREL	
Material	Aluminum alloy with austenitic iron liner
Bore size (standard)	67 mm
Stroke	70 mm
Oversizes	½ mm and 1 mm
CYLINDER HEAD	
Material	Aluminum alloy
Inlet port size	1.125 in. (28.575 mm)
Exhaust port size	1.25 in. (31.75 mm)
CAMSHAFT	
Journal diameter (right- and left-hand)	0.7480–0.7485 in. (18.9992–19.0119 mm)
Cam lift (inlet)	0.345 in. (8.763 mm)
Cam lift (exhaust)	0.336 in. (8.534 mm)
Base circle radius	0.906 in. (23.0124 mm)
CAMSHAFT BUSHINGS	
Bore diameter (fitted)	0.7492–0.7497 in. (19.0297–19.04238 mm)
Outside diameter	0.908–0.909 in. (23.0632–23.0886 mm)
Camshaft clearance	0.0007–0.0017 in. (0.01778–0.04318 mm)
CRANKSHAFT	
End float	0.002–0.005 in. (0.0508–0.127 mm)
VALVES	
Seat angle (inclusive)	90°
Head diameter (inlet)	1.450–1.455 in. (36.830–36.957 mm)
Head diameter (exhaust)	1.312–1.317 in. (33.3248–33.4518 mm)
Stem diameter (inlet)	0.3095–0.3100 in. (7.861–7.874 mm)
Stem diameter (exhaust)	0.3090–0.3095 in. (7.848–7.861 mm)
VALVE GUIDES	
Material	Hidural 5
Bore diameter	0.3120–0.3130 in. (7.9248–7.950 mm)
Outside diameter	0.5005–0.5010 in. (12.7127–12.7254 mm)
Length	1.844 in. (46.8376 mm)
Cylinder head interference fit	0.0015–0.0025 in. (0.0381–0.0635 mm)
VALVE SPRINGS	
Free length (inner)	1.400 in. (35.56 mm)
Free length (outer)	1.750 in. (44.45 mm)
Fitted length (inner)	1.262 in. (32.0548 mm)
Fitted length (outer)	370 in. (34–798 mm)
VALVE TIMING	
Tappets set to 0.015 in. (0.381 mm) for checking purposes only:	
Inlet opens BTDC	51°
Inlet closed ABDC	68°
Exhaust opens BBDC	78°
Exhaust closes ATDC	37°
BEARING DIMENSIONS	
Clutch roller (25)	0.1875 x 0.1875 in. (4.7025 x 4.7025 mm)
Con-rod big-end bearing—running clearance	0.0005–0.0015 in. (0.0127–0.0381 mm)
Con-rod big-end—crank diameter	1.4375–1.4380 in. (36.5125–36.5252 mm)
Crank undersizes	0.010, 0.020, and 0.030 in. (0.254, 0.508, and 0.762 mm)
Con-rod small-end bush (bore	0.6890–0.6894 in. (17.5006–17.6108 mm)
Crankcase bearing (drive-side)	25 x 62 17 mm
Crankcase bearing (timing-side)	25 x 62 x 17 mm
Crankcase diameter (drive-side and timing side)	0.9841–0.9844 in. (24.9961–22.0038 mm)
Gearbox layshaft bearings (drive-side and timing side)	0.5 x 0.625 x 0.8125 in .(12.7 x 15.875 x 20.6375 mm)
Gearbox layshaft diameter (drive-side and timing side)	0.6245–0.625 in. (15.8623–15.8750 mm)
Gearbox mainshaft bearing (drive-side)	30 x 62 x 16 mm
Gearbox mainshaft bearing (timing-side)	0.625 x 1.5625 x 0.4375 in. (15.875 x 39.2875 x 11.1125 mm)
Gearbox mainshaft diameter (drive-side)	0.7485–0.749 in. (19.0119–19.0246 mm)
Gearbox mainshaft diameter (timing-side)	0.6245–0.625 in. (15.8623–15.8750 mm)
Gearbox sleeve pinion (internal diameter)	0.752–0.753 in. (19.1008–19.1262 mm)
Gearbox sleeve pinion (external diameter)	1.179–1.180 in. (29.9466–29.9720 mm)
Piston pin diameter	0.6882–0.6885 in. (17.4803–17.4879 mm)

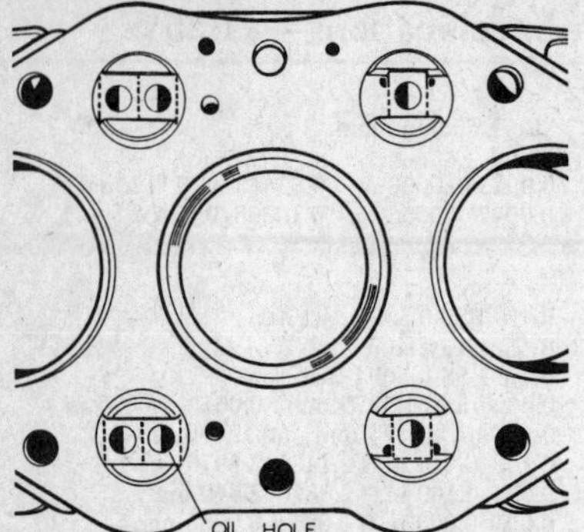

Correct cam follower positions (Trident)

4. Install the tappets in their original positions. Wrap a piece of tape around the top of each tappet stem to prevent it from falling into the crankcase as the cylinder is installed. Make sure that the oil holes in the tappet stems line up with the oil holes in the guide blocks, as shown.

5. Install a new cylinder base gasket on the crankcase flange. Stagger the end gaps of the piston rings 120° apart and oil the rings liberally. Bring the center piston up to top dead center and install a ring compressor. Slide the cylinder down over the piston. Raise the outside pistons as far as possible without accidentally pulling the center piston out of its bore. Install the outer pistons and seat the cylinder against the crankcase. Tighten the cylinder retaining nuts gradually, in the proper sequence, to 20-22 ft lbs.

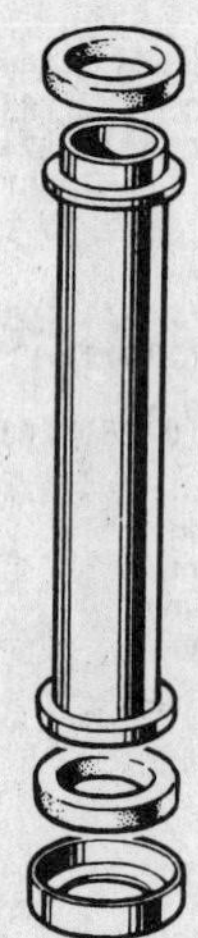
Pushrod tube assembly (Trident)

6. Remove the tape from the tappets and fit the pushrod tubes over the tappet guides. Make sure that the rubber seals at either end of the tubes are in good condition.

7. Install a new head gasket on the cylinder with the ribs facing down (toward the cylinder). Install the cylinder head carefully over the studs and onto the cylinder. Fit the four outer head bolts loosely. Insert the pushrods onto their tubes. Make sure that the pushrods line up evenly. *This is very important.*

8. Install the rocker boxes on the head using new gaskets. Coat only one side of the gaskets with cement. Make sure that the pushrods are properly seated in the rocker arms.

Engine and Transmission Specifications—TR25W (cont.)

CLUTCH	
Type	Multi-plate with integral cush drive
Number of plates:	
Driving (bonded segments)	4
Driven (plain)	5
Overall thickness of driving plate and segments	0.167 in. (4.242 mm)
Clutch springs	4
Free length of springs	1.65685 in. (42.0687 mm)
Clutch pushrod (length)	9.0 in. (228.6 mm)
Clutch pushrod (diameter)	0.1875 in. (4.7025 mm)

Engine Specifications—T100C and T100R

PISTONS		
Material	Aluminum alloy die casting	
Clearance:	*From H.49833*	*Before H.49833*
Top of skirt	0.0050–0.0072 in.	0.0075–0.0085 in.
Bottom of skirt	0.0030–0.0045 in.	0.002–0.003 in.
Piston pin hole diameter	0.6882–0.6886 in.	0.6882–0.6886 in.
PISTON RINGS		
Material	Cast iron	
Compression rings (taper faced):		
Width	0.0615–0.0625 in.	
Thickness	0.092–0.100 in.	
Fitted gap	0.010–0.014 in.	
Clearance in groove	0.001–0.003 in.	
Oil control ring:		
Width	0.124–0.125 in.	
Thickness	0.092–0.100 in.	
Fitted gap	0.010–0.014 in.	
Clearance in groove	0.0005–0.0025 in.	
VALVES		
Seat angle (included)	90°	
Head diameter:		
Inlet	1 17/32 in.	
Inlet (Before H.49833)	1 7/16 in.	
Exhaust	1 5/16 in.	
Stem diameter:		
Inlet	0.3095–0.3100 in.	
Exhaust	0.3090–0.3095 in.	
VALVE GUIDES		
Material	Hidural	
Bore diameter (Inlet and exhaust)	0.312–0.313 in.	
Outside diameter (Inlet and exhaust)	0.5005–0.5010 in.	
Length:		
Inlet	1¾ in.	
Exhaust	1¾ in.	
VALVE SPRINGS (Inner—Yellow, Outer—L/Blue Spot)	*Outer*	*Inner*
Free length	1½ in.	1 19/32 in.
Total number of coils	6	8¼
Total fitted load:		
Valve open	136 lbs	
Valve closed	63 lbs	
VALVE TIMING		
Set all tappet clearances at 0.020 in (0.5 mm) for checking:		
Inlet opens	34° before top center	
Inlet closes	55° after bottom center	
Exhaust opens	48° before bottom center	
Exhaust closes	27° after top center	
ROCKERS		
Material	High tensile steel forging	
Bore diameter	0.4375–0.4380 in.	
Rocker spindle diameter	0.4355–0.4360 in.	
Tappet clearance (cold):		
Inlet	0.002 in. (0.05 mm)	
Exhaust	0.004 in. (0.10 mm)	
TAPPETS		
Material	High tensile steel forging—Stellite Tip	
Tip radius	¾ in. (T100C), 1⅛ in. (T100R)	
Tappet diameter	0.3110–0.3115 in.	
Clearance in guide block	0.0005–0.0015 in.	
TAPPET GUIDE BLOCK		
Diameter of bores	0.3120–0.3125 in.	
Outside diameter	1.000–0.9995 in.	
Interference fit in cylinder block	0.0005–0.0015 in.	

Engine Specifications—T100C and T100R (cont.)

CAMSHAFTS	
Journal diameter:	
Left	0.8100–0.8105 in.
Diametrical clearance:	
Left	0.0010–0.0025 in.
End float	0.005–0.008 in.
Cam lift:	
Inlet	0.314 in.
Exhaust	0.296 in. (T100C), 0.314 in. (T100R)
Base circle diameter:	
Inlet and exhaust	0.812 in.
CAMSHAFT BEARING BUSHES	
Material	Steel-backed bronze
Bore diameter (fitted):	
Left	0.8125–0.8135 in.
Outside diameter:	
Left	0.906–0.907 in.
Length:	
Left inlet	1.114–1.094 in.
Left exhaust	0.922–0.942 in.
Interference fit in crankcase:	
Left	0.002–0.003 in.
TIMING GEARS	
Inlet and exhaust camshaft pinions:	
Number of teeth	50
Interference fit on camshaft	0.000–0.001
Intermediate timing gear:	
Number of teeth	42
Bore diameter	0.5618–0.5625
Intermediate timing gear bush:	
Material	Phosphor bronze
Outside diameter	0.5635–0.5640 in.
Bore diameter	0.4990–0.4995 in.
Length	0.6775–0.6825 in.
Working clearance on spindle	0.0005–0.0015 in.
Intermediate wheel spindle:	
Diameter	0.4980–0.4985 in.
Interference fit in crankcase	0.0005–0.0015 in.
Crankcase pinion:	
Number of teeth	25
Fit on crankcase	+0.0003 in. −0.0005 in.
CYLINDERS	
Material	Cast iron
Bore size	2.7160–2.7165 in.
Maximum oversize	2.7360–2.7365 in.
Tappet guide block housing diameter	0.9985–0.9990 in.
CYLINDER HEAD	
Material	DTD 424 Aluminum Alloy
Inlet port size	1 in. dia (T100C), 1 1/16 in. dia. (T100R)
Exhaust port size	1¼ in. dia.
Valve seatings:	
Type	Cast-in
Material	Cast iron
CRANKSHAFT	
Type	Forged two-throw crank with bolt-on flywheel
Left main bearing size and type	72 x 30 x 19 mm. Ball Journal
Right crankshaft main-bearing journal diameter	1.4375–1.4380 in.
Right main-bearing more, size, and type	1.4390–1.4385 in. Steel-backed copper lead-lined bush Under sizes available: −0.010 in. −0.020 in., −0.030 in.
Left main bearing housing diameter	2.8321–2.8336 in.
Right main bearing housing diameter	1.8135–1.8140 in.
Big-end journal diameter	1.4375–1.4380 in.
Min. regrind diameter	1.4075–1.4080 in.
Crankshaft end float	0.008–0.017 in.
CONNECTING RODS	
Material	Alloy 'H' Secton RR .56
Length (Centers)	5.311–5.313 in.
Big-end bearings type	Steel-backed white metal
Bearing side clearance	0.013–0.017 in.
Bearing diametrical clearance	0.005–0.0020 in. minimum
PISTON PIN	
Material	High tensile steel
Fit in small end bush	0.0005–0.0012 in.
Diameter	0.6882–0.6885 in.
Length	2.151–2.156 in.
SMALL-END BUSHING	
Material	Phosphor Bronze
Outer diameter	0.782–0.783 in.
Length	0.890–0.910 in.
Finished bore diameter	0.6905–0.6910 in.

9. Install the remaining eight, cylinder head bolts and tighten all twelve nuts and bolts evenly, in the sequence shown, to 18 ft lbs. Refit the remaining rocker box mounting bolts and nuts.

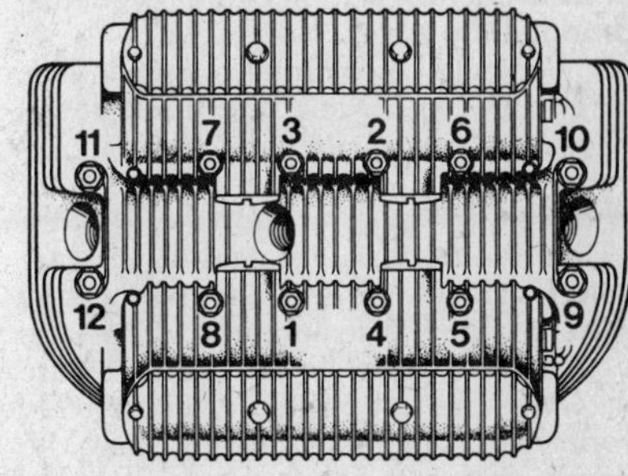

Cylinder head bolt tightening sequence

10. Reconnect the rocker oil lines using new copper washers. Install the top engine mount and exhaust headerpipes. Install the carburetors on the head and connect the throttle and choke cables. Bolt the oil cooler onto the frame, taking care to install the rubber bushings correctly, and connect the oil lines. Install the fuel tank.

Clutch

DISASSEMBLY

1. Drain the oil from the primary chaincase.
2. Take out the four screws and remove the clutch inspection cover. Unscrew the large locknut and the adjuster nut from the end of the clutch release rod.
3. Back off the primary chain adjuster, remove the fourteen screws, and pull off the primary cover. Note that the screws are of different lengths; they must be replaced in their original positions.
4. Bend back the locktab, install oil seal protector 61-6051, and unscrew the engine sprocket retaining nut. Remove the transmission sprocket (clutch hub), retaining nut and pull both sprockets off together using Triumph tools D1860 and 61-6046—or suitable gear pullers.

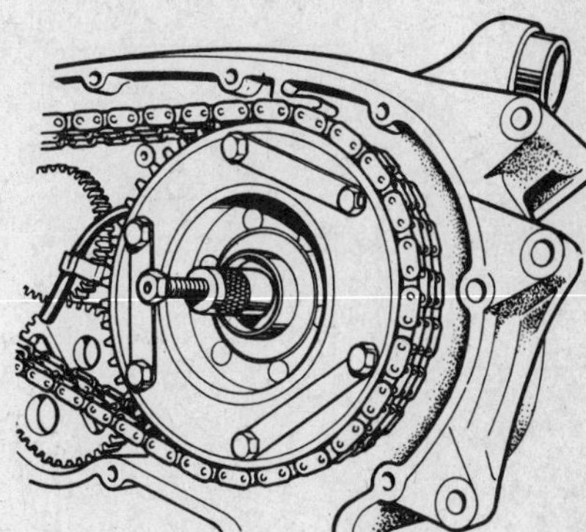

Removing the clutch hub

5. To remove the inner crankcase (clutch) cover, first take out the screws and bolts that secure the cover, noting their positions to facilitate reassembly. Pull off the inner cover, taking care not to damage or lose the oil pump O-rings.
6. Take off the spacer and pull the

clutch unit off the shaft.

7. Mark the relative positions of the clutch cover, drive plate, and pressure plate. Bend back the locktabs on the twelve cover bolts and loosen the bolts gradually, a turn at a time, to prevent distortion of the cover.

8. Separate the clutch components, taking care not to lose the three dowel pins in the cover.

INSPECTION

Examine the drive plate and pressure plate for cracks, scoring, and overheating (extreme blue discoloration). Check to see that the drive plate slots and pressure plate tabs are not broken or excessively worn. The diaphram spring may be reused unless it shows signs of being overheated, in which case it may have been weakened. If the bearing is worn and/or the oil seal damaged, replace both components.

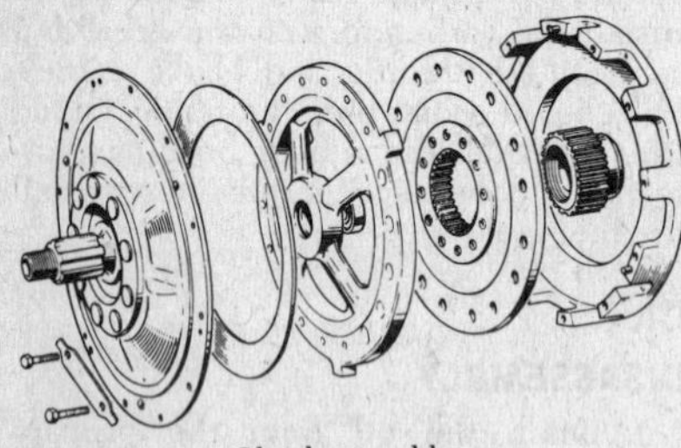

Clutch assembly

ASSEMBLY

1. Apply a small amount of high temperature grease to the sides of the three pressure plate tabs and assemble the pressure plate, disc, and drive plate (aligning the positioning marks).
2. Apply a small amount of grease to the machined ridge on the pressure plate and install the diaphram on the ridge with the outer edge of the spring upward.
3. Lightly grease the ridge inside the cover and install the cover (in alignment with the drive plate and pressure plate positioning marks) and install the twelve bolts using new locktabs. Tighten finger-tight only.

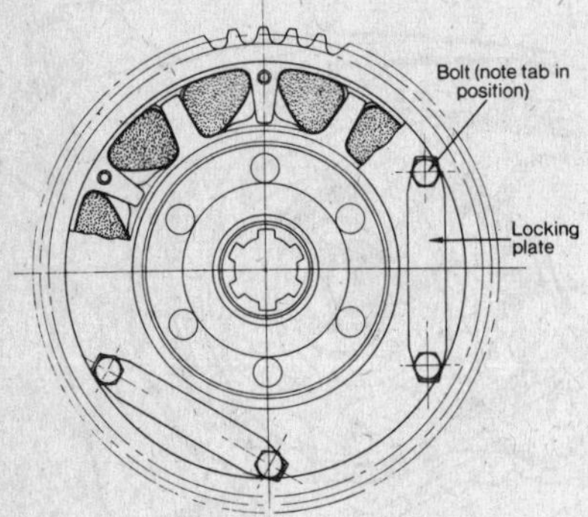

Late type shock absorber rubbers

4. Install a centering tool from the rear of the clutch and tighten the twelve bolts one-half turn at a time, working around the cover, until the cover meets the drive plate. Fully tighten the bolts and lock them with the locktabs.

Clutch and Transmission Specifications—T100C and T100R

CLUTCH	
Type	Multiplate with integral shock absorber
Number of plates:	
Driving (bonded)	6
Driven (plain)	6
Pressure Springs:	
Number	3
Free-length	$1\frac{31}{32}$ in.
Number of working coils	$9\frac{1}{2}$
Spring rate	$58\frac{1}{2}$ lbs/in.
Approximate fitted load	42 lbs
Bearing rollers:	
Number	20
Diameter	0.2495–0.2500 in.
Length	0.231–0.236 in.
Clutch hub bearing diameter	1.37–1.3743 in.
Clutch sprocket bore diameter	1.0745–1.0755 in.
Thrust washer thickness	0.052–0.054 in.
Engine sprocket teeth	26
Clutch sprocket teeth	58
Chain details	Duplex endless—$\frac{3}{8}$ in. pitch x 78 links
CLUTCH OPERATING MECHANISM	
Conical spring:	
Number of working coils	2
Free length	$\frac{13}{32}$ in.
Diameter of balls	$\frac{3}{8}$ in.
Clutch operating rod:	
Diameter of rod	$\frac{3}{16}$ in.
Length of rod	9.562–9.567 in.
RATIOS	
Internal ratios (Std)	
4th (Top)	1.00 : 1
3rd	1.22 : 1
2nd	1.61 : 1
1st (Bottom)	2.47 : 1
Overall ratios:	
4th (Top)	5.70
3rd	6.95
2nd	9.18
1st (Bottom)	14.09
Engine rpm @ 10 mph in 4th (Top) gear	763
Gearbox sprocket teeth	18
GEARS	
Mainshaft high gear:	
Bore diameter (Bush fitted)	0.7520–0.7530 in.
Working clearance on shaft	0.0020–0.0035 in.
Bush length	$2\frac{19}{32}$ in.
Bush protrusion length	$\frac{3}{8}$ in. (nil after H.57083)
GEARS	
Layshaft low gear:	
Bore diameter (bush fitted)	0.689–0.690 in.
Working clearance on shaft	0.0015–0.003 in.
GEARBOX SHAFTS	
Mainshaft:	
Left end diameter	0.7495–0.7500 in.
Right end diameter	0.6685–0.6689 in.
Length	$9\frac{1}{64}$ in.
Length (before H.49833)	$8\frac{51}{64}$ in.
Layshaft:	
Left-end diameter	0.6845–0.6850 in.
Right-end diameter	0.6870–0.6875 in.
Length	$5\frac{3}{8}$ in.
Camplate plunger spring:	
Free-length	$2\frac{1}{2}$
Number of working coils	22
Spring rate	5–6 lbs/in.
BEARINGS	
High gear bearing	30 x 62 x 16 mm Ball journal
Mainshaft bearing	17 x 47 x 14 mm Ball journal
Layshaft bearing (left)	$\frac{11}{16}$ x $\frac{7}{8}$ x $\frac{3}{4}$ in. Needle roller
Layshaft bearing (right)	$\frac{5}{8}$ x $\frac{13}{16}$ x $\frac{3}{4}$ in. Needle roller
KICK-START OPERATING MECHANISM	
Ratchet spring free-length	$\frac{1}{2}$ in.
GEARCHANGE MECHANISM	
Plungers:	
Outer diameter	0.3402–0.3412 in.
Working clearance in bore	0.0015–0.0035 in.
Plunger springs:	
Number of working coils	16
Free-length	$1\frac{1}{16}$ in.
Outer bush bore diameter	0.623–0.624 in.
Clearance on shaft	0.001–0.003 in.
Quadrant return springs:	
Number of working coils	18
Free-length	$1\frac{7}{8}$ in.

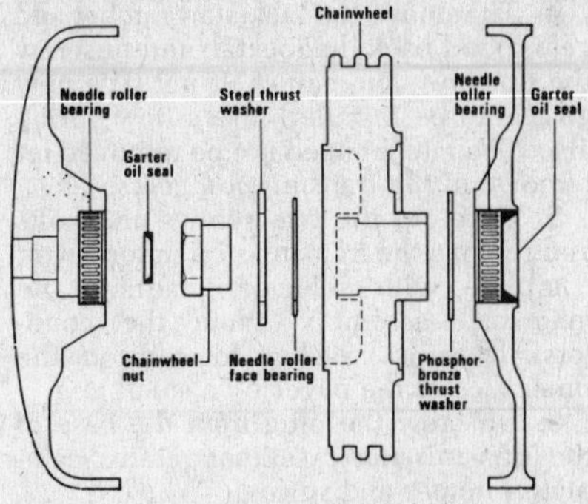

Clutch assembly order

5. Remove the centering tool, install the release rod, lightly grease the disc splines, and install the clutch on the engine.

6. Install the oil pump O-rings and check the clutch hub needle bearing for excessive play. Check the oil seal and replace if worn or deformed.

7. Apply gasket-sealing compound to the crankcase and inner cover mating surfaces. Install the cover on the crankcase using a new gasket, and tighten the screws evenly.

8. Install the twelve damper rubbers and then the outer plate. Apply thread-lock compound to the six plate-retaining screws.

NOTE: *Later models use six bolts with locktabs and a modified plate. If the screws on earlier models were found to be in need of replacement, replace the screws and plate with the later components.*

9. Install the thrust washer on the back of the damper hub, fit the primary chain over the sprockets, and install the sprockets, on the shafts. Tighten the crankshaft sprocket nut to 60 ft lbs and lock in position with the locktab. Install the spacer and tighten the mainshaft sprocket nut to 60 ft lbs.

10. Install the thrust bearing and replace the primary cover using gasket cement and a new gasket.

11. Adjust primary chain tension.

12. Install the large clutch adjusting nut, taking care not to damage the oil seal on the release rod threads. Insert an 0.005 in. feeler gauge between the bearing and large nut, and tighten the small locknut while holding the release rod from turning. Refill the primary chaincase with oil and check the clutch for correct operation.

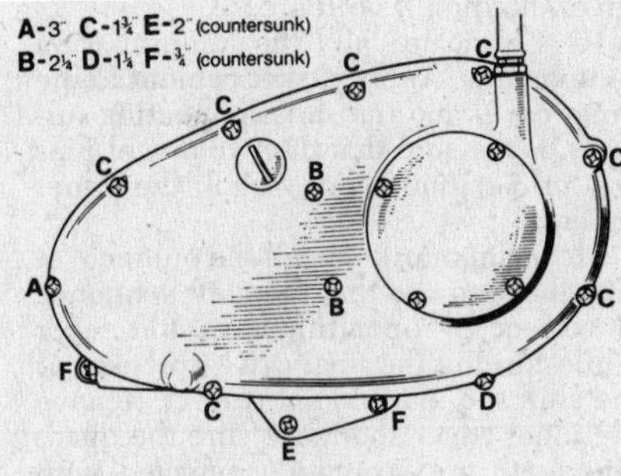

Primary chaincase screws

Engine Specifications—TR6R, TR6C, and T120R

PISTONS		
Clearance:		
Top of skirt	0.0106–0.0085 in.	
Bottom of skirt	0.0061–0.0046 in.	
Piston pin hole diameter	0.6882–0.6886 in.	
PISTON RINGS		
Material	Cast iron	
Compression rings (tapered):		
Width	0.0615–0.0625 in.	
Thickness	0.092–0.100 in.	
Fitted gap	0.010–0.014 in.	
Clearance in groove	0.001–0.003 in.	
Oil control ring:		
Width	0.092–0.100 in.	
Thickness	0.124–0.125 in.	
Fitted gap	0.010–0.014 in.	
Clearance in groove	0.0005–0.0025 in.	
VALVES		
Stem diameter:		
Intake	0.3095–0.3100 in.	
Exhaust	0.3090–0.3095 in.	
Head diameter:		
Intake	1.592–1.596 in.	
Exhaust	1.434–1.440 in.	
Exhaust valve material	21–4NS	
VALVE GUIDES		
Material	Aluminum-bronze	
Bore diameter (Inlet and exhaust)	0.3127–0.3137 in.	
Outside diameter (Inlet and exhaust)	0.5005–0.5010 in.	
Length:		
Inlet	$1\frac{31}{32}$ in.	
Exhaust	$1\frac{11}{64}$ in.	
VALVE SPRINGS (RED SPOT INNER, GREEN SPOT OUTER)		
	Outer	*Inner*
Free-length	$1\frac{1}{2}$ in.	$1\frac{17}{32}$
Number of coils	$5\frac{1}{2}$	$7\frac{1}{4}$
Total fitted load:	*Intake*	*Exhaust*
Valve open	143 lbs	155 lbs
Valve closed	75 lbs	87 lbs
Fitted length (valve closed):		
Inner	$1\frac{3}{16}$ in.	$1\frac{1}{8}$ in.
Outer	$1\frac{7}{32}$ in.	$1\frac{5}{32}$ in.
ROCKERS		
Material	High tensile steel forging	
Bore diameter	0.5002–0.5012 in.	
Rocker spindle diameter	0.4990–0.4995 in.	
Tappet clearance (cold):		
Inlet	0.002 in. (0.05 mm)	
Exhaust	0.004 in. (0.10 mm)	
CAMSHAFTS		
Journal diameter:		
Left	0.8100–0.8105 in.	
Right	0.8730–0.8735 in.	
Diametrical clearance:		
Left	0.0010–0.0025 in.	
Right	0.0005–0.0020 in.	
End float	0.013–0.020 in.	
Cam lift: Inlet and exhaust	0.314 in.	
Base circle diameter	0.812 in.	

Primary Drive Service

Follow steps 1-4, above, for clutch disassembly. Inspect the sprockets for worn and broken teeth. If the sprockets are to be replaced, the chain should be replaced also or else the new sprockets will be ruined in a short time.

Transmission Countershaft Sprocket

1. Remove the small clutch hub and clutch housing.

2. Remove the clutch hub retaining nut and pull the hub using a suitable gear puller.

3. Remove the clutch housing from the crankcase. Check the oil seal for wear and distortion, and replace if necessary. Unscrew the sprocket nut and then remove the final, drive-chain master link. Pull the sprocket off the shaft.

4. To replace the sprocket, install it on the shaft using hardening gasket cement on the sleeve gear splines to prevent oil from leaking between the sprocket and sleeve gear.

5. The remainder of installation is in reverse order of removal.

Gearbox, Shifter, and Kick-Starter, Mechanisms

4-SPEED

Disassembly

1. Drain the primary chaincase and transmission.

2. Remove the clutch.

3. Take out the five screws and the acorn nut, and remove the transmission outer cover complete with kick-start assembly and shifter mechanism. The kick-start half-gear is a press fit onto the shaft. If the return spring is to be replaced, load it $1\frac{1}{4}$ turns before slipping the hook over the dowel pin. The kick-start seal is accessible after the kick-start lever is removed.

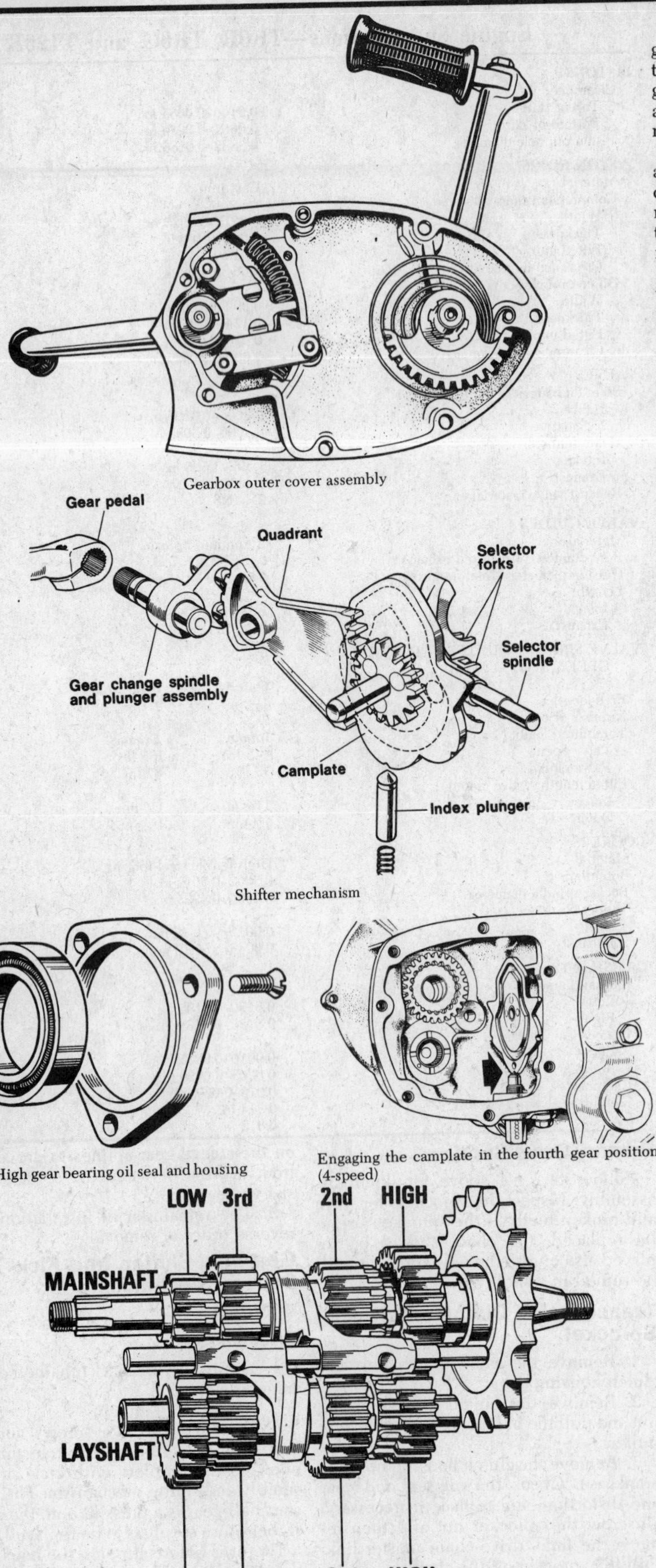

Gearbox outer cover assembly

Shifter mechanism

High gear bearing oil seal and housing

Engaging the camplate in the fourth gear position (4-speed)

Gearbox components

4. To remove the kick-start ratchet and gear, bend back the locktab and unscrew the transmission mainshaft nut. If a new gear is to be installed, use a new spring also. The ratchet need not be removed for removal of the transmission gears.

5. Take out the two screws and bolts and remove the transmission inner cover, complete with selector quadrant and mainshaft assembly. Note the countershaft thrust washer located on the inner face of the cover by a small peg.

6. Unscrew the plug from the base of the transmission case that retains camplate plunger and spring.

7. Pull out the shift fork shaft and remove the countershaft first gear. Remove the sliding gears and selector forks from the case.

8. Pull the countershaft assembly out of the case and then remove the shift camplate. The countershaft top gear or sleeve pinion is attached to the final drive sprocket by a large nut.

Assembly

1. Install the high gear into the bearing and then the final drive sprocket into the case.

2. Lubricate and install the camplate shaft into the case.

3. Install the camplate plunger and spring, with retaining plug, under the transmission case, and the fiber washer.

4. Set the camplate with the plunger located in the high gear notch. Install the the thrust washer over the inner needle bearing. The grooved surface of the washer should face the countershaft. The washer can be held in place with grease.

5. Lubricate the components and assemble the countershaft and mainshaft gear clusters.

6. Place the camplate rollers on the shift forks, holding them in position with grease. Install the shift forks in their respective gears. The fork with the smaller radius is for the mainshaft cluster.

7. Install the mainshaft and countershaft gears, align the gears so that the shift fork rollers are located in the camplate tracks, and align the shift fork bores as closely as possible.

8. Lubricate the fork shaft and install it through the forks, shouldered end first, until it is fully engaged in the case. (The mainshaft shift fork should be at the innermost position).

9. Make sure the camplate quadrant is able to move freely in the inner cover. Position the countershaft thrust washer over the needle bearing in the inner cover, holding it with grease.

10. Lubricate all the transmission components. Apply gasket cement to the inner cover and transmission mating surfaces, make sure that the two dowel pins are in position, and install the inner cover.

11. Temporarily install the outer cover and check to see that the shift sequence is correct by operating the shift lever while turning the final drive sprocket. If the shift sequence is not correct, remove the inner cover and make sure the quadrant teeth are accurately engaged with the camplate gear. When reinstalling the inner cover, sure the top of the first tooth

is on the centerline of the mainshaft.

12. Reassemble the kick-shaft ratchet and gear, tightening the nut 40–45 ft lbs. To facilitate this, install the final drive chain, put the transmission in gear, and apply the rear brake.

13. Install the outer cover using gasket cement on both mating surfaces.

14. Install the clutch.

5-SPEED

The Trident T150V (5-speed) utilizes a transmission which is quite similar to the 5-speed found in the TR7V and T140V. For service procedures, refer to the earlier section dealing with the transmission for the 750 Twins.

One difference between the 750 Twin transmission and that for the T150V is that the latter has a high gear bearing oil seal which is found in a housing secured by three screws.

Engine Specifications—TR6R, TR6C, and T120R (cont.)

TAPPETS	
Material	High tensile steel body—Stellite tip
Tip radius	1.125 in.
Tappet diameter	0.3110–0.3115 in.
Clearance in guide block	0.0005–0.0015 in.
TAPPET GUIDE BLOCK	
Diameter of bores	0.3120–0.3125 in.
Outside diameter	1.000–0.9995 in.
Interference fit in cylinder block	0.0005–0.0015 in.
CAMSHAFT BEARING BUSHES	
Material	High density sintered bronze
Bore diameter (fitted):	
Left	0.8125–0.8135 in.
Right	0.874–0.875 in.
Outside diameter:	
Left	1.0010–1.0015 in.
Right	1.126–1.127 in.
Length:	
Left inlet	1.104–1.114 in.
CAMSHAFT BEARING BUSHES	
Left exhaust	0.932–0.942 in.
Right inlet and exhaust	1.010–1.020 in.
Interference fit in crankcase:	
Left	0.001–0.002 in.
Right	0.0010–0.0025 in.
TIMING GEARS	
Inlet and exhaust camshaft pinions:	
Number of teeth	50
Interference fit on camshaft	0.000–0.001 in.
Intermediate timing gear:	
Number of teeth	47
Bore diameter	0.5618–0.5625 in.
Intermediate timing gear bush:	
Material	Phosphor bronze
Outside diameter	0.5635–0.5640 in.
Bore diameter	0.4990–0.4995 in.
Length	0.6775–0.6825 in.
Working clearance on spindle	0.0005–0.0015 in.
Intermediate wheel spindle:	
Diameter	0.4980–0.4985 in.
Interference fit in crankcase	0.0005–0.0015 in.
Crankshaft pinion:	
Number of teeth	25
Fit on crankshaft	+0.0003/−0.0005 in.
CYLINDER BLOCK	
Material	Cast iron
Bore size	2.7984–2.7953 in.
Maximum oversize	2.8348–2.8353 in.
Tappet guide block housing diameter	0.9990–0.9985 in.
CYLINDER HEAD	
Material	D.T.D. 424 Aluminum
Inlet port size	$1\frac{3}{16}$ in. dia tapering to $1\frac{1}{8}$ in.
Exhaust port size	$1\frac{3}{8}$ in. dia
Valve seating:	
Type	Cast-in
Material	Cast iron
CRANKSHAFT	
Crankshaft type	Forged two-throw crank with bolt-on flywheel Located by the timing side main bearing
Main bearing (drive-side) size and type	$2\frac{13}{16}$ x $1\frac{1}{8}$ x $\frac{13}{16}$ in. Ball Journal
Main Bearing (timing side) size and type	$2\frac{13}{16}$ x $1\frac{1}{8}$ x $\frac{13}{16}$ in. Ball Journal
Main bearing journal diameter	1.1247–1.1250 in.
Main bearing housing diameter	2.8095–2.8110 in.
Big-end journal diameter	1.6235–1.6240 in.
Minimum regrind diameter	1.6035–1.6040 in.
Crankshaft end float	0.003–0.017 in.
Balance factor	85 per cent (using 689 gramme weights)
CONNECTING RODS	
Length (centers)	6.499–6.501 in.
Big-end bearings—type	Steel-backed white metal
Bearing side clearance	0.012–0.016 in.
Bearing diametrical clearance	0.0005–0.0020 in.

Bottom End

DISASSEMBLY

1. Drain the oil from the crankcase, transmission, and primary drive. Remove the engine.

2. Remove the cylinder head, barrel, and pistons.

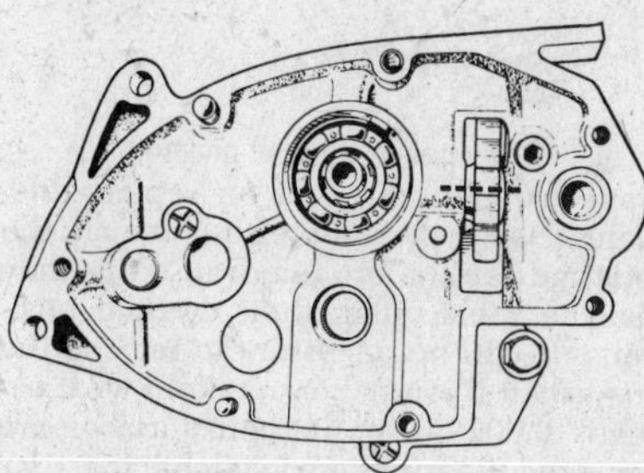

Inner cover installed with quadrant aligned

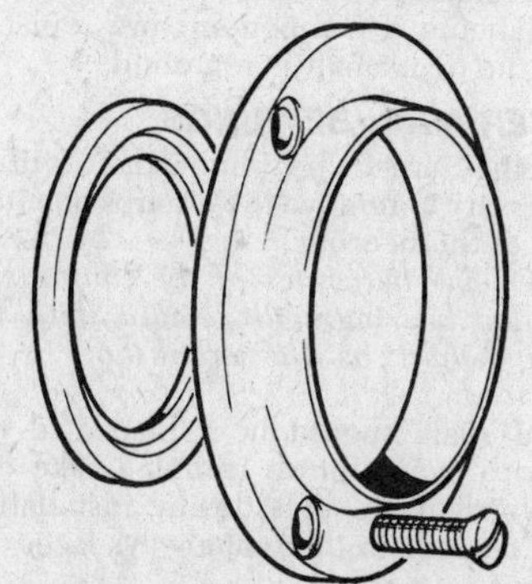

Mainshaft high gear oil seal and housing (5-speed)

3. Remove the primary drive and clutch assembly.

4. Remove the transmission gear cluster.

5. Remove the ignition points cover. Scribe a line on the breaker plate housing to facilitate reassembly, take out the three bolts, and remove the breaker plate assembly. Unscrew the bolt in the center of the breaker cam and remove the ignition advance unit with tool no. D782, or by screwing in a bolt that fits the threads in the cam until the advance unit is broken loose.

6. Take out the screws and remove the timing gear cover (right crankcase cover).

7. Unscrew the three nuts and pull the alternator stator off the studs. Unscrew the cable sleeve nut (covered by a rubber grommet) and pull the cable through.

8. Bend back the locktab and unscrew the alternator rotor retaining nut. Pull the rotor off the shaft, leaving the key in place to prevent the crankshaft timing gear from turning.

9. Before removing the timing gears, take note of the marks on the gear teeth that will line up if the gears are installed correctly. Pull the crankshaft pinion off using tool no. 61-6019 or a suitable gear puller.

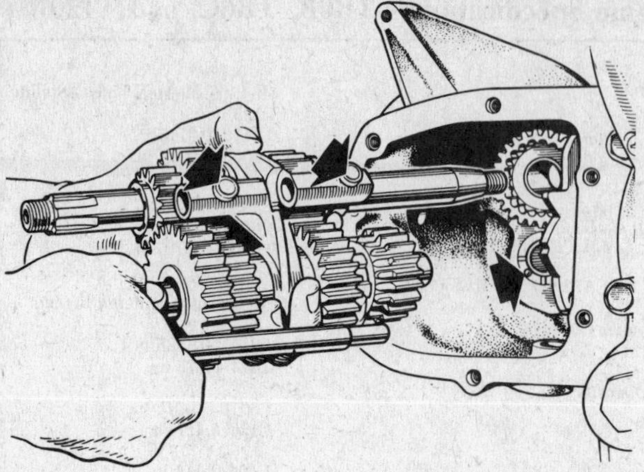
Installing the gearbox components

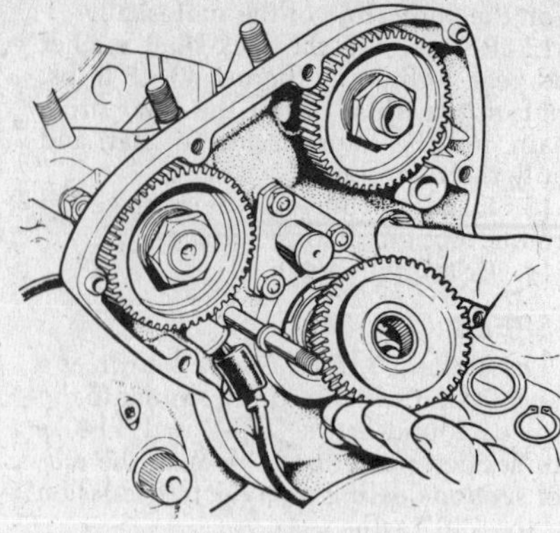
Removing the idler timing gear

10. Remove the circlip and pull off the idler (center) timing gear and its thrust washer.

11. To unscrew the two camshaft, timing-gear retaining nuts, it will be necessary to lock the crankshaft in position by inserting a bar through two of the connecting rods. Take care not to damage the crankcase. Unscrew the nuts, *which have left-hand threads,* and pull off the camshaft timing gears using tool no. D2213 or a suitable gear puller. Remove the woodruff keys.

12. Take out the three bolts and remove the tachometer drive which is located just above the front engine mount.

13. Remove the oil filter from the bottom of the crankcase, held in place by a large brass plug.

14. To separate the crankcases, first take out the hex bolts, allen bolt, and the six nuts from the timing side crankcase as shown in the illustration.

15. Next, remove the hex-head bolts from the drive-side crankcase. Tap off the drive-side crankcase using a soft metal drift. Place the drift against the lug at the rear of the case.

CAM SHAFTS

Withdraw the camshafts from the timing side crankcase and examine the lobes for wear and damage. Examine the tachometer drive gear on the exhaust camshaft for broken or worn teeth. Replace the camshafts if they do not appear to be in perfect condition.

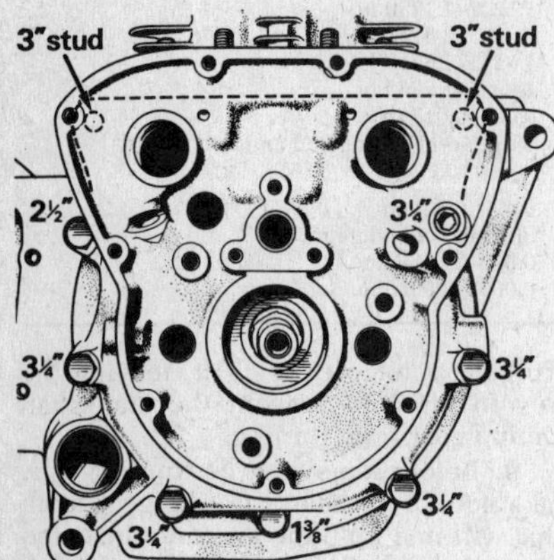

Right case securing bolts

Kickstarter return spring installation

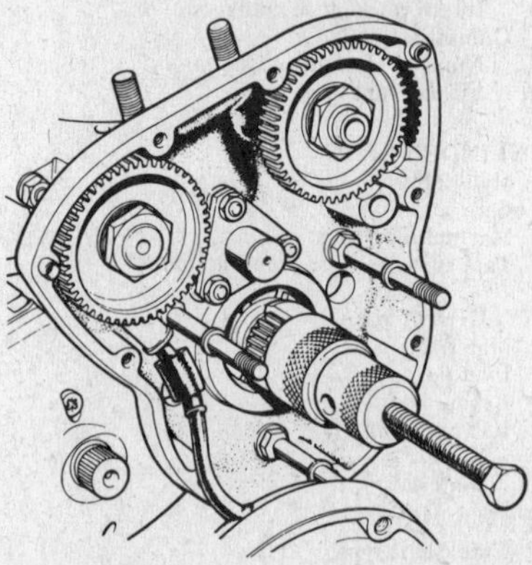
Removing the crankshaft pinion

CRANKSHAFT REMOVAL

1. Remove the retaining screws from the two small oil lines on top of the main bearing journal caps, pull the lines up, turn them away from the caps, and push them down and out of the crankcase.

2. Remove the locknuts from the main bearing caps. To remove the caps, screw the oil line screws, with washers, back into them and pry the caps off the studs with levers.

3. The crankshaft assembly can now be removed.

CENTER MAIN BEARINGS AND CONNECTING ROD BEARINGS

The crankpins and the two center crankshaft journals run on replaceable, plain bearing inserts. Be sure to mark the rods and caps before removal so that they may be replaced in their original positions. It will be necessary to regrind the crankshaft if journal or crankpin wear exceeds 0.002 in. or if their surfaces are damaged. Bearings are available in 0.010, 0.020, 0.030, and 0.040 in. undersizes. The crankshaft assembly will *not* require rebalancing if components are replaced or if the crankshaft is reground.

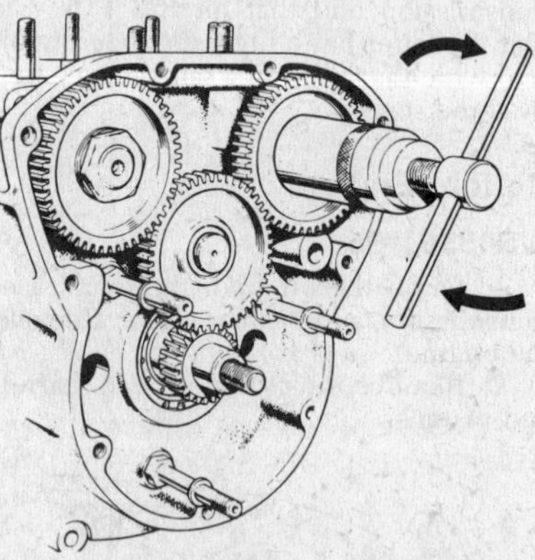
Removing the camshaft pinions

OUTER MAIN BEARINGS

If they are to be removed, it will be necessary to remove the circlips on either side of the bearing.

NOTE: *The center of the timing side roller bearing will remain with the crankshaft as the crankshaft is removed.*

Oil seals should be replaced at this time to avoid future trouble. Take care not to damage seals during installation. The flat side of the seal always faces outside.

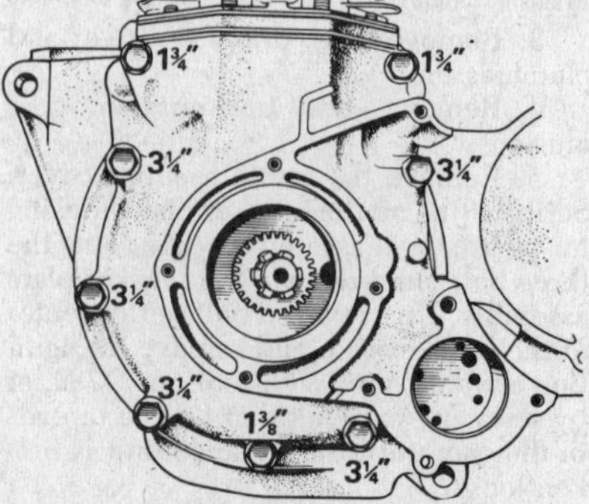

Left case securing bolts

ASSEMBLY

1. Fit the rod and main bearing inserts into their seats and lubricate them with fresh engine oil. Install the connecting rods and caps in their original positions and tighten the nuts to 18 ft lbs. Use new nuts if possible. Make sure that all components are completely clean and well lubricated during assembly.

2. Place the crankshaft in position in the crankcase, with the splined end on the drive side. Install the main bearing caps, making sure that the marks on the caps and lower bearing seats correspond. Install the washers and nuts (new nuts should be used) and tighten to 18 ft lbs. Check to see that the crankshaft is free to rotate easily. If it will not, switch the main bearing inserts around, make sure they are seated properly and re-oil them. Too tight a fit will require turning down the crankshaft journals slightly.

3. Install new rubber seals for the tappet oil lines (connecting at the main bearing caps) and install the lines as removed, taking care not to damage the seals.

4. Replace the oil filter O-rings in the center crankcase.

5. Apply a thin coat of gasket cement to the crankcase mating surfaces and install the crankcases (with the camshafts installed in the turning side case) in reverse order of removal. Take care to avoid damaging tappet oil lines with the exhaust camshaft as the turning side case is installed. Tighten the nuts and bolts evenly to 15 ft lbs.

6. Check that the crankshaft and camshafts are free to rotate freely. If not, alignment is incorrect somewhere and must be corrected.

7. Install the crankshaft spacer on the timing side and then install the special key and crankshaft timing gear (with the mark facing out).

8. Install the camshaft timing gears with the no. 1 keyway (in line with the timing mark) located on the key in the shaft, and with the timing marks facing out. Install and tighten the left-handed-threaded retaining nuts.

9. Install the idler timing gear, aligning the timing marks as shown.

10. Install the alternator rotor, tightening the nut to 50 ft lbs. Install the stator and tighten the nuts to 8 ft lbs.

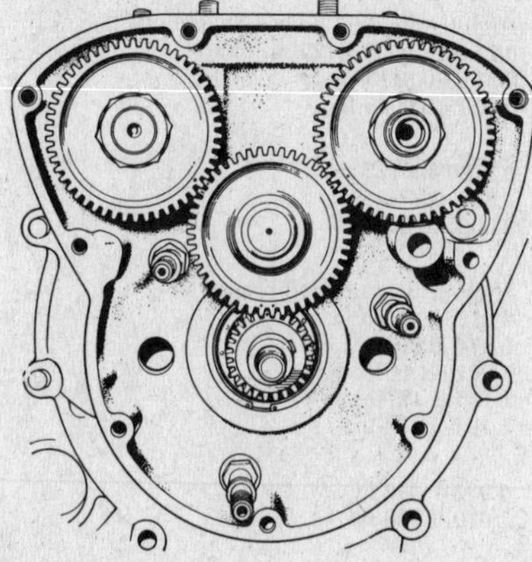

Timing gear marks properly aligned

Engine Specifications—TR6R, TR6C, and T120R (cont.)

PISTON PIN	
Material	High tensile steel
Fit in small-end bush	0.0005–0.0012 in. clearance
Diameter	0.6882–0.6885 in.
Length	2.151–2.156 in.
SMALL END BUSHING	
Material	Phosphor bronze
Outer diameter	0.8140–0.8145 in.
Length	1.030–1.031 in.
Finished bore diameter	0.6890–0.6894 in.

Clutch and Transmission Specifications—TR6R, TR6C, and T120R

CLUTCH	
Type	Multiplate with integral shock absorber
Number of plates:	
Driving (bonded)	6
Driven (plain)	6
Pressure springs:	
Number	3
Free-length	1$^{13}/_{16}$ in.
Number of working coils	9½
Spring rate	113 lbs/in.
Approximate fitted load	62 lbs
Bearing rollers:	
Number	20
Diameter	0.2495–0.2500 in.
Length	0.231–0.236 in.
Clutch hub bearing diameter	1.3733–1.3743 in.
Clutch sprocket bore diameter	1.8745–1.8755 in.
Thrust washer thickness	0.052–0.054 in.
Engine sprocket teeth	29
Clutch sprocket teeth	58
Chain details	Duplex endless—⅜ in. pitch x 84 links
CLUTCH OPERATING MECHANISM	
Conical spring:	
Number of working coils	2
Free-length	$^{13}/_{32}$ in.
Diameter of balls	⅜ in.
Clutch operating rod:	
Diameter of rod	$^{7}/_{32}$ in.
Length of rod	11.822–11.812 in.
GEARS	
Mainshaft high gear:	
Bore diameter (bush fitted)	0.8135–0.8145 in.
Working clearance on shaft	0.0032–0.0047 in.
Bush length	2$^{19}/_{32}$ in.
Layshaft low gear:	
Bore diameter (bush fitted)	0.8135–0.8145 in.
Working clearance on shaft	0.0025–0.0045 in.
GEARBOX SHAFTS	
Mainshaft:	
Left end diameter	0.8098–0.8103 in.
Right end diameter	0.7494–0.7498 in.
Length	11$^{19}/_{64}$ in.
Layshaft:	
Left end diameter	0.6845–0.6850 in.
Right end diameter	0.6845–0.6850 in.
Length	6$^{31}/_{64}$ in.
Camplate plunger spring:	
Free-length	2½ in.
Number of working coils	22
Spring rate	5–6 lb/in.
BEARINGS	
High gear bearing	1¼ x 2½ x ⅝ in. Ball Journal
Mainshaft bearing	¾ x 1⅞ x $^{9}/_{16}$ in. Ball Journal
Layshaft bearing (right and left)	$^{11}/_{16}$ x ⅞ x ¾ in. Needle Roller
KICK START OPERATING MECHANISM	
Bush bore diameter	0.751–0.752 in.
Spindle working clearance in bush	0.003–0.005 in.
Ratchet spring free-length	½ in.
GEARCHANGE MECHANISM	
Plungers:	
Outer diameter	0.4315–0.4320 in.
Working clearance in bore	0.0005–0.0015 in.
GEARCHANGE MECHANISM	
Plunger springs:	
Number of working coils	12
Free-length	1¼ in.
Inner bush bore diameter	0.6245–0.6255 in.
Clearance on shaft	0.0007–0.0032 in.
Outer bush bore diameter:	0.7495–0.7505 in.
Clearance on shaft	0.0005–0.0025 in.
Quadrant return springs:	
Number of working coils	9½
Free-length	1¾ in.

Replacement Piston and Suitable Bore Sizes

500

Piston Marking in. (mm)	Bore (in.)	Bore (mm)
Standard	2.716	60.000
+0.010 (0.254)	2.726	69.254
+0.020 (0.508)	2.736	69.508
+0.040 (1.016)	2.756	70.000

650

Piston Marking in.(mm)	Suitable Bore Sizes (in.)	Suitable Bore Sizes (mm)
Standard	2.7948 2.7953	70.993 71.006
Oversizes		
+0.010 (0.254)	2.8048 2.8053	71.247 71.260
+0.020 (0.508)	2.8148 2.8153	71.501 71.514
+0.040 (1.016)	2.8348 2.8353	72.009 72.022

750—2

Piston Marking in. (mm)	Suitable Bore Sizes (in.)	Suitable Bore Sizes (mm)
Standard (L, M, H)	see "Cylinder and Piston Grading"	
+0.010 (0.254)	3.0010– 3.0021	76.2254– 76.2533
+0.020 (0.508)	3.0110– 3.0121	76.4794– 76.5073
+0.030 (0.726)	3.0210– 3.0221	76.7334– 76.7613
+0.040 (1.016)	3.0310– 3.0321	76.9514– 76.9793

750—3

Piston Size in. (mm)	Bore (in.)	Size (mm)
Standard	2.6368 2.6363	66.975 66.962
+0.010 (0.254)	2.6468 2.6463	67.229 67.215
+0.020 (0.508)	2.6568 2.6563	67.483 67.470
+0.040 (1.016)	2.6768 2.6763	67.990 67.980

Cylinder and Piston Grading

750—2

	"L"	"M"	"H"
Piston Diameter in.	2.9871– 2.9874	2.9875– 2.9878	2.9879– 2.9882
mm	75.872– 75.880	75.883– 75.890	75.893– 75.900
Cylinder Bore in.	2.9911– 2.9913	2.9914– 2.9917	2.9918– 2.9921
mm	75.973– 75.980	75.983– 75.990	75.993– 76.000

Engine Specifications—TR7V, T140V

PISTONS	
Material	Aluminum alloy die cast
Clearance	see piston grading chart
Top of Skirt	—
Bottom of Skirt	—
Piston pin hole diameter	0.7502–0.7504 in.
PISTON RINGS	
Material	cast iron
Compression rings (tapered)	
Width	0.113–0.121 in.
Thickness	0.0615–0.0625 in.
Fitted gap	0.008–0.013 in.
Clearance in groove	0.0015–0.0025 in.
Oil control ring	
Width	0.121 in.
Thickness	0.125 in.
Fitted gap	0.010–0.040 in.
Clearance in groove	0.0015–0.0025 in.
VALVES	
Stem diameter: Intake	0.3095–0.3100 in.
Exhaust	0.3090–0.3095 in.
Head diameter: Intake	1.592–1.596 in.
Exhaust	1.434–1.440 in.
Exhaust valve material	21/4NS
VALVE GUIDES	
Material	Aluminum-bronze
Bore diam. (Inlet & exhaust)	0.3127–0.3137 in.
Outside diameter (Inlet and exhaust)	0.5005–0.5010 in.
Length: Inlet	$1\frac{31}{32}$
Exhaust	$2\frac{11}{64}$
VALVE SPRINGS (Red spot inner, Green spot outer)	
Free-length	Out. $1\frac{1}{2}$ in. In. $1\frac{17}{32}$ in.
Number of coils	Out. $5\frac{1}{2}$ In. $7\frac{1}{4}$
Total fitted load	
Valve open	Int. 143 lbs. Ex. 155 lbs.
Valve closed	Int. 75 lbs. Ex. 87 lbs.
Fitted length (valve closed)	
Inner	$1\frac{3}{16}$ in. $1\frac{1}{8}$ in.
Outer	$1\frac{7}{32}$ in. $1\frac{5}{32}$ in.
ROCKERS	
Material	High tensile steel forging
Bore diameter	0.5002–0.5012 in.
Rocker spindle diameter	0.4990–0.4995 in.
Tappet clear. (cold): Inlet	0.008 in. (0.203 mm)
Exhaust	0.006 in. (0.15 mm)
CAMSHAFTS	
Journal diam.: Left	0.8100–0.8105 in.
Right	0.8730–0.8735 in.
Diametrical clear.: Left	0.0010–0.0025 in.
Right	0.0005–0.0020 in.
End float	0.013–0.020 in.
Cam lift: Inlet and exhaust	0.347 and 0.305 in.
Base circle diameter	0.812 in.
CRANKSHAFT	
Crankshaft type	Forged two-throw crank with bolt-on flywheel located by the timing side main bearing
Main bearing (drive side) size and type	$2\frac{13}{16}$ x $1\frac{1}{8}$ x $\frac{13}{16}$ in. roller bearing
Main bearing (timing side) size and type	72 x 30 x 19 mm ball race
Main bearing journal diameter (timing side)	1.1808–1.1812 in.
Main bearing journal diameter (drive side)	1.1247–1.250 in.
Main bearing housing diameter	2.8095–2.8110 in.
Big end journal diameter	1.6235–1.6240 in.
Minimum regrind diameter	1.6035–1.6040 in.
Crankshaft end float	0.003–0.017 in.
TAPPETS	
Material	High tensile steel body—Stellite tip
Tip radius	0.75 in. (In.); 1.125 in. (Ex.)
Tappet diameter	0.3110–0.3115 in.
Clearance in guide block	0.0005–0.0015 in.
TAPPET GUIDE BLOCK	
Diameter of bores	0.3120–0.3125 in.
Outside diameter	1.000–0.9995 in.
Interference fit in cyl. block	0.0005–0.0015 in.
CAMSHAFT BEARING BUSHES	
Material	High density sintered bronze
Bore diam. (fitted): Left	0.8125–0.8135 in.
Right	0.874–0.875 in.
Outside diameter: Left	1.0010–1.0015 in.
Right	1.126–1.127 in.
Length: Left inlet	1.104–1.114 in.
CAMSHAFT BEARING BUSHES	
Left exhaust	0.932–0.942 in.
Right inlet and exhaust	1.010–1.020 in.
Interference fit in crankcase	
Left	0.001–0.002 in.
Right	0.0010–0.0025 in.

750—3 Center Bearing Sizes

Shell Bearing Marking	Suitable Crankshaft Size (in.)	(mm)
Standard	1.9170 1.9175	48.692 48.705
Undersize −0.010	1.9070 1.9075	48.438 48.451
−0.020	1.8970 1.8975	48.184 48.197
−0.030	1.8870 1.8875	47.930 47.943
−0.040	1.8770 1.8775	47.676 47.689

11. Loosely install the ignition advance unit and then install the breaker plate assembly, aligning the marks. Coat the crankcase and cover mating surfaces with gasket cement and install the timing side crankcase cover, using a new gasket.
12. Install the oil filter in the bottom of the engine.
13. Install the tachometer drive unit, coating the gasket with gasket cement on both sides. Tachometer drive components generally do not require replacement unless an obvious fault is visible.
14. Install the transmission gear cluster as detailed earlier.
15. Install the primary drive and clutch.

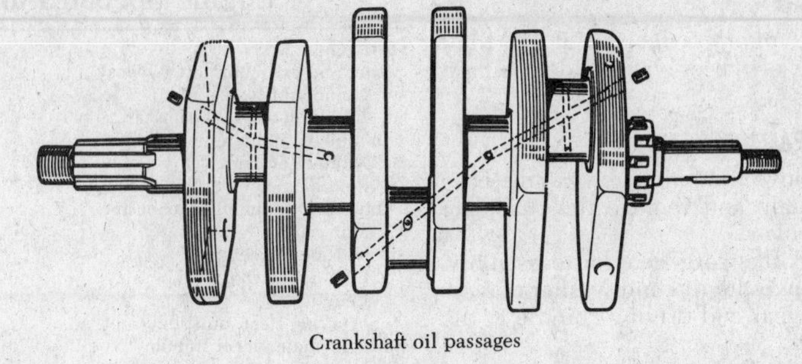

Crankshaft oil passages

Big-End Journal Sizes

Shell Bearing Marking	Journal Size 250 (in.)	250 (mm)	500 (in.)	500 (mm)	650, 750—2 (in.)	650, 750—2 (mm)	750—3 (in.)	750—3 (mm)
Standard	1.4375 1.4380	36.5125 36.5252	1.4375 1.4380	36.512 36.525	1.6235 1.6240	41.237 41.250	1.6235 1.6240	41.237 41.250
Undersize −0.010	1.4275 1.4280	36.2585 36.2712	1.4365 1.4370	36.258 36.271	1.6135 1.6140	40.983 40.996	1.6135 1.6140	40.983 40.996
−0.020	1.4175 1.4180	36.0045 36.0172	1.4355 1.4360	36.004 36.017	1.6035 1.6040	40.729 40.742	1.6035 1.6040	40.729 40.742
−0.030	1.4075 1.4080	35.7505 35.7632	1.4345 1.4350	35.750 35.763	— —	— —	1.5935 1.5940	40.475 40.488
−0.040	— —	— —	— —	— —	— —	— —	1.5833 1.5840	40.221 40.234

LUBRICATION SYSTEMS

TR25W

Scavenge Non-return Valve

The scavenge non-return valve is located within the oil return pipe in the engine sump. It's a good idea to check its operation whenever the sump strainer screen is removed.

Scavenge non-return valve (250)

Poke a piece of wire into the pipe and force the check ball out of its seat. Allow it to drop back down of its own weight. If the ball does not seat itself properly, this indicates a sludge buildup in and around the valve. If necessary, immerse the return pipe in gasoline and let it sit until the check ball operates freely.

Feed Non-return Valve

The oil feed non-return valve is located in the inner timing cover of the engine. Check its operation as described above and, if necessary, clean it with gasoline.

If you have a problem with the engine sump filling with oil whenever the bike is left to sit, chances are that a malfunction of this valve is the cause.

Crankcase Oil Line Union

The oil line union is secured to the crankcase with one nut. If a leak has developed at this junction, disconnect the oil lines and inspect the union sealing O-rings. Replace if necessary.

When reinstalling the union, note that the oil lines are correctly connected when they are crossed (i.e., outer line from the oil tank to the inner connection of the union).

Oil Pressure Relief Valve

The oil pressure relief valve is located at the front right side of the crankcase. Should oil pressure exceed a pre-set limit, the valve routes the excess oil directly back into the sump.

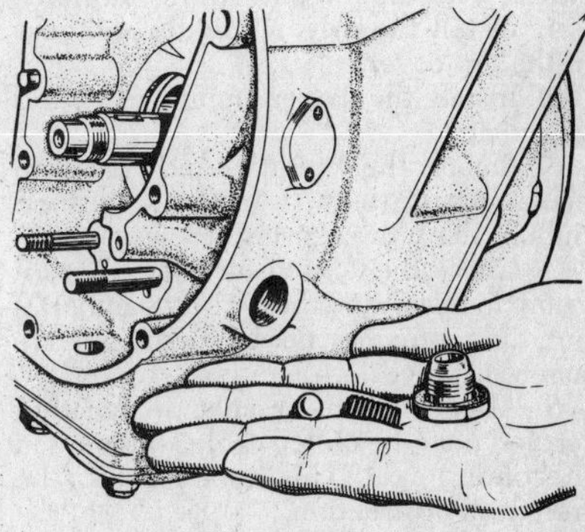

Oil pressure relief valve (250)

To remove the valve, unscrew the hexagonal plug and withdraw the ball and spring. Inspect them for corrosion etc., and replace them if necessary. The spring will, in time, lose its strength, so it is advisable to replace it if the machine has accumulated high mileage. Also replace the fiber washer if it is in less than perfect condition.

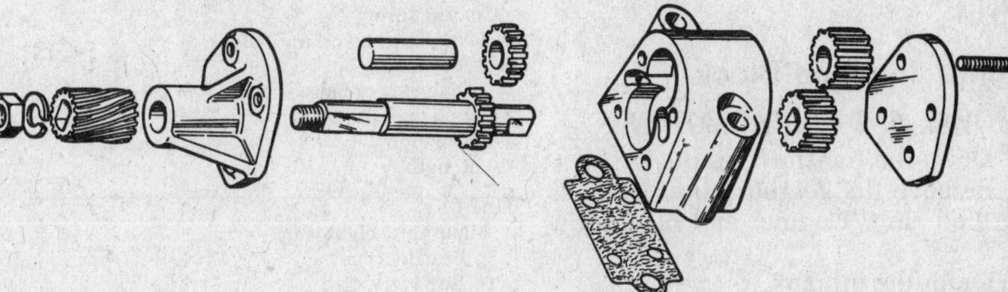

Oil pump (250)

Oil Pump

The oil pump is located at the front right side of the engine inside the case cover.

DISASSEMBLY

1. Remove the four screws at the base of the pump and remove the baseplate and top cover.
2. Mark the worm gear for reassembly, then remove the nut and washer that secure the gear and driving spindle to the top cover.
3. Clean all parts thoroughly in kerosine or a cleaning solvent and blow them dry with compressed air.

INSPECTION

Examine the oil pump parts for excessive scoring and foreign object damage. If oil changes have been neglected, it will be evident by the damage done to the pump gear teeth and pump body. Small scratches can be ignored, but any more substantial wear calls for parts replacement.

Inspect the pump gears for worn or broken teeth. If formerly sharp edges have become rounded off, the gear should be replaced.

ASSEMBLY

1. Make sure all parts are absolutely clean and bathed in engine oil or assembly lube.
2. Insert the driving spindle into the pump top cover.
3. Install the worm drive gear and secure it with the nut and spring washer.
4. Install the driven spindle and gear in the top cover.
5. Install the lower pump gears and baseplate.
6. Rotate the spindle and gears to make certain there is no binding, then tighten the four securing screws.
7. Check the joining surfaces of the oil pump to make sure they are all parallel. If not, the pump may not be free to operate when installed in the engine.
8. Also check the crankcase breather located near the clutch cable abutment in the timing case. This breather *must* be free from obstruction.

500, 650, 750 TWINS

Checking Oil Pressure

Normal oil pressure at idle is about 20 to 25 psi, but may rise as high as 80 psi when the engine is cold. Normal running pressure is 65 to 80 psi.

Oil pressure can be checked by connecting a gauge and adaptor in place of the relief valve.

Oil Line Junction Block

REMOVAL AND INSTALLATION

1. Drain the transmission oil.
2. Remove the gearbox outer cover as described in "Engine and Transmission."
3. Drain the oil tank.
4. Disconnect the rubber lines from

Engine Specifications—TR7V, T140V (cont.)

TIMING GEARS	
Inlet and exh. camshaft pinions	
Number of teeth	50
Interference fit on camshaft	0.000–0.001 in.
Intermediate timing gear	
Number of teeth	47
Bore diameter	0.5618–0.5625 in.
Intermediate timing gear bush	
Material	Phosphor bronze
Outside diameter	0.5635–0.5640 in.
Bore diameter	0.4990–0.4995 in.
Length	0.6775–0.6825 in.
Working clear. on spindle	0.0005–0.0015 in.
Intermediate wheel spindle	
Diameter	0.4980–0.4985 in.
Interference fit in crank.	0.0005–0.0015 in.
Crankshaft pinion	
Number of teeth	25
Fit on crankshaft	+0.0003/−0.0005 in.
CYLINDER BLOCK	
Material	Cast iron
Bore size	2.9911–2.9921 in.
Maximum oversize	+0.040 in.
Tappet guide block housing diameter	0.9990–0.9985 in.
CYLINDER HEAD	
Material	D.T.D. 424 Aluminum
Inlet port size	1.12 in.
Exhaust port size	1⅜ in. diam.
Valve seatings	
Type	Cast-in
Material	Cast iron
CONNECTING RODS	
Length (centers)	5.999–6.001 in.
Big-end bearings—type	Steel backed with white metal
Bearing side clearance	0.012–0.016 in.
Bearing diametrical clearance	0.005–0.0020 in.
PISTON PIN	
Material	High tensile steel
Fit in small-end bush	0.0005–0.0012 in. clear.
Diameter	0.6882–0.6885 in.
Length	2.151–2.156 in.
SMALL END BUSHING	
Material	Phosphor bronze
Outer diameter	0.8140–0.8145 in.
Length	1.030–1.031 in.
Finished bore diameter	0.6890–0.6894 in.

Clutch and Transmission Specifications—TR7V, T140V

CLUTCH	
Type	Multiplate with integral shock absorber
Number of plates	
Driving (bonded)	6
Driven (plain)	6
Pressure springs	
Number	3
Free length	1.75 in.
No. working coils	7½
Spring rate	169 lbs.
Approximate fitted load	83 lbs.
Bearing rollers	
Number	20
Diameter	0.2495–0.2500 in.
Length	0.231–0.236 in.
Clutch hub bearing diameter	1.3733–1.3743 in.
Clutch sprocket bore diameter	1.8745–1.8755 in.
Thrust washer thickness	0.052–0.054 in.
Engine sprocket teeth	29
Clutch sprocket teeth	58
Chain	Triplex endless—⅜ in. pitch x 84 links
CLUTCH OPERATING MECHANISM	
Conical spring	
Number of working coils	2
Free length	1³⁄₃₂ in.
Diameter of balls	⅜ in.
Clutch operating rod	
Diameter	7/32 in.
Length	11.812–11.822 in.
GEARS	
Mainshaft, high gear	
Bearing type	Needle roller (Torrington B1314)
Bearing length	0.865–0.875 in.
Spigot diameter (high gear)	1.5072–1.5077 in.

Clutch and Transmission Specifications—TR7V, T140V (cont.)

GEARBOX SHAFTS	
Mainshaft	
Left end diameter	0.8089–0.8103 in.
Right end diameter	0.7494–0.7498 in.
Length	11.23 in.
Layshaft	
Left end diameter	0.6870–0.6875 in.
Right end diameter	0.6870–0.6875 in.
Length	6.47 in.
GEARBOX BEARINGS	
Mainshaft bearing (left)	1½ x 2½ x ⅝ in. Roller bearing
Mainshaft bearing (right)	¾ x 1⅞ x 9⁄16 in. Ball Journal
Layshaft bearing (left)	11⁄16 x ⅞ x ¾ in. Needle roller
Layshaft bearing (right)	11⁄16 x ⅞ x ¾ in. Needle roller
Layshaft 1st gear bush	
Bore diameter	0.795–0.800 in.
Shaft diameter	0.8070–0.8075 in.
Layshaft 2nd gear bush	
Bore diameter	0.795–0.800 in.
Shaft diameter	0.8070–0.8075 in.
KICK START OPERATING MECHANISM	
Bush bore diameter	0.751–0.752 in.
Spindle working clearance in bush	0.003–0.005 in.
Ratchet spring free-length	½ in.
GEARCHANGE MECHANISM	
Plungers	
Outer diameter	0.4315–0.4320 in.
Working clearance in bore	0.0005–0.0015 in.
Plunger springs	
Number of working coils	12
Free-length	1¼ in.
Inner bush bore diameter	0.6245–0.6255 in.
Clearance on shaft	0.0007–0.0032 in.
Outer bush bore diameter	0.7495–0.7505 in.
Clearance on shaft	0.0005–0.0025 in.
Quadrant return springs	
Number of working coils	9½
Free-length	1¾ in.

Engine Specifications—T150

PISTONS	
Material	Aluminum Alloy-die casting
Clearance:	
Top of skirt	0.0056–0.0035 in. (0.42–0.089 mm)
Bottom of skirt	0.0033–0.0018 in. (0.084–0.0457 mm)
Piston pin hole diameter	0.6885–0.6883 in. (17.9879–17.4828 mm)
PISTON RINGS	
Material	Cast iron HG10
Compression rings (tapered):	
Width	2.729–2.577 in.
Thickness	0.0625–0.0615 in. (1.5875–1.5621 mm)
Fitted gap	0.009–0.013 in. (0.2286–0.3302 mm)
Clearance in groove	0.0035–0.0015 in. (0.89–0.038 mm)
Oil control ring:	
Width	2.729–2.577 mm
Thickness	0.125–0.124 in. (3.175–3.1496 mm)
Fitted gap	0.010–0.040 in. (0.254–1.016 mm)
Clearance in groove	0.0105–0.0065 in. (0.266–0.165 mm)
CYLINDER	
Material	Austenitic steel liner Aluminum Alloy
Bore size	2.6368–2.6363 in. (66.9747–66.062 mm)
Maximum oversize	0.040 in. (1.016 mm)
Tappet guide block housing diameter	1.1562–1.1557 in. (29.3675–29.3548 mm)
CYLINDER HEAD	
Material	Alum. alloy die casting
Inlet port size	1 in. dia (25.4 mm)
Exhaust:	
Valve seatings	1¼ in. dia (31.75 mm)
Type	Cast-in
Material	Cast iron
VALVES	
Stem diameter:	
Intake	0.3100–0.3095 in. (7.8740–7.8613 mm)
Exhaust	0.3095–0.3090 in. (7.8613–7.8495 mm)
Head diameter:	
Intake	1.534–1.528 in. (38.9636–38.812 mm)
Exhaust	1.315–1.309 in. (33.401–33.2486 mm)
Exhaust valve material	21-4 'N' heat treated
VALVE GUIDES	
Material	Hidural 5
Bore diameter (Inlet and exhaust)	0.3115–0.3110 in. (7.9121–7.8994 mm)
Outside diameter (Inlet and exhaust)	0.5005–0.5010 in. (12.7127–12.7254 mm)
Length:	
Intake	1.875 in. (47.625 mm)
Exhaust	1.875 in. (47.625 mm)

the oil tank.

5. Remove the junction block and clean it thoroughly in kerosine.

6. Check all lines for chafing and signs of decomposition. Replace as necessary.

7. Installation is basically a reversal of the removal procedure. Use a new gasket between the junction block and crankcase, and reconnect the oil lines carefully.

Rocker Oil Feed Line

REMOVAL AND INSTALLATION

1. Remove the two domed nuts securing the feed line to the rocker spindle.

2. Disconnect the feed line at the oil tank.

3. Remove the clips securing the feed line to the frame.

NOTE: *Take care not to bend the feed line when removing it from the frame beecause it may cause a future rupture.*

4. Thoroughly clean the oil feed line with kerosine, then blow it out with compressed air.

5. Check the line for proper sealing by holding your thumb over the banjo fitting

Pressure relief valve (Twins)

at one end of the line and blowing through the other.

6. To install the rocker oil feed-line, reverse the removal procedure and replace the banjo fitting washers.

Oil Pressure Relief Valve

The valve is located at the front of the engine on the right side, adjacent to the timing cover.

REMOVAL AND DISASSEMBLY

1. Remove the valve body by unscrewing the hexagonal cap.

2. Separate the cap from the valve body and withdraw the piston and spring.

3. Thoroughly clean all parts in kerosine, then inspect the piston and spring for signs of wear. Also check to make sure the valve filter is free from obstruction.

4. If the bike has accumulated high mileage it is advisable to check spring pressure with the standard figure given in specifications.

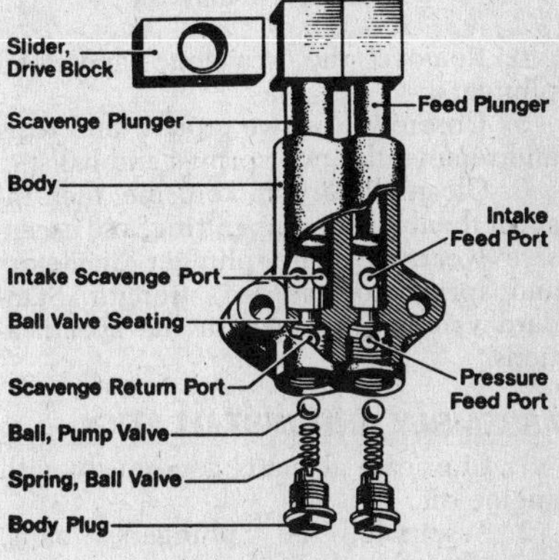

Oil pump (Twins)

ASSEMBLY AND INSTALLATION

1. Replace both fiber washers with new ones.
2. Assemble the valve body, piston, and spring.

NOTE: *The open end of the piston should face toward the spring and cap.*

3. Install the valve body and screw on the hexagonal cap.

Oil Pump

The oil pump is located inside the timing cover and is driven off the end of the intake camshaft. Since the pump itself is totally immersed in oil, wear on internal parts should be negligible. The oil pump drive block slider is not as well lubricated, however, and therefore should be replaced when the machine has accumulated high mileage.

REMOVAL AND DISASSEMBLY

1. Remove the timing cover.
2. Remove the two oil pump securing nuts.
3. Lift the oil pump off the mounting studs.

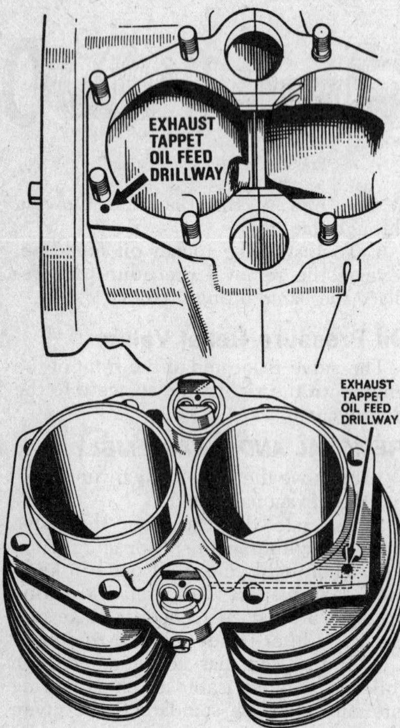

Tappet oil feed drillways

4. Remove the scavenge and feed plungers.
5. Unscrew the two square end caps and remove the two springs and balls.
6. Clean all parts in kerosine, then inspect them for scoring, pitting, and excessive wear. Measure plunger diameters and spring compressed strength. Standard values are given in the specifications.

ASSEMBLY AND INSTALLATION

1. Lubricate all parts generously with engine oil.
2. Assemble the plungers, balls, springs, and end caps.

Engine Specifications—T150 (cont.)

VALVE SPRINGS (RED AND WHITE)	
Free-length:	
Inner	1.468 in. (37.2872 mm)
Outer	1.600 in. (40.64 mm)
Total number of coils:	
Inner	6
Outer	5½
Total fitted load	
Valve open:	
Inner	82 lbs (37.228 kgm)
Outer	115 lbs (51.31 kgm)
Valve closed:	
Inner	37–40 lbs (16.798–18.144 kgm)
Outer	43–53 lbs (21.792–24.062 kgm)
VALVE LIFT	
Set all tappet clearances @ nil for checking Measure valve lift at TBC with cold engine	Valve lift: Inlet 0.152 in. (3.86 mm) Exhaust 0.146 in. (3.71 mm)
ROCKERS	
Material	NI. CH. Steel stamping (EN33)
Bore diameter	0.5002–0.5012 in. (12.7051–12.7305 mm)
Rocker spindle diameter	0.4990–0.4995 in. (12.6746–12.6873 mm)
Tappet clearance (cold):	
Inlet	0.006 in. (0.1524 mm)
Exhaust	0.008 in. (0.2032 mm)
CAMSHAFTS	
Journal diameter	1.0615–1.0605 in. (26.9621–26.9367 mm)
Diametrical clearance	0.0005–0.0020 in. (0.0127–0.0508 mm)
End float	0.007–0.014 in. (0.178–0.356 mm)
Cam lift: Inlet and exhaust	0.3045 in. (7.7343 mm)
Base circle diameter	0.812 in. dia (20.6248 mm)
TAPPETS	
Material	EN32B (Stellite tip)
Tip radius	1.125 in. (28.575 mm)
Tappet diameter	0.3115–0.3110 in. (7.9121–7.8994 mm)
Clearance in guide block	0.0005–0.0015 in. (0.0127–0.0381 mm)
TAPPET GUIDE BLOCK	
Diameter of bores	0.3125–0.3120 in. (7.9375–7.9248 mm)
Outside diameter	1.153–1.148 in. (29.2862–29.1592 mm)
Interference fit in cylinder block	0.0027–0.0082 in. (0.06858–0.20828 mm)
ROCKER SPINDLE BUSHINGS	
Bush D/S:	
Bore diameter	0.497–0.498 in. (12.624–12.649 mm)
Outside diameter	0.6260–0.6265 in. (15.9004–15.913 mm)
Bush T/S:	
Bore diameter	0.375–0.374 in. (9.525–9.4996 mm)
Outside diameter	0.501–0.502 in. (12.725–12.751 mm)
TIMING GEARS	
Inlet and exhaust camshaft pinions:	
Number of teeth	50
Interference fit on camshaft	0.000–0.001 in. (0.000–0.0254 mm)
Intermediate timing gear	
Number of teeth	42
Bore diameter	0.5618–0.5625 in. (14.2697–14.2875 mm)
Intermediate timing gear needle roller	11/16 x 7/8 x 5/8 in. (17.46 x 22.225 x 15.87 mm)
Intermediate wheel spindle	
Diameter	0.6888–0.6885 in. (17.4955–17.4879 mm)
Crankcase pinion:	
Number of teeth	25
Fit on crankcase	−0.00003 in. (−.00762 mm) −0.0005 in. (−0.0127 mm)
CRANKSHAFT	
Crankshaft type	EN16B hardened and tempered stamping—one piece
Main bearing (drive side) size and type	1 1/8 x 2 13/16 x 13/16 in. (caged ball) (28.58 x 71.43 x 20.63 mm)
Main bearing (center) running clearance	0.0005–0.0022 in. (0.0127–0.05588 mm)
Main bearing (timing side) size and type	1 1/4 x 2 13/16 x 13/16 in. (roller) (28.58 x 71.43 x 20.62 mm)
Right main bearing housing diameter	2.8110–2.8095 in. (71.3994–71.3613 mm)
Right main bearing journal diameter	1.1248–1.1245 in. (28.5699–28.5623 mm)
Center main bearing housing diameter	2.0630–2.0625 in. (52.4002–52.3875 mm)
Center main bearing journal diameter	1.9170–1.9175 in. (48.6918–48.7045 mm)
Left main bearing housing diameter	2.0447–2.0457 in. (51.9344–51.9608 mm)
Left main bearing journal diameter	0.9843–0.9840 in. (25.0012–24.9936 mm)
Big-end journal diameter	1.6240–1.6235 in. (41.2496–41.2369 mm)
Minimum regrind diameter	1.6200–1.6185 in. (41.148–44.1099 mm)
Crankshaft end float	0.0015–0.0145 in. ((0.038–0.368 mm)
CONNECTING RODS	
Material	Alloy 'H' Section RR.56
Length (centers)	5.751–5.749 in. (14.6075–14.6024 mm)
Big-end bearings type	Steel-backed white metal
Con rod side clearance	0.013–0.019 in. (0.3302–0.4826 mm)
Bearing diametrical clearance	0.0005–0.0020 in. minimum (0.0127–0.0508 mm)
PISTON PIN	
Material	High tensile steel
Fit in small-end	0.0005–0.0011 in. (0.0127–0.0279 mm)

3. Add approximately 1 cc of oil in each plunger bore, then press the plungers until the oil is forced through both outlet ports.

NOTE: *The outlet ports are the two holes nearest the square end caps.*

4. Hold your thumb over the intake ports (nearest the plunger tops) and pull the plungers out slightly. If the oil level drops in either outlet port, the ball and spring in that port are not seated properly, and the end cap should be removed and the cleaning process repeated.

NOTE: *On machines equipped with a brass body oil pump, the balls can be lightly, but sharply, tapped to ensure a good seal. On machines equipped with the cast iron pump body, however, this should not be attempted since a bad seal indicates a warped body that should be replaced.*

5. Check the oil pump drive block slider for excessive wear, then install the pump with a new gasket. Make sure that the conical securing nuts are positioned so that they fit into the countersunk holes in the pump body.

6. Clean the timing cover and crankcase mating surfaces, then apply fresh sealing compound and install the cover.

T150, T150V

Checking Oil Pressure

Normal running oil pressure at 3,000 rpm is 75–90 psi, but may rise above that when the engine is cold. Pressure can be checked by installing an oil pressure gauge in one of the blanking plugs at the front of the center crankcase.

If the oil pressure is unsatisfactory, check the following:

1. Faulty or dirty oil pressure relief valve.
2. Insufficient amount of lubricant in the oil tank.
3. Dirty or incorrectly installed oil filters.
4. Faulty oil pump.
5. Obstructed crankcase drillings.
6. Excessively worn main or connecting rod bearings.
7. Leaking crankcase union O-rings.

Oil Pressure Relief Valve

The oil pressure relief valve is located in the primary chaincase. Triumph special tool no. D2135 can be used to remove the valve with only the primary cover removed, but if this tool is not available,

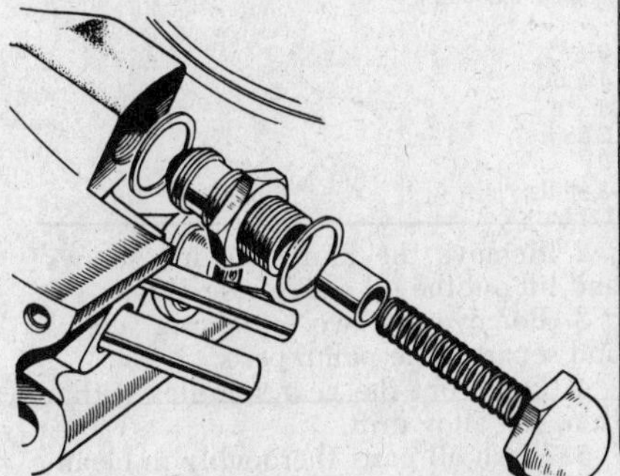

Pressure relief valve (Trident)

Clutch and Transmission Specifications—T150

CLUTCH DETAILS	
Single diaphragm spring-clutch spring rate	1,000 lb (approx) (453.6 kgm)
Minimum travel to disengage	0.035 in. (0.889 mm)
Minimum wear of friction plate	0.06 in. (1.524 mm)
Bearing-Outer thrust plate—Size and type	1/2 x 1 1/8 x 1/4 in. (12.7 x 28.575 x 6.35 mm)
Needle race—Size and type	(2 off) 1 3/8 x 1 5/8 x 1/2 in. (34.93 x 41.28 x 12.7 mm)
Thrust race—Size and type	1 3/8 x 2 1/16 x 5/64 in. (34.93 x 52.39 x 1.984 mm)
GEAR	
Mainshaft high gear:	
Bore diameter (bush fitted)	0.8135–0.8145 in. (20.6629–20.6883 mm)
Working clearance on shaft	0.0032–0.0047 in. (0.08128–0.1194 mm)
Bush length	2 1/4 in. (57.15 mm)
Layshaft low gear:	
Bore diameter	0.8135–0.8145 in. (20.6629–20.6883 mm)
Working clearance	0.0025–0.0045 in. (0.0635–0.127 mm)
GEARBOX SHAFTS	
Mainshaft:	
Left end diameter	0.8098–0.8103 in. (20.5689–20.5816 mm)
Right end diameter	0.7494–0.7498 in. (19.0348–19.044 mm)
Length	10 13/64 in. (262.3337 mm)
Layshaft:	
Left end diameter	0.6845–0.6850 in. (17.4063–17.419 mm)
	0.6845–0.6850 in. (17.4063–17.419 mm)
Length	6 41/64 in. (168.6941 mm)
Camplate plunger spring:	
Free-length	2 21/32 in. (67.4675 mm)
Number of working coils	27
Spring rate	9 lbs/in. (0.633 kg/sq cm)
Working range	7.5 to 11.5 lbs (3.405 kgm–5.220 kgm)
BEARINGS	
High gear bearing	1 1/4 x 2 1/2 x 5/8 in. Ball Journal 31.75 x 63.5 x 15.875 mm)
Mainshaft bearing	3/4 x 1 7/8 x 9/16 in. Ball Journal (19.05 x 47.625 x 14.282 mm)
Layshaft bearing (left)	11/16 x 7/8 x 3/4 in. Needle Roller (17.463 x 22.227 x 19.05 mm)
Layshaft bearing (right)	11/16 x 7/8 x 3/4 in. Needle Roller (17.463 x 22.227 x 19.05 mm)
KICK-START OPERATING MECHANISM	
Bush bore diameter	0.751–0.752 in. (19.0754–19.1008 mm)
Spindle working clearance in bush	0.003–0.005 in. (0.0762–0.127 mm)
Ratchet spring free-length	1/2 in. (12.7 mm)
GEARCHANGE MECHANISM	
Plungers:	
Outer diameters	0.4315–0.4320 in. (10.9601–10.9728 mm)
Working clearance in bore	0.0005–0.005 in. (0.0127–0.127 mm)
Plunger springs:	
Number of working coils	12
Free-length	1 1/4 in. (31.75 mm)
Inner bush bore diameter	0.6245–0.6255 in. (15.7423–15.8877 mm)
Clearance on shaft	0.0007–0.0032 in. (0.01778–0.08128 mm)
Outer bush bore diameter	0.7495–0.7505 in. (19.0373–19.0627 mm)
Clearance on shaft	0.0005–0.0025 in. (0.0127–0.0635 mm)
Quadrant return springs:	
Number of working coils	9 1/2
Free-length	1 3/4 in. (44.45 mm)

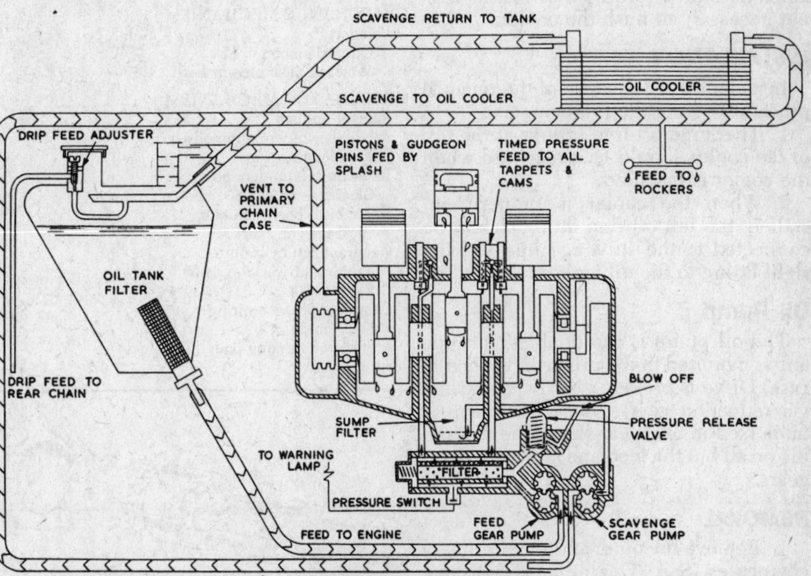

Trident lubrication system

the chaincase must be disassembled to gain access.

Disassemble and inspect the valve as described for the 500, 650 and 750 cc Twins.

Rocker Oil Feed Line

Service the rocker oil feed line as described for the twins.

Oil Cooler

The Trident is equipped with an oil cooler mounted below the gas tank on two support brackets. Great care should be taken when handling this component.

REMOVAL

1. Remove the gas tank.
2. Mark both oil lines for reassembly, then disconnect the clips. Take care not to tilt the cooler as it still contains approximately one-half pint of oil.
3. Loosen the top support bracket bolts and remove the bracket corner packings.

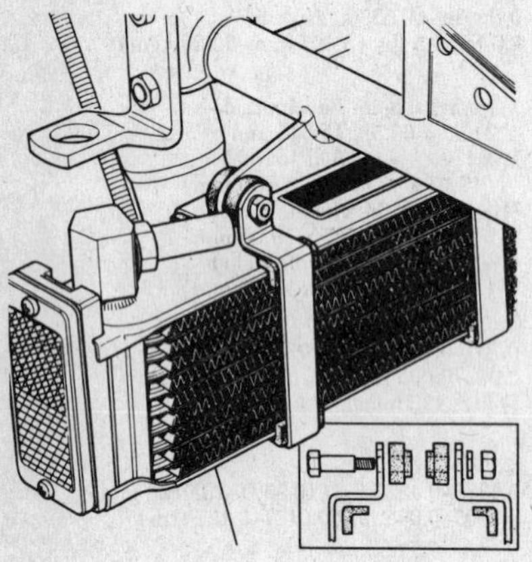

Oil cooler installation

4. Hold the cooler upright and remove the bracket bolts, nuts, and washers.
5. Lift out the cooler, then drain the remaining oil by inverting the cooler over a suitable container.
6. Clean the outside of the cooler with kerosine and a soft-bristled brush. It is not necessary to flush the cooler.

INSTALLATION

Installation is a reversal of the removal procedure. Note the following:

1. The large oil line fittings at the top of the cooler should face rearward when the cooler is installed.
2. When the cooler is properly installed, the left oil line fitting should be connected to the scavenge line and the right fitting to the oil tank return line.

Oil Pump

The oil pump is the double-gear type and is mounted in the primary side crankcase. Drive is provided by the crankshaft via reduction gears. Since the pump is immersed in oil, wear should be negligible on all but the feed and scavenge drive gears.

REMOVAL

1. Remove the outer and inner primary chaincases (See "Engine and Transmission").

Engine Specifications—T150V①

MAIN BEARINGS	
Right main bearing size	25 x 52 x 15 mm
Right main bearing journal diameter	2.0447–2.0457 in. (51.934–51.961 mm)
Left main bearing journal diameter	2.8095–2.8110 in. (71.3613–71.3994 mm)
Left main bearing journal diameter	1.1245–1.1248 in. (28.563–28.5699 mm)
Minimum regrind diameter	1.5833–1.5840 in. (40.221–40.234 mm)
CONNECTING RODS	
Big end bearing material	Lead-bronze
CYLINDER HEAD	
Intake port size	1 1/16 in. (27 mm)
CAMSHAFTS	
Cam lift (In. and Ex.)	0.329 in. (8.356 mm)

① With the exception of the specifications on this chart T150V information may be obtained from the T150 Engine Specifications chart.

Clutch and Transmision Specifications—T150V

CLUTCH DETAILS	
Single diaphragm spring-clutch spring rate	1,000 lb (approx) (453.6 kmg)
Minimum travel to disengage	0.035 in. (0.889 mm)
Minimum wear to friction plate	0.06 in. (1.524 mm)
Bearing-Outer thrust plate—Size and type	½ x 1⅛ x ¼ in. (12.7 x 28.575 x 6.35 mm)
Needle race—Size and type	(2 off) 1⅜ x 1⅝ x ½ in. (34.93 x 41.28 x 12.7 mm)
Thrust race—Size and type	1⅜ x 2 1/16 x 5/64 in. (34.93 x 52.39 x 1.984 mm)
GEARS	
Mainshaft, high gear	
Bearing type	Needle roller (Torrington B1314)
Bearing length	0.865–0.875 in.
Spigot diameter (high gear)	1.5072–1.5077 in.
GEARBOX SHAFTS	
Mainshaft	
Left end diameter	0.8089–0.8103 in.
Right end diameter	0.7494–0.7498 in.
Length	10.33 in.
Layshaft	
Left end diameter	0.6870–0.6875 in.
Right end diameter	0.6870–0.6875 in.
Length	6.47 in.
GEARBOX BEARINGS	
Mainshaft bearing (left)	1½ x 2½ x ⅝ in. Roller bearing
Mainshaft bearing (right)	¾ x 1⅞ x 9/16 in. Ball journal
Layshaft bearing (left)	11/16 x ⅞ x ¾ in. Needle roller
Layshaft bearing (right)	11/16 x ⅞ x ¾ in. Needle roller
Layshaft 1st gear bush	
Bore diameter	0.795–0.800 in.
Shaft diameter	0.8070–0.8075 in.
Layshaft 2nd gear bush	
Bore diameter	0.795–0.800 in.
Shaft diameter	0.8070–0.8075 in.
KICK START OPERATING MECHANISM	
Bush bore diameter	0.751–0.752 in.
Spindle working clearance in bush	0.003–0.005 in.
Ratchet spring free-length	½ in.
GEARCHANGE MECHANISM	
Plungers	
Outer diameter	0.4315–0.4320 in.
Working clearance in bore	0.0005–0.0015 in.
GEARCHANGE MECHANISM	
Plunger springs	
Number of working coils	12
Free-length	1¼ in.
Inner bush bore diameter	0.6245–0.6255 in.
Clearance on shaft	0.0007–0.0032 in.
Outer bush bore diameter	0.7495–0.7505 in.
Clearance on shaft	0.0005–0.0025 in.
Quadrant return springs	
Number of working coils	9½
Free-length	1¾ in.
Camplate plunger spring:	
Free length	2.28 in.
Number of working coils	21
Spring rate	8.80 lbs./in.

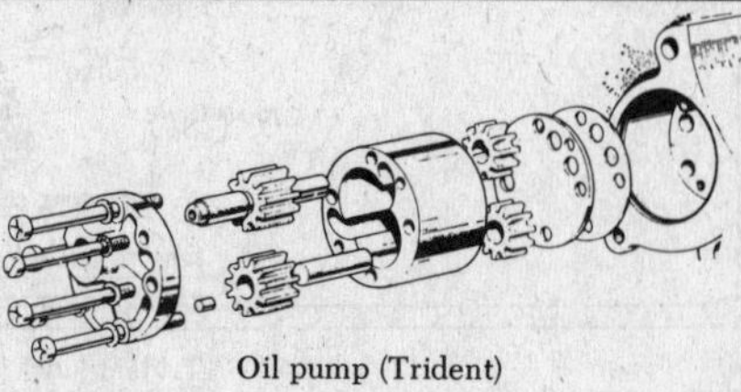

Oil pump (Trident)

2. Remove the four attaching screws and lift out the oil pump assembly.
3. Remove the two remaining screws and separate the pump parts.
4. Drive out the gear spindles with a thin, soft alloy drift.
5. Wash all parts thoroughly in cleaning solvent or kerosine, then blow them dry with compressed air.

INSPECTION

Examine the gear teeth for scoring or rounded out edges. Check the spindles and spindle bores in the gears and pump body. Replace any parts that are excessively worn.

Engine Torque Specifications

TR25W

Carburetor flange nuts	10 ft lbs (1.383 kg/m)
Clutch center nut	60–65 ft lbs (8.295–8.998 kg/m)
Con. rod end cap nuts	25–27 ft lbs (3.456–3.733 kg/m)
Crankshaft pinion nut	35–40 ft lbs (4.839–5.530 kg/m)
Cylinder barrel nuts	26–28 ft lbs (3.595–3.871 kg/m)
Cylinder head stud nuts	18–20 ft lbs (2.489–2.765 kg/m)
Kick-start ratchet nut	50–55 ft lbs (6.913–7.604 kg/m)
Oil pump stud nuts	5–7 ft lbs (691–968 kg/m)
Rotor fixing nut	60 ft lbs 8.295 kg/m)
Valve cover nuts (large)	10 ft lbs (1.383 kg/m)
Valve cover nuts (small)	5–7 ft lbs (691–869 kg/m)

T100C, T100R

Flywheel bolts	33 ft lbs
Con. rod bolts	27 ft lbs
Crankcase junction bolts	15 ft lbs
Crankcase junction studs	20 ft lbs
Cylinder block nuts	35 ft lbs
Cylinder head bolts (3/8 in. dia.)	18 ft lbs
Rocker box nuts	5 ft lbs
Rocker box bolts	5 ft lbs
Rocker spindle-domed nuts	25 ft lbs
Oil pump nuts	6 ft lbs
Kickstart ratchet pinion nut	40 ft lbs
Clutch center nut	50 ft lbs
Rotor fixing nut	30 ft lbs
Stator fixing nuts	20 ft lbs
Twin carburetor manifold socket screws	10 ft lbs

TR6R, TR6C, T120R

Flywheel bolts	33 ft lbs (4.6 kg/m)
Con. rod bolts	28 ft lbs (3.9 kg/m)
Crankcase junction bolts	13 ft lbs (1.8 kg/m)
Crankcase junction studs	20 ft lbs (2.8 kg/m)
Cylinder block nuts	35 ft lbs (4.8 kg/m)
Cylinder head bolts (3/8 in. dia.)	18 ft lbs (2.49 kg/m)
Cylinder head bolt (5/16 in. dia.)	15 ft lbs (2.1 kg/m)
Rocker box nuts	5 ft lbs (0.7 kg/m)
Rocker box bolts	5 ft lbs (0.7 kg/m)
Rocker spindle-domed nuts	22 ft lbs (3.0 kg/m)
Oil pump nuts	5 ft lbs (0.7 kg/m)
Kick-start ratchet pinion nut	45 ft lbs (6.3 kg/m)
Clutch center nut	50 ft lbs (7 kg/m)
Rotor fixing nut	30 ft lbs (4.1 kg/m)
Stator fixing nuts	20 ft lbs (2.8 kg/m)
Primary cover domed nuts	10 ft lbs (1.4 kg/m)

TR7V, T140V

Flywheel bolts	33 ft lbs (4.6 kg/m)
Con. rod bolts	22 ft lbs (3.9 kg/m)
Crankcase junction bolts	13 ft lbs (1.8 kg/m)
Crankcase junction studs	20 ft lbs (2.8 kg/m)
Rocker box bolts—inner (5/16 in. dia.)	10 ft lbs (1.38 kg/m)
Cylinder head bolts—outer (3/8 in. dia.)	18 ft lbs (2.49 kg/m)
Cylinder head bolt—center (5/16 in dia.)	16 ft lbs (2.07 kg/m)
Cylinder head bolt—inner (3/8 in. dia.)	18 ft lbs (2.49 kg/m)
Rocker box nuts	5 ft lbs (7 kg/m)
Rocker box bolts (1/4 in. dia.)	5 ft lbs (7 kg/m)
Rocker spindle-domed nuts	22 ft lbs (3.0 kg/m)
Oil pump nuts	5 ft lbs (7 kg/m)
Kick-start ratchet pinion nut	45 ft lbs (6.3 kg/m)
Clutch center nut	70 ft lbs (7 kg/m)
Rotor fixing nut	40 ft lbs (4.1 kg/m)
Stator fixing nuts	20 ft lbs (2.8 kg/m)
Primary cover domed nuts	10 ft lbs (1.4 kg/m)

T150, T150V

Con. rod bolts	18 ft lbs (2.489 kg/m)
Crankcase junction bolts	12 ft lbs (1.659 kg/m)
Crankcase junction studs	15 ft lbs (2.074 kg/m)
Cylinder block nuts	20–22 ft lbs (2.765–3.042 kg/m)
Cylinder head bolts	18 ft lbs (2.489 kg/m)
Rocker box nuts	6 ft lbs (0.691 kg/m)
Rocker box bolts	6 ft lbs (0.691 kg/m)
Rocker spindle-domed nuts	22 ft lbs (3.042 kg/m)
Kick-start ratchet pinion nut	40–45 ft lbs (5.530–6.221 kg/m)
Rotor fixing nut	50 ft lbs (6.913 kg/m)
Stator fixing nuts	8 ft lbs (1.106 kg/m)
Clutch center nut	60 ft lbs (8.295 kg/m)
Gearbox sprocket—Lock nut	58 ft lbs (8.019 kg/m)
Center bearing nuts	18 ft lbs (2.489 kg/m)

INSTALLATION

Installation is a reversal of the removal procedure. Note the following:

1. Replace the gasket that fits between the pump and crankcase.
2. Make certain that the two screws holding the pump body together are sufficiently tightened.
3. Make sure the pump is correctly located over the dowel in the crankcase recess.
4. Replace the O-ring that fits around the pump body in the inner primary chaincase.
5. When installing the oil pump drive gear, apply a thread-locking compound to the securing screw.

Oil Pump and Pressure Relief Valve Specifications

TR25W

OIL PUMP	
Pump body material	Zinc base alloy
Type	Double gear
Drive ratio	1 : 4
Non-return valve spring (free-length)	0.625 in. (15–875 mm)
Non-return valve spring ball (diameter)	0.25 in. (6.35 mm)
Oil pressure relief valve spring (free-length)	0.6094 in. (15.4781 mm)
Oil pressure relief valve ball (diameter)	0.3125 in. (7.9375 mm)

T100C and T100R

OIL PUMP	
Body material	Brass
Bore diameter:	
Feed	0.3748–0.3753 in.
Scavenge	0.4372–0.4377 in.
Scavenge (Bef. H.49833)	0.4877–0.4872 in.
Plunger diameter:	
Feed	0.3744–0.3747 in.
Scavenge	0.4369–0.4372 in.
Scavenge (Bef H.49833)	0.4872–0.4869 in.
Valve spring length	1/2 in.
Ball diameter	7/32 in.
Aluminum cross-head width	0.497–0.498 in.
Working clearance in plunger heads	0.0015–0.0045 in.
OIL PRESSURE RELIEF VALVE	
Piston diameter	0.5605–0.5610 in.
Working clearance	0.001–0.002 in.
Pressure relief operates	60 lb/sq in. (4.22 kg/sq cm)
Spring length (Free)	1 3/8 in.
Load at 1 3/16 in.	8 lbs
Rate	42.3 lbs
OIL PRESSURE	
Normal running	60 lb/sq in.
Idling	20–25 lb/sq in.

Oil Pump and Pressure Relief Valve Specifications (cont.)

TR6R, TR6C, T120R, TR7V, T140V

OIL PUMP	
Body material	Brass
Bore diameter:	
Feed	0.40675–0.40625 in.
Scavenge	0.4877–0.4872 in.
Plunger diameter:	
Feed	0.40615–0.40585 in.
Scavenge	0.4872–0.4869 in.
Valve spring length	½ in.
Ball diameter	7/32 in.
Aluminum cross-head width	0.497–0.498 in.
Working clearance in plunger heads	0.0015–0.0045 in.
OIL PRESSURE RELIEF VALVE	
Piston diameter	0.5605–0.5610 in.
Working clearance	0.001–0.002 in.
Presure relief operates	60 lb/sq in. (4.22 kg/sq cm
Spring length	1 17/32 in.
Load at 1 3/16 in.	12–12½ lbs
Rate	37 lb/in.
OIL PRESSURE	
Normal running	68–80 lb/sq in.
Idling	20–25 lb/sq in.
OIL PRESSURE SWITCH	
Operating pressure	7–11 lb/sq in.

T150, T150V

OIL PUMP	
Body material	Cast iron
Bore diameter	0.3438–0.3433 in. (8.7325–8.7198 mm)
Scavenge gear-bore diameter	0.3438–0.3448 in. (8.7325–8.7579 mm)
Feed gear-bore diameter	0.3438–0.3448 in. (8.7325–8.7579 mm)
Spindle diameter	0.3433–0.3428 in. (8.7198–8.70712 mm)
Cover plate bore diameters:	
Spindle	0.3433–0.3438 in. (8.7198–8.7325 mm)
Drive scavenge gear	0.4375–0.4370 in. (11.1125–11.0998 mm)
Pump drive ratio	1.9 : 1 (engine to pump)
OIL PUMP DRIVE	
Intermediate gear-bore diameter	0.5625–0.5620 in. (14.287–14.2748 mm)
Bush-bore	0.4387–0.4382 in. (11.143–11.1302 mm)
-length	0.755–0.745 in. (19.177–18.923 mm)
Spindle-diameter	0.4360–0.4355 in. (11.0744–11.0617 mm)
OIL PRESSURE RELIEF VALVE	
Piston diameter	0.5605–0.5610 in. (14.2367–14.2494 mm)
Working clearance	1.001–0.002 in. (0.0254–0.0508 mm)
Pressure relief operates	90 lb/sq in. (6.328 kg/sq cm)
Spring length (Free)	1⅜ in. (34–925 mm)
Lead at 1 3/16 in.	8 lbs (3.632 kgm)
Rate	42.3 lbs (19–2042 kgm)
OIL PRESSURE	
Normal running	75–85 lb/sq in. (5.273–5.624 kg/sq cm)
Idling	20–25 lb/sq in. (1.406–1.758 kg/sq cm)
Oil pressure switch: Working range	7–11 lbs (3.178–4.994 kgm)

FUEL SYSTEMS

Triumph motorcycles were fitted with one or two Amal Monobloc carburetors prior to 1967, and from that date have been equipped with the Concentric version.

NOTE: *For carburetor theory, inspection, and service, refer to "Carburetors" under the "General Information" section.*

MONOBLOC

Removal and Disassembly

1. Remove the air cleaner(s).
2. Disconnect the fuel feed line at the carburetor banjo. Disconnect the feed line between the carburetors.
3. Gradually loosen the two carburetor flange nuts, and remove the carburetor.
4. Unscrew and remove the carburetor cap, and pull out the choke and throttle slide assembly. To disassemble, remove the needle clip, compress the spring, disengage the cable from the slide, and separate the components.
5. Remove the banjo bolt, and take off the banjo and filter screen.
6. Unscrew and remove the float needle seat. Take out the needle.
7. Remove the main jet cover nut. Unscrew and remove the main jet holder complete with main and needle jets.
8. Remove the pilot jet cover nut. Unscrew and remove the pilot jet.
9. Remove the float bowl cover (3 screws). Remove the float spindle, float, and spindle bush.
10. Remove the pilot air and throttle stop screws.
11. Remove the locating peg, and shake out the jet block.

Assembly and Installation

1. Assembly is the reverse of disassembly. Use new gaskets, O-rings, and fiber washers.
2. Install the throttle slide(s) in the carburetor(s) before tightening the flange nuts. Tighten these nuts slowly and evenly. Check for free slide movement as the nuts are tightened. If the slide sticks, the nuts are overtightened, warping the carburetor body.
3. After connecting the fuel line(s), check for leaks.

CONCENTRIC (EXCEPT TRIDENT)

Removal and Disassembly

1. Remove the air cleaner(s).
2. Disconnect the fuel feed lines at the carburetor(s).
3. Loosen the carburetor flange nuts evenly, then remove them and pull off the carburetor.
4. Remove the carburetor top and pull out the slide assembly. To disassemble, remove the needle and clip by compressing the return spring against the cap, compress the return spring and disengage the cable from the slide.
5. Remove the float bowl banjo bolt, with banjo and filter.
6. Remove the float bowl screws, tapping the bowl lightly to free it if stuck.

   NOTE: *Hold the carburetor in the upright position when removing the float bowl.*
7. Remove the float assembly from the float bowl. The float spindle is pressed lightly into the bowl.
8. Unscrew and remove the main jet holder complete with main and needle jets.
9. Unscrew and remove the pilot jet (if fitted), pilot air screw, and throttle stop screw.

Assembly and Installation

1. Assembly is the reverse of disassembly. Use new O-rings (the condition of the flange O-ring is critical), float bowl gasket, and washers.
2. If plastic banjos are fitted, do not overtighten them, or they may leak.
3. Put the throttle slide assemly in the carburetor body before bolting it down. Be sure the flange O-ring is seated in its groove and hold the carburetor against its manifold while screwing on the nuts.
4. Tighten the flange nuts gradually and evenly, checking for free slide movement as this is done. Overtightening or uneven tightening of the nuts may cause the slide to stick because it may warp the body.
5. After connecting the fuel line(s), check for leaks.

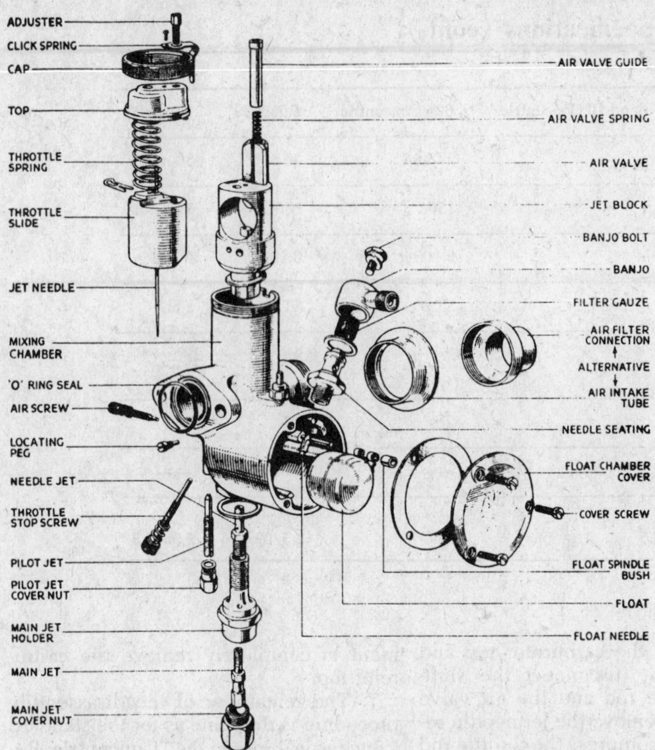

Monobloc carburetor with float bowl

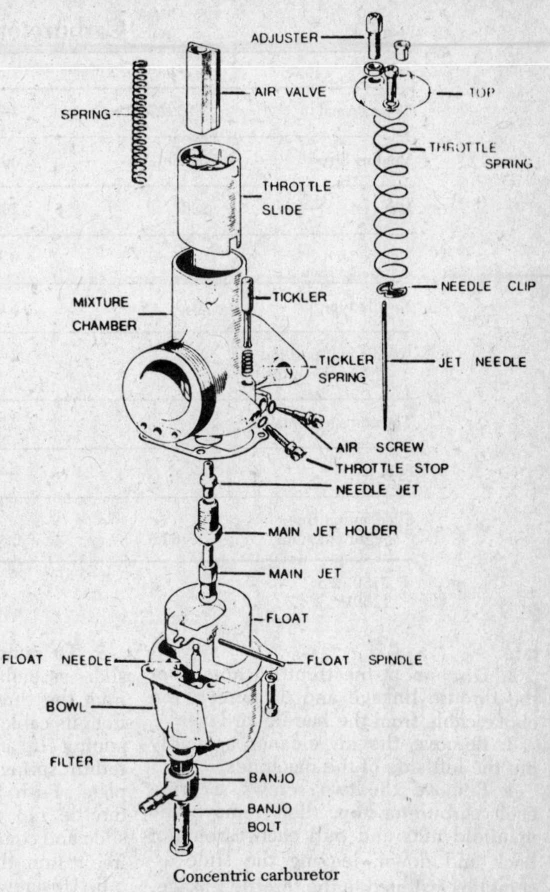

Concentric carburetor

Removing the main jet, holder, and needle jet

TRIDENT

The Trident is equipped with three, Model 600 Concentric carburetors. These units differ from the other Concentric carburetors in that the throttle slide has no conventional throttle spring, but is returned by a scissor spring located on the external throttle linkage.

Removal and Disassembly

1. Remove the side panels and the fuel

Carburetor Specifications

	TR25W	T100C (before H57083)	T100C (H57083 and later)	T100R (before H57083)	T100R (H57083 and later)
Type (Amal)	928/1 Concentric	376/273	628/8 Concentric	376/324 and 325	626/9 and 10 Concentric
Venturi Size	28 mm	1 in. (25.4 mm)	26 mm	1¹⁄₁₆ in.	26 mm
Main jet	160	190	180	200	140
Needle jet	0.106 in.	0.106 in.	0.106 in.	0.106 in.	0.106 in.
Needle type	—	C	—	C	—
Needle clip position (groove from top)	1	3	2	3	2
Throttle slide cutaway	3	3.5	4	3.5	3
Pilot jet	—	25	—	25	—
Slide spring free length (in./mm)	2.5/63.5	—	2.5/63.5	—	2.5/63.5

Carburetor Specifications (cont.)

	TR6R and TR6C	T120R	T150, T150V	TR7V	T140V
Type (Amal)	R930/23 Concentric	R930/9 and 10 Concentric	626 Concentric	R930/89	L930/93
Venturi Size	30 mm	30 mm	27 mm	30 mm	30 mm
Main jet	230	220	150	280	190
Needle jet	0.106 in.	0.106 in.	0.106 in.	0.106 in.	0.106 in.
Needle type	STD	STD	STD	STD	STD
Needle clip position (groove from top)	2	2	2	2	1
Throttle slide cutaway	3	2.5	①	3.5	3
Pilot jet	—	—	—	—	—
Slide spring free length (in./mm)	2.5/63.5	2.5–63.5	—	2.5/63.5	2.5/63.5

① T150: 2.5
T150V: 3.5

tank.

2. Disconnect the throttle cable from the throttle linkage and disconnect the choke cable from the handlebar lever.

3. Remove the air cleaner assembly out the left side of the machines.

4. Remove the two screws securing each carburetor top, then remove the manifold nuts and pull each carburetor back and down, leaving the slide assemblies fastened to the throttle linkage.

5. To remove the carburetor top and slide assemblies, disconnect the slide from the throttle rod and the air valve from its cable. Remove the jet needle retaining clip and compress the throttle rod return spring to free the top retaining plate. Push the bottom nipple of the throttle rod down to clear the throttle slide and compress the air valve spring to free it from the cable end nipple.

6. Unscrew the air valve cable abutment to completely remove the carburetor top.

7. The remainder of the disassembly procedure is the same as for the standard Concentric. Refer to the "Concentric: Removal and Disassembly" section preceding, Steps 5–9.

Assembly and Installation

Refer to "Concentric: Assembly and Installation" section preceding.

ELECTRICAL SYSTEMS

IGNITION SYSTEM

Troubleshooting

TR25W

1. Make sure the contact breaker is clean and correctly gapped. Also make certain the battery terminals are tight and in good condition.

2. Check the main wiring harness fuse.

3. Turn the ignition switch on and slowly turn the engine over while watching the ammeter needle. As the contact breaker opens and closes, the needle should flick between zero and a slight discharge. If it does not, there is a fault somewhere in the low tension circuit.

4. Recheck the condition of the points to make sure you aren't getting a false indication due to dirt, oil, or an incorrect adjustment.

500 AND 650 TWINS

1. Check the condition and gap of the contact breaker points and the tightness of the battery terminals.

2. Remove the gas tank.

3. Disconnect the white lead that connects the "SW" terminals of both ignition coils.

4. Connect the white lead to the left coil "SW" terminal, then turn on the ignition switch and slowly turn over the engine while observing the ammeter needle. As the contact breaker opens and closes, the needle should flick between zero and a slight discharge.

5. Disconnect the white lead from the left coil and connect the "SW" terminal of the right coil. Turn the ignition switch on and observe the ammeter needle as described above.

6. If the ammeter needle does not flick in the described manner for both the right and left ignition coils, a fault exists in the low tension circuit.

T150

1. Lift up the seat and disconnect the white lead that connects the "SW" terminal of all three ignition coils.

NOTE: *Lucas coils are marked "SW" and "CB." SIBA coils are marked "1" instead of "SW" and "15" instead of "CB."*

2. Connect the white lead to one coil at a time and check ammeter needle deflection as previously described for the other models.

750 TWINS, T150V

Procedures are essentially as described above, except that the coil wires are white/yellow.

Low Tension Circuit Tests

If the above tests showed that the fault exists somewhere in the low tension circuit, isolate the problem source in the following manner:

NOTE: *On 12 volt machines, disconnect the zener diode center terminal.*

1. Place a piece of non-conducting material between the contact breaker points. Turn the ignition switch on.

2. Using a 0–15 volt DC voltmeter (0–10 volts for 6 volt machines) and the appropriate wiring diagram for reference, make point-to-point checks as described below.

3. Check the battery by connecting the voltmeter between the negative terminal of the battery and ground (frame). No reading indicates a blown main, or a faulty red, battery lead; a low reading indicates a poor ground.

4. Connect the voltmeter between the ignition coil negative terminal (SW or 1) and ground (one at a time on twins and triples). No reading indicates a faulty lead between the battery and coil terminal, or a faulty switch or ammeter connection.

5. Connect the voltmeter between ground and one ammeter terminal at a time. No reading at the "load" terminal indicates either a faulty ammeter or a break in the blue/brown lead from the battery; no reading on the battery side in-

dicates a faulty ammeter.

6. Connect the voltmeter between the ignition switch "feed" terminal and ground. No reading indicates a break or faulty terminal along the brown/white lead. Check for voltage readings between ground and the brown/white lead terminals at the rectifier, ammeter and lighting switch (on singles and twins.)

7. Connect the voltmeter between the ignition switch "load" terminal and ground. No reading indicates a faulty switch. A positive reading at this point, but not in step 4, indicates a break or faulty connection along the white lead.

8. Disconnect the ignition coil lead from the positive (CB or 15) terminal and connect one voltmeter lead in its place (one coil at a time on twins and triples). Connect the other voltmeter lead to ground. No reading indicates a faulty primary coil winding.

9. Reconnect the ignition coil lead(s) and connect the voltmeter across the contact breaker points one set at a time. Leave the rubber insulator in place. No reading indicates a faulty connection, faulty insulation, or a faulty condenser.

10. On 12 volt machines, reconnect the zener diode center terminal and connect the voltmeter to this terminal and ground. The meter should read battery output voltage.

High Tension Circuit Tests

If the preliminary ignition system checks showed that the problem lay in the high tension circuit, check the following:

1. Test the ignition coil(s) as described in component tests. If the coils are in satisfactory condition, either the high tension cables or spark plug cap(s) are at fault.

2. Remove the spark plug cap(s) from the cable(s) and turn the ignition switch on. Hold the cable about ⅛ in. away from the cylinder cooling fins and kick the engine over. A bright blue spark should jump across the gap; if not, the cable is defective. If the spark does appear, the spark plug cap is faulty.

Component Tests

IGNITION Coil

1. Check the coil in the machine by removing the spark plug cap and holding the high tension cable end about ⅛ in. away from the cylinder cooling fins. Turn the ignition on and kick the engine over.

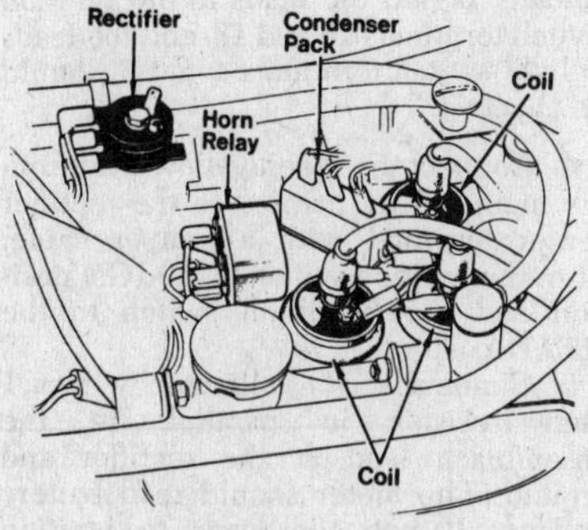

Component location (Trident)

2. Check primary winding resistance by removing the coil and connecting an ohmmeter to the low tension terminals. The readings obtained should be:

TR25W

3.0 ohms minimum
3.4 ohms maximum

T100C, T100R, TR6C, TRGR, and T120R
MA6 type

1.8 ohms minimum
2.4 ohms maximum

MA12 type

3.0 ohms minimum
3.4 ohms maximum

T150, T150V

3.3 ohms minimum
3.8 ohms maximum

TR7V, T140V

3.0 ohms minimum
3.4 ohms maximum

3. Inspect the high tension cables for any signs of insulator deterioration.

CONDENSERS

A faulty condenser is usually indiated by burning or arcing of the points. On the TR25W, the consenser is located under the ignition plate in the primary chaincase; on twins and triples, they are located under the gas tank.

To check the condenser(s), first turn the ignition switch on, then take readings across the contact breaker(s) (open position) with a voltmeter. No reading indicates that the condenser insulation has broken down, and the unit should be replaced.

CHARGING SYSTEM

The charging system consists of an alternator and a full-wave bridge rectifier that converts the AC pulses in DC for recharging the battery and powering the lights. 12 volt machines are also equipped with a zener diode to absorb any excess charge.

Alternator Output Test

TR525W

1. Disconnect the two or three alternator output leads.

NOTE: *Earlier machines have three leads; later machines have two.*

2. Start and run the engine at 3,000 rpm.

3. Connect a 0–15 volt AC voltmeter with a 1 ohm load resitor in parallel with each of the alternator leads as described below.

4. Three-lead-type stator:

a. White/green and green/black leads—minimum voltmeter reading 4.0 volts.

b. White/green and green/yellow leads—minimum voltmeter reading 6.5 volts.

c. White/green and green/black with green/yellow leads—minimum voltmeter reading 8.5 volts.

5. Two-lead-type stator:

a. White/green and green/yellow leads—minimum voltmeter reading 8.5 volts, for all except 47205 stator (9.0V).

6. If low or no readings are obtained, inspect the leads for damage and make sure they have tight connections. Check the alternator output again, and if the same results are obtained the difficulty lies in the alternator itself and it must be replaced.

7. To check for grounded coils within the stator, connect the voltmeter to each terminal and ground. If a reading is obtained, the coil connected to the lead being tested is grounded.

T100C, T100R, TR64, TR6C, AND T120R

Test the alternator output as described for the TR25W. Correct output readings are given in the following chart.

T150

Check alternator output for the Trident in the same manner as described for the three-lead TR25W stator. Correct output readings are given.

TR7V , T140V, T150V

These models use a 47205 stator. Procedures are same as for TR25W. Minimum voltmeter reading is 9.0 volts.

	Alternator Output Minimum AC Volts @ 3,000 rpm		
RM20 stator 47209 (12 volt)	green/white and green/black connected 5.0	green/white and green/yellow connected 8.0	green/white green/black and green/yellow connected 10.0

Rectifier Test

Two precautions should be taken whenever handling the rectifier for testing or for any other purpose.

1. When removing or installing the rectifier, prevent any possibility of twisting the rectifier plates, which could result in broken internal wiring.

2. *Never* disturb the nuts that hold the rectifier plates together.

To test the rectifier in the machine:

1. Disconnect the brown/white lead from the center terminal and wrap the end in tape to prevent a short-circuit to ground.

2. Connect a DC voltmeter in parallel with a 1 ohm load resistor between the center rectifier terminal and ground.

3. On twins, disconnect the alternator green/yellow lead and connect it to the rectifier green/black lead by using the appropriate jumper cable. Make sure this connection is insulated to prevent a short-circuit.

4. Start and run the machine at 3,000 rpm and observe the voltmeter reading. It must be 7.5 volts minimum.

5. If the reading is higher than specified, check the rectifier ground. If the ground is OK, replace the rectifier. If the reading was zero or less than specified, the problem lies in the rectifier or charging system wiring. First check the rectifier on a bench.

Stator Number	System Voltage	DC Input to Battery amp @ 3,000 rpm Off	Pilot	Head	Alternator Output Minimum AC Volts @ 3,000 rpm A	B	C	Stator Coil Details No. of Coils	Turns per coil	S.W.G.
	6V	2.75	2.0	2.0						
47162	12V	2.0°	2.1°	1.5°	4.0	6.5	8.5	6	140	22
		4.8†	3.8†	1.8†						
47164	6V	2.7	0.9	1.6	4.5	7.0	9.5	6	122	21
47167	6V	6.6‡	6.6‡	13.6‡	7.7	11.6	13.2	6	74	19
								2	250	25 IGN
47188	6V	Not applicable			5.0	1.5	3.5	2	98	20 LIGHT
								1	98	20 LIGHT
								1	98	21
47204	12V						8.5	as 47162		

Coil Ignition Machines
A—Green/White and Green/Black
B—Green/White and Green/Yellow
C—Green/White and {Green/Black, Green/Yellow} connected

° Zener in Circuit
† Zener disconnected
‡ With Boost Switch in Circuit

NOTE: *On machines fitted with two-lead-stator, only test C is applicable as leads are colored green/white and green/yellow.*

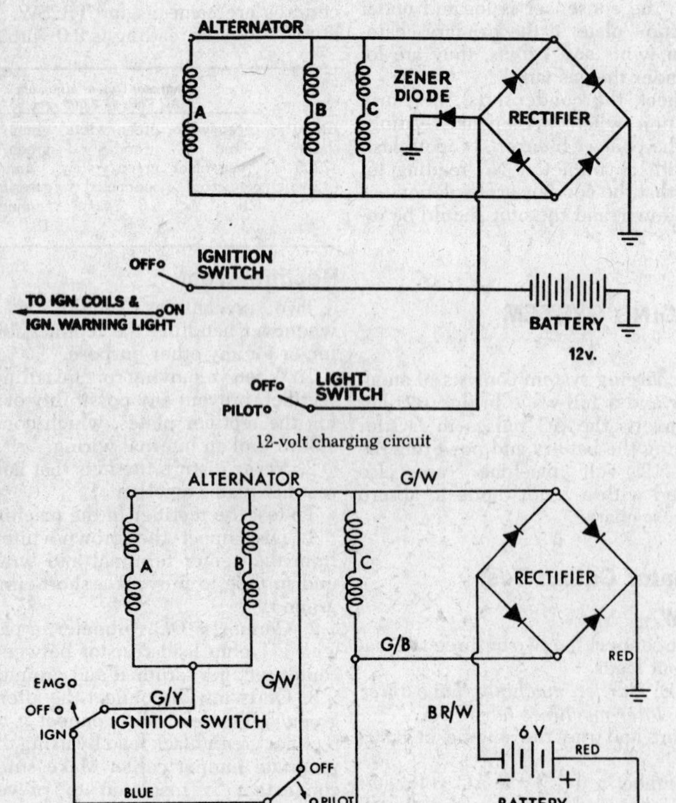

12-volt charging circuit

6-volt charging circuit

Rectifier Bench Test

1. Disconnect and remove the rectifier. Observe the note on handling the unit.
2. Connect the rectifier to a 12 volt battery and a 1 ohm load resistor.
3. Connect a DC voltmeter in the V position as shown in the accompanying illustration. The meter should read 12 volts.

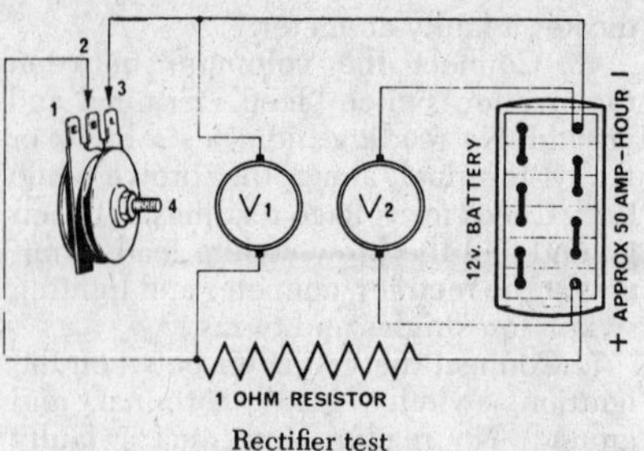

Rectifier test

4. Disconnect the voltmeter and, using the accompanying illustrations for guidance, test each of the diodes with the voltmeter leads. Keep the testing time as short as possible so that the rectifier does not overheat. No reading should be greater than 2.5 volts in Test 1, and no reading should be more than 1.5 volts less than the battery voltage in Test 2 (i.e., 10.5 volts minimum).
5. If the rectifier does not meet specifications, it should be replaced.

Charging Circuit Continuity Test

If the rectifier tests did not pinpoint the problem, it must be located somehere within the charging circuit wiring. For checking continuity, the battery must be in a good state of charge and the alternator leads must be disconnected at their snap connectors.

TR25W

1. Make sure there is power at the rectifier by connecting a DC voltmeter, with a 1 ohm load resistor in parallel, between the center rectifier terminal and ground. The meter should read battery voltage.
2. If there is no voltage at the rectifier, repeat steps 3, 5, and 6 under "Low Tension Circuit Tests" to isolate the problem in the wiring.

500 AND 650 TWINS

6 Volt Machines

1. Repeat steps 1 and 2 given for the TR25W.
2. Connect the green/yellow lead from the main wiring harness (under the engine) to the rectifier center terminal with a jumper cable. Turn the ignition switch on.
3. Connect a DC voltmeter, with a 1 ohm resistor in parallel, between the green/white lead at the rectifier and ground. With the light switch in the "off" position, the meter should read battery voltage. If not, the leads to the ignition switch terminals 16 and 18, and the leads to light switch terminals 4 and 5, should be checked.
4. Connect the green/yellow lead from the main wiring harness to the rectifier center terminal with a jumper cable. Turn the ignition switch to the IGN position and the headlight switch to the HEAD position.
5. Connect a DC voltmeter, with a 1 ohm resistor in parallel, to the green/black lead at the rectifier and ground. The meter should read battery voltage. If not, the leads to ignition switch terminals 16 and 17, and the leads

to light switch terminals 5 and 7, should be checked. With the light switch in the PILOT position, there should be no voltage reading between ground and the rectifier green/black or green/white leads.

12 Volt Machines

1. Check the battery to make sure the fuse is intact and that the battery is correctly connected to ground (positive).
2. Check to see that there is voltage at the rectifier center terminal as previously described. If there is not, disconnect the alternator leads at their snap connectors under the engine.
3. Wire a jumper lead between the center and green/yellow rectifier terminals and check the voltage between the snap connector and ground. If there is no reading, the alternator harness lead is faulty.
4. Repeat the above for the rectifier green/white lead.
5. If there is voltage at the center rectifier terminal, check the ammeter terminal. If it is satisfactory here, the brown/white lead to the rectifier center connector is faulty.
6. If there is no voltage at either the rectifier or the ammeter, the blue/brown wire from the battery is faulty.

T150

Perform the charging circuit continuity test for the Trident in the same manner as described for the 500 and 650 twins.

TR7V, T150V, T150V

The test is similar to that for the 500 and 650 Twins as described above except that the wire color codes have changed. The rectifier center terminal for these models is fitted with a brown/blue wire instead of the brown/white wire for the earlier models.

Load Resistor

A 1 ohm load resistor has been referred to in several steps of the charging system test procedures. This resistor is easily obtainable from a local electrical supply outlet, or can be constructed as follows:

1. Materials:

4 yards of 18, S.W.G. (0.048 in.) Nichrome wire

1 foot of flexible, heavy gauge wire

1 alligator clip

1 piece of asbestos approximately 2 in. in diameter

2. Instructions:

Fold the thin wire double and connect the heavy wire to the folded end. Connect the other end of the heavy wire to the positive terminal of a 6 volt battery. Connect a 0–10 volt DC voltmeter between the battery terminals and an ammeter between the negative terminal of the battery and the free ends of the thin wire. Make this last connection with the alligator clip. Move the clip along the two thin wires until the ammeter reading is numerically equal to the voltmeter reading. Cut the thin wires at this point and wrap them around the piece of asbestos, making sure the wires do not touch each other.

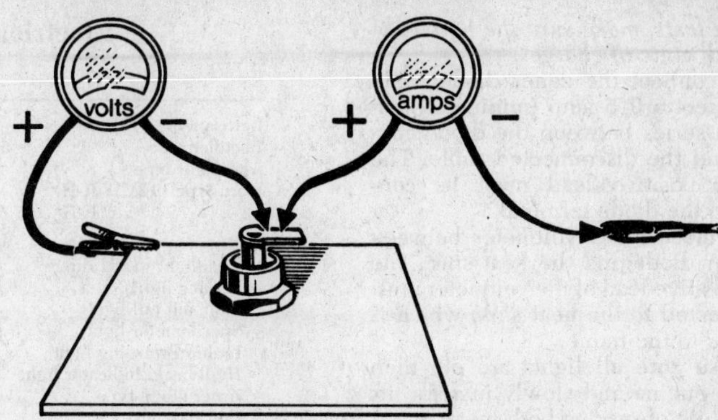

Zener diode test

Zener Diode

The zener diode serves the functions of a voltage regular, tapping off excess alternator current output and rerouting it to a heat sink. It is very important that the diode be kept clean and free from obstruction in the cooling airstream at all times. Other than this, if you make sure that the base of the diode and heat sink have firm metal-to-metal contact, the diode is a maintenance free item.

NOTE: *Before making any of the fol-*

Electrical Specifications

TR25W

Battery	Lucas PUZ5A
Coil	Lucas MA.12
Contact breaker unit	Lucas 6CA
Generator	Lucas RM.19
Generator output	115 watt
Horn	Lucas 6H
Rectifier	Lucas 2DS.506
Zener diode	Lucas ZD.715
Bulbs: headlamp (main)	40/27 watt
headlamp (pilot)	6 watt
main beam indicator	2 watt
stop and tail lamp	6/21 watt

T100C and T100R

Battery	1 Lucas 12 volt battery PUZ5A or earlier 2 Lucas batteries connected in series (MKZ9E)	
Rectifier	Lucas 2DS506	
Alternator type	Lucas RM19	
Horn	27899 12 volt	
Bulbs:	No.	Type
Headlight	Lucas 414	50/40 watts
Parking light	Lucas 989	6 watts MCC
Stop and tail light	Lucas 380	6/21 watts offset
Speedometer light	Lucas 987	2 watts MES
Ignition warning light	Lucas 281	2 watts (BA7S)
Main beam indicator light (where fitted)	Lucas 281	2 watts (BA7S)
Zener diode type	ZD 715	
Coil type	Lucas MA12 (12V) 2 off	
Contact breaker type	Lucas 4CA (12° range) After H.57083 Lucas 6CA (12° range)	
Fuse rating	35 amp	

TR6C, TR6R, and T120R

Battery (12V)	PUZ5A	
Rectifier type	2DS 506	
Alternator type	RM.19	
Horn type (12V)	6H	
Cutout switch	151SA	
Bulbs:	No.	Type
Headlight (L/H dip)	464	40/27 watts vert-dip pre-focus
Parking light	989	6 watts—MCC
Stop and tail light	380	L679 21/6 watts—offset pin
Speedometer light	989	6 watts—MCC
Ignition warning light	281	2 watts (BA7S)
High beam indicator light	281	2 watts (BA7S)
Zener diode type	ZD 715	
Coil type (2 off)	Siba 3200/1 2 off or later, 17M12 (12V) 2 off	
Contact breaker type	6CA	
Fuse rating	35 amp	

lowing tests, make sure the battery is in a full state of charge.

1. Disconnect the zener diode cable and connect a 0–5 amp (minimum) ammeter in series between the diode connector and the disconnected cable. The ammeter positive lead must be connected to the diode terminal.

2. Connect a DC voltmeter between the zener diode and the heat sink. The red or positive lead of the voltmeter must be connected to the heat sink, which is grounded to the frame.

3. Make sure all lights are off, then start the engine and slowly increase its speed while observing both meters.

4. Until the voltmeter reaches 12.75 volts, the ammeter should read zero.

5. Continue increasing the engine speed until the ammeter reads 2.0 amps, at which time the voltmeter should be reading 13.5 to 15.3 volts.

6. If the ammeter registers before the voltmeter reaches 12.75 volts in step 4, or if the voltage is higher than stated in step 5 when the ammeter reads 2.0 amps, the zener diode should be replaced.

CAPACITOR IGNITION SYSTEM

A capacitor ignition system kit is available to make it possible to run the machine without a battery. The kit consists only of a mounting spring and the capacitor unit itself. The system uses the same equipment as the coil ignition/battery type, with the exception of the battery.

In operation, the capacitor stores the current from the alternator and releases it at the moment of contact breaker opening. This produces an adequate spark for starting, although not as healthy a spark as it produced by a battery. When running, the capacitor also helps to reduce DC voltage ripple. The lighting system will also operate normally, except that the parking light will not function when the engine is not running.

In addition to the obvious advantage of not requiring a battery, this system has several other points in its favor: cold weather does not affect the capacitor mounted so that it can be connected in an emergency starting situation.

INSTALLATION

1. The capacitor terminals can be identified s follows:

Single terminal—positive (ground) marked with a red dot on the mounting rivet. Double terminal—negative.

2. Install the capacitor in its spring with the terminals facing down. Push the unit into the spring until the last coils fit into the capacitor body groove.

3. Connect the capacitor negative terminal *and* zener diode to the center (brown/white lead) connector of the rectifier.

4. Connect the positive terminal of the capacitor to the rectifier center ground bolt terminal.

5. Mount the capacitor spring in any convenient spot near the battery carrier.

Before putting the machine into operation, a few precautions should be taken to avoid any damage to the capacitor or wiring system.

1. If the battery is to remain in the machine, it is essential that the negative lead be very carefully insulated to prevent it from shorting to the frame. This can be done by either wrapping the lead in electrical tape or, better yet, by replacing the battery fuse with a wooden dowel of similar dimensions.

2. If the capacitor is being used as a back-up system in case of battery failure, take the time to check it occasionally to ensure that it's still operational.

3. Do not run the engine with the zener diode disconnected as the capacitor will be destroyed due to excessive voltage.

Capacitor Ignition Test

The capacitor has a limited storage life of approximately 18 months at 68° F, or 9 to 12 months at 86° F. Therefore, it would be wise to check its condition regularly if it is not in use.

1. Connect the capacitor to a 12 volt battery for approximately 5 seconds. Make sure the terminal polarity is correct or the capacitor will be ruined.

2. Let the capacitor stand for at least 5 minutes, then connect a DC voltmeter to the terminals. Note the steady reading of the meter. A good capacitor will register at least 9 volts.

Electrical Specifications (cont.)

T150

Battery type (12V)	PUZ5A	
Rectifier type	54048008 (Lucas)	
Alternator type	RM20	
Horn type (12V): R-H	P201	
L-H	P101	
Bulbs:	No.	Type
Headlight (L/H dip)	446	50/40 watts—pre-focus
Parking light	989	6 watts—MCC
Stop and tail light	380	6/21 watts—offset pin
Speedometer light	987	2.2 watts—MES
Ignition warning light	281	2 watts (BA7S)
High beam indicator light	283	2 watts (BA7S)
Zener diode type	ZD 71S	
Coil type (3)	Siba 32000 3 off	
Contact breaker type	Lucas 7CA (12°)	
Oil warning light	281 2 watts (BA7S)	
Fuse rating	35 amps	

T150V

Battery type (12V)	PUZ5A	
Rectifier type	Lucas 2DS.506	
Alternator	RM 20/21	
Horn	Clearhooter HF 80 High/low	
Bulbs:	No.	Type
Headlight	370	45/40 watts
Parking light	989	6 watts
Stop and tail light	380	21/6 watts
Instrument lights	643	2.2 watts
Zener diode	ZD.715	
Coils (3)	17M12	
Contact breakers	7CA	
Fuse rating	35 amps	

TR7V, T140V

Batery type (12V)	PUZ5A	
Rectifier	2DS 506	
Alternator	RM21	
Horn	Lucas 6H	
Zener diode	2D715	
Coils (2)	17M12	
Bulbs:	No.	Type
Headlight	370	45/35 watts
Parking light	989	6 watts
Stop and tail light	380	5/21 watts
Warning lights	281	2 watts
Instrument lights	987	3 watts

WIRING DIAGRAMS

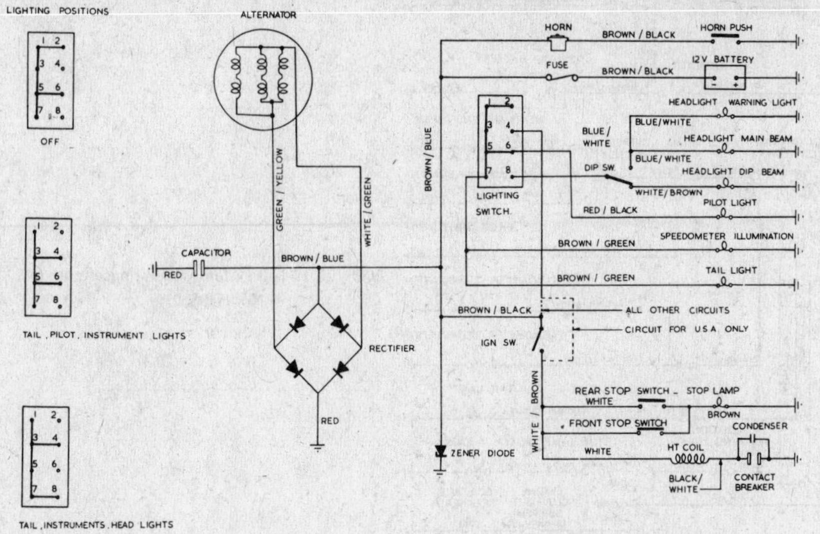

LIGHTING POSITIONS

OFF

TAIL, PILOT, INSTRUMENT LIGHTS

TAIL, INSTRUMENTS, HEAD LIGHTS

250

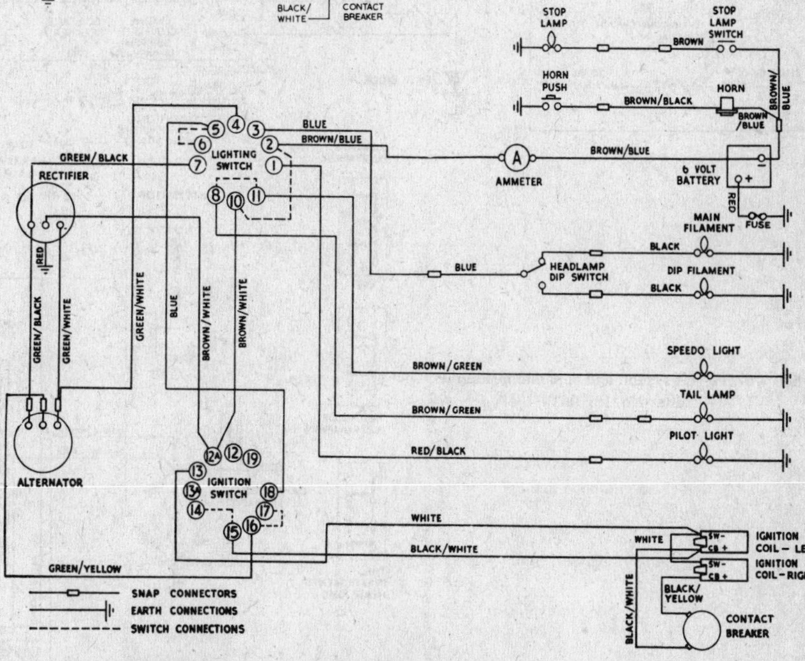

500 with 6-volt system

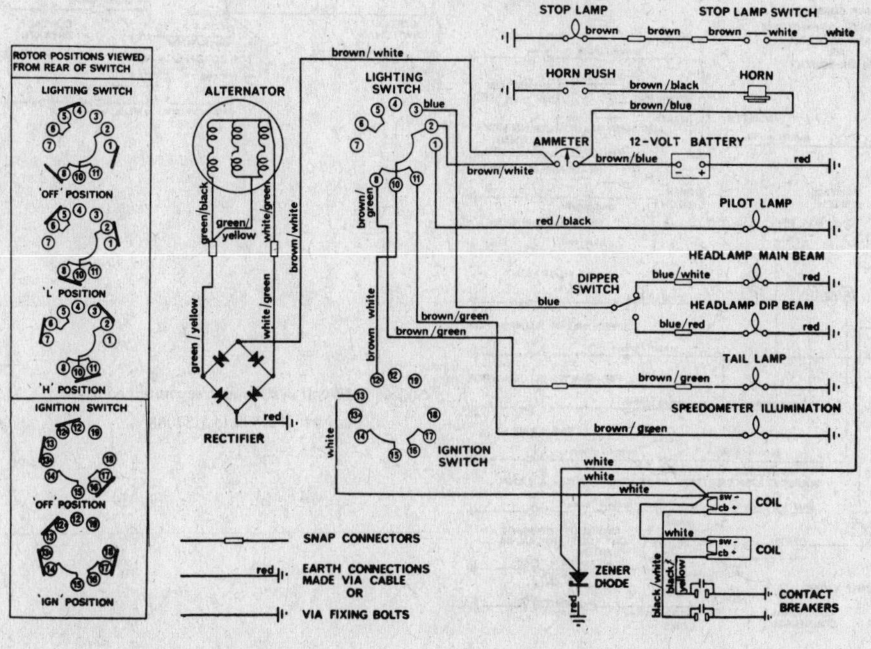

SNAP CONNECTORS
EARTH CONNECTIONS
SWITCH CONNECTIONS

ROTOR POSITIONS VIEWED FROM REAR OF SWITCH

LIGHTING SWITCH

'OFF' POSITION

'L' POSITION

'H' POSITION

IGNITION SWITCH

'OFF' POSITION

'IGN' POSITION

SNAP CONNECTORS
EARTH CONNECTIONS MADE VIA CABLE OR
VIA FIXING BOLTS

500 with 12-volt system and nacelle to No. H49832

WIRING DIAGRAMS

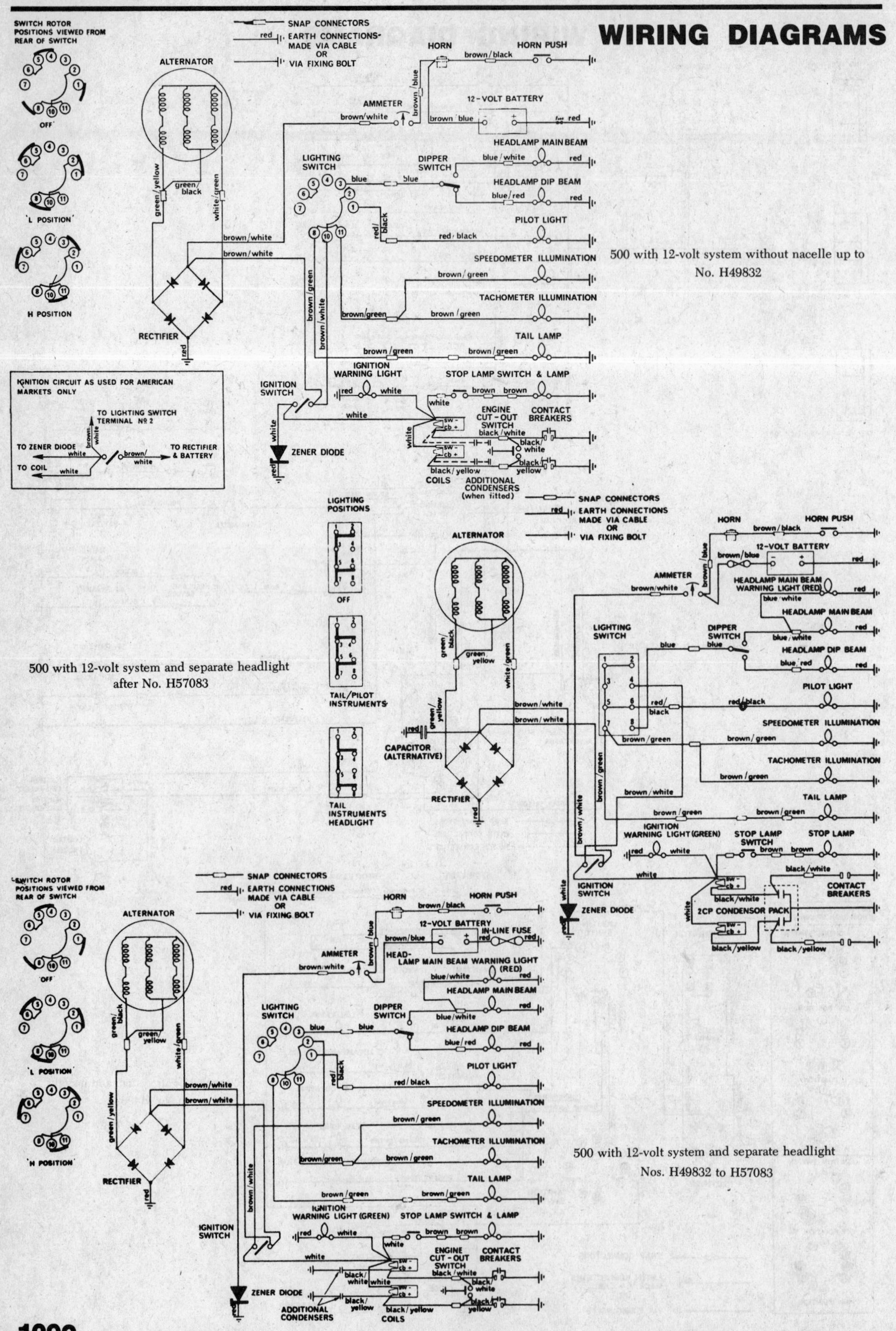

500 with 12-volt system without nacelle up to No. H49832

500 with 12-volt system and separate headlight after No. H57083

500 with 12-volt system and separate headlight Nos. H49832 to H57083

WIRING DIAGRAMS

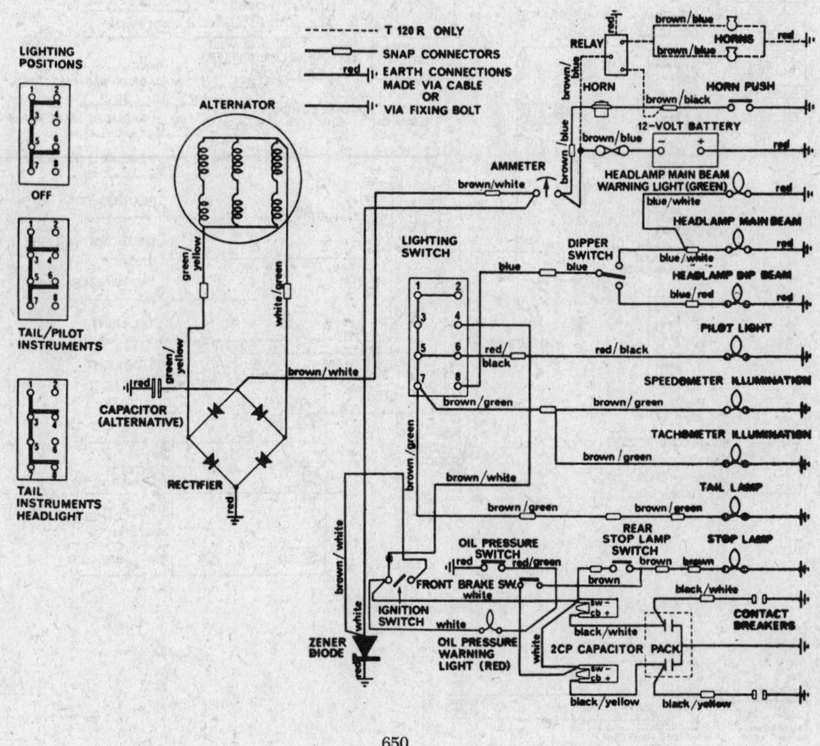
LIGHTING POSITIONS
OFF
TAIL/PILOT INSTRUMENTS
TAIL INSTRUMENTS HEADLIGHT
T 120 R ONLY
SNAP CONNECTORS
EARTH CONNECTIONS MADE VIA CABLE OR VIA FIXING BOLT
ALTERNATOR
CAPACITOR (ALTERNATIVE)
RECTIFIER
RELAY
HORNS
HORN
HORN PUSH
12-VOLT BATTERY
AMMETER
HEADLAMP MAIN BEAM WARNING LIGHT (GREEN)
HEADLAMP MAIN BEAM
DIPPER SWITCH
HEADLAMP DIP BEAM
LIGHTING SWITCH
PILOT LIGHT
SPEEDOMETER ILLUMINATION
TACHOMETER ILLUMINATION
TAIL LAMP
OIL PRESSURE SWITCH
REAR STOP LAMP SWITCH
STOP LAMP
FRONT BRAKE SW.
IGNITION SWITCH
OIL PRESSURE WARNING LIGHT (RED)
CONTACT BREAKERS
2CP CAPACITOR PACK
ZENER DIODE

650

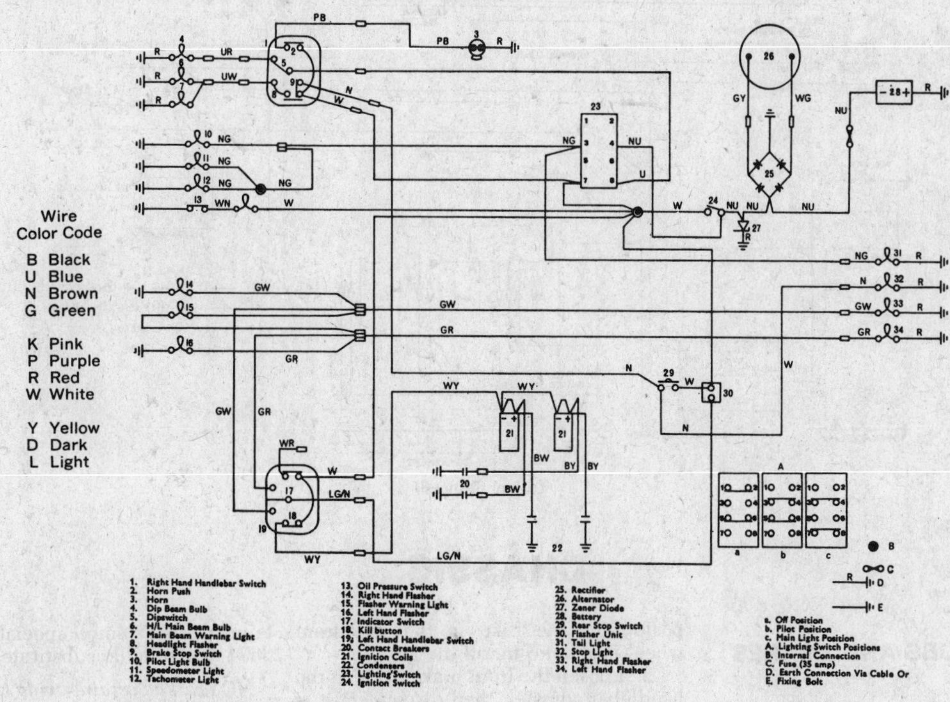
Wire Color Code
B Black
U Blue
N Brown
G Green
K Pink
P Purple
R Red
W White
Y Yellow
D Dark
L Light
1. Right Hand Handlebar Switch
2. Horn Push
3. Horn
4. Dip Beam Bulb
5. Dipswitch
6. H/L Main Beam Bulb
7. Main Beam Warning Light
8. Headlight Flasher
9. Brake Stop Switch
10. Pilot Light Bulb
11. Speedometer Light
12. Tachometer Light
13. Oil Pressure Switch
14. Right Hand Flasher
15. Flasher Warning Light
16. Left Hand Flasher
17. Indicator Switch
18. Kill button
19. Left Hand Handlebar Switch
20. Contact Breakers
21. Ignition Coils
22. Condensers
23. Lighting Switch
24. Ignition Switch
25. Rectifier
26. Alternator
27. Zener Diode
28. Battery
29. Rear Stop Switch
30. Flasher Unit
31. Tail Light
32. Stop Light
33. Right Hand Flasher
34. Left Hand Flasher
a. Off Position
b. Pilot Position
c. Main Light Position
A. Lighting Switch Positions
B. Internal Connection
C. Fuse (35 amp)
D. Earth Connection Via Cable Or
E. Fixing Bolt

TR7V, T140V

WIRING DIAGRAMS

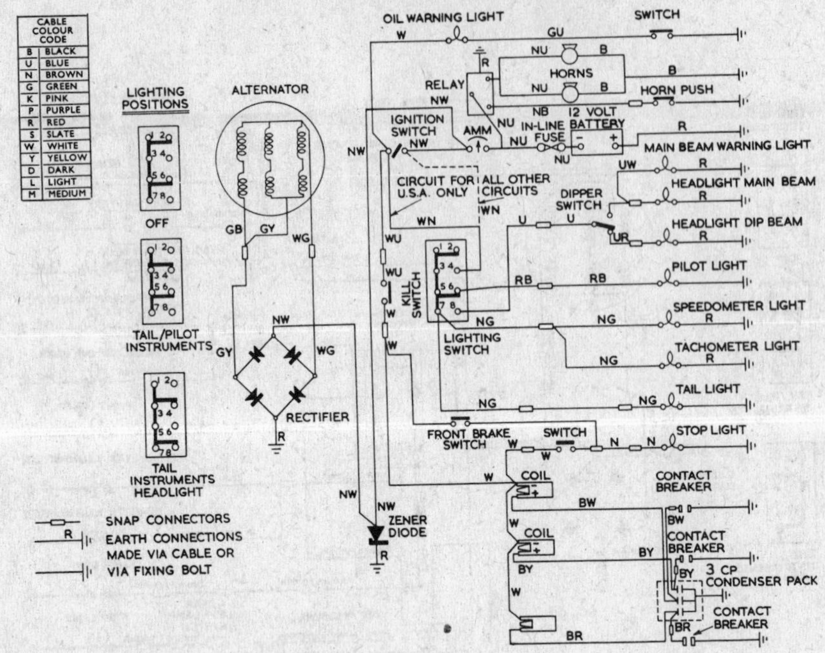

Trident (4-speed)

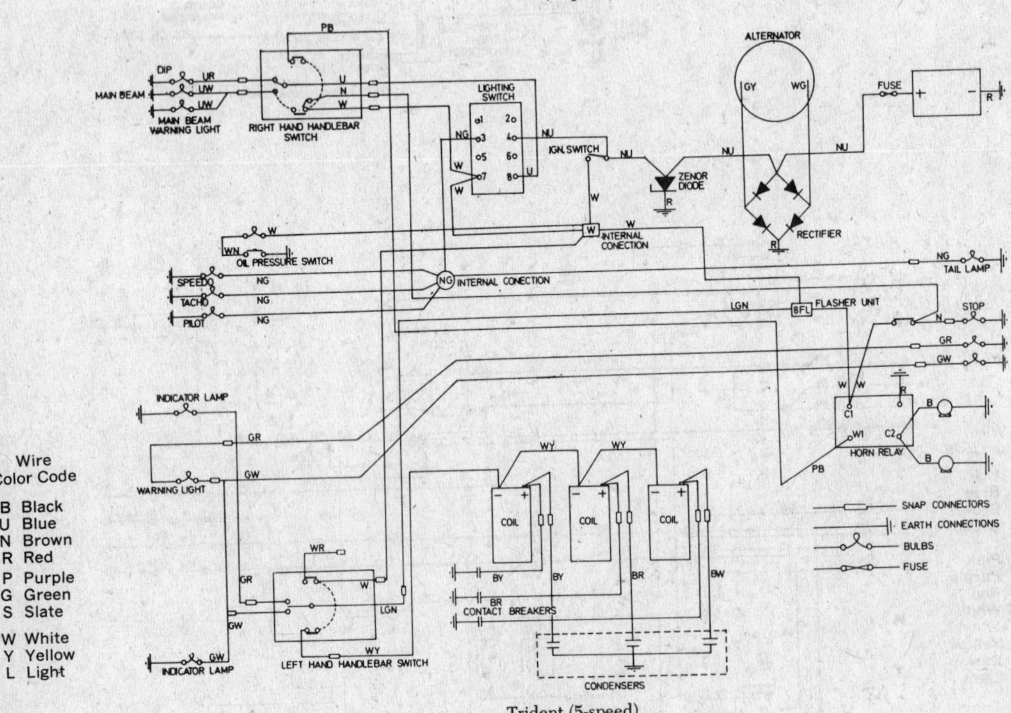

Trident (5-speed)

CHASSIS

WHEELS, HUBS AND BRAKES

TR25W

FRONT

Removal and Disassembly

1. Support the bottom of the engine with a wooden box or wire milk basket, positioning the bike so that the front wheel is about 6 in. off the ground.

2. Loosen the front brake cable at the handlebar adjuster, then disconnect it at the brake backing plate.

3. Remove the two axle securing nuts, slide the axle through the hub, then remove the front wheel assembly.

4. Separate the front anchor plate from the wheel and remove the right retainer with Triumph special tool no. 61-3694 or a suitable substitute.

NOTE: *The retainer ring has left-hand threads.*

5. Remove the right wheel bearing by driving it out from the left side with the axle used as a drift.

6. Remove the backing ring and the inner retainer disc.

Rear wheel bearing retainer

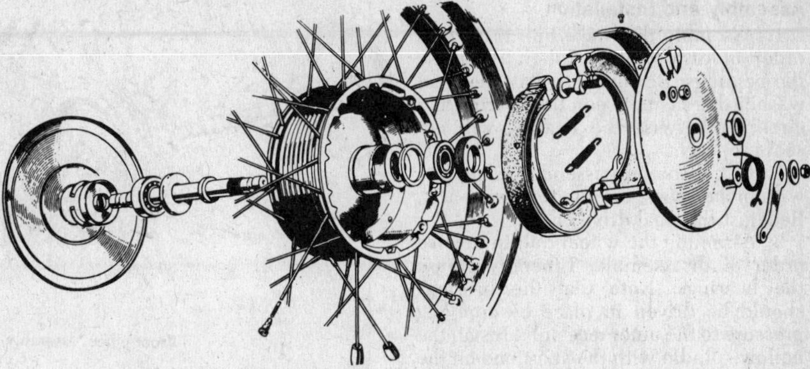

Front wheel assembly, single-leading shoe brake

NOTE: *On machines equiped with double leading shoe brakes, the backing ring and retainer disc are replaced by a single part.*

7. Remove the left wheel bearing circlip and drive the bearing (with retaining plates) out from the right side with the axle.

8. Remove the brake backing plate center nut and withdraw the brake shoe assembly.

9. On machines equipped with double leading shoes, lift up the edge of one shoe until it is free of the backing plate. Disconnect one end of each brake return spring and then remove the second shoe. Remove the pivot pin cotter key at each end of the lever adjustment rod and lift out the pivot pin. Remove the brake cam securing nuts and washers and disconnect the return spring from the front cam. Prey off the levers one at a time and remove the brake cams.

10. On machines equipped with single leading shoes, turn the brake operating lever to relieve the pressure of the shoes against the drum, then pull out the brake and backing plate assembly. Slowly release the operating lever until the return springs can be removed, then remove the springs and the brakes shoes as shown in the accompanying illustration. Remove the operating lever securing nut and washers, then remove the lever and cam spindle.

11. Thoroughly clean all parts (except brake shoes) in kerosine or a cleaning solvent and blow them dry with compressed air.

Inspection

Examine the ball bearings for any signs of pitting or excessive wear. Replace them both if there is any doubt as to their condition.

Inspect the anchor plate for any cracks or signs of distortion, particularly in the area of the brake cam housing. Check the return springs for general condition and signs of fatigue. Measure the drum diameter in several places and check for scoring, etc. If drum diameter is 0.010 in. greater than specified, replacement is in order.

Check the condition of the brake shoes. If oil-soaked, cracked, badly scored, or if the lining is worn down to the rivets, replace the shoes.

If possible check wheel rim runout on a wheel stand. Tighten any loose spokes.

Assembly and Installation

1. On machines with single leading shoes, install the operating lever, cam spindle, and pivot pin. Fasten the return springs to their respective hooks on the brake shoes, then position the shoes over the cam and pivot pin. Snap the shoes in place by pressing on the outer edges of the shoes. Position the operating lever in a counterclockwise location then connect the return spring.

2. On machines with double leading shoes, first lubricate the spindles lightly, then install both cams—wedge shape out. Install the outside return spring on the front cam, then reinstall both brake cam levers and secure them with washers and nuts. Install the abutment plates on the anchor plate the tag side toward the anchor plate. Position the shoes with the radiused end toward the pivot pin and connect the return springs. This is most easily accomplished by installing one shoe, connecting the springs, and snapping the other shoe into place.

3. Coat the wheel bearings and retainers liberally with the recommended grease, then install the left inner retainer, bearing, and outer dust cap. Install the retaining circlip and then drive the bearing up against the circlip, using the shouldered end of the axle as a drift.

4. Install the right retainer disc and backing ring (one piece on machines with double leading brakes).

5. Using the shouldered end of the axle as a drift, drive the right bearing into place, then install the left-hand thread retainer ring.

6. The remainder of the assembly and installation procedure is a reversal of the removal and disassembly instructions.

7. Adjust the front brake.

Removal and Disassembly

1. Disconnect the speedometer drive cable, then remove the securing nut and the rear axle.

2. The distance collar that fits between the hub and the swing arm should drop out when the axle is removed, thereby facilitating wheel removal.

3. Remove the speedometer drive unit and unscrew the end cover.

4. Withdraw the wheel, leaving the brake hub assembly fastened to the swing arm.

5. Remove the left side bearing retainer.

NOTE: *This bearing retainer has lefthand threads.*

6. Using a drift slightly under ¾ in. diameter, drive out the hollow hub spindle. This will release the right bearing, inner collar, and washers.

7. Drive out the left bearing and thrust washer from the right side. Do not disturb the bearing oil seal unless it must be replaced.

8. To remove the brake hub assembly from the swing arm, disconnect the final drive chain and unscrew the brake adjusting rod sleeve. Remove the axle nut and disconnect the torque arm at the hub. Lift out the brake assembly.

9. The brake assembly can now be disassembled and inspected as previously described for the front brakes.

10. To remove the brake hub bearing, first drive out the hollow spindle from the left side and remove the bearing circlip. The bearing can then be driven out with a suitable drift.

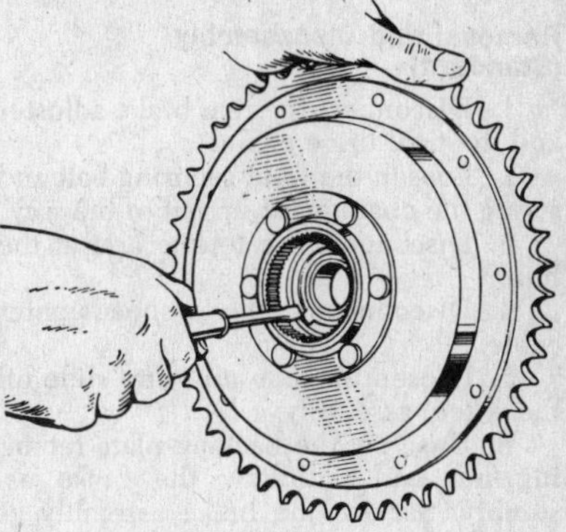

Removing the rear hub bearing circlip

11. Do not disturb the chain sprocket unless it must be replaced. To remove it, bend back the locking tabs and remove the six securing bolts.

12. Thoroughly clean all parts (except brake shoes) in solvent and blow them dry with compressed air. *Do not spin the bearings until they have been completely dried and lubricated.*

Inspection

Examine all parts as previously described for the front wheel and hub. Replace the chain sprocket if the teeth points have become hooked or rounded.

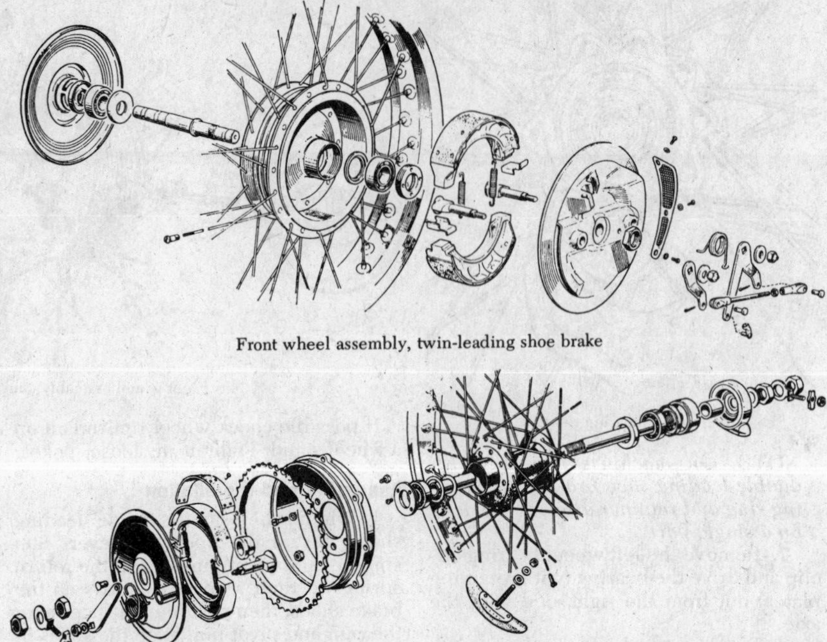

Front wheel assembly, twin-leading shoe brake

Standard rear wheel (500 and 650)

Assembly and Installation

1. Assemble the brake hub in reverse order of disassembly. Liberally grease the bearings. Be sure to install the steel washer that fits between the bearing and circlip, otherwise the bearing will not seat properly.
2. Install the hub assembly, complete with brake shoes, etc., on the swing arm. Readjust the final drive chain.
3. Assemble the wheel hub in reverse order of disassembly. Liberally grease the bearings. Note that the bearings should be driven in place by applying pressure to the outer race only. Install the hollow spindle with the short end on the left-hand side, and install the bearing seals facing outward.
4. Install all the wheel and hub assembly in the reverse of the removal procedure. Do not forget the distance collar between the swing arm and hub. If the brake hub assembly was not removed, it will not be necessary to readjust the chain.

T100C, T100R, TR6R, TR6C, and T120R

FRONT

The front wheel assembly on the 500 and 650 cc models is basically the same as the arrangement used on the TR25W. It can be serviced in the same manner, except that on 500s, Triumph special tool no. Z76 must be used to remove the left bearing retainer ring, rather than tool no. 61-3694.

Use the accompanying illustrations for refrence.

REAR

NOTE: *The 500 and 650 cc models are equipped with either standard or quickly detachable rear wheels.*

Removal and Disassembly (Standard)

1. Disconnect the rear brake adjuster and the final drive chain.
2. Loosen the front securing bolt and swing the chainguard up out of the way.
3. Disconnect the torque arm at the hub.
4. Disconnect the speedometer cable.
5. Loosen the axle nuts and slide off the wheel assembly.
6. Unscrew the backing plate retaining nut and withdraw the brake assembly. Service the brake assembly as described in the TR25W section.
7. Remove the wheel spindle, complete with speedometer drive, out of the right side.
8. Remove the slotted screw that locks the left bearing retainer ring in place.
9. Remove the retainer ring with tool no. 276 or a suitable substitute. The ring has left-hand threads.
10. To gain access to remove the left bearing, drive the central distance piece from the left side until the grease retainer collapses. The bearing can now be driven out from the right side, using a suitable, soft drift.
11. Remove the backing ring, collapsed grease retainer and central distance piece.
12. Drive out the right bearing and dust cap with a drift approximately 1⅝ in. in diameter.
13. Thoroughly clean all parts (except brake shoes) in kerosine or cleaning solvent and blow them dry with compressed air.

Inspection

Examine all parts carefully as described in the TR25W section.

Assembly and Installation

1. Liberally grease the bearings and retainers.
2. Drive in the right grease retainer (new or straightened) and bearing. Install the dust cap after making sure that the bearing and the cavities on either side of the bearing are filled with grease.
3. Install the distance piece, right grease retainer and right bearing. Make sure everything is well packed in grease.
4. Bring the distance piece in line with the axle, then install the threaded (left-hand) retainer ring.
5. Install the retainer locking screw.
6. The remainder of the assembly and installation procedure is a reversal of the removal and disassembly instructions.

Removal and Disassembly (Quickly Detachable)

1. Disconnect the speedometer cable.
2. Unscrew the axle from the right side of the machine and pull out the distance collar.
3. Pull the wheel clear of the engaging splines and remove it out the back of the machine.
4. Remove the locknut on the right side of the axle sleeve and lift off the speedometer drive unit.
5. Disassemble the wheel hub and bearings as previously described for the standard rear wheel.
6. Disconnect the final drive chain, brake operating rod and torque arm, and then remove the axle sleeve nut.
7. Disassemble the brake components as previously described in the TR25W section.
8. Press out the axle sleeve, then remove the bearing circlip located in the brake drum.
9. Pry out the retainer and felt washer, then drive out the bearing with a suitable drift.
10. Thoroughly clean all metal parts in kerosine or cleaning solvent, then blow them dry with compressed air. *Do not spin the bearings until they have been completely dried and lubricated.*

Inspection

Examine all parts as previously described and make any necessary replacements.

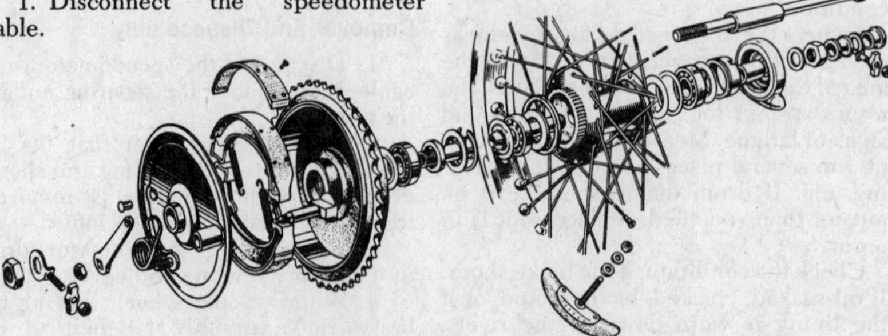

Quickly detachable rear wheel (500 and 650)

Assembly and Installation

Assembly and installation is a reversal of the removal and disassembly instructions. If brake work was performed and the hub was removed from the swing arm, it will be necessary to adjust the rear brake and the final drive chain. Make sure the bearings and retainers are thoroughly packed with grease and remember to soak the felt washer in oil before reassembly.

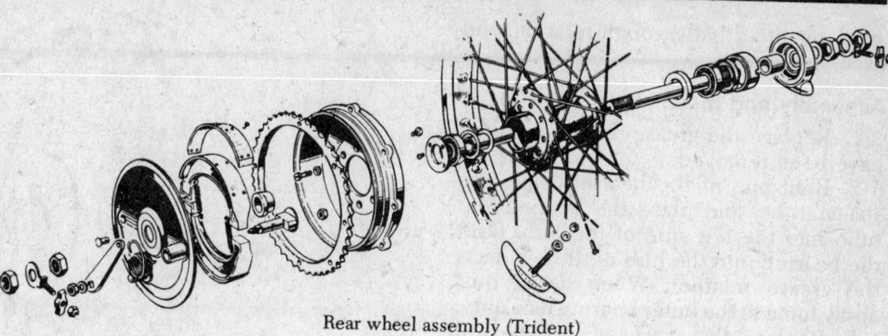

Rear wheel assembly (Trident)

T150

Early models use a front hub not dissimilar to that described above for the TR25W. These models also used a rear hub like that of the 650 Twins (standard hub). Refer to the section above.

Note that some later model Tridents are equipped with the newer type forks (without external fork springs or fork gaitors), and these forks have four nuts on each axle cap which must be removed to remove the front wheel.

When refitting the wheel with this type of fork, place the front wheel assembly into the forks while engaging the brake anchor stud in the slot in the right fork slider. Refit the axle caps and replace all of the cap nuts, tightening them evenly until they are just a bit more than hand tight. Slacken all of them ½ turn.

Pull the wheel to the right side of the machine until the brake anchor plate facing boss touches the mating lug on the fork leg. Holding the wheel in this position, tighten the axle cap nuts *evenly* to 15 ft lbs. Check that no gap exists between the facing boss and the fork slider. Retighten the anchor stud nut.

TR7V, T140V, T150V

FRONT

Removal and Disassembly

These models are equipped with a front disc brake and the latest type of front fork. This fork is easily distinguished from earlier units in that it is *not* fitted with either external fork springs or fork gaitors. The fork tubes are chromed, and the top of each slider is fitted with a small dust seal.

1. Support the machine so that the front wheel is off of the ground.
2. Remove the four axle cap nuts at the bottom of each fork leg, remove the caps, and take away the front wheel assembly. Do not apply the front (disc) brake with the wheel removed.
3. Remove the axle nut on the left side, then unscrew the bearing retainer ring with the Triumph tool 61-3694 or a suitable substitute. The retainer has a standard right-hand thread.
4. Remove the left side wheel bearing by driving the axle through the wheel from the right side. Remove the grease seal beneath the bearings.
5. Take off the circlip on the right hand side of the wheel, and insert the axle into the left hand side, driving out the right hand bearing along with its two grease seals (one on each side of the bearing).

Inspection

1. Clean all parts thoroughly in a solvent and blow them dry.
2. Check the bearings for wear, pitting, play in the bearing races, and rough or uneven rotation. Replace as necessary.

Assembly and Installation

1. Refit the inner grease seal for the right side wheel bearing. Lubricate the bearing thoroughly and refit it and the outer grease seal.
2. Replace the circlip for the right side bearing. Insert the shouldered end of the axle into the left side of the wheel, and use it to drift the bearing assembly up aginast the circlip.
3. Take out the axle, and then reinsert it into the wheel from the left in its normal position.
4. Replace the left-hand bearing grease seal, the lubricated bearing, and the retainer. Screw in the retainer until tight. Tap the axle from the right until the axle shoulder contacts the left side bearing. Replace the axle nut and tighten securely.
5. Engage the brake disc into the caliper and replace the fork caps. Tighten the four nuts on the left fork slider *first*, then tighten the nuts on the right slider. In both cases, tighten the nuts evenly and in an "X" pattern. Torque the cap nuts to 25 ft lbs.

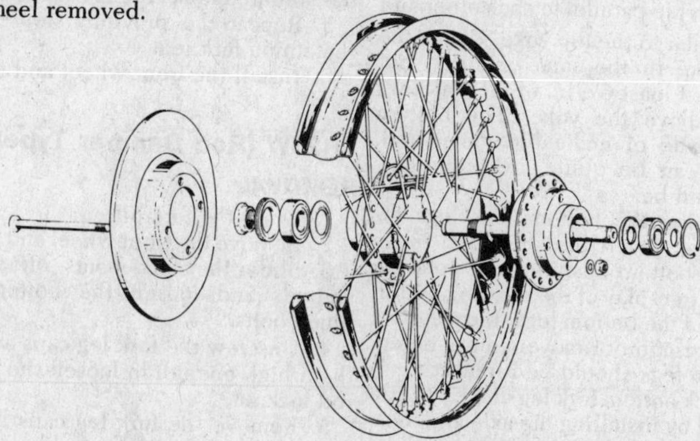

Front wheel assembly (disc brake)

REAR

Removal and Disassembly

1. Support the machine so that the wheel is about 12 in. off the ground.
2. Disconnect the rear chain and disengage it from the rear wheel sprocket.
3. Disconnect the speedometer cable at the rear wheel. Disconnect the brake anchor at the brake plate and remove the anchor from the machine after removing the nut and bolt at the other end.
4. Loosen the bolt securing the left side shock absorber to the swing arm. Lift the chainguard so that the sprocket will clear it.
5. Loosen the axle nut (right side) and pull the wheel assembly out of the machine. Remove the axle, brake assembly, and speedometer drive.
6. To remove the bearings, remove the speedometer drive ring from the right side of the wheel.

   NOTE: *This ring has a left-hand thread.*
7. Remove the bearing retainer from the left side. Use Triumph tool No. 61-3694 to remove this retainer.
8. A drift is needed to remove the bearings and spacer. This drift should have dimensions as shown in the illustration. If this drift is not used, the spacer tube may be damaged, and will have to be replaced. Using the drift, insert it into either side of the wheel and knock out one of the bearings and the spacer tube out of the wheel.
9. Note that the bearing is an interference fit on the end of the spacer tube. Use the drift again to separate the bearing and the spacer tube, then reinsert the spacer tube in the hub, and use it and the drift to remove the remaining bearing. Separate this bearing from the spacer tube after removal.
10. Grease retainers behind each bearing may be left in place, but can be removed with a drift if desired by driving them out from the inside of the hub.

Inspection

1. Check the condition of the bearings and seals. If the latter have been removed, they must be replaced.
2. Wash the bearings in a solvent and blow them dry. Check for worn, dam-

aged, or pitted balls, rough rotation, and excessive play.

Assembly and Installation

1. Replace the grease retainers if they have been removed.
2. Refit one of the bearings onto the spacer tube, and place the bearing and tube into the left side of the hub. Drift the bearing into the hub until it contacts the grease retainer. When doing this, apply force to the outer bearing race only.
3. Replace the washers and the left side retainer ring and tighten it securely. Refit the other wheel bearing driving it home as with the first, and replace and tighten the speedometer drive ring (left-hand thread).
4. The remainder of the procedure is a reversal of the removal instructions.

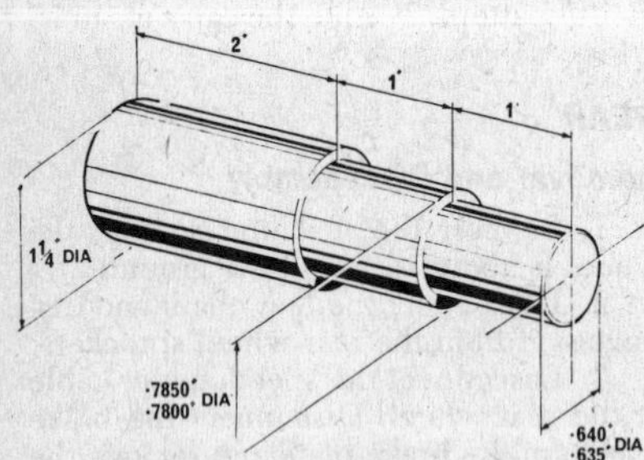

Drift for removing rear wheel bearings (1973 and later)

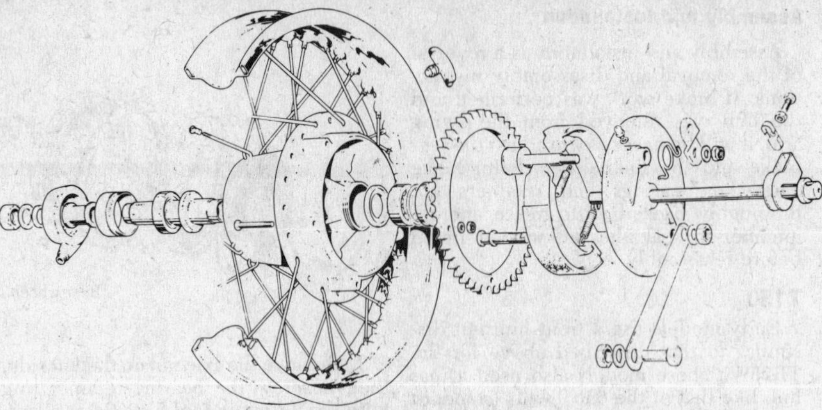

Rear wheel assembly (1973 and later)

FRONT FORK

Late models (including the TR7V, T140V, an T150V) are equipped with a telescopic fork of the "slim-line" pattern easily noticeable because of its chromed fork tubes and the absence of external springs and fork gaitors.

Other models have either rod damper or shuttle valve-type forks. In general, the shuttle valve types can be identified by its longer and narrower spring, and by its overall slimmer appearance.

TR25W (Shuttle Valve Type)

REMOVAL

1. Drain the fork oil.
2. Remove the front wheel and fender.
3. Slide the boots clear of the top fork shrouds.
4. Remove the fork leg caps along with cable brackets.
5. Loosen the bottom yoke, fork pinch-bolts and screw Triumph special tool no. 61-3824 or a suitable substitute into the top of the fork stanchion.
6. Hit the tool sharply with a mallet and the stanchion taper will be freed of the top yoke.
7. The fork legs can now be removed.
8. After removing the fork legs, lift off the boots and main springs.

DISASSEMBLY

1. Wrap a piece of rubber around the fork leg and clamp the leg in a soft-jawed vise.
2. Remove the oil seal holder, using Triumph special tool no. 61-6017 or a suitable substitute. Turn the tool counterclockwise.
3. Firmly grasp the stanchion tube and move it back and forth against the top bushing until the bushing is driven out of the lower fork leg. At this time, the stanchion, complete with bushings and shuttle valve, can be removed.
4. To free the shuttle valve, remove the bottom retaining circlip, and let the valve slide out the top end of the stanchion.
5. Do not disturb the bottom bushing unless it is to be replaced. If it is, then remove the bottom bearing retaining nut and drive the bushing out with a hammer and chisel. Take care not to slip and damage the stanchion tube.
6. If it is necessary to remove the restricter at the bottom of the leg, unscrew the bolt in the spindle cutaway.
7. To remove the oil seals from their holders, take out the loose backing washer from the threaded end of the holder, and drive the seal out through the exposed slot. Note the O-ring in the threaded end of the seal holder.

INSPECTION

1. Check the stanchion tubes for straightness by rolling them along a known flat surface. Any bow greater than 5/32 in. requires that the stanchion be replaced. If less than 5/32 in., the stanchion may be straightened.
2. Examine the top fork yoke for cracks and then insert the fork legs (if true) and tighten them down with the top caps. Take several measurements to ensure that the legs are parallel to each other and perpendicular to the top yoke. Check the bottom yoke in the same manner, but make sure at least 6½ in. of the fork legs protrude above the yoke. The bottom yoke is made of malleable metal and, therefore, can be quite easily straightened if need be.
3. Examine the bottom fork legs for any damage. Insert the stanchion tubes (with new bottom bushing) and note the amount of free-play of the bushing within the bores of the bottom legs. If excessive, or any restriction of movement is noted, the bottom legs should be replaced.
4. Check bottom fork leg and front axle alignment by installing the axle and measuring their inclusive angle with a square. Check one leg at a time, then both simultaneously.
5. Inspect the condition of the top and bottom bushings, and measure their inside or outside diameters (see specifications). Excessive wear, or too great a clearance between the bushing and its mating surface, indicates that the bushings should be replaced.
6. Check the main springs for any stress cracks etc., and measure its free-standing height. Both springs must be within ¼ in. of their original dimension.

ASSEMBLY

Assembly is basically a reversal of the disassembly procedure. Note the following:

1. Make sure the new bottom bushing is correctly seated before installing the retaining nut.
2. Note that the large end of the shuttle valve fits into the stanchion.
3. Thoroughly lubricate all parts in the fork before reassembly.
4. Replace the oil seals and apply locking compound to the holder threads.

INSTALLATION

1. Slide the fork leg boots over the oil seal holders and install the main springs.
2. Insert one leg through the bottom and top yoke bores and install Triumph special tool no. 61-3824 on the top of the stanchion. Install the collar and nut, and tighten the nut until the stanchion is firmly locked in its taper.
3. Tighten the bottom yoke pinch bolts and then remove the special tool.
4. Slide the top of the fork boot over the shroud and secure it in place.
5. Repeat the previous steps for the remaining fork leg.
6. Install the front wheel and fender.

TR25W (Rod Damper Type)

REMOVAL

1. Drain the fork oil.
2. Remove the front wheel and fender.
3. Slide the fork boots off the top shrouds and loosen the bottom yoke pinch bolts.
4. Unscrew the fork leg caps and raise them high enough to loosen the damper rod locknut.
5. Remove the fork leg caps from the top of the rod damper.
6. Install Triumph special tool no.

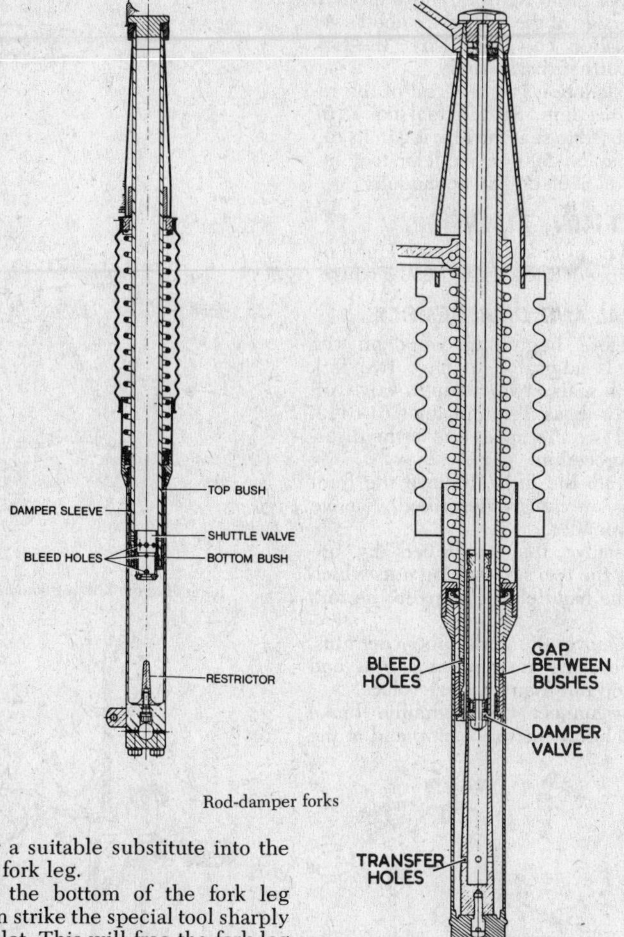

Rod-damper forks

61-3350 or a suitable substitute into the top of one fork leg.

7. Hold the bottom of the fork leg firmly, then strike the special tool sharply with a mallet. This will free the fork leg from its taper in the top yoke.

8. Remove the other fork leg in the same manner.

9. Remove the fork boots and main springs.

DISASSEMBLY

1. Clamp the fork leg in a soft-jawed vise at the axle lug.

2. Slide Triumph special tool no. 61-3005 over the main tube and engage the dogs at the bottom of the oil seal holder.

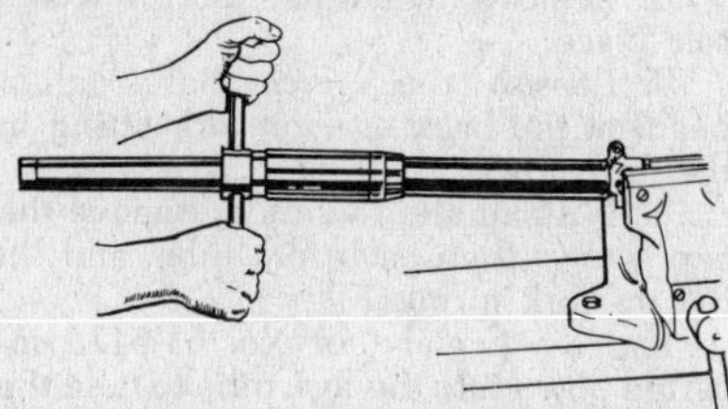

Removing the oil seal holder (rod-damper forks)

3. While applying pressure to the end of the tool, turn it counterclockwise and free the seal holder.

4. Remove the special tool and slide the seal holder to the end of the tube. Do not attempt to entirely remove the seal holder as damage may result.

5. The main tube assembly and lower sliding leg can now be separated.

6. Clamp the un-machined portion of the tube in a soft-jawed vise and remove the large nut at the base of the shaft. Remove the bushings, spacer, and oil seal assembly.

7. Remove the allen screw that secures the damper tube to the lower portion of the fork leg.

8. Remove the two circlips at the top of the damper tube. This will free the damper rod with valve and bushing.

9. Remove the nut that secures the damper valve to the rod. Do not disturb the sealing washer and special retainer located just below the nut unless they require replacement.

10. If an oil seal requires replacement, position the holder with the bottom edge on a wooden block and drive out the seal with Triumph special tool no. 61-3007 or a suitable substitute.

INSPECTION

Examine all parts as generally described for the shuttle-valve-type fork. Compare measurements with those given in specifications at the end of this section and made any necessary replacements.

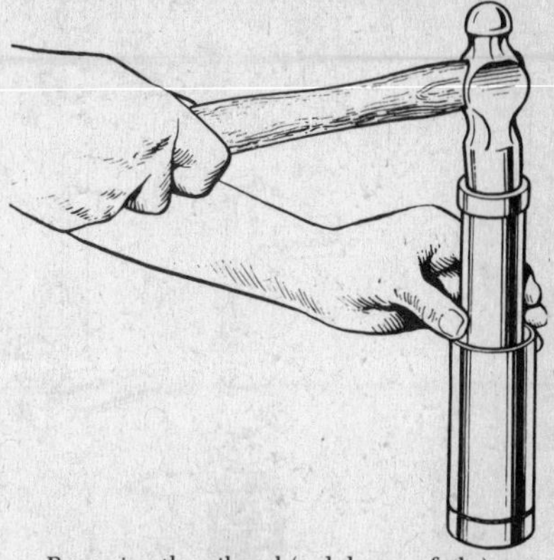

Removing the oil seal (rod-damper forks)

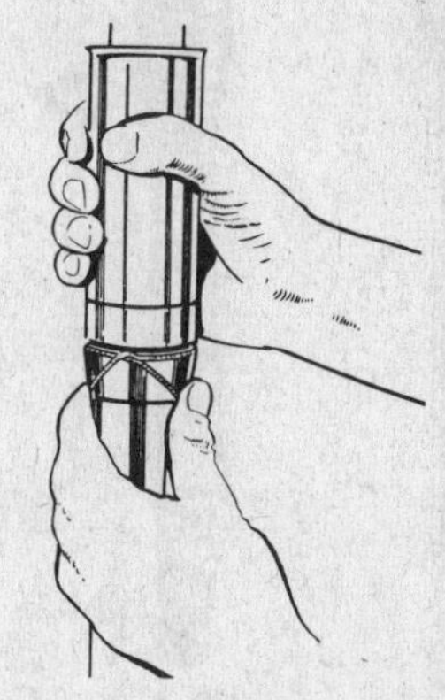

Installing twine for added protection (rod-damper forks)

ASSEMBLY AND INSTALLATION

1. Coat the outside of the oil replacement seals with gasket sealer and drive them into their holders with Triumph special tool no. 61-3007 or a suitable substitute. Grease the feather edge of the seal before further assembly.

2. Make certain all parts are completely clean, then reassemble the remaining parts in reverse order of disassembly.

NOTE: *When tightening down the oil seal holders, it's a good idea to wrap a piece of no. 5 twine around one of the last threads. This will provide additional protection for the seals.*

3. Triumph special tool no. 61-3350 must be used to set the fork leg in its taper, and special tool no. 61-3765 must be used to raise the damper high enough in the tube to screw on the fork leg cap.

T100C, T100R, TR6R, T120R, and T150

These machines are equipped with fork assemblies nearly, if not exactly, identical to those used on the TR25W.

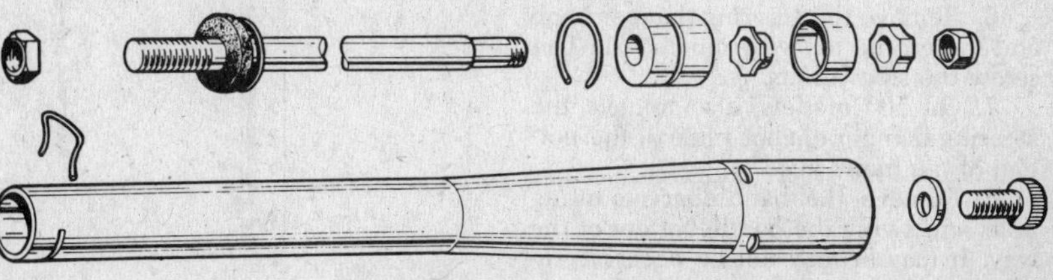

Rod and damper assembly

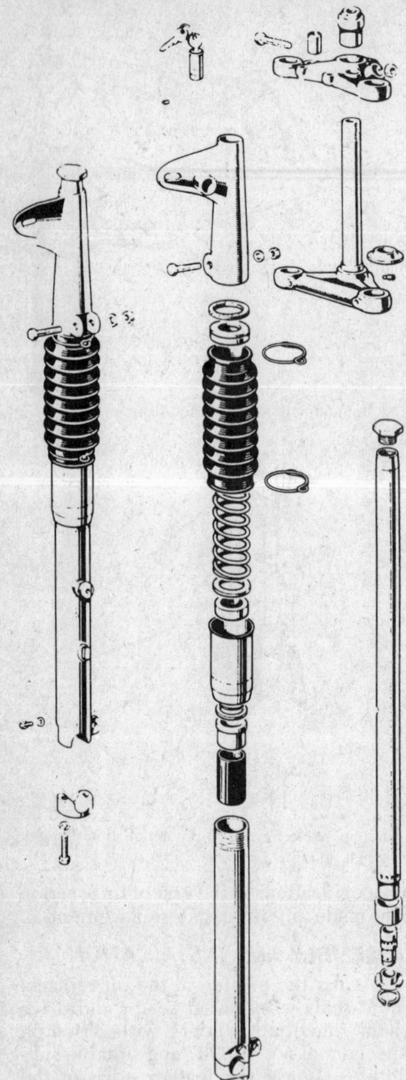

500 and 650 front forks

Disassembly, inspection, and assembly procedures remain the same, but the removal and installation instructions vary slightly to suit various instrument arrangements and the use of a steering damper.

NOTE: *Some late models 650 Twins and Tridents may use the "slim-line" forks. See below.*

REMOVAL AND INSTALLATION

1. Drain the fork oil.
2. Remove the front wheel and fender.
3. Remove the headlight assembly.
4. Disconnect throttle, choke, and front brake cables.
5. Disconnect any instrument and/or diode wiring.
6. Remove the steering damper knob and loosen the top yoke pinch bolt. Unscrew the sleeve nuts.
7. On 500 models, also remove the steering damper anchor plate at the bottom of the frame head.
8. Remove the handlebar mounting bolts and swing the handlebar out of the way. It may or may not be necessary to disconnect all controls.
9. Hold on to the fork and then give the underside of the top yoke a good swat with a mallet. This should free the fork legs for further disassembly.
10. Installation is a reversal of the removal procedure. Special tool no. Z161 must be used to seat the fork leg in its top yoke taper on 500 cc models; tool no. 61-3824 on 650 and 750 cc models.

TR7V, T140V, T150V

This type of fork may also be found on some 4-speed Tridents and 650 Twins.

REMOVAL AND DISASSEMBLY

1. Before beginning work on the forks, it is advisable to have two fork slider oil seals, two damper valve oil seals as well as Triumph tool 61-6113. This tool is quite necessary to the disassembly procedure.
2. Drain the forks, remove the front wheel as previously described, remove the front fender.
3. Remove the handlebars by unscrewing the two self-locking nuts which secure the handlebar clamps to the fork crown.
4. Remove the fork tube cap nuts. Disconnect the instrument cables and lights, and put them in a safe place.
5. Disconnect the hydraulic brake line at the lower triple clamp and at the fork slider.
6. Remove the caliper and put it in a safe place.
7. Loosen the pinch bolts (allen head) at the back of each fork fitting in the fork crown.
8. With an allen wrench, remove the cap screws from each fork tube, and lift out the fork springs.
9. Use special tool No. 61-6113 inserted down into the fork tube to hold the damper valve assembly in place while the allen bolt is removed from the bottom of the slider.
10. Remove the slider from the fork tube. Remove the fork tubes from the triple clamps by first loosening the pinch bolts on the lower triple clamp and yanking down on the tubes until free.
11. Lift the rubber dust cover off of the top of the slider. Remove the nut at the bottom of the damper assembly.
12. Take out the damper assembly. The damper assembly should not be taken apart unless absolutely necessary.

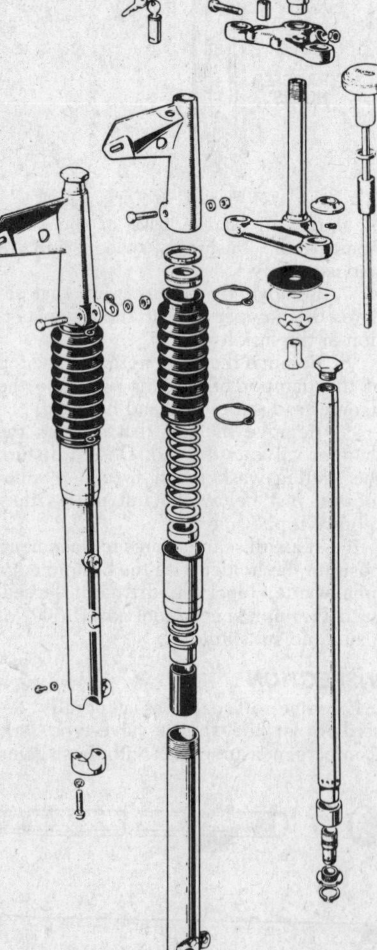

Trident front fork assembly

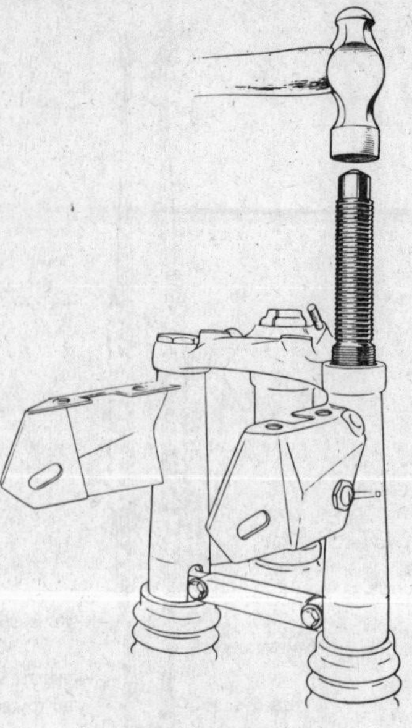

Removing the fork leg stanchion

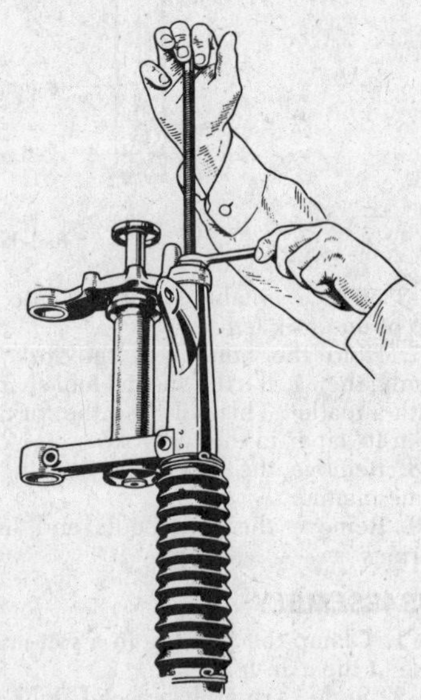

Installing the fork leg with toll no. Z161

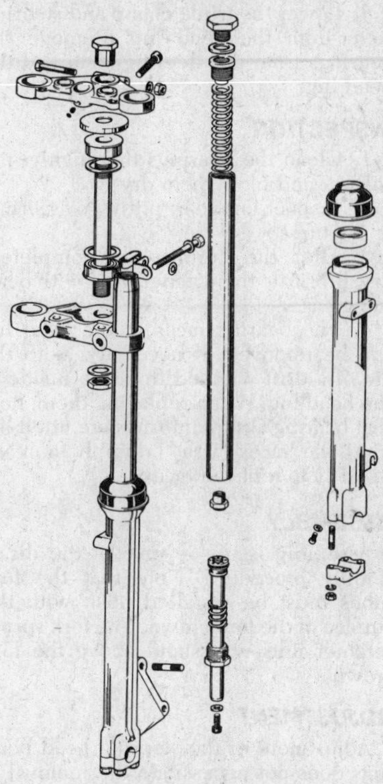

Late model "slim-line" front forks

The O-ring oil seal on the damper bleed valve should be removed and a new one fitted by hand.

13. Account for the sealing washer at the very bottom of each fork slider.

INSPECTION

1. Check all parts for wear or damage. Replace as necessary.
2. To replace the fork slider oil seal, use a tool similar to the one shown or a suitable substitute. The important thing is that the soft aluminum of the slider not be touched by the tool when removing the oil seal. Pry all around the circumference of the seal, gradually lifting it off its seat.
3. To replace the seal, cover the top of the fork tube with a thin plastic "sandwich bag" or something similar. Oil the lips of the seal, and slide it down over the top of the fork tube. Be very careful that the seal is not forced in any way. It is extremely easy to damage the seal.

Place the fork slider in position at the bottom of the fork tube, and bring the seal down to meet it.

A drift is needed to properly seat the oil seal in the slider or it will leak. After installation, remove the slider from the fork tube.

4. Clean all components thoroughly before reassembly.

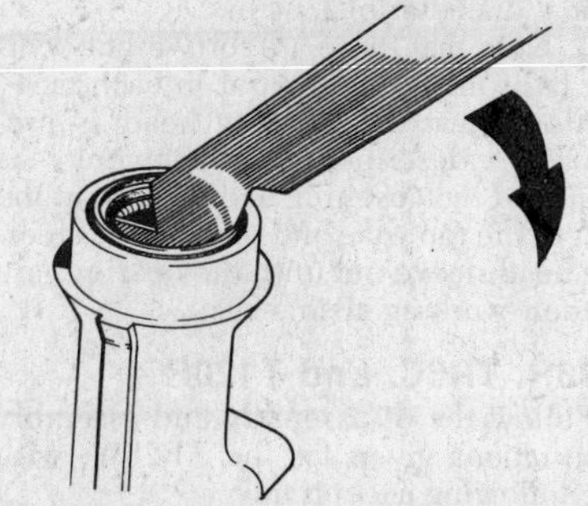

Removing the slider oil seal

ASSEMBLY AND INSTALLATION

1. Refit the damper valve assembly into the bottom of the fork leg. Use a bit of thread locking compound on the damper retainer nut and tighten the nut to 25 ft lbs.
2. Locate the small sealing washer in the very bottom of the fork slider. Replace the dust cover atop the slider, and replace the slider on the fork leg.
3. Bring the slider up to meet the damper assembly and insure that the end of the damper rests on top of the sealing washer. Replace and tighten the allen screw in the bottom of the fork slider with the aid of the special tool.
4. Replace the fork leg assembly in the triple clamps. Push upward until the top of the fork tube is exactly flush with the top of the fork crown. Tighten the pinch bolts on the lower triple clamp and the fork crown to 20 ft lbs.
5. Replace the fork springs. Refill each leg with the correct grade and quantity of oil.
6. Smear the threads of the cap screws with a gasket compound, and tighten the screws to 40 ft lbs. Replace the instruments and the fork cap nuts. Tighten them to 40 ft lbs as well.
7. The remainder of the assembly procedure is the reverse of disassembly. Refer to "Front Wheel Installation" if necessary. Remember that the axle cap nuts on the left slider are tightened first.

ALIGNMENT

In the event that the fork alignment is not correct, loosen the axle cap nuts on the left slider, and tighten those on the right. Loosen the pinch bolts on the lower triple and the fork crown, including the pinch bolt just behind the fork crown center nut.

Pump the forks up and down several times and then retighten the axle cap nuts, the lower triple clamp pinch bolts, the fork crown pinch bolts at the fork tubes, and finally the fork crown pinch bolt behind the center nut. The nuts and bolts must be tightened in that order.

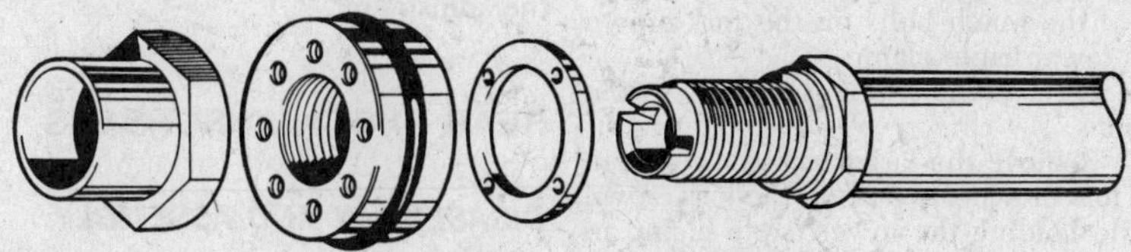

Damper assembly (1973 and later)

STEERING HEAD

TR25W

DISASSEMBLY

1. Remove the headlight assembly and speedometer head.
2. Disconnect the front brake cable and remove the zener diode and heat sink.
3. Protect the gas tank with a piece of cloth, then remove the handlebar mounting bolts and lay the handlebar on the tank.
4. Loosen the steering head clamp bolt and top yoke pinch bolt.
5. Remove the steering head adjusting nut.
6. Unscrew the fork leg caps and disconnect them from the damper rod (if so equipped).
7. Strike the underside of the top yoke smartly with a mallet. This should free the fork legs from their tapers in the top yoke.

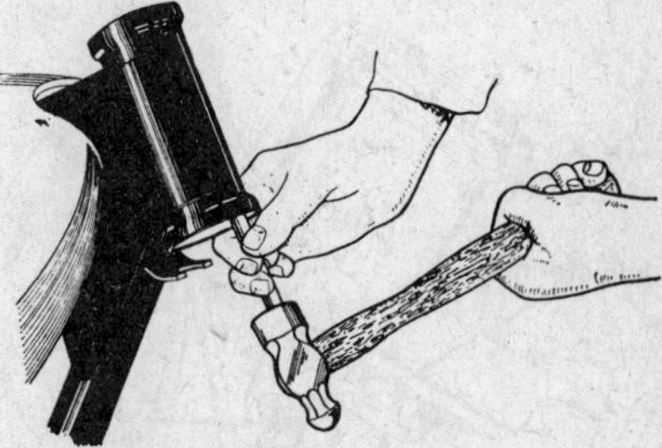

Removing the top bearing cone race

8. Locate the top yoke somewhere out of the way, then pull steering stem down and out of the head. Take care not to lose the bottom ball bearings as the stem is withdrawn.
9. Drive out the top cone race with a long narrow drift and mallet.
10. Pry out the bottom cone race by forcing it up with two levers.
11. Remove the cups by installing special tool no. 61-306.

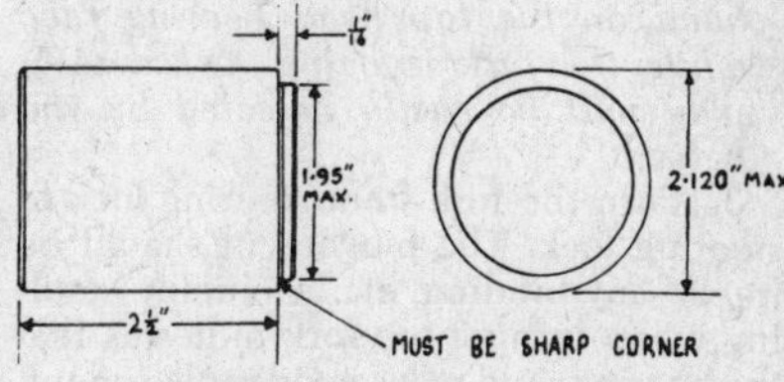

Drift for cup removal (250)

INSPECTION

Examine the bearing balls for pitting, scoring, or flat spots and, if necessary, replace the bearings, cups, and cones.

Clean out the steering head bore and remove any burrs, etc., with emery cloth. Also clean up and inspect the stem itself.

ASSEMBLY

1. Install the bearing cups by driving them into position with a drift. Make sure the cups are square in their housings.
2. Drive the bottom cone into position

with a piece of pipe 1¼ in. in diameter and long enough to clear the column. Make sure it is squarely seated.

3. Liberally grease the bearing cups with the recommended lubricant and install the bearing balls.

NOTE: *There should be forty bearing balls all together; twenty for each race.*

4. Slide the stem back into the head and assemble the top cone and dust cover.

5. Install the top yoke and screw on the adjuster cap.

6. The remainder of assembly is a reversal of the removal procedure.

7. Adjust the steering head as described below.

ADJUSTMENT

1. Place a strong support under the engine so that the front wheel is about 6 in. off the ground.

2. Standing in front of the bike, attempt to rock the front fork back and forth. If there is any play, an adjustment will be necessary.

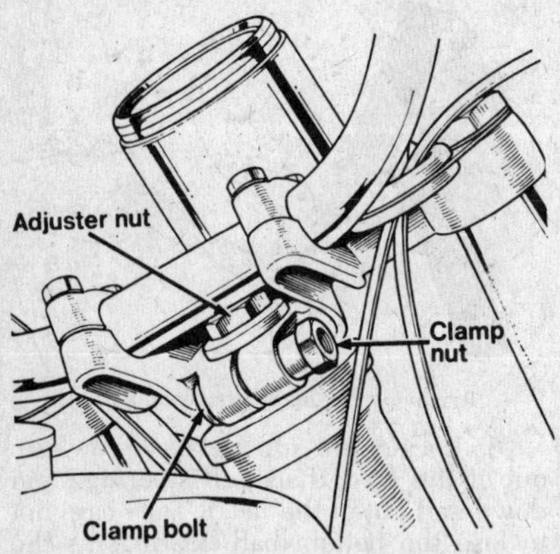

Steering head adjustment (250)

NOTE: *It is very difficult to distinguish between steering head play and front fork bushing wear, so a more accurate method of determining whether an adjustment is necessary is by having a helper hold the fingers of one hand on the top head bearing race while the fork is being rocked. Any play will be easily detected by the helper.*

3. Turn the fork from steering lock to steering lock. The movement should be free of any binding, etc. A "lumpy" feeling when turning the fork indicates that the bearings and races need replacement.

4. If an adjustment is necessary, loosen the steering head clamp bolt and the top yoke pinch bolt.

5. Turn the adjuster bolt until there is no rocking free-play. Make sure the bearings aren't *too* tight by centering the front fork and giving it a slight push to one side. The fork should fall freely until it reaches the steering lock.

T100C and T100R

Follow the disassembly and assembly instructions given for the TR25W, with the following exceptions:

1. When driving the bearing cones into position, use Triumph special tool no. Z24 or a piece of tubing 9 in. long with a diameter of 1¹/₁₆ in.

2. Note that there are forty-eight bearing balls total; twenty-four in each race.

Also adjust the steering head as previously described. Adjustment is achieved by loosening a pinch bolt at the rear of the top yoke and turning the steering head sleeve nut until the bearings are at their working clearances.

TR6R, TR6C, and T120R

Follow the disassembly and assembly instructions given for the TR25W, with the following exception:

1. When installing the bearing cones, use Triumph special tool no. 61-6009 or a piece of tubing 9 in. long with a diameter of 1¹/₁₆ in.

Adjust the steering head as described above for the T100C and T100R.

T150

Follow the disassembly and assembly instructions given for the TR25W, with the following exception:

1. When driving the bearing cones into position use Triumph special tool no. D2218 or a piece of tubing 9 in. long with a diameter of 1¹/₁₆ in.

Adjust the steering head as described above for the T100C and T100R.

TR7V, T140V, T150V

DISASSEMBLY

1. Disconnect the brake line from the fork crown and lower triple clamp.

2. Disconnect the zener diode wires and remove the diode and heat sink from the machine.

3. Remove the headlight and the handlebar assembly. Remove the fork cap nuts. Place the instruments aside.

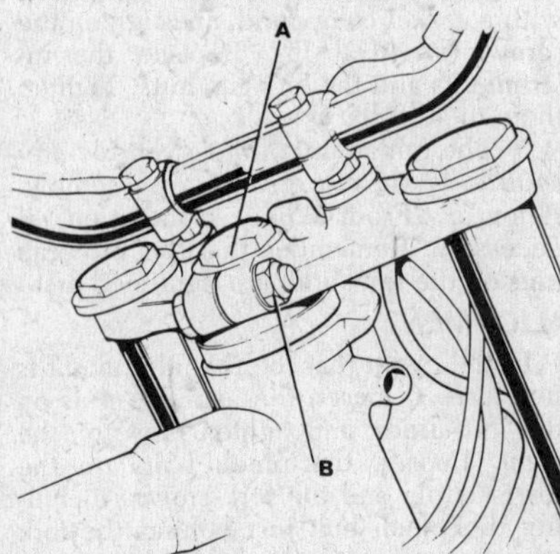

Steering head adjustment nut A and pinch bolt B (TR7V, T140V)

4. Support the machine so that the front wheel is far off the ground. Remove the front wheel and fender as described above.

5. Loosen the fork crown pinch bolt in back of the large adjuster nut, and loosen all of the pinch bolts on the fork crown and lower triple clamp.

6. Remove the fork legs from the triple clamps.

7. Remove the large adjuster nut from the fork crown and take off the fork crown while holding the lower triple clamp in place. Strike the underside of the crown with a soft-faced mallet if necessary.

8. Lower the triple clamp and steering stem from the head lug. Remove the bearings from the steering stem and the head lug.

INSPECTION

1. Clean the bearings thoroughly in a solvent and blow them dry.

2. Inspect for wear, pitting or scoring, or fractures.

3. After the barings are completely dry, lubricate them generously with bearing grease.

4. The bearing races in the head lug can be removed, if necessary, with the aid of a drift wielded from the inside of the head lug. When replacing them, note that bearing abutment rings are fitted behind the races. Use Triumph tool No. 61-6121 to refit the races.

ASSEMBLY

Assembly is the reverse of the disassembly procedure. Note that the fork tubes must be installed flush with the surface of the fork crown. The fork spring retainer nuts will stand above the fork crown.

ADJUSTMENT

Adjustment of the steering head bearings does not necessitate the removal of any components.

1. Support the front wheel off of the ground.

2. Grasp the fork sliders, and attempt to move them forward and back, noting any movements as you do so.

3. Another method, which is also recommended, is to grasp the tip of the front fender and attempt to move the fork assembly up and down. Your other hand should be positioned beneath the steering head feeling for any movement of the lower triple clamp relative to the steering head.

4. The presence of play in the forks in either of these tests would indicate that the bearings must be adjusted.

5. Also note that the forks should be able to be turned from side to side without any binding or a "lumpy" feeling. The latter may indicate worn or broken roller bearings or dented races. See section above for bearing replacement.

6. To adjust the steering head bearings, loosen the fork crown pinch bolt just behind the large bearing adjuster nut, and loosen the adjuster nut itself.

Then tighten the adjuster nut until bearing adjustment is correct. Be certain that the adjustment is not made too tight. This will be noticeable by a wobbly feeling at low road speeds, the same as though a steering damper was tightened down too much. The forks should swing from side to side very easily.

After adjusting the bearings, retighten the fork crown pinch bolt, and recheck the adjustment.

REAR SHOCK ABSORBERS

DISASEMBLY AND ASSEMBLY

The shock absorber consists of a sealed hydraulic damper unit, coil spring, dust covers, and rubber end bushings.

1. Position the cam ring or adjusting ring in its lowest (light load) setting.
2. Clamp the bottom lug of the shock in a soft-jawed vise, then compress the spring by hand and have a helper remove the spring retaining collars.
3. If the rubber end bushings require replacement, drive them out with a suitable drift.
4. Inspect the damper unit for any signs of oil leakage, bending of the plunger rod, etc. Replace it if necessary. Examine the coil spring for any stress cracks, then measure its freestanding height and compare with specifications.
5. Assembly is a reversal of the disassembly procedure. If installing new end bushings, smear them with soapy water to aid assembly.

SWING ARM

The swing arm is mounted to the rear of the frame by a spindle supported in plain bushings. In conjunction with the rear shock absorbers, it serves as the rear wheel suspension system.

TR25W

REMOVAL AND DISASSEMBLY

1. Remove the rear wheel, chainguard, shock absorbers, and rear brake pedal.
2. Disconnect the brake light switch connectors and remove the switch with its bracket.
3. Remove the large spindle nut and washer on the right side of the machine.
4. Drive the spindle out of the swing arm bore with a suitable drift and mallet.
5. Tap the left side of the swing arm down and the right side up, using a mallet. This will free the swing arm from the frame plates.
6. Each swing arm bushing consists of two steel sleeves bonded together with rubber. The inner sleeves are slightly longer than half the width of the swing arm and are locked together, thereby putting the rubber under tension when the arm swings through its arc.

If it is necessary to replace the bushings, the rubber must first be burned out to facilitate removal. This can be done with a thin rod or strip of metal heated until cherry red.

7. When enough rubber has been removed, drive out the inner sleeves and then the outer sleeves.

ASSEMBLY AND INSTALLATION

Assembly and installation is a reversal of the removal and disassembly procedure. Do not tighten the swing arm spindle nut until after the shock absorbers have been installed.

T100C and T100R (Before Serial No. H49832)

REMOVAL AND DISASSEMBLY

1. Remove the front chainguard bolt, disconnect the stoplight switch wiring and remove the switch operating clip from the brake rod.

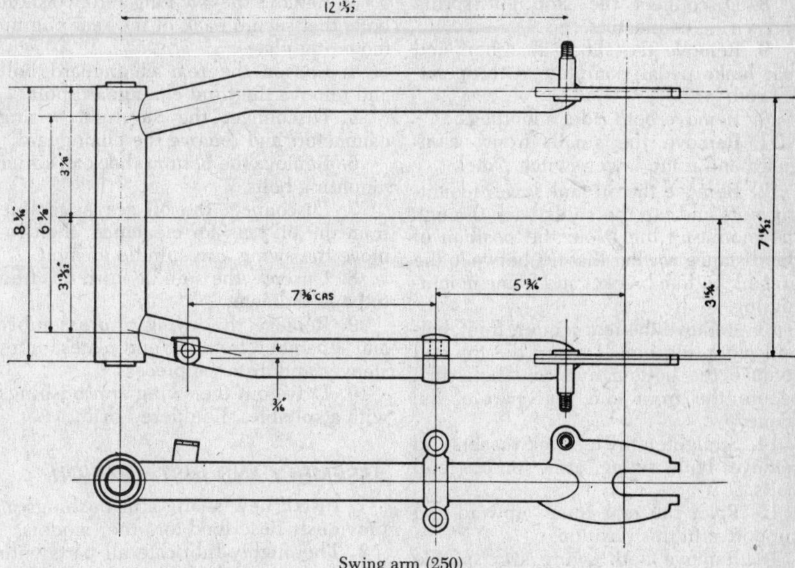

Swing arm (250)

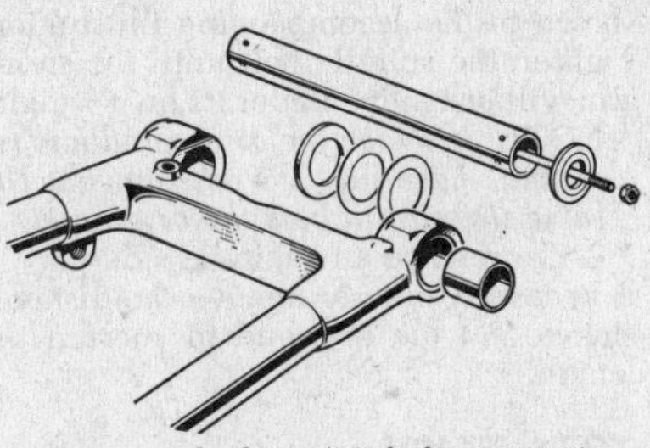

Swing arm bushings (500 before H49832)

2. Disconnect the shock absorbers from the swing arm.
3. Remove the swing arm spindle retaining rod and caps.
4. Using a threaded extractor (see illustration), draw the spindle out the right side of the machine.
5. Disconnect the chain and rear brake torque arm.
6. Disconnect the brake operating rod.
7. Remove the rear chainguard bolt and swing the chainguard out of the way. Disconnect the speedometer cable, loosen the rear axle nuts and remove the rear wheel.
8. Remove the swing arm from the frame lugs. Take care to mark and separate the spacers.
9. Remove the swing arm bushings by driving them out with a suitable drift and mallet.

ASSEMBLY AND INSTALLATION

1. Press or drive in the new swing arm bushings. A drift can be fabricated out of $^{31}/_{32}$ in. bar stock by machining 1 in. of one end to ⅞ in. diameter.
2. Line-ream the bushings to the bore size given in specifications, using Triumph special tool no. Z126 or a suitable substitute.
3. Assemble the swing arm to the frame lugs, using the same spacers that were removed. Lift the arm up and let it drop: the arm should just be able to move under its own weight. If movement was restricted, remove a spacer on each side and try again; if movement was too free, add spacers until the correct working clearance is obtained.

NOTE: *Spacers are available in 0.003 and 0.005 in. sizes.*

4. When the correct clearance has been obtained, grease the bushings and spindle, then press the spindle into position with the extractor tool used for removal.
5. Lubricate the swing arm grease nipple with the recommended lubricant, then assemble the remaining parts in reverse order of disassembly.

T100C and T100R (After Serial No. H49832)

REMOVAL AND DISASSEMBLY

1. Support the machine on its side stand or a wooden box, then disconnect the center stand spring.
2. Disconnect the chain and remove the rear brake adjuster.
3. Disconnect the brake torque arm from the hub.
4. Remove the rear chainguard bolt and swing the chainguard up out of the way.
5. Disconnect the speedometer cable, then remove the rear wheel.
6. Disconnect the rubber chain oiler tube.
7. Remove the exhaust pipes and mufflers.

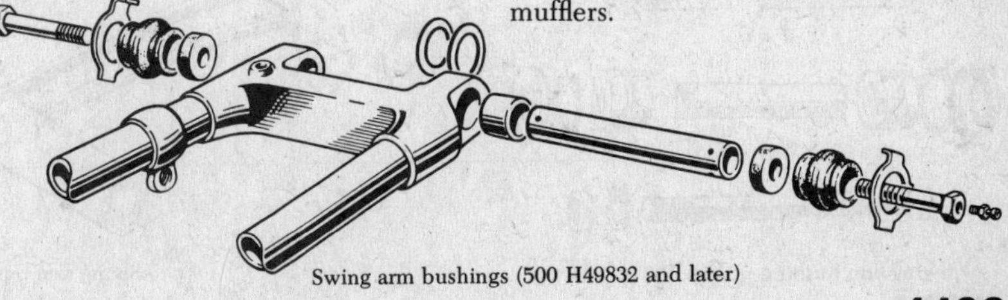

Swing arm bushings (500 H49832 and later)

8. Disconnect the stoplight spring and wiring connectors.

9. Remove the shock absorbers and rear brake pedal, complete with operating rod.

10. Remove both rider's footpegs.

11. Remove the small, front chainguard and front, lower switch panel.

12. Remove the oil tank lower mounting nuts and tap the studs back through the mounting lug. Note the position of the distance washer that fits between the oil tank bottom bracket and frame mounting lug.

13. Remove the rear fender, front, bottom mounting bolt. Loosen the top and remove the bottom nuts and bolts that secure the front and rear part of the frame.

14. Straighten the tab lockwashers and remove both swing arm spindle end bolts.

15. Pivot the rear frame upward and support it in this position.

16. Remove both swing arm spindle distance pieces noting that the thicker one fits on the chain side.

17. Remove the swing arm spindle by tapping it out with a suitable, shouldered drift. The chain side of the spindle has an extra hole that will accept a C-wrench, should it become needed on reassembly.

18. Drive out the swing arm bushings with a suitable drift.

ASSEMBLY AND INSTALLATION

1. Install new bushings as described for the "T100C and T100R before serial no. H49832."

2. The remainder of assembly and installation is a reversal of the removal and disassembly procedure. Note that when installing the swing arm distances pieces, the ribbed sides must face the rear frame side plates.

TR6C, TR6R, T120R and T120 and T150V

REMOVAL AND DISASSEMBLY

1. Disconnect the chain and rear brake torque arm, then remove the brake rod adjuster.

2. Loosen the rear axle nuts and remove the rear wheel.

3. Remove the two long and two short bolts that secure each of the rear engine mounting plates.

4. Loosen the rear chainguard bolt and remove the front chainguard bolt.

5. Disconnect the stoplight wiring connectors and remove the chainguard.

6. Remove the bottom shock absorber mounting bolts.

7. Disconnect the oil scavenge line from the oil tank for clearance, then remove the swing arm spindle locknut.

8. Unscrew the spindle until it is free to be withdrawn.

9. Remove the swing arm assembly and separate it from the end plates, outer sleeves and distance pieces.

10. Drive out the swing arm bushings with a suitable, shouldered drift.

ASSEMBLY AND INSTALLATION

1. Install new swing arm bushings as previously described for other models.

2. Thoroughly lubricate all parts with grease, then assemble them in the order shown in the accompanying illustration. Tighten the spindle bolt until the swing arm will just move under its own weight.

NOTE: *If the swing arm spindle is replaced, make sure the new one has the same thread pitch as the original.*

3. To remove any spindle side-play, it is necessary only to remove the distance sleeve and file one end to shorten the length.

TR7V, T140V

REMOVAL AND DISASSEMBLY

1. Remove the rear wheel and the chainguard. Remove the shock absorbers.

2. Remove the swing arm spindle nut on the right side and pull out the spindle.

3. Take the swing arm out of the frame.

4. Remove the four dust covers (one on each side of the swing arm bush housings).

5. Note the location of the thrust washers (the thicker of the two is fitted to the right side of the swing arm); remove the spacers.

INSPECTION

1. Clean all parts thoroughly.

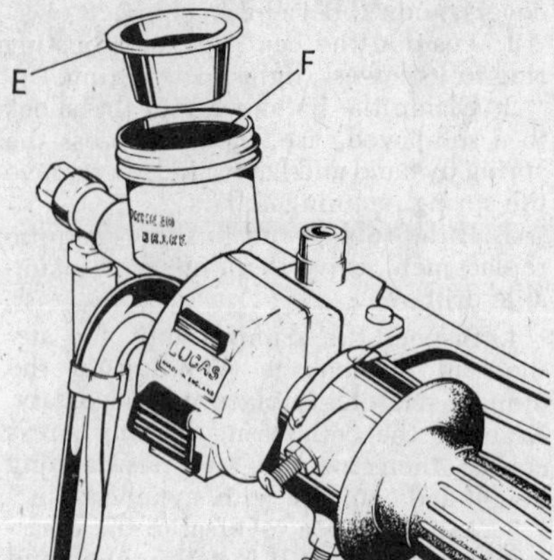

Fluid reservoir diaphragm (E) and fluid level (F)

2. Check the bushes for wear or damage.

3. Check the dimensions of the bushes and spacer tubes against the standard values given at the end of this section. Replace any worn parts as is necessary.

4. A special tool (No. 61-6117) is used to remove and install the bushes in their housings. Note its operation in the accompanying illustrations. A drift can also be used, provided that it has a narrow section 1 in. in diameter and a 1⅛ in. shoulder.

Use some grease on the bushings to facilitate reassembly. Note that new bushes are pre-sized and need not be reamed to fit correctly.

ASSEMBLY

Assembly is the reverse of the disassembly procedure. Refer to the exploded diagram for the correct placement of the parts. Replace the dust covers in their proper positions, then place the swing arm in the frame. Fit the thrust washers (they are of different thickness: the thicker is fitted to the right side of the swing arm). Replace the spindle and the spindle nut.

Replace the chainguard and rear wheel.

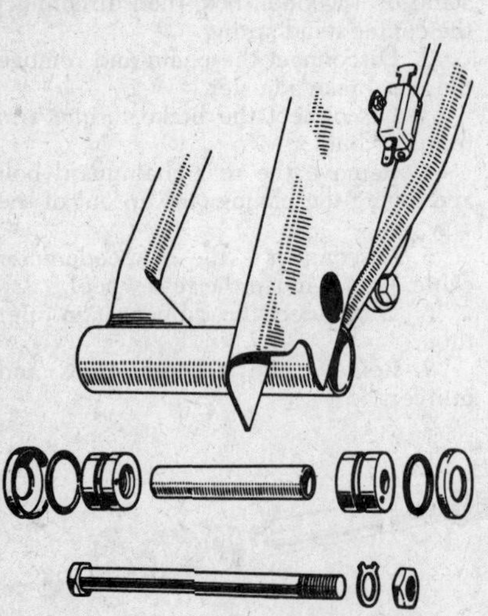

Swing arm bushings (650 and Trident)

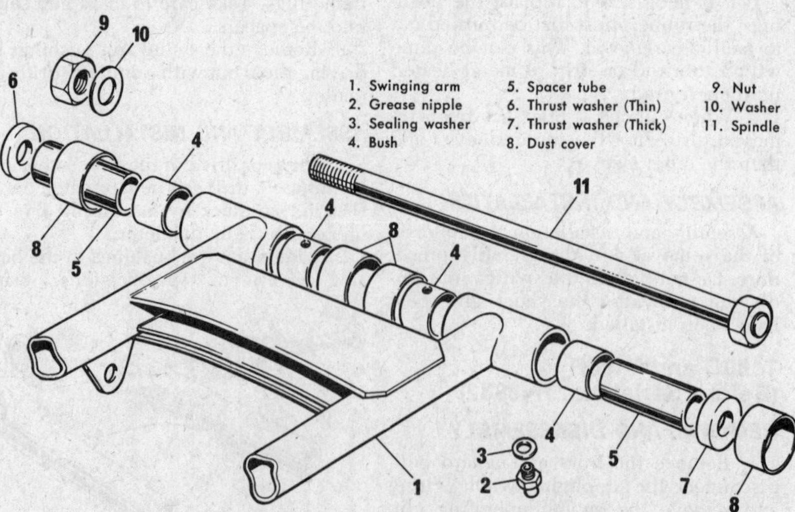

Swing arm bushings (TR7V, T140V)

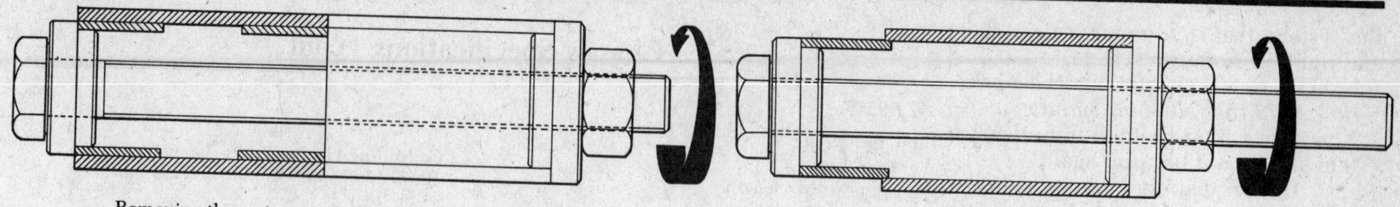

Removing the swing arm bushings with the special tool (750 Twins)

Installing the swing arm bushings (750 Twins)

DISC BRAKE SERVICE

Maintenance

1. The hydraulic brake fluid level should be set at about ¼ in. from the top of the reservoir after the system has been bled. It is not necessary to add fluid to the system provided that there are no leaks in the lines. The fluid level in the reservoir will drop slightly as the brake pads wear.

2. The brake pads should be examined for wear at regular intervals. To do this, it will be necessary to remove them.

   a. Remove the caliper's aluminum cover by removing the two phillips head screws.

   b. Remove the two cotter pins. (These are indicated by the letter "B" in the illustration).

   c. Pull out both pads.

   d. Pads are bonded to the brake lining material. They must be replaced when the lining thickness is 1/16 in. (1.6 mm) or less.

   e. It is recommended that new cotter pins be used upon reassembly.

Bleeding

Any time any part of the brake system has been removed or the line is disconnected, it will be necessary to "bleed"

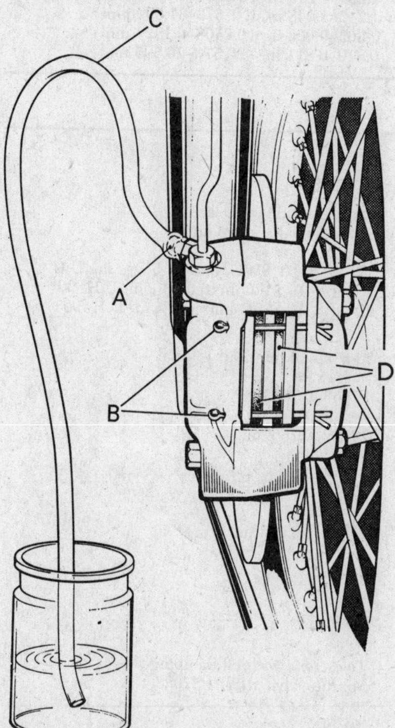

Bleeding the brake system. Note bleed nipple (A), brake pad cotter pins (B), and brake pads (D)

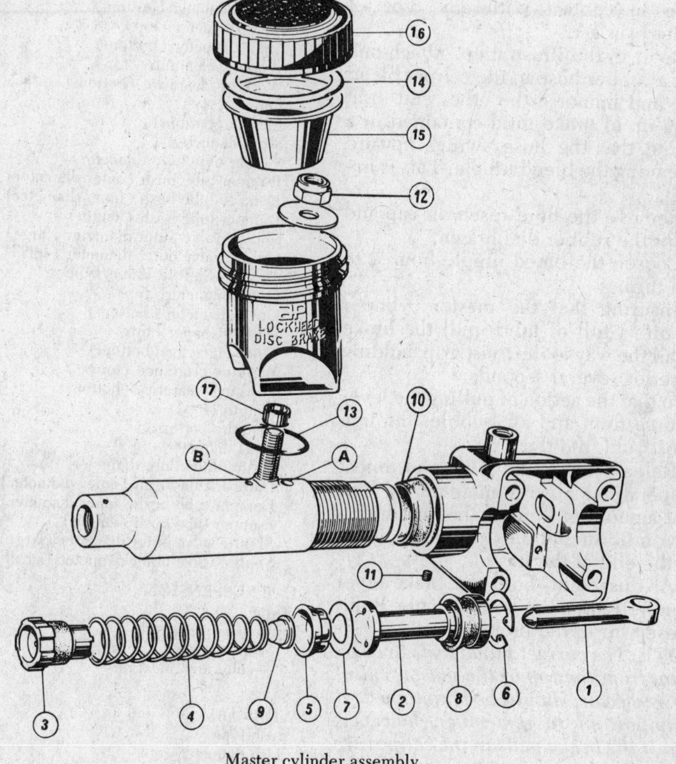

Master cylinder assembly

1. Pushrod
2. Piston
3. Check valve
4. Return spring
5. Primary seal
6. Circlip
7. Piston washer
8. Secondary seal
9. Spring retainer
10. Dust cover
11. Set screw
12. Reservoir securing nut
13. O-ring
14. Paper washer
15. Diaphragm
16. Cap
17. Spacer

Chassis Specifications

TR25W	
WHEELS	
Rim size and type (front)	WM2-18
Rim size and type (rear)	WM3-18
Spoke sizes:	
Front (long) 20	10 s.w.g. x 6 in. (3.251 x 152.4 mm)
Front (medium) 10	10 s.w.g. x 5 7/32 in. (3.251 x 132.55 mm)
Front (short) 10	10 s.w.g. x 5 3/16 in. (3.251 x 131.76 mm)
Rear (long) 20	10 s.w.g. x 7.4375 in. (3.251 x 188.9125 mm)
Rear (short) 20	10 s.w.g. x 7.375 in. (3.251 x 187.325 mm)
WHEEL BEARINGS	
Front (left- and right-hand)	20 x 47 x 14 mm Ball Journal
Rear (left- and right-hand)	20 x 47 x 14 mm Ball Journal
Rear brake drum	20 x 47 x 14 mm Ball Journal
Spindle diameter (front)	0.8740–0.8745 in. (22.199–22.212 mm)
Spindle diameter (rear, left-hand)	0.8745–0.8750 in. (22.212–22.225 mm)
Spindle diameter (rear, right-hand)	0.685–0.686 in. (17.399–17.424 mm)
BRAKES	
Front (diameter) twin leading shoe	—
Front (diameter) single leading shoe	7 in. (177.8 mm)
Front (width) twin leading shoe	1.557 in. (39.6875 mm)
Front (width) single leading shoe	1.125 in. (28.575 mm)
Rear (diameter)	7 in. (177.8 mm)
Rear (width)	1.125 in. (28.575 mm)
Lining thickness (front and rear)	0.146–0.166 in. (3.96 mm)

the system, that is, to remove air pockets and bubbles from the system.

NOTE: *Before beginning the operation, read the following points:*

a. Brake fluid drained from the system should not be used again.

b. Insure that the master cylinder reservoir is kept at least half full during the entire bleeding operation.

c. Take all precautions necessary to insure that the brake fluid does not come in contact with any type of painted surface.

1. Refer to the illustration. Attach one end of a rubber hose to the caliper bleed nipple and immerse the other end in at least ½ in. of brake fluid contained in a jar. Note that the hose swings upward after leaving the bleed nipple. This is important.

2. Remove the fluid reservoir cap and take out the rubber diaphragm.

3. Loosen the bleed nipple from ½ to ¾ of a turn.

4. Insuring that the master cylinder reservoir is full of fluid, pull the brake lever all the way to the twist grip, holding it there for several seconds.

Note that the action of pulling the lever will force fluid and air bubbles through the hose and into the jar.

5. Release the brake lever and repeat the operation, always maintaining sufficient amount of fluid in the master cylinder, until air bubbles no longer issue from the end of the hose.

6. At this point, hold the brake lever *on*, and retighten the bleed nipple. Refill the reservoir to the proper level.

NOTE: *The correct fluid level, given as ¼ in. from the top of the master cylinder reservoir, should be maintained. It is important to remember, however, that if the brake pads in the caliper are not new when the system is bled, the fluid level will rise in the reservoir when new pads are installed. Therefore, it may be necessary to remove some fluid from the reservoir when this is done.*

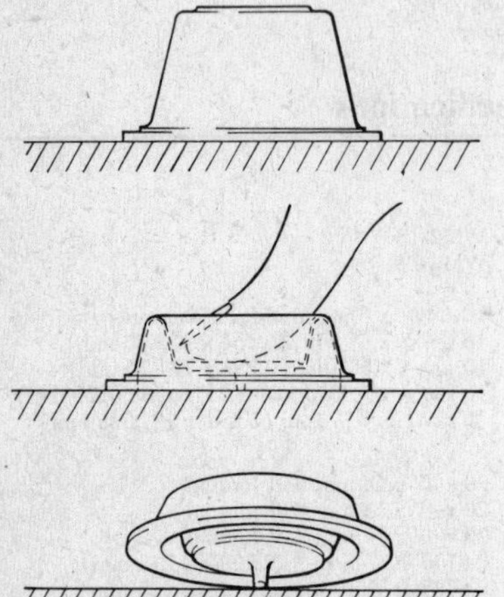

Compressing diaphragm prior to installation

7. Refer to the illustrations, and fold the diaphragm, as shown, before replacing it in the master cylinder reservoir. Install the paper washer in the cap, and screw on and tighten the cap securely.

Chassis Specifications (cont.)

TR25W

FRONT FORK	
Type	Coil-spring (hydraulically damped)
Springs—free length	10.75–10.875 in. (273.05–276.225 mm)
—spring rate	34 in. lbs
—number of coils	20½
—color identification	Red-green
Bushings—Rod Damper Type	
Outer diameter (top)	1.4750–1.4755 in. (37.465–37.477 mm)
Outer diameter (bottom)	1.473–1.474 in. (37.414–37.439 mm)
Inner diameter (top)	1.250–1.251 in. (31.750–31.755 mm)
Inner diameter (bottom)	1.2485–1.2495 in. (31.711–31.737 mm)
Working clearance (top)	0.0005 in. (0.0127 mm)
Working clearance (bottom)	0.002–0.003 in. (0.0508–0.0762 mm)
Length (top)	2.125 in. (53.975 mm)
Length (bottom)	1.25 in. (31–75 mm)
Shaft diameter	1.248–1.249 in. (31.699–31.7246 mm)
Sliding tube bore diameter	1.475–1.477 in. (31.699–31.7246 mm)
Damper tube bush (outer diameter)	0.6165–0.6185 in. (15.6591–15.7099 mm)
Damper tube bush (inner diameter)	0.399–0.340 in. (8.6106–8.636 mm)
Damper tube bush (length)	0.53125 in. (13.4937 mm)
Shuttle valve outer diameter (large)	——
Shuttle valve outer diameter (small)	——
Bushings—Shuttle Valve Type	
Outer diameter (top)	1.498–1.499 in. (3.805–3.808 mm)
Outer diameter (bottom)	1.4935–1.4945 in. (3.792–3.799 mm)
Inner diameter (top)	1.3065–1.3075 in. (3.318–3.32 mm)
Inner diameter (bottom)	1.2485–1.2495 in. (3.168–3.172 mm)
Working clearance (top)	0.0035–0.0050 in. (0.0889–0.127 mm)
Working clearance (bottom)	1.0035–0.0065 in. (0.0889–0.165 mm)
Length (top)	1 in. (25.4 mm)
Length (bottom)	0.870–0.875 in. (2.221 mm)
Shaft diameter	1.3025–1.3030 in. (3.309–3.312 mm)
Sliding tube bore diameter	1.498–1.500 in. (3.802–3.81 mm)
Damper tube bush (outer diameter)	——
Damper tube bush (inner diameter)	——
Damper tube bush (length)	——
Shuttle valve outer diameter (large)	1.018–1.016 in. (2.583–2.58 mm)
Shuttle valve outer diameter (small)	0.875–0.874 in. (2.221–2.22 mm)
REAR SUSPENSION	
Type	Coil-spring (hydraulically damped)
Springs—free length	8.40 in. (213.36 mm)
—spring rate	100 in. lbs
—color identification	Green-pink (applies both to chrome or black springs)
SWING ARM	
Bush type	Bonded rubber
Bush diameter	1.250–1.253 in. (31.75–31.8262 mm)
Housing diameter	1.247–1.248 in. (31.673–31.699 mm)
Interference fit	0.002–0.006 in. (0.0508–0.1524 mm)
Spindle diameter	0.810–0.811 in. (20.570–20.595 mm)

T100, T100R

WHEELS	
Rim size: Front and rear	WM2-18
Type:	
Front	Spoke—single cross lacing
Rear	Spoke—double cross lacing
Spoke details:	
Front	40 off 8–10 SWG butted 5 17/32 in. U.H.
Rear: left-side	20 off 8–10 SWG butted 7 9/16 in. U.H. 90°
right-side	20 off 8–10 SWG butted 7 7/8 in. U.H. 90°
WHEEL BEARINGS	
Front and rear, dimensions and type	20 x 47–14 mm Ball Journal
Front spindle diameter (at bearing journals)	0.7868–0.7873 in.
Rear spindle diameter (at bearing journals)	0.7862–0.7867 in.
BRAKES	
Type	Internal Expanding
Drum diameter:	
Front	8 in. } ±0.002 in.
Rear	7 in. } ±0.002 in.
Lining thickness:	
Front and rear	0.183/0.197 in.
Lining area:	
Front and rear	23.4/14.6
FRONT FORK	
Type	Telescopic with oil damping Shuttle valve after H.57083
Spring details:	
Free length	9¾ in.
No. of working coils	12½
Spring rate	26½ in. lbs
Color code	Yellow-blue

Chassis Specifications (cont.)

T100, T100R

Bushing details: Material	*Top bush*	*Bottom bush*
Length	1 in.	0.870–0.875 in.
Outer diameter	1.498–1.499 in.	1.4935–1.4945 in.
Inner diameter	1.3065–1.3075 in.	1.2485–1.2495 in.
Stanchion diameter	1.3025–1.3030 in.	
Working clearance in top bush	0.0035–0.0050 in.	
Fork leg bore diameter	1.498–1.500 in.	
Working clearance of bottom bush	0.0035–0.0065 in.	
Shuttle valve:		
outer diameter (large)	1.018–1.106 in.	
outer diameter (small)	0.875–0.874 in.	
REAR SUSPENSION		
Type	Swing fork controlled by combined spring-hydraulic damper units. (Bolted up after H.49833).	
SPRING DETAILS:		
Fitted length	8 in.	
Free length	8 3/16 in.	
Mean coil diameter	1 3/4 dia	
Spring rate	145 in. lbs	
Color code	Blue-Yellow	
Load at fitted length	38 lbs	
SWING ARM		
Bush type	Phosphor bronze strip	
Bush bore diameter	0.8745–0.8750 in.	
Spindle diameter	0.8735–0.8740 in.	
Distance between fork ends	7 7/16 in.	

TR6R, TR6C, T120R

WHEELS		
Rim size: Front and rear	WM12–19 front	WM3–18 rear
Type: Front	Spoke-single cross lacing	
Rear	Spoke-double cross lacing	
Spoke details:		
Front: left-side	20 off 8/10 SWG butted 5 5/8 in. U.H. straight	
right-side	10 off 8/10 SWG butted 4 25/32 in. U.H. 78° head	
right-side	10 off 8/10 SWG butted 4 7/8 in. U.H. 100° head	
Rear: left-side	20 off 8/10 SWG butted 7 9/16 in. U.H. 90° head	
right-side	20 off 8/10 SWG butted 7 7/8 in. U.H. 90° head	
WHEEL BEARINGS		
Front and rear, dimensions and type	20 x 47 x 14 mm—Ball Journal	
Front and rear, spindle diameter (at bearing journals)	0.7862–0.7867 in.	
Q.D. REAR WHEEL		
Bearing type	3/4 x 1 7/8 x 9/16 in. Ball Journal	
Bearing sleeve: journal diameter	0.7500–0.7495 in.	
Brake drum bearing	7/8 x 2 x 9/16 in. Ball Journal	
Bearing sleeve: journal diameter	0.8745–0.8740 in.	
Bearing housing: internal diameter	1.9890–1.9980 in.	
BRAKES		
Type	Internal expanding twin leading shoes	
Drum Diameter:		
Front	8 in. ± 0.002 in.	
Rear	7 in. ± 0.002 in.	
Lining thickness:		
Front	0.183–0.193 in.	
Rear	0.177–0.187 in.	
Lining area:		
Front	24.4 sq in.	
Rear	14.6 sq in.	
Pre-set length of adjustable cam lever rod	6 1/2 in. between centers	
FRONT FORK		
Type	Telescopic-Shuttle valve damping	
Spring details:	Solo	Sidecar
Free length	9 3/4 in.	9 3/4
No. working coils	12 1/2	15 1/2
Spring rate	26 1/2 lb in.	32 1/2 lb in.
Gauge	6 SWG	5 SWG
Color code	Yellow/blue	Yellow/green
Damper sleeve		
Length	2 1/8 in.	
Internal diameter	1.387–1.393 in.	
Material	Black polypropylene	
Bush details:	*Top bush*	*Bottom bush*
Length	1 in.	0.870–0.875 in.
Outer diameter	1.498–1.499 in.	1.4935–1.4945 in.
Inner diameter	1.3065–1.3075 in.	1.2485–1.2495 in.
Stanchion diameter	1.3025–1.3030 in.	
Working clearance in top bush	0.0035–0.0050 in.	
Bleed holes	8 holes 3/16 in. dia	
Fork leg bore diameter	1.498–1.500 in.	
Working clearance of bottom bush	0.0035–0.0065 in.	
Shuttle valve:		
Outer diameter (large)	1.018–1.016 in.	
Outer diameter (small)	0.875–0.874 in.	

Flushing

Every three years, or if the system has accumulated any foreign matter, it should be flushed out as directed below:

1. Connect a hose to the bleed nipple, running the other end into a container, and squeeze the brake lever until all of the fluid in the system has been pumped out.
2. Fill the master cylinder reservoir with denatured alcohol and pump it out through the system in the same manner.
3. After all of the alcohol has been removed, fill the master cylinder with brake fluid, and bleed the system as described above.

Master Cylinder

REMOVAL AND DISASSEMBLY

1. Drain the brake fluid. Disconnect the brake line at the master cylinder.
2. Remove the brake lever and then the pushrod.
3. Remove the four screws which hold the master cylinder assembly on the handlebar, and remove the assembly.
4. Remove the reservoir cap, if this has not already been accomplished, and the paper washer and diaphragm.
5. Remove the nut inside the reservoir, and separate it from the master cylinder. Note the location of the spacer and O-ring beneath the reservoir.
6. Remove the set screw which locks the cylinder into the rest of the assembly, and unscrew the cylinder.
7. Remove the dust cover from the end of the cylinder. Use the pushrod, inserting it into the master cylinder, to push down the piston and remove the circlip.
8. Remove the secondary seal and piston, the piston washer, primary seal, return spring retainer, spring, and check valve. If the primary seal will not come out of the piston, try blowing into the brake line end of the piston.
9. Remove the secondary seal from the piston by stretching it over the piston flange.

INSPECTION

1. All seals and O-rings must be replaced.
2. Check the inside of the cylinder for scoring. Replace if necessary.
3. Clean all parts thoroughly in *brake fluid only.*

CAUTION: *Do not clean the parts in any sort of solvent such as gasoline.*

ASSEMBLY AND INSTALLATION

1. Fit the new secondary seal onto the piston noting that the seal lip faces the drilled end of the piston. Work the seal around the groove in the piston until it is properly seated.
2. Fit the check valve onto the large end of the return spring, and the spring retainer onto the other end. Insert the assembly into the cylinder, check valve first.
3. Fit the primary seal into the cylinder, inserting the lip end of the seal first. Do not force the seal, and make sure that the lip is not folded back upon installation.

4. Install the piston washer, convex side *outward* (towards the piston), and then the piston (drilled end piston), and then the piston (drilled end first). Depress the piston with the pushrod as on removal, and replace the circlip. Be sure the circlip is properly seated.

5. Fit the dust cover boot over the end of the cylinder.

6. Install the reservoir O-ring, spacer, and the reservoir.

7. Fill the reservoir with brake fluid, insert the pushrod into its place, and push inwards on the piston. The pushrod should be pushed in several times and then brake fluid should begin to flow out of the brake line connection at the end of the cylinder.

8. Drain the fluid.

9. The master cylinder must be properly located in the housing. Proceed as follows:

a. Remove the reservoir from the cylinder.

b. Insert the pushrod in place and install the brake lever and bolt.

c. Screw the cylinder into the housing while holding the brake lever *on* until the cylinder can no longer be turned.

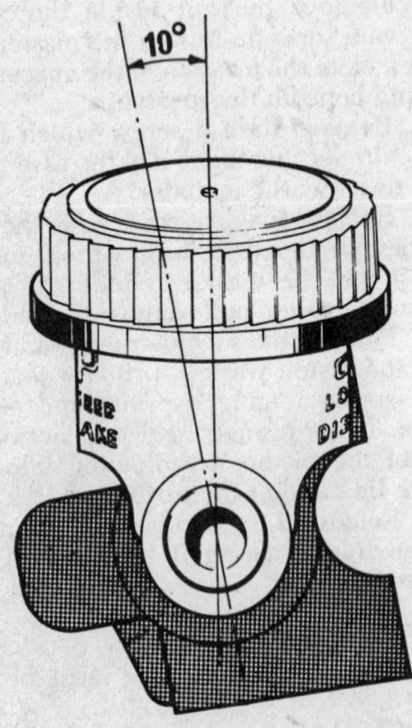

Fluid reservoir installation angle

d. Refer to the exploded diagram of the master cylinder assembly. Note that the cylinder has two ports, designated "A" and "B" which flank the reservoir mounting stud. "A" is the main feed port, and "B" the breather port.

e. Place a finger over the main feed port "A" and blow through the brake line end of the cylinder. No air should escape.

f. Unscrew the cylinder while blowing through the cylinder until air just begins to escape from the breather port "B."

g. Unscrew the cylinder one full turn, and set the reservoir stud at about 10° from the vertical. This will allow the flat section on the threaded end of the cylinder to line up with the set screw.

Chassis Specifications (cont.)

T150

WHEELS	
Rim size: Front and rear	WM2–19 front WM3–19 rear
Type:	
Front	Spoke-single cross lacing
Rear	Spoke-double cross lacing
Spoke details:	
Front: left-side	20 off 8–10 SWG butted 5⅝ in. U.H. straight (219.075 mm)
right-side	10 off 8–10 SWG butted 4 11/16 in. U.H. 95° head (118.0625 mm)
right-side	10 off 8–10 SWG butted 4 11/16 in. U.H. 80° head (118.0625 mm)
Rear: left-side	20 off 8–10 SWG butted 8 in. U.H. 90° head (203.2 mm)
right-side	20 off 8–10 SWG butted 8⅜ in. U.H. 90° head (212–725 mm)
WHEEL BEARINGS	
Front and rear, dimensions and type	20 x 47 x 14 mm—Ball Journal
Front and rear, spindle diameter (at bearing journals)	0.7862–0.7867 in. (19.9695 x 19.9822 mm)
BRAKES	
Type	Internal expanding 2 leading shoe
Drum diameter:	
Front	8 in. ± 0.002 in. (203.2 mm) ± 0.0508 mm
Rear	7 in. ± 0.002 in. (177.8 mm) ± 0.0508 mm
Lining thickness:	
Front	0.181–0.188 in.
Rear	0.165–0.175 in.
Lining area:	
Front	23.4 sq in. (150.967 sq cm)
Rear	14.6 sq in. (94–193 sq cm)
FRONT FORK	
Type	Telescopic-Oil damping
Spring details:	
Free-length	9.688–9.812 in. (246.075–249.225 mm)
Number working coils	15½
Spring rate	32½ in. lbs (4.485 kg mm)
Gauge	5 swg
Color code	Yellow-green
Damper sleeve	
Length	2⅓ in. (53.975 mm)
Internal diameter	1.387–1.393 in. (35.2298–35.3822 mm)
Bush details: Material	Sintered bronze
	Top bush
Length	1 in. (25.4 mm)
Outer diameter	1.498–1.499 in. (38.0492–38.0746 mm)
Inner diameter	1.3065–1.3075 in. (33.185–33.2105 mm)
STANCHION DIAMETER	1.3025–1.3030 in. (33.0889–0.127 mm)
Working clearance in top bush	0.0035–0.0050 in. (10889–0.127 mm)
	Bottom Bush
Length	0.870–0.875 in. (22.098–22.225 mm)
Outer diameter	1.4935–1.4945 in. (37.945–37.960 mm)
Inner diameter	1.2485–1.2495 in. (31.712–31.7373 mm)
FORK LEG BORE DIAMETER	1.498–1.500 in. (38.049–38.1 mm)
Working clearance of bottom bush	0.0035–0.0065 in. (0.0889–0.165 mm)
REAR SUSPENSION	
Type	Swinging fork controlled by combined coil spring-hydraulic damper units
Color code	Black
Extended distance between center	12.875 in. (32.66 mm)
Compressed distance between center	10.375 in. (23.36 mm)
SWING ARM	
Bush type	Pre-sized steel-backed-phosphor bronze
Bush bore diameter	1.4460–1.4470 in. (36.7284–36.7538 mm)
Sleeve diameter	1.445–1.4450 in. (36.6903–36.702 mm)
Distance between fork ends	7½ in. (190.5 mm)
REAR SUSPENSION	
Type	Swinging fork controlled by combined coil spring/hydraulic damper units
Spring details:	
Fitted length	8⅜ in.
Free-length	8⅜ in.
Mean coil diameter	1¾ in.
Spring coil diameter	100 lb/in.
Color code	Green/green
Load at fitted length	28 lbs
SWING ARM	
Bush type	Pre-sized, steel-backed—phosphor bronze
Bush bore diameter	1.4460–1.4470 in.
Sleeve diameter	1.4445–1.4450 in.
Distance between fork ends	7½ in.

h. Thread in the set screw and tighten it.

i. Refit the reservoir spacer, O-ring, and reservoir.

10. Install the master cylinder assembly on the handlebar and bleed the system as previously described.

Brake Caliper

REMOVAL AND DISASSEMBLY

1. Remove the caliper cover (2 screws), drain the brake fluid; disconnect the brake line from the caliper.
2. Remove the nuts which secure the caliper to the fork slider, and remove the caliper.
3. Remove the cotter pins which hold the brake pads, and remove the pads from the caliper.
4. Pry out the dust seal and the metal dust seal housing from both halves of the caliper.
5. With the aid of compressed air applied to the brake fluid inlet, eject each piston from its bore.

NOTE: *Mark each piston for location after removal. Each must be reinserted into its own bore.*

6. Pry out the fluid seals in each piston bore with a small, blunted screwdriver, being extremely careful not to damage the seal grooves.

CAUTION: *The brake caliper halves must never be separated. If this has been done, the fluid passage seal should be renewed if damaged, and the caliper mating surface and bolts thoroughly cleaned.*

Tighten the bolts to 35–40 ft lbs, and check the caliper for fluid tightness under maximum braking pressure.

The caliper should be returned to the manufacturer for an overhaul if the halves have been split.

INSPECTION

1. The dust seals and metal housings *must* be replaced.
2. The brake fluid seals must be replaced if they have been removed.
3. Inspect the pistons and piston bores for scoring or signs of seizure.
4. Clean all parts thoroughly.

ASSEMBLY AND INSTALLATION

1. Smear the fluid seals with brake fluid and replace them in their grooves in the cylinder bores. Note that the larger side faces outward, toward the open end of the bore. Be sure the seals are properly seated.
2. Coat the pistons with brake fluid, and insert each of them, closed end first, squarely into its bore. Press them in as far as possible.
3. Coat one of the dust seals with brake fluid and fit it into a metal housing. Place this assembly into one of the bores with the dust seal on the inside (facing the piston in that bore). Place a suitable shaped plate over the dust seal assembly, and use a "C" clamp to press the assembly into the bore until the outer edges of the metal housing are flush with the bore surface.
4. Repeat this procedure with the other dust seal.

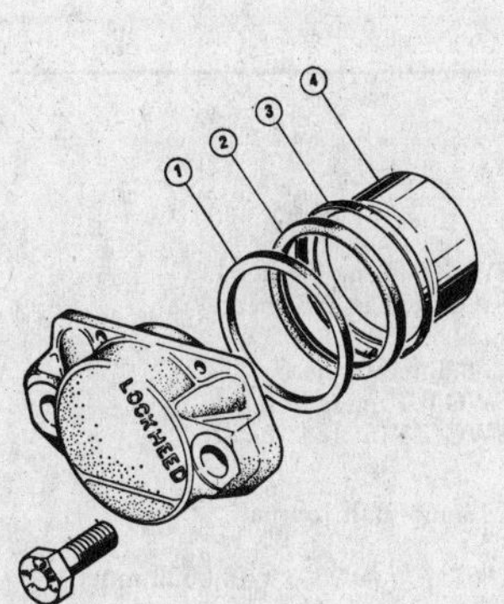

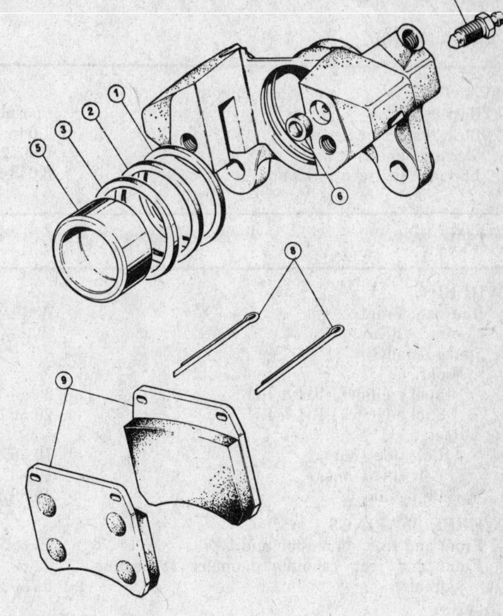

Caliper assembly

5. Replace the brake pads, securing them with new cotter pins.
6. Secure the caliper to the fork slider, tightening the nuts securely. Reconnect the lines, and bleed the system as previously described.

Brake Disc

1. Check the disc for scoring or other damage.
2. Check for run-out with a dial gauge. Run-out should not exceed 0.0035 in. (0.089 mm). Run-out can be corrected for somewhat by loosening the four disc nuts and repositioning the disc. Retighten the nuts in an "X" pattern to 20 ft lbs.

Chassis Specifications (cont.)

TR7V, T140V	
WHEELS	
Rim size: Front	WM2–19
Rear	WM3–18
Spoke details:	
Front	
Spoke (inner) RH & LH	20 off 10 SWG 7.75 in. 96° head
Spoke (outer) RH & LH	20 off 10 SWG 7.85 in. 80° head
Rear	
Left side (outer)	10 off 10 SWG 5.8 in. 10° head
Left side (inner)	10 off 10 SWG 5.7 in. 102° head
Right side	20 off 10 SWG 7.2 in. 135° head
WHEEL BEARINGS	
Front and rear, dimensions and type	20 x 47 x 14 mm—Ball Journal
Front and rear, spindle diameter (at bearing journals)	0.7862–7.7867 in.
BRAKES	
Front, type	Hydraulic disc
Disc diameter	10 in.
Friction pads, type	Mintex M64
Lining thickness	0.25 in.
Rear, type	Internal expanding, single leading shoe
Lining thickness	0.187.0.197 in.
Drum diameter	7.0 in.
FRONT FORK	
Type	Telescopic, hydraulic damped
Spring:	
Free length	19.1 in.
Compressed length	11.4 in.
Fitted length	18.5 in.
Maximum load	194 lbs
Color code	Orange
Stanchion diameter (top)	1.350–1.355 in.
(bottom)	1.3605–1.3610 in.
Outer member bore diameter	1.363–1.365 in.
REAR SUSPENSION	
Type	Swing arm/hydraulically damped springs
Fitted length	8.0 in. (mid position)
Free length	9.5 in.
Spring rate	88 lbs/in.
Mean coil diameter	1.98 in.

Chassis Specifications (cont.)

TR7V, T140V

SWING ARM	
Bush type	Phosphor bronze
Bush bore diameter	1.0 in.
Sleeve diameter	0.9972–0.9984 in.
Distance between fork ends	8.018 in.

T150V

WHEELS	
Rim size: Front	WM2–19
Rear	WM3–19
Spoke details:	
Front	
Spoke (inner) RH & LH	20 off 10 SWG 7.75 in. 96° head
Spoke (outer) RH & LH	20 off 10 SWG 7.85 in. 80° head
Rear	
Left side (outer)	10 off SWG 6.3 in. 90° head
Left side (inner)	10 off 10 SWG 6.1 in. 101° head
Right side	20 off 10 SWG 7.5 in. 134° head
WHEEL BEARINGS	
Front and rear, dimension and type	20 x 47 x 14 mm—Ball Journal
Front and rear (spindle diameter at bearing journals)	0.7862–0.7867 in. (19.9695 x 19.9822 mm)
BRAKES	
Front, type	Hydraulic disc
Disc diameter	10 in.
Friction pads, type	Mintex M64
Lining thickness	0.25 in.
Rear, type	Internal expanding
Lining thickness	0.187–0.197 in.
Drum diameter	7.0 in.
FRONT FORK	
Type	Telescopic, oil damping
Spring:	
Free length	19.50 in.
No. working coils	63
Spring rate	32.5 lbs/in.
Color code	Orange
Fork leg diameter: top	1.350–1.355 in.
bottom	1.3605–1.3610 in.
Outer member bore diameter	1.363–1.365 in.
REAR SUSPENSION	
Type	Swing arm/hydraulically damped springs
Fitted length	8.0 in.
Free length	8.810 in.
Spring rate	110 lbs/in.
Mean coil diameter	1.98 in.
SWING ARM	
Bush type	Steel backed phosphor-bronze
Bush bore diameter	1.4460–1.4470 in.
Sleeve diameter	1.4445–1.4450 in.
Distance between fork ends	7.5 in.

Chassis Torque Specifications

T150, T150V

Headlamp pivot bolts	10 ft lbs (1.383 kg/m)
Headrace sleeve nut pinch bolt	15 ft lbs (2.074 kg/m)
Stanchion pinch bolts	25 ft lbs (3.456 kg/m)
Front wheel axle cap bolts	25 ft lbs (3.456 kg/m)
Brake cam spindle nuts	20 ft lbs (2.756 kg/m)
Zener diode fixing nut	2–2.3 ft lbs (0.277–0.3174 kg/m)
Fork cap nut	80 ft lbs (11.06 kg/m)

TR25W

Fork leg cap nuts	50–55 ft lbs (6.913–7.604 kg/m)
Fork leg pinch bolts	18–20 ft lbs 2.489–2.765 kg/m)

T100C, T100R

Headlamp pivot bolts	10 ft lbs
Headrace sleeve nut pinch bolt	15 ft lbs
Stanchion pinch bolts	25 ft lbs
Front wheel axle cap bolts	25 ft lbs
Brake cam spindle nuts	20 ft lbs
Zener diode fixing nut	1½ ft lbs

TR6R, TR6C, T120R

Headlamp pivot bolts	10 ft lbs (1.4 kg/m)
Headrace sleeve nut pinch bolt	15 ft lbs (2.1 kg/m)
Stanchion pinch bolts	25 ft lbs (3.5 kg/m)
Front wheel axle cap bolts	25 ft lbs (3.5 kg/m)
Rear brake drum to hub bolts	15 ft lbs (2.1 kg/m)
Brake cam spindle nuts	20 ft lbs (2.8 kg/m)
Zener diode fixing nut	1.5 ft lbs (0.21 kg/m)
Fork cap nut	80 ft lbs (11.1 kg/m)

TR7V, T140V

Headlamp pivot bolts	10 ft lbs (1.4 kg/m)
Steering head bearing adjuster nut pinch bolt	15 ft lbs (2.1 kg/m)
Fork leg pinch bolts	25 ft lbs (3.4 kg/m)
Front wheel axle cap bolts	25 ft lbs (3.5 kg/m)
Rear brake drum to hub bolts	15 ft lbs (2.1 kg/m)
Brake cam spindle nuts	20 ft lbs (2.8 kg/m)
Zener diode fixing nut	1.5 ft lbs (21 kg/m)
Fork cap nut	80 ft lbs (11.1 kg/m)
Brake disc retaining bolts	20 ft lbs (2.8 kg/m)

Yamaha YTM 200/225

MODEL COVERAGE

YTM 200K-N
YTM 200 EK/EL/ERN Yamahauler
YTM 225 DX K/L/N

INDEX

SERIAL NUMBER LOCATION

In order to prevent possible confusion when purchasing parts, always refer to the engine and frame serial numbers on the machine.

The frame serial number is stamped into the right side of the steering head lug.

The engine serial number is located on the top of the crankcase at the right side rear of the engine.

MAINTENANCE

NOTE: *Common maintenance procedures are explained in detail in the "General Information" section.*

LUBRICATION

Motor Oil

When average air temperature is above 41°F (5°C), use Yamalube 4-Cycle or SAE 20W-40, service rating "SE" or "SF."

When the air temperature is consistently below freezing, use SAE 10W-30, service rating "SE" or "SF."

All manufacturers recommend a certain grade and viscosity of motor oil for their engines, and this recommendation should be followed to ensure long engine life.

Checking Oil Level

1. A dipstick is provided to check oil level.
2. The machine should be parked on level ground.

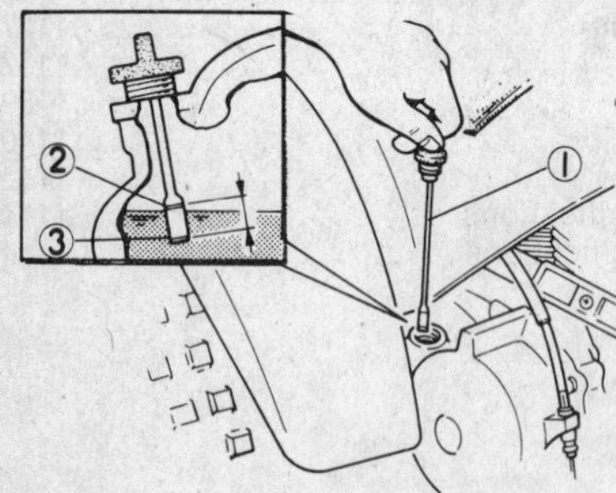

Checking oil: dipstick (1); maximum and minimum level marks (2,3)

3. Let the engine run for a few minutes then shut it off.
4. Unscrew and remove the dipstick from the right side of the engine. Wipe it off.
5. Reinsert the dipstick, allowing the cap to rest on the threads of the hole.
6. Pull it out. Oil level should be between the maximum and minimum marks on the dipstick. If level is too low, add enough of the recommended oil to bring it up to the specified level. Do not overfill.
7. When level is correct, screw the dipstick in and tighten it securely.

Changing Oil

1. The recommended change interval is every 6 mos. after initial break-in is over.
2. Oil should be changed when the engine is warm. This ensures more complete draining and makes it more likely that the oil will carry off any particulates with it.

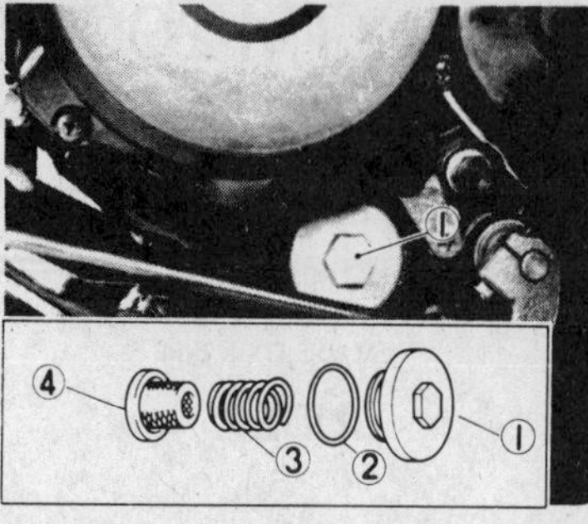

Draining oil: drain plug (1); o-ring (2); spring (3); strainer (4)

3. Place a suitably-sized container (over 2 qts. capacity) beneath the drain plug on the left side of the engine.
4. Remove the dipstick.
5. Remove the drain plug. When it is removed, the O-ring, compression spring and strainer will come out as well. Take care that they are not misplaced.
6. On the right side of the engine, remove the oil filter cover drain bolt which is the lowest of the three bolts on the cover.
7. If the filter is to be cleaned, see "Oil Filter/Oil strainer," below.
8. When the oil has drained completely, install the filter cover drain bolt. Install the oil stainer, compression spring, and drain plug with O-ring.
9. Tighten the filter cover drain bolt to about 7 ft. lbs. Tighten the drain plug to 31 ft. lbs.
10. Add about 1.6 qts. of the recommended oil to the crankcase. Check level with the dipstick. When level seems correct, start the engine and let it run for a few minutes, then shut it off and check again after it has been sitting for a short period. Top up if necessary.

Check Oil Flow

CAUTION: *This procedure should be done after every oil change.*

1. Change the oil and check for proper level of refill as outlined above.
2. Loosen the oil passage bolt at the top of the cylinder head on the right side of the engine. A slight loosening is all that it required.

Oil passage bolt (1)

3. Start the engine.
4. After about a minute, oil seepage at the bolt should be noted, showing that the head is getting lubricant.
5. If no oil appears, shut the engine off immediately and determine the cause.
6. Tighten the oil passage bolt to 5 ft. lbs.

Oil Filter/Oil Strainer

1. These components should be serviced at every other oil change or once a year.
2. Drain the oil as outlined in the "Changing Oil" procedure.
3. Remove the oil filter cover drain bolt and the two remaining filter cover bolts. Remove the cover and take out the filter element.
4. Clean both the filter element and the strainer screen in clean solvent and dry.
5. Check for damage such as punctures or excessively clogged pores. Replace the element or stariner if any defect is apparent.
6. Check condition of the O-rings and replace them if chipped, deformed or otherwise damaged.

Filter cover bolts (1); filter cover drain bolt (2)

7. Carefully refit the strainer, compression spring and drain plug with O- ring.
8. Install the filter element, cover and bolts.
9. Tighten the drain bolt on the cover and the cover bolts to 7 ft. lbs.
10 Tighten the drain plug to 31 ft. lbs.
11. Add oil. It may be necessary to add a bit more than the 1.6 qts. called for in the oil change procedure, above.
12. Check level and oil flow as outlined in the prior procedures.

Final Gearbox

1. Oil level should be checked periodically and changed once a year.

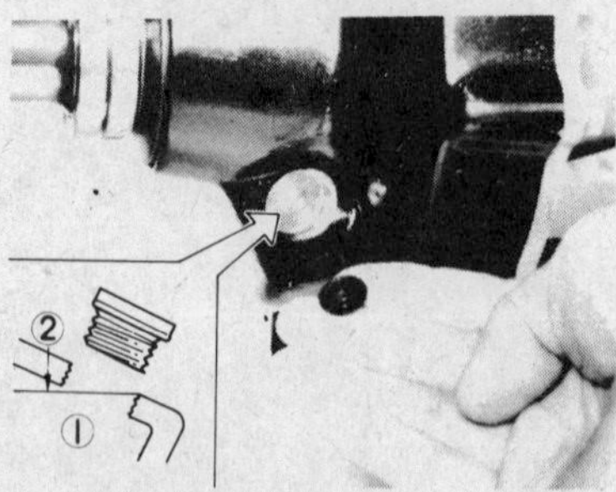

Final gearbox level plug: oil (1); level (2)

2. The gearbox uses SAE 80 API "GL-4" hypoid gear oil or SAE 80W90 hypoid gear oil.

CHECKING GEARBOX OIL

1. The machine should be parked on a level surface. The engine should be cold.

2. Remove the level plug on the left side of the gearbox.

3. Oil level should be the top of the threads at the lower part of the plug hole. In other words, it should just be about to seep out.

4. If level is too low, top up with the recommended oil.

5. Check gasket condition before fitting level plug.

CHANGING GEARBOX OIL

1. The machine should be parked on a level surface.
2. Place a drain pan beneath the gearbox.
3. Remove the level plug.
4. Remove the drain plug.
5. Check drain plug gasket condition.
6. After the oil has had several minutes to drain, install the drain plug and tighten it to 17 ft. lbs.
7. Add the recommended oil to the gearbox. Capacity is about 0.14 qts. Wait of few minutes after adding to give the thick oil a change to find its level. The oil should cover the threads at the lower part of the level plug hole.
8. When level is correct, fit the level plug and tighten it securely.

Front Forks

Fork oil should be changed every year after the initial break-in period. Removal of the forks is required. Refer to the "Chassis" section.

Chassis Lubrication

1. Wheel and steering head bearings should be lubricated with medium weight wheel bearing grease. The service interval is one year for the wheels and two years for the steering head. See "Chassis" for procedures.
2. The brake lever and brake cams should be lubricated with lithium-based grease. The service interval is 6 months. Refer to "Chassis" for brake service procedures.

Drive Chain

1. Drive chains require lubrication at 1 month intervals.
2. The chain can be cleaned at lubricated through the inspection hole on the chain case.
3. The chain uses O-ring seals between the plates. Commercial chain lubes should never be used as they may cause damage. Use only motor oil, such as SAE 20-50 or similar grades, to lubricate the chain.
4. Before lubricating the chain, wipe it off with kerosene if it appears dirty. Never use gasoline or other solvents.
5. Keep steam cleaning and spray car wash wands away from the chain.

SERVICE CHECKS AND ADJUSTMENTS

Drive Chain

On models with chain drive, adjust as follows:

1. The chain should have about 10-15mm (0.4-0.6 in.) of free-play when checked at the inspection hole.
2. When checking, the rear wheels must be on the ground.
3. The chain should be cleaned and lubricated before checking free-play. Dirty chain tend to get tight.

Wheel hub bolts and tightening torques

4. If a way can be found to safely support the wheels off the ground, rotate them and check the chain at several places for tight spots. If a tight spot exists, chain tension should be adjusted to the proper value at that point. Note, however, that such a condition is indicative of a worn chain and/or worn sprockets and replacement will probably be required in the near future.
5. If the chain needs adjustment, loosen the four rear wheel hub bolts.
6. Turn the chain adjuster puller in or out until tension is correct.
7. Tighten the rear wheel hub bolts. Recheck tension.
8. The upper left hand hub bolt should be tightened to 43 ft. lbs. The other three should be tightened to 32 ft. lbs.

NOTE: *"Left" and "right" are referenced from the rear of the machine.*

Clutch

1. Locate the clutch adjuster on the right side of the engine near the oil filter cover.
2. Loosen the locknut slightly.
3. Carefully turn the adjuster screw counterclockwise until resistance is felt; then turn it 1/8 turn clockwise.
4. As marked on the crankcase cover, turning the adjuster screw CCW will decrease lever play and vice-versa.
5. Tighten the locknut to 11 ft. lbs.

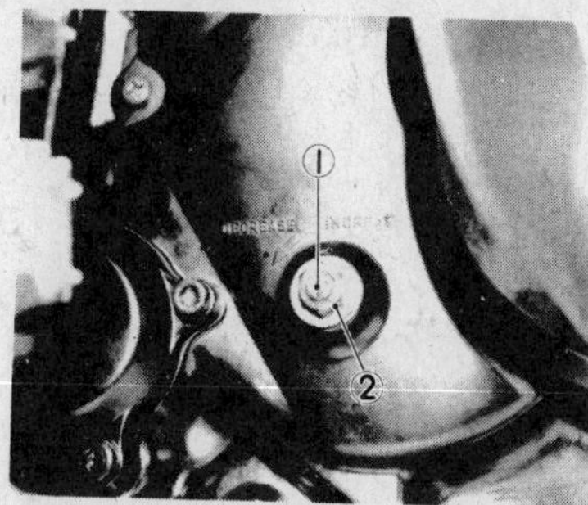

Clutch adjuster (1); locknut (2)

Throttle Cable

1. The throttle lever should have 3-5mm (0.12-0.20 in.) of free movement before the throttle slide begins to open.
2. Make this adjustment with the adjuster near the top of the throttle cable. Loosening the adjuster locknut and turning it in or out will affect lever free-lay.
3. Start the engine and turn the forks slowly from lock-to-lock. Idle speed must not increase. If it does, the throttle cable has insufficient free-play, is incorrectly routed, or is binding at some point. Find the trouble before riding.

Starter Lever

On models equipped with a starter lever, adjust as follows:

1. Pull the starter lever up by hand until resistance is felt and check the gap between the bottom of the lever and the lever holder.
2. It should be 1-2mm (0.04-0.08 in.).
3. Adjust, if required, with the cable adjuster.

Brakes

FRONT

1. The brakes should be adjusted so that the lever has 5-8mm of free movement measured between the lever and the lever holder before the linings contact the drum.
2. The brake can be adjusted with either the cable adjuster at the brake plate or with the adjuster on the handle bar. Loosen the locknut and turn the hand lever adjuster out to decrease lever free-play. At the brake plate, turning the wing nut in will accomplish the same thing.
3. It is recommended that major adjustments be made at the brake plate and finer adjustments with the handle bar adjuster.
4. After adjustment, lift the front wheel slightly and check that it can spin freely.
5. Apply the brake and check that the wear indicator on the brake plate is in the safe zone.

REAR

1. Pump the brake pedal and hand lever several times before adjustment.
2. At the hand lever, loosen the adjuster locknut and screw in the adjuster to give maximum cable freeplay.
3. Loosen the brake pedal wing nut and the brake hand lever wing nut at the caliper.
4. Loosen the locknut and adjusting bolt.
5. Screw in the brake hand lever wing nut so that the caliper lever can be positioned as shown in the illustration.
6. Slowly screw the adjusting bolt in by hand until resistance is felt, then back it off 1/4 turn.

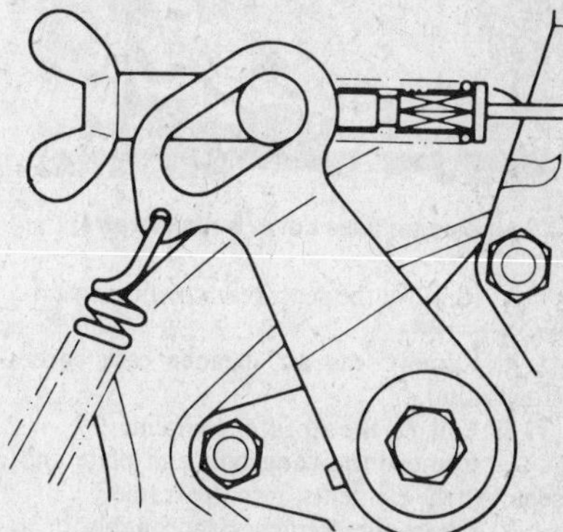
Rear brake preliminary position

7. Hold the adjusting bolt with a wrench so that it doesn't move. Tighten the locknut.
8. Screw in the brake pedal cable adjuster until the pin just touches the upper end of the lever slot. Clearance between the pin and the brake lever should be 0-1mm (0-0.04 in.).

9. Support the rear wheels off the ground and check that they spin freely. If they are tight, or if noise is heard, repeat the adjustment procedure.

10. Check free-play at the brake pedal. It should be less than 50mm (2.0 in.) Use the adjuster at the pedal to make this adjustment. On average, freeplay should be about 25mm (1.0 in.)

11. Check free-play at the rear brake hand lever. It should be about 5mm (0.2 in.). Use the cable adjuster at the hand lever to make this adjustment.

CAUTION: *Both pedal and lever should be adjusted when performing rear brake adjustments. Do not adjust one without checking the other.*

REAR PAD WEAR

When the head of the adjusting bolt comes close to touching its locknut, replace the brake pads.

Headlight Adjustment

Vertical adjustment of the headlight can be made by turning the screw below the lamp.

Turning the screw clockwise will move the beam higher.

Turning the screw counterclockwise will lower the beam.

FUEL SYSTEM

The fuel system consists of the carburetor, fuel petcock and air cleaner.

These items should be serviced about every six months under normal operating conditions.

Air Cleaner

1. A wet-foam air filter element is used.
2. Loosen the rear carrier knob, if fitted, and pull the carrier back.

Air cleaner case cover bolts (arrows)

3. Remove the seat/rear cowling assembly.
4. Remove the air cleaner case cover (four bolts).
5. Pull out the air filter element.
6. Remove the wing bolt and plate and separate the elements from the frame.
7. Clean the elements thoroughly in a safe solvent.
8. Dry the elements after cleaning by squeezing. Do not wring them out as the pores may be damaged.
9. Soak the elements in SAE 10W30 motor oil.
10. Squeeze off the excess oil. Elements should be wet, but not dripping with oil.
11. Assemble the filter elements on the frame and install the plate and wing bolt.
12. Clean the inside of the air cleaner case if it is wet or dirty.
13. Fit the air cleaner to the case. Be sure that the carburetor side of the air cleaner mates perfectly with the case surface to prevent unfiltered air from entering the engine.
14. Check air passages in the intake system for condition. The inlet to the case must be free of obstructions. The hose running to the carburetor from the case must have a tight seal at both the case and the carb.
15. Inspect the hose at the bottom of the air cleaner case. Remove the hose cap and drain off any water which may have collected.

Petcock

1. The petcock has filter screens inside the tank which should be cleaned periodically- about every 6 mos. under normal conditions.
2. Remove the gas tank.
3. Drain the gas.
4. Remove the lines from the petcock.
5. Remove the petcock securing screws and pull the assembly out of the tank.
6. Check gasket condition. Replace it if it appears damaged leaking prior to removal. removal.
7. Remove the filter screens and clean them in a safe solvent.
8. If foreign matter cannot be removed, or if the screens are punctured, crushed, other otherwise damaged, replace them.
9. Check the petcock mating surface. Replace the unit if any is noted.
10. Flush out the gas tank before installing the petcock to get rid of any residual dirt.
11. When fitting the petcock to the tank, be sure the gasket is in place.
12. After gas is added, check for leaks before operation. Be sure that all lines are tightly connected.

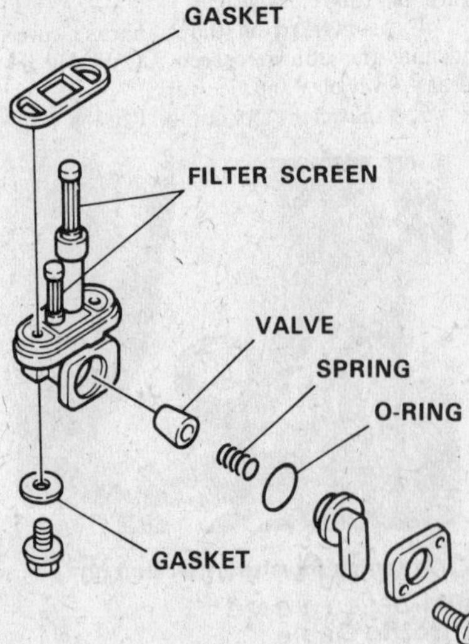

Petcock

Carburetor

1. Carburetor service procedure are detailed in the "Fuel System" section.
2. Carburetor float bowls are fitted with a drain screw which can be used periodically to remove water or any other foreign matter which may have passed through the system. Before draining float bowls, be sure that the petcock is "off," and that the fuel will be collected in a suitable container.

CHASSIS INSPECTIONS

Steering Head Bearings

1. Support the front wheel off the ground.
2. Grasp the lower end of the forks and try to move them back and forth in line with the machine.
3. If any looseness is felt, adjust the steering head bearings.
4. Turn the forks slowly from lock-to-lock. Movement should be smooth. If rough or binding, adjust the bearings.
5. Loosen the upper and lower triple clamp pinch bolts. Loosen the carrier bolts, if one is fitted.
6. Loosen the steering stem bolt on the upper triple clamp.
7. Use a pin wrench on the bearing adjuster nut beneath the upper triple clamp and turn the nut to remove any looseness from the bearings.
8. Tighten the lower triple clamp pinch bolts to 22 ft. lbs.
9. Tighten the upper triple clamp pinch bolts to 14 ft. lbs. Tighten carrier bolts to 11 ft. lbs.
10. Tighten the steering stem bolt on the upper triple clamp to 61 ft. lbs.

Wheel Bearings

1. Wheel bearing problems may make themselves known by a rumbling sound which increases with speed.
2. Support the wheel you are checking off the ground.
3. Spin the wheel and listen for any unusual noise. Place your hand on the front forks or the rear hub while the wheel is turning.
4. If you feel any vibration, suspect wheel bearing damage.
5. Refer to "Chassis" for disassemble procedures.

Tires

1. Special low pressure tires require special consideration.
2. Tire pressures are critical. The pressure must be maintained at the recommended pressure as shown on the stickers on the machine.
3. Pressure should be checked with a suitable low-pressure tire gauge.
4. Never allow pressure to fall below 2 psi. The tire can separate from the rim if pressure is too low.
5. Maximum allowable pressure is 10 psi. Overinflation is dangerous.
6. When adding air to tires, do so very slowly and carefully. Unregulated service station air lines should not be used. Rapid inflation can cause the tire to burst.
7. Be sure that pressure at all three tires is equal.
8. Check pressures when tires are cold.
9. Tires should be replaced when the tread depth at any point falls below 3mm (0.12 in.).
10. Rear tires should be replaced in pairs.

CAUTION: *Replacement tires must always meet manufacturer's size and performance specifications.*

PERIODIC MAINTENANCE INTERVALS①

Before each ride
- Safety items
- Lights
- Chain adjustment (if equipped)
- Control cable adjustment
- Tightness of critical fasteners

Monthly
- Clean and lubricate drive chain (if equipped)
- Check chain tension (if equipped)

Every 3 Months
- Check brake system

Every 6 Months
- Tune-up engine
- Service fuel system
- Check battery level
- Check tire pressure
- Check wheel bearings
- Check steering head bearings
- Change engine oil
- General chassis lubrication

Annually
- Clean oil filter and strainer
- Change fork oil
- Repack wheel bearings
- Change gearbox oil (if equipped)

Every 2 Years
- Check/repack steering head bearings

① Based on normal usage after initial service and break-in are completed.

RECOMMENDED LUBRICANTS

Engine
- Above 41°F (5°C): Yamalube 4-Cycle or SAE 20W-40, service rating "SE" of "SF"
- Below freezing: SAE 10W-30, service rating "SE" or "SF"

Final Gearbox
- SAE 80 API "GL-4" hypoid gear oil
- SAE 80W90 hypoid gear oil

Wheel/Steering Head Bearings
- Medium weight wheel bearing grease

Brake Components/Throttle Twist grip
- Lithium-based grease

Front Forks
- Yamaha Fork Oil
- SAE 10W motor oil

Drive Chain
- Medium weight motor oil

RECOMMENDED LUBRICANTS

Control cables
- Light motor oil
- Graphite-based lubricants
- Commercial cable lubes

Air Clean Elments
- SAE 10W30 motor oil

MAINTENANCE DATA

Fuel Capacity	**2.4 gal./9 L**
Engine Oil	
When changing	1.6 qts./1.5 L
After rebuilding	1.9 qts./1.8 L
Final Gearbox Oil	
Level	Check by level plug
Capacity	0.14 qt./0.13 L
Front Fork Capacity (each leg)	
DX	4.0 oz./117 cc
Other models	6.5 oz./193 cc
Tire pressure (f/r)	2.2 psi
Battery (if used)	12 v/14 ah

TUNE-UP

NOTE: *Common tune-up procedures are explained in detail in the "General Information" section. This includes a full description of spark plug service and analysis.*

REQUIRED MATERIALS

In addition to common hand tools, the procedures detailed in this section require:

a. A set of feeler gauges for valve adjustment;

b. A compression gauge for the compression test;

c. A tachometer for idle speed adjustments 2nd ignition timing check;

d. A stroboscopic timing light for ignition timing.

Connection of the tachometer and timing light will depend on make and/or model.

VALVE ADJUSTMENT

NOTE: *Valves must be adjusted when the engine is cold.*

1. If a carrier is fitted, loosen the knob and pull it backward.
2. Remove the seat/rear cowling assembly.
3. Remove the intake and exhaust valve covers.
4. Remove the timing window plug from the left crankcase cover.
5. Slowly pull the recoil starter knob until the "T" mark on the flywheel aligns with the stationary timing mark.
6. Check for clearance at both valves. If both are not free, rotate the engine 360° until the "T" mark appears again and check for clearance. Valves are adjusted when the engine is at Top Dead Center on the compression stroke.

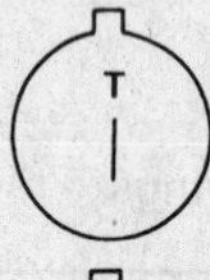

TOP DEAD CENTER

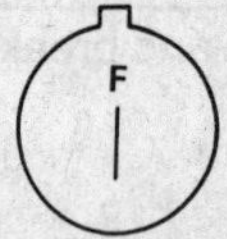

IGNITION TIMING MARK

Flywheel timing marks

7. With the proper thickness feeler gauge, check clearance. Clearances are:
   Intake: 0.05- 0.09mm/0.002-0.004 in.
   Exhaust: 0.11- 0.15mm/0.004-0.006 in.
8. If the valve is correctly adjusted, the gauge blade will be a light slip fit. If fit is too tight or loose, adjust the valve(s).
9. Loosen the valve adjuster locknut.
10. With the feeler gauge blade between the valve adjuster and the valve, turn the adjuster and the valve, turn the adjuster in or out until the blade is a light slip fit.
11. Hold the adjuster in place and tighten the locknut.
    Torque: 10 ft. lbs.
12. Install the valve covers. Fit the covers so that the ribs on the inside are at the top.
13. On models with a compression release, adjust the cable (see below).
14. Install timing window plug, and seat/rear cowling assembly.

COMPRESSION RELEASE

NOTE: *This adjustment must be made any time the valves are adjusted.*

Compression release lever (3); adjuster and locknut (1,2)

1. With the seat/rear cowling assembly and the timing window plug removed, check that the piston is at TDC on the compression stroke: the "T" flywheel mark must be aligned with the stationary timing mark with clearance at both valves.
2. Pull the recoil starter knob, if necessary, to achieve alignment.
3. Check for free- play at the compression release lever on the engine. It should move 2-3mm (0.08-0.12 in.) before contacting the rocker arm.
4. Use the cable adjuster at the engine to effect this adjustment.
5. When free-play is correct, tighten the adjuster locknut.
6. Fit the timing window plug, seat/rear cowling assembly, etc.

CAM CHAIN ADJUSTMENT

1. Remove the timing windown plug from the left crankcase cover.
2. Pull the recoil starter knob to align the "T" mark on the flywheel witht he stationary timing mark on the crankcase.

Cam chain adjuster: pushrod (1); adjuster (2); locknut (3)

3. Locate the cam chain adjuster behind the cylinder. Remove the adjuster cap.
4. Loosen the adjuster locknut a few turns.
5. Turn the adjuster in until the pushrod inside is flush with the adjuster end.
6. Start the engine.
7. Observe pushrod movement. The rod should move slightly when the engine is idling. If it does not, loosen the adjuster slightly until movement is noted.
8. Stop at this point and tighten the locknut (torque: 22 ft. lbs.).
9. Install the adjuster cap. Install timing windown plug.

COMPRESSION TEST

Refer to the "General Information" section under "Tune-Up" for compression test procedures.

1. The compression test should be made after valves and compression release (if fitted) are adjusted.
2. Engine should be run for several minutes before the test.
3. Remove the spark plug. Connect the plug to its cap and ground it against the engine case to prevent sparking during the test.

CAUTION: *Be sure the plug is properly grounded when cranking the engine.*

4. Screw- in type compression gauges need a 12mm thread for these machines.
5. Hold the throttle open while cranking the engine.
6. Compression should be about 128 psi. This is the standard value. The upper and lower limits are 142 psi and 114 psi.
7. If compression is too low, check that the valves are properly adjusted and that the compression release is not holding the exhaust valve open.

IGNITION TIMING

Ignition timing is not adjustable. A strobe timing light and a tachometer are needed to make this check.

1. Remove the timing window plug from the left crankcase cover.
2. Connect the tach and timing light according to the manufacturer's instructions.
3. Start the engine and let it run at the specified idle speed (1,400 ± 50 rpm).
4. Aim the light through the timing window. At idle, the "F" mark on the flywheel should appear to be aligned witht he stationary timing mark on the crankcase cover.
5. If alignment is not correct, check the pickup coil for looseness on its mount.

CARBURETORS

Carburetor adjustments to be made during a tune-up include float height, idle speed and mixture.

Float Height

1. Float height determines the level of gasoline in the float bowl during operation. While it is a critical setting, it will not normally need frequent attention once it is properly set. Although it need not be done at every tune-up, it should be checked from time to time.
2. The machine must be parked on a level surface.
3. Place a stand or jack under the engine and raise it until the carburetor is positioned vertically.
4. Disconnect the drain line from the bottom of the float bowl and connect a transparent vinyl tube (6mm/0.24 in. inside diameter) to the bowl fitting.
5. Set the petcock "ON" and start the engine, letting it run for a few minutes.
6. Hold the vinyl tube alongside the carburetor body. Open the drain screw. Gasoline will flow into the tube.
7. Shut the engine off.
8. Note the level of the gasoline in the tube relative to the carburetor body. The gas should be 3.0mm/0.12 in. below the edge of the carb body. The tolerance is ±0.1mm/0.04 in.
9. If correct, close the drain screw and disconnect the tube. Reconnect the drain line.
10. If not correct, disassemble and check float height as follows:
   a. Remove the carburetor from the engine. Refer to "Fuel System" for procedures.
   b. Remove the float bowl. Remove the float bowl gasket.
   c. With the carburetor positioned vertically, lower the float until the float arm tang just touches, but does not depress the float needle tip.
   d. Float height is the distance from the top of the float to the float bowl mating surface ("A" in the illustration).
   e. The specification is 21.5mm/0.85 in. for all models.

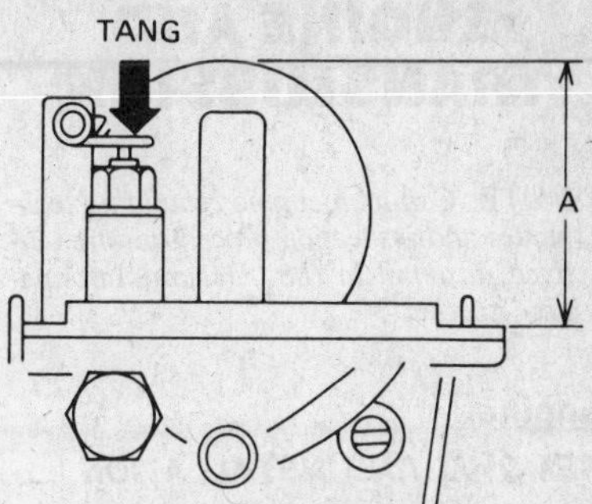

Carburetor float level (A)

   f. The tolerance is ±0.5mm/0.02 in. If adjustment is necessary, push out the float pivot pin and remove the float assembly.
   g. Carefully bend the tang on the float arm to adjust height. Bending the tang away from the carb body will decrease float height, and vice-versa.

18. After adjustment, recheck fuel level as outlined in the beginning of this procedure.
19. After adjustment, check for leaks and proper operation of the machine before riding.

Idle Speed and Mixture

NOTE: *These adjustments must be made when the engine is at operating temperature. They should also be made after all other tune-up procedures have been carried out, if a full tune-up is intended.*

1. Turn the pilot screw in *carefully* until it is lightly seated. Back it out the number of turns shown in the "Tune-UP Specifications" chart for your machine.
2. Fit a tachometer. Use the idle adjustment screw on the carburetor until engine speed is 1,400 rpm.
3. Smooth out idle, if necessary, by fine adjustments to the pilot air screw. About 1/2 turn in either direction from the specification should produce a good, smooth idle. If it doesn't, there may be a carburetor or engine fault.
4. Check the throttle cable adjustment. Turn the handle bars from side to side. If idle speed changes when this is done, the cable is too tight.

TUNE-UP SPECIFICATIONS

COMPRESSION	
Standard (psi)	128
Allowable range (psi)	114-142
VALVE CLEARANCE	
Intake (mm/in.)	0.05-0.09/0.002-0.004
SPARK PLUGS	
OEM (standard)	NGK/ND
Type (NGK/ND)	D-7EA/X22ES-U
Gap (mm/in.)	0.6-0.7/0.0240.028
Torque (ft. lbs.)	14
CARBURETOR	
Fuel level (mm/in.)	3.0/0.12
Float height (mm/in.)	21.5/0.85
Pilot screw setting (turns out)	①
Idle speed (rpm)	1,400

① Tri-Moto 200: 2¼ ± 1/2; Yamahauler: 2 ± 1/2; 225 DX: 1½ ± 1/2.

ENGINE AND TRANSMISSION

NOTE: *Common engine rebuilding techniques and inspection procedures are outlined in detail in the "General Information" section.*

Engine

REMOVAL AND INSTALLATION

YTM 200K-N

NOTE: *Top end components can be removed with the engine still in the frame.*

1. Clean the machine thoroughly before engine removal.
2. Remove the rear seat/cowling assembly.
3. Remove the gas cap and fuel tank cover bracket bolts. Remove the cover.
4. Remove the gas tank bolt at the front of the tank.
5. Shut the petcock off and disconnect the lines.
6. Disengage the rubber band at the rear of the tank and remove the gas tank.
7. Remove the exhaust pipe flange bolts at the engine.
8. Remove the muffler bolts on the frame.
9. Remove the exhaust system.
10 Loosen the shift linkage pinch bolt and pull the lever off the splined shaft on the engine.
11. Loosen the drive chain tensioner to give as much chain free-play as possible.
12. Remove the engine sprocket cover.
13. Remove the engine sprocket bolts (3); remove the lock plate. Remove the sprocket.
14. Disconnect the carburetor lines.
15. Remove the carburetor from the engine.
16. Disconnect the spark plug cable from the plug.
17. Disconnect the CDE leads at the connector near the ignition coil. Disengage them from the strain reliefs and arrange the wiring so that it will be out of the way when the engine is removed.
18. Disconnect the foot brake cable at the pedal.
19. Remove the bolt which secures the rear brake cable holder on the clutch cover.
20. Disconnect the compression release cable at the cylinder head.
21. Disconnect the vent pipe from the crankcase.
22. Remove the rear engine mounting bolts (upper and lower).
23. Remove the mounting brackets at the front of the engine.
24. Remove the cylinder head bracket.
25. Remove the engine from the right side of the frame.
26. Installation is basically the reverse of the removal procedure. Note the following points.
27. Place the engine on a suitable stand and lower the frame over it.
28. Install the rear upper and lower engine mounting bolts. Do not tighten them fully just yet. Bolts should be inserted from the right side of the machine.
29. Locate the front engine mounting brackets. Note that they differ (the left side bracket is flat). Fit the brackets on the proper side. Install the bolts and keep nuts only finger tight at this point.
30. Install the cylinder head bracket.
31. Tighten all engine mounting bolts now:

 Cylinder head bracket: 24 ft. lbs.
 Front brackets: 24 ft. lbs.
 Rear mounting bolts: 32 ft. lbs.

32. Remaining torques which should be noted are:

 Exhaust pipe at engine: 7 ft. lbs.
 Muffler at frame: 19 ft. lbs.
 Engine sprocket: 7 ft. lbs.

33. Be sure that all cables are properly adjusted, all fasteners correctly tightened and all connections tight before attempting operation.

CAUTION: *Do not forget to add engine oil.*

Other Models

NOTE: *Top end components can be removed witht he engine still in the frame.*

1. Clean the machine thoroughly before engine removal.
2. Loosen the rear brake cable adjusters at the caliper lever.
3. Disconnect the cables from the lever, brake pedal, holder and guides.
4. Jack the rear end of the machine off the ground using standard safety precautions and remove the rear wheels.
5. Remove the trailer hitch bracket, if fitted.
6. Disconnect the final gear breather pipe from the housing.
7. Remove the four nuts and two bolts which secure the housing.
8. Remove the wheel housing bolts.
9. Remove the rear wheel assembly.
10. Disconnect the negative lead from the battery; then disconnect the positive lead.
11. Loosen the rear carrier knob and pull the carrier back.
12. Remove the rear seat/cowling assembly.
13. Remove the gas cap. Remove the gas tank cover bracket bolts. Remove the cover.
14. Remove the tank bolt at the front of the tank.
15. Shut off the petcock. Disconnect the lines at the tank.
16. Remove the gas tank after disengaging the rubber band at the rear.
17. Remove the muffler bolts at the cylinder head. Remove the bolts on the frame. Remove the exhaust system.
18. Disconnect the fuel line from the cylinder head clamp.
19. Remove the carburetor and manifold.
20. Disconnect the spark plug lead from the plug.
21. Disconnect the CDI leads at the connector near the ignition coil. Disengage the wiring from the strain reliefs and arrange wiring so that it will not be damaged when the engine is removed.
22. Disconnect the compression release at the cylinder head, if fitted.
23. Disconnect the vent pipe from the top of the crankcase.
24. Loosen the shift linkage pinch bolt and pull the lever off the splined engine shaft.
25. Disconnect the foot brake pedal return spring.

Front engine mounting brackets

26. Remove the four starter motor/bracket screws. Remove the bracket.
27. Disconnect the starter motor high tension cable from the motor. Remove the starter motor.
28. Remove the rear engine mounting bolts, upper and lower.
29. Remove the front engine mounting brackets.
30. Remove the cylinder head bracket.
31. Remove the engine from the right side of the frame.
32. Installation is basically the reverse of the removal procedure. Note the following points.
33. Place the engine on a suitable stand and lower the frame over it.
34. Install the upper and lower rear mounting bolts. Do not tighten the bolts. yet.

NOTE: *All engine mounting bolts should be inserted from the right side of the frame.*

35. Note that the two front mounting brackets are different. They must be installed on the correct sides. Refer to the illustration to identify them. Install the brackets and nuts and bolts. Do not tighten the fasteners yet.
36. Install the cylinder head brackets.
37. Install the coupling gear joint into the bearing housing. Engage it with the coupling gear.
38. Install the rear wheel assembly.
39. Install the final gear housing. Tighten the nuts to 17 ft. lbs. and the bolts to 32 ft. lbs.
40. Tighten the engine mounting nuts and bolts as follows:

 Cylinder head bracket: 24 ft. lbs.
 Front brackets: 24 ft. lbs.
 Rear mounting bolts: 32 ft. lbs.

41. Tighten the wheel hub bolts evenly and torque to 36 ft. lbs.
42. The remainder of the procedure is the reverse of removal. Important torque settings are:

 Upper tow hitch: 11 ft. lbs.
 Lower tow hitch: 22 ft. lbs.
 Manifold-to- engine: 8.7 ft. lbs.
 Carburetor-to-manifold: 5.8 ft. lbs.
 Exhaust pipe at engine: 7.2 ft. lbs.
 Muffler at frame: 19 ft. lbs.

43. When fitting the gear shift linkage, align the punch mark on the shaft with the slot on the lever.
44. Be sure that all cables are correctly routed and properly connected. Be sure that all fasteners are tight. Check all electrical wiring connections. Check that fuel system lines are tight.

CAUTION: *Be sure to add engine oil.*

TOP END

Cylinder head, cylinder and piston can be removed with the engine in the frame.

Cylinder Head

REMOVAL

1. Disconnect the spark plug lead and remove the plug.
2. Remove the seat/rear cowling.
3. Remove the tank cover.
4. Remove the gas tank.
5. Disconnect and remove the ignition coil on the frame.
6. Disconnect the compression release at the cylinder head, if fitted.
7. Remove the carburetor.
8. Remove the cam chain tensioner cap.
9. Loosen the tensioner locknut.
10. Unscrew and remove the tensioner assembly. Note the locations of all parts.
11. Remove the cam sprocket cover screws.
12. Remove the cam sprocket cover.
13. Remove the neutral switch lead (if fitted) and the recoil starter assembly.
14. Remove the cam sprocket bolt. The crankshaft will have to be held with a special tool to do this in most cases. Secure the crank with a holder on the rotor.
15. Disengage the cam sprocket from the cam chain and remove it. Secure the chain so that it does not fall into the crankcase.
16. Take the pin out of the camshaft.
17. Gradually loosen the cylinder head bolts. When they are all loose, remove them.
18. Remove the cylinder head.

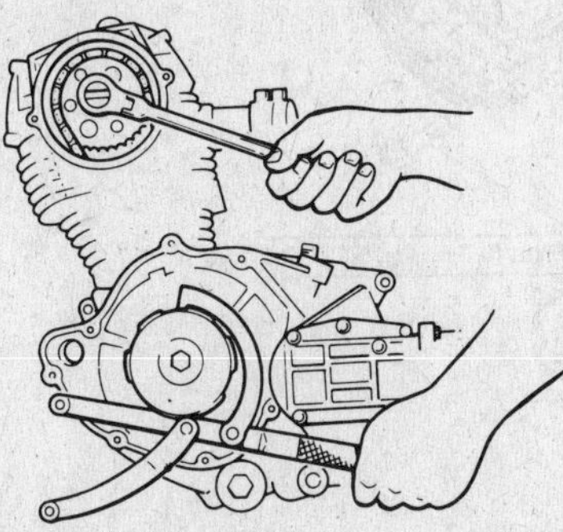

Removing the cam sprocket bolt

Cylinder head bolts

DISASSEMBLY

1. Remove the valve covers.
2. Bend down the lock tabs on the cam bearing retainer. Remove the bolts. Remove the retainer.
3. Thread a suitably sized bolt into the rocker arm shafts and pull the shafts out of the head. Mark the rocker arms for position. Do not mix shafts and rocker arms.

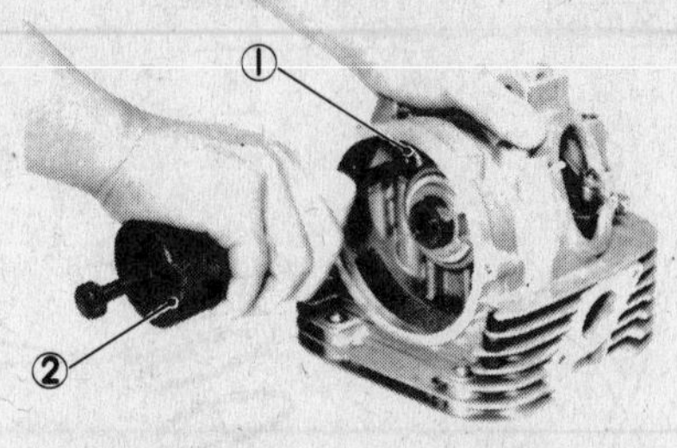

Removing the rocker arm shafts (1) with a slide hammer (2)

4. Thread a 10mm bolt into the camshaft and pull it out.
5. Remove the valve assemblies with a spring compressor.

INSPECTION

NOTE: Refer to "General Information" for a guide to engine component inspection procedures. Engine specifications for these machines are summarized in a chart at the end of this section.

1. Check valve condition.
2. Measure valve stem diameter and valve guide inside diameter. Subtract the readings for valve- to-guide clearance.
3. Check valve run- out.
4. Check valve seat width in the head.
5. Use a machinist's dye to check the width and position of the valve seat. Apply the dye to the valve's beveled seating area and a very small amount of grinding compound to the valve seat in the head. Spin the valve back and forth against the seat for several seconds, then remove the grinding compoind and inspect the pattern of the seat, from which the dye will have been removed.
6. The valve seat should be about 1.0mm (0.04 in.) wide and even in width all around the valve. The maximum acceptable seat width is 1.5mm (0.06 in.).
7. If the seat is uniform in width but is too wide (A), use a flat cutter, the a 30° cutter to reduce the seat width to within specification.
8. If the seat is centered on the valve face, but is too narrow (B), use a 45° cutter to increase the width to the proper specification.
9. If the seat is too narrow, and is towards the top edge of the face (C), first use a flat cuter, and then the 45° cutter.
10. If the seat is too narrow and positioned towards the bottom edge of the face (D), use a 30° cutter first, then a 45° cutter.
11. Check valve spring condition and free length.
12. Measure rocker arm shaft diameters and the inside diameters of the rocker arm bores.
13. Visually inspect the camshaft and replace it if damage is noted. Measure the cam lobe height.
14. Check the camshaft bushing for wear.
15. Check cam sprocket condition.

ASSEMBLY

1. Be certain that all parts are reinstalled in their original locations.
2. Valve springs are progressively wound. Install the close coils against the cylinder head. Note direction of winding.
3. Oil valves before installation. Use new valve seals.

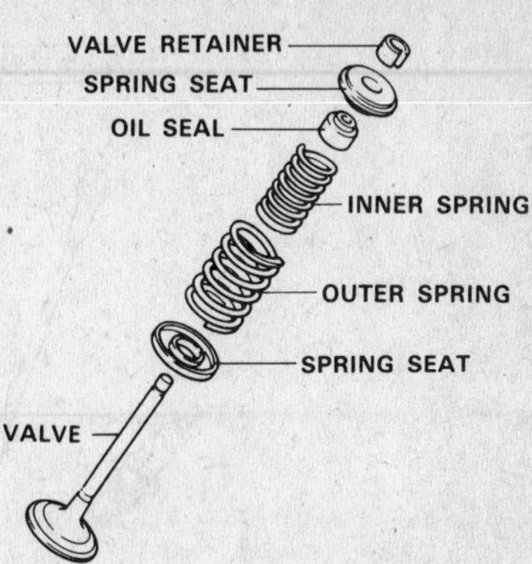

Valve spring assembly

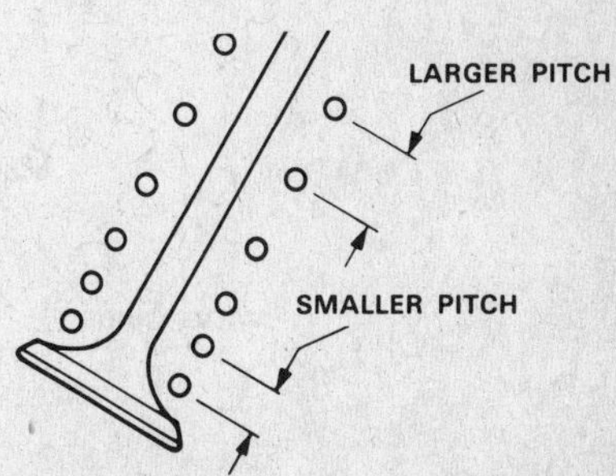

Install springs with close coils against the head

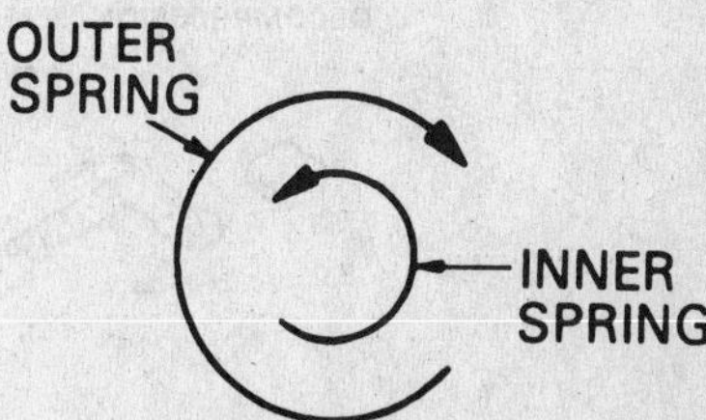

Spring winding directions when viewed from top

4. After valves are fitted, rap the stem once with a plastic mallet to seat the keepers.
5. Be sure that rocker arms and shafts are fitted tot heir original locations. Lubricate the shafts before insertion.
6. Rocker arm shafts must be installed with the threaded end facing out.
7. The intake rocker shaft is the longer of the two. It should be installed so that the bevel at the end of the shaft is positioned to clear the cylinder head bolt hole.
8. Lubricate the camshaft and bushings before installation. Install the cam and turn it so that the timing pin aligns with the mark on the cylinder head.
9. The camshaft bushing cutout must be flush with the cylinder head. Install. the retainer plate and tighten the bolts to 7.2 ft. lbs.

INSTALLATION

1. Be sure that the three dowel pins and the O-ring are in place on the cylinder mating surface.
2. Fit a new cylinder head gasket.
3. Fit the cylinder head, pulling the cam chain through the head as this is done.
4. Lightly oil the cylinder head bolt cop-

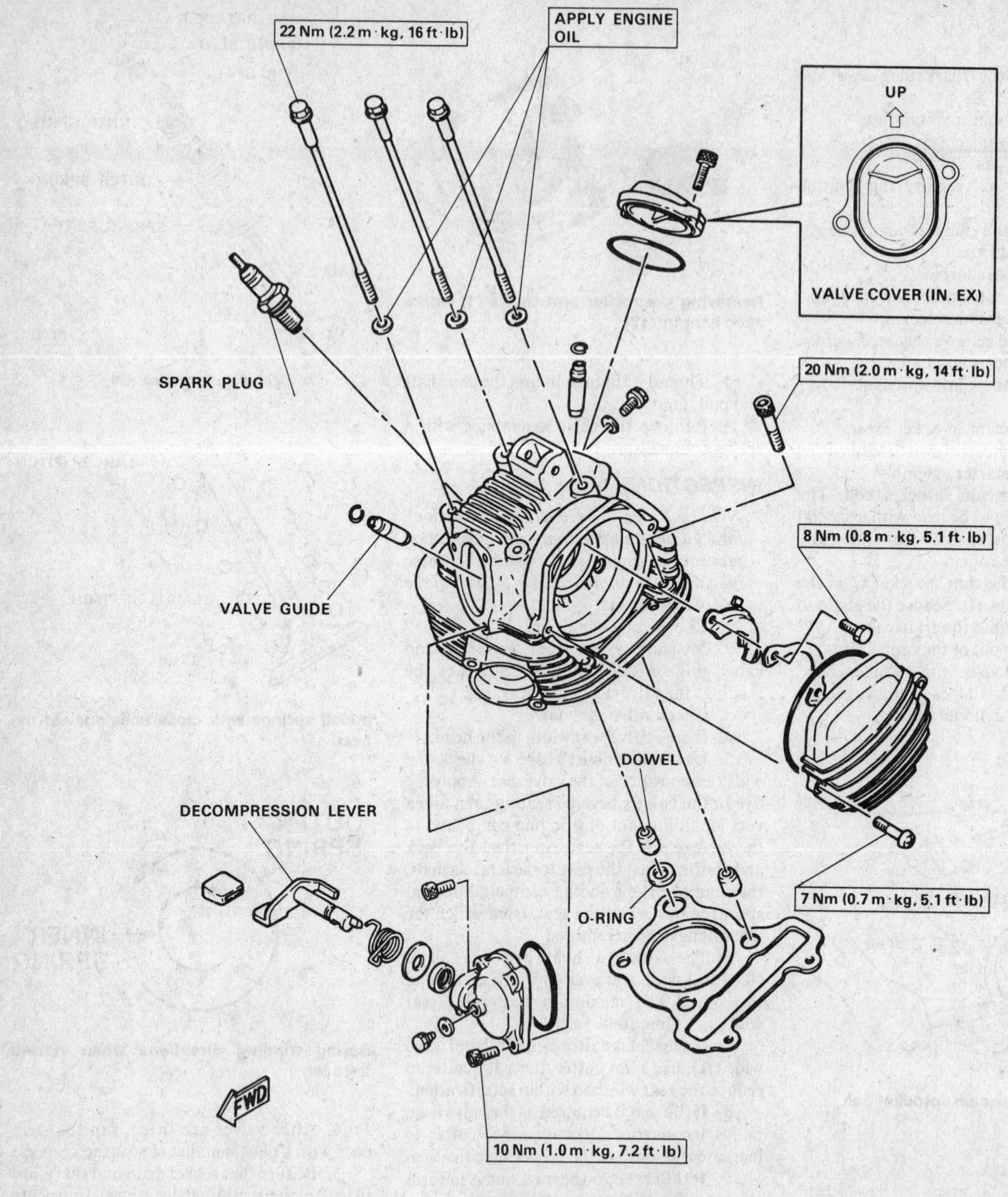

22 Nm (2.2 m · kg, 16 ft · lb)
APPLY ENGINE OIL
UP
VALVE COVER (IN. EX)
SPARK PLUG
20 Nm (2.0 m · kg, 14 ft · lb)
8 Nm (0.8 m · kg, 5.1 ft · lb)
VALVE GUIDE
DOWEL
DECOMPRESSION LEVER
7 Nm (0.7 m · kg, 5.1 ft · lb)
O-RING
FWD
10 Nm (1.0 m · kg, 7.2 ft · lb)

Cylinder head components

CUTAWAY
(EX-SIDE)
(IN-SIDE)
THREADS MUST FACE OUT

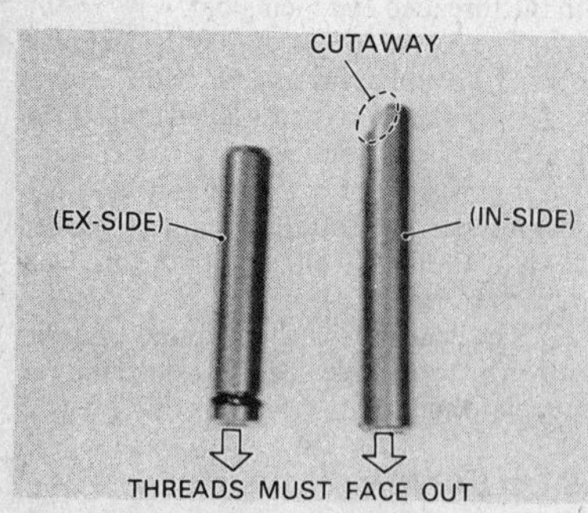

Rocker arm shafts

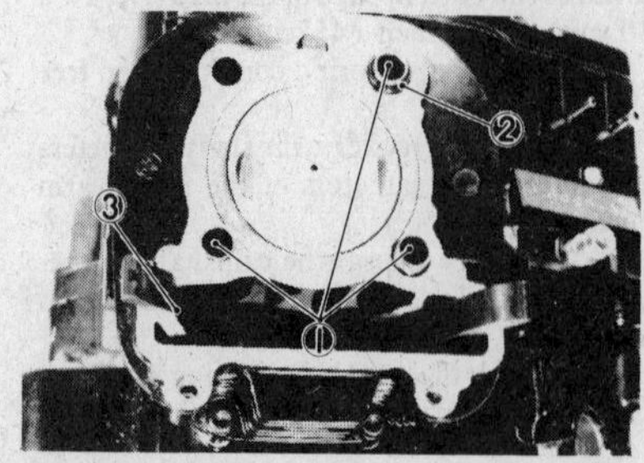

Cam chain guide (3); dowel pin (1) and o-ring (2) positions

per washers and the bolt seat near the compression release.

5. Install the cylinder head bolts and washers.

6. Proper torque the cylinder head bolts is 16 ft. lbs. for the long ones and 14 ft. lbs. for the short ones.

7. Tighten the bolts gradually and in a cross pattern until the correct torque values are reached.

8. Remove the timing window plug from the left crankcase cover.

9. Align the "T" mark on the flywheel with the mark on the crankcase.

10. Check that the timing pin is installed in the end of the camshaft. Align it with the head timing mark.

11. Install the cam sprocket. Pull the sprocket so that the front run of the chain is taut. Slip the sprocket onto the end of the camshaft, engaging the hole with the timing pin.

12. Check that the flywheel "T" mark is still lined up.

13. The line scribed on the sprocket must align with the mark at the very top of the cylinder head.

14. If timing is correct, install the cam bolt and tighten it to 43 ft. lbs.

15. Install the sprocket cover. Note that

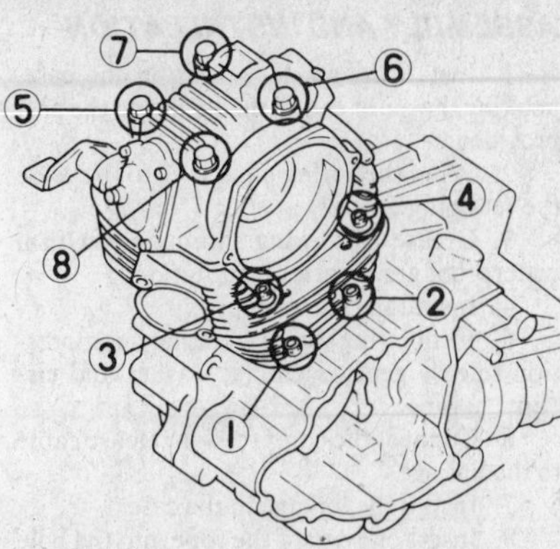

Cylinder head bolt tightening sequence

Position cam pin upwards before fitting sprocket

Align sprocket mark with head timing mark

Timing is set with flywheel "T" mark aligned with stationary timing mark

the fuel line clamp goes towards the rear of the cylinder head, if one is fitted.

16. Install the cam chain adjuster and set it as outlined in "Maintenance."

17. Install the valve covers so that the ridge is towards the top.

18. The remainder of the procedure is straight forward.

Cylinder and Piston

REMOVAL

1. Remove the cylinder head.
2. Remove the two securing bolts on the left side of the cylinder head.
3. Lift off the cylinder.
4. Remove the base gasket.
5. Account for all dowel pins and O-rings between the cylinder and the head and between the cylinder and crankcase.
6. Remove the piston wrist pin circlips. Push out the wrist pin. Remove the piston.

INSPECTIONS

1. Measure the diameter of the cylinder bore at three places front-to-rear and side-to-side. Compare the readings with each other and with the specifications at the end of this section. Maximum allowable variation between any two readings is 0.005mm (0.0002 in.). Reboring is necessary in the event of any greater variation.
2. Measure piston diameter 7.5mm (0.3 in.) above the edge of the skirt.
3. Check piston ring side clearance and end-gap.
4. Check all components for visible signs of wear.
5. If reboring is necessary, piston clearance is 0.025-0.045mm (0.0010-0.0018) in.

INSTALLATION

1. Install the piston so that the arrow on the crown points towards the exhaust port.
2. Press in the wrist pin. It may be necessary to heat the piston crown gently so that the pin can be pushed in.
3. Use new circlips for the wrist pin. Be certain they are properly seated.
4. Stagger the ring end-gaps around the piston as shown in the illustration. Manufacturer's marks on the rings must face up.

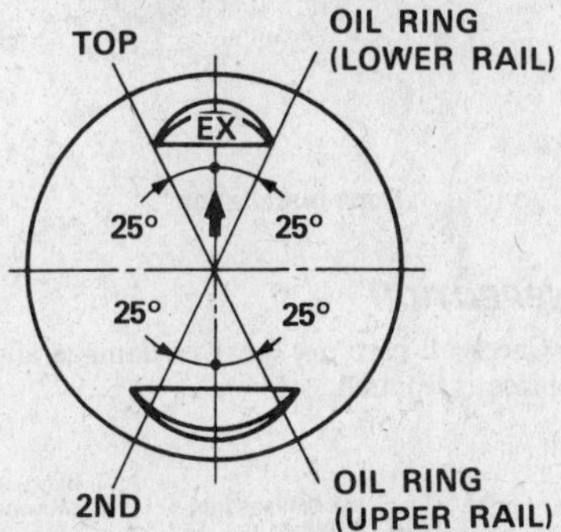

Piston ring end-gap alignments

Cylinder dowel pin (1) and o-ring (2) positions

5. Check that the dowel pins and O-ring are in place in the cylinder base.
6. Use a new base gasket.
7. Coat piston and rings with oil before the cylinder is installed.
8. Compress the rings and install the cylinder.
9. Install the two cylinder bolts. Do not tighten the bolts until the cylinder head bolts are torqued. At that time, tighten them to 14 ft. lbs.

CRANKCASE COVER COMPONENTS

Recoil Starter (Yamahauler, DX)

REMOVAL AND DISASSEMBLY

1. Remove the recoil starter assembly from the crankcase by removing the cover screws.
2. Pull the starter knob out about a foot and hold the sheave drum in place. Fit the rope into the but-out in the drum. Allow the drum to wind back gradually.
3. Remove the starter knob cap.
4. Pull out the rope and untie the knot. Remove the knob.
5. Remove the drive housing securing nut.
6. Remove the housing, drive pawl and and drive pawl spring.
7. Remove the sheave drum from the case.
8. Remove the starter spring.

INSPECTIONS

Check all parts for wear and replace as required.

ASSEMBLY AND INSTALLATION

1. Install the starter spring.
2. Wind the spring clockwise to fit inside the retaining posts. Hook the loop on the outer end of the spring onto the spring hook on the case.
3. Grease the spring thoroughly with a waterproof grease.
4. Insert the end of the rope into the sheave drum hole. Knot the end.
5. Wind the rope around the drum as shown in the illustration. When you have about 16 inches of rope left, hook it into the drum cut-out.
6. Install the sheave drum into the starter case. Be sure the inner hook in the spring engages the cutout in the drum.
7. When first placed in the case, the sheave drum will be resting on the spring. Rotate the drum until it drops slightly, then rotate it clockwise until spring tension is felt.
8. Insert the rope end into the case hole.
9. Install the knob and knot the rope.
10. When installing the drive pawl spring, note that the longer end of the spring is inserted into the hole in the sheave drum.
11. Carefully install the drive pawl onto the spring so that the spring end fits a notch in the drive pawl.
12. Rotate the drive pawl one turn CCW to preload the spring, then push the drive pawl into the cutout in the sheave drum.
13. Install the spring clip onto the drive housing. Tighten the nut to 7.2 ft. lbs.
14. Rotate the drum four turns CW.
15. Check operation. The sheave drum should rotate clockwise and the drive pawl

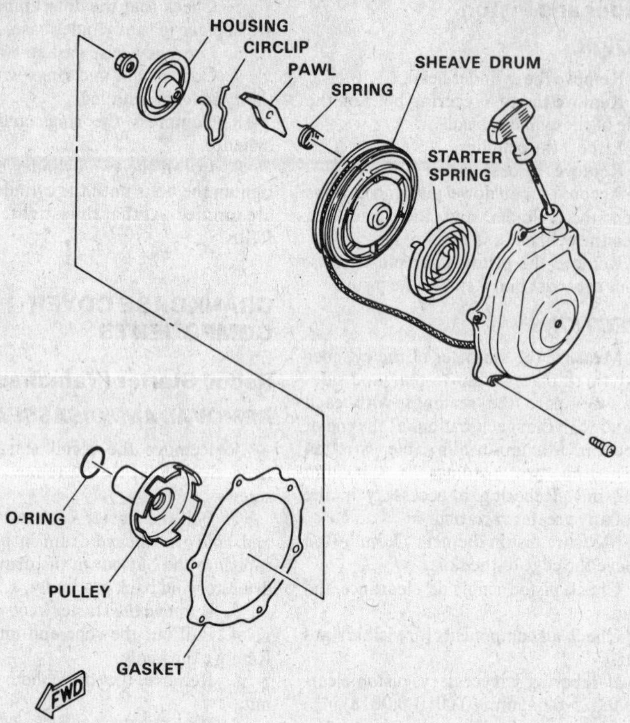

Recoil starter (Yamahauler, DX)

Starter spring installation

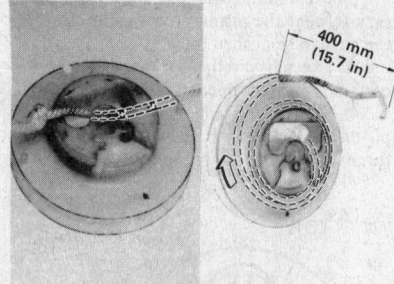

Starter spring installation

should emerge from the sheave drum when the rope is pulled.

Rope installation

INSPECTION

Check all parts for wear or damage and replace as required.

Recoil Starter (Tri-Moto)

REMOVAL AND DISASSEMBLY

1. Remove the recoil starter assembly from the crankcase by removing the cover screws.
2. Remove the knob cap.
3. Untie the knot in the rope and remove the knob.
4. Remove the drive housing securing nut.
5. Remove the housing, drive pawl and drive pawl spring.
6. Remove the sheave drum and starter spring from the case.
7. Remove the circlip, washer and compression release linkage.

NOTE: *Springs are not identical. Mark them so that they can be installed in their original locations.*

10. Remove the starter spring guide and starter spring from the case.

ASSEMBLY AND INSTALLATION

1. Install the starter spring in the case, hooking the outer end of the spring on the post provided.
2. Wind the spring clockwise to fit inside the retaining posts.
3. Grease the spring thoroughly with a waterproof grease after installation.
4. Install the stopper spring.
5. Install the spring retainer, compression release gear assembly, washer and circlip.
6. Connect the compression release cable to the linkage.
7. Install the linkage in the case.
8. Insert one end of the rope into the hole in the sheave drum. Knot the end.
9. Wind the rope clockwise around the drum.
10. When there is about 26 in. of rope left, engage it with the drum cut-out.
11. Install the sheave drum in the case.
12. Be sure the inner hook in the spring engages the cutout in the sheave drum.
13. When first installed, the drum will be resting on the spring. Rotate the drum until it drops slightly, then rotate it clockwise until spring tension is felt.
14. Insert the end of the rope into the hole in the starter case. Fit the free end through the starter knob and knot it. Install the knob cap.
15. Install the drive pawl spring and drive pawl.
16. The longer end of the spring should be inserted into the hole in the sheave drum.
17. Carefully install the drive pawl onto the spring so the spring end fits a notch in the drive pawl.
18. Rotate the drive pawl one turn CCW

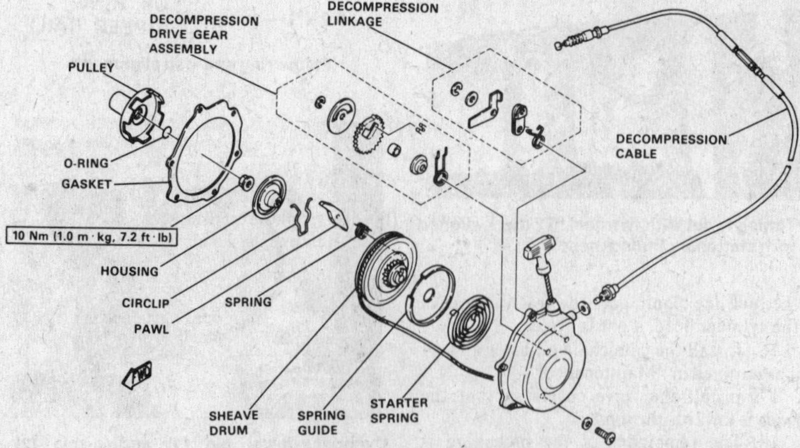

Recoil starter (Tri-Moto 200)

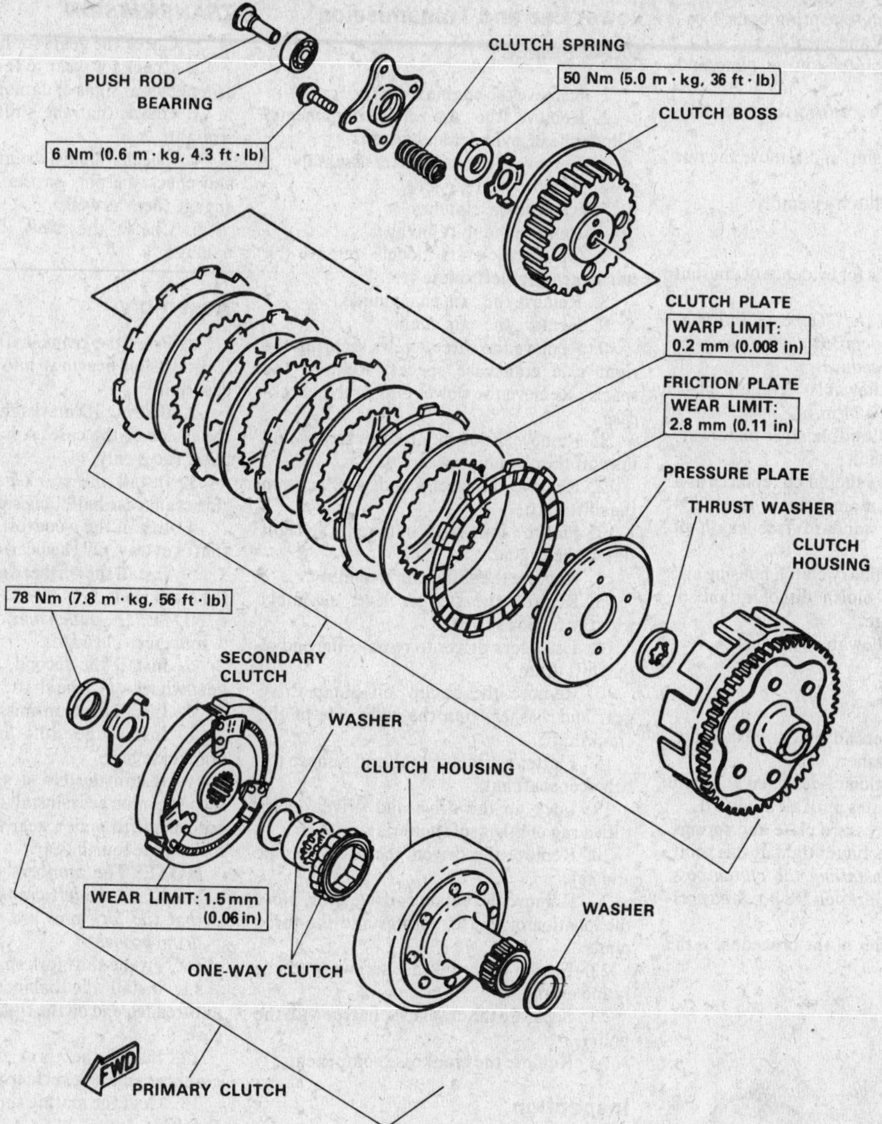

Clutch assemblies

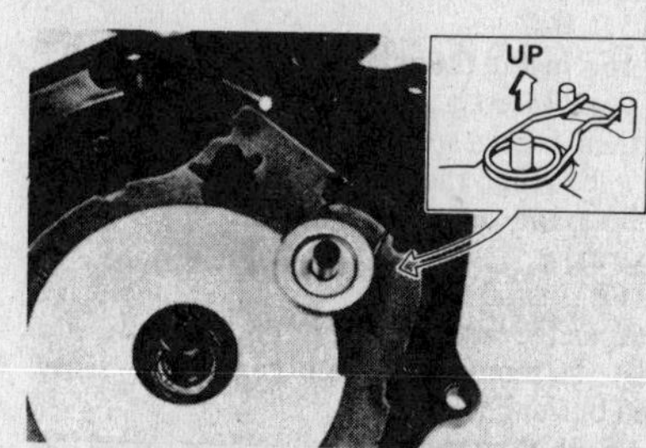

Pawl spring installation

to preload the spring, then push the drive pawl into the cutout in the sheave drum.

19. Install the spring clip onto the drive housing.

20. Tighten the drive housing securing nut to 7.2 ft. lbs.

21. Rotate the drum four turns CW to preload the spring.

22. Check operation of the starter. The sheave drum should rotate clockwise and the drive pawl should emerge from the drum when the rope is pulled.

Magneto

REMOVAL

1. Remove the recoil starter assembly.
2. Remove the recoil starter pulley bolt. It may be necessary to hold the pulley steady with a special tool to do this.
3. Remove the pulley.
4. Remove the left side crankcase spacer screws.
5. Remove the spacer, noting the dowel pins in the crankcase.
6. Use a puller to remove the magneto flywheel from the crankshaft.
7. Remove the woodruff key.

INSTALLATION

1. Installation is the reverse of removal.
2. Use a new crankcase spacer gasket.
3. Tighten the pulley bolt to 36 ft. lbs.

Clutches

REMOVAL

1. Drain the engine oil
2. Remove the oil filter cover bolts.
3. Remove the filter cover, filter and O-rings.
4. Remove the clutch adjuster locknut, washer and O-ring.
5. Remove the clutch cover screws.
6. Tap around the cover carefully with a plastic mallet to break it free, then remove it.
7. Note the dowel pins in the crankcase.
8. Remove the clutch lever spring, the clutch lever, shift guide No. 1, the pawl holder and shift guide No. 2.
9. Flatten the lock tab on the primary clutch nut.
10. Hold the clutch and remove the nut and washer.
11. Turn the secondary clutch so that one of the clearance notches will allow the primary gear to pass. Then remove the primary clutch assembly.
12. Note that there is a washer beneath the primary gear. Locate it and place in a safe location.
13. Remove the pushrod and bearing from the secondary clutch spring plate.

14. Remove the clutch spring bolts, loosening them gradually and evenly.

15. Remove the clutch spring plate and the springs.

16. Flatten the tab securing the secondary clutch hub nut.

17. Hold the housing and remove the nut and lockwasher.

18. Remove the clutch assembly.

INSPECTION

1. Check all parts for evidence of unusual wear.

NOTE: *Refer to the "General Information" section for detailed engine component inspection procedures.*

2. Minimum allowable friction plate thickness is 2.8mm (0.11 in.).

3. Maximum allowable steel plate warpage is 0.2mm (0.008 in.).

4. Clutch springs should be replaced as a set if any measures more than 1.0mm (0.04 in.) less than the standard free-length of 34.9mm (1.37 in.).

5. Check the primary clutch housing and shoe assembly for bluish discoloration indicating heat damage.

6. Maximum allowable clutch shoe wear is 1.5mm (0.06 in.).

INSTALLATION

1. Install the secondary clutch housing. Install the thrust washer.

2. Install a friction plate. Then alternate steel and friction plates until all are fitted.

3. Install the pressure plate and springs. Tighten the bolts finger tight at this point.

NOTE: *When installing the clutch boss, align the arrow marks on the boss and pressure plate.*

4. The remainder of the procedure is the reverse of disassembly. Note the following points:

a. Tighten the secondary clutch hub bolt to 36 ft. lbs. Be sure to bend up the lock tab.

b. Tighten the spring bolts to 4.3 ft. lbs.

c. When installing the one-way assembly of the primary clutch, ensure that the flange side faces inward.

d. Torque the primary clutch nut to 56 ft. lbs.

e. When installing the shift linkage, the slot in shift guide No. 1 must engage the shift shaft projection, and the shift guide No. 2 slot must engage the projection of the right-side spacer.

f. Be sure that the two dowel pins are in place before fitting the cover.

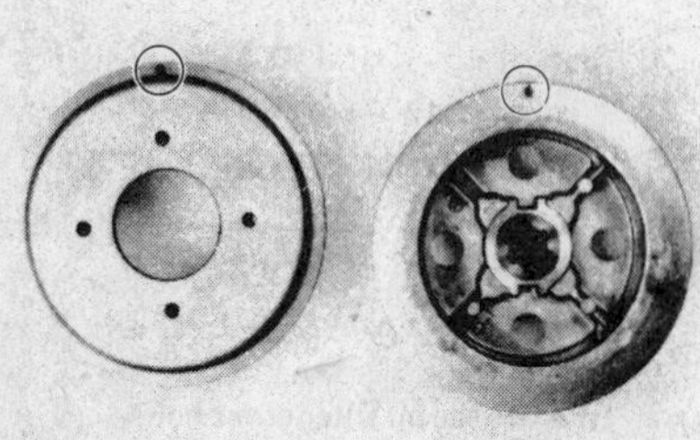

Align pressure plate and hub marks when installing

Lower End and Transmission

DISASSEMBLY

1. Remove the engine from the frame.

2. Remove the top end components: cylinder head, cylinder and piston.

3. Remove the recoil starter assembly.

4. Remove the magneto.

5. Remove the clutches.

6. Remove the shift linkage.

7. On electric-start models, remove the starter gearing (left side).

8. Remove the cam chain guide.

9. Remove the cam chain.

10. Remove the three screws securing the right side crankcase spacer. Remove the spacer. Remove the dowel pins in the crankcase.

11. Remove the oil pump cover screws and take off the oil pump assembly.

12. Remove the circlip and washer from the shift shaft.

13. Pull the shift shaft out from the right side of the engine.

14. Remove the shift lever assembly.

15. Remove the stopper lever assembly with the torsion spring.

16. Use a torx driver to remove the end of the shift drum.

17. Remove the circlip, oil pump drive gear and washer from the right side of the crankshaft.

18. Flatten the locking tab and remove the balancer shaft nut.

19. Lock up the drive and driven gears with a rag or other soft material.

20. Remove the driven gear nut, washer and key.

21. Remove the balancer drive gear. Note the location of the six springs and the three pins.

22. Loosen the crankcase screws gradually and evenly.

23. Separate the crankcase halves with the puller.

24. Remove the crankcase components.

Inspection

OIL PUMP

1. Rotor bore in the body must not exceed 6mm (0.24 in.).

2. Inner-to-outer rotor clearance must not exceed 0.15mm (0.0059 in.).

3. If either specification is not met, the pump must be replaced.

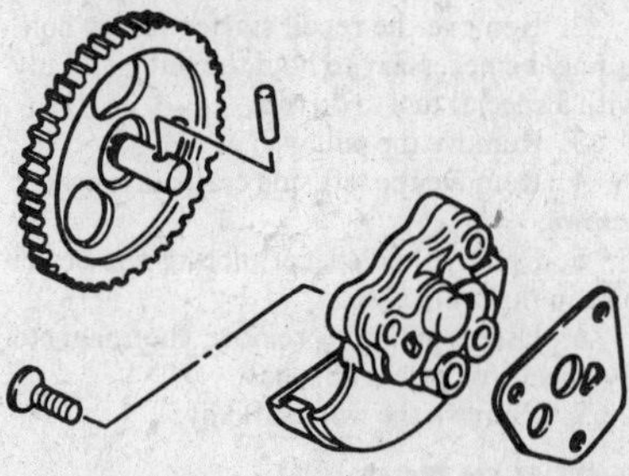

Oil pump assembly

CRANKSHAFT

1. Refer to the "Engine Specifications" chart at the end of this section.

2. The crankshaft should be inspected for rod play, run-out and bearing condition.

TRANSMISSION

1. Check the gears for heat damage.

2. Check for wear to the teeth, pitting or other obvious signs of damage.

3. Check that the shift fork shafts are straight.

4. Check the shift drum grooves for wear and check the pins on the shift forks which engage them as well.

5. Check the shift fork fingers for damage.

Assembly

1. Press the crankshaft bearing and the transmission bearings into the right crankcase half.

2. Bearing ID marks should face towards the inside of the case. Apply pressure to the outer races only.

3. Install the crankshaft into the right side crankcase half, long side first.

4. Install the woodruff key in the crankshaft keyway. Oil the bearings and taper.

5. Install the washer and buffer boss onto the crankshaft.

NOTE: *The punch mark on the buffer boss must face outwards.*

6. Install the second, fourth and third-gear wheels onto the shaft.

7. Install the transmission shafts.

8. Install the shift drum in the right crankcase half.

9. Install the No. 1 shift fork onto the second pinion gear; install the No. 2 shift fork onto the fifth pinion gear the the No. 3 shift fork on the fourth gear.

NOTE: *The numbers on the shift forks must face the left crankcase half. Be sure that the fork pins are seated in the shift drum grooves.*

10. Fit the shift fork shaft.

11. Install the balancer shaft with the unthreaded end on the right side of the crankcase.

12. Install the three dowel pins on the crankcase mating surface.

13. Coat the mating surface with Yamaha Bond No. 4.

14. Join the case halves.

15. Tighten the screws gradually and in a cross pattern. When all are tight, torque them to 5 ft. lbs.

16. Install the balancer drive gear:

a. Insert a spring into the buffer boss, then insert a spring with a pin in it.

b. Align the punch marks on the buffer boss and drive gear and install the drive gear.

17. Install the washer and oil pump drive gear on the crankshaft. Fit the circlip. Be sure that the pump gear tab engages the washer and buffer boss slots.

18. Fit the balancer driven gear. Align the punch marks on the two gears.

19. Fit the key to the balancer shaft.

20. Install the washer and the nut.

21. Lock the gears in place and tighten the nut to 36 ft. lbs.

22. Use a non-permanent thread-locking compound on the shift drum end plate. When installing the plate, align the match mark with the longer pin.

23. Tighten the torx bolt to 8.7 ft. lbs.

24. Lightly grease the lips of the shift shaft oil seal.

25. Install the shaft. Hook the spring onto the crankcase boss provided. Be sure that the

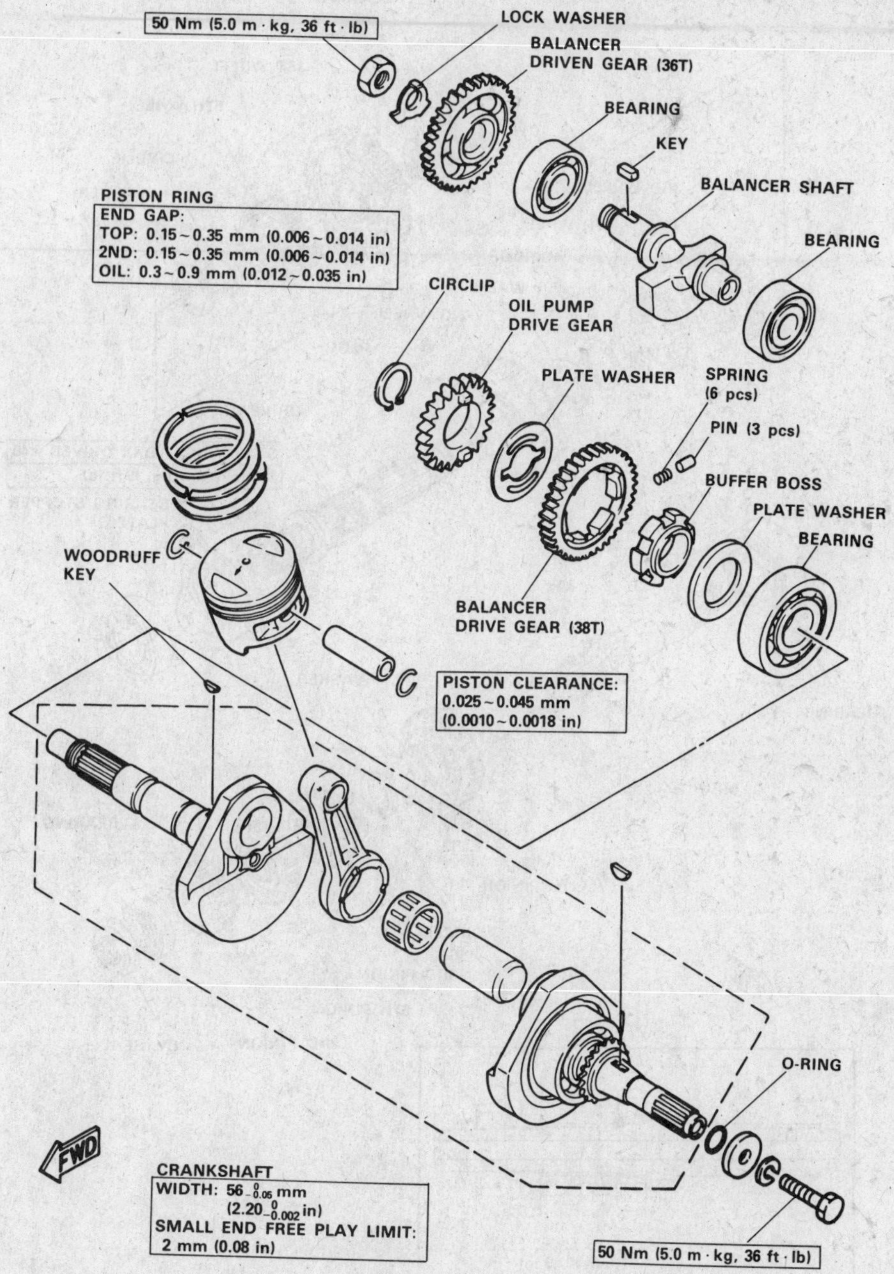

50 Nm (5.0 m · kg, 36 ft · lb)

LOCK WASHER

BALANCER DRIVEN GEAR (36T)

BEARING

KEY

BALANCER SHAFT

BEARING

PISTON RING
END GAP:
TOP: 0.15 ~ 0.35 mm (0.006 ~ 0.014 in)
2ND: 0.15 ~ 0.35 mm (0.006 ~ 0.014 in)
OIL: 0.3 ~ 0.9 mm (0.012 ~ 0.035 in)

CIRCLIP

OIL PUMP DRIVE GEAR

PLATE WASHER

SPRING (6 pcs)

PIN (3 pcs)

BUFFER BOSS

PLATE WASHER

BEARING

WOODRUFF KEY

BALANCER DRIVE GEAR (38T)

PISTON CLEARANCE:
0.025 ~ 0.045 mm
(0.0010 ~ 0.0018 in)

O-RING

FWD

CRANKSHAFT
WIDTH: $56_{-0.05}^{\ 0}$ mm
($2.20_{-0.002}^{\ 0}$ in)
SMALL END FREE PLAY LIMIT:
2 mm (0.08 in)

50 Nm (5.0 m · kg, 36 ft · lb)

Crankshaft assembly

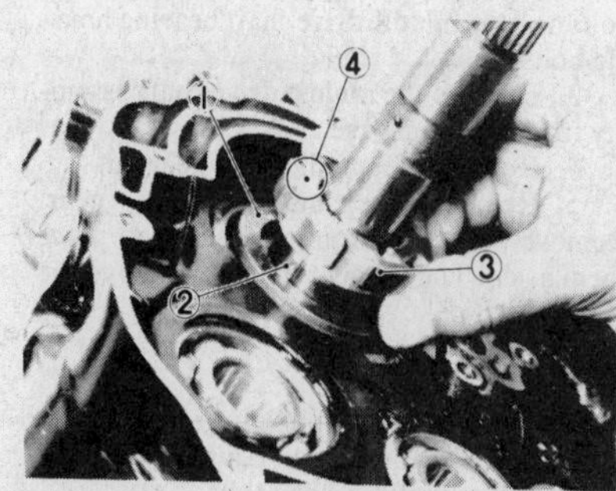
Plate washer (1); key (2); buffer boss (3); punch mark (4)

Buffer boss (1); springs (2); pins (3)

Drive gear alignment marks

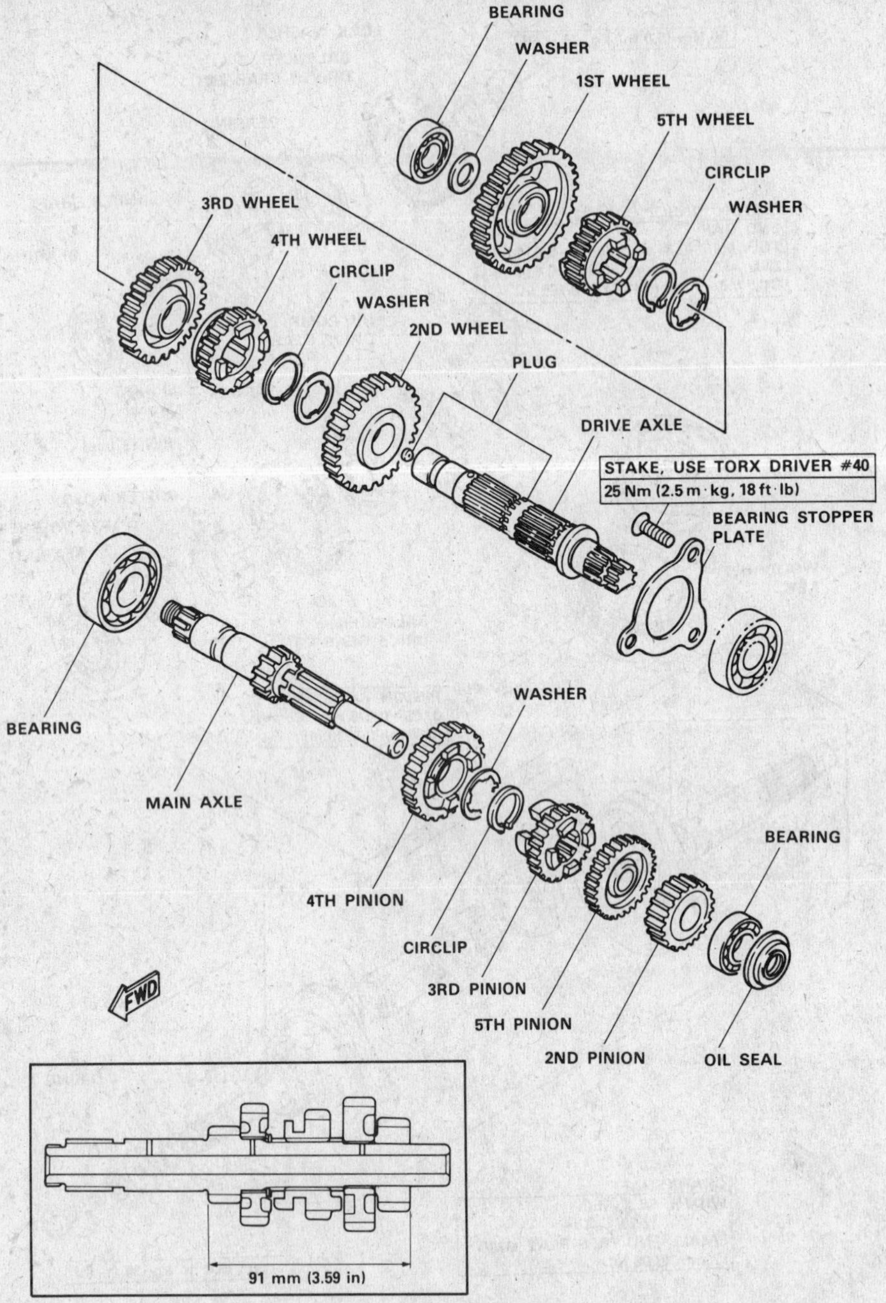

BEARING
WASHER
1ST WHEEL
5TH WHEEL
CIRCLIP
WASHER
3RD WHEEL
4TH WHEEL
CIRCLIP
WASHER
2ND WHEEL
PLUG
DRIVE AXLE
STAKE, USE TORX DRIVER #40
25 Nm (2.5 m·kg, 18 ft·lb)
BEARING STOPPER PLATE
BEARING
MAIN AXLE
WASHER
BEARING
4TH PINION
CIRCLIP
3RD PINION
5TH PINION
2ND PINION
OIL SEAL
FWD
91 mm (3.59 in)

Transmission assembly

Drive and driven gear alignment marks

shift lever correctly engages the shift drum pins.

26. Install the shift shaft washer and circlip.

27. Install the oil pump, using a new gasket. Tighten the bolts to 5 ft. lbs.

28. Remaining procedures are contained in the relevant component sections.

MIDDLE GEAR CASE

Removal

1. Remove the engine from the frame.
2. Remove the middle gear case cover bolts and the middle drive shaft bearing housing bolts.
3. Remove the middle drive shaft assembly from the crankcase.
4. Remove the middle drive gear nut.
5. Remove the middle drive gear. Remove the shims from the shaft and place them aside. The number and thickness of the shims is critical.

Disassembly

1. Remove the coupling gear nut.
2. Remove the washer, coupling gear and middle drive shaft subassembly.
3. Remove the washers and the collapsible collar from the middle drive axle.

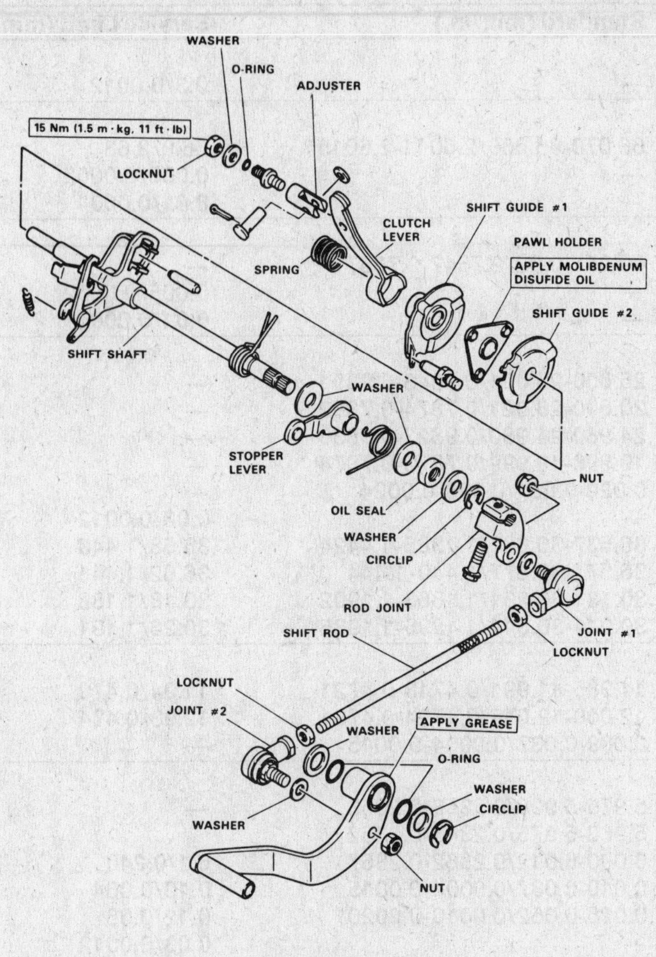

Shift assembly

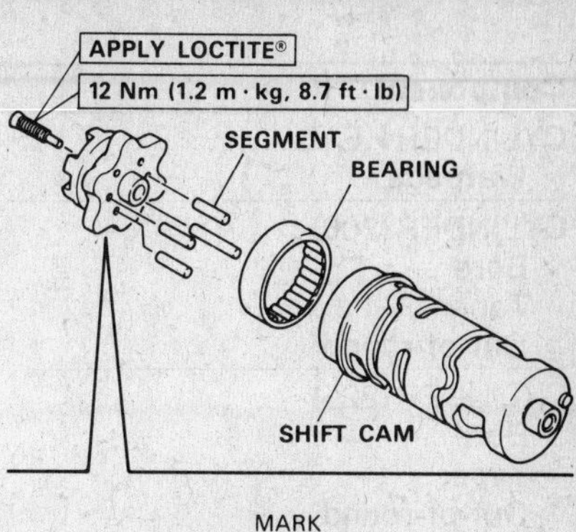

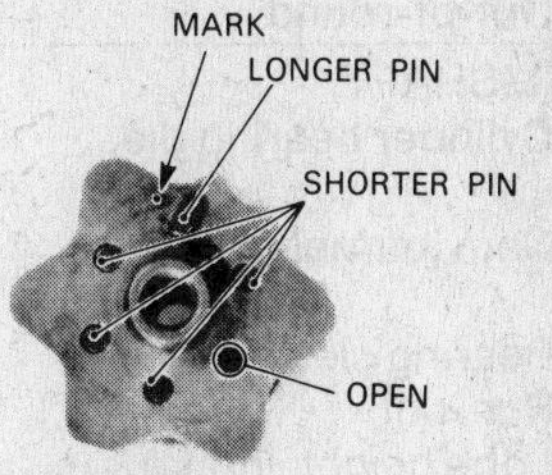

Shift drum plate installation

Inspection

1. Check all parts for wear or damage. Further disassembly requires special tools and should only be entrusted to trained specialists.

Assembly And Installation

1. Reverse the previous procedures.
2. Be sure that all of the original shims are installed behind the middle drive gear.
3. Tighten the middle drive gear nut to 43 ft. lbs.
4. Refer to the exploded view of the middle gear assembly for additional information.

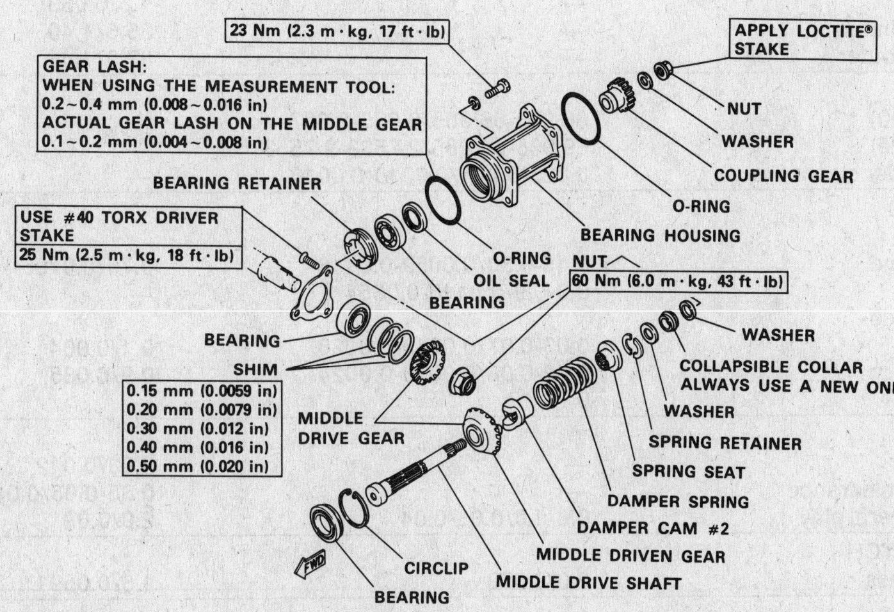

Middle drive gear assembly

ENGINE SPECIFICATIONS

Component	Standard (mm/in.)	Service Limit (mm/in.)
CYLINDER HEAD		
Warpage	—	0.3/0.0012
CYLINDER (200)		
Bore	66.070-66.080/2.6011-2.6015	66.9/2.63
Taper	—	0.005/0.0002
Out-of-round	—	0.01/0.0004
CYLINDER (225)		
Bore	69.97-70.02/2.7547-2.7567	—
Taper	—	0.005/0.0002
Out-of-round	—	0.01/0.0004
CAMSHAFT		
Cylinder bearing dia.	25.000-25.021/0.9843-0.9851	—
	20.000-20.021/0.7874-0.7882	—
Cam journal dia.	24.960-24.980/0.9827-0.9835	—
	19.998-19.999/0.7873-0.7874	—
Bearing clearance	0.020-0.061/0.008-0.0024	—
Run-out	—	0.03/0.0012
Lobe height, intake	36.537-36.637/1.4385-1.4424	36.58/1.440
Lobe height, exhaust	36.577-36.677/1.440-1.444	36.62/1.441
Base circle dia., intake	30.131-30.231/1.1863-1.1902	30.18/1.188
Base circle dia., exhaust	30.214-30.314/1.1895-1.1935	30.26/1.191
ROCKER ARMS		
Rocker arm shaft OD	11.985-11.991/0.4718-0.4721	11.94/0.470
Rocker arm ID	12.000-12.018/0.4724-0.4731	12.03/0.474
Arm-shaft clearance	0.009-0.037/0.0004-0.0015	—
VALVES		
Stem OD, intake	5.975-5.990/0.2353-0.2358	—
Stem OD, exhaust	5.960-5.975/0.2346-0.2352	
Guide ID, in & ex	6.000-6.012/0.2362-0.2367	6.1/0.240
Stem-to-guide clearance, intake	0.010-0.037/0.0004-0.0015	0.10/0.004
Stem-to-guide clearance, exhaust	0.025-0.052/0.0010-0.0020	0.12/0.05
Run-out	—	0.03/0.0012
Head dia., intake	33.9-34.1/1.3346-1.3425	—
Head dia., exhaust	28.4-28.6/1.1181-1.1260	—
Seat width	0.9-1.1/0.0354-0.0433	1.6/0.063
VALVE SPRINGS		
Tilt	—	1.6/0.063
Free length, inner	—	35.5/1.40
Free length, outer	—	37.2/1.46
PISTON		
Diameter (200)	66.935-66.985/2.635-2.637	—
Diameter (225)	69.935-69.985/2.7533-2.7553	—
Piston-cylinder clearance	0.025-0.045/0.0010-0.0018	—
PISTON RINGS		
End-gap		
Top, second	0.15-0.30/0.0059-0.0118	0.75/0.0295
Oil	0.3-0.9/0.0118-0.0354	—
Side clearance		
Top	0.03-0.07/0.0012-0.0028	0.1/0.004
Second	0.02-0.06/0.0008-0.0024	0.9/0.035
Oil	0	—
CRANKSHAFT		
Run-out	—	0.03/0.012
Big end side clearance	—	0.35-0.65/0.0138-0.0256
Small end lateral play	0.8-1.0/0.03-0.04	2.0/0.08
PRIMARY CLUTCH		
Shoe thickness	2.0/0.079	1.5/0.0591

ENGINE SPECIFICATIONS

Component	Standard (mm/in.)	Service Limit (mm/in.)
SECONDARY CLUTCH		
Friction plate thickness	3.0/0.12	2.8/0.11
Steel plate thickness	1.6/0.06	—
Steel plate warp limit	—	0.2/0.008
Spring free length	34.9/1.37	33.9/1.33
TRANSMISSION		
Shaft run-out	—	0.08/0.0031
Middle gear lash	—	0.1-0.2/0.004-0.008
Final gear lash	—	0.1-0.2/0.004-0.008

ENGINE TORQUE SPECIFICATIONS

Part	Torque (ft lbs)
Cylinder head bolts	
Long	16.0 (oiled)
Short	14.0 (oiled)
Cam sprocket cover	5.1
Valve covers	7.2
Rocker arm shafts	5.8
Spark plug	14.0
Cylinder bolts	7.2
Balancer shaft nut	36.0
Starter pulley bolt	36.0
Valve adjuster nut	10.0
Cam sprocket bolt	43.0
Cam chain tensioner nut	22.0
Cam chain tensioner cap nut	3.6
Chain guide #2 retainer	5.8
Oil drain plug	31.0
Filter cover bolts	7.2
Crankcase screws	5.1
R/H bearing retainer	7.2
Primary clutch nut	56.0
Clutch springs	4.3
Clutch hub nut	36.0
Clutch adjuster	11.0
Middle gear case cover	7.2
Drive axle bearing retainer	18.0 (staked in place)
Housing bearing retainer	43.0
Bearing housing	17.0
Starter clutch screw	22.0 (staked in place)

FUEL SYSTEM

NOTE: *For carburetor theory and operation, refer to the "General Information" section.*

GAS TANK

Removal And Installation

1. If a rear carrier is fitted, remove the carrier securing knob and pull the carrier backwards.
2. Remove the seat/rear cowling assembly.
3. Remove the gas cap. Remove the tank cover bracket bolts at the sides. Remove the cover.
4. Be sure the petcock is "OFF." Disconnect the lines at the petcock and tank.
5. Remove the tank mounting bolt at the front of the tank. Disconnect the band at the rear of the tank. Remove the gas tank.
6. Installation is the reverse of removal. Be sure that all fuel lines are tightly connected before operating the machine.

CARBURETOR

Removal And Installation

TRI-MOTO 200

1. Remove the gas tank as outlined above.
2. Fold back the carburetor's rubber cap.
3. Unscrew the cap and carefully pull out the throttle slide assembly, watching that the needle is not damaged during the removal procedure.
4. If throttle slide service is required, disengage the cable from the slide. If not, wrap the assembly in a clean cloth and position it out of the way to prevent damage to it.
5. Unscrew and remove the starter plunger from the carburetor body.
6. Disconnect the overflow line from the carburetor body. Disengage the fuel line from the clamp on the cylinder head.
7. Loosen the air cleaner and engine side clamp screws and carefully pull the carb free.

CAUTION: *Drain gasoline into a suitable container and dispose of properly.*

8. Installation is the reverse of removal. Be sure that the carburetor is correctly mounted in the hoses on both air cleaner and engine side and that they are not folded or partially obstructing the intake or outlets of the carb.
9. Position the carb straight up. Be sure it is not tilted. Tighten the clamp screws.
10. Carefully insert the throttle slide assembly. Be sure the needle enters the needle jet without forcing it. Check that the slide enters the carb body easily and that the movement is free.

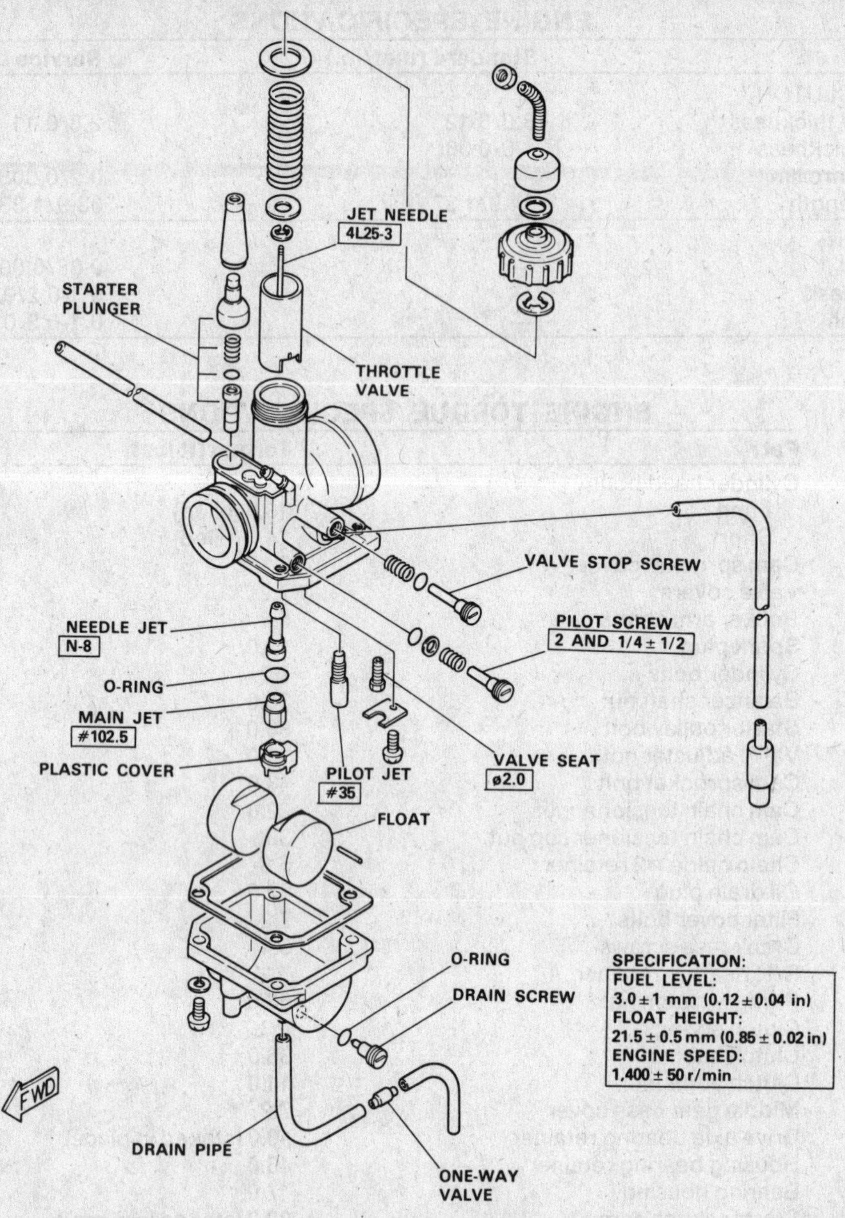

Carburetor (Tri-Moto 200)

11. Tighten the cap. Position the rubber cap so that foreign matter cannot enter. Check for proper throttle action.
12. Screw in and tighten the starter plunger.
13. Connect the overflow line to float bowl. Secure the fuel line with the clamp on the cylinder head.
14. Install the gas tank and connect all lines. Be sure that gas and vacuum lines are securely connected.
15. Turn on the fuel and check for air or gas leaks before operating the machine.
16. Start the engine and check for proper operation of starter plunger and throttle and for proper idle speed before riding.

YAMAHAULER, 225 DX

1. Remove the gas tank as outlined above.
2. Fold back the carburetor's rubber cap.
3. Unscrew the cap and carefully pull out the throttle slide assembly, ensuring that the needle is not damaged during the removal procedure.
4. If throttle slide service is required, disengage the cable from the slide and separate the components. If not, wrap the assembly in a clean cloth and position it out of the way.
5. Unscrew and remove the starter plunger from the carburetor body.
6. Disconnect the overflow line from the float bowl. Disengage the fuel line clamp on the cylinder head.
7. Loosen the air cleaner hose clamp.
8. Remove the carburetor mounting nuts.
9. Pull the carburetor free of the manifold and remove it.

CAUTION: *Drain gasoline into a suitable container and dispose of properly.*

10. Installation is the reverse of removal. Be sure that the carb mounting O-ring is secure in its groove and that it is not lost, damaged or moved out of the proper position when the carb is fitted to the manifold.
11. Tighten manifold nuts gradually and evenly.
12. Check that the air cleaner hose is properly fitted over the carb intake and not folded or partially obstructing the intake. Tighten the clamp.
13. Carefully insert the throttle slide assembly. Be sure that the needle enters the needle jet without forcing it. Check that the slide enters the carb body easily and that the movement is free.
14. Tighten the cap. Position the rubber cap so that foreign matter cannot enter. Check for proper throttle action.
15. Screw in and tighten the starter plunger.
16. Connect the overflow line to the float bowl. Secure the fuel feed line with the clamp on the cylinder head.

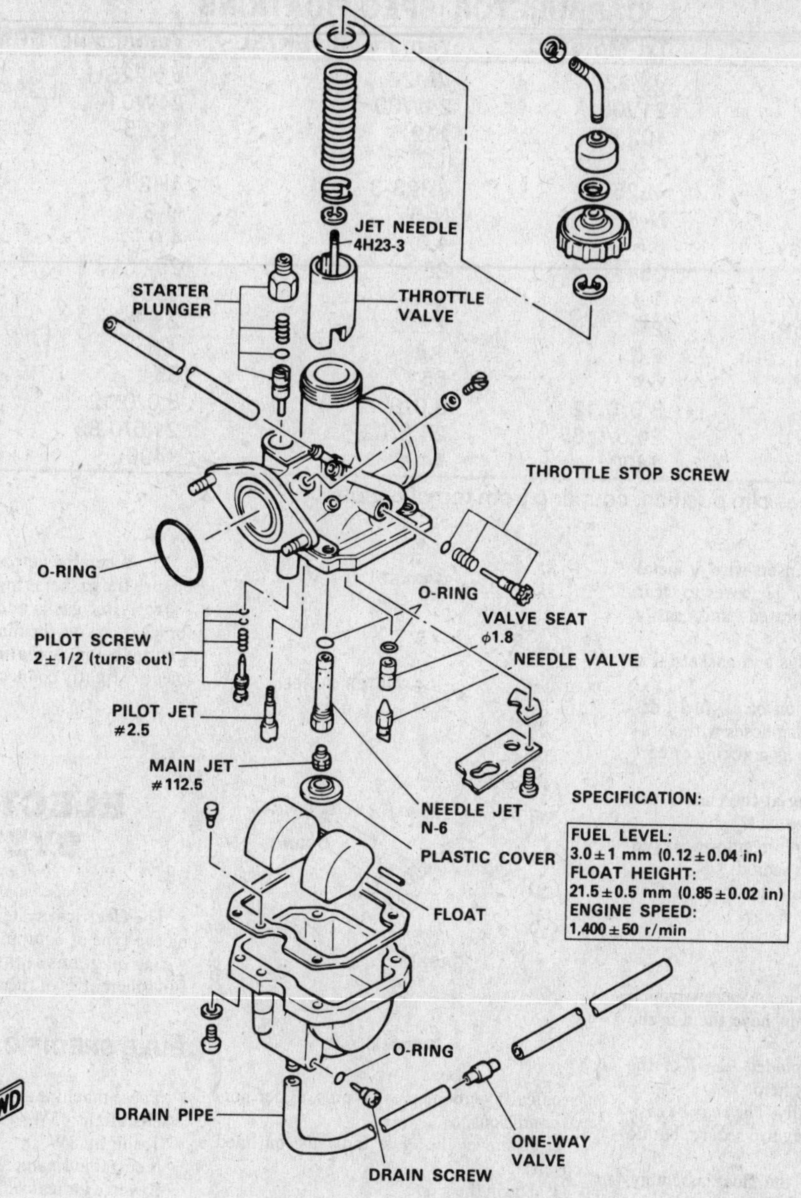

Carburetor assembly (Yamahauler, 225 DX)

17. Install the gas tank and connect all lines. Be sure that gas and vacuum lines are securely connected.

18. Turn on the fuel and check for air or gas leaks before operating the machine.

19. Start the engine and check for proper operation of the starter plunger and throttle and for proper idle speed. Before all systems are in normal working order before riding.

Disassembly

ALL MODELS

1. To disassembly the throttle slide, pull the spring out of the slide and compress it while disengaging the cable from the slide. Shake out the needle and clip. Some models have a keeper clip which must be removed before the cable will come out.

CAUTION: *Do not remove the clip from the needle. Position is critical. See the "Carburetor Specifications" chart.*

2. Turn the carb upside down and remove the four float bowl scres.

3. Carefully remove the float bowl and the gasket. If the bowl will not come off, rap the sides with the screwdriver handle, but hold the bowl while you do this so it doesn't come off and hit the float assembly. When the bowl is free, lift it off carefully.

4. Push out the float pivot pin and lift out the float and needle assembly.

5. Remove the plastic cover from the main jet.

6. Unscrew and remove the main jet.

7. Unscrew and remove the pilot jet.

8. On some models, the needle jet can be unscrewed for removal. On others, it must be pushed out from the top of the carburetor with a wooden dowel. Note any O-rings which may be on the jets or in the carburetor body.

9. Unscrew and remove the pilot screw and the throttle stop screw. Note spring and O- ring(s). Remember that adjustment of these components is required when assembling.

10. Needle valve seats are secured by keeper plates held by screws. If removal is required, remove the screws and take out plate and seat.

11. Disconnect fuel feed and vacuum lines from the carburetor body.

12. Remove the manifold O-ring, if one is fitted.

13. Unscrew and remove the drain screw from the float bowl. Note the O- ring.

Inspection

ALL MODELS

1. Refer to the "General Information" section for carburetor inspection tips.

2. Clean the body and other metal parts in a clean, non-caustic solvent intended for carburetor cleaning.

3. Blow air and fuel passages clear with

CARBURETOR SPECIFICATIONS

	Tri-Moto 200	Yamahauler EK/EL	Yamahauler ERN	225 DX
Type	VM22	VM22	VM22SH	VM22
ID Mark	21V00	24W00	24W01	29U00
Main jet	102.5	112.5	112.5	112.5
Main air jet	1.5	1.7	1.7	1.6
Jet needle①	4L25-3	4H23-3	4H23-3	5L10-3
Needle jet	N-8	N-6	N-6	N-8
Throttle slide cutaway	3.5	4.0	4.0	3.5
Pilot jet	35	25	25	20
Pilot air jet	1.3	130	130	60
Pilot screw (turns out)	2¼ ± ½	2 ± ½	2 ± ½	1½ ± ½
Float needle seat	2.0	1.8	1.8	1.8
Starter jet	65	65	85	65
Fuel level (mm/in.)	3.0/0.12	3.0/0.12	3.0/0.12	3.0/0.12
Float height (mm/in.)	21.5/0.85	21.5/0.85	21.5/0.85	21.5/0.85
Idle speed (rpm)	1400	1400	1400	1400

① Last digit indicates clip position, counting from top of needle.

low pressure air. Do not insert wire or metal objects into carburetor or jet bores to clear them. Bores are calibrated and easily damaged.

4. Use all new O-rings and gaskets as a matter of safety.

5. Check the condition of all fuel lines and vacuum lines. Replace hoses with abrasion or age damage such as cracking or hardening.

6. Check for splitting at the ends of the hoses. Replace if damaged.

7. Check the starter plunger for wear and replace it if the plunger is scored.

8. Check for wear on the throttle slide and the carburetor bore.

Assembly

1. Be sure that all jets and screws which are equipped with O-rings have them in the proper positions.

2. Refer to the exploded views of the carburetors for assembly help.

3. Install jets carefully. They can be easily damaged. Be sure they are secure, but do not overtighten.

4. When installing the float assembly, carefully lower the needle into the seat with the floats attached. Position the float so the pivot pin can be inserted. Check for free movement.

6. Install a new manifold O-ring, on models so equipped. Be sure that the O-ring is pushed into the groove and firmly seated.

7. When installing the pilot screw, turn it in very carefully until resistance is felt, then back it out the number of turns shown in the "Carburetor Specifications" chart.

CAUTION: *Do not overtighten this screw when installing it. Stop turning it the moment some resistance is felt. Otherwise, it will be damaged.*

8. After the carburetor is installed, check float level and adjust idle speed and mixture. These procedures are outlined in the "Tune-Up" section.

FUEL PETCOCK

All Models

1. The fuel petcock has filter screens inside the tank which should be cleaned periodically—about every 6 mos. under normal conditions.

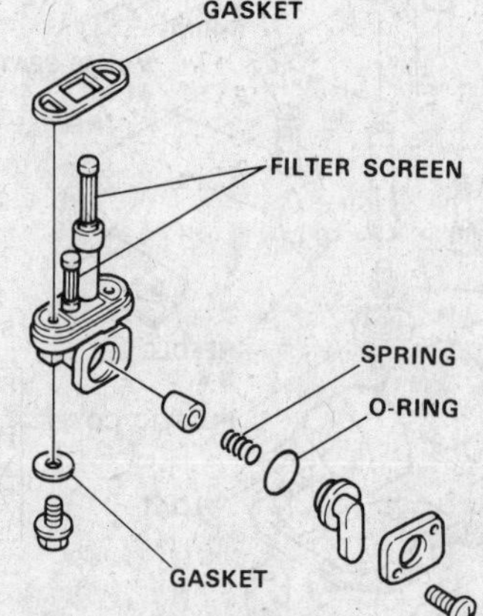

Petcock

2. Remove the gas tank as outlined above.

3. Drain the gas.

4. Remove the lines from the petcock.

5. Remove the petcock securing screws and pull the assembly out of the tank.

6. Check the gasket condition. Replace it if it appears damaged or if it was leaking prior to removal.

7. Remove the filter screens and clean them in a safe solvent.

8. If foreign matter cannot be removed, or if the screens are punctured, crushed, or otherwise damaged, replace them.

9. Check the petcock mating surface for damage. Replace the unit if any is noted.

10. Flush out the gas tank before installing the petcock to get rid of any residual dirts.

11. If the petcock does not operate properly, remove the two screws which secure the lever plate. Remove the plate, lever, O-ring, gaskets, spring and diaphragm.

12. Check the diaphragm for damage. Replace the unit if any is noted.

13. Clean all metal parts thoroughly in solvent. If corrosion cannot be removed from the petcock body, the unit must be replaced.

14. Use new gaskets and O-ring when assembling.

15. When the petcock is fitted to the tank, be sure the gasket is in place.

16. After gas is added to the tank, check for leaks. Allow the machine to sit for several minutes before operation. Be sure that all fuel lines are tightly connected.

ELECTRICAL SYSTEM

The electrical system may vary depending on the type of equipment fitted. Refer to the wiring diagrams at the end of this section for full schematics of the specific machines.

BULB SPECIFICATIONS

These machines use the following bulbs:
Headlight:45W/45W
Taillight: 8W
Neutral indicator: 3.4W
Reverse indicator: 3.4W

CHARGING SYSTEM

Battery-equipped models have a charging system which consists of a 12 V battery, a regulator/ rectifier unit and charging coils in the CDI magneto.

System Check

1. Connect a DC voltmeter across the battery terminals.

2. Start the engine and run it up to 5,000 rpm.

3. The meter should show 14-15 V across the battery terminals.

4. If the voltage is not within this specification, determine the cause. Check battery condition; check wiring connections for corrosion. Check other system components as outlined below.

CAUTION: *Never disconnect the battery from the system when the engine is running. Charging system components will be damaged.*

Charging Coil

1. Remove the seat/cowling assembly.
2. Locate and disconnect the CDI magneto wiring at the platic connecotor.
3. Check the resistance of charging coil across the white lead and ground on engine or frame.
4. Resistance should be 0.4 ohms.
5. If the reading obtained is not within 10% of this specification, the charging coil must be replaced.

Regulator/Rectifier

1. This unit can be checked with an ohmmeter.
2. Locate and disconnect the regulator-/rectifier wiring at the plastic connector.
3. Connect the ohmmeter across the red and white leads (low range on meter) and note reading.
4. Reverse the meter leads and note reading.
5. There should be continuity in one direction only.
6. If the ohmmeter shows continuity in both directions, or neither direction, the unit must be replaced.

CAUTION: *The regulator/rectifier can be damaged by careless handling. Be sure that the battery connections are never reversed. Be sure that the engine is never run with the battery disconnected.*

LIGHTING SYSTEM

1. The output of the lighting coil (AC) can be checked between any point in the lighting circuit and ground. This procedure checks output at the headlight.
2. Disconnect the yellow and black wires at the headlight.
3. Connect an AC voltmeter set to the 20 V AC range (or equivalent) to the leads. Yellow is positive.
4. Start the engine.
5. Voltage should be 12-18 V AC with engine speeds 3000-8000 rpm. Voltage increases gradually with speed.
6. Locate the lighting coil wiring beneath the seat/cowling and disconnect it at the plastic connector.
7. Connect an ohmmeter across the coil wires: positive meter lead to yellow/red and negative meter lead to ground.
8. Resistance should be 0.78 ohms for machines without a battery and 0.34 ohms for battery-equipped machines.
9. If the reading is not within 10% of this specifications, the lighting coil must be replaced.
10. If the lighting coil resistance is correct, but system voltage is not, the problem is probably with the voltage regulator (fitted to battery-equipped machines only).

SWITCHES

1. Switch operation can be checked with an ohmmeter set to the low scale or with a simple continuity tester (self- powered).

2 Disconnect the switch you wish to test at the plastic connector to isolate it.

Engine Stop Switch

1. There should be continuity between black and black/white wires when the switch is in either of the "OFF" or "STOP" positions.
2. There should be no continuity when the switch is in the "RUN" position.

Starter Button

1. On machines equipped with an electric starter, check for continuity across the red/white and brown switch leads.
2. There should be continuity when the starter button is pushed: No continuity when the button is released.

Main Switch

1. When in the "OFF" position, there should be continuity only between the black/white and black leads.
2. In the "ON" position, there should be continuity only between the red and brown leads and between the blue/black and blue leads.
3. When switched to "LIGHT," there should be continuity between the black/white and black leads and between the red and blue/black leads.
4. Any other continuities indicate a defective switch.

Dimmer Switch

1. At least two types are fitted, depending on whether the machine is fitted with a battery.
2. On machines without a battery, there should be no continuity between switch leads when it is "OFF." In the "LO" position, there should be continuity across green, blue and yellow/red. In the "HI" position, there should be continuity across yellow, blue and yellow/red.
3. On battery equipped machines, there should be no continuities when the switch is in the "OFF" position. When in the "LO" position, there should be continuity across yellow red and blue and across blue/black and green. In the "HI" position, there should be continuity across blue/black and yellow and between yellow/red and blue.

IGNITION SYSTEM

The major components of the ignition system are the CDI magneto, the CDI unit, the ignition coil and the spark plugs.

Ignition Coil

1. The ignition coil is located beneath the gas tank and can be accessed by removing the engine mounting bracket cover from the front of the cylinder.
2. Disconnect the ignition coil wires (orange).
3. Check primary coil resistance across orange wire and chassis ground. It should be 0.85 ohms.
4. Check secondary coil resistance across orange wire and high tension lead. It should be 5.9 ohms.
5. If both readings are not within 10% of these values, the ignition coil must be replaced.

Pickup Coil

1. Remove the seat/cowling assembly.
2. Disconnect the CDI magneto lead.
3. Check resistance across the pickup coil leads (magneto side of the connector).
4. Resistance between the white/green and white/red leads should be 196 ohms.
5. If the reading is not within 10% of this figure, replace the pickup coil.

Charge Coil

1. The charge coil leads are brown and black and are accessed by disconnecting the plastic CDI magneto connector as outlined for the pickup coil, above.
2. Resistance across the brown and black leads should be 381 ohms.
3. If the reading is not within 10% of this specification, replace the unit.

ELECTRIC START SYSTEM

Operation

The electric start system consists of a starter motor, located on the front of the engine, a starter solenoid, neutral switch, and starter circuit cut-off relay.

When the main switch is on, the starter motor will operate only if the transmission is in neutral. The cut-off relay prevents starting in gear.

If the engine stop switch is in the "OFF" position, the starter motor will turn the engine over, but the ignition will not be on in any case.

Testing

If the starter will not operate, switch on the headlight and observe its intensity. If it is dim when the starter is not being operated, check the battery connections and recharge the battery. If the headlight doesn't light, check the fuse, the battery connections, the ignition switch and its connections, and check the continuity of the wire between the ignition switch and the battery.

If the headlight is normally bright, press the starter button and observe any changes. If the headlight dims when the button is pushed, it indicates that the starter motor is drawing current. If it does not dim (i.e. nothing happens), the starter motor is probably not getting any current. In this case, suspect the starter solenoid.

To check the solenoid and starter button, the easiest test is to bypass the unit completely by disconnecting the battery lead from the solenoid and connecting it directly (with the aid of a high-tension jumper cable) to the starter motor terminal. If the starter motor works, the solenoid or starter button is defective and must be replaced.

If the motor still fails to work, the motor itself may be the cause of the trouble.

Starter motor faults are rare, but several things can go wrong.

If the starter spins freely, but the engine doesn't turn over, suspect the starter motor clutch.

If the engine will turn over only very slowly and without a great degree of predictability, some possible causes include: a low or almost dead battery, oil which is too thick for weather conditions (extreme cold), or bad bearings in the motor itself. Worn bearings could cause the armature to contact the field coils which will effectively short out the starter. Usually, repeated attempts at starting will result in the starter motor getting very hot. Other possible causes of starter motor trouble include worn brushes, a worn or dirty commutator, or a defective armature.

Starter Solenoid

The solenoid is located beneath the seat on the left side of the frame.

1. If the battery is in reasonably good condition, and nothing at all happens when the starter button is pushed, check the solenoid.
2. Disconnect the starter cable at the solenoid. When the button is pushed, there should be an audible "click" which indicates that the solenoid is opening.
3. If further testing is necessary, remove the solenoid from the machine.

CAUTION: *Be sure to disconnect the cables at the battery before disconnecting the solenoid terminals.*

4. Connect a fully charged 12-volt battery across the solenoid low-tension leads and check for continuity across the high-tension terminals with an ohmmeter or self-contained test light. If there is no continuity, replace or repair the solenoid.
5. Check for continuity across the low-tension terminals with an ohmmeter or self-powered test light. Resistance should be 3.5 ohms. If there is no continuity, the primary winding of the solenoid is broken, and the unit must be replaced.
6. If starter trouble began just after the starter button housing was disassembled or moved for any reason, check the connections at the switch as they may have come adrift.

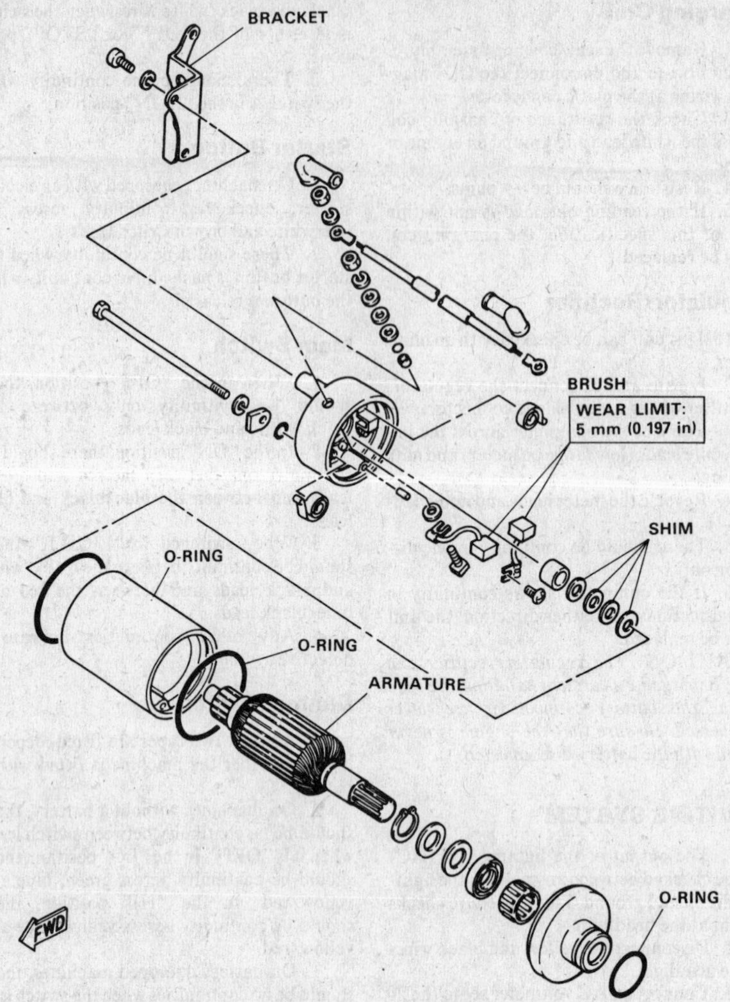

Electric starter motor

Starter Motor

REMOVAL

1. Disconnect the high tension lead at the starter motor.
2. Disconnect the brake pedal return spring.
3. Remove the starter motor bracket screws (4) and take off the bracket.
4. Remove the starter motor.

INSPECTION

1. Take out the two screws and remove the starter side cover.
2. Check electrical continuity between the commutator and armature core using a multitester or test light and battery. If continuity exists, the armature coil is grounded and the complete starter motor unit must be replaced.
3. Check for continuity between all of the commutator segments. Continuity must exist in each case (maximum allowable resistance: 0.023 ohms).
4. Check continuity between the brush that is wired to the stator coil and the starter motor cable. Lack of continuity indicates an open circuit in the stator coil, and the starter motor unit should be replaced. Resistance should not exceed 0.05 ohms.
5. Examine the carbon brushes for damage to the contact surfaces and measure their length. Replace the brushes as a set if either one measures less than 5.0mm (0.2 in.), or if they are damaged in any way.
6. Brush spring tension should be measured with a small pull-scale. Replace the springs if they have weakened to less than 400g tension.
7. The mica undercut of the commutator should be maintained at 0.7mm (0.027 in.). Any carbon deposits should be cleaned out of the commutator grooves, and a piece of hacksaw blade or the like used to increase the undercut depth if necessary.
8. Polish the commutator with fine emery cloth and then clean it thoroughly before installing.
9. Measure the diameter of the commutator. The armature should be replaced if the measurement is less than 22mm (0.87 in.).
10. Check the condition of the armature bearings and replace them as a set if any damage is noted.
11. Check the condition of the oil seal and replace it if the seal lips are cracked or worn.
12. Unsealed bearings should be lubricated with 20W or 30W motor oil before assembly. Coat the lips of the oil seal with white grease before assembly.

INSTALLATION

1. When installing the starter motor, be sure that the O-ring is not damaged.
2. Tighten the mounting screws to 5 ft. lbs.

Cut-Off Relay

The relay is located beneath the seat/cowling on the right side of the frame.

1. Remove the relay from the rubber clamp. Disconnect the wiring at the plastic connector.
2. Check the resistance of the relay windings. Reading should be about 75 ohms. If reading is not correct, replace the relay.
3. Put 12 VDC across the windings. Make a voltage reading as shown. If the voltmeter does not show 12 V, replace the relay.

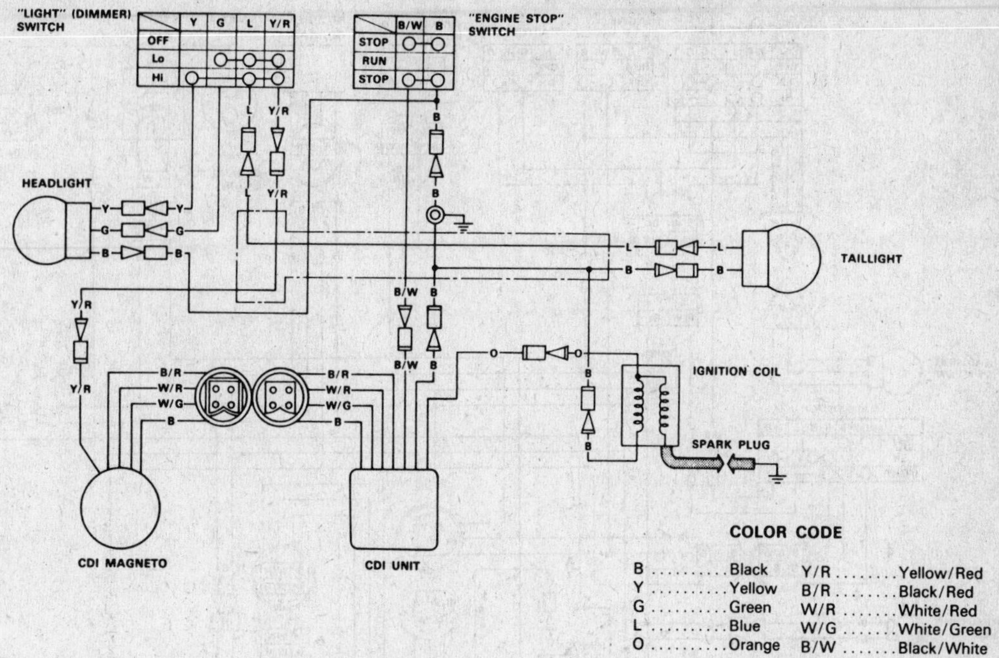

YTM 200K-N

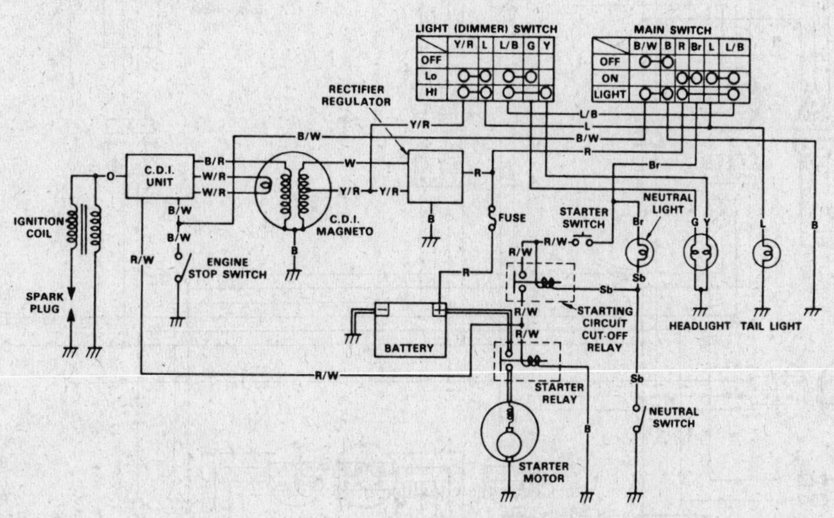

COLOR CODE

B ....Black	Y ....Yellow	Y/R .....Yellow/Red
O ....Orange	W.......White	R/W ....Red/White
L ....Blue	Sb ......Sky blue	W/R ....White/Red
R ....Red	Br.......Brown	B/R.....Black/Red
G ....Green	L/B .....Blue/Black	B/W ....Black/White

YTM 200EK, EL, EN

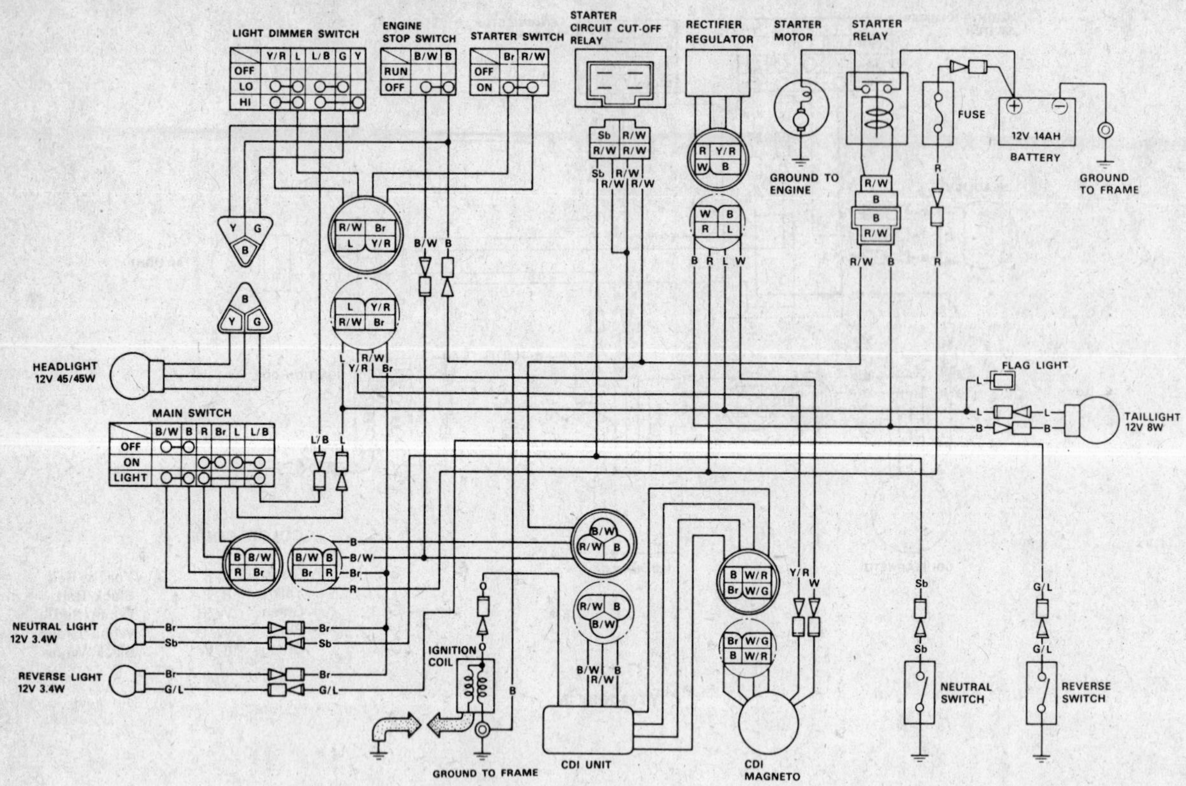

YTM 200ERN

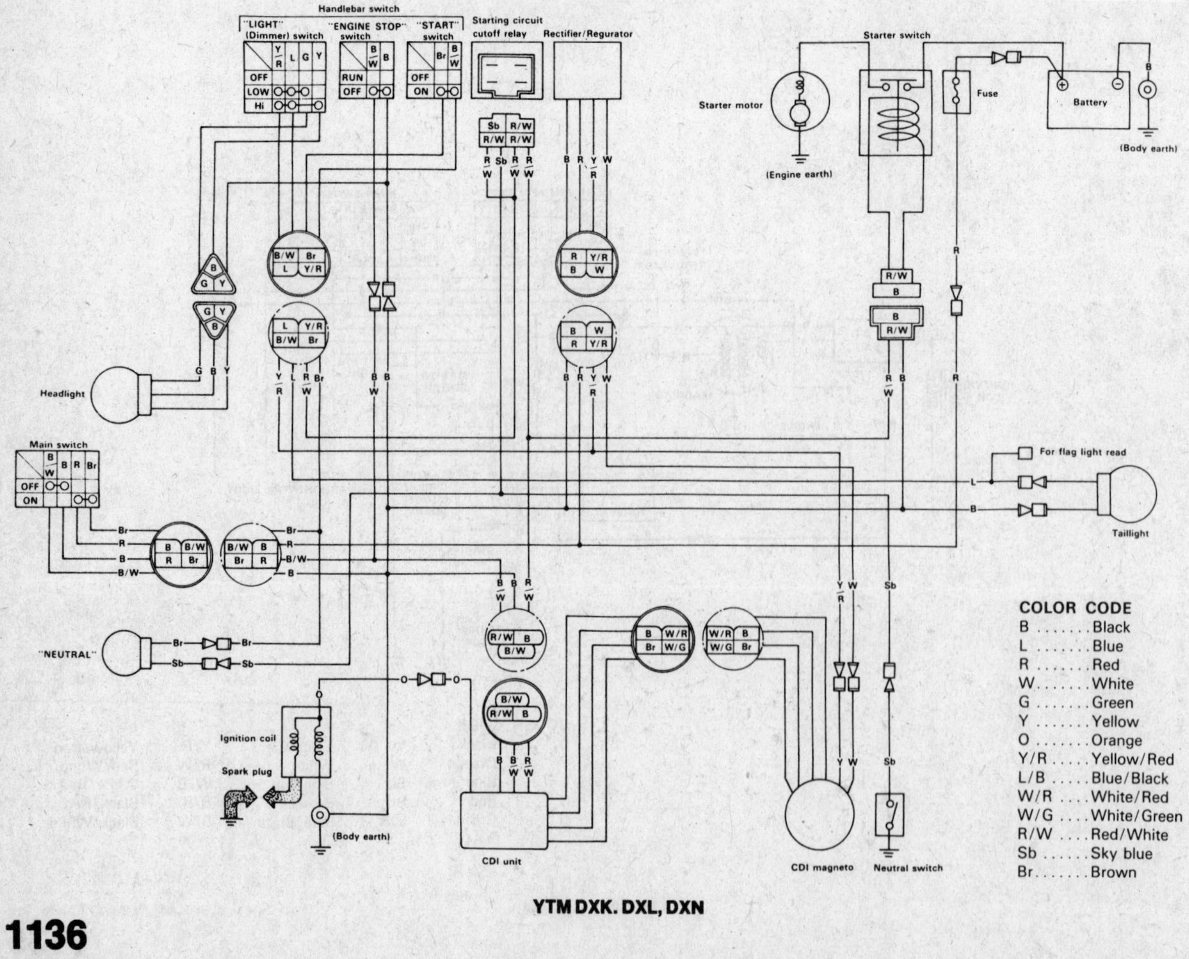

YTM DXK. DXL, DXN

COLOR CODE

B .... Black
L .... Blue
R .... Red
W .... White
G .... Green
Y .... Yellow
O .... Orange
Y/R ..... Yellow/Red
L/B ..... Blue/Black
W/R ..... White/Red
W/G ..... White/Green
R/W ..... Red/White
Sb ...... Sky blue
Br ...... Brown

CHASSIS

FRONT WHEEL

Removal

1. Place safety stands or similar devices beneath the engine to support the front wheel a few inches off the ground.
2. Disconnect the brake cable by running the adjuster at the hand lever all the way in and the wing nut. Disconnect the cable from the hand lever and then from the brake plate.
3. Remove the cotter pin from the axle nut.
4. Remove the axle nut.
5. Support the wheel to take the weight off the axle and pull the axle out.
6. Remove the wheel from the forks.

Inspection

1. Remove any rust or corrosion from the axle with fine emery cloth.
2. Check axle run-out. If there is any at all, replace the axle.

CAUTION: *Do not attempt to straighten a bent axle. Replace it.*

3. Check the rim for damage.
4. Check wheel run-out. Maximum allowable run-out in both vertical (up and down) and lateral (side-to-side) directions is 2.0mm (0.08 in.).
5. Replace any rim which is damaged or which exceeds run-out limits.

Installation

1. Put a light coating of lithium-based soap grease on the lips of the wheel grease seals.
2. Install the wheel in the forks, engaging the brake anchor with the lug on the forks.
3. Install the axle.
4. Tighten the axle nut to 36 ft. lbs.
5. Install a new cotter pin.
6. Connect the brake cable and adjust lever play as outlined in "Maintenance."

FRONT BRAKE

1. Take the brake plate assembly out of the wheel.
2. Check the thickness of the brake shoe linings at the middle and the ends. If less than 2mm (0.08 in.) at any point, both shoes should be replaced.
3. Check the linings for scoring or other evidence of unusual wear. Damaged linings must be replaced. If the linings are scored, check the brake drum as well.
4. Linings should be sandpapered to remove any glaze or dirt, then cleaned thoroughly prior to installation.

CAUTION: *Do not allow any type of solvent or lubricant to contact the linings.*

5. The linings can be removed from the brake plate by pulling them off together.
6. Check the spring for damage, rust and corrosion, etc.
7. After removing the shoes, the brake cam can be removed from the brake plate.
8. Remove any old grease with solvent, then remove any rust or corrosion with medium grade sandpaper.
9. Lubricate the cam with a lithium-based grease before installation.

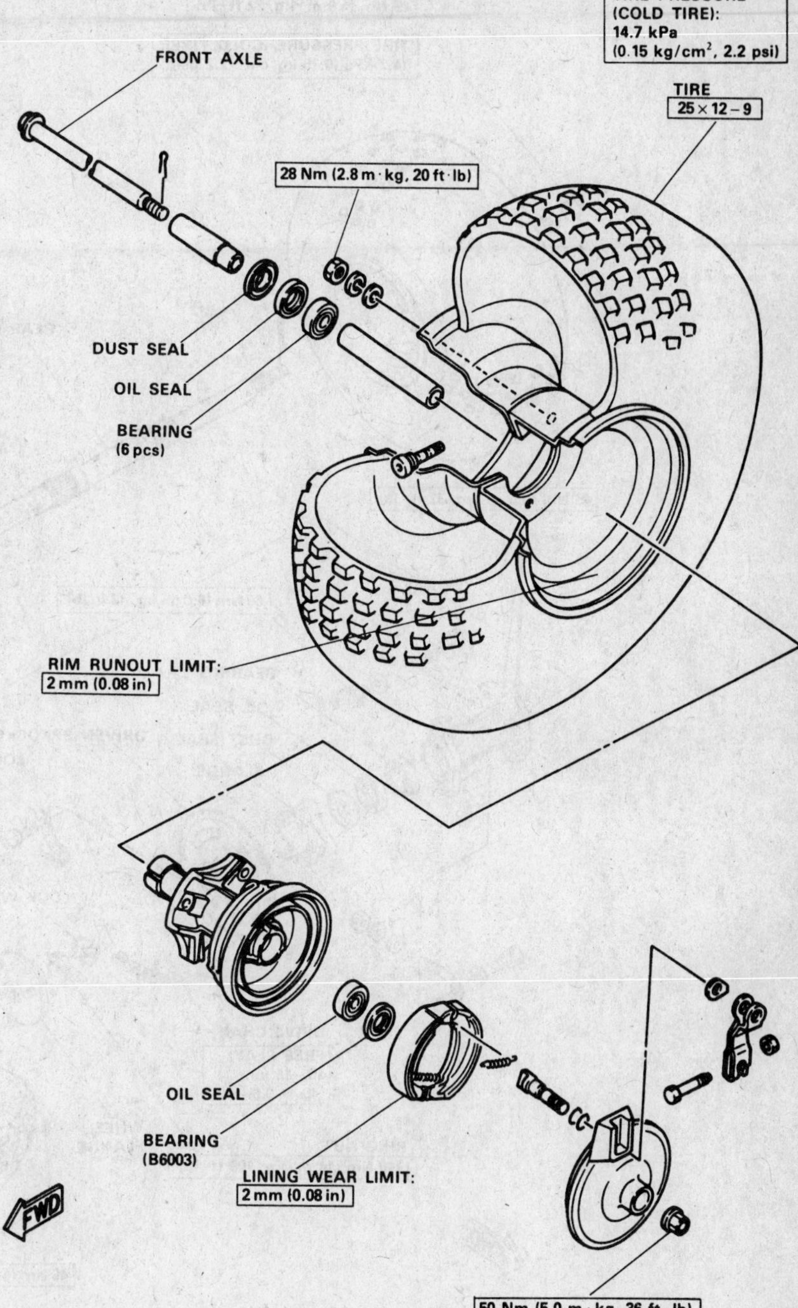

Front wheel assembly

10. Check that the brake drum surface is smooth and featureless. If scoring is noted, the drum should be turned down on a lathe.

FRONT WHEEL BEARINGS

Removal

1. Wheel bearings should be checked before removal is attempted. Rotate the wheel and listen for unusual noise. Place your hand on the fork tube and see if you can feel any vibration while the wheel is spinning.
2. After removing the wheel from the machine, remove the brake plate.
3. Pry out the grease seals on both sides of the hub.

Front wheel brake anchor

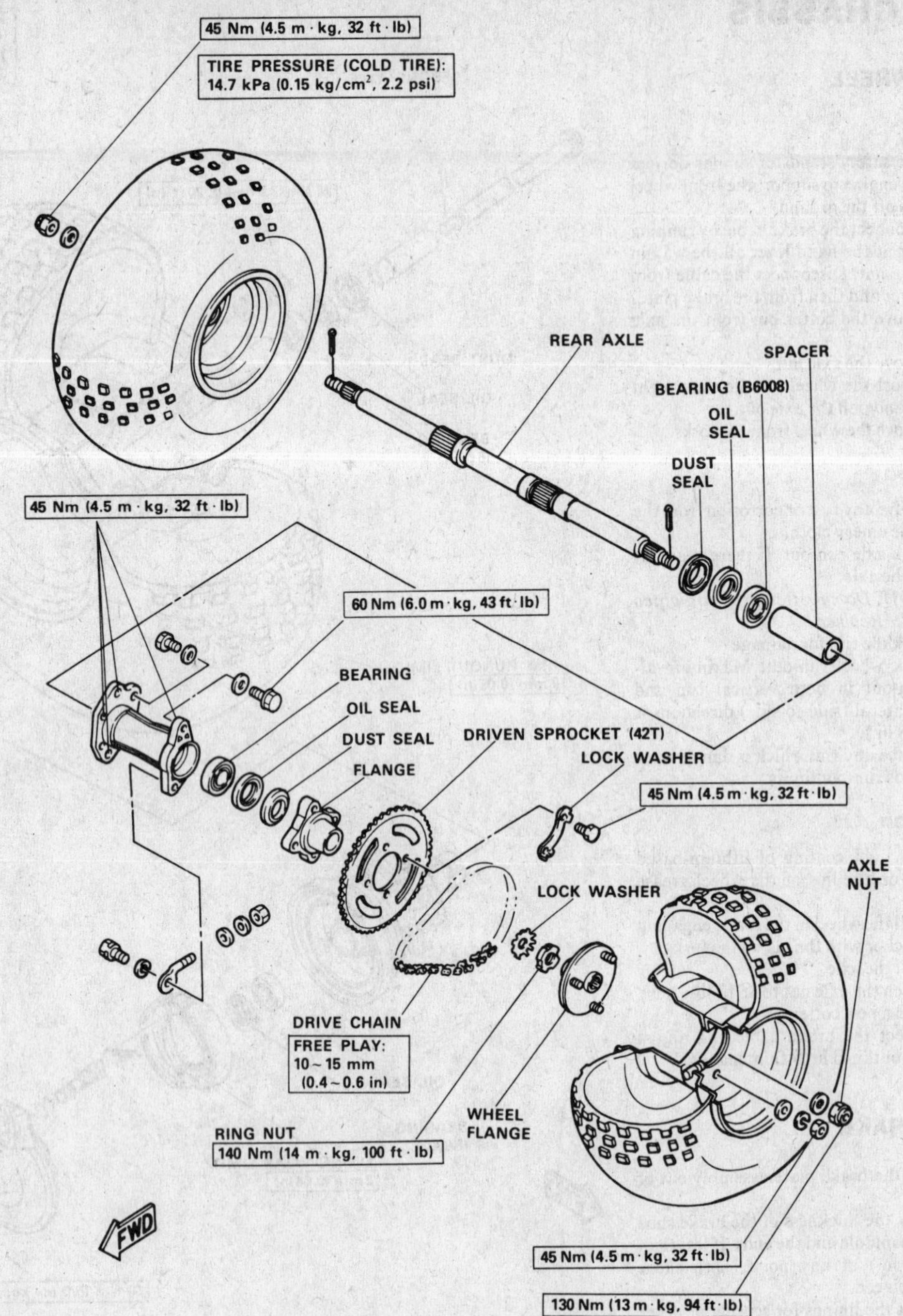

Rear wheel assembly (chain drive)

4. Reach through the hub with a suitable punch. Move the wheel bearing spacer as far as possible to one side to achieve a purchase on the wheel bearing and drive it out.
5. Remove the spacer.
6. Remove the other bearing in the same manner.

Inspection

1. Wash the wheel bearings thoroughly in a solvent to remove all of the old grease.
2. Inspect the general condition of the bearings. There should be not rust, pitting, or obvious signs of wear or damage on either balls or races.
3. Slowly rotate the bearings. Rotation should be smooth, noiseless, and free of binding or unevenness. If any of the above conditions exist, both bearings should be replaced.
4. Place each bearing on a flat surface and hold the inner race firmly in place. Attempt to move the outer race up and down. If any play is evident, the bearings should be replaced.
5. If equipment is available, a dial gauge can be used to check bearing run-out. Pass the axle through each bearing in turn and check the axial and diametrical run-out with the gauge. If axial run-out exceeds 0.1mm (0.004 in.) or if diametrical run-out is greater than 0.05mm (0.002 in.), the bearings should be replaced.

Installation

Assembly is the reverse of the above. Note the following points:

a. Pack the bearings with a good grade of wheel bearing grease. Put a small handful of the grease in the hub as well.

b. Do not forget to install the spacer in the hub before installing the bearing.

c. Bearings may be driven into place using a suitably sized socket or a bearing driver. If one side of the bearing is sealed, install it with the sealed side facing outward.

d. Use new grease seals and lubricate them with oil to make installation easier.

CAUTION: *Do not strike the center race when installing bearings. The driver should contact the outer race only. Be sure that the bearings are driven straight into the hub and not cocked or tilted.*

REAR WHEELS

Removal

1. Block the front tire so the machine won't move.
2. Apply the parking brake.
3. Jack up the rear wheel you wish to remove so that it is an inch or so off the ground.
4. Remove the lug nuts.
5. Pull off the wheel.

Installation

1. If three lug nuts are used on the wheel, tightening torque is 32 ft. lbs.
2. If four lug nuts are used, tightening torque is 20 ft. lbs.

REAR BRAKE

Removal

1. Block the front wheel so that the machine cannot move.
2. Raise the rear of the machine so that the rear wheel are off the ground.
3. Back off the rear brake cable adjuster wing nuts.
4. Disconnect the rear brake cables and springs from the caliper lever.
5. Remove the caliper securing nuts.
6. Remove the caliper lever assembly and outer pad from the caliper body.
7. Remove the brake cover securing screws and take off the brake cover.
8. Remove the caliper securing bolts.
9. Pull out the disc plate.
10. Remove the caliper body from the rear wheel hub.

Pad Inspection

1. Replace the pads as a set if either is worn to a thickness of 1.5mm (0.06 in.) or less.

Brake Inspection

1. Inspect the caliper piston and replace it if it is rusted or otherwise damaged.
2. Check the brake disc. If there are score marks on the surface, the disc can be turned down, but only if the minimum thickness of 3mm (0.12 in.) is maintained.
3. Check disc thickness. If it is worn below 3mm (0.12 in.), it must be replaced.
4. Check disc run-out. Maximum allowable run-out is 0.5mm (0.02 in.).

Installation

1. Installation is the reverse of removal. Note the following torques.

CAUTION: *When installing the caliper, be sure that bolts are installed in their original locations. The longer body bolt is installed in the higher position.*

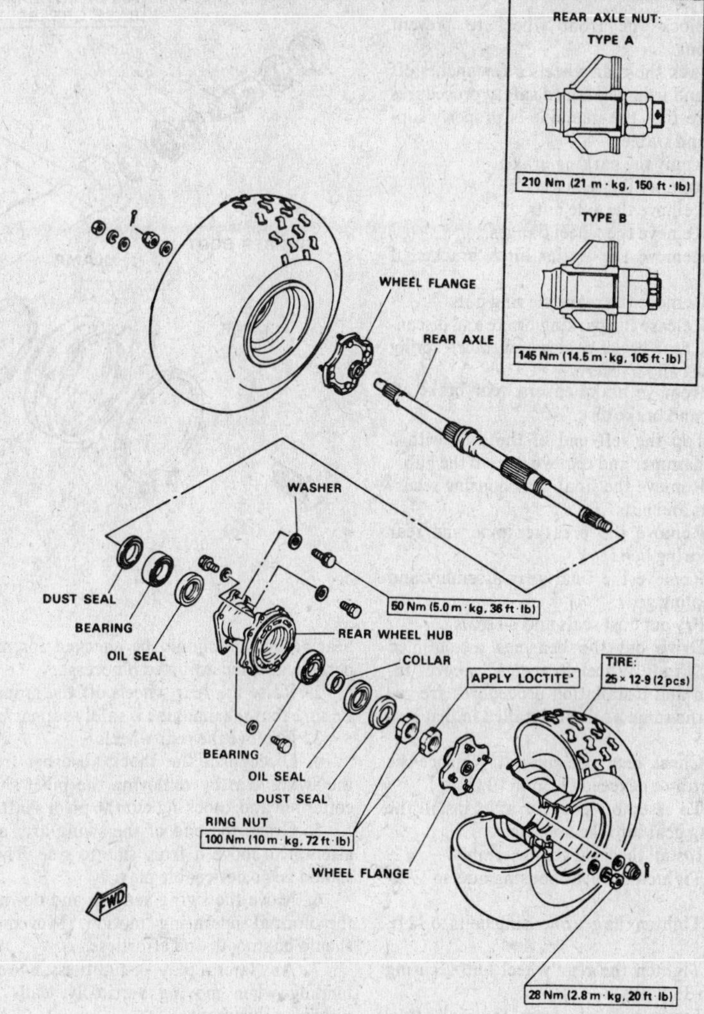

Rear wheel assembly (shaft drive)

2. Tighten the caliper body bolts to 32 ft. lbs.
3. Tighten the caliper nuts to 6.5 ft. lbs.
4. Adjust the brake after installation as outlined in "Maintenance."

REAR AXLE (CHAIN DRIVE)

1. Block the front wheel to prevent movement.
2. Jack the rear wheels a few inches off the ground using standard safety procedures to ensure that the machine is properly supported and stable. Apply the parking brake.
3. Remove the rear wheels.
4. Remove the axle nuts.
5. Remove the wheel flanges.
6. Remove the sprocket bolts after bending down the lock tabs which secure them.
7. Remove the axle ring nut.
8. Remove the chain cover. Disconnect the drive chain, or remove the engine sprocket cover and take off chain and both sprockets together.
9. Remove the sprocket and sprocket flange.
10. Disconnect the brake cables at the caliper.
11. Remove the rear brake assembly and brake disc.
12. Tap the left end of the axle with a plastic mallet and remove it from the hub.
13. To remove bearings from the hub, move the spacer aside and tap around the inner race with a suitable drift. Remove one bearing, the spacer and the remaining bearing.
14. Bearing inspection procedures are detailed under "Front Wheel Bearings," above.
15. Bearing installation is basically the same as outlined for the front wheel bearings.
16. Check rear axle run-out. Replace it if run-out exceeds 1.5mm (0.06 in.).
17. Assembly is the reverse of disassembly. Note the following points:
    a. Use new cotter pins and lockwashers and lock tabs.
    b. Tighten the axle ring nut to 100 ft. lbs.
    c. Tighten the brake caliper bolts to 32 ft. lbs.
    d. Tighten the sprocket bolts to 32 ft. lbs.
    e. Tighten the axle nut to 94 ft. lbs.
18. Adjust the drive chain and brakes. See "Maintenance."

REAR AXLE (SHAFT DRIVE)

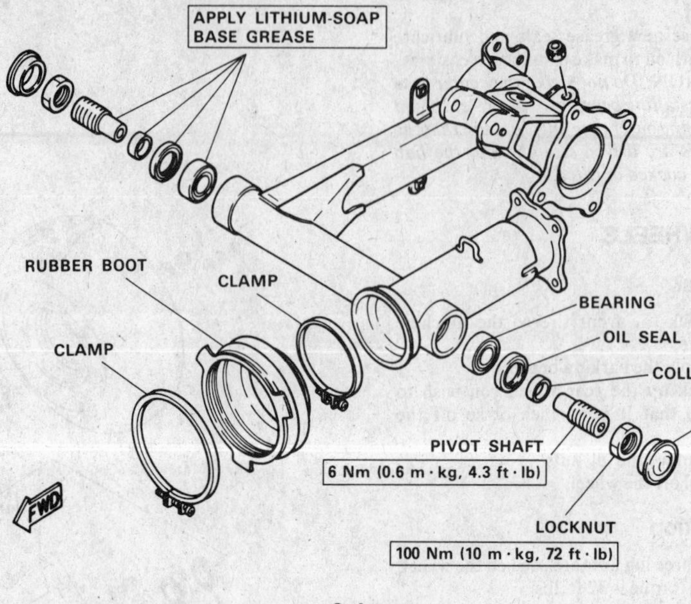

1. Block the front wheel to prevent movement.
2. Jack the rear wheels a few inches off the ground using standard safety procedures to ensure that the machine is properly supported and stable.
3. Apply the parking brake.
4. Remove the rear wheels.
5. Remove the axle nuts.
6. Remove the wheel flanges.
7. Remove the trailer hitch bracket, if fitted.
8. Remove the rear axle ring nuts.
9. Release the parking brake and disconnect the rear brake cables and return spring from the caliper lever.
10. Remove brake covers, rear brake assembly and brake disc.
11. Tap the left end of the axle with a plastic hammer and remove it from the hub.
12. Remove the final gear housing securing bolts and nuts.
13. Remove the breather pipe and rear hub securing bolts.
14. Remove the final gear assembly and the coupling gear.
15. Pry out dust seals and oil seals.
16. Drive out the bearings as outlined under "Front Wheel Bearings," above. Inspection and installation procedures are basically the same as those detailed in that section.
17. Check rear axle run-out. Replace the axle if run-out exceeds 1.5mm (0.06 in.).
18. To assembly the rear axle, install the coupling gear into the housing.
19. Install the final gear assembly.
20. Tighten the gear housing nuts to 17 ft. lbs.
21. Tighten the gear housing bolts to 32 ft. lbs.
22. Tighten the rear wheel hub securing bolts to 36 ft. lbs.
23. Insert the axle from the right side, again tapping with a plastic mallet as on removal.
24. Grease and install the hub dust seals.
25. Install the rear axle ring nuts finger tight.
26. Install and adjust the rear brake assembly. See "Maintenance" for adjustment procedures.

NOTE: *Caliper body bolts are tightened to 36 ft. lbs. The nuts are tightened to 6.5 ft. lbs. Be sure that the long body bolt is installed in the upper position.*

27. Apply the parking brake.
28. Tighten the inside ring nut to 71 ft. lbs.
29. Using a non-permanent thread-locking compound on the threads of the outer ring nut, tighten it to 72 ft. lbs. as well.

NOTE: *Do not use thread-lock on the inner ring nut. Hold the inside ring nut with a wrench while the outer is tightened.*

30. Install and tighten the rear axle nuts to 150 ft. lbs. (Type A) or 105 ft. lbs. (Type B). See illustration to distinguish types. Use new cotter pins.
31. Tighten the wheel lug nuts to 20 ft. lbs.

Swing arm

SWING ARM (DX)

Bearing Adjustment

1. The swing arm is mounted on tapered bearings which should be checked for play periodically and adjusted if necessary.
2. Raise the rear wheels off the ground. Be sure that the machine is safely supported.
3. Remove the rear wheels.
4. Disconnect the shock absorber from the swing arm by removing the pivot shaft cotter pin and knocking out the pivot shaft.
5. Grasp the end of the swing arm and attempt to move it from side to side. There should be no noticeable play.
6. Move the swing arm up and down in the normal operating motion. Movement should be smooth and effortless.
7. Any lateral play, or tightness, noise or binding when moving vertically, calls for bearing adjustment.
8. Remove the rubber caps from the pivot on left and right sides of the swing arm.
9. Loosen the pivot shaft locknut on the right side.
10. Loosen the pivot shaft locknut on the left side.
11. Tighten the left side pivot shaft adjuster to 4.3 ft. lbs.
12. Hold the adjuster in place and tighten its locknut to 72 ft. lbs.
13. Repeat the procedure on the right side.
14. Check bearing action again as outlined above. If no improvement is noted, replace the bearings.

Removal

NOTE: *The entire rear axle assembly may be removed along with the swing arm. If no service is required, this is the easiest way to take the rear end of the machine off.*

1. Disconnect the shock absorber from the swing arm.
2. Loosen the locknuts and unscrew the pivot shaft adjusters.
3. Remove the swing arm assembly.

Inspection

1. Remove the bearing oil seal collars.
2. Remove the bearings.
3. Check for wear or damage. Bearings must be replaced in pairs.
4. Use lithium soap-based grease to lubricate the bearings.
5. Use new oil seals.

Installation

1. Reverse the removal procedure.
2. Tighten the bearings and check operation as outlined above.

Disassembly

Disassembly of the swing arm is basically the same as described for "Rear Axle (Shaft Drive)", above.

FRONT FORKS

DX Models

REMOVAL

1. Use safety stands or the like to support the front wheel a few inches off the ground.
2. Remove the front wheel.
3. Remove the fender.
4. Loosen the upper and lower triple clamp pinch bolts.
5. Pull each fork leg out of the triple clamps.

DISASSEMBLY

1. Loosen the rubber boot clamp screws and remove the boot from each leg.
2. Remove the rubber cap from the top of the fork.
3. Remove the circlip beneath the cap. This is done by pressing down on the spring seat and prying the circlip out of its groove with a small screwdriver.

CAUTION: *Discard the circlips once removed. New ones must be used when assembling the forks.*

4. When the circlip is removed, the spring seat and fork spring can be taken out.
5. Pour off the old fork oil.
6. Remove the Allen bolt from the bottom of the fork leg.
7. Take out the damper rod assembly.

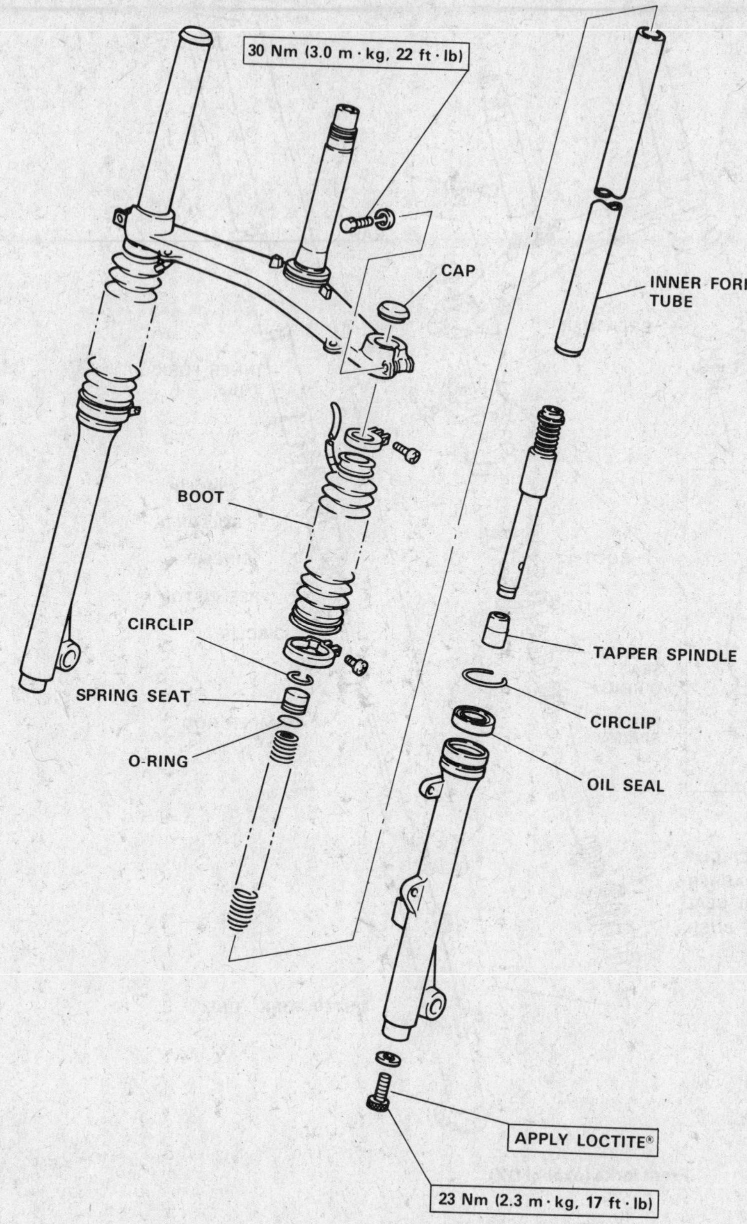

Front forks (DX)

8. Remove the oil seal retainer from the fork slider.
9. Pry out the slider oil seal. New seals must be used on reassembly.

INSPECTION

1. Check the fork tube for a bent condition. If bent, the fork tube must be replaced.
WARNING: *Do not attempt to straighten bent fork tubes.*
2. Check the fork slider for dents or other damage. Replace as required.
3. Check the fork tubes for corrosion or rust, especially in the area on which the slider oil seal rides. Remove any deposits with fine emery cloth.
4. Check fork spring free length. Replace springs, as a set, if either is less than 501.1mm (19.73 in.) in length.
5. Check the spring seat O- ring. Replace it if knicked or otherwise damaged.

ASSEMBLY

1. Clean all metal parts in a solvent.
2. Using new slider oil seals, press each into its slider with a large socket. Ensure that the seal is driven straight in and that it is fully seated.
3. Install the oil seal retainer. Be sure it is seated in the groove provided.
4. Lightly grease the lips of the slider oil seal and insert the fork tube into the slider.
5. Install the taper spindle and damper rod assembly.
6. Secure the damper rod with the Allen bolt at the bottom of the slider. Do not forget the copper washer. The Allen bolt should be secured with a non-permanent threadlocking compound. Bolt torque is 71 ft. lbs.
7. Add 4.0 oz. (117cc) of Yamaha fork oil or SAE 10 motor oil to each fork leg.
8. Install the fork spring. Note that the spring is installed so that the close coils are at the top of the fork.
9. Fit the spring seat.
10. Press down on the spring seat and install the circlip. Be sure it is properly seated.
CAUTION: *A new circlip should always be used.*
11. Install the boots. Install the rubber caps.

INSTALLATION

1. Push the fork legs into the triple clamps.
2. Align the top of each for leg with the top of the upper triple clamp.
3. Tighten the lower triple clamp pinch bolts to 22 ft. lbs.
4. Tighten the upper triple clamp pinch bolts to 14 ft. lbs.
5. Tighten the boot clamps.
6. Install the front fender. Be sure that the breather tubes are correctly routed.
7. Install the front wheel.

Other Models

REMOVAL

1. Use safety stands or the like to support the front wheel a few inches off the ground.
2. Remove the front wheel.
3. Remove the front fender.
4. Loosen the upper and lower triple clamp pinch bolts/carrier bolts.
5. Pull the fork legs down and out of the triple clamp and remove the carrier, if fitted.

DISASSEMBLY

1. Loosen the clamp screws and take the boot off each fork leg.
2. Remove the rubber cap from the top of the fork tube.
3. Press down on the spring seat and pry out the retaining circlip with a small screwdriver.
NOTE: *New circlips must be used during final assembly.*
4. Remove the spring seat and the fork spring.
5. Remove the fork slider oil seal circlip and washer.
6. Position the inner tube about 2 in. from the end of its travel range.
7. Fill the fork completely with a suitable fork oil. The purpose of this procedure is to use the oil pressure to force out the fork seals.
8. Install the spring seat and circlip.
9. Slowly press the inner tube into the fork slider until the oil seal comes out.
CAUTION: *Apply pressure slowly and gradually.*
10. Remove the oil seal and guide bush.
11. Separate fork tube and slider.
12. Pour off the old oil.
13. Separate the components.

INSPECTION

1. Check the fork tubes for a bent condition. If bent, the tubes must be replaced.
CAUTION: *Do not attempt to straighten bent fork tubes.*
2. Check the fork slider for dents or other damage. Replace as required.
3. Check the guide bush for wear or scoring. Replace it if it shows signs of damage.
4. Check the fork tubes for rust or corro-

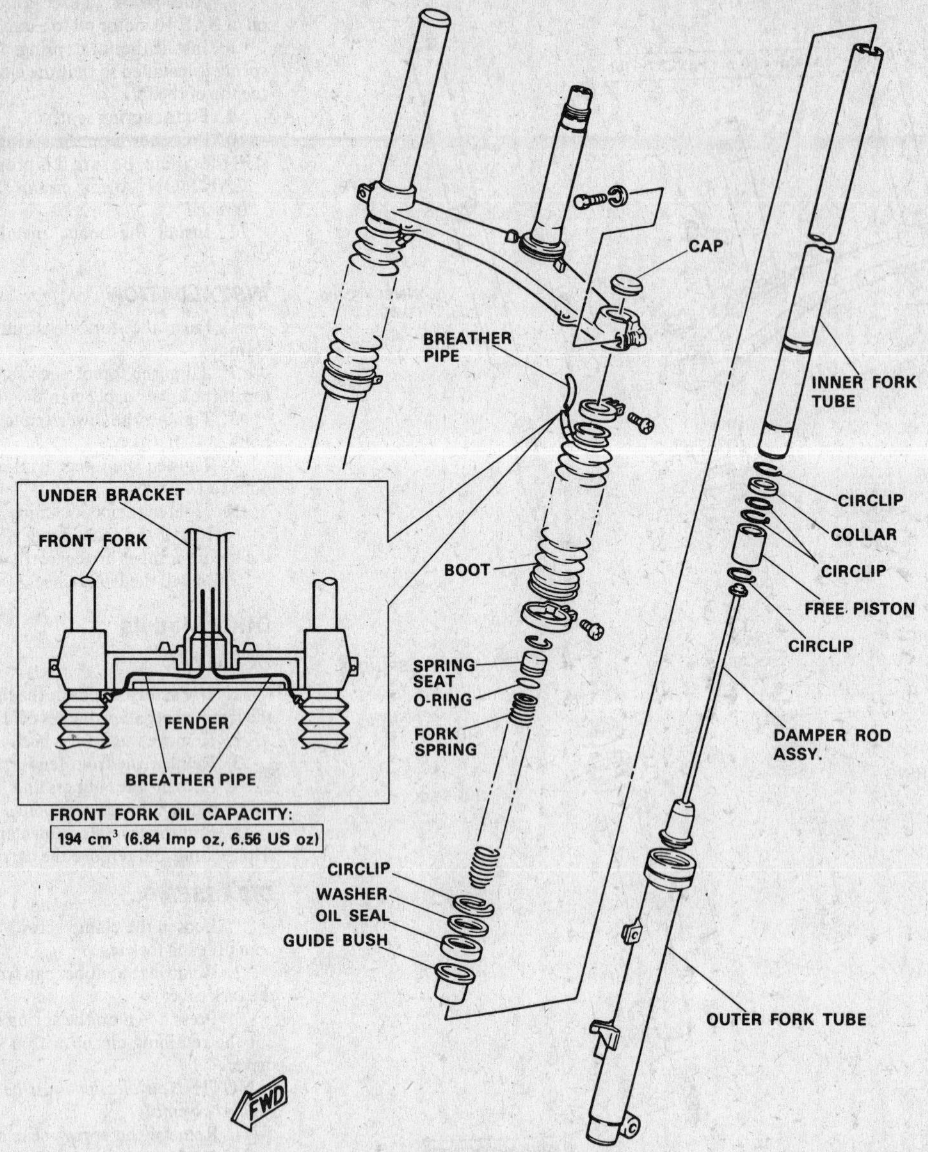

Front forks (except DX)

sion, especially in those areas on which the slider oil seal and the guide bush ride. Remove any deposits with fine emery cloth.

5. Check fork spring free length. Replace the fork springs as a set if either measures less than 395.1mm (15.56 in.).

6. Check the spring seat O-ring. Replace it if knicked or otherwise damaged.

ASSEMBLY

1. Clean all metal parts in a suitable solvent.
2. Insert the damper rod into the fork slider.
3. Install the guid bush and the slider oil seal on the fork tube.
4. Position the tube in the slider.
5. Press the oil seal into the slider.
6. Install the slider washer.
7. Install the seal circlip. Ensure that it is properly seated.
8. Pour 6.6 oz. (194cc) of fork oil into each fork leg. Use Yamaha fork oil or equivalent, such as SAE 10 or 10W30 motor oil.
9. Install the fork spring. Note that the tapered end of the spring goes at the lower end of the fork.
10. Install the spring seat.
11. Fit the spring seat circlip. New circlips must always be used. Be sure the circlip is properly seated.
12. Install the boot on each fork leg.

INSTALLATION

1. Push each fork leg up into the triple clamps, positioning the carrier in its place, if one is fitted.
2. Position the fork legs so that the top of the fork tube is 9mm (0.35 in.) above the surface of the upper triple clamp.
3. Tighten the lower triple clamp bolts to 22 ft. lbs.
4. Tighten the upper triple clamp bolts to 14 ft. lbs.
5. Tighten carrier bolts, if equipped, to 11 ft. lbs.
6. Install the fork rubber caps.
7. Install the front fender. Be sure the breather tubes are correctly routed.
8. Install the front wheel.

STEERING STEM

Adjustment

Refer to "Maintenance" for steering stem bearing adjustment.

Removal

1. Remove the front panel/headlight securing bolts.
2. Disconnect headlight wiring at the connector.
3. Remove the front wheel.
4. Remove the fender.
5. Remove the front forks.

6. Remove the upper triple clamp steering stem bolt.

7. Take off the upper triple clamp.

8. While supporting the steering stem assembly with one hand, carefully unscrew the ring nut.

CAUTION: *The uncaged balls are liable to come out as this is done.*

9. Lower the steering stem until clear of the frame lug. Note the uncaged balls in the frame lug and the steering stem.

Inspection

1. Check all of the bearing balls after washing them thoroughly in solvent.

2. The balls should be replaced if rusted, pitted, dented, or scored.

3. Inspect the condition of the ball races checking for pitting, a rippled surface, or dents.

4. Replace all of the balls if any wear or damage is noted, and the races as well.

The bearing races in the frame lug are a press- fit and should not be removed unless replacement is necessary. If replacement is necessary, the old races can be removed by reaching through the frame lug with a suitable punch and tapping the race evenly around it circumference to remove it from the inside of the frame lug. Be sure that the race does not become cocked in its seat upon removal.

New races are installed with a suitably sized bearing driver, i.e., one which will drive the race squarely into its seat. Be certain that the race goes straight in.

These races can also be installed using a block of hard wood or a large socket of sufficient size to cover the race in place of a bearing driver.

Assembly

1. The steering stem bearing specifications are:

Upper race: 1/4 in., 22 ea.

Lower race: 3/16 in., 19 ea.

2. Use a good grade, medium-weight bearing grease for lubrication.

3. Apply a coating of grease to the steering stem race. Imbed 19 of the 3/16 in. bearing balls in it.

4. Grease the race in the frame lug. Place 22 of the 1/4 in. balls in it.

5. Slip the steering stem up into the frame lug.

6. Once in place, hold it so none of the balls can slip out.

7. Install the upper bearing cover.

8. Thread the ring nut on. Screw it on as far as possible by hand, then adjust it to take all the play out of the steering stem. The bearing adjustment procedure is outlined in "Maintenance."

9. The remainder of the procedure is the reverse of disassembly.

NOTE: *The handle bar clamps are installed with the gap towards the rear. Tighten the forward most bolts first (14 ft. lbs.).*

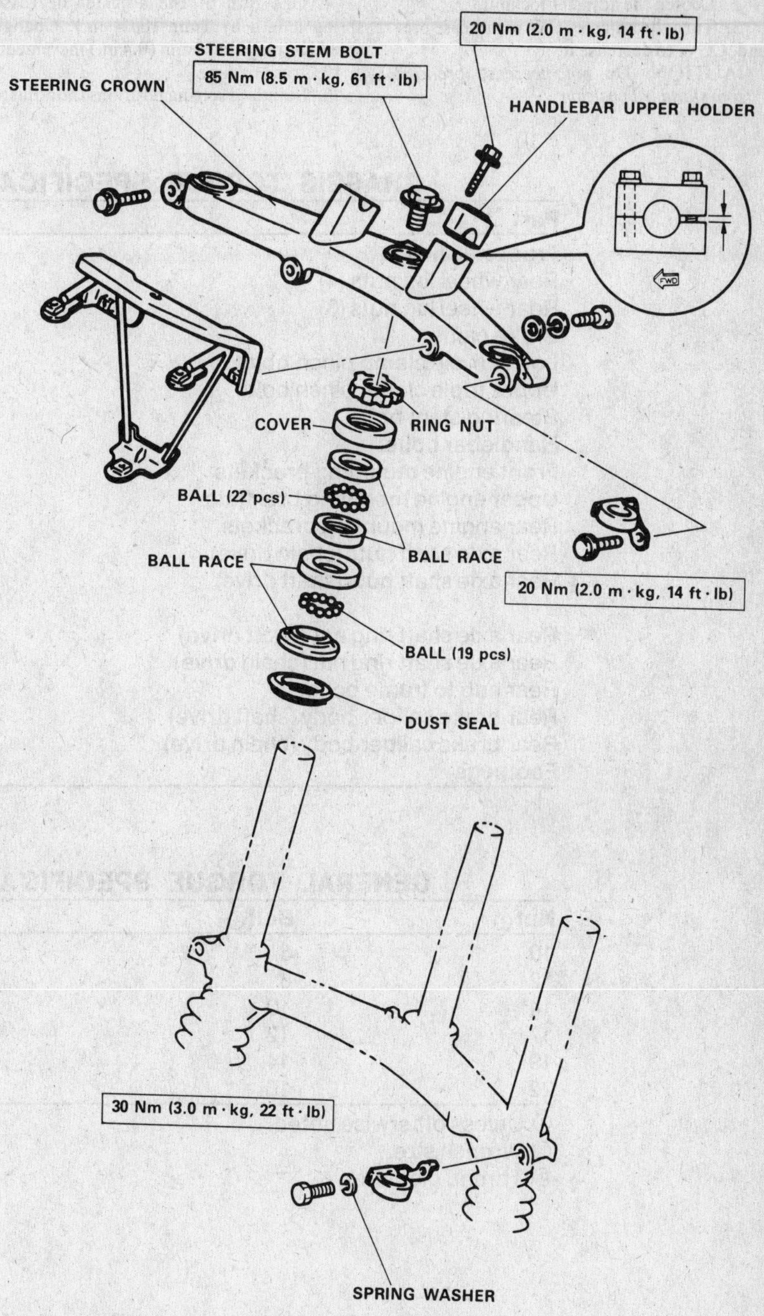

Steering stem assembly

REAR SHOCK ABSORBER

Removal

1. Place a suitable stand beneath the engine and raise the rear wheels a few inches off the ground. Block the front wheel so that the machine cannot move. Be sure that the machine is secure and safely supported.

2. Remove the seat and rear fender.

3. Remove the upper shock absorber mounting bolt.

4. Remove the cotter pin on the lower shock absorber mount.

5. Drive out the pivot shaft.

6. Disengage the shock absorber from the swing arm and remove it from the machine.

Inspection

Repair is not possible. If the shock absorber leaks or has been damaged, it must be replaced.

CAUTION: *Gas filled shocks must be depressurized before disposal. This procedure must be left to qualified service personnel.*

Installation

1. Grease the pivot shaft and upper mounting bolt lightly with lithium soap-based lubricant.

2. Tighten the upper mounting bolt to 18 ft. lbs.

Adjustment

1. Spring pre-load can be adjusted by turning the adjuster at the lower end of the unit.

2. Loosen the adjuster locknut.
3. Turn the adjuster CW to increase pre-load, CCW to decrease it.
CAUTION: *Do not decrease pre-load from standard position.*

4. One turn of the adjuster decreases spring length by 1mm (0.04 in.). Changes should be made in 10mm (0.4 in.) increments, or 10 turns at a time.
5. Standard setting positions the adjuster 57.8mm (2.28 in.) above the centerline of the pivot pin (punch mark).
6. Maximum allowable distance is 67.8mm (2.67 in.).

CHASSIS TORQUE SPECIFICATIONS

Part	Torque (ft lbs)
Front axle nut	36
Rear wheel lug nuts (4)	20
Rear wheel lug nuts (3)	32
Brake cams	6.5
Lower triple clamp pinch bolts	22
Upper triple clamp pinch bolts	14
Steering stem bolt	65
Handlebar bolts	14
Front engine mounting brackets	24
Upper engine mounting brackets	24
Rear engine mounting brackets	32
Rear axle shaft nuts (chain drive)	94
Rear axle shaft nuts (shaft drive)	150 (Type A) 105 (Type B)
Rear axle shaft ring nut (shaft drive)	72
Rear axle shaft ring nut (chain drive)	100
Rear hub to frame bolts	36
Rear brake caliper body (shaft drive)	36
Rear brake caliper body (chain drive)	32
Footpegs	24

GENERAL TORQUE SPECIFICATIONS ①

Nut ②	Bolt ③	Torque (ft lbs)
10	6	4.3
12	8	11
14	10	22
17	12	40
19	14	61
22	16	94

① Unless otherwise noted.
② Wrench size.
③ Thread diameter.

Yamaha Moto 4 80/200

MODEL COVERAGE

YFM80 YFM200

INDEX

GENERAL SPECIFICATIONS

	80	200
ENGINE		
Type	4-stroke, ohc	4-stroke, ohc
Displacement (cc)	79	196.3
Bore × Stroke (mm/in.)	47.0 × 45.6/1.850 × 1.795	67.0 × 55.7/2.6 × 2.2
Compression ratio	9.6:1	8.5:1
Starting system	Electric	Electric and recoil
CHASSIS		
Fuel capacity (L/gal)	5.4/1.4	9.5/2.5
Tank reserve (L/gal)	1.1/0.3	1.9/0.5
Weight (wet) (kg/lbs.)	99/218	169/373
Overall length (mm/in.)	1415/55.7	1850/72.8
Overall width (mm/in.)	825/32.5	995/39.2
Overall height (mm/in.)	865/34.1	985/38.8
Minimum ground clearance (mm/in.)	105/4.1	120/4.7
Wheelbase (mm/in.)	945/37.2	1125/44.3
Tires		
Front	17 × 7-7	22 × 8-10
Rear	18 × 9-7	22 × 11-8
TRANSMISSION		
Primary reduction	gear	gear
Primary reduction ratio	65/20 (3.250)	73/22 (3.318)
Secondary reduction	shaft	shaft
Secondary reduction ratio	19/18 × 34/10 (3.588)	19/18 × 46/11 (4.414)
Type	constant mesh, 4-speed	constant mesh, 5-speed
1st	39/11 (3.545)	35/11 (3.181)
2nd	35/17 (2.059)	31/15 (2.066)
3rd	31/22 (1.409)	30/21 (1.428)
4th	27/24 (1.125)	26/25 (1.040)
5th	—	23/28 (0.821)
Reverse	—	35/11 (3.181)
ELECTRICAL SYSTEM		
Ignition	CDI Magneto	CDI Magneto
Generator	Flywheel Magneto	Flywheel Magneto

SERIAL NUMBER LOCATION

In order to prevent possible confusion when purchasing parts, always refer to the engine and frame serial numbers on the machine.

The frame serial number is stamped on the lower frame tube, left side of the chassis.

The engine serial number is located on the top of the crankcase at the right side rear of the engine.

MAINTENANCE

NOTE: *Common maintenance procedures are explained in detail in the "General Information" section.*

LUBRICATION

Motor Oil

When average air temperature is above 41°F (5°C), use Yamalube 4-Cycle or SAE 20W-40, service rating "SE" or "SF."

When the air temperature is consistently below freezing, use SAE 10W-30, service rating "SE" or "SF."

All manufacturers recommend a certain grade and viscosity of motor oil for their engines, and this recommendation should be followed to ensure long engine life.

Checking Oil Level

1. A dipstick is provided to check oil level.
2. The machine should be parked on level ground.
3. Let the engine run for a few minutes then shut it off.
4. Unscrew and remove the dipstick from the right side of the engine. Wipe it off.
5. Reinsert the dipstick, allowing the cap to rest on the threads of the hole.
6. Pull it out. Oil level should be between the maximum and minimum marks on the dipstick. If level is too low, add enough of the recommended oil to bring it up to the specified level. Do not overfill.
7. When level is correct, screw the dipstick in and tighten it securely.

Changing Oil

80

1. The recommended change interval is every 6 mos. after initial break-in is over.

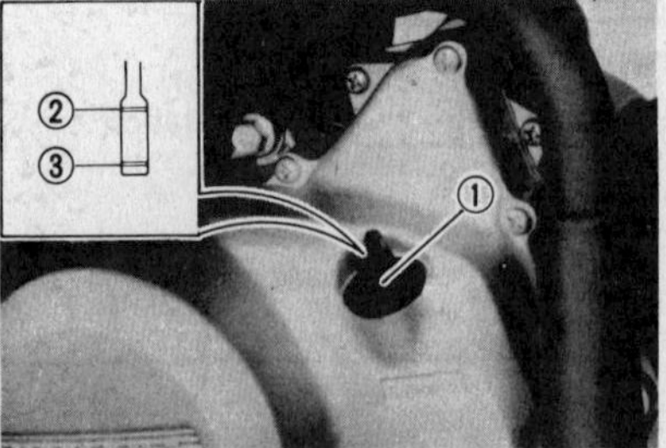

Dipstick (1) with upper and lower oil level marks (80)

Oil drain plug (1)(80)

2. Oil should be changed when the engine is warm. This ensures more complete draining and makes it more likely that the oil will carry off any particulates with it.

3. Place a suitable container (over 1 qt. capacity) beneath the drain plug.

4. Remove the dipstick.

5. Remove the drain plug. Allow the oil to drain completely.

6. Check the condition of the drain plug gasket. Replace it if necessary.

7. Refit the drain plug. Tighten to 14 ft. lbs.

8. Add engine oil. The proper amount at routine changes is 0.9 qts. (0.85 liters). Do not overfill.

9. After oil is added, let the engine run for a few minutes, then check level with the dipstick. Top up to the indicated upper level if necessary.

10. Check for leaks before operating the machine.

200

1. The recommended change interval is every 6 mos. after break-in is over.

2. Oil should be changed when the engine is warm. This ensures more complete draining and makes it more likely that the oil will carry off any particulates with it.

3. Place a suitably-sized container (over 2 qts. capacity) beneath the drain plug on the left side of the engine.

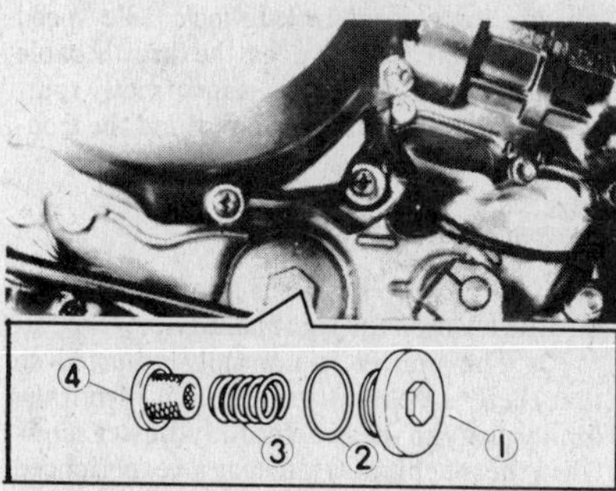

Oil drain plug (1); o-ring (2); spring (3) and oil strainer (4)(200)

4. Remove the dipstick.

5. Remove the drain plug. When it is removed, the O-ring, compression spring and strainer will come out as well. Take care that they are not misplaced.

6. On the right side of the engine, remove the oil filter cover drain bolt which is the lowest of the three bolts on the cover.

7. If the filter is to be cleaned, see "Oil Filter/Oil Strainer," below.

8. When the oil has drained completely, install the filter cover drain bolt. Install the oil strainer, compression spring, and drain plug with O-ring.

9. Tighten the filter cover drain bolt to about 7 ft. lbs. Tighten the drain plug to 31 ft. lbs.

10. Add about 1.6 qts, of the recommended oil to the crankcase. Check level with the dipstick. When level seems correct, start the engine and let it run for a few minutes, then shut it off and check again after it has been sitting for a short period. Top up if necessary.

Check Oil Flow (200)

CAUTION: *This procedure should be done after every oil change.*

Oil filter cover drain bolt (2)(200)

1. Change the oil and check for proper level of refill as outlined above.

2. Loosen the oil passage bolt at the top of the cylinder head on the right side of the engine. A slight loosening is all that it required.

3. Start the engine.

4. After about a minute, oil seepage at the bolt should be noted, showing that the head is getting lubricant.

5. If no oil appears, shut the engine off immediately and determine the cause.

6. Tighten the oil passage bolt to 5 ft. lbs.

Oil Filter/Oil Strainer

80

1. There is a filter screen inside the right crankcase cover. The screen should be cleaned at every other oil change or once a year.

2. Drain the oil as outlined in the "Changing Oil" procedure, above.

3. Remove the seat.

4. Remove the battery.

5. Remove the rear fender.

6. Remove the muffler, unbolting it from the cylinder head and from the chassis.

7. Place a drip pan beneath the right crankcase cover to catch the oil which will come out when the cover is taken off.

8. Remove the nine screws which secure the crankcase cover. Remove the cover. If it is stuck, tap around the sides very carefully with a plastic mallet to break it free.

9. Pull the oil strainer out of its slot.

10. Clean the strainer thoroughly in a clean, safe solvent.

11. Check the screen for punctures or other damage. If the screen is damaged in any way, or if foreign matter cannot be removed, replace it.

12. Install the strainer.

13. Install the crankcase cover. Using a new gasket is recommended.

Oil passage bolt (1)

14. Note the following torques:
Crankcase cover screws: 5.1 ft. lbs.
Drain plug: 14 ft. lbs.
Exhaust pipe at head: 7.2 ft. lbs.
Muffler bracket: 18 ft. lbs.

15. Refill the engine with the proper grade of oil. It may be necessary to add slightly more than the 0.9 qts. which is added at a routine change because of oil loss when the cover is taken off. Be sure to check level with the dipstick and top up to the upper level mark before riding.

200

1. Filter and strainer should be serviced at every other oil change, or once a year.

2. Drain the oil as outlined in the "Changing Oil" procedure.

Crankcase cover screws (80)

Removing the oil strainer (4)(80)

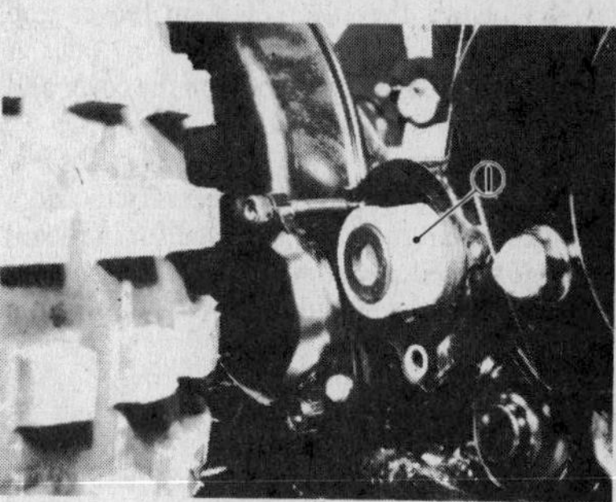

Oil filter element (1)(200)

3. Remove the oil filter cover drain bolt and the two remaining filter cover bolts. Remove the cover and take out the filter element.

4. Clean both the filter element and the strainer screen in clean solvent and dry.

5. Check for damage such as punctures or excessively clogged pores. Replace the element or strainer if any defect is apparent.

6. Check condition of the O-rings and replace them if chipped, deformed or otherwise damaged.

7. Carefully refit the strainer, compression spring and drain plug with O-ring.

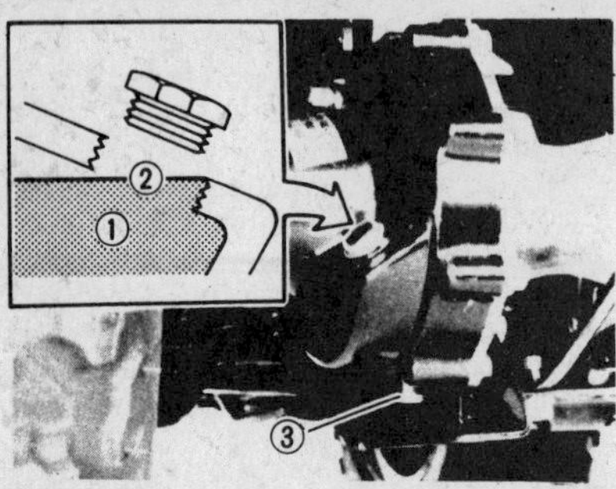

Final gearbox oil (1); level (2) and drain plug (3)

Knuckle grease fitting

Steering shaft grease fitting

8. Install the filter element, cover and bolts.
9. Tighten the drain bolt on the cover and the cover bolts to 7 ft. lbs.
10. Tighten the drain plug to 31 ft. lbs.
11. Add oil. It may be necessary to add a bit more than the 1.6 qts. called for in the oil change procedure, above.
12. Check level and oil flow as outlined in the prior procedures.

Final Gearbox (200)

1. Oil level should be checked periodically and changed once a year.
2. The gearbox uses SAE 80 API "GL-4" hypoid gear oil or SAE 80W-90 hypoid gear oil.

CHECKING GEARBOX OIL

1. The machine should be parked on a level surface. The engine should be cold.
2. Remove the level plug on the left side of the gearbox.
3. Oil level should be to the top of the threads at the lower part of the plug hole. In other words, it should just be about to seep out.
4. If level is too low, top up with the recommended oil.
5. Check gasket condition before fitting level plug.

CHANGING GEARBOX OIL

1. The machine should be parked on a level surface.
2. Place a drain pan beneath the gearbox.
3. Remove the level plug.
4. Remove the drain plug.
5. Check drain plug gasket condition.
6. After the oil has had several minutes to drain, install the drain plug and tighten it to 17 ft. lbs.
7. Add the recommended oil to the gearbox. Capacity is about 0.14 qts. Wait a few minutes after adding to give the thick oil a chance to find its level. The oil should cover the threads at the lower part of the level plug hole.
8. When level is correct, fit the level plug and tighten it securely.

Chassis Lubrication

1. There is a grease fitting at the bottom of the steering shaft and one on each front wheel steering knuckle. These items should be lubricated with lithium soap-based grease. The service interval is every 6 mos. under normal conditions.
2. Wheel bearings should be lubricated with medium weight wheel bearing grease. The service interval is one year. See "Chassis" for procedures.
3. The brake levers and brake cams should be lubricated with lithium soap-based grease. The service interval is 6 mos. Refer to "Chassis" for brake service procedures.

SERVICE CHECKS AND ADJUSTMENTS

Clutch

80

1. The clutch adjuster is located on the left crankcase cover.
2. Remove the adjuster cap.
3. Loosen the locknut.
4. Carefully turn the adjuster screw clockwise until resistance is felt; then turn it 1/8 turn counterclockwise.
5. Turning the adjuster CCW will decrease clutch lever free-play and vice-versa.
6. Tighten the locknut to 5.8 ft. lbs.
7. Install the cap.

200

1. Locate the clutch adjuster on the right side of the engine near the oil filter cover.
2. Loosen the locknut slightly.

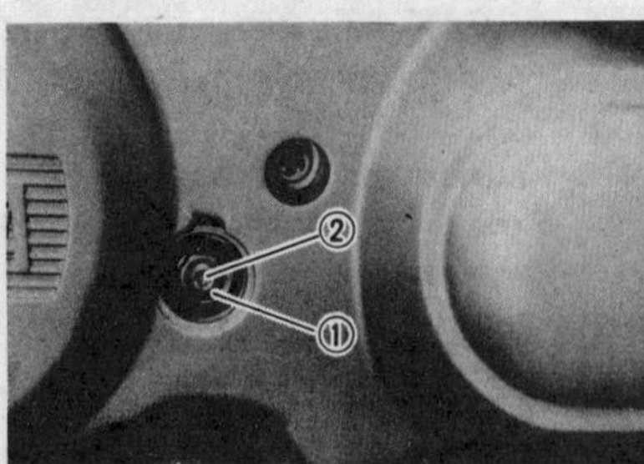

Clutch adjuster screw (2) and adjuster locknut (1)(80)

Clutch adjuster screw (1) and locknut (2)(200)

3. Carefully turn the adjuster screw counterclockwise until resistance is felt; then turn it 1/8 turn clockwise.
4. As marked on the crankcase cover, turning the adjuster screw CCW will decrease lever play and vice-versa.
5. Tighten the locknut to 11 ft. lbs.

Throttle Cable

1. The throttle lever should have 3-5mm (0.12-0.20 in.) of free movement before the throttle slide begins to open.
2. Make the adjustment with the adjuster near the top of the throttle cable. Loosening the adjuster locknut and turning it in or out will affect lever free-play.
3. Start the engine and turn the handlebars slowly from lock-to-lock. Idle speed must not increase. If it does, the throttle cable has insufficient free-play, is incorrectly routed, or is binding at some point. Find the trouble before riding.

Speed Limiter (80)

1. The speed limiter is located above the throttle lever on the right handgrip.
2. The limiter is normally adjusted so that there is 8-9mm (0.31-0.35 in.) from the limiter body to the head of the adjuster screw when the machine is ridden by an experienced individual.

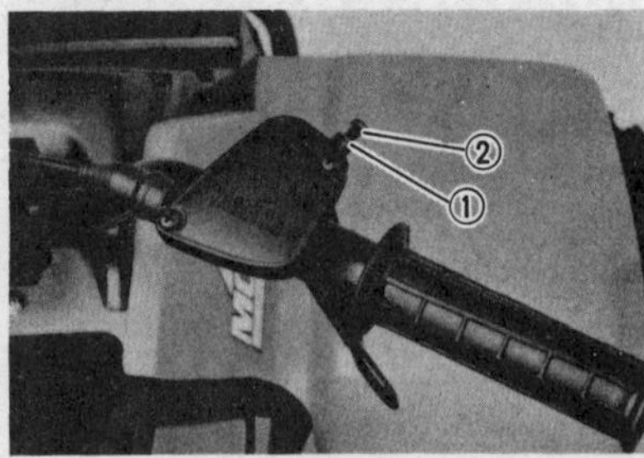

Speed limiter screw and locknut (1,2)

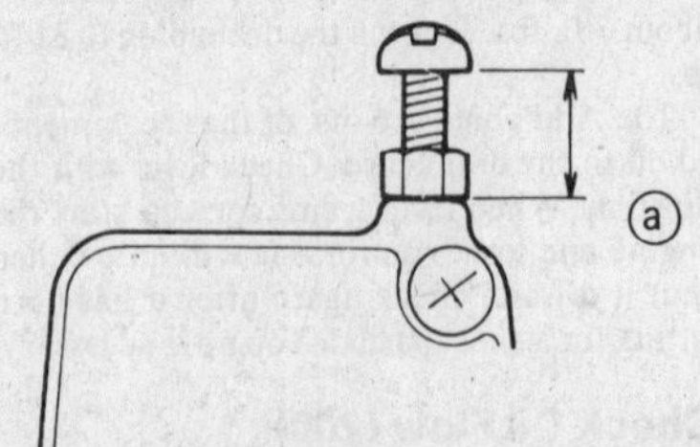

Limiter should be adjusted so that "a" equals 8-9 mm (0.31-0.35 in.)

3. Loosen the adjuster screw locknut and turn the screw to make this adjustment. Then tighten the locknut.

4. Check throttle cable free-play as outlined above.

CAUTION: *The factory recommends that the speed limiter be screwed in completely for beginning riders. This adjustment is a critical safety factor which must be determined by the machine's rider(s) and/or their guardians.*

Brakes (80)

WEAR LIMIT

When the brake lever or pedal is applied, check the position of the brake wear indicator relative to the limit notch cast into the drum. When the indicator reaches the limit, replace the brake shoes.

ADJUSTMENT

CAUTION: The brake hand lever and the brake pedal must be adjusted at the same time.

1. The brake hand lever should have 10-20mm (0.40-0.8 in.) of free movement before the linings contact the drum. This distance is measured at the ball end of the hand lever.

2. The brake can be adjusted with either the cable adjuster at the handlebar or with the wing nut at the drum. Make minor adjustments at the handlebar. If a major adjustment is required, use the wing nut.

3. The cable adjuster at the handlebar is used by loosening the locknut and screwing the adjuster out. Tighten the locknut.

4. If you use the wing nut to make brake adjustments, first screw the handlebar adjuster in several turns. The hand lever is connected to the wing nut on the left, when the machine is viewed from the rear. Turn the wing nut clockwise to decrease hand lever free-play.

5. The brake foot pedal should have 20-30mm (0.8-1.2 in.) of free-play before the linings contact the drum.

6. The pedal is adjusted with the right-side wing nut on the drum.

7. When brake adjustments are correct, apply the brakes and check position of the wear indicator as directed above.

Brakes (200)

FRONT

1. The brakes should be adjusted so that the lever has 5-8mm (0.2-0.3 in.) of free movement measured between the levger and the lever holder before the linings contact the drum.

2. The brake can be adjusted with either the cable adjusters at the brake plates or with the adjuster on the handlebar. Loosen the locknut and turn the hand lever adjuster out to decrease lever free-play. At the brake plates, turning the wing nuts in will accomplish the same thing.

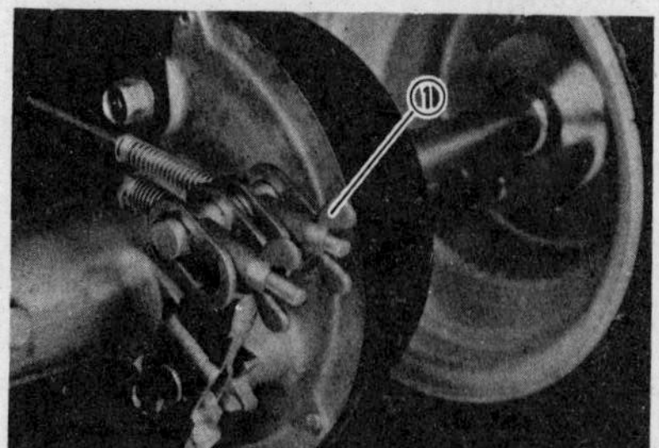

Brake adjuster wing nuts (80)

3. It is recommended that major adjustments be made at the brake plates and finer adjustments with the handlebar adjuster.

CAUTION: *When making adjustments at the brake plates, be sure that both wheels are adjusted equally. Check the brake cable joint. It should be horizontal, indicating that both cables have equal tension. If it is tilted, one brake will pull when the lever is activated.*

4. After adjustment, check that the wheels can turn freely without dragging.

5. Apply the brake and check the positions of the brake wear indicators on the drums. When the wear indicator reaches the limit line, replace the brake shoes. Both wheels should be serviced if either shows excessive brake wear.

REAR

1. Pump the brake pedal and hand lever several times before adjustment.

2. At the hand lever, loosen the adjuster locknut and screw in the adjuster to give maximum cable free-play.

3. Loosen the brake pedal wing nut and the brake hand lever wing nut at the caliper.

4. Loosen the locknut and adjusting bolt.

5. Screw in the brake hand lever wing nut so that the caliper lever can be positioned as shown in the illustration.

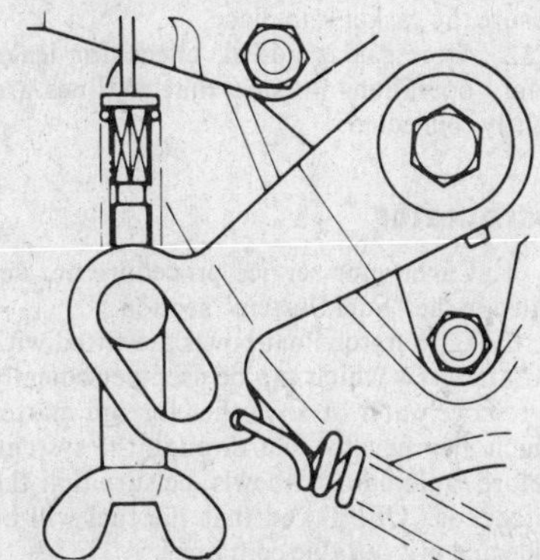

Rear brake preliminary adjustment position (200)

6. Slowly screw the adjusting bolt in by hand until resistance is felt, then back it off 1/4 turn.

7. Hold the adjusting bolt with a wrench so that it doesn't move. Tighten the locknut.

8. Screw in the brake pedal cable adjuster until the pin just touches the upper end of the lever slot. Clearance between the pin and the brake lever should be 0-1mm (0-0.04 in.).

9. Support the rear wheels off the ground and check that they spin freely. If they are tight, or if noise is heard, repeat the adjustment procedure.

10. Check free-play at the brake pedal. It should be less than 50mm (2.0 in.) Use the adjuster at the pedal to make this adjustment. On average, free-play should be about 25mm (1.0 in.).

11. Check free-play at the rear brake hand lever. It should be about 5mm (0.2 in.). Use the cable adjuster at the hand lever to make this adjustment.

CAUTION: *Both pedal and lever should be adjusted when performing rear brake adjustments. Do not adjust one without checking the other.*

READ PAD WEAR

When the head of the adjusting bolt comes close to touching its locknut, replace the brake pads.

Headlight Adjustment (200)

Vertical adjustment of the headlight can be done by loosening the body mounting nuts and moving the body up or down as required.

Bulb Replacement

1. Remove the two screws beneath the lens which secure it to the body.

2. Take out the lens assembly.

3. Turn the bulb holder CCW and take out the bulb.

4. Replace the burned out unit with an identical bulb: 45/45W, 12V.

5. Insert the holder into the lens and turn it CW to lock it.

6. Install the lens assembly in the body and install and tighten the two screws.

FUEL SYSTEM

The fuel system consists of the carburetor, fuel petcock and air cleaner.

These items should be serviced about every six months under normal operating conditions.

Air Cleaner

80

1. Remove the four screws securing the front cover and take it off.

2. Disconnect the band securing the filter element frame and pull out the element assembly.

3. Clean the element thoroughly in a safe solvent.

Air filter front cover (80)

4. Dry the element after cleaning by squeezing. Do not wring it out as the pores may be damaged.

5. Soak the element in SAE 10W-30 motor oil.

6. Squeeze off the excess oil. Elements should be wet, but not dripping with oil.

7. Clean the inside of the air filter housing.

8. Apply a light coat of grease to the element seat.

9. Install the filter element. Be sure that mating surfaces match to prevent air leaks.

200

1. The air cleaner is accessed from the rear of the machine.

2. Remove the air cleaner case cover (four screws).

3. Pull out the air filter element.

4. Turn the element plate 90° and separate the element and element guide.

5. Clean the element thoroughly in a safe solvent.

6. Dry the element after cleaning by squeezing. Do not wring it out as the pores may be damaged.

7. Soak the element in SAE 10W-30 motor oil.

Air filter element location (200)

8. Squeeze off the excess oil. The element should be wet, but not dripping with oil.

9. Assemble the filter element and guide. Install and secure the plate.

10. Clean the inside of the air cleaner case if it is wet or dirty.

11. Install the element, making sure that all mating surfaces match to prevent unfiltered air from entering the engine.

12. Check air passages in the intake system for condition. The inlet to the case must be free of obstructions. The hose running to the carburetor from the case must have a tight seal at both the case and the carb.

13. Inspect the hose at the bottom of the air cleaner case. Remove the hose cap and drain off any water which may have collected.

Petcock

1. The petcock has filter screens inside the tank which should be cleaned periodically—about every 6 mos. under normal conditions.

2. Remove the gas tank.

3. Drain the gas.

4. Remove the lines from the petcock.

5. Remove the petcock securing screws and pull the assembly out of the tank.

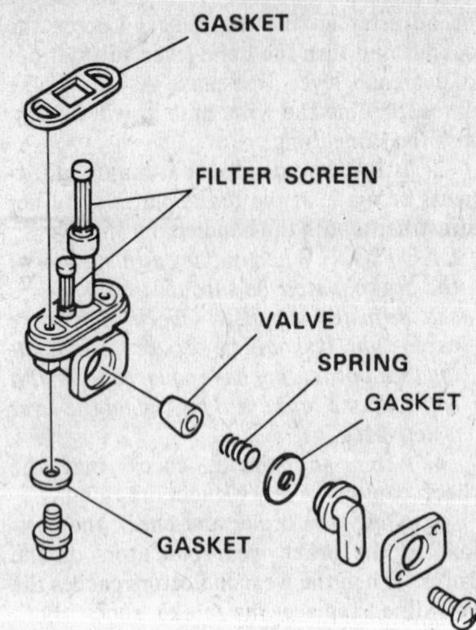

Fuel petcock

6. Check gasket condition. Replace it if it appears damaged or if it was leaking prior to removal.

7. Remove the filter screens and clean them in a safe solvent.

8. If foreign matter cannot be removed, or if the screens are punctured, crushed, other otherwise damaged, replace them.

9. Check the petcock mating surface. Replace the unit if any defect is noted.

10. Flush out the gas tank before installing the petcock to get rid of any residual dirt.

11. When fitting the petcock to the tank, be sure the gasket is in place.

12. After gas is added, check for leaks before operation. Be sure that all lines are tightly connected.

Carburetor

1. Carburetor service procedure are detailed in the "Fuel System" section.

2. Carburetor float bowls are fitted with a drain screw which can be used periodically to remove water or any other foreign matter which may have passed through the system. Before draining float bowls, be sure that the petcock is "OFF," and that the fuel will be collected in a suitable container.

CHASSIS INSPECTION

Wheel Bearings

1. Wheel bearing problems may make themselves known by a rumbling sound which increases with speed.

Check the front wheels for lateral play

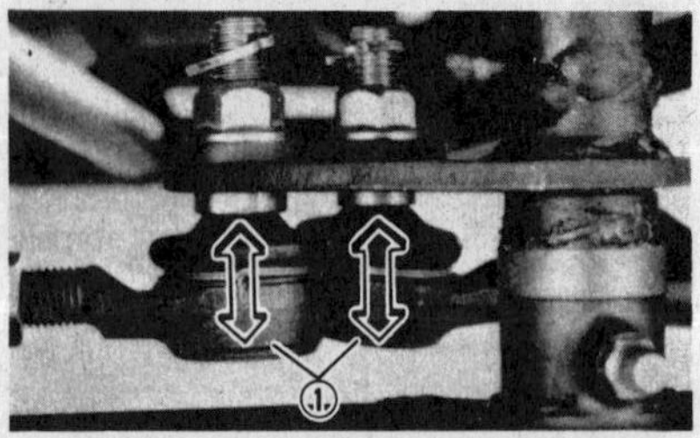

Check tie-rod ends for vertical play

2. Support the wheel you are checking off the ground.

3. Spin the wheel and listen for any unusual noise. Place your hand on the (front) knuckle or the (rear) hub while the wheel is turning.

4. If you feel any vibration, suspect wheel bearing damage.

5. Refer to "Chassis" for disassembly procedures.

Steering System

1. The steering system should be checked periodically for accident-related damage as well as for normal wear.

2. Check for play in the handlebars. Attempt to move the bars back and forth and up and down. If there is any play, replace the steering shaft bushings. See the "Chassis" section.

3. Turn the handlebars completely to either left or right, then move them slightly back in the opposite direction.

4. While shaking the handlebars back and forth in this range, check for any vertical play in the tie-rod ends. If there is any, the tie-rod ends must be replaced.

5. Support the front of the machine with a jack or suitable, safe method of support. Grasp the tires and try to move them in and out. Check for looseness in any direction. If any free-play is found, check wheel bearings, knuckle bushings, knuckle shafts, collars, thrust covers and cotter pins.

MAINTENANCE DATA

	80	200
Fuel capacity gal./L)	1.4/5.4	2.5/9.5
Engine oil		
When changing (qts./L)	0.9/0.85	1.6/1.5
After rebuilding (qts./L)	1.1/1.0	1.9/1.8
Final Gearbox Oil		
Level	—	Check by level plug
Capacity (qts./L)	—	0.14/0.13
Tire pressure (f/r) (psi)	2.4-2.8	2.2
Battery	12V/7 ah	12v/14 ah

Tires

1. Special low pressure tires require special consideration.
2. Tire pressures are critical. The pressure must be maintained at the recommended pressure as shown on the stickers on the machine.
3. Pressure should be checked with a suitable low-pressure tire gauge.
4. Never allow pressure to fall below the minimum shown on the machine sticker. The tire can separate from the rim if pressure is too low.
5. Maximum allowable pressure is 10 psi for the YFM 200, 20 psi for the YFM 80.
6. When adding air to tires, do so very slowly and carefully. Unregulated service station air lines should not be used. Rapid inflation can cause the tire to burst.
7. Be sure that pressure at all four tires is equal.
8. Check pressures when tires are cold.
9. Tires should be replaced when the tread depth at any point falls below 3mm (0.12 in.).
10. Tires should be replace in pairs (left and right) if one is worn or damaged.

CAUTION: *Replacement tires must always meet manufacturers size and performance specifications.*

TUNE-UP

NOTE: *Common tune-up procedures are explained in detail in the "General Information" section. This includes a full description of spark plug service and analysis.*

REQUIRED MATERIALS

In addition to common hand tools, the procedures detailed in this section require:

a. A set of feeler gauges for valve adjustment;

b. A compression gauge for the compression test;

c. A tachometer for idle speed adjustment and ignition timing check:

d. A stroboscopic timing light for ignition timing. Connection of the tachometer and timing light will depend on make and/or model.

VALVE ADJUSTMENT

80

NOTE: *Valves must be adjusted when the engine is cold.*

1. Remove the seat.
2. Remove the battery.
3. Remove the rear fender securing bolts and take off the fender.

Remove the gearshift pedal from its shaft.

5. Remove the three screws which secure the left crankcase cover. Take off the cover.
6. Remove the intake and exhaust valve adjuster covers.
7. Turn the crankshaft CW with a Wrench on the flywheel nut until the "T" mark on the flywheel aligns with the timing mark on the crankcase.
8. Check for play at both rocker arms. Play ensures that both valves are closed and

PERIODIC MAINTENANCE INTERVALS①

Before each ride
- Safety items
- Lights (200)
- Control cable adjustments
- Tightness of critical fasteners
- Brake operation
- Fuel/oil leaks

Every 3 Months
- Brake system

Every 6 Months
- Tune up engine
- Service fuel system
- Check battery level
- Check tire pressure
- Check wheel bearings
- Check steering for play
- Change engine oil
- Lubricate steering system
- General chassis lubrication

Annually
- Clean oil filter and strainer
- Repack wheel bearings
- Change gearbox oil (200)

① Based on normal usage after initial service and break-in are completed.

RECOMMENDED LUBRICANTS

Engine
- Above 41°F (5°C): Yamalube 4-Cycle or SAE 20W-40, service rating "SE" or "SF"
- Below freezing: SAE 10W-30, service rating "SE" or "SF"

Final Gearbox (200)
- SAE 80 API "GL-4" hypoid gear oil
- SAE 80W-90 hypoid gear oil

Wheel Bearings
- Medium weight wheel bearing grease

Steering System
- Lithium-based grease

Brake Components/Throttle
- Lithium-based grease

Control Cables
- Light motor oil
- Graphite-based lubricants
- Commercial cable lubes

Air Cleaner Element
- SAE 10W-30 motor oil

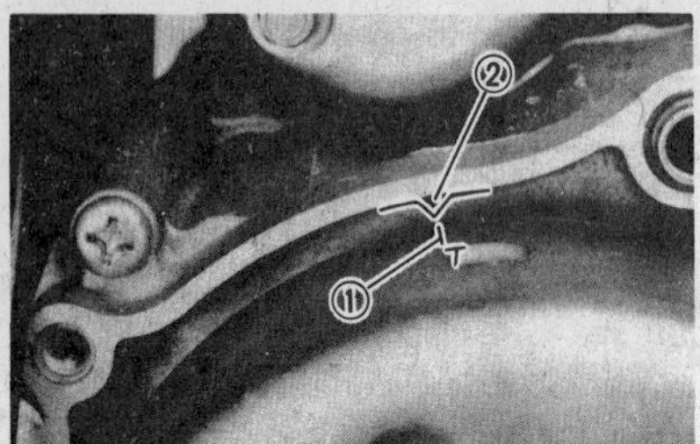

Align the "T" mark to position the piston at TDC

Match mark (3) and timing mark (4) will align when the piston is at TDC on the compression stroke

the piston is at Top Dead Center on the compression stroke. If play is not evident at both valves, turn the flywheel 360° and align the "T" mark again. Recheck the play. The piston must be at TDC on the compression stroke.

NOTE: *If there is any doubt, remove the cam sprocket cover and turn the flywheel to align its "T" mark at the same time aligning the match mark on the cam sprocket with the timing mark on the head.*

9. With feeler gauge blades of the proper thickness, check the clearance between the valve and its adjuster.

Clearances are:
Intake: 0.05-0.10mm/0.002-0.004 in.
Exhaust: 0.08-0.13mm/0.003-0.005 in.

10. If the valve is correctly adjusted, the gauge blade will be a light slip fit. If the fit is too tight or too loose, adjust the valve(s).

11. Loosen the valve adjuster locknut.

12. With the feeler gauge blade between the adjuster and the valve, turn the adjuster in or out until the blade shows a light slip fit.

13. Hold the adjuster in place and tighten the locknut.

Torque: 5.1 ft. lbs.

14. Install the crankcase cover, valve adjuster covers and remaining components.

200

NOTE: *Valves must be adjusted when the engine is cold.*

1. Remove the front carrier mounting bolts and pull the carrier forward to remove it.
2. Remove the two screws which secure the front panel. Remove the panel.
3. Remove the seat.
4. Remove the fuel tank cover bolts. Unhook the cover and pull forward to remove it.
5. Remove the intake and exhaust valve covers.
6. Remove the timing window plug from the left crankcase cover.
7. Slowly pull the recoil starter knob until the "T" mark on the flywheel aligns with the stationary timing mark.
8. Check for clearance at both valves. If both are not free, rotate the engine 360° until the "T" mark appears again and check for clearance. Valves are adjusted when the engine is at Top Dead Center on the compression stroke.
9. With the proper thickness feeler gauge, check clearance. Clearances are:
   Intake: 0.05-0.09mm/0.002-0.004 in.
   Exhaust: 0.11-0.15mm/0.006 in.
10. If the valve is correctly adjusted the gauge blade will be a light slip fit. If fit is too tight or loose, adjust the valve(s).
11. Loosen the valve adjuster locknut.
12. With the feeler gauge blade between the valve adjuster and the valve, turn the adjuster in or out until the blade is a light slip fit.
13. Hold the adjuster in place and tighten the locknut.
   Torque: 10 ft. lbs.
14. Install the valve covers. Fit the covers so that the ribs on the inside are at the top.
15. Assemble the remaining components in the reverse of the order of removal.

CAM CHAIN ADJUSTMENT

80

1. Remove the seat.
2. Remove the battery.
3. Remove the rear fender bolts and take off the fender.
4. Remove the gearshift pedal.
5. Remove the left crankcase cover screws and take off the cover.
6. Remove the cam sprocket cover.
7. Remove the cam chain tensioner crown nut.
8. Loosen the cam chain tensioner locknut. Back the adjusting screw off several turns.
9. With a wrench on the flywheel nut, turn the crankshaft CCW until the "T" mark on the flywheel aligns with the pointer on the crankcase and the match mark on the cam sprocket aligns with the mark on the cylinder head.
10. Continue turning the crankshaft in the same direction until the sprocket match mark is directly in line with the cam chain tensioner and at the lowest point it can reach (see illustration).
11. Tighten the cam chain tensioner adjusting screw.
12. Tighten the adjusting screw locknut. Proper torque is 5.1 ft. lbs.
13. Install and secure the crown nut (torque to 3.6 ft. lbs.).
14. Install remaining components in the reverse of the removal order.

200

1. Remove the timing window plug from the left crankcase cover.
2. Pull the recoil starter knob to align the "T" mark on the flywheel with the stationary timing mark on the crankcase.
3. Locate the cam chain tensioner behind the cylinder. Remove the tensioner cap.
4. Loosen the adjuster locknut a few turns.
5. Turn the adjuster in until the pushrod inside is flush with the adjuster end.
6. Start the engine.
7. Observe pushrod movement. The rod should move slightly when the engine is

Align the "T" mark with the stationary timing mark to position the piston at TDC

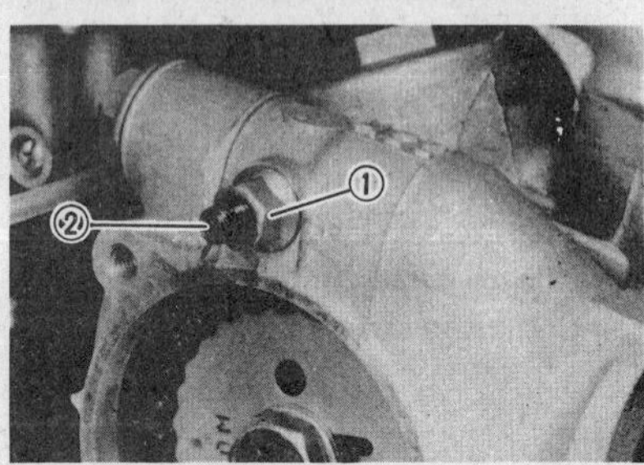

Cam chain tensioner locknut (1) and adjusting screw (2) (80)

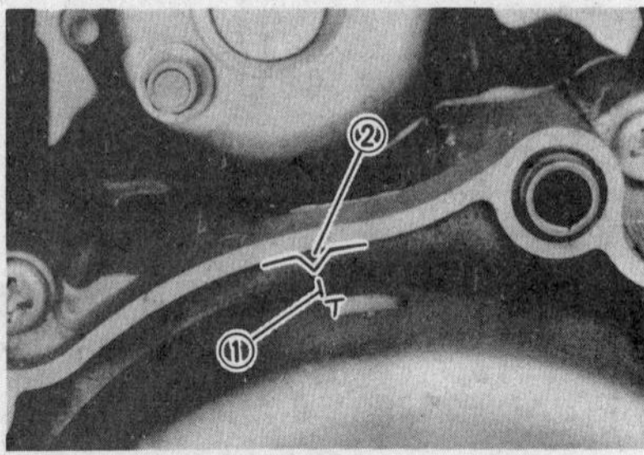

Align the "T" mark with the pointer

Align the match mark with the cylinder head mark, then . . .

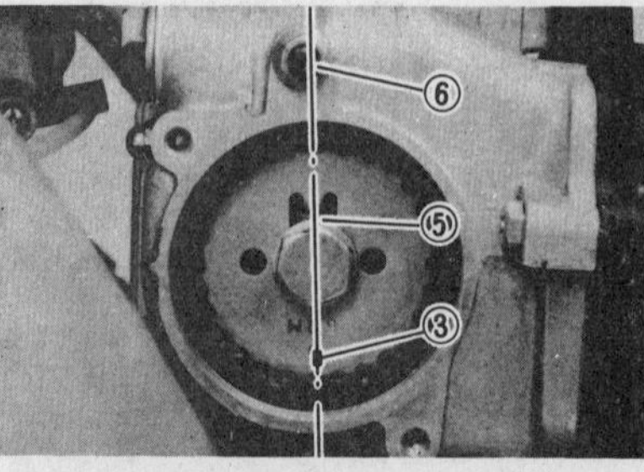

Position the match mark as shown to make cam chain tension adjustment

Cam chain tensioner pushrod (1), adjuster (2), locknut (3)

idling. If it does not, loosen the adjuster slightly until movement is noted.

8. Stop at this point and tighten the locknut (torque: 22 ft. lbs.).

9. Install the tensioner cap. Install timing window plug.

COMPRESSION TEST

Refer to the "General Information" section under "Tune-Up" for compression test procedures.

1. The compression test should be made after valves are adjusted.

2. Engine should be run for several minutes before the test.

3. Remove the spark plug. Connect the plug to its cap and ground it against the engine case to prevent sparking during the test. CAUTION: *Be sure the plug is properly grounded when cranking the engine.*

4. Screw-in type compression gauges need a 12mm thread for 20cc machines, 10mm for 80cc units.

5. Hold the throttle open while cranking the engine.

6. For 200cc machines, compression should be about 128 psi. This is the standard value. The upper and lower limits are 142 psi and 114 psi.

7. For 80cc machines, standard compression is about 171 psi. The upper and lower service limits are 185 psi and 142 psi, respectively.

8. If compression is too low, and the valves were just adjusted, first check that clearances are correct.

IGNITION TIMING

Ignition timing is not adjustable. A strobe timing light and a tachometer are needed to make this check.

1. On 80cc models, remove the seat, battery, rear fender, gearshift pedal and left crankcase cover.

Ignition timing mark on flywheel (200)

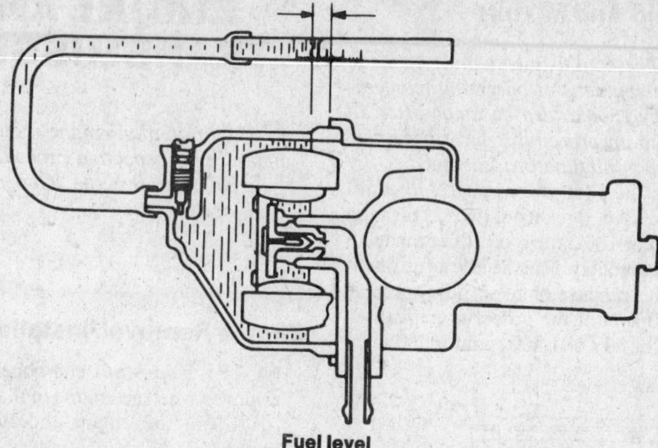

Fuel level

2. On 200cc models, remove the timing window plug from the left crankcase cover.

3. Connect the tach and timing light according to the manufacturer's instructions.

4. Start the engine and let it run at the specified idle speed: 1400 ± 50 rpm for the 200 and 1800 ± 50 rpm for the 80.

5. On 200cc models, aim the light through the timing window. At idle, the "F" mark on the flywheel should appear to be aligned with the stationary timing mark on the crankcase cover.

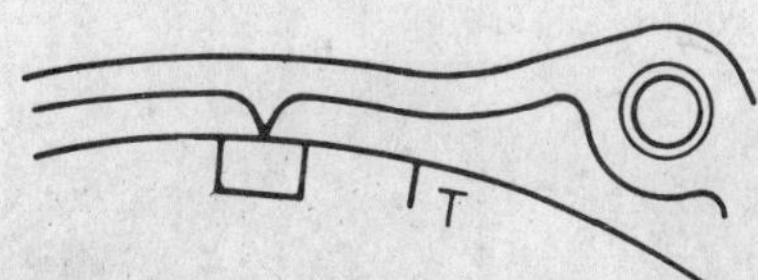

Ignition firing range mark on flywheel (80)

6. On 80cc models, check that the firing range mark on the flywheel aligns with the stationary timing mark on the crankcase.

7. If alignment is not correct, check the pickup coil for looseness on its mount.

CARBURETORS

Carburetor adjustments to be made during a tune-up include float height, and idle speed and mixture.

Float Height

1. Float height determines the level of gasoline in the float bowl during operation. While it is a critical setting, it will not normally need frequent attention once it is properly set. Although it need not be done at every tune-up, it should be checked from time to time.

2. The machine must be parked on a level surface.

3. Place a stand or jack under the engine and raise it until the carburetor is positioned vertically.

4. Disconnect the drain line from the bottom of the float bowl and connect a transparent vinyl tube (6mm/0.24 in. inside diameter) to the bowl fitting.

5. Set the petcock "ON" and start the engine, letting it run for a few minutes.

6. Hold the vinyl tube alongside the carburetor body. Open the drain screw. Gasoline will flow into the tube.

7. Shut the engine off.

8. Note the level of the gasoline in the tube relative to the carburetor body.

On 80cc models, the gas should be 3.5mm (0.14 in.) below the edge of the carb body. The tolerance is ±1.0mm (0.04 in.).

On 200cc models, the gas should be 3.0mm (0.12 in.) below the edge of the carb body. The tolerance is ±1.0mm (0.04 in.)

9. If correct, close the drain screw and disconnect the tube. Reconnect the drain line.

10. If not correct, disassemble and check float height as follows.

11. Remove the carburetor from the engine. Refer to "Fuel System" for procedures.

12. Remove the float bowl. Remove the float bowl gasket.

13. With the carburetor positioned vertically, lower the float until the float arm tang just touches, but does not depress the float needle tip.

14. Float height is the distance from the top of the float to the float bowl mating surface ("a" in the illustration).

15. The specification is 21.5mm/0.85 in. for 200cc models and 21.0mm/0.83 in. For 80cc units.

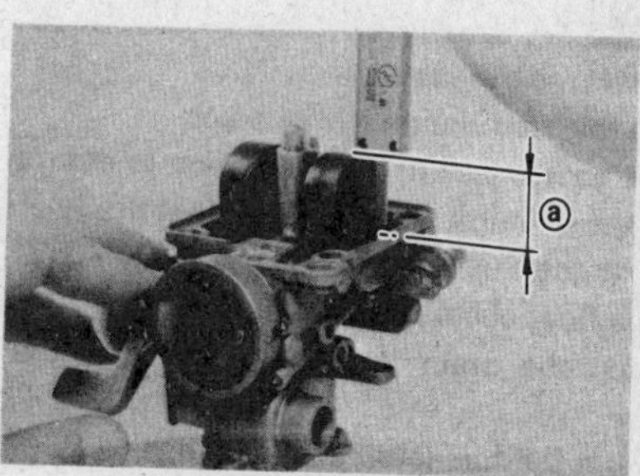

Float height ("a")

16. The tolerance is ±0.5mm/0.02 in. If adjustment is necessary, push out the float pivot pin and remove the float assembly.

17. Carefully bend the tang on the float arm to adjust height. Bending the tang away from the carb body will decrease float height, and vice-versa.

18. After adjustment, recheck fuel level as outlined in the beginning of this procedure.

19. After adjustment, check for leaks and proper operation of the machine before riding.

Idle Speed And Mixture

NOTE: *These adjustments must be made when the engine is at operating temperature. They should also be made after all other tune-up procedures have been carried out, if a full tune-up is intended.*

1. Turn the pilot screw in *carefully* until it is lightly seated. Back it out two (2) turns on 80cc models or 1 1/2 turns on 200cc models.

Fit a tachometer. Use the idle adjustment screw on the carburetor to set idle speed to within ±50 rpm of the proper specification: 1,800 rpm for 80's or 1,400 rpm for 200's.

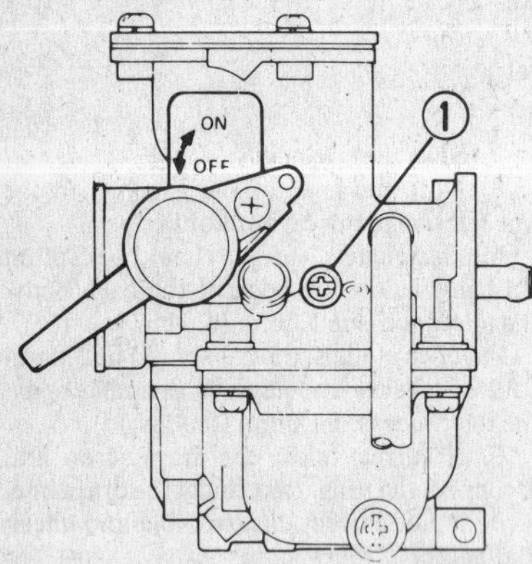

Idle speed screw (80)

3. Smooth out idle, if necessary, by fine adjustments to the pilot air screw. About 1/2 turn in either direction from the specification should produce a good, smooth idle. If it doesn't, there may be a carburetor or engine fault.

4. Check the throttle cable adjustment. Turn the handlebars from side to side. If idle speed changes when this is done, the cable is too tight.

ENGINE AND TRANSMISSION

NOTE: *Common engine rebuilding techniques and inspection procedures are explained in detail in the "General Information" section.*

YFM 80

Engine Removal/Installation

NOTE: *Top end components can be removed with the engine in the frame.*

1. Clean the engine thoroughly before removal.
2. Drain the engine oil.
3. Remove the seat.
4. Remove the battery.
5. Remove the bolts securing the rear fender. Remove the fender.
6. Remove the muffler bracket bolts.
7. Remove the exhaust pipe nuts at the cylinder head. Remove the exhaust pipe assembly.
8. Remove the carburetor. See "Fuel System" for procedures.
9. Disconnect the spark plug lead from the plug.

Engine mounting bolts

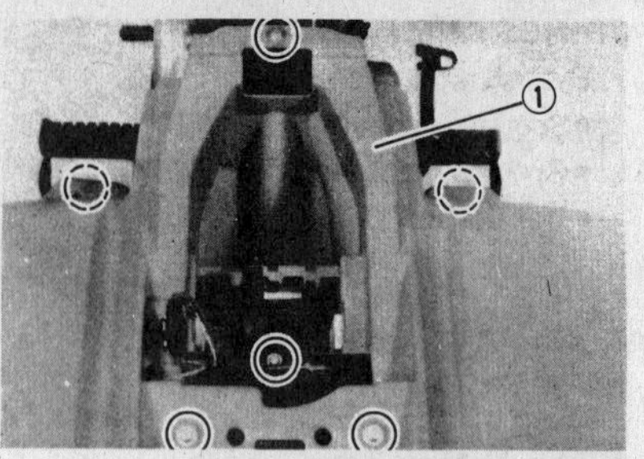

Rear fender fasteners

10. Disconnect the magneto wires just above the electric starter.
11. Disconnect the crankcase vent pipe from the crankcase.
12. Loosen the gearshift lever pinch bolt and pull the lever off the shaft.
13. Remove the three screws securing the left crankcase cover. Remove the cover.
14. Remove the drive shaft rubber boot.
15. Disconnect the starter motor lead at the starter motor.
16. Remove the two starter motor mounting screws and remove it.
17. Remove the engine mounting bolts.
18. Take the engine out to the left side of the chassis.
19. Installation is the reverse of removal. Note the following points:
   a. Torque engine mounting bolts to 17 ft. lbs.
   b. Starter motor screws are to be tightened to 5.1 ft. lbs.
   c. Muffler bracket bolt torque is 18 ft. lbs. Exhaust pipe nuts at the cylinder head are tightened to 7.2 ft. lbs.
   d. When installing the left crankcase cover, be sure that the dowel pins are in place. Use a new gasket. Tighten the screws gradually and evenly.
   e. Tighten carburetor nuts to 5.1 ft. lbs.
   f. Do not forget to add oil before starting the engine.

TUNE-UP SPECIFICATIONS

	80	200
COMPRESSION		
Standard (psi)	171	128
Minimum (psi)	142	114
Maximum (psi)	185	142
VALVE CLEARANCE		
Intake (mm/in.)	0.05-0.10/0.002-0.004	0.05-0.09/0.002-0.004
Exhaust (mm/in.)	0.08-0.13/0.003-0.005	0.11-0.15/0.004-0.006
SPARK PLUGS		
OEM	NGK/ND	NGK/ND
Type (NGK/ND)	C-7HSA/U22FS-U	D-7EA/X22ES-U
Gap (mm/in.)	0.6-0.7/0.024-0.028	0.6-0.7/0.024-0.028
Torque (ft lbs)	9	14
CARBURETOR		
Fuel level (mm/in.)	3.5/0.14	3.0/0.12
Float height (mm/in.)	21.0/0.83	21.5/0.85
Pilot screw setting (turns out)	2 ± ½	1½ ± ½
Idle speed (rpm)	1,800	1,400 + 50

Top End

Cylinder head, cylinder and piston can be removed with the engine in the frame.

CYLINDER HEAD

Removal

1. Remove the seat, battery and rear fender.
2. Remove the exhaust system by removing the muffler bracket bolts and the exhaust pipe nuts at the cylinder head.
3. Remove the carburetor. See "Fuel System" for procedures.
4. Remove the carburetor manifold from the cylinder head.
5. Disconnect the spark plug lead and remove the spark plug.
6. Remove the gearshift lever by loosening the pinch bolt and pulling the lever off the shaft.
7. Remove the three screws which secure the left crankcase cover. Remove the cover.
8. Remove the intake and exhaust valve adjuster covers.
9. Remove the cam sprocket cover (2 screws).

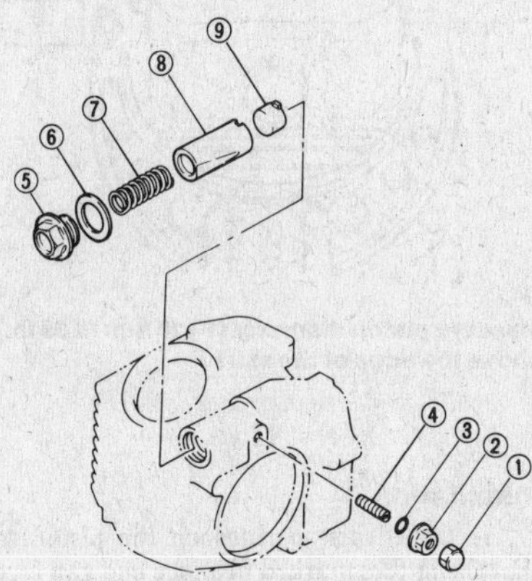

1. Crown nut
2. Locknut
3. O-ring
4. Adjusting screw
5. Tensioner end plug
6. Gasket
7. Compression spring
8. Tensioner rod
9. Straight plug

Cam chain tensioner components

10. Remove the cam chain tensioner crown nut. Loosen the locknut. Unscrew and remove the chain tensioner adjusting screw with O-ring and locknut.
11. Remove the tensioner end plug from the cylinder head. Remove the gasket, spring, tensioner rod and straight plug.
12. Secure the flywheel with a rotor holder or similar method.
13. Remove the cam sprocket bolt.
14. Remove the sprocket from the cam.
15. Disengage the sprocket from the chain.
16. Remove the four cylinder head nuts. Remove the two screws on the left side of the head.
17. Remove the cylinder head.
18. Remove the head gasket.
19. Note the location of the dowel pins on the left side cylinder head studs.

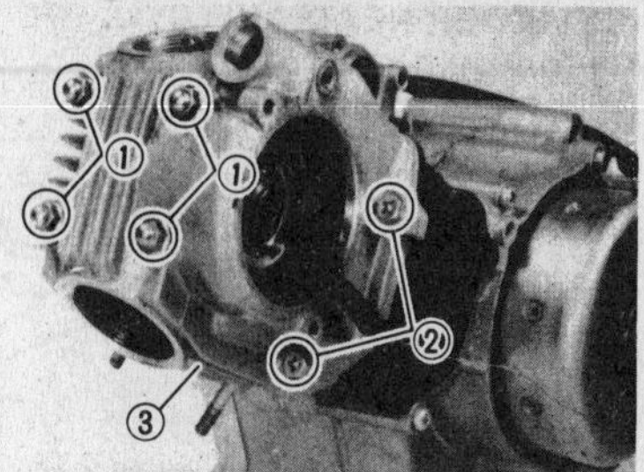

Cylinder head nuts (1) and screws (2)

Disassembly

1. Back off the valve adjusters.
2. Thread a slide hammer or a suitable bolt into each rocker arm shaft and pull them out to the left.
3. Mark each rocker arm and shaft "IN" or "EX" and do not mix shafts and their arms.
4. Thread a slide hammer or a suitable bolt into the camshaft and pull it out to the left side.
5. Use a spring compressor to remove the intake and exhaust valve assemblies.

Inspection

NOTE: *Refer to "General Information" for a guide to engine component inspection procedures. Engine specifications for these machines are summarized in a chart at the end of this section.*

1. Use machinist's dye to check the width and position of the valve seat on the valve. The valve seat should be about 1.0mm (0.04 in.) wide all around the valve and centered on the valve face. Maximum acceptable seat width is 1.5mm (0.06 in.).
   a. If the valve seat is uniform in width around the valve, but too wide, use a 30° or 60° seat cutter to reduce the width. Use the cutter lightly.
   b. If the seat is in the middle of the face, but too narrow, use a 45° cutter to increase the width.
   c. If the valve seat is too narrow and too high, first use a 30° cutter, then a 45° cutter.
   d. If the seat is too narrow and too low on the face, use a 60° cutter first, then a 45° cutter.
   e. After cutting valve seats, lap valves into their seats.
2. Check valve condition. Check for runout, pitted or burnt edges, bluish discoloration and other obvious signs of damage. Replace if any imperfections are evident.
3. Measure the valve stem diameter at three places along its length. Measure the inside diameter of each valve guide and compare the readings with the valve stem diameters to calculate valve-to-guide clearance. Compare the measured value with the specification.

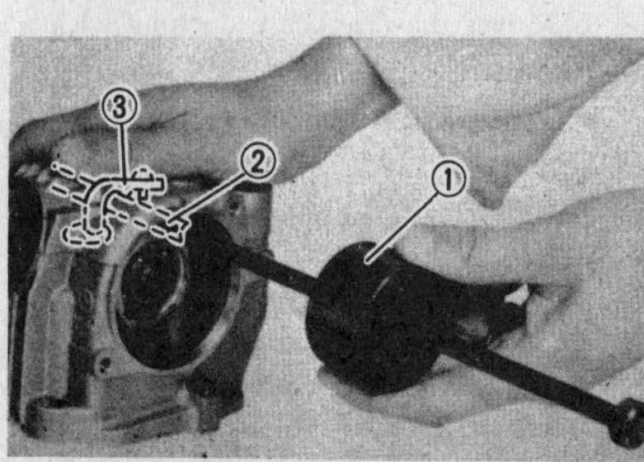

Removing a rocker arm shaft

4. Check each rocker arm shaft for scoring, wear or bluish discoloration. Check each rocker arm bore for similar signs of damage. Measure inside and outside diameters of bores and shafts and compare them to the specifications.
5. Measure the free length of each valve spring and compare the measurement against the specification given.
6. Check the cam lobes for pitting, scoring, discoloration or other obvious signs of wear. Measure the height of each cam lobe as well as the base circle diameters and compare the readings to the standard specifications.
7. Slowly rotate the cam bearings and check for noise, roughness and other indications of damage.
8. Check cam sprocket condition. Replace the sprocket and the chain if the teeth show any signs of unusual wear.

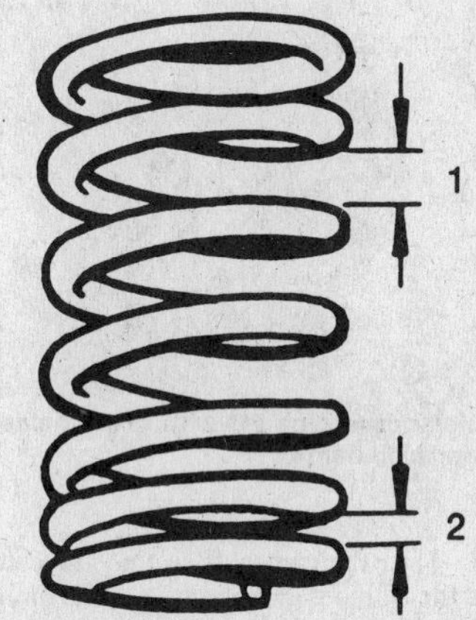

Install valve springs with the close coils (2) against the head

Assembly

1. Lightly oil all parts before assembly.
2. Be sure that all parts are installed in their original locations.
3. Oil valves before inserting them in the guides. Install new valve seals.

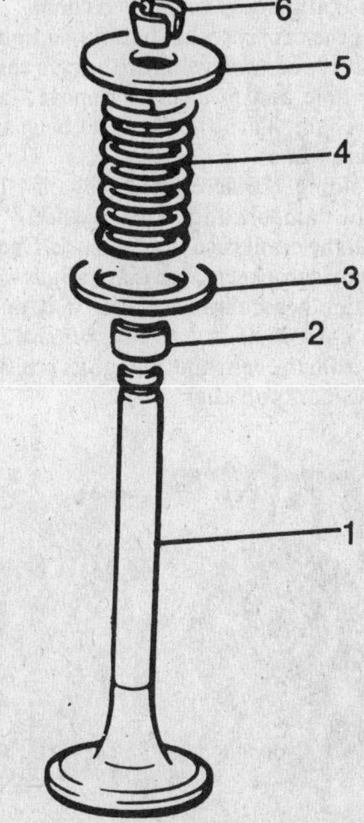

Valve (1), spring seat (2), oil seal (3), spring (4), spring seat (5) and keepers (6)

4. When installing valve springs, note that they are progressively wound. The close pitch coils go against the head.

5. After valves are installed, rap the stem once with a plastic mallet to seat the keepers.

Installation

1. Check that the dowel pins are in place on the left side cylinder head studs.

2. Use a new cylinder head gasket.

3. Pull the cam chain out and make sure it is properly engaged with the crankshaft sprocket.

4. Install the head, pulling the cam chain through.

5. Install the cylinder head nuts and the two screws on the left side. Tighten the fasteners gradually and in a cross pattern until the required torque is reached. Torque is 7.2 ft. lbs.

Cylinder dowel pins (1) with chain guides (2,3) and cylinder (4)

6. Turn the camshaft so that the notch faces the cylinder and aligns with the timing mark on the cylinder head.

7. Turn the flywheel so that the "T" mark aligns with the crankcase timing pointer.

8. Pull the cam chain taut. Install the sprocket onto the chain and then onto the camshaft engaging sprocket pawl with cam groove so that the sprocket match mark aligns with the timing mark on the cylinder head. Neither the camshaft nor the flywheel must move out of alignment when this is done.

9. Fit the cam sprocket bolt finger tight.

10. Insert a screwdriver into the cam chain tensioner hole and push in to remove slack from the chain. Turn the flywheel back and forth several times.

11. Holding the screwdriver against the cam chain damper, align the flywheel "T" mark with the crankcase timing mark. Check that the cam sprocket match mark aligns with the cylinder head timing mark. If it does, timing is correct. If it does not, remove the sprocket from the cam and change its position until these marks all align.

Align the cam notch (1) with the timing mark (2). The cam notch must face the cylinder

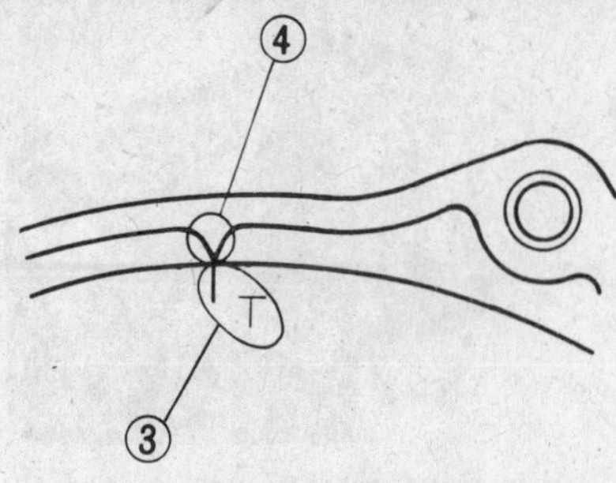

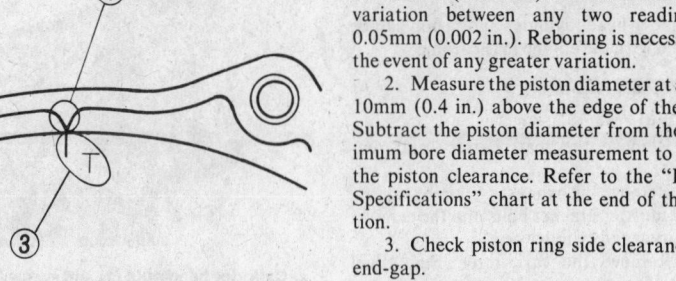

Align the flywheel "T" mark (3) with the crankcase timing pointer (4)

12. When alignment is correct, tighten the sprocket bolt to 14 ft. lbs.

13. Install the cam chain tensioner. Note that the flat surface on the tensioner rod should face the adjusting screw hole.

14. Tighten the chain tensioner end plug to 11 ft. lbs.

15. Adjust cam chain tension as outlined in "Tune-Up."

16. Adjust valve clearance. See "Tune-Up."

17. The cam sprocket cover screws are tightened to 7.2 ft. lbs.

18. Tighten valve adjuster covers to 5.1 ft. lbs.

19. Tighten the spark plug to 9.1 ft. lbs.

20. Tighten the carburetor manifold bolts to 5.1 ft. lbs.

21. The remainder of the procedure is the reverse of disassembly. See the "Engine Torque Specifications" chart for tightness of critical fasteners.

Align cam sprocket match mark (7) with cylinder head timing mark (8)

CYLINDER AND PISTON

Removal

1. Remove the cylinder head.
2. Remove the cam chain dampers.
3. Pull off the cylinder.
4. Check the dowel pins between the cylinder and crankcase.
5. Remove the cylinder base gasket.
6. Cover the crankcase opening with a clean rag so that the piston wrist pin circlips will not fall in.
7. Remove the wrist pin circlips.
8. Push out the wrist pin. It may be helpful to heat the piston crown gently to facilitate removal.
9. Remove the piston.

Inspection

1. Measure the diameter of the cylinder bore at three places front-to-rear and side-to-side. Compare the readings with each other and with the maximum bore diameter of 47.1mm (1.854 in.). Maximum allowable variation between any two readings is 0.05mm (0.002 in.). Reboring is necessary in the event of any greater variation.

2. Measure the piston diameter at a point 10mm (0.4 in.) above the edge of the skirt. Subtract the piston diameter from the maximum bore diameter measurement to obtain the piston clearance. Refer to the "Engine Specifications" chart at the end of this section.

3. Check piston ring side clearance and end-gap.

4. Check the wrist pin for wear. Check wrist pin clearance in both the piston and the rod small end.

5. Check all components for visible signs of wear, such as scuffing on the piston skirt which would indicate a seizure in the past.

6. If reboring is necessary, set piston-to-cylinder clearance to 0.025-0.045mm (0.0010-0.0018 in.).

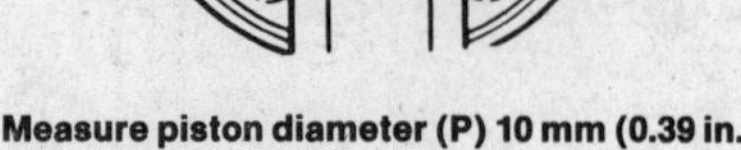
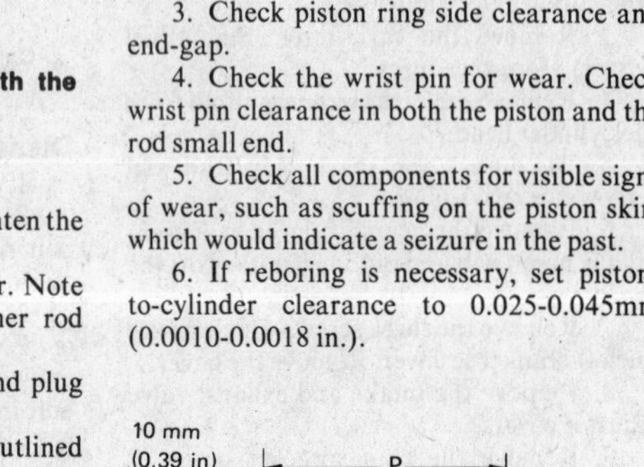

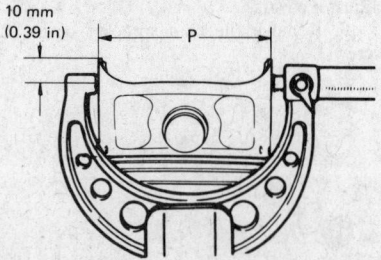

Measure piston diameter (P) 10 mm (0.39 in.) above the edge of the skirt

Installation

1. Install piston rings on the piston so that the letters marked near the end gap face up.

NOTE: *Compression rings are not interchangeable. The upper compression ring has a plain profile; the lower (second) compression ring is wedge-shaped.*

2. Install the piston on the rod so that the arrow on the crown points towards the exhaust port.

3. Press in the wrist pin. The piston crown may be heated, as on removal, to make insertion easier.

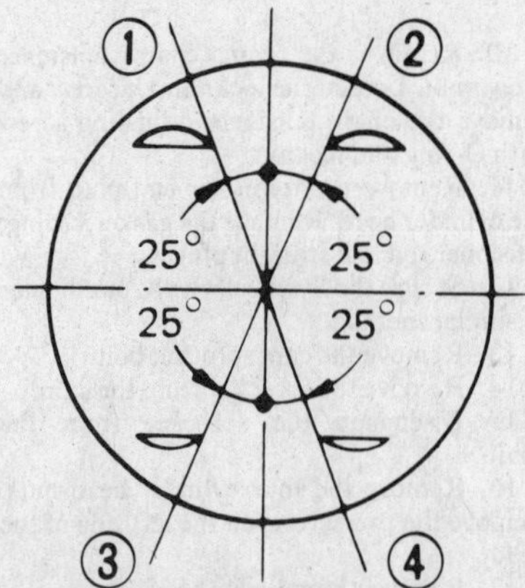

Stagger ring end-gaps around the piston: 1, top ring; 2, lower oil ring rail; 3, upper oil ring rail; 4, second ring

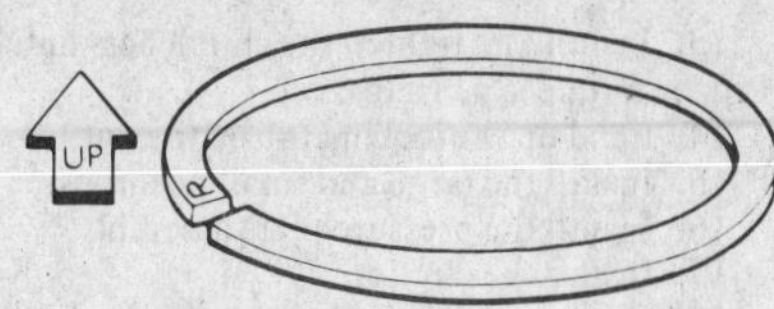

Install piston rings with the manufacturer's mark up

Crankcase dowel pins (1) and cylinder base gasket (2)

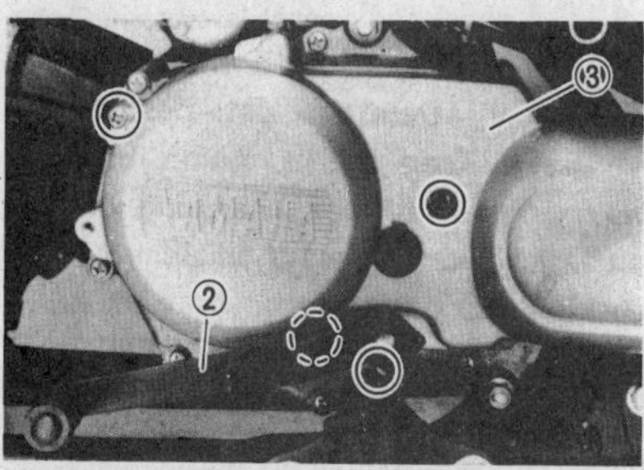

Gearshift lever (2) and left crankcase cover screws

Magneto base plate (1), screw locations and neutral switch (200)

Right crankcase cover screws

4. Use new wrist pin circlips. Be sure they are properly seated in their grooves.

5. Stagger the piston ring end gaps around the piston as shown in the illustration.

6. Check that the crankcase dowel pins are in place.

7. Fit a new cylinder base gasket.

8. Slip the cylinder onto the studs. Carefully compress the rings with your fingers and slide the cylinder over them.

9. Seat the cylinder.

10. Install the dowel pins on the left side cylinder head studs.

Crankcase Cover Components

CDI MAGNETO

Removal

1. Remove the gearshift lever from its shaft.

2. Remove the three screws which hold the left crankcase cover. Remove the cover.

3. Hold the magneto rotor with a suitable tool and remove the rotor nut.

4. Use the rotor puller to remove the rotor. Remove the woodruff key from its slot in the crankshaft.

5. Remove the two screws which secure the magneto base plate.

6. Remove the base plate.

7. Note the O-rings which are installed in the mounting screw holes. Be sure that they are in place when assembling.

Installation

1. Check that the base plate mounting screw O-rings are in place.

2. Install the base plate.

3. Install the screws. Tighten to 5.1 ft. lbs.

4. Fit the rotor woodruff key carefully into its slot in the crankshaft. Be sure it is fully seated or it may be dislocated when the rotor is installed.

5. Lightly oil the crankshaft taper.

6. Line up the rotor key slot with the key and push the rotor into place.

7. Install the rotor nut. Hold the rotor with a suitable tool and tighten the nut to 29 ft. lbs.

CLUTCH

Removal

1. Drain the crankcase oil.

2. Place a drip pan beneath the right crankcase cover to catch any oil which will come out when the crankcase cover is removed.

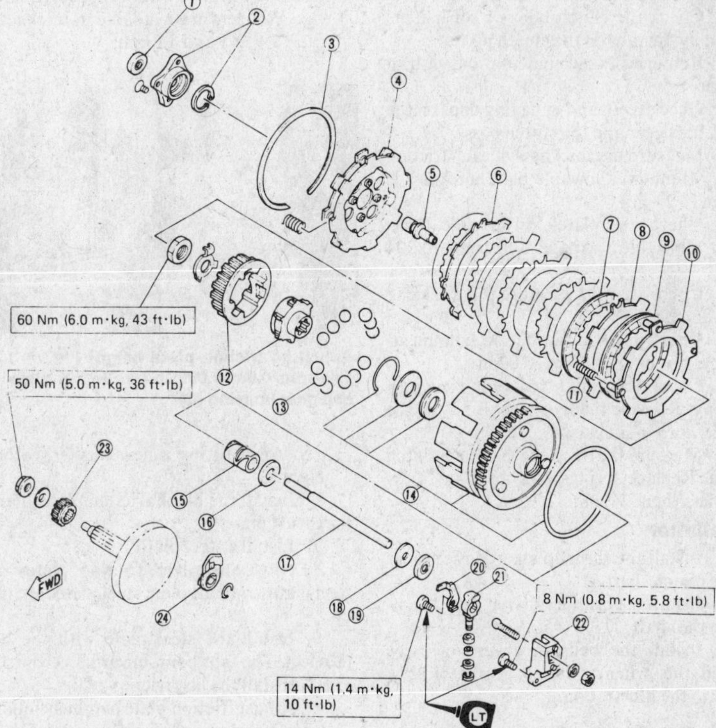

1. Oil seal
2. Push plate assembly
3. Circlip
4. Pressure plate assembly
5. Pushrod (short)
6. Clutch plate (bent tabs)
7. Friction plate (silver)
8. Steel plate
9. Friction plate (black)
10. Thrust plate
11. Spring
12. Clutch boss
13. Clutch balls
14. Primary driven gear assembly
15. Spacer
16. Thrust washer
17. Pushrod (long)
18. Bushing
19. Oil seal
20. Boss spring
21. Push lever
22. Push rod guide
23. Primary drive gear
24. Push lever #2

Clutch assembly

3. Remove the nine crankcase cover screws.
4. Carefully pull off the cover, noting the dowel pins between the cover and crankcase.

NOTE: *If the case will not come off readily, tap carefully around the edges with a plastic mallet to break it loose.*

5. Remove the gasket. A new one must be used when assembling.
6. Remove the clutch circlip.
7. Remove the pressure plate assembly.
8. Remove the short and long pushrods.
9. Remove the friction and steel plates from the clutch hub.
10. Bend down the locking tab on the clutch boss nut.
11. Holding the clutch either with the special tool or by engaging the transmission, remove the boss nut.
12. Carefully remove the clutch boss assembly. Separate the boss from the primary driven gear assembly. Note the clutch balls.
13. Remove the spacer and thrust plate from the shaft.

Inspection

1. Check all parts for evidence of unusual wear.

NOTE: *Refer to the "General Information" section for detailed engine component inspection procedures.*

2. Check the primary driven gear teeth for wear or damage. Check for pitting.
3. Check the clutch housing for indents caused by the tabs on the clutch plates.
4. Remove any such indentations with an oilstone.
5. Check teeth and engaging dogs on the clutch boss gear and the clutch boss.
6. Measure the thickness of each friction plate. Minimum allowable plate thickness is 2.9mm (0.11 in.).
7. Check steel plates for warpage. Maximum allowable warpage is 0.1mm (0.004 in.).
8. Check that the pressure plate bearing is not damaged.
9. Check pushrod run-out. Maximum allowable run-out is 0.5mm (0.02 in.).
10. Check the clutch balls for pitting or scuffing. Replace them as a set if any of the balls is worn in such a way.
11. Measure the free-length of each clutch spring. Replace springs as a set if any measures less than 29.1mm (1.15 in.).

Installation

1. Install the thrust plate and the spacer on the clutch shaft.
2. Install the primary driven gear assembly on the shaft.
3. Install the balls in groups of three around the primary driven gear assembly. Refer to the illustration.

Adjusting clutch boss height ("a" = 0.2-0.4 mm/0.008-0.016 in.) with thrust plate (1) and clutch boss (2)

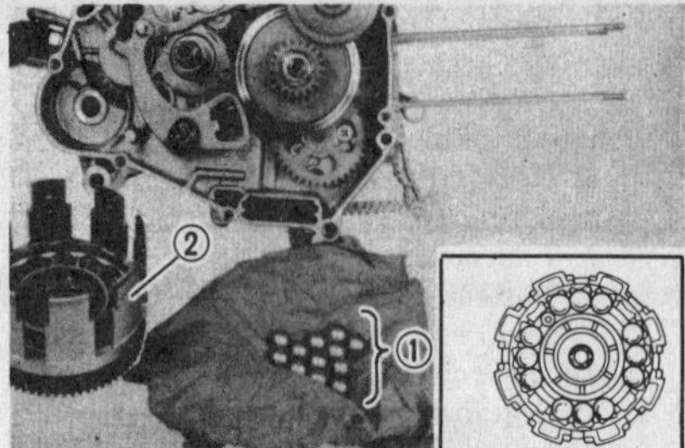

Clutch ball installation (1) on primary driven gear assembly (2)

4. Install the thrust plate followed by the clutch boss assembly.
5. Adjust clutch boss height as follows:
   a. Push down on the thrust plate.
   b. Measure the distance between the thrust plate and the clutch boss.
   c. It should be 0.2-0.4mm (0.009-0.016 in.).
   d. If the measured distance is not within specification, remove the boss and the primary driven gear assembly.
   e. Remove the circlip, adjusting washer and bearing from the primary driven gear assembly.
   f. Replace the adjusting washer with another of a thickness which will bring the measured distance within specification.
   g. Washers are available in thicknesses of 1.7, 1.9, 2.1 and 2.3mm.

Adjusting friction plate height ("a" = 1.30-1.65 mm/0.051-0.065 in.) with top plate (1) and gear housing (2)

   h. After fitting a new washer, recheck height.
6. Install the black friction plate against the thrust plate.
7. Install a steel plate.
8. Alternate silver friction plates and steel plates until all plain steel plates are used up.
9. Install the steel plate with the bent tabs last. The tabs point inward.
10. Install the last friction plate.
11. Adjust friction plate height as follows:
   a. Push down on the plate assembly.
   b. Measure the distance between the step on the driven gear housing and the top plate.
   c. It should be 1.30-1.65mm (0.051-0.065 in.).
   d. If the distance is not within specification, remove the clutch assembly.
   e. Steel plates are available in three thicknesses. Choose one which will give the proper clearance. Thicknesses are 1.2, 1.4 and 1.6mm.
   f. Install the new steel plates and repeat the check.
12. Remove the clutch plates.
13. Install and tighten the clutch boss nut. Proper torque is 43 ft. lbs.
14. Bend up the locking tab on the nut.
15. Install the large and small pushrods.
16. Install the pressure plate assembly.
17. Install the circlip.
18. Be sure the dowel pins are in place between the crankcase cover and the crankcase.
19. Use a new gasket.
20. Tighten the screws in a cross pattern to 5.1 ft. lbs.
21. Refill the crankcase with oil.

GEARSHIFT SHAFT

Removal

1. Remove the right side crankcase cover.
2. Remove the clutch assembly.
3. Remove the gearshift lever.
4. Remove the left side crankcase cover.
5. Remove the gearshift shaft circlip.
6. Remove the push lever.
7. Remove the pin.
8. Remove the plain washers.
9. Remove the thrust bearing.
10. Disengage the fingers of the gearshift shaft from the shift drum and pull the shaft assembly out.
11. Unhook the stopper lever spring from the stopper lever.
12. Unbolt and remove the stopper lever.

Inspection

1. Check shift fingers for wear or for a bent condition.
2. Check the stopper lever spring and the pawl spring for weakness or obvious damage.
3. Check the pins of the shift drum for condition.

Installation

1. When installing the stopper lever, ensure that the spring is engaged with the boss in the crankcase.
2. Use a non-permanent thread-locking compound on the threads of the stopper lever bolt. Torque it to 10 ft. lbs.
3. When installing the gearshift shaft assembly, be sure to engage the fingers with the pins on the shift drum.

Stopper lever spring (1) must engage the crankcase boss. The lever bolt must be secured with non-permanent thread-locking compound

4. Be sure that the pawl spring is properly seated on its pin on the crankcase and positioned to tension the assembly.
5. On the left side, install:
   a. Thrust bearing
   b. Plain washers
   c. Pin
   d. Push lever
   e. Gearshift shaft circlip.

Circlip (1), push lever #2 (2), pin (3), washers (4), thrust bearing (5)

DRIVE AND STARTER GEARS

Removal

1. Remove the clutch. Remove the left crankcase cover.
2. Use the special rotor holder or a similar device to lock the magneto rotor in place.
3. Remove the primary drive gear nut.
4. Remove the spring washer.
5. Remove the primary drive gear.
6. Remove the starter clutch assembly.
7. Remove the spacer and idler gear.
8. Remove the starter wheel assembly.

Spring washer (1), primary drive gear (2), starter clutch (3), spacer (4), idle gear (5) and starter wheel assembly (6)

Inspection

1. Inspect all parts for wear or damage.
2. Check condition of gear teeth.
3. Check for bluish discoloration caused by overheating.

Installation

1. Fit components in this order:
   a. Starter wheel assembly
   b. Idler gear
   c. Spacer
   d. Starter clutch assembly
   e. Primary drive gear
   f. Spring washer
   g. Nut
2. Tighten the nut to 36 ft. lbs.

OIL PUMP

Removal

1. Remove the clutch assembly.
2. Remove the drive and starter gear assembly.
3. Remove the oil pump driven gear circlip.
4. Remove the driven gear from the pump and the drive gear from the crankshaft.
5. Remove the two screws which secure the oil pump and remove the pump from the crankcase.

Inspection

1. Check drive and driven gears for any wear or damage to the teeth. Replace both if any irregularities are noted on either.
2. Check the clearance between the pump outer rotor and the pump housing. If it exceeds 0.10mm (0.0039 in.), replace the oil pump.
3. Check the clearance between the inner rotor and the outer rotor. If it exceeds 0.20mm (0.0079 in.), replace the oil pump.

Installation

1. Thoroughly clean pump components in clean motor oil.

Circlip (1), oil pump driven gear (2) and drive gear (3)

2. Thoroughly clean the oil pump mounting area on the crankcase.
3. With an oil can, pump the crankcase oil passages full of clean motor oil.
4. Oil all pump components before installation.
5. Be sure the mating surface is perfectly clean.
6. Use a new gasket.
7. Fit the pump. Tighten the screws to 5.1 ft. lbs.
8. Fit the drive gear. Fit the driven gear and secure it with the circlip.

Lower End And Transmission

NOTE: *To service these components, the engine must be removed from the chassis.*

SPLITTING THE CRANKCASES

1. Refer to the preceding sections for detailed instructions.
2. Remove the engine from the frame.
3. Remove the cylinder head, cylinder and piston.
4. Remove the left crankcase cover.
5. Remove the magneto rotor and the basplate with components.
6. Remove the gearshift shaft parts on the left side.
7. Remove the clutch.
8. Remove the gearshift shaft.

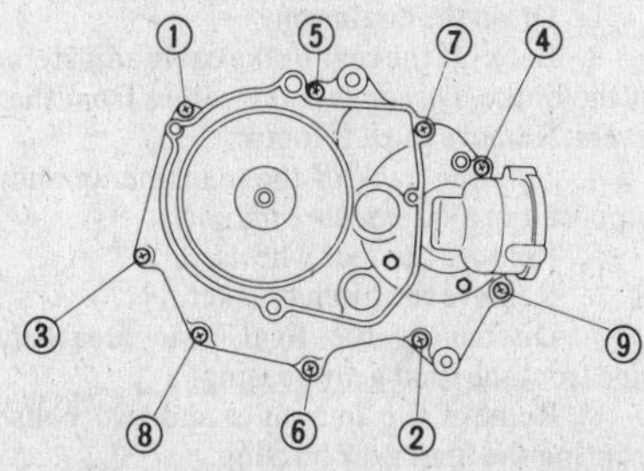

Crankcase screw loosening and tightening sequence

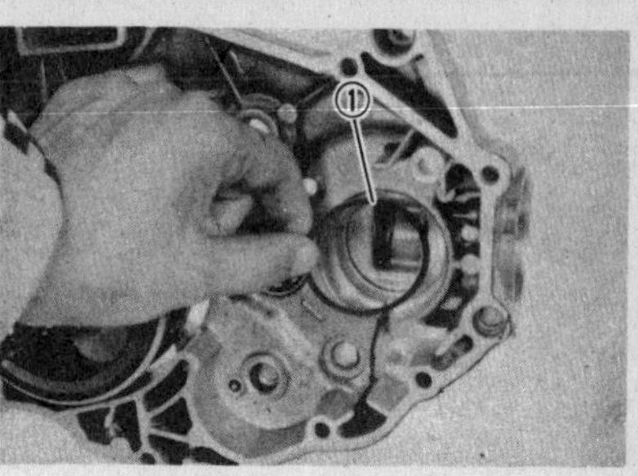

Middle drive gear shim

9. Remove the primary drive and starter gear assembly.
10. Remove the oil pump gears.
11. Remove the oil pump.
12. Remove the oil strainer.
13. Remove the middle gear housing bolts. Remove the components, noting any shims. These are critical and all of them must be put back when assembling.
14. Remove the shift drum stopper plate (two screws).
15. Remove the nine crankcase screws. Screws should be loosened in a cross pattern before removal.
16. Separate the crankcase by prying them apart with a screwdriver applied to the two pry slots. While this is being done, tap the end of the crankshaft and transmission shaft with a plastic mallet. Do not use force. Do not get the crankcase halves cocked. Do not pry at the mating surfaces, or strike a mating surface with the mallet.
17. Remove the shift drum.
18. Remove the shift fork shaft. Take out the shift forks.
19. Remove the gear clusters.
20. Remove the middle drive gear shim.
21. Tap the crankshaft lightly to remove it from the case.

CRANKSHAFT

1. Measure the width of the assembly between the outer faces of the two flywheels. If it is not 40.20-40.25mm (1.583-1.585 in.), replace the crankshaft.
2. Check clearance between the connecting rod big end and the flywheel. It must not exceed 0.5mm (0.02 in.).
3. Crankshaft run-out, when measured at either end of the shaft, must not exceed 0.05mm (0.002 in.).
4. Connecting rod small end play must not exceed 2.0mm (0.08 in.).
5. Check bearing condition. Replace bearings if they show any heat damage, signs of wear, or rough rotation.

TRANSMISSION

1. Check the gears for heat damage.
2. Check for wear or pitting of the gear teeth.
3. Check that the shift fork shaft is not bent.
4. Check shift drum grooves for wear.
5. Check shift fork fingers for a bent condition, chipping or other signs of damage.
6. Check the pin on the shift forks which engages the shift drum for condition.
7. Check transmission shaft run-out. If it exceeds, 0.08mm (0.0031 in.), replace the shaft.
8. Check shaft bearings for heat damage, rough rotation, noise, pitted or crushed balls.

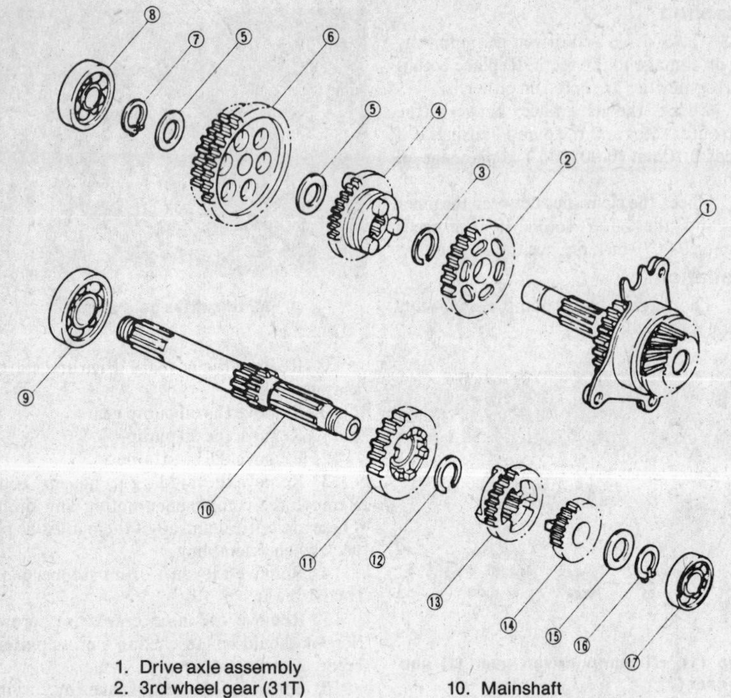

Transmission assembly

ASSEMBLING THE CRANKCASES

1. Clean all parts thoroughly before assembly.
2. Lubricate all bearings with clean motor oil.
3. Install the crankshaft into the left crankcase half. Hold the connecting rod and tap the end of the crankshaft with a plastic mallet to seat it.
4. Install the middle drive gear shim.
5. Install the gear clusters.
6. Install the shift drum.
7. Install the shift forks and their shaft. Be sure that the number "29" embossed on the one fork faces the shaft O-ring end, while the number "29F" on the other fork faces away from the O-ring end of the shaft.
8. Be sure that the two dowel pins are in place on the crankcase mating surface.
9. Apply a liquid gasket compound to the mating surface and mate the case halves.

Shift fork shaft o-ring (1) and fork (2,3) installations

10. Tap the cases together to ensure that they are fully mated. Do not attempt to force them together.
11. After the cases are mated, check that the crankshaft rotates freely and that the transmission shafts are free to turn.
12. Install the crankcase screws and bolts. Tighten them in a cross pattern (see illustration) until the proper torque is reached:
    Crankcase screws: 5.1 ft. lbs.
    Crankcase bolts: 7.2 ft. lbs.
13. Install the shift drum stopper.
14. The remainder of the assembly procedure is the reverse of disassembly.

YFM 200

Engine Removal/Installation

NOTE: *Top end components can be removed with the engine in the frame.*

1. Clean the engine thoroughly before removal.
2. Drain the engine oil.
3. Back off the rear brake cable adjusters at the brake. Disconnect the cables from the levers. Remove the left footrest.
4. Jack the back of the machine up and support it in a safe, secure manner.
5. Remove the rear wheels.
6. Remove the hitch bracket.
7. Disconnect the final gear breather pipe from the final gear housing.
8. Remove the four nuts and two bolts securing the final gear housing.
9. Remove the rear wheel housing mounting bolts.

Final gear housing mounting hardware

10. Remove the rear wheel assembly.
11. Disconnect the battery leads. Remove the battery.
12. Remove the front and rear carriers.
13. Remove the front panel.
14. Remove the fuel tank cover.
15. Turn off the petcock. Disconnect the fuel line at the petcock. Detach the retaining band and remove the fuel tank.
16. Remove the front fender.
17. Remove the exhaust pipe bolts at the cylinder head. Remove the two muffler bracket bolts. Remove the exhaust system.
18. Remove the carburetor. Refer to "Fuel System" for procedures.
19. Disconnect the spark plug lead from the plug.
20. Disconnect the CDI leads at the connector on the frame. Arrange the leads so that they will not become entangled when the engine is taken out.
21. Disconnect the crankcase ventilation hose from the crankcase.
22. Disconnect the high tension lead from the starter motor.
23. Remove the starter motor bracket.
24. Remove the starter motor.
25. Remove the upper and lower mounting bolts at the rear of the engine.
26. Remove the mounting bracket bolts at the cylinder head.
27. Remove the mounting bracket bolts in the front of the engine.
28. Remove the engine from the left side of the frame.

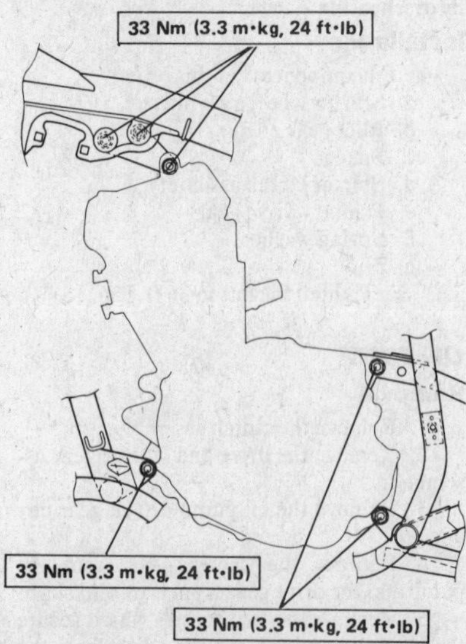

Engine mounting bolt locations and torques

Cam chain tensioner (1) and locknut (2)

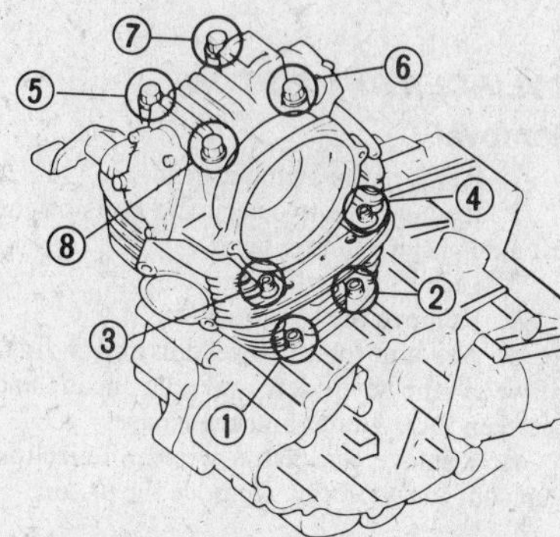
Cylinder head bolt loosening and tightening sequence. 1 and 2 are cylinder screws

Cylinder head dowel pins (1), o-ring (2) and chain guide (3)

Cam bearing retainer bolts (1) and retainer (2)

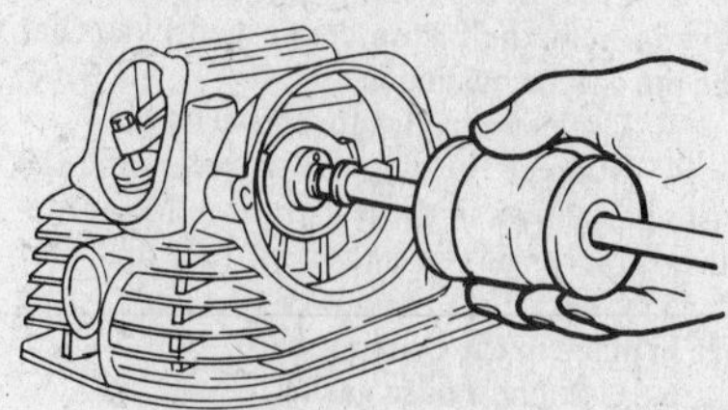
Removing the camshaft

29. To install the engine, reverse the removal procedure with reference to the following points.

30. Fit the engine into the frame from the left side.

31. Install the upper and lower mounting bolts at the rear of the engine. Do not tighten them at this point.

32. Install the engine mounting brackets and bolts at the front of the engine.

33. Install the brackets and bolts at the cylinder head.

NOTE: *All engine mounting bolts should be inserted from the right side.*

34. Install the coupling gear joint to the driveshaft.

35. Install the rear wheel assembly.

36. Install the final gear housing nuts and bolts and the rear wheel hub fasteners. Do not tighten the fasteners at this point.

37. Tighten all the final gear housing mounting hardware gradually and evenly and them torque them to the proper values:

Nuts: 17 ft. lbs.
Bolts: 32 ft. lbs.

38. Tighten all of the engine mounting bolts. All of them should be torqued to 24 ft. lbs.

39. Tighten the rear wheel hub bolts to 36 ft. lbs.

40. Install the hitch bracket and tighten the bolts as follows:

Upper (8mm): 11 ft. lbs.
Lower (10mm): 22 ft. lbs.

41. Grease the starter motor O-ring before installing the unit. Note that the terminal should face downwards.

42. The remainder of the procedure is the reverse of disassembly. Note the following torque values:

Carburetor manifold at cylinder head: 8.7 ft. lbs.
Carburetor-to-manifold: 5.8 ft. lbs.
Exhaust pipe at head: 7.2 ft. lbs.
Muffler bracket: 19 ft. lbs.
Footrest: 58 ft. lbs.
Rear wheel panel: 32 ft. lbs.

43. Do not forget to add oil before starting the engine.

Top End

Cylinder head, cylinder and piston can be removed with the engine in the frame.

CYLINDER HEAD

Removal

1. Disconnect the spark plug lead and remove the plug.
2. Remove the seat.
3. Remove the rear fender.
4. Remove the front panel.
5. Remove the fuel tank cover.
6. Remove the fuel tank.
7. Remove the carburetor.
8. Remove the exhaust system by taking off the two screws at the cylinder head and the two bolts at the muffler bracket.
9. Remove the cylinder head brackets.
10. Remove the cam chain tensioner cap.
11. Loosen the tensioner locknut.
12. Unscrew and remove the tensioner assembly. Note the locations of all parts.
13. Remove the cam sprocket cover screws.
14. Remove the cam sprocket cover.
15. Remove the forward/reverse change pedal assembly.
16. Remove the recoil starter assembly.
17. Remove the cam sprocket bolt. The crankshaft will have to be held with a special tool to do this in most cases. Secure the crank with a holder on the rotor.
18. Disengage the cam sprocket from the cam chain and remove it. Secure the chain so that it does not fall into the crankcase.
19. Take the pin out of the camshaft.
20. Gradually loosen the cylinder head bolts. When all are loose, remove them.
21. Remove the cylinder head.

Disassembly

1. Remove the valve covers.
2. Bend down the lock tabs on the cam bearing retainer. Remove the bolts. Remove the retainer.
3. Thread a suitably sized bolt into the rocker arm shafts and pull the shafts out of the head. Mark the rocker arms for position. Do not mix shafts and rocker arms.
4. Thread a 10mm bolt into the camshaft and pull it out.
5. Remove the valve assemblies with a spring compressor.

Inspection

1. Use machinist's dye to check the width and position of the valve seat on the valve. The valve seat should be about 1.0mm (0.04 in.) wide all around the valve and centered on the valve face. Maximum acceptable seat width is 1.5mm (0.06 in.).

a. If the valve seat is uniform in width around the valve, but too wide, use a 30° or 60° seat cutter to reduce the width. Use the cutter lightly.

b. If the seat is in the middle of the face, but too narrow, use a 45° cutter to increase the width.

c. If the valve seat is too narrow and too high, first use a 30° cutter, then a 45° cutter.

d. If the seat is too narrow and too low on the face, use a 60° cutter first, then a 45° cutter.

e. After cutting valve seats, lap valves into their seats.

2. Check valve condition. Check for run-out, pitted or burnt edges, bluish discoloration and other obvious signs of damage. Replace if any imperfection are noted.

3. Measure the valve stem diameter at three places along its length. Measure the inside diameter of each valve guide and compare the readings with the valve stem diameters to calculate valve-to-guide clearance. Compare the measured value with the specification.

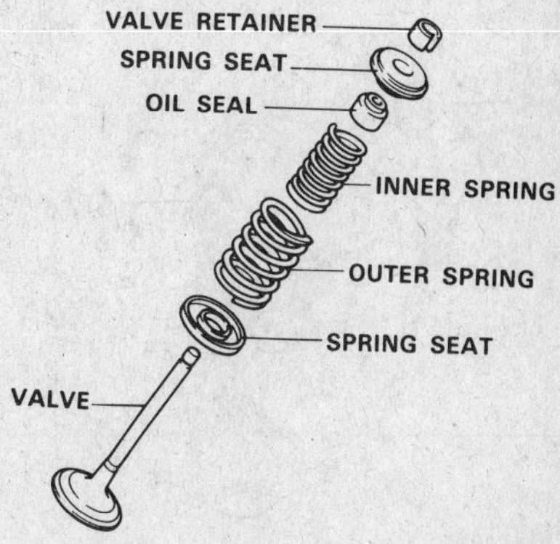

Valve assembly

4. Check each rocker arm shaft for scoring, wear or bluish discoloration. Check each rocker arm bore for similar signs of damage. Measure inside and outside diameters of bores and shafts and compare them to the specifications.

5. Measure the free length of each valve spring and compare the measurement against the specification given.

6. Check the cam lobes for pitting, scoring, discoloration or other obvious signs of wear. Measure the height of each cam lobe as well as the base circle diameters and compare the readings to the standard specifications.

7. Check the cam bushings for scoring or other indications of damage.

8. Check cam sprocket condition. Replace the sprocket and the cam chain if the teeth show any signs of unusual wear.

Assembly

1. Be certain that all parts are reinstalled in their original locations.

2. Valve springs are progressively wound. Install the close coils against the cylinder head.

3. Oil valves before installation. Use new valve seals.

4. After valves are fitted, rap the stem once with a plastic mallet to seat the keepers.

5. Thoroughly lubricate the camshaft and bushings before installation.

6. Install the bearing retainer plate and secure the two bolts (torque: 5.8 ft. lbs.).

7. When installing the rocker arm shafts, note that they must be fitted with the threaded ends facing out. The longer shaft, the one without the O-ring, is the intake shaft. When fitting the intake shaft, position the cut-away on the end so that the cylinder head bolt will clear it when installed.

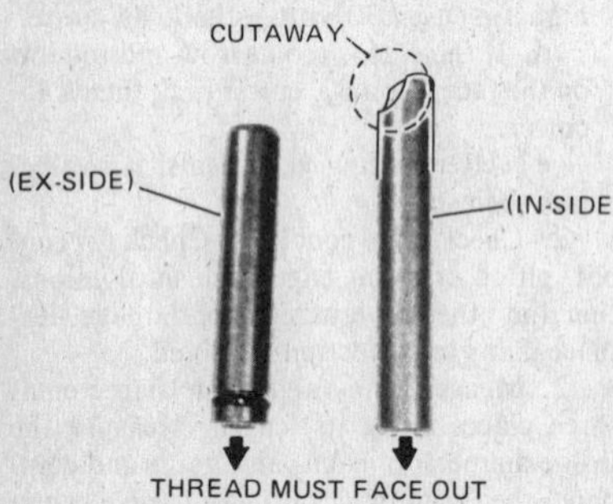

Rocker arm shaft installation notes

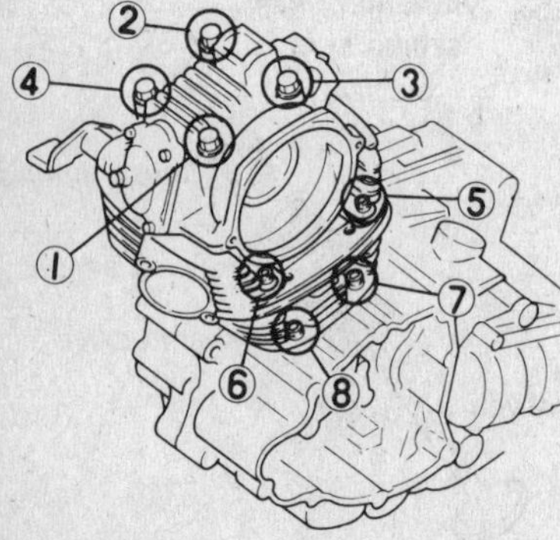

Cylinder head bolt tightening sequence

Position cam pin up and aligned with the cylinder head timing mark

Align the flywheel mark with the crankcase timing mark

Installation

1. Be sure that the three dowel pins and the O-ring are in place on the cylinder mating surface.

2. Fit a new cylinder head gasket.

3. Fit the cylinder head, pulling the cam chain through the head as this is done.

4. Lightly oil the cylinder head bolt copper washers and the bolt seat near the compression release.

5. Install the cylinder head bolts and washers.

6. Proper torque the cylinder head bolts is 16 ft. lbs. for the long ones and 14 ft. lbs. for the short ones.

7. Tighten the bolts gradually and in a cross pattern until the correct torque values are reached.

8. Remove the timing window plug from the left crankcase cover.

9. Align the "T" mark on the flywheel with the mark on the crankcase.

10. Check that the timing pin is installed in the end of the camshaft. Position the pin to align with the cylinder head timing mark.

11. Install the cam sprocket. Pull the sprocket so that the front run of the chain is taut. Slip the sprocket onto the end of the camshaft, engaging the hole with the timing pin.

Align the cam sprocket match mark with the cylinder head timing mark

12. Check that the flywheel "T" mark is still lined up.

13. The line scribed on the sprocket must align with the mark at the very top of the cylinder head.

14. If timing is correct, install the cam bolt and tighten it to 43 ft. lbs.

15. Install the sprocket cover. Note that the fuel line clamp goes towards the rear of the cylinder head, if one is fitted.

16. Install the cam chain adjuster and set it as outlined in "Maintenance."

17. Install the valve covers so that the ridge is towards the top.

18. The remainder of the procedures is straightforward.

CYLINDER AND PISTON

Removal

1. Remove the cylinder head.

2. Remove the two securing bolts on the left side of the cylinder head.

3. Lift off the cylinder.

4. Remove the base gasket.

5. Account for all dowel pins and O-rings between the cylinder and the head and between the cylinder and crankcase.

6. Remove the piston wrist pin circlips. Push out the wrist pin. Remove the piston.

Inspection

1. Measure the diameter of the cylinder bore at three places front-to-rear and side-to-side. Compare the readings with each other and with the specifications at the end of this section. Maximum allowable variation between any two readings is 0.005mm (0.0002 in.). Reboring is necessary in the event of any greater variation.

2. Measure piston diameter 7.5mm (0.3 in.) above the edge of the skirt.

3. Check piston ring side clearance and end-gap.

4. Check for wrist pin fit in both piston and small end.

5. Check all components for visible signs of wear.

6. If reboring is necessary, piston clearance is 0.025-0.045mm (0.0010-0.0018 in.).

7. If fitting new piston rings is required, be sure to exercise appropriate precautions when fitting them. Using a ring expander is recommended as this is the surest way to avoid breaking them when expanding them to fit over the piston.

NOTE: *Be sure to install rings so that the manufacturer's mark near the end gap faces up. Compression rings are not interchangeable. Both have plain profiles, but the second (lower) ring has a more pronounced profile taper.*

Installation

1. Install the piston so that the arrow on the crown points towards the exhaust port.

2. Press in the wrist pin. It may be necessary to heat the piston crown gently so that the pin can be pushed in.

3. Use new circlips for the wrist pin.

4. Stagger the ring end-gaps around the piston as shown in the illustration. Manufacturer's marks on the rings must face up.

5. Check that the dowel pins and O-ring are in place in the cylinder base.

6. Use a new base gasket.

7. Coat piston and rings with oil before the cylinder is installed.

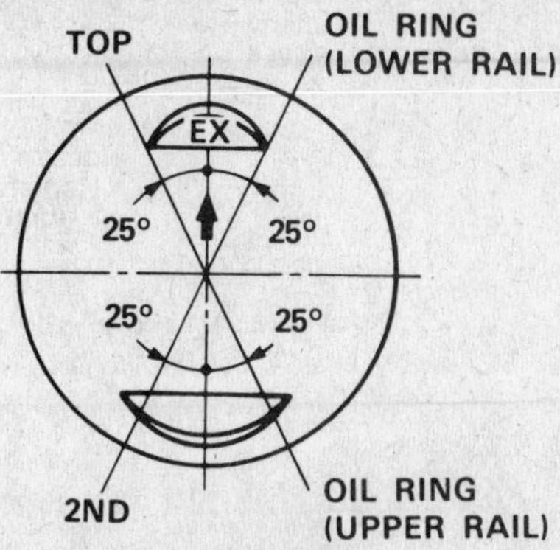

Stagger ring end-gaps around the piston

Cylinder dowel pins (1) and o-ring (2)

8. Compress the rings and install the cylinder.

9. Install the two cylinder bolts. Do not tighten the bolts until the cylinder head bolts are torqued. At that time, tighten them to 14 ft. lbs.

Crankcase Cover Components

RECOIL STARTER

Removal And Disassembly

1. Remove the recoil starter assembly from the crankcase by removing the cover screws.
2. Pull the starter knob out about a foot and hold the sheave drum in place. Fit the rope into the indent in the drum. Allow the drum to wind back gradually.
3. Remove the starter knob cap.
4. Pull out the rope and untie the knot. Remove the knob.

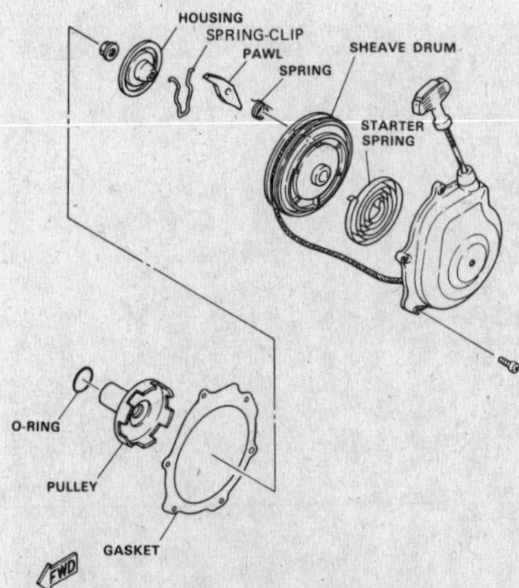

Recoil starter assembly

5. Remove the drive housing securing nut.
6. Remove the housing, drive pawl and and drive pawl spring.
7. Remove the sheave drum from the case.
8. Remove the starter spring.

Inspection

Check all parts for wear and replace as required.

Assembly And Installation

1. Install the starter spring.
2. Wind the spring clockwise to fit inside the retaining posts. Hook the loop on the outer end of the spring onto the spring hook on the case.
3. Grease the spring thoroughly with a waterproof grease.
4. Insert the end of the rope into the sheave drum hole. Knot the end.
5. Wind the rope around the drum as shown in the illustration. When you have about 16 inches of rope left, hook it into the drum detent.
6. Install the sheave drum into the starter case. Be sure the inner hook in the spring engages the cutout in the drum.
7. When first placed in the case, the sheave drum will be resting on the spring. Rotate the drum until it drops slightly, then rotate it clockwise until spring tension is felt.
8. Insert the rope end into the case hole.
9. Install the knob and knot the rope.
10. When installing the drive pawl spring, note that the longer end of the spring is inserted into the hole in the sheave drum.
11. Carefully install the drive pawl onto the spring so that the spring end fits a notch in the drive pawl.
12. Rotate the drive pawl one turn CCW to preload the spring, then push the drive pawl into the cutout in the sheave drum.
13. Install the spring clip onto the drive housing. Tighten the nut to 7.2 ft. lbs.
14. Rotate the drum four turns CW.
15. Check operation. The sheave drum should rotate clockwise and the drive pawl should emerge from the sheave drum when the rope is pulled.

MAGNETO

Removal

1. Remove the recoil starter assembly.
2. Remove the recoil starter pulley bolt. It may be necessary to hold the pulley steady with a special tool to do this.
3. Remove the pulley.
4. Remove the left side crankcase spacer screws.
5. Remove the spacer, noting the dowel pins in the crankcase.
6. Use a puller to remove the magneto flywheel from the crankshaft.
7. Remove the woodruff key.

Installation

1. Installation is the reverse of removal.
2. Use a new crankcase spacer gasket.
3. Tighten the pulley bolt to 36 ft. lbs.

CLUTCHES

Removal

1. Drain the engine oil.
2. Remove the oil filter cover bolts.
3. Remove the filter cover, filter and O-rings..

Spring installation

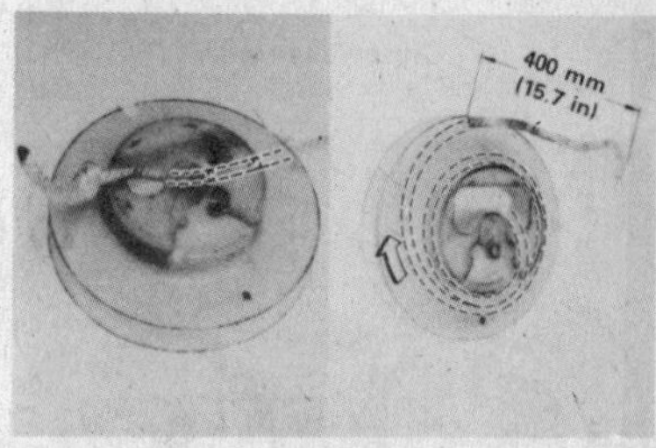

Rope installation

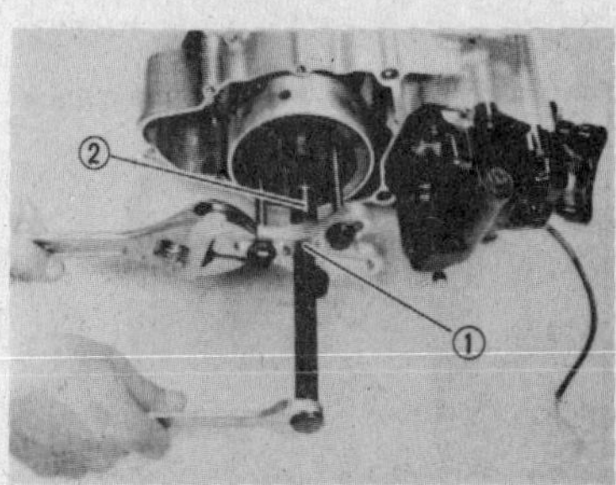

Removing the magneto flywheel

4. Remove the clutch adjuster locknut, washer and O-ring.
5. Remove the clutch cover screws.
6. Tap around the cover carefully with a plastic mallet to break it free, then remove it.
7. Note the dowel pins in the crankcase.
8. Remove the clutch lever spring, the clutch lever, shift guide No. 1, the pawl holder and shift guide No. 2.
9. Flatten the lock tab on the primary clutch nut.
10. Hold the clutch and remove the nut and washer.

Crankcase cover screws

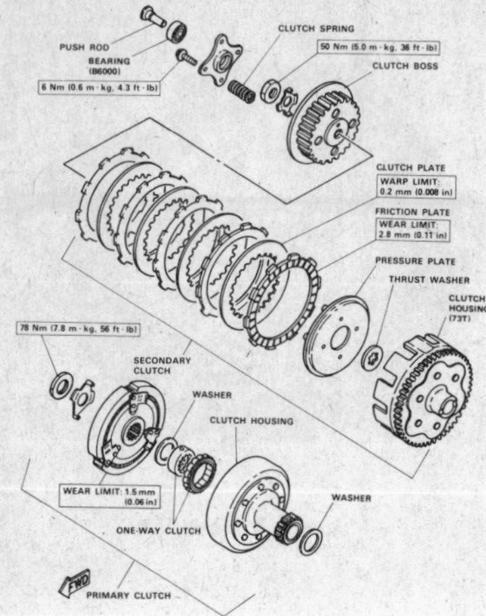

Clutch assembly

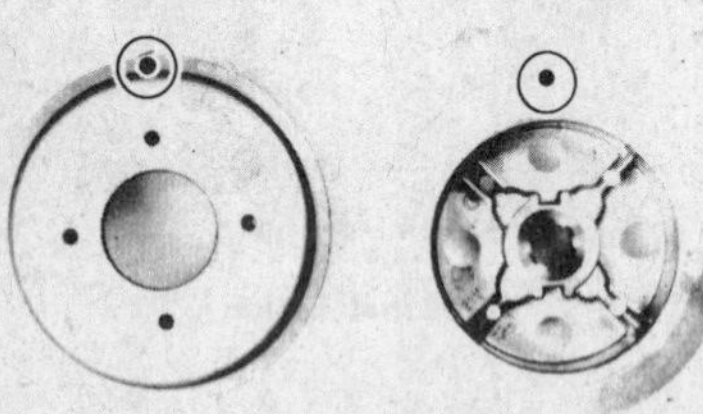

Align clutch boss and pressure plate marks when assembling

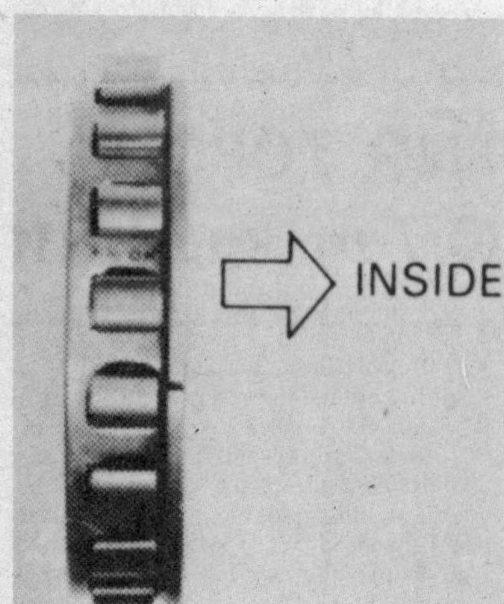

One-way assembly is installed with the flanged side inward

11. Turn the secondary clutch so that one of the clearance notches will allow the primary gear to pass. Then remove the primary clutch assembly.

12. Note that there is a washer beneath the primary gear. Locate it and place in a safe location.

13. Remove the pushrod and bearing from the secondary clutch spring plate.

14. Remove the clutch spring bolts, losening them gradually and evenly.

15. Remove the clutch spring plate and the springs.

16. Flatten the tab securing the secondary clutch hub nut.

17. Hold the housing and remove the nut and lockwasher.

18. Remove the clutch assembly.

Inspection

1. Check all parts for evidence of unusual wear.

NOTE: *Refer to the "General Information" section for detailed engine component inspection procedures.*

2. Minimum allowable friction plate thickness is 2.8mm (0.11 in.).

3. Maximum allowable steel plate warpage is 0.2mm (0.008 in.).

4. Clutch springs should be replaced as a set if any measures more than 1.0mm (0.04 in.) less than the standard free-length of 34.9mm (1.37 in.).

5. Check the primary clutch housing and shoe assembly for bluish discoloration indicating heat damage.

6. Maximum allowable clutch shoe wear is 1.5mm (0.06 in.).

Installation

1. Install the secondary clutch housing. Install the thrust washer.

2. Install a friction plate. Then alternate steel and friction plates until all are fitted.

3. Install the pressure plate and springs. Tighten the bolts finger tight at this point.

NOTE: *When installing the clutch boss, align the arrow marks on the boss and pressure plate.*

4. The remainder of the procedure is the reverse of disassembly. Note the following points:

a. Tighten the secondary clutch hub bolt to 36 ft. lbs. Be sure to bend up the lock tab.

b. Tighten the spring bolts to 4.3 ft. lbs.

c. When installing the one-way assembly of the primary clutch, ensure that the flange side faces inward.

d. Torque the primary clutch nut to 56 ft. lbs.

e. When installing the shift linkage, the slot in shift guide No. 1 must engage the shift shaft projection, and the shift guide No. 2 slot must engage the projection of the right-side spacer.

f. Be sure that the two dowel pins are in place before fitting the cover.

Lower End And Transmission

DISASSEMBLY

1. Remove the engine from the frame.
2. Remove the top end components: cylinder head, cylinder and piston.
3. Remove the recoil starter assembly.
4. Remove the magneto.
5. Remove the clutches.
6. Remove the shift linkage.
7. Remove the starter gearing (left side).
8. Remove the cam chain guide.
9. Remove the cam chain.
10. Remove the three screws securing the right side crankcase spacer. Remove the spacer. Remove the dowel pins in the crankcase.
11. Remove the oil pump cover screws and take off the oil pump assembly.
12. Remove the circlip and washer from the shift shaft.
13. Pull the shift shaft out from the right side of the engine.

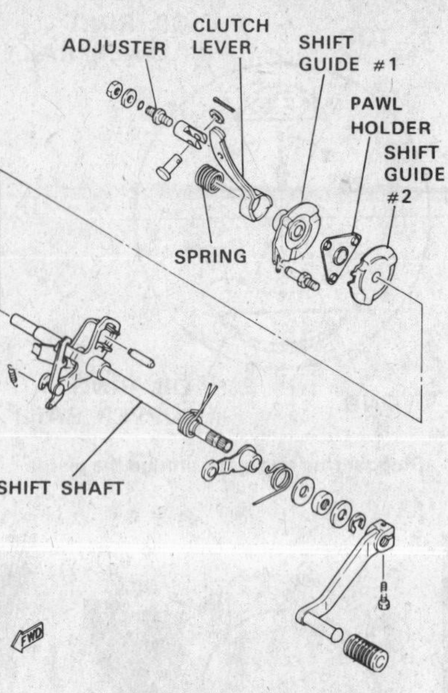

Gearshift lever assembly

14. Remove the shift lever assembly.
15. Remove the stopper lever assembly with the torsion spring.
16. Use a torx driver to remove the end of the shift drum.
17. Remove the circlip, oil pump drive gear and washer from the right side of the crankshaft.
18. Flatten the locking tab and remove the balancer shaft nut.
19. Lock up the drive and driven gears with a rag or other soft material.
20. Remove the drive gear nut, washer and key.

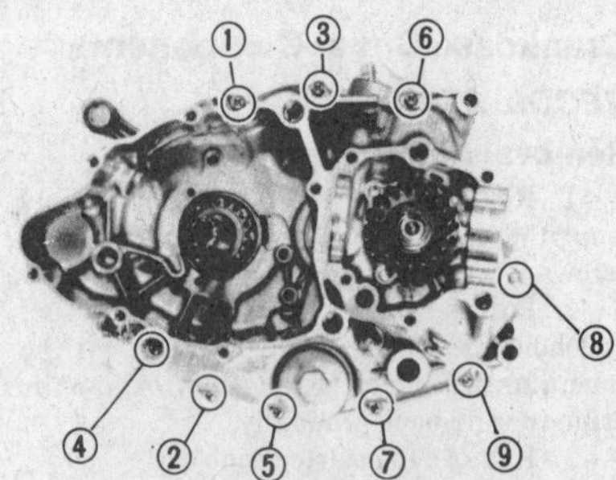

Left side crankcase screws

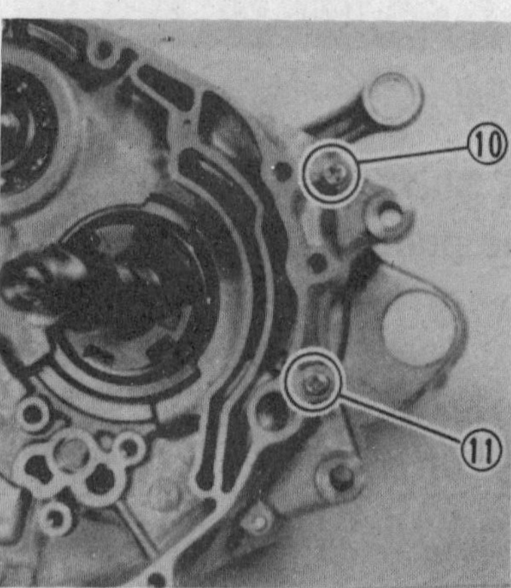

Right side crankcase screws

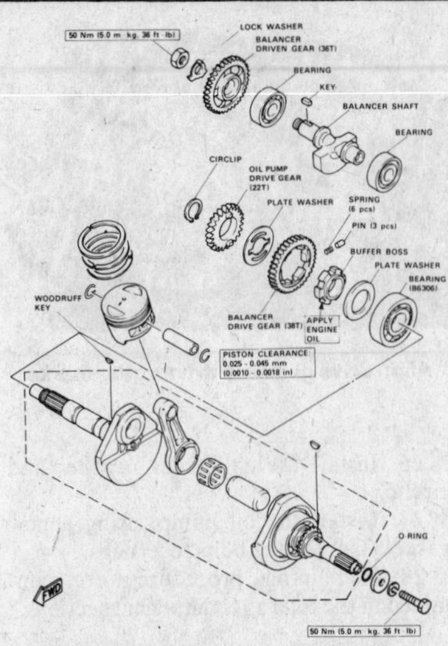

Crankshaft and balancer assemblies

21. Remove the balancer drive gear. Note the location of the six springs and the three pins.

22. Disconnect the neutral and reverse switch leads.

23. Remove the middle gear case cover.

24. Remove the middle gear assembly.

25. Loosen the crankcase screws 1/4 turn each. The screws should be loosened in a cross pattern.

26. When all of the scres are loosened, remove them.

27. Separate the crankcase halves with the flywheel puller and attachment.

28. Major components will remain in the right crankcase half.

INSPECTION

Oil Pump

1. Rotor bore in the body must not exceed 6mm (0.24 in.).

2. Inner-to-outer rotor clearance must not exceed 0.15mm (0.0059 in.).

3. If either specification is not met, the pump must be replaced.

Crankshaft

1. Refer to the "Engine Specifications" chart at the end of this section.

2. The crankshaft should be inspected for rod play, run-out and bearing condition.

Transmission

1. Check the gears for heat damage.

2. Check for wear to the teeth, pitting or other obvious signs of damage.

3. Check that the shift fork shafts are straight.

4. Check the shift drum grooves for wear and the pins on the shift forks which engage them as well.

5. Check the shift fork fingers for damage.

6. Refer to the "Engine Specifications" chart for specifications.

ASSEMBLY

1. Press the crankshaft bearing and the transmission bearings into the right crankcase half.

2. Bearing ID marks should face towards the inside of the case. Apply pressure to the outer races only.

3. Install the crankshaft into the right side crankcase half, long side first.

4. Install the woodruff key in the crankshaft keyway. Oil the bearings and taper.

5. Install the washer and buffer boss onto the crankshaft.

NOTE: *The punch mark on the buffer boss must face outwards.*

6. Install the second, forth and third-gear wheels onto the shaft.

7. Install the transmission shafts.

8. Install the shift drum in the right crankcase half.

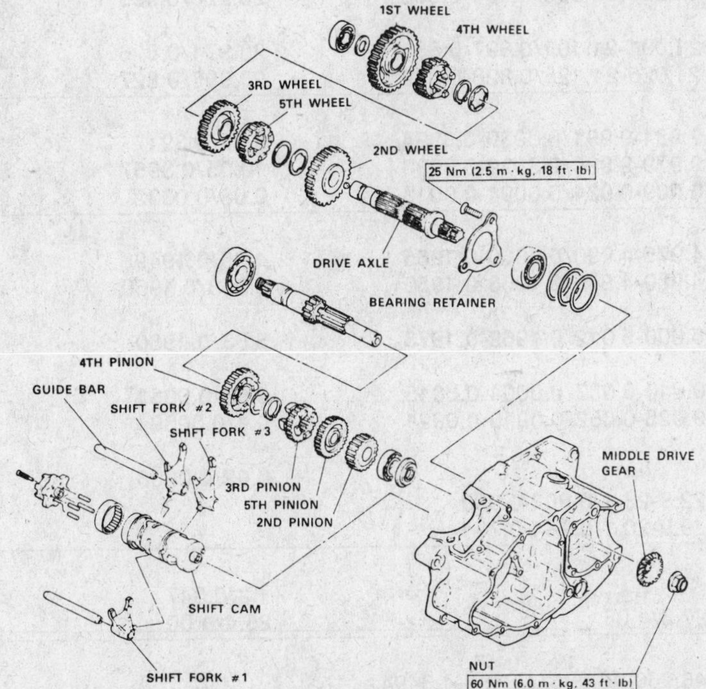

Transmission assembly

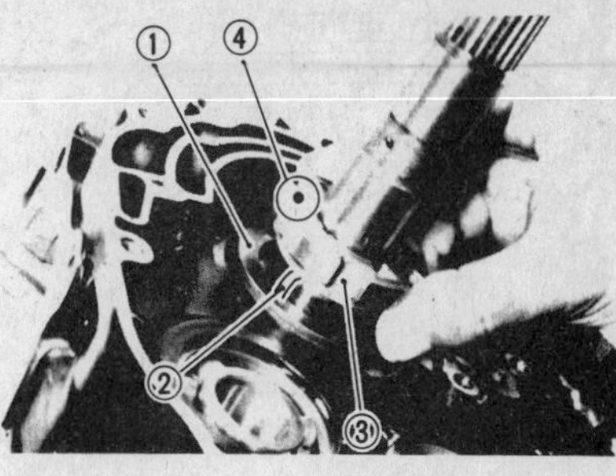

Install buffer boss (3) with punch mark (4) facing out.

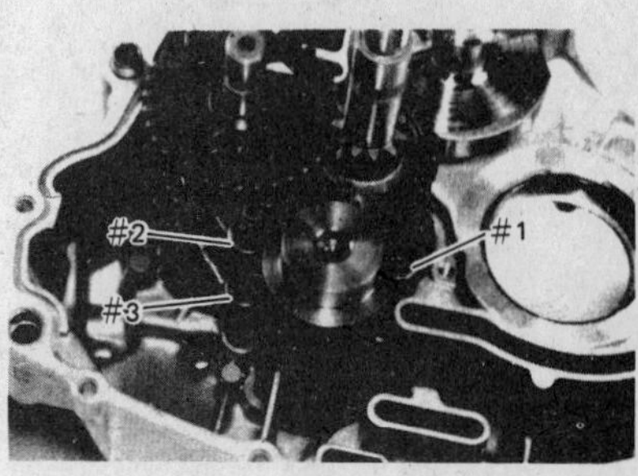

Shift fork shaft installation

9. Install the No. 1 shift fork onto the second pinion gear; install the No. 2 shift fork onto the fifth pinion gear and the No. 3 shift fork on the fourth gear.

NOTE: *The numbers on the shift forks must face the left crankcase half. Be sure that the fork pins are seated in the shift drum grooves.*

10. Fit the shift fork shaft.

11. Install the balancer shaft with the unthreaded end on the right side of the crankcase.

Align buffer boss and drive gear marks

12. Install the three dowel pins on the crankcase mating surface.

13. Coat the mating surface with Yamaha Bond No. 4.

14. Join the case halves.

15. Tighten the screws gradually and in a cross pattern. When all are tight, torque them to 5 ft. lbs.

16. Install the balancer drive gear:

a. Insert a spring into the buffer boss, then insert a spring with a pin in it.

b. Align the punch marks on the buffer boss and drive gear and install the drive gear.

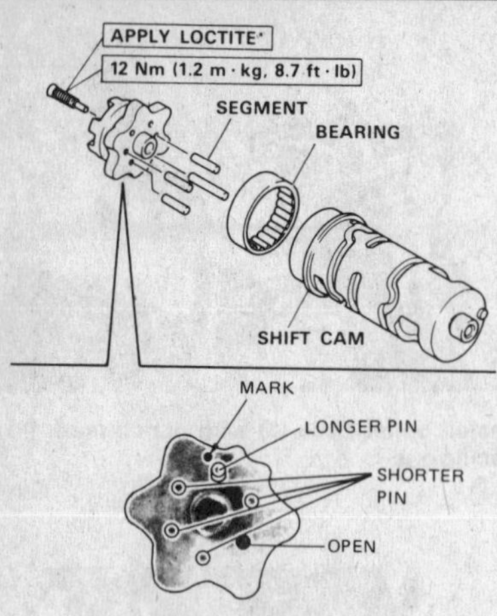

Shift drum plate installation

17. Install the washer and oil pump drive gear on the crankshaft. Fit the circlip. Be sure that the pump gear tab engages the washer and buffer boss slots.

18. Fit the balancer driven gear. Align the punch marks on the two gears.

19. Fit the key to the balancer shaft.

20. Install the washer and the nut.

21. Lock the gears in place and tighten the nut to 36 ft. lbs.

22. Use a non-permanent thread-locking compound on the shift drum end plate. When installing the plate, align the match mark with the longer pin.

23. Tighten the torx bolt to 8.7 ft. lbs.

24. Lightly grease the lips of the shift shaft oil seal.

25. Install the shaft. Hook the spring onto the crankcase boss provided. Be sure that the shift lever correctly engages the shift drum pins.

Align drive gear and driven gear marks

26. Install the shift shaft washer and circlip

27. Install the oil pump, using a new gasket. Tighten the bolts to 5 ft. lbs.

28. Remaining procedures are contained in the relevant component sections.

ENGINE SPECIFICATIONS
YFM 80

Component	Standard (mm/in.)	Service limit (mm/in.)
CYLINDER HEAD		
Warpage	—	0.05/0.02
CYLINDER		
Bore	47.000-47.005/1.850-1.851	47.1/1.854
Taper	—	0.05/0.002
Out-of-round	—	0.01/0.004
CAMSHAFT		
Run-out	—	0.03/0.0012
Lobe height, intake	25.258-25.358/0.994-0.998	25.227/0.993
Lobe height, exhaust	25.258-25.358/0.994-0.998	25.228/0.993
Base circle dia., intake	21.001-21.101/0.827-0.831	20.971/0.826
Base circle dia., exhaust	21.025-21.125/0.828-0.832	20.995/0.827
ROCKER ARMS		
Rocker arm shaft OD	9.981-9.991/0.3930-0.3934	9.95/0.3917
Rocker arm ID	9.979-9.990/0.3929-0.3933	10.05/0.3957
Arm-shaft clearance	0.009-0.034/0.0004-0.0013	0.08/0.0032
VALVES		
Stem OD, intake	4.975-4.990/0.1960-0.1965	4.95/0.1949
Stem OD, exhaust	4.980-4.975/0.1953-0.1959	4.953/0.1950
Guide ID, IN & EX	5.000-5.012/0.1969-0.1973	5.03/0.1980
Stem-to-guide clearance, intake	0.010-0.037/0.0004-0.0015	0.08/0.0031
Stem-to-guide clearance, exhaust	0.025-0.052/0.0010-0.0021	0.1/0.0039
Run-out	—	0.02/0.0008
Head diameter, intake	22.9-23.1/0.902-0.909	—
Head diameter, exhaust	19.9-20.1/0.784-0.791	—
VALVE SPRINGS		
Tilt	—	1.2/0.047
Free length	27.3/1.08	25.4/1.00
PISTON		
Diameter	46.960-46.975/1.8488-1.8494	—
Piston-cylinder clearance	0.025-0.045/0.0010-0.0018	0.045/0.0018

ENGINE SPECIFICATIONS
YFM 80

Component	Standard (mm/in.)	Service limit (mm/in.)
PISTON RINGS		
End-gap		
Top, second	0.10-0.25/0.004-0.010	0.4/0.016
Oil	0.2-0.7/0.008-0.028	—
Side clearance		
Top	0.030-0.065/0.0012-0.0026	0.12/0.0047
Second	0.020-0.055/0.0008-0.0022	0.12/0.0047
Oil	0	—
CRANKSHAFT		
Width	40.20-40.25/1.583-1.585	—
Big end side clearance	0.1-0.4/0.004-0.016	0.5/0.020
Small end lateral play	0.8-1.0/0.03-0.04	2.0/0.08
Run-out	—	0.05/0.002
CLUTCH		
Friction plate thickness	2.92-3.08/0.115-0.121	2.9/0.114
Steel plate thickness	1.2-1.6/0.047-0.063	—
Steel plate warp limit	—	0.1/0.004
Spring free length	30.1/1.19	29.1/1.15
TRANSMISSION		
Shaft run-out	—	0.08/0.0031
Middle gear lash	—	0.17-0.31/0.007-0.012
Final gear lash	—	0.17-0.31/0.007-0.012

ENGINE SPECIFICATIONS
YFM 200

Component	Standard (mm/in.)	Service limit (mm/in.)
CYLINDER HEAD		
Warpage	—	0.03/0.0012
CYLINDER		
Bore	66.070-66.080/2.6011-2.6015	67.1/2.64
Taper	—	0.005/0.0002
Out-of-round	—	0.01/0.004
CAMSHAFT		
Cylinder bearing dia.	25.000-25.021/0.9843-0.9851	—
	20.000-20.021/0.7874-0.7882	—
Cam journal dia.	24.960-24.980/0.9827-0.9835	—
	19.998-19.999/0.7873-0.7874	—
Bearing clearance	0.020-0.061/0.008-0.0024	—
Run-out	—	0.03/0.0012
Lobe height, intake	36.537-36.637/1.4385-1.4424	36.58/1.440
Lobe height, exhaust	36.577-36.677/1.440-1.444	36.62/1.441
Base circle dia., intake	30.131-30.231/1.1863-1.1902	30.18/1.188
Base circle dia., exhaust	30.214-30.314/1.1895-1.1935	30.26/1.191
ROCKER ARMS		
Rocker arm shaft OD	11.985-11.991/0.4718-0.4721	11.94/0.470
Rocker arm ID	12.000-12.018/0.4724-0.4731	12.03/0.474
Arm-shaft clearance	0.009-0.037/0.0004-0.0015	—

ENGINE SPECIFICATIONS
YFM 200

Component	Standard (mm/in.)	Service limit (mm/in.)
VALVES		
Stem OD, intake	5.975-5.990/0.2352-0.2358	—
Stem OD, exhaust	5.960-5.975/0.2346-0.2352	—
Guide ID, in & ex	6.000-6.012/0.2362-0.2367	6.1/0.240
Stem-to-guide clearance, intake	0.010-0.037/0.0004-0.0015	0.10/0.004
Stem-to-guide clearance, exhaust	0.025-0.052/0.0010-0.0020	0.12/0.05
Run-out	—	0.03/0.0012
Head dia., intake	33.9-34.1/1.3346-1.3425	—
Head dia., exhaust	28.4-28.6/1.1181-1.1260	—
Seat width	0.9-1.1/0.0354-0.0433	1.6/0.063
VALVE SPRINGS		
Tilt	—	1.6/0.063
Free length, inner	—	35.5/1.40
Free length, outer	—	37.2/1.46
PISTON		
Diameter (200)	66.935-66.985/2.635-2.637	—
Diameter (225)	69.935-69.985/2.7533-2.7553	—
Piston-cylinder clearance	0.025-0.045/0.0010-0.0018	
PISTON RINGS		
End-gap		
Top, second	0.15-0.30/0.0059-0.0118	0.75/0.0295
Oil	0.3-0.9/0.0118-0.0354	—
Side clearance		
Top	0.03-0.07/0.0012-0.0028	0.1/0.004
Second	0.02-0.06/0.0008-0.0024	0.9/0.035
Oil	0	—
CRANKSHAFT		
Run-out	—	0.03/0.012
Big end side clearance	—	0.35-0.65/0.0138-0.0256
Small end lateral play	0.8-1.0/0.03-0.04	2.0/0.08
PRIMARY CLUTCH		
Shoe thickness	2.0/0.079	1.5/0.0591
SECONDARY CLUTCH		
Friction plate thickness	3.0/0.12	2.8/0.11
Steel plate thickness	1.6/0.06	—
Steel plate warp limit	—	0.2/0.008
Spring free length	34.9/1.37	33.9/1.33
TRANSMISSION		
Shaft run-out	—	0.08/0.0031
Middle gear lash	—	0.1-0.2/0.004-0.008
Final gear lash	—	0.1-0.2/0.004-0.008

ENGINE TORQUE SPECIFICATIONS YFM 80

Part	Torque (ft lbs)
Cylinder head	
Nuts	7.2
Bolts	7.2
Tappet cover	5.1
Spark plug	9.1
Cam sprocket cover	7.2
Magneto rotor nut	29
Valve adjuster locknuts	5.1
Cam sprocket bolt	14
Cam chain tensioner plug	11
Cam chain tensioner nut	5.1
Cam chain tensioner crown nut	3.6
Cam chain tensioner bolt	2.9
Crankcase oil drain plug	14
Carburetor manifold	5.1
Muffler bracket bolts	18
Exhaust pipe at cylinder head	7.2
Crankcase half screws	5.1 (thread locking compound)
Crankcase half bolts	7.2
Starter clutch screws	7.2 (thread locking compound)
Primary drive gear nut	36
Clutch boss nut	43
Bearing housing (middle)	43 (thread locking compound)
Shift drum stopper lever bolt	10 (thread locking compound)

ENGINE TORQUE SPECIFICATIONS YFM 200

Part	Torque (ft lbs)
Cylinder head bolts	
Long	16.0 (oiled)
Short	14.0 (oiled)
Cam sprocket cover	5.1
Valve covers	7.2
Rocker arm shafts	5.8
Spark plug	14.9
Cylinder bolts	7.2
Balancer shaft nut	36.0
Starter pulley bolt	36.0
Valve adjuster nut	10.0
Cam sprocket bolt	43.0
Cam chain tensioner nut	22.0
Cam chain tensioner cap nut	3.6
Chain guide #2 retainer	5.8
Oil drain plug	31.0
Filter cover bolts	7.2
Crankcase screws	5.1
R/H bearing retainer	7.2
Primary clutch nut	56.0
Clutch springs	4.3
Clutch hub nut	36.0
Clutch adjuster	11.0
Middle gear case cover	7.2
Drive axle bearing retainer	18.0 (staked in place)
Housing bearing retainer	43.0
Bearing housing	17.0
Starter clutch screw	22.0 (staked in place)

FUEL SYSTEM

NOTE: *For carburetor theory and operation, refer to the "General Information" section.*

GAS TANK

Removal and Installation (80)

1. Remove the seat.
2. Remove the gas cap.
3. Shut the fuel petcock "OFF."
4. Disconnect the fuel line at the petcock.
5. Remove the gas tank fasteners and band and take off the tank.
6. Installation is the reverse of removal. Be certain that the fuel line is tight before turning the petcock "ON."

Removal and Installation (200)

1. Remove the front and rear carriers by removing the securing bolts and pulling the carriers up and clear of the machine.
2. Remove the two screws which secure the front panel and take off the panel.
3. Remove the fuel tank cover screws beneath the front panel. Note washers and collars.
4. Unhook the cover from the tank, then pull it forward to remove it.
5. Shut the fuel petcock "OFF."
6. Disconnect the fuel line at the petcock.
7. Remove the gas tank bolts.
8. Disconnect the band at the rear of the tank.
9. Remove the gas cap.
10. Remove the gas tank.
11. Installation is the reverse of removal. Be sure that the fuel line is tightly connected to the petcock before turning it "ON."

CARBURETOR (80)

Removal and installation

1. Shut the fuel petcock "OFF."
2. Disconnect the fuel line from the carburetor.
3. Disconnect the breather pipe from the carburetor.
4. Disconnect the carburetor overflow line.
5. Remove the carburetor cap screws.
6. Carefully pull out the throttle slide assembly.
7. If throttle slide or needle service is required, disconnect the throttle cable from the slide and separate the components. Otherwise, wrap the assembly in a clean shop rag and position it out of the way to guard against damage.
8. Loosen the air cleaner hose clamp at the carburetor.
9. Remove the carburetor mounting nuts and pull the unit clear of the manifold to remove it.

CAUTION: *Drain float bowl gasoline into a suitable container and dispose of properly.*

10. Installation is the reverse of removal. Note the following points:
    a. A new gasket and O-rings should be used.
    b. When fitting the carburetor, be sure the O-rings are firmly seated in their

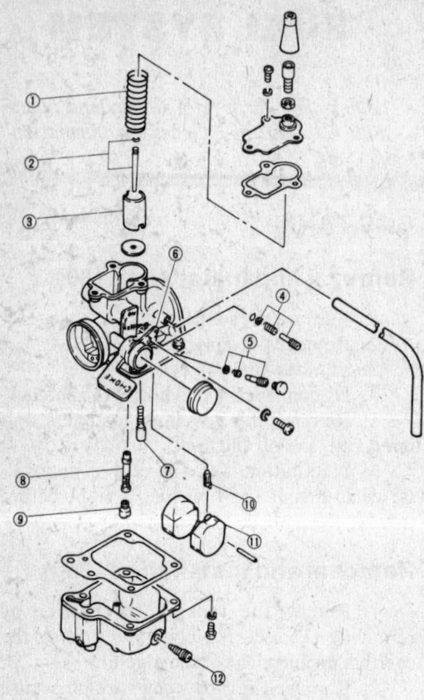

1. Throttle slide spring
2. Needle and clip
3. Throttle slide
4. Idle speed screw assembly
5. Pilot air screw assembly
6. Choke lever
7. Pilot jet
8. Needle jet
9. Main jet
10. Float needle
11. Float
12. Drain screw

Carburetor (YFM 80)

grooves in the carb body and the manifold and that they are not knocked out of place when the carburetor is positioned.

c. Check that the air cleaner hose is correctly located around the carburetor intake and not folded or otherwise obstructing the intake. Also be sure that the hose has not been pulled out of the air cleaner box through mishandling.

d. Tighten the carb mounting nuts gradually and evenly. Proper torque is 5.1 ft. lbs.

e. Carefully insert the throttle slide assembly. Be sure that the needle enters the needle jet without forcing it in. Check that the slide enters the carb body easily and that movement is free.

f. Check for proper throttle slide action before operating the machine.

g. Be sure that all lines are securely connected. Turn the fuel petcock "ON" and check carefully for leaks before operating the machine.

Disassembly

1. To disassemble the throttle slide, pull the spring out of the slide and compress it while disengaging the cable from the slide. Shake out the needle and clip.

CAUTION: *Do not remove the clip from the needle. Position is critical. See the "Carburetor Specifications" chart.*

2. Turn the carb upside down and remove the four float bowl screws.

3. Carefully remove the float bowl and the gasket. If the bowl will not come off, rap the sides with the screwdriver handle, but hold the bowl while you do this so it doesn't come off and hit the float assembly. When the bowl is free, lift it off carefully.

4. Push out the float pivot pin and lift out the float and needle assembly.

5. Unscrew and remove the main jet.

6. Unscrew and remove the pilot jet.

7. Unscrew and remove the pilot air screw from the carburetor body. Note spring and O-ring.

8. Remove the throttle stop screw. Note spring and O-ring.

9. Push out the needle jet from the top of the carburetor. Use a wooden dowel to do this.

10. Remove the O-ring from the manifold flange.

11. Unscrew and remove the float bowl drain screw.

Inspection

1. Refer to the "General Information" section for carburetor inspection tips.

2. Clean the body and other metal parts in a clean, non-caustic solvent intended for carburetor cleaning.

3. Blow fuel and air passages clear with low pressure air. Do not insert wire or metal objects into carburetor jets or jet bores to clear them. Bores are calibrated and easily damaged.

4. Use new O-rings and gaskets.

5. Check the condition of all fuel system lines. Replace any with abrasion or age damage such as cracking or hardening.

6. Check for splitting at the ends of the hoses. Replace if damaged.

7. Check for wear on the throttle slide and the carburetor bore.

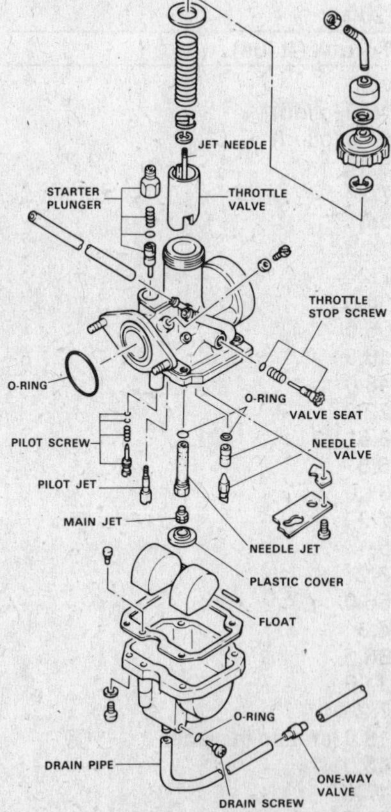

Carburetor (YFM 200)

Assembly

1. Be sure that all jets and screws which are equipped with O-rings have them in the proper positions.

2. Refer to the exploded view of the carburetor for assembly help.

3. Install jets carefully. They can be easily damaged. Be sure they are secure,but do not overtighten.

4. When installing the float assembly, carefully lower the needle into the seat with the floats attached. Position the float so that the pivot pin can be inserted. Check for free movement.

5. Use a new float bowl gasket. Tighten the float bowl screws gradually and evenly.

6. Use new manifold O-rings and gasket. Be certain that the O-rings are pushed into their grooves and firmly seated.

7. When installing the pilot screw, apply a tiny bit of grease tot he O-ring. Carefully turn the screw in until resistance is felt, then back it out 2 1/2 turns.

CAUTION: *Do not overtighten this screw when installing it. Stop turning the moment some resistance is felt. Otherwise, it will be damaged.*

8. After the carburetor is installed, check fuel level and adjust idle speed and mixture. These procedures can be found in the "Tune-Up" section.

CARBURETOR (200)

Removal and Installation

1. Remove the seat.

2. Fold back the carburetor's rubber cap.

3. Unscrew the cap and carefully pull out the throttle slide assembly, ensuring that the needle is not damaged during the removal procedure.

4. If throttle slide service is required, disengage the cable from the slide and separate the components. If not, wrap the assembly in a clean cloth and position it out of the way.

5. Unscrew and remove the starter plunger from the carburetor body.

6. Disconnect the overflow line from the float bowl.

7. Be sure that the fuel petcock is "OFF" and disconnect the fuel line from the carburetor.

8. Disconnect the vacuum line from the carburetor body.

9. Loosen the air cleaner hose clamp.

10. Remove the carburetor mounting nuts.

11. Pull the carburetor free of the manifold and remove it.

WARNING: *Drain gasoline into a suitable container and dispose of properly.*

12. Installation is the reverse of removal. Be sure that the carb mounting O-ring is secure in its groove and that it is not lost, damaged or moved out of the proper position when the carb is fitted to the manifold.

13. Tighten manifold nuts gradually and evenly. Proper torque is 5.8 ft. lbs.

14. Check that the air cleaner hose is properly fitted over the carb intake and not folded or partially obstructing the intake. Tighten the clamp.

15. Carefully insert the throttle slide assembly. Be sure that the needle enters the needle jet without forcing it. Check that the slide enters the carb body easily and that the movement is free.

16. Tighten the cap. Position the rubber cap so that foreign matter cannot enter. Check for proper throttle action.

17. Screw in and tighten the starter plunger.

18. Connect the overflow line to the float bowl.

19. Connect all lines. Be sure that gas and vacuum lines are securely connected.

20. Turn on the fuel and check for air or gas leaks before operating the machine.

Disassembly

1. To disassemble the throttle slide, pull the spring out of the slide and remove the spring clip. Disengage the cable from the slide.

2. Shake out the needle and clip.

CAUTION: *Do not remove the clip from the needle. Position is critical.*

See the "Carburetor Specifications" chart for proper clip position if it is removed.

3. Turn the carb upside down and remove the four float bowl screws.

4. Carefully remove the float bowl and the gasket. If the bowl will not come off, rap the sides with the screwdriver handle, but hold the bowl while you do this so it doesn't come off unexpectedly. When the bowl is free, lift it off carefully.

5. Push out the float pivot pin and lift out the float and needle assembly.

6. Remove the plastic cover from the main jet.

7. Unscrew and remove the main jet.

8. Unscrew and remove the pilot jet.

9. Unscrew the needle jet. Note any O-rings which may be on the jets or in the carburetor body.

10. Unscrew and remove the pilot screw and the throttle stop screw. Note spring and O-ring(s). Remember that adjustment of these components is required when assembling.

11. Needle valve seats are secured by a keeper plate held by a screw. If removal is required, remove the screw and take out plate and seat.

12. Remove the manifold O-ring.

13. Unscrew and remove the drain screw from the float bowl. Note the O-ring.

Inspection

1. Refer to the "General Information" section for carburetor inspection tips.

2. Clean the body and other metal parts in a clean non-caustic solvent intended for carburetor cleaning.

3. Blow air and fuel passages clear with low pressure air. Do not insert wire or metal objects into carburetor or jet bores to clear them. Bores are calibrated and easily damaged.

4. Use all new O-rings and gaskets as a matter of safety.

5. Check the condition of all fuel lines and vacuum lines. Replace hoses with abrasion or age damage such as cracking or hardening.

6. Check for splitting at the ends of the hoses. Replace if damaged.

7. Check the starter plunger for wear and replace it if the plunger is scored.

8. Check for wear on the throttle slide and the carburetor bore.

Assembly

1. Be sure that all jets and screws which are equipped with O-rings have them in the proper positions.

2. Refer to the exploded view of the carburetor for assembly help.

3. Install jets carefully. They can be easily damaged. Be sure they are secure, but do not overtighten.

4. When installing the float assembly, carefully lower the needle into the seat with the floats attached. Position the float so the pivot pin can be inserted. Check for free movement. Install the keeper plate.

5. Use a new float bowl gasket. Tighten the float bowl screws gradually and evenly.

6. Install a new manifold O-ring.

7. When installing the pilot screw, turn it in very carefully until resistance is felt, then back it out 1 1/2 turns.

CAUTION: *Do not overtighten this screw when installing it. Stop turning it the movement some resistance is felt. Otherwise, it will be damaged.*

8. After the carburetor is installed, check fuel level and adjust idle speed and mixture. These procedures are outlined in the "Tune-Up" section.

FUEL PETCOCK

All Models

1. The fuel petcock has filter screens inside the tank which should be cleaned periodically—about every 6 mos. under normal conditions.

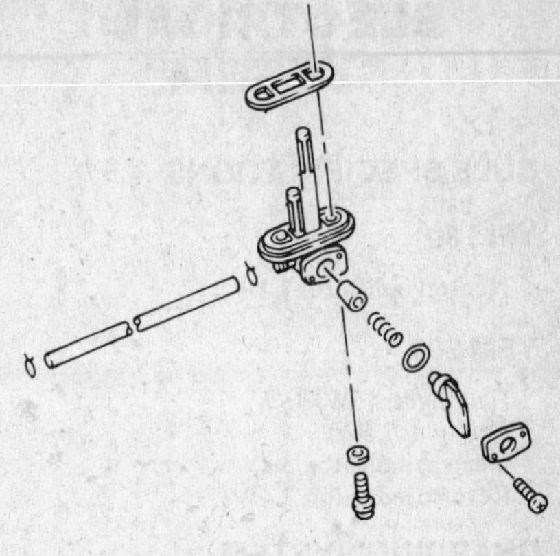

Fuel petcock

2. Remove the gas tank as outlined above.

3. Drain the gas.

4. Remove the lines from the petcock.

5. Remove the petcock securing screws and pull the assembly out of the tank.

6. Check the gasket condition. Replace it if it appears damaged or if it was leaking prior to removal.

7. Remove the filter screens and clean them in a safe solvent.

8. If foreign matter cannot be removed, or if the screens are punctured, crushed, or otherwise damaged, replace them.

9. Check the petcock mating surface for damage. Replace the unit if any is noted.

10 Flush out the gas tank before installing the petcock to get rid of any residual dirt.

11. If the petcock does not operate properly, remove the two screws which secure the lever plate. Remove the plate, lever, O-ring and spring.

12. Clean all metal parts thoroughly in solvent. If corrosion cannot be removed from the petcock body, the unit must be replaced.

13. Use a new O-ring when assembling.

14. When the petcock is fitted to the tank, be sure the gasket is in place.

15. After gas is added to the tank, check for leaks. Allow the machine to sit for several minutes before operation. Be sure that all fuel lines are tightly connected.

CARBURETOR SPECIFICATIONS

	80	200
Carburetor type	VM16SH	VM22SH
ID mark	55X00	52H-00
Main jet	80	115
Main air jet	1.2	1.7
Needle	3HP9-3①	4DH1-3①
Needle jet	E-2	N-6
Throttle slide cutaway	3.0	4.0
Pilot jet	12.5	27.5
Pilot air jet	na	130
Pilot screw (turns out)	2 ± ½	1 to 2
Float needle seat	1.2	1.8
Fuel level (mm/in.)	3.5 ± 1.0/0.14 ± 0.04	3.0 ± 1.0/0.12 ± 0.04
Float height (mm/in.)	21.9 ± 0.5/0.83 ± 0.02	21.5 ± 0.85 ± 0.02
Idle speed (rpm)	1,800 ± 50	1,400 ± 50

① Last digit indicates clip position, counting from top of needle.

ELECTRICAL SYSTEM

BULB SPECIFICATIONS

YFM 80

Neutral indicator: 3.4W

YFM 200

Headlight: 45W/45W
Taillight: 7.5W
Neutral indicator: 3.4W
Reverse indicator: 3.4W

CHARGING SYSTEM

YFM 80

The charging system consists of the charging coil in the CDI magneto, a regulator/rectifier unit and the battery.

CAUTION: *Never run the engine when the battery is disconnected. This may damage charging system components.*

SYSTEM CHECK

1. Remove the seat.
2. Disconnect the battery positive (red) lead.
3. Connect an ammeter from the positive terminal of the battery to the red lead.
4. Start the engine. Note current readings at the specified engine speeds:
   0.7 a (or higher) @ 3,000 rpm
   3.0 a (or lower) @ 8,000 rpm
5. If the charging current is not within specification, check charging coil resistance.
6. Remove the battery.
7. Remove the rear fender.
8. Disconnect the DCI magneto black lead. Disconnect the 4-pin connector.
9. Check the resistance between the black lead and the white lead in the 4-pin connector.
10. Resistance should be 0.9 ohms. If the measured resistance is not within 10% of this value, replace the charging coil.
11. The regulator/rectifier can be checked with an ohmmeter.
12. Locate and disconnect the regulator /rectifier wiring at the plastic connector.
13. Connect the ohmmeter across the red and white leads (low range on meter) and note reading.
14. Reverse the meter leads. Note reading.
15. There should be continuity in one direction only. If the meter shows continuity in both directions, or in neither direction, the regulator/rectifier must be replaced.

CAUTION: *This unit can be damaged by careless handling. Never run the engine with the battery disconnected. Always take precautions not to reverse battery leads.*

YFM 200

The charging system consists of a 12 v battery, a regulator/rectifier unit and a charging coil in the CDI magneto.

SYSTEM CHECK

1. Connect a DC voltmeter across the battery terminals.
2. Start the engine and run it up to 5,000 rpm.
3. The meter should show 12.0-16.5 across the battery terminals.
4. If the voltage is not within this specification, determine the cause. Check battery condition; check wiring connections for corrosion. Check other system components as outlined below.

CAUTION: *Never disconnect the battery from the system when the engine is running. Charging system components will be damaged.*

CHARGING COIL

1. Remove the seat, rear carrier and rear fender.
2. Locate and disconnect the CDI magneto wiring at the plastic connector.
3. Check the resistance of the charging coil across the white lead and ground on the engine or frame.
4. Resistance should be 0.4 ohms.
5. If the reading obtained is not within 10% of this figure, the charging coil must be replaced.

REGULATOR/RECTIFIER

1. This unit can be checked with an ohmmeter.
2. Locate and disconnect the regulator/rectifier wiring at the plastic connector.
3. Connect the ohmmeter across the red and white leads (low range on meter) and note reading.
4. Reverse the meter leads and note the readings.
5. There should be continuity in one direction only.
6. If the ohmmeter shows continuity in both directions, or in neither direction, the regulator/rectifier must be replaced.

CAUTION: *The regulator/rectifier can be damaged by careless handling. Be sure that battery connections are never reversed. Be sure the engine is never run with the battery disconnected.*

LIGHTING SYSTEM (YFM 200)

1. The output of the lighting coil (AC) can be checked between any point in the lighting circuit and ground. This procedure checks output at the headlight.
2. Disconnect the yellow and black wires at the headlight.
3. Connect an AC voltmeter set to the 20 VAC range (or equivalent) to the leads. yellow is positive.
4. Start the engine.
5. Voltage should be 12-18 VAC with engine speeds 3000-8000 rpm. Voltage increases gradually with speed.
6. Locate the lighting coil wiring beneath the seat/cowling and disconnect it at the plastic connector.
7. Connect an ohmmeter across the coil wires: positive meter lead to yellow/red and negative meter lead to ground.
8. Resistance should be 0.34 ohms.
9. If the reading is not within 10% of this specifications, the lighting coil must be replaced.
10. If the lighting coil resistance is correct, but system voltage is not, the problem is probably with the voltage regulator.

SWITCHES

1. Switch operation can be checked with an ohmmeter set to the low scale or with a simple continuity tester (self-powered).
2. Disconnect the switch you wish to test at the plastic connector to isolate it.

Engine Stop Switch

1. There should be continuity between black and black/white wires when the switch is in either of the "OFF" or "STOP" positions.
2. There should be no continuity when the switch is in the "RUN" position.

Starter Button

1. On machines equipped with an electric starter, check for continuity across the red/white and brown switch leads.
2. There should be continuity when the starter button is pushed: No continuity when the button is released.

Main Switch

1. When in the "OFF" position, there should be continuity only between the black/white and black leads.
2. In the "ON" position, there should be continuity only between the red and brown leads.
3. Any other continuities indicate a defective switch.

Dimmer Switch

1. In the "OFF" position, there should be no continuities in the switch.
2. In the "LO" position, there should be continuity between the yellow/red, blue and the green leads.
3. In the "HI" position, there should be continuity between the yellow/red, blue and yellow leads.

IGNITION SYSTEM

YFM 80

The major components of the ignition system are the CDI magneto, the CDI unit, the ignition coil and the spark plug.

IGNITION COIL

1. Remove the seat.
2. Remove the battery.
3. Remove the rear fender.
4. Remove the fuel tank.
5. Disconnect the ignition coil lead (orange).
6. Disconnect the spark plug lead.
7. Check primary coil resistance across the orange wire and a chassis ground. It should be 1.6 ohms.
8. Check secondary coil resistance across the orange wire and the high tension lead. It should be 6.6 K ohms.
9. If both readings are not within 10% of these values, the ignition coil must be replaced.

PICKUP COIL

1. Remvoe the seat.
2. Remove the battery.
3. Remove the rear fender.
4. Disconnect the single, black CDI lead.
5. Disconnect the 3-pin plastic connector with white/red, green/white and Sky blue wires.

6. Check resistance across the pickup coil black and white/red leads. It should be 330 ohms.

7. Replace the coil if the reading is not within 10% of this specification.

SOURCE COIL

1. Remove the seat.
2. Remvoe the battery.
3. Remove the rear fender.
4. Disconnect the single, black CDI lead.
5. Disconnect the 4-pin CDI connector.
6. Check the resistance between the single, black lead and the black/red lead in the connector.
7. Reistance should be 380 ohms.
8. If the measurement is not within 10% of this value, the source coil must be replaced.

YFM 200

The major components of the ignition system are the CDI magneto, the CDI unit, the ignition coil and the spark plug.

IGNITION COIL

1. Remove the seat.
2. Remove the front carrier.
3. Remove the front panel.
4. Remove the fuel tank cover.
5. Remove the fuel tank.
6. Disconnect the ignition coil wires (orange).
7. Check primary coil resistance across orange wire and chassis ground. It should be 0.85 ohms.
8. Check secondary coil resistance across orange wire and high tension lead. It should be 5.9 K ohms.
9. If both readings are not within 10% of these values, the ignition coil must be replaced.

PICKUP COIL

1. Remvoe the seat.
2. Remove the rear carrier.
3. Remove the rear fender.
4. Disconnect the CDI magneto lead.
5. Check resistance across the pickup coil leads (magneto side of the connector).
6. Resistance between the white/green and white/red leads should be 196 ohms.
7. If the reading is not within 10% of this figure, replace the pickup coil.

CHARGE COIL

1. The charge coil leads are brown and black and are accessed by disconnecting the plastic CDI magneto connector as outlined for the pickup coil, above.
2. Resistance across the brown and black leads should be 381 ohms.
3. If the reading is not within 10% of this specification, replace the unit.

ELECTRIC START SYSTEM

YFM 80

OPERATION

The electric start system consists of the starter motor, a starter solenoid, neutral switch ans circuit cut-off relay. When the main switch is on, the starter motor will operate only if the transmission is in neutral. The cut-off switch prevents starting in gear.

If the engine stop switch is in the "OFF" position, the starter motor will turn the engine over, but the ignition will not be on.

TESTING

1. To check the solenoid and starter button, the easiest method is to bypass these components completely by disconnecting the battery high tension lead from the solenoid and connecting it directly to the starter motor terminal. If the motor turns over, the solenoid or starter button is defective.

2. If the starter motor fails to operate, the unit itself may be the cause of the problem.

3. If the starter motor spins freely when the button is pushed, but the engine does not turn over, suspect the starter motor clutch or gearing.

4. If the engine will turn over only very slowly and without a great degree of predictability, some possible causes include: a low or almost dead battery, oil which is too thick for weather conditions or bad starter motor bearings. Worn bearings could cause the armature to contact the field coils which will effectively short out the starter. Usually, repeated attempts at starting will result in the starter motor getting very hot. Other possible causes of starter motor trouble include worn brushes, a worn or dirty commutator or a defective armature.

STARTER SOLENOID

1. Remove the seat.
2. Remove the battery.
3. Remove the rear fender.
4. Remove the solenoid wires. Remove the solenoid.
5. Connect a fully charged 12 v battery across the solenoid low tension terminals and check for continuity across the high tension terminals. If there is none, the solenoid is defective and must be replaced.
6. Check the resistance across the low tension terminals with an ohmmeter. Resistance must be within 10% of 4.6 ohms. If it is not, replace the solenoid.

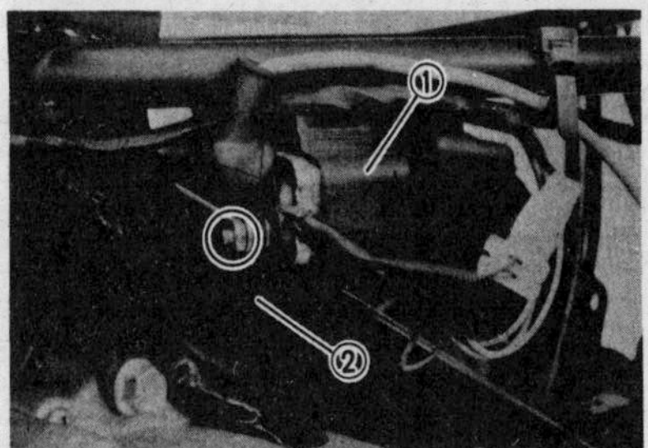

Starter solenoid location (YFM 80)

STARTER MOTOR

Removal

1. Disconnect the high tension lead from the starter motor terminal.
2. Remove the two screws and take out the starter motor.

Inspection

1. Remove the through-screws and separate the starter motor components.

2.Check for continuity between the commutator and the armature core. If there is any, the starter motor must be replaced.

3. Check for continuity between all of the commutator segments. Continuity must exist in every case. The maximum allowable resistance between the segments is 0.043 ohms.

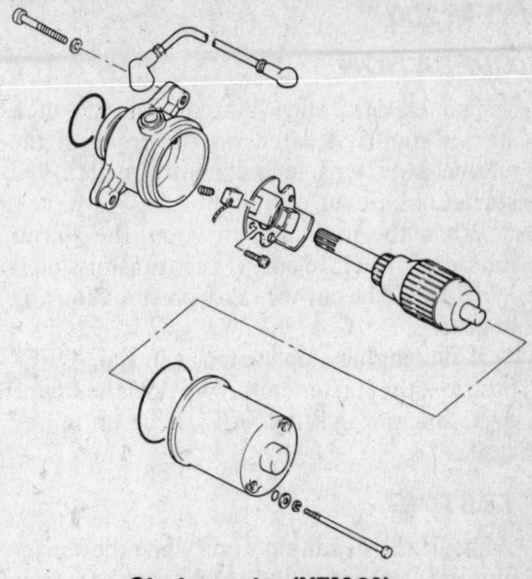

Starter motor (YFM 80)

4. Examine the carbon brushes for wear or damage. Replace both if either measures less than 3.5mm (0.14 in.).

5. Check brush spring tension. it should be 310-450 g.

6. The mica undercut of the commutator should be maintained at 1.0mm (0.04 in.). Any carbon deposits should be cleaned out of the commutator grooves, and a piece of hacksaw blade or the like used to increase the undercut depth, if necessary.

7. Polish the commutator with fine emery cloth and then clean it thoroughly before installation.

8. Measure the diameter of the commutator. Replace the motor is it measures less than 15.5mm (0.61 in.).

9. Check the condition of the armature bearing and replace it if it is damaged.

10. Check oil seal condition. Check O-ring condition. Replace them if cracked, knicked or worn or if there is any evidence or oil leakage.

Installation

1. Lightly oil the lips of the oil seal before assembling the motor.
2. When assembling the cases, align the groove and tab on the cases.
3. Lightly lubricate the O-ring before installation.

CUT-OFF RELAY

1. Remove the seat.
2. Remove the battery.
3. Remove the rear fender.
4. Disconnect the relay at the plastic coupling.
5. Check the resistance of the windings. The reading should be about 80 ohms.

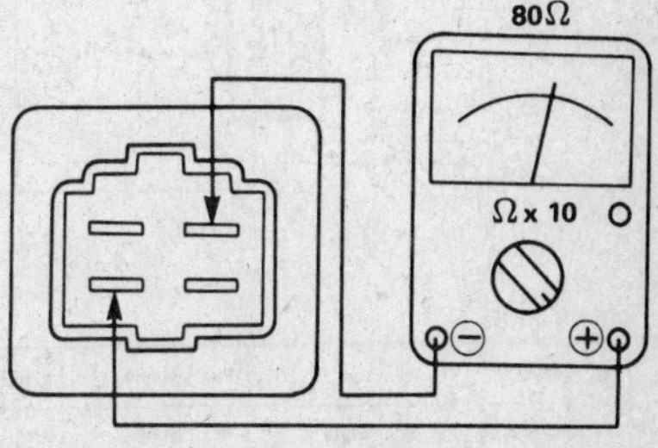

Checking cut-off relay (YFM 80)

YFM 200

OPERATION

The electric start system consists of a starter motor, located on the front of the engine, a starter solenoid, neutral switch, and starter circuit cut-off relay.

When the main switch is on, the starter motor will operate only if the transmission is in neutral. The cut-off relay prevents starting in gear.

If the engine stop switch is in the "OFF" position, the starter motor will turn the engine over, but the ignition will not be on in any case.

TESTING

1. If the headlight dims when the starter button is pushed, it indicates that the starter motor is drawing current.
2. If nothing happens when the button is pushed, the starter motor is not getting any current. Suspect a defective starter button or starter solenoid.
3. To check the starter solenoid and starter button, the easiest method is to by pass them by disconnecting the battery high tension lead from the solenoid and connecting battery directly to the starter motor high tension terminal with the aid of a suitable jumper. If the motor still fails to work, the starter motor itself is probably the source of the trouble. But if it does, suspect the starter button or solenoid.
4. If the starter motor spins freely, but the engine doesn't turn over suspect the starter motor clutch.
5. If the engine will turn over only very slowly and without a great degree of predictability, some possible causes include: a low or almost dead battery, oil which is too thick for weather conditions (extreme cold), or bad bearings in the motor itself. Worn bearings could cause the armature to contact the field coils which will effectively short out the starter. Usually, repeated attempts at starting will result in the starter motor getting very hot.Other possible causes of starter motor trouble include worn brushes, a worn or dirty commutator, or a defective armature.

STARTER SOLENOID

To access the solenoid, remove the seat, rear carrier and rear fender.

1. If the battery is in reasonably good condition, and nothing at all happens when the starter button is pushed, check the solenoid.
2. Disconnect the starter cable at the solenoid. When the button is pushed, there should be an audible "click" which indicates that the solenoid is opening.
3. If further testing is necessary, remove the solenoid from the machine.

CAUTION: *Be sure to disconnect the cables at the battery before disconnecting the solenoid terminals.*

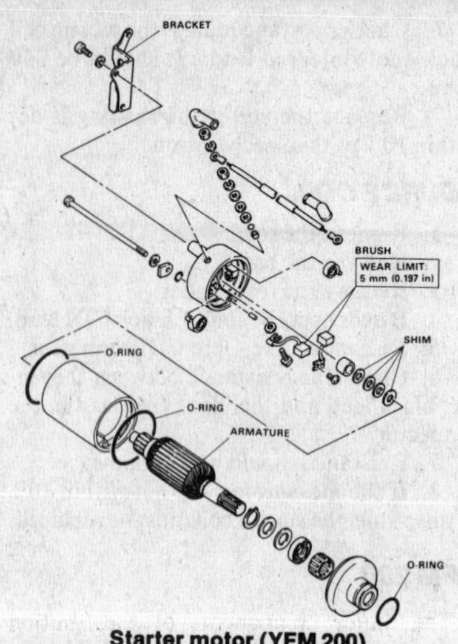

Starter motor (YFM 200)

Connect a fully charged 12-volt battery across the solenoid low-tension leads and check for continuity across the high-tension terminals with an ohmmeter or self-contained test light. If there is not continuity, replace or repair the solenoid.

4. Check for continuity across the low-tension terminals with an ohmmeter or self-powered test light. Resistance should be 3.5 ohms. If there is not continuity, the primary

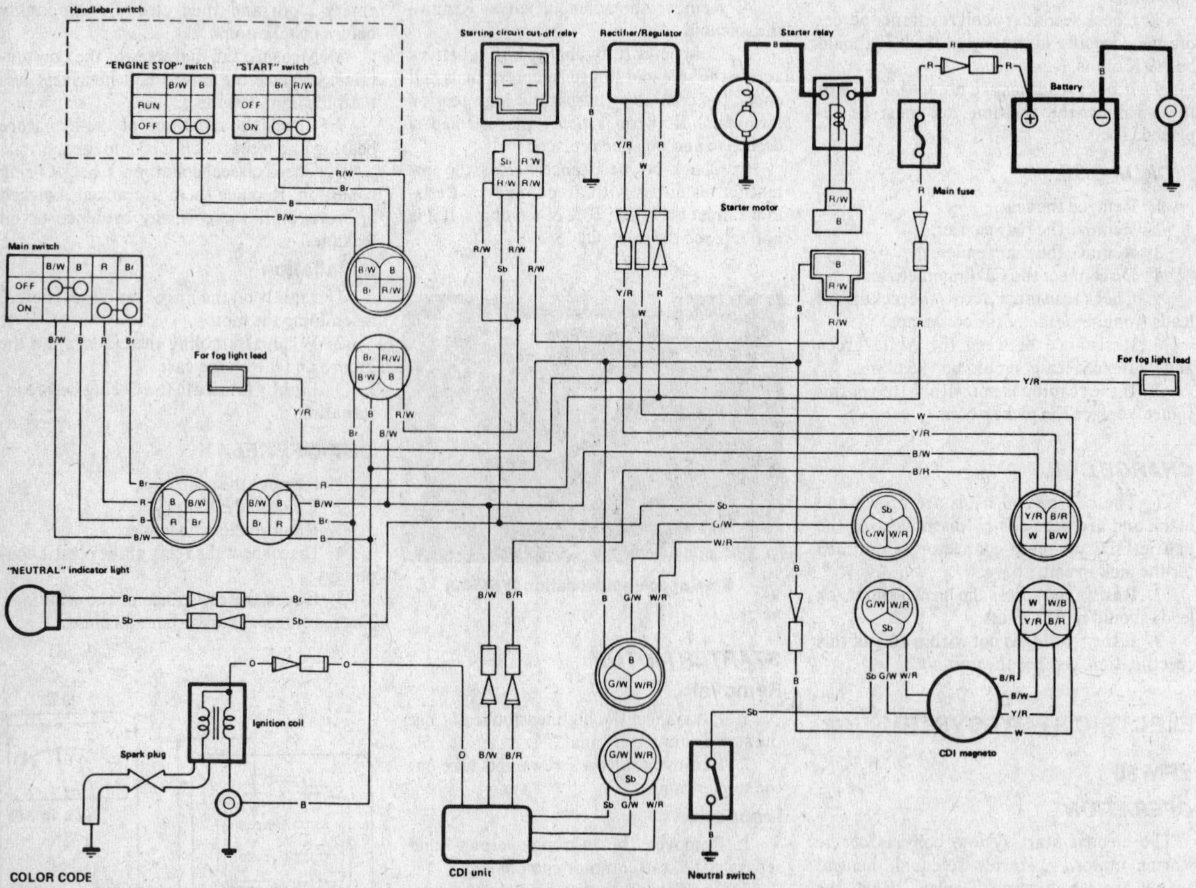

COLOR CODE

B	Black	R	Red	Sb	Sky blue	Y/R	Yellow/Red	W/R	White/Red	G/W	Green/White
O	Orange	W	White	Br	Brown	R/W	Red/White	B/W	Black/White	B/R	Black/Red

YFM 80

winding of the solenoid is broken, and the unit must be replaced.

5. If starter trouble began just after the starter button housing was disassembled or moved for any reason, check the connections at the switch as they may have come adrift.

STARTER MOTOR

Removal

1. Disconnect the high tension lead at the starter motor.
2. Remove the starter motor bracket screws (4) and take off the bracket.
3. Remove the starter motor.

Inspection

1. Take out the two scres and remove the starter side cover.
2. Check electrical continuity between the commutator and armature core using a multitester or test light and battery. If continutiy exists, the armature coil is grounded and the complete starter motor unit must be replaced.
3. Check for continuity between all of the commutator segments. Continuity must exist in each case (maximum allowable resistance: 0.023 ohms).
4. Check continuity between the brush that is wired to the stator coil and the starter motor cable. Lack of continuity indicates an open circuit in the stator coil, and the starter motor unit should be replaced. Resistance should not exceed 0.05 ohms.
5. Examine the carbon brushes for damage to the contact surfaces and measure their length. Replace the brushes as a set if either one measures less than 5.0mm (0.2 in.), or if they are damaged in any way.
6. Brush spring tension should be measured with a small pull-scale. Replace the springs if they have weakened to less than 400 g tension.
7. The mica undercut of the commutator should be maintained at 0.7mm (0.027 in.). Any carbon deposits should be cleaned out of the commutator grooves, and a piece of hacksaw blade or the like used to increase the undercut depth if necessary.
8. Polish the commutator with fine emery cloth and then clean it thoroughly before installing.
9. Measure the diameter of the commutator. The armature should be replaced if the measurement is less than 22mm (0.87 in.).
10. Check the condition of the armature bearings and replace them as a set if any damage is noted.
11. Check the condition of the oil seal and replace it if the seal lips are cracked or worn.
12. Unsealed bearings should be lubricated with 20W or 30W motor oil before assembly. Coat the lips of the oil seal with white grease before assembly.

Installation

1. When installing the starter motor, be sure that the O-ring is not damaged.
2. Tighten the mounting screws to 5 ft. lbs.

CUT-OFF RELAY

1. Remove the seat, rear carrier and rear fender.
2. Remove the relay from the rubber clamp. Disconnect the wiring at the plastic connector.

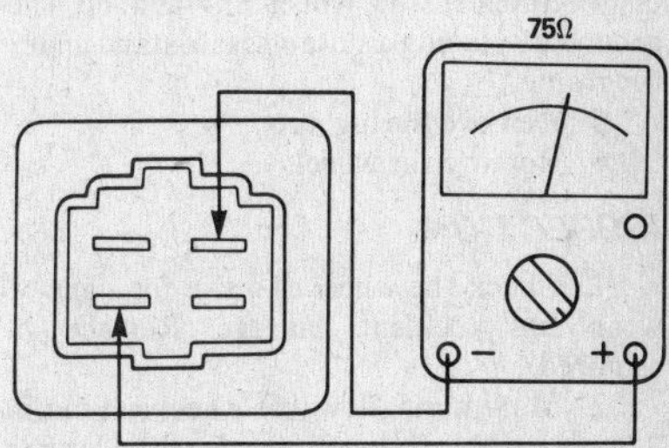

Checking cut-off relay (YFM 200)

3. Check the resistance of the relay windings. Reading should be about 75 ohms. If reading is not correct, replace the relay.
4. Put 12 VDC across the windings. Make a voltage reading as shown. If the voltmeter does not show 12 V, replace the relay.

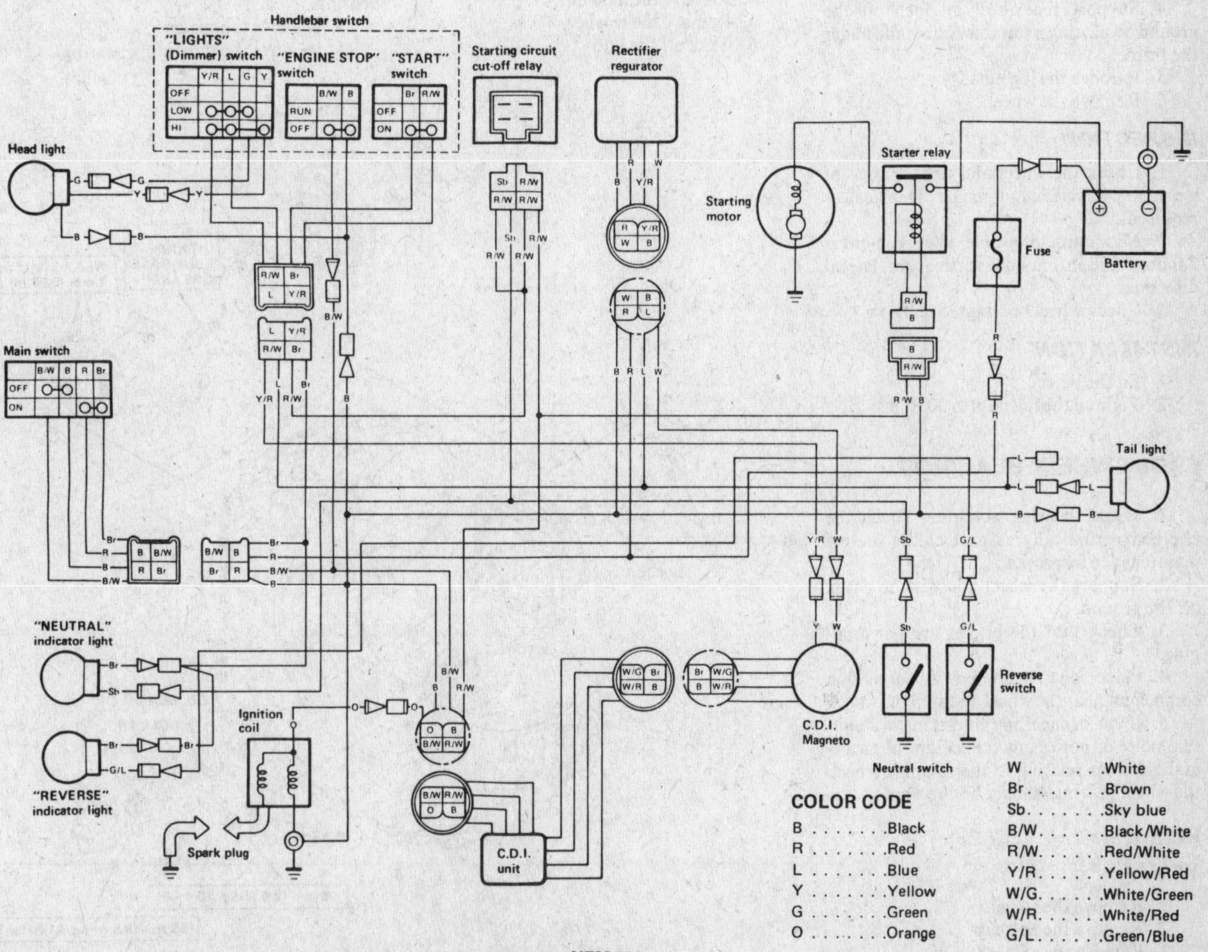

COLOR CODE

B	Black
R	Red
L	Blue
Y	Yellow
G	Green
O	Orange
W	White
Br	Brown
Sb	Sky blue
B/W	Black/White
R/W	Red/White
Y/R	Yellow/Red
W/G	White/Green
W/R	White/Red
G/L	Green/Blue

YFM 200

CHASSIS

FRONT WHEELS

YFM 80

REMOVAL

1. Park the machine on a level surface.
2. Apply the parking brake.
3. Loosen the three wheel lug nuts.
4. Support the wheel an inch off the ground by placing a suitable, safe stand under the frame.
5. Remove the lug nuts.
6. Remove the wheel.

INSPECTION

1. Check the wheel and tire for signs of wear and accident damage. Replace as required.
2. Maximum allowable wheel run-out is 2.0mm (0.08 in.) in both vertical and lateral directions.
3. Check wheel bearings. See below.

INSTALLATION

1. Fit the wheel.
2. Tighten the lug nuts to 20 ft. lbs.

YFM 200

REMOVAL

1. Park the machine on a level surface.
2. Apply the parking brake.
3. Loosen the four wheel lug nuts.
4. Support the wheel an inch off the ground by placing a suitable, safe stand under the frame.
5. Remove the lug nuts.
6. Remove the wheel.

INSPECTION

1. Check the wheel and tire for signs of wear and accident damage. Replace as required.
2. Maximum allowable wheel run-out is 2.0mm (0.08 in.) in both vertical and lateral directions.
3. Check wheel bearings. See below.

INSTALLATION

1. Fit the wheel.
2. Tighten the lug nuts to 20 ft. lbs.

FRONT WHEEL BEARINGS

1. Wheel bearing condition should be checked periodically as part of the routine maintenance inspection.
2. Support the wheel you wish to check off the ground.
3. Check that the brakes are not dragging.
4. Place one hand on a suspension component near the wheel and spin the wheel.
5. If you can feel any vibration, hear unusual noise or notice any other signs of abnormal behavior relating to the spinning wheel, the wheel bearings should be checked.

Removal

YFM 80

1. Remove the wheel.
2. Remove the hub cap.
3. Remove the axle cotter pin.

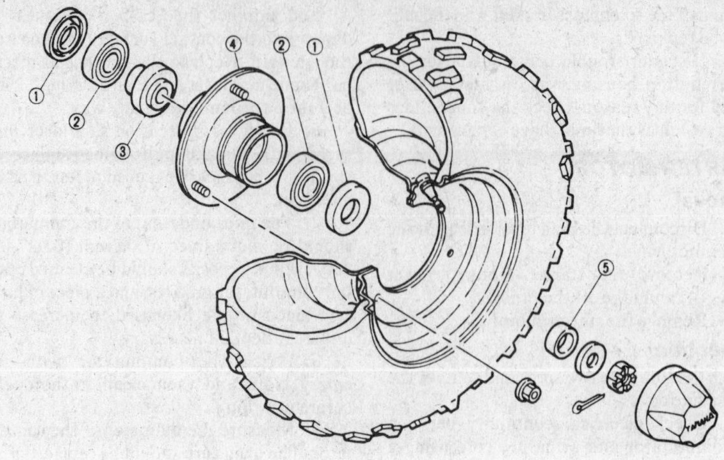

YFM 80 front wheel: 1, oil seals; 2, bearings, 3, spacer; 4, hub; 5, collar

4. Remove the axle nut.
5. Remove the washer.
6. Take off the hub.
7. Remove the axle collar from the hub.
8. Wheel bearings are pressed in to the hub and protected by grease seals on each side.

YFM 200

1. Remove the wheel.
2. Remove the hub cap.
3. Remove the axle cotter pin.
4. Remove the axle nut.
5. Remove the washer.
6. Take off the hub.
7. The wheel bearings are pressed into the wheel and protected by grease seals on each side.

Inspection

ALL MODELS

1. Pry out the grease seals from the hub.
2. Reach into the hub with a suitable punch. Attempt to move the bearing spacer aside as far as possible to achieve purchase on the outer race of the bearing. Drive out the bearing.
3. Remove the spacer.
4. Remove the remaining bearing.

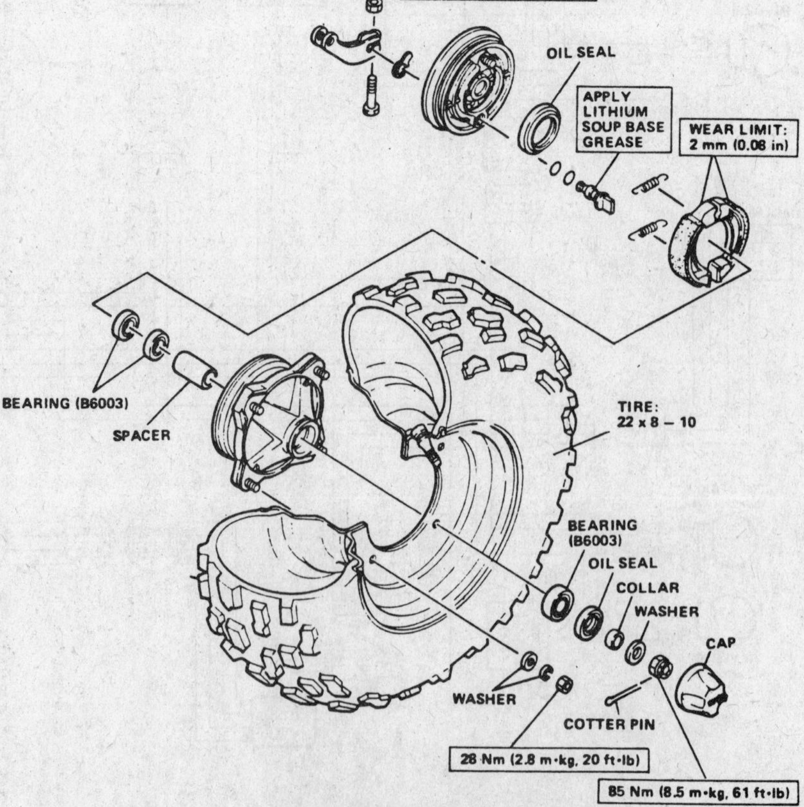

YFM 200 front wheel assembly

5. Clean bearings thoroughly in a safe solvent.

6. Check for obvious signs of wear or damage; scored or crushed balls, deformed cage, etc.

7. Lubricate bearings lightly and rotate slowly. Check for roughness, noise, and so on.

8. Hold the outer race firmly and attempt to move the inner race. There must be no play evident.

9. Replace both wheel bearings if either is damaged.

Installation

1. Pack the bearings with a good quality bearing grease. Place a quantity in the hub as well.

2. Clean the bearing seats thoroughly.

3. Drive in one bearing. Bearings may be installed with a bearing driver, a large block of wood or the like.

CAUTION: *Do not strike the center race when installing bearings. The driver should contact the outer race only. Be sure the bearings are driven straight into the hub and not cocked or tilted.*

4. Instill the spacer.

5. Drive in the remaining bearing.

6. Press in the grease seals. New grease seals should be used. Lightly lubricate the seal lips with lithium soap-based grease.

YFM 80

1. Lubricate the axle lightly.
2. Install the hub.
3. Be sure the collar is in place.
4. Install the washer.
5. Fit the axle nut. Torque to 47 ft. lbs.
6. Use a new axle nut cotter pin. Fit the hub cap. Install the wheel. Lug nut torque is 20 ft. lbs.

YFM 200

1. Lubricate the axle lightly.
2. Install the hub.
3. Install the washer.
4. Fit the axle nut. Torque it to 61 ft. lbs.
5. Install a new axle nut cotter pin.
6. Fit the hub cap.
7. Install the wheel. Torque lug nuts to 20 ft. lbs.

FRONT BRAKE (YFM 200)

1. Remove the front wheel.

2. Remove the hub cap, cotter pin and axle nut and washer.

3. Remove the hub.

4. Check the thickness of the brake shoe linings at the middle and the ends. If less than 2mm (0.08 in.) at any point, both shoes should be replaced.

5. Check the linings for scoring or other evidence of unusual wear. Damaged linings must be replaced. If the linings are scored, check the brake drum as well.

6. Linings should be sandpapered to remove any glaze or dirt, then cleaned thoroughly prior to installation.

CAUTION: *Do not allow any type of solvent or lubricant to contact the linings.*

7. Check that the brake hub surface is smooth and featureless. Remove dirt, oil or foreign matter from the drum surface. Remove minor imperfections with emery cloth. Clean the hub thoroughly. Scoring which cannot be removed by hand may have to be cut away by mounting the hub on a lathe.

8. To remove the brake plate assembly, back off and remove the brake cable adjuster at the plate.

9. Remove the cable pin, washer and springs and disconnect the cable from the brake plate.

10. Remove the brake plate from the axle.

11. Remove the shoes by pulling them off.

12. Match-mark the brake cam and cam lever so it will be easier to put the lever back in the right position when assembling.

13. Remove the brake lever. Remove the cam.

14. Check the return springs for weakness, corrosion or more obvious damage.

15. Remove any old grease from the brake cam with solvent. Remove any rust or corrosion with a medium grade sandpaper.

16. Lubricate the cam with a lithium-based grease before installation.

17. When fitting the brake plate, be sure to engage the brake anchor on the plate with the lug of the front suspension knuckle.

18. The remainder of the installation procedure is the reverse of removal.

REAR WHEELS

YFM 80

REMOVAL

1. Park the machine on a level surface.
2. Apply the parking brake.
3. Loosen the three wheel lug nuts.
4. Support the wheel an inch off the ground by placing a suitable, safe stand under the frame.
5. Remove the lug nuts.
6. Remove the wheel.

INSPECTION

1. Check the wheel and tire for signs of wear and accident damage. Replace as required.

2. Maximum allowable wheel run-out is 2.0mm (0.08 in.) in both vertical and lateral directions.

3. Check wheel bearings.

INSTALLATION

1. Fit the wheel.
2. Tighten the lug nuts to 20 ft. lbs.

YFM 200

REMOVAL

1. Park the machine on a level surface.
2. Apply the parking brake.
3. Loosen the three wheel lug nuts.
4. Support the wheel an inch off the ground by placing a suitable stand under the frame.
5. Remove the lug nuts.
6. Remove the wheel.

INSPECTION

1. Check the wheel and tire for signs of wear and accident damage. Replace as required.

2. Maximum allowable wheel run-out is 2.0mm (0.08 in.) in both vertical and lateral directions.

3. Check wheel bearings.

Front brake anchor engaged with lug (1)

INSTALLATION

1. Fit the wheel.
2. Torque lug nuts to 32 ft. lbs.

REAR WHEEL BEARINGS

YFM 80

Refer to the "Front Wheel Bearing" procedure, above. Front and rear hubs on these machines are identical.

NOTE: *Rear axle nut torque is 61 ft. lbs.*

YFM 200

Wheel bearing service requires virtual disassembly of the axle. Refer to the "Rear Axle" section, below.

REAR BRAKES

YFM 80

REMOVAL

1. Apply the parking brake.
2. Remove the rear wheels.
3. Remove the hub cap, cotter pin, axle nut and washer.
4. Remove the hub.
5. Remove the two axle ring nuts.
6. Release the parking brake.
7. Remove the pedal and hand lever cable adjusters.
8. Unhook the brake lever spring.
9. Remove the brake cover.
10. Remove the brake drum.
11. The linings are now accessible for inspection.

INSPECTION

1. Check the thickness of the brake linings at the middle and at the ends. If less than 2mm (0.08 in.) at any point, both shoes must be replaced.

2. Check the linings for scoring or other evidence of unusual wear. Damaged linings must be replaced. If the linings are scored, check the drum for similar damage.

3. Check the linings for glaze or dirt. Sandpaper them lightly. Clean thoroughly before installing the drum.

CAUTION: *Do not allow any type of solvent or lubricant to contact the linings.*

4. Check that the brake drum surface is smooth and featureless. Remove dirt, oil or foreign matter from the drum. Remove minor imperfections with emery cloth. Clean the hub thoroughly. Scoring which cannot be removed by hand may have to be cut away by a lathe.

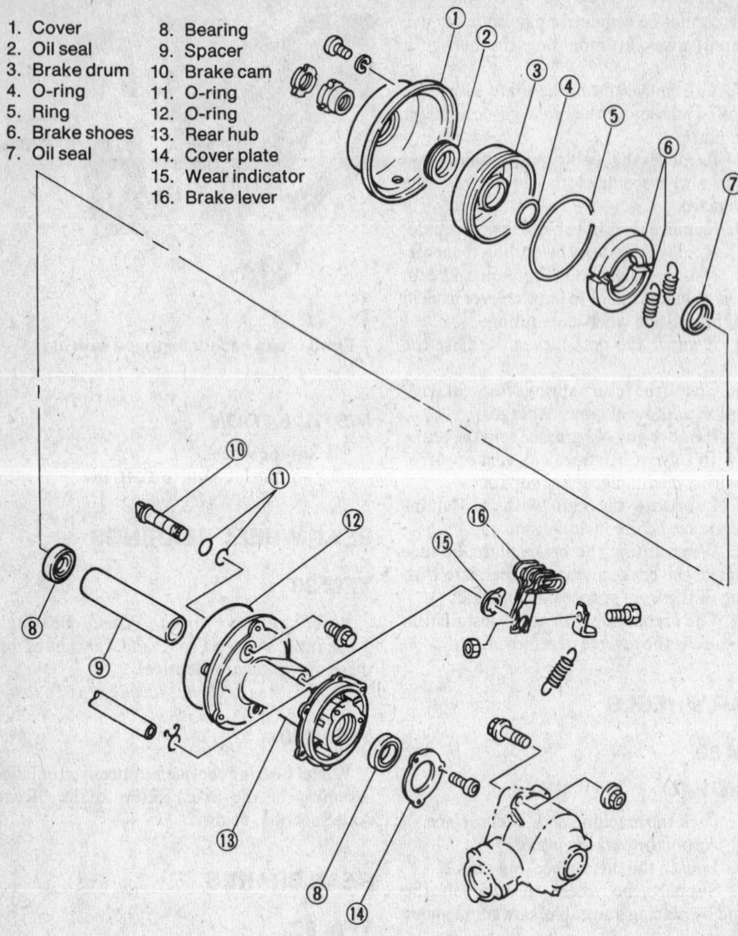

Rear brake assembly (YFM 80)

5. To remove the brake shoes, pull them off the brake plate together.

6. Check the return springs for weakness, corrosion or more obvious damage.

7. Match-mark the brake cam and the cam lever so it will be easier to put the lever back in the right position when assembling.

8. Remove the lever. Remove the cam.

9. Remove any old grease from the cam with solvent. Remove any rust or corrosion with a medium grade sandpaper.

10. Lubricate the cam with a lithium-based grease before installation.

INSTALLATION

1. Installation is basically the reverse of the removal procedure. Note the following points.

Caliper inner body (1), inner pad (2) and brake disk (3)

2. To install the axle ring nuts, first be sure that they are fitted with the tapered side facing inward.

3. Thread the inner ring nut on and make it finger tight.

4. Install the outer ring nut.

5. Holding the inner ring nut in place, tighten the outer nut to 80 ft. lbs.

6. Hold the outer nut in place and tighten the inner nut to 105 ft. lbs.

7. Refer to the preceding sections for wheel installation.

YFM 200

REMOVAL

1. Block the front wheel so that the machine cannot move.

2. Raise the rear of the machine so that the rear wheels are off the ground.

3. Back off the rear brake cable adjuster wing nuts.

4. Disconnect the rear brake cables and springs from the caliper lever.

5. Remove the caliper securing nuts.

6. Remove the caliper lever assembly and outer pad from the caliper body.

7. Remove the brake cover securing screws and take off the brake cover.

8. Remove the caliper securing bolts.

9. Pull off the brake disk.

10. Remove the caliper body from the rear wheel hub.

PAD INSPECTION

1. Replace the pads as a set if either is worn to a thickness of 1.5mm (0.06 in.) or less.

BRAKE INSPECTION

1. Inspect the caliper piston and replace it if it is rusted or otherwise damaged.

2. Check the brake disk. If there are score marks on the surface, the disk can be turned down, but only if the minimum thickness of 3mm (0.12 in.) is maintained.

3. Check disk thickness. If it is worn below 3mm (0.12 in.), it must be replaced.

4. Check disk run-out. Maximum allowable run-out is 0.5mm (0.02 in.).

INSTALLATION

1. Installation is the reverse of removal. Note the following torques.

CAUTION: *When installing the caliper, be sure that bolts are installed in their original locations. The longer body bolt is installed in the higher position.*

2. Tighten the caliper body bolts to 36 ft. lbs.

3. Tighten the caliper nuts to 6.5 ft. lbs.

4. Adjust the brake after installation as outlined in "Maintenance."

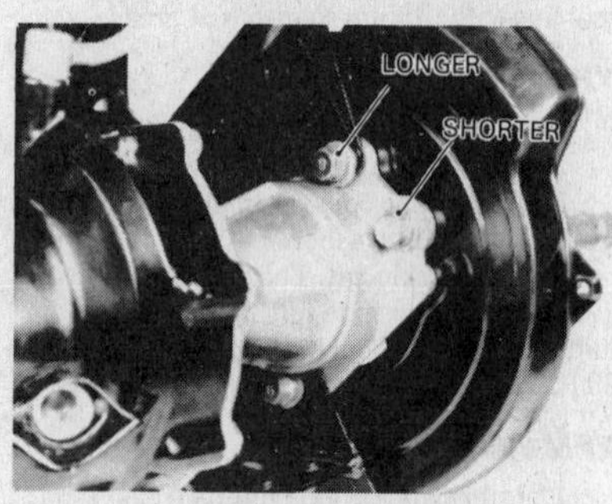

Correct bolt installation

TIE-RODS/STEERING KNUCKLES

YFM 80

REMOVAL

1. Remove the front wheels.

2. Remove the hub assemblies.

3. Remove the tie-rod cotter pins and nuts.

4. Remove the tie-rods.

5. Remove the steering knuckle cotter pin.

6. Remove the steering knuckle nut, then the washer, thrust covers, bushings, spacer, bolt and the knuckle itself.

INSPECTION

1. Check the fit of the spacer and bushings in the knuckle. If they are loose, replace them. There must be no play between knuckle, spacer and bushings.

2. Check the bushings for damage. Bushings must be replaced as a set.

3. Check the tie-rod end for free-play. If there is any, replace the tie-rod end.

4. Check the tie-rod end for rough rotation. If rotation is rough, replace the tie-rod end.

5. Check the thrust covers for wear or damage and replace if necessary.

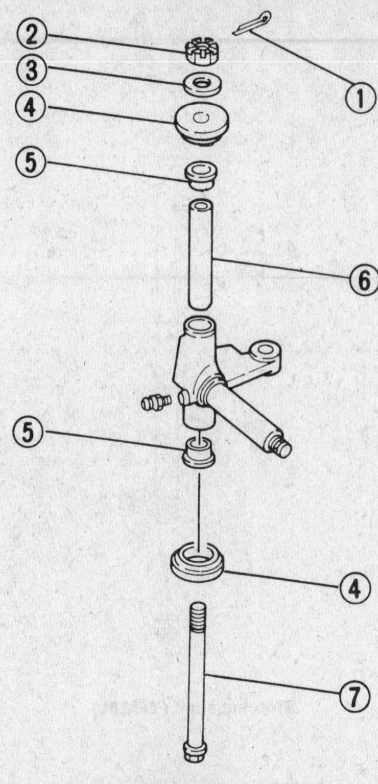

1. Cotter pin
2. Steering knuckle nut
3. Plain washer
4. Thrust covers
5. Bushings
6. Spacer
7. Knuckle shaft

Knuckle assembly (YFM 80)

INSTALLATION

1. Lubricate the knuckle shaft, bushings and thrust covers with lithium-based grease.
2. Install the steering knuckle and its components.
3. Tighten the steering knuckle nut to 22 ft. lbs.

CAUTION: *Do not overtighten.*

4. Use a new cotter pin.

Checking tie-rod end for rough rotation

5. Adjust tie-rod length as follows:

a. Refer to the illustration of the tie-rod. "A" is a right-hand thread; "B" is a left-hand thread.

b. The distance between the center lines of the rod end threads ("a") must be 240mm (9.45 in.).

c. To make this adjustment, loosen both rod end locknuts and turn both ends by equal amounts until the rod length is correct.

d. Exposed threads ("b") for each rod end must be equal.

e. When these conditions are met, locknuts "A" and "B" can be tightened to 22 ft. lbs. Be sure that the rod end threaded studs are properly positioned before tightening.

6. Install the tie-rods. The rod with the white paint mark goes on the right.
7. Tighten the rod mounting nuts to 32 ft. lbs.
8. Use new cotter pins.

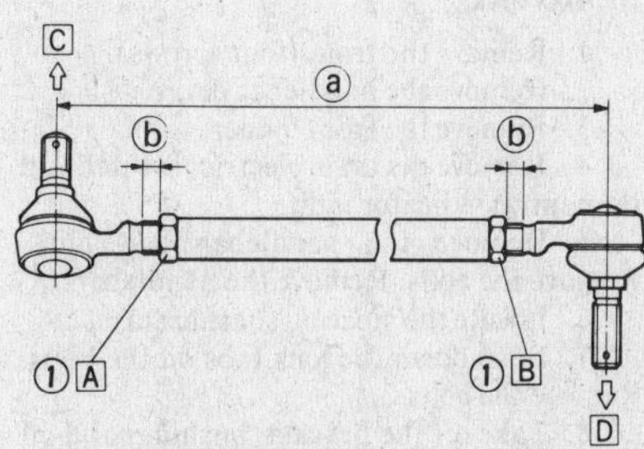

Tie-rod installation (see text)

TIE-ROD ADJUSTMENT

1. Park the machine on a level surface.
2. Mark the center of the thread on the left and right tires.
3. Measure the distance between the marks.
4. Turn both tires 180°.
5. Measure the distance between the marks.
6. Subtract the first measurement from the second.
7. The calculation must give 0-3mm (0-0.12 in.). This is the toe-in specification.
8. If the calculated value is not within this specification, adjust rod length as outlined above.

NOTE: *When the tie-rods are installed on the machine, length can be adjusted by loosening both rod end locknuts and turning the rod. Flat are provided for an open-end wrench.*

CAUTION: *Toe-in is an important setting which will affect handling. This procedure should be done by someone with the experience to do it properly.*

9. If toe-in adjustment or rod length adjustments are made, carefully test machine handling before normal riding.
10. Be sure the handlebars point straight ahead. When toe-in is adjusted, both rods must be adjusted by similar amounts or misalignment may occur.
11. Ride the machine slowly in a straight line on a smooth surface with the hands resting lightly on the handlebars. The machine must run in a straight line. Handling must be normal. If the machine pulls to one side or handlebar response seems faulty, check rod length, toe-in and the front end components.

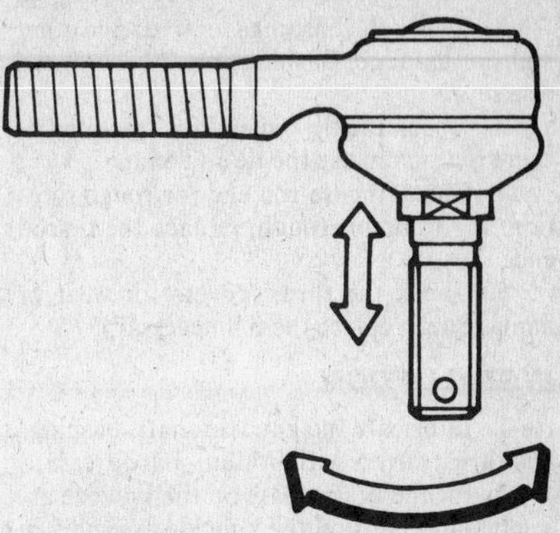

Checking tie-rod end for free-play

YFM 200

REMOVAL

1. Remove the front wheels.
2. Remove the hub assemblies.
3. Remove the tie-rod cotter pins and nuts.
4. Remove the tie-rods.
5. Remove the steering knuckle cotter pin.
6. Remove the steering knuckle nut.

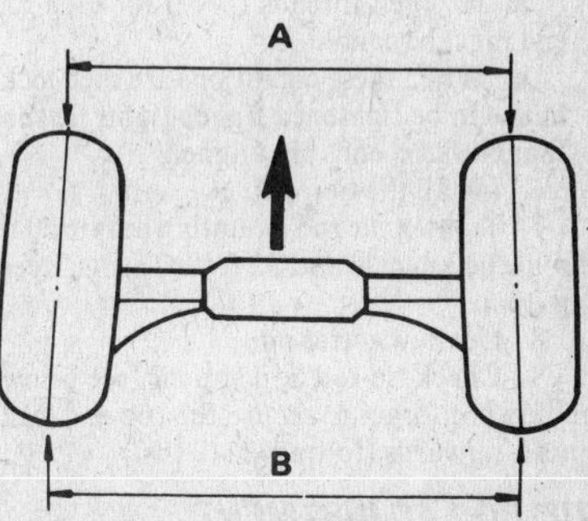

Toe-in is calculated by subtracting "A" from "B"

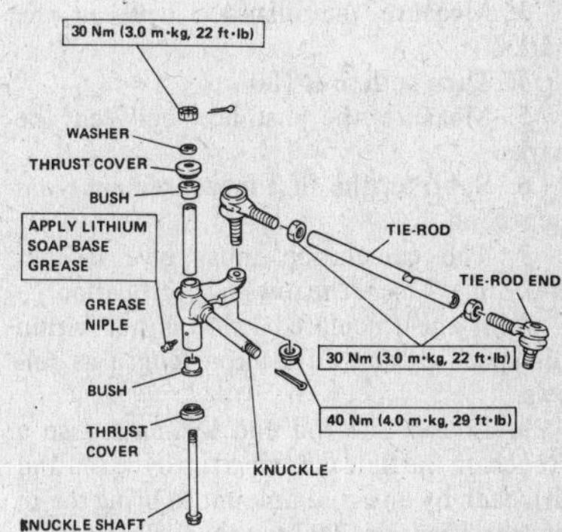

Knuckle and tie-rod assembly (YFM 200)

7. Pull the knuckle/brake assembly out and separate the brake plate from the knuckle.
8. Separate knuckle components: thrust covers, spacer, bushings and bolt.

INSPECTION

1. Fit the spacer and bushings in the knuckle and check for free-play or looseness. There must be no play. If there is, replace the bushings.

2. Check the bushings for wear and other signs of damage. Bushings must be replaced as a set.

3. Check the tie-rod end for free-play. If there is any, replace the tie-rod end.

4. Check the tie-rod end for rough rotation. If rotation is rough, replace the tie-rod end.

5. Check the thrust covers for wear or damage and replace them if necessary.

INSTALLATION

1. Lubricate the knuckle shaft, bushings and thrust covers with lithium- base grease.

2. Fit the brake plate on the knuckle assembly and position the knuckle assembly in the frame.

3. Tighten the steering knuckle nut to 22 ft. lbs.

CAUTION: *Do not overtighten.*

4. Use a new cotter pin.

5. Adjust tie-rod length as follows:

a. Refer to the illustration of the tie-rod. Note right-hand and left hand threads.

b. The distance between the center lines of the rod end threads must be 285mm (11.22 in.).

c. To make this adjustment, loosen both rod end locknuts and turn both ends by equal amounts until rod length is correct.

d. Exposed threads ("A") for each rod end must be equal.

e. When these conditions are met, locknuts can be tightened finger-tight. Be sure that both rod ends are aligned.

6. Install the tie-rods.

7. Tighten the rod mounting nuts to 29 ft. lbs. at the knuckle and 32 ft. lbs. at the steering stem.

8. Use new cotter pins.

9. Check tie-rod adjustment (see below) and do not forget to secure the rod end locknuts afterwards (torque: 22 ft. lbs.).

TIE-ROD ADJUSTMENT

1. Park the machine on a level surface.

2. Mark the center of the tread on the left and right tires.

3. Measure the distance between the marks.

4. Turn both tires 180°.

5. Measure the distance between the marks.

6. Subtract the first measurement from the second.

7. The calculation must give 0-5mm (0-0.2 in.). This is the tow-in specification.

8. If the calculated value is not within this specification, adjust rod length as follows.

9. Loosen the rod end locknuts. Use a wrench on the flats machined into the rod and turn each by an equal amount to bring toe-in into specification. Tighten the locknuts to 22 ft. lbs.

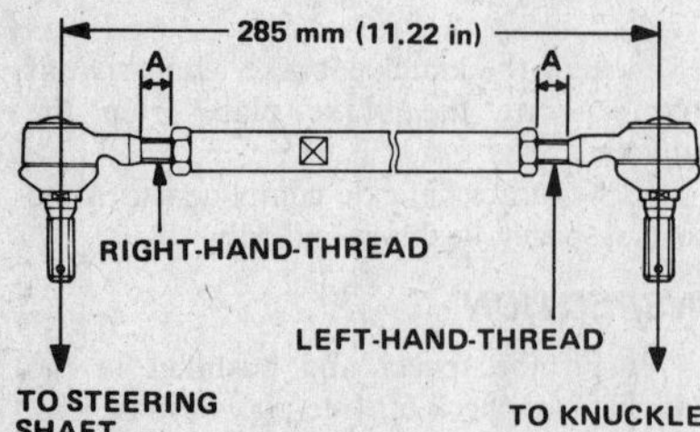

Tie-rod installation points (see text)

CAUTION: *Toe-in is an important setting which will affect handling. This procedure should be done by someone with the experience to do it properly.*

10. If toe-in adjustment or rod length adjustments are made, carefully test machine handling before normal riding.

11. Be sure the handlebars point straight ahead. When toe-in is adjusted, both rods must be adjusted by similar amounts or misalignment may occur.

12. Ride the machine slowly in a straight line on a smooth surface with the hands resting lightly on the handlebars. The machine must run in a straight line. Handling must be normal. If the machine pulls to one side, or handlebar response seems faulty, check rod length, toe-in and the front end components.

STEERING STEM

YFM 80

REMOVAL

1. Remove the front (four screws).

2. Remove the handlebar cover.

3. Remove the front fender.

4. Remove the main electrical switch and the neutral indicator light.

5. Remove the handlebar bolt clips. Remove the bolts. Remove the handlebars.

6. Locate the steering shaft bracket.

7. Bend down the lock tabs on the bolts. Remvoe the bolts.

8. Take off the bracket, bushings and oil seals.

9. Remove the front frame guard (four bolts).

10. At the bottom of the steering shaft, remove the cotter pin. Take off the nut and washer.

11. Disconnect both tie-rods from the steering shaft.

12. Remove the steering shaft.

INSPECTION

1. Check the shaft for a bent condition. If it is bent, replace it.

CAUTION: *Do not attempt to straighten a bent shaft. This may weaken it and cause a dangerous operating condition.*

2. Check the bushings for wear. Replace them if any wear or other damage is noted.

3. Check the oil seals for damage and replace them as required.

4. With the steering stem installed, check for shaft free-play. There must be none. If there is, the bushings (upper and lower) must be replaced.

INSTALLATION

1. Be sure that all cables and wiring are on the correct sides of the shaft when it is installed.

2. Tighten the tie-rod end nuts to 32 ft. lbs. Use new cotter pins.

3. Tighten the bottom steering shaft nut to 22 ft. lbs. Use a new cotter pin.

4. Lubricate the bushings and oil seals with lithium-base grease. Be sure the seals are not damaged when installing them.

5. Fit the bushings, ensuring that the seals go into the grooves provided.

6. Install the bracket.

7. Fit new lock tabs.

8. Install the bracket bolts and torque to 17 ft. lbs.

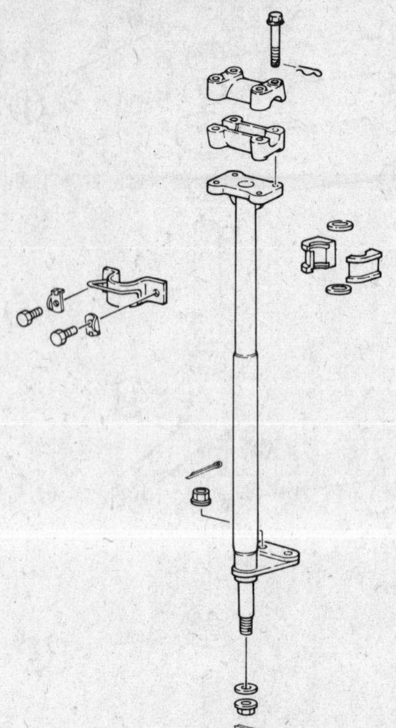

Steering shaft (YFM 80)

9. Bend up the lock tabs.

10. Tighten the handlebar bolts to 17 ft. lbs.

11. Use new handlebar bolt clips.

12. Use a grease gun with lithium-base grease on the fitting at the bottom of the steering shaft.

YFM 200

REMOVAL

1. Remove the seat.

2. Remove the front carrier.

3. Remove the fuel tank cover.

4. Remove the front fender.

5. Remove the handlebar cover.

6. Remove the headlight bracket bolts.

7. Remove the clips on the handlebar holders. Remove the nuts and take off the handlebar assembly.

8. Flatten the lock tabs on the steering shaft bracket bolts.

9. Remove the bracket bolts.

10. Remove the bracket.

11. Remove the guides and O-rings.

12. Remove the front frame guard.

13. Remove the tie-rod cotter pins and nuts and disconnect the rods from the steering shaft.

14. Remove the cotter pin, nut and washer from the bottom of the steering shaft.

15. Remove the steering shaft from the frame.

INSPECTION

1. Check the shaft for a bent condition. If it is bent, replace it.

CAUTION: *Do not attempt to straighten a bent shaft. This may weaken it and cause a dangerous operating situation.*

1. Check the upper guides and lower (frame) bushings for wear. Replace them as a set if there is any obvious damage.

3. Check the oil seals for damage and replace them as required.

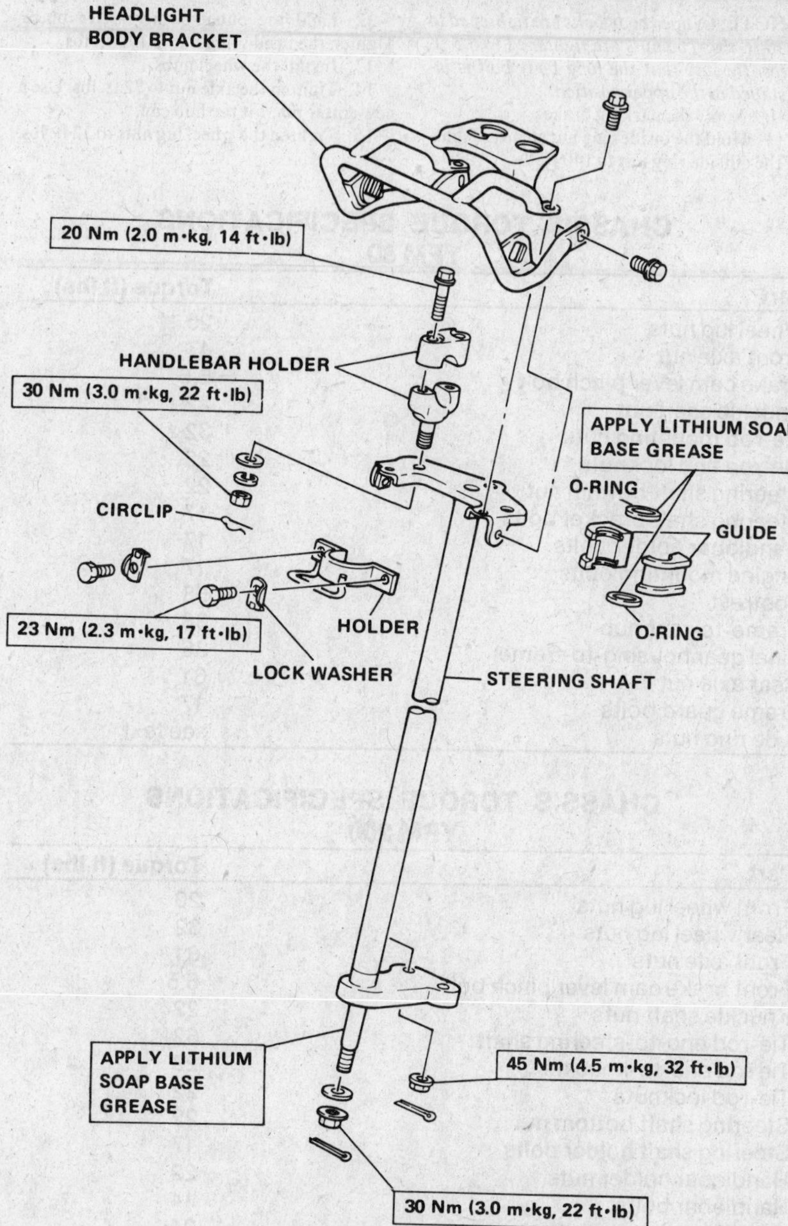

Steering shaft (YFM 200)

4. With the steering stem installed, check for free-play. Any looseness or play in the shaft will require replacement of the upper guides and lower frame bushings.

INSTALLATION

1. Be sure that all cables and wiring are on the correct side of the shaft when it is installed.
2. Install the shaft.
3. Connect the tie-rod ends. tighten the nuts to 32 ft. lbs. Use new cotter pin.
4. Install the washer and steering stem bottom nut. Tighten the nut to 22 ft. lbs. Use a new cotter pin.
5. Lubricate the upper guides and O-rings with lithium-base grease.
6. Install the components, ensuring that the seals go into the grooves provided in the guides.
7. Install the bracket.
8. Fit new lock tabs.
9. Install and tighten bracket bolts to 14 ft. lbs.
10. Bend up the locking tabs.
11. Tighten the handlebar holder nuts to 22 ft. lbs. Use new clips.
12. Torque the headlight bracket bolts to 7.2 ft. lbs.
13. The remainder of the procedure is the reverse of disassembly.

REAR AXLE

YFM 80

REMOVAL

1. Remove the rear wheels.
2. Remove the rear wheel hubs.
3. Remove the two axle ring nuts.
4. Remove the brake adjusters and disconnect brake cables from the levers.
5. Unhook the brake lever spring.
6. Remove the brake cover.
7. Remove the brake drum.
8. Remove the brake shoes.
9. Remove the three bolts which secure the final gear housing to the drive shaft tube.
10. Disconnect the breather hose.
1. Remove the mounting hardware and take off the rear hub assembly.

INSTALLATION

1. Position the final gear housing so that the breather hose fitting is on the top.
2. Tighten the rear hub bolts to 7.2 ft. lbs.
3. Apply a liquid gasket sealant to the final gear housing-drive shaft tube mating surface.
4. Tighten the three bolts to 18 ft. lbs.
5. Tighten the rear hub mounting nuts to 36 ft. lbs.
6. Fit the axle ring nuts with the tapered side facing inwards.
7. Tighten the inner ring nut finger tight. Hold it with a pin wrench or suitable substitute and tighten the outer nut to 80 ft. lbs. Then hold the outer nut and tighten the inner nut to 105 ft. lbs.
8. The remainder of the procedure is the reverse of disassembly.

YFM 200

REMOVAL

1. Block the front wheel to prevent movement.
2. Jack the rear wheels a few inches off the ground using standard safety procedures to ensure that the machine is properly supported and stable.
3. Apply the parking brake.

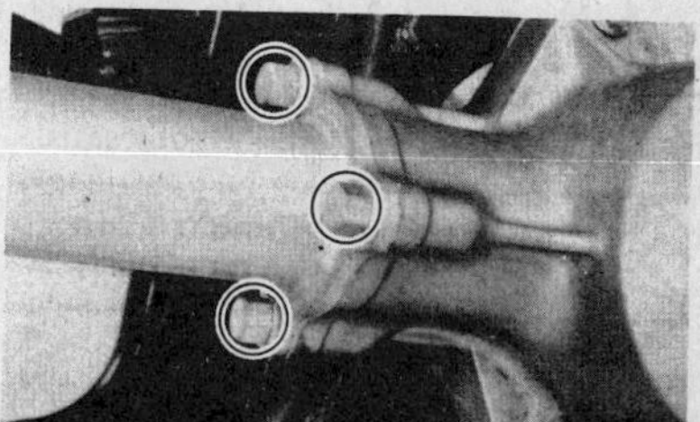

Final gear housing-to-drive shaft bolts

Final gear housing mounting hardware

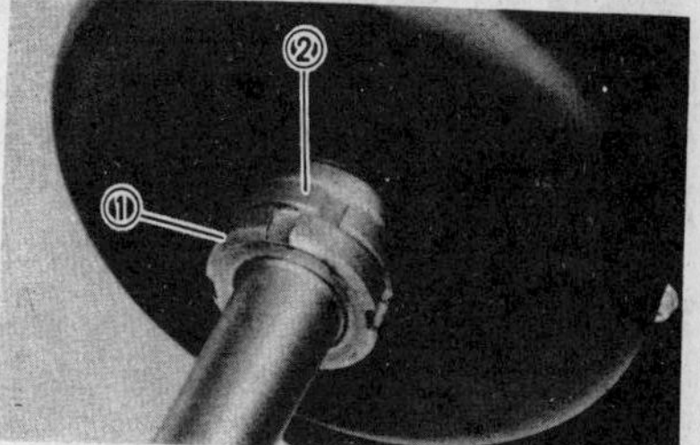

Outer (1) and inner (2) axle ring nuts

4. Remove the rear wheels.
5. Remove the axle nuts.
6. Remove the wheel hubs.
7. Remove the trailer hitch bracket.
8. Remove the rear axle ring nuts.
9. Release the parking brake and disconnect the rear brake cables and return spring from the caliper lever.
10. Remove the brake covers, rear brake assembly and brake disk.
11. Tap the left end of the axle with a plastic hammer and remove it from the hub.
12. Remove the final gear housing securing bolts and nuts.
13. Remove the breather pipe and rear hub securing bolts.
14. Remove the final gear assembly and the coupling gear.

INSPECTION

1. Pry out dust seals and oil seals.
2. Drive out the bearings as outlined under "Front Wheel Bearings," above. Inspection and installation procedures are basically the same as those detailed in that section.
3. Check rear axle run-out. Replace the axle if run-out exceeds 1.5mm (0.06 in.).

INSTALLATION

1. To assemble the rear axle, install the coupling gear into the housing.
2. Install the final gear assembly.
3. Tighten the gear housing nuts to 17 ft. lbs.
4. Tighten the gear housing bolts to 32 ft. lbs.
5. Tighten the rear wheel hub securing bolts to 36 ft. lbs.
6. Insert the axle from the right side, again tapping with a plastic mallet as on removal.
7. Grease and install the hub dust seals.
8. Install the rear axle ring nuts finger tight.
9. Install and adjust the rear brake assembly. See "Maintenance" for adjustment procedures.

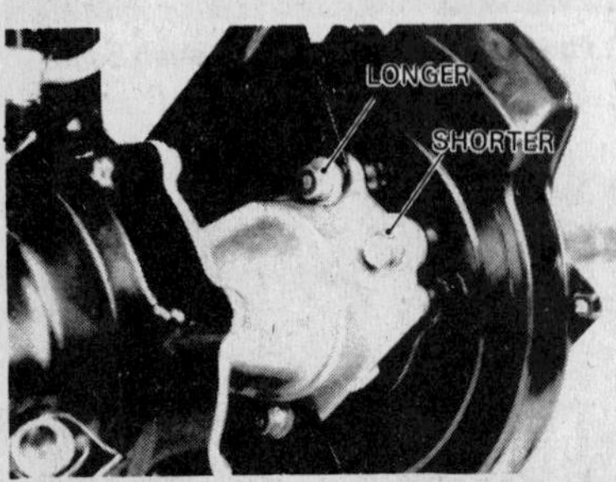

Correct bolt installation

Axle ring nuts (1)

NOTE: *Caliper body bolts are tightened to 36 ft. lbs. The nuts are tightened to 6.5 ft. lbs. Be sure that the long body bolt is installed in the upper position.*

10. Apply the parking brake.
11. Hold the inside ring nut steady. Tighten the outside ring nut to 140 ft. lbs.
12. Hold the outside ring nut in place. Tighten the inside ring nut to 170 ft. lbs.
13. Install the wheel hubs.
14. Tighten the axle nut to 72 ft. lbs. Use a new cotter pin. Fit the hub cap.
15. Tighten the wheel lug nuts to 32 ft. lbs.

CHASSIS TORQUE SPECIFICATIONS YFM 80

Part	Torque (ft lbs)
Wheel lug nuts	20
Front axle nut	47
Brake cam lever pinch bolt	6.5
Knuckle shaft nut	22
Tie-rod mounting nuts	32
Tie-rod end locknuts	22
Steering shaft bottom nut	22
Steering shaft bracket bolts	17
Handlebar holder bolts	17
Engine mounting bolts	17
Footrest	58
Frame-to-rear hub	36
Final gear housing-to-frame	36
Rear axle nut	61
Frame guard bolts	17
Axle ring nuts	see text

CHASSIS TORQUE SPECIFICATIONS YFM 200

Part	Torque (ft lbs)
Front wheel lug nuts	20
Rear wheel lug nuts	32
Front axle nuts	61
Front brake cam lever pinch bolt	6.5
Knuckle shaft nuts	22
Tie-rod end-to-steering shaft	32
Tie rod end-to-knuckle	29
Tie-rod locknuts	22
Steering shaft bottom nut	22
Steering shaft holder bolts	17
Handlebar holder nuts	22
Handlebar bolts	14
Engine mounting bolts	24
Footrest	58
Rear wheel hub-to-frame bolts	36
Final gear housing mounting bolts	32
Rear axle nut	72
Axle ring nuts	see text
Brake caliper nut	6.5
Brake caliper bolts	36
Caliper pad adjuster locknut	11
Frame guards	17
Final gear housing nuts	17

GENERAL TORQUE SPECIFICATIONS ①

Nut ②	Bolt ③	Torque (ft lbs)
10	6	4.3
12	8	11
14	10	22
17	12	40
19	14	61
22	16	94

① Unless otherwise noted ② Wrench size ③ Thread diameter

Yamaha Street Two-Strokes

MODEL COVERAGE

G5, G6, G6S/B, G7S	AS2C	RD250/A/B
RD60/A/B	CS3/B/C, CS5	RD350/A/B
U5E/L	DS6/B/C, DS7	YAS1/C
YA6	HS1/B	YCS1/C
RD125	LS2	YDS3/C, YDS5
YGS1	R3/C	YL1/E
YG5S/T	R5/B/C	YM1, YM2C
YJ2	RD200B/C	YR2/C
YL2/C/CM		RD400

INDEX

General Specifications

	U5/U5L/U5E	RD60	Early YJ2	Late YJ2	U7/U7E
DIMENSIONS					
Net Weight (lbs)	190	163	190	190	170
Overall Length (in.)	71.1	71.9	71.3	71.3	—
Overall Width (in.)	24.8	24.8	25.4	25.4	—
Overall Height (in.)	37.2	38.0	38.4	38.4	—
Ground Clearance (in.)	5.1	5.9	5.5	5.5	—
Wheelbase (in.)	44.9	46.7	45.1	45.1	—
Tire Size (in.): front	2.25 x 17	2.50 x 17	2.25 x 17	2.25 x 17	2.25 x 17
rear	2.25 x 17	2.50 x 17	2.25 x 17	2.25 x 17	2.50 x 17
ENGINE					
Displacement (cc)	50	55	58	58	72
No. of Cylinders	1	1	1	1	1
Bore X Stroke (mm)	40 x 40	42 x 39.7	42 x 42	42 x 42	47 x 42
Compression Ratio (:1)	6.8	6.9	6.6	7.5	6.8
Torque @ RPM (ft lbs)	3.76 @ 5000	3.4 @ 6500	3.9 @ 6000	3.98 @ 6000	4.7 @ 4500
Fuel Induct.①	RV	RD	RV	RV	RD
Carburetion (Mikuni)	VM14SC	VM16SH	VM14SC	VM16SC	VM15SC
Lubrication②	OI	OI	OI	OI	OI
TRANSMISSION					
Clutch	Auto	Manual	Manual	Manual	Auto
Reduction (pri/sec)	3.895/2.715	3.578/3.500	3.895/2.600	3.895/2.533	3.578/2.571
Transmission Ratio: 1st	3.083	3.250	3.083	3.083	3.250
2nd	1.722	2.000	1.882	1.882	1.833
3rd	1.174	1.428	1.338	1.333	1.200
4th	—	1.125	1.000	1.000	—
5th	—	0.961	—	—	—
6th	—	—	—	—	—
ELECTRICS					
Ignition	Magneto	Magneto	Magneto	Magneto	Generator
Starting	Kick/Electric	Kick	Kick	Kick	Kick/Electric

	YGSI/YGSIT	YG5S/T	G5S/G6S/ G6SB/G7S	HSI/HSIB	YL2
DIMENSIONS					
Net Weight (lbs)	190	175	170	199	200
Overall Length (in.)	71.7	70.9	71.3	70.9	75.4
DIMENSIONS					
Overall Width (in.)	24.6/30.5	31.7	31.1	30.3	28.1
Overall Height (in.)	37.8/38.8	40.0	39.2	39.6	41.7
Ground Clearance (in.)	5.9	6.3	5.3	6.1	5.5

General Specifications (cont.)

	YGS1/YGS1T	YG5S/T	G5S/G6S/ G6SB/G7S	HS1/HS1B	YL2
Wheelbase (in.)	45.1	46.3	45.9	47.0	46.9
Tire Size (in.): front	2.50 x 17	2.50 x 17	2.50 x 17	2.50 x 18	2.50 x 18
rear	2.50 x 17	3.00 x 17	2.50 x 17	2.50 x 18	2.50 x 18
ENGINE					
Displacement (cc)	73	73	73	89	97
No. of Cylinders	1	1	1	2	1
Bore X Stroke (mm)	47 x 42	47 x 42	47 x 42	36.5 x 43	52 x 45.6
Compression Ratio (:1)	6.8	6.8	6.8	7.5	7.0
Torque @ RPM (ft lbs)	5.78 @ 6500	5.2 @ 6000	4.1 @ 5500	3.1 @ 5500	6.8 @ 5500
Fuel Induct.①	RV	RV	RV	PP	RV
Carburetion (Mikuni)	VM15SC-1	VM16SC	VM16SC	VM16SC (2)	VM17SC
Lubrication②	OI	OI	OI	OI	OI
TRANSMISSION					
Clutch	Manual	Manual	Manual	Manual	Manual
Reduction (pri/sec)	3.895/2.467	3.895/2.740	3.895/2.643	3.895/3.077	3.895/2.335
Transmission Ratio: 1st	3.083	3.077	3.077	3.182	3.077
2nd	1.882	1.889	1.889	1.813	1.889
3rd	1.333	1.304	1.304	1.300	1.304
4th	1.000	0.963	0.963	1.045	0.963
5th	—	—	—	0.840	—
6th	—	—	—	—	—
ELECTRICS					
Ignition	Magneto	Generator	Magneto	Alternator	Generator
Starting	Kick	Electric	Kick	Kick	Kick

	YL2C	YL2CM③	LS2	YL1/YL1E	YA6
DIMENSIONS					
Net Weight (lbs)	200	200	209	180	245
Overall Length (in.)	73.2	73.2	—	71.6	75.6
Overall Width (in.)	28.1	28.1	—	24.8	28.5
Overall Height (in.)	42.5	42.5	—	37.3	41.1
Ground Clearance (in.)	7.9	6.9	—	5.1	5.3
Wheelbase (in.)	48.5	48.5	—	45.1	49.0
Tire Size (in.): front	3.00 x 18	3.00 x 18	2.50 x 18	2.50 x 17	3.00 x 16
rear	3.00 x 18	3.00 x 18	2.50 x 18	2.50 x 17	3.00 x 16
ENGINE					
Displacement (cc)	97	97	97	98	123
No. of Cylinders	1	1	2	2	1
Bore X Stroke (mm)	52 x 45.6	52 x 45.6	38 x 40	38 x 43	56 x 50
Compression Ratio (:1)	7.0	6.6	7.0	7.1	6.8

	YL2C	YL2CM③	LS2	YL1/YL1E	YA6
Torque @ RPM (ft lbs)	7.24 @ 6000	7.24 @ 6000	6.95 @ 7500	6.0 @ 8000	9 @ 5000
Fuel Induct.①	RV	RV	PP	PP	RV
Carburetion (Mikuni)	VM17SC	VM20SC	VM17SC (2)	VM16SC (2)	VM22SC
Lubrication②	OI	OI	OI	OI	OI
TRANSMISSION					
Clutch	Manual	Manual	Manual	Manual	Manual
Reduction (pri/sec)	3.895/2.335	3.895/2.334	3.894/3.000	3.895/2.335	3.833/2.600
Transmission Ratio: 1st	3.077	3.077	3.181	3.077	2.533
2nd	1.889	1.889	1.812	1.889	1.524
3rd	1.304	1.304	1.300	1.304	1.120
4th	0.963	0.963	1.045	0.963	0.828
5th	—	—	0.840	—	—
6th	—	—	—	—	—
ELECTRICS					
Ignition	Generator	Generator	Alternator	Generator	Generator
Starting	Electric	Electric	Kick	Kick/Electric	Electric

	YAS1/YAS1C AS2C	RD125	YCS1C	YCS1	CS3C
DIMENSIONS					
Net Weight (lbs)	220	228	260	260	262
Overall Length (in.)	73.0	76.2	75.6	75.6	76.0
Overall Width (in.)	31.9	38.1	30.1	30.1	32.1
Overall Height (in.)	39.6	41.7	39.2	39.2	40.2
Ground Clearance (in.)	5.9	6.1	6.1	6.1	6.9
Wheelbase (in.)	47.2	48.8	49.0	49.0	49.0
Tire Size (in.): front	2.75 x 18	2.75 x 18	2.75 x 18	3.00 x 18	2.75 x 18
rear	3.00 x 18	3.00 x 18	3.00 x 18	3.00 x 18	3.00 x 18
ENGINE					
Displacement (cc)	124	124	180	180	195
No. of Cylinders	2	2	2	2	2
Bore X Stroke (mm)	43 x 43	43 x 43	50 x 46	50 x 46	52 x 46
Compression Ratio (:1)	7.0	7.0	7.0	6.8	6.2
Torque @ RPM (ft lbs)	9.4 @ 7500	NA	14.6 @ 7000	14.6 @ 7000	15.7 @ 7000
Fuel Induct.①	PP	RD	PP	PP	PP
Carburetion (Mikuni)	VM17SC (2)	Y18P-1C⑤	VM20SC (2)	VM18SC (2)	VM20SC (2)
Lubrication②	OI	OI	OI	OI	OI
TRANSMISSION					
Clutch	Manual	Manual	Manual	Manual	Manual
Reduction (pri/sec)	3.895/2.600	3.894/2.785	3.313/2.667	3.313/2.466	3.313/2.857
Transmission Ratio: 1st	3.182	3.181	2.833	2.833	2.833
2nd	1.875	1.812	1.875	1.875	1.875
3rd	1.300	1.300	1.421	1.421	1.421
4th	1.045	1.045	1.045	1.045	1.045
5th	0.840	0.840	0.840	0.840	0.840
6th	—	—	—	—	—

	YASI YASIC AS2C	RD125	YCSIC	YCSI	CS3C
ELECTRICS					
Ignition	Alternator	Alternator	Generator	Generator	Generator
Starting	Kick	Kick	Electric	Electric	Electric

	CS3B/CS5	RD200	YDS3	YDS3C	YDS5
DIMENSIONS					
Net Weight (lbs)	258	256	320	320	325.6
Overall Length (in.)	76.0	77.0	79.0	79.0	78.4
Overall Width (in.)	32.1	29.0	31.2	31.2	30.3
Overall Height (in.)	40.2	39.8	42.0	42.0	41.4
Ground Clearance (in.)	6.9	6.1	5.8	5.8	6.1
Wheelbase (in.)	49.0	49.0	51.9	51.9	50.8
Tire Size (in.): front rear	2.75 x 18 3.00 x 18	2.75 x 18 3.00 x 18	3.00 x 18 3.25 x 18	3.00 x 18 3.50 x 18	3.00 x 18 3.25 x 18
ENGINE					
Displacement (cc)	195	195	246	246	246
No. of Cylinders	2	2	2	2	2
Bore X Stroke (mm)	52 x 46	52 x 46	56 x 50	56 x 50	56 x 50
Compression Ratio (:1)	7.1	7.1	7.5	7.5	7.5
Torque @ RPM (ft lbs)	15.7 @ 7000	15.7 @ 7000	18.1 @ 7500	18.1 @ 7500	19.7 @ 7500
Fuel Induct.①	PP	RD	PP	PP	PP
Carburetion (Mikuni)	VM20SC (2)	Y20P-1A⑤	VM24SC (2)	VM24SC (2)	VM26SC (2)
Lubrication②	OI	OI	OI	OI	OI
TRANSMISSION					
Clutch	Manual	Manual	Manual	Manual	Manual
Reduction (pri/sec)	3.313/2.857	3.312/2.571	3.250/2.600	3.250/2.733	3.250/2.733
Transmission Ratio: 1st 2nd 3rd 4th 5th 6th	2.833 1.875 1.421 1.045 0.840 —	2.833 1.705 1.250 1.045 0.916 —	2.545 1.533 1.167 0.950 0.773 —	2.545 1.533 1.167 0.950 0.773 —	2.545 1.533 1.167 0.950 0.773 —
ELECTRICS					
Ignition	Generator	Generator	Generator	Generator	Generator
Starting	Electric	Electric	Kick	Kick	Electric

	DS6C	DS6/B	DS7	RD250/A/B	YM1
DIMENSIONS					
Net Weight (lbs)	309	304	304	309	340
Overall Length (in.)	78.3	78.3	80.3	80.3	78.9
Overall Width (in.)	32.9	32.9	32.9	32.9	31.2

	DS6C	DS6/B	DS7	RD250/A/B	YM1
Overall Height (in.)	41.9	41.9	42.7	43.7	42.0
Ground Clearance (in.)	5.9	6.1	5.9	5.9	5.9
Wheelbase (in.)	50.8	50.8	52.0	52.0	50.7
Tire Size (in.): front rear	3.00 x 18 3.50 x 18	3.00 x 18 3.25 x 18	3.00 x 18 3.25 x 18	3.00 x 18 3.25 x 18	3.00 x 18 3.25 x 18
ENGINE					
Displacement (cc)	246	246	247	247	305
No. of Cylinders	2	2	2	2	2
Bore X Stroke (mm)	56 x 50	56 x 50	54 x 54	54 x 54	60 x 54
Compression Ratio (:1)	7.3	7.3	7.1	6.7 : 1	6.7
Torque @ RPM (ft lbs)	21.1 @ 7000	21.1 @ 7000	21.1 @ 7000	21.1 @ 7000	19.9 @ 6000
Fuel Induct.①	PP	PP	PP	RD	PP
Carburetion (Mikuni)	VM26SC (2)	VM26SC (2)	VM26SC (2)	VM28SC (2)	VM24SC (2)
Lubrication②	OI	OI	OI	OI	OI
TRANSMISSION					
Clutch	Manual	Manual	Manual	Manual	Manual
Reduction (pri/sec)	3.250/2.929	3.250/2.733	3.238/2.666	3.238/2.666	3.250/2.353
Transmission Ratio: 1st 2nd 3rd 4th 5th 6th	2.545 1.533 1.167 0.950 0.773 —	2.545 1.533 1.167 0.950 0.773 —	2.562 1.590 1.192 0.965 0.806 —	2.571 1.777 1.318 1.040 0.888 0.785	2.545 1.533 1.167 0.950 0.773 —
ELECTRICS					
Ignition	Generator	Generator	Alternator	Alternator	Generator
Starting	Kick	Kick	Kick	Kick	Kick

	YM2/2C	YR2/YR2C	R3/R3C	R5/R5B/R5C	RD350/A/B	RD400
DIMENSIONS						
Net Weight (lbs)	326	348	340	308	315	342
Overall Length (in.)	73.3	81.2	80.3	80.3	80.3	79.3
Overall Width (in.)	31.2	28.9	35.2	32.9	32.9	32.7
Overall Height (in.)	38.1	39.4	42.7	42.7	43.7	42.9
Ground Clearance (in.)	6.1	5.7	5.9	6.1	6.1	6.1
Wheelbase (in.)	51.0	52.6	52.8	52.0	52.0	51.8
Tire Size (in.): front rear	3.00 x 18 3.25 x 18	3.00 x 18 3.50 x 18	3.00 x 18 3.50 x 18	3.00 x 18 3.50 x 18	3.00 x 18 3.50 x 18	3.25 x 18 3.50 x 18
ENGINE						
Displacement (cc)	305	348	348	347	347	398
No. of Cylinders	2	2	2	2	2	2
Bore X Stroke (mm)	60 x 54	61 x 59.6	61 x 59.6	64 x 54	64 x 54	64 x 62
Compression Ratio (:1)	7.5	6.9	7.5	6.9	6.6 : 1	6.2 : 1
Torque @ RPM (ft lbs)	23.4 @ 6500	27.8 @ 6000	28 @ 6000	28 @ 6500	28.0 @ 7000	NA

	YM2/2C	YR2/YR2C	R3/R3C	R5/R5B/R5C	RD350/A/B	RD400
Fuel Induct.①	PP	PP	PP	PP	RD	RD
Carburetion (Mikuni)	VM26SC (2)	VM28SC (2)	VM28SC (2)	VM28SC (2)	VM28SC (2)	VM28SC (2)
Lubrication②	OI	OI	OI	OI	OI	OI
TRANSMISSION						
Clutch	Manual	Manual	Manual	Manual	Manual	Manual
Reduction (pri/sec)	3.250/2.500	2.870/2.563④	2.870/2.730	2.869/2.666	2.869/2.666	NA
Transmission Ratio: 1st	2.545	2.545	2.545	2.562	2.571	2.571
2nd	1.533	1.600	1.600	1.590	1.777	1.777
3rd	1.167	1.167	1.167	1.192	1.318	1.318
4th	0.950	0.950	0.950	0.965	1.040	1.083
5th	0.773	0.773	0.773	0.806	0.888	0.961
6th	—	—	—	—	0.785	0.888
ELECTRICS						
Ignition	Generator	Generator	Generator	Alternator	Alternator	Alternator
Starting	Kick	Kick	Kick	Kick	Kick	Kick

① RV—Rotary Valve
PP—Piston Port
RD—Reed Valve
② OI—Oil Injection
③ YL2C after Serial No. 550101
④ YR2C—2.870/2.730
⑤ Teikei carburetor
NA Not available

MAINTENANCE

NOTE: *Common maintenance procedures are explained in detail in "General Information."*

LUBRICATION

Engine

The crankshaft bearings, cylinder(s) and piston(s) are lubricated by the Yamaha "Autolube" oil injection system.

The system does not require maintenance except for a periodic check on oil pump cable adjustment and stroke provided that the Autolube tank is kept full of oil. A level glass is provided for this purpose.

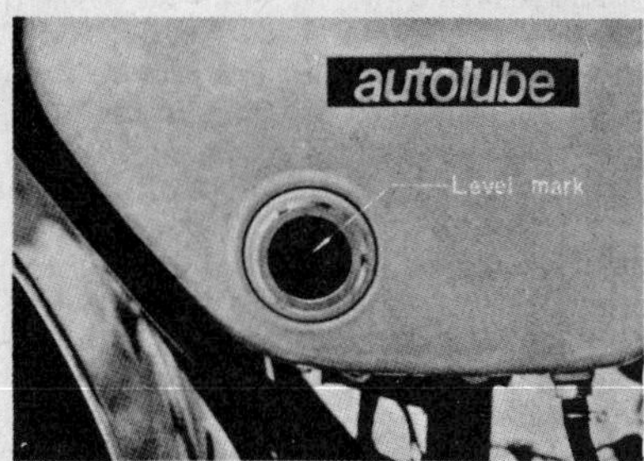

Autolube tank oil level mark (Courtesy Yamaha Int. Corp.)

"Yamalube" oil is recommended by the factory. If this is not available, one of the following types of oil can also be used:

a. Any high-quality two-stroke oil labeled "BIA certified for service TC-W.";

b. Any high-quality SAE 30W two-stroke oil designed for air cooled engines;

c. A high-quality detergent-type motor oil, SAE 30W, rated "SE." This should be used only if two-stroke oil is not available.

In extremely cold weather (average temperature below 15° F) use a high-quality detergent motor oil rated "SE," with a viscosity of SAE 10W-30. Each time you add oil, check that the oil tank cap breather hole is not clogged, or that the tank breather tube is not clogged or pinched at any point.

NOTE: *If the tank ever runs out of oil, or if the feed line is disconnected for any reason, it will be necessary to bleed the system before operating the motorcycle. Refer to the "Lubrication System" chapter for procedures.*

Transmission

The transmission and clutch are lubricated by an oil bath. Yamalube 4-cycle oil, SAE 10W–3, or SAE 30W service rating "SE" is recommended for all models.

CHECKING OIL

1. The machine should be on the center stand, preferably on a level surface, when checking the transmission oil level.

2. The engine should be warm.

3. If a dipstick is provided, unscrew it and wipe it off. Reinsert, allowing the dipstick cap to rest on top of the threads of its hole. The oil level should be between the maximum and minimum marks on the dipstick. If too low, add oil until the level is correct.

4. On some older models, the dipstick and cap are separate. Remove the inspection cap, and then check the oil level as outlined above. A separate plug may be fitted to add oil. On machines such as the YA6, this plug is accessible after removing the left air cleaner cover. Refer to the illustration. On this type of machine, oil *must not* be added through the level inspection hole because of the difference between transmission and clutch oil levels.

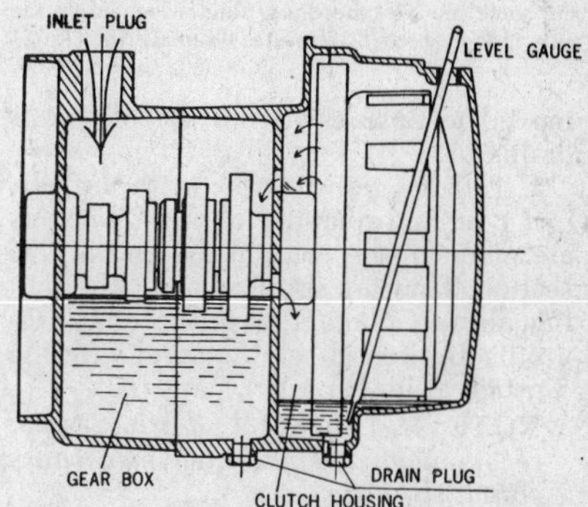

On early models such as the YA6, transmission oil must be added to the crankcases only. If oil is added through the level gauge hole in the clutch cover, an incorrect level reading will be obtained (Courtesy Yamaha Int. Corp.)

5. If no dipstick is supplied, the oil level is checked by means of a level screw or bolt near the bottom of the clutch cover. When the screw or bolt is removed the oil should just begin to seep out if the level is correct. If necessary, add oil through the filler hole on top of the crankcases or clutch cover until the oil just begins to come out of the level plug hole.

CHANGING OIL

The transmission oil should be changed at least every 2,000 miles after break-in is over.

1. The machine should be on the center stand and parked on a level surface.

2. Remove the dipstick (or the inlet plug on older models).

3. Remove the drain plug(s) and allow the oil to drain off for several moments. Most late model machines have one drain

plug located at the bottom of the crankcases. Others have the drain plug located at the bottom side of the clutch case. Still others (DS6, R3) have plugs at both of these locations, and both should be re-

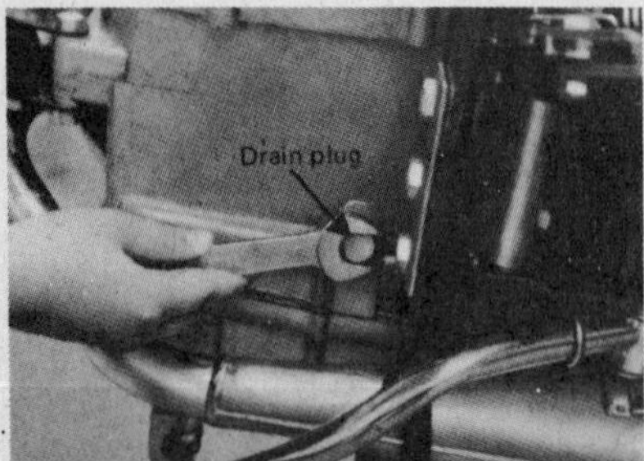

Removing the transmission drain plug (Courtesy Yamaha Int. Corp.)

On some models, the drain plug is located on the side of the cases (R3) (Courtesy Yamaha Int. Corp.)

moved to ensure that all the old oil is drained.

4. Fill the transmission with the correct type and quantity of oil. Capacities are given in the chart at the end of this section. They are approximates. After filling, allow a moment for the oil to distribute itself, then check the level with the dipstick or level plug.

NOTE: *The use of oil additives is not recommended, since they may cause clutch slippage.*

Front Forks

1. Yamaha fork oil is recommended for the front forks.

2. Fork oil should be changed every 2,000 miles.

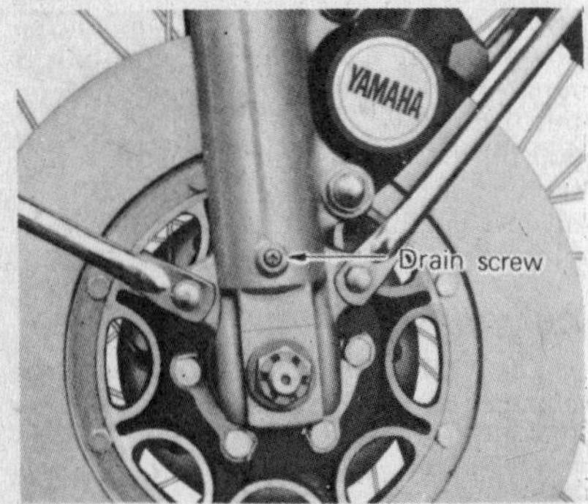

Front fork drain screw location (RD350 shown) (Courtesy Yamaha Int. Corp.)

3. To drain the fork oil, remove the drain plug at the lower portion of one of the fork sliders. Allow the oil to drain into a suitable container; pump the slider up and down several times. (Sit on the machine after taking it off the center stand, apply the front brake, and push forward). After most of the oil is expelled, turn the forks all the way to the right to completely drain the right fork leg, or to the left for the left fork leg. Check the condition of the drain plug gasket. Replace it if necessary. Refit and tighten the drain plug.

4. Repeat the procedure with the other fork leg.

5. Remove the fork filler bolt from the top of each fork leg. If a large filler bolt is fitted (as on most twins), the handlebar clamps may have to be loosened and the bars pulled back to allow access to the fork bolts. Loosening the triple clamp pinch-bolts may make removal easier.

Removing the fork filler bolt (Courtesy Yamaha Int. Corp.)

6. Add the correct quantity and viscosity of oil to each fork leg. Capacities for each model are given in the "Maintenance Data" chart at the end of this section.

7. Inspect the condition of the fork bolt O-rings, if they are fitted to your model, and replace them if torn or cracked. Fit the bolts and tighten them securely. Tighten the handlebar and pinch-bolts if they were loosened. Allow a moment for the oil to settle in the forks before operation.

Chassis Lubrication

1. The swing arm pivot is fitted with a grease nipple. This item should be lubricated with a good grade of chassis grease every 2,000 miles. Grease should be applied until some of it shows at either end of the swing arm.

2. Some older models are fitted with grease fitting for the brake cams. These should receive no more than one shot of a good quality chassis grease approximately every 2,000 miles.

3. Wheel and steering head bearings are lubricated with bearing grease. This should be accomplished every 4,000 miles. Refer to the "Chassis" section for procedures.

SERVICE CHECKS AND ADJUSTMENTS

Drive Chain

1. The chain should have about ¾ in. (20 mm) of total up-and-down free-play measured in the middle of the lower chain run.

2. *Before* checking or adjusting the chain slack, the following conditions should be met:

a. The machine should be off the center stand, and with a rider sitting on the seat;

b. The chain should be clean and well lubricated;

c. The chain should have been checked for any tight spots by slowly rotating the wheel and checking for variances in the chain tension at different points. If a tight spot exists, the chain should be adjusted to the prescribed free-play at the tight spot. Note, however, that such a condition is indicative of a worn chain and probably sprockets which should be replaced as soon as possible.

3. To adjust the chain, first back off the rear brake adjuster nut if a rod-operated brake is fitted.

4. Remove the axle nut cotter pin and loosen the axle nut several turns. On RD400C models, loosen the caliper bracket shaft nut; loosen the tension bar locknut. Loosen the sprocket hub securing nut. Loosen the locknut on each adjuster bolt.

To adjust the chain, loosen the axle nut (1), loosen the adjuster locknut (2), and turn the adjuster bolts (3) clockwise to move the wheel back (Courtesy Yamaha Int. Corp.)

5. Turn each of the adjuster bolts in by equal amount until chain tension is approximately correct.

6. Check wheel alignment by means of the adjusting marks inscribed on both sides of the swing arm. Be sure that both adjusters are lined up with the same mark on each side. If not, turn one of the adjuster bolts in or out so that alignment is achieved.

7. Tighten the sprocket nut and the axle nut and check the chain tension. Correct if necessary. After adjustment is correct, torque the axle nut to 42–50 ft lbs (under 350cc) or about 100 ft lbs on larger machines. On the RD400C, tighten the caliper bracket shaft nut to 58 ft lbs and the tension bar locknut to 10–16 ft lbs. Fit a new cotter pin. Tighten the adjuster locknuts. Readjust the rear brake.

Clutch

1. The clutch lever should be able to be moved 2–3 mm (1/16–⅛ in.) away from the lever holder before the clutch begins

to disengage.

2. If your model is equipped with an adjuster and locknut at the clutch lever, use these to effect the proper adjustment. If not, an adjuster is fitted to the clutch

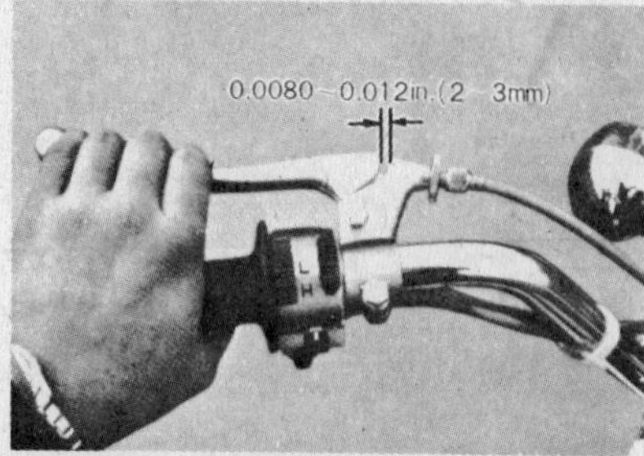

Clutch cable free-play adjustment (Courtesy Yamaha Int. Corp.)

Adjusting clutch cable free-play with the adjuster on the engine

cable where it enters the crankcase cover. Loosen the locknut, and turn the adjuster in or out to increase or decrease lever free-play as needed.

3. If adjusting the cable does not provide satisfactory clutch performance, the pushrod should be adjusted.

On most twins, the pushrod is accessible after removing the cover plate from the left crankcase cover. On the RD60, the alternator cover is removed. On G-series machines, remove the right crankcase cover. On some older models, the pushrod is covered by a rubber plug on the crankcase cover.

Adjusting the clutch pushrod

Clutch pushrod locknut and adjusting screw (RD350) (Courtesy Yamaha Int. Corp.)

4. Run down the cable adjuster until a good amount of free-play exists in the cable.

5. Remove the cover or plug to gain access to the pushrod adjuster. Loosen the pushrod adjuster locknut and back it off several turns.

6. Turn the pushrod adjuster screw in until it just touches the clutch pushrod (a slight resistance will be felt). Back off the screw ¼ turn. Holding this adjustment, tighten the locknut.

7. Adjust the cable to give the proper lever free-play, and check clutch operation.

Throttle Cables

ALL MODELS EXCEPT RD400

1. Throttle cables should be adjusted *after* the idle speed. This procedure is given in the "Tune-Up" section.

2. The oil pump cable must be adjusted after adjusting the throttle cable(s).

3. A cable adjuster is fitted to the top of the carburetor and another at the twist-grip. One throttle cable runs from the twist-grip to a junction box. There, it is connected to the oil pump cable and one or two (on twins) shorter throttle cables which run to the carburetor(s). Therefore, each cable must be adjusted.

4. After setting the idle speed, use the adjuster on the carburetor cap to give 1 mm (0.04 in.) of cable free-play. This can be measured by gently lifting the cable out of the adjuster. It should come out no

Checking throttle cable free-play by lifting the cable out of the adjuster until tension is felt

more than the amount shown before the throttle slide begins to rise. On twins, adjust both cables. Loosen the locknut and

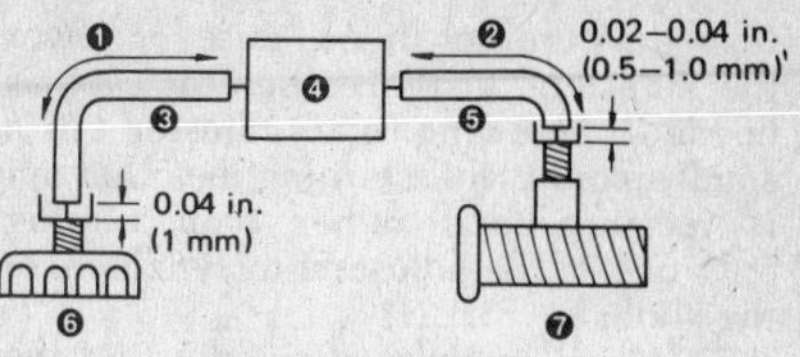

Throttle cable free-play

1. Short throttle cable free-play
2. Long throttle cable free-play
3. Short throttle cable
4. Junction block
5. Long throttle cable
6. Carburetor cap
7. Twist-grip

screw the adjuster clockwise (in) to increase the slack and counterclockwise (out) to decrease it. Tighten the locknut.

5. Adjust the long throttle cable with the adjuster at the twist-grip. This cable should be adjusted to give 0.5–1.0 mm (0.02–0.04 in.) of free-play.

6. On twins, the throttle slides must now be synchronized. Remove the air

INCORRECT

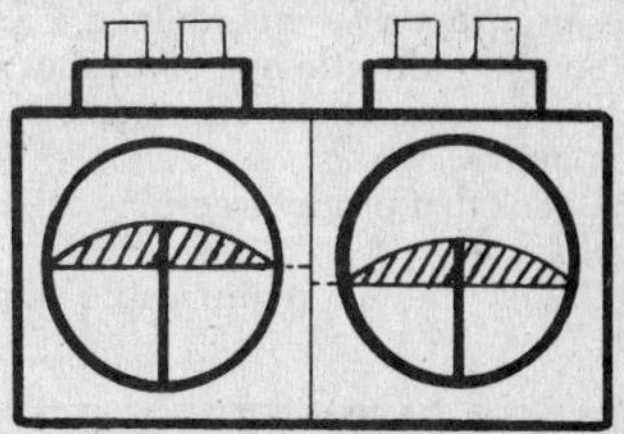

CORRECT

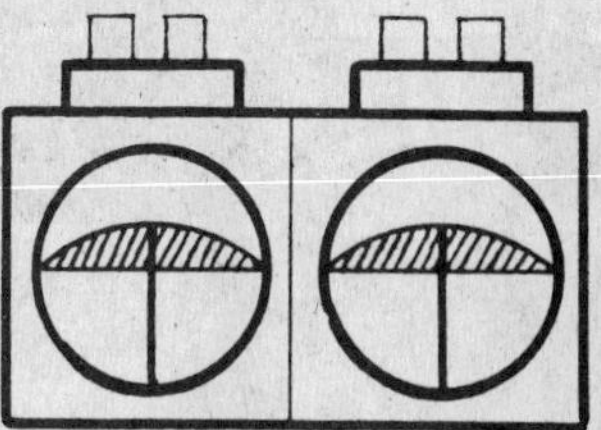
On twins, the throttle slides must be synchronized as shown (Courtesy Yamaha Int. Corp.)

cleaner. Turn the twist-grip until the throttle slides just begin to move. Both must begin to move at the same time.

Another synchronization method is to insert your fingers into the carburetor bores to ensure that both throttle slides clear the bore at the same time. You will be able to feel when one slide becomes just flush with the uppermost part of the bore. The other slide must be in exactly the same position. See the illustration.

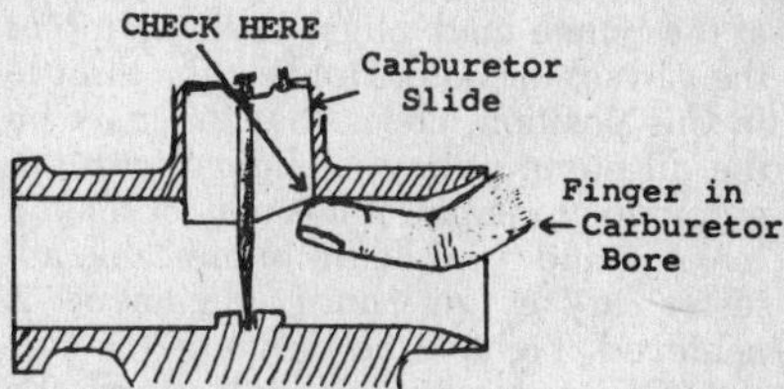

Throttle slide synchronization may be checked by noting when each slide clears the carburetor bore. When one slide is in this position, the other must be also (Courtesy Yamaha Int. Corp.)

If adjustment is necessary to synchronize the throttle slides, raise or lower the adjusters on the carburetor caps as needed. Screwing one adjuster in a small amount while turning the other out is recommended rather than turning only one of the adjusters to synchronize the slides.

7. On all models, after adjusting the throttle cables, start the engine and turn the forks slowly from lock-to-lock, noting any variation in idle speed. If the revs change, either the cables are adjusted too tightly or are binding somewhere along their routing.

8. Adjust the oil pump cable.

RD400

1. Refer to Steps 1–5 for other models, above.
2. Remove the inspection plugs from the carburetors.
3. Turn the twist-grip fully open. In this position, the punch marks on the throttle slides should align with the lower edge of the inspection holes.
4. If they do not, use the cable adjusters atop each carburetor so that the slides are properly synchronized.
5. Snap the throttle open and shut several times and recheck alignment of the punch marks.
6. Check that proper free-play exists in the cables.
7. Check the oil pump cable adjustment.

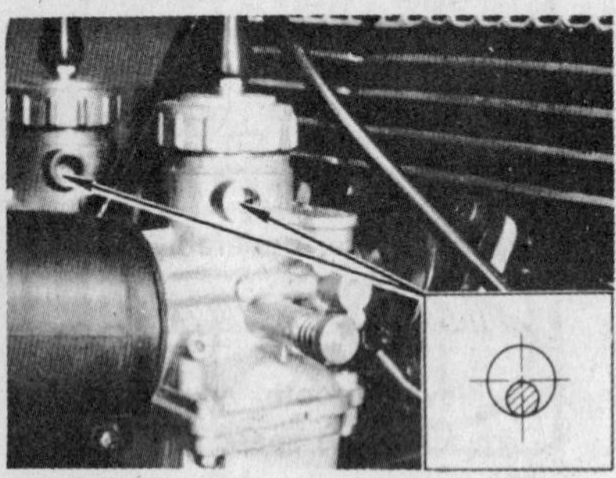

Throttle slide punch marks aligned (RD400C) (Courtesy Yamaha Int. Corp.)

Oil Pump Cable

ALL MODELS EXCEPT RD400

1. Set the throttle cable adjustments as previously described.
2. Remove the oil pump cover. On rotary valve models, this will expose the carburetor as well.
3. On rotary valve models, note the punch mark on the throttle slide. Turn the throttle twist-grip until the upper part of the punch mark aligns with the top of the carburetor bore. Holding the throttle in this position, check that the mark on the oil pump pulley is aligned with the oil pump guide pin. If it is not, loosen the locknut, and turn the oil pump cable adjuster in or out until alignment is achieved. Tighten the locknut.
4. On piston-port models, turn the throttle twist-grip until all slack is taken out of the cables, but the throttle slide(s) have not moved. At this point, the raised mark on the oil pump pulley should align with the oil pump guide pin. If it does

Throttle slide punch mark aligned with the upper portion of the carburetor bore to adjust the oil pump cable (rotary valve models)

Oil pump pulley (Courtesy Yamaha Int. Corp.)

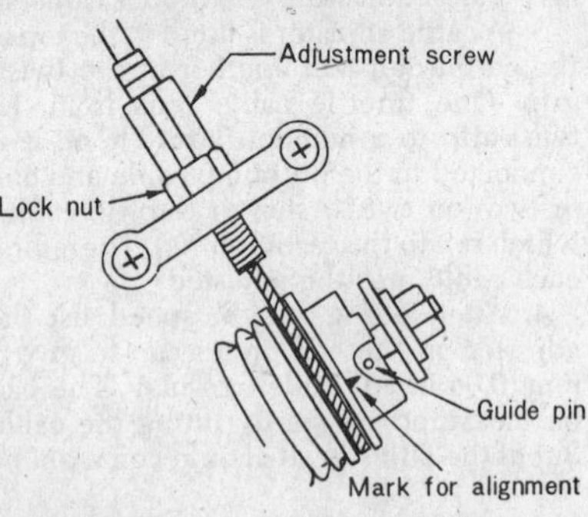

Oil pump alignment marks and cable adjuster (Courtesy Yamaha Int. Corp.)

not, loosen the locknut on the oil pump cable adjuster located in the sidecover and turn the adjuster in or out until adjustment is achieved.

5. Periodically, the oil pump minimum stroke should be checked. Refer to the "Lubrication System" section.

RD400

1. Set the throttle cable adjustments as previously described. Remove the oil pump cover.
2. With the throttle held fully open, the plunger pin on the oil pump should align with the mark on the pump pulley.
3. If it does not, adjust with the oil pump cable adjuster threaded into the crankcase cover until the plunger pin and pulley mark are aligned.

Brakes

FRONT DISC

1. The brake lever is fitted with an adjusting screw. The lever should have

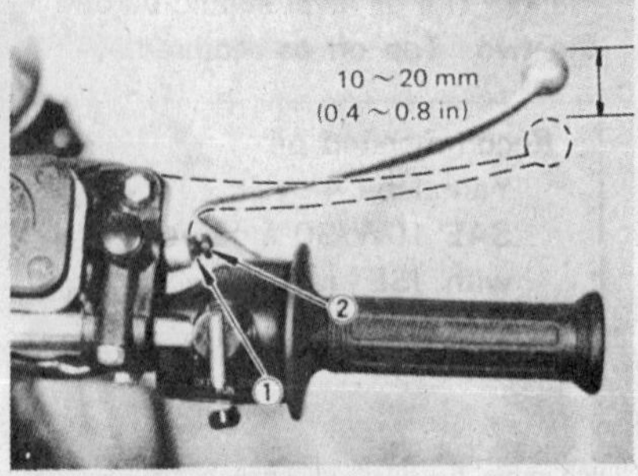

Front disc brake lever adjustment (Courtesy Yamaha Int. Corp.)

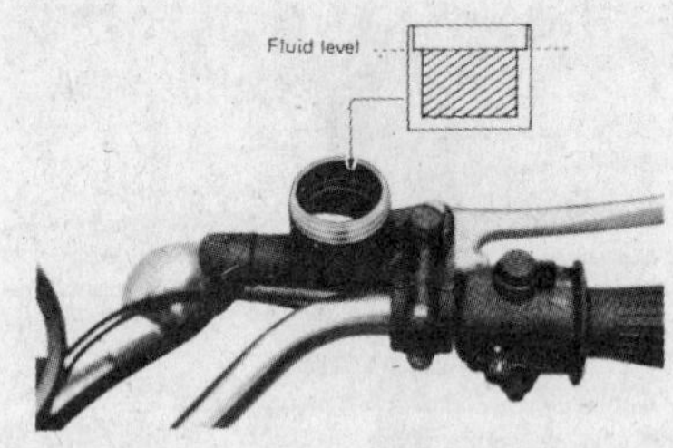

Master cylinder fluid level (Courtesy Yamaha Int. Corp.)

about 20 mm (0.8 in.) of free-play, measured as shown in the illustration. To adjust, loosen the locknut and turn the adjusting screw in or out. Then tighten the locknut.

2. Maintain the brake fluid level in the master cylinder at the level line inscribed on the master cylinder. Although the fluid level may drop slightly as the pads wear, this drop should not be significant.

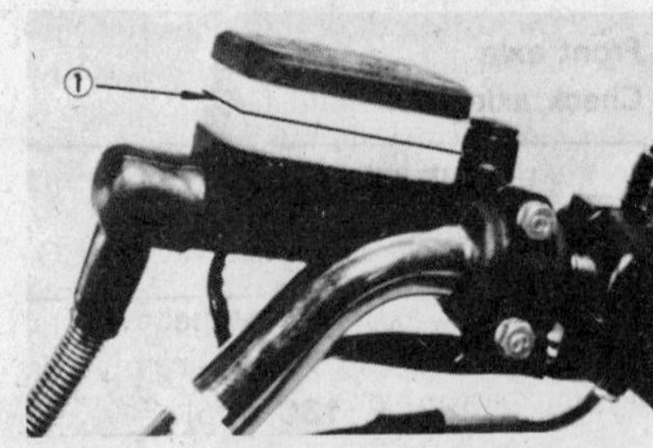

Brake fluid lower level mark (1) (RD400C) (Courtesy Yamaha Int. Corp.)

Rear disc brake lower fluid level mark (1) (RD400C) (Courtesy Yamaha Int. Corp.)

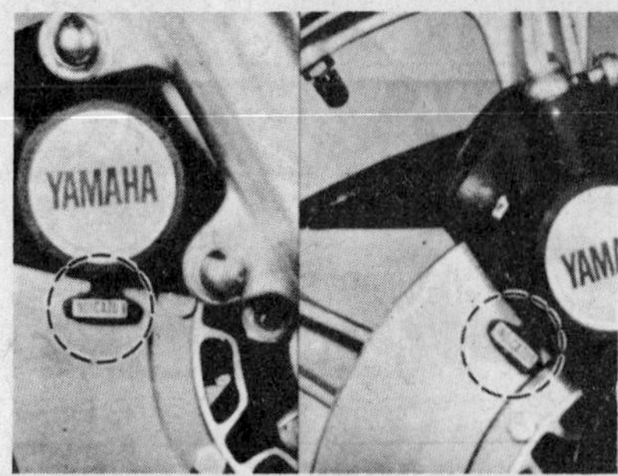

Front and rear brake pad wear indicators (Courtesy Yamaha Int. Corp.)

3. Pads should be checked periodically for wear. Replace them when worn to or near the red limit line or when the wear indicator shows the need for replacement. Refer to the "Chassis" section for pad replacement procedures.

4. The brake hoses should be checked for seepage or abrasion damage often, and should be replaced if they show wear or leakage of any kind. Make sure that the lines touch the frame or forks at the mounting points only.

5. Every 8,000 miles or 1 year, the brake system should be flushed and refilled with fresh fluid. Refer to the "Chassis" section for procedures.

FRONT DRUM

1. Use the cable adjuster on the brake plate to allow about ¼ in. (6 mm) of brake handlebar lever free-play before the shoes contact the drum. This free-play is to be measured between the lever and the lever holder.

Front drum brake lever adjustment is measured between the lever and the holder (Courtesy Yamaha Int. Corp.)

2. This free-play can be maintained as the shoes wear by using the adjuster at the handlebar lever.

3. The linkage of twin-leading shoe front brakes ordinarily does not need adjustment. If the backing plate has been disassembled, or adjustment is felt to be necessary because of weak brakes, proceed as follows:

a. Loosen the locknut on the rod connecting the two brake cam levers on the brake plate;

b. Use a vise-grip pliers (protecting the rod with a rag) to turn the rod so that the distance between the ends of the two levers *decreases;*

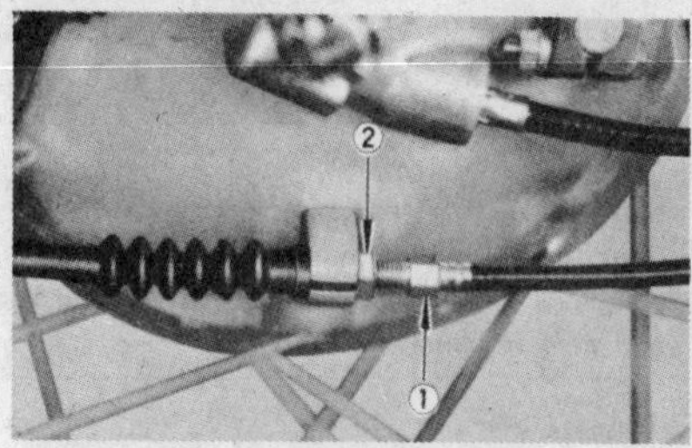

Front brake adjuster on the brake plate (Courtesy Yamaha Int. Corp.)

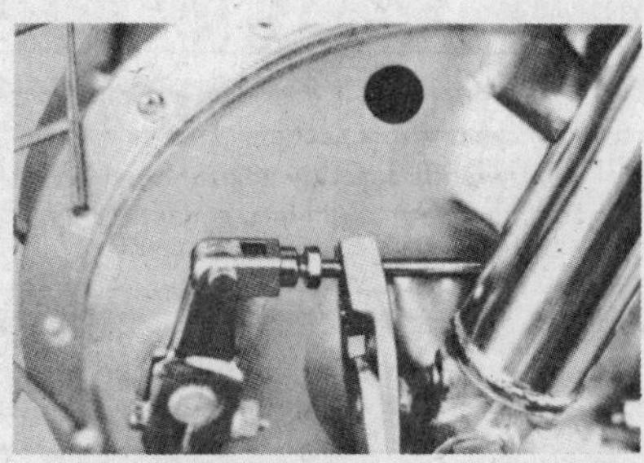

Adjusting the twin-leading shoe brake rod (Courtesy Yamaha Int. Corp.)

c. Apply the brake. The lever which is connected directly to the cable will raise its brake shoe to contact the drum;

d. Turn the connecting rod so that the distance between the two levers *increases,* and continue until it is no longer possible to turn the rod. The second lever will have raised its shoe against the brake drum at this point and the linkage is adjusted. Tighten the rod locknut.

e. Adjust the brake cable.

REAR DRUM

Use the adjusting nut on the end of the cable or rod so that the brake pedal has 25 mm (1 in.) of free-play before the linings contact the drum. On models with rod-operated brakes, make the adjustment with a rider on the machine.

NOTE: *If the angle between the brake cable or rod and the lever on the brake plate exceeds 90° when the brake is applied, the lining thickness should be checked. On some models, this can be done by removing the brake plate inspection cap.*

Rear brake adjusting nut (Courtesy Yamaha Int. Corp.)

REAR DISC

The RD400C is fitted with a rear disc. All points noted above for front disc brakes are applicable. A wear indicator is fitted to check pad condition.

To adjust the brake pedal, loosen the brake rod locknut and turn the adjuster in or out so that the brake has 5–10 mm (0.2–0.4 in.) of free pedal movement. Tighten the locknut.

BRAKE LIGHT SWITCH

The switches should be checked for operation after the brake is adjusted. The rear brake light switch is mounted in a slotted bracket and secured by locknuts. Moving the light switch up on the bracket allows the brake light to turn on sooner. Moving it down allows it to come on later. Generally, the brake light should come on just before the linings contact the drum.

Steering Stem Bearings

The steering stem bearings should be checked periodically and adjusted if necessary. Refer to the "Chassis" section.

Generator

1. Begin inspection of the carbon brushes on machines with (DC) generators after 4,000 miles. Brushes will usually have a wear limit line marked on them. Refer to the "Electrical Systems" section for wear limits.

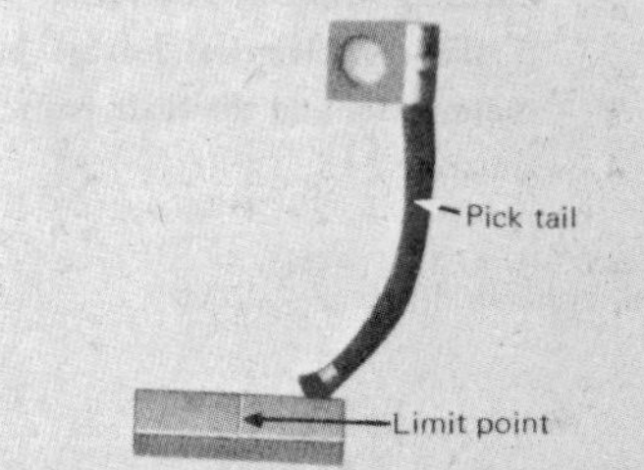

Generator brush wear limit line (Courtesy Yamaha Int. Corp.)

2. Clean off the generator commutator with a gasoline-soaked rag. The commutator surface can be polished with #400–600 sandpaper or fine emery cloth. After polishing, clean the commutator thoroughly. Check the mica undercut. Refer to the "Electrical Systems" section for specifications.

Polishing the commutator segments (Courtesy Yamaha Int. Corp.)

FUEL SYSTEM

1. Fuel system maintenance involves cleaning the petcock and filter, cleaning

Yamaha Street 2-Strokes

Periodic Maintenance

Mileage intervals indicate maintenance under average riding conditions. Services should be performed more often under adverse conditions or hard usage.

Daily (before each ride)
- Check lighting equipment and horn operation
- Check operation and adjustment of the brakes
- Tire condition
- Chain tension
- Cable adjustments
- Autolube tank oil level

Weekly
- Transmission oil level
- Tire pressure (cold)
- Spoke tension
- Battery electrolyte level
- Chain condition
- Critical nuts and bolts

Monthly
- Trickle charge stored battery

Every 200 miles
- Lubricate chain

Every 2000 miles
- Change transmission oil
- Remove, clean, and lubricate chain
- Lubricate grease fittings
- Lubricate control and instrument cables
- Decarbonize engine
- Check oil pump adjustment
- Clean fuel petcock
- Check brake fluid level (disc brake)
- Grease speedometer drive mechanism
- Change fork oil

Every 3000 miles
- Clean or replace air cleaner

Every 4000 miles
- Disassemble and clean carburetors
- Check generator brushes
- Check brake linings
- Pack wheel and steering head bearings

Every 8000 miles
- Flush hydraulic disc brake system

Recommended Lubricants

Autolube
- Yamalube 2-cycle
- Two-stroke oil (TC-W)
- Two-stroke oil SAE 30W (for air-cooled engines)
- Motor oil SAE 30 service rating "SE" (detergent)
- Motor oil SAE 10W-30 service rating "SE" (detergent) (below 15° F)

Transmission
- Yamalube 4-cycle
- SAE 10W-30 service rating "SE"
- SAE 30W service rating "SE"

Forks
- Yamaha fork oil
  - 10W
  - 20W
  - 30W
- SAE 10W-30
- SAE 30
- SAE 20

Grease Fittings
- High-quality lithium or moly-based chassis grease

Drive Chain
- High-quality chain lube specifically developed for motorcycle drive chains

Wheel and Steering Head Bearings
- Lithium or moly-based bearing grease

Cables
- Light motor oil
- Graphite-based lubricant
- Molybdenum disulphide-based lubricant

Maintenance Data

	Fuel Tank Capacity (Gal)	Autolube Oil Capacity (Qt)	Transmission⑤ Oil Capacity (Qt)	Front Fork① Oil Capacity (cc)	(oz)	Tire Pressure Front/Rear (psi)
U5, U5L, U5E	0.90	1.60	0.50	—	—	22/28
U7E	1.20	1.50	0.65	—	—	20/28
YJ2	1.38	1.16	0.50	130	4.4	22/28
RD60, RD60A	2.10	1.10	0.47	135	4.5	22/28
YG1K, YG1TK, YGS1, YGS1T	1.72	1.15	0.50	130	4.4	22/28
YG5S/T	1.60	1.48	0.65	140	4.7	25/27
G5S	1.60	1.50	0.65	②		26/28
G6S	1.60	1.50	0.65	130	4.4	26/28
G6SB, G7S	1.60	1.50	0.65	②		20/28
HS1, HS1B, LS2	2.00	③	0.85	147	5.0	20/28
YL2, YL2C, YL2CM	2.20	1.70	0.75	145	4.9	25/27
YL1, YL1E	1.95	1.16	0.75	130	4.4	25/27
YA6	2.38	1.90	1.40	170	5.8	22/28
YAS1, YAS1C	2.50	1.59	0.85	160	5.4	25/27
AS2C	2.00	1.59	0.85	160	5.4	26/28
RD125B	3.00	1.60	0.85	137	4.6	26/28
YCS1	3.40	2.10	0.85	170	5.8	25/32
YCS1C	3.00	2.00	0.85	170	5.8	25/32
CS3C, CS3B, CS5	2.40	2.00	0.85	170	5.8	25/32
RD200B	3.00	1.60	0.85	157	5.3	25/32
RD200C	3.0	2.1	0.85	④	④	23/29
Early YDS3, YDS3C	3.70	1.70	1.50	200	6.7	22/28
Late YDS3, YDS3C	3.70	1.70	1.75	200	6.7	22/28
YDS5	4.00	2.50	1.75	200	6.7	22/28
DS6, DS6C, DS6B	2.90	1.60	1.75	200	6.7	26/28
YM1	3.70	1.70	1.75	200	6.7	22/28
YM2C	4.00	2.50	1.75	200	6.7	22/28
YR2, YR2C	3.80	3.40	1.27	240	8.1	22/28
R3C	4.00	3.40	1.27	240	8.1	23/28
R5, R5B, R5C, DS7	3.20	2.10	1.60	145	4.9	22/28
RD250, RD250A/B	3.20	2.10	1.60	145	4.9	23/29
RD350, RD350A/B	3.20	2.10	1.60	145	4.9	23/29
RD400	3.4	2.1	1.60	145	4.9	26/28

① Each leg
② Right leg—154 cc (5.2 oz); left leg—136 cc (4.6 oz)
③ HS1, HS1B—1.6; LS2—1.5
④ Normal change: 173 cc/5.9 oz
After rebuild: 181 cc/6.1 oz
⑤ Values are approximates. Use dipstick or level plug when adding oil.

or replacing the air cleaner, and cleaning the carburetor(s).

2. The carburetor(s) should be removed, disassembled, and cleaned every 4,000 miles. The procedures are outlined in the "Fuel Systems" section.

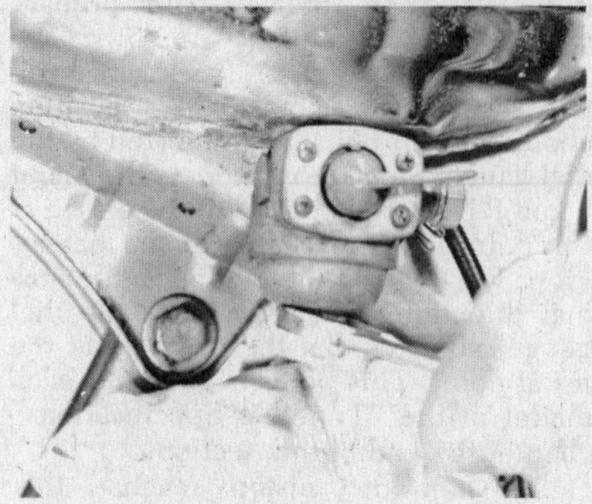

Removing the petcock sediment bowl

3. The petcock should be serviced every 2,000 miles. Shut the fuel off, then unscrew and remove the petcock sediment bowl. Take out the fuel filter. Clean the parts in a solvent and reinstall. Check for leaks.

4. The air cleaner should be serviced or replaced every 2–3,000 miles, depending on conditions. If the air cleaner is the paper type, it should be kept free of water, solvents, etc.

The paper filters can be cleaned, after a fashion, by tapping off heavy dirt deposits, or brushing off the outside, and blowing compressed air through the inside of the filter element. These techniques, however, are limited in usefulness, and it is really preferable to replace the element every 5,000 miles or so (once again, depending on conditions).

Where filters are a tight fit in their housings, some liquid detergent or a bit of oil can be applied to the end plates to facilitate installation.

If a foam-type air cleaner is used, wash it in gasoline to remove dirt, and squeeze until it is dry. Immerse the filter in light motor oil (20 or 30 W) and squeeze off the excess oil. Then install on the machine.

TUNE-UP

NOTE: *Common tune-up procedures are explained in detail in "General Information." A dial gauge and "Points Checker" (ohmmeter) are necessary for ignition timing. On battery-ignition machines, a test or continuity light can be used in place of the Points Checker.*

CONTACT BREAKER POINTS

Location

1. On single-cylinder machines with magneto ignition, breaker points are located beneath magneto flywheel (rotor) on the left-side of the engine. Remove the left-side engine cover to gain access to the points. Cutouts are provided in the rotor to allow the points to be cleaned and gapped.

2. On single-cylinder machines with electric starters, the points are located beneath a cover plate on the left-side engine cover.

3. Twin-cylinder machines have two sets of points which run off the crankshaft. Except for YDS and DS6 models, the points are located on the left-side of the engine and are accessible for cleaning and gapping or replacing after removing the point cover.

On YDS and DS6 models, the points are located on the right-side of the engine.

Gapping

Points should be filed (if necessary) or cleaned before gapping.

SINGLES—MAGNETO IGNITION

1. After removing the magneto cover, turn the magneto rotor so that the breaker points are visible through one of the cutouts.

2. Position the rotor so that the breaker points are fully open, then check the gap with a feeler gauge. Refer to the "Tune-Up Specifications" chart at the end of this section for the proper point gap for your model. The feeler gauge should be a light slip fit between the open points.

3. If the gap is not within specification, adjust by loosening the locknut and screwing the fixed point in or out on its bracket to increase or decrease the gap until it is correct. Retighten the locknut and recheck the gap.

SINGLES—BATTERY IGNITION

1. Remove the points cover and turn the engine over until the points are fully open.

2. With the proper feeler gauge, check the point gap. Be sure to use the correct gap for your machine as given in the "Tune-Up Specifications" chart at the end of this section.

3. The feeler gauge should be a light slip fit between the points.

On early models, the point gap is adjusted by loosening the locknut and turning the adjuster screw (black arrow) so that the fixed point (white arrow) is the correct distance from the moveable point

4. If the gap is not within specification, loosen the locknut, and screw the fixed point in or out on its bracket to increase or decrease the gap as needed. Retighten the locknut and recheck the gap.

TWINS

Two sets of points are used and they are adjusted independently. Be sure that both sets are set to exactly the same gap.

1. After removing the breaker point cover plate, rotate the engine so that either set of points is fully open.

2. Check the gap with the proper feeler gauge. Refer to the "Tune-Up Specifications" chart at the end of this section for the proper point gap for your machine.

3. If the gap is not within specification, it must be adjusted. On older models (those with a fixed point secured by a locknut), loosen the locknut and screw the fixed point in or out on its bracket so that the gap is correct. Secure the locknut.

On all newer models, the fixed point is a part of a plate and is secured with a screw; refer to the accompanying illustration. Loosen the fixed point securing screw and with a thin screwdriver applied to the pry slot provided, move the fixed point towards or away from the

On recent twins, the point gap is adjusted after loosening the screws (1 and 2). Screws 3, 4, 5, and 6 are used to adjust the ignition timing. The white arrows indicate the points' primary wire terminals (Courtesy Yamaha Int. Corp.)

movable point until the gap is correct.

4. Tighten the fixed point securing screw and recheck the gap.

5. Turn the engine over until the other set of points is open, and repeat the procedure.

Replacement

MAGNETO IGNITION

Two special tools are needed to replace the points on magneto-ignition machines. A holder is used to hold the magneto rotor steady while the nut is removed, and a special puller, threaded

Removing the magneto rotor (Courtesy Yamaha Int. Corp.)

into the center of the rotor, is used to pull it off its tapered shaft.

CAUTION: *The rotor puller is essential for this job. It is not wise to attempt to remove the rotor in any other way.*

1. Remove the left-side engine cover, after loosening the pinch-bolt and pulling the gearshift lever off its shaft. The use of an impact driver to remove and install phillips head case screws is recommended.

2. Holding the magneto rotor with the special tool, or a suitable substitute, loosen and remove the rotor nut.

NOTE: *Alternately, engage the transmission and apply the rear brake to hold the rotor if a shop holder is not available.*

3. Thread the rotor puller into the rotor. The puller bolt should be backed off enough so that the puller outer has a good number of threads in the rotor.

NOTE: *The puller outer has a left-hand thread. Thread it into the rotor in a counterclockwise direction.*

4. Tighten the puller bolt against the end of the crankshaft to remove the rotor. The rotor should come off the taper. If it is stuck, tighten the puller bolt as much as possible and give it a sharp rap with a hammer. This should free the rotor. Note the key fitted to the crankshaft.

CAUTION: *Never use heat in an attempt to remove the rotor, since this may affect its magnetic properties. Handle the rotor with care: avoid dropping or striking it, as this, too, will affects its magnetism.*

5. Disconnect the primary wire from the breaker point terminal, then remove the securing screw. Remove the old points set.

6. Clean the contact surfaces of the new set of points to remove any protective coating present. Install the points and reconnect the primary wire.

7. Grease or oil the crankshaft taper slightly before fitting the rotor to make removal easier next time. Line up the slot in the rotor with the key in the crankshaft. Push the rotor into place. If the puller is still fitted back off the puller bolt, and strike the puller bolt once or twice to ensure that the rotor is firmly seated, but do not strike the rotor itself. Refit the rotor nut and tighten it securely. Reset the point gap and check the ignition timing.

BATTERY AND COIL IGNITION

1. Remove the breaker point cover.

2. Disconnect the primary wire at the breaker points terminal, and remove the securing screw. Remove the old points. On twins, install one set of new points before removing the other old set.

3. Before installing new points, be sure to clean off the breaker point surfaces with a solvent to remove any protective coating.

4. Install the new points, tightening the securing screw lightly. Reconnect the terminal primary wire. Be sure that the small nut is firmly secured.

5. Adjust the point gap and recheck the ignition timing.

Lubrication

1. Whenever the point gap is checked or points replaced, it is necessary to lubricate the cam follower fiber heel and the pivot point of the contact breaker. This minimizes wear and ensures that the timing will remain accurate for a longer period. A worn heel will retard the timing.

2. A small dab of grease (high melting point, if possible) or oil should be applied to the lubricator felt so that the lubricator can distribute it onto the breaker cam. A drop of engine oil should be applied to the pivot point.

3. In both cases it is imperative that care be taken to keep the lubricant away from the points.

4. The lubricating felt should be adjusted so that it just contacts the breaker cam.

5. If the felt is missing, or the model not equipped with it, the grease can be sparingly applied to the cam itself.

IGNITION TIMING

NOTE: *Points must be cleaned and gapped before checking the timing. Dirty points will cause inaccurate readings.*

Magneto Ignition

The timing on magneto ignition models is adjusted by changing the point gap. A dial indicator and a points checker are necessary for ignition timing.

1. Clean and gap the points.

2. Remove the spark plug and fit the dial gauge in its place.

3. Slowly rotate the engine until the gauge indicates its highest reading and begins to reverse. The highest reading is top dead center. Turn the engine a few degrees in either direction to recheck your finding. Then zero the gauge.

4. Attach the negative (black) lead of the ohmmeter or Point Checker to the engine case (ground), and the positive (red) lead to the breaker point primary wire.

5. Turn the engine "backward" (rotate the rotor clockwise) to a position about 3–4 mm BTDC as indicated by the dial gauge. Since most models fire about 2 mm BTDC, the points will be closed at this point. (Zero resistance on the meter).

6. Slowly turn the engine in the normal direction of rotation until the dial gauge indicates that the piston is at the firing point. This point is given for each model in the "Tune-Up Specifications" chart at the end of this section.

7. When the piston reaches this point, the points should open (as indicated by the reaction of the checker (if the ignition is correctly timed. If the points open before the correct position, the timing is too advanced. If they open when the piston is past it, the timing is retarded.

8. If adjustment is necessary, increase or decrease the point gap until the timing is right on. It should be possible to change the gap to correct the timing while still staying within the limits outlined under "Gapping."

9. If the timing was advanced, loosen the fixed point locknut and turn the fixed point to *decrease* the gap. If the timing was retarded, turn the point to *increase* the gap.

10. Repeat the procedure until the points open at the instant the piston reaches the correct distance BTDC. Timing should be within 0.1 mm of the given value. After adjustment, recheck the point gap in the fully open position. As noted above, it should still be within the proper specification. If not, the points should be replaced.

Battery Ignition

On battery ignition machines, a dial gauge is used to find piston position, while the moment of points opening can be determined either with the Point Checker or with a test or continuity light.

On twins, the timing is adjusted for each cylinder independently. Be sure that both sets of points are gapped to the same value, and that the ignition timing is the same for both when you are through.

1. Remove the points cover and clean and gap the breaker points.

2. If a timing advance mechanism is fitted, wedge the counterweights in the OPEN (fully advanced) position.

3. Remove the spark plug(s) and fit the dial gauge. On twins, either cylinder may be timed first.

4. Position the piston at top dead center by turning the engine over by hand until the dial gauge indicates the highest reading and then begins to reverse. The highest reading is top dead center. Turn the crankshaft a few degrees in either direction to check your finding,

On models so equipped, the timing advance weights should be propped open (full advance) when setting the timing

then position the piston at TDC and zero the gauge.

5. Refer to the "Tune-Up Specifications" chart at the end of this section for the proper timing for your machine. Ordinarily, the firing point will be 2 mm or more BTDC.

6. Hook up the test light or Point Checker: one lead to ground on the engine or frame, the other to the primary wire terminal of the points. On twins, the "LH" point set (orange wire) fires the left cylinder, and the "RH" (gray wire) the right cylinder.

7. Turn the crankshaft opposite the normal direction of rotation to about 3–4 mm BTDC. The points should be closed at this position.

8. Slowly rotate the engine in the normal direction of rotation. When the dial indicator shows that the piston is at the proper distance BTDC, the points should open.

9. If the points open before the piston reaches this distance, the timing is too advanced; if they open after it passes the timing distance, the timing is retarded.

10. To adjust the timing, loosen the two timing screws which hold the point mounting plate to the generator housing just enough to allow the points to be moved. Move the points in the direction of crankshaft rotation to correct advanced timing; move them opposite the direction of crankshaft rotation to correct retarded timing.

11. After adjustment, recheck the timing. The points should open at the precise instant which the dial gauge indicates that the piston is correctly positioned. Accuracy must be within 0.1 mm of the given specification.

NOTE: *Tightening the timing screws may change the timing slightly. So check your setting after they are secured.*

12. On twin-cylinder machines, repeat this procedure for the other set of points.

Adjusting the ignition timing: a screwdriver is used to move the points plate as shown (Courtesy Yamaha Int. Corp.)

The timing of the two cylinders must be as nearly identical as possible. They must be at least within 0.05–0.10 mm of each other.

NOTE: *Although not recommended except for emergency situations, the timing marks on the breaker assembly and generator housing can be used as a rough approximation of piston position in the event that a dial gauge is not available. When these marks are aligned (see illustration), the piston is at the firing point and the breaker points should just begin to open. This can be verified with a test light as above or by trapping a very thin piece of paper or cellophane between the points. Tug gently on the paper while slowly rotating the engine. As the timing marks align, the paper should come free. If the points open before the marks align, the timing is too advanced; if they open after the moving mark passes the stationary mark, the timing is retarded. Adjust the points as described above to correct.*

Ignition timing marks can be used to approximate ignition timing

Note that this procedure is not as accurate as that using a dial indicator.

CARBURETOR

Three adjustments to be made to the carburetor are float height, idle mixture, and idle speed. For the first of these, the carburetor(s) must be removed from the machine.

Adjusting Float Height

1. Remove the carburetor(s) as outlined in the "Fuel Systems" section.

2. Turn the carburetor upside down, and remove the four float bowl screws carefully lifting off the float bowl.

3. Remove the float bowl gasket.

4. Float height can be measured with a steel rule or a vernier caliper. Float height is defined as the distance from the float bowl gasket surface to the top of the float, when the tang of the float arm is just touching the float needle.

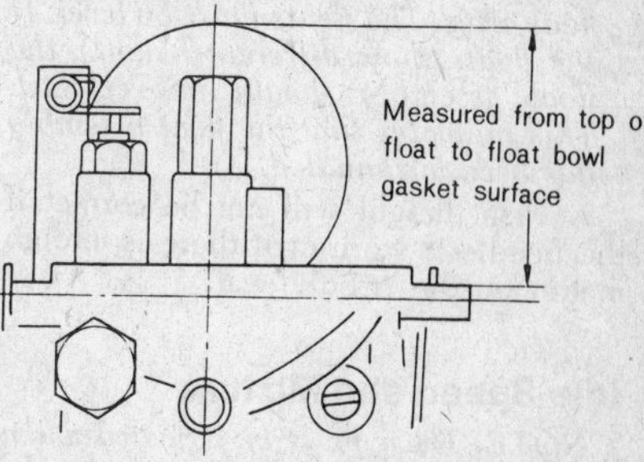

The float level is measured from the top of the float to the gasket surface. The gasket itself must be removed before checking (Courtesy Yamaha Int. Corp.)

NOTE: *Lower the float down until the tang just contacts the float needle. Hold the float in this position, then measure the float height.*

5. Compare the value obtained with the correct specification for your machine given at the end of this section. If the float height is too high or low, pull out the pin which holds the float in place, and bend the tang very slightly to correct the adjustment.

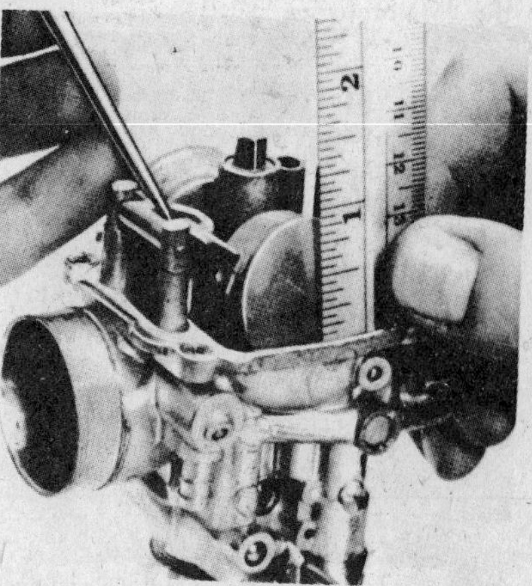

Checking float height

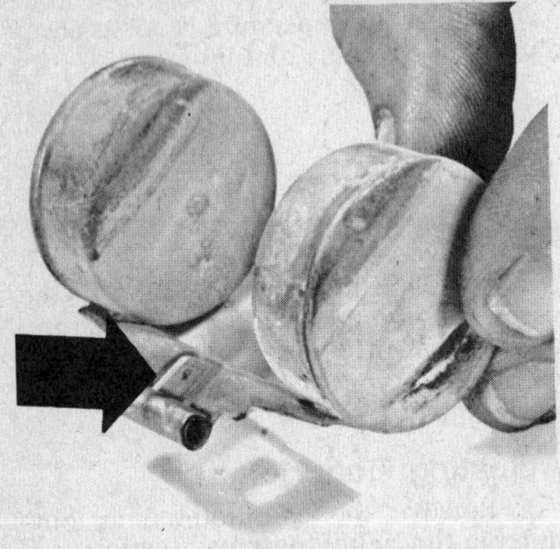

To adjust the float height, bend only the small tang indicated

NOTE: *If float height is too high, bend the tang away from the carburetor body. If too low, bend it toward the carburetor body.*

6. Refit the float and recheck the adjustment.

CAUTION: *Bend only the float tang to make an adjustment. Do not bend the float arms. The floats must be level. If the floats show different heights, the float assembly should be replaced. This indicates that the float assembly has been mishandled.*

7. Float height will not be correct if the needle is worn or if there is foreign matter on the needle seat.

Idle Speed and Mixture

NOTE: *These must be adjusted when the engine is at operating temperature.*

1. On all rotary valve, and the smaller piston-port models, the idle speed (or throttle stop) screw is located on the carburetor top. On other models it is located on one side of the carburetor body.

2. On some rotary valve models, the pilot air screw is located in the carburetor mouth, and is accessible after removing the carb cover plate (see the illustration). On all other models it is located on one side of the carburetor body.

3. The throttle cable(s) should be adjusted after making the idle speed and mixture adjustments. After adjusting the throttle cables, adjust the oil pump cable. Both of these operations are covered in the "Maintenance" section.

Rotary valve models pilot air and idle adjustment screws

Tune-Up Specifications

	Breaker Point Gap (mm)	*Ignition① Timing (BTDC)*	*Spark Plug (NGK)*	*Spark Plug Gap (mm)*	*Carburetor② Air Screw (Turns Out)*	*Idle Speed (rpm)*	*Float Height (mm)*
U5, U5L, U5E	0.20–0.40	1.7–1.9	B7HZ	0.6–0.7	1¼	1200–1400	22.5
U7E	0.30–0.40	1.7–1.9	B6HS	0.5–0.6	1¾	1200–1400	22.5
Early YJ2	0.20–0.40	1.7–1.9	B7HZ	0.6–0.7	1½	1200–1400	23.0
Late YJ2	0.20–0.40	1.7–1.9	B8HC	0.6–0.7	1¾	1200–1400	23.0
YG1, YG1T	0.20–0.40	2.0–2.2	B7HZ	0.6–0.7	1½	1200–1400	23.0
YG1K, YG1KT	0.20–0.40	2.0–2.2	B7HZ	0.6–0.7	1¾	1200–1400	23.0
YG5S/T	0.30–0.35	1.7–1.9	B7HZ	0.6–0.7	1½	1200–1400	20.5
G5S	0.30–0.35	1.7–1.9	B7HZ	0.5–0.6	1¾	1200–1400	20.5
G6S	0.30–0.35	1.7–1.9	B7HZ	0.5–0.6	1¾	1200–1400	20.5
G6SB, G7S	0.30–0.40	1.7–1.9	B7HS	0.5–0.6	1¾	1200–1400	22.5
RD60, RD60A	0.30–0.40	1.7–1.9	B7HS	0.5–0.6	1¾	1200–1400	22.5
HS1	0.30–0.35	1.7–1.9	B7HZ	0.5–0.6	1½	1100–1200	22.5
HS1B	0.30–0.40	1.7–1.9	B9HC	0.5–0.6	1½	1100–1200	22.5
LS2	0.30–0.40	1.7–1.9	B7HS	0.5–0.6	1¾	1200–1400	22.5
YL2, YL2C	0.30–0.35	1.7–1.9	B7HZ	0.5–0.6	1½	1300–1500	22.0
YL2CM	0.30–0.35	1.7–1.9	B8HC	0.5–0.6	1¾	1300–1500	22.0
YL1, YL1E	0.30–0.35	1.7–1.9	B7HZ	0.5–0.6	2½	1200–1500	23.0
YA6	0.30–0.35	2.5–2.6	B7HZ	0.6–0.7	1¼	1300–1500	25.0
YAS1, YAS1C	0.30–0.35	1.7–1.9	B9HC	0.5–0.6	1¾	1200–1400	22.5
AS2C	0.30–0.35	1.7–1.9	B9HC	0.5–0.6	1¾	1100–1200	25.3
RD125	0.30–0.40	1.8	B8HS	0.6–0.7	1½	1150–1250	20.0
YCS1	0.30–0.35	1.7–1.9	B8HC	0.6–0.7	2	1100–1200	21.0
YCS1C	0.30–0.35	1.7–1.9	B8HC	0.5–0.7	2¼	1100–1200	21.0
CS3C	0.30–0.35	1.7–1.9	B9HC	0.5–0.6	2¼	1100–1200	21.0
RD200B	0.30–0.40	1.8	B8HS	0.6–0.7	1¼	1150–1250	20.0
RD200C	0.30–0.40	1.8	B8ES	0.6–0.7	1½	1150–1250	20.0
CS3B, CS5	0.30–0.40	1.7–1.9	③	0.5–0.6	2	1100–1200	21.7
YDS3	0.30–0.35	1.8–1.9	B77HC	0.6–0.7	1½	1100–1200	25.0
YDS3C	0.30–0.35	1.7–1.9	B8HC	0.6–0.7	1½	1100–1200	25.0
YDS5	0.30–0.35	1.7–1.9	B8HC	0.6–0.7	1½	1000–1200	25.5
DS6, DS6B, DS6C	0.30–0.35	1.7–1.9	B9HC	0.5–0.6	1½	1100–1300	25.7
DS7	0.30–0.40	1.9–2.1	B8HCS	0.6–0.7	1½	1100–1200	15.1
RD250, RD250A/B	0.30–0.40	2.0	B9HS	0.5–0.6	1¼	1300–1500	15.0
YM1	0.30–0.35	1.9–2.0	B8HC	0.6–0.7	1½	1100–1200	25.1

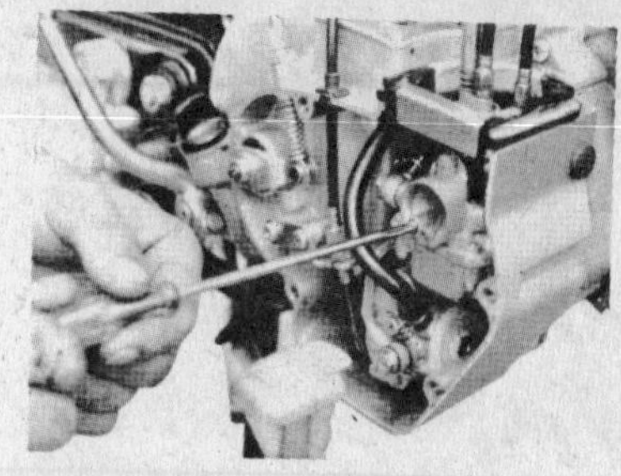

Adjusting the pilot air screw (rotary valve models) (Courtesy Yamaha Int. Corp.)

SINGLES

1. Ensure that the throttle cable adjustment is approximately correct so that the cable has enough slack to allow the throttle slide to be fully closed.

2. Screw the pilot air screw in (carefully) until it bottoms lightly, then turn it out the number of turns shown in the "Tune-Up Specifications" chart at the end of this section.

3. Start the engine. When operating temperature is reached, adjust the throttle stop screw (if necessary) so that the engine idles as slowly as possible. Then turn the pilot air screw in or out until the engine runs smoothly. It should not be necessary to vary the air screw more than ½ turn in either direction from the given setting.

4. Adjust the throttle stop screw so that the engine idles at the desired rpm.

Piston port models pilot air and idle adjustment (throttle stop) screws (Courtesy Yamaha Int. Corp.)

5. After idle speed and mixture are set, adjust the throttle cable and oil pump cable as outlined in the "Maintenance" section.

TWINS

1. Check that sufficient slack exists in the throttle cables to allow the throttle slides to be fully closed.

2. Refer to the chart at the end of this section giving the pilot air screw settings, and turn each air screw in carefully until it bottoms lightly, then screw each out the proper number of turns.

3. Start the engine and allow it to reach operating temperature. Remove one of the spark plug leads, and turn the throttle stop screw on the carburetor of the running cylinder so that the engine will idle (as slowly as possible) on the one cylinder. Turn the pilot air screw for that cylinder in or out until the engine idles smoothly. It should not be necessary to vary the air screw setting more than ½ turn in either direction from the setting given in the chart.

4. Connect the spark plug lead for the disconnected cylinder, then remove the lead from the cylinder just adjusted. Repeat the above procedure for the second cylinder.

5. When both carburetors have been adjusted, run the engine with both plug wires connected. Idle speed will be high. Decrease idle speed by turning the throttle stop screws on each carburetor *equal* amounts until the desired idle speed is obtained.

6. After setting the idle speed and mixture, adjust the throttle cables, synchronize the throttle slides, and adjust the oil pump cable. These procedures are outlined in the "Maintenance" section.

Tune-Up Specifications (cont.)

	Breaker Point Gap (mm)	Ignition① Timing (BTDC)	Spark Plug (NGK)	Spark Plug Gap (mm)	Carburetor② Air Screw (Turns Out)	Idle Speed (rpm)	Float Height (mm)
YM2C	0.30–0.35	2.0–2.2	B8HC	0.6–0.7	1½	1000–1200	25.5
YR2, YR2C	0.30–0.35	2.0–2.2	B9HC	0.5–0.6	1½	1200–1400	25.5
R3, R3C	0.30–0.35	2.0–2.2	B9HC	0.5–0.6	1½	1200–1400	25.5
R5/R5B	0.30–0.40	1.9–2.1	B9HC	0.5–0.6	1¾	1300–1400	15.0
R5C	0.30–0.40	2.0	B8HS	0.6–0.7	1¾	1300–1500	15.0
RD350, RD350A/B	0.30–0.40	2.0	B9HS	0.5–0.6	1¾	1300–1500	15.0
RD400	0.30–0.40	2.3	B8ES	0.6–0.7	1½	1100–1200	23.0

① in mm
② May vary according to atmospheric conditions
③ CS3B—B9HC; CS5—B9HS

ENGINE AND TRANSMISSION

NOTE: For engine component inspection techniques and procedures, refer to "Engine Rebuilding" under the General Information section.

SERVICE NOTES

NOTE: *If the oil pump has been removed or any of the lines disconnected, the pump must be bled before starting the engine. On rebuilt engines, the oil pump should be held wide open by means of the cable for several seconds after starting. This to ensure sufficient lubrication to critical moving parts.*

In-Frame Service

Service to the following components can be carried out with the engine in the frame:

a. top end (cylinder head, cylinder, piston, rings, small end bearing);
b. clutch;
c. magneto, generator, or alternator;
d. countershaft sprocket;
e. rotary valve (where fitted);
f. oil pump;
g. kick-starter;
h. shifter shaft and shift arm.

Service to the crankshaft, transmission, shift drum, kick-starter shaft or crank and transmission bearings will necessitate splitting the cases.

ENGINE REMOVAL

Clean the engine thoroughly before removal to take away as much grease and road grime as possible. Be especially attentive to the cylinder base and crankcase mating areas.

Piston-Port Singles

1. Warm the engine and drain off the transmission oil. Replace the drain plug hand-tight. Remove the fairing, if fitted. Remove the spark plug.

Removing the exhaust pipe ring nut (Courtesy Yamaha Int. Corp.)

2. Remove the muffler and exhaust pipe. The exhaust pipe ring nut at the cylinder (and on some models at the muffler as well) should be removed with the special pin wrench.

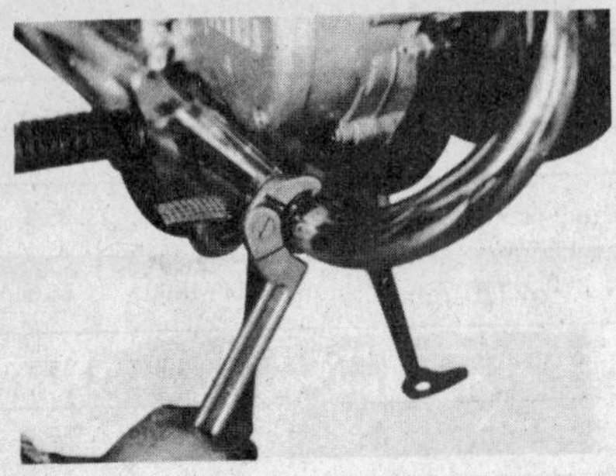

Loosening the muffler nut (Courtesy Yamaha Int. Corp.)

Frozen or balky ring nuts should be loosened first with some penetrating oil or fluid applied to the threads.

3. Remove the gearshift lever. Remove the left crankcase cover.

4. On magneto ignition machines, remove the magneto rotor nut, holding the rotor either with the special tool, or by placing the motorcycle in gear and applying the rear brake.

Removing the magneto rotor nut (Courtesy Yamaha Int. Corp.)

5. Back off the puller bolt on the rotor puller, and thread in the puller (left-hand thread) until it is firmly attached to the rotor. Tighten the puller bolt (standard right-hand thread) until it draws the rotor off the crankshaft. If trouble is encountered, tighten the bolt as much as possible, then strike it sharply with a hammer. This should serve to pop the rotor off the shaft.

CAUTION: *Do not strike the rotor; do not attempt to remove the rotor without the puller.*

6. Put the rotor in a safe place.

7. Unscrew and remove the magneto stator securing screws. Remove the stator assembly from the engine, take the rubber wiring grommet out of its cutout in the crankcase, and place the stator aside, tieing it out of the way if necessary.

Removing the magneto stator (Courtesy Yamaha Int. Corp.)

8. With a small punch, remove the rotor woodruff key from the crankshaft taper. Place the key with the rotor to be sure it is replaced upon installation.

9. On generator-equipped motorcycles, disconnect the wiring harness terminals on the generator.

NOTE: *On some early models, the wiring harness must be disconnected in the battery compartment because the generator terminals are soldered.*

10. Remove the chain guard.

11. Rotate the rear wheel so that the masterlink is accessible. Use pliers to remove the masterlink spring clip; remove the cover plate and the masterlink. Disengage the chain from the countershaft sprocket.

NOTE: *Assemble the masterlink on one end of the disconnected chain to avoid loss.*

12. Remove the oil pump cover. Disconnect the pump cable from the pump, then detach the cable from the engine case (in some cases the adjuster must be unscrewed from the crankcase).

13. Unscrew the carburetor cap and pull out the throttle slide assembly. Tie it out of the way to avoid damage. Disconnect the carburetor from the air cleaner.

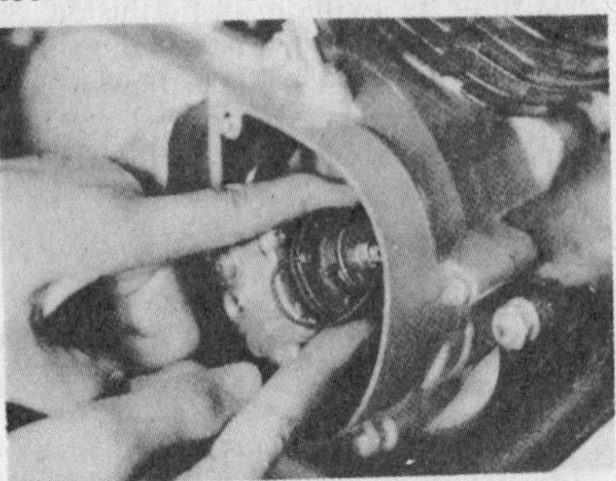

Disconnecting the oil pump cable (Courtesy Yamaha Int. Corp.)

14. Disconnect the tachometer cable from the engine. If the clutch cable adjuster is threaded into the crankcase itself, remove the clutch release lever cover and disconnect the cable from the lever. Unscrew the adjuster from the crankcase.

15. Shut the fuel petcock "off" and disconnect the fuel line at the petcock. Disconnect the oil line at the Autolube tank, plugging the tank to prevent loss of oil. Disconnect the neutral indicator wire if fitted.

16. Remove the engine mounting bolts and take the engine out of the frame.

Rotary-Valve Engines

1. Warm up the engine and drain off the transmission oil. Replace the drain plug(s) and tighten hand-tight. Remove the spark plug.

2. Remove the muffler and exhaust pipe. These are usually secured with ring nuts which are removed with a pin wrench.

3. Remove the gearshift lever.

4. Remove the left crankcase cover.

For magneto-equipped bikes, refer to Steps 5–9; if generator-equipped, see Step 10.

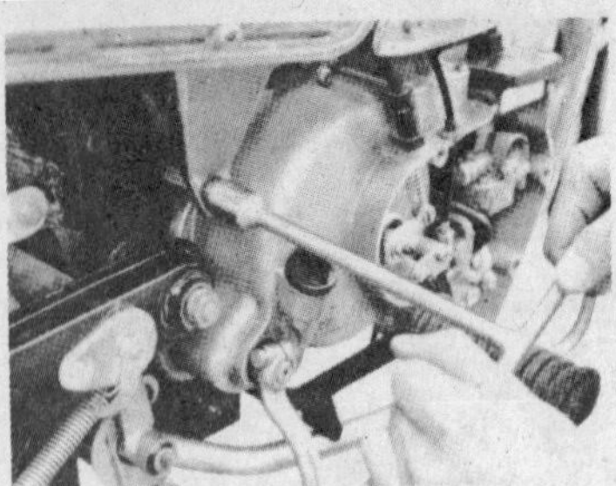

Removing the muffler mounting bolt (Courtesy Yamaha Int. Corp.)

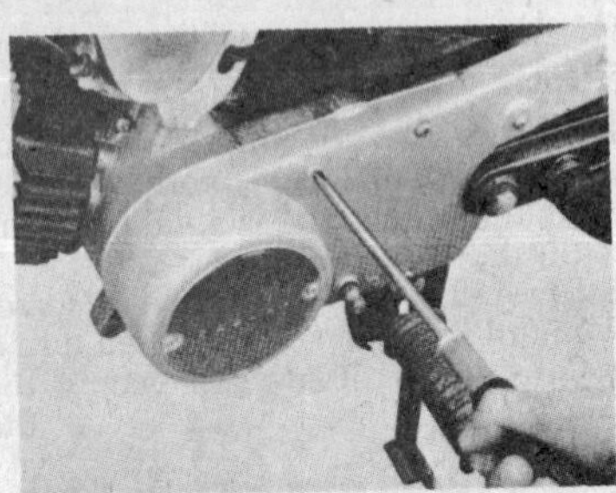

Removing the left crankcase cover (Courtesy Yamaha Int. Corp.)

5. On magneto-ignition machines, remove the magneto rotor nut, holding the rotor either with the special tool, or by

Removing the magneto rotor nut (Courtesy Yamaha Int. Corp.)

placing the motorcycle in gear and applying the rear brake.

6. Back off the puller bolt on the rotor puller, and thread in the puller (left-hand thread) until it is firmly attached to the rotor. Tighten the puller bolt (standard right-hand thread) until it draws the rotor off the crankshaft. If trouble is encountered, tighten the bolt as much as possible, then strike it sharply with a hammer. This should serve to pop the rotor off the shaft.

CAUTION: *Do not strike the rotor; do not attempt to remove the rotor without the puller.*

7. Put the rotor in a safe place.

8. Unscrew and remove the magneto stator securing screws. Remove the stator assembly from the engine, take the rubber wiring grommet out of its cutout in the crankcase, and place the stator aside, tieing it out of the way if necessary.

9. With a small punch, remove the rotor woodruff key from the crankshaft taper. Place the key with the rotor to be sure it is replaced upon installation.

10. On generator-equipped motorcycles, disconnect the wiring harness terminals on the generator.

NOTE: *On some early models, the wiring harness must be disconnected in the battery compartment because the generator terminals are soldered.*

11. Remove the drive chain masterlink spring clip with pliers, remove the cover plate and the masterlink. Disengage the chain from the countershaft sprocket. Install the masterlink on one end of the chain to avoid loss.

12. Remove the carburetor cover. Use an impact driver to loosen the cover screws.

Removing the right-side engine cover (Courtesy Yamaha Int. Corp.)

13. Remove the small rubber plug at the side of the carburetor/oil pump compartment. Insert a screwdriver through the hole and loosen the carburetor clamp. Shut off the fuel petcock. Disconnect the carburetor overflow line. Disconnect the fuel feed line at the carburetor. Pull the carb off the mounting spigot and tie it safely out of the way.

Loosening the carburetor clamp screw (Courtesy Yamaha Int. Corp.)

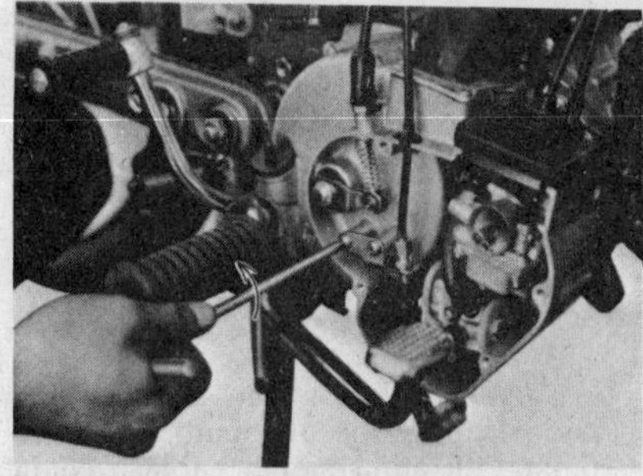

Removing the oil pump cable adjuster holder (Courtesy Yamaha Int. Corp.)

14. Remove the screws which secure the oil pump cable adjuster holder, and disconnect the cable from the oil pump.

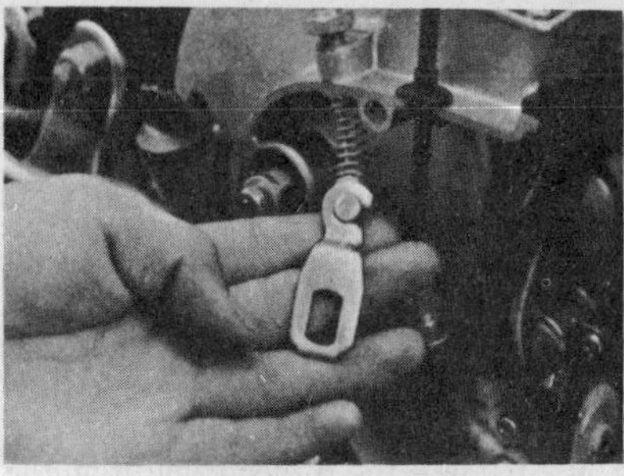

Clutch cable lever disconnected from engine (Courtesy Yamaha Int. Corp.)

15. If the clutch cable adjuster is threaded into the crankcase itself, remove the clutch release lever cover (if necessary), disconnect the cable from the lever, and unscrew the cable adjuster from the crankcase.

16. Disconnect the oil pump feed line at the Autolube tank and plug the tank to prevent oil loss.

Disconnect and plug the autolube tank feed line (Courtesy Yamaha Int. Corp.)

17. Remove the air cleaner and disconnect the air cleaner housing from the hose.

18. Disconnect the neutral indicator wire, if accessible; if not (as on G-series machines) proceed to the next step.

19. Remove the upper engine mounting bolts. Loosen the footpeg bolts. Tilt the engine forward until the neutral indicator switch on top of the crankcase is accessible. Disconnect the wire.

Disconnecting the neutral switch wire (Courtesy Yamaha Int. Corp.)

20. Remove the footpegs and take the engine out of the frame.

TWINS

1. Warm the engine up and drain the transmission oil. Replace the drain plug(s) hand-tight. Remove the spark plugs.

2. Shut off the fuel petcock and disconnect the fuel lines at the carburetors.

3. Remove the exhaust pipes. On late models, the headers are unbolted from the cylinder and the mufflers from the frame. On some early models, the header is connected to the cylinder and muffler with ring nuts. Use a pin wrench to loosen ring nuts.

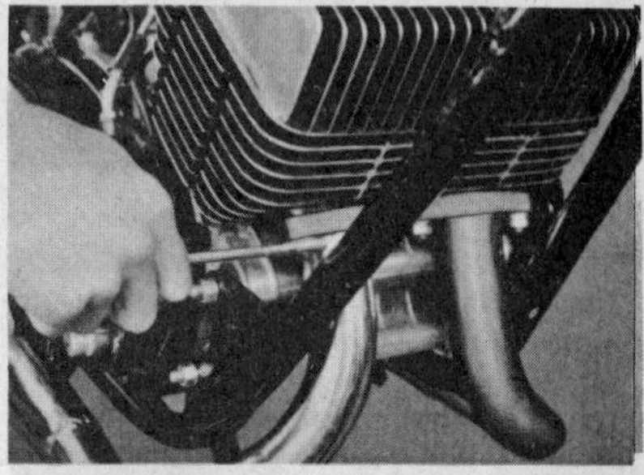

Disconnecting the exhaust pipes from the cylinder (Courtesy Yamaha Int. Corp.)

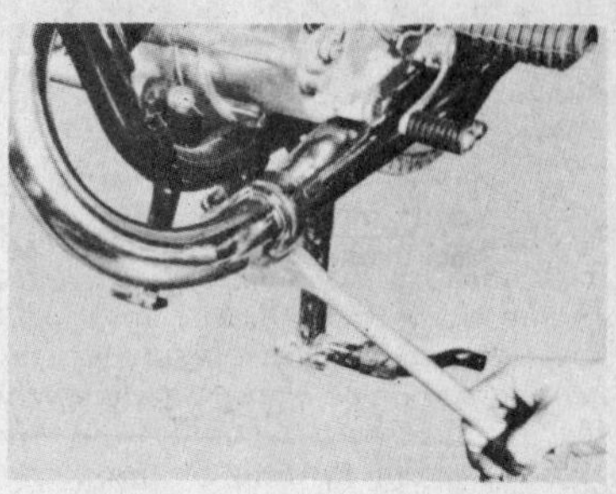

Loosening the muffler nut (Courtesy Yamaha Int. Corp.)

4. Remove the footpegs and the gearshift lever, pulling it carefully off the splined shaft after the pinch-bolt is removed. Remove the shift lever dust seal if fitted.

Removing the oil pump cover (Courtesy Yamaha Int. Corp.)

5. Remove the oil pump cover. Remove the alternator or generator cover and the countershaft sprocket cover. On some machines this side cover is one piece; on others, the sprocket and generator have separate covers.

6. Disconnect the clutch cable at the clutch release lever at the engine and detach the cable from the side cover.

7. Disconnect the alternator or generator wires at the connectors. Disconnect the neutral indicator switch as well.

8. Remove the alternator/generator stator mounting screws and remove the stator assembly.

Removing the alternator cover (Courtesy Yamaha Int. Corp.)

Left-side engine cover removed (Courtesy Yamaha Int. Corp.)

NOTE: *If the countershaft sprocket will have to be removed after the engine is out of the frame, loosen the sprocket nut or bolts before disconnecting the drive chain. Applying the rear brake hard should stop the sprocket from turning so the nut or bolts can be removed. Use a chisel to bend down the tab on the nut lockwasher if fitted.*

Disconnecting the alternator wires at the plastic connectors (Courtesy Yamaha Int. Corp.)

Removing the alternator stator (Courtesy Yamaha Int. Corp.)

9. Disconnect the drive chain. On older models this can be done by removing the spring clip with a pair of pliers, taking off the masterlink plate and removing the masterlink. On newer machines (RD-series), the masterlink is pressed on and the chain must be "broken" at the masterlink with the special tool. This tool, or a substitute, must also be used to press the link together for installation. If the special tool is not available and the chain will not come apart, move the rear wheel forward on the adjusters, apply the rear brake hard, bend down the tab on the sprocket lockwasher with a chisel, remove the countershaft sprocket nut, and remove the countershaft sprocket from the shaft.

10. Remove the oil feed line from the tank, plugging the outlet to prevent oil loss. Disconnect the oil pump cable from the pump, then lift up the rubber cover, loosen the locknut, and unscrew the pump cable adjuster from the engine. Some models have the oil pump cable adjuster fitted onto a bracket inside the oil pump compartment. In this case, remove the adjuster bracket screws and arrange the cable out of the way.

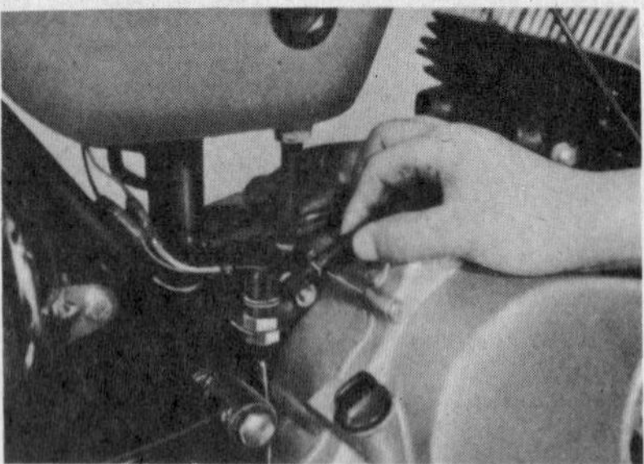
Disconnect and plug the oil tank feed line (Courtesy Yamaha Int. Corp.)

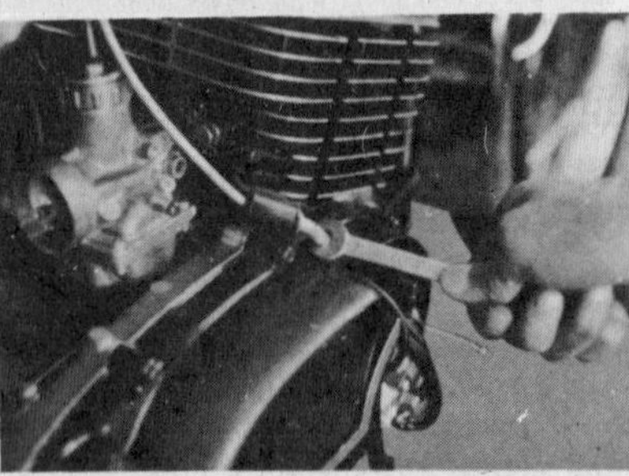
Removing the oil pump cable adjuster from the engine (Courtesy Yamaha Int. Corp.)

11. Loosen the carburetor cap ring nuts and pull the throttle slide assemblies out of the carburetors. Tie the assemblies out of the way so that they will not be damaged during the engine removal procedure.

Disconnecting the air filter hose at the carburetor (Courtesy Yamaha Int. Corp.)

12. Loosen the carburetor air cleaner clamp screws. On the HS1/B, YAS1/C, AS2 and early YDS models, remove the air cleaners.

13. Loosen the carburetor manifold clamp screws; remove the carburetors from their manifolds together. On most models the carburetors will be connected by a balance tube and starter linkage. Put the carburetors in a safe place after draining off the gasoline in the float bowls.

14. Disconnect the tachometer cable at the engine.

15. On 250, 305, 350 and 400cc models:

a. Remove the engine mounting bolts;

b. On the DS7, R5, and RD-series, remove the upper right rear engine mounting plate;

c. Straddle the machine, grasping the engine by the cooling fins on one side and the kick-starter lever on the other. Pull the engine back slightly, then remove it from the right-side of the frame.

16. On other models:

a. Support the engine with a crate or by having an assistant hold it;

b. Remove the engine mounting bolts, and lower the engine from the frame.

17. On the 100 cc YL1 models:

a. Loosen the upper downtube bolt;

b. Remove the front mounting bolts, and swing the downtube out of the way;

c. Support the front of the engine; remove the upper rear mounting bolt and lower the engine down onto a crate or scisssors jack;

d. Remove the rear mounting bolt and remove the engine from the frame.

Engine Installation

ALL MODELS

1. Installation is basically the reverse of the removal procedure, but the following points should be noted:

a. Engine mounting bolts should be properly torqued. Refer to the chart at the end of this section;

b. On magneto-ignition machines, apply a bit of grease to the crankshaft taper before refitting the magneto rotor. This will make removal easier next time;

c. On all machines, do not forget to install the crankshaft woodruff key for the rotor/armature;

d. Coat the threads of engine case screws with anti-seize compound or a general purpose lubricant to prevent them from seizing in the engine cases. Install them with an impact driver;

e. Replace any worn or damaged exhaust pipe ring nut gaskets;

f. Make sure that all fuel and oil lines are properly seated and secured with circlips;

g. After refilling the transmission and bleeding the oil pump, check all points of adjustment: cables, chain rear brake, ignition timing, carburetor synchronization, oil pump stroke, pump cable adjustment, etc. Install the drive chain masterlink spring clip with the closed end facing the direction of rotation.

TOP END

Cylinder Head, Cylinder and Piston

REMOVAL

1. Clean the engine thoroughly to remove any dirt or deposits. The area around the cylinder base is especially important.
2. Remove the spark plug.
3. Disconnect the exhaust pipe from the cylinder. Refer to "Engine Removal" for details.
4. On piston-port motorcycles, remove the carburetor from the cylinder.
5. Loosen the four cylinder head nuts ¼ turn at a time in an "X" pattern until they are loose, then remove them and their washers from the studs.
6. Remove the cylinder head and the aluminum cylinder head gasket as well.

NOTE: *The cylinder head may become stuck to the cylinder due to carbon build-up. In this case, tap around the lower edge of head with a plastic mallet until the head is free. Do not strike the cooling fins.*

7. On piston-port models, disconnect the oil feed banjo at the cylinder. Wrap a piece of plastic around the banjo, bolt, and washers. Secure it with a rubber band to prevent the entry of dirt.

Disconnecting the oil line banjo bolts at the cylinders (Courtesy Yamaha Int. Corp.)

8. Place the piston at top dead center and lift the cylinder off the crankcases until there is enough room to stuff a clean rag between the cylinder and the cases. This will serve to catch any pieces of broken piston ring or dirt which may drop into the cases when the cylinder is removed. Pull the cylinder straight up, catching the piston with one hand when the cylinder is free so that the piston won't hit the studs.

NOTE: *If the cylinder is stuck, it may be freed by tapping around the fins with a plastic mallet.*

9. Remove and discard the cylinder base gasket.
10. Remove the piston wrist pin snap-rings with a needlenose pliers. The rag should remain in place while doing this to prevent one of the snap-rings from falling into the crankcase. Grasp the piston with one hand and push out the wrist pin with a suitable drift. If the pin will not come out, the piston crown may be heated, evenly and gently, with a propane torch. If the pin still resists, it is ad-

Removing the piston wrist pin snap-rings (Courtesy Yamaha Int. Corp.)

visable to use the shop wrist pin removal tool. This consists of a steel band or bands which fit around the piston while the attached screw device is used to push out the pin.

11. When the wrist pin is about ¾ in. out of the piston, grasp the exposed end with a needlenose pliers, and pull it out until it is clear of the connecting rod. Remove the piston from the engine.

CAUTION: *Never strike the wrist pin or attempt to use brute force to drive it out. The connecting rod may be bent in the attempt.*

Cylinder and Piston

INSPECTION AND SERVICE

1. To check for wear of the bore, use an inside micrometer and take bore diameter measurements at the following points, holding the instrument in line with the intake and exhaust ports: just below the top edge of the cylinder; just above the exhaust port; just below the lower edge of the exhaust port; just above the top edge of the cylinder spigot. Record the diameters. Then turn the micrometer 90° and take another set of readings at the same points.

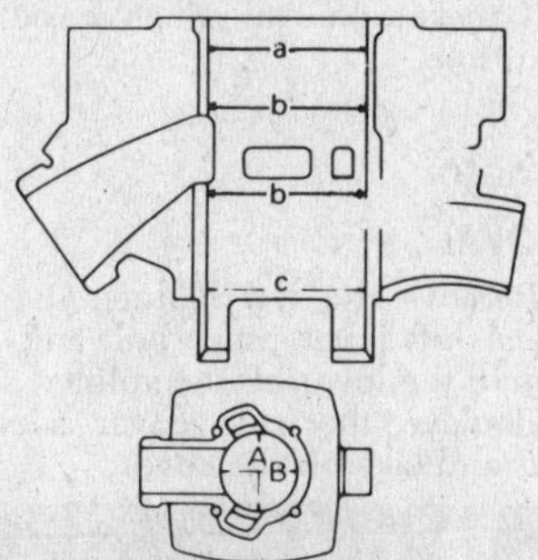

Measure the diameter of the cylinder bore at the four places shown and in directions "A" and "B" (Courtesy Yamaha Int. Corp.)

2. If the difference between the highest and lowest of these eight measurements exceeds 0.05 mm (0.0019 in.), the cylinder should be bored and the next oversize piston fitted (see below).
3. With a micrometer, measure the diameter of the piston perpendicular to the wrist pin at a point 10 mm above the bottom edge of the piston skirt. Compare this reading of the piston diameter with the *smallest* of the cylinder bore measurements made earlier. Subtracting the piston diameter from the smallest of the bore measurements will give the piston-to-cylinder clearance. If the measured value is more than 0.1 mm (0.0039 in.), the cylinder should be bored and the next oversize piston fitted.

If the wear has occurred primarily on the piston, fitting a new piston of the same original size you have might serve to bring the clearance into tolerance. This is, however, not often the case.

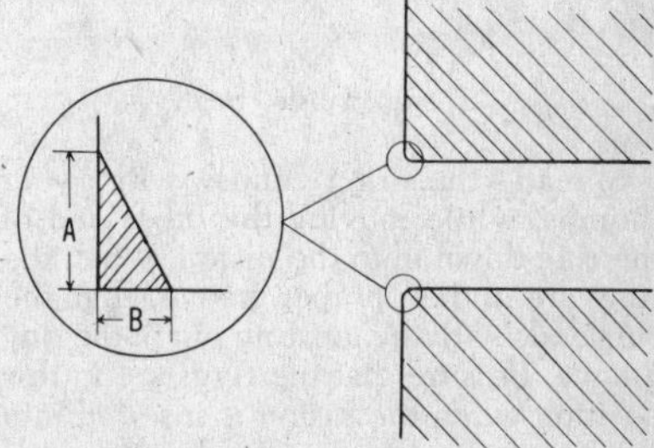

After boring, the edges of the ports should be chamfered so that there are no sharp edges

After boring, the difference between the largest and smallest cylinder bore diameters should not exceed 0.01 mm (0.0004 in.).

After the cylinder is bored, use a small file to put a slight chamfer on the edges of all the ports. This is important since rings will catch on the edges of unchamfered ports.

4. Check ring side clearance by inserting the proper size feeler gauge between the ring and the top of the ring groove. Clearance should be 0.04–0.08 mm (0.0016–0.0032 in.) for the top ring, and 0.03–0.07 mm (0.0012–0.0028 in.) for the bottom. If old rings do not have the correct side clearance, they will have to be replaced. If new rings show the wrong clearance, the piston will have to be replaced since either the ring grooves are worn (clearance too large), or have been closed up by a piston seizure. If the rings are not on the piston, roll each around the piston in its own groove as shown and check that it neither sticks nor binds in its groove.
5. Check the ring end gap with the proper feeler gauge. Refer to the "Piston Specifications" chart at the end of this section for the correct gaps for your machine.

Cylinder Head, Cylinder, and Piston

ASSEMBLY

1. Assemble the piston and rings. Pistons which use keystone rings have a "K" marked on the piston crown. Keystone rings are marked with a number (1 or 2) and a letter: "1N," "2N," etc. The number is the ring position. "1" is the top ring, and "2" is the bottom ring. The rings are not interchangeable.

The RD200 uses an "L" shaped top ring.

On models with two plain rings, the chrome plated ring is installed in the TOP groove.

All rings are installed with the stamped mark facing *up*.

"L"-shaped piston ring

Spread the ring ends with your thumbs, while moving the other end of the ring down onto the piston. When the rings are in their proper groove, align the ring ends with the locating pin in the ring groove. Be sure that the rings are in this position when the piston is inserted into the bore.

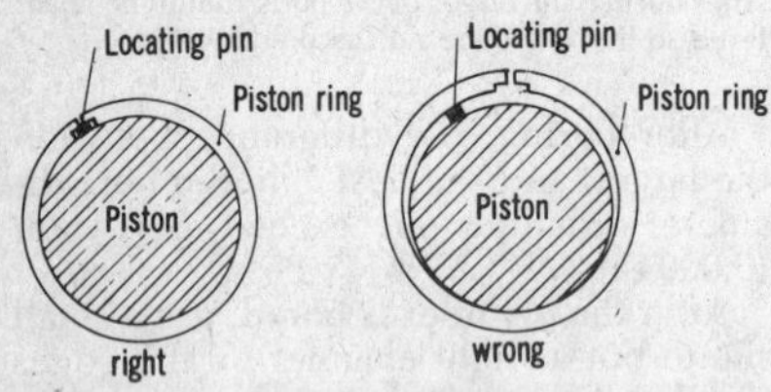

Ensure that the ring ends are located on either side of the locating pin in the ring grooves (Courtesy Yamaha Int. Corp.)

2. Lubricate the connecting rod small end with two-stroke oil. Place the piston over the rod with the arrow on the piston crown pointing towards the *exhaust* port. Push the wrist pin into the piston until it is located between the snap-ring grooves.

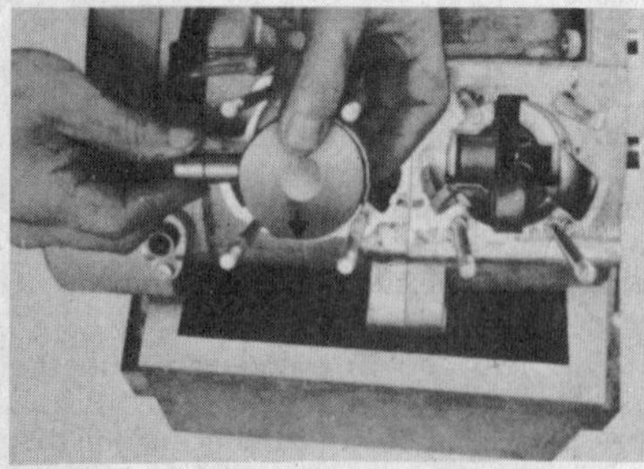

Install the pistons so that the arrow stamped on the crown faces the exhaust port (Courtesy Yamaha Int. Corp.)

3. Install *new* wrist pin snap-rings.

4. Clean off the crankcase mating surface and fit a new cylinder base gasket. Check again to ensure that the piston is correctly installed, and the ring ends are on either side of the locating pins.

5. Lubricate the piston rings and skirt and the cylinder bore with two-stroke oil. Place the piston at top dead center. Move the cylinder down on the studs until the piston begins to enter the bore. Then carefully compress the rings with your fingers until they enter the bore. Continue moving the cylinder downward until it is seated in the crankcase.

6. Clean off the top of the cylinder. Apply some clean oil to both sides of the head gasket and install it on the cylinder. Apply a bit of oil to the threads of each of the studs.

7. Install the cylinder head; tighten the head nuts gradually and evenly in an "X" pattern until the proper torque is reached. Refer to the "Torque Specifications" chart at the end of this chapter.

8. The remainder of the procedure is the reverse of removal. Use new exhaust pipe gaskets where applicable.

ENGINE COVER ASSEMBLIES

On all models with the exception of the YM, YDS, and DS6 series, the magneto, generator or alternator is located on the left-side of the crankshaft; the clutch is on the right-side of the engine, as is the primary drive, and the countershaft sprocket is on the left.

On all models so equipped, the rotary valve is located on the right end of the crankshaft.

On YM, YDS, and DS6 motorcycles, the generator is on the right, and the clutch on the left.

Before beginning work on the side cover assemblies, note the following points:

a. A puller will be needed to remove the magneto rotor, generator armature, or alternator rotor;

b. The clutch on all models is the wet-type. Transmission oil must be drained before removing the clutch cover. In addition, a new clutch cover gasket should be used upon reassembly;

c. All phillips head engine cover screws should be removed and installed with an impact driver. Additionally, coat the threads of engine case screws with a lubricant or anti-seize compound before installing, as this will make removal much easier the next time.

Magneto

REMOVAL

1. Remove the left footpeg. Remove the gearshift lever pinch-bolt and carefully pull the lever off the splined shaft.

2. Remove the side cover securing screws and take off the cover.

Removing the left crankcase cover (Courtesy Yamaha Int. Corp.)

3. Hold the magneto rotor in place either with the special holder (if the engine is out of the frame), or by placing the transmisssion in First gear and applying the rear brake hard. Then remove the rotor nut. An impact driver can also be used to break this nut loose.

Removing the magneto rotor nut (Courtesy Yamaha Int. Corp.)

4. Use the special puller to remove the magneto rotor. Back the puller bolt off several turns so that the puller can be threaded a good way into the rotor. Thread in the puller (left-hand thread). When it is in as far as possible, hold the puller with a wrench and turn the puller bolt clockwise until the rotor comes off the crankshaft.

Removing the rotor with the special puller (Courtesy Yamaha Int. Corp.)

NOTE: *If the rotor resists removal, tighten the puller bolt as much as possible, then give the end of the bolt a sharp rap with a hammer which should break it loose.*

CAUTION: *Do not strike the rotor itself.*

5. Unscrew and remove the stator securing screws and take off the magneto stator.

6. With a hammer and punch, remove the rotor woodruff key from the crankshaft.

INSPECTION

1. Magneto electrical tests can be found in "Electrical Systems."

2. Handle the magneto rotor carefully. Do not drop or strike it as this may decrease its magnetic properties.

3. Check the rotor for loose hub rivets or cracks. Check the inside of the rotor and note any scoring which may have been caused by contact with the stator coil cores. If such scoring exists, the cause must be determined and remedied.

4. Check the stator assembly for any damage visible to the eye such as scored coil core ends, broken or frayed wiring, loose coils, etc.

5. The tapered portion of the crankshaft should be smooth and free of corrosion, rust, etc. Finish off any scratches

or scores with fine emery cloth. Clean the area thoroughly.

6. Check the end of the crankshaft for play which would indicate a bad crank bearing. This is one thing which would cause the rotor to strike the coil cores.

7. Check the woodruff key for condition and replace it if step-wear has taken place or if the key is too loose in the keyway.

INSTALLATION

1. Installation is the reverse of removal.

2. Do not forget to install the woodruff key. Apply some oil or grease to the crankshaft taper.

3. Push the rotor on by hand after lining up the rotor slot with the key.

4. Use the rotor nut to seat the rotor. Do not strike the rotor.

Generator

REMOVAL

1. Remove the generator cover screws and then the generator cover.

Removing the generator cover (DS6) (Courtesy Yamaha Int. Corp.)

2. Disconnect the generator wiring at the generator terminals, and the neutral switch wire (if fitted) at the connector.

Disconnecting the generator wires (Courtesy Yamaha Int. Corp.)

Removing the armature bolt (Courtesy Yamaha Int. Corp.)

3. Unscrew and remove the armature bolt and take off the timing plate. Place

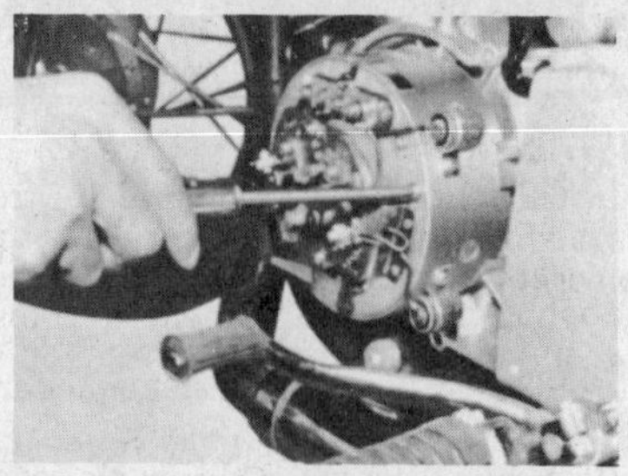

Removing the generator stator (Courtesy Yamaha Int. Corp.)

the transmission in gear and apply the rear brake to hold the armature if necessary. If the engine is out of the frame, secure the countershaft sprocket.

4. Remove the stator screws and take off the stator.

5. Thread a suitable bolt into the end of the armature to pull it off the crankshaft.

6. Use a hammer and punch to remove the armature woodruff key from the crankshaft.

INSPECTION

1. Refer to "Electrical Systems for component test procedures.

2. Check the woodruff key for wear and replace it if worn or loose in the keyway.

3. Inspect the generator armature for wear or scoring of the commutator segments. If the armature has been rubbing against the stator, the cause must be determined. This may be caused by an improperly mounted stator, a bent crankshaft, damaged crank bearing, etc. When the armature rotates it must not touch the stator at any point.

4. Clean up the armature with a solvent-soaked rag.

INSTALLATION

1. Installation is the reverse of the removal procedure.

2. When installing the stator, ensure that the carbon brushes are not crushed against the armature.

3. Arrange the wires so that they won't be pinched when the cover is refitted.

Alternator

REMOVAL

1. Remove the pinch-bolt and pull the gearshift lever carefully off the splined shaft.

2. Remove the alternator cover and the crankcase side cover screws and remove the covers.

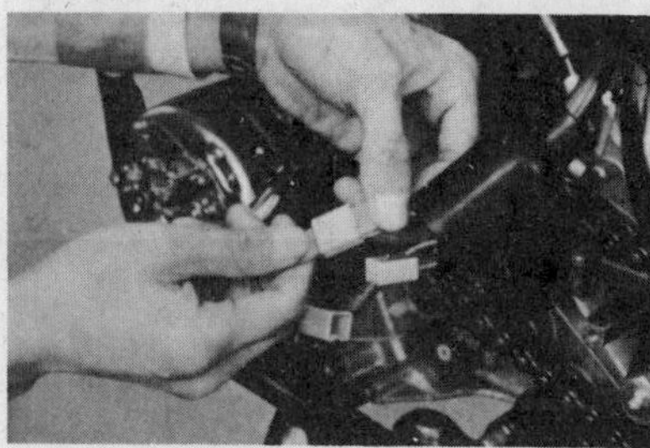

Disconnecting the alternator wires (Courtesy Yamaha Int. Corp.)

3. Disconnect the alternator wires and the neutral switch wire at the plastic couplers. On some older models, unscrew the neutral switch wire at the switch.

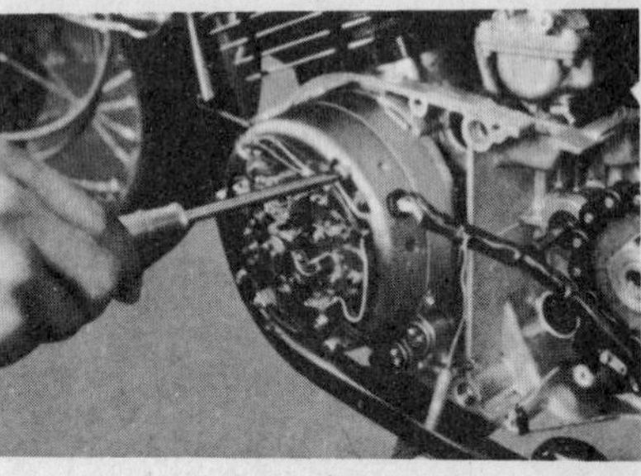

Removing the alternator stator (Courtesy Yamaha Int. Corp.)

4. Remove the alternator stator mounting screws and take away the stator.

5. Hold the rotor by placing the transmission in First gear and applying the rear brake hard. If the engine is out of the frame, loop a length of drive chain around the countershaft sprocket and lock the ends in a vise.

Removing the alternator rotor bolt (Courtesy Yamaha Int. Corp.)

6. Remove the rotor bolt and breaker cam.

7. Thread the special puller bolt into the rotor and pull it off the crankshaft.

8. Use a hammer and punch to remove the woodruff key from the crankshaft.

Pulling off the alternator rotor (Courtesy Yamaha Int. Corp.)

INSPECTION

1. Refer to "Electrical Systems" for component tests.

2. Check the rotor for scoring or wear which would indicate that the rotor has been contacting the stator. If this is the case, the cause must be determined. Either the stator is improperly mounted, the crankshaft is bent, or the crankshaft bearing is damaged.

3. Check the end of the crankshaft for

play which would indicate a damaged bearing.

4. Most models are fitted with rotor slip rings and these should be cleaned off with a solvent and rag.

5. Check the condition and length of the carbon brushes. Replace them if shorter than the specification given in the "Electrical Systems" section or if they are worn near the limit line scribed on them.

6. Check the condition of the crankshaft woodruff key and replace it if worn or if it is a loose fit in the keyway.

INSTALLATION

1. Reverse the removal procedure to install the components. Ensure that the rotor does not contact the stator at any point.

2. When fitting the stator, be careful that the carbon brushes are not crushed.

3. Arrange the wiring so that none of the wires will be pinched when the cover is refitted.

Countershaft Sprocket

REMOVAL

1. Remove the sprocket side crankcase cover.

2. With a hammer and punch, bend down the tab on the countershaft sprocket nut washer.

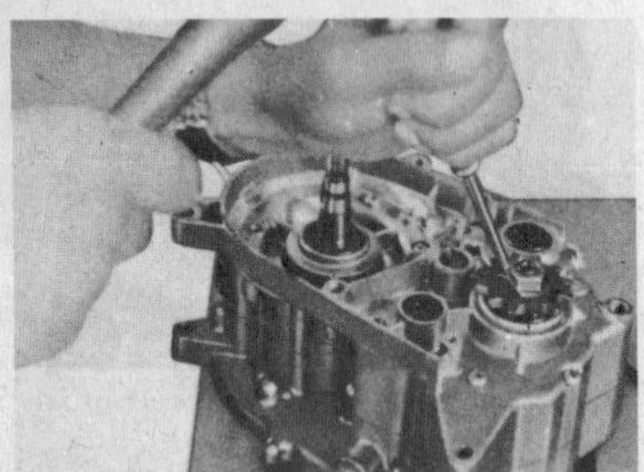

Bending down the locking tab on the sprocket nut washer (Courtesy Yamaha Int. Corp.)

3. Loosen the sprocket nut. If the engine is in the frame, the sprocket may be held while this is done by applying the rear brake hard. If the engine is not in the frame, loop a length of old drive chain around the sprocket and clamp the ends in a vise. Then remove the nut.

4. If the drive chain is still connected, disconnect it at this point. If a pressed-on masterlink is fitted and no chain-breaker is available, move the rear wheel all the way forward in the adjustment slots, then pull the sprocket off the countershaft. Remove the felt seal.

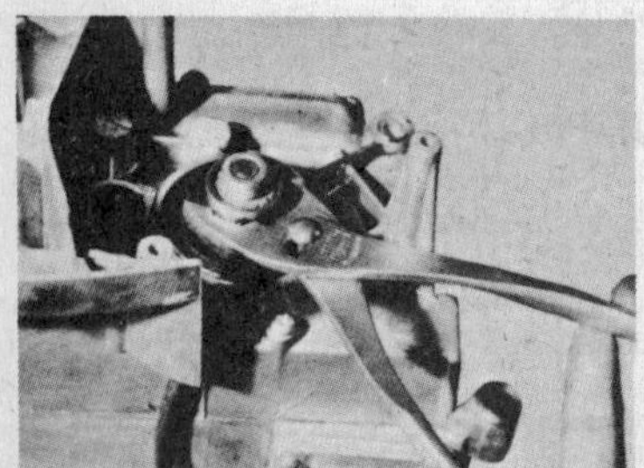

Removing the sprocket spacer (Courtesy Yamaha Int. Corp.)

5. Check for any spacers or thrust washers fitted behind the sprocket.

INSTALLATION

Installation is the reverse of the removal procedure. Ensure that the sprocket nut is firmly tightened and that the tab on the washer is bent up across one of the nut flats.

Clutch

Removing the clutch-side engine cover on rotary-valve models entails removing the carburetor. Refer to "Carburetor Removal" in "Fuel System" for procedures.

On all models, the oil pump may be left in place when the clutch-side cover is removed.

REMOVAL

1. Drain the transmission oil.

2. Remove the oil pump compartment cover.

3. Disconnect the oil feed line at the oil tank and plug the tank outlet.

4. On rotary-valve machines, remove the carburetor. Disconnect the air cleaner hose.

5. Disconnect the oil pump cable from the pump and the adjuster holder or adjuster from the cover. Disconnect the oil pump feed line(s) from the engine. On piston-port models, this is on the cylinder at the intake manifold; on rotary valve engines it is located in the oil pump compartment (see the illustration). Cover the banjo bolt(s) and washers with a plastic bag to prevent the entry of dirt.

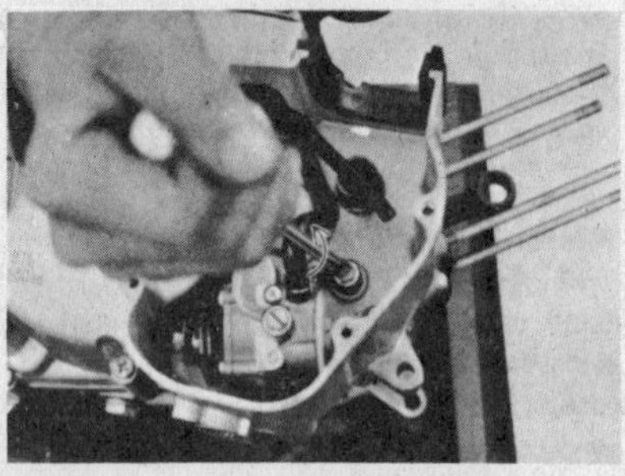

Removing the oil pump feed line banjo bolt from the engine (rotary valve models) (Courtesy Yamaha Int. Corp.)

6. Remove the kick-starter pinch-bolt and carefully pull the kick-starter off the shaft.

Removing the kick-starter shaft oil seal (DS6) (Courtesy Yamaha Int. Corp.)

7. On machines which have a kick-starter shaft oil seal accessible from the outside of the cover (such as the DS6-series) remove the oil seal now.

8. Disconnect the clutch cable and lever from the side cover if fitted. On most models, the cable is on the other side of the engine and can be left in place.

9. Place a drip pan beneath the cover to catch any oil residue. Loosen all of the phillips head cover screws with an impact driver and remove them. Tap around the edges of the cover with a plastic mallet to free it, if stuck, and remove the cover. Pull off the cover gasket; it should be replaced with a new one upon assembly.

10. The clutch is now accessible for disassembly and service.

NOTE: *If the primary drive (crankshaft) gear must be removed, it is advisable to loosen the primary drive gear nut with the clutch installed. Stuff a rag between the clutch and primary gears to lock them in place, then loosen the nut. Using impact rather than steady pressure on this nut will make removal easier.*

11. On centrifugal clutches only, bend in the stopper ring and lift out the ring, clutch, and friction plates. On YDS3 models, remove the clutch push crown.

12. On manual clutches, loosen the clutch pressure plate screws gradually and evenly, then remove them.

Removing the clutch pressure plate screws (Courtesy Yamaha Int. Corp.)

13. Remove the clutch pressure plate. Remove the springs; take out the pushrod.

Removing the pushrod (Courtesy Yamaha Int. Corp.)

14. Remove the clutch steel and friction plates. Note the cushion bands fitted between each pair of friction and steel plates. Handle them carefully. Note the order of the plates and bands as they are removed. All components must be installed in the same order.

15. Remove the clutch hub nut after bending down the nut washer tab with a hammer and chisel (if fitted).

To remove the hub nut, either hold the

Removing the hub nut (Courtesy Yamaha Int. Corp.)

hub stationary with the special tool, as shown, or engage the transmission and lock the countershaft sprocket in place using a method described earlier.

16. Remove the clutch hub, noting any thrust washers behind it.

17. Remove the clutch housing. The housing bushing will remain in the housing in most cases. Note any thrust washers which may be fitted to the shaft after the housing is removed.

INSPECTION

Centrifugal Clutch

Clutch plate—With the assembly mounted on the shaft, measure the clearance between the stopper ring and clutch plate. Adjust the clearance to 1.0–1.2 mm (0.040–0.047 in.) by installing replacement clutch plates of an appropriate thickness.

NOTE: *Clutch plates are available in 1.2 mm(0.047 in.), 1.4 mm (0.055 in.), and 1.6 mm (0.063 in.) thicknesses.*

Spacer—Install the bushing in the primary driven gear and check it for radial play. If any play is present, replace the bushing because it will cause premature clutch wear and excessive noise.

Rollers and retainer—Check the rollers and retainer for scratches, burrs, or rough spots. Place the rollers in the retainer grooves and roll them back and forth to make sure that their movement is smooth.

Manual Clutch

1. Refer to the "Clutch Specifications" chart at the end of this section for individual model specifications.

2. With a vernier caliper, check the thickness of each friction plate. If any of them is 0.3 mm (or more) less than the standard value, replace the friction plates as a set.

Clutch springs should be replaced as a set if any is 1.0 mm (0.04 in.) less than the standard free length.

3. If any steel plate is warped more than 0.1 mm (0.004 in.) on early machines, or 0.05 mm (0.002 in.) on recent models, all of the plates should be replaced.

4. Remove the bushing from the housing and inspect both inner and outer surfaces for scoring, scratches, or wear. Remove any such imperfections with emery cloth or sandpaper. If the damage cannot be remedied in this way, replace the bushing.

5. Insert the bushing into the housing and check for play. If the clearance is excessive, replace the bushing. If a new bushing yields an excess of play, replace the housing.

6. Place the bushing on the mainshaft. If excessive play is noted here, the bushing should be replaced.

A worn or scored bushing will cause excessive clutch noise and possibly impair operation.

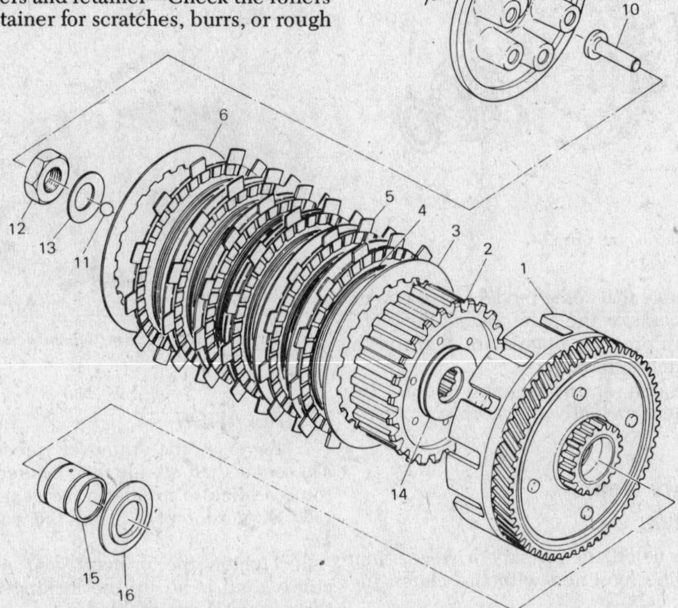

Clutch assembly (DS7, RD-models) (Courtesy Yamaha Int. Corp.)

1. Clutch housing
2. Clutch hub
3. Steel plate
4. Cushion band
5. Friction plate
6. Steel plate
7. Pressure plate
8. Clutch spring screw
9. Clutch spring
10. Pushrod
11. Ball bearing (5/16 in.)
12. Clutch hub nut
13. Spring washer
14. Thrust washer
15. Bushing
16. Thrust washer

Some early models are fitted with a needle bearing in place of this bushing.

Checking the clutch bushing for exesssive play in the housing (Courtesy Yamaha Int. Corp.)

Checking the bushing for excessive play in mainshaft (Courtesy Yamaha Int. Corp.)

The bearing should be checked for wear, discoloration, or damage to the needles or cage, and replaced if necessary.

Some models may be fitted with ball bearing-mounted clutch housings. This bearing can be removed from the housing after removing its securing snap-rings. This bearing should be checked for rough or binding rotation or obvious signs of damage to the balls or races. Replace the bearing if damaged.

INSTALLATION

1. Clean all metal parts in a solvent. Lubricate them with transmission oil before assembly.

Fitting a clutch cushion band (Courtesy Yamaha Int. Corp.)

2. Install the clutch components in the reverse of the removal procedure, referring to the accompanying illustrations if necessary. Be certain that all thrust washers are correctly located. Note that the plates on the RD400 have a cutaway edge. Install the plates so that these cut-aways are about 60° apart, all around the clutch hub.

3. Be sure all of the cushion bands are in place between the friction and steel plates.

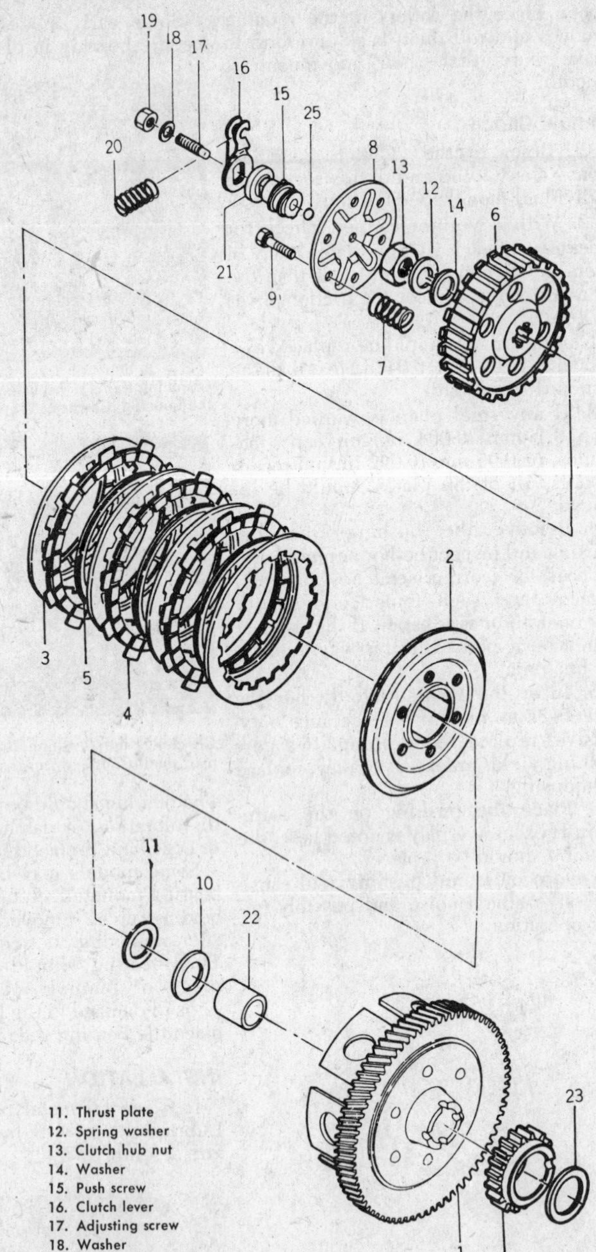

Clutch assembly (YG5S/T) (Courtesy Yamaha Int. Corp.)

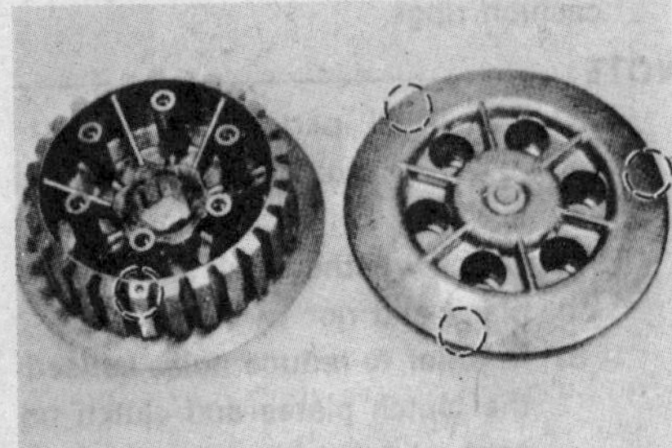

On the RD400C, install the pressure plate, aligning one of the punch marks with the mark on the clutch hub

4. Tighten the clutch hub nut securely. Bend up the tab on the washer (if fitted). When installing the pressure plate, note that some models have one or more marks on the plate. Install the plate so that a pressure plate mark aligns with the clutch hub mark.

5. Clutch spring screws should be tightened gradually and evenly.

Primary Gear

REMOVAL

1. As noted, the primary drive gear nut should be loosened with the clutch installed.

2. Bend down the locking tab on the gear nut washer (if so equipped).

3. Stuff a rolled up rag between the primary and clutch housing gears to lock them in place, then remove the nut.

Removing the primary gear nut (Courtesy Yamaha Int. Corp.)

Removing the primary gear (Courtesy Yamaha Int. Corp.)

4. Some models have the oil pump drive gear mounted on the outboard side of the primary gear. This gear should be pried off with two small pry bars. Remove the woodruff key as well.

5. The primary drive gear may be secured either with splines or with a woodruff key. To remove the gear, use two small pry bars or long, thin screwdrivers.

CAUTION: *Do not use the crankcase as a lever point. Protect it with rags. Take care that the oil seal beneath the primary gear is not damaged.*

6. Remove the primary gear woodruff key from the crankshaft (if fitted), and the spacer (RD60).

The oil pump drive gear in the crankcase cover (Courtesy Yamaha Int. Corp.)

INSTALLATION

1. Reverse the removal procedure. The crankshaft should be smeared with some oil before installing the gear.

2. Do not forget to install the woodruff key.

3. Tighten the primary gear nut securely, and bend up the locking tab on the washer if one is fitted.

Rotary Valve Assembly

REMOVAL

1. Remove the engine side cover, pri-

mary drive gear, and clutch assembly as outlined in the preceding sections.

2. Remove the phillips head screws which hold the rotary valve cover to the engine. Carefully remove the valve cover.

Removing the rotary valve cover (Courtesy Yamaha Int. Corp.)

3. Remove the rotary valve and the rotary valve collar.

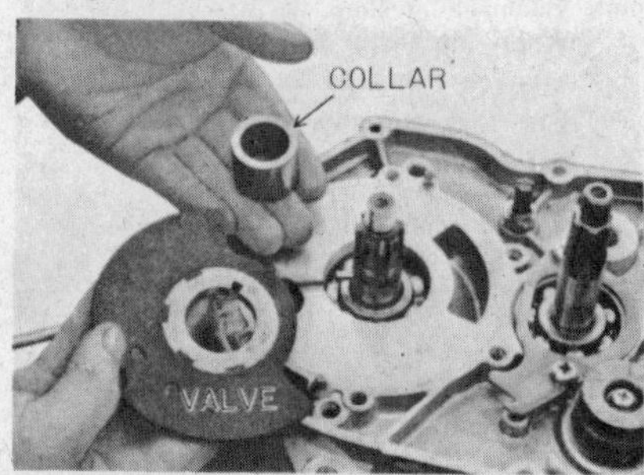

Rotary valve and valve collar (Courtesy Yamaha Int. Corp.)

Removing the crankshaft O-ring (Courtesy Yamaha Int. Corp.)

4. Remove the rotary valve locating pin from the crankshaft either by pulling it out with pliers, or by tapping it out.

CAUTION: *Take care not to damage the crankcase or rotary valve mating surfaces during this operation.*

5. Remove the O-ring from the crankshaft and discard it; a new one must be fitted on assembly.

INSPECTION

1. The rotary valve must be close to perfectly flat. If warped, replace it.

2. Inspect the valve collar for step-wear caused by the valve locating pin. Replace the collar if wear shows at this point.

3. Insert the collar into the valve. If play is excessive, replace the valve.

4. Place the collar onto the crankshaft; if play is excessive here, the collar must be replaced.

5. Remove any score marks from the collar surfaces with emery cloth. Check

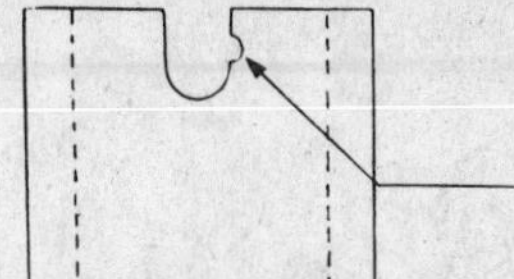

Check the collar for step-wear caused by the pin (Courtesy Yamaha Int. Corp.)

for excessive clearances after polishing.

6. Check the cover oil seal for cracked or damaged lips and replace it if necessary.

7. Replace the locating pin if it is bent or damaged in any way.

INSTALLATION

1. The crankshaft and rotary valve cover O-rings should be replaced if they

Fitting the valve cover O-ring (Courtesy Yamaha Int. Corp.)

have been disturbed. The valve cover O-ring must be replaced if it will no longer fit properly in its groove.

2. Grease the O-rings thoroughly before installing them. The valve cover O-ring should be seated in the cover groove. The crankshaft O-ring should be located in the crankshaft groove.

3. Grease the lips of the valve cover oil seal before installing the cover.

Kick-Starter Mechanism

On all late model machines the kick-starter mechanism can be removed (complete) from the right (clutch) side of the engine after the engine cover is removed.

On machines such as the DS6, R3, YM, and YR-series, the kick-starter return spring can be inspected or replaced after removing the side cover. Removal of the shaft and gear, however, requires splitting the crankcases. If the cases are to be split, remove the clutch assembly, the kick-starter idler gear, and the kick-starter assembly. The clutch must be removed to remove the idler gear.

REMOVAL AND DISASSEMBLY

1. On DS6, YM, R3, and YR-series machines, remove the kick-starter return spring cover; disconnect the return spring from the case and remove it from the shaft.

2. On all late models, disconnect the kick-starter return spring from the engine and pull off the kick-starter assembly complete, if desired. Note the location of any thrust washers which may be fitted to the engine side of the kick-starter shaft.

NOTE: *If the kickstarter is to be disassembled, this is made somewhat easier by leaving the shaft in place and removing one component at a time.*

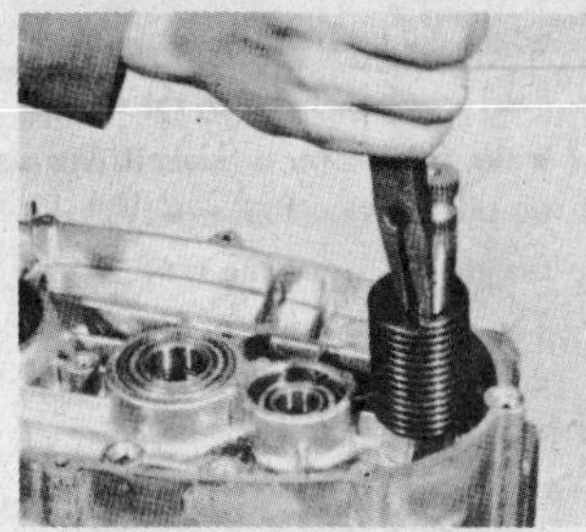

Removing the kick-starter return spring (Courtesy Yamaha Int. Corp.)

Detaching the return spring from the engine (Courtesy Yamaha Int. Corp.)

Removing the kick-starter shaft assembly (Courtesy Yamaha Int. Corp.)

Removing the kick-starter idle gear circlip (Courtesy Yamaha Int. Corp.)

Removing the kick-starter shaft circlip (Courtesy Yamaha Int. Corp.)

3. Remove the kick-starter idler gear circlip and remove the idler gear from the shaft. This is only necessary if the cases are to be split. The clutch assembly must be removed before removing the idler gear.

Disassembly procedures will vary slightly depending on model.

Singles (except YL2)

a. Remove the kick-starter shaft circlip.

b. Remove the spring cover, spring, spring guide from the shaft.

c. Remove the second circlip. Remove the shim, kick-starter shaft gear wishbone-shaped clip, and separate the kick-starter gear from the shaft.

Small Displacement Twins, YL2

a. For models such as the HS1, RD125, RD200, and CS-series, refer to "Singles," above. The same type of assembly is used.

b. On the YL1 and YL2, the procedure is essentially the same except that no wishbone clip is fitted. After removing the kick-starter gear circlip, remove the shim(s), spring washer, and slide the gear off the shaft.

CAUTION: *The gear holds down the kick pawl which is spring-loaded. Remove it carefully and note the position of the pawl pin and spring on the kick-starter shaft.*

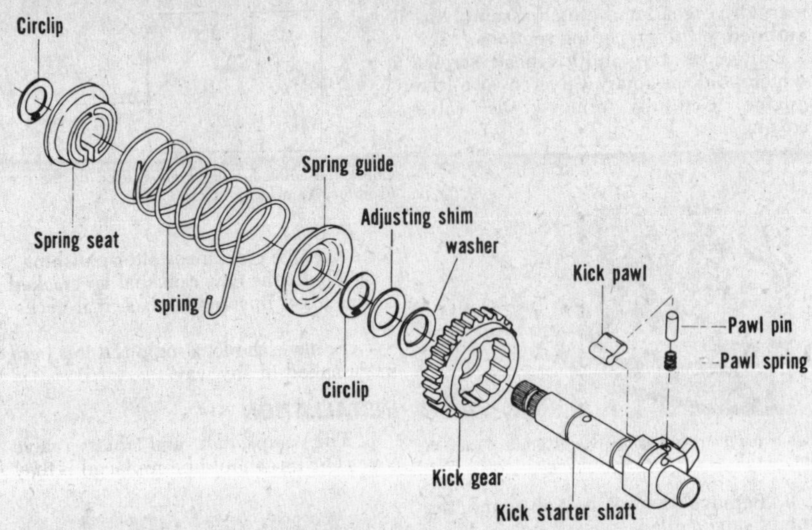

Kick-starter assembly (YL1) (Courtesy Yamaha Int. Corp.)

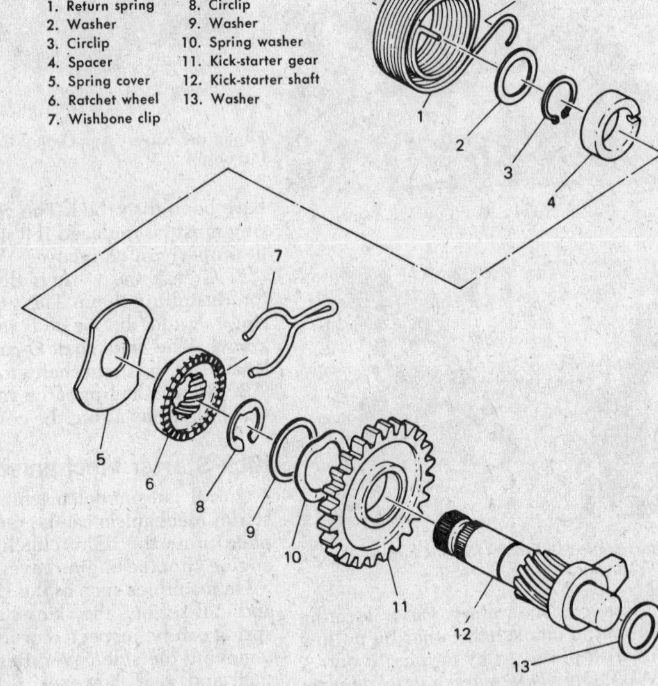

Kick-starter assembly (RD250/350) (Courtesy Yamaha Int. Corp.)

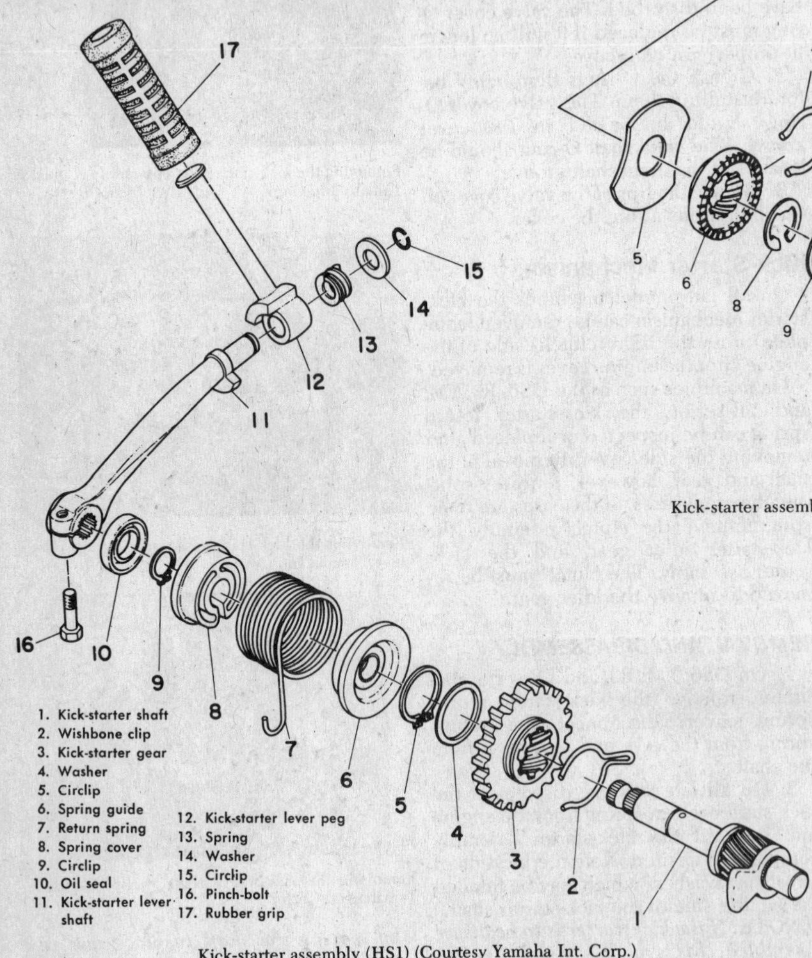

Kick-starter assembly (HS1) (Courtesy Yamaha Int. Corp.)

Large Displacement Twins

a. On models such as the DS7 and RD250/350/400, remove the return spring.

b. Remove the shim, kick-starter shaft circlip, spacer, and spring cover.

c. Remove the ratchet wheel wishbone clip and take off the ratchet wheel.

d. Remove the shaft circlip, shim, and spring washer, and remove the kick-starter gear from the shaft.

INSPECTION

All Models

Follow the inspection procedures applicable to your model.

1. Check the splines on the kick-starter shaft. If torn, worn, or splintered to the extent that they will not hold the kick-starter lever in place, replace the shaft.
2. Check the gear teeth on the shaft. If any are broken or worn, the shaft should be replaced.
3. Check the condition of the kick-starter pawl on models so equipped. If the edge of the pawl is chipped, grooved, or shows signs of wear, it should be replaced.
4. Check the condition of the ratchet wheel on models so equipped. The inside gear teeth should be in good condition. Replace the gear if they are worn or broken. Make a close inspection of the ratchet teeth (on the sides of the gear). The gear must be replaced if these show signs of wear. If they are worn, check the condition of the ratchet teeth on the kick-starter gear in the same manner. Replace this gear as well if the teeth are worn.
5. If the kick-starter gear has a plain bore, check it for scoring and finish up any defects with a fine emery cloth. Check that the gear does not have excessive play on the shaft.
6. Check kick-starter gear teeth for wear, chipping, and other damage, and replace the gear if the teeth are damaged.
7. Inspect the kick-starter idler gear in the same ways (Steps 5–6).
8. If a pawl-type kick-starter mechanism is fitted, check the inside surfaces of the kick-starter gear. If the internal ribs are worn or chipped, replace the gear and the pawl as well.
9. Check the wishbone clip and replace it if twisted or deformed.
10. Check the condition of the kick-starter return spring. If the spring has fatigued or twisted ends, it should be replaced.
11. Replace any broken or twisted circlips.
12. Check the kick-starter shaft for wear in any area a gear rides on. Insert the shaft into its bushing. If there is excessive play, either the shaft or the bushing should be replaced.

INSTALLATION

All Models

1. Installation is the reverse of the removal procedure.
2. Models using a ratchet wheel should have the extension in the ratchet wheel wishbone clip positioned in the recess in the crankcase.
3. When installing the return spring, ensure that the inner end of the spring is inserted into the hole in the crankcase. Then turn the spring in the direction required to engage the outer (hooked) end onto its stud. The spring should have some tension in this position to hold the kick-starter lever in place.

CAUTION: *Failure to preload the spring may cause damage to the kick-starter gear during operation.*

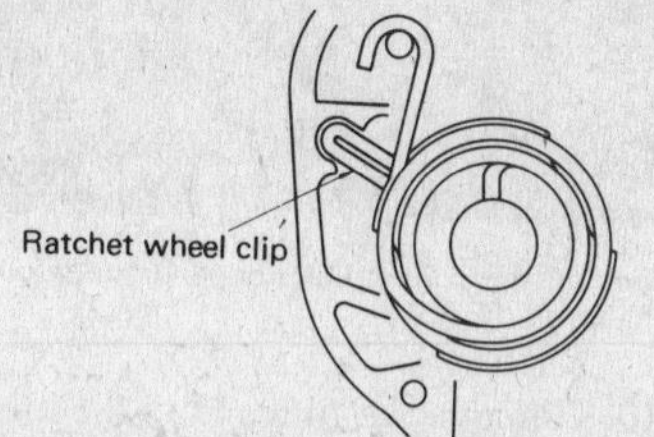

Fit the wishbone clip into the recess in the crankcase (Courtesy Yamaha Int. Corp.)

Shifter Mechanism

On most models, with the exception of YDS, DS6, YM and YR-series machines, the shift arm and shaft can be removed and inspected with the engine in the frame. On these models, a different type of shift mechanism is used.

REMOVAL

DS7, RD250/350/400, R5

1. Remove the right-side cover, the clutch, and kick-starter assemblies.
2. Remove the gearshift lever and the countershaft sprocket cover.
3. Remove the gearshift shaft boot. Remove the circlip and shim from the left-side of the gearshift shaft.

Removing the gearshift shaft boot (Courtesy Yamaha Int. Corp.)

Removing the gearshift shaft circlip (Courtesy Yamaha Int. Corp.)

Removing the gearshift shaft (Courtesy Yamaha Int. Corp.)

4. Pull out the gearshift shaft and shift arm from the right-side of the engine.
5. Remove the circlip which secures the gearshift linkage and remove the linkage complete with shift fingers and shifter return spring.

Removing the gearshift linkage circlip (Courtesy Yamaha Int. Corp.)

Other Models

1. Remove the right-side cover, clutch, and kick-starter mechanism. Remove the countershaft sprocket cover after removing the gearshift lever from its shaft.

Removing the gearshift shaft circlip and washer (Courtesy Yamaha Int. Corp.)

2. Remove the circlip and washers from the left (countershaft) side of the shift shaft. On the RD60, remove the circlip from the right-side shift linkage and remove the linkage.
3. Disengage the shift arm from the shift drum and pull the shift shaft out of the engine from the right-side.

Removing the shift shaft and arm from the engine (Courtesy Yamaha Int. Corp.)

INSPECTION

Follow those procedures applicable to your type of shift mechanism.

1. Check the splines on the gearshift shaft for wear or splintering, and replace the shaft if they are too badly damaged to properly secure the gearshift lever.
2. Check the shaft for a bent condition and replace it if bent.
3. Check the shift arm for straightness. Check the shift fingers for straightness, and especially for wear at the tips.
4. Inspect the shifter return spring and replace it if broken, or if the ends of the spring show signs of twisting or fatigue.
5. Check the other springs in the shift

linkage and replace any that are deformed or damaged.

6. Inspect the shift arm roller and replace it if worn.

INSTALLATION

1. Installation is the reverse of the removal procedure.

2. When installing the return spring, be sure that both ends of the spring bear tightly against the pin. the spring ends should be parallel to one another. This will provide the tension needed to keep the (foot) shift lever in position after each shift.

3. Adjust the linkage, after installation, with the adjusting screw.

a. Place DS7 and RD250/350/400 models in Second gear;

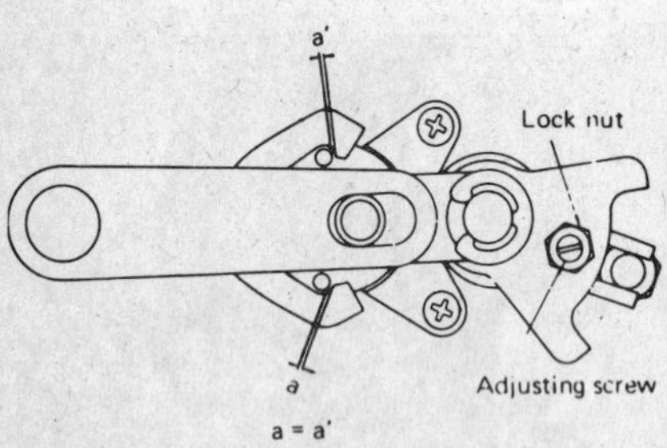

Gearshift linkage adjustment: "a" must equal distance "a' " (DS7, R5C, RD250/350/400)

b. Check that the distance between the shift arm fingers and the shift drum pins is equal in both cases. Refer to the illustrations.

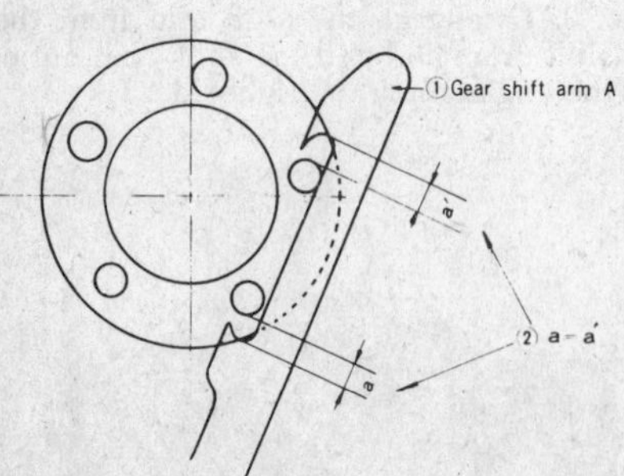

Gearshift linkage adjustment: "a" must equal "a' " (Courtesy Yamaha Int. Corp.)

LOWER END AND TRANSMISSION

The following section deals with service to the crankshaft, transmission, shifter drum assembly, crankcase bearings and seals. Removing the engine and splitting the crankcases is necessary to service these components.

Splitting the Crankcases

LATE MODEL TWINS

The following procedure is applicable to the DS7, R5, and RD250/350/400 models. These machines have horizontally split crankcases. No special tools are needed to split the cases.

1. Remove the engine from the frame. Remove the top end assembly. Remove the side cover components: alternator, countershaft sprocket, clutch, primary drive gear, kick-starter assembly, shift mechanism. See previous sections for procedures. Remove any bearing stopper plates which are fitted. Turn the engine upside down. The crankcase bolts are numbered. Beginning with the highest number, turn each bolt ¼ turn until all are loose, then remove them. (To assemble the cases, tighten the bolts in the same way, but begin with the lowest numbered bolt.)

Removing the crankcase bolts (Courtesy Yamaha Int. Corp.)

2. Turn the engine right side up. Tap all around the crankcase mating surface with a soft-face or plastic mallet. When the upper case comes free, remove it. The crankshaft and gear clusters will remain in the lower case half.

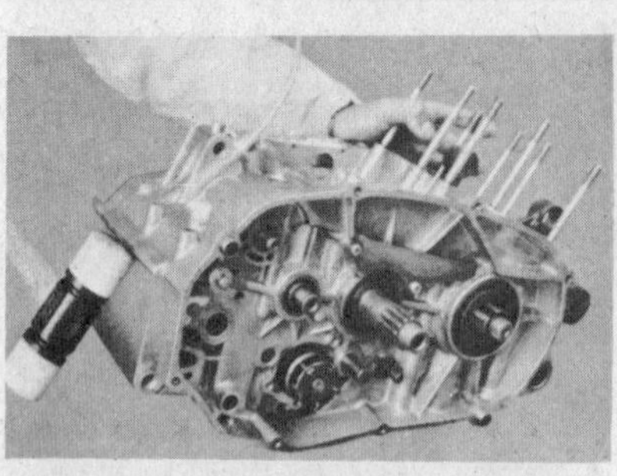

Splitting the crankcases (Courtesy Yamaha Int. Corp.)

3. To remove the crankshaft from the crankcase, tap upwards on one end of the shaft with a plastic mallet. Lift out the crank carefully. Note the clutch side crank bearing locating ring in the case half. Be sure that they are in place upon installation.

Crankcase components (Courtesy Yamaha Int. Corp.)

Removing the crankshaft bearing locating ring (Courtesy Yamaha Int. Corp.)

4. Inspection of the transmission gears can be carried out with the gear clusters in place. Do not remove the gear clusters unless it is necessary to do so.

5. Lift out the mainshaft, complete with gears, tapping upwards on the clutch end of the shaft with a plastic mallet to free it if necessary.

6. Remove the countershaft and gears in the same manner.

NOTE: *Check the location of the transmission shaft bearing locating rings in the crankcase: rings are found on both sides of the countershaft and the clutch side of the mainshaft. Locating rings must be in place when the shafts are installed.*

7. Before removing the shift drum and forks, mark the location of each fork so that they may be reinstalled in their proper locations.

8. Remove the neutral switch from the left-side of the shift drum.

Removing the neutral switch (Courtesy Yamaha Int. Corp.)

9. Remove the shift lever guide, and the shift drum stopper plate (mounted at the right end of the shift drum). Both are secured with phillips screws.

Removing the shift drum stopper plate (Courtesy Yamaha Int. Corp.)

10. Remove the plugs from the ends of the shift fork shafts. Remove the circlips from the shift fork shafts. Note that one of

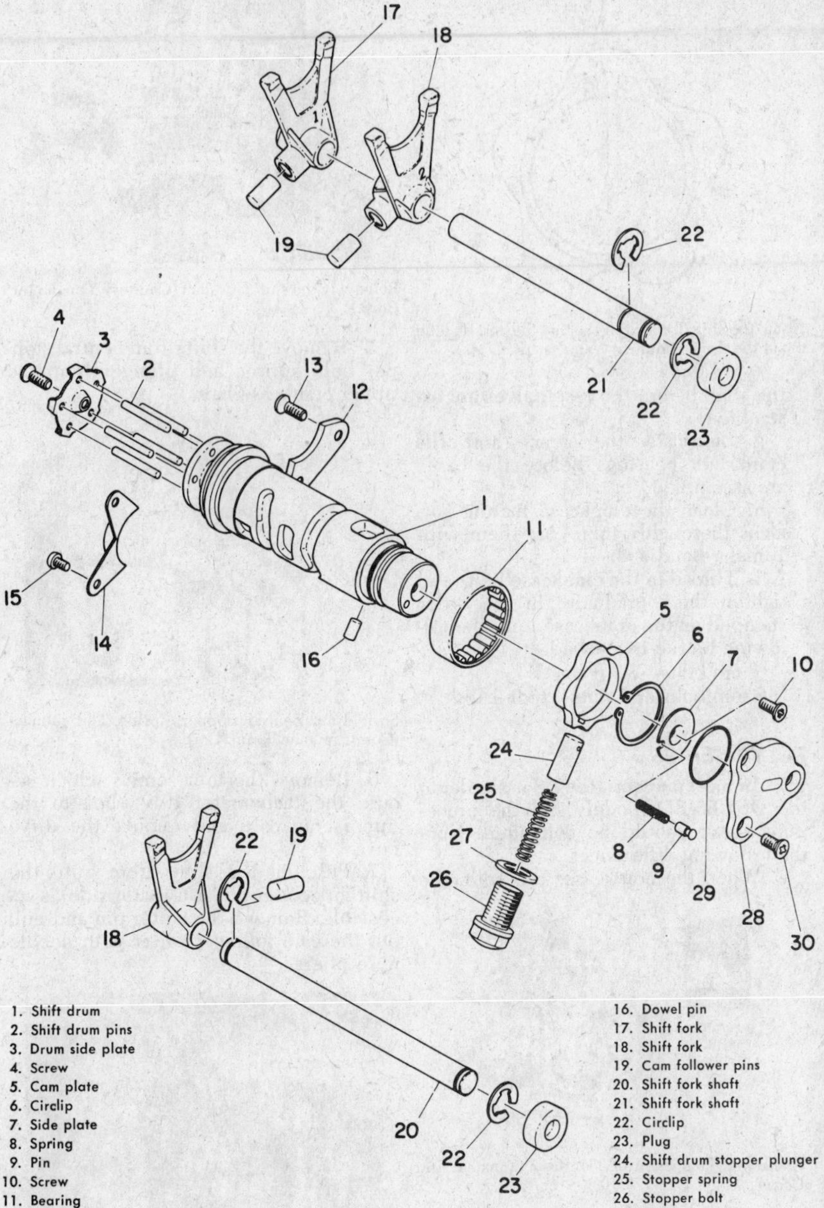

1. Shift drum
2. Shift drum pins
3. Drum side plate
4. Screw
5. Cam plate
6. Circlip
7. Side plate
8. Spring
9. Pin
10. Screw
11. Bearing
12. Stopper plate
13. Screw
14. Shift arm guide
15. Screw
16. Dowel pin
17. Shift fork
18. Shift fork
19. Cam follower pins
20. Shift fork shaft
21. Shift fork shaft
22. Circlip
23. Plug
24. Shift drum stopper plunger
25. Stopper spring
26. Stopper bolt
27. Washer
28. Neutral switch
29. O-ring
30. Screw

Shift drum assembly (Courtesy Yamaha Int. Corp.)

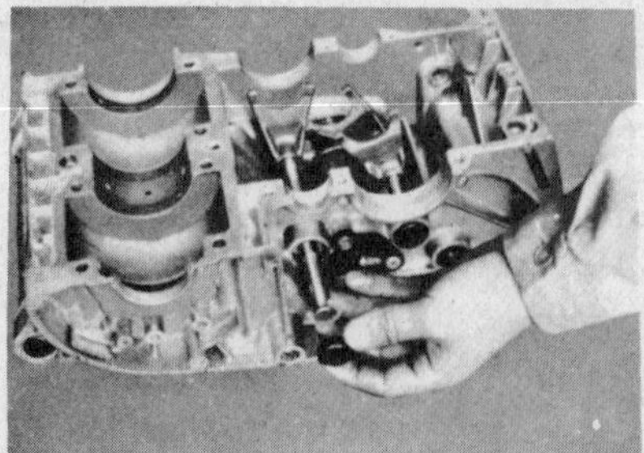

Shift fork shaft and plug (Courtesy Yamaha Int. Corp.)

the circlips is located on the inside of the crankcase.

11. Gently tap out the shift fork shafts from the right-side of the case. Remove the forks.

12. Remove the shift drum neutral stopper bolt, spring, and plunger from the bottom of the crankcase.

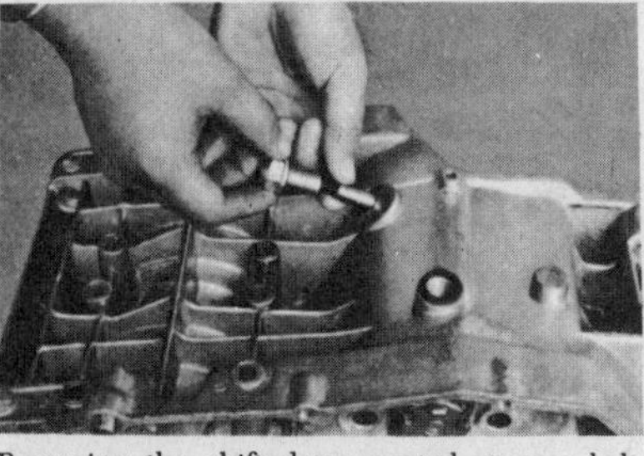

Removing the shift drum neutral stopper bolt, spring, and plunger (Courtesy Yamaha Int. Corp.)

Removing the shift drum circlip (Courtesy Yamaha Int. Corp.)

13. Move the shift drum over to the right of the case; remove the drum cam circlip, take off the cam, and remove the shift drum from the crankcase.

14. Unscrew the tachometer drive gear from the top crankcase half. Remove the circlip and pull off the nylon tachometer gear.

Removing the tachometer drive gear circlip (Courtesy Yamaha Int. Corp.)

Removing the tach drive shaft stopper plate (Courtesy Yamaha Int. Corp.)

15. Remove the tach drive shaft stopper plate from the shaft. Remove the drive shaft circlips on the inside of the crankcase and remove the shaft.

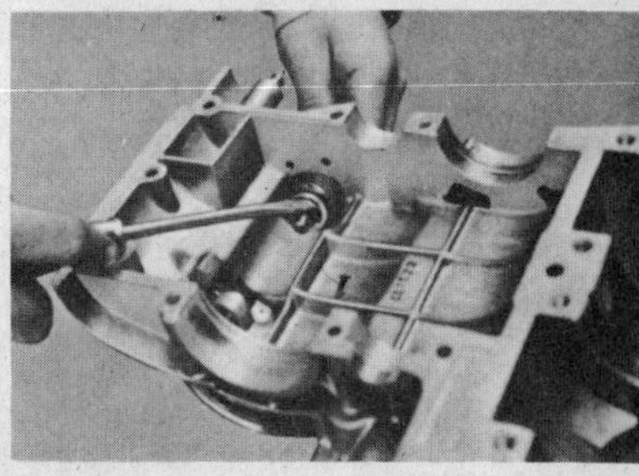

Removing the tach drive shaft circlips (Courtesy Yamaha Int. Corp.)

Assembly

1. Inspect the components as outlined in the sections following.

2. Note the following points upon assembly:

a. When installing the crankshaft, be sure that the bearing locating rings are in place in the cases;

b. Fit the bearing locating pin on each crankshaft bearing into the pin hole at the forward end of the crankcase;

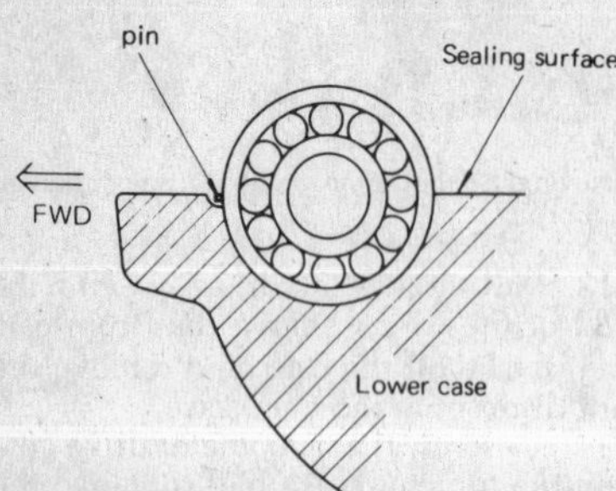

Ensure that the bearing locating pin is fitted into the recess in the crankcase (Courtesy Yamaha Int. Corp.)

c. Crankshaft oil seals should be installed as follows: the clutch side seal should be installed so that the lip on the inner side of the seal touches the outer race of the bearing. The alternator side seal should be installed so that the outer edge of the seal is flush with the crankcase surface;

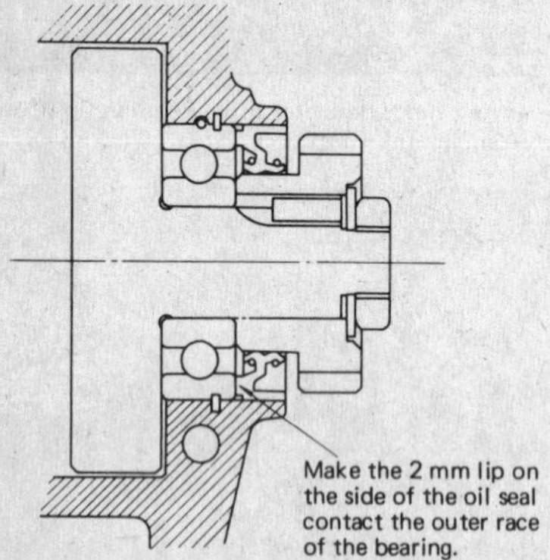

Installation of the clutch-side crankshaft oil seal (Courtesy Yamaha Int. Corp.)

d. Position the shift drum cam circlip so that the ends are at the top of the drum;

e. When installing the transmission

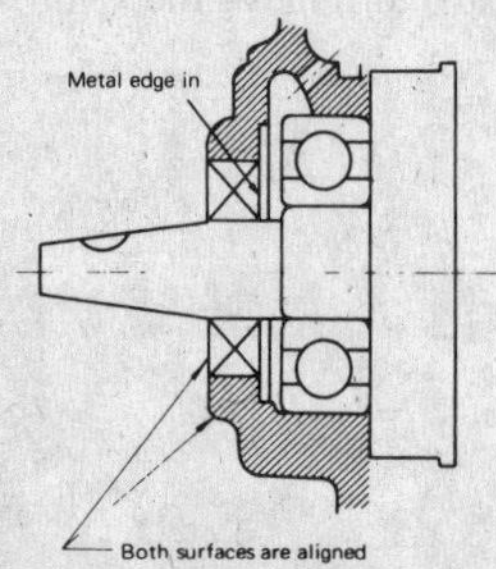

Installation of the alternator-side oil seal (Courtesy Yamaha Int. Corp.)

shafts, be sure that the bearing retainer rings are correctly installed in the crankcase;

f. Install the countershaft oil seal on

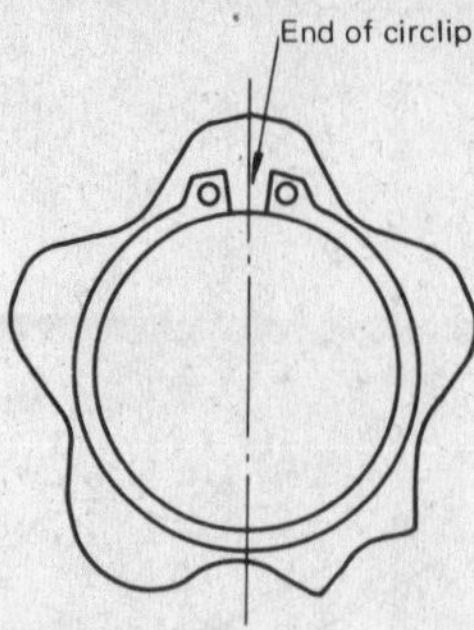

Install the shift drum circlip so that the end is at the top of the drum (Courtesy Yamaha Int. Corp.)

the shaft before the case halves are assembled;

g. Lubricate the gears and the crankshaft bearings before the cases are assembled;

h. Clean the crankcase mating surfaces thoroughly then coat them with Yamaha Bond # 4;

i. Thread in the crankcase bolts and tighten them gradually in the order stamped on the crankcase until the following torque is reached:

6 mm bolts—7.5 ft lbs
8 mm bolts and nuts—15.0 ft lbs

R3, YR-SERIES

1. In most respects, the R3 is similar to the DS7/R5/RD models and the procedure above should be consulted. Note the following differences:

2. When the crankcases are split, the

Crankcase components (Courtesy Yamaha Int. Corp.)

gear clusters and crankshaft will remain in the *upper* crankcase half.

3. The kick-starter shaft assembly should be removed and inspected as outlined in the "Kick-starter Mechanism" section.

4. To remove the shift mechanism, remove the two circlips which secure the shift fork shaft. One of the clips is on the right-side of the shaft and the other is inside the crankcase. Tap out the shaft and remove the shift fork.

Removing the shift fork shaft circlips (Courtesy Yamaha Int. Corp.)

Removing the shift fork shaft (Courtesy Yamaha Int. Corp.)

5. Remove the shift drum neutral stopper bolt, spring, and plunger from the upper crankcase half.

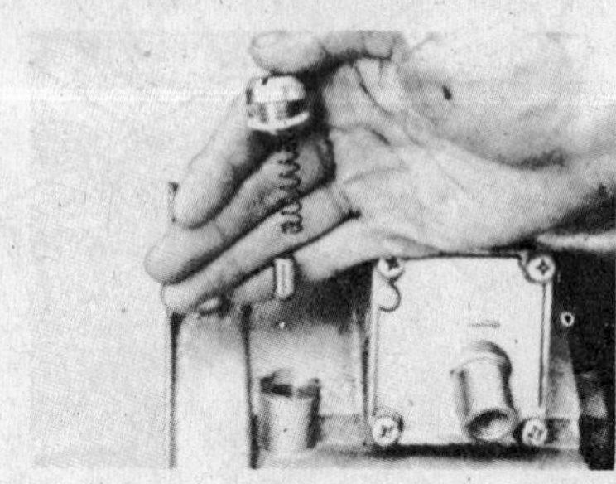

Shift drum neutral stopper, spring, and plunger (Courtesy Yamaha Int. Corp.)

6. Remove the four screws which secure the tachometer drive box to the upper crankcase and remove the drive box.

7. Pull out the shift drum until the shift fork cotter pin (alternator side) is accessible. Remove the cotter pin and pull out the cam follower roller with needle nose pliers.

Removing the shift drum cam follower roller (Courtesy Yamaha Int. Corp.)

8. Remove the cotter pin and roller from the center and clutch side shift forks in the same manner, moving the shift drum as necessary to gain access to the cotter pin.

9. Remove the shift drum.

Assembly

1. Refer to the assembly section for the late model twins, above. Note the following differences:

a. The upper crankcase half is fitted with locating pins for the crankshaft bearings and the center crankshaft oil seal. When installing the crank, line up the scribed marks on the bearing races with the crankcase mating surface and ensure that each bearing locating pin is seated in its bearing. Make sure that

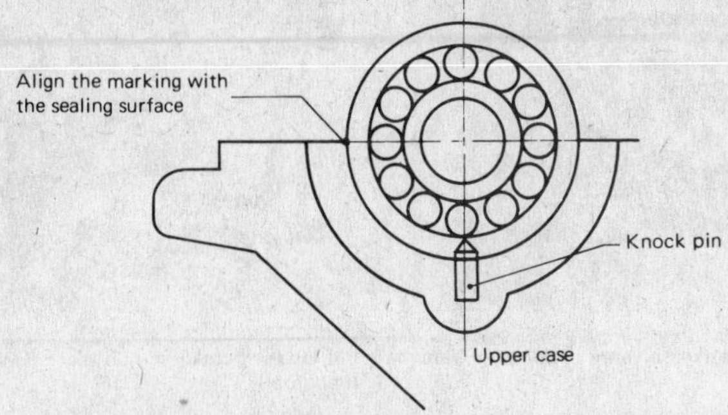

Install the crank bearings with the marks facing the front of the engine (Courtesy Yamaha Int. Corp.)

the center oil seal locating pin is fitted into the hole in the seal;

CAUTION: *Do not attempt to force the crankshaft to seat properly.*

Bearing marks should be aligned with the crankcase mating surface (Courtesy Yamaha Int. Corp.)

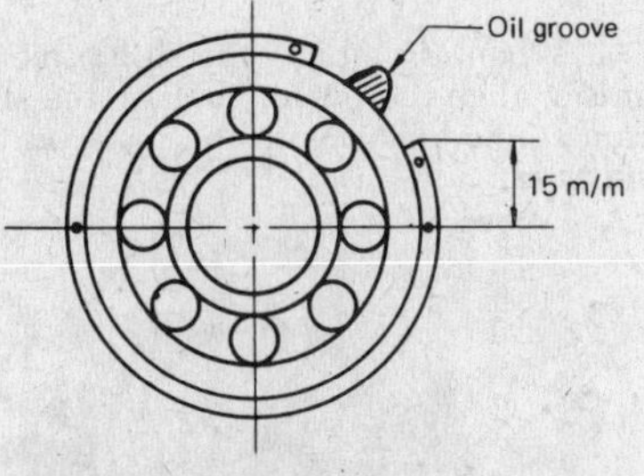

Position the snap-ring of the right-side crank bearing so that the oil groove machined into the upper crankcase is halfway between the snap-ring ends (Courtesy Yamaha Int. Corp.)

b. Align the snap-ring on the right-side crankshaft bearing so that the oil groove machined into the upper crankcase half is halfway between the snap-ring ends;

Bend down the ends of the cotter pins so that they will not touch the shift forks or crankcase when the forks move (Courtesy Yamaha Int. Corp.)

c. When installing the shifter mechanism, bend down the ends of the cotter pins so that they will not touch other forks or the crankcase when the forks move. Check clearances by shifting the gears by hand. New cotter pins should always be used.

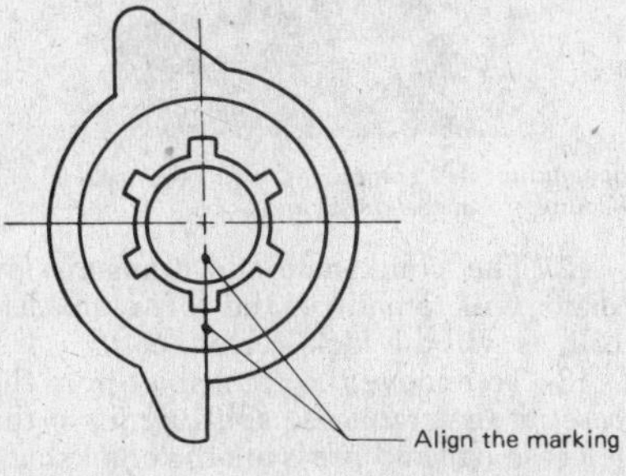

Align the marks on the kick-starter shaft and ratchet wheel (Courtesy Yamaha Int. Corp.)

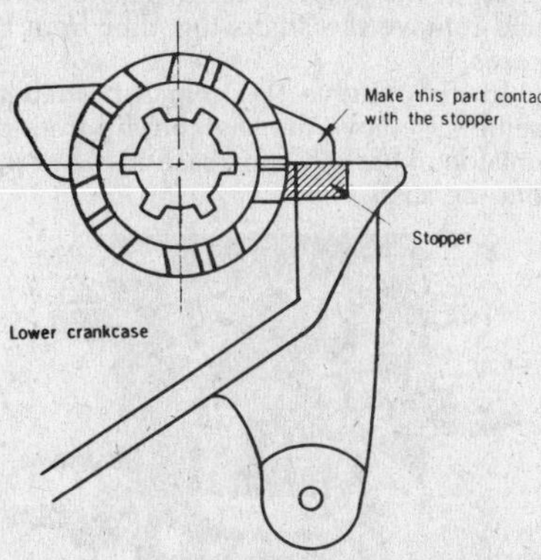

The ratchet wheel arm should rest against the stopper on the lower crankcase (Courtesy Yamaha Int. Corp.)

d. When installing the kick-starter mechanism, fit the ratchet wheel onto the shaft so that the punch marks align. Install the shaft into the crankcase so that the ratchet wheel arm bears against the stopper in the lower crankcase half;

e. Adjust the shifter mechanism with the adjusting screw so that the fingers of the shift arm are equidistant from the pins on the shift drum.

EARLY TWINS

The following procedure is applicable to machines such as the DS6, YDS, and YM-series. A special jig is needed to split the cases, which are vertically mated. Another shop tool is required to seat the crankshaft in the crankcase.

1. Remove the engine from the frame; remove the top end, clutch generator, kick-stater, and primary drive assemblies.
2. Remove the four phillips head screws which secure the tachometer drive box on top of the crankcase.

Tachometer drive box removed (Courtesy Yamaha Int. Corp.)

3. Turn the engine over and remove the gearshift linkage cover from the bottom of the crankcase.
4. Stuff a clean rag into the crankcase around the shift linkage. Carefully remove the clip securing the shift arm to the cam assembly. Remove the washer and spring and disconnect the shift arm.
5. Remove the phillips screws, and lift out the shifter cam assembly.
6. Remove the shift shaft circlip and pull the shaft out of the cases.
7. Mark the shift forks for position so that they may be installed in the same locations.

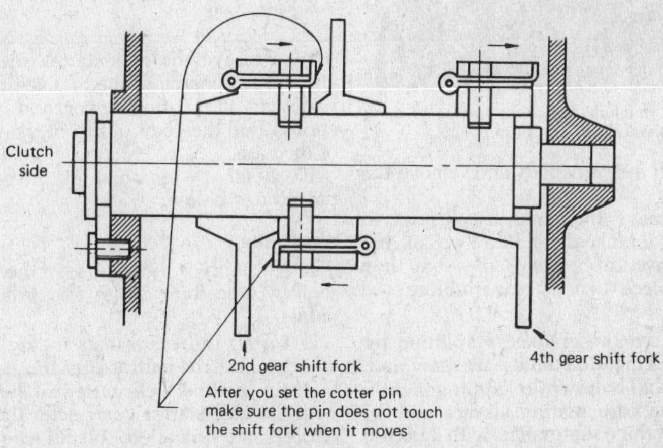

(Courtesy Yamaha Int. Corp.)

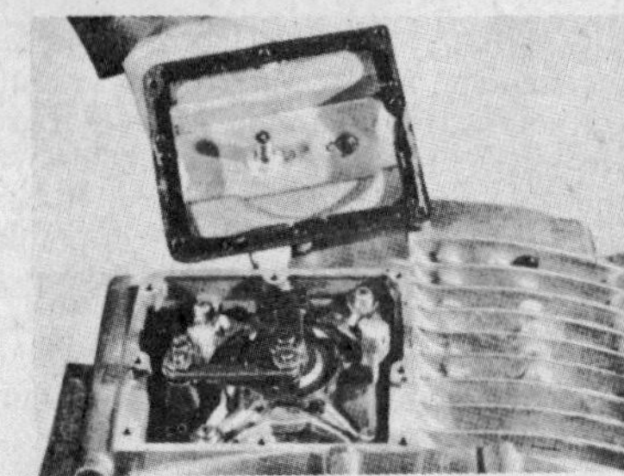

Removing the gearshift linkage cover (Courtesy Yamaha Int. Corp.)

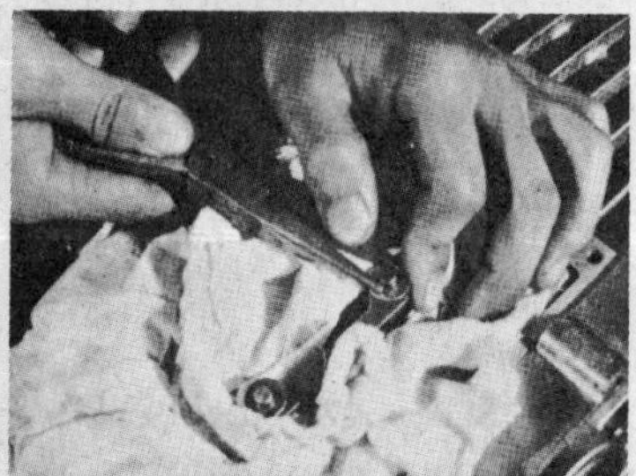

Removing the shift arm clip (Courtesy Yamaha Int. Corp.)

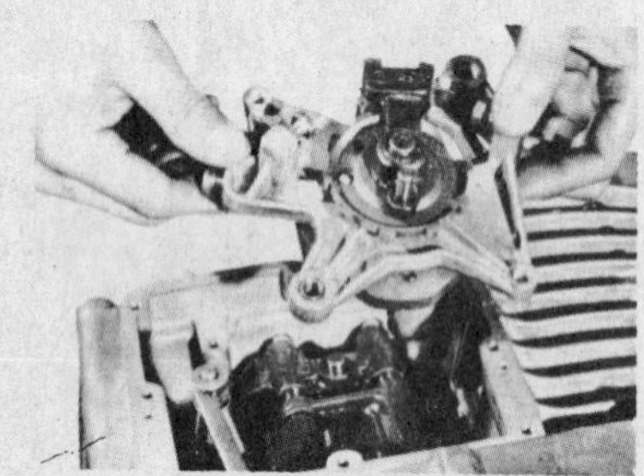

Removing the shifter cam assembly (Courtesy Yamaha Int. Corp.)

8. Remove the shift fork shaft circlips on the outside of the crankcase. Push the shafts in, then remove the shaft circlips on the inside of the case.

Remove the shift fork shaft circlips inside the crankcase (Courtesy Yamaha Int. Corp.)

9. Pull out the shafts and remove the shift forks.

10. Remove tne crankcase screws in the right crankcase half. Two of the screws have rubber caps. Be sure they are in place when reassembling the engine.

11. Secure the crankcase splitting jig in place. Threaded holes are provided. Tighten the bolt while tapping lightly around the case mating surface and on the end of the countershaft with a plastic mallet. Separate the cases evenly.

Removing the crankcase screws (Courtesy Yamaha Int. Corp.)

Separating the crankcases with the special jig (Courtesy Yamaha Int. Corp.)

12. The crankshaft and transmission shafts will remain in the left crankcase half, as will the kick-starter shaft.

13. To remove the crankshaft from the case, fit the crankcase splitting jig to the left case half and press out the crankshaft.

14. Check the gear clusters in place. If removal is required, tap lightly on the ends of the shafts with a plastic mallet and remove the shafts together from the cases.

15. To remove the gearshift shaft assembly, remove the shaft circlip from the outside of the left crankcase half and pull out the shaft.

Removing the gearshift shaft assembly (Courtesy Yamaha Int. Corp.)

16. Remove the kick-starter shaft circlip on the outside of the crankcase after removing the spring cover and return spring. Pull the shaft out from the inside of the case.

17. Refer to component inspection procedures below.

Assembly

1. Assembly is the reverse of the disassembly procedure. Note the following points.

2. Install the crankshaft in the right-side crankshaft half using the special tool. Engage the kick-starter ratchet gear with the kick-starter gear. After the gear clusters are installed, install the shift forks to the gears and slide in the shift

Pulling the crankcase into place (Courtesy Yamaha Int. Corp.)

fork shafts. Secure them with the snap-rings.

3. When ready to assemble the cases, coat the mating surface of the right-side crankcase with Yamaha Bond #5. Tap the cases together with a plastic mallet with the con rod at top dead center.

Kick-starter ratchet gear and kick-starter gear installed (Courtesy Yamaha Int. Corp.)

4. When assembling the shifter mechanism, align the punch mark on the shift cam splined shaft with the mark on the shift cam.

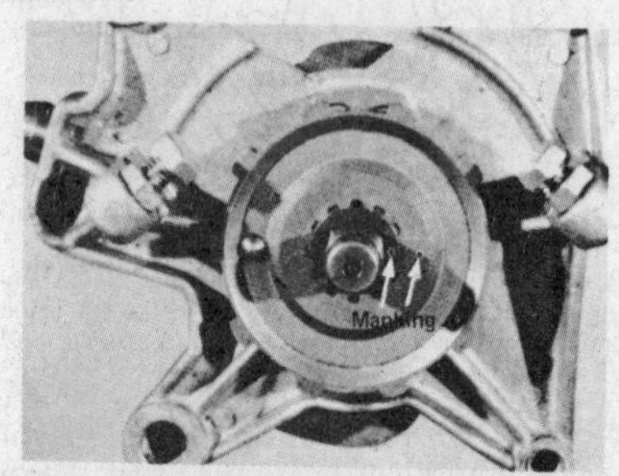

Line up the punch mark on the shift cam with that on the splined shaft (Courtesy Yamaha Int. Corp.)

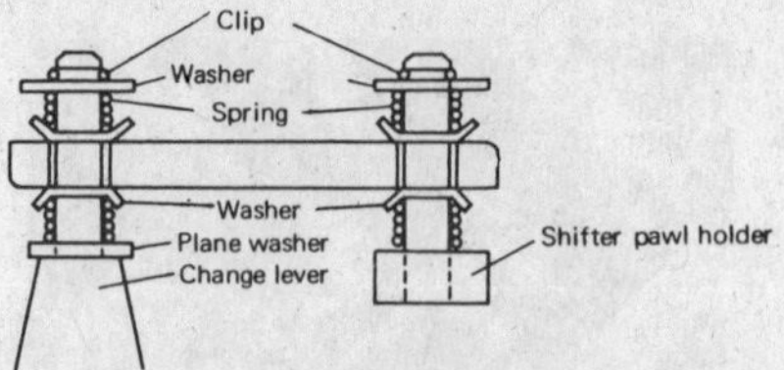

Shift arm installation (Courtesy Yamaha Int. Corp.)

5. Place the transmission in Neutral then install the cam in the engine. Install the shift arm, fitting a spring, washer, and clip to the end of the shift arm. Adjust the shift linkage so that with the stopper ball engaged in the cam stopper notch, the gap between the pawl and stop is about 1 mm.

6. Use a new gasket on the gearshift linkage cover.

Shift linkage adjustment: the gap between the pawl and stop should be about 1mm (Courtesy Yamaha Int. Corp.)

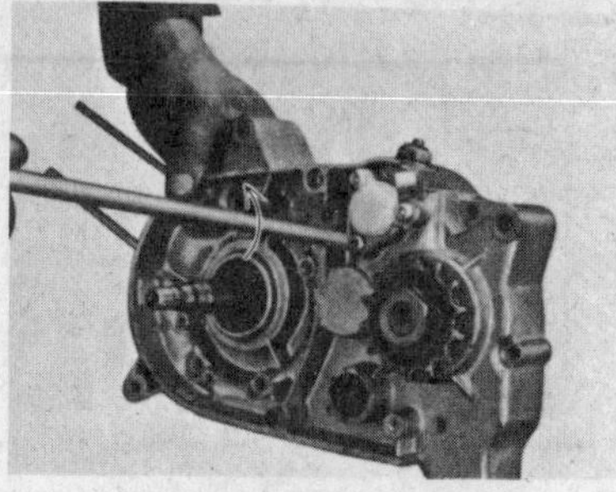
Removing the neutral switch from the shift drum (Courtesy Yamaha Int. Corp.)

Shift drum and gear clusters assembled (Courtesy Yamaha Int. Corp.)

SINGLES AND SMALL DISPLACEMENT TWINS

The following procedure is applicable to all machines with vertically mated crankcases. Examples: G-series, RD60, YL, YA, YAS, AS2, RD125, YCS, RD200, HS1, LS2, and CS-series machines. A jig to separate the cases is needed.

1. Remove the engine from the frame.
2. Remove the top end; remove the left and right-side covers, clutch assembly, primary drive gear, electrical generator, countershaft sprocket, shift arm, kick-starter shaft and gears, rotary valve (if fitted), etc.
3. Remove the gearshift drum stopper spring and lever.
4. Unscrew and remove the crankcase screws in the right or left crankcase half. Fit the crankcase separating jig to the right case half, and tighten the jig bolt, while tapping lightly on the end of the countershaft sprocket with a plastic mallet. Separate the cases gradually and evenly.
5. The crankshaft and transmission components will remain in the left case half.
6. Remove the gearshift drum neutral switch. Remove the neutral stopper bolt, spring and plunger from the top of the case half.
7. Remove the shift drum circlip, washer, and keeper.
8. With a plastic mallet, tap out the countershaft while holding the shift drum and mainshaft. The transmission and shift mechanism should be removed as an assembly.

Removing the crankcase screws (Courtesy Yamaha Int. Corp.)

Splitting the crankcases while tapping on the mainshaft to ensure that the cases come apart evenly (Courtesy Yamaha Int. Corp.)

Shift drum circlip, washer, and keeper (Courtesy Yamaha Int. Corp.)

9. Fit the crankcase splitting tool to the left case half and use it to press out the crankshaft.
10. Refer to component inspection procedures, below, for service work on the crank, bearings or seals, transmission or shifter.

Assembly

1. When assembling the cases, note the following points:
   a. Draw the crankshaft into the left case half with the special puller, while holding the connecting rod at TDC;

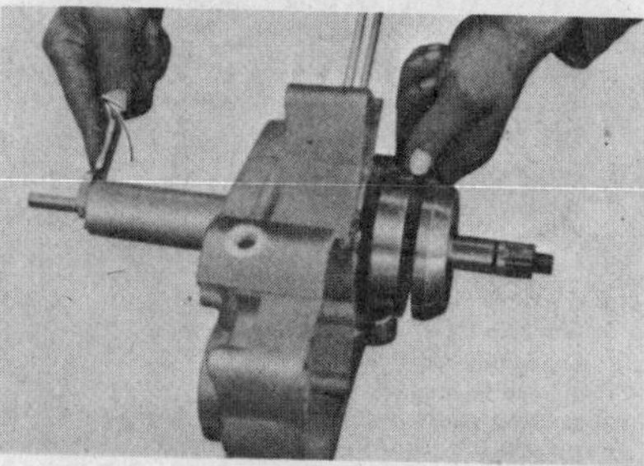
Pulling the crankshaft into place (Courtesy Yamaha Int. Corp.)

   b. Assemble the shift drum and gear clusters as an assembly. Be sure that the shift drum is positioned in Neutral while refitting the assembly to the cases;
   c. Coat the mating surface of the left case half with Yamaha Bond #4. Join the cases with care. Tighten the crankcase screws securely.

CAUTION: *Do not use the crankcase screws to force the cases together. They should be tightened only after the cases have been mated.*

Crankshaft

1. Crankshafts on all models are pressed together. To disassemble any crankshaft (which would be necessary in the event of a bent connecting rod, worn big end bearing, or worn inner crank bearings on twins), a special tool is needed.
2. Lubricate the big end bearing with two-stroke oil. Rotate the rod slowly around the crankpin. The movement should be smooth and noiseless.
3. With the crankshaft mounted in a jig, and a dial indicator mounted to bear against the small end of the connecting rod, check the lateral movement of the small end. It should not exceed 2.0 mm (0.08 in.). If the movement exceeds this figure, the con rod big end bearing is worn, and it must be replaced.

When new, rod small end movement should be 0.8—1.0 mm (0.032–0.04 in.).

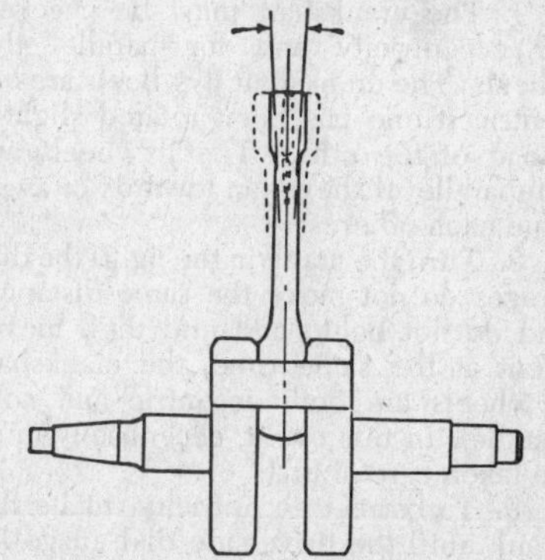
Small end lateral play is an indication of big end bearing wear (Courtesy Yamaha Int. Corp.)

Checking big end side clearance with a feeler gauge (Courtesy Yamaha Int. Corp.)

4. Check the connecting rod big end side clearance with a feeler gauge placed between the rod big end and one of the flywheels. Side clearance should be 0.1–0.3 mm (0.004–0.012 in.) (RD400: 0.25–0.75 mm/0.01–0.03 in.). If side clearance exceeds this figure, the crank should be disassembled and inspected.

5. Mount the crankshaft in a set of V-blocks, and attach dial indicators to each end of the crank and to the center main bearing on twins.

Rotate the crank slowly and note the indicator readings. The maximum allowable run-out is 0.03 mm (0.0011 in.) (RD400: 0.05 mm/0.002 in.). If run-out exceeds this figure, the crankshaft is either bent, or the flywheels are out of alignment.

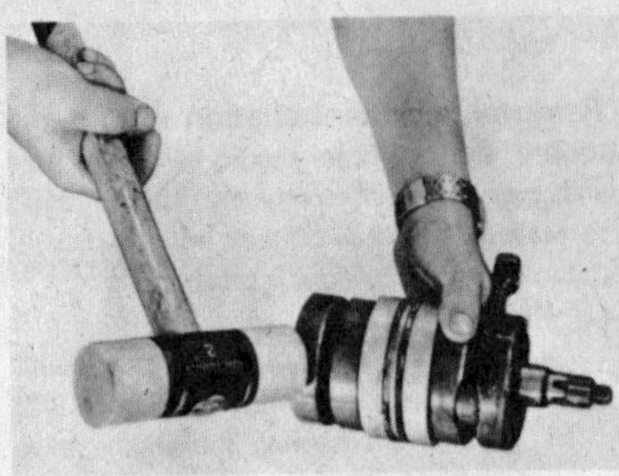

Aligning crankshaft flywheels (Courtesy Yamaha Int. Corp.)

crankpin lies along an imaginary line drawn between the ends of the two dial gauge shafts, the flywheels are evidently pinched together opposite the crankpin.

To correct this condition, insert a wedge, preferably of wood or soft metal, between the flywheels at a point opposite

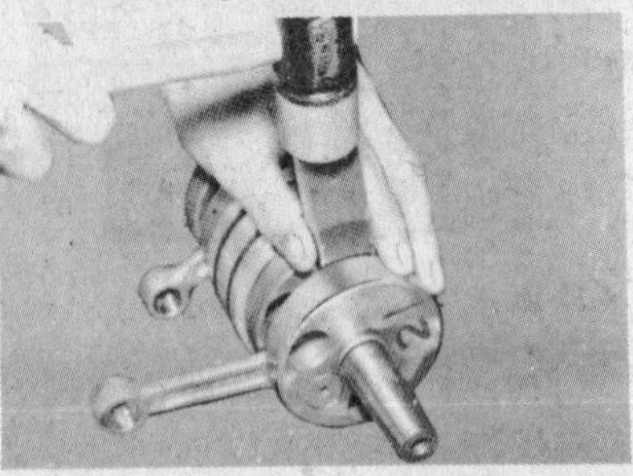

Spreading pinched flywheels with a soft drift (Courtesy Yamaha Int. Corp.)

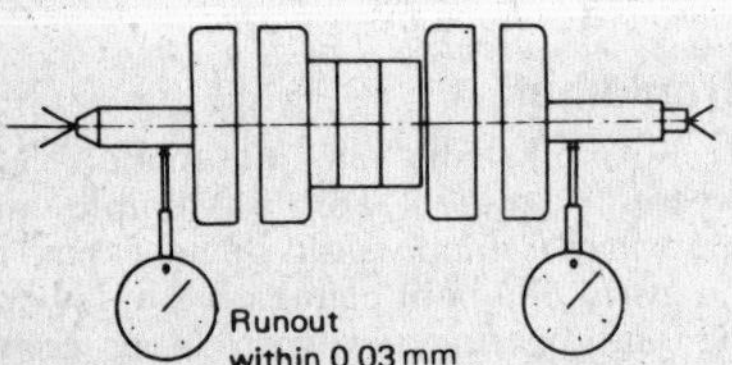

Checking crankshaft run-out with dial gauges (Courtesy Yamaha Int. Corp.)

6. The following procedure concerning crankshaft truing should only be undertaken by an experienced mechanic. The information is supplied, however, for the purpose of providing general information.

NOTE: *The procedure is written for single-cylinder machines. It is, however, applicable to twins as well, if each side of the crank is treated as a "single" first: check alignment and run-out of each side; then overall alignment.*

7. The crankshaft must be checked for eccentricity and for parallel flywheels. The crankshaft flywheels are eccentric if one has been rotated slightly ahead of the other. The flywheels are nonparallel if they lean towards or away from each other.

8. Turn the crank in the jig. If the dial gauges do not move the same distance, and do not begin and end their movement at the same time, the crankshaft flywheels are both eccentric and nonparallel. In this event, eccentricity must be taken care of first.

9. To correct eccentricity, rotate the crank until the drive-side dial guage indicates the high point of its travel. Stop at this point. Imagine a line drawn from one of the dial gauge shafts to the other. Mark the spot on the drive-side flywheel at the spot this line would cross it. Remove the crankshaft from the aligning jig, and, with the brass hammer, strike this spot on the drive-side flywheel smartly. Be sure you are holding the crank assembly by the generator/magneto-side shaft while doing this. Recheck alignment, and repeat this procedure as long as necessary until the dial gauge needles begin and end their travel at the same time.

10. Replace the crankshaft assembly in the jig, and rotate it until the needles reach their highest point of travel. If the

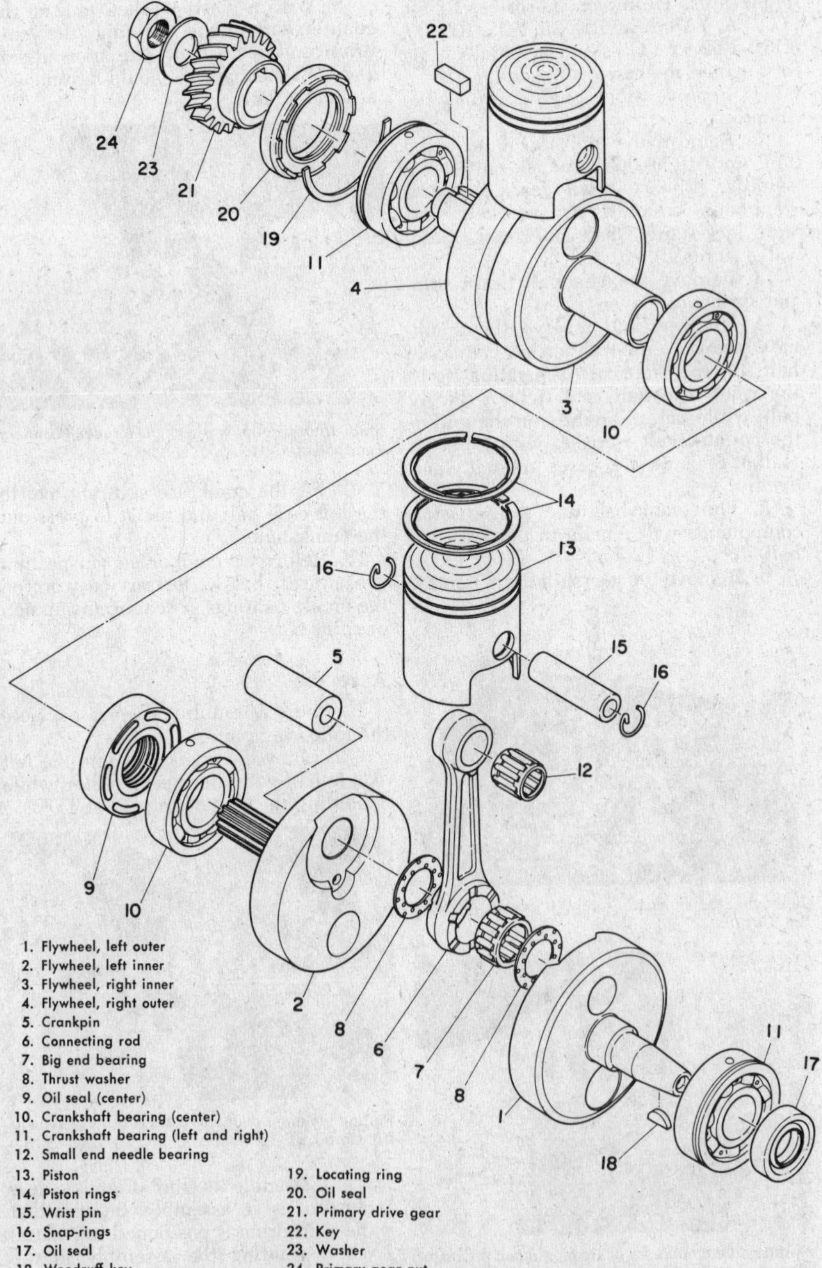

1. Flywheel, left outer
2. Flywheel, left inner
3. Flywheel, right inner
4. Flywheel, right outer
5. Crankpin
6. Connecting rod
7. Big end bearing
8. Thrust washer
9. Oil seal (center)
10. Crankshaft bearing (center)
11. Crankshaft bearing (left and right)
12. Small end needle bearing
13. Piston
14. Piston rings
15. Wrist pin
16. Snap-rings
17. Oil seal
18. Woodruff key
19. Locating ring
20. Oil seal
21. Primary drive gear
22. Key
23. Washer
24. Primary gear nut

Crankshaft assembly (Courtesy Yamaha Int. Corp.)

the crankpin, and, supporting the crank in one hand, strike the wedge with a hammer to spread the flywheels apart. Continue until the flywheels are parallel within specifications.

11. If, when checking for parallelism, the crankpin was *not* along or near the line drawn between the ends of the dial gauge shafts, if it was opposite this line, then the flywheels are too far apart, opposite the crankpin. In this case, once again make a mark on either flywheel where the imaginary line would cross it. (Note that the crank should be positioned so that the dial gauges are at the highest point of their travel). Remove the crank, and, with the brass hammer, strike the flywheel sharply on the *side* to bring the flywheels closer together. Check again, and repeat the procedure until crank runout is within specification.

12. Clean the crank assembly thoroughly, and oil the big end bearing well.

Transmission

1. The gears should not be removed from their shafts unless absolutely necessary. If the gears are being removed, be sure that each gear, thrust washer, shim, and snap-ring is laid out in the order of removal so that it can be installed in the proper location.

NOTE: *When referring to the exploded diagrams, note that the number of thrust washers may vary for individual machines.*

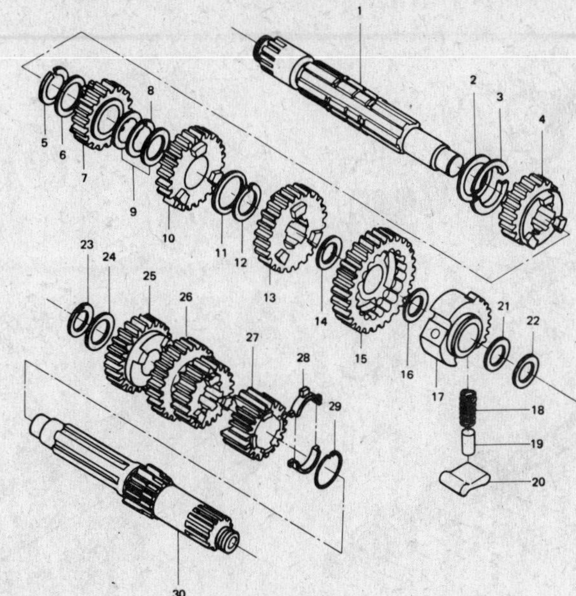

Transmission (DS6, YM2) (Courtesy Yamaha Int. Corp.)

1. Countershaft
2. Shim
3. Countershaft set rings
4. 4th gear
5. Circlip
6. Washer
7. 5th gear
8. Circlip
9. Washer
10. 3rd gear
11. Washer
12. Circlip
13. 2nd gear
14. Spacer
15. Kick-starter gear
16. Thrust washer
17. Kick-starter ratchet gear
18. Pawl spring
19. Pawl pin
20. Pawl
21. Shim
22. Shim
23. Mainshaft circlip
24. Washer
25. 4th gear
26. 3rd and 5th gears
27. 2nd gear
28. Set rings
29. Circlip
30. Mainshaft

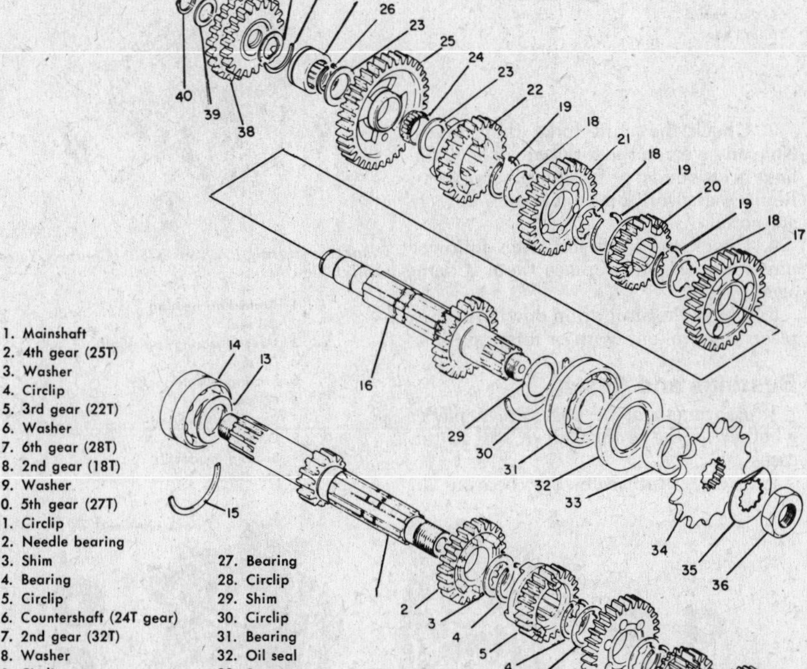

1. Mainshaft
2. 4th gear (25T)
3. Washer
4. Circlip
5. 3rd gear (22T)
6. Washer
7. 6th gear (28T)
8. 2nd gear (18T)
9. Washer
10. 5th gear (27T)
11. Circlip
12. Needle bearing
13. Shim
14. Bearing
15. Circlip
16. Countershaft (24T gear)
17. 2nd gear (32T)
18. Washer
19. Circlip
20. 6th gear (22T)
21. 3rd gear (29T)
22. 4th gear (26T)
23. Washer
24. Bearing
25. 1st gear (36T)
26. Circlip
27. Bearing
28. Circlip
29. Shim
30. Circlip
31. Bearing
32. Oil seal
33. Spacer
34. Sprocket (countershaft)
35. Lockwasher
36. Locknut
37. Spring washer
38. Idler gear
39. Shim
40. Circlip

Transmission (RD250/350) (Courtesy Yamaha Int. Corp.)

2. Check each of the gears for chipped, broken, or worn teeth. If any gear shows evidence of such damage, it should be replaced. In addition, the gear with which it

Gear clusters and shift drum assembly (CS3) (Courtesy Yamaha Int. Corp.)

meshes should be replaced as well, since it has undoubtedly been overstressed.

3. Check the inner splines on those gears so equipped, and replace the gear if the splines are worn or broken. Inspect the corresponding splines on the shafts. The shafts should be replaced if damaged.

4. Inspect the engaging dogs on gears which have them. The dogs must not be worn, chipped, or broken. Replace the the gear if they are.

5. Inspect the transmission shafts for damage to the sprocket nut threads, and wear or damage to the clutch gear, or sprocket splines. Make sure that the shafts are not bent. Inspect the shaft bearings (see below).

6. Where applicable, check the transmission gears for smooth rotation on their

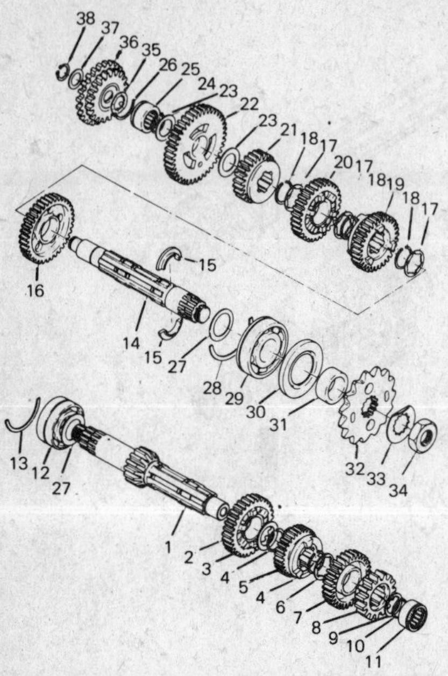

Transmission (DS7, R5) (Courtesy Yamaha Int. Corp.)

1. Mainshaft	20. 5th gear
2. 5th gear	21. 5th gear
3. Washer	22. 1st gear
4. Circlip	23. Washer
5. 3rd gear	24. Circlip
6. Washer	25. Bearing
7. 4th gear	26. Circlip
8. 2nd gear	27. Shim
9. Washer	28. Circlip
10. Circlip	29. Bearing
11. Bearing	30. Oil seal
12. Bearing	31. Spacer
13. Circlip	32. Countershaft sprocket
14. Countershaft	33. Lockwasher
15. Spacer	34. Locknut
16. 2nd gear	35. Spring washer
17. Washer	36. Idler gear assembly
18. Circlip	37. Shim
19. 4th gear	38. Circlip

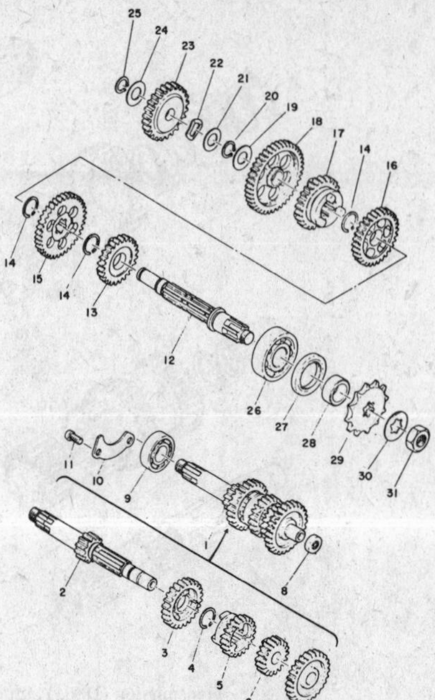

Transmission (RD60) (Courtesy Yamaha Int. Corp.)

1. Mainshaft assembly	17. 4th gear
2. Mainshaft	18. 1st gear
3. 4th gear	19. Shim
4. Clip	20. Circlip
5. 3rd gear	21. Thrust washer
6. 2nd gear	22. Spring washer
7. 5th gear	23. Kick-starter idler gear
8. Oil seal	24. Washer
9. Bearing	25. Circlip
10. Bearing retainer	26. Bearing
11. Screw	27. Oil seal
12. Countershaft	28. Spacer
13. 5th gear	29. Countershaft sprocket
14. Clip	30. Lockwasher
15. 2nd gear	31. Locknut
16. 3rd gear	

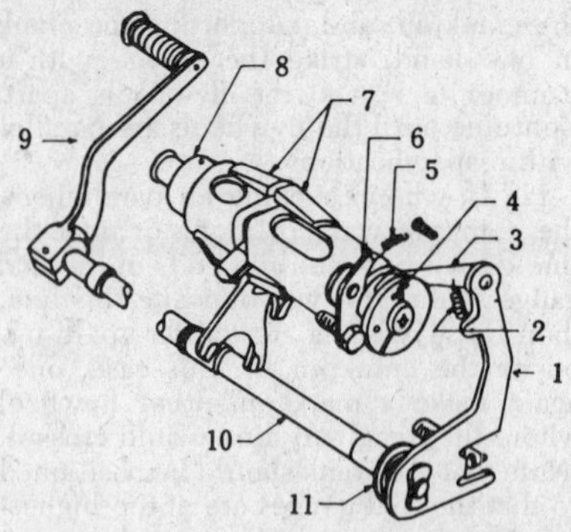

Gearshift assembly (G6S) (Courtesy Yamaha Int. Corp.)

1. Gearshift arm	7. Shift fork
2. Spring	8. Gearshift drum
3. Gearshift pivot arm	9. Gearshift lever
4. Shift drum pins	10. Gearshift shaft
5. Shift drum stopper spring	11. Gearshift return spring
6. Shift drum stopper lever	

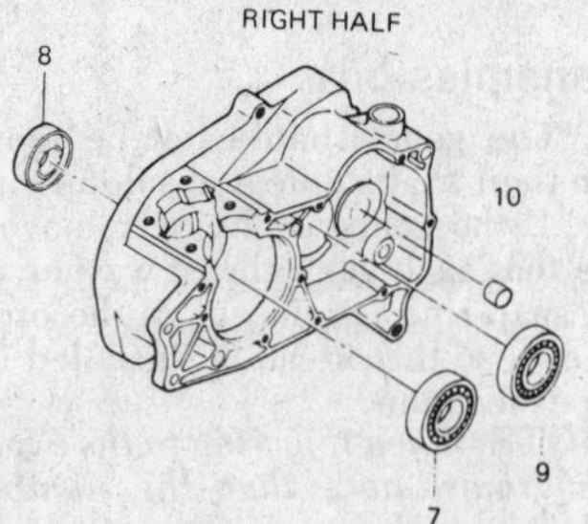

LEFT HALF

Crankcase bearing locations (CS3) (Courtesy Yamaha Int. Corp.)

1. Crankshaft bearing
2. Oil seal
3. Needle bearing (mainshaft)
4. Oil seal
5. Bearing (countershaft)
6. Oil seal
7. Crankshaft bearing
8. Oil seal
9. Bearing (mainshaft)
10. Needle bearing (countershaft)

shafts. If rotation is rough or noisy, replace the gear needle bearing (where fitted) or the gear itself.

Shift Drum

1. The shift drum itself should be inspected for wear in the shift fork cam follower pin grooves, wear to the cam plate, and scoring or wear of the bearing surfaces.

2. The shift fork shafts should be inspected for wear in those areas on which the shift forks ride. Roll the shafts along a flat surface to check them for a bent condition. Replace the shafts if bent.

Check the shift drum grooves for wear (Courtesy Yamaha Int. Corp.)

3. Check the shift forks themselves. Note any wear to the fork bore. Check the fingers for bends, or for chipping or wear. Replace any fork on which such defects are noted.

4. Check the shift fork cam follower pins for wear, and replace them if damaged.

5. Check the shift drum dowl pins. Replace any broken, worn or missing pins.

Bearings and Seals

1. Bearings can be checked in place, whether on the crankshaft or still in the cases.

2. Lightly lubricate the bearing in

Crankcase bearings and oil seals (G5S) (Courtesy Yamaha Int. Corp.)

question with some two-stroke oil, and rotate it slowly. Movement must be smooth, effortless, and quiet.

3. If the bearing movement is halting, or noisy, the bearing should be replaced.

4. Check the general condition of the bearing in place, if possible. Note any damaged bearings or scored races.

5. If the bearings must be replaced, note the following:

a. Crankshaft bearings should be replaced in sets, along with the oil seals. Outer bearings on twins can be removed from the crankshaft with a puller, but renewing the inner crank bearing requires splitting the crankshaft;

Removing a crankshaft bearing retainer snap-ring (DS6) (Courtesy Yamaha Int. Corp.)

b. Bearings, either crankshaft or transmission, which remain in the crankcases can be removed after taking away any bearing retainer plates, snaprings or oil seals which are fitted;

Prying out a crankshaft bearing oil seal (Courtesy Yamaha Int. Corp.)

c. Bearing removal from crankcases is facilitated by gently heating the crankcase around the bearing boss. Tap out the old bearing, and drive new ones straight in (after heating the case) with a bearing driver, or a sturdy block of wood.

6. Oil seals should be replaced as a matter of course. Oil seals can be pried out of the cases with a screwdriver using a block of wood as a leverage point. Alternately, use a hooked tool to remove the seals. Seals with damaged or torn lips must be replaced.

Installing a crankcase bearing with a bearing driver (Courtesy Yamaha Int. Corp.)

7. Once seals are removed, they should not be reused for any reason.

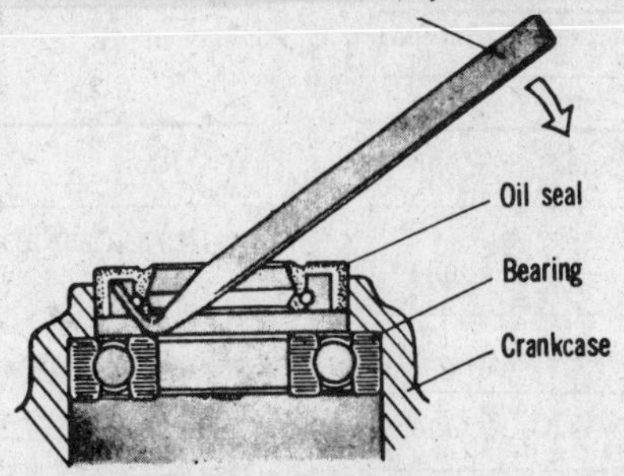

Removing an oil seal with a hooked lever

8. Upon assembly, lubricate the bearing before installation with the type of oil usually supplied to it (i.e., either transmission or two-stroke oil). Grease the lips of all oil seals before inserting any shafts into them.

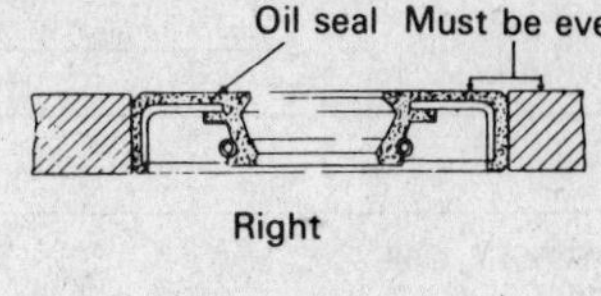

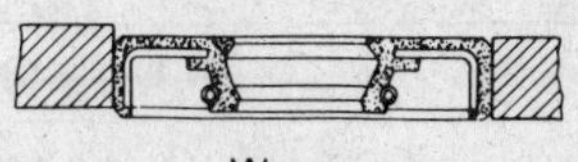

Oil seal installation

9. Where applicable, all bearings and seals should be installed with the manufacturer's mark facing outward.

Piston Specifications

Model		Piston-Cylinder Clearance (mm)	Piston-Cylinder Clearance (in.)	Ring End Gap (mm)	Ring End Gap (in.)
U5/E/L, U7/E		0.030–0.035	0.0012–0.0014	0.15–0.35	0.006–0.014
YJ2		0.035–0.040	0.0014–0.0016	0.15–0.35	0.006–0.014
YGS1, YG5S/T		0.038–0.040	0.0015–0.0016	0.15–0.35	0.006–0.014
RD60/A		0.040–0.045	0.0016–0.0018	0.15–0.35	0.006–0.014
G5S, G6S, G6SB, G7S		0.040–0.045	0.0016–0.0018	0.15–0.35	0.006–0.014
HS1, HS1B, LS2		0.035–0.040	0.0014–0.0016	0.15–0.35	0.006–0.014
YL2, YL2C, YL2CM		0.025–0.030	0.0011–0.0012	0.15–0.35	0.006–0.014
YL1, YL1E		0.035–0.040	0.0014–0.0016	0.15–0.35	0.006–0.014
YA6		0.030–0.040	0.0012–0.0016	Top 0.15–0.30 Bottom 0.10–0.20	0.006–0.012 0.004–0.008
YAS1, YAS1C, AS2C		0.040–0.045	0.0016–0.0018	0.15–0.45	0.006–0.018
RD125		0.035–0.040	0.0014–0.0016	0.20–0.40	0.008–0.016
YCS1, YCS1C		0.030–0.035	0.0012–0.0014	0.15–0.35	0.006–0.014
CS3, CS3B/C, CS5		0.030–0.035	0.0012–0.0014	0.15–0.35	0.006–0.014
RD200B/C		0.040–0.045	0.0016–0.0018	0.15–0.35	0.006–0.014
YDS3, YDS3C, YM1		0.050–0.055	0.0020–0.0022	Top 0.15–0.30 Bottom 0.10–0.20	0.006–0.012 0.004–0.008
DS6, DS6B/C		0.035–0.040	0.0014–0.0016	0.15–0.35	0.006–0.014
DS7, RD250/A/B		0.040–0.045	0.0016–0.0018	0.15–0.35	0.006–0.014
YM2C, YDS5		0.035–0.040	0.0014–0.0016	Top 0.15–0.30 Bottom 0.10–0.20	0.006–0.012 0.004–0.008
YR2/C		0.035–0.040	0.0014–0.0016	0.15–0.35	0.006–0.014
R3, R3C		0.030–0.035	0.0012–0.0014	0.15–0.35	0.006–0.014
R5, R5B		0.040–0.045	0.0016–0.0018	0.45–0.65	0.018–0.026
R5C		0.040–0.045	0.0016–0.0018	0.30–0.50	0.012–0.020
RD350/A/B		0.040–0.045	0.0016–0.0018	0.20–0.40	0.008–0.016
RD400	0.30–0.40	0.030–0.035	0.0012–0.0014	0.3–0.5	0.012–0.020

Clutch Specifications

Model	Clutch Spring Free Length (mm)	(in.)	Friction Plate Thickness (new) (mm)	(in.)
YJ2	34.0	1.34	3.5	0.14
YGS1, YG5S/T, G5S, G6S/B, G7S	27.0	1.06	3.5	0.14
RD60/A	31.5	1.26	3.5	0.14
HS1/B, LS2	31.5	1.26	4.0	0.16
YL2, YL2C, YL2CM	28.2	1.30	3.5	0.14
YL1/E	25.5	1.00	4.0	0.16
YA6	31.5	1.26	4.0	0.16
YAS1/C, AS2C	34.0	1.34	4.0	0.16
RD125	31.5	1.24	3.2	0.12
YCS1/C	34.0	1.34	4.0	0.16
CS3/C/B, CS5, RD200	34.0	1.34	4.0	0.16
YDS3/C, YM1	25.5	1.00	4.3	0.17
YDS5, YM2C	25.5	1.00	3.0	0.12
DS6/B/C	44.0	1.72	3.0	0.12
YR2/C, R3/C	36.4	1.43	3.0	0.12
DS7, RD250/A/B	36.0	1.40	3.0	0.12
R5/B/C	36.0	1.40	3.0	0.12
RD350/A/B	36.0	1.40	3.0	0.12
RD400	36.4	1.43	3.0	0.12

Torque Specifications

size①	ft lbs
6 mm	7
7 mm	11
8 mm	15
10 mm	26–29
12 mm	29–33
14 mm	33–37
17 mm	40–50

① Refers to thread diameter; not socket size

LUBRICATION SYSTEM

All of the Yamahas covered in this section use the "Autolube" automatic oil injection system.

The Autolube system includes an oil reservoir, oil feed line, oil pump, and oil delivery lines. The pump is of the plunger type and is driven by the crankshaft or clutch (early models) through reduction gears. The amount of oil fed to the crankcase delivery line is determined by two variables—the speed of plunger operation and the length of plunger stroke. These variables are set by the engine rpm and the degree of throttle opening, respectively. The pump effectively meters the amount of oil according to engine speed and load and, as a result, no more and no less than the required amount is consumed. The pump also houses a check valve that keeps the oil output pressure constant and seals the delivery line when the engine is not operating.

The lubrication system is virtually maintenance-free except for checks on the oil pump cable adjustment (covered in the "Maintenance" section), the minimum pump stroke setting (see below), and pump bleeding (necessary only if the Autolube tank has run dry, or the oil lines disconnected for any reason).

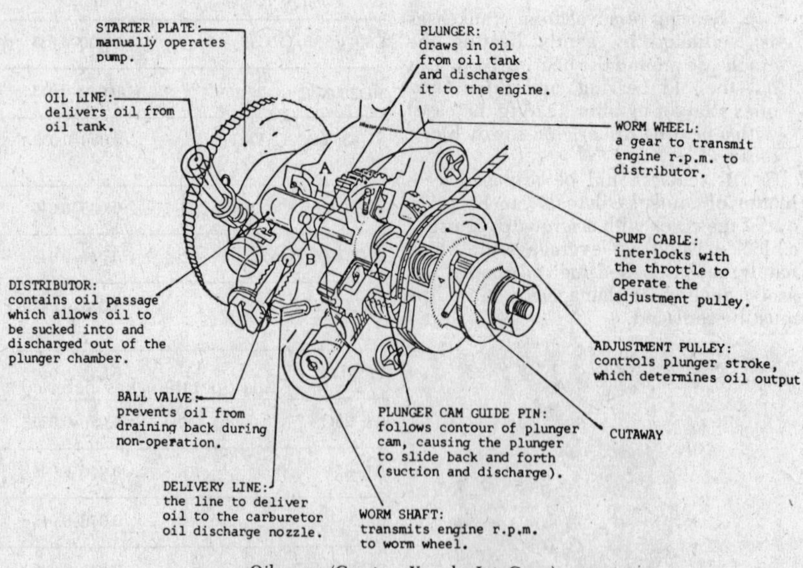

STARTER PLATE: manually operates pump.
OIL LINE: delivers oil from oil tank.
PLUNGER: draws in oil from oil tank and discharges it to the engine.
WORM WHEEL: a gear to transmit engine r.p.m. to distributor.
A
B
PUMP CABLE: interlocks with the throttle to operate the adjustment pulley.
DISTRIBUTOR: contains oil passage which allows oil to be sucked into and discharged out of the plunger chamber.
ADJUSTMENT PULLEY: controls plunger stroke, which determines oil output
BALL VALVE: prevents oil from draining back during non-operation.
PLUNGER CAM GUIDE PIN: follows contour of plunger cam, causing the plunger to slide back and forth (suction and discharge).
CUTAWAY
DELIVERY LINE: the line to deliver oil to the carburetor oil discharge nozzle.
WORM SHAFT: transmits engine r.p.m. to worm wheel.

Oil pump (Courtesy Yamaha Int. Corp.)

OIL PUMP

The oil pump must never be disassembled for any reason. To do so will render the pump unserviceable. If lubrication problems are traced to the pump, it must be replaced with a new one.

Removal and Installation

1. Remove the oil pump cover.
2. Disconnect the pump cable from the adjusting pulley. Disconnect the oil tank-to-pump line and plug it to avoid oil loss.
3. Disconnect the pump-to-engine line(s). These may be either simple hose fittings or banjo fittings secured with a screw and sealed with gaskets on either side of the banjo.

   CAUTION: *If oil pump inlet and outlet fittings are identical, mark the location of each hose before disconnecting it, so that the hook-ups will be correct when the pump is refitted. If banjo fittings are used for the outlet lines, take care that the gaskets are not misplaced.*
4. Remove the securing screws and remove the pump.

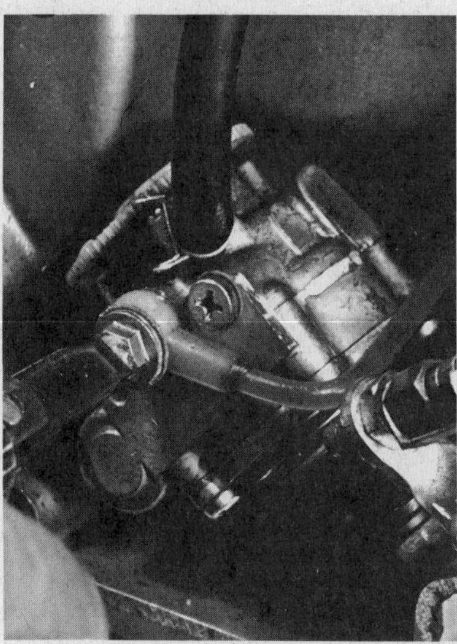

Removing an oil pump banjo bolt

5. Cover the oil line ends with small plastic bags secured by rubber bands to prevent the entry of dirt or other foreign matter in the event that the pump will be out of the machine for some time.
6. Check the condition of all oil lines. Replace any that are cracked, torn, or which show signs of damage. Check the banjo gaskets for condition and replace them if cracked.
7. The oil pump mating surface may be fitted with either an O-ring or a gasket, and this item should be replaced each time the pump is removed.
8. Installation is the reverse of the disassembly procedure. Ensure that all hose fittings are correct. Do not overtighten banjo connection screws.
9. After installation, turn the throttle twist-grip from closed to full open. Note that the guide pin should not touch the adjustment pulley at any point in its travel.
10. Before starting the engine, bleed the pump (see below), adjust the pump cable and minimum stroke.
11. When replacing the oil pump cover, ensure that it does not pinch any oil lines.

Bleeding

As noted above, bleeding the pump is necessary any time that the oil pump has been removed from the machine, whenever any of the oil lines has been disconnected, or if the Autolube tank has been drained or run dry.

Before beginning, ensure that the oil tank has a sufficient supply of oil.

1. Remove the oil pump cover. Place a suitable receptacle beneath the oil pump compartment to catch the drained oil.
2. The pump is equipped with a plastic starter plate on one end. This is used to bleed the system.

Loosening the oil pump bleed screw. The arrow indicates the pump starter plate

3. Loosen and remove the bleeder screw on the pump body.
4. Open the throttle fully and hold it open during the bleeding operation.
5. With your other hand, turn the starter plate in the direction of rotation indicated by the arrow on the plate.
6. Continue turning the starter plate while observing the flow of oil from the bleeder hole. When the oil is completely free of air bubbles, replace and tighten the bleeder screw. The system has now been bled.
7. After this operation has been completed, start the engine and allow it to idle for a few seconds while holding the oil pump open with the cable. This is only necessary on newly rebuilt engines to ensure sufficient lubrication during the first moments of operation. If the pump is held open too long, the plug(s) may foul.
8. After bleeding, check the pump minimum stroke and the cable adjustment.
9. If the bleeding procedure does not work (i.e., air bubbles continue to come out of the bleeder hole), check for air leaks at the hose junctions. With the engine running, squirt some clean Autolube oil at the hose connections. If bubbles form, there is an air leak at that point.

Minimum Oil Pump Stroke

Before beginning, have a feeler gauge of the correct size at hand. The minimum pump stroke on most recent models is 0.20–0.25 mm (0.008–0.010 in.), although on some older models it is slightly greater. Refer to the specifications chart at the end of this section for the correct minimum pump stroke for your machine.

Note the following terms: the *starter plate* is the plastic disc at one side of the oil pump and is used to operate the pump by hand. The *adjustment pulley* is that to which the oil pump cable is attached. The *adjustment plate* is the small plate at the opposite end of the pump from the starter plate. It is secured by a locknut.

1. Remove the oil pump cover plate. Make sure that the throttle twist-grip is fully closed.
2. Slowly turn the starter plate by hand in the direction of rotation indicated by the arrow on the plate. As the starter plate is turned, a gap will be created between the adjusting plate and the adjusting pulley. Continue to turn the starter plate until this gap is at its maximum width. This can be done by gauging the gap with your eye.

Turn the starter plate slowly until the gap between the adjusting plate and pulley is as wide as possible (Courtesy Yamaha Int. Corp.)

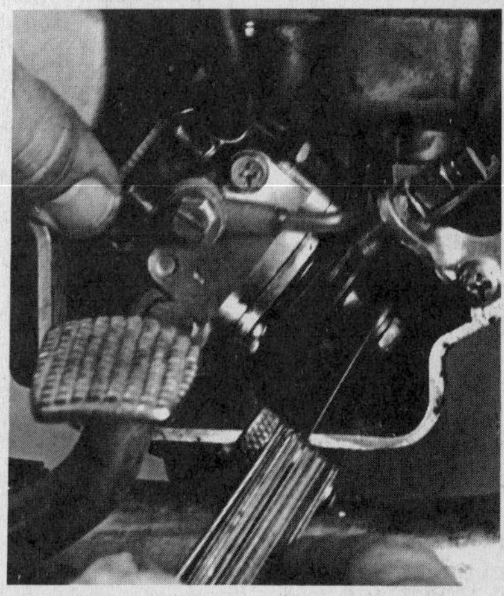

Checking the minimum oil pump stroke with a feeler gauge inserted between the adjusting pulley and plate

3. Insert the correct sized feeler gauge between the adjusting pulley and the adjusting plate. The clearance between the two should be within the specification shown for the individual models in the chart.

Removing the adjusting plate locknut (Courtesy Yamaha Int. Corp.)

4. If the clearance is not correct, remove the adjusting plate locknut, then the adjusting plate. Add or remove the 0.1 mm adjusting shims (supplied for this purpose) to the oil pump shaft to correct the adjustment, then refit the adjusting plate and tighten the locknut securely. Recheck the clearance.

NOTE: *If the original adjusting plate to pulley clearance was too great, remove a shim; if it was too small, add a shim or shims.*

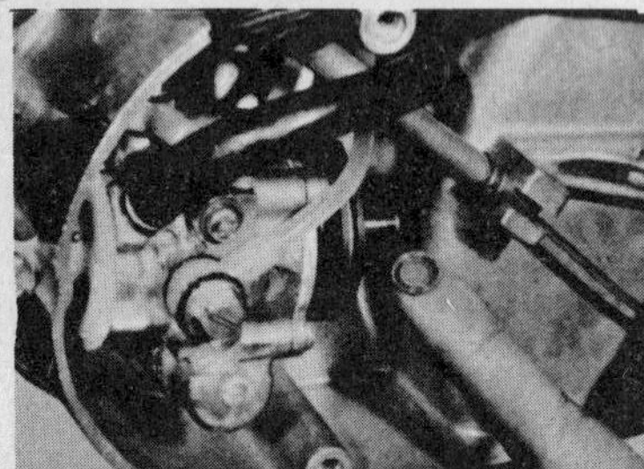

Adjusting shim (Courtesy Yamaha Int. Corp.)

Pump Output Check

1969, 1970 AND 1971 MODELS AND RD400

The delivery output of the oil pump should be measured on the above models after all other possible causes of trouble have been eliminated (see "Troubleshooting," below).

Needed for this operation are: a laboratory tube graduated in cubic centimeters, and an extra oil pump-to-engine delivery line.

NOTE: *This check can be performed with the pump mounted on the bike or on a bench.*

1. Cut one end off the extra delivery line and slide it over the end of the graduated tube (see the illustration).

2. Disconnect the oil pump delivery line banjo bolt and connect the extra one in its place with the graduated tube attached.

3. Make sure that there is sufficient oil in the oil tank, then set the pump at the minimum or maximum stroke.

NOTE: *When checking maximum output, turn the pump pulley so that the ramp moves along the guide pin to the maximum position. Do not push the pulley straight into position because the plunger stroke may then be longer than when in actual operation.*

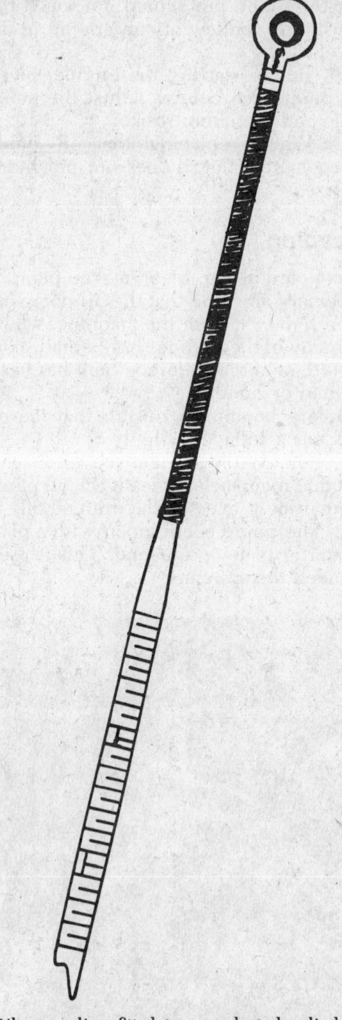

Oil pump line fitted to a graduated cylinder to check pump output (Courtesy Yamaha Int. Corp.)

4. Turn the starter plate 200 revolutions in the direction of rotation indicated by the arrow on the plate. Measure the amount of oil in the graduated tube, and compare this figure with the standard value given in the chart at the end of this section.

5. To check at minimum pump stroke, reset the pulley to the minimum output position and repeat the operation.

Troubleshooting

Before proceeding, first check that the oil tank has a sufficient supply of oil.

1. In the event of piston seizure or overheating not caused by component failure or incorrect timing or carburetor settings, check the oil pump cable adjustment, the oil pump minimum stroke, the quality of oil being used (poor quality oil will cause this); check that the breather hole in the oil tank cap is open or that the oil tank breather tube (if fitted) is not blocked. Check for air in the lines by bleeding the pump. Check for air or oil leaks in the lines from the tank and to the engine.

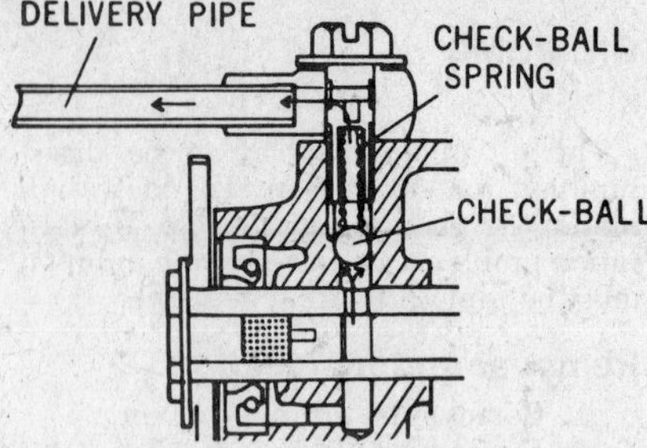

Oil pump check valve cutaway view (Courtesy Yamaha Int. Corp.)

2. In the case of excessive smoking or oil consumption, check the oil pump cable adjustment. Check for leakage at banjo fittings, and cracked or broken oil lines. Make sure that the oil is of good quality.

3. Check that the oil pump is feeding oil to the engine by removing a banjo fitting, turning the throttle twist-grip fully open, and turning the starter plate by hand in the direction of rotation indicated by the arrow on the starter plate. Oil should dribble out of the banjo bolt hole. If it does not, either the pump is not getting any oil because of an empty tank, blocked feed line, or blocked tank breather, or the pump is defective. The latter would be an extremely rare occurrence.

Minimum Oil Pump Stroke

Model	Stroke (mm)
YG5S/T, G5S, G6S/B, HS1/B, LS2, YL2/C/CM, YL1/E, YAS1/C, AS2C, RD125, YCS1/C, CS3/C/B, CS5, RD200, YDS5, DS6/B/C, DS7, YM1/2C, YR1/2/2C, R3/C, R5/B, RD250/A/B, RD350/A/B, RD400C	0.20–0.25
U5/E/L, YG1 (all), YJ2, YA6, YDS3/C	0.22–0.26
U7/E	0.25–0.29
RD60/A	0.30–0.35

Autolube Pump Output

	Minimum Stroke (cc @ 200 rev)	Maximum Stroke (cc @ 200 rev)
G5S, G6S, G6SB	0.50–0.63	4.65–5.15
HS1, HS1B, YL1/E, AS2C	0.50–0.63	4.20–4.80
CS1C, CS3B, CS3C, DS6B, DS6C, R3/C, R3, R5, R5B, RD400C	0.50–0.63	5.15–5.70

FUEL SYSTEMS

NOTE: *Refer to "Carburetors" in the General Information section for an explanation of carburetory theory, inspection, and troubleshooting.*

All Yamaha models covered in this manual are equipped with Mikuni carburetors, except for the RD125 and 200 which have Teikei units that are quite similar. Although similar in basic operation (all are concentric float bowl with cable-controlled throttle slides), working procedures vary slightly depending on the model of the carburetor.

CARBURETOR SERVICE

Removal and Installation

ROTARY VALVE MODELS

The carburetor is located beneath the cover at the forward end of the right-side engine case.

1. Lift up the rubber carburetor cover. Remove the rubber plug on the front of the right engine case. Using an impact driver, if necessary, unscrew and remove the carburetor cover.

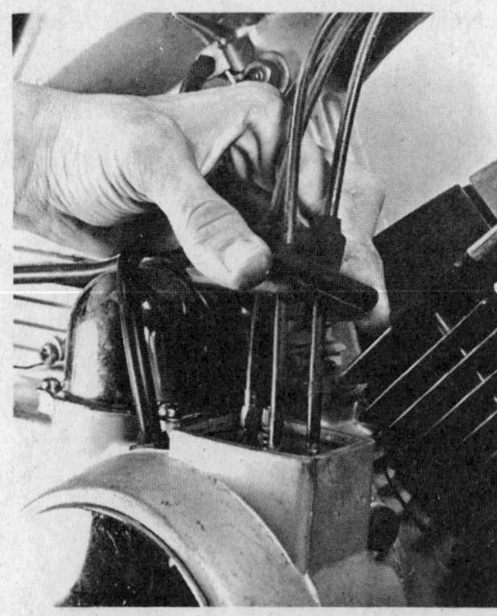

Removing the rubber cover

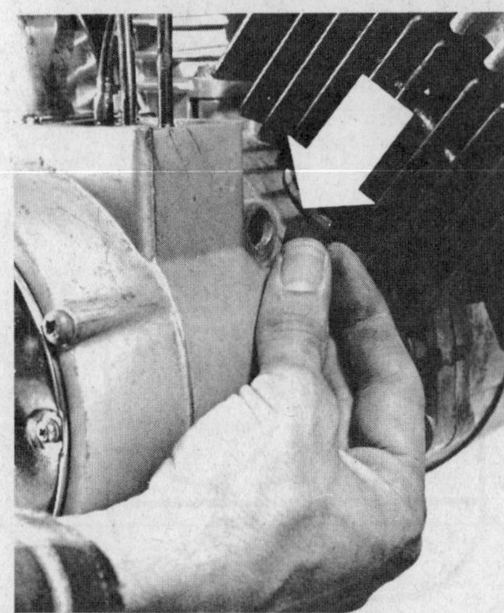

Removing the carburetor clamp access plug

Removing the carburetor cover

2. Unscrew the carburetor cap and pull out the throttle slide assembly.
3. Shut the fuel petcock off. Disconnect the fuel line from the carburetor.

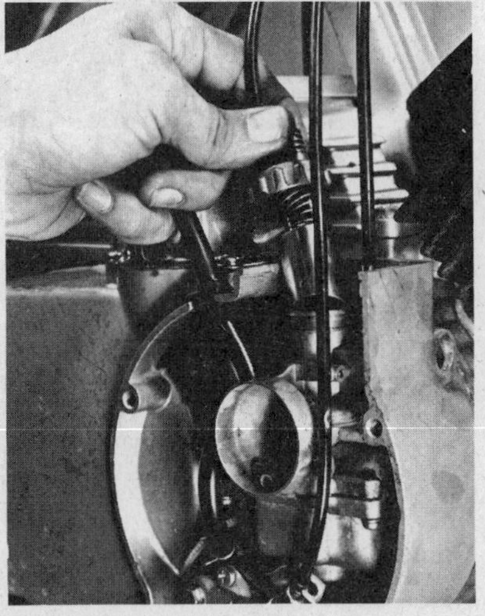

Unscrew the carburetor cap and lift out the throttle slide assembly

4. With a screwdriver (slot head) loosen the carburetor mounting clamp which is accessible through the plug hole at the front of the carburetor case.

Loosening the carburetor clamp screw

5. Pull the carburetor off its spigot.
6. Disconnect the overflow tube from the float bowl. Unscrew the starter plunger and pull it out of the carburetor body.
7. Drain the gasoline out of the carburetor before disassembly.
8. Installation is the reverse of the removal procedure. Be sure that all lines are firmly attached, and that the rubber grommets are properly seated.

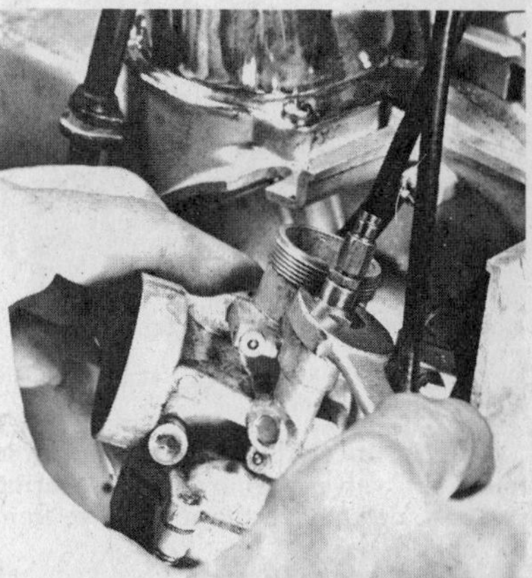

Unscrew and remove the starter plunger

Removing the starter plunger

PISTON PORT SINGLES

1. Shut off the fuel petcock. Disconnect the fuel line at the carburetor.
2. Loosen the air cleaner clamp screw at the carburetor.

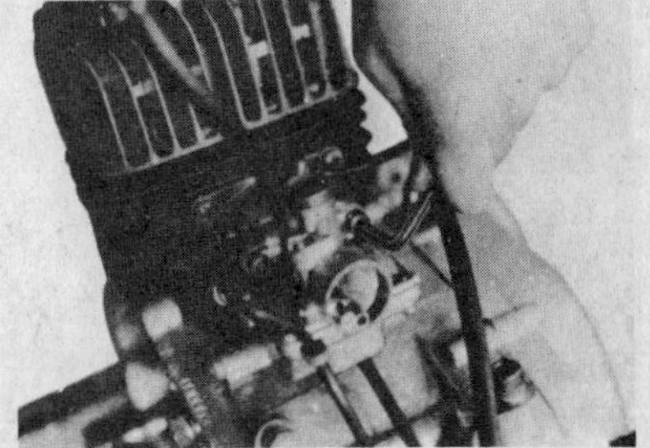

Removing the carburetor (RD60) (Courtesy Yamaha Int. Corp.)

3. Disconnect the overflow tube from the float bowl and the breather tube from the carburetor body. Slip the breather tube free of the clamp on the carburetor body.

4. Unscrew the carburetor cap and pull the throttle slide assembly out.

5. Loosen each of the carburetor bolts one turn, then unscrew and remove them, and remove the carburetor from the manifold.

Disconnecting the oil feed line at the manifold (Courtesy Yamaha Int. Corp.)

6. Disconnect the oil feed line from the reed valve. Remove the securing screws, and remove the reed valve from the cylinder.

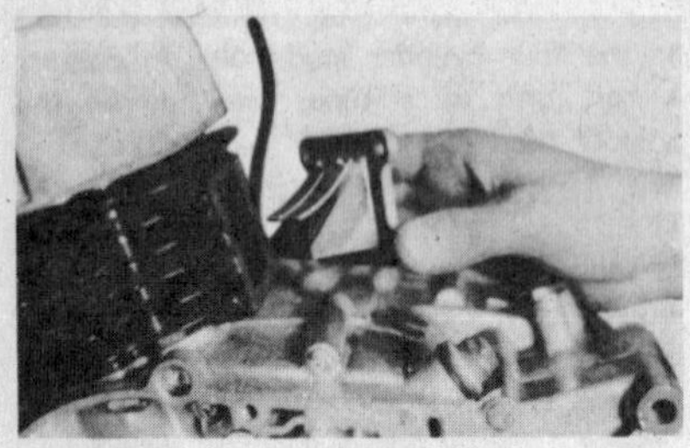

Removing the reed valve (Courtesy Yamaha Int. Corp.)

7. Drain the gas out of the carburetor before disassembly.

8. Installation is the reverse of the removal procedure. Check the condition of the reed valve and carburetor mounting flange gaskets, and replace them if damaged or if condition is doubtful. Tighten the carburetor mounting bolts evenly. Do not overtighten.

PISTON PORT TWINS

1. Loosen the air cleaner clamp screw at each carburetor and remove the rubber air cleaner hoses.

2. Shut off the fuel petcock and disconnect the fuel lines at the carburetors.

3. Unscrew the carburetor caps and pull out the throttle slide assembly for each carburetor.

Disconnecting the air cleaner hose at the carburetor (Courtesy Yamaha Int. Corp.)

4. Disconnect the starter lever linkage.

5. Disconnect the overflow tube from the float bowl for each carb. Disconnect the breather tube from each carburetor body. Slip the breather tubes free of the small clamp on each carburetor.

6. Loosen the clamp screw which secures each carburetor to the manifold, and pull them free together. On late models with the carburetors mounted in rubber spigots, a slot-and-pin arrangement is used to ensure correct vertical alignment of the carburetors. Therefore, be sure that the carbs are pulled straight out of the spigots, and are not twisted or turned to free them. When removing, note that in most cases the two carbs will still be connected by a balance tube, which may be disconnected after removal.

Loosening the carburetor clamp at the manifold (Courtesy Yamaha Int. Corp.)

7. Drain the gasoline out of the float bowls after removal.

8. If removal of the reed valves is desired, disconnect the oil feed line at the banjo on each rubber spigot. Unbolt and remove the spigots and the reed valves.

9. Installation is the reverse of the removal procedure. Be certain that all carburetor lines are secured before operation.

Disassembly

ALL MODELS

Disassembly procedures will vary slightly depending on the type of carburetor fitted.

IMPORTANT: *Note the location of all O-rings, washers, and gaskets when disassembling the carburetors. Refer to the exploded views if necessary.*

If disassembly of the throttle slide assembly is desired, refer to the procedures below. If a throttle stop rod is used to adjust the idle speed (rotary valve and some piston port models), see Step 1 and following. On all other models, begin with Step 2.

1. The idle speed adjuster screw on the carburetor cap has a small cotter pin at the top. Removing this pin will allow the throttle stop rod to be taken out of the bottom of the throttle slide.

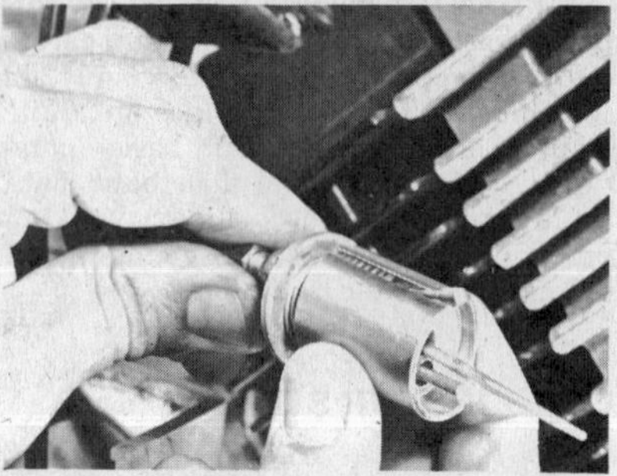

Detaching the throttle cable from the slide

2. Compress the throttle slide against the carburetor cap until the end of the cable protrudes from the bottom of the slide. Slip the cable end up along the slot in the slide until free, then remove the spring and the throttle slide.

3. Remove the spring seat or circlip from the inside of the slide, then turn it upside down to remove the needle and clip.

NOTE: *Do not remove the needle clip unless its position is to be changed.*

4. Turn the carburetor upside down, and remove the four float bowl screws. Remove the float bowl.

NOTE: *If the carburetor is old and has*

Removing the float bowl screws

POOR

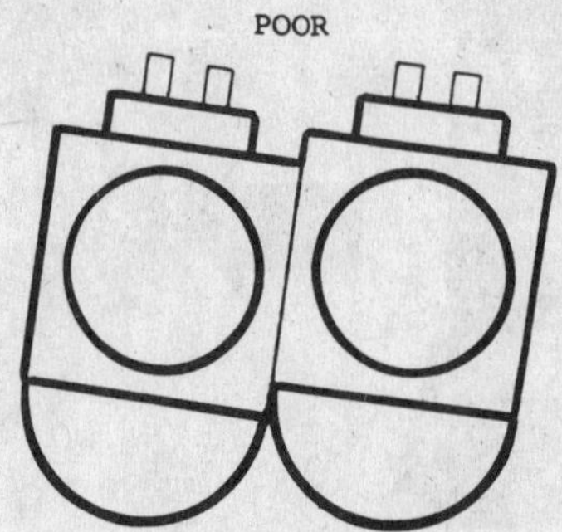

GOOD

When installing the carburetors, ensure that they are vertically aligned (Courtesy Yamaha Int. Corp.)

Removing the float bowl

never been disassembled, the float bowl may be stuck to the gasket. Use a soft-faced (plastic) mallet to tap around the bowl until it is free. Restraint should be exercised while doing this.

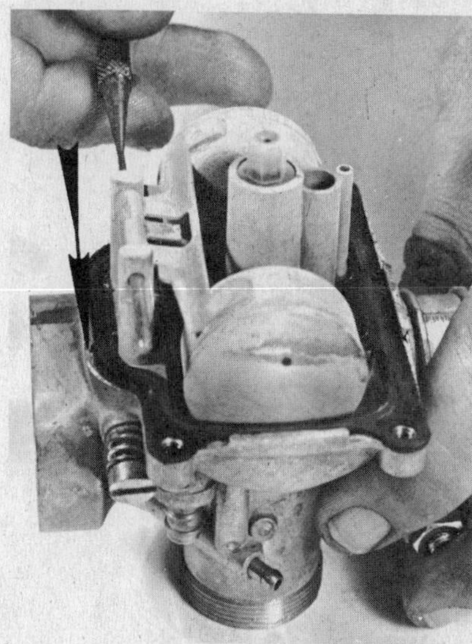

Push out the float pivot pin

5. Push out the float pivot pin by hand or with a small punch, and remove the float assembly.

CAUTION: *Carefully note or mark the top side of the float assembly, since damage could occur if the attempt were made to install the floats incorrectly.*

6. Remove the float needle.
7. With a suitable socket, unscrew and remove the float needle seat.
8. Unscrew and remove the main jet.

CAUTION: *All fuel jets are very malleable and must be removed and installed with care to avoid damage.*

9. The needle jet is of two types, depending on model. If a hex-head is provided, simply unscrew and remove the needle jet in the same manner as the main jet.

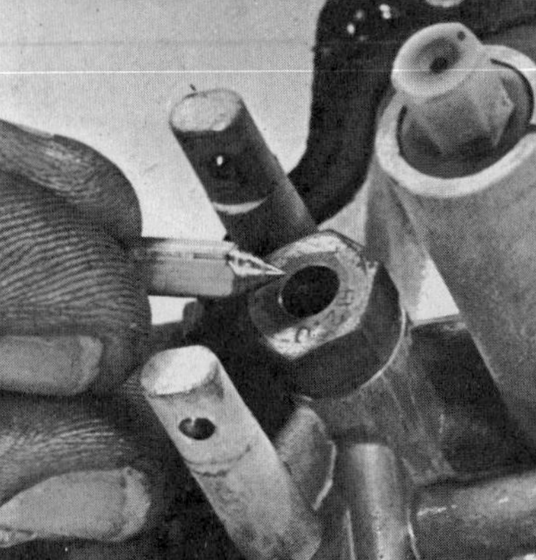

Take out the float needle

Removing the float needle seat

Removing the main jet

If this is not the case, the needle jet is recessed into a holder in the carburetor body. After removing the main jet, use a thin knife blade or something similar to remove the washer which is press-fitted at the bottom of the needle jet.

The needle jet is pressed into the carburetor body. To remove it, a wooden dowl should be used as a drift. Tap lightly at the bottom of the needle jet (the float bowl end) to force the jet into the carburetor bore.

10. Unscrew and remove the pilot jet.
11. If the starter plunger is still in place, unscrew the large nut on the carburetor body and remove the plunger assembly.
12. Unscrew and remove the pilot air jet. On most models, this is located on the side of the carburetor, but on some rotary valve models it is threaded into a passage just below the carb air intake.

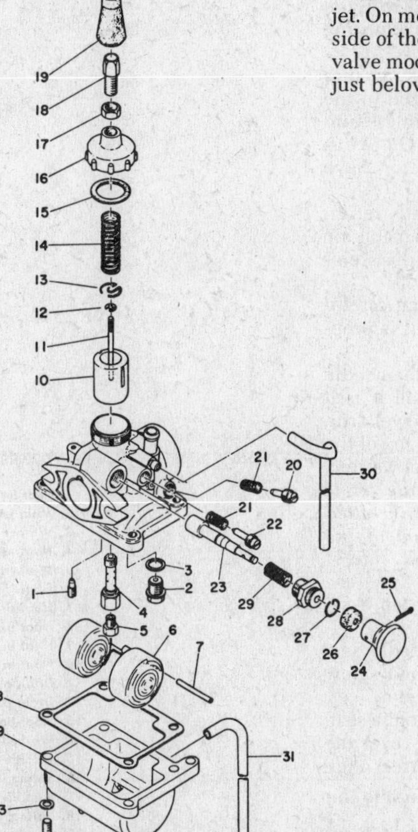

1. Pilot jet
2. Float needle seat
3. Needle seat washer
4. Needle jet
5. Main jet
6. Float assembly
7. Float pivot pin
8. Float bowl gasket
9. Float bowl
10. Throttle slide
11. Needle
12. Needle clip
13. Return spring seat
14. Throttle return spring
15. Gasket
16. Carburetor cap
17. Cable adjuster locknut
18. Cable adjuster
19. Cap
20. Pilot air screw
21. Spring
22. Throttle stop screw
23. Starter plunger
24. Holder
25. Pin
26. Plunger cap cover
27. Clip
28. Plunger cap
29. Spring
30. Breather tube
31. Float bowl overflow tube
32. Float bowl screw
33. Washer

VM16SH carburetor (Courtesy Yamaha Int. Corp.)

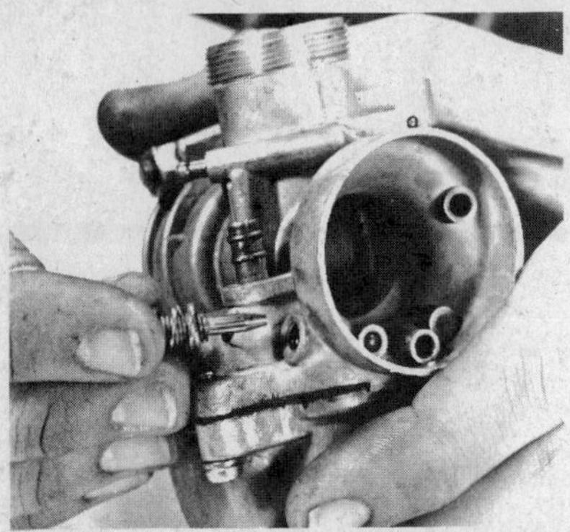

Removing the pilot air screw

13. Unscrew and remove the throttle stop screw. Both the pilot air screw and throttle stop screws are held in adjustment by small springs. Be careful that these are not lost when the screws are removed.

Assembly

1. The following parts should be replaced each time the carburetor is disassembled:
   a. Manifold gasket and manifold O-ring (if fitted);
   b. Float bowl gasket;
   c. Float needle seat gasket;
   d. Throttle stop rod cotter pin (if fitted).
2. On rotary valve models, assemble the throttle slide assembly by first fitting the carburetor cap onto the throttle cable. Install the throttle stop rod through the bottom of the slide and attach it with the cotter pin to the top of the idle adjusting screw on the carburetor cap.
3. Install the needle, making sure that the needle clip is positioned in the same groove as it was found, unless tuning changes have been made. On twins, double check that both carburetors have the same needle setting.
4. Install the spring seat, return spring, and engage the throttle cable on the slide in the reverse of the disassembly procedure.
5. Install the pilot jet, being careful when screwing the jet in that it is properly seated.
6. Install the needle jet. If the needle jet is the pressed-in type, install it as it was removed with a wooden dowel drift, tapping it into its seat from the top of the carburetor. Install the needle jet washer.
   NOTE: *If this type of needle jet is used, make sure that it is installed with the cutaway at the top of the needle jet facing the ENGINE side of the carburetor.*
7. Install the main jet; tighten it securely.
8. Install the fiber float needle seat gasket onto the needle seat, and screw the needle seat into the carburetor.
9. Place the float needle into the seat, and position the float assembly over the needle, ensuring that the correct side faces up. Slip the float pivot pin into the holder.
10. Adjust the float height.
11. Fit a new float bowl gasket. Install

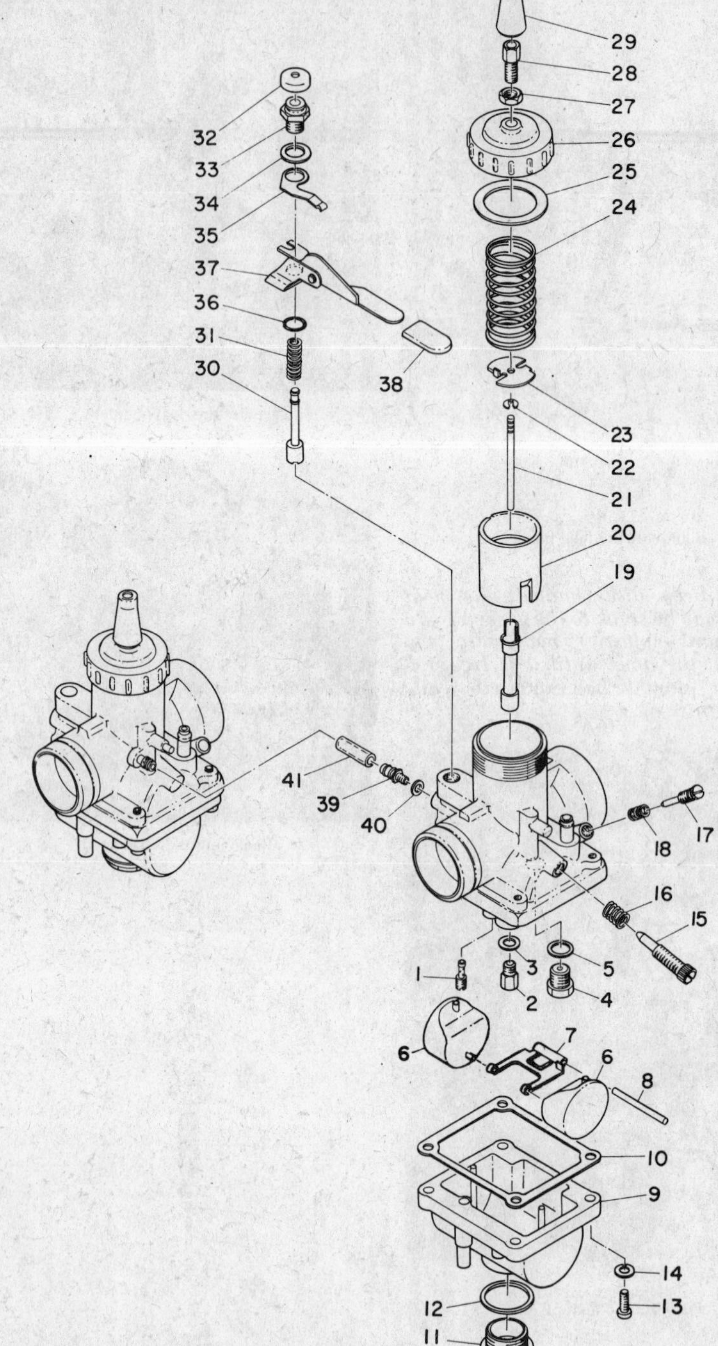

VM28SC carburetor (Courtesy Yamaha Int. Corp.)

1. Pilot jet
2. Main jet
3. Washer
4. Float needle seat
5. Washer
6. Float
7. Float arm
8. Float pivot pin
9. Float bowl
10. Float bowl gasket
11. Drain plug
12. Drain plug gasket
13. Float bowl screw
14. Washer
15. Throttle stop screw
16. Spring
17. Pilot air screw
18. Spring
19. Needle jet
20. Throttle slide
21. Needle
22. Needle clip
23. Spring seat
24. Throttle return spring
25. Gasket
26. Carburetor cap
27. Cable adjuster locknut
28. Cable adjuster
29. Cap
30. Starter plunger
31. Spring
32. Plunger cap cover
33. Plunger cap
34. Washer
35. Plate
36. O-ring
37. Starter lever
38. Starter lever rubber tip
39. Balance fitting
40. Washer
41. Balance tube

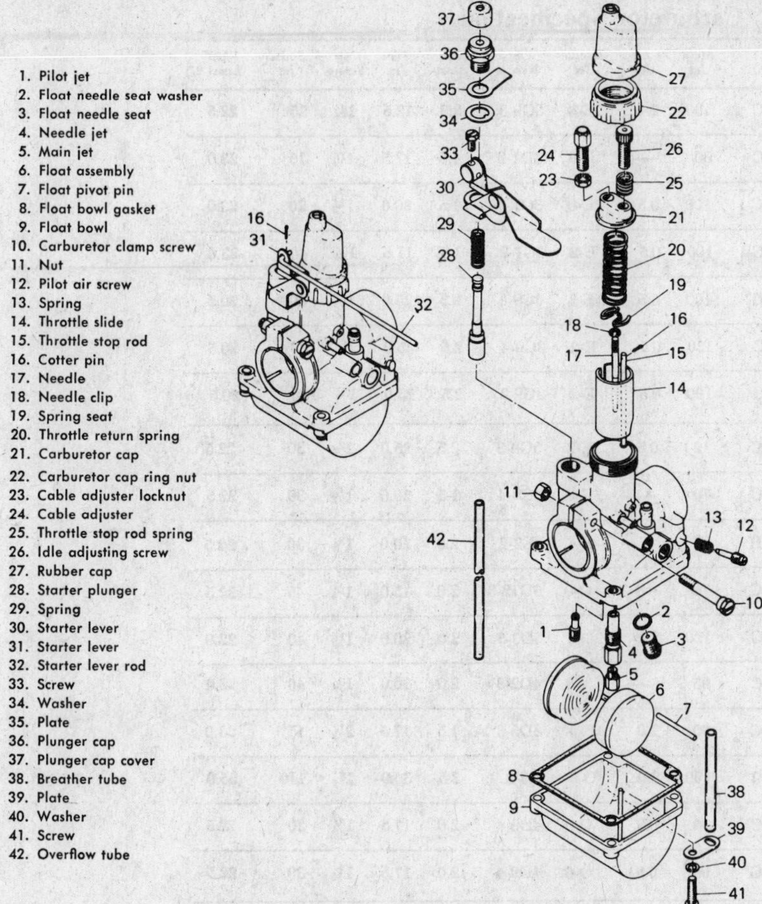

Mikuni type "SC" carburetor (Courtesy Yamaha Int. Corp.)

the float bowl, and install the four phillips head screws, tightening them gradually, and in an "X" pattern.

12. Refit the pilot air screw and spring. Screw in the pilot air screw until lightly seated, then back it off the prescribed number of turns given in the "Carburetor Specifications" chart at the end of this section. This is an approximate setting and may have to be readjusted when the engine is started. Install the throttle stop screw and spring.

13. Install the starter plunger in the carburetor body and secure it.

14. Install the carburetor on the manifold and install the throttle slide assembly.

15. Refer to the "Maintenance" and "Tune-Up" sections if necessary to adjust pilot air and throttle stop screws, throttle cables, and throttle slide synchronization.

Reed Valve

The valve must not be handled excessively. Salt from the hands may damage the valve. Do not expose it to the sun and store it in a cool dry place if it is removed.

REMOVAL

1. Remove the carburetor.
2. Remove the four valve securing screws.
3. Gently remove the valve assembly from the cylinder. Do not pry the valve off.

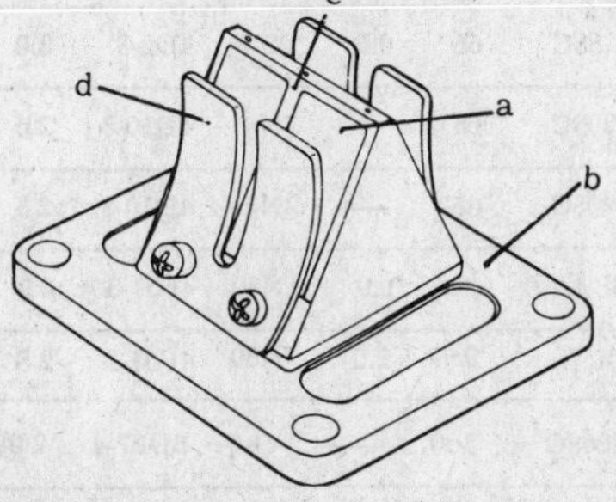

Reed valve: a, valve; b, case; c, gasket; d, valve stopper (Courtesy Yamaha Int. Corp.)

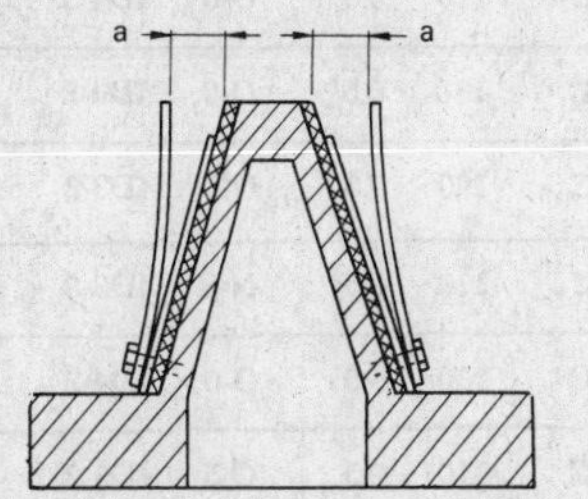

Valve stopper clearance (a) should be about 9 mm (0.35 in.) (Courtesy Yamaha Int. Corp.)

INSPECTION

1. If the reeds and the stopper plate must be removed from the case use the cut in the lower corner of the reed and stopper plate as a guide to reassembly.
2. Reinstall the reeds and stopper plates in their original locations.
3. Check the rubber parts of valve for cracking and other signs of deterioration.
4. Inspect the reed petals for signs of fatigue cracks. The reeds should seat flush against their neoprene seats, or nearly so. Apply a suction to the carburetor side of the reed valve: the leakage should be very slight.

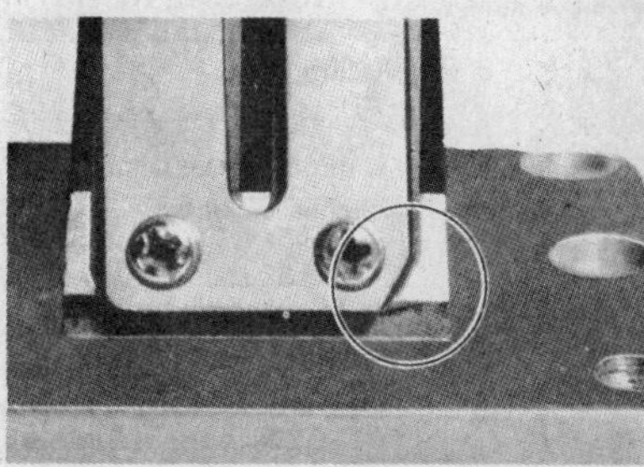

Note the cut edge of the reed as an aide to installation (Courtesy Yamaha Int. Corp.)

INSTALLATION

1. Apply Lock-Tite® or some similar thread bonder to the reed securing screws so that they will not fall into the engine during operation. Torque the screws to 0.6 in. lbs.
2. Install the valve carefully into the cylinder and tighten the valve securing bolts in a cross pattern.
3. Torque bolts to 5.1–7.2 ft lbs.

FUEL PETCOCK

1. The fuel petcock contains a wire mesh filter which should be removed and cleaned every 2,000 miles or every few months.
2. Unscrew the sediment bowl after shutting the fuel off.
3. Remove the filter from the petcock, and clean the bowl and the filter in a solvent.
4. Make sure that the petcock can fully shut off the gas. If leakage is noted when the petcock is in the "OFF" position, the petcock should be replaced.
5. Check the condition of the sediment bowl O-ring and replace it if damaged.
6. Replace the filter and sediment bowl. Do not overtighten the bowl. After installation, turn on the petcock and check for leaks.

If water has been getting into the carburetor from the gas tank, some or most of it can be removed by disconnecting the fuel line(s) at the carburetor(s) or petcock, placing a suitable container underneath to catch the gasoline, and turning the petcock to the "Reserve" position. Letting the gasoline run out for several seconds in this manner should remove any water present around the petcock line inside the gas tank.

7. Late models may have a fuel filter above the petcock which is accessible after removing the petcock from the tank.

Carburetor Specifications

	Type (Mikuni)	Main Jet	Air Jet	Needle Jet	Jet Needle	Cut Away	Pilot Jet	Air Screw	Starter Jet	Float Level ②
U5/E/L, U7, U7E	VM15SC	100	2.4	E-8	3G9-3	2.5	12.5	1¾	25	22.5
YJ2	VM16SC	60	—	E-0	3D1-3	1.5	17.5	1½	15	23.0
YG1, YG1T	VM15SC-1	100	0.5	E-0	3G1-3	1.5	20.0	1½	20	23.0
YG1K, YGS1, YGS1T	VM15SC-1	100	0.5	E-2	3G1-2	1.5	17.5	1¾	40	23.0
G5S	VM16SC	100	0.5	E-2	3G9-3	2.5	25.0	1¾	30	20.5
YG5T, YG5S	VM16SC	120	0.5	E-2	3G9-4	2.5	25.0	1½	30	20.5
G6S	VM16SC	100	0.5	E-2	3G9-3	2.5	25.0	1¾	30	20.5
G6SB, G7S	VM16SC	120	0.5	E-2	3G9-3	2.5	25.0	1¾	30	22.5
HS1, HS1B	VM16SC	70	—	E-0	3G9-4	1.5	20.0	1½	30	22.5
RD60, RD60A	VM16SH	95	—	E-4	3E2-2	2.0	20.0	1¾	30	22.5
LS2	VM17SC	70	0.8	O-0	3D12-3	2.0	15.0	1¾	40	22.5
YL2, YL2C	VM17SC	120	2.0	D-0	3D3-3	2.0	20.0	1½	40	22.0
YL2CM	VM20SC	95	—	N-8	4D2-3	2.0	30.0	1¾	40	22.0
YL1, YL1E	VM16SC	60	2.0	E-0	3D3-3	1.5	17.5	2½	15	23.0
YA6	VM22SC	190	2.0	O-0	4J6-3	2.5	30.0	1¾	110	25.0
YAS1	VM17SC	90	0.8	O-0	4D9-4	2.0	17.5	1¾	30	22.5
YAS1C	VM17SC	95	0.8	O-0	4D9-4	2.0	17.5	1¾	30	22.5
AS2C	VM17SC	95	—	O-0	4D9-4	2.0	17.5	1¾	30	25.3
RD125	Y18P-1C③	94	2.0	N30	4D50-2	2.5	44.0	1½	70	20.0
YCS1	VM18SC	65	0.5	O-0	4D2-3	3.0	20.0	2	40	21.0
YCS1C, CS3C	VM20SC	65	—	N-6	4D10-3	2.5	30.0	2¼	40	21.0
CS3B, CS5	VM20SC	65	—	N-6	4D10-3	2.5	30.0	2	40	21.7
RD200	Y20P-1A③	94	0.9	N80	4F51-3	2.0	42.0	1¼	70	20.0
RD200C	Y20P	94	2.0	N80	4F51-2	2.5	44	1½	70	20.0
DS7	VM26SC	100	—	O-0	5DP7-4	2.0	40.0	1½	100①	15.1
Early YDS3	VM24SC	120	0.5	O-0	4D4-2	2.0	20.0	1½	40	25.0
Early YDS3C	VM24SC	120	0.5	O-0	4D4-3	2.0	20.0	1½	40	25.0
Late YDS3, YDS3C	VM24SC	130	0.5	O-0	4D4-2	2.0	20.0	1½	40	25.0
YDS5	VM26SC	120	0.5	O-5	4D3-2	2.5	30.0	1½	40	25.5
DS6, DS6B, DS6C	VM26SC	110	0.5	N-8	4D3-3	2.0	30.0	1½	40	25.7
YM1	VM24SC	130	0.5	O-0	4D4-2	2.0	20.0	1½	40	25.1
YM2C	VM26SC	110	0.5	O-5	4D3-2	2.5	30.0	1½	40	25.5
YR2, YR2C, R3, R3C	VM28SC	170	0.5	O-2	5D1-3	2.0	30.0	1½	40	25.5
R5, R5B	VM28SC	110	—	O-0	5DP7-4	2.0	40.0	1¾	100①	15.0
R5C	VM28SC	120	—	O-4	5DP7-4	2.0	30.0	1¼	100	15.0
RD 250A/B	VM28SC	120	—	O-8	5I4-3	2.5	30.0	1¼	100	15.0

Carburetor Specifications (cont.)

	Type (Mikuni)	Main Jet	Air Jet	Needle Jet	Jet Needle	Cut Away	Pilot Jet	Air Screw	Starter Jet	Float Level ②
RD350 A/B	VM28SC	140	—	O-8	5I4-3	2.5	25.0	1¾	100	15.0
RD400	VM28SC	115	0.5	P-2	5LI-3	2.5	25.0	1½	70	23.0

① Left carburetor only
② Measured in mm
③ Teikei carburetor

ELECTRICAL SYSTEMS

COMPONENT TESTS

Use the following procedures in conjunction with the electrical specifications at the end of this section to determine faulty components.

DC Generator Voltage Output

1. Disconnect the generator wiring from the other components.
2. Connect a voltmeter to the armature terminal "A" (red) and ground field terminal "F" (black).

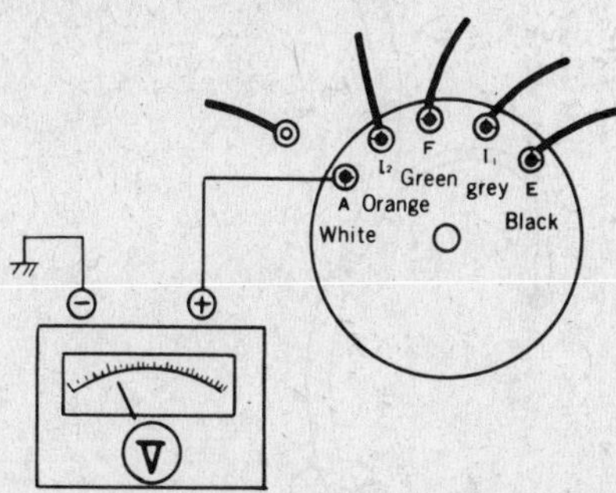

Checking generator output (Courtesy Yamaha Int. Corp.)

3. Run the engine up to about 2,500 rpm and check the voltmeter reading. If within reasonable bounds of the necessary output (6 or 12 volts), the generator is not likely to be the source of your problem. If the output is nil or minimal, isolate the cause by checking the carbon brushes and field winding insulation.

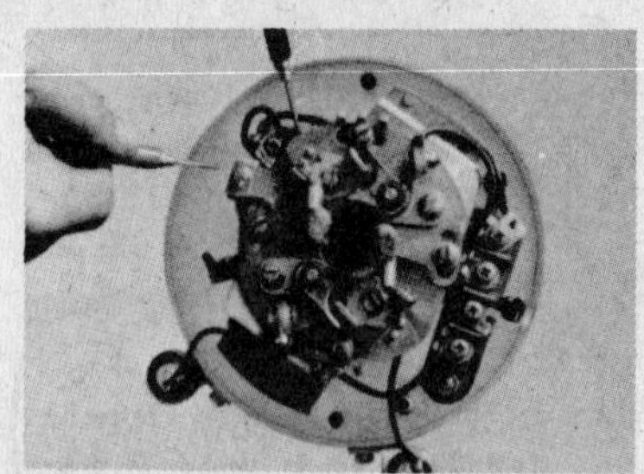

Checking positive brush insulation (Courtesy Yamaha Int. Corp.)

a. Check all brush wire connections.
b. Measure brush length and spring tension.
c. Make sure the positive carbon brush is properly insulated.

NOTE: *Disconnect the negative brush before checking for a positive brush short.*

d. Check for any dirt, oil, etc. that may be shorting out part of the stator assembly.
e. Check for proper continuity between the armature and field windings (terminals "A" and "F").

NOTE: *Lift the carbon brushes off the commutator before checking field winding resistance.*

Checking field winding insulation (Courtesy Yamaha Int. Corp.)

f. Check field winding insulation with an ohmmeter set at the highest scale. Readings between the housing and terminal "A" and housing and terminal "F" should be infinite (3 megohms or more).

4. If the preceding tests didn't reveal the problem, perform the following checks on the armature:

a. Clean the commutator in a solvent. Make sure that the mica gaps are free from carbon dust which could short out the individual segments;

Checking for continuity between the armature and the field windings (Courtesy Yamaha Int. Corp.)

b. Check the mica undercut; refer to the specifications for each machine at the end of this section. If necessary, increase the mica undercut with a piece of hacksaw blade or thin screwdriver. Clean thoroughly afterwards;
c. If the commutator segments are corroded or scored, remove imperfections with sandpaper or a fine grade of emery cloth. Clean thoroughly with a solvent after this operation and check the undercut.

Increasing the mica undercut (Courtesy Yamaha Int. Corp.)

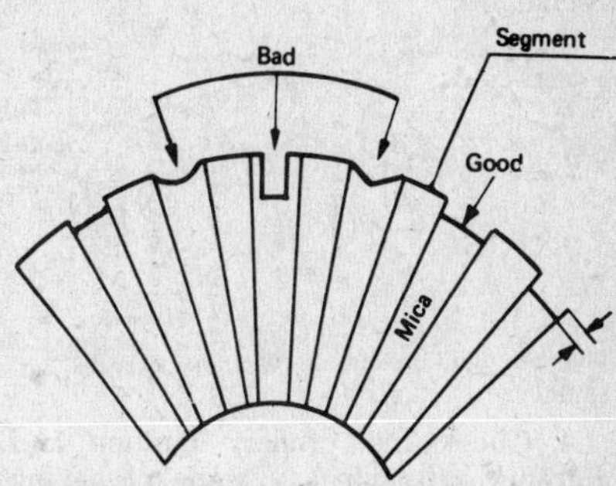

Mica undercut conditions (Courtesy Yamaha Int. Corp.)

d. Check for continuity between the commutator segments and armature *core.* Resistance should be infinite (no continuity). If continuity exists, the commutator is shorted against the core and the whole armature will have to be replaced.
e. Check for continuity between each of the individual commutator segments. There should be no resistance. If there is, the armature has an open circuit and must be replaced.

Checking for insulation between the commutator segments and the armature core (Courtesy Yamaha Int. Corp.)

Starter Generator Brushes and Coil

1. Disconnect the negative starter brush and check the positive brush for insulation.

2. Disconnect the voltage regulator wiring and lift the positive brushes off the commutator. Make sure that there is continuity between terminals "A" and "M." No resistance indicates a broken starter winding.

3. Disconnect the heavy motor winding wire from the positive brush and make sure the windings are insulated.

NOTE: *On early models, the fields and motor windings are internally connected. The readings on these machines must be exactly as specified.*

4. With the heavy motor winding wire still disconnected from the positive brush, make sure there is an open circuit between the "M" terminal and ground (at least 3 megohms).

Magneto Assembly

1. Make sure that all connections are tight.

2. Check all parts for any oil or water spots.

3. The flywheel magnets eventually weaken. If the points and condenser are good, but lighting and spark are weak, replace the flywheel or have the magnets recharged.

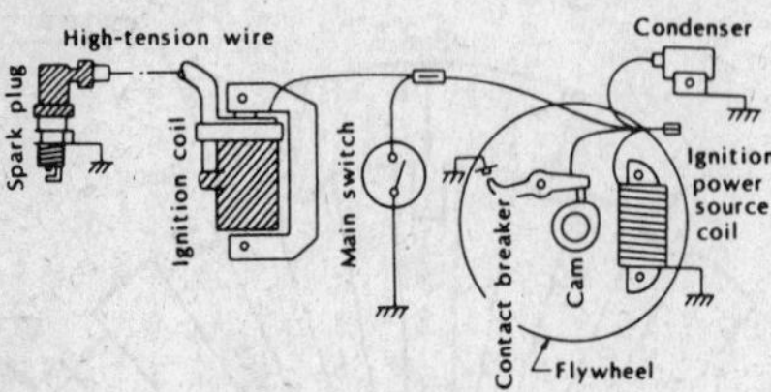

Magneto ignition circuit (Courtesy Yamaha Int. Corp.)

4. Check the primary ignition and lighting coils for any signs of having burnt out.

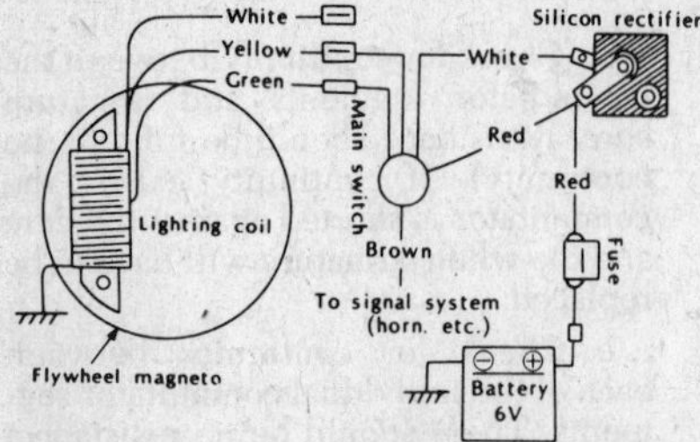

Magneto lighting circuit (Courtesy Yamaha Int. Corp.)

5. Make sure that the lighting coil wires all have continuity with each other.

6. Make sure that there is no continuity between the primary ignition coil leads and the coil core.

7. Check for continuity between the primary ignition coil lead and the coil mounting plate. Continuity must be present. If it is not, check for poor contact between the coil core and the plate or suspect a broken coil wire.

8. Check for continuity between the lighting coil lead and the coil mounting plate. If there is no continuity, check for poor contact between the coil core and the plate or a broken wire.

9. Check the ends of the coil cores and the inner surface of the magneto rotor to ensure that there has been no contact between the two as indicated by worn or scored marks. If contact has been made, check the crankshaft for play which would indicate a bad crankshaft bearing. Check that the coils are properly mounted on the plate and that the plate is secure. Any contact between the magneto rotor and the coil cores must be eliminated.

Alternator No Load Voltage Check

CAUTION: *Never disconnect the battery from an AC generating system during operational tests.*

1. Connect a voltmeter across the battery terminals. The battery must be in good condition and have a full charge. Start and run the engine to about 3,000 rpm. The voltmeter should read 14–16v depending on model. If the voltage output is too high and the battery is overcharging, suspect the voltage regulator. If the voltage is too low, check the regulator, rectifier, and the alternator.

To check the alternator, proceed as follows:

2. Check for continuity between each of the alternator wires and the others. If there is not continuity, the stator has a broken wire and must be replaced.

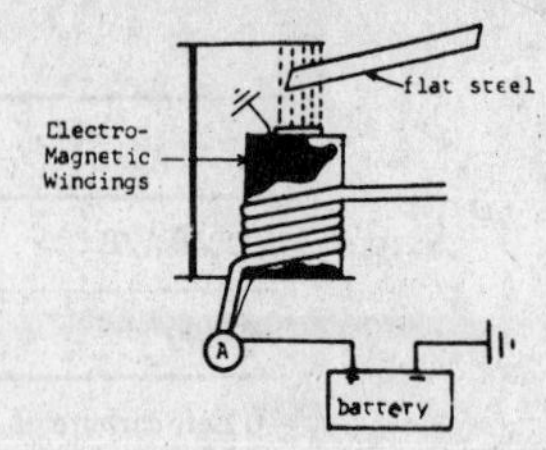

Checking the voltage regulator relay coil (Courtesy Yamaha Int. Corp.)

3. Check for continuity between each stator lead and the stator housing. Each lead must be insulated (no continuity). If there is continuity, the stator wiring is internally shorted and must be replaced.

4. If the alternator is in the machine, check for continuity between the two (black and green) field coil leads. More than a few ohms resistance here indicates that the field coil is defective, one of the wire leads is broken, or one of the brushes is damaged.

5. After removing the alternator rotor, clean the slip rings thoroughly and check the resistance across them. If more than a

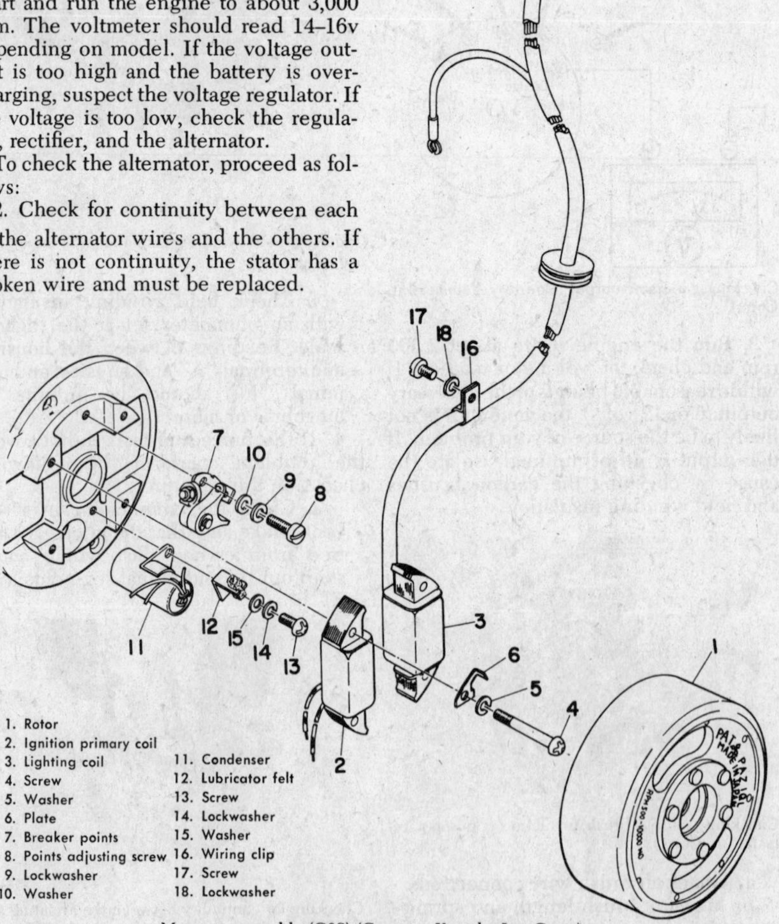

Magneto assembly (G6S) (Courtesy Yamaha Int. Corp.)

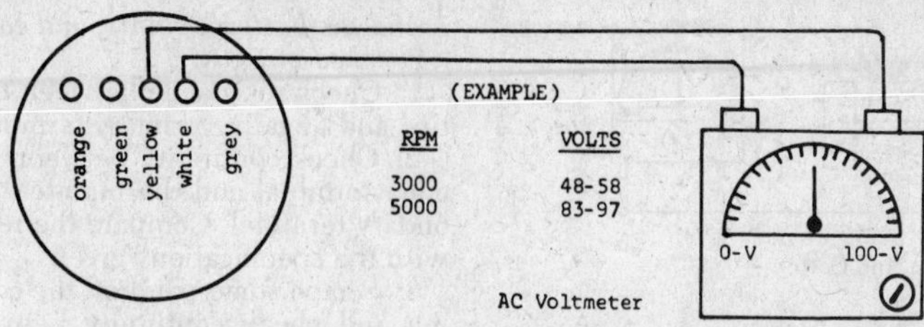

Checking alternator output (nighttime circuit) (Courtesy Yamaha Int. Corp.)

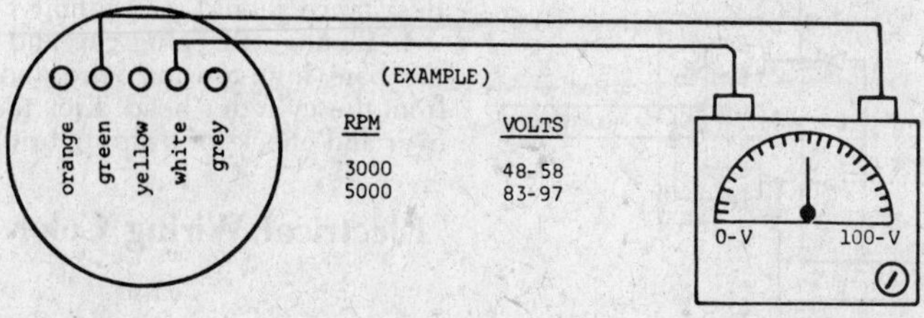

Checking alternator output (daytime circuit) (Courtesy Yamaha Int. Corp.)

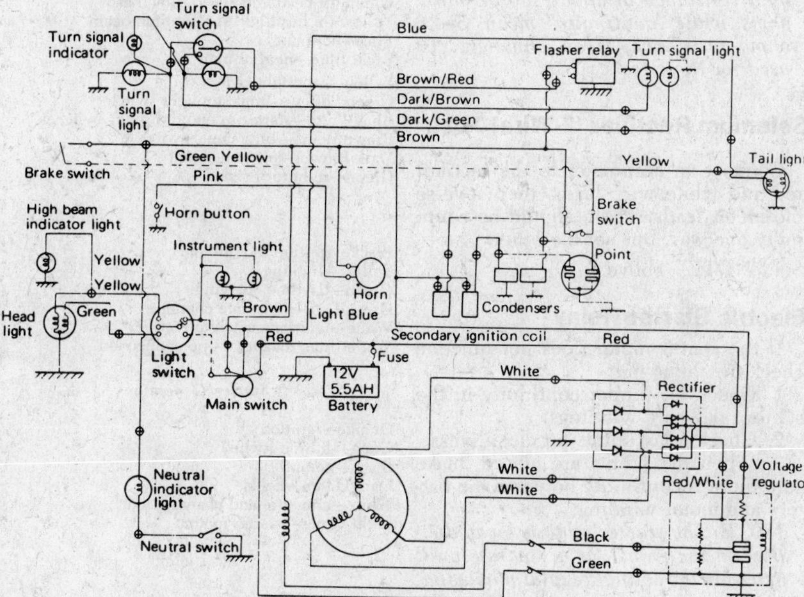

Alternator schematic (Courtesy Yamaha Int. Corp.)

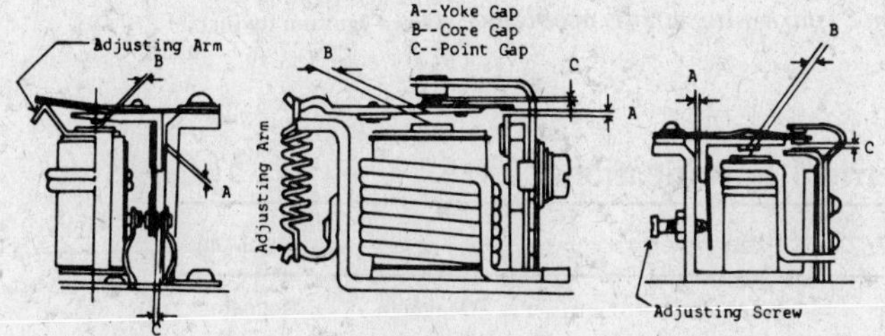

Voltage regulator relay adjustments (Courtesy Yamaha Int. Corp.)

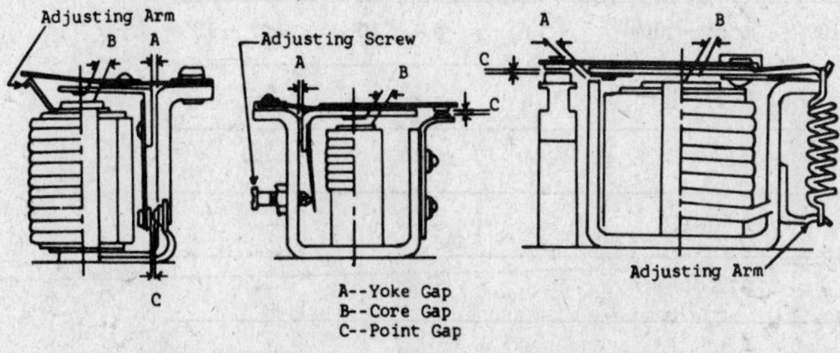

Cut-out relay adjustments (Courtesy Yamaha Int. Corp.)

few ohms, the field coil is broken and the rotor must be replaced.

6. Check for continuity between each slip ring and the rotor core. If continuity exists, replace the rotor.

Alternator Average Amperage Check

1. Disconnect the rectifier red wire.
2. Connect a DC ammeter positive lead to the red wire and connect the ammeter negative lead to the red wire connector.
3. Output at 3,000 rpm should be 2.8 ± 0.5A—day position, 6.7 ± 0.5A—night position; at 5,000 rpm, 3.2 ± 0.5A—day position and 7.1 ± 0.5A—night position.

Voltage Regulator Relay

NOTE: *If isolating a problem source, first check the generator as previously described, then check this relay.*

1. Check for any loose connections, broken solder, dirty points, etc.
2. Connect the correct voltage battery to the regulator coil as shown in the illustration, then insert a flat piece of steel into the electromagnetic field. If the steel is attracted by the field, the coil is OK.
3. Check the shunt resistors by connecting an ohmmeter positive lead to the "A" terminal and the negative lead to the "F" terminal. Manually operate the relay—each of the shunt positions should show a different resistance. If any of the positions indicate infinite resistance, one of the shunts is open.
4. Check the yoke, core, and point gap with specifications if given. Adjust if necessary.
5. Check the regulator no-load voltage by starting the engine, disconnecting the wire at regulator terminal "B," connecting the positive lead of a voltmeter to the terminal and the negative lead to ground. Increase engine speed to the specified rpm and check the reading against specifications. The voltage can be adjusted by bending the spring hook or turning the adjusting screw so that the point pressure is increased or decreased.

NOTE: *Increasing the pressure raises the voltage.*

Voltage Cut-Out Relay

NOTE: *Check the cut-out relay if the generator and voltage regulator relay are in good condition.*

1. Check the relay magnetic field as previously described.
2. Check and adjust yoke, core, and point gap as previously described.
3. Check the relay cut-out voltage in the same manner as the regulator relay no-load voltage. If necessary, bend the point spring hook so that the cut-out voltage meets specifications.

Full-Wave Recifier Test

An ohmmeter or continuity tester can be used to check the rectifier. The rectifier consists of a diode pack and is used to change the alternating current produced by the alternator to direct current to charge the battery. A diode will pass current in only one direction if it is

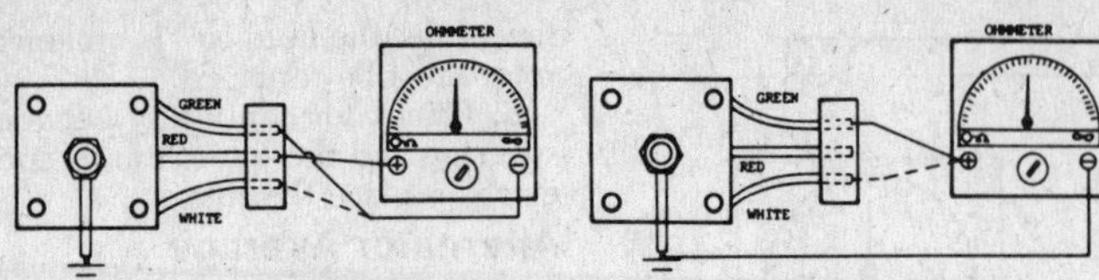

Checking the rectifier (Courtesy Yamaha Int. Corp.)

operating properly, which is the key to the following tests.

3-WIRE RECTIFIER

This type is used on the smaller alternator machines.

1. Connect the positive tester lead to the red rectifier lead and the negative tester lead to each of the other leads in turn. Check for continuity. Now reverse the tester leads and repeat the test. For each pair of leads, there should be continuity in one direction only. If there was continuity in both directions, or in neither direction, the rectifier is defective and must be replaced.
2. Repeat the test, connecting one tester lead to ground and the other to each lead in turn. Replace the rectifier if any test does not conform to the one-way continuity rule.

5-WIRE RECTIFIER

This rectifier is fitted to larger machines such as the RD250/350/400.

1. Check for continuity between each of the white leads and the red rectifier lead. Then reverse the tester leads and repeat the test. In each case there must be continuity in one direction only. If any pair of leads show continuity in both, or in neither, directions, replace the rectifier.
2. Check for continuity between each white lead and the red/white lead. Reverse the tester leads and repeat the test. The findings must conform to the one-way continuity rule as in Step 1, or replace the rectifier.
3. Check for continuity between each lead and ground. In all cases there must be continuity in one direction only.

NOTE: *"No continuity" is indicated by a resistance of about 100 or more ohms, while "continuity" means 5–40 ohms resistance, if an ohmmeter is used for these tests.*

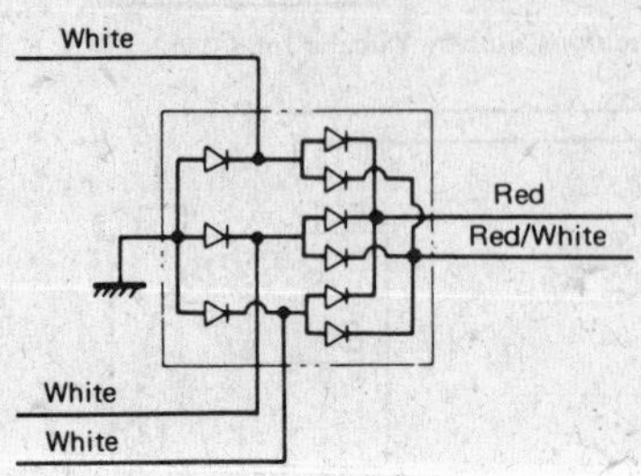

5-wire rectifier schematic (Courtesy Yamaha Int. Corp.)

Selenium Rectifier (2-Wire) Test

Connect an ohmmeter to the rectifier red and white wire leads, then reverse the meter leads. There should be continuity one way, but not the other.

See "NOTE," above.

Electric Starter Relay

If the starter motor does not function check the following:

1. Check for proper continuity in the starter relay core windings.
2. Check relay points for cleanliness.
3. When the points are closed, make sure there is continuity between the battery and motor windings.

NOTE: *The starter relay is located either on the frame, as a separate unit, or within the voltage regulator housing.*

Ignition Coil

NOTE: *Check the ignition coil if you are having spark plug firing problems and the battery, points, and condenser checked out OK.*

1. Check resistance between the positive and negative primary terminals.
2. Check continuity between one primary terminal and the high-tension secondary terminal. Compare the resistance with the specifications given.
3. Scrape some paint off the coil housing and check continuity between the primary winding and the coil housing. Resistance should read infinity.
4. Remove the plug cap and position the bare high-tension wire about ¼ in. from the cylinder head. Kick the engine over and check for a strong bright spark.

Electrical Wiring Color Codes

Chassis

Red—battery
Brown—current source wire
Dark Blue—lighting, switches
Green (in headlight shell)—low beam
Yellow (in headlight shell)—high beam
Pink—horn
Light Blue—neutral light
Yellow—stoplight switch
Green/Yellow—front stoplight switch
Blue/White—starter solenoid or light switches
Brown/White—turn signal switch
Dark Brown—left turn signal
Green—right turn signal

Magneto

Black—ignition (not ground)
Yellow—lighting
Green—daytime charging
Green/Red—nighttime charging
White—ignition switch to rectifier
White (from magneto)—no connection

Starter/Generator

Orange—ignition
Gray—ignition (twins)
Black—ground
Dark Green—fields
White—armature and charging light
Light Green—starter motor

Alternator

White (3)—AC output
Black—ground brush
Green—positive brush
Orange—ignition
Gray—ignition (twins)

Electrical Specifications

Generator and Magneto	*U5/U5L*	*U5E/U7E*	*YJ2*	*YG1 (all)*
Type	Magneto	Starter Gen.	Magneto	Magneto
Contact Press. (kg)	0.83 ± 10%	0.5–0.7	0.83 ± 10%	0.7–0.9
Condenser Cap. (μf)	0.3 ± 10%	0.22 ± 10%	0.3 ± 10%	0.27 ± 10%
Stand. Brush Dimen. (mm)	—	5 x 8 x 20	—	—
Min. Brush Length (mm)	—	11.8	—	—
Brush Spring Strength (kg)	—	0.40–0.56	—	—
Commutator Dia. (mm)	—	37.5	—	—
Commutator Wear Limit (mm)	—	2.0	—	—

Electrical Specifications (cont.)

Generator and Magneto	*U5/U5L*	*U5E/U7E*		*YJ2*	*YG1 (all)*
Stand. Mica Undercut (mm)	—	0.5–1.0		—	—
Min. Mica Undercut (mm)	—	0.2		—	—
Field Coil Resist. (ohms)	—	5.0		—	—
REGULATOR	*U5 U5L*	*U5E*	*U7E*	—	—
Model No.	—	T10-6-52	T106-52A	—	—
No Load Adj. (v @ rpm)	—	15.8–16.5 @ 2500	15.8–16.5 @ 2500	—	—
Yoke Gap (mm)	—	0.6–0.7	0.6–0.7	—	—
Core Gap (mm)	—	0.4–0.7	0.4–0.5	—	—
Point Gap (mm)	—	0.4–0.5	11.8	—	—
Coil Resistance (ohms)	—	17.0	13.0	—	—
CUT-OUT RELAY					
Cut-In Voltage	—	13 ± 0.5	0.2	—	—
Yoke Gap (mm)	—	0.2	0.8–1.0	—	—
Core Gap (mm)	—	0.8–1.0	0.6–0.8	—	—
Point Gap (mm)	—	0.6–0.8	—	—	—
IGNITION COIL					
Min. Spark Test (mm @ rpm)	6 @ 500	6 @ 100	8 @ 300	6 @ 500	6 @ 500
Sec. Wind. Resist. (ohms)	8K–9K	8K–9K	11K	8K–9K	4K
Prim. Wind. Resist. (ohms)	4.5	4.5	4.0	4.9	—
STARTER RELAY					
Core Gap (mm)	—	1.4–1.5	1.3–1.4	—	—
Point Gap (mm)	—	1.3–1.4	1.4–1.5	—	—
Wind. Resistance (ohms)	—	4.6	—	—	—
Activating Voltage (min)	—	10	12	—	—
BATTERY					
Capacity	6V-7AH	12V–5.5AH	12V–7AH	6V–4AH	6V–4AH

Generator and Magneto	*YG5S/ YG5T*	*G5S*	*G6S/G6SB/ GS7*	*RD60/A*	*HS1/HS1B*
Type	Starter Gen.	Magneto	Magneto	Magneto	Alternator
Contact Press. (kg)	0.70 ± 10%	0.70 ± 10%	0.65–0.85	0.65–0.85	0.60–0.80
Condenser Cap. (μf)	0.22 ± 10%	0.22 ± 10%	0.22	0.22	0.22
Stand. Brush Dimen. (mm)	4.5 x 8 x 20	—	—	—	—
Min. Brush Length (mm)	12.0	—	—	—	—
Brush Spring Strength (kg)	0.6 ± 15%	—	—	—	—

Generator and Magneto	YG5S YG5T	G5S	G6S/G6SB/ GS7	RD60/A	HS1/HS1B
Commutator Dia. (mm)	40.0	—	—	—	—
Commutator Wear Limit (mm)	2.0	—	—	—	—
Stand. Mica Undercut (mm)	0.5–1.0	—	—	—	—
Min. Mica Undercut (mm)	0.2	—	—	—	—
Field Coil Resist. (ohms)	6.1	—	—	—	—
REGULATOR					
Model No.	RC2332W	—	—	—	—
No Load Adj. (v @ rpm)	15.8–16.5 @ 2500	—	—	—	—
Yoke Gap (mm)	—	—	—	—	—
Core Gap (mm)	1.1–1.2	—	—	—	—
Point Gap (mm)	0.3–0.4	—	—	—	—
Coil Resistance (ohms)	18.5	—	—	—	—
CUT-OUT RELAY					
Cut-In Voltage	13 ± 0.5	—	—	—	—
Yoke Gap (mm)	—	—	—	—	—
Core Gap (mm)	0.5–0.7	—	—	—	—
Point Gap (mm)	0.6–0.8	—	—	—	—
Type	Starter Gen.	Magneto	Magneto	Magneto	Alternator
IGNITION COIL					
Min. Spark Test (mm @ rpm)	7 @ 500	7 @ 500	7 @ 500	7 @ 500	7 @ 500
Sec. Wind. Resist. (ohms)	7K–8K	5K	5.8K ± 10%	6K	5K–8K
Prim. Wind. Resist. (ohms)	0.6	0.6	0.6 ± 10%	1.7	4.2–5.2
STARTER RELAY					
Core Gap (mm)	1.2–1.4	—	—	—	—
Point Gap (mm)	1.3–1.5	—	—	—	—
Wind. Resistance (ohms)	11.2	—	—	—	—
Activating Voltage (min)	8	—	—	—	—
BATTERY					
Capacity	6V–4AH	6V–4AH	6V–4AH	6V–4AH	12V–5.5AH

Generator and Magneto	LS2	YL2	YL2/C/CM	YL1	YL1E
Type	Magneto	Generator	Starter Gen.	Generator	Starter Gen.
Contact Press. (kg)	0.5–0.7	0.7 ± 10%	0.7 ± 10%	0.5–0.7	0.5–0.7
Condenser Cap. (μf)	0.22	0.22 ± 10%	0.22 ± 10%	0.22 ± 10%	0.22 ± 10%

Generator and Magneto	*LS2*	*YL2*	*YL2/C/CM*	*YL1*	*YL1E*
Stand. Brush Dimen. (mm)	—	4.5 x 8 x 20	4.5 x 8 x 20	4.5 x 8 x 20	5 x 8 x 20
Min. Brush Length (mm)	—	12.0	12.0	12.0	11.5
Brush Spring Strength (kg)	—	0.6 ± 15%	0.6 ± 15%	0.6 ± 10%	0.40–0.56
Commutator Dia. (mm)	—	40.0	40.0	40.0	37.5
Commutator Wear Limit (mm)	—	2.0	2.5	2.0	2.0
Stand. Mica Undercut (mm)	—	0.5–1.0	0.5–1.0	0.5–0.8	0.5–1.0
Min. Mica Undercut (mm)	—	0.2	0.2	0.2	0.2
Type	Magneto	Generator	Starter Gen.	Generator	Starter Gen.
Field Coil Resist. (ohms)	—	5.2	5.2	5.2	5.2
REGULATOR					
Model No.	—	RN226J2	RC2332W	T106-01	T106-53
No Load Adj. (v @ rpm)	—	15.6–16.3 @ 2500	15.8–16.5 @ 2500	15.6–16.3 @ 2500	15.8–16.5 @ 3000
Yoke Gap (mm)	—	0.3	0.3	0.6–0.7	0.6–0.7
Core Gap (mm)	—	1.0–1.2	1.0–1.2	0.4–0.7	0.4–0.7
Point Gap (mm)	—	0.3–0.4	0.3–0.4	0.4–0.5	0.4–0.5
Coil Resistance (ohms)	—	18.5	18.5	17.0	17.0
CUT-OUT RELAY					
Cut-In Voltage	—	13 ± 0.5	13 ± 0.5	13 ± 0.5	13 ± 0.5
Yoke Gap (mm)	—	0.3	0.3	0.2	0.2
Core Gap (mm)	—	0.5–0.7	0.5–0.7	0.8–1.0	0.8–1.0
Point Gap (mm)	—	0.6–0.8	0.6–0.8	0.6–0.8	0.6–0.8
IGNITION COIL					
Min. Spark Test (mm @ rpm)	8 @ 300	6 @ 100	6 @ 100	6 @ 100	6 @ 100
Sec. Wind. Resist. (ohms)	11K	7K–8K	7K–8K	5K–6K	5K–6K
Prim. Wind. Resist. (ohms)	4.0	4.8	4.8	4.7	4.7
STARTER RELAY					
Core Gap (mm)	—	—	1.2–1.4	—	1.4–1.5
Point Gap (mm)	—	—	1.3–1.5	—	1.3–1.4
Wind. Resistance (ohms)	—	—	11	—	4.6
Activating Voltage (min)	—	—	8	—	10
BATTERY					
Capacity	12V–5.5AH	12V–5.5AH	12V–7AH	12V–5.5AH	12V–5.5AH

Yamaha Street 2-Strokes

Generator and Magneto	*YA6*	*YAS1/C AS2C*	*RD125*	*YCS1/C*	*CS3C/CS3B*	*CS5*	*RD200*	*RD200C*
Type	Starter Gen.	Alternator	Alternator	Starter Gen.	Starter Gen.	Starter Gen.	Starter Gen.	Starter Gen.
Contact Press. (kg)	0.5–0.7	0.6 ± 10%	—	0.7 ± 10%	0.7 ± 10%	0.7 ± 10%	0.7 ± 10%	0.7 ± 10%
Condenser Cap. (μf)	0.22 ± 10%	0.22 ± 10%	0.15	0.22 ± 10%	0.22 ± 10%	0.22	0.22	0.22
Stand. Brush Dimen. (mm)	4.5 x 8 x 19.5	—	—	4.5 x 8 x 20	4.5 x 8 x 20	4.5 x 8 x 20	4.5 x 8 x 21	4.5 x 8 x 21
Min. Brush Length (mm)	11.5	—	—	12.0	12.0	8.0	9.0	9.0
Brush Spring Strength (kg)	0.40–0.50	—	—	0.6 ± 15%	0.6 ± 15%	0.6 ± 15%	0.6 ± 15%	0.6 ± 15%
Commutator Dia. (mm)	37.5	—	—	40.0	40.0	40.0	38.5	38.5
Commutator Wear Limit (mm)	2.0	—	—	2.0	2.0	2.0	2.0	2.0
Stand. Mica Undercut (mm)	0.5–0.8	—	—	0.5–1.0	0.5–1.0	0.5	0.5	0.5
Min. Mica Undercut (mm)	0.2	—	—	0.2	0.2	0.2	0.2	0.2
Field Coil Resist. (ohms)	6.8	—	—	5.0	4.9	4.9	4.6	4.6
REGULATOR								
Model No.	T167-52	—	K108–12	RC2333V	T107-S5	RC2333V	T107–58	T107–58
No Load Voltage (v @ rpm)	15.8–16.2 @ 3000	—	15.8–16.5 @ 2500	15.6–16.3 @ 2500	15.6–16.3 @ 2500	15.6–17.2 @ 4000	15.8–16.5 @ 2500	15.8–16.5 @ 2500
Yoke Gap (mm)	0.6–0.7	—	0.6–0.7	0.3	0.3	1.0–1.2	0.6–0.7	0.6–0.7
Core Gap (mm)	0.4–0.5	—	0.4–0.7	1.0–1.2	1.0–1.2	—	0.4–0.7	0.4–0.7
Point Gap (mm)	0.4–0.5	—	0.4–0.5	0.3–0.4	0.3–0.4	0.3–0.4	0.4–0.5	0.4–0.5
Coil Resistance (ohms)	14.4	—	11.8	18.5	8.1 @ 20° C	8.1 @ 20° C	11.8	11.8
CUT-OUT RELAY								
Cut-In Voltage (v)	13 ± 0.5	—	12.5–13.5	13 ± 0.5	13 ± 0.5	14.0	12.5–13.5	12.5–13.5
Yoke Gap (mm)	0.6–0.7	—	—	0.3	0.3	0.3–0.5	—	—
Core Gap (mm)	—	—	0.8–1.0	0.3–0.5	0.3–0.5	—	0.8–1.0	0.8–1.0
Point Gap (mm)	0.6–0.7	—	0.6–0.8	0.7–0.9	0.7–0.9	0.7–0.9	0.6–0.8	0.6–0.8
IGNITION COIL								
Min. Spark Test (mm @ rpm)	6 @ 100	7 @ 500	6 @ 1500	6 @ 100	7 @ 500	7 @ 1500	6 @ 1500	6 @ 500
Sec. Wind. Resist. (ohms)	5.5K	6K–7K	11K	7K–8K	7.2K	11K	11K	8K
Prim. Wind. Resist. (ohms)	4.9	4.7	4.0	4.8	4.8	4.0	4.0	3.9
STARTER RELAY								
Core Gap (mm)	1.4–1.5	—	—	1.2–1.4	1.2–1.4	1.3–1.5	—	—
Point Gap (mm)	1.3–1.4	—	—	1.3–1.5	1.3–1.5	1.2–1.4	—	—
Wind. Resistance (ohms)	11.3	—	—	11.2	11.2	11.2	—	—
Activating Voltage (min)	8	—	—	8	8	12	—	—
BATTERY								
Capacity	12V–10AH	12V–5.5AH	12V–5.5AH	12V–9AH	12V–9AH	12V–9AH	12V–9AH	12V–9AH

Generator and Magneto	*YDS3/C/ YM1*	*DS6C*	*DS6B*	*DS7*	*YM2/C*
Type	Generator	Generator	Generator	Alternator	Generator
Contact Press. (kg)	0.7 ± 10%	0.7 ± 10%	0.7 ± 10%	0.7 ± 10%	0.7 ± 10%
Condenser Cap. (μf)	0.22 ± 10%	0.22 ± 10%	0.22 ± 10%	0.22	0.22 ± 10%
Stand. Brush Dimen. (mm)	5 x 9 x 17	4.5 x 8 x 20	4.5 x 8 x 20	6 x 7 x 11	4.5 x 8 x 20
Min. Brush Length (mm)	11.0	8.0	12.0	6.0	12.0
Brush Spring Strength (kg)	0.6 ± 15%	0.6	0.6	0.62	0.6
Commutator Dia. (mm)	35.0	40.0	40.0	—	40.0
Commutator Wear Limit (mm)	1.0	2.0	2.0	—	2.0
Stand. Mica Undercut (mm)	0.5–1.0	0.5–1.0	0.5–1.0	—	0.5–1.0
Min. Mica Undercut (mm)	0.2	0.2	0.2	—	0.2
Field Coil Resist. (ohms)	4.2	5.57	5.6	4.2	5.6
REGULATOR					
Model No.	RN6225K	RN2226J	RN2226J	RL215	RN2226J
No Load Adj. (v @ rpm)	7.7–8.1 @ 2500	15.6–16.3 @ 2500	15.6–16.3 @ 2500	14.0–15.5 @ 4000	15.6–16.3 @ 2500
Yoke Gap (mm)	0.3	—	—	0.7–1.2	—
Core Gap (mm)	1.1–1.4	1.0–1.2	1.0–1.2	0.8–1.1	1.0–1.2
Point Gap (mm)	0.3–0.4	0.3–0.4	0.3–0.4	0.3–0.4	0.3–0.4
Coil Resistance (ohms)	5.6	18.5	18.5	10.8	18.5
CUT-OUT RELAY					
Cut-In Voltage	6.5–7.0	13 ± 0.5	13 ± 0.5	—	13 ± 0.5
Yoke Gap (mm)	0.3	—	—	—	—
Core Gap (mm)	0.3–0.5	0.3–0.5	0.3–0.5	—	0.3–0.5
Point Gap (mm)	0.7–0.9	0.7–0.9	0.7–0.9	—	0.7–0.9
IGNITION COIL					
Min. Spark Test (mm @ rpm)	6 @ 100	7 @ 100	7 @ 700	7 @ 500	6 @ 100
Sec. Wind. Resist. (ohms)	5K–6K	8.2K	8.2K	11K	7K–8K
Prim. Wind. Resist. (ohms)	1.6	4.6	4.6	4.0	4.8
STARTER RELAY					
Core Gap (mm)	—	—	—	—	—
Point Gap (mm)	—	—	—	—	—
Wind. Resistance (ohms)	—	—	—	—	—
Activating Voltage (min)	—	—	—	—	—
BATTERY					
Capacity	6V–7AH	12V–5AH	12V–5AH	12V–5.5AH	12V–5.5AH

Generator and Magneto	YR1/YR2/C/R3/C	R5/R5B	R5C	RD250/A/B	RD350A/B	RD400
Type	Generator	Alternator	Alternator	Alternator	Alternator	Alternator
Contact Press. (kg)	0.7 ± 10%	0.6–0.8	0.65–0.75	—	—	—
Condenser Cap. (μf)	0.22 ± 10%	0.22	0.22	0.22	0.22	0.22
Stand. Brush Dimen. (mm)	4.5 x 8 x 20	11.5 x 7 x 6	11.0 x 7 x 6	11.0 x 7 x 6	11.0 x 7 x 6	11.0 x 7 x 6
Min. Brush Length (mm)	12.0	6.0	6.0	6.0	6.0	6.0
Brush Spring Strength (kg)	0.6	—	—	—	—	0.54
Commutator Dia. (mm)	40.0	—	—	—	—	—
Commutator Wear Limit (mm)	2.0	—	—	—	—	—
Stand. Mica Undercut (mm)	0.5–1.0	—	—	—	—	—
Min. Mica Undercut (mm)	0.2	—	—	—	—	—
Field Coil Resist. (ohms)	5.6	—	—	5.5②	5.5②	5.5②
REGULATOR						
Model No.	RN2226J①	—	—	—	—	RFT12M②
No Load Adj. (v @ rpm)	15.6–16.3 @ 2500	15.5–16.5 @ 2000	14.0–15.0 @ 2000	14.0–15.0 @ 2000	14.0–15.0 @ 2000	14.5
Yoke Gap (mm)	—	—	—	—	—	
Core Gap (mm)	1.0–1.2	—	—	—	—	—
Point Gap (mm)	0.3–0.4	—	—	—	—	—
Coil Resistance (ohms)	18.5	—	—	—	—	—
CUT-OUT RELAY						
Cut-In Voltage	13 ± 0.5	—	—	—	—	—
Yoke Gap (mm)	—	—	—	—	—	—
Core Gap (mm)	0.3–0.5	—	—	—	—	—
Point Gap (mm)	0.7–0.9	—	—	—	—	—
IGNITION COIL						
Min. Spark Test (mm @ rpm)	6 @ 100	7 @ 2000	7 @ 2000	7 @ 2000	7 @ 2000	6 @ 2000
Sec. Wind. Resist. (ohms)	7K–8K	11K	6.5K	—	6.6K	6.6K
Prim. Wind. Resist. (ohms)	4.8	5.0	0.9	—	1.4	1.4
STARTER RELAY						
Core Gap (mm)	—	—	—	—	—	—
Point Gap (mm)	—	—	—	—	—	—
Wind. Resistance (ohms)	—	—	—	—	—	—
Activating Voltage (min)	—	—	—	—	—	—
BATTERY						
Capacity	12V–5.5AH	12V–5.5AH	12V–5.5AH	12V–5.5AH	12V–5.5AH	12V–5.5AH

① R3—R2220J

② Stator coil: 0.46 ohms

WIRING DIAGRAMS

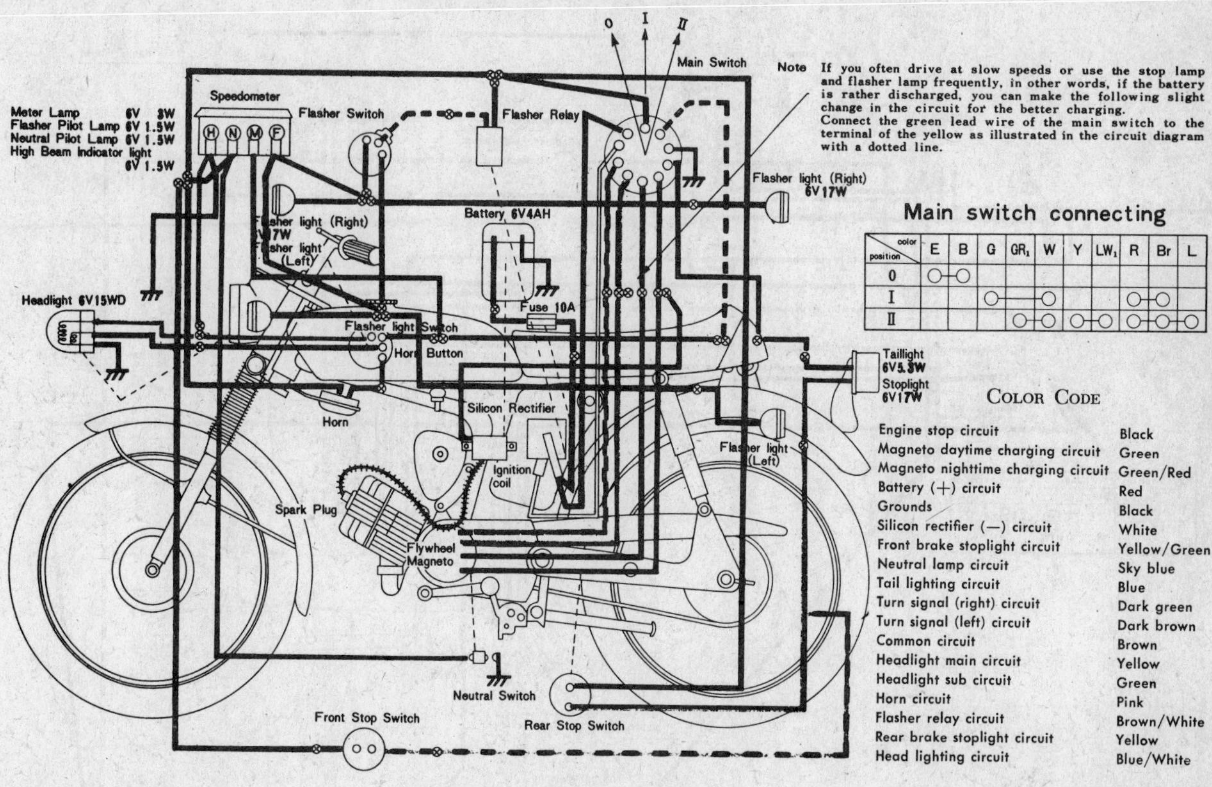

Main switch connecting

position \ color	E	B	G	GR₁	W	Y	LW₁	R	Br	L
0	○	○								
I			○	—	○			○	○	
II				○	○	○	○	○	○	○

COLOR CODE

Engine stop circuit	Black
Magneto daytime charging circuit	Green
Magneto nighttime charging circuit	Green/Red
Battery (+) circuit	Red
Grounds	Black
Silicon rectifier (—) circuit	White
Front brake stoplight circuit	Yellow/Green
Neutral lamp circuit	Sky blue
Tail lighting circuit	Blue
Turn signal (right) circuit	Dark green
Turn signal (left) circuit	Dark brown
Common circuit	Brown
Headlight main circuit	Yellow
Headlight sub circuit	Green
Horn circuit	Pink
Flasher relay circuit	Brown/White
Rear brake stoplight circuit	Yellow
Head lighting circuit	Blue/White

G5, G6/S/SB, G7S, RD60/A (Courtesy Yamaha Int. Corp.)

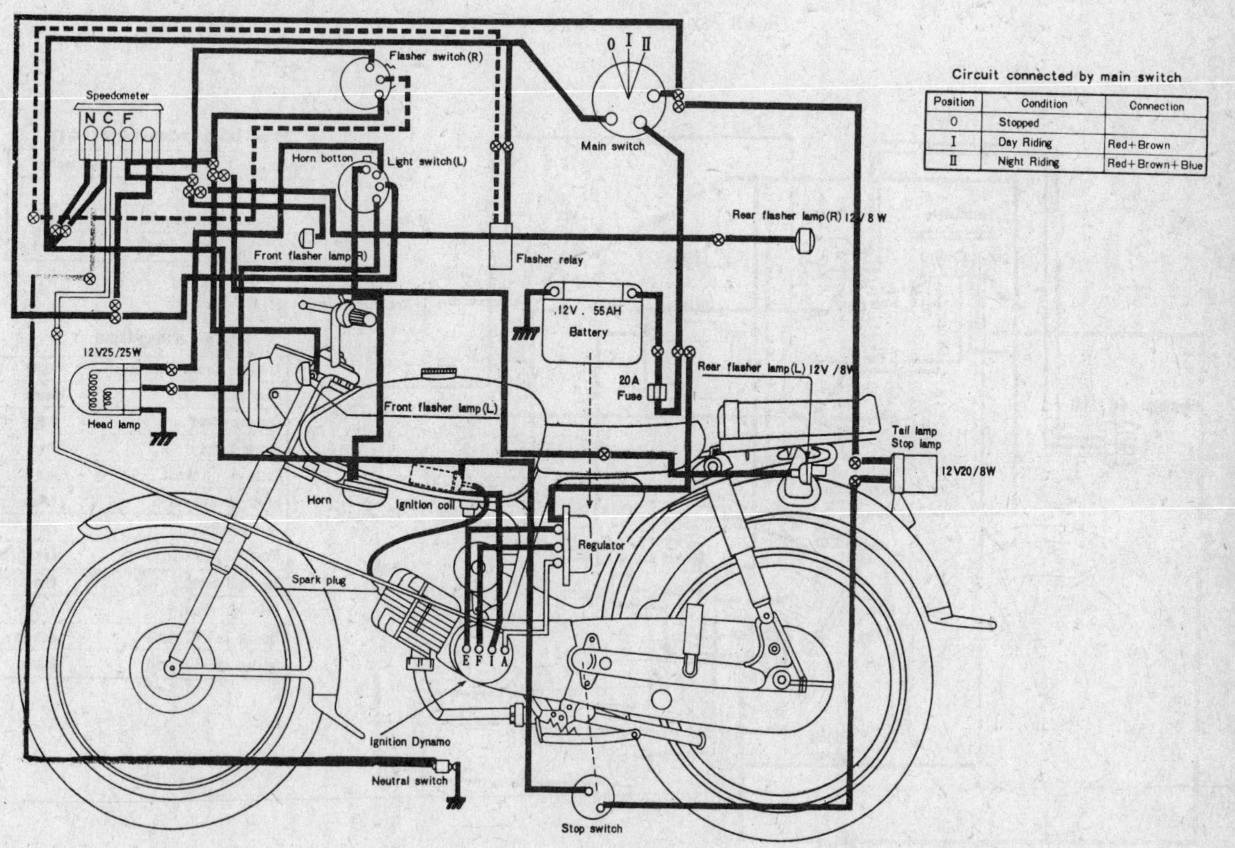

Circuit connected by main switch

Position	Condition	Connection
0	Stopped	
I	Day Riding	Red+Brown
II	Night Riding	Red+Brown+Blue

YL2, YL2C

WIRING DIAGRAMS

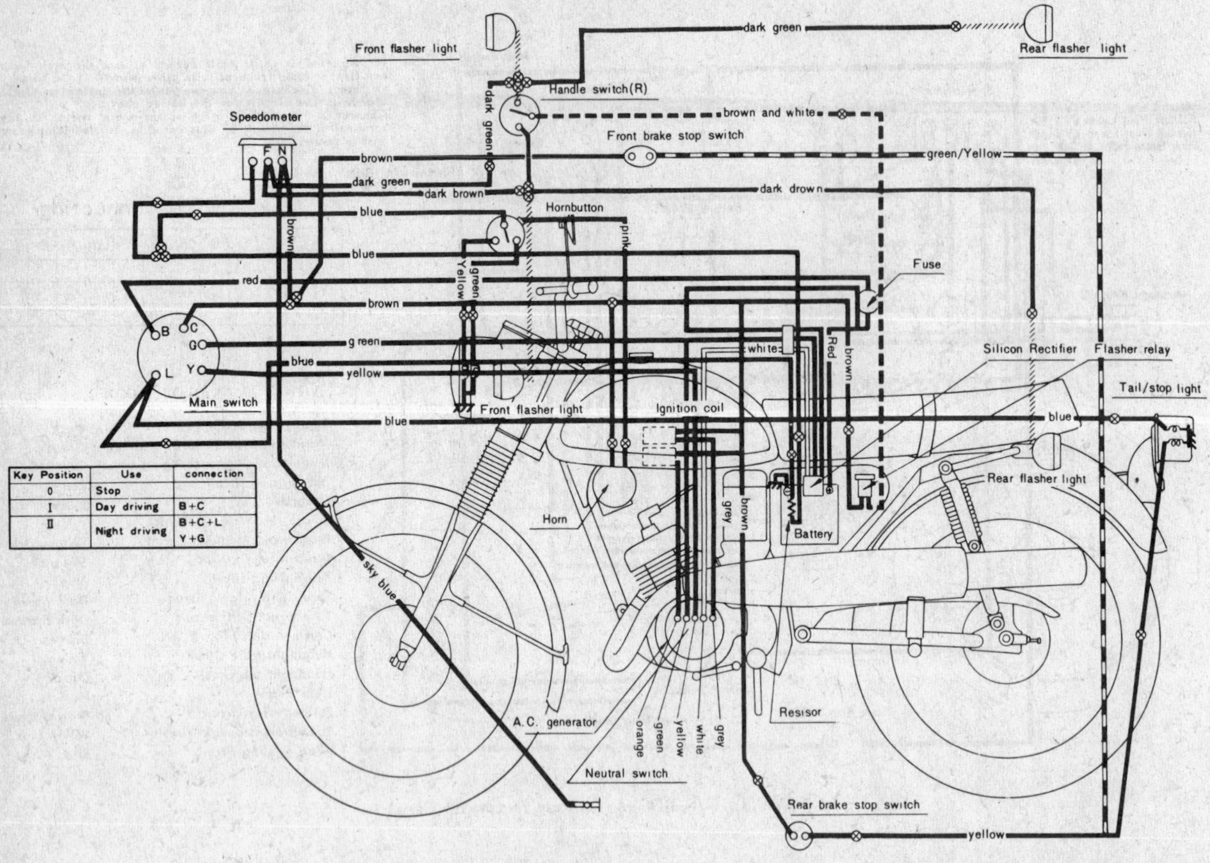

Front flasher light
dark green
Rear flasher light
Handle switch (R)
brown and white
Speedometer
Front brake stop switch
green/Yellow
brown
dark green
dark brown
dark drown
blue
Hornbutton
pink
Fuse
red
brown
Yellow
green
Main switch
white
Red
brown
Silicon Rectifier
Flasher relay
yellow
Front flasher light
Ignition coil
Tail/stop light
Rear flasher light
Horn
grey
Battery
sky blue
Resisor
A.C. generator
orange
green
yellow
white
grey
Neutral switch
Rear brake stop switch
yellow

Key Position	Use	connection
0	Stop	
I	Day driving	B+C
II	Night driving	B+C+L Y+G

HS1/B, AS2C (Courtesy Yamaha Int. Corp.)

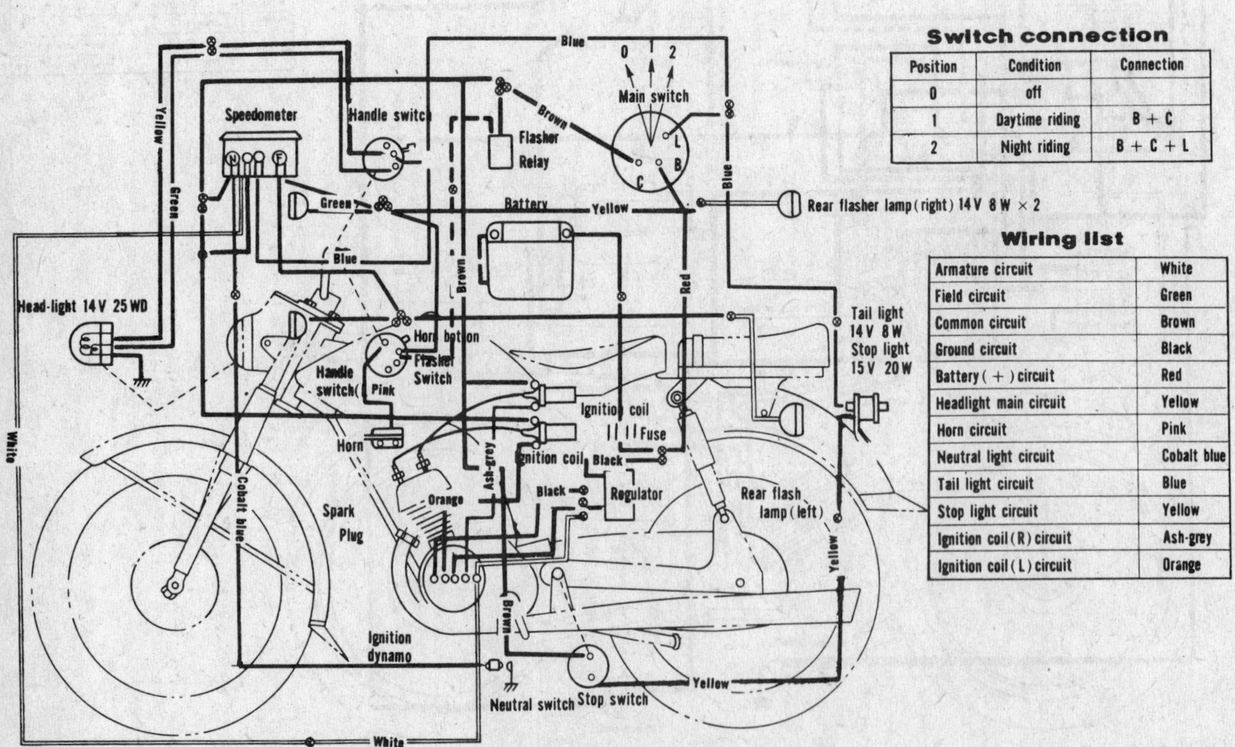

Switch connection

Position	Condition	Connection
0	off	
1	Daytime riding	B + C
2	Night riding	B + C + L

Wiring list

Armature circuit	White
Field circuit	Green
Common circuit	Brown
Ground circuit	Black
Battery (+) circuit	Red
Headlight main circuit	Yellow
Horn circuit	Pink
Neutral light circuit	Cobalt blue
Tail light circuit	Blue
Stop light circuit	Yellow
Ignition coil (R) circuit	Ash-grey
Ignition coil (L) circuit	Orange

YL1 (Courtesy Yamaha Int. Corp.)

WIRING DIAGRAMS

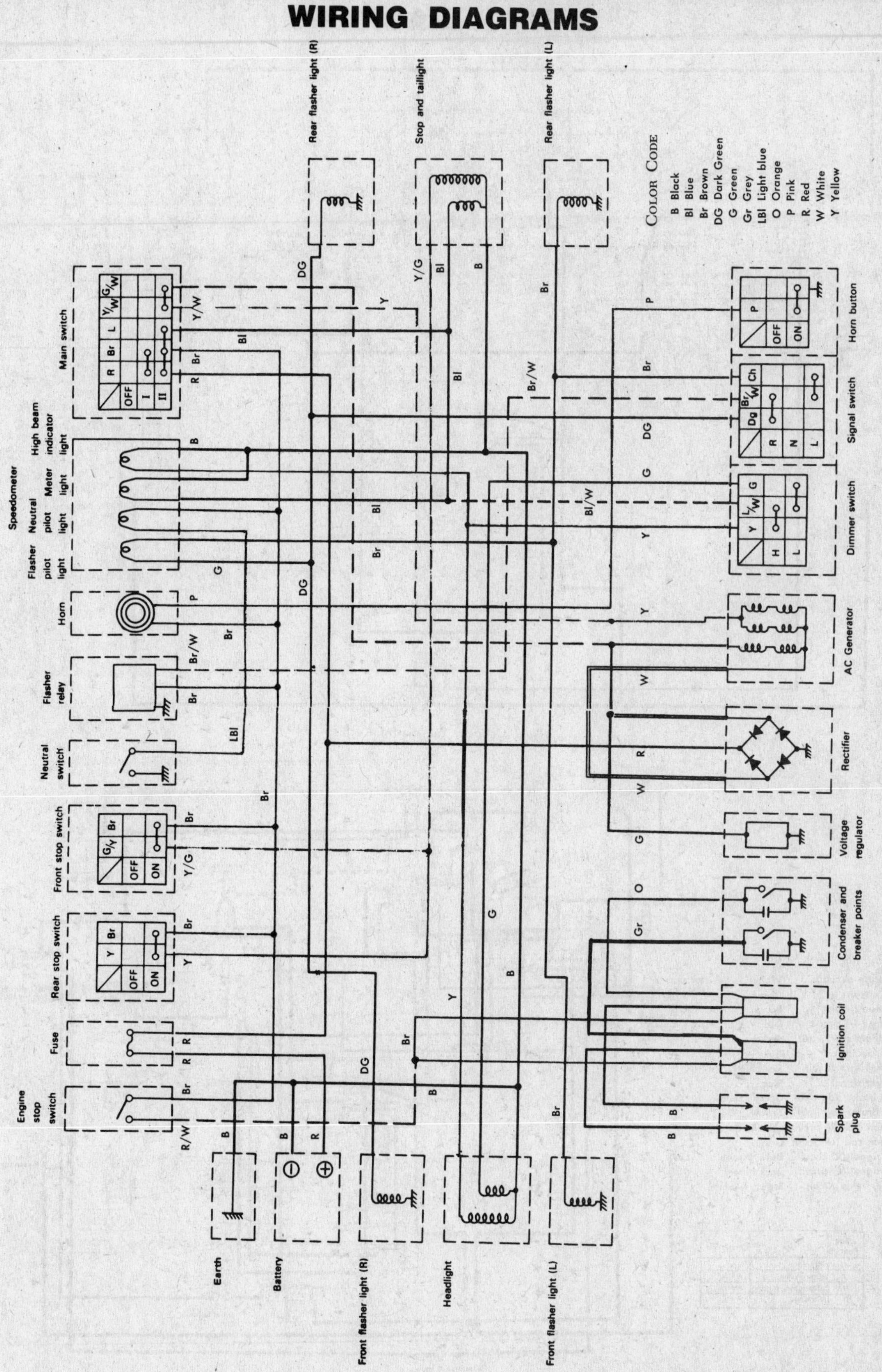

RD125 (Courtesy Yamaha Int. Corp.)

WIRING DIAGRAMS

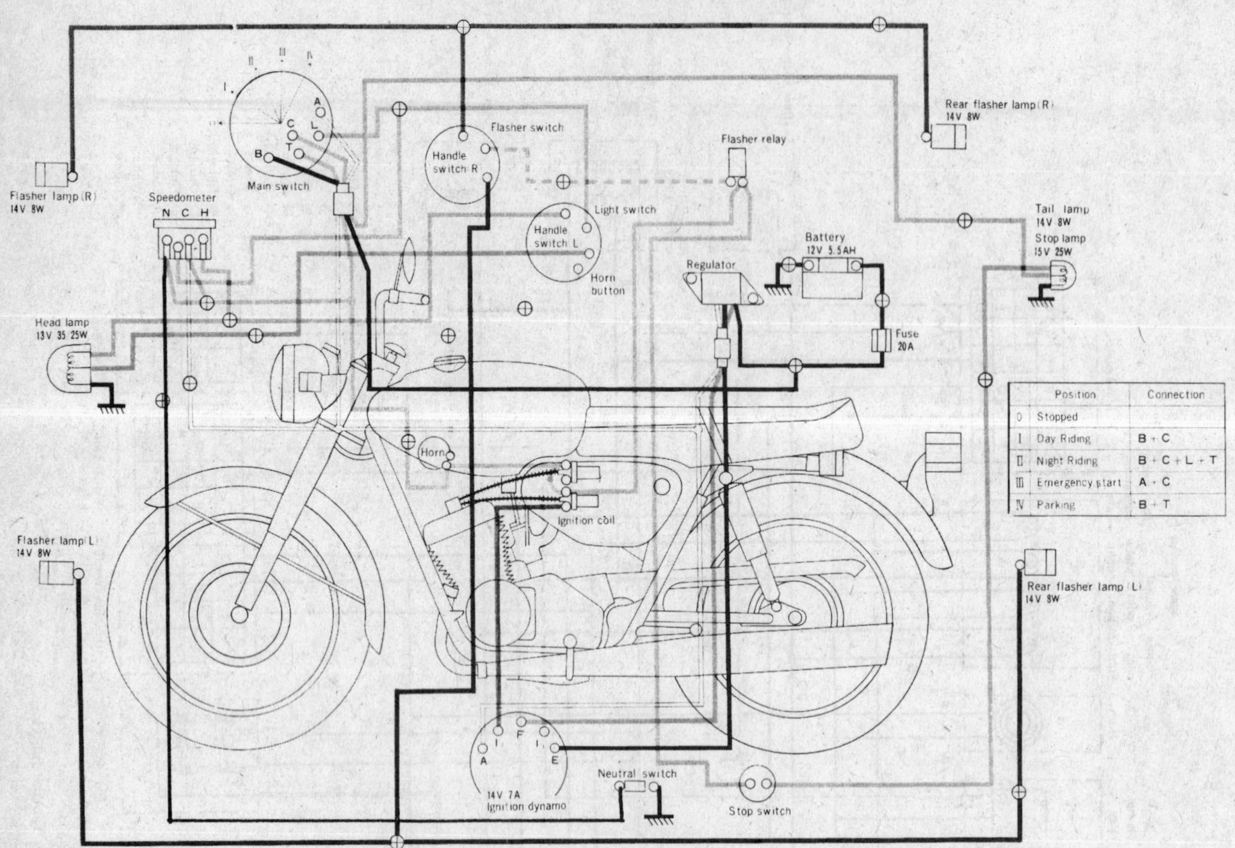

	Position	Connection
0	Stopped	
I	Day Riding	B + C
II	Night Riding	B + C + L + T
III	Emergency start	A + C
IV	Parking	B + T

YR2/C (Courtesy Yamaha Int. Corp.)

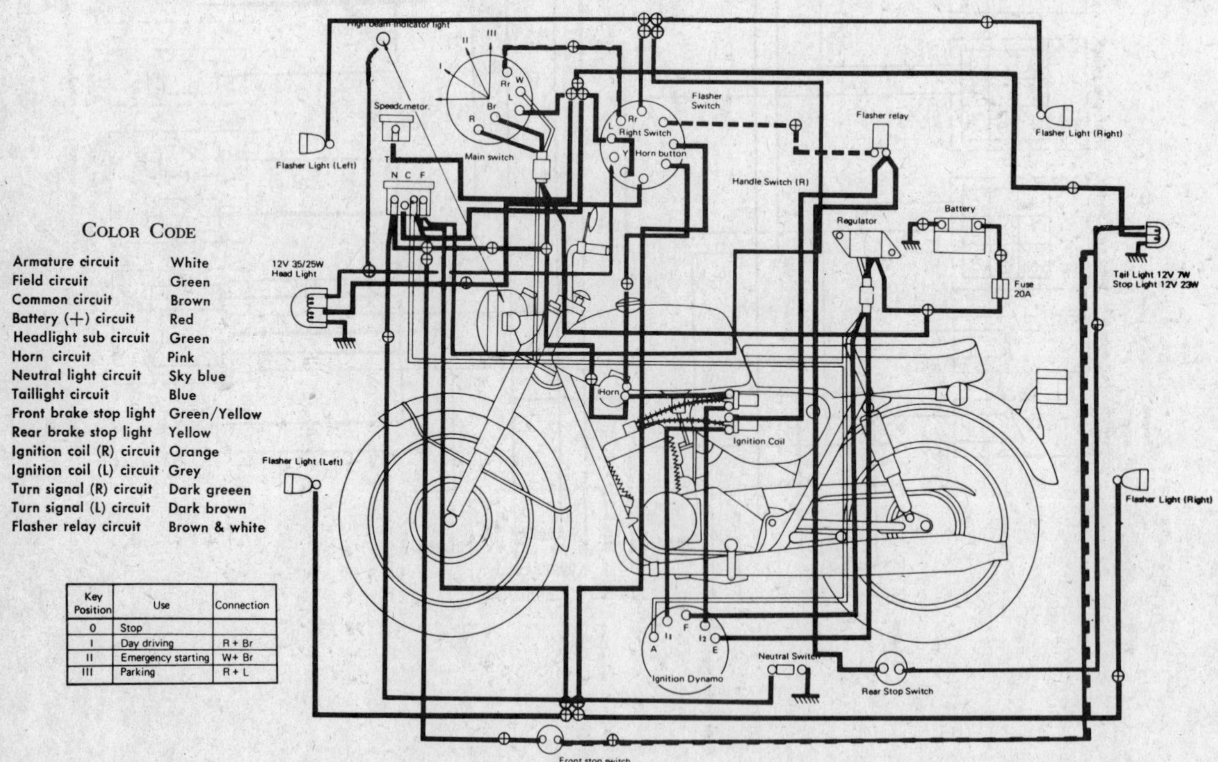

Color Code

Armature circuit	White
Field circuit	Green
Common circuit	Brown
Battery (+) circuit	Red
Headlight sub circuit	Green
Horn circuit	Pink
Neutral light circuit	Sky blue
Taillight circuit	Blue
Front brake stop light	Green/Yellow
Rear brake stop light	Yellow
Ignition coil (R) circuit	Orange
Ignition coil (L) circuit	Grey
Turn signal (R) circuit	Dark greeen
Turn signal (L) circuit	Dark brown
Flasher relay circuit	Brown & white

Key Position	Use	Connection
0	Stop	
I	Day driving	R + Br
II	Emergency starting	W + Br
III	Parking	R + L

R3 (Courtesy Yamaha Int. Corp.)

WIRING DIAGRAMS

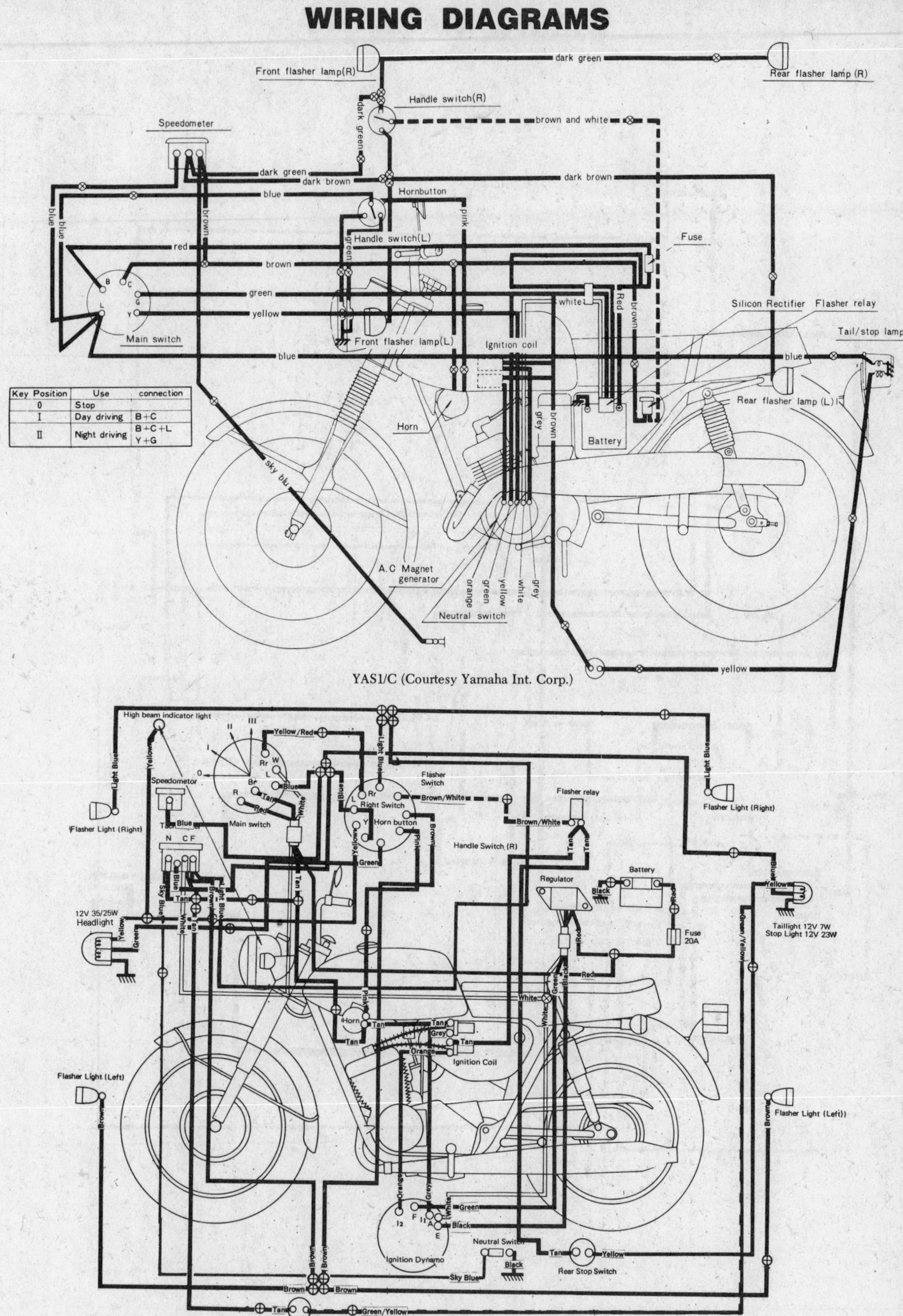

Key Position	Use	connection
0	Stop	
I	Day driving	B+C
II	Night driving	B+C+L Y+G

YAS1/C (Courtesy Yamaha Int. Corp.)

DS6/B/C (Courtesy Yamaha Int. Corp.)

WIRING DIAGRAMS

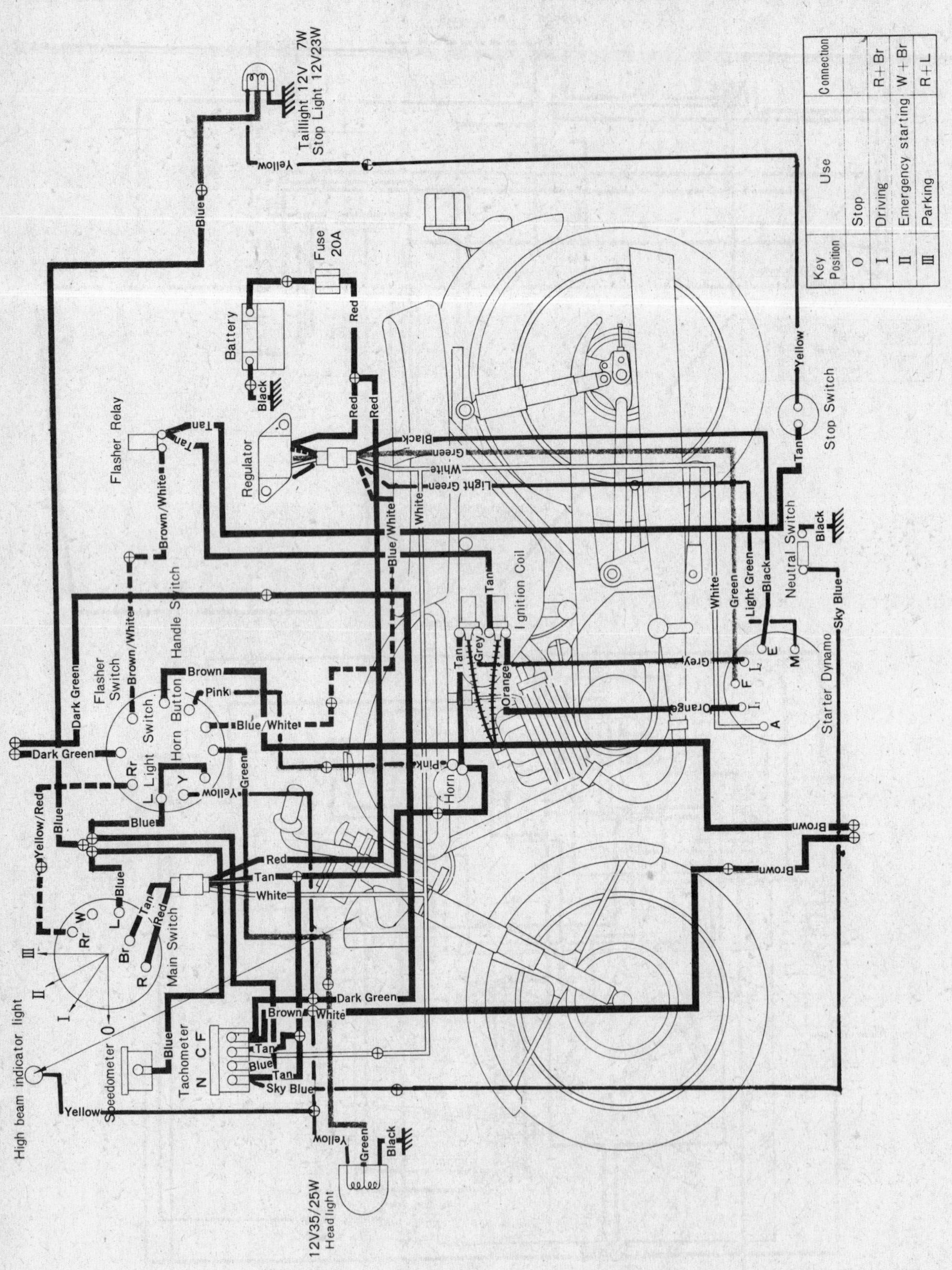

Key Position	Use	Connection
O	Stop	
I	Driving	R+Br
II	Emergency starting	W+Br
III	Parking	R+L

WIRING DIAGRAMS

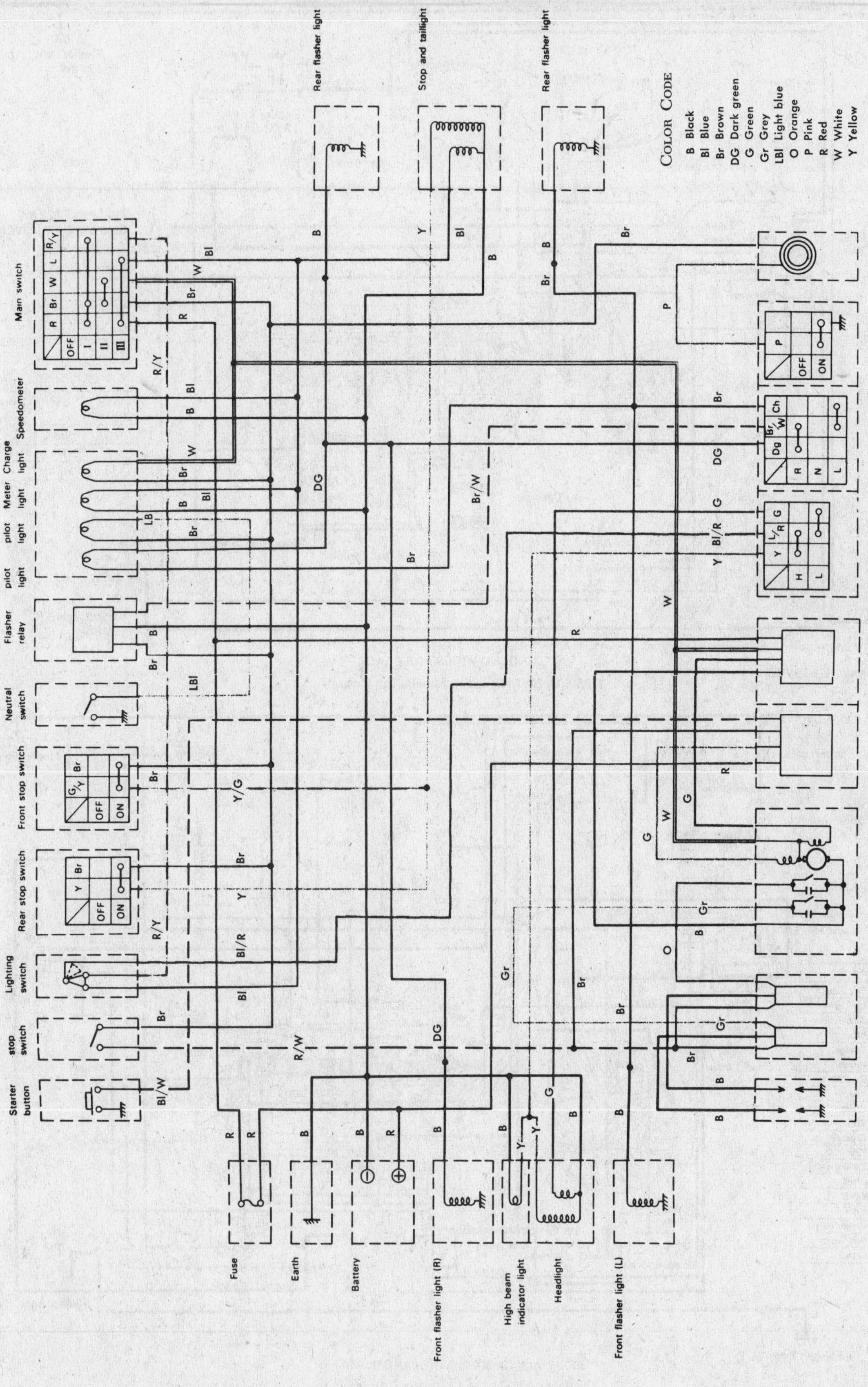

COLOR CODE

- B Black
- Bl Blue
- Br Brown
- DG Dark green
- G Green
- Gr Grey
- LBl Light blue
- O Orange
- P Pink
- R Red
- W White
- Y Yellow

RD200 (Courtesy Yamaha Int. Corp.)

WIRING DIAGRAMS

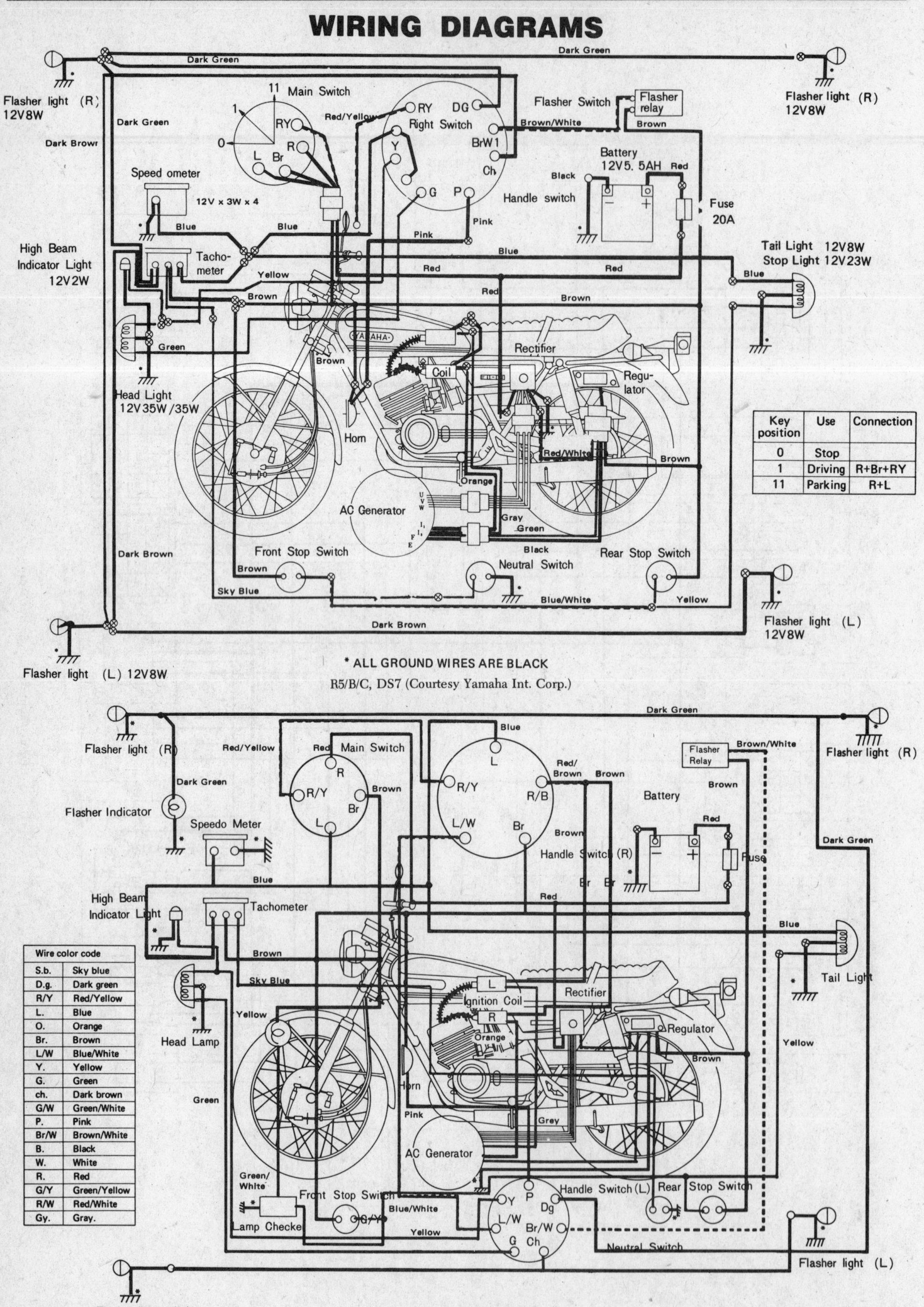

Key position	Use	Connection
0	Stop	
1	Driving	R+Br+RY
11	Parking	R+L

Wire color code	
S.b.	Sky blue
D.g.	Dark green
R/Y	Red/Yellow
L.	Blue
O.	Orange
Br.	Brown
L/W	Blue/White
Y.	Yellow
G.	Green
ch.	Dark brown
G/W	Green/White
P.	Pink
Br/W	Brown/White
B.	Black
W.	White
R.	Red
G/Y	Green/Yellow
R/W	Red/White
Gy.	Gray.

* ALL GROUND WIRES ARE BLACK

R5/B/C, DS7 (Courtesy Yamaha Int. Corp.)

* ALL GROUND WIRES ARE BLACK

RD250, 350 (Courtesy Yamaha Int. Corp.)

WIRING DIAGRAMS

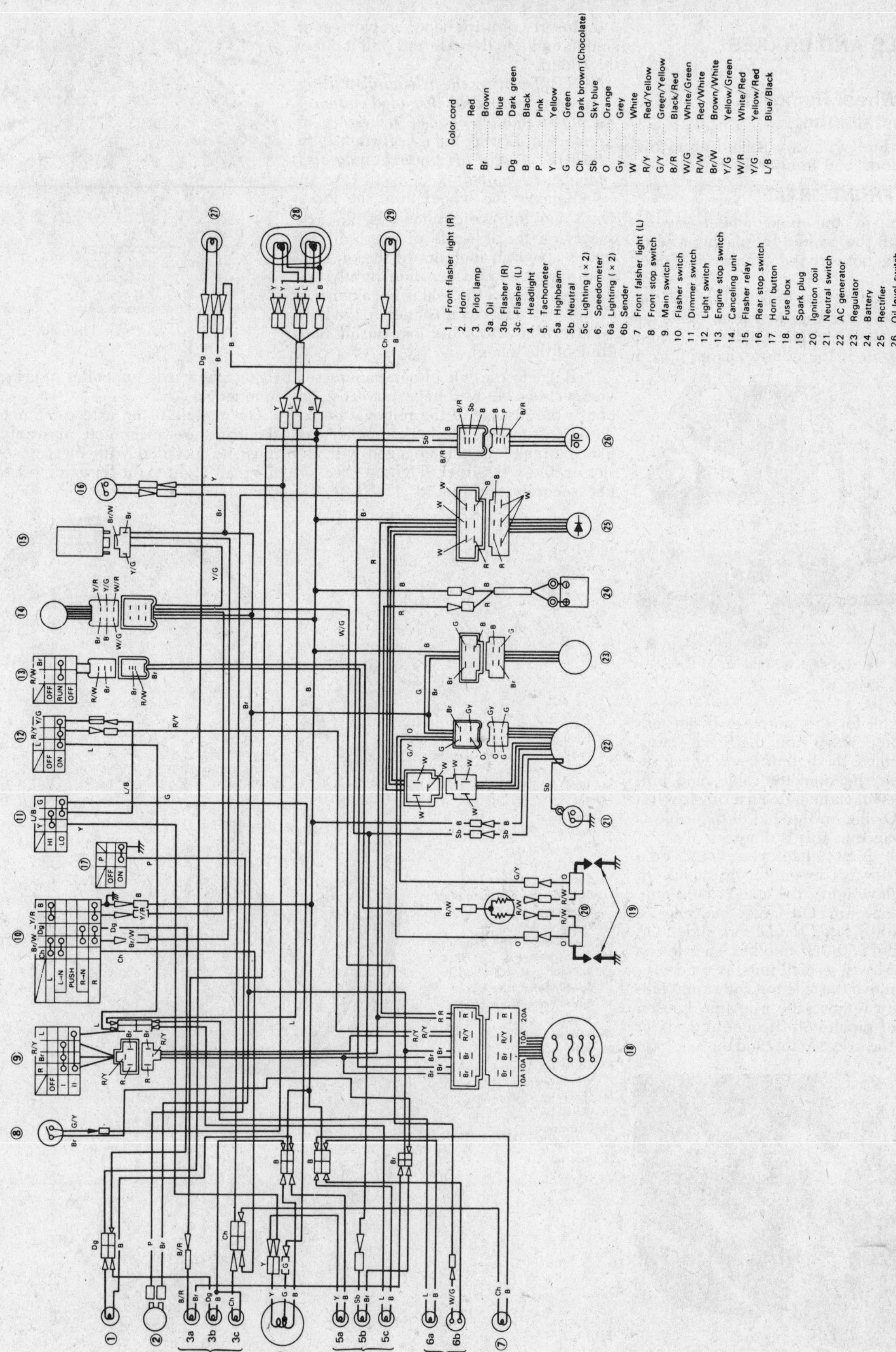
1 Front flasher light (R)
2 Horn
3 Pilot lamp
3a Oil
3b Flasher (R)
3c Flasher (L)
4 Headlight
5 Tachometer
5a Highbeam
5b Neutral
5c Lighting (×2)
6 Speedometer
6a Lighting (×2)
6b Sender
7 Front falsher light (L)
8 Front stop switch
9 Main switch
10 Flasher switch
11 Dimmer switch
12 Light switch
13 Engine stop switch
14 Canceling unit
15 Flasher relay
16 Rear stop switch
17 Horn button
18 Fuse box
19 Spark plug
20 Ignition coil
21 Neutral switch
22 AC generator
23 Regulator
24 Battery
25 Rectifier
26 Oil level switch
27 Rear flasher light (R)
28 Tail/Stoplight
29 Rear flasher light (L)
Color cord
R Red
Br Brown
L Blue
Dg Dark green
B Black
P Pink
Y Yellow
G Green
Ch Dark brown (Chocolate)
Sb Sky blue
O Orange
Gy Grey
W White
R/Y Red/Yellow
G/Y Green/Yellow
B/R Black/Red
W/G White/Green
R/W Red/White
Br/W Brown/White
Y/G Yellow/Green
W/R White/Red
Y/G Yellow/Red
L/B Blue/Black

RD400 (Courtesy Yamaha Int. Corp.)

CHASSIS

WHEELS AND BRAKES

Front Wheel Removal and Installation

Procedure will vary according to the type of forks and front brake fitted.

DRUM FRONT BRAKE

1. Support the front wheel several inches off the ground by placing a crate or the like beneath the motorcycle if necessary.
2. Disconnect the brake cable from the handlebar lever and then from the lever on the brake plate. Detach the cable from the adjuster if the adjuster is equipped

Detaching the speedometer cable from the brake plate

with a slot for this purpose. If not, unscrew the adjuster from the brake plate.

3. Remove the bolt or screw which secures the speedometer cable, and pull the cable out of the hub, ensuring that the rubber O-ring on the end of the cable is not damaged as this is done.
4. The front wheel is secured in a number of ways depending on model. On most lightweights, the axle is held only by the axle nut. On larger machines, a pinch-bolt is fitted to one fork slider. On late model 250–350 cc bikes, an axle cap (secured by two small nuts) is used.
5. Remove the axle nut cotter pin if fitted. Then remove the axle nut. Loosen the slider pinch-bolt (if so equipped), or remove the axle capnuts and the axle cap.

Loosening the slider pinch-bolt

6. Insert a phillips head screwdriver or similar tool into the axle and pull it out of the sliders.

NOTE: *Twisting the axle while pulling it out or tapping the threaded end with a plastic mallet may be necessary to remove it. Lifting the wheel slightly to take the weight off the axle may also facilitate removal.*

7. Remove the wheel from the forks. On some lightweight models, an axle spacer on the left-side of the hub protrudes about an inch out of the oil seal. This spacer should be oiled lightly and then taken out of the seal using a twisting motion. If a dust cover is fitted to the hub, remove it now to avoid loss during handling of the wheel.

Removing the wheel dust cover

8. Refer to the wheel component service sections below if necessary. Installation is the reverse of the removal procedure. Ensure that the brake anchor cast into the brake plate is engaged with the slot on the fork slider. Tighten the axle nut securely; torque to 42–50 ft lbs. Using a new axle nut cotter pin is recommended.

On models using axle caps, note that the caps are machined unevenly, and must be installed with the gap towards the rear. Tighten the forwardmost cap nut first.

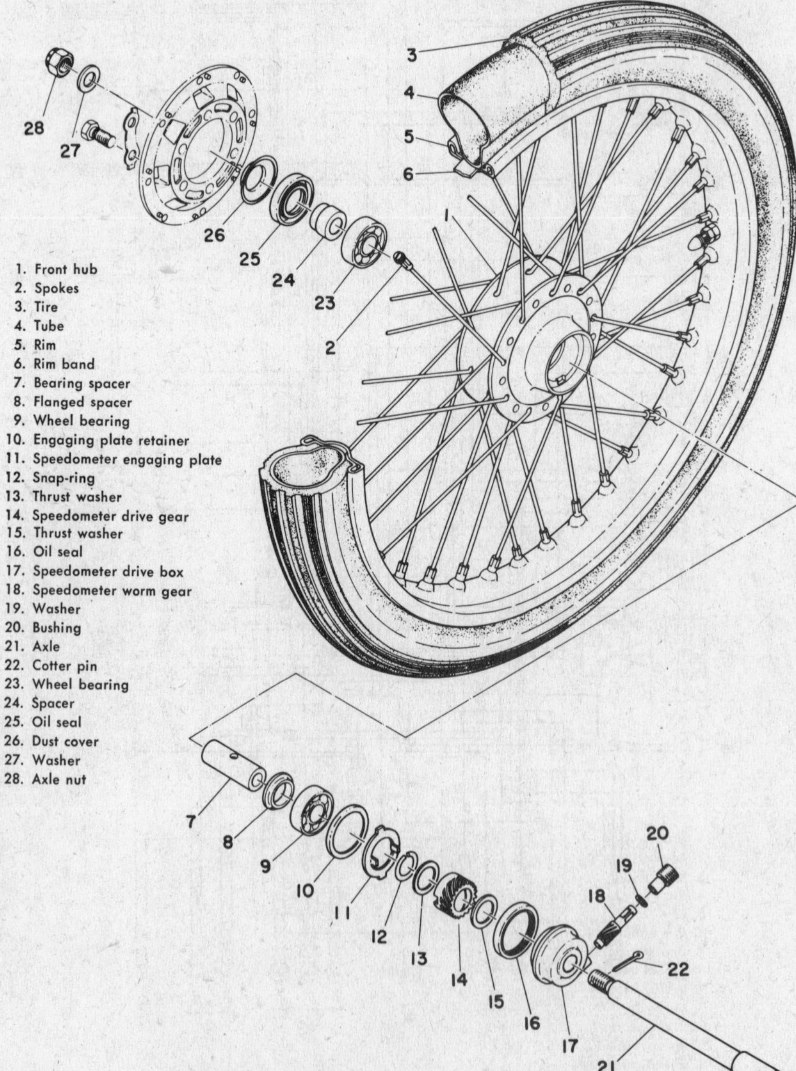

Front wheel assembly (disc brake models) (Courtesy Yamaha Int. Corp.)

DISC BRAKE

1. Support the front wheel off the ground. Unscrew the speedometer cable from the drive mechanism.
2. Remove the axle nut cotter pin and remove the axle nut.
3. Loosen the two nuts on the axle cap.

Removing the axle capnuts (Courtesy Yamaha Int. Corp.)

Install axle caps so that the gap is towards the rear. Tighten the front nut first (Courtesy Yamaha Int. Corp.)

Insert a phillips head screwdriver or similar tool into the hole in the axle and pull it out of the sliders.

NOTE: *Using a twisting motion while pulling it out or tapping the threaded end with a plastic mallet may be necessary. Lifting the wheel slightly to take the weight off the axle may also facilitate removal.*

4. Remove the wheel from the forks.
5. Installation is the reverse of the removal procedure. Slip the brake disc into the caliper carefully. Tighten the axle cap nuts securely. Position the speedometer drive mechanism so that the speedometer cable is not subjected to any kinks or sudden bends. Tighten the axle nut to 42–50 ft lbs. (RD400:60–94 ft lbs.) Using a new axle nut cotter pin is recommended. Tighten axle cap nuts to 8–13 ft lbs. Note that the axle caps are machined unevenly and *must* be installed with the gap towards the rear. Tighten the forwardmost cap nut first.

Rear Wheel Removal and Installation

DRUM BRAKE

All models are fitted with a single-leading shoe rear brake which may be either rod or cable activated. The rear wheel can be removed without disturbing the sprocket and chain. On some models it is necessary to remove the muffler(s) to allow the axle to be taken out.

1. Remove the brake anchor cotter pin. Remove the anchor nut and detach the anchor from the brake plate.
2. Unscrew and remove the brake adjuster nut. Depress the brake pedal and disconnect the brake cable or rod from the brake plate lever. On cable-operated brakes, disconnect the cable from the brake lever and the cable adjuster from the holder on the brake plate. Remove the spring and place it along with the adjuster nut and clevis pin fitting in a safe place.

Removing the brake anchor clip (Courtesy Yamaha Int. Corp.)

3. Loosen the chain adjuster locknut on each adjuster. Then back off the adjuster bolts to allow some free-play of the rear wheel.

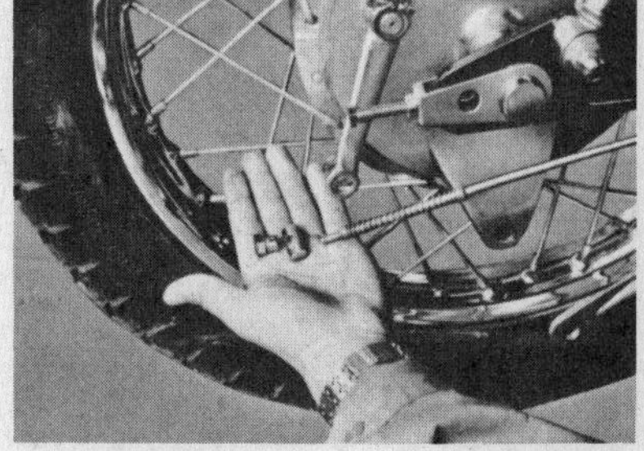

Brake rod nut and clevis pin fitting (Courtesy Yamaha Int. Corp.)

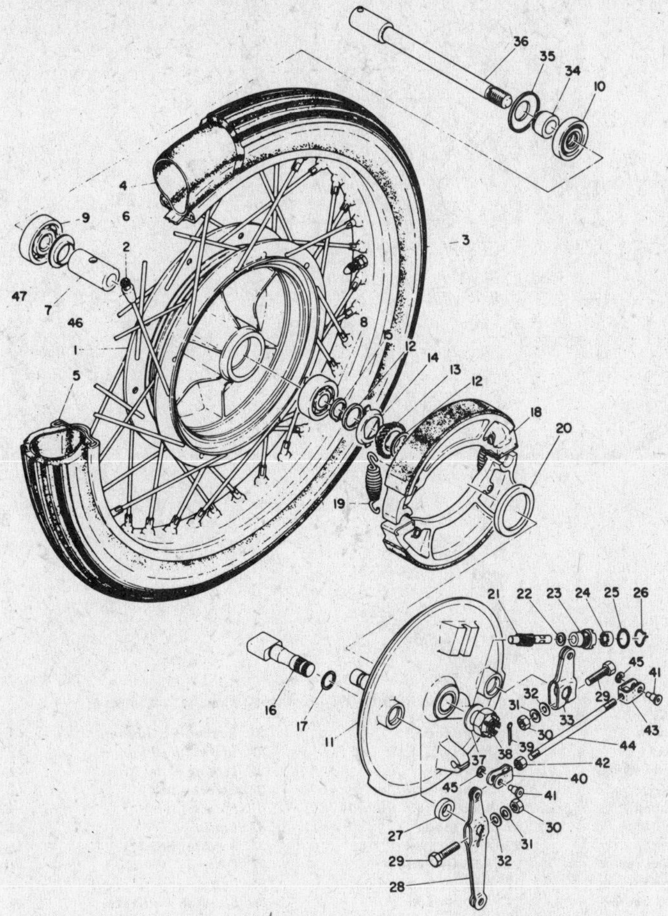

Front wheel assembly (late model twins) (Courtesy Yamaha Int. Corp.)

1. Front hub
2. Spokes
3. Tire
4. Tube
5. Rim
6. Rim band
7. Bearing spacer
8. Wheel bearing
9. Wheel bearing
10. Oil seal
11. Brake plate
12. Thrust washer
13. Speedometer drive gear
14. Engaging plate
15. Circlip
16. Brake cam
17. Shim
18. Brake shoes
19. Return spring
20. Oil seal
21. Speedometer worm gear
22. Thrust washer
23. Bushing
24. Oil seal
25. O-ring
26. Snap-ring
27. Dust seal
28. Brake lever
29. Pinch-bolt
30. Nut
31. Lockwasher
32. Washer
33. Brake lever
34. Spacer
35. Dust cover
36. Axle
37. Washer
38. Nut
39. Cotter pin
40. Connecting rod fitting
41. Pin
42. Rod locknut
43. Connecting rod fitting
44. Connecting rod
45. Circlip
46. Wheel balance weight
47. Flanged spacer

4. Remove the muffler if necessary to allow removal of the axle. Remove the axle nut cotter pin, the axle nut, and tap the axle using a plastic mallet while pulling it out with a twisting motion.

Removing the rear axle nut (Courtesy Yamaha Int. Corp.)

5. After the axle is removed, remove the axle spacer on the right-side of the wheel, and the right-side chain adjuster. Pull off the brake plate and remove it from the machine. Pull the wheel as far as possible to the right, and remove it from the machine. On some models it may be necessary to lean the motorcycle slightly to the left to remove the wheel.

6. Installation is the reverse of the removal procedure. When fitting the wheel, ensure that the driving tabs on the sprocket assembly are engaged with the slots in the hub's rubber dampers. Adjust

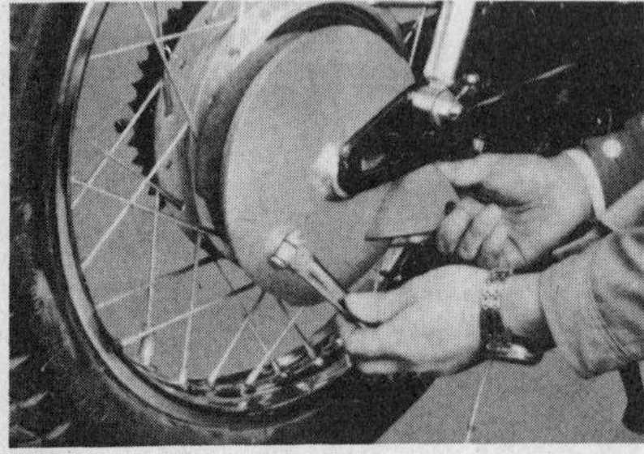

Removing the brake plate (Courtesy Yamaha Int. Corp.)

chain tension and the rear brake in that order. Tighten the axle nut securely; recommended torque is 42–50 ft lbs.

DISC BRAKE

1. With the motorcycle on the center stand, disconnect the drive chain. Remove the rear axle nut cotter pin and the axle nut.

2. Pull out the axle and remove the rear wheel.

3. Grease the oil seal lips before installation. Installation is the reverse of removal.

SPROCKET ASSEMBLY, DRUM BRAKE

The rear sprocket assembly consists of the sprocket, sprocket hub, and sprocket hub bearing. Also included are the rubber hub dampers which will remain in the wheel when it is removed.

Removal and Disassembly

1. Disconnect the drive chain. Unscrew the large sprocket hub nut and remove the assembly from the swing arm.

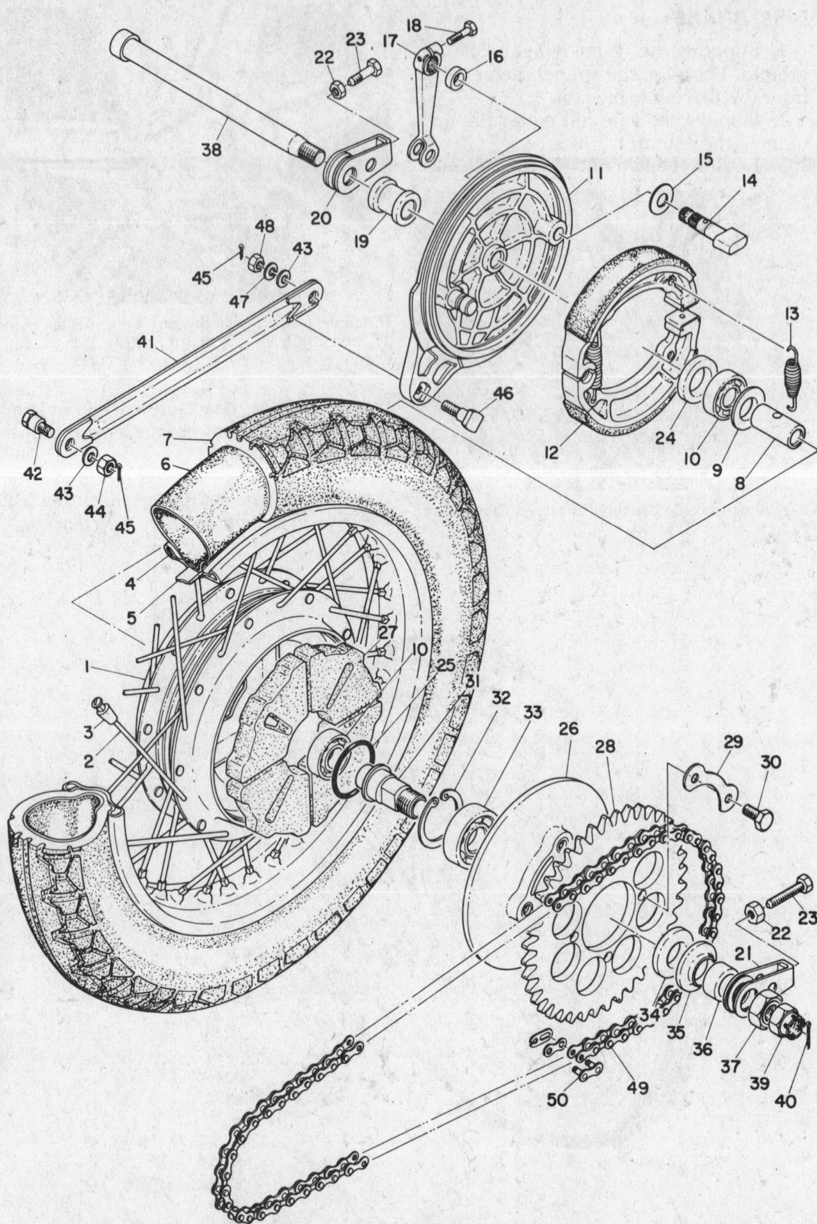

Rear wheel assembly (R3) (Courtesy Yamaha Int. Corp.)

1. Rear hub
2. Spokes
3. Balance weight
4. Rim
5. Rim band
6. Tube
7. Tire
8. Bearing spacer
9. Flanged spacer
10. Wheel bearing
11. Brake plate
12. Brake shoes
13. Return spring
14. Brake cam
15. Shim
16. Dust seal
17. Brake lever
18. Brake lever pinch-bolt
19. Axle spacer
20. Adjuster (right)
21. Adjuster (left)
22. Adjuster bolt locknut
23. Adjuster bolt
24. Oil seal
25. O-ring
26. Sprocket hub
27. Rubber hub dampers
28. Sprocket
29. Locking plate
30. Sprocket bolt
31. Sprocket shaft
32. Circlip
33. Sprocket bearing
34. Oil seal
35. Dust cover
36. Sprocket shaft collar
37. Nut
38. Axle
39. Axle nut
40. Cotter pin
41. Brake anchor
42. Bolt
43. Washer
44. Nut
45. Clip
46. Bolt
47. Lockwasher
48. Nut
49. Chain
50. Masterlink

Removing the sprocket hub nut (Courtesy Yamaha Int. Corp.)

Bending down the sprocket bolt locking tabs (Courtesy Yamaha Int. Corp.)

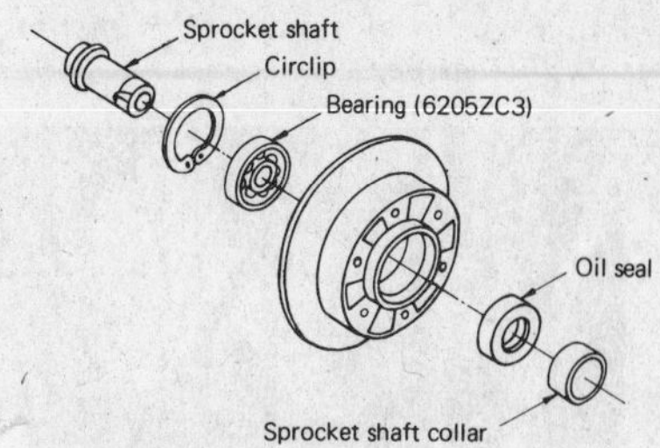

Sprocket hub assembly (DS7) (Courtesy Yamaha Int. Corp.)

2. Bend down the tabs on the sprocket bolt locking plates. Unscrew the bolts, and remove the sprocket from the hub.
3. To remove the hub bearing, first remove the sprocket shaft by tapping it out from the sprocket side of the hub. Use a plastic mallet or wood block so that the sprocket shaft threads will not be damaged when struck.
4. Take off the sprocket shaft collar by hand, then the dust seal (fitted to late models).
5. Use an elbow-shaped tool to pry out the oil seal. If the oil seal is damaged on removal, as is likely, a new one must be fitted.
6. Remove the circlip on the inside of the hub. Drive the bearing out toward the sprocket side of the hub with a suitable drift or bearing driver.

Assembly

1. Assembly is the reverse of the disassembly procedure.
2. Lubricate the bearing as described in "Wheel Bearings," below. The bearing should be driven into place with a bearing driver or a suitable substitute.
3. Grease the lips of the oil seal before installation. The seal should be pressed into the hub with care.
4. Tap the sprocket shaft into the hub from the wheel side.
5. When connecting the chain masterlink, install the spring clip facing the direction of chain rotation. Tighten the sprocket hub nut securely.

SPROCKET (DISC BRAKE)

The sprocket is removed together with the wheel.

After bending down the lockwasher tabs, remove the sprocket bolts, circlip, plate washer, and sprocket.

Assembly is the reverse of disassembly. Note that the circlip has a bevelled inside edge and must be installed so that the high point of the bevel is towards the swing arm.

Be sure the sprocket/wheel mating surface is clean. Tighten bolts in a cross pattern to 43–54 ft lbs.

Drum Brake Service

All models use a single-leading shoe rear brake, while, with the exception of the disc brake models, a single or twin-leading shoe is used on the front brake. Yamahas use brakes in which the lining is bonded to the brake shoe. Lining and shoe, therefore, are purchased and replaced as a single unit.

1. Brakes can be inspected in place on the brake plate.
2. Inspect the shoes for wear. There should be at least 0.03 in. (0.77 mm) of lining material left (measured at the lining's thinnest point) or the shoes must be replaced.
3. An alternate method of checking brake wear is to use a large vernier caliper to measure the outer diameters of the shoes as shown in the illustration. For most twins the shoes must measure at least 175 mm (6.9 in.), or they should be replaced. For single-cylinder machines, the minimum acceptable reading is 105 mm (4.1 in.). This applies to both front and rear brakes.
4. Inspect the linings for scoring or grooves. These may be caused by particles of dirt which have entered the drum. If badly scored, the shoes should be replaced. If scoring of the shoes is evident, it would be wise to inspect the brake drum for the same type of damage.

Be sure that there is no oil or grease present on the linings. Oil-impregnated linings must be replaced.

5. If the linings are usable, rough up the surface with sandpaper. Then clean the linings thoroughly with alcohol or lacquer thinner. Clean the brake drum with the same solvent.
6. To disassemble the brake plate, simply grasp each shoe and fold them towards the center of the brake plate as shown. They may be installed using the same methed.

Installing shoes onto the brake plate

7. Remove the brake springs. Remove the brake lever pinch-bolt(s) and pull the lever(s) off the splined brake camshaft(s).

NOTE: *The plurals refer to twin-leading shoe brakes.*

8. Push the brake cam(s) out of the plate from the outside using hand p sure or by tapping with a plastic mallet. Note the presence of any shims on the cam(s) and be sure they are in place when the brake plate is reassembled. Remove the dust seal(s) from the brake plate.
9. Check that the brake lever pinch-bolts are not bent.
10. Inspect the splines on the brake cam(s). These should be in good condition. Check that the brake cams are not bent and that they can rotate freely in the brake plate passage. If it will not, use a fine grade of sandpaper on the camshaft and the surface of the brake plate passage.
11. Clean the cam(s) thoroughly in a solvent to remove any old grease, rust or corrosion. Use sandpaper or emery cloth to polish the cams. Clean off any residue; before reassembly, smear the cams with chassis grease.
12. Inspect the brake plate for cracks or fractures, and replace it if necessary.
13. On twin-leading shoe brakes, the brake plate linkage should be checked. The connecting rod is secured to each brake lever by a clevis pin and circlip. These pins can be removed after the circlips are taken off. They should be checked for wear, especially on high mileage machines, and replaced if necessary.
14. Check the condition of the brake springs, noting any twisted or fatigued hooks. Replace any broken, rusted, or old springs with new ones.
15. Clean all parts thoroughly with a suitable solvent, making a special effort to remove the dust and built-up dirt from the backing plate.
16. When reassembling the hub, note the following points:
   a. Ensure that the brake cams are lubricated with chassis grease and that any shims which were on the cams are in place;
   b. The use of new dust seals is recommended;
   c. Lubricate the brake shoe pivot points with a little grease;
   d. Install the shoes as on removal. Hook them together with the springs, and fold them down over the brake cam(s) and pivot(s).

BRAKE DRUMS

1. Upon disassembly of the hub, inspect the brake drum surface for condition. The drums must be clean and free from score marks or rust.
2. Rust can be removed from the drum surface with sandpaper. Polish the surface until it is shiny, then clean it thoroughly.
3. Alcohol or lacquer thinner can be used to remove dirt or deposits from the drum.
4. The drum should be checked for concentricity. An out-of-round condition is usually noticeable as an on-off-on feel-ing when the brake is applied while riding.
5. An out-of-round condition and most scoring can be removed by having the drum turned on a lathe.

Disc Brake Service (250/350/400 cc)

When handling disc brake fluid, observe the following cautions:

   a. Brake fluid absorbs moisture very quickly, and then becomes useless. Therefore, never use fluid from an old or unsealed container;
   b. Brake fluid will quickly damage paint. Place a protective cover on the gas tank;
   c. Use only DOT #3 or DOT #4 brake fluid.

FLUSHING

The brake system should be flushed out every 8,000 miles, or once a year.

1. Attach a length of vinyl tube, about 4 mm in diameter, to the bleed screw on the brake caliper, and put the other end into a small container.
2. Remove the master cylinder cap, and the diaphragm. Loosen the bleed screw. Pull the brake lever slowly to the handgrip or pump the brake pedal (rear disc). Repeat until the master cylinder is almost empty.
3. Add new brake fluid to the master cylinder and continue squeezing and releasing the brake lever until the new fluid begins to come out of the vinyl tube. Bleed the system as outlined below.

BLEEDING

1. Needed for this operation are a torque wrench, a small cup, and a vinyl tube with an inside diameter of 4 mm.
2. Be sure that the reservoir is topped up. After checking the reservoir level, replace the diaphragm.
3. Connect the vinyl tube to the bleed screw on the caliper, making sure that it is a tight fit; then insert the other end of the tube into a small container with several inches of brake fluid in it. Be sure that the end of the tube is below the level of the fluid in the container.

Bleeding the disc brake (Courtesy Yamaha Int. Corp.)

4. Apply the brake lever *slowly* several times, then hold it ON.
5. While holding the brake lever on, loosen the bleed screw. The brake lever will be pulled toward the handgrip or brake pedal will be pushed down (rear disc). Close the bleed screw BEFORE the lever bottoms out on the handgrip.
6. Repeat the procedure until the fluid issuing from the lower end of the tube is completely free of air bubbles.

   NOTE: *During the operation, keep a check on the reservoir fluid level, maintaining it near its normal position.*
7. Tighten the bleed screw to 4.5–6.7 ft lbs.
8. Top up the reservoir to the level line.

PAD REPLACEMENT

1. Pads must be removed to check for wear except on late models with wear indicators on the pads. Remove the front wheel and use a screwdriver to pry out each pad as shown. On newer models, the wear indicator obviates the need to pry out the pads.

Removing the brake pads from the caliper (Courtesy Yamaha Int. Corp.)

Removing brake pads on machines with wear indicators (Courtesy Yamaha Int. Corp.)

2. Minimum allowable pad thickness is shown in the accompanying illustration. This should be measured with an accurate instrument, and the pads replaced when thickness falls below 0.5 mm (0.0196 in.) or 4.5 mm (0.177 in.) depending on where the measurement is taken.

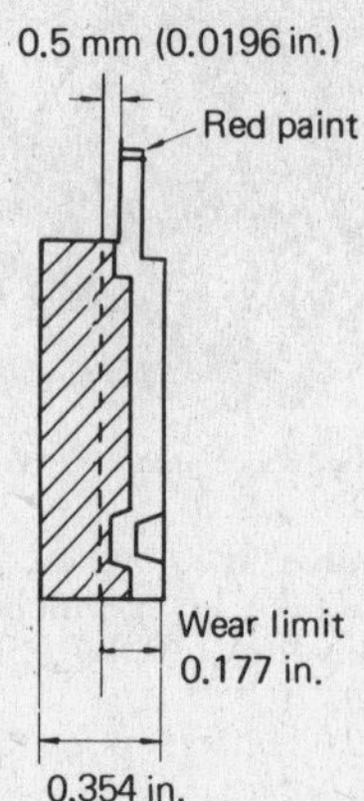

Brake pad wear limits (Courtesy Yamaha Int. Corp.)

3. Nominal thickness of new pads is 9.0 mm (0.354 in.).
4. Note that fitting new pads in place of a pair which were considerably worn will result in a rise in the reservoir fluid level. If it gets too high, drain off any excess fluid via the caliper bleed screw.
5. After installing new pads, avoid hard application of the brake for at least 50 miles.

CALIPER (FRONT)

Removal and Disassembly

NOTE: *A compressed air supply will be necessary to remove the pistons from the caliper.*

Disconnecting the brake line from the caliper (Courtesy Yamaha Int. Corp.)

1. Use a length of tape to hold the brake lever in the "on" position.
2. Disconnect the brake line from the caliper. Cover the end of the line with a small plastic bag, which will keep out dirt or foreign matter.
3. Unbolt the caliper, lift it up, and remove it from the slider.

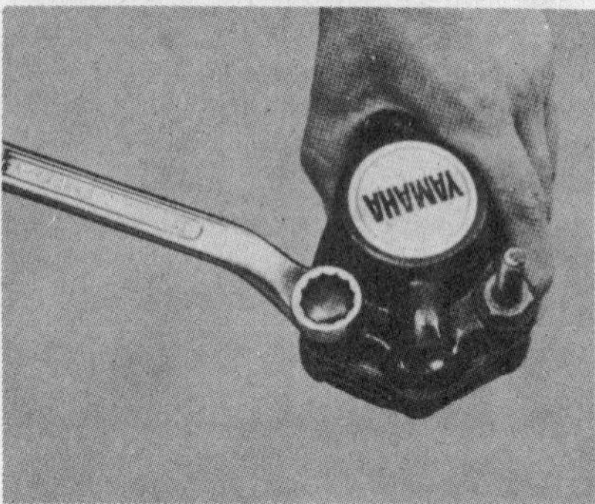

Removing the caliper bolts (Courtesy Yamaha Int. Corp.)

4. Remove the pads. Remove the bridge bolts and the hex-head caliper bolts, and separate the caliper halves.
5. Remove the seal from the fluid passage.

Removing the fluid passage seal (Courtesy Yamaha Int. Corp.)

6. Apply compressed air to the fluid passage in each caliper half to force out the pistons.

   NOTE: *This is the only recommended method of removing the pistons.*
7. Remove the piston seal and the dust seal from each caliper half.

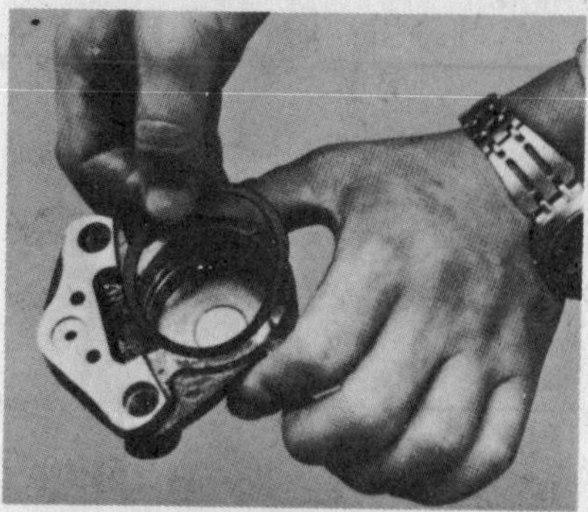

Removing the dust seal from the caliper (Courtesy Yamaha Int. Corp.)

Inspection

NOTE: *Caliper components should be kept free of any solvent. Parts should be cleaned only in brake fluid.*

1. Check the pads for scoring and replace them if scored. Check pad thickness as directed above.
2. Inspect the pistons for scoring along the sides or for other signs of wear. Replace as necessary.
3. Replace any damaged seal in the unit. All seals should be replaced every two years regardless of appearance.
4. The two bridge bolts *must* be replaced each time they are removed.

Assembly and Installation

1. Clean all parts in new brake fluid.
2. Install the dust seal and piston seal in the caliper halves.
3. Coat the caliper cylinder walls and the pistons with new brake fluid, and then carefully insert each piston into its own caliper half.

 Be sure that the piston goes in smoothly.
4. Install the caliper seals.
5. Fit the two caliper halves together, and replace the two hex-head bolts and tighten them to 13–19 ft lbs.
6. Install new bridge bolts and tighten them to 56–71 ft lbs.
7. Install the pads. It will be necessary to push the pistons back by hand when installing the pads.
8. Replace the caliper on the fork slider, tightening the nuts to 30–37.2 ft lbs.
9. Refit the brake line to the caliper and tighten it to 10–13.4 ft lbs.

CALIPER (REAR)

Removal

1. Disconnect the brake line at the caliper. Wrap the banjo with a cloth or plastic bag to prevent fluid loss.
2. Remove the caliper mounting bolts and take off the caliper.
3. For service, refer to "Caliper (Front)". The units are virtually identical.

Installation

1. Tighten mounting bolts to 22–35 ft lbs.
2. Tighten brake line-to-caliper bolt to 22–35 ft lbs.

BRAKE DISC

1. Check the disc for run-out by securing a dial gauge to the fork slider. If run-out is 0.15 mm or more, remove the disc and check for warpage. If the disc is not warped, suspect the wheel bearings.
2. Measure the thickness of the disc. Minimum allowable thickness is 6.5 mm.
3. To remove the disc, remove the front wheel, bend down the locking tabs on the disc securing bolts, and remove the bolts.
4. When installing the disc, care should be taken to tighten the bolts evenly and gradually until the proper torque (250/350: 5.7–7.2 ft lbs; 400: 12.3–16.0 ft lbs) is reached. Ensure that the locking tabs are bent up against the flats on the disc bolts.

MASTER CYLINDER (FRONT)

Removal and Disassembly

CAUTION: *A special guide is needed to install the piston cylinder cup once it has been removed. Do not disassemble the piston unless this guide is available.*

1. Remove the brake light switch at the master cylinder, and remove the brake lever, watching for the return spring.

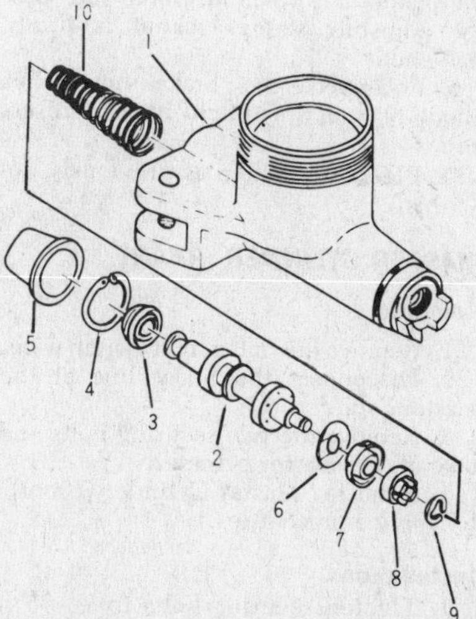

Master cylinder (Courtesy Yamaha Int. Corp.)

1. Master cylinder body
2. Piston
3. Cup
4. Circlip
5. Boot
6. Spacer
7. Cup
8. Retainer
9. Clip
10. Spring

2. Disconnect the brake hose at the master cylinder.
3. Remove the master cylinder mounting bolts, and remove the assembly from the handlebar.
4. Remove the reservoir cap, take out the diaphragm, and drain off the fluid.
5. Remove the boot.
6. Remove the snap-ring with a pair of snap-ring pliers.
7. Take out the piston. Take out the spring behind the piston.
8. Remove the circlip from the piston assembly, and take off the cylinder cup retainer, then the cylinder cup.

Removing the master cylinder boot (Courtesy Yamaha Int. Corp.)

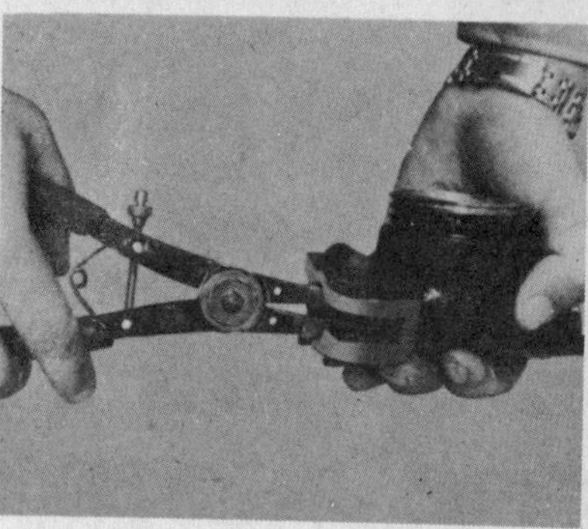

Removing the snap-ring (Courtesy Yamaha Int. Corp.)

Inspection

1. Wash all parts in new brake fluid only.

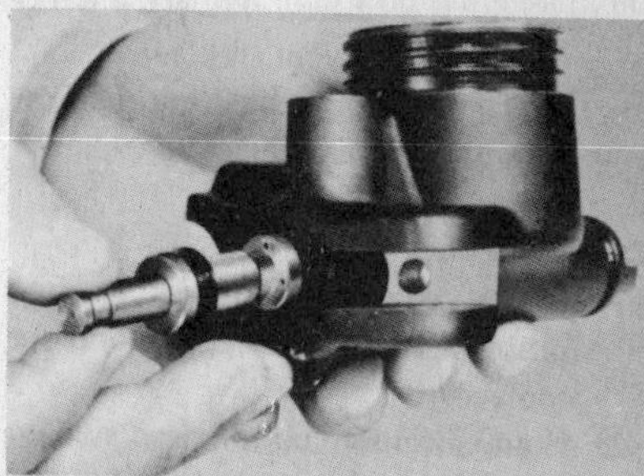

Removing the piston assembly (Courtesy Yamaha Int. Corp.)

2. Check the master cylinder port for clogging due to foreign matter.
3. Be sure that the reservoir is clean.
4. Check the walls of the master cylinder for grooves or score marks.
5. Check the outlet end for dents or other damage.

Piston cup spacer (1) and spring (2) (Courtesy Yamaha Int. Corp.)

In the event of any permanent damage, replace the master cylinder body.

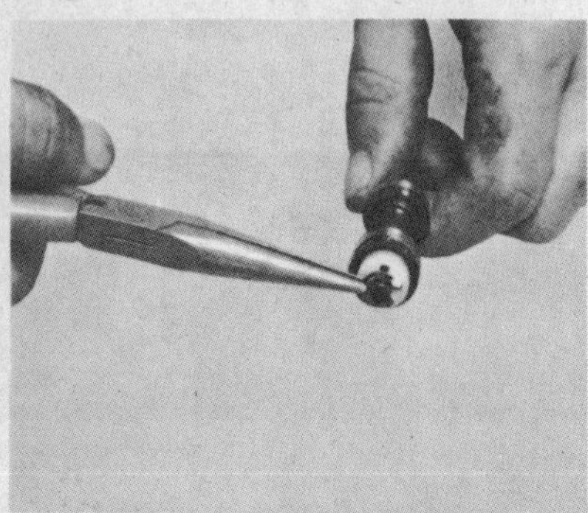

Removing the piston circlip (Courtesy Yamaha Int. Corp.)

6. Check the piston for wear or rust and replace as necessary.

7. Check the condition of the cylinder cup noting any evidence of groove wear on the contact surface. Replace if any is evident.

8. Check all rubber parts for wear damage, or swelling. Replace as necessary. Note that all rubber parts should be replaced every two years regardless of appearance.

9. Check the reservoir diaphragm for cracks or damage to the edges and the accordion pleats. Check the diaphragm and the boot for swelling.

These components should be replaced if damaged or worn, and replaced every two years regardless of appearance.

10. The master cylinder spring minimum length is 60.4 mm. Replace it if it is shorter than this or if it shows signs of damage.

11. Check the brake hose and line for cracks or seepage. The brake hose should be replaced every four years regardless of condition.

12. When installing the hose and line, note that they should not contact the forks or frame at any point except where attachment clips are fitted.

Assembly and Installation

1. Dip the cylinder cup in new brake fluid, and, using the special guide, install the cup on the piston.

2. Install the spacer. Note the correct position. Fit the cup retainer and circlip.

3. Fit the conical spring into the master cylinder body. Then carefully insert the piston assembly into the cylinder. Do not force the piston in.

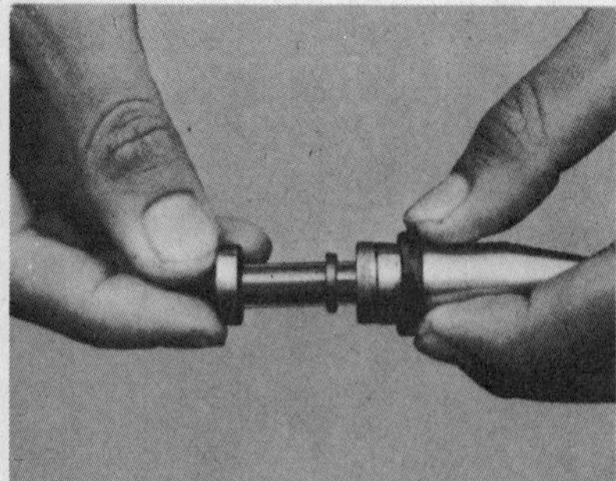

Fitting the cylinder cup (Courtesy Yamaha Int. Corp.)

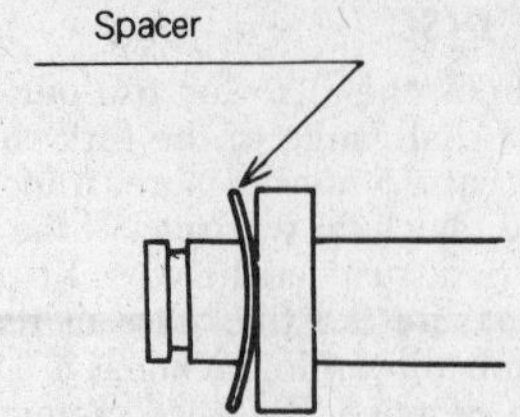

Correct spacer installation (Courtesy Yamaha Int. Corp.)

4. Install the snap-ring. Refit the boot, being sure that it is correctly installed in the cylinder and piston grooves.

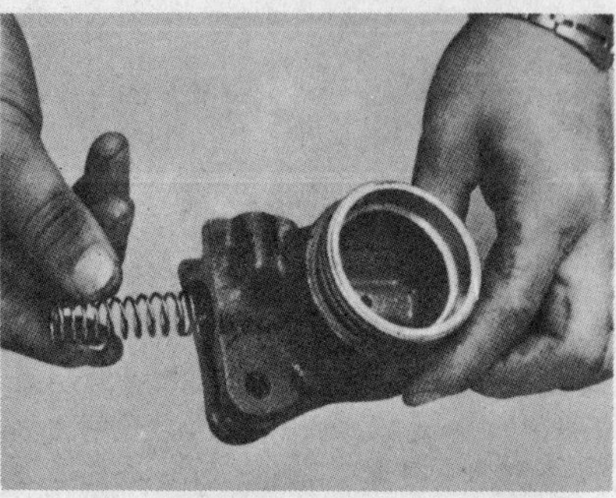

Fitting the spring (Courtesy Yamaha Int. Corp.)

5. Install the master cylinder on the handlebar. Adjust the clearance between the piston and pushrod. Make sure that the adjusting screw locknut is firmly tightened.

6. Reconnect the brake hose. Put about 30 cc of brake fluid into the reservoir.

7. Bleed the system as previously described.

MASTER CYLINDER (REAR)

Removal

1. Remove the brake light switch wire.

2. Disconnect the brake line at the master cylinder.

3. Remove the two securing bolts and take off the master cylinder.

4. Refer to "Master Cylinder (Front)" for service procedures.

Installation

1. Tighten securing bolts to 22–35 ft lbs.

Disc Brake Service (RD200C)

The RD200C is fitted with a front disc brake slightly different in construction from that used on 250/350/400cc machines.

Observe precautions outlined at the beginning of the 250/350/400 disc brake section.

Flushing and Bleeding procedures are the same as outlined for the larger machines.

Use DOT #3 or #4 brake fluid.

PAD REPLACEMENT

1. Remove the front wheel.

2. Remove the phillips screw from the wheel side of the caliper, taking out the metal pad support and the outer pad. Remove the inner pad.

Remove the screw to remove the pad (RD200C) (Courtesy Yamaha Int. Corp.)

Pads removed (RD200C) (Courtesy Yamaha Int. Corp.)

3. Check pad thickness. Standard thickness is 15 mm (0.6 in.) for the inner pad and 12 mm (0.48 in.) for the outer.

Replacement limit is 11 mm (0.44 in.) inner, and 7.5 mm (0.3 in.) outer.

4. Smear the sides of the pads with a light coat of silicon grease before installation.

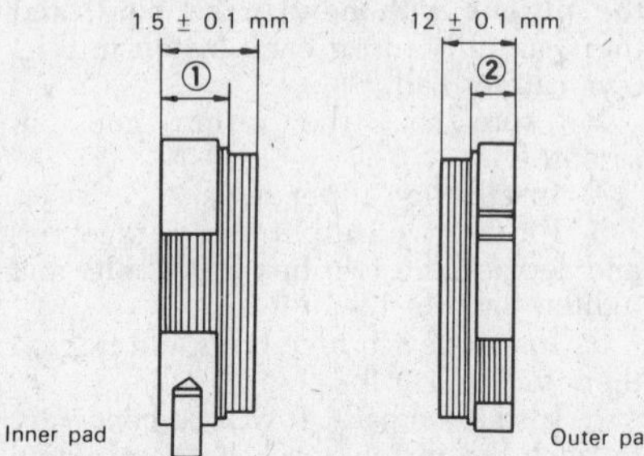

Brake pad dimensions (Courtesy Yamaha Int. Corp.)

CALIPER

The caliper is a one-piece type.

Removal and Disassembly

1. Remove the front wheel. Remove the brake pads.

2. Disconnect the brake line at the caliper, blocking the end of the line to prevent fluid loss.

NOTE: *Apply the brake lever, keeping it on with tape or the like to prevent fluid leakage from the master cylinder.*

3. Unbolt and remove the caliper.

4. Remove the rubber boot retaining ring from the caliper. Remove the boot.

5. Remove the blind plugs from the wheel side of the caliper. Remove the circlips revealed by plug removal.

6. Screw a 5 mm screw into the pins and pull them out. Remove the caliper bracket.

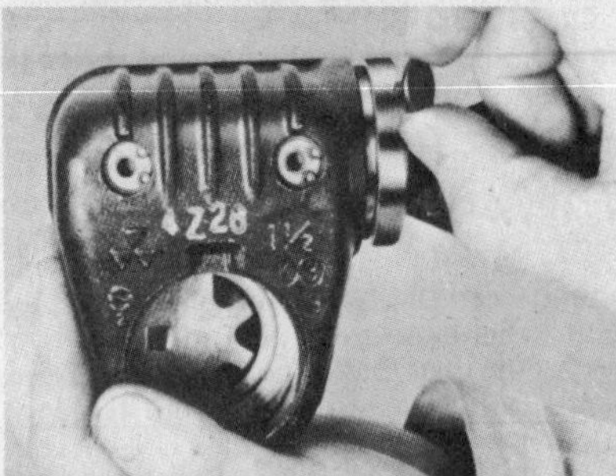
Removing the blind plugs (Courtesy Yamaha Int. Corp.)

Removing the circlips (Courtesy Yamaha Int. Corp.)

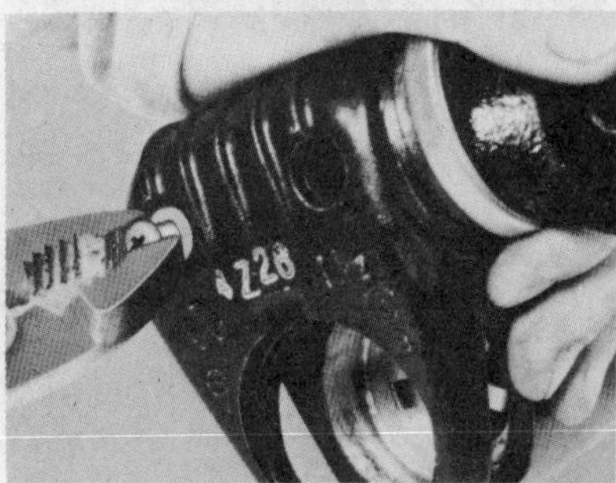
Using a 5 mm screw to pull out the caliper pins (Courtesy Yamaha Int. Corp.)

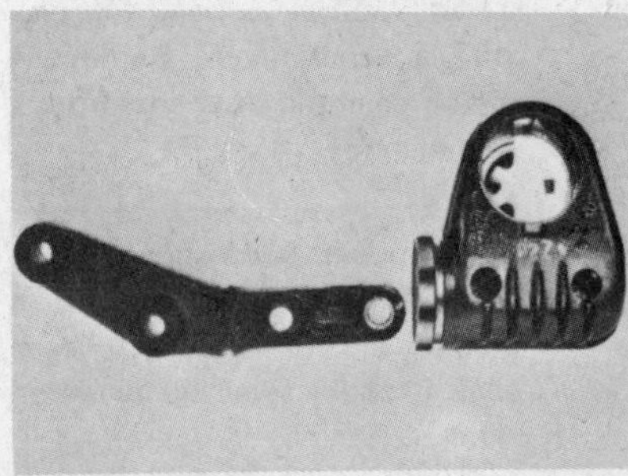
Caliper bracket and caliper (Courtesy Yamaha Int. Corp.)

Anti-rattle spring (Courtesy Yamaha Int. Corp.)

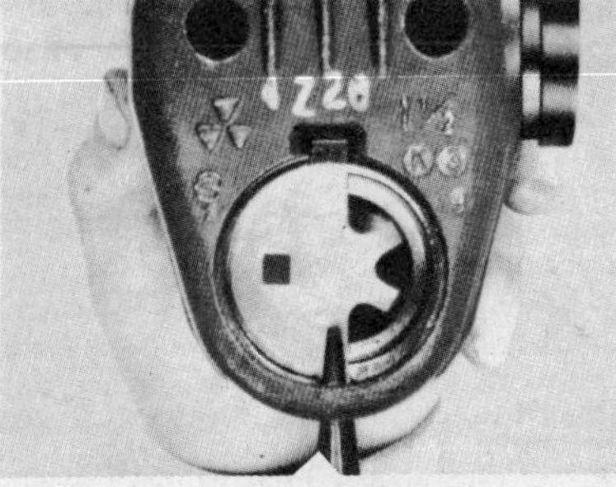
Removing the anti-squeak shim (Courtesy Yamaha Int. Corp.)

7. Remove the anti-rattle spring. Remove the anti-squeak shim.
8. Apply compressed air at brake line fitting on the caliper to force out the piston. Remove the piston dust seal and fluid seal.

Inspection

Refer to "Inspection" for the 250/350/400 caliper, above.

Assembly and Installation

1. Assembly is the reverse of disassembly. Coat caliper walls, piston, and seals with clean brake fluid.

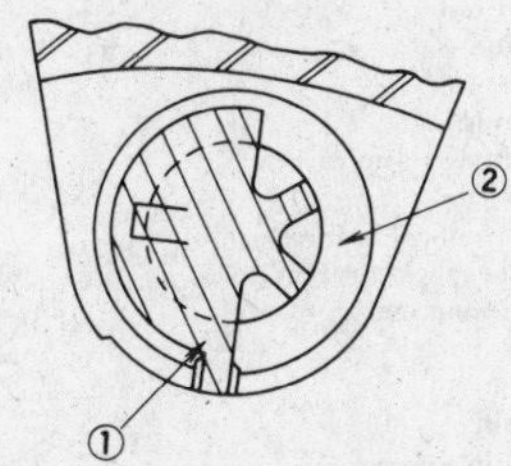

Anti-squeak shim (1) and piston (2) (Courtesy Yamaha Int. Corp.)

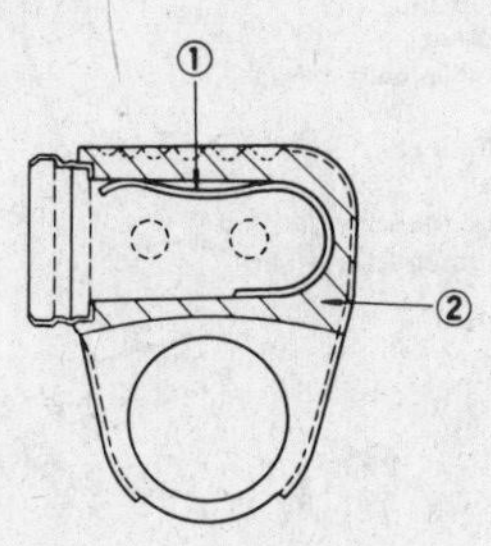

Anti-rattle spring (1) and caliper (2) (Courtesy Yamaha Int. Corp.)

2. Use silicon grease on both sides of the anti-squeak shim. Install the anti-rattle spring as illustrated. Lubricate rubber/metal contact areas and caliper pins with silicon grease.
3. Tighten caliper mounting bolts to 16–23 ft lbs.

MASTER CYLINDER

Refer to "Master Cylinder (Front)" for 250/350/400 models, above. Procedures are similar.

Wheel Bearings

Removal of the wheel bearings necessitates removing the hub oil seals. These must be replaced with new ones upon reassembly. In addition, a drift with a hooked end should be used to remove the bearings. Refer to the illustration. Clean the outside of the hub before removal.

DISASSEMBLY

1. Remove the wheel and take out the brake plate (drum brakes). On disc brake wheels, remove the speedometer drive mechanism.
2. Remove any dust covers, dust seals, or axle spacers fitted to either side of the hub.
3. Pry out the oil seals on either side of the hub using a small screwdriver, or, preferably, an elbow-shaped tool.

Prying out a wheel bearing oil seal

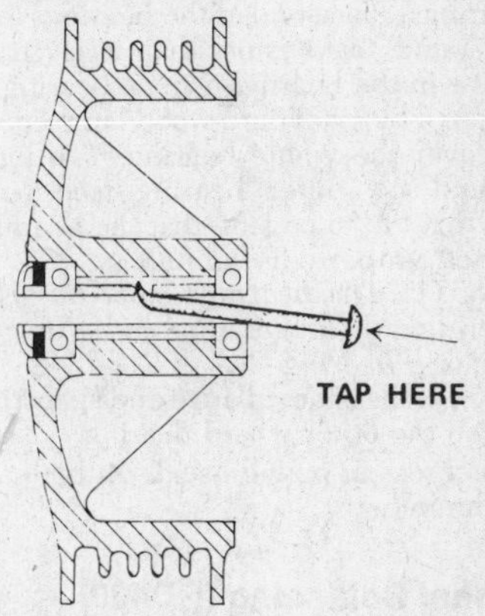

Removing a wheel bearing from the hub with a hooked tool (Courtesy Yamaha Int. Corp.)

4. Using the bearing removal tool, or a suitable substitute, engage the hole drilled into the bearing spacer. Striking the removal tool with a hammer will drive out one wheel bearing. Alternatively, a straight punch may be used to remove the bearing. Move the spacer to one side as shown in the illustration and tap it out.
5. Take out the bearing spacer and spacer flange. Drive out the other bearing with a suitable drift.

NOTE: *On some models, especially high mileage machines, the hub should be heated gently with a propane torch in the vicinity of the bearing bosses to facilitate removal.*

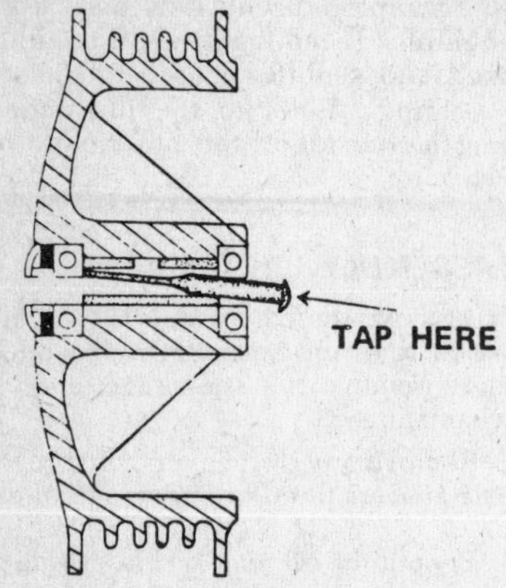

Alternate method of removing the wheel bearings (Courtesy Yamaha Int. Corp.)

ASSEMBLY

1. Obtain a good grade of wheel bearing grease to lubricate the wheel bearings.
2. Pack the grease in the bearing. A common method of doing this is to place a goodly amount of the grease in the palm of one hand. Taking the clean, dry, bearing, press one section of it into the grease. Turn the bearing until the grease has been deposited around the entire circumference. The packing process is complete when the grease begins to come out of the upper side of the bearing. Place an amount of grease in the hub as well.
3. Heat either side of the wheel hub with a propane torch as on removal of the bearings. Place one of the bearings in the hub, and make sure that it is seated. Drive in the bearing using a bearing driver, or a block of hard wood large enough to cover the whole bearing. Tap lightly around the outer bearing race before driving it in to be sure that the bearing is started properly in the hub.

NOTE: *The bearings must be driven straight in; do not attempt to force in a cocked bearing.*

4. Fit the spacer flange and spacer, and install the other wheel bearing.
5. Press in new oil seals on both sides of the hub.

Wheel Balancing (RD400)

Balancing of the alloy wheels on the RD400C is performed in the same manner as for conventional spoked wheels (See "Chassis" in the General Information section), except that balance weights must not be installed closer than 40 mm to the center line of the spokes.

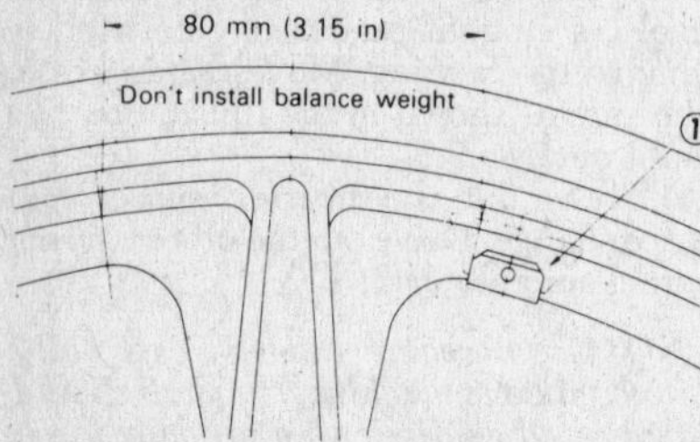

Balance weight placement, RD400C cast wheels (Courtesy Yamaha Int. Corp.)

FRONT FORKS

Two basic types of forks are used: one for lightweights (200 cc and under) and most older bikes, and another type for the larger machines, including the RD200.

The chief distinctions are the use of external fork springs on most of the light-weight forks with the exception of machines such as the RD125 and 200B, and the method of securing the slider to the fork leg. Larger machines use an allen bolt in the bottom of the slider which threads into the damper, while others have a circular nut fitted to the top of the slider. The slider oil seal is pressed into the top of the slider nut, while on newer models an O-ring is also fitted to the lower end of the nut.

The "heavyweight" fork type is used on such machines as the RD200C, DS7, R5/B/C, RD250-350A/B, and RD400.

On all forks, the fork slider oil seals must be replaced each time the slider is removed from the fork inner tube.

Removal and Disassembly

HEAVYWEIGHT TYPE

1. Support the front end of the machine well off the ground. Remove the front wheel and the front fender.
2. On disc brake models, unbolt and remove the brake caliper from the fork slider.
3. Loosen the handlebar bolts just enough to allow the bars to be pulled back towards the rider to give access to the fork cap bolts.
4. Each fork leg assembly is removed separately from the triple clamps. Loosen the fork cap bolt on one of the fork legs. As the bolt is removed, press down on it with your hand to prevent it from popping off due to spring pressure. Remove the cap bolt, the washer (if fitted), and

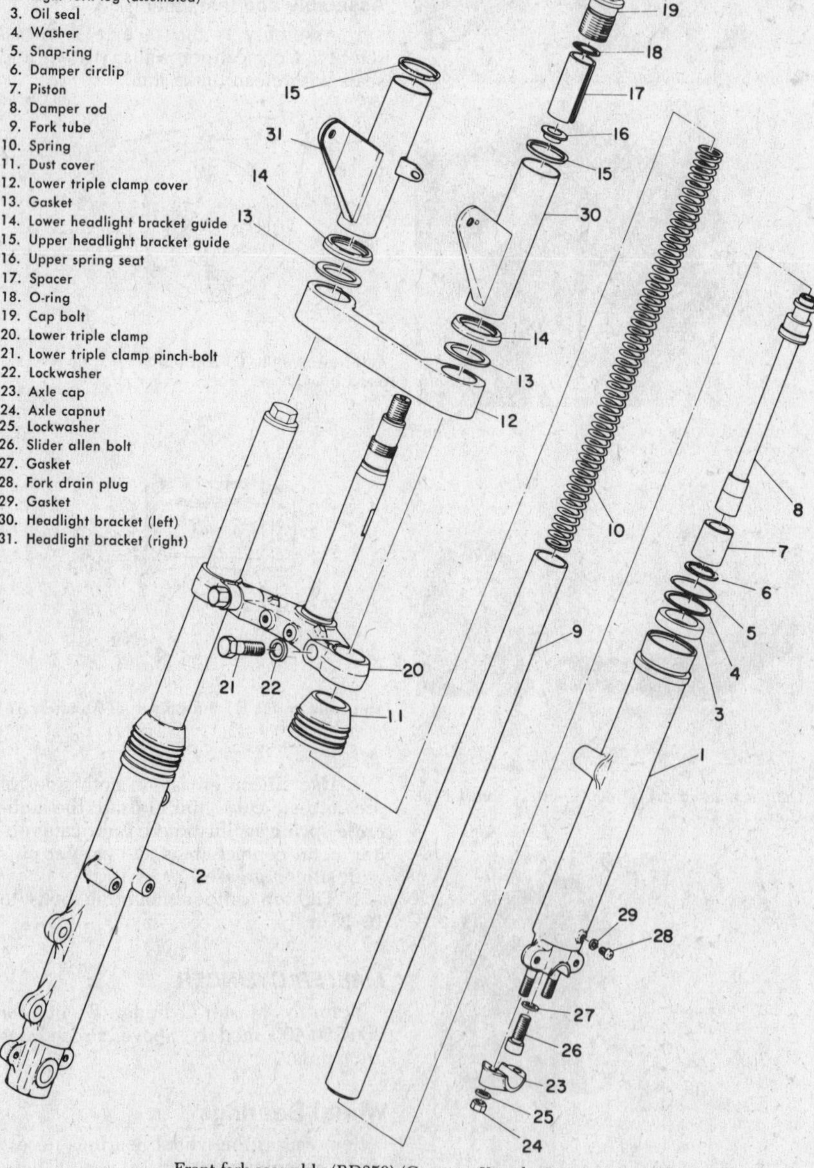

Front fork assembly (RD350) (Courtesy Yamaha Int. Corp.)

spring spacer. Take out the upper spring seat and the fork spring.

5. Loosen the upper and lower triple clamp pinch-bolts for the partially disassembled fork leg.

6. Grasp the fork slider for that fork leg and pull it sharply downward to free the fork tube from the triple clamps. Remove the dust seal cover (DS7, R5) and the dust seal, by prying them off the top of the slider.

7. Turn the fork leg upside down to drain off the fork oil.

8. Remove the axle cap from the bottom of the slider if fitted. The fork slider is secured to the fork tube by an allen bolt in the very bottom of the slider. Pull the slider and fork tube as far apart as possible, extending the assembly to its full length. Remove the slider allen bolt. An impact driver may be necessary.

9. Pull the slider free of the fork tube.

10. The slider oil seal will remain in place in the slider. To remove it, remove the snap-ring, the washer, and pry the seal out of the slider with a small screwdriver or hooked tool.

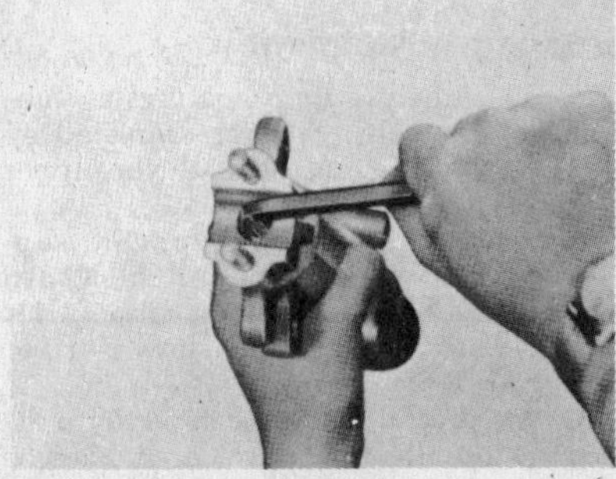

Removing the fork slider allen bolt (Courtesy Yamaha Int. Corp.)

11. Remove the circlip from the bottom of the damper, take off the piston, and remove the damper from the top of the fork tube.

12. Repeat the procedure with the other fork leg.

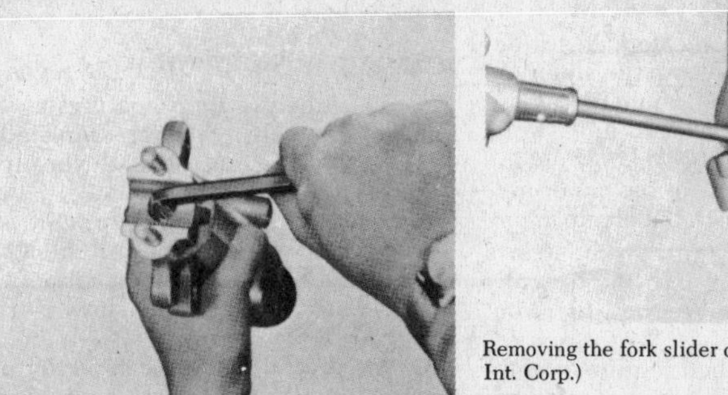

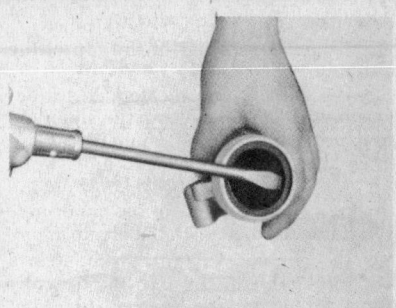

Removing the fork slider oil seal (Courtesy Yamaha Int. Corp.)

13. If only the fork slider oil seals need attention, the slider may be removed while leaving the fork tube assembly in place as follows:

a. Drain the fork oil;

b. Remove the front wheel, fender, and the caliper on disc brake models;

c. Pry up the dust seal cover (if fitted), and the rubber dust cover from the top of the fork slider;

d. Remove the axle cap if it is fitted;

e. Pry out the oil seal snap-ring; remove the washer;

f. Remove the allen screw from the bottom of the fork slider and remove the slider from the fork tube;

g. Assembly will be made easier if the fork cap bolts are removed to relieve fork spring tension.

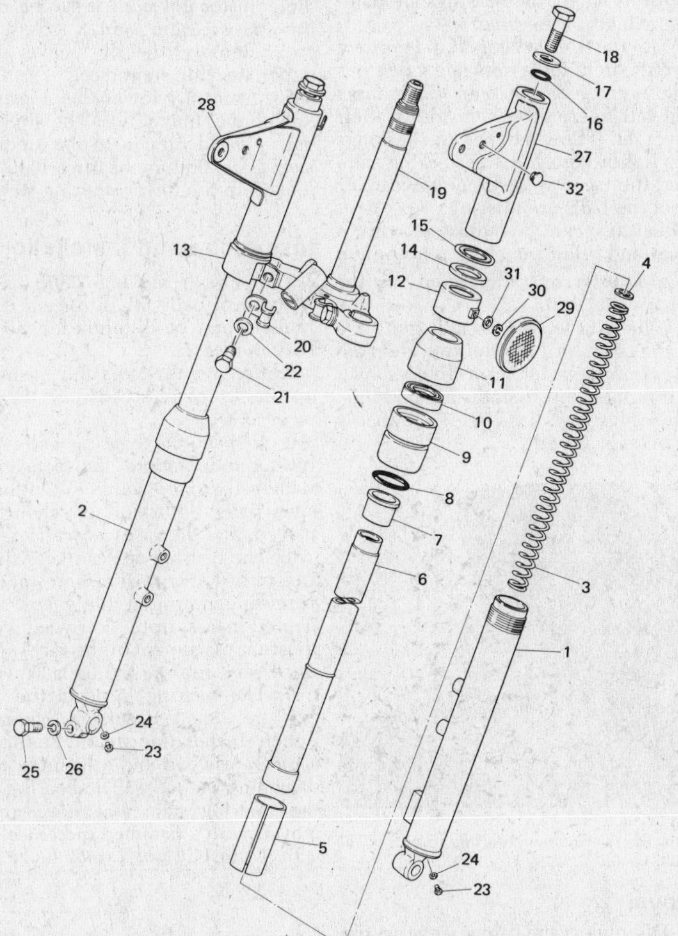

Front fork assembly (RD125B/RD200B) (Courtesy Yamaha Int. Corp.)

1. Fork slider, left
2. Fork slider, right
3. Fork spring
4. Spring washer
5. Spacer (200B)
6. Fork tube
7. Sliding bushing
8. O-ring
9. Circular nut
10. Oil seal
11. Dust seal
12. Cover, left
13. Cover, right
14. Gasket
15. Grommet
16. O-ring
17. Washer
18. Fork filler bolt
19. Lower triple clamp
20. Cable bracket
21. Bolt
22. Washer
23. Drain plug
24. Gasket
25. Pinch bolt
26. Lockwasher
27. Headlight bracket, left
28. Headlight bracket, right
29. Reflector
30. Lockwasher
31. Washer
32. Plug

EXTERNAL FORK SPRING AND LIGHTWEIGHT TYPE

With minor constructional variations, this type of fork is used on lightweight machines and on early 200–350 cc models such as the R3, DS6, YDS-series, CS-series, RD125 and 200B.

The fork slider is secured to the fork inner tube by a large circular nut. The slider oil seal is also located in this nut. Some models have an 0-ring in the bottom of the nut as well.

1. Support the front wheel well off the ground. Remove the front wheel and fender.

2. Remove the fork cap filler bolt, washer, and O-ring (if fitted).

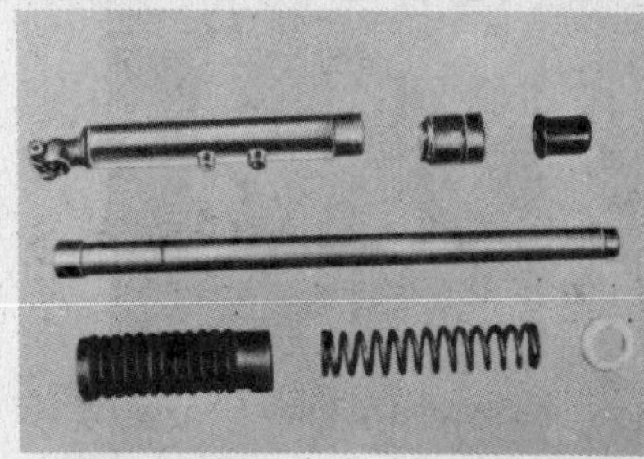

External spring fork components (Courtesy Yamaha Int. Corp.)

3. Loosen the upper and lower triple clamp pinch-bolts for one of the fork legs. Grasp the slider and pull sharply downward to free the fork leg from the triple clamps.

4. Remove the fork boot or slider dust seal, upper spring seat, fork spring, spring guide (if fitted), and lower spring seat from the fork tube, or remove the

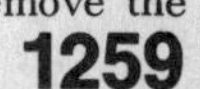

inner fork spring from the fork tube.

5. Drain the oil out of the top of the fork tube.

6. To disassemble the fork leg, a device must be used to clamp the slider nut so that it can be turned. In many cases, a large heater hose clamp will work. Tighten the heater hose clamp around the slider nut; a piece of old inner tube should be used beneath the clamp to protect the chrome. Clamp the slider in a vise, preferably by the axle lug. Unscrew the slider nut and remove the slider from the fork tube.

An alternative method requires clamping the slider nut in a vise (protected with rubber padding or the like), and unscrewing the slider from it as shown in the illustration.

A strap wrench on the slider nut, if one is available, is the easiest method.

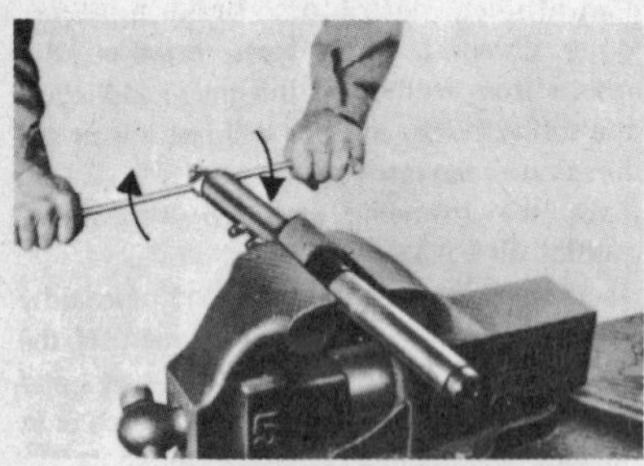

Removing the fork slider circular nut (Courtesy Yamaha Int. Corp.)

7. Remove the slider nut with the oil seal by the top of the fork tube, followed by the sliding bushing. The oil seal, which must be replaced, can be pried out of the circular nut with a small screwdriver or hooked tool.

8. Repeat the procedure with the other fork leg.

Assembly and Installation

ALL MODELS

1. Assembly is the reverse of the disassembly procedure. Note the following points.

2. All O-rings, oil seals, and felt washers must be replaced.

3. Slider oil seals should be pressed directly into the slider or circular nut (depending on fork type) with a suitable drift which will cover the whole seal. This will minimize chances of distorting the seal when installing it and will allow it to be fully seated. On some models, the old seals can be used to drive in the new.

4. Grease the lips of the oil seals before installing on the fork tubes. After installing the slider on the fork tube, check that it can move smoothly up and down.

5. When installing the tubes in the triple clamps, ensure that the top of the tubes are flush with the top surface of the upper triple clamp. Tighten the upper and lower triple clamp pinch-bolts securely.

6. Refill each fork leg with the proper viscosity and quantity of oil.

STEERING STEM

Bearing Adjustment

1. The steering stem bearings are uncaged ¼ in. balls. They are adjusted by means of a ring nut beneath the upper triple clamp.

2. To check bearing adjustment, support the front wheel off the ground. Grasp the tip of the front fender, place your other hand beneath the lower triple clamp at the frame lug.

3. Attempt to move the forks by pulling up on the front fender. If play or movement can be felt at the lower triple clamp, the bearings are too loosely adjusted or worn.

4. Turn the forks slowly from lock-to-lock. Movement should be smooth, silent, and effortless. If any binding or uneven movement is felt, the balls and races are either too tightly adjusted or are worn. If the steering feels uniformly stiff, the bearings are too tightly adjusted. If any noise is noted, the bearings are damaged, or some are missing.

5. With the front wheel off the ground, release the front forks from a few degrees off the centered position. The forks should fall freely to either side of their own weight. If they will not, the bearings are too tightly adjusted, the steering stem is bent, the races are extremely worn, or some of the balls are missing.

6. Bearings can be adjusted with a hammer and blunt punch or pin wrench on the adjuster nut after removing the upper triple clamp.

7. Tighten or loosen the adjuster nut a little at a time until the steering stem adjustment conforms to that outlined above.

8. If proper adjustment is not possible, the bearings and races will probably need to be replaced.

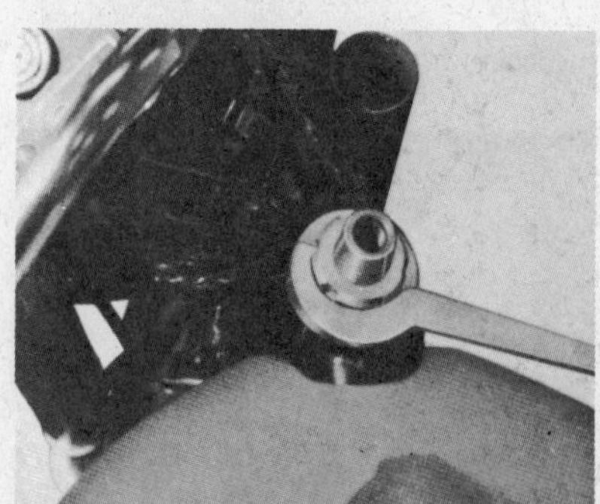

Adjusting the steering stem bearings (Courtesy Yamaha Int. Corp.)

Removal

1. Disconnect the cables, remove the electrical switches from the handlebars; unbolt and remove the handlebars from the motorcycle.

2. Unbolt the instruments from the upper triple clamp and lay them carefully aside. Unbolt the headlight from the brackets and allow it to hang by the wiring harness.

3. Remove the front wheel, fender, brake caliper (if disc brake), and remove both fork legs from the triple clamps.

4. If a friction steering damper is fitted, remove the damper plate cotter pin beneath the lower triple clamp. Unscrew the damper rod and remove it. Remove the damper plate bolt and lockwasher and the damper plates.

5. Loosen the upper triple clamp pinch-bolt behind the large triple clamp nut. Then remove the nut, the spring on models with a steering damper, and the large washer.

6. The upper triple clamp can now be removed. Tap upwards on the underside of the triple clamp with a plastic mallet until it is free.

7. Remove the headlight brackets. Since the steering head ball bearings are uncaged, it is likely that some will drop out of the races when the steering stem is lowered. Therefore, if the bearings are going to be reused, cover the ground beneath the assembly with a drop cloth.

8. With a hammer and punch, loosen the bearing adjuster nut until it can be turned by hand. Support the lower triple clamp with one hand while unscrewing the adjuster nut until it can be removed from the steering stem.

9. Remove the dust cover and the upper steering stem race.

10. Carefully lower the steering stem out of the frame lug. The top bearing balls should remain in the steering lug race. The bottom bearing balls should remain in the lower steering stem race.

Inspection and Installation

1. Before removing them, note the number of balls fitted to each race. The number may be different for the top and bottom races.

2. Remove the balls and wash them in a suitable solvent. Clean off the bearing races as well.

3. Inspect the bearing balls for rust, pitting, indentations, flat spots, or cracks. Rather than replacing individual damaged balls, both ball sets should be replaced, and the races as well.

4. The bearing race surfaces should be free of rust or corrosion, and smooth. Run your finger around the races. Any indented marks, ripples, or wear would indicate replacement of the races. If this is necessary, replace the balls as well.

5. The bearing races in the steering lug are removed with a hammer and punch. Installation should be made with a block of wood and a hammer to avoid damaging the races. The bearing race on the steering stem may have to be removed with a hammer and chisel.

6. To install, put a thick layer of bear-

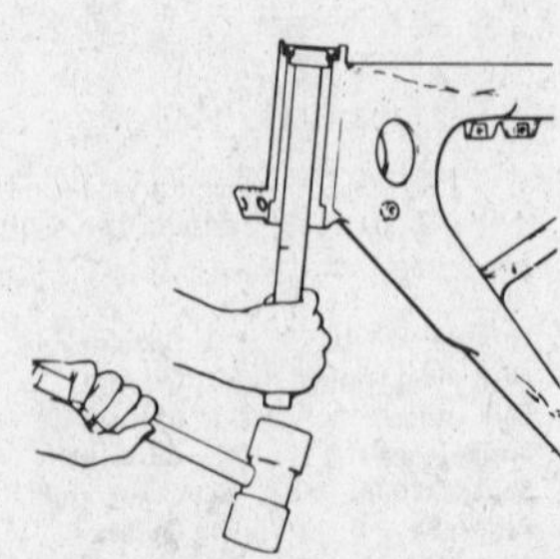

Removing the top frame lug race

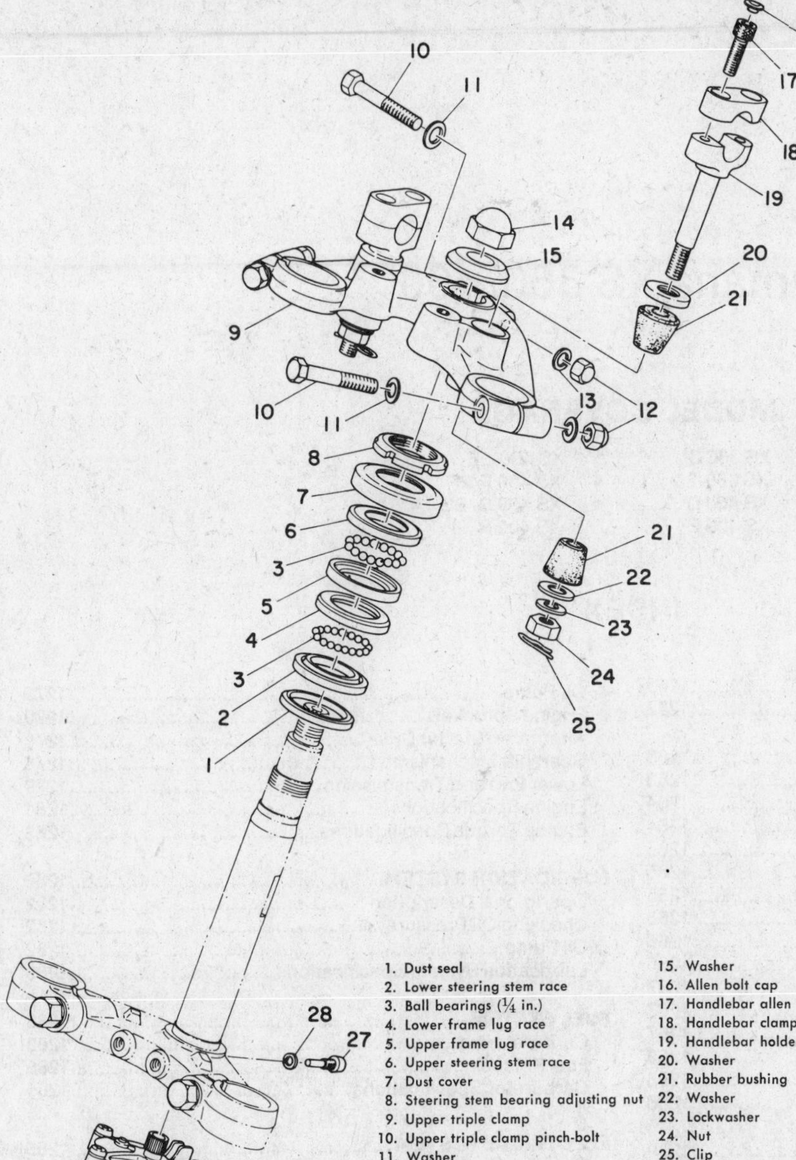

1. Dust seal
2. Lower steering stem race
3. Ball bearings (¼ in.)
4. Lower frame lug race
5. Upper frame lug race
6. Upper steering stem race
7. Dust cover
8. Steering stem bearing adjusting nut
9. Upper triple clamp
10. Upper triple clamp pinch-bolt
11. Washer
12. Capnuts
13. Lockwasher
14. Triple clamp crown nut
15. Washer
16. Allen bolt cap
17. Handlebar allen bolt
18. Handlebar clamp
19. Handlebar holder
20. Washer
21. Rubber bushing
22. Washer
23. Lockwasher
24. Nut
25. Clip
26. Steering damper
27. Bolt
28. Lockwasher

Steering stem assembly (RD250, 350) (Courtesy Yamaha Int. Corp.)

ing grease on the top frame lug race and on the lower steering stem race. Embed the bearings in the grease, ensuring that the correct number of balls are fitted. Install the steering stem replacing the top race, dust cover, and adjuster nut. Tighten the nut until slight resistance is felt, then adjust it so the steering stem will fall to either side of its own weight when released from a few degrees from the centered position.

7. Reassemble the rest of the front end in the reverse of the removal procedure. Check bearing adjustment as described above.

SWING ARM

The swing arm is mounted by means of bushings which tend to wear after many miles. The rate of wear will increase if the machine is used over rough terrain. For street machines, Yamaha recommends replacement of the swing arm bushings every 6,000 miles. However, if a check of the bushings reveals that wear is minimal, this interval can be extended.

Inspection

1. To check the condition of the swing arm bushings, remove the rear wheel and sprocket and unbolt the lower shock absorber mounts.
2. Check for play by grasping the end of the swing arm firmly and attempting to move it from side-to-side. Play should be nil. If there is any, the swing arm should be removed and the bushings replaced.
3. Measure the distance between the top and bottom shock absorber mounts on both sides. The two measurements must be identical, or the swing arm will have to be replaced or fixed.
4. Check that the rear wheel mounting plates are parallel.

The swing arm is most likely to be damaged if the machine is operated for any length of time with a broken or otherwise defective shock absorber.

Removal and Installation

1. Remove the rear wheel, sprocket hub, and chain guard. Unbolt the shock absorbers from the swing arm.
2. Remove the swing arm pivot shaft nut. Push or tap out the shaft; turn the swing arm sideways, and remove it from the machine.
3. Remove the dust covers from the ends of the swing arm tube if fitted. Note the location and number of any shims beneath the dust covers.
4. Remove the bushings, tapping them out with a long punch and hammer if necessary. Remove the spacer. Once bushings are removed, they should be replaced. Check the shaft for wear and replace it if there is any evident.
5. Lubricate new bushings with a good chassis grease. Press in one bushing, refit the spacer, and install the other bushing.
6. Install the swing arm on the machine. After tightening the swing arm pivot shaft nut, move the swing arm up and down to ensure that movement is smooth and effortless.

REAR SHOCK ABSORBERS

1. Shock absorbers are sealed units which cannot be disassembled. If defective, they must be replaced.
2. If a shock leaks oil or is damaged in an accident (such as bent shaft, dented body, etc.), replace it.
3. To check a shock which is removed from the machine, place the bottom end on the ground and use the weight of your body to compress it as much as possible. Release the shock and note the rebound behavior. If the shock returns quickly at first, then slowly returns to the normal length, it is serviceable. If it returns to its normal length all at once, it should be replaced. Note that shock absorbers should always be replaced in pairs.

Torque Specifications

Stud Size (mm)	*Torque (ft lbs)*
6	7.5
7	11.3
8	15.0
10	25.0–28.2
12	28.2–33.5
14	33.5–37.5
17	41.7–50.0
Axle Nuts	41.7–50.0

Yamaha XS 360/400

MODEL COVERAGE

XS 360 C
XS 360-2D
XS 400 D
XS 400 E
XS 400-2E
XS 400 F/2F
XS 400 G/SG
XS 400 H

INDEX

General Specifications

	XS360	XS400D	XS400E	XS400-2E	XS400F/2F	XS400G/SG,H
Engine						
Type	air cooled, SOHC twin	air cooled, SOHC twin	air cooled, SOHC twin	air cooled, SOHC twin	air cooled, SOHC twin	air cooled, SOHC twin
Displacement (cc/ci)	358/21.6	392/23.9	392/23.9	392/23.9	392/23.9	392/23.9
Bore x Stroke (mm/in.)	66.0 x 52.4/2.53 x 2.06	69.0 x 52.4/2.72 x 2.06	69.0 x 52.4/2.72 x 2.06	69.0 x 52.4/2.72 x 2.06	69.0 x 52.4/2.72 x 2.06	69.0 x 52.4/2.72 x 2.06
Compression ratio	8.7 : 1	9.2 : 1	9.3 : 1	9.4 : 1	9.3 : 1	9.3 : 1
Starting system	①	electric and kick	electric and kick	kick	③	electric and kick
Ignition system	battery and coil	battery and coil	battery and coil	battery and coil	battery and coil	transistor
Lubrication system	wet sump	wet sump	wet sump	wet sump	wet sump	wet sump
Carburetion	Mikuni BS34	Mikuni BS34	Mikuni BS34	Mikuni BS34	Mikuni BS34	Mikuni BS34
Transmission						
Clutch type	wet, multi-plate	wet, multi-plate	wet, multi-plate	wet, multi-plate	wet, multi-plate	wet, multi-plate
No. speeds	6	6	6	6	6	6
Primary reduction	78/24 (3.250)	78/24 (3.250)	78/24 (3.250)	78/24 (3.250)	78/24 (3.250)	78/24 (3.250)
Secondary reduction	40/16 (2.500)	37/16 (2.312)	37/16 (2.312)	37/16 (2.312)	37/16 (2.312)	36/16 (2.312)
Gear ratios						
1st	35/14 (2.500)	35/14 (2.500)	35/14 (2.500)	35/14 (2.500)	35/14 (2.500)	35/14 (2.500)
2d	32/18 (1.777)	32/18 (1.777)	32/18 (1.777)	32/18 (1.777)	32/18 (1.777)	32/18 (1.777)
3rd	29/21 (1.380)	29/21 (1.380)	29/21 (1.280)	29/21 (1.380)	29/21 (1.380)	29/21 (1.380)
4th	27/24 (1.125)	27/24 (1.125)	27/24 (1.125)	27/24 (1.125)	27/24 (1.125)	27/24 (1.125)
5th	25/26 (0.961)	25/26 (0.961)	25/26 (0.961)	25/26 (0.961)	25/26 (0.961)	25/26 (0.961)
6th	26/30 (0.8666)	26/30 (0.866)	26/30 (0.866)	26/30 (0.866)	26/30 (0.866)	26/30 (0.866)
Chassis						
Frame	semi-double cradle	semi-double cradle	semi-double cradle	semi-double cradle	semi-double cradle	semi-double cradle
Caster	26° 30′	26° 30′	27°	26° 30′	27°	27° 30′
Trail (mm/in.)	81/3.2	85/3.4	84/3.3	81/3.2	84/3.3	87/3.4
Front suspension	telescopic fork	telescopic fork	telescopic fork	telescopic fork	telescopic fork	telescopic fork
Rear suspension	swing arm/shock absorber	swing arm/shock absorber	swing arm/shock absorber	swing arm/shock absorber	swing arm/shock absorber	swing arm/shock absorber
Tire size						
front	3.00 x 18	3.50 x 18	3.00 x 18	3.00 x 18	3.00 x 18	3.00 x 18 (tubeless)
rear	3.50 x 18	3.50 x 18	3.50 x 18	3.50 x 18	3.50 x 18	120/90-16 63S (tubeless)
Fuel capacity (gal/1)	2.9/11	2.9/11	3.7/14	2.9/11	3.7/14	3.7/14
Overall Dimensions						
Length (mm/in.)	2045/80.5	2025/79.7	2065/81.2	2025/79.5	2065/81.2	2065/81.2
Width (mm/in.)	845/33.3	845/33.3	865/34.1	845/33.3	④	⑦
Height (mm/in.)	1100/43.3	1100/43.3	1140/44.9	1100/43.3	⑤	⑧
Seat Height (mm/in.)	800/31.5	815/32.1	780/30.7	815/32.1	780/30.7	770/30.3
Ground clearance (mm/in.)	155/6.1	150/5.9	150/5.9	150/5.9	150/5.9	135/5.3
Dry Weight (kg/lbs)	②	164/367	168/370	155/342	⑥	⑨

① XS360C: electric and kick
XS360-2D: kick
② XS360C: 159/350
XS360-2D: 153/337
③ XS400F: electric and kick
XS400-2F: kick
④ XS400F: 865/34.1
XS400-2F: 845/33.3
⑤ XS400F: 1140/44.9
XS400-2F: 1130/44.5
⑥ XS400F: 168/370
XS400-2F: 159/351
⑦ XS400G: 860/33.9
XS400SG: 870/34.3
XS400H: 860/33.9
⑧ XS400G: 1105/43.5
XS400SG: 1140/44.9
XS400H: 1105/43.5
⑨ XS400G: 166/366
XS400SG: 169/373
XS400H: 167/366

SERIAL NUMBER LOCATION

In order to prevent possible confusion when ordering parts, always refer to the engine and frame serial numbers.

The frame number is stamped on the right side of the steering lug, while the engine number is located on a raised boss just behind the right cylinder on the top of the crankcases.

Frame serial number location

Engine serial number location

MAINTENANCE

NOTE: *Common maintenance procedures are explained in detail in "General Information."*

LUBRICATION

Motor Oil

When the average air temperature is above 5° C (41° F), use Yamalube 4-stroke oil, or SAE 20W-40, service rating "SE." or "SF."

When the air temperature is consistently below 15°C (59°F), use SAE 10W-30, service rating "SE" or "SF."

Straight grades can also be used according to ambient air temperatures as given in the "Recommended Lubricants" chart at the end of this section.

Maintain the oil level between the upper and lower dipstick marks (A and B)

Checking Oil Level

XS400G/SG-ON

1. A sight glass in the crankcase is provided to enable the rider to check oil level at a glance. When checking, the motorcycle should be parked on the centerstand on a level surface.

2. Oil should be checked when the engine is warm. After shutting it off, let the machine sit for a few minutes.

3. Maintain the oil level between the

Oil level sight glass

upper and lower level marks inscribed on the crankcase. If the oil level is too low, remove the filler cap and add enough oil to bring the level up to the upper level mark. Do not overfill.

OTHER MODELS

1. A dipstick is provided to check the oil level.

2. The motorcycle should be parked on level ground and put on the centerstand.

3. Unscrew and remove the dipstick and wipe it off. Reinsert the dipstick, allowing it to rest on the treads of the hole. Oil level should be between the maximum and minimum marks on the stick. If the oil level is too low, add enough oil to bring the level up to between the marks. Do not overfill the crankcase.

Changing Oil

1. The recommended oil change interval is 2,000 miles or every 3 months, whichever comes first.

2. Oil should be changed when the engine is warm. This ensures more complete draining and makes it more likely that the oil will carry off any particulate matter with it.

3. Remove the dipstick. Place a suitable container (at least 2½ qt. capacity) beneath the engine and remove the drain plug. Allow the oil to drain off for several minutes, then install the drain plug and tighten it securely. Proper torque is 25–29 ft lbs.

4. Remove the oil filter screen and the oil filter if it is time to service them (see below).

5. Add 2.1 qts. (2.0 l) of the recommended grade and viscosity oil to the crankcase. If the filter has been changed, add 2.4 qts. (2.3 l).

6. Start the engine and let it run for a few minutes. Then shut it off and check the oil level with the dipstick. Add additional oil, if necessary, to bring the level to between the level marks on the dipstick.

Oil Filter

1. The disposable oil filter element should be replaced at every other oil change: 4,000

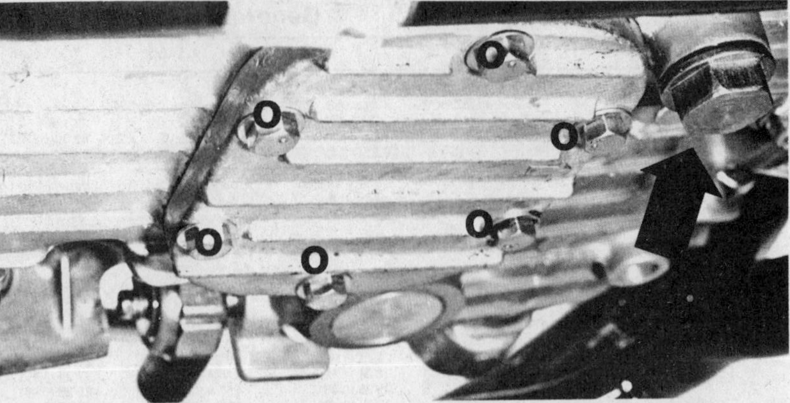

Crankcase drain plug (arrow). Filter screen bolts (0)

miles or every 6 months, whichever comes first.

2. Drain the oil as outlined above.

3. Remove the oil filter housing bolt and remove the housing and filter element. Have a container placed beneath the filter housing prior to removal to catch any oil which might drip out.

4. Clean the inside of the filter housing prior to fitting a new filter element.

5. Install the new element and refit the housing. Tighten the housing bolt to 10–12 ft lbs. *Do not overtighten.*

6. Fill the crankcase with 2.4 qts. (2.3 l) of the recommended grade and viscosity oil.

7. Run the engine for several minutes and check for leaks.

Filter Screen

1. The XS360 and XS400 are fitted with an oil filter screen in the sump. The screen should be removed and cleaned every other time the oil is changed: every 4,000 miles or 6 months, whichever comes first.

2. Drain the oil as outlined above.

3. Remove the six bolts which secure the

Oil filter bolt

oil filter screen and pull it out. Have a container beneath the screen cover to catch any oil which will drip out.

4. Clean the screen in a safe solvent and

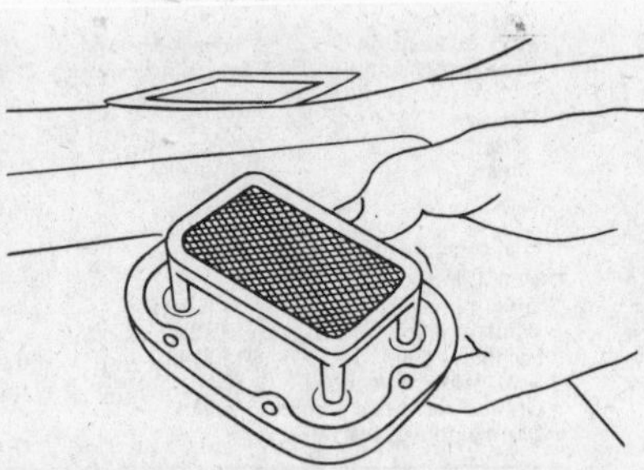

Removing the filter screen

use a reasonably soft brush, if necessary, to remove any foreign matter trapped on it. Check the condition of the gasket and replace it if necessary. Blow dry and reinstall, tightening the cover bolts gradually and evenly. Proper torque is 4.5–6.0 ft lbs.

5. Refill the crankcase with oil. Check for leaks.

Front Forks

1. Yamaha fork oil, SAE 20W motor oil, or SAE 10W-30 motor oil is recommended for all forks.

Front fork oil drain plug

Oil viscosity can be varied if slightly stiffer or less stiff fork action is desired. Special types of oil designed specifically for motorcycle forks can also be used, although care must be taken to flush the forks thoroughly when changing types or brands of fork fluid, since some may be incompatible with others.

2. After an initial change at 2,000 miles, the fork oil should be changed at 10,000 miles intervals.

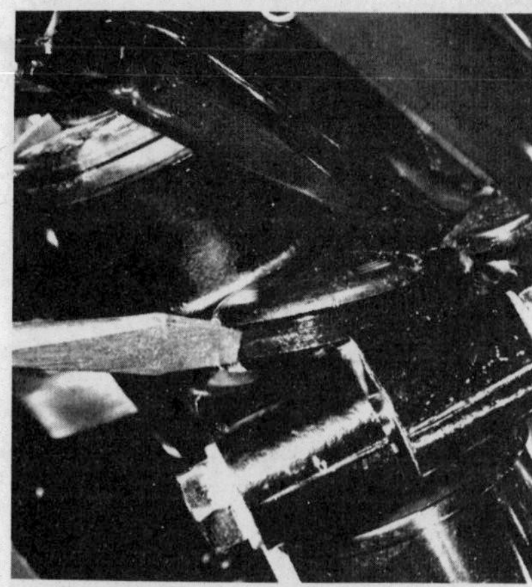

Removing the rubber fork cap

3. Fork capacities are as follows:

XS360 XS400D XS400-2E	130 cc (4.4 oz.)
XS400E XS400F, 2F XS400G, SG-ON	142 cc (4.8 oz.)

Note that the amounts shown are to be added to each fork leg.

4. Support the front wheel off the ground by placing a jack or the like beneath the engine.

5. Remove the rubber caps at the tops of the fork legs. Press down the fork caps slightly with a screwdriver or similar instrument, and remove the snap rings. Remove the fork caps. Pull out the fork springs.

6. Place a suitable container beneath one of the fork sliders and remove the drain screw. After most of the oil has drained off, pump the slider up and down a few times to

Fork filler cap

remove any oil remaining in the forks. Check the condition of the drain plug gasket and replace it with a new one if necessary. Refit the drain screw and tighten it securely.

Repeat the procedure with the other fork leg.

7. Examine the drained oil. If it contains water or is exceptionally dirty, it may be that the fork dust covers are damaged and allowing foreign matter to get past. This will also damage the fork seals quickly. Check that the dust covers are properly secured and replace them if they are cracked, ripped, or otherwise damaged.

8. Add the proper quantity of oil to each fork leg.

9. Check the condition of the fork cap o-rings, and replace them if they are damaged. Refit the springs, fork caps, snap rings and rubber caps.

10. After several miles of operation, check the area around the fork slider seals for leaks or seepage. Even a minimal amount of seepage will require replacement of the seals. A coating of grime building up in this area over a period of time is also indicative of ineffective seals.

Chassis Lubrication

1. The swing arm pivot is fitted with two grease nipples which should be lubricated with chassis grease every 2,000 miles. Apply grease until it shows at both ends of the swing arm pivot.

Swing arm grease fitting

2. Wheel and steering head bearings are lubricated with bearing grease, the service interval being 8,000 miles.

SERVICE CHECKS AND ADJUSTMENTS

Drive Chain

1. On 1976-78 models, the chain should have about 10-20 mm (0.4-0.8 in.) of total up-and-down free-play measured in the middle of the lower chain run.

On 1979 and later models, chain free-play should be 30-35 mm (1.2-1.4 in.).

2. Before checking or adjusting the chain slack, the following conditions should be met:

a. The motorcycle should be placed on both wheels with a rider sitting with his weight on the seat.

b. The transmission should be placed in neutral;

c. The chain should be clean and well-lubricated;

d. The chain should have been checked for any tight spots by slowly rotating the wheel and checking for variances in the chain tension at different points. If a tight spot exists, the chain tension should be adjusted to the prescribed free-play at the tight spot. Note, however, that such a con-

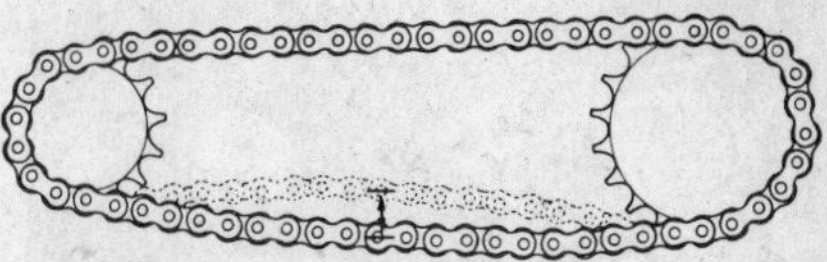

Chain play is the total up and down movement measured in the middle of the lower chain run

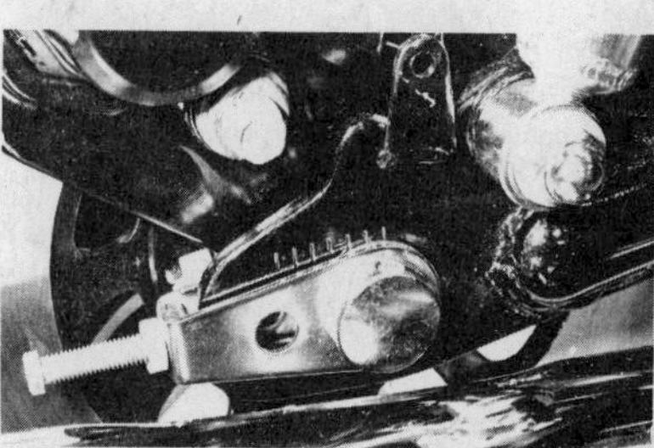

Chain adjusting bolt and swing arm alignment marks

dition is indicative of a worn chain and probably worn sprockets, which should be replaced as soon as possible.

3. To adjust the chain, first back off the rear brake adjuster nut on drum rear brakes.

4. Remove the axle nut cotter pin and loosen the axle nut several turns. Loosen the locknut on each chain adjuster bolt.

5. Turn each of the adjuster bolts in or out by equal amounts until the chain tension is approximately correct.

6. Check wheel alignment by means of the aligning marks inscribed on both sides of the swing arm. Be sure that both adjusters are lined up with the same mark on each side. If not, turn one of the adjuster bolts in or out so that alignment is achieved.

7. Tighten the axle nut and adjuster bolt nuts and check the chain tension. Correct if necessary. After adjustment is correct, torque the axle nut to 50–72 ft lbs.

Fit a new cotter pin. Readjust the rear brake on drum brake models.

Clutch

1. Cable adjustment must always be maintained at the proper specification. If the cable has insufficient free-play, the clutch will slip and rapidly burn out. If it has too much play, the clutch will not completely disengage, resulting in hard shifting and creeping at stops.

2. Use the cable adjuster at the handlebar to maintain the correct amount of cable slack. The clutch hand lever should be able to be moved 2–3 mm (0.08–0.12 in.) measured between the lever and the lever holder before the clutch begins to disengage.

If clutch operation is not satisfactory after making this adjustment, proceed as follows:

3. Screw the cable adjuster at the lever in all the way thus increasing cable free-play.

4. Remove the clutch adjuster cover plug. Loosen the clutch adjusting screw locknut.

5. Turn the adjusting screw clockwise until a slight resistance is felt, then turn it counterclockwise ¼ turn. Holding the screw in this position, tighten the locknut.

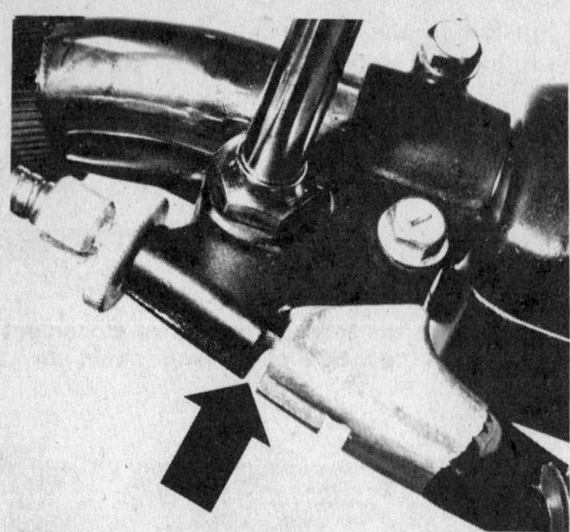
Clutch cable free-play (arrow) should be 2–3 mm (0.08–0.12 in.)

6. Turn the cable adjuster out until there is about 2–3 mm (0.08–0.12 in.) of free-play in the hand lever. Tighten the locknut on the cable adjuster.

Clutch adjuster screw and locknut

Throttle Cable

1. The throttle cable is fitted with an adjuster at the twist-grip. The twist-grip should be able to be rotated approximately 10–15° (3–5 mm [0.12–0.20 in.]) before the throttle slides begin to open.

2. Use the cable adjuster at the handlebar to make and maintain this adjustment. To check that the cable has sufficient slack, start the engine and turn the forks slowly from lock-to-lock. Idle speed must not increase. If it does, it indicates that the cable has insufficient free-play, is incorrectly routed, or is binding at some point.

3. For complete carburetor adjustments, refer to "Tune-Up."

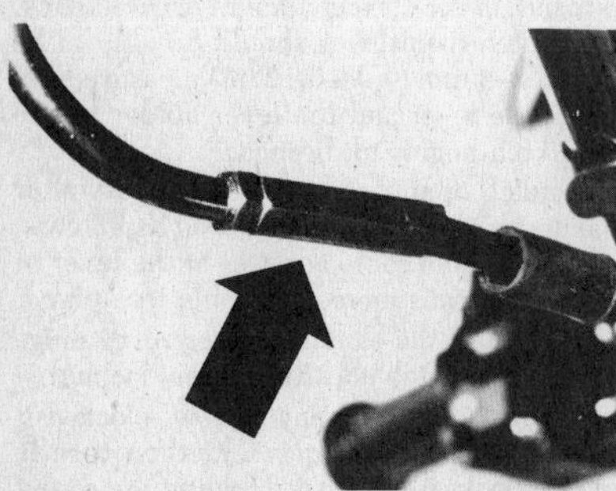
Throttle cable adjuster

Brakes

FRONT DISC

Disc brakes need little attention other than a periodic check of the fluid level and of pad wear:

1. Check the brake fluid level relative to the lower level line inscribed on the see-through master cylinder reservoir. If the fluid level is below the inscribed line, add enough DOT 3 type brake fluid to bring the level up to the mark. Reinstall the master cylinder reservoir cap and tighten the screws securely.

NOTE: *The fluid level will drop slightly as the pads wear.*

2. To check brake pad wear, remove the wear indicator cap on the caliper. The pads should be replaced as a set if either of them is worn to the red limit line inscribed on them.

Refer to "Chassis," for brake system service procedures.

3. If the brake lever feels spongy, or if brake effectiveness has been reduced, a possible cause is air bubbles in the lines. To remedy this, bleed the system. This procedure can also be found in the "Chassis," section.

4. The brake lever should have about 13–25 mm (0.5–1.0 in.) of movement which is measured at the tip of the lever.

Lever movement is adjustable by means of an adjusting screw near the lever holder. Once set properly, the lever travel will not ordinarily need readjustment. If lever travel becomes excessive, it is more probable that the system needs to be bled or has some other fault. Adjusting brake lever travel will not remedy any brake system shortcomings.

Front master cylinder brake fluid level line

Check brake pad wear here

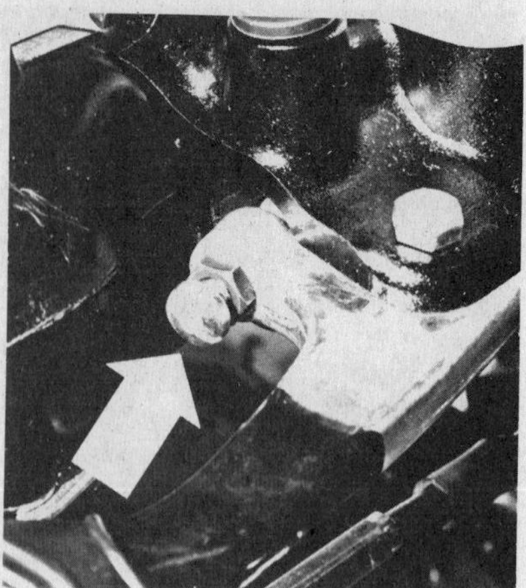
Brake lever adjusting screw

REAR DISC

1. The transparent master cylinder allows inspection of the fluid level without removing the master cylinder cap. If the fluid level is below the level mark, remove the cap and diaphragm and add enough DOT 3 brake fluid to bring the level up to the mark. Reinstall the diaphragm and cap and tighten it securely.

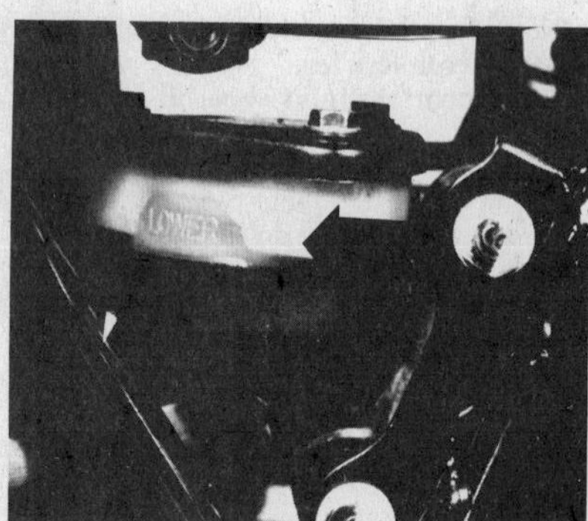

Rear master cylinder brake fluid level line

Brake pedal height adjusting bolt (lower) and brake rod adjuster locknut

2. Pad wear can easily be checked by visual inspection. Replace the pads as a set if either of them is worn to the red limit line.

3. To adjust brake pedal height and free-play, loosen the height adjuster bolt locknut.

Turn the adjuster bolt in or out so that the top of the pedal is about 12–18 mm (0.5–0.7 in.) below the top surface of the footpeg rubber. Tighten the adjuster bolt locknut.

Loosen the brake rod adjuster locknut and turn the brake rod until there is noticeable free-play between the rod and the master cylinder. Turn the brake rod in until it just touches the master cylinder, than back it out about 1½ turns. Tighten the locknut.

CAUTION: *The pin hole mark on the brake rod must not show above the locknut.*

This adjustment should yield brake pedal free-play of 13–15 mm (0.5–0.6 in.).

FRONT DRUM

1. The brake should be adjusted so that the lever has 5–8 mm (0.2–0.3 in.) of free movement measured between the lever and the lever holder before the linings contact the drum.

2. The brake can be adjusted with either the cable adjustor at the brake plate or the adjustor on the handlebar. Loosen the locknut and turn the adjustor out to decrease brake lever movement. It is recommended that major adjustments be made with the adjuster at the brake plate and finer adjustments with the handlebar adjustor.

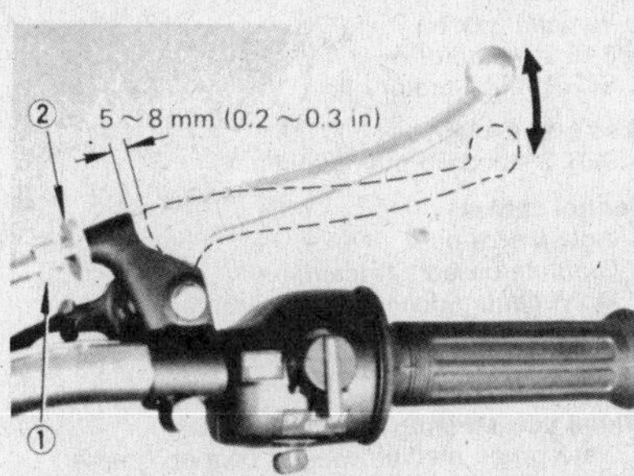

Brake lever free-play showing cable adjuster and locknut (1 and 2)

Brake plate adjuster and locknut (1 and 2)

REAR DRUM

1. On early models with rear drum brakes, brake lining wear can be determined by means of the wear indicator pointer fitted to the brake lever on the hub. If the pointer lines up with the red slash mark when the brake pedal is fully applied, the linings are worn as far as possible for effective braking and should now be replaced.

On late drum-brake models, an inspection plug is fitted to the brake plate to allow direct inspection of the linings. They should be replaced when worn to less than 2 mm (0.08 in.). Thickness of new linings is 4 mm (0.16 in.).

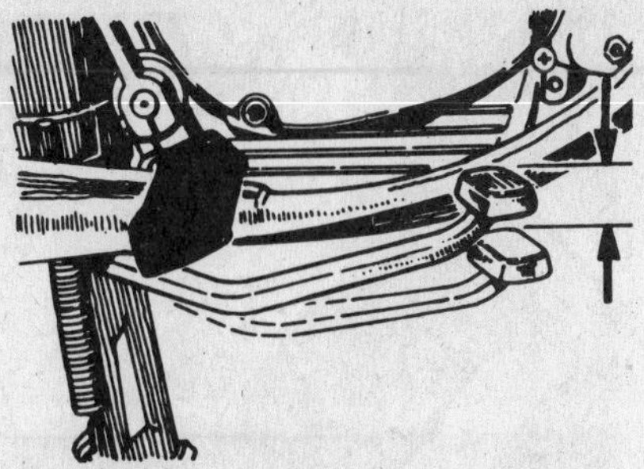

The brake pedal should have about 1 inch of movement before the linings contact the drum

Rear brake adjusting nut

2. Observe the angle formed by the brake lever on the hub and the brake rod when the brake is fully applied. When the lever and rod form an angle greater than 90°, the shoes should be checked for wear as they probably are worn to the point of needing replacement.

3. The rear brake should be adjusted so that there is approximately 25 mm (1.0 in.) free-play at the pedal before the linings contact the drum. Adjust by turning the nut on the brake rod. When adjustment has been made, be sure that the nut is seated properly on the brake lever pin. Also, check the operation of the brake light switch.

4. Brake pedal height can be adjusted by means of the stopper bolt and locknut provided. The pedal height can be adjusted to suit personal preference, but it should generally be about ½ in. measured between the top of the rubber footpeg and the top of the brake pedal.

Be sure to check brake adjustment and brake light operation after making any change in the pedal height.

Brake Light Switches

The switches should be checked for operation after the brakes are adjusted. The rear brake light switch and adjuster nut are mounted on a slotted bracket. The rear switch is adjusted by holding the switch and turning the adjuster nut to effect adjustment. Moving the switch up on the bracket allows the brake light to turn on sooner. Moving it down allows the light to turn on later. Do not turn the switch to effect adjustment as the wires will become twisted and may break.

The front disc brake switch is activated by the pressure of the brake fluid in the brake line. This switch is not adjustable; if defective, it must be replaced.

Headlight Adjustment

1. Set the machine about 25 feet away from a wall, preferably of a color which reflects light well.

The machine should be off the stand, and with a rider putting his weight on the machine as in operation.

2. Switch on the high beam. The headlight high beam should be parallel to the ground and should hit the wall directly in front of the machine.

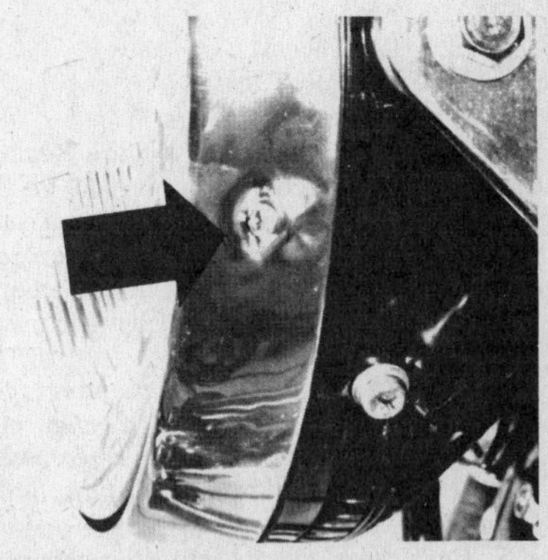

Headlight lateral adjustment screw

3. Vertical adjustment is made by first removing the headlight rim anchor screw and removing the headlight by prying at the point provided at the bottom. Slightly loosen the two headlight shell mounting nuts and install the headlight. Adjust the headlight by pivoting the shell up or down as needed. Remove the headlight and tighten the two mounting bolts. Install the headlight and tighten the anchor screw.

4. Lateral adjustment is accomplished by turning the adjusting screw on the side of the headlight. Tighten the screw to move the beam to the right; loosen it to move the beam towards the left.

FUEL SYSTEM

Fuel system maintenance involves cleaning the petcock fuel filter screen, cleaning or replacing the air filter elements, and cleaning the carburetors.

The normal service interval is 2,000 miles.

Petcock

The petcock is the vacuum-activated type which incorporates a mesh filter inside the gas tank.

Petcock securing screws

1. Set the petcock to the "RES" position. Disconnect the fuel line from the petcock and the vacuum line from the manifold.
2. Remove the gas tank. Drain off the fuel.
3. Unscrew the petcock securing nut or two phillips screws depending upon the method of fastening, and pull off the petcock.
4. Clean the filter screen in a solvent. Be sure to remove any foreign matter trapped in the screen as this will impede fuel flow. If the screen cannot be cleaned, or if it is punctured or otherwise damaged, it should be replaced.
5. Check the sealing washer and replace it if it is damaged.
6. Install the petcock. After the tank is refitted, check for leaks before operating the motorcycle.

Air Filters

1. Remove the side covers.
2. Loosen the carburetor clamp. Remove the element case holder screw, take off the securing band, and remove the element case.
3. Remove the case screws and separate the case halves, removing the filter element.
4. Blow out the elements from the inside with compressed air.

NOTE: *After several such cleanings, the elements should be replaced with new ones. The service interval for replacement will depend upon the amount of dirt build-up on the elements.*

5. Refit the elements into their cases and install them.

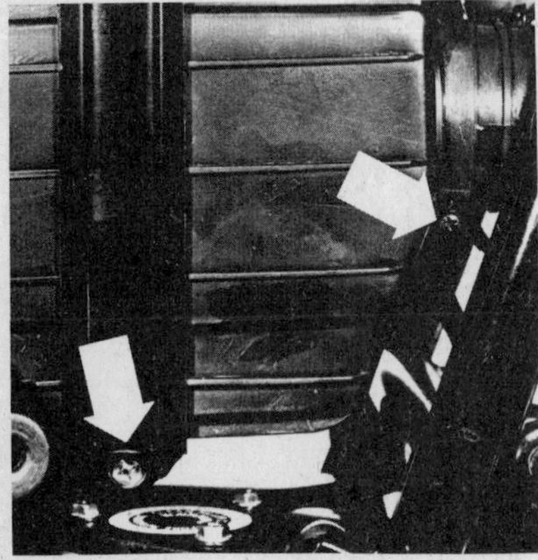

Air filter case holder and hose clamp screw

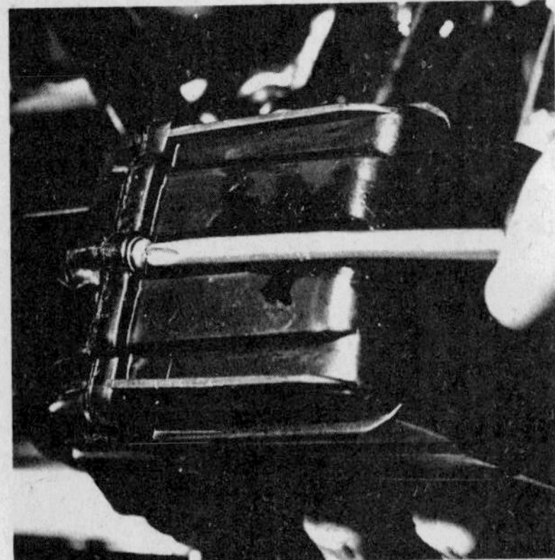

Separating the air cleaner case

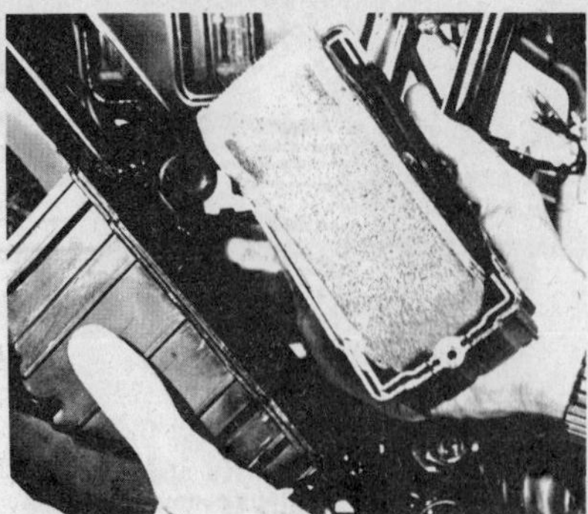

Air filter element

Carburetors

1. Although major overhaul of the carburetors requires their removal as a unit, the float bowls and jets can be cleaned with the units in place.
2. Make sure that the petcock is shut off ("RES" position). Drain the fuel from the carburetor float bowls by removing the main jet cover bolt from the bottom of the float bowls.

CAUTION: *Do not let gasoline spill on a hot engine.*

3. Remove the four screws which secure each float bowl and carefully lower the bowls until they are clear of the float mechanism.

Carburetor float bowl drain plug

4. Unscrew and remove the main and pilot jets. These are fitted to the float bowl on 360 models and are on the carburetor bodies on 400 models. Blow the jets clear, then reinstall. Clean any foreign matter out of the float bowls. When installing, position the bowls carefully to avoid damage to the floats. Tighten the screws gradually and evenly. Check for fuel leaks before operation.

Periodic Maintenance Intervals ①

Before each ride
- Safety items
- Operation of lights
- Chain adjustment
- Control cable adjustment

Weekly
- Engine oil level
- Tire pressure (check when cold)
- Battery electrolyte level

Every 200 miles
- Lubricate chain

Every 1,000 miles
- Clean chain

Every 2,000 miles/3 months
- Change engine oil
- Clean air filter
- Check swing arm
- Lubricate cables
- Check steering bearing adjustment
- Lubricate swing arm pivot
- Check rim run-out and spoke tension
- Check wheel bearings
- Clean fuel petcock and carburetors
- Check and adjust ignition timing
- Check spark plugs

Every 4,000 miles/6 months
- Change oil filter
- Clean oil strainer
- Check compression
- Check cylinder head bolt torque
- Check oil pressure

Every 10,000 miles
- Change fork oil

Every 12,000 miles/24 months
- Flush and refill hydraulic disc brake system
- Repack wheel and steering head bearings

① Based on normal usage after initial service and break-in are completed.

Recommended Lubricants

Engine
At ambient temperatures above 5° C (41° F):
- Yamalube 4-cycle oil
- SAE 20W-40 service rating "SE" or "SF"

At ambient temperatures below 15° C (59° F):
- SAE 10W-30 service rating "SE" or "SF"

Front forks
- Yamaha fork oil
- SAE 20W motor oil
- SAE 10W-30 motor oil

Disc brake systems
- DOT 3 standard brake fluid

Control cables
- Light motor oil
- Graphite-based lubricant
- Molybdenum-disulphide-based lubricant

Tach, speedometer cables; throttle twist-grip
- Light duty grease

Wheel and steering head bearings
- Waterproof, medium-weight bearing grease

Grease fittings
- Waterproof, medium-weight chassis grease

Drive chain
- Lubricant developed specifically for motorcycle drive chains

Maintenance Data

	XS360	*XS400*
Fuel capacity (gal/1)	2.9/11	①
Oil capacity (qt/1)		
Routine change	2.1/2.0	2.1/2.0
Oil and filter change	2.4/2.3	2.4/2.3
After rebuilding engine	2.7/2.6	2.7/2.6
Front forks (oz/cc)	4.4/130	②
Tire pressure (psi)		
Solo (front/rear)	26/28	26/28
Two-up or extended high speed (front/rear)	28/33	28/33
Battery		
Voltage	12	12
Output (ah)	③	12
Continuous charging rate (amps)	④	1.2

① XS400D, 2E: 2.9/11
XS400E,F,2F,G,SG: 3.7/14
② XS400D, 2E: 4.4/130
XS400E,F,2F,G,SG,H: 4.8/142
③ XS360C:12
XS360-2D:7
④ XS360C:1.2
XS360-2D:0.7

TUNE-UP

NOTE: *Common tune-up procedures are explained in detail in the "General Information" section.*

COMPRESSION TEST

1. A compression check should be made before each tune-up since this will provide a general idea of engine condition.
2. It is necessary to have a gauge with the proper adapter (plug holes are 14 mm) if a screw-in type gauge is used. The less expensive "hold in" type gauges can also be used. Use some oil on the rubber tip to ensure a good seal.
3. The engine should be at operating temperature when checking compression.
4. Remove both of the spark plugs and fit the gauge to one of the plug holes.
5. Close the choke and hold the throttle wide open while spinning the engine with the starter motor or the kickstarter. Note the highest compression reading and repeat the test with the remaining cylinder.
6. Compression may vary according to gauge tolerance and several other factors. However, it should normally be between 140 and 170 psi. Both cylinders must be within 15 psi of this range and of each other.

CAM CHAIN ADJUSTMENT

The cam chain tension is automatically regulated. No routine adjustment is required.

VALVE ADJUSTMENT

NOTE: *Valves must be adjusted when the engine is cold.*

1. Turn the fuel petcock to the "RES" position. Disconnect the fuel feed line and the vacuum line from the petcock.
2. Remove the gas tank.
3. Remove the intake and exhaust tappet covers.
4. Remove the alternator rotor cover.
5. The valves for each cylinder are adjusted when the piston for the cylinder is at top dead center on the compression stroke. Use a wrench on the rotor nut so that the "LT" mark on the rotor is aligned with the stationary timing mark on the crankcase cover. Check that there is clearance at both valves for the left cylinder. There should be a little movement in both rocker arms. If there is not, it indicates that the piston is at TDC on the *exhaust* stroke. If this is the case, rotate the engine through one full turn of the rotor and align the "LT" mark again. This should be TDC on the compression stroke.

Alternator rotor cover allen bolts

Checking valve adjustment

Alternator rotor aligned with timing mark to position right-side piston at top dead center

6. Check the clearance between the rocker arm and the top of the valve for both intake and exhaust valves using the appropriate feeler gauges.

Clearances should be 0.08-0.12 mm (0.003-0.005 in.) for the intake, and 0.16-0.20 mm (0.006-0.008 in.) for the exhaust.

If the clearance is correct, a feeler gauge of the proper thickness will be a light slip fit between the rocker arm and valve.

7. If adjustment is necessary, loosen the adjuster locknut and turn the adjuster screw so that clearance is correct. Again, the feeler gauge should be a slip fit between the rocker arm and valve. Hold the adjuster in place and tighten the locknut securely. Recheck the clearance.
8. Turn the rotor one full turn so that the "RT" mark (for the right cylinder) is aligned with the stationary timing mark. Check that the piston is at TDC on the compression stroke by noting clearance at both valves as before. Check the right cylinder valves in the same manner.

NOTE: *When the engine is at operating temperature, the valves should be very quiet. Ticking from properly adjusted valves is sometimes due to the valve stem becoming indented by the valve adjuster screw. This should be confined to older machines, since the valve ends are stellite-coated. Indentations on the valve stem will give a false feeler gauge reading: the clearance will be too large. Valves can be checked by visual inspection by unscrewing the adjuster.*

While more annoying than harmful, the only safe remedy for this situation is replacement of the valves.

CONTACT BREAKER POINTS

Location

The contact breaker points are opened and closed by a cam on the end of the camshaft and are located beneath a cover on the left side of the cylinder head.

The timing advance mechanism is located behind the breaker point plate.

The condensers are mounted near the coils.

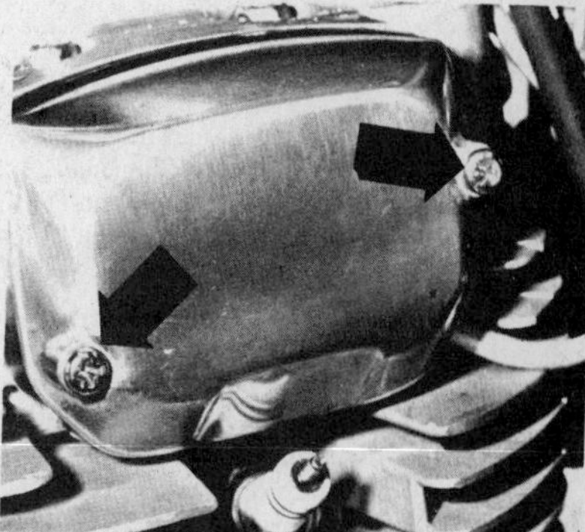
Breaker point cover screws

Replacement

1. Points sets purchased complete with the breaker plate can be easily replaced by disconnecting the primary wires at the connectors beneath the gas tank, removing the two large breaker plate securing screws, and carefully pulling off the old plate and points. After installing the new points and plate, the breaker point gaps and the ignition timing must be set (see below).
2. If the points are purchased separately, disconnect the primary wire at each point set, remove the securing screws, and remove the old points. When installing new points, note that the proper installation of the insulating washers at the primary terminal is critical. If improperly installed, no spark will occur. There is a small insulating tube which fits around the terminal bolt and two insulating washers, one immediately on either side of the terminal bracket. All connectors (primary wire, points spring) are made on the outer sides of these washers (i.e., no connector must touch the bracket, which is a ground).
3. New points may have a protective coating on the contact surfaces to prevent oxidation. Clean off these surfaces with a non-oily

Primary wire connectors beneath the gas tank

solvent before attempting to start the machine.

4. If the motorcycle will not start immediately after installation of new points, check that the primary wire connections under the gas tank are tight, that the insulating washers at the primary terminal are properly installed, and that the contact surfaces are thoroughly cleaned.

5. Condensers are easily replaced after disconnecting the lead near the coils and removing the screw which secures the condenser.

Gapping

Periodic gapping is necessary to compensate for erosion of the contact surfaces due to electrical arcing and for wear of the fiber heel. As the heel wears, the points will open later relative to the rotation of the crankshaft, thus retarding the timing slightly.

Points should be filed (if necessary) and cleaned before gapping.

1. Remove the points cover.
2. Turn the engine over until one of the two sets of points is fully open.
3. With the proper feeler gauge blade, check the gap. The proper specification is 0.3–0.4 mm (0.012–0.016 in.), and the blade should be a slip fit between the points if the gap is correct.

Checking point gap

4. If adjustment is necessary, loosen the screws which secure the point set to its plate, and use a small screwdriver at the pry point provided to adjust the gap.

CAUTION: *Loosen the screws just enough to allow the points to be moved. If loosened too much, the points will snap shut instead of holding the gap.*

5. Tighten the screws and recheck the gap. It may change slightly when the screws are tightened.
6. Repeat the procedure with the remaining points set. Try to adjust both sets so that the feeler gauge blade has the same "feel" in both sets. This will help to ensure accurate timing.
7. If it is not possible to gap the points correctly, the fiber heel is evidently worn; the points should then be replaced.

Loosen the screws indicated by arrows to adjust the point gap for both point sets

Lubrication

1. On all models it is necessary to occasionally lubricate the cam follower fiber heel and the pivot point of the contact breaker. This minimizes wear and ensures that the timing will remain accurate for a longer period. A worn heel will retard the timing.
2. A small dab of grease (high melting point, if possible) should be applied to the lubricator wick so that the lubricator can distribute it onto the breaker cam. A drop of engine oil should be applied to the pivot point.
3. In both cases it is imperative that care be taken to keep the lubricant away from the points contact surface.
4. The lubricating wick should be adjusted so that it just contacts the breaker cam.

IGNITION TIMING (BREAKER POINT MODELS)

All models except the XS400G/SG and H models are fitted with contact breaker points. Procedures for the transistorized ignition found on the G/SG and H models are given in the next section.

The rotor marks are interpreted as follows: "LT" indicates top dead center for the left piston, "RT" for the right piston. "LF" and "RF" are the fixed-advance firing points for the two pistons, which is about 10° before TDC. There are, in addition, two other marks, and these represent the full-advance firing points, which is about 36° before TDC. Timing advance begins at about 2500 rpm.

NOTE: *Points must be cleaned and gapped before checking timing. Dirty points will cause inaccurate readings.*

Remove the points cover and observe the breaker plate. Note that the points for the left cylinder (orange lead) are mounted directly to the large breaker plate, while the points for the right cylinder (grey lead) are mounted on a smaller moveable plate. Therefore, the *left* cylinder timing must be set *first*, since adjustment involves turning the entire breaker plate, which will alter the timing of the right cylinder as well. The points for the right cylinder are adjusted by moving only the points themselves.

Dynamic Timing

1. Park the bike on the centerstand in a well-ventilated area.

Static firing point for the left-side cylinder

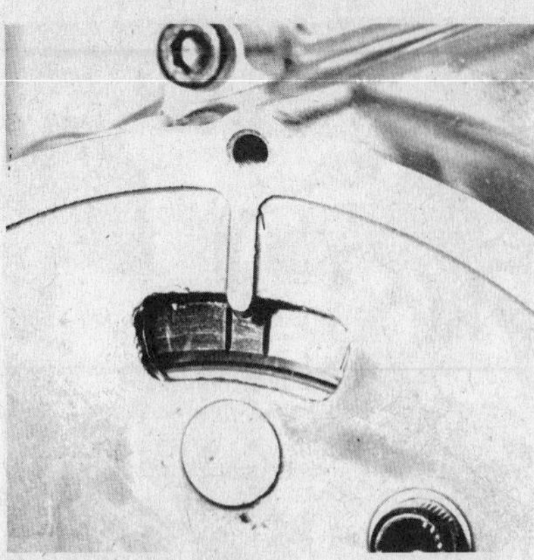

Full advance firing point is indicated by two lines

2. Remove the points cover and the alternator rotor cover. Clean and gap both sets of points as previously described.

3. Hook up the strobe light according to the manufacturer's instructions to pick up impulses from the left cylinder.

4. Start the engine and adjust the idle speed, if necessary, to 1,200 rpm.

5. Aim the timing light at the marks on the alternator rotor visible through the cutout. At idle, the "LF" mark on the rotor should align with the stationary timing mark.

6. To check the ignition timing at full advance, increase engine speed until the motor is turning 2,500–3,000 rpm. At this point, the stationary timing mark should be between the two full advance marks scribed onto the alternator rotor.

7. If adjustment is necessary, loosen the two large base plate screws, and rotate the entire plate so that the proper marks align at the specified rpm. Establishing this alignment at full advance is recommended. Tighten the base plate screws.

To adjust the timing for the left cylinder, loosen the two breaker plate screws (large arrows) and rotate the entire plate. To adjust the right cylinder, loosen the two point screws (smaller arrows) and move the right cylinder's points

8. Repeat the procedure, this time having the strobe light pick up the *right* cylinder. If adjustment is necessary, loosen the two small phillips screws which secure the points set to its plate, and use a small screwdriver at the pry point provided to move the set so that proper mark alignment is achieved. Tighten the screws.

9. If it is not possible to achieve full advance alignment without moving the base plate or the right points set all the way to the end of their range of allowable travel, it is possible that the points are either incorrectly gapped, or that they are worn to the point where they must be replaced.

Static Timing

1. Remove the points cover and the alternator rotor cover.

2. Clean and gap both sets of points as described previously.

3. Connect one lead of the tester or test light to the primary wire terminal for the left cylinder (orange lead), and the other tester lead to ground on the engine or frame.

4. If the test device is not self-powered, turn the ignition switch *on* and be sure the kill switch is in the middle position.

5. Turn the engine over in the normal direction of rotation until the "LF" mark aligns with the stationary timing mark. The test instrument should react at the instant these marks align, indicating that the points have opened. If they do not, loosen the two large screws which secure the points base plate and rotate the plate so that the points just open when the timing marks are in alignment. Tighten the base plate screws and recheck the timing.

6. Repeat the procedure with the right points set. If adjustment is necessary, loosen the two screws which secure these points to their mounting plate and use a small screwdriver at the pry point provided. Tighten the screws and recheck the timing.

IGNITION TIMING (XS400G/SG,H)

Because of the transistorized spark unit which is used in place of the more conventional breaker points, ignition timing for these models need not be checked unless the pick-up unit is removed.

If a check is required, note that the "LF" timing mark on the rotor should align with the index mark at 1200 rpm. Dynamic timing (using a strobe light) is the only method of checking the timing. Adjustment is not possible. If the marks are not properly aligned at the given speed, the only cause would be a loose spark unit rotor bolt.

CARBURETORS

Carburetor adjustments to be made during a tune-up include setting float level, synchronization, and idle speed and mixture.

Adjusting Float Level

1. Float level is a measure of the amount of gasoline which will be in the float bowls during operation. While it is a critical specification, it will not normally need readjustment once properly set. Float level, therefore, need not be checked at every tune-up, but should be attended to from time to time.

2. Remove the carburetors.

3. Remove the float bowls. Remove the gasket. With the carburetor(s) positioned vertically, lower the float until the float arm just touches but does not depress the tip of the float needle. Float level is the measured distance from the bottom of the float to the float bowl mating surface.

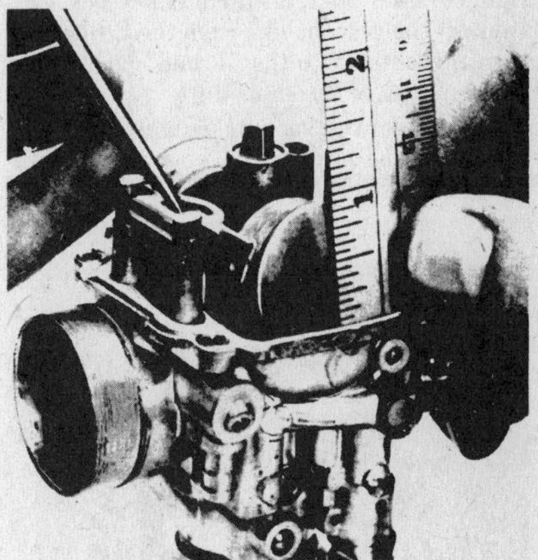

Checking float level

4. Float level for each model is given in the "Tune-Up Specifications" chart at the end of this section. Adjust, if necessary, by pushing out the float pivot pin, removing the floats, and bending the float arm tang. Bending the tang towards the carburetor body will increase the float level measurement and vice-versa.

5. Both carburetors must have the same float level. Measure both before changing either. Note that the measured float level will be inaccurate if the float needle tip is worn or if there is foreign matter on the needle seat.

Adjusting the float tang

Synchronization

Vacuum gauges are necessary to properly synchronize the carburetors, although a rough approximation can be made by visually aligning the butterflies (see below).

The butterflies are synchronized by means of a single screw located between the two carburetors. Turning the screw simultaneously closes one butterfly while opening the other.

1. Run the engine until operating temperature is reached.

2. Remove the gas tank's rear mounting bolt and raise the tank (fitting a longer fuel

feed line if necessary, so that the synchronization screw between the carburetors is accessible.

3. The vacuum gauge fittings are on the manifolds. The vacuum gauge fitting for the right cylinder operates the fuel petcock. Disconnect the petcock line from the fitting, and turn the petcock to the "Prime" position for the duration of the procedure.

4. Connect the vacuum gauges.

5. Start the engine and note the vacuum readings. At idle (1,200 rpm) the two cylinders must be within 5 cm Hg (0.2 in. Hg). Adjust, if necessary, by turning the synchronization screw in or out until the vacuum readings for the two cylinders is as identical as possible.

NOTE: *If the vacuum gauges read more than 5 cm Hg (0.2 in. Hg) at 1,200 rpm, check the compression, spark plugs, ignition timing, and valve clearance.*

6. If vacuum gauges are not available, a rough method of synchronizing the carburetors may be carried out. Remove the carburetors as a unit from the motorcycle. Look into the engine side of the carburetors and note the relative positions of the edges of the butterflies in relation to the small by-pass passages in the bottom of the bores. Both butterflies should be in the same position relative to these by-pass holes.

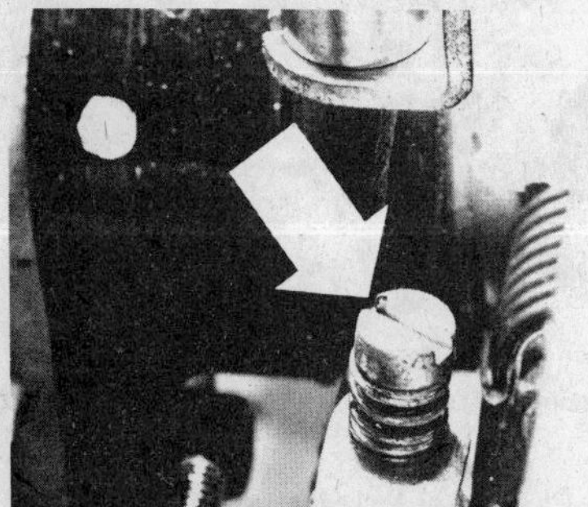

Carburetor synchronizing screw

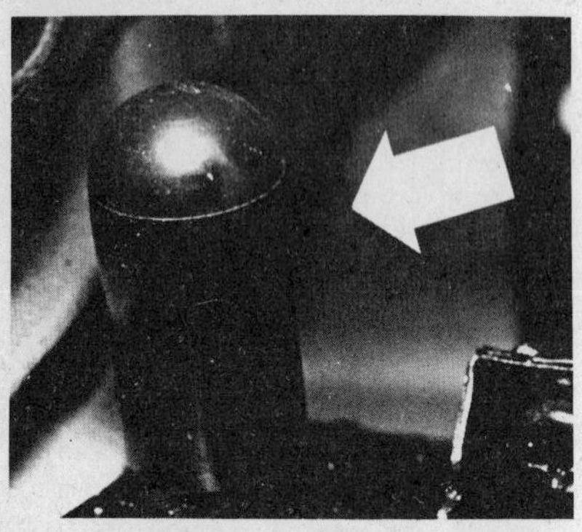

Manifold vacuum fitting (left side)

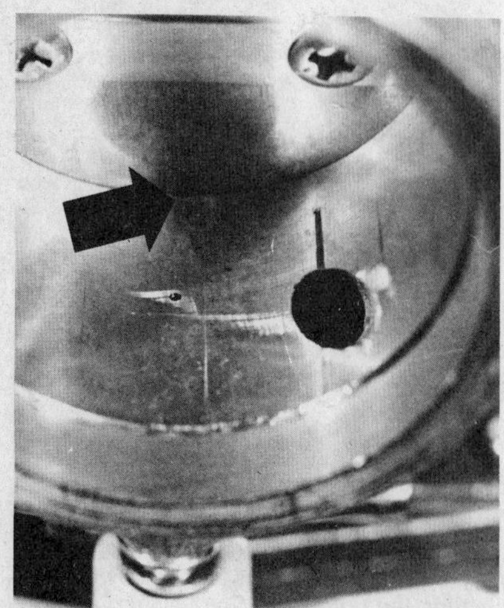

Aligning both butterflies relative to the bypass outlet is a rough way to synchronize the carburetors

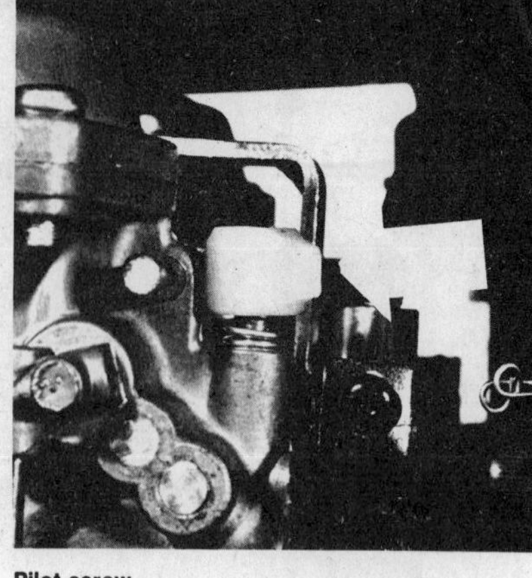

Pilot screw

Idle Speed and Mixture

1. The idle mixture is controlled by a pilot screw fitted to each carburetor. The screws are fixed in position by means of idle limiter caps. This is designed to reduce emissions. Therefore, it is not generally necessary to adjust the pilot screws.

2. If the limiter caps are missing, or if the pilot screws have been removed (as during a carburetor overhaul), pilot screw adjustment is accomplished by screwing the pilot screws in (very carefully) until lightly seated, then backing them out 1½ turns on 360 models and 1¼ turns on 400 models.

3. Idle speed is set by means of the throttle stop screw between the carburetors. Idle speed is 1,200 rpm, and must be adjusted when the engine is at operating temperature.

Throttle stop screw

Tune-Up Specifications

Item	*XS360*	*XS400D/E*	*Other Models*
Compression			
Cranking pressure (psi)	140–170	140–170	140–170
Max allowable variation (psi)	15	15	15
Valve clearance			
Intake (mm/in.)	0.08–0.12/0.003–0.005	0.08–0.12/0.003–0.005	0.08–0.12/0.003–0.005
Exhaust (mm/in.)	0.16–0.20/0.006–0.008	0.16–0.20/0.006–0.008	0.16–0.20/0.006–0.008
Ignition			
Spark plugs			
OEM	NGK/Champion	NGK/Champion	NGK/Champion
Standard	BP-6ES/N-7Y	BP-7ES/N-7	BP-6ES/N-7Y
Hot	BP-5ES/N-13Y	BP-6ES/N-13Y	BP-5ES/N-13Y
Cold	BP-7ES/N-8Y	BP-8ES/N-8Y	BP-7ES/N-8Y
Spark plug gap (mm/in.)	0.7–0.8/0.028–0.032	0.7–0.8/0.028–0.032	0.7–0.8/0.028–0.032
Breaker point gap (mm/in.)	0.3–0.4/0.012–0.016	0.3–0.4/0.012–0.016	0.3–0.4/0.012–0.016
Ignition timing			
Static (degrees BTDC)	10	10	10
Maximum (degrees BTDC @ 2500 rpm)	36	36	36
Carburetion			
Idle speed (rpm)	1,200	1,200	1,200
Pilot screws (turns out)	1½	1¼	not adjustable
Vacuum uniformity (cm/in. Hg)	5/0.2	5/0.2	5/0.2
Float level (mm/in.)	26.6/1.05	32.0/1.26	①

① XS400-2E: 25.7/1.0
XS400F/2F: 32.0/1.26
XS400G/SG,H: 27.3/1.1

ENGINE AND TRANSMISSION

NOTE: *Common engine rebuilding techniques and inspection procedures are given under "Engine Rebuilding" in the General Information section.*

ENGINE SERVICE

1. The cylinder head, barrels, and pistons can be removed with the engine in the frame.
2. Crankcase cover components such as the clutch, oil pump, kickstarter assembly, alternator, etc., can also be serviced without removing the engine.
3. Service to the crankshaft, transmission, and gear shift components requires removal of the engine.
4. Read each procedure carefully before beginning so that replacement items such as gaskets, o-rings, etc., can be purchased before-hand.

ENGINE REMOVAL AND INSTALLATION

1. Clean and degrease the engine thoroughly before removal. This will minimize chances of foreign matter getting into the crankcase during the disassembly procedure.
2. Disconnect the fuel line from the petcock, the vacuum line from the right manifold, the bolt from the rear of the tank, and remove the gas tank.
3. Drain the crankcase oil. Remove the oil filter housing.
4. Remove the side covers. Remove the air filter boxes. Remove the air filter hoses from the carburetors.
5. Disconnect the throttle cable from the linkage, loosen the carburetor clamps, and remove the two carburetors as a unit.
6. Remove the mufflers and header pipes.
7. Remove the rider footpegs.
8. Remove the rear brake pedal.
9. Remove the gearshift lever from its shaft.
10. Disconnect the spark plug caps and loosen the plugs.
11. Disconnect the tachometer cable from the cylinder head.
12. Remove the engine sprocket cover. Disconnect the clutch cable.
13. Disconnect the breaker point leads and the alternator wires at the connectors.
14. Disconnect the started motor lead from the solenoid.
15. Disconnect the battery ground lead.
16. To remove the engine sprocket, temporarily fit the gear shift lever, engage the transmission, fit the rear brake pedal, apply the brake, and remove the engine sprocket nut. Remove the sprocket from its shaft. It may be necessary to move the rear wheel forward to yield sufficient chain slack to allow this.
17. Remove the engine mounting bolts and take the engine out of the frame.
18. Installation is the reverse of removal. Note the following points:
   a. Install the engine in the frame from the right side.
   b. Tighten the 10 mm nuts to 18-30 ft lbs. Tighten the 8 mm nuts and bolts to 10–21 ft lbs.

TOP END

Cylinder Head Removal

1. Remove the gas tank by disconnecting the fuel line from the petcock and the vacuum line from the manifold and the rear tank mounting bolt.
2. Disconnect the throttle cable at the carburetors. Loosen the carburetor manifold and air cleaner hose clamp screws and remove the carburetors as a unit.
3. Remove the exhaust system. Disconnect the spark plug caps. Remove the plugs.
4. On breaker point-equipped models, disconnect the point leads at the connectors. Remove the breaker point cover. Remove the point assembly. Pull off the timing mechanism. Disconnect the tachometer cable from the cylinder head.

On transistorized ignition models, a special procedure is necessary. Proceed as follows to remove the pick-up coil which is fitted in place of the breaker points:

   a. Centerpunch the blind plug which secures the pick-up coil cover. Use a 5 mm drill bit to drill the plug.

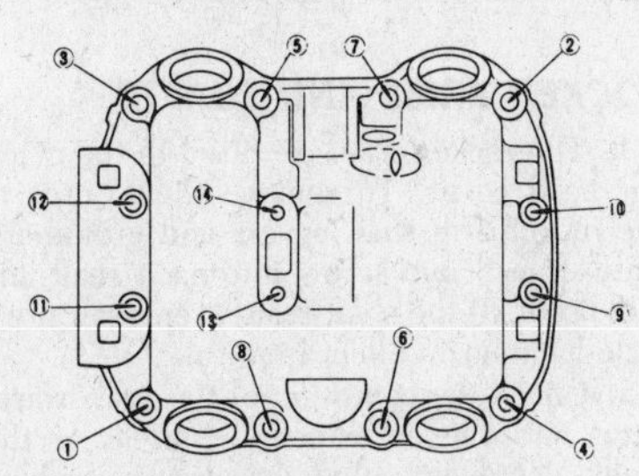

Cylinder head cover bolt loosening order

Removing the cam chain tensioner assembly

Camshaft sprocket bolt

Removing the camshaft. Note cam chain secured by wire

Removing the cam chain guide

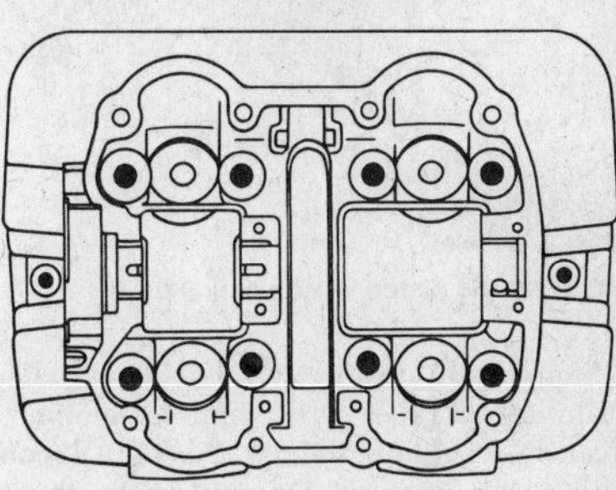
Cylinder head nuts and bolts

   b. Cut internal threads 6 mm diameter x 1.0 mm pitch in the blind plug with a proper size tap. Thread in the special slide hammer or a suitable metric bolt, and pull out the plug.
   c. Remove the cover screws and take off the cover.
   d. Remove the rotor bolt and the rotor.
   e. Remove the pick-up coil screws and remove the assembly.

5. Remove the cylinder head-to-frame mounting nuts and bolts.
6. Remove the cylinder head cover bolts. Loosen the bolts gradually and in a cross pattern. If the cover is stuck, tap around the sides with a plastic mallet to free it.
7. Remove the alternator rotor cover.
8. Take out the cam chain tensioner assembly. Note the location of each part.
9. Turn the engine over, if necessary, so that one of the cam chain sprocket bolts is acessible. Remove the bolt. Turn the engine over so that the other bolt can be removed.
10. Loop a length of wire through one of the cam chain sprocket holes and anchor the wire to the engine. Remove the camshaft.
11. Remove the cam chain guides.
12. Remove the cylinder head nuts and bolts. Remove the cylinder head.

Cylinder and Piston Removal

1. Lift the cylinder a few inches off its seat and stuff a clean, lint-free rag or rags beneath the pistons. This is to prevent any foreign matter or pieces of broken piston ring from falling into the crankcase when the cylinders are removed.

2. Lift the cylinder straight up and free of the studs.

3. With a needle-nosed pliers, remove the wrist pin circlips from the pistons. Push out the piston wrist pins and remove the pistons from the rods.

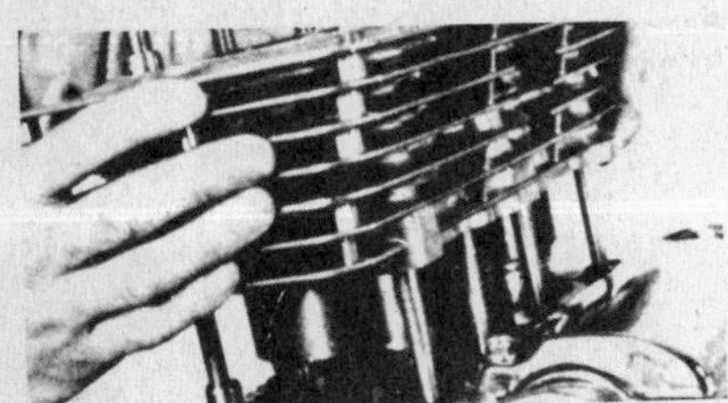

Removing the cylinders

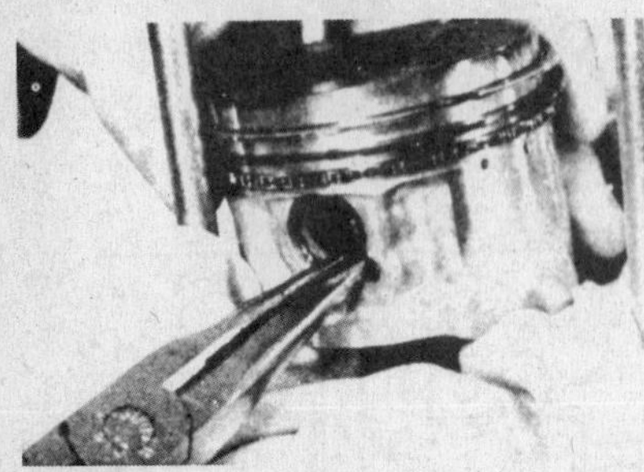

Removing the piston wrist pin circlip

Support the piston with one hand while pushing out the wrist pin to minimize chances of bending the rod. Push the pin out with stead pressure. Do *not* use an impact method. If the wrist pins resist removal, heat the piston crown gently and evenly with a propane torch until the pins can be easily pushed out.

Disgard the wrist pin circlips. New circlips must be used on assembly.

4. Mark each piston so that it can be installed in its original cylinder on reassembly.

Inspection

CAMSHAFT

1. Check the cam lobes for flaking, scoring, or blue discoloration, and replace the cam if any of these signs of damage are present.

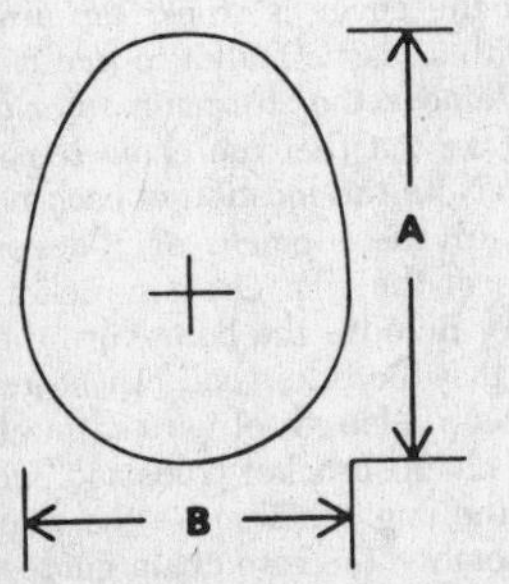

Measure cam lobe height (A) and base circle diameter (B)

2. With a micrometer, measure the height of each cam lobe and compare the measurement with the specifications given in the chart at the end of this section.

3. Measure the base circle of each cam lobe. This measurement is taken in a plane perpendicular to the cam height measurement through the camshaft centerline. Refer

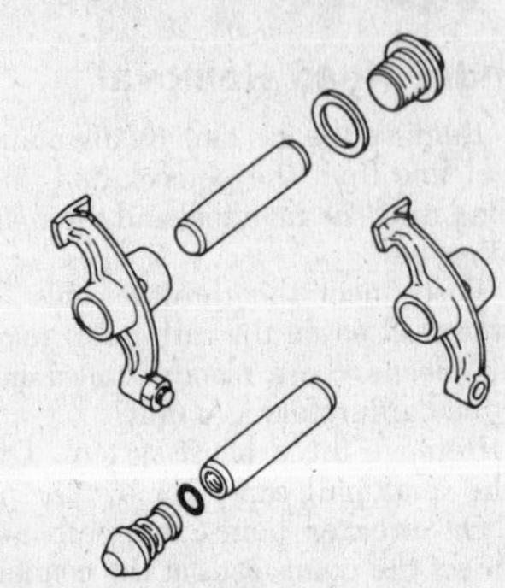

Rocker arm assembly

to the specifications chart at the end of this section.

4. Mount the camshaft in a set of v-blocks and measure run-out with a dial gauge. If run-out exceeds 0.03 mm (0.0012 in.), the cam should be replaced.

5. Check the cam bearings for scoring and wear. Check the journals as well. Measure the journal diameters, referring to the specifications chart at the end of this section.

ROCKER ARMS AND SHAFTS

1. The rocker arms are fitted to the cylinder head cover. To remove them, remove the rocker arm shaft covers and grommets. Thread an 8 mm screw into each shaft and pull it out. If the shaft resists removal, use a slide-hammer to effect removal.

2. Check the condition of the rocker arm bores and the corresponding areas of the shafts. Note any blue discoloration which might be due to excessive heat or lack of lubricant. Replace the rocker arms and shafts if this condition exists, or if there are obvious signs of damage, such as scoring.

3. Check the cam contacting pad of each rocker arm for pitting or wear. Replace the arm if wear is evident.

4. Measure the inside diameter of the rocker arm bore and the outside diameter of the shaft. Standard clearance is 0.016–0.054 mm (0.00063–0.00212 in.). If the clearance exceeds 0.1 mm (0.004 in.), replace the components.

CYLINDER HEAD

1. Clean any traces of head gasket material from the cylinder head mating surface. Place a straight edge across the mating surface and check for warpage by attempting to slip feeler gauge blades between the head and straight edge. Standard head warpage is about 0.05 mm (0.002 in.), and maximum allowable warpage is 0.1 mm (0.004 in.). At this point, the head should be milled to restore a flat mating surface.

2. Use a wire brush fitting on a power drill to decarbonize the combustion chambers. The valves should be left in place as this is done, as it minimizes the chance of causing damage to the valve seats.

VALVE ASSEMBLY

Before removing the valves, check their sealing ability by pouring a small quantity of gasoline into each port and allowing the head to sit for about five minutes. If the valves are properly seating, leakage into the combustion chamber will be minimal.

1. To remove the valves, and install them properly, a suitable C-clamp is necessary. Compress the valve springs and remove the split collars, retainers, springs, seals, and spring seats. Inspect the valves, guides, springs, and valve seats in the following manner. Keep each assembly separate so that every piece can be installed in its original location. New valve seals must always be used on assembly.

2. If considerable mileage has been covered, the valve springs should be replaced as a matter of course. Always replace valve springs as a set.

Measure the free-length of each valve spring with a vernier caliper. If any of the springs is more than 2 mm (0.08 in.) less than the standard free-length given in the specifications chart at the end of this section, the springs should all be replaced.

3. Each valve must be free to move up and down in its guide with little resistance. Any sticking or binding as the valve is moved in the guide will indicate that the valve stem or guide is in poor condition.

4. Inspect the valve, paying close attention to the edges of the valve head for pitting, burnt or broken edges, excessive carbon build-up, etc. A certain amount of carbon and lead deposits on the valve face and the top of the exhaust valve are inevitable. Heavy deposits should be carefully scraped off with a dull knife, or a wire wheel, and the valve finished up with very fine emery cloth.

Do not touch the valve seating area during these operations.

If the valve has burnt or broken edges, it must be replaced.

5. Check the end of the valve stem for indented wear caused by the valve adjuster. Although rare, it may occur after long mileage. Since an indentation here will make proper valve adjustments impossible, the valve should be replaced.

NOTE: *The tips and edges of the valves are stellite-coated. Machining for any reason is not recommended. In case of wear, replace the valve.*

6. Carbon deposits should not extend too far up along the valve stem. This would indicate a worn or cracked valve guide.

7. Wet, oily deposits on the back of the valve head is indicative of a worn guide or bad seal. Less severe wear to these components show up as brown oil stains on the valve stem.

8. Holding a valve in your fingers, spin it while observing the head. A wobble is indicative of a bent valve. If a dial gauge is available, check the run-out of the head. Replace the valve if run-out exceeds 0.03 mm (0.0012 in.). Run-out is the total indicated dial gauge reading.

Attempt to rotate the valve by hand when it is fully inserted into the guide. If the valve will not rotate easily, or if it sticks as it is turned, it is probably bent.

9. Check valve-to-stem clearance and compare to the specification given. Insert the valve in the guide, holding it about ½ in. off

the seat; check the total amount of allowable movement in two directions using a dial gauge.

Maximum allowable clearances are 0.08 mm (0.003 in.) for the intake valves and 0.1 mm (0.004 in.) for the exhaust valves. If the measured clearances exceed these amounts, replace both valve and guide.

A quick check of the operational worthiness of a valave and guide can be accomplished by dipping the valve stem in oil and inserting it into its guide. Place a finger over the other end of the guide. Pull the valve a little way out of the guide and release it. The valve should be drawn back into the guide by suction if the components are in serviceable condition.

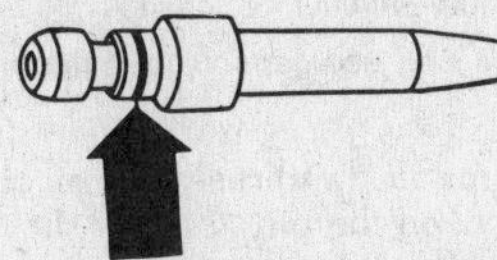

Oversized valve guides are identified by a groove around the upper part of the guide

Valve springs are installed with the close coils (arrows) towards the head

10. Measure the diameter of each valve stem at three places along the length of the valve. Check the measurement against the standard diameter given in the chart at the end of this section, and replace the valve if any of the measurements is below the standard.

11. To replace a valve guide, heat the cylinder head in an oven to a temperature of 212°F (100°C). Drive out the old guide(s) with a suitable drift. Drive in the new guide(s) until fully seated. Use new o-rings.

NOTE: *When replacing valve guides, use the special oversized guides. These are easily identified since they have a groove around the upper part of the guide.*

After installation, ream the new guide(s) with a 7 mm reamer. Clean the inside of the guide thoroughly afterwards.

12. After installing new guides, the valve seat should be recut and the valve lapped in.

13. Check the width of the valve seat on the valve. It should be about 1.0 mm (0.04 in.) all the way around. If narrower or wider than this, or if width varies around the valve, the seat should be recut and the valve lapped in.

NOTE: *Valve springs are progressively wound. When installing them, be sure they are fitted with the close coils towards the cylinder head.*

SEAT CUTTING

1. Use a machinist's dye to check the width and position of the valve seat. Apply the dye to the valve's beveled seating area and a very small amount of grinding compound to the valve seat in the head. Spin the valve back and forth against the seat for several seconds, then remove the grinding compound and inspect the pattern of the seat, from which the dye will have been removed.

2. The valve seat should be about 1.0 mm (0.04 in.) wide and even in width all around the valve. The maximum acceptable seat width is 1.5 mm (0.06 in.).

3. If the seat is uniform in width but is too wide, use a flat cutter, then a 30° cutter to reduce the seat width to within specification.

4. If the seat is centered on the valve face, but is too narrow, use a 45° cutter to increase the width to the proper specification.

5. If the seat is too narrow, and is towards the top edge of the face, first use a flat cutter, and then the 45° cutter.

6. If the seat is too narrow and positioned towards the bottom edge of the face, use a 30° cutter first, then a 45° cutter.

LAPPING

1. Valves should be lapped into their seats if the leakage test shows poor sealing, if the seat has been recut, if the valve edges or seat in the head are pitted, if the motorcycle has covered considerable mileage, or if new valves or guides are fitted.

2. Clean off all carbon build-up on the surface of the combustion chamber. Place three small dabs of valve lapping paste around the circumference of the valve head and place the valve into the guide.

3. If you have a lapping tool, use it as the manufacturer directs. Usually the tool will turn the valve back and forth while rotating it around the seat at the same time. Do not use excessive pressure during the operation.

If you do not have such a tool, a piece of thick fuel line placed over the valve stem works just as well. Turn the valve back and forth and rotate it to a new position every few seconds.

NOTE: *Check the condition of the valve face and seat frequently. When a smooth, even finish is evident, stop lapping. Excessive lapping may lead to a pocketed valve.*

4. Remove the valve and clean it thoroughly. Remove any traces of lapping compound from the seat and the combustion chamber. Swab out the guide with a cotton swab soaked in a solvent. Squirt a little oil into the guide so that it may carry away any particles inside.

CYLINDERS AND PISTONS

1. Make a visual inspection of the cylinder bore, noting any imperfections. The cylinder walls should be uniformly smooth.

2. With an inside micrometer, measure the diameter of each bore at the top, middle, and bottom. Make measurements in two directions, 90° apart, both parallel and perpendicular to the piston wrist pins.

If the difference between the high and lower measurement in any one direction (taper) is greater than 0.05 mm (0.002 in.), or if the difference between two measurements at any point on the cylinder (out-of-round) exceeds 0.01 mm (0.0004 in.), the cylinders should be bored to the next oversize and fitted with new pistons.

3. Make a visual inspection of the pistons. Scoring, scuffing, or seizure marks on the piston skirts may be removed with a fine grade of emery or crocus cloth if they are not too severe. Sanding should be done in a cross-hatch pattern. If the damage is severe (more than about ½ in. wide), the pistons should be replaced.

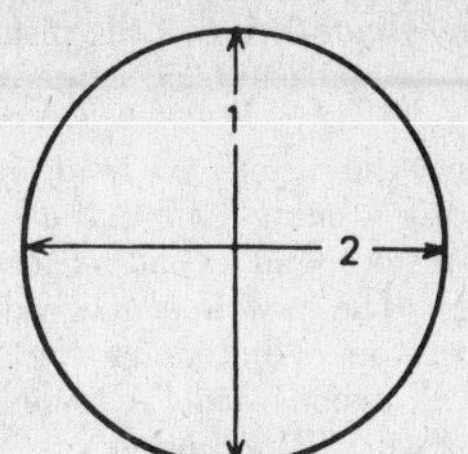

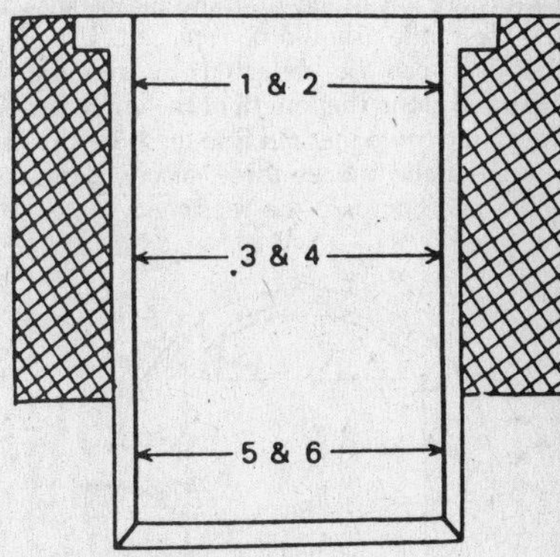

Cylinder bore measurement points

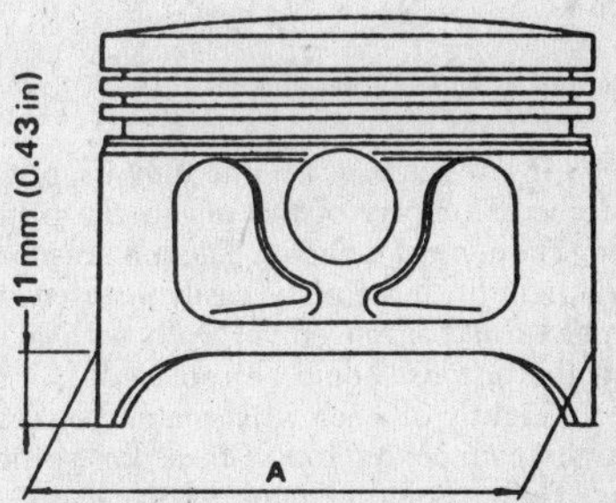

Measure the piston diameter 11 mm (0.43 in.) above the bottom edge of the skirt and perpendicular to the wrist pin

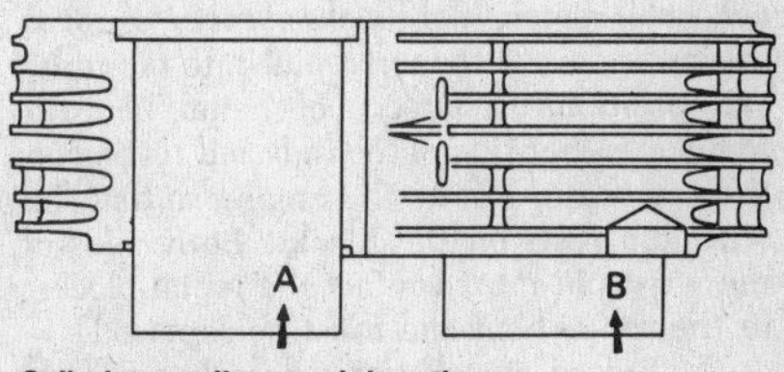

Cylinder grading mark locations

4. The rings must be free to move in the piston grooves. If they cannot, either they are carbon clogged (which necessitates replacing the rings and cleaning out the grooves), or metal has been pushed into the grooves by a piston seizure. In this event, pistons and rings must be replaced. Carbon-clogged rings are almost always broken when an attempt is made to remove or free them, so be prepared to buy a new set.

5. Pistons are available in four oversizes in increments of 0.25 mm.

To determine piston diameter, use a micrometer and measure the diameter in a direction perpendicular to the wrist pin at a point about 11 mm (0.43 in.) above the bottom edge of the skirt.

Bore the cylinders so that the piston clearance will be 0.030–0.050 mm (0.0012–0.0020 in.).

6. If only the pistons are being replaced, and no boring is being done to the cylinders, note that pistons and cylinders are graded "A" or "B". The piston is marked on the crown, and the cylinders at the cylinder base. Fit "A" pistons with "A" cylinders and "B" pistons with "B" cylinders.

7. Check the condition of the wrist pins. If the pins are blued or show indications of step-wear, they should be replaced. Usually, step-wear can be detected by running a fingernail along the length of the wrist pin. A more conclusive method is to measure the diameter of the pin at three places along its length and compare the readings.

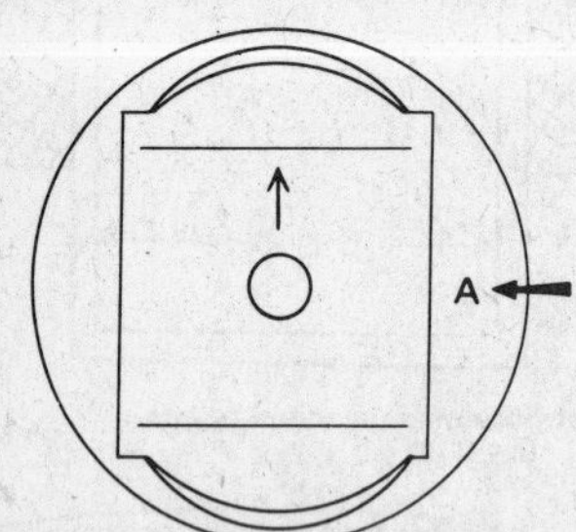

Piston grading mark locations

8. Insert each wrist pin into its piston and check for play of the pin in the piston hole. There must be none. The pin must be a fairly tight fit. If the pin is easily inserted and can be turned or moved vertically with no effort, the pistons should be replaced.

9. Lightly oil each wrist pin and insert it into its connecting rod. Check for vertical play. There should be none. If play exists, or if the rod small end is discolored, the rod and/or pin should be replaced.

10. Check the connecting rods for a bent condition. This can be accomplished with two small rectangular blocks of metal of equal thickness. Insert the wrist pins into the rods, and position the pieces of metal beneath them on either side of the rods and resting on the crankcase. Rotate the engine so that the wrist pin rests on the blocks. Both sides of the wrist pin must contact the metal blocks, or the rod is bent and must be replaced.

11. Before installation, decarbonize the piston crowns. Remove any carbon from the ring grooves with a piece of broken ring or a very thin screwdriver. Be careful not to scratch the grooves.

Carefully check the cylinder, cleaning the bore thoroughly. If considerable mileage has been covered, honing the cylinders and fitting new rings is recommended. If the cylinders are honed, make a strenuous effort to clean them thoroughly afterwards, preferably with very hot soapy water and a stiff brush. This is to remove any abrasive particles deposited by the hone in the course of the operation.

Remove any traces of gasket material from the cylinder base and the head mating surface.

12. Be sure that all oil passages in the cylinder are clear. Check the condition of the cam chain tensioner guides and replace them if damaged.

13. Replace the cylinder base o-rings. Check that any o-rings and the important dowel pins fitted to the cylinders are in their proper locations before installation.

PISTON RINGS

Two checks to be made on the piston rings are side clearance and end-gap. These checks should be made on both new and used rings.

1. Piston ring side clearance for compression rings is checked with the rings installed on the piston. Insert a feeler gauge blade between the ring and the ring groove and check that the clearance is within the specification given for your machine in the "Engine Specifications" chart at the end of this section. If the clearance is too large, the rings or grooves are worn. If too small, metal may have been pushed into the grooves due to a piston seizure. Check that the grooves are not just carboned up. If new rings do not bring the clearance to the proper value, the pistons must be replaced.

2. To remove the rings from the piston, use a ring spreader as illustrated. They are available at most auto stores. Decarbonize the ring grooves.

3. To check the ring end-gap, ensure first that the cylinder bore is not excessively worn. Place each ring, in turn, into the bottom of its cylinder and push it in an inch or more using the piston skirt to align the ring in the bore. Measure the end-gap with a feeler gauge. If the end-gap is larger than the service limit, the rings must be replaced. If the measured end-gap of new rings is too large, the cylinder is worn and should be bored to the next oversize.

Removing piston rings with an expander makes breakage unlikely

If new rings are fitted and the end-gap is too small, the ring ends must be filed. Hold the ring steady as illustrated, closing the ends over a thin, fine file. Do not squeeze the ring, as this is the easiest way to break it. A few strokes of the file will increase the end-gap.

CAUTION: *Do not make more than a few strokes before checking the end-gap again. It is easy to remove too much metal.*

Do not allow the file to slip out of the ring, as this risks breaking it.

4. Roll each ring around its own groove and ensure that this can be done easily. If a ring sticks or binds in the groove, the pistons must be replaced.

Cylinder and Piston Installation

1. When installing piston rings, note that all rings are installed with the manufacturer's mark (the small letter near the end-gap) facing *up*.

NOTE: *Oversize compression rings are stamped "25" "50" "75" or "100" and must be fitted to the correct oversized piston! Oversized oil rings have painted expanders. Red is standard and the four oversizes are brown, blue, black, and yellow in ascending order.*

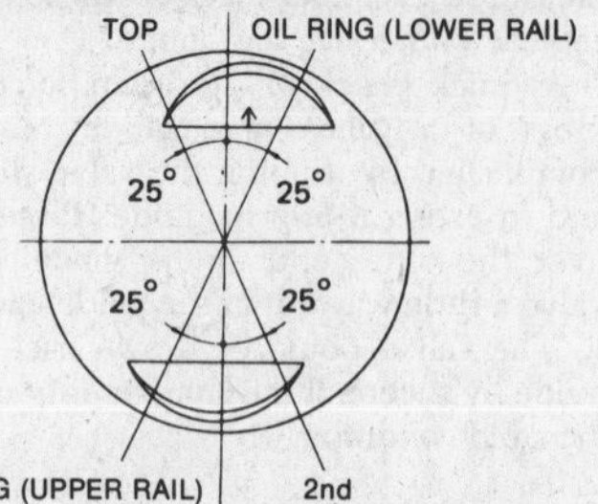

Stagger the ring end-gaps around the piston as shown

2. To install the three-piece oil ring, install one rail on the piston below the oil ring groove, fit the expander, then move the rail into place. Install the top rail.

3. Use a ring expander to install the rings to reduce the chance of breaking them.

4. Ring end-gaps must be staggered around the piston so that they do not overlap. Position the end-gaps as shown in the illustration. Note that none of the end-gaps are positioned at the very front or sides of the piston.

5. Install the pistons on their connecting rods so that the arrow marks on the crown face the front (exhaust side) of the engine.

NOTE: *Be sure to use new wrist pin circlips.*

6. Slip the wrist pins into place, heating the piston crown as on removal if necessary. Install the wrist pin circlips with a needle-nosed pliers. Be sure each circlips is firmly seated in its groove and arranged so that the circlip end-gap and the cut-out in the piston do *not* align.

7. Lubricate the rings and piston skirts with clean motor oil.

8. Install the o-ring on the oil delivery passage which is around the right rear stud.

9. Install the cylinder base gasket. Check that the cam chain is properly engaged with the crankshaft sprocket.

10. Install the cylinder, routing the cam chain up through its passage as the cylinders are lowered. Compress the piston rings with your fingers as the pistons enter the bores. Be sure the cylinders are firmly seated.

Cylinder Head Installation

1. Be sure that the oil delivery passage o-ring is fitted to the right rear stud. Check that the dowel pins are fitted to the right and left front studs. Install the cylinder head gasket.

2. Fit the cylinder head over the studs and gradually lower it into position while pulling the cam chain through the cut-out.

3. Install and tighten the cylinder head bolts and nuts. Bolts should be torqued to 7 ft lbs, nuts to 24 ft lbs. Tightening should be done gradually and in a cross pattern beginning with the centermost nuts. Refer to the illustration showing tightening sequence. Lubricate the cam bearings on the head.

4. Pull up the cam chain and slip the cam through. Fit the cam sprocket, so that the

sprocket marks face the left side of the engine, and set the valve timing as described in the following steps.

NOTE: *Using a new camshaft oil seal is recommended. Lubricate the seal lips before assembly.*

Be sure the O-ring is in place around the right rear cylinder stud

Install the O-ring and dowel pins on the cylinder studs

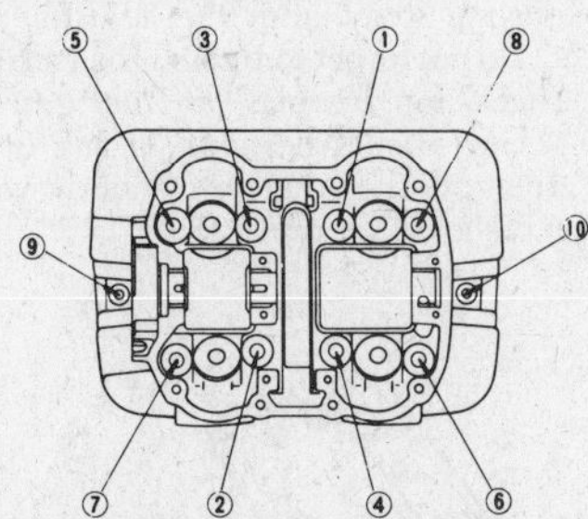

Tighten the cylinder head nuts and bolts in the order shown

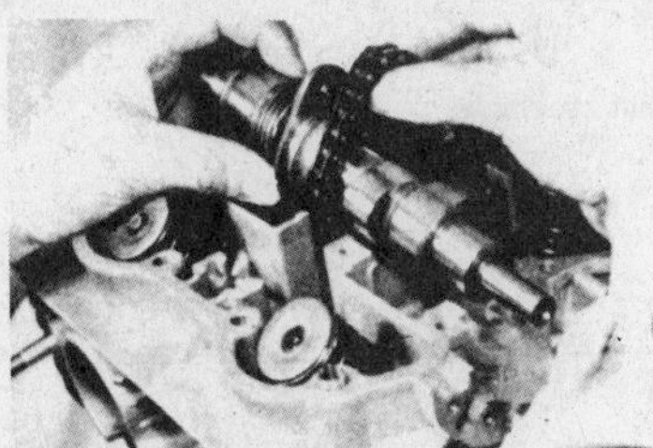

Installing the camshaft

Install the cam sprocket so that the lines are flush with the head surface

Use a pin to hold the cam chain tensioner spring in place

5. To set the cam timing, first turn the crankshaft so that the alternator rotor "LT" mark aligns with the timing mark.

6. Position the camshaft so that the locating pin faces upwards. Position the camshaft sprocket so that the two lines on the sprocket align with the cylinder head surface and the "O" mark on the sprocket is at the top.

7. Fit the cam chain over the sprocket without altering the sprocket's alignment.

8. The sprocket bolt holes should be aligned with the cam bolt holes at this point. Fit one of the cam sprocket bolts, tightening it to 13–16 ft lbs. Use a small quantity of a nonpermanent thread-locking compound on the bolt threads is recommended. Turn the engine over until the other bolt hole is accessible, and fit that bolt, torquing it to the same value.

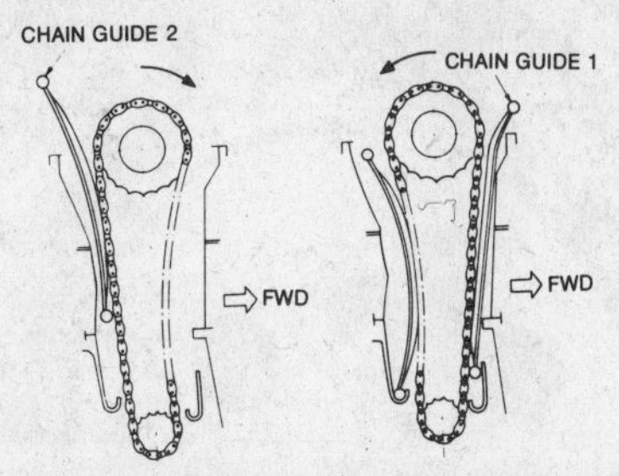

Rotate the crankshaft as shown to install the cam chain guides

9. Thoroughly lubricate the cam lobes and bearings with motor oil.

10. Compress the cam chain tensioner spring and hold it in place with a pin inserted into the hole provided. Install the tensioner, tightening the bolts to 6–9 ft lbs. After properly tightening the bolts, remove the pin.

11. Fit the cam chain guides. It is necessary to rotate the crankshaft to do this, as this will slacken one side or the other of the chain to allow the guides to be slipped into place.

12. If the rocker arms have been disassembled, lubricate the arms and shafts thorougly and install them in the head cover. Note that the threaded end of the shafts must face outwards. Use new o-rings.

13. Use a liquid gasket on the head cover mating surface, then install the cover. Tighten the head bolts gradually and in a cross pattern.

Proper torque is 6–9 ft lbs. for the 6 mm bolts and 15–17 ft lbs. for the 8 mm bolts.

14. Install and secure the rocker arm shaft plugs.

15. Adjust the valve clearance.

16. Carefully turn the engine over to ensure that the valve timing is correct. If resistance is felt when turning the crankshaft, stop immediately and determine the cause. Do not force the crankshaft or bent valves may result.

17. On breaker point models, install the timing advance mechanism, being sure to engage the hole in the mechanism with the pin on the camshaft. Tighten the bolt to 6–9 ft lbs. Fit the breaker point plate. The lead wires pass beneath the top cooling fin. Adjust the ignition timing after assembly is completed.

18. On transistor ignition models, install the pick-up coil assembly. Install the rotor and tighten the rotor bolt to 7 ft lbs. Check the ignition timing. If it is not correct, rotate the pick-up coil base plate until the timing marks align at the specified rpm as outlined in chapter 3. After fitting the pick-up coil cover, install a new blind plug. Do not force the plug in against determined resistance, or the cover may be cracked.

CRANKCASE COVER COMPONENTS

The following sections deal with the removal, inspection, and installation of those components found beneath the left and right crankcase covers. These include the clutch, alternator, starter drive, shift mechanism, kickstarter, and engine sprocket. These components can be serviced with the engine in the frame.

Note the following points:

a. Crankcase covers are secured with allen screws. When installing these screws, coat the threads with a bit of lubricant or antiseize paste to facilitate future removal. Tighten the screws evenly.

b. New cover gaskets (where applicable) should always be used. Remove any traces of old gasket or gasket sealing compound from the cover and crankcase mating surface.

c. During the disassembly procedure it may be necessary to keep the engine from turning over while a component is removed. There are several ways to do this. If the engine is in the frame, place the transmission in gear and apply the rear brake. If the engine has been removed from the frame, loop a length of old drive chain around the engine sprocket and secure the end in a vise. Engage the transmission and the engine will not turn over.

Clutch

REMOVAL

1. Drain the oil.

2. Remove the right-side exhaust system, the rider's footpeg, and the rear brake pedal.

3. Unscrew and remove the right crankcase cover bolts. Remove the cover. If it is stuck, tap around the cover with a plastic mallet until it is freed.

4. Gradually, and in a cross-pattern, unscrew and remove the clutch pressure plate screws. Remove the springs, the pressure

Clutch hub circlip and thrust washer

plate, and the steel and friction plates. Note the order of the steel and friction plates.

5. Remove the pushrod.

6. Remove the clutch hub circlip, thrust washer, and remove the clutch hub.

7. Remove the clutch housing, noting any thrust washers on the engine or hub side of the housing.

INSPECTION

1. Check the condition of the kick-start shaft oil seal. If it leaks, or if the lips show signs of damage, pry the old seal out with a small screwdriver. Press the new seal straight into the cover. Apply some oil or grease to the seal lips before installation.

2. Check the condition of the clutch cover mating surface. Remove any burrs or imperfections with an oilstone.

3. Measure the thickness of the friction plates, and replace them if they are less than 2.7mm (0.106 in.) thick.

4. Place the steel clutch plates on a flat surface, such as a piece of glass, and check for excessive warpage by attempting to slip a feeler gauge blade between the surface and the plate. Replace the steel and friction plates as a set if warpage exceeds 0.05 mm (0.002 in.).

5. Measure the free-length of each clutch spring and replace them as a set if any are found to be less than 34.6 mm (1.36 in.) long, or if their length varies. If the latter is true, be sure that all of the screws are evenly tightened on assembly.

6. Check the friction plate tabs for wear or damage. Check the clutch housing for indented wear caused by the tabs. Remove any burrs with a file or oilstone.

7. Check the corresponding splines of the clutch hub and steel plates for indented wear.

8. Using a dial indicator, check the pushrod for a bent condition. Replace the pushrod if it is bent more than 0.2 mm (0.008 in.).

9. Check the condition of the clutch gear teeth. Note any pitting or chipping. Check the primary gear teeth as well. If damage to either is noted, replace both. The primary gear is replaced by removing the securing bolt and pulling off the gear.

10. Note the lash letters stamped on the clutch gear and primary gear. The gears should be replaced with reference to these lash letters. Gears should be paired as follows:

Primary gear	Clutch gear
A	C
B	D
C	E
D	F

Primary gear lash notation

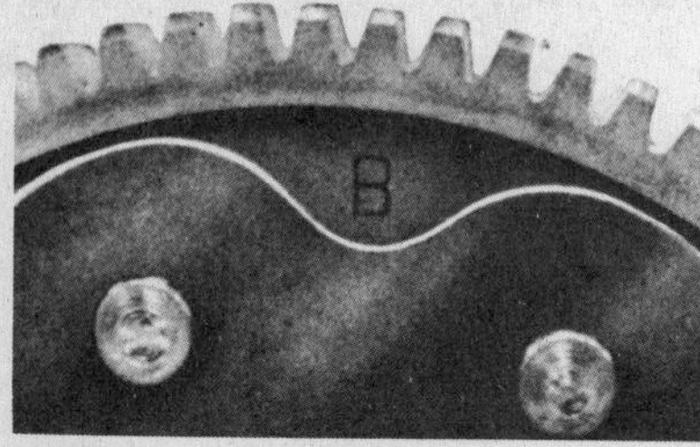

Clutch gear lash letter location

INSTALLATION

1. Installation is the reverse of disassembly. When fitting the clutch plates, alternate steel and friction plates. The last plate installed should be a friction plate.

2. Install the pressure plate so that the arrow on the plate aligns with the arrow on the clutch hub.

3. Tighten the pressure plate screws gradually and evenly.

4. Tighten the primary gear bolt to 29–33 ft lbs.

Kickstarter Shaft

REMOVAL

1. After removing the right crankcase cover, the kickstarter shaft can be removed by pulling it out.

When installing the pressure plate, align the arrow on the plate with that on the clutch hub

Removing the kickstarter assembly

2. When disassembling the shaft components, lay each one out in the order removed to facilitate assembly.

INSPECTION

1. Check the condition of the kickstarter shaft splines.

2. Check the kickstarter gear teeth for chipping or other damage, and replace it if such damage is noted.

3. Check the condition of the shaft return spring. The spring should be replaced if it will not return the shaft quickly to the rest position and hold it securely in place.

INSTALLATION

1. Set the kickstarter gear clip into the groove in the crankcase.

2. Rotate the return spring clockwise and hook it onto the projection.

Gearshift Mechanism

REMOVAL

1. Remove the right crankcase cover. Remove the clutch assembly.

2. Remove the engine sprocket cover (left side).

3. Remove the circlip from the gearshift shaft on the left side of the engine and pull out the gearshift assembly from the right.

INSPECTION

1. Check the gearshift shaft for a bent condition and replace it if it is bent. Check the condition of the gearshift shaft splines.

2. Check the condition of the shift fingers. Note any chipping or wear to the finger ends. Replace the fingers if they are bent or worn.

3. Inspect the shift mechanism springs and replace them if weakened or broken.

INSTALLATION

1. Installation is the reverse of removal. After fitting the mechanism, temporarily install the gearshift lever and test shifting action through the gears.

2. In each gear, check that the shift fingers are equidistant from the shift drum pins. Refer to the illustration. If they are not, loosen the adjusting screw locknut and turn the screw to equalize the distances. Use a non-permanent thread-locking compound on the adjusting screw after the adjustment is correct. Do not forget to tighten the locknut.

3. Check for freeplay in the gearshift lever. There should be none. If any is evident, the return spring is evidently weakened and should be replaced.

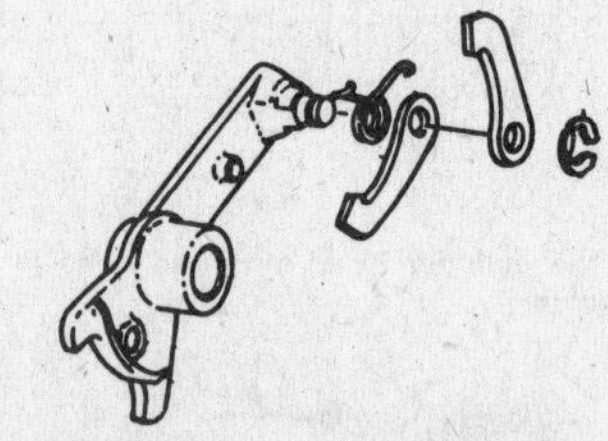

Gearshift assembly

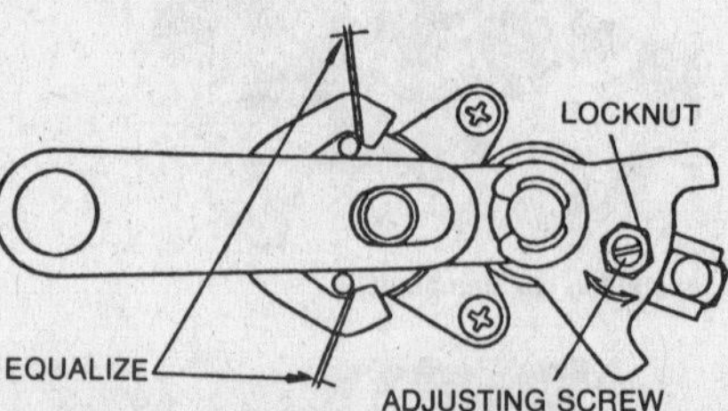

Use the adjusting screw to equalize the two clearances indicated

4. Check that the shift finger return spring will hold the fingers firmly against the shift drum pins. If not, replace the spring.

Oil Pump

Refer to "Lubrication System," for oil pump removal, inspection, and installation procedures.

Engine Sprocket

REMOVAL

1. Remove the left-side rider's footpeg. Remove the gearshift lever.
2. Remove the engine sprocket cover screws and take off the cover.
3. Place the transmission in gear and apply the rear brake. Unscrew and remove the engine sprocket nut. Remove the lockwasher and sprocket. It may be necessary to move the rear wheel forward to remove the sprocket from its shaft.

INSTALLATION

Installation is the reverse of removal. Tighten the sprocket nut to 36–58 ft lbs.

Alternator/Starter Drive

REMOVAL

1. Drain the crankcase oil.
2. Remove the alternator cover.
3. Remove the rotor bolt. Remove the rotor with the special puller. Take out the woodruff key.
4. Remove the sprocket guide and chain guide.
5. Pull off the starter and crankshaft sprocket and chain.

INSPECTION

1. Check the sprockets for wear such as hooking of the teeth. Replace them, along with the chain, as necessary.

INSTALLATION

Installation is the reverse of removal. The alternator rotor must be turned onto its shaft because of the starter clutch rollers.

Tighten the rotor bolt to 22–25 ft lbs.

Removing the alternator rotor

Starter drive

LOWER END AND TRANSMISSION

Splitting the Crankcases

Splitting the crankcases is necessary for service to the crankshaft and connecting rods, transmission gears, and internal shift mechanism.

Removal of the engine is required.

1. Drain the oil. Remove the engine from the frame.
2. Remove the top end components.
3. Remove the left and right crankcase covers and the components therein: clutch, primary drive gear, kickstarter shaft, oil pump assembly, gearshift mechanism, engine sprocket, alternator/starter drive assembly, etc.
4. Remove the starter motor. Remove the breather cover.
5. Disconnect the neutral switch lead and the oil pressure switch lead.
6. Remove the neutral switch cover.
7. Remove the shift drum cam stopper plate and the change lever guide (right side).

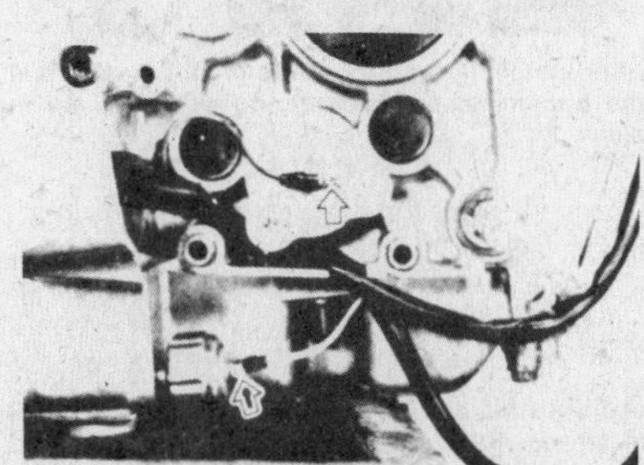

Neutral and oil pressure switch leads

Removing the neutral switch cover

8. Remove the upper and lower crankcase bolts. Loosen each bolt ¼ turn, then remove all of them.
9. Remove the upper crankcase half. If it is stuck, first check that all fasteners have been removed. Then tap around the case mating surface with a plastic mallet to break the case free.

Case Assembly

1. Be sure that the crankcase mating surface is clean and free of all traces of old gasket compound. Minor scratches or burrs can be removed with an oilstone, although care must be taken that the surface is not grooved when doing this.

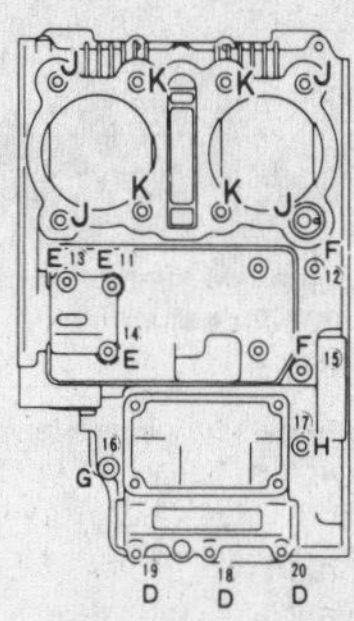

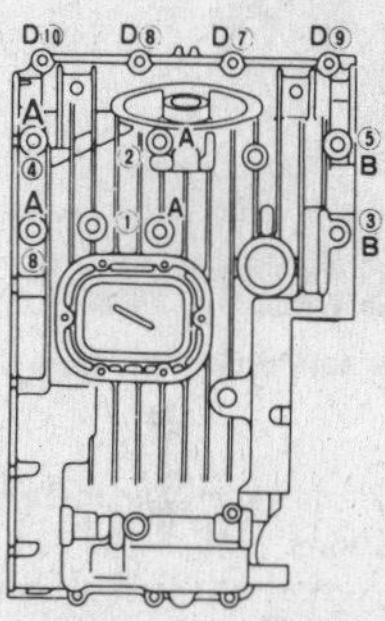

Crankcase bolt locations

2. Lubricate all bearing surfaces with motor oil.
3. Be sure that the crankshaft and transmission shafts are properly seated. The transmission shaft bearings are located with set rings. Be sure the shift forks are engaged with their gears.
4. Be sure that all dowel pins between the cases are in place.
5. Apply a thin coat of a liquid gasket compound to the case mating surface. Install the upper case half. After ensuring that it is properly seated, install the crankcase bolts and tighten them gradually and in a cross pattern.

Tighten the 8 mm bolts to 15–17 ft lbs.

Tighten the 6 mm bolts to 6–9 ft lbs.

Transmission/Gear Shift Assembly

REMOVAL

1. Lift the transmission shafts out of the case.
2. Before removing the shift forks, mark

Separating the crankcase halves

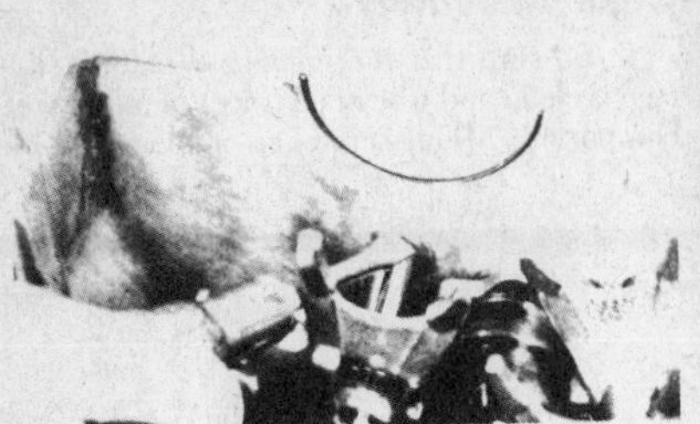
Removing the shift fork shaft circlip

Removing the shift drum cam plate circlip

them so that they can be installed in their original locations.

3. Remove the shift fork shaft circlips and push out the shafts with grommets.

4. Move the shift drum as far as possible to one side, then remove the cam plate circlip and the cam plate. Remove the shift drum.

INSPECTION

NOTE: *Do not disassemble the gear set unless inspection shows that replacement of individual gears is necessary. Gear shaft circlips are not reusable and must be replaced with new ones whenever the gear set is taken apart.*

If the gear set is disassembled, carefully lay out each piece in the order it is removed to facilitate reassembly.

1. Flush the transmission shaft bearings with clean motor oil and check operation. Bearing rotation must be smooth, effortless, and quiet. There must be no play between the inner and outer bearing races. If damage is noted, replace the bearings as a set.

2. Check the gear teeth for damage, wear, or pitting. Pay close attention to the very base of the teeth. Gears are surfacehardened, and if this hardened layer is damaged, what is left will not last long. Check the engaging dogs and/or dog slots on each gear for chipping or wear. Check that splined gears are a good fit on their shaft (neither too loose nor too tight) and that the splines on the shafts and on the gears are in good condition. Check that gears with plain bores can rotate freely but are not too loose on their shafts.

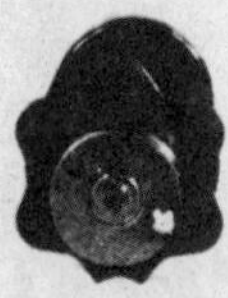
Install the cam plate on the shift drum as shown

Shift fork installation

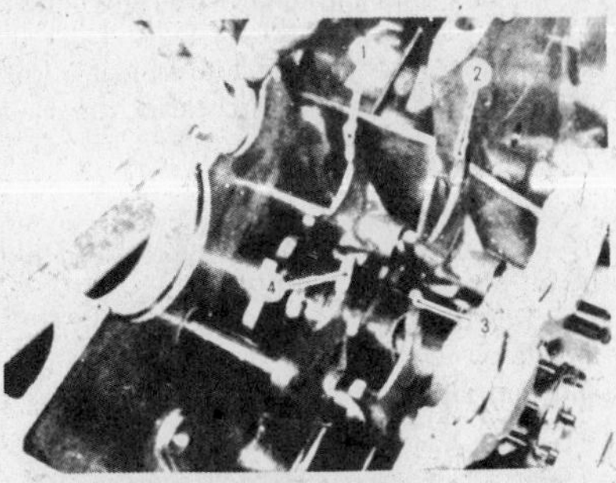
After installing the shift forks (1-4), be sure that the transmission shaft bearing set rings are in place

Check all parts for damage due to overheating or lack of lubricant.

NOTE: *Gears should always be replaced in pairs.*

3. Check that the gear shift fork fingers are not chipped, worn, or bent. If any damage is noted, replace the shift fork in question.

4. Check that each shift fork moves freely on its shaft. If sticking or binding is noted, determine the cause. Check the shafts for a bent condition. Replace any shafts which are even slightly bent.

5. Check the shift fork guide pins for wear. Also inspect the corresponding grooves in the shift drum.

ASSEMBLY

1. Assemble the gear sets onto their shafts. Use *new* circlips.

2. Install the shift drum, fitting the cam plate on the drum as illustrated.

3. Install the shift forks, shafts, and grommets.

4. Be sure that the bearing locater rings are in place in the crankcase.

5. Use new oil seals. Install the output shaft oil seal on the shaft before installation.

6. Install the transmission shafts, engaging the shift fork fingers with the proper gears as this is done. Assembly is facilitated by ensuring that the transmission is in neutral.

7. Install the shift drum cam stopper plate and the change lever guide. Use a non-permanent thread-locking compound on these screws.

Crankshaft

REMOVAL

The crankshaft can be lifted out after the cases have been split.

INSPECTION

1. Mount the crank in a set of v-blocks and measure run-out with a dial gauge. If run-out exceeds 0.02 mm (0.0008 in.), the crank is bent and must be replaced.

Checking the crankshaft for run-out

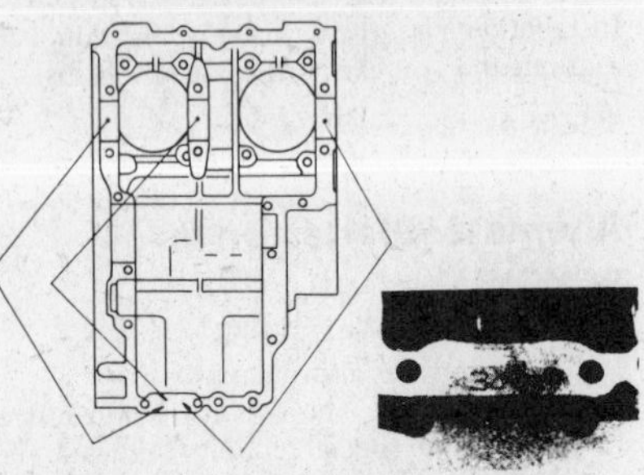
Crankshaft bearing insert number locations

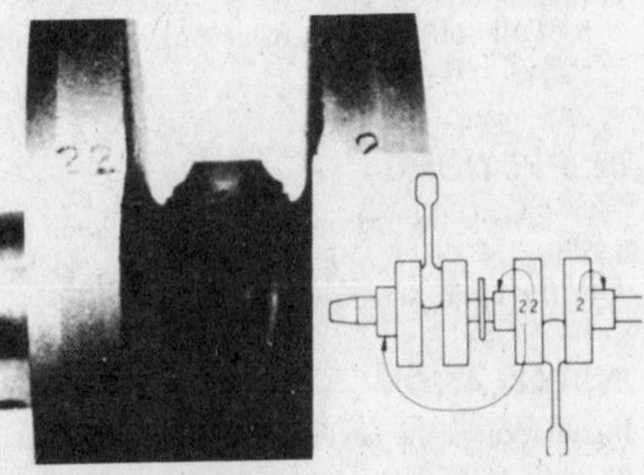

Crankshaft bearing insert number locations on the crank flywheels

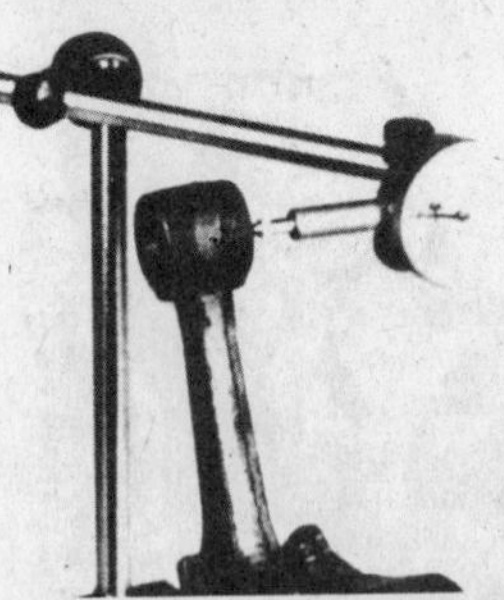
Checking big end axial play

2. Check the crankshaft bearing inserts in the crankshaft for scoring or obvious signs of wear and replace the inserts if the surfaces are not in good condition. The inserts must be free of any defects or they should be replaced.

3. Crankshaft bearings are replaced as a set, and the correct color insert should be selected. Replace bearing inserts with others of the same color. If the color of the old bearing is no longer visible, refer to the following chart:

Note the crankcase number which is stamped on the case and the crank journal number inscribed on the crank flywheel. Compare the two numbers to select the proper bearing insert.

Crankcase No.	Journal No.	Insert
3	1	Blue
4	2	Black
5	-	Brown
-	-	Green

Big end bearing insert number location

Be sure that both rods have the same identification numbers and that the numbers on rods and caps align

When installing the rods, be sure that the "YAMAHA" mark faces the left side of the crank

4. With a dial gauge, check connecting rod side play at the small end. If the movement exceeds 0.5 mm (0.019 in.), the big end bearing should be replaced.

5. Replace big end bearing inserts with inserts of the same color code. If the color is no longer visible on the old insert, select a replacement according to the following chart.

Big End Bearing No.	Crankpin No.	Insert
3	1	Blue
4	2	Black
5	-	Brown
-	-	Green

6. If one or both of the connecting rods is going to be replaced, be sure that the weight codes stamped on the rod and cap match for both rods.

7. Before installing connecting rods on the crankpins, thoroughly lubricate the bearings with motor oil. Install the rods so that the "YAMAHA" mark on both rods faces the *left* end of the crankshaft and the bearing protuberance is towards the *intake* side of the engine. Be sure that the rods are installed so that the cap numbers align with the rod numbers.

8. Coat the con rod bolt threads with a molybdenum disulphide lubricant and torque them to 24–28 ft lbs.

Engine Specifications XS360

CYLINDER	
Bore	66.00–66.02 mm/2.5900–2.5908 in.
Max allowable taper	0.05 mm/0.002 in.
Max allowable out-of-round	0.01 mm/0.0004 in.
PISTON	
Piston skirt-to-cylinder clearance	0.030–0.050 mm/0.0012–0.0019 in.
Piston oversizes	66.25 mm/2.608 in.
	66.50 mm/2.618 in.
	66.75 mm/2.628 in.
	67.00 mm/2.638 in.
Wrist pin diameter	15.995–16.000 mm/0.6298–0.6300 in.
PISTON RINGS	
Piston ring end-gap (installed)	
Compression	0.2–0.4 mm/0.008–0.016 in.
Oil	0.2–0.9 mm/0.008–0.035 in.
Groove side clearance	
Top compression	0.04–0.08 mm/0.0016–0.0032 in.
Lower compression	0.03–0.07 mm/0.0012–0.0028 in.
CAMSHAFT	
Bearing clearance	0.020–0.054 mm/0.00079–0.00213 in.
Intake lobe height service limit	38.70 mm/1.527 in.
Exhaust lobe height service limit	38.74 mm/1.525 in.
Intake lobe base circle service limit	32.08 mm/1.263 in.
Exhaust lobe base circle service limit	31.90 mm/1.256 in.
Max allowable run-out	0.03 mm/0.0012 in.
ROCKER ASSEMBLY	
Rocker arm bore diameter	13.000–13.018 mm/0.5120–0.5127 in.
Rocker arm shaft diameter	12.964–12.984 mm/0.51199859–0.51199937 in.
Shaft-to-bore clearance	0.016–0.054 mm/0.00063–0.00122
VALVES	
Valve seat width	1.0–1.1 mm/0.03937–0.04330 in.
Intake valve stem diameter	6.975–6.990 mm/0.2741–0.2746 in.
Exhaust valve stem diameter	6.955–6.970 mm/0.2732–0.2738 in.
Valve-to-stem clearance	
Intake	0.010–0.037 mm/0.00039–0.00145 in.
Exhaust	0.030–0.057 mm/0.0012–0.0022 in.
Max allowable run-out	0.03 mm/0.0012 in.
VALVE SPRINGS	
Free length	
Inner	39.3 mm/1.547 in.
Outer	42.8 mm/1.685 in.
Tilt replacement limit	
Inner	1.7 mm/0.067 in. (2.5°)
Outer	1.9 mm/0.075 in. (2.5°)
CRANKSHAFT	
Max allowable run-out	0.02 mm/0.0008 in.
Crank bearing clearance	0.020–0.044 mm/0.00079–0.00157 in.
Con rod big end clearance	0.021–0.045 mm/0.00080–0.00180 in.

Engine Specifications XS400

CYLINDER	
Bore	69.00–69.02 mm/2.7200–2.7208 in.
Max allowable taper	0.05 mm/0.002 in.
Max allowable out-of-round	0.01 mm/0.0004 in.
PISTON	
Piston skirt-to-cylinder clearance	0.030–0.050 mm/0.0012–0.0019 in.
Piston oversizes	69.25 mm/2.727 in.
	69.50 mm/2.736 in.
	69.75 mm/2.746 in.
	70.00 mm/2.756 in.
Wrist pin diameter	15.995–16.000 mm/0.6298–0.6300 in.
PISTON RINGS	
Piston ring end-gap (installed)	
Compression	0.2–0.4 mm/0.008–0.016 in.
Oil	0.2–0.9 mm/0.008–0.035 in.
Groove side clearance	
Top compression	0.04–0.08 mm/0.0016–0.0032 in.
Lower compression	0.03–0.07 mm/0.0012–0.0028 in.
CAMSHAFT	
Bearing clearance	0.020–0.054 mm/0.00079–0.00213 in.
Intake lobe height service limit	39.38 mm/1.550 in.
Exhaust lobe height service limit	39.42 mm/1.552 in.
Intake lobe base circle service limit	32.12 mm/1.265 in.
Exhaust lobe base circle service limit	31.97 mm/1.259 in.
Max allowable run-out	0.03 mm/0.0012 in.

INSTALLATION

Lubricate the crank and rod bearings throroughly before installation.

Engine Torque Specifications

Part	Torque (ft lbs)
Cylinder head	
10 mm	22–25
6 mm	6–9
Tappet cover	7–10
Rocker arm plug	9–15
Spark plug	13–16
Connecting rod bolts	24–28
Valve adjusting screw	9–11
Cam sprocket bolts	13–16
Oil filter housing bolt	10–12
Exhaust pipe ring nut	15–17
Crankcase bolts	
8 mm	15–17
6 mm	6–9
Oil drain bolt	25–29
Primary gear	29–33
Engine sprocket	36–58
Alternator rotor bolt	21–25
Oil pressure switch	7–11
Neutral switch	2–3
Shift drum stopper	9–15

Engine Specifications (cont.) XS400

ROCKER ASSEMBLY	
Rocker arm bore diameter	13.000–13.018 mm/0.5120–0.5127 in.
Rocker arm shaft diameter	12.964–12.984 mm/0.51199859–0.51199937 in.
Shaft-to-bore clearance	0.016–0.054 mm/0.00063–0.00122
VALVES	
Valve seat width	1.0–1.1 mm/0.03937–0.04330 in.
Intake valve stem diameter	6.975–6.990 mm/0.2741–0.2746 in.
Exhaust valve stem diameter	6.955–6.970 mm/0.2732–0.2738 in.
Valve-to-stem clearance	
Intake	0.010–0.037 mm/0.00039–0.00145 in.
Exhaust	0.030–0.057 mm/0.0012–0.0022 in.
Max allowable run-out	0.03 mm/0.0012 in.
VALVE SPRINGS	
Free length	
Inner	39.3 mm/1.547 in.
Outer	42.8 mm/1.685 in.
Tilt replacement limit	
Inner	1.7 mm/0.067 in. (2.5°)
Outer	1.9 mm/0.075 in. (2.5°)
CRANKSHAFT	
Max allowable run-out	0.02 mm/0.0008 in.
Crank bearing clearance	0.020–0.044 mm/0.00079–0.00157 in.
Con rod big end clearance	0.021–0.045 mm/0.00080–0.00180 in.

LUBRICATION SYSTEM

OPERATIONAL DESCRIPTION

The oil pump is housed beneath the right crankcase cover and is driven by the crankshaft through a reduction gear. The pump is the "trochoidal" type, meaning that it consists of one rotor turning inside another. The shape of the rotors gives the pump its name and the action of one working against the other pumps the oil.

The oil pump sucks oil from the sump. The oil passes through a course wire-mesh filter before reaching the pump, which removes any large impurities which might damage the pump rotors. This filter is made course so as not to restrict the passage of oil in low temperatures.

The oil pressure relief valve is fitted in conjunction with the pump. The relief valve is pre-set to operate at a pressure above about 70 psi. If the oil pressure reaches this value, the relief valve opens and returns some of the oil to the sump.

After passing through the oil pump, the oil is forced through the replaceable oil filter where microscopic impurities are removed. The oil filter housing is equipped with a by-pass valve. In the event that the filter becomes clogged with filtered material, oil will flow around it to reach the engine's moving parts. This oil, however, will not be filtered, so it is imperative to change the filter at the prescribed intervals to ensure long engine life.

Oil pressure switch location

Oil pressure gauge fitting

After leaving the filter, the oil enters the main oil gallery. Here, oil passages allow it to be fed directly to the crankshaft main bearings, connecting rod bearings, and transmission shafts. An oil passage running up through the cylinders and head feeds oil to the camshaft and valve assemblies. The main oil passage is also equipped with an oil pressure switch which monitors the system for pressure failure, and it includes a fitting to attach an oil pressure gauge.

After lubricating the various components, the oil is returned to the sump and the cycle is repeated.

CHECKING OIL PRESSURE

1. A special gauge is needed to check the oil pressure. It is attached to a fitting on the left side of the crankcase sump (see illustration).

2. Oil pressure should be checked when the engine is at operating temperature. Before checking, be sure that the oil level is between the two dipstick marks.

3. At 3,000 rpm, the oil pressure should be about 42 psi (3 kg/cm²).

4. If the pressure is significantly lower than this, remove and inspect the oil pump. If the oil pump condition is satisfactory, the lack of oil pressure may be caused by worn or damaged bearings.

OIL PUMP

Removal

1. Drain the oil.

2. Remove the kickstarter pinch bolt and carefully pull the kickstarter off the splined shaft.

3. Remove the right-side footpeg and the rear brake pedal.

4. Remove the allen bolts which secure the right side crankcase cover and take off the cover. If the cover is stuck, tap around the sides with a plastic mallet to free it. Pull the cover straight off and do it carefully to avoid damage to the kickstarter shaft oil seal.

5. Remove the three allen bolts which hold the oil pump and pump gear and take off the assembly.

Inspection

1. Carefully loosen and remove the three phillips screws which secure the oil pump rotor cover plate. Remove the plate.

2. Measure the clearance between the rotor tips with a feeler gauge. The specified

Oil pump assembly allen bolts

Oil pump (1), cover screws (2), drive gear (3), and cover (4)

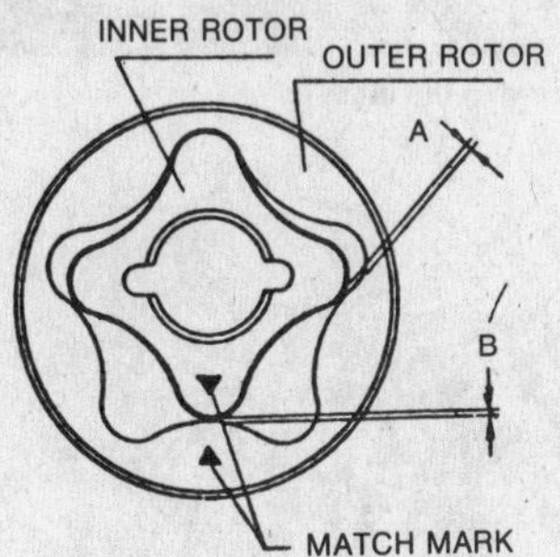

Rotor tip clearance (A,B) and rotor match marks

clearance is 0.03–0.09 mm (0.0012–0.0035 in.). If the measured clearance is not within this specification, replace the rotors.

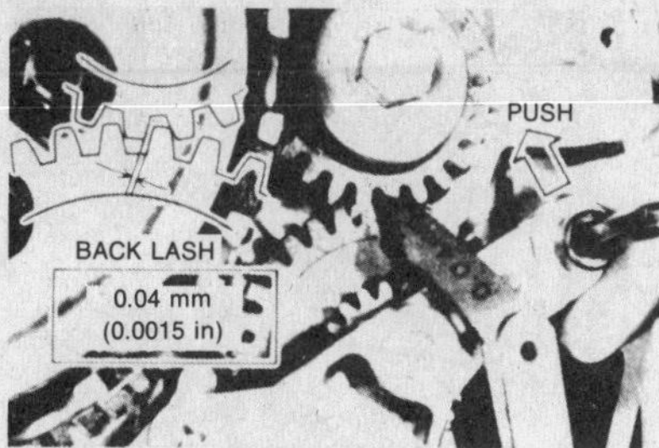

Adjusting the gear backlash

3. Measure the clearance between the outer rotor and the oil pump housing. Specified clearance is 0.03–0.09 mm (0.0012–0.0035 in.). If the measured clearance exceeds this amount, replace the rotors or housing.

4. Lay a straight edge across the top of the rotors and measure the side clearance with a feeler gauge. Side clearance should be 0.010–0.18 mm (0.0039–0.0071 in.). If the measured clearance is greater than this, replace the rotors.

5. The rotors have match marks on one side. If the pump is disassembled, be sure that the rotors are installed so that the match marks line up.

6. Use a small amount of a non-permanent thread-locking compound on the oil pump rotor cover plate.

Installation

1. Installation is the reverse or removal. The primary gear-pump idler gear backlash must be adjusted.

2. Fit the oil pump assembly and install, but do not tighten, the mounting bolts. Measure the clearance between the primary gear and the oil pump idler gear. It should be 0.04 mm (0.0015 in.). To obtain the correct backlash push or pull on the oil pump assembly. When clearance is correct, hold the assembly in place and tighten the mounting bolts securely.

Lubrication System Specifications

Oil pump type	Trochoid
Rotor side clearance	0.10–0.18 mm (0.0039–0.0071 in.)
Rotor tip clearance	0.03–0.09 mm (0.0012–0.0035 in.)
Outer rotor-to-pump body clearance	0.03–0.09 mm (0.0012–0.0035 in.)
Pump output	1.2 l (1.3 qt) per minute @ 500 rpm
Relief valve operating pressure	5 kg/cm² (71 psi)
Filter by-pass valve operating pressure	1 kg/cm² (14 psi)

FUEL SYSTEM

CARBURETORS

Removal

1. Disconnect the fuel line at the petcock. Disconnect the petcock vacuum line at the right manifold.

2. Lift the seat. Remove the gas tank bolt. Lift up the rear of the tank and slide it back until it is clear of its rubber mounts. Remove the gas tank from the motorcycle.

3. Disconnect the throttle cable from the lever between the carburetors.

4. Loosen the screws on the manifold clamps and the air cleaner hose clamps.

5. Carefully pull the carburetors back until they are free of the manifolds, then move them out to the side and off the motorcycle.

Carburetor manifold and air cleaner hose clamp screws

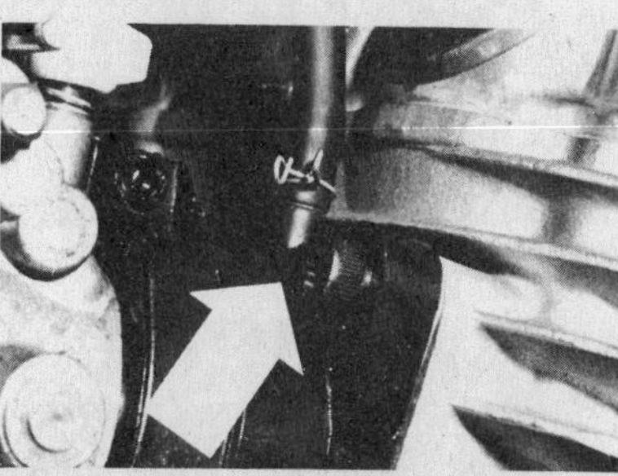
Petcock vacuum line connection

Removing the carburetors

Installation

1. Installation is basically the reverse of removal.

Removing the drain plug

2. Position the carburetors on the manifolds and be sure they are properly seated. Work the air cleaner hoses around the carburetor mouths and be sure they are not folded are creased. Tighten the clamps. Connect the throttle cable. Check twist-grip action.

3. After fitting the gas tank and connecting the lines, turn the petcock to the "Prime" position for a few moments to fill the float bowls. Check for leaks before starting the motorcycle.

Disassembly

1. Remove the drain plug at the bottom of each float bowl. Holding the carburetors in the normal operational position, allow the gas to drain off. Refit the drain plugs to prevent loss.

2. Remove the angle-iron bracket which runs by the float bowls and holds the carburetors together.

3. Loosen the choke rod securing screws and disconnect the choke rod from the starter plungers. Pull out the rod. Take care that the shaft positioning balls on the left and right do not pop out.

4. Remove the bracket which holds the carburetors together at the caps.

5. Separate the two carburetors.

6. Remove the carburetor cap. Take out the return spring. Carefully, so as to avoid damage to the rubber diaphragm, lift out the throttle slide assembly.

7. Remove the float bowl screws and carefully lift off the float bowl until it clears the floats. If the bowl is stuck, rap it once on the side with the screwdriver handle. This should be sufficient to break it free.

8. Using a small punch, push out the float pivot pin and remove the float bulbs.

9. Lift out the float needle.

10. Unscrew and remove the float needle seat and gasket.

11. Unscrew and remove the pilot and main jets. On XS360 models, these are fitted to the float bowl, but on the 400 they are on the carburetor body. Jets are brass and should be removed carefully to avoid damage.

12. Pry out the washer beneath the needle jet, and remove this jet by tapping it out with a wooden dowel or the like from the top of the carburetor.

13. Remove the float bowl gasket.

14. Remove the banjo bolt for the fuel feed line from the left carburetor.

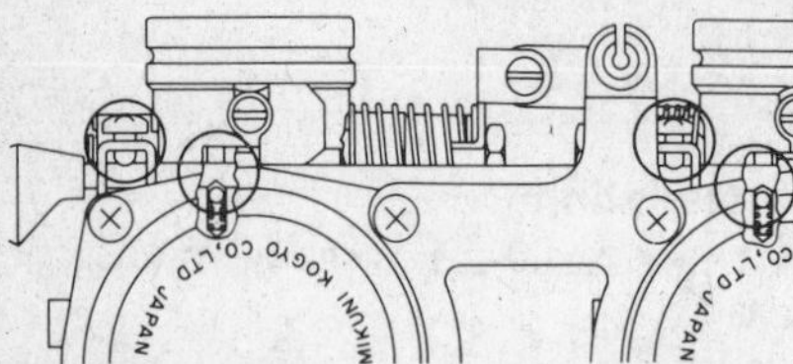

Choke shaft securing screw and plunger location

Carburetor top and throttle slide assembly

Removing the float bowl screws

Removing the float bowl

Removing the float assembly

Removing the float needle

Unscrewing the main jet

Removing the plunger assembly

15. Remove the idle limiter caps from the pilot screws and remove the screws.

16. Unscrew and remove the starter plunger from the carburetor.

Inspection

1. Clean the carburetor body and float bowl in a carburetor cleaner or solvent which is safe for plastic parts and dry thoroughly.

2. Use compressed air to blow air and fuel passages clear.

3. Clean all fuel jets in the same manner.

CAUTION: *Do not insert anything into the jet passages to clear them; use air pressure only.*

4. Inspect the carburetor body for any vibration or stress cracks.

5. Check the condition of the throttle slide. Smooth movement of the slide on the carburetor body is imperative. If the slide sticks or binds at any point from full closed to wide open, replace it.

6. Inspect the needle jet and the needle. The needle must be free of nicks or score marks along its tapered portion. More often, however, these components will need to be replaced because of normal wear. As the throttle slide moves up and down while the machine is in operation, the needle is rubbing against the jet. Eventually, these components will wear enough to cause a noticeable rich running condition in the mid-throttle range. If this occurs, both the needle and the jet should be replaced. If the components are more than four years old, new ones should be fitted before attempting to tune the carburetor, or taking remedial action to correct a rich condition (such as lowering the needle).

7. Carefully inspect the float. Shake the float close to your ear; listen for any gasoline trapped inside. If the float assembly leaks, or if any puncture is noted, replace it; do not attempt repairs.

8. Inspect the tip of the float needle and the needle seat for dirt or corrosion. Check the needle tip for wear. If worn, the needle should be replaced.

If there is any corrosion or deposits evident on the needle or needle seat, the deposits must be removed, or the parts replaced.

NOTE: *Do not attempt to clean the needle or needle seat by lapping one against the other.*

To check the efficiency of the float needle valve, proceed as follows:

a. With the carburetor assembled except for the float bowl, connect it to its fuel line;

b. Place a number of dry rags beneath the carburetor, and hold it upright (in its normal operating position) with one hand;

c. With the other hand, gently raise the float assembly until the float needle is seated. Have an assistant turn the fuel petcock on ("Prime" position);

d. If the needle and seat are in good condition and forming a good seal, no gasoline will flow out of the carburetor;

e. If a leak is noted, replace the needle and seat.

CAUTION: *While performing this test, be sure that adequate precautions are taken in the event of spillage.*

The float level should be checked prior to assembly.

9. Check that the tapered portion of the pilot screw is smooth and clean. Replace it if it is crushed or blunted.

10. Inspect the float bowl for a warped gasket surface, or stress cracks (especially around the screw holes).

11. Check the throttle slide diaphragm for rips. Replace the assembly if the diaphragm is damaged. Repairs are not possible.

Assembly

Assembly is basically the reverse of the disassembly procedure. Note the following points:

1. Always use new gaskets and O-rings.

2. Exercise care when installing jets—they are made of soft brass and are easily damaged if overtightened.

3. If the throttle slide and needle have been disassembled, check that both needle clips are installed in the correct groove from the top of the needle. Refer to the "Carburetor Specifications" chart at the end of this section for the correct needle clip position.

Be sure that the diaphragm tab is properly seated

4. When installing the pilot screws, turn them in gently until they are lightly seated, then back them out 1½ turns on XS360 models and 1¼ turns on XS400 models. Fit the idler limiter caps.

5. When fitting the throttle slide, be sure to engage the tab on the diaphragm with the cut-out in the carburetor body.

6. Check the float level as outlined in the "Tune-Up" section.

7. When installing the choke rod, be sure that the securing screws fit into the shaft detents.

FUEL PETCOCK

The petcock is the vacuum-activated type which incorporates a mesh filter inside the gas tank.

1. Set the petcock to the "RES" position. Disconnect the fuel line from the petcock and the vacuum line from the manifold.

2. Remove the gas tank. Drain off the fuel.

3. Unscrew the petcock securing nut or two phillips screws depending upon the method of fastening, and pull off the petcock.

4. Clean the filter screen in a solvent. Be sure to remove any foreign matter trapped in the screen as this will impede fuel flow. If the screen cannot be cleaned, or if it is punctured or otherwise damaged, it should be replaced.

5. Check the sealing washer and replace it if it is damaged.

6. Install the petcock. After the tank is refitted, check for leaks before operating the motorcycle.

7. Check operation of the petcock after disconnecting the fuel feed line. No fuel should flow out when the lever is in the "On" or "RES" positions. This should happen only when the lever is set to the "Prime" position. If fuel does flow in the other positions, replace the petcock.

8. In the event that fuel flow is a problem, check that the vacuum line is tightly secured at both ends, and is free from dry-rotting or other damage. Replace the vacuum line if any damage is noted.

Carburetor Specifications

	XS360	*XS400D*	*XS400E, F/2F*	*XS400-2E*	*XS400G/SG,H*
Type	Mikuni BS34	Mikuni BS34	Mikuni BS34	Mikuni BS34	Mikuni BS34
Main jet	135	142.5	132.5	137.5	135
Air jet	0.6	45	45	45	45
Jet Needle	4FP21-3	5Z1-4	5Z1-3	5Z1-3	5GZ9
Needle clip position (from top)	3	4	3	3	na
Needle jet	X-6	X-4	X-6	X-6	Y-2
Throttle slide	145	135	135	135	na
Pilot jet	17.5	42.5	42.5	42.5	42.5
Pilot screw (turns out)	1½	1¼	1¼	Preset	Preset
Float level (mm/in.)	26.6/1.05	32.0/1.26	32.0/1.26	25.7/1.0	27.3/1.1

ELECTRICAL SYSTEM

CHARGING SYSTEM

Alternator

OUTPUT CHECK

NOTE: *To give accurate results, the battery must be in good condition and fully charged before performing the output test.*

1. Connect a D.C. voltmeter across the battery terminals.

2. Start the engine and let it run at about 2,000 or more rpm.

3. Battery voltage on the meter should be 14.5 v with a maximum allowable variation of 0.3 v.

4. If the voltage is greater than this, check the voltage regulator (see below). If it is less, check the alternator wiring, the regulator, and the rectifier.

CAUTION: *Never run the engine with the battery leads disconnected. To do so risks ruining the other charging system components.*

FIELD COIL/ARMATURE TESTS

1. With the engine *off,* disconnect the alternator wiring at the connector. With an ohmmeter, check the resistance between each of the three white leads. Resistance should be 0.72 ohms.

2. If the resistance is not within 10% of this value, the problem is probably with the alternator armature wiring. If the resistance is too high, the wiring is probably broken; if it is too low, the windings may be breaking down. In either event, the armature must be replaced.

3. Check the resistance across the two field coil leads (green-green). Resistance should be 4.0 ohms. If the measured resistance is not within 15% of this figure, replace the field coil.

NOTE: *Resistance figures are taken at 20° C (68° F). Therefore, it is preferable to*

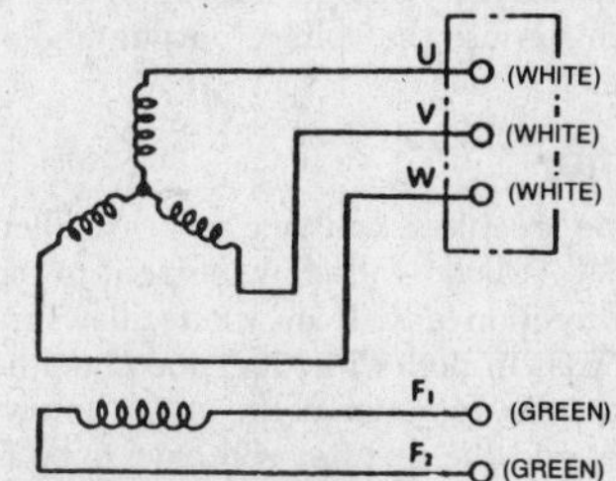

Alternator wiring schematic

Voltage regulator

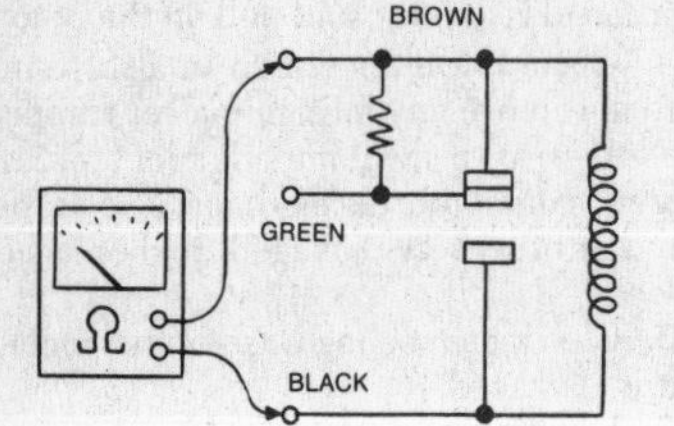

Checking resistance between the brown lead and ground

check them when the engine is cold to ensure accuracy.

Regulator

A mechanical voltage regulator is used on all models. The regulator is adjustable, although this procedure (given below) should not be attempted until the regulator has first been checked for defects.

1. Perform the alternator output test and field coil/armature tests first. If the alternator proves satisfactory, check the regulator.
2. Disconnect the wiring and remove the regulator from the motorcycle.
3. With an ohmmeter, check the resistance between the black regulator lead and the regulator base (black). Resistance should be 10.5 ohms. If the measured resistance is not within 2 ohms of this figure, replace the regulator.
4. Check the resistance between the green and the brown regulator leads. Resistance should be 140 ohms. If the measured resistance is not within 10 ohms of this figure, replace the regulator.
5. If the resistance tests indicate that the regulator winding and resistor are satisfactory, but the charging system is not developing the standard 14.5 v across the battery, the regulator may be in need of adjustment. However, it would be wise to check the rectifier first.
6. Remove the regulator cover. Install the unit on the motorcycle, checking that all wiring connections are correct.
7. Disconnect the fuse box wire leading to the battery. Connect a voltmeter from the fuse box to ground. Start the engine and allow it to run at 2,500 rpm. At this point, the voltmeter should read 14.5–15.0 v. If it does not, turn the regulator adjusting screw to obtain the correct voltage output. Turn the screw *in* to raise the voltage output, and *out* to lower it.

Rectifier

1. The rectifier consists of a six-diode "bridge." A diode will allow current to pass in one direction only. If any diode allows current to pass in both directions, or in neither direction, the operation of the entire unit will be upset and the rectifier will have to be replaced.
2. It is the ability of the diodes to pass current one way and stop it in the other which is tested when checking the rectifier.
3. The rectifier can be checked with an ohmmeter or a self-powered low-voltage test light. Disconnect the rectifier wiring and remove it from the motorcycle.
4. Connect the positive lead of the tester to the rectifier red lead and the negative tester lead to each of the three white leads in turn. Note whether or not there is continuity in each case. Now reverse the tester connections so that the negative tester lead is connected to the red rectifier lead and the positive tester lead is connected to each white lead in turn. Note whether or not there is continuity.

If there was continuity for a certain connection during the first test, there should not be any when the tester leads are reversed. If there was continuity in both cases, or lack of continuity in both cases, a diode is defective and the rectifier must be replaced.

5. Connect the positive lead of the tester to the rectifier black lead and the negative tester lead to each of the three white leads in turn. Repeat the test with these connections. Replace the rectifier if all tests are not satisfactory.

BREAKER POINT IGNITION

Troubleshooting

1. In the event of failure of the ignition system, first check the fuses; if all are in working order, check that the snap connectors for the coils and breaker points are all clean and tight.
2. At this point refer to chapters 2 and 3 for inspection procedures for the breaker points, plugs, and battery. If these items are all in working order, the problem may be isolated to the coils, condensers, or plug caps.
3. If only one cylinder fails to fire, and the problem is not a loose connection or defective spark plug, suspect the plug cap. The caps are fitted with a resistor to prevent radio interference while in operation, and heat and vibration may cause the value of this resistor to increase considerably, even to becoming an open circuit.

The easiest way to see if a misfire is due to a defective cap is to switch the plug cap of the non-firing cylinder with the other cap. If the dead cylinder begins to fire and the other cylinder ceases, the problem is the plug cap. The caps should be replaced as a set.

Functional caps will have a resistance of 9,000 ohms. Usually, when resistance exceeds this valve significantly, the plug for that cap will no longer fire.

Caps are easily removable by unscrewing them from their cables.

4. Defective condensers are seldom a problem, since these are now usually replaced along with the breaker points. Defective condensers will cause considerable arcing or sparking between the breaker point contacts while the machine is running, and this should be cause for replacement before they fail completely. Badly burned or pitted point contact surfaces can also be caused by defective condensers, as well as by improper adjustment. If the points are in bad condition, replace them and the condensers as well.
5. Condenser capacity can be checked with electrical test equipment (if available) in place on the machine, provided the condenser is first disconnected from the primary terminal. Capacitance should be 0.24 MFD. The resistance of the condensers should be in excess of 3 MΩ. A variation of 10% in either reading is allowable.
6. If the condensers are not suspect, check the ignition coils. Coils should be checked for continuity of the windings. First remove the gas tank. Disconnect the red/white coil lead and the other lead which is orange for the left cylinder's coil, or grey for the right. Check resistance across the leads. It should be about 4 ohms. If the resistance is not very close to this figure, the primary winding is defective and the coil must be replaced.
7. To check the secondary coil, first remove the spark plug cap from the plug lead. Check the resistance between the plug lead and the orange or grey lead. Secondary winding resistance should be 9.5 K ohms. If the measured resistance is not very close to this value, the secondary winding is breaking down, and the coil must be replaced.

TRANSISTORIZED IGNITION

Troubleshooting

1. In the event of spark failure, first check the entire electrical system for loose connections.
2. Check that the battery is fully charged. Recharge if necessary.
3. Check all fuses.
4. If all of the above elements are found satisfactory, check the resistance of the ignition coil primary and secondary windings. Primary winding resistance should be about 3 ohms. Secondary resistance should be about 8.6 K ohms.

The primary winding leads at the coils are red/white and orange. The secondary winding resistance is checked between the spark plug lead (minus cap) and the re/white lead.

5. Check the pick-up coils' resistance. It should be about 700 plus/minus 150 ohms.
6. If all of the above elements are satisfactory, replace the TCI unit.

Pick-up Coil

REMOVAL AND INSTALLATION

The pick-up coils are located beneath the cover on the left side of the cylinder head.

1. Centerpunch the blind plug which secures the cover. Use a 5 mm drill bit to drill the plug.
2. Cut internal threads 6 mm diameter x 1.0 mm pitch in the blind plug with a proper sized tap. Thread in the special slide hammer, or a suitable metric bolt, and pull out the plug.
3. Remove the cover screws and take off the cover.
4. Remove the rotor bolt and rotor.
5. Remove the pick-up coil screws and take off the assembly.
6. Installation is the reverse of removal. Install the rotor and tighten the rotor bolt to 7 ft lbs. Check the ignition timing as outlined in "Tune-Up." Rotate the pick-up coil base plate, if necessary, until the timing marks align as specified. After fitting the pick-up coil cover, install a new blind plug. Do not

force the plug in if it is too tight, as this may crack the cover.

STARTING SYSTEM

The starting system consists of the starter motor and clutch, the solenoid, and the handlebar-mounted starter switch. When the button is pressed, the electrical circuit to the solenoid is closed and the solenoid is activated, sending the battery current directly to the starter motor. The starting system is quite reliable and it is unlikely that any major problems will arise.

Testing

If the starter will not operate, switch on the headlight and observe its intensity. If it is dim when the starter is not being operated, check the battery connections and recharge the battery. If the headlight doesn't light, check the fuse, the battery connections, the ignition switch and its connections, and check the continuity of the wire between the ignition switch and the battery.

If the headlight is normally bright, press the starter button and observe any changes. If the headlight dims when the button is pushed, it indicates that the starter motor is drawing current. If it does not dim (i.e. nothing happens), the starter motor is probably not getting any current. In this case, suspect the starter solenoid.

To check the solenoid and starter button, the easiest test is to bypass the unit completely by disconnecting the battery lead from the solenoid and connecting it directly (with the aid of a high-tension jumper cable) to the starter motor terminal. If the starter motor works, the solenoid or starter button is defective and must be replaced.

If the motor still fails to work, the motor itself may be the cause of the trouble.

Starter motor faults are rare, but several things can go wrong.

If the starter spins freely, but the engine doesn't turn over, suspect the starter motor clutch.

If the engine will turn over only very slowly and without a great degree of predictability, some possible causes include: a low or almost dead battery, oil which is too thick for weather conditions (extreme cold), or bad bearings in the motor itself. Worn bearings could cause the armature to contact the field coils which will effectively short out the starter. Usually, repeated attempts at starting will result in the starter motor getting very hot. Other possible causes of starter motor trouble include worn brushes, a worn or dirty commutator, or a defective armature.

Starter Motor Service

REMOVAL AND INSTALLATION

1. Remove the gas tank. Remove the carburetors.
2. Remove the starter motor cover. Disconnect the starter lead.
3. Remove the alternator cover.
4. Remove the starter motor bolts.
5. Remove the gear from the starter motor shaft and take out the starter motor.
6. Installation is the reverse of removal.

INSPECTION

1. Take out the two screws and remove the starter side cover.
2. Check electrical continuity between the commutator and armature core using a multitester or test light and battery. If continuity exists, the armature coil is grounded and the complete starter motor unit must be replaced.
3. Check for continuity between all of the commutator segments. Continuity must exist in each case.
4. Check continuity between the brush that is wired to the stator coil and the starter motor cable. Lack of continuity indicates an open circuit in the stator coil, and the starter motor unit should be replaced. Resistance should not exceed 0.05 ohms.
5. Examine the carbon brushes for damage to the contact surfaces and measure their length. Replace the brushes as a set if either one measures less than 6 mm (0.24 in.), or if they are damaged in any way.

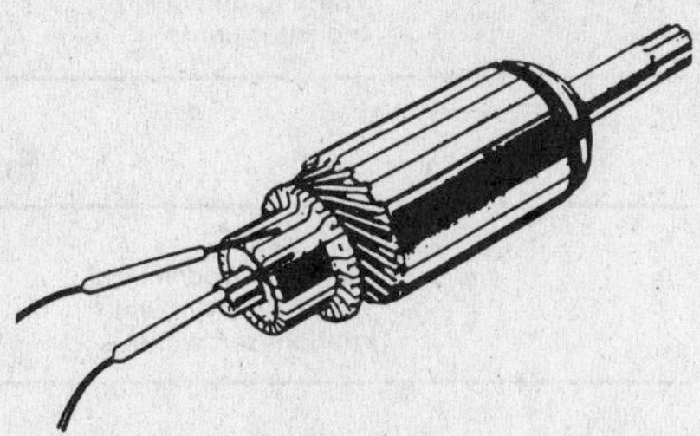

Checking for continuity between commutator segments

6. Brush spring tension should be measured with a small pull-scale. Replace the springs if they have weakened to less than 550 g tension.
7. The mica undercut of the commutator should be maintained at 0.7 mm (0.027 in.). Any carbon deposits should be cleaned out of the commutator grooves, and a piece of hacksaw blade or the like used to increase the undercut depth if necessary.
8. Polish the commutator with fine emery cloth and then clean it thoroughly before installing.
9. Measure the diameter of the commutator. The armature should be replaced if the measurement is less than 27 mm (1.06 in.).
10. Check the condition of the armature bearings and replace them as a set if any damage is noted.
11. Check the condition of the oil seal and replace it if the seal lips are cracked or worn.
12. Unsealed bearings should be lubricated with 20W or 30W motor oil before assembly. Coat the lips of the oil seal with white grease before assembly.

Starter Solenoid

1. If the battery is in reasonably good condition, and nothing at all happens when the starter button is pushed, check the solenoid.
2. Disconnect the starter cable at the solenoid. When the button is pushed, there should be an audible "click" which indicates that the solenoid is opening.
3. If further testing is necessary, remove the solenoid from the machine.

CAUTION: *Be sure to disconnect the cables at the battery before disconnecting the solenoid terminals.*

Connect a fully charged 12-volt battery across the solenoid low-tension leads and check for continuity across the high-tension terminals with an ohmmeter or self-contained test light. If there is no continuity, replace or repair the solenoid.

4. Check for continuity across the low-tension terminals with an ohmmeter or self-powered test light. Resistance should be 3.5 ohms. If there is no continuity, the primary winding of the solenoid is broken, and the unit must be replaced.
5. If starter trouble began just after the starter button housing was disassembled or moved for any reason, check the connections at the switch as they may have come adrift.

ELECTRICAL COMPONENTS

Horn

1. If the horn fails to sound, check that there is 12 v on the brown horn lead. If there isn't, check for a broken wire.
2. If the brown lead checks out, check that the pink wire is grounded when the horn button is pressed. If it isn't, check the horn button.
3. If the wiring is satisfactory, replace the horn.

Brake Light

1. If only one of the two brakes fails to activate the brake light, the problem is probably confined to that switch.
2. If neither switch will activate the brake light, first check the brake light bulb. If it is in workable condition, check that there is 12 v on the yellow brake light lead.
3. If there is voltage on the yellow lead, check for voltage on each brown lead at the brake light switches.

Taillight

1. If the taillight will not work, check the bulb first.
2. If it is satisfactory, check for voltage on the blue lead. If there is voltage on this wire, check for a good ground (black wire).

Turn Signals

1. If only one side fails to work, check both bulbs on that side first.
2. If the bulbs are operable, check for voltage on the green (right) or brown (left) leads. If there is voltage here, check the grounds (black leads).
3. If neither side will work, check for voltage on the brown/white lead at the handlebar turn signal switch. Then check for voltage on the brown lead at the turn signal flasher relay.
4. If these checks are satisfactory, replace the flasher relay. If the turn signals still will not operate, replace the flasher switch. If this will not work, the entire self-cancelling system must be checked out (see below).

Neutral Indicator

1. If indicator light fails to come on, check the bulb first.
2. If the bulb is satisfactory, check that there is voltage on the blue wire at the switch. If there is, replace the switch itself.

Oil Pressure Indicator

1. Check the bulb first.
2. If the bulb is satisfactory, check for voltage on the black/red lead to the switch.
3. If the wiring checks out, replace the oil pressure indicator switch.

Self-Cancelling Turn Signal System

1. In the event that the self-cancelling system fails to operate properly, first disconnect the 6-prong connector from the flasher cancelling unit and try the turn signals. If both sides operate normally, the trouble can be confined to the cancelling unit itself, the handlebar switch reset circuit, or the speedometer sensor circuit.
2. Connect an ohmmeter set to the R x 100 range across the white/green and black wires on the wiring harness side of the 6-prong connector. Turn the speedometer shaft. The ohmmeter needle should swing back and forth between zero and infinity four times. If this happens, it indicates that the speedometer sensor circuit is functioning properly. If the meter does not function in this manner, either the sensor or the wiring harness is defective.
3. Check for continuity between the yellow/red lead of the 6-prong connector on the wiring harness side and ground on the chassis. When the turn signal switch is *off*, there should be infinite resistance. When the switch is pushed to either "L" or "R", there should be no resistance. If this is not the case, check the wiring harness and the handlebar switch circuit.
4. If no defective operation is apparent in the above tests, replace the self-cancelling unit.
5. If the turn signals operate only when the turn signal button is pushed to "L" or "R" and they shut off immediately when the button is released, replace the self-cancelling unit.

Note the following concerning the self-cancelling turn signal system:

a. Yamaha recommends that the turn signals be shut off manually after a turn is completed.

b. If the self-cancelling unit fails, the turn signals can be used manually by simply disconnecting the 6-prong connector from the unit.

Bulbs

Headlight	40/30W
Tail/Brake light	8/27W
Turn signals	27W
Meter lights	3.4W
Warning lights	3.4W
Indicator lights	3.4W

Fuses

Main (red)	20A
Headlight (red/yellow)	10A
Turn signal (brown)	10A
Ignition (red/white)	10A

WIRING DIAGRAMS

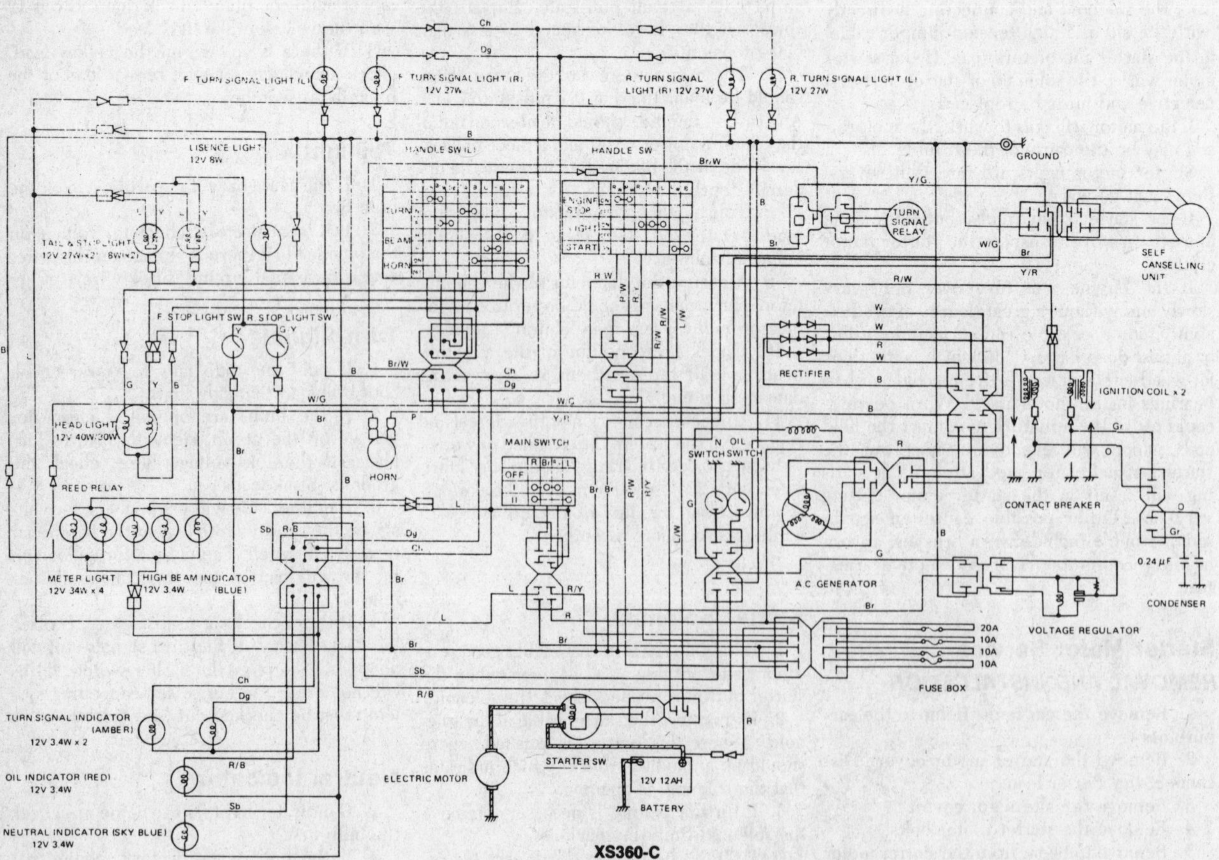

XS360-C

WIRING DIAGRAMS

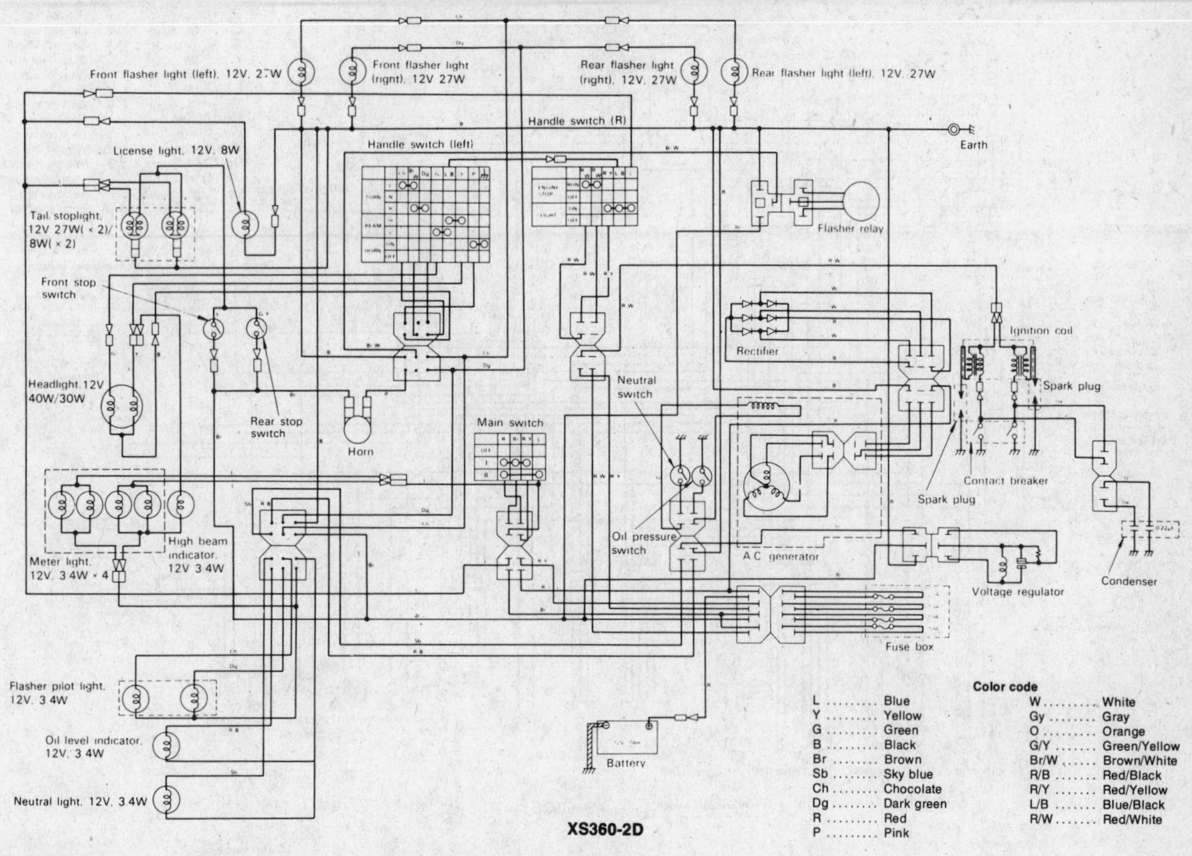

XS360-2D

Color code

L	Blue	W	White
Y	Yellow	Gy	Gray
G	Green	O	Orange
B	Black	G/Y	Green/Yellow
Br	Brown	Br/W	Brown/White
Sb	Sky blue	R/B	Red/Black
Ch	Chocolate	R/Y	Red/Yellow
Dg	Dark green	L/B	Blue/Black
R	Red	R/W	Red/White
P	Pink		

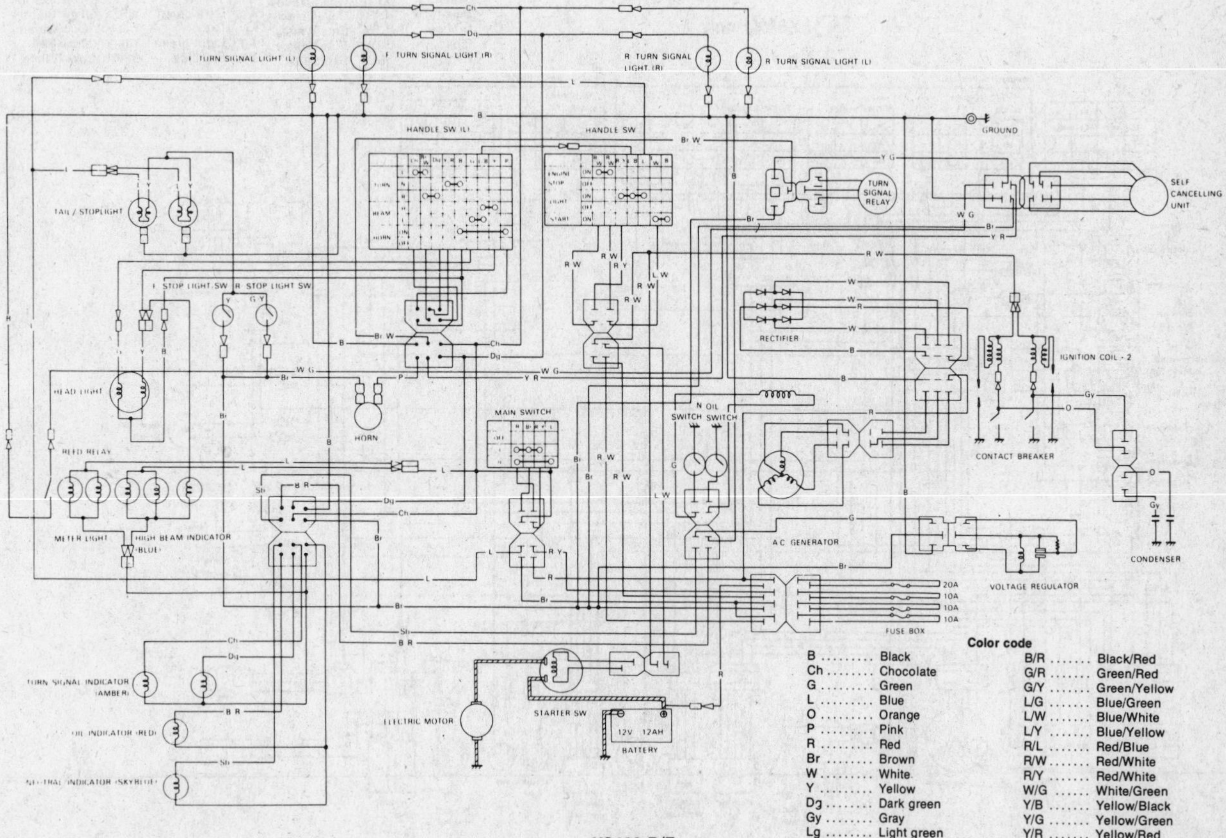

F TURN SIGNAL LIGHT (L)
F TURN SIGNAL LIGHT (R)
R TURN SIGNAL LIGHT (R)
R TURN SIGNAL LIGHT (L)
GROUND
HANDLE SW (L)
HANDLE SW
TURN SIGNAL RELAY
SELF CANCELLING UNIT
TAIL / STOPLIGHT
F STOP LIGHT SW
R STOP LIGHT SW
RECTIFIER
IGNITION COIL - 2
HEAD LIGHT
HORN
MAIN SWITCH
N SWITCH
OIL SWITCH
CONTACT BREAKER
REED RELAY
METER LIGHT
HIGH BEAM INDICATOR (BLUE)
A.C. GENERATOR
CONDENSER
VOLTAGE REGULATOR
20A
10A
10A
10A
FUSE BOX
TURN SIGNAL INDICATOR (AMBER)
OIL INDICATOR (RED)
NEUTRAL INDICATOR (SKYBLUE)
ELECTRIC MOTOR
STARTER SW
12V 12AH
BATTERY

XS400-D/E

Color code

B	Black	B/R	Black/Red
Ch	Chocolate	G/R	Green/Red
G	Green	G/Y	Green/Yellow
L	Blue	L/G	Blue/Green
O	Orange	L/W	Blue/White
P	Pink	L/Y	Blue/Yellow
R	Red	R/L	Red/Blue
Br	Brown	R/W	Red/White
W	White	R/Y	Red/White
Y	Yellow	W/G	White/Green
Dg	Dark green	Y/B	Yellow/Black
Gy	Gray	Y/G	Yellow/Green
Lg	Light green	Y/R	Yellow/Red
Sb	Sky blue	Br/W	Brown/White

WIRING DIAGRAMS

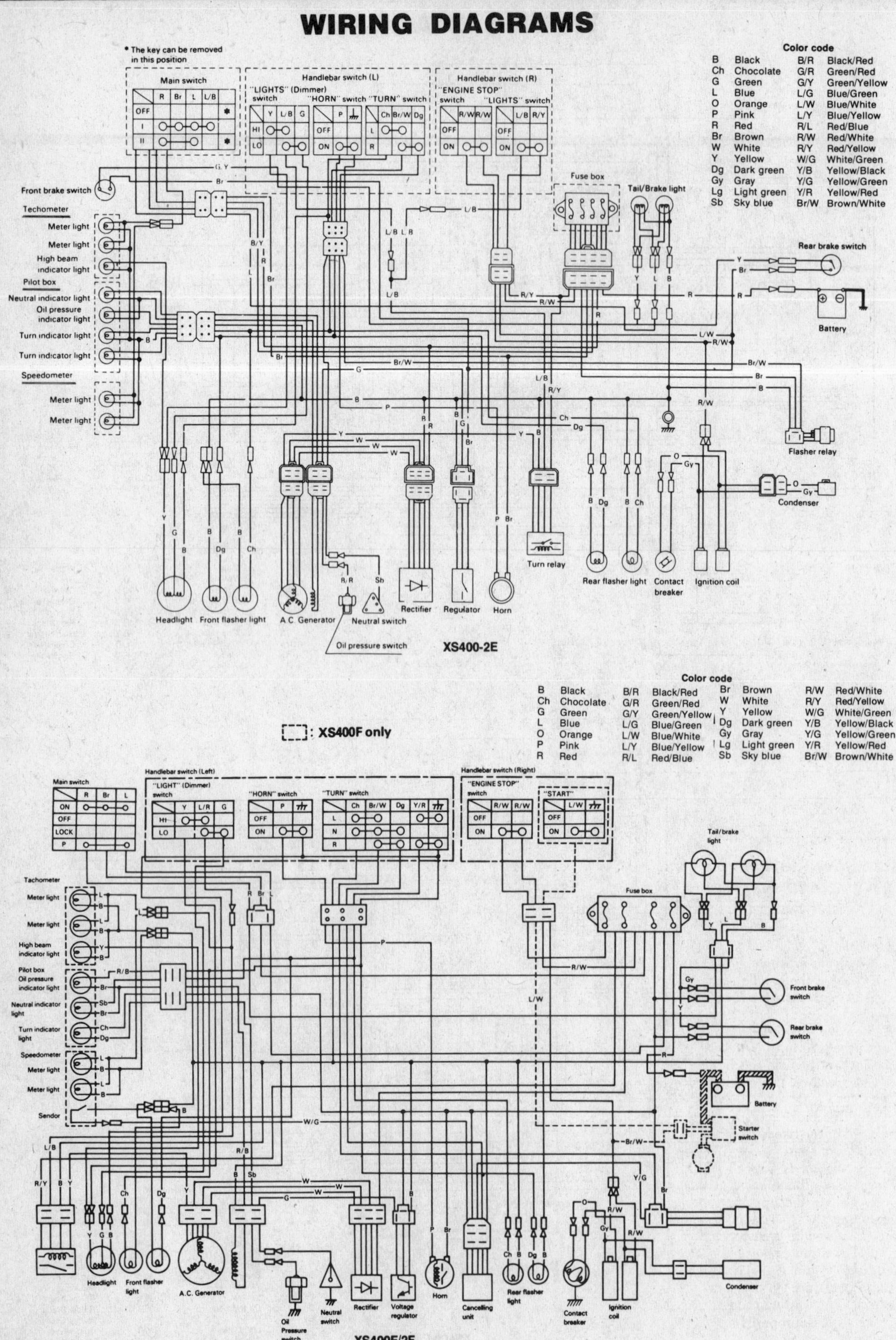

WIRING DIAGRAMS

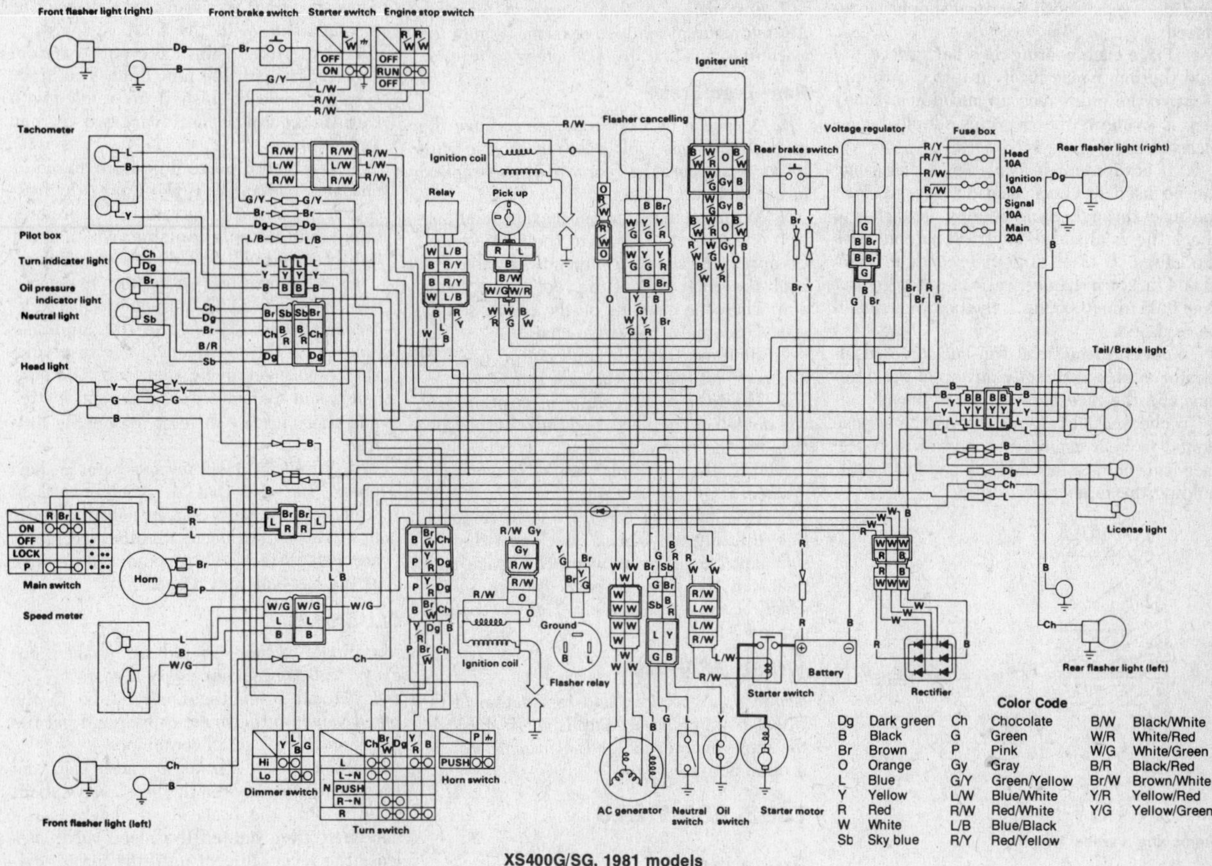

XS400G/SG, 1981 models

CHASSIS

WHEELS

Front Wheel Assembly

REMOVAL AND INSTALLATION

1. Support the front wheel several inches off the ground by placing a support beneath the engine.
2. On drum brake models, disconnect the brake cable at the handlebar.
3. Disconnect the speedometer cable at the wheel.
4. Remove the axle nut cotter pin and remove the axle nut.
5. Loosen the axle cap nuts. Pull out the axle and remove the wheel from the machine.
6. On disc brake models, place a piece of cardboard or the like between the brake pads to keep them apart.
7. Installation is basically the reverse of removal. Note the following points:

   a. Grease the lips of the wheel grease seals and the speedometer drive mechanism with white grease.

   b. On drum brake models, be sure to engage the brake anchor with the slot on the fork slider. On disc brake models, be careful when fitting the wheel so that the brake disc is properly installed between the pads.

   c. If the axle cap has been removed, install it so that the arrow on it points towards the front of the motorcycle.

   d. When tightening the axle cap nuts, tighten the frontmost one first. Torque it to 15 ft lbs. Then tighten the rear one to the same torque. The cap is machined unevenly. There should be a small gap between the cap and the fork slider visible above the rearmost nut.

   e. Tighten the axle nut to 72 ft lbs on drum brake models and 77 ft lbs on disc brake machines. Use a new cotter pin.

Tighten the forwardmost axle cap nut first: there should be a gap between the cap and the slider at the rear (arrow)

   f. Check brake operation *before* riding the motorcycle.

WHEEL BEARINGS

Removal

1. After removing the front wheel, remove the brake plate on drum brake models, or the brake disc on disc brake machines.
2. Remove the speedometer drive box on disc brake machines.
3. Remove any wheel bearing covers or retainers fitted to either side of the hub.
4. Pry out the grease seals. Once removed, the seals should be replaced with new ones.
5. Reach through the hub with a suitable punch, move the wheel bearing spacer as far as possible to one side to achieve a purchase on the wheel bearing, and drive it out. Remove the spacer. Drive out the remaining wheel bearing from the other side of the hub.

Inspection

1. Wash the wheel bearings thoroughly in a solvent to remove all of the old grease.
2. Inspect the general condition of the bearings. There should be no rust, pitting, or obvious signs of wear or damage on either balls or races.
3. Slowly rotate the bearings. Rotation

should be smooth, noiseless, and free of binding or unevenness. If any of the above conditions exist, both bearings should be replaced.

4. Place each bearing on a flat surface and hold the inner race firmly in place. Attempt to move the outer race up and down. If any play is evident, the bearings should be replaced.

5. If equipment is available, a dial gauge can be used to check bearing run-out. Pass the axle through each bearing in turn and check the axial and diametrical run-out with the gauge. If axial run-out exceeds 0.1 mm (0.004 in.) or if diametrical run-out is greater than 0.05 mm (0.002 in.), the bearings should be replaced.

To check diametrical run-out, the dial indicator is placed directly on top of the outer race and the race moved up and down.

To check axial run-out, the gauge is positioned to bear against the side of the outer race and the race moved back and forth while holding the inner race in place.

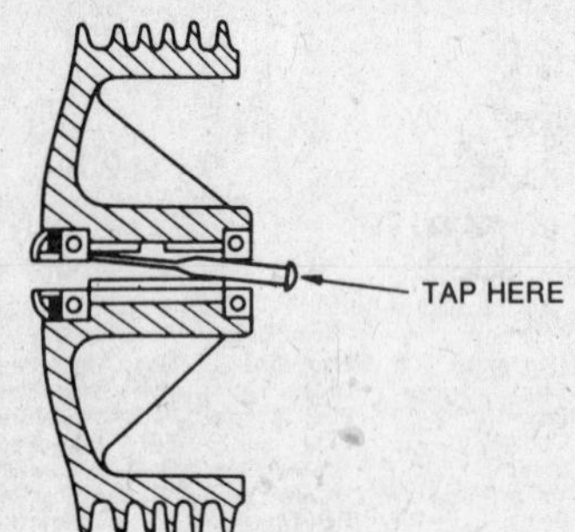

Removing a wheel bearing

Installation

Assembly is the reverse of the above.

Note the following points:

a. Pack the bearings with a good grade of wheel bearing grease. Put a small handful of the grease in the hub as well.

b. Do not forget to install the spacer in the hub before installing the bearing.

c. Bearings may be driven into place using a suitably sized socket or a bearing driver. If one side of the bearing is sealed, install it with the sealed side facing outward.

d. Use new grease seals and lubricate them with oil to make installation easier.

Rear Wheel Assembly

REMOVAL AND INSTALLATION

Rear Drum Brake

1. Park the motorcycle on the center stand.

2. Remove the brake rod adjusting nut and disconnect the brake rod from the lever on the brake plate.

3. Disconnect the brake anchor from the brake plate.

4. Remove the cotter pin and loosen the axle nut. Loosen the chain adjuster bolt locknuts. Back off the adjuster bolts.

5. On models with a masterlink chain, disconnect the chain. On models with an endless chain, fold down the adjuster plates and push the wheel as far forward as possible. Disengage the chain from the sprocket.

6. Remove the axle nut and pull out the axle. Remove the wheel from the motorcycle, noting the locations of any spacers or collars.

7. Installation is the reverse of removal. After adjusting the chain tension, tighten the axle nut to 50–72 ft lbs. Use a new cotter pin.

Rear Disc Brake

1. A special tool is needed to remove the rear wheel. This tool, a length of wire with hooks to support the rear wheel, is supplied in the tool kit.

2. With the machine on the side stand, attach one end of the tool to the frame hook. Compress the shocks as much as possible and hook the other end of the tool to the swing arm. Place the machine on the center stand.

3. Disconnect the drive chain.

4. Remove the axle nut cotter pin and unscrew and remove the axle nut.

5. Hold the brake caliper in position so it will not fall out of place, and pull out the axle. Remove the rear wheel assembly.

NOTE: *Do not apply the brake while the wheel is off the machine.*

6. Installation is the reverse of removal. Before fitting the wheel, check that there is sufficient clearance between the brake pads to install the disc. Grease the lips of the wheel bearing grease seals. Tighten the axle nut to 77 ft lbs.

WHEEL BEARINGS

Removal, inspection, and installation of the wheel bearings is accomplished in basically the same manner as for the front wheel described above.

TUBELESS TIRES

Precautions

Some models are equipped with aluminum wheels which are compatible with either tube or tubeless tires. Tubeless tires are installed at the factory. Obey the following precautions when dealing with tubeless tires.

1. Do not attempt to use tubeless tires on wheels which are not specifically designed for them.

WARNING: *Injury or tire failure may result from using tubeless tires with incompatible wheels.*

2. Tire pressure is critical. Always maintain pressure at the proper specification.

3. Check tire condition before riding.

4. Aluminum wheels cannot be repaired. If the wheel is bent or cracked, it must be replaced.

5. After changing or fitting a new tire, ride with caution for several miles to allow the tire to seat itself properly on the wheel.

6. Be sure that the valve stem locknut is securely fastened.

7. Changing a tubeless tire is basically the same as described for tube types in the "General Information" section.

8. The tubeless wheels fitted to these motorcycles will accept a tube and tube type tire if so desired. Be sure, however, that the tube is the proper size for the tire and that the tire matches the rim.

9. Do not attempt to fit oversized (wider) tires to the standard wheels.

DISC BRAKE SERVICE

When handling disc brake fluid, observe the following precautions:

a. Use DOT #3 brake fluid only. Do not mix types or brands of brake fluid. Since the fluid in the motorcycle may be incompatable with the fluid you wish to add, it is wise to flush the entire system and refill it with the new fluid. The brake system should be flushed and refilled with fresh brake fluid about every two years in any case.

b. Never use brake fluid from an old or unsealed container. Brake fluid is hydroscopic: it absorbs moisture. Therefore, brake fluid left in a container which is not tightly sealed will quickly become useless.

c. When working on the disc brake system, be sure that all components are scrupulously clean. Clean the tops of brake fluid cans, the master cylinder reservoir, etc., before removing their caps. Be sure hands and tools are free of foreign matter and that rags are at least reasonably dirt-free.

d. Brake fluid will remove paint in short order. Be sure that all painted surfaces which can come in contact with the brake fluid through spillage or other accidents are well covered. This includes items such as the gas tank and frame.

FLUSHING

The brake system should be flushed out every 12,000 miles, or every 2 years.

1. Attach a length of vinyl tube to the bleed valve on the brake caliper and put the other end into a small container.

2. Remove the master cylinder cap, and the diaphragm. Loosen the bleed valve about ½ turn. Pull the brake lever slowly to the handgrip, then tighten the bleed valve. Release the lever. Repeat until the master cylinder is almost empty.

3. Add new brake fluid to the master cylinder and continue squeezing and releasing the brake lever slowly until the new fluid begins to come out of the vinyl tube. Bleed the system as outlined below.

BLEEDING

The brake hydraulic system must be bled whenever any part of the system has been disconnected or removed for service. When refilling the master cylinder reservoir, use only brake fluid conforming to DOT 3 specifications. Any brand meeting this requirement is acceptable. The brake fluid container of all reputable brands will be plainly marked with the standards the fluid meets or exceeds.

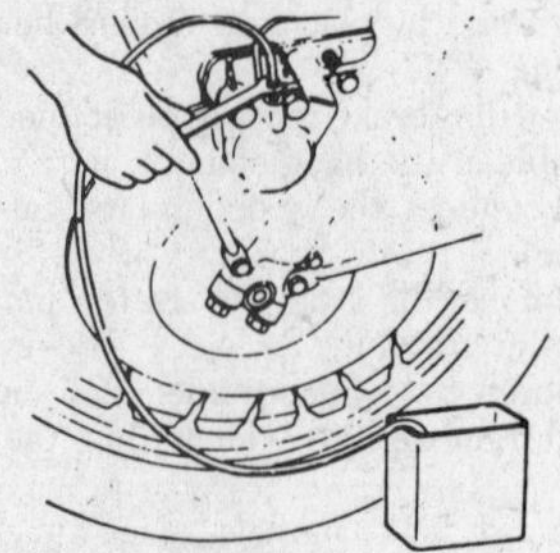

Bleeding the brake system

NOTE: *It is sometimes helpful to let the cycle sit for several hours before bleeding the system. Pulling and tapping on the lines will help expel any air bubbles trapped in the system. If you find that you can't get the system bled properly and the master cylinder has been dry for awhile, the seals inside the cylinder may have become dried and cracked. In this case rebuild the master cylinder.*

1. Top up the reservoir with brake fluid and replace the cap to keep dirt and moisture out and the fluid in. Cover the gas tank with a thick cloth to avoid damage due to spilled brake fluid.

2. Attach one end of a small diameter rubber hose to the bleed valve on the caliper, and place the other end in a jar which contains several inches of clean, new brake fluid. Be sure that the end of the hose is submerged in this fluid. Arrange the hose so that it loops upward after leaving the bleed valve, and see that it has no kinks or sharp bends.

3. Pump the brake lever rapidly several times until some resistance is felt and, holding the lever against the resistance, open the bleed valve about one-half turn. When the lever bottoms, close the valve (do not overtighten) and then release the lever.

4. Repeat the operation until no more air is released out of the hose and the brake lever is firm in operation. Check the fluid level in the reservoir often to make sure that it doesn't go dry and draw more air into the system. Do not reuse fluid that has been pumped out of the system. Do not use fluid that has been stored for more than a few weeks after the seal on its container has been opened, as brake fluid will absorb moisture from the air and may corrode the master cylinder and caliper.

5. Refill the reservoir to the level mark when through (but do not overfill). Avoid overtightening the cap or fluid will weep around the cap edge.

Front Disc Brake

PAD REPLACEMENT

1. Unbolt the caliper from the fork slider.
2. Remove the pad screw which secures the fixed pad on the wheel side of the caliper. Remove the fixed pad.
3. Remove the piston pad.
4. Installation is the reverse of removal. Secure the fixed pad phillips screw with a non-permanent thread-locking compound.

CALIPER

Removal

1. Disconnect the brake line from the caliper. Plug the end of the brake line to prevent loss of brake fluid.
2. Remove the mounting bolts and take the caliper from the fork slider.

Disassembly

1. Remove the phillips screw which secures the fixed pad and take out the pad and pad spring.
2. Remove the piston pad.
3. Remove the caliper support bolt. Separate the caliper and support bracket. Remove the piston dust seal and retaining ring.
4. Apply compressed air to the brake line fitting on the caliper and force out the piston.

Caution: Be sure your fingers are clear of the piston, as it may come out with some force.

5. Remove the piston seal.

Inspection

1. Clean all parts in new brake fluid. Do not use gasoline or other solvents.
2. All rubber parts should be replaced with new ones once the caliper has been disassembled. These parts should also be replaced every two years as a matter of preventive maintenance.
3. Check the piston for scoring or other obvious signs of wear, and replace it if damage is noted. Check the caliper bore as well.

Assembly

1. Using a new caliper support bolt is recommended. As noted above, all rubber parts must be replaced as well.
2. Lightly lubricate the piston seal with fresh brake fluid and install it in the caliper. Be sure that the seal is properly seated.
3. Lubricate the sides of the piston with brake fluid and install it.
4. Fit the caliper and support bracket together, not forgetting the bushing and bushing boot. Install the support bolt and tighten it to 11–15 ft lbs.
5. Install the brake pads. Secure the fixed pad phillips screw with a non-permanent thread-locking compound. Grease the pad-shim contact area before installation. Bend each tab of the shim over the piston pad.

Caliper mounting bolts

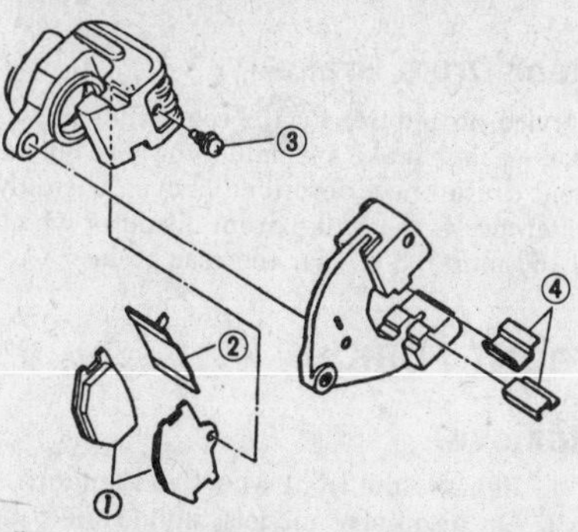

Caliper pad components: 1, pads; 2, pad spring; 3, screw; 4, retainers

Installation

1. Tighten the caliper mounting bolts to 21–29 ft lbs.

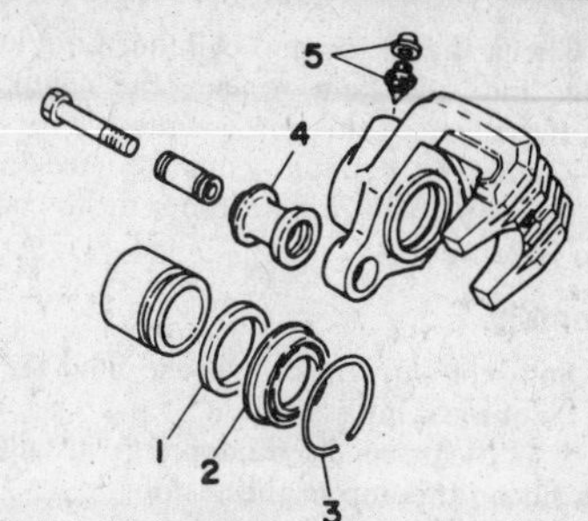

Caliper components: 1, piston seal; 2, boot; 3, dust cover clip; 4, bushing boot; 5, bleed screw

2. Tighten the brake line banjo bolt to 18–25 ft lbs. Bleed the system.

MASTER CYLINDER

Removal

1. Disconnect the front brake light switch leads.
2. Remove the brake lever. Note the return spring.
3. Disconnect the brake line from the master cylinder. Take adequate precautions to avoid spillage.
4. Remove the two master cylinder handlebar clamp bolts and remove the master cylinder assembly.

Disassembly

1. Remove the master cylinder cap and diaphragm and drain off and disgard the brake fluid.
2. Remove the master cylinder rubber boot.
3. Remove the snap-ring. Take out the piston assembly. The spring will remain in the master cylinder.
4. Remove the spring and stopper valve.
5. Remove the stopper plate and the cylinder cups.

Inspection

1. Clean all parts in fresh brake fluid.
2. Check the master cylinder port for clogging.

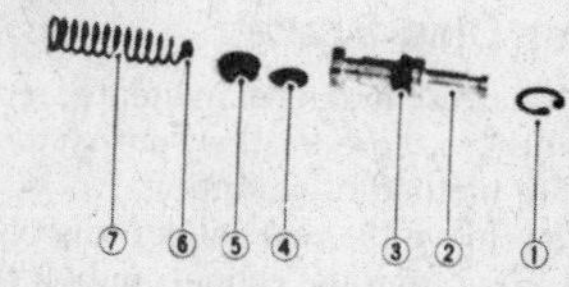

Master cylinder components

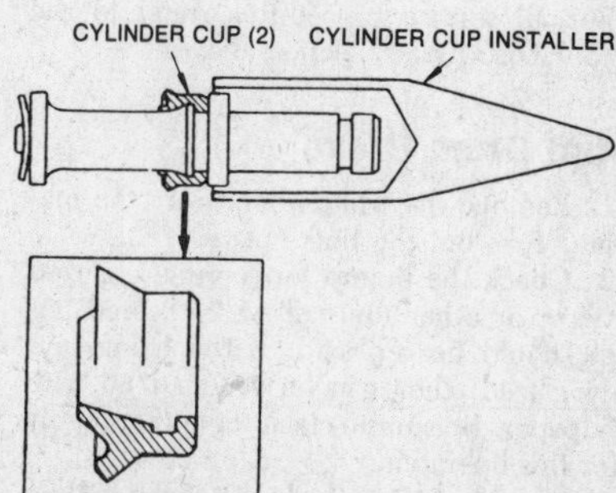

Installing the cylinder cup

3. Check the piston and cylinder bore for scoring and wear and replace the components if damage of this sort is noted.

4. Check the cylinder cups for cracking and dry-rotting and replace them if this condition is present.

Assembly

1. Soak the cups in new brake fluid for a time before assembly.

2. Use the special cylinder cup installer when fitting the cup to the piston.

3. Install the stopper plate into the master cylinder. Insert the spring and valve.

4. Insert the piston into the master cylinder. Take care not to scratch the piston or cylinder wall. Fit the snap-ring. Be sure that it is firmly seated.

5. Fit the boot into the grooves of the master cylinder and piston.

Installation

Bolt the master cylinder to the haldlebar. Connect the brake and tighten the banjo bolt to 17–20 ft lbs. Fill the master cylinder with fresh brake fluid and bleed the system.

DISC SERVICE

The brake disc normally requires no service of any kind. However, if the disc becomes scored for any reason, it should be replaced and a new set of pads should be installed. A badly scored disc will reduce the effectiveness of the brake and shorten pad life considerably. If the front brake lever oscillates or fluctuates when the brake is applied at speed, the indication is that the brake disc is warped or bent. Check the run-out of the disc with a dial indicator and replace it if run-out exceeds 0.15 mm (0.006 in.). Measure disc thickness. If it is less than 4.5 mm (0.18 in.), it should be replaced. To replace the disc:

1. Remove the wheel.

2. Bend back the locktabs, unscrew the bolts, and remove the disc from the hub.

3. Mount the new disc on the hub and tighten the bolts evenly, using new locktabs or thread-locking compound to secure them. Proper torque is 12–16 ft lbs.

4. Examine the brake pads and replace them if they are close to the limit of wear or have worn in an unusual pattern.

Rear Disc Brake

The rear disc brake components are virtually identical to those for the front system except for the method of mounting.

To remove the rear caliper, disconnect the brake line from the caliper, unbolt the brake anchor, and remove the rear axle.

For all service procedures, refer to the "Front Disc Brake" section above.

Front Drum Brake

1. Remove the front wheel from the machine. Take out the brake plate.

2. Check the linings for scoring, a glazed surface, or other unusual wear. Scored linings should be replaced. If the linings are only glazed, they can be roughed up with sandpaper. Be sure to clean them thoroughly after this operation.

3. Measure lining thickness at the middle and ends of each brake shoe. Minimum acceptable lining thickness is 2 mm (0.08 in.). New linings will have a thickness of 4 mm (0.16 in.).

4. Remove the shoes from the brake plate by folding them in towards the center.

5. Check the condition of the brake return springs. Standard free length of the springs is 68 mm (2.68 in.), and they should be replaced if they are stretched over this standard. Also check the springs for rust, damaged ends, or other obvious signs of age.

6. Measure the diameter of the brake drum in at least two directions. Standard diameter is 180 mm (7.1 in.). If the measured diameter exceeds this standard by more than a small amount, the drum should be replaced.

7. Rough up the surface of the brake drum with sandpaper. Clean the drum out thoroughly before assembly.

LINING THICKNESS

8. Check for excessive play in the brake rod linkage. If play exists, the most obvious cause is wear wear of the clevis pins. Replace the pins as necessary.

9. The brake cams can be removed from the brake plate after removing the shoes and brake linkage. Mark the brake levers and cams before disassembly so the levers can be reinstalled in their original positions. Clean the cams in solvent. Remove any rust or corrosion with medium grade emery cloth. Check that the cams can rotate freely in their holes. Check the condition of the splines. Replace any bent or otherwise damaged cams. Before installation, smear the cams with a good grade of chassis grease.

Rear Drum Brake

Service procedures for the rear drum single-leading shoe brake are similar to those for the front drum brake described above. The only difference is the brake drum diameter which is 160 mm (6.3 in.) for the rear brake.

FRONT FORKS

Removal

1. Remove the front wheel and fender.

2. On disc brake models, unbolt the caliper from the fork slider. Disconnect the brake line from the fork leg.

3. Loosen the upper and lower triple clamp pinch bolts. Pull each fork leg down and free of the triple clamps.

Dissassembly

1. Remove the rubber fork caps, press down on the metal caps and remove the snap-ring. Take out the cap and fork spring. Drain off the fork oil.

2. Remove the allen bolt from the bottom of the fork slider.

3. Separate the fork slider from the fork tube.

4. Remove the clip from the bottom of the fork tube and remove the piston assembly.

5. To remove the slider oil seal, remove the dust cover and the snap-ring and pry the old seal out. New seals must always be used on assembly.

Upper triple clamp pinch bolts

Inspection

1. Inspect the fork tubs for bends such as might have been incurred in an accident. Replacement is recommended rather than attempting to straighten bend fork tubes.

2. The chrome plating on the fork tubes must be in perfect condition in the area along which the slider oil seal rides. If the plating is chipped or flaking, the seal will leak. Damage to the plating requires replacement of the fork tube.

Removing a fork slider oil seal

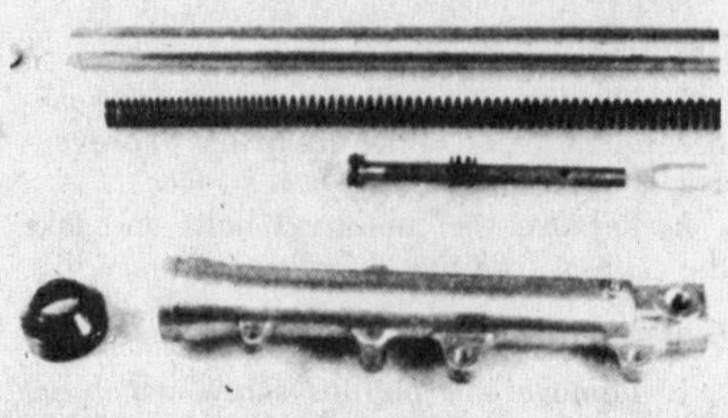

Fork components

3. Compare the spring heights of the fork springs from each fork leg. They should be equal. Standard spring free length is 484 mm (19.1 in.). If the spring heights are unequal, or if either or both of them has been compressed through use, both should be replaced.

4. Clean the damper components thoroughly in a safe solvent. Be sure that all bleed holes are clear. Clean out the inside of the fork sliders with solvent as well.

Assembly

Assembly is the reverse of disassembly. Note the following points:

a. New slider oil seals must always be used. Drive the new seals straight into the slider (sealed side up) until there is sufficient room to install the snap-ring in its groove. Use a large socket or the like to install the seal. Be sure it is not cocked or twisted during the installation procedure. Install the snap-ring. Oil the lips of the seal before assembling the fork components.

b. Tighten the fork slider allen bolt securely. The threads of the allen bolt should be coated with a non-permanent thread-locking compound before installation.

c. The fork springs are progressively wound. They are installed so that the close coils are towards the *top*.

Installation

1. Fit each fork leg up through the triple clamps until the top edge of the fork tube is flush with the upper surface of the upper triple clamp.
2. Tighten the lower triple clamp pinch bolts to 22–29 ft lbs.
3. Tighten the upper triple clamp pinch bolts to 7–10 ft lbs.

4. Fill each fork leg with 130 cc (4.4 oz) of the proper fork oil. Refer to the "Maintenance" section for oil recommendations.

5. Install the front wheel and fender and caliper assembly, if applicable.

STEERING STEM ASSEMBLY

Bearing Adjustment

1. The steering stem bearings are uncaged ¼-in. balls. They are adjusted by means of a ring nut beneath the upper triple clamp.
2. To check bearing adjustment, support the front wheel off the ground. Grasp the tip of the front fender and place your other hand beneath the lower triple clamp at the frame lug.
3. Attempt to move the fork by pulling up on the tip of the fender. If play or movement can be felt at the lower triple clamp, the bearings are adjusted too loosely or are worn. An alternate method is to grasp the fork sliders and attempt to move them back and forth in line with the motorcycle. No play should be noted.
4. Turn the forks slowly from lock-to-lock. Movement should be smooth, silent, and effortless. If any binding or uneven movement is felt, the balls and races are either too tightly adjusted or they are worn. If the steering feels uniformly stiff, the bearings are too tightly adjusted. If any noise is noted, the bearings are damaged or some are missing.
5. With the front wheel off the ground, release the front forks from a few degrees off the centered position. The fork should fall freely to either side of their own weight. If they will not, the bearings are too tightly adjusted, the steering stem is bent, the races are extremely worn, or some of the bearings are missing.
6. To adjust the bearings, remove the gas tank. The bearings are adjusted by means of the adjuster nut under the upper triple clamp.
7. Tighten or loosen the adjuster nut a little at a time until the steering stem adjustment conforms to that outlined above.
8. If proper adjustment is not possible, the bearings and races will probably need to be replaced.

Disassembly

1. Remove the front wheel, front fender, and the fork legs.
2. Remove the headlight bracket.
3. Remove the gas tank. Disconnect the headlight wires beneath the tank.
4. Disconnect the wires between the handlebar switches and the main wiring harness.
5. Disconnect the clutch and throttle cables at the handlebars and the instrument cables at the instruments. On disc brake models, unbolt the master cylinder from the handlebar.
6. Loosen the steering stem pinch bolt. Remove the upper triple clamp fitting bolt and crown washer.

Steering head bearing adjuster nut

7. Remove the upper triple clamp complete with instruments.
8. Hold the lower triple clamp in place to prevent the lower race balls from falling out, and unscrew and remove the bearing adjuster nut. Remove the bearing cover.
9. Carefully lower the lower triple clamp/steering stem assembly out of the frame lug. Note that the lower race balls may fall out as the assembly is lowered.
10. Remove the top bearing cover and race and remove the ball bearings.
11. Remove the bottom cone race, dust seal, and dust seal washer from the steering stem if they are to be replaced. These will have to be pried off with a chisel; therefore only remove them if necessary.
12. The bearing races in the frame lug are a press-fit and should not be removed unless replacement is necessary. If replacement is necessary, the old races can be removed by reaching through the frame lug with a suitable punch and tapping the race evenly around its circumference to remove it from the inside of the frame lug. Be sure that the race does not become cocked in its seat upon removal.

New races are installed with a suitably sized bearing driver, i.e., one which will drive the race squarely into its seat. Be certain that the race goes straight in.

These races can also be installed using a block of hard wood of sufficient size to cover the race in place of a bearing driver.

Inspection

1. Wash the ball bearings in a suitable solvent.
2. Clean all of the old grease from the bearing race surfaces, steering stem, and frame lug.
3. Inspect the bearing race surfaces. They must be clean and smooth and free of any cracks, scoring, rust, or indentations. Run your finger around each of the bearing races.

Checking steering head bearing play

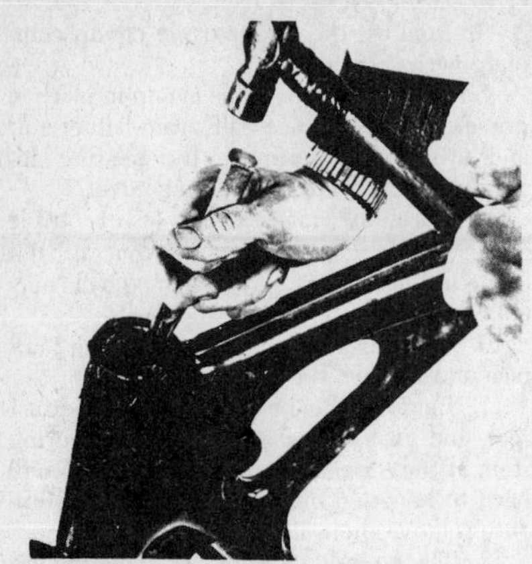
Removing the frame races

Note any roughness or ripples on the race surface. If any imperfections are noted, both sets of races and all of the balls must be replaced.

4. Check the balls themselves for rust, pitting, scoring, or flat spots. If the balls are found to be defective in any way, the balls and both sets of races must be replaced.

NOTE: *Balls and races must always be replaced in a set because worn races will destroy new balls and worn balls will destroy new races.*

5. Check the dust seal for condition and replace if torn or cracked.

6. Check the steering stem for cracks or a bent condition; this is especially important if the bike has been involved in a spill.

Assembly

1. Put a coat of a good grade of bearing grease on the steering stem race and the upper frame race.

2. Imbed the ball bearings in the grease. There are 19 balls in each race.

3. Install the steering stem assembly in the frame, holding it in place so that the balls cannot fall out. Fit the top bearing race and bearing cover. Install the bearing adjuster nut. Tighten the nut until all the play is taken out of the steering stem, but insure that the stem can turn freely.

4. The remainder of the procedure is the reverse of disassembly. Tighten the upper triple clamp fitting bolt to 26–29 ft lbs., and the steering stem pinch bolt to 10–16 ft lbs.

5. If the handlebars have been removed, tighten the clamp bolts evenly to yield a gap on both sides of the clamps. Tighten the clamp bolts to 10–16 ft lbs.

REAR SHOCKS

1. The rear shock absorbers are sealed units. No service is possible. If the shocks leak oil, have a bent damper rod, damaged damper case, or other damage, they should be replaced.

Shock absorbers should be replaced in sets to ensure equal damping characteristics.

2. Shocks can be removed by removing the upper and lower mounts. To remove the spring, set the load adjuster on the softest setting, compress the spring, and remove the spring retainers.

3. With the spring removed, check the damping characteristics of the unit. The damper rod should be able to be pushed into the damper body with considerably less effort than it takes to pull it out. If little or no resistance is felt when pulling a damper rod out, the shock should be replaced. Shocks should have equal damping characteristics.

4. Tighten the mounting bolts to 16–25 ft lbs when installing the shock absorbers.

SWING ARM

Inspection

1. Remove the mufflers.

2. Remove the rear wheel, shock absorbers, and chain guard.

3. Measure the distance between the top and bottom shock absorber mounts on both sides. The two measurements must be identical, or the swing arm will have to be replaced.

4. Check that the rear wheel mounting plates are parallel.

5. Grasp the legs of the swing arm and attempt to move it from side to side. Any noticeable side-play (more than 1 mm/0.04 in.) will indicate that the swing arm bushings need replacement.

The swing arm is most likely to be damaged if the machine is operated for any length of time with a broken or otherwise defective shock absorber.

Removal and Installation

1. Proceed as above. Then remove the swing arm pivot bolt nut and tap out the pivot with a long drift.

2. Remove the swing arm by pulling it straight back. Note the locations of any spacers or shims which may come off. They must be installed in their original locations.

3. The swing arm should be inspected for cracks or fractures, especially around the welds.

4. Remove the bushings, tapping them out with a hammer and punch. Once the bushings are removed, they should be replaced.

5. Lubricate new bushings with a good chassis grease. Press the bushings into the swing arm.

6. Clean out the pivot bolt and ensure that all grease passages are clear. Install the swing arm on the machine. Grease and install the pivot bolt. After tightening the swing arm pivot bolt nut, move the swing arm up and down to ensure that movement is smooth and effortless.

7. Pivot bolt torque is 36–58 ft lbs.

Yamaha 650 Twins

MODEL COVERAGE

XS 1	TX 650
XS 1B	TX 650 A
XS 2	XS 650 B-H

INDEX

General Specifications

	XS1/1B/2	TX/XS650B-F	XS650 G-H
ENGINE			
Type	4-s, sohc twin	4-s, sohc twin	4-s, sohc twin
Displacement (cc)	653	653	653
Bore x Stroke (in.)	2.95 x 2.91	2.95 x 2.91	2.95 x 291
Compression ratio (: 1)	①	8.4	8.7
Lubrication	wet sump	wet sump	wet sump
Ignition	battery/coil	battery/coil	TCI
TRANSMISSION			
No. Speeds	5	5	5
Reduction			
primary	2.666	2.666	2.666
secondary	2.000	2.000	2.000
Gear ratios			
first	②	2.461	2.461
second	1.588	1.588	1.588
third	1.300	1.300	1.300
fourth	1.095	1.095	1.095
fifth	0.956	0.956	0.956
DIMENSIONS			
Wheelbase (in.)	55.5	56.5	56.5
Ground clearance (in.)	5.9	5.5	5.3
Overall length (in.)	85.4	85.8	83.5
Overall width (in.)	35.6	35.4	36.4
Overall height (in.)	45.3	45.7	48.0
Dry weight (lbs)	409	467	459
CARBURETION	BS38	BS38	BS34
TIRE SIZE			
Front	③	3.50 x 19	3.50 x 19
Rear	4.00 x 18	4.00 x 18	130/905 x 16

① XS1/1-B: 8.7 XS2: 8.4 ② XS1/1-B: 2.214 XS2: 2.461 ③ XS1/1-B: 3.25 x 19 XS2: 3.50 x 19

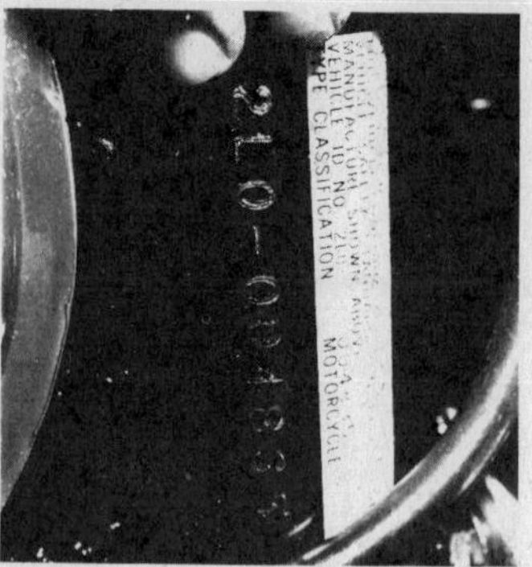

Frame serial number location

Engine serial number location

SERIAL NUMBER LOCATION

In order to prevent possible confusion when ordering parts, always refer to the engine and frame serial numbers.

The frame number is stamped on the right side of the steering head lug; the engine number is stamped on the crankcase behind the right cylinder.

MAINTENANCE

NOTE: *Common maintenance procedures are explained in detail in the "General Information" section.*

LUBRICATION

Motor Oil

When the average air temperature is above 5°C (41°F), use Yamalube® 4-stroke oil, or SAE 20W-40, service rating, "SE" or "SF."

When the air temperature is consistently below 15°C (59°F), use SAE 10W-30, service rating "SE" or "SF." All manufacturers recommend a certain grade and viscosity of motor oil for their engines, and this recommendation should be adhered to in order to ensure long engine life.

Checking Oil Level

XS650H

1. A sight glass is provided on the right side of the crankcase which provides an immediate check on oil level.
2. The motorcycle should be parked on the centerstand on a level surface to insure an accurate reading.
3. Maintain the oil level between the marks inscribed on the crankcase. The engine should be run for a few minutes before checking.
4. If the level is low, add enough oil of the recommended grade to bring the level up to the upper mark. Do not overfill.

OTHER MODELS

1. A dipstick is provided to check the oil level.
2. The motorcycle should be parked on level ground and put on the centerstand.

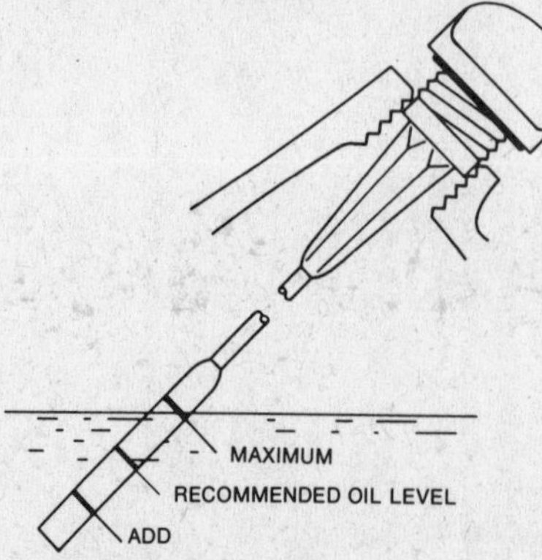

Dipstick marks

3. Unscrew and remove the dipstick and wipe it off. Reinsert the dipstick, allowing it to rest on the threads of the hole. Oil level should be between the maximum and minimum marks on the stick. If the oil level is too low, add enough oil to bring the level up to between the marks. Do not overfill the crankcase.

Note that the oil capacity for the 650 motor has been revised for 1974 and later models. 1975 650s after Engine No. 103747 have a modified dipstick to accommodate this change. Recommended oil level is midway between the max and min marks.

TX650A or early XS650B models which blow oil mist from the breather pipes should use the new lower level. Refer to the illustration of the modified dipstick.

Changing Oil

1. The recommended oil change interval is 2,000 miles or three months, whichever comes first.

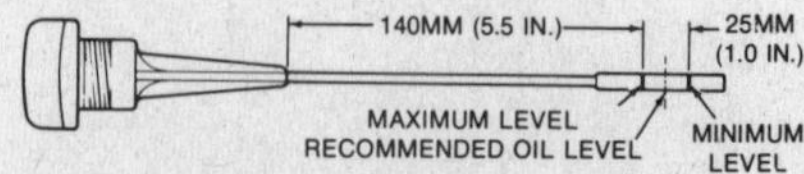

Modified dipstick for 1975 and later models

Crankcase drain plugs (remove both when changing the oil)

2. Oil should be changed when the engine is warm. This ensures more complete draining, and makes it more likely that the oil will carry off any particular matter with it.

3. Place a suitably-sized container (at least 3 qt. capacity) beneath the crankcase drain plug. Remove both of the drain plugs and allow the oil to drain for several minutes.

4. Clean the drain plugs thoroughly, removing any metal particles or foreign matter. Check the condition of the drain plug gaskets. Replace the gaskets if damaged. Install the drain plugs and tighten them securely. Proper torque is 25–30 ft lbs.

5. If the oil filter is to be serviced and/or the filter screen cleaned, refer to the procedures outlined below. Note that the quantity of oil to be added to the crankcase will depend on whether or not the filter is being serviced.

6. Refer to the "Maintenance Data" chart at the end of this section for the proper quantity of oil. Add the oil to the crankcase, start the engine and allow it to idle for about one minute. Stop the engine and let it sit for a minute. Then check the oil level with the dipstick (see above for procedures if necessary) or at the level glass.

Top up the crankcase, if necessary, so that the oil level is between the two lines on the dipstick or at the level sight glass.

Oil Filter

The crankcase cover oil filter should be cleaned every 4,000 miles or every other oil change.

1. Drain the crankcase oil as outlined in Steps 1–4, above.

2. Remove the allen bolts which secure the oil filter cover plate to the right side crankcase cover and remove the cover plate.

3. Separate the sealing O-ring from the cover plate and inspect it for damage. Replace it if necessary, as a good seal is essential.

Oil filter retaining bolt

4. Remove the oil filter retaining bolt and pull out the filter.

5. Clean the filter in a clean, safe solvent and dry it with compressed air. Check for damage or for any particulate matter lodged in the outer mesh.

6. Clean out the filter cavity in the crankcase cover.

7. Reinstall the filter, securing bolt, and the cover plate and O-ring.

CAUTION: *Do not overtighten the filter securing bolt, as this could cause the filter to collapse.*

8. Tighten the cover plate allen bolts evenly. After refilling the crankcase with the proper grade and quantity of oil, start the engine and check for leaks.

Filter Screen

The oil filter screen is fitted to the bottom of the crankcase. The filter screen should be removed and cleaned every 4,000 miles or at every other oil change. A new cover plate gasket should be used.

1. Drain the crankcase oil as outlined in Steps 1–4 under "Changing Oil," above.

2. Remove the six filter screen cover plate bolts from the bottom of the crankcase. Remove the cover plate, gasket, and filter screen.

Filter screen cover plate bolts

3. Clean the filter screen of any foreign matter with a safe solvent. Blow it dry with compressed air.

4. When reinstalling the filter screen and cover plate, the use of a new cover plate gasket is recommended.

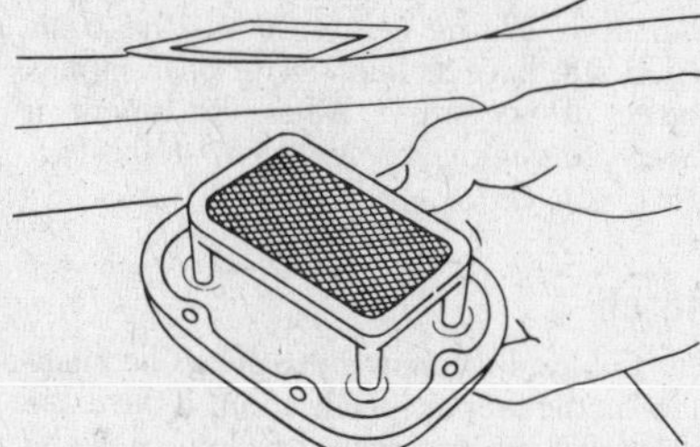

Removing the filter screen

5. Tighten the cover plate securing bolts gradually and evenly and in a cross pattern until all are tight.

6. Fill the crankcase with the correct grade and quantity of oil as given in the charts at the end of this section. Start the engine and check for leaks.

Front Forks

The oil in the forks should be changed every 4,000 miles, or more frequently if the machine is operated under extremely dusty conditions.

1. Yamaha fork oil, SAE 10W-30 motor oil (service-rated "SE" or "SF"), or any other high-quality special motorcycle fork oil can be used.

1. Yamaha fork oil, SAE 10W-30 motor oil (service-rated "SE"), or any other high quality special motorcycle fork oil can be used.

Oil viscosity can be varied if slightly stiffer or less stiff fork action is desired. While special types of oil designed specifically for motorcycle forks can be used, care must be taken to flush the forks thoroughly when changing types or brands of fork fluid, since some may be incompatible with others.

2. Refer to the "Maintenance Data" chart at the end of this section for fork capacity. This will vary according to model year.

3. Support the front wheel off the ground by placing a jack or the like beneath the engine.

CAUTION: *Be sure that the motorcycle is properly supported.*

4. Remove the rubber caps fitted to the tops of each fork leg, if applicable. Unscrew and remove each of the fork filler caps.

5. Remove the fork springs on later-type internal spring forks.

6. Place a suitable container beneath one of the fork sliders and remove the drain screw. After most of the oil has drained off, pump the slider up and down a few times to remove all of the oil in it. Check the condition of the drain screw gasket and replace it with a new one if necessary. Refit the drain screw and tighten it securely.

7. Repeat the procedure with the remaining fork leg.

8. Examine the drained oil. If it contains water or is exceptionally dirty, it may be that the fork dust covers or gaitors are damaged and allowing foreign matter to get past. This will also damage the fork seals quickly. Check that the dust covers are properly secured, or replace them if they are cracked, ripped, or otherwise damaged.

9. Add the proper grade and quantity of oil to each of the fork legs.

10. Check the condition of the fork filler cap O-rings and replace them if they are cracked or ripped. Refit the springs on internal fork spring forks and install the filler caps. Tighten the filler caps securely.

11. After several miles of operation, check the area around the fork slider seals for leaks or seepage. Even a minimal amount of seepage will require replacement of the seals. A

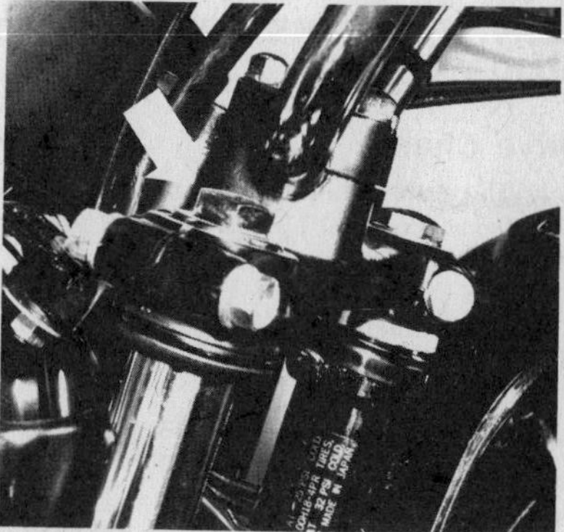

Front fork filler cap

coating of grime building up in this area over a period of time is also indicative of ineffective seals.

Front fork oil drain plug

Chassis Lubrication

1. The swing arm pivot is fitted with one or two grease nipples which should be lubricated with a good grade of chassis grease every 2,000 miles. Apply grease until it shows at both ends of the swing arm pivot. Wipe off the excess.

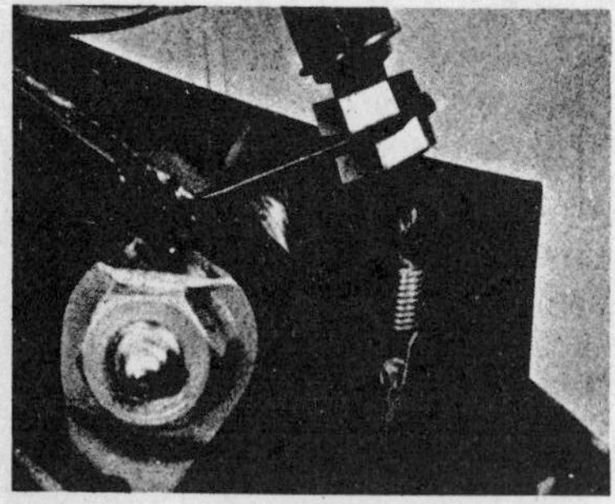

Swing arm pivot grease fitting

2. Wheel and steering head bearings are lubricated with bearing grease, the service interval being 8,000 miles. Be sure to obtain a good quality bearing grease. The older types are often not suitable for use.

SERVICE CHECKS AND ADJUSTMENTS

Drive Chain

1. The chain should have about 10–20 mm (0.4–0.8 in.) of total up-and-down free-play measured in the middle of the lower chain run.

2. Before checking or adjusting the chain slack, the following conditions should be met:

a. The motorcycle should be placed on both wheels with a rider sitting with his weight on the seat.

b. The transmission should be placed in neutral;

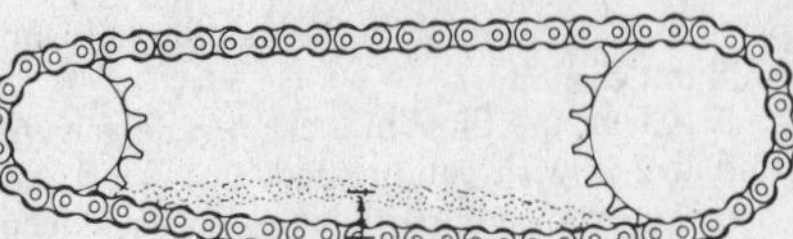

Drive chain slack is measured in the middle of the lower chain run

c. The chain should be clean and well-lubricated;

d. The chain should have been checked for any tight spots by slowly rotating the wheel and checking for variances in the chain tension at different points. If a tight spot exists, the chain tension should be adjusted to the prescribed free-play at the tight spot. Note, however, that such a condition is indicative of a worn chain and

Chain adjusting bolt and swing arm alignment marks

probably worn sprockets, which should be replaced as soon as possible.

3. Remove the axle nut cotter pin and loosen the axle nut several turns. Loosen the locknut on each chain adjuster bolt.

4. Turn each of the adjuster bolts in or out by equal amounts until the chain tension is approximately correct.

5. Check wheel alignment by means of the aligning marks inscribed on both sides of the swing arm. Be sure that both adjusters are lined up with the same mark on each side. If not, turn one of the adjuster bolts in or out so that alignment is achieved.

6. Tighten the axle nut and adjuster bolt nuts and check the chain tension. The chain tension should also be checked with the weight of a rider sitting on the motorcycle when it is off the center stand; the chain should still have at least ½ in. of free-play. Correct if necessary. After adjustment is correct, torque the axle nut to 87–130 ft lbs. Fit a new cotter pin.

Clutch

1. Cable adjustment must always be maintained at the proper specification. If the cable has insufficient free-play, the clutch will slip and rapidly burn out. If it has too much play, the clutch will not completely disengage, resulting in hard shifting and creeping at stops.

2. Use the cable adjuster at the handlebar to maintain the correct amount of cable slack. The clutch hand lever should be able to be moved 2–3 mm (0.08–0.12 in.) measured between the lever and the lever holder before the clutch begins to disengage.

If clutch operation is not satisfactory after making this adjustment, proceed as follows:

3. Screw the cable adjuster at the lever in all the way thus increasing cable free-play.

Clutch cable free-play (arrow) should be 2–3 mm (0.08–0.12 in.)

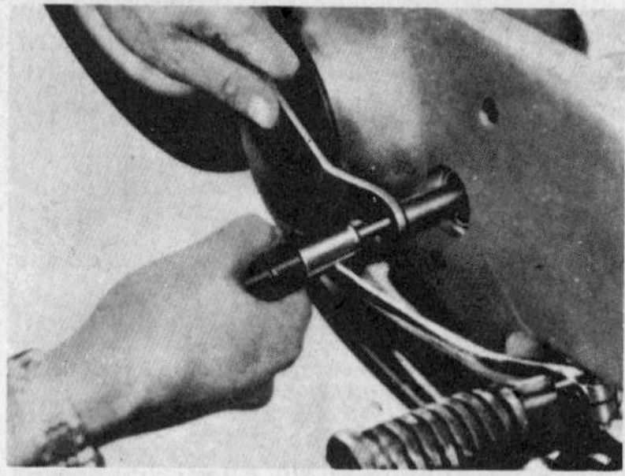

Adjusting the clutch

4. Remove the clutch adjuster cover plug on the left crankcase cover. Loosen the clutch adjusting screw locknut.

5. Turn the adjusting screw clockwise until a slight resistance is felt, then turn it counterclockwise ¼ turn. Holding the screw in this position, tighten the locknut.

6. Turn the cable adjuster out until there is about 2–3 mm (0.08–0.12 in.) of free-play in the hand lever. Tighten the locknut on the cable adjuster.

Throttle Cables

1. The throttle cable is fitted with an adjuster at the twist-grip. The twist-grip should be able to be rotated approximately 10–15° before the butterflies begin to open.

2. Use the cable adjusters at the handlebar to make and maintain this adjustment. To check that the cable has sufficient slack, start the engine and turn the forks slowly from lock-to-lock. Idle speed must not increase. If it does, it indicates that the cable has insufficient free-play, is incorrectly routed, or is binding at some point.

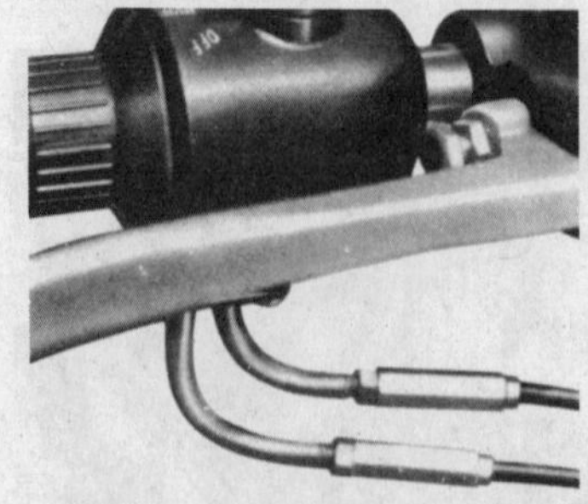

Throttle cable adjusters

Brakes

FRONT DISC

Disc brakes need little attention other than a periodic check of the fluid level and of pad wear.

1. Check the brake fluid level in the master cylinder reservoir. On older models, the master cylinder cap and diaphragm must be removed. The fluid level line is inscribed on the inside of the reservoir. Later models

Front master cylinder brake fluid level line

have a see-through plastic reservoir which can be checked at a glance. If the fluid level is below the inscribed level mark, add enough DOT 3 type hydraulic disc brake fluid to bring the level up to the mark. Reinstall the diaphragm and cap and tighten it securely.

NOTE: *To keep the brake fluid clean, wipe any dirt or foreign matter off of the reservoir before removing the cap. Do not leave the cap off for extended periods of time. Do not allow water to get into the reservoir. Do not apply the brake while the cap is removed. Do not overfill the reservoir. Fluid level will drop slightly as the pads wear. Fitting new pads will usually restore the fluid level to its original line . .*

2. Brake pads should be replaced, as a set, if either or both are worn. Late models have a red wear indicator line inscribed on the pads. Replace them when they are worn to the red line. On earlier models the pads should be replaced when they are worn to a thickness of 0.18 in. or less.

3. If the brake levers feels spongy, or if brake effectiveness has been reduced, a possible cause is air bubbles in the lines. To remedy this, bleed the system. This procedure can also be found in the Chassis section.

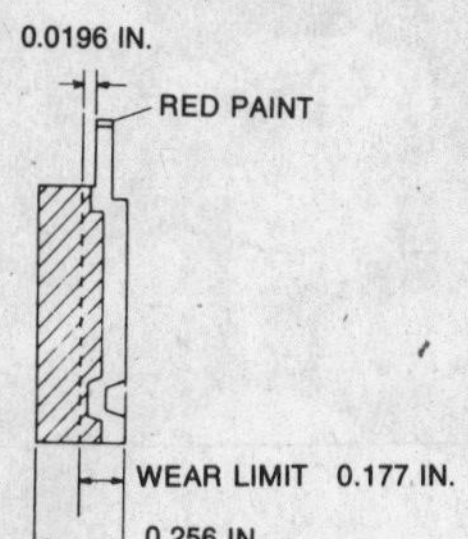

Old style brake pad wear limit

Check brake pad wear here

4. The brake lever should have about 13–25 mm (0.5–1.0 in.) of movement which is measured at the tip of the lever.

Lever movement is adjustable by means of an adjusting screw near the lever holder. Once set properly, the lever travel will not ordinarily need readjustment. If lever travel becomes excessive, it is more probable that the system needs to be bled or has some other fault. Adjusting the brake lever travel will not remedy any brake system faults.

REAR DISC

Refer to the "Front Disc" section preceeding for general information. On late models, front and rear brake calipers are identical units.

1. The transparent master cylinder reservoir allows inspection of the fluid level without removing the master cylinder cap. If the fluid level is below the level mark, remove the cap and diaphragm and add enough DOT 3 brake fluid to bring the level up to the mark. Reinstall the diaphragm and cap and tighten it securely.

2. Pad wear can easily be checked by visual inspection. Replace the pads, as a set, if either of them is worn to the red limit line.

3. To adjust brake pedal height and free-play, loosen the height adjuster bolt locknut. Turn the adjuster bolt in or out so that the top of the pedal is about 12–18 mm (0.5–0.7 in.) below the top surface of the footpeg rubber. Tighten the adjuster bolt locknut.

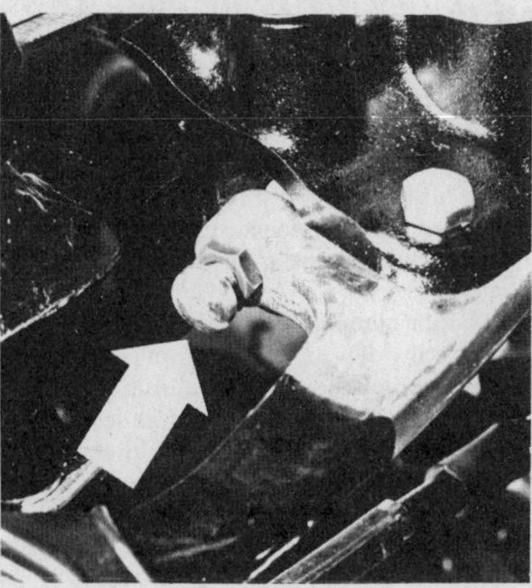

Brake lever adjusting screw

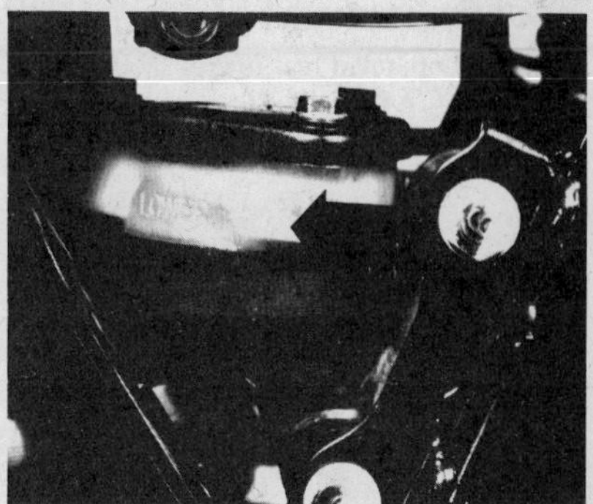

Rear master cylinder brake fluid level line

Loosen the brake rod adjuster locknut and turn the brake rod until there is noticeable free-play between the rod and the master cylinder. Turn the brake rod in until it just touches the master cylnder, than back it out about 1½ turns. Tighten the locknut.

CAUTION: *The pin hole mark on the brake rod must not show above the locknut.*

The adjustment should yield brake pedal free-play of 13–15 mm (0.5–0.6 in.).

FRONT DRUM

1. The brake should be adjusted so that the lever has 5–8 mm (0.2–0.3 in.) of free movement measured between the lever and the lever holder before the linings contact the drum.

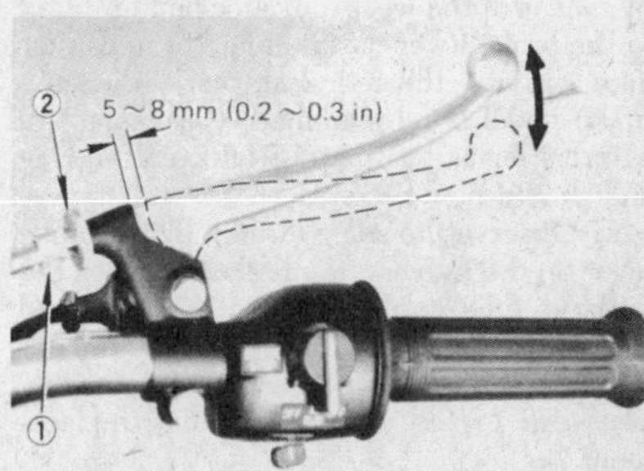

Brake lever free-play showing cable adjuster and locknut (1 and 2)

Brake plate adjuster and locknut (1 and 2)

2. The brake can be adjusted with either the cable adjustor at the brake plate or the adjustor on the handlebar. Loosen the locknut and turn the adjustor out to decrease brake lever movement. It is recommended that major adjustments be made with the adjuster at the brake plate and finer adjustments with the handlebar adjustor.

REAR DRUM (EARLY)

1. Rod-operated rear brakes should be adjusted with a rider on the machine and the machine off the center stand. In this position, the brake should be adjusted by means of the adjuster nut on the brake rod to yield ½–1 in. of brake pedal travel before the brake linings fully contact the drum.

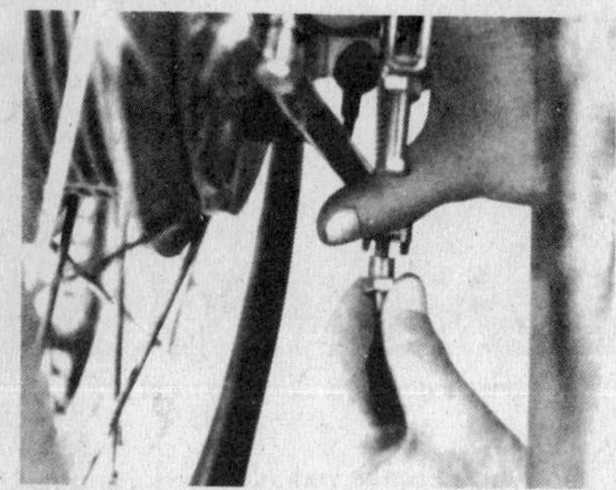

Adjusting the rear brake

2. On drum brakes, the angle formed by the brake rod of brake cable and the actuating lever on the brake drum should not exceed 90° when te brake is fully applied. If it does, it is time to replace the linings. Late models are fitted with wear indicators.

3. After adjusting the brakes, be sure to check operation of the brake light.

REAR DRUM (LATE)

1. Brake lining wear can be determined by means of the wear indicator pointer fitted to the brake lever on the hub. If the pointer lines up with the red slash mark when the brake pedal is fully applied, the linings are worn as far as possible for effective braking and should now be replaced.

2. Observe the angle formed by the brake lever on the hub and the brake rod when the brake is fully applied. When the lever and rod form an angle greater than 90°, the shoes should be checked for wear as they probably are worn to the point of needing replacement.

3. The rear brake should be adjusted so that there is approximately 25 mm (1.0 in.) free-play at the pedal before the linings contact the drum. Adjust by turning the nut on the brake rod. When adjustment has been made, be sure that the nut is seated properly on the brake lever pin. Also, check the operation of the brake light switch.

Brake Light Switches

The switches should be checked for operation after the brakes are adjusted. The rear brake light switch and adjuster nut are mounted on a slotted bracket. The rear switch is adjusted by holding the switch and turning the adjuster nut to effect adjustment. Moving the switch up on the bracket allows the brake light to turn on sooner. Moving it down allows the light to turn on later. Do not turn the switch to effect adjustment as the wires will become twisted and may break.

The front disc brake switch is activated by the pressure of the brake fluid in the brake line. This switch is not adjustable; if defective, it must be replaced.

Headlight Adjustment

1. Set the machine about 25 feet away from a wall, preferably of a color which reflects light well.

The machine should be off the stand, and with a rider putting his weight on the machine as in operation.

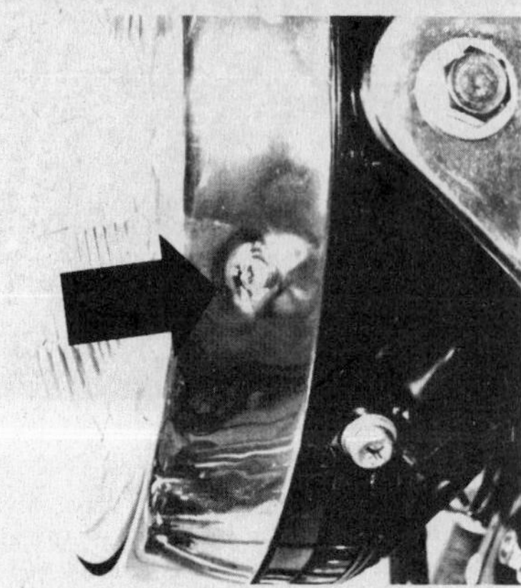

Headlight lateral adjustment screw

2. Switch on the high beam. The headlight high beam should be parallel to the ground and should hit the wall directly in front of the machine.

3. Vertical adjustment is made by first removing the headlight rim anchor screw and removing the headlight by prying at the point provided at the bottom. Slightly loosen the two headlight shell mounting nuts and install the headlight. Adjust the headlight by pivoting the shell up or down as needed. Remove the headlight and tighten the two mounting bolts. Install the headlight and tighten the anchor screw.

4. Lateral adjustment is accomplished by turning the adjusting screw on the side of the headlight. Tighten the screw to move the beam to the right; loosen it to move the beam towards the left.

FUEL SYSTEM

The fuel system consists of the carburetors, petcock(s), and air cleaner(s).

These items should be serviced every 2,000 miles when the machine is used under normal conditions.

Air Cleaner

1. The air filter may be either a pleated paper element or a foam-type cleaner depending on model and year.

2. While the normal maintenance interval for air filters is 2,000 miles, cleaning or replacement may be necessary more frequently if the machine is used in a dusty environment.

3. Paper elements can only be cleaned by brushing any deposits of dirt from the outside of the filter elements with a stiff, non-metallic brush. If compressed air is available, blow through the inside of the filter to remove any dirt from the paper pores.

This procedure is only marginally effective. After 3 or 4 such cleanings, the filter should be replaced with a new one.

Paper filters must be kept dry. Do not attemp to clean them in solvents or any other liquid.

Blowing dirt out of a paper element filter with compressed air

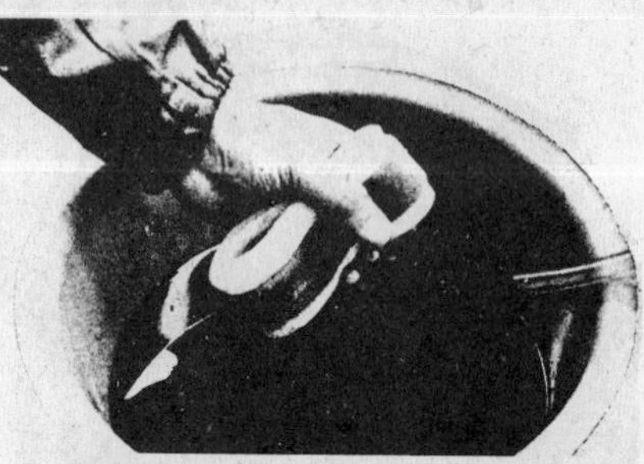

Squeeze, do not wring, foam-type filter elements

4. Foam-type air filters depend upon oil-coated pores to catch dirt particles. These filters are semi-permanent, and may be cleaned by immersing them in a solvent such as kerosene and then squeezing them dry.

Do not wring the filter as the fabric may be damaged.

Soak the element in clean SAE 10W-30 motor oil and squeeze out the excess. Then refit the filter to the motorcycle.

5. XS650C and later models use a dry-foam element which is serviced in the same manner as the paper-type filters.

Petcock

1. One or two petcocks are used, depending on model year. The petcock contains the fuel filter screen(s) which should be cleaned every 2,000 miles.

2. Several different types of petcock have been fitted over the years. The most common type has a sediment trap incorporated into it as well as a fuel filter screen on the outlet pipe.

3. After ensuring that the petcock lever is in the "off" position, place a small container beneath the petcock and remove the sediment trap drain bolt. After the trap has drained, inspect the bolt gasket, replace it if

Removing the petcock sediment trap drain bolt

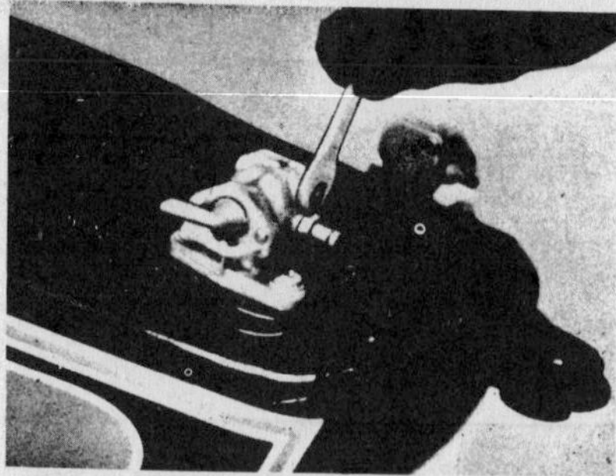
Removing the outlet pipe and filter

necessary, and refit the bolt, securing it tightly.

4. Check that the outlet pipe is the removable type by noting the presence of a hex fitting on the pipe. Disconnect the fuel line from the outlet pipe, after first ensuring that the petcock lever is in the "off" position. Unscrew and remove the outlet pipe. Clean the filter screen in gasoline and blow dry. Remove any foreign matter trapped in the screen. Check the screen for holes or other damage. If the screen is punctured, or if it cannot be properly cleaned, replace it with a new one.

After reassembly, turn on the fuel and check for leaks before operating the motorcycle. Be sure that the fuel line is tightly secured to the outlet pipe with its spring clip or with safety wire.

5. The petcock is usually secured to the gas tank by two screws. Sealing is accomplished by means of a rubber O-ring. The petcock can be removed from the tank when it is empty by removing the two securing screws. Disassemble the petcock by removing the outlet pipe, the sediment trap

Petcock securing screws

bolt, and the two screws which secure the plate to the petcock body. Clean all metal components thoroughly in gasoline. Before installation, check the condition of the rubber O-ring and replace it if it is chipped or cracked, or if it fails to form an effective seal.

Carburetors

Thorough cleaning of the carburetors, which should be carried out every 2,000 miles under normal conditions, requires removal of the units from the machine.

On some models, the carburetor float bowls are fitted with drain plugs which can be removed periodically to flush out any water or other foreign matter which may have passed through the system.

Before removing carburetor float bowl drain plugs, be sure that the fuel petcock(s) are in the "off" position. This operation should also be avoided when the engine is hot due to the danger of fire from gasoline spilling on the hot engine.

Carburetor float bowl drain plug

Recommended Lubricants

Engine
- At ambient temperatures above 5° C (41° F):
  - Yamalube 4-cycle oil
  - SAE 20W-40 service rating "SE" or "SF"
- At ambient temperatures below 15° C (59° F):
  - SAE 10W-30 service rating "SE" or "SF"

Front forks
- Yamaha fork oil
- SAE 20W motor oil
- SAE 10W-30 motor oil

Disc brake systems
- DOT 3 standard brake fluid

Control cables
- Light motor oil
- Graphite-based lubricant
- Molybdenum-disulphide-based lubricant

Tach, speedometer cables; throttle twist-grip
- Light duty grease

Wheel and steering head bearings
- Waterproof, medium-weight bearing grease

Grease fittings
- Waterproof, medium-weight chassis grease

Drive chain
- Lubricant developed specifically for motorcycle drive chains

Periodic Maintenance Intervals①

Before each ride
- Safety items
- Operation of lights
- Chain adjustment
- Control cable adjustment

Weekly
- Engine oil level
- Tire pressure (check when cold)
- Battery electrolyte level

Every 200 miles
- Lubricate chain

Every 1,000 miles
- Clean chain

Every 2,000 miles/3 months
- Change engine oil
- Clean air filter
- Check swing arm
- Lubricate cables
- Check steering bearing adjustment
- Lubricate swing arm pivot
- Check rim run-out and spoke tension
- Check wheel bearings
- Clean fuel petcock and carburetors
- Check and adjust ignition timing
- Check spark plugs

Every 4,000 miles/6 months
- Clean oil strainer and filter
- Check compression
- Check cylinder head bolt torque
- Check oil pressure
- Change fork oil

Every 8,000 miles/12 months
- Flush and refill hydraulic disc brake system
- Repack wheel and steering head bearings

① Based on normal usage after initial service and break-in are completed.

Maintenance Data

	XS1/1B/2	*TX650/A*	*XS650B-H*
Crankcase oil (qts)			
Routine oil change	2.7	2.1	2.1
Oil and filter	2.9	2.3	2.3
After engine rebuild	3.2	2.6	2.6
Front forks (@ leg) (oz/cc)	①	②	③
Tire pressure (psi)			
Front	23	26	26
Rear	28	28	30
Battery			
Model No.	12N12-4A-1④	YB14L	YB14L
Capacity	12v, 12ah	12v, 14ah	12v, 14ah
Continuous charging rate (amps)	1.2	1.4	1.4

① XS1: 8.1/240
XS1B: 7.5/223
XS2: 4.6/135
② TX650: 5.8/173
TX650A: 5.2/155
③ XS650B/C: 5.2/155
XS650D-H: 5.7/168
④ Without electric starter:
12v, 5.5ah; 0.5 amps charging rate

TUNE-UP

NOTE: *Common tune-up procedures are explained in detail in the "General Information" section.*

COMPRESSION TEST

1. A compression check should be made before each tune-up since this will provide a general idea of engine condition.
2. It is necessary to have a gauge with the proper adapter (plug holes are 14 mm) if a screw-in type gauge is used. The less expensive "hold in" type gauges can also be used. Use some oil on the rubber tip to ensure a good seal.
3. The engine should be at operating temperature when checking compression.
4. Remove both of the spark plugs and fit the gauge to one of the plug holes.
5. Close the choke and hold the throttle wide open while spinning the engine with the starter motor or the kickstarter. Note the higest compression reading and repeat the test with the remaining cylinder.
6. Compression may vary according to gauge tolerance and several other factors. However, it should normally be between 130 and 145 psi. Both cylinders must be within 15 psi of this range and of each other.

CAM CHAIN ADJUSTMENT

1970-75

1. The cam chain tensioner is located at the rear of the cylinders, between and below the intake ports.
2. The cam chain tension should be checked every 2,000 miles.

1. Rubber guide
2. Pushrod
3. Gasket
4. Lock nut
5. Adjuster
6. Cover
7. Pivot point
8. Spring

Cam chain tensioner assembly

3. Slowly rotate the engine in the normal direction of rotation (counterclockwise when viewed from the engine's left side). One rotation should be sufficient to place all of the cam chain slack on the tensioner side.
4. Remove the tensioner cover. Loosen the tensioner locknut, then turn the adjuster

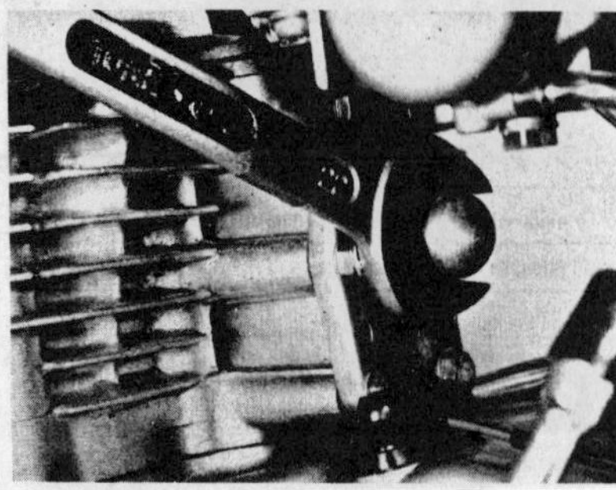

Removing the tensioner cover

in until the end of the tensioner pushrod is flush with the end of the adjuster.

5. Tighten the locknut. Install the tensioner cover.

1976 and Later

1. The cam chain adjuster is located between and at the rear of the cylinders.
2. Remove the adjuster cap nut.

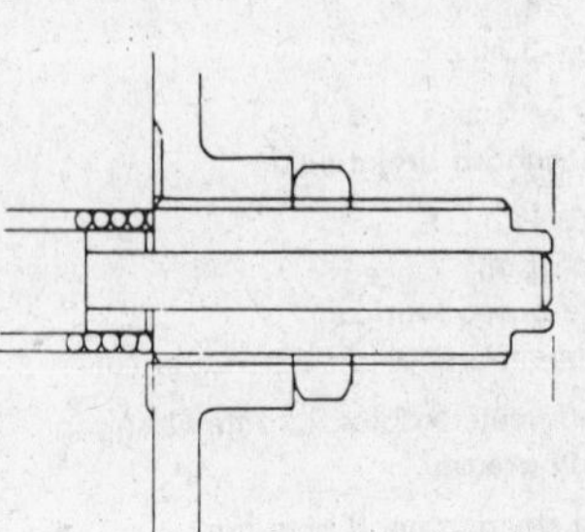

TENSIONER CORRECT

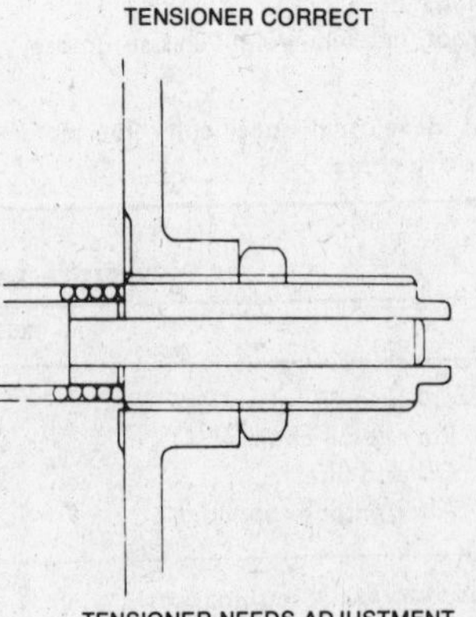

TENSIONER NEEDS ADJUSTMENT

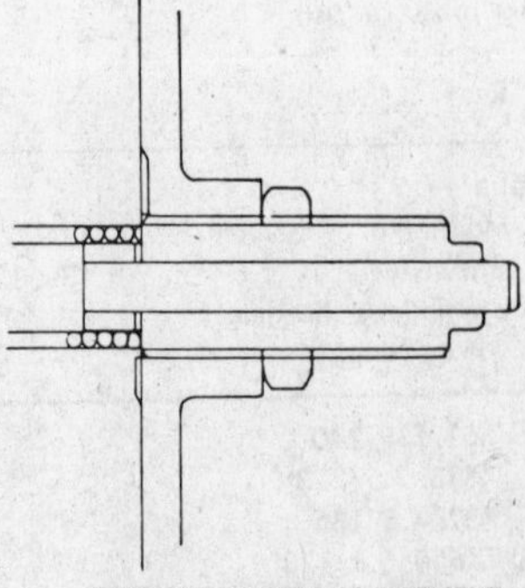

TENSIONER NEEDS ADJUSTMENT

3. The end of the pushrod should be flush with the end of the adjuster bolt.
4. If it is not, turn the adjuster bolt until it is flush with the end of the pushrod.
5. Install the cap nut.

VALVE ADJUSTMENT

NOTE: *Valves must be adjusted when the engine is cold.*

1. Remove the intake and exhaust valve covers, and the alternator cover. Remove the spark plugs.
2. Place a thumb over each spark plug hole, and kick the engine over slowly until compression is felt in one of the cylinders.
3. Continue turning the engine over (in the normal direction of rotation) using a

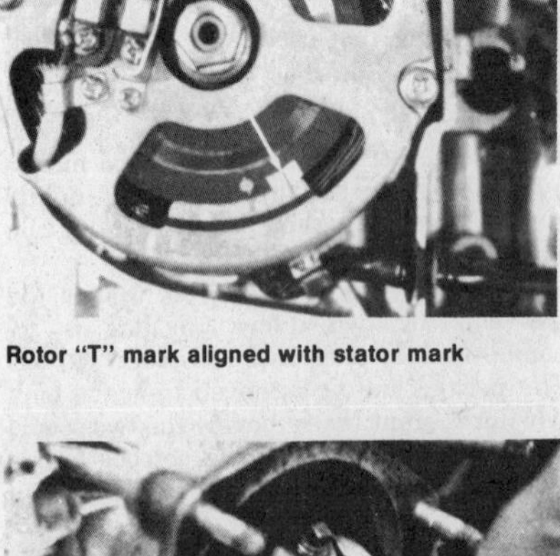

Rotor "T" mark aligned with stator mark

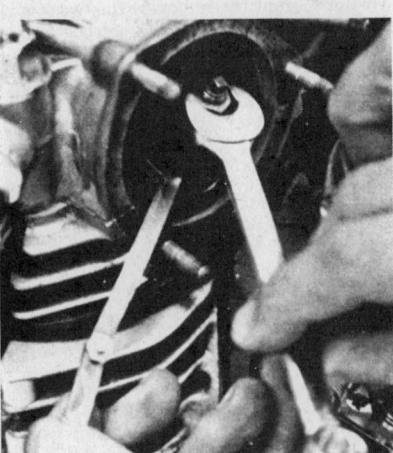

Adjusting the valve clearance

wrench on the alternator rotor nut until the reference mark on the rotor lines up with the "T" mark on the stator. The pistons are now at top dead center, and the cylinder in which you felt compression should be at the top of its compression stroke. Both valves for this cylinder will be closed, and these are to be adjusted first. Verify that this cylinder is at TDC on the compression stroke by checking for slack at its intake and exhaust valve adjusters.

4. Insert the proper size feeler gauge between valve stem and tappet. There should be a light drag when pulling out the feeler gauge blade, if the valve is correctly adjusted.

Proper valve clearances are as follows:

Model	Intake (in./mm)	Exhaust (in./mm)
XS1/1B/2, TX650	0.003/0.08	0.006/0.15
TX650A, XS650B	0.002/0.05	0.004/0.10
XS650C/D	0.002/0.05	0.006/0.15
XS650E/F/G/H	0.004/0.10	0.006/0.15

5. If adjustment is necessary, loosen the adjuster locknut, and turn the adjuster in or out until the proper clearance is obtained. Hold the adjuster securely and tighten the locknut.

6. Rotate the crankshaft 360° and repeat the procedure with the other cylinder.

NOTE: *An alternative method is to adjust each valve when it is closed without regard to piston position. To do this, remove the valve covers and spark plugs, and turn the engine over slowly with the kick-starter while watching the valve action. When the left intake valve is open (the rocker arm will be depressed), the* RIGHT *intake valve will be closed, and can be adjusted for the proper clearance. When the left exhaust valve is opened, the* RIGHT *exhaust valve can be adjusted, etc.*

CONTACT BREAKER POINTS

Location

The contact breaker points are opened and closed by a cam on the end of the camshaft and are located beneath a cover on the left side of the cylinder head.

The timing advance mechanism is located on the opposite side of the cylinder head beneath its own cover.

Replacement

1. Points sets are available already mounted on the breaker plate, or may be purchased separately.

2. If the points are purchased separately, disconnect the primary wire at each point set, remove the securing screw, and remove the old points. When installing new points, note that the proper installation of the insulating washers at the primary terminal is critical. If improperly installed, no spark will occur. There is a small insulating washer which fits around the terminal bolt and two insulating washers, one immediately on either side of the terminal bracket. All connectors (condenser, primary wire, points spring) are made on the outer sides of these washers (i.e., no connector must touch the bracket, which is a ground).

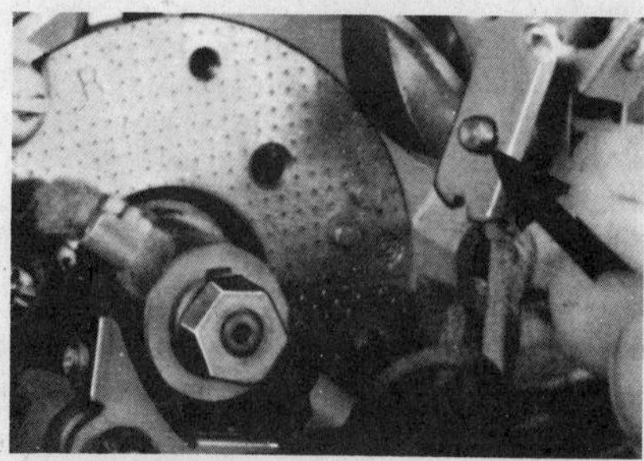

Be sure that the locating pin is seated in its hole

3. New points may have a protective coating on the contact surfaces to prevent oxidation. Clean off these surfaces with a non-oily solvent before attempting to start the machine.

4. If the motorcycle will not start immediately after installation of new points, check that the primary wire connections are tight, that the insulating washers at the primary terminal are properly installed, and that the contact surfaces are thoroughly cleaned.

5. The condensers are mounted on the left side of the top engine mounting bracket. They must be replaced as a set.

Gapping

Points should be filed (if necessary) and cleaned before gapping.

1. Remove the points cover.

2. Turn the engine over until one of the two sets of points is fully open.

3. With the proper feeler gauge blade, check the gap. The proper specification is 0.3–0.4 mm (0.012–0.016 in.), and the blade should be a slip fit between the points if the gap is correct.

4. If adjustment is necessary, loosen the screw which secures the point set to its plate, and use a small screwdriver at the pry point provided to adjust the gap.

CAUTION: *Loosen the screw just enough to allow the points to be moved. If loosened too much, the points will snap shut instead of holding the gap.*

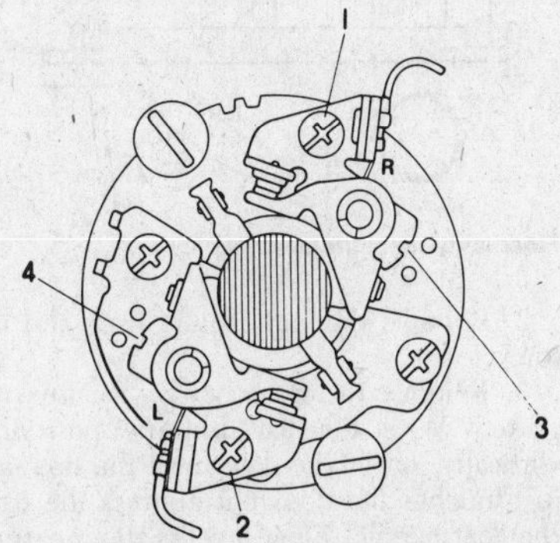

Point gap adjustment screws (1,2) and pry points (3,4)

5. Tighten the screw and recheck the gap. It may change slightly when the screw is tightened.

6. Repeat the procedure with the remaining points set. Try to adjust both sets so that the feeler gauge blade has the same "feel" in both sets. This will help to ensure accurate timing.

7. If it is not possible to gap the points correctly, the fiber heel is evidently worn; the points should then be replaced.

Lubrication

1. On all models it is necessary to occasionally lubricate the cam follower fiber heel and the pivot point of the contact breaker. This minimizes wear and ensures that the timing will remain accurate for a longer period. A worn heel will retard the timing.

2. A small dab of grease (high melting point, if possible) should be applied to the lubricator wick so that the lubricator can distribute it onto the breaker cam. A drop of engine oil should be applied to the pivot point.

3. In both cases it is imperative that care be taken to keep the lubricant away from the points contact surface.

4. The lubricating wick should be adjusted so that it just contacts the breaker cam.

IGNITION TIMING

Breaker-Point Models

NOTE: *Points must be cleaned and gapped before checking timing. Dirty points will cause inaccurate readings.*

Remove the points cover and observe the breaker plate. Note that the points for the right cylinder (grey lead) are mounted directly to the large breaker plate, while the points for the left cylinder (orange lead) are mounted on a small moveable plate. Therefore, the right cylinder timing must be set *first,* since adjustment involves turning the entire breaker plate, which will alter the timing of the left cylinder as well. The points for the left cylinder are adjusted by moving only the points themselves.

NOTE: *Be sure the cam chain is properly adjusted.*

1. Remove the alternator inspection plate, ignition points cover, and centrifugal advance unit cover.

2. Inspect, clean and gap the points.

3. Ignition timing is set by matching the marks on the alternator stator and rotor. The

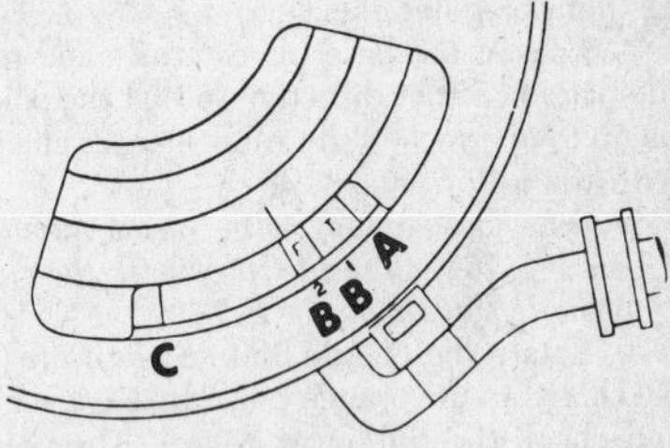

A-TOP DEAD CENTER
B[1] & B[2]—IGNITION FIRE MARKS
C-MARK FOR "FULLY ADVANCED" IGNITION TIMING

Alternator rotor reference marks

rotor has one reference timing mark and the stator has four: the first mark (to right of the letter "T") identifies Top Dead Center, the next two marks (either side of the letter "F") identify idle timing (fully retarded) and the remaining mark identifies high speed timing (fully advanced).

4. Secure the centrifugal advance coun-

Timing advance mechanism weights held in the retarded position

terweights in the fully retarded idle position (held inward).

5. Connect an ignition timing light or point checker as follows:

(+) RED lead—to grey point wire connector

(−) BLACK lead—to ground (frame or engine case)

Right and left cylinder point sets are marked "R" (grey wire) and "L" (orange wire), respectively.

NOTE: *The right cylinder timing MUST be set first. The right cylinder points are mounted directly to the base plate, the left cylinder points are mounted on a separate plate; therefore, setting the left side first would cause a position shift when timing the right.*

6. Turn the crankshaft in the direction of normal rotation until the right cylinder

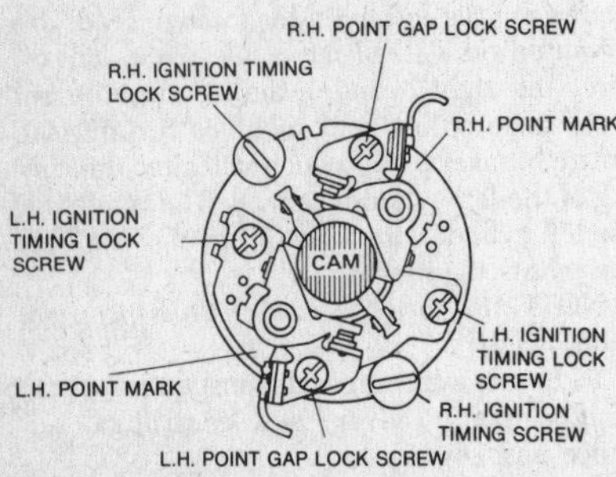

Breaker point ignition timing screws

points begin to open (as indicated by the timing light or point checker).

7. Loosen the base plate screws and turn the plate in either direction so that the points begin to open when the rotor mark is aligned with the letter "F."

NOTE: *On engines with serial numbers below 11764, align the rotor with the mark to the left of the letter F.*

8. Rotate the engine 360°. Switch the (+) RED lead to the orange point wire connector and check the timing as before. The points should just begin to open when the "F" mark is aligned with the rotor mark. If adjustment is necessary, loosen the screws which secure the left cylinder's points to the base plate, and turn the points as needed to adjust the timing.

9. After idle timing has been set on both cylinders, secure the centrifugal advance counterweights in the fully advanced (held outward) position: the points should open at the full advance stator mark or within 3 mm of the mark. Make any necessary adjustments and recheck the idle timing.

Timing advance mechanism

NOTE: *If the correct marks align at the idle timing position, but full advance timing is not correct, the ignition advance weight stoppers can be bent slightly to increase or decrease the amount of full advance. Bend them out to increase the amount of full advance, in to decrease it.*

TCI Models

Transistorized ignition models do not require periodic ignition adjustments or maintenance.

CARBURETORS

Carburetor adjustments to be made during a tune-up include setting float level, synchronization, and idle speed and mixture.

Adjusting Float Level

1. Float level is a measure of the amount of gasoline which will be in the float bowls during operation. While it is a critical specification, it will not normally need readjustment once properly set. Float level, therefore, need not be checked at every tune-up, but should be attended to from time to time.

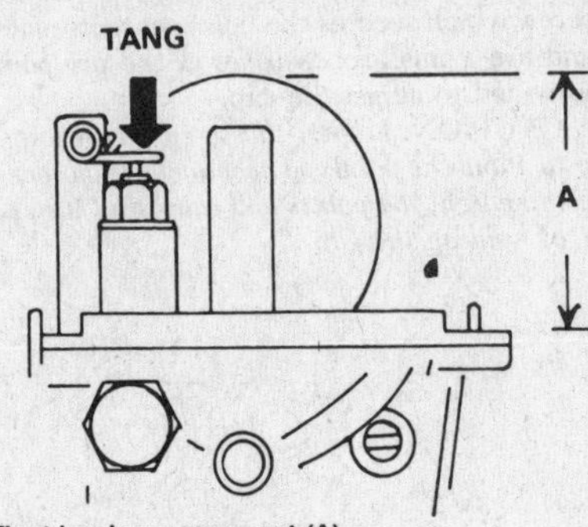

Float level measurement (A)

2. Remove the carburetors from the motorcycle.

3. Remove the float bowls. Remove the gasket. With the carburetor(s) positioned vertically, lower the float until the float arm just touches but does not depress the tip of the float needle. Float level is the measured distance from the bottom of the float to the float bowl mating surface.

4. Float levels are as follows: XS650C-H: 25.0 mm/0.98 in.

Adjusting the float tang

All other models: 24.0 mm/0.94 in. Adjust, if necessary, by pushing out the float pivot pin, removing the floats, and bending the float arm tang. Bending the tang towards the carburetor body will increase the float level measurement and vice-versa.

5. Both carburetors must have the same float level. Measure both before changing either. Note that the measured float level will be inaccurate if the float needle tip is worn or if there is foregn matter on the needle seat.

Idle Speed and Mixture

NOTE: *Idle speed and idle mixture adjustments must be made when the engine is at operating temperature.*

1. Except on XS650E-H models which have factory-installed idle mixture limiter caps on the screw heads, turn each pilot screw in until it bottoms lightly, then back each one out the proper number of turns:

Adjusting the pilot screw

XS1/1B: ½ turn
XS2, TX650/A, XS650B: ¾ turn
XS650C/D: 1½ turns

XS650E-H models are preset at 2¼ turns out and adjustment is not necessary unless the pilot screws have been removed for carburetor rebuilding.

Adjusting the throttle stop screw

2. Use the throttle stop screw on each carburetor so that the engine idles at 1,000–1,200 rpm and both cylinders run evenly.

3. To check that both cylinders run evenly, turn up each throttle stop screw so that the engine idles at about 1,500 rpm. Disconnect one spark plug lead. Back out the throttle stop screw of the running cylinder until the engine just dies. Connect the spark plug lead, restart the engine, and disconnect the plug lead of the cylinder which has just been adjusted. Back out the throttle stop screw of the running cylinder until the engine just dies. Restart the engine with both plugs connected, rev it a few times to clean off the plugs, and back out each throttle

stop screw in small, even increments until the desired idle speed is obtained.

Synchronization

1970-77

The easiest method of synchronizing the carburetors is to operate the twist-grip slowly and observe the movement of the throttle arms on each carburetor.

The throttle arms should begin and end their movements at the same time. If they do not, adjust the throttle cable free-play so that synchronized movement is achieved.

NOTE: *The idle speed must be properly set before synchronization is attempted.*

After adjusting cable free-play, check that they are not too tightly adjusted by moving the forks slowly from lock-to-lock with the engine idling. Idle speed must not vary. If it does, this indicates that one or both of the throttle cables is too tightly adjusted. The twist-grip should have 10–15° of free rotation before the throttle arms begin to move.

NOTE: *If trouble is encountered during the idle speed or synchronization procedures, first check that the throttle cables have sufficient free-play. Make sure that the throttle stop screw for each carburetor is resting against its stop when the throttle is closed. If the trouble persists, check for air leaks at the manifolds. If this fails to reveal the problem, the fuel system may need an overhaul. Check for poor fuel flow, clogged filters, air leaks, and so on.*

1978 and Later

Vacuum gauges are necessary to properly synchronize the carburetors, although a rough approximation can be made by visually aligning the butterflies (see below).

The butterflies are synchronized by means of a single screw located between the carburetors. Turning the screw simultaneously closes one valve while opening the other.

1. Run the engine until operating temperature is reached.
2. Remove the gas tank's rear mounting bolt and raise the tank (fitting a longer fuel feed line if necessary, so that the synchronization screw between the carburetors is accessible).
3. The vacuum gauge fittings are on the sides of the carburetors. Connect the vacuum gauges.
4. Turn the fuel petcock to the "Prime" position.
5. Start the engine and note the vacuum gauge readings. At idle (1000-1200 rpm), the two cylinders must be within 5 cm Hg (0.2 in. Hg). Adjust by turning the synchronization screw in or out until the vacuum readings for the two carburetors are as equal as possible.

   NOTE: *If the gauges read more than 5 cm Hg (0.2 in. Hg) at 1200 rpm, check the compression, spark plugs and valve clearances.*
6. If vacuum gauges are not available, a rough method of synchronizing the carburetors may be carried out. Remove the carburetors as a unit from the motorcycle. Look into the engine side of the carburetors and note the positions of the butterflies relative to the small by-pass passages at the bottoms of the carburetor bores. Both butterflies should be the same distance from these holes. Turn the synchronization screw to equalize the distance.

Tune-Up Specifications

	XS1/1B	XS2	TX650	TX650A	XS650B	XS650C/D	XS650E/F	XS650G/H
Valve clearance								
Intake (in./mm)	0.003/0.08	0.003/0.08	0.003/0.08	0.002/0.05	0.002/0.05	0.002/0.05	0.004/0.10	0.004/0.10
Exhaust (in./mm)	0.006/0.15	0.006/0.15	0.006/0.15	0.004/0.10	0.004/0.10	0.006/0.15	0.006/0.15	0.006/0.15
Breaker point gap (in./mm)	0.012–0.016/ 0.3–0.4	0.012–0.016/ 0.3–0.4	0.012–0.016/ 0.3–0.4	0.012–0.016/ 0.3–0.4	0.012–0.016/ 0.3–0.4	0.012–0.016/ 0.3–0.4	0.012–0.016/ 0.3–0.4	na
Spark plugs								
Type (NGK standard)	B-8ES	B-8ES	B-8ES	B–7ES	B–8ES	BP-7ES	BP-7ES	BP-7ES
Gap (in./mm)	0.024–0.028/ 0.6–0.7	0.024–0.028/ 0.6–0.7	0.024–0.028/ 0.6–0.7	0.024–0.028/ 0.6–0.7	0.020–0.024/ 0.5–0.6	0.024–0.028/ 0.6–0.7	0.024–0.028/ 0.6–0.7	0.024–0.028/ 0.6–0.7
Cranking compression (psi)	130–145	130–145	130–145	130–145	130–145	130–145	130–145	130–145
Max allowable variation (psi)	15	15	15	15	15	15	15	15
Carburetors								
Pilot screw (turns out)	½	¾	¾	¾	¾	1½	2¼	pre-set
Float level (in./mm)	0.94/24.0	0.94/24.0	0.94/24.0	0.94/24.0	0.94/24.0	0.98/25.0	0.98/25.0	0.98/25.0
Idle speed (rpm)	1,000–1,200	1,000–1,200	1,000–1,200	1,000–1,200	1,000–1,200	1,000–1,200	1,000–1,200	1,000–1,200

***NOTE:** Part numbers listed in this reference are not recommendations by Chilton for any product by brand name. They are references that can be used with interchange manuals and aftermarket supplier catalogs to locate each brand name supplier's discrete part number.*

ENGINE AND TRANSMISSION

NOTE: *Common engine rebuilding techniques and inspection procedures are outlined in detail in the "General Information" section.*

ENGINE REMOVAL AND INSTALLATION

NOTE: *Degrease the engine thoroughly before removal.*

1. Warm up the engine and drain the oil.

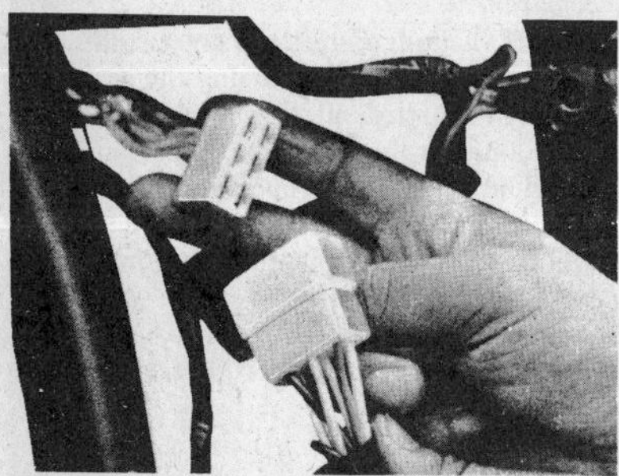

Disconnecting the alternator wiring

2. Turn off both fuel petcocks and disconnect the fuel crossover tube.
3. Lift the seat, then remove the attaching bolts and the gas tank.
4. Remove both side covers.
5. Disconnect the alternator wiring harness at the center connector.
6. Disconnect both throttle cables.
7. Disconnect the air cleaner mounting bolts.

Neutral indicator wire connection

8. Disconnect the fuel balance tube and remove the carburetors.
9. Disconnect the engine breather tube.
10. Disconnect the neutral switch wire.
11. Disconnect the spark plug leads.
12. Disconnect the tachometer drive cable.
13. Disconnect ignition point and ignition switch wires.

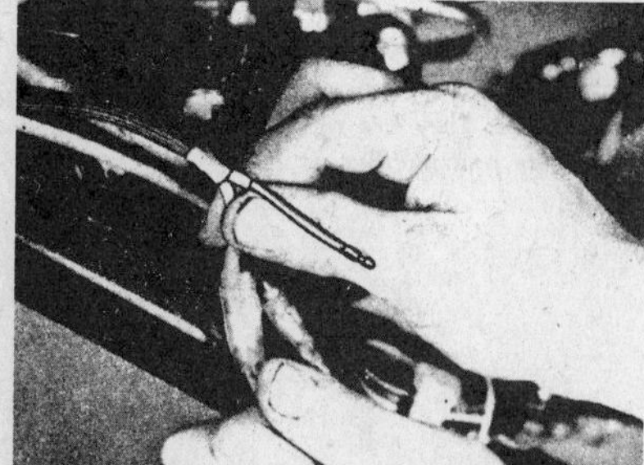

Disconnecting the breaker point wires

Removing the head bracket

14. Remove the horn and mounting bracket.
15. Remove the left case over.
16. Disconnect the master link and remove the final drive chain. "Endless" chains require a chain breaker for removal.
17. Remove the left footrest.
18. Remove both exhaust header pipes.
19. Remove the engine cylinder head mounting brackets.
20. Remove the brake pedal.
21. Remove the engine mounting bolts in the order shown in the illustration, then left the engine out the left-side of the frame.
22. Installation is the reverse of removal. Tighten the 10 mm mounting bolts to 26 ft lbs., and 8 mm mounting bolts to 15 ft lbs.

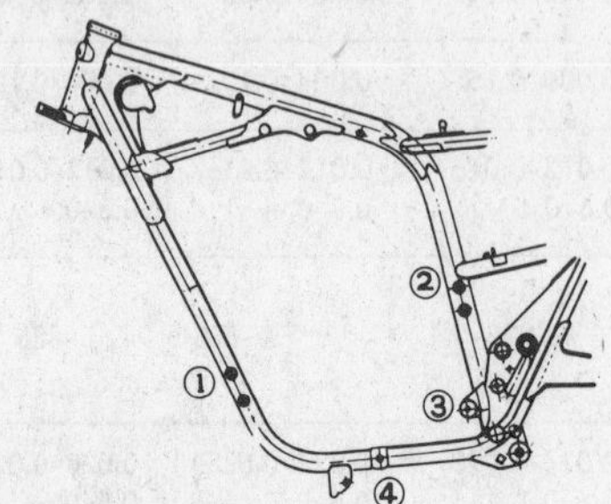

Engine mounting bolts

TOP END

To remove the cylinder head cover and/or cylinder head, it is necessary to remove the engine from the frame. Refer to the section above for the procedure.

Cylinder Head Cover

REMOVAL

1. Remove the oil delivery line at the front of the engine between the cylinders.
2. Remove the points and base plate by removing the two securing screws.
3. Remove the advance mechanism locknut and plate.
4. Pull the advance rod out the left (point) side.
5. Tap loose the advance mechanism ring nut, then slide out the unit. Also, remove the advance locating pin.
6. Remove the 3 attaching screws and the advance mechanism housing.

Removing the breaker plate

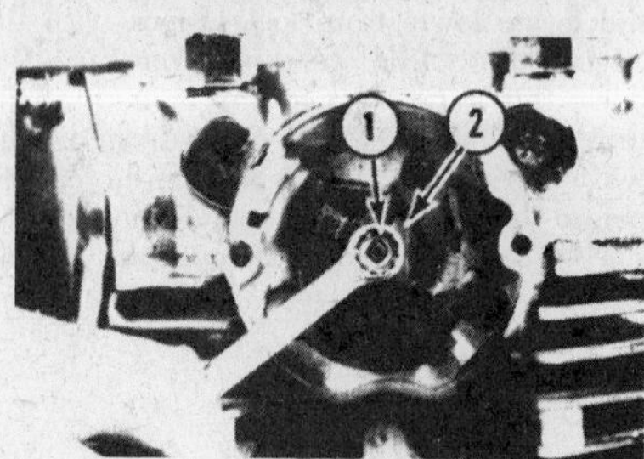

Removing the timing advance mechanism locknut (1) and plate (2)

Removing the timing advance mechanism ringnut

Removing the advance mechanism locating pin

7. Remove the 4 tappet covers.
8. Remove the 8 retainer nuts, 4 retainer bolts, and the head cover. Make certain to remove the nuts and bolts in the sequence shown in the illustration.
9. Remove the rocker shaft covers, sleeves, and O-rings.
10. Remove the rocker arm shafts and arms using a 6 mm extracting screw.

INSPECTION

1. Check the rocker arm for excessive wear at the two points indicated in the illus-

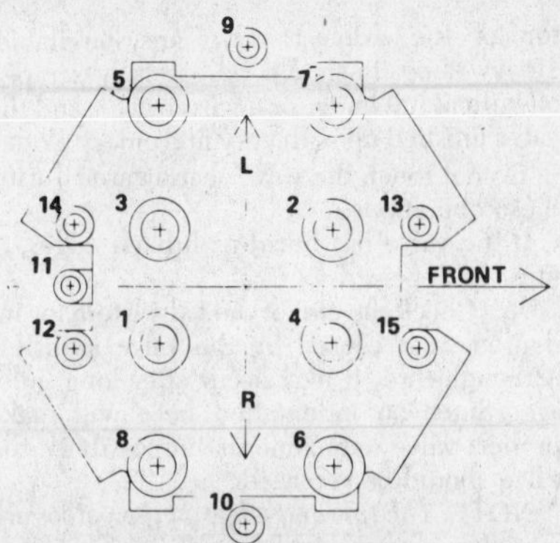

Cylinder head cover fastener loosening sequence

Rocker arm shaft sleeves and O-rings

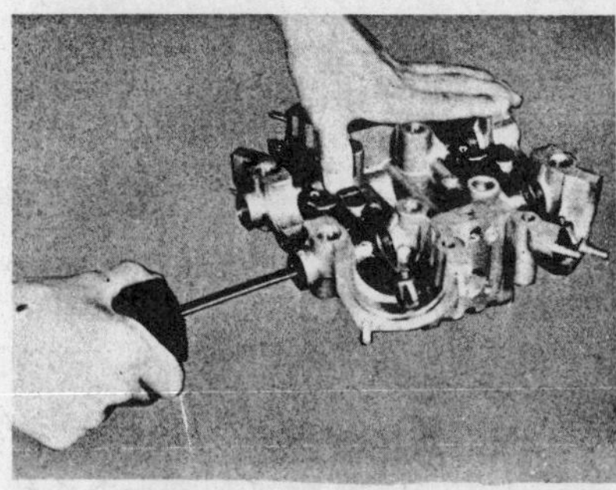

Removing the rocker arm shafts

tration. Look for any grooves, scratches, discoloration, or flaking of the hardened surfaces.

2. Measure the rocker shaft hole with an inside micrometer. Standard size is 15.03 mm. Also measure the rocker shaft diameter and check for step wear or discoloration. Standard diameter is 14.98 mm.

3. Normal shaft-to-rocker arm clearance is 0.05 mm. The maximum clearance is 0.10 mm.

INSTALLATION

Reverse the removal procedure and note the following:

1. Coat all parts with oil before assembling.

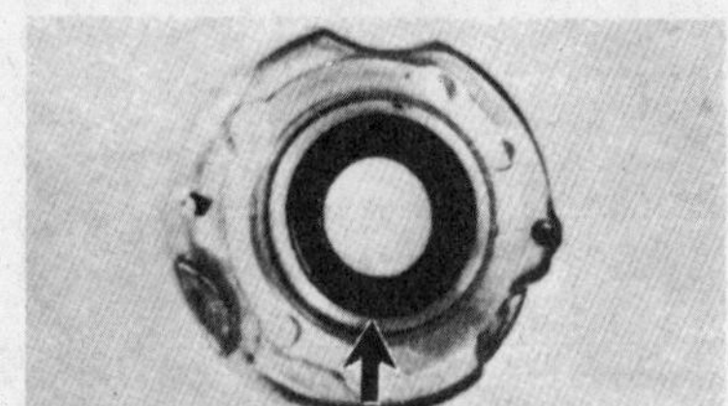

New O-ring installed in housing. Grease the seal lips before installation

Note the positioning notch in the back of the timing advance unit housing

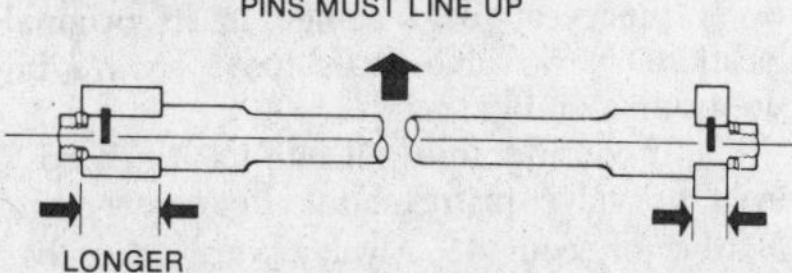

Ignition advance rod installation

Be sure to align the advance arm and disc color marks

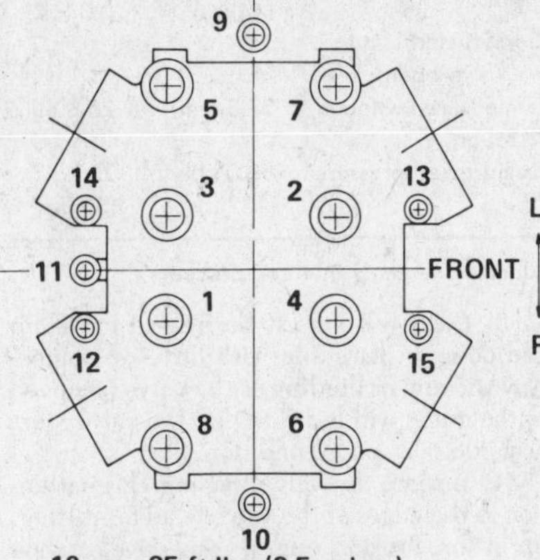

10 mm. 25 ft-lbs. (3.5 m-kgs.)
8 mm. 14 ft-lbs. (2.0 m-kgs.)
6 mm. 7 ft-lbs. (1 m-kg.)

Cylinder head cover fastener tightening sequence and torque settings

2. Make sure that the rocker arms are installed with the tapped end pointed outward.

3. Coat mating head and cover surfaces with Yamaha Bond #4.

4. Torque 10 mm nuts to 22–25 ft lbs, 10 mm stud bolts to 11–15 ft lbs, 8 mm bolts to 15–18 ft lbs and 6 mm bolts to 8–11 ft lbs in the order shown in the illustration.

5. Install a new O-ring between the advance unit housing and head cover, and grease the oil seal lip before positioning.

6. Ignition point and advance mechanism housings are identical, but can be installed in only one position.

NOTE: *When installing the timing advance mechanism, make sure that the disc face with the arrow showing direction of rotation faces outward. The timing advance mechanism arm with the color mark must be installed in the slot with the color mark next to it.*

Cylinder Head

REMOVAL

1. Stuff a rag under the cam chain sprocket, then break the link marked with slots and punch holes, using a chain breaker.

NOTE: *Before breaking the chain, fasten wire to the links on either side of the marked link, so that the chain won't drop into the case.*

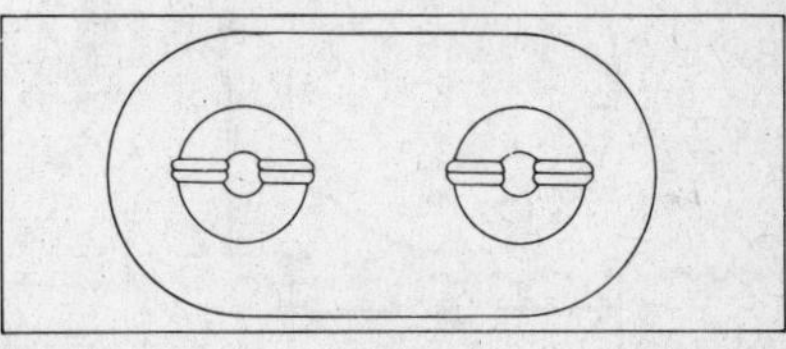

The cam chain must be separated at this marked link

Breaking the cam chain

2. Remove the chain, feeding the attaching wire into the case in its place.

3. Remove the camshaft.

4. Remove the camshaft bearings.

5. Remove the carburetor manifolds.

6. Disconnect the manifold equalizer tube.

7. Remove the two attaching bolts under

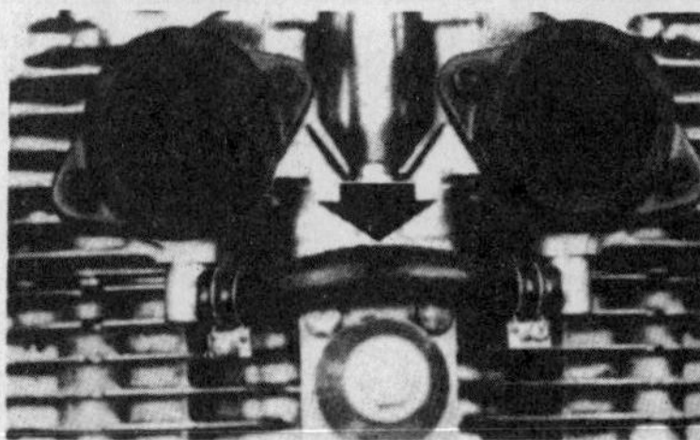

Manifold equalizer tube

the spark plugs and the screw between the intake manifold openings.

8. Lift off the cylinder head, making sure that the cam chain leader wire doesn't drop into the case.

INSPECTION

Cylinder Head

1. Clean any traces of head gasket material from the cylinder head mating surface. Place a straight edge across the mating surface and check for warpage by attempting to slip feeler gauge blades between the head and

straight edge. Standard head warpage is about 0.05 mm (0.002 in.), and maximum allowable warpage is 0.1 mm (0.004 in.). At this point, the head should be milled to restore a flat mating surface.

2. Use a wire brush fitting on a power drill to decarbonize the combustion chambers. The valves should be left in place as this is done, as it minimizes the chance of causing damage to the valve seats.

Camshaft

1. Check the cam lobes for flaking, scoring, or blue discoloration, and replace the cam if any of these signs of damage are present.

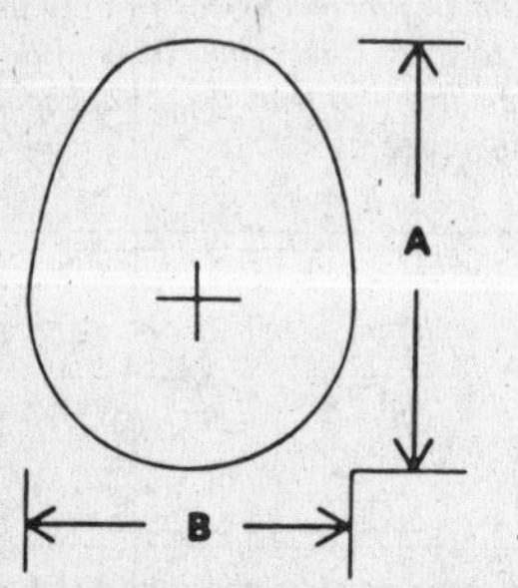

Measure cam lobe height (A) and base circle diameter (B)

2. With a micrometer, measure the height of each cam lobe and compare the measurement with the specifications given below.

3. Measure the base circle of each cam lobe. This measure is taken in a plane perpendicular to the cam height measurement through the camshaft centerline. Refer to the speiifications chart below.

4. Mount the camshaft in a set of v-blocks and measure run-out with a dial gauge. If run-out exceeds 0.03 mm (0.0012 in.), the cam should be replaced.

Cam Lobe Dimensions

1970–72

	Cam Lift (A) (mm)		Base Circle Diameter (B) (mm)	
	Stand Value *	Wear Limit	Stand Value *	Wear Limit
Intake	39.63	39.39	32.19	32.12
Exhaust	39.36	39.39	32.24	32.17

1973–81

	Cam Lift (A) (mm)		Base Circle Diameter (B) (mm)	
	Stand Value *	Wear Limit	Stand Value *	Wear Limit
Intake	39.99	39.88	32.24	32.02
Exhaust	40.03	39.88	32.30	32.15

* ± 0.05

5. Rotate each of the camshaft bearings slowly noting any roughness, binding, or clicking as this is done. The outer race should rotate smoothly and silently. Try to move the outer race up and down. There should be no movement possible. Make a visual inspection of the bearing balls, noting any denting or blue discoloration.

If any defects are noted in any bearing, replace them as a set.

Valve Assembly

Before removing the valves, check their sealing ability by pouring a small quantity of gasoline into each port and allowing the head to sit for about five minutes. If the valves are properly seating, leakage into the combustion chamber will be minimal.

1. To remove the valves, and install them properly, a suitable C-clamp is necessary. Compress the valve springs and remove the split collars, retainers, springs, seals, and spring seats. Inspect the valves, guides, springs, and valve seats in the following manner. Keep each assembly separate so that every piece can be installed in its original location. New valve seals must always be used on assembly.

2. If considerable mileage has been covered, the valve springs should be replaced as a matter of course. Always replace valve springs as a set.

Measure the free-length of each valve spring with a vernier caliper. If any of the springs is more than 2 mm (0.08 in.) in.) less than the standard free-length given in the specifications chart below, the springs should all be replaced.

Valve Spring Specifications

	Outer	Inner
Direction of winding	Right-hand	Left-hand
Total windings	6.0	7.25
Free-length	41.8 mm	41.0 mm
Installed length (Valve closed)	37 mm	35 mm
Installed pressure	20.1 kg (44 lbs)	9.7 kg (20 lbs)
Compressed length (Valve open) Measured without collar	27.8 mm	25.8 mm
Compressed pressure	60.0 kg. (132 lbs)	25 kg (55 lbs)

All measurements ± three percent

3. Each valve must be free to move up and down in its guide with little resistance. Any sticking or binding as the valve is moved in the guide will indicate that the valve stem or guide is in poor condition.

4. Inspect the valve, paying close attention to the edges of the valve head for pitting, burnt or broken edges, excessive carbon build-up, etc. A certain amount of carbon and lead deposits on the valve face and the top of the exhaust valve are inevitable. Heavy deposits should be carefully scraped off with a dull knife, or a wire wheel, and the valve finished up with very fine emery cloth.

Do not touch the valve seating area during these operations.

If the valve has burnt or broken edges, it must be replaced.

5. Check the end of the valve stem for indented wear caused by the valve adjuster. Although rare, it may occur after long mileage. Since an indentation here will make proper valve adjustments impossible, the valve should be replaced.

NOTE: *The tips and edges of the valves are stellite-coated. Machining for any reason is not recommended. In case of wear, replace the valve.*

6. Carbon deposits should not extend too far up along the valve stem. This would indicate a worn or cracked valve guide.

7. Wet, oily deposits on the back of the valve head is indicative of a worn guide or bad seal. Less severe wear to these components show up as brown oil stains on the valve stem.

8. Holding a valve in your fingers, spin it while observing the head. A wobble is indicative of a bent valve. If a dial gauge is available, check the run-out of the head. Replace the valve if run-out exceeds 0.03 mm (0.0012 in.). Run-out is the total indicated dial gauge reading.

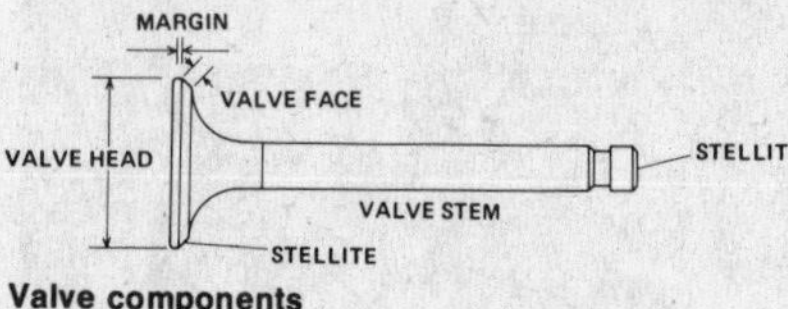

Valve components

Attempt to rotate the valve by hand when it is fully inserted into the guide. If the valve will not rotate easily, or if it sticks as it is turned, it is probably bent.

9. If inside and outside micrometers are available, measure the diameter of each valve stem at three places along the length of the valve, and compare this measurement to the inside diameter of the respective guide, also measure at three places. Subtract the smallest stem diameter obtained from the largest of the guide measurements to obtain the clearance. Compare your clearance to the "Replacement Clearance" given in the following chart:

Valve Guide Specifications

			Original Clearance	Clearance Replacement
Intake	Valve Guide ID	8.010–8.019 mm	0.020–0.044 mm	0.100 mm
	Valve Stem OD	7.975–7.790 mm		
Exhaust	Valve Guide ID	8.010–8.019 mm	0.035–0.059 mm	0.120 mm
	Valve Stem OD	7.960–7.975 mm		

Checking valve run-out with a dial gauge

10. To replace a valve guide, heat the cylinder head in an oven to a temperature of 212° F (100° C). Drive out the old guide(s) with a suitable drift. Drive in the new guide(s) until fully seated. Use new O-rings.

NOTE: *Replacement valve guides are available in two oversizes. The valve guide hole in the cylinder head must be reamed before attempting to install the guide. The reamer diameter should be 15.107–15.115 mm for the first oversize and 15.207–15.215 mm for the second.*

A new valve must always be used when a new guide is fitted.

11. After installing new guides, the valve seat should be recut and the valve lapped in.

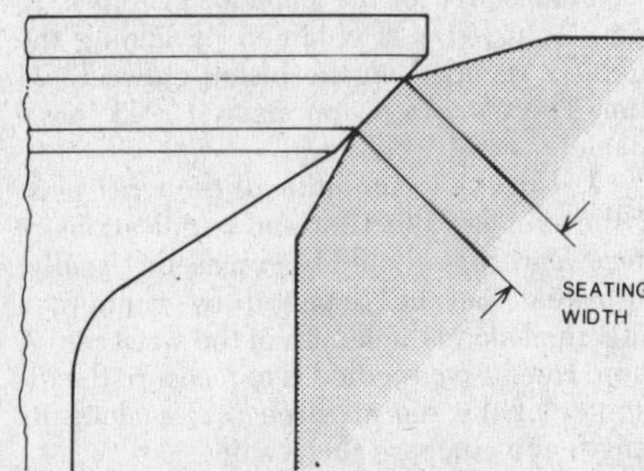

Valve seat width measurement point

Valve springs are installed with the close coils (arrows) towards the head

12. Check the width of the valve seat on the valve. It should be about 1.0 mm (0.04 in.) all the way around. If narrower or wider than this, or if width varies around the valve, the seat should be recut and the valve lapped in.

NOTE: *Valve springs are progressively wound. When installing them, be sure they are fitted with the close coils towards the cylinder head.*

SEAT CUTTING

1. Use a machinist's dye to check the width and position of the valve seat. Apply the dye to the valve's beveled seating area and a very small amount of grinding compound to the valve seat in the head. Spin the valve back and forth against the seat for several seconds,

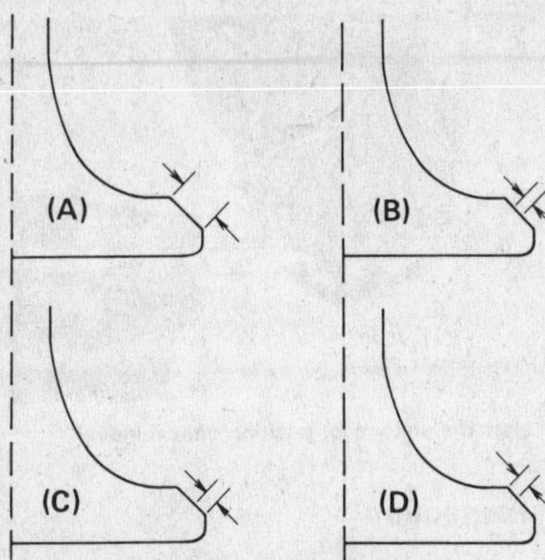

Valve seat patterns (see text for explanation)

then remove the grinding compound and inspect the pattern of the seat, from which the dye will have been removed.

2. The valve seat should be about 1.0 mm (0.04 in.) wide and even in width all around the valve. The maximum acceptable seat width is 1.5 mm (0.06 in.).

3. If the seat is uniform in width but is too wide (A), use a flat cutter, then a 30° cutter to reduce the seat width to within specification.

4. If the seat is centered on the valve face, but is too narrow (B), use a 45° cutter to increase the width to the proper specification.

5. If the seat is too narrow, and is towards the top edge of the face (C), first use a flat cutter, and then the 45° cutter.

6. If the seat is too narrow and positioned towards the bottom edge of the face (D), use a 30° cutter first, then a 45° cutter.

LAPPING

1. Valves should be lapped into their seats if the leakage test shows poor sealing, if the seat has been recut, if the valve edges or seat in the head are pitted, if the motorcycle has covered considerable mileage, or if new valves or guides are fitted.

2. Clean off all carbon build-up on the surface of the combustion chamber. Place three small dabs of valve lapping paste around the circumference of the valve head and place the valve into the guide.

3. If you have a lapping tool, use it as the manufacturer directs. Usually the tool will turn the valve back and forth while rotating it around the seat at the same time. Do not use excessive pressure during the operation.

If you do not have such a tool, a piece of thick fuel line placed over the valve stem works just as well. Turn the valve back and forth and rotate it to a new position every few seconds.

NOTE: *Check the condition of the valve face and seat frequently. When a smooth, even finish is evident, stop lapping. Excessive lapping may lead to a pocketed valve.*

4. Remove the valve and clean it thoroughly. Remove any traces of lapping compound from the seat and the combustion chamber. Swab out the guide with a cotton swab soaked in a solvent. Squirt a little oil into the guide so that it may carry away any particles inside.

INSTALLATION

1. Slide all the cam bearings in toward the center, then position the camshaft on the head.

2. Align the camshaft chain sprocket with the crankshaft sprocket by sliding the shaft back and forth. Both bearings must be equidistant in the cam bearing bosses.

3. Install a new cylinder head gasket, pull the cam chain lead wires through the cylinder head and slide the head over the studs. Install and tighten the retaining bolts and screw.

4. Position the pistons at top dead center by lining up the "T" mark as shown.

5. Align the camshaft sprocket as shown in the illustration, then draw around and reconnect the cam chain with a new link. Use a chain riveter to secure the new link.

6. Adjust the cam chain tensioner to remove the excess chain slack.

7. Adjust the valves to the correct clearances.

8. Mount a degree wheel to the crankshaft.

9. Insert a wooden dowel pin in a spark plug hole and position the degree wheel to read zero with the piston at top dead center on the compression stroke.

10. Mount a dial indicator over an intake valve adjuster.

11. Rotate the crankshaft counterclockwise and watch when the valve begins to open. The degree wheel should indicate 47° BTDC. If necessary, reposition the cam

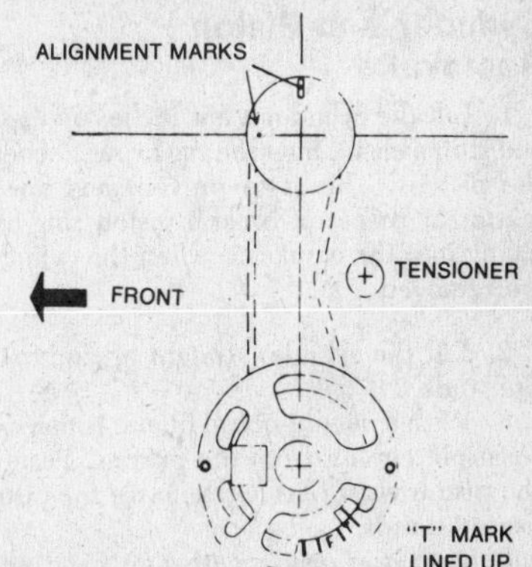

Valve timing positions

Degree wheel in place

Dial gauge positioned to check valve movement

chain so that the valve opens at the correct point.

NOTE: *Each chain link equals approximately 10° of crankshaft rotation.*

Cam Chain Tensioner and Vibration Damper

REMOVAL

1. Remove the 4 attaching screws and the vibration damper (see illustration).

NOTE: *Note the position of the two slotted screws.*

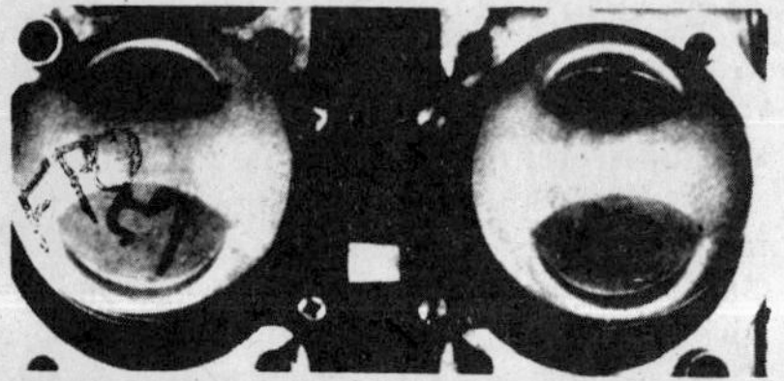

Vibration damper screws

2. Remove the attaching bolts and the tensioner housing.
3. Pull out the tensioner unit.

INSTALLATION

Installation is a reversal of the removal procedure. Replace the tensioner housing gasket and apply Yamaha Bond #4 to the mating surfaces.

Cylinder and Piston Removal

1. Lift the cylinder a few inches off its seat and stuff a clean, lint-free rag or rags beneath the pistons. This is to prevent any foreign matter or pieces of broken piston ring from falling into the crankcase when the cylinders are removed.

2. Lift the cylinder straight up and free of the studs.
3. With a needle-nosed pliers, remove the wrist pin circlips from the pistons. Push out the piston wrist pins and remove the pistons from the rods.

Support the piston with one hand while pushing out the wrist pin to minimize chances of bending the rod. Push the pin out with steady pressure. Do *not* use an impact method. If the wrist pins resist removal, heat the piston crown gently and evenly with a propane torch until the pins can be easily pushed out.

Discard the wrist pin circlips. New circlips must be used on assembly.

4. Mark each piston so that it can be installed in its original cylinder on reassembly.

Removing the piston wrist pin circlip

Mark the pistons for position after removal

Inspection

1. Make a visual inspection of the cylinder bore, noting any imperfections. The cylinder walls should be uniformly smooth.
2. With an inside micrometer, measure the diameter of each bore at the top, middle, and bottom. Make measurements in two directions, 90° apart, both parallel and perpendicular to the piston wrist pins.

If the difference between the high and lower measurement in any one direction (taper) is greater than 0.05 mm (0.002 in.), or if the difference between two measurements at any point on the cylinder (out-of-round) exceeds 0.01 mm (0.004 in.), the cylinders should be bored to the next oversize and fitted with new pistons.

3. Make a visual inspection of the pistons. Scoring, scuffing, or seizure marks on the piston skirts may be removed with a fine grade of emery or crocus cloth if they are not too severe. Sanding should be done in a cross-hatch pattern. If the damage is severe (more than about ½ in. wide), the pistons should be replaced.

4. The rings must be free to move in the piston grooves. If they cannot, either they are carbon clogged (which necessitates replacing the rings and cleaning out the grooves), or metal has been pushed into the grooves by a piston seizure. In this event, pistons and rings must be replaced. Carbon-clogged rings are almost always broken when an attempt is made to remove or free them, so be prepared to buy a new set.

5. Pistons are available in four oversizes in increments of 0.25 mm.

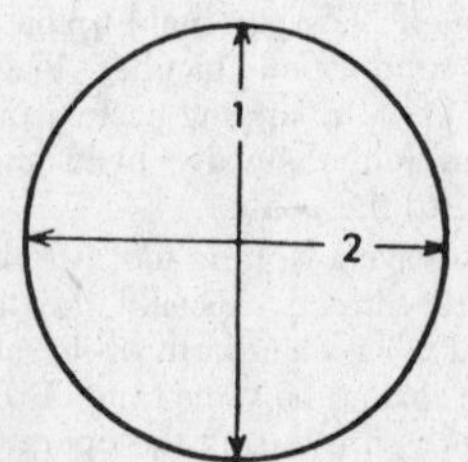

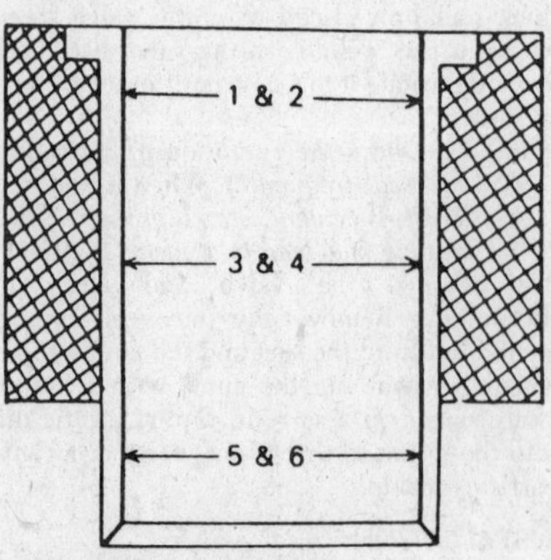

Cylinder measurement points

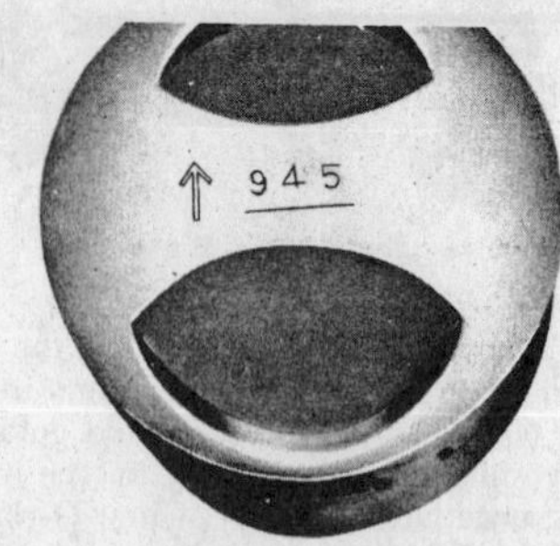

Install pistons with the arrow mark on the crown pointing towards the exhaust port. The number indicates size

To determine piston diameter, use a micrometer and measure the diameter in a direction perpendicular to the wrist pin at a point about 11 mm (0.43 in.) above the bottom edge of the skirt.

6. Standard piston-to-cylinder clearance is 0.050–.060 mm (0.0020–0.0024 in.).

Nominal size for the standard pistons is 75 mm. Actual size is obtained by adding the number stamped on the piston crown to 74 mm. Therefore, a piston marked "945" has a diameter of 74.945 mm.

7. Check the condition of the wrist pins. If the pins are blued or show indications of step-wear, they should be replaced. Usually, step-wear can be detected by running a fingernail along the length of the wrist pin. A more conclusive method is to measure the diameter of the pin at three places along its length and compare the readings.
8. Insert each wrist pin into its piston and check for play of the pin in the piston hole. There must be none. The pin must be a fairly tight fit. If the pin is easily inserted and can be turned or moved vertically with no effort, the pistons should be replaced.
9. Lightly oil each wrist pin and insert it into its connecting rod. Check for vertical play. There should be none. If play exists, or if the rod small end is discolored, the rod and/or pin should be replaced.
10. Check the connecting rods for a bent condition. This can be accomplished with two small rectangular blocks of metal of equal thickness. Insert the wrist pins into the rods, and position the pieces of metal beneath them on either side of the rods and resting on the crankcase. Rotate the engine so that the wrist pin rests on the blocks. Both sides of

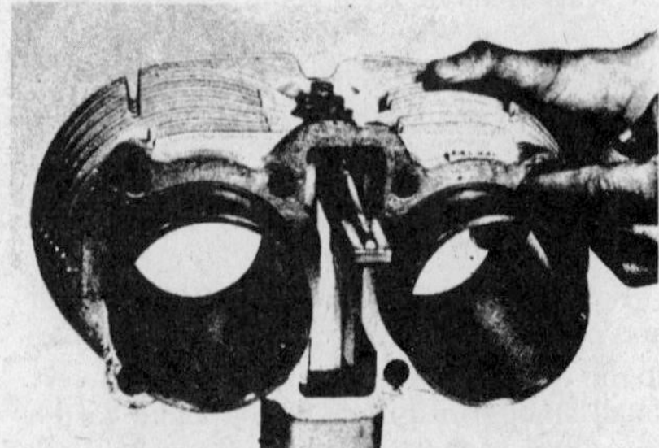

Use new cylinder base O-rings upon reassembly

the wrist pin must contact the metal blocks, or the rod is bent and must be replaced.

11. Before installation, decarbonize the piston crowns. Remove any carbon from the ring grooves with a piece of broken ring or a very thin screwdriver. Be careful not to scratch the grooves.

Carefully check the cylinder, cleaning the bore thoroughly. If considerable mileage has been covered, honing the cylinders and fitting new rings is recommended. If the cylinders are honed, make a strenuous effort to clean them thoroughly afterwards, preferably with very hot soapy water and a stiff brush. This is to remove any abrasive particles deposited by the hone in the course of the operation.

Remove any traces of gasket material from the cylinder base and the head mating surface.

12. Be sure that all oil passages in the cylinder are clear. Check the condition of the cam chain tensioner guides and replace them if damaged.

13. Replace the cylinder base O-rings. Check that any O-rings and the important dowel pins fitted to the cylinders are in their proper locations before installation.

Piston Rings

Two checks to be made on the piston rings are side clearance and end-gap. These checks should be made on both new and used rings.

1. Piston ring side clearance for compression rings is checked with the rings installed on the piston. Insert a feeler gauge blade between the ring and the ring groove and check that the clearance is within the specification. Standard clearance is 0.04–0.08 mm (0.0016–0.0032 in.). The service limit is 0.15 mm (0.006 in.). If the clearance is too large, the rings or grooves are worn. If too small, metal may have been pushed into the grooves due to a piston seizure. Check that the grooves are not just carboned up. If new rings do not bring the clearance to the proper value, the pistons must be replaced.

A ring expander reduces the chances of breaking a ring

Checking piston ring end-gap

2. To remove the rings from the piston, use a ring spreader as illustrated. They are available at most auto stores. Decarbonize the ring grooves.

3. To check the ring end-gap, ensure first that the cylinder bore is not excessively worn. Place each ring, in turn, into the bottom of its cylinder and push it in an inch or more using the piston skirt to align the ring in the bore. Measure the end-gap with a feeler gauge. Standard end-gap is 0.2–0.4 mm (0.008–0.016 in.) for the compression rings and 0.3–0.6 mm (0.012–0.024 in.) for the oil rings. The service limit is 0.8 mm (0.032 in.) for the compression rings and 1.0 mm (0.04 in.) for the oil rings. If the end-gap is larger than the service limit, the rings must be replaced. If the measured end-gap of new rings is too large, the cylinder is worn and should be bored to the next oversize.

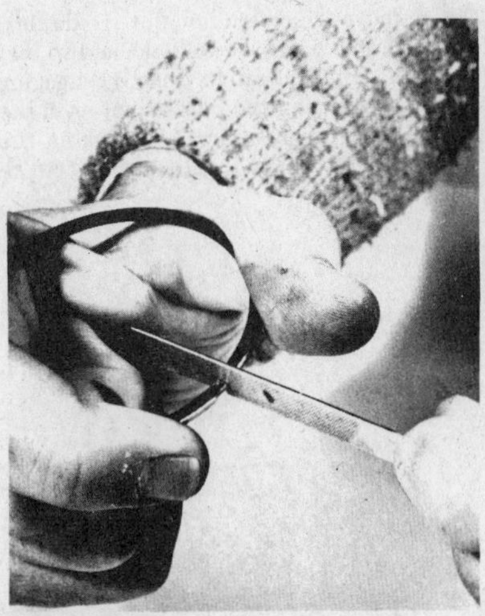
Filing ring ends

If new rings are fitted and the end-gap is too small, the ring ends must be filed. Hold the ring steady as illustrated, closing the ends over a thin, fine file. Do not squeeze the ring, as this is the easiest way to break it. A few strokes of the file will increase the endgap.

CAUTION: *Do not make more than a few strokes before checking the end-gap again. It is easy to remove too much metal.*

Do not allow the file to slip out of the ring, as this risks breaking it.

Roll each ring around the piston in its own groove to check for free movement

4. Roll each ring around its own groove and ensure that this can be done easily. If a ring sticks or binds in the groove, the pistons must be replaced.

Cylinder and Piston Installation

Note that there are differences in the compression rings. The earlier type were used on XS1 and XS2 models and the TX650 to No. 010152. Later TX650s and all XS650 models use the later type ring. Refer to the illustration of ring profiles. The new rings must be used on new type pistons.

1. When installing piston rings, note that all rings are installed with the manufacturer's mark (the small letter near the end-gap) facing *up*.

NOTE: *Oversized rings, which must be used only with the proper oversized piston, are marked as follows:*

Compression Rings

Size (mm)	Mark
Standard	None
Oversize 1st	25
2nd	50
3rd	75
4th	100

Oil Rings

	Size	Color
Standard		Blue (1 mark)
Oversize 1st	25 (0.25 mm)	Blue (2 marks)
2nd	50 (0.50 mm)	Red (1 mark)
3rd	75 (0.75 mm)	Red (2 marks)
4th	100 (1.0 mm)	Yellow (1 mark)

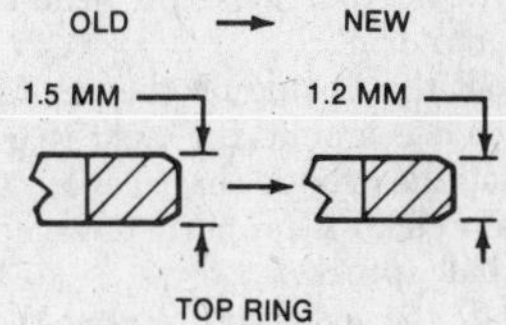

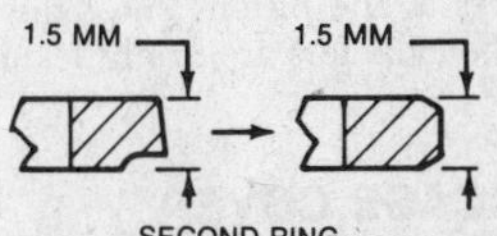

Old and newer model compression ring profiles

Always install rings on the piston with the mark facing up

2. To install the three-piece oil ring, install one rail on the piston below the oil ring groove, fit the expander, then move the rail into place. Install the top rail.

3. Use a ring expander to install the rings to reduce the chance of breaking them.

4. Ring end-gaps must be staggered around the piston so that they do not overlap. Position the end-gaps as shown in the illustration. Note that none of the end-gaps are positioned at the very front or sides of the piston.

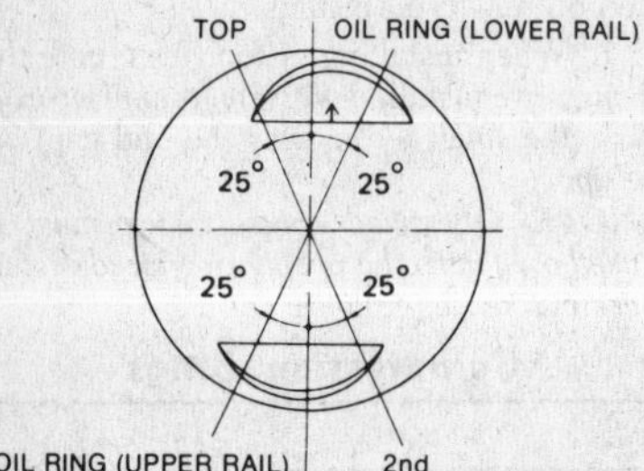

Stagger the ring end-gaps around the piston as shown

5. Install the pistons on their connecting rods so that the arrow marks on the crown face the front (exhaust side) of the engine.

NOTE: *Be sure to use new wrist pin circlips.*

6. Slip the wrist pins into place, heating the piston crown as on removal if necessary. Install the wrist pin circlips with a needle-nosed pliers. Be sure each circlip is firmly seated in its groove and arranged so that the circlip end-gap and the cut-out in the piston do *not* align.

7. Lubricate the rings and piston skirts with clean motor oil.

8. Install the O-ring on the oil delivery passage which is around the right rear stud.

9. Install the cylinder base gasket. Check that the cam chain is properly engaged with the crankshaft sprocket.

10. Install the cylinder, routing the cam chain up through its passage as the cylinders are lowered. Compress the piston rings with your fingers as the pistons enter the bores. Be sure the cylinders are firmly seated.

CRANKCASE COVER COMPONENTS

Right Crankcase Cover

REMOVAL AND INSTALLATION

1. Drain the oil. Disconnect the tach cable. Remove the right-side rider's footpeg and the kickstarter crank.

2. Remove the attaching allen screws and the primary case cover.

If the cover resists removal, tap carefully around it with a plastic mallet.

3. Unscrew the tachometer shaft locknut.

4. Drive out the tachometer housing with a hammer and drift.

5. Lift out the tachometer gear.

6. Remove the oil pump (see "Lubrication System.").

7. Remove the oil filter.

8. Installation is the reverse of removal. Make sure that the copper washer is seated under the shaft, and replace the O-ring if it is worn or damaged.

Clutch and Primary Gear

REMOVAL

1. Remove the right crankcase cover as outlined above.

2. Loosen the six clutch spring screws gradually and evenly until they can be removed, then take off the springs and pressure plate.

3. Remove the clutch pushrod, then tilt the unit to the right to remove the pushrod ball. There is another pushrod behind the ball which is more easily removed from the other side of the mainshaft.

4. Remove the clutch friction and steel plates. Keep them in the order in which they are removed.

5. Remove the clutch hub nut. To do this, the clutch hub will have to be locked so that it will not turn. This can be done by engaging a gear and applying the rear brake, or, if the engine is out of the frame, by locking the engine sprocket with a length of chain. An alternative method is to bolt together an old friction plate and steel plate.

6. Remove the clutch hub. Note the two thrust washers and the thrust bearing behind the hub.

7. Remove the clutch housing, clutch bushing spacer and thrust washer(s) behind it. Carefully note the number and location of the thrust washers. They must be installed correctly.

INSPECTION

1. Check the condition of the clutch cover mating surface. Remove any burrs or imperfections with an oilstone.

2. Measure the thickness of the friction plates, and replace them if they are less than 3.1mm (0.12 in.) thick.

3. Place the steel clutch plates on a flat surface, such as a piece of glass, and check for excessive warpage by attempting to slip a feeler gauge blade between the surface and

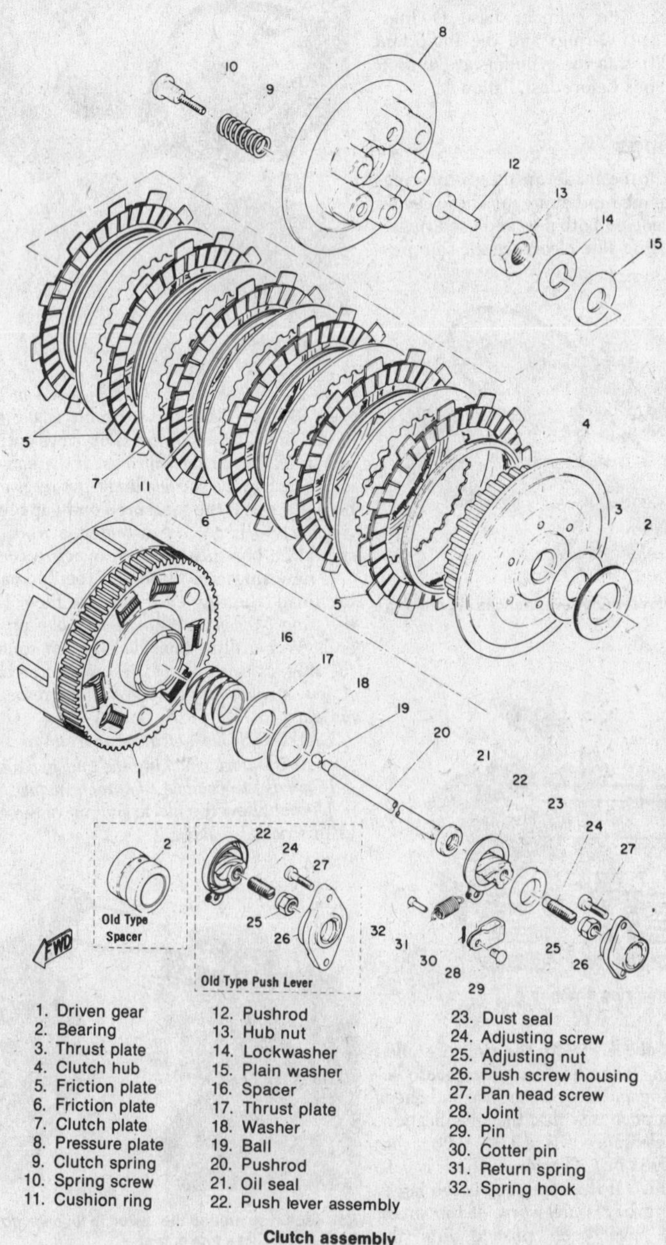

Clutch assembly

the plate. Replace the steel and friction plates as a set if warpage exceeds 0.2 mm (0.008 in).

4. Measure the free-length of each clutch spring and replace them as a set if any are found to be less than 33.6 mm (1.32 in.) long, or if their length varies. If the latter is true, be sure that all of the screws are evenly tightened on assembly.

5. Check the friction plate tabs for wear or damage. Check the clutch housing for indented wear caused by the tabs. Remove any burrs with a file or oilstone.

6. Check the corresponding splines of the clutch hub and steel plates for indented wear.

7. Using a dial indicator, check the pushrod for a bent condition. Replace the pushrod if it is bent more than 0.2 mm (0.008 in.).

8. Check the condition of the clutch gear teeth. Note any pitting or chipping. Check the primary gear teeth as well. If damage to either is noted, replace both. The primary gear is replaced by removing the securing bolt and pulling off the gear.

INSTALLATION

1. If the primary gear was removed, be sure that the securing nut is tightened to 85 ft lbs. The gear is keyed to the crankshaft. Be sure that the key is in place before fitting the gear to the shaft.

2. Install the thrust washers and spacer, followed by the clutch housing.

3. Use some heavy grease to hold the thrust bearing and washer, then install the clutch hub.

Tighten the clutch hub to 54–58 ft lbs.

4. Friction plates are alternated with steel plates in the housing. There are two kinds of friction plate—fiber-backed (4) or alloy-backed (2). The fiber-backed plates are installed first. A friction plate is fitted to the housing first, then a steel plate, and so on. After the four fiber-backed plates are used, install the alloy-backed plates, alternating them with the steel plates as before.

5. Fit the clutch pushrod ball, the pushrod, and the pressure plate. Install the clutch springs and screws. Tighten the screws gradually and evenly until all are secured.

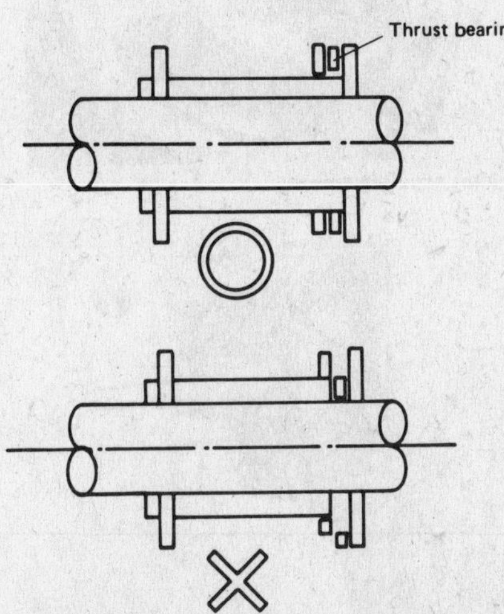

Correct thrust bearing installation (top)

Shift mechanism

Gearshift Mechanism

REMOVAL

1. Remove the right crankcase cover. Remove the clutch assembly.

2. Remove the left crankcase cover, shift lever and footpeg.

3. Remove the chain guide nut, wire clamp and the guide. Remove the circlip from the gearshift shaft on the left side of the engine and pull out the gearshift assembly from the right.

INSPECTION

1. Check the gearshift shaft for a bent condition and replace it if it is bent. Check the condition of the gearshift shaft splines.

2. Check the condition of the shift fingers. Note any chipping or wear to the finger ends.

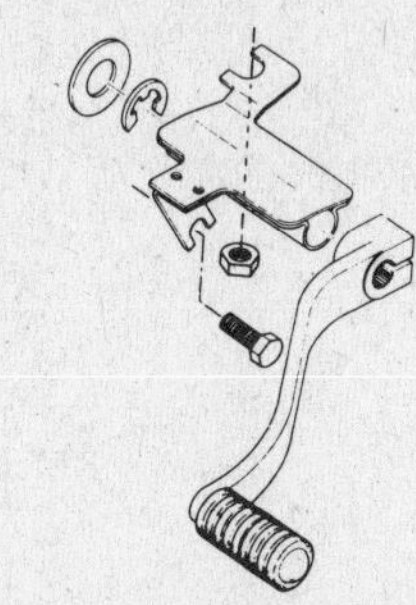

Shift lever and chain guide assembly

Replace the fingers if they are bent or worn.

3. Inspect the shift mechanism springs and replace them if weakened or broken.

INSTALLATION

1. Installation is the reverse of removal. After fitting the mechanism, temporarily install the gearshift lever and test shifting action through the gears.

2. In each gear, check that the shift fingers

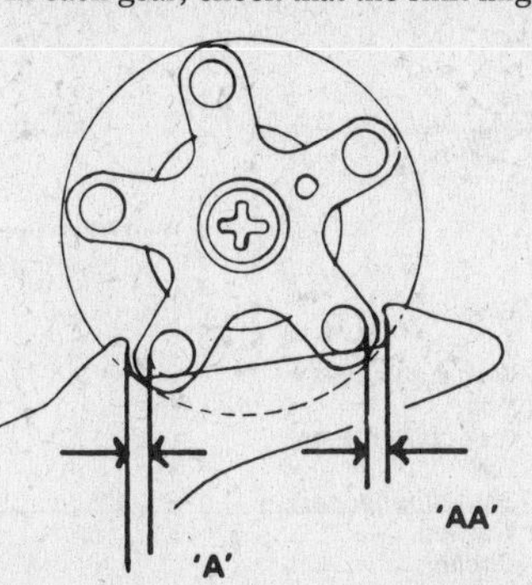

Use the adjuster screw to equalize distances "A" and "AA"

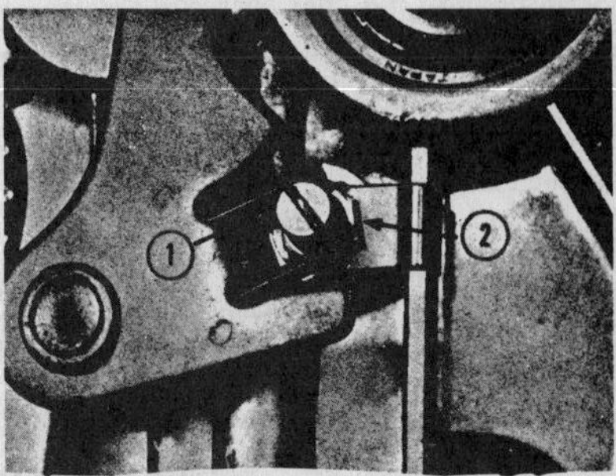

Adjusting screw (1) and locknut (2)

are equidistant from the shift drum pins. Refer to the illustration. If they are not, loosen the adjusting screw locknut and turn the screw to equalize the distances. Do not forget to tighten the locknut and bend up the locktab.

3. Check for freeplay in the gearshift lever. There should be none. If any is evident, the return spring is evidently weakened and should be replaced.

Kickstarter Shaft

REMOVAL

1. After removing the right crankcase cover, the kickstarter shaft can be removed by pulling it out.

2. When disassembling the shaft components, lay each one out in the order removed to facilitate assembly.

INSPECTION

1. Check the condition of the kickstarter shaft splines.

Be sure that the kickstarter return spring is hooked over the boss as shown

2. Check the kickstarter gear teeth for chipping or other damage, and replace it if such damage is noted.

3. Check the condition of the shaft return spring. The spring should be replaced if it will not return the shaft quickly to the rest position and hold it securely in place.

INSTALLATION

1. Set the kickstarter gear clip into the groove in the crankcase.

2. Rotate the return spring clockwise and hook it onto the projection.

Starter Reduction Gears

REMOVAL

1. Drain the engine oil.

2. Remove the left and right crankcase covers.

3. Remove the gear train cover.

4. Remove the idler gear.
5. Remove the clutch.
6. Remove the stopper plate.
7. Remove the outer gear ("2" in the illustration), then the gear circlip and the other reduction gears.

Starter reduction gear train compartment

INSPECTION

1. Check all the gear teeth for wear, pitting, or broken teeth, and replace any if necessary.
2. Check the return spring tension, and replace it if it is fatigued, weakened, or broken.

INSTALLATION

Installation is the reverse of removal. Be sure that the starter clip is firmly seated in the crankcase groove. Use a non-permanent thread-locking compound on the stopper plate screw.

Left Crankcase Cover

The cover is easily removed after removing the left footpeg mounting bolts, the gearshift lever, and the cover securing screws. It is not necessary to drain the oil from the crankcase.

Alternator

For alternator output tests, refer to "Electrical System,"

REMOVAL

1. Remove the left crankcase cover.
2. Remove the two stator securing screws. Carefully remove the stator assembly, being careful that the wires are not ripped during the process.

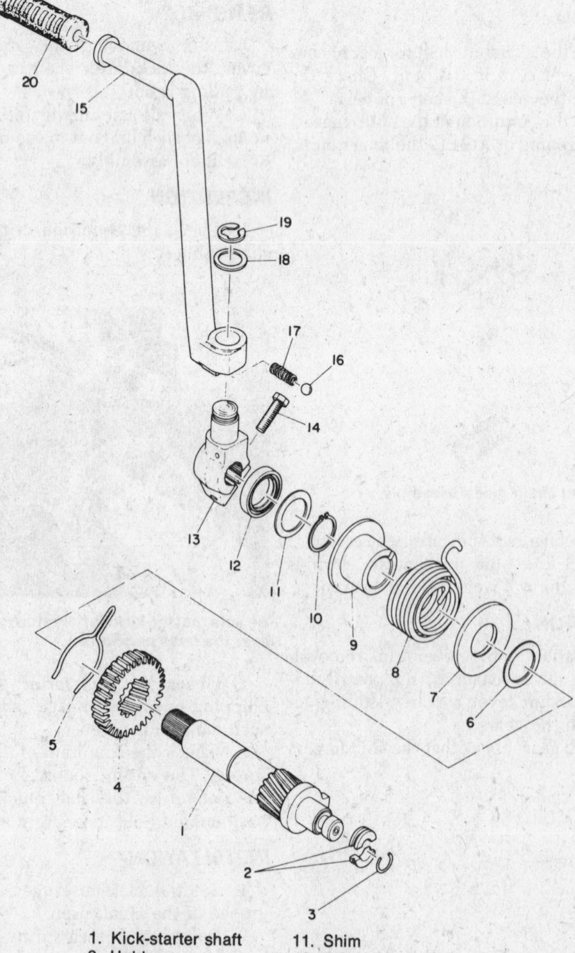

1. Kick-starter shaft
2. Holder
3. Clip
4. Kick-starter gear
5. Wishbone clip
6. Shim
7. Spacer
8. Return spring
9. Spring guide
10. Circlip
11. Shim
12. Oil seal
13. Kick crank boss
14. Bolt
15. Kick-starter lever
16. Ball
17. Boss stopper spring
18. Washer
19. Circlip
20. Rubber grip

Kickstarter assembly

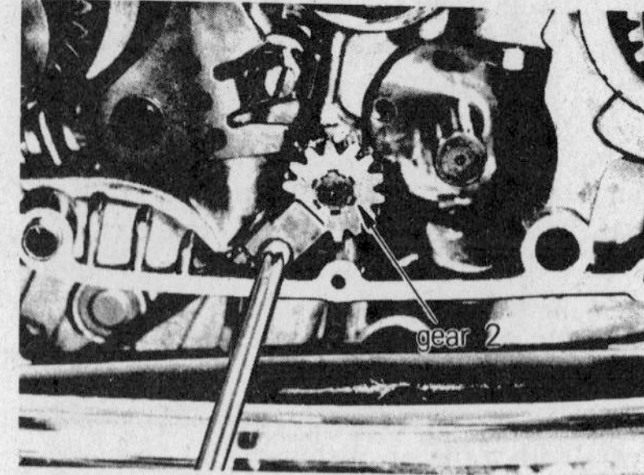

Removing the stopper plate

Removing the gear circlip

Removing the reduction gears

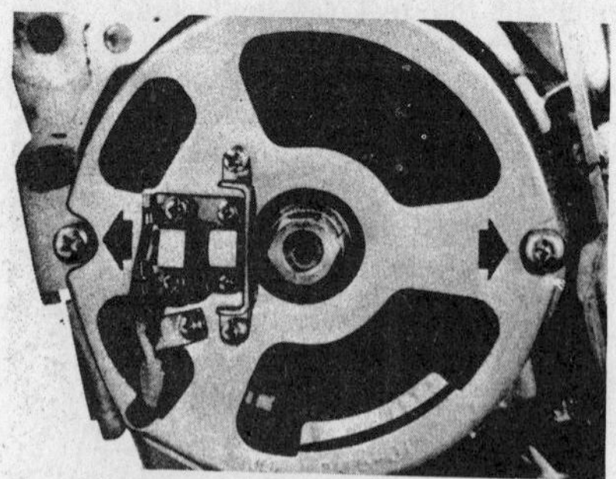
Stator securing screws

Removing the rotor

3. To remove the rotor, a special puller is needed. Remove the rotor securing nut and washer. Fit the special tool, and remove the rotor.

4. Remove the woodruff key from the crankshaft.

INSTALLATION

1. Installation is the reverse of removal. Lightly grease the rotor woodruff key and install it in its seat on the crankshaft. Be sure that the key is fully seated before attempting to install the rotor.

2. Lightly grease the crankshaft taper. Line up the rotor slot with the key and push the rotor on as far as possible by hand. Tightening the rotor nut will seat the rotor fully.

CAUTION: *Do not tap the rotor into place with a hammer or other instrument as damage may result.*

3. Tighten the rotor nut 50–54 ft lbs.

Engine Sprocket

REMOVAL

1. Remove the left-side rider's footpeg. Remove the gearshift lever.

2. Remove the left side crankcase cover screws and take off the cover.

3. Place the transmission in gear and apply the rear brake. Unscrew and remove the engine sprocket nut. Remove the lockwasher and sprocket. It may be necessary to move the rear wheel forward to remove the sprocket from its shaft.

INSTALLATION

Installation is the reverse of removal. Tighten the sprocket nut to 72–87 ft lbs.

Bend up the locktabs over one of the nut flats.

LOWER END AND TRANSMISSION

Splitting the Crankcases

Splitting the crankcases is necessary for service to the crankshaft and connecting rods, transmission gears, and internal shift mechanism.

Removal of the engine is required.

All top end components (cylinder head, cylinders, pistons) must be removed in order to split the cases. When disassembly is complete, the top half of the crankcase will lift off, the crankshaft and transmission gears remaining in the lower case half.

1. Drain the engine oil. Degrease the engine as thoroughly as possible, especially the lower crankcase half area. This will to some extent prevent foreign matter from entering the engine when it is disassembled.

Removing the starter motor

2. Remove the engine from the frame.

3. Remove the top end components.

4. Remove the left and right crankcase covers and the components therein: clutch, primary drive gear, kickstarter shaft assembly, gearshift mechanism, engine sprocket, alternator stator and rotor, starter drive reduction gears on electric start models, etc.

5. Remove the electric starter motor, if fitted.

6. Turn the engine upside down and loosen the crankcase nuts and bolts. The fasteners are numbered. Start with #18 and loosen them in descending order.

7. When the nuts and bolts have been removed, carefully turn the engine upright and lift off the upper crankcase half. If the case is stuck, tap around the mating surfaces very gently with a plastic mallet. Be sure that all fasteners have been removed before attempting to split the cases.

CAUTION: *Do not use a steel hammer to do this, and do not strike the left crankcase cover mounting flange (see illustration).*

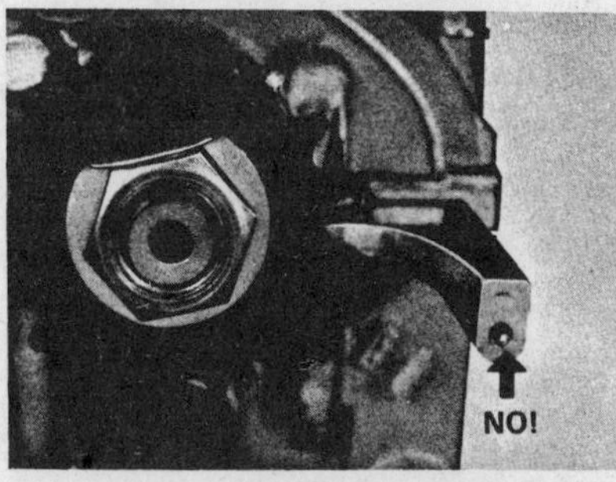

Do not strike this flange when attempting to split the cases

Case Assembly

1. Be sure that the crankcase mating surface is clean and free of all traces of old gasket compound. Minor scratches or burrs can be removed with an oilstone, although care must be taken that the surface is not grooved when doing this.

2. Lubricate all bearing surfaces with motor oil.

3. Be sure that the crankshaft and transmission shafts are properly seated. The transmission shaft bearings are located with set rings. Be sure the shift forks are engaged with their gears.

4. Be sure that all dowel pins between the cases are in place.

5. Apply a thin coat of a liquid gasket compound to the case mating surface. Install the upper case half. After ensuring that it is properly seated, install the crankcase bolts and nuts and tighten them gradually and in a cross pattern.

Tighten the 8 mm bolts and nuts to 15–17 ft lbs.

Transmission/Gear Shift Assembly

REMOVAL

1. Split the crankcases as described in the preceding section.

2. Lift the transmission shafts and gear clusters out of the lower case, tapping lightly with a plastic mallet if necessary to free them.

3. Before removing the shift forks, mark them so that they can be installed in their proper locations without confusion later.

4. Check for free movement of the shift drum before removal. If movement is rough or balky, inspect the shift drum and/or shift fork shaft for grooves or wear after disassembly.

5. Disconnect the shift drum stopper spring (#1 in the illustration), bend down the

Disconnect the shift drum stopper spring (1) and remove the locating plate (2)

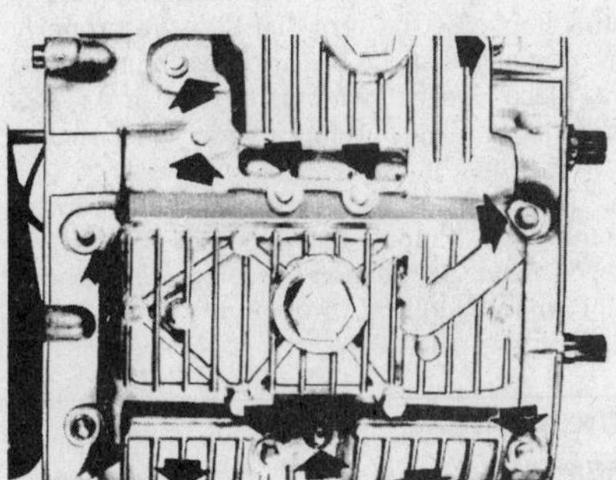

Lower crankcase securing nuts and bolts

Removing the upper crankcase half

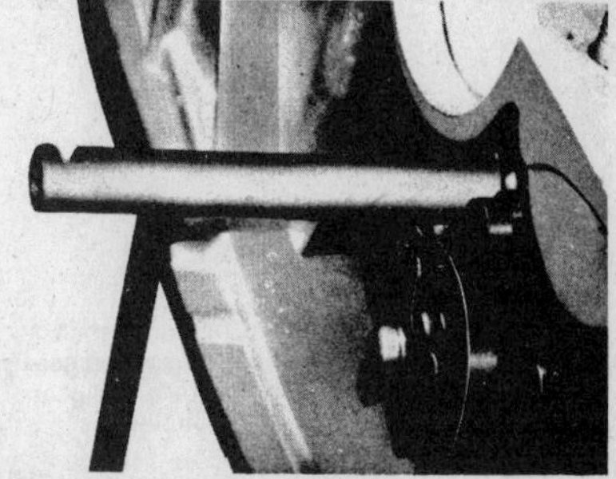

Removing the shift fork shaft

locktabs and remove the locating plate bolts and the locating plate (#2).

6. Remove the shift fork shaft.

7. Unscrew and remove the neutral stopper bolt and plunger assembly from the crankcase.

Neutral stopper bolt

8. Remove the cotter pin on each shift fork, and take out the cam follower roller.

9. Pull out the shift drum, being careful not to lose the cam follower rollers.

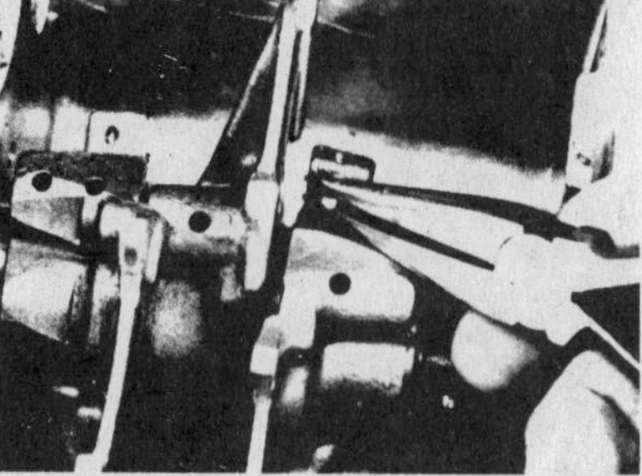

Removing the shift fork roller pins

INSTALLATION

1. If the gears have been removed from their shafts, install them in the correct locations, referring to the illustration of the transmission assembly if necessary. Note that *new* transmission shaft circlips must always be used.

2. Lubricate the shaft drum and fit it to the crankcase sliding it through the shift forks. Be sure that the shift forks are correctly installed. The fifth gear shift fork has a notch matched into it for the neutral light switch. The fourth gear fork is also notched to provide clearance for the neutral stopper. Use new cotter pins. Be sure that the cam follower rollers are in place.

Removing the shift drum

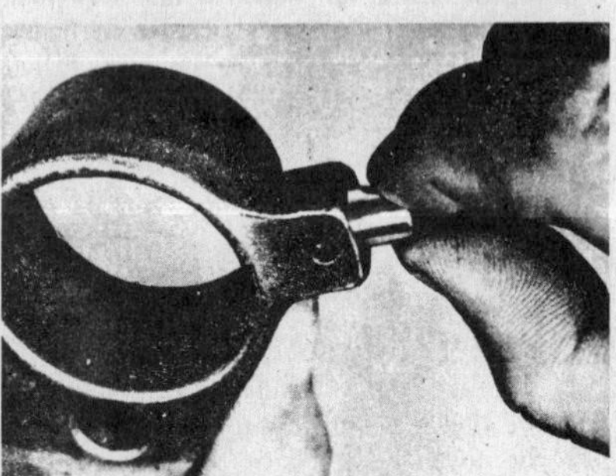

Checking shift fork roller pin fit

3. When installng the shift drum locating plate bolts, use a non-permanent thread-locking compound on the threads. Bend up the locktabs against the flats of the bolt heads.

4. Turn the shift drum so that it is in the neutral position, and install the shift drum stopper plunger and bolt assembly.

Shift fork assembly properly installed

5. Install the transmission shaft assembly into the upper case half.

The use of new oil seals is important.

6. When fitting the transmission shafts to the crankcase, be sure that they are properly seated and that the bearing locating rings are in place. Do not attempt to force the shafts into place. The shift fork fingers must engage their gears.

7. Lubricate the gears and shaft bearings with clean motor oil.

8. After installation is completed, check for smooth shifting throughout the range.

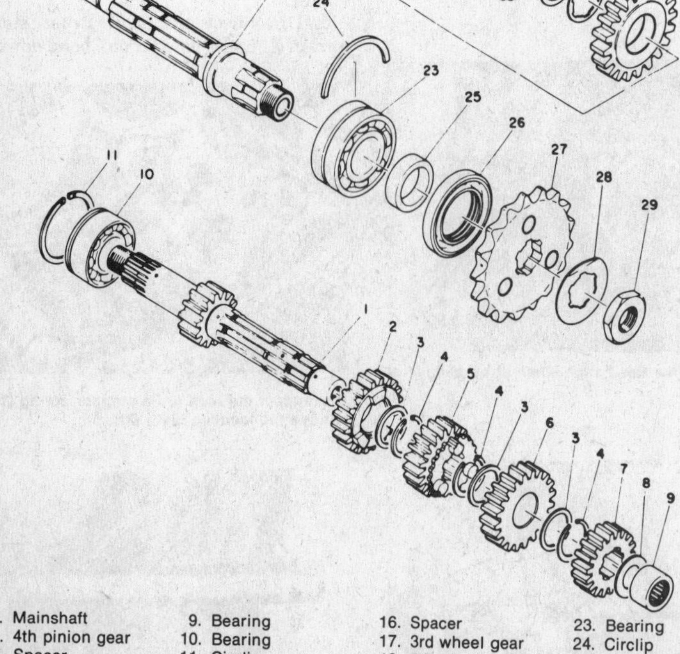

1. Mainshaft
2. 4th pinion gear
3. Spacer
4. Circlip
5. 3rd pinion gear
6. 5th pinion gear
7. 2nd pinion gear
8. Shim
9. Bearing
10. Bearing
11. Circlip
12. Countershaft
13. 2nd wheel gear
14. 4th wheel gear
15. Circlip
16. Spacer
17. 3rd wheel gear
18. 5th wheel gear
19. 1st wheel gear
20. Washer
21. Circlip
22. Bearing
23. Bearing
24. Circlip
25. Distance collar
26. Oil seal
27. Drive sprocket
28. Lockwasher
29. Locknut

Transmission assembly

Crankshaft

REMOVAL

1. Split the crankcases as outlined above.

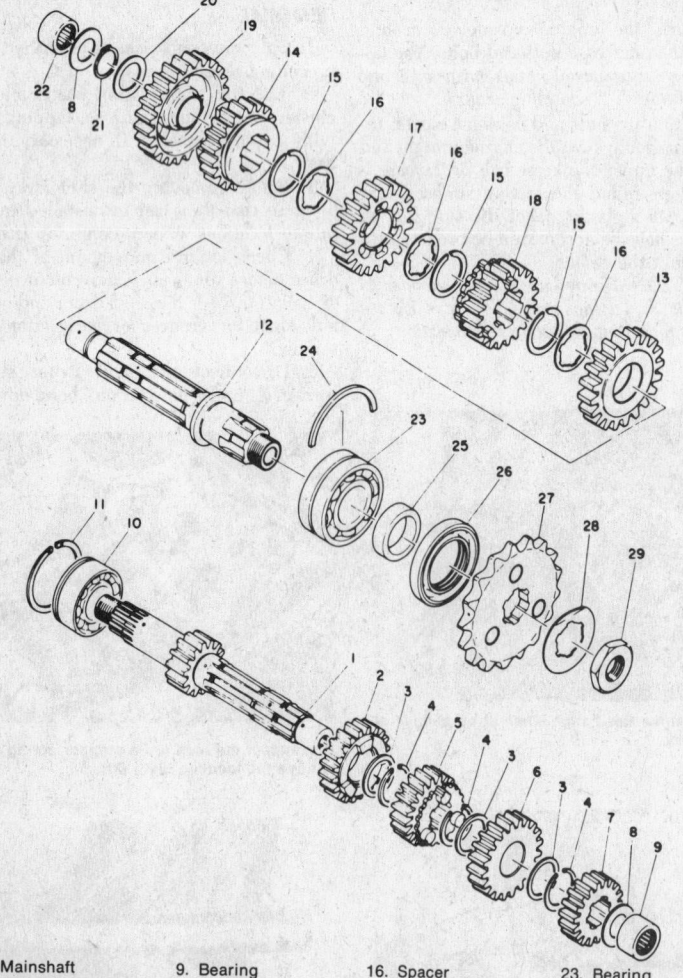

2. Carefully lift out the crankshaft, tapping upwards on the end of the shaft with a plastic mallet to free the crankshaft if necessary.

INSPECTION

1. Check each of the crankshaft bearings for wear. Oil the bearings with motor oil, then turn the outer race slowly. Movement must be smooth, effortless, and noiseless. If the rotation of any of the bearings is halting, or if clicking noises or binding is noted, the bearings should be replaced.

Bearings should always be replaced as a set, and disassembly of the pressed-together crankshaft is necessary to remove the inner bearings.

This operation requires a great deal of special equipment and must be left to a trained expert.

2. Check each bearing for visible damage to the bearing balls such as denting or blue discoloration due to heat damage. Replace the bearings if either of these conditions is present.

3. Mount the crankshaft assembly in a pair of v-blocks and check the run-out at a point just outboard of the outer bearings with a dial indicator. Run-out should not exceed 0.03 mm (0.0012 in.). If it does, the crank is bent and must be replaced.

4. With a dial gauge, measure the total amount of lateral movement (back and forth) in the connecting rod small end. Be sure to hold the big end steady to obtain an accurate reading. The maximum amount of small end movement allowable is 2 mm (0.08 in.). If this side play exceeds this specification, it is probable that the big end bearings are worn. Disassembly of the crankshaft is required for replacement.

5. Use a feeler gauge to measure con rod big end side clearance. Standard clearance is 0.30–0.36 mm (0.012–0.024 in.). Replace the rods and bearings if the side clearance exceeds 0.26 mm (0.010 in.).

1. Crank 1 (left)
2. Crank 1 (right)
3. Crank 2 (left)
4. Crank 2 (right)
5. Connecting rod
6. Con-rod big end bearing
7. Crank pin washer
8. Crank pin
9. Crank pin
10. Crank shim
11. Bearing
12. Circlip
13. Cam chain sprocket
14. Bearing
15. Piston
16. Piston ring set
17. Piston wrist pin
18. Piston pin clip
19. Dowel pin
20. Oil seal
21. Spring washer
22. Crank shaft nut
23. Woodruff key
24. Circlip
25. Primary drive gear
26. Drive gear
27. Spring washer
28. Crank shaft nut
29. Dowel pin
30. Woodruff key

Crankshaft assembly

Engine Torque Specifications

Part	*Torque (ft lbs)*
Cylinder head	
10 mm nut	22–25
10 mm stud bolt	11–15
8 mm bolt	15–18
6 mm bolt	8–11
Strainer cover	6–7
Oil line banjos	15–16
Drain plugs	25–29
Pump cover	5–7
Kickstarter pinch bolt	11–18
Alternator rotor nut	50–54
Alternator stator screws	5–7
Clutch hub nut	54–58
Engine sprocket nut	72–87
Crankcase bolts and nuts	15–17
Primary drive gear nut	51–72
Spark plugs	20–21
Breaker cam nut	6–7
Engine mounting nuts	25–35

6. Lightly oil the connecting rod big end bearings and rotate the rod slowly around the crankpin. Movement must be firm and smooth with no noticeable roughness, binding, or noise. If any of these conditions are noted, the big end bearings are probably in need of replacement.

7. Using a dial gauge, check the amount of connecting rod radial movement (up and down) on the crankpin. Movement should be almost nil. If any appreciable movement is noted, the big end bearings may be worn to the point of replacement.

INSTALLATION

1. Use an oil can to flush out all of the bearings by squirting clean motor oil into the races. Check for free movement of all bear-

Crank bearings must be seated by means of the locating pins (arrows)

ings before installation. Sometimes foreign matter will get into a ball bearing race and cause binding. Be sure that there is none of this.

2. Use a new seal on the left side of the crankshaft, installing it so that the teflon lip faces outwards.

3. Position the crankshaft over the case, and carefully lower it into place so that the cam chain does not drop down and get caught beneath the crank.

4. Each of the crank bearings is located by a pin fitted to the crankcase. The bearing outer races are marked to facilitate installation. Line up the punch mark on each bearing outer race with the crankcase mating surface and lower the crankshaft into position. Be sure that each locating pin enters the hole in each bearing race. Do not attempt to force the crank into place. If it will not seat, turn each bearing race slowly a few degrees in either direction until the locating pin enters the hole in the bearing.

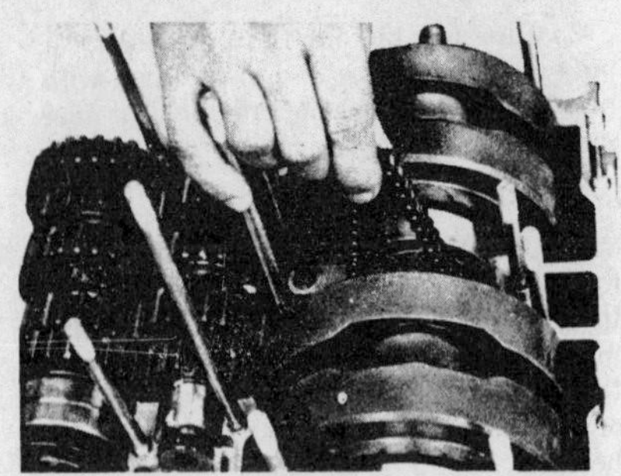

Be sure the cam chain is properly engaged on the drive sprocket

LUBRICATION SYSTEM

OIL PUMP

Removal

1. Remove the tachometer shaft locknut, then drive out the tachometer housing with a punch.

2. Remove the tachometer gear, washer, and O-ring.

3. Remove the oil pump gear and woodruff key.

4. Remove the pump housing retaining screws and, while tapping the housing with a soft-faced mallet, lift out the pump.

Oil pump drive gear

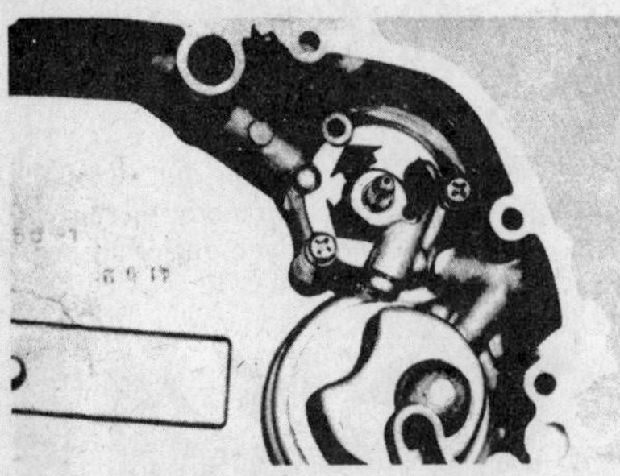

Oil pump housing retainer screws

inner rotor and driveshaft are correctly aligned. Rotor marks should face the engine.

b. Install the pump as a unit, using the locating pin provided for alignment.

c. Replace the tachometer gear O-ring

Inspection

1. Check for wear or damage.

2. Oil all parts thoroughly before installation.

Installation

1. Installation is the reverse of removal. Note the following points:

Removing the oil pump

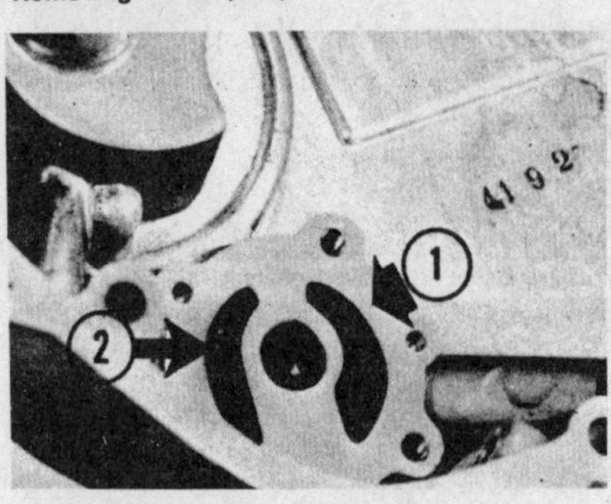

Oil pump inlet and outlet passages

a. Make sure that the notches in the inner rotor and driveshaft are correctly aligned.

b. Install the pump fully assembled using the locating pin provided for alignment.

c. Replace the tachometer gear O-ring.

Rotor marks should face the engine

Note the locating pin when installing the pump

FUEL SYSTEM

CARBURETORS

Removal

1. Disconnect the fuel line(s) from the petcock(s) after first ensuring that they are set to the "off" position.
2. Raise the seat and remove the gas tank mounting bolt. Disconnect the gas tank balance tube, if so equipped, and remove the gas tank.
3. Remove the side covers.
4. Disconnect the throttle cables from the carburetors.
5. Remove the air cleaner housing mounting bolts. Loosen the air cleaner-to-carburetor clamp screws.
6. Remove the balance tube between the carburetors from one of the float bowls.
7. Loosen the manifold clamp screws and remove the carburetors from the motorcycle. On late models, the carburetors are connected by a piece of angle iron and they must be removed together.

Installation

Installation is the reverse of removal. Be sure that both carburetors are firmly seated in their manifolds and are vertically positioned before tightening the clamp screws. If the units have been disassembled, turn on the petcock(s) and check for fuel leaks before operating the motorcycle.

Be sure that all fuel lines are properly secured with safety clips.

Disassembly

1. Remove the 4 screws which secure the vacuum chamber cover; take off the cover, lift out the spring.
2. Carefully disengage the diaphragm from the carburetor body, and pull the slide assembly straight out.
3. Remove the needle retainer and the needle.
4. Remove the float bowl screws, and take off the float bowl.
5. Remove the float pivot pin, take away the float assembly, and the float needle.
6. Unscrew the main jet. Pull out the needle jet.
7. Remove the pilot jet.

Carburetor top and throttle slide assembly

Removing the float bowl

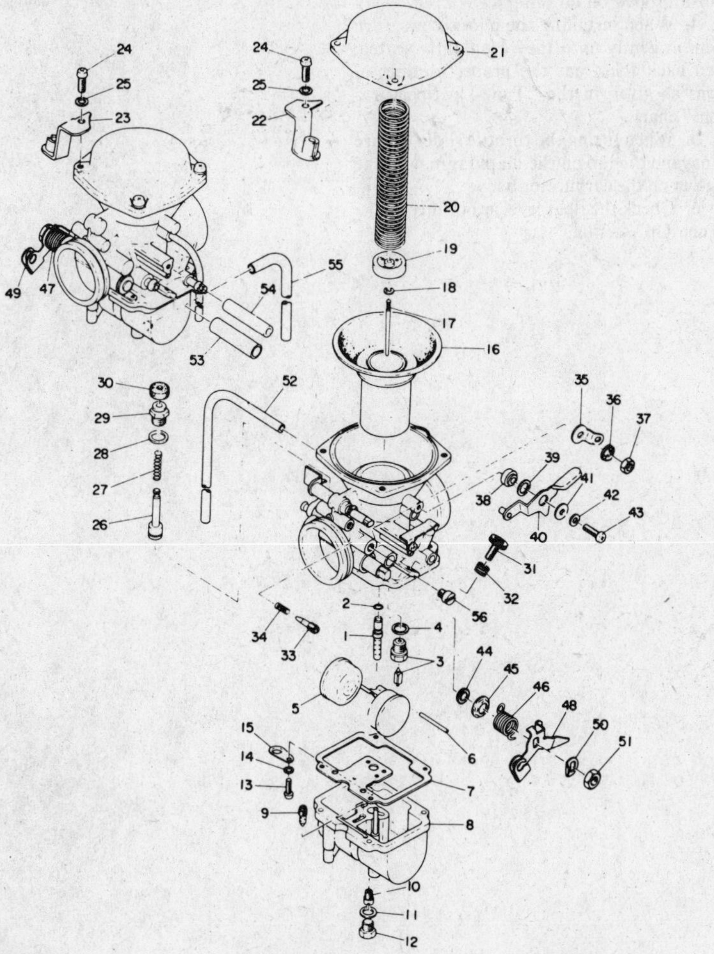

1. Needle jet
2. O-ring
3. Float needle and seat ass'y
4. Washer
5. Float
6. Float pivot pin
7. Float bowl gasket
8. Float bowl
9. Pilot jet
10. Main jet
11. Washer
12. Plug screw
13. Float bowl screw
14. Lockwasher
15. Plate
16. Diaphragm and slide ass'y
17. Needle
18. Clip
19. Needle set plate
20. Diaphragm spring
21. Vacuum chamber cover
22. Left bracket throttle ass'y
23. Right bracket throttle ass'y
24. Screw
25. Spring washer
26. Starter plunger
27. Plunger spring
28. Washer
29. Plunger cap
30. Plunger cap cover
31. Throttle stop screw
32. Throttle stop spring
33. Pilot screw
34. Pilot screw spring
35. Starter lever
36. Washer
37. Nut
38. Ring
39. Washer
40. Lever ass'y
41. Washer
42. Spring washer
43. Roundhead screw
44. Seal
45. Cap
46. Left throttle spring
47. Right throttle spring
48. Left throttle lever
49. Right throttle lever
50. Washer
51. Nut
52. Overflow tube
53. Hose
54. Balance tube
55. Fuel line
56. Vacuum gauge plug

Carburetor components

Assembly

Assembly is basically the reverse of the disassembly procedure. Note the following points:

1. Always use new gaskets and O-rings.
2. Exercise care when installing jets—they are made of soft brass and are easily damaged if overtightened.
3. If the throttle slide and needle have

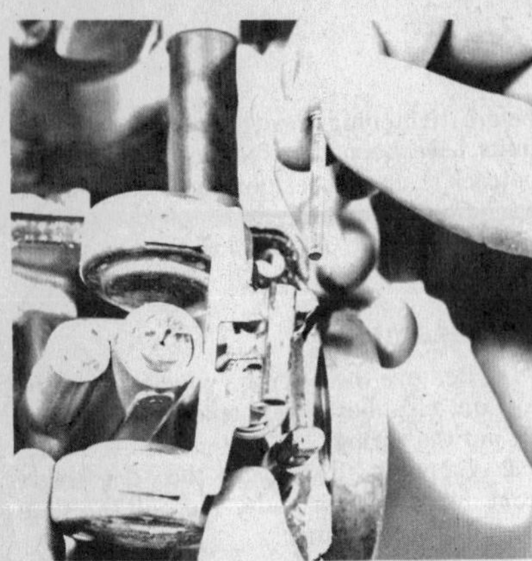
Removing the float assembly

Unscrewing the main jet

Removing the needle jet

been disassembled, first check that both needle clips are installed in the third groove from the top on XS650 C-F models, and the fourth groove on all others.

4. When installing the pilot screws, turn them in gently until they are lightly seated, then back them out the proper number of turns as given in the "Tune-Up Specifications" chart.

5. When fitting the throttle slide, be sure to engage the tab on the diaphragm with the cut-out on the carburetor body.

6. Check the float level as outlined in the "Tune-Up" section.

Be sure that the diaphragm tab is properly seated

ELECTRICAL SYSTEM

CHARGING SYSTEM

CAUTION: *The following precautions should be taken when carrying out electrical system tests.*

1. Be positive that the battery connections are not reversed. This will burn out the rectifier almost immediately.
2. Be certain all electrical connections are noted before disconnecting them so that they can be reconnected properly.
3. Do not run the engine at high rpm with the "P" terminal circuit of the rectifier disconnected.
4. When quick-charging the battery, always disconnect the rectifier at the "P" terminal.
5. Never disconnect the battery while the engine is running.
6. When testing the regulator, be sure to keep the battery connected.
7. When testing the regulator, be sure that the battery has a full charge.

Alternator

OUTPUT CHECK

NOTE: *To give accurate results, the battery must be in good condition and fully charged before performing the output test.*

1. Connect a D.C. voltmeter across the battery terminals.

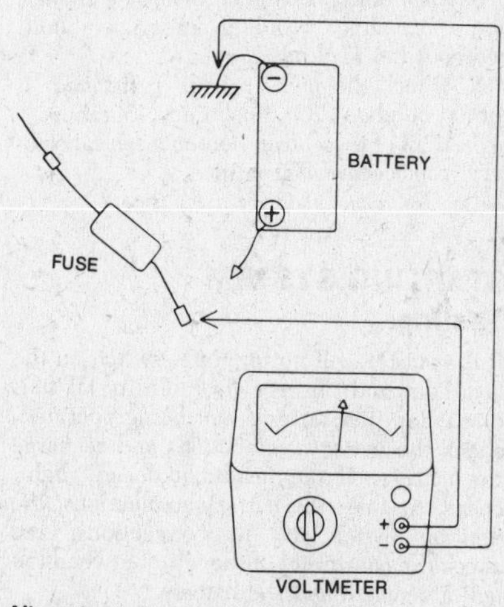

Alternator output test connections

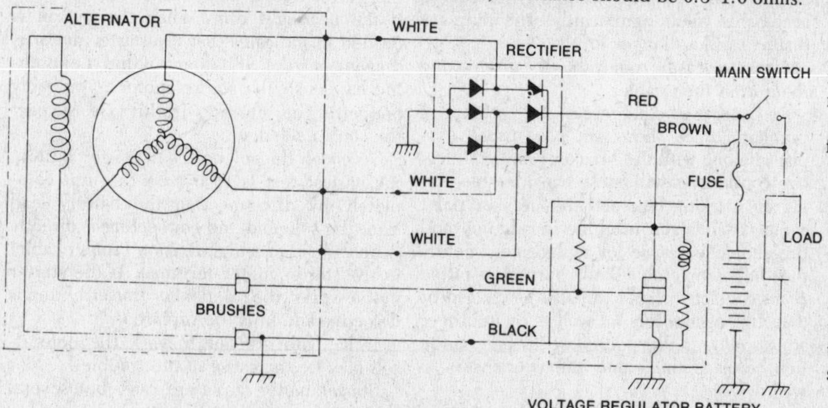

Charging circuit

2. Start the engine and let it run at about 2,000 or more rpm.
3. Battery voltage on the meter should be 14.5 v with a maximum allowable variation of 0.3 v.
4. If the voltage is greater than this, check the voltage regulator (see below). If it is less, check the alternator wiring, the regulator, and the rectifier.

CAUTION: *Never run the engine with the battery leads disconnected. To do so risks ruining the other charging system components.*

FIELD COIL/ARMATURE CHECKS

1. Disconnect the alternator wiring at the plastic connector.
2. There are six wires joined at the connector. Note the following tests.

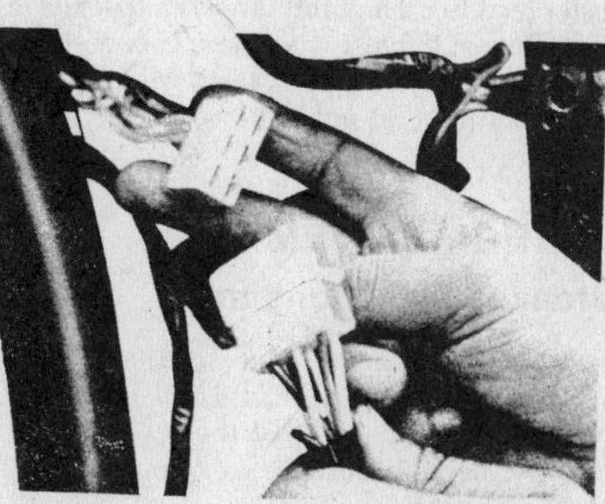

Disconnecting the alternator wiring

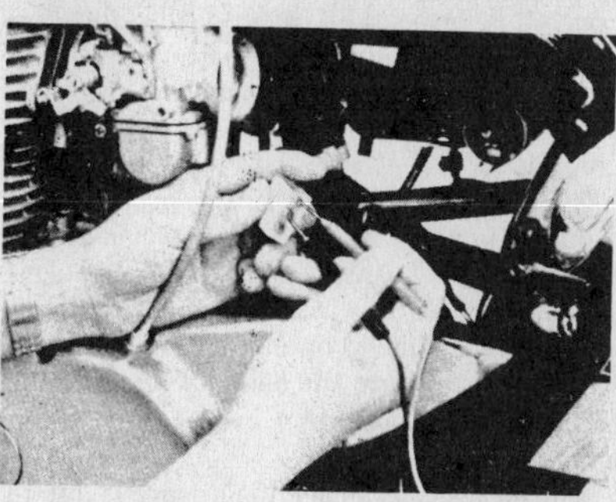

Checking armature continuity

3. Connect ohmmeter leads across the white wires. Do two wires at a time. If the wires are lettered "A", "B", and "C", readings are taken across A–B, A–C, and B–C. In all cases, resistance should be 0.8–1.0 ohms.
4. Adjust the ohmmeter scale to the highest range and attach one meter lead to the stator housing and the other to each white wire, one at a time.

In each case, the resistance should be infinite.

5. If resistance readings vary from the above, the entire alternator stator winding assembly must be replaced.
6. Visually inspect the condition of the carbon brushes for wear or flaking. Brush length (new) is 14.5 mm (0.57 in.). Replace the brushes if they are shorter than 7.0 mm (0.28 in.).
7. The carbon brushes are connected to

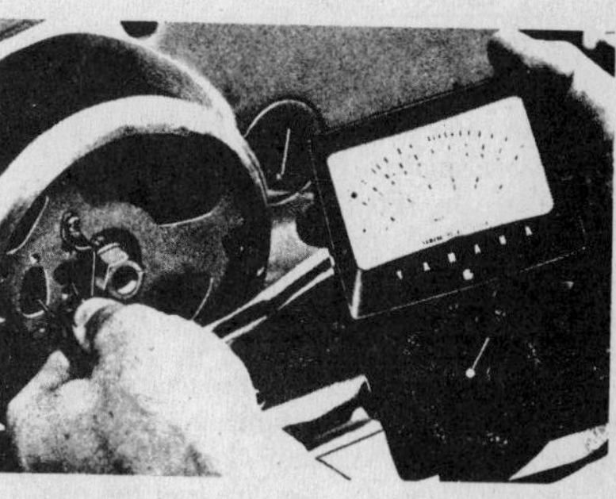

Checking slip ring resistance

the black and green alternator wires. After disconnecting the alternator wires at the plastic junction, check the resistance between the green wire and the carbon brush and then the black wire and its carbon brush. In both cases resistance should equal zero ohms, or the wire(s) will have to be replaced.

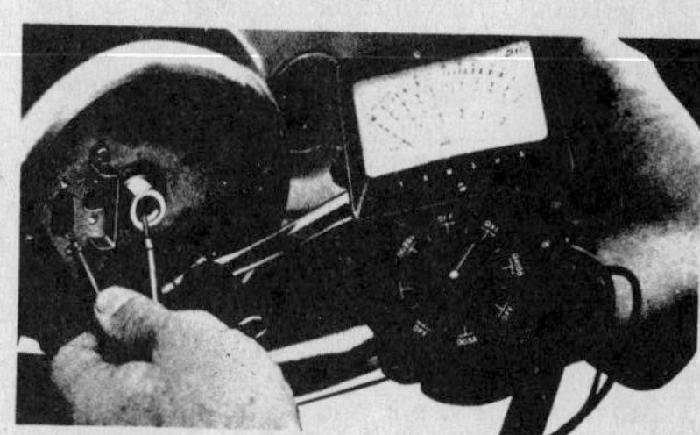

Checking slip ring to rotor core resistance

8. Check the resistance between the slip rings. Resistance should be 5–7 ohms. Note that both slip rings must be clean for an accurate reading. Clean them with an electrical contact cleaner if necessary.
9. Using the ohmmeter's highest scale, measure the resistance between each slip ring and the rotor core. Resistance must be infinite.
10. If readings vary from those above, the field coil winding should be replaced.

Voltage Regulator

The voltage regulator is reached by removing the right side cover.

A mechanical voltage regulator is used on all models. The regulator is adjustable, although this procedure should not be undertaken until the alternator has first been inspected for faults.

1. Disconnect the red wire at the fuse box (as above), start the engine, and hook up the voltmeter positive lead to the red wire.

Ground the voltmeter negative lead. Voltage reading should be 14.5–15v. If voltage is either too low or too high, proceed as described below.

2. Remove the regulator housing. Note the adjusting screw which bears on a flat spring steel plate.

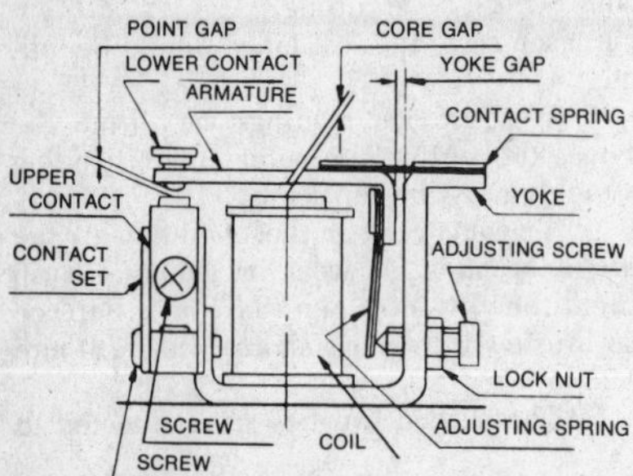

Voltage regulator components

3. Turn the screw in or out to adjust the voltage to the proper value. Turning the screw IN raises the charging voltage, while turning the screw OUT decreases the charging voltage.

4. If this does not bring the charging voltage to within specification, make a visual inspection of the regulator. Note any pitting of the contact points. Be sure that the points are not stuck together. Replace the regulator as necessary.

5. For further tests, make sure that the engine and electrical system are off. Disconnect the regulator wires at the plastic connector junction.

6. Attach an ohmmeter to the black regulator wire and to the regulator base (ground). It should read zero resistance.

7. Attach the ohmmeter leads to the brown and green regulator leads. Remove the regulator housing if this has not already been done.

8. Move the central contact point as indicated below and note the readings.

   a. When the central contact point is held against the top point, resistance should be zero.

   b. When the central contact point is midway between the top and bottom points, resistance should be 9–10 ohms.

   c. When the central point is held against the bottom point, resistance should be 7–8 ohms.

9. Connect the ohmmeter leads across the black and brown regulator wires. Hold the central point against the top point. Resistance should be 36–38 ohms.

If any of the readings vary from these figures, and the cause is not dirty points and broken or frayed wires, the regulator should be replaced.

Rectifier

1. The rectifier consists of a six-diode "bridge." A diode will allow current to pass in one direction only. If any diode allows current to pass in both directions, or in neither direction, the operation of the entire unit will be upset and the rectifier will have to be replaced.

2. It is the ability of the diodes to pass current one way and stop it in the other which is tested when checking the rectifier.

3. The rectifier can be checked with an ohmmeter or a self-powered low-voltage test light. Disconnect the rectifier wiring and remove it from the motorcycle.

4. Connect the positive lead of the tester to the rectifier red lead and the negative tester lead to each of the three white leads in turn. Note whether or not there is continuity in each case. Now reverse the tester connections so that the negative tester lead is connected to the red rectifier lead and the positive tester lead is connected to each white lead in turn. Note whether or not there is continuity.

If there was continuity for a certain connection during the first test, there should not be any when the tester leads are reversed. If there was continuity in both cases, or lack of continuity in both cases, a diode is defective and the rectifier must be replaced.

5. Connect the positive lead of the tester to the rectifier black lead and the negative tester lead to each of the three white leads in turn. Repeat the test with these connections. Replace the rectifier if all tests are not satisfactory.

IGNITION SYSTEM

Breaker Point Ignition

1. In the event of failure of the ignition system, first check the fuses; if all are in working order, check that the snap connectors for the coils and breaker points are all clean and tight.

2. At this point refer to "General Information" for inspection procedures for the breaker points, plugs, and battery. If these items are all in working order, the problem may be isolated to the coils, condensers, or plug caps.

3. If only one cylinder fails to fire, and the problem is not a loose connection or defective spark plug, suspect the plug cap. The caps are fitted with a resistor to prevent radio interference while in operation, and heat and vibration may cause the value of this resistor to increase considerably, even to becoming an open circuit.

The easiest way to see if a misfire is due to a defective cap is to switch the plug cap of the non-firing cylinder with the other cap. If the dead cylinder begins to fire and the other cylinder ceases, the problem is the plug cap. The caps should be replaced as a set.

Functional caps will have a resistance of 9,000 ohms. Usually, when resistance exceeds this value significantly, the plug for that cap will no longer fire.

Caps are easily removable by unscrewing them from their cables.

4. Defective condensers are seldom a problem, since these are now usually replaced along with the breaker points. Defective condensers will cause considerable arcing or sparking between the breaker point contacts while the machine is running, and this should be cause for replacement before they fail completely. Badly burned or pitted point contact surfaces can also be caused by defective condensers, as well as by improper adjustment. If the points are in bad condition, replace them and the condensers as well.

5. Condenser capacity can be checked with electrical test equipment (if available) in place on the machine, provided the condenser is first disconnected from the primary terminal. Capacitance should be 0.24 MFD. The resistance of the condensers should be in excess of 3 MΩ. A variation of 10% in either reading is allowable.

6. If the condensers are not suspect, check the ignition coils. Coils should be checked for continuity of the windings. First remove the gas tank. Disconnect the red/white coil lead and the other lead which is orange for the left cylinder's coil, or grey for the right. Check resistance across the leads. It should be about 4 ohms. If the resistance is not very close to this figure, the primary winding is defective and the coil must be replaced.

7. To check the secondary coil, first remove the spark plug cap from the plug lead. Check the resistance between the plug lead and the orange or grey lead. Secondary winding resistance should be 9.5 K ohms. If the measured resistance is not very close to this value, the secondary winding is breaking down, and the coil must be replaced.

TCI

1. In the event of spark failure, first check the entire electrical system for loose connections.

2. Check that the battery is fully charged. Recharge if necessary.

3. Check all fuses.

4. If all of the above elements are found satisfactory, check the resistance of the ignition coil primary and secondary windings. Primary winding resistance should be about 3 ohms. Secondary winding resistance should be about 8.6 K ohms.

5. Check the pick-up coils' resistance. It should be about 700 plus/minus 150 ohms.

6. If all of the above elements are satisfactory, replace the TCI unit.

STARTING SYSTEM

Testing

If the starter will not operate, switch on the headlight and observe its intensity. If it is dim when the starter is not being operated, check the battery connections and recharge the battery. If the headlight doesn't light, check the fuse, the battery connections, the ignition switch and its connections, and check the continuity of the wire between the ignition switch and the battery.

If the headlight is normally bright, press the starter button and observe any changes. If the headlight dims when the button is pushed, it indicates that the starter motor is drawing current. If it does not dim (i.e. nothing happens), the starter motor is probably not getting any current. In this case, suspect the starter solenoid.

To check the solenoid and starter button, the easiest test is to bypass the unit completely by disconnecting the battery lead from the solenoid and connecting it directly (with the aid of a high-tension jumper cable) to the starter motor terminal. If the starter motor works, the solenoid or starter button is defective and must be replaced.

If the motor still fails to work, the motor itself may be the cause of the trouble.

Starter motor faults are rare, but several things can go wrong.

If the starter spins freely, but the engine

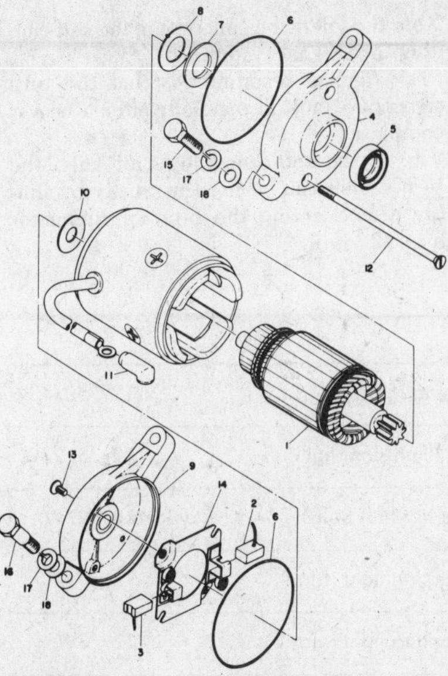

1. Armature
2. Brush 1
3. Brush 2
4. Cover
5. Oil seal
6. O-ring
7. Special washer
8. Thrust washer
9. Cover
10. Thrust washer
11. Cap
12. Special screw
13. Flat head screw
14. Brush holder
15. Reamer bolt
16. Bolt
17. Spring washer
18. Plain washer

Starter motor components

doesn't turn over, suspect the starter motor clutch.

If the engine will turn over only very slowly and without a great degree of predictability, some possible causes include: a low or almost dead battery, oil which is too thick for weather conditions (extreme cold), or bad bearings in the motor itself. Worn bearings could cause the armature to contact the field coils which will effectively short out the starter. Usually, repeated attempts at starting will result in the starter motor getting very hot. Other possible causes of starter motor trouble include worn brushes, a worn or dirty commutator, or a defective armature.

Starter Motor Service

REMOVAL AND INSTALLATION

The starter motor is bolted to the underside of the crankcase.

1. Drain the engine oil.
2. Remove the four 8 mm starter motor mounting bolts. Pull the starter motor straight back to remove it.
3. When refitting the starter motor, be sure that the gear shaft properly engages the reduction gear.
4. Tighten the mounting bolts to 15 ft lbs.
5. Fill the crankcase with oil.

INSPECTION

1. Take out the two screws and remove the starter side cover.
2. Check electrical continuity between the commutator and armature core using a multitester or test light and battery. If continuity exists, the armature coil is grounded and the complete starter motor unit must be replaced.
3. Check for continuity between all of the commutator segments. Continuity must exist in each case.
4. Check continuity between the brush that is wired to the stator coil and the starter motor cable. Lack of continuity indicates an open circuit in the stator coil, and the starter motor unit should be replaced. Resistance should not exceed 0.05 ohms.

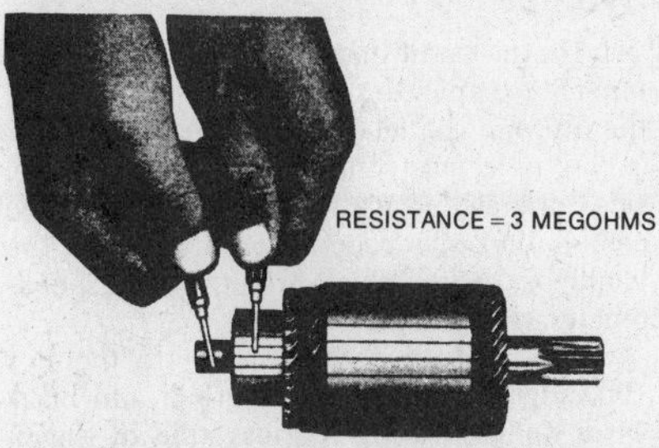

Checking resistance between the commutator and armature core

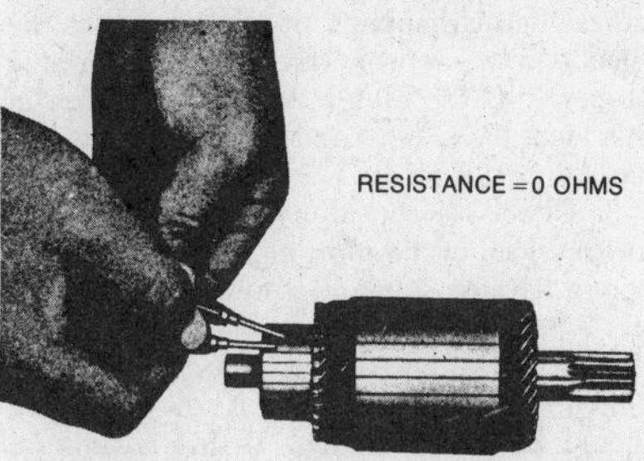

Checking resistance between the commutator segments

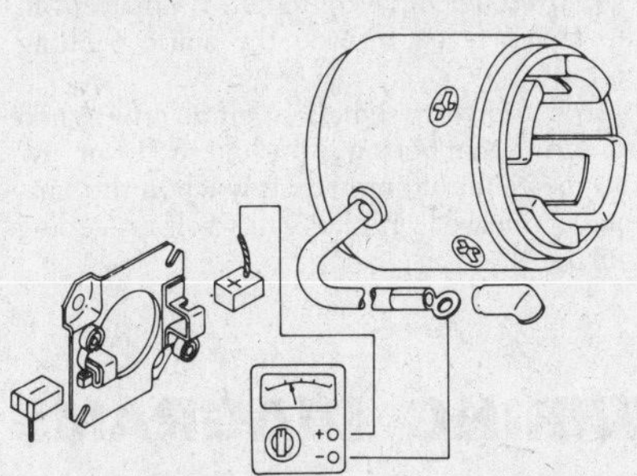

Checking resistance between the brush and starter motor cable

5. Examine the carbon brushes for damage to the contact surfaces and measure their length. Replace the brushes as a set if either one measures less than 4.5 mm (0.18 in.), or if they are damaged in any way.
6. Brush spring tension should be measured with a small pull-scale. Replace the springs if they have weakened to less than 550 g tension.
7. The mica undercut of the commutator should be maintained at 0.7 mm (0.027 in.). Any carbon deposits should be cleaned out of the commutator grooves, and a piece of hacksaw blade or the like used to increase the undercut depth if necessary.
8. Polish the commutator with fine emery cloth and then clean it thoroughly before installing.
9. Measure the diameter of the commutator. The armature should be replaced if the measurement is less than 27 mm (1.06 in.)
10. Check the condition of the armature bearings and replace them as a set if any damage is noted.
11. Check the condition of the oil seal and replace it if the seal lips are cracked or worn.
12. Unsealed bearings should be lubricated with 20W or 30W motor oil before assembly. Coat the lips of the oil seal with white grease before assembly.

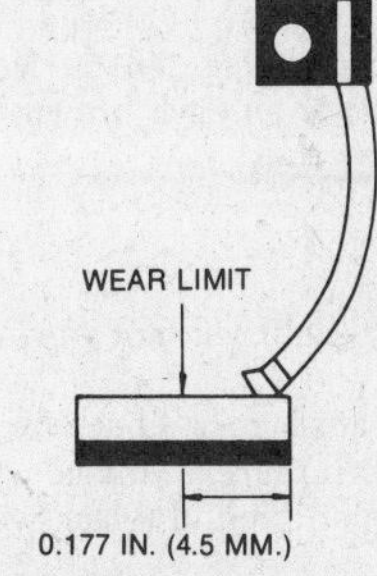

Carbon brush length

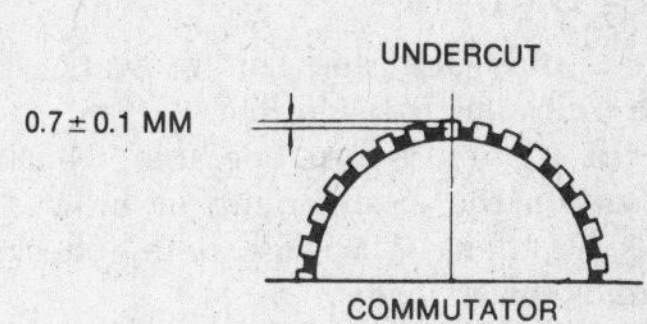

Commutator undercut specifications

Starter Solenoid

1. If the battery is in reasonably good condition, and nothing at all happens when the starter button is pushed, check the solenoid.
2. Disconnect the starter cable at the solenoid. When the button is pushed, there should be an audible "click" which indicates that the solenoid is opening.
3. If further testing is necessary, remove the solenoid from the machine.

CAUTION: *Be sure to disconnect the cables at the battery before disconnecting the solenoid terminals.*

Connect a fully charged 12-volt battery across the solenoid low-tension leads and check for continuity across the high-tension terminals with an ohmmeter or self-contained test light. If there is no continuity, replace or repair the solenoid.

4. Check for continuity across the low-tension terminals with an ohmmeter or self-powered test light. Resistance should be 3.5 ohms. If there is no continuity, the primary winding of the solenoid is broken, and the unit must be replaced.
5. If starter trouble began just after the starter button housing was disassembled or moved for any reason, check the connections at the switch as they may have come adrift.

ELECTRICAL COMPONENTS

Horn

1. If the horn fails to sound, check that there is 12 v on the brown horn lead. If there isn't, check for a broken wire.
2. If the brown lead checks out, check that the pink wire is grounded when the horn button is pressed. If it isn't, check the horn button.
3. If the wiring is satisfactory, replace the horn.

Brake Light

1. If only one of the two brakes fails to activate the brake light, the problem is probably confined to that switch.
2. If neither switch will activate the brake light, first check the brake light bulb. If it is in workable condition, check that there is 12 v on the yellow brake light lead.
3. If there is voltage on the yellow lead, check for voltage on each brown lead at the brake light switches.

Taillight

1. If the taillight will not work, check the bulb first.
2. If it is satisfactory, check for voltage on the blue lead. If there is voltage on this wire, check for a good ground (black wire).

Turn Signals

1. If only one side fails to work, check both bulbs on that side first.
2. If the bulbs are operable, check for voltage on the green (right) or brown (left) leads. If there is voltage here, check the grounds (black leads).
3. If neither side will work, check for voltage on the brown/white lead at the handlebar turn signal switch. Then check for voltage on the brown lead at the turn signal flasher relay.
4. If these checks are satisfactory, replace the flasher relay. If the turn signals still will not operate, replace the flasher switch. If this will not work, the entire self-cancelling system must be checked out (see below).

Neutral Indicator

1. If indicator light fails to come on, check the bulb first.
2. If the bulb is satisfactory, check that there is voltage on the blue wire at the switch. If there is, replace the switch itself.

Self-Cancelling Turn Signal System

1. In the event that the self-cancelling system fails to operate properly, first disconnect the 6-prong connector from the flasher cancelling unit and try the turn signals. If both sides operate normally, the trouble can be confined to the cancelling unit itself, the handlebar switch reset circuit, or the speedometer sensor circuit.
2. Connect an ohmmeter set to the R x 100 range across the white/green and black wires on the wiring harness side of the 6-prong connector. Turn the speedometer shaft. The ohmmeter needle should swing back and forth between zero and infinity four times. If this happens, it indicates that the speedometer sensor circuit is functioning properly. If the meter does not function in this manner, either the sensor or the wiring harness is defective.
3. Check for continuity between the yellow/red lead of the 6-prong connector on the wiring harness side and ground on the chassis. When the turn signal switch is *off*, there should be infinite resistance. When the switch is pushed to either "L" or "R", there should be no resistance. If this is not the case, check the wiring harness and the handlebar switch circuit.
4. If no defective operation is apparent in the above tests, replace the self-cancelling unit.
5. If the turn signals operate only when the turn signal button is pushed to "L" or "R" and they shut off immediately when the button is released, replace the self-cancelling unit.

Note the following concerning the self-cancelling turn signal system:

a. Yamaha recommends that the turn signals be shut off manually after a turn is completed.

b. If the self-cancelling unit fails, the turn signals can be used manually by simply disconnecting the 6-prong connector from the unit.

Bulbs

Headlight	12v, 50/40W
Taillight-Stoplight	12v, 8/27W
Turn signal bulbs	12v, 27W
Parking light, front	12v, 5W
Parking light, rear	12v, 8W
Neutral indicator	12v, 3W
High beam indicator	12v, 3W
Charging light	12v, 3W
Turn signal pilot	12v, 3W
Instrument lights	12v, 3W
Taillight warning light	12v, 3W
Brake lining warning light	12v, 3W
Stoplight warning light	12v, 3W

WIRING DIAGRAMS

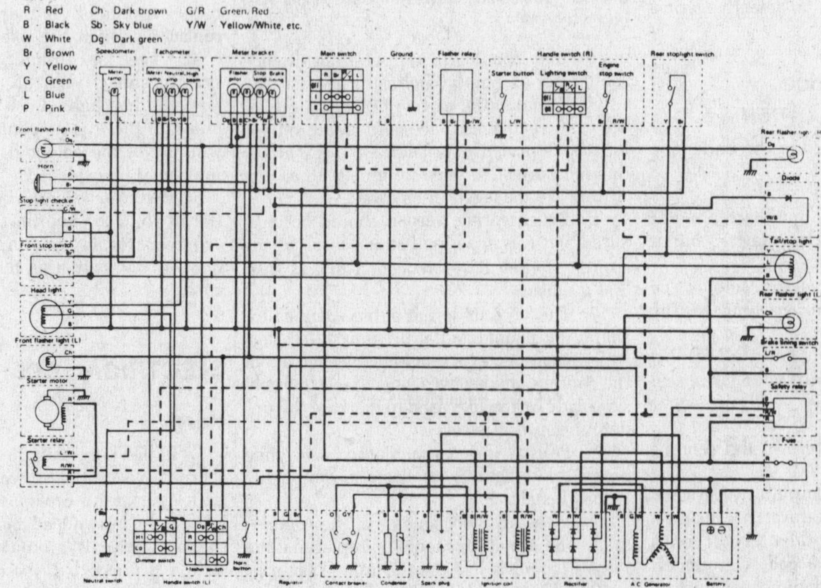

XS650B/C

WIRING DIAGRAMS

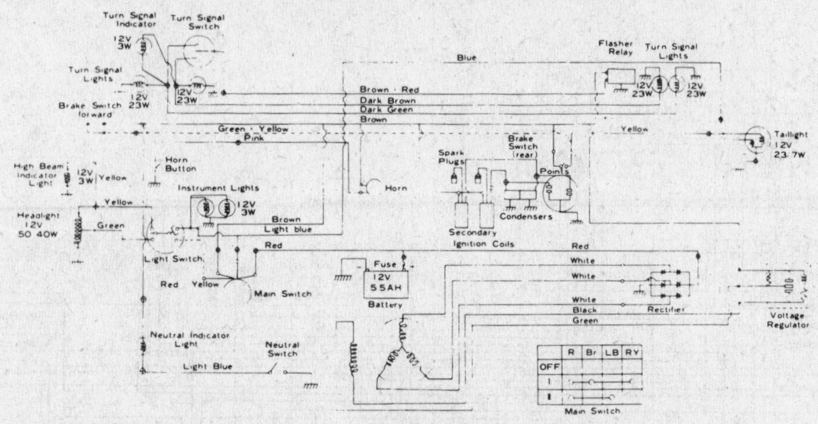

XS1/1B2

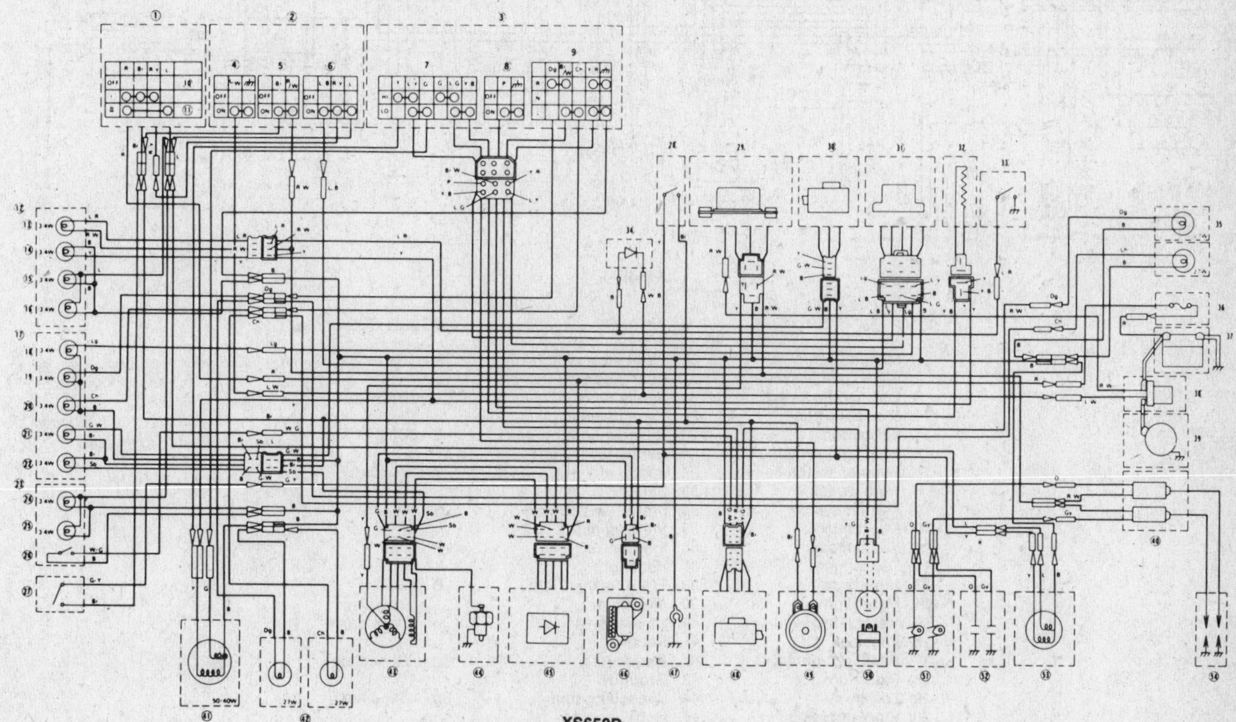

XS650D

COMPONENT CODE

1. Main switch
2. Right handle switch
3. Left handle switch
4. Starter button
5. Kill button
6. Headlight switch
7. Dimmer
8. Horn button
9. Flasher
10. Key removal
11. Key removal
12. Tach
13. Brake wear
14. High beam
15. Meter light
16. Meter light
17. Pilot box
18. Headlight outage
19. Right turn signal
20. Left turn signal
21. Stoplight
22. Neutral indicator
23. Speedometer
24–25. Meter lights
26. Speedometer sensor
27. Front stop switch
28. Rear stop switch
29. Safety relay
30. Light checker
31. Reverse lighting
32. Resistor
33. Brake wear
34. Diode
35. Rear flasher
36. Fuse
37. Battery
38. Starter switch
39. Starter motor
40. Ignition coil
41. Headlight
42. Front flasher light
43. Alternator
44. Neutral switch
45. Rectifier
46. Regulator
47. Ground
48. Cancelling unit
49. Horn
50. Flasher relay
51. Points
52. Condenser
53. Taillight
54. Spark plugs

COLOR CODE

R = Red
Br = Brown
L = Blue
Y = Yellow
G = Green
P = Pink
B = Black
Dg = Dark green
Ch = Chocolate
Sb = Sky blue
W = White
Gy = Gray
O = Orange
Lg = Light green

WIRING DIAGRAMS

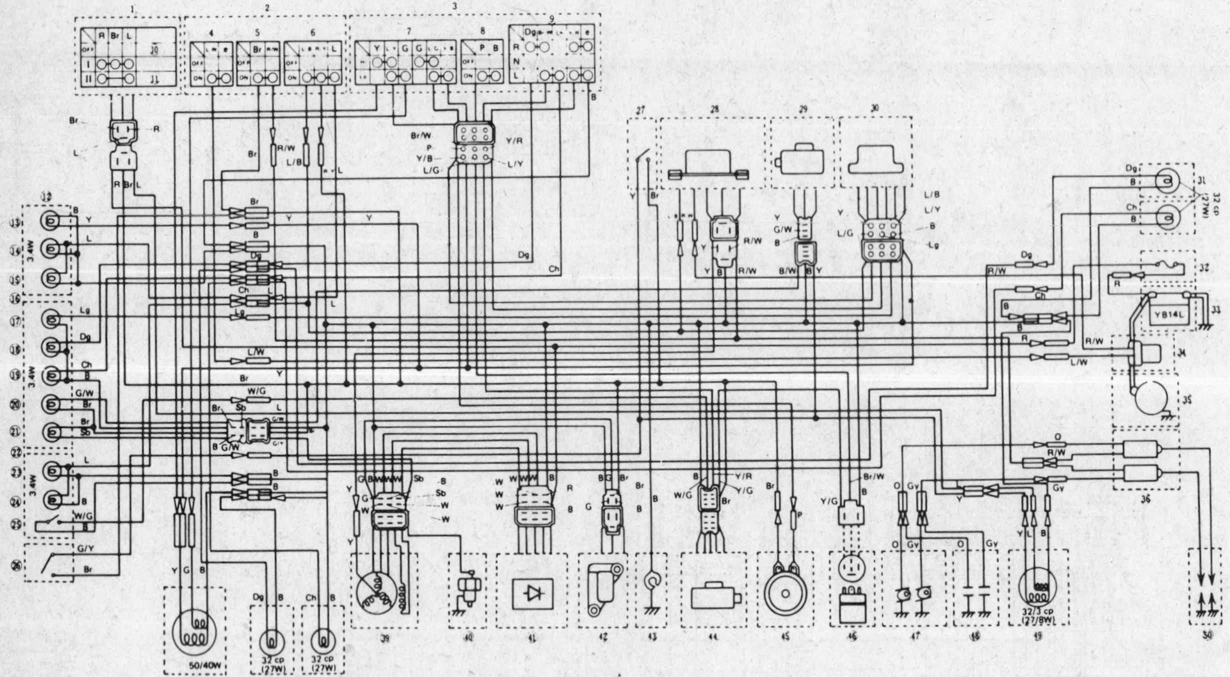

XS650E-F

COMPONENT CODE

1. Main switch
2. Right handle switch
3. Left handle switch
4. Starter button
5. Kill button
6. Headlight switch
7. Dimmer switch
8. Horn switch
9. Flasher switch
10. Key removal
11. Key removal
12. Tachometer
13. High beam
14. Meter light
15. Meter light
16. Pilot box
17. Headlight outage
18. Right turn
19. Left turn
20. Stoplight
21. Neutral
22. Speedometer
23. Meter light
24. Meter light
25. Lead switch
26. Front stop switch
27. Rear stop switch
28. Safety relay
29. Light checker
30. Reverse lighting unit
31. Rear flasher light
32. Fuse
33. Battery
34. Starter switch
35. Starting motor
36. Ignition coil
37. Headlight
38. Front flasher light
39. Alternator
40. Neutral switch
41. Rectifier
42. Regulator
43. Ground
44. Cancelling unit
45. Horn
46. Flasher relay
47. Points
48. Condenser
49. Taillight
50. Spark plugs

COLOR CODE

R = Red

Br = Brown

L = Blue

Y = Yellow

G = Green

P = Pink

B = Black

Dg = Dark green

Ch = Chocolate

Sb = Sky blue

W = White

Gy = Gray

O = Orange

Lg = Light green

CHASSIS

WHEELS

Front

REMOVAL AND INSTALLATION

1. Support the front wheel off the ground by placing a jack or similar support beneath the engine.

CAUTION: *Be sure that the motorcycle is firmly supported.*

2. Remove the axle nut.
3. Disconnect the speedometer cable at the hub. On drum brake models, disconnect the brake cable.
4. Loosen the axle cap nuts on forks so equipped, or the axle pinch-bolt on the right fork slider on earlier model forks. Pull out the axle and remove the wheel.

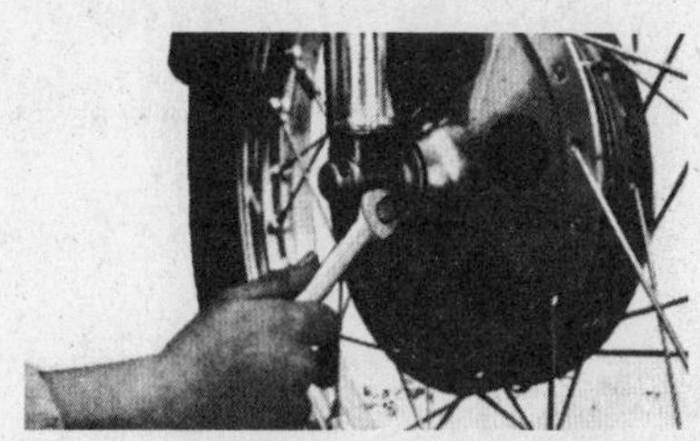

Loosening the pinch bolt

Loosening the axle cap nuts

5. On disc brake models, place a small sheet of cardboard between the brake pads to prevent residual line pressure from forcing them together.

NOTE: *Do not apply the brake while the wheel is removed.*

6. Installation is the reverse of removal. When installing the wheel on drum-brake models, be sure that the brake plate is engaged with the brake anchor on the slider. Position the speedometer drive box so that the cable has no sharp bends.

Tighten the axle nut to 50–72 ft lbs. Tighten the axle cap nuts (if fitted) to 15 ft lbs. Be sure to tighten the forwardmost nut first.

Fit the speedometer drive so that the cable is not sharply bent

Rear

REMOVAL AND INSTALLATION

Rear Drum Brake

1. Disconnect the rear drive chain.
2. Pull out the clip which secures the brake anchor to the brake plate, remove the nut and washers, and detach the anchor from the plate.
3. Disconnect the rear brake rod from the lever on the brake plate by removing the brake adjuster nut and depressing the pedal.
4. Remove the axle nut cotter pin (use a new one when installing the wheel), and remove the axle nut.
5. Loosen the chain adjuster bolt locknuts, back off the adjuster bolts, and bend them down and out of the way.
6. Pull out the axle. Remove the spacer on the right side. Remove the right-side chain adjuster plate.
7. Take out the brake plate, and have an assistant lean the machine to the left while pulling the rear wheel assembly back and out of the frame.
8. Installation is the reverse of removal. Tighten the rear axle nut to 87–130 ft lbs.

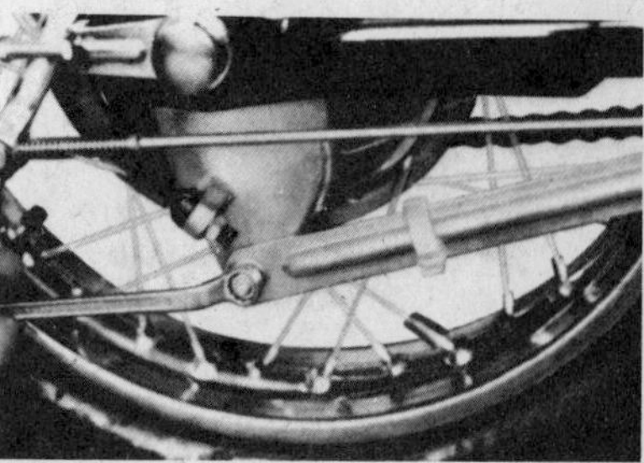

Removing the brake anchor bolt

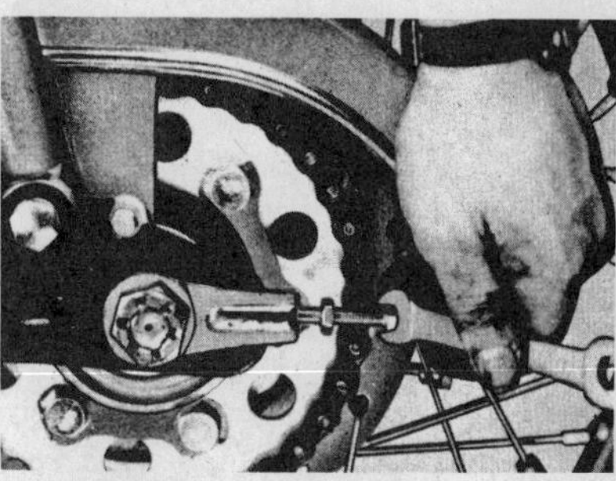

Loosening the chain adjuster bolt

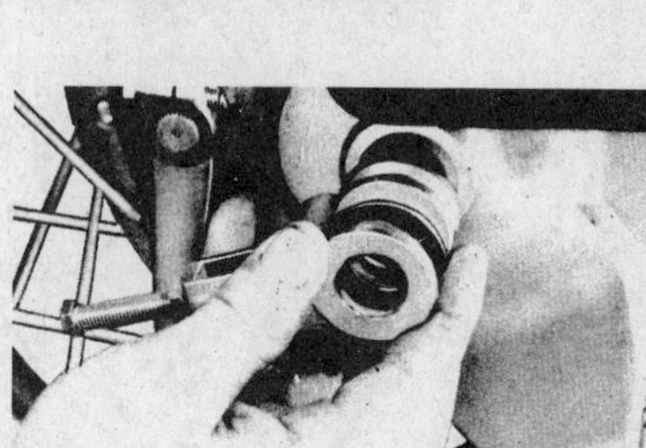

Removing the chain adjuster and spacer

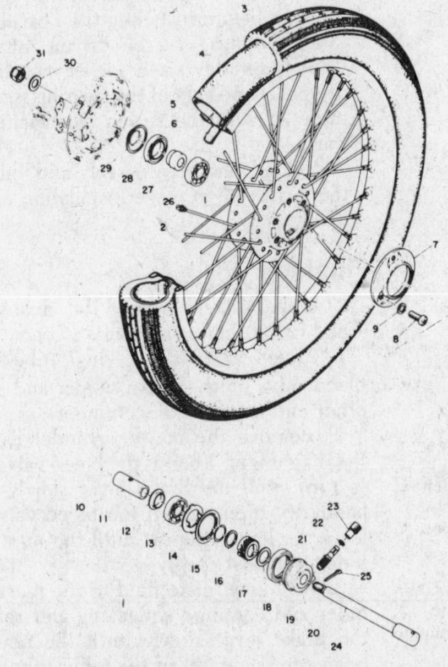

1. Front hub
2. Spoke set
3. Front tire
4. Tube
5. Rim
6. Rim band
7. Housing cover
8. Screw
9. Lockwasher
10. Bearing spacer
11. Spacer flange
12. Wheel bearing
13. Meter clutch
14. Clutch meter retainer
15. Stop ring
16. Thrust 2 washer
17. Speedometer drive gear
18. Thrust 1 washer
19. Oil seal
20. Gear unit housing
21. Speedometer worm gear
22. Washer
23. Bushing
24. Axle
25. Cotter pin
26. Wheel bearing
27. Axle spacer
28. Oil seal
29. Hub dust cover
30. Washer
31. Axle nut

Front wheel assembly

Rear Disc Brake

1. A special tool is needed to remove the rear wheel. This tool, a length of wire with hooks to support the rear wheel, is supplied in the tool kit.
2. With the machine on the side stand, attach one end of the tool to the frame hook. Compress the shocks as much as possible and hook the other end of the tool to the swing arm. Place the machine on the center stand.
3. Disconnect the drive chain.
4. Remove the axle nut cotter pin and unscrew and remove the axle nut.

5. Hold the brake caliper in position so it will not fall out of place, and pull out the axle. Remove the rear wheel assembly.

NOTE: *Do not apply the brake while the wheel is off the machine.*

6. Installation is the reverse of removal. Before fitting the wheel, check that there is sufficient clearance between the brake pads to install the disc. Grease the lips of the wheel bearing grease seals. Tighten the axle nut to 87–130 ft lbs.

Wheel Bearings

REMOVAL

1. After removing the wheel, remove the brake plate on drum brake models, or the brake disc on disc brake machines.
2. Remove the speedometer drive box on disc brake machines.
3. Remove any wheel bearing covers or retainers fitted to either side of the hub.
4. Pry out the grease seals. Once removed, the seals should be replaced with new ones.
5. Reach through the hub with a suitable punch, move the wheel bearing spacer as far as possible to one side to achieve a purchase on the wheel bearing, and drive it out. Remove the spacer. Drive out the remaining wheel bearing from the other side of the hub.

INSPECTION

1. Wash the wheel bearings thoroughly in a solvent to remove all of the old grease.
2. Inspect the general condition of the bearings. There should be no rust, pitting, or obvious signs of wear or damage on either balls or races.
3. Slowly rotate the bearings. Rotation should be smooth, noiseless, and free of binding or unevenness. If any of the above conditions exist, both bearings should be replaced.
4. Place each bearing on a flat surface and hold the inner race firmly in place. Attempt to move the outer race up and down. If any play is evident, the bearings should be replaced.
5. If equipment is available, a dial gauge can be used to check bearing run-out. Pass the axle through each bearing in turn and check the axial and diametrical run-out with the gauge. If axial run-out exceeds 0.1 mm (0.004 in.) or if diametrical run-out is greater than 0.05 mm (0.002 in.), the bearings should be replaced.

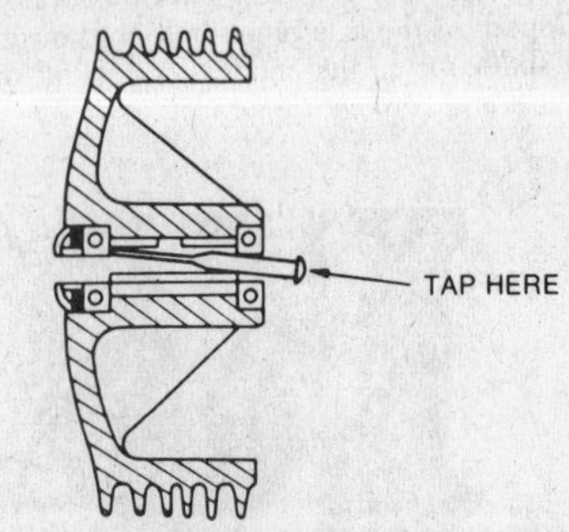

Removing a wheel bearing

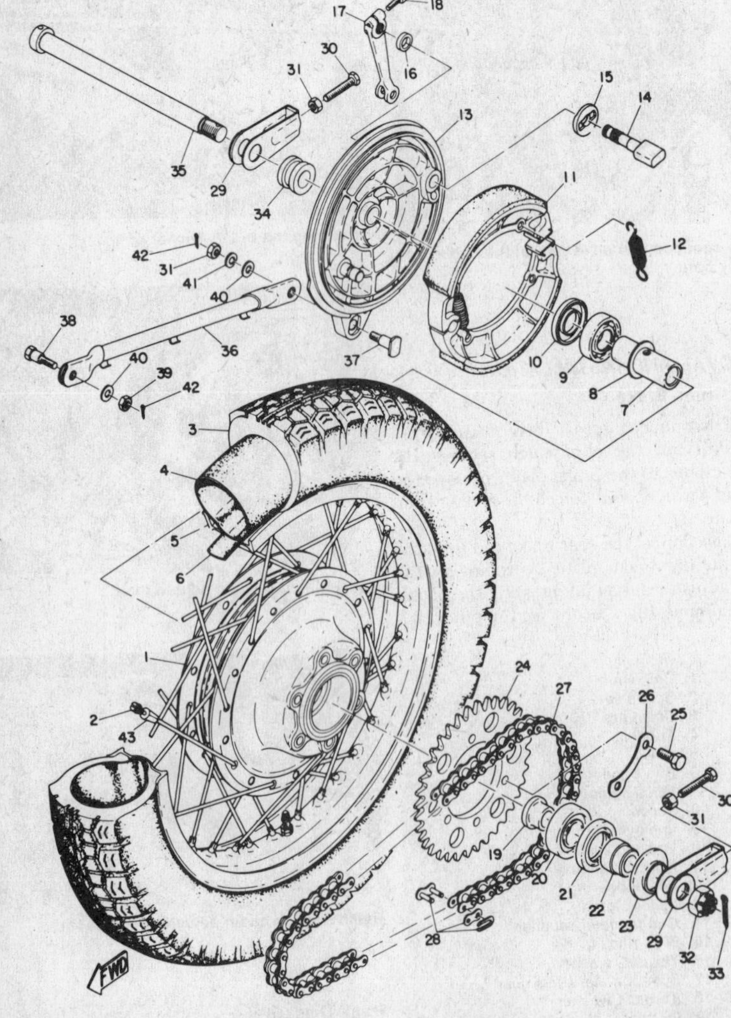

1. Rear hub
2. Spoke set
3. Rear tire
4. Tube
5. Rim
6. Rim band
7. Bearing spacer
8. Spacer flange
9. Bearing
10. Oil seal
11. Brake shoe comp.
12. Return spring
13. Brake shoe backing plate
14. Brake camshaft
15. Camshaft shim
16. Camshaft seal
17. Camshaft lever
18. Bolt
19. Spacer
20. Bearing
21. Oil seal
22. Axle spacer
23. Dust cover
24. Sprocket
25. Fitting bolt
26. Lockplate
27. Chain
28. Master link
29. Chain puller
30. Chain adjusting bolt
31. Adjusting locknut
32. Axle nut
33. Cotter pin
34. Axle spacer
35. Axle
36. Brake anchor
37. Anchor bolt
38. Anchor bolt
39. Nut
40. Washer
41. Spring washer
42. Cotter pin
43. Wheel balancer weight

Rear wheel assembly

DISC BRAKE SERVICE

To check diametrical run-out, the dial indicator is placed directly on top of the outer race and the race moved up and down.

To check axial run-out, the gauge is positioned to bear against the side of the outer race and the race moved back and forth while holding the inner race in place.

INSTALLATION

Assembly is the reverse of the above.

Note the following points:

a. Pack the bearings with a good grade of wheel bearing grease. Put a small handful of the grease in the hub as well.

b. Do not forget to install the spacer in the hub before installing the bearing.

c. Bearings may be driven into place using a suitably sized socket or a bearing driver. If one side of the bearing is sealed, install it with the sealed side facing outward.

d. Use new grease seals and lubricate them with oil to make installation easier.

Flushing

The brake system should be flushed out every 12,000 miles, or every 2 years.

1. Attach a length of vinyl tube to the bleed valve on the brake caliper and put the other end into a small container.
2. Remove the master cylinder cap, and the diaphragm. Loosen the bleed valve about ½ turn. Pull the brake lever slowly to the handgrip, then tighten the bleed valve. Release the lever. Repeat until the master cylinder is almost empty.
3. Add new brake fluid to the master cylinder and continue squeezing and releasing the brake lever slowly until the new fluid begins to come out of the vinyl tube. Bleed the system as outlined below.

Bleeding

The brake hydraulic system must be bled whenever any part of the system has been disconnected or removed for service. When refilling the master cylinder reservoir, use only brake fluid conforming to DOT 3 specifications. Any brand meeting this requirement is acceptable. The brake fluid container of all reputable brands will be plainly marked with the standards the fluid meets or exceeds.

NOTE: *It is sometimes helpful to let the cycle sit for several hours before bleeding the system. Pulling and tapping on the lines will help expel any air bubbles trapped in the system. If you find that you can't get the system bled properly and the master cylinder has been dry for awhile, the seals inside the cylinder may have become dried and cracked. In this case rebuild the master cylinder.*

1. Top up the reservoir with brake fluid and replace the cap to keep dirt and moisture out and the fluid in. Cover the gas tank with a thick cloth to avoid damage due to spilled brake fluid.
2. Attach one end of a small diameter rubber hose to the bleed valve on the caliper, and place the other end in a jar which contains several inches of clean, new brake fluid. Be sure that the end of the hose is submerged in this fluid. Arrange the hose so that it loops upward after leaving the bleed valve, and see that it has no kinks or sharp bends.
3. Pump the brake lever rapidly several times until some resistance is felt and, holding the lever against the resistance, open the bleed valve about one-half turn. When the lever bottoms, close the valve (do not overtighten) and then release the lever.
4. Repeat the operation until no more air is released out of the hose and the brake lever is firm in operation. Check the fluid level in the reservoir often to make sure that it doesn't go dry and draw more air into the system. Do not reuse fluid that has been pumped out of the system. Do not use fluid that has been stored for more than a few weeks after the seal on its container has been opened, as brake fluid will absorb moisture from the air and may corrode the master cylinder and caliper.
5. Refill the reservoir to the level mark when through (but do not overfill). Avoid overtightening the cap or fluid will weep around the cap edge.

FRONT DISC BRAKE

Pad Replacement (Early Models)

Brake pads are easily removed and replaced after removing the front wheel and prying the pads carefully out of the caliper with a screwdriver.

Bleeding the brake

Note that fitting new pads in place of a pair which were considerably worn will result in a rise in the reservoir fluid level. Excess fluid may be drained off by temporarily loosening the bleed screw on the caliper.

Removing the brake pads

Pad Replacement (Late Models)

1. Unbolt the caliper from the fork slider.
2. Remove the pad screw which secures the fixed pad on the wheel side of the caliper. Remove the fixed pad.
3. Remove the piston pad.
4. Installation is the reverse of removal. Secure the fixed pad phillips screw with a non-permanent thread-locking compound.

Caliper (Early Models)

REMOVAL AND DISASSEMBLY

NOTE: *A compressed air supply will be necessary to remove the pistons from the caliper.*

1. Use a length of tape to hold the brake lever in the ON position.
2. Disconnect the brake line from the caliper. Cover the end of the line with a small plastic bag.
3. Unbolt the caliper from the fork slider, lift it up, and remove it.
4. Remove the pads. Remove the two bridge bolts and the hex-head caliper bolts, and separate the caliper halves.
5. Remove the seal from the fluid passage.
6. Apply compressed air to the fluid passage in each caliper half to force out the pistons.

Fixed pad securing screws

Removing the caliper bolts

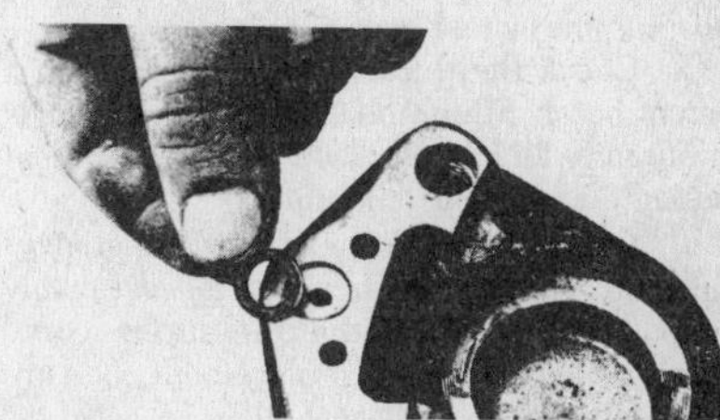
Removing the fluid seal. This seal must be replaced when assembling

Removing the pistons from the caliper with compressed air

NOTE: *This is the only recommended method of removing the pistons.*

7. Remove the piston seal and the dust seal from each caliper half.

INSPECTION

NOTE: *Caliper components should be kept free of any solvent. Parts should be cleaned in fresh, clean brake fluid only.*

1. Check the pads for wear or scoring and replace them as a set if necessary.
2. Inspect the pistons for scoring or other signs of wear. Replace as necessary.
3. Replace any damaged seal in the unit. All seals should be replaced every two years regardless of appearance.
4. The two bridge bolts must be replaced each time that they are removed.

ASSEMBLY AND INSTALLATION

1. Clean all parts in new brake fluid.
2. Install the dust seal and piston seal in the caliper halves.
3. Coat the caliper cylinder walls and the pistons with new brake fluid, and then carefully insert each piston into its own caliper half.

Be sure that the piston goes in smoothly.

4. Install the caliper seals.
5. Fit the two caliper halves together, and replace the two hex-head bolts and tighten them to 16–23 ft lbs.
6. Install new bridge bolts and tighten them to 56–71 ft lbs.
7. Install the pads. It will be necessary to

push the pistons back by hand when installing the pads.

8. Replace the caliper on the fork slider, tightening the bolts to 30–37.2 ft lbs.

9. Refit the brake line to the caliper and tighten it to 10–13.4 ft lbs.

Brake Disc (Early Models)

1. Check the disc for run-out by securing a dial gauge to the fork slider. If run-out is 0.15 mm (0.006 in.) or more, remove the disc and inspect it closely. If the disc is not warped, suspect the wheel bearings.

2. Check the thickness of the disc with a micrometer. Minimum allowable thickness is 6.5 mm (0.26 in.). Replace the disc if it measures less than this amount.

3. Check the disc for scoring or grooves and replace it if the surface is not reasonably smooth. In the event that the disc is scored badly enough to need replacement, be sure to fit new brake pads as well.

4. Clean the disc surfaces as thoroughly as possible, removing any dirt or grease. Use a quickly evaporating disc cleaning agent, several brands of which are readily available in spray cans.

Caliper (Late Models)

REMOVAL

1. Disconnect the brake line from the caliper. Plug the end of the brake line to prevent loss of brake fluid.

2. Remove the mounting bolts and take the caliper from the fork slider.

DISASSEMBLY

1. Remove the phillips screw which secures the fixed pad and take out the pad and pad spring.

2. Remove the piston pad.

3. Remove the caliper support bolt. Separate the caliper and support bracket. Remove the piston dust seal and retaining ring.

4. Apply compressed air to the brake line fitting on the caliper and force out the piston.

CAUTION: *Be sure your fingers are clear of the piston, as it may come out with some force.*

5. Remove the piston seal.

Caliper mounting bolts

INSPECTION

1. Clean all parts in new brake fluid. Do not use gasoline or other solvents.

2. All rubber parts should be replaced with new ones once the caliper has been disassembled. These parts should also be replaced every two years as a matter of preventive maintenance.

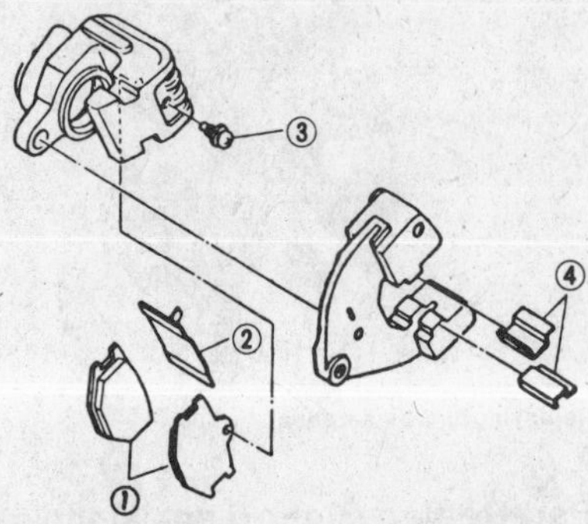

Caliper pad components: 1, pads; 2, pad spring; 3, screw; 4, retainers

3. Check the piston for scoring or other obvious signs of wear, and replace it if damage is noted. Check the caliper bore as well.

ASSEMBLY

1. Using a new caliper support bolt is recommended. As noted above, all rubber parts must be replaced as well.

2. Lightly lubricate the piston seal with fresh brake fluid and install it in the caliper. Be sure that the seal is properly seated.

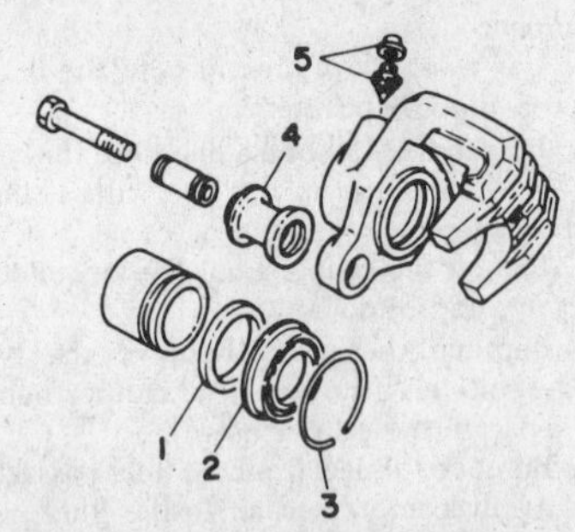

Caliper components: 1, piston seal; 2, boot; 3, dust cover clip; 4, bushing boot; 5, bleed screw

3. Lubricate the sides of the piston with brake fluid and install it.

4. Fit the caliper and support bracket together, not forgetting the bushing and bushing boot. Install the support bolt and tighten it to 11–15 ft lbs.

5. Install the brake pads. Secure the fixed pad phillips screw with a non-permanent thread-locking compound. Grease the pad-shim contact area before installation. Bend each tab of the shim over the piston pad.

INSTALLATION

1. Tighten the caliper mounting bolts to 21–29 ft lbs.

2. Tighten the brake line banjo bolt to 18–25 ft lbs. Bleed the system.

Brake Disc (Late Models)

The brake disc normally requires no service of any kind. However, if the disc becomes scored for any reason, it should be replaced and a new set of pads should be installed. A badly scored disc will reduce the effectiveness of the brake and shorten pad life considerably. If the front brake lever oscillates or fluctuates when the brake is applied at speed, the indication is that the brake disc is warped or bent. Check the run-out of the disc with a dial indicator and replace it if run-out exceeds 0.15 mm (0.006 in.). Measure disc thickness. If it is less than 4.5 mm (0.18 in.), it should be replaced. To replace the disc:

1. Remove the wheel.

2. Bend back the locktabs, unscrew the bolts, and remove the disc from the hub.

3. Mount the new disc on the hub and tighten the bolts evenly, using new locktabs or thread-locking compound to secure them. Proper torque is 12–16 ft lbs.

4. Examine the brake pads and replace them if they are close to the limit of wear or have worn in an unusual pattern.

Master Cylinder (All Models)

REMOVAL

1. Disconnect the front brake light switch leads.

2. Remove the brake lever. Note the return spring.

3. Disconnect the brake line from the master cylinder. Take adequate precautions to avoid spillage.

Removing the brake lever and spring

4. Remove the two master cylinder handlebar clamp bolts and remove the master cylinder assembly.

DISASSEMBLY

1. Remove the master cylinder cap and diaphragm and drain off and discard the brake fluid.

2. Remove the master cylinder rubber boot.

3. Remove the snap-ring. Take out the piston assembly. The spring will remain in the master cylinder.

4. Remove the spring and stopper valve.

5. Remove the stopper plate and the cylinder cups.

INSPECTION

1. Wash all parts in new brake fluid only.

2. Check the master cylinder port for clogging due to foreign matter.

3. Be sure that the reservoir is clean.

4. Check the walls of the master cylinder for grooves or score marks.

5. Check the outlet end for dents or other damage.

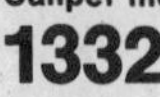

In the event of any permanent damage, replace the master cylinder body.

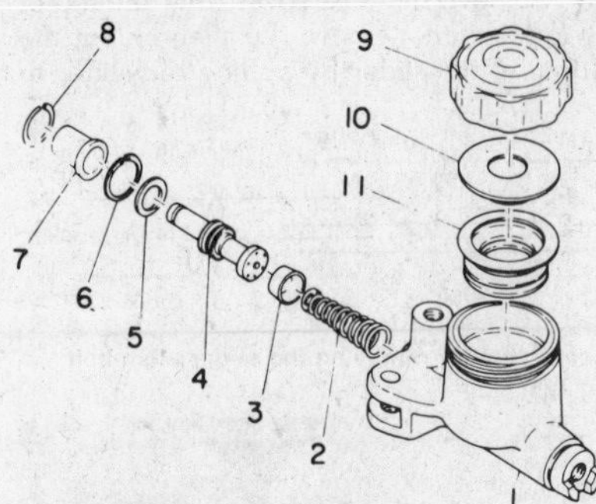

1. Master cylinder reservoir body
2. Spring
3. Cup
4. Piston assembly
5. Seal
6. Lockring
7. Boot
8. Snapring
9. Reservoir cap
10. Washer
11. Diaphragm

Master cylinder components

Removing the snap-ring

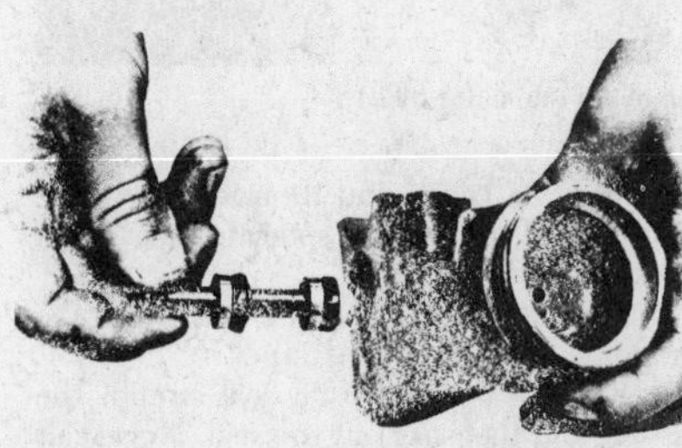

Removing the piston assembly

6. Check the piston for wear or rust, and replace as necessary.

7. Check the condition of the cylinder cup noting any evidence of grooved wear on the contact surface. Replace if any is evident.

8. Check all rubber parts for wear, damage, or swelling and replace them as necessary. Note that all rubber parts should be replaced every two years regardless of appearance.

9. Check the reservoir diaphragm for cracks or damage to the edges and the accordion pleats. Check the diaphragm and the boot for swelling.

These components should be replaced if damaged or worn, and replaced every two years regardless of appearance.

10. The master cylinder spring minimum length is 60.4 mm. Replace it if it is shorter than this or if it shows signs of damage.

11. Check the brake hose and line for cracks or seepage. The brake hose should be replaced every 4 years regardless of condition.

12. When installing the hose and line, note that they should not contact the forks or frame at any point except where attachment clips are fitted.

ASSEMBLY

1. Soak the cups in new brake fluid for a time before assembly.

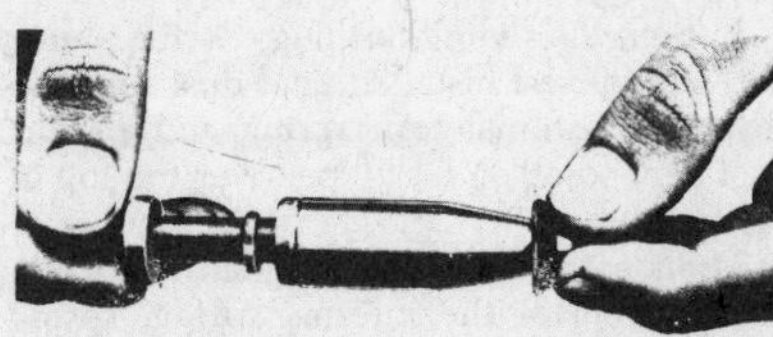

Using the special tool to install the cylinder cup

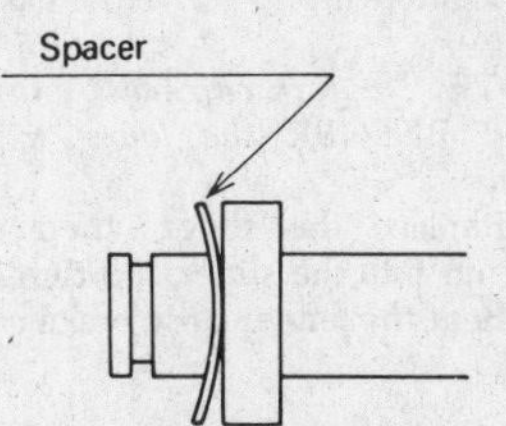

Be sure that the spacer is properly installed

2. Use the special cylinder cup installer when fitting the cup to the piston.

3. Install the stopper plate into the master cylinder. Insert the spring and valve.

4. Insert the piston into the master cylinder. Take care not to scratch the piston or cylinder wall. Fit the snap-ring. Be sure that it is firmly seated.

5. Fit the boot into the grooves of the master cylinder and piston.

INSTALLATION

Bolt the master cylinder to the handlebar. Connect the brake and tighten the banjo bolt to 17–20 ft lbs. Fill the master cylinder with fresh brake fluid and bleed the system.

REAR DISC BRAKE

The rear disc brake components are virtually identical to those for the late model front system except for the method of mounting.

To remove the rear caliper, disconnect the brake line from the caliper, unbolt the brake anchor, and remove the rear axle.

For all service procedures, refer to the "Front Disc Brake" section above.

DRUM BRAKES

1. All rear drum brakes are single-leading shoe units, while the drum fitted to the front of early 650 cc models is a twin-leading shoe unit.

Removing the brake shoes from the plate

2. Brake shoes should be inspected for wear. Lining thickness, when new, is 4 mm (0.16 in.), and brakes should be replaced if lining is less than 2 mm (0.08 in.) thick.

3. Brake shoes should also be checked for scoring or for an oil-soaked condition. If scored, the linings should be replaced and the drum checked for scoring as well. If oil soaked, replace.

4. Even minor imperfections of the brake drum should be removed by having the drum turned on a lathe.

5. Linings should be sandpapered to remove any glaze or dirt, then cleaned thoroughly prior to installation.

6. The brake shoes can be removed from the backing plate by pulling them up and off, after disengaging them from the anchor pin. Check the brake springs for distortion, corrosion, or other damage.

7. After removing the brake shoes, the brake cam (or cams on twin-leading shoe brakes) should be tapped out of the backing plate. Remove any old grease from the cams and then take off any rust or corrosion with medium grade sandpaper. Clean the cams thoroughly in a solvent; lubricate with chassis grease before installing in the backing plate. Check the condition of the cam seal and replace if necessary.

8. An off-on-off feeling while applying the brake may be due to a warped drum. Most often it is possible to correct this condition by having the drum turned down on a lathe. Most machine shops have the facilities to accomplish this task.

FRONT FORKS

XS1, XS1B

Two different styles of forks are fitted. Early model forks have an external fork spring covered by a rubber boot.

Later model forks have an internal spring, chrome fork tubes, and a dust cover over the top of the fork slider.

In the following procedures, make allowances for the differences in each type.

REMOVAL AND DISASSEMBLY

1. Remove the front wheel and fender. On disc brake models, remove the caliper from the fork slider.

2. Lift up the dust cover from the top of the slider, or move the boot out of the way, and use a strap wrench to unscrew the outer nut from the slider. Use the axle, inserted through the sliders, to keep them from turning while the nut is unscrewed.

The chrome may be protected with a piece of rubber before fitting the strap wrench.

If a strap wrench is not available, it may be possible to remove the outer nut by tightening a large heater hose clamp on it (with a piece of rubber beneath it to protect the chrome). A vise-grips or large pliers can then be used on the clamp worm screw to turn the nut. The slider must be held in place while removing the nut.

3. Pull the slider down and free of the fork tube. Drain out the fork oil.

4. Take out the springs, if they are the internal type.

5. To remove the fork tube, remove the handlebars, the fork crown bolts, and loosen the lower triple clamp pinch-bolt. Pull the tube down and free of the triple clamps.

6. Remove the external fork spring and boot, if fitted. Remove the dust cover and dust seal, if fitted.

7. Remove the outer nut, O-ring, sliding bushing, spacer, and spring seat.

INSPECTION

1. The fork oil seals are pressed into the top of the outer nuts. Seals should be replaced every time the fork is disassembled.

NOTE: *Grease the lips of new seals before installation.*

2. Check the straightness of the fork tubes. Slightly bent tubes may be straightened with a press, but if the tubes are kinked or the metal buckled, replacement is the only solution.

3. Check the oil seal contact area on the outside of each tube and make sure that it is free of dents, scoring, rust or other surface irregularities which would make oil sealing impossible.

4. Check the fit of the sliding bushing on the fork tube. When new, the bushing should have a clearance of 0.2 mm (0.008 in.). If clearance exceeds 0.5 mm (0.020 in.), replace the sliding bush.

5. Note any scoring on the inner surface of the sliding bushing, or score marks on the surface of the fork tube where the bushing contacts it.

6. Check the condition of each fork spring, noting any collapsed coils, fatigue cracks, or other damage, and replace them as necessary. Springs for each leg should be of equal length.

7. Check the condition of the slider and fork crown bolt O-rings, and replace them if necessary.

ASSEMBLY AND INSTALLATION

1. Wash all metal parts thoroughly in solvent.

2. Refit the sliding bushing, O-ring, outer nut with oil seal installed, and dust seal and cover, or external fork spring and rubber boot depending on fork type, over the top of the fork tube.

3. Slide the fork tube through the triple clamps, replace the internal spring, spring seat, and spacer; refit the fork cap bolt and tighten it.

4. Tighten the lower triple clamp pinch-bolt.

NOTE: *The fork cap bolts must be tightened* BEFORE *the lower triple clamp bolts.*

5. Replace the slider, then screw the outer nut into the slider and tighten it.

6. Refit the fender, disc brake caliper, and wheel.

All Other Models

REMOVAL AND DISASSEMBLY

1. Remove the front wheel and fender. Remove the caliper from the right fork slider. Remove the fork cap bolts.

2. Loosen the upper and lower triple clamp pinch-bolts for one of the fork legs, then pull down on the fork leg and remove it from the machine. Drain the oil out of the top of the fork tube. Remove the other fork leg in the same way.

3. Remove the dust cover from the top of the fork slider. Remove the allen bolt at the bottom of the slider by pulling the slider to the end of its travel and then loosening the allen bolt. If this fails, a special socket must be made as shown.

4. Separate the fork slider from the tube assembly. Take out the damper.

5. Remove the slider oil seal circlip, the washer, and then pry out the seal. New seals must always be used upon reassembly.

INSPECTION

1. Check that the fork tubes are perfectly true. If bent, they may be straightened with a press. If the tubes are kinked, or the metal creased, the tube must be replaced.

Check the outer surface of the fork tubes along the oil seal contact area. Any rust, nicks or grooves on the tube must be removed or the seals will leak.

2. Check the fork spring for general condition, noting any closed coils or fatigue wear. Both fork springs must be of equal length.

3. Check the damper piston for wear or damage.

ASSEMBLY AND INSTALLATION

1. Clean all parts thoroughly.

2. New fork seals must be used.

3. Drive in the new seal with a suitably sized socket or drift, refit the circlip, and install the slider onto the tube assembly. Replace and tighten the allen bolt in the fork slider bottom.

NOTE: *Lubricating the seal lips will aid in installation.*

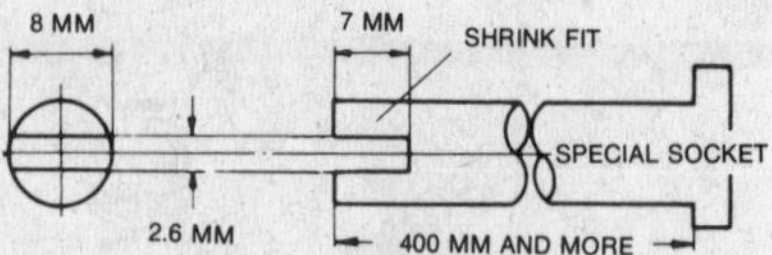

Special tool for removing the slider allen bolt

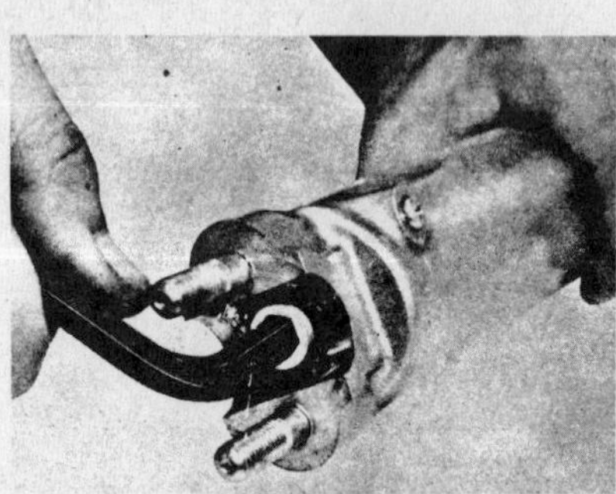

Removing the slider allen bolt

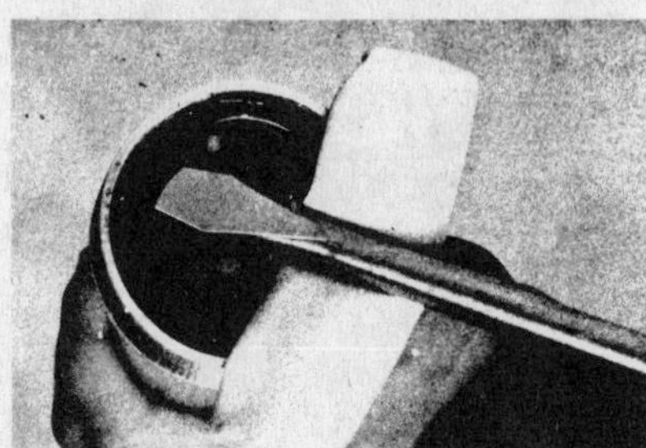

Removing the slider oil seal

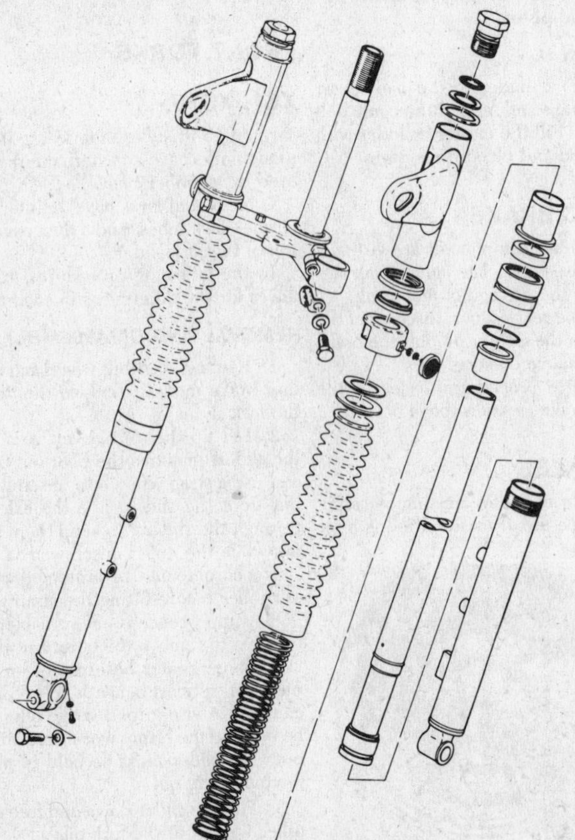

Early XS1 front fork assembly

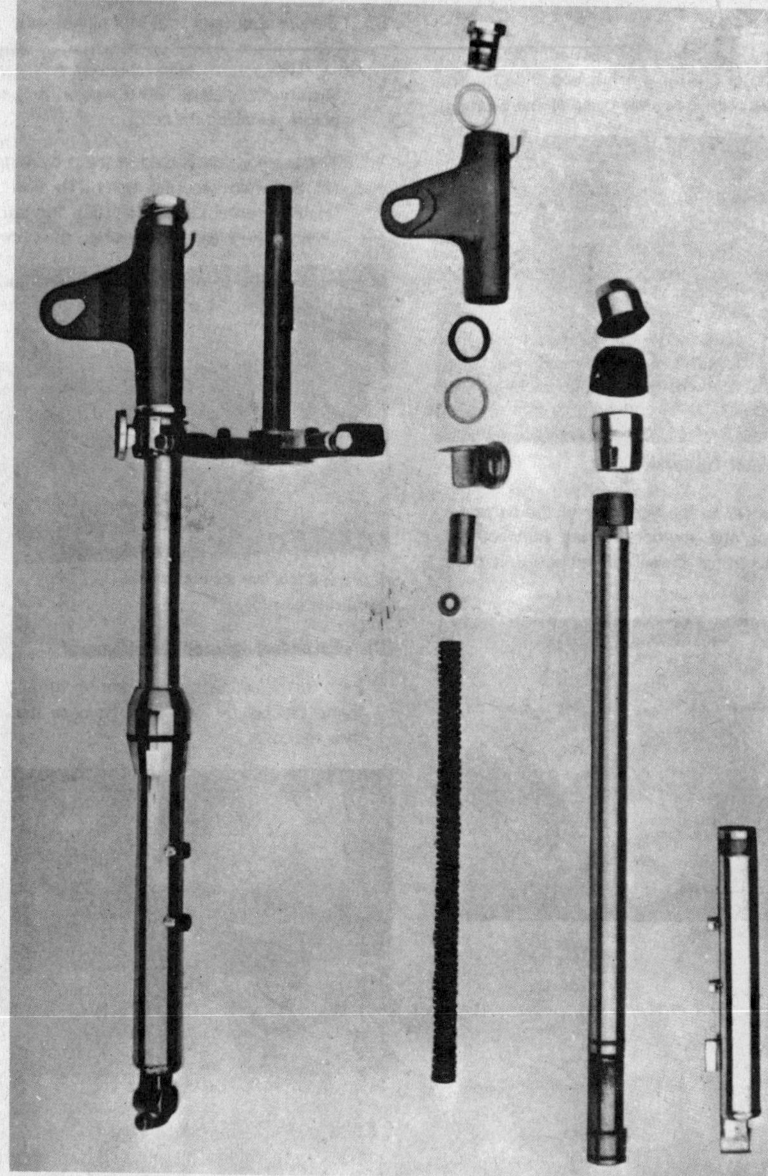

Later XS1B fork assembly

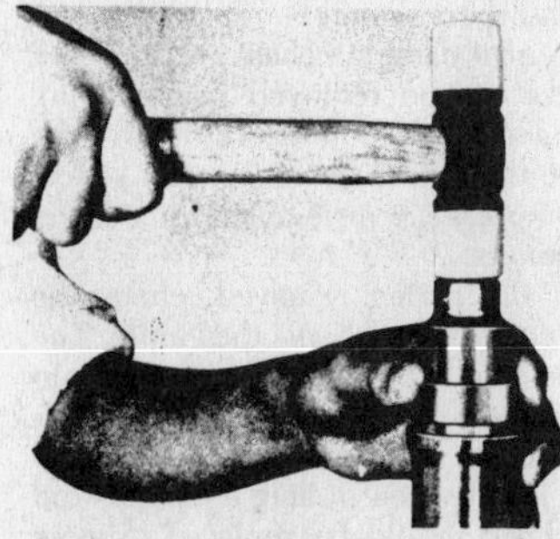

Installing a slider oil seal

4. Put the dust cover into position over the top of the slider.

5. Install the assembled fork leg up through the triple clamps. Tighten the pinch-bolts to 5.8–9 ft lbs.

6. Add the correct amount and grade of fork oil (see the "Maintenance Data" chart and install the fork cap bolts.

STEERING STEM ASSEMBLY

Bearing Adjustment

1. The steering stem bearings are uncaged $^{3}/_{16}$ in. (upper) or ¼ in. (lower) balls. They are adjusted by means of a ring nut beneath the upper triple clamp.

2. To check bearing adjustment, support the front wheel off the ground. Grasp the tip of the front fender and place your other hand beneath the lower triple clamp at the frame lug.

3. Attempt to move the fork by pulling up on the tip of the fender. If play or movement can be felt at the lower triple clamp, the bearings are adjusted too loosely or are worn. An alternate method is to grasp the fork sliders and attempt to move them back and forth in line with the motorcycle. No play should be noted.

4. Turn the forks slowly from lock-to-lock. Movement should be smooth, silent, and effortless. If any binding or uneven movement is felt, the balls and races are either too tightly adjusted or they are worn. If the steering feels uniformly stiff, the bearings are too tightly adjusted. If any noise is noted, the bearings are damaged or some are missing.

5. With the front wheel off the ground, release the front forks from a few degrees off the centered position. The fork should fall freely to either side of their own weight. If they will not, the bearings are too tightly adjusted, the steering stem is bent, the races are extremely worn, or some of the bearings are missing.

Steering head bearing adjuster nut

6. To adjust the bearings, remove the gas tank. The bearings are adjusted by means of the adjuster nut under the upper triple clamp.

7. Tighten or loosen the adjuster nut a little at a time until the steering stem adjustment conforms to that outlined above.

8. If proper adjustment is not possible, the bearings and races will probably need to be replaced.

Removal

1. The steering stem may be removed with the forks intact provided that the machine is supported well off the ground.

2. Remove the handlebars after removing the nuts (1) beneath the upper triple clamp which secure the assembly in its rubber mounts (2). (See illustration)

3. Remove the steering damper knob and rod.

4. Loosen the lower triple clamp pinch-bolts, and the upper triple clamp pinch-bolts where fitted.

5. Loosen the upper triple clamp pinch-bolt behind the steering stem nut.

6. Remove the steering stem bolt and both fork top bolts, then remove the upper triple clamp.

7. Loosen the ring nut on the steering stem.

8. As the ring nut is loosened, the steering stem will begin to drop away from the frame. Remove the nut, and take away the assembly.

NOTE: *A special wrench is used on the ring nuts although a blunt punch and hammer can also be used if care is exercised.*

Inspection

1. Check all of the bearing balls after washing them thoroughly in solvent.

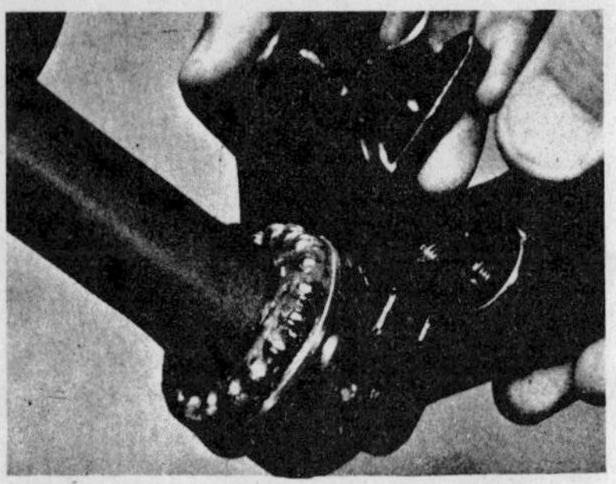

Lower bearing race

2. The balls should be replaced if rusted, pitted, dented, or scored.

3. Inspect the condition of the ball races checking for pitting, a rippled surface, or dents.

4. Replace all of the balls if any wear or damage is noted, and the races as well.

The bearing races in the frame lug are a press-fit and should not be removed unless replacement is necessary. If replacement is necessary, the old races can be removed by reaching through the frame lug with a suitable punch and tapping the race evenly around its circumference to remove it from the inside of the frame lug. Be sure that the race does not become cocked in its seat upon removal.

New races are installed with a suitably sized bearing driver, i.e., one which will drive the race squarely into its seat. Be certain that the race goes straight in.

These races can also be installed using a block of hard wood or a large socket of sufficient size to cover the race in place of a bearing driver.

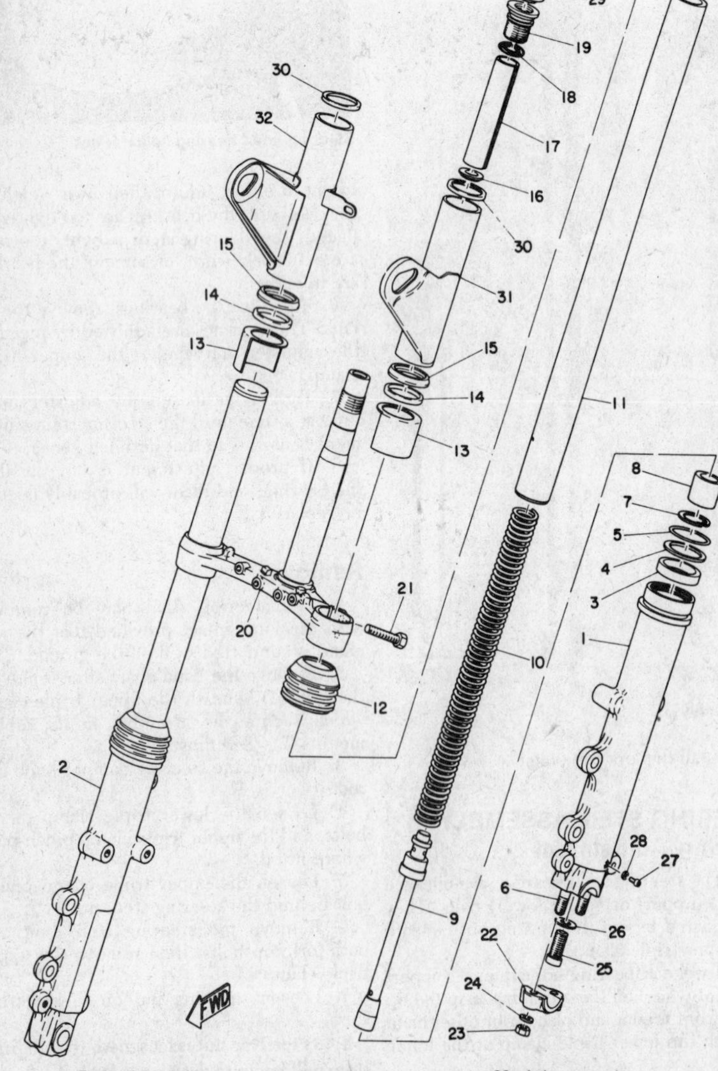

1. Fork slider (left)
2. Fork slider (right)
3. Slider oil seal
4. Washer
5. Clip
6. Stud
7. Circlip
8. Piston
9. Cylinder assembly
10. Spring
11. Fork tube
12. Dust seal
13. Cover
14. Gasket
15. Guide
16. Upper spring seat
17. Spacer
18. O-ring
19. Filler cap bolt
20. Lower triple clamp
21. Pinch bolt
22. Axle cap
23. Axle cap nut
24. Lockwasher
25. Slider allen bolt
26. Gasket
27. Drain plug
28. Gasket
29. Cap
30. Bracket guide
31. Left headlight bracket
32. Right headlight bracket

Fork assembly for XS2 and following models

Assembly

1. Grease the lower race on the steering stem with a good grade of bearing grease, then arrange the balls on the lower race. There are 19 balls on the lower race.

2. Arrange the balls into the race on the frame. The upper race has 22 balls. Insert the steering stem, and replace the ring nut(s)

3. Continue to tighten the ring nut until all steering stem play has been eliminated but assure that the steering stem still pivots freely. With the front wheel off the ground, the forks should be able to swing to either side of their own weight.

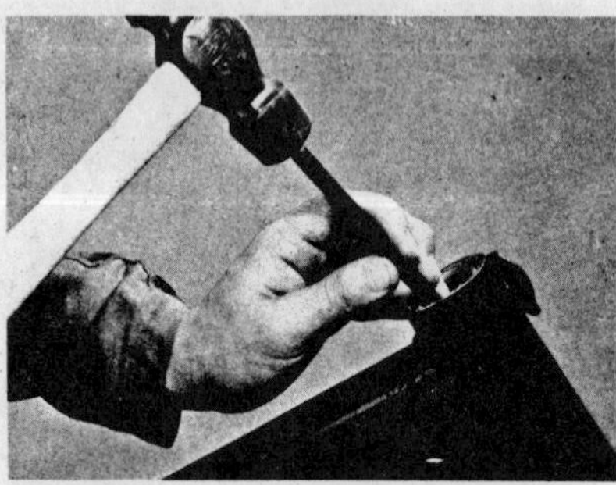

Removing the frame races

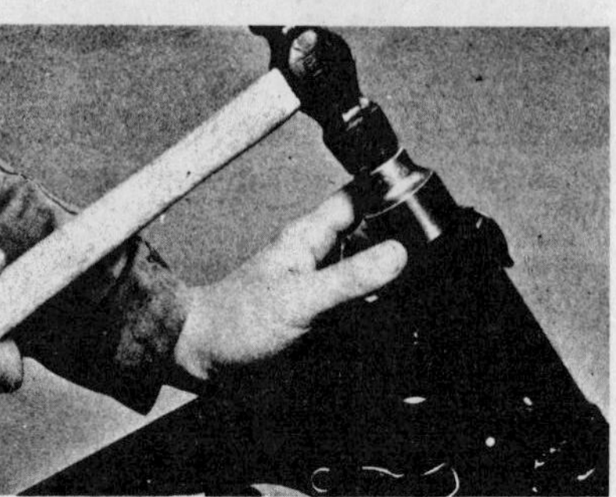

Installing the frame races

REAR SHOCK ABSORBERS

1. The rear shock absorbers are sealed units. No service is possible. If the shocks leak oil, have a bent damper rod, damaged damper case, or other damage, they should be replaced.

Shock absorbers should be replaced in sets to ensure equal damping characteristics.

2. Shocks can be removed by removing the upper and lower mounts. To remove the spring, set the load adjuster on the softest setting, compress the spring, and remove the spring retainers.

3. With the spring removed, check the damping characteristics of the unit. The damper rod should be able to be pushed into the damper body with considerably less effort than it takes to pull it out. If little or no resistance is felt when pulling a damper rod out, the shock should be replaced. Shocks should have equal damping characteristics.

4. Tighten the mounting bolts to 17–26 ft lbs when installing the shock absorbers.

SWING ARM

Inspection

1. Remove the mufflers.

2. Remove the rear wheel, shock absorbers, and chain guard.

3. Measure the distance between the top and bottom shock absorber mounts on both sides. The two measurements must be identical, or the swing arm will have to be replaced.

4. Check that the rear wheel mounting plates are parallel.

5. Grasp the legs of the swing arm and attempt to move it from side to side. Any noticeable side-play (more than 1 mm/0.04 in.) will indicate that the swing arm bushings need replacement.

The swing arm is most likely to be damaged if the machine is operated for any length of time with a broken or otherwise defective shock absorber.

Removal and Installation

1. Proceed as above. Then remove the swing arm pivot bolt nut and tap out the pivot with a long drift.

2. Remove the swing arm by pulling it straight back. Note the locations of any spacers or shims which may come off. They must be installed in their original locations.

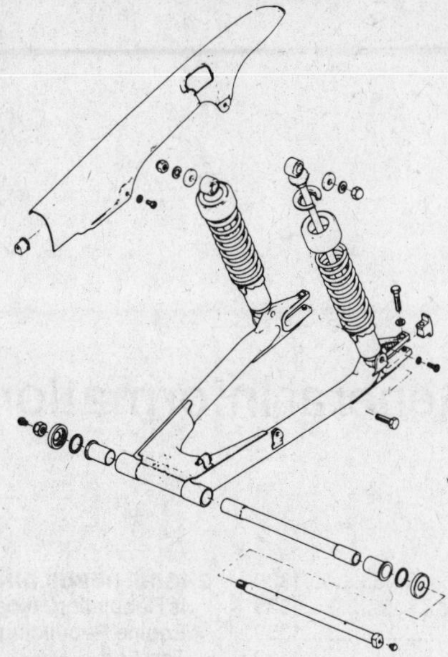

Swing arm assembly

3. The swing arm should be inspected for cracks or fractures, especially around the welds.

4. Remove the bushings, tapping them out with a hammer and punch. Once the bushings are removed, they should be replaced.

5. Lubricate new bushings with a good chassis grease. Press the bushings into the swing arm.

6. Clean out the pivot bolt and ensure that all grease passages are clear. Install the swing arm on the machine. Grease and install the pivot bolt. After tightening the swing arm pivot bolt nut, move the swing arm up and down to ensure that movement is smooth and effortless.

7. Pivot bolt torque is 36–58 ft lbs.

Torque Specifications

Part	Torque (ft lbs)	Part	Torque (ft lbs)
Front axle nut	50–72	Caliper halves	54–68
Rear axle nut	87–130	Caliper mounting bolts	29–36
Front axle cap nuts	15	Bleed screw	4.3–6.5
Steering stem nut pinch-bolt	5.8–8.6	Disc-to-disc bracket	5.8–7.2
Steering stem nut	30–47	Disc bracket-to-hub	12–16
Upper triple clamp fork tube pinch-bolts	5.8–8.6	Engine mounting, front upper	19–24.5
Swing arm spindle nut	36–58	Engine mounting, front lower	19–24.5
Shock absorber, top	17–26	Engine mounting, rear upper	19–24.5
Shock absorber, bottom	17–26	Engine mounting, rear lower	36–51
Master cylinder-to-brake hose	17–20	Front engine bracket-to-frame	10–16
Brake hose and pipe junctions	9.4–13	Rear engine bracket-to-frame	10–16

General Information

GENERAL INFORMATION

The "General Information" section following is intended to provide an overview of the various motorcycle component systems and the maintenance and service procedures pertinent to them. Because of the similarity of these systems among motorcycles in general, most of the material here is applicable to the overwhelming majority of machines currently on the road. There are always some exceptions to the rules, however, and this must be borne in mind when applying this material to individual bikes.

The subsections under "General Information," such as "Maintenance," or "Tune-Up," correspond to the organization of each of the individual model sections. We recommend that the novice mechanic or new owner first master the general principles in this portion of the book, and then apply them to the specific machine in question. For specific information on your machine, however, always refer to the individual model procedures. This section is provided not only to avoid repetition of common procedures, but to allow easier and faster information retrieval when using the model sections.

INTRODUCTION

There is no guarantee that every motorcycle owner will be able to perform every procedure contained in this book, nor is this even likely. Some jobs require special tools which may be extremely expensive, while others will require a great deal of experience and skill which comes only with ample practice or a gift for the job at hand. There is no reason to be discouraged, however, since every motorcycle owner of even modest mechanical skills can use this manual to help keep his or her motorcycle in peak condition—a state of affairs which is not only financially important, but, from the aspect of riding safety, absolutely imperative.

Routine tune-up and maintenance procedures on many machines can be carried out by the owner with only a few simple hand tools and careful attention to detail.

We recommend that the novice read the following sections carefully before beginning any work.

USING THIS MANUAL

Individual model procedures are divided to group similar or related operations under convenient headings.

Be sure your machine is listed there before you begin work. The following subsections are designed to cover the various component systems which comprise the motorcycle.

The "Maintenance" section deals with those routine operations necessary at periodic intervals to keep the machine on the road: lubrication of the engine, drive line, forks, and controls; adjustments of cables, brakes, and chains; and checks of tires, wheels, lights, brakes, and other related and safety items. At the end of each "Maintenance" section is a list of the manufacturer's recommended lubricants, factory recommended maintenance intervals, and other data such as oil capacities, tire pressures, etc.

The "Tune-Up" section involves periodic adjustments or checks of the valve assembly, ignition system, and carburetors. In this portion is information relating to plugs and points, cam chains, valve clearances, and so on. Tune-up specifications are summarized in a chart at the end of the section.

"Engine and Transmission" gives detailed instructions for the removal, repair, and installation of the motor and its parts, including checks for wear, replacement limits, and other necessary specifications.

The oil pump, pressure relief valves (where applicable) and other oil-related components can be found in the "Lubrication System."

The "Fuel System" deals with carburetor rebuilding and petcock service.

"Electrical Systems" is concerned with the charging components (alternator/generator, rectifier, voltage regulator), ignition parts which are not a cause or routine maintenance (coils, etc.), and switches, safety devices, or other electrical items applicable.

"Chassis" includes rebuilding procedures and service operations on forks, brakes, and other parts of the rolling frame.

Since service procedures for many items are similar regardless of their design or manufacturer, basic information common to all or most of the machines covered in this manual has been deleted from the individual sections, and has been collected in this "General Information" section. This has been done not only to avoid repetition of material, but to make the manual easier to use.

Less experienced owners are urged to refer to this section first before attempting any of the operations outlined in the manual.

Before beginning any job with which you are not familiar, read the given procedures thoroughly. This will not only give you a good idea of what is involved, but will prepare you for any unexpected occurences. It will also allow you to have all of the necessary tools and spare parts on hand at the outset. Some parts, such as gaskets or seals, must always be replaced if they are disturbed. Have them ready before beginning. Any work is made easier if all of the necessary materials are readily available.

Of special importance are the so-called "special tools" which may be necessary in any given operation. Sometimes these are general purpose items such as gear or flywheel pullers which are usable in a number of different places, while at other times they are single purpose items designed and made for a specific job on a particular motorcycle. The latter type may be very expensive or difficult to obtain, or it may just not be cost efficient for the individual owner to purchase one which he or she may use only rarely. Occasionally it is possible to get around using the special factory tool, but very often it is not. The frustration that the lack of the proper tool can cause, and the damage to fragile components which can be done with improper working procedures, must be experienced to be believed. We have attempted to make things as easy as possible for the owner without special equipment by mentioning alternatives to special tools in those cases where they exist and can be employed without danger to the mechanic or the machine. In most cases, however, there is simply no safe substitute for the factory-recommended equipment, and these instances, too, are pointed out in the working instructions. All users of this manual are urged to abide by this commonsense approach and avoid "shade tree" methods of working on the motorcycle. There are simply too many variables which can lead to mechanical damage and/or personal injury if the correct methods and the proper tools are not used.

SAFETY PRECAUTIONS

Several steps must be taken, depending on the nature of the job you are doing, to avoid the risk of personal injury either to yourself or to other persons in the vicinity of the motorcycle or work area. Once again, a commonsense approach is the safest path to follow. Generally, however, the following precautions are always applicable although this list is not all inclusive.

1. Make sure that the motorcycle is securely parked on a hard, level surface, and is on the centerstand unless the job requires the sidestand to be used.

2. If the engine is to be started or run as part of the operation, be sure that the bike is in an open, well-ventilated area. Doing a tune-up in a closed garage is simply not safe. Keep the door open regardless of how cold it is outside.

3. Take care to keep children and other innocents away from the work area—especially if the engine is running. Never leave a running motorcycle unattended.

4. Keep gasoline or other flammable fluids well clear of a running motorcycle. Have plenty of rags on hand to mop up any gas or oil spills immediately.

5. Keep a fire extinguisher on hand in your work place. Be sure to get one which is suitable for fuel and electrical fires. This should be considered an absolute necessity—especially if you do most of your work in the garage or basement.

6. Study the nature of unfamiliar materials before you try to use them. For example, adding the hardening catalyst to fiberglass resin produces an *exothermic* reaction: it gives off a great deal of heat. It is vital that this be considered before you try mixing up a batch. Other materials produce noxious fumes. Be sure to read all of the warning labels and instructions for use on all containers.

7. Always use protective clothing or devices if they are called for. Safety glasses should be in every work area. Protective face mask filters are also a good idea if the operation you are performing is going to produce a fair amount of fine particulate matter.

8. Misusing tools can cause personal injury. Never attempt to use a tool for a job for which it was not intended just because it is handy or looks like it might work.

9. Try to work in a place which allows you to move around the motorcycle without tripping over things. Try to move safety hazards out of the way. Be careful when moving around in a close space. Remember that it is relatively easy to lose your balance when jumping up and trying to get from one

spot to another in an undue hurry. This is not meant to be amusing. For example, crouching by the side of a bike, it is easy to forget that the end of the handlebar is just a few inches above your head. Getting up suddenly can get you a nasty bump or worse.

10. Never forget that the engine gets very hot when running, and it gets especially hot if it is sitting still. The hottest part of a running engine exposed to touch is the exhaust pipe header. Remember this when reaching around an engine to make an adjustment.

11. If it becomes necessary to rig a potentially unstable device such as a fuel tank propped up to allow access to vacuum screws, be absolutely certain that the tank is firmly secured while the adjustments are being made.

Above all, let common sense be your guide. There is nothing inherently dangerous about working on a motorcycle provided that proper precautions are taken.

NECESSARY TOOLS

This topic is included for the benefit of the owner who is working on his or her own motorcycle or those of friends. A long-time owner/mechanic may have already accumulated a large selection of tools over a period of years. A relative newcomer, however, is faced with the problem of what to buy. This can be an expensive investment, since good tools cost money, and it is really not economical to buy things you may seldom or never use. Your tool requirements will largely depend on the type of work you are willing or able to do yourself, and, of course, on the kind of machine you ride. The toolkits which come with motorcycles vary in quality from "fair" to very good. In general, however, most consist of only a few open-end wrenches and a number of special sockets for items such as axle nuts and spark plugs, and screwdriver bits. Unfortunately, these tools are not always of the highest possible quality.

Most riders will profit from the purchase of a basic set of high-quality hand tools. We recommend that you spend the extra money for a good set of tools now, rather than trying to save a little on cheaper items which may have to be replaced in a few years. Well-known brand name tools got that way because of their quality, and investing in this type will seldom be disappointing.

Your tools will more than likely be metric since all Japanese, Italian, and German motorcycles are built to metric specifications.

For those who intend to do more than the most basic work, the following items are recommended:

a. A set of open-end wrenches;

b. A set of twelve-point sockets with ⅜ in. drive ratchet. Get a set which includes a couple of extensions. As your need for more sophisticated equipment becomes available, you will find that there are any number of attachments, adapters, and swivels which will make your socket set extremely flexible;

c. A selection of Phillips and slot-head screwdrivers;

d. A set of allen keys if your bike is fitted with these fasteners as many of the newer models are;

e. An impact driver with Phillips and slot head bits. This is the one "special tool" to buy if you are only going to buy one. It will repay your initial investment almost immediately, since you will find that it is virtually impossible to remove engine screws on most motorcycles without one. These screws are put on very tightly to begin with, and may sometimes seize in the alloy engine cases. Most attempts to remove them without an impact driver will only succeed in stripping the screw heads. The driver should also be used when installing these screws, since it is hard to get them tight enough to stay on with only a screwdriver. Once the head of a screw is stripped, removing it can be very expensive. Don't take the chance. Get an impact driver.

f. A pair of good tire irons. To remove or install tires, always use tire irons designed for motorcycle tires. Two irons are usually sufficient, although a third can be helpful. Never use screwdrivers, crowbars, or anything else which may pinch the tube, rip the tire carcass, or damage the wheel (which is just about everything else other than a genuine tire iron). When the proper tire lubricant is used, almost any tire can be removed or fitted with the smallish tire irons sold in any motorcycle shop.

g. A tire pressure gauge. Many different types are available at relatively inexpensive prices. Since the meters attached to the hoses in filling stations are not particularly accurate, a tire gauge is a worthwhile investment. Proper inflation of your tires not only affects tire wear, fuel mileage, and traction, but the safety aspects of the subject should be obvious—especially if you are generally riding two-up or carrying luggage.

These tools may be considered as basic necessities. As you progress in your knowledge of the motorcycle or of motorcycles in general, you may be willing to take on increasingly difficult tasks which may require more specialized equipment. As one example, note that we have recommended twelve-point sockets for a start. Really heavy-duty sockets of the six-point type are also available. These fit directly over the hex bolt or nut giving greater purchase, which is important on slightly rounded nuts or bolts, but will not slip over the fastener as readily as the twelve point type. This may be a disadvantage when working in tight places. In addition, the six-point sockets are usually a bit more expensive.

A ⅜ in. drive ratchet will be suitable for most work which you will encounter. For heavy-duty jobs, a sturdier ½ in. drive ratchet is better. Of course, you will still be able to use the ⅜ in. sockets provided that you purchase an adapter.

Large adjustable wrenches are useful for items like axle nuts or situations in which the nut or bolt size is larger and a lot of torque is required. However, adjustable wrenches should not be used in place of precision-sized sockets or open-end wrenches, since they can easily round off a nut or bolt head if not used correctly.

When using an adjustable wrench, always position it on the nut or bolt so that the force will bear against the fixed jaw of the wrench.

You may find that your machine requires one or more "special tools" which will make a job much easier. For example, a thin-walled socket might be used to get at the cylinder head bolts. You will probably learn these tricks and others like them as you do more work on your own machine.

Insofar as factory special tools are concerned, your needs will depend, again, upon the kind of motorcycle you own, and the type of work you intend to do.

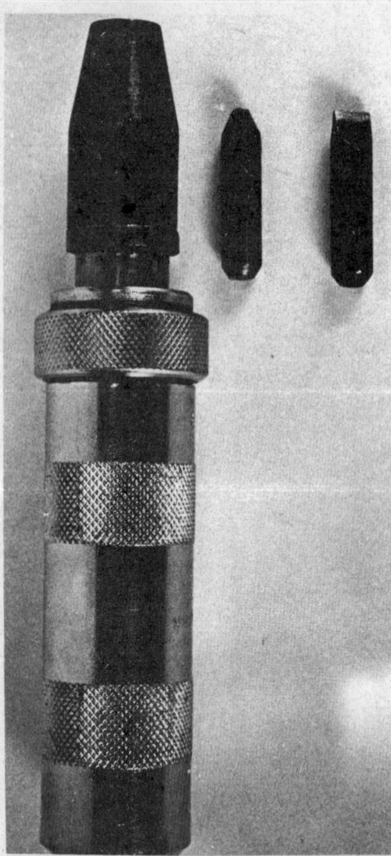

Impact driver and bits

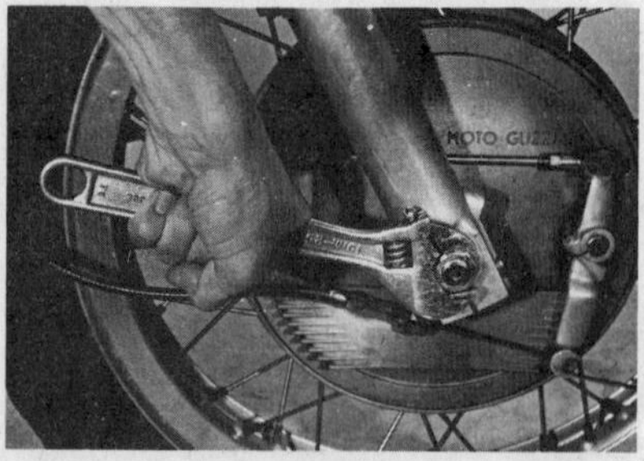

Incorrect use of an adjustable wrench (loosening nut)

Correct use (loosening nut): stress applied to fixed jaw

A *magneto flywheel puller* is a basic item which any owner of a motorcycle equipped with a flywheel magneto should consider. Removal of the flywheel is usually required to replace the contact breaker points, and sometimes to adjust the ignition timing, both procedures being within the capabilities of the majority of owners. So a device to remove the flywheel, which is usually press-fit onto a tapered portion of the crankshaft, is handy to have.

The motorcycle manufacturers supply these pullers for their own motorcycles, so this tool will be available at your dealers'.

On some motorcycles, the exhaust pipes are secured at the engine by circular nuts which thread into the cylinder or cylinder head. These nuts are often finned, sometimes not, but always require a *pin wrench* for removal or tightening. A pin wrench which will fit these fasteners is a wise investment.

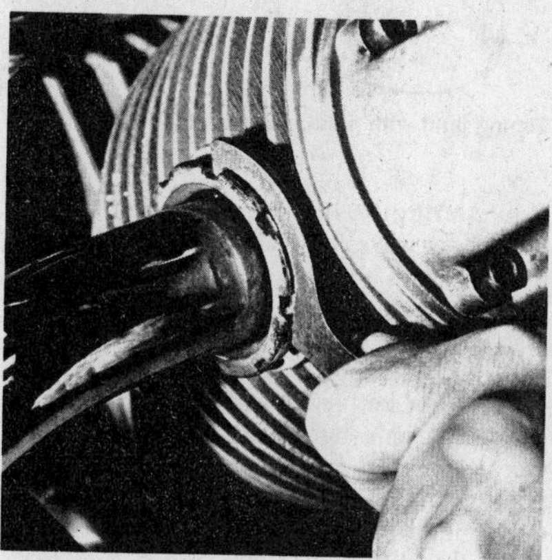

A pin wrench is a necessity when loosening or securing exhaust pipe nuts such as this

Be sure the wrench fits the nut properly (left)

Another helpful tool, which is becoming increasingly more necessary, is a "*chain breaker*" for use on machines with pressed-on masterlinks on the final drive chain. The masterlink, with its spring-clipped side plate, is the weakest point of the chain, and to remedy the problem of broken chains on the larger motorcycles, more manufacturers are fitting "endless" chains which require a chain breaker to remove and to install the masterlink.

Other tools, which might be worth the initial investment depending upon how often you use them, include a *plastic mallet*. There are numerous uses for this tool, for example, breaking loose a clutch cover, oil pan, or other alloy casting which stays put even after its screws have been removed. A steel hammer will certainly damage parts like this, and prying it off may damage the gasket mating surface.

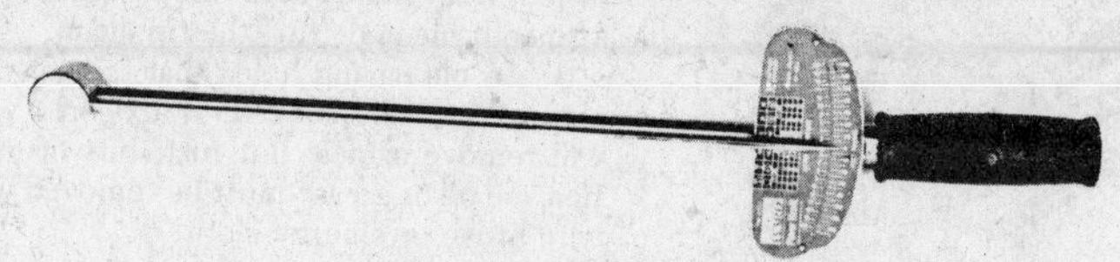

A beam-type torque wrench

Keep your screwdriver tips in good shape (left)

A *torque wrench* is a necessity for installing cylinder heads and any other large parts which are secured by a number of bolts. Proper tightening of the fasteners is required due to the stresses involved, and an *even* tightening is required to prevent warpage or distortion and ensure a good seal. Proper torquing of axle nuts and suspension parts is a safety item. On two-strokes, which will require relatively frequent removal of the cylinder head(s) for routine decarbonization, a torque wrench is an essential tool. Distortion of the head due to improperly tightened bolts is a very real danger, and proper installation become even more imperative on multi-cylinder motorcycles in which the head is a single casting.

There are two types of torque wrenches—the beam type and the click type. Click-type (or breakaway) torque wrenches can be set to any desired setting and will automatically release once the setting is reached. These are used mostly by professionals, and are not really necessary for the backyard mechanic. The beam-type torque wrench, while not quite as accurate or as fast to use as the click-type, is perfectly adequate for everyday use, and quite inexpensive. When using a torque wrench on any fasteners, keep the socket as straight as possible on the fastener. Trying to torque something on an angle just won't work.

Feeler Gauges

Feeler gauges are needed for jobs like adjusting valves, setting breaker point gaps, gapping spark plugs and so on.

Blade-type feeler gauges are suitable for valves and points, but spark plugs should be gapped with wire-type gauges, most of which also come with a small lever for bending the side electrode.

Most feeler gauges are stamped with their thickness in both English and metric measure. One type, which is known as a "go-no-go" gauge is very easy to use since each blade has two thicknesses. It is therefore obvious whether the gap being set is within tolerance.

No matter what gap you are setting with a feeler gauge, the proper method is to adjust it so that a blade of the proper size is a light drag when pulled through.

It is important that feeler gauges be properly cared for and kept out of the weather as much as possible. Long exposure will cause corrosion to build up on the blade, which will affect the thickness. It may be impossible to remove this corrosion without abrasive methods, which is, of course, not practical since this will also affect blade thickness.

If your tools sits out in a garage, it may be profitable to spray your feeler gauge with a demoisturizing agent from time to time in order to protect the blades. Naturally, make sure you clean off any blade thoroughly before using it.

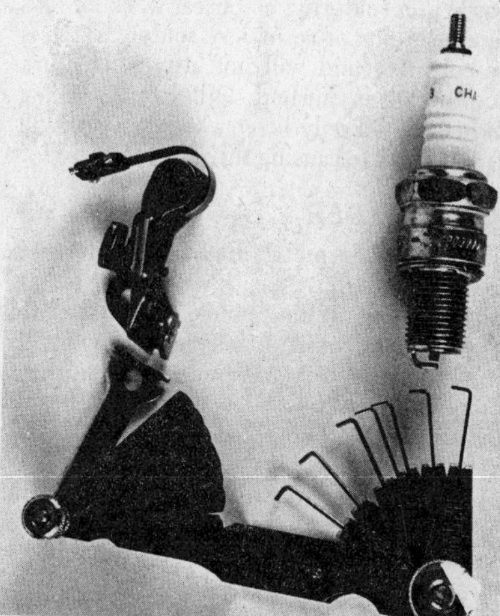

Combination feeler gauge for spark plugs and points

Go-no-go feeler gauge

Soldering Gun

Soldering is a quick, efficient method of joining metals permanently. Everyone who has the occasion to make electrical repairs should know how to solder. Electrical connections that are soldered are far less likely to come apart and will conduct electricity far better than connections that are only "pig-tailed" together.

The most popular (and preferred) method

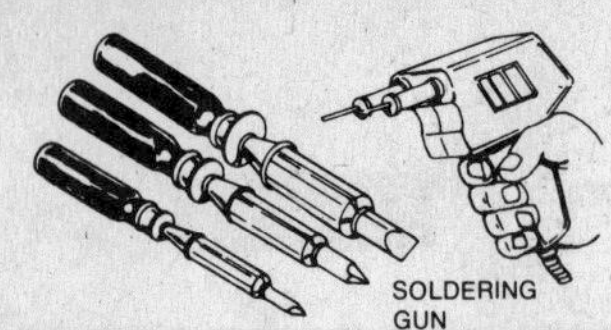

Soldering irons are available in many sizes and wattage ratings

of soldering is with an electric soldering gun. Soldering irons are available in many sizes and wattage ratings. Irons with high wattage ratings deliver higher temperatures and recover lost heat faster. A small soldering iron rated for no more than 50 watts is recommended for home use, especially on electrical projects where excess heat can damage the components being soldered.

There are 3 ingredients necessary for successful soldering—proper flux, good solder and sufficient heat.

FLUX

A soldering flux is necessary to clean the metal of tarnish, prepare it for soldering and to enable the solder to spread into tiny crevices. When soldering electrical work, always use a resin flux or resin core solder, which is non-corrosive and will not attract moisture once the job is finished. Other types of flux (acid-core) will only leave a residue that will attract moisture causing the wires to corrode.

GOOD SOLDER

Tin is a unique metal. In a molten state, it dissolves and alloys easily with many metals and has a low melting point. Solder is made by mixing tin (which is very expensive) with lead (which is very inexpensive). The most common proportions are 40/60, 50/50 and 60/40, the percentage of tin always being listed first.

Low priced solders often contain less tin and this makes them very difficult for a beginner to use, because more heat is required to melt the solder. A common solder is 40/60 which is well suited for all-around general use, but 60/40 melts easier, has more tin for a better joint and is preferred for electrical work.

SUFFICIENT HEAT

Successful soldering requires enough heat to raise the areas of the metals to be joined to a temperature that will melt the solder, usually somewhere around 360–460°F., depending on the tin content of the solder. Contrary to popular belief, the purpose of the soldering iron is not to melt the solder itself, but to heat the parts being soldered to a temperature high enough to melt solder when it is touched to the work. Melting flux-cored solder on the soldering iron will usually destroy the effectiveness of the flux.

How to Solder

1. Soldering tips are made of copper for good heat conductance, but must be "tinned" regularly for quick transference of heat to the project and to prevent the solder from sticking to the iron. To "tin" the iron, simply heat it and touch flux-cored solder to the tip; the solder will flow over the tip. Wipe the excess off with a rag.

2. After some use, the tip may become pitted. If so, simply dress the tip smooth with a smooth file and "tin" the tip again.

3. An old saying holds that "metals well-cleaned are half soldered." Flux-cored solder will remove oxides, but rust, bits of insulation and oil or grease must be removed with a wire brush or emergy cloth.

4. For maximum strength in soldered parts, the joint must start off clean and tight. Weak joints will result in gaps too wide for the solder to bridge.

5. If a separate soldering flux is used, it should be brushed or swabbed on only those areas that are to be soldered. Most solders contain a core of flux and separate fluxing is unnecessary.

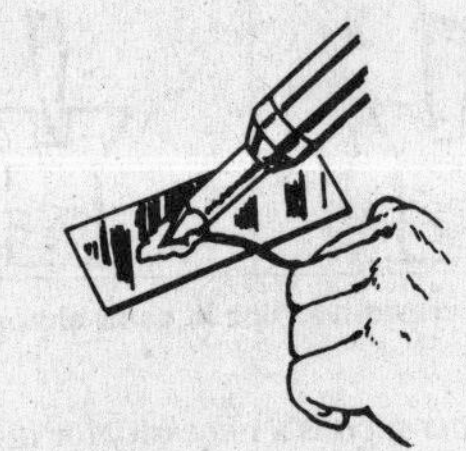

Tinning the soldering iron

Wipe the excess tin from the iron while hot

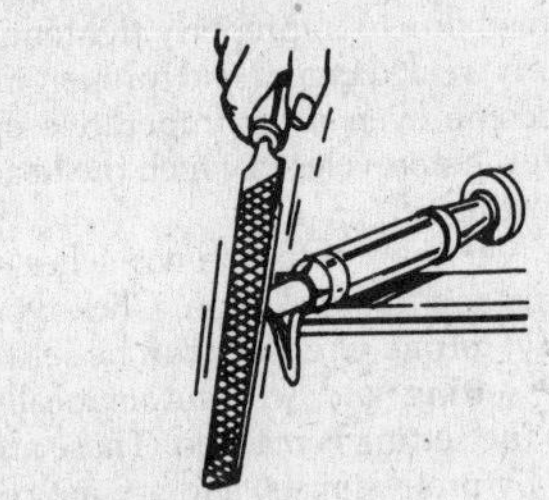

Dress the tip with a fine file

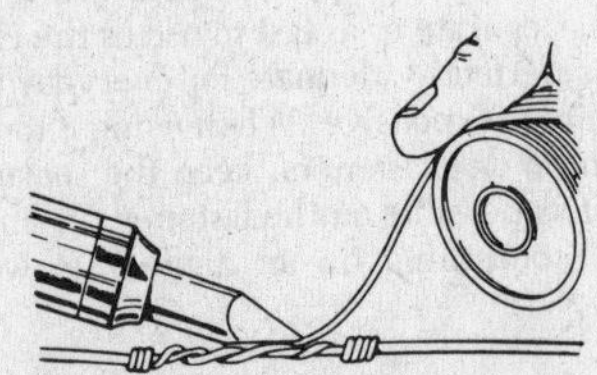

The correct method of soldering. Let the heat transferred to the work melt the solder

Test Equipment

Continuity lights and *test lights* are very handy to have for any number of tasks. In addition to tracing electrical troubles such as shorts and open circuits, either can be used for static (engine off) ignition timing, for battery-ignition motorcycles.

A test light need be nothing more than a small bulb of the same voltage as your motorcycle's electrical system (6 or 12V) with two leads attached. Alligator clips are necessary if you intend to time the bike with this light, since your hands will be otherwise occupied during this procedure.

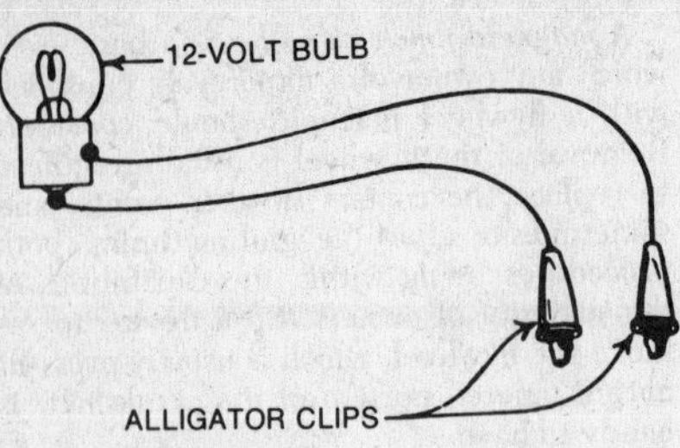

Simple continuity light

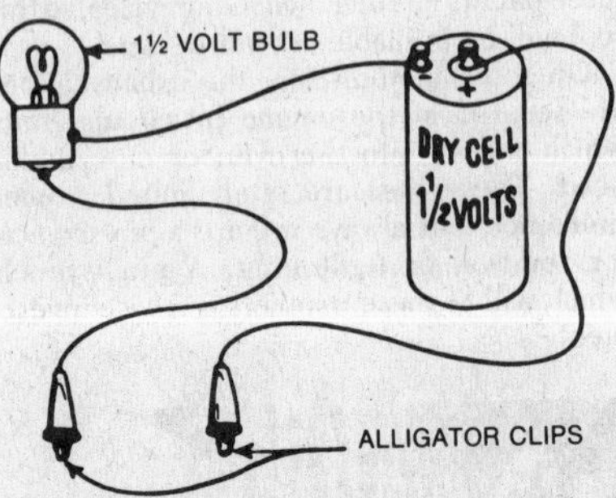

Timing light with a self-contained power source

A continuity light can be rigged in a number of ways. Basically, it is a bulb wired in series with a battery. You can use a flashlight battery and bulb providing the bulb is matched to the battery voltage.

With the simpler test light, ignition can be checked on battery-ignition motorcycles by connecting one light lead to ground on the engine case, and the other to the breaker point primary terminal or spring. The motorcycle's ignition must be *on*. When the points open, the bulb will go *on*.

A continuity light used for ignition timing is connected in the same manner as the test light. The difference is that the bike's ignition must be turned *off* when setting the timing. When the points open, the continuity light bulb will go *off*.

On many motorcycles, it is preferable to set the ignition timing *dynamically*, that is, with the engine running. For this job, a stroboscopic timing light is necessary, and suitable strobes through a wide range of prices can be obtained almost anywhere.

Neither of these methods may work on a large number of magneto-ignition motorcycles, however, due to the characteristics of magneto construction. For many of these machines, the moment of point opening must be checked with an *ohmmeter*. Yamaha dealers sell a sensitive ohmmeter called a "Points Checker" for this very purpose.

In addition, a dial indicator may be needed for your bike. When setting the ignition timing it is necessary to know just where the piston is at the time the points open. On many battery-ignition machines, this is indicated by top dead center and firing marks on the alternator rotor. On some magneto-ignition bikes, however, this is not the case, and a dial gauge is needed.

A *voltmeter* is used to measure the difference in electrical "pressure" between two points in a circuit. Just as water pressure is measured in pounds per square inch, electrical pressure is measured in volts. When a voltmeter's two probes are placed on two "live" portions of an electrical circuit with different electrical pressures, current will

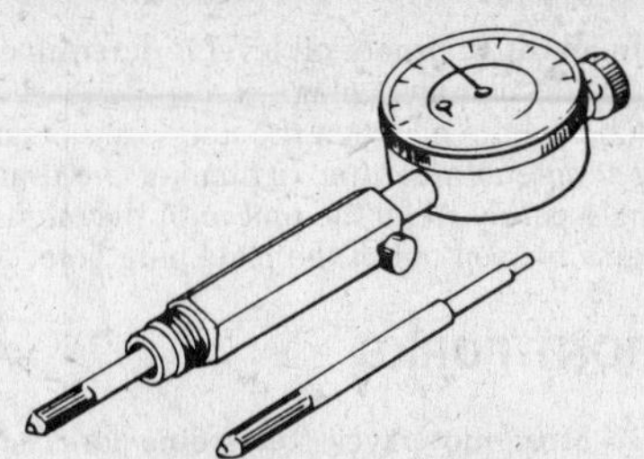

A dial gauge for finding piston position

flow through the voltmeter and produce a reading which indicates the difference in electrical pressure between the two parts of the circuit. An ohmmeter differs from a voltmeter in that it incorporates its own source of power so that a standard voltage is always presednt. An *ohmmeter* is connected in the same way as a voltmeter, but since it is self-powered, all the power in the circuit should be off and the portion of the circuit to be measured contacted at either end by the probes of the meter. Remember that a voltmeter is measuring volts or electrical pressure, while an ohmmeter is measuring ohms, or circuit resistance. Volt/ohmmeters are only useful if you have some knowledge of electricity and of course have the factory specifications for whatever you are testing. It does you no good to know that a certain circuit has, say, twelve volts, unless you know what the factory specification for that circuit is. They are not used very often but are handy in certain situations.

Miscellaneous

There are a few other items which will make life a little easier when you are working on the bike. A *points file* is used to remove burned marks or flash-over from points surfaces and can also be used to square off spark plug electrodes.

A *wire brush* is useful for cleaning plugs, removing corrosion from bolt threads, etc.

You should also have a selection of emery cloth, sandpaper, and the like, as well as penetrating oil, parts-easing fluid, spray solvents, and thread-locking compound (non-permanent).

Of course, we cannot possibly list *all* of the tools you will ever need, but you may eventually run into the need for most of the ones mentioned above.

ORDERING PARTS

We recommend that you replace any necessary parts on your motorcycle with original factory equipment. This is the safest course. Other parts may differ slightly in quality, and using them may void your warranty. In addition, purchasing parts from an authorized dealer of your motorcycle will ensure that you get the right part for your bike.

When ordering parts, always provide the model, year, and engine and frame numbers where necessary.

Compare the new part with the old one where possible before trying to install it. Then, if a mistake has been made, you can return the incorrect item at no cost.

Be careful when buying electrical components, especially expensive charging system items such as regulators or rectifiers, or the even more expensive electronic ignition units. Almost all dealers and parts outlets have a standing policy against any returns or exchanges on electrical parts. The reason for this is that these items can be easily damaged or destroyed by such a simple mistake as reversing two connecting wires, or by another defective part in the circuit. There is usually no way of telling if the component is ruined just by looking at it either.

Buying Used Parts

Replacing worn or broken parts of your machine with acceptable used parts from a wreck, salvage yard, or other source is certainly a simple way to save money, but you had better know what you are doing before you try it.

Parts which are subject to normal wear such as pistons or clutch plates should never be purchased to replace what you have no matter how good they look. The same goes for bearings or bushings. They will only continue to wear at the normal rate, and before you know it you will be doing the same job again.

Some parts, however, do not normally wear out in the short run, and if you have had a spill, accident damage, or a freak occurrence such as a hole punched in the crankcase, some used items may cut the cost of repair significantly.

Before even considering used parts, first find out where they come from. A set of carburetors from a motorcycle which was wrecked in a collision may be a good buy, but carburetors from a motorcycle with a blown engine may not be. Did the carburetors themselves cause engine failure because of air leaks, bad casting, or some other hidden defect? You should ask yourself questions such as this before you commit yourself.

Rolling chassis components such as forks, shocks, wheels, and brakes often make good purchases since new items are very expensive, and the condition of the used parts will probably be evident at first examination.

Used electrical components are a very chancy proposition. It is impossible to determine how long they have been in service, or whether failure is imminent.

Major items, such as cylinder heads, can cost enormous sums if purchased new, so buying a used one might be considered. The part must be examined closely, however, and it helps, once again, to know where it came from and what kind of service it has seen. A part like a cylinder head will have to be reconditioned in any case, so barring unusual damage such as cracks in the casting or battered valve seats, you can save money if you are cautious. If you do not know what to look for in an engine component, however, it is best not to take the chance. Always remember that, aside from the money you invest in your bike, every part on the machine affects your personal safety when you ride. What kind of price can you put on that?

Another point to keep in mind when buying used parts is applicability. Be sure that the part comes from your exact model and year. Manufacturers very often make minor changes in parts from year to year or between similar models. Even if the differences are not immediately apparent, they may be very significant especially when, as is almost always the case, the part you are replacing has to work in close conjunction with another part. Even a minor difference here may cause a malfunction.

MAINTENANCE

OILS AND ADDITIVES

The Functions of Engine Oil

What does oil do in your engine? If you answered "lubricate," you're only partially right. While oil is primarily a lubricant, it also performs a number of other functions which are vital to the life and performance of your engine.

In addition to being a lubricant, oil also dissipates heat and makes parts run cooler; it helps reduce engine noise; it combats rust and corrosion of metal surfaces; it acts as a seal for pistons, rings, and cylinder walls; it combines with the oil filter to remove foreign substances from the engine.

Types of Engine Oil

Engine oil service classifications have been provided by the American Petroleum Institute and include "S" (normal gasoline engine use) and "C" (commercial and fleet) applications. The following chart compares the latest API oil classification with those previously used:

API Engine Service (Classification)	*Replaces*	*Previous API Engine (Service Application)*
Service Station Applications:		
SA		ML
SB		MM
SC		MS (1964)
SD		MS (1968)
SE		None
SF		None
Commercial and Fleet Applications:		
CA		DG
CB		DM
CC		DM
CD		DS

Oil Viscosity

In addition to meeting the SE or SF classification of the American Petroleum Institute, your oil should be of a viscosity suitable for the outside temperature in which you'll be driving.

Oil must be thin enough to get between the close-tolerance moving parts it must lu-

types of chain lube. For this reason, SAE 90W oil should be used to lubricate the chain. Check the "Recommended Lubricants" chart at the end of the applicable "Maintenance" section for the proper recommendation.

General Lubrication

For control cables, pivoting parts such as kickstands or folding footpegs, etc., light motor oil can be used. Alternatives include graphite or molybdenum disulphide lubricants which are readily available in small dispensers from your dealer or an auto supply store.

ENGINE OIL CHANGES

Oil changes should always be performed according to the recommended intervals, or more frequently under certain circumstances.

An often overlooked fact about oil change intervals is that they depend not only on mileage, but upon *time*, that is, how long the oil has been in the crankcase, regardless of how much the machine has been ridden.

Oil wears out in time and loses its lubricating properties. Gradually the oil begins to be filled with acids from combustion as well as the more widely feared particles of dirt or metal.

As noted previously, oil oxidizes during exposure to air, and this naturally affects its efficiency. Acids get into the oil when the engine is started from cold. While the cylinder walls are not yet at operating temperature, the acids formed by the combustion process may condense on them and then get into the oil. Unless the lubricant is changed, these acids may destroy the oil's lubricating properties in time.

The recommended oil-change interval is based upon normal usage, and should probably be done more frequently if the bike is used under adverse conditions.

These conditions include extended periods of high-speed riding at high air temperatures, operation in an extremely dusty environment, extended periods of stop-and-go riding, extended short hops (such as commuting a short distance), infrequent operation, especially during the winter months, and so on.

The correct oil as recommended by the manufacturer is given in the "Recommended Lubricants" chart at the end of each "Maintenance" section. Note that motor oil service-rated "SE" or "SF" is recommended for all four-strokes. Oil of lesser quality should never be used.

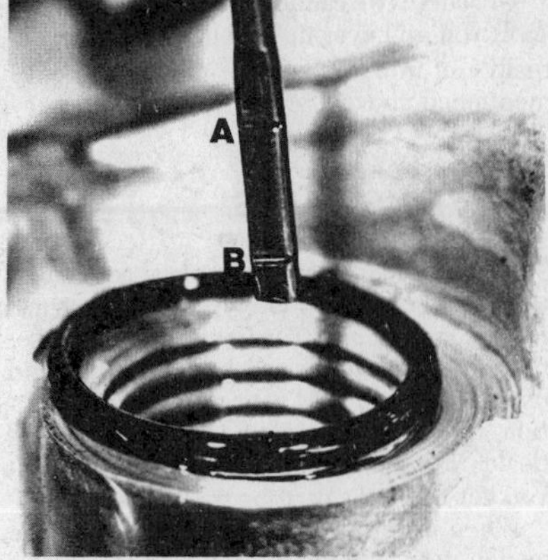

Maintain the oil level between the upper and lower dipstick marks (A and B)

Oil level sight glass

Most motorcycles are fitted with a dipstick to check the engine or transmission oil level. Some have a level plug. The dipstick or level plug must be the final determination as to whether the level is correct.

When checking any oil level, the engine should be warm, parked on the center stand, and on a level surface. Note that most manufacturer's specify that the dipstick rest on the threads of the dipstick hole when checking the level, although on some models, the dipstick must be threaded all the way into the hole.

On four-stroke motorcycles with a wet-sump lubrication system, oil level is checked at the tank. It is important that machines of this type be run for several minutes before checking the oil level, as the oil has a tendency to seep into the engine while the machine is at rest for any length of time, resulting in a false reading.

When changing oil, the engine should be close to operating temperature. This makes it easier for the oil leaving the engine to carry particulate matter with it. Be sure that all appropriate drain plugs are removed. On dry-sump machines, oil must be drained from both the oil tank and the crankcase.

After adding the correct amount of oil, allow the engine to run for a minute or so and recheck the level. Top up if necessary.

The use of oil additives is not specifically recommended by any manufacturer. Some types of additive may cause clutch slippage on machines with a "wet" clutch.

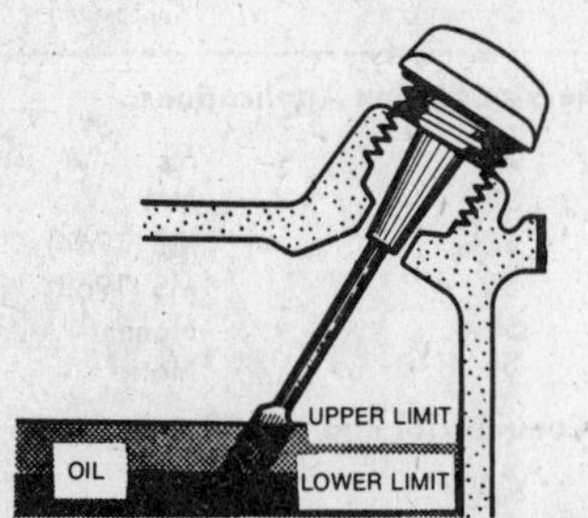

On most bikes, the dipstick should rest on the threads of the inspection hole when checking the level

TRANSMISSIONS/DRIVE BOXES

Motorcycles with separate gearboxes and shaft drive bikes with rear wheel drive boxes need oil changes at these points.

In all cases, proper oil level is determined by means of a level plug.

Change the oil when the unit is at operating temperature. After tightening the drain plug securely, refill the unit until the oil just begins to seep out of the level plug hole.

FRONT FORKS

1. Most motorcycle telescopic forks are similar as far as routine maintenance is concerned, using with a drain plug at the lower end of the slider and a filler cap on top of the fork tube.
2. Refer to the individual sections for the type of fork oil recommended for your motorcycle.

Many motorcycles can use ATF (automatic transmission fluid) in the forks. Others take various weights of motor oil. Although it is often possible to change the damping characteristics of the forks by filling them with a different viscosity oil, care must be taken to ensure that the oil you are adding is compatible with that which was previously in the fork. If you are not sure, flush the forks with a solvent before adding the new oil. On almost all motorcycle forks, *some* of the old oil will remain in the fork even if the slider is pumped after the drain plug is removed. This fact should also be taken into consideration when rebuilding forks. Note that many models give two fork capacities: one for routine changes, one for after disassembly of the fork

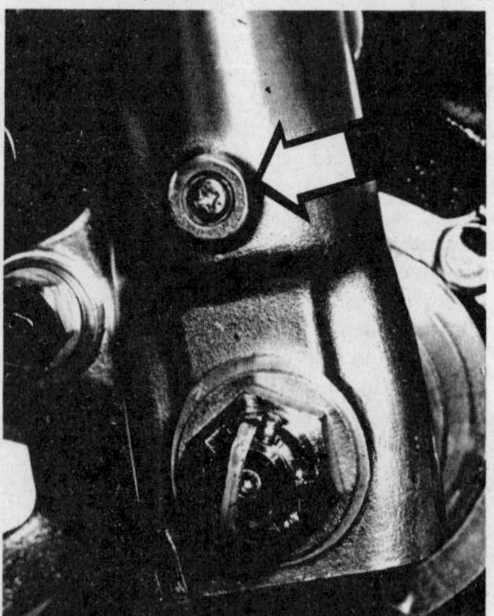

Front fork oil drain plug

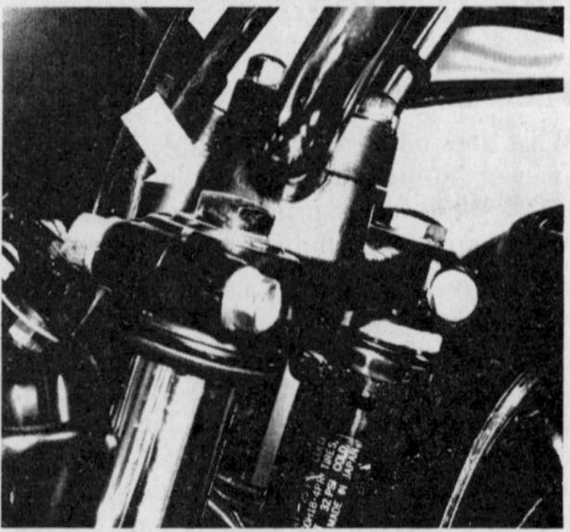

Front fork filler cap

leg. The latter figure is roughly 10% greater than the former.

3. Care must be taken when changing fork oil.

To drain the oil, remove the drain plug from the bottom of the fork slider. On most forks, it will be necessary to pump the slider up and down several times to get it all out.

Inspect the drained oil. If the oil is very dirty, or if it contains water; it is probable that the slider seals are ineffective and should be replaced.

After refitting the drain plugs, remove the filler caps.

CAUTION: *On most forks, removal of both filler caps will allow the forks to collapse, possibly tipping the machine over. Therefore, either support the front wheel off the ground by placing a scissors jack or sturdy crate beneath the engine (if necessary), or leave one of the filler caps in place while the other is removed.*

4. On some models, special procedures are necessary to remove the filler caps (such as moving the handlebars).

5. Adding oil to the forks is easy on some machines, but not so on others. Sometimes, the internal fork components necessitate that the oil be added very slowly since they impede it as it flows down through the fork leg. On some models it is possible to lift out the fork spring to speed filling.

A plastic baby bottle with the nipple cut off is a handy device for filling fork legs, since these are calibrated in ounces or "cc's."

6. After tightening the filler caps very securely, check fork operation. Check for leaks or seepage around the fork slider seals after several miles of operation. Even a small amount will necessitate replacement of the seals. A coating of grime building up in this area over a period of time is also indicative of ineffective seals.

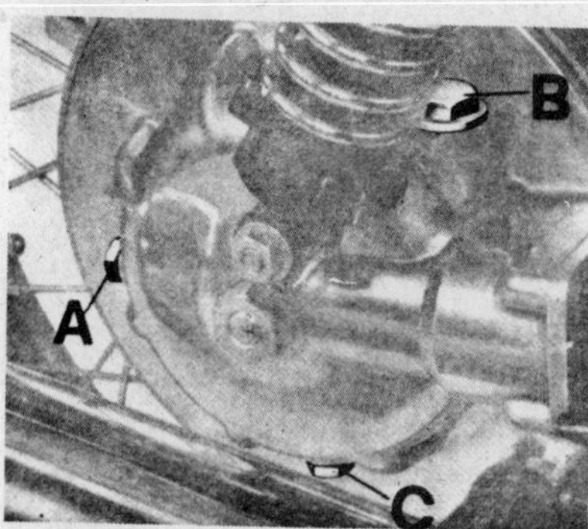

Typical drive box level plug (A), filler plug (B) and drain plug (C)

CHASSIS

Most modern motorcycles have only a single grease fitting—at the swing arm pivot.

Chassis grease is injected here to lubricate the swing arm bushings.

On the majority of designs, the fitting is easily visible on the side of the pivot. On others, it is located in the middle of the swing arm pivot tube.

In either case, chassis grease should be applied with a grease gun until some grease appears at both ends of the swing arm. Wipe off the excess grease.

Swing arm grease fitting

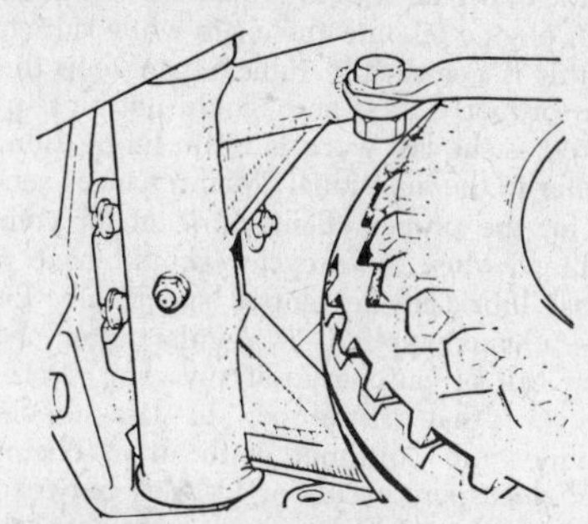

Swing arm grease fitting location

CABLES AND CONTROLS

1. The throttle, clutch and drum brake cables should be lubricated about every 3,000 miles either with a light or medium grade of motor oil or with the newer graphite or molybdenum-based lubricants sold for this purpose.

2. Disconnect the cable from the lever or twist-grip and dribble the lubricant down between the inner cable and the sheath until you think the lubricant is coming out of the other end. If you are using motor oil, a few drops of gasoline added to the cable first will make the surface of the cable slicker so that the oil will flow into the cable somewhat faster.

3. After lubricating the cables, apply some chassis grease to the exposed upper portion of each cable, and attempt to get some into the sheath. This will help prevent the entry of dirt and water.

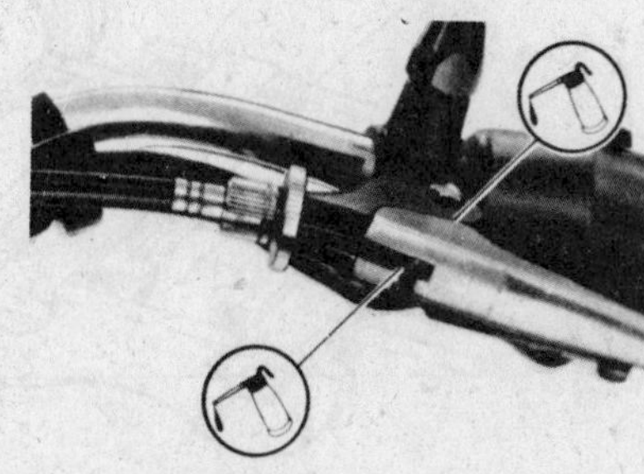

Control lever lubrication points

4. A few drops of oil should be applied to the cable fitting in the clutch lever. Lack of lubricant here may cause a snatching feeling when the lever is pulled, due to the cable fitting binding in the lever. Since the lever's hole is on the lower side and hard to lubricate, one solution is to smear the cable fitting with grease before reconnecting it.

5. After fitting the clutch cable to the lever, readjust it, but to keep out water and foreign matter, try to position the slot in the cable adjuster so that it points downward.

6. The throttle twist-grip should be taken apart and the drum lubricated with a light-weight, multi-purpose grease.

CAUTION: *When working on the twist-grip, take care not to disturb the wiring connections in the twist-grip housing.*

7. When assembling the twist-grip, tighten the screws slowly and evenly while operating the throttle to ensure free movement.

8. A few drops of motor oil should be applied to drum brake pedal pivots. At more extended intervals, the drum brake cam should be lubricated with chassis grease. Disassembly of the brake plate will be required.

9. The tachometer and speedometer cables should be disconnected, removed from the sheaths, and smeared with a light coating of chassis grease. This should be done about every 3,000 miles. Use very little of the grease on the portion of the cable closest to the instrument to avoid getting any inside the works.

10. At about 12,000 mile intervals, the speedometer drive mechanism should be lubricated with chassis grease.

Lubricating the twist-grip

DRUM BRAKES

Drum brakes have one point which should receive periodic lubrication, and that is the brake cam or cams which open and close the brake shoes.

In most cases, the cams ride directly in holes in the aluminum brake plate. They are often protected by dust washers to keep out dirt and water.

To lubricate the cams, remove the wheel from the motorcycle and take out the brake plate.

Remove the brake shoes from the plate.

Loosen the brake lever pinch bolt and carefully pry the lever from the splined cam shaft. It might be helpful to punch mark the lever and shaft for position before removal to facilitate reassembly, although on some designs the punch marks are there already.

Remove any dust washers or spacers and tap out the cam shaft.

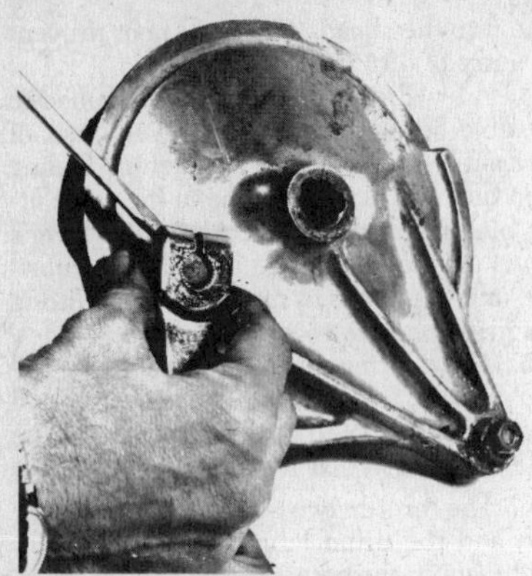

Removing the brake plate lever

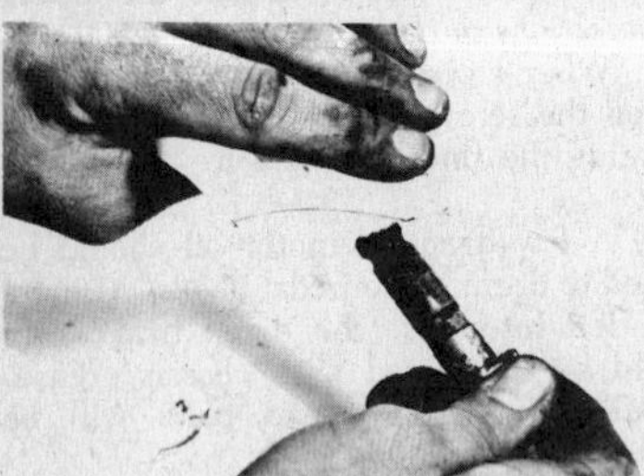

Removing corrosion from the brake cam

Clean the shaft thoroughly in a solvent to remove any old grease. Remove any rust or corrosion with a fine grade of emery paper. Clean out the hole in the brake plate as well.

Before installing the shaft, lubricate it thoroughly with a good grade of chassis grease. Check for free movement of the shaft before assembling the remaining components.

Typical brake cam grease fitting

Brake linkage, footpeg, and kickstarter lubrication points

On some older bikes, the brake cam is fitted with a grease nipple which allows the cam to be lubricated without disassembly. On set-ups like this, the cam nipple should receive no more than one shot of chassis grease from the grease gun.

MOVING PARTS

There are a number of moving parts on the motorcycle which should receive periodic lubrication with motor oil or light grease. These include drum brake rod pivots, folding footpegs, side and center stands, carburetor linkages, brake pedals, and kickstarter pivots.

DRIVE CHAIN LUBRICATION

Some models now come with permanently lubricated drive chains, but most do not. Automatic oiling devices found on some models meter engine oil onto the chain while riding, but this is not usually sufficient to keep the chain properly oiled and should not be considered as the last word in chain lubrication.

Refer to the individual "Maintenance" section for the proper chain lubricant for your machine. Most motorcycles should have a special lubricant developed specifically for drive chains applied at regular intervals. These can be purchased at any shop. Note, however, that a number of late model machines are equipped with drive chains which incorporate rubber O-rings between the chain plates which serve as a kind of seal. Some of these O-rings can be damaged by synthetic or petroleum-based chain lubes. In this case, the manufacturer recommends lubricating the chain with 80 or 90W oil. The recommended lubricant for your machine can be found in the "Recommended Lubricants" chart of the applicable section.

Frequency of lubrication is dependent upon the type of lubricant used, riding habits, average speeds, weather conditions, and so on.

The rider should check chain condition frequently until he or she finds the maintenance interval compatible with his or her riding style. As in the case of engine oil, maintenance will be necessary at shorter intervals if the chain is subjected to severe use: high speeds, off-road riding, jack-rabbit acceleration, etc.

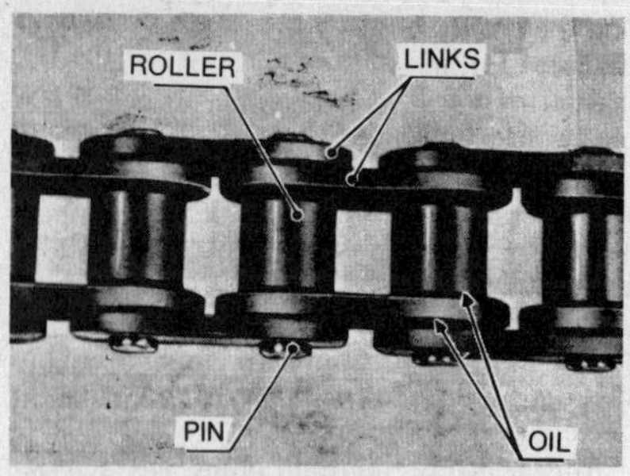

Drive chain lubrication points

Many riders find that an application of chain lube every 300 miles or so gives satisfactory chain life.

When applying a chain lube, be sure to follow the manufacturer's instructions for use. Many lubes are dispensed in a very fluid state. This facilitates their penetration into the chain. In a few minutes they become thick and sticky, enabling them to adhere to the chain as it spins around the sprockets while riding.

When applying the lubricant, direct it towards the edges of the chain plates so it will reach the pins beneath the rollers.

At extended intervals, about every 2000 miles, the chain should be removed from the motorcycle for cleaning.

NOTE: *Models with endless chains will require a special tool to break the chain. On all models, removal and installation of the masterlink spring clip should be done with a pliers—not a screwdriver—to avoid deforming the spring clip.*

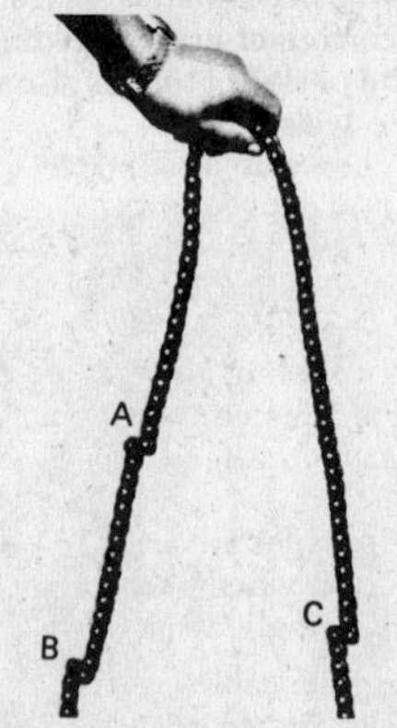

Check for kinked or frozen links (A,B,C)

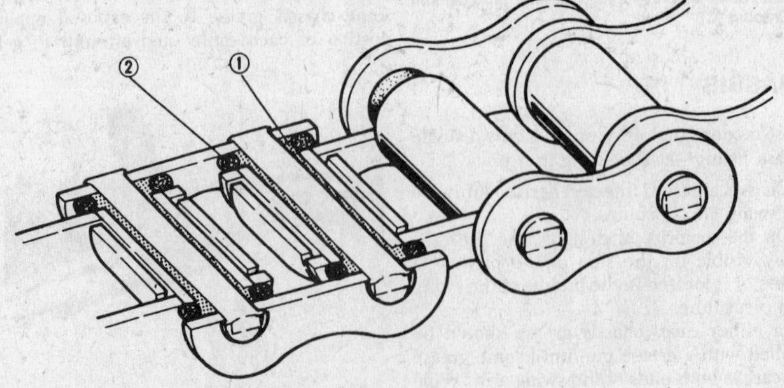

Drive chain lubricant (1) and sealing O-rings (2)

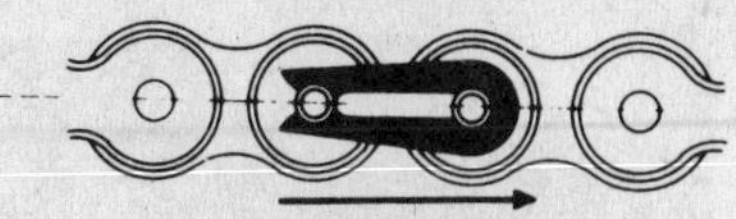

Install masterlink spring clips so that the closed end is facing the direction of chain rotation

Having an old chain on hand makes chain removal somewhat simpler, since the old chain can be attached to one end of the chain on the bike and pulled through over the engine sprocket, so that it is not necessary to remove the sprocket cover or other components.

Remove heavy deposits of dirt and grease with a stiff brush and solvent. Then soak the chain for several hours in a light motor oil. Hang it up to drain.

Check that each chain link can pivot freely. If there are any kinked or binding links which cannot be freed, or if the chain is rusted or has suffered damage from corrosion (such as might happen if it is touched by acid from an incorrectly routed battery overflow tube), replace it.

After cleaning the chain, refit it to the machine, lubricate it in the usual way, and adjust the tension.

When joining the chain, note the following points: models which use an endless type chain will require a new masterlink. On other models, the masterlink may be reused if in good condition. Also, check the condition of the masterlink spring clip. Be sure to install the spring clip with the closed end facing the direction of chain rotation. Also, if the clip is "sprung," the concave side must face the chain.

NOTE: *When washing the machine, especially at high-pressure car washes, keep water and detergents off the chain if possible. Never use high-pressure spray units to remove grease or dirt from the chain. This may damage O-rings on sealed chains or will allow water to get between the pins and rollers on other types of chain.*

ROUTINE ADJUSTMENTS

CARBURETOR CONTROLS

One often-overlooked cause of poor fuel system operation can be found in the throttle controls: twist-grip, cables, and the linkage arrangements found on multi-carburetor motorcycles.

Proper lubrication of the carburetor controls is essential.

Twist-grips are usually of the split type in which the drum is contained in a two-piece housing. The housing top half can be removed for lubrication. Since many machines incorporate various electrical switches in the twist-grip, exercise care when removing to avoid damage to wiring and connections. Use a light grease in the throttle twist-grip. Apply some lubricant to the part of the grip which contacts the handlebar to ensure smooth movement. When putting the housing back together, note that on most motorcycles, there is a locating pin somewhere on the twist-grip to prevent it from rotating around the handlebar. This pin fits into a hole in the handlebar. Be sure it is engaged before tightening the housing.

When installing the top of the housing, tighten the fasteners slowly and evenly, checking for free throttle movement as you go along.

Throttle cables are arranged in many ways depending on whether the engine is a two or four-stroke, single, twin, or multi, and so on.

All throttle cables should be lubricated periodically in accordance with the recommended maintenance interval.

In addition, cables must be adjusted to the recommended free-play, an adjustment which is usually performed in conjunction with a tune-up.

Throttle cables must be arranged as the manufacturer intended. The cables must not be bent sharply or kinked anywhere along their length. Ensure that the cables are clipped to the frame only at those points determined by the factory. Removal and installation of the gas tank is one instance in which the cable(s) may be disturbed.

When separating the twist-grip, be careful of the electrical wiring

Check that cables are long enough, especially if new ones have been installed, or handlebars changed. With the engine idling, turn the handlebars from lock-to-lock. Any rise in the idle speed indicates that the cables are either too short, improperly adjusted, or are improperly installed.

On some motorcycles, especially multicylinder ones, the throttle cables must be routed in specific ways over or under the top frame tubes. Altering this arrangement even in a seemingly minor fashion can cause improper operation. Memorize or make a sketch of the original cable routes before any work is done on the system.

Throttle linkages at the carburetors, such as the pulley arrangements now in wide use, are in most cases best left alone. Some of these linkages have grease fittings which should be lubricated with a light-weight grease at intervals recommended by the manufacturer. Systems of this sort also have the adjustments for throttle slide synchronization, and should therefore be approached with caution, unless you have the proper vacuum gauges to synchronize the slides.

Throttle slides must snap closed from any position except in those rare instances in which the linkage is the non-return type.

Pulley linkages as found on many machines are usually not prone to trouble in this regard. If the throttle slide(s) will not close when the twist-grip is released, first check that the tensioner sometimes fitted to the twist-grip for touring is not in play. Next, check cable lubrication. Inner cables which are sharply bent or kinked can cause the slide(s) to hang up.

Also, check the condition of the inner cable. A cable which is frayed or has even a single broken strand must be replaced at once.

The most common troublespot for throttle cables is at the twist-grip. Since on most motorcycles the cable is bent around the throttle drum when the twist-grip is turned, metal fatigue is only natural and the cable will eventually suffer one or more broken strands at this point. A broken strand can seize in the cable housing making it impossible to close the throttle slide(s). The frequency of cable damage at the twist-grip is dependent to some extent upon the diameter of the drum. A cable which must be bent around a small diameter drum will be more likely to break eventually than one which is not bent to such a great degree. Some machines which suffer frequent cable failure at this point may benefit from the installation of a "quick throttle," which has a large diameter drum.

Another problem which might cause control malfunction is seizing of the slide in the carburetor. Although relatively rare, this can happen on some models. Especially prone to this phenomenon are carburetors which are bolted to their manifolds with a flange. Uneven tightening or overtightening of the mounting nuts or bolts can warp the carburetor body and cause the slide to stick.

On carburetors of this sort, it is sometimes helpful to install the complete slide assembly with carburetor cap in the carb before bolting the unit to the manifold. Constantly operating the slide while tightening the fasteners is recommended. If the slide sticks suddenly, the nuts or bolts are either over-tight, or the carburetor body is warped. This presents a problem, since the fasteners must be relatively tight to form an effective seal at the manifold. If the body is warped, it should be replaced.

Adjust the throttle cable adjuster at the twist-grip so that the throttle has about 10–15° of free rotation before the slides begin to open.

After making this adjustment, start the engine and let it idle while turning the front forks from lock-to-lock. There should be no change in the idle speed. If there is, the cable is too tightly adjusted or is misrouted.

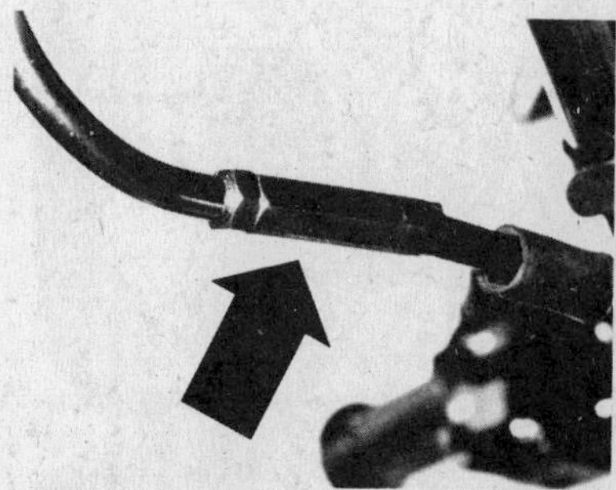

Throttle cable adjuster

HEADLIGHT ADJUSTMENT

The adjustment procedure is similar for all motorcycles.

1. Set the machine about 25 feet away from and perpendicular to a wall, preferably of a color which reflects light well.

The bike should be on its wheels, with a rider putting his weight on the seat as he would when riding.

2. Switch on the high beam. The headlight high beam should be parallel to the ground and should hit the wall directly in front of the machine.

3. Vertical adjustment is made by loosening the headlight shell mounting bolts slightly and pivoting the shell up or down.

4. For lateral adjustment, most makes have an adjusting screw at one side or the other.

Headlight lateral adjustment screw

BRAKES

Drum Brakes

1. Drum brakes are operated by either cable or rod. In most cases, front brakes have cable adjusters at the brake plate and at the hand lever. Rear brakes usually have an adjuster at the brake plate.

Generally, brake adjustment should be maintained so that the brake hand lever or brake pedal has about 1 in. of movement before the linings contact the drum.

In the case of rod-operated rear brakes, this adjustment should be made with the machine off the stands and with a rider sitting on it. The reason for this is that the movement of the swing arm may vary the distance

Adjusting the brake at the brake plate

Rear brake adjusting nut

between the brake cam and the pedal pivot, thereby changing the brake adjustment as the machine is operated.

2. On front brakes, the adjustment is usually made at the brake plate, with fine adjustments made at the hand lever.

3. Twin-leading shoe brakes are fitted with a linkage connecting the two cams, and the linkage may not need routine adjustment unless the brake plate has been disassembled or new shoes have been fitted. One type of the linkage has both brake levers connected with a cable and the levers are pulled together when the brake is applied. This type is self-adjusting.

A more common method is to have the brake cable connected to one brake level, the remaining lever being connected to the first by means of a rod and clevises. The rod is usually threaded and means of varying the length of the rod to make an adjustment is possible.

This is done in one of two ways, depending upon how the rod is attached.

To check the adjustment, disconnect the rod at the main brake lever. There is usually a retaining clip or cotter pin at the clevis pin. Apply the brake hand lever until the shoe contacts the drum. Holding this position, apply the secondary brake lever with your

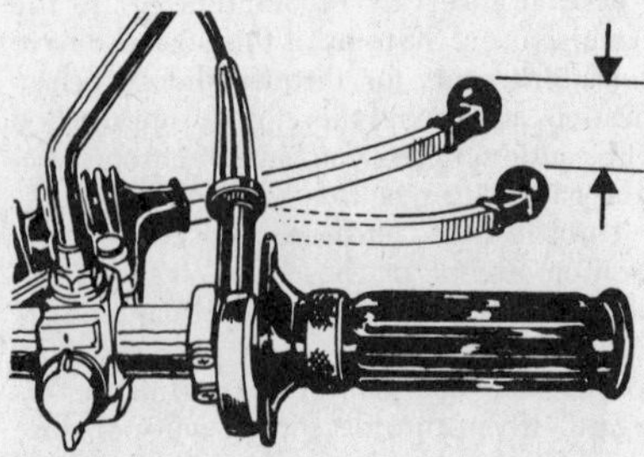

The brake lever should have about 1 inch of movement before the linings contact the drum

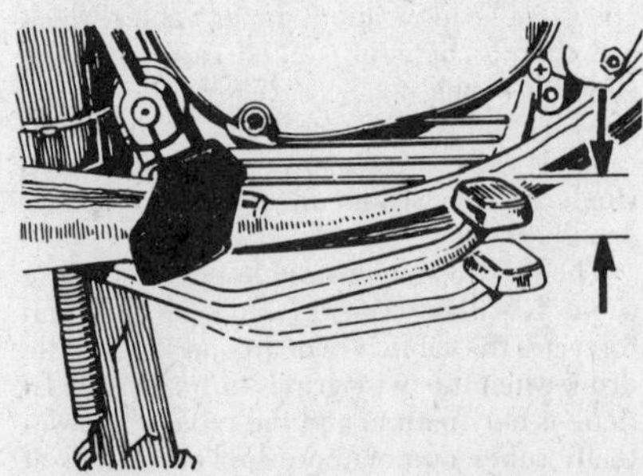

The brake pedal should have about 1 inch of movement before the linings contact the drum

When the brake hand lever is applied so that one brake shoe fully contacts the drum, pushing the other shoe's lever until it too is in contact should result in the alignment of the lever and clevis holes, If not, the brake linkage is improperly adjusted

hand until that shoe contacts the drum. The clevis holes should line up at this point. If they do not, lengthen or shorten the brake rod so that the holes align.

4. Brake lining wear on newer models can be determined by means of the wear indicator pointer fitted to the brake lever on the hub. If the pointer lines up with the red slash mark when the brake pedal is fully applied, the linings are worn as far as possible for effective braking and should now be replaced.

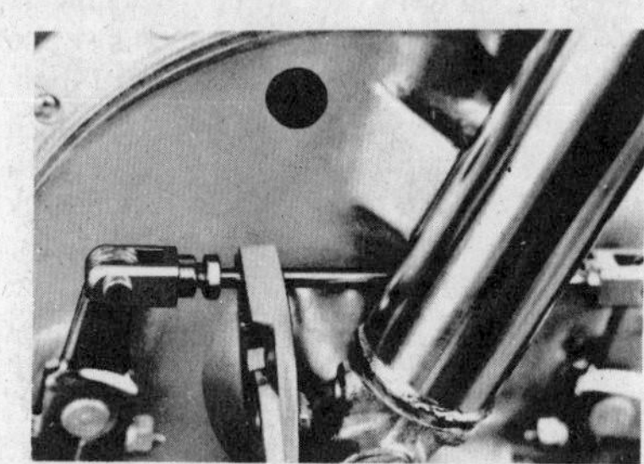

Adjusting the brake rod

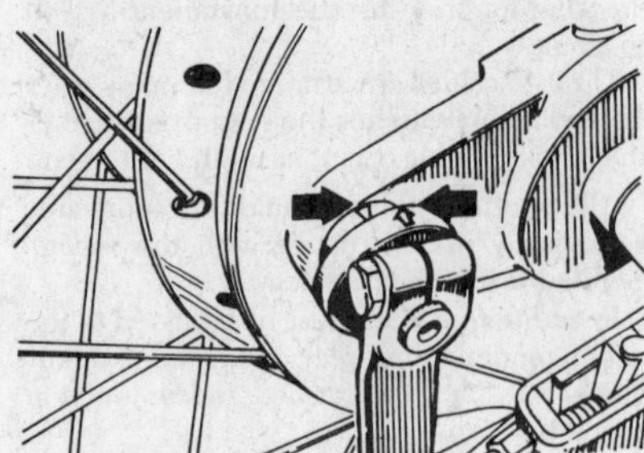

Brake wear indicator marks

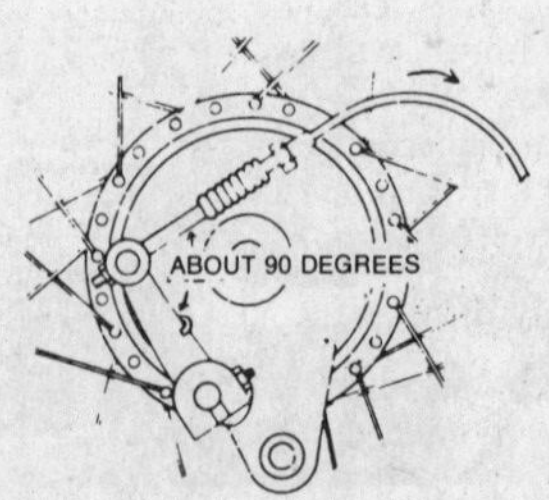

With the brake applied, the angle between the lever and cable or rod should be about 90°

5. On older models, observe the angle formed by the brake lever on the hub and the brake rod or cable when the brake is fully applied. When the lever and rod or cable form an angle greater than 90°, the shoes should be checked for wear as they probably are worn to the point of needing replacement.

Brake Light Switches

The switches should be checked for operation after the brakes are adjusted. The rear brake light switch and adjuster nut are mounted on a slotted bracket. The rear switch is adjusted by holding the switch and turning the adjuster not to effect adjustment. Moving the switch upon the bracket allows the brake light to turn on sooner. Moving it down allows the light to turn on later. Do not turn the switch to effect adjustment as the wires will become twisted and may break. Generally, the brake light should come on just as the linings contact the drum.

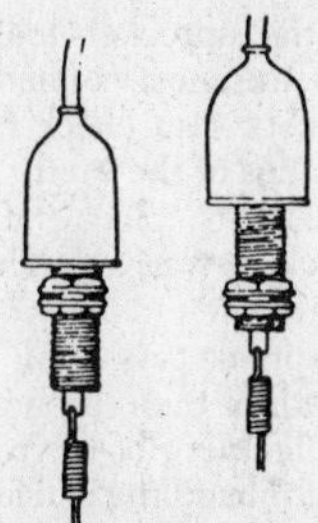

Typical rear brake light switch adjustments

Rear brake light switch

Disc Brakes

1. Disc brake systems need little routine maintenance other than an occasional check on pad wear and fluid level.

2. Pads should be replaced when they are worn to the limit lines. These are fitted to most types of disc brakes. Other types will have tab-type wear indicators. On others, the manufacturer will specify minimum pad thickness.

3. The master cylinder fluid level is usually inscribed on the master cylinder. The fluid level may drop slightly over a period of time as the pads wear, but this drop will be slight. Do not top up a master cylinder reservoir whose level has dropped slightly due to pad wear, since the level will return to the normal level when new pads are fitted. An exception, of course, will be made if braking effectiveness is reduced due to a low level.

Brake pad inspection slot

4. Brake pedal or hand lever travel should be about 1 in. measured at the end of the pedal or lever—the same as for drum brakes. On some systems, there is an adjustment for lever travel. Once properly set, no readjustment should be necessary. If lever travel becomes excessive, the system should be checked over.

5. Periodically check condition of hoses and lines. Be sure that all hoses are arranged as the manufacturer intended, and are properly mounted. Check for abrasion damage. Check banjo fittings for signs of seepage.

CAUTION: *Working with brake fluid requires special precautions. Refer to the "Chassis" section following for information.*

Maintain brake fluid level at the inscribed line

See-through type master cylinder with level mark

CLUTCH

Unsatisfactorily rough action of the clutch hand lever is almost always due to improper lubrication of the hand lever, clutch cable, or release mechanism.

Like all control cables, the clutch cable must be free of sharp bends or kinks along its route. If lever pull is hard, check this first.

Always keep the cable well lubricated by dribbling oil or a special cable lubricant between cable and sheath. Be sure that the lever itself has a well-lubricated pivot. Also, check the fit of the cable end in the lever. The cable end must turn slightly when the lever is pulled toward the handgrip, and if it cannot do so, lever action will be stiff and cable life short. An uneven or snatching feeling when the lever is pulled towards the handgrip is often due to the cable end fitting binding in the lever. This can usually be remedied by thoroughly lubricating the cable end fitting. If this does not work, the lever cut-out can be enlarged slightly with a file so that the cable end fitting is free to rotate in it.

The release mechanism on some machines requires occasional service. On some Hondas, the mechanism is fitted with a grease fitting easily accessible on the engine case. One or two shots of chassis grease every year or so should suffice here.

On some other makes no grease nipple is fitted, and the release mechanism must be removed for service. This is especially true of those makes in which the release mechanism is installed in the engine sprocket cover. In this location the mechanism can get very dirty due to its exposure, and rough clutch action will be the result.

The clutch cable on almost all designs has an adjuster fitted at the clutch hand lever. Clutch cable adjustment must always be maintained at the proper specification. If the cable has insufficient free-play, the clutch will slip and rapidly burn out. If it has too much play, the clutch will not disengage completely, resulting in hard shifting and creeping at stops.

Use the adjuster at the hand lever to maintain the correct amount of cable slack. The

Clutch cable free-play (arrow) should be 2-3 mm (0.08–0.12 in.)

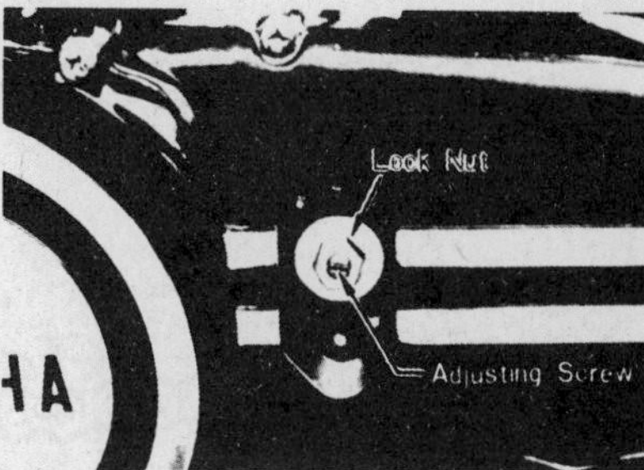

Typical clutch adjusting screw and locknut

clutch lever should be able to be moved 2–3 mm (0.08–0.12 in.) measured between the lever and the lever holder before the clutch begins to disengage.

If clutch operation is not satisfactory after making this adjustment, the clutch itself must probably be adjusted.

Note that there is a large difference between adjusting the *cable*, and adjusting the *clutch*. Cable adjustment is not the way to get rid of clutch maladies. On the other hand, no amount of clutch adjustment will compensate for an incorrectly adjusted cable.

On most bikes, the clutch is adjusted by means of a screw which bears against the clutch pushrod. To adjust this type of set-up, first run down the cable adjuster or adjusters to give as much slack as possible in the cable.

Next, loosen the clutch adjuster locknut and back it off several turns.

Carefully screw the adjuster *in* until resistance is felt. This resistance will be the adjuster bearing against the pushrod(s) which in turn bear against the clutch pressure plate.

Back the adjuster off ½–¾ turns and tighten the locknut. Adjust the cable to give the proper amount of free-play.

CHAIN AND SPROCKETS

1. First make a visual inspection of the chain and its sprockets. If the chain is rust red in color, it has probably suffered too long without proper lubrication, and should be replaced as the damage done to the pin bushings (which you cannot see) is already beyond repair. The chain must also be replaced if it has any broken or cracked rollers.

If the chain is very dirty, covered with grease and dirt, it should be removed and cleaned.

2. Check the battery overflow tube, and ensure that it has been so routed as to avoid the chain completely. White deposits on the links is a sign that sulfuric acid from the battery has come in contact with the chain. If this has happened, the acid has probably damaged one or more of the links. This will weaken them to the point where the chain can no longer be trusted. The chain should be replaced immediately.

3. After lubrication and adjustment road test the bike to check chain operation. If the motorcycle vibrates at intervals, it could be that the chain is too tight, or that one of the sprockets is warped or worn. If the chain slaps the chainguard or swing arm, it is too loose and must be adjusted. Another symptom of a badly adjusted or worn chain or sprockets is noise while coasting. This can be checked by simply rolling the bike down hill for a short distance.

If the chain slaps the chainguard or swing

Attempt to pull the chain off the sprocket to check for wear

arm, it is too loose and must be adjusted. Another symptom of a badly adjusted or worn chain or sprockets is noise while coasting. This can be checked by simply rolling the bike down hill for a short distance.

4. The drive chain slack is the total up and down movement of the chain measured at a point midway between the sprockets. The specifications may differ for various machines, but is usually about 20mm (¾ in.).

5. Conditions under which the chain slack is measured differ from make to make. Some manufacturer's specify that the machine be on the center stand with the rear wheel off the ground, while others state that the slack is measured with the weight of a rider on the bike. Refer to the individual model section for the correct method.

6. On all machines, however, it is imperative that the chain be clean and well lubricated before checking slack.

7. The chain must be checked for tight spots before making this adjustment. Rotate the wheel slowly and note any variances in chain tension. If the tension varies greatly, it is probable that the chain or the sprockets are worn to the point of replacement. If a tight spot is found, make a mark on the rear sprocket relative to some fixed point. Continue to rotate the wheel. If the chain becomes tight each time the sprocket mark passes the point you chose, the sprocket is warped and should be replaced. If there is no relation between the periods of chain tightness and the rotation of the sprocket, chances are that the chain itself is the problem.

8. Although a chain with a tight spot must soon be replaced, if it must remain in service for a period of time be sure to adjust the chain tension to the given specification at the tight spot. This will probably mean that the chain will have some very loose spots at which it may slap and hit the chainguard, but the potential of breaking the chain will be somewhat reduced.

9. After adjusting the chain to the manufacturer's specification, check for wear by attempting to pull the chain off the rear wheel sprocket. If you can see more than ½ of the sprocket tooth at the point this is done, the chain is worn and should be replaced as soon as possible.

10. Other methods of checking the chain for wear involve first removing it from the machine. Stretch the chain out to its full length and measure it. Then compress the links so that the chain is as short as possible, but not bent. Measure the chain again. If the difference between the two measurements amounts to more than ¼ in. per foot of chain, or more than 3% of its total length, the chain should be replaced.

11. In the event of a worn chain, the sprockets should be inspected closely. A worn chain can ruin sprockets, and conversely, worn sprockets will quickly wear out a new chain.

Check that the sprocket teeth are not hooked. This is the most common sign of a damaged sprocket. Also check for wear on the edges and sides of the teeth. If possible, remove the sprockets, place them on a flat surface and check for warpage. The sprockets must be perfectly flat.

If one of the sprockets is worn, it is recommended that both of them be replaced.

12. Proper alignment of the rear wheel is very important for handling and for chain and sprocket life. Most motorcycles have axle alignment marks on the swing arm, and care should be taken when adjusting the chain that the index on the adjuster are lined up

Normal (top) and worn sprocket

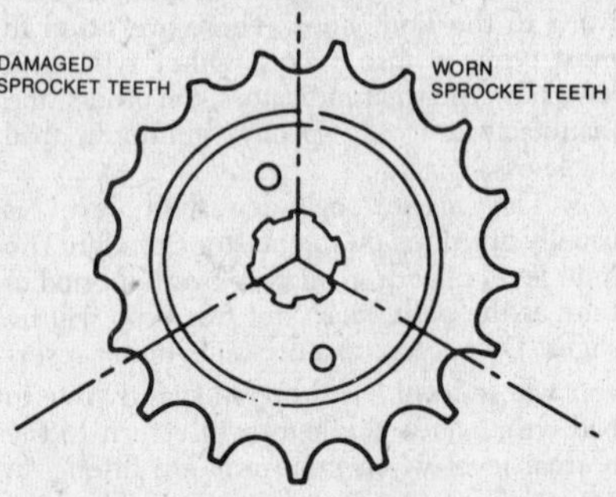

Sprocket wear patterns

Chain play should be measured in the middle of the lower run

with the same mark on both sides of the wheel.

If such alignment marks are not fitted, it is possible to align the wheel by "eyeballing" it using the front wheel as a reference. Alternately, if there is not too much in the way, you can measure the distance from the swing arm pivot to the center of the axle and make sure it is the same on both sides.

TWO-STROKE DECARBONIZATION

Decarbonization of the top end of two-stroke engines is a very important service which must be done regularly and thoroughly if engine performance is to be maintained. The cylinder head, piston crown, exhaust port, and exhaust system should all be cleaned at the same time.

Each manufacturer has their own recommended service interval for decarbonization, but this is only an approximation since the amount of carbon build-up on engine components is largely dependent upon carburetor settings, the type of two-stroke oil used, riding habits, and several other factors.

A substantial loss of power, especially in the higher gears, is usually a signal that decarbonization is necessary. Also, the presence of carbon deposits 1/16 in. or more in depth on the exhaust system baffles indicates that service is required.

To perform a routine decarbonization, it is usually only necessary to remove the exhaust system baffle(s), the exhaust pipe(s), and the cylinder head(s). After an extended period, however, removal of the cylinder itself may be required to check or replace the piston rings. These may also become carbon-fouled.

The following items are needed for this procedure:

a. A blunted screwdriver, or broken hacksaw blade, or other unsharpened device for scraping off carbon;

b. A propane torch;

c. Some steel wool and a wire brush;

d. A quantity of solvent;

e. A torque wrench to refit the cylinder head;

f. Replacement parts: Exhaust pipe gasket(s), cylinder head gasket(s), and cylinder base gasket(s) if the cylinder is to be removed. If the cylinder is going to come off, it is recommended that the rings be replaced in any event. Piston rings not only wear rapidly on some machines, they often tend to become carbon-clogged after extended mileage. Rings in this condition are usually impossible to free without breaking them, and replacement is the only solution. The relatively small expense involved in fitting new rings makes this operation worthwhile from a maintenance standpoint.

1. Remove the set screw or bolt which secures the baffle at the rear of the exhaust pipe(s). Grasp the baffle with a large pliers and pull it out.

2. Unbolt the exhaust pipe(s) from the cylinder and from the frame and remove it from the machine.

3. Loosen each cylinder head nut or bolt ¼ turn at a time, and in a cross pattern, until they are loose, then remove them and the cylinder head. If the head is stuck, tap it with

Removing the baffle securing bolt

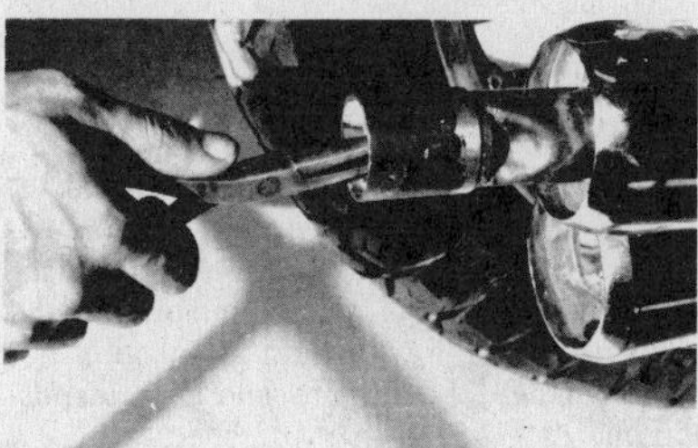

Pulling out the baffle

a plastic mallet to free it. Remove the head gasket.

4. To clean exhaust pipe baffles, first heat them with a propane torch until quite hot. Grasping the baffle with a pliers, tap it against a wooden block to knock off heavy carbon deposits. After it cools, remove any remaining deposits with a wire brush and solvent.

5. Check the amount of carbon buildup on the inside of the exhaust pipe. If substantial, much of it can be removed on some types of exhaust systems by running an old

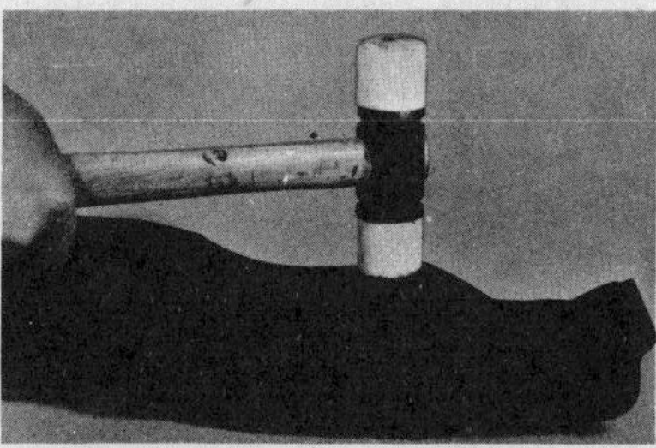

Heating the exhaust pipe and then tapping the outside with a plastic mallet can remove some otherwise inaccessible carbon deposits

Remove deposits with a wire brush

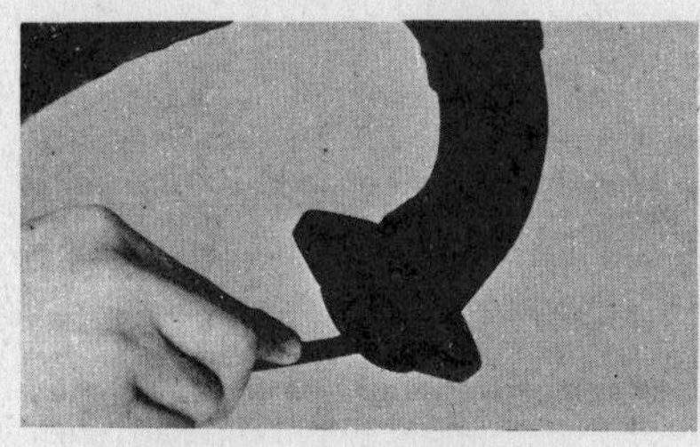

Scraping exhaust pipe carbon deposits

length of drive chain back and forth inside the pipe. Alternatively, a bent up coat hanger should remove most deposits at the engine end of the pipe.

Carbon can sometimes be removed from exhaust systems which are not chromed by heating the pipe itself with a torch and tapping the outside with care with a plastic mallet to break carbon loose.

If exhaust pipe deposits are heavy, and especially if they show a wet, oily appearance, check the adjustments of the carburetor, oil pump, etc.

6. Remove carbon deposits from the combustion chamber using a blunt tool.

CAUTION: *Take care not to scratch the combustion chamber as this may cause localized "hot-spots" during operation.*

Remove as much carbon as possible, then finish up with steel wool and solvent. Leaving stubborn deposits in place is not recommended. Be sure to clean out any carbon chips which may have accumulated in the spark plug hole.

7. Remove carbon from the piston crown in the same manner. The piston must be placed at top dead center while this is done. Still, care must be taken to remove any particles which may become trapped between the piston and cylinder wall. Use compressed air

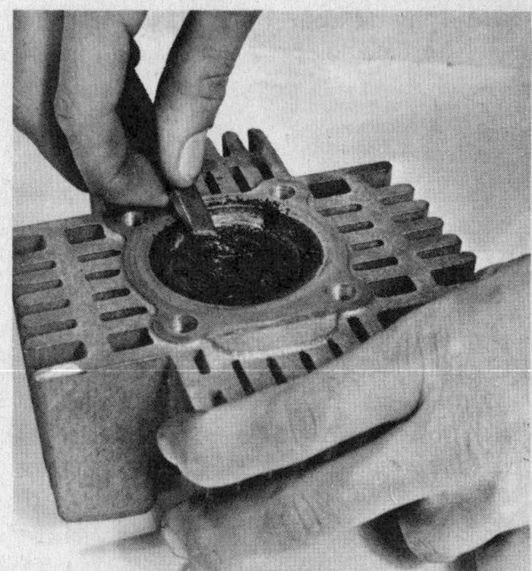

Decarbonizing the cylinder head

Removing carbon from the piston crown

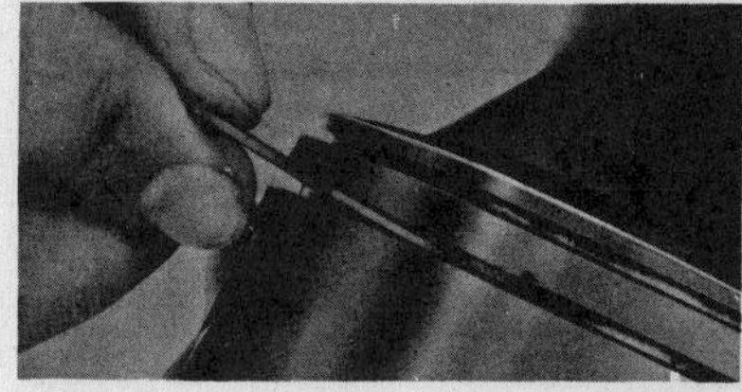

Use a piece of a broken ring to clean out the piston ring grooves

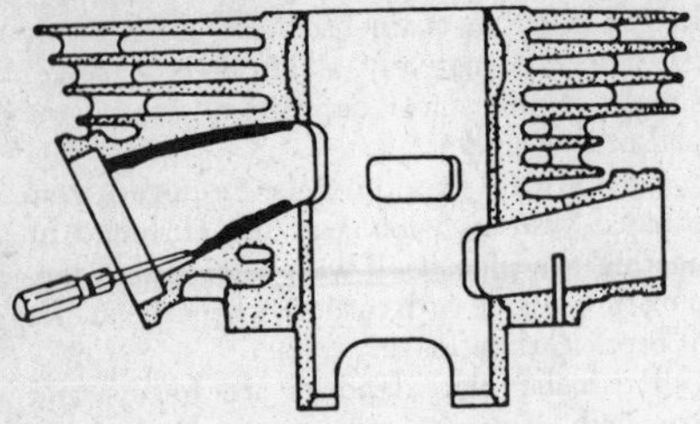

Removing exhaust port carbon buildup

to blow out such particles, or imbed grease between the piston and cylinder. When the piston is lowered in the bore, the grease will retain the particles which may then be wiped off. This procedure must be repeated several times to be effective.

8. To decarbonize the exhaust port, position the piston at the bottom of its stroke. Stuff a clean rag into the cylinder so that it covers the piston and blocks the exhaust port. Use a blunted instrument to scrape carbon from the exhaust port, being careful to prevent particles from entering the cylinder. If possible, parts can be decarbonized with a solvent specifically designed for this purpose, such as Gunk "Hydro-Seal."® Parts to be cleaned are immersed in the fluids for periods ranging from 4 to 24 hours. Be sure the solvent you choose is safe for aluminum.

9. If the cylinder is removed, check that the piston rings are free to move. If they are stuck, they must be freed or replacement is necessary. If the old rings are removed, clean out the ring grooves with a thin screwdriver, once again being careful not to gouge the metal.

10. When assembling, be sure that the cylinder head studs or bolts are clean. Use a torque wrench to tighten the nuts or bolts to the recommended tightness. Tighten the nuts or bolts in a cross pattern and in increments of a few ft. lbs.

STORAGE

Storage procedures will depend to some extent on the length of duration and the place where the machine is kept. Some or all of the following precautions should be taken:

1. Change the engine and/or transmission oil.

2. On two-strokes, drain the oil injection tank and stuff a clean, lint-free rag into the filler neck to keep out foreign matter and help prevent condensation.

3. Drain the fuel from the carburetor(s), fuel lines, and petcock.

4. If the machine is to be stored out-of-doors, fill the gas tank to the top. If it is to be stored in a closed area, drain the tank. Leave a small amount of gasoline in the tank and add a cup or more of oil. Slosh this mixture around inside the tank so the oil will coat the tank walls to prevent rust. These precautions are not necessary on machines with fiberglass or alloy tanks which need only be drained.

5. Remove the spark plug(s) and add an ounce or two of oil to each cylinder. Turn the engine over slowly several times, then add a little more oil. If possible, position the piston(s) at top dead center, and add a little more oil. Repeat this procedure every few weeks of storage. Stuff a piece of a clean, lint-free rag into the spark plug hole(s).

6. Place a piece of business card which has been coated with clean oil between the contact breaker points to retard oxidation.

7. Remove the battery from the motorcycle. Store it in a cool, dry place and trickle charge it monthly.

8. Put a coat of wax on all plated surfaces.

9. Support the machine vertically, preferably with both tires off the ground. Decrease tire pressure by a few psi.

10. Cover the machine with a breathable cover.

11. Before restoring the machine to service flush the gas tank and refill with fresh gasoline. Change the oil. Clean the oil out of the cylinder(s) by kicking the engine over briskly several times with the plug(s) out. Continue kicking the engine over to circulate the oil thoroughly before starting the engine (especially important on ohc models). Clean the points, check tire pressure, etc.

TUNE-UP

NOTE: *Specific tune-up procedures for individual motorcycles are given in the respective sections. Common operations applicable to all or most motorcycles follow.*

What constitutes a "tune-up" will vary according to what you ride. In general, some or all of the following items should be considered:

a. A compression test;

b. Spark plug inspection, cleaning, gapping, or replacement;

c. Breaker point inspection and gapping (if applicable);

d. Ignition timing;

e. Cam chain adjustment (if applicable);

f. Valve adjustment for four-strokes;

g. Carburetor synchronization, idle speed and mixture adjustments;

h. Carburetor cable adjustments and oil pump adjustments for injected two-strokes;

i. A road test to determine whether settings are correct or should be rechecked.

Some of these procedures are not necessary on certain models. Obviously, you do not have to worry about breaker points on CDI-equipped machines. On most magneto-ignition bikes, changing the point gap is the way ignition timing changes are made, so this will be one procedure, rather than two separate operations.

In other cases, the operation may require special equipment which you do not have, or be extremely complex. Setting valve clearances on a Triumph is easy. Hondas use somewhat smaller clearances, and are therefore a bit more difficult to do with great accuracy. Motorcycles with camshafts which ride directly on the valves have clearances adjusted with shims, and this can be a painstaking operation, and far from the ability of the average owner.

In general, however, you might need some or all of the following equipment for a complete tune-up:

A wire brush for removing spark plug deposits;

A points' file;

Wire-type feeler gauges for gapping spark plugs;

A good set of blade-type feeler gauges for gapping breaker points and checking valve clearances;

A micrometer for adjusting valve clearances on dohc engines where the cams ride directly on the valves;

A timing light or ohmmeter for checking ignition timing;

Vacuum gauges for synchronizing carburetors;

A dial gauge for determining piston position of some two-strokes;

A torque wrench for cylinder head installation if decarbonization is necessary prior to the tune-up;

A compression gauge;

A selection of small screwdrivers and wrenches.

In many cases, poor running or hard starting are due to the fact that routine adjustments which should be checked periodically have not been carried out.

If a competent tune-up is performed, and the machine still fails to run correctly, then you can begin to check more serious items.

Tune-up related items, though, are very common sources of trouble. Replacement items such as spark plugs and breaker points are subject to harsh conditions. Points will become worn just in normal use due to the job they perform. They must make and break electrical connections for spark to occur. They also have a fiber heel which is constantly in contact with the breaker cam, and this will wear.

The points will become unserviceable even faster if they are not properly adjusted, or if the condenser is bad.

Spark plugs can last 15000 miles in some motorcycles under some conditions. They can also become fouled after only 1500 miles in other bikes under other conditions. The number of factors which affect spark plug life are legion. If the fuel/air mixture is too lean or too rich, the plugs may burn or foul. Two-stroke oil pump adjustments will naturally come into play here. If the plug is too hot or too cold for the type of riding you do, this will also have an adverse affect not only on performance, but also on the life span of the plugs.

If you have a two-stroke, even the brand of injection oil you use will have a bearing on the matter.

All these items should be kept in mind when attempting a tune-up. Manufacturers give recommended change intervals for things like points and plugs, but these are really only estimates based on their experience with machines used under "normal" conditions. "Normal" for you, certainly, may be another matter.

COMPRESSION TEST

1. A compression check should be made before each tune-up, as this will give a general clue to engine condition.
2. The engine should be at operating temperature.
3. Insert the gauge into the spark plug hole. If the gauge is the "hold-in" type, use a quantity of oil on the rubber tip to give a good seal.
4. Hold the throttle wide open and kick the engine over briskly. Note the compression reading.
5. Although not all manufacturers provide compression specifications, most four-strokes will average about 160 psi, and most two-strokes about 110 psi.
6. On multi-cylinder machines, the difference between cylinders is important. Cylinders must have compression within 10% of each other. If they vary more than this, suspect some sort of mechanical damage to the low cylinder(s).
7. On four-strokes with low compression, squirt a small quantity of motor oil into the cylinder and check compression again. If it is now higher than the original reading, the piston rings or cylinder are worn. If the second compression reading is not higher than the first, suspect worn, damaged, or improperly adjusted valves.
8. On two-strokes especially, if the compression increases over a series of several tune-ups, the piston crown and combustion chamber are becoming carboned up and should be decarbonized.

Checking compression

SPARK PLUGS

1. Spark plug deposits may be cleaned with a wire brush. Remove deposits from the center and side electrodes. Clean out any trapped particles with solvent or air pressure. If a commercial "plug cleaner" (sandblaster) is used, note that oily or oilfouled plugs should not be cleaned with these devices as the oil will catch and hold the abrasive cleaning particles.
2. Check electrode condition. Replace the plugs if they are worn, rounded or partially melted. "Square off" electrodes with a thin file.

NOTE: *Do not attempt to file plugs with a fine wire center electrode. This will only bend or damage the electrode making the plug useless.*

3. Adjust the gap by bending the side electrode. Plugs should be gapped with a wire-type feeler gauge, rather than the blade type, since they are more accurate.

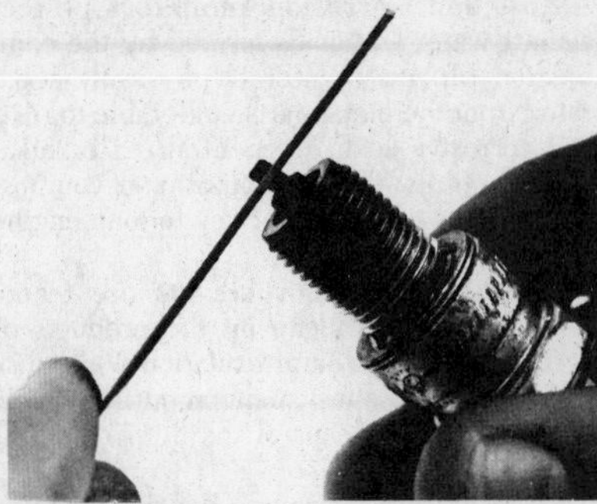

Squaring off the center electrode

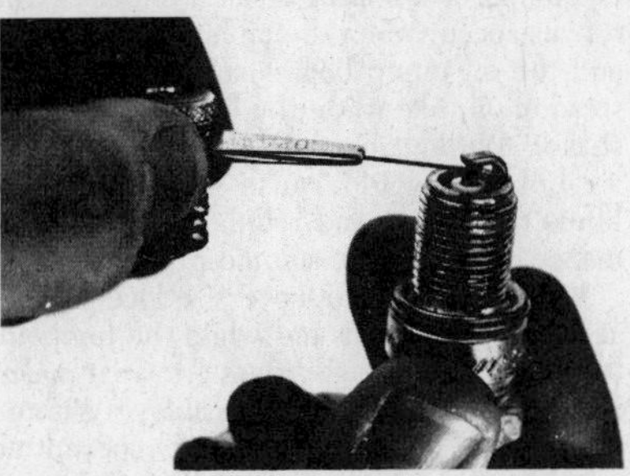

Checking spark plug gap

4. If new plugs are being fitted, be sure they are the correct heat range and reach. The latter is especially important. If plug reach is too long, the lower threads will protrude into the combustion chamber. Even if the piston does not hit the plug when the engine is turned over, these threads will become carbon coated during operation, and it will become impossible to remove the plug.

If a plug with too short a reach is fitted, the plug hole will shield the spark with adverse effects on the combustion process. Additionally, the lower plug hole threads will become carbon covered, making it difficult or impossible to fit the correct reach plug later.

5. Spark plug heat range refers to the plug's ability to dissipate heat, and is dependent upon the amount of insulation around the center electrode.

Spark plugs of a certain heat range are recommended by the various factories after extensive testing, and should therefore be suitable for most riders.

There is, however, some range of choice if performance of the standard plugs is not satisfactory. If the machine is run constantly at high speeds or under heavy loads, a plug one heat range colder than standard may be used. Note that the colder plug may tend to load up during low speed operation, however.

If the machine is run at predominately slow speeds and low loads, a plug one heat range hotter than standard can be used.

CAUTION: *Fittings of plugs more than one heat range step in either direction from the recommended plug is not recommended.*

6. Before fitting spark plugs, check that the sealing gasket is in good condition. Lightly lubricate the threads with oil or light grease. Use a torque wrench, where possible, to install the plugs. Take care not to overtighten the plugs. Plugs with 14 mm diameter threads should be torqued to about 18 ft lbs. Smaller plugs (10–12 mm) should

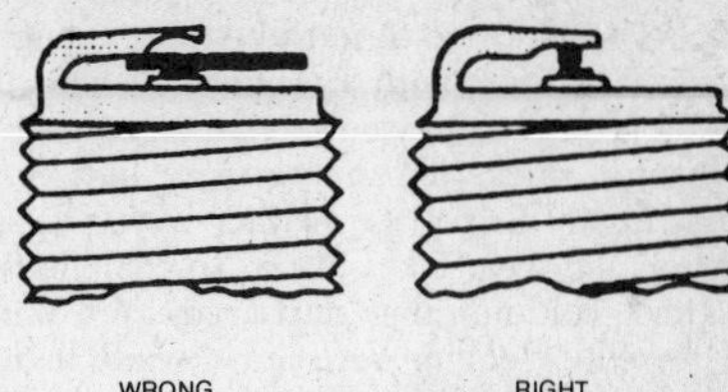

Use a wire-type feeler gauge to gap used plugs

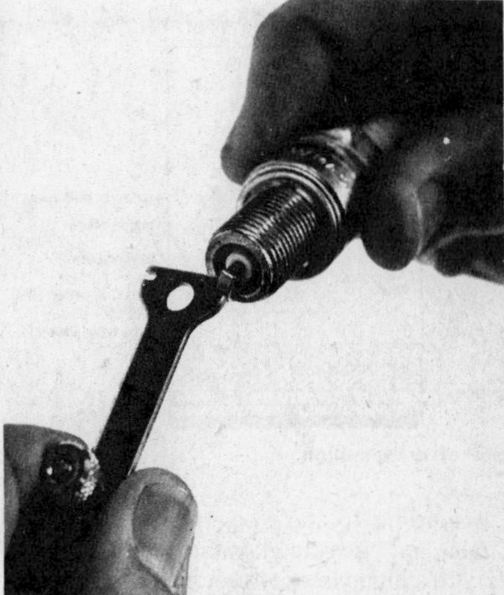

Bending the side electrode

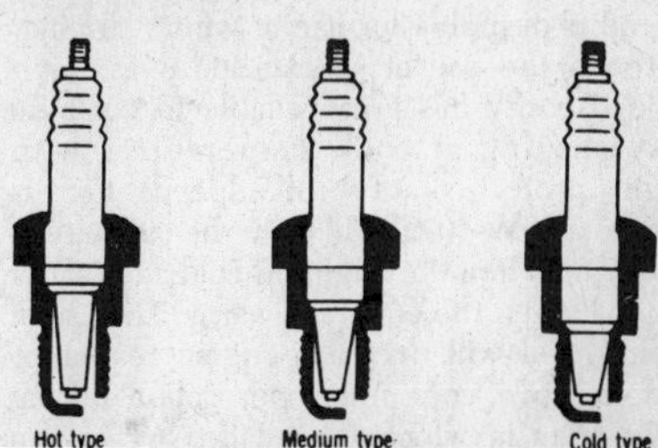

Spark plug heat range is a function of the length of the center electrode insulator

Normal (left) and projected tip center electrodes

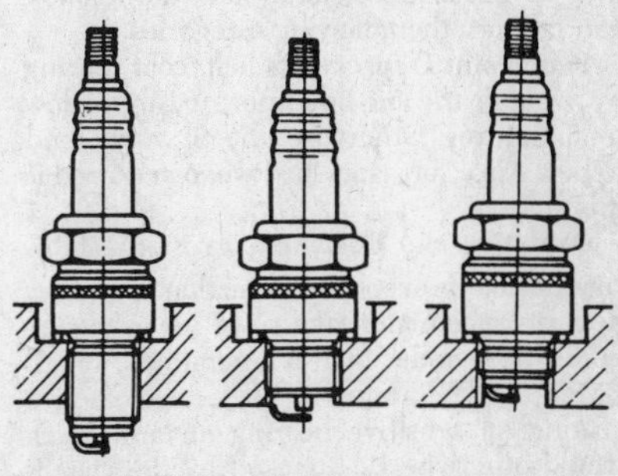

Be sure that plugs of the proper reach (center) are fitted

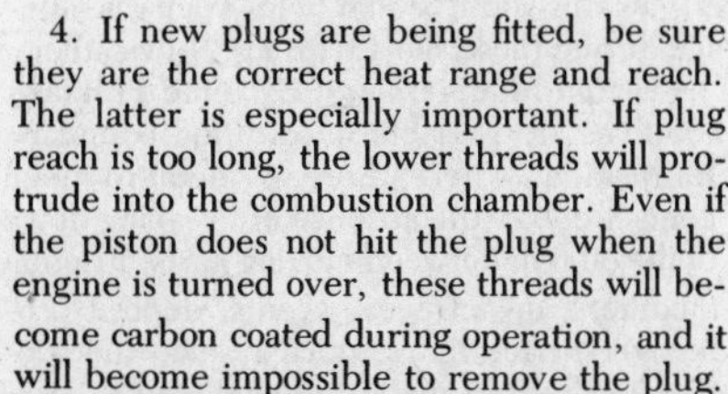

bricate. Once there, it must be thick enough to separate them with a slippery oil film. If the oil is too thin, it won't separate the parts; if it's too thick, it can't squeeze between them in the first place—either way, excess friction and wear takes place. To complicate matters, cold-morning starts require a thin oil to reduce engine resistance, while high-speed driving requires a thick oil which can lubricate vital engine parts at temperatures up to 250° F.

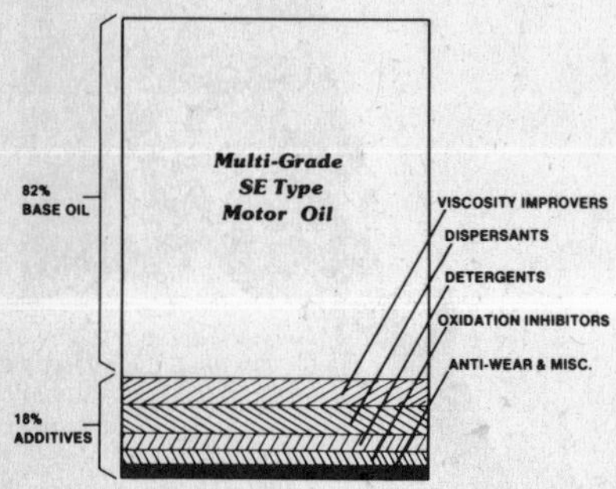

"SE" oil composition

According to the Society of Automotive Engineers' viscosity classification system, an oil with a high viscosity number (e.g., 40) will be thicker than one with a lower number (e.g., 10W). The "W" in 10W indicates that the oil is desirable for use in winter driving. Through the use of special additives, multiple-viscosity oils are available to combine easy starting at cold temperatures with engine protection at turnpike speeds. For example, a 10W-40 oil will have the viscosity of a 10W oil when the engine is cold and that of a 40 oil when the engine is warm. The use of such an oil will decrease engine resistance and improve your miles per gallon during short trips in which the oil doesn't have a chance to warm up.

Some of the more popular multiple-viscosity oils are 5W-20, 5W-30, 10W-30, 10W-40, 20W-40, 20W-50, and 10W-50. In general, a 5W-20 or 5W-30 oil is suitable for temperatures below 0°F, 10W-30 or 10W-40 whenever the lowest temperature expected is 0° F., and 20W-40 whenever the lowest temperature expected is 32° F. However, consult your owner's manual or the "Recommended Lubricants" chart at the end of each "Maintenance" section for the recommended viscosity range for your motorcycle and the outside temperature in which it operates.

Additives

A high-quality engine oil will include a number of chemical compounds known as additives. These are blended in at the refinery and fall into the following categories.

Pour Point Depressants help cold starting by making the oil flow more easily at low temperatures. Otherwise, the oil would tend to be a waxy substance just when you need it the most.

Oxidation and Bearing Corrosion Inhibitors help to prevent the formation of gummy deposits which can take place when engine oil oxidizes under high temperatures. In addition, these inhibitors place a protective coating on sensitive bearing metals, which would otherwise be attacked by the chemicals formed by oil oxidation.

Rust and Corrosion Inhibitors protect against water and acids formed by the combustion process. Water is physically separated from the metal parts vulnerable to rust, and corrosive acids are neutralized by alkaline chemicals. The neutralization of combustion acids is an important key to long engine life.

Detergents and Dispersants use teamwork. Detergents clean up the products of normal combustion and oxidation while dispersants keep them suspended until they can be removed by means of the filter or an oil change.

Foam Inhibitors prevent the tiny air bubbles which can be caused by fast-moving engine parts whipping air into the oil. Foam can also occur when the oil level falls too low and the oil pump begins sucking up air instead of oil (like when the kids finish a milkshake). Without foam inhibitors, these tiny air bubbles would cause hydraulic valve lifters to collapse and reduce engine performance and economy significantly.

Viscosity Index Improvers reduce the rate at which an oil thins out when the temperature climbs. These additives are what makes multiple-viscosity oils possible. Without them, a single-weight oil which permitted easy starting on a cold morning might thin out and cause you to lose your engine on a hot afternoon. If you use a multiple-viscosity oil, it's this additive that helps your gas mileage during those short trips in cold weather.

Friction Modifiers and Extreme Pressure additives are valuable in so-called boundary lubrication, where there is metal-to-metal contact due to the absence or breaking down of the oil film between moving parts. Friction modifiers, or anti-wear agents, deposit protective surface films which reduce the friction and heat of metal-to-metal contact. Extreme pressure additives work by reacting chemically with metal surfaces involved in high pressure contact.

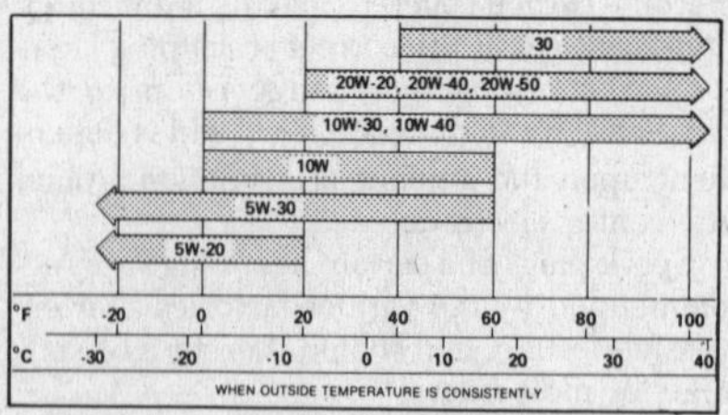

Oil recommendation chart

Synthetic Oils

Recently, a number of major oil companies have introduced synthetic oils, which are composed of manmade hydrocarbons instead of petroleum based hydrocarbons. There are quite a few claims being made for synthetic oils, including increased gas mileage, extended oil drain intervals, improved hot and cold weather engine performance, and less wear and tear on engines. Whether or not these claims are true has yet to be decided. One thing is certain, however. Synthetic oil is inexpensive. At prices that range up to three dollars a quart, synthetic oils will have to live up to every one of their claims to be cost-effective but, as long as it has an SE or SF rating, synthetic oil certainly will not harm your engine.

Transmission Lubricants

Four-strokes with transmissions which use a separate oil supply and two-strokes may require special oil for the gears.

Most four-strokes specify SAE 80 or SAE 90 "EP" (extreme pressure) lubricant for this purpose. This is a gear oil viscosity and has nothing to do with motor oil viscosity. For example, an SAE 80W gear oil can have the same viscosity characteristics as an SAE 40 or 50 motor oil.

Two-strokes generally use a lighter oil in their transmissions. This may be 10W-30 or 20W-50 motor oil. Check the "Recommended Lubricants" chart at the end of each "Maintenance" section for the proper oil for your bike.

Drive Box Lubricants

All shaft-drive motorcycles currently in production recommend SAE 90 EP gear lube for the rear drive box. In winter, SAE 80 EP may be used.

Front Fork Oil

Refer to the "Recommended Lubricants" chart included in each "Maintenance" section for fork oil recommendations. Depending on make and model, fork oils may range from ATF (Automatic Transmission Fluid) to SAE 30W motor oil or specially designed fork oils.

NOTE: *When fork capacities are given, the quantities shown always refer to the amount needed in each fork leg.*

Chassis Grease

Chassis grease is generally needed for the swing arm pivot, drum brake cams, exposed pivoting parts, and anywhere else that grease fittings occur.

Other uses include lubrication of speedometer drive boxes, internal lubrication of instrument cables, waterproofing control cables, throttle drums, etc.

There is not much differentiation among chassis lube. Generally, anything that will fit your cartridge-type grease gun should do the job.

Wheel Bearing Grease

Wheel bearing grease should be of the long fiber (high temperature) type, especially for motorcycles with disc brakes.

Bearing grease is also used for steering head bearings.

Disc Brake Fluid

DOT 3 or DOT 4 hydraulic disc brake fluid is recommended for most motorcycles. The SAE standard is J1709. The rating can be found on the can. Any exceptions will be noted in the applicable section.

Drive Chain Lubricant

A good brand of lubricant developed and marketed specifically for motorcycle drive chains is recommended in most cases. Follow the manufacturer's instructions when applying the lube.

Some drive chains now in use have rubber o-rings between the side plates and rollers. These o-rings may be damaged by certain

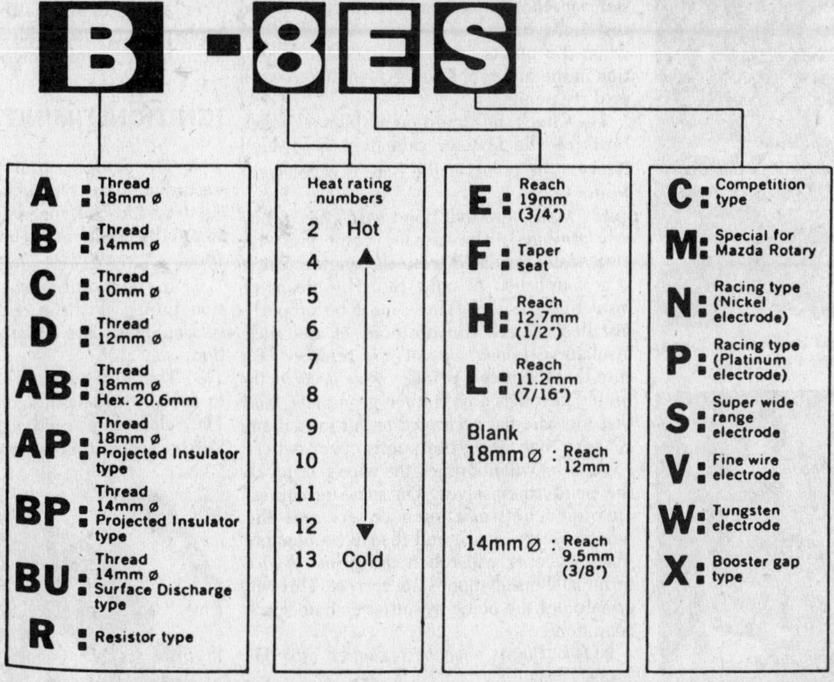

The letters and numbers that make up the spark plug type are the manufacturers' code for various characteristics of the plug. This is NGK's system

be tightened to about 12 ft lbs. If it is not possible to use a torque wrench, turning the plugs about ¼ to ½ turn after they are hand-tight should secure them sufficiently.

NOTE: *Plugs for individual models as recommended by the manufacturer are given in the "Tune-Up Specifications" chart of each section. Comparable plugs of different makes may also be used provided heat range and reach are the same.*

BREAKER POINTS

The breaker points and the condensers wired to them are one of the most critical parts of the ignition system. The points are subjected to wear through electrical arcing and wear of the heel or rubbing block which bears against the breaker cam. For this reason, the points are worthy of close attention.

Inspection

1. Make visual inspection of the breaker point surfaces. A slight graying of the surfaces is normal.
2. Check for pitting or burned spots on the points.
3. If the surfaces are the normal gray, or if burnt spots are small, the point surfaces may be restored by running a thin, flat points file through them. This file should be designed specifically for contact breaker points, and the points should be open when using the file.
4. A too vigorous use of the file may render the points unusable. Do not remove any more material than is necessary to eliminate pitting or other irregularities.
5. After filing, clean off the points with a solvent. Finish up by allowing the points to close on a piece of business card, and then pulling it out. Continue doing this until the points no longer leave a mark on the card.
6. It is also possible to restore points by working them on an oilstone, which of course will require their removal from the machine. In this case care must be taken to avoid removing too much metal.
7. If pitting or burning is severe, the points should be replaced rather than filed.

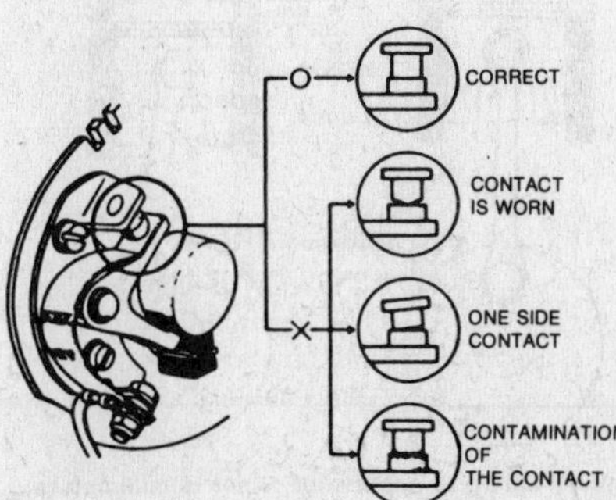

Breaker point conditions

Points should be aligned when closed as shown

Points incorrectly aligned

Unserviceable points. Note deeply pitted area, cracked contact, and the fact that the pitted area is off center indicating misalignment

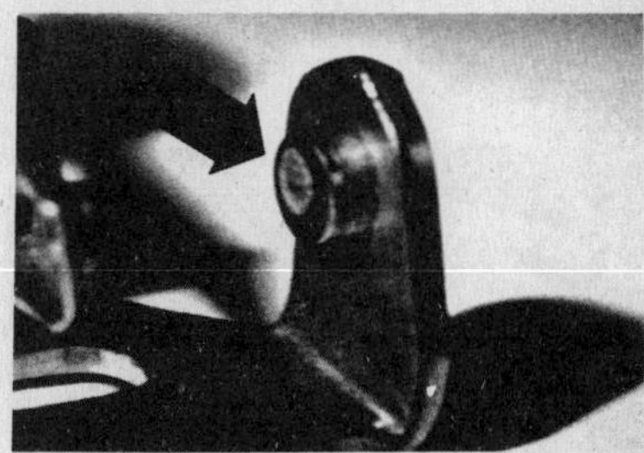

Check contact surface for pitting as shown

Extremely dirty points must be cleaned. Excess breaker cam lubricant is often the cause

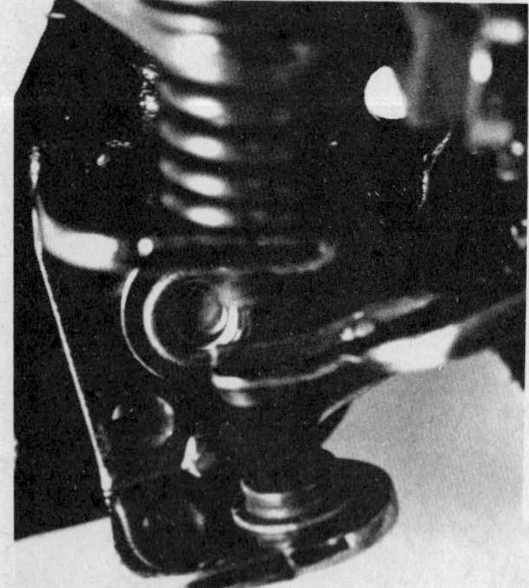
These points show normal wear and require only cleaning to stay in use

NOTE: *New points may have a preservative coating on them to retard oxidation. This must be removed with a solvent before the points are installed.*

The condenser(s) should be replaced as well.

8. When closed, points should lie flat against one another. If they do not, it is possible that one of them is unevenly worn or that one or the other is bent out of alignment. In this case, replace the points.

9. On battery-ignition motorcycles, an ohmmeter can be used to give a further clue to point condition. When closed, the resistance across the points should be zero. If resistance is somewhat higher than this value, the points should be replaced.

10. If the ignition timing is being set by a static method, note that the reaction of the test light or meter should be immediate when the points open. A noticeable hesitation in the meter or light is often due to worn or dirty points.

Filing breaker points

11. Check the condition of the heel which bears on the breaker cam (if it is visible). Replace the points if the heel is excessively worn.

12. Make sure that point wire(s) are properly arranged. The moving point must be electrically insulated from the engine which is accomplished in most cases by means of insulating washers. These must be properly installed. Check the positions of any such insulators whenever points are replaced. Be sure that the points primary wire is correctly routed through any rubber grommets, and that the wire has no frayed or cut insulation. Be sure that fitting the points cover (where applicable) will not pinch the wire(s) or touch the points themselves. On some machines, clearance between such covers and the points is very small, and it may be possible that the cover will touch the primary wire terminal if installation is not correct. This will ground out the points resulting in a no-spark condition.

NOTE: *Points must be regapped after filing.*

Checking point gap

Lubrication

1. It is necessary to lubricate the point breaker cam occasionally to minimize wear to the breaker point heel, which will eventually cause retarded ignition timing.

2. Most motorcycles have one or two felt wicks so mounted that they gradually apply lubricant to the cam. A small amount of high melting-point grease should be applied to the felt, and the felt arranged to that it bears lightly on the breaker cam.

3. On a few motorcycles, the felt does not contact the breaker cam directly, but sits in the breaker cam shaft. Lubricators of this type should get a few drops of oil.

4. If the felt wick is missing, a small quantity of grease should be applied to the cam itself. Care must be taken in either case, however, not to overlubricate, or the points may be fouled.

5. A drop of oil, or other lubricant such as molybdenum disulphide, can also be applied to the moving point pivot.

IGNITION TIMING

1. The ignition timing procedure varies according to the type of ignition system fitted (battery-and-coil, magneto, CDI) and according to the number of cylinders, and other factors.

2. In the most basic sense, however, ignition timing is the procedure whereby the spark plug is set to fire at an exact piston position.

3. There are two ways the plug is signaled to fire: by mechanical or electronic means. The "electronic" method refers to Capacitor Discharge Ignition systems. The more com-

Typical timing marks: "T" for top dead center, "F" for the fixed advance firing point, and two slash marks for the full advance firing point

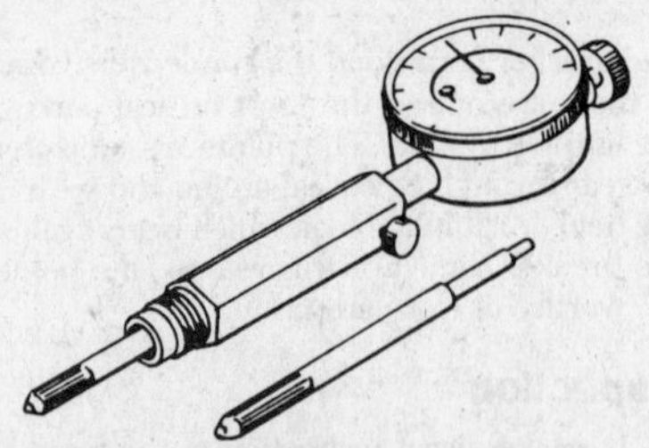
Dial indicator for finding piston position when there are no marks provided

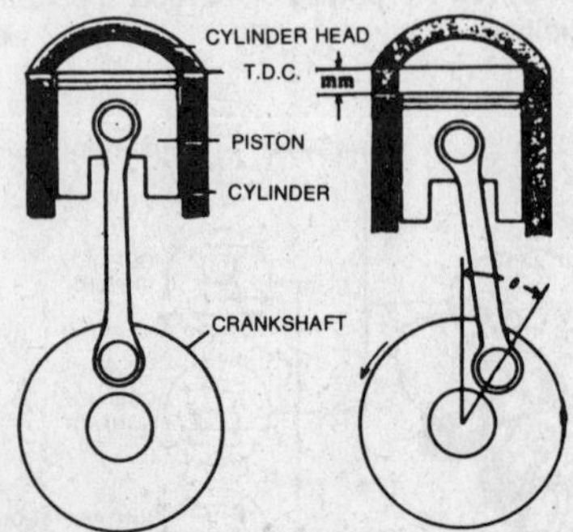

Ignition timing is expressed either in millimeters before top dead center (TDC), or degrees of crankshaft rotation before TDC

mon mechanical signal device refers to the familiar contact breaker points found on most motorcycles.

The spark plug fires at the instant the breaker points begin to separate.

4. To check the ignition timing, then, one must know when the points open, and where the piston is at this point.

Piston position can be determined in a number of ways, depending on model. On many motorcycles, timing reference marks are provided on the alternator or magneto rotor. These usually indicate piston Top Dead Center, the plug firing point at fixed advance, and the firing point at full advance.

On other models, however, piston position must be determined by means of a dial gauge or a degree wheel. Since in these cases the ignition timing specification is given in millimeters or inches before top dead center, or in degrees of crankshaft revolution before top dead center, the dial gauge or degree wheel is used to position the piston at the proper spot and to check if the points open at that point.

5. When piston position has been established by one of the above methods, the next step is to determine when the points open. This can be accomplished in several ways.

On magneto-ignition motorcycles, an ohmmeter or "points checker" is the simplest method of determining when the points open. One lead of the test instrument is connected to ground on the engine, and the other to the points primary wire, or primary wire terminal.

When the points begin to open, the meter will register an increase in resistance.

A device known as a "buzz-box" accomplished the same thing, but allows the mechanic to hear when the points open, since it changes the pitch of its signal when this happens.

Battery ignition motorcycles can be timed with a simple test or continuity light.

6. On the large majority of four-strokes, and on most two-strokes which are equipped with an electric starter, a timing advance mechanism is incorporated into the breaker cam. As the name implies, this device automatically advances the ignition timing (allowing the spark plug to fire sooner relative to the piston position) as the engine revolutions increase. This is the reason for the two sets of firing marks found on some alternator and magneto rotors mentioned previously. If an ohmmeter, test light, or continuity light is used to check the timing, the engine will not be running and you will be checking the timing at the fixed advance point unless you open the advance mechanism manually. This is "static timing." On some motorcycles, "dynamic timing" is also possible. This is done with the engine running, and it is possible to

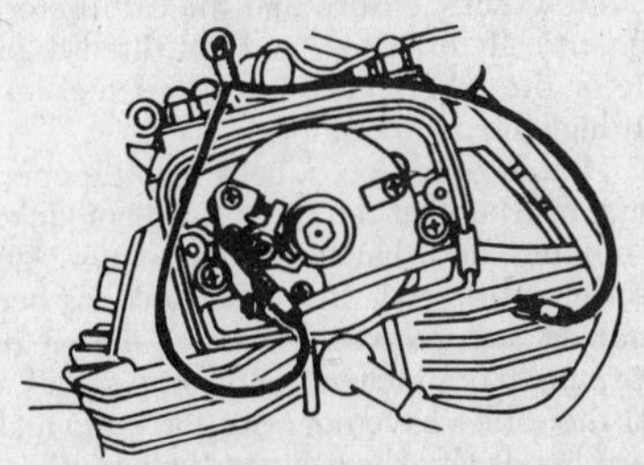

Test light in use

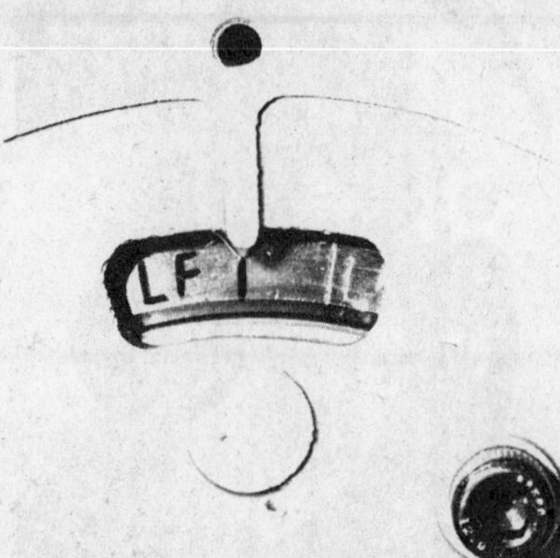

Static firing point for the left-side cylinder

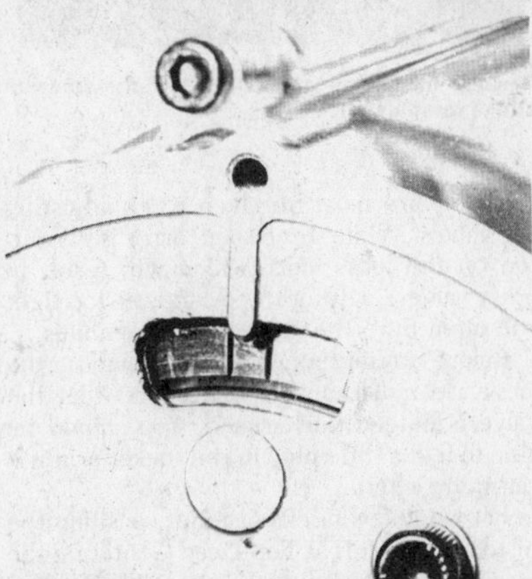

Full advance firing point is indicated by two lines

check the timing both at the fixed advance *and* the fully advanced points. To do this, an automotive-type strobe light is used. Checking the timing at the full advanced position is preferred, since this is more critical to proper engine operation.

7. On most models, the ignition timing is changed by rotating the plate on which the points are mounted, or by moving the points themselves. This allows them to open sooner or later relative to the piston movement. On others, notably two-strokes, ignition timing can only be changed by changing the point gap.

8. Breaker points should be inspected, filed and cleaned if necessary, and gapped before checking the ignition timing.

Timing Troubleshooting

If trouble is encountered during the ignition timing procedure, check the following possibilities:

1. If the points have been replaced, check that the contact surfaces are cleaned. Some points are coated with a preservative to prevent oxidation which must be removed with solvent when the points are put into service.

2. If new points have been installed, check that all insulating washers, grommets, etc., are correctly installed. On battery-ignition systems the moving points must be electrically insulated from the engine (ground) when the points are open. On magneto ignition motorcycles there will be some continuity here in any case.

3. If there is a no-spark condition after the points have been gapped, the feeler gauge blade probably deposited some foreign matter on the contact surfaces. Clean them and try again. Such a condition may also cause sparking at the points when the engine is running, but this may also be caused by a bad condenser.

4. If it is not possible to set the gap wide enough, the breaker points heel is worn.

5. If it is not possible to set the timing correctly, a severely worn breaker point heel may be the cause. Alternately, a sticking or otherwise defective timing advance mechanism may be the trouble.

6. Using the dynamic method of ignition timing allows the operation of the timing advance mechanism to be checked. On many machines, the mechanism is fitted behind the breaker point mounting plate and is easily accessible after this plate is removed. On those magneto machines which use this mechanism, it is probably incorporated into the back of the flywheel.

Timing advance mechanisms consist of spring-controlled weights which are pivoted at one end. As engine speed increases, the centrifugal force exerted on the weights gradually overcomes the spring tension, and the weights swing out from their pivot point, carrying the cam along with them.

As shown in the illustration, turning the breaker cam in the advance direction will swing the weights out. When released the cam should return to its original position.

Sticking or frozen advance mechanisms must be replaced. It may be possible to free them with penetrating oil. The most common problem is loss of spring tension which occurs after extended mileage and which allows the advance to come on too soon.

Checking the auto advance mechanism

Electronic Ignition

Electronic ignition systems (those not using breaker points) have been used for several years on a number of two-stroke motorcycles, and have recently been seen on some four-strokes as well.

Point-less systems are usually referred to as "CDI" (Capacitor Discharge Ignition) or, as in the case of Suzuki, "PEI," or Pointless Electronic Ignition.

In either case the principle is the same: the substitution of a solid-state electrical component system in place of the breaker points.

The advantages are obvious: usually, the system needs only periodic inspection of the timing which should never vary, and it obviates the need to gap, clean, or replace the breaker points. A hotter spark and more accurate ignition timing can also be obtained.

Although similar in theory, these electronic systems differ widely from make to make and it is not possible to generalize about them.

In practice, they offer either low maintenance or no maintenance once set properly, and it is usually not necessary to recheck the ignition timing as a part of the tune-up procedure. For more specific information, refer to the individual sections.

VALVE ADJUSTMENTS

For valve adjustment procedures for four-stroke engines, refer to the individual sections.

In all cases, valves must be adjusted on a cold engine.

Most motorcycles use a simple screw fitting on the end of the rocker arm to make this adjustment, although there are exceptions. Some machines, like the 350 Honda, have the rocker arms mounted on eccentric shafts, and these shafts are rotated to provide more or less clearance, the clearance being measured between the valve stem and the rocker arm. Some others use shims between the cam lobes and the valve stems to adjust the clearance, and in these instances you will need a micrometer and a selection of shims of the proper thicknesses.

On machines on which clearance can be adjusted with feeler gauge blades, note that the blade should be a slip fit in a correctly adjusted valve.

Checking valve clearance

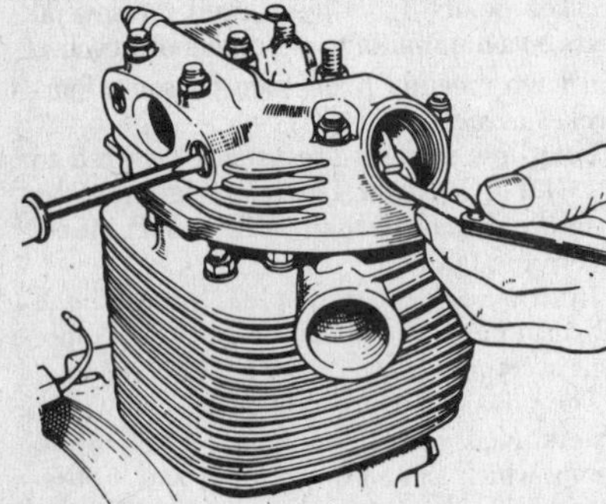

Some models use eccentric shafts to adjust clearance

Position the piston at TDC on the compression stroke to adjust the valves

Great care must be taken when adjusting the valves. While some small error is permitted on the loose side (which will result in noisy valves), setting the clearances too tight will often burn the valves after few miles.

Before attempting to check or adjust the valve clearance, always check first that the valve is indeed fully closed. You should be able to feel a little play in the rocker arm if it can be reached.

For single-cylinder machines, position the piston so that it is at Top Dead Center on the *compression* stroke. This will allow all valves to be adjusted, since all will be closed. Piston position marks can be found on the alternator or generator rotor, and "T" will indicate top dead center when it is aligned with the stationary timing mark. Note, however, that this is no guarantee that the piston is on the compression stroke: it may be on the *exhaust* stroke. Therefore, check for clearance at the valves before going further. If one valve seems to be open, rotate the engine 360° until the "T" mark is again aligned with the timing mark and recheck for play.

For twins, the procedure is essentially the same. If rotor marks are there, they will probably be differentiated "T" and "LT", the first being TDC for the right cylinder, the second for the left cylinder.

If the twin has a 360° crankshaft (meaning that the pistons rise and fall together), there may be only one set of marks. What can be done in this case is to turn the engine over until the right (or left) intake or exhaust valve is opened by the rocker arm, then you can be sure that the corresponding valve for the other cylinder is closed, and can be adjusted. Continue to turn the engine over in like manner until all valves have been checked.

Three- and four-cylinder engines are somewhat more complicated and information regarding them can be found in the individual model sections.

CAM CHAINS

Occasional adjustment of cam chains is necessary on most overhead-cam motorcycles in which the cam is driven by this method. Some, however, have hydraulically-tensioned chains which need no attention.

On most designs, the chain tensioner consists of a spring-loaded rod with a chain slipper at one end. When the crankshaft is positioned at the point yielding the most slack at the point on the chain where the tensioner is located, a nut or bolt is loosened which releases the rod and allows the spring tension to take up the chain slack. The locknut or bolt is then tightened securing the rod in this position.

Obviously, the most important part of the procedure is ensuring that the crankshaft is properly positioned. Usually, the position will be given with reference to the timing marks on the alternator rotor.

Refer to the individual model section for specific cam chain adjustment procedures.

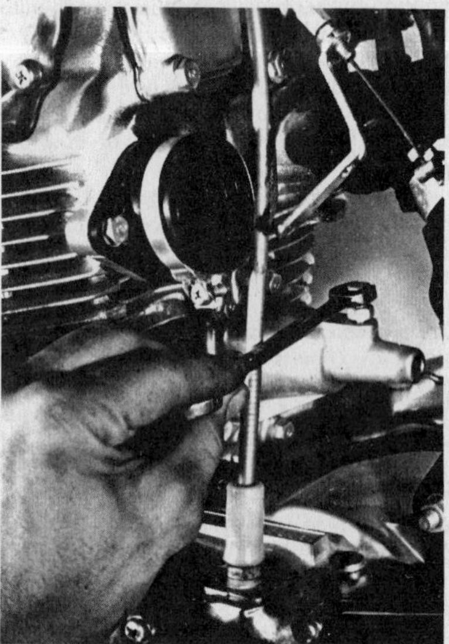

Adjusting cam chain tension

CARBURETORS

Carburetor tune-up procedure will largely depend upon the type of engine, the type and number of carburetors, what kind of carburetor controls are fitted, and ancillary systems, if fitted, such as oil pumps and the like which operate in conjunction with the carbureator.

Carburetor adjustments must always be made when the engine is at operating temperature.

Pre-Adjustment Checks

Before attempting to make carburetor adjustments, all of the following points should be checked:

1. Carburetor alignment. On flexible-mounted units, ensure that the carburetor(s) are vertically oriented, and not tilted to one side or the other. This may effect fuel level and high-speed operation.

2. Cable condition. Check throttle operation, ensuring that the cable(s) are not kinked or binding, and that they and the twist-grip are well-lubricated. If the gas tank has been removed and reinstalled, check that it has not trapped or pinched the throttle cables, or that the cables have not been forced to make sharp bends anywhere along their route.

3. Ancillary systems. Carburetor adjust-

ments should be made last after all other systems have been attended to in order to prevent misleading symptoms. Check that the air clean is serviceable, the spark plugs are in good condition, valves (four-stroke) are correctly adjusted, and the ignition timing at least approximately correct. Also ensure that the gasoline is reasonably fresh, of the correct octane, and that foreign material, such as water or dirt, has been purged from the fuel system. Check fuel filters, if applicable.

Cable Adjustment

1. On most motorcycles, provision is made for adjusting the throttle cable to compensate for stretching. The adjuster is usually found at or near the twist-grip. This device should be adjusted so that the twist-grip has a small amount of noticeable free-play when turned. In general, this free-play should amount to about 10–15° of grip rotation before the slides begin to lift.

2. On oil-injection two-strokes, the oil pump cable adjustment must be checked any time the throttle cable is adjusted.

3. After adjustment, turn the forks slowly from side to side with the engine idling. Idle speed must not change or the cable is too tightly adjusted or too short. Check routing.

Idle Speed and Mixture

Idle speeds which are recommended by the manufacturer should be adhered to in most cases. The idle running of a motorcycle engine is usually the most unsatisfactory carburetor range. There are many reasons for this. For one, the quantities of fuel and air which are going into the engine are relatively small, and are controlled by equally smallish passages. These are more likely to become clogged with dirt or varnish than the much larger jets, and the mixture will then be upset. Further, the relative quantities of gas and air are more critical at idle, a situation which is compounded by the fact that one or the other can be adjusted by means of a knob or screw on the outside of the carburetor, and can easily be adjusted incorrectly.

Direct-control carburetor. Pilot air screw (left) and throttle stop screw (center)

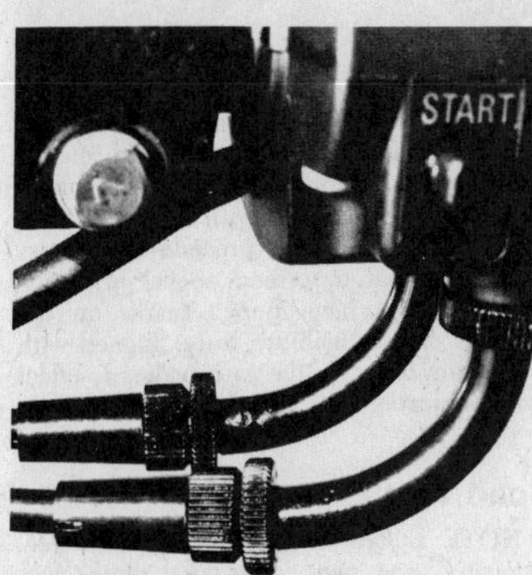

Throttle cable adjusters

Finally, since the engine is turning slowly, and is not under load, any irregularities in the mixture flow cause an erratic idle which may be irritating.

On most motorcycles, a satisfactory idle can be obtained by carefully setting the carburetors, ignition, and plugs to the recommended specifications. As noted, above, idle speed should be set to the recommended specification. An idle speed which is too low may cause trouble by making smooth transition to the slow or mid-range circuit impossible. On some motorcycles, too low an idle may cause damage to bearings and other moving parts due to the great lapse between power pulses.

CV carburetor. The throttle lever screw (arrow) adjusts idle speed while the pilot fuel screw (near manifold clamp) controls idle mixture

On the other hand, too high an idle speed may cause the rpm to hang up for a moment or so when the throttle is closed. It may also make engaging the gears noisy or difficult, or result in excessive brake lining wear by negating the effects of engine braking.

Because of the low engine speeds involved, minor misadjustments or slightly defective components will be much more noticeable at idle.

The idle mixture is determined largely by the *pilot air screw* which controls the amount of air mixing with the idle circuit jets, or the *pilot fuel screw* which controls the amount of gasoline passing into the circuit.

Carburetors may be equipped with one or the other of these screws. While exceptions exist, on most carburetors the location of the screw will indicate whether it is an air screw or a fuel screw. Generally, pilot *air* screws are located on the intake side of the carburetor, while most pilot fuel screws are located between the throttle slide and the engine manifold. Most "CV" carburetors use pilot fuel screws.

It is only important to know whether you have an "air screw" or a "fuel screw" if you intend to make mixture changes based on plug readings or road tests. Turning an *air* screw *in* will give a richer mixture, while turning it *out* will lean the mixture out. For pilot *fuel* screws, exactly the opposite is true.

Regardless of type, pilot screw settings are given by the manufacturer, and should be adhered to, at least to within certain limits. The pilot screw settings are expressed in *turns out from the seated position.* The pilot screw's tip is tapered and is mated to an air or fuel passage. To make the adjustment, the screw is turned in gently until you can feel that it is *lightly* seated, then backed out the given number of turns. For example, if your specification for the pilot screw setting is "2½," you will back the screw out this number of times.

When turning these screws in, it is best to be very careful, as it is possible to ruin the tapered portion of the screw if it is turned down too tightly.

When performing a tune-up, always turn the pilot screws out to the given specification, then make any necessary adjustments. It should not be necessary to vary the screw setting more than ½ turn from the given setting unless changes have been made to the intake, engine, or exhaust systems. If it is not possible to obtain satisfactory performance with the settings as specified, suspect clogged carburetor passages or air leaks, etc.

NOTE: *On many late-model motorcycles, the pilot screws are covered with limiter caps or other devices which will prevent any readjustment. These caps are fitted to conform with clean air regulations, and they should not be removed, nor should the pilot screw setting be changed.*

Due to the large number of differing throttle linkage and carburetor assemblies used

If flexibly-mounted carburetors are fitted, be sure they are vertically aligned

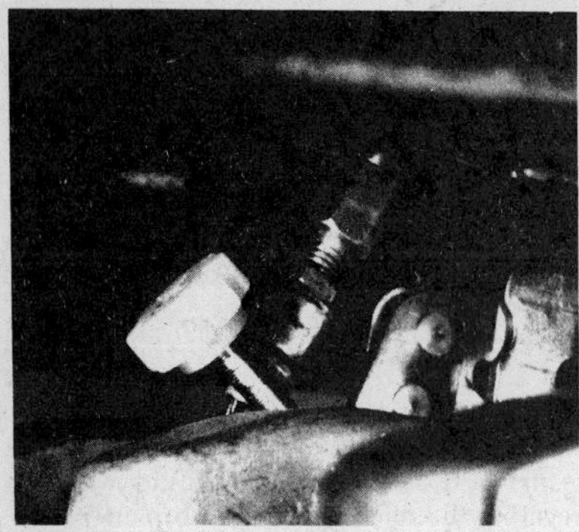

Throttle stop screw

today, no general procedure will be able to provide all of the information necessary to properly adjust the carburetors on most motorcycles.

A few of the easier procedures are given below, but on most multi-cylinder machines, idle speed and mixture are controlled by complex linkages and are accomplished in many cases in conjunction with throttle slide synchronization, a procedure which requires a vacuum gauge. Therefore, detailed procedures for tuning these machines can be found in the applicable model section.

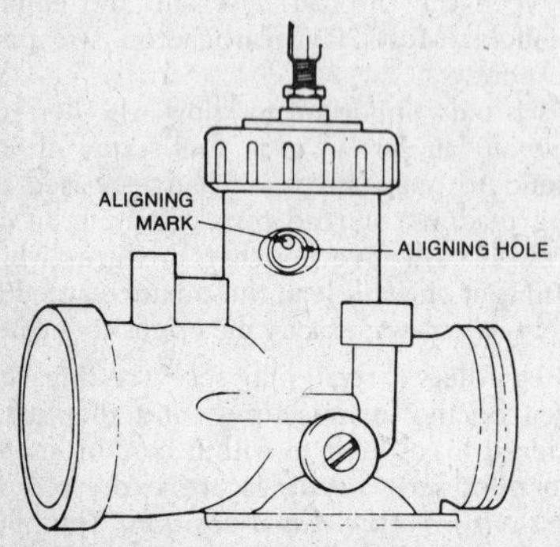

Some carburetors have slide alignment marks to facilitate synchronization

SINGLES

1. Single-cylinder machines, whether two- or four-stroke are easily adjusted in the following manner.
2. After setting the pilot screw to the given specification, allow the engine to warm up, then use the throttle-stop (or idle speed) screw so that the engine turns over at the specified rpm.
3. Smooth out the idle, if necessary, by making careful adjustments to the pilot screw, but do not turn the pilot screw more than ½ turn in either direction from the recommended specification.
4. If satisfactory performance cannot be obtained using the given specifications, check for clogged carburetor passages, air leaks, plug condition and gap, timing, damaged components, etc.

TWINS

For single-carburetor models, refer to "Singles," above. For dual carburetor machines, the procedure is as follows:

1. Adjust the pilot screws for both carburetors to the recommended specification.
2. To ensure that one cylinder is not "leading" the other it is necessary to equalize the idle speed.
3. With the engine at operating temperature, disconnect one plug lead and turn the idle speed screw on the running cylinder in until the engine will run on one cylinder. Adjust the running cylinder's idle so that it is as low as possible, then try to get it as smooth as is feasible using the pilot screw.

Do not turn the pilot screw more than ½ turn in either direction from the recommended setting.

4. Connect the disconnected plug lead. Rev the engine a few times to clean off the spark plugs, then disconnect the plug lead for the cylinder which has already been adjusted.
5. Repeat Step 3 for the other cylinder.
6. Connect both leads. Idle speed will be very high. Back out each carburetor's idle speed screw in small, equal increments until the desired idle speed is arrived at.

NOTE: *On twins using a single ignition coil, disconnecting one lead will kill both cylinders. To get the engine to run on one cylinder it will be necessary to allow the disconnected lead to ground its spark against the cylinder head.*

7. Synchronize the throttle plates (CV) or slides.

On CV carburetors this can be done by opening the throttle slightly and checking that both throttle arms begin to move at the same time.

On direct-control carburetors, remove the air cleaner(s) and check that both slides begin to move at the same time.

On some late-model twins, the throttle slides are fitted with a punch mark which can be aligned with inspection holes on the carburetor bodies for synchronization.

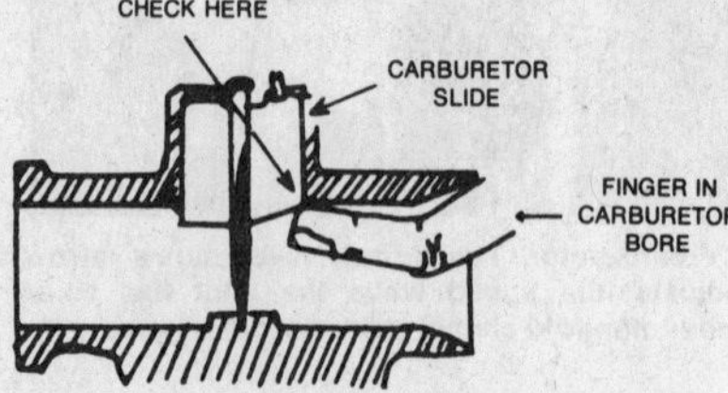

Check for carburetor synchronization by ensuring that both slides clear the carburetor bores at the same time

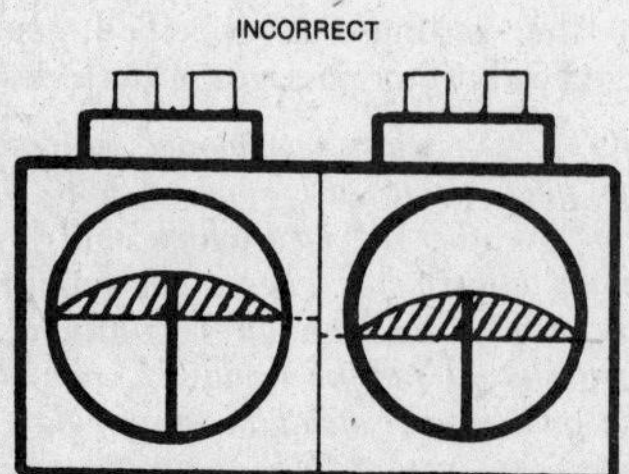

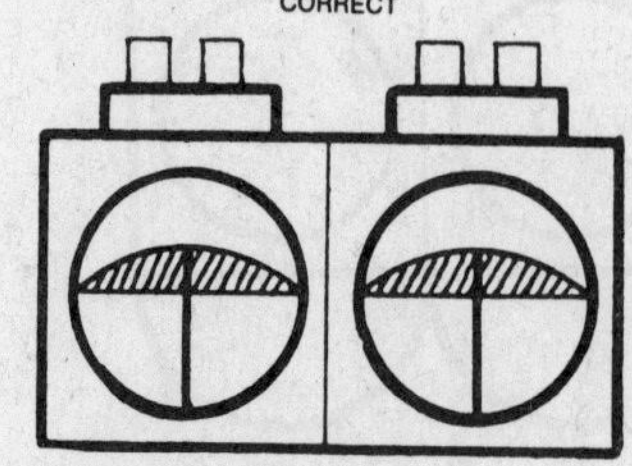

On multi-cylinder machines, throttle slides must be synchronized

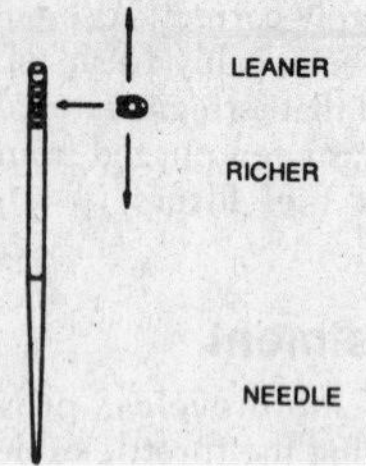

Carburetor metering components. If the unit has a pilot fuel screw, reverse the direction of those arrows to lean or enrichen the idle mixture

An alternate method is possible on some machines. Turn the throttles open until one of the slides just clears the carburetor bore. Check by feeling the top edge of the bore with your finger. The other slide must be in exactly the same position.

Slide synchronization is adjusted on most units by means of he the cable adjusted atop each carburetor, or at the side on CV units.

Carburetors can also be synchronized with vacuum gauges if appropriate fittings are there.

TRIPLES AND FOURS

Late-model triples and fours utilize throttle pulleys and linkages and you should refer to the specific section for precise adjustment procedures. For others with separate cables to each carburetor, the procedures are very similar to that described above for twins. Many models have punch marks on the throttle slides which are to be aligned with inspection holes on the carb bodies to effect synchronization.

Road Test

NOTE: *Before carrying out any of the following tests, new spark plugs of the factory-recommended heat range should be fitted. Before making any alterations to the carburetor jetting based on the tests below, be sure that the carburetor does not have any air leaks, or that the engine is not carbon-choked, or running with worn rings, bad valves or seals, etc. Deceptive readings will be obtained in these cases, and if the unbalanced mixture is being caused by mechanical malfunction such as a leaking carburetor float needle, wrong float level, punctured float, blocked or obstructed fuel lines or gas tank vent.*

The following test is for the main jet.

1. Warm up the engine and accelerate through at least the first three gears at full throttle. When the engine is pulling high rpm, shut off the throttle, pull in the clutch,

and kill the ignition, all as simultaneously as possible.

2. Remove the plugs and note the color. The plugs should be light tan to dark brown in color if the carburetor settings are correct.

3. If the plugs are black and wet with gas or oil, the mixture is too rich, and smaller size main jets should be installed. If the plugs are white, the mixture is too lean and larger main jets should be fitted. Main jets are sized accordingly: the larger the number on the jet, the more fuel it will pass in a given time, and the richer the mixture will be.

NOTE: *Never change main jet sizes more than one increment at a time; each time new jets are fitted, repeat the test until the plugs show the proper color. All plugs must show the same reading. The use of caution is advised when fitting smaller main jets. Too lean a mixture will cause overheating and probable piston seizure.*

4. Once main jet size is determined to be correct, mid-range operation should be checked. Mid-range mixture is controlled by the needle jet and the needle. Repeat the test above, but do not use more than half-throttle when testing. Adjust the mixture by moving the needle clip up or down.

NOTE: *After considerable mileage, the needle and needle jet will become worn. This will cause a rich mid-range condition. If this occurs, replace both the jet and the needle.*

5. Mixture at idle and just above idle is controlled by the pilot screw. This adjustment is covered above.

CAUTION: *The effect that other badly adjusted or worn engine components can have on spark plug color cannot be overemphasized. Since main jets and other carburetor settings are determined by the factory after extensive testing, it is wise to suspect that things other than the jet sizes are causing misleading plug readings.*

Throttle Opening	*Mixture too Rich*	*Mixture too Lean*
0–1/8	Turn pilot air screw out, pilot fuel screw in	Turn pilot air screw in, pilot fuel screw out
1/8–1/4	Enlarge throttle slide cutout	Reduce throttle slide cutout
1/4–3/4	Lower the jet needle	Raise the jet needle
3/4–full	Use smaller no. main jet	Use larger no. main jet

ENGINE REBUILDING

The following section is provided to give the novice some idea of the methods and techniques used in rebuilding an engine and/or servicing various engine components, as well as indicating to a certain degree the kinds of tools necessary for this kind of work.

The model sections, of course, provide step-by-step procedures for specific motorcycles as well as giving all necessary specifications.

IS REBUILDING NECESSARY?

Before beginning any procedure like engine rebuilding which will necessarily entail a good deal of time and money, it is worthwhile to determine first whether rebuilding is indeed necessary. Of course, if there is a major component failure (such as a sudden and total loss of compression) the answer is obvious. In most cases, however, rebuilding is undertaken to cure less obvious malfunctions, or to repair damage due to normal wear which takes place over a long period of time and many miles.

Even in the event of seemingly serious engine or transmission trouble, it is important to do a bit of preoperative testing or diagnosis prior to simply tearing the engine down. For example, if the transmission jumps out of gear, the cause may be due to worn or damaged engaging dogs on the gears themselves—and this will require splitting the crankcases: a major undertaking. On the other hand, this sort of problem may also be caused by a defect in the shift linkage. It then becomes a relatively simple job which in many cases can be fixed with the engine in the frame.

Another example is poor engine performance. While this can be caused by worn out rings or cylinders, it is equally likely to be due to dirty or out-of-adjustment components in the tune-up system: points, air filters, carburetors, etc. Obviously, these simple parts should be checked before jumping to conclusions.

If you think you need an engine rebuild, it may save a great deal of time and money to first refer to the "Troubleshooting" diagnostic charts in this manual. Also, examine the motorcycle itself closely and take into consideration its past life: mileage, maintenance history, etc.

Some of the most obvious needs for an engine rebuild are given below.

Mechanical Noise

Few engines stop suddenly without providing some sort of warning in the form of unusual mechanical noise. Of course, some do. Piston seizure is one example, although if this happens you will know right away what the problem is.

Noises can usually be isolated, and to some extent analyzed, by determining when they occur and from what part of the engine they come.

Top end noise is perhaps the most common. This can arise from badly adjusted valves, but you must determine whether the valve noise is a result of the need for periodic readjustment or something more serious such as indented valve stems, worn or damaged adjusters, worn cam lobes, scored or worn camshaft bearings, bent valves or damaged valves or seats.

If the noise is confined to one valve (and you can usually tell, since the ticking will be unmistakable) some sort of mechanical damage is likely. In any event, check the clearance and proceed from there.

Another common top end noise is due to a loose or worn cam chain. Readjust the chain according to the given procedures. If the noise persists the chain may have to be replaced. This type of problem is almost always confined to very high mileage motorcycles, or those on which the chain was improperly adjusted. You can check this on some machines on which the cam chain also drives the breaker points. If the ignition timing marks seem to jump all over the place when strobe-timing, chances are that a worn cam chain is the cause.

A grinding or whinning noise from the top end of ohc engines may be due to worn or scored camshaft bearings.

Lower end noises are a bit harder to identify, since there are many more potential causes.

A clicking or 'snapping' noise, especially noticed when the engine is cold or just when the clutch is let out and the engine put under load, may be due to piston slap-worn pistons and/or cylinders.

Roller bearing lower ends can sometimes give indications that they are damaged by a rumbling sound which increases in pitch as the engine speed increases. Under heavy load, a badly damaged ball or roller bearing may produce a rapid thumping.

Plain bearing lower ends are usually a little quieter, but they, too, will whine or bang under load.

A knocking sound in the lower end, especially when the engine changes speed, may be due to worn or damaged connecting rod plain bearings. If the rod bearings are roller-type, the noises may be similar to those of a ball or roller lower end as described above.

Transmission noises are usually easier to identify. About the only really serious symptom is gear noise which indicates worn gear teeth. Chattering or grinding sounds may be due to worn or damaged transmission shaft bearings, but this is very unusual.

Performance Loss

Loss in performance is difficult to notice since it most often occurs over a long period of time, and is intrinsically tied up with tune-up adjustments and service procedures which are often ignored.

Before taking an engine apart because of loss in performance, first go over all of the tune-up operations and maintenance items relating to the ignition and fuel systems. On two-strokes, decarbonize the engine and exhaust system.

Make a compression check (see "Tune-Up," above). This is one of the most revealing tests you can carry out without dismantling the engine.

Oil Consumption

Oil consumption is one of the most common symptoms of worn engine components and one of the easiest to identify.

The only problem is determining how much oil consumption you can live with. Many people are willing to put up with an oil burner until the tell-tale blue-white smoke from the exhaust pipes becomes embarassing.

All engines will consume some oil under certain conditions. Four-strokes, however, are not supposed to smoke noticeably, and when this happens you can be sure that wear in the engine has become excessive.

Note that oil smoke is blue or blue-white. Black smoke is carbon or unburned fuel, and may be caused by excessive carbon build-up on the piston crown or combustion chamber, an excessively rich fuel/air mixture, incorrect ignition timing, or other causes.

Oil burning may be due to worn rings, worn pistons or cylinder bores, worn valves or valve guides, damaged valve seals, or broken rings.

Wet, black, oily spark plugs will confirm oil burning. If all of the plugs of a multi-cylinder high-mileage machine are in this condition, normal, long-term wear is the cause. If only one plug is oil-fouled, suspect mechanical damage to that cylinder.

ENGINE REBUILDING METHODS

General Service

1. Engine work requires extra care and attention to detail especially during disassembly and assembly procedures. While largely a matter of common sense, the following points should be noted.

2. It is important that no undue force be used when removing or installing engine parts. If a part resists removal, be sure you are using the correct procedure and the right tool. Use a parts loosener or penetrating oil whenever necessary.

3. Phillips-head engine screws should always be removed and installed with an impact driver. Not only are these screws put on tightly to begin with, on some models they tend to seize in the cases due to corrosion on the threads.

4. When threading and screw or bolt into an allow casting (such as crankcases or cylinder heads), it is recommended that the threads be coated with an antiseize paste. Alternately, oil or grease can be used, but these may not work as well as the paste. The reason for this is to prevent the screw or bolt from seizing in the alloy casting which makes future removal easier and minimizes the chance of damaging the threads or snapping the screw or bolt while attempting removal.

5. A torque wrench is a necessity for most engine work, especially if the cylinder head is removed. Because of the high temperatures at which cylinder heads run, and the resultant expansion, an improperly torqued head may allow compression leaks, blown head gaskets, and/or a warpage of the head itself. It should be noted that a compression leak will very often cause the engine to seize in a short time.

6. When tightening a bolt or nut for which a torque specification is given, be sure that the threads are clean. Oil them lightly where possible to ensure an accurate torque reading.

7. When securing a component which is held by two or more bolts or nuts or screws, tighten them gradually and in a cross pattern so that the component goes on straight. Cylinder head bolt or nut tightening orders are given in the individual sections, and for some motorcycles, crankcase bolt tightening orders are given as well.

8. In most cases, gaskets should be replaced rather than reused. This is especially true of metal gaskets which derive part of their sealing ability from being compressed when the part is torqued. Once disturbed, the gasket may not provide the same seal as when new.

Sometimes, however, it may be easier to leave paper gaskets alone if they are in no way damaged.

Copper sealing washers can often be renewed by heating them until they are red-hot, then allowing them to cool. This will soften the copper, allowing it to form a better seal.

9. The use of gasket compounds or sealing agents is sometimes recommended by the manufacturers, and when this is the case, it will be noted in the text of the individual sections. In other cases the uses of such compounds is optional, but they are usually not needed. On the majority of modern motorcycles, the thickness of gaskets and the width of mating surfaces make gasket compound unnecessary. Oil leaks are therefore not inherent in the design, and if the engine does leak, it is probably due to a damaged gasket, a knicked or warped mating surface, or an improperly installed part. Determine the cause before attempting to stem the leak with gasket compound.

Additionally, the use of such compounds may make future removal of the gasket a chore, since all traces of the old gasket and compound must be removed from the mating surface.

If gasket compound is used, it must be applied carefully, to avoid clogging oil passages or being squeezed into the engine when the part is tightened.

Be sure to follow manufacturer's instructions for suitability and use.

10. For some operations, special tools are required. For safety and reliability, it is suggested that you purchase these tools where possible.

11. Whenever engine components are removed, they should be marked for position whenever the potential for incorrect installation exists. This is especially true for parts like pistons, valves, valve springs, etc., which must always be installed in the same location from which they were removed.

12. All engine components should be lubricated by hand before the engine is started after work has been done. For example, piston rings and skirts should have a coating of motor oil on them before the cylinder is installed. The same holds true of crankshaft and connecting rod bearings, cams, rocker arms, etc.

13. The replacement of parts which are not reusable should be considered before disassembly. Gaskets and oil seals are obvious. In many cases, however, the reuse of snap-rings and circlips is specifically not recommended. These items are often deformed by removal and should be replaced. Of special importance in this regard are piston wrist pin and transmission shaft circlips.

14. While most engine components can be cleaned in a safe solvent after removal, this procedure is not recommended for roller and ball bearings which are going to continue in use. Immersion in any but the purest solvent may allow minute particles to enter the bearing, causing a rough movement and possible damage. It is preferable to clean ball and roller bearings by squirting clean motor oil through them. This will serve to carry away the greater part of any particles which may have entered the bearing.

15. Some components are pressed into place, and heat or cold may be used to facilitate removal. An example is bearings or bushings which are tight fits in an alloy case. Since the expansion rate of an alloy when subjected to heat is greater than that of steel or iron, the case can be heated before removing the bushing or bearing. This can be done with a propane torch, but care must be taken to heat the alloy gently and evenly, and to keep the flame off the bearing. However, since uneven heating may cause the alloy part to warp, it is somewhat safer to heat it in an oven or on a hot plate. Extreme heat should not be necessary. Since some of the heat will be transfered to the bearing or bushing, removal can be made even easier in some cases by running a damp rag or an ice cube around the bearing. The chill will cause it to contract very slightly, and, since the heat caused the alloy to expand, the bearing or bush should come right out.

This handy aid cannot be used in other situations. For example, it is not possible to remove a ball or roller bearing from a steel shaft by heating. The expansion rate will be about the same and the swelling of the shaft will nullify any expansion of the bearing. In addition, as noted above, bearings should not be heated by contact with a flame.

There are some instances in which heat will not work. For example, when pressing a bushing into a case. Although the normal procedure would be to heat the case, sometimes the bushing may be made from a substance with like characteristics. The heat may be transferred to the bushing as soon as it contacts the case. It will then expand making installation very difficult. Such occurences are rare, but the possibility should be recognized.

16. After a four-stroke engine has been rebuilt, and all settings checked, it should be run for several miles, allowed to cool, and the head should be retorqued. Readjust valves and cam chain, if applicable.

17. Follow owner's manual instructions for the care of a new engine if extensive rebuilding was done. Keep a close watch on engine temperature for the first several miles after the rebuild.

Bearings and Seals

1. Many bearings (such as for the crankshaft and transmission shafts) are fitted with an oil seal. If removed, these seals must be replaced. Seals which are pressed into their housing may be pried out with a hooked tool,

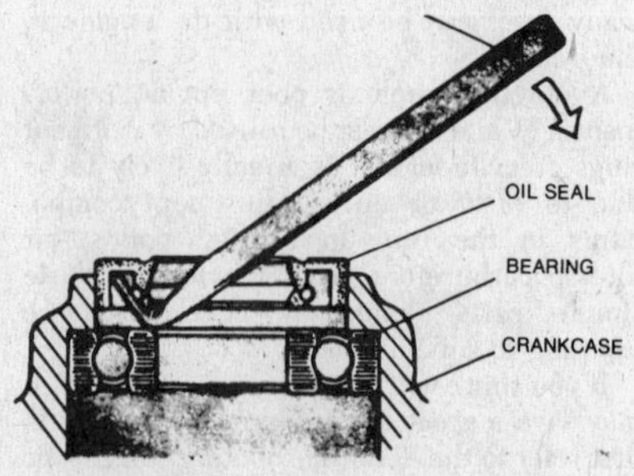

Removing an oil seal

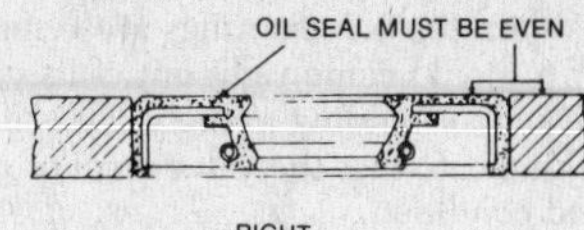

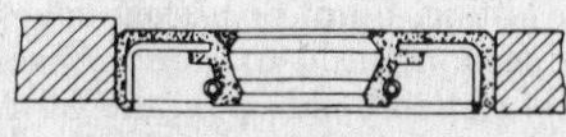

Correct and incorrect seal installation

as illustrated. When fitting a new seal, be sure it is not cocked or tilted in the housing. Lubricate the lips of all seals before inserting any shaft into them.

2. A rough check of the condition of ball and roller bearings can be obtained by lubricating them with oil, and noting any binding, roughness, or noise during rotation. Binding may be due to foreign particles which found their way into the bearing during the disassembly procedure, and they can sometimes be removed by squirting clean oil through the bearing. If roughness persists, or if the bearing is obviously damaged with pitted or discolored balls or rollers or scored races, it must be replaced.

3. Some bearings can also be checked by holding the outer race firmly in place, as illustrated, and attempting to move the inner race back and forth. No movement should be possible.

Check bearing races for imperfections

Checking a bearing for excessive play

Checking bearing clearance with a dial indicator

4. A more precise method of checking bearing clearance involves the use of a dial gauge.

5. Plain bearings must exhibit a perfectly smooth, featureless surface, or they must be replaced. Clearance of plain bearings is best checked with Plastiguage® or by measuring the bearing journal and subtracting this value from the diameter of the bearing itself.

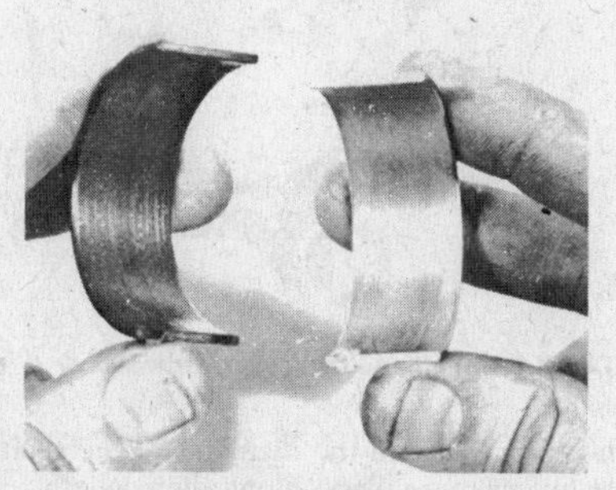

Plain bearings should be featureless as on the right

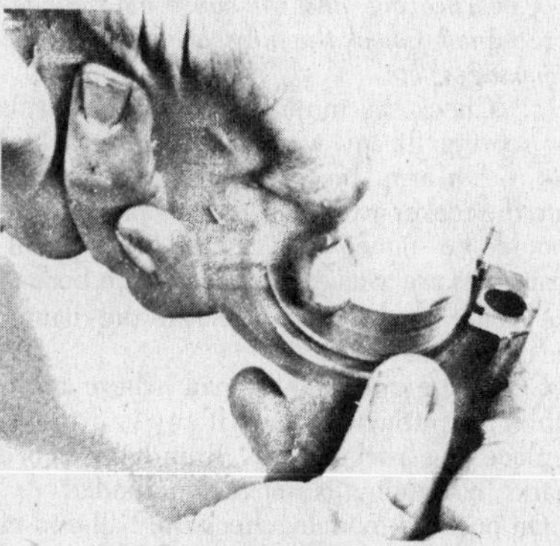

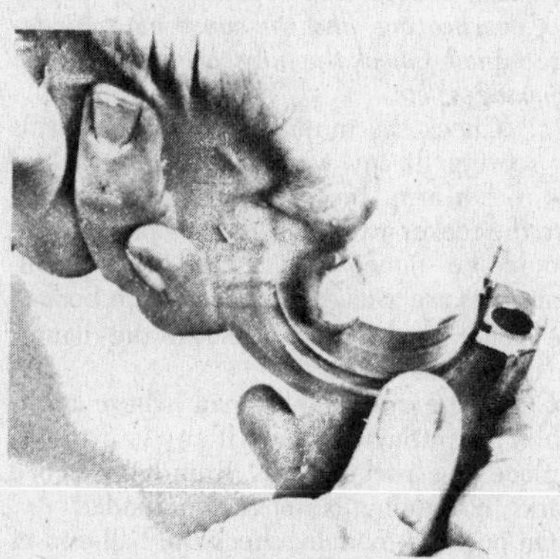

Removing a con rod plain bearing

Top End

The following procedures are common to most motorcycles.

While most of the following inspections are written in the singular, bear in mind that any work done to one cylinder must be done to all of them in a twin or multi. Some parts, such as valve springs, piston rings, pistons, etc., must of course be replaced in sets, even if only one is unserviceable. Boring, honing, valve lapping, etc., must be done to all of the cylinders for the same reason.

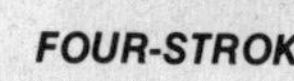

FOUR-STROKE

Cylinder Head

1. Clean carbon deposits from the cylinder head using a wire wheel or a blunt instrument such as a butter knife or the rounded edge of an old hacksaw blade. Do not use a pointed instrument.

NOTE: *Dec::rbonizing the head with the valves in place is recommended as this minimizes chances of damaging the valve seats.*

2. Make a check of valve seating efficiency by pouring a small quantity of gasoline into each of the ports and allowing it to stand for about five minutes. If the valves are seating properly, leakage into the combustion chamber will be minimal. If the gasoline leaks in quickly, the valves should be lapped.

Before removing the valves, note that most models and that progressively wound valve springs and that these types of springs are always installed with the close pitch side toward the head. Also, each spring should be assembled to its own valve, and each valve to its guide. Mark the pieces for location as they are removed.

3. Valves can be removed after compressing the valve springs with a spring compressor. On some machines, they can be removed with a suitably sized socket. Turning the head upside down and pressing the valve spring against the socket while holding the valve against its seat should allow the valve keepers to fall out. When they do so, the spring assembly and valve can be removed. Remove the retainer, springs, spring seats and any washers fitted. Remove the valve guide oil seals, if so equipped.

NOTE: *New valve guide oil seals should be used on assembly.*

4. Check the cylinder head for warpage, where possible, by placing it on a very flat suface such as a piece of plate glass and prob-

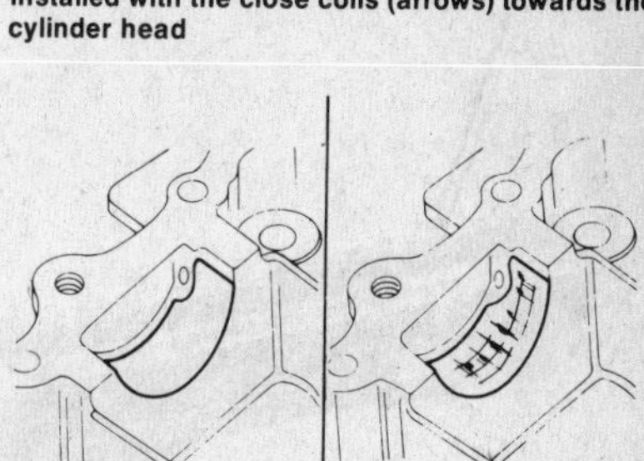

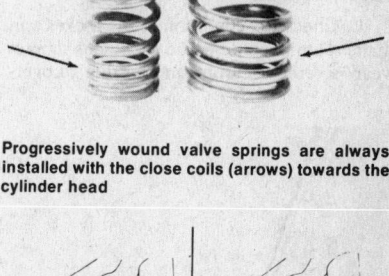

Progressively wound valve springs are always installed with the close coils (arrows) towards the cylinder head

Check the bearing surfaces for scoring or marks as on the right

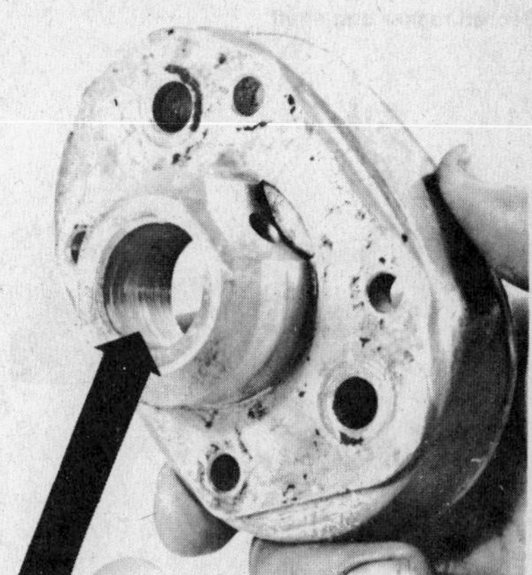

Scored cam bearing cap must be replaced

ing around the cylinder mating surface with a thin feeler gauge. The head mating surface should be very flat (i.e., it should not be possible to slip the feeler gauge between the head and the glass). If it is warped, the head can be lapped. Be sure to remove only enough metal to rectify the warpage. If warpage is slight, it can sometimes be remedied by putting a quantity of valve lapping paste on the glass and working the head back and forth in a figure-eight motion until the mating surface is flat. A sheet of emery cloth placed on a flat surface can also be used. Ensure that the head is cleaned up very thoroughly after this operation. Check oil passages especially.

5. Some overhead camshaft motorcycles have the camshaft(s) riding directly on journals cast as part of the cylinder head. Others use cam bearing housings which are removable. In either case the bearing surfaces must be smooth and featureless. Removing any imperfections from these surfaces by abrasive methods may make the cam-to-bearing clearance unacceptable.

6. Where applicable, check that the rocker arm shafts are a snug fit in the cylinder head, not excessively loose.

7. Check that all head and valve cover gasket surfaces are clean and smooth. Remove all traces of old gaskets or gasket compound.

Valve Assembly

1. Check the condition of the rocker arm shafts. They should be free of obvious signs of wear, scoring, or discoloration due to overheating. Measure the diameter of the shafts at two or three places along their length.

NOTE: *If any top end components show signs of discoloration it is usually the result of overheating, and the cause must be determined. Check the lubrication system, oil passages, etc.*

2. Check the inner bore of rocker arms for scoring. If any wear is evident, replace the rocker arm. Insert the rocker arm shaft into the rocker arm and check for play. There should be none. Or, if the proper instruments are available, measure the bore of the rocker arm and compare it to the diameter of the shaft.

Check the cam follower pad (where applicable) for pitting or wear. If any is present, replace the rocker arm. Removing score marks by grinding is not recommended.

On pushrod models, check the ball-end of the rocker arm for damage. The ball should be smooth and shiny.

3. With a vernier caliper or a short steel rule, measure the free-length of both the inner and outer valve springs. Replace springs in sets if any of them has been compressed beyond the serviceable limit.

4. When the valve springs are removed, the valve should come right out of its guide. Any sticking or binding as the valve is pulled out will indicate that the valve stem or guide is in bad condition.

5. Inspect the valve paying close attention to the condition of the edges of the valve head for pitting, burnt or broken edges, excessive carbon build-up, etc. A certain amount of carbon build-up on the valve face and on the top of the exhaust valve head is inevitable. These deposits should be carefully scraped off with a dull knife, or with a wire wheel, and the valve finished with a fine emery cloth.

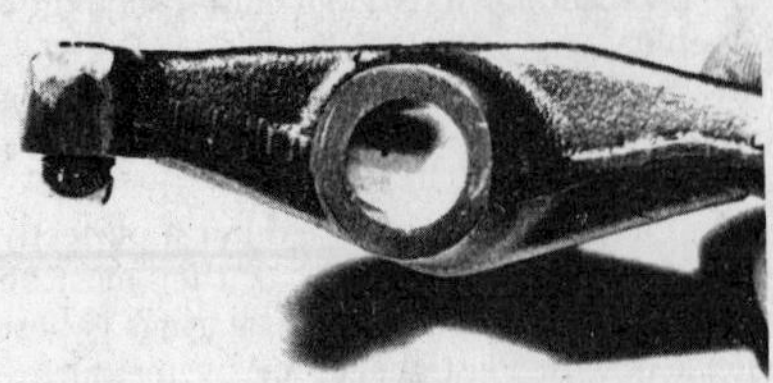

Check the shaft bore for scoring and the ball end for blueing or imperfections

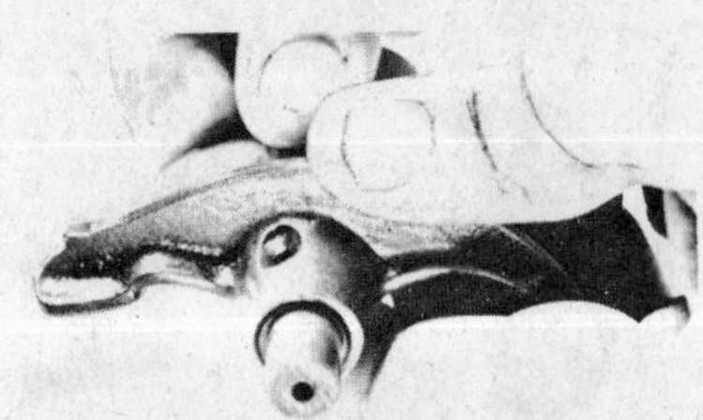

Check the shaft and rocker for vertical play

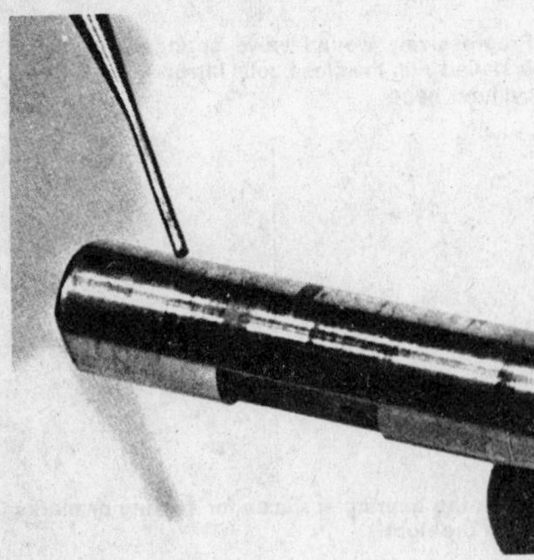

Scored rocker arm shaft

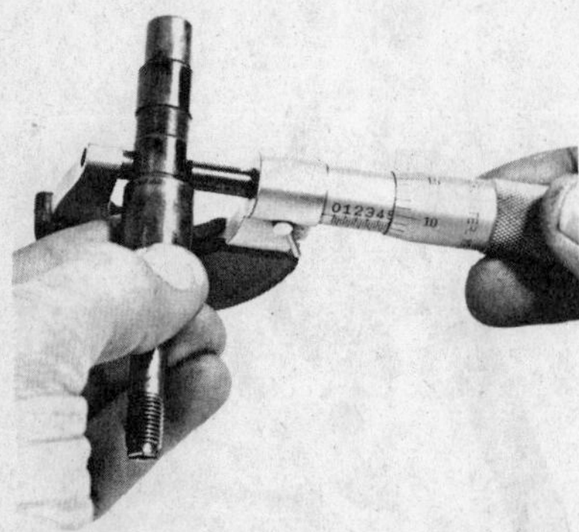

Measuring rocker arm shaft diameter

Pitted rocker arm pad

Measuring valve spring free length

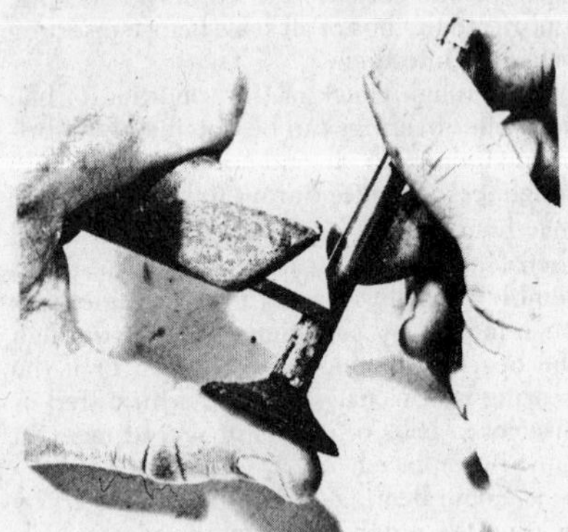

Decarbonizing a valve

A burnt valve. Note chipped edges

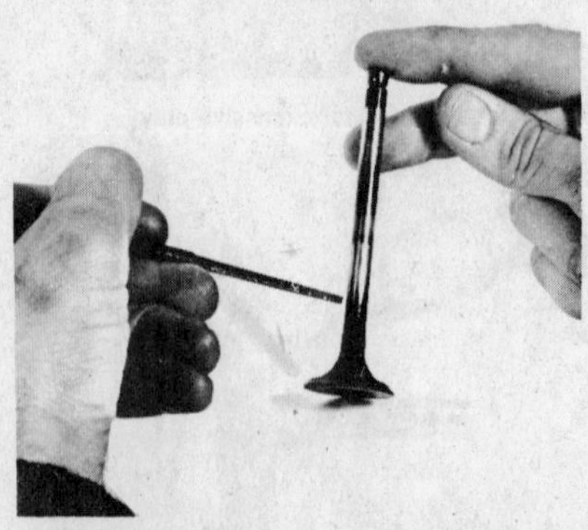

Deposits should not extend too far up along the valve stem

Do not touch the valve seating area during these operations.

Carbon deposits, however, should not extend too far up along the exhaust valve stem. This would indicate a worn or cracked valve guide.

Wet oil on the back of the valve head is indicative of a worn guide (which must be replaced) or bad seal.

Check for a bent valve

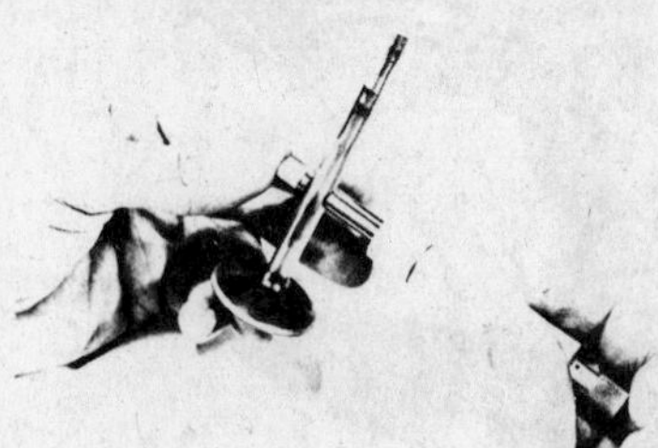

Measuring valve stem diameter

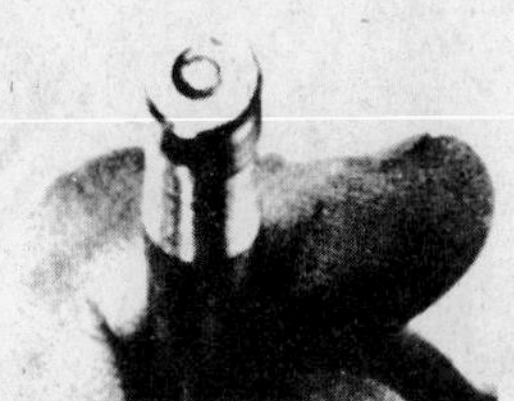

Indented valve stem

Holding the valve stem, spin the valve in your fingers and watch the head. A wobble in the rotation of the head is indicative of a bent valve. Valve head runout can also be measured with a dial gauge.

6. Check the diameter of the valve stem with a micrometer.

A quick check of the operational worthiness of valve and guide can be done by putting a small amount of engine oil on the stem and inserting the valve into the guide. Place a finger over the other end of the guide and pull out the valve. A slight "pop" should be heard.

A valve should move smoothly in the guide. If any tightness or sticking is encountered as the valve is pushed into or rotated in the guide, it is probable that the valve is bent.

A bent valve must be replaced, and if one is found, it is wise to inspect its guide very carefully, as it is likely to be cracked.

7. Check the end of the valve stem for indented wear which may be caused by some types of rocker arms. Although this damage can be remedied on some machines by grinding the end of the valve, this procedure is not recommended since many manufacturers use stellite-tipped valves. Grinding may remove the hardened stellite surface and the indentation will reoccur more quickly.

8. Valve-to-guide clearance can be measured by comparing the diameter of the valve stem with the inside diameter of the guide. Or, by placing the valve into the guide, holding it about ½ inch off its seat, and checking movement in two directions with a dial gauge.

9. Valve guides are replaced by driving them out with a drift. It is often necessary to heat the head before driving out the guides to avoid scuffing or enlarging the guide bores. Do not exceed 300° F.

If the guide is cracked, it may be necessary to chisel off the portion which extends into the port to allow removal.

10. Most models have oversize guides available. Installation is accomplished by pressing the guide in until it is fully seated.

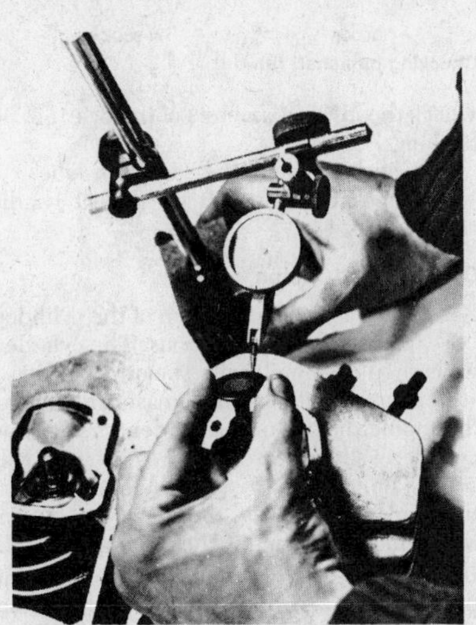

Checking valve-to-guide clearance

11. After installation of a new guide, the guide must be reamed to the proper size and the valve seat must be recut.

Valve Seats

1. Valve seats can be checked by applying a thin coat of lapping paste to the valve seat and a coat of dye to the valve. Lap the valve lightly and check the pattern remaining on the valve.

2. On most models, the valve seat should be 1.0–1.5mm wide and must be of the same width all the way around. The seat contact area must be centered on the valve bevel.

3. If the valve seat does not conform to these standards, or if it is badly pitted, or if new guides have been fitted, the seat should be recut.

Lapping

1. Valves must be lapped into their seats if the valve seat has been recut, a new valve has been fitted, the leakage test shows poor sealing, or minor pitting on the seat or valve are noted.

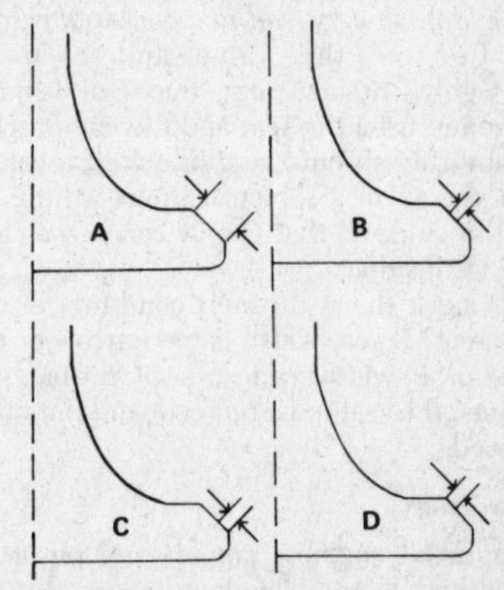

Valve seats: A, too wide; B, too narrow; C, too low; D, too high

It should also be done as a routine operation on high-mileage machines.

2. Clean off all carbon build-up on the surface of the combustion chamber. Place three small dabs of valve lapping paste around the circumference of the valve head and place the valve into the guide.

3. If you have a lapping tool, use it as the manufacturer directs. Usually, the tool will turn the valve back and forth while rotating it around the seat at the same time. Do not use excessive pressure during the operation.

If you do not have such a tool, a piece of

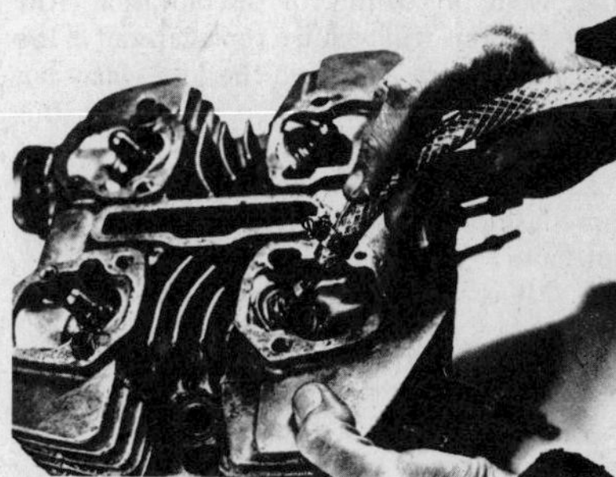

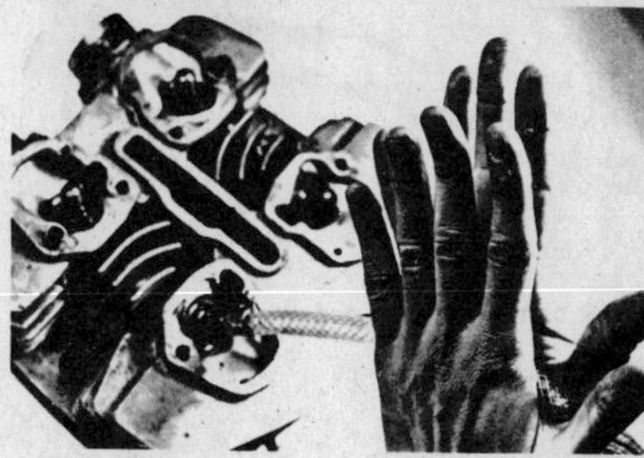

Hand lapping the valves

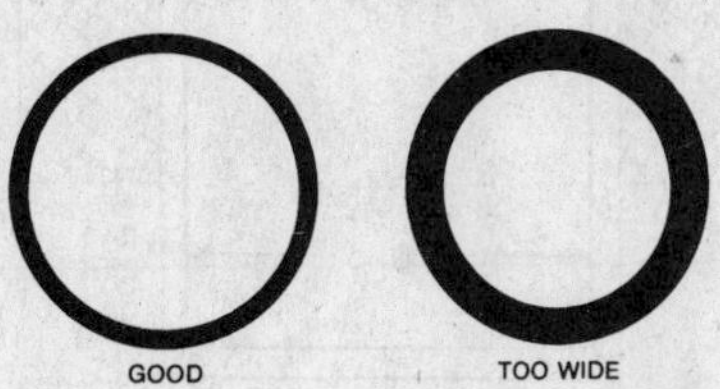

Valve seat patterns

thick fuel line placed over the valve stem works just as well. Turn the valve back and forth and rotate it to a new position every few seconds.

NOTE: *Check the condition of the valve face and seat frequently. When a smooth, even finish is evident, stop lapping. Excessive lapping may lead to a pocketed valve.*

4. Remove the valve and clean it thoroughly. Remove any traces of lapping compound from the seat and the combustion chamber. Swab out the guide with a cotton swab soaked in a solvent. Squirt a little oil into the guide so that is may carry away any particles inside.

5. Check the width and condition of the valve seat. If seat width is too narrow or too large, or if width varies, or if pitting still remains, the seat must be recut and the valve replaced.

Valve Train

On pushrod engines, tappets and pushrods should be checked as follows:

1. Check the condition of the tappet pad which contacts the camshaft. It must be smooth and without score marks. If damaged, the tappet should be replaced, since in most cases the pad is specially hardened and grinding the pad flat is therefore not recommended. Check the pushrod cup for damage. Check the sides of the tappet for scoring, and replace it if damaged.

2. Pushrods must be perfectly straight, as is obvious. Also check the condition of the pushrod ends, making sure that any ball end is perfectly smooth and not discolored.

Camshaft

1. Closely inspect the cam lobes for pitting, wear or scoring, or discoloration. Any imperfections will require replacement of the camshaft. Score marks on the lobes may not be removed by an abrasive method as this will affect the valve timing.

2. Check the camshaft journals in the same fashion. Bearing surfaces must be without flaws.

3. Measure the diameters of the journals.

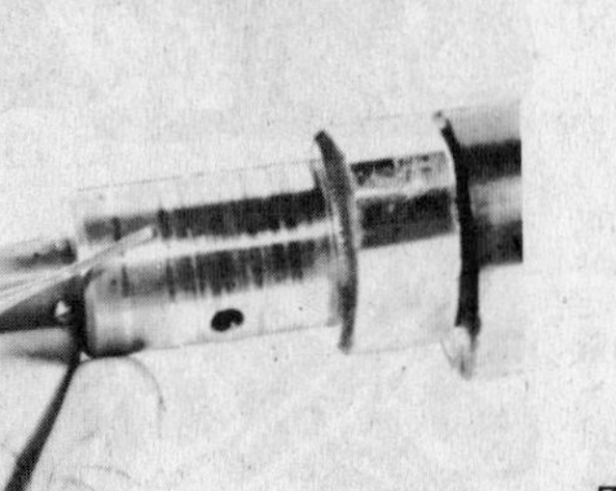

Check cam journal for scoring

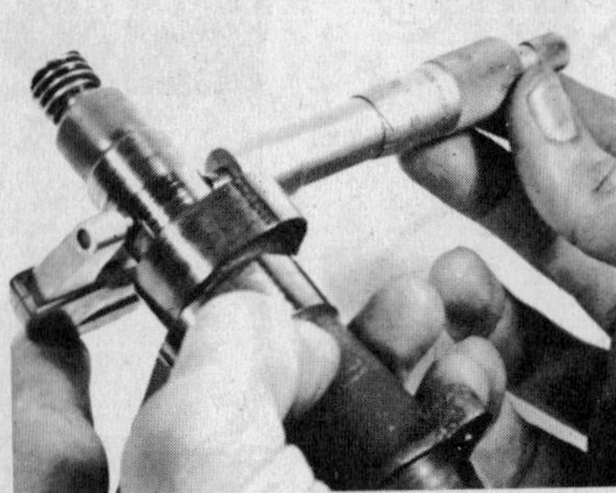

Measuring cam journal diameter

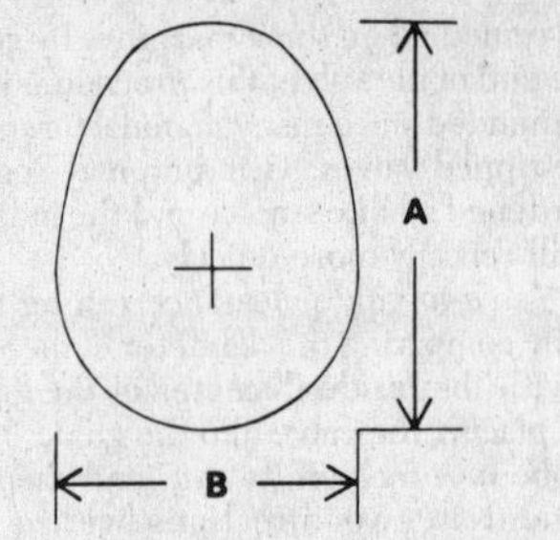

Cam lobe height (A) and base circle diameter (B)

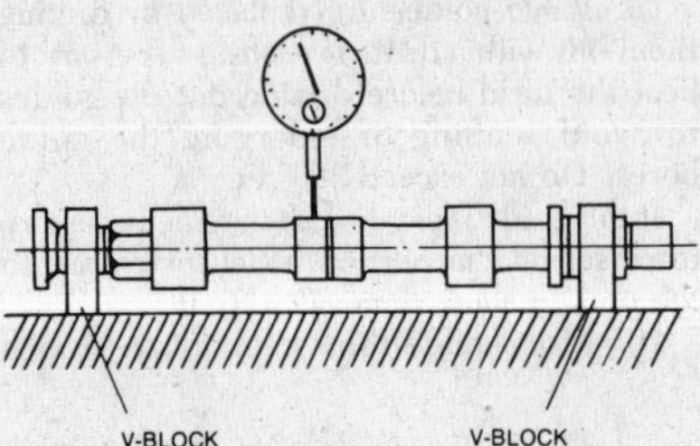

Checking camshaft run-out

Check the inside diameters of the bearings or bushings.

4. Check the height of each cam lobe.

5. Check the camshaft for a bent condition.

Cylinder and Piston

1. Make a visual inspection of the cylinder bore, noting any imperfections. The cylinder walls should be uniformly smooth.

Perform the following measurements to determine the extent of cylinder wear. If the cylinder walls are chromed, wear beyond the service limit requires replacement of the pistons and cylinders. On the much commoner iron cylinders, boring is the usual remedy. If boring is necessary, obtain the replacement pistons first, and bore the cylinders to the piston diameter plus the standard piston clearance. After boring, hone the cylinder(s) to produce a light cross-hatch pattern.

2. Measure the diameter of the cylinder(s) at the top, middle, and bottom of the bore making all measurements in the same direction (i.e. from the front to rear of the cylinder). The difference between the smallest and largest of the three readings is the cylinder taper. The largest of the readings is to be compared with the bore service limit if given for your machine.

3. Turn the micrometer 90° and measure the bore at the top, middle, and bottom as before. The difference between readings taken in different directions yields cylinder ovality.

4. Make a visual inspection of the piston(s). Scoring, scuffing, or seizure marks on the piston skirt may be removed with a fine grade of crocus or emery cloth if not severe. Sanding should be done to produce a cross-

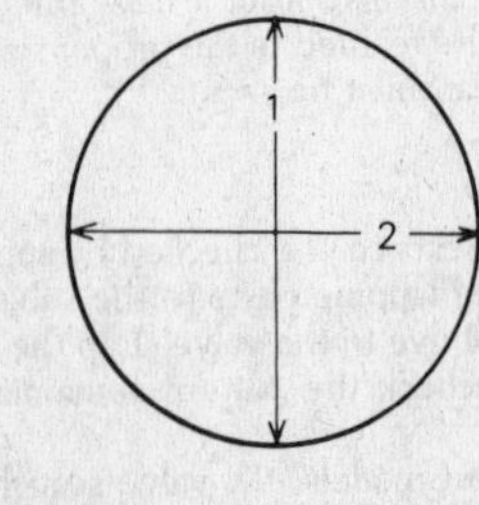

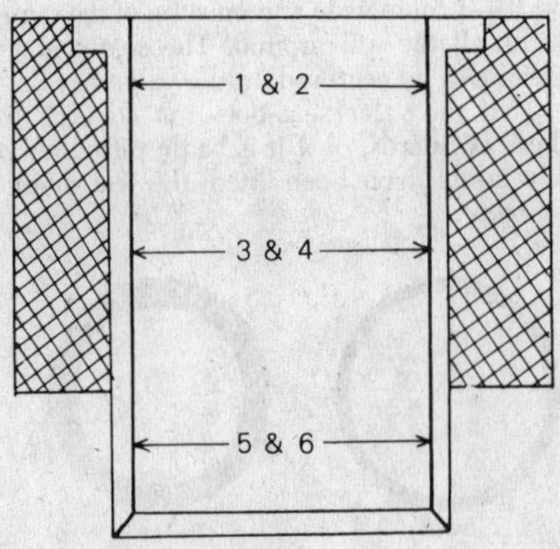

Cylinder measurement points

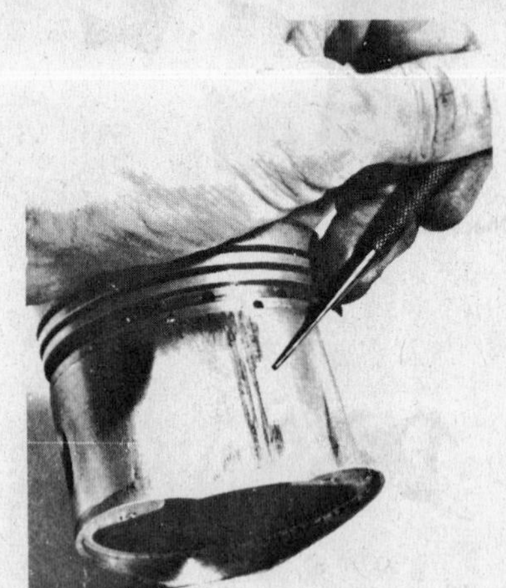

Score marks caused by piston seizure

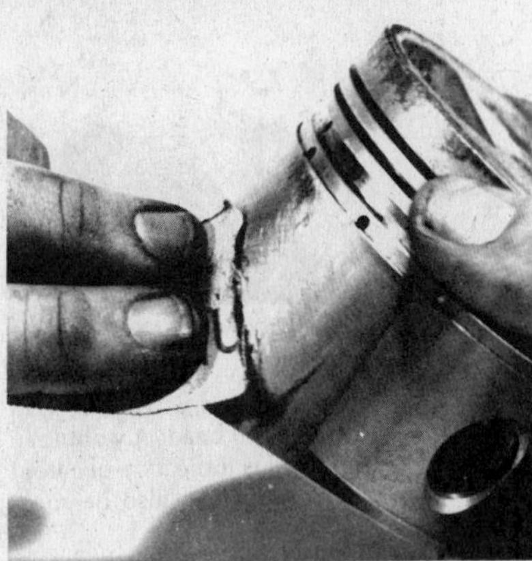

Remove minor scoring by sanding lightly and in a cross-pattern

Cylinders should be smooth

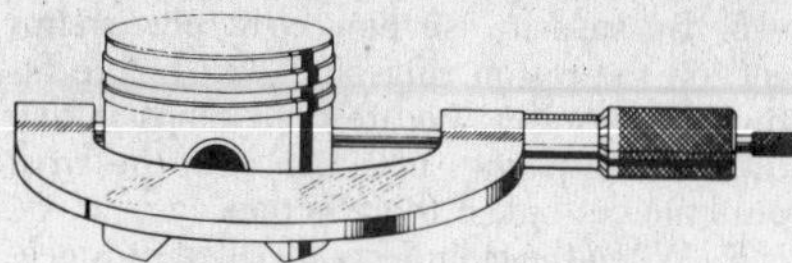
Measuring piston diameter

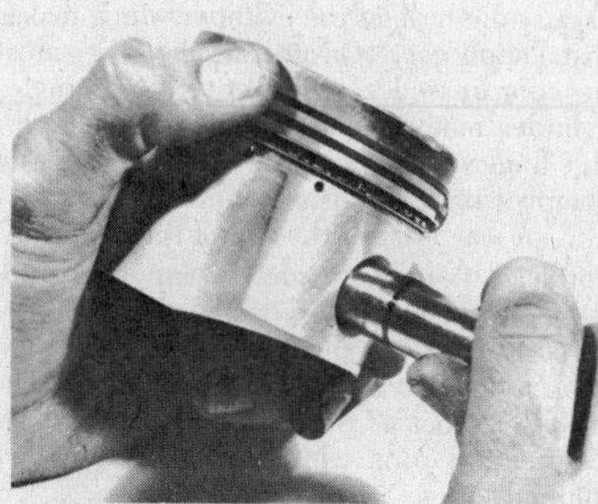
Checking wrist pin fit

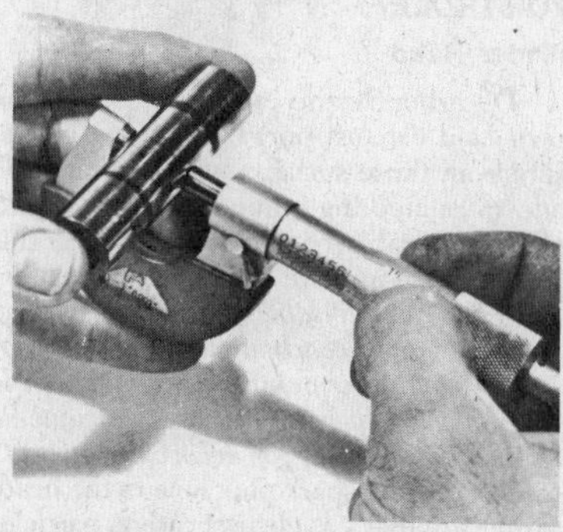
Measuring wrist pin diameter

hatch pattern. If the score marks are more than about ½ in. wide, or if the skirt has deep scratches, the piston(s) must be replaced.

5. The rings must be free to move in their grooves. If they cannot, either they are carbon clogged (which necessitates removing the rings and cleaning out the grooves), or metal has been pushed into the grooves by a piston seizure. In this case, piston and rings must be replaced. Since it is virtually impossible to remove frozen rings without breaking them, new rings will usually be required if the present set are carboned up.

6. Measure the diameter of the piston(s) at the bottom of the skirt perpendicular to the wrist pin, or at the specified distance from the bottom if given. Compare the reading with the standard piston diameter, if given, and with the bore diameter.

7. If possible, measure the inside diameter of the wrist pin holes. Check the fit of the wrist pin in the piston. It should be a tight fit with no play at all evident. If the wrist pin fits loosely in the piston, either the piston or the pin is worn.

8. Check the diameter of the wrist pin at three places along its length. Check for stepwear.

Replacement of the pin is also required if it is in any way scored or discolored.

9. Check the fit of the wrist pin in the connecting rod small end. There should be no vertical play. Check the condition of the small end, noting any scoring or discoloration. Some motorcycles have a replaceable bush in the con rod small end eye, while on most, the wrist pin rides directly on the rod. Movement of the wrist pin or scoring of the small end will require replacing the bush or rod itself.

Piston Rings

Two checks to be made to the piston rings are side clearance and ring end-gap.

1. Side clearance is checked with the rings installed on the piston. Insert a feeler gauge of the proper thickness between the ring and ring groove. If the clearance is too large, the rings or grooves are worn. If not sufficient, metal may have been pushed into the grooves due to a piston seizure. Check that the grooves are not just carboned up before replacing the piston. If new rings do not bring the clearance to the proper value, the piston must be replaced.

Checking ring side clearance

2. To remove rings from a piston, a ring expander is recommended. Removing the rings by hand risks breaking them.

3. To check ring end-gap, ensure first that the bore is not worn to the service limit. Place each ring, in turn, into its own cylinder at the bottom of the bore and push it in an inch or more. Use the piston to correctly align the ring in the bore.

NOTE: *Oil the rings before this operation to prevent scratching them on the bore*

Removal and installation of rings should be done with a ring expander

Measure the end-gap with a feeler gauge of the proper thickness. If the endgap is larger than the given value, replace the rings as a set. If the measured gap of new rings is larger than the standard value, the cylinder is worn and should be bored to the next oversize.

If new rings are being checked, and the end-gap is too small, the ring ends must be filed. Hold the ring steady, closing the ends over a thin, flat file. Do not squeeze the ring, or allow the file to slip out from the ring ends, as this is the easiest way to break it. A few strokes of the file will increase the end-gap.

Measuring ring end-gap

Use the piston to align the ring in the bore

CAUTION: *Do not make more than a few strokes before rechecking the end-gap. It is easy to remove too much metal.*

4. Roll each ring around the piston in its own groove. If a ring sticks or binds in a groove, the grooves must be cleaned. If this does not remedy the problem, replace the piston.

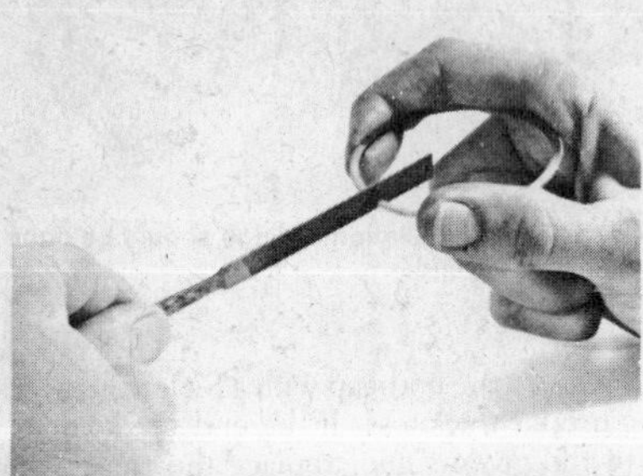

Filing ring ends

Roll the ring around the groove to check for free movement

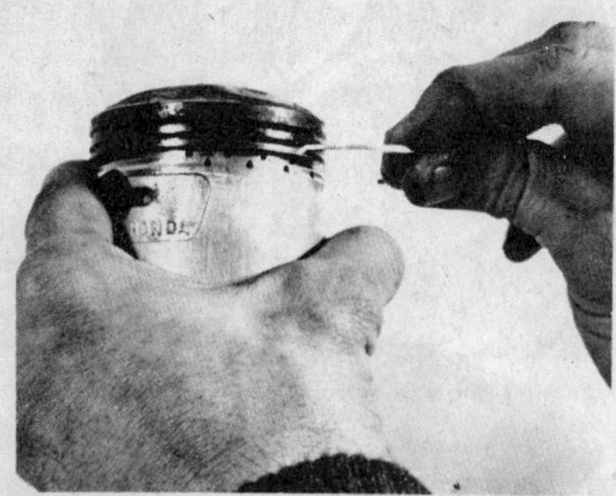

Cleaning out piston ring grooves

5. Before fitting new rings, the ridge at the top of the cylinder must be removed. This ridge forms on all cylinders eventually because the top compression ring never reaches the very top of the cylinder, while the rest of the bore wears slightly. Fitting new rings on high-mileage machines without removing the ridge may cause the top compression ring to break when it contacts the ridge.

6. The cylinder(s) should be honed before fitting new rings. Honing should be done to put a light cross-hatch pattern on the walls.

Piston Installation

1. When fitting rings to pistons first note that the two compression rings are usually not interchangeable.

2. Rings are always installed with the marked side *up*. On some rings this is marked "Top," while on most others the top side is indicated by the manufacturer's mark near the ring end.

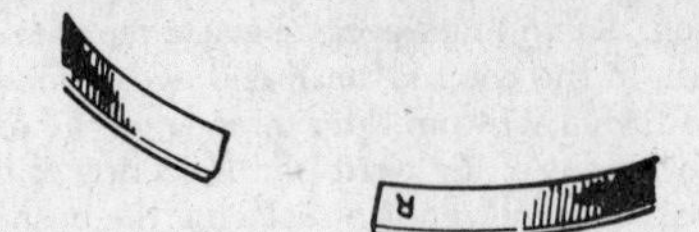

Rings are always installed with the stamped mark facing up

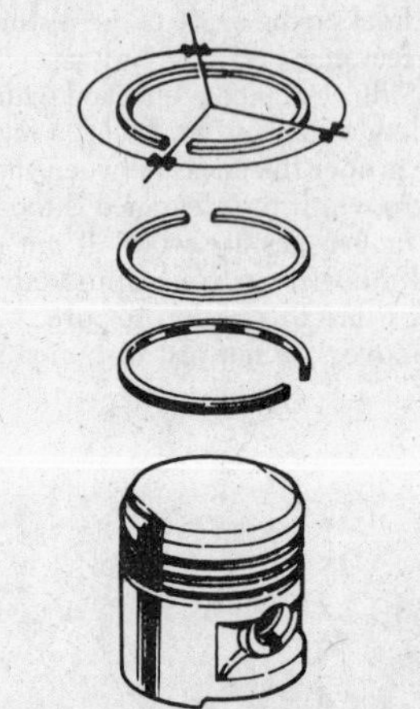

Stagger ring end-gaps. Note piston position mark

3. Ring ends must be staggered around the piston since alignment would cause compression and oil leaks. Unless specific instructions to the contrary are given, on models with a single-piece oil ring, arrange the end-gaps 120° apart. On models with a two-rail oil ring, the end-gap of the rail expander should be 120° from the gap of the lower compression ring and the end gaps of the oil rails should be about 45° on either side of the expander gap.

In both cases the rings should be arranged so that none of the end gaps is at the very front or back of the piston or directly above the wrist pin hole, unless the manufacturer specifically states to do so.

4. In almost all cases the piston crown is marked for proper installation. If "IN" is stamped on the crown, it must be located on the intake side, and the opposite is of course true if "EX" is marked. On pistons marked with arrows, the arrow almost always points towards the exhaust port.

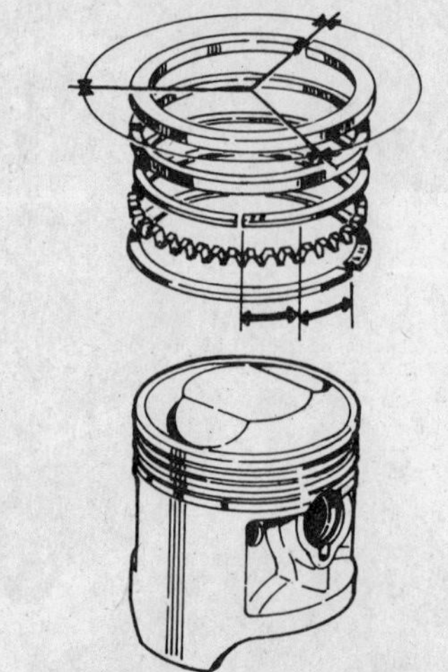

Ring end-gap positions with three piece oil ring

5. Be sure to use new wrist pin circlips and oil the piston rings and skirt before fitting the cylinder. Locate the circlips so that their end gap does not align with the wrist pin hole cut-out, if there is one.

6. When the cylinder is installed, it is necessary to pay some attention to the piston rings so that they will enter the bore without breaking. Many machines have a beveled area at the base of the cylinder which makes installation easy. On others, the rings must be compressed as they enter. On single-cylinder motorcycles this can be done with the fingers, but on twins and multis, ring compressors must usually be used.

7. A way around the use of ring compressors can be used on some twins. Using this method, the pistons are installed in the bores as far as the wrist pin holes, the inside wrist pin circlips having already been fitted. The cylinder block is then supported above the connecting rods while the wrist pins are slipped in.

If this method is used, care must be taken not to install the pistons backwards.

TWO-STROKE

Cylinder Head

1. Decarbonize the cylinder head, piston crown, and exhaust port by scraping off deposits from these surfaces with a blunt knife blade or something similar. After as much carbon as possible has been removed in this manner, finish up with #400 grit sandpaper.

NOTE: *It is advisable to exercise extreme caution when decarbonizing these components to avoid scratching or scraping of the metal itself. Therefore, sharp instruments should not be used for decarbonization.*

2. Inspect the spark plug hole in the head, making sure that it is clear of carbon particles and the like. The threads may be cleaned out with a tap if necessary.

3. Inspect the combustion chamber surface for smoothness. It should be free of any major surface imperfections as might have been caused by a botched decarbonization job.

4. Check that the cylinder head mating surface is as smooth as possible. Clean off any foreign matter with a very fine abrasive emery paper. Place the head on a known flat surface, such as a piece of glass to check it for warpage.

One method of installing the cylinder without ring compressors

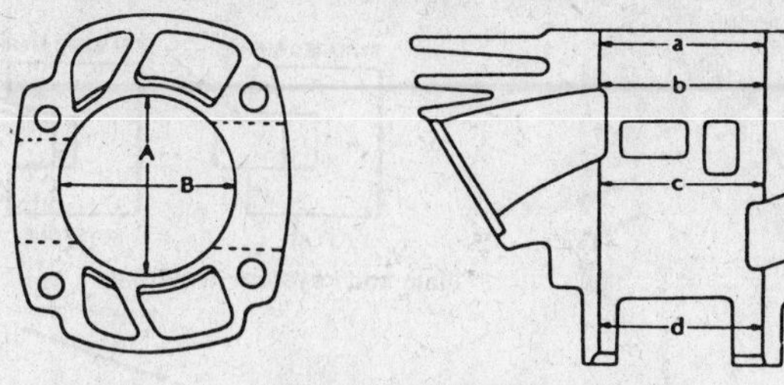

Cylinder bore measurement points

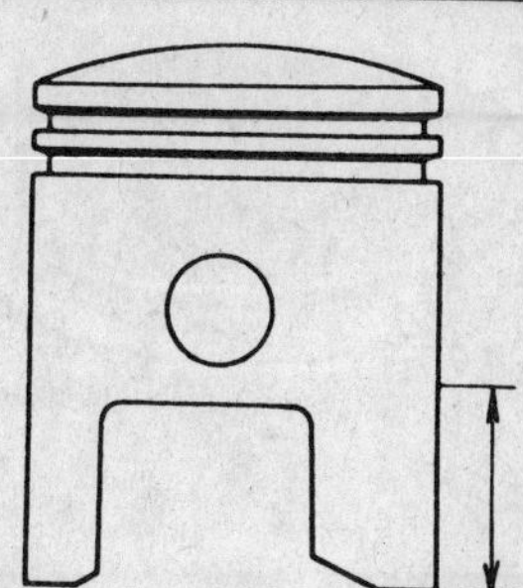

Most makes give a certain distance above the edge of the skirt at which diameter is measured

The head should contact the glass all around. Using very thin feeler gauges, try to slip them in between the cylinder head mating surface and the glass. Ideally, you would not be able to do this. If you can, however, it indicates that the head is slightly warped. A straight-edge can also be used.

Head warpage can sometimes be remedied, or mating surface imperfections removed, by placing the head on a perfectly flat surface which has an amount of valve grinding paste or a sheet of emery cloth on it. The head can then be worked back and forth, or lapped, in a figure 8 pattern, until the warpage is eliminated or the imperfections removed.

CAUTION: *The most important consideration is that the lapping operation not be carried to extremes. It is very easy to remove too much metal from the head.*

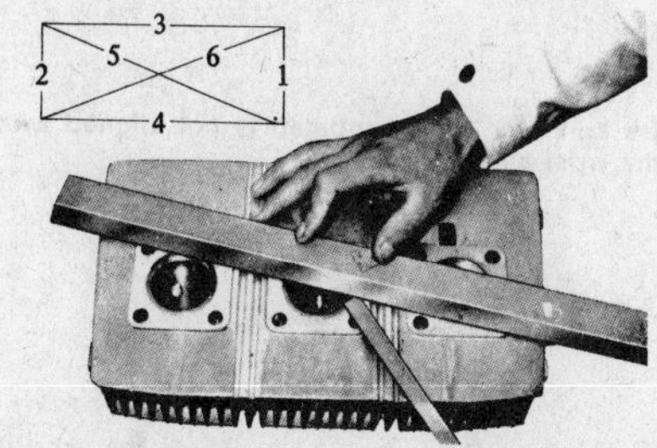

Checking head warpage with a straightedge and feeler gauge

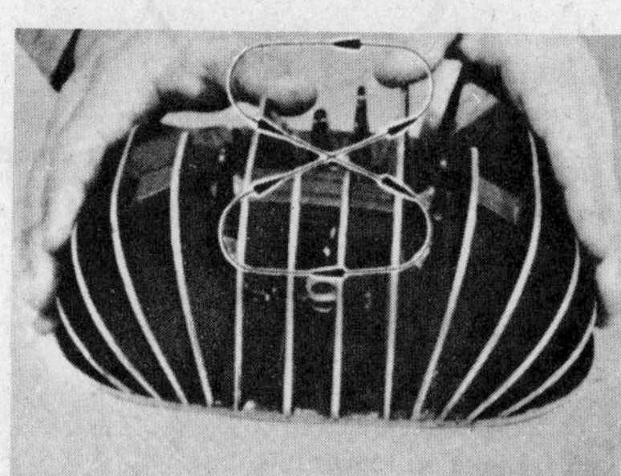

When lapping the head, move it in a figure-eight motion

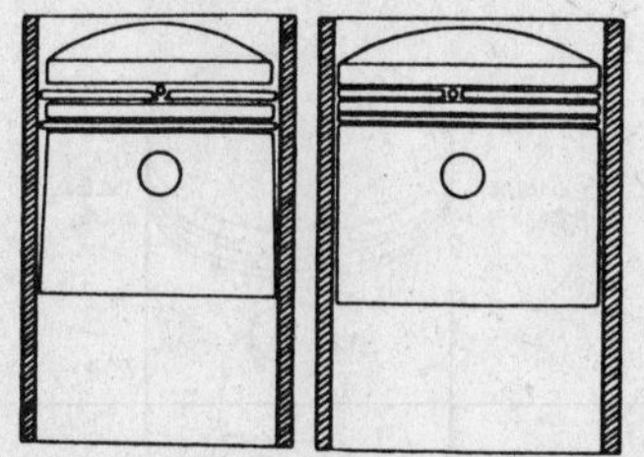

Unsymmetrical piston (left) expands to circular shape during operation (right)

5. If hand lapping does not restore the flatness of the mating surface, it can be done on a machine designed for this purpose.

Cylinder and Piston

1. This piston is "cam-turned" in the same way, and for the same reasons, as the four-stroke piston described in the preceeding section.

2. Wear of the cylinder bore is checked by making a series of readings at three or four places along the bore in one direction, and then turning the gauge 90° and measuring at the same places. The measurements are taken at the top, middle, and bottom of the bore, but most manufacturers give exact points at which the readings are to be taken.

3. Make a visual inspection of the piston. The skirt must be free of scoring or seizure marks. If present, it may be possible to save the piston by polishing the damaged area with emery or crocus cloth. Sand lightly to produce a cross-hatch pattern.

If the scored area was wider than ½ in., or if deep scratches remain after sanding, the piston should be replaced.

4. Piston diameter is measured perpendicular to the wrist pin near the bottom edge of the piston skirt. Some manufacturers give a precise measurement point.

Maximum allowable piston-to-cylinder clearance for most models is 0.1mm (0.0039 in.), and after this point the cylinder must be bored to the next oversize, unless it is a chrome-plated bore.

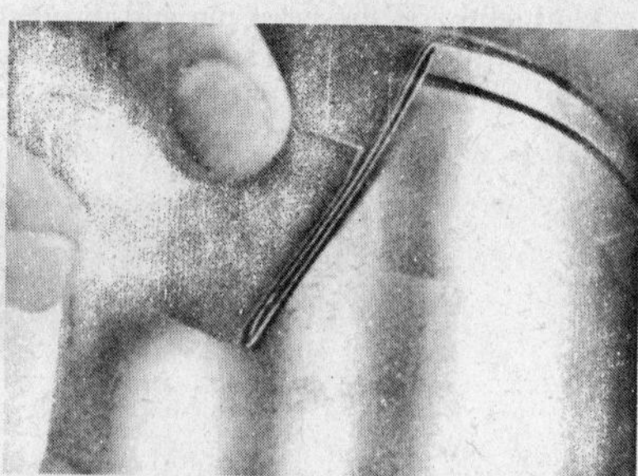

Removing scuff marks from skirt. Sand to produce a cross-hatch pattern

Measuring piston diameter

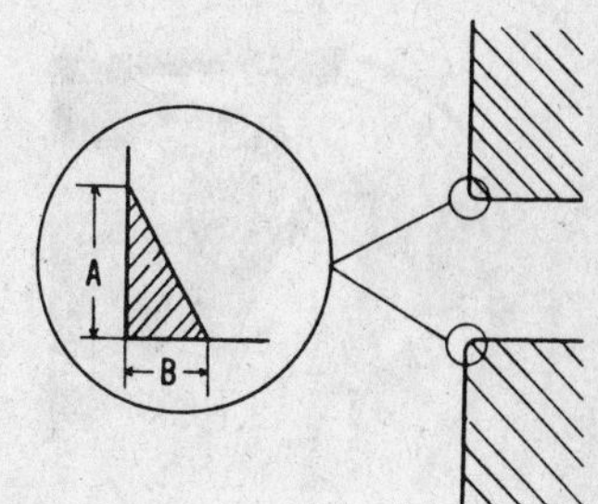

After boring, the edges of all ports should be bevelled

If the cylinder is bored, it is necessary to chamfer all the edges of the ports with a file to remove any sharp edges.

5. Piston rings must be free to move on the piston. If frozen, they may be carbon-clogged, or the ring grooves may have been ruined by a seizure. If carbon-clogged, it will only be necessary to replace the rings, but deformed grooves necessitate replacement of the piston.

6. Check ring side clearance by inserting the proper size feeler gauge between the ring and the bottom of the ring groove. If used rings do not have the correct side clearance, replace them and recheck. If new rings show the incorrect clearance, replace the piston.

7. To check ring end-gap, remove the rings from the piston by spreading the ends with the thumbs. After removal, check the rings for a twisted or warped condition. Such rings must be replaced.

Some manufacturers give a "free end-gap" specification. As the name implies, this is a measurement of the ring end-gap as the ring sits after removal from the piston and is not to be confused with the more common "ring end-gap" which is measured with the ring in the cylinder bore (see Step 8, following). "Free end-gap" should be measured after a ring has been removed from its piston, and is intended to indicate whether the ring has been deformed by removal.

8. Place each ring, in turn, into the top or bottom of its bore and push it in an inch or so using the piston skirt. This will ensure that the ring is aligned perpendicular to the cylinder wall.

First check that the ring is contacting the cylinder wall at all points. Place a piece of white paper beneath the cylinder and see if anything is visible between the cylinder wall and the ring. If you can see the white paper,

Checking ring side clearance

Removing a piston ring

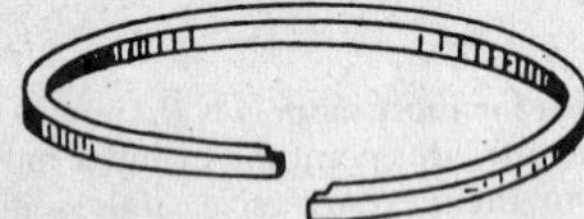
Check for warped rings

the ring is not touching the wall either because the ring is worn or deformed, or because the cylinder itself has become ovalized through wear.

9. Check ring end-gap with the proper feeler gauge. If the gap is larger than the given specification, the rings must be replaced. If too small, hold the ring carefully, closing both ends against a thin, flat file. After a few strokes of the file, recheck the gap.

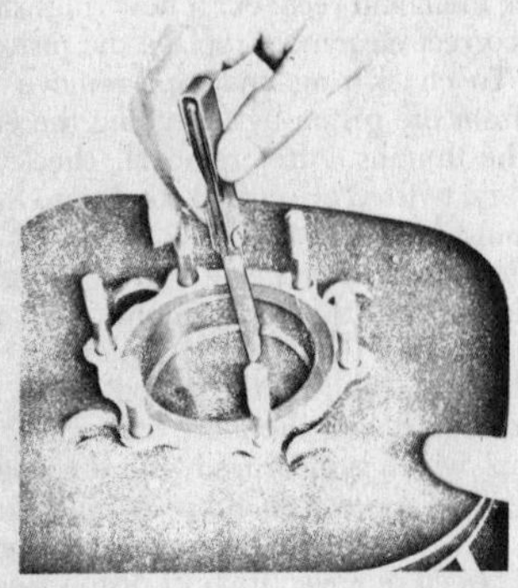
Measuring ring end-gap

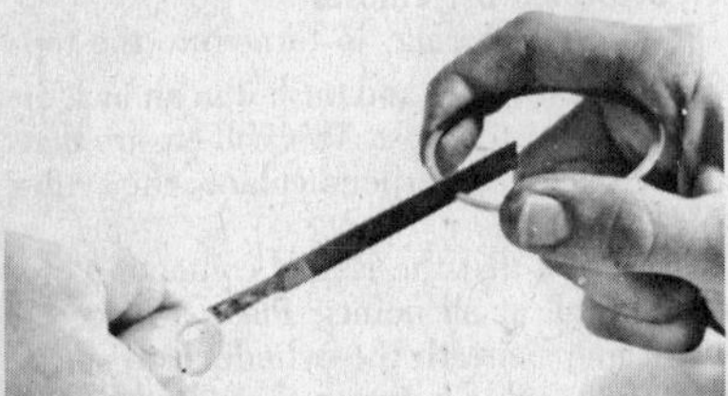
Filing ring ends

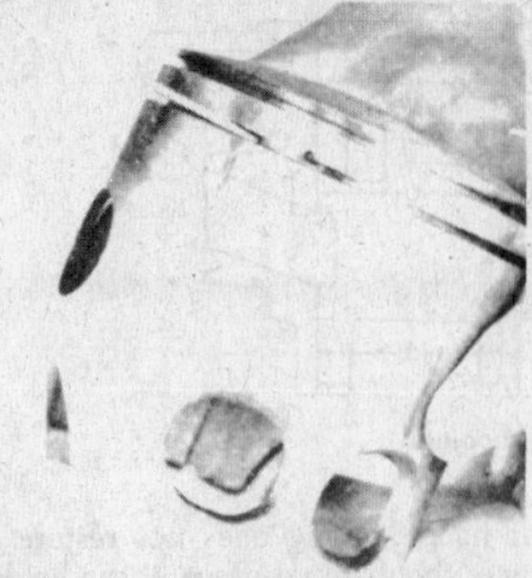
Decarbonizing ring grooves

Checking fit of wrist pin in piston

CAUTION: *Check the end-gap frequently during this operation as it is easy to remove too much metal. Do not allow the file to slip out while filing as it is very easy to break the ring in this way.*

10. Clean out the piston ring grooves. Use a small screwdriver or thin instrument for this operation, but take care that the metal of the piston is not scratched.

Plain-type ring grooves may be cleaned out with a piece of broken piston ring. Other types of grooves, however, should not be cleaned in this manner, as the groove may be scratched.

11. Check the wrist pin for discoloration or step-wear. If damaged in this manner, the wrist pin and needle bearing (if fitted) should be replaced.

12. Lightly oil the wrist pin and insert it into the piston. There should be a fair amount of drag on the wrist pin while at-

Checking small end bearing and wrist pin for play

Inspect the small-end needle bearing for condition

STAMPED MARK STAMPED MARK

FLAT KEYSTONE

Plain and keystone-type rings

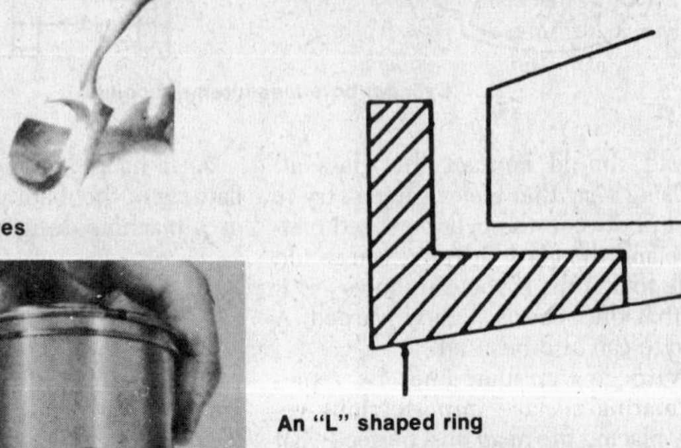
An "L" shaped ring

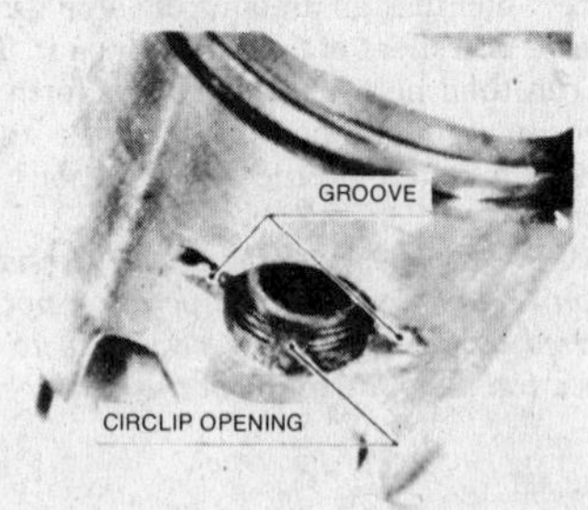

Be sure the circlip end-gap is not aligned with the wrist pin hole grooves

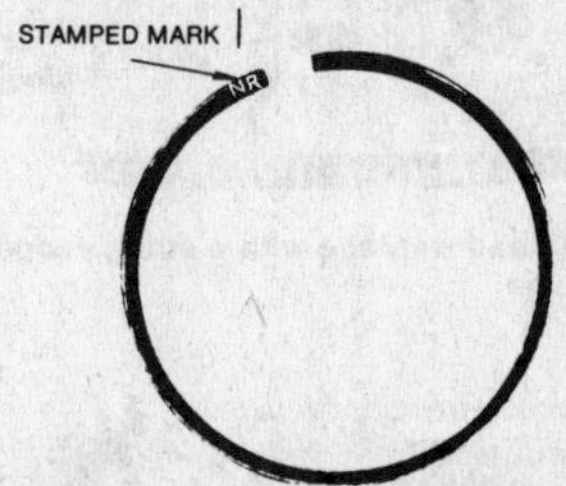

Rings are always installed with the stamped mark facing up

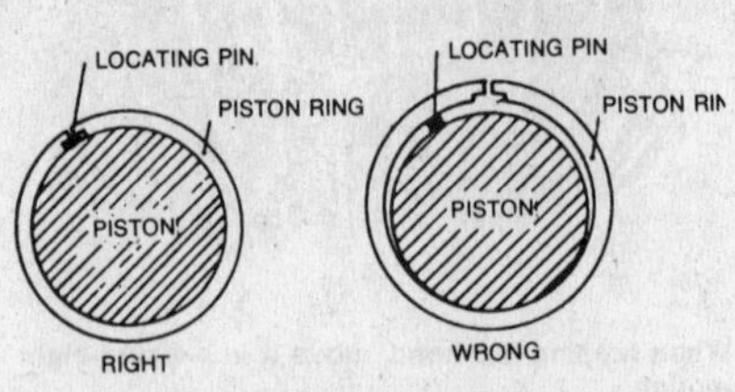

Be sure that the rings are installed with the end-gap on either side of the locating pin

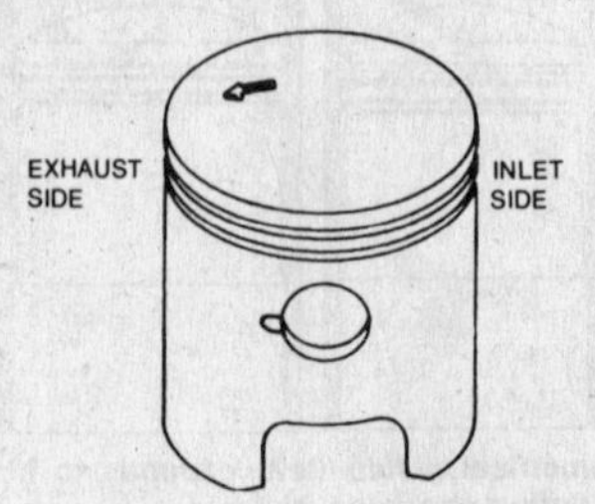

Check the piston crown for installation marks

tempting to push it in by hand. If the pin goes in easily, or can be turned with ease after insertion, either it or the piston will have to be replaced.

13. Insert the wrist pin into the con rod small end. Check for vertical play. If there is any at all, the wrist pin and the small end bearing must be replaced.

14. To check for connecting rod straightness, fit the piston, minus the rings, onto the connecting rod and install the wrist pin. Install the cylinder. The piston should be dead center in the cylinder bore. If moved to either side, it should return to the center position after the engine is turned over once or twice. If it does not, or if it appears to be to one side or the other in the bore, the connecting rod is probably bent.

15. On models with caged needle bearing small ends, check the condition of the needle bearing. Replace it if the needles are pitted, discolored, or otherwise damaged, or if the wrist pin or piston rings are replaced.

Piston Installation

1. Piston rings may be "plain," "keystone," or "L-shaped" depending on make and model and in some cases the top and bottom rings may not be interchangeable.

2. Rings are always installed with the identification marks facing *up*.

3. Be sure that the ring end gaps are located on either side of the locating pin in the ring groove.

4. The piston must be properly installed on the rod, and in most cases an arrow is stamped on the piston crown. This must point towards the exhaust port. Some models may have other ways of determining piston position.

5. Always use new wrist pin circlips. Position the circlip end-gaps so that they do not align with the wrist pin hole cutout.

CLUTCH

1. Check the condition of the friction plates noting any scoring or damage to the material. Check the condition of the engaging tabs. Measure the thickness of the plates and compare to the standard specification.

Friction plates are replaced in sets.

2. Check the steel plates for scoring or discoloration. Check plate warpage.

3. Check clutch spring free length and replace springs as a set if any one spring is compressed.

Checking clutch spring free-length

Checking a steel plate for warpage

4. Check the clutch housing for indented wear caused by the engaging tabs of the plates. Indentations here, and minor wear to the engaging tabs, can usually be remedied with an oilstone or file. Indentations on the housing may catch the plates and not allow them to disengage properly, and should therefore be removed, or the housing replaced.

5. Either the clutch hub or the housing will engage the shaft splines, depending on the design of the clutch. Check for excessive backlash, and damage or wear to the clutch and shaft splines.

6. Check the clutch housing gear, if applicable, for wear or damage to the teeth. If the gear teeth are worn, check those of the primary gear as well. Gears which mesh should always be replaced in pairs. If the clutch is chain-driven, check the teeth for hooking or wear in the same manner as for countershaft and rear wheel sprockets.

7. Check the clutch pushrod, if applicable, for a bent condition. Replace or straighten it if bent.

Inspect the clutch hub bushing for wear

8. The clutch lifter mechanism is not ordinarily subject to wear. However, the component should be thoroughly cleaned, especially on those models where it shares the crankcase cover with the engine sprocket, and should be well lubricated.

TRANSMISSION

1. Gears may be inspected in place on their shafts on models which allow the gear clusters to be removed as a unit. On many makes, the transmission gears are located with circlips. Once removed, these circlips should be replaced with new ones. If disassembly of the gears is undertaken, lay out each circlip thrust washer, shim, or gear in order to facilitate installation.

2. Check each of the gears for heat damage (discoloration), or for chipped, broken, or worn teeth. Pitting or wear of the hardened surface of the teeth will be most obvious at the very base of the teeth. Replace any gear showing such signs, and replace the gear with which it meshes as well.

3. Check the inner splines on gears so equipped, and replace the gear if the splines are worn or broken. Inspect the corresponding splines on the transmission shaft. Check for excessive play of the gear(s) on the shaft(s).

4. On gears with a plain bore, check for scoring. Check that the gear fits easily on the shaft, and turns freely, but it must not have

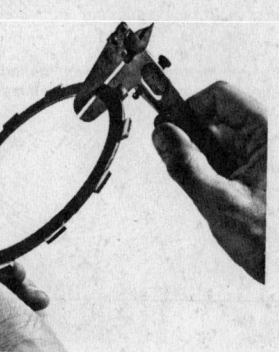

Measuring friction plate thickness

Check the hub for indented wear caused by the plates

Check the gears for wear of the teeth

Checking gear backlash

any up-and-down play. On gears with replaceable bushings, check for score or scratch marks, discoloration, etc., and replace the bushes if necessary.

5. Check the engaging dogs on gears which have them. Dogs must not be vorn, chipped, or borken, or the gear must be replaced.

6. Check that the transmission shafts are not bent. Check the condition of the splines, surfaces, and bearing journals, if applicable.

7. Check the transmission shaft bearings. If ball or roller bearings, check for discoloration, damage to the balls or rollers, noisy or halting rotation, etc. If plain-type bearings or bushings, check for score marks.

8. If the means are available, check gear backlash. If the backlash for any two gears is excessive, both gears of that set must be replaced.

9. During reassembly, check gear side-clearance if applicable.

Inspect each gear for worn or chipped engaging dogs

SHIFTER

To change gears, it is necessary to move certain gears back and forth on their shafts, and this is accomplished by the use of "shift forks." The shift forks are themselves moved either by a "shift drum" or a "camplate," the later being found primarily on British motorcycles.

1. Check shift forks for wear at the ends of the fingers. Some models have a finger thickness specification given. Check that the fingers are not chipped or bent. Check the shifter shaft or shift drum bore in the fork for wear. The forks should be a close fit on the shaft or drum. Check the shift fork pin (which rides in the drum or camplate grooves) for chipping or other damage.

2. If the transmission has a shift fork shaft, check that is is not bent by rolling it along a flat surface.

3. If a camplate is fitted, check that it is perfectly flat. Check for wear to the grooves. Check the detent plunger notches for condition.

4. If a shift drum is fitted, check the shift fork pin grooves for wear or damage. If the shift fork(s) ride on the shift drum, check for wear at that point. Check for wear of the bearing surfaces, if applicable.

FUEL SYSTEM

The fuel system is made up of the carburetor(s), fuel filter, and air filter. The following information encompasses the great majority of components currently in use.

Of course, in actual practice, carburetors are not quite that simple. The basic unit described above has no provisions for throttle control, cold starting, or the varying needs of the engine.

The operating stages of a "real" carburetor are described below.

Construction

Most carburetors consist of a one-piece body cast from cheap pot metal, although some "racing" units are made from more expensive materials such as magnesium. The body incorporates the venturi, a bore for the movement of the throttle slide, and provides a mounting point for various fuel and air jets.

Primary air passage. flanked by idle air passage on left

In addition, the body is drilled with a number of fuel and air passages. Among these are the primary air passage, pilot air passage, and pilot outlet or by-pass.

The *primary air passages* can usually be found just beneath the carburetor intake, and is drilled through to the needle jet. The air taken in through this passage helps to atomize, or mix, the gasoline passing through the needle jet before it enters the venturi. Unless the gasoline is atomized, raw fuel will reach the combustion chamber, resulting in wet-fouled spark plugs, inefficient combustion, and generally poor operation.

The *pilot air passage* is located alongside the primary air passage on most carburetors. The air taken in through this drilling is used for idle and low-speed operation.

The *pilot outlet* is a very small drilling which can be seen on the engine side of the throttle slide bore. The fuel/air mixture for idling pass through here and then to the engine.

The carburetor body also has a place for the attachment of the *float bowl.* The float bowl houses the float assembly and carries the carburetor's gasoline supply. A part of the float assembly is the float valve which usually consists of a small needle and a needle seat. The floats rise and fall according to the amount of gasoline in the float bowl, alternately pressing the needle against its seat and releasing it, thence controlling the fuel flow. The float bulbs may be made of various materials. Most early carburetors used brass bulbs, but plastic has been used more frequently in recent years. Float needles can be plastic, brass, or neoprene-tipped brass, the last proving most effective. Needle seats are almost always brass, and on most carburetors can be unscrewed for cleaning or replacement.

The great majority of modern carburetors mount the float bowl directly beneath the carburetor body. In this position the fuel supply surrounds the main jet ensuring an accurately metered supply of fuel during ac-

Pilot outlet and by-pass passages

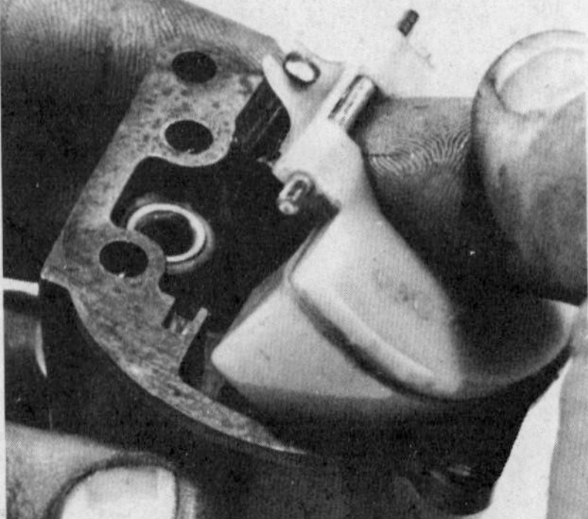
Float bowl components: float, needle, spindle, and needle seat

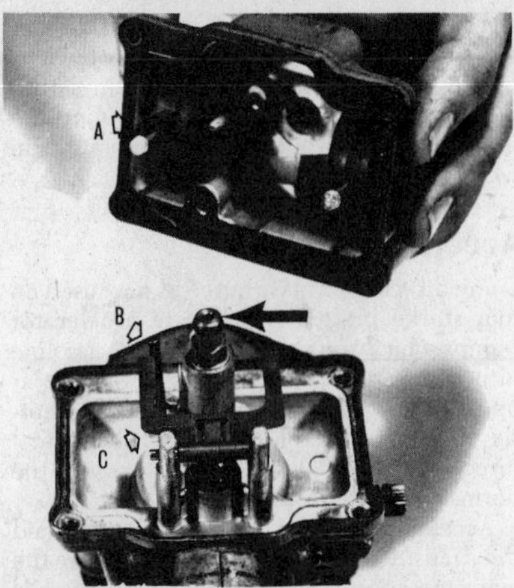

Mikuni SH-type carburetor. Floats (A), starter jet (B), float arm (C), and needle jet set bolt (arrow). The main jet is in the float bowl

celeration, braking, or banking to either side. This type of carburetor is usually known as "concentric." Not all carburetors were constructed in this manner, and separate float bowl carburetors were the rule for many years.

The *throttle slide* is the chief metering component of the carburetor. It is controlled directly by the throttle cable which runs to the twist grip on direct-control type carburetors. On "CV" units, the throttle cable opens and closes a throttle plate, and the slide proper opens and closes by venturi vacuum (this is explained later).

The throttle slide determines the size of the carburetor venturi and therefore meters the amount of air in the fuel/air mixture at most of the operating range. Additionally, the *needle* or *jet needle* is attached to the slide. This needle works in conjunction with the *needle jet* and determines the amount of gasoline allowed to pass into the engine primarily in the mid-range.

The throttle slide is cylindrical in most carburetors, although there are examples of "square slides" such as used by some Dell 'Orto carburetors. The slide has a cutaway at the intake side of the carburetor to allow the entry of air in sufficient quantities to mix with the gasoline when the throttle is closed. The higher the cutaway, the leaner the mixture will be when the slide is just opened. If the size of the cutaway is not matched to the other metering components and the particular needs of the engine, the transition from idle to the main metering system will be greatly impaired. This is a particularly critical period, since the load on the engine is changing as the clutch is engaged, and smooth starts from a dead stop must be considered a matter of safety in many cases.

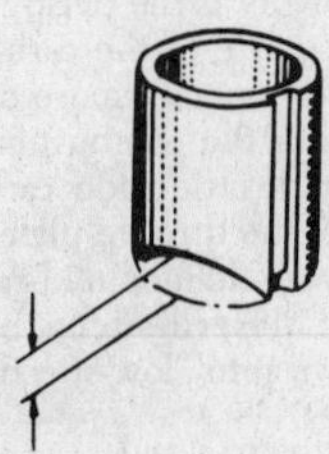
Throttle slide cutaway

Formerly, throttle slides were cast from the same material as the carburetor body, but this was found to cause greatly accelerated wear on both slide and body. Today, the slide is commonly steel, often chromed, bringing wear into more acceptable limits. In CV carburetors, where the slide must be moved by venturi vacuum, the slides must be light in weight so light alloys are used.

CV carburetor slides are light in weight and must be closely fitted to the carb bore

OPERATION

The operation of a practical carburetor can best be described by dividing it into five circuits, and the components which control each one.

Direct-Control Carburetor

STARTING CIRCUIT (0 THROTTLE OPENING)

The engine needs a rich mixture for starting when cold. Since this need is only temporary and the mixture must be balanced when the engine warms up, a manually operated

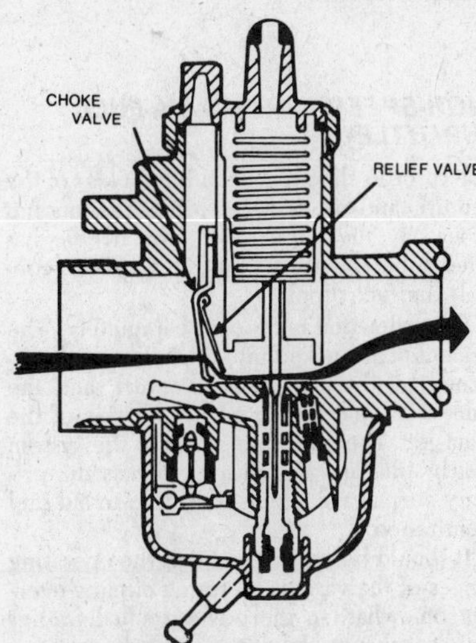

Typical choke plate operation

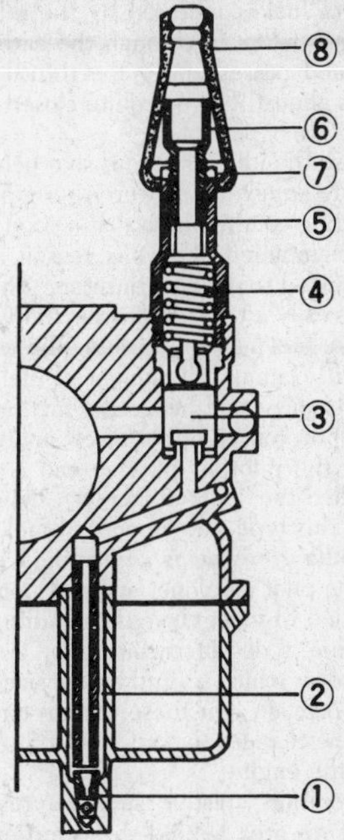

1. Starter jet
2. Starter pipe
3. Plunger
4. Plunger spring
5. Plunger cap
6. Adjuster
7. Locknut
8. Dust cover

Starter circuit

"choke" is incorporated into most carburetors and is controlled by the operator.

There are various ways of creating this rich mixture. The most simple is to reduce the amount of air available to the carb by closing off the mouth with a plate. This method is most often found on Honda motorcycles and on some others as well.

On some units, notably the Amal Monoblocs and Concentrics, a temporary rich mixture is obtained by flooding or overfilling the float bowl. "Ticklers" are provided on the carburetor. When pushed, they depress the float, allowing the float needle to rise from its seat. The fuel level in the float bowl then exceeds its normal level and rises through the jets into the venturi where it provides a rich starting mixture.

Other carburetors, such as Mikuni and Dell'Orto use a refined version of the tickler. A starter jet is fitted which is activated by a cable or lever. When activated, the jet is opened (in most cases a spring-loaded plunger does the opening and closing), and fuel from the float bowl can bypass the normal fuel jets and pass into the carburetor bore.

Once the engine is started and warmed up, the choke is switched off, and the fuel/air metering is turned over to the idle circuit components.

IDLE CIRCUIT (0–1/8 THROTTLE OPENING)

At idle under normal operating conditions, the engine requires very little fuel and air. It does, however, require more accurate metering than pure venturi action can provide while the engine is turning relatively slowly and intake air velocity is low.

The idle circuit on most popular carburetors consists of a pilot jet, pilot air passage, and the throttle slide.

Fuel is provided by the float bowl. The

amount of fuel is metered by the pilot jet, while air is taken in through the carburetor venturi and passes under the throttle slide (which is almost, but not quite closed at this point).

Because the idle mixture is so crucial, it is possible to adjust the mixture to compensate for changing conditions so that a good idle is always maintained. For this reason a pilot screw is fitted to most carburetors. The pilot screw is really a tapered needle and is fitted to an air or fuel passage. Turning the screw in or out will change the amount of fuel or air allowed to pass, and hence the mixture. On some carburetors the pilot screw is fitted directly to the pilot air passage and is sometimes called the "pilot air screw." On carburetors of this type, the amount of fuel entering the idling engine is determined by the size of the pilot jet alone, and the amount of air is varied to meet changing conditions.

On other types of carburetors, it is the amount of air which is fixed by the size of the pilot air passage. On these carburetors, the pilot screw changes the amount of *fuel* passing into the engine.

In operation, piston suction creates a low-pressure area behind the throttle slide. To equalize this low pressure, air rushes through the pilot air passage, mixes with fuel from the pilot jet. This mixture is bled into the carburetor's intake tract through the pilot outlet. The air coming in under the throttle slide is added to this mixture and delivers it to the combustion chamber.

LOW-SPEED CIRCUIT (1/8–1/4 THROTTLE OPENING)

This circuit uses the same components as the idle circuit. There is, however, an increase in the airflow as the throttle slide rises, and in fuel flow as the needle begins to come out of the needle jet. This effects a transition to the mid-range circuit, since the increased amounts of fuel and air delivered by the needle jet and the venturi overshadow the smaller amounts coming from the pilot outlet, eventually eliminating the idle circuit from the metering system.

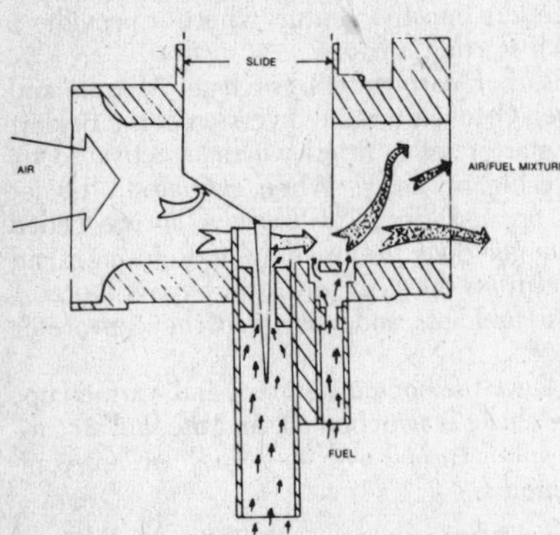

Carburetor low-speed operation

MID-RANGE CIRCUIT (1/4–3/4 THROTTLE OPENING)

In this circuit, air is supplied by two sources: the venturi and the primary air passage. The more important reason for the air going through the primary air passage, however, is that it mixes with the gasoline in the needle jet (the needle jet has a number of holes drilled in it), and this helps to atomize the fuel before it enters the venturi.

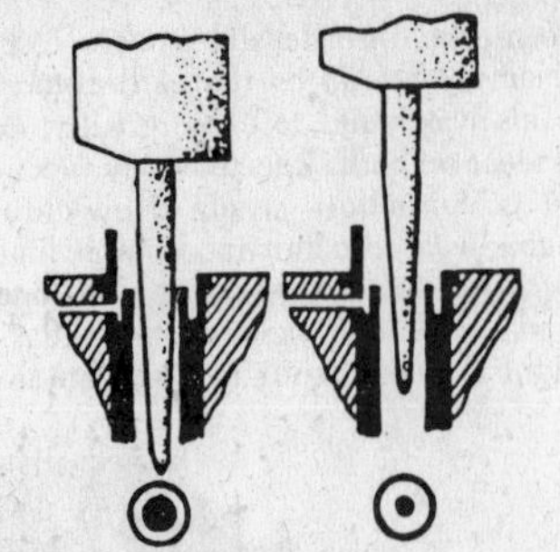

Needle/needle jet operation as the throttle slide is raised

Fuel is supplied by the float bowl and metered by the needle jet and needle. The needle jet on most carburetors is located just above the main jet and works in conjunction with the needle suspended from the throttle slide.

As the slide rises, the air flow through the carburetor is increased, and at the same time the tapered needle allows more and more fuel to pass through the needle jet.

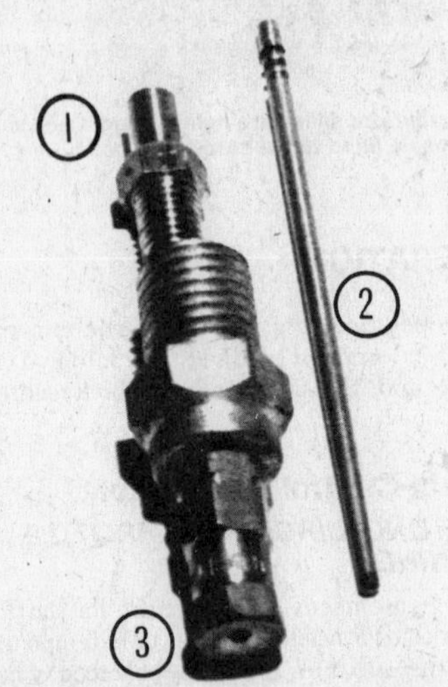

Mid and high range metering: 1, needle jet; 2, needle; 3, main jet

HIGH-SPEED CIRCUIT (3/4-FULL THROTTLE)

The throttle slide has been lifted clear of the venturi, and no longer controls the amount of air. By the same token, the needle has lifted out of the needle jet, and no longer controls the fuel supply.

Venturi action takes over completely. The amount of air sucked into the engine is determined by the size of the venturi, and the amount of fuel delivered by the size of the main jet. The only other part of the system which still has a significant effect is the primary air passage which continues to aid fuel atomization.

It should be understood that the operating ranges of the various metering circuits overlap somewhat, so there is a gradual, rather than an abrupt, transition from one to another as the throttle is operated.

The relative independence of the various circuits, however, should explain why it is fruitless to make random changes in carburetor settings without first determining the nature of the problem, and the range in which it occurs.

Accelerator Pumps

Some direct-control carburetors now used on four-stroke motors incorporate accelerator pumps which squirt a stream of raw gasoline into the venturi whenever the throttle is opened. The pumps usually consist of a throttle slide-activated plunger which takes fuel directly from the float bowl, bypassing the normal metering components.

Accelerator pumps are incorporated to aid the transition from the idle system to the main metering system. Throttle response is therefore much improved. One disadvantage of the system, however, is that it may have an adverse effect on fuel economy.

Constant-Velocity Carburetors

The constant-velocity carburetor is basically the same as the direct-control type carburetor, except that the throttle twist-grip is not connected directly to the throttle slide. Instead, in the CV carburetor, the throttle grip and cable are connected to a throttle plate located between the intake manifold and throttle slide. As the throttle plate is opened, the manifold vacuum evacuates air from the top of the slide chamber through a passage in the slide. Consequently, on demand from the engine, the slide is raised and more air is admitted, and the tapered needle is proportionally lifted out of the jet tube to admit more fuel.

The term "constant-velocity" (or constant vacuum) refers to the speed of the air passing over the main jet tube and the vacuum in the carburetor throat which remains constant due to the movement of the piston in relation to the vacuum. As the engine demands more air and the manifold vacuum increases, the slide responds by lifting in proportion to the vacuum. Thus the carburetor air speed and vacuum remain constant, because an increase in vacuum means an increase in slide lift, which in turn increases the amount of air passing through the carburetor by altering the size of the air passage (venturi), and compensating for the increased engine demands with a larger flow of air. A constant vacuum indicates a constant-velocity, and vice versa.

Throttle-Plate Carburetors

The "throttle-plate" carburetor is little different in theory from the throttle-slide types considered above except, of course, that there is no moving slide. In its place is a flat plate which pivots as the twist-grip is rotated to increase the size of the carburetor throat and allow progressively more of the fuel/air mixture to enter the combustion chamber.

Unlike the throttle-slide carburetors described above, the throttle-plate units do not usually have well-defined mid-range circuits, and are best described by breaking the operation down into "low-speed" and "high-speed" circuits.

The Bendix 16P12 carburetor is typical of this type and is used to illustrate the following explanation. This carburetor was used on most Harley-Davidson V-Twins after 1970, with the exception of late models fitted with a very similar Keihin unit.

STARTING CIRCUIT

A choke plate on the intake side of the carburetor closes off the mouth to yield a rich mixture needed for starting. A hole in the choke plate allows some air to enter to prevent flooding the engine. In addition, an accelerator pump is fitted which injects a stream of gasoline into the venturi when the throttle is opened.

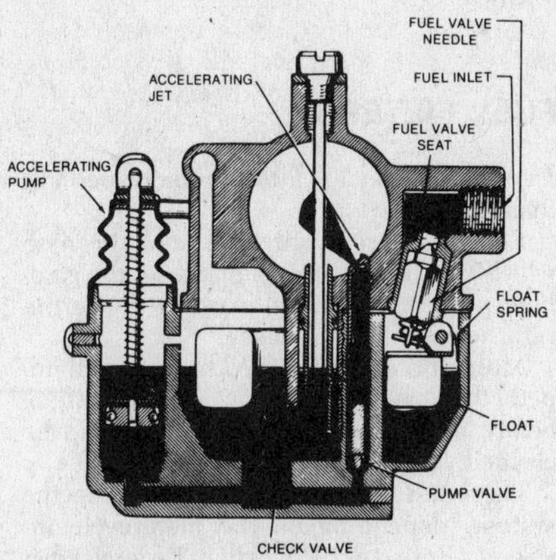

Starting circuit

LOW-SPEED CIRCUIT

There are three or four idle discharge holes located at the top engine side of the venturi. The main idle discharge hole (No. 1 in the illustration) is variable in size as it works in conjunction with a tapered idle adjusting needle. At idle, the throttle plate stop screw holds the throttle plate open just enough so that this passage is able to discharge its fuel into the engine.

Drawn by piston suction, gasoline rises from the float bowl through the idle tube. As the fuel passes the idle discharge holes (Nos. 2, 3, and 4), air is drawn in and mixed with it.

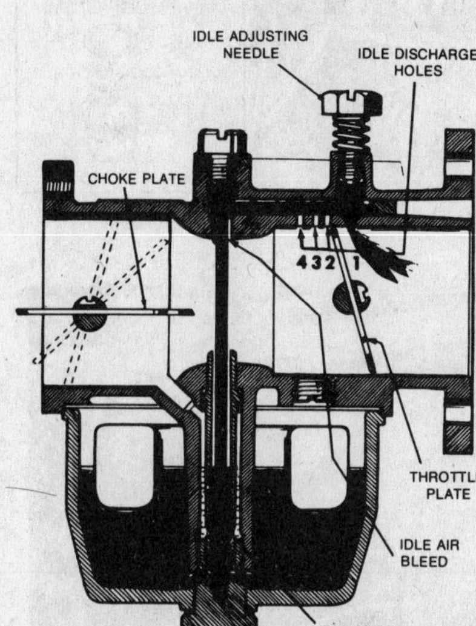

Low-speed circuit

The mixture is then bled into the intake port through the idle hole No. 1.

The mixture is determined by the idle adjusting needle. If the needle is turned IN, the mixture will be leaned out, and it will be richened if the needle is turned out.

As the throttle is opened slightly, the other idle discharge holes are exposed in turn, each allowing progressively more fuel and air into the intake port.

Eventually, the throttle plate is opened enough so that engine suction is powerful enough to draw gasoline from the main discharge tube and the transition to the high-speed circuit begins.

HIGH-SPEED CIRCUIT

The high-speed circuit begins when all idle discharge holes are exposed, and can no longer supply sufficient gasoline and air for the engine's needs.

As the throttle plate is opened the velocity of the incoming air passing through the venturi is increased, and, as this happens, this air exerts an increasingly powerful suction on the gasoline in the discharge tube just below the venturi. This gasoline is already partially atomized by the air drawn through the well vent.

When the throttle is fully opened, the amount of air in the mixture is determined by the size of the carburetor venturi and the amount of fuel by the size of the main jet.

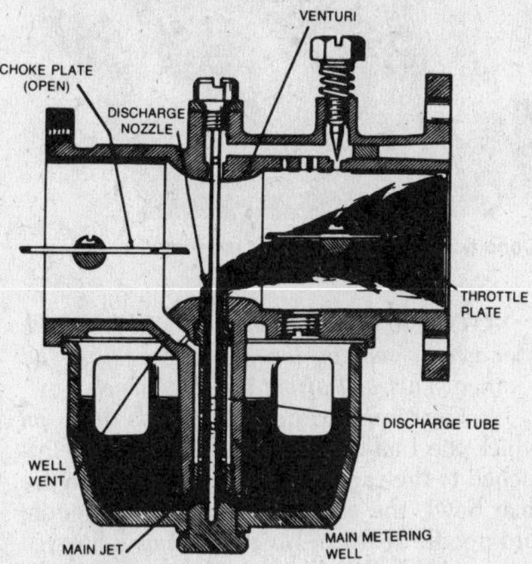

High-speed circuit

CARBURETOR REBUILDING

The following guidelines are applicable to all carburetors in use today. For specific disassembly procedures, refer to the individual model section.

1. After disassembly, clean all metal parts with a solvent or a commercial carburetor cleaner. Blow dry.

CAUTION: *Clean carburetors in a solvent which is safe for plastic. Many units are fitted with non-removable parts of this material which may be damaged if a harsh solvent is used.*

2. Use compressed air to clean out the air and fuel passages in the carburetor body. On some units, the primary air and pilot air passages may be large enough to permit the entry of a cotton swab if necessary to remove dirt and varnish.

3. Check the main body casting carefully for vibration or stress cracks. If the carburetor is bolted to the cylinder head or manifold, check the mounting flange for warpage by placing a straight edge across it or by placing it on a flat surface such as a piece of glass. The flange must be very close to a perfectly flat condition, or possible air leaks may be the result. Minor warpage or surface imperfections can be corrected by placing a piece of emery cloth on the glass and working the carburetor flange on it. Move the carburetor in a figure-8 motion. Alternatively, an oilstone can be used.

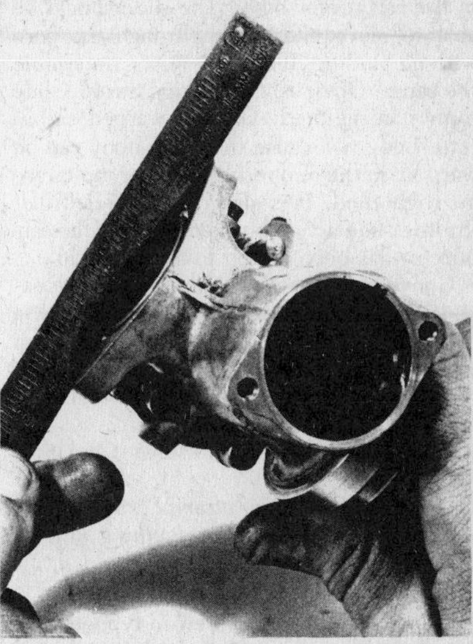

Checking for a warped flange

Be sure to wash the carburetor thoroughly afterwards.

4. Check the condition of the throttle slide. Check for scratches or score marks on the sides of the slide. On most direct-control type carburetors the slides are chromed, so wear or scoring should not be a problem. Some carburetors use slides which are made from the same material as the carburetor body, and therefore wear is sometimes a problem. Check for corresponding wear in the throttle slide bore of the carburetor body.

5. On CV carburetors, slide condition is critical, and no imperfections of the sides of the slide can be allowed. If a rubber diaphragm is fitted on the carb slide, check it carefully for punctures or tears.

6. Check the action of the throttle slide

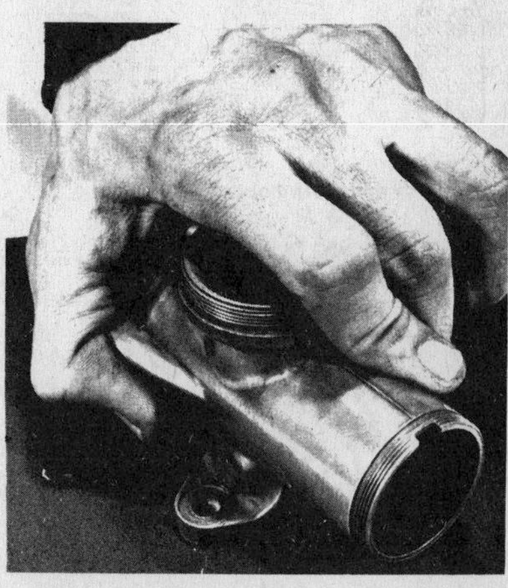

Working carburetor flange on emery cloth

in the carburetor body. The slide should be able to move effortlessly through the bore with no binding. If binding exists, determine the cause. Obviously, a sticking throttle slide cannot be ignored. Often a warped carburetor body will cause this. The body can be warped if the mounting nuts or bolts are overtightened. It is also recommended that throttle slide action be checked after the carburetor has been bolted to the manifold.

Conversely, the slide should not have excessive clearance in the bore. Often, such a condition will cause a clattering sound at idle. Replace either the slide or the carburetor body (or both) depending on what parts are worn.

7. Clean the fuel jets in solvent and blow them clear.

CAUTION: *Never attempt to clear a blocked jet by inserting anything into its bore. Clear by blowing through with air pressure only.*

8. When installing screw-in type jets, do not overtighten them. Jets are brass and are easily damaged.

9. Inspect the needle jet and needle. The needle must be free of knicks or any signs of wear along its length. Often, these components will need to be replaced because of normal wear. As the throttle slide moves up and down while the machine is in operation, the needle rubs against the inside of the jet. Eventually, these components may wear enough to cause a noticeable rich running condition in the mid-range. If this occurs, both the needle and the jet should be replaced.

10. Make a careful inspection of the float(s). Some floats are solid, but most are hollow, being either brass or plastic. Check for leaks by shaking the float close to your ear and listening for any gas trapped inside. If semi-transparent plastic, gasoline can be detected by holding the float up to a strong light.

If the float leaks, replace it; do not attempt repairs.

On models with two connected float bulbs, check that they are level, and that the assembly is not twisted or out of alignment.

11. Check the tip of the float needle for wear or corrosion. Inspect the float needle seat as well. If there is any foreign matter on the needle or seat, remove it.

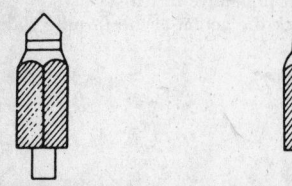

Normal (left) and worn float needle

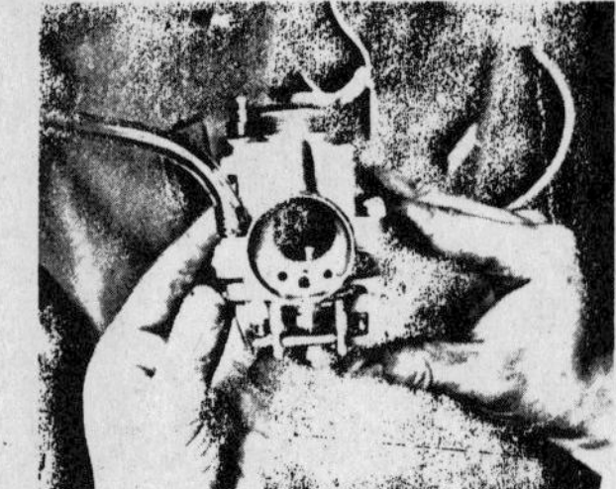

Checking needle sealing ability

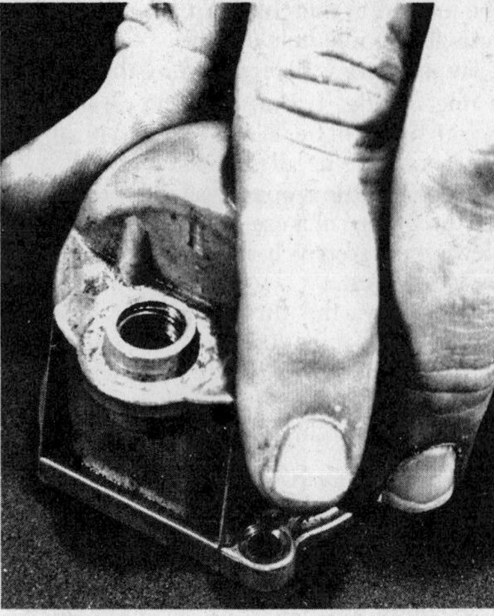

Cleaning up a float bowl mating surface

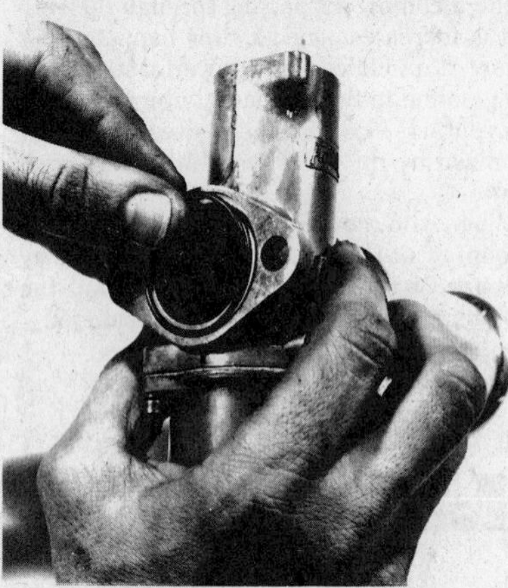

Condition of rubber o-rings is critical

NOTE: *Do not attempt to clean the needle or needle seat by lapping one against the other. This will affect the float level.*

12. On some carburetors, that is those on which the fuel feed line and the float are attached to the carburetor body rather than the float bowl, the efficiency of the float needle and needle seat can be checked as follows:

a. With the float, needle, and seat installed on the carburetor body, connect the fuel line to the carburetor;

b. Place a number of dry rags beneath the carburetor, and hold it upright (in its normal operating position) with one hand;

c. With the other hand, gently raise the float assembly until the float needle is seated. Have an assistant turn the petcock to a fuel flow position (if a diaphragm-type petcock is fitted, it must be turned to the "Prime" position);

d. If the needle and seat are in good condition, and forming a good seal, no gasoline will flow out of the carburetor;

e. If a leak is noted, replace the needle and seat.

f. The test may not be valid if the needle is pressed into its seat with more than a few ounces of pressure.

CAUTION: *While performing this test, be sure that adequate precautions are taken in the event of spillage.*

13. Check that the tapered portion of the pilot screw is smooth and clean. Replace it if it is crushed or blunted.

14. On models which use a starter-plunger, be sure the plunger is clean. If neoprene-tipped, clean it only in gasoline.

15. Clean out the float bowl thoroughly. Check for stress cracks around screw holes. If the bowl has a flat gasket surface, any imperfections on the surface can be removed by working the bowl on a piece of emery cloth or an oilstone. This, of course, cannot be done on float bowls with an o-ring or gasket groove at the mating surface.

16. New gaskets, fiber washers, and O-rings should always be used when reassembling. O-rings are especially important as they may be used as air or fuel seals and even slight damage or deformation may affect the mixture.

FUEL FILTERS

Fuel filters, like air filters, require periodic maintenance.

Fuel filters are usually wire or plastic mesh which trap dirt or foreign matter in the gasoline, preventing it from clogging the carburetor jets and fuel passages.

After a time, this trapped material will impede the flow of gasoline through the system; before this happens, the filter(s) should be cleaned.

There are one or more fuel filters in the system, depending on the motorcycle involved. Prior to 1975, when Federal edict redesigned the fuel petcock, most motorcycles had a sediment bowl fitted to the petcock with a wire mesh filter just above it. After shutting off the gas, unscrew and remove the sediment bowl. Pull out the o-ring and filter screen. Wash the screen and bowl in gasoline, and reinstall.

If the petcock has no sediment bowl, the filter is probably located on the petcock intake pipe inside the gas tank. Some petcocks with sediment bowls have an additional filter here as well. Access to these filters can only

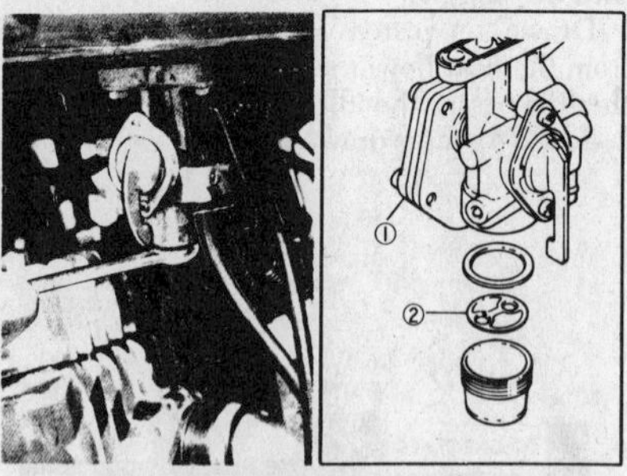

Petcock sediment bowl and filter screen

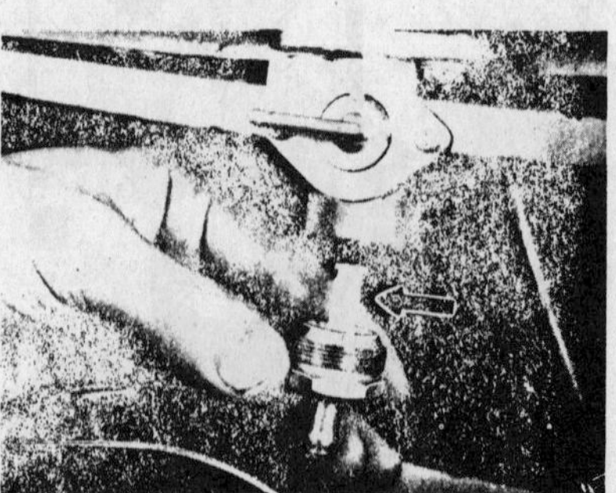

On some models, the filter is inside the tank

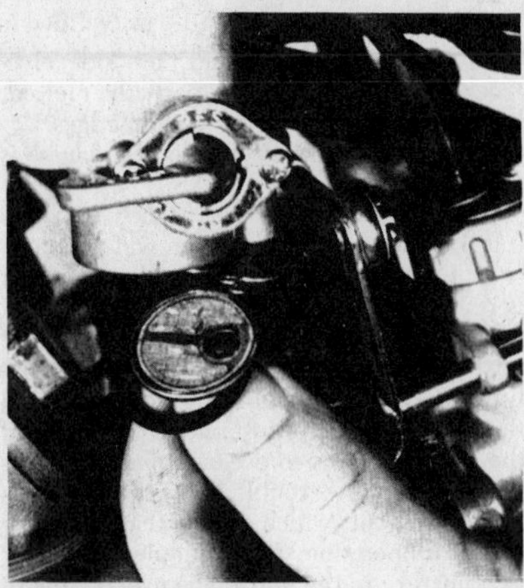

Petcock filter screen and o-ring

be gained by first draining all gasoline in the tank. Removal of the tank from the motorcycle first is the quickest and safest way to do this.

Petcocks are secured either with a single large nut which screws onto a fitting on the tank, or by two or more screws. In either case care must be taken on removal, since certain sealing devices are in use, such as rubber O-rings.

Clean the fuel filter(s) is gasoline and check condition. If the filter is very old, enough foreign matter may have accumulated on it to make thorough cleaning impossible. In this event, replace it.

Clogged fuel filters may cause a lean running condition at high speeds, since the engine may be using gasoline faster than it can flow through the filters. In addition, if clogged badly enough, the filters may cause hard starting, especially when the supply of fuel in the tank is low.

AIR FILTERS

Because it is designed to be replaced or cleaned at periodic intervals, the air filter is a likely source of trouble.

As it fills up with dirt, the air filter will cause the mixture to become increasingly rich. If it is not serviced, the mixture will become so rich that performance will be greatly impaired.

The oil-foam air cleaner is the most popular type in use today, although there are a multitude of different kinds.

The dry "paper element" air filter has been standard equipment on most motorcycles until very recently. The paper is porous, and will therefore allow air to pass more or less freely, while retaining foreign matter.

Most paper elements are pleated to afford maximum intake area in a given space.

Paper elements can be serviced, after a fashion, by brushing dirt deposits off the outside and using compressed air to blow out remaining fine dirt from the inside of the filter box. This technique, however, is very limited in effect, and it makes more sense to simply replace the element after several thousand miles.

"Oil-foam" filter elements are now in wide use, and have many advantages over the paper filters they are replacing. First, the foam elements can capture much smaller bits of foreign matter, and yet are less restrictive to air. Secondly, the foam elements are easy to service and can be reused.

Foam filters depend upon an oil film for filtering effectiveness.

Service oil-foam filters by first washing thoroughly in a solvent. Let the filter soak up the solvent like a sponge. Squeeze it dry. Repeat the procedure until the solvent being squeezed off ceases carrying off dirt. Be sure to *squeeze* the element: do not wring it out, as this risks tearing it, or at least damaging the close-knit pores.

Soak the cleaned element in the type of oil recommended by the manufacturer. In most cases, standard motor oil (20W/50 or 30W) can be used, but some filters specify 80W or 90W gear lubricant.

Squeeze off the excess oil, and the filter is ready to use again.

Another kind of air filter which is coming into use today can best be described as the "wet-paper" type. At the present time, this kind of filter is not standard equipment on any popular motorcycle, but is available as an accessory item. This filter is composed of a special type of paper which offers almost no resistance to air but, when treated with a special oil supplied by the manufacturer, offers an extremely high degree of filtering. This filter must not be treated with motor oil or the like—only with the special oil. Cleaning is accomplished with lacquer thinner, and the filter is reusable.

Blowing dirt out of a paper-type air filter

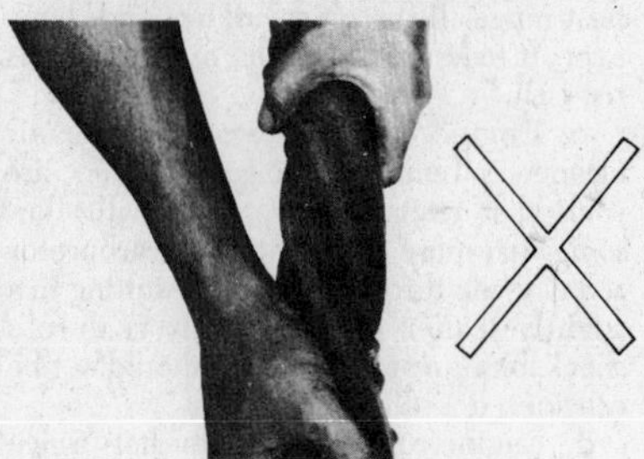

Do not wring out foam-type air filters

Squeezing off the excess oil

Service Intervals

Air filter service intervals will depend entirely upon the environment in which the machine is ridden, although the "Periodic Maintenance" chart in each section will give a guide to service under routine conditions. This is usually about 5000 miles for road bikes, and about 2500 miles for off-road machines, but this can be far too long if there is a lot of dust in the air.

The outward appearance of the air filter element is no reliable indicator of its condition. Some oil-foam filters tend to take on a dirty appearance after only a few miles, while filtering ability is unimpaired. Some paper elements never look too bad, but may be almost fully clogged.

Fitting Accessory Filters

Non-stock or accessory air filters are a popular item, and may benefit your machine. Often, such filters claim less intake restriction as well as improve filtering properties, and, if this is true, it may be necessary to rejet the carburetor(s) to avoid a lean mixture. Generally, the manufacturer of the accessory air filter will provide this information.

The filter you choose should be made specifically for your machine, as this will help you avoid numerous troubles in adapting and mounting the new filter. Even a reputable element may cause a decrease in performance if it is incorrectly mounted or simply too small to do the job. Additionally, foam air cleaners depend on a wire mesh or a coil spring to keep their shape. If incorrectly installed, engine suction can cause them to contract at high rpm, effectively cutting down the amount of air supplied.

HOSES/CLAMPS/MANIFOLDS

Periodic inspection of the fuel lines and manifolds is an important safety item which should not be overlooked.

Take the time to check the following points:

Be sure that all fuel-carrying lines are tightly secured by safety clips or clamps at both ends.

Be sure that the lines are fitted on to their respective spigots as far as they will go.

Check that the lines are properly routed. Fuel lines must not touch the cylinder head or any other part of the engine. Be sure that the lines are long enough. Lines which are too short are subject to abrasion damage and cracking which may cause leaks.

Check fuel lines for any sort of damage or wear. Lines which are cracked, hardened, or otherwise unserviceable must be replaced at once. The lines should not be allowed to get to the point where they actually leak. Preventive maintenance will require replacement of old lines before they get to this point. The safety implications of gasoline leaking onto a hot engine are obvious.

On twins and multis, check that manifold balance tubes, where fitted, are tightly secured. The balance tubes should be subjected to the same rigorous inspection as the fuel lines themselves. On some models, balance tubes are a prime source of air leaks which will cause erratic performance, or perhaps even engine overheating and/or piston seizure.

On models with diaphragm-type fuel petcocks, you should note that proper fuel flow depends on the condition of the vacuum line from the petcock to the manifold. Air leaks due to loose connections, cracks in the line, etc., will impede fuel flow or stop it all together.

On models with carburetor float bowl overflow tubes, be sure that the tubes are firmly secured to the carburetors and are properly routed to spill any gasoline well clear of the engine or other motorcycle parts.

Carburetor air leaks are a very serious matter since they will cause an extremely lean mixture which can and will damage the engine due to the heat generated in the combustion process.

The most common area in which air leaks occur is at the manifold.

Air leaks very often cause an extremely erratic idle which cannot be smoothed out by any degree of adjustment. Also, the mixture may vary depending on how hot the engine is. Therefore, settings which let the engine idle smoothly when it is cold will cause erratic operation as it heats up, and vice-versa.

To check for air leaks, warm the engine up to operating temperature and allow it to idle. Squirt motor oil carefully around potential areas of leakage such as the carburetor mount on the manifold or where the manifold mounts to the engine. If the idle changes, there is an air leak at that spot.

Manifold service checks will depend upon the type of mounting employed.

The most common type of carburetor mounting in use today involves fitting the carburetor spigot into a rubber sleeve. With this type of set-up, it is only necessary to ensure that the carburetor is fitted into the manifold sleeve as far as it will go, and that the carburetor clamp is properly tightened.

Also, be sure that the carburetor is perfectly vertical.

On some models, the carburetor(s) are rigidly mounted on the manifold by bolts or nuts. With fixtures of this sort, it is imperative that the sealing o-ring in the carburetor flange is in good condition. This can be checked by unbolting the carburetor and inspecting the o-ring. Replace it if it is chipped, cracked, hardened, or deformed. When installing a new o-ring, use of small quantity of grease in the carburetor groove and on the o-ring to hold it in place and provide a good air seal.

When installing the carburetor, be sure that the o-ring does not slip out of place.

When tightening the carburetor bolts or nuts, be sure to do so evenly and gradually.

Do not overtighten the nuts or bolts. Check throttle slide action while tightening these fasteners. If the slide suddenly sticks, the mounting flange may be warped. This condition must be remedied (see "Carburetor Rebuilding").

A third type of carburetor mounting consists of a clamp around the carburetor spigot which secures it to the manifold. With this type, there is usually a plastic gasket inside the carburetor. If the clamp is properly tightened, and the gasket is in good condition, there should be no trouble is obtaining a good seal.

CARBURETOR TROUBLESHOOTING

For the most part, the carburetor(s) will become a troublespot when something occurs which upsets the balance of gas and air going into the engine.

When there is an excess of gasoline in the mixture, it is said to be "rich." An excess of air, and the mixture is said to be too "lean."

If you have read the "Operational Description" above, it should be obvious that it is possible for the mixture to be "lean" or "rich" at one throttle opening, but normal at others. This is often caused by the installation of the wrong size jets, rather than a defect in the components themselves.

Like all other aspects of troubleshooting, an approach to a carburetor problem must in large measure depend on the nature and the history of the ailment.

Probably the most common carburetor malady is simple dirt which has gotten past the fuel or air filters and has clogged or even partially obstructed the various passages in the carburetor.

Again, individual cases must be taken into account. If the trouble has developed slowly over a number of miles, this could be the cause. If the unit(s) have simply stopped functioning correctly, however, there is probably another reason. The following may serve as a rough guide to determine whether the mixture is lean or rich.

Indications of a Rich Mixture

An excess of gasoline in the fuel/air mix is often indicated by one or more of the following:

a. Visible exhaust emissions without oil consumption. This refers primarily to four-strokes, since some visible smoke is characteristic of two-stroke engines. These emissions will be black, as opposed to the blue-white color of burning oil.

b. Spark plug(s) black or carbon-fouled. When checking the plugs for mixture, the color of the side electrode is the key. The center electrode is more of a guide to plug heat range. If the plugs are too cold, however, it may seem that the fuel mixture is too rich.

c. Engine runs better when the air cleaner is removed. Since air filters are somewhat restrictive, removal will allow somewhat more air to enter the carburetor at any given throttle opening resulting in a slightly leaner mixture. This is only a check for a rich mixture, and should not be considered a solution.

d. Engine runs worse when hot. Since engines need a slightly rich mixture when they are cold, a faulty fuel/air mix may go unnoticed until the engine is at operating temperature.

e. Performance is sluggish.

f. Engine misfires at high rpm.

g. Excessive fuel consumption.

Indications of a Lean Mixture

a. Engine is hard to start when cold, or requires excessive choking.

b. Engine refuses to idle smoothly, or rpm fluctuates at steady throttle openings.

c. Engine runs hot.

d. Spark plugs are white or yellow in color. In extreme instances, the side electrode may be eroded or partially melted, both electrodes showing rounded edges.

e. Engine runs better when the choke is engaged.

f. Engine runs better at slightly less than full throttle than it does when wide open.

g. Engine runs worse when the air cleaner is removed.

In addition to determining whether the mixture is rich or lean, you should also analyze whether the imbalance occurs at all throttle openings, or just one in particular. If the malady seems to occur at one spot, it is probable that the trouble lies with the metering components which control that particular range of operation. For example, an overly rich mixture in the mid-range may be due to a worn needle and needle jet.

Carburetor Flooding

Flooding of the carburetor will cause an overly-rich mixture at all throttle openings if not too severe, or leakage of fuel from the float bowl if it is really bad.

Minor flooding, which may not be immediately recognizable as such, can be caused by an incorrect float level. Another cause can be a worn float needle. Checking and adjusting the float level varies from carburetor to carburetor and procedures and specifications should be obtained from the model sections. As a rule, two-strokes are somewhat more sensitive to float level than are four-strokes.

Major flooding of the carburetor(s) is usually indicated by the discharge of gasoline. Most carburetors are equipped with float bowl overflow tubes, and if fuel is being discharged from here after the machine has been sitting for a few minutes with the petcock open, there is undoubtedly something amiss with the float assembly.

On models which do not have overflow tubes, removal of the air cleaner hose may give an indication of excess fuel in the float bowl. If raw gasoline appears at their air passages in the carburetor mouth, either the float level is far too high, or the float needle and seat are not forming an effective seal.

The most common float malady is caused by the failure of the float needle to form an effective seal with its seat. The float bowl then becomes overfilled with gasoline. Often, a routine cleaning of the float needle and seat is all that is required, assuming that the needle is being held off the seat by a transient bit of foreign matter.

On older machines, however, this problem can be caused by corrosion built up on the needle or the seat. If this is the case, both components should be replaced. The needle

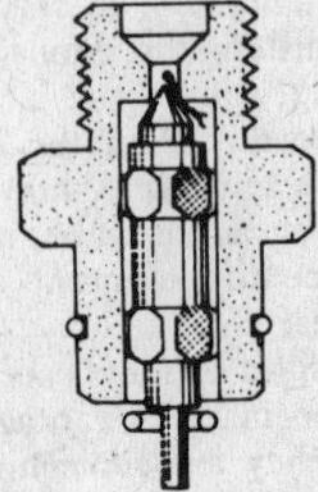

Float needle seat blocked by foreign matter

seat on most carburetors can be unscrewed for replacement. Never attempt to reform a seal by lapping the needle against the seat. This will cause wear on one or the other, and will change the float level. Needle seats are almost always brass, and therefore highly resistant to corrosion. Long periods of disuse, however, can caused the build-up of foreign matter which is almost irremovable. Float needles can be brass or plastic, or neoprene-tipped. Any foreign matter on the tip of the needle can be removed with solvents (on neoprene needles only gasoline should be used to clean the tip) and compressed air, but no attempt should be made to scrape the tip clean.

High-mileage machines may show wear of the needle tip. However, wear must be severe to be easily noticeable, and can be present though scarcely visible. If flooding is a problem, replacement of the needle is advisable.

On carburetors on which the float assembly is mounted on the carburetor body and the fuel feed is on the body as well, the efficacy of the float needle and seat can be checked as follows:

Remove the float bowl. Place a suitable container beneath the carburetor to catch any gasoline which may spill.

Carefully raise the float bulbs with your finger until the needle is gently seated. Do not use excessive pressure.

Turn on the fuel. No leakage should be apparent. If fuel leaks from the needle seat, replace or clean the needle and seat. When the needle is seated, fuel flow must be entirely cut off.

A less common cause of flooding, but one which should be checked, is failure of the float bulbs. If gasoline leaks into the bulbs, they will allow float level to become higher. Eventually, enough gasoline may leak in to "sink" the bulbs, at which time the needle will remain open at all times.

It is easy enough to check for a defective float: just shake it next to your ear and listen for trapped gasoline. Alternatively, semi-transparent plastic floats can be held up to a strong light and any gasoline inside will become visible.

Punctured or leaking floats must always be replaced. No repairs are possible.

Troubles of this sort have been largely sorted out by modern carburetors, many of which use solid buoyant float bulbs of plastic or resin as distinguished from older floats of brass or hollow plastic.

Effect of Altitude on Carburetion

Increased altitude tends to produce a rich mixture; the greater the altitude, the smaller the main jet required. Most standard jetting is suitable for use in altitudes up to approximately 3,000 feet. If you use your machine constantly in altitudes between 3,000 and 6,000 feet, the main jet size should be reduced about 5 percent. A further reduction of 4 percent should be made for every 3,000 feet in excess of 6,000 feet altitude. No adjustment can be made to compensate for the loss of power due to rarefied air.

CHASSIS

TIRES

Checking Pressure

1. Tire pressures are recommended by the manufacturer and you should abide by the recommended pressure unless the motorcycle is being put to some special use, such as competition.

These pressures are determined by considering the design of the motorcycle, tire sizes, the weight of an average rider, and several other factors. The resultant pressure should give a comfortable ride, reasonable tire life, and, most importantly, safe handling. It is therefore not wise to deviate from the recommended pressures unless you really know what you are doing.

2. On most late-model motorcycles, the tire pressure is given somewhere on the motorcycle. If it isn't here, check the "Maintenance Data" chart of the applicable section.

You will note that pressure may be different for the front and rear wheels. Also, pressure variations may be necessary if you carry luggage, ride two-up, or will ride at high speeds for extended intervals (no longer very wise). In general, you might add 4–6 psi to the rear wheel and 2–3 psi to the front over normal pressure to compensate for these conditions.

3. Tire pressure should be checked every two weeks or so. A hand-held gauge is recommended, since it is a fact that the pressure meters on the air hoses found in service stations are not particularly accurate in many instances.

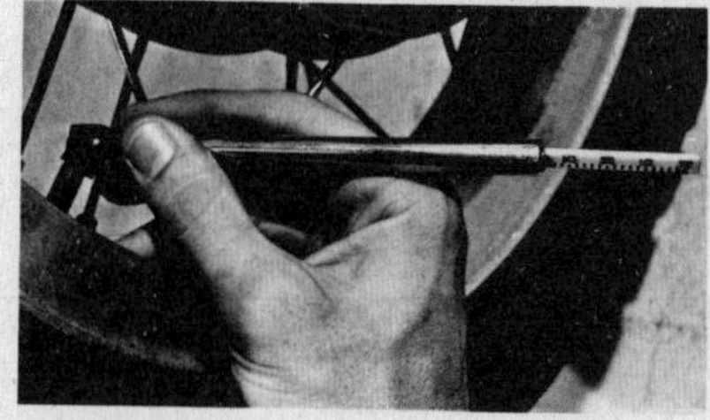
Checking tire pressure

Check pressures when the tires are *cold*. Tire pressure will build up as you ride. The tire gets hot, and the air inside tries to expand. A ride of a mile or so probably will not affect pressure significantly, however, so you can ride to the local gas station before checking the tires.

4. Overinflated tires will wear rapidly, give a harsh ride, and may decrease braking ability. Underinflated tires may cause "squirrely" handling.

Tire Inspection

1. Tire tread depth is one of the most critical items you can check. Since many states have their own laws in this regard however, it is not possible to generalize with a great degree of accuracy as to what depth constitutes the "safe" limit. The following is provided only as a rough guide based on a survey of various manufacturers' recommendations:

For road machines: 1.5 mm (0.06 in.) front
2.0 mm (0.08 in.) rear

For light-weight off-road bikes: 1.0 mm (0.04 in.)

For Superbike-class machines used at high speeds: 2.0 mm (0.08 in.) front
3.0 mm (0.12 in.) rear

This measurement is taken at the center of the tire tread, and at the point of minimum depth if the tire is unevenly worn.

2. Occasionally spin each tire and remove any pebbles, nails, etc., which may have become stuck in the tread grooves.

3. Check for uneven or unusual tire wear or feathering of the tread. Any number of things may cause uneven tire wear: a misaligned wheel due to clumsy rear chain adjustment or bent forks; a rim out of true; an unbalanced wheel; or worn or damaged bearings.

4. Occasionally, loosen the valve stem locknut. If the valve stem tilts to one side when this is done, it indicates that the tire has slipped around the rim during use.

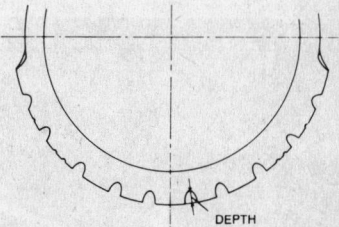

DEPTH

Tire tread depth

This condition must be corrected, or the tire may slip enough to pull the stem out of the inner tube causing a blow-out. Deflate the tire and move it back so that the stem protrudes at right angles to the rim. If a rim lock is fitted, do not forget to loosen this first and push it off the tire bead. If it isn't possible to move the tire by hand, you should remove the wheel and break the tire off the rim by walking around on the sidewall.

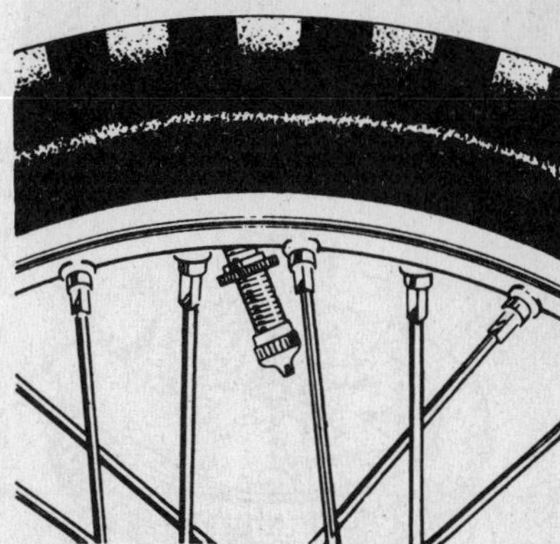
If the valve stem tilts to one side when the locknut is loosened, the tire has slipped around the rim

Tire Changing

To change a tire you will need two motorcycle tire irons, a lubricant such as soapy water or dishwashing liquid, and a plastic mallet which, while not entirely necessary, is certainly helpful.

You can purchase suitable tire irons at any motorcycle shop, or it is possible that they may have been included in your bike's toolkit. Tire irons are specifically designed for the job. They are angled to provide good leverage and have smooth, rounded spoons to prevent pinching the tube. Although some irons may seem small, if you are using the right method they should provide sufficient leverage to get the tire off the rim. There is no acceptable substitute for good tire irons. Attempting to use screwdrivers or other levers for this job is only asking for trouble.

If you have cast alloy wheels, tire irons should be used with care to avoid damaging the wheel. The same is true to a lesser extent with alloy spoked rims which can be scratched. It may be possible to cover the shaft of the irons with a piece of an old inner tube or the like to obviate the chances of damage.

A large sheet of cardboard can also decrease chances of damage to the wheel or brake disc (if fitted). Changing the tire on a concrete surface can easily chip chrome or scratch the rim or brake disc, while changing it on the lawn will certainly get dirt or grass into the wheel bearings unless a rag is placed under the hub.

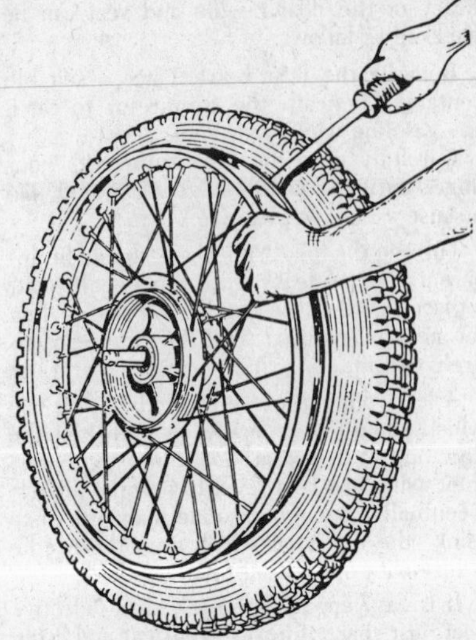

Removing the tire from the rim

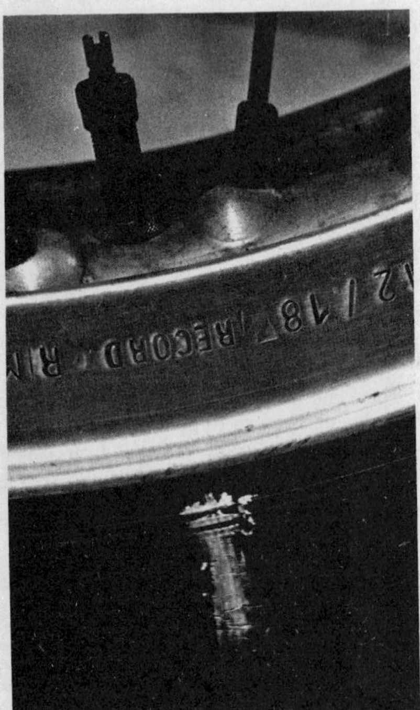

Mark the location of the valve stem before removing the tire

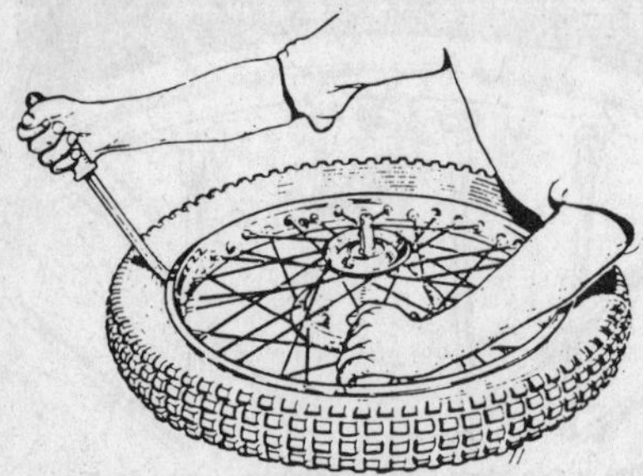

Prying off the first bead

1. After removing the wheel from the motorcycle, take out the valve core. Remove the valve stem nut(s). If a rimlock is fitted, remove its nut and push the rimlock down off the tire bead. If the same tire is to be refitted, mark the location of the valve stem and the direction of rotation on the tire sidewall.
2. Place the wheel on the ground and walk around the tire to break the bead off the rim. This may be necessary if the tire has been on the rim for some time.
3. Smear some soapy water or dishwashing liquid around the beads on both sides of the tire.
4. Beginning at the valve stem, use the tire irons to lever one bead off the rim. The tire bead opposite the valve stem should be pressed well down into the rim well. Kneel on the tire, if necessary to hold the bead down. Start by inserting both tire irons under the bead a few inches apart. Do not insert them too deeply or you may catch the tube. Pull back on both irons simultaneously until a portion of the bead is over the rim. Then remove one of the irons and use it again several inches away from its first position. Continue around the tire until one side is completely free of the rim.
5. Pull out the tube. If the tire is to be replaced, remove the rimlock and lever the remaining bead off the rim.
6. Check the tube for leaks. Patching the tube is not recommended except in emergency situations. The patch may leak or may upset tire balance. Get a new tube if a puncture is evident.
7. Carefully remove the rim band and, using a wire brush, remove any rust deposits here with the wire brush.
8. Check the spokes for looseness and tighten if necessary. If this is done, check that no spoke end protrudes from its nipple. Grind down any protruding spoke ends to obviate the chances of a puncture. Carefully refit the rim band so that it covers all the nipples.
9. The tire must be mounted so that the mark on the sidewall aligns with the valve stem. New tires will have this alignment mark painted near the bead. Also note direction of rotation, if applicable. On some tires the direction of rotation will be different depending on whether the tire is mounted on the front or the rear of the motorcycle. If a rimlock is fitted, be sure to install it before the tube, but do not fit its locknut.
10. If you have only replaced the tube, and the tire is still on the rim, care must be exercised when stuffing the tube into the tire since it is possible to twist it. If the tire has been completely removed, the easiest method is to mount tire and tube together. Install the valve core into the stem and put just a few lbs of air in the tube. You should inflate the tube just enough so that it holds its shape, but not so much that the tube expands. Place the inflated tube into the tire. Approximately aligning the valve stem and the hole in the rim, lever tire and tube together over the rim. Be sure to lubricate the tire beads as on removal.
11. If it is very difficult to lever the tire bead on, use a plastic mallet to strike the bead, thus forcing it over the edge of the rim as you move around the tire with the tire irons.

Note the direction of rotation marked on the sidewall

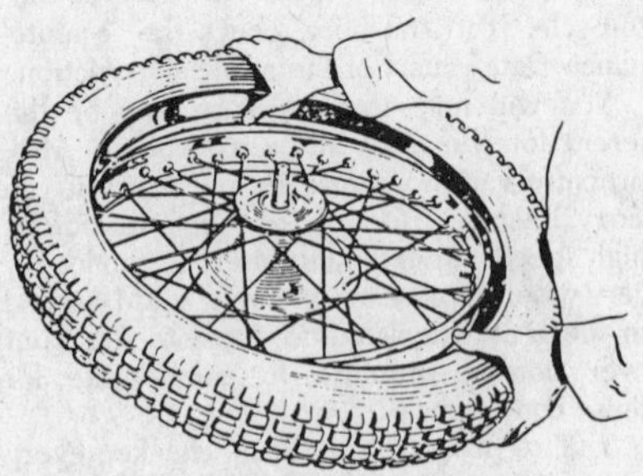

Fitting tire and tube together

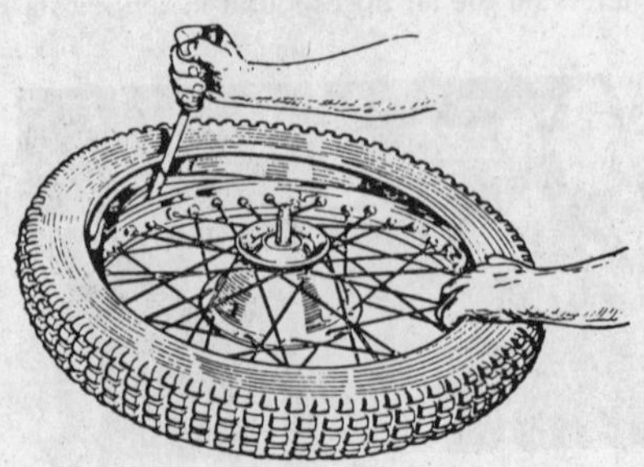

Levering on the first bead

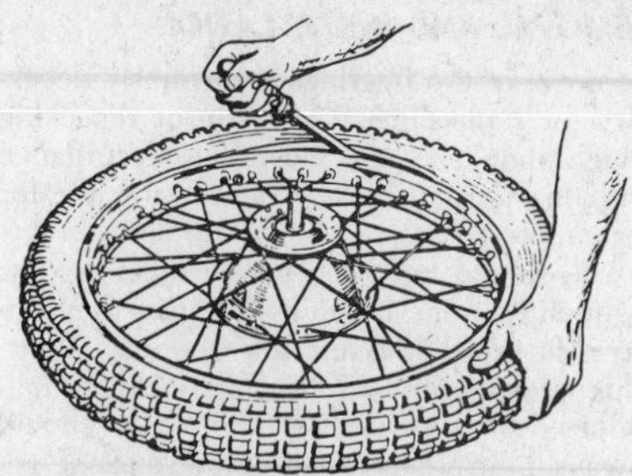
Levering on the second bead

Check that the alignment mark is equidistant from the rim all the way around

12. After the tire and tube are installed, temporarily overinflate the tube to seat the tire. The tire will have an aligning mark which is a thin line molded into the sidewall and which will appear just above the edge of the rim. This line should be equidistant from the rim edge all the way around the tire. If it is not concentric, the tire is not properly seated. This is sometimes caused by rust on the rim and can often be remedied by thoroughly lubricating the beads and temporarily overinflating the tube.

13. After the tube has been inflated to the correct pressure, tighten the valve stem locknut(s) and the nut on the rimlock if one is fitted.

14. The wheel should be balanced after completing this operation.

WHEELS

Spokes

1. Spokes should be checked periodically for proper tension. Spin the wheel slowly while striking each spoke lightly with a screwdriver. Each one should emit a "ping" of approximately the same pitch.

2. A loose spoke will emit a dull sound. Such spokes should be tightened. The nipple, however, should not be turned more than two revolutions. To exceed this risks puncturing the tube with the end of the spoke. If two turns will not tighten the spoke, remove the tire and tube before continuing.

Spoke nipples should be turned only with a genuine spoke nipple wrench which you should be able to purchase from your dealer.

3. If more than two adjacent spokes are found to be loose, the rim should be checked for run-out, and trued if necessary. On-bike tightening of loose spokes is intended only to secure spokes which may have loosened from vibration or setting. It is not intended to true up rims which have been knocked out of kilter. Continuous loosening of spokes should be remedied by removing the wheel and having it properly trued.

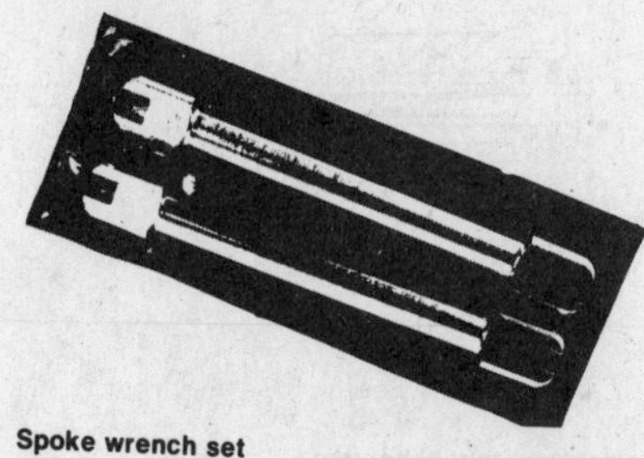
Spoke wrench set

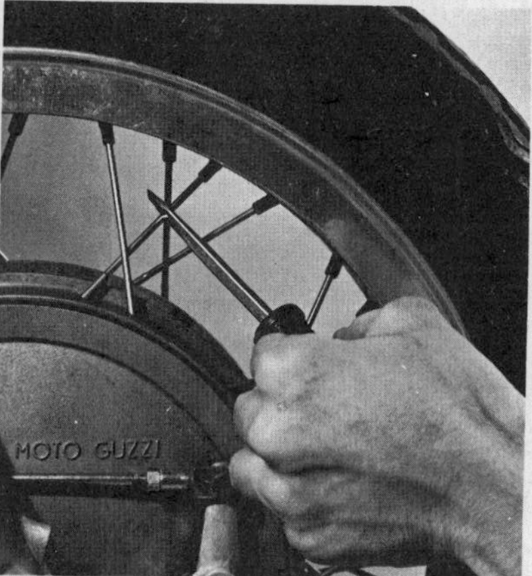

Each spoke should emit a "ping" of about the same pitch

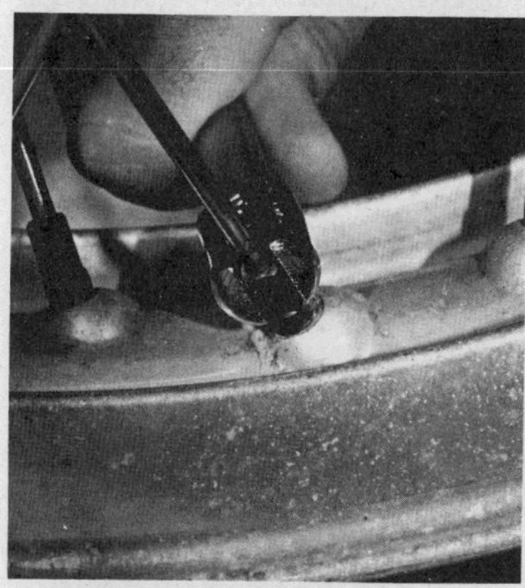
Securing a spoke with the special wrench

Wheel Balancing

Wheels should be balanced each time the tire is removed or replaced. A badly balanced tire may make itself evident by vibration (especially if the front tire is out-of-balance) or by unusual tire wear.

1. Wheels should be balanced on a wheel stand. Balancing on the machine is not recommended due to drag imposed by chains, brake pads, and even wheel bearing grease seals. If a stand is not available, it is permissible to hang the wheel by the axle between two benches or chairs. Only make sure that both surfaces are of equal height. To obtain the most accurate balance it is necessary to remove as much rotation friction as possible. On some designs, wheel bearing grease seals contribute to friction, and really should be removed if possible. It may also be helpful to oil the axle as the wheel is turned. If the wheel will not rotate freely, determine the cause (i.e. bad bearings) before balancing.

Installing a balance weight

2. The tire and tube must be in place and properly installed during balancing. If the wheel has a disc brake, leave it in place. Drum brake hubs should be removed.

3. If there are tire balancing weights already on the spokes, leave them there. Remove or reposition these weights once you are into the procedure.

4. Spin the wheel slowly several times in succession, marking the tire with a grease pencil or the like at the lowest part of the wheel each time it stops. If the same mark rotates to the lowest position several times in succession, this is the heaviest part of the assembly. Ideally, the wheel would stop rotating at random locations. If a heavy point is noted, attach a tire balance weight to a spoke directly opposite the heavy point. Repeat the procedure, adding or repositioning weights so that the wheel will not stop at any one point in particular when it is spun.

5. Balance weights are available in several forms, the most popular being the type which fits over the spoke nipple and is secured with pliers. Another kind is an almost-flat piece of lead which attaches to steel rims by means of adhesive. Cast alloy wheels may require special kinds of balance weights. On this kind of wheel, always install the balance weight on the outer part of the rim, not on the sides of the spokes.

Balance weights may be available in dif-

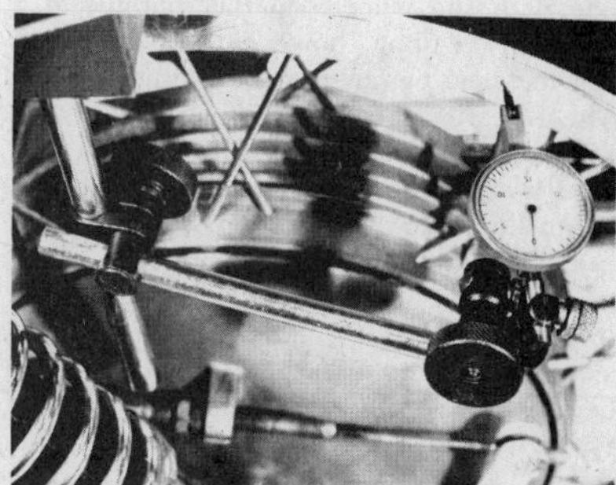
Measuring rim run-out with a dial gauge

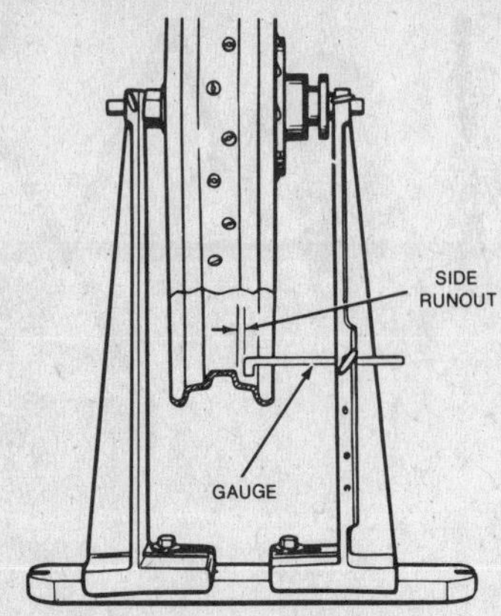

Checking side run-out on a wheel stand

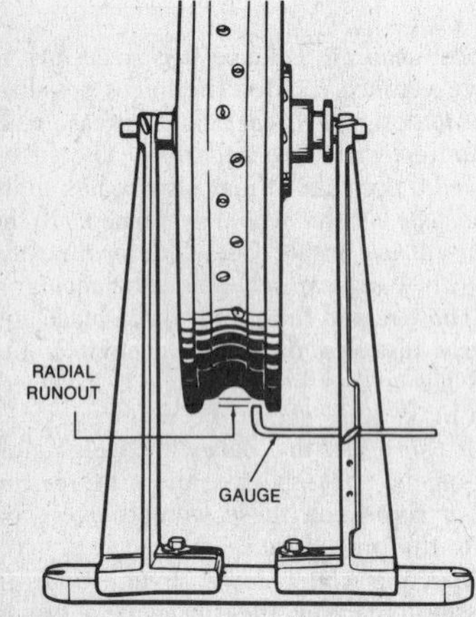

Checking radial run-out

ferent weights. Use the lightest ones to start. If you have to add more than three or four weights to correct balance, there is probably something amiss.

As an alternative to balance weights, there are several brands of balancing *fluid* currently on the market. This is added to the tube and automatically balances the tire when the machine is ridden. It will also change as changes are made to the system, so that fitting a new tire will bring about an automatic compensation on the part of the fluid.

Rim Run-Out

1. Rim run-out can be checked with a dial gauge or a simple pointer. This check can be made with the wheels on the motorcycle. Before this is done, however, be sure that the wheel bearings are in good condition (see "Wheel Bearings"), misleading results may be obtained. All spokes must be secure.

2. Rims should be checked for lateral (side-to-side) run-out, and for concentricity (up-and-down movement). In both cases, the maximum acceptable variance is 2.0 mm (0.08 in.). If either lateral or vertical run-out exceeds this amount, the rim should be trued. To true a rim, the tire and tube must be removed, and a wheel stand should be used.

3. It is not possible to true rims which are bent, even if the damage is slight, since the spokes cannot exert enough force to bend the rim back into shape. Such rims must be replaced.

4. If the rim shows both lateral and vertical run-out, the vertical run-out should be corrected first. This can be done by first loosening those spokes opposite the high-spot, and then tightening the spokes at the high-spot. Spokes should be loosened or tightened in small, even increments since lateral run-out will be affected while correcting vertical run-out.

5. If a new rim is being fitted, it is necessary to have the rim at least approximately centered on the hub before attempting to true it. This can be accomplished in most cases by tightening the spoke nipples by approximately the same amount: that is, so that about the same number of spoke threads show at each nipple. File off the ends of any protruding spokes.

6. The fitting of a new rim can be facilitated by securing each set of two spokes loosely with lengths of wire or tape before removing the old rim.

Wheel Bearings

Most motorcycle wheels are fitted with ball bearings, although a few use roller or tapered roller bearings.

Each wheel has two bearings which in most cases are press-fit into the hub and are separated by a spacer tube. Some wheels use threaded retainers or perhaps circlips to secure one or both bearings. Grease seals are usually fitted to both sides of the hub to keep the bearing grease in and dirt and moisture out.

Some larger bikes also have a "wheel bearing" in the rear wheel sprocket assembly for added rigidity.

Wheel bearings can usually be inspected on the bike simply by grasping either side of the tire and checking for play. There should be none.

If play is evident, the bearings may be worn and replacement will be in order. Bearings are always replaced in pairs.

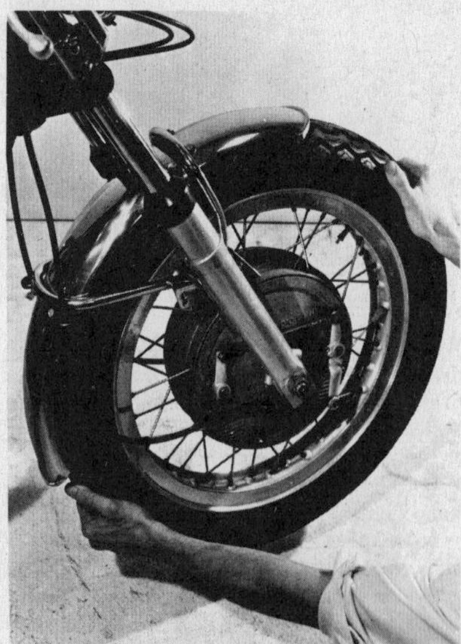

Checking wheel bearings for play

REMOVAL AND INSTALLATION.

Removal of the bearings is obviously necessary for replacement and also for repacking which should be carried out in accordance with the periodic maintenance schedule for your motorcycle.

You should note that the removal process frequently ruins bearings because they are press-fit in the hub and must be driven out. This is especially true on high-mileage machines. In addition, grease seals should always be replaced with new ones if removed.

1. Remove the wheel from the motorcycle.

2. Remove any dust covers, spacers, etc. from either side of the hub.

3. Pry out the grease seals, if accessible. Machines with tapered-roller bearings use the seals to hold the bearings, and once the seals are removed, the bearings will come out.

Prying out a grease seal

4. Remove any retainers or circlips from the hub. Note that some threaded retainers are *left-hand thread.*

5. Wheel bearings are driven out with a drift in most cases. It is sometimes helpful to heat the hub very gently to facilitate removal. Heating the hub with a rag soaked in boiling water is one way to do this. Some manufactures specify that the hub should not be heated to more than 212° F (100° C).

6. The best way to remove wheel bearings is to tap around the *outer* race with a punch and hammer. This is not possible in most cases, however. If the axle is suitable, it can be inserted into the bearings. A sharp

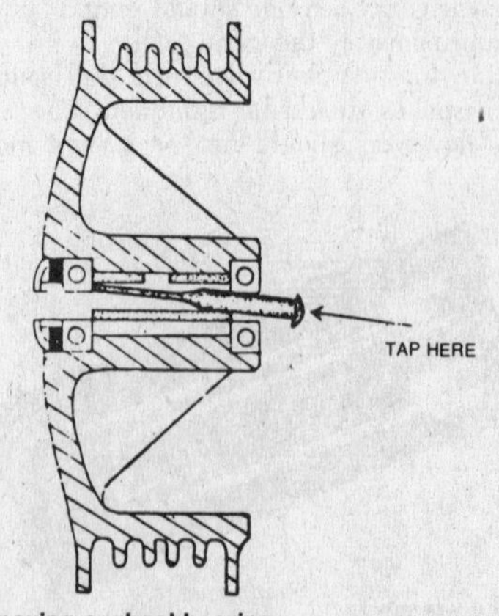

Removing a wheel bearing

Wheel bearing removal

blow on one side of the axle may then be used to dislodge the bearing on the opposite side. It is possible that the bearing will not even look like it moved, but check anyway. In some instances a slight movement is all that is necessary, and the bearings will be free.

If this is not possible, the bearing can be removed by reaching through the hub with a long punch. Try to move the spacer tube to one side so that ample purchase can be obtained. Tap the bearing out evenly, alternating your blows around the circumference of the race.

Yamaha motorcycles are equipped with a hole in the spacer tube which allows the bearing to be removed without striking the bearing directly. If a properly hardened hooked tool is available, it can be used as illustrated to remove the bearings.

7. Once one bearing is removed, you can take out the spacer tube. If this is only a routine repacking, leave the other bearing in place if possible. As noted, removal risks ruining the bearings, and repacking is possible with one removed.

8. Remove old grease from the hub and

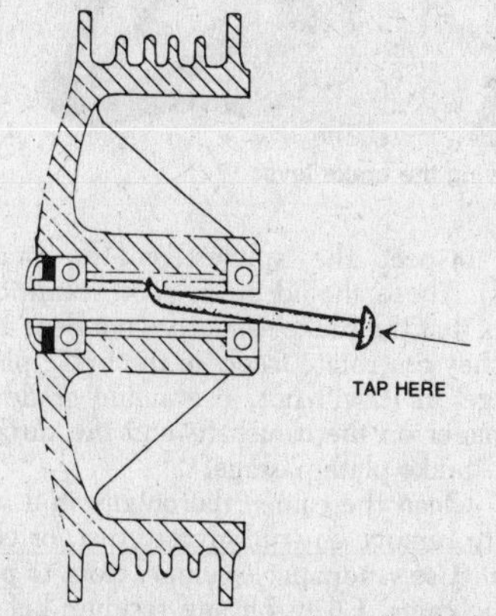

Removing a wheel bearing with a hooked tool (Yamaha)

the bearings with a solvent. After the bearing is clean, lubricate it with oil and check for smooth rotation. Any roughness, binding or clicking sounds which appear indicate that both bearings should be replaced. Place each bearing on a flat surface and hold the outer race firmly in place. Attempt to move the inner race back and forth. Little or no movement should be noted, or a worn bearing is indicated.

9. Repack bearings with a good grade of wheel bearing grease of the type recommended for your motorcycle. Grease should be pressed into the bearing until it is full. Place a quantity of grease into the hub as well.

Play or movement of the inner race indicates a worn bearing

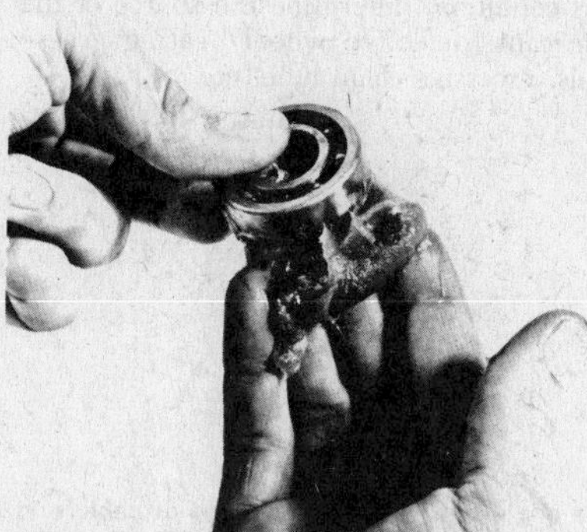

Packing a wheel bearing

10. Bearings should be installed by tapping them into place. Drive the bearing in squarely and evenly. Do not allow the bearing to become cocked while entering the hub. Tap on the *outer* bearing race only.

Bearings which have one side sealed are always installed with the sealed side facing *out*.

If a retainer or circlip is fitted to one side of the hub, the bearing on that side should be installed first. After the bearing is installed, fit the retainer or circlip. This will ensure proper location of the bearing to ease fitting the other one.

11. Install new grease seals.

DISC BRAKES

Bleeding

A mushy feeling at the brake lever or pedal is most often due to air in the lines. This can happen if the fluid level drops too low, or if any line or hose is disconnected for any reason. This requires bleeding of the brake to remove the air.

NOTE: *Sometimes the bleeding procedure is easier if the motorcycle is allowed to sit for several hours without operating the brakes. This allows the tiny air bubbles to concentrate into fewer large ones which may be bled off more quickly and thoroughly.*

PRECAUTIONS

Certain precautions should be taken when working with disc brake fluid.

a. Brake fluid absorbs moisture very quickly, and then becomes useless. Therefore, never use fluid from an old or unsealed container.

b. Do not mix brake fluids of different types. If the fluid in the system is the original factory fluid, it may be incompatible with what you can purchase. In this case, the entire system should be flushed and refilled with the new fluid.

c. DOT #3 or #4 hydraulic disc brake fluid is recommended for almost all motorcycles at this time. However, you should check the applicable model section.

d. Brake fluid will quickly remove paint. Avoid damage to the gas tank by placing a protective cover over it.

To bleed the brake system, obtain a length of transparent plastic hose, the inside diameter of which is such that the hose will fit tightly over the bleed nipple of the brake caliper.

Also needed is a small cup.

Fit the plastic hose to the bleed nipple, and put the other end in the cup which should have an inch or so of new brake fluid in it. Be sure that the end of the hose is below the surface of the fluid in the cup.

The hose should not have any sharp bends or kinks in it. It should loop up from the bleed nipple, and then down towards the cup.

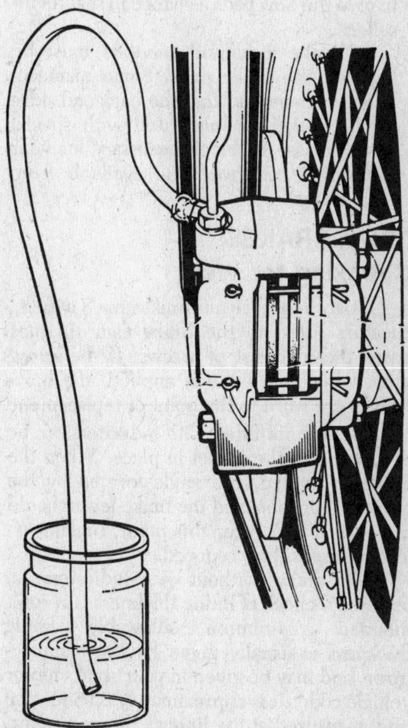

Bleeding the brake system

The motorcycle should be on the center stand with the forks centered.

Remove the master cylinder cap and diaphragm and check that the fluid level is topped up to the indicated line.

Apply the brake lever slowly several times, then hold it on.

While holding the brake lever on, loosen the caliper bleed nipple. The brake lever will be pulled towards the handgrip (or if a rear brake, will bottom out), and fluid will be forced through the plastic hose. Try to tighten the bleed nipple before the lever bottoms out.

Note the brake fluid being forced out of the plastic hose. If there was air in the lines, air bubbles will be noted coming out of the hose.

Pump up the lever again, and loosen the nipple as before, once again checking the fluid being forced out. When air bubbles no longer issue from the plastic hose, the system is bled.

Be sure that the master cylinder reservoir is kept topped up during the bleeding procedure.

Flushing

The procedure for flushing a brake system is identical to that for bleeding, except that the process should be continued until new brake fluid begins to issue from the plastic hose. You will begin by pumping out the old fluid with the lever while adding the new fluid in its place. After the new fluid starts coming out, begin checking for air bubbles as outlined above.

Installing Brake Pads

This procedure will vary according to the make and model of the motorcycle, but all have certain points in common.

a. When new pads are fitted, avoid hard braking if possible for at least 50 miles to give the new pads a chance to seat themselves.

b. Brake fluid and solvents must be kept off the brake pads. Some manufacturers recommend that the back and sides of the pad(s) be lubricated with special PBC grease. If this is necessary for your motorcycle, it should be available from your dealer.

DRUM BRAKES

Checking for Wear

1. Late model drum brakes have wear indicators fitted to the brake cam. In most cases these consist of arrows. If the arrows align when the brake is applied, the brake linings are worn to the point of replacement.

2. Brakes not fitted with indicators can be checked with the wheel in place. When the brake is applied, the angle formed by the brake rod or cable and the brake lever should not exceed 90°. After this point, braking effectiveness will be reduced.

3. On brakes without wear indicators, an occasional check of lining thickness is recommended. Minimum allowable lining thickness is usually given by the manufacturer, and may be given in your state's motor vehicle code. It is approximately 0.08 in. (2.0 mm) measured at the lining's thinnest point, but this value is only a generalization, and the exact figure must be obtained from your owner's handbook or shop manual, as it differs from bike to bike.

On machines with riveted brake shoes, the thickness of the lining must be measured from the top of the rivets. On bonded shoes, it is measured from the surface of the shoe casting.

Brake Service

The following procedure is to be considered a general guide to inspecting and servicing a drum brake assembly. The procedure may vary in detail depending upon the design of the brake assembly in question.

1. Remove the wheel from the motorcycle and separate the hub from the brake plate assembly.

2. Wear of brake linings can be checked with the linings in place. Be sure to measure brake lining thickness at the linings' thinnest points. On riveted brakes, measure the distance from the top of the rivets to the lining surface.

3. Check the linings for grooves, scoring, or other signs of unusual wear. Most damage of this sort is caused by particles of dirt, which have entered the brake drum. If badly scored, the shoes must be replaced. If the shoes are scored, the drum should be checked for the same type of damage.

Be sure that there is no oil or grease present in the linings. Oil-impregnated linings must be replaced. If the linings show this condition, determine the source of the lubricant: defective wheel bearing grease seals, excessive chain lube, etc.

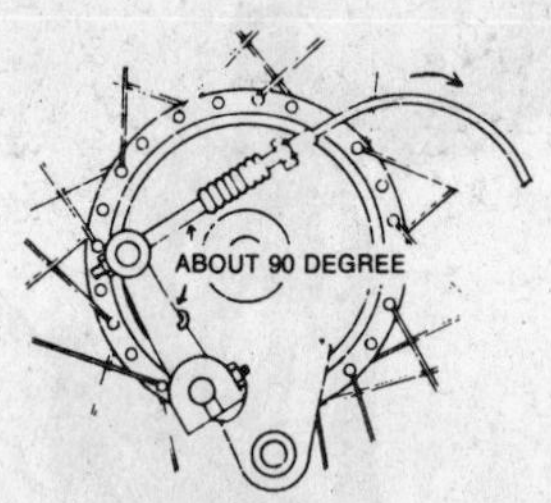

The angle between the brake rod or cable and brake lever should not exceed 90° when the brake is applied. If it does, check the linings for wear

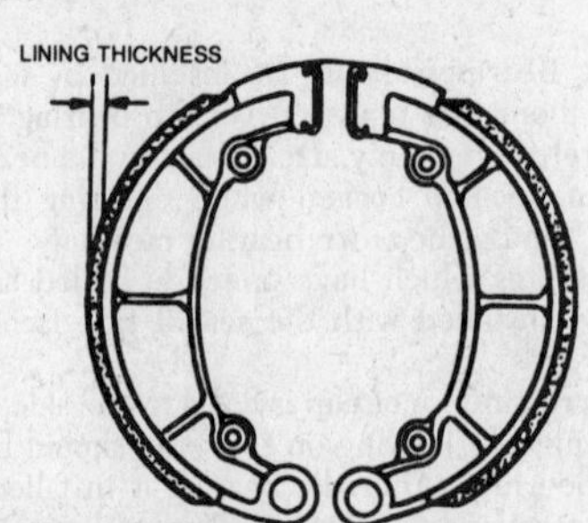

Check lining thickness with a caliper

Removing the glaze from brake linings

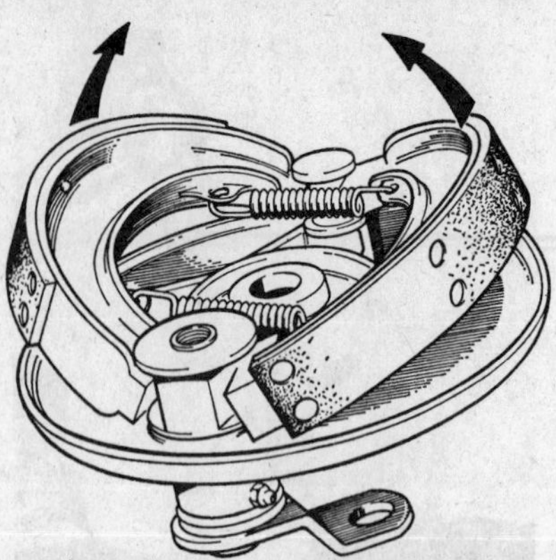

Prying linings off the brake plate

4. If the linings are usable, rough up their surface with sandpaper. Then clean them with alcohol or lacquer thinner. Polish the brake drum surface removing any rust or dirt and clean the drum thoroughly.

5. To disassemble the brake plate, remove the shoes. On some models, this is possible simply by grasping both shoes and folding them towards the center of the brake plate. Other models, however, are fitted with retainers or guards. Remove any cotter pins and washers from the brake cam(s), then remove the shoes.

NOTE: *The plurals refer to the twin-leading shoe brakes.*

6. To remove the cam(s) from the brake plate, remove the brake lever pinch bolt(s). Most brake levers are fitted on splines and will have to be pried off carefully. After the lever is removed, the brake cam can be tapped or pushed out of the brake plate. Note any dust seals or washers on the brake cam.

7. Check that the brake lever pinchbolts are not bent. This can easily happen if they are overtightened. Replace any bolts in this condition. Inspect the brake lever splines and replace the lever(s) if these are worn or stripped.

Removing the brake lever

8. Inspect the splines on the brake cam(s). These should be in good condition. Check that the brake cam(s) are not bent and that they can rotate freely in the brake plate passage. If it will not, use a fine grade of sandpaper on the camshafts and the surface of the brake plate passage.

9. Clean the cam(s) thoroughly in a solvent to remove any old grease, rust, or corrosion. Use sandpaper or emery cloth to polish the cams. Clean off any residue; before reassembly, smear the cams with chassis grease.

10. Inspect the brake plate for cracks or fractures, and replace it if necessary.

11. On twin-leading shoe brakes, the brake plate linkage should be checked. The connecting rod is secured to each brake lever by a clevis pin and cotter pin or clip. They should be checked for wear, especially on high mileage machines, and replaced if necessary.

12. Check the condition of the brake springs, noting any twisted or fatigued hooks. Replace any broken, rusted, or old springs with new ones. Check spring free length if specified for your bike.

13. Clean all metal parts thoroughly with a suitable solvent, making a special effort to remove the dust and built-up dirt from the backing plate.

14. When reassembling the brake plate, note the following points:

a. Ensure that the brake cams are lubricated with chassis grease;

b. The use of new dust seals is recommended;

c. Lubricate the brake shoe pivot points with a little grease;

d. Install the shoes as on removal. Hook them together with the springs, and fold them down over the brake cam(s) and pivot(s). Install new cotter pins to the pivot points;

e. When installing the brake lever on the brake cam, be sure that the punch marks on the lever and cam align, if applicable.

15. The drum should be checked for concentricity. An out-of-bound condition is usually noticeable as an on-off-on feeling when the brake is applied while riding. With the wheel assembly mounted on the machine, spin the wheel while applying the brake very lightly. The rubbing noise of the brakes against the drum should be heard for the entire revolution of the wheel.

16. An out-of-round condition and most scoring can be removed by having the drum turned on a lathe. This operation should be entrusted to a qualified specialist with the proper equipment. Usually, the tire and wheel bearings will have to be removed so that the wheel can be checked to the lathe. If the rim needs to be trued, have this done before any work on the drum is performed, as the action of the spokes while truing the rim may further aggravate the drum warpage.

FRONT FORKS

Seal Replacement

1. Fork slider oil seals may simply wear out over a period of time and then begin to leak. Some causes of *rapid* wear of the seal lips include damage during installation, dirty, contaminated fork oil, damaged dust seals or fork gaiters, rust, corrosion, or scratches on the fork tube, a bent fork tube, or rubber-damaging oil in the forks.

Seals may also leak if the forks are overfilled.

2. On most motorcycles, the seals can be replaced simply by removing the fork sliders. It is necessary to remove the front wheel, fender, brake caliper (if applicable), etc. Refer to a shop manual for removal procedures. These will of course vary depending on the make and model of the machine.

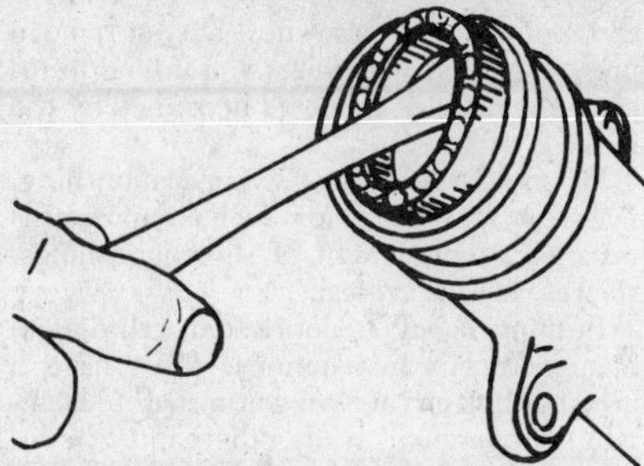

Prying out a front fork oil seal

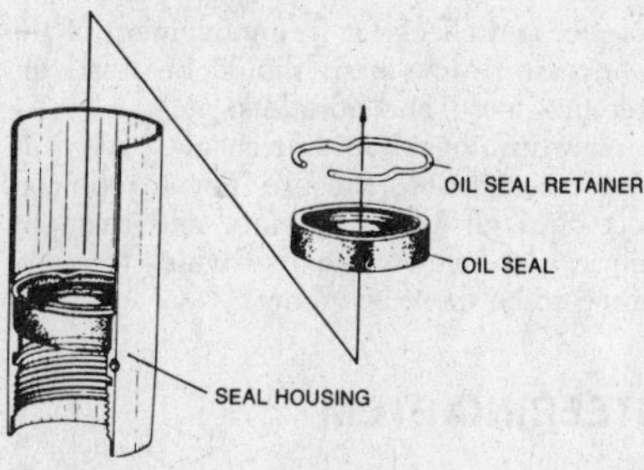

Typical slider oil seal mounting

3. The slider seals are pressed into the top of the fork slider on most bikes, although on a few, the seals may be in the circular nut threaded onto the top of the slider.

Seals must be pried out with a suitable lever. Seals should always be replaced once the slider is removed from the fork tube. Condition of the seals cannot be determined from examination of the lips.

When prying out the seals, be sure to protect the upper lip of the fork slider. This can be accomplished by placing a soft metal pad beneath your lever. Also take care that the end of the lever does not score the inner wall of the slider.

Install new seals by pressing them straight into the slider. Often, one of the old seals can be used, placing it on top of the new seal and tapping around the edges to force the new seal into place. Alternately, a suitably sized socket can be placed over the seal to use as a drift.

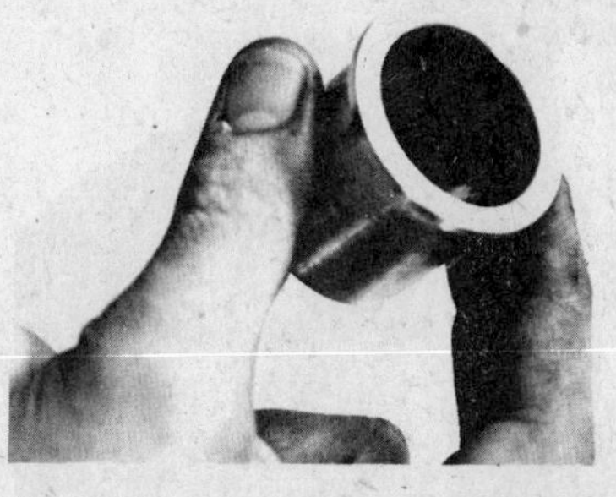

Check slider bushings for scoring or wear

4. Always coat the lips of seals with the type of oil you are going to put in the forks.

Component Inspection

1. As previously noted, fork disassembly procedures vary from model to model. There are, however, two popular methods of holding the forks together, and these are by means of a large circular nut at the top of the slider, and by means of a bolt at the bottom of the slider which will be accessible after removing the axle. Some forks have both.

2. Drain fork oil before disassembly is attempted. Be sure the motorcycle is firmly supported with the front wheel off the ground.

3. Some forks require special tools for disassembly. On models with a bolt under the slider, you should note that often this bolt is threaded into the fork damper, which may turn with the bolt when you attempt to remove it. A special tool is used, inserted through the top of the fork, to hold the damper while the slider bolt is removed. It is often possible to work around this tool by leaving the filler cap and inner fork spring in place, the spring tension being used to hold the damper.

4. Forks with sliders secured by circular nuts may be somewhat easier to disassemble. The slider must be secured when attempting to remove the nut, and this can be accomplished by inserting the axle through the fork legs. Removal of the nut itself is done with a special strap wrench or pin wrench in most cases. It is possible to remove the nut by wrapping a piece of inner tube around the nut, securing a large heater-hose clamp over it, and using a vise-grip pliers on the clamp screw to turn off the nut.

5. In the event that the fork tubes are to be removed from the triple clamps, be sure that all applicable pinchbolts are loosened. If the fork tubes are stuck, try spreading the lower triple clamp slot with a wedge, if such a slot is provided. Alternately, install the filler cap, turning it in several turns, then strike it sharply with a plastic mallet. This should serve to free the tube. This treatment should not be carried to extremes, however, since it is possible to crush the filler cap threads.

6. Fork tubes should be checked for condition. If chromed, all plating in the area on which the slider or slider oil seals ride must be in good condition. If the plating is scratched, flaking, or worn, the tube must be replaced.

On fork tubes which are not plated, check for rust or corrosion on the surface of the tubes on which the slider seals ride. Any roughness or build-up must be removed with a low-abrasive method. Pitting or extreme

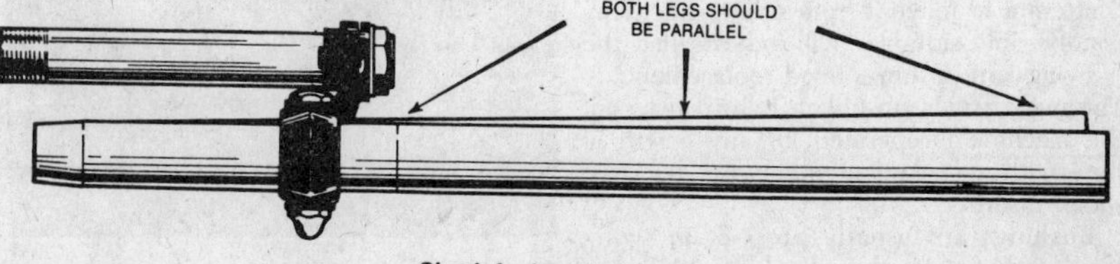

Check for bent fork legs

rust would necessitate replacement of the fork tubes.

7. Check the fork tubes for a bent condition. Minor bends may not be visible to the eye, and run-out should be checked with a dial gauge. If a tube is only slightly bent, it may be possible to return it to its original condition with a large press, but it is usually necessary to replace tubes which are bent.

8. Check the fork springs for a compressed condition by comparing their measured free length with the standard free length if given in the specifications.

9. Check the condition of the fork slider and its fit on the fork tubes. Some forks use a replaceable bronze slider bushing. Check this bushing for scoring or wear on the inner surface. Check its fit on the fork tube. The bushing should move freely, but any wobbling or play from side-to-side would indicate that replacement is necessary.

10. Clean all damper components, blowing clear any oil passages.

REAR SHOCK ABSORBERS

Almost all production motorcycle rear shock absorbers are sealed, and cannot be disassembled. In fact, on some models, it is dangerous to attempt to do so.

If the shock leaks oil, looses its damping ability, is damaged through collision or extreme use, both units should be replaced. The springs, however, should have an unlimited life.

To check a shock absorber, remove it from the motorcycle, and compress the spring so that the spring keepers or collars can be removed. Take off the spring and dust cover, if fitted.

Push the damper rod into the damper body and pull it out. There should be considerable resistance when attempting to pull out the rod. If movement is easy, or if the two shocks show different characteristics, both should be replaced.

SWING ARM

Except on shaft-drive motorcycle, swing arms are very simple components and usually free of trouble.

Swing arms are usually attached to the frame by means of a heavy shaft which may ride in bushings or needle bearings. Wear to these bushings is the prime trouble spot of the swing arm.

To check your swing arm, proceed as follows:

a. Remove the rear wheel, shock absorbers, and chain guard.

b. Measure the distance between the top and bottom shock absorber mounts on both sides. The two measurements must be identical, or the swing arm will have to be replaced.

c. Check that the rear wheel mounting plates are parallel.

d. Grasp the legs of the swing arm and attempt to move it from side-to-side. Any noticeable side-play will indicate that the swing arm bushings need replacement.

The swing arm is most likely to be damaged if the machine is operated for any length of time with a broken or otherwise defective shock absorber.

Bushings are usually press-fit in swing arms, and, if worn, they should be driven out and replaced with new ones. Do not remove pressed-in bushings unless you intend to replace them, since they will be ruined by the removal process.

When disassembling a swing arm bushing, make careful note of how each component is installed as placement of shims, bushings, sleeves, etc., is critical.

Bushings should be lubricated according to manufacturer's instructions. Most have a grease fitting on the swing arm shaft to facilitate the operation, while others must be lubricated by hand.

After a rebuilt swing arm is installed, tighten the shaft nut (if fitted) to the proper torque, and check for free movement of the swing arm. Movement should be relatively free (not loose) and noiseless.

New bushings should be checked carefully before installation. Be sure they are the correct ones for your machine, and that any lubrication holes or grooves which are supposed to be there are there.

STEERING STEM

The steering stem assembly consists of the upper and lower triple clamps, their connecting shaft, and the bearings on which the assembly rides in the frame lug.

The bearings in most cases are uncaged balls which ride on bearing races, the inner halves of which are pressed into the frame lug.

The condition of the steering stem bearings should be checked periodically in the following manner:

a. Support the front wheel of the motorcycle off the ground.

b. Grasp the fork sliders, and attempt to move them back and forth in line with the motorcycle. No play should be noted here. An alternate method, applicable to machines with a sturdy front fender is to grasp the tip of the fender and pull upwards, placing your other hand at the junction of the triple clamp and frame to feel for play.

Checking steering stem bearings for adjustment

Checking steering stem bearings for play

Ordinarily, play indicated by either of these two methods can be remedied by simply adjusting the bearings. There is, in most cases, a nut or nuts beneath the upper triple clamp which are used to make this adjustment.

c. With the front wheel free of the ground, and any steering damper loosened or disconnected, turn the forks slowly from lock to lock. Movement should be smooth, effortless, and without noise. If fork movement is rough, or if there seems to be a detent spot somewhere during the movement of the forks, the bearings or races may be worn.

d. Position the forks about 5–10° off the centered position and release them. The forks should fall to either side of their own weight. If they do not, the bearings may be too tightly adjusted.

In general, bearings which cannot be properly adjusted, or will not hold an adjustment for any length of time, can be said to be worn to the point of replacement.

For uncaged ball bearings, all of the balls and all races must be replaced at the same time.

Removal procedures vary for different types of assemblies. In all cases, however, the frame races must be driven out with a drift, and installed with a block of wood until firmly seated in the frame lug.

The outer race of the lower bearing is usually a tight fit on the steering stem and will have to be chiseled off.

If you have disassembled the steering stem for routine lubrication, you can check the condition of the balls and races after cleaning them thoroughly in solvent to remove all the old grease.

Any balls which are pitted, rusted, or

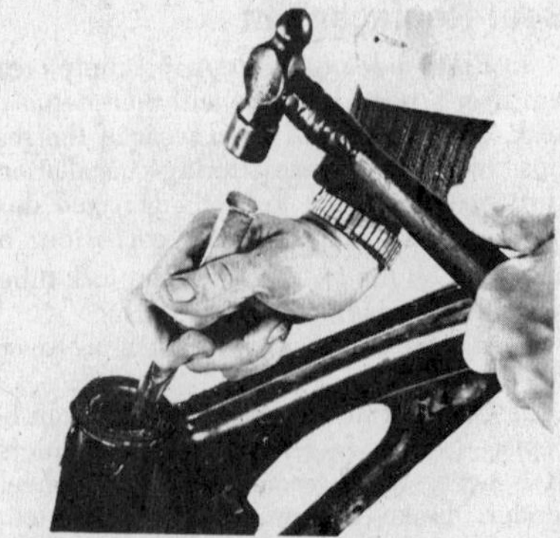

Driving out a steering head bearing race

dented will necessitate replacement of the entire bearing and race assembly.

Races themselves should be checked for a rippled surface, indentations, and other imperfections. Frame races should not be removed unless defective, since they will probably be rendered useless by the removal procedure. The same is true of the steering stem lower race.

When installing a steering stem assembly, always be sure that the proper number of balls are fitted to each race. Imbed the balls in a high grade bearing grease.

Adjust the bearings so that fork action conforms to those standards outlined above. If new frame races have been installed, make frequent checks of adjustment during the first several hundred miles, since the frame races will probably settle over a period of time.

BATTERY

GENERAL MAINTENANCE

1. The battery electrolyte level should be checked about once every two weeks, more often in warm weather.

2. Maintain the electrolyte level between the maximum and minimum marks on the battery case. This refers to batteries with transparent plastic cases which are found on the majority of motorcycles today. If the battery does not have this type of case, check level by removing the caps from each cell. Maintain the electrolyte level just above the tops of the plates.

3. Never add acid to a battery. Add *distilled water* only. Tap water in some areas contains chemical or mineral impurities which may shorten battery life.

4. Do not overfill the battery. This may cause spillage of the electrolyte while riding.

5. Check the condition of the battery terminals. On some small batteries, the terminals are sealed and need no service. On most batteries, however, this is not the case. Terminals must be free of corrosion. Check that the connections are tight.

6. Check the battery overflow tube. It must not be blocked or pinched at any point, and must be arranged to that it will discharge any electrolyte well below any painted or plated surface. On most late models, a plate is provided on the motorcycle showing the correct routing of the overflow tube. Follow the manufacturer's instructions.

7. Check that the battery is securely mounted and that any and all straps, rubber pads, etc. provided by the manufacturer are in place and in good condition.

8. Any battery service such as cleaning, charging, etc., should not be carried out with the battery in the motorcycle. Se following sections for procedures.

9. During cold weather, keep the battery fully charged. A low battery will freeze much quicker than one with a charge. Freezing will ruin the plates even if it doesn't harm the case.

Charging

1. Battery state-of-charge is checked with an hydrometer. These are available in several sizes and prices, and range from professional models which provide a numerical specific gravity reading to less expensive units which check battery condition by indicating how many colored balls will float in the hydrometer tube.

For motorcycle use, the smaller type is recommended, since the larger model's hose may not fit through the smallish filler cap holes, and the cell may not have enough electrolyte above the plates to operate the float.

The measure of battery state-of-charge is the *specific gravity* of the electrolyte, which is nothing more than the weight of the electrolyte relative to an equal volume of water. Electrolyte with a specific gravity of 1.230, for example, is 1.230 times as heavy as water.

Note the following relations between specific gravity and battery state-of-charge, these figures being applicable at room temperature (20° C/68° F):

Electrolyte Specific Gravity	*Battery State-of-Charge*
1.260	100%
1.230	75%
1.200	50%
1.170	25%
1.140	almost none
1.110	dead

2. The battery should be recharged if the specific gravity of one or more cells shows that the battery is charged only 50% of its capacity or less (specific gravity 1.200 or less).

3. Batteries should not be charged on the motorcycle. This risks damage due to splashing electrolyte on painted or plated surfaces. It also makes it difficult to clean the case thoroughly, which should be accomplished after the battery is charged. In addition, some systems can be damaged unless the battery terminals are disconnected during charging.

4. When removing the battery, disconnect the ground side *first*. This will be the negative terminal on most motorcycles, although the positive terminal is the ground on British machines. Disconnect the battery overflow tube before removing the battery.

5. Before charging, remove the cell caps. During charging, keep a check on the electrolyte level, topping it up from time to time if necessary.

If the battery draws a lot of current from the charger, or if it gets very hot during the charging period, replacement of the battery will be necessary. Electrolyte temperatures should never exceed 110° F.

6. It is recommended that batteries be trickle-charged only at no more than 10% of their amp-hour rating. Therefore, the continuous charging rate for a 6 amp battery should be 0.6 amps. The amp-hour rating of a battery is stamped on the battery case for most batteries. Example: Yuasa battery No. 12N12A-4A indicates that the battery is a 12-volt, 12-amp-hour unit.

7. After charging, shake the battery gently to allow any trapped air bubbles to escape. Allow the battery to cool to normal temperature before checking state-of-charge.

8. After charging is completed, top up the electrolyte level if necessary, and install the cell caps. Clean off the top and sides of the battery case with a solution of warm water and baking soda. Be extremely careful that this solution does not enter the cells, since it will neutralize the acid.

9. Dirty or corroded battery terminals should be cleaned with a wire brush to ensure good contact. After the battery is installed and the terminal connections are secured, coat the terminals with petroleum jelly to reduce future corrosion.

10. When installing the battery, be sure that the overflow tube is connected and properly routed. Be sure that the battery is properly fitted. The polarity of each terminal will be clearly stamped or painted on the battery case. Even a momentary reversal of connections can destroy some electrical components.

11. Before connecting the battery, check that the cable connections are free of corrosion or oxidation. If possible, clean up the cable connectors with sandpaper.

Connect the power side of the battery first. This will be the positive terminal except on positive-ground (British) systems.

12. Ensure that the connections are tight. Check that the ground cable is securely fastened to the frame or engine. A poor ground may not prevent the motorcycle from running, but it may eventually damage electrical components on some types of systems.

Storage

1. If the motorcycle is to be out of service for any length of time, the battery should be removed and stored in a cool, dry location.

2. Trickle-charge stored batteries every month.

Troubleshooting

1. If the electrical system goes completely dead suddenly, chances are that the trouble is either a fuse or a bad electrical connection somewhere in the circuit.

Most motorcycles are fitted with an in-line fuse on the battery positive lead usually right in the neighborhood of the battery itself. Check this fuse first.

Next, check that the battery terminal connections are clean and tight. It is possible for a bad connection to show up here for seemingly no reason all of a sudden. Even if the connections seem okay, disconnect the wires at the terminals and clean them off. Sometimes you will find that the electrical system suddenly has power again while you are in the process of disconnecting the battery. In this event you can be sure that a poor electrical connection was causing the trouble.

Other electrical connections should also be checked before suspecting the battery itself in case of a sudden failure such as we are discussing here. Most motorcycles have a large number of male-female connectors either in the headlight, under the gas tank, or under one of the side covers. These connectors can come apart, corrode, or fill with water.

2. If the battery self-discharges, check that the battery case has not become impregnated with sulphuric acid. This can be done by checking the resistance of the case with an ohmmeter. Hold one probe against the case near the positive terminal, the other to the case near the negative terminal. Resistance must be infinite. Sometimes acid on the top of the battery will form a current path between the terminals, causing the battery to discharge itself. If this is the case, it may be possible to save the battery for a while by sprinkling baking soda over the top, letting it set for several minutes, and then washing it off with warm water. Take care not to let any of this get into the cells.

3. If one cell seems to lose more electrolyte than the others, check its charge with an hydrometer. It is probably shorted. Replace the battery if any cell is shorted or will not hold a charge.

4. Whitish sulfate deposits on the battery plates is a usual sign of battery age indicating that replacement will be in order soon. It may be possible to prolong the life of a sulfated battery by charging it at half the usual rate for twice the normal time.

TROUBLESHOOTING

Troubleshooting Tune-Up Items

Problem	*Possible Causes*	*Inspection/Remedy*
Engine fails to start (no spark at plugs)	Ignition switched off	Turn on ignition.
	Kill button switched off	Reset.
	Battery dead	Charge battery.
	Blown fuse	Check fuse and replace if necessary.
	Loose or corroded battery terminals	Clean and secure connections.
	Spark plugs too old; worn or fouled	Clean or replace plugs.
	Spark plugs wet	Kick engine over after removing plugs to clear it. Blow plugs dry.
	Plug gap incorrect	Set to correct gap.
	Points wires disconnected; loose or corroded snap connectors	Check wiring; clean and tighten wire connectors.
	Points incorrectly gapped pitted, worn or dirty	Inspect points. Replace or clean and adjust gap.
	Spark plug cap resistors defective	Replace spark plug caps.
	Plug leads dirty, damaged, wet, or defective	Replace leads and coils.
	Ignition coils defective	Replace.
	Condenser defective	Replace.
	Points grounding out against point plate	Inspect. Check that the point wire is insulated.
	Damaged insulators at points terminal	Replace.
Engine fails to start (has spark at plugs)	Lack of fuel	Make sure petcock is on; check for fuel in the tank.
	Fuel starvation: fuel lines clogged; petcock or filter dirty; vent in gas tank cap closed up; carburetor float valve closed off	Check for fuel at the float bowl and then back through the system.
	Carburetor adjustments incorrect	Adjust.
	Ignition timing incorrect	Adjust.
	Incorrect valve adjustment	Adjust.
	Carburetor float punctured	Replace.
	Low compression: worn rings or cylinder; bent or poorly seated valves; broken or worn valve guides	Inspect top end.
	Low compression due to blown head gasket, warped head	Rebuild.
	Incorrect valve timing	Reset.
Engine is hard to start	Worn, dirty or improperly gapped plugs, or plugs too cold	Clean or replace and gap plugs or replace with correct heat range.

Troubleshooting

Problem	Possible Causes	Inspection/Remedy
	Points dirty, pitted, or out ot adjustment	Clean or replace and gap points.
	Carburetor idle setting wrong; pilot air or fuel passages clogged	Adjust idle settings or clean carburetor.
	Battery low	Recharge or replace battery.
	Ignition timing out of adjustment	Adjust.
	Valves adjusted incorrectly	Adjust valves.
	Spark plug leads cracked or dirty	Replace plug leads.
	Loss or intermittently grounded wires at coil, points, or connectors	Check all connections and condition of wiring.
	Defective coils or condensers	Replace.
	Worn or improperly seating valves	Perform top end overhaul; inspect and lap valves.
	Low compression due to worn or damaged top end components	Overhaul top end.
Engine starts but refuses to run	Fuel feed problem	Check fuel supply; check fuel petcock, lines, carburetor for blocked passages; check gas tank cap vent.
	Spark plugs too cold or worn	Replace with proper heat range plugs.
	Valve clearance incorrect	Set valve clearance.
	Ignition timing incorrect	Adjust.
Engine idles poorly	Carburetor idle adjustments incorrect	Adjust idle circuit.
	Spark plugs worn, dirty, or gap too wide	Clean or replace and gap plugs.
	Spark plugs too cold	Fit the proper heat range plugs.
	Breaker point gaps incorrect	Adjust.
	Ignition timing incorrect	Adjust.
	Valves improperly adjusted	Adjust.
	Water in carburetors	Drain float bowls and gas tank if necessary and fill with fresh gas.
	Carburetor float levels wrong	Adjust.
	Air leaks at manifolds	Determine cause and rectify.
	Leaking valves	Lap valves (four-stroke).
	Worn valve, valve guides, valve seats	Check valve train (four-stroke)
	Weak spark	Check coils and condensers.
	Petcock clogged	Clean.
	Float bowl fuel level too low	Check float height.
Engine misfires when accelerating	Loose or intermittent connections in the ignition circuit	Check all connections; make sure that they are clean and tight.
	Ignition timing incorrect	Adjust.
	Gas tank cap vent clogged	Clear.
	Water in float bowls	Drain and refill with fresh mixture.
	Carburetor main jet clogged	Remove and clean.
	Air leaks at carburetor manifolds	Determine cause and remedy.
	Defective ignition coils or condensers	Replace.
	Carburetor setting wrong	Take plug readings and reject carbs if necessary.
	Very low or dead battery	Recharge or replace battery.
Engine surges or runs unevenly at steady throttle openings	Carburetor fault; mixture too lean, erratic fuel flow	Remove and inspect carburetors.
	Air leaks at carburetor manifolds	Determine cause and remedy.
	Valves improperly adjusted	Adjust.
Engine breaks up or misfires while running	Battery very low or dead	Recharge or replace battery.
	Loose or intermittent connections in the ignition circuit	Check and secure connections.
	Battery terminal come adrift	Clean and secure battery connections.

Troubleshooting

Problem	Possible Causes	Inspection Remedy
Poor low-speed operation	Incorrect ignition timing	Adjust timing.
	Carburetor idle circuit poorly adjusted	Adjust pilot screws and idle speed.
	Spark plug gap too great or plugs too cold	Use correct heat range and gap to proper specifications.
	Poor breaker point contact	Clean or replace breaker points.
	Valves improperly adjusted	Adjust.
	Carburetor fault	See Chapter 8.
Poor high-speed operation	Ignition timing too retarded	Adjust timing.
	Spark plug gap too small	Adjust gap.
	Plugs too cold	Fit plugs of the correct heat range.
	Carburetor float level too low	Adjust float level.
	Partially blocked fuel lines or petcock	Clean.
	Dirty air cleaner	Clean or replace element.
	Weak breaker point arm spring	Replace points.
	Defective ignition coils or condensers	Replace.
	Weakened valve springs	Inspect springs.
	Incorrect valve timing	Reset.
Loss of power	Incorrect valve adjustment	Adjust tappets.
	Clogged or dirty air cleaner	Clean or replace the element.
	Incorrect ignition timing	Adjust.
	Dirty carburetors	Clean.
	Valves not sealing	Lap valves.
	Valve springs weakened	Replace.
	Rings or cylinder worn	Rebuild.
	Valve timing incorrect	Reset.
	Carburetor float level incorrect	Adjust.
	Spark plug gap incorrect	Adjust.
	Engine or muffler carbon choked	Decarbonize.
	Exhaust pipe broken or loose	Secure or replace.

Spark Plug Analysis—4-Stroke Engines

Condition	Appearance	Recommendation
NORMAL 	Brown to grayish tan color and slight electrode wear. Correct heat range for engine and operating conditions.	Service and reinstall. Replace if over 10,000 miles of service.
MODIFIER DEPOSITS 	Powdery white or yellow deposits that build up on shell, insulator and electrodes. This is a normal appearance with certain branded fuels. These materials are used to modify the chemical nature of the deposits to lessen misfire tendencies.	Plugs can be cleaned. If replaced, use same heat range.

Spark Plug Analysis—4-Stroke Engines

Condition	*Appearance*	*Recommendation*
OIL DEPOSITS 	Oily coating.	Caused by poor oil control. Oil is leaking past worn valve guides or piston rings into the combustion chamber. Hotter spark plug may temporarily relieve problem, but positive cure is to correct the condition with necessary engine repairs.
CARBON DEPOSITS 	Dry soot.	Dry deposits indicate rich mixture or weak ignition. Check for clogged air cleaner, high float level, sticky choke or worn breaker contacts. Hotter plugs will temporarily provide additional fouling protection.
PREIGNITION 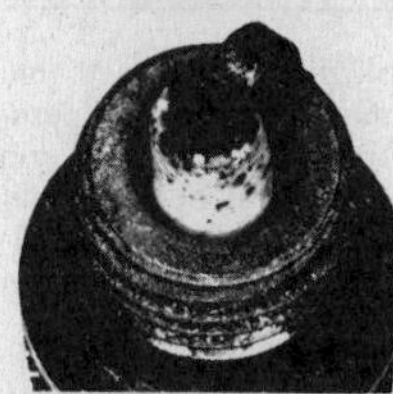	Melted electrodes. Center electrode generally melts first and ground electrode follows. Normally, insulators are white, but may be dirty due to misfiring or flying debris in combustion chamber.	Check for correct plug heat range, overadvanced ignition timing, lean fuel mixtures, leaking intake manifold, and lack of lubrication.
TOO HOT 	Blistered, white insulator, eroded electrodes and absence of deposits.	Check for correct plug heat range, overadvanced ignition timing, lean fuel/air mixtures, leaking intake manifold, sticking valves, and if bike is driven at high speeds most of the time.
HIGH SPEED GLAZING 	Insulator has yellowish, varnish-like color. Indicates combustion chamber temperatures have risen suddenly during hard, fast acceleration. Normal deposits do not get a chance to blow off, instead they melt to form a conductive coating.	If condition recurs, use plug type one step colder.
SPLASHED DEPOSITS 	Spotted deposits. Occurs shortly after long delayed tune-up. After a long period of misfiring, deposits may be loosened when normal combustion temperatures are restored by tune-up. During a high-speed run, these materials shed off the piston and head and are thrown against the hot insulator.	Clean and service the plugs properly and reinstall.

Spark Plug Analysis—2-Stroke Engines

Condition	*Appearance*	*Recommendation*
NORMAL 	Correct heat range. Insulator is light tan to gray color. Few deposits present. Electrodes are not burned.	Change plugs at regular intervals, using the same heat range.

Spark Plug Analysis—2-Stroke Engines

Condition	*Appearance*	*Recommendation*
CORE BRIDGING GAP BRIDGING  	Combustion particles wedged or fused between electrodes or core nose.	Both core bridging and gap bridging are caused by excessive combustion chamber deposits striking and adhering to the spark plug's firing end. They originate from the piston and cylinder head surfaces. These deposits are formed by one or a combination of the following: Excessive carbon in cylinder. Use of non-recommended oils. Immediate high-speed operation after prolonged and excessive idling. Improper ratio of fuel/oil mix.
WET FOULING 	Damp or wet, black carbon coating over entire firing end. Forms sludge in some cases.	Wrong spark plug heat range (too cold). Prolonged slow speed operation. Carburetor adjustment is too rich. Improper ratio of fuel-to-oil mixture. Induction manifold bleed-off return passage obstructed. Worn or defective breaker points, resulting in lack of voltage.
ALUMINUM THROW-OFF 	Aluminum deposits adhering to electrodes and plug core.	Caused by pre-ignition source within cylinder melting aluminum alloy off piston. Do not install new plugs until piston is examined and the source of pre-ignition is determined.
OVERHEATING 	Electrodes badly eroded. Premature gap wear. Insulator has gray or white "blistered" appearance.	Incorrect spark plug heat range (too hot). Ignition timing overadvanced. "Sticky" piston rings. Engine constantly operated at slow speeds.
LOW TEMPERATURE FOULING	Soft, sooty deposits indicate incomplete combustion. Probable causes: rich carburetion; weak ignition; retarded timing or low compression. Continuous low-speed operation or, with oil injection systems, gunning throttle at idle.	Clean or replace.

Two-Stroke Engine Troubleshooting

Problem	Possible Causes	Inspection/Remedy
Abnormal engine noise	Piston slap; piston-to cylinder clearance too great	Check clearance.
	Knock, especially noticable at idle: worn con rod big end bearing	Replace.
	Worn small end bearing	Replace.
	Rumble at idle developing into whine at high rpm: crankshaft main bearings worn or damaged	Replace bearing(s).
	Defective or worn transmission gears or shaft bearings	Inspect and replace worn parts.
	Pinging or spark knock	Timing too advanced; Low quality gasoline.
Engine fails to start (has spark at plug)	No gas in tank; fuel petcock turned off; fuel lines clogged	Refuel; turn on petcock; check for fuel at the carburetor; disconnect and blow out fuel line.
	Engine flooded	Remove spark plug and crank engine to clear it.
	Crankcase flooded	Remove spark plug; shut off petcock; crank engine.
	Ignition timing incorrect	Reset timing.
	Improper fuel/oil mixture	Drain fuel tank and refill with proper mixture.
	Low or no compression	Blown head gasket; warped head; Worn or damaged crankshaft seals; poor seal at crankcase mating surfaces. Worn piston rings; worn bore.
	Carburetor adjustments wrong, or carburetor flooded	Adjust carburetor. Check float height.
Engine fails to start (no spark at plug)	Ignition switched off	Turn on ignition
	Kill button switched off	Reset.
	Spark plug too old; worn or fouled	Clean or replace plug.
	Spark plug heat range too cold	Replace with proper heat range plug.
	Spark plug gap incorrect	Reset gap.
	Spark plug cap resistor defective	Replace cap.
	Plug lead damaged or defective	Replace.
	Ignition coil defective	Replace.
	Condenser defective	Replace.
	Points dirty, pitted, worn, or improperly gapped	Clean and adjust or replace points.
	Breaker points wires disconnected; loose or corroded snap connectors	Check wiring; clean and tighten connections.
	Dead battery (battery-and-coil ignition)	Recharge or replace battery.
	Blown fuse	Replace.
	Loose or corroded battery terminals	Clean and secure terminals.
Engine is hard to start	Worn, dirty, or improperly gapped plug, or plug too cold	Clean or replace and gap plug or replace with correct heat range.
	Points dirty, pitted, or out of adjustment	Clean or replace and gap points.
	Carburetor idle settings wrong; pilot air or fuel passages clogged	Adjust idle settings or clean carburetor.
	Battery low (battery ignition)	Recharge or replace battery.
	Ignition timing out of adjustment	Adjust.

Two-Stroke Engine Troubleshooting

Problem	Possible Causes	Inspection/Remedy
	Spark plug lead cracked or dirty	Replace plug lead.
	Loose or intermittently grounded wires at coil, points, or connectors	Check all connections and condition of wiring.
Engine is hard to start	Defective coils or condensers	Replace.
	Leaking of crankshaft oil seals or crankcase mating surfaces yielding low compression. Worn rings or cylinder bore	Rebuild.
Engine idles poorly and misfires under acceleration	Incorrect carburetor adjustment	Adjust.
	Spark plug dirty, fouled, or improperly gapped	Replace or clean plug and set gap.
	Poor wiring connections in ignition circuit	Check connections at plugs, points, and coils.
	Defective ignition coils or condensers	Replace.
	Ignition timing incorrect	Adjust.
	Air leaks at carburetor manifolds	Refer to "Fuel System"
	Water in carburetors	Drain float bowls and gas tank if necessary.
	Carburetor main jet clogged	Remove and clean.
	Gas tank cap vent clogged	Blow clear.
	Petcock clogged	Clean.
	Float bowl fuel level too low	Check float height.
Spark plugs foul repeatedly	Plug gap too narrow	Adjust to proper value.
	Plug too cold for conditions	Fit plug one heat range hotter.
	Fuel mixture too rich	Adjust carburetor.
	Too much oil in mixture	Check oil pump cable adjustment.
	Piston rings badly worn	Replace.
Engine surges or runs unevenly at standard throttle openings	Air leaks at carburetor manifolds	Check as described in "Fuel System"
	Partial seizure occurring due to overheating.	See below.
Engine breaks up or misfires while running	Battery dead (battery ignition)	Recharge or replace battery.
	Loose or intermittent connections in the ignition circuit	Check connections.
	Carburetor float level incorrect	Check that float needle is sealing properly; check float height.
Loss of compression or power	Holed or damaged piston	Replace.
	Piston partially seizing	Determine cause.
	Badly worn piston rings	Replace rings.
	Blown or leaking head gasket	Check gasket.
	Muffler or exhaust port carbon clogged	Decarbonize.
	Air filter clogged with dirt	Clean or replace.
Poor low-speed operation	Incorrect ignition timing	Adjust timing.
	Poor breaker point contact	Adjust or replace points.
	Defective coil or condenser	Replace.
	Carburetor float level incorrect	Adjust float level.
	Pilot screw not adjusted properly	Adjust carburetor.
	Spark plug gap too great	Adjust.

Two-Stroke Engine Troubleshooting

Problem	Possible Causes	Inspection/Remedy
Poor high speed operation	Ignition timing incorrect	Adjust timing.
	Spark plug gap too small	Adjust gap.
	Defective ignition coil	Replace.
	Carburetor float level incorrect	Adjust float level.
	Low compression	Check head gasket for leakage as well as crankcase mating surfaces. Check rings and cylinder for wear.
	Engine carbon fouled; exhaust pipe carbon-fouled or broken	Decarbonize engine and exhaust pipe; check exhaust pipe for leaks.
	Pipe loose at cylinder	Tighten.
	Weak breaker point spring	Replace points.
	Air cleaner dirty or clogged	Clean or replace element.
Engine partially seizes or slows after high-speed operation	Spark plug too hot	Use plugs one heat range colder.
	Piston seizure	Determine cause.
	Carburetor mixture too lean	Take plug readings. Adjust carburetor as needed.
	Insufficient lubricant in mixture	Check oil pump cable adjustment or gas/oil mixture percentage.
	Air leaks at carburetor manifolds	Check manifold.
Engine overheats	Heavy carbon deposits on piston, exhaust port, and muffler	Decarbonize.
	Ignition timing too retarded	Adjust timing.
Engine detonates or preignites	Spark plugs too hot for application	Replace with plugs one heat range colder.
	Ignition timing too advanced	Adjust.
	Insufficient oil in fuel	Adjust oil pump cable or fuel/oil mixture percentage. Bleed oil line if necessary.
	Carburetor mixture too lean	Adjust.
	Air leaks at carb manifolds	See "Fuel System"
	Engine carbon-choked	Decarbonize head, piston, and muffler.
	Fuel octaine rating too low	Use fuel with higher octaine rating.
Engine backfires or kickstarter kicks back	Ignition timing too advanced	Adjust.
Rapid piston and cylinder wear	Ineffective or leaking air filter	Clean or replace filter element.

Four-Stroke Engine Troubleshooting

Problem	Possible Causes	Inspection/Remedy
Abnormal engine noise (top end)	Excessive tappet clearance	Adjust.
	Piston knock due to worn cylinder	Inspect and have cylinder bored if necessary.
	Excessive carbon build-up in combustion chamber	Decarbonize.
	Worn wrist pin or con rod small end	Inspect and replace if necessary.
	Misadjusted or worn cam chain	Adjust. Replace if adjustment does not quiet the chain.
	Worn cam or crankshaft sprocket	Inspect.
	Pinging or spark knock	Timing too advanced; Low quality gasoline; drain and refill tank with fresh gas.

Four-Stroke Engine Troubleshooting

Problem	Possible Causes	Inspection/Remedy
	Rumble at idle developing into whine at higher rpm: crankshaft main bearings worn or damaged	Inspect and replace if necessary.
	Knock, especially noticeable at idle, increasing with rpm: worn con rod big end bearing	Replace.
Engine fails to start (no spark at plugs)	Ignition switched off	Turn on ignition.
	Kill button switched off	Reset.
	Battery dead	Charge battery.
	Blown fuse	Check fuse and replace if necessary.
	Loose or corroded battery terminals	Clean and secure connections.
	Spark plugs too old; worn or fouled	Clean or replace plugs.
	Spark plugs wet	Kick engine over after removing plugs to clear it. Blow plugs dry.
	Plug gap incorrect	Set to correct gap.
	Points wires disconnected; loose or corroded snap connectors	Check wiring; clean and tighten wire connectors.
	Points incorrectly gapped, pitted, worn or dirty	Inspect points. Replace or clean and adjust gap.
	Spark plug cap resistors defective	Replace spark plug caps.
	Plug leads dirty, damaged, wet, or defective	Replace leads and coils.
	Ignition coils defective	Replace.
	Condenser defective	Replace.
	Points grounding out against point plate	Inspect. Check that the point wire is insulated.
	Damaged insulators at points terminal	Replace.
Spark at one plug	Defective, worn, dirty, or fouled spark plug	Switch the nonfunctioning plug to the other lead. If spark is evident, the plug is not at fault. If no spark, replace the plug.
	Defective resistor spark plug cap	Replace.
	Defective, cracked, wet or dirty plug lead	Replace along with coil.
	Dirty, misadjusted, pitted or burned breaker points	Replace.
	Breaker point wire disconnected, broken; snap connector loose or corroded; insulation torn	Check point wiring; clean and secure connector.
	One set of points grounding out against point cover or mounting plate. Damaged insulators on point wire terminal	Check point assemblies.
	Defective condenser	Replace.
	Defective ignition coil	Replace.
Engine fails to start (has spark at plugs)	Lack of fuel	Make sure petcock is on; check for fuel in the tank.
	Fuel starvation: fuel lines clogged; petcock or filter dirty; vent in gas tank cap closed up; carburetor float valve closed off	Check for fuel at the float bowl and then back through the system.
	Carburetor adjustments incorrect	Adjust.
	Ignition timing incorrect	Adjust.
	Incorrect valve adjustment	Adjust.
	Carburetor float punctured	Replace.

Four-Stroke Engine Troubleshooting

Problem	Possible Causes	Inspection/Remedy
	Low compression: worn rings or cylinder; bent or poorly seated valves; broken or worn valve guides	Inspect top end.
	Low compression due to blown head gasket, warped head	Rebuild.
	Incorrect valve timing	Reset.
Engine is hard to start	Worn, dirty, or improperly gapped plugs, or plugs too cold	Clean or replace and gap plugs or replace with correct heat range.
	Points dirty, pitted, or out of adjustment	Clean or replace and gap points.
	Carburetor idle settings wrong; pilot air or fuel passages clogged	Adjust idle settings or clean carburetor.
	Battery low	Recharge or replace battery.
	Ignition timing out of adjustment	Adjust.
	Valves adjusted incorrectly	Adjust valves.
	Spark plug leads cracked or dirty	Replace plug leads.
	Loss of intermittently grounded wires at coil, points, or connectors	Check all connections and condition of wiring.
	Defective coils or condensers	Replace.
	Worn or improperly seating valves	Perform top end overhaul; inspect and lap valves.
	Low compression due to worn or damaged top end components	Overhaul top end.
Engine starts but refuses to run	Fuel feed problem	Check fuel supply; check fuel petcock, lines, carburetor for blocked passages; check gas tank cap vent.
	Spark plugs too cold or worn	Replace with proper heat range plugs.
	Valve clearance incorrect	Set valve clearance.
	Ignition timing incorrect	Adjust.
Engine idles poorly	Carburetor idle adjustments incorrect	Adjust idle circuit.
	Spark plugs worn, dirty, or gap too wide	Clean or replace and gap plugs.
	Spark plugs too cold	Fit the proper heat range plugs.
	Breaker point gaps incorrect	Adjust.
	Ignition timing incorrect	Adjust.
	Valves improperly adjusted	Adjust.
	Water in carburetors	Drain float bowls and gas tank if necessary and fill with fresh gas.
	Carburetor float levels wrong	Adjust.
	Air leaks at manifolds	Determine cause and rectify.
	Leaking valves	Lap valves.
	Worn valves, valve guides, valve seats	Check valve train.
	Weak spark	Check coils and condensers.
	Petcock clogged	Clean.
	Float bowl fuel level too low	Check float height.
Engine misfires when accelerating	Loose or intermittent connections in the ignition circuit	Check all connections; make sure that they are clean and tight.
	Ignition timing incorrect	Adjust.
	Gas tank cap vent clogged	Clear.
	Water in float bowls	Drain and refill with fresh mixture.
	Carburetor main jet clogged	Remove and clean.
	Air leaks at carburetor manifolds	Determine cause and remedy.
	Defective ignition coils or condensers	Replace.
	Carburetor settings wrong	Take plug readings and rejet carbs if necessary.

Four-Stroke Engine Troubleshooting

Problem	*Possible Causes*	*Inspection/Remedy*
	Very low or dead battery	Recharge or replace battery.
Engine surges or runs unevenly at steady throttle openings	Carburetor fault; mixture too lean, erratic fuel flow	Remove and inspect carburetors.
	Air leaks at carburetor manifolds	Determine cause and remedy.
	Valves improperly adjusted	Adjust.
Engine breaks up or misfires while running	Battery very low or dead	Recharge or replace battery.
	Loose or intermittent connections in the ignition circuit	Check and secure connections.
	Battery terminal come adrift	Clean and secure battery conections.
Poor low-speed operation	Incorrect ignition timing	Adjust timing.
	Carburetor idle circuit poorly adjusted	Adjust pilot screws and idle speed.
	Spark plug gap too great or plugs too cold	Use correct heat range and gap to proper specifications.
	Poor breaker point contact	Clean or replace breaker points.
	Valves improperly adjusted	Adjust.
	Carburetor fault	See "Fuel System"
Poor high-speed operation	Ignition timing too retarded	Adjust timing.
	Spark plug gap too small	Adjust gap.
	Plugs too cold	Fit plugs of the correct heat range.
	Carburetor float level too low	Adjust float level.
	Partially blocked fuel lines or petcock	Clean.
	Dirty air cleaner	Clean or replace element.
	Weak breaker point arm spring	Replace points.
	Defective ignition coils or condensers	Replace.
	Weakened valve springs	Inspect springs.
	Incorrect valve timing	Reset.
Loss of power	Incorrect valve adjustment	Adjust tappets.
	Clogged or dirty air cleaner	Clean or replace the element.
	Incorrect ignition timing	Adjust.
	Dirty carburetors	Clean.
	Valves not sealing	Lap valves.
	Valve springs weakened	Replace.
	Rings or cylinder worn	Rebuild.
	Valve timing incorrect	Reset.
	Carburetor float level incorrect	Adjust.
	Spark plug gap incorrect	Adjust.
	Engine or muffler carbon choked	Decarbonize.
	Exhaust pipe broken or loose	Secure or replace.
Engine overheats	Insufficient engine oil	Top up.
	Too lean a mixture	See "Fuel System"
	Timing too advanced	Adjust.
	Oil pump defective; oil passage blocked	Clear system.
	Engine carbon choked	Decarbonize.
Engine backfires or kickstarter kicks back	Timing too advanced	Adjust.
	Advance unit stuck	Lubricate; check for free movement.
Popping at muffler after shutting off throttle	Air leaks in muffler	Secure clamps or nuts.
	Mixture too lean	Adjust idle circuit and float level. Check for air leaks.
Exhaust smoke accompanied by oil consumption	Too much oil in engine	Set to correct level.
	Worn rings or bore	Rebuild.
	Worn valve guides or seals	Replace.
	Scored cylinder	Bore to oversize.

Four-Stroke Engine Troubleshooting

Problem	Possible Causes	Inspection/Remedy
Black smoke from exhaust pipes	Engine carboned up	Decarbonize.
Piston seizure	Low oil level	Maintain oil at proper level.
	Engine overheating due to too advanced ignition timing, insufficient tappet clearance, stuck valves	Check settings.
	Insufficient oil	Check oil pump.
Burned valves	Clearances adjusted too tightly	Replace valves; check guides; maintain adjustment.
	Timing too retarded	Adjust.
Bent valves or broken valve guides	Valve hitting piston because of incorrect valve timing, overrevving the engine, or weak valve springs	Check top end components.
Bad connecting rod bearings	Insufficient or contaminated oil	Check oil, filter, and oil pump.
	Overrevving engine	Abide by tachometer red line
	Extended use of the engine with ignition timing too advanced, high-speed misfire, etc.	
Bad crankshaft bearings	Insufficient or contaminated oil	Replace bearings.
	Overrevving engine	Abide by tachometer red line.
	Extended use of the motorcycle with one weak or misfiring cylinder	
Worn cam lobes or bearings	Insufficient or contaminated oil	Maintain oil at proper level; change filter when directed.
	Failure to allow engine sufficient warm-up	Allow at least one minute of warm-up when starting cold eninge.
	Defective oil pump or clogged oil passages in engine	Replace.
Worn cylinder and rings	Damaged or leaking air cleaner	Replace element; secure connections.
	Low oil level or contaminated oil	Maintain oil at proper level; change oil and filter at proper intervals.
	Defective oil pump	Replace.
	Failure to allow engine sufficient warm-up	Allow at least one minute for warm-up when starting cold engine.

Clutch and Transmission Troubleshooting

Problem	Possible Causes	Inspection/Remedy
Clutch slips	Clutch improperly adjusted	Adjust.
	Clutch springs weak or damaged	Replace.
	Clutch springs not correctly secured	Tighten spring bolts.
	Friction discs worn or oil-impregnated	Check disc width and condition. Replace if necessary.
	Friction discs warped	Inspect and replace discs if necessary.
	Clutch cable has insufficient play	Adjust cable.

Clutch and Transmission Troubleshooting

Problem	Possible Causes	Inspection/Remedy
Clutch drags	Clutch cable or clutch improperly adjusted	Adjust cable and clutch.
	Friction discs gummy	Replace friction discs.
	Steel plates warped	Replace.
	Uneven spring tension	Check springs and replace as a set if necessary.
	Transmission oil too heavy for climate, or dirty	Change oil.
Clutch noisy	Clutch hub bearing worn	Replace.
	Clutch housing gear worn or damaged	Inspect and replace if necessary.
	Excessive clearance between disc tabs and housing	Check clearance.
	Worn or damaged clutch or mainshaft splines	Replace if necessary.
Transmission grinds when shifting or shifting is difficult	Clutch improperly adjusted	Adjust.
	Engine oil too heavy for temperature	Drain and refill with correct grade of oil.
	Worn or damaged shift forks, fork pins, shift drum, shift lever, shift arm	Inspect all components.
	Mainshaft or countershaft bearings worn or shafts bent	Inspect shafts and bearings.
Excessive gear noise	Insufficient lubricant in engine	Check level and refill to proper level.
	Gears worn (excessive backlash)	Inspect all gears.
	Worn transmission shaft bearings	Inspect and if necessary replace bearings.
Shift lever does not return	Weak or broken return spring	Inspect spring and replace if necessary.
Transmission will not shift	Clutch dragging	Check adjustment and condition of clutch assembly.
	Bent shift forks	Inspect and replace shift forks.
	Broken shifter return spring	Replace.
Transmission jumps out of gear	Worn transmission gear engaging dogs	Inspect gears and replace if damaged.
	Worn or bent shift forks or shift drum	Inspect and replace if necessary.
	Worn splines on countershaft or mainshaft	Inspect and replace if necessary.
	Bent gearshift shaft or damaged shift arm	Inspect components and replace if necessary.
	Worn or broken gear teeth	Inspect gears and replace any damaged or worn gears.
	Weak shift drum stopper spring	Replace.

Carburetor Troubleshooting

Problem	Possible Causes	Inspection/Remedy
Carburetor floods repeatedly.	Float sticking due to misalignment	Correct.
	Fuel petcock left open with engine shut off	Shut off the fuel after you stop engine.
	Float punctured	Replace.

Carburetor Troubleshooting

Problem	Possible Causes	Inspection/Remedy
Idle mixture too lean	Pilot jet too small	Replace with larger jet.
	Worn throttle slide	Replace.
	Pilot screw out of adjustment	Adjust.
Idle mixture too rich	Pilot jet too large	Replace with smaller jet.
	Dirt or foreign matter in idle passage	Dismantle and clean carburetor.
	Pilot screw out of adjustment	Adjust.
Lean mixture at sustained mid-range speeds	Jet needle set too lean	Reset needle clip at lower notch.
	Needle or main jet clogged	Remove and clean jets.
	Intake manifold air leak	Find leak and rectify.
Lean mixture at sustained high-speeds	Main jet too small	Replace with larger jet.
	Main jet clogged	Remove and clean.
	Float level too low	Remove float and adjust level.
Lean mixture during acceleration	Jets clogged	Remove and clean.
	Damaged or worn throttle slide	Replace.
	Float level too low	Adjust float height.
Lean mixture throughout throttle range	Fuel filters clogged or dirty	Remove and clean.
	Gas cap vent blocked	Blow clear.
	Damaged or worn throttle slide	Replace.
	Air leaks at carb manifold	Find leak and rectify.
Rich mixture at sustained mid-range speeds	Air cleaner dirty	Clean or replace.
	Main jet too large	Replace with smaller jet.
	Carburetor flooding	See above.
	Needle or needle jet worn	Replace.
Rich mixture at sustained high-speeds	Main jet too large	Replace with smaller size jet.
	Carburetor flooding	See above.
	Air cleaner dirty	Replace or clean.
Rich mixture throughout throttle range	Carburetor flooding	See above.
	Air cleaner dirty	Replace or clean.
Erratic idle	Air leaks	Determine source and recify.
	Dirty or blocked idle passages	Clean carburetor.
	Idle settings incorrect	Adjust to specifications.
	Damage to pilot screw	Replace.
	Worn or damaged air seals such as o-rings or gaskets	Rebuild carburetor.
	Unsynchronized carburetors on multi-carb machines	Adjust and synchronize carburetors.
	Defective auto timing advancer	Repair or replace.
	Mixture too lean	Adjust carburetor.
Engine dies when throttle is opened	Fuel flow problem	Check for sufficient fuel supply, clogged petcock or lines, clogged filters, proper float level.
	Idle mixture incorrect	Set idle speed and pilot screw to specifications; if correct, check pilot passages for clogged condition, pilot screw for damage.
	Idle mixture too lean	Check pilot screw and idle jet settings. Check throttle slide cutaway.
Engine misfires when accelerating	Fuel feed problem	Check for clogged tank cap vent, petcock filter, lines.
	Water in float bowls	Drain bowls and, if necessary, drain gas tank.
	Carburetor main jet clogged	Remove and blow clear.
	Main jet too large	Fit smaller jet and run plug check.
	Air leaks at manifolds	Determine source and rectify.

Carburetor Troubleshooting

Problem	*Possible Causes*	*Inspection/Remedy*
Engine misfires at high rpm	Main jet too large or too small	Change size after plug readings.
	Air cleaner clogged	Clean or replace air cleaner element.
	Air leaks	Determine cause and rectify.
	Throttle slide diaphragm ripped (CV carbs)	Replace.

Electrical Troubleshooting

Problem	*Possible Causes*	*Inspection/Remedy*
Battery does not charge	Defective battery	Test each cell. Replace if shorted cell(s) are evident. See chapter 2.
	Battery electrolyte level low	Top up.
	Broken or shorting wires in charging circuit	Check continuity and condition or insulation of all wires.
	Loose or dirty battery terminals	Clean terminals and secure connections.
	Defective voltage regulator	Test and adjust if necessary. See chapter 7.
	Defective alternator	Replace.
	Defective rectifier	Replace.
Excessive battery charging	Defective battery (shorted plates)	Replace battery.
	Voltage regulator not properly grounded	Secure.
	Regulator defective	Adjust or replace. See chapter 7.
Unstable charging voltage	Intermittent short	Check wiring for frayed insulation.
	Defective key switch	Replace.
	Intermittent coil in alternator	Replace.
Electric starter spins, but engine does not	Broken starter clutch	Replace.
Starter does not turn over, but warning lights dim when starter button is pushed, or engine turns over slowly	Low battery, or battery connections loose or corroded	Charge or replace battery; clean and tighten terminals.
	Starter armature bushings worn	Replace starter.
Clicking sound when starter button is pushed; engine does not turn over	Battery low or terminals loose or corroded	Charge or replace battery; clean and tighten connections.
	Defective starter solenoid	Replace.
Nothing happens when starter button is pushed	Loose or broken connections in the starter switch or battery leads	Check switch connections, check battery terminals; clean and tighten battery leads.
Engine turns over slowly when starter button is pushed (cold weather)	Low or dead battery	Recharge or replace battery.
	Engine oil too heavy	Use correct viscosity oil.
Turn signal will not light	Burned out bulb	Replace.
Turn signal will not flash	One bulb burned out	Replace.
	Low battery	Charge or replace battery.
Speed of flasher varies with engine rpm	Low battery	Charge or replace battery.
	Defective flasher unit	Replace.
No spark or weak spark	Defective ignition coil(s)	Replace.
	Defective spark plug(s)	Replace.
	Plug lead(s) or wires damaged or disconnected	Check condition of leads and wires; check all connections.
Breaker points pitted or burned	Defective condenser	Replace points and condenser.

Electrical Troubleshooting

Problem	Possible Causes	Inspection/Remedy
Carbon-fouled spark plugs	Mixture too rich	Adjust carburetors; check air cleaner.
	Plugs too cold for conditions	Use hotter plugs.
	Idle speed set too high	Adjust carburetors.
Oil-fouled spark plugs	Worn rings, cylinders, or valve guides	See chapter 4.
Spark plug electrodes burned or overheated	Spark plugs too hot for conditions	Use colder plugs.
	Engine overheating	See "Engine Troubleshooting" chart, above.
Spark plug electrodes burned or overheated	Ignition timing incorrect	Adjust. Refer to chapter 3.
	Mixture too lean	See above.

Chassis Troubleshooting

Problem	Possible Causes	Inspection/Remedy
Excessive vibration	Engine mounting bolts loose	Secure mounting bolts.
	Broken frame	Replace frame or have damage recified by competent welder.
	Drive chain badly worn, unlubricated, or too tight; worn sprockets	Replace, lubricate, or adjust drive chain; replace sprockets.
	Loose spokes	Tighten spokes; have rim trued as soon as possible.
	Rims out-of-true	Have rims trued.
	Wheels unbalanced, especially front wheel	Balance wheels.
	Loose axle nuts	Tighten.
	Worn or loose steering head bearings	Adjust or replace bearings as necessary
	Crankshaft bearing failure	Inspect and replace if necessary.
	Carburetor out of synchronization	Perform tune-up.
Poor front fork operation	Weak, collapsed, or broken fork springs	Inspect and replace.
	Insufficient oil in forks	Refill with correct amount.
	Too much oil in forks	Drain and refill with correct amount.
	Oil of wrong viscosity being used	Use higher or lower viscosity oil to stiffen or weaken fork action.
	Noisy fork operation	Check oil level.
	Excessive clearance in slider bushings	Replace.
	Bent fork tubes	Replace.
	Dirty or contaminated fork oil	Change oil.
	Worn or leaky seals as evidenced by dirt in the fork oil or leaking around the seals	Replace oil seals.
Uncertain or wobbly handling	Worn or improperly adjusted steering head bearings	Adjust or replace the bearings.
	Low tire pressure	Inflate to recommended pressure.
	Worn or defective rear shocks (insufficient damping), or weak rear shock springs; spring not properly adjusted for load	Replace rear shocks; replace or adjust springs.
	Loose spokes	Tighten spokes; have rim trued as soon as possible.
	Rims out-of-true	Have rims trued.
	Loose axle	Secure axle nut and axle mounting hardware.
	Worn swing arm bushings	Replace.
Heavy or stiff steering	Low front tire pressure	Inflate to recommended pressure.
	Steering head bearings too tightly adjusted	Adjust.
	Steering damper too tightly adjusted	Loosen damper.
	Steering stem bent	Replace.
	Steering stem ball bearings unlubricated or damaged	Replace bearings and races.

Chassis Troubleshooting

Problem	Possible Causes	Inspection/Remedy
Pull to one side	Unequal suspension spring tension	Replace springs.
	Bent front fork or axle	Replace.
Excessive level or pedal travel with loss of braking power (disc brakes)	Air in hydraulic system	Bleed system.
	Master cylinder low on fluid	Fill master cylinder to level line and bleed system.
	Loose lever or pedal adjusting bolt	Adjust travel and secure bolt.
	Leak in hydraulic system	Rebuild system seals or hoses.
	Worn pads	Replace.
Brakes squeal (disc brakes)	Glazed pads	Clean up or replace pads.
	Improperly adjusted caliper (Honda)	Adjust caliper.
	Extremely dusty brake assembly	Thoroughly blow out assembly.
Brakes shudder (disc brakes)	Warped disc	Replace disc and pads.
	Distorted pads	Replace.
	Oil or brake fluid impregnated pads	Replace pads.
	Loose caliper or disc mounting bolts	Secure all fasteners.
Brake pads remain on disc (disc brakes)	Piston seized in bore	Rebuild caliper.
	Relief port blocked by piston in master cylinder	Rebuild master cylinder.
	Caliper out of adjustment (Honda)	Adjust.
	Caliper pivot frozen (Honda)	Clean and lubricate pivot.
Brakes do not hold (drum brakes)	Brake shoes glazed or worn	Repair or replace shoes.
	Brake shoes oil or grease impregnated	Replace shoes.
	Brake linings worn away	Replace linings.
	Brake drum worn or damaged	Replace or have drum turned down.
	Insufficient hydraulic fluid or air in brake lines	Drain system and refill with fresh fluid, then bleed system.
	Brake linkage incorrectly adjusted	Adjust linkage as necessary.
	Brake control cables insufficiently lubricated or binding	Lubricate or replace cables as necessary.
Brakes drag (drum brakes)	Lack of play in the linkage	Adjust linkage as necessary.
	Weak or damaged return springs	Replace springs as a set.
	Rusted cam and lever shaft	Replace as necessary.
Unadjustable brakes (drum brakes)	Worn brake shoe linings	Replace shoes or rotate the actuating lever a few degrees on its splined shaft (if applicable).
	Worn brake shoe cam	Replace the cam as necessary.
	Worn or damaged brake drum	Replace the drum or have it turned down.
Brakes make scraping sounds (drum brakes)	Linings worn down to the rivets	Replace the linings and have the drum turned or replaced as necessary.
	Broken brake shoe	Replace the shoes and repair or replace the drum as necessary.
	Dirt in the drum	Blow the assembly out with compressed air and replace or repair the drum as necessary.
	Scored or out of round brake drum	Repair or replace the drum as necessary.
	Broken pivot	Replace the pivot.
Brake shudder (drum brakes)	Unevenly worn shoes	Replace shoes.
	Out of round brake drum	Repair or replace drum.
Brake squeal (drum brakes)	Dirt on the linings or brake drum	Remove and clean the linings and drum.
	Worn or damaged brake linings	Replace.
	Linings glazed or hardened	Replace.
Brake gives on-off-on feeling when applied (drum brakes)	Braking on rough road surface (rod-operated brake)	None.
	Drum warped out-of-round	Have drum turned down on a lathe.

APPENDIX

Conversion Table

To change			Multiply			
cc	⟶	cu in.	cc	×	0.0610	= cubic inches
cc	⟶	oz (Imp)	cc	×	0.02816	= ounces (Imperial)
cc	⟶	oz (U.S.)	cc	×	0.03381	= ounces (U.S.)
cu in	⟶	cc	cu in.	×	16.39	= cubic centimeters
°C	⟶	°F	°C + 17.8	×	1.8	= °F
ft-lb	⟶	in. lbs	ft-lb	×	12	= inch pounds
ft-lb	⟶	kg-M	ft-lb	×	0.1383	= kilogram-meters
gal (Imp)	⟶	liter	Imp gal	×	4.546	= liters
gal (U.S.)	⟶	liter	U.S. gal	×	3.785	= liters
in	⟶	mm	in	×	25.40	= millimeters
kg	⟶	lbs	kg	×	2.205	= pounds
kg-M	⟶	ft lbs	kg-M	×	7.233	= foot-pounds
kg/sq cm	⟶	lbs/sq in	kg/sq cm	×	14.22	= pounds/square inch
km	⟶	mi	km	×	0.6214	= miles
lb	⟶	kg	lb	×	0.4536	= kilograms
lb/sq in	⟶	kg/sq cm	lb/sq in.	×	0.0703	= kilograms/square centimeter
liter	⟶	cc	liter	×	1,000	= cc
liter	⟶	oz (U.S.)	liter	×	33.81	= ounces (U.S.)
liter	⟶	qt (Imp)	liter	×	0.8799	= quarts (Imperial)
liter	⟶	qt (U.S.)	liter	×	1.0567	= quarts (U.S.)
mi	⟶	km	mi	×	1.6093	= kilometers
mm	⟶	in	mm	×	0.03937	= inches
qt (Imp)	⟶	liter	Imp qt	×	1.1365	= liters
qt (U.S.)	⟶	liter	U.S. qt	×	0.9463	= liters

Conversion—Millimeters to Decimal Inches

mm	inches	mm	inches	mm	inches	mm	inches	mm	inches
1	.039 370	31	1.220 470	61	2.401 570	91	3.582 670	210	8.267 700
2	.078 740	32	1.259 840	62	2.440 940	92	3.622 040	220	8.661 400
3	.118 110	33	1.299 210	63	2.480 310	93	3.661 410	230	9.055 100
4	.157 480	34	1.338 580	64	2.519 680	94	3.700 780	240	9.448 800
5	.196 850	35	1.377 949	65	2.559 050	95	3.740 150	250	9.842 500
6	.236 220	36	1.417 319	66	2.598 420	96	3.779 520	260	10.236 200
7	.275 590	37	1.456 689	67	2.637 790	97	3.818 890	270	10.629 900
8	.314 960	38	1.496 050	68	2.677 160	98	3.858 260	280	11.032 600
9	.354 330	39	1.535 430	69	2.716 530	99	3.897 630	290	11.417 300
10	.393 700	40	1.574 800	70	2.755 900	100	3.937 000	300	11.811 000
11	.433 070	41	1.614 170	71	2.795 270	105	4.133 848	310	12.204 700
12	.472 440	42	1.653 540	72	2.834 640	110	4.330 700	320	12.598 400
13	.511 810	43	1.692 910	73	2.874 010	115	4.527 550	330	12.992 100
14	.551 180	44	1.732 280	74	2.913 380	120	4.724 400	340	13.385 800
15	.590 550	45	1.771 650	75	2.952 750	125	4.921 250	350	13.779 500
16	.629 920	46	1.811 020	76	2.992 120	130	5.118 100	360	14.173 200
17	.669 290	47	1.850 390	77	3.031 490	135	5.314 950	370	14.566 900
18	.708 660	48	1.889 760	78	3.070 860	140	5.511 800	380	14.960 600
19	.748 030	49	1.929 130	79	3.110 230	145	5.708 650	390	15.354 300
20	.787 400	50	1.968 500	80	3.149 600	150	5.905 500	400	15.748 000
21	.826 770	51	2.007 870	81	3.188 970	155	6.102 350	500	19.685 000
22	.866 140	52	2.047 240	82	3.228 340	160	6.299 200	600	23.622 000
23	.905 510	53	2.086 610	83	3.267 710	165	6.496 050	700	27.559 000
24	.944 880	54	2.125 980	84	3.307 080	170	6.692 900	800	31.496 000
25	.984 250	55	2.165 350	85	3.346 450	175	6.889 750	900	35.433 000
26	1.023 620	56	2.204 720	86	3.385 820	180	7.086 600	1000	39.370 000
27	1.062 990	57	2.244 090	87	3.425 190	185	7.283 450	2000	78.740 000
28	1.102 360	58	2.283 460	88	3.464 560	190	7.480 300	3000	118.110 000
29	1.141 730	59	2.322 830	89	3.503 903	195	7.677 150	4000	157.480 000
30	1.181 100	60	2.362 200	90	3.543 300	200	7.874 000	5000	196.850 000

To change decimal millimeters to decimal inches, position the decimal point where desired on either side of the millimeter measurement shown and reset the inches decimal by the same number of digits in the same direction. For example, to convert 0.001 mm into decimal inches, reset the decimal behind the 1 mm (shown on the chart) to 0.001; change the decimal inch equivalent (0.039" shown) to 0.000039".

Conversion—Common Fractions to Decimals and Millimeters

Inches			Inches			Inches		
Common Fractions	*Decimal Fractions*	*Millimeters (approx.)*	*Common Fractions*	*Decimal Fractions*	*Millimeters (approx.)*	*Common Fractions*	*Decimal Fractions*	*Millimeters (approx.)*
1/128	.008	0.20	11/32	.344	8.73	43/64	.672	17.07
1/64	.016	0.40	23/64	.359	9.13	11/16	.688	17.46
1/32	.031	0.79	3/8	.375	9.53	45/64	.703	17.86
3/64	.047	1.19	25/64	.391	9.92	23/32	.719	18.26
1/16	.063	1.59	13/32	.406	10.32	47/64	.734	18.65
5/64	.078	1.98	27/64	.422	10.72	3/4	.750	19.05
3/32	.094	2.38	7/16	.438	11.11	49/64	.766	19.45
7/64	.109	2.78	29/64	.453	11.51	25/32	.781	19.84
1/8	.125	3.18	15/32	.469	11.91	51/64	.797	20.24
9/64	.141	3.57	31/64	.484	12.30	13/16	.813	20.64
5/32	.156	3.97	1/2	.500	12.70	53/64	.828	21.03
11/64	.172	4.37	33/64	.516	13.10	27/32	.844	21.43
3/16	.188	4.76	17/32	.531	13.49	55/64	.859	21.83
13/64	.203	5.16	35/64	.547	13.89	7/8	.875	22.23
7/32	.219	5.56	9/16	.563	14.29	57/64	.891	22.62
15/64	.234	5.95	37/64	.578	14.68	29/32	.906	23.02
1/4	.250	6.35	19/32	.594	15.08	59/64	.922	23.42
17/64	.266	6.75	39/64	.609	15.48	15/16	.938	23.81
9/32	.281	7.14	5/8	.625	15.88	61/64	.953	24.21
19/64	.297	7.54	41/64	.641	16.27	31/32	.969	24.61
5/16	.313	7.94	21/32	.656	16.67	63/64	.984	25.00
21/64	.328	8.33						

Tap Drill Sizes

National Fine or S.A.E.		
Screw & Tap Size	Threads Per Inch	Use Drill Number
No. 5	44	37
No. 6	40	33
No. 8	36	29
No. 10	32	21
No. 12	28	15
1/4	28	3
5/16	24	1
3/8	24	Q
7/16	20	W
1/2	20	29/64
9/16	18	33/64
5/8	18	37/64
3/4	16	11/16
7/8	14	13/16
1 1/8	12	1 3/64
1 1/4	12	1 11/64
1 1/2	12	1 27/64

National Coarse or U.S.S.		
Screw & Tap Size	Threads Per Inch	Use Drill Number
No. 5	40	39
No. 6	32	36
No. 8	32	29
No. 10	24	25
No. 12	24	17
1/4	20	8
5/16	18	F
3/8	16	5/16
7/16	14	U
1/2	13	27/64
9/16	12	31/64
5/8	11	17/32
3/4	10	21/32
7/8	9	49/64
1	8	7/8
1 1/8	7	63/64
1 1/4	7	1 7/64
1 1/2	6	1 11/32

Decimal Equivalent Size of the Number Drills

Drill No.	Decimal Equivalent	Drill No.	Decimal Equivalent	Drill No.	Decimal Equivalent
80	.0135	53	.0595	26	.1470
79	.0145	52	.0635	25	.1495
78	.0160	51	.0670	24	.1520
77	.0180	50	.0700	23	.1540
76	.0200	49	.0730	22	.1570
75	.0210	48	.0760	21	.1590
74	.0225	47	.0785	20	.1610
73	.0240	46	.0810	19	.1660
72	.0250	45	.0820	18	.1695
71	.0260	44	.0860	17	.1730
70	.0280	43	.0890	16	.1770
69	.0292	42	.0935	15	.1800
68	.0310	41	.0960	14	.1820
67	.0320	40	.0980	13	.1850
66	.0330	39	.0995	12	.1890
65	.0350	38	.1015	11	.1910
64	.0360	37	.1040	10	.1935
63	.0370	36	.1065	9	.1960
62	.0380	35	.1100	8	.1990
61	.0390	34	.1110	7	.2010
60	.0400	33	.1130	6	.2040
59	.0410	32	.1160	5	.2055
58	.0420	31	.1200	4	.2090
57	.0430	30	.1285	3	.2130
56	.0465	29	.1360	2	.2210
55	.0520	28	.1405	1	.2280
54	.0550	27	.1440		

Decimal Equivalent Size of the Letter Drills

Letter Drill	Decimal Equivalent	Letter Drill	Decimal Equivalent	Letter Drill	Decimal Equivalent
A	.234	J	.277	S	.348
B	.238	K	.281	T	.358
C	.242	L	.290	U	.368
D	.246	M	.295	V	.377
E	.250	N	.302	W	.386
F	.257	O	.316	X	.397
G	.261	P	.323	Y	.404
H	.266	Q	.332	Z	.413
I	.272	R	.339		

Comparison of Wrench Sizes

U.S.	Metric	Whitworth	Decimal Inches
5/32			.156
	4 mm		.157
		7BA	.172
3/16			.187
		6BA	.193
	5 mm		.197
13/64			.203
7/32			.218
		5BA	.220
15/64			.234
	6 mm		.236
		4BA	.248
1/4			.250
17/64			.265
	7 mm		.276
9/32			.281
		3BA	.282
5/16			.312
	8 mm		.315
		2BA	.324
		1/8W	.338
11/32			.343
	9 mm		.354
		1BA	.365
3/8			.375
	10 mm		.393
		OBA	.413
	11 mm		.433
7/16			.437
		3/16W	.448
15/32			.468
	12 mm		.472
1/2			.500
	13 mm		.512
		1/4W	.525
17/32			.531
	14 mm		.551
9/16			.562
	15 mm		.591
19/32			.593
		5/16W	.600

U.S.	Metric	Whitworth	Decimal Inches
5/8			.625
	16 mm		.630
21/32			.656
	17 mm		.669
11/16			.687
	18 mm		.709
		3/8W	.710
	19 mm		.748
3/4			.750
25/32			.781
	20 mm		.787
13/16			.812
		7/16W	.820
	21 mm		.827
	22 mm		.866
7/8			.875
	23 mm		.906
29/32			.906
		1/2W	.920
15/16			.937
	24 mm		.945
31/32			.968
	25 mm		.984
1			1.000
		9/16W	1.010
	26 mm		1.024
1 1/16			1.062
	27 mm		1.063
		5/8W	1.100
	28 mm		1.102
1 1/8			1.125
	29 mm		1.142
	30 mm		1.181
1 3/16			1.187
		11/16W	1.200
	31 mm		1.220
1 1/4			1.250
	32 mm		1.260
	33 mm		1.299

Common Abbreviations

ABDC .... after bottom dead center
ATDC .... after top dead center
BBDC .... before bottom dead center
BDC .... bottom dead center
BTDC .... before top dead center
cc .... cubic centimeters
cu in. .... cubic inches
ft .... foot, feet
ft lbs .... foot-pounds
gal .... gallon
hp .... horsepower
in. .... inch
in. lbs .... inch-pounds
kg .... kilogram, kilograms
kg/cm² .... kilograms per square centimeter
kg/m .... kilogram meters
km .... kilometer
kph .... kilometers per hour
lbs .... pounds
lbs/sq in. .... pounds per square inch
l .... liter
m .... meter
mi .... mile
mm .... millimeters
mph .... miles per hour
oz .... ounce
psi .... pounds per square inch
pt .... pint
qt .... quart
rpm .... revolutions per minute
sec .... second
TDC .... top dead center

Spark Plug Comparison Chart

Thread Size	Heat Range	NGK Standard Type	NGK Projected Type	Champion Y—Projected Type G—Gold Palladium Electrode	AC S—Projected Type	Denso (ND)	Bosch	KLG P—Projected Type	Auto-Lite
	hot			J14J, J14Y, UJ18Y	C49, 46S		W45T3	FS20	A82
				J12J, UJ12	48, C47, C47W, M47			FS30, FS45P	A11, AT10,
		B—4	BP—4	J11, J11J	46, C46, M46	W14	W145T3		AZ9, A9
									AT8, A9XM
				J13Y, UJ12Y, J11Y, J12Y	45, C45, C45W, M45, 45S	W17	W175T3	FS50, FS55P	A7, AT6, A42
		B—6S	BP—6S	J10Y, UJ10Y, J8, J8J	44, C44, M44, M44B, 44S			FS70	AT4
14 mm				J7, J7J, UJ8	MC44				
				J6, UJ6, J6J	43, C42-4, C43, 43S, MC42	W22	W225T3	FS75	A3, AT3
		B—7S		J5	M44C, M43				
		B—7C °							
		B—77C °		J62R					A23
		B—8S		J4, J4J, J61Y, J60R	42, C42-1, M42	W24	W240T3	FS100	AT2
⅜ in.		B—9S		J2J, J57R	41				AT1
Reach	cold	B—10						FS100-2	A901
	hot			H12	47L				AL11
14 mm		B—4L		H11	45L, C45L, TC45L				AL9, ATL8
				H10, H10J, H18Y			W125T4	FA50, FA50H	AL7, A7
7/16 in.		B—6L		H8, H8J	43L, C43L, C43LY			FA70	ATL4, ATL3
Reach	cold			H14Y					
	hot	B—4H	BP—4H	L14, UL15Y, L10	46FF, 46FFS, 45FFS, 45FF	W9FP	W95T1	F20, F50	AE52, AE6
		B—5HS		L90	45F, M45FF	W14F	W145T1	F55P	
		B—6HS	BP—6HS	L86, L85, L95Y	44FFS, 44FF, M43FF	W17F	W175T1, W175T7	F70, F65P	AE4, AE42
				UL12Y, L88	44F, 43F, 43FFS		W200T7, W200T35	F75	AE3, AE32
				L7, L87Y, UL87Y	42F, 42FF, 42FS	W22F	W225T1, W225T35		AE2, AE22
14 mm		B—7HS	BP—7HS	L81, L82Y, UL82Y	M42FF, MC42F		W225T7	F80	
				L5					
		B—7HC °				W24F	W240T1, W240T16	F100	
		B—7HZ							
		B—77HC °		L62R			W260T1		
		B—8HS		L4J, L64Y, L66Y			W270T16		AE903
		B—8HC °							
		B—8HCS °		L60R, L3G			W280M1		
		B—9HS		L2G			W310T16		AE603
		B—9HC °							
		B—9HCS °		L57R					
½ in.		BUHX °°		L54R					
Reach	cold	B—10H							
				N21, N16Y	47XL	W9EP	W95T2, W125T2	FE20	AG9
	hot	B—4E	BP—4E	N18	46XLS			FE30	
		B—5ES	BP—5ES	N8, N14Y, N13Y	46N, 46XL, 45XLS	W14E	W145T2	FE50, FE45P	AG7, AC52
			BP—5ESL	N84, N88		W14EP	W145T30, W160T2		AG5
14 mm		B—6ES	BP—6ES	N6, N12Y, UN12Y	45N, 45XL, C45XL	W17E	W175T2, W175T30	FE70, FE55P	AG4, AG42
				N11Y, N10Y, N5	44N, 44XL, 44XLS	W20EP	W200T27, W200T30	FE75	AG3, AG32
		B—7ES	BP—7ES	N9Y, N8Y	44XLS, 43XLS, 43N, 43XL	W22E, W22ES	W225T2, W230T30	FE80, FE65P	AG2, AG23
		B—7EC °		N4					
		B—77EC °		N62R	C42N		W240T2, W240T28	FE100	
				N6Y, N7Y			W250P21, WG250T28	FE220	
		B—8ES	BP—8ES	N3, N3G	42XL, 42XLS	W24E, W24ES	W260T28, W265P21	FE250	
¾ in.		B—9ES/EV		N60R, N2	41XLS	W27E	W280M2, W300M2		
Reach	cold	B—10E				W31E			AG701
14 mm	hot		BP—6FS	UBL13Y	46TS, 45TS		WA125T40		AF52
Taper				BL11Y	44TS				AF42
Seat									
	cold		BP—7FS	BL7Y, BL9Y	43TS, 42TS, 40TS		WA200T40		AF32
	hot	D—4H							
12 mm		D—5HS				X17F	X175T1		
		D—6HS		P—8Y	S124FS	X20FS	X260T1	TW270	HE3
½ in.		D—8HS		P—7	S122F	X24FS	X300T1	TW275	HE2
Reach	cold	D—10HS		P—6	S121F	X28FS	X320T1	TW280	HE1
	hot								
		D—4E							
		D—6ES							
		D—7E				X20E	X240T17		
		D—7ES							
12 mm		D—8E		R—61		X22E, X22ES	X270T17		
¾ in.		D—8ESL							
Reach		D—8ES		R—6, R—6G	S123XL	X24E, X24ES	X300T2		
		D—10E							
	cold	D—10ES			S121XL				
	hot								
10 mm		C—4H							
		C—6H		Z—10	S104F	U20FS	U175T1	T30	PE3
		C—7HS		Z—8		U22FS	U260T1	T70	
½ in.		C—9H						T90	
Reach		C—10H		Z—6	S102F	U24F			
	cold								

° Competition type with short side electrode

°° Surface-gap type for CDI systems

GLOSSARY OF COMMON TERMS

Accelerator pump—A small pump fitted to some carburetors which injects a charge of fuel into the intake tract in addition to that supplied by the normal metering components. Most accelerator pumps are activated by the movement of the throttle slide and are intended to aid transition from the pilot system to the mid-range system for smoother acceleration

Advance—Setting the ignition timing so that spark occurs before the piston reaches top dead center (TDC)

Alternating current (AC)—Electric current that flows first, in one direction, then in the opposite direction, continually reversing flow

Alternator—A device which produces AC (alternating current) which is converted to DC (direct current) by the rectifier to charge the car battery

Ammeter—A gauge which measures current flow (amps). Ammeters show whether the battery is charging or discharging

Ampere (amp)—Unit to measure the rate of flow of electrical current

Amp/hr. rating (battery)—Measurement of the ability of a battery to deliver a stated amount of current for a stated period of time. The higher the amp/hr. rating, the more powerful the battery

Antifreeze—A substance (ethylene glycol) added to the coolant to prevent freezing in cold weather

ATDC—After Top Dead Center

Bead—The portion of the tire which holds it onto the rim

Breaker points (or simply, "points")—An electrical switch operated by a cam which make and break the ignition coil circuit. When the circuit is broken by the opening points, the spark plug fires

BTDC—Before Top Dead Center. Spark occurs on the compression stroke, before the piston reaches top dead center

Bezel—Piece of metal surrounding headlights, gauges or similar components; sometimes used to hold the glass face of a gauge in the dash

Brake caliper—The housing that fits over the brake disc. The caliper holds the brake pads which are pressed against the discs by the caliper pistons, when the brake lever or pedal is depressed

Brake horsepower—Usable horsepower of an engine measured at the crankshaft

Brake fade—Loss of braking power, usually caused by excessive heat after repeated brake applications

Brake pad—The friction pad on a disc brake system

Brake shoe—The friction lining on a drum brake system

Block—The basic engine casting containing the cylinders

Bore—Diameter of a cylinder

Bushing—A plain, replaceable bearing of soft metal or rubber

Camshaft—A shaft that rotates at ½ engine speed, used to operate the intake and exhaust valves

Carbon monoxide (CO)—One of the by-products of the combustion process. Carbon monoxide is odorless and deadly

Choke—Usually, plate near the top of the carburetor that is closed to restrict the amount of air taken into the carburetor, making the fuel mixture richer. Some carburetors use a fuel plunger in lieu of a plate. Operating the choke lever raises the plunger from its seat, uncovering a fuel passage which allows gasoline to enter the intake tract bypassing the usual metering components and thus enrichening the mixture

Clutch—Part of the power train used to connect/disconnect power to the rear wheel

Combustion chamber—The part of the engine in the cylinder head where combustion takes place

Compression check—A test involving removing each spark plug and inserting a gauge. When the engine is cranked, the gauge will record a pressure reading in the individual cylinder. General operating condition can be determined from a compression check

Compression ratio—The ratio of the volume between the piston and cylinder head when the piston is at the bottom of its stroke (bottom dead center) and when the piston is at the top of its stroke (top dead center)

Condenser—A small device in the ignition system which absorbs the momentary surge of current produced when the breaker points open. It protects the points from burning

Coil—Part of the ignition system that boosts the relatively low voltage supplied by the battery to the high voltage required to fire the spark plugs

Connecting rod—The connecting link between the crankshaft and piston

Conventional ignition—Ignition system which uses breaker points

Coolant—Mixture of water and antifreeze circulated through the engine to carry off heat produced by the engine

Crankshaft—Engine component (connected to pistons by connecting rods) which converts the reciprocating (up and down) motion of pistons to rotary motion used to turn the driveshaft

Crankcase—The part of the engine that houses the crankshaft

Curb weight—The weight of a vehicle without passengers or payload, but including all fluids (oil, gas, coolant, etc.) and other equipment specified as standard

Detergent—An additive in engine oil to improve its operating characteristics

Detonation—Instantaneous combustion of fuel, resulting in excessive heat and pressure which can damage engine components. Fuel should burn in the cylinders in a controlled manner, rather than exploding immediately

Diode—An electrical component which allows current to flow through it in only one direction. When connected in a certain way (i.e. "bridged") four diodes will convert AC to DC, thus the rectifier

Direct current (DC)—Electrical current that flows in one direction only

Distributor—Device containing the breaker points which distributes high voltage to the proper spark plug at the proper time. Rarely used in motorcycles

DOHC—Double overhead camshaft engine. Two overhead camshafts are used—one operates exhaust valves, and the other operates intake valves

Dry charged battery—Battery to which electrolyte is added when the battery is placed in service

Dwell angle—The number of degrees on the breaker cam that the points are closed

Electrode—Conductor (positive or negative) of electric current

Electrolyte—A solution of water and sulphuric acid used to activate the battery. Electrolyte is extremely corrosive

Electronic ignition—Type of ignition system which uses no breaker points

Enamel—Type of paint that dries to a smooth, glossy finish

Ethyl—A substance added to gasoline to improve its resistance to knock, by slowing down the rate of combustion

EP lubricant—EP (extreme pressure) lubricants are specially formulated for use with gears involving heavy loads (transmission, drive boxes etc.)

Ethylene glycol—The base substance of antifreeze

Fast idle—The speed of the engine when the choke is on. Fast idle speeds engine warm-up

Filament—The part of a bulb that glows; the filament creates high resistance to current flow and actually glows from the resulting heat

Firing order—The numerical sequence in which an engine's cylinders fire

Flame front—The term used to describe certain aspects of the fuel explosion in the cylinders. The flame front should move in a controlled pattern across the cylinder, rather than simply exploding immediately

Flat spot—A point during acceleration when the engine seems to lose power for an instant

Flooding—A condition created when too much fuel reaches the cylinders; starting will be difficult or impossible

Flywheel—A heavy disc of metal attached to the crankshaft. It smooths the firing impulses of the engine and keeps the crankshaft turning during periods when no firing takes place

Foot pound—A measurement of torque (turning force)

Fuse—A device containing a piece of metal rated to pass a given number of amps. If more current than the rated amperage passes through the fuse, the metal will melt and interrupt the circuit

Gearbox—Transmission

Gear ratio—A ratio expressing the number of turns a smaller gear will make to turn a larger gear through one revolution. The ratio is found by dividing the number of teeth in the smaller gear into the number of teeth on the larger gear

Gel coat—A thin coat of plastic resin covering fiberglass panels

Generator—A device which produces direct current (DC) necessary to charge the battery

Heat range—A term used to describe the ability of a spark plug to carry away heat. Plugs with longer nosed insulators take longer to carry heat off effectively

Hydrocarbon (HC)—A combination of hydrogen and carbon atoms found in all petroleum based fuels. Unburned hydrocarbons (those not burned during normal combustion) are about .1% of exhaust emissions

Hydroplaning—A phenomenon of driving when water builds up under the tire tread, causing it to lose contact with the road. Slowing down will usually restore normal tire contact with the road

Idle mixture—The mixture of air and fuel (usually about 14:1) being fed to the cylinders. The idle mixture screw(s) are sometimes adjusted as part of a tune-up

Lacquer—A quick drying automotive paint

Lithium base grease—Chassis and wheel bearing grease using lithium as a base. Not compatible with sodium base grease

Load range—Indicates the number of plies at which a tire is rated. Load range B equals 4 ply rating; C equals 6 ply rating; and, D equals an 8 ply rating

Manifold—A casting connecting a series of outlets to a common opening, usually referring to mounts for the carburetor(s) in motorcycle use

Master cylinder—Reservoir containing hydraulic brake fluid which forces brake fluid to the caliper pistons as the brake lever or pedal is depressed

Misfire—Condition occurring when the fuel mixture in a cylinder fails to ignite, causing the engine to run roughly

Multiweight—Type of oil that provides adequate lubrication at both high and low temperatures

Nitrous oxide (NOx)—One of the 3 basic pollutants found in the exhaust emission of an internal combustion engine. The amount of NOx usually varies in an inverse proportion to the amount of HC and CO

Octane rating—A number, indicating the quality of gasoline based on its ability to resist knock. The higher the number, the better the quality. Higher compression engines require higher octane gas

OEM—Original Equipment Manufactured. OEM equipment is that furnished standard by the manufacturer

Ohm—Unit used to measure the resistance to flow of direct current

Oscilloscope—A piece of test equipment that shows electric impulses as a pattern on a screen. Engine performance can be analyzed by interpreting these patterns

Overhead camshaft—Camshaft mounted above the combustion chamber

Oxides of nitrogen—See nitrous oxide (NOx)

Percolation—A condition in which the fuel actually "boils," due to excess heat. Percolation prevents proper atomization of the fuel causing rough running

Pick-up coil—The coil in which voltage is induced in an electronic ignition

Ping—A metallic rattling sound produced by the engine under acceleration. It is usually due to incorrect ignition timing or a poor grade of gasoline

Pinion—The smaller of 2 meshing gears

Piston ring—Metal rings (usually 3) installed in grooves in the piston. Piston rings seal the small space between the piston and wall of the cylinder

Ply rating—A rating given a tire which indicates strength (but not necessarily actual plies). A 2 ply/4 ply rating has only 2 plies, but the strength of a 4 ply tire

Polarity—Indication (positive or negative) of the 2 poles of a battery

Power-to-weight ratio—Ratio of horsepower to weight of a vehicle

Ppm—Parts per million; unit used to measure exhaust emissions

Preignition—Early ignition of fuel in the cylinder, sometimes due to glowing carbon deposits in the combustion chamber. Preignition can be damaging since combustion takes place prematurely

Psi—Pounds per square inch; a measurement of pressure

Pushrod—A steel or aluminum rod between the valve lifter and the valve rocker arm in overhead valve (OHV) type engines

Rectifier—A diode or series of diodes which change Alternating to Direct Current for battery charging. Although some small motorcycles may use a single diode for this purpose (half-wave rectifiers), the overwhelming majority use four diodes connected in a bridge which yields full-wave rectification

Resin—A liquid plastic used in body work

Resistor spark plug—A spark plug incorporating a resistor to shorten the spark duration. This suppresses radio interference and lengthens plug life

Retard—Set the ignition timing so that spark occurs later (fewer degrees before TDC)

Rocker arm—A lever which rotates around a shaft pushing down (opening) the valve with an end when the other end is pushed up by the pushrod. Spring pressure will later close the valve

Rpm—Revolutions per minute (usually indicates engine speed)

Run-on—Condition when the engine continues to run, even when the key is turned off. See dieseling

Sealed beam—A modern automotive headlight. The lens, reflector and filament from a single unit

Shimmy—Vibration (sometimes violent) in the front end caused by misaligned front end, out of balance tires or worn suspension components

Short circuit—An electrical malfunction where current takes the path of least resistance to ground (usually through damaged insulation). Current flow is excessive from low resistance resulting in a blown fuse

Sludge—Thick, black deposits in engine formed from dirt, oil, water, etc. It is usually formed in engines with neglected oil changes

SOHC—Single overhead camshaft

Solenoid—An electrically operated, magnetic switching device

Specific gravity (battery)—The relative weight of liquid (battery electrolyte) as compared to the weight of an equal volume of water

Spongy lever or pedal—A soft or spongy feeling when the brake lever or pedal is depressed. It is usually due to air in the brake lines

Sprung weight—The weight of a vehicle supported by the suspension

Straight weight—Term designating motor oil as suitable for use within a narrow range of temperatures. Outside the narrow temperature range its flow characteristics will not adequately lubricate

Stroke—The distance the piston travels from bottom dead center to top dead center

Synthetic oil—Non-petroleum based oil

Tachometer—Instrument which measures engine speed in rpm

TDC—Top dead center. The exact top of the piston's stroke

Thermostat—A temperature sensitive device in the cooling system that regulates the flow of coolant

Timing chain (belt)—A chain or belt that is driven by the crankshaft and operates the camshaft

Torque—Measurement of turning or twisting force, expressed as foot-pounds or inch-pounds

Tread wear indicator—Bars molded into the tire at right angles to the tread that appear as horizontal bars when 1/16th in. of tread remains

Tread wear pattern—The pattern of wear on tires which can be "read" to diagnose problems in the front suspension

Turbocharged—A system to increase engine power by using exhaust gas to drive a compressor. As engine speed and load increases, the compressor forces a greater air/fuel mixture into the cylinder. Under light load, or cruising conditions, the turbocharger "idles" and a normal air/fuel mixture reaches the cylinders

Unsprung weight—The weight of vehicle components not supported by the springs (wheels, tires, brakes, etc.)

Vacuum advance—A method of advancing the ignition timing by applying engine vacuum to a diaphragm mounted on the distributor

Valve guides—The guide through which the stem of the valve passes. The guide is designed to keep the valve in proper alignment

Valve clearance—The operating clearance in the valve train

Valve timing—The relationship between the opening and closing of the intake and exhaust valves relative to crankshaft (and hence, piston) position

Valve train—The system that operates intake and exhaust valves, consisting of camshaft, valves and springs, lifters, pushrods, and rocker arms, where applicable

Varnish—Term applied to the residue formed when gasoline gets old and stale

Viscosity—The ability of a fluid to flow. The lower the viscosity rating, the easier the fluid will flow. 10 weight motor oil will flow much easier than 40 weight motor oil

Volt—Unit used to measure the force or pressure of electricity. It is defined as the pressure needed to move 1 amp through a resistance of 1 ohm

Voltage regulator—A device that controls the current output of the alternator or generator

Wankel engine—An engine which uses no pistons. In place of pistons triangular shaped rotors revolve in specially shaped housings

Wheelbase—Distance between the center of front wheel and the center of rear wheel

Wheel weight—Small weights attached to the wheel to balance the wheel and tire assembly. Out of balance tires quickly wear out and also give erratic handling when installed on the front

Zener diode—A semiconductor used on British motorcycles for many years as a voltage regulator. When the voltage across the zener diode reached a certain point, the element would begin to conduct current, routing it to ground, thus preventing the battery from overcharging

Mechanics' Data

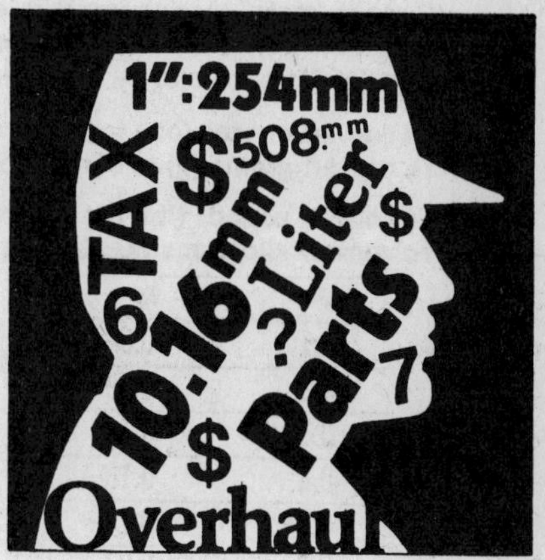

SI METRIC TABLES

The following tables are given in SI (International System) metric units. SI units replace both customary (English) and the older gavimetric units. The use of SI units as a new worldwide standard was set by the International Committee of Weights and Measures in 1960. SI has since been adopted by most countries as their national standard.

These tables are general conversion tables which will allow you to convert customary units, which appear in the text, into SI units.

The following are a list of SI units and the customary units, used in this book, which they replace:

To measure:	Use SI units:	Which replace (customary units):
mass	kilograms (kg)	pounds (lbs)
temperature	Celsius (°C)	Fahrenheit (°F)
length	millimeters (mm)	inches (in.)
force	newtons (N)	pounds force (lbs)
capacities	liters (l)	pints/quarts/gallons (pts/qts/gals)
torque	newton-meters (N·m)	foot pounds (ft lbs)
pressure	kilopascals (kPa)	pounds per square inch (psi)
volume	cubic centimeters (cm^3)	cubic inches (cu in.)
power	kilowatts (kW)	horsepower (hp)

If you have had any prior experience with the metric system, you may have noticed units in this chart which are not familiar to you. This is because, in some cases, SI units differ from the older gravimetric units which they replace. For example, newtons (N) replace kilograms (kg) as a force unit, kilopascals (kPa) replace atmospheres or bars as a unit of pressure, and, although the units are the same, the name Celsius replaces centigrade for temperature measurement.

If you are not using the SI tables, have a look at them anyway; you will be seeing a lot more of them in the future.

ENGLISH TO METRIC CONVERSION: MASS (WEIGHT)

Current mass measurement is expressed in pounds and ounces (lbs. & ozs.). The metric unit of mass (or weight) is the kilogram (kg). Even although this table does not show conversion of masses (weights) larger than 15 lbs, it is easy to calculate larger units by following the data immediately below.

To convert ounces (oz.) to grams (g): multiply th number of ozs. by 28
To convert grams (g) to ounces (oz.): multiply the number of grams by .035

To convert pounds (lbs.) to kilograms (kg): multiply the number of lbs. by .45
To convert kilograms (kg) to pounds (lbs.): multiply the number of kilograms by 2.2

lbs	kg	lbs	kg	oz	kg	oz	kg
0.1	0.04	0.9	0.41	0.1	0.003	0.9	0.024
0.2	0.09	1	0.4	0.2	0.005	1	0.03
0.3	0.14	2	0.9	0.3	0.008	2	0.06
0.4	0.18	3	1.4	0.4	0.011	3	0.08
0.5	0.23	4	1.8	0.5	0.014	4	0.11
0.6	0.27	5	2.3	0.6	0.017	5	0.14
0.7	0.32	10	4.5	0.7	0.020	10	0.28
0.8	0.36	15	6.8	0.8	0.023	15	0.42

ENGLISH TO METRIC CONVERSION: TEMPERATURE

To convert Fahrenheit (°F) to Celsius (°C): take number of °F and subtract 32; multiply result by 5; divide result by 9

To convert Celsius (°C) to Fahrenheit (°F): take number of °C and multiply by 9; divide result by 5; add 32 to total

Fahrenheit (F)		Celsius (C)		Fahrenheit (F)		Celsius (C)		Fahrenheit (F)		Celsius (C)	
°F	°C	°C	°F	°F	°C	°C	°F	°F	°C	°C	°F
−40	−40	−38	−36.4	80	26.7	18	64.4	215	101.7	80	176
−35	−37.2	−36	−32.8	85	29.4	20	68	220	104.4	85	185
−30	−34.4	−34	−29.2	90	32.2	22	71.6	225	107.2	90	194
−25	−31.7	−32	−25.6	95	35.0	24	75.2	230	110.0	95	202
−20	−28.9	−30	−22	100	37.8	26	78.8	235	112.8	100	212
−15	−26.1	−28	−18.4	105	40.6	28	82.4	240	115.6	105	221
−10	−23.3	−26	−14.8	110	43.3	30	86	245	118.3	110	230
−5	−20.6	−24	−11.2	115	46.1	32	89.6	250	121.1	115	239
0	−17.8	−22	−7.6	120	48.9	34	93.2	255	123.9	120	248
1	−17.2	−20	−4	125	51.7	36	96.8	260	126.6	125	257
2	−16.7	−18	−0.4	130	54.4	38	100.4	265	129.4	130	266
3	−16.1	−16	3.2	135	57.2	40	104	270	132.2	135	275
4	−15.6	−14	6.8	140	60.0	42	107.6	275	135.0	140	284
5	−15.0	−12	10.4	145	62.8	44	112.2	280	137.8	145	293
10	−12.2	−10	14	150	65.6	46	114.8	285	140.6	150	302
15	−9.4	−8	17.6	155	68.3	48	118.4	290	143.3	155	311
20	−6.7	−6	21.2	160	71.1	50	122	295	146.1	160	320
25	−3.9	−4	24.8	165	73.9	52	125.6	300	148.9	165	329
30	−1.1	−2	28.4	170	76.7	54	129.2	305	151.7	170	338
35	1.7	0	32	175	79.4	56	132.8	310	154.4	175	347
40	4.4	2	35.6	180	82.2	58	136.4	315	157.2	180	356
45	7.2	4	39.2	185	85.0	60	140	320	160.0	185	365
50	10.0	6	42.8	190	87.8	62	143.6	325	162.8	190	374
55	12.8	8	46.4	195	90.6	64	147.2	330	165.6	195	383
60	15.6	10	50	200	93.3	66	150.8	335	168.3	200	392
65	18.3	12	53.6	205	96.1	68	154.4	340	171.1	205	401
70	21.1	14	57.2	210	98.9	70	158	345	173.9	210	410
75	23.9	16	60.8	212	100.0	75	167	350	176.7	215	414

ENGLISH TO METRIC CONVERSION: LENGTH

To convert inches (ins.) to millimeters (mm): multiply number of inches by 25.4

To convert millimeters (mm) to inches (ins.): multiply number of millimeters by .04

Inches	Decimals	Milli-meters	Inches to millimeters inches	mm	Inches	Decimals	Milli-meters	Inches to millimeters inches	mm
1/64	0.051625	0.3969	0.0001	0.00254	33/64	0.515625	13.0969	0.6	15.24
1/32	0.03125	0.7937	0.0002	0.00508	17/32	0.53125	13.4937	0.7	17.78
3/64	0.046875	1.1906	0.0003	0.00762	35/64	0.546875	13.8906	0.8	20.32
1/16	0.0625	1.5875	0.0004	0.01016	9/16	0.5625	14.2875	0.9	22.86
5/64	0.078125	1.9844	0.0005	0.01270	37/64	0.578125	14.6844	1	25.4
3/32	0.09375	2.3812	0.0006	0.01524	19/32	0.59375	15.0812	2	50.8
7/64	0.109375	2.7781	0.0007	0.01778	39/64	0.609375	15.4781	3	76.2
1/8	0.125	3.1750	0.0008	0.02032	5/8	0.625	15.8750	4	101.6
9/64	0.140625	3.5719	0.0009	0.02286	41/64	0.640625	16.2719	5	127.0
5/32	0.15625	3.9687	0.001	0.0254	21/32	0.65625	16.6687	6	152.4
11/64	0.171875	4.3656	0.002	0.0508	43/64	0.671875	17.0656	7	177.8
3/16	0.1875	4.7625	0.003	0.0762	11/16	0.6875	17.4625	8	203.2
13/64	0.203125	5.1594	0.004	0.1016	45/64	0.703125	17.8594	9	228.6
7/32	0.21875	5.5562	0.005	0.1270	23/32	0.71875	18.2562	10	254.0
15/64	0.234375	5.9531	0.006	0.1524	47/64	0.734375	18.6531	11	279.4
1/4	0.25	6.3500	0.007	0.1778	3/4	0.75	19.0500	12	304.8
17/64	0.265625	6.7469	0.008	0.2032	49/64	0.765625	19.4469	13	330.2
9/32	0.28125	7.1437	0.009	0.2286	25/32	0.78125	19.8437	14	355.6
19/64	0.296875	7.5406	0.01	0.254	51/64	0.796875	20.2406	15	381.0
5/16	0.3125	7.9375	0.02	0.508	13/16	0.8125	20.6375	16	406.4
21/64	0.328125	8.3344	0.03	0.762	53/64	0.828125	21.0344	17	431.8
11/32	0.34375	8.7312	0.04	1.016	27/32	0.84375	21.4312	18	457.2
23/64	0.359375	9.1281	0.05	1.270	55/64	0.859375	21.8281	19	482.6
3/8	0.375	9.5250	0.06	1.524	7/8	0.875	22.2250	20	508.0
25/64	0.390625	9.9219	0.07	1.778	57/64	0.890625	22.6219	21	533.4
13/32	0.40625	10.3187	0.08	2.032	29/32	0.90625	23.0187	22	558.8
27/64	0.421875	10.7156	0.09	2.286	59/64	0.921875	23.4156	23	584.2
7/16	0.4375	11.1125	0.1	2.54	15/16	0.9375	23.8125	24	609.6
29/64	0.453125	11.5094	0.2	5.08	61/64	0.953125	24.2094	25	635.0
15/32	0.46875	11.9062	0.3	7.62	31/32	0.96875	24.6062	26	660.4
31/64	0.484375	12.3031	0.4	10.16	63/64	0.984375	25.0031	27	690.6
1/2	0.5	12.7000	0.5	12.70					

ENGLISH TO METRIC CONVERSION: TORQUE

To convert foot-pounds (ft. lbs.) to Newton-meters: multiply the number of ft. lbs. by 1.3

To convert inch-pounds (in. lbs.) to Newton-meters: multiply the number of in. lbs. by .11

in lbs	N-m	in lbs	N-m	in lbs	N-m	in lbs	N-m	in lbs	N-m
0.1	0.01	1	0.11	10	1.13	19	2.15	28	3.16
0.2	0.02	2	0.23	11	1.24	20	2.26	29	3.28
0.3	0.03	3	0.34	12	1.36	21	2.37	30	3.39
0.4	0.04	4	0.45	13	1.47	22	2.49	31	3.50
0.5	0.06	5	0.56	14	1.58	23	2.60	32	3.62
0.6	0.07	6	0.68	15	1.70	24	2.71	33	3.73
0.7	0.08	7	0.78	16	1.81	25	2.82	34	3.84
0.8	0.09	8	0.90	17	1.92	26	2.94	35	3.95
0.9	0.10	9	1.02	18	2.03	27	3.05	36	4.07

ENGLISH TO METRIC CONVERSION: TORQUE

Torque is now expressed as either foot-pounds (ft./lbs.) or inch-pounds (in./lbs.). The metric measurement unit for torque is the Newton-meter (Nm). This unit—the Nm—will be used for all SI metric torque references, both the present ft./lbs. and in./lbs.

ft lbs	N-m	ft lbs	N-m	ft lbs	N-m	ft lbs	N-m
0.1	0.1	33	44.7	74	100.3	115	155.9
0.2	0.3	34	46.1	75	101.7	116	157.3
0.3	0.4	35	47.4	76	103.0	117	158.6
0.4	0.5	36	48.8	77	104.4	118	160.0
0.5	0.7	37	50.7	78	105.8	119	161.3
0.6	0.8	38	51.5	79	107.1	120	162.7
0.7	1.0	39	52.9	80	108.5	121	164.0
0.8	1.1	40	54.2	81	109.8	122	165.4
0.9	1.2	41	55.6	82	111.2	123	166.8
1	1.3	42	56.9	83	112.5	124	168.1
2	2.7	43	58.3	84	113.9	125	169.5
3	4.1	44	59.7	85	115.2	126	170.8
4	5.4	45	61.0	86	116.6	127	172.2
5	6.8	46	62.4	87	118.0	128	173.5
6	8.1	47	63.7	88	119.3	129	174.9
7	9.5	48	65.1	89	120.7	130	176.2
8	10.8	49	66.4	90	122.0	131	177.6
9	12.2	50	67.8	91	123.4	132	179.0
10	13.6	51	69.2	92	124.7	133	180.3
11	14.9	52	70.5	93	126.1	134	181.7
12	16.3	53	71.9	94	127.4	135	183.0
13	17.6	54	73.2	95	128.8	136	184.4
14	18.9	55	74.6	96	130.2	137	185.7
15	20.3	56	75.9	97	131.5	138	187.1
16	21.7	57	77.3	98	132.9	139	188.5
17	23.0	58	78.6	99	134.2	140	189.8
18	24.4	59	80.0	100	135.6	141	191.2
19	25.8	60	81.4	101	136.9	142	192.5
20	27.1	61	82.7	102	138.3	143	193.9
21	28.5	62	84.1	103	139.6	144	195.2
22	29.8	63	85.4	104	141.0	145	196.6
23	31.2	64	86.8	105	142.4	146	198.0
24	32.5	65	88.1	106	143.7	147	199.3
25	33.9	66	89.5	107	145.1	148	200.7
26	35.2	67	90.8	108	146.4	149	202.0
27	36.6	68	92.2	109	147.8	150	203.4
28	38.0	69	93.6	110	149.1	151	204.7
29	39.3	70	94.9	111	150.5	152	206.1
30	40.7	71	96.3	112	151.8	153	207.4
31	42.0	72	97.6	113	153.2	154	208.8
32	43.4	73	99.0	114	154.6	155	210.2

ENGLISH TO METRIC CONVERSION: FORCE

Force is presently measured in pounds (lbs.). This type of measurement is used to measure spring pressure, specifically how many pounds it takes to compress a spring. Our present force unit (the pound) will be replaced in SI metric measurements by the Newton (N). This term will eventually see use in specifications for electric motor brush spring pressures, valve spring pressures, etc.

To convert pounds (lbs.) to Newton (N): multiply the number of lbs. by 4.45

lbs	N	lbs	N	lbs	N	oz	N
0.01	0.04	21	93.4	59	262.4	1	0.3
0.02	0.09	22	97.9	60	266.9	2	0.6
0.03	0.13	23	102.3	61	271.3	3	0.8
0.04	0.18	24	106.8	62	275.8	4	1.1
0.05	0.22	25	111.2	63	280.2	5	1.4
0.06	0.27	26	115.6	64	284.6	6	1.7
0.07	0.31	27	120.1	65	289.1	7	2.0
0.08	0.36	28	124.6	66	293.6	8	2.2
0.09	0.40	29	129.0	67	298.0	9	2.5
0.1	0.4	30	133.4	68	302.5	10	2.8
0.2	0.9	31	137.9	69	306.9	11	3.1
0.3	1.3	32	142.3	70	311.4	12	3.3
0.4	1.8	33	146.8	71	315.8	13	3.6
0.5	2.2	34	151.2	72	320.3	14	3.9
0.6	2.7	35	155.7	73	324.7	15	4.2
0.7	3.1	36	160.1	74	329.2	16	4.4
0.8	3.6	37	164.6	75	333.6	17	4.7
0.9	4.0	38	169.0	76	338.1	18	5.0
1	4.4	39	173.5	77	342.5	19	5.3
2	8.9	40	177.9	78	347.0	20	5.6
3	13.4	41	182.4	79	351.4	21	5.8
4	17.8	42	186.8	80	355.9	22	6.1
5	22.2	43	191.3	81	360.3	23	6.4
6	26.7	44	195.7	82	364.8	24	6.7
7	31.1	45	200.2	83	369.2	25	7.0
8	35.6	46	204.6	84	373.6	26	7.2
9	40.0	47	209.1	85	378.1	27	7.5
10	44.5	48	213.5	86	382.6	28	7.8
11	48.9	49	218.0	87	387.0	29	8.1
12	53.4	50	224.4	88	391.4	30	8.3
13	57.8	51	226.9	89	395.9	31	8.6
14	62.3	52	231.3	90	400.3	32	8.9
15	66.7	53	235.8	91	404.8	33	9.2
16	71.2	54	240.2	92	409.2	34	9.4
17	75.6	55	244.6	93	413.7	35	9.7
18	80.1	56	249.1	94	418.1	36	10.0
19	84.5	57	253.6	95	422.6	37	10.3
20	89.0	58	258.0	96	427.0	38	10.6

ENGLISH TO METRIC CONVERSION: LIQUID CAPACITY

Liquid or fluid capacity is presently expressed as pints, quarts or gallons, or a combination of all of these. In the metric system the liter (l) will become the basic unit. Fractions of a liter would be expressed as deciliters, centiliters, or most frequently (and commonly) as milliliters.

To convert pints (pts.) to liters (l): multiply the number of pints by .47
To convert liters (l) to pints (pts.): multiply the number of liters by 2.1
To convert quarts (qts.) to liters (l): multiply the number of quarts by .95

To convert liters (l) to quarts (qts.): multiply the number of liters by 1.06
To convert gallons (gals.) to liters (l): multiply the number of gallons by 3.8
To convert liters (l) to gallons (gals.): multiply the number of liters by .26

gals	liters	qts	liters	pts	liters
0.1	0.38	0.1	0.10	0.1	0.05
0.2	0.76	0.2	0.19	0.2	0.10
0.3	1.1	0.3	0.28	0.3	0.14
0.4	1.5	0.4	0.38	0.4	0.19
0.5	1.9	0.5	0.47	0.5	0.24
0.6	2.3	0.6	0.57	0.6	0.28
0.7	2.6	0.7	0.66	0.7	0.33
0.8	3.0	0.8	0.76	0.8	0.38
0.9	3.4	0.9	0.85	0.9	0.43
1	3.8	1	1.0	1	0.5
2	7.6	2	1.9	2	1.0
3	11.4	3	2.8	3	1.4
4	15.1	4	3.8	4	1.9
5	18.9	5	4.7	5	2.4
6	22.7	6	5.7	6	2.8
7	26.5	7	6.6	7	3.3
8	30.3	8	7.6	8	3.8
9	34.1	9	8.5	9	4.3
10	37.8	10	9.5	10	4.7
11	41.6	11	10.4	11	5.2
12	45.4	12	11.4	12	5.7
13	49.2	13	12.3	13	6.2
14	53.0	14	13.2	14	6.6
15	56.8	15	14.2	15	7.1
16	60.6	16	15.1	16	7.6
17	64.3	17	16.1	17	8.0
18	68.1	18	17.0	18	8.5
19	71.9	19	18.0	19	9.0
20	75.7	20	18.9	20	9.5
21	79.5	21	19.9	21	9.9
22	83.2	22	20.8	22	10.4
23	87.0	23	21.8	23	10.9
24	90.8	24	22.7	24	11.4
25	94.6	25	23.6	25	11.8
26	98.4	26	24.6	26	12.3
27	102.2	27	25.5	27	12.8
28	106.0	28	26.5	28	13.2
29	110.0	29	27.4	29	13.7
30	113.5	30	28.4	30	14.2

ENGLISH TO METRIC CONVERSION: PRESSURE

The basic unit of pressure measurement used today is expressed as pounds per square inch (psi). The metric unit for psi will be the kilopascal (kPa). This will apply to either fluid pressure or air pressure, and will be frequently seen in tire pressure readings, oil pressure specifications, fuel pump pressure, etc.

To convert pounds per square inch (psi) to kilopascals (kPa): multiply the number of psi by 6.89

Psi	kPa	Psi	kPa	Psi	kPa	Psi	kPa
0.1	0.7	37	255.1	82	565.4	127	875.6
0.2	1.4	38	262.0	83	572.3	128	882.5
0.3	2.1	39	268.9	84	579.2	129	889.4
0.4	2.8	40	275.8	85	586.0	130	896.3
0.5	3.4	41	282.7	86	592.9	131	903.2
0.6	4.1	42	289.6	87	599.8	132	910.1
0.7	4.8	43	296.5	88	606.7	133	917.0
0.8	5.5	44	303.4	89	613.6	134	923.9
0.9	6.2	45	310.3	90	620.5	135	930.8
1	6.9	46	317.2	91	627.4	136	937.7
2	13.8	47	324.0	92	634.3	137	944.6
3	20.7	48	331.0	93	641.2	138	951.5
4	27.6	49	337.8	94	648.1	139	958.4
5	34.5	50	344.7	95	655.0	140	965.2
6	41.4	51	351.6	96	661.9	141	972.2
7	48.3	52	358.5	97	668.8	142	979.0
8	55.2	53	365.4	98	675.7	143	985.9
9	62.1	54	372.3	99	682.6	144	992.8
10	69.0	55	379.2	100	689.5	145	999.7
11	75.8	56	386.1	101	696.4	146	1006.6
12	82.7	57	393.0	102	703.3	147	1013.5
13	89.6	58	399.9	103	710.2	148	1020.4
14	96.5	59	406.8	104	717.0	149	1027.3
15	103.4	60	413.7	105	723.9	150	1034.2
16	110.3	61	420.6	106	730.8	151	1041.1
17	117.2	62	427.5	107	737.7	152	1048.0
18	124.1	63	434.4	108	744.6	153	1054.9
19	131.0	64	441.3	109	751.5	154	1061.8
20	137.9	65	448.2	110	758.4	155	1068.7
21	144.8	66	455.0	111	765.3	156	1075.6
22	151.7	67	461.9	112	772.2	157	1082.5
23	158.6	68	468.8	113	779.1	158	1089.4
24	165.5	69	475.7	114	786.0	159	1096.3
25	172.4	70	482.6	115	792.9	160	1103.2
26	179.3	71	489.5	116	799.8	161	1110.0
27	186.2	72	496.4	117	806.7	162	1116.9
28	193.0	73	503.3	118	813.6	163	1123.8
29	200.0	74	510.2	119	820.5	164	1130.7
30	206.8	75	517.1	120	827.4	165	1137.6
31	213.7	76	524.0	121	834.3	166	1144.5
32	220.6	77	530.9	122	841.2	167	1151.4
33	227.5	78	537.8	123	848.0	168	1158.3
34	234.4	79	544.7	124	854.9	169	1165.2
35	241.3	80	551.6	125	861.8	170	1172.1
36	248.2	81	558.5	126	868.7	171	1179.0

ENGLISH TO METRIC CONVERSION: PRESSURE

The basic unit of pressure measurement used today is expressed as pounds per square inch (psi). The metric unit for psi will be the kilopascal (kPa). This will apply to either fluid pressure or air pressure, and will be frequently seen in tire pressure readings, oil pressure specifications, fuel pump pressure, etc.

To convert pounds per square inch (psi) to kilopascals (kPa): multiply the number of psi by 6.89

Psi	kPa	Psi	kPa	Psi	kPa	Psi	kPa
172	1185.9	216	1489.3	260	1792.6	304	2096.0
173	1192.8	217	1496.2	261	1799.5	305	2102.9
174	1199.7	218	1503.1	262	1806.4	306	2109.8
175	1206.6	219	1510.0	263	1813.3	307	2116.7
176	1213.5	220	1516.8	264	1820.2	308	2123.6
177	1220.4	221	1523.7	265	1827.1	309	2130.5
178	1227.3	222	1530.6	266	1834.0	310	2137.4
179	1234.2	223	1537.5	267	1840.9	311	2144.3
180	1241.0	224	1544.4	268	1847.8	312	2151.2
181	1247.9	225	1551.3	269	1854.7	313	2158.1
182	1254.8	226	1558.2	270	1861.6	314	2164.9
183	1261.7	227	1565.1	271	1868.5	315	2171.8
184	1268.6	228	1572.0	272	1875.4	316	2178.7
185	1275.5	229	1578.9	273	1882.3	317	2185.6
186	1282.4	230	1585.8	274	1889.2	318	2192.5
187	1289.3	231	1592.7	275	1896.1	319	2199.4
188	1296.2	232	1599.6	276	1903.0	320	2206.3
189	1303.1	233	1606.5	277	1909.8	321	2213.2
190	1310.0	234	1613.4	278	1916.7	322	2220.1
191	1316.9	235	1620.3	279	1923.6	323	2227.0
192	1323.8	236	1627.2	280	1930.5	324	2233.9
193	1330.7	237	1634.1	281	1937.4	325	2240.8
194	1337.6	238	1641.0	282	1944.3	326	2247.7
195	1344.5	239	1647.8	283	1951.2	327	2254.6
196	1351.4	240	1654.7	284	1958.1	328	2261.5
197	1358.3	241	1661.6	285	1965.0	329	2268.4
198	1365.2	242	1668.5	286	1971.9	330	2275.3
199	1372.0	243	1675.4	287	1978.8	331	2282.2
200	1378.9	244	1682.3	288	1985.7	332	2289.1
201	1385.8	245	1689.2	289	1992.6	333	2295.9
202	1392.7	246	1696.1	290	1999.5	334	2302.8
203	1399.6	247	1703.0	291	2006.4	335	2309.7
204	1406.5	248	1709.9	292	2013.3	336	2316.6
205	1413.4	249	1716.8	293	2020.2	337	2323.5
206	1420.3	250	1723.7	294	2027.1	338	2330.4
207	1427.2	251	1730.6	295	2034.0	339	2337.3
208	1434.1	252	1737.5	296	2040.8	240	2344.2
209	1441.0	253	1744.4	297	2047.7	341	2351.1
210	1447.9	254	1751.3	298	2054.6	342	2358.0
211	1454.8	255	1758.2	299	2061.5	343	2364.9
212	1461.7	256	1765.1	300	2068.4	344	2371.8
213	1468.7	257	1772.0	301	2075.3	345	2378.7
214	1475.5	258	1778.8	302	2082.2	346	2385.6
215	1482.4	259	1785.7	303	2089.1	347	2392.5

TAP DRILL SIZES

NATIONAL COARSE OR U.S.S.

Screw & Tap Size	Threads Per Inch	Use Drill Number
No. 5	40	39
No. 6	32	36
No. 8	32	29
No. 10	24	25
No. 12	24	17
1/4	20	8
5/16	18	F
3/8	16	5/16
7/16	14	U
1/2	13	27/64
9/16	12	31/64
5/8	11	17/32
3/4	10	21/32
7/8	9	49/64
1	8	7/8
1 1/8	7	63/64
1 1/4	7	1 7/64
1 1/2	6	1 11/32

NATIONAL FINE OR S.A.E.

Screw & Tap Size	Threads Per Inch	Use Drill Number
No. 5	44	37
No. 6	40	33
No. 8	36	29
No. 10	32	21
No. 12	28	15
1/4	28	3
5/16	24	1
3/8	24	Q
7/16	20	W
1/2	20	29/64
9/16	18	33/64
5/8	18	37/64
3/4	16	11/16
7/8	14	13/16
1 1/8	12	1 3/64
1 1/4	12	1 11/64
1 1/2	12	1 27/64

DECIMAL EQUIVALENT SIZE OF THE NUMBER DRILLS

Drill No.	Decimal Equivalent	Drill No.	Decimal Equivalent	Drill No.	Decimal Equivalent
80	.0135	53	.0595	26	.1470
79	.0145	52	.0635	25	.1495
78	.0160	51	.0670	24	.1520
77	.0180	50	.0700	23	.1540
76	.0200	49	.0730	22	.1570
75	.0210	48	.0760	21	.1590
74	.0225	47	.0785	20	.1610
73	.0240	46	.0810	19	.1660
72	.0250	45	.0820	18	.1695
71	.0260	44	.0860	17	.1730
70	.0280	43	.0890	16	.1770
69	.0292	42	.0935	15	.1800
68	.0310	41	.0960	14	.1820
67	.0320	40	.0980	13	.1850
66	.0330	39	.0995	12	.1890
65	.0350	38	.1015	11	.1910
64	.0360	37	.1040	10	.1935
63	.0370	36	.1065	9	.1960
62	.0380	35	.1100	8	.1990
61	.0390	34	.1110	7	.2010
60	.0400	33	.1130	6	.2040
59	.0410	32	.1160	5	.2055
58	.0420	31	.1200	4	.2090
57	.0430	30	.1285	3	.2130
56	.0465	29	.1360	2	.2210
55	.0520	28	.1405	1	.2280
54	.0550	27	.1440		

DECIMAL EQUIVALENT SIZE OF THE LETTER DRILLS

Letter Drill	Decimal Equivalent	Letter Drill	Decimal Equivalent	Letter Drill	Decimal Equivalent
A	.234	J	.277	S	.348
B	.238	K	.281	T	.358
C	.242	L	.290	U	.368
D	.246	M	.295	V	.377
E	.250	N	.302	W	.386
F	.257	O	.316	X	.397
G	.261	P	.323	Y	.404
H	.266	Q	.332	Z	.413
I	.272	R	.339		

DECIMAL EQUIVALENTS OF THE COMMON FRACTIONS

Fraction	Decimal
1/64	.0156
1/32	.0313
3/64	.0469
1/16	.0625
5/64	.0781
3/32	.0938
7/64	.1094
1/8	.1250
9/64	.1406
5/32	.1563
11/64	.1719
3/16	.1875
13/64	.2031
7/32	.2188
15/64	.2344
1/4	.2500
17/64	.2656
9/32	.2813
19/64	.2969
5/16	.3125
21/64	.3281
11/32	.3438
23/64	.3594
3/8	.3750
25/64	.3906
13/32	.4063
27/64	.4219
7/16	.4375
29/64	.4531
15/32	.4688
31/64	.4844
1/2	.5000
33/64	.5156
17/32	.5313
35/64	.5469
9/16	.5625
37/64	.5781
19/32	.5938
39/64	.6094
5/8	.6250
41/64	.6406
21/32	.6563
43/64	.6719
11/16	.6875
45/64	.7031
23/32	.7188
47/64	.7344
3/4	.7500
49/64	.7656
25/32	.7813
51/64	.7969
13/16	.8125
53/64	.8281
27/32	.8438
55/64	.8594
7/8	.8750
57/64	.8906
29/32	.9063
59/64	.9219
15/16	.9375
61/64	.9531
31/32	.9688
63/64	.9844

GENERAL CONVERSION TABLE

Multiply By	To Convert	To	
		Length	—
2.54	Inches	Centimeters	.3937
25.4	Inches	Millimeters	.03937
30.48	Feet	Centimeters	.0328
.304	Feet	Meters	3.28
.914	Yards	Meters	1.094
1.609	Miles	Kilometers	.621
		Volume	
.473	Pints	Liters	2.11
.946	Quarts	Liters	1.06
3.785	Gallons	Liters	.264
.016	Cubic inches	Liters	61.02
16.39	Cubic inches	Cubic cms.	.061
28.3	Cubic feet	Liters	:0353
		Mass (Weight)	
28.35	Ounces	Grams	.035
.4536	Pounds	Kilograms	2.20
		Area	
.645	Square inches	Square cms.	.155
.836	Square yds.	Square meters	1.196
		Force	
4.448	Pounds	Newtons	.225
.138	Ft./lbs.	Kilogram/meters	7.23
1.36	Ft./lbs.	Newton-meters	.737
.112	In./lbs.	Newton-meters	8.844
		Pressure	
.068	Psi	Atmospheres	14.7
6.89	Psi	Kilopascals	.145
		Other	
1.104	Horsepower (DIN)	Horsepower (SAE)	.9861
.746	Horsepower (SAE)	Kilowatts (KW)	1.34
1.60	Mph	Km/h	.625
.425	Mpg	Km/1	2.35
—	**To obtain**	**From**	**Multiply by**

TAP DRILL SIZES

NATIONAL COARSE OR U.S.S.						NATIONAL FINE OR S.A.E.					
Screw & Tap Size	Threads Per Inch	Use Drill Number	Screw & Tap Size	Threads Per Inch	Use Drill Number	Screw & Tap Size	Threads Per Inch	Use Drill Number	Screw & Tap Size	Threads Per Inch	Use Drill Number
No. 5	40	39	1/2	13	27/64	No. 5	44	37	1/2	20	29/64
No. 6	32	36	9/16	12	31/64	No. 6	40	33	9/16	18	33/64
No. 8	32	29	5/8	11	17/32	No. 8	36	29	5/8	18	37/64
No. 10	24	25	3/4	10	21/32	No. 10	32	21	3/4	16	11/16
No. 12	24	17	7/8	9	49/64	No. 12	28	15	7/8	14	13/16
1/4	20	8	1	8	7/8	1/4	28	3	1 1/8	12	1 3/64
5/16	18	F	1 1/8	7	63/64	5/16	24	1	1 1/4	12	1 11/64
3/8	16	5/16	1 1/4	7	1 7/64	3/8	24	Q	1 1/2	12	1 27/64
7/16	14	U	1 1/2	6	1 11/32	7/16	20	W